OF CONTE

This edition of the MOTOR Auto Repair Manual, Vol. 2, covers specifications and service procedures on 2000-2004 DaimlerChrysler Corporation, Ford Motor Company and General Motors Corporation models available at time of publication. Volume 2 covers Dash Gauges, Speed Controls, Wiper Systems, Passive Restraints, Dash Panel Service, Anti-Lock Brakes, Tire Pressure Monitoring Systems and Active Suspension Systems. The remaining vehicle information is located in Volume 1.

This manual is divided into four sections using three tabs. The section before Tab 1 covers Vehicle Identification, Air Bag System Precautions, Computer Relearn Procedures, Service Reminder & Warning Lamp Reset Procedures, Vehicle Lift Points, Non-Standard Tire & Wheel Size Adjustment To Ride Height Specifications & Tire Size Adjustment Charts, Electrical Symbol & Wire Color Code Identification and Vehicle Maintenance Schedules. Tab 1 covers DaimlerChrysler Corporation vehicles. Tab 2 covers Ford Motor Company vehicles. Tab 3 covers General Motors Corporation vehicles. Each tabbed section starts on page 1-1. Data reported in this manual is subject to change.

DAIMLERCHRYSLER CORP.—TAB 1

FORD MOTOR CO.—TAB 2

TABLE OF CONTENTS-Continued

GENERAL MOTORS CORP.—TAB 3

VEHICLE IDENTIFICATION

INDEX

DIGIT 1 Country Of Origin
- 1 = USA
- 2 = Canada
- 3 = Mexico
- 4 = USA

DIGIT 2 Manufacturer
- G = General Motors

DIGIT 3 Make
- 4 = Buick

DIGIT 4 Restraint System
- A = Manual Belts
- B = Automatic Belts
- C = Passive/Inflatable

DIGIT 4-5 Carline/Series
- AG = Century
- AG = Century Special & Wagon
- AG = Century T-Type
- AG = Century Special
- AH = Century Custom
- AL = Century Estate Wagon
- AL = Century Limited
- BN = Roadmaster
- BN = LeSabre Custom
- BP = LeSabre Limited
- BR = Roadmaster Estate Wagon
- BR = LeSabre Estate Wagon
- BT = Roadmaster Limited
- BV = Electra Estate Wagon
- CF = Electra T-Type
- CU = Electra Park Avenue Ultra
- CU = Park Avenue Ultra
- CW = Electra Park Avenue
- CW = Park Avenue
- CX = Electra
- CX = Electra Limited
- EC = Reatta
- EY = Riviera T-Type
- EZ = Riviera
- GD = Riviera
- GJ = Regal
- GK = Regal T-Type
- GM = Regal Limited
- HH = LeSabre
- HP = LeSabre Custom
- HR = LeSabre Limited
- JE = Skyhawk T-Type
- JS = Skyhawk
- JS = Skyhawk Custom
- JT = Skyhawk Limited
- NC = Skylark 4D Custom
- ND = Skylark Limited
- ND = Skylark 4D Luxury
- NJ = Skylark Limited
- NJ = Skylark
- NJ = Somerset
- NJ = Skylark 2D Custom
- NJ = Skylark Custom
- NK = Somerset T-Type
- NM = Somerset Limited
- NM = Skylark Limited
- NM = Skylark 2D Limited
- NM = Skylark Gran Sport
- NV = Skylark Custom
- NV = Skylark
- WB = Regal Custom
- WB = Regal LS
- WB = Regal 2D Gran Sport
- WD = Regal Limited
- WF = Regal 4D Gran Sport
- WF = Regal GS

DIGIT 4-5 Carline/Series
- WF = Regal Gran Sport
- WS = Century Custom
- WY = Century Limited
- XB = Skylark Custom
- XC = Skylark Limited

DIGIT 5 Carline/Series
- B = Skylark Custom
- B = Skylark
- C = Skylark Limited
- D = Skylark Sport
- D = Skylark T-Type
- E = Skyhawk T-Type
- E = Century Wagon
- G = Century T-Type
- H = Century
- H = Century Custom
- J = Regal
- K = Regal T-Type
- K = Regal Sport
- L = Century Limited
- M = Regal Limited
- N = LeSabre
- N = LeSabre Custom
- P = LeSabre Limited
- R = Electra Limited
- R = LeSabre Estate Wagon
- S = Skyhawk
- S = Skyhawk Custom
- T = Skyhawk Limited
- U = Electra Park Avenue
- V = Electra Estate Wagon
- W = Electra Park Avenue
- X = Electra Limited
- Y = Riviera T-Type
- Z = Riviera

DIGIT 6 Body Style
- 1 = 2D Coupe
- 2 = 2D Hatchback
- 2 = 2D Coupe
- 3 = 2D Convertible
- 5 = 4D Sedan
- 8 = 4D Station Wagon
- 8 = 4D Wagon

DIGIT 6-7 Body Style
- 11 = 2D Sedan
- 19 = 4D Sedan
- 27 = 2D Coupe
- 35 = 4D Wagon
- 37 = 2D Coupe
- 47 = 2D Coupe
- 57 = 2D Coupe
- 67 = 2D Convertible
- 69 = 4D Sedan
- 77 = 2D Hatchback

DIGIT 7 Restraint System
- 1 = Manual Belts
- 2 = Dual Front Airbags w/Manual Belts
- 3 = Driverside Airbag w/Manual Belts
- 4 = Automatic Belts
- 4 = 2nd Generation Dual Front & Side Airbags w/Manual Belts
- 5 = Driverside Airbag w/Automatic Belts
- 5 = Dual Front & Side Airbags w/Manual Belts

DIGIT 8 Engine
- 0 = 1.8L I-4 EFI
- 1 = 2.0L I-4 EFI
- 1 = 3.8L V6 MPI S/C
- 3 = 2.3L I-4 EFI OHC
- 3 = 3.8L V6 FI TBO

ARM0300000000364

Fig. 1 VIN Identification (Part 1 of 2). Buick

DIGIT 8 Engine
3 = 3.8L V6 SFI
3 = 3.8L V6 2BBL
3 = 3.8L V6 4BBL T/C
4 = 2.2L I-4 MPI
4 = 4.1L V6 4BBL
5 = 2.5L I-4 2BBL
7 = 5.7L V8 TBI
7 = 3.8L V6 SFI
8 = 3.8L V6 2BBL
9 = 3.8L V6 SFI
A = 3.8L V6 2BBL
B = 2.0L I-4 2BBL
B = 3.8L V6 SFI
C = 3.8L V6 MPI
D = 2.3L I-4 EFI Quad
E = 3.0L V6 2BBL
E = 5.0L V8 TBI
G = 1.8L I-4 2BBL
H = 5.0L V8 4BBL
J = 1.8L I-4 MPI
J = 3.1L V6 SFI
K = 3.8L V6 MPI
K = 2.0L I-4 EFI
K = 3.8L V6 SFI
L = 3.8L V6 MPI
L = 3.0L V6 MPI
M = 3.1L V6 MPI
M = 2.0L I-4 EFI
M = 3.1L V6 SFI
N = 5.7L V8 Dsl
N = 5.7L V8 4BBL Dsl
N = 3.3L V6 MPI
P = 5.7L V8 MPI
P = 2.0L I-4 EFI
R = 2.5L I-4 TBI
S = 4.3L V8 2BBL
T = 3.1L V6 MPI
T = 4.3L V6 Dsl
T = 2.4L I-4 SFI DOHC
U = 2.5L I-4 TBI
V = 4.3L V6 Dsl
W = 2.8L V6 2BBL
W = 2.8L V6 MPI
X = 2.8L V6 2BBL
Y = 5.0L V8 4BBL
Z = 2.8L V6 2BBL HO

DIGIT 9 CHECK DIGIT
= 0-9 or X

DIGIT 10 Model Year
1 = 2001
2 = 2002
3 = 2003
B = 1981
C = 1982
D = 1983
E = 1984
F = 1985
G = 1986
H = 1987
J = 1988
K = 1989
L = 1990
M = 1991
N = 1992
P = 1993
R = 1994
S = 1995
T = 1996
V = 1997
W = 1998
X = 1999
Y = 2000

DIGIT 11 Assembly Plant Location
1 = Oshawa #2, ON, Canada
1 = Wentzville, MO, USA
2 = Ste. Therese, PQ, Canada
4 = Orion, MI, USA
6 = Oklahoma City, OK, USA
A = Lakewood, GA, USA
B = Lansing, MI, USA
C = Lansing, MI, USA
D = Doraville, GA, USA
E = Linden, NJ, USA
G = Framingham, MA, USA
H = Flint, MI, USA
J = Janesville, WI, USA
K = Leeds, MO, USA
K = Linden, NJ, USA
M = Lansing, MI, USA
P = Pontiac, MI, USA
R = Arlington, TX, USA
S = Ramos Arizpe, Mexico
T = Tarrytown, NY, USA
U = Hamtramck, MI, USA
W = Willow Run, MI, USA
X = Fairfax, Ks, USA
Z = Fremont, CA, USA

ARM0300000000365

Fig. 1 VIN Identification (Part 2 of 2). Buick

DIGIT 1 Country Of Origin
1 = USA
W = Germany

DIGIT 2 Manufacturer
0 = Opel
G = General Motors

DIGIT 3 Make
6 = Cadillac

DIGIT 4 Restraint System
A = Manual Belts

DIGIT 4-5 Carline/Series
CB = Fleetwood
CB = DeVille Sixty Special
CD = DeVille
CG = Fleetwood Sixty Special
CS = Fleetwood Sixty Special
CT = DeVille Touring
DG = CTS
DM = CTS
DW = Fleetwood RWD
DW = Fleetwood Brougham RWD
DW = Brougham RWD
EC = Eldorado ETC Collector's Edition
EL = Eldorado ESC
EL = Eldorado
ET = Eldorado ETC
ET = Eldorado Touring
JG = Cimarron
KD = DeVille
KE = DeVille DHS
KE = DeVille D'Elegance
KF = DeVille DTS
KF = DeVille Concours
KS = Seville
KS = Seville SLS
KY = Seville STS
KY = Seville Touring
VR = Allante
VR = Allante Convertible w/Hardtop
VR = Catera
VS = Allante Convertible

DIGIT 5 Carline/Series
B = Fleetwood
B = Fleetwood, Brougham
D = DeVille
F = Fleetwood Limousine
G = Cimarron
L = Eldorado
M = DeVille RWD
S = Seville

DIGIT 6 Body Style
1 = 2D Coupe
3 = 2D Convertible
5 = 4D Sedan

DIGIT 6-7 Body Style
23 = 4D Sedan Limousine
33 = 4D Sedan Limousine
47 = 2D Coupe
57 = 2D Coupe
67 = 2D Convertible
69 = 4D Sedan

DIGIT 7 Restraint System
1 = Manual Belts
2 = Dual Front Airbags w/Manual Belts
3 = Driverside Airbag w/Manual Belts
4 = Automatic Belts
4 = Dual Front & Side Airbags w/Manual Belts
5 = Dual Front & Side Airbags w/Manual Belts
7 = Dual Front, Front & Rear Side Airbags & Manual Belts

DIGIT 8 Engine
1 = 2.0L I-4 EFI
3 = 4.5L V8 DFI
4 = 4.1L V6 4BBL
5 = 4.5L V8 DFI
5 = 4.5L V8 EFI
6 = 6.0L V8 4BBL
7 = 5.7L V8 TBI
7 = 5.7L V8 MPI
7 = 4.1L V8 SFI
8 = 4.1L V8 DFI
8 = 4.1L V8 TBI
8 = 4.5L V8 MPI
9 = 5.0L V8 4BBL
9 = 4.6L V8 MPI
9 = 6.0L V8 MPI
B = 4.9L V8 MPI
E = 5.0L V8 TBI
G = 1.8L I-4 2BBL
N = 3.2L V6 DOHC
N = 5.7L V8 Dsl
P = 5.7L V8 MPI
P = 2.0L I-4 EFI
R = 3.0L V6 MPI
T = 4.3L V6 Dsl
W = 2.8L V6 MPI
Y = 4.6L V8 MPI DOHC
Y = 5.0L V8 4BBL

DIGIT 9 CHECK DIGIT
= 0-9 or X

DIGIT 10 Model Year
1 = 2001
2 = 2002
3 = 2003
B = 1981
C = 1982
D = 1983
E = 1984
F = 1985
G = 1986
H = 1987
J = 1988
K = 1989
L = 1990
M = 1991
N = 1992
P = 1993
R = 1994
S = 1995
T = 1996
V = 1997
W = 1998
X = 1999
Y = 2000

DIGIT 11 Assembly Plant Location
0 = Lansing, MI, USA
4 = Orion, MI, USA
9 = Detroit, MI, USA
C = Southgate, CA, USA
E = Pontiac East, MI, USA
E = Linden, NJ, USA
J = Janesville, WI, USA
K = Leeds, MO, USA
R = Arlington, TX, USA
R = Russelsheim, Germany
U = Hamtramck, MI, USA

ARM0300000000366

Fig. 2 VIN Identification. Cadillac

DIGIT 1 Country Of Origin

1	= USA
2	= Canada
3	= Mexico
4	= USA
J	= Japan

DIGIT 2 Manufacturer

8	= Isuzu
C	= Cami
G	= General Motors
Y	= Nummi

DIGIT 3 Make

1	= Chevrolet

DIGIT 4 Restraint System

A	= Manual Belts

DIGIT 4-5 Carline/Series

AW	= Celebrity
BL	= Impala SS
BL	= Impala
BL	= Caprice Classic
BL	= Caprice
BN	= Impala SS
BN	= Caprice Classic LS
BN	= Caprice Classic
BU	= Caprice Brougham
FP	= Camaro
FS	= Camaro Berlinetta
GZ	= Monte Carlo
JC	= Cavalier RS
JC	= Cavalier Base
JC	= Cavalier VL
JC	= Cavalier
JD	= Cavalier CS
JE	= Cavalier Type 10 & Conv
JE	= Cavalier RS
JF	= Cavalier LS
JF	= Cavalier Z24
JF	= Cavalier LS Sedan
JF	= Cavalier RS
JH	= Cavalier LS Sport
JS	= Cavalier LS Coupe
LD	= Corsica
LT	= Corsica LT
LT	= Corsica
LV	= Beretta
LW	= Beretta Z26
LW	= Beretta GT
LZ	= Corsica LTZ
LZ	= Beretta GTZ
MR	= Metro
MR	= Sprint
MS	= Sprint ER
ND	= Malibu
NE	= Malibu LS
RF	= Spectrum
RF	= Spectrum Coupe
RG	= Spectrum Sedan
SK	= Nova
SK	= Prizm
TB	= Chevette CS
WF	= Impala
WH	= Impala LS
WL	= Lumina LS
WL	= Lumina
WN	= Lumina LTZ
WN	= Lumina LS
WN	= Lumina Euro
WP	= Lumina Z34
WW	= Monte Carlo LS
WX	= Monte Carlo SS

DIGIT 4-5 Carline/Series

WX	= Monte Carlo Z34
XX	= Citation II
YY	= Corvette
YZ	= Corvette ZR1
ZL	= Lumina LS

DIGIT 5 Car Line/Series

T	= Malibu

DIGIT 5* Carline/Series

B	= Chevette
B	= Chevette CS
C	= Cavalier
D	= Cavalier CS
D	= Cavalier
E	= Cavalier Type 10
H	= Citation Coupe
J	= Chevette
J	= Chevette Scooter
L	= Impala
N	= Caprice Classic
P	= Camaro Sport Coupe
S	= Camaro Berlinetta
W	= Malibu Classic
W	= Celebrity
W	= Malibu
X	= Citation
Y	= Corvette
Z	= Monte Carlo

DIGIT 6 Body Style

1	= 2D Coupe/Sedan
1	= 2D Coupe
2	= 2D Hatchback
2	= 2D Liftback
2	= 2D Hatchback/Liftback
3	= 2D Convertible
5	= 4D Sedan
6	= 4D Hatchback, Sedan
6	= 4D Hatchback
8	= 4D Station Wagon

DIGIT 6-7 Body Type

07	= 2D Coupe
08	= 2D Hatchback
11	= 2D Coupe
19	= 4D Sedan/Hatchback
27	= 2D Coupe
27	= 2D Coupe/Hatchback
35	= 4D 2-Seat Wagon
37	= 2D Coupe/Hatchback
47	= 2D Hatchback Sport
67	= 2D Convertible
68	= 4D Hatchback
68	= 4D Sedan/Hatchback
69	= 4D Sedan
69	= 4D Seadn/Hatchback
77	= 2D Hatchback
77	= 2D Coupe/Hatchback
87	= 2D Hatchback
87	= 2D Sedan/Hatchback

DIGIT 7 Restraint System

1	= Manual Belts
2	= Dual Front Airbags w/Manual Belts
3	= Driverside Airbag w/Manual Belts
4	= Dual Front & Side Airbags w/Manual Belts
4	= Automatic Belts
4	= Passive Automatic Belts
5	= Driverside Airbag w/Automatic Belts
5	= Dual Front & Driver's Side Airbags w/Manual Belts

ARM0300000000367

Fig. 3 VIN Identification (Part 1 of 3). Chevrolet

DIGIT 8 Engine

1	= 2.8L V6 2BBL
1	= 2.0L I-4 EFI
2	= 1.3L I-4 EFI SOHC
2	= 2.5L I-4 TBI
2	= 1.0L I-3 Turbo
2	= 2.5L I-4 EFI
3	= 3.8L V6 2BBL
4	= 2.2L I-4 MPI
4	= 1.6L I-4 2BBL
5	= 1.0L I-3 2V
5	= 1.6L I-4 MPI
5	= 2.5L I-4 2BBL
5	= 5.7L V8 SFI DOHC
6	= 5.7L V8 4BBL
6	= 1.0L I-3 EFI SOHC
7	= 1.5L I-4 2BBL
7	= 5.7L V8 EFI
7	= 5.7L V8 TBI
7	= 6.0L V8 CPI
8	= 1.8L I-4 SFI DOHC
8	= 5.7L V8 TPI
9	= 1.5L I-4 FI TBO
9	= 1.6L I-4 2BBL
9	= 1.3L I-4 EFI
9	= 3.8L V6 2BBL
A	= 2.3L I-4 MPI
A	= 3.8L V6 2BBL
C	= 1.6L I-4 2BBL
D	= 2.3L I-4 MFI
D	= 1.8L I-4 Dsl
E	= 5.0L V8 TBI
E	= 3.4L V6 SFI
F	= 2.5L I-4 2BBL
F	= 2.2L I-4 MPI DOHC
F	= 5.0L V8 MPI
G	= 2.2L I-4 TBI
G	= 5.7L V8 MPI
G	= 1.8L I-4 2BBL
G	= 5.0L V8 4BBL
H	= 5.0L V8 4BBL
J	= 4.4L V8 2BBL
J	= 5.7L V8 MFI
J	= 5.7L V8 SFI
J	= 5.7L V8 MPI
J	= 3.1L V6 SFI
K	= 1.5L I-4 2BBL
K	= 3.8L V6 2BBL
K	= 3.8L V6 SFI
L	= 2.8L V6 2BBL
L	= 5.7L V8 4BBL
M	= 1.0L I-3 2BBL
M	= 3.1L V6 SFI
N	= 5.7L V8 Dsl
N	= 5.7L V8 FI Dsl
P	= 5.7L V8 SFI
P	= 5.7L V8 MPI
P	= 2.0L I-4 EFI
R	= 2.5L I-4 TBI
S	= 5.7L V8 SFI HO
S	= 2.8L V6 EFI
S	= 5.0L V8 TBI
S	= 3.4L V6 MPI
T	= 4.3L V6 DSL
T	= 2.4L I-4 SFI DOHC
T	= 3.1L V6 MPI
T	= 4.3L V6 EFI
V	= 4.3L V6 Dsl
V	= 4.3L V6 FI Dsl
W	= 2.8L V6 MPI
W	= 3.1L V6 MPI
W	= 4.3L V8 SFI

DIGIT 8 Engine

X	= 3.4L V6 SFI DOHC
X	= 2.8L V6 2BBL
Y	= 5.0L V8 4BBL
Z	= 2.8L V6 2BBL HO
Z	= 4.3L V6 EFI

DIGIT 9 CHECK DIGIT

	= 0-9 or X

DIGIT 10 Model Year

1	= 2001
2	= 2002
3	= 2003
4	= 2004
B	= 1981
C	= 1982
D	= 1983
E	= 1984
F	= 1985
G	= 1986
H	= 1987
J	= 1988
K	= 1989
L	= 1990
M	= 1991
N	= 1992
P	= 1993
R	= 1994
S	= 1995
T	= 1996
V	= 1997
W	= 1998
X	= 1999
Y	= 2000

DIGIT 11 Assembly Plant Location

0	= Lansing, MI, USA
1	= Oshawa, ON, Canada
1	= Oshawa #2, ON, Canada
2	= Ste. Therese, PQ, Canada
3	= Kawasaki, Japan
5	= Bowling Green, KY, USA
6	= Oklahoma City, OK, USA
6	= Ingersoll, ON, Canada
7	= Fujisawa, Japan
7	= Lordstown, OH, USA
8	= Fujisawa, Japan
9	= Oshawa #1, ON, Canada
9	= Detroit, MI, USA
A	= Lakewood, GA, USA
B	= Lansing, MI, USA
B	= Baltimore, MD, USA
C	= South Gate, CA, USA
D	= Doraville, GA, USA
E	= Linden, NJ, USA
G	= Framingham, MA, USA
H	= Flint, MI, USA
J	= Janesville, WI, USA
K	= Leeds, MO, USA
K	= Kosai, Japan
L	= Van Nuys, CA, USA
M	= Lansing, MI, USA
M	= Toluca, Mexico
N	= Norwood, OH, USA
P	= Pontiac, MI, USA
R	= Arlington, TX, USA
S	= Ramos Arizpe, Mexico
T	= Tarrytown, NY, USA
W	= Willow Run, MI, USA
W	= Iwata, Japan
X	= Fairfax, KS, USA
Y	= Wilminton, DE, USA

ARM0300000000368

Fig. 3 VIN Identification (Part 2 of 3). Chevrolet

DIGIT 11 **Assembly Plant Location**
Y = Wilmington, DE, USA
Z = Fremont, CA, USA

ARM0300000000369

Fig. 3 VIN Identification (Part 3 of 3). Chevrolet

DIGIT 1 Country Of Origin
1 = USA
2 = Canada
3 = Mexico
4 = USA - MMMA
J = Japan

DIGIT 2 Manufacturer
A = Imperial
C = Chrysler
J = Chrysler

DIGIT 3 Vehicle Type
3 = Passenger Car
4 = Multipurpose Passenger Vehicle
8 = Multipurpose Passenger Vehicle w/Side Airbags
A = PT Cruiser w/Side Airbags

DIGIT 4 Restraint System
A = Dual Airbags w/Manual Belts
A = Active Front & Side Airbags
A = Dual Front Airbags w/Manual Belts
A = Driverside Airbag w/Motorized Passenger Belt
B = Manual Seat Belts
C = Automatic Seat Belts
E = Dual Front Airbags w/Manual Belts
E = Dual Airbags w/Manual Belts
H = Hybrid Airbags
H = Dual Front Airbags w/Manual Belts
H = Dual Airbags w/Manual Belts
X = Driverside Airbag w/Manual Belts
Y = Driverside Airbag w/Automatic Passenger Belt

DIGIT 4* GVWR
C = Automatic Seat Belts
C = Automatic Seat Belts
F = 4001-5000 Lbs
F = 4001-5000 Lbs

DIGIT 5 Carline
A = Lebaron 4D
A = Laser
C = New Yorker
C = LHS
C = Conquest
C = Lebaron 4D
C = Lebaron
D = LHS
D = Concorde
D = New Yorker
E = 300M
F = New Yorker
F = Fifth Avenue
G = Sebring Coupe
H = Lebaron GTS
J = Cirrus
J = Cordoba
J = Lebaron 2D
L = Sebring Convertible
L = Sebring
L = Concorde
M = Fifth Avenue
M = Lebaron
R = Newport
R = New Yorker
S = Cordoba
T = E Class
T = New Yorker
T = New Yorker Turbo
U = New Yorker
U = Lebaron 2D
U = Sebring
V = Imperial
V = Fifth Avenue

DIGIT 5 Carline
W = Prowler
Y = Fifth Avenue
Y = Imperial
Y = PT Cruiser

DIGIT 6 Series
3 = Medium
4 = High Line
4 = High
5 = Premium Line
5 = Premium
6 = Special
7 = Performance
7 = X Series

DIGIT 7 Body Style
1 = 2D Sedan
1 = 2D Coupe
2 = 2D Hardtop
2 = 2D Pillared Hardtop
2 = 2D Specialty Hardtop
3 = 2D Specialty Hardtop
4 = 2D Hatchback
5 = 2D Convertible
5 = 2D Convertible/Open Body
6 = 4D Sedan
7 = 4D Pillared Hardtop
8 = 4D Hatchback
9 = 4D Wagon

DIGIT 7* Body
8 = Hatchback
B = Hatchback

DIGIT 8 Engine
3 = 3.0L V6 TBI
3 = 3.0L V6 MPI
A = 2.2L I-4 Turbo
B = 2.2L I-4 2BBL
B = 2.4L I-4 MPI
C = 2.2L I-4 EFI Turbo
C = 2.2L I-4 2BBL
C = 2.0L I-4 SFI SOHC
C = 2.2L I-4
D = 2.6L I-4 2BBL
D = 2.2L I-4 TBI
D = 2.2L I-4 EFI
E = 2.2L I-4 Turbo
E = 3.7L I-6 1BBL
E = 2.2L I-4 FI Turbo
F = 3.5L V6 MPI
F = 3.7L I-6 1BBL
G = 2.6L I-4 2BBL
G = 2.6L I-4
G = 3.5L V6 EFI HO SOHC
G = 3.5L V6 MPI HO
G = 3.5L V6 EFI SOHC HO
G = 2.4L I-4 EFI DOHC
G = 3.5L V6 MPI SOHC HO
H = 3.7L I-6 1BBL
H = 2.5L V6 SFI SOHC
H = 3.0L V6 MPI SOHC
J = 2.5L I-4 FI Tbo
J = 3.2L V6 EFI SOHC
J = 5.2L V8 EFI
K = 2.5L I-4 TBI
K = 5.2L V8 2BBL
K = 3.5L V6 MPI
L = 5.2L V8 2BBL HD
L = 5.2L V8 EFI
L = 3.8L V6 MPI
L = 5.2L V8 2BBL
M = 5.2L V8 4BBL

ARM0300000000370

Fig. 4 VIN Identification (Part 1 of 2). Chrysler

DIGIT 8 Engine
M = 5.2L V8 2BBL
M = 3.5L V6 MPI SOHC
N = 2.6L I-4 T/C I/C
N = 5.2L V8 2BBL
N = 5.2L V8 4BBL
N = 5.2L V8 4BBL HD
N = 2.5L V6 SFI SOHC
P = 5.2L V8 2BBL
R = 2.7L V6 SFI DOHC
R = 3.3L V6 EFI
T = 2.7L V6 MPI FFV
T = 3.3L V6 MPI
U = 2.7L V6 SFI DOHC
U = 2.7L V6 MPI DOHC
U = 3.0L V6 MPI
V = 3.5L V6 EFI HO SOHC
V = 3.5L V6 EFI SOHC
X = 2.4L I-4 EFI DOHC
X = 2.4L I-4 SFI DOHC
Y = 2.0L I-4 SFI DOHC

DIGIT 9 CHECK DIGIT
= 0-9 or X

DIGIT 10 Model Year
1 = 2001
2 = 2002
3 = 2003
4 = 2004
B = 1981
C = 1982
D = 1983
E = 1984
F = 1985
G = 1986
H = 1987
J = 1988
K = 1989
L = 1990
M = 1991
N = 1992
P = 1993
R = 1994
S = 1995
T = 1996
V = 1997
W = 1998
X = 1999
Y = 2000

DIGIT 11 Assembly Plant Location
A = Lynch RD, USA
A = Auburn Hills, MI, USA
C = Jefferson, MI, USA
D = Belvidere, IL, USA
E = Normal, IL, USA
F = Newark, DE, USA
G = St. Louis #1, MO, USA
H = Bramalea, ON, Canada
N = Sterling Heights, MI, USA
R = Windsor, Canada
T = Toluca, Mexico
U = Mizushima, Japan
V = Conner Ave, Detroit, MI, USA
W = Kenosha #1, USA
X = St. Louis #2, MO, USA
Y = Kenosha #2, USA
Y = Nagoya 1, Japan
Z = Okazaki, Japan

ARM0300000000371

Fig. 4 VIN Identification (Part 2 of 2). Chrysler

DIGIT 1 Country Of Origin
1 = USA
2 = Canada
3 = Mexico
4 = USA - MMMA
J = Japan

DIGIT 2 Manufacturer
B = Dodge

DIGIT 3 Vehicle Type
3 = Passenger Car
4 = Multi-Purpose Passenger Vehicle

DIGIT 4 Restraint
A = Active Front & Side Airbags
A = Dual Front Airbags w/Manual Belts
A = Dual Airbags w/Manual Belts
A = Driverside Airbag w/Motorized Passenger Belt
B = Automatic Belts
B = Manual Seat Belts
C = Automatic Seat Belts
C = Automatic Seat Belt
E = Driverside Airbag
E = Dual Front Airbags w/Manual Belts
H = Dual Front Airbags w/Manual Belts
H = Dual Airbags, Passenger Hybrid w/Manual Belts
X = Driverside Airbag w/Manual Seat Belts
X = Driverside Airbag w/Manual Passenger Belt
Y = Driverside Airbag w/Automatic Passenger Belt

DIGIT 5 Carline
A = Colt
A = Daytona
A = Spirit
B = Monaco
C = Conquest
C = Dynasty
D = Stealth
D = Intrepid
D = Challenger
D = Aries
E = 600
E = Stealth
E = Colt
G = Stratus Coupe
G = Diplomat
G = Colt Wagon
G = Daytona
H = Colt Wagon AWD
H = Lancer
J = Mirada
J = Stratus
J = Stratus Sedan
K = Aries
L = Stratus Sedan
L = Omni
L = 024 Omni
M = Stealth
M = Stealth FWD
M = Diplomat
N = Stealth Turbo
N = Stealth AWD
P = Shadow
R = St. Regis
R = Viper
S = Neon
S = Shadow
U = Colt
U = Dynasty
U = Avenger
V = 600 2D Coupe/Convertible
V = Colt Wagon
V = 400

DIGIT 5 Carline
W = Colt Wagon AWD
W = Daytona
X = Lancer
X = Mirada
Z = Omni

DIGIT 6 Series
1 = Economy
2 = Low
2 = Base
3 = High
3 = Medium
4 = Base
4 = ES
4 = High
5 = Pacifica
5 = Premium
6 = Turbo
6 = Shelby Z
6 = Special
6 = ES Turbo
6 = IROC R/T
6 = Turbo Z
7 = R/T
7 = IROC
7 = Shelby
7 = Performance
8 = R/T Turbo

DIGIT 7 Body Style
1 = 2D Coupe
2 = 2D Pillared Hardtop
4 = 2D Hatchback
5 = 2D Convertible / Open Body
5 = 2D Convertible
5 = 2D Convertible/Open Body
6 = 4D Sedan
7 = 4D Pillared Hardtop
8 = 4D Hatchback
9 = 4D Wagon
9 = 2D Specialty Coupe

DIGIT 7* Body Type
1 = 4D Wagon AWD
1 = 2D Sedan
1 = 4D Wagon
4 = 2D Hatchback
6 = 4D Sedan
8 = 4D Wagon
8 = 4D Hatchback
9 = 4D Wagon

DIGIT 8 Engine
2 = 1.4L I-4 2BBL
3 = 3.0L V6 MPI
3 = 1.6L I-4 2BBL
4 = 5.2L V8 2BBL
4 = 5.2L V8 EFI
7 = 2.6L I-4
A = 2.2L I-4 FI Turbo
A = 1.6L I-4 2BBL
A = 2.2L I-4 MPI Turbo
A = 1.7L I-4 2BBL
A = 1.5L I-4 MPI
A = 1.4L I-4 2BBL
A = 2.2L I-4 Turbo
B = 1.8L I-4 MPI
B = 1.6L I-4 2BBL
B = 1.7L I-4 2BBL
B = 3.0L V6 MPI
C = 2.2L I-4 2BBL
C = 2.2L I-4
C = 2.2L I-4 EFI Turbo

ARM0300000000372

Fig. 5 VIN Identification (Part 1 of 2). Dodge

DIGIT 8	Engine
C	= 3.0L V6 MPI Turbo
C	= 2.0L I-4 SFI SOHC
C	= 1.8L I-4 MPI
D	= 2.2L I-4 FI Turbo
D	= 2.2L I-4 Turbo
D	= 2.0L I-4 MPI
D	= 2.6L I-4
D	= 2.2L I-4 EFI
E	= 2.2L I-4 Turbo
E	= 3.7L I-6
E	= 8.0L V10 SFI
F	= 3.7L I-6
F	= 2.0L I-4 SFI SOHC HP
F	= 1.6L I-4 Turbo
F	= 2.2L I-4 2BBL HO
F	= 2.0L I-4 SFI SOHC
F	= 3.7L I-6 HD
F	= 3.5L V6 MPI
G	= 2.6L I-4
G	= 3.5L V6 EFI SOHC HO
H	= 2.5L I-4 EFI
H	= 3.7L I-6
H	= 3.0L V6 MPI SOHC
H	= 2.5L V6 SFI SOHC
H	= 2.6L I-4 Tbo
H	= 2.5L V6 SFI
J	= 3.0L V6 MPI DOHC
J	= 3.2L V6 SFI SOHC
J	= 2.5L I-4 FI Turbo
J	= 2.5L I-4 MPI Turbo
K	= 5.2L V8 2BBL
K	= 2.5L I-4 TBI
K	= 1.5L I-4
K	= 3.0L V6 MPI Tbo DOHC
M	= 5.2L V8
M	= 3.5L V6 MPI
N	= 5.2L V8 HD
N	= 5.2L V8
N	= 2.5L V6 SFI SOHC
P	= 5.2L V8
P	= 5.2L V8 2BBL
R	= 2.7L V6 MPI FFV
R	= 2.7L V6 SFI DOHC
R	= 3.3L V6 MPI
R	= 5.2L V8 4BBL
S	= 3.0L V6 MPI
T	= 2.7L V6 MPI FFV
T	= 1.8L I-4 MPI
T	= 3.3L V6 MPI
U	= 3.0L V6 MPI
U	= 3.3L V6 SFI Flex
U	= 2.7L V6 SFI DOHC
V	= 3.5L V6 MPI SOHC
V	= 2.5L I-4 TBI Flex Fuel
V	= 3.5L V6 EFI SOHC HO
V	= 2.0L I-4 MPI
X	= 1.5L I-4 MPI
X	= 2.4L I-4 SFI DOHC HOT
X	= 2.4L I-4 SFI DOHC
Y	= 2.0L I-4 SFI DOHC
Z	= 8.3L V10 MPI
Z	= 1.5L I-4 MPI
Z	= 1.6L I-4 Turbo

DIGIT 9	CHECK DIGIT
	= 0-9 or X

DIGIT 10	Model Year
1	= 2001
2	= 2002
3	= 2003
4	= 2004

DIGIT 10	Model Year
B	= 1981
C	= 1982
D	= 1983
E	= 1984
F	= 1985
G	= 1986
H	= 1987
J	= 1988
K	= 1989
L	= 1990
M	= 1991
N	= 1992
P	= 1993
R	= 1994
S	= 1995
T	= 1996
V	= 1997
W	= 1998
X	= 1999
Y	= 2000

DIGIT 11	Assembly Plant Location
A	= Mizushima 2, Japan
B	= St. Louis South, MO, USA
C	= Jefferson North Assembly, Detroit, MI, USA
D	= Belvidere, IL, USA
E	= Normal, IL, USA
F	= Newark, NJ, USA
G	= St. Louis #1, MO, USA
H	= Bramalea, ON, Canada
J	= Nagoya 3, Japan
N	= Sterling Heights, MI, USA
P	= Nagoya 2, Japan
R	= Windsor, On, Canada
T	= Toluca, Mexico
U	= Mizushima 1, Japan
U	= Mizushima, Japan
V	= Detroit, MI, USA
W	= Kenosha #1, WI, USA
X	= St. Louis #2, MO, USA
Y	= Kenosha #2, WI, USA
Y	= Nagoya 1, Japan
Z	= Okazaki, Japan

ARM0300000000373

Fig. 5 VIN Identification (Part 2 of 2). Dodge

DIGIT 1-3	World Manufacturer Identifier
1FA	= Ford Motor Company, USA
1ZV	= AutoAlliance International
2FA	= Ford Motor Company of Canada
2FD	= Ford Motor Company of Canada
3FA	= Ford Motor Company of Mexico
3FA	= Ford Motor Company, USA
KNJ	= Kia Motors Inc., Korea

DIGIT 4	Restraint System
A	= Driverside Airbag w/Driver & Rear Manual Belts & Front Pas
B	= Manual Belts
C	= Driverside Airbag w/Manual Belts
F	= 2nd Generation Dual Airbags w/Manual Belts
H	= Dual Front & Front Side Airbags w/Manual Belts
H	= 2nd Generation Front & Side Airbags w/Manual Belts
K	= 2nd Generation Dual Airbags w/Manual Belts
L	= Dual Front Airbags w/Manual Belts
P	= Front Automatic Belts & Rear Manual Belts
R	= Driverside Airbag w/Front Automatic Belts & Rear Manual E
S	= Dual Airbags w/Front Automatic Belts & Rear Manual Belts

DIGIT 5	Designation
P	= Passenger Car - Ford Make
T	= Passenger Car

DIGIT 6-7	Carline/Series/Body Style
01	= EXP 2D Hatchback
04	= Escort Base 2D Hatchback
04	= Escort L 2D Hatchback
05	= Escort GL 2D Hatchback
05	= Aspire 2D Hatchback
05	= Festiva L 2D Hatchback
05	= Escort 2D Hatchback
06	= Aspire 4D Hatchback
06	= Festiva GL 2D Hatchback
06	= Festiva L Plus 2D Hatchback
06	= Festiva L 2D Hatchback
06	= Escort GLX 4D Hatchback
06	= Escort 4D Hatchback
07	= Aspire SE 2D Hatchback
07	= Festiva LX 2D Hatchback
07	= Escort GT 2D Hatchback
08	= Escort 4D Wagon
09	= Escort L 4D Wagon
10	= Escort Base 2D Hatchback
10	= Escort Pony 2D Hatchback
10	= Escort GL 4D Wagon
10	= Mustang 2D Coupe
10	= Mustang GL 2D Coupe
10	= Mustang L 2D Coupe
10	= Escort LX 4D Sedan
10	= Escort Base LX 4D Sedan
10	= Escort Base 4D Sedan
11	= Escort GLX 4D Wagon
11	= Escort LX 4D Wagon
11	= Escort ZX2 2D Coupe
11	= Escort LX 2D Hatchback
12	= Mustang GLX 2D Coupe
12	= Mustang Ghia 2D Coupe
12	= Escort GT 2D Hatchback
13	= Mustang GLX 2D Hatchback
13	= Escort LX 4D Sedan
13	= Escort Base 4D Hatchback
13	= Escort 4D Sedan
13	= Escort L 4D Hatchback
13	= Mustang Ghia 2D Hatchback
13	= Escort SE 4D Sedan
14	= Escort GL 4D Hatchback
14	= Escort LX 4D Hatchback
15	= Escort LX 4D Hatchback
15	= Escort LX 4D Wagon
15	= Escort SE 4D Wagon
15	= Mustang 2D Hatchback
15	= Escort GLX 4D Hatchback
16	= Escort LX-E 4D Sedan
16	= Mustang GLX 2D Hatchback
16	= Mustang GL 2D Hatchback
17	= Escort Exp Luxury 2D Coupe
18	= Escort Exp Sport 2D Coupe
18	= Tempo L 2D Coupe
19	= Tempo GL 2D Coupe
20	= Probe GL 2D Hatchback
20	= Fairmont Futura 2D Sedan
20	= Escort Pony 2D Hatchback
20	= Probe SE 2D Hatchback
20	= Fairmont 2D Coupe
20	= Tempo GLX 2D Coupe
20	= Probe Base 2D Hatchback
21	= Escort GL 2D Hatchback
21	= Tempo L 4D Sedan
21	= Escort LX 2D Hatchback
21	= Fairmont 4D Sedan
21	= Probe LX 2D Hatchback
21	= Fairmont Futura 4D Sedan
22	= Tempo GL 4D Sedan
22	= Probe GT 2D Hatchback
22	= Fairmont Futura 2D Coupe
23	= Tempo LX 4D Sedan
23	= Tempo GLX 4D Sedan
23	= Fairmont 4D Wagon
23	= Escort GT 2D Hatchback
25	= Escort GL 4D Hatchback
25	= Escort LX 4D Hatchback
26	= Mustang 2D Coupe
26	= Granada 2D Sedan
26	= Mustang L 2D Coupe
26	= Mustang LX 2D Coupe
27	= Mustang GT 2D Convertible
27	= Mustang 2D Convertible
27	= Granada 4D Sedan
27	= Mustang LX 2D Convertible
28	= Escort LX 4D Wagon
28	= Escort GL 4D Wagon
28	= Mustang SVO 2D Hatchback
28	= Mustang L 2D Hatchback
28	= Mustang LX 2D Hatchback
28	= Mustang 2D Hatchback
28	= Mustang GT 2D Hatchback
28	= Granada 4D Wagon
29	= Taurus 4D Sedan
30	= Focus SVT 4D Hatchback
30	= Taurus 4D Wagon
30	= Tempo L 2D Coupe
31	= Focus ZX3 2D Hatchback
31	= Escort L 2D Hatchback
31	= Tempo GL 2D Coupe
31	= LTD S 4D Sedan
31	= Escort Pony 2D Hatchback
31	= Escort Base 2D Hatchback
32	= Escort GL 2D Hatchback
32	= LTD 2D Sedan
32	= Escort LX 2D Hatchback
32	= Tempo LX 2D Coupe
33	= Tempo GLS 2D Coupe
33	= LTD 4D Sedan
33	= Focus LX 4D Sedan
33	= Tempo Sport GL 2D Coupe
33	= Escort GT 2D Hatchback
34	= Escort L 4D Wagon
34	= Tempo AWD 2D Coupe
34	= LTD Crown Victoria 2D Sedan
34	= Focus SE 4D Sedan
35	= Focus ZTW 4D Wagon

ARM0300000000374

Fig. 6 VIN Identification (Part 1 of 3). Ford

DIGIT 6-7	Carline/Series/Body Style
35	= Escort GL 4D Wagon
35	= Fairmont Futura 2D Sedan
35	= Escort LX 4D Wagon
35	= LTD Crown Victoria 4D Sedan
35	= Tempo L 4D Sedan
36	= Focus SE 4D Wagon
36	= Tempo GL 4D Sedan
36	= Escort L 4D Wagon
36	= Escort Base 4D Hatchback
36	= Fairmont Futura 4D Sedan
36	= Focus ZTW 4D Wagon
36	= Escort L 4D Hatchback
37	= Escort LX 4D Hatchback
37	= Escort GL 4D Hatchback
37	= Fairmont Futura 2D Coupe
37	= LTD S 4D Wagon
37	= Tempo LX 4D Sedan
37	= LTD S 4D Sedan
37	= Focus ZX5 4D Hatchback
38	= Focus ZTS 4D Sedan
38	= Tempo GLS 4D Sedan
38	= LTD 4D Wagon
38	= Tempo Sport GL 4D Sedan
39	= Tempo AWD 4D Sedan
39	= Focus SVT 2D Hatchback
39	= LTD 4D Squire Wagon
39	= LTD 4D Sedan
40	= LTD 4D Wagon
40	= Mustang Base 2D Coupe
40	= Mustang LX 2D Coupe
41	= Mustang LX 2D Hatchback
42	= Mustang Cobra 2D Coupe
42	= Mustang GTS 2D Coupe
42	= Mustang GT 2D Coupe
42	= Mustang GT 2D Hatchback
42	= LTD Crown Victoria 2D Sedan
42	= Thunderbird 2D Coupe
42	= Mustang Cobra 2D Hatchback
43	= LTD Crown Victoria 4D Sedan
44	= Mustang Base 2D Convertible
44	= Mustang LX Limited Edition 2D Convertible
44	= Mustang LX 2D Convertible
44	= LTD Crown Victoria 4D Wagon
44	= LTD Crown Victoria 4D Squire Wagon
45	= Mustang GT 2D Convertible
45	= Mustang Cobra 2D Convertible
46	= Mustang Cobra 2D Convertible
46	= Thunderbird 2D Coupe
47	= Mustang Cobra 2D Coupe
48	= Mustang Cobra 2D Coupe
49	= Mustang Cobra 2D Convertible
50	= Taurus L 4D Sedan
51	= Taurus G 4D Sedan
51	= Taurus MT5 4D Sedan
52	= Taurus LX 4D Sedan
52	= Taurus SE 4D Sedan
52	= Taurus GL 4D Sedan
53	= Taurus SE 4D Sedan - 2V
53	= Taurus SE Comfort 4D Sedan
53	= Taurus SE 4D Sedan
53	= Taurus LX 4D Sedan
54	= Taurus SHO 4D Sedan
54	= Taurus SE 4D Sedan - 4V
55	= Taurus SES 4D Sedan
55	= Taurus L 4D Wagon
56	= Taurus SEL 4D Sedan
56	= Taurus MT5 Wagon
57	= Taurus GL 4D Wagon
57	= Taurus SE 4D Wagon
58	= Taurus LX 4D Wagon
58	= Taurus SE Comfort 4D Wagon

DIGIT 6-7	Carline/Series/Body Style
58	= Taurus SE 4D Wagon
59	= Taurus SEL 4D Wagon
60	= Thunderbird 2D Coupe
60	= Thunderbird Sport 2D Coupe
60	= Thunderbird 2D Convertible
60	= Thunderbird 2D Sport Coupe
60	= Thunderbird Base 2D Coupe
61	= Thunderbird Sport 2D Coupe
62	= Thunderbird 2D Convertible
62	= Thunderbird LX 2D Coupe
63	= Thunderbird Pacific Coast Roadster
64	= Thunderbird 2D Convertible Neiman Marcus
64	= Thunderbird Super Coupe
64	= Thunderbird 2D Super Coupe
64	= Thunderbird Turbo 2D Coupe
65	= Contour GL 4D Sedan - Early Production
65	= Contour Base 4D Sedan - Early Production
65	= Contour GL 4D Sedan
65	= Contour LX 4D Sedan
65	= Contour Base 4D Sedan
66	= Contour Sport 4D Sedan
66	= Contour SE 4D Sedan
66	= Contour LX 4D Sedan - Early Production
66	= Contour LX 4D Sedan
67	= Contour SE V6 4D Sedan - Early Production
67	= Contour SE 4D Sedan
68	= Contour SVT 4D Sedan
70	= Crown Victoria 4D Sedan LWB - Fleet
70	= LTD Crown Victoria 2D Coupe
71	= Crown Victoria 4D Sedan w/Police Interceptor Package
71	= LTD Crown Victoria LX 2D Coupe
72	= LTD Crown Victoria S 4D Sedan
72	= Crown Victoria 4D Sedan - Fleet
72	= LTD Crown Victoria Base 4D Sedan
73	= LTD Crown Victoria Base 4D Sedan
73	= Crown Victoria 4D Sedan
74	= Crown Victoria LX 4D Sedan
74	= LTD Crown Victoria LX 4D Sedan
75	= Crown Victoria Touring 4D Sedan
76	= LTD Crown Victoria Base 4D Wagon
77	= LTD Crown Victoria LX 4D Wagon
78	= LTD Crown Victoria Country Squire 4D Wagon
79	= LTD Crown Victoria Country Squire LX 4D Wagon
90	= Escort Pony 2D Hatchback
91	= Escort LX 2D Hatchback
93	= Escort GT 2D Hatchback
95	= Escort LX 4D Hatchback
98	= Escort LX 4D Wagon

DIGIT 8	Engine
1	= 3.0L V6 SFI FFV - Methanol
2	= 3.0L V6 EFI FFV
2	= 1.6L I-4 2BBL
2	= 3.0L V6 SFI FFV - Ethanol
3	= 3.8L V6 CFI
3	= 2.0L I-4 EFI DOHC
3	= 3.8L V6 2BBL
3	= 2.0L I-4 SFI DOHC
4	= 1.6L I-4 2BBL HO
4	= 3.8L V6 EFI
5	= 2.0L I-4 SFI HO
5	= 1.6L I-4 EFI
6	= 4.6L V8 EFI SOHC
6	= 2.3L I-4 1BBL OHC LPG
8	= 1.6L I-4 EFI Tbo
8	= 1.6L I-4 FI Turbo
8	= 1.8L I-4 EFI DOHC
9	= 1.9L I-4 CFI
9	= 4.6L V8 EFI SOHC CNG
9	= 1.9L I-4 2BBL
A	= 3.9L V8 EFI DOHC
A	= 2.0L I-4 EFI DOHC

ARM0300000000375

Fig. 6 VIN Identification (Part 2 of 3). Ford

DIGIT 8	Engine
A	= 2.3L I-4 1BBL
A	= 2.3L I-4 2BBL
A	= 2.3L I-4 1BBL OHC
A	= 2.3L I-4 EFI SOHC
B	= 3.3L V6 1BBL
B	= 2.5L V6 EFI DOHC
B	= 3.3L I-6 1BBL
C	= 3.8L V6 EFI S/C
C	= 2.2L I-4 EFI
D	= 4.2L V8 2BBL
D	= 5.0L V8 EFI SHP
D	= 2.5L I-4 CFI HSC
E	= 5.0L V8 EFI HO
F	= 5.0L V8 2BBL
F	= 5.0L V8 EFI
F	= 5.0L V8 4BBL
G	= 2.5L V6 EFI DOHC HO
G	= 5.8L V8 2BBL HO
H	= 2.0L I-4 FI Dsl
H	= 1.3L I-4 EFI SOHC
H	= 1.3L I-4 EFI
J	= 1.9L I-4 EFI
J	= 1.9L I-4 EFI HO
K	= 1.3L I-4 2BBL
L	= 2.5L V6 EFI DOHC
L	= 2.2L I-4 EFI T/C I/C
M	= 2.3L I-4 EFI
M	= 5.0L V8 EFI HO
N	= 2.5L I-4 EFI
N	= 3.4L V8 EFI DOHC SHO
P	= 3.2L V6 EFI DOHC SHO
P	= 2.0L I-4 SPI
R	= 2.3L I-4 1BBL HSC
R	= 4.6L V8 EFI DOHC Ram Air
R	= 3.8L V6 EFI S/C
S	= 2.3L I-4 EFI HSO
S	= 2.3L I-4 CFI HSC+
S	= 3.0L V6 EFI DOHC
T	= 2.3L I-4 EFI T/C I/C
T	= 5.0L V8 EFI HO
U	= 3.0L V6 EFI
V	= 4.6L V8 EFI DOHC
W	= 4.6L V8 EFI SOHC
W	= 2.3L I-4 EFI SOHC T/C
W	= 2.3L I-4 EFI SOHC Turbo
X	= 4.6L V8 EFI SOHC
X	= 2.3L I-4 CFI HSC
X	= 2.3L I-4 EFI HSC
X	= 3.3L I-6 1BBL
Y	= 4.6L V8 EFI DOHC SC
Y	= 3.0L V6 EFI DOHC SHO
Z	= 2.0L I-4 DOHC PZEV
Z	= 2.0L I-4 EFI DOHC GFP

DIGIT 9	CHECK DIGIT
	= 0-9 or X

DIGIT 10	Model Year
1	= 2001
2	= 2002
3	= 2003
4	= 2004
B	= 1981
C	= 1982
D	= 1983
E	= 1984
F	= 1985
G	= 1986
H	= 1987
J	= 1988
K	= 1989
L	= 1990

DIGIT 10	Model Year
M	= 1991
N	= 1992
P	= 1993
R	= 1994
S	= 1995
T	= 1996
V	= 1997
W	= 1998
X	= 1999
Y	= 2000

DIGIT 11	Assembly Plant Location
5	= AAI - Flat Rock, MI, USA
6	= Mazda-Kia, Korea
A	= Atlanta, GA, USA
B	= Oakville, ON, Canada
F	= Dearborn, MI, USA
G	= Chicago, IL, USA
H	= Lorain, OH, USA
K	= Kansas City, MO, USA
M	= Cuautitlan, Mexico
R	= Hermosillo, Mexico
R	= San Jose, CA, USA
T	= Edison, NJ, USA
U	= Louisville, KY, USA
W	= Wayne, MI, USA
X	= St. Thomas, ON, Canada
Y	= Wixom, MI, USA
Z	= St. Louis, MO, USA

ARM0300000000376

Fig. 6 VIN Identification (Part 3 of 3). Ford

DIGIT 1-3 World Manufacturer Identifier

1L1 = Ford Motor Company, USA - Lincoln, Limousine
1LJ = Ford Motor Company, USA - Lincoln, Hearse
1LN = Ford Motor Company, USA - Lincoln
1MR = Ford Motor Company, USA - Continental

DIGIT 4 Restraint System

B = Manual Belts
C = Driverside Airbag w/Manual Belts
F = 2nd Generation Dual Front Airbags w/Manual Belts
H = 2nd Generation Front & Side Airbags w/Manual Belts
L = Dual Front Airbags w/Manual Belts

DIGIT 5 Designation

L = Passenger Car - Lincoln Make
M = Passenger Car - Lincoln Make
P = Passenger Car

DIGIT 6-7 Carline/Body Style

81 = Town Car Executive 4D Sedan
81 = Town Car 4D Sedan
82 = Town Car Signature 4D Sedan
83 = Town Car Cartier 4D Sedan
83 = Town Car Ultimate 4D Sedan
84 = Town Car Executive L 4D Sedan
84 = Town Car Signature Special Edition 4D Sedan
85 = Town Car Ultimate L 4D Sedan
85 = Town Car Cartier L 4D Sedan
86 = LS V6
87 = LS V8
91 = Mark VIII Base 2D Coupe
91 = Mark VII Base 2D Coupe
92 = Mark VII Bill Blass Designer 2D Coupe
92 = Mark VIII LSC 2D Coupe
93 = Mark VII LSC 2D Coupe
93 = Town Car 2D Sedan
94 = Town Car 4D Sedan
95 = Mark VI 2D Coupe
96 = Town Car 4D Sedan
96 = Mark VI 4D Sedan
97 = Continental 4D Sedan
98 = Continental Givenchy Designer 4D Sedan
98 = Mark VII 2D Coupe
98 = Mark VI 2D Coupe
98 = Continental Signature 4D Sedan
99 = Mark VI 4D Sedan

DIGIT 8 Engine

3 = 3.8L V6 EFI
4 = 3.8L V6 EFI
A = 3.9L V8 EFI DOHC
E = 5.0L V8 EFI HO
F = 5.0L V8 EFI
L = 2.4L I-6 FI TDsl
M = 5.0L V8 SFI HO
S = 3.0L V6 EFI DOHC
V = 4.6L V8 EFI DOHC
W = 4.6L V8 EFI SOHC

DIGIT 9 CHECK DIGIT

= 0-9 or X

DIGIT 10 Model Year

1 = 2001
2 = 2002
3 = 2003
4 = 2004
B = 1981
C = 1982
D = 1983
E = 1984
F = 1985
G = 1986
H = 1987

DIGIT 10 Model Year

J = 1988
K = 1989
L = 1990
M = 1991
N = 1992
P = 1993
R = 1994
S = 1995
T = 1996
V = 1997
W = 1998
X = 1999
Y = 2000

DIGIT 11 Assembly Plant Location

Y = Wixom, MI, USA

ARM0300000000377

Fig. 7 VIN Identification. Lincoln

DIGIT 1-3 World Manufacturer Identifier

1ME = Ford Motor Company, USA - Mercury
1ZW = Auto Alliance International, Inc
2ME = Ford Motor Company of Canada - Mercury
3MA = Ford Motor Company of Mexico - Mercury
3ME = Ford Motor Company of Mexico - Mercury
6MP = Ford Motor Company of Australia, Ltd.
WF1 = Merkur

DIGIT 4 Restraint System

A = Driverside Airbag w/Manual Driver & Rear Belts & Automati
B = Manual Belts
C = Driverside Airbag w/Manual Belts
F = 2nd Generation Dual Front Airbags w/Manual Belts
H = 2nd Generation Dual Front & Side Airbags w/Manual Belts
H = Dual Front & Front Side Airbags w/Manual Belts
L = Dual Front Airbags w/Manual Belts
P = Automatic Front Belts & Manual Rear Belts
R = Driverside Airbag w/Automatic Front Belts & Manual Rear E
S = Dual Front Airbags w/Automatic Front Belts and Manual Re

DIGIT 5 Designation

M = Passenger Car - Mercury Make
P = Passenger Car
P = Ford Make
T = Ford Import

DIGIT 6-7 Carline/Body Style

01 = Capri Base 2D Convertible
03 = Capri XR2 2D Convertible
10 = Tracer Base 4D Sedan
10 = Tracer GS 4D Sedan
11 = Tracer Base 2D Hatchback
12 = Tracer Base 4D Hatchback
13 = Tracer LS 4D Sedan
13 = Tracer Base 4D Wagon
14 = Tracer LTS 4D Sedan
15 = Tracer LS 4D Wagon
15 = Tracer Base 4D Wagon
20 = Lynx L 2D Hatchback
21 = Lynx GS 2D Hatchback
23 = Lynx XR3 2D Hatchback
25 = Lynx GS 4D Hatchback
28 = Lynx GS 4D Wagon
31 = Topaz GS 2D Coupe
33 = Topaz GS Sport 2D Coupe
33 = Topaz XR5 2D Coupe
36 = Topaz GS 4D Sedan
37 = Topaz LS 4D Sedan
38 = Topaz GS Sport 4D Sedan
38 = Topaz LTS 4D Sedan
50 = Sable LS 4D Sedan
50 = Sable GS 4D Sedan
51 = LN7 2D Hatchback
51 = Lynx L 2D Hatchback
51 = Lynx Base 2D Hatchback
51 = Sable G 4D Sedan
52 = Lynx GS 2D Hatchback
53 = Sable LS 4D Sedan
53 = Lynx XR3 2D Hatchback
53 = Sable LS Premium 4D Sedan
54 = Lynx L 2D Hatchback
54 = Lynx Base 2D Hatchback
55 = Lynx GS 2D Hatchback
55 = Sable GS 4D Wagon
55 = Sable LS Premium 4D Sedan
55 = Sable LS 4D Wagon
57 = Lynx RS 2D Hatchback
58 = Lynx LS 2D Hatchback
58 = Sable LS 4D Wagon
58 = Sable GS 4D Wagon
58 = Lynx L 4D Wagon
58 = Sable LS Premium 4D Wagon

DIGIT 6-7 Carline/Body Style

59 = Sable LS Premium 4D Wagon
59 = Lynx GS 4D Wagon
60 = Cougar LS 2D Coupe
60 = Cougar I-4 2D Coupe
60 = Lynx L 4D Wagon
61 = Cougar V6 2D Coupe
61 = Lynx GS 4D Wagon
61 = LN7 2D Hatchback
62 = Cougar S 2D Coupe
62 = Cougar V6 2D Coupe
62 = Cougar XR-7 2D Coupe
63 = Lynx 2D Hatchback
63 = Lynx L 4D Hatchback
63 = Lynx LS 4D Wagon
64 = Lynx GS 4D Hatchback
64 = Lynx 4D Hatchback
65 = Lynx 4D Wagon
65 = Lynx 4D Liftgate
65 = Lynx L 4D Hatchback
65 = Mystique Base 4D Sedan
65 = Mystique GS 4D Sedan
65 = Lynx Base 4D Hatchback
66 = Mystique LS 4D Sedan
66 = Lynx GS 4D Hatchback
67 = Capri 2D Hatchback
68 = Lynx LTS 4D Hatchback
68 = Capri GS 2D Hatchback
70 = Zephyr 2D Sedan
71 = Zephyr 4D Sedan
72 = Grand Marquis LS 2D Sedan
72 = Zephyr Z-7 2D Sedan
72 = Topaz GS 2D Coupe
73 = Zephyr 4D Wagon
73 = Topaz LS 2D Coupe
74 = Grand Marquis GS 4D Sedan
75 = Grand Marquis LS 4D Sedan
75 = Topaz GS 4D Sedan
75 = Grand Marquis LSE 4D Sedan
75 = Grand Marquis Marauder 4D Sedan
76 = Topaz LS 4D Sedan
76 = Cougar 2D Coupe
77 = Cougar 4D Sedan
78 = Cougar GS 4D Wagon
78 = Grand Marquis Colony Park GS 4D Wagon
79 = Grand Marquis Colony Park LS 4D Wagon
79 = Capri 2D Hatchback
81 = Marquis 4D Sedan
82 = Marquis Brougham 2D Sedan
83 = Marquis Brougham 4D Sedan
84 = Grand Marquis 2D Sedan
85 = Grand Marquis 4D Sedan
86 = Zephyr 4D Sedan
87 = Zephyr Z-7 2D Sedan
87 = Sable 4D Sedan
87 = Zephyr Z 2D Coupe
87 = Marquis 4D Wagon
88 = Sable 4D Wagon
88 = Marquis Colony Park 4D Wagon
89 = Marquis 4D Sedan
90 = Marquis 4D Wagon
90 = Cougar XR-7 2D Coupe
92 = Cougar 2D Coupe
93 = Grand Marquis 2D Sedan
94 = Grand Marquis Colony Park 4D Wagon
95 = Grand Marquis 4D Sedan

DIGIT 8 Engine

2 = 3.0L V6 EFI FFV
2 = 1.6L I-4 2BBL
2 = 3.0L V6 EFI FFV Ethanol
3 = 3.8L V6 EFI
3 = 2.0L I-4 EFI DOHC

ARM0300000000378

Fig. 8 VIN Identification (Part 1 of 2). Mercury

DIGIT 8 Engine

3 = 3.8L V6 2BBL
4 = 1.6L I-4 2BBL HO
4 = 3.8L V6 EFI
5 = 1.6L I-4 EFI
6 = 2.3L I-4 1BBL LPG
6 = 1.6L I-4 EFI Turbo
6 = 4.6L V8 EFI SOHC
8 = 1.8L I-4 EFI DOHC
9 = 1.9L I-4 2BBL
9 = 1.9L I-4 EFI
A = 2.3L I-4 1BBL SOHC
A = 2.3L I-4 2BBL
B = 3.3L I-6 1BBL
D = 4.2L V8 2BBL
D = 2.5L I-4 EFI HSC
D = 4.2L V8 1BBL
F = 5.0L V8 4BBL HO
F = 5.0L V8 2BBL
F = 5.0L V8 EFI
G = 2.5L V6 EFI DOHC HO
G = 5.8L V8 2BBL HO
H = 2.0L I-4 Dsl
J = 1.9L I-4 EFI HO
J = 1.9L I-4 EFI
L = 2.5L V6 EFI DOHC
M = 5.0L V8 EFI HO
M = 5.0L V8 4BBL
P = 2.0L I-4 SPI
R = 2.3L I-4 1BBL HSC
R = 3.8L V6 EFI S/C
S = 3.0L V6 EFI DOHC
S = 2.3L I-4 EFI HSO
T = 5.0L V8 EFI HO
U = 3.0L V6 EFI
V = 4.6L V8 EFI DOHC
V = 2.9L V6 EFI
W = 4.6L V8 EFI SOHC
W = 4.6L V8 EFI
W = 2.3L I-4 EFI T/C I/C
W = 2.3L I-4 EFI Turbo
X = 2.3L I-4 EFI HSC
X = 3.3L I-6 1BBL
Z = 1.6L I-4 EFI DOHC

DIGIT 9 CHECK DIGIT

= 0-9 or X

DIGIT 10 Model Year

1 = 2001
2 = 2002
3 = 2003
4 = 2004
B = 1981
C = 1982
D = 1983
E = 1984
F = 1985
G = 1986
H = 1987
J = 1988
K = 1989
L = 1990
M = 1991
N = 1992
P = 1993
R = 1994
S = 1995
T = 1996
V = 1997
W = 1998
X = 1999
Y = 2000

DIGIT 11 Assembly Plant Location

5 = AAI: Flat Rock, MI, USA
8 = Broadmeadows: Campbellfield, Australia
A = Atlanta, GA, USA
B = Oakville, ON, Canada
F = Dearborn, MI, USA
G = Chicago, IL, USA
H = Lorain, OH, USA
K = Kansas City, MO, USA
M = Cuautitlan, Mexico
R = Hermosillo, Mexico
R = San Jose, CA, USA
T = Edison, NJ, USA
T = Metuchen, NJ, USA
W = Wayne, MI, USA
X = St. Thomas, ON, Canada
Z = St. Louis, MO, USA

ARM0300000000379

Fig. 8 VIN Identification (Part 2 of 2). Mercury

DIGIT 1 Country Of Origin

1 = USA
2 = Canada
3 = Mexico

DIGIT 2 Manufacturer

G = General Motors

DIGIT 3 Make

3 = Oldsmobile

DIGIT 4 Restraint System

A = Manual Belts

DIGIT 4-5 Carline/Series

6K = Cutlass Salon 442
AG = Cutlass Clera S
AJ = Cutlass Clera LS
AJ = Cutlass Clera S
AJ = Cutlass Clera Base
AJ = Cutlass Clera SL
AJ = Cutlass Clera S Cruiser Wagon
AL = Cutlass Clera Base
AL = Cutlass Clera S
AM = Cutlass Clera Brougham
AM = Cutlass Clera SL
AS = Cutlass Clera International
BN = Eighty Eight Royale
BP = Eighty Eight Custom Cruiser
BY = Eighty Eight Brougham
CV = Ninety Eight Touring Sedan
CW = Ninety Eight Regency Brougham
CW = Ninety Eight Regency Elite
CX = Ninety Eight Regency Elite
CX = Ninety Eight Regency
EV = Toranado Trofeo
EZ = Toranado
GK = Cutlass Salon Coupe
GM = Cutlass Supreme Brougham RWD
GR = Aurora
GR = Cutlass Salon 442
GR = Cutlass Supreme RWD
GS = Aurora
HC = Regency
HC = Eighty Eight Anniversary Edition
HN = Eighty Eight Royale
HN = Eighty Eight LS
HN = Eighty Eight Base
HY = Eighty Eight Royale LSS
HY = Eighty Eight LSS
HY = Eighty Eight Royale Brougham
HY = Eighty Eight Royale LS
JC = Firenza Base
JC = Firenza S
JD = Firenza GT
JD = Firenza LC
JD = Firenza LX
JD = Firenza SX
NB = Cutlass GL
NF = Achieva SL & SC
NF = Achieva SL
NF = Alero GLS
NF = Cutlass Calais S
NF = Cutlass Calais
NF = Calais
NG = Cutlass GLS
NK = Cutlass Calais International
NK = Alero GX
NK = Calais International
NL = Cutlass Calais
NL = Achieva SL
NL = Achieva
NL = Alero GL
NL = Achieva S

DIGIT 4-5 Carline/Series

NL = Achieva SL & SC
NT = Cutlass Calais Supreme
NT = Calais Supreme
NT = Cutlass Calais SL
WH = Intrigue
WH = Intrigue GX
WH = Cutlass Supreme Base
WH = Cutlass Supreme SL
WH = Cutlass Supreme S
WR = Cutlass Supreme International
WS = Intrigue GL
WS = Cutlass Supreme SL
WT = Cutlass Supreme Convertible
WX = Intrigue GLS

DIGIT 5 Carline

B = Omega
C = Firenza
D = Firenza LX
D = Firenza Brougham
D = Firenza SX
E = Omega Brougham
G = Cutlass Clera
G = Ninety Eight Regency
G = Cutlass
H = Cutlass Cruiser
H = Ninety Eight Brougham
J = Cutlass Clera LS
K = Cutlass Calais
L = Delta Eighty Eight
M = Ninety Eight Brougham
M = Cutlass Clera Brougham
M = Cutlass Supreme Brougham
N = Delta Eighty Eight Royale
P = Eighty Eight Custom Cruiser
R = Cutlass LS
R = Cutlass Supreme
V = Ninety Eight Luxury
V = Delta Eighty Eight Royale Brougham LS
W = Ninety Eight Regency Brougham
X = Ninety Eight Regency
Y = Delta Eighty Eight Royale Brougham
Z = Toranado Brougham

DIGIT 6 Body Style

1 = 2D Sedan
1 = 2D Coupe
1 = 2D Coupe/Sedan
2 = 2D Hatchback
3 = 2D Convertible
5 = 4D Sedan
6 = 4D Sedan
8 = 4D Station Wagon

DIGIT 6-7 Body Type

11 = 2D Notchback Sedan
19 = 4D Sedan
27 = 2D Coupe
35 = 4D 2-Seat Wagon
37 = 2D Notchback Special Coupe
47 = 2D Coupe
47 = 2D Notchback Special Coupe
57 = 2D Notchback Special Coupe
69 = 4D Sedan
69 = 4D Notchback Sedan
77 = 2D Coupe

DIGIT 7 Restraint System

1 = Manual Belts
2 = Dual Front Airbags w/Manual Belts
3 = Driverside Airbag w/Manual Belts
4 = Dual Front & Side Airbags w/Manual Belts
4 = Automatic Belts

ARM0300000000380

Fig. 9 VIN Identification (Part 1 of 2). Oldsmobile

DIGIT 7 Restraint System
5 = Driverside Airbag w/Automatic Belts
6 = Dual Front & Side Airbags, Auto Passenger Sensor w/Manu

DIGIT 8 Engine
0 = 1.8L I-4 TBI
1 = 2.0L I-4 EFI
1 = 3.8L V6 MPI
1 = 3.8L V6 SFI S/C
3 = 3.8L V6 MPI
3 = 2.3L I-4 MPI
4 = 4.1L V6 4BBL
4 = 2.2L I-4 MPI
5 = 2.5L I-4 2BBL
7 = 5.7L V8 TBI
8 = 4.3L V8 2BBL
9 = 5.0L V8 4BBL
A = 3.8L V6 2BBL
A = 2.3L I-4 HO Quad 4
B = 2.0L I-4 EFI
B = 3.8L V6 SFI
C = 3.8L V6 MPI
C = 4.0L V8 SFI
D = 2.3L I-4 Quad 4
E = 5.0L V8 TBI
E = 3.0L V6 2BBL
E = 3.4L V6 SFI
F = 4.3L V8 2BBL
F = 2.0L I-4 MPI DOHC
G = 1.8L I-4 2BBL
H = 5.0L V8 4BBL
H = 3.5L V6 MPI
K = 3.8L V6 MPI S/C
K = 2.0L I-4 EFI
L = 3.8L V6 MPI
L = 3.0L V6 MPI
M = 2.0L I-4 EFI
M = 3.1L V6 MPI
N = 5.7L V8 Dsl
N = 3.3L V6 MPI
P = 2.0L I-4 EFI
R = 2.5L I-4 TBI
T = 4.3L V6 Dsl
T = 2.4L I-4 MPI
T = 3.1L V6 MPI
U = 2.5L I-4 TBI
V = 4.3L V6 Dsl
W = 2.8L V6 MPI
X = 3.4L V6 MPI
X = 2.8L V6 2BBL
Y = 5.0L V8 4BBL
Z = 2.8L V6 2BBL HO

DIGIT 9 CHECK DIGIT
= 0-9 or X

DIGIT 10 Model Year
1 = 2001
2 = 2002
3 = 2003
B = 1981
C = 1982
D = 1983
E = 1984
F = 1985
G = 1986
H = 1987
J = 1988
K = 1989
L = 1990
M = 1991
N = 1992
P = 1993

DIGIT 10 Model Year
R = 1994
S = 1995
T = 1996
V = 1997
W = 1998
X = 1999
Y = 2000

DIGIT 11 Assembly Plant Location
1 = Wentzville, MO, USA
2 = Ste. Therese, PQ, Canada
4 = Orion, MI, USA
6 = Oklahoma City, OK, USA
9 = Oshawa #1, ON, Canada
9 = Detroit, MI, USA
B = Lansing, MI, USA
C = Lansing, MI, USA
D = Doraville, GA, USA
E = Linden, NJ, USA
F = Fairfax II, KS, USA
G = Framingham, MA, USA
H = Flint, MI, USA
K = Leeds, MO, USA
K = Linden, NJ, USA
M = Lansing, MI, USA
P = Pontiac, MI, USA
R = Arlington, TX, USA
S = Ramos Arizpe, Mexico
U = Hamtramck, MI, USA
W = Willow Run, MI, USA
X = Fairfax, KS, USA
Y = Wilmington, DE, USA

ARM0300000000381

Fig. 9 VIN Identification (Part 2 of 2). Oldsmobile

DIGIT 1 Country Of Origin
1 = USA
2 = Canada
3 = Mexico
4 = USA - MMMA
J = Japan

DIGIT 2 Make
P = Plymouth

DIGIT 3 Vehicle Type
3 = Passenger Car
4 = Multi-Purpose Passenger Vehicle

DIGIT 4 Restraint
A = Dual Front & Side Airbags w/Manual Belts
A = Driverside Airbag w/Automatic Passenger Belt
B = Manual Seat Belts
B = Driverside Airbag w/Manual Belts
B = Manual Belts
C = Automatic Seat Belts
C = Automatic Belts
E = Driverside Airbag
E = Dual Airbags w/Manual Belts
H = Dual Airbags w/Manual Belts
X = Driverside Airbag w/Manual Belts
Y = Driverside Airbag w/Automatic Passenger Belt

DIGIT 4* GVW Range
B = Manual Seat Belts
B = Manual Seat Belts
E = 3001-4000 Lbs, Hydraulic
E = 3001-4000 Lbs, Hydraulic
F = 4001-5000 Lbs, Hydraulic Brakes
F = 4001-5000 Lbs, Hydraulic Brakes
P = Manual Seat Belts
P = Manual Seat Belts

DIGIT 5 Carline
A = Colt
B = Gran Fury Salon
C = Conquest
D = Sapporo
E = Colt
G = Colt Vista
J = Caravelle
K = Reliant
L = Horizon
M = Horizon
P = Reliant

DIGIT 5* Model
E = Champ

DIGIT 5-6 Carline
A4 = Acclaim
A5 = Acclaim LE
A7 = Acclaim LX
B1 = Gran Fury Special
B2 = Gran Fury Salon
F3 = Laser
F4 = Laser RS & RS Turbo FWD
G4 = Laser RS Turbo AWD
J3 = Caravelle
J4 = Caravelle SE
J4 = Breeze
K4 = Reliant
L1 = Horizon
M1 = Horizon
M2 = Gran Fury Salon
M3 = Gran Fury Special
M4 = Horizon Turismo
P2 = Sundance America
P2 = Sundance
P4 = Sundance

DIGIT 5-6 Carline
P4 = Sundance Highline
P6 = Sundance RS
P6 = Sundance Duster
S2 = Neon Competition
S2 = Neon Base
S3 = Laser
S4 = Neon Highline
S4 = Sundance
S4 = Laser RS 2WD
S6 = Neon Sport
T4 = Laser RS AWD
W6 = Prowler

DIGIT 6 Series
1 = Miser
1 = Base
2 = Base
2 = Low
3 = DLX
3 = High
3 = Medium
4 = Custom
4 = SE
4 = Turismo
4 = High
4 = DLX
4 = Base
5 = Euro
5 = Premium
5 = Custom
5 = Turismo 2.2
5 = Turismo

DIGIT 7 Body Style
1 = 2D Sedan
2 = 2D Pillared Hardtop
3 = 2D Hardtop
4 = 2D Hatchback
5 = 2D Convertible
6 = 4D Sedan
7 = 4D Pillared Hardtop
7 = 4D Sedan
8 = 4D Hatchback
9 = 4D Wagon

DIGIT 7* Body Type
0 = Wagon
1 = 2D Sedan
1 = Wagon
4 = 2D Hatchback
6 = 4D Sedan
8 = 4D Hatchback
9 = Wagon

DIGIT 8 Engine
2 = 1.4L I-4 2BBL
3 = 3.0L V6 MPI
3 = 1.6L I-4 2BBL
4 = 5.2L V8 2BBL
7 = 2.6L I-4 2BBL
A = 1.6L I-4 2BBL
A = 1.5L I-4 MPI
A = 1.4L I-4 2BBL
A = 1.7L I-4 2BBL
B = 1.7L I-4 2BBL
B = 2.2L I-4 2BBL
B = 1.8L I-4 MPI
B = 1.6L I-4 2BBL
C = 2.2L I-4 Turbo
C = 2.0L I-4 SFI SOHC
C = 1.8L I-4 MPI
D = 2.2L I-4 TBI
D = 2.6L I-4 2BBL

ARM0300000000382

Fig. 10 VIN Identification (Part 1 of 2). Plymouth

DIGIT 8	Engine
D	= 2.0L I-4
D	= 1.8L I-4 MPI
D	= 2.0L I-4 2BBL
D	= 2.0L I-4 MPI
E	= 2.2L I-4 Turbo
E	= 2.0L I-4 MPI DOHC
E	= 3.7L 6 Cyl 1BBL
F	= 1.6L I-4 Turbo
F	= 2.0L I-4 DOHC T/C I/C
F	= 3.7L 6 Cyl 1BBL
F	= 3.5L V6 MPI
G	= 2.4L I-4 MPI
G	= 2.4L I-4 MPI SOHC
G	= 2.6L I-4 2BBL
G	= 3.5L V6 MPI SOHC HO
H	= 3.7L 6 Cyl 1BBL
H	= 2.5L I-4 EFI
H	= 2.6L I-4 Tbo
J	= 2.5L I-4 Turbo
K	= 2.5L I-4 TBI
K	= 1.5L I-4
K	= 5.2L V8 2BBL
L	= 5.2L V8 2BBL
M	= 5.2L V8 4BBL
N	= 5.2L V8 4BBL
N	= 2.6L I-4 Tbo
P	= 5.2L V8 2BBL
R	= 5.2L V8 4BBL
R	= 2.0L I-4 MPI DOHC
S	= 5.2L V8 4BBL
T	= 1.8L I-4 MPI
U	= 2.0L I-4 MPI DOHC Turbo
V	= 2.0L I-4 MPI
V	= 2.5L I-4 TBI Flex Fuel
W	= 2.4L I-4 MPI
X	= 1.5L I-4 MPI
X	= 2.4L I-4 SFI
Y	= 2.0L I-4 SFI DOHC
Z	= 1.6L I-4 Turbo
Z	= 1.5L I-4 MPI

DIGIT 9	CHECK DIGIT
	= 0-9 or X

DIGIT 10	Model Year
1	= 2001
B	= 1981
C	= 1982
D	= 1983
E	= 1984
F	= 1985
G	= 1986
H	= 1987
J	= 1988
K	= 1989
L	= 1990
M	= 1991
N	= 1992
P	= 1993
R	= 1994
S	= 1995
T	= 1996
V	= 1997
W	= 1998
X	= 1999
Y	= 2000

DIGIT 11	Assembly Plant
U	= Mizushima, Japan
Y	= Nagoya, Japan
Z	= Okazaki, Japan

DIGIT 12	Transmission
4	= 5-Speed Manual - Federal
5	= 5-Speed Manual - California
7	= Automatic - Federal
8	= Automatic - California

ARM0300000000383

Fig. 10 VIN Identification (Part 2 of 2). Plymouth

DIGIT 1	Country Of Origin
1	= USA
2	= Canada
3	= Mexico
4	= USA
K	= Korea

DIGIT 1-3	Manufacturer Identification
5Y2	= Pontiac, Nummi

DIGIT 2	Manufacturer
G	= General Motors
L	= Daewoo

DIGIT 3	Make
2	= Pontiac

DIGIT 4	Restraint System
A	= Manual Belts

DIGIT 4-5	Carline/Series
AE	= 6000 SE
AF	= 6000
AF	= 6000 LE
AG	= 6000 LE
AH	= 6000 STE
AJ	= 6000 SE
BL	= Parisienne
BT	= Parisienne Brougham
FS	= Firebird
FV	= Trans AM
FV	= Formula
FW	= Trans AM GTA
FW	= Trans AM
FX	= Firebird SE
GJ	= Grand Prix
GK	= Grand Prix LE
GN	= Bonneville
GP	= Grand Prix Brougham
GR	= Bonneville Brougham
GS	= Bonneville LE
HX	= Bonneville
HX	= Bonneville SLE
HX	= Bonneville LE
HX	= Bonneville SE
HY	= Bonneville SLE
HY	= Bonneville SSE
HY	= Bonneville SSEi
HZ	= Bonneville SE
HZ	= Bonneville LE
HZ	= Bonneville SSE
HZ	= Bonneville SSEi
JB	= Sunbird LE & Convertible
JB	= Sunbird LE
JB	= Sunfire GT Convertible
JB	= Sunfire SE
JB	= Sunfire SE Convertible
JB	= Sunbird SE & Convertible
JB	= Sunbird
JC	= Sunbird
JC	= Sunbird LE
JD	= Sunbird SE
JD	= Sunbird GT
JD	= Sunfire GT
JL	= Sunbird SE
JU	= Sunbird GT
NE	= Grand AM
NE	= Grand AM SE
NE	= Grand AM LE
NF	= Grand AM SE1
NG	= Grand AM SE2
NG	= Grand AM
NV	= Grand AM LE
NV	= Grand AM GT1

DIGIT 4-5	Carline/Series
NW	= Grand AM SE
NW	= Grand AM GT
PE	= Fiero Formula
PE	= Fiero Coupe
PF	= Fiero SE Coupe
PG	= Fiero GT Coupe
PM	= Fiero Sport Coupe
TL	= 1000
TN	= Lemans SE
TN	= Lemans
TN	= Lemans LE
TR	= Lemans SE
TS	= Lemans GSE
TX	= Lemans Coupe
TX	= Lemans Aerocoupe
WH	= Grand Prix LE
WJ	= Grand Prix SE
WJ	= Grand Prix
WJ	= Grand Prix LE
WK	= Grand Prix LE
WK	= Grand Prix SE1
WP	= Grand Prix SE
WP	= Grand Prix GT
WR	= Grand Prix GTP
WT	= Grand Prix STE

DIGIT 5	Carline
B	= J2000
B	= Sunbird 2000
C	= J2000 LE
C	= Sunbird 2000 LE
D	= J2000 SE
D	= Sunbird 2000 SE
D	= Lemans
E	= J2000 S
E	= Fiero Coupe
F	= 6000
F	= Grand Lemans
F	= Fiero SE Coupe
G	= 6000 LE
H	= 6000 STE
J	= Grand Prix
K	= Grand Prix LJ
K	= Grand Prix LE
L	= Catalina
L	= Parisienne
L	= 1000
M	= Fiero Sport Coupe
M	= 1000
N	= Bonneville
P	= Grand Prix Brougham
R	= Bonneville Brougham
S	= Bonneville LE
S	= Firebird
T	= Parisienne Brougham
T	= Phoenix SJ
T	= Firebird Esprit
T	= Phoenix SE
V	= Formula
W	= Trans AM
X	= Trans AM Turbo Special
X	= Firebird SE
Y	= Phoenix
Z	= Phoenix LJ
Z	= Phoenix LE

DIGIT 6	Body Style
1	= 2D Coupe
1	= 2D Coupe/Sedan
2	= 2D Hatchback
2	= 2D Hatchback/Liftback
3	= 2D Convertible

ARM0300000000384

Fig. 11 VIN Identification (Part 1 of 3). Pontiac

DIGIT 6	Body Style
5	= 4D Sedan
6	= 4D Hatchback
6	= 4D All Purpose w/Liftgate
8	= Station Wagon

DIGIT 6-7	Body Type
08	= 2D Hatchback
19	= 4D Notchback Sedan
27	= 2D Notchback Coupe
35	= 4D Wagon
37	= 2D Notchback Special Coupe
67	= 2D Convertible
68	= 4D Hatchback
69	= 4D Notchback Sedan
77	= 2D Hatchback
87	= 2D Coupe
97	= 2D Notchback Sport Coupe

DIGIT 7	Restraint System
1	= Manual Belts
2	= Dual Front Airbags w/Manual Belts
3	= Driverside Airbag w/Manual Belts
3	= Dual Front Airbags w/Manual Belts
4	= Dual Front & Side Airbags w/Manual Belts
4	= Automatic Belts
4	= Dual Front & Front Side Airbags w/Manual Belts
5	= Dual Front & Driver's Side Airbags w/Manual Belts
5	= Driverside Airbag w/Automatic Belts
6	= Dual Front Airbags w/Automatic Belts

DIGIT 7*	Restraint
2	= Dual Front Airbags w/Manual Belts
4	= Dual Front & Front Side Airbags w/Manual Belts

DIGIT 8	Engine
0	= 1.8L I-4 TBI
1	= 2.8L V6 2BBL
1	= 3.8L V6 SFI S/C
2	= 2.5L I-4 TBI
3	= 3.8L V6 SFI
3	= 2.3L I-4 MPI
4	= 4.1L V6 4BBL
4	= 2.2L I-4 MPI SOHC
5	= 2.5L I-4 2BBL
6	= 1.6L I-4 TBI
7	= 5.0L V8 CPI
8	= 2.5L I-4 EFI
8	= 1.8L I-4 MPI
8	= 5.7L V8 MPI
9	= 2.8L V6 MPI
A	= 2.3L I-4 MPI Quad HO
A	= 3.8L V6 2BBL
C	= 1.6L I-4 2BBL
C	= 3.8L V6 MPI
D	= 2.3L I-4 MPI DOHC
D	= 2.3L I-4 MPI Quad 4
D	= 2.3L I-4 EFI Quad 4
E	= 5.0L V8 TBI
E	= 3.4L V6 SFI
F	= 2.5L I-4 2BBL
F	= 2.2L I-4 MPI DOHC
F	= 5.0L V8 MPI
G	= 1.8L I-4 2BBL
G	= 5.0L V8 4BBL
G	= 5.7L V8 MPI
G	= 2.5L I-4 EFI
H	= 5.0L V8 4BBL
H	= 2.0L I-4 MPI
J	= 1.8L I-4 Turbo
J	= 3.1L V6 SFI
J	= 1.8L I-4 FI Turbo
K	= 2.0L I-4 TBI
K	= 3.8L V6 MPI

DIGIT 8	Engine
K	= 3.8L V6 EFI
K	= 3.8L V6 SFI
K	= 3.8L V6 2BBL
L	= 3.8L V6 MPI
L	= 2.8L V6 2BBL
L	= 1.8L I-4 SFI DOHC
L	= 3.0L V6 EFI
M	= 2.0L I-4 FI Turbo
M	= 2.0L I-4 Turbo
M	= 2.0L I-4 TBO
M	= 3.1L V6 SFI
M	= 2.0L I-4 MPI
N	= 3.3L V6 MPI
N	= 5.7L V8 Dsl
P	= 5.7L V8 MPI
P	= 5.7L V8 EFI
P	= 2.8L V6 MPI
P	= 2.0L I-4 TBI
P	= 2.0L I-4 EFI
R	= 2.5L I-4 TBI
S	= 2.8L V6 MPI
S	= 3.4L V6 SFI HO
S	= 4.3L V8 2BBL
T	= 2.4L I-4 EFI DOHC
T	= 2.4L I-4 MPI DOHC
T	= 3.1L V6 MPI
T	= 4.3L V6 Dsl
T	= 4.9L V8 4BBL
U	= 2.5L I-4 TBI
V	= 3.1L V6 EFI
V	= 3.0L V6 TBI
W	= 4.9L V8 4BBL
W	= 2.8L V6 MPI
X	= 3.4L V6 EFI DOHC
X	= 2.8L V6 2BBL
Y	= 5.0L V8 4BBL
Z	= 2.8L V6 2BBL
Z	= 4.3L V6 EFI

DIGIT 9	CHECK DIGIT
	= 0-9 or X

DIGIT 10	Model Year
1	= 2001
2	= 2002
3	= 2003
4	= 2004
B	= 1981
C	= 1982
D	= 1983
E	= 1984
F	= 1985
G	= 1986
H	= 1987
J	= 1988
K	= 1989
L	= 1990
M	= 1991
N	= 1992
P	= 1993
R	= 1994
S	= 1995
T	= 1996
V	= 1997
W	= 1998
X	= 1999
Y	= 2000

DIGIT 11	Assembly Plant Location
1	= Oshawa, ON, Canada
1	= Oshawa #2, ON, Canada
1	= Wentzville, MO, USA

ARM0300000000385

Fig. 11 VIN Identification (Part 2 of 3). Pontiac

DIGIT 11	Assembly Plant Location
2	= Ste. Therese, PQ, Canada
4	= Orion, MI, USA
6	= Oklahoma City, OK, USA
7	= Lordstown, OH, USA
9	= Oshawa #1, ON, Canada
A	= Lakewood, GA, USA
B	= Lansing, MI, USA
B	= Baltimore, MD, USA
B	= Pupyong, Korea
C	= Lansing, MI, USA
F	= Fairfax II, KS, USA
G	= Framingham, MA, USA
H	= Flint, MI, USA
J	= Janesville, WI, USA
K	= Leeds, MO, USA
L	= Van Nuys, CA, USA
M	= Lansing, MI, USA
N	= Norwood, Oh, USA
P	= Pontiac, MI, USA
S	= Ramos Arizpe, Mexico
T	= Tarrytown, NY, USA
W	= Willow Run, MI, USA
X	= Fairfax I, KS, USA
X	= Fairfax, KS, USA
Y	= Wilmington, DE, USA

ARM0300000000386

Fig. 11 VIN Identification (Part 3 of 3). Pontiac

DIGIT 1 Country Of Origin
1 = USA

DIGIT 2 Manufacturer
G = General Motors

DIGIT 3 Make
8 = Saturn

DIGIT 4-5 Carline/Series
AF = Level 1 5sp
AG = Level 1 at
AJ = Level 2 at
AK = Level 3 5sp
AL = Level 3 at
AZ = Level 2 5sp
JR = LS 5sp
JR = L100 5sp
JS = L100 at
JS = LS at
JT = LS1 5sp
JT = L200 5sp
JT = LW200 5sp
JU = LW200 at
JU = LW1 at
JU = LS1 at
JU = L200 at
JW = LW300 at
JW = L300 at
JW = LS2 at
JW = LW2 at
ZE = SC1 5sp
ZF = SC1 at
ZF = SL 5sp
ZG = SW1 5sp
ZG = SC2 5sp
ZG = SC 5sp
ZG = SL1 5sp
ZH = SC at
ZH = SC2 at
ZH = SW1 at
ZH = SL1 at
ZJ = SW2 5sp
ZJ = SL2 5sp
ZK = SW2 at
ZK = SL2 at
ZN = SC1 5sp
ZN = SW2 at
ZP = SC1 at
ZR = SC2 5sp
ZY = SC2 at

DIGIT 6 Body Style
1 = 2D Coupe
5 = 4D Sedan
8 = 4D Wagon

DIGIT 7 Restraint System
2 = Dual Front Airbags w/Manual Belts
4 = Dual Front & Side Airbags w/Manual Belts
4 = Automatic Belts
5 = Driverside Airbag w/Automatic Belts

DIGIT 8 Engine
7 = 1.9L I-4 MPI DOHC
8 = 1.9L I-4 TBI
9 = 1.9L I-4 TBI
F = 2.2L I-4 MPI DOHC
R = 3.0L V6 EFI DOHC

DIGIT 9 CHECK DIGIT
= 0-9 or X

DIGIT 10 Model Year
1 = 2001

DIGIT 10 Model Year
2 = 2002
3 = 2003
4 = 2004
M = 1991
N = 1992
P = 1993
R = 1994
S = 1995
T = 1996
V = 1997
W = 1998
X = 1999
Y = 2000

DIGIT 11 Assembly Plant Location
Y = Wilmington, DE, USA
Z = Spring Hill, TN, USA

ARM0300000000387

Fig. 12 VIN Identification. Saturn

AIR BAG SYSTEM PRECAUTIONS

INDEX

DAIMLERCHRYSLER

Disarming

It may be required to access and record Diagnostic Trouble Codes (DTCs) prior to disarming the air bag system.

1. Place ignition switch in Lock position.
2. **On Avenger, Breeze, Cirrus, Neon, Sebring and Stratus models,** disconnect and isolate battery ground cable.
3. **On Concorde, Intrepid, LHS and 300M models,** disconnect and isolate battery ground cable remote terminal at remote battery post, **Fig. 1.**
4. **On all models except Sebring and Stratus Coupe, wait at least two minutes after disconnection before doing any further work on vehicle. The air bag system is designed to retain enough voltage to deploy air bags for short time even after battery has been disconnected.**
5. **On Sebring and Stratus Coupe, wait at least sixty seconds after disconnection before doing any further work on vehicle. The air bag system is designed to retain enough voltage to deploy air bags for short time even after battery has been disconnected.**

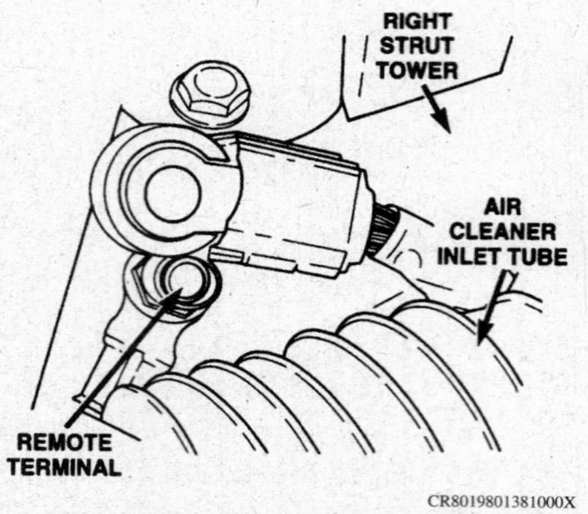

Fig. 1 Battery ground remote terminal. Concorde, Intrepid, LHS & 300M

Arming

1. **Ensure no one is inside vehicle and ignition switch is in Lock position.**
2. Connect battery ground or negative remote cable or terminal.
3. **From safe location at sides or below air bag modules,** turn ignition switch to On position.
4. SRS lamp should light for 7–10 seconds and remain off for at least 45 seconds to indicate SRS is functioning properly.

FORD MOTOR CO.

Disarming

CONTINENTAL

1. Disconnect and isolate battery ground cable.
2. **On models equipped with auxiliary batteries and power supplies,** disconnect and isolate these items.
3. **On all models,** wait one minute for back-up power supply to deplete.
4. Remove two steering wheel spoke bolt covers, if equipped.
5. Remove two air bag module to steering wheel mounting bolts.
6. Lift air bag module away from steering wheel, then disconnect air bag module and horn to clockspring electrical connectors. **When carrying live air bag module, ensure bag and trim cover are pointed away from your body. Place module on bench with trim cover facing upward.**
7. Remove driver's air bag module.
8. Attach Rotunda air bag simulator tool No. 105-R0012, or equivalent, to vehicle harness connector at top of steering column.

9. Open glove compartment, push tabs in and turn door downward past stops.
10. Disconnect passenger's air bag module electrical connector.
11. Attach Rotunda air bag simulator tool No. 105-R0012, or equivalent, to passenger's air bag module electrical connector on vehicle wiring harness side.
12. Disconnect side impact air bag module electrical connector located beneath driver's seat.
13. Attach Rotunda air bag simulator tool No. 105-R0012, or equivalent, to side impact air bag connector under driver's seat on vehicle wiring harness side
14. Disconnect side impact air bag module electrical connector located beneath passenger's seat.
15. Attach Rotunda air bag simulator tool No. 105-R0012, or equivalent, to side impact air bag connector under passenger's seat on vehicle wiring harness side
16. If side impact air bag diagnosis or service is to be performed, remove front seats as follows:
    a. Move front seat all way rearward, then remove covers and seat track front bolts.
    b. Move front seat all way forward, then remove covers and seat track rear bolts.
    c. Disconnect front seat electrical connectors and remove front seats.
17. Connect battery ground cable.

CONTOUR & MYSTIQUE

1. Disconnect and isolate battery ground cable.
2. Allow at least one minute for back-up power supply to deplete.
3. Remove two driver's air bag module Torx mounting screws at rear of steering wheel.
4. Lift driver's air bag module upward and disconnect air bag module electrical connector.
5. Remove air bag module. **When carrying live air bag module, ensure bag and trim cover are pointed away from your body. Place module on bench with trim cover facing upward.**
6. Connect Rotunda air bag simulator tool No. 105-R0012, or equivalent, to vehicle harness at top of steering column.
7. Open and lower glove compartment to floor by pressing inward on sides.
8. Remove four upper panel screws and disconnect glove compartment lamp.
9. Remove glove compartment upper panel.
10. Remove passenger's air vent duct.
11. Disconnect passenger's air bag module electrical connector.
12. Connect second Rotunda air bag simulator tool No. 105-R0012, or equivalent, to wiring harness in place of passenger's air bag.
13. Connect battery ground cable.

COUGAR

Prior to disconnecting battery, record preset radio frequencies.

1. Disconnect and isolate battery ground cable, then the positive cable.
2. **On models equipped with auxiliary batteries and power supplies,** disconnect and isolate these items.
3. **On all models,** allow at least one minute for back-up power supply to deplete.
4. Remove two driver's air bag module Torx mounting screws at rear of steering wheel.
5. Lift driver's air bag module upward and disconnect air bag module electrical connector.
6. Remove air bag module. **When carrying live air bag module, ensure bag and trim cover are pointed away from your body. Place module on bench with trim cover facing upward.**
7. Connect Rotunda air bag simulator tool No. 105-R0012, or equivalent, to vehicle harness at top of steering column.
8. Remove three glove compartment Torx mounting screws.
9. Open glove compartment and depress side stops to detach sides.
10. Remove four Torx screws and glove compartment finish panel.
11. Remove passenger's air register duct.
12. Disconnect passenger's air bag module electrical connector.
13. Remove two passenger's air bag module to crossbeam mounting bolts.
14. Lower front edge of passenger's air bag module, roll air bag module around crossbeam. Lower air bag module to passenger's foot well and remove it. **When carrying live air bag module, ensure bag and trim cover are pointed away from your body. Place module on bench with trim cover facing upward.**
15. Connect second Rotunda air bag simulator tool No. 105-R0012, or equivalent, to wiring harness in place of passenger's air bag.
16. **On models equipped with side impact air bags,** proceed as follows:
    a. From driver's and passenger's seats, remove seat back rest, cover and pad.
    b. Depress retaining tang at each side and disconnect side impact air bag module electrical connector at driver's and passenger's seats.
    c. Remove side impact air bag module mounting nuts from driver's and passenger's seats.
17. **On all models,** connect battery ground cable.

CROWN VICTORIA & GRAND MARQUIS

2000

1. Disconnect and isolate battery ground cable, then wait one minute for back-up power supply to deplete.
2. **On models equipped with auxiliary batteries and power supplies,** disconnect and isolate these items also.
3. **On all models,** wait one minute for back-up power supply to deplete.
4. Remove two air bag module to steering wheel mounting bolts.
5. Lift air bag module from steering wheel, then disconnect air bag module and horn switch electrical connectors. **When carrying live air bag module, ensure bag and trim cover are pointed away from your body. Place module on bench with trim cover facing upward.**
6. Connect Rotunda air bag simulator tool No. 105-00012, or equivalent, to air bag wiring harness at top of steering column.
7. Open and disconnect glove compartment locator.
8. Push inward on glove compartment door tabs and position door downward.
9. Disconnect passenger's air bag module electrical connector.
10. Remove two air bag module mounting bolts and screws.
11. Place one hand in glove compartment opening and push air bag module from instrument panel. **When carrying live air bag module, ensure bag and trim cover are pointed away from your body. Place module on bench with trim cover facing upward.**
12. Attach Rotunda air bag simulator tool No. 105-00012, or equivalent, to harness side of passenger's air bag module connector.
13. Connect battery ground cable.

2001–04

1. Disconnect battery ground cable.
2. Wait at least one minute for back-up power supply in restraints control module (RCM) to deplete its' stored energy.
3. Remove two steering wheel back cover plugs and two air bag module bolts.
4. Release two air bag retaining tabs. Label driver air bag squib number on air bag module connector before disconnecting.
5. Remove wire harness from holder.
6. Disconnect horn switch electrical connector.
7. Remove air bag module.
8. Attach restraint system diagnostic tools 418-F395, or equivalent, to clockspring side of driver air bag module electrical connectors.
9. Disconnect rear window defroster switch, clock and air bag deactivation lamp electrical connectors, then remove trim panel.
10. Open glove compartment and disconnect glove compartment isolator.
11. While pushing in on two glove compartment door tabs, lower glove compartment door.
12. Remove air bag module bolts through glove compartment opening,
13. Place one hand in glove compartment opening and push air bag module out from instrument panel. **Do not handle passenger air bag module by grabbing edges of deployment doors.**
14. Attach restraint system diagnostic tools 418-F395, or equivalent, to vehicle harness side of passenger air bag module electrical connectors.
15. Remove front seats.
16. Access passenger safety belt retractor

and pretensioner located behind passenger side B-pillar.
17. Disconnect passenger safety belt retractor and pretensioner electrical connector.
18. Attach restraint system diagnostic tool 418-F088, or equivalent, to passenger safety belt retractor and pretensioner electrical connector.
19. Access driver safety belt retractor and pretensioner located behind driver side B-pillar.
20. Disconnect driver safety belt retractor and pretensioner electrical connector.
21. Attach restraint system diagnostic tool 418-F088, or equivalent, to driver safety belt retractor and pretensioner electrical connector.
22. Connect battery ground cable.

ESCORT & ZX2

1. Disconnect and isolate battery ground cable. Allow at least one minute for back-up power supply to deplete.
2. **On models equipped with auxiliary batteries and power supplies,** disconnect and isolate these items also.
3. **On all models,** remove two air bag module mounting bolts, then disconnect air bag and horn electrical connectors.
4. Remove driver's air bag module from steering wheel. **When carrying live air bag module, ensure bag and trim cover are pointed away from your body. Place module on bench with trim cover facing upward.**
5. Connect air bag simulator tool No. 105–00012, or equivalent, to air bag wiring harness at top steering column.
6. Open glove compartment, push in on two door tabs and roll door downward.
7. Remove four passenger's air bag module mounting bolts.
8. Pull passenger's air bag module from instrument panel and disconnect electrical connector. **When carrying live air bag module, ensure bag and trim cover are pointed away from your body. Place module on bench with trim cover facing upward.**
9. Connect Rotunda air bag simulator tool No. 105-R00010, or equivalent, to wiring harness in place of passenger's air bag module.
10. Connect battery ground cable.

FOCUS

1. Disconnect and isolate battery ground cable.
2. **On models equipped with auxiliary batteries and power supplies,** disconnect and isolate these items also.
3. **On all models,** wait one minute for back-up power supply to deplete.
4. Remove two air bag module mounting bolts, then disconnect air bag and horn electrical connectors.
5. Remove driver's air bag module from steering wheel. **When carrying live air bag module, ensure bag and trim cover are pointed away from your body. Place module on bench with trim cover facing upward.**
6. Connect air bag simulator tool No. 418-037, or equivalent, to air bag wiring harness at top steering column.
7. Remove mounting screws and glove compartment.
8. Disconnect passenger's air bag module electrical connector.
9. Connect Rotunda air bag simulator tool 418–138, or equivalent, to wiring harness in place of passenger's air bag module.
10. From beneath driver's seat, disconnect side impact air bag module electrical connector. Connect Rotunda air bag simulator tool 418–139, or equivalent, to connector on wiring harness side of side impact air bag harness.
11. From beneath passenger's seat, disconnect side impact air bag module electrical connector. Connect Rotunda air bag simulator tool 418–139, or equivalent, to connector on wiring harness side of side impact air bag harness.
12. Disconnect driver's seat belt pretensioner electrical connector. Connect Rotunda air bag simulator tool 418–139, or equivalent, to connector on wiring harness side of seat belt pretensioner harness.
13. Disconnect passenger's seat belt pretensioner electrical connector. Connect Rotunda air bag simulator tool 418–139, or equivalent, to connector on wiring harness side of seat belt pretensioner harness.
14. Connect battery ground cable.

LS

1. Disconnect and isolate battery ground cable.
2. **On models equipped with auxiliary batteries and power supplies,** disconnect and isolate these items.
3. **On all models,** wait one minute for back-up power supply to deplete.
4. Remove two rear cover plugs from steering wheel in order to access air bag module screws.
5. Remove driver's air bag module mounting bolts and disconnect electrical connector.
6. Remove air bag module. **When carrying live air bag module, ensure bag and trim cover are pointed away from your body. Place module on bench with trim cover facing upward.**
7. Connect Rotunda air bag simulator tool No. 418-F395, or equivalent, to air bag wiring harness at top steering column.
8. Remove glove compartment.
9. Reaching over cross-car beam, slide passenger's air bag connector lock downward. Squeeze connector lock tabs and pull connector from air bag.
10. Connect Rotunda air bag simulator tool No. 418-F395, or equivalent, to vehicle side of passenger's air bag wiring harness connector.
11. From beneath driver's seat, disconnect side impact air bag module electrical connector. Connect Rotunda air bag simulator tool 418–133, or equivalent, to connector on wiring harness side of side impact air bag harness.
12. From beneath passenger's seat, disconnect side impact air bag module electrical connector. Connect Rotunda air bag simulator tool 418–133, or equivalent, to connector on wiring harness side of side impact air bag harness.
13. Remove driver's side B-pillar pillar trim.
14. Access and disconnect driver's side seat belt pretensioner electrical connector. Connect Rotunda seat belt pretensioner simulator tool 105-R0012, or equivalent, to seat belt pretensioner electrical connector.
15. Remove passenger's side B-pillar pillar trim.
16. Access and disconnect passenger's side seat belt pretensioner electrical connector. Connect Rotunda seat belt pretensioner simulator tool 105-R0012, or equivalent, to seat belt pretensioner electrical connector.
17. Connect battery ground cable.

MUSTANG

1. Disconnect battery ground cable.
2. Allow at least one minute for back-up power supply to deplete.
3. **On models equipped with auxiliary batteries and power supplies,** disconnect and isolate these items also.
4. **On all models,** remove two rear cover plugs from steering wheel in order to access air bag module screws.
5. Remove driver's air bag module mounting screws and washers, then disconnect electrical connector.
6. Remove air bag module. **Place module on bench with trim cover facing upward.**
7. Connect Rotunda air bag simulator tool, or equivalent, to air bag wiring at top of steering column.
8. Open glove compartment, press sides inward to release it from instrument panel and lower glove compartment to floor.
9. Remove righthand air conditioning duct and passenger's air bag mounting bolts from instrument panel steel reinforcement.
10. Disconnect electrical connector at lower lefthand corner of passenger's air bag module and remove connector from instrument panel reinforcement.
11. Gently pull upon each corner of air bag cover to disconnect from instrument panel and push air bag module out from behind instrument panel. **Place module on bench with trim cover facing upward.**
12. Install second air bag simulator Rotunda air bag simulator tool, or equivalent, on passenger's air bag harness.
13. Connect battery ground cable.

SABLE & TAURUS

1. Move front seat to full rear and highest position.
2. Disconnect and isolate battery ground cable.
3. **On models equipped with auxiliary batteries and power supplies,** disconnect and isolate these items also.
4. **On all models,** wait one minute for back-up power supply to deplete.

5. Remove mounting screws and pull out release clips, then remove lower steering column cover with reinforcement.
6. Disconnect driver's air bag sliding contact electrical connect at base of steering column.
7. Connect driver's air bag restraint system diagnostic tool 418-F403, or equivalent, to vehicle side of driver's air bag sliding contact four-pin electrical connector.
8. Open glove compartment, push in on tabs and release glove compartment.
9. Through glove compartment opening, remove two passenger's air bag module mounting bolts.
10. Pull lefthand corner of passenger's air bag trim cover away from instrument panel.
11. From left to right, slide across seam between instrument panel and trim cover to release trim cover retaining clips.
12. Pull passenger's air bag module and trim cover away from instrument panel.
13. Disconnect passenger's air bag module electrical connector and remove harness retainer from air bag module.
14. Remove passenger's air bag module. **When carrying live air bag module, ensure bag and trim cover are pointed away from your body. Place module on bench with trim cover facing upward.**
15. Connect passenger's air bag restraint system diagnostic tool 418-F403, or equivalent, to vehicle side of passenger's air bag electrical connector.
16. **On models equipped with side impact air bags,** disconnect passenger's seat air bag electrical connector and attach side impact air bag restraint system diagnostic tool 418-133, or equivalent, to side impact air bag floor electrical connector on passenger's side.
17. **On all models,** disconnect passenger's seat belt pretensioner electrical connector.
18. Attach passenger's seat belt pretensioner restraint system diagnostic tool 418-F407, or equivalent, to floor electrical connector.
19. **On models equipped with side impact air bags,** disconnect driver's seat air bag electrical connector and attach side impact air bag restraint system diagnostic tool 418-133, or equivalent, to side impact air bag floor electrical connector on driver's side.
20. **On all models,** disconnect driver's seat belt pretensioner electrical connector.
21. Attach driver's seat belt pretensioner restraint system diagnostic tool 418-F405, or equivalent, to floor electrical connector.
22. Connect battery ground cable.

THUNDERBIRD

1. Disconnect battery ground cable and wait at least one minute for back-up power supply to deplete.
2. Remove two pin-type retainers from lower steering column opening finish panel, pull out on finish panel far enough to access and disconnect electrical connectors.
3. Remove lower steering column finish panel.
4. Remove two pin-type retainers from driver side lower insulator panel.
5. Remove light socket from insulator panel and panel from instrument panel.
6. Remove mounting screws and disconnect hood latch from steering column reinforcement.
7. Remove mounting screw and heater duct.
8. Position carpet aside and loosen two driver side instrument panel tunnel brace bolts.
9. Remove mounting screws and lower steering column reinforcement from instrument panel.
10. Disconnect clockspring electrical connector located at base of steering column.
11. Attach restraint system diagnostic tool No. 418-F088, or equivalent, to clockspring electrical connector.
12. Remove glove compartment and door.
13. Locate passenger air bag module electrical connector by reaching through glove compartment opening towards center of instrument panel and above cross-car beam. **Passenger air bag module connector is not visible because of its mounting position in instrument panel.**
14. Disconnect passenger air bag module electrical connector.
15. Attach restraint system diagnostic tool No. 418-F395, or equivalent, to vehicle harness side of passenger air bag electrical connector.
16. Connect battery ground cable and move front seats to highest and most forward positions.
17. Disconnect battery ground cable and wait at least one minute for back-up power supply to deplete.
18. Disconnect passenger seat side impact air bag electrical connector located under passenger seat.
19. Attach restraint system diagnostic tool No. 418-F133, or equivalent, to passenger seat side impact air bag electrical connector.
20. Remove passenger side door scuff plate and weather stripping.
21. Remove safety belt from passenger seat guide.
22. Remove speaker grille from passenger side rear trim panel.
23. Remove snap screws and passenger side rear trim panel.
24. Disconnect passenger safety belt retractor pretensioner electrical connector.
25. Attach restraint system diagnostic tool No. 418-F395, or equivalent, to passenger safety belt retractor pretensioner electrical connector.
26. Disconnect driver seat side impact air bag electrical connector located under driver seat.
27. Attach restraint system diagnostic tool No. 418-F133, or equivalent, to driver seat side impact air bag electrical connector.
28. Remove driver side door scuff plate and weather stripping.
29. Remove safety belt from driver seat guide.
30. Remove speaker grille from driver side rear trim panel.
31. Remove snap screws and driver side rear trim panel.
32. Disconnect driver safety belt retractor pretensioner electrical connector.
33. Attach restraint system diagnostic tool No. 418-F395, or equivalent, to driver safety belt retractor pretensioner electrical connector.
34. Connect battery ground cable.

TOWN CAR

2000

1. Disconnect and isolate battery ground cable.
2. **On models equipped with auxiliary batteries and power supplies,** disconnect and isolate these items, too.
3. **On all models,** wait one minute for back-up power supply to deplete.
4. Remove two steering wheel spoke bolt covers, if equipped.
5. Remove two air bag module to steering wheel mounting bolts.
6. Lift air bag module away from steering wheel, then disconnect air bag module and horn to clockspring electrical connectors. **When carrying live air bag module, ensure bag and trim cover are pointed away from your body. Place module on bench with trim cover facing upward.**
7. Remove air bag module and attach Rotunda air bag simulator tool No. 105-R0012, or equivalent, to vehicle harness connector at top of steering column.
8. Open glove compartment, push tabs in and turn door downward past stops.
9. Disconnect passenger's air bag module electrical connector.
10. Attach Rotunda air bag simulator tool No. 105-R0012, or equivalent, to passenger's air bag module electrical connector on vehicle wiring harness side.
11. Disconnect side impact air bag module electrical connector located beneath driver's seat.
12. Attach Rotunda air bag simulator tool No. 105-R0012, or equivalent, to side impact air bag connector under driver's seat on vehicle wiring harness side
13. Disconnect side impact air bag module electrical connector located beneath passenger's seat.
14. Attach Rotunda air bag simulator tool No. 105-R0012, or equivalent, to side impact air bag connector under passenger's seat on vehicle wiring harness side
15. If side impact air bag diagnosis or service is to be performed, remove front seats as follows:
    a. Move front seat all way rearward, then remove covers and seat track front bolts.
    b. Move front seat all way forward, then remove covers and seat track rear bolts.

   c. Disconnect front seat electrical connectors and remove front seats.
16. Connect battery ground cable.

2001-04

1. Disconnect and isolate battery ground cable.
2. **On models equipped with auxiliary batteries and power supplies,** disconnect and isolate these items, too.
3. **On all models,** wait one minute for back-up power supply to deplete.
4. Remove steering column opening lower finish panel by removing parking brake release then pulling out at top of panel to release retaining clips.
5. Remove mounting bolts and steering column lower reinforcement.
6. Remove lefthand lower instrument panel insulator.
7. Pushing in on release tab, disconnect clockspring electrical connector at base of steering column.
8. Attach restraint system diagnostic tool No. 418-F403, or equivalent to vehicle harness side of clockspring electrical connector.
9. Remove audio unit.
10. Remove instrument panel cluster finish panel from instrument panel.
11. Open glove compartment and disconnect glove compartment isolator.
12. While pushing in on two glove compartment door tabs, position glove compartment downward.
13. Through glove compartment opening, remove passenger air bag module wire harness pin type fasteners from instrument panel.
14. Through glove box opening, remove passenger air bag module bolts.
15. Placing one hand in glove compartment opening, push passenger air bag module out from instrument panel. **Do not handle air bag module by grabbing edges of deployment doors.**
16. Disconnect passenger air bag module electrical connector and remove air bag module.
17. Attach restraint system diagnostic tool No. 418-F403, or equivalent, to vehicle harness side of passenger side impact air bag module electrical connector.
18. Connect battery ground cable.
19. Move and tilt front seats to highest and most forward position.
20. Disconnect battery ground cable and wait at least one minute for back-up power supply to deplete.
21. **On models equipped less side impact air bags,** proceed as follows:
    a. **Do not deactivate side impact air bags module circuit by removing side impact air bag bridge resistor from side impact air bag floor electrical connector.**
    b. If side impact air bag bridge resistor is removed, an open circuit fault will be generated by restraints control module (RCM)
    c. If restraint system diagnostic tool is installed at side impact air bag floor electrical connector, low resistance fault will be generated by RCM.
22. **On models equipped with side impact air bags,** proceed as follows:
    a. From under front passenger seat, release tab and disconnect passenger seat side impact air bag electrical connector.
    b. Attach restraint system diagnostic tool No. 418-FO88, or equivalent, to vehicle harness side of passenger seat side impact air bag electrical connector.
23. **On all models,** remove passenger side B-pillar lower trim panel.
24. Push in on release tab and disconnect passenger safety belt retractor pretensioner electrical connector.
25. Attach restraint system diagnostic tool No. 418-FO88, or equivalent, to vehicle harness side of passenger safety belt retractor pretensioner electrical connector
26. **On models equipped with side impact air bags,** proceed as follows:
    a. From under driver seat, release tab and disconnect driver seat side impact air bag electrical connector.
    b. Attach restraint system diagnostic tool No. 418-FO88, or equivalent, to vehicle harness side of driver seat air bag electrical connector.
27. **On all models,** remove driver side B-pillar lower trim panel.
28. Push in on release tab and disconnect driver safety belt retractor pretensioner electrical connector.
29. Attach restraint system diagnostic tool to vehicle harness side of driver side safety belt retractor pretensioner electrical connector.
30. Connect battery ground cable.
31. With restraint system diagnostic tools installed on all deployable devices, prove out supplemental restraint system.
32. Turn ignition switch from Off to Run position and visually monitor air bag indicator with air bag modules and pretensioners or restraint system diagnostic tools installed.
33. Air bag lamp will illuminate for approximately six seconds and turn off.
34. If air bag supplemental restraint system fault is present, air bag indicator will either fail to illuminate, remain illuminate continuously or flash.
35. Disconnect battery ground cable and wait for at least one minute for back-up power supply to deplete.

Arming

CONTINENTAL

1. Disconnect and isolate battery ground cable.
2. **On models equipped with auxiliary batteries and power supplies,** disconnect and isolate these items.
3. **On all models,** wait one minute for back-up power supply to deplete.
4. Remove air bag simulator harness connector at top of steering column.
5. **When carrying live air bag module, ensure bag and trim cover are pointed away from your body. Place module on bench with trim cover facing upward.**
6. Connect driver's air bag module and horn to clockspring electrical connectors.
7. Position driver's air bag module to steering wheel.
8. Install two driver's air bag module to steering wheel mounting bolts.
9. **Torque** mounting bolts to 108 inch lbs.
10. Install two steering wheel spoke bolt covers, if equipped.
11. Remove air bag simulator at passenger's air bag connector.
12. Connect passenger's air bag electrical connector and close glove compartment.
13. Remove air bag simulator from side impact air bag connector located beneath driver's seat and connect side impact air bag electrical connector.
14. Remove air bag simulator from side impact air bag connector located beneath passenger's seat and connect side impact air bag electrical connector.
15. If front seats were removed, install as follows:
    a. Disconnect side air simulator tools from side impact air bag module floor connectors at driver's and passenger's sides.
    b. Position front seat in vehicle.
    c. Move front seat all way forward, then install seat track rear bolts and covers.
    d. Move front seat all way rearward, then install seat track front bolts and covers.
    e. Disconnect side air simulator tools from side impact air bag module floor connectors at driver's and passenger's sides.
    f. Connect driver's and passenger's front seat electrical connectors.
16. Connect battery ground cable.
17. **From safe location at sides or below air bag modules,** place ignition switch in Run position and observe air bag warning lamp operating. Indicator lamp should light for approximately six seconds and turn off.

CONTOUR & MYSTIQUE

1. Disconnect and isolate battery ground cable.
2. Allow at least one minute for back-up power supply to deplete.
3. Remove air bag simulator tool from driver's air bag sliding contact connector.
4. Connect driver's air bag module electrical connector.
5. Position driver's air bag module to steering wheel.
6. Install two air bag module bolt and washer assemblies at rear or sides of steering wheel.
7. **Torque** mounting bolts/nuts to 44 inch lbs.
8. Remove air bag simulator tool from passenger's air bag wiring harness.
9. Connect passenger's air bag module electrical connector.
10. Install passenger's air vent duct and glove compartment upper cover, connect glove compartment lamp and install screws.

11. Install glove compartment in instrument panel.
12. Connect battery ground cable.
13. **From safe location at sides or below air bag modules,** place ignition switch in Run position and observe air bag warning lamp operating. Indicator lamp should light for approximately six seconds and turn off.

COUGAR

1. Disconnect and isolate battery ground cable.
2. Allow at least one minute for back-up power supply to deplete.
3. Remove air bag simulator tool from driver's air bag sliding contact connector.
4. Connect driver's air bag module electrical connector.
5. Position driver's air bag module to steering wheel.
6. Install driver's air bag module Torx mounting screws.
7. **Torque** mounting screws to 44 inch lbs.
8. Remove air bag simulator tool from passenger's air bag wiring harness.
9. From passenger's foot well, roll passenger's air bag module around crossbeam.
10. Position air bag module and install two air bag module to crossbeam mounting bolts.
11. **Torque** mounting bolts/nuts to 12 ft. lbs.
12. Connect passenger's air bag module electrical connector.
13. Install passenger's air register duct.
14. Install glove compartment finish panel and secure with four Torx mounting screws.
15. Depress side stops to attach glove compartment sides and close glove compartment.
16. Install three glove compartment Torx mounting screws.
17. **On models equipped with side impact air bags,** proceed as follows:
    a. Install side impact air bag module.
    b. **Torque** side impact air bag module mounting bolts/nuts to 12 ft. lbs.
    c. Connect side impact air bag module electrical connector at driver's and passenger's seats.
    d. Install seat pads, covers and back rests.
18. **On all models,** connect battery ground cable.
19. **From safe location at sides or below air bag modules,** place ignition switch in Run position and observe air bag warning lamp operating. Indicator lamp should light for approximately three seconds and turn off.

CROWN VICTORIA & GRAND MARQUIS

2000

1. Disconnect and isolate battery ground cable, then wait one minute for back-up power supply to deplete.
2. Remove air bag simulator from harness on top of steering column.
3. Connect driver's air bag and horn electrical connectors.
4. Position driver's air bag on steering wheel and secure with two mounting bolts.
5. **Torque** driver's air bag module mounting bolts/nuts to 108 inch lbs.
6. Remove air bag simulator from passenger side impact air bag harness connector.
7. Position air bag module in instrument panel.
8. Install two passengers air bag module mounting screws and bolts.
9. **Torque** passenger air bag module mounting bolts/nuts to 80 inch lbs.
10. Connect passenger's air bag module electrical connector.
11. Connect clock electrical connector and position trim panel to instrument panel. Attach trim panel by pulling inward to seat clips.
12. Push inward on glove compartment door tabs then position door upward
13. Install glove compartment locator.
14. Connect battery ground cable.
15. **From safe location at sides or below air bag modules,** place ignition switch in Run position and observe air bag warning lamp operating. Indicator lamp should light for approximately six seconds and turn off.
16. Reset radio stations and clock.

2001–04

1. Disconnect battery ground cable.
2. Wait at least one minute for back-up power supply to deplete.
3. Remove restraint system diagnostic tool from driver safety belt retractor and pretensioner electrical connector.
4. Connect driver safety belt retractor and pretensioner electrical connectors.
5. Remove restraint system diagnostic tool from passenger safety belt retractor and pretensioner electrical connectors.
6. Connect passenger safety belt retractor and pretensioner electrical connectors.
7. Install front seats.
8. Remove restraint system diagnostic tools from passenger air bag module electrical connectors.
9. Install passenger air bag module electrical connector.
10. Remove restraint system diagnostic tools from driver air bag module electrical connectors.
11. Install driver air bag module electrical connector.
12. Connect battery ground cable.
13. Turn ignition switch from OFF to RUN position and visually monitor air bag indicator with air bag modules and safety belt pretensioners or restraint system diagnostic tools installed.
14. Air bag indicator will light continuously for approximately six seconds and then turn off.
15. If air bag supplemental restraint system (SRS) fault is present, air bag indicator will either fail to light, remain lit continuously, or flash.
16. Flashing might not occur until approximately 30 seconds after ignition switch has been turned from OFF to RUN position. This is time required for restraints control module (RCM) to complete testing of SRS.
17. If air bag indicator is inoperative and SRS fault exists, chime will sound in pattern of five sets of five beeps. If this occurs, air bag indicator will need to be repaired before diagnosis can continue.

ESCORT & ZX2

1. Disconnect battery ground cable. Allow one minute for back-up power supply to deplete.
2. **On models equipped with auxiliary batteries and power supplies,** disconnect and isolate these items also.
3. **On all models,** remove air bag simulator from harness on top of steering column.
4. Connect driver's air bag connector.
5. Position driver's air bag on steering wheel and secure with two bolts.
6. **Torque** mounting bolts to 70–86 inch lbs.
7. Remove air bag simulator from passenger's air bag harness connector.
8. Connect air bag module electrical connector and position module in instrument panel.
9. Install four air bag module bolts.
10. **Torque** air bag module mounting bolts to 72–103 inch lbs.
11. Push glove compartment door back into instrument panel.
12. Connect battery ground cable.
13. **From safe location at sides or below air bag modules,** place ignition switch in Run position and observe air bag warning lamp operating. Indicator lamp should light for approximately six seconds and turn off. If air bag indicator is inoperative and SRS fault exists, chime will sound in pattern of five sets of beeps. If this occurs, air bag indicator will need to be repaired before diagnosis can continue
14. Reset radio stations and clock.

FOCUS

1. Disconnect and isolate battery ground cable.
2. **On models equipped with auxiliary batteries and power supplies,** disconnect and isolate these items, too.
3. **On all models,** wait one minute for back-up power supply to deplete.
4. Remove air bag simulator from harness on top of steering column.
5. Connect driver's air bag connector.
6. Position driver's air bag on steering wheel and secure with two bolts. **When carrying live air bag module, ensure bag and trim cover are pointed away from your body. Place module on bench with trim cover facing upward.**
7. **Torque** mounting screws to 44 inch lbs.
8. Remove air bag simulator from passenger's air bag harness connector.
9. Connect passenger's air bag module electrical connector.
10. Remove air bag simulator from driver's side seat belt pretensioner connector.

11. Connect driver's side seat belt pretensioner electrical connector.
12. Remove air bag simulator from driver's side impact air bag connector.
13. Connect driver's side impact air bag electrical connector.
14. Remove air bag simulator from passenger's side seat belt pretensioner connector.
15. Connect passenger's side seat belt pretensioner electrical connector.
16. Remove air bag simulator from passenger's side impact air bag connector.
17. Connect passenger's side impact air bag electrical connector.
18. Install glove compartment.
19. Connect battery ground cable.
20. **From safe location at sides or below air bag modules,** place ignition switch in Run position and observe air bag warning lamp operating. Indicator lamp should light for approximately six seconds and turn off.
21. Reset radio stations and clock.

LS

1. Disconnect and isolate battery ground cable.
2. **On models equipped with auxiliary batteries and power supplies,** disconnect and isolate these items also.
3. **On all models,** wait one minute for back-up power supply to deplete.
4. Remove seat belt pretensioner simulator tool from passenger's seat belt pretensioner harness connector.
5. Connect passenger's seat belt pretensioner electrical connector.
6. Install passenger side B-pillar pillar trim.
7. Remove seat belt pretensioner simulator tool from driver's seat belt pretensioner harness connector.
8. Connect driver's seat belt pretensioner electrical connector.
9. Install driver side B-pillar pillar trim.
10. Remove air bag simulator tool from harness connector at top of steering column.
11. Connect driver's air bag electrical connector.
12. Position driver's air bag on steering wheel and secure with its bolts. **When carrying live air bag module, ensure bag and trim cover are pointed away from your body. Place module on bench with trim cover facing upward.**
13. **Torque** mounting bolts to 108 inch lbs.
14. Remove air bag simulator from passenger's air bag harness connector.
15. Connect passenger's air bag module electrical connector.
16. Install glove compartment.
17. Remove air bag simulator from passenger's side impact air bag connector.
18. Connect passenger's side impact air bag electrical connector.
19. Remove air bag simulator from driver's side impact air bag connector.
20. Connect driver's side impact air bag electrical connector.
21. Connect battery ground cable.
22. **From safe location at sides or below air bag modules,** place ignition switch in Run position and observe air bag warning lamp operating. Indicator lamp should light for approximately six seconds and turn off.
23. Reset radio stations and clock.

MUSTANG

1. Disconnect battery ground cable.
2. **On models equipped with auxiliary batteries and power supplies,** disconnect and isolate these items also.
3. **On all models,** allow at least one minute for back-up power supply to deplete.
4. Remove air bag simulator tool from harness connector at top of steering column.
5. Connect driver's air bag connector.
6. Position driver's air bag on steering wheel and secure with four nut and bolt assemblies.
7. **Torque** driver's air bag module mounting bolts/nuts to 80 inch lbs.
8. Remove air bag simulator tool from passenger's air bag module harness then position module in instrument panel.
9. Attach connector to instrument panel reinforcement and wiring harness.
10. Install passenger's air bag mounting bolt.
11. **Torque** passenger's air bag module mounting bolts to 80 inch lbs.
12. Press gently on air bag module corners to engage with instrument panel trim and install righthand side air conditioning duct.
13. Press sides of glove compartment together and lift into position in instrument panel. Close glove compartment door.
14. Connect battery ground cable.
15. Place ignition switch in Run position and observe air bag warning lamp operating. Warning lamp should illuminate for approximately six seconds and turn off.

SABLE & TAURUS

1. Disconnect and isolate battery ground cable.
2. **On models equipped with auxiliary batteries and power supplies,** disconnect and isolate these items also.
3. **On all models,** wait one minute for back-up power supply to deplete.
4. Disconnect driver's air bag restraint system diagnostic tool from vehicle side of driver's air bag sliding contact electrical connector.
5. Connect driver's air bag sliding contact electrical connector.
6. Install steering column lower cover and reinforcement.
7. Disconnect passenger's air bag restraint system diagnostic tool from vehicle side of passenger's air bag electrical connector.
8. Inspect position of passenger's air bag module J-nuts.
9. Position air bag module and trim cover to instrument panel. **When carrying live air bag module, ensure bag and trim cover are pointed away from your body. Place module on bench with trim cover facing upward.**
10. Install wiring harness pin retaining to air bag module.
11. Connect passenger's air bag module electrical connector.
12. Align air bag module channels with instrument panel rails.
13. Starting at lefthand side of air bag module trim cover, install upper and lower alignment pins into instrument panel.
14. Working from left to right, install trim cover alignment pins and retainers into instrument panel. When all channels and rails are aligned, gap around perimeter of air bag module trim cover will be even.
15. Through glove compartment opening, install passengers air bag module mounting bolts.
16. **Torque** mounting bolts to 71 inch lbs.
17. Close glove compartment.
18. Disconnect passenger's seat belt pretensioner restraint system diagnostic tool from 10 pin floor electrical connector.
19. Connect passenger's seat belt pretensioner electrical connector.
20. **On models equipped with side impact air bags,** disconnect side impact air bag restraint system diagnostic tool from side impact air bag floor electrical connector on passenger's side. Connect side impact air bag electrical connector on passenger's side.
21. **On all models,** disconnect driver's seat belt pretensioner restraint system diagnostic tool from 10 pin floor electrical connector.
22. Connect driver's seat belt pretensioner electrical connector.
23. **On models equipped with side impact air bags,** disconnect side impact air bag restraint system diagnostic tool from side impact air bag floor electrical connector on driver's side.
24. **On models equipped with side impact air bags,** connect side impact air bag electrical connector on driver's side.
25. **On all models,** connect battery ground cable.
26. **From safe location at sides or below air bag modules,** place ignition switch in Run position and observe air bag warning lamp operating. Indicator lamp should light for approximately six seconds and turn off.

THUNDERBIRD

1. Disconnect battery ground cable and wait at least one minute for back-up power supply to deplete.
2. Remove diagnostic tool No. 418-F395, or equivalent, from driver side safety belt retractor pretensioner electrical connector.
3. Connect driver side safety belt retractor pretensioner electrical connector.
4. Install driver side rear trim panel and speaker grille.
5. Position safety belt back into driver seat guide, then install driver side door weather stripping and scuff plate.
6. Remove diagnostic tool No. 418-F133,

or equivalent, from driver seat side impact air bag module electrical connector located under driver seat.
7. Connect driver seat side impact air bag module electrical connector.
8. Remove diagnostic tool No. 418-F395, or equivalent, from passenger side safety belt retractor pretensioner electrical connector.
9. Connect passenger side safety belt retractor pretensioner electrical connector.
10. Install passenger side rear trim panel and speaker grille.
11. Position safety belt back into passenger seat guide, then install passenger side door weatherstripping and scuff plate.
12. Remove diagnostic tool No. 418-F133, or equivalent, from passenger seat side impact air bag module electrical connector located under passenger seat.
13. Connect passenger seat side impact air bag module electrical connector.
14. Connect battery ground cable and move seats as far rearward as possible.
15. Disconnect battery ground cable and wait at least one minute for back-up power supply to deplete.
16. Reach through glove compartment opening and remove diagnostic tool No. 418-F395, or equivalent, from passenger air bag module electrical connector located behind center of instrument panel, above cross-car brace.
17. Connect passenger air bag module electrical connector, then install glove compartment and door.
18. Remove diagnostic tool No. 418-F088, or equivalent, from clockspring electrical connector located at base of steering column.
19. Connect clockspring electrical connector and install steering column reinforcement.
20. Tighten two driver side instrument panel tunnel brace bolts and position carpet back in place.
21. Install heater duct and hood latch.
22. Install driver side insulator panel and light socket.
23. Connect electrical connectors and install lower steering column opening finish panel.
24. Connect battery ground cable.
25. **From safe location at sides or below air bag modules,** place ignition switch in RUN position and observe air bag warning lamp operating. Indicator lamp should light for approximately six seconds and turn off.

TOWN CAR

2000

1. Disconnect and isolate battery ground cable.
2. **On models equipped with auxiliary batteries and power supplies,** disconnect and isolate these items also.
3. **On all models,** wait one minute for back-up power supply to deplete.
4. Remove air bag simulator from harness connector at top of steering column.
5. Connect driver's air bag module and horn to clockspring electrical connectors. **When carrying live air bag module, ensure bag and trim cover are pointed away from your body. Place module on bench with trim cover facing upward.**
6. Position driver's air bag module to steering wheel.
7. Install two driver's air bag module to steering wheel mounting bolts.
8. **Torque** driver's air bag module mounting bolts/nuts to 108 inch lbs.
9. Install two steering wheel spoke bolt covers, if equipped.
10. Remove air bag simulator at passenger's air bag connector.
11. Connect passenger's air bag electrical connector and close glove compartment.
12. Remove air bag simulator from side impact air bag connector located beneath driver's seat and connect side impact air bag electrical connector.
13. Remove air bag simulator from side impact air bag connector located beneath passenger's seat and connect side impact air bag electrical connector.
14. If front seats were removed, install as follows:
    a. Position front seat in vehicle.
    b. Move front seat all way forward, then install seat track rear bolts and covers.
    c. Move front seat all way rearward, then install seat track front bolts and covers.
    d. Disconnect side air simulator tools from side impact air bag module floor connectors at driver's and passenger's sides.
    e. Connect driver's and passenger's front seat electrical connectors.
15. Connect battery ground cable.
16. **From safe location at sides or below air bag modules,** place ignition switch in Run position and observe air bag warning lamp operating. Indicator lamp should light for approximately six seconds and turn off.

2001–04

1. Disconnect and isolate battery ground cable.
2. **On models equipped with auxiliary batteries and power supplies,** disconnect and isolate these items also.
3. **On all models,** wait one minute for back-up power supply to deplete.
4. Remove air bag simulator from harness connector at top of steering column.
5. Connect driver's air bag module and horn to clockspring electrical connectors. **When carrying live air bag module, ensure bag and trim cover are pointed away from your body. Place module on bench with trim cover facing upward.**
6. Position driver's air bag module to steering wheel.
7. Install two driver's air bag module to steering wheel mounting bolts, **torque** to 108 inch lbs.
8. Install two steering wheel spoke bolt covers, if equipped.
9. Remove air bag simulator at passenger's air bag connector.
10. Connect passenger's air bag electrical connector and close glove compartment.
11. Remove air bag simulator from side impact air bag connector located beneath driver's seat and connect side impact air bag electrical connector.
12. Remove air bag simulator from side impact air bag connector located beneath passenger's seat and connect side impact air bag electrical connector.
13. If front seats were removed, install as follows:
    a. Position front seat in vehicle.
    b. Move front seat all way forward, then install seat track rear bolts and covers.
    c. Move front seat all way rearward, then install seat track front bolts and covers.
    d. Disconnect side air simulator tools from side impact air bag module floor connectors at driver's and passenger's sides.
    e. Connect driver's and passenger's front seat electrical connectors.
14. Connect battery ground cable.
15. **From safe location at sides or below air bag modules,** place ignition switch in Run position and observe air bag warning lamp operating. Indicator lamp should light for approximately six seconds and turn off.

GENERAL MOTORS

The Diagnostic Energy Reserve Module or Sensing and Diagnostic Module (DERM/SDM) can maintain enough voltage to cause air bag deployment for up to 10 minutes after the ignition is turned Off and the battery is disconnected. Servicing the SIR system during this period may result in accidental deployment and personal injury.

Disarming

ALERO, CUTLASS, GRAND AM & MALIBU

2000–02

1. Ensure front wheels are pointed straight-ahead.
2. Ensure ignition switch is in Off or Lock position. Remove key.
3. Remove lefthand instrument panel wiring harness junction block access panel.
4. Remove AIR BAG fuse from lefthand instrument panel fuse junction block.
5. Disconnect Connector Position Assurance (CPA) located above lefthand instrument panel wiring harness junction block.
6. Disconnect steering wheel module coil connector.
7. Remove righthand instrument panel wiring harness junction block access panel.

8. Disconnect CPA located above righthand instrument panel wiring harness junction block.
9. Disconnect passenger's air bag module connector.

2003-04

Zone 3

1. Ensure front wheels are pointed straight-ahead.
2. Turn ignition key off and remove ignition key from switch.
3. Remove access panel from lefthand instrument panel wiring harness junction block.
4. Remove AIR BAG fuse from junction block.
5. Remove Connector Position Assurance (CPA) cover from steering wheel module coil connector. Connector is located above lefthand instrument panel wiring harness junction block.
6. Disconnect steering wheel module coil connector.

Zone 5

1. Ensure front wheels are pointed straight-ahead.
2. Turn ignition key off and remove ignition key from switch.
3. Remove access panel from lefthand instrument panel wiring harness junction block.
4. Remove AIR BAG fuse from junction block.
5. Remove access panel from righthand instrument panel wiring harness junction block.
6. Remove Connector Position Assurance (CPA) cover from instrument panel module connector. Connector is located above righthand instrument panel wiring harness junction block.
7. Disconnect instrument panel module electrical connector.

AURORA

2001-02

1. Ensure front wheels are pointing straight ahead.
2. Turn ignition switch to Off position and remove key.
3. Remove SIR fuse from rear fuse block located under rear seat.
4. Remove instrument panel lefthand side sound insulator.
5. Remove Connector Position Assurance (CPA) from driver's air bag module yellow connector located next to steering column.
6. Disconnect driver's air bag module yellow connector from harness yellow connector.
7. Remove instrument panel righthand side sound insulator.
8. Remove CPA from passenger's air bag module yellow connector located above instrument panel righthand side sound insulator.
9. Disconnect passenger's air bag module yellow connector from harness yellow connector.
10. Remove CPA from lefthand side impact air bag module yellow connector located under driver's seat.
11. Disconnect lefthand side impact air bag module yellow connector from harness yellow connector.
12. Remove CPA from righthand side impact air bag module yellow connector located under righthand front seat.
13. Disconnect righthand side impact air bag module yellow connector from harness yellow connector.

2003-04

Zone 1

1. Position steering wheel in straight ahead position.
2. Turn ignition switch to Off position and remove key.
3. Remove rear seat lower cushion.
4. Remove SIR fuse from rear fuse center.
5. Remove Connector Position Assurance (CPA) lock from Electronic Frontal Sensor (EFS) connector. EFS is located on front lefthand side of engine compartment.
6. Disconnect EFS connector.

Zone 2

1. Position steering wheel in straight ahead position.
2. Remove rear seat lower cushion.
3. Remove SIR fuse from rear fuse center.
4. Remove front and rear carpet retainers from lefthand center pillar trim panel.
5. Remove lefthand center pillar trim panel from pillar.
6. Remove Connector Position Assurance (CPA) lock from lefthand Side Impact Sensor (SIS) connector.
7. Disconnect SIS connector.

Zone 3

1. Position steering wheel in straight ahead position.
2. Turn ignition switch to Off position and remove key.
3. Remove rear seat lower cushion.
4. Remove SIR fuse from rear fuse center.
5. Remove lefthand closeout/insulator panel from under lefthand side of instrument panel.
6. Remove Connector Position Assurance (CPA) lock from steering wheel module yellow connector.
7. Disconnect steering wheel module connector from yellow harness connector.

Zone 5

1. Position steering wheel in straight ahead position.
2. Turn ignition switch to Off position and remove key.
3. Remove rear seat lower cushion.
4. Remove SIR fuse from rear fuse center.
5. Remove righthand closeout/insulator panel from under righthand side of instrument panel.
6. Remove Connector Position Assurance (CPA) lock from instrument panel module yellow connector.
7. Disconnect instrument panel module connector from yellow harness connector.

Zone 6

1. Position steering wheel in straight ahead position.
2. Turn ignition switch to Off position and remove key.
3. Remove rear seat lower cushion.
4. Remove SIR fuse from rear fuse center.
5. Remove front and rear carpet retainers from righthand center pillar trim panel.
6. Remove righthand center pillar trim panel from pillar.
7. Remove Connector Position Assurance (CPA) lock from righthand Side Impact Sensor (SIS) connector.
8. Disconnect SIS connector.

Zone 7

1. Turn steering wheel to straight-ahead position.
2. Turn ignition switch to Off position and remove key.
3. Remove steering column upper and lower covers.
4. Disconnect inflatable restraint steering wheel module coil connector from inflatable restraint steering wheel module coil.
5. Remove passenger's air bag module cover.
6. Disconnect Connector Position Assurance (CPA) from passenger's air bag module electrical connector.
7. Disconnect passenger's air bag module electrical connector.
8. Remove driver's outer seat track cover.
9. Disconnect driver's seat belt pretensioner two-way electrical connector from inline connector C315.
10. Disconnect CPA from lefthand side impact air bag module electrical connector.
11. Disconnect lefthand side impact air bag module electrical connector.
12. Remove righthand front outer seat track cover.
13. Disconnect passenger's seat belt pretensioner two-way electrical connector from inline connector C316.
14. Remove CPA from righthand side impact air bag module electrical connector.
15. Disconnect righthand side impact air bag module electrical connector.
16. Remove rear seat lower cushion.
17. Remove SIR fuse from rear fuse center.
18. Remove Connector Position Assurance (CPA) lock from lefthand driver side impact module and seat belt pretensioner yellow connector. Connector is located under driver's seat.
19. Disconnect lefthand driver side impact module and seat belt pretensioner yellow connector from harness connector.

Zone 8

1. Position steering wheel in straight ahead position.

2. Turn ignition switch to Off position and remove key.
3. Remove steering column upper and lower covers.
4. Disconnect inflatable restraint steering wheel module coil connector from inflatable restraint steering wheel module coil.
5. Remove passenger's air bag module cover.
6. Disconnect Connector Position Assurance (CPA) from passenger's air bag module electrical connector.
7. Disconnect passenger's air bag module electrical connector.
8. Remove driver's outer seat track cover.
9. Disconnect driver's seat belt pretensioner two-way electrical connector from inline connector C315.
10. Disconnect CPA from lefthand side impact air bag module electrical connector.
11. Disconnect lefthand side impact air bag module electrical connector.
12. Remove righthand front outer seat track cover.
13. Disconnect passenger's seat belt pretensioner two-way electrical connector from inline connector C316.
14. Remove CPA from righthand side impact air bag module electrical connector.
15. Disconnect righthand side impact air bag module electrical connector.
16. Remove rear seat lower cushion.
17. Remove SIR fuse from rear fuse center.
18. Remove Connector Position Assurance (CPA) lock from righthand side impact module and seat belt pretensioner yellow connector. Connector is located under passenger's front seat.
19. Disconnect righthand side impact module and seat belt pretensioner yellow connector from harness connector.
20. Remove righthand closeout/insulator panel from under righthand side of instrument panel.
21. Remove CPA lock from instrument panel module yellow connector.
22. Disconnect instrument panel module connector from yellow harness connector.
23. Remove lefthand closeout/insulator panel from under lefthand side of instrument panel.
24. Remove CPA lock from steering wheel module yellow connector.
25. Disconnect steering wheel module connector from yellow harness connector.
26. Remove CPA lock from lefthand driver side impact module and seat belt pretensioner yellow connector. Connector is located under driver's seat.
27. Disconnect lefthand driver side impact module and seat belt pretensioner yellow connector from harness connector.

Zone 9

1. Position steering wheel in straight ahead position.
2. Remove rear seat lower cushion.
3. Remove SIR fuse from rear fuse center.
4. Remove Connector Position Assurance (CPA) lock from righthand passenger side impact module and seat belt pretensioner yellow connector. Connector is located under passenger's seat.
5. Disconnect righthand side impact module and seat belt pretensioner yellow connector to vehicle harness connector.

BONNEVILLE, EIGHTY-EIGHT & LESABRE

2000–02

1. Ensure front wheels are pointed straight-ahead.
2. Turn ignition switch to Off position and remove key.
3. Remove SIR fuse from rear fuse block located under rear seat.
4. Remove instrument panel lefthand sound insulator.
5. Disconnect Connector Position Assurance (CPA) from driver's air bag module yellow two-way connector at base of steering column.
6. Disconnect driver's air bag module yellow two-way connector from harness yellow connector.
7. Remove righthand sound insulator.
8. Disconnect CPA and yellow two-way connector from passenger's air bag module yellow connector located above righthand sound insulator.
9. Disconnect passenger's air bag module yellow connector from harness yellow connector.
10. Disconnect CPA from lefthand side impact air bag module yellow electrical connector located under driver's seat.
11. Disconnect lefthand side impact air bag module yellow electrical connector from harness yellow connector.
12. Remove CPA from righthand side impact air bag module electrical connector located under righthand front seat.
13. Disconnect righthand side impact air bag module yellow electrical connector from harness yellow connector.

2003–04

For disarming procedures on these models, refer to "2003–04" in "Aurora."

CAMARO & FIREBIRD

1. Ensure front wheels are pointed straight-ahead.
2. Turn ignition switch to Off position and remove key.
3. Remove instrument panel fuse block access door.
4. Remove AIR BAG fuse from instrument panel fuse box.
5. Remove lefthand instrument panel insulator.
6. Disconnect Connector Position Assurance (CPA) from inflatable restraint steering wheel module coil connector located at base of steering column.
7. Disconnect steering wheel module coil connector located at base of steering column.
8. Remove righthand instrument panel insulator.
9. Disconnect CPA from passenger's air bag module connector located behind instrument panel compartment door.
10. Disconnect yellow two-way connector from passenger's air bag module located behind glove compartment.

CATERA

1. Turn steering wheel to straight-ahead position.
2. Turn ignition switch to Off position and remove key.
3. Remove steering column upper and lower covers.
4. Disconnect inflatable restraint steering wheel module coil connector from inflatable restraint steering wheel module coil.
5. Remove passenger's air bag module cover.
6. Disconnect Connector Position Assurance (CPA) from passenger's air bag module electrical connector.
7. Disconnect passenger's air bag module electrical connector.
8. Remove driver's outer seat track cover.
9. Disconnect driver's seat belt pretensioner two-way electrical connector from inline connector C315.
10. Disconnect CPA from lefthand side impact air bag module electrical connector.
11. Disconnect lefthand side impact air bag module electrical connector.
12. Remove righthand front outer seat track cover.
13. Disconnect passenger's seat belt pretensioner two-way electrical connector from inline connector C316.
14. Remove CPA from righthand side impact air bag module electrical connector.
15. Disconnect righthand side impact air bag module electrical connector.

CAVALIER & SUNFIRE

2000–02

1. Ensure front wheels are pointed straight-ahead.
2. Turn ignition switch to Off position and remove key.
3. Remove lefthand instrument panel junction block access panel.
4. Remove SIR or AIR BAG fuse from lefthand instrument panel fuse block.
5. Disconnect Connector Position Assurance (CPA) from driver's air bag module coil connector located above lefthand instrument panel wiring harness junction block.
6. Disconnect steering wheel module coil connector.
7. Remove righthand instrument panel wiring harness junction block access panel.
8. Disconnect CPA from passenger's air bag module connector located above righthand instrument panel wiring harness junction block.
9. Disconnect passenger's air bag module connector.

2003-04

Zone 1

1. Position steering wheel in straight ahead position.
2. Ensure ignition switch is Off and key is removed.
3. Remove lefthand instrument panel outer trim cover.
4. Remove AIR BAG fuse from lefthand instrument panel junction block.
5. Remove hood closeout filler panel from front of engine compartment.
6. Remove Connector Position Assurance (CPA) cover from inflatable restraint Electronic Front Sensor (EFS) connector.
7. Disconnect connector from EFS.

Zone 2, Coupe

1. Position steering wheel in straight ahead position.
2. Ensure ignition switch is Off and key is removed.
3. Remove lefthand instrument panel outer trim cover.
4. Remove AIR BAG fuse from lefthand instrument panel junction block.
5. Remove window regulator handle from lefthand door trim panel.
6. **On models equipped with power door locks,** remove power door lock switch from lefthand door trim panel.
7. **On all models,** remove lefthand door trim panel mounting screws and pull trim panel away from door.
8. Remove inflatable restraint Side Impact Sensor (SIS) from door.
9. Remove Connector Position Assurance (CPA) cover from SIS connector.
10. Disconnect SIS connector.

Zone 2, Sedan

1. Position steering wheel in straight ahead position.
2. Ensure ignition switch is Off and key is removed.
3. Remove lefthand instrument panel outer trim cover.
4. Remove AIR BAG fuse from lefthand instrument panel junction block.
5. Remove upper trim from lefthand center pillar.
6. Remove inflatable restraint Side Impact Sensor (SIS) from center pillar.
7. Remove Connector Position Assurance (CPA) cover from SIS connector.
8. Disconnect SIS connector.

Zone 3

1. Position steering wheel in straight ahead position.
2. Ensure ignition switch is Off and key is removed.
3. Remove lefthand instrument panel outer trim cover.
4. Remove AIR BAG fuse from lefthand instrument panel junction block.
5. Remove Connector Position Assurance (CPA) cover from inflatable restraint steering wheel module coil connector. Connector is located under lefthand side of instrument panel, left of steering column.
6. Disconnect steering wheel module coil connector.

Zone 5

1. Position steering wheel in straight ahead position.
2. Ensure ignition switch is Off and key is removed.
3. Remove lefthand instrument panel outer trim cover.
4. Remove AIR BAG fuse from lefthand instrument panel junction block.
5. Remove Connector Position Assurance (CPA) cover from inflatable restraint instrument panel module inline connector. Connector is located under lefthand side of instrument panel, left of steering column.
6. Disconnect instrument panel module inline connector.

Zone 6, Coupe

1. Position steering wheel in straight ahead position.
2. Ensure ignition switch is Off and key is removed.
3. Remove lefthand instrument panel outer trim cover.
4. Remove AIR BAG fuse from lefthand instrument panel junction block.
5. Remove window regulator handle from righthand door trim panel.
6. **On models equipped with power door locks,** remove power door lock switch from righthand door trim panel.
7. **On all models,** remove righthand door trim panel mounting screws and pull trim panel away from door.
8. Remove inflatable restraint Side Impact Sensor (SIS) from door.
9. Remove Connector Position Assurance (CPA) cover from SIS connector.
10. Disconnect SIS connector.

Zone 6, Sedan

1. Position steering wheel in straight ahead position.
2. Ensure ignition switch is Off and key is removed.
3. Remove lefthand instrument panel outer trim cover.
4. Remove AIR BAG fuse from lefthand instrument panel junction block.
5. Remove upper trim from righthand center pillar.
6. Remove inflatable restraint Side Impact Sensor (SIS) from center pillar.
7. Remove Connector Position Assurance (CPA) cover from SIS connector.
8. Disconnect SIS connector.

Zone 7

1. Position steering wheel in straight ahead position.
2. Ensure ignition switch is Off and key is removed.
3. Remove lefthand instrument panel outer trim cover.
4. Remove AIR BAG fuse from lefthand instrument panel junction block.
5. Remove Connector Position Assurance (CPA) cover from inflatable restraint side impact module connector. Connector is located under driver's seat.
6. Disconnect side impact module connector.

Zone 9

1. Position steering wheel in straight ahead position.
2. Ensure ignition switch is Off and key is removed.
3. Remove lefthand instrument panel outer trim cover.
4. Remove AIR BAG fuse from lefthand instrument panel junction block.
5. Remove Connector Position Assurance (CPA) cover from inflatable restraint side impact module connector. Connector is located under passenger's front seat.
6. Disconnect side impact module connector.

CENTURY & REGAL

2000-02

1. Ensure front wheels are pointed straight-ahead.
2. Turn ignition to Off position and remove ignition key.
3. Remove instrument panel fuse block access door.
4. Remove AIR BAG fuse from instrument panel fuse block.
5. Remove lefthand underdash trim panel.
6. Disconnect Connector Position Assurance (CPA) from driver's air bag module coil connector located at base of steering column.
7. Disconnect driver's air bag module coil connector.
8. Disconnect passenger's air bag module CPA located to right of steering column.
9. Disconnect passenger's air bag module yellow air bag module connector.
10. **On models equipped with side impact air bag modules,** proceed as follows:
    a. Remove CPA from lefthand side impact air bag module impact module.
    b. Disconnect lefthand side impact air bag module.

2003-04

Zone 2

1. Position steering wheel in straight ahead position.
2. Ensure ignition switch is Off and key is removed.
3. Remove instrument panel fuse block cover.
4. Remove SIR fuse from fuse block.
5. Remove lefthand center pillar trim panel.
6. Remove Side Impact Sensor (SIS) from center pillar.
7. Remove Connector Position Assurance (CPA) cover from SIS connector.
8. Disconnect SIS connector.

Zone 3

1. Position steering wheel in straight ahead position.
2. Ensure ignition switch is Off and key is removed.

3. Remove instrument panel fuse block cover.
4. Remove SIR fuse from fuse block.
5. Remove insulator panel from under lefthand side of instrument panel.
6. Remove Connector Position Assurance (CPA) cover from inflatable restraint steering wheel module coil connector. Connector is located at base of steering column.
7. Disconnect steering wheel module coil connector.

Zone 5

1. Position steering wheel in straight ahead position.
2. Ensure ignition switch is Off and key is removed.
3. Remove instrument panel fuse block cover.
4. Remove SIR fuse from fuse block.
5. Remove insulator panel from under lefthand side of instrument panel.
6. Remove Connector Position Assurance (CPA) cover from inflatable restraint instrument panel module connector. Connector is located on righthand side of steering column.
7. Disconnect instrument panel module connector.

Zone 7

1. Position steering wheel in straight ahead position.
2. Ensure ignition switch is Off and key is removed.
3. Remove instrument panel fuse block cover.
4. Remove SIR fuse from fuse block.
5. Remove Connector Position Assurance (CPA) cover from lefthand side impact module connector. Connector is located under driver's seat.
6. Disconnect side impact module connector.

Zone 9

1. Position steering wheel in straight ahead position.
2. Ensure ignition switch is Off and key is removed.
3. Remove instrument panel fuse block cover.
4. Remove SIR fuse from fuse block.
5. Remove insulator panel from under lefthand side of instrument panel.
6. Remove Connector Position Assurance (CPA) cover from inflatable restraint steering wheel module coil connector. Connector is located at base of steering column.
7. Disconnect steering wheel module coil connector.
8. Remove CPA cover from inflatable restraint instrument panel module connector. Connector is located on righthand side of steering column.
9. Disconnect instrument panel module connector.
10. Remove lefthand center pillar trim panel.
11. Remove Side Impact Sensor (SIS) from center pillar.
12. Remove CPA cover from SIS connector.
13. Disconnect SIS connector.

CORVETTE

2000-02

1. Place front wheels in straight-ahead position.
2. Turn ignition switch to Off position and remove key.
3. Remove front floor kick-up panel.
4. Remove SDM fuse from instrument panel fuse block.
5. Remove lefthand sound insulator.
6. Disconnect Connector Position Assurance (CPA) from driver's air bag module coil connector located at base of steering column.
7. Disconnect driver's air bag module coil yellow two-way SIR electrical connector at base of steering column.
8. Disconnect CPA from passenger's air bag module coil connector located at base of steering column.
9. Disconnect passenger's air bag module coil yellow two-way SIR electrical connector at base of steering column.

2003-04

Zone 3

1. Position steering wheel in straight ahead position.
2. Ensure ignition switch is Off and key is removed.
3. Remove kick-up panel from under instrument panel.
4. Remove SDM fuse from instrument panel fuse block.
5. Remove sound insulator panel from under lefthand side of instrument panel.
6. Remove Connector Position Assurance (CPA) cover from inflatable restraint steering wheel module coil connector. Connector is located at base of steering column.
7. Disconnect steering wheel module coil connector.

Zone 4

1. Position steering wheel in straight ahead position.
2. Ensure ignition switch is Off and key is removed.
3. Remove kick-up panel from under instrument panel.
4. Remove SDM fuse from instrument panel fuse block.
5. Remove sound insulator panel from under lefthand side of instrument panel.
6. Remove Connector Position Assurance (CPA) cover from inflatable restraint steering wheel module coil connector. Connector is located at base of steering column.
7. Disconnect steering wheel module coil connector.
8. Remove CPA cover from inflatable restraint instrument panel module connector. Connector is located near base of steering column.
9. Disconnect instrument panel module connector.

Zone 5

1. Position steering wheel in straight ahead position.
2. Ensure ignition switch is Off and key is removed.
3. Remove kick-up panel from under instrument panel.
4. Remove SDM fuse from instrument panel fuse block.
5. Remove sound insulator panel from under lefthand side of instrument panel.
6. Remove Connector Position Assurance (CPA) cover from inflatable restraint instrument panel module connector. Connector is located near base of steering column.
7. Disconnect instrument panel module connector.

CTS

ZONE 1

1. Position steering wheel in straight ahead position.
2. Turn ignition to Off position and remove key.
3. Remove rear seat lower cushion.
4. Remove SIR fuse from righthand rear fuse center.
5. Remove Connector Position Assurance (CPA) lock from Electronic Frontal Sensor (EFS) connector. EFS is located on front lefthand side of engine compartment.
6. Disconnect EFS connector.

ZONE 2

1. Position steering wheel in straight ahead position.
2. Turn ignition to Off position and remove key.
3. Remove rear seat lower cushion.
4. Remove SIR fuse from righthand rear fuse center.
5. Release lefthand rear sail panel retaining clips.
6. Remove lefthand rear sail panel from lefthand side of rear window.
7. Remove Connector Position Assurance (CPA) lock from lefthand roof rail module yellow electrical connector.
8. Disconnect lefthand roof rail module connector.
9. Remove front and rear carpet retainers from lefthand center pillar trim panel.
10. Remove lefthand center pillar trim panel from pillar.
11. Remove Connector Position Assurance (CPA) lock from lefthand Side Impact Sensor (SIS) connector.
12. Disconnect SIS connector.

ZONE 3

1. Position steering wheel in straight ahead position.
2. Turn ignition to Off position and remove key.
3. Remove rear seat lower cushion.
4. Remove SIR fuse from righthand rear fuse center.
5. Remove lefthand closeout/insulator panel from far lefthand side of instrument panel.
6. Remove Connector Position Assurance (CPA) lock from steering wheel

module yellow connector.
7. Disconnect steering wheel module connector from yellow harness connector.

ZONE 5

1. Position steering wheel in straight ahead position.
2. Turn ignition to Off position and remove key.
3. Remove rear seat lower cushion.
4. Remove SIR fuse from righthand rear fuse center.
5. Remove righthand closeout/insulator panel from far righthand side of instrument panel.
6. Remove Connector Position Assurance (CPA) lock from instrument panel module yellow connector.
7. Disconnect instrument panel module connector from yellow harness connector.

ZONE 6

1. Position steering wheel in straight ahead position.
2. Turn ignition to Off position and remove key.
3. Remove rear seat lower cushion.
4. Remove SIR fuse from righthand rear fuse center.
5. Release righthand rear sail panel retaining clips.
6. Remove righthand rear sail panel from righthand side of rear window.
7. Remove Connector Position Assurance (CPA) lock from righthand roof rail module yellow electrical connector.
8. Disconnect righthand roof rail module connector.
9. Remove front and rear carpet retainers from righthand center pillar trim panel.
10. Remove righthand center pillar trim panel from pillar.
11. Remove Connector Position Assurance (CPA) lock from righthand Side Impact Sensor (SIS) connector.
12. Disconnect SIS connector.

ZONE 7

1. Position steering wheel in straight ahead position.
2. Turn ignition to Off position and remove key.
3. Remove rear seat lower cushion.
4. Remove SIR fuse from righthand rear fuse center.
5. Remove Connector Position Assurance (CPA) lock from lefthand driver side impact module and seat belt pretensioner yellow connector. Connector is located under driver's seat.
6. Disconnect lefthand driver side impact module and seat belt pretensioner yellow connector from harness connector.

ZONE 8

1. Position steering wheel in straight ahead position.
2. Turn ignition to Off position and remove key.
3. Remove rear seat lower cushion.
4. Remove SIR fuse from righthand rear fuse center.
5. Release righthand rear sail panel retaining clips.
6. Remove righthand rear sail panel from righthand side of rear window.
7. Remove Connector Position Assurance (CPA) lock from righthand roof rail module yellow electrical connector.
8. Disconnect righthand roof rail module connector.
9. Remove righthand closeout/insulator panel from far righthand side of instrument panel.
10. Remove Connector Position Assurance (CPA) lock from instrument panel module yellow connector.
11. Disconnect instrument panel module connector from yellow harness connector.
12. Remove Connector Position Assurance (CPA) lock from righthand driver side impact module and seat belt pretensioner yellow connector. Connector is located under passenger's front seat.
13. Disconnect righthand driver side impact module and seat belt pretensioner yellow connector from harness connector.
14. Remove lefthand closeout/insulator panel from far lefthand side of instrument panel.
15. Remove Connector Position Assurance (CPA) lock from steering wheel module yellow connector.
16. Disconnect steering wheel module connector from yellow harness connector.
17. Remove Connector Position Assurance (CPA) lock from lefthand driver side impact module and seat belt pretensioner yellow connector. Connector is located under driver's seat.
18. Disconnect lefthand driver side impact module and seat belt pretensioner yellow connector from harness connector.
19. Release lefthand rear sail panel retaining clips.
20. Remove lefthand rear sail panel from lefthand side of rear window.
21. Remove Connector Position Assurance (CPA) lock from lefthand roof rail module yellow electrical connector.
22. Disconnect lefthand roof rail module connector.

ZONE 9

1. Position steering wheel in straight ahead position.
2. Turn ignition to Off position and remove key.
3. Remove rear seat lower cushion.
4. Remove SIR fuse from righthand rear fuse center.
5. Remove Connector Position Assurance (CPA) lock from righthand passenger side impact module and seat belt pretensioner yellow connector. Connector is located under passenger's seat.
6. Disconnect righthand driver side impact module and seat belt pretensioner yellow connector to vehicle harness connector.

DEVILLE

2000-02

1. Place front wheels in straight-ahead position.
2. Turn ignition to Off position and remove key.
3. Remove rear seat cushion.
4. Remove SIR fuse from fuse block under rear seat.
5. Remove instrument panel lefthand sound insulator.
6. Disconnect Connector Position Assurance (CPA) from driver's air bag module yellow connector located next to steering column.
7. Disconnect driver's air bag module connector from harness yellow connector.
8. Remove instrument panel righthand sound insulator.
9. Disconnect CPA from passenger's air bag module yellow connector located above righthand sound insulator.
10. Disconnect passenger's air bag module yellow connector from harness yellow connector.
11. Remove both CPAs locks from lefthand side impact air bag module and pretensioner yellow electrical connectors located under seat.
12. Disconnect lefthand side impact air bag module and pretensioner yellow electrical connectors from harness yellow connector.
13. Disconnect both CPAs from righthand side impact air bag module and pretensioner yellow electrical connectors located under seat.
14. Disconnect righthand side impact air bag module and pretensioner yellow electrical connectors.
15. **On models equipped with rear side impact air bag modules,** proceed as follows:
    a. Remove rear seatback.
    b. Disconnect CPA from righthand rear side impact air bag module yellow electrical connector.
    c. Disconnect righthand rear side impact air bag module yellow electrical connector.
    d. Disconnect CPA from lefthand rear side impact air bag module yellow electrical connector.
    e. Disconnect lefthand rear side impact air bag module yellow electrical connector.

2003-04

Zone 1

1. Position steering wheel in straight ahead position.
2. Turn ignition to Off position and remove key.
3. Remove rear seat lower cushion.
4. Remove SIR fuse from rear fuse center.
5. Remove Connector Position Assurance (CPA) lock from Electronic Frontal Sensor (EFS) connector. EFS is located on front lefthand side of engine compartment.
6. Disconnect EFS connector.

Zone 2

1. Position steering wheel in straight ahead position.
2. Turn ignition to Off position and remove key.
3. Remove rear seat lower cushion.
4. Remove SIR fuse from rear fuse center.
5. Remove front and rear carpet retainers from lefthand center pillar trim panel.
6. Remove lefthand center pillar trim panel from pillar.
7. Remove Connector Position Assurance (CPA) lock from lefthand Side Impact Sensor (SIS) connector.
8. Disconnect SIS connector.

Zone 3

1. Position steering wheel in straight ahead position.
2. Turn ignition to Off position and remove key.
3. Remove rear seat lower cushion.
4. Remove SIR fuse from rear fuse center.
5. Remove lefthand closeout/insulator panel from under lefthand side of instrument panel.
6. Remove Connector Position Assurance (CPA) lock from steering wheel module yellow connector. Connector is located near steering column.
7. Disconnect steering wheel module connector from yellow harness connector.

Zone 5

1. Position steering wheel in straight ahead position.
2. Turn ignition to Off position and remove key.
3. Remove rear seat lower cushion.
4. Remove SIR fuse from rear fuse center.
5. Remove righthand closeout/insulator panel from under righthand side of instrument panel.
6. Remove Connector Position Assurance (CPA) lock from instrument panel module yellow connector. Connector is located under righthand side of instrument panel.
7. Disconnect instrument panel module connector from yellow harness connector.

Zone 6

1. Position steering wheel in straight ahead position.
2. Turn ignition to Off position and remove key.
3. Remove rear seat lower cushion.
4. Remove SIR fuse from rear fuse center.
5. Remove front and rear carpet retainers from righthand center pillar trim panel.
6. Remove righthand center pillar trim panel from pillar.
7. Remove Connector Position Assurance (CPA) lock from righthand Side Impact Sensor (SIS) connector.
8. Disconnect SIS connector.

Zone 7

1. Position steering wheel in straight ahead position.
2. Turn ignition to Off position and remove key.
3. Remove rear seat lower cushion.
4. Remove SIR fuse from rear fuse center.
5. Remove Connector Position Assurance (CPA) lock from lefthand driver side impact module and seat belt pretensioner yellow connector. Connector is located under driver's seat.
6. Disconnect lefthand driver side impact module and seat belt pretensioner yellow connector from harness connector.

Zone 8

1. Position steering wheel in straight ahead position.
2. Turn ignition to Off position and remove key.
3. Remove rear seat lower cushion.
4. Remove SIR fuse from rear fuse center.
5. Remove righthand rear passenger seat back.
6. Remove Connector Position Assurance (CPA) lock from rear righthand side impact module and seat belt pretensioner yellow connector. Connector is located near righthand rear door jamb.
7. Disconnect rear righthand side impact module connector.
8. Remove CPA lock from righthand front side impact module yellow connector. Connector is located under passenger's front seat.
9. Disconnect righthand side impact module and seat belt pretensioner yellow connector from harness connector.
10. Remove righthand closeout/insulator panel from under righthand side of instrument panel.
11. Remove CPA lock from instrument panel module yellow connector.
12. Disconnect instrument panel module connector from yellow harness connector.
13. Remove lefthand closeout/insulator panel from under lefthand side of instrument panel.
14. Remove CPA lock from steering wheel module yellow connector.
15. Disconnect steering wheel module connector from yellow harness connector.
16. Remove CPA lock from lefthand driver side impact module and seat belt pretensioner yellow connector. Connector is located under driver's seat.
17. Disconnect lefthand driver side impact module and seat belt pretensioner yellow connector from harness connector.
18. Remove lefthand rear passenger seat back.
19. Remove Connector Position Assurance (CPA) lock from rear lefthand side impact module and seat belt pretensioner yellow connector. Connector is located near lefthand rear door jamb.
20. Disconnect rear lefthand side impact module connector.

Zone 9

1. Position steering wheel in straight ahead position.
2. Turn ignition to Off position and remove key.
3. Remove rear seat lower cushion.
4. Remove SIR fuse from rear fuse center.
5. Remove Connector Position Assurance (CPA) lock from righthand passenger side impact module and seat belt pretensioner yellow connector. Connector is located under passenger's seat.
6. Disconnect righthand side impact module and seat belt pretensioner yellow connector to vehicle harness connector.

Zone 10

1. Position steering wheel in straight ahead position.
2. Turn ignition to Off position and remove key.
3. Remove rear seat lower cushion.
4. Remove SIR fuse from rear fuse center.
5. Remove lefthand rear passenger seat back.
6. Remove Connector Position Assurance (CPA) lock from rear lefthand side impact module and seat belt pretensioner yellow connector. Connector is located near lefthand rear door jamb.
7. Disconnect rear lefthand side impact module connector.

Zone 12

1. Position steering wheel in straight ahead position.
2. Turn ignition to Off position and remove key.
3. Remove rear seat lower cushion.
4. Remove SIR fuse from rear fuse center.
5. Remove righthand rear passenger seat back.
6. Remove Connector Position Assurance (CPA) lock from rear righthand side impact module and seat belt pretensioner yellow connector. Connector is located near righthand rear door jamb.
7. Disconnect rear righthand side impact module connector.

ELDORADO

1. Place front wheels in straight-ahead position.
2. Turn ignition to Lock position and remove key.
3. Remove SIR fuse from trunk compartment fuse block.
4. Remove instrument panel lefthand sound insulator.
5. Disconnect CPA and both yellow two-way SIR electrical connectors at base of steering column.
6. Remove glove compartment.

7. Disconnect CPA and yellow two-way connector from passenger's air bag module pigtail behind instrument panel.

GRAND PRIX & INTRIGUE

2000-02

1. Ensure front wheels are pointed straight-ahead.
2. Turn ignition switch to Lock position and remove ignition key.
3. Remove AIR BAG or SIR system fuse from instrument panel fuse block.
4. Remove lefthand underdash trim panel.
5. Disconnect Connector Position Assurance (CPA) and yellow air bag module connectors at base of steering column.
6. Disconnect passenger's air bag module CPA and yellow air bag module connectors located to right of steering column.

2003-04

Zone 3

1. Position steering wheel in straight ahead position.
2. Turn ignition Off and remove key from ignition switch.
3. Remove instrument panel fuse block cover.
4. Remove SIR fuse from instrument panel fuse block.
5. Remove lefthand insulator panel from under lefthand side of instrument panel.
6. Remove Connector Position Assurance (CPA) cover from inflatable restraint steering wheel module coil connector. Connector is located at base of steering column.
7. Disconnect steering wheel module coil connector.

Zone 5

1. Position steering wheel in straight ahead position.
2. Turn ignition Off and remove key from ignition switch.
3. Remove instrument panel fuse block cover.
4. Remove SIR fuse from instrument panel fuse block.
5. Remove lefthand insulator panel from under lefthand side of instrument panel.
6. Remove Connector Position Assurance (CPA) cover from inflatable restraint instrument panel module connector. Connector is located on righthand side of steering column.
7. Disconnect instrument panel module connector.

Zone 9

1. Position steering wheel in straight ahead position.
2. Turn ignition Off and remove key from ignition switch.
3. Remove instrument panel fuse block cover.
4. Remove SIR fuse from instrument panel fuse block.
5. Remove lefthand insulator panel from under lefthand side of instrument panel.
6. Remove Connector Position Assurance (CPA) cover from inflatable restraint steering wheel module coil connector. Connector is located at base of steering column.
7. Disconnect steering wheel module coil connector.
8. Remove CPA cover from inflatable restraint instrument panel module connector. Connector is located on righthand side of steering column.
9. Disconnect instrument panel module connector.
10. Remove CPA cover from Sensing and Diagnostic Module (SDM). Connector is located under front righthand seat.
11. Disconnect SDM wiring harness connector.

IMPALA & MONTE CARLO

2000-02

1. Ensure front wheels are pointed straight-ahead.
2. Turn ignition switch to Off position and remove ignition key.
3. Remove lefthand instrument panel fuse access cover.
4. Remove SRS fuse from fuse block.
5. Disconnect Connector Position Assurance (CPA) from driver's air bag module coil connector, located at lefthand side of instrument panel.
6. Disconnect driver's air bag module coil connector.
7. Remove instrument panel righthand access hole cover.
8. Unclip driver's and passenger's air bag modules' yellow four-way electrical connector from metal rail.
9. Disconnect CPA from passenger's air bag module connector, located at righthand side if instrument panel.
10. Disconnect passenger's air bag module connector.
11. Disconnect CPA from side impact air bag module, located under driver's seat.
12. Disconnect side impact module.

2003-04

Zone 1

1. Position steering wheel in straight ahead position.
2. Turn ignition Off and remove key from ignition switch.
3. Remove instrument panel fuse block cover.
4. Remove SIR fuse from instrument panel fuse block.
5. Remove upper air baffle and deflector from radiator.
6. Remove orange Connector Position Assurance (CPA) cover from yellow sensor harness.
7. Disconnect sensor harness from sensor.

Zone 2, Impala

1. Position steering wheel in straight ahead position.
2. Turn ignition Off and remove key from ignition switch.
3. Remove instrument panel fuse block cover.
4. Remove SIR fuse from instrument panel fuse block.
5. Remove trim panel from lefthand center pillar.
6. Remove Side Impact Sensor (SIS) from center pillar.
7. Remove Connector Position Assurance (CPA) cover from SIS connector.
8. Disconnect SIS connector.

Zone 2, Monte Carlo

1. Position steering wheel in straight ahead position.
2. Turn ignition Off and remove key from ignition switch.
3. Remove instrument panel fuse block cover.
4. Remove SIR fuse from instrument panel fuse block.
5. Remove door handle trim bezel from lefthand front door trim panel.
6. Remove door trim panel to door mounting screws.
7. Pry trim panel away from door and disconnect power door lock and power window switch electrical connectors.
8. Remove trim panel from door.
9. Remove Side Impact Sensor (SIS) from mounting bracket on door impact beam.
10. Remove Connector Position Assurance (CPA) cover from SIS connector.
11. Disconnect SIS connector.

Zone 3

1. Position steering wheel in straight ahead position.
2. Turn ignition Off and remove key from ignition switch.
3. Remove instrument panel fuse block cover.
4. Remove SIR fuse from instrument panel fuse block.
5. Remove insulator panel from under lefthand side of instrument panel.
6. Remove Connector Position Assurance (CPA) cover from inflatable restraint steering wheel module coil connector. Connector is located at base of steering column.
7. Disconnect steering wheel module coil connector.

Zone 5

1. Position steering wheel in straight ahead position.
2. Turn ignition Off and remove key from ignition switch.
3. Remove instrument panel fuse block cover.
4. Remove SIR fuse from instrument panel fuse block.
5. Remove access panel from far righthand side of instrument panel.
6. Remove Connector Position Assurance (CPA) cover from instrument panel module connector.
7. Disconnect instrument panel module connector.

Zone 7

1. Position steering wheel in straight ahead position.

2. Turn ignition Off and remove key from ignition switch.
3. Remove instrument panel fuse block cover.
4. Remove SIR fuse from instrument panel fuse block.
5. Remove Connector Position Assurance (CPA) cover from lefthand side impact module connector. Connector is located under driver's seat.
6. Disconnect side impact module connector.

Zone 9

1. Position steering wheel in straight ahead position.
2. Turn ignition Off and remove key from ignition switch.
3. Remove instrument panel fuse block cover.
4. Remove SIR fuse from instrument panel fuse block.
5. Remove insulator panel from under lefthand side of instrument panel.
6. Remove Connector Position Assurance (CPA) cover from inflatable restraint steering wheel module coil connector. Connector is located at base of steering column.
7. Disconnect steering wheel module coil connector.
8. Remove access panel from far righthand side of instrument panel.
9. Remove Connector Position Assurance (CPA) cover from instrument panel module connector.
10. Disconnect instrument panel module connector.
11. Remove Connector Position Assurance (CPA) cover from lefthand side impact module connector. Connector is located under driver's seat.
12. Disconnect side impact module connector.

LUMINA

1. Ensure front wheels are pointed straight-ahead.
2. Turn ignition to Lock position and remove ignition key.
3. Remove instrument panel fuse block door.
4. Remove Fuse 21 from fuse block.
5. Remove instrument panel lefthand sound insulator.
6. Disconnect CPA and yellow air bag module electrical connectors at base of steering column.
7. Remove instrument panel righthand sound insulator.
8. Open glove compartment door.
9. Disconnect passenger's air bag module CPA and yellow electrical connector.

METRO

1. Ensure front wheels are pointed straight-ahead.
2. Turn ignition to Lock position.
3. Remove AIR BAG fuse from fuse block near steering wheel base.
4. Remove steering wheel side cap.
5. Remove Connector Position Assurance (CPA) and disconnect yellow two-way electrical connector for driver's air bag module.
6. Pull glove compartment out while pushing inward on left and righthand stoppers.
7. Remove CPA and disconnect passenger's air bag module electrical connector.

PARK AVENUE

2000–02

1. Ensure front wheels are pointed straight-ahead.
2. Turn ignition to Lock position and remove key.
3. Remove SIR fuse from underhood fuse block.
4. Remove lefthand sound insulator.
5. Disconnect Connector Position Assurance (CPA) and driver's air bag module yellow two-way connector at base of steering column.
6. Remove righthand sound insulator.
7. Disconnect CPA and yellow two-way connector from passenger's air bag module wiring.
8. Disconnect CPA and yellow two-way connector from righthand side impact air bag module electrical connector under front seat.

2003–04

Zone 2

1. Position steering wheel in straight ahead position.
2. Turn ignition Off and remove key from ignition switch.
3. Remove SIR fuse from underhood fuse center.
4. Remove trim panel from lefthand center pillar.
5. Remove Connector Position Assurance (CPA) cover from Side Impact Sensor (SIS) connector.
6. Disconnect SIS connector.

Zone 3

1. Position steering wheel in straight ahead position.
2. Turn ignition Off and remove key from ignition switch.
3. Remove SIR fuse from underhood fuse center.
4. Remove insulator panel from under lefthand side of instrument panel.
5. Remove Connector Position Assurance (CPA) cover from steering wheel module coil yellow connector. Connector is located near steering column.
6. Disconnect steering wheel module coil yellow connector.

Zone 5

1. Position steering wheel in straight ahead position.
2. Turn ignition Off and remove key from ignition switch.
3. Remove SIR fuse from underhood fuse center.
4. Remove insulator panel from under righthand side of instrument panel.
5. Remove Connector Position Assurance (CPA) cover from instrument panel module connector. Connector is located under righthand side of instrument panel.
6. Disconnect instrument panel module connector.

Zone 6

1. Position steering wheel in straight ahead position.
2. Turn ignition Off and remove key from ignition switch.
3. Remove SIR fuse from underhood fuse center.
4. Remove trim panel from righthand center pillar.
5. Remove Connector Position Assurance (CPA) cover from Side Impact Sensor (SIS) connector.
6. Disconnect SIS connector.

Zone 7

1. Position steering wheel in straight ahead position.
2. Turn ignition Off and remove key from ignition switch.
3. Remove SIR fuse from underhood fuse center.
4. Remove Connector Position Assurance (CPA) cover from driver side impact module connector. Connector is located under driver's seat.
5. Disconnect driver side impact module connector.

Zone 9

1. Position steering wheel in straight ahead position.
2. Turn ignition Off and remove key from ignition switch.
3. Remove SIR fuse from underhood fuse center.
4. Remove Connector Position Assurance (CPA) cover from passenger side impact module connector. Connector is located under passenger's front seat.
5. Disconnect passenger side impact module connector.
6. Remove insulator panel from under righthand side of instrument panel.
7. Remove CPA cover from instrument panel module connector. Connector is located under righthand side of instrument panel.
8. Disconnect instrument panel module connector.
9. Remove insulator panel from under lefthand side of instrument panel.
10. Remove CPA cover from steering wheel module coil yellow connector. Connector is located near steering column.
11. Disconnect steering wheel module coil yellow connector.
12. Remove CPA cover from driver side impact module connector. Connector is located under driver's seat.
13. Disconnect driver side impact module connector.

PRIZM

1. Ensure front wheels are pointed straight-ahead.
2. Turn ignition to Lock position.
3. Remove IGN and CIG fuses from junction block No. 1 near base of steering column.

4. Remove steering column lower trim cover.
5. Remove Connector Position Assurance (CPA) and disconnect yellow two-way electrical connector at base of steering column.
6. Remove glove compartment from instrument panel.
7. Remove CPA and disconnect yellow two-way connector from passenger's air bag module.
8. Release, unlock and disconnect side impact air bag modules' electrical connectors.

SEVILLE

2000-02

Refer to "2000–02" under "DeVille" for disarming procedure.

2003-04

Zone 2

1. Position steering wheel in straight ahead position.
2. Turn ignition switch to Off position and remove key.
3. Remove rear seat lower cushion.
4. Remove SIR fuse from rear fuse center.
5. Remove trim panel front lefthand center pillar.
6. Remove Connector Position Assurance (CPA) cover from Side Impact Sensor (SIS) connector.
7. Disconnect SIS connector.

Zone 3

1. Position steering wheel in straight ahead position.
2. Turn ignition switch to Off position and remove key.
3. Remove rear seat lower cushion.
4. Remove SIR fuse from rear fuse center.
5. Remove insulator panel from under lefthand side of instrument panel.
6. Remove Connector Position Assurance (CPA) cover from steering wheel module coil yellow connector. Connector is located near steering column.
7. Disconnect steering wheel module coil yellow connector.

Zone 5

1. Position steering wheel in straight ahead position.
2. Turn ignition switch to Off position and remove key.
3. Remove rear seat lower cushion.
4. Remove SIR fuse from rear fuse center.
5. Remove insulator panel from under righthand side of instrument panel.
6. Remove Connector Position Assurance (CPA) from instrument panel module to vehicle harness yellow connector. Connector is located under righthand side of instrument panel.
7. Disconnect instrument panel module yellow connector.

Zone 6

1. Position steering wheel in straight ahead position.
2. Turn ignition switch to Off position and remove key.
3. Remove rear seat lower cushion.
4. Remove SIR fuse from rear fuse center.
5. Remove trim panel from righthand center pillar.
6. Remove Connector Position Assurance (CPA) cover from Side Impact Sensor (SIS) connector.
7. Disconnect SIS connector.

Zone 7

1. Position steering wheel in straight ahead position.
2. Turn ignition switch to Off position and remove key.
3. Remove rear seat lower cushion.
4. Remove SIR fuse from rear fuse center.
5. Remove Connector Position Assurance (CPA) covers from lefthand side impact module and pretensioner connectors. Connectors are located under driver's seat.
6. Disconnect lefthand side impact and pretensioner connectors.

Zone 9

1. Position steering wheel in straight ahead position.
2. Turn ignition switch to Off position and remove key.
3. Remove rear seat lower cushion.
4. Remove SIR fuse from rear fuse center.
5. Remove Connector Position Assurance (CPA) covers from righthand side impact module and pretensioner connectors. Connectors are located under passenger's front seat.
6. Disconnect righthand side impact and pretensioner connectors.
7. Remove insulator panel from under righthand side of instrument panel.
8. Remove CPA from instrument panel module to vehicle harness yellow connector. Connector is located under righthand side of instrument panel.
9. Disconnect instrument panel module yellow connector.
10. Remove insulator panel from under lefthand side of instrument panel.
11. Remove CPA cover from steering wheel module coil yellow connector. Connector is located near steering column.
12. Disconnect steering wheel module coil yellow connector.
13. Remove CPA covers from lefthand side impact module and pretensioner connectors. Connectors are located under driver's seat.
14. Disconnect lefthand side impact and pretensioner connectors.

VIBE

ZONE 1

1. Ensure front wheels are pointed straight-ahead.
2. Turn ignition switch to Off position and remove key.
3. Remove SIR Fuse from junction block, located near base of steering column.
4. Locate righthand front end discriminating sensor electrical connector.
5. Remove Connector Position Assurance (CPA) from righthand front end discriminating sensor connector.
6. Remove righthand front end discriminating sensor electrical connector from front end discriminating sensor.
7. Open hood and locate lefthand front end discriminating sensor electrical connector.
8. Remove Connector Position Assurance (CPA) from lefthand front end discriminating sensor connector.
9. Remove lefthand front end discriminating sensor electrical connector from front end discriminating sensor.

ZONE 2

1. Ensure front wheels are pointed straight-ahead.
2. Turn ignition switch to Off position and remove key.
3. Remove SIR Fuse from junction block, located near base of steering column.
4. Remove lefthand front seat belt lower anchor bolt trim cover and front seat belt lower anchor bolt.
5. Remove lefthand front door and rear door sill plates.
6. Remove lefthand center pillar lower trim panel.
7. Remove front seat shoulder belt guide adjuster trim cover and bolt and lefthand front seat shoulder belt guide adjuster.
8. Disconnect pretensioner electrical connector, then remove bolts and front seat belt retractor.
9. Remove side impact sensor electrical connector.

ZONE 3

1. Ensure front wheels are pointed straight-ahead.
2. Turn ignition switch to Off position and remove key.
3. Remove SIR Fuse from junction block, located near base of steering column.
4. Remove lower steering column trim cover.
5. Release inflatable restraint steering wheel module coil connector locking mechanism.
6. Disconnect inflatable restraint steering wheel module coil connector.

ZONE 4

1. Ensure front wheels are pointed straight-ahead.
2. Turn ignition switch to Off position and remove key.
3. Remove SIR Fuse from junction block, located near base of steering column.
4. Release inflatable restraint steering wheel module coil connector locking mechanism.
5. Disconnect inflatable restraint steering wheel module coil connector.
6. Open instrument panel compartment door and remove screw .
7. Compress each side of compartment, until upper tabs release and remove compartment by pulling out to disconnect lower tabs.
8. Release and unlock instrument panel module connector, then disconnect

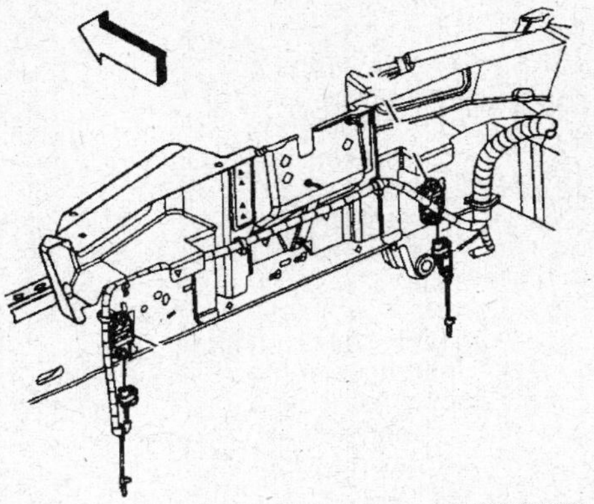

Fig. 2 Zone 1 component removal. XLR

module pigtail.
9. Release, then unlock driver and passenger seat module connectors.
10. Disconnect driver and passenger seat modules.

ZONE 5

1. Ensure front wheels are pointed straight-ahead.
2. Turn ignition switch to Off position and remove key.
3. Remove SIR Fuse from junction block, located near base of steering column.
4. Open instrument panel compartment door and remove screw .
5. Compress each side of compartment, until upper tabs release and remove compartment by pulling out to disconnect lower tabs.
6. Release and unlock instrument panel module connector, then disconnect module pigtail.

ZONE 6

1. Ensure front wheels are pointed straight-ahead.
2. Turn ignition switch to Off position and remove key.
3. Remove SIR Fuse from junction block, located near base of steering column.
4. Remove righthand front seat belt lower anchor bolt trim cover and front seat belt lower anchor bolt.
5. Remove righthand front door and rear door sill plates.
6. Remove righthand center pillar lower trim panel.
7. Remove front seat shoulder belt guide adjuster trim cover and bolt and righthand front seat shoulder belt guide adjuster.
8. Disconnect pretensioner electrical connector, then remove bolts and front seat belt retractor.
9. Remove side impact sensor electrical connector.

ZONE 7

1. Ensure front wheels are pointed straight-ahead.
2. Turn ignition switch to Off position and remove key.
3. Remove SIR Fuse from junction block, located near base of steering column.
4. Release, then unlock driver and passenger seat module connectors.
5. Disconnect driver and passenger seat modules.

ZONE 9

1. Ensure front wheels are pointed straight-ahead.
2. Turn ignition switch to Off position and remove key.
3. Remove SIR Fuse from junction block, located near base of steering column.
4. Release, then unlock driver and passenger seat module connectors.
5. Disconnect driver and passenger seat modules.

XLR

ZONE 1

1. Ensure that steering wheel is pointed in straight ahead position.
2. Ensure ignition is in Off position.
3. Remove kick panel to access I/P fuse block.
4. Remove SIR fuse (#16) from fuse block.
5. Open hood and remove air cleaner assembly.
6. Locate and remove lefthand and righthand electronic frontal sensors as indicated, **Fig. 2.**
7. Remove lefthand and righthand CPA's from connecting EFS as indicated, **Fig. 2.**
8. Remove lefthand and righthand EFS connector from EFS.

ZONE 2

1. Ensure that steering wheel is pointed in straight ahead position.
2. Ensure ignition is in Off position.
3. Remove kick panel to access I/P fuse block.
4. Remove SIR fuse (#16) from fuse block.
5. Open lefthand and righthand doors, then remove door trim panels.
6. Locate and remove CPA from SIS connector, then the SIS connector from SIS, **Fig. 3.**

ZONE 3

1. Ensure that steering wheel is pointed in straight ahead position.
2. Ensure ignition is in Off position.
3. Remove kick panel to access I/P fuse block.
4. Remove SIR fuse (#16) from fuse block.
5. Remove lefthand driver side sound insulator from I/P.
6. Remove CPA from vehicle harness yellow connector.
7. Disconnect steering wheel module coil yellow connector from vehicle harness yellow connector, **Fig. 4.**

ZONE 4

1. Ensure that steering wheel is pointed in straight ahead position.
2. Ensure ignition is in Off position.
3. Remove kick panel to access I/P fuse block.

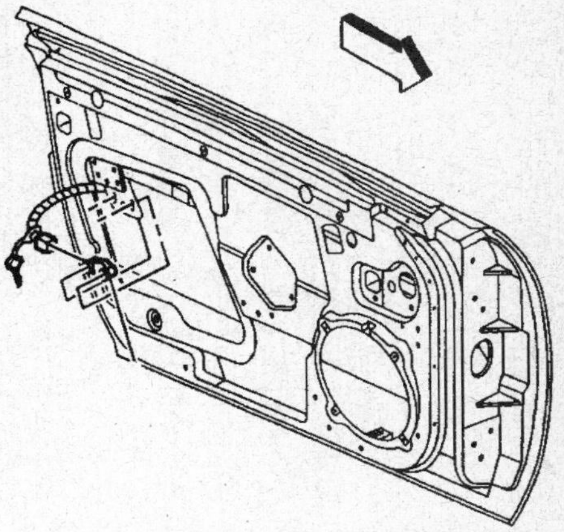

Fig. 3 Zone 2 component removal. XLR

4. Remove SIR fuse (#16) from fuse block.
5. Remove righthand sound insulator from I/P.
6. Remove CPA from vehicle harness yellow connector.
7. Disconnect I/P module yellow connector from vehicle harness yellow connector, **Fig. 5.**
8. Remove both CPA's from righthand front passenger's side impact air bag module and seat belt pretensioner yellow connector under passenger's seat, **Fig. 6.**
9. Remove lefthand driver's side sound insulator from I/P.
10. Remove CPA from vehicle yellow harness from under steering column.
11. Disconnect steering wheel module coil yellow connector from vehicle harness yellow connector.
12. Remove both CPA's from lefthand front driver's side impact air bag module and pretenstioner yellow connector under driver's seat, **Fig. 7.**
13. Disconnect vehicle harness yellow connector from lefthand front side impact air bag module and pretensioner yellow connector.

ZONE 5

1. Ensure that steering wheel is pointed in straight ahead position.
2. Ensure ignition is in Off position.
3. Remove kick panel to access I/P fuse block.
4. Remove SIR fuse (#16) from fuse block.
5. Remove righthand passenger's side sound insulator panel.
6. Remove and disconnect CPA from vehicle harness yellow connector.

ZONE 6

1. Ensure that steering wheel is pointed in straight ahead position.
2. Ensure ignition is in Off position.
3. Remove kick panel to access I/P fuse block.
4. Remove SIR fuse (#16) from fuse block.
5. Open righthand side passenger door

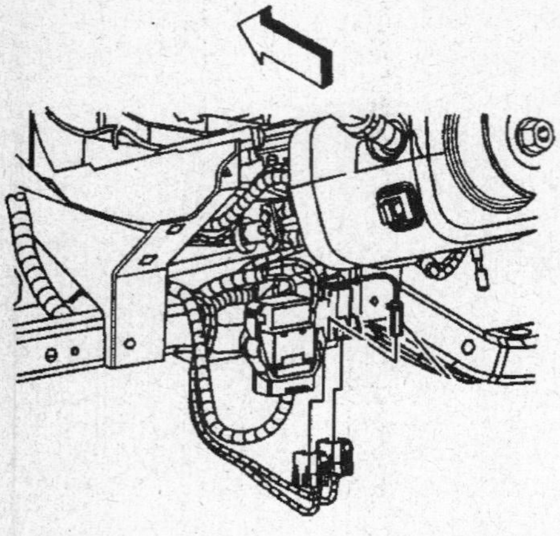

ARM0300000000804

Fig. 4 Zone 3 component removal. XLR

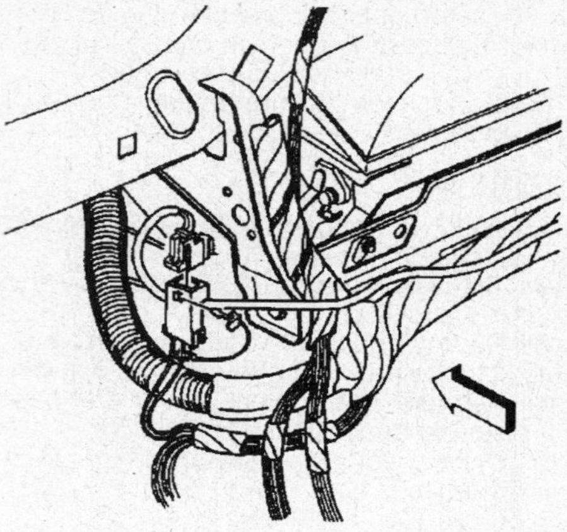

ARM0300000000805

Fig. 5 Vehicle harness location. XLR

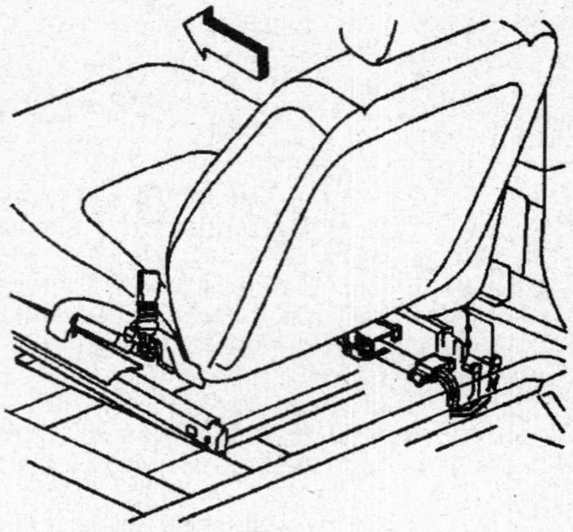

ARM0300000000806

Fig. 6 Passenger's side impact air bag module connector. XLR

and remove door trim panel using suitable removal tool.

6. Remove CPA from SIS connector, then the SIS connector from SIS, **Fig. 3.**

ZONE 7

1. Ensure that steering wheel is pointed in straight ahead position.
2. Ensure ignition is in Off position.
3. Remove kick panel to access I/P fuse block.
4. Remove SIR fuse (#16) from fuse block.
5. Remove both CPA's from lefthand from driver's side impact air bag module and pretensioner yellow connector from under driver's seat, **Fig. 7.**

ZONE 9

1. Ensure that steering wheel is pointed in straight ahead position.
2. Ensure ignition is in Off position.
3. Remove kick panel to access I/P fuse block.
4. Remove SIR fuse (#16) from fuse block.
5. Remove and disconnect both CPA's from righthand front passenger's side impact air bag module and seat belt pretensioner yellow connector from under passenger's seat, **Fig. 6.**

Arming

ALERO, CUTLASS, GRAND AM & MALIBU

2000–02

1. Ensure front wheel are in straight ahead position.
2. Place ignition in Lock position and remove ignition key.
3. Connect yellow two-way connector to passenger's air bag module pigtail and install CPA.
4. Connect yellow two-way SIR electrical connector and install CPA.
5. Install AIR BAG fuse into fuse block.
6. **From safe location at sides or below air bag modules,** turn ignition switch to On position.

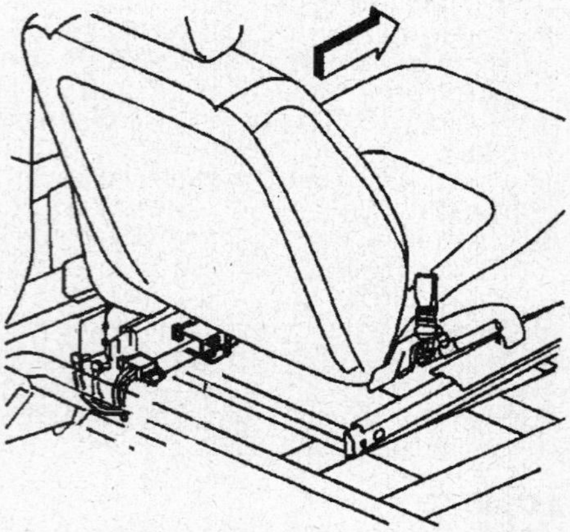

ARM0300000000807

Fig. 7 Driver's seat electrical components. XLR

7. Ensure SIR lamp flashes seven times and turns off.

2003–04

Zone 3

1. Connect steering wheel module coil connector.
2. Install Connector Position Assurance (CPA) cover onto steering wheel module coil connector. Connector is located under lefthand side of instrument panel.
3. Install AIR BAG fuse into junction block.
4. Install junction block access panel onto lefthand side of instrument panel.
5. **From safe location at sides or below air bag modules,** turn ignition switch to On position.
6. Ensure SIR lamp flashes seven times and turns off.

Zone 5

1. Connect instrument panel module electrical connector.
2. Install Connector Position Assurance (CPA) cover onto instrument panel module connector. Connector is located above righthand instrument panel wiring harness junction block.
3. Install junction block access panel onto righthand side of instrument panel.
4. Install AIR BAG fuse into lefthand junction block.
5. Install junction block access panel onto lefthand side of instrument panel.
6. **From safe location at sides or below air bag modules,** turn ignition switch to On position.
7. Ensure SIR lamp flashes seven times and turns off.

AURORA

2001–02

1. Remove key from ignition switch.
2. Connect righthand side impact air bag module yellow connector to vehicle harness yellow connector located under righthand front seat.
3. Install connector position assurance (CPA) to righthand side impact air bag module yellow connector.
4. Connect lefthand side impact air bag module yellow connector to vehicle harness yellow connector located under driver's seat.
5. Install CPA to lefthand side impact air bag module yellow connector.
6. Connect passenger's air bag module yellow connector to vehicle harness yellow connector located above righthand sound insulator.
7. Install CPA to passenger's air bag module yellow connector.
8. Install instrument panel righthand side sound insulator.
9. Connect driver's air bag module yellow connector to vehicle harness yellow connector located next to steering column.
10. Install CPA to driver's air bag module yellow connector.
11. Install instrument panel lefthand side sound insulator.
12. Install SIR fuse to rear fuse block located under rear seat.
13. Staying well away from air bag modules and turn ignition switch to ON position.

14. AIR BAG warning lamp will flash seven times and turn OFF.

2003-04

Zone 1

1. Connect EFS connector. EFS is located on front lefthand side of engine compartment.
2. Install Connector Position Assurance (CPA) lock onto Electronic Frontal Sensor (EFS) connector.
3. Install SIR fuse into rear fuse center.
4. Install rear seat lower cushion.
5. **From safe location at sides or below air bag modules,** turn ignition switch to On position.
6. Ensure SIR lamp flashes seven times and turns off.

Zone 2

1. Connect lefthand Side Impact Sensor (SIS) connector.
2. Install Connector Position Assurance (CPA) lock onto SIS connector.
3. Install lefthand center pillar trim panel onto pillar.
4. Install front and rear carpet retainers onto lefthand center pillar trim panel.
5. Install SIR fuse into rear fuse center.
6. Install rear seat lower cushion.
7. **From safe location at sides or below air bag modules,** turn ignition switch to On position.
8. Ensure SIR lamp flashes seven times and turns off.

Zone 3

1. Connect steering wheel module yellow harness connector.
2. Install Connector Position Assurance (CPA) lock onto steering wheel module yellow connector.
3. Install lefthand closeout/insulator panel under lefthand side of instrument panel.
4. Install SIR fuse into rear fuse center.
5. Install rear seat lower cushion.
6. **From safe location at sides or below air bag modules,** turn ignition switch to On position.
7. Ensure SIR lamp flashes seven times and turns off.

Zone 5

1. Connect instrument panel module yellow harness connector.
2. Install Connector Position Assurance (CPA) lock onto instrument panel module yellow connector.
3. Install righthand closeout/insulator panel under righthand side of instrument panel.
4. Install SIR fuse into rear fuse center.
5. Install rear seat lower cushion.
6. **From safe location at sides or below air bag modules,** turn ignition switch to On position.
7. Ensure SIR lamp flashes seven times and turns off.

Zone 6

1. Connect righthand Side Impact Sensor (SIS) connector.
2. Install Connector Position Assurance (CPA) lock onto SIS connector.
3. Install righthand center pillar trim panel onto pillar.
4. Install front and rear carpet retainers onto righthand center pillar trim panel.
5. Install SIR fuse into rear fuse center.
6. Install rear seat lower cushion.
7. **From safe location at sides or below air bag modules,** turn ignition switch to On position.
8. Ensure SIR lamp flashes seven times and turns off.

Zone 7

1. Connect lefthand driver side impact module and seat belt pretensioner yellow connector from harness connector. Connector is located under driver's seat.
2. Install Connector Position Assurance (CPA) lock onto lefthand driver side impact module and seat belt pretensioner yellow connector.
3. Install fuse into rear fuse center.
4. Install rear seat lower cushion.
5. **From safe location at sides or below air bag modules,** turn ignition switch to On position.
6. Ensure SIR lamp flashes seven times and turns off.

Zone 8

1. Connect lefthand driver side impact module and seat belt pretensioner yellow connector to vehicle harness connector. Connector is located under driver's seat.
2. Install Connector Position Assurance (CPA) lock onto lefthand driver side impact module and seat belt pretensioner yellow connector.
3. Connect steering wheel module connector to yellow harness connector.
4. Install CPA lock onto steering wheel module yellow connector.
5. Install lefthand closeout/insulator panel under lefthand side of instrument panel.
6. Connect instrument panel module connector to yellow harness connector.
7. Install CPA lock onto instrument panel module yellow connector.
8. Install righthand closeout/insulator panel under righthand side of instrument panel.
9. Connect righthand side impact module and seat belt pretensioner yellow connector to vehicle harness connector. Connector is located under passenger's front seat.
10. Install CPA lock onto righthand side impact module and seat belt pretensioner yellow connector.
11. Install SIR fuse into rear fuse center.
12. Install rear seat lower cushion.
13. **From safe location at sides or below air bag modules,** turn ignition switch to On position.
14. Ensure SIR lamp flashes seven times and turns off.

Zone 9

1. Connect righthand side impact module and seat belt pretensioner yellow connector to vehicle harness connector. Connector is located under passenger's seat.
2. Install Connector Position Assurance (CPA) lock onto righthand passenger side impact module and seat belt pretensioner yellow connector.
3. Install SIR fuse into rear fuse center.
4. Install rear seat lower cushion.
5. **From safe location at sides or below air bag modules,** turn ignition switch to On position.
6. Ensure SIR lamp flashes seven times and turns off.

BONNEVILLE, EIGHTY-EIGHT & LESABRE

2000-02

1. Turn steering wheel to straight-ahead position.
2. Turn ignition to Lock position and remove key.
3. Connect yellow two-way connector and CPA at righthand side impact air bag module electrical connector under front seat.
4. Connect yellow two-way connector and CPA at lefthand side impact air bag module electrical connector under front seat.
5. Connect yellow two-way connector to passenger's air bag module wiring and install CPA.
6. Install righthand sound insulator.
7. Connect yellow two-way SIR electrical connector at base of steering column and install CPA.
8. Install lefthand sound insulator.
9. Install SIR fuse into rear fuse block.
10. **From safe location at sides or below air bag modules,** turn ignition switch to On position.
11. Ensure SIR lamp flashes seven times and turns off.

2003-04

For arming procedures on these models, refer to "2003–04" in "Aurora."

CAMARO & FIREBIRD

1. Turn ignition key to Lock and remove key.
2. Connect yellow two-way connector to passenger's air bag module and install CPA.
3. Install righthand instrument panel insulator.
4. Connect driver's air bag module yellow two-way SIR electrical connector.
5. Install CPA near base of steering column.
6. Install lefthand sound insulator.
7. Install AIR BAG fuse.
8. **From safe location at sides or below air bag modules,** turn ignition switch to On position.
9. Ensure SIR lamp flashes seven times and turns off.

CATERA

1. Turn steering wheel to straight-ahead position.
2. Turn ignition to Lock position.
3. Connect SDM electrical connectors if required.

4. Connect righthand side impact air bag module electrical connector and install CPA.
5. Connect righthand front seat belt pretensioner electrical connector.
6. Install righthand front seat track trim cover.
7. Connect lefthand side impact air bag module electrical connector and install CPA.
8. Connect driver's seat belt pretensioner electrical connector.
9. Install driver's front seat track trim cover.
10. Connect passenger's front air bag module electrical connector and install CPA.
11. Install passenger's front air bag module cover.
12. Connect driver's air bag module electrical connector to SRS coil (clockspring).
13. Install steering column lower and upper covers.
14. **From safe location at sides or below air bag modules,** turn ignition switch to On position.
15. Ensure AIR BAG warning lamp flashes seven times and turns off.

CAVALIER & SUNFIRE

2000-02

1. Turn ignition to Lock position and remove key.
2. Connect both yellow SIR connectors at base of steering column.
3. Install CPAs and lefthand lower trim panel.
4. Install SIR AIR BAG fuse into fuse block.
5. Install instrument panel lefthand end cap.
6. **From safe location at sides or below air bag modules,** turn ignition switch to On position.
7. Ensure AIR BAG warning lamp flashes seven times and turns off.

2003-04

Zone 1

1. Connect Electronic Front Sensor (EFS) connector. Connector is located on front righthand side of engine compartment.
2. Install Connector Position Assurance (CPA) cover onto inflatable restraint EFS connector.
3. Install hood closeout filler panel onto front of engine compartment.
4. Install AIR BAG fuse into lefthand instrument panel junction block.
5. Install lefthand instrument panel outer trim cover.
6. **From safe location at sides or below air bag modules,** turn ignition switch to On position.
7. Ensure SIR lamp flashes seven times and turns off.

Zone 2, Coupe

1. Connect Side Impact Sensor (SIS) connector. Connector is located behind lefthand door panel.
2. Install Connector Position Assurance (CPA) cover onto SIS connector.
3. Install inflatable restraint Side Impact Sensor (SIS) onto door.
4. Install lefthand door trim panel and trim panel mounting screws.
5. Install window regulator handle.
6. **On models equipped with power door locks,** install power door lock switch.
7. **On all models,** install AIR BAG fuse into lefthand instrument panel junction block.
8. Install lefthand instrument panel outer trim cover.
9. **From safe location at sides or below air bag modules,** turn ignition switch to On position.
10. Ensure SIR lamp flashes seven times and turns off.

Zone 2, Sedan

1. Connect lefthand Side Impact Sensor (SIS) connector. Connector is located behind lefthand center pillar upper trim panel.
2. Install Connector Position Assurance (CPA) cover onto SIS connector.
3. Remove inflatable restraint Side Impact Sensor (SIS) from center pillar.
4. Install lefthand center pillar upper trim panel.
5. Install AIR BAG fuse into lefthand instrument panel junction block.
6. Install lefthand instrument panel outer trim cover.
7. **From safe location at sides or below air bag modules,** turn ignition switch to On position.
8. Ensure SIR lamp flashes seven times and turns off.

Zone 3

1. Connect steering wheel module coil connector. Connector is located under lefthand side of instrument panel, left of steering column.
2. Install Connector Position Assurance (CPA) cover onto inflatable restraint steering wheel module coil connector.
3. Install AIR BAG fuse into lefthand instrument panel junction block.
4. Install lefthand instrument panel outer trim cover.
5. **From safe location at sides or below air bag modules,** turn ignition switch to On position.
6. Ensure SIR lamp flashes seven times and turns off.

Zone 5

1. Connect inflatable restraint instrument panel module inline connector. Connector is located under lefthand side of instrument panel, left of steering column.
2. Install Connector Position Assurance (CPA) cover onto inflatable restraint instrument panel module inline connector.
3. Install AIR BAG fuse into lefthand instrument panel junction block.
4. Install lefthand instrument panel outer trim cover.
5. **From safe location at sides or below air bag modules,** turn ignition switch to On position.
6. Ensure SIR lamp flashes seven times and turns off.

Zone 6, Coupe

1. Connect righthand Side Impact Sensor (SIS) connector.
2. Install Connector Position Assurance (CPA) cover onto SIS connector.
3. Install SIS into righthand door.
4. Install righthand door trim panel and trim panel mounting screws.
5. **On models equipped with power door locks,** install power door lock switch.
6. **On all models,** install window regulator handle.
7. Install AIR BAG fuse into lefthand instrument panel junction block.
8. Install lefthand instrument panel outer trim cover.
9. **From safe location at sides or below air bag modules,** turn ignition switch to On position.
10. Ensure SIR lamp flashes seven times and turns off.

Zone 6, Sedan

1. Connect righthand Side Impact Sensor (SIS) connector.
2. Install Connector Position Assurance (CPA) cover onto SIS connector.
3. Install inflatable restraint SIS onto center pillar and pillar upper trim panel.
4. Install AIR BAG fuse into lefthand instrument panel junction block.
5. Install lefthand instrument panel outer trim cover.
6. **From safe location at sides or below air bag modules,** turn ignition switch to On position.
7. Ensure SIR lamp flashes seven times and turns off.

Zone 7

1. Connect inflatable restraint side impact module connector. Connector is located under driver's seat.
2. Install Connector Position Assurance (CPA) cover onto module connector.
3. Install AIR BAG fuse into lefthand instrument panel junction block.
4. Install lefthand instrument panel outer trim cover.
5. **From safe location at sides or below air bag modules,** turn ignition switch to On position.
6. Ensure SIR lamp flashes seven times and turns off.

Zone 9

1. Connect inflatable restraint side impact module connector. Connector is located under passenger's front seat.
2. Install Connector Position Assurance (CPA) cover onto side impact module connector.
3. Install AIR BAG fuse into lefthand instrument panel junction block.
4. Install lefthand instrument panel outer trim cover.
5. **From safe location at sides or below air bag modules,** turn ignition switch to On position.

6. Ensure SIR lamp flashes seven times and turns off.

CENTURY & REGAL

2000-02

1. Ensure front wheels are in straight-ahead position and key is removed from ignition.
2. Connect side impact air bag module connector located under driver's seat.
3. Install Connector Position Assurance (CPA) to side impact module.
4. Connect passenger's air bag module CPA and air bag module yellow connectors located to right of steering column.
5. Connect driver's air bag module CPA and yellow air bag module connectors at base of steering column.
6. Install AIR BAG or SIR fuse into fuse block.
7. **From safe location at sides or below air bag modules,** turn ignition switch to On position.
8. Ensure AIR BAG warning lamp flashes seven times and turns off.

2003-04

Zone 2

1. Connect lefthand Side Impact Sensor (SIS) connector.
2. Install Connector Position Assurance (CPA) cover onto SIS connector.
3. Install SIS on center pillar.
4. Install lefthand center pillar trim panel.
5. Install SIR fuse into fuse block.
6. Install instrument panel fuse block cover.
7. **From safe location at sides or below air bag modules,** turn ignition switch to On position.
8. Ensure SIR lamp flashes seven times and turns off.

Zone 3

1. Connect inflatable restraint steering wheel module coil connector. Connector is located at base of steering column.
2. Install Connector Position Assurance (CPA) cover onto steering wheel module coil connector.
3. Install lefthand insulator panel from under lefthand side of instrument panel.
4. Install SIR fuse into fuse block.
5. Install instrument panel fuse block cover.
6. **From safe location at sides or below air bag modules,** turn ignition switch to On position.
7. Ensure SIR lamp flashes seven times and turns off.

Zone 5

1. Connect instrument panel module connector. Connector is located on righthand side of steering column.
2. Install Connector Position Assurance (CPA) cover onto instrument panel module connector.
3. Install insulator panel under lefthand side of instrument panel.
4. Install SIR fuse into fuse block.
5. Install instrument panel fuse block cover.
6. **From safe location at sides or below air bag modules,** turn ignition switch to On position.
7. Ensure SIR lamp flashes seven times and turns off.

Zone 7

1. Connect side impact module connector. Connector is located under driver's seat.
2. Install Connector Position Assurance (CPA) cover onto side impact module connector.
3. Install SIR fuse into fuse block.
4. Install instrument panel fuse block cover.
5. **From safe location at sides or below air bag modules,** turn ignition switch to On position.
6. Ensure SIR lamp flashes seven times and turns off.

Zone 9

1. Connect Side Impact Sensor (SIS) connector.
2. Install Connector Position Assurance (CPA) cover onto SIS connector.
3. Install lefthand Side Impact Sensor (SIS) on center pillar.
4. Install lefthand center pillar trim panel.
5. Connect instrument panel module connector. Connector is located on righthand side of steering column.
6. Install CPA cover onto instrument panel module connector.
7. Connect steering wheel module coil connector. Connector is located at base of steering column.
8. Install CPA cover onto steering wheel module coil connector.
9. Install insulator panel under lefthand side of instrument panel.
10. Install SIR fuse into fuse block.
11. Install instrument panel fuse block cover.
12. **From safe location at sides or below air bag modules,** turn ignition switch to On position.
13. Ensure SIR lamp flashes seven times and turns off.

CORVETTE

2000-02

1. Turn ignition to Lock position and remove key.
2. Connect both yellow SIR connectors and install CPA.
3. Insert courtesy lamp through panel and install lefthand sound insulation panel.
4. Install push-on nut to steering column bracket stud and twist rivets clockwise to secure.
5. Align courtesy lamp and push into place.
6. Install SDM fuse into instrument panel fuse block.
7. Install front floor kick-up panel.
8. **From safe location at sides or below air bag modules,** turn ignition switch to On position.
9. Ensure AIR BAG warning lamp flashes seven times and turns off.

2003-04

Zone 3

1. Connect steering wheel module coil connector. Connector is located at base of steering column.
2. Install Connector Position Assurance (CPA) cover onto inflatable restraint steering wheel module coil connector.
3. Install sound insulator panel under lefthand side of instrument panel.
4. Install SDM fuse into fuse block.
5. Install kick-up panel.
6. **From safe location at sides or below air bag modules,** turn ignition switch to On position.
7. Ensure SIR lamp flashes seven times and turns off.

Zone 4

1. Connect steering wheel module coil connector. Connector is located at base of steering column.
2. Install Connector Position Assurance (CPA) cover onto inflatable restraint steering wheel module coil connector.
3. Connect inflatable restraint instrument panel module connector. Connector is located near base of steering column.
4. Install CPA cover onto inflatable restraint instrument panel module connector.
5. Install sound insulator panel under lefthand side of instrument panel.
6. Install SDM fuse into fuse block.
7. Install kick-up panel.
8. **From safe location at sides or below air bag modules,** turn ignition switch to On position.
9. Ensure SIR lamp flashes seven times and turns off.

Zone 5

1. Connect inflatable restraint instrument panel module connector. Connector is located near base of steering column.
2. Install Connector Position Assurance (CPA) cover onto inflatable restraint instrument panel module connector.
3. Install sound insulator panel under lefthand side of instrument panel.
4. Install SDM fuse into fuse block.
5. Install kick-up panel.
6. **From safe location at sides or below air bag modules,** turn ignition switch to On position.
7. Ensure SIR lamp flashes seven times and turns off.

CTS

ZONE 1

1. Ensure ignition is Off.
2. Connect Electronic Frontal Sensor (EFS) connector and install Connector Position Assurance (CPA) cover onto connector.
3. Install SIR fuse into righthand rear fuse center.
4. Install rear seat.
5. **From safe location at sides or below air bag modules,** turn ignition switch to On position.
6. Ensure AIR BAG warning lamp flashes seven times and turns off.

ZONE 2

1. Connect lefthand Side Impact Sensor (SIS) electrical connector.
2. Install Connector Position Assurance (CPA) cover onto lefthand Side Impact Sensor (SIS) connector.
3. Install lefthand center pillar trim panel onto pillar.
4. Instal front and rear carpet retainers onto lefthand center pillar trim panel.
5. Connect lefthand roof rail module connector.
6. Install Connector Position Assurance (CPA) cover onto lefthand roof rail module yellow electrical connector.
7. Install lefthand rear sail panel.
8. Install SIR fuse into righthand rear fuse center.
9. Install rear seat lower cushion.
10. **From safe location at sides or below air bag modules,** turn ignition switch to On position.
11. Ensure AIR BAG warning lamp flashes seven times and turns off.

ZONE 3

1. Connect steering wheel module connector to yellow harness connector.
2. Install Connector Position Assurance (CPA) cover onto steering wheel module yellow connector.
3. Install lefthand closeout/insulator panel on to lefthand side of instrument panel.
4. Install SIR fuse into righthand rear fuse center.
5. Install rear seat lower cushion.
6. **From safe location at sides or below air bag modules,** turn ignition switch to On position.
7. Ensure AIR BAG warning lamp flashes seven times and turns off.

ZONE 5

1. Connect instrument panel module connector to yellow harness connector.
2. Install Connector Position Assurance (CPA) cover onto instrument panel module yellow connector.
3. Install righthand closeout/insulator panel on to righthand side of instrument panel.
4. Install SIR fuse into righthand rear fuse center.
5. Install rear seat lower cushion.
6. **From safe location at sides or below air bag modules,** turn ignition switch to On position.
7. Ensure AIR BAG warning lamp flashes seven times and turns off.

ZONE 6

1. Connect righthand Side Impact Sensor (SIS) electrical connector.
2. Install Connector Position Assurance (CPA) cover onto righthand Side Impact Sensor (SIS) connector.
3. Install righthand center pillar trim panel onto pillar.
4. Instal front and rear carpet retainers onto righthand center pillar trim panel.
5. Connect righthand roof rail module connector.
6. Install Connector Position Assurance (CPA) cover onto righthand roof rail module yellow electrical connector.
7. Install righthand rear sail panel.
8. Install SIR fuse into righthand rear fuse center.
9. Install rear seat lower cushion.
10. **From safe location at sides or below air bag modules,** turn ignition switch to On position.
11. Ensure AIR BAG warning lamp flashes seven times and turns off.

ZONE 7

1. Connect lefthand driver side impact module and seat belt pretensioner yellow connector to vehicle harness connector. Connector is located under driver's seat.
2. Install Connector Position Assurance (CPA) cover on to lefthand driver side impact module and seat belt pretensioner yellow connector.
3. Install SIR fuse into righthand rear fuse center.
4. Install rear seat lower cushion.
5. **From safe location at sides or below air bag modules,** turn ignition switch to On position.
6. Ensure AIR BAG warning lamp flashes seven times and turns off.

ZONE 8

1. Connect lefthand roof rail module connector.
2. Install Connector Position Assurance (CPA) lock onto lefthand roof rail module yellow electrical connector.
3. Install lefthand rear sail panel.
4. Install lefthand rear sail panel retaining clips.
5. Connect lefthand driver side impact module and seat belt pretensioner yellow connector from harness connector. Connector is located under driver's seat.
6. Install CPA lock onto lefthand driver side impact module and seat belt pretensioner yellow connector.
7. Connect steering wheel module connector to yellow harness connector.
8. Install CPA lock onto steering wheel module yellow connector.
9. Install lefthand closeout/insulator panel onto far lefthand side of instrument panel.
10. Connect righthand driver side impact module and seat belt pretensioner yellow connector to vehicle harness connector. Connector is located under passenger's front seat.
11. Install CPA lock onto righthand driver side impact module and seat belt pretensioner yellow connector.
12. Connect instrument panel module connector to yellow harness connector.
13. Install CPA lock onto instrument panel module yellow connector.
14. Install righthand closeout/insulator panel onto far righthand side of instrument panel.
15. Connect righthand roof rail module connector.
16. Install CPA lock onto righthand roof rail module yellow electrical connector.
17. Install righthand rear sail panel.
18. Install righthand rear sail panel retaining clips.
19. Install SIR fuse into righthand rear fuse center.
20. Install rear seat lower cushion.
21. **From safe location at sides or below air bag modules,** turn ignition switch to On position.
22. Ensure AIR BAG warning lamp flashes seven times and turns off.

ZONE 9

1. Connect righthand passenger side impact module and seat belt pretensioner yellow connector to vehicle harness connector. Connector is located under passenger's seat.
2. Install Connector Position Assurance (CPA) cover on to righthand side impact module and seat belt pretensioner yellow connector.
3. Install SIR fuse into righthand rear fuse center.
4. Install rear seat lower cushion.
5. **From safe location at sides or below air bag modules,** turn ignition switch to On position.
6. Ensure AIR BAG warning lamp flashes seven times and turns off.

DEVILLE

2000-02

1. Turn ignition to Lock and remove key.
2. **On models equipped with rear side impact air bag modules (AW9),** proceed as follows:
   a. Connect lefthand rear side impact air bag module yellow electrical connector.
   b. Install CPA for lefthand rear side impact air bag module yellow electrical connector.
   c. Connect righthand rear side impact air bag module yellow electrical connector.
   d. Install CPA for righthand rear side impact air bag module yellow electrical connector.
   e. Install rear seatback.
3. **On all models,** connect yellow two-way connector to passenger's air bag module pigtail and install CPA.
4. Connect yellow two-way connector to driver's air bag module pigtail and install CPA.
5. Connect yellow two-way SIR electrical connector at base of steering column and install CPA.
6. Install lefthand sound insulator.
7. Install SIR fuse into fuse block.
8. **From safe location at sides or below air bag modules,** turn ignition switch to On position.
9. Ensure SIR lamp flashes seven times and turns off.

2003-04

Zone 1

1. Connect EFS connector. EFS is located on front lefthand side of engine compartment.
2. Install Connector Position Assurance (CPA) lock onto Electronic Frontal Sensor (EFS) connector.

3. Install SIR fuse into rear fuse center.
4. Install rear seat lower cushion.
5. **From safe location at sides or below air bag modules,** turn ignition switch to On position.
6. Ensure SIR lamp flashes seven times and turns off.

Zone 2

1. Connect lefthand Side Impact Sensor (SIS) connector.
2. Install Connector Position Assurance (CPA) lock onto SIS connector.
3. Install lefthand center pillar trim panel onto pillar.
4. Install front and rear carpet retainers onto lefthand center pillar trim panel.
5. Install SIR fuse into rear fuse center.
6. Install rear seat lower cushion.
7. **From safe location at sides or below air bag modules,** turn ignition switch to On position.
8. Ensure SIR lamp flashes seven times and turns off.

Zone 3

1. Connect steering wheel module yellow harness connector.
2. Install Connector Position Assurance (CPA) lock onto steering wheel module yellow connector.
3. Install lefthand closeout/insulator panel under lefthand side of instrument panel.
4. Install SIR fuse into rear fuse center.
5. Install rear seat lower cushion.
6. **From safe location at sides or below air bag modules,** turn ignition switch to On position.
7. Ensure SIR lamp flashes seven times and turns off.

Zone 5

1. Connect instrument panel module yellow harness connector.
2. Install Connector Position Assurance (CPA) lock onto instrument panel module yellow connector.
3. Install righthand closeout/insulator panel under righthand side of instrument panel.
4. Install SIR fuse into rear fuse center.
5. Install rear seat lower cushion.
6. **From safe location at sides or below air bag modules,** turn ignition switch to On position.
7. Ensure SIR lamp flashes seven times and turns off.

Zone 6

1. Connect righthand Side Impact Sensor (SIS) connector.
2. Install Connector Position Assurance (CPA) lock onto SIS connector.
3. Install righthand center pillar trim panel onto pillar.
4. Install front and rear carpet retainers onto righthand center pillar trim panel.
5. Install SIR fuse into rear fuse center.
6. Install rear seat lower cushion.
7. **From safe location at sides or below air bag modules,** turn ignition switch to On position.
8. Ensure SIR lamp flashes seven times and turns off.

Zone 7

1. Connect lefthand driver side impact module and seat belt pretensioner yellow connector from harness connector. Connector is located under driver's seat.
2. Install Connector Position Assurance (CPA) lock onto lefthand driver side impact module and seat belt pretensioner yellow connector.
3. Install fuse into rear fuse center.
4. Install rear seat lower cushion.
5. **From safe location at sides or below air bag modules,** turn ignition switch to On position.
6. Ensure SIR lamp flashes seven times and turns off.

Zone 8

1. Connect rear lefthand side impact module connector. Connector is located near lefthand rear door jamb.
2. Install Connector Position Assurance (CPA) lock onto rear lefthand side impact module and seat belt pretensioner yellow connector.
3. Install lefthand rear passenger seat back.
4. Connect lefthand driver side impact module and seat belt pretensioner yellow connector to vehicle harness connector. Connector is located under driver's seat.
5. Install CPA lock onto lefthand driver side impact module and seat belt pretensioner yellow connector.
6. Connect steering wheel module connector to yellow harness connector.
7. Install CPA lock onto steering wheel module yellow connector.
8. Install lefthand closeout/insulator panel under lefthand side of instrument panel.
9. Connect instrument panel module connector to yellow harness connector.
10. Install CPA lock onto instrument panel module yellow connector.
11. Install righthand closeout/insulator panel under righthand side of instrument panel.
12. Connect righthand side impact module and seat belt pretensioner yellow connector to vehicle harness connector. Connector is located under passenger's front seat.
13. Remove CPA lock onto righthand front side impact module yellow connector.
14. Connect rear righthand side impact module connector. Connector is located near righthand rear door jamb.
15. Install Connector Position Assurance (CPA) lock onto rear righthand side impact module and seat belt pretensioner yellow connector.
16. Install righthand rear passenger seat back.
17. Install SIR fuse into rear fuse center.
18. Install rear seat lower cushion.
19. **From safe location at sides or below air bag modules,** turn ignition switch to On position.
20. Ensure SIR lamp flashes seven times and turns off.

Zone 9

1. Connect righthand side impact module and seat belt pretensioner yellow connector to vehicle harness connector. Connector is located under passenger's seat.
2. Install Connector Position Assurance (CPA) lock onto righthand passenger side impact module and seat belt pretensioner yellow connector.
3. Install SIR fuse into rear fuse center.
4. Install rear seat lower cushion.
5. **From safe location at sides or below air bag modules,** turn ignition switch to On position.
6. Ensure SIR lamp flashes seven times and turns off.

Zone 10

1. Connect rear lefthand side impact module connector. Connector is located near lefthand rear door jamb.
2. Install Connector Position Assurance (CPA) lock onto rear lefthand side impact module and seat belt pretensioner yellow connector.
3. Install lefthand rear passenger seat back.
4. Install SIR fuse into rear fuse center.
5. Install rear seat lower cushion.
6. **From safe location at sides or below air bag modules,** turn ignition switch to On position.
7. Ensure SIR lamp flashes seven times and turns off.

Zone 12

1. Connect rear righthand side impact module connector. Connector is located near righthand rear door jamb.
2. Install Connector Position Assurance (CPA) lock onto rear righthand side impact module and seat belt pretensioner yellow connector.
3. Install righthand rear passenger seat back.
4. Install SIR fuse into rear fuse center.
5. Install rear seat lower cushion.
6. **From safe location at sides or below air bag modules,** turn ignition switch to On position.
7. Ensure SIR lamp flashes seven times and turns off.

ELDORADO

1. Turn ignition to Lock position and remove key.
2. Connect yellow two-way connector to passenger's air bag module pigtail and install CPA.
3. Install glove compartment.
4. Connect yellow two-way SIR electrical connectors at base of steering column and install CPA.
5. Install lefthand sound insulator.
6. Install SIR fuse into fuse block.
7. **From safe location at sides or below air bag modules,** turn ignition switch to On position.
8. Ensure SIR lamp flashes seven times and turns off.

GRAND PRIX & INTRIGUE

2000-02

1. Ensure front wheels are in straight-ahead position and key is removed from ignition switch.
2. Connect passenger's air bag module CPA and air bag module yellow connectors located to right of steering column.
3. Connect driver's air bag module CPA and yellow air bag module connectors at base of steering column.
4. Install AIR BAG or SIR fuse into fuse block.
5. Staying well away from both air bag modules, turn ignition On.
6. Ensure AIR BAG warning lamp flashes seven times and turns off.

2003-04

Zone 3

1. Connect steering wheel module coil connector. Connector is located at base of steering column.
2. Install Connector Position Assurance (CPA) cover onto inflatable restraint steering wheel module coil connector.
3. Install lefthand insulator panel under lefthand side of instrument panel.
4. Install SIR fuse into fuse block.
5. Install instrument panel fuse block cover.
6. **From safe location at sides or below air bag modules,** turn ignition switch to On position.
7. Ensure SIR lamp flashes seven times and turns off.

Zone 5

1. Connect inflatable restraint instrument panel module connector. Connector is located on righthand side of steering column.
2. Install Connector Position Assurance (CPA) cover onto inflatable restraint instrument panel module connector.
3. Install lefthand insulator panel under lefthand side of instrument panel.
4. Install SIR fuse into fuse block.
5. Install instrument panel fuse block cover.
6. **From safe location at sides or below air bag modules,** turn ignition switch to On position.
7. Ensure SIR lamp flashes seven times and turns off.

Zone 9

1. Connect SDM wiring harness connector. Connector is located under front righthand seat.
2. Install CPA cover onto Sensing and Diagnostic Module (SDM) connector.
3. Connect instrument panel module connector. Connector is located on righthand side of steering column.
4. Install CPA cover onto inflatable restraint instrument panel module connector.
5. Connect steering wheel module coil connector. Connector is located at base of steering column.
6. Install Connector Position Assurance (CPA) cover onto inflatable restraint steering wheel module coil connector.
7. Install lefthand insulator panel under lefthand side of instrument panel.
8. Install SIR fuse into fuse block.
9. Install instrument panel fuse block cover.
10. **From safe location at sides or below air bag modules,** turn ignition switch to On position.
11. Ensure SIR lamp flashes seven times and turns off.

IMPALA & MONTE CARLO

2000-02

1. Ensure front wheels are in straight-ahead position and key is removed from ignition.
2. **On models equipped with lefthand side impact air bag module,** connect yellow electrical connector under driver's seat and install CPA.
3. **On all models,** connect driver's air bag module CPA and yellow air bag module connector.
4. Install instrument panel righthand access hole cover.
5. Install SDM fuse into fuse block.
6. Install instrument panel fuse access cover.
7. **From safe location at sides or below air bag modules,** turn ignition switch to On position.
8. Ensure AIR BAG warning lamp flashes seven times and turns off.

2003-04

Zone 1

1. Connect front sensor to harness connector. Connector is located on front center of engine compartment.
2. Install orange Connector Position Assurance (CPA) cover onto yellow sensor harness connector.
3. Install upper air baffle and deflector onto radiator.
4. Install SIR fuse into fuse block.
5. Install instrument panel fuse block cover.
6. **From safe location at sides or below air bag modules,** turn ignition switch to On position.
7. Ensure SIR lamp flashes seven times and turns off.

Zone 2, Impala

1. Disconnect Side Impact Sensor (SIS) connector. Connector is located on lefthand center pillar.
2. Install Connector Position Assurance (CPA) cover onto SIS connector.
3. Install SIS onto center pillar.
4. Install lefthand center pillar trim panel.
5. Install SIR fuse into fuse block.
6. Install instrument panel fuse block cover.
7. **From safe location at sides or below air bag modules,** turn ignition switch to On position.
8. Ensure SIR lamp flashes seven times and turns off.

Zone 2, Monte Carlo

1. Connect Side Impact Sensor (SIS) connector. Sensor is located on lefthand front door impact beam.
2. Install Connector Position Assurance (CPA) cover onto SIS connector.
3. Install SIS onto door impact beam mounting bracket.
4. Install door trim panel, then connect power door lock and power window switch electrical connectors.
5. Install door trim panel to door mounting screws.
6. Install door handle trim bezel.
7. Install SIR fuse into fuse block.
8. Install instrument panel fuse block cover.
9. **From safe location at sides or below air bag modules,** turn ignition switch to On position.
10. Ensure SIR lamp flashes seven times and turns off.

Zone 3

1. Connect steering wheel module coil connector. Connector is located at base of steering column.
2. Install Connector Position Assurance (CPA) cover onto steering wheel module coil connector.
3. Install insulator panel under lefthand side of instrument panel.
4. Install SIR fuse into fuse block.
5. Install instrument panel fuse block cover.
6. **From safe location at sides or below air bag modules,** turn ignition switch to On position.
7. Ensure SIR lamp flashes seven times and turns off.

Zone 5

1. Connect instrument panel module connector. Connector is located behind access panel on far righthand side of instrument panel.
2. Install Connector Position Assurance (CPA) cover onto instrument panel module connector.
3. Install access panel on far righthand side of instrument panel.
4. Install SIR fuse into fuse block.
5. Install instrument panel fuse block cover.
6. **From safe location at sides or below air bag modules,** turn ignition switch to On position.
7. Ensure SIR lamp flashes seven times and turns off.

Zone 7

1. Connect lefthand side impact module connector. Connector is located under driver's seat.
2. Install Connector Position Assurance (CPA) cover onto lefthand side impact module connector.
3. Install SIR fuse into fuse block.
4. Install instrument panel fuse block cover.
5. **From safe location at sides or below air bag modules,** turn ignition switch to On position.
6. Ensure SIR lamp flashes seven times and turns off.

Zone 9

1. Connect lefthand side impact module connector. Connector is located under driver's seat.
2. Install Connector Position Assurance (CPA) cover onto lefthand side impact module connector.
3. Connect instrument panel module connector. Connector is located behind access panel on far righthand side of instrument panel.
4. Install CPA cover onto instrument panel module connector.
5. Install access panel onto far righthand side of instrument panel.
6. Connect steering wheel module coil connector. Connector is located at base of steering column.
7. Install CPA cover onto steering wheel module coil connector.
8. Install insulator panel under lefthand side of instrument panel.
9. Install SIR fuse into fuse block.
10. Install instrument panel fuse block cover.
11. **From safe location at sides or below air bag modules,** turn ignition switch to On position.
12. Ensure SIR lamp flashes seven times and turns off.

LUMINA

1. Ensure front wheels are in straight-ahead position and key is removed from ignition.
2. Connect passenger's air bag module CPA and yellow air bag module connector, then close glove compartment door.
3. Install righthand sound insulator.
4. Connect CPA and yellow air bag module connectors at base of steering column.
5. Install lefthand sound insulator.
6. Install Fuse 21 into fuse block.
7. Install instrument panel fuse block door.
8. **From safe location at sides or below air bag modules,** turn ignition switch to On position.
9. Ensure AIR BAG warning lamp flashes seven times and turns off.

METRO

1. Turn ignition key to Lock position and remove key.
2. Connect passenger's air bag module yellow electrical connector.
3. Install passenger's air bag module CPA and close glove compartment.
4. Connect yellow two-way electrical connector inside steering wheel air bag module housing.
5. Install driver's air bag module CPA and steering wheel side cap.
6. Install AIR BAG fuse into Air Bag fuse block.
7. **From safe location at sides or below air bag modules,** turn ignition switch to On position.
8. Ensure AIR BAG lamp flashes seven times and turns off.

MONTE CARLO

2000–02

1. Ensure front wheels are in straight-ahead position and key is removed from ignition.
2. **On models equipped with driver's side impact air bag module,** connect yellow electrical connector under driver's seat and install CPA.
3. **On all models,** connect frontal air bag module CPA and yellow air bag connector.
4. Install instrument panel Passenger's access hole cover.
5. Install SDM fuse into fuse block.
6. Install instrument panel fuse access cover.
7. **From safe location at sides or below air bag modules,** turn ignition switch to On position.
8. Ensure AIR BAG warning lamp flashes seven times and turns off.

2003–04

Refer to "2003–04" in "Impala" for procedures on these vehicles.

PARK AVENUE

2000–02

1. Turn steering wheel to straight-ahead position.
2. Turn ignition switch to Lock position and remove key.
3. Connect yellow two-way connector to passenger's air bag module wiring and install CPA.
4. Install righthand sound insulator.
5. Connect yellow two-way SIR electrical connector at base of steering column and install CPA.
6. Install lefthand sound insulator.
7. Install SIR fuse into under hood bussed electrical center.
8. Staying well away from both air bag modules, turn ignition On.
9. Ensure SIR lamp flashes seven times and turns off.

2003–04

Zone 2

1. Connect lefthand Side Impact Sensor (SIS) connector.
2. Install Connector Position Assurance (CPA) cover onto SIS connector.
3. Install lefthand center pillar trim panel.
4. Install SIR fuse into underhood fuse center.
5. **From safe location at sides or below air bag modules,** turn ignition switch to On position.
6. Ensure SIR lamp flashes seven times and turns off.

Zone 3

1. Connect steering wheel module coil yellow connector. Connector is located near steering column.
2. Install Connector Position Assurance (CPA) cover onto steering wheel module coil yellow connector.
3. Install insulator panel under lefthand side of instrument panel.
4. Install SIR fuse into underhood fuse center.
5. **From safe location at sides or below air bag modules,** turn ignition switch to On position.
6. Ensure SIR lamp flashes seven times and turns off.

Zone 5

1. Connect instrument panel module connector. Connector is located under righthand side of instrument panel.
2. Install Connector Position Assurance (CPA) cover onto instrument panel module connector.
3. Install insulator panel under righthand side of instrument panel.
4. Install SIR fuse into underhood fuse center.
5. **From safe location at sides or below air bag modules,** turn ignition switch to On position.
6. Ensure SIR lamp flashes seven times and turns off.

Zone 6

1. Connect righthand Side Impact Sensor (SIS) connector.
2. Install Connector Position Assurance (CPA) cover onto SIS connector.
3. Install righthand center pillar trim panel.
4. Install SIR fuse into underhood fuse center.
5. **From safe location at sides or below air bag modules,** turn ignition switch to On position.
6. Ensure SIR lamp flashes seven times and turns off.

Zone 7

1. Connect driver side impact module connector. Connector is located under driver's seat.
2. Install Connector Position Assurance (CPA) cover onto driver side impact module connector.
3. Install SIR fuse into underhood fuse center.
4. **From safe location at sides or below air bag modules,** turn ignition switch to On position.
5. Ensure SIR lamp flashes seven times and turns off.

Zone 9

1. Connect driver side impact module connector. Connector is located under driver's seat.
2. Remove Connector Position Assurance (CPA) cover onto driver side impact module connector.
3. Connect steering wheel module coil yellow connector. Connector is located near steering column.
4. Install CPA cover onto steering wheel module coil yellow connector.
5. Install insulator panel under lefthand side of instrument panel.
6. Connect instrument panel module connector. Connector is located under righthand side of instrument panel.
7. Install CPA cover onto instrument panel module connector.
8. Install insulator panel under righthand

side of instrument panel.
9. Connect passenger side impact module connector. Connector is located under passenger's front seat.
10. Install CPA cover onto passenger side impact module connector.
11. Install SIR fuse into underhood fuse center.
12. **From safe location at sides or below air bag modules,** turn ignition switch to On position.
13. Ensure SIR lamp flashes seven times and turns off.

PRIZM

1. Turn ignition to Lock position and remove key.
2. Connect side impact air bag modules electrical connectors.
3. Connect passenger's air bag module yellow two-way connector and secure with CPA.
4. Install glove compartment.
5. Connect yellow two-way connector on lower steering column and secure with CPA.
6. Install steering column lower trim cover.
7. Install CIG and IGN fuses in junction block.
8. **From safe location at sides or below air bag modules,** turn ignition switch to On position.
9. Ensure AIR BAG lamp lights for approximately six seconds and turns off.

SEVILLE

2000-02

1. Turn ignition to Lock and remove key.
2. **On models equipped with rear side impact air bag modules (AW9),** proceed as follows:
   a. Connect lefthand rear side impact air bag module yellow electrical connector.
   b. Install CPA for lefthand rear side impact air bag module yellow electrical connector.
   c. Connect righthand rear side impact air bag module yellow electrical connector.
   d. Install CPA for righthand rear side impact air bag module yellow electrical connector.
   e. Install rear seatback.
3. **On all models,** connect yellow two-way connector to passenger's air bag module pigtail and install CPA.
4. Connect yellow two-way connector to driver's air bag module pigtail and install CPA.
5. Connect yellow two-way SIR electrical connector at base of steering column and install CPA.
6. Install lefthand sound insulator.
7. Install SIR fuse into fuse block.
8. **From safe location at sides or below air bag modules,** turn ignition switch to On position.
9. Ensure SIR lamp flashes seven times and turns off.

2003-04

Zone 2

1. Connect Side Impact Sensor (SIS connector.)
2. Install Connector Position Assurance (CPA) cover onto SIS connector.
3. Install lefthand center pillar trim panel.
4. Install SIR fuse into rear fuse center.
5. Install rear seat lower cushion.
6. **From safe location at sides or below air bag modules,** turn ignition switch to On position.
7. Ensure SIR lamp flashes seven times and turns off.

Zone 3

1. Connect steering wheel module coil yellow connector. Connector is located near steering column.
2. Install Connector Position Assurance (CPA) cover onto steering wheel module coil yellow connector.
3. Install insulator panel under lefthand side of instrument panel.
4. Install SIR fuse into rear fuse center.
5. Install rear seat lower cushion.
6. **From safe location at sides or below air bag modules,** turn ignition switch to On position.
7. Ensure SIR lamp flashes seven times and turns off.

Zone 5

1. Connect instrument panel module yellow connector. Connector is located under righthand side of instrument panel.
2. Install Connector Position Assurance (CPA) onto instrument panel module to vehicle harness yellow connector.
3. Install insulator panel under righthand side of instrument panel.
4. Install SIR fuse into rear fuse center.
5. Install rear seat lower cushion.
6. **From safe location at sides or below air bag modules,** turn ignition switch to On position.
7. Ensure SIR lamp flashes seven times and turns off.

Zone 6

1. Connect Side Impact Sensor (SIS) connector.
2. Install Connector Position Assurance (CPA) cover onto SIS connector.
3. Install righthand center pillar trim panel.
4. Install SIR fuse into rear fuse center.
5. Install rear seat lower cushion.
6. **From safe location at sides or below air bag modules,** turn ignition switch to On position.
7. Ensure SIR lamp flashes seven times and turns off.

Zone 7

1. Connect lefthand side impact and pretensioner connectors. Connectors are located under driver's seat.
2. Install Connector Position Assurance (CPA) covers onto lefthand side impact module and pretensioner connectors.
3. Install SIR fuse into rear fuse center.
4. Install rear seat lower cushion.
5. **From safe location at sides or below air bag modules,** turn ignition switch to On position.
6. Ensure SIR lamp flashes seven times and turns off.

Zone 9

1. Connect lefthand side impact and pretensioner connectors. Connectors are located under driver's seat.
2. Install Connector Position Assurance (CPA) covers onto lefthand side impact module and pretensioner connectors.
3. Connect steering wheel module coil yellow connector. Connector is located near steering column.
4. Install CPA cover on steering wheel module yellow connector.
5. Install insulator panel under lefthand side of instrument panel.
6. Connect instrument panel module yellow connector. Connector is located under righthand side of instrument panel.
7. Install CPA onto instrument panel module to vehicle harness yellow connector.
8. Install insulator panel under righthand side of instrument panel.
9. Connect righthand side impact and pretensioner connectors. Connectors are located under passenger's front seat.
10. Install CPA covers onto righthand side impact module and pretensioner connectors.
11. Install SIR fuse into rear fuse center.
12. Install rear seat lower cushion.
13. **From safe location at sides or below air bag modules,** turn ignition switch to On position.
14. Ensure SIR lamp flashes seven times and turns off.

VIBE

ZONE 1

1. Connect lefthand front end discriminating sensor electrical connector from front end discriminating sensor.
2. Connect Connector Position Assurance (CPA) from lefthand front end discriminating sensor connector.
3. Connect righthand front end discriminating sensor electrical connector from front end discriminating sensor.
4. Connect Connector Position Assurance (CPA) from righthand front end discriminating sensor connector.
5. Install SIR Fuse into junction block.
6. **From safe location at sides or below air bag modules,** turn ignition switch to On position.
7. SIR indicator will flash then turn OFF.

ZONE 2

1. Install side impact sensor electrical connector.
2. Install lefthand front seat belt retractor to vehicle with mounting bolts.
3. Connect pretensioner electrical connector and install lefthand front seat shoulder belt guide adjuster bolt.
4. Install front seat shoulder belt guide trim cover.
5. Install center pillar lower trim panel,

then lefthand front and rear side door sill trim plates.
6. Install lefthand front seat belt lower anchor bolt and trim cover to front lower anchor.
7. Install SIR Fuse into junction block.
8. **From safe location at sides or below air bag modules,** turn ignition switch to On position.
9. SIR indicator will flash then turn OFF.

ZONE 3

1. Install yellow two-way connector for inflatable restraint steering wheel module coil.
2. Connect connector and lock connector with connector lock lever.
3. Install lower steering column trim cover.
4. Install SIR Fuse into junction block.
5. **From safe location at sides or below air bag modules,** turn ignition switch to On position.
6. SIR indicator will flash then turn OFF.

ZONE 4

1. Remove key from ignition switch.
2. Install yellow two-way connectors to driver and passenger seat modules.
3. Connect connectors and lock connectors with connector lock levers.
4. Install yellow two-way connector to inflatable restraint instrument panel module pigtail.
5. Connect connectors and lock connectors with connector lock levers.
6. Install instrument panel compartment and secure compartment until lower tabs engage.
7. Compress each side of compartment, until upper tabs engage, install screw and close door.
8. Install yellow two-way connector for inflatable restraint steering wheel module coil.
9. Install lower steering column trim cover.
10. Install SIR Fuse into junction block.
11. **From safe location at sides or below air bag modules,** turn ignition switch to On position.
12. SIR indicator will flash then turn OFF.

ZONE 5

1. Install yellow two-way connector to inflatable restraint instrument panel module pigtail.
2. Connect connector and lock connector with connector lock lever.
3. Install instrument panel compartment and secure compartment until lower tabs engage.
4. Compress each side of compartment, until upper tabs engage, install screw and close door.
5. Install SIR Fuse into junction block.
6. **From safe location at sides or below air bag modules,** turn ignition switch to On position.
7. SIR indicator will flash then turn OFF.

ZONE 6

1. Install side impact sensor electrical connector.
2. Install righthand front seat belt retractor to vehicle with mounting bolts.
3. Connect pretensioner electrical connector, then install righthand front seat shoulder belt guide adjuster bolt.
4. Install front seat shoulder belt guide trim cover.
5. Install center pillar lower trim panel, then the righthand front and rear side door sill trim plates.
6. Install righthand front seat belt lower anchor bolt and trim cover to front lower anchor.
7. Install SIR Fuse into junction block.
8. **From safe location at sides or below air bag modules,** turn ignition switch to On position.
9. SIR indicator will flash then turn OFF.

ZONE 7

1. Install yellow two-way connectors to driver and passenger seat modules.
2. Connect connectors and lock connectors with connector lock levers.
3. Install SIR Fuse into junction block.
4. **From safe location at sides or below air bag modules,** turn ignition switch to On position.
5. SIR indicator will flash then turn OFF.

ZONE 9

1. Install yellow two-way connectors to driver and passenger seat modules.
2. Connect connectors and lock connectors with connector lock levers.
3. Install SIR Fuse into junction block.
4. **From safe location at sides or below air bag modules,** turn ignition switch to On position.
5. SIR indicator will flash then turn OFF.

XLR

ZONE 1

Refer to "Disarming" procedure for component locations.

1. Ensure ignition is in Off position.
2. Connect lefthand and righthand EFS connector to appropriate sensor.
3. Connect lefthand and righthand CPA to appropriate EFS connector.
4. Install SIR fuse into fuse block.
5. Install block cover.
6. Use caution while placing ignition to On position from below or side.
7. The AIR BAG indicator will flash, then turn Off. Refer to "Diagnosis & Testing" in **MOTOR's "Air Bag Manual" or "Air Bag Diagnostics CD"** for information.

ZONE 2

Refer to "Disarming" procedure for component locations.

1. Ensure ignition is in Off position.
2. Connect SIS connector to SIS, then the CPA to SIS connector.
3. Install door trim panel.
4. Install SIR fuse into fuse block.
5. Install fuse block cover and kick panel to I/P.
6. Use caution while placing ignition to On position from below or side.
7. The AIR BAG indicator will flash, then turn Off. Refer to "Diagnosis & Testing" in **MOTOR's "Air Bag Manual" or "Air Bag Diagnostics CD"** for information.

ZONE 3

Refer to "Disarming" procedure for component locations.

1. Ensure ignition is in Off position.
2. Connect wheel module coil yellow connector to vehicle harness yellow connector.
3. Install CPA to vehicle harness yellow connector.
4. Install lefthand sound insulator to I/P.
5. Install SIR fuse into fuse block.
6. Install kick panel and cover to I/P.
7. Use caution while placing ignition to On position from below or side.
8. The AIR BAG indicator will flash, then turn Off. Refer to "Diagnosis & Testing" in **MOTOR's "Air Bag Manual" or "Air Bag Diagnostics CD"** for information.

ZONE 4

Refer to "Disarming" procedure for component locations.

1. Ensure ignition is in Off position.
2. Connect vehicle harness yellow connector to lefthand side impact air bag module and pretensioner yellow connector.
3. Install CPA's to lefthand side impact air bag module and pretensioner yellow connector.
4. Connect steering wheel module coil yellow connector to vehicle harness yellow connector.
5. Install CPA to harness yellow connector.
6. Install lefthand sound insulator panel to I/P.
7. Connect vehicle harness yellow connector to lefthand side impact air bag module and pretensioner yellow connector.
8. Install both CPA's to lefthand side imapct air bag module and pretensioner yellow connector.
9. Connect I/P module yellow connector to vehicle harness yellow connector.
10. Install CPA to vehicle harness yellow connector.
11. Install righthand sound insulator to I/P.
12. Install SIR fuse to fuse block.
13. Install kick panel to cover I/P.
14. Use caution while placing ignition to On position from below or side.
15. The AIR BAG indicator will flash, then turn Off. Refer to "Diagnosis & Testing" in **MOTOR's "Air Bag Manual" or "Air Bag Diagnostics CD"** for information.

ZONE 5

Refer to "Disarming" procedure for component locations.

1. Ensure ignition is in Off position.
2. Connect I/P module yellow connector to vehicle harness yellow connector.
3. Install CPA to vehicle harness yellow connector.
4. Install righthand sound insulator to I/P.
5. Install SIR fuse to fuse block.
6. Install I/P fuse block cover, then the kick panel to cover I/P fuse block.
7. Use caution while placing ignition to On position from below or side.
8. The AIR BAG indicator will flash, then

turn Off. Refer to "Diagnosis & Testing" in **MOTOR's "Air Bag Manual" or "Air Bag Diagnostics CD"** for information.

ZONE 6

Refer to "Disarming" procedure for component locations.

1. Ensure ignition is in Off position.
2. Connect SIS connector to SIS, then the CPA to SIS connector.
3. Install door trim panel(s).
4. Install SIR fuse to fuse block.
5. Install kick panel and cover to I/P fuse block.
6. Use caution while placing ignition to On position from below or side.
7. The AIR BAG indicator will flash, then turn Off. Refer to "Diagnosis & Testing" in **MOTOR's "Air Bag Manual" or "Air Bag Diagnostics CD"** for information.

ZONE 7

Refer to "Disarming" procedure for component locations.

1. Ensure ignition is in Off position.
2. Connect vehicle harness yellow connector to lefthand side impact air bag module and pretensioner yellow connector.
3. Install both CPA's to lefthand side impact air bag module and pretensioner yellow connector.
4. Install SIR fuse into fuse block.
5. Install I/P fuse block cover, then the kick panel to cover I/P.
6. Use caution while placing ignition to On position from below or side.
7. The AIR BAG indicator will flash, then turn Off. Refer to "Diagnosis & Testing" in **MOTOR's "Air Bag Manual" or "Air Bag Diagnostics CD"** for information.

ZONE 9

Refer to "Disarming" procedure for component locations.

1. Ensure ignition is in Off position.
2. Connect and install vehicle harness yellow connector to righthand side impact air bag module and pretensioner yellow connector.
3. Install SIR fuse to I/P fuse block.
4. Install I/P fuse block cover, then the kick panel to I/P fuse block.
5. Use caution while placing ignition to On position from below or side.
6. The AIR BAG indicator will flash, then turn Off. Refer to "Diagnosis & Testing" in **MOTOR's "Air Bag Manual" or "Air Bag Diagnostics CD"** for information.

SATURN

Disarming

ION

ZONE 2

Coupe

1. Ensure front wheels are pointed straight-ahead.
2. Turn ignition key off and remove ignition key from switch.
3. Remove Air Bag fuse from Body Control Module (BCM) fuse center. Fuse center is located under center of instrument panel.
4. Remove coat hooks from headliner.
5. Pull trim panel from around high mount stop lamp.
6. Pull back headliner to access lefthand pretensioner connector.
7. Remove Connector Position Assurance (CPA) cover from lefthand pretensioner connector.
8. Disconnect lefthand pretensioner connector.
9. Remove garnish molding from lefthand upper lock pillar.
10. Remove CPA cover from lefthand roof rail module yellow connector.
11. Disconnect lefthand roof rail module yellow connector.

Sedan

1. Ensure front wheels are pointed straight-ahead.
2. Turn ignition key off and remove ignition key from switch.
3. Remove Air Bag fuse from Body Control Module (BCM) fuse center. Fuse center is located under center of instrument panel.
4. Remove trim panel from lefthand center pillar.
5. Remove Connector Position Assurance (CPA) cover from lefthand pretensioner yellow connector.
6. Disconnect lefthand pretensioner yellow connector.
7. Remove garnish molding from lefthand upper lock pillar.
8. Remove CPA cover from lefthand roof rail module yellow connector.
9. Disconnect lefthand roof rail module yellow connector.

ZONE 3

1. Ensure front wheels are pointed straight-ahead.
2. Turn ignition key off and remove ignition key from switch.
3. Remove Air Bag fuse from Body Control Module (BCM) fuse center. Fuse center is located under center of instrument panel.
4. Remove outer trim cover from lefthand side of instrument panel.
5. Remove Connector Position Assurance (CPA) cover from steering wheel module coil yellow connector.
6. Disconnect steering wheel module coil yellow connector.

ZONE 5

1. Ensure front wheels are pointed straight-ahead.
2. Turn ignition key off and remove ignition key from switch.
3. Remove Air Bag fuse from Body Control Module (BCM) fuse center. Fuse center is located under center of instrument panel.
4. Remove outer trim cover from righthand side of instrument panel.
5. Remove Connector Position Assurance (CPA) cover from instrument panel module yellow connector.
6. Disconnect instrument panel module yellow connector.

ZONE 6

Coupe

1. Ensure front wheels are pointed straight-ahead.
2. Turn ignition key off and remove ignition key from switch.
3. Remove Air Bag fuse from Body Control Module (BCM) fuse center. Fuse center is located under center of instrument panel.
4. Remove coat hooks from headliner.
5. Pull trim panel from around high mount stop lamp.
6. Pull back headliner to access righthand pretensioner connector.
7. Remove Connector Position Assurance (CPA) cover from righthand pretensioner connector.
8. Disconnect righthand pretensioner connector.
9. Remove garnish molding from righthand upper lock pillar.
10. Remove CPA cover from righthand roof rail module yellow connector.
11. Disconnect righthand roof rail module yellow connector.

Sedan

1. Ensure front wheels are pointed straight-ahead.
2. Turn ignition key off and remove ignition key from switch.
3. Remove Air Bag fuse from Body Control Module (BCM) fuse center. Fuse center is located under center of instrument panel.
4. Remove trim panel from righthand center pillar.
5. Remove Connector Position Assurance (CPA) cover from righthand pretensioner yellow connector.
6. Disconnect righthand pretensioner yellow connector.
7. Remove garnish molding from righthand upper lock pillar.
8. Remove CPA cover from righthand roof rail module yellow connector.
9. Disconnect righthand roof rail module yellow connector.

ZONE 8

Coupe

1. Ensure front wheels are pointed straight-ahead.
2. Turn ignition key off and remove ignition key from switch.
3. Remove Air Bag fuse from Body Control Module (BCM) fuse center. Fuse center is located under center of instrument panel.
4. Remove garnish molding from righthand upper lock pillar.
5. Remove Connector Position Assurance (CPA) cover from righthand roof rail module yellow connector.
6. Disconnect righthand roof rail module yellow connector.
7. Remove outer trim cover from righthand side of instrument panel.
8. Remove CPA cover from instrument

panel module yellow connector.
9. Disconnect instrument panel module yellow connector.
10. Remove coat hooks from headliner.
11. Pull trim panel from around high mount stop lamp.
12. Pull back headliner to access righthand pretensioner connector.
13. Remove CPA cover from righthand pretensioner connector.
14. Disconnect righthand pretensioner connector.
15. Remove outer trim cover from lefthand side of instrument panel.
16. Remove CPA cover from steering wheel module coil yellow connector.
17. Disconnect steering wheel module coil yellow connector.
18. Pull back headliner to access lefthand pretensioner connector.
19. Remove CPA cover from lefthand pretensioner connector.
20. Disconnect lefthand pretensioner connector.
21. Remove garnish molding from lefthand upper lock pillar.
22. Remove CPA cover from lefthand roof rail module yellow connector.
23. Disconnect lefthand roof rail module yellow connector.

Sedan

1. Ensure front wheels are pointed straight-ahead.
2. Turn ignition key off and remove ignition key from switch.
3. Remove Air Bag fuse from Body Control Module (BCM) fuse center. Fuse center is located under center of instrument panel.
4. Remove garnish molding from righthand upper lock pillar.
5. Remove Connector Position Assurance (CPA) cover from righthand roof rail module yellow connector.
6. Disconnect righthand roof rail module yellow connector.
7. Remove outer trim cover from righthand side of instrument panel.
8. Remove CPA cover from instrument panel module yellow connector.
9. Disconnect instrument panel module yellow connector.
10. Remove trim panel from righthand center pillar.
11. Remove CPA cover from righthand pretensioner yellow connector.
12. Disconnect righthand pretensioner yellow connector.
13. Remove outer trim cover from lefthand side of instrument panel.
14. Remove CPA cover from steering wheel module coil yellow connector.
15. Disconnect steering wheel module coil yellow connector.
16. Remove trim panel from lefthand center pillar.
17. Remove CPA cover from lefthand pretensioner yellow connector.
18. Disconnect lefthand pretensioner yellow connector.
19. Remove garnish molding from lefthand upper lock pillar.
20. Remove CPA cover from lefthand roof rail module yellow connector.
21. Disconnect lefthand roof rail module yellow connector.

L-SERIES

1. Place front wheels in straight-ahead position.
2. Turn ignition to Lock position and remove key.
3. Remove IGN1 mini-fuse from underhood fuse block.
4. Remove instrument panel lefthand lower close-out panel.
5. Push out clips securing yellow two-way SIR connectors to instrument panel brace.
6. Disconnect SIR connectors.

S-SERIES

1. Place front wheels in straight-ahead position.
2. Turn ignition to Lock position and remove key.
3. Remove AIR BAG fuse from instrument panel fuse block.
4. Disconnect driver's air bag module two-way yellow electrical connector clipped to steering column brace.
5. Reach under instrument panel on righthand side and detach clip which retains yellow two-way SIR electrical connector to metal brace near HVAC fan.
6. Disconnect passenger's air bag module connector.

Arming

ION

ZONE 2

Coupe

1. Connect lefthand roof rail module yellow connector.
2. Install Connector Position Assurance (CPA) cover onto lefthand roof rail module yellow connector.
3. Install lefthand upper lock pillar garnish molding.
4. Connect lefthand pretensioner connector.
5. Install CPA cover onto lefthand pretensioner connector.
6. Push headliner and high mount stop lamp trim panel back into place.
7. Install coat hooks.
8. Install Air Bag fuse into Body Control Module (BCM) fuse panel.
9. **From safe location at sides or below air bag modules,** turn ignition switch to On position.
10. Ensure air bag lamp flashes seven times and turns off.

Sedan

1. Connect lefthand roof rail module yellow connector.
2. Install Connector Position Assurance (CPA) cover onto lefthand roof rail module yellow connector.
3. Install lefthand upper lock pillar garnish molding.
4. Connect lefthand pretensioner yellow connector.
5. Install CPA cover onto lefthand pretensioner yellow connector.
6. Install lefthand center pillar trim panel.
7. Install Air Bag fuse into Body Control Module (BCM) fuse panel.
8. **From safe location at sides or below air bag modules,** turn ignition switch to On position.
9. Ensure air bag lamp flashes seven times and turns off.

ZONE 3

1. Connect steering wheel module coil yellow connector.
2. Install Connector Position Assurance (CPA) cover onto steering wheel module coil yellow connector.
3. Install lefthand side of instrument panel outer trim cover.
4. Install Air Bag fuse into Body Control Module (BCM) fuse panel.
5. **From safe location at sides or below air bag modules,** turn ignition switch to On position.
6. Ensure air bag lamp flashes seven times and turns off.

ZONE 5

1. Connect instrument panel module yellow connector.
2. Install Connector Position Assurance (CPA) cover onto instrument panel module yellow connector.
3. Install righthand side of instrument panel outer trim cover.
4. Install Air Bag fuse into Body Control Module (BCM) fuse panel.
5. **From safe location at sides or below air bag modules,** turn ignition switch to On position.
6. Ensure air bag lamp flashes seven times and turns off.

ZONE 6

Coupe

1. Connect righthand roof rail module yellow connector.
2. Install Connector Position Assurance (CPA) cover onto righthand roof rail module yellow connector.
3. Install righthand upper lock pillar garnish molding.
4. Connect righthand pretensioner connector.
5. Install CPA cover onto righthand pretensioner connector.
6. Push headliner and trim panel around high mount stop lamp back into place.
7. Install coat hooks into headliner.
8. Install Air Bag fuse into Body Control Module (BCM) fuse panel.
9. **From safe location at sides or below air bag modules,** turn ignition switch to On position.
10. Ensure air bag lamp flashes seven times and turns off.

Sedan

1. Connect righthand roof rail module yellow connector.
2. Install Connector Position Assurance (CPA) cover from righthand roof rail module yellow connector.
3. Install righthand upper lock pillar garnish molding.
4. Connect righthand pretensioner yellow connector.

5. Install CPA cover onto righthand pretensioner yellow connector.
6. Install righthand center pillar trim panel.
7. Install Air Bag fuse into Body Control Module (BCM) fuse panel.
8. **From safe location at sides or below air bag modules,** turn ignition switch to On position.
9. Ensure air bag lamp flashes seven times and turns off.

ZONE 8

Coupe

1. Connect lefthand roof rail module yellow connector.
2. Install Connector Position Assurance (CPA) cover onto lefthand roof rail module yellow connector.
3. Install lefthand upper lock pillar garnish molding.
4. Connect lefthand pretensioner connector.
5. Install CPA cover onto lefthand pretensioner connector.
6. Connect steering wheel module coil yellow connector.
7. Install CPA cover onto steering wheel module coil yellow connector.
8. Install lefthand side of instrument panel outer trim cover.
9. Connect righthand pretensioner connector.
10. Install CPA cover onto righthand pretensioner connector.
11. Push headliner and trim panel around high mount stop lamp back into place.
12. Install coat hooks.
13. Connect instrument panel module yellow connector.
14. Install CPA cover onto instrument panel module yellow connector.
15. Install righthand side of instrument panel outer trim cover.
16. Connect righthand roof rail module yellow connector.
17. Install CPA cover onto righthand roof rail module yellow connector.
18. Install righthand upper lock pillar garnish molding.
19. Install Air Bag fuse into Body Control Module (BCM) fuse panel.
20. **From safe location at sides or below air bag modules,** turn ignition switch to On position.
21. Ensure air bag lamp flashes seven times and turns off.

Sedan

1. Connect lefthand roof rail module yellow connector.
2. Install Connector Position Assurance (CPA) cover onto lefthand roof rail module yellow connector.
3. Install lefthand upper lock pillar garnish molding.
4. Connect lefthand pretensioner yellow connector.
5. Install CPA cover onto lefthand pretensioner yellow connector.
6. Install lefthand center pillar trim panel.
7. Connect steering wheel module coil yellow connector.
8. Install CPA cover onto steering wheel module coil yellow connector.
9. Install instrument panel lefthand outer trim cover.
10. Connect righthand pretensioner yellow connector.
11. Install CPA cover onto righthand pretensioner yellow connector.
12. Install righthand center pillar trim panel.
13. Connect instrument panel module yellow connector.
14. Install CPA cover onto instrument panel module yellow connector.
15. Install instrument panel righthand outer trim cover.
16. Connect righthand roof rail module yellow connector.
17. Install CPA cover onto righthand roof rail module yellow connector.
18. Install righthand upper lock pillar garnish molding.
19. Install Air Bag fuse into Body Control Module (BCM) fuse panel.
20. **From safe location at sides or below air bag modules,** turn ignition switch to On position.
21. Ensure air bag lamp flashes seven times and turns off.

L-SERIES

1. Turn ignition to Lock position and remove key.
2. Connect SIR connectors.
3. Push in clips securing yellow two-way SIR connectors to instrument panel brace.
4. Install instrument panel lefthand lower close-out panel.
5. Install IGN1 mini-fuse in underhood fuse block.
6. **From safe location at sides or below air bag modules,** turn ignition switch to On position.
7. Ensure air bag lamp flashes seven times and turns off.

S-SERIES

1. Turn ignition to Lock position and remove key.
2. Connect passenger's air bag module connector.
3. Reach under instrument panel on righthand side and install clip which retains yellow two-way SIR electrical connector to metal brace near HVAC fan.
4. Connect driver's air bag module two-way yellow electrical connector clipped to steering column brace.
5. Install AIR BAG fuse into instrument panel fuse block.
6. **From safe location at sides or below air bag modules,** turn ignition switch to On position.
7. Ensure air bag lamp flashes seven times and turns off.

COMPUTER RELEARN PROCEDURE

INDEX

DAIMLERCHRYSLER

Powertrain Control Module (PCM)

Anytime the PCM is replaced the VIN and vehicle mileage must be programmed into the new PCM. If the PCM is not programmed, Diagnostic Trouble Codes (DTCs) will set. To program the PCM, connect a DRB or suitably programmed scan tool to the Data Link Connector (DLC) and follow scan tool manufacturers' instructions. On models equipped with the Sentry Key Immobilizer System (SKIS), refer to "Sentry Key Immobilizer System (SKIS)" to program secret key into the PCM.

Sentry Key Immobilizer System (SKIS)

When replacing the PCM on these models, it will be required to program the SKIS I.D. code into the new PCM. The new PCM will not allow the engine to operate unless it receives the correct I.D. code from the Sentry Key Immobilizer Module (SKIM). Use the following procedure to program the secret key into the PCM.

1. Obtain vehicle's four-digit PIN number.
2. Ensure transmission or transaxle is in Park or Neutral and turn ignition to ON position.
3. Connect DRB or suitably programmed scan tool to Data Link Connector (DLC).
4. Select THEFT ALARM, SKIM, MISCELLANEOUS and PCM REPLACED from scan tool menu.
5. Enter secured access mode by entering vehicle's four-digit PIN number.
6. Press ENTER to transfer secret key code to PCM.
7. **If incorrect code is entered three times, secured access mode will be locked out for one hour. To exit lockout mode, turn ignition key to RUN position for one hour and enter correct PIN (ensure accessories are turned off and monitor state of battery charge, connect battery charger).**

FORD MOTOR CO.

Powertrain Control Module (PCM)

AUTOMATIC DATA TRANSFER

1. Prior to removing old PCM, connect suitably programmed scan tool to Data Link Connector (DLC).
2. Follow scan tool manufacturers' instructions to download data from old PCM.
3. Install new PCM and connect scan tool to DLC.
4. Follow scan tool manufacturers' instructions to download data from scan tool to replacement PCM.

MANUAL DATA ENTRY

1. Install new PCM.
2. Connect suitably programmed scan tool to Data Link Connector (DLC).
3. Follow scan tool manufacturers' instructions to manually program VID block data to PCM. If instructed by scan tool to contact "AS BUILT" data center, proceed as follows.
   a. Contact Fed World website at "fedworld.gov."
   b. Select auto service information and search for "Calibrations" or "Vehicle Calibrations."
   c. Specify vehicle manufacturer, model name and model year as required.

GENERAL MOTORS

Body Control Module (BCM)

ALERO & GRAND AM

This procedure must be performed if the BCM, Passlock sensor or PCM is replaced. If BCM is not properly programmed, it will not control the features properly.

1. Ensure battery is fully charged and ignition switch is in ON position.
2. Connect suitably programmed scan tool to Data Link Connector (DLC).
3. Access scan tool "Special Functions" menu and follow scan tool instructions to program BCM.
4. If BCM fails to accept program, inspect BCM connections and ensure scan tool is equipped with latest software.

AURORA

Refer to "Dash Integration Module (DIM)," "Instrument Panel Integration Module (IPM)" and "Rear Integration Module (RIM)" for programming procedures.

BONNEVILLE

Refer to "Dash Integration Module (DIM)," "Instrument Panel Integration Module (IPM)" and "Rear Integration Module (RIM)" for programming procedures.

CAMARO & FIREBIRD

This customer key learn procedure must be performed anytime the BCM is replaced.

1. Insert customer key into ignition cylinder and turn to ON position.
2. Start engine to ensure system operation.
3. Observe SECURITY indicator lamp, noting the following:
   a. If indicator lamp lights for approximately five seconds and then goes out, BCM is properly programmed.
   b. If indicator lamp flashes at rate of one flash per second, BCM is not properly programmed, inspect BCM wiring and connectors for fault.

CATERA

Anytime battery power is disconnected the following accessory programing procedure must be performed.

ELECTRONIC THROTTLE CONTROL (ETC)

1. Turn ignition switch to RUN position, but do not start engine.
2. Leave ignition switch in RUN position for approximately three minutes to allow ETC to cycle and relearn its home position.
3. Turn ignition switch off, start engine and allow to run for 30 seconds.

POWER SUNROOF

1. Turn ignition switch to RUN position.
2. Turn power sunroof switch to CLOSED position.
3. After sunroof fully closes and motor stops, press and hold switch in CLOSED position for three seconds.
4. Turn power sunroof switch to TILT position.
5. After sunroof reaches tilt position and motor stops, press and hold switch in TILT position for three seconds.
6. Turn power sunroof switch to FULL OPEN position.
7. After sunroof reaches full open position and motor stops, press and hold switch in FULL OPEN position for three seconds.
8. Turn power sunroof switch to CLOSED position.
9. After sunroof fully closes and motor stops, press and hold switch in CLOSED position for three seconds.

POWER WINDOWS

1. Turn ignition switch to RUN position.
2. Press power window switch to DOWN position.
3. After window reaches full down position, press and hold switch in DOWN position for three seconds.
4. Press power window switch to UP position.
5. After window reaches full up position, press and hold switch in UP position for three seconds.
6. Repeat procedure for each window.

HEAT & AIR CONDITIONING CONTROL HEAD

1. Turn ignition switch to RUN position.
2. Simultaneously press and hold AUTO and OFF buttons for at least five seconds.
3. Stepper motors should cycle from one stop to another while calibrating.
4. Ensure heater and air conditioning head operates correctly.

CAVALIER & SUNFIRE

This procedure must be performed if the BCM Is replaced. If BCM is not properly programmed with the proper RPO configurations, it will not control the features properly.

1. Ensure battery is fully charged.
2. Connect suitably programmed scan tool to Data Link Connector (DLC).
3. Turn ignition switch to ON position.
4. Access "SPECIAL FUNCTIONS" from scan tool menu, select "NEW BCM SETUP" and follow scan tool instructions to program new BCM.
5. If BCM fails to accept program, inspect BCM connections and ensure scan tool is equipped with latest software.
6. Anytime BCM is replaced, it will required for PCM to learn new fuel continue password, as follows:
   a. Turn ignition switch to ON position.
   b. Attempt to start engine and release key to ON (vehicle will not start).
   c. Observe "SECURITY" telltale lamp. After approximately 10 minutes lamp will turn off.
   d. Turn off ignition switch and wait five seconds.
   e. Repeat procedure two more times for total of three cycles/30 minutes.
   f. Turn ignition switch to OFF position.
   g. Start engine, vehicle has now learned Passlock sensor data password.

CENTURY

The following procedure must be performed anytime the BCM is replaced. After performing the BCM programming procedure, program the theft deterrent system as outlined in "Theft Deterrent Systems."

1. Connect suitably programmed scan tool to Data Link Connector (DLC).
2. Turn ignition switch to ON position.
3. Select "Diagnostics" from scan tool menu and enter vehicle data when prompted by scan tool.
4. Select "Body," then "Body Control Module" from scan tool menu.
5. Select "Special Functions" and "New VIN" from scan tool menu, then follow scan tool instructions to input required data.
6. Exit back to "Special Functions" menu and select "BCM Reprogramming."
7. Scan tool should inquire "Do you want to setup a Body Control Module?"
8. At prompt, select "Setup BCM" on scan tool.
9. Scan tool will display "Now setting up the new Body Control Module."
10. When successful programming is complete, scan tool will display "Body Control Module setup is complete."
11. Program theft deterrent system as outlined in "Theft Deterrent Systems."

CORVETTE

1. Ensure battery is fully charged.
2. Connect suitably programmed scan tool to Data Link Connector (DLC).
3. Select NEW BCM SETUP and program BCM with proper RPO configuration.
4. Turn ignition On and leave on for 11 minutes.
5. Turn ignition Off position for 30 seconds.
6. Turn ignition On for 11 minutes or until DTC P1630 sets.
7. Turn ignition Off for 30 seconds.
8. Turn ignition On for 30 seconds and start engine.
9. If engine starts, proceed as follows:
   a. Clear DTCs and turn ignition Off for 30 seconds.
   b. Ensure engine starts and runs.
10. If engine cranks but will not start, refer to **MOTOR's Domestic Engine Performance & Driveability Manual.**

CUTLASS & MALIBU

This procedure must be performed if the BCM, Passlock sensor or PCM is replaced. If BCM is not properly programmed, it will not control the features properly.

1. Ensure battery is fully charged and ignition switch is in ON position.
2. Connect suitably programmed scan tool to Data Link Connector (DLC).
3. Access scan tool "Special Functions" menu and follow scan tool instructions to program BCM.
4. If BCM fails to accept program, inspect BCM connections and ensure scan tool is equipped with latest software.

DEVILLE

Refer to "Dash Integration Module (DIM)," "Instrument Panel Integration Module (IPM)" and "Rear Integration Module (RIM)" for programming procedures.

GRAND PRIX & REGAL

2000

The following procedure must be performed anytime the BCM is replaced.

1. Connect suitably programmed scan tool to Data Link Connector (DLC).

2. Input required data when prompted by scan tool.
3. Turn ignition switch to RUN position.
4. Select "SPECIAL FUNCTIONS" from "MAIN MENU" screen.
5. Select "NEW VIN" and input required data.
6. Exit back to "SPECIAL FUNCTION" menu and select "BCM REPROGRAMMING."
7. Scan tool will display "DO YOU WANT TO SETUP A BODY CONTROL MODULE?" Select "SETUP BCM" hotspot on scan tool.
8. Scan tool will display "NOW SETTING UP THE BODY CONTROL MODULE."
9. When BCM has been setup successfully, scan tool will display "BODY CONTROL MODULE SETUP IS COMPLETE."
10. Program theft deterrent system as outlined in "Theft Deterrent Systems."

2001-04

The following procedure must be performed anytime the BCM is replaced. After performing the BCM programming procedure, program the theft deterrent system as outlined in "Theft Deterrent Systems."

1. Connect suitably programmed scan tool to Data Link Connector (DLC).
2. Turn ignition switch to ON position.
3. Select "Diagnostics" from scan tool menu and enter vehicle data when prompted by scan tool.
4. Select "Body," then "Body Control Module" from scan tool menu.
5. Select "Special Functions" and "New VIN" from scan tool menu, then follow scan tool instructions to input required data.
6. Exit back to "Special Functions" menu and select "BCM Reprogramming."
7. Scan tool should inquire "Do you want to setup a Body Control Module?"
8. At prompt, select "Setup BCM" on scan tool.
9. Scan tool will display "Now setting up the new Body Control Module."
10. When successful programming is complete, scan tool will display "Body Control Module setup is complete."
11. Program theft deterrent system as outlined in "Theft Deterrent Systems."

IMPALA & MONTE CARLO

The following procedure must be performed anytime the BCM is replaced. After performing the BCM programming procedure, program the theft deterrent system as outlined in "Theft Deterrent Systems."

1. Connect suitably programmed scan tool to Data Link Connector (DLC).
2. Turn ignition switch to ON position.
3. Select "Diagnostics" from scan tool menu and enter vehicle data when prompted by scan tool.
4. Select "Body Control Module" from scan tool menu.
5. Select "Special Functions" and "New VIN" from scan tool menu, then follow scan tool instructions to input required data.
6. Exit back to "Special Functions" menu and select "BCM Reprogramming."
7. Scan tool should inquire "Do You Want To Setup A Body Control Module?"
8. At prompt, select "Setup BCM" on scan tool.
9. Scan tool will display "Now Setting Up The New Body Control Module."
10. When successful programming is complete, scan tool will display "Body Control Module Setup Is Complete."
11. Exit back to "Special Functions" menu and select "Set Options."
12. Select "Point Of Sale" and input required data when prompted by scan tool.
13. Exit back to "Set Options" menu and select "Option Configuration."
14. Input required data when prompted by scan tool.
15. After BCM, VIN, Point Of Sale and Option Configuration have been entered, program theft deterrent system as outlined in "Theft Deterrent Systems."

INTRIGUE

The following procedure must be performed anytime the BCM is replaced. After performing the BCM programming procedure, program the theft deterrent system as outlined in "Theft Deterrent Systems."

1. Connect suitably programmed scan tool to Data Link Connector (DLC).
2. Turn ignition switch to ON position.
3. Select "Diagnostics" from scan tool menu and enter vehicle data when prompted by scan tool.
4. Select "Body," then "Body Control Module" from scan tool menu.
5. Select "Special Functions" and "New VIN" from scan tool menu, then follow scan tool instructions to input required data.
6. Exit back to "Special Functions" menu and select "BCM Reprogramming."
7. Scan tool should inquire "Do you want to setup a Body Control Module?"
8. At prompt, select "Setup BCM" on scan tool.
9. Scan tool will display "Now setting up new Body Control Module."
10. When successful programming is complete, scan tool will display "Body Control Module setup is complete."
11. Program theft deterrent system as outlined in "Theft Deterrent Systems."

LESABRE

Refer to "Dash Integration Module (DIM)," "Instrument Panel Integration Module (IPM)" and "Rear Integration Module (RIM)" for programming procedures.

PARK AVENUE

The following procedure must be performed anytime the BCM is replaced.

1. Connect suitably programmed scan tool to Data Link Connector (DLC).
2. Turn ignition switch to ON position.
3. Select "Body Control Module" from scan tool menu.
4. Select "Special Functions," then "Setup SDM Serial Number In BCM," follow scan tool instructions to input required data.
5. Exit back to "Special Functions" menu and select "Setup BCM."
6. Scan tool should inquire "Do You Want To Setup A Body Control Module?"
7. At prompt, select "Setup BCM" on scan tool.
8. Scan tool will display "Now Setting Up The New Body Control Module."
9. When successful programming is complete, scan tool will display "Body Control Module Setup Is Complete."
10. Exit back to "Special Functions" menu and select "Set Options."
11. Select "Point Of Sale" and input required data when prompted by scan tool.
12. Exit back to "Set Options" menu and select "Load Management Option."
13. Input required data when prompted by scan tool.
14. Exit back to "Special Functions."

SEVILLE

Refer to "Dash Integration Module (DIM)," "Instrument Panel Integration Module (IPM)" and "Rear Integration Module (RIM)" for programming procedures.

Crankshaft Position System Variation Learn

2.2L & 2.4L ENGINES

The following procedure must be performed when any of the following procedures are performed; PCM is replaced, engine is replaced, crankshaft is replaced, crankshaft position sensor is replaced, or any engine repair that disturbs the crankshaft/harmonic balancer to the crankshaft position sensor relationship.

1. Ensure battery is fully charged, parking brake is applied and vehicle wheels are blocked.
2. Place transaxle in Park or Neutral position.
3. Turn accessories off and connect suitably programmed scan tool to Data Link Connector (DLC).
4. Start and run engine until it reaches operating temperature of at least 185°F.
5. With engine running, enable "Crankshaft Position System Variation Learning" procedure with scan tool.
6. Press and hold brake pedal firmly and raise engine speed to 3,920 RPM, release throttle as soon as engine cuts out.
7. With scan tool, ensure crankshaft variation has been learned.
8. Perform this procedure up to 10 times. If PCM will not learn variation, DTC 1336 should set. Refer to **Motors' "Domestic Engine Performance & Driveability Manual"** for DTC P1336 diagnosis.

3.1L, 3.4L, 3800, 4.0L & 4.6L ENGINES

The crankshaft position system values are stored within PCM memory after a learn procedure is performed. If crankshaft position system variation is not within value stored in PCM memory, DTC P0300 may be set.

The crankshaft variation learn procedure must be performed under the following conditions: DTC P1336, PCM replacement, PCM reprogramming, engine replacement, crankshaft replacement, crankshaft damper replacement and crankshaft position sensor replacement.

When performing this procedure, ensure vehicle is at operating temperature, no DTCs other than P1336 are present and that no camshaft position sensor faults are present. Proceed as follows for CKP learn procedure:

1. Set parking brake and block drive wheels.
2. Start and run engine until it reaches operating temperature.
3. Turn engine off and turn ignition key to ON position.
4. Connect suitably programmed scan tool to Data Link Connector (DLC) and select "CKP Variation Learn Procedure" from scan tool function list.
5. Start engine and when instructed by scan tool, apply brake pedal firmly.
6. Ensure transaxle is in PARK and increase pedal position until CKP system variation learn fuel cut-off is reached at 5150 RPM.
7. Release accelerator pedal after second fuel cut-off is reached.
8. CKP system variation compensating values are learned when RPM decreases back to idle.
9. Monitor scan tool for DTC P1336. If scan tool indicates DTC P1336 ran and passed, learn procedure is complete. If scan tool indicates DTC P1336 failed or did not run, inspect for DTCs. If no DTCs other than P1336 exist, repeat learn procedure.

3.5L ENGINE

The crankshaft position system values are stored within PCM memory after a learn procedure is performed. If crankshaft position system variation is not within value stored in PCM memory, DTC P0300 may be set.

The crankshaft variation learn procedure must be performed under the following conditions: DTC P1336, PCM replacement, PCM reprogramming, engine replacement, crankshaft replacement, crankshaft damper replacement and crankshaft position sensor replacement.

When performing this procedure, ensure vehicle is at operating temperature, no DTCs other than P1336 are present and that no camshaft position sensor faults are present. Proceed as follows for CKP learn procedure:

1. Set parking brake and block drive wheels.
2. Start and run engine until it reaches operating temperature.
3. Turn engine off and turn ignition key to ON position.
4. Connect suitably programmed scan tool to Data Link Connector (DLC) and select "CKP Variation Learn Procedure" from scan tool function list.
5. Start engine and when instructed by scan tool, apply brake pedal firmly.
6. Ensure transaxle is in PARK.
7. **On 2000 models,** increase pedal position until CKP system variation learn fuel cut-off is reached at 4300 RPM.
8. **On 2001–04 models,** increase pedal position until CKP system variation learn fuel cut-off is reached at 4050 RPM.
9. **On all models,** release accelerator pedal after second fuel cut-off is reached.
10. CKP system variation compensating values are learned when RPM decreases back to idle.
11. Monitor scan tool for DTC P1336. If scan tool indicates DTC P1336 ran and passed, learn procedure is complete. If scan tool indicates DTC P1336 failed or did not run, inspect for DTCs. If no DTCs other than P1336 exist, repeat learn procedure.

5.7L ENGINE

CAMARO & FIREBIRD

1. Connect suitably programmed scan tool to Data Link Connector (DLC).
2. Apply parking brake, block drive wheels and close hood.
3. **On models equipped with automatic transmission,** place selector lever in PARK position.
4. **On models equipped with manual transmission,** place shift lever in NEUTRAL position.
5. **On all models,** start and run engine until coolant temperature is at least 150°F.
6. Turn off accessories and apply brakes.
7. Enable "Crankshaft Variation Learn Procedure" with scan tool.
8. Slowly raise engine speed to 4000 RPM and immediately release throttle when engine speed decreases.
9. Turn ignition off for 15 seconds after learn procedure is completed.

CORVETTE

Refer to "3.1L, 3.4L, 3800, 4.0L & 4.6L Engines" for CKP variation learn procedures on this engine.

Dash Integration Module (DIM)

AURORA, BONNEVILLE, DEVILLE, LESABRE & SEVILLE

1. Ensure battery is fully charged and modules on serial data line are connected.
2. Connect suitably programmed scan tool to Data Link Connector (DLC).
3. Turn ignition switch to ON position.
4. Access DIM menu on scan tool and select "Special Functions."
5. Select "New VIN" from special functions menu and follow scan tool instructions.
6. Select "Setup SDM Serial Number In DIM," scan tool should ask "Do you want to set up a Dash Integration Module?" Answer yes to set up module.
7. When scan tool displays "Module Initialized," DIM module is setup.
8. To program vehicle options, access "Special Functions" menu and select "Set Options."
9. Select "Automatic/Manual HVAC" and follow scan tool instructions to select RPO configuration.
10. Select "Options" and follow scan tool instructions to Select Headlamp Type option configuration.
11. Select "LH Drvr. Personalization" and follow scan tool instructions to select LH Drvr. Personalization option configuration.
12. Select "Magna Steer Option" and follow scan tool instructions to select RPO configuration.
13. Select "Miscellaneous Options No. 1" and follow scan tool instructions to select RPO configuration.
14. Select "Miscellaneous Options No. 2" and follow scan tool instructions to select RPO configuration.
15. Select "Universal Theft Deterrent" and follow scan tool instructions to select RPO configuration.
16. Exit back to "Special Functions" menu.

Engine Control Module (ECM)

CATERA

This procedure should only be performed when the ECM is replaced, when requested by the ECM or when informed by a service bulletin. In order to perform this programming procedure, access to a General Motors' Techline Information System 2000 PC Techline Terminal will be required.

1. Turn ignition switch off.
2. Select "Service Programming System" from Techline Terminal.
3. Select "Programming Process" and "Vehicle" for ECU location.
4. Turn ignition switch to ON position.
5. connect suitably programmed scan tool to Data Link Connector (DLC).
6. Connect cable tool No. RS-232, between Techline Terminal and scan tool.
7. Turn scan tool on and wait for start screen.
8. Ensure VIN displayed on Techline Terminal matches VIN.
9. Select type of module to be programmed and type of programming needed.
10. Select appropriate calibration file and ensure current calibration with selected calibration.
11. Select "Next" to initiate download of calibration files.
12. After download is complete, turn ignition switch off for at least 30 seconds and activate theft deterrent system immobilizer as follows:
    a. Select "Special Functions" from scan tool "Immobilizer" menu.
    b. Select "Program Immobilizer," then follow scan tool instructions to activate immobilizer.
13. After activating immobilizer, select "EXIT" service programming.

Instrument Panel Integration Module (IPM)

AURORA, BONNEVILLE, DEVILLE, LESABRE & SEVILLE

1. Connect suitably programmed scan tool to Data Link Connector (DLC).
2. Turn ignition switch to ON position.
3. Select "Instrument Panel Module," then "Special Functions" from scan tool menu.
4. Select "Miscellaneous Test" and "IPM Recalibration."
5. After scan tool recalibrates IPM, ensure latest version has been installed by selecting "Data Display" and "Module Information", then view calibration ID number. ID number must match version loaded on scan tool.

Powertrain Control Module (PCM)

ALERO & GRAND AM

The following procedure must be performed anytime the PCM is replaced or Diagnostic Trouble Code (DTC) P0601 is set. Code P0601 indicates that EEPROM programming has faulted.

1. Ensure battery is fully charged.
2. Connect suitably programmed scan tool to Data Link Connector (DLC).
3. Follow scan tool instructions to program EEPROM.
4. If PCM will not program properly, replace PCM.
5. Perform CKP system variation learn procedure as outlined in "Crankshaft Position System Variation Learn."
6. Program theft deterrent system as outlined in "Theft Deterrent System Programming."

AURORA, BONNEVILLE, CAMARO, CENTURY, EIGHTY EIGHT, FIREBIRD, GRAND PRIX, IMPALA, INTRIGUE, LESABRE, LUMINA, MONTE CARLO, PARK AVENUE & REGAL

2000

The following procedure must be performed anytime the PCM is replaced or Diagnostic Trouble Code (DTC) P0602 is set. Code P0602 indicates that the EEPROM is not programmed or has faulted.

1. Ensure battery is fully charged.
2. Connect suitably programmed scan tool to Data Link Connector (DLC).
3. Follow scan tool instructions to program EEPROM.
4. If PCM will not program properly, replace PCM.

2001-04

This procedure should only be performed when the PCM is replaced, when requested by the PCM or when informed by a service bulletin. In order to perform this programming procedure, access to a General Motors' Techline Information System 2000 PC Techline Terminal will be required.

1. Turn ignition switch to OFF position.
2. Connect suitably programmed scan tool to Data Link Connector (DLC).
3. Turn ignition switch to ON position and turn accessories off.
4. Select "Service Programming" from scan tool menu.
5. Input vehicle information requested by scan tool.
6. Select type of module to be programmed and type of programming to be performed.
7. Compare VIN displayed on scan tool with VIN. If VIN does not match, write down actual VIN and correct at Techline terminal.
8. Exit "Service Programming" and turn off scan tool.
9. Disconnect scan tool from DLC connector and turn off ignition switch.
10. Connect scan tool to Techline Terminal and select "Service Programming."
11. Select type of scan tool and type of programming to be performed.
12. Ensure displayed VIN with VIN.
13. Select type of module to be programmed and identify type of programming to be performed as follows:
    a. Normal: This type of programming is for updating existing calibration or programming new controller.
    b. Vehicle Configuration Index (VCI): This selection is used if VIN is unavailable or is not recognized by Techline Terminal. Techline Customer Support center will have to be contacted to use this option.
    c. Reconfigure: This type of programming is used to reconfigure vehicle, such as tire size or axle ration changes.
14. Select appropriate calibration file and ensure connections are secure.
15. Select "Reprog" to initiate download of new calibration to scan tool.
16. After download is complete, turn off scan tool and disconnect from Techline Terminal.
17. Connect scan tool to DLC.
18. Turn scan tool and ignition switch to ON position.
19. Select "Service Programming" and "Select Program."
20. After download is complete, exit "Service Programming."
21. Turn ignition switch off for 30 seconds.
22. Turn scan tool off.
23. If control module was replaced, perform the following service procedures:
    a. CKP system variation learn.
    b. GM Oil Life System resetting.
    c. Program theft deterrent system.

CORVETTE

2000

The following procedure must be performed anytime the PCM is replaced, when requested by the PCM or when informed by service bulletin.

1. Ensure battery is fully charged.
2. Connect suitably programmed scan tool to Data Link Connector (DLC).
3. Turn ignition switch off and remove passenger side floor access panel.
4. Remove splice pack/star connector shorting bars from both splice pack/star connectors, **Fig. 1.** It may be required to remove splice pack/star connectors from mounting positions.
5. Connect Star connector cable No. 1 of Serial Data Link Tester tool No. J-42236-A, or equivalent, to 12-pin splice pack connector No. 3 (8 or 9 wires).
6. Connect Star connector cable No. 2 of Serial Data Link Tester tool No. J-42236-A, or equivalent, to 12-pin splice pack connector No. 2 (4 wires).
7. Select Star connector No. 1 on Serial Data Link Tester tool toggle switch.
8. Select position "B" on Serial Data Link Tester.
9. Turn ignition switch to ON position.
10. Program PCM using latest software matching vehicle.
11. Enter "Service Programming System (SPS)" with scan tool.
12. Enter vehicle information requested.
13. Choose "Request Info" soft key on scan tool and select "Done."
14. Follow instructions on scan tool vehicle set-up screen.
15. Disconnect scan tool from DLC and connect scan tool to Techline Terminal.
16. Select "Service Programming System" at Techline Terminal.
17. Select terminal to Tech II programming method.
18. Select "Done," then follow remaining instructions from Techline Terminal.
19. Select "Vehicle Theft Re-Learn" option.
20. Select "Program" at summary screen, Techline Terminal will download information to Tech II.
21. Return scan tool to vehicle and connect to DLC.
22. Select "Service Programming" from scan tool main menu.
23. Answer prompts regarding model year and vehicle type.
24. Press "Theft Re-Learn" soft key on scan tool and follow instructions.
25. BCM and PCM will be prepared for relearn, security timer will be on for approximately 11 minutes or until DTC code P1630 sets. **It is important to keep scan tool connected to DLC during 11 minute wait.**
26. After 11 minute wait, turn ignition switch off for 30 seconds and start engine.
27. **On models equipped with automatic transmission,** perform idle learn procedure as follows:
    a. Turn off ignition switch and restore PCM battery feed.
    b. Turn off air conditioning controls, set parking brake and block drive wheels.
    c. Start and run engine until it reaches operating temperature of 176°F.

d. Shift transmission into Drive and allow engine to idle for approximately five minutes.
e. Shift transmission into Park and allow engine to idle for approximately five minutes.
f. Turn off engine for 30 seconds.

28. **On models equipped with manual transmissions,** perform idle learn procedure as follows:
   a. Turn off ignition switch and restore PCM battery feed.
   b. Turn off air conditioning controls, set parking brake and block drive wheels.
   c. Place transmission in Neutral.
   d. Start and run engine until it reaches operating temperature of 176°F.
   e. Allow engine to idle for approximately five minutes.
   f. Turn off engine for 30 seconds.

2001-04

Refer to "2001–04" in "Aurora" for PCM programming.

CUTLASS & MALIBU

DEVILLE, ELDORADO & SEVILLE

Refer to "Aurora" for PCM programming.

Rear Integration Module

AURORA, BONNEVILLE, DEVILLE, LESABRE & SEVILLE

1. Connect suitably programmed scan tool to Data Link Connector (DLC).
2. Turn ignition switch to ON position.
3. Access "Chassis Main" menu and select "Rear Integration Module."
4. Select "Recalibration" and follow scan tool instructions to calibrate automatic level control.

Theft Deterrent System Programming

ALERO, GRAND AM & MALIBU

The following procedure must be performed anytime the BCM, PCM or Passlock sensor is replaced.

1. Ensure battery is fully charged and there are no Diagnostic Trouble Codes (DTCs) present.
2. Turn ignition switch from OFF position to CRANK position attempting to start vehicle. Vehicle should start and then stall.
3. After vehicle stalls, leave ignition in ON position and observe security indicator on instrument cluster.
4. When security indicator turns off, turn ignition switch off and wait 10 seconds.
5. Repeat procedure two more times (three times total).
6. BCM and PCM will learn new code on next start attempt.

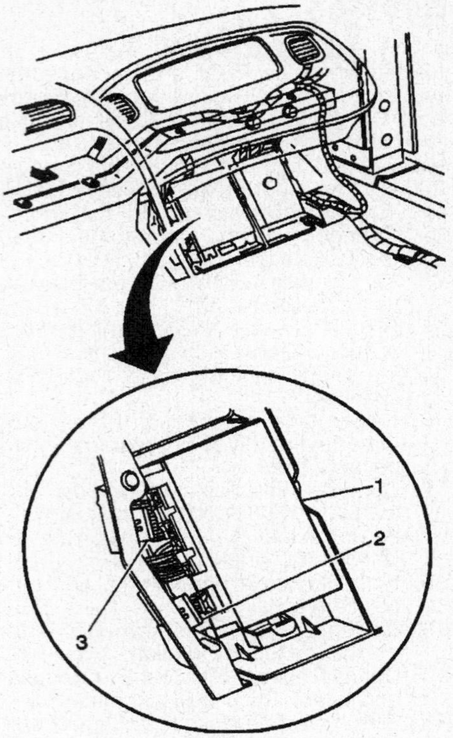

Fig. 1 Splice pack/star connectors. 2000 Corvette

AURORA, BONNEVILLE, CTS, DEVILLE, GRAND PRIX, LESABRE, PARK AVENUE & SEVILLE

The following procedure must be performed when any of the following components are replaced; ignition keys, theft deterrent control module or PCM.

1. Connect suitably programmed scan tool to Data Link Connector (DLC).
2. Turn ignition switch to ON position.
3. Select "Setup New VTD Module" from scan tool special functions menu.
4. Follow scan tool instructions to setup theft deterrent control module.
5. Turn ignition switch to ON position, using master Passkey III key.
6. Observe instrument cluster security lamp, after approximately 10 minutes, lamp should turn off.
7. After lamp turns off, turn ignition switch to OFF position and wait five seconds.
8. Repeat procedure two more times (three times total).
9. With master Passkey III key, start vehicle.
10. Vehicle has now learned key transponder information and PCM has now learned fuel continue password.
11. Clear any Diagnostic Trouble Codes (DTCs) with scan tool.

CATERA

The following procedure must be performed anytime the theft deterrent control module is replaced.

Programming a new theft control module means the consecutive programming of the security code, engine type, key cylinder number, VIN number and ECM to learn the new frequency code. The engine type, VIN number and key cylinder number may also be programmed individually.

The security code and key cylinder number can be obtained by contacting GM TRACS 2000, phone number 1-800-433-6961.

1. Connect suitably programmed scan tool to Data Link Connector (DLC).
2. Access theft deterrent system on scan tool menu.
3. Use arrow keys on scan tool to enter security code obtained from General Motors. **Security code is four alpha numeric character combination and can only be programmed once. After it is entered, combination can not be altered or erased. However, security code is always entered twice for cross check. Scan tool will compare entered codes and evaluate results. If mismatch occurs, security code input must be repeated.**
4. If mistake is made when entering security code (more than two times), module will internally activate security wait time. After first and second attempts, waiting time of 10 seconds each will occur. After third attempt, waiting time of approximately 10 minutes occurs. Each attempt after that will double wait time. Any attempt to enter security code during wait time will fail.
5. Security wait time can be viewed through scan tool menu.
6. Access engine type on scan tool and follow scan tool instructions to program engine type.
7. Enter key cylinder number obtained from General Motors.
8. Program VIN number with scan tool.
9. New ECMs are delivered with immobilizer function deactivated, to activate immobilizer, proceed as follows:
   a. Select "Special Functions" from scan tool "Immobilizer" menu.
   b. Select "Program Immobilizer," then follow scan tool instructions to activate immobilizer.

CAVALIER & SUNFIRE

In order for a theft deterrent vehicle to run, a password is communicated between the PCM and Instrument Panel Cluster (IPC). If the PCM is replaced, the new PCM needs to learn the correct password for the vehicle. When the new PCM is installed, the EEPROM calibration is flashed into the PCM and the vehicle will learn its' new password upon initial ignition ON. If the IPC is replaced, the PCM needs to learn the new password from the IPC. Use the following procedure to learn the new password.

1. Attempt to start vehicle and leave ignition on.
2. Telltale "THEFT SYSTEM" lamp will flash for approximately 10 minutes.
3. When lamp stops flashing, start vehicle.
4. When vehicle is running, password is learned.

CENTURY, IMPALA, INTRIGUE, MONTE CARLO & REGAL

The following procedure must be performed anytime the BCM or PCM is replaced.

1. Ensure battery is fully charged and there are no Diagnostic Trouble Codes (DTCs) present.
2. Turn ignition switch from OFF position to CRANK position attempting to start vehicle. Vehicle should start and then stall.
3. After vehicle stalls, leave ignition in ON position and observe security indicator on instrument cluster.
4. When security indicator turns off, turn ignition switch off and wait five seconds.
5. Repeat procedure two more times (three times total).
6. Start engine, BCM and PCM have now learned new code.
7. Clear any Diagnostic Trouble Codes (DTCs) present.

CORVETTE

2000

The following procedure must be performed anytime the BCM or ignition key is replaced.

1. Connect suitably programmed scan tool to Data Link Connector (DLC).
2. Program BCM as outlined in "Body Control Module (BCM)."
3. Turn ignition switch to ON position for 11 minutes and turn ignition switch off for 30 seconds.
4. Turn ignition switch to ON position for 11 minutes and turn ignition switch off for 30 seconds.
5. Turn ignition switch to ON position for 11 minutes or until DTC P1630 sets and turn ignition switch off for 30 seconds.
6. Turn ignition switch to ON position for 30 seconds and attempt to start engine.
7. Engine should start, indicating password has been learned.
8. If engine still will not start, diagnose engine control system as outlined in **Motors' "Domestic Engine Performance & Driveability Manual."**
9. Clear Diagnostic Trouble Codes (DTCs).

2001-04

To program the theft deterrent system on these models, refer to "Century, Impala, Intrigue, Monte Carlo & Regal."

ELDORADO

The following procedure must be performed anytime the Instrument Panel Cluster (IPC) or PCM is replaced.

1. Turn ignition switch to ON position.
2. Attempt to start engine and release key to ON position.
3. Observe SECURITY telltale lamp, after approximately 10 minutes lamp should turn off.
4. After lamp turns off, turn ignition switch off and wait five seconds.
5. Repeat procedure two more times (total of three).
6. Start engine, vehicle has now learned password.
7. Clear any Diagnostic Trouble Codes (DTCs) with suitably programmed scan tool.

SATURN

Crankshaft Learn Procedure

The PCM uses crankshaft velocity calculations to determine engine misfire and to run misfire self-diagnostics. The PCM must know precisely the variability in crankshaft notches for this function. The PCM has a notch learn process that learns the variability between notches which must be reset if the crankshaft has been replaced. Using a suitably programmed scan tool, the "Crankshaft Learn Procedure" can be set to "Relearn."

Crankshaft Relearn Procedure

Any time a PCM or crankshaft position sensor is replaced the PCM must relearn the crankshaft notches. Using a suitably programmed scan tool, select Crankshaft Position Variation Learn under the SPECIAL FUNCTIONS menu and follow the on screen prompts. This procedure will not be initiated if a misfire has been detected. If misfire DTCs are present, diagnose and repair before proceeding with crankshaft relearn procedure.

Crankshaft Position System Variation Learn

ION

The following procedure must be performed when any of the following procedures are performed; ECM is replaced, engine is replaced, crankshaft is replaced, crankshaft position sensor is replaced, or any engine repair that disturbs the crankshaft/harmonic balancer to the crankshaft position sensor relationship.

1. Ensure battery is fully charged, parking brake is applied and vehicle wheels are blocked.
2. Place transaxle in Park or Neutral position.
3. Turn accessories off and connect suitably programmed scan tool to Data Link Connector (DLC).
4. Enable "Crankshaft Position System Variation Learning" procedure with scan tool.
5. Start and idle engine until it reaches operating temperature of at least 185°F.
6. Press and hold brake pedal firmly, then raise engine speed to 3,920 RPM, release throttle as soon as engine cuts out.
7. Ensure parking brake is set. **Do not apply brake pedal.**
8. Cycle ignition switch off to on, apply and hold brake pedal.
9. Start and run engine at idle speed.
10. Ensure air conditioning is off.
11. With scan tool, enable crankshaft variation system learn procedure.
12. Accelerate to Wide Open Throttle (WOT), release accelerator as soon as fuel cut-off occurs.
13. Scan tool will display learned procedure is complete by indicating DTC P0315 has been run and passed. If scan tool indicates DTC P0315 has failed or did not run. Refer to **Motors' "Domestic Engine Performance & Driveability Manual"** for DTC P0315 diagnosis.

L SERIES

2.2L ENGINE

Refer to "2.2L & 2.4L Engines" in "Crankshaft Position System Variation Learn" in "General Motors."

3.1L ENGINE

On these engines the Powertrain Control Module (PCM) will program crankshaft position variation automatically.

PCM/ECM Learning Procedure

If the battery is disconnected or if the PCM is replaced, the PCM must go through the learning process. To allow the PCM to relearn, proceed as follows:

1. Start vehicle and run until engine reaches normal operating temperature.
2. Drive vehicle at part throttle, with moderate acceleration and idle conditions until normal performance returns.
3. Park vehicle and engage parking brake with engine running.
4. **On models equipped with automatic transaxle,** place transaxle in Drive position.
5. **On models equipped with manual transaxle,** place transaxle in Neutral position.
6. **On all models,** allow vehicle to idle for

approximately two minutes until engine idle stabilizes. Ensure engine is at normal operating temperature.

Passlock Theft Deterrent Relearn Procedure

There are two methods used to reprogram the Passlock security system, the Seed and Key method and the Auto Learn method. If no components were replaced or the Passlock sensor was the only component replaced, the Auto Learn technique may be used to program the security system. If the BCM or PCM were replaced then the "Seed & Key" method must be used.

SEED & KEY METHOD

1. Turn ignition On.
2. Inspect for body control module (BCM) or powertrain control module (PCM) diagnostic trouble codes (DTCs) using suitably programmed scan tool.
3. Record and repair DTCs.
4. Turn ignition Off.
5. Select "Passlock Relearn" option using suitably programmed scan tool.
6. Wait for 10 minutes and observe security telltale changing from Flashing to On to Off.
7. If ignition is turned Off before telltale changes state, relearn procedure must be performed again.
8. Turn ignition Off.
9. Vehicle should start on next ignition switch cycle.

AUTO LEARN METHOD

1. Turn ignition On.
2. Momentarily turn ignition to Crank position, but do not start vehicle.
3. Wait for 10 minutes.
4. Observe SECURITY telltale changing from Flashing to On to Off.
5. If ignition is turned Off before telltale changes state, procedure will have to be performed again.
6. Turn Ignition Off.
7. Repeat procedure two more times.
8. If vehicle does not start on next ignition switch cycle, repeat procedure.

Remote Keyless Entry Synchronization

The remote keyless entry system does not send the same signal twice. The body control module (BCM) will not execute a signal if it has been sent previously. To synchronize a transmitter with the BCM, simultaneously press and hold the Lock and Unlock buttons on the transmitter for approximately ten seconds near the vehicle. The doors locks will cycle to confirm synchronization.

SERVICE REMINDER & WARNING LAMP RESET PROCEDURES

TABLE OF CONTENTS

DaimlerChrysler

INDEX

AIR BAG WARNING LAMP

If the Air Bag warning lamp lights and stays on, diagnosis and repair of the air bag system will be required to reset the lamp.

ANTI-LOCK BRAKE SYSTEM WARNING LAMP

This lamp should light when the ignition is turned On. The lamp may light for as long as 30 seconds as a bulb and system inspection. If the lamp remains lit or lights while operating the vehicle, a fault condition in the anti-lock brake system is indicated. When the lamp is lit, turn ignition Off and start the engine again. If the lamp still remains lit, the anti-lock brake system should be serviced. The brake system will remain functional, but without the anti-lock function. After servicing the anti-lock brake system, the lamp will automatically reset. On some models, it may be required to operate the vehicle at a speed over 18 mph and make several hard brake applications from 40 mph to reset the lamp.

CHECK ENGINE LAMP

The Check Engine lamp should light for approximately 3 seconds after the ignition has been turned On as a bulb inspection. If improper or no signals are received by the Single Board Engine Controller (SBEC) from various sensors or if the PCM enters its Limp-In mode, the SBEC will light the Check Engine lamp. After diagnosing and servicing the fuel injection system or emission related systems, the SBEC memory will be cleared after approximately 40–100 ignition key On-Off cycles.

The Check Engine lamp may light if the fuel filler cap has not been completely tightened. The lamp should turn off after the cap has been properly tightened and the vehicle has successfully completed a predetermined number of trip cycles.

On Monaco and Premier models, this lamp should light during engine starting as a bulb inspection. Once the engine has started, the lamp should go off. If the lamp remains lit, the fuel injection and emission control system diagnosis should be performed using tester DRB II. During the diagnosis and repair procedure with tester DRB II, the Check Engine lamp will be reset.

CHECK ENGINE OR MALFUNCTION INDICATOR LAMP

Except Colt & Summit

The powertrain control module monitors a variety of sensors in the fuel injection, ignition, emission and engines systems. Each time the ignition is turned On, the instrument panel MIL should light for approximately two seconds and then go out. If the PCM senses a fault condition with a monitored circuit often enough to indicate an actual fault condition or if it enters its Limp-In mode, it stores a Diagnostic Trouble Code (DTC) in the PCM's memory. If the code applies to a non-emissions related components or system and the fault condition is repaired or ceases to exist, the PCM cancels the code after 40 warm-up cycles. DTCs that affect vehicle emissions light the MIL. Use a suitably programmed scan tool to retrieve and erase DTC's and to reset the MIL.

On 1998 and newer models, the Check Engine lamp may light if the fuel filler cap has not been completely tightened. The lamp should turn off after the cap has been properly tightened and the vehicle has successfully completed a predetermined number of trip cycles.

Colt & Summit

This lamp is used to monitor fuel injection and emission control system components for faults. When the ignition is turned On, the lamp will light for 2–3 seconds as a bulb inspection. If the lamp remains on, a fault in the fuel injection or emission control system is indicated. If fault is intermittent, the lamp will go off when the Electronic Control Unit (ECU) receives a normal signal from the faulting component. If the ECU receives an improper signal from a faulting component for a time longer than that programmed into the ECU, a code will be stored in the ECU memory and the Malfunction Indicator Lamp should light. After

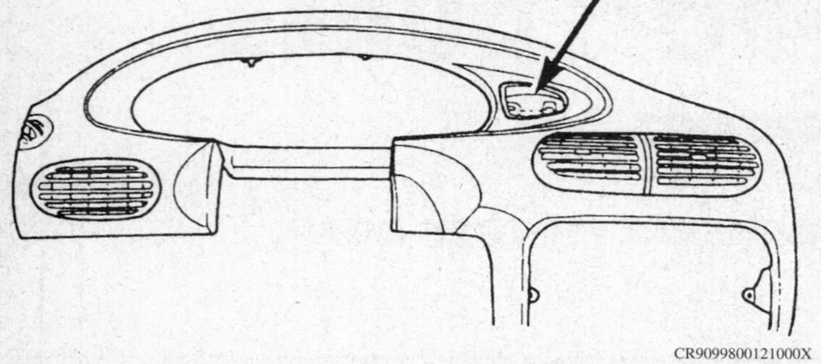

Fig. 1 Compass/temperature mini trip computer. Concorde, Intrepid, LHS, Vision, 300M & 1994–96 New Yorker

servicing the indicated component, the Malfunction Indicator Lamp can be reset by clearing the ECU memory. The ECU memory is cleared by using a suitable scan tool or disconnecting the battery ground cable for approximately 10 seconds.

COMPASS & TEMPERATURE MINI TRIP COMPUTER

Concorde, Intrepid, LHS, Vision, 300M & 1994–96 New Yorker

1. Set mini trip computer to Compass/ Temperature mode, **Fig. 1.**
2. Press US/M and STEP buttons simultaneously until VAR and current variance zone number is displayed.
3. Press STEP until proper variance zone number is displayed, **Fig. 2.**
4. After 5 seconds of inactivity, displayed zone will be set automatically. Ensure accuracy of compass by pointing vehicle in N, S, E and W directions.

Sebring Convertible

If the CAL indicator lights, the compass will need to be calibrated. This should be done on a level surface free of large metal objects such as other vehicles, bridges, buildings, railroads and underground cables. Proceed as follows:

1. Drive in complete circles, keeping steering wheel in fixed position, at speeds of 7–10 mph until CAL indicator turns Off. This may require two to six turns.
2. When CAL indicator turns Off, compass has been calibrated and should now display proper headings.
3. Inspect for proper calibrations by selecting North, South, East and West.
4. If compass does not appear to be reading accurately, calibration procedure should be repeated in another area.

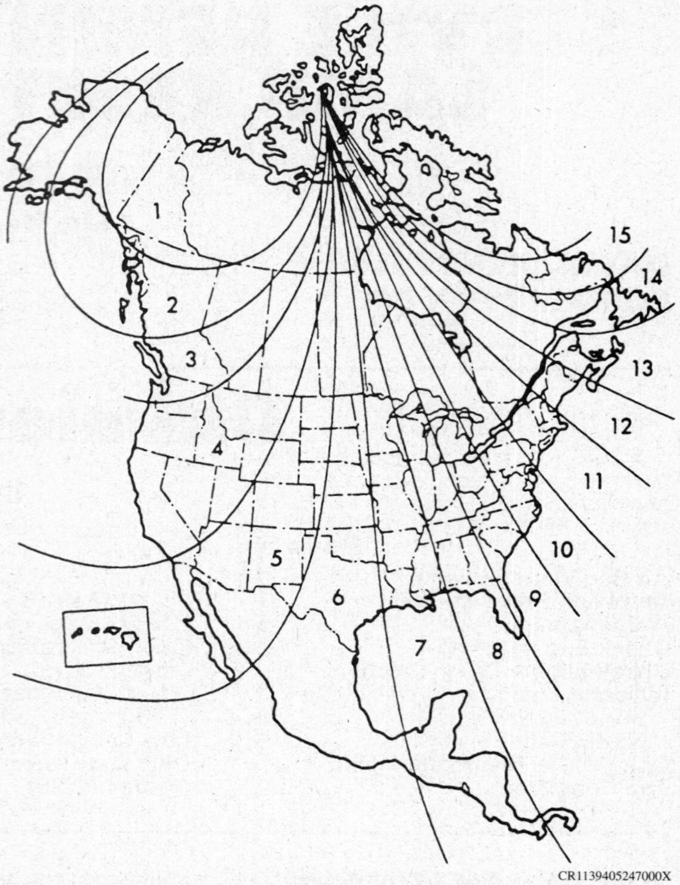

Fig. 2 Variance zone map. Concorde, Intrepid, LHS, Vision, 300M & 1994–96 New Yorker

ELECTRONIC VEHICLE INFORMATION CENTER

1992–93 Dynasty, Fifth Avenue, Imperial & New Yorker

The Electronic Vehicle Information Center is a computer controlled warning system which monitors various sensors used on the vehicle. The system supplements the warning indicators in the instrument cluster. When a warning message has been activated, a tone will sound to attract the driver's attention. The warning message will then be displayed on the overhead console until the condition has been corrected or a new display function is called up, **Fig. 3.** A tone will announce each new warning condition. The "Service Reminder" warning message will be indicated at 7,500 mile or 12 month intervals to indicate that required service is to be performed. After performing the required service, the Service Reminder message can be reset by using a DRB II diagnostic readout tool.

OVERHEAD TRAVEL INFORMATION SYSTEM (OTIS)

Concorde, Intrepid, LHS, Vision, 300M & 1994–96 New Yorker

Overhead Travel Information System (OTIS) is a module with six informational displays and four buttons. When the ignition is turned ON, OTIS blanks the display for one second and returns to the display active when the vehicle was last turned OFF.

LOW OIL PRESSURE—This message will be displayed when a low engine oil pressure condition exists. If message is encountered with vehicle operating at idle speed, increase engine RPM. If message remains or if message is encountered while operating vehicle, the engine lubricating system should be inspected and serviced immediately. After engine lubricating system has been serviced, the message will be automatically cancelled.

SERVICE REMINDER—This message will be indicated at 7,500 mile or 12 month intervals to indicate that required service is to be performed. After performing the required service, with the Service Reminder message displayed, depress the Vehicle Electronic Information Center Reset button.

TURN SIGNAL ON—This message will be indicated when the turn signal is on and the vehicle has traveled a distance over ½ mile at a speed more than 15 mph. The message will be reset when the turn signal lever has been returned to Off.

VOLTAGE IMPROPER—When this message is displayed, a fault condition in the charging or electrical system exists. After servicing, the message will be reset after the ignition has been cycled to the OFF position.

WASHER FLUID LOW—When this message is displayed, bring washer fluid to proper level. This message will be reset after the ignition has been cycled to the OFF position.

The six informational displays are:

1. Compass/temperature.
2. Average fuel economy.
3. Distance to empty.
4. Instantaneous fuel economy.
5. Trip odometer.
6. Elapsed time.

The four buttons on the OTIS are:

1. STEP—Depress this button to select display modes except Compass/temperature.
2. C/T—Depress this button to display compass (vehicle direction) and temperature.
3. U/SM—Switches display information between English and Metric readings.
4. RESET—Depress this button to reset current display (for displays that can be reset.)

COMPASS CALIBRATION

Do not attempt to set compass calibration near large metal objects, such as other vehicles, buildings or bridges.

1. Remove magnetic devices from roof panel.
2. Turn ignition On.
3. Press C/T button to select Compass/temperature display.
4. Depress and hold RESET button for approximately five seconds. VAR symbol will light during this time.
5. Continue to hold RESET button for approximately 10 seconds until CAL symbol lights.
6. Drive vehicle through three complete 360° turns in no less than 48 seconds. Compass will be calibrated when CAL symbol is extinguished.
7. Press and hold RESET button for approximately five seconds until VAR symbol is lit.
8. OTIS will display variance zone and VAR.
9. Press STEP button to display variance zone, **Fig. 2.**
10. Press RESET button to set new variance zone and resume normal operation.

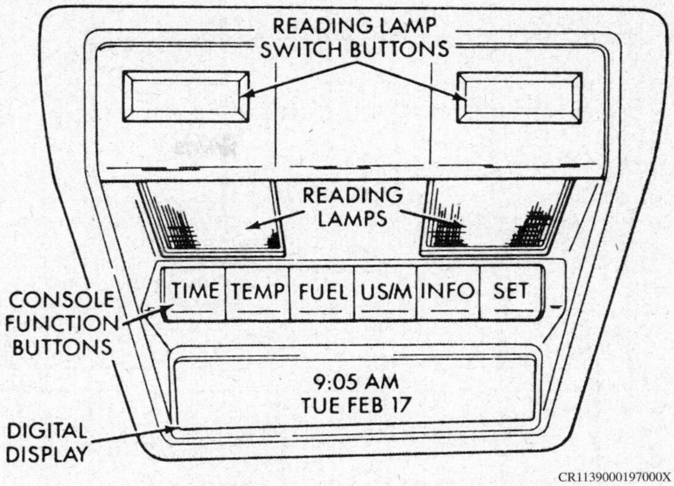

Fig. 3 Electronic Vehicle Information Center display console. 1992–93 Dynasty, Fifth Avenue, Imperial & New Yorker

LOW COOLANT WARNING LAMP

The Low Coolant warning lamp should light whenever coolant level in the coolant reservoir is below a predetermined level. Add coolant to bring reservoir to proper level to turn lamp off.

POWER LOSS/LIMIT LAMP

The Power Loss/Limit lamp should light for approximately 3 seconds after the ignition has been turned On as a bulb inspection. If improper or no signals are received by the logic module from various sensors, the logic module will light the Power Loss/Limit lamp. After diagnosing and servicing the fuel injection system or EGR system (California models with EGR sensor), the logic module memory can be cleared by disconnecting and connecting the battery quick-disconnect.

VEHICLE MAINTENANCE MONITOR (VMM) SYSTEM

This system, **Fig. 4,** monitors regular service and maintenance intervals, engine oil level, engine coolant level, windshield washer fluid level, brake and tail lamps, door ajar and oil, coolant and washer sensors.

When the vehicle is started and no faults are present, the display will indicate "MONITOR." If the monitor detects a fault, it will be noted on the display. If more than one fault is noted, the fault of the highest priority will be displayed first. The display will then note all existing faults and return to the fault of highest priority. The VMM fault messages are as follows:

DOOR—Door Ajar—Close door indicated on vehicle outline display to reset monitor.

LAMP—Brake or Tail Lamp Outage—The display should light when brake is applied or headlamp switch is in the On position and a burned out lamp bulb is present. To reset monitor, replace burned out bulb.

COOLANT—Low Engine Coolant Level—Bringing coolant to proper level will reset monitor.

OIL—Low Engine Oil Level—The system will inspect engine oil level approximately 12 minutes after the ignition has been turned Off. A low oil level condition must be indicated three consecutive times before the monitor will display "Oil." To reset monitor, add oil to bring to proper level. Then, while display is indicating the "Oil" message, depress RESET select switch until a beep is noted. Even if RESET select switch is not depressed, the system will automatically reset monitor after three proper oil level readings have been obtained.

WASHER—Low Washer Fluid Level—Bringing washer fluid to proper level will reset monitor.

SERVICE—Perform Required Service and Maintenance—This message will be indicated at 7,500 mile intervals to indicate that required service is to be performed. After performing required service, depress the Reset select switch until a beep is noted.

SENSOR—This message will be indicated when a defect in the oil, coolant or washer sensor circuit is noted. Refer to "Self Diagnosis."

MILES (KMS)—Mile to next scheduled service interval.

Self Diagnosis

To diagnose, depress and hold the Check and List select switches, then turn ignition On. With the instrument cluster

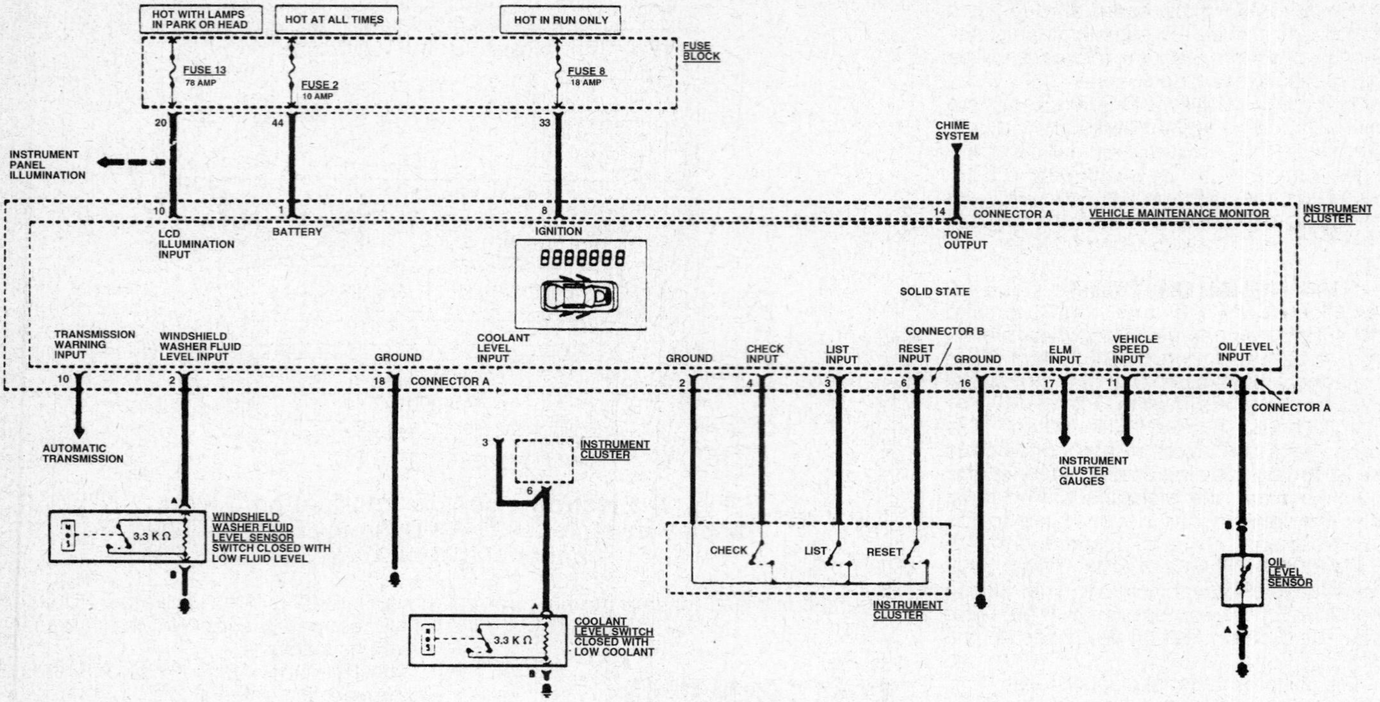

CR1138900204010X

Fig. 4 Vehicle Maintenance Monitor (VMM) System wiring schematic (Part 1 of 2). Monaco & Premier

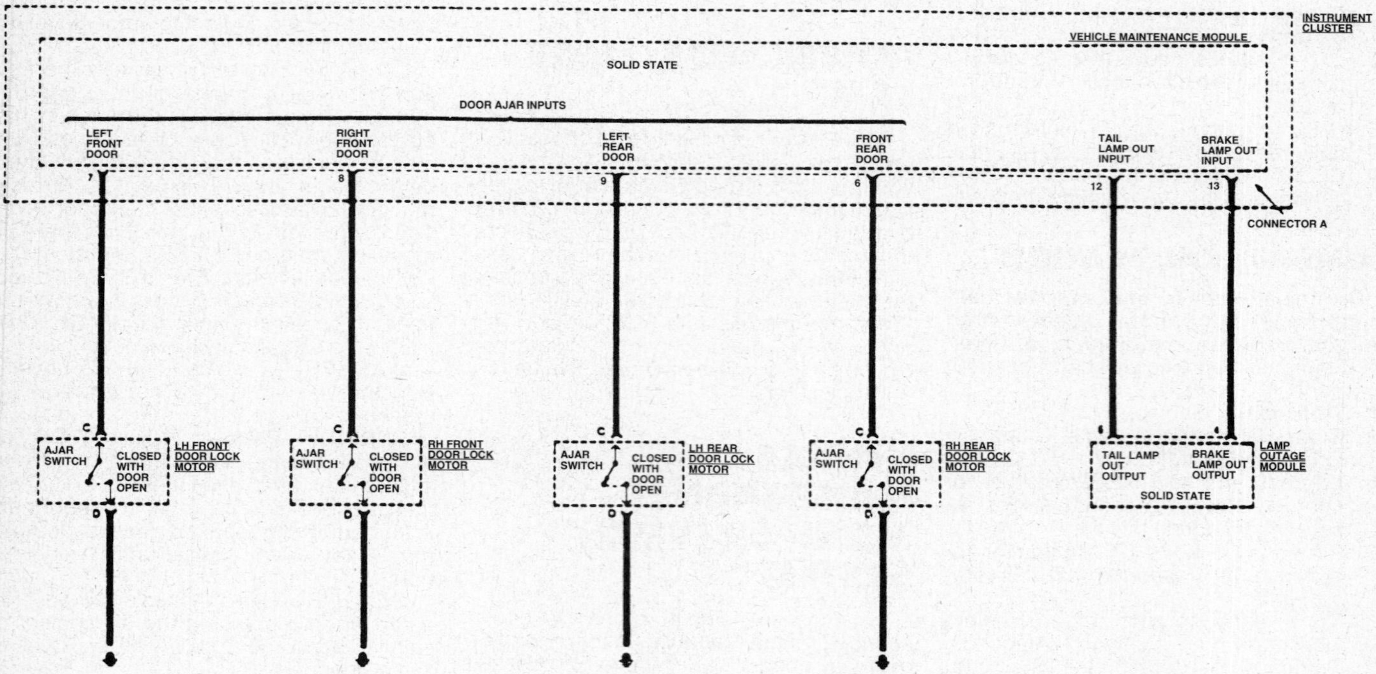

CR1138900204020X

Fig. 4 Vehicle Maintenance Monitor (VMM) System wiring schematic (Part 2 of 2). Monaco & Premier

switch in the English mode, all diagnosis will be performed automatically in sequence. With the instrument cluster in the Metric mode, the Check select switch will have to be depressed to proceed to the next test. The display will indicate which components are faulty or satisfactory. Refer to **Fig. 5.** After completing diagnosis, depress Check and List select switches to exit diagnosis mode.

Troubleshooting

1. If a condition of no display or improper information exists, start engine and inspect the following:
   a. **On models less passive restraint,** inspect fuses 8 and 19 in fuse panel. **On models with passive restraint,** inspect fuses 2 and 8 in fuse panel. Replace any blown fuses.
   b. **On all models,** inspect terminal Nos. 1 and 5 of connector A using a suitable voltmeter, **Fig. 4.** Voltmeter should indicate battery voltage. If not, inspect for open circuit to fuse panel.
   c. Connect a suitable ohmmeter between terminal Nos. 15 and 18 of connector A, **Fig. 4.** Ohmmeter should indicate zero ohms. If a no display condition is present, replace monitor. If an improper information condition is present, refer to "Self Diagnosis." If reading is other than zero ohms, inspect for open circuit.
   d. With all doors closed, connect an ohmmeter between terminal Nos. 6, 7, 8 and 9 of connector A, **Fig. 4.** Ohmmeter should indicate an infinite reading. If reading is other than infinite, inspect for short circuit to ground.
2. If monitor fails to change modes, disconnect electrical connector B, **Fig. 4,** and proceed as follows:
   a. With Check select switch depressed, connect ohmmeter between terminal Nos. 2 and 4 of connector B. If ohmmeter reading is zero ohms, proceed to step b. If ohmmeter reading is other than zero ohms, replace mode select switches.
   b. With List select switch depressed, connect ohmmeter between terminal Nos. 2 and 3 of connector B. If ohmmeter reading is zero ohms, proceed to step c. If ohmmeter reading is other than zero ohms, replace mode select switches.
   c. With Reset select switch depressed, connect ohmmeter between terminal Nos. 2 and 5 of connector B. Ohmmeter reading should be zero ohms. If ohmmeter reading is other than zero ohms, replace mode select switches.

Ford Motor Co.

INDEX

AIR BAG WARNING LAMP

If the Air Bag warning lamp lights and stays on, diagnosis and repair of the air bag system will be required to reset the lamp.

ANTI-LOCK BRAKE WARNING LAMP

This lamp should light when the ignition is turned On. It may light for as long as 30 seconds as a bulb and system inspect. If the lamp remains lit or lights while operating the vehicle, a fault condition in the anti-lock brake system is indicated. When the lamp is lit, turn ignition Off and start engine again. If the lamp still remains lit, the anti-lock brake system should be serviced. The brake system will remain functional, but without the anti-lock function. After servicing the anti-lock brake system, the lamp will automatically reset when the vehicle is operated at a speed over 25 mph.

CHECK ENGINE LAMP

EEC-IV

1992–93

EXCEPT FESTIVA, PROBE w/ 2.2L ENGINE & ESCORT & TRACER w/1.8L ENGINE

This lamp should light when the ignition is turned On. After the engine is started, the lamp should go off, unless a fault condition is detected by the EEC-IV system. Following diagnosis and repair, the Check Engine/MIL lamp will automatically reset when the stored codes are cleared from the EEC-IV system memory. After diagnosis and repair, the EEC-IV memory may be cleared of stored codes as follows:

1. With ignition turned Off, connect a jumper wire between Self Test and Self Test Input (STI) connectors, **Fig. 1. On Crown Victoria, Grand Marquis and Town Car models,** the Self Test and STI connectors are gray in color and are located on the front of the lefthand fender apron, near the Electronic Engine Control (EEC) relay. **On Mustang models,** the Self Test and STI connectors are gray in color and are located on the lefthand fender apron. **On Tempo and Topaz models,** the Self Test connector is gray in color and the STI connector is black in color and they are both located on the righthand fender apron, near the front of the strut tower. **On Taurus and Sable models,** the Self Test and STI connectors are gray in color and are located on the righthand fender apron, near the front of the engine in the area of the AIR pump and alternator. **On 1992–93 Thunderbird and Cougar models,** the Self Test and STI connectors are gray in color and are located on the righthand fender apron, near the strut tower.
2. **On all models,** turn ignition On, then disconnect jumper wire from test connector terminals. Disconnect jumper as soon as Check Engine lamp starts flashing.

FESTIVA

The Check Engine Indicator lamp should light when the ignition is in the RUN position with the engine not operating. When the engine is started, the Check Engine lamp should go off. If the lamp remains on, a service code has been stored in the EEC-IV self test system memory. After diagnosis and repair, the self test memory may be cleared of stored codes as follows:

1. With ignition turned Off, connect a jumper wire between Self Test Input (STI) connector terminal and ground. The STI connector is located in rear lefthand side of engine compartment, **Fig. 2.**
2. Turn ignition On, then disconnect and reconnect jumper wire connected between STI connector and ground.
3. Disconnect jumper from STI connector as soon as Check Engine lamp stops flashing.
4. Disconnect battery ground cable and depress brake pedal for approximately 5–10 seconds.
5. Connect battery ground cable.

PROBE w/2.2L ENGINE & ESCORT & TRACER w/1.8L ENGINE

This lamp should light when the ignition is turned On. After engine is started, the lamp should go off, unless a fault condition is detected by the system. After diagnosis and repair, the Check Engine lamp will automatically reset when stored codes are cleared from the system memory. After diagnosis and repair, memory may be cleared of stored codes as follows:

1. Disconnect battery ground cable, then depress brake pedal for approximately 5–10 seconds.
2. Connect battery ground cable again.

1995–97

This lamp should light when the ignition is turned On. After engine starts, the lamp should go off, unless a fault condition is detected by the EEC-IV system. A diagnostic trouble code is stored in the PCM. Following diagnosis and repair, the Check Engine/MIL lamp will automatically reset when stored diagnostic trouble codes are cleared from PCM memory. The PCM reset procedure allows the scan tool to command the PCM to clear all diagnostic trouble codes.

PCM RESET USING STAR TESTER

1. Turn ignition Off.
2. Perform required vehicle preparation and visual inspection.
3. Connect Star tester, then select vehicle model and year.
4. Follow operating instructions on tester screen. Select Generic OBD II Functions.

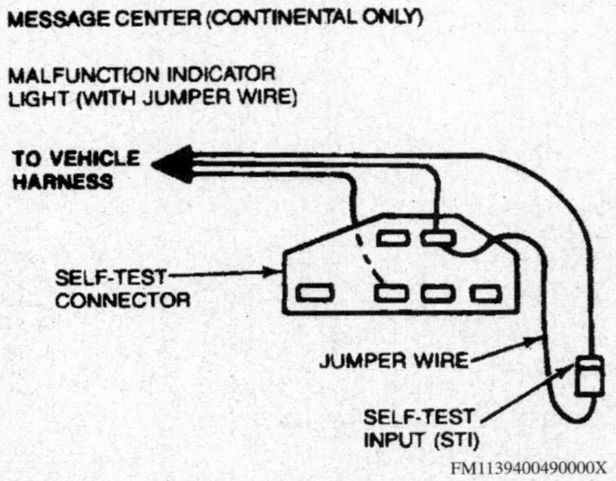

Fig. 1 Jumper wire connections for resetting Check Engine lamp. EEC-IV Except Festiva, Probe w/2.2L Engine & Escort & Tracer w/1.8L Engine

5. Press CONT button if all OBD II monitors are not complete.
6. Turn ignition On.
7. Select Clear Diagnostic Codes and press Start key.

PCM RESET USING GENERIC SCAN TOOL

1. Turn ignition Off.
2. Connect scan tool to DLC.
3. Turn ignition On.
4. Perform scan tool reset, then turn ignition Off.

KEEP ALIVE MEMORY (KAM) RESET & PCM RESET LESS ELECTRONIC TESTER

To clear KAM, disconnect battery ground cable for at least 5 minutes. This will also result in PCM reset.

EEC-V

1. Turn ignition Off.
2. Connect scan tool to DLC.
3. Turn ignition On.
4. Perform scan tool reset and turn ignition Off.
5. **On 1998 and newer models,** Check Engine lamp may light if fuel filler cap has not been completely tightened. Lamp should turn off after cap has been properly tightened and vehicle has successfully completed predetermined number of trip cycles.

CHECK FUEL CAP LAMP

The Check Fuel Cap Lamp will illuminate momentarily when the ignition switch is placed in ON position as a bulb check. If the lamp remains On, inspect fuel cap for proper installation. After properly installing the fuel cap the lamp should go off after a normal period of driving.

ELECTRONIC COMPASS

Continental

1. Determine magnetic zone, **Fig. 3.**
2. Insert suitable rod into compass module, **Fig. 4,** and press internal switch until ZONE and current zone setting are displayed.
3. Turn ignition On and release switch.
4. Press internal switch until proper zone number is displayed, release to exit zone setting mode and lock in zone.

Mark VIII

1. Press and hold COMPASS button, then the RESET button until ECO-ZONE and RSETCAL is displayed.
2. Press FUEL ECONOMY button to enter the zone set mode.
3. Refer to **Fig. 3,** for proper compass zone selection.
4. Press RESET until correct zone is selected.
5. Press COMPASS button to end zone adjustment.

Town Car

The compass module is located at the back of the rearview mirror.

1. Select compass magnetic zone, **Fig. 3.**
2. Press and hold reset button on top of compass module until message center display reads current magnetic zone setting.
3. Press calibration button on compass module to select proper zone setting.
4. To exit zone setting mode, do not press any buttons for 10 seconds.

LOW COOLANT WARNING SYSTEM

The low coolant warning lamp should light whenever the coolant level in the coolant recovery bottle is ¼ to ¾ inch or more below the cold full mark. Raise coolant level in recovery bottle to the cold full mark to turn lamp off.

On models equipped with GEM module and low coolant level warning system, the low coolant level indicator lights for two seconds during engine startup or when ignition is turned to RUN. If coolant level falls below specification for more than 15 seconds, the GEM module generates a single one second tone. Raise coolant level in recovery bottle to specified level to turn lamp off.

LOW OIL LEVEL WARNING INDICATOR

This system is used to indicate when the engine oil level is 1½ quarts or more below the specified level. The lamp should light during engine starting. If the oil level is sufficient, the lamp will go off when the engine is operating. If the oil level is low, the lamp will remain on until engine oil is added and the ignition is turned Off. The module will take approximately 5 minutes to reset. If the engine is started during this period, the last recorded reading will be displayed.

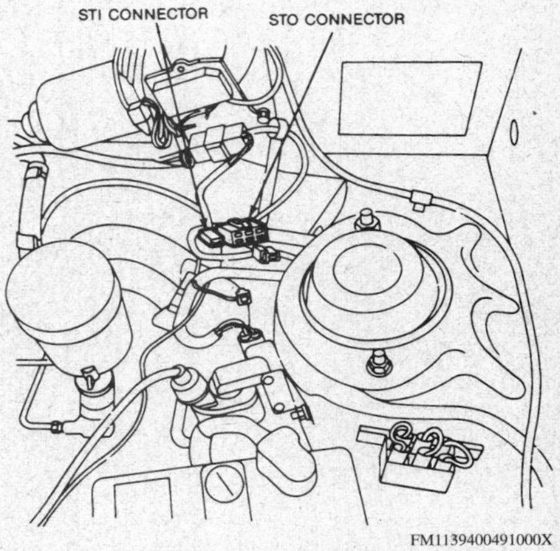

Fig. 2 STI connector location. Festiva

MALFUNCTION INDICATOR LAMP (MIL)

Refer to "Check Engine Lamp" for lamp reset procedure.

MESSAGE CENTER

Crown Victoria, Grand Marquis & Town Car

The message center may be located to the right of the instrument cluster, or it may be a part of the cluster itself. It consists of three buttons: Select, E/M and Reset. The E/M button switches the display between English and Metric. The Reset button set data to zero of instantaneous information. The Select button cycles the message display through the following selections:

1. Average speed.
2. Fuel remaining.
3. Average fuel economy and instantaneous fuel economy.
4. Distance to empty.
5. Trip distance.

Mark VIII

AIR RIDE SWITCH OFF

This warning message is displayed when the air suspension service switch, located in the luggage compartment, is turned Off.

CHECK AIR RIDE SYSTEM

This warning message is displayed when an air suspension system diagnostic trouble code is detected by the air suspension/EVO control module.

CHECK CHARGING SYSTEM

This warning message is displayed when the electrical system is not maintaining a proper voltage at the message center.

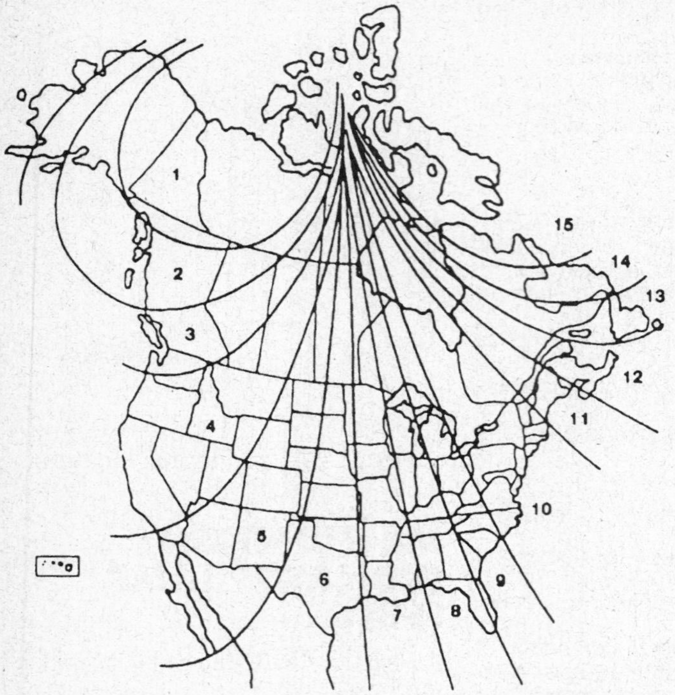

FM9099800928000X

Fig. 3 Magnetic zone map. Continental & Town Car

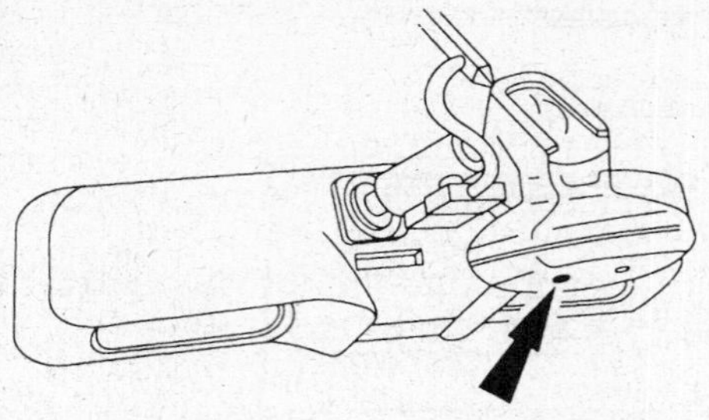

FM9099800929000X

Fig. 4 Compass module location. Continental

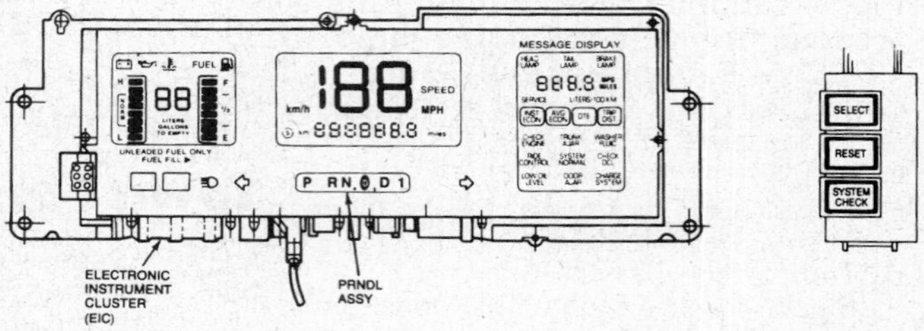

FM1138800151000X

Fig. 5 Instrument cluster & message center. Continental

CHECK ENGINE TEMP

This warning message is displayed when the coolant is overheating.

LOW ENGINE COOLANT

This warning message is displayed when the engine coolant level is below the cold line of the coolant recovery reservoir.

CHECK EXTERIOR LAMPS

This warning message is displayed when one of the following lamps is turned on and at least one is burned out: stop lamp, rear parking lamp or low beam headlamp.

CHANGE OIL SOON OR OIL CHANGE REQUIRED

The oil life functions include oil life, change oil soon and oil change required. The oil life is determined by three functions: Smart Tach pulses, miles driven and time elapsed.

When the oil life drops down to the range of 1–5%, the "Change Oil Soon" message will appear. When oil life is 0%, the "Oil Change Required" message will appear.

Depressing the oil change reset button will reset the oil life to 100%.

SERVICE INTERVAL REMINDER

Continental

After performing the required interval service, the service interval reminder mileage display on the instrument cluster can be reset as follows:

1. Depress System Check button on instrument panel. Service interval reminder mileage should be displayed on fuel computer display, **Fig. 5.**
2. Depress Reset button. Service interval reminder mileage should start flashing.
3. Depress Reset and System Check buttons at same time to reset mileage.

Cougar

1992-93

At approximately 7,500 miles, for models less super charged engine, the engine oil change indicator on the Vehicle Maintenance Monitor will indicate an oil change is needed. On models with super charged engine, the need for engine oil change will be indicated at 5,000 miles. After completing the required service, the oil change indicate can be reset by depressing the reset switch, **Fig. 6.**

1999

Some of these models are equipped with an optional overhead warning lamp system which includes a Service Interval reminder. This will light after approximately 358 days or 4800 miles to indicate that routine service is needed.

After service has been performed, the lamp can be reset by holding the trip computer SELECT and UNITS buttons for 5 seconds. The Service Interval lamp will light, then turn off after approximately four seconds.

2000-02

The maintenance interval warning indicator is controlled by the HEC. The HEC illuminates the indicator advising a scheduled maintenance (which is dependant on time of distance). The indicator is reset by placing the ignition switch in position II and depressing SELECT & UNITS buttons simultaneously for five seconds until maintenance light extinguishes.

LS

CHANGE OIL SOON OR OIL CHANGE REQUIRED

The oil life functions include "Oil Life OK, Change Oil Soon" and "Oil Change Required." The oil life is determined by the engine oil level and temperature sensors, ABS control module, odometer data and PCM RPM data.

When the oil life reaches the range of 1–5%, the "Change Oil Soon" message will appear. When oil life is 0%, the "Oil Change Required" message will appear.

Depressing the oil change RESET button will reset the oil life to 100%.

Mark VIII

CHANGE OIL SOON OR OIL CHANGE REQUIRED

The oil life functions include "Oil Life OK, Change Oil Soon" and "Oil Change Required." The oil life is determined by the engine oil level and temperature sensors, ABS control module, odometer data and PCM RPM data.

When the oil life reaches the range of 1–5%, the "Change Oil Soon" message will appear. When oil life is 0%, the "Oil Change Required" message will appear.

Depressing the oil change RESET button will reset the oil life to 100%.

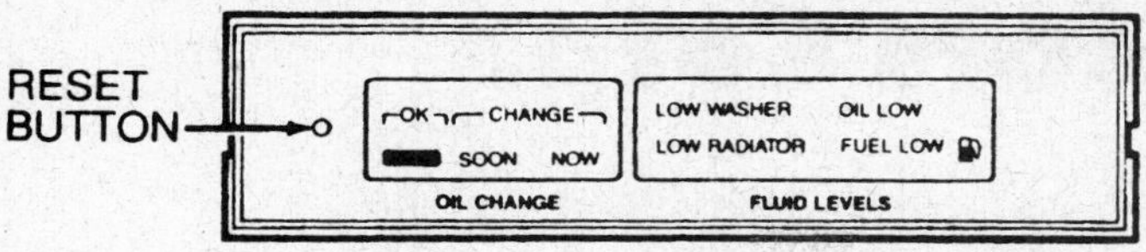

FM1138900150000X

Fig. 6 Oil change interval indicator reset switch access hole location. 1992–93 Cougar & Thunderbird

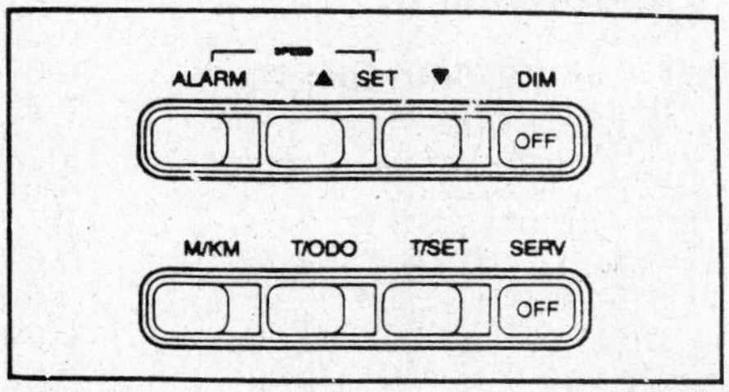

FM1138900153000X

Fig. 8 Speed alarm keyboard. Probe

Probe

ELECTRONIC INSTRUMENT CLUSTER

At 7,500 mile intervals, a Service Check message will be displayed under the System Scanner nomenclature on the instrument cluster for 3 minutes after engine starts, **Fig. 7.** After performing the required interval service, reset the service interval by depressing and holding the Service reset button, located on the speed alarm keyboard, until three tones have sounded, **Fig. 8.**

VEHICLE MAINTENANCE MONITOR

At 7,500 mile intervals a Service lamp, located on the overhead map lamp console, should light for 3 minutes after engine start, **Fig. 9.** After performing the required interval service, reset the service interval. **On models equipped with speed alarm keypad,** depress and hold the Service reset button, until three tones have sounded. **On models less speed alarm keypad,** locate reset hole in overhead console, then use a suitable tool to depress the reset button located behind the hole.

Thunderbird

1992–93

At approximately 7,500 miles, for models less super charged engine, the engine oil change indicator on the Vehicle Maintenance Monitor will indicate an oil change is needed. On models with super charged engine, the need for engine oil change will be indicated at 5,000 miles. After completing the required service, the oil change indicate can be reset by depressing the reset switch, **Fig. 6.**

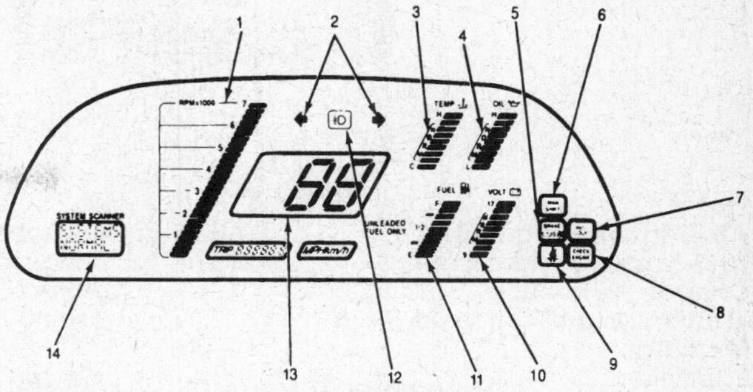

1. TACHOMETER
2. TURN INDICATORS
3. TEMPERATURE GAUGE
4. OIL PRESSURE GAUGE
5. BRAKE WARNING LIGHT
6. MANUAL SHIFT INDICATOR (ATX ONLY)
7. ANTILOCK BRAKE WARNING LIGHT
8. ENGINE WARNING LIGHT
9. SEAT BELT WARNING LIGHT
10. VOLTMETER
11. FUEL GAUGE
12. HIGH BEAM INDICATOR
13. SPEEDOMETER
14. ELECTRONIC SYSTEM SCANNER

FM1138900152000X

Fig. 7 Electronic instrument cluster. Probe

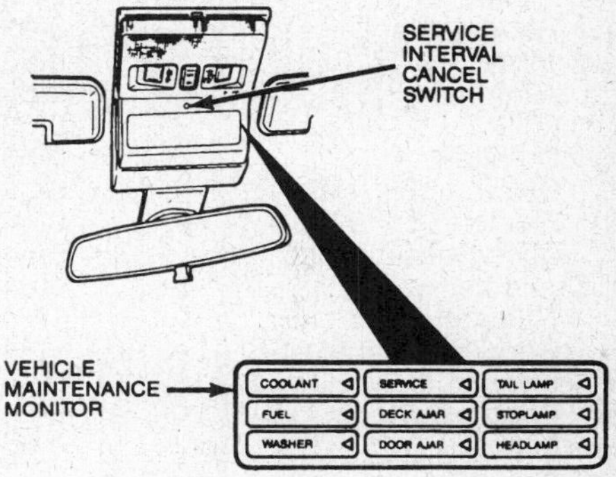

FM1138900154000X

Fig. 9 Vehicle maintenance monitor. Probe

General Motors Corp.

INDEX

AIR BAG WARNING LAMP

If the air bag warning lamp lights and stays on, diagnosis and repair of the air bag system will be required to reset the lamp.

ANTI-LOCK WARNING LAMP

This lamp should light when the ignition is turned On. The lamp may light for as long as 30 seconds as a bulb and system inspection. If lamp remains lit or lights while operating the vehicle, a fault condition in the anti-lock brake system is indicated. When lamp is lit, turn ignition Off and restart engine. If lamp still remains lit, the anti-lock brake system should be serviced. The brake system will remain functional, but without the anti-lock function. After servicing the anti-lock brake system the lamp will automatically reset. **On some models,** it may be required to operate vehicle at a speed over 18 mph to reset lamp.

CHANGE AUTOMATIC TRANSMISSION/ TRANSAXLE FLUID INDICATOR

DeVille & Seville

1. Turn ignition switch to ON position.
2. Press INFO button on Driver Information Center (DIC) button to display "Trans Fluid Life."
3. Press and hold Info RESET button on DIC until display reads "100% Trans Fluid Life."
4. Place ignition switch in Off position

Eldorado

2000

1. Turn ignition switch to ON position.
2. Press INFO button on Driver Information Center (DIC) button to display "Trans Fluid Life."
3. Press and hold Info RESET button on DIC until display reads "100% Trans Fluid Life."
4. Place ignition switch in Off position

2001-02

1. Turn ignition switch to ON position.
2. Press and hold OFF and REAR DEFOG buttons on climate control until "Trans Fluid Life Reset" appears on DIC
3. Place ignition switch in Off position

CHANGE ENGINE OIL MESSAGE

Buick

CENTURY & REGAL

1997

The Driver Information Center (DIC) engine oil life monitor indicates when to change oil. The "Change Oil" or "Change Oil Soon" messages might appear before 2,000 miles when operating under severe conditions.

To reset the oil change indicator after an oil change, proceed as follows:

1. Turn ignition On.
2. Fully depress and release accelerator pedal three times in 5 seconds.
3. If "Change Oil" or "Change Oil Soon"

message flashes twice, indicator has properly reset.
4. If "Change Oil" or "Change Oil Soon" message stays on for 5 seconds, indicator has not properly reset and must be reset again.
5. **On models equipped with Oil Life Monitor,** press and hold RESET button for more than 5 seconds while oil monitor is being displayed or until oil life percentage reaches 100%.

1999

The Engine Oil Life monitor indicates when an oil and filter change are needed, usually from 3000–10,000 miles since the last change. The CHANGE OIL SOON indicator may light even before 3000 miles if the vehicle has been operated under severe service.

The monitor will not detect dust in the oil. If operating in dusty conditions be sure to change the oil and filter every 3000 miles or sooner if the CHANGE OIL SOON lamp lights.

To reset the Engine Oil Life monitor proceed as follows:

1. Turn ignition On, but do not start engine.
2. Fully depress and release accelerator pedal three times within 5 seconds.
3. If CHANGE OIL SOON lamp flashes twice, this means system is properly reset.
4. If CHANGE OIL SOON lamp lights and stays lit for 5 seconds, system did not reset. Repeat reset procedure.

2000-04

To reset the Engine Oil Life monitor proceed as follows:

1. Turn ignition On, but do not start engine.
2. Fully depress and release accelerator pedal three times within 5 seconds. The oil life indicator will begin to flash indicating the system is resetting.
3. Place ignition switch in Off position, then start engine.
4. The engine oil change light should illuminate as a bulb check and then go Off.
5. If oil change light remains On, repeat reset procedure.

LESABRE & PARK AVENUE

1992-95

After the engine oil has been changed, the "Change Oil Soon" lamp must be reset. With ignition On, use a pencil to depress the RESET button, located under the righthand side of the instrument panel, for 5 seconds. The lamp should flash four times to indicate the Oil Life Monitor System has been reset.

1996-97

After the engine oil has been changed, display the oil life index on the DIC, then hold the RESET button for 5 seconds. When a DIC message of RESET is displayed and the oil life index equals 100%, the reset is complete.

1998

1. Turn ignition to Run.
2. Press TRIP button on driver information center until OIL LIFE REMAINING is displayed.
3. Press and hold RESET for 6 seconds, then turn ignition off.

1999

1. Turn ignition On, then press TRIP button on driver information center (DIC) switch to view various menu choices and stop on OIL LIFE REMAINING. A message will display percentage of oil life remaining.
2. Press and hold RESET button on DIC switch for at least two seconds. A message will display the percentage of oil life remaining as 99%. The engine oil life monitor is now reset.
3. Turn ignition Off.

2000-04

1. Turn ignition switch to On position.
2. Display Oil Life Index on Driver Information Center (DIC), then press and hold RESET button for more than 5 seconds until display reads 100%.
3. Turn ignition Off.

ROADMASTER

1994

After engine oil has been changed, the Change Oil lamp must be reset. Remove the instrument panel fuse box cover. With ignition On, depress the OIL RESET button for 5 seconds. The Change Oil lamp should go off.

1995-96

1. Turn ignition On, without starting engine.
2. Within 5 seconds, depress accelerator pedal to wide open position and release three times.
3. When lamp goes out, engine oil life monitor is reset. PCM will acknowledge if reset was successful by flashing Change Oil lamp twice, then will turn lamp off. If lamp does not reset, turn ignition Off and repeat procedure.

RIVIERA

1997-98

1. Turn ignition to Run.
2. Press TRIP button on driver information center until OIL LIFE REMAINING is displayed.
3. Press and hold RESET for 6 seconds, then turn ignition off.

1999

1. Turn ignition to On, then press TRIP button on driver information center (DIC) switch to view various menu choices and stop on OIL LIFE REMAINING. A message will display percentage of oil life remaining.
2. Press and hold RESET button on DIC switch for at least two seconds. A message will display percentage of oil life remaining as 99%. The engine oil life monitor is now reset.
3. Turn ignition Off.

Cadillac

ALLANTE

Press RANGE button until oil index appears, then simultaneously press and hold the AVG SPD and RANGE buttons for a minimum of 5 seconds.

CTS

LESS NAVIGATION SYSTEM

1. Access Driver Information Center (DIC) menu by pressing arrow key on INFO button located on righthand side of DIC.
2. When "100% ENGINE OIL LIFE" is highlighted, press and hold CLR button.
3. Percentage will return to 100 and oil life indicator will be reset.
4. If percentage will not return to 100, repeat procedure.

WITH NAVIGATION SYSTEM

1. Turn system on by pressing PWR/VOL knob once. PWR/VOL knob is located on lefthand side of Driver Information Center (DIC).
2. Access vehicle information menu by pressing INFO button on lefthand side DIC.
3. Turn TUNE/SEL knob on righthand side of DIC until "Engine Oil Life" is highlighted and press knob to select it.
4. When "100% Engine Oil Life" is displayed, press multi-function button next to "Reset" prompt in upper righthand corner of display.
5. Percentage will return to 100 and oil life indicator will reset.
6. If percentage does not return to 100, repeat procedure.

DEVILLE

1992

Press RANGE and FUEL USED buttons simultaneously to display oil life index, then press the RANGE and RESET buttons until "Change Oil Soon" light flashes (approximately 5 seconds). The oil life index will not remain displayed.

1993

Reset the Engine Oil Life Index (EOLI) after each oil change by pressing the RANGE and RESET keys on the Fuel Data Center for 5–50 seconds. The "Change Oil Soon" lamp will flash four times to indicate that the index has been reset.

1994-98

Press the INFORMATION button until Oil Life Index is displayed, then press and hold RESET button until Oil Life Index resets to 100 (approximately 5 seconds).

1999

1. Turn ignition On, then press TRIP button on driver information center (DIC) switch to view various menu choices and stop on OIL LIFE REMAINING. A message will display percentage of oil life remaining.
2. Press and hold RESET button on DIC

switch for at least two seconds. A message will display the percentage of oil life remaining as 99%. The engine oil life monitor is now reset.
3. Turn ignition Off.

2000-04

1. Turn ignition On, press Gauge Info button on Driver Information Center (DIC) switch to view various menu choices and stop on OIL LIFE REMAINING. Message will display percentage of oil life remaining.
2. Press and hold RESET button on DIC switch until display reads Oil Life Index 100% Normal.
3. Turn ignition Off.

FLEETWOOD (RWD)

REAR WHEEL DRIVE

1. Turn ignition On, without starting engine.
2. Press accelerator pedal to wide open throttle (WOT) position and release three times within 5 seconds.
3. If "Change Oil" warning indicator goes out, system has been reset.
4. If "Change Oil" warning indicator does not reset, turn ignition Off and repeat procedure.

1992 FRONT WHEEL DRIVE

Press RANGE and FUEL USED buttons simultaneously to display oil life index, then press the RANGE and RESET buttons until "Change Oil Soon" light flashes (approximately 5 seconds). The oil life index will not remain displayed.

ELDORADO & SEVILLE

1992

Press and hold the ENG DATA and RANGE buttons for a minimum of 5 seconds.

1993

Press the INFORMATION button until oil life index is displayed, then press STORE/RECALL until oil life index resets to 100 (approximately 5 seconds).

1994-98

Press the INFORMATION button until Oil Life Index is displayed, then press and hold RESET button until Oil Life Index resets to 100 (approximately 5 seconds).

1999

1. Turn ignition On, then press TRIP button on driver information center (DIC) switch to view various menu choices and stop on OIL LIFE REMAINING. A message will display percentage of oil life remaining.
2. Press and hold RESET button on DIC switch for at least two seconds. A message will display the percentage of oil life remaining as 99%. The engine oil life monitor is now reset.
3. Turn ignition Off.

2000-04

1. Turn ignition On, press Gauge Info button on Driver Information Center (DIC) switch to view various menu choices and stop on OIL LIFE REMAINING. Message will display percentage of oil life remaining.
2. Press and hold RESET button on DIC switch until display reads Oil Life Index 100% Normal.
3. Turn ignition Off.

SIXTY SPECIAL

1993

Reset the Engine Oil Life Index (EOLI) after each oil change by pressing the RANGE and RESET keys on the Fuel Data Center for 5–50 seconds. The "Change Oil Soon" lamp will flash four times to indicate that the index has been reset.

Chevrolet

CAMARO

1. Turn ignition to Run, engine Off.
2. Press TRIP/OIL RESET button on instrument panel for 12 seconds. OIL CHANGE lamp will start to flash to confirm system is reset. When reset is complete lamp will go out.
3. Turn ignition Off.

CORVETTE

1992-96

1. Turn ignition key to On position, without starting engine.
2. Press ENG MET button on the trip monitor and release, then press and release again within 5 seconds.
3. Within 5 seconds of previous step, press and hold GAUGES button on trip monitor. "Change Oil" lamp will flash.
4. Hold GAUGES button until "Change Oil" lamp stops flashing and goes out.
5. When lamp goes out, engine oil life monitor is reset. If it does not reset, turn ignition Off and repeat procedure.

1997

1. Turn ignition to Run.
2. Press TRIP button on the Driver Information Center (DIC) switch to view menu. Stop at OIL LIFE REMAINING. A message will display percentage of oil life remaining.
3. Press and hold the DIC switch RESET button for at least two seconds. A message will display the percentage of oil life remaining as 100%. Oil life monitor has been reset.
4. Turn ignition Off.

1998-2000

The Driver Information Center (DIC) engine oil life monitor indicates when to change oil, usually 3000–7500 miles, although the "Change Oil" message might appear before 3000 miles when operating under severe conditions.

To reset the oil life monitor after an oil change, proceed as follows:
1. Turn ignition On.
2. Press TRIP button on DIC to view menu choices and stop on "Oil Life Remaining."
3. Press and hold RESET button for more than two seconds. When remaining oil life percentage changes to 99%, monitor has been properly reset.
4. Turn ignition Off.

2001-02

1. Turn ignition switch On with engine off.
2. Press TRIP button until "OIL LIFE" percentage is displayed.
3. Press RESET button and hold for two seconds, "OIL LIFE REMAIN" percent will appear.

IMPALA & MONTE CARLO

LESS DE SERIES RADIO

The Engine Oil Life monitor indicates when an oil and filter change are needed, usually 3000–10,000 miles since the last change. The CHANGE OIL SOON indicator may light even before 3000 miles if the vehicle has been operated under severe service.

The monitor will not detect dust in the oil. If operating in dusty conditions, change the oil and filter every 3000 miles, or less, if the CHANGE OIL SOON lamp lights.

To reset the Engine Oil Life monitor proceed as follows:
1. Turn ignition On, but do not start engine.
2. Fully depress and release accelerator pedal three times within five seconds.
3. If CHANGE OIL SOON lamp flashes twice, this means system is properly reset.
4. If CHANGE OIL SOON lamp lights and stays lit for five seconds, system did not reset. Repeat reset procedure.

WITH DE SERIES RADIO

1. Place ignition switch in On position with radio Off.
2. Press and hold Disp button on radio for at least five seconds until Settings is displayed.
3. Press Seek up or down arrow to scroll though main menu.
4. Scroll until Oil Life appears on display.
5. Press Prev or Next button to enter submenu. Reset will be displayed.
6. Press Disp button to reset. A chime will be heard to ensure new setting and Done will be displayed for one second.
7. Once message has been reset, scroll until Exit appears on display.
8. Press Disp button to exit programming. A chime will be heard to ensure exit.

CAPRICE & IMPALA SS

1994

After engine oil has been changed, the "Change Oil" lamp must be reset. Remove the instrument panel fuse box cover. With ignition On, depress the OIL RESET button for 5 seconds. The lamp should go off.

1995-96

1. Turn ignition On, without starting engine.
2. Within 5 seconds, depress accelerator pedal to wide open position and release three times.
3. When lamp goes out, engine oil life

monitor is reset. PCM will acknowledge if reset was successful by flashing "Change Oil" lamp twice, then will turn lamp off. If lamp does not reset, turn ignition Off and repeat procedure.

LUMINA

1998–2001

The Engine Oil Life monitor indicates when an oil and filter change are needed, usually 3000–10,000 miles since the last change. The CHANGE OIL SOON indicator may light even before 3000 miles if the vehicle has been operated under severe service.

The monitor will not detect dust in the oil. If operating in dusty conditions, change the oil and filter every 3000 miles, or less, if the CHANGE OIL SOON lamp lights.

To reset the Engine Oil Life monitor proceed as follows:

1. Turn ignition On, but do not start engine.
2. Fully depress and release accelerator pedal three times within five seconds.
3. If CHANGE OIL SOON lamp flashes twice, this means system is properly reset.
4. If CHANGE OIL SOON lamp lights and stays lit for five seconds, system did not reset. Repeat reset procedure.

Oldsmobile

ALERO

The Engine Oil Life monitor indicates when an oil and filter change are needed, usually 3000–7500 miles since the last change. The indicator may light even before 3000 miles if the vehicle has been operated under severe service.

The monitor will not detect dust in the oil. If operating in dusty conditions, change the oil and filter every 3000 miles, or less, if the CHANGE OIL SOON lamp lights.

To reset the Engine Oil Life monitor proceed as follows:

1. Turn ignition On, but do not start engine.
2. Press and release RESET button. RESET button is located in driver's side instrument panel fuse block. CHANGE OIL indicator will begin flashing.
3. Press and release RESET button again.
4. Reset is complete when light goes out and chime sounds.

AURORA

1995

When the engine oil life index has reached 10 or less, the Driver Information System display will indicate distance to oil change and sound a beep when the ignition is placed in the RUN or ACC position for the first time each day. When the engine oil life index has reached zero, the Driver Information System display will indicate "Change Oil Now" and sound a beep, when ignition is turned to RUN or ACC for the first time each day. After engine oil change has been performed, the oil life index may be reset as follows:

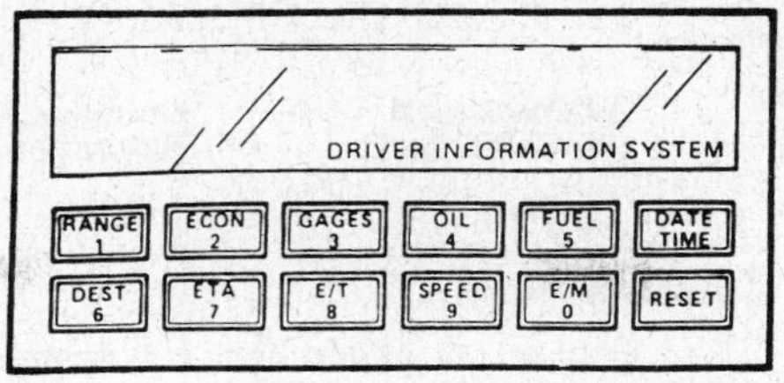

GC1138800168000X

Fig. 1 Driver Information Center. Oldsmobile except Alero, Aurora, Eighty Eight, Intrigue, LSS, Ninety-Eight & Toronado

1. Depress TEST button and release, then depress OIL button and release.
2. Depress and hold the RESET button for 5–7 seconds.

1996–99

After the engine oil has been changed, display the oil life index on the DIC, then hold the RESET button for 5 seconds. When a DIC message of RESET is displayed and the oil life index equals 100%, the reset is complete.

2001–03

1. Place ignition switch in On position.
2. Press the Select right arrow button on the driver information center until the Oil Life % is displayed.
3. Press and hold the RESET button until the display indicates Oil Life 100%.
4. Engine oil life monitor is reset.

INTRIGUE

The "Change Oil" lamp will light when the engine oil's useful life is close to its expiration. This lighting may appear earlier than outlined in the owner's manual, depending on driving patterns.

To reset the oil life monitor after an oil change, proceed as follows:

1. Turn ignition On.
2. Fully depress and release accelerator pedal three times in five seconds.
3. If "Change Oil" message flashes, monitor has properly reset.
4. If "Change Oil" message stays on for five seconds, monitor has not properly reset and must be reset again.
5. **On models equipped with U20 option,** reset oil life low indicator as follows:
   a. Press and hold MODE button until light appears next to OIL LIFE.
   b. Press and hold trip RESET button until oil life percentage changes to 99%.

EIGHTY EIGHT, LSS, NINETY-EIGHT & REGENCY

1992–95

When the engine oil life index has reached 10 or less, the Driver Information System display will indicate distance to oil change and sound a beep when the ignition is placed in the RUN or ACC position for the first time each day. When the engine oil life index has reached zero, the Driver Information System display will indicate "Change Oil Now" and sound a beep, when ignition is turned to RUN or ACC for the first time each day. After engine oil change has been performed, the oil life index may be reset as follows:

1. **On 1992–93 models,** depress TEST button and release, then depress OIL button and release.
2. **On 1994–95 models,** select OIL menu by depressing MODE button.
3. **On all models,** depress and hold the RESET button for 5–7 seconds.

1996–97

After the engine oil has been changed, display the oil life index on the DIC, then hold the RESET button for 5 seconds. When a DIC message of RESET is displayed and the oil life index equals 100%, the reset is complete.

1998–99

The Driver Information Center (DIC) engine oil life monitor indicates when to change oil, usually between 3000–7500 miles, although the "Change Oil" message might appear before 3000 miles when operating under severe conditions.

To reset the oil life monitor after an oil change, proceed as follows:

1. Turn ignition On.
2. Press TRIP button on DIC to view menu choices, then stop on "Oil Life Remaining."
3. Press and hold RESET button for more than 5 seconds. Monitor has been properly reset when remaining oil life percentage changes to 100%.
4. Turn ignition Off.

EXCEPT ALERO, AURORA, EIGHTY EIGHT, INTRIGUE, LSS, NINETY-EIGHT & TORONADO

When the engine oil life index has reached 10 or less, the Driver Information System display will indicate distance to oil change and sound a beep when ignition is turned to Run or Accessory for the first time each day. When the engine oil life index has reached 0, the Driver Information System display will indicate Change Oil Now and sound a beep when ignition is turned to Run or Accessory for the first time each day. After engine oil change has been performed, the oil life index may be reset by depressing and holding the Oil and Reset buttons for approximately 5 seconds, **Fig. 1.**

TORONADO

1992

Less CRT Driver Information Display

Oil life is displayed by pressing the ENG DATA button on the Driver Information System (DIS) keypad several times. To reset the oil life index, press and hold the RESET/ENTER key for 5 seconds while the oil life is displayed.

With Driver Information Display

Oil life may be displayed by pressing the INFO button and then selecting the OIL LIFE option. Oil life is reset is reset by pressing RESET on the oil life display and then pressing YES on the confirmation screen. This will reset the oil life index and OIL LIFE INDEX 100. The Change Oil message will remain off until the next oil change is needed.

Pontiac

BONNEVILLE

1992-95

After changing engine oil and filter, if required, reset service interval indicator by depressing and releasing the service reminder button until the desired item is displayed. When the desired item is displayed, do not release service reminder button. After button has been depressed for approximately 10 seconds, the service interval mileage display will begin to count down in 500 mile intervals. When desired service interval mileage is reached, release button. The service interval reminder indicates miles to service, not miles from last service.

1996-97

After the engine oil has been changed, display the oil life index on the DIC, then hold the RESET button for 5 seconds. When a DIC message of RESET is displayed and the oil life index equals 99% or 100%, the reset is complete.

1998

1. Turn ignition switch to RUN position.
2. Press TRIP button on driver information center (DIC) switch to view menu choices.
3. Select OIL LIFE REMAINING.
4. Press and hold RESET button on DIC for more than 5 seconds until oil life changes to 100%.
5. Turn ignition switch to OFF position.

1999

1. Turn ignition switch to RUN position.
2. Press and hold reset button in glove compartment for at least 5 seconds but not more than 60 seconds.
3. After 5 seconds, observe the CHANGE OIL SOON light flash four times before light turns OFF.
4. Engine oil life monitor has been reset.

2000-04

1. Turn ignition switch to On position.
2. Press MODE button on driver information center (DIC) until VIEW DATA is visible.
3. Press SELECT button until OIL LIFE % is visible.
4. Press and hold RESET button on DIC until display reads OIL LIFE 100% NORMAL.
5. Engine oil life monitor is now reset.

FIREBIRD

1. Turn ignition to Run, engine Off.
2. Press TRIP/OIL RESET button on instrument panel for 12 seconds. OIL CHANGE lamp will start to flash to confirm system is reset. When reset is complete lamp will go out.
3. Turn ignition Off.

GRAND AM

The Engine Oil Life monitor indicates when an oil and filter change are needed. Usually 3000–7500 miles for 1999–2000 models, from 3000–12,500 miles for 2001 models, since the last change. The indicator may light even before 3000 miles if the vehicle has been operated under severe service.

The monitor will not detect dust in the oil. If operating in dusty conditions, change the oil and filter every 3000 miles, or less, if the CHANGE OIL SOON lamp lights.

To reset the Engine Oil Life monitor proceed as follows:

1. Turn ignition On, but do not start engine.
2. Press and release RESET button. CHANGE OIL indicator will begin flashing.
3. Press and release RESET button again.

GRAND PRIX

1992-96

Ensure oil life indicator is displayed by pressing Driver Information System SYSTEMS CHECK button. Press and hold the RESET button until oil life display is returned to 100%.

1997-99

Change Oil Soon Indicator

1. Turn ignition On, but do not start engine.
2. Fully depress and release accelerator three times within 5 seconds.
3. If "Change Oil Soon" lamp flashes this means system is resetting.
4. Turn ignition Off, then start engine.
5. If "Change Oil Soon" lamp lights, repeat procedure.

Oil Life Monitor

Press trip calculator MODE button until light appears next to "Oil Life," then press and hold RESET button until oil life percentage reaches 100%.

2000-04

To reset the Engine Oil Life monitor proceed as follows:

1. **On models equipped with DIC,** proceed as follows:
   a. Turn ignition On, but do not start engine.
   b. Fully depress and release accelerator pedal three times within five seconds. Oil life indicator will begin to flash indicating system is resetting.
   c. Place ignition switch in Off position and start engine.
   d. Engine oil change light should illuminate as bulb check and then go Off.
   e. If oil change light remains On, repeat reset procedure.
2. **On models equipped with trip computer,** proceed as follows:
   a. Depress Mode button until light appears next to Oil Life.
   b. Depress Trip Reset button until oil life percentage reads 99%.

Saturn

ION

1. Turn ignition key to RUN position.
2. Press trip odometer reset stem once or twice until "OIL LIFE" message is flashing on message center.
3. Press and hold instrument panel trip odometer button for few seconds until chime sounds five times.
4. When reset is complete "OIL LIFE" message will stay on without flashing.
5. Turn ignition switch off.
6. Turn ignition switch ON, if "OIL LIFE" lamp comes on and stays on for 30 seconds, lamp did not reset. Repeat procedure.

L SERIES

1. Turn ignition switch to RUN position.
2. Remove underhood fuse block cover, press red OIL RESET button and hold for five seconds.
3. Turn ignition switch off.
4. Turn ignition switch to RUN position and ensure "SERVICE OIL SOON" lamp turns off after 30 seconds.
5. If lamp does not turn off, repeat procedure.

S SERIES

The PCM has the ability to calculate when the engine oil needs to be changed based on vehicle mileage, engine revolutions and engine coolant temperature. The PCM bases the engine oil change interval within a window of 3000–6000 miles regardless of engine revolutions and engine coolant temperature. To reset the PCM oil life monitor, proceed as follows:

1. Remove cover from underhood fuse relay center.
2. Place ignition switch in On position.
3. Press red Oil Reset Button and hold for five seconds.
4. If "Change Engine Oil Soon" lamp is flashing, system is reset. Lamp will flash for 30 seconds or until ignition switch is placed in Off position.
5. If lamp comes On and remains On for 30 seconds at next ignition On cycle, lamp did not reset. Reset procedure must be performed again.

CHECK ENGINE OR SERVICE NOW/SOON ENGINE INDICATOR LAMPS

The Check Engine lamp may light if the fuel filler cap has not been completely tightened. This lamp should turn off after the cap has been properly tightened and the vehicle has successfully completed a predetermined number of trip cycles.

Except LeMans, Metro, Prizm & Storm

The Check Engine lamp should light when the ignition is turned On. When the engine is started, the lamp should go off. If the lamp remains On for 10 seconds or constantly after the engine is started, the self diagnosis system has detected a fault condition and has stored a code in the system Electronic Control Module (ECM) or Powertrain Control Module (PCM). After diagnosis and repair, the ECM memory can be cleared of codes as follows:

1. **On models except Cadillac with DEFI,** proceed as follows:
   a. Remove ECM/PCM fuse or disconnect battery ground cable for approximately 30 seconds, with ignition turned Off.
   b. If battery ground cable is disconnected to clear codes, components such as clocks, electronically tuned radios etc., will have to be reset.
2. **On Cadillac models equipped with DEFI,** the ECM/PCM power feed is connected by a pigtail, inline fuse holder, at the positive battery terminal. To clear codes within ECM/PCM system and protect components that need resetting, disconnect inline fuse.
3. **On Eldorado and Seville models,** stored codes are cleared during self-diagnostic procedure.

LeMans

The Check Engine lamp should light when the ignition is turned On. When the engine is started, them should go off. If the lamp remains On for 10 seconds or constantly after the engine is started, the self diagnosis system has detected a fault condition and has stored a code in the system Electronic Control Module (ECM). After diagnosis and repair, the ECM memory can be cleared of codes, by disconnecting battery ground cable for 10 seconds, with ignition turned Off.

Metro

The Check Engine lamp should light when the ignition is turned On with engine not operating. When engine is started, the Check Engine lamp should go off. If lamp remains on, a code has been stored by the Electronic Control Module (ECM) memory. After diagnosis and repair, turn ignition Off and clear codes stored in the ECM memory by disconnecting the battery ground cable, for approximately 20 seconds.

The Check Engine lamp may light if the fuel filler cap has not been completely tightened. This lamp should turn off after the cap has been properly tightened and the vehicle has successfully completed a predetermined number of trip cycles.

Prizm

The Check Engine lamp should light when the ignition is in ON position with engine not operating. When engine is started, the Check Engine lamp should go off. If lamp remains on, a code has been stored by the Electronic Control Unit (ECU) memory. After diagnosis and repair, turn ignition Off and clear codes stored in the ECU memory by removing the Stop Fuse. The Stop fuse is located in a fuse panel, in the passenger compartment, on driver's side, behind kick panel. The fuse must be removed for 10 seconds or longer, depending on ambient temperature. The lower the ambient temperature, the longer the fuse will have to be removed.

Storm

The Check Engine lamp should light when the ignition is in the On position with engine not operating. When engine is started, the Check Engine lamp should go off. If lamp remains on, a code has been stored by the Electronic Control Module (ECM) memory. After diagnosis and repair, turn ignition Off, then clear codes stored in the ECM memory by disconnecting the battery ground cable for approximately 30 seconds.

CHECK GAUGE WARNING LAMP

The Check Gauge warning lamp will light to warn the driver to inspect the oil pressure gauge, engine coolant temperature gauge and the voltmeter. When lit, the "Check Gauge" lamp indicates that one of these gauges is operating in an abnormal range.

CHECK INFO CENTER WARNING LAMP

Eldorado & Seville

1992

This lamp will light for a few seconds when the ignition is turned On as a bulb inspection. If lamp remains lit, a message is stored in the Driver Information Center. Refer to "Driver Information Center."

DRIVER INFORMATION CENTER

Aurora

1995-99

The Driver Information Center Display is located on the instrument panel (Eighty-Eight and Ninety-Eight models with digital cluster or touring sedan gauge cluster). It provides traveling and performance information on the following:

1. Date and Time—This information is displayed for 5 seconds when the ignition is turned On. The DT/TM button may be depressed at any time to display current date and time.
2. Fuel Economy—The ECON button displays average fuel economy.
3. Remaining Fuel/Fuel Used—Depressing FUEL button displays amount of fuel used since reset button was last pressed. Depressing FUEL button a second time displays amount of fuel remaining.
4. Fuel Range—Depress RANGE to display distance that may be driven before refueling. To display amount of fuel used from a specific starting point, depress FUEL then RESET.
5. Average Speed—Depress SPEED to display average speed. To reset average speed, depress SPEED then RESET.
6. Remaining Oil Life and Oil Change Information—The OIL button displays information on oil life. Refer to "Change Oil Or Change Oil Now Message" for reset procedure.
7. Engine Coolant Temperature, Oil Pressure, Battery Voltage and Tachometer—Depressing GAGES once displays coolant temperature. Pressing GAGES a second time displays oil pressure. Pressing GAGES a third time displays battery voltage. Pressing GAGES a fourth time displays tachometer RPM.
8. Distance To Destination—Depress DEST then RESET and enter length of trip. Display will then count backwards to zero distance remaining. When the display reaches zero, "TRIP COMPLETE" is displayed. This message will clear when the TEST button is depressed or the ignition is turned Off.
9. Estimated Time of Arrival—After entering distance to destination, Press ETA button to display time remaining to destination (based on average speed).
10. Elapsed Time—Depressing the E/T button activates a stopwatch that records up to 100 hours.

Bonneville

The Driver Information Center Display is located on the instrument panel. When the ignition is turned On, the display will go through a bulb inspection in which the vehicle graph and message title will be displayed in sequence. After the sequence has been completed, all messages and vehicle graph will remain lit for approximately two seconds. After approximately two seconds, if all monitored systems are functioning properly, the message titles should go off and only the vehicle outline should be lit. If a fault condition in any of the monitored systems is present, the particular title for the monitored system should light and its approximate location on the vehicle graphic display should light. The following messages will be displayed:

1. **Function Monitor**—The coolant level, fuel level and windshield washer levels are monitored when ignition is turned On.
   a. Coolant Level—This message will be indicated when engine coolant level in the radiator drops below a predetermined level. To cancel message, inspect cooling system, then add coolant to bring system to proper level.
   b. Fuel Level—This message will be

indicated when fuel level is 5 gallons or less. To cancel message add fuel to fuel tank.

c. Washer Fluid—This message will be indicated when windshield washer fluid is at about 40% of capacity. To cancel message, add washer fluid to reservoir.

2. **Lamp Check**—The headlamps, tail lamps, brake lamps and turn signal lamps will be inspected whenever the lamp system is activated. To cancel this message, replace bulb or inspect and repair electrical system as required for lamp system indicated.
3. **Security**—Door, Hood Or Trunk Ajar are monitored. This message will appear when the indicated component is open or improperly closed. To cancel message, properly close indicated component.
4. **Service Reminder**—Oil change, oil filter change, engine tune-up and tire rotation intervals are monitored.
   a. After the bulb inspection sequence has been completed, the service interval can be inspected by depressing the service reminder button. Depressing the button once will display the Change Oil indication and mileage remaining to service interval. Depressing the button a second time, will display the Change Oil Filter indication and mileage remaining to service interval. Depressing the button a third time will display the Rotate Tires and mileage to service interval. Depressing the button a fourth time will display Tune-Up indication and mileage to service interval.
   b. After completing the required service, reset service interval indicator by depressing and releasing the service reminder button until the desired item is displayed. When the desired item is displayed, do not release service reminder button. After button has been depressed for approximately 10 seconds, the service interval mileage display will begin to count down in 500 mile intervals. When desired service interval mileage is reached, release button. The service interval reminder indicates miles to service, not miles from last service.

Eldorado & Seville

1992

This system incorporates a warning lamp, located on the instrument cluster, that is lit when the ignition is in the On position. After a few seconds the lamp should go off, unless a message in The Driver Information System is present. The driver information center will display the following messages:

A/C Overheated—A/C Compressor Off—This message is displayed when excessive pressure in the refrigerant system is encountered. When this condition is encountered, the A/C Compressor clutch will be de-energized and cool air will not be delivered to the vehicle interior. The message will continue to appear and the A/C compressor clutch will continue to be de-energized until the system pressure returns to normal range. If this message frequently appears, the A/C system should be serviced.

A/C Sensor Fault—This message will be displayed when the sensor controlling A/C compressor clutch cycling has failed. When this sensor has failed, the A/C compressor will not operate and the A/C system will emit warmer air. After servicing system and replacing sensor, the display message will be cancelled.

Battery Volts High—This message will appear when the charging system is overcharging the battery. After completing charging system diagnosis and repair, the message will be cancelled when battery voltage returns to 11.5–15.5 volts with engine operating. Battery voltage can be displayed on the Drive Information Center Display by depressing the Eng-Data button three times.

Battery Volts Low—If this message is displayed while driving the vehicle or after vehicle has been started, a fault condition in the charging system is present or battery has been drained. After diagnosing charging system or electrical system for cause of battery drain, the message will be cancelled when engine is operating and battery voltage is between 11.5–15.5 volts. Battery voltage can be displayed on the Drive Information Center Display by depressing the Eng-Data button three times.

Change Engine Oil—When the engine oil life index has reached 0, the Change Engine Oil message will be indicated. After performing the engine oil change, the engine Oil Life Index may be reset by depressing and holding the Engine Data and Range buttons for at least 5 seconds

Cooling Fan Fault—This message will appear when the engine cooling fan system inoperative. After repairing cooling fan system the message will be automatically cancelled.

Engine Hot—A/C Compressor Off—This message will appear when A/C system is Auto or Defrost and engine coolant temperature is excessive. The A/C compressor clutch will be automatically de-energized when excessive engine coolant temperatures are encountered. When engine coolant temperature returns to normal, the A/C compressor clutch will be energized and the message on the display will be cancelled.

Front Or Rear Door Ajar—This message will appear when the transmission selector lever is moved out of the Park position and a door is not properly closed. The message can be cancelled by properly closing the indicated door.

Fuel Level Very Low—When low fuel level conditions are encountered this message will appear. To cancel message, add fuel.

Gear Select Problem—This message will appear if a fault condition in the transaxle gear select system is encountered while operating vehicle. After performing required service, the message will automatically be cancelled.

Headlamps Or Parking Lamps On—This message will be displayed when the headlamp switch is On, vehicle is moving and the sensed level of outside light indicates that headlamps should not be lit. This message may be cancelled by turning the headlamp switch Off.

Headlamps Suggested—This message will be displayed when the Twilight Sentinel is in the Off position, vehicle is moving and the sensed level of outside light indicates that headlamps should be lit. This message may be cancelled by activating the Twilight Sentinel System.

Low A/C Refrigerant—A/C Compressor Off—This message will be displayed when the A/C system detects a refrigerant charge low enough to cause compressor damage. When this condition is encountered, the A/C compressor clutch is de-energized and the A/C system is switched from AUTO to ECON. The system will remain in ECON until required repairs are made and system is recharged. After completing required repairs and recharging the system, A/C system operation will return to normal and the message on the display will be cancelled.

Low A/C Refrigerant—Service A/C Soon—This message will be displayed when the A/C system detects that refrigerant charge is low enough to cause a reduction in cooling capacity. This message will be displayed until system has been recharged.

Low Washer Fluid—This message will appear when windshield washer fluid level is low. To cancel message, refill windshield washer fluid reservoir.

Oil Life Index—The oil life index is a series of numerals ranging from 0–100. The 100 is indicated when engine oil has been drained and replacement engine oil has been installed. The 0 is an indication that the engine oil should be changed. The oil life index is accessed by depressing the Engine Data button four times.

Service Electrical System—This message will appear when a fault condition in the charging system is present. After repairing charging system, the message will be automatically cancelled.

Set Timing Mode—This message will appear if ignition timing is improperly set. After performing required service, the message will be automatically cancelled.

Starting Disabled/Due to Theft System/Remove Ignition Key—This message is an indication of a fault condition in the vehicle security system that may prohibit the vehicle from being restarted after the ignition has been turned Off. After servicing the vehicle security system the message will be automatically cancelled.

System Satisfactory—This message will be displayed for approximately 5 seconds after ignition has been turned On, unless a fault condition in the system has been detected. After approximately 5 seconds the display will return to the last display function selected.

System Problem—Service Car Soon—This message will be displayed when one or more of the vehicle computers supplying information to the Driver Information Center become faulty. After diagnosis

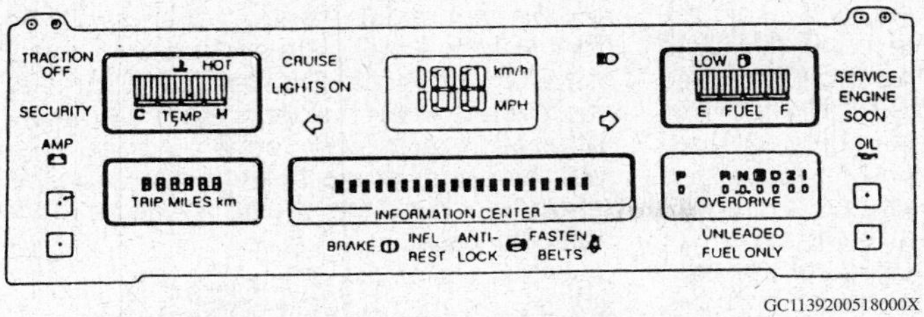

Fig. 2 Driver information center. 1992–93 Eighty-Eight & Ninety-Eight

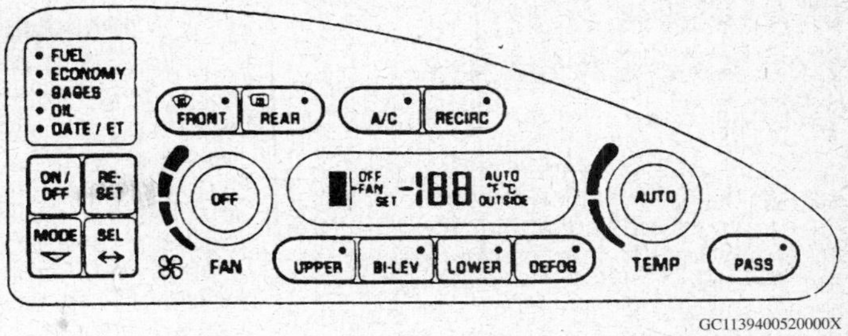

Fig. 3 Driver information center. LSS, 1994–96 Eighty Eight & Ninety Eight

and repair of the faulty computer, the message will be automatically cancelled.

Theft System Problem/Car May Not Start—This message will appear when the vehicle security system senses an improper ignition key has been placed in the ignition. After removing key from ignition, the Driver Information Center display will indicate "Wait 3 Minutes," "Wait 2 Minutes," Wait 1 Minute and then "Start Car." When the "Start Car" message appears, insert ignition key and attempt to start vehicle. If message appears again, inspect ignition key for damage and replace as required. If key appears to be satisfactory, clean pellet contacts with a soft cloth and attempt to restart vehicle.

Trunk Open—This message will appear when the ignition is the Run position and the trunk is not properly closed. The message can be cancelled by properly closing the trunk.

Eighty-Eight, LSS & Ninety-Eight

1992-93

The Driver Information Center Display, **Fig. 2,** is located on the instrument panel (Eighty-Eight and Ninety-Eight models with digital cluster or touring sedan gauge cluster). It provides traveling and performance information on the following:

1. Date and Time—This information is displayed for 5 seconds when the ignition is turned On. The DT/TM button may be depressed at any time to display current date and time.
2. Fuel Economy—The ECON button displays average fuel economy.
3. Remaining Fuel/Fuel Used—Depressing FUEL button displays amount of fuel used since reset button was last pressed. Depressing FUEL button a second time displays amount of fuel remaining.
4. Fuel Range—Depress RANGE to display distance that may be driven before refueling. To display amount of fuel used from a specific starting point, depress FUEL then RESET.
5. Average Speed—Depress SPEED to display average speed. To reset average speed, depress SPEED then RESET.
6. Remaining Oil Life and Oil Change Information—The OIL button displays information on oil life. Refer to "Change Oil Or Change Oil Now Message" for reset procedure.
7. Engine Coolant Temperature, Oil Pressure, Battery Voltage and Tachometer—Depressing GAGES once displays coolant temperature. Pressing GAGES a second time displays oil pressure. Pressing GAGES a third time displays battery voltage. Pressing GAGES a fourth time displays tachometer RPM.
8. Distance To Destination—Depress DEST then RESET and enter length of trip. Display will then count backwards to zero distance remaining. When the display reaches zero, "TRIP COMPLETE" is displayed. This message will clear when the TEST button is depressed or the ignition is turned Off.
9. Estimated Time of Arrival—After entering distance to destination, Press ETA button to display time remaining to destination (based on average speed).
10. Elapsed Time—Depressing the E/T button activates a stopwatch that records up to 100 hours.

1994-96

The Driver Information Center Display, **Fig. 3,** is located on the instrument panel. When the ignition is turned On, the display will go through a system inspection while the message "Monitored Systems OK" is displayed. If no fault conditions are detected, the screen returns to the mode displayed before the ignition was turned Off.

There are four buttons that control the functions of the driver information center:

1. The MODE button, when pressed, cycles through a series of displays in the following order:
   a. ECON—Average fuel economy and instantaneous fuel economy.
   b. FUEL—Amount of fuel used since last fuel-used reset, and fuel remaining.
   c. RANGE—Fuel range and low fuel range.
   d. OIL—Oil life index and next required oil change.
   e. GAGES—Oil pressure, tachometer and battery voltage information.
   f. ET—Elapsed time since last reset.
   g. DT/TM—Date and time.
2. The ON/OFF button is used to input numbers and to blank out the display.
3. The RESET button is used with other buttons to reset the system. Depressing this button once enters the reset mode. Pressing this button again aborts the reset.
4. The SEL button is used to select different displays within a specific mode. For example, when the SEL button is depressed while in the GAGES mode, the display will cycle from oil pressure to battery voltage to tachometer.

ENGINE COOLANT TEMPERATURE TELLTALE LAMP

If the engine coolant temperature if more than 244°F, or if the transaxle fluid temperature if more than 284°F, the coolant temperature telltale lamp will light. The PCM will turn the cooling fan on if an ECT DTC is active.

LOW COOLANT LAMP

This lamp should light when engine coolant level in the radiator drops below a predetermined level. To turn lamp off, inspect cooling system and add coolant to bring system to proper level.

LOW OIL DIPSTICK

The Low Oil indicator ground is controlled by the PCM. To inspect for a low oil condition, the PCM inspects the low oil level sensor after the ignition has been turned to the Off or Lock position. The PCM inspects for a low oil condition 32 minutes after the ignition is turned Off if the previous ignition cycle was less than 12 minutes. The PCM inspects for a low oil condition 3 minutes after the ignition is turned off if the previous ignition cycle was less than 12 minutes.

LOW OIL PRESSURE TELLTALE LAMP

The engine oil pressure switch is normally closed and open when engine oil pressure is 1.4–5.8 psi. If the lamp is lit with engine running, inspect wiring for oil pressure switch circuit and the engine lubrication system for proper oil pump output pressure.

LOW WASHER FLUID INDICATOR

The windshield washer solvent tank has a switch that closes when the washer solvent level becomes low, illuminating the "Low Washer Fluid" indicator.

MALFUNCTION INDICATOR LAMP (MIL)

As a bulb and system check, the lamp will light with the ignition On and the engine not running. When the engine is started, the lamp will turn off. If the lamp remains On, the self diagnostic system has detected a fault. If the fault is intermittent or the system is repaired, the lamp will go Off after three trips but a diagnostic trouble code (DTC) will be stored in the PCM. Use a suitably programmed scan tool to retrieve and erase any DTCs using the "Clear DTC Information" option. If the lamp remains lit while the engine is running or when a fault is suspected because of a driveability problem, perform an OBD system inspection. Scan the serial data stream using a suitably programmed scan tool.

PASSLOCK TELLTALE LAMP

The instrument panel cluster contains the security telltale lamp. The security telltale has three modes of operation: Off, Flashing & On. The security telltale will be off if ignition is in the Off position or if the ignition is in the Run, Start or ACC position and the security system diagnostics have all passed. The security telltale will be on if the body control module (BCM) is performing a bulb test at vehicle start up, the security system diagnostics have not yet completed at vehicle start up or if a security system diagnostic trouble code (DTC) is set in the BCM or PCM. The security telltale will be flashing if the tamper hall effect has been triggered, there was improper Passlock sensor data to the BCM for more than five seconds during vehicle start, there was no Passlock sensor data to the BCM for more than five seconds during vehicle start or there was improper password from the BCM to the PCM after five seconds during vehicle start. Repair or replace components. Retrieve and clear any associated DTCs to reset the telltale lamp.

SERVICE AIR COND LAMP

This lamp should light when the air conditioning system detects a low refrigerant charge. The lamp should light for approximately two seconds after ignition has been turned On as a bulb inspection.

If while operating vehicle, the lamp lights for approximately 60 seconds and then goes off, the refrigerant level is low enough to cause reduced cooling capacity. At this point the blower motor will increase speed to try to offset the loss in cooling capacity. The lamp will be automatically reset after system has been inspected and refrigerant charge has been brought to proper level.

If lamp is lit for approximately 60 seconds after engine start up, the refrigerant charge may be low enough to cause air conditioning compressor damage. When this condition is encountered, the air conditioning compressor clutch is de-energized and the air conditioning system is switched from Auto to Econ. The system will remain in ECON until required repairs are made and system is recharged. After completing required repairs and recharging the system, air conditioning system operation will return to normal and the lamp will be automatically reset.

SERVICE ELECTRICAL SYSTEM LAMP

This lamp should light when a fault condition in the charging system is present. The lamp should light during engine starting as a bulb inspection. If lamp is lit while engine is operating, the charging system should be inspected. After repairing charging system, the lamp will be automatically reset.

SERVICE TELLTALE LAMP

The service telltale lamp is used for non-emissions related failures which without being serviced could lead to component damage to other sub systems. As a bulb check, the lamp will light for 2–3 seconds and then turn off. If the lamp remains lit, the system has detected a fault condition. If the condition is intermittent or the system is repaired, the lamp will turn off 3 seconds after the PCM diagnostic test passes. Any DTCs will be stored in the freeze frame/failure records. Use a suitably programmed scan tool to retrieve and erase any DTCs using the "Clear DTC Information" option.

VEHICLE LIFT POINTS

TABLE OF CONTENTS

DaimlerChrysler

INDEX

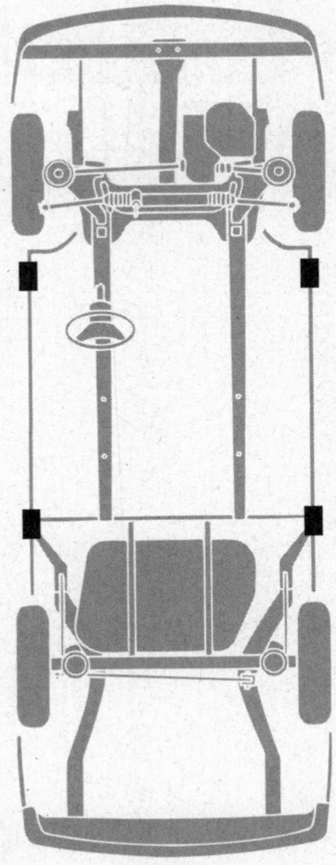

CH-8

ALCR00008

Fig. 1 Vehicle Lift Points. Avenger & Sebring Coupe

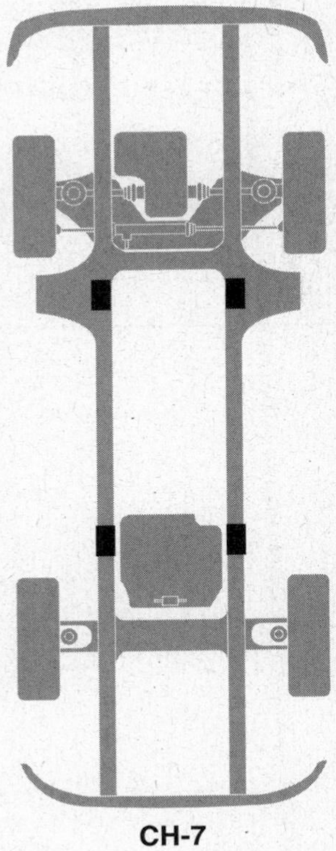

CH-7

ALCR00007

Fig. 2 Vehicle Lift Points. Breeze, Cirrus, Sebring Sedan, Sebring Convertible & Stratus Sedan

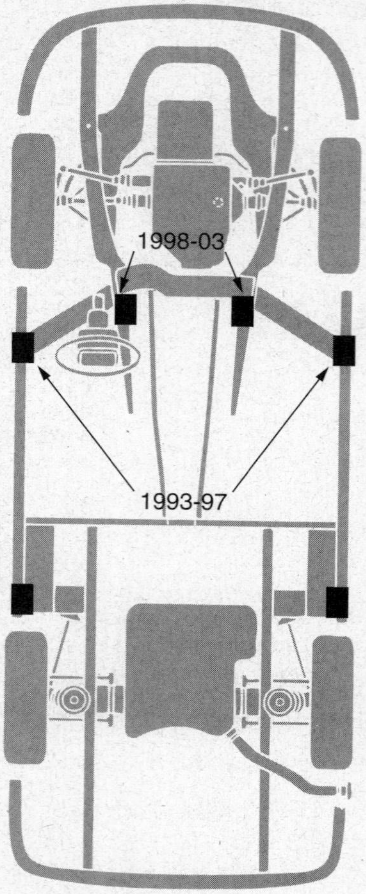

Fig. 3 Vehicle Lift Points. Concode, Intrepid, LHS, & 300M

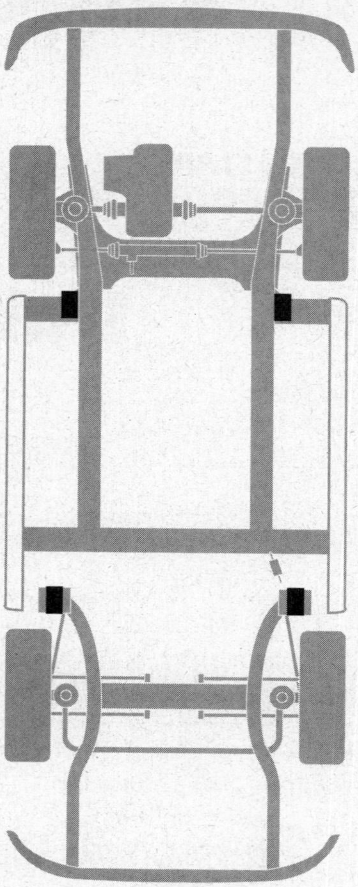

Fig. 4 Vehicle Lift Points. Neon

Ford Motor Co.

INDEX

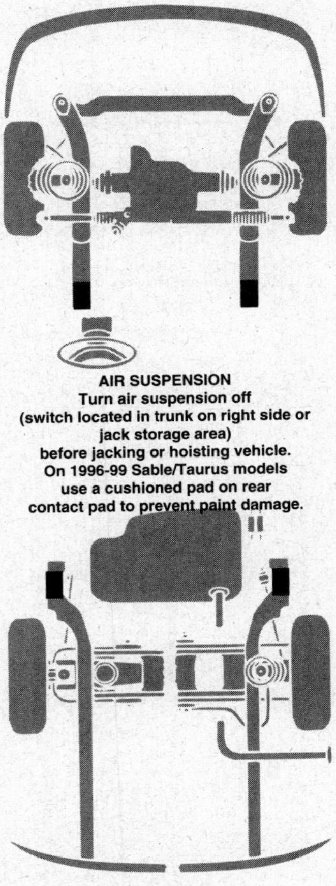
AIR SUSPENSION
Turn air suspension off
(switch located in trunk on right side or
jack storage area)
before jacking or hoisting vehicle.
On 1996-99 Sable/Taurus models
use a cushioned pad on rear
contact pad to prevent paint damage.
FO-7
ALFD00007

Fig. 1 Vehicle Lift Points. Contrinental, Sable & Taurus

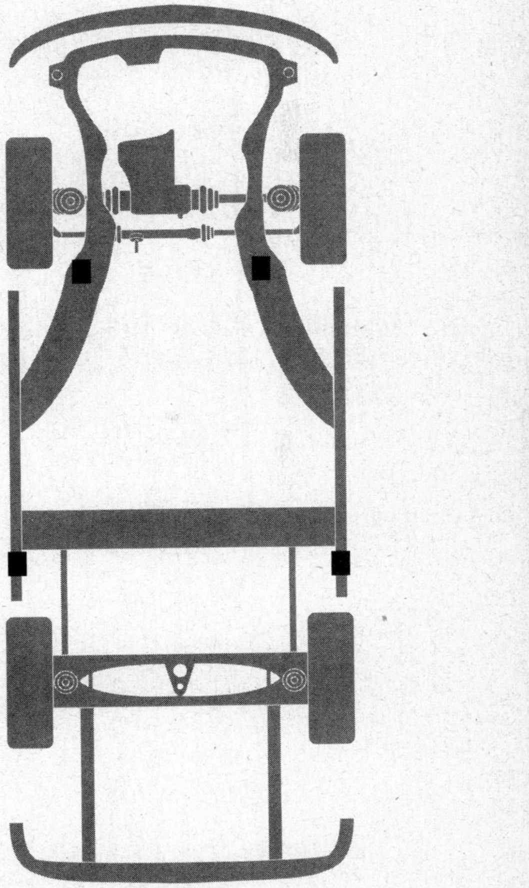
FO-10
ALFD00010

Fig. 2 Vehicle Lift Points. Contour, Cougar & Mystique

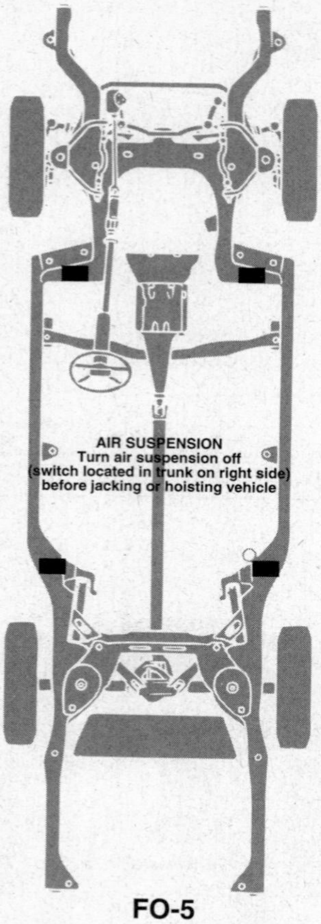
AIR SUSPENSION
Turn air suspension off
(switch located in trunk on right side)
before jacking or hoisting vehicle
FO-5

ALFD00005

Fig. 3 Vehicle Lift Points. Crown Victoria, Grand Marquis, Marauder & Town Car

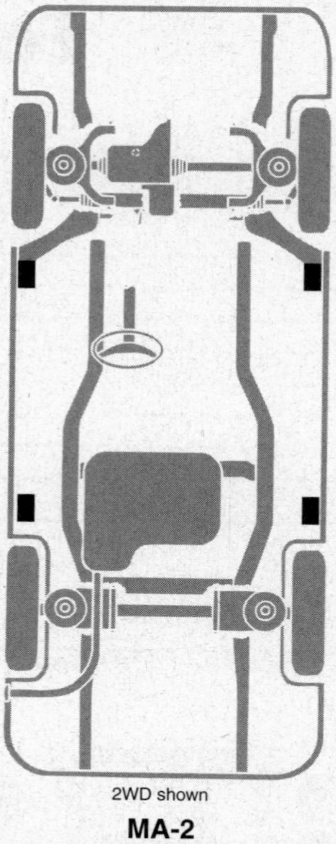
2WD shown
MA-2

ALMA00002

Fig. 4 Vehicle Lift Points. Escort, Focus & ZX2

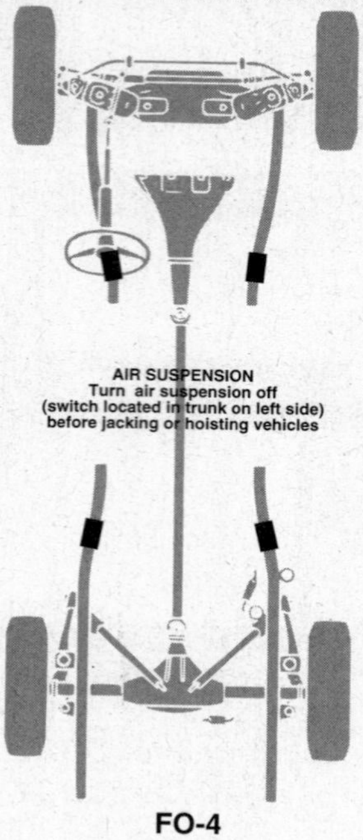
AIR SUSPENSION
Turn air suspension off
(switch located in trunk on left side)
before jacking or hoisting vehicles
FO-4

ALFD00004

Fig. 5 Vehicle Lift Points. Mustang

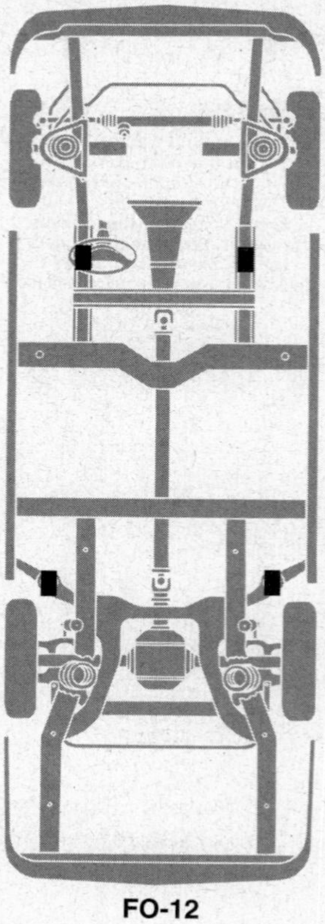
FO-12

ALFD00012

Fig. 6 Vehicle Lift Points. LS & Thunderbird

General Motors Corp.

INDEX

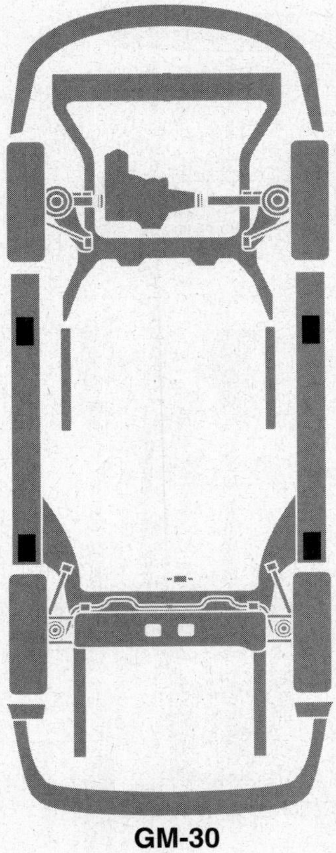

Fig. 1 Vehicle Lift Points. Alero, Grand Am & Malibu

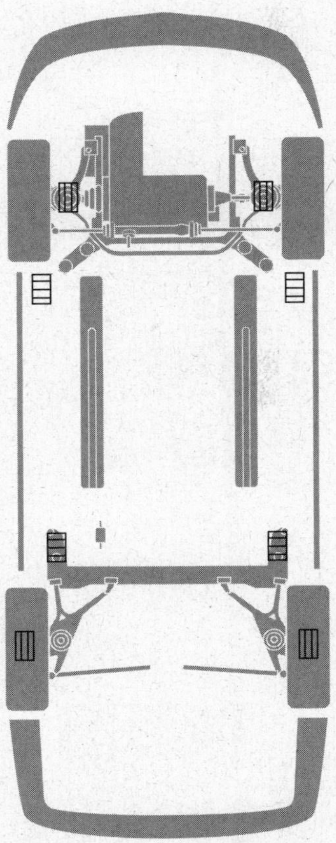

Fig. 2 Vehicle Lift Points. Aurora, Bonneville, DeVille & Seville

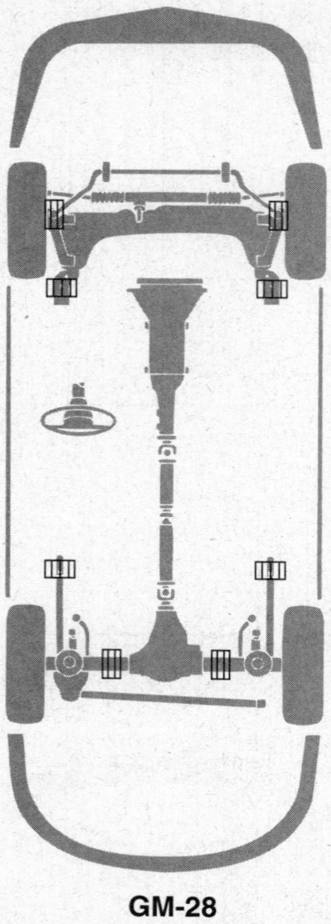

ALGM00028

Fig. 3 Vehicle Lift Points. Camaro & Firebird

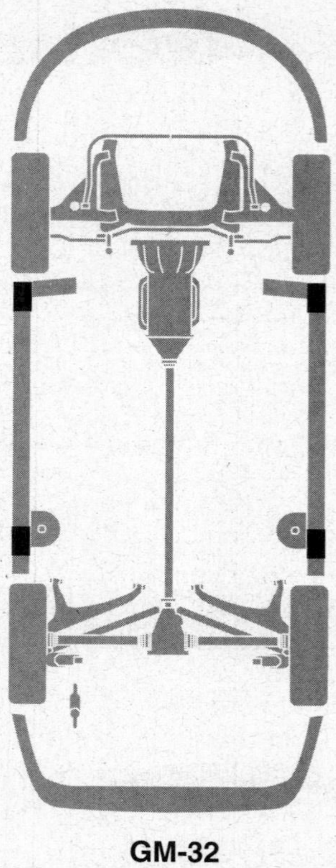

ALGM00032

Fig. 4 Vehicle Lift Points. Catera

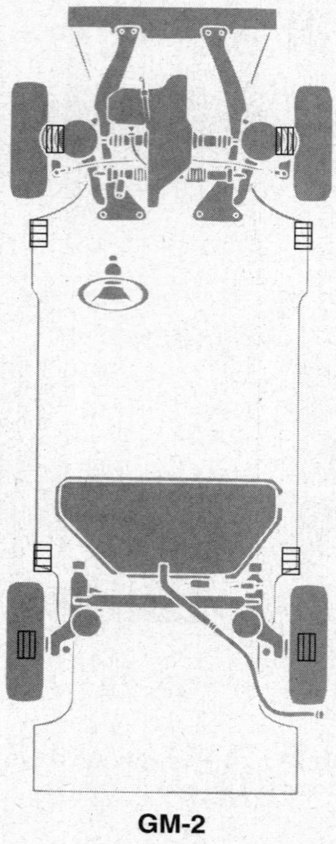

ALGM00002

Fig. 5 Vehicle Lift Points. Cavalier & Sunfire

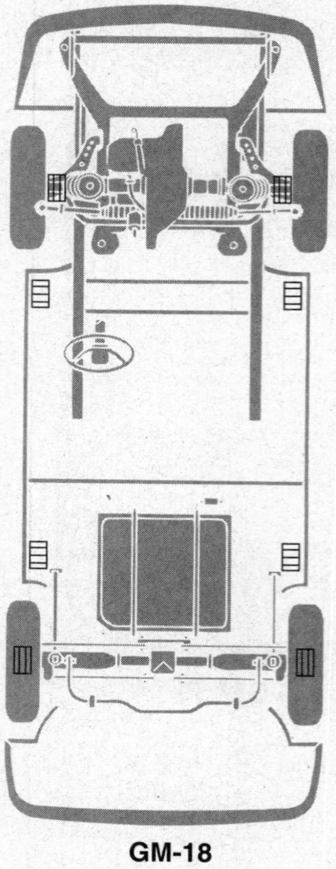

ALGM00018

Fig. 6 Vehicle Lift Points. Century, Grand Prix, Impala, Intrigue, Lumina, Monte Carlo & Regal

GM-33

Position lift pad as follows:
Front, immediately forward of the front frame rail shipping slot reinforcements.
Rear, install GM tool J 43625 into rear frame rail shipping slots, lock into place.
Then position rear hoist pad under J 43625.

ALGM00033

Fig. 7 Vehicle Lift Points. Corvette

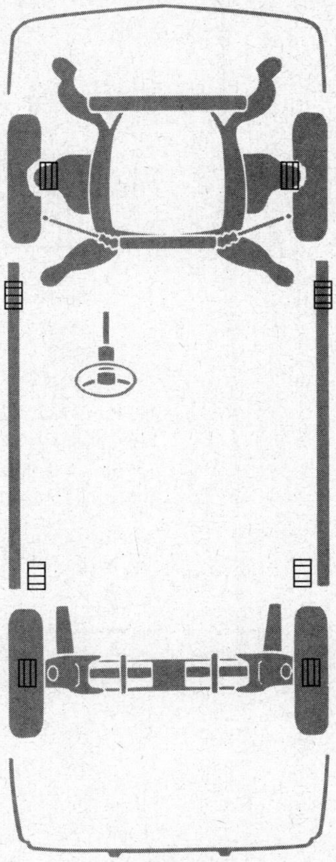

GM-12

ALGM00012

Fig. 8 Vehicle Lift Points. Eldorado

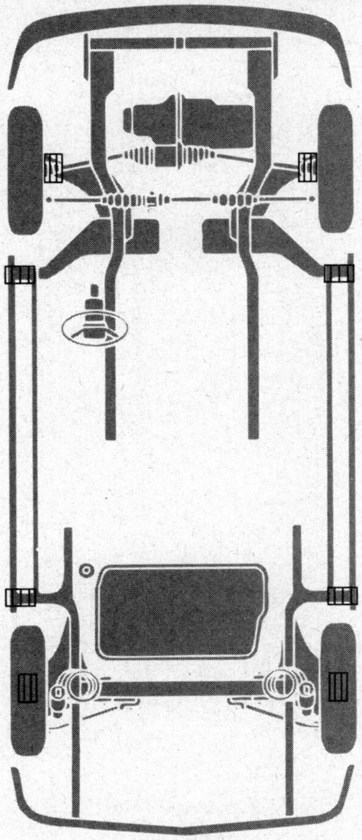

GM-34

ALGM00034

Fig. 9 Vehicle Lift Points. Metro

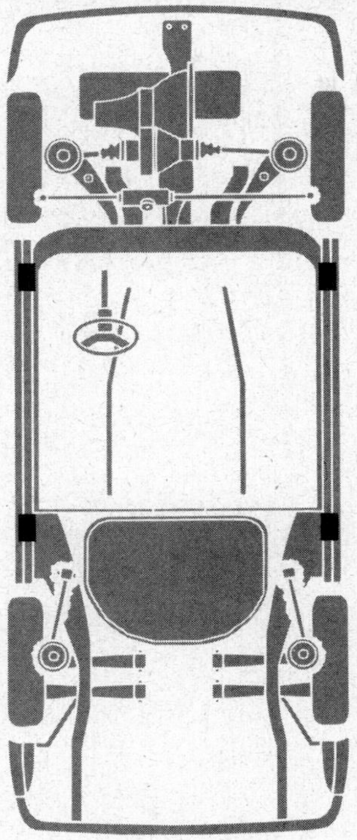

TO-3

ALTA00003

Fig. 10 Vehicle Lift Points. Prizm

VEHICLE LIFT POINTS

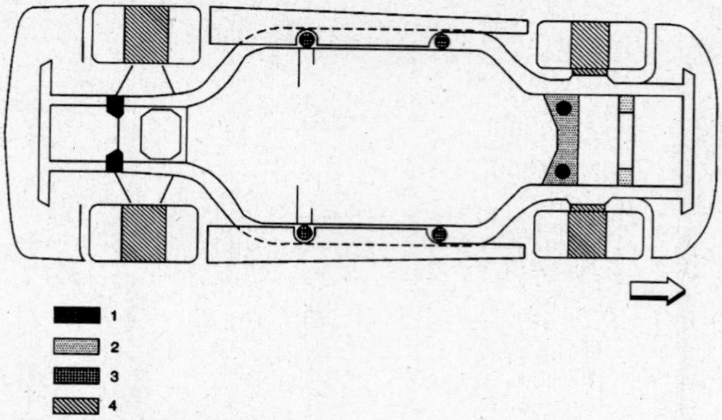

(1) Preferred Vehicle Jacking Locations
(2) Optional Vehicle Jacking Locations
(3) Frame Contact Hoist Locations, Optional Vehicle Jacking Locations
(4) Suspension Contact Hoist Locations

ARM0300000000689

Fig. 11 Vehicle Lift Points. XLR

Saturn

INDEX

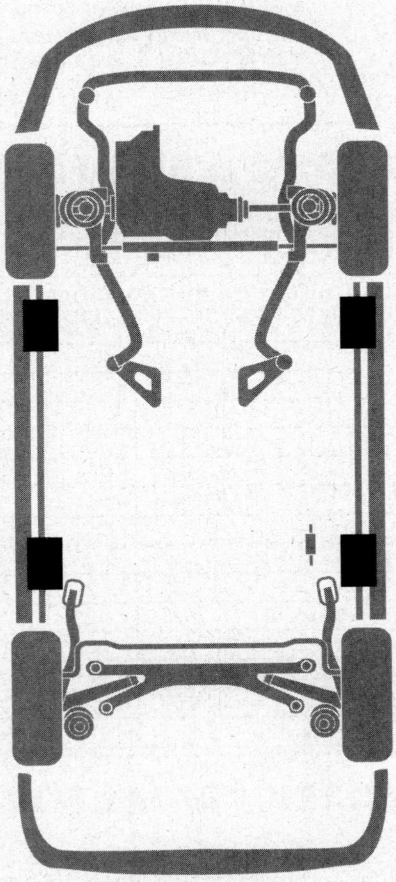

Fig. 1 Vehicle Lift Points. L-Series

Fig. 2 Vehicle Lift Points. S-Series

NON-STANDARD TIRE & WHEEL SIZE ADJUSTMENT TO RIDE HEIGHT SPECIFICATIONS & TIRE SIZE ADJUSTMENT CHARTS

INDEX

SECTION WIDTH ADJUSTMENT FOR METRIC RADIAL & BIAS PLY TIRES

These specifications are approximate and are only intended for use in making approximate ride height inspections and adjustments on models with non-standard tires. These specifications should not be used in place of those recommended by the vehicle manufacturer.

Standard Tire	Optional Tire, Tire Section Width Change Adjustment To Ride Height Specification, Inch													
	P145	P155	P165	P175	P185	P195	P205	P215	P225	P235	P245	P255	P265	P275
P145	0	+.25	+.50											
P155	–.25	0	+.25	+.50										
P165	–.50	–.25	0	+.25	+.50									
P175		–.50	–.25	0	+.25	+.50								
P185			–.50	–.25	0	+.25	+.50							
P195				–.50	–.25	0	+.25	+.50						
P205					–.50	–.25	0	+.25	+.50					
P215						–.50	–.25	0	+.25	+.50				
P225							–.50	–.25	0	+.25	+.50			
P235								–.50	–.25	0	+.25	+.50		
P245									–.50	–.25	0	+.25	+.50	
P255										–.50	–.25	0	+.25	+.50
P265											–.50	–.25	0	+.25
P275												–.50	–.25	0

ASPECT RATIO ADJUSTMENT FOR P145-215 METRIC RADIAL & BIAS PLY TIRES

These specifications are approximate and are only intended for use in making approximate ride height inspections and adjustments on models with non-standard tires. These specifications should not be used in place of those recommended by the vehicle manufacturer.

Standard Tire	Optional Tire, Tire Aspect Ratio Change to Ride Height Specification, Inch				
	60	65	70	75	80
60	0	+.38	+.75	—	—
65	–.38	0	+.38	+.75	—
70	–.75	–.38	0	+.38	+.75
75	—	–.75	–.38	0	+.38
80	—	—	–.75	–.38	0

ASPECT RATIO ADJUSTMENT FOR P225-275 METRIC RADIAL & BIAS PLY TIRES

These specifications are approximate and are only intended for use in making approximate ride height inspections and adjustments on models with non-standard tires. These specifications should not be used in place of those recommended by the vehicle manufacturer.

Standard Tire	Optional Tire, Tire Aspect Ratio Change to Ride Height Specification, Inch				
	60	65	70	75	80
60	0	+.50	+1.00	—	—
65	–.50	0	+.50	+1.00	—
70	–1.00	–.50	0	+.50	+1.00
75	—	–.75	–.50	0	+.50
80	—	—	–1.00	–.50	0

SECTION WIDTH ADJUSTMENT FOR ALPHA-NUMERIC RADIAL PLY TIRES

These specifications are approximate and are only intended for use in making approximate ride height inspections and adjustments on models with non-standard tires. These specifications should not be used in place of those recommended by the vehicle manufacturer.

Standard Tire	Optional Tire, Tire Section Width Change Adjustment To Ride Height Specification, Inch						
	DR	ER	FR	GR	HR	JR	LR
DR	0	+.19	+.44	—	—	—	—
ER	–.19	0	+.25	+.50	—	—	—
FR	–.44	–.25	0	+.25	+.63	—	—
GR	—	–.50	–.25	0	+.31	+.50	—
HR	—	—	–.63	–.31	0	+.19	+.44
JR	—	—	—	–.50	–.19	0	+.25
LR	—	—	—	—	–.44	–.25	0

ASPECT RATIO ADJUSTMENT FOR ALPHA-NUMERIC RADIAL PLY TIRES

These specifications are approximate and are only intended for use in making approximate ride height inspections and adjustments on models with non-standard tires. These specifications should not be used in place of those recommended by the vehicle manufacturer.

Standard Tire	Optional Tire, Change Adjustment to Ride Height Specification, Inch		
	60	70	78
60	0	+.50	+.62
70	–.50	0	+.13
78	–.62	–.13	0

SECTION WIDTH ADJUSTMENT FOR ALPHA-NUMERIC BIAS PLY TIRES

These specifications are approximate and are only intended for use in making approximate ride height inspections and adjustments on models with non-standard tires. These specifications should not be used in place of those recommended by the vehicle manufacturer.

Standard Tire	Optional Tire, Change Adjustment To Ride Height Specifications, Inch							
	A	B	C	D	E	F	G	H
A	0	+.25	+.50	—	—	—	—	—
B	–.25	0	+.25	+.38	—	—	—	—
C	–.50	–.25	0	+.13	+.37	—	—	—
D	—	–.37	–.13	0	+.25	+.50	—	—
E	—	—	–.38	–.25	0	+.25	+.50	—
F	—	—	—	–.50	–.25	0	+.25	+.56
G	—	—	—	—	–.50	–.25	0	+.31
H	—	—	—	—	—	–.56	–.31	0

ELECTRICAL SYMBOL & WIRE COLOR CODE IDENTIFICATION

TABLE OF CONTENTS

Electrical Symbol Identification

INDEX

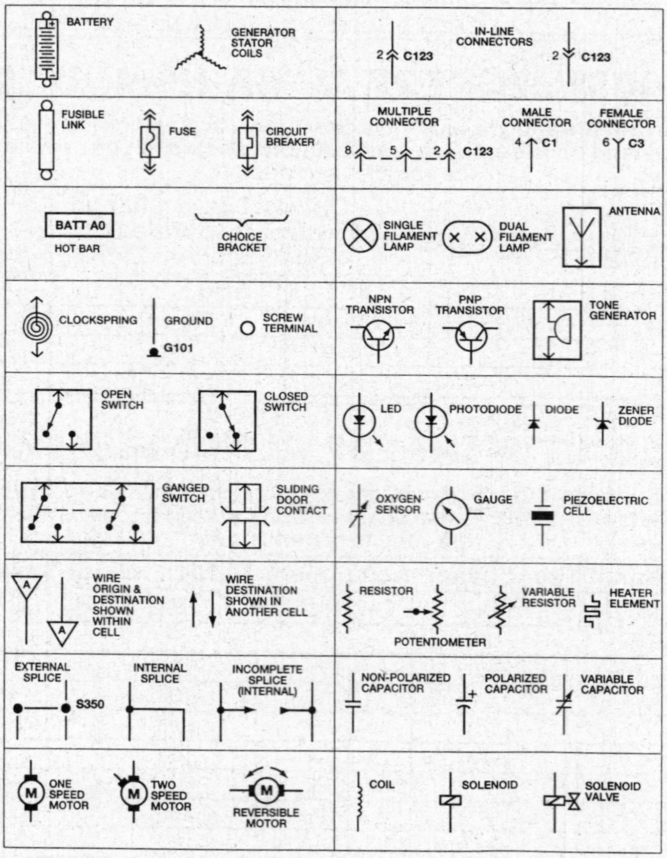

Fig. 1 Symbol Identification. DaimlerChrysler

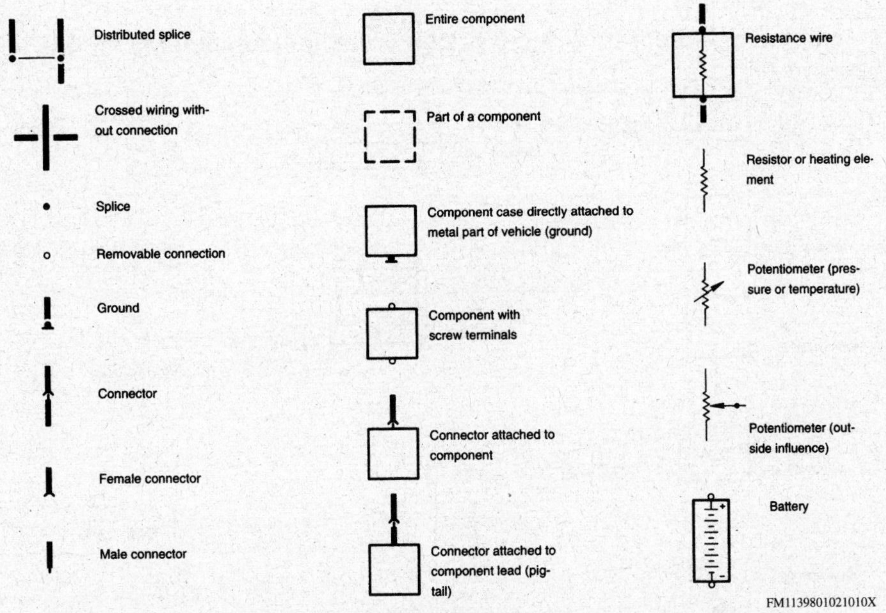

Fig. 2 Symbol Identification (Part 1 of 6). Ford Motor Co. w/New Style Wiring

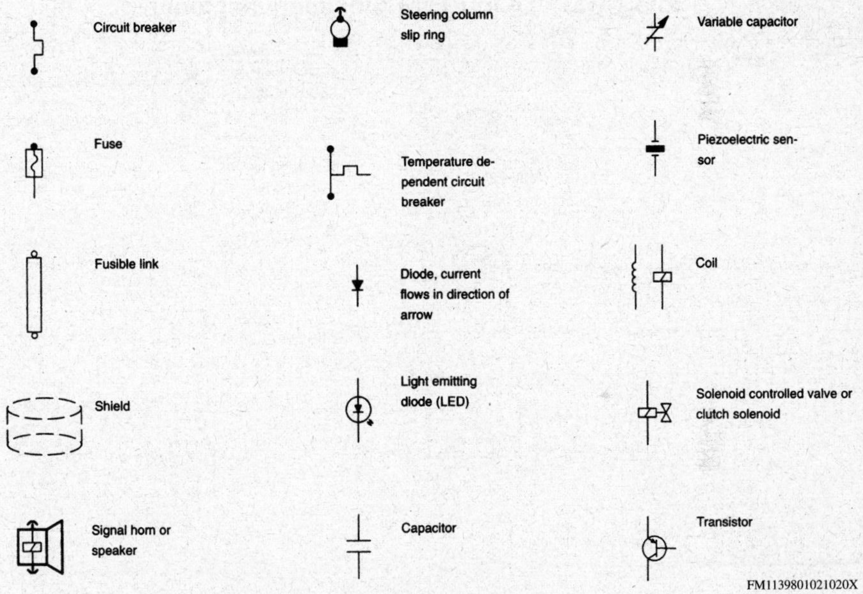

Fig. 2 Symbol Identification (Part 2 of 6). Ford Motor Co. w/New Style Wiring

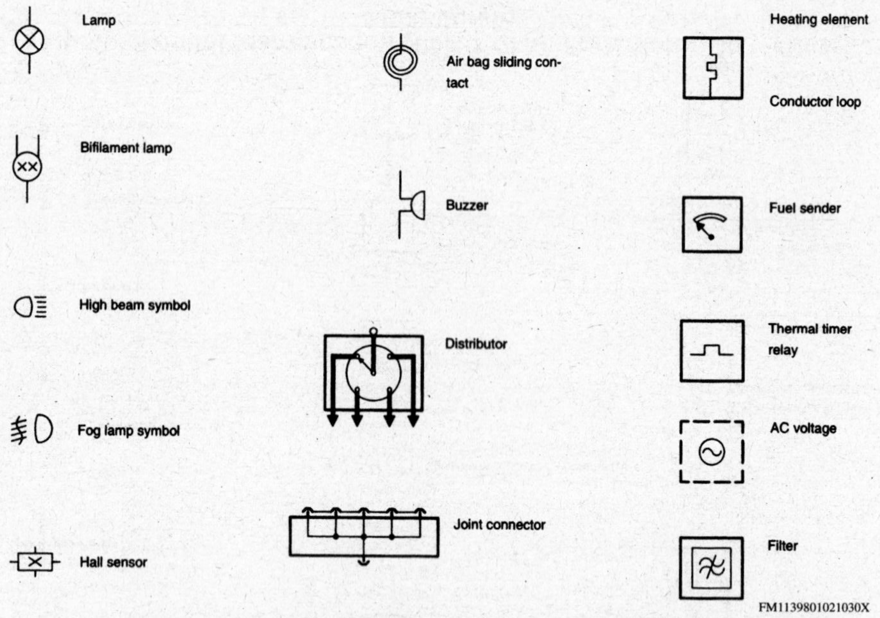

Fig. 2 Symbol Identification (Part 3 of 6). Ford Motor Co. w/New Style Wiring

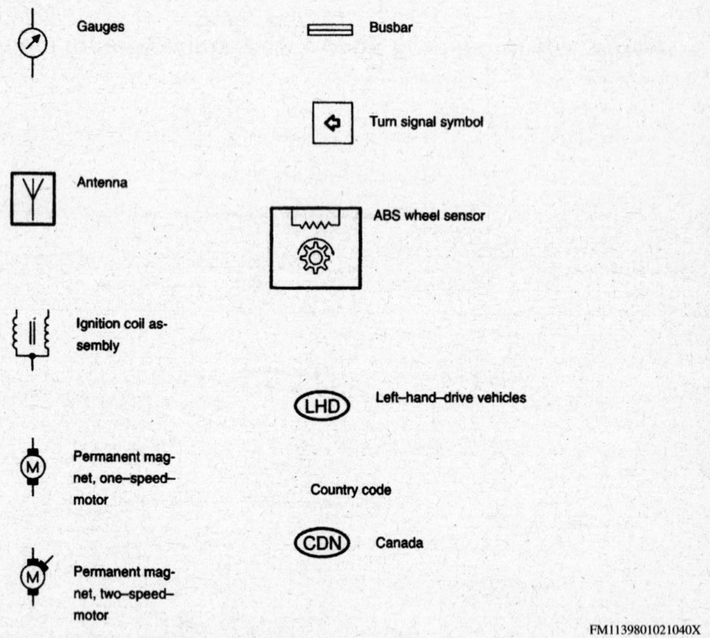

Fig. 2 Symbol Identification (Part 4 of 6). Ford Motor Co. w/New Style Wiring

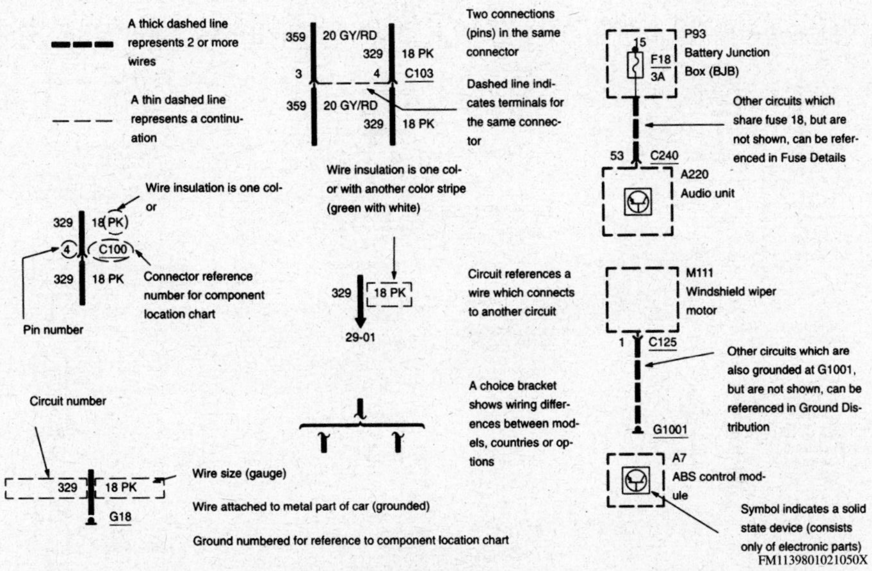

Fig. 2 Symbol Identification (Part 5 of 6). Ford Motor Co. w/New Style Wiring

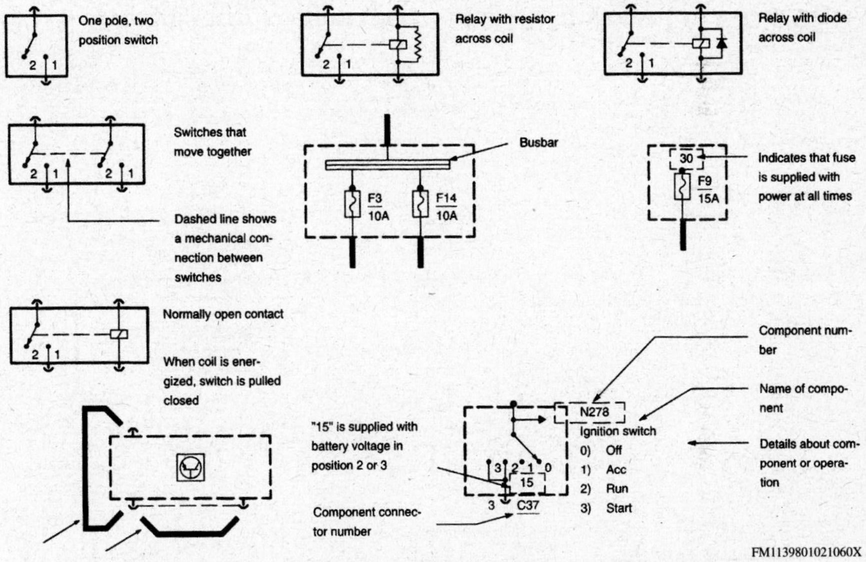

Fig. 2 Symbol Identification (Part 6 of 6). Ford Motor Co. w/New Style Wiring

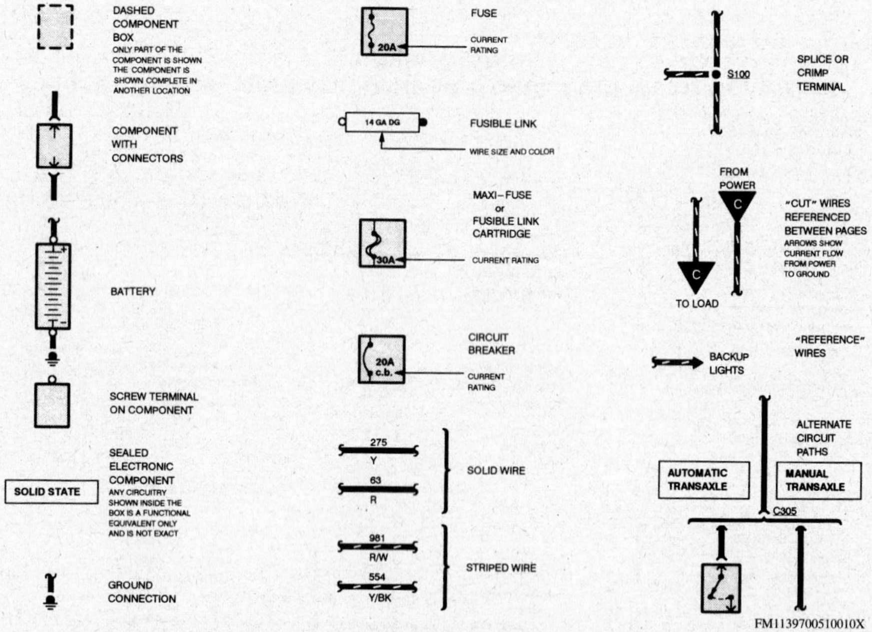

Fig. 3 Symbol Identification (Part 1 of 2). Ford Motor Co. w/Old Style Wiring

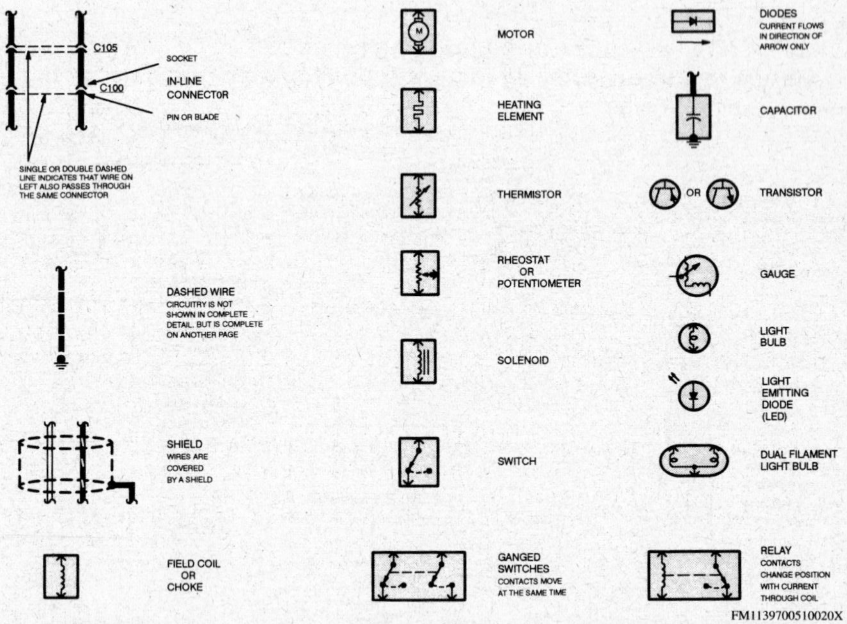

Fig. 3 Symbol Identification (Part 2 of 2). Ford Motor Co. w/Old Style Wiring

Symbol	Description	Symbol	Description
	Supplemental Inflatable Restraint (SIR) or Supplemental Restraint System (SRS) Icon This icon is used to alert the technician that the system contains SIR/SRS components that require certain precautions before servicing.	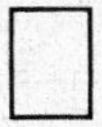	Entire Component When a component is represented in a solid box the component or its wiring is shown in its entirety.
	On-Board Diagnostic (OBD II) Icon This icon is used to alert the technician that the circuit is essential for proper OBD II emission controls circuit operation. Any circuit which, if it fails, causes the malfunction indicator lamp (MIL) to turn on, is identified as an OBD II circuit.	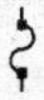	Fuse
	Important Icon This icon is used to alert the technician that there is additional information that will aid in servicing a system.		Circuit Breaker
Hot At All Times Hot In Run Hot In Start Hot In Acc And Run Hot In Run And Start Hot In Run, Bulb Test And Start Hot With Headlamp Switch In Park Or Head Hot In Retained Accessory Power (RAP)	Voltage Indicator Boxes These boxes are used on schematics to indicate when voltage is present at a fuse.		Fusible Link
	Partial Component When a component is represented in a dashed box, the component or its wiring is not shown in its entirety.	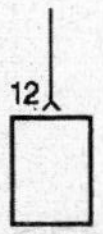	Connector Attached to Component

GC1139801141010X

Fig. 4 Symbol Identification (Part 1 of 4). General Motors

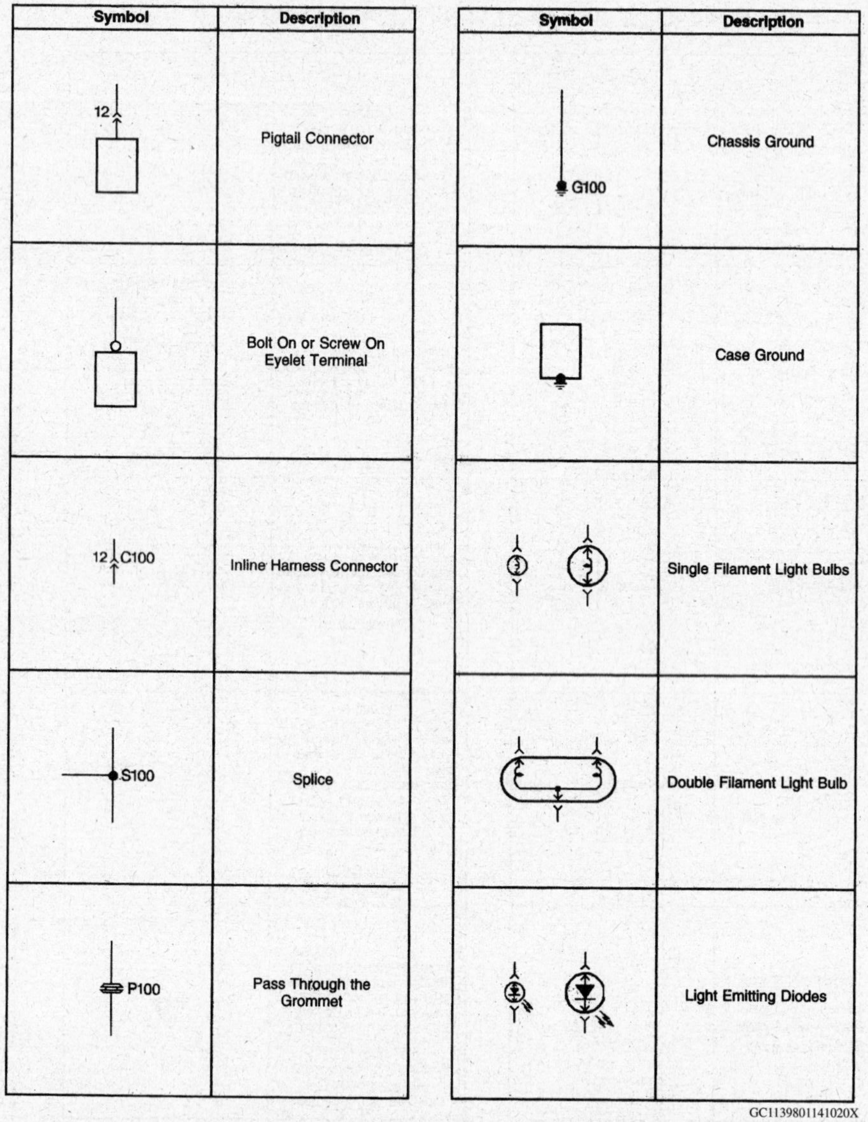
Symbol
Description
12
Pigtail Connector
Bolt On or Screw On
Eyelet Terminal
12
C100
Inline Harness Connector
S100
Splice
P100
Pass Through the
Grommet
Symbol
Description
G100
Chassis Ground
Case Ground
Single Filament Light Bulbs
Double Filament Light Bulb
Light Emitting Diodes
GC11398011141020X

Fig. 4 Symbol Identification (Part 2 of 4). General Motors

Symbol	Description
	Capacitor
	Battery
	Variable Battery
	Resistor
	Variable Resistor

Symbol	Description
	Position Sensor
	I/O Resistors
	I/O Switches
	Diode
	Crystal

GC1139801141030X

Fig. 4 Symbol Identification (Part 3 of 4). General Motors

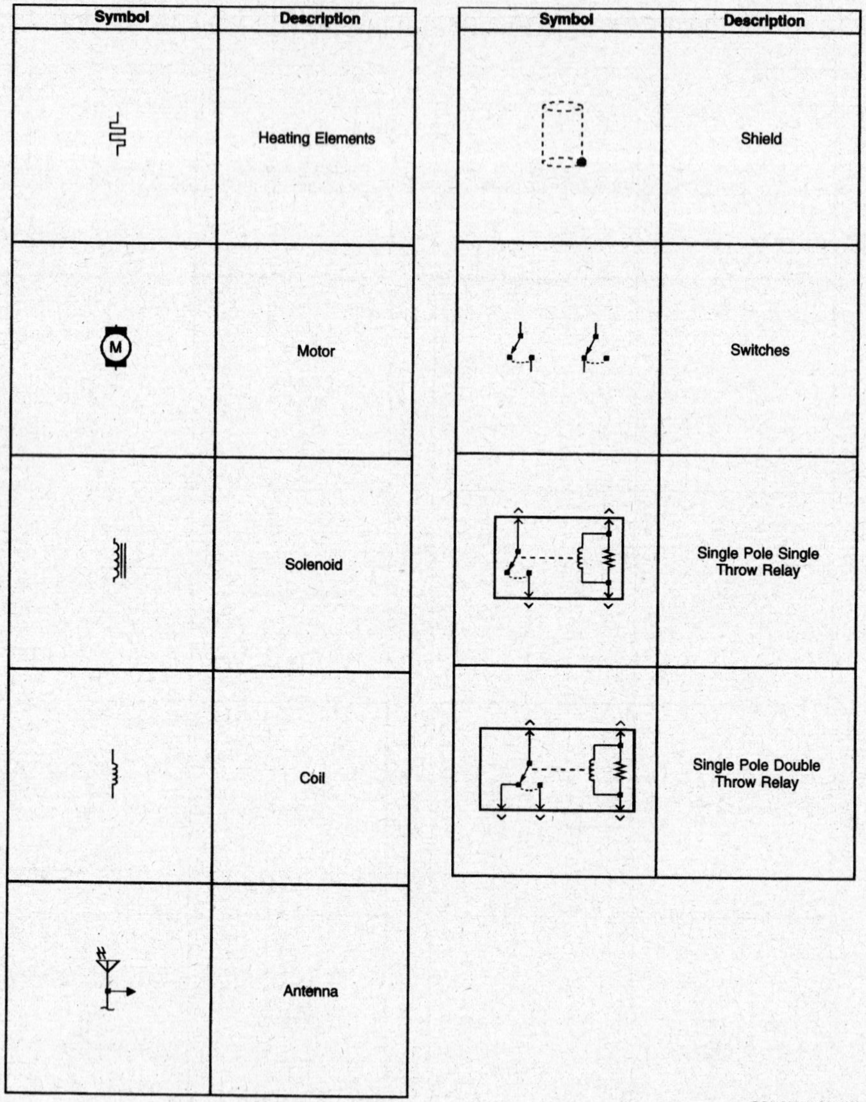

Description	Symbol
Shield	
Switches	
Single Pole Single Throw Relay	
Single Pole Double Throw Relay	
Description	Symbol
Heating Elements	
Motor	
Solenoid	
Coil	
Antenna	

Fig. 4 Symbol Identification (Part 4 of 4). General Motors
GC113980114/040X

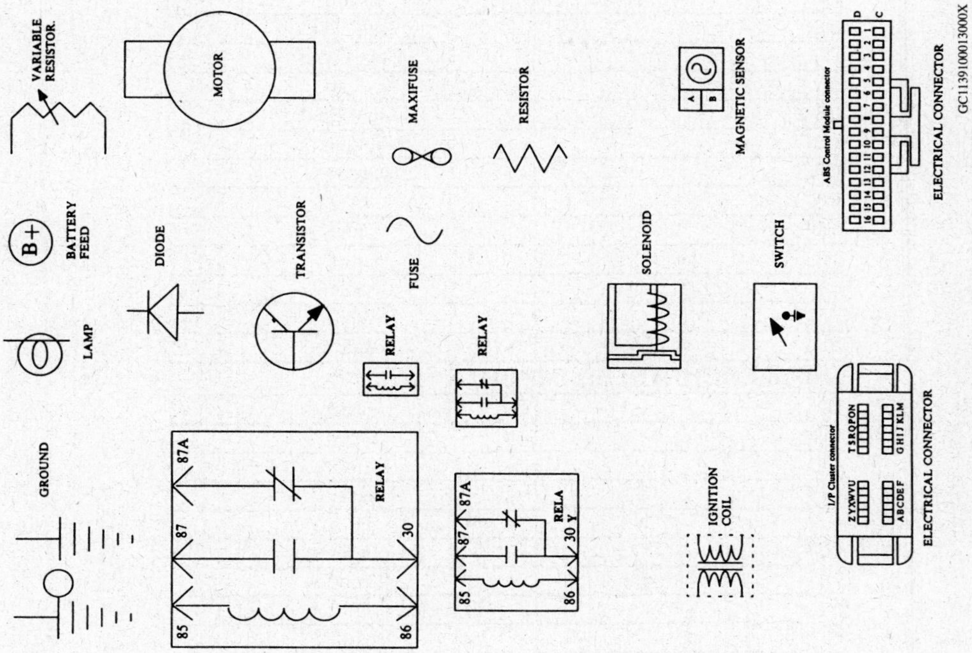

Fig. 5 Symbol Identification. Saturn

Wire Color Code Identification

Abbreviation	Wire Color
DAIMLERCHRYSLER DOMESTIC	
BL	Blue
BK	Black
BR	Brown
DB	Dark Blue
DG	Dark Green
GY	Gray
LB	Light Blue
LG	Light Green
OR	Orange
PK	Pink
RD	Red
TN	Tan
VT	Violet
WT	White
YL	Yellow
DAIMLERCHRYSLER IMPORTS	
B	Black
BR	Brown
G	Green
GR	Gray
L	Blue
LG	Light Green
O	Orange
P	Pink
R	Red
SB	Sky Blue
V	Violet
W	White
Y	Yellow
FORD MOTOR CO. w/NEW STYLE WIRING	
BK	Black
BN	Brown
BR	Brown
BU	Blue
GN	Green
GY	Gray
LG	Light Green
NA	Natural
OG	Orange
P	Purple
PK	Pink
RD	Red
SR	Silver
VT	Violet
WH	White
YE	Yellow
FORD MOTOR CO. w/OLD STYLE WIRING	
BL	Blue
BK	Black
BN	Brown
BR	Brown
DB	Dark Blue
DG	Dark Green
GN	Green
GY	Gray

Continued

Abbreviation	Wire Color
LB	Light Blue
LG	Light Green
N	Natural
O	Orange
P	Purple
PK	Pink
R	Red
T	Tan
W	White
Y	Yellow
GENERAL MOTORS & SATURN	
Black	BLK
Blue	BLU
Brown	BRN
DK BLU	Dark Blue
DK GRN	Dark Green
GRA/GRY	Gray
GRN	Green
LT BLU	Light Blue
LT GRAY	Light Gray
LT GRN	Light Green
ORN	Orange
PNK	Pink
PPL	Purple
RED	Red
TAN	Tan
WHT	White
YEL	Yellow

VEHICLE MAINTENANCE SCHEDULES

TABLE OF CONTENTS

Chrysler Cirrus, Sebring Convertible, Sebring Sedan, Dodge Neon, Stratus Sedan, Plymouth Breeze & Neon

Recommended Service & Intervals (Months)	Service Interval In Miles①																																							
	3000	6000	7500	9000	12000	15000	18000	21000	22500	24000	27000	30000	33000	36000	37500	39000	42000	45000	48000	51000	52500	54000	57000	60000	63000	66000	67500	69000	72000	75000	78000	81000	82500	84000	87000	90000	93000	96000	97500	99000
BODY																																								
Inspect Supplemental Restraint System												X												X												X				
BRAKES																																								
Inspect Brake Connections, Hoses & Lines	Normal Service Every 6 Months Or 7500 Miles, Severe Service Every 3000 Miles																																							
Inspect Brake Drums & Rotors (Normal Service Every 18 Mos.)					S				N	S				S				N		S				S			N		S					S		N		S		
Inspect Brake Pads, Linings & Wheel Bearings, 2000–02	Normal Service Every 22,500 Miles; Severe Every 12,000 Miles																																							
Inspect Brake Pads, Linings & Wheel Bearings, 2003	Normal Service Every 18,000 Miles; Severe Every 9000 Miles																																							
Inspect Brake Pads, Linings & Wheel Bearings, 2004	Normal Service Every 18,000 Miles; Severe Every 12,000 Miles																																							
CLUTCH & TRANSMISSION																																								
Change Automatic Transaxle Filter, Fluid & Adjust Bands, Breeze, Cirrus, Stratus & 2000 Neon	Normal Service Every 30,000 Miles; Severe Service Every 15,000 Miles																																							
Change Automatic Transaxle Filter, Fluid & Adjust Bands, Sebring Convertible, Breeze, Cirrus & Stratus	Normal Service Every 100,000 Miles; Severe Service Every 48,000 Miles																																							
Change Automatic Transaxle Filter, Fluid & Adjust Bands, 2001–03	Severe Service Every 48,000 Miles																																							
Change Automatic Transaxle Filter, Fluid & Adjust Bands, 2004	Severe Service Every 60,000 Miles																																							
DRIVESHAFT																																								
Inspect CV Joints	S	S	X	S	S	X	S	S	X	S	S	X	S	S	X	S	S	X	S	S	X	S	S	X	S	S	X	S	S	X	S	S	X	S	S	X	S	S	X	S

Recommended Service & Intervals (Months)	Service Interval In Miles①																																							
	3000	6000	7500	9000	12000	15000	18000	21000	22500	24000	27000	30000	33000	36000	37500	39000	42000	45000	48000	51000	52500	54000	57000	60000	63000	66000	67500	69000	72000	75000	78000	81000	82500	84000	87000	90000	93000	96000	97500	99000
ENGINE																																								
Change Engine Coolant, 2000	At 36 Months Or 45,000 Miles, Then Every 30,000 Miles Thereafter																																							
Change Engine Coolant, 2001–04	At 60 Months Or 100,000 Miles, Whichever Comes First																																							
Change Engine Oil (Normal Service Every 6 Mos.), 2000–02	S	S	N	S	S	X	S	S	N	S	S	X	S	S	N	S	S	X	S	S	N	S	S	X	S	S	N	S	S	X	S	S	N	S	S	X	S	S	N	S
Change Engine Oil (Normal Service Every 6 Mos.), 2003–04	Normal Service Every 6000 Miles; Severe Service Every 3000 Miles																																							
Change Engine Oil Filter, 2000–02	Normal Service Every 7500 Miles; Severe Service Every 3000 Miles																																							
Change Engine Oil Filter, 2003–04	Normal Service Every 6000 Miles; Severe Service Every 3000 Miles																																							
Inspect Air Filter, 2003②						S						X						S						X						S						X				
Inspect Air Filter, 2004②	Normal Service Every 6000 Miles; Severe Service Every 3000 Miles																																							
Inspect Coolant Level	At Every Engine Oil Change																																							
Inspect EVAP & Fuel Systems Filler Pipe, Hoses, Lines, Tank & Cap												X												X												X				
Inspect Exhaust System	S	S	N	S	S	X	S	S	N	S	S	X	S	S	N	S	S	X	S	S	N	S	S	X	S	S	N	S	S	X	S	S	N	S	S	X	S	S	N	S
Inspect PCV Valve②	Normal Service Every 48 Months Or 60,000 Miles; Severe Service Every 30,000 Miles																																							
Inspect & Adjust Drive Belts,						X						X						X						X						X						X				
Replace Drive Belts Except 2001–04 Sebring Convertible 2.7L	Every 60,000 Miles																																							
Replace Drive Belts, 2001–04 Sebring Convertible 2.7L	Normal Service Inspect & Adjust At 60,000 Miles, Replace At 105,000 Miles; Severe Service Every 60,000 Miles																																							
Replace Air Filter	Every 30,000 Miles																																							
Replace Spark Plugs, 2.0L & 2.4L												X												X												X				
Replace Spark Plugs, 2000 2.5L	Normal Service Every 100,000 Miles; Severe Service Every 75,000 Miles																																							
Replace Spark Plugs, 2001 2.7L	Normal Service At 100,000 Miles; Severe Service Replace at 60,000 Miles Then Every 40,000 Miles Thereafter																																							
Replace Spark Plugs, 2002–04 2.7L	Every 100,000 Miles																																							
Replace Ignition Cables, 2002–04 2.4L	Every 60,000 Miles																																							
Replace Timing Belt, 2000–01	At 105,000 Miles																																							
Replace Timing Belt, 2002	Normal Service At 105,000 Miles; Severe Service At 90,000 Miles																																							

Recommended Service & Intervals (Months)	Service Interval In Miles①																																							
	3000	6000	7500	9000	12000	15000	18000	21000	22500	24000	27000	30000	33000	36000	37500	39000	42000	45000	48000	51000	52500	54000	57000	60000	63000	66000	67500	69000	72000	75000	78000	81000	82500	84000	87000	90000	93000	96000	97500	99000
ENGINE																																								
Replace Timing Belt, 2003 2.0L	Normal Service At 105,000 Miles; Severe Service At 102,000 Miles																																							
Replace Timing Belt, 2003–04 2.4L	Normal Service At 102,000 Miles; Severe Service At 90,000 Miles																																							
STEERING, SUSPENSION & TIRES																																								
Inspect Ball Joints												X												X												X				
Lubricate Suspension & Steering Linkage												X												X												X				
Rotate Tires & Adjust Pressure, 2000–02	Inspect And Rotate Tires Normal Service Every 7500 Miles; Severe Service Every 6000 Miles																																							
Rotate Tires & Adjust Pressure, 2003–04	Inspect And Rotate Tires Every 6000 Miles																																							

Mos. — Months
N — Normal Service
S — Severe Service
X — Normal Or Severe Service
① — After vehicles passes 99,000 mile mark return to beginning of mileage table & start cycle over again.
② — This maintenance is recommended by DaimlerChrysler Corporation to the owner but is not required to maintain the emissions warranty.

Chrysler Concorde, LHS, 300M, Dodge Intrepid

Recommended Service & Intervals (Months)	Service Interval In Miles①																																							
	3000	6000	7500	9000	12000	15000	18000	21000	22500	24000	27000	30000	33000	36000	37500	39000	42000	45000	48000	51000	52500	54000	57000	60000	63000	66000	67500	69000	72000	75000	78000	81000	82500	84000	87000	90000	93000	96000	97500	99000
BODY																																								
Inspect Supplemental Restraint System												X												X												X				
BRAKES																																								
Inspect Brake Connections, Hoses & Lines, 2000–02	Normal Service Every 6 Mos. Or 7500 Miles; Severe Service Every 3000 Miles																																							
Inspect Brake Connections, Hoses & Lines, 2003	Normal Service Every 6 Mos. Or 6000 Miles; Severe Service Every 3000 Miles																																							
Inspect Brake Connections, Hoses & Lines, 2004	Normal Service Every 12,000 Miles; Severe Service Every 9000 Miles																																							
Inspect Brake Drums & Rotors					S				N	S				S				N	S					S			N		S					S		N		S		
Inspect Brake Pads, Linings					S				N	S				S				N	S					S			N		S					S		N		S		
CLUTCH & TRANSMISSION																																								
Change Automatic Transaxle Fluid & Filter, 2000	Normal Service At 100,000 Miles; Severe Service Every 48,000 Miles																																							
Change Automatic Transaxle & Differential Fluid & Filter, 2001–03	Severe Service Every 48,000 Miles																																							
Change Automatic Transaxle Fluid & Filter, 2004	Severe Service Every 60,000 Miles																																							
Change Differential Fluid, 2004	Severe Service Every 48,000 Miles																																							
DRIVESHAFT & CV JOINTS																																								
Inspect CV Joints	S	S	N	S	S	X	S	S	N	S	S	X	S	S	N	S	S	X	S	S	N	S	S	X	S	S	N	S	S	X	S	S	N	S	S	X	S	S	N	S
ENGINE																																								
Change Engine Coolant	Every 60 Months Or 100,000 Miles																																							
Change Engine Oil (Normal Service Every 6 Mos.), 2000–02	S	S	N	S	S	X	S	S	N	S	S	X	S	S	N	S	S	X	S	S	N	S	S	X	S	S	N	S	S	X	S	S	N	S	S	X	S	S	N	S
Change Engine Oil (Normal Service Every 6 Mos.), 2003–04	Normal Service Every 6000 Miles; Severe Service Every 3000 Miles																																							
Change Engine Oil Filter (Normal Service Every 6 Mos.), 2000–02	Normal Service Every 7500 Miles; Severe Service Every 3000 Miles																																							
Change Engine Oil Filter (Normal Service Every 6 Mos.), 2003–04	Normal Service Every 6000 Miles; Severe Service Every 3000 Miles																																							
Inspect Air Filter	At Every Oil Change																																							

Recommended Service & Intervals (Months)	Service Interval In Miles①																																							
	3000	6000	7500	9000	12000	15000	18000	21000	22500	24000	27000	30000	33000	36000	37500	39000	42000	45000	48000	51000	52500	54000	57000	60000	63000	66000	67500	69000	72000	75000	78000	81000	82500	84000	87000	90000	93000	96000	97500	99000
ENGINE																																								
Inspect EVAP & Fuel Systems Filler Pipe, Hoses, Lines, Tank & Cap												X												X												X				
Inspect Exhaust System	S	S	N	S	S	X	S	S	N	S	S	X	S	S	N	S	S	X	S	S	N	S	S	X	S	S	N	S	S	X	S	S	N	S	S	X	S	S	N	S
Inspect PCV Valve	Normal Service Replace at 60,000 Miles & Inspect Every 30,000 Thereafter; Severe Service Replace Every 30,000 Miles																																							
Inspect & Adjust Drive Belts						X						X						X						X						X						X				
Replace Air Filter						S						X						S						X						S						X				
Replace Drive Belts																								S																
Replace Spark Plugs, 2000–02	Every 100,000 Miles																																							
Replace Spark Plugs, 2003–04	Normal Service Every 102,000 Miles; Severe Service Every 100,000 Miles																																							
Replace Timing Belt, 3.2L & 3.5L, 2000–02②	At 100,000 Miles																																							
Replace Timing Belt, 3.2L & 3.5L, 2003–04	Normal Service Every 102,000 Miles; Severe Service Federal Emissions Every 100,000 Miles; California Emissions Every 105,000 Miles																																							
Replace Timing Belt, 3.2L & 3.5L, 1999–2004③	At 105,000 Miles																																							
STEERING, SUSPENSION & TIRES																																								
Inspect Ball Joints	At Every Oil Change																																							
Lubricate Suspension & Steering Linkage						S						S						S						X						S						S				
Rotate Tires & Adjust Pressure, 2000–02		S	N		S	N	S		N	S		X		S	N		S	N	S		N	S		X		S	N		S	N	S		N	S		X		S	N	
Rotate Tires & Adjust Pressure, 2003–04	Every 6000 Miles																																							

Mos. — Months
N — Normal Service
S — Severe Service
X — Normal Or Severe Service
① — After vehicles passes 99,000 mile mark return to beginning of mileage table & start cycle over again.
② — 2000–01 models w/Federal emissions.
③ — 2000–01 models w/California emissions.

Chrysler Sebring Coupe, Dodge Avenger & Stratus Coupe

Service Interval In Miles①

Recommended Service & Intervals (Months)	3000	6000	7500	9000	12000	15000	18000	21000	22500	24000	27000	30000	33000	36000	37500	39000	42000	45000	48000
BODY																			
Inspect Supplemental Restraint System Components	Every 10 Years From Vehicle Build Date																		
BRAKES																			
Inspect Brake Connections, Hoses & Lines	Every 12 Months Or 15,000 Miles																		
Inspect Disc Brake Pads (Every 12 Mos.), 2000–03	Normal Service Check for Wear Every 15,000 Miles; Severe Service Every 6000 Miles																		
Inspect Drum Brake Shoes (Every 24 Mos.), 2000–03	Normal Service Check For Wear Every 30,000 Miles; Severe Service Every 15,000 Miles																		
CLUTCH & TRANSMISSION																			
Change Or Inspect Automatic Transaxle Fluid & Filter, 2000	Normal Service, Inspect Every 15,000 Miles; Severe Service, Change Fluid Every 15,000 Miles, Change Filter Every 30,000 Miles																		
Change Or Inspect Automatic Transaxle Fluid & Filter, 2001–03	Normal Service, Inspect Every 15,000 Miles; Severe Service, Inspect Every 15,000 Miles, Change Fluid & Filter Every 30,000 Miles																		
Change Manual Transaxle Lubricant												S							
DRIVESHAFT & CV JOINTS																			
Inspect CV Joint Boots (Every 12 Mos.)						X						X						X	
ENGINE																			
Change Engine Coolant, 2000	Every 24 Months Or 30,000 Miles																		
Change Engine Coolant, 2001–03	At 48 Months Or 60,000 Miles Then Every 24 Months Or 30,000 Miles																		
Change Engine Oil (Normal Service Every 6 Mos./Severe Service Every 3 Mos.)	S	S	N	S	S	X	S	S	N	S	S	X	S	S	N	S	S	X	S
Change Engine Oil & Filter		S			S	N	S			S		X		S			S	N	S
Inspect Air Filter						S						X						S	
Inspect Coolant Level	At Every Engine Oil Change																		
Inspect Distributor Cap & Rotor																			
Inspect EVAP System																			

Recommended Service & Intervals (Months)	51000	52500	54000	57000	60000	63000	66000	67500	69000	72000	75000	78000	81000	82500	84000	87000	90000	93000	96000	97500	99000
BODY																					
Inspect Supplemental Restraint System Components	Every 10 Years From Vehicle Build Date																				
BRAKES																					
Inspect Brake Connections, Hoses & Lines	Every 12 Months Or 15,000 Miles																				
Inspect Disc Brake Pads (Every 12 Mos.), 2000–03	Normal Service Check for Wear Every 15,000 Miles; Severe Service Every 6000 Miles																				
Inspect Drum Brake Shoes (Every 24 Mos.), 2000–03	Normal Service Check For Wear Every 30,000 Miles; Severe Service Every 15,000 Miles																				
CLUTCH & TRANSMISSION																					
Change Or Inspect Automatic Transaxle Fluid & Filter, 2000	Normal Service, Inspect Every 15,000 Miles; Severe Service, Change Fluid Every 15,000 Miles, Change Filter Every 30,000 Miles																				
Change Or Inspect Automatic Transaxle Fluid & Filter, 2001–03	Normal Service, Inspect Every 15,000 Miles; Severe Service, Inspect Every 15,000 Miles, Change Fluid & Filter Every 30,000 Miles																				
Change Manual Transaxle Lubricant					S												S				
DRIVESHAFT & CV JOINTS																					
Inspect CV Joint Boots (Every 12 Mos.)					X						X						X				
ENGINE																					
Change Engine Coolant, 2000	Every 24 Months Or 30,000 Miles																				
Change Engine Coolant, 2001–03	At 48 Months Or 60,000 Miles Then Every 24 Months Or 30,000 Miles																				
Change Engine Oil (Normal Service Every 6 Mos./Severe Service Every 3 Mos.)	S	N	S	S	X	S	S	N	S	S	X	S	S	N	S	S	X	S	S	N	S
Change Engine Oil & Filter			S		X		S			S	N	S			S		X		S		
Inspect Air Filter					X						S						X				
Inspect Coolant Level	At Every Engine Oil Change																				
Inspect Distributor Cap & Rotor					X																
Inspect EVAP System					X																

Recommended Service & Intervals (Months)	Service Interval In Miles①																																							
	3000	6000	7500	9000	12000	15000	18000	21000	22500	24000	27000	30000	33000	36000	37500	39000	42000	45000	48000	51000	52500	54000	57000	60000	63000	66000	67500	69000	72000	75000	78000	81000	82500	84000	87000	90000	93000	96000	97500	99000
ENGINE																																								
Inspect Exhaust System & Heat Shields	S	S	N	S	S	X	S	S	N	S	S	X	S	S	N	S	S	X	S	S	N	S	S	X	S	S	N	S	S	X	S	S	N	S	S	X	S	S	N	S
Inspect Fuel Filler Cap																								X																
Inspect Fuel Hoses, Lines & Connections																								X																
Inspect Fuel Tank																								X																
Inspect & Adjust Drive Belts						X						X						X						X						X						X				
Replace Air Filter	Every 30,000 Miles																																							
Replace Spark Plugs, DOHC						S						X						S						X						S						X				
Replace Spark Plugs, 2000–03 SOHC	Normal Service Every 100,000 Miles; Severe Service Every 15,000 Miles																																							
Replace Timing Belt																								X																
STEERING, SUSPENSION & TIRES																																								
Inspect Ball Joints & Steering Linkage Grease Seals (Every 24 Mos.)												X												X												X				
Lubricate Suspension & Steering Linkage (Every 24 Mos.)												X												X												X				
Rotate Tires & Adjust Pressure (Every 6 Mos.)			X			X			X			X			X			X			X			X			X			X			X			X			X	

Mos. — Months
N — Normal Service
S — Severe Service
X — Normal Or Severe Service
① — After vehicles passes 99,000 mile mark return to beginning of mileage table & start cycle over again.

Crossfire

Recommended Service & Intervals (Months)	Service Interval In Miles①																																						
	3000	6000	7500	9000	12000	15000	18000	21000	22500	24000	27000	30000	33000	36000	37500	39000	42000	45000	48000	51000	52500	54000	57000	60000	63000	66000	67500	69000	72000	75000	78000	81000	82500	84000	87000	90000	93000	96000	97500	99000
BODY																																								
Replace Cabin Air Filter	Every 18,500 Miles																																							
BRAKES																																								
Inspect Brake Connections, Hoses & Lines	Normal Service Every 6 Months Or 7000 Miles; Severe Service Every 3 Months Or 3000 Miles																																							
Inspect Brake Drums & Rotors					S		S		N		S			S				X				S			S		N		S			S				X				
Inspect Brake Drum	Normal Service Every 18,000 Miles; Severe Service Every 12,000 Miles																																							
Inspect Brake Pads & Linings					S		S		N		S			S				X				S			S		N		S			S				X				
Replace Brake Fluid																			S																			S		
CLUTCH & TRANSMISSION																																								
Change Automatic Transmission Fluid & Filter	Replace Every 80,000 Miles																																							
Check Transmission Lubricant & Level Condition	Severe Service At Every Oil Change																																							
DRIVE AXLE & DRIVESHAFT																																								
Inspect CV & Driveshaft Joint Boots			X			X			X			X			X			X			X			X			X			X			X			X			X	
ENGINE																																								
Change Engine Coolant	Every 60 Months Or 100,000 Miles																																							
Change Engine Oil & Filter	Every 7000 Miles																																							
Inspect Coolant Level, Hoses & Clamps	At Every Oil Change																																							
Inspect Drive Belts						S						X						S						X						S						X				
Inspect Exhaust System	At Every Oil Change																																							
Adjust Alternator Drive Belt Tension	Every 24 Months Or 30,000 Miles																																							
Replace Air Filter	Normal Service 60,000 Miles																																							
Replace Fuel Filter	Normal Service 60,000 Miles																																							
Replace Spark Plugs	Every 60 Months Or 100,000 Miles																																							
STEERING, SUSPENSION & TIRES																																								
Inspect Bushings, Arms, CV Joints, Seals, Springs & Jounce Bumpers	S	X		S	X	S	X	S		X	S	X	S	X		S	X	S	X	S		X	S	X	S	X		S	X	S	X	S		X	S	X	S	X		S
Inspect Tie Rod Ends & Boot Seals	Every 50,000 Miles																																							

Recommended Service & Intervals (Months)	Service Interval In Miles①																																						
	3000	6000	7500	9000	12000	15000	18000	21000	22500	24000	27000	30000	33000	36000	37500	39000	42000	45000	48000	51000	52500	54000	57000	60000	63000	66000	67500	69000	72000	75000	78000	81000	82500	84000	87000	90000	93000	96000	97500	99000
STEERING, SUSPENSION & TIRES																																								
Lubricate Ball Joints (Every 18 Mos.)									X									X									X									X				
Lubricate Steering Linkage (Every 12 Mos.)						X						X						X						X						X						X				
Rotate Tires & Adjust Pressure	Every 7000 Miles																																							

① — After vehicles passes 99,000 mile mark return to beginning of mileage table & start cycle over again.N — Normal Service
S — Severe Service
X — Normal Or Severe Service

Ford Contour & Mercury Mystique

Service Interval In Miles①

Recommended Service	3000	5000	6000	7500	9000	10000	12000	15000	18000	20000	21000	22500	24000	25000	27000	30000	33000	35000	36000	37500	39000	40000	42000	45000	48000	50000	51000	52500	54000	55000	57000	60000
BODY																																
Inspect A/C Refrigerant Charge & System Operation	Every 12 Months Or 15,000 Miles, Before Warm Season Arrives																															
Inspect Instrument Panel Warning Lamps & Gauges	At Every Engine Oil Change																															
Lubricate Body Hardware & Hinges								X								X								X								X
Lubricate Hood Latch Pivot Points & All Contact Areas				X				X				X				X				X				X				X				X
Replace Passenger Compartment Pollen Filter								X								X								X								X
BRAKES																																
Inspect Brake Drums, Linings, Pads, Rotors, Lubricate Caliper Slide Rails	Normal Service Every 15,000 Miles; Severe Service Every 5000 Miles																															
Inspect Parking Brake System Operation								X								X								X								X
CLUTCH & TRANSMISSION																																
Change Automatic Transmission Fluid & Filter	Normal Service Inspect Every 15,000 Miles; Severe Service Change Every 30,000 Miles.																															
Lubricate Transmission Control Linkage								X								X								X								X
DRIVESHAFT																																
Inspect CV Joint Boots (Every 6 Mos.)								X								X								X								X
ENGINE																																
Change Engine Coolant	Replace Green Coolant If Equipped, Every 45,000 Miles, Then Every 30,000 Miles Thereafter; Replace Orange Coolant If Equipped, Every 150,000 Miles																															
Change Engine Oil & Filter	S	N	S		S	N	S	X	S	N	S		S	N	S	X	S	N	S		S	N	S	X	S	N	S		S	N	S	X
Inspect Cooling & Protection Level	Annually Or Every 15,000 Miles																															
Inspect Drive Belts	Every 100,000 Miles																															
Inspect Exhaust Heat System																X																X
Inspect Fluid & Lubricant Levels	At Every Engine Oil Change																															
Inspect Fuel System Connections, Hoses & Lines								X								X								X								X
Replace Air Filter																X																X
Replace Fuel Filter②	Every 30,000 Miles																															
Replace PCV Valve	4 Cylinder Every 60,000 Miles; 6 Cylinder Every 100,000 Miles																															
Replace Spark Plugs, 2.5L	Normal Service Every 100,000 Miles; Severe Service Every 60,000 Miles																															
Replace Spark Plugs, 2.0L	Every 100,000 Miles																															
STEERING, SUSPENSION & TIRES																																
Rotate Tires,	Inspect For Wear And Rotate Every 5000 Miles																															

Mos. — Months
N — Normal Service
S — Severe Service
X — Normal Or Severe Service
① — After vehicle has passed 60,000 mile mark return to beginning of mileage table & start cycle over again.
② — On vehicles equipped with California emissions.

Ford Crown Victoria, Mercury Grand Marquis & Marauder

Recommended Service	Service Interval In Miles①																														
	3000	5000	6000	7500	9000	10000	12000	15000	18000	20000	21000	22500	24000	25000	27000	30000	33000	35000	36000	37500	39000	40000	42000	45000	48000	50000	51000	52500	54000	55000	57000	60000
BODY																																
Inspect A/C Refrigerant Charge & System Operation	Every 12 Months Or 15,000 Miles																															
Inspect Instrument Panel Warning Lamps & Gauges	At Every Engine Oil Change																															
Lubricate Body Hardware & Hinges								X								X								X								X
Lubricate Hood Latch Pivot Points & All Contact Areas				X				X				X				X				X				X				X				X
Replace Cabin Air Filter	Every 15,000 Miles If Equipped																															
BRAKES																																
Inspect Brake Drums, Linings, Pads, Rotors, Lubricate Caliper Slide Rails	Normal Service Every 15,000 Miles; Severe Service Every 5000 Miles																															
Inspect Parking Brake System Operation								X								X								X								X
CLUTCH & TRANSMISSION																																
Change Automatic Transmission Fluid & Filter	Normal Service Inspect Every 15,000 Miles; Change Every 30,000 Miles																															
Lubricate Transmission Control Linkage								X								X								X								X
DRIVE AXLE & DRIVESHAFT																																
Change Differential Lubricant	②																															
Lubricate Driveshaft								X								X								X								X
ENGINE																																
Change Engine Coolant, 2000–03	Replace Green Coolant, Every 45,000 Miles, Then Every 30,000 Miles Thereafter, Orange Coolant, Every 150,000 Miles, Yellow Coolant Every 5 Years Or 100,000 Miles																															
Change Engine Coolant, 2004	Replace Premium Gold Coolant, Every 5 Years Or 100,000 Miles Thereafter Replace Every 36 Months Or 50,000 Miles																															
Change Engine Oil & Filter, 2000–03	S		S	N	S		S	X	S		S	N	S		S	X	S		S	N	S		S	X	S		S	N	S		S	X
Change Engine Oil & Filter, 2004	Normal Service Every 5000 Miles; Severe Service Every 3000 Miles																															
Inspect Cooling System & Protection Level	Annually Or Every 15,000 Miles																															
Inspect Drive Belts	Every 100,000 Miles																															
Inspect Exhaust System																X																X
Inspect Fluid & Lubricant Levels	At Every Engine Oil Change																															
Inspect Fuel System Connections, Hoses & Lines								X								X								X								X
Inspect & Replace Engine Air Filter								S								X								S								X
Replace Engine Air Filter	Every 30,000 Miles																															
Replace Fuel Filter Element & Housing O-Ring Seal, Drain Coalescent Filter Bowl, 2002–04 NGV	Every 15 Years From Date On Tank From Manufacturer																															
Replace Fuel Filter Element & Housing O-Ring Seal, Drain Coalescent Filter Bowl, 2000–01 NGV	Every 120,000 Miles																															

Recommended Service	Service Interval In Miles①																															
	3000	5000	6000	7500	9000	10000	12000	15000	18000	20000	21000	22500	24000	25000	27000	30000	33000	35000	36000	37500	39000	40000	42000	45000	48000	50000	51000	52500	54000	55000	57000	60000
ENGINE																																
Replace Fuel Filter	Normal Service Every 30,000 Miles; Severe Service Every 15,000 Miles																															
Replace PCV Valve	Every 100,000 Miles																															
Replace Spark Plugs, Except NGV	Normal Service Every 100,000 Miles; Severe Service Every 60,000 Miles																															
Replace Spark Plugs, NGV																																X
STEERING, SUSPENSION & TIRES																																
Inspect & Repack Front Wheel Bearings																X																X
Lubricate Steering & Suspension Components								X								X								X								X
Rotate Tires	Normal Service Inspect for Wear & Rotate Every 5,000 Miles																															

N — Normal Service
NGV — Natural Gas Vehicle
S — Severe Service
X — Normal Or Severe Service
① — After vehicle has passed 60,000 mile mark return to beginning of mileage table & start cycle over again.
② — Normal Vehicle Axle Maintenance: Rear axle units containing synthetic lubricant are lubricated for life. These lubricants are not to be checked or changed unless a leak is suspected, service is required or the axle assembly has been submerged in water. The axle lubricant should be changed anytime the axle has been submerged in water. Non-synthetic rear axle lubricants should be replaced every 100,000 miles under normal operating conditions. Non-synthetic rear axle lubricants should be replaced every 3000 miles or 3 months, whichever occurs first, during extended trailer tow operation above (70°F) ambient and wide open throttle for extended periods above 45 mph. The 3000 mile lube change interval may be waived if the axle was filled with 75W140 synthetic gear lubricant meeting Ford specification WSL-M2C192-A. Add four ounces of additive friction modifier C8AZ-19B546-A or equivalent for complete refill of Traction-Lok rear axles. The rear axle lubricant should be changed anytime the axle has been submerged in water. Police and Taxi Vehicle Axle Maintenance: Replace rear axle lubricant every 160,000 km (100,000 miles). Rear axle lubricant change may be waived if the axle was filled with 75W140 synthetic gear lubricant meeting Ford specification WSL-M2C192-A. Add four ounces of additive friction modifier C8AZ-19B546-A or equivalent for complete refill of Traction-Lok rear axles. The rear axle lubricant should be changed anytime the axle has been submerged in water.

Ford Mustang

Recommended Service	Service Interval In Miles①																															
	3000	5000	6000	7500	9000	10000	12000	15000	18000	20000	21000	22500	24000	25000	27000	30000	33000	35000	36000	37500	39000	40000	42000	45000	48000	50000	51000	52500	54000	55000	57000	60000
BODY																																
Inspect A/C Refrigerant Charge & System Operation	Every 12 Months Or 15,000 Miles																															
Inspect Instrument Panel Warning Lamps & Gauges	At Every Engine Oil Change																															
Lubricate Body Hardware & Hinges								X								X								X								X
Lubricate Hood Latch Pivot Points & All Contact Areas				X				X				X				X				X				X				X				X
Replace Cabin Air Filter	Every 15,000 Miles, If Equipped																															
BRAKES																																
Inspect Brake Drums, Linings, Pads, Rotors, Lubricate Caliper Slide Rails	Normal Service Every 15,000 Miles; Severe Service Every 5,000 Miles																															
Inspect Parking Brake System Operation								X								X								X								X
CLUTCH & TRANSMISSION																																
Change Automatic Transmission Fluid & Filter	Inspect Every 15,000 Miles; Change Every 30,000 Miles.																															
Lubricate Transmission Control Linkage								X								X								X								X
DRIVE AXLE & DRIVESHAFT																																
Change Differential Lubricant	③																															
Lubricate Driveshaft								X								X								X								X
ENGINE																																
Change Engine Coolant, 2000–03	Green Coolant, Every 45,000 Miles, Then Every 30,000 Miles Thereafter. Replace Orange Coolant, Every 150,000 Miles, Replace Yellow Coolant Every 5 Years Or 100,000 Miles																															
Change Engine Coolant, 2004	Replace Premium Gold Coolant, Every 5 Years Or 100,000 Miles Thereafter Replace Every 36 Months Or 50,000 Miles																															
Change Engine Oil & Filter	S	N	S		S	N	S	X	S	N	S		S	N	S	X	S	N	S		S	N	S	X	S	N	S		S	N	S	X
Inspect Cooling System & Protection Level	Annually Or Every 15,000 Miles																															
Inspect Drive Belts	Every 100,000 Miles																															
Inspect Engine Air Filter								S								X								S								X
Inspect Exhaust System																X																X
Inspect Fluid & Lubricant Levels	At Every Engine Oil Change																															
Inspect Fuel System Connections, Hoses & Lines								X								X								X								X
Replace Engine Air Filter	Every 30,000 Miles																															
Replace Fuel Filter②	Normal Service Every 30,000 Miles; Severe Service Every 15,000 Miles																															
Replace PCV Valve	Every 100,000 Miles																															
Replace Spark Plugs	Normal Service Every 100,000 Miles; Severe Service Every 60,000 Miles																															
STEERING, SUSPENSION & TIRES																																
Inspect & Repack Front Wheel Bearings																X																X
Lubricate Steering & Suspension Components								X								X								X								X
Rotate Tires	Normal Service Inspect for Wear And Rotate Every 5,000 Miles																															

N — Normal Service
S — Severe Service
X — Normal Or Severe Service
① — After vehicle has passed 60,000 mile mark return to beginning of mileage table & start cycle over again.
② — On All vehicles equipped with California emissions.
③ — Normal Vehicle Axle Maintenance: Rear axle units containing synthetic lubricant are lubricated for life. These lubricants are not to be checked or changed unless a leak is suspected, service is required or the axle assembly has been submerged in water. The axle lubricant should be changed anytime the axle has been submerged in water. Non-synthetic rear axle lubricants should be replaced every 100,000 miles under normal operating conditions. Non-synthetic rear axle lubricants should be replaced every 3000 miles or 3 months, whichever occurs first, during extended trailer tow operation above (70°F) ambient and wide open throttle for extended periods above 45 mph. The 3000 mile lube change interval may be waived if the axle was filled with 75W140 synthetic gear lubricant meeting Ford specification WSL-M2C192-A. Add four ounces of additive friction modifier C8AZ-19B546-A or equivalent for complete refill of Traction-Lok rear axles. The rear axle lubricant should be changed anytime the axle has been submerged in water.

Ford Escort & ZX2

Recommended Service	Service Interval In Miles①																														
	3000	5000	6000	7500	9000	10000	12000	15000	18000	20000	21000	22500	24000	25000	27000	30000	33000	35000	36000	37500	39000	40000	42000	45000	48000	50000	51000	52500	54000	55000	57000	60000
BODY																																
Inspect A/C Refrigerant Charge & System Operation	Every 12 Months Or 15,000 Miles																															
Inspect Instrument Panel Warning Lamps & Gauges	At Every Engine Oil Change																															
Lubricate Body Hardware & Hinges								X								X								X								X
Lubricate Hood Latch Pivot Points & All Contact Areas				X				X				X				X				X				X				X				X
Replace Cabin Air Filter	Every 15,000 Miles If Equipped																															
Tighten Body Fasteners								S								X								S								X
BRAKES																																
Inspect Brake Drums, Linings, Pads, Rotors, Lubricate Caliper Slide Rails	Normal Service Every 15,000 Miles; Severe Service Every 5000 Miles																															
Inspect Parking Brake System Operation								X								X								X								X
CLUTCH & TRANSMISSION																																
Change Automatic Transmission Fluid & Filter	Normal Service Inspect Every 15,000 Miles Change Every 150,000 Miles; Severe Service Change Every 30,000 Miles																															
Inspect Clutch Pedal Operation																X																X
Lubricate Transmission Control Linkage								X								X								X								X
DRIVESHAFT																																
Inspect CV Joint Boots								X								X								X								X
ENGINE																																
Change Engine Coolant, 2000–03	Replace Green Coolant, Every 45,000 Miles, Then Every 30,000 Miles Thereafter, Replace Orange Coolant, Every 150,000 Miles, Replace Yellow Coolant, Every 5 Years Or 100,000 Miles																															
Change Engine Coolant, 2004	Replace Premium Gold Coolant, Every 5 Years Or 100,000 Miles Thereafter Replace Every 36 Months Or 50,000 Miles																															
Change Engine Oil & Filter	Normal Service Every 5000 Miles; Severe Service Every 3000 Miles																															
Inspect Cooling System & Protection Level	Annually Or Every 15,000 Miles																															
Inspect Drive Belts	Every 100,000 Miles																															

Recommended Service	Service Interval In Miles①																														
	3000	5000	6000	7500	9000	10000	12000	15000	18000	20000	21000	22500	24000	25000	27000	30000	33000	35000	36000	37500	39000	40000	42000	45000	48000	50000	51000	52500	54000	55000	57000	60000
ENGINE																																
Inspect Engine Air Filter																X																X
Inspect Exhaust System																X																X
Inspect Fuel System Connections, Hoses & Lines								X								X								X								X
Replace Fuel Filter, 2000②	Every 30,000 Miles																															
Replace Fuel Filter, 2001–04	Normal Service Every 30,000 Miles; Severe Service Every 15,000 Miles																															
Replace PCV Valve, 2000–01	Every 60,000 Miles																															
Replace PCV Valve, 2002–04	Every 100,000 Miles																															
Replace Spark Plugs	Every 100,000 Miles																															
Replace Timing Belt	Every 120,000 Miles																															
STEERING, SUSPENSION & TIRES																																
Inspect & Repack Rear Wheel Bearings																X																X
Lubricate Steering & Suspension Components								X								X								X								X
Rotate Tires	Normal Service Inspect For Wear And Rotate Every 5000 Miles																															
Tighten Chassis Fasteners								S								X								S								X

N — Normal Service
S — Severe Service
X — Normal Or Severe Service
① — After vehicle has passed 60,000 mile mark return to beginning of mileage table & start cycle over again.
② — On vehicles equipped with California emissions.

Ford Focus

Recommended Service	Service Interval In Miles① 3000	5000	6000	7500	9000	10000	12000	15000	18000	20000	21000	22500	24000	25000	27000	30000	33000	35000	36000	37500	39000	40000	42000	45000	48000	50000	51000	52500	54000	55000	57000	60000
BODY																																
Inspect A/C Refrigerant Charge & System Operation	Every 12 Months Or 15,000 Miles																															
Inspect Instrument Panel Warning Lamps & Gauges	At Every Engine Oil Change																															
Lubricate Body Hardware & Hinges								X								X								X								X
Lubricate Hood Latch Pivot Points & All Contact Areas				X				X				X				X				X				X				X				X
Replace Cabin Air Filter	Every 15,000 Miles																															
Tighten Body Fasteners								S								X								S								X
BRAKES																																
Inspect Brake Drums, Linings, Pads, Rotors, Lubricate Caliper Slide Rails	Normal Service Every 15,000 Miles; Severe Service Every 5000 Miles																															
Inspect Parking Brake System Operation								X								X								X								X
CLUTCH & TRANSMISSION																																
Change Automatic Transmission Fluid & Filter	Inspect Every 15,000 Miles; Change Every 30,000 Miles																															
Inspect Clutch Pedal Operation																X																X
Lubricate Transmission Control Linkage								X								X								X								X
DRIVESHAFT																																
Inspect CV Joint Boots								X								X								X								X
ENGINE																																
Change Engine Coolant, 2000–2003	Replace Green Coolant, Every 45,000 Miles, Then Every 30,000 Miles Thereafter, Orange Coolant, Every 150,000 Miles, Yellow Coolant Every 5 Years Or 100,000 Miles																															
Change Engine Coolant, 2004	Replace Premium Gold Coolant, Every 5 Years Or 100,000 Miles Thereafter Replace Every 36 Months Or 50,000 Miles																															
Change Engine Oil & Filter	Normal Service Every 5000 Miles; Severe Service Every 3000 Miles																															
Inspect Cooling System & Protection Level	Annually Or Every 15,000 Miles																															
Inspect Drive Belts	Every 100,000 Miles																															
Inspect Exhaust System																X																X
Inspect Fuel System Connections, Hoses & Lines								X								X								X								X
Inspect Engine Air Filter																X																X
Replace Fuel Filter	Normal Service Every 30,000 Miles; Severe Service Every 15,000 Miles																															
Replace PCV Valve, 2000–01	Every 60,000 Miles																															
Replace PCV Valve, 2002–04	Every 100,000 Miles																															
Replace Spark Plugs	Every 100,000 Miles																															
Replace Timing Belt	Every 120,000 Miles																															
STEERING, SUSPENSION & TIRES																																
Inspect & Repack Rear Wheel Bearings																X																X
Lubricate Steering & Suspension Components								X								X								X								X

Recommended Service	Service Interval In Miles①																														
	3000	5000	6000	7500	9000	10000	12000	15000	18000	20000	21000	22500	24000	25000	27000	30000	33000	35000	36000	37500	39000	40000	42000	45000	48000	50000	51000	52500	54000	55000	57000	60000
STEERING, SUSPENSION & TIRES																																
Rotate Tires	Normal Service Inspect For Wear And Rotate Every 5000 Miles																															
Tighten Chassis Fasteners								S								X								S								X

N — Normal Service
S — Severe Service
X — Normal Or Severe Service
① — After vehicle has passed 60,000 mile mark return to beginning of mileage table & start cycle over again.

Ford Taurus & Mercury Sable

Recommended Service	Service Interval In Miles①																														
	3000	5000	6000	7500	9000	10000	12000	15000	18000	20000	21000	22500	24000	25000	27000	30000	33000	35000	36000	37500	39000	40000	42000	45000	48000	50000	51000	52500	54000	55000	57000	60000
BODY																																
Inspect A/C Refrigerant Charge & System Operation	Every 12 Months Or 15,000 Miles, Before Warm Season Arrives																															
Inspect Instrument Panel Warning Lamps & Gauges	At Every Engine Oil Change																															
Lubricate Body Hardware & Hinges								X								X								X								X
Lubricate Hood Latch Pivot Points & All Contact Areas				X				X				X				X				X				X				X				X
Replace Passenger Compartment Pollen Filter								X								X								X								X
BRAKES																																
Inspect Brake Drums, Linings, Pads, Rotors, Lubricate Caliper Slide Rails	Normal Service Every 15,000 Miles; Severe Service Every 5000 Miles																															
Inspect Brake Lines & Hoses							S						S			N			S						S							X
Inspect Parking Brake System Operation								X								X								X								X
CLUTCH & TRANSMISSION																																
Change Automatic Transmission Fluid & Filter	Inspect Every 15,000 Miles; Change Every 30,000 Miles																															
Lubricate Transmission Control Linkage								X								X								X								X
DRIVESHAFT																																
Inspect CV Joint Boots								X								X								X								X
ENGINE																																
Change Engine Coolant, 2000–03	Green Coolant, Every 45,000 Miles, Then Every 30,000 Miles Thereafter Replace Orange Coolant, Every 150,000 Miles, Replace Yellow Coolant, Every 5 Years Or 100,000 Miles																															
Change Engine Coolant, 2004	Replace Premium Gold Coolant, Every 5 Years Or 100,000 Miles Thereafter Replace Every 36 Months Or 50,000 Miles																															
Change Engine Oil & Filter	S	N	S		S	N	S	X	S	N	S		S	N	S	X	S	N	S		S	N	S	X	S	N	S		S	N	S	X
Inspect Cooling System & Protection Level	Annually Or Every 15,000 Miles																															
Inspect Drive Belts	Inspect Accessory Drive Belts Every 100,000 Miles																															
Inspect Exhaust System																X																X
Inspect Fluid & Lubricant Levels	At Every Engine Oil Change																															
Inspect Fuel System Connections, Hoses & Lines								X								X								X								X
Inspect Engine Air Filter																X																X
Replace Fuel Filter, 2000②	Every 30,000 Miles																															
Replace Fuel Filter, 2001–04	Normal Service Every 30,000 Miles; Severe Service Every 15,000 Miles																															
Replace PCV Valve	Every 100,000 Miles																															
Replace Spark Plugs	Normal Service Every 100,000 Miles; Severe Service Every 60,000 Miles																															

Recommended Service	Service Interval In Miles①																															
	3000	5000	6000	7500	9000	10000	12000	15000	18000	20000	21000	22500	24000	25000	27000	30000	33000	35000	36000	37500	39000	40000	42000	45000	48000	50000	51000	52500	54000	55000	57000	60000
ENGINE																																
STEERING, SUSPENSION & TIRES																																
Lubricate Steering & Suspension Components								X								X								X								X
Rotate Tires	Normal Service Inspect For Wear And Rotate Every 5000 Miles																															

N — Normal Service
S — Severe Service
X — Normal Or Severe Service
① — After vehicle has passed 60,000 mile mark return to beginning of mileage table & start cycle over again.
② — On vehicles equipped with California emissions.

Ford Thunderbird

Recommended Service	Service Interval In Miles①																															
	3000	5000	6000	7500	9000	10000	12000	15000	18000	20000	21000	22500	24000	25000	27000	30000	33000	35000	36000	37500	39000	40000	42000	45000	48000	50000	51000	52500	54000	55000	57000	60000
BODY																																
Inspect A/C Refrigerant Charge & System Operation	Every 12 Months Or 15,000 Miles																															
Inspect Instrument Panel Warning Lamps & Gauges	At Every Engine Oil Change																															
Lubricate Body Hardware & Hinges								X								X								X								X
Lubricate Hood Latch Pivot Points & All Contact Areas				X				X				X				X				X				X				X				X
BRAKES																																
Inspect Brake Drums, Linings, Pads, Rotors, Lubricate Caliper Slide Rails	Normal Service Every 15,000 Miles; Severe Service Every 5000 Miles																															
Inspect Parking Brake System Operation								X								X								X								X
CLUTCH & TRANSMISSION																																
Change Automatic Transmission Fluid & Filter	Normal Service Inspect Every 15,000 Miles, Change Every 150,000 Miles; Severe Service Every 30,000 Miles																															
Lubricate Transmission Control Linkage								X								X								X								X
DRIVE AXLE & DRIVESHAFT																																
Lubricate Driveshaft								X								X								X								X
ENGINE																																
Change Engine Coolant	Green Coolant, Every 45,000 Miles, Then Every 30,000 Miles Thereafter. Replace Orange Coolant, Every 150,000 Miles, Replace Yellow Coolant Every 5 Years Or 100,000 Miles																															
Change Engine Oil & Filter,	S	N	S		S	N	S	X	S	N	S		S	N	S	X	S	N	S		S	N	S	X	S	N	S		S	N	S	X
Inspect Cooling System & Protection Level	Annually Or Every 15,000 Miles																															
Inspect Drive Belts	Every 100,000 Miles																															
Inspect Exhaust System																X																X
Inspect Fluid & Lubricant Levels	At Every Engine Oil Change																															
Inspect Fuel System Connections, Hoses & Lines								X								X								X								X
Inspect & Replace Engine Air Filter								S								X								S								X
Replace Engine Air Filter	Every 30,000 Miles																															
Replace Fuel Filter	Normal Service Every 30,000 Miles; Severe Service Every 15,000 Miles																															
Replace PCV Valve	4 Cylinder Every 60,000 Miles; V6 Every 100,000 Miles																															
Replace Spark Plugs	Normal Service Every 100,000 Miles; Severe Service Every 60,000 Miles																															

Recommended Service	Service Interval In Miles①																															
	3000	5000	6000	7500	9000	10000	12000	15000	18000	20000	21000	22500	24000	25000	27000	30000	33000	35000	36000	37500	39000	40000	42000	45000	48000	50000	51000	52500	54000	55000	57000	60000
STEERING, SUSPENSION & TIRES																																
Lubricate Steering & Suspension Components								X								X								X								X
Rotate Tires	Normal Service Inspect For Wear And Rotate Every 5000 Miles																															

N — Normal Service
NGV — Natural Gas Vehicle
S — Severe Service
X — Normal Or Severe Service
① — After vehicle has passed 60,000 mile mark return to beginning of mileage table & start cycle over again.

Lincoln Continental, LS & Town Car

Recommended Service	Service Interval In Miles①																														
	3000	5000	6000	7500	9000	10000	12000	15000	18000	20000	21000	22500	24000	25000	27000	30000	33000	35000	36000	37500	39000	40000	42000	45000	48000	50000	51000	52500	54000	55000	57000	60000
BODY																																
Inspect A/C Refrigerant Charge & System Operation	Every 12 Months Or 15,000 Miles, Before Warm Season Arrives																															
Inspect Instrument Panel Warning Lamps & Gauges	At Every Engine Oil Change																															
Lubricate Body Hardware & Hinges								X								X								X								X
Lubricate Hood Latch Pivot Points & All Contact Areas				X				X				X				X				X				X				X				X
Replace Passenger Compartment Pollen Filter	Normal Service Every 15,000 Miles																															
BRAKES																																
Inspect Brake Drums, Linings, Pads, Rotors, Lubricate Caliper Slide Rails	Normal Service Every 15,000 Miles; Severe Service Every 5000 Miles																															
Inspect Brake Lines & Hoses	Normal Service Every 30,000 Miles; Severe Service Every 12,000 Miles																															
Inspect Parking Brake System Operation								X								X								X								X
CLUTCH & TRANSMISSION																																
Change Automatic Transmission Fluid & Filter, Continental & Town Car	Inspect Every 15,000 Miles; Change Every 30,000 Miles																															
Change Automatic Transmission Fluid & Filter, LS	Normal Service Inspect Every 15,000 Miles, Change Every 150,000 Miles; Severe Service Change Every 30,000 Miles																															
Change Manual Transmission Fluid, Lincoln LS	Every 60,000 Miles																															
Lubricate Transmission Control Linkage								X								X								X								X
DRIVE AXLE & DRIVESHAFT																																
Change Differential Lubricant, Town Car, 2000–03	②																															
Inspect CV Joint Boots								X								X								X								X
Lubricate Driveshaft								X								X								X								X
ENGINE																																
Change Engine Coolant, 2000–03	Green Coolant, Every 45,000 Miles, Then Every 30,000 Miles Thereafter. Replace Orange Coolant, Every 150,000 Miles, Replace Yellow Coolant, Every 5 Years Or 100,000 Miles																															
Change Engine Coolant, 2004	Replace Premium Gold Coolant, Every 5 Years Or 100,000 Miles Thereafter Replace Every 36 Months Or 50,000 Miles																															
Change Engine Oil & Filter, 2000–02	S	N	S		S	N	S	X	S	N	S		S	N	S	X	S	N	S		S	N	S	X	S	N	S		S	N	S	X
Inspect Cooling System & Protection Level	Annually Or Every 15,000 Miles																															
Inspect Drive Belts	Every 100,000 Miles																															
Inspect Exhaust System																X																X
Inspect Fuel System Connections, Hoses & Lines								X								X								X								X
Inspect Engine Air Filter																X																X
Replace Fuel Filter	Normal Service Every 30,000 Miles; Severe Service Every 15,000 Miles																															
Replace PCV Valve	Every 100,000 Miles																															
Replace Spark Plugs	Normal Service Every 100,000 Miles; Severe Service Every 60,000 Miles																															

Recommended Service	Service Interval In Miles①																															
	3000	5000	6000	7500	9000	10000	12000	15000	18000	20000	21000	22500	24000	25000	27000	30000	33000	35000	36000	37500	39000	40000	42000	45000	48000	50000	51000	52500	54000	55000	57000	60000
STEERING, SUSPENSION & TIRES																																
Inspect & Repack Front Wheel Bearings, Town Car																X																X
Lubricate Steering & Suspension Components								X								X								X								X
Rotate Tires	Normal Service Inspect for Wear And Rotate Every 5000 Miles																															

N — Normal Service
S — Severe Service
X — Normal Or Severe Service
① — After vehicle has passed 60,000 mile mark return to beginning of mileage table & start cycle over again.
② — Normal Vehicle Axle Maintenance: Rear axle units containing synthetic lubricant are lubricated for life. These lubricants are not to be checked or changed unless a leak is suspected, service is required or the axle assembly has been submerged in water. The axle lubricant should be changed anytime the axle has been submerged in water. Non-synthetic rear axle lubricants should be replaced every 100,000 miles under normal operating conditions. Non-synthetic rear axle lubricants should be replaced every 3000 miles or 3 months, whichever occurs first, during extended trailer tow operation above (70°F) ambient and wide open throttle for extended periods above 45 mph. The 3000 mile lube change interval may be waived if the axle was filled with 75W140 synthetic gear lubricant meeting Ford specification WSL-M2C192-A. Add four ounces of additive friction modifier C8AZ-19B546-A or equivalent for complete refill of Traction-Lok rear axles. The rear axle lubricant should be changed anytime the axle has been submerged in water.

Mercury Cougar

Recommended Service	Service Interval In Miles①																															
	3000	5000	6000	7500	9000	10000	12000	15000	18000	20000	21000	22500	24000	25000	27000	30000	33000	35000	36000	37500	39000	40000	42000	45000	48000	50000	51000	52500	54000	55000	57000	60000
BODY																																
Inspect A/C Refrigerant Charge & System Operation	Every 12 Months Or 15,000 Miles																															
Inspect Instrument Panel Warning Lamps & Gauges	At Every Engine Oil Change																															
Lubricate Body Hardware & Hinges								X								X								X								X
Lubricate Hood Latch Pivot Points & All Contact Areas				X				X				X				X				X				X				X				X
Replace Cabin Air Filter	Every 15,000 Miles																															
BRAKES																																
Inspect Brake Drums, Linings, Pads, Rotors, Lubricate Caliper Slide Rails	Normal Service Every 15,000 Miles; Severe Service Every 5000 Miles																															
Inspect Parking Brake System Operation								X								X								X								X
CLUTCH & TRANSMISSION																																
Change Automatic Transmission Fluid & Filter	Normal Service Inspect Every 15,000 Miles, Change Every 150,000 Miles; Severe Service Every 30,000 Miles																															
Lubricate Transmission Control Linkage								X								X								X								X
ENGINE																																
Change Engine Coolant	Green Coolant, Every 45,000 Miles, Then Every 30,000 Miles Thereafter. Replace Orange Coolant, Every 150,000 Miles, Replace Yellow Coolant Every 5 Years Or 100,000 Miles																															
Change Engine Oil & Filter,	S	N	S		S	N	S	X	S	N	S		S	N	S	X	S	N	S		S	N	S	X	S	N	S		S	N	S	X
Inspect Cooling System & Protection Level	Annually Or Every 15,000 Miles																															
Inspect Drive Belts	Every 100,000 Miles																															
Inspect Exhaust System																X																X
Inspect Fluid & Lubricant Levels	At Every Engine Oil Change																															
Inspect Fuel System Connections, Hoses & Lines								X								X								X								X
Inspect & Replace Engine Air Filter								S								X								S								X
Replace Engine Air Filter	Every 30,000 Miles																															
Replace Fuel Filter, 2000②	Every 30,000 Miles																															
Replace Fuel Filter, 2001–02	Normal Service Every 30,000 Miles; Severe Service Every 15,000 Miles																															
Replace PCV Valve	4 Cylinder Every 60,000 Miles; V6 Every 100,000 Miles																															
Replace Spark Plugs	Normal Service Every 100,000 Miles; Severe Service Every 60,000 Miles																															
Replace Timing Belt, 2.0L	Every 120,000 Miles																															

Recommended Service	Service Interval In Miles①																															
	3000	5000	6000	7500	9000	10000	12000	15000	18000	20000	21000	22500	24000	25000	27000	30000	33000	35000	36000	37500	39000	40000	42000	45000	48000	50000	51000	52500	54000	55000	57000	60000
STEERING, SUSPENSION & TIRES																																
Lubricate Steering & Suspension Components								X								X								X								X
Rotate Tires	Normal Service Inspect For Wear And Rotate Every 5000 Miles																															

N — Normal Service
NGV — Natural Gas Vehicle
S — Severe Service
X — Normal Or Severe Service
① — After vehicle has passed 60,000 mile mark return to beginning of mileage table & start cycle over again.
② — On vehicles equipped with California emissions.

Buick Century, Regal, Chevrolet Impala, Lumina, Monte Carlo, Oldsmobile Intrigue & Pontiac Grand Prix

Recommended Service	Service Interval In Miles①																																							
	3000	6000	7500	9000	12000	15000	18000	21000	22500	24000	27000	30000	33000	36000	37500	39000	42000	45000	48000	51000	52500	54000	57000	60000	63000	66000	67500	69000	72000	75000	78000	81000	82500	84000	87000	90000	93000	96000	97500	99000
BODY																																								
Inspect Lamps, Seat Belts & Warning Devices	At Least Once Every 6 Months																																							
Lubricate Hinges, Latches, Lock Cylinders & Strikers	At Engine Oil Changes Or At Least Every 12 Months																																							
Replace Passenger Compartment Air Filter						X						X						X						X						X						X				
BRAKES																																								
Inspect Brake System,	Every 6 Months																																							
Inspect Disc Brake Pads, Rotors, Shoes & Drums	At 7500 Miles, Then Every 15,000 Miles																																							
Inspect Parking Brake Operation	At Least Once Every 12 Months																																							
Lubricate Parking Brake Cable Guides		S	N		S	N	S		N	S		X		S	N		S	N	S		N	S		X		S	N		S	N	S		N	S		X		S	N	
CLUTCH & TRANSAXLE																																								
Change Automatic Transmission Fluid & Filter, Except Regal CNG	No Normal Service; Severe Service Every 50,000 Miles																																							
Change Automatic Transmission Fluid & Filter, Regal CNG	Normal Service Every 100,000 Miles; Severe Service Every 50,000 Miles																																							
Inspect Neutral Safety & BTSI & Lubricate Shift Linkage		S	N		S	N	S		N	S		X		S	N		S	N	S		N	S		X		S	N		S	N	S		N	S		X		S	N	
DRIVE AXLE & DRIVESHAFT																																								
Inspect CV Joint Boots	At Tire Rotations																																							
ENGINE																																								
Add Fuel Injector Cleaner, 2000 Regal CNG	Every 7500 Miles																																							
Change Engine Coolant	Every 60 Months Or 150,000 Miles																																							
Change Engine Oil & Filter, Less Turbo②	S	S	N	S	S	X	S	S	N	S	S	X	S	S	N	S	S	X	S	S	N	S	S	X	S	S	N	S	S	X	S	S	N	S	S	X	S	S	N	S
Change Engine Oil & Filter, w/Turbo②	X	X		X	X	X	X	X		X	X	X	X	X		X	X	X	X	X		X	X	X	X	X		X	X	X	X	X		X	X	X	X	X		X

Recommended Service	Service Interval In Miles①																																							
	3000	6000	7500	9000	12000	15000	18000	21000	22500	24000	27000	30000	33000	36000	37500	39000	42000	45000	48000	51000	52500	54000	57000	60000	63000	66000	67500	69000	72000	75000	78000	81000	82500	84000	87000	90000	93000	96000	97500	99000
ENGINE																																								
Inspect Drive Belts & EGR System, 2000–02	Inspect Every 60,000 Miles																																							
Inspect Exhaust System	At Engine Oil Changes																																							
Inspect Fuel Filter & PCV System												X												X												X				
Inspect Fuel Tank, Cap, Lines & Gasket For Damage Or Leaks, 2000 Regal CNG												X												X												X				
Inspect Spark Plug Wires	At Spark Plug Changes																																							
Inspect Supercharger Oil Level, 3.8L Supercharged VIN 1	Every 30,000 Miles Or 36 Months																																							
Inspect TBI Unit Mounting Fastener Security		S	N																																					
Inspect Throttle Linkage Operation	At Air Cleaner Element Changes																																							
Replace Air Filter & PCV Filter						S						X						S						X						S						X				
Replace Air Filter, 2000 Regal CNG	Every 30,000 Miles																																							
Replace Spark Plugs Except Regal CNG	Every 100,000 Miles																																							
Replace Spark Plugs, 2000, Regal CNG	Every 15,000 Miles																																							
STEERING, SUSPENSION & TIRES																																								
Inspect Steering & Suspension System	At Tire Rotations																																							
Lubricate Chassis & Suspension		S	N		S	N	S		N	S		X		S	N		S	N	S		N	S		X		S	N		S	N	S		N	S		X		S	N	
Rotate Tires③	Inspect For Wear And Rotate Every 7500 Miles																																							

CNG — Compressed Natural Gas
N — Normal Service
S — Severe Service
X — Normal Or Severe Service
BTSI — Brake Transmission Shift Interlock
IAC — Idle Air Control
ISC — Idle Speed Control System
① — After vehicle passes 99,000 mile mark return to beginning of mileage table & start cycle over again.
② — If equipped, the engine oil life monitor will indicate when to change engine oil, usually 3000–10,000 miles. Under severe driving conditions, engine oil may need to be changed before 3000 miles. If vehicle is driven in a dusty area, change engine oil every 3000 miles.
③ — 2001, Tire Inflation Monitor System, if equipped, must be reset when tires are rotated.

Buick LeSabre, Park Avenue & Pontiac Bonneville

Recommended Service	Service Interval In Miles①																																						
	3000	6000	7500	9000	12000	15000	18000	21000	22500	24000	27000	30000	33000	36000	37500	39000	42000	45000	48000	51000	52500	54000	57000	60000	63000	66000	67500	69000	72000	75000	78000	81000	82500	84000	87000	90000	93000	96000	97500	99000
BODY																																								
Clean Power Antenna Mast		S	N		S	N	S		N	S		X		S	N		S	N	S		N	S		X		S	N		S	N	S		N	S		X		S	N	
Flush Vehicle Underside, Inspect Drain Holes	At Least Every 12 Months																																							
Inspect Lamps & Seat Belts & Warning Devices	At Least Once Every 6 Months																																							
Lubricate Hinges, Latches, Lock Cylinders & Strikers	At Engine Oil Changes Or At Least Every 12 Months																																							
Replace Passenger Compartment Air Filter, 2000–01						X						X						X						X						X						X				
Replace Passenger Compartment Air Filter, 2002–03	Normal Service Every 15,000 Miles; Severe Service Every 12,000 Miles																																							
BRAKES																																								
Inspect Brake Fluid Level	Every 6 Months																																							
Inspect Brake System 2000	Every 6,000 Miles																																							
Inspect Brake System 2001–03	Normal Service Every 7500 Miles; Severe Service Every 6000 Miles																																							
Inspect Parking Brake Operation	At Least Once Every 12 Months																																							
Lubricate Parking Brake Cable Guides		S	N		S	N	S		N	S		X		S	N		S	N	S		N	S		X		S	N		S	N	S		N	S		X		S	N	
CLUTCH & TRANSAXLE																																								
Change Automatic Transmission Fluid & Filter③	Normal Service Every 100,000 Miles; Severe Service Every 50,000 Miles																																							
Inspect Neutral Safety & BTSI & Lubricate Shift Linkage		S	N		S	N	S		N	S		X		S	N		S	N	S		N	S		X		S	N		S	N	S		N	S		X		S	N	
DRIVESHAFT																																								
Inspect CV Joint Boots	At Engine Oil Changes & Tire Rotations																																							
ENGINE																																								
Change Engine Coolant ④	Every 60 Months Or 150,000 Miles																																							
Change Engine Oil & Filter②	S	S	N	S	S	X	S	S	N	S	S	X	S	S	N	S	S	X	S	S	N	S	S	X	S	S	N	S	S	X	S	S	N	S	S	X	S	S	N	S
Inspect Drive Belts & EGR System																								X																
Inspect Exhaust System	At Engine Oil Changes																																							

Service Interval In Miles① (columns 3000–51000)

Recommended Service	3000	6000	7500	9000	12000	15000	18000	21000	22500	24000	27000	30000	33000	36000	37500	39000	42000	45000	48000	51000
ENGINE																				
Inspect Fuel System & PCV Valve & Supercharger Lubricant Level④												X								
Inspect Spark Plug Wires	At Spark Plug Changes																			
Inspect TBI Unit Mounting Fastener Security		S	N																	
Inspect Thermostatically Controlled Air Cleaner Operation												X								
Inspect Throttle Linkage Operation	At Engine Oil Or Air Cleaner Element Changes																			
Replace Air Filter & PCV Filter④	Every 30,000 Miles																			
Replace Spark Plugs④	Every 100,000 Miles																			
STEERING, SUSPENSION & TIRES																				
Inspect Power Steering Fluid Level & Suspension System	At Engine Oil Changes & Tire Rotations																			
Lubricate Chassis & Suspension		S	N		S	N	S		N	S		X		S	N		S	N	S	
Rotate Tires	Normal Service Inspect For Wear & Rotate Every 7500 Miles; Severe Service Every 6000 Miles																			

Service Interval In Miles① (columns 52500–99000)

Recommended Service	52500	54000	57000	60000	63000	66000	67500	69000	72000	75000	78000	81000	82500	84000	87000	90000	93000	96000	97500	99000
ENGINE																				
Inspect Fuel System & PCV Valve & Supercharger Lubricant Level④				X												X				
Inspect Spark Plug Wires	At Spark Plug Changes																			
Inspect TBI Unit Mounting Fastener Security																				
Inspect Thermostatically Controlled Air Cleaner Operation				X												X				
Inspect Throttle Linkage Operation	At Engine Oil Or Air Cleaner Element Changes																			
Replace Air Filter & PCV Filter④	Every 30,000 Miles																			
Replace Spark Plugs④	Every 100,000 Miles																			
STEERING, SUSPENSION & TIRES																				
Inspect Power Steering Fluid Level & Suspension System	At Engine Oil Changes & Tire Rotations																			
Lubricate Chassis & Suspension	N	S		X		S	N		S	N	S		N	S		X		S	N	
Rotate Tires	Normal Service Inspect For Wear & Rotate Every 7500 Miles; Severe Service Every 6000 Miles																			

N — Normal Service
S — Severe Service
X — Normal Or Severe Service
BTSI — Brake Transmission Shift Interlock
IAC — Idle Air Control
ISC — Idle Speed Control System
① — After vehicle passes 99,000 mile mark return to beginning of mileage table & start cycle over again.
② — If equipped, the engine oil life monitor will indicate when to change engine oil, usually 3,000–10,000 miles. Under severe driving conditions, engine oil may need to be changed before 3000 miles. If vehicle is driven in a dusty area, change engine oil every 3000 miles.
③ — If vehicle is used in hilly or mountainous terrain, heavy city traffic where outside temperature reaches 90°F or higher or uses such as high performance operation.
④ — The U.S. Environmental Protection Agency or the California Air Resources Board has determined the failure to perform this maintenance item will not nullify the emission warranty or limit recall liability prior to the completion of the vehicle's useful life. We, however, urge that all recommended maintenance services be performed at the indicated intervals and the maintenance be recorded.

Cadillac Catera

Recommended Service	Service Interval In Miles①																																							
	3000	6000	7500	9000	12000	15000	18000	21000	22500	24000	27000	30000	33000	36000	37500	39000	42000	45000	48000	51000	52500	54000	57000	60000	63000	66000	67500	69000	72000	75000	78000	81000	82500	84000	87000	90000	93000	96000	97500	99000
BODY																																								
Flush Vehicle Underside, Inspect Drain Holes	At Least Every 12 Months, Especially In Winter & Springtime																																							
Inspect Lamps, Seat Belts & Warning Devices	At Least Once Every 6 Months																																							
Lubricate Hinges, Latches, Lock Cylinders & Strikers	At Engine Oil Changes Or At Least Every 12 Months																																							
Replace Passenger Compartment Air Filter						X						X						X						X						X						X				
BRAKES																																								
Inspect Brake System	Every 5000 Miles																																							
Inspect Parking Brake Operation	At Least Once Every 12 Months																																							
Lubricate Parking Brake Cable Guides		S	N		S	N	S		N	S		X		S	N		S	N	S		N	S		X		S	N		S	N	S		N	S		X		S	N	
CLUTCH & TRANSAXLE																																								
Change Automatic Transmission Fluid & Filter, 2000	No Normal Service; Severe Service Every 50,000 Miles																																							
Change Automatic Transmission Fluid & Filter, 2001	Normal Service Every 100,000 Miles; Severe Service Every 50,000 Miles																																							
Inspect Neutral Safety & BTSI Operation		S	N		S	N	S		N	S		X		S	N		S	N	S		N	S		X		S	N		S	N	S		N	S		X		S	N	
Lubricate Transmission Shift Linkage		S	N		S	N	S		N	S		X		S	N		S	N	S		N	S		X		S	N		S	N	S		N	S		X		S	N	
ENGINE																																								
Change Engine Coolant	Every 60 Months Or 150,000 Miles																																							
Change Engine Oil & Filter	Normal Service Initially At 5000 Miles, Then Every 10,000 Miles Thereafter; Severe Service Every 5000 Miles																																							
Inspect Air Cleaner Element						X												X												X						X				
Inspect Drive Belts	Every 60,000 Miles																																							
Inspect EGR System												X												X												X				
Inspect Exhaust System	At Engine Oil Changes																																							
Inspect Fuel Filler Cap												X												X												X				
Inspect Fuel System Hoses, Lines & Connections												X												X												X				
Inspect PCV Valve												X												X												X				

Recommended Service	Service Interval In Miles①																																							
	3000	6000	7500	9000	12000	15000	18000	21000	22500	24000	27000	30000	33000	36000	37500	39000	42000	45000	48000	51000	52500	54000	57000	60000	63000	66000	67500	69000	72000	75000	78000	81000	82500	84000	87000	90000	93000	96000	97500	99000
ENGINE																																								
Inspect Spark Plug Wires	At Spark Plug Changes																																							
Replace Air Filter & PCV Filter	Every 30,000 Miles																																							
Replace Fuel Filter	Every 100,000 Miles																																							
Replace Spark Plugs	Every 100,000 Miles																																							
Replace Timing Belt	Replace Every 100,000 Miles Under Normal Operating Conditions; Replace Every 60,000 Miles If Driven Without An Engine Coolant Heater At Ambient Temperatures Of −20°F Or Less, Then Inspect At 15,000 Mile Intervals																																							
Replace Timing Belts, Reset Counter,②	Every 60,000 Miles																																							
STEERING, SUSPENSION & TIRES																																								
Inspect Steering & Suspension System	At Tire Rotations																																							
Lubricate Chassis & Suspension		S	N		S	N	S		N	S		X		S	N		S	N	S		N	S		X		S	N		S	N	S		N	S		X		S	N	
Rotate Tires	Initial Service At 5000 Miles, Then Every 10,000 Miles Thereafter																																							

N — Normal Service
S — Severe Service
X — Normal Or Severe Service
BTSI — Brake Transmission Shift Interlock
IAC — Idle Air Control
ISC — Idle Speed Control System
① — After vehicle passes 99,000 mile mark return to beginning of mileage table & start cycle over again.
② — If equipped.

Cadillac DeVille, Eldorado & Seville

Recommended Service	Service Interval In Miles① 3000	6000	7500	9000	12000	15000	18000	21000	22500	24000	27000	30000	33000	36000	37500	39000	42000	45000	48000	51000	52500	54000	57000	60000	63000	66000	67500	69000	72000	75000	78000	81000	82500	84000	87000	90000	93000	96000	97500	99000
BODY																																								
Flush Vehicle Underside, Inspect Drain Holes	At Least Every 12 Months																																							
Inspect Lamps, Seat Belts & Warning Devices	At Least Once Every 6 Months																																							
Replace Passenger Compartment Air Filter						X						X						X						X						X						X				
BRAKES																																								
Inspect Brake System	Every 7500 Miles																																							
Inspect Parking Brake Operation	At Least Once Every 12 Months																																							
Lubricate Parking Brake Cable Guides		S	N		S	N	S		N	S		X		S	N		S	N	S		N	S		X		S	N		S	N	S		N	S		X		S	N	
CLUTCH & TRANSAXLE																																								
Change Automatic Transmission Fluid & Filter, 2000	No Normal Service Required; Severe Service Every 50,000 Miles																																							
Change Automatic Transmission Fluid & Filter, 2001–02 Eldorado	Normal Service Every 100,000 Miles; Severe Service Every 50,000 Miles																																							
Change Automatic Transmission Fluid & Filter, 2001–03 Except Eldorado②	No Normal Service Required; Severe Service Every 50,000 Miles																																							
Inspect Neutral Safety & BTSI Operation		S	N		S	N	S		N	S		X		S	N		S	N	S		N	S		X		S	N		S	N	S		N	S		X		S	N	
Lubricate Transmission Shift Linkage		S	N		S	N	S		N	S		X		S	N		S	N	S		N	S		X		S	N		S	N	S		N	S		X		S	N	
DRIVESHAFT																																								
Inspect CV Joint Boots	At Engine Oil Changes & Tire Rotations																																							
ENGINE																																								
Change Engine Coolant	Every 60 Months Or 150,000 Miles																																							
Change Engine Oil & Filter	S	S	N	S	S	X	S	S	N	S	S	X	S	S	N	S	S	X	S	S	N	S	S	X	S	S	N	S	S	X	S	S	N	S	S	X	S	S	N	S
Inspect Drive Belts & EGR System, 2000–02	Every 60,000 Miles																																							
Inspect Exhaust System	At Engine Oil Changes																																							
Inspect Fuel & PCV System												X												X												X				
Inspect Spark Plug Wires	At Spark Plug Changes																																							

Recommended Service	3000	6000	7500	9000	12000	15000	18000	21000	22500	24000	27000	30000	33000	36000	37500	39000	42000	45000	48000	51000	52500	54000	57000	60000	63000	66000	67500	69000	72000	75000	78000	81000	82500	84000	87000	90000	93000	96000	97500	99000
	Service Interval In Miles①																																							
ENGINE																																								
Inspect Thermostatically Controlled Air Cleaner Operation												X												X												X				
Inspect Throttle Linkage Operation	At Engine Oil Or Air Cleaner Element Changes																																							
Replace Air Filter	Every 30,000 Miles																																							
Replace PCV Valve												X												X												X				
Replace Spark Plugs	Every 100,000 Miles																																							
STEERING, SUSPENSION & TIRES																																								
Inspect Steering & Suspension System	At Tire Rotations																																							
Lubricate Chassis & Suspension		S	N		S	N	S		N	S		X		S	N		S	N	S		N	S		X		S	N		S	N	S		N	S		X		S	N	
Rotate Tires, 2000	Normal Service Inspect For Wear & Rotate Every 7500 Miles; Severe Service Every 6000 Miles																																							
Rotate Tires, 2001–03	Inspect For Wear & Rotate Every 7500 Miles																																							

N — Normal Service
S — Severe Service
X — Normal Or Severe Service
BTSI — Brake Transmission Shift Interlock
IAC — Idle Air Control
ISC — Idle Speed Control System
① — After vehicle passes 99,000 mile mark return to beginning of mileage table & start cycle over again.
② — No normal service required until message Change Trans Fluid appears on the drivers information center.

Chevrolet Camaro & Pontiac Firebird

Service Interval In Miles①

Recommended Service	3000	6000	7500	9000	12000	15000	18000	21000	22500	24000	27000	30000	33000	36000	37500	39000	42000	45000	48000	51000	52500	54000	57000	60000	63000	66000	67500	69000	72000	75000	78000	81000	82500	84000	87000	90000	93000	96000	97500	99000
BODY																																								
Clean Power Antenna Mast		S	N		S	N	S		N	S		X		S	N		S	N	S		N	S		X		S	N		S	N	S		N	S		X		S	N	
Flush Vehicle Underside, Inspect Drain Holes	At Least Every 12 Months																																							
Inspect Lamps, Seat Belts & Warning Devices	At Least Once Every 6 Months																																							
Lubricate Hinges, Latches, Lock Cylinders & Strikers	At Engine Oil Changes Or At Least Every 12 Months																																							
Replace Passenger Compartment Air Filter						X						X						X						X						X						X				
BRAKES																																								
Inspect Brake System, 2000–01	Normal Service At 7500 Miles, Then Every 10,000 Miles Thereafter; Severe Service Every 7500 Miles																																							
Inspect Parking Brake Operation	At Least Once Every 12 Months																																							
Lubricate Parking Brake Cable Guides		S	N		S	N	S		N	S		X		S	N		S	N	S		N	S		X		S	N		S	N	S		N	S		X		S	N	
CLUTCH & TRANSAXLE																																								
Change Automatic Transmission Fluid & Filter, 2000	Normal Service Every 100,000 Miles; Severe Service Every 50,000 Miles																																							
Change Automatic Transmission Fluid & Filter, 2001–02	Normal Service Every 50,000 Miles; Severe Service Every 15,000 Miles																																							
Inspect Neutral Safety & BTSI Operation		S	N		S	N	S		N	S		X		S	N		S	N	S		N	S		X		S	N		S	N	S		N	S		X		S	N	
Lubricate Transmission Shift Linkage		S	N		S	N	S		N	S		X		S	N		S	N	S		N	S		X		S	N		S	N	S		N	S		X		S	N	
ENGINE																																								
Change Engine Coolant, 2000	Every 60 Months Or 150,000 Miles																																							
Change Engine Coolant, 2001–02	Every 60 Months Or 240,000 Miles																																							
Change Engine Oil & Filter	S	S	N	S	S	X	S	S	N	S	S	X	S	S	N	S	S	X	S	S	N	S	S	X	S	S	N	S	S	X	S	S	N	S	S	X	S	S	N	S
Inspect Drive Belts	Every 60,000 Miles																																							
Inspect EGR System												X												X												X				
Inspect Exhaust System	At Engine Oil Changes																																							
Inspect Fuel Filler Cap												X												X												X				

Recommended Service	Service Interval In Miles①																																							
	3000	6000	7500	9000	12000	15000	18000	21000	22500	24000	27000	30000	33000	36000	37500	39000	42000	45000	48000	51000	52500	54000	57000	60000	63000	66000	67500	69000	72000	75000	78000	81000	82500	84000	87000	90000	93000	96000	97500	99000
ENGINE																																								
Inspect Fuel System Hoses, Lines & Connections												X												X												X				
Inspect PCV Valve												X												X												X				
Inspect Spark Plug Wires	At Spark Plug Changes																																							
Inspect TBI Unit Mounting Fastener Security		S	N																																					
Inspect Thermostatically Controlled Air Cleaner Operation												X												X												X				
Inspect Throttle Linkage Operation	At Air Cleaner Element Changes																																							
Replace Air Filter & PCV Filter, 2000②	Inspect & Replace If Necessary Every 10,000 Miles																																							
Replace Air Filter, 2001–02	Inspect & Replace If Necessary Every 15,000 Miles																																							
Replace Spark Plugs	Every 100,000 Miles																																							
STEERING, SUSPENSION & TIRES																																								
Inspect Steering & Suspension System	At Tire Rotations																																							
Lubricate Chassis & Suspension		S	N		S	N	S		N	S		X		S	N		S	N	S		N	S		X		S	N		S	N	S		N	S		X		S	N	
Rotate Tires		S	N				S		N			S			N		S				N	S					X					S	N				S		N	

N — Normal Service
S — Severe Service
X — Normal Or Severe Service
BTSI — Brake Transmission Shift Interlock
IAC — Idle Air Control
ISC — Idle Speed Control System
① — After vehicle passes 99,000 mile mark return to beginning of mileage table & start cycle over again.
② — The U.S. Environmental Protection Agency or the California Air Resources Board has determined the failure to perform this maintenance item will not nullify the emission warranty or limit recall liability prior to the completion of the vehicle's useful life. The vehicle manufacturer however, urge that all recommended maintenance services be performed at the indicated intervals & the maintenance be recorded.

Chevrolet Cavalier & Pontiac Sunfire

Service Interval In Miles①

Recommended Service	3000	6000	7500	9000	12000	15000	18000	21000	22500	24000	27000	30000	33000	36000	37500	39000	42000	45000	48000	51000	52500	54000	57000	60000	63000	66000	67500	69000	72000	75000	78000	81000	82500	84000	87000	90000	93000	96000	97500	99000
BODY																																								
Inspect Lamps, Seat Belt & Warning Devices	At Least Once Every 6 Months																																							
Lubricate Hinges, Latches, Lock Cylinders & Strikers	At Engine Oil Changes Or At Least Every 12 Months																																							
Replace Passenger Compartment Air Filter						X						X						X						X						X						X				
BRAKES																																								
Inspect Brake System, 2000	Normal Service At 7500 Miles, Then Every 10,000 Miles Thereafter; Severe Service Every 7500 Miles																																							
Inspect Brake System, 2001	Normal Service At 7500 Miles, Then Every 10,000 Miles Thereafter; Severe Service Every 6000 Miles																																							
Inspect Brake System, 2002–04	Normal Service At 7500 Miles; Severe Service Every 6000 Miles																																							
Inspect Parking Brake Operation	At Least Once Every 12 Months																																							
Lubricate Parking Brake Cable Guides		S	N		S	N	S		N	S		X		S	N		S	N	S		N	S		X		S	N		S	N	S		N	S		X		S	N	
CLUTCH & TRANSAXLE																																								
Change Automatic Transmission Fluid & Filter	No Normal Service Required; Severe Service Every 50,000 Miles																																							
Inspect Neutral Safety & BTSI Operation & Lubricate Shift Linkage		S	N		S	N	S		N	S		X		S	N		S	N	S		N	S		X		S	N		S	N	S		N	S		X		S	N	
DRIVESHAFT																																								
Inspect CV Joint Boots	At Tire Rotations																																							
ENGINE																																								
Change Engine Coolant	Every 60 Months Or 150,000 Miles																																							
Change Engine Oil & Filter, Less Turbo	S	S	N	S	S	X	S	S	N	S	S	X	S	S	N	S	S	X	S	S	N	S	S	X	S	S	N	S	S	X	S	S	N	S	S	X	S	S	N	S
Change Engine Oil & Filter, w/Turbo	X	X		X	X	X	X	X		X	X	X	X	X		X	X	X	X	X		X	X	X	X	X		X	X	X	X	X		X	X	X	X	X		X
Inspect Drive Belt, 2004	Every 150,000 Miles																																							
Inspect Drive Belts & EGR System & Fuel & PCV System												X												X												X				
Inspect Exhaust System	At Engine Oil Changes																																							
Inspect CNG Fuel Lines & Fittings 2000, Cavalier CNG	Every 7500 Miles																																							

Recommended Service	Service Interval In Miles①																																							
	3000	6000	7500	9000	12000	15000	18000	21000	22500	24000	27000	30000	33000	36000	37500	39000	42000	45000	48000	51000	52500	54000	57000	60000	63000	66000	67500	69000	72000	75000	78000	81000	82500	84000	87000	90000	93000	96000	97500	99000
ENGINE																																								
Inspect CNG Fuel Hoses & Clamps 2000, Cavalier CNG	Every 7500 Miles																																							
Inspect Fill Valve O-Ring 2000, Cavalier CNG	Every 7500 Miles																																							
Inspect HPR Filter 2000, Cavalier CNG	Every 60,000 Miles																																							
Inspect Spark Plug Wires	At Spark Plug Changes																																							
Inspect Thermostatically Controlled Air Cleaner Operation												X												X												X				
Inspect Throttle Linkage Operation	At Engine Oil Or Air Cleaner Element Changes																																							
Replace Air Filter & PCV Filter, 2000–01						S						X						S						X						S						X				
Replace Air Filter, 2002–04												X												X												X				
Replace Spark Plugs, Except CNG	Every 100,000 Miles																																							
Replace Spark Plugs, 2000, Cavalier CNG	Every 60,000 Miles																																							
STEERING, SUSPENSION & TIRES																																								
Inspect Steering & Suspension System	At Tire Rotations																																							
Lubricate Chassis & Suspension		S	N		S	N	S		N	S		X		S	N		S	N	S		N	S		X		S	N		S	N	S		N	S		X		S	N	
Rotate Tires	Normal Service Inspect For Wear & Rotate Every 7500 Miles; Severe Service Every 6000 Miles																																							

CNG — Compressed Natural Gas
N — Normal Service
S — Severe Service
X — Normal Or Severe Service
BTSI — Brake Transmission Shift Interlock
IAC — Idle Air Control
ISC — Idle Speed Control System
① — After vehicle passes 99,000 mile mark return to beginning of mileage table & start cycle over again.

Chevrolet Corvette

Recommended Service	Service Interval In Miles① 3000	6000	7500	9000	12000	15000	18000	21000	22500	24000	27000	30000	33000	36000	37500	39000	42000	45000	48000	51000	52500	54000	57000	60000	63000	66000	67500	69000	72000	75000	78000	81000	82500	84000	87000	90000	93000	96000	97500	99000
BODY																																								
Clean Power Antenna Mast		S	N		S	N	S		N	S		X		S	N		S	N	S		N	S		X		S	N		S	N	S		N	S		X		S	N	
Inspect Lamps, Seat Belts & Warning Devices	At Least Once Every 6 Months																																							
Lubricate Hinges, Latches, Lock Cylinders & Strikers	At Engine Oil Changes Or At Least Every 12 Months																																							
Replace Passenger Compartment Air Filter						X						X						X						X						X						X				
BRAKES																																								
Inspect Brake System	Normal Service At 7500 Miles, Then Every 10,000 Miles Thereafter; Severe Service Every 7500 Miles																																							
Inspect Parking Brake Operation	At Least Once Every 12 Months																																							
Lubricate Parking Brake Cable Guides		S	N		S	N	S		N	S		X		S	N		S	N	S		N	S		X		S	N		S	N	S		N	S		X		S	N	
CLUTCH & TRANSAXLE																																								
Change Automatic Transmission Fluid & Filter	Normal Service Every 100,000 Miles; Severe Service Every 50,000 Miles																																							
Inspect Neutral Safety & BTSI Operation & Lubricate Shift Linkage		S	N		S	N	S		N	S		X		S	N		S	N	S		N	S		X		S	N		S	N	S		N	S		X		S	N	
ENGINE																																								
Change Engine Coolant	Every 60 Months Or 150,000 Miles																																							
Change Engine Oil & Filter, ②	Normal Service Every 12 Months Or As Indicated By Oil Life Monitor; Severe Service Every 3000 Miles																																							
Inspect Air Cleaner Element	Every 15,000 Miles																																							
Inspect Drive Belts, EGR, Fuel & PCV System												X												X												X				
Inspect Exhaust System	At Engine Oil Changes																																							
Inspect Fuel System	Every 25,000 Miles																																							
Inspect Spark Plug Wires	At Spark Plug Changes																																							
Inspect TBI Unit Mounting Fastener Security		S	N																																					
Inspect Thermostatically Controlled Air Cleaner Operation												X												X												X				
Inspect Throttle Linkage Operation	At Air Cleaner Element Changes																																							
Replace Air Filter	Every 30,000 Miles																																							

Recommended Service	Service Interval In Miles①																																							
	3000	6000	7500	9000	12000	15000	18000	21000	22500	24000	27000	30000	33000	36000	37500	39000	42000	45000	48000	51000	52500	54000	57000	60000	63000	66000	67500	69000	72000	75000	78000	81000	82500	84000	87000	90000	93000	96000	97500	99000
ENGINE																																								
Replace Spark Plugs	Every 100,000 Miles																																							
STEERING, SUSPENSION & TIRES																																								
Inspect Steering & Suspension System	At Tire Rotations																																							
Lubricate Chassis & Suspension		S	N		S	N	S		N	S		X		S	N		S	N	S		N	S		X		S	N		S	N	S		N	S		X		S	N	

N — Normal Service
S — Severe Service
X — Normal Or Severe Service
BTSI — Brake Transmission Shift Interlock
IAC — Idle Air Control
ISC — Idle Speed Control System
① — After vehicle passes 99,000 mile mark return to beginning of mileage table & start cycle over again.
② — If equipped, the engine oil life monitor will indicate when to change engine oil, usually 3000–10,000 miles. Under severe driving conditions, engine oil may need to be changed before 3000 miles. If vehicle is driven in a dusty area, change engine oil every 3000 miles.

Chevrolet Malibu, Oldsmobile Alero & Pontiac Grand Am

Recommended Service	Service Interval In Miles①																																							
	3000	6000	7500	9000	12000	15000	18000	21000	22500	24000	27000	30000	33000	36000	37500	39000	42000	45000	48000	51000	52500	54000	57000	60000	63000	66000	67500	69000	72000	75000	78000	81000	82500	84000	87000	90000	93000	96000	97500	99000
BODY																																								
Clean Power Antenna Mast		S	N		S	N	S		N	S		X		S	N		S	N	S		N	S		X		S	N		S	N	S		N	S		X		S	N	
Inspect Lamps, Seat Belts & Warning Devices	At Least Once Every 6 Months																																							
Lubricate Hinges, Latches, Lock Cylinders & Strikers	At Engine Oil Changes Or At Least Every 12 Months																																							
BRAKES																																								
Inspect Brake System	Every 7500 Miles																																							
Inspect Parking Brake Operation	At Least Once Every 12 Months																																							
Lubricate Parking Brake Cable Guides		S	N		S	N	S		N	S		X		S	N		S	N	S		N	S		X		S	N		S	N	S		N	S		X		S	N	
CLUTCH & TRANSAXLE																																								
Change Automatic Transmission Fluid & Filter	No Normal Service Required; Severe Service Every 50,000 Miles																																							
Inspect Neutral Safety & BTSI Operation & Lubricate Shift Linkage		S	N		S	N	S		N	S		X		S	N		S	N	S		N	S		X		S	N		S	N	S		N	S		X		S	N	
DRIVESHAFT																																								
Inspect CV Joint Boots	At Engine Oil Changes & Tire Rotations																																							
ENGINE																																								
Change Engine Coolant	Every 60 Months Or 150,000 Miles																																							
Change Engine Oil & Filter, Less Turbo②	S	S	N	S	S	X	S	S	N	S	S	X	S	S	N	S	S	X	S	S	N	S	S	X	S	S	N	S	S	X	S	S	N	S	S	X	S	S	N	S
Change Engine Oil & Filter, w/Turbo②	X	X		X	X	X	X	X		X	X	X	X	X		X	X	X	X	X		X	X	X	X	X		X	X	X	X	X		X	X	X	X	X		X
Inspect Accessory Drive Belts, 2004	Every 150,000 Miles																																							
Inspect Drive Belts & EGR System, 2000–03	Every 60,000 Miles																																							
Inspect Exhaust System, 2000–03	At Engine Oil Changes																																							
Inspect Exhaust System, 2004	Every 25,000 Miles																																							
Inspect Fuel System, 2000–03	At Each Oil Change																																							

Recommended Service	Service Interval In Miles① 3000	6000	7500	9000	12000	15000	18000	21000	22500	24000	27000	30000	33000	36000	37500	39000	42000	45000	48000	51000	52500	54000	57000	60000	63000	66000	67500	69000	72000	75000	78000	81000	82500	84000	87000	90000	93000	96000	97500	99000
ENGINE																																								
Inspect Fuel System, 2004	Every 25,000 Miles																																							
Inspect Spark Plug Wires	At Spark Plug Changes																																							
Inspect Thermostatically Controlled Air Cleaner Operation & Fuel & PCV System												X												X												X				
Inspect Throttle Linkage Operation	At Air Cleaner Element Changes																																							
Replace Air Filter & PCV Filter, 2003③	Normal Service Every 30,000 Miles; Severe Service Inspect Every 15,000 Miles, Replace Every 30,000 Miles																																							
Replace Air Filter & PCV Filter, 2004③	Every 25,000 Miles																																							
Replace Spark Plugs③	Every 100,000 Miles																																							
Replace Timing Belt																								X																
STEERING, SUSPENSION & TIRES																																								
Inspect Steering & Suspension System	At Tire Rotations																																							
Lubricate Chassis & Suspension		S	N		S	N	S		N	S		X		S	N		S	N	S		N	S		X		S	N		S	N	S		N	S		X		S	N	
Rotate Tires	Inspect for Wear and Rotate Every 7500 Miles																																							

N — Normal Service
S — Severe Service
X — Normal Or Severe Service
BTSI — Brake Transmission Shift Interlock
IAC — Idle Air Control
ISC — Idle Speed Control System

① — After vehicle passes 99,000 mile mark return to beginning of mileage table & start cycle over again.

② — If equipped, the engine oil life monitor will indicate when to change engine oil, usually 3,000–10,000 miles. Under severe driving conditions, engine oil may need to be changed before 3000 miles. If vehicle is driven in a dusty area, change engine oil every 3000 miles.

③ — The U.S. Environmental Protection Agency or the California air Resources Board has determined the failure to perform this maintenance item will not nullify the emission warranty or limit recall liability prior to the completion of the vehicle's useful life. The vehicle manufacturer, however, urge that all recommended maintenance services be performed at the indicated intervals & the maintenance be recorded.

Chevrolet Metro

Recommended Service	Service Interval In Miles①																																							
	3000	6000	7500	9000	12000	15000	18000	21000	22500	24000	27000	30000	33000	36000	37500	39000	42000	45000	48000	51000	52500	54000	57000	60000	63000	66000	67500	69000	72000	75000	78000	81000	82500	84000	87000	90000	93000	96000	97500	99000
BODY																																								
Inspect Seat Belts & Related Components & Lubricate Lock Cylinders	At Least Once Every 12 Months																																							
Inspect Supplemental Restraint System	10 Years From Vehicle Build Date																																							
Inspect Warning Lamps & Devices	S	S	N	S	S	X	S	S	N	S	S	X	S	S	N	S	S	X	S	S	N	S	S	X	S	S	N	S	S	X	S	S	N	S	S	X	S	S	N	S
Lubricate Door Hinges	At Every Engine Oil Change																																							
BRAKES																																								
Change Brake Fluid																								X																
Inspect Brake System		S	N		S				N	S				S	N				S		N			S			N		S				N	S				S	N	
CLUTCH & TRANSAXLE																																								
Change Automatic Transaxle Fluid & Filter	No Normal Service Interval Recommended By Manufacturer; Severe Service Every 50,000 Miles																																							
Change Manual Transaxle Lubricant					S					S		N		S					S					X					S					S		N		S		
Inspect Clutch Pedal Freeplay		S	N		S	N	S		N	S		X		S	N		S	N	S		N	S		X		S	N		S	N	S		N	S		X		S	N	
Inspect Neutral Safety & Shift Interlock Switch Operation	At Least Once Every 12 Months																																							
Inspect Transaxle Fluid & Shift Control Operation	At Every Engine Oil Change																																							
Replace Automatic Transaxle Fluid Cooler Hoses																		X																		X				
DRIVESHAFT																																								
Inspect CV Joint Boots		S	N		S	N	S		N	S		X		S	N		S	N	S		N	S		X		S	N		S	N	S		N	S		X		S	N	
ENGINE																																								
Change Engine Coolant & Inspect Ignition Coils												X												X												X				
Change Engine Oil & Filter	S	S	N	S	S	X	S	S	N	S	S	X	S	S	N	S	S	X	S	S	N	S	S	X	S	S	N	S	S	X	S	S	N	S	S	X	S	S	N	S
Inspect Air Filter Element	S	S		S	S	S	S	S		S	S	S	S	S		S	S	S	S	S		S	S	S	S	S		S	S	S	S	S		S	S	S	S	S		S
Inspect Distributor Cap & Rotor & Drive Belts & PCV Valve						S						S						S						X						S						S				
Inspect Engine Valve Clearance						X						X						X						X						X						X				
Inspect Exhaust, Fuel & EVAP System & Coolant						X						X						X						X						X						X				

Recommended Service	Service Interval In Miles① 3000	6000	7500	9000	12000	15000	18000	21000	22500	24000	27000	30000	33000	36000	37500	39000	42000	45000	48000	51000	52500	54000	57000	60000	63000	66000	67500	69000	72000	75000	78000	81000	82500	84000	87000	90000	93000	96000	97500	99000
ENGINE																																								
Inspect Spark Plug Wires						S						S						S												S						S				
Inspect Warning Lamps	S	S	N	S	S	X	S	S	N	S	S	X	S	S	N	S	S	X	S	S	N	S	S	X	S	S	N	S	S	X	S	S	N	S	S	X	S	S	N	S
Replace Engine Air Filter Element & PCV Filter	Normal Service Every 30,000 Miles; More Frequently In Severe Service Or Dusty Conditions																																							
Replace EVAP Canister Filter	Every 10 Years Or 120,000 Miles																																							
Replace Spark Plugs												X												X												X				
Replace Spark Plug Wires																								X																
Replace Timing Belt	Every 100,000 Miles																																							
STEERING, SUSPENSION & TIRES																																								
Inspect Power Steering, Steering & Suspension & Wheel Bearings		S	N		S	N	S		N	S		X		S	N		S	N	S		N	S		X		S	N		S	N	S		N	S		X		S	N	
Lubricate Chassis & Suspension	At Every Engine Oil Change																																							
Rotate Tires	Normal Service Every 7500 Miles; Severe Service Every 6000 Miles																																							

N — Normal Service
S — Severe Service
X — Normal Or Severe Service
① — After vehicle passes 99,000 mile mark return to beginning of mileage table & start cycle over again.
② — The U.S. Environmental Protection Agency or the California Air Resources Board has determined the failure to perform this maintenance item will not nullify the emission warranty or limit recall liability prior to the completion of the vehicle's useful life. The vehicle manufacturer however, urge that all recommended maintenance services be performed at the indicated intervals & the maintenance be recorded.

Chevrolet Prizm

Recommended Service	Service Interval In Miles①																																						
	3000	6000	7500	9000	12000	15000	18000	21000	22500	24000	27000	30000	33000	36000	37500	39000	42000	45000	48000	51000	52500	54000	57000	60000	63000	66000	67500	69000	72000	75000	78000	81000	82500	84000	87000	90000	93000	96000	97500	99000
BODY																																								
Inspect Body Fastener Security	Severe Service Every 5000 Miles																																							
Inspect Lamps & Warning Devices	S	S	N	S	S	X	S	S	N	S	S	X	S	S	N	S	S	X	S	S	N	S	S	X	S	S	N	S	S	X	S	S	N	S	S	X	S	S	N	S
Inspect Seat Belts & Related Components	At Least Once Every 12 Months																																							
Supplemental Restraint System	10 Years From Vehicle Build Date, Then Every 24 Months Thereafter																																							
Lubricate Lock Cylinders	At Least Once Every 12 Months																																							
BRAKES																																								
Inspect Brake System Hoses, Lines & Connections	Normal Service Every 15,000 Miles; Severe Service Every 5000 Miles																																							
CLUTCH & TRANSAXLE																																								
Change Automatic Transmission Fluid & Filter						S						S						S						S						S						S				
Change Differential & Manual Transaxle Lubricant												S												S												S				
Inspect Neutral Safety & Shift Interlock Switch Operation	At Least Once Every 12 Months																																							
Inspect Transaxle Lubricant Level	At Every Engine Oil Change																																							
DRIVESHAFT																																								
Inspect CV Joint Boots & Tighten Driveshaft Flange	Normal Service Every 15,000 Miles; Severe Service Every 5000 Miles																																							
ENGINE																																								
Change Engine Coolant	Every 24 Months Or 30,000 Miles																																							
Change Engine Oil & Filter	Normal Service Every 7500 Miles; Severe Service Every 3000 Miles																																							
Inspect Cooling System & Drive Belts						X						X						X						X						X						X				
Inspect Engine Valve Clearance																								X																
Inspect EVAP Charcoal Canister	Every 72 Months Or 60,000 Miles																																							
Inspect EVAP & Fuel System						X						X						X						X						X						X				
Inspect Exhaust System					X						X						X						X						X						X					
Inspect Thermostatic Air Cleaner System Operation												X												X												X				

Recommended Service	Service Interval In Miles①																																							
	3000	6000	7500	9000	12000	15000	18000	21000	22500	24000	27000	30000	33000	36000	37500	39000	42000	45000	48000	51000	52500	54000	57000	60000	63000	66000	67500	69000	72000	75000	78000	81000	82500	84000	87000	90000	93000	96000	97500	99000
ENGINE																																								
Replace Air Filter Element & PCV Filter	Normal Service Every 30,000 Miles; More Frequently In Severe Service Or Dusty Conditions																																							
Replace Spark Plugs (Standard Type), 2000–01												X												X												X				
Replace Spark Plugs (Platinum Tip Type), 2000–01																								X																
Replace Spark Plugs, 2002	Every 120,000 Miles																																							
Replace Timing Belt																								X																
STEERING, SUSPENSION & TIRES																																								
Inspect Chassis Fastener Security	Severe Service Every 5000 Miles																																							
Inspect Steering & Suspension			S			X			S			X			S			X			S			X			S			X			S			X			S	
Lubricate Chassis & Suspension	At Every Engine Oil Change																																							
Rotate Tires	Normal Service Every 7500 Miles; Severe Service Every 6000 Miles																																							

N — Normal Service
S — Severe Service
X — Normal Or Severe Service
① — After vehicle passes 99,000 mile mark return to beginning of mileage table & start cycle over again.

Oldsmobile Aurora

Recommended Service	Service Interval In Miles①																																						
	3000	6000	7500	9000	12000	15000	18000	21000	22500	24000	27000	30000	33000	36000	37500	39000	42000	45000	48000	51000	52500	54000	57000	60000	63000	66000	67500	69000	72000	75000	78000	81000	82500	84000	87000	90000	93000	96000	97500	99000
BODY																																								
Clean Power Antenna Mast		S	N		S	N	S		N	S		X		S	N		S	N	S		N	S		X		S	N		S	N	S		N	S		X		S	N	
Inspect Lamps, Seat Belts & Warning Devices	At Least Every 6 Months																																							
Lubricate Hinges, Latches, Lock Cylinders & Strikers	At Engine Oil Changes Or At Least Every 12 Months																																							
Replace Passenger Compartment Air Filter						X						X						X						X						X						X				
BRAKES																																								
Inspect Brake System	Every 7500 Miles																																							
Inspect Parking Brake Operation	At Least Once Every 12 Months																																							
Lubricate Parking Brake Cable Guides		S	N		S	N	S		N	S		X		S	N		S	N	S		N	S		X		S	N		S	N	S		N	S		X		S	N	
CLUTCH & TRANSAXLE																																								
Change Automatic Transmission Fluid & Filter	Normal Service Every 100,000 Miles; Severe Service Every 50,000 Miles																																							
Inspect Neutral Safety & BTSI Operation		S	N		S	N	S		N	S		X		S	N		S	N	S		N	S		X		S	N		S	N	S		N	S		X		S	N	
Lubricate Transmission Shift Linkage		S	N		S	N	S		N	S		X		S	N		S	N	S		N	S		X		S	N		S	N	S		N	S		X		S	N	
DRIVESHAFT																																								
Inspect CV Joint Boots	At Tire Rotations																																							
ENGINE																																								
Change Engine Coolant	Every 60 Months Or 150,000 Miles																																							
Change Engine Oil & Filter, ②	S	S	N	S	S	X	S	S	N	S	S	X	S	S	N	S	S	X	S	S	N	S	S	X	S	S	N	S	S	X	S	S	N	S	S	X	S	S	N	S
Inspect Drive Belts												X												X												X				
Inspect EGR System												X												X												X				
Inspect Exhaust System	At Engine Oil Changes																																							
Inspect Fuel Filler Cap												X												X												X				
Inspect Fuel System Hoses, Lines & Connections												X												X												X				
Inspect PCV Valve												X												X												X				
Inspect Spark Plug Wires	At Spark Plug Changes																																							
Inspect Throttle Body Bores & Plates, Remove Any Deposits						X												X												X										

Recommended Service	Service Interval In Miles①																																							
	3000	6000	7500	9000	12000	15000	18000	21000	22500	24000	27000	30000	33000	36000	37500	39000	42000	45000	48000	51000	52500	54000	57000	60000	63000	66000	67500	69000	72000	75000	78000	81000	82500	84000	87000	90000	93000	96000	97500	99000
ENGINE																																								
Inspect Throttle Linkage Operation	At Air Cleaner Element Changes																																							
Replace Air Filter & PCV Filter						S						X						S						X						S						X				
Replace Spark Plugs	Every 100,000 Miles																																							
STEERING, SUSPENSION & TIRES																																								
Inspect Steering & Suspension System	At Tire Rotations																																							
Lubricate Chassis & Suspension		S	N		S	N	S		N	S		X		S	N		S	N	S		N	S		X		S	N		S	N	S		N	S		X		S	N	
Rotate Tires	Inspect For Wear & Rotate Every 7500 Miles																																							

N — Normal Service
S — Severe Service
X — Normal Or Severe Service
BTSI — Brake Transmission Shift Interlock
IAC — Idle Air Control
ISC — Idle Speed Control System
① — After vehicle passes 99,000 mile mark return to beginning of mileage table & start cycle over again.
② — The Aurora is equipped with a GM Oil Life System which indicate when to change the engine oil & filter. Reset Oil Life System when oil & filter have been changed.

Saturn

Recommended Service	Service Interval In Miles①																																							
	3000	6000	7500	9000	12000	15000	18000	21000	22500	24000	27000	30000	33000	36000	37500	39000	42000	45000	48000	51000	52500	54000	57000	60000	63000	66000	67500	69000	72000	75000	78000	81000	82500	84000	87000	90000	93000	96000	97500	99000
BODY																																								
Inspect Seat Belts & Restraint Systems	At Least Once Every 6 Months																																							
Inspect Wiper Blades & Inserts	At Least Once Every 6 Months																																							
Lubricate Door Check Straps & Hinges		X		X		X		X		X		X		X		X		X		X		X		X		X		X		X		X		X		X		X		X
Lubricate Hood Latch		X		X		X		X		X		X		X		X		X		X		X		X		X		X		X		X		X		X		X		X
Lubricate Headlamp Doors		X		X		X		X		X		X		X		X		X		X		X		X		X		X		X		X		X		X		X		X
Lubricate Sunroof		X		X		X		X		X		X		X		X		X		X		X		X		X		X		X		X		X		X		X		X
Replace Cabin Air Filter, L-Series 2000–03	Every 12 Months Or 12,000 Miles. In Dusty Areas Change More Often																																							
Replace Cabin Air Filter, 2003 Ion	Every 18,000 Miles. In Dusty Areas Change More Often																																							
BRAKES																																								
Add DEX-CVT Additive to VTi Variable Transmission, Ion	Every 50,000 Miles																																							
Inspect Brake Drums & Shoes		X				X				X				X				X				X				X				X				X				X		
Inspect Disc Brake Calipers For Freedom Of Movement (Lubricate If Required)		X				X				X				X				X				X				X				X				X				X		
Inspect Disc Brake Pads & Rotors		X				X				X				X				X				X				X				X				X				X		
Inspect Brake Hoses, Lines & Connections		X				X				X				X				X				X				X				X				X				X		
CLUTCH & TRANSAXLE																																								
Change Automatic Transaxle Fluid & Filter, S-Series 2000	No Normal Service; Severe Every 30,000 Miles																																							
Change Automatic Transaxle Fluid & Filter, L-Series 2004	Normal Service Every 100,000 Miles; Severe Every 50,000 Miles																																							
Change Automatic Transaxle Fluid & Filter, L-Series 2000–03	No Normal Service; Severe Every 50,000 Miles																																							
Change Automatic Transaxle Fluid & Filter, S-Series 2001	No Normal Service; Severe Every 50,000 Miles																																							
Change Automatic Transaxle Fluid & Filter, S-Series 2002	Normal Service Every 100,000 Miles; Severe Every 50,000 Miles																																							
Change Automatic Or VTi Transaxle Fluid & Filter, Ion & Vue 2003	No Normal Service; Severe Every 50,000 Miles																																							

Recommended Service	Service Interval In Miles①																																							
	3000	6000	7500	9000	12000	15000	18000	21000	22500	24000	27000	30000	33000	36000	37500	39000	42000	45000	48000	51000	52500	54000	57000	60000	63000	66000	67500	69000	72000	75000	78000	81000	82500	84000	87000	90000	93000	96000	97500	99000
CLUTCH & TRANSAXLE																																								
Change Automatic Or VTi Transaxle Fluid & Filter, Ion & Vue 2004	Normal Service Every 100,000 Miles; Severe Every 50,000 Miles																																							
DRIVESHAFT																																								
Inspect CV Joint Boots		X		X		X		X		X		X		X		X		X		X		X		X		X		X		X		X		X		X		X		X
ENGINE																																								
Change Engine Coolant & Inspect Pressure Cap, 2000–03	Every 60 Months Or 100,000 Miles																																							
Change Engine Coolant & Inspect Pressure Cap, 2004	Every 60 Months Or 150,000 Miles																																							
Change Engine Oil & Filter②	S	X	S	X	S	X	S	X	S	X	S	X	S	X	S	X	S	X	S	X	S	X	S	X	S	X	S	X	S	X	S	X	S	X	S	X	S	X	S	X
Inspect Air Filter	Severe Service Every 15,000 Miles																																							
Inspect Cooling System & Protection Level						X						X						X						X						X						X				
Inspect Drive Belts & Coolant Hoses, 2000–03	Every 18,000 Miles																																							
Inspect Drive Belts & Coolant Hoses, 2004	Every 25,000 Miles																																							
Inspect Emission Hoses, Lines & Connections, 2000–03	Every 30,000 Miles																																							
Inspect Exhaust System, 2000–03		X		X		X		X		X		X		X		X		X		X		X		X		X		X		X		X		X		X		X		X
Inspect Exhaust System, 2004	Every 25,000 Miles																																							
Inspect Fuel System, 2004	Every 25,000 Miles																																							
Inspect Fuel Hoses, Lines & Connections										X										X										X										X
Inspect Fuel Tank Filler Cap										X										X										X										X
Replace Air Filter, 2000–03	Normal Service Every 30,000 Miles; More Frequently In Severe Service Or Dusty Conditions																																							
Replace Air Filter, 2004	Every 25,000 Miles																																							
Replace Fuel Filter, 2002 S-Series																				X																				X
Replace Fuel Filter, 2000–01, 2002–03 L-Series, Vue & 2003 Ion	Every 100,000 Miles																																							
Replace Fuel Filter, 2004 L-Series	Every 25,000 Miles																																							
Replace Spark Plugs, S-Series 2000–02												X												X												X				
Replace Spark Plugs, L-Series 2000	3.0L V6 At 100,000 Miles; 2.2L L4 At 150,000 Miles																																							

Recommended Service	Service Interval In Miles①																																						
	3000	6000	7500	9000	12000	15000	18000	21000	22500	24000	27000	30000	33000	36000	37500	39000	42000	45000	48000	51000	52500	54000	57000	60000	63000	66000	67500	69000	72000	75000	78000	81000	82500	84000	87000	90000	93000	96000	97500	99000
ENGINE																																								
Replace Spark Plugs, 2001–04 L-Series, 2002–04 Vue & 2003–04 Ion	Every 100,000 Miles																																							
Replace Timing Belt, L-Series 3.0L V6, 2000–04	At 100,000 Miles																																							
STEERING, SUSPENSION & TIRES																																								
Inspect Ball Joint Seals		X		X		X		X		X		X		X		X		X		X		X		X		X		X		X		X		X		X		X		X
Inspect Suspension		X		X		X		X		X		X		X		X		X		X		X		X		X		X		X		X		X		X		X		X
Rotate Tires, 2000–01 & 2002 S-Series		X				X				X				X				X				X				X				X				X				X		
Rotate Tires, 2002 L-Series	Every 12 Months Or 12,000 Miles																																							
Rotate Tires, 2002 Vue & 2003–04 All	Every 6000 Miles																																							

N — Normal Service
S — Severe Service
X — Normal Or Severe Service
BTSI — Brake Transaxle Shift Interlock

① — 2000–S-Series After vehicle passes 100,000 mile mark return to beginning of mileage table & start cycle over again. L-Series After vehicle passes 150,000 mile mark return to beginning of mileage table & start cycle over again. 2001–after vehicle passes 120,000 mile mark return to beginning of mileage table & start cycle over again.

② — On models equipped with Engine Oil Life Monitor, change engine oil when message appears in message display center. Never drive vehicle more then 6000 miles or 6 months without changing oil and filter.

DASH GAUGES & WARNING INDICATORS

NOTE: On Air Bag Equipped Models, Refer To "Air Bag System Precautions" Located In The Front Of This Manual For System Disarming & Arming Procedures.

NOTE: Refer To "Computer Relearn Procedures" Located In The Front Of This Manual When Battery Power To The Computer Has Been Interrupted.

NOTE: "Electrical Symbol & Wire Color Code Identification" Located In The Front Of This Manual May Be Used As An Aid When Using Wiring Circuits Found In This Section.

NOTE: Refer To The "Dash Panel Service" Section For Dash Panel Removal Procedures.

NOTE: Prior To Performing Any Service Operations Listed In This Section, Consult The "Technical Service Bulletins" Section For Related Information.

INDEX

PRECAUTIONS

Air Bag Systems

Refer to "Air Bag System Precautions" in the front of this manual for system disarming and arming procedures.

Battery Ground Cable

Prior to service, disconnect battery ground cable and isolate as required.

TROUBLESHOOTING

Air Bag Warning Lamp

Air bag warning lamp illuminates when there is an air bag system fault.

Refer to **"Diagnosis & Testing" in MOTOR's "Air Bag Manual" or "Air Bag Diagnosis CD"** for diagnosis and testing.

Anti-Lock Brake Warning Lamp

The Anti-lock brake warning lamp will illuminate if the system controller detects any fault in the anti-lock brake system. Normal brake system operation will remain operational, but wheels could lock during panic stop. Refer to "Anti-Lock Brake" chapter.

Brake System Warning Lamp

1. Brake fluid level switch.
2. Low brake fluid level.
3. Park brake system.
4. Wiring circuits and bulb.
5. Instrument cluster printed circuits.

Charging System Warning Lamp

1. Wiring circuits and bulb.
2. Inspect BCM.
3. Inspect for corroded terminals.
4. Alternator (Generator).
5. Instrument cluster printed circuits.

Check Engine Warning Lamp

Check engine or Malfunction Indicator Lamp (MIL) indicator is illuminated by Powertrain Control Module (PCM). Refer to

MOTOR's "Domestic Engine Performance & Driveability Manual" for lamp diagnosis.

Low Fuel Warning Lamp

1. Fuel gauge and indicator bulb.
2. Low fuel level switch.
3. Inspect sensor.
4. Instrument cluster printed circuits.

Oil Pressure Indicator Lamp

1. Wiring circuits, bulb and fuse.
2. Oil pressure switch.
3. Low engine oil level.
4. Instrument cluster printed circuits.

Safety Belt Warning Lamp

1. Seat belt switch and fuse.
2. Wiring circuits and bulb.
3. Instrument cluster printed circuits.

DIAGNOSIS & TESTING

Accessing Diagnostic Trouble Codes

Connect a suitably programmed scan tool to Data Link Connector (DLC), and follow manufacturer's instructions.

Wiring Diagrams

AVENGER

Refer to **Fig. 1,** for wiring diagrams.

BREEZE & CIRRUS

Refer to **Fig. 2,** for wiring diagrams.

CONCORDE, INTREPID, LHS & 300M

Refer to **Figs. 3 through 5,** for wiring diagrams.

NEON

Refer to **Figs. 6 through 8,** for wiring diagrams.

SEBRING & STRATUS

CONVERTIBLE

2000

Refer to **Fig. 9,** for wiring diagrams.

2001-04

Refer to **Figs. 10 and 11,** for wiring diagrams.

COUPE

2000

Refer to **Fig. 1,** for wiring diagrams.

2001-2003

Refer to **Figs. 12 and 13,** for wiring diagrams.

SEDAN

2000

Refer to **Fig. 2,** for wiring diagrams.

2001-04

Refer to **Figs. 10 and 11,** for wiring diagrams.

Symptom Tests

AVENGER

Refer to **Figs. 14 through 19,** for diagnostic tests.

BREEZE & CIRRUS

Refer to **Figs. 20 through 29,** for diagnostic tests.

CONCORDE, INTREPID, LHS & 300M

Refer to **Figs. 30 through 67,** for diagnostic tests.

NEON

2000

Refer to **Figs. 68 through 86,** for diagnostic tests.

2001-04

Refer to **Figs. 87 through 117,** for diagnostic tests.

SEBRING & STRATUS

CONVERTIBLE

2000

Refer to **Figs. 20 through 29,** and **Fig. 118,** for diagnostic tests.

2001

Refer to **Figs. 119 through 145,** for diagnostic tests.

2002-04

Refer to **Figs. 146 through 165,** for diagnostic tests.

COUPE

2000

Refer to **Figs. 14 through 19,** for diagnostic tests.

2001-03

Refer to **Figs. 166 through 174,** for diagnostic tests.

SEDAN

2000

Refer to **Figs. 20 through 29,** for diagnostic tests.

2001

Refer to **Figs. 119 through 145,** for diagnostic tests.

2002-04

Refer to **Figs. 146 through 165,** for diagnostic tests.

Component Tests

FUEL GAUGE SENDING UNIT

AVENGER

1. Measure resistance between fuel gauge sending unit and ground terminals, **Fig. 175.**
2. Resistance at highest point should be 2–6 ohms; at lowest point, 105–119 ohms.
3. Ensure resistance changes smoothly are float slowly moves between highest and lowest points.
4. Measure distance float highest and lowest points touching stopper, **Fig. 176.**
5. If highest measurement is not 1.13 inches and lowest 6.3 inches, adjust arm.
6. Connect thermistor to battery using suitable test lamp and immerse it in water, **Fig. 177.**
7. If lamp goes off when thermistor is in water, gauge is working satisfactory.
8. If lamp does not turn off, replace fuel gauge sending unit.

SEBRING & STRATUS COUPE

2000

Refer to "Avenger" for testing procedures.

2001-03

1. Measure resistance between fuel gauge sending unit and ground terminals, **Fig. 178.**
2. Resistance at highest point should be 3–5 ohms; at lowest point, 110–112 ohms.
3. Ensure resistance changes smoothly are float slowly moves between highest and lowest points.
4. Measure distance float highest and lowest points touching stopper, **Fig. 179.**
5. If highest measurement is not 7.1 inches and lowest .74 inch, adjust arm.

FUEL GAUGE

AVENGER

1. Remove instrument cluster as outlined under "Electrical" section in chassis chapter of **MOTOR's "Auto Repair Manual."**
2. Remove power supply screw.
3. **Do not touch printed board with testing probe.**
4. Measure resistance between power supply and ground terminals. Resistance should be 219–279 ohms.
5. Measure resistance between power supply and fuel gauge terminals. Resistance should be 102–152 ohms.
6. Measure resistance between fuel gauge and ground terminals. Resistance should be 112–132 ohms.

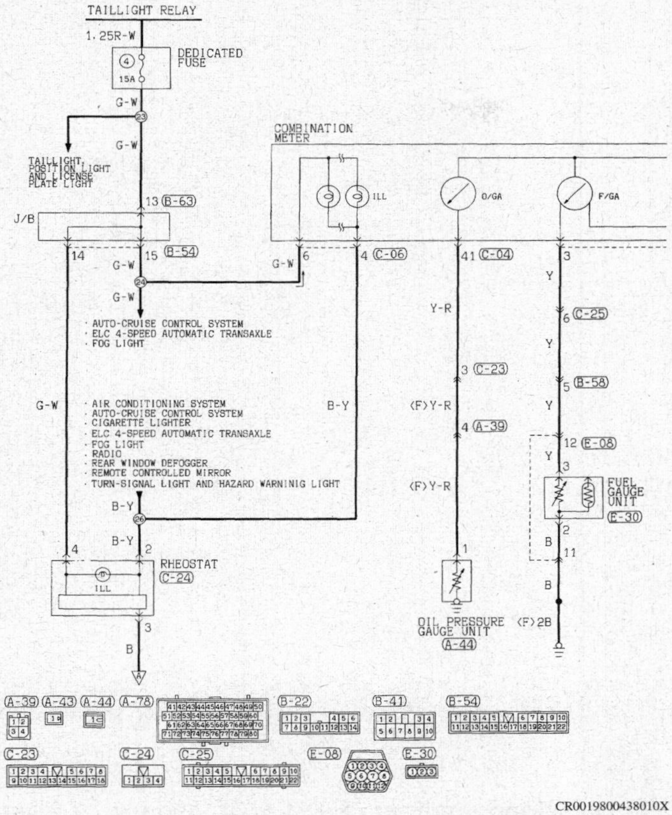

Fig. 1 Wiring diagram (Part 1 of 4). Avenger & 2000 Sebring Coupe

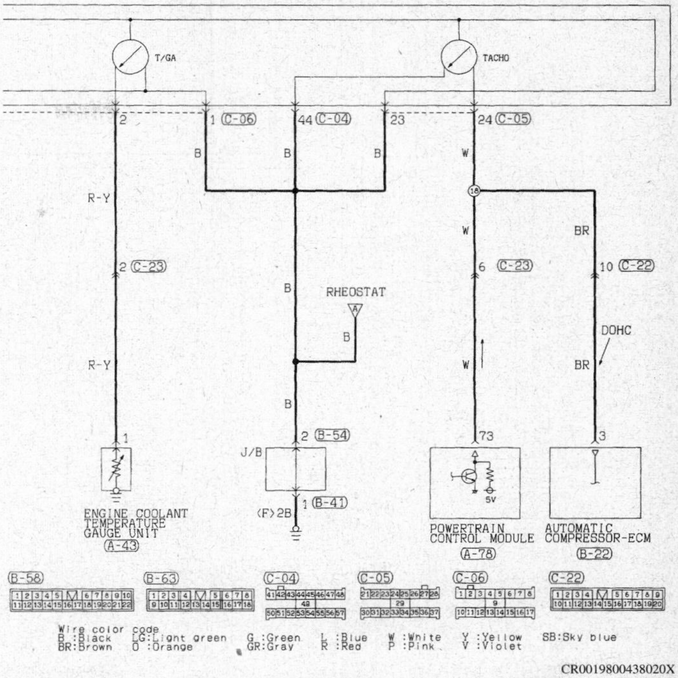

Fig. 1 Wiring diagram (Part 2 of 4). Avenger & 2000 Sebring Coupe

7. If resistance is not as specified, replace fuel gauge.

SEBRING COUPE & STRATUS COUPE

2000

Refer to "Avenger" for testing procedures.

2001-03

1. Remove instrument cluster as outlined under "Electrical" section in chassis chapter of **MOTOR's "Auto Repair Manual."**
2. Remove power supply screw.
3. **Do not touch printed board with testing probe.**
4. Measure resistance between power supply and ground terminals. Resistance should be approximately 233 ohms.
5. Measure resistance between power supply and fuel gauge terminals. Resistance should be approximately 108 ohms.
6. Measure resistance between fuel gauge and ground terminals. Resistance should be approximately 125 ohms.
7. If resistance is not as specified, replace fuel gauge.

ENGINE COOLANT TEMPERATURE (ECT) SENDING UNIT

AVENGER

1. Drain engine coolant into suitable container.
2. Remove ECT sending unit.
3. Immerse unit in 158°F water and measure resistance, **Fig. 180.**
4. If resistance is not 90.5–117.5°F replace sending unit.
5. Apply suitable adhesive to treads and install sending unit and **torque** to 87–102 inch lbs.
6.

SEBRING COUPE & STRATUS COUPE

2000

Refer to "Avenger" for testing procedures.

ENGINE COOLANT TEMPERATURE (ECT) GAUGE

AVENGER

1. Remove instrument cluster as outlined under "Electrical" section in chassis chapter of **MOTOR's "Auto Repair Manual."**
2. Remove power supply screw.
3. **Do not touch printed board with testing probe.**
4. Measure resistance between power supply and ground terminals. Resistance should be 160.9–196.9 ohms.
5. Measure resistance between power supply and ECT gauge terminals. Resistance should be 51.3–56.7 ohms.
6. Measure resistance between ECT gauge and ground terminals. Resistance should be 209.9–255.9 ohms.
7. If resistance is not with in specifications, replace ECT gauge.

SEBRING COUPE & STRATUS COUPE

2000

Refer to "Avenger" for testing procedures.

2001-03

1. Remove instrument cluster as outlined under "Electrical" section in chassis chapter of **MOTOR's "Auto Repair Manual."**
2. Remove power supply screw.
3. **Do not touch printed board with testing probe.**
4. Measure resistance between power supply and ground terminals. Resistance should be approximately 176 ohms.
5. Measure resistance between power supply and ECT gauge terminals. Resistance should be approximately 54 ohms.
6. Measure resistance between ECT

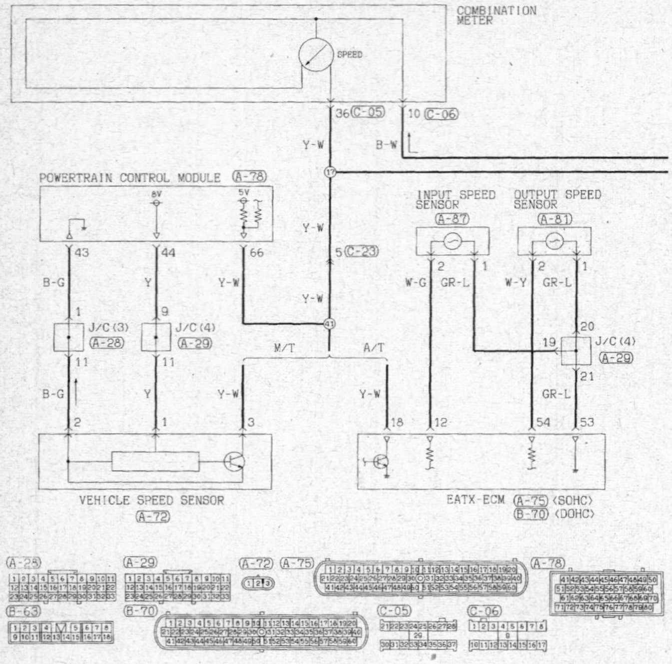

CR0019800438030X

Fig. 1 Wiring diagram (Part 3 of 4). Avenger & 2000 Sebring Coupe

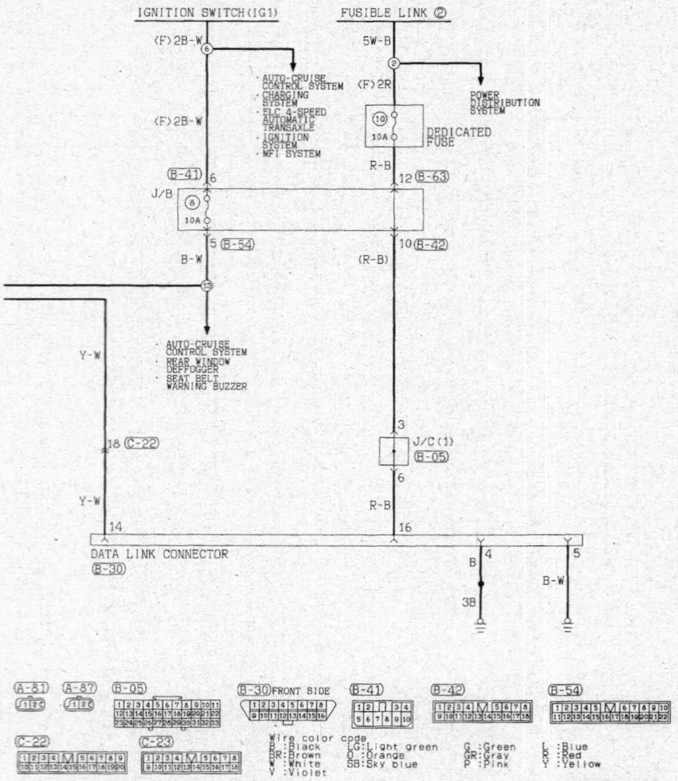

CR0019800438040X

Fig. 1 Wiring diagram (Part 4 of 4). Avenger & 2000 Sebring Coupe

gauge and ground terminals. Resistance should be approximately 230 ohms.

7. If resistance is not with in specifications, replace ECT gauge.

SPEED SENSOR

AVENGER

1. Disconnect input or output speed sensor connector.
2. Measure resistance between input speed sensor connector terminals.
3. If resistance is not .3–1.2 kohms, replace sensor.

SEBRING COUPE & STRATUS COUPE

2000

Refer to "Avenger" for testing procedures.

2001-03

1. Remove vehicle speed sensor.
2. Connect suitable 3–20 kohms resistor, **Fig. 181.**
3. Turn shaft and ensure there are four pulses of voltage every full turn between terminals Nos. 2 and 3.
4. If voltage pulses are not as specified, replace sensor.

OIL PRESSURE GAUGE

AVENGER

1. Remove instrument cluster as outlined under "Electrical" section in chassis chapter of **MOTOR's "Auto Repair Manual."**
2. Remove power supply screw.
3. **Do not touch printed board with testing probe.**
4. Measure resistance between oil pressure gauge terminals.
5. If resistance is not 40–44 ohms, replace gauge.

SEBRING COUPE & STRATUS COUPE

2000

Refer to "Avenger" for testing procedures.

Clearing Diagnostic Trouble Codes

Connect a suitably programmed scan tool to Data Link Connector (DLC), and follow manufacturer's instructions.

Diagnostic Trouble Codes (DTC) will be automatically cleared after 50 key cycles.

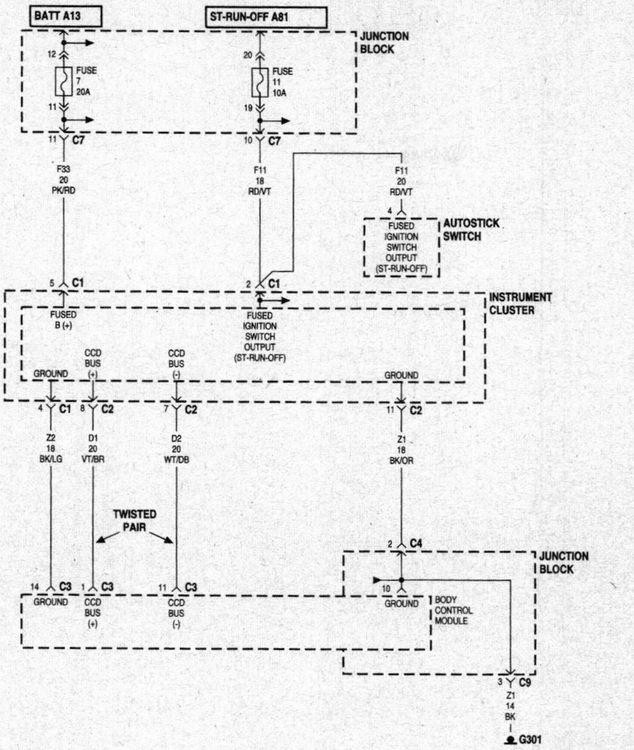

CR4099900439010X

Fig. 2 Wiring diagram (Part 1 of 7). Breeze, Cirrus & 2000 Stratus

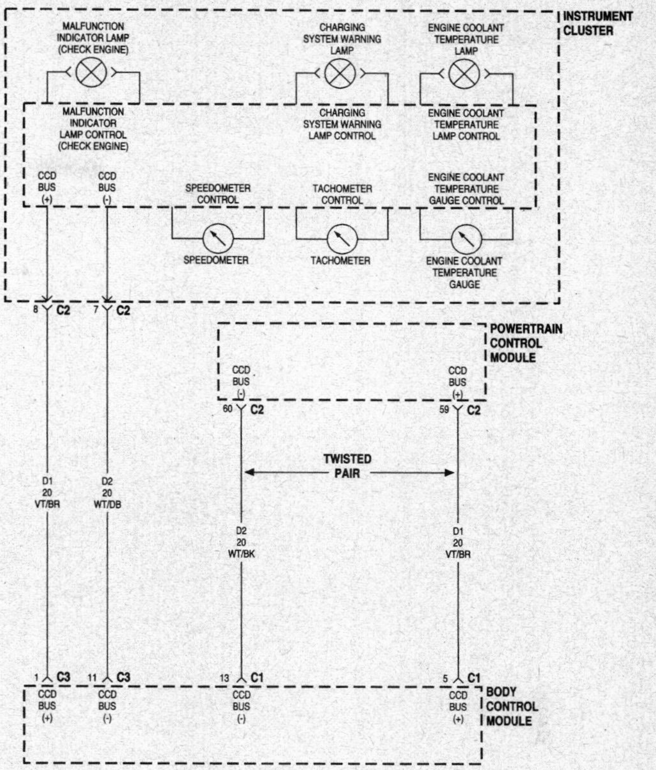

CR4099900439020X

Fig. 2 Wiring diagram (Part 2 of 7). Breeze, Cirrus & 2000 Stratus

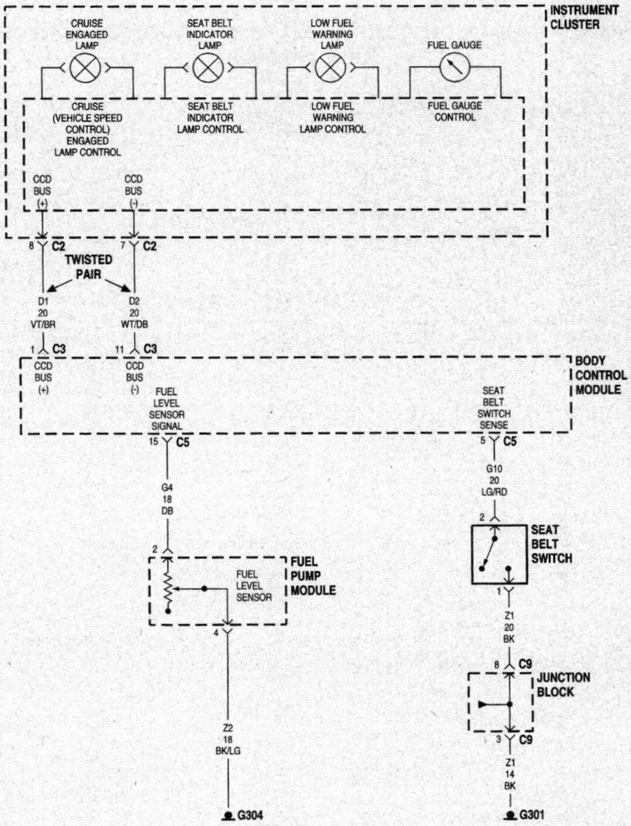

CR4099900439030X

Fig. 2 Wiring diagram (Part 3 of 7). Breeze, Cirrus & 2000 Stratus

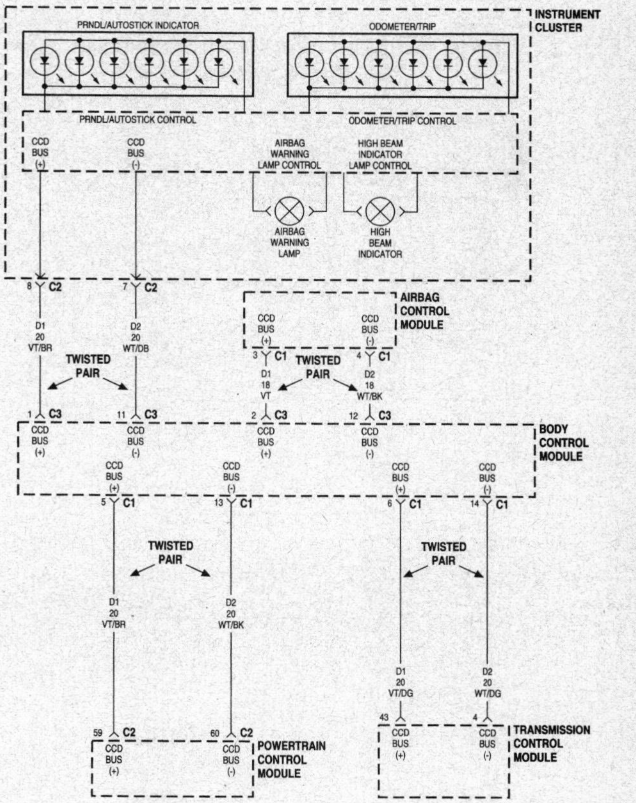

CR4099900439040X

Fig. 2 Wiring diagram (Part 4 of 7). Breeze, Cirrus & 2000 Stratus

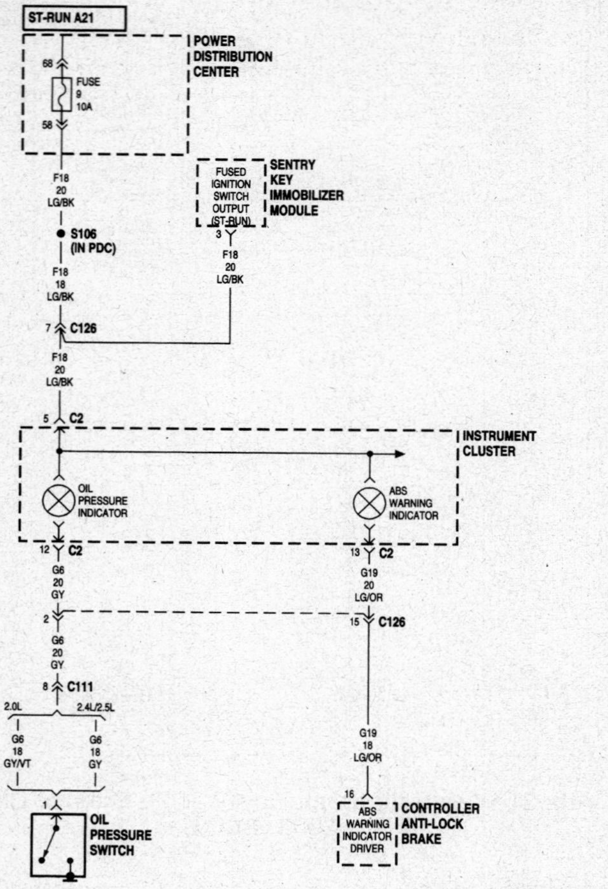

CR4099900439050X

Fig. 2 Wiring diagram (Part 5 of 7). Breeze, Cirrus & 2000 Stratus

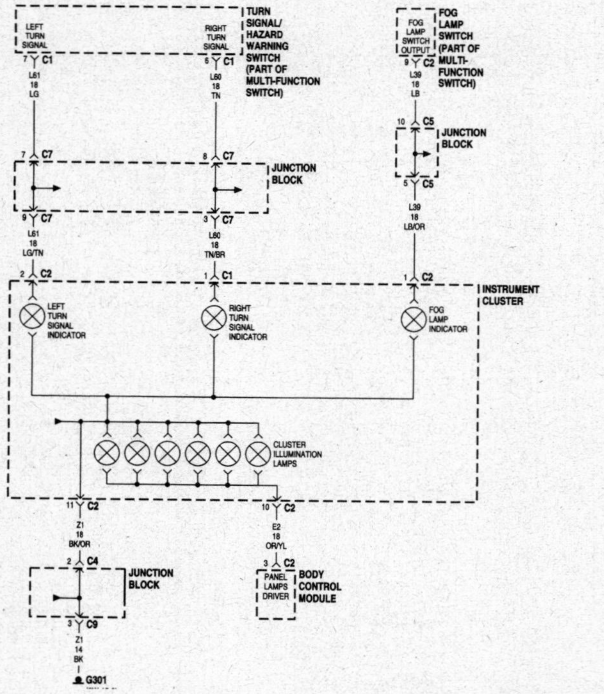

CR4099900439070X

Fig. 2 Wiring diagram (Part 7 of 7). Breeze, Cirrus & 2000 Stratus

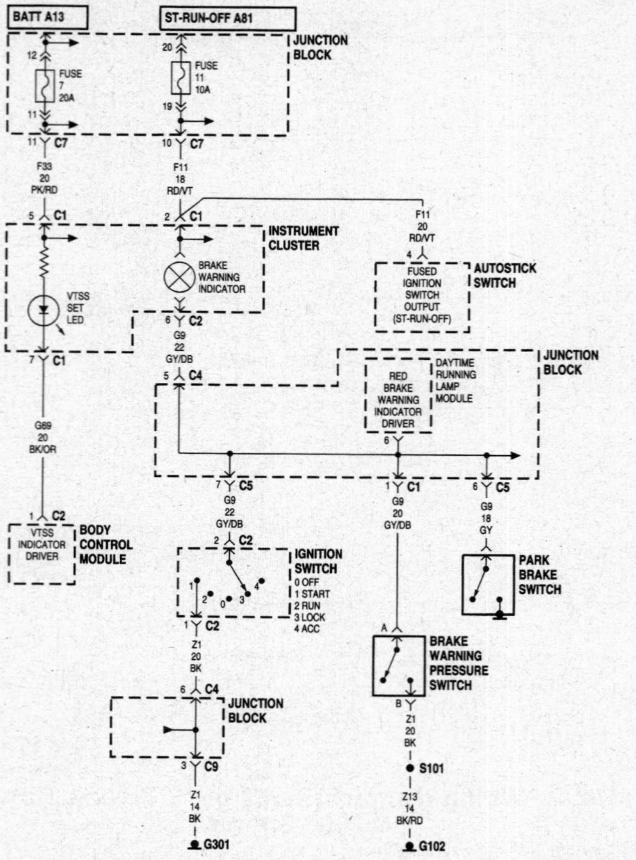

CR4099900439060X

Fig. 2 Wiring diagram (Part 6 of 7). Breeze, Cirrus & 2000 Stratus

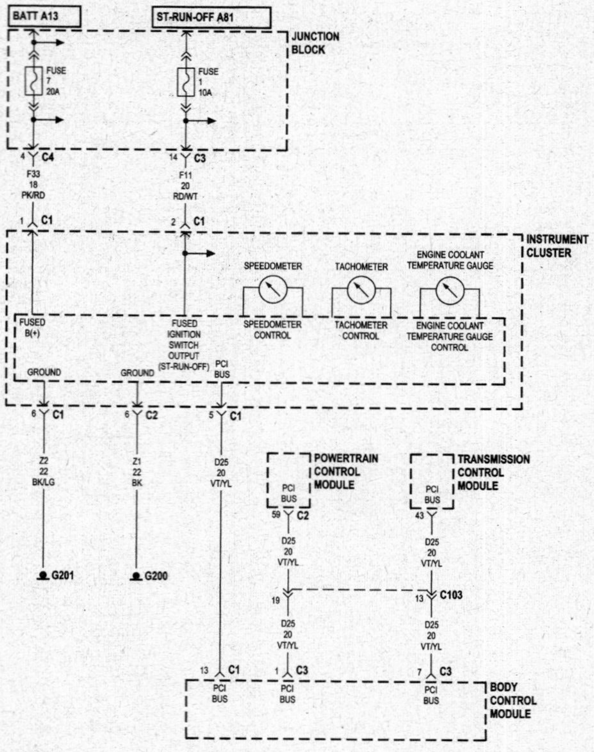

CR9049900467010X

Fig. 3 Wiring diagram (Part 1 of 8). 2000 Concorde, Intrepid, LHS & 300M

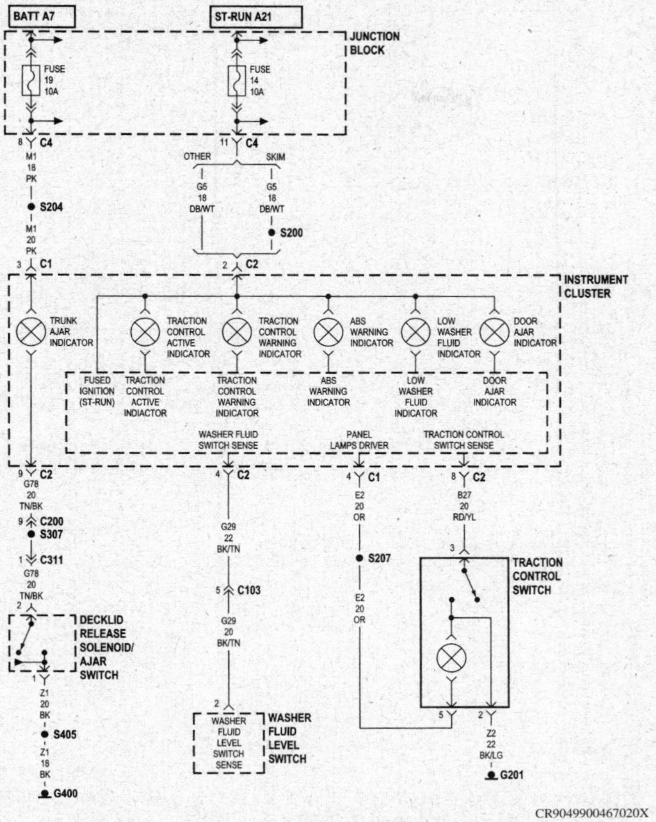

Fig. 3 Wiring diagram (Part 2 of 8). 2000 Concorde, Intrepid, LHS & 300M

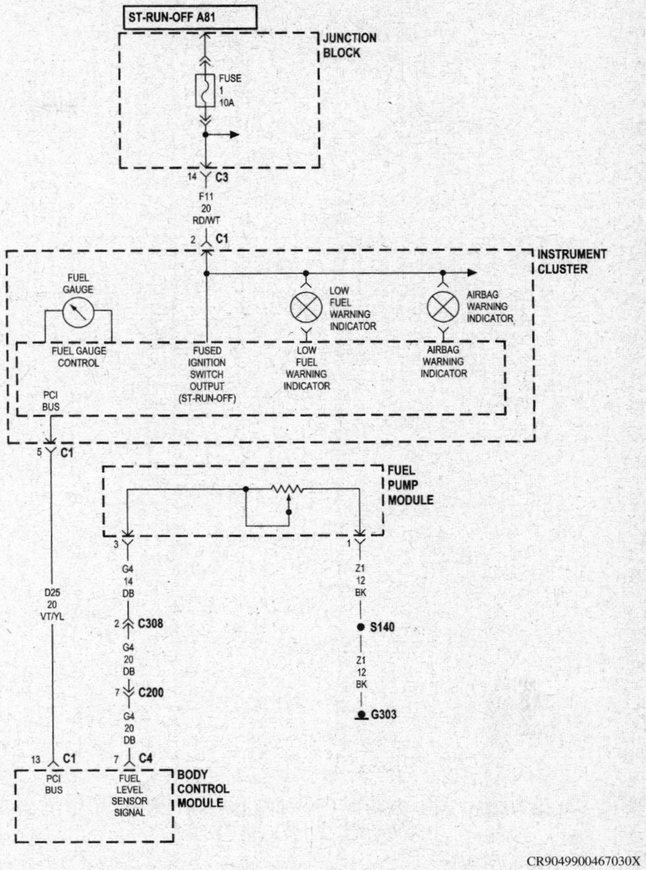

Fig. 3 Wiring diagram (Part 3 of 8). 2000 Concorde, Intrepid, LHS & 300M

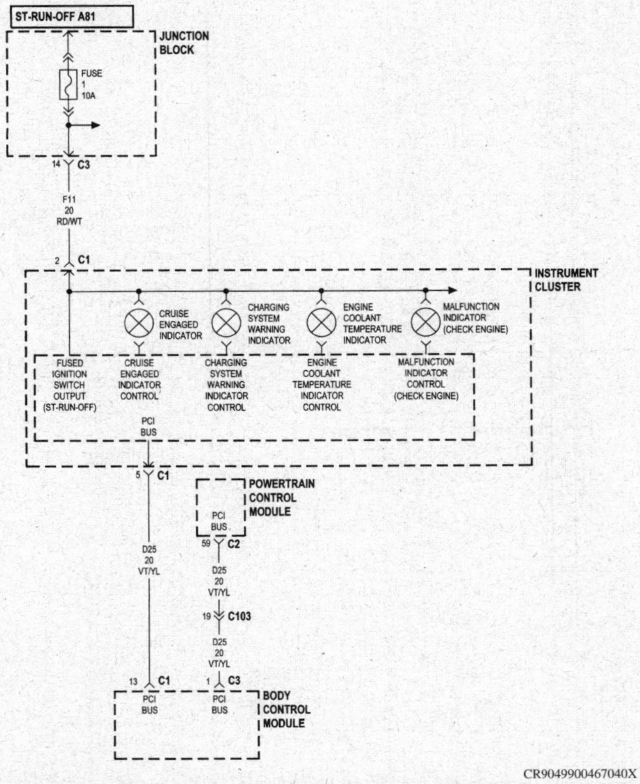

Fig. 3 Wiring diagram (Part 4 of 8). 2000 Concorde, Intrepid, LHS & 300M

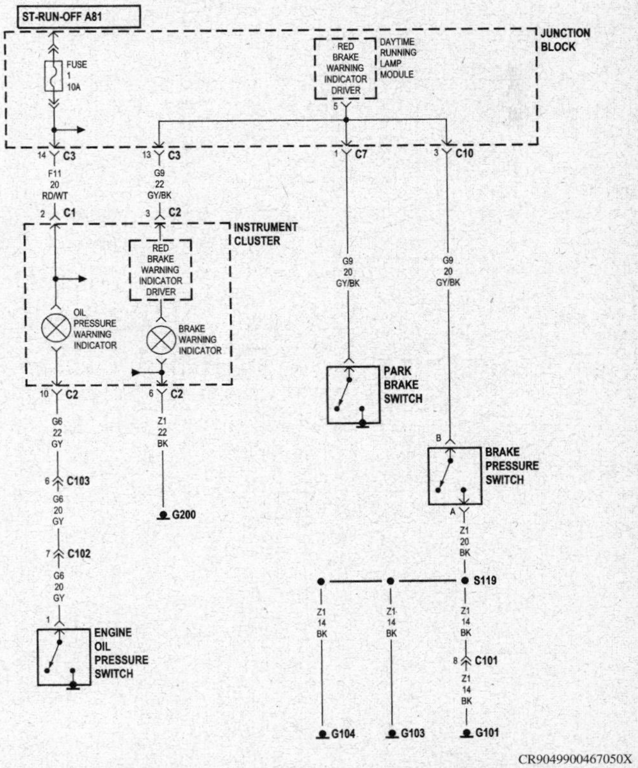

Fig. 3 Wiring diagram (Part 5 of 8). 2000 Concorde, Intrepid, LHS & 300M

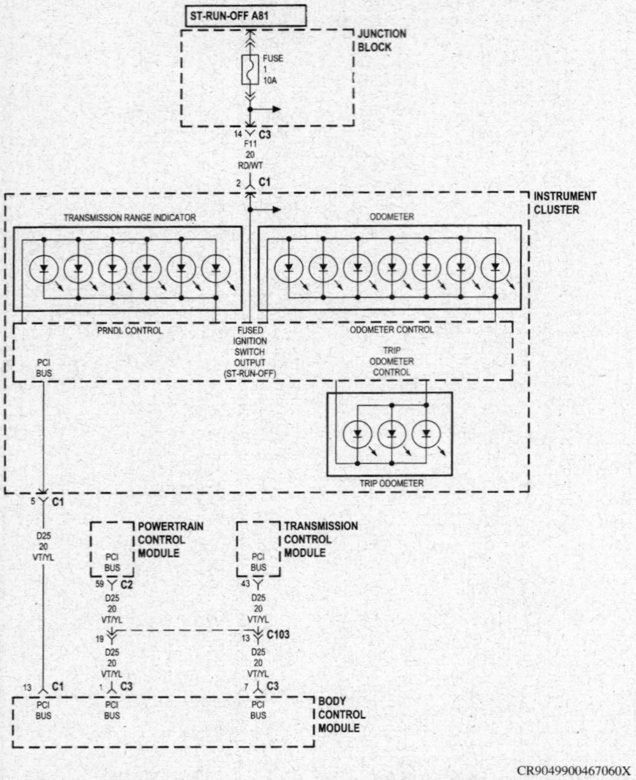

Fig. 3 Wiring diagram (Part 6 of 8). 2000 Concorde, Intrepid, LHS & 300M

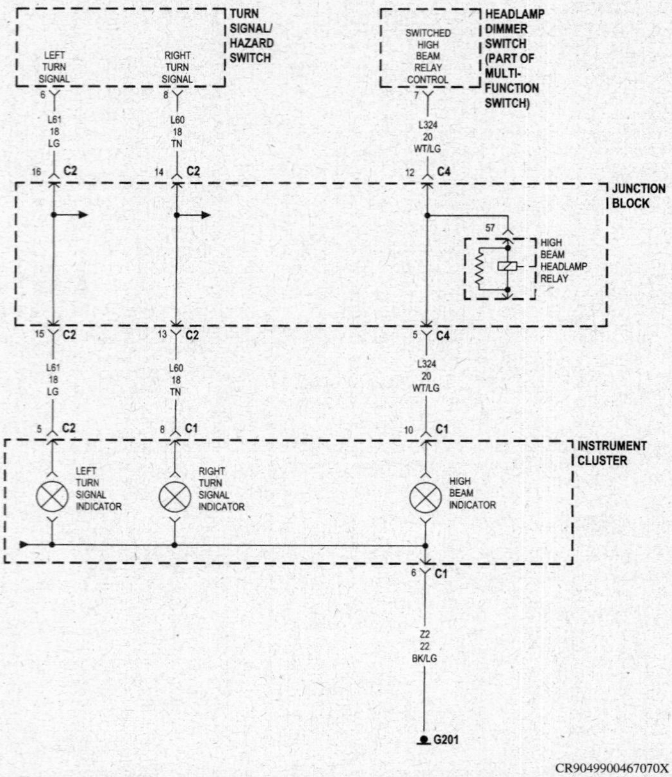

Fig. 3 Wiring diagram (Part 7 of 8). 2000 Concorde, Intrepid, LHS & 300M

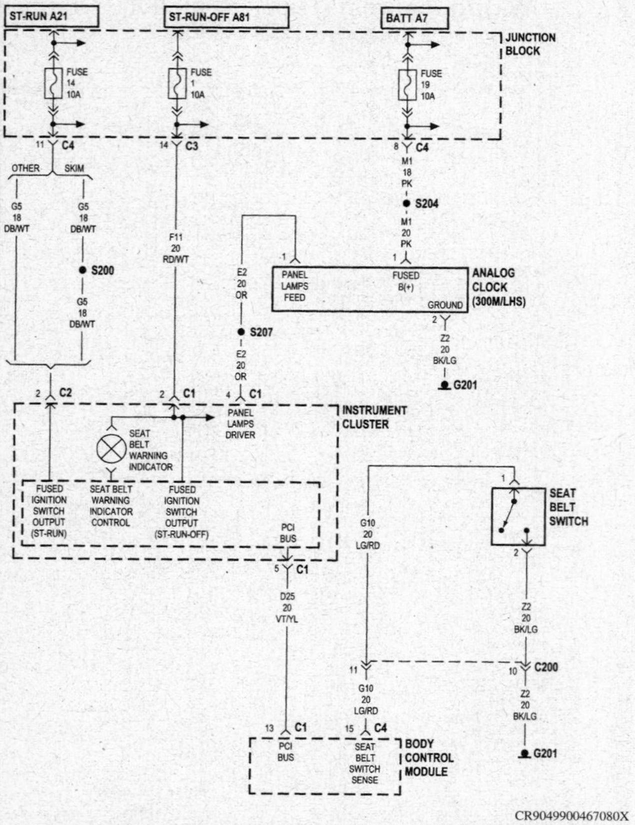

Fig. 3 Wiring diagram (Part 8 of 8). 2000 Concorde, Intrepid, LHS & 300M

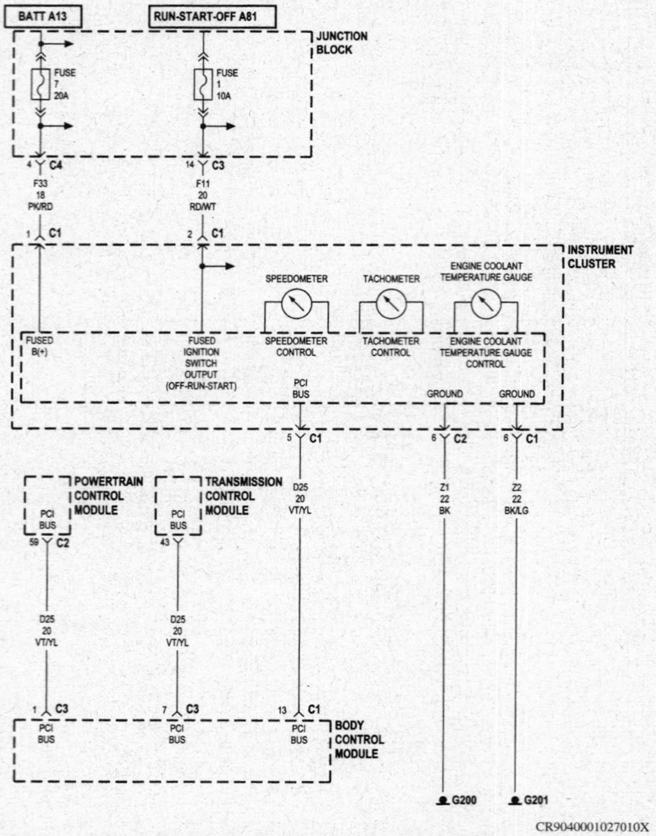

Fig. 4 Wiring diagram (Part 1 of 8). 2001 Concorde, Intrepid, LHS & 300M

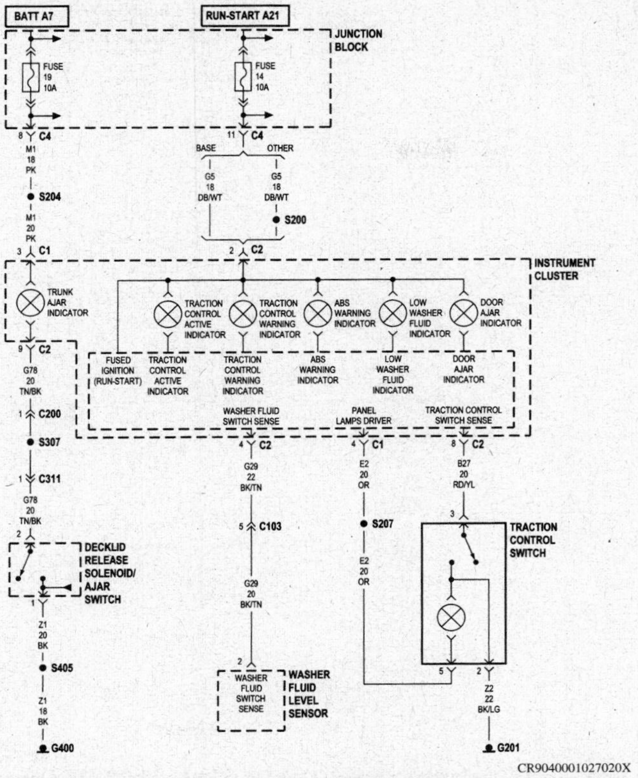

Fig. 4 Wiring diagram (Part 2 of 8). 2001 Concorde, Intrepid, LHS & 300M

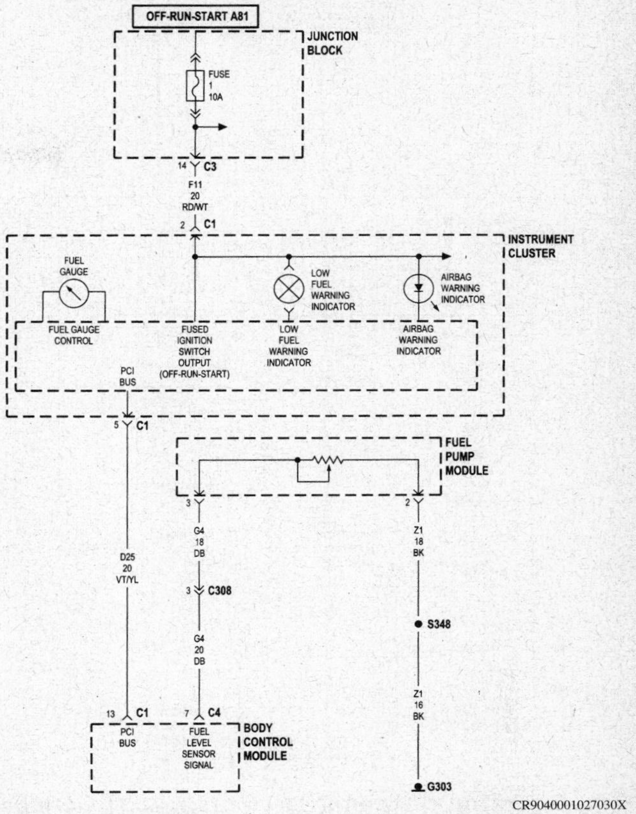

Fig. 4 Wiring diagram (Part 3 of 8). 2001 Concorde, Intrepid, LHS & 300M

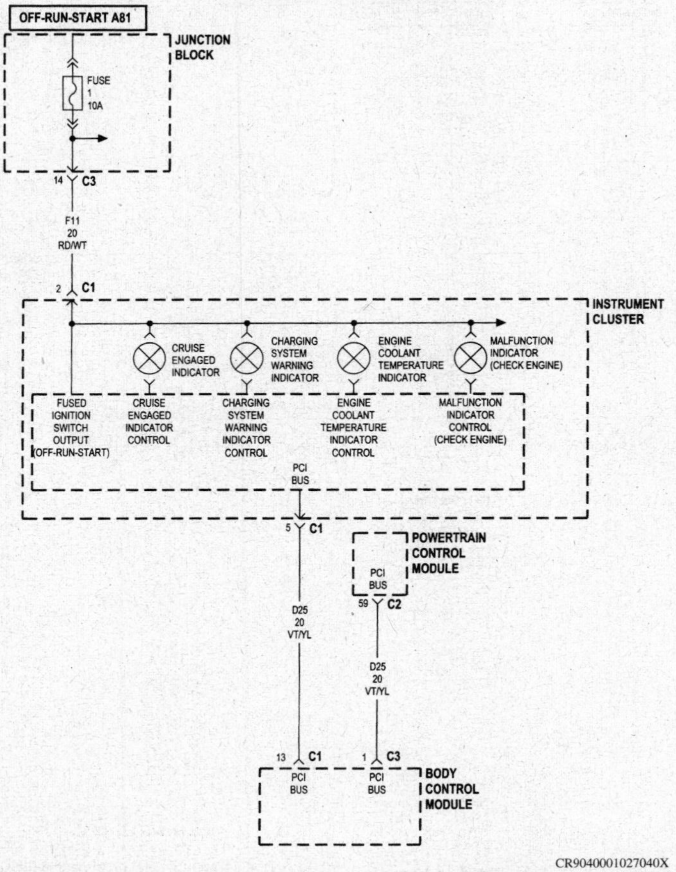

Fig. 4 Wiring diagram (Part 4 of 8). 2001 Concorde, Intrepid, LHS & 300M

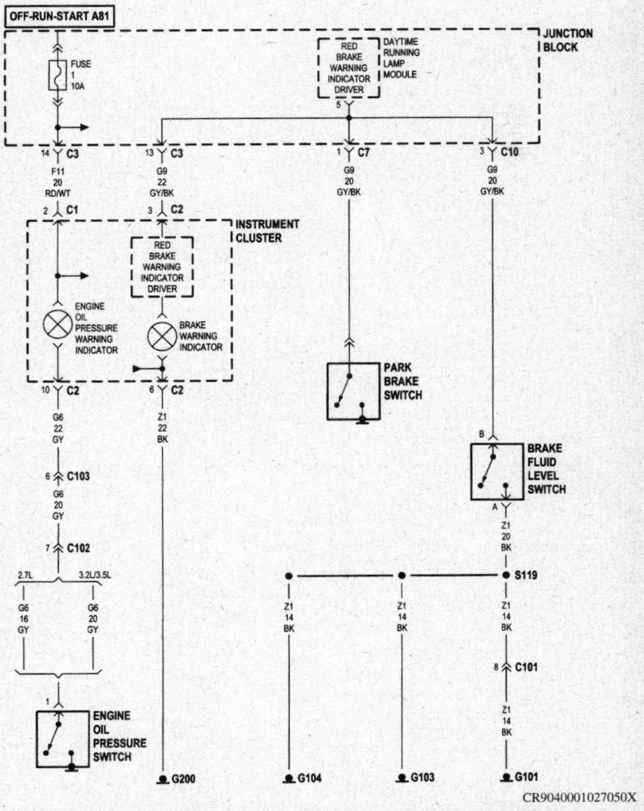

Fig. 4 Wiring diagram (Part 5 of 8). 2001 Concorde, Intrepid, LHS & 300M

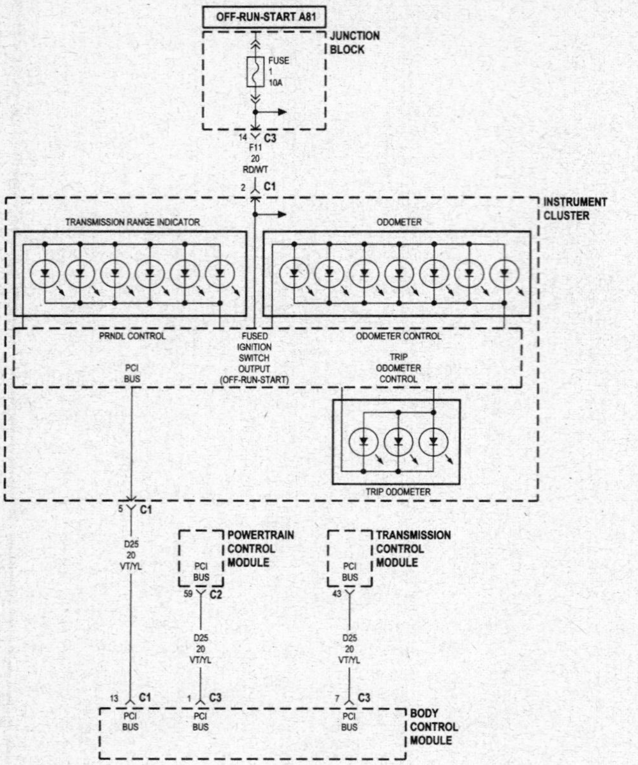

CR9040001027060X

Fig. 4 Wiring diagram (Part 6 of 8). 2001 Concorde, Intrepid, LHS & 300M

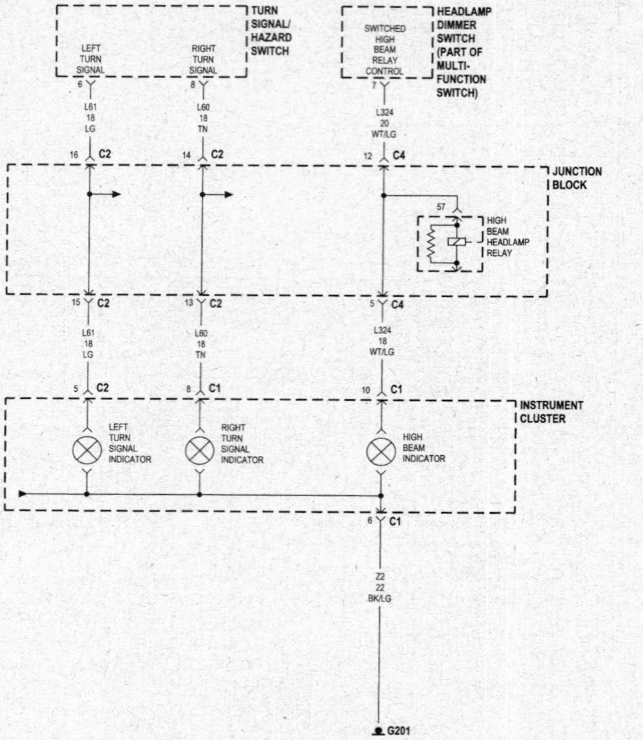

CR9040001027070X

Fig. 4 Wiring diagram (Part 7 of 8). 2001 Concorde, Intrepid, LHS & 300M

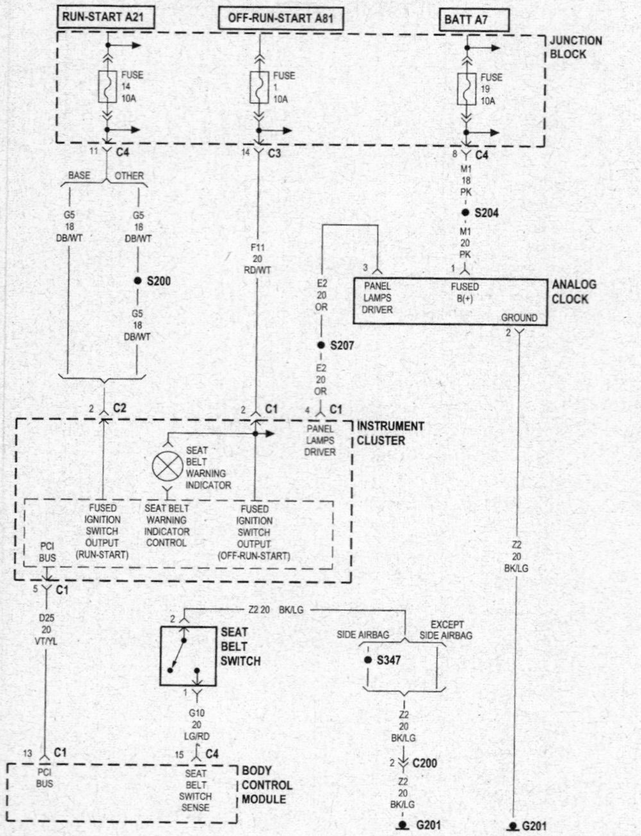

CR9040001027080X

Fig. 4 Wiring diagram (Part 8 of 8). 2001 Concorde, Intrepid, LHS & 300M

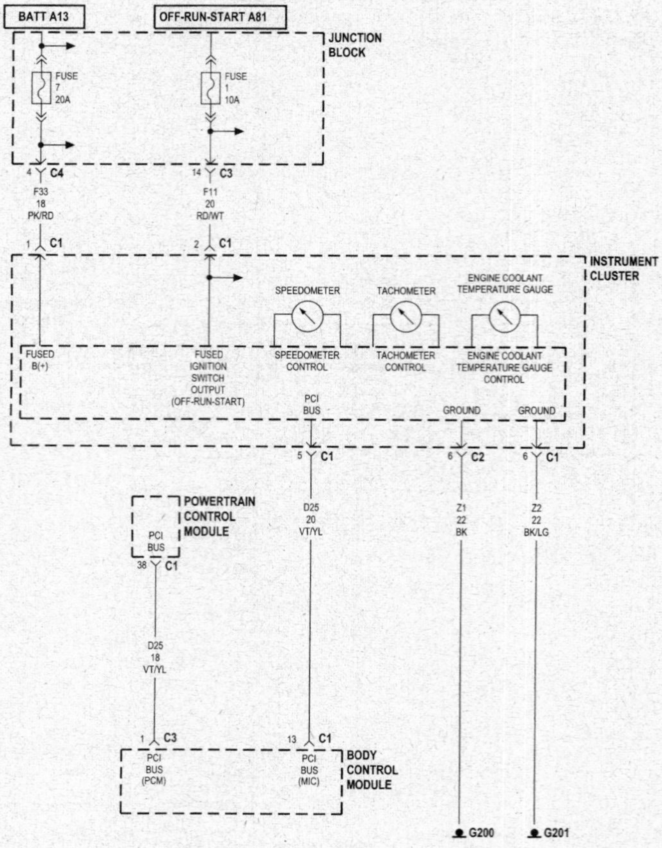

CR9040202503010X

Fig. 5 Wiring diagram (Part 1 of 8). 2002–04 Concorde, Intrepid & 300M

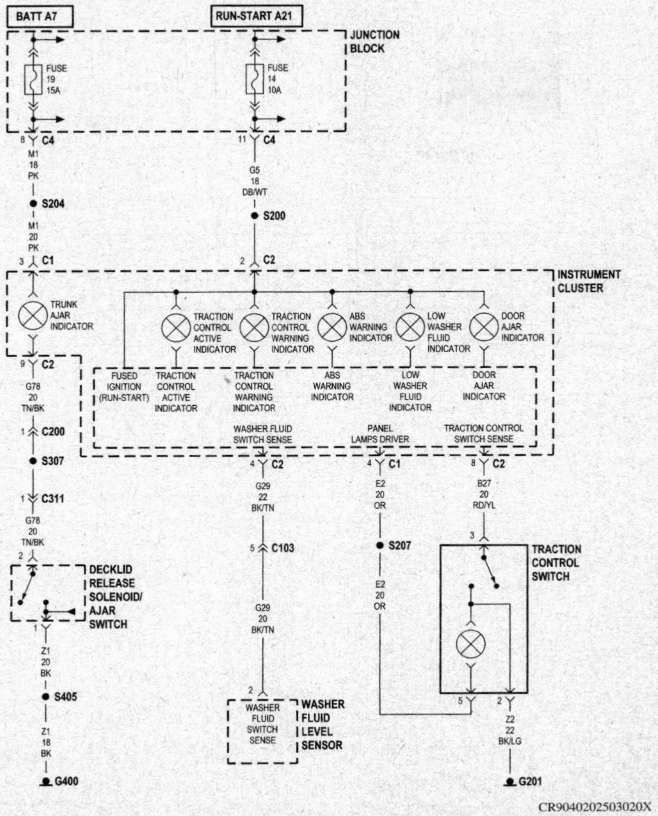

Fig. 5 Wiring diagram (Part 2 of 8). 2002–04 Concorde, Intrepid & 300M

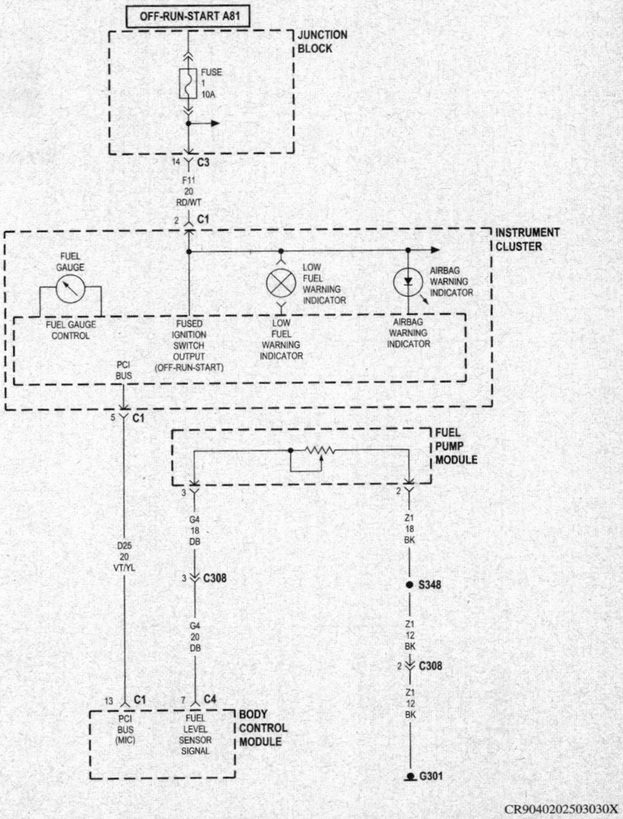

Fig. 5 Wiring diagram (Part 3 of 8). 2002–04 Concorde, Intrepid & 300M

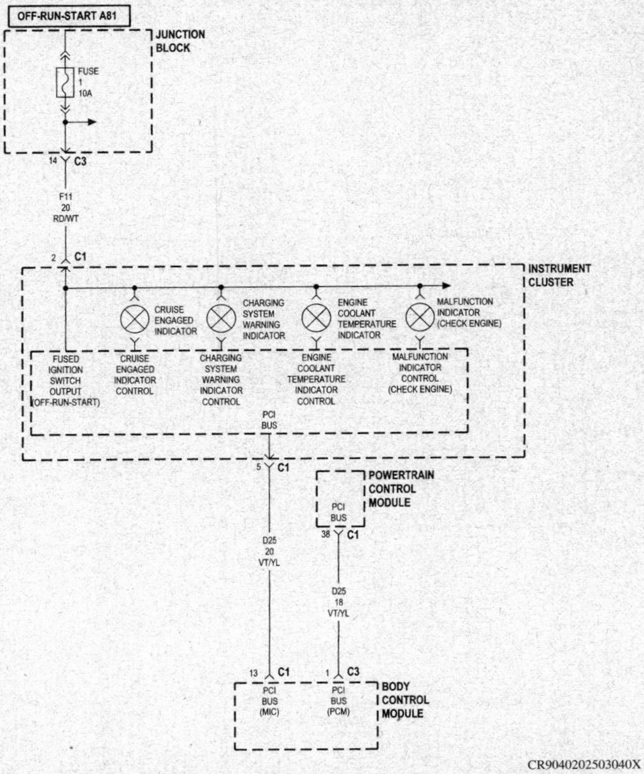

Fig. 5 Wiring diagram (Part 4 of 8). 2002–04 Concorde, Intrepid & 300M

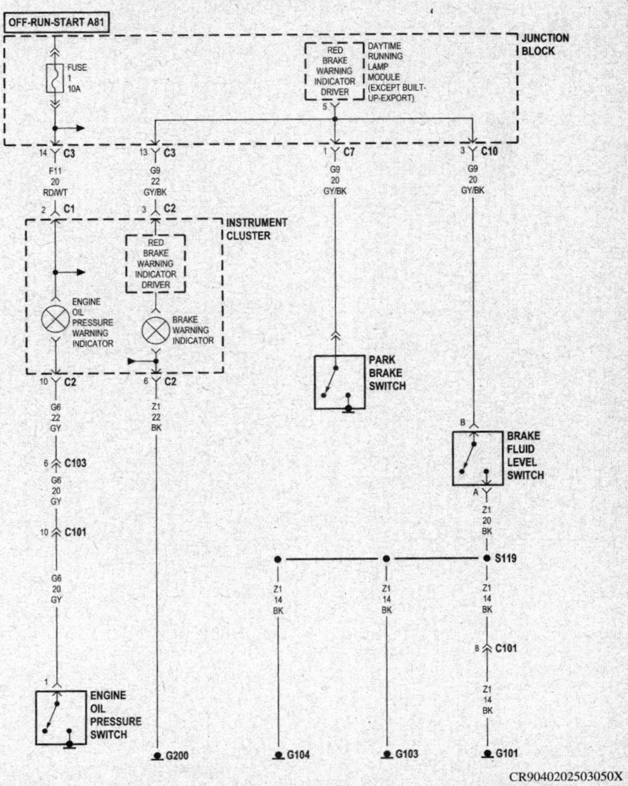

Fig. 5 Wiring diagram (Part 5 of 8). 2002–04 Concorde, Intrepid & 300M less police package/ special service

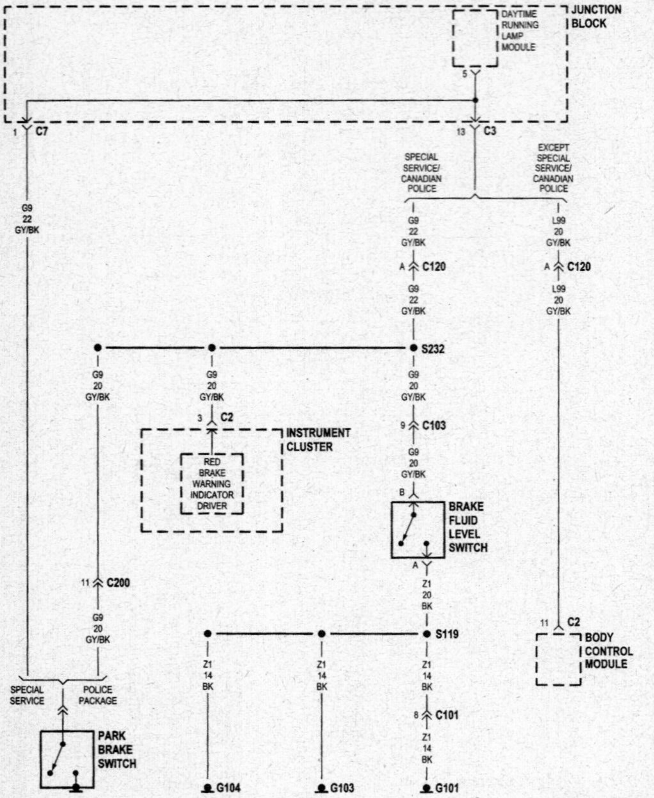

CR9040302503050X

Fig. 5 Wiring diagram (Part 5 of 8). 2003–04 Intrepid w/police package/special service

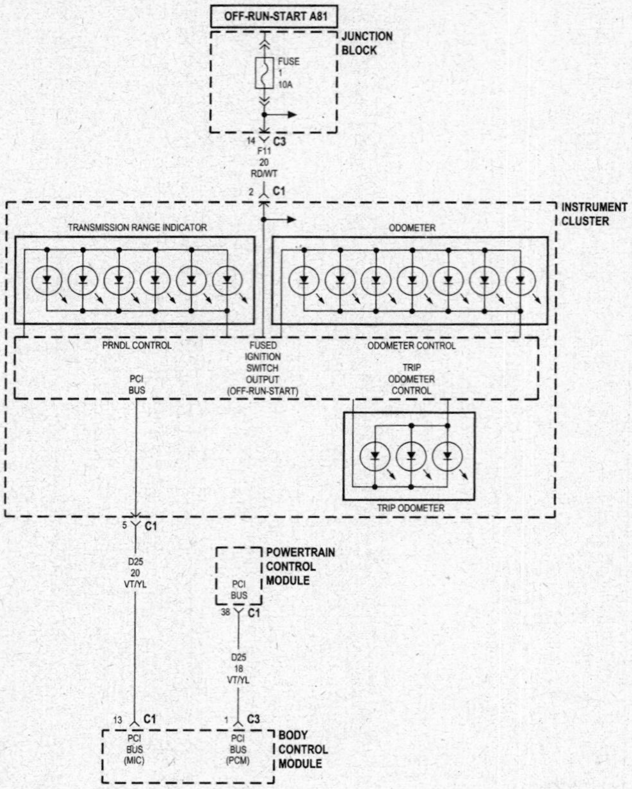

CR9040202503060X

Fig. 5 Wiring diagram (Part 6 of 8). 2002–04 Concorde, Intrepid & 300M

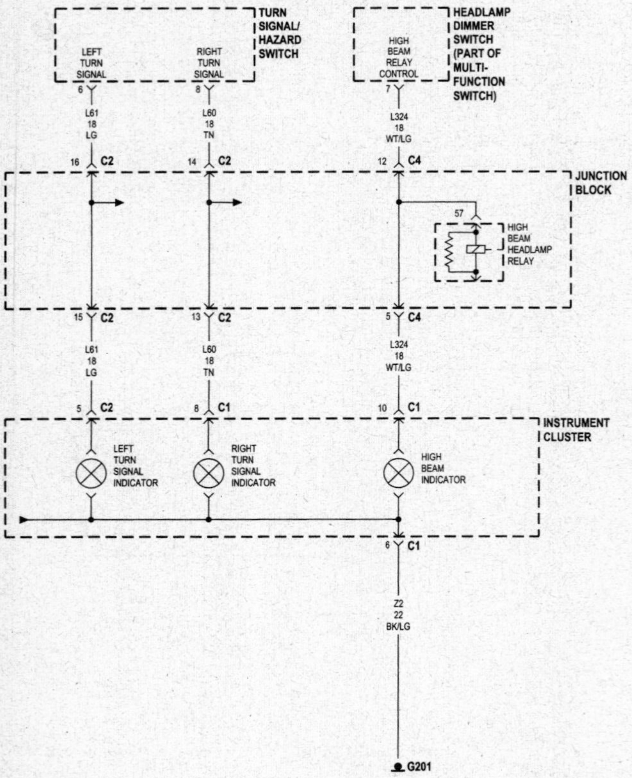

CR9040202503070X

Fig. 5 Wiring diagram (Part 7 of 8). 2002–04 Concorde, Intrepid & 300M

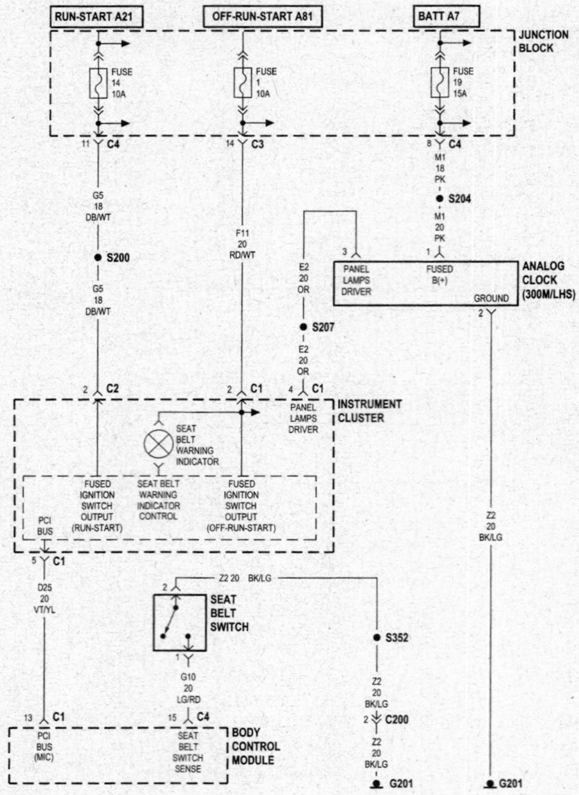

CR9040202503080X

Fig. 5 Wiring diagram (Part 8 of 8). 2002–04 Concorde, Intrepid & 300M

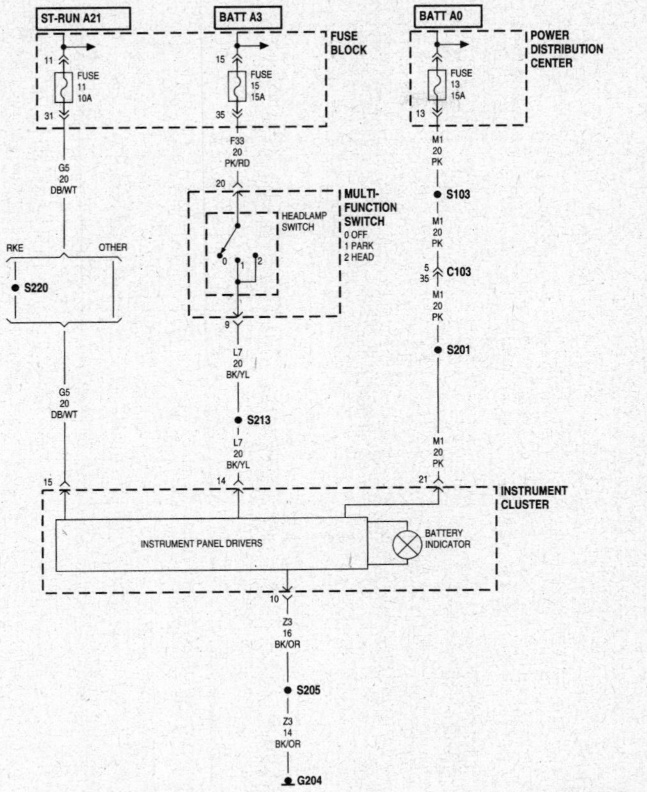

CR9040001029010X

Fig. 6 Wiring diagram (Part 1 of 10). 2000 Neon

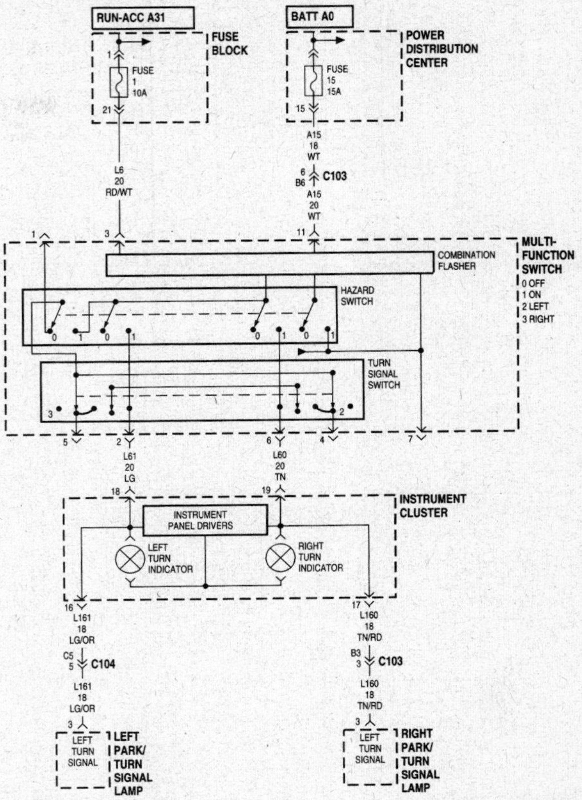

CR9040001029020X

Fig. 6 Wiring diagram (Part 2 of 10). 2000 Neon less daylight running lamps

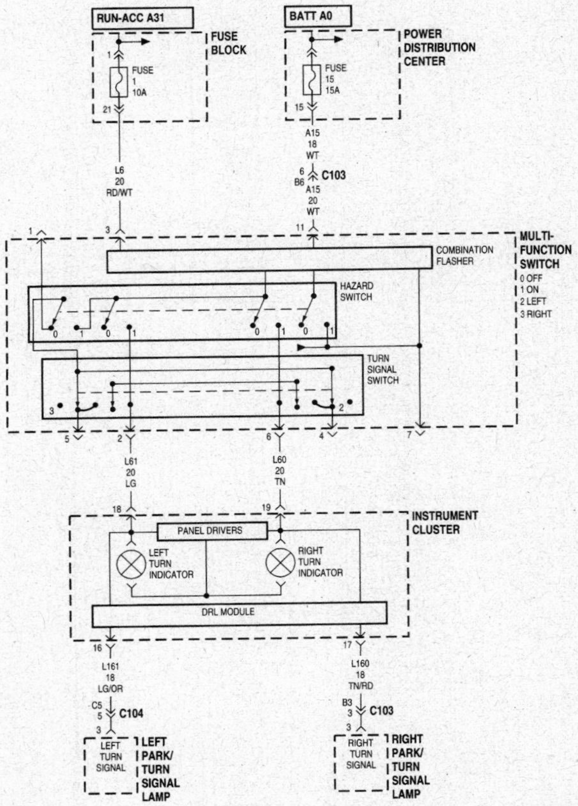

CR9040001029030X

Fig. 6 Wiring diagram (Part 2 of 10). 2000 Neon w/daylight running lamps

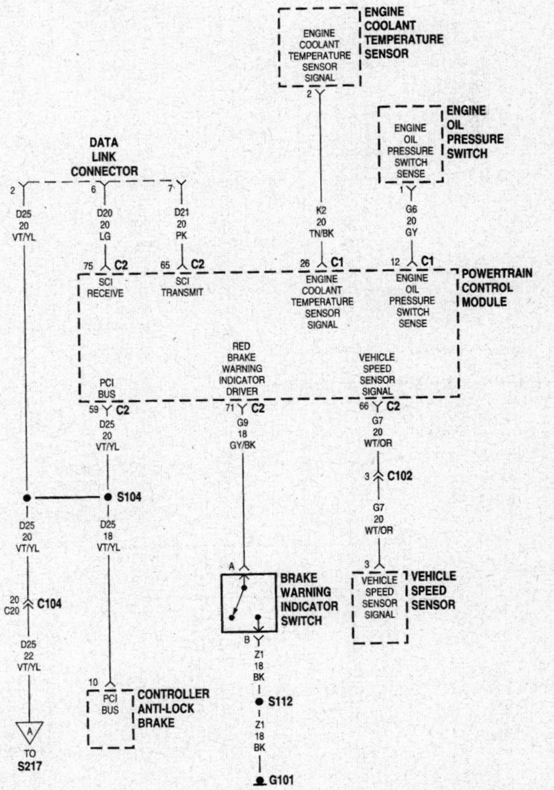

CR9040001029040X

Fig. 6 Wiring diagram (Part 3 of 10). 2000 Neon

DASH GAUGES & WARNING INDICATORS

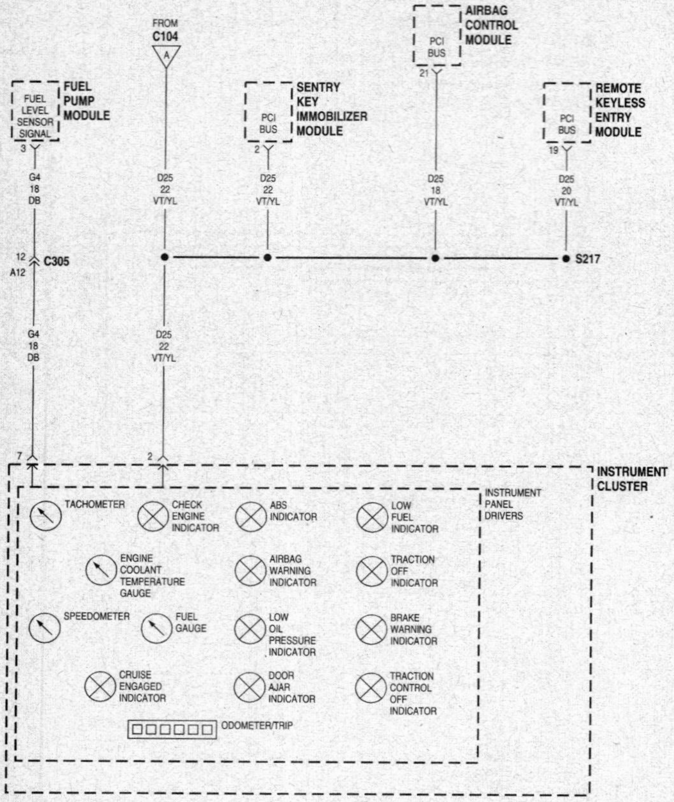

CR9040001029050X

Fig. 6 Wiring diagram (Part 4 of 10). 2000 Neon

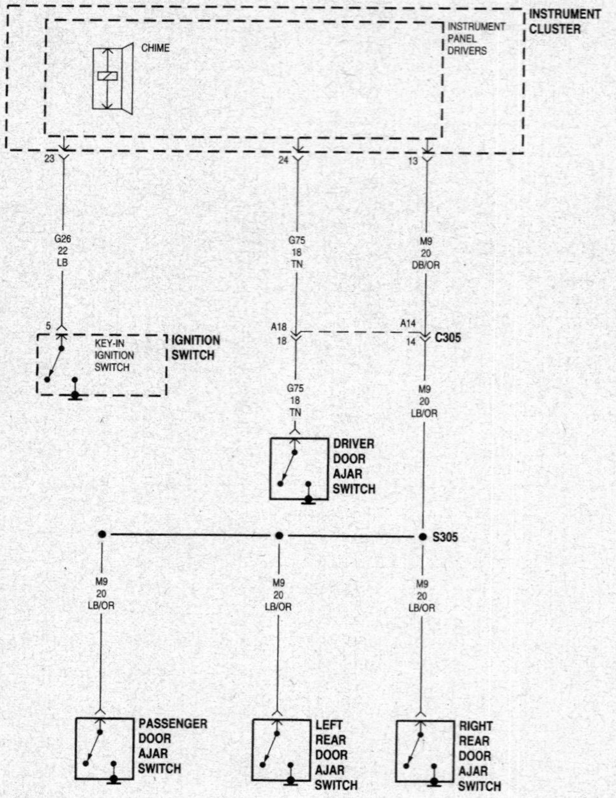

CR9040001029060X

Fig. 6 Wiring diagram (Part 5 of 10). 2000 Neon less remote keyless entry

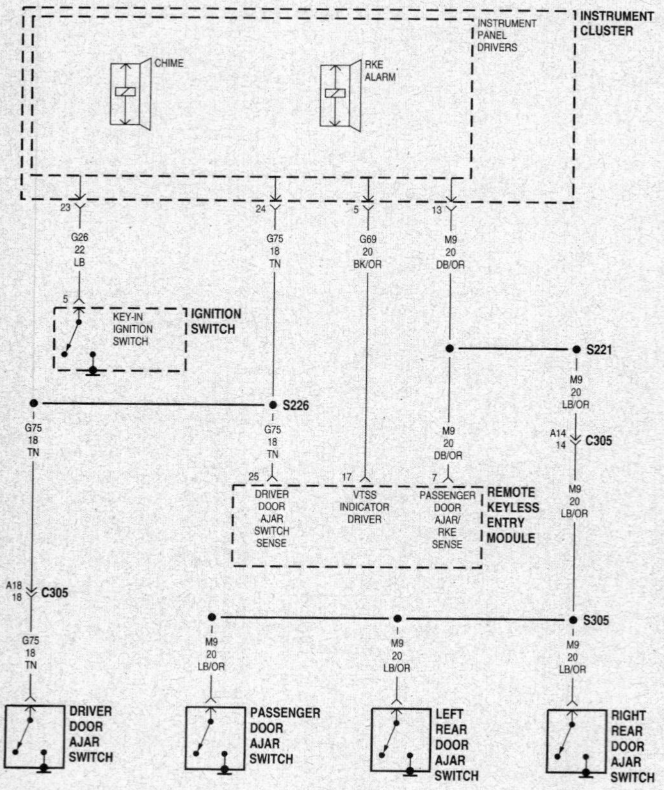

CR9040001029070X

Fig. 6 Wiring diagram (Part 5 of 10). 2000 Neon w/remote keyless entry

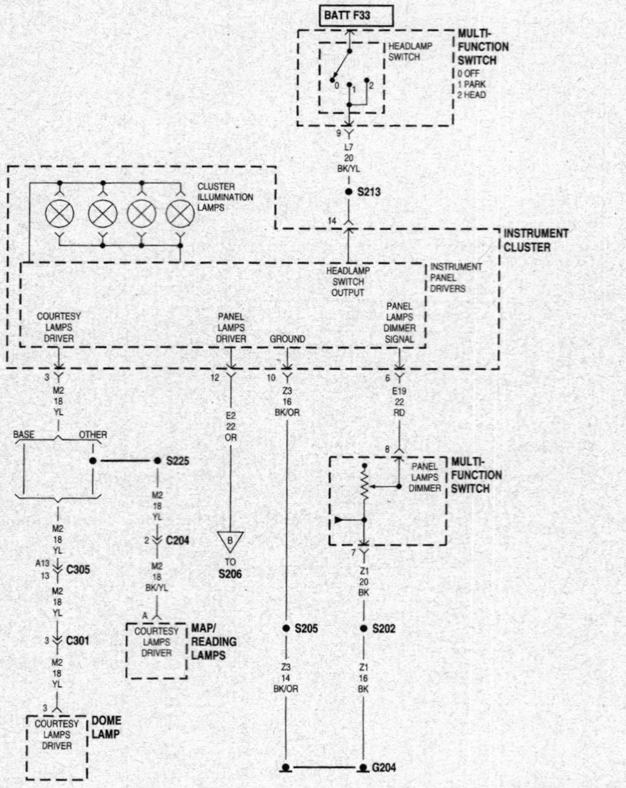

CR9040001029080X

Fig. 6 Wiring diagram (Part 6 of 10). 2000 Neon

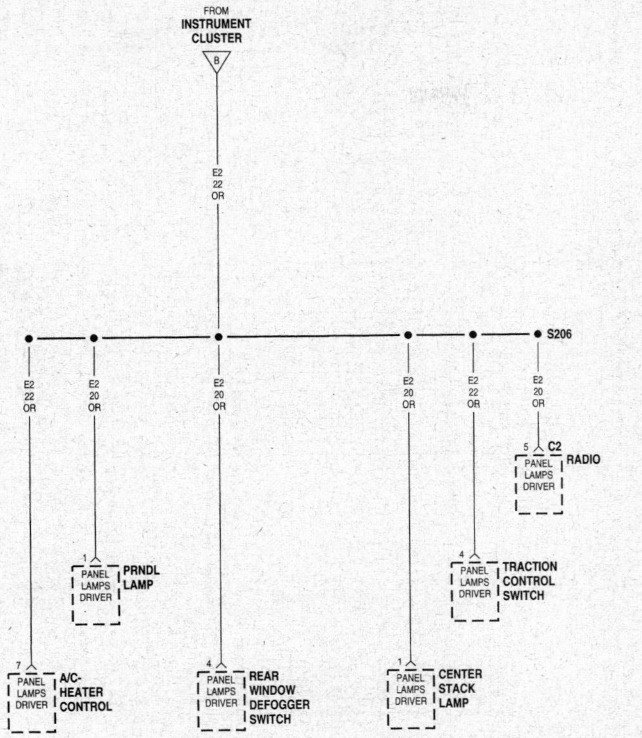

CR9040001029090X

Fig. 6 Wiring diagram (Part 7 of 10). 2000 Neon

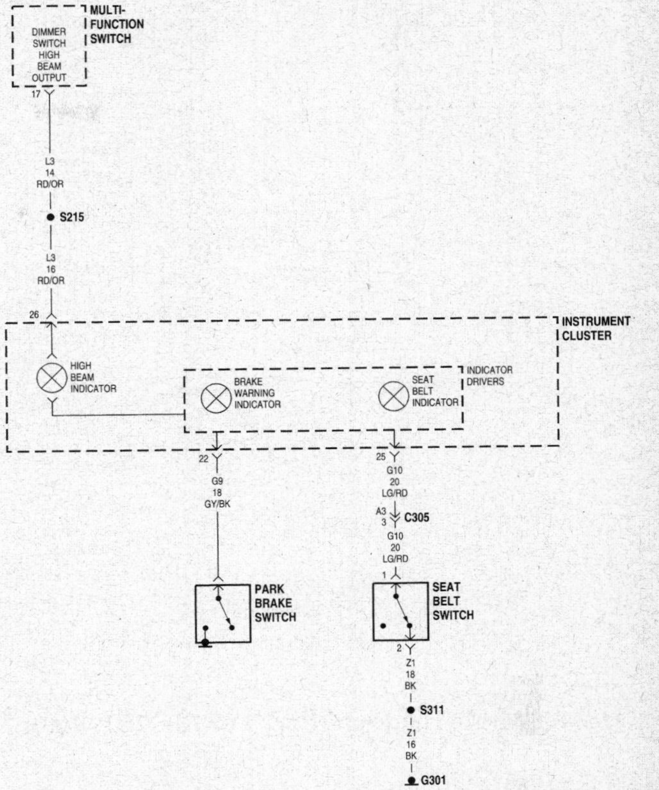

CR9040001029100X

Fig. 6 Wiring diagram (Part 8 of 10). 2000 Neon

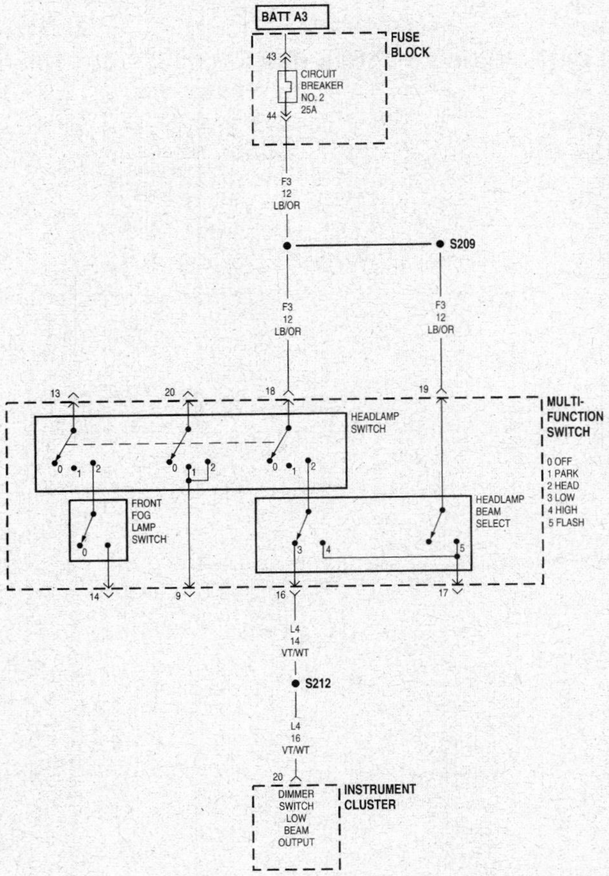

CR9040001029110X

Fig. 6 Wiring diagram (Part 9 of 10). 2000 Neon

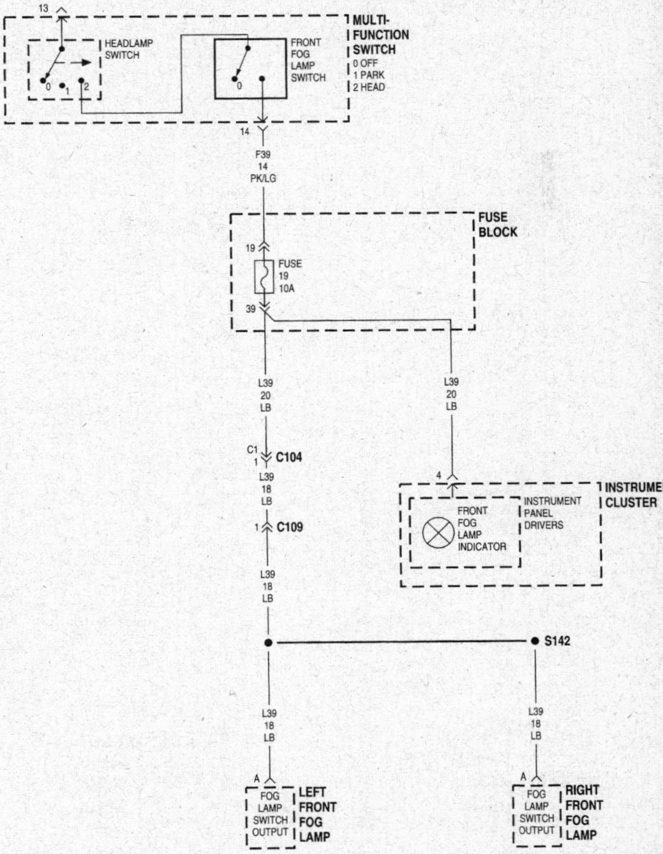

CR9040001029120X

Fig. 6 Wiring diagram (Part 10 of 10). 2000 Neon

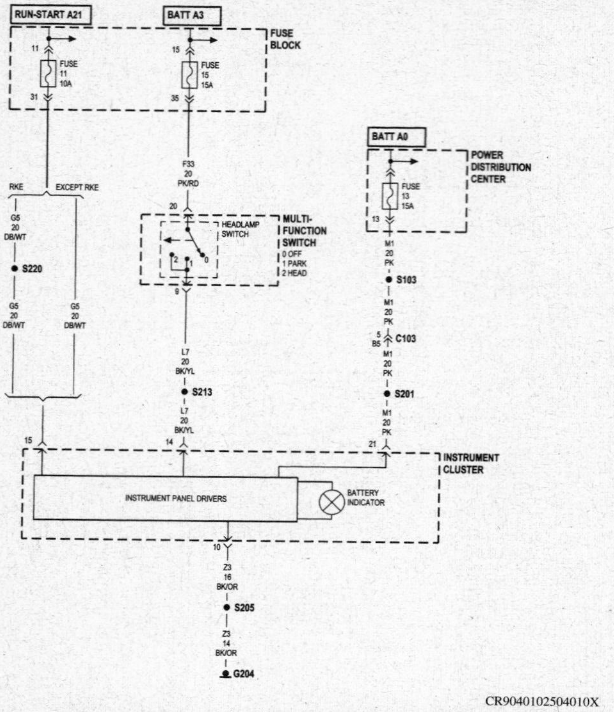

Fig. 7 Wiring diagram (Part 1 of 13). 2001 Neon

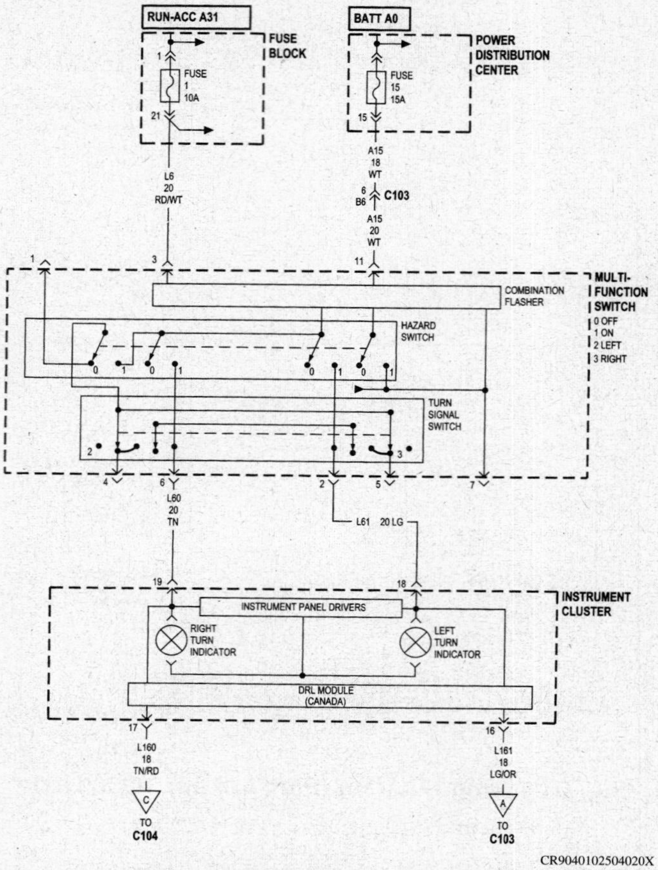

Fig. 7 Wiring diagram (Part 2 of 13). 2001 Neon

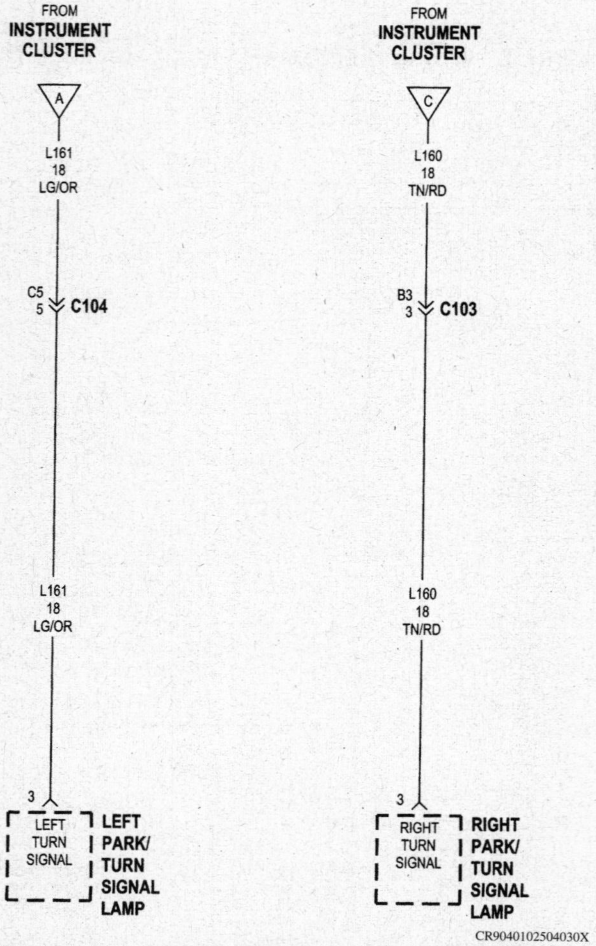

Fig. 7 Wiring diagram (Part 3 of 13). 2001 Neon

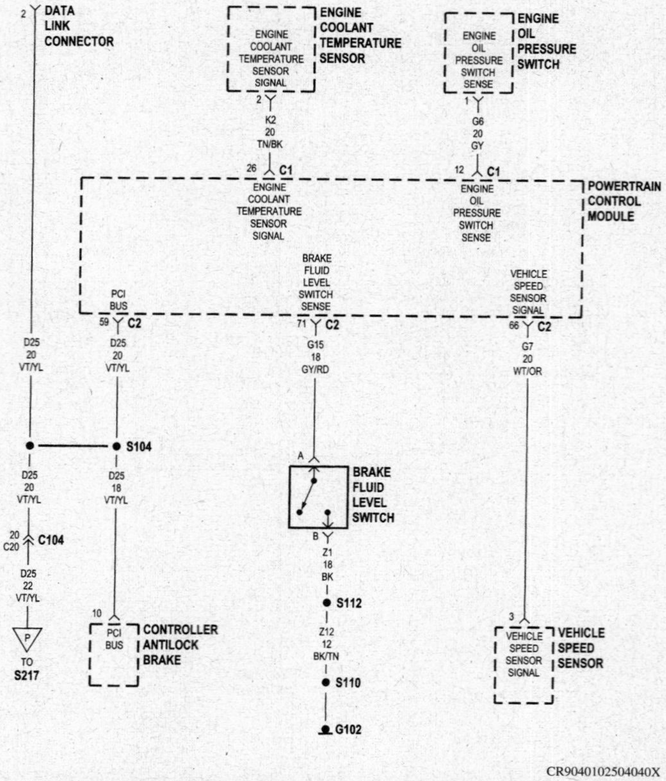

Fig. 7 Wiring diagram (Part 4 of 13). 2001 Neon

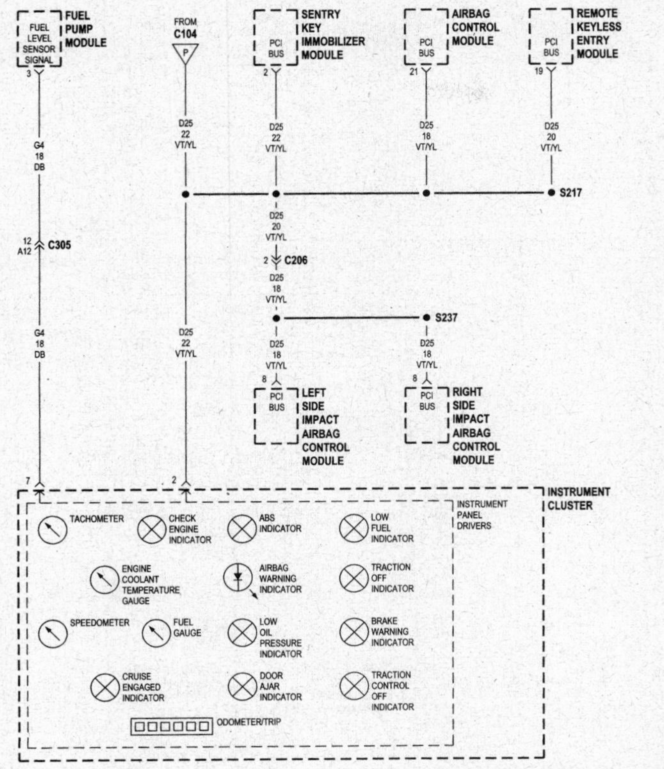

CR9040102504050X

Fig. 7 Wiring diagram (Part 5 of 13). 2001 Neon

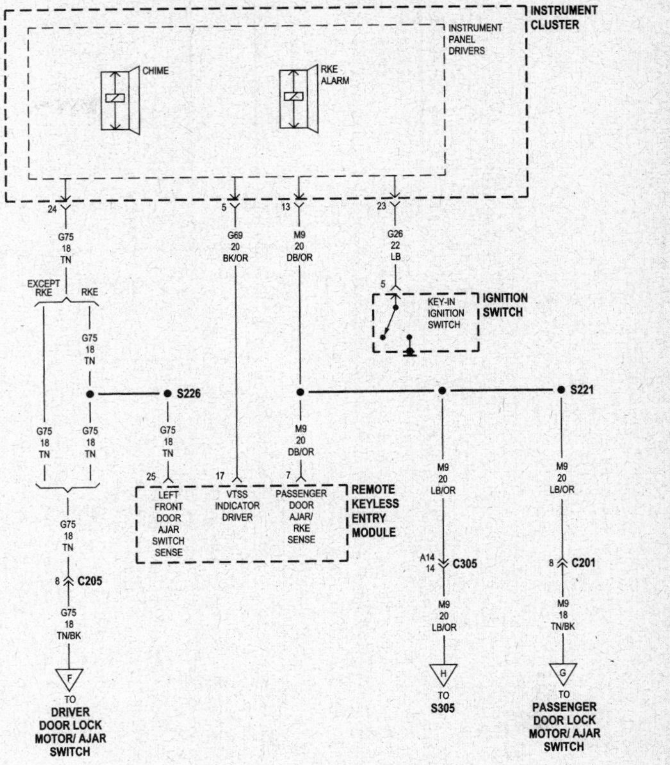

CR9040102504060X

Fig. 7 Wiring diagram (Part 6 of 13). 2001 Neon

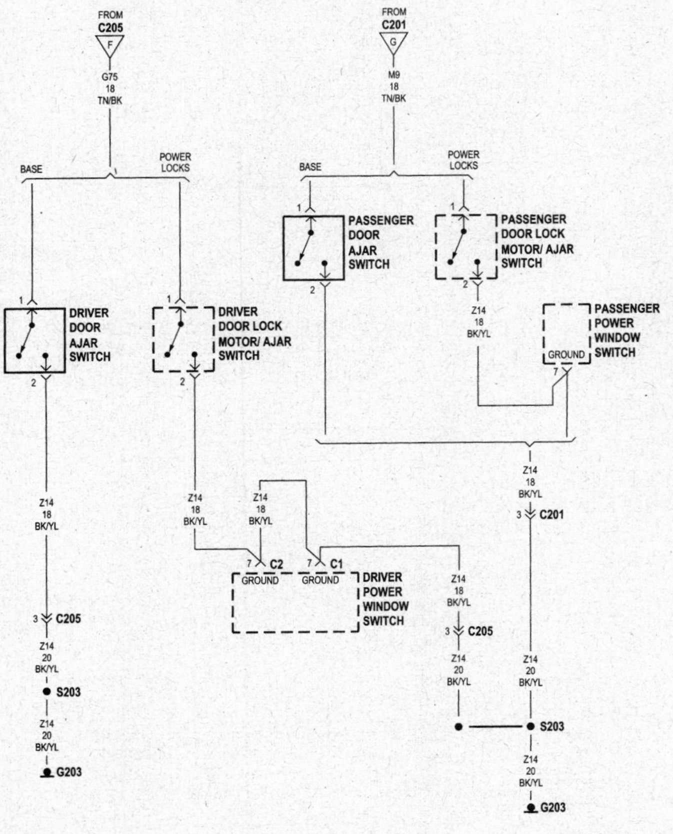

CR9040102504070X

Fig. 7 Wiring diagram (Part 7 of 13). 2001 Neon

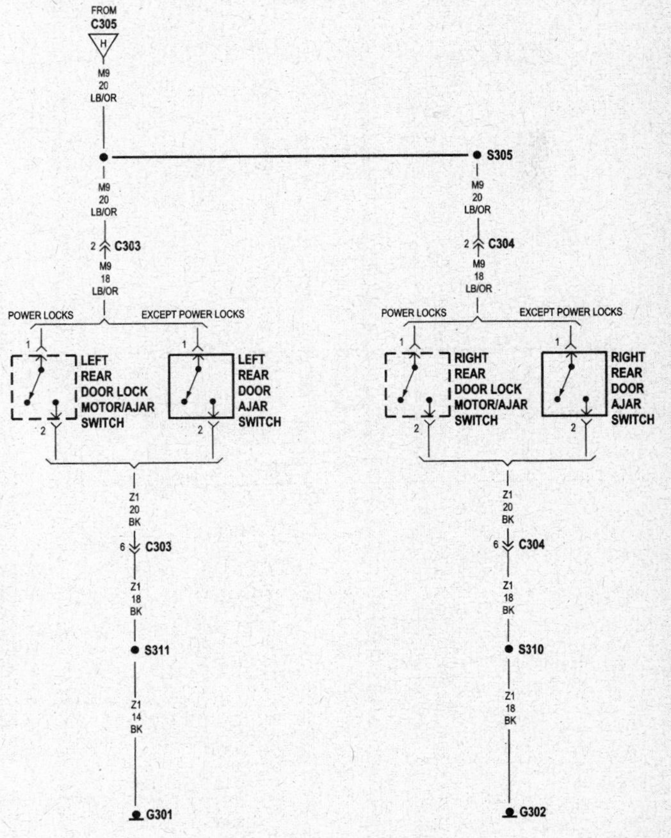

CR9040102504080X

Fig. 7 Wiring diagram (Part 8 of 13). 2001 Neon

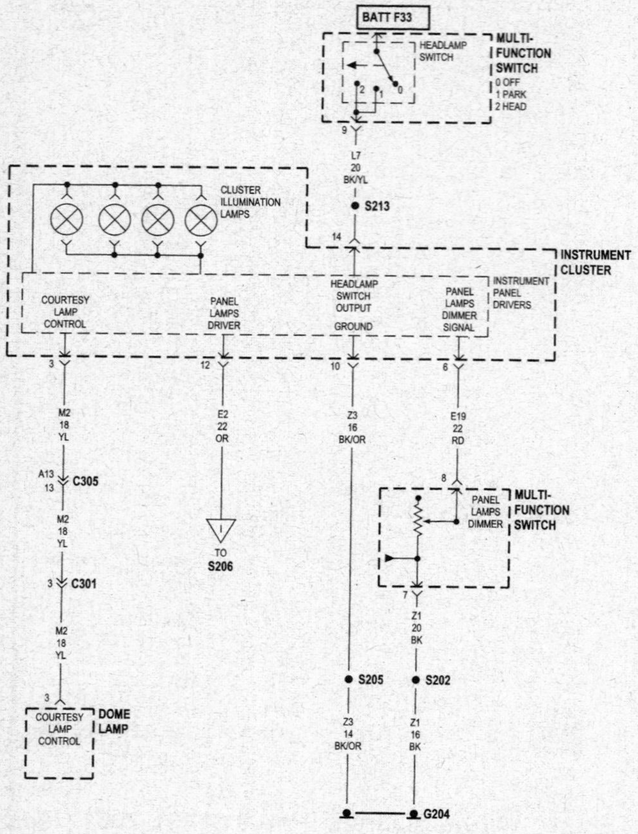

CR9040102504090X

Fig. 7 Wiring diagram (Part 9 of 13). 2001 Neon

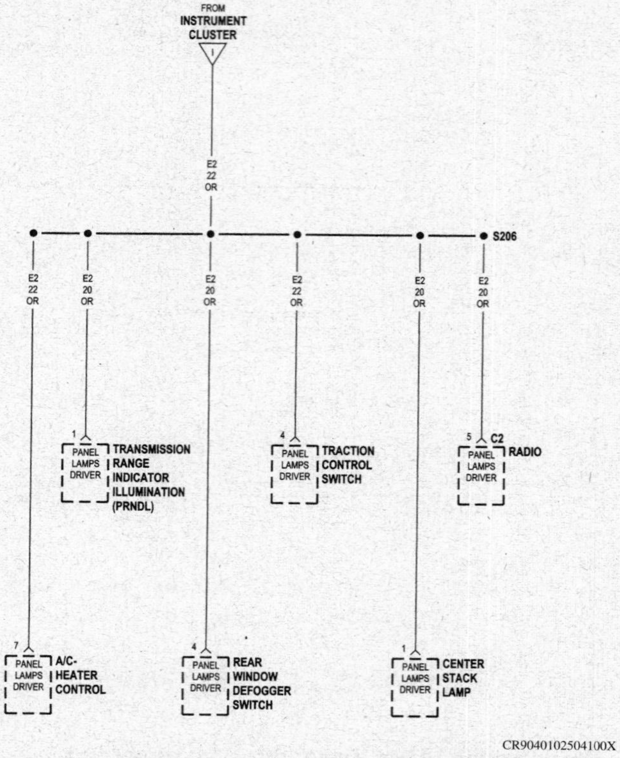

CR9040102504110X

Fig. 7 Wiring diagram (Part 11 of 13). 2001 Neon

CR9040102504100X

Fig. 7 Wiring diagram (Part 10 of 13). 2001 Neon

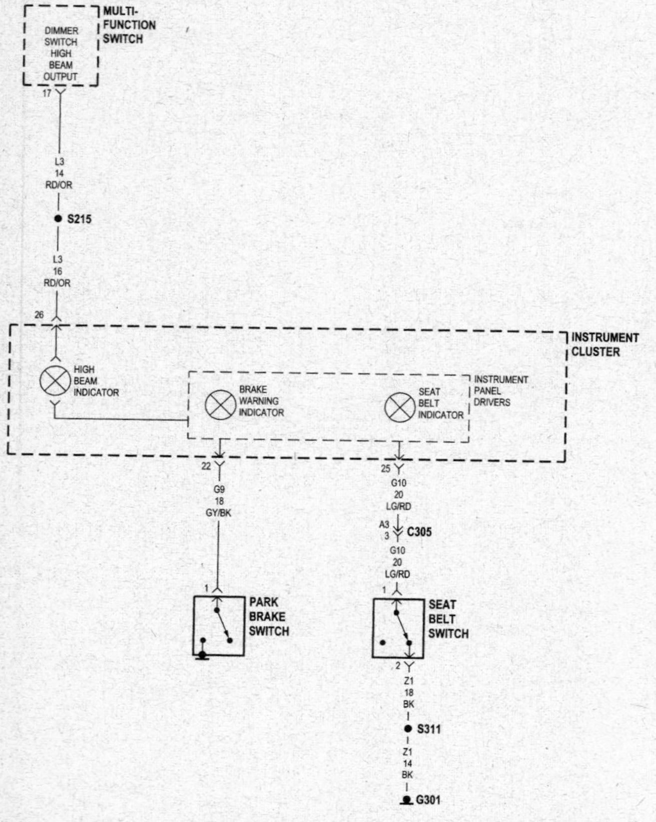

CR9040102504120X

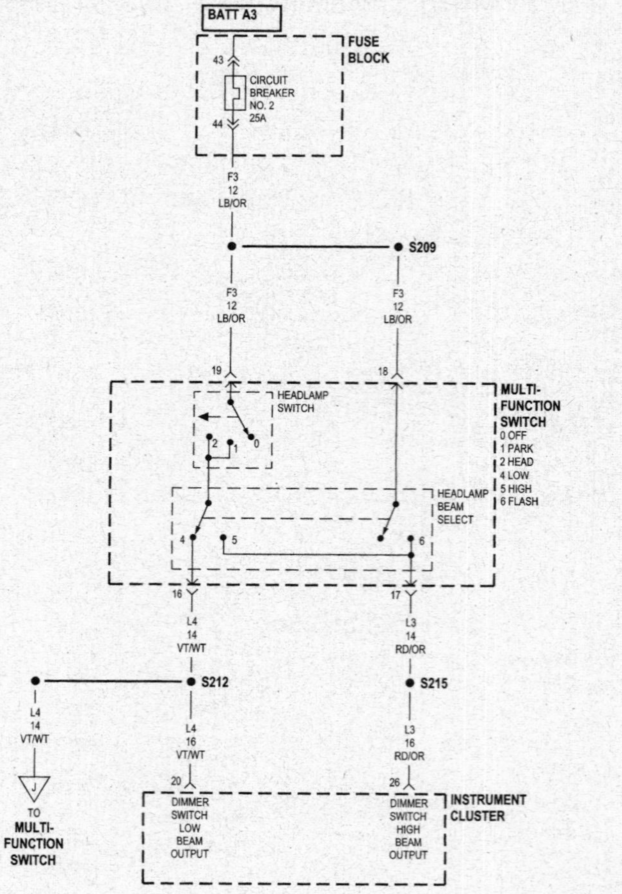

Fig. 7 Wiring diagram (Part 12 of 13). 2001 Neon

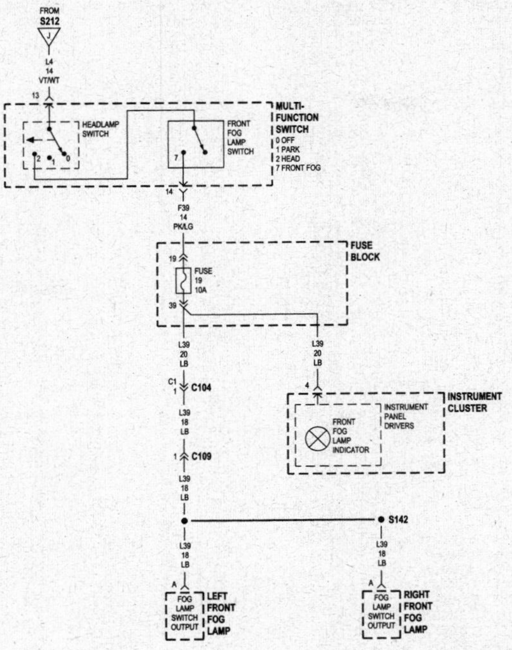

CR9040102504130X

Fig. 7 Wiring diagram (Part 13 of 13). 2001 Neon

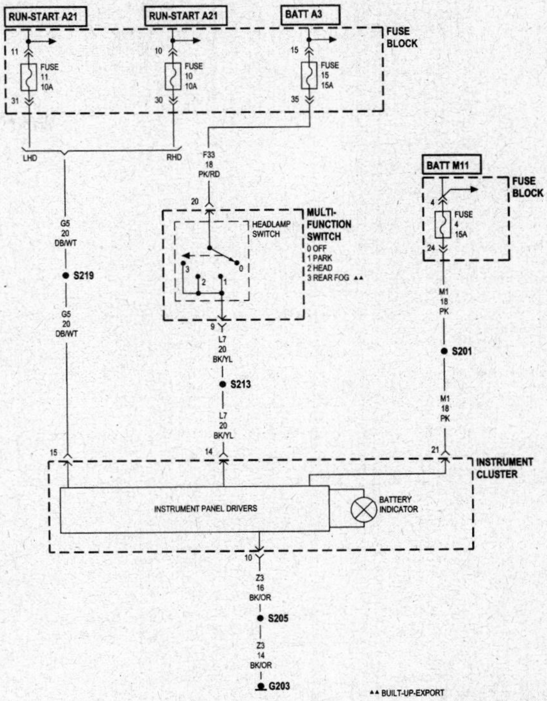

CR9040202505010X

Fig. 8 Wiring diagram (Part 1 of 13). 2002–03 Neon less autostick

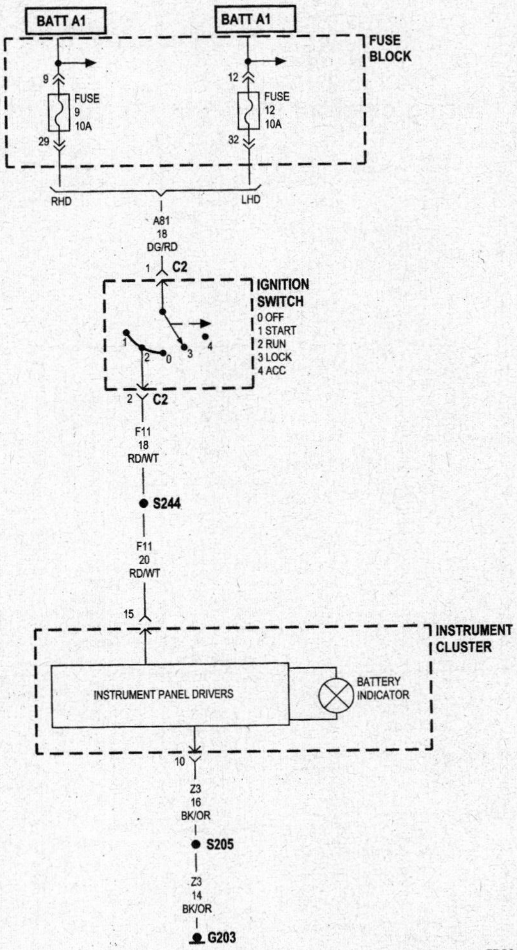

CR9040202505020X

Fig. 8 Wiring diagram (Part 1 of 13). 2002 Neon w/autostick

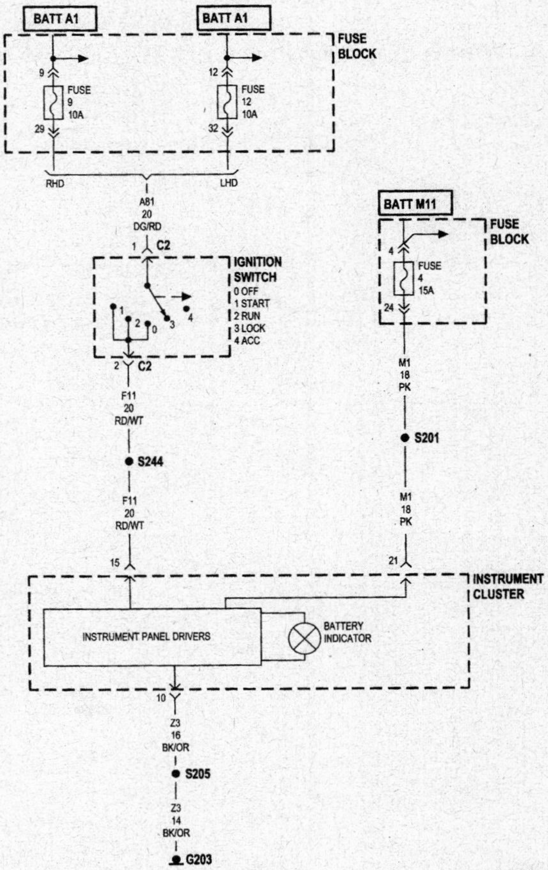

CR9040302505020X

Fig. 8 Wiring diagram (Part 1 of 13). 2003–04 Neon w/autostick

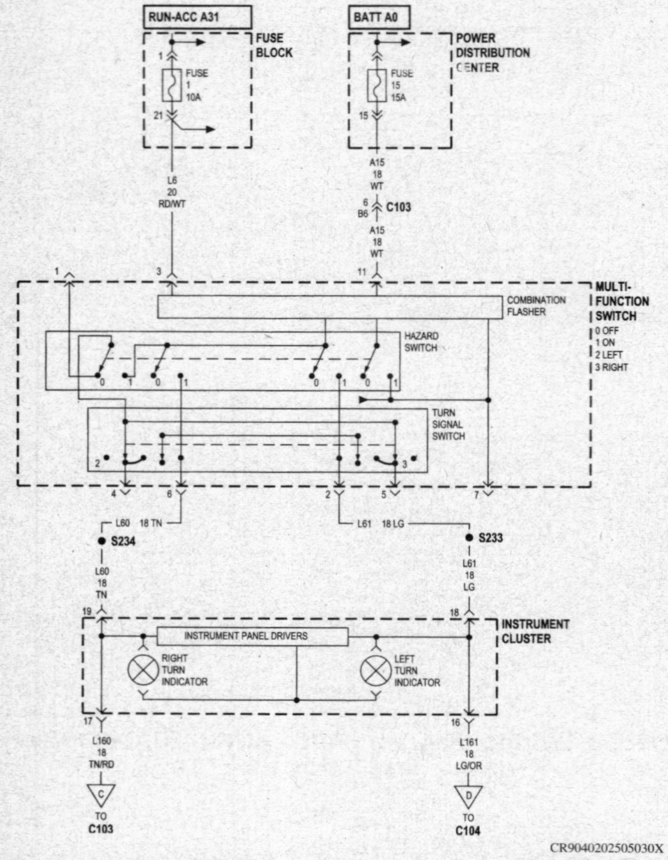

Fig. 8 Wiring diagram (Part 2 of 13). 2002–04 Neon

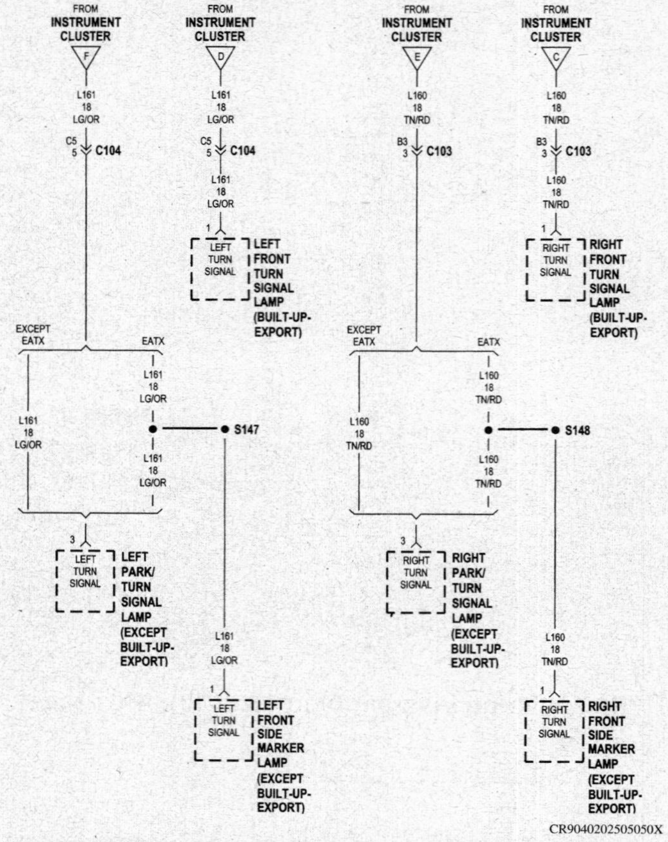

Fig. 8 Wiring diagram (Part 3 of 13). 2002–04 Neon

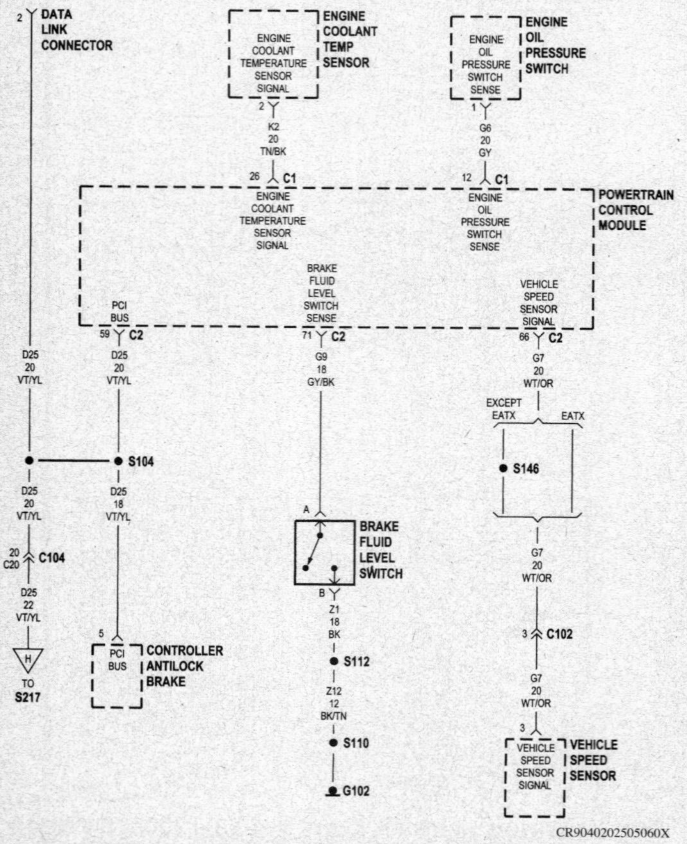

Fig. 8 Wiring diagram (Part 4 of 13). 2002–04 Neon

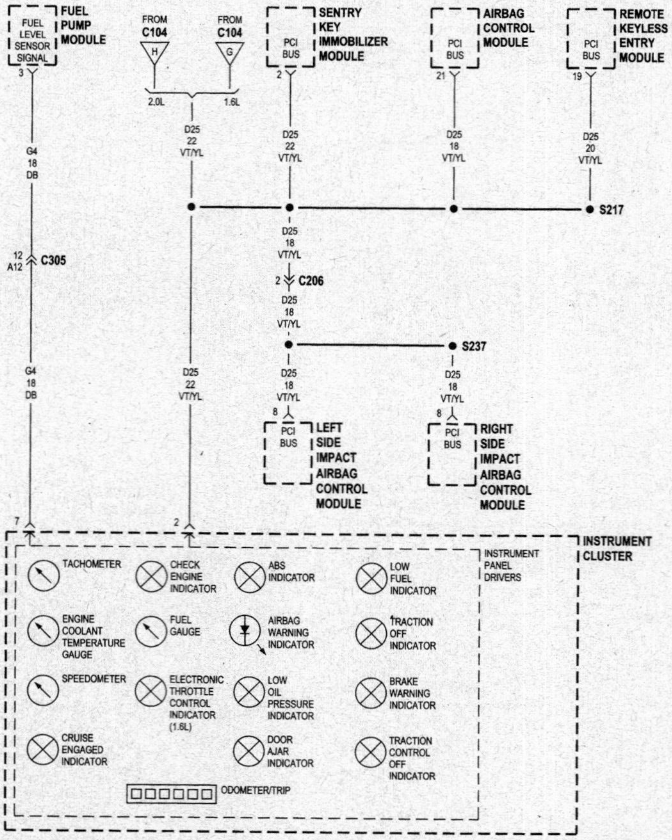

Fig. 8 Wiring diagram (Part 5 of 13). 2002 Neon

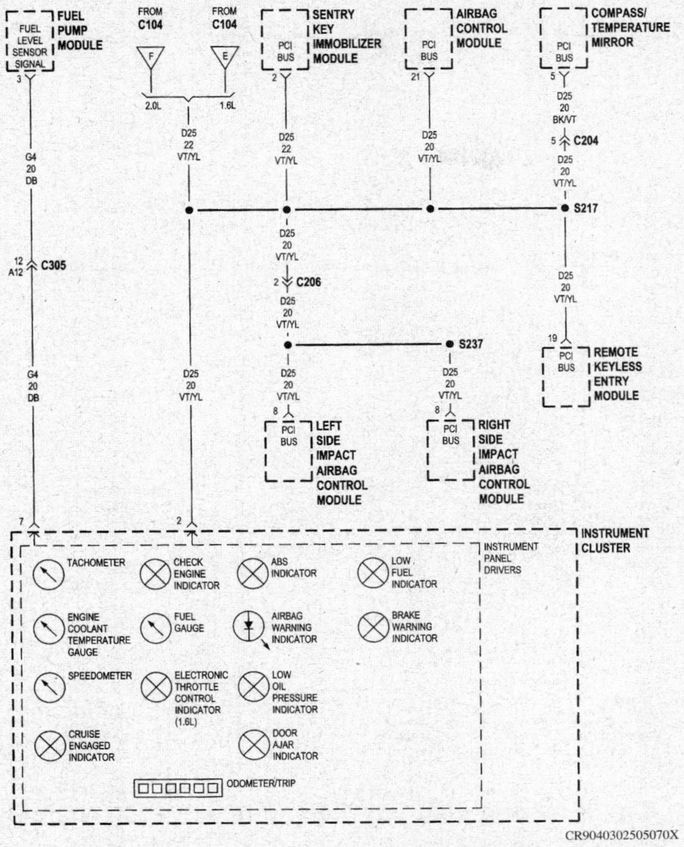

Fig. 8 Wiring diagram (Part 5 of 13). 2003–04 Neon

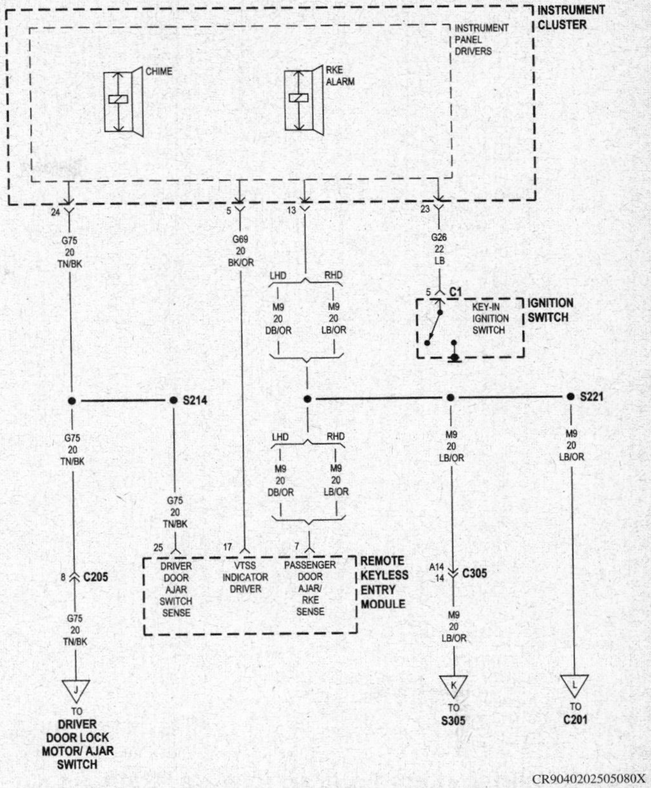

Fig. 8 Wiring diagram (Part 6 of 13). 2002–04 Neon

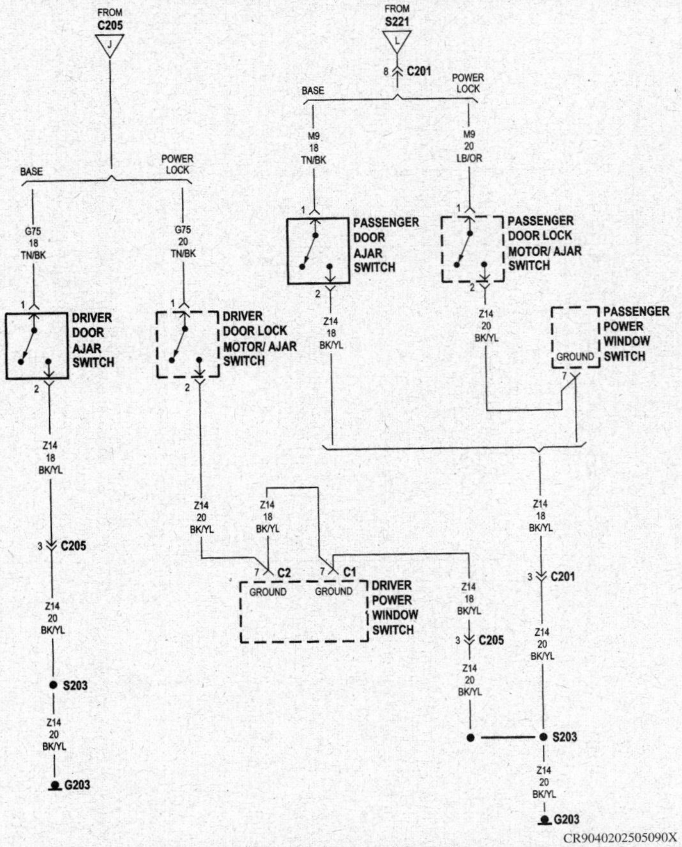

Fig. 8 Wiring diagram (Part 7 of 13). 2002–04 Neon

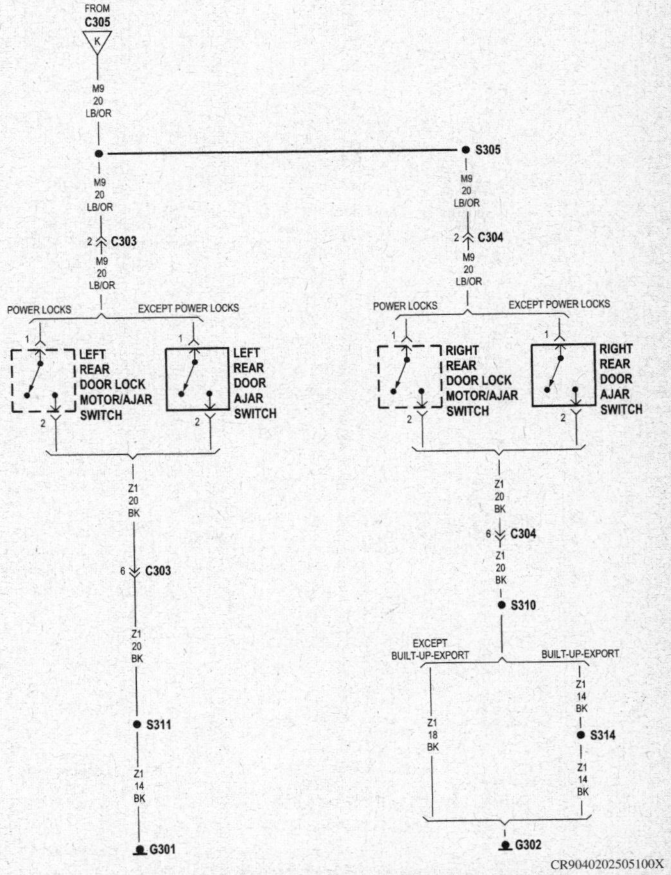

Fig. 8 Wiring diagram (Part 8 of 13). 2002–04 Neon

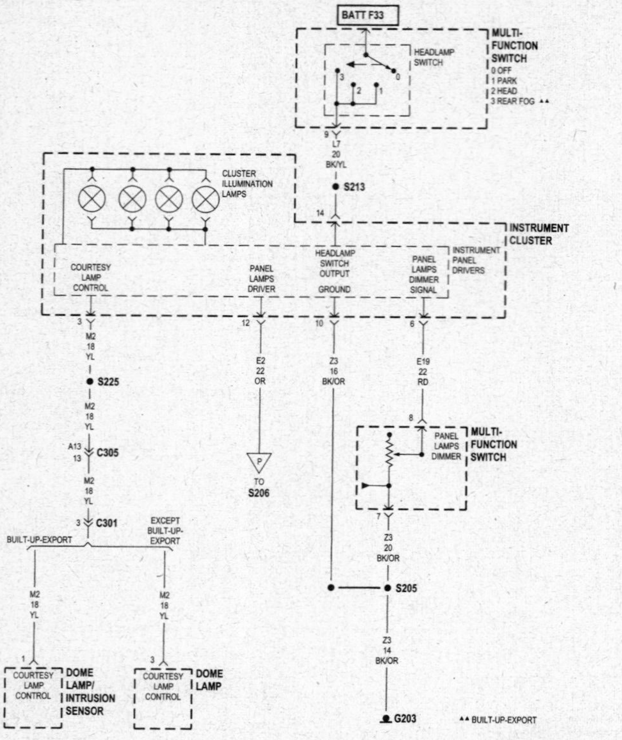

CR9040202505110X

Fig. 8 Wiring diagram (Part 9 of 13). 2002–04 Neon

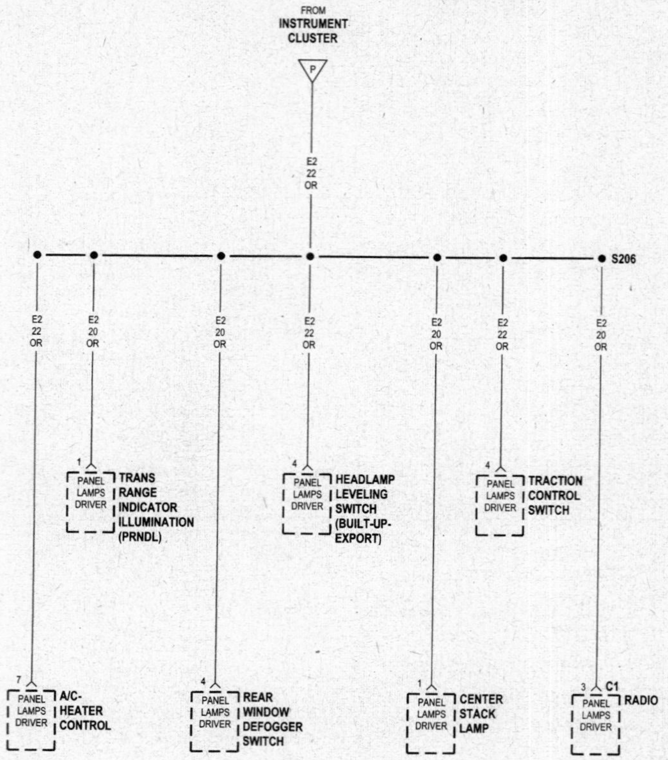

CR9040202505120X

Fig. 8 Wiring diagram (Part 10 of 13). 2002 Neon

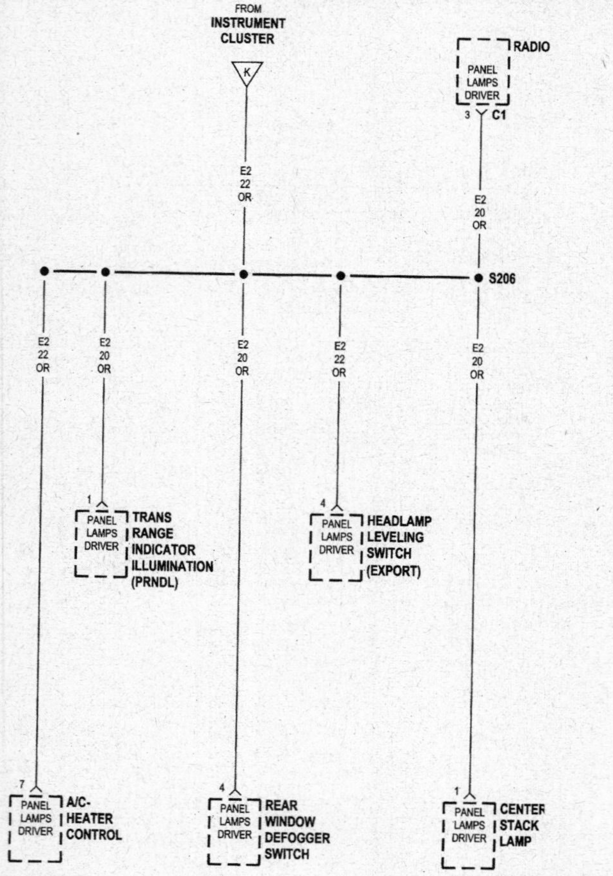

CR9040302505120X

Fig. 8 Wiring diagram (Part 10 of 13). 2003–04 Neon

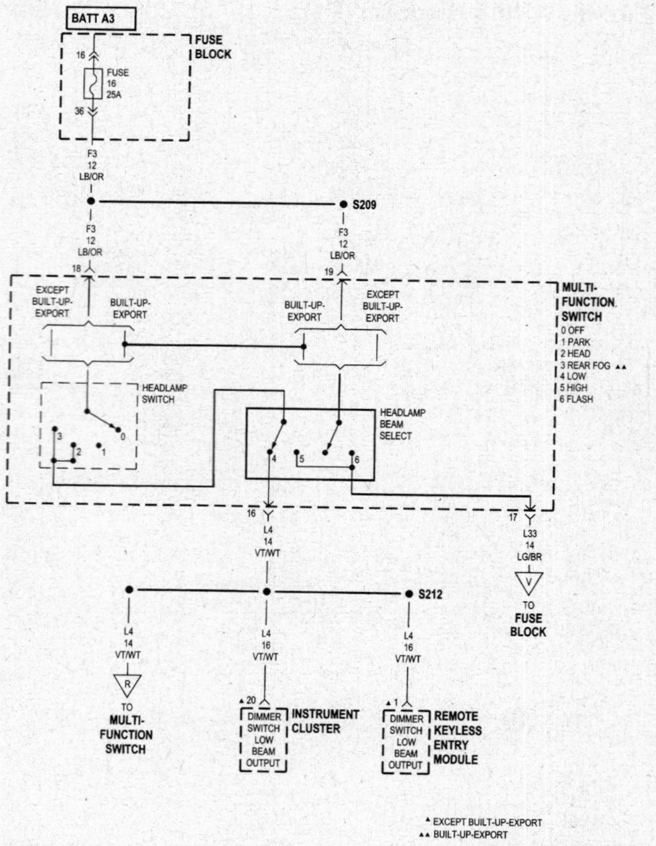

CR9040202505130X

Fig. 8 Wiring diagram (Part 11 of 13). 2002–04 Neon

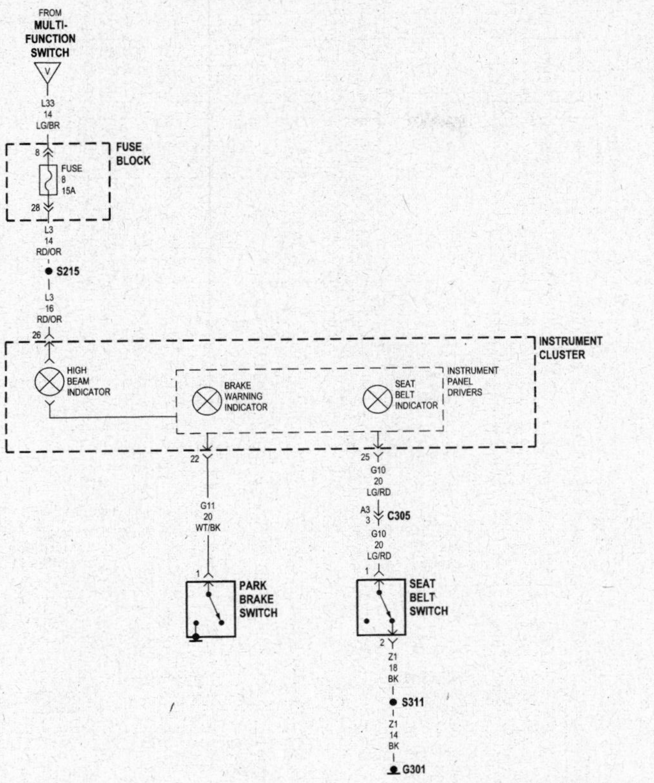

CR9040202505140X

Fig. 8 Wiring diagram (Part 12 of 13). 2002–04 Neon

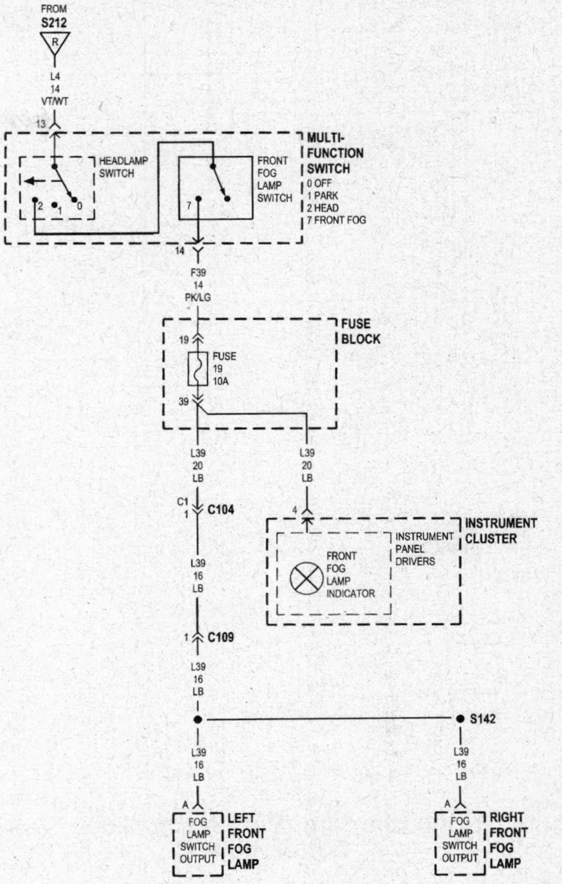

CR9040202505150X

Fig. 8 Wiring diagram (Part 13 of 13). 2002–04 Neon

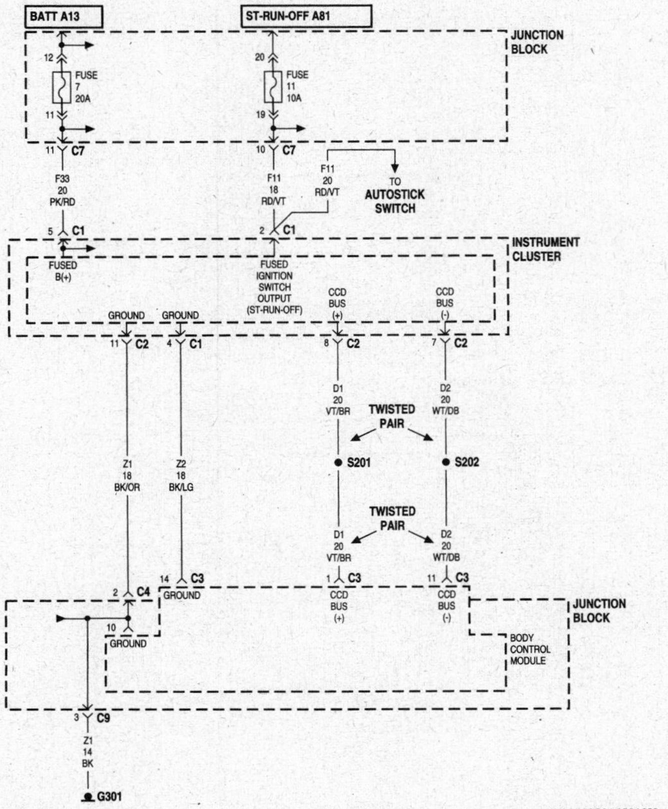

CR9049900165010X

Fig. 9 Wiring diagram (Part 1 of 9). 2000 Sebring Convertible

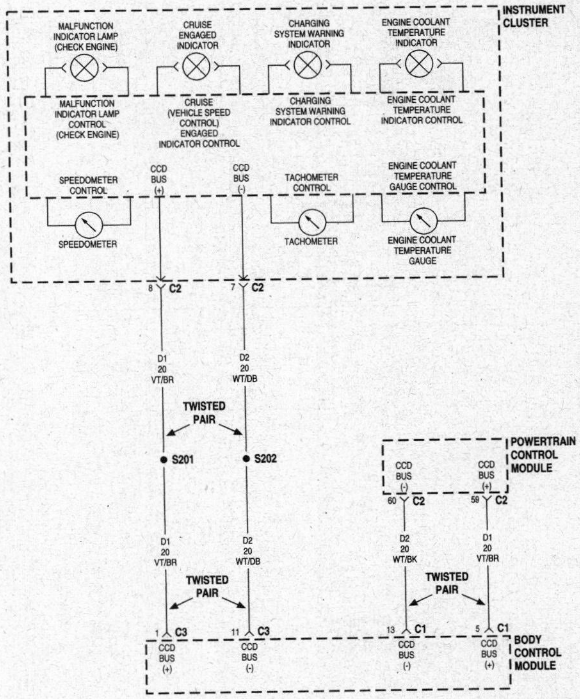

CR9049900165020X

Fig. 9 Wiring diagram (Part 2 of 9). 2000 Sebring Convertible

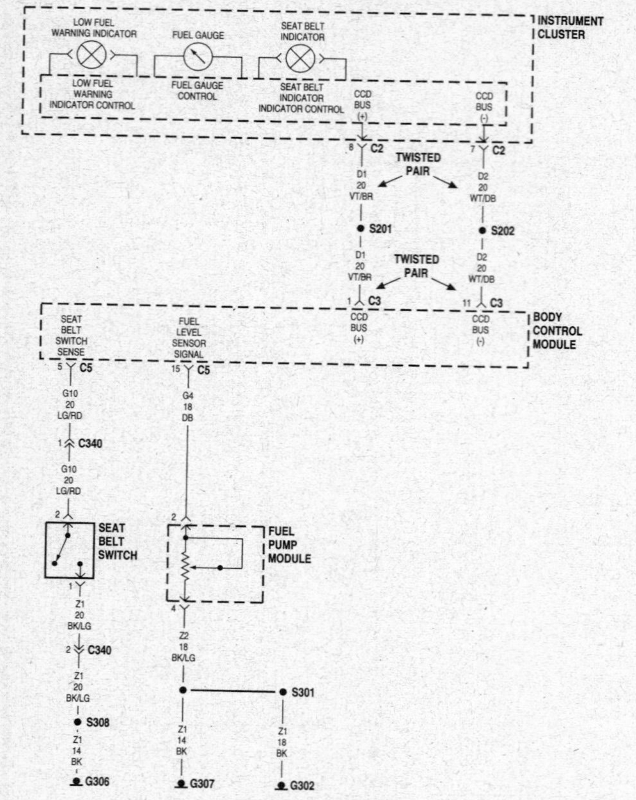

Fig. 9 Wiring diagram (Part 3 of 9). 2000 Sebring Convertible

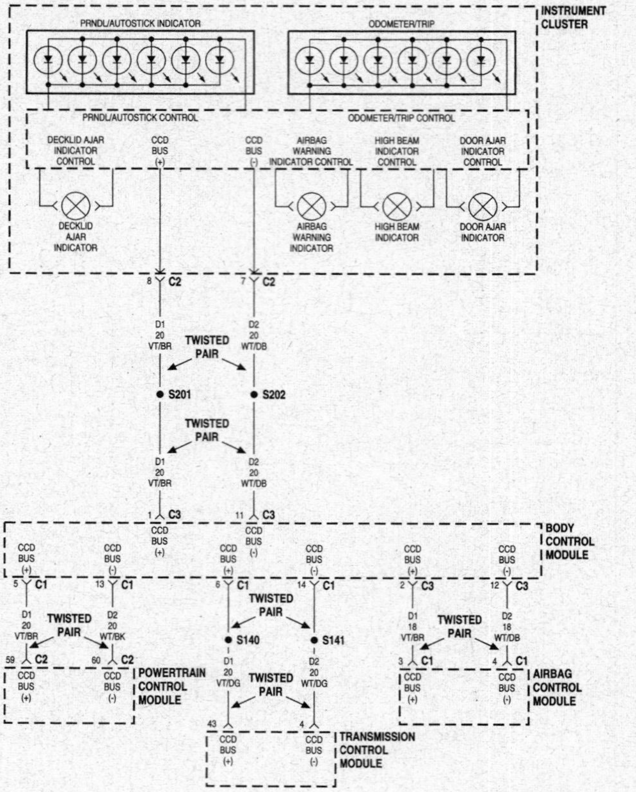

Fig. 9 Wiring diagram (Part 4 of 9). 2000 Sebring Convertible

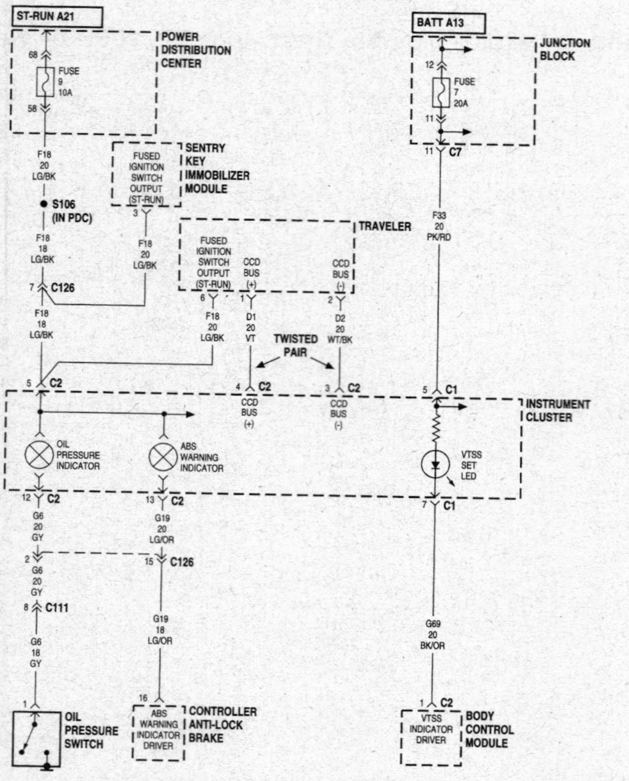

Fig. 9 Wiring diagram (Part 5 of 9). 2000 Sebring Convertible

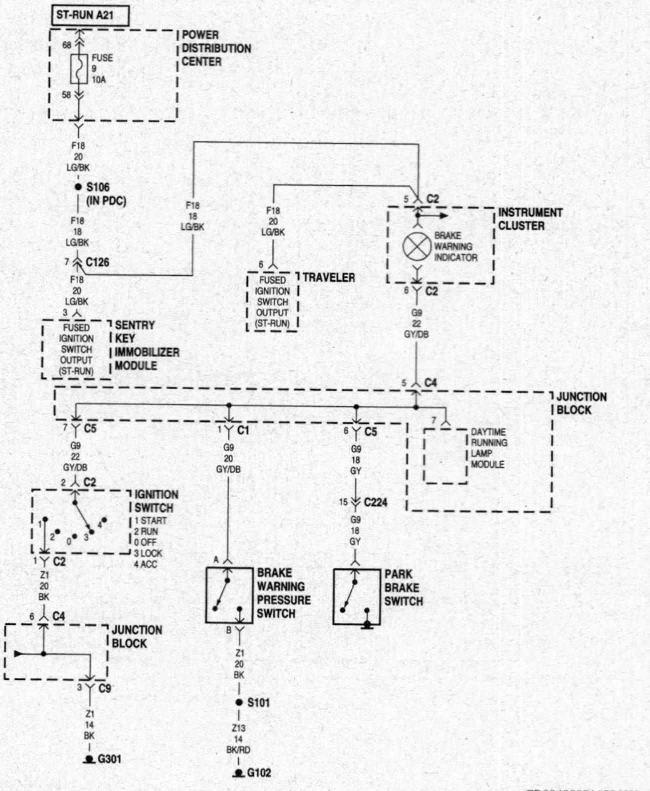

Fig. 9 Wiring diagram (Part 6 of 9). 2000 Sebring Convertible

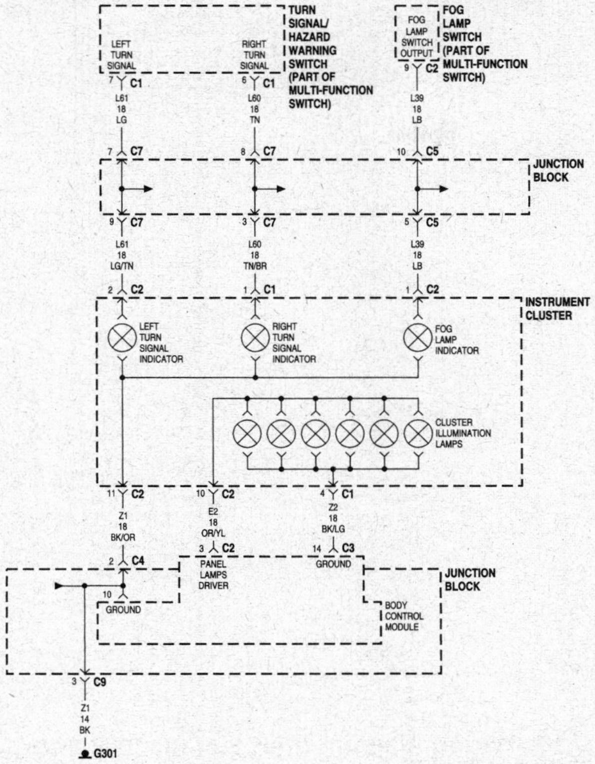

CR9049900165070X

Fig. 9 Wiring diagram (Part 7 of 9). 2000 Sebring Convertible

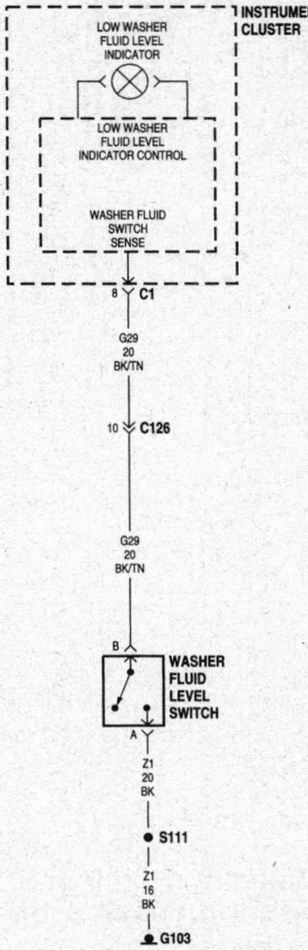

CR9049900165080X

Fig. 9 Wiring diagram (Part 8 of 9). 2000 Sebring Convertible

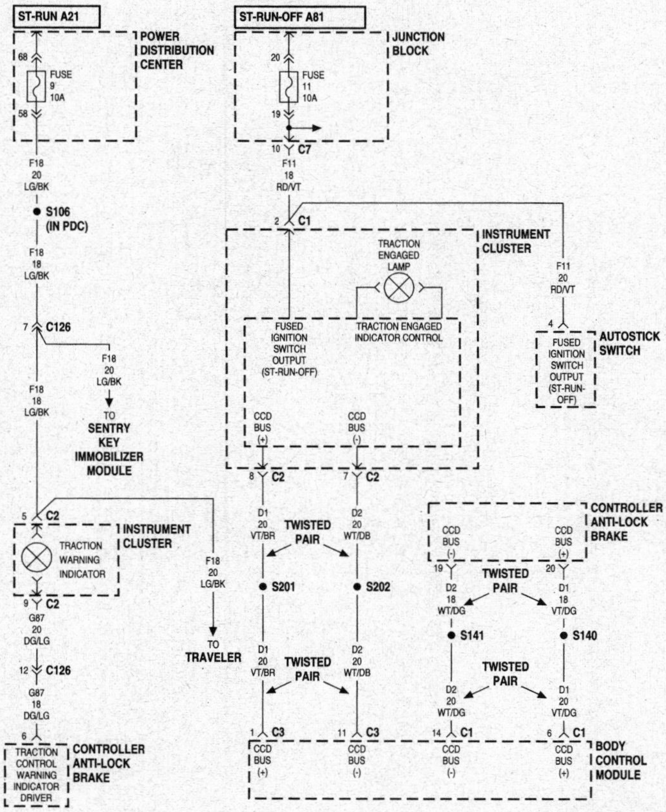

CR9049900165090X

Fig. 9 Wiring diagram (Part 9 of 9). 2000 Sebring Convertible

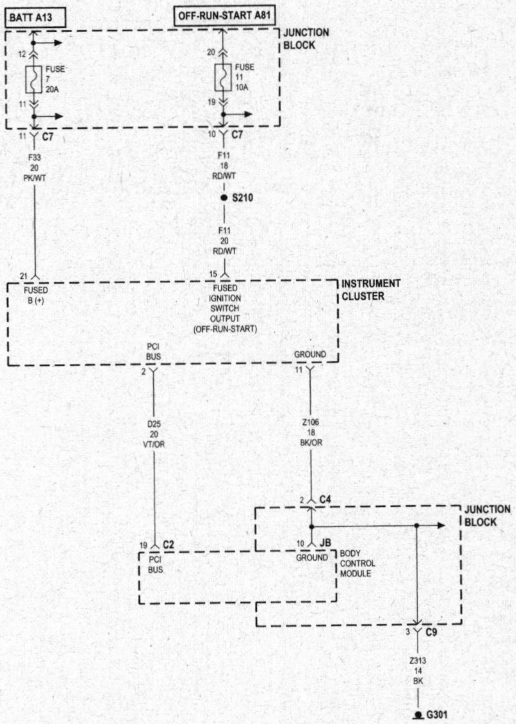

CR9040001025010X

Fig. 10 Wiring diagram (Part 1 of 8). 2001 Sebring Convertible, Sebring Sedan & Stratus Sedan

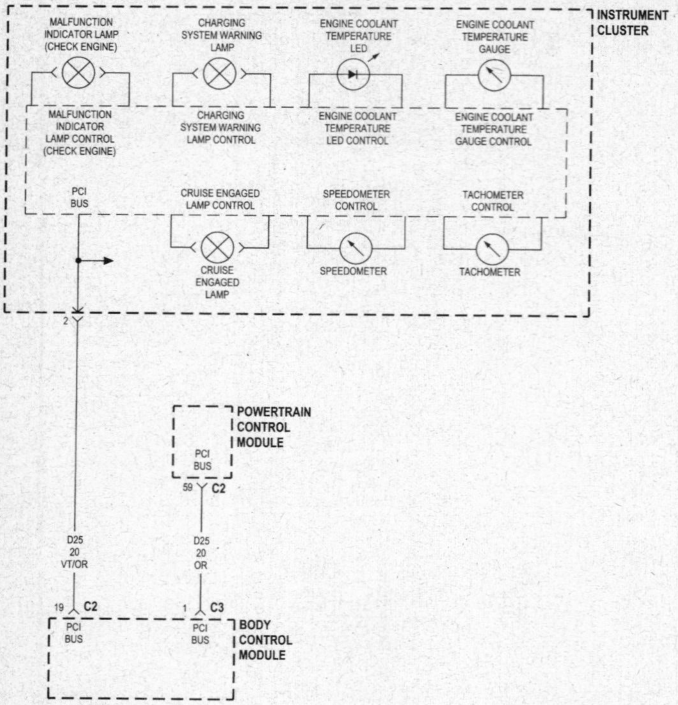

CR9040001025020X

Fig. 10 Wiring diagram (Part 2 of 8). 2001 Sebring Convertible, Sebring Sedan & Stratus Sedan

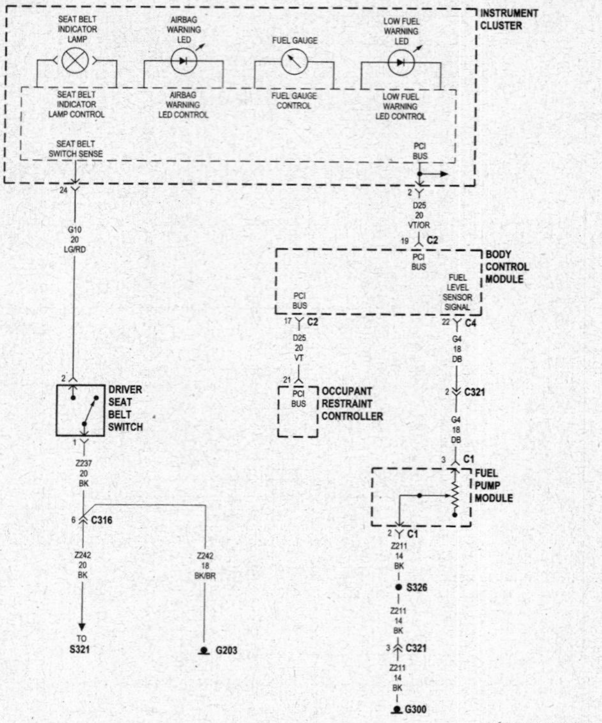

CR9040001025030X

Fig. 10 Wiring diagram (Part 3 of 8). 2001 Sebring Convertible, Sebring Sedan & Stratus Sedan

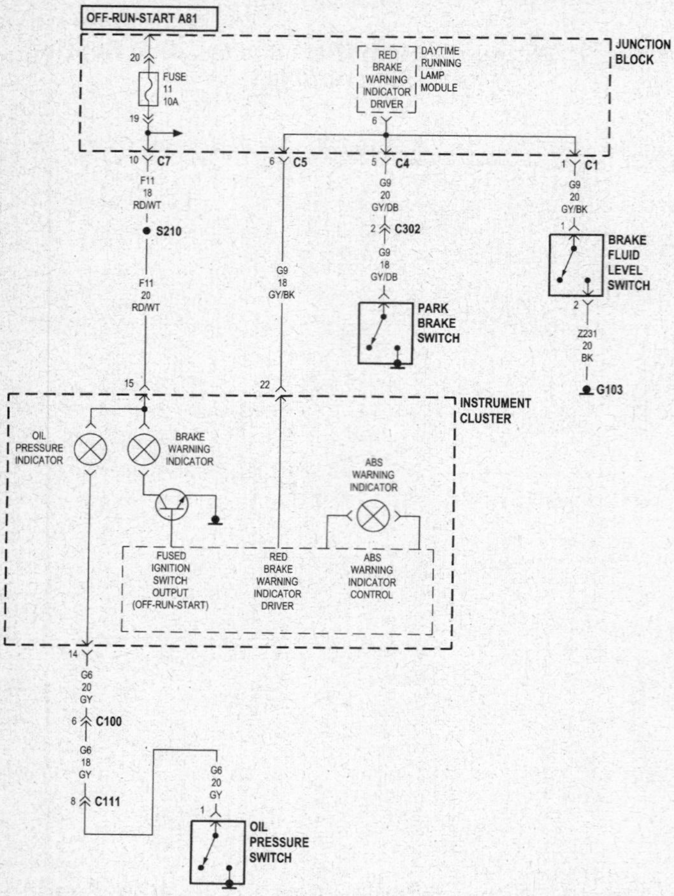

CR9040001025040X

Fig. 10 Wiring diagram (Part 4 of 8). 2001 Sebring Convertible, Sebring Sedan & Stratus Sedan

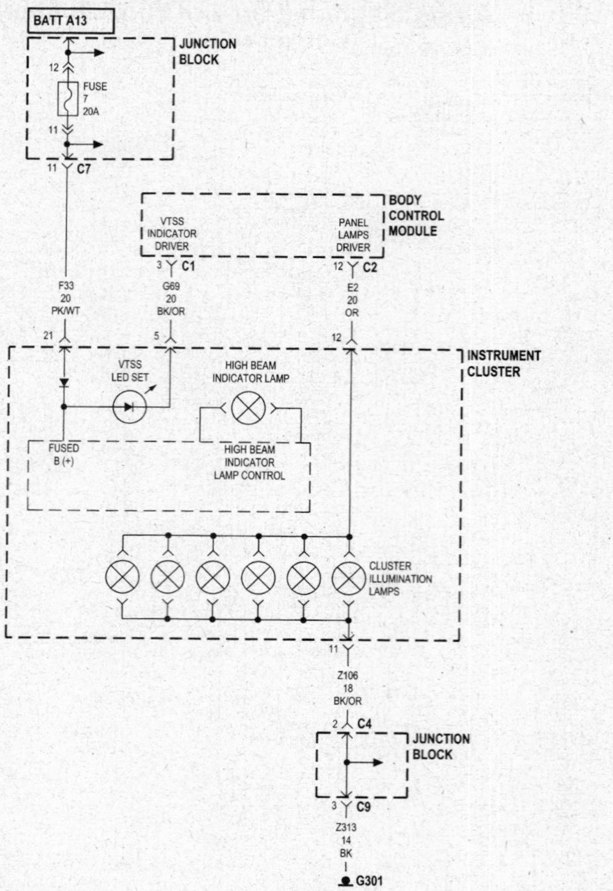

CR9040001025050X

Fig. 10 Wiring diagram (Part 5 of 8). 2001 Sebring Convertible, Sebring Sedan & Stratus Sedan

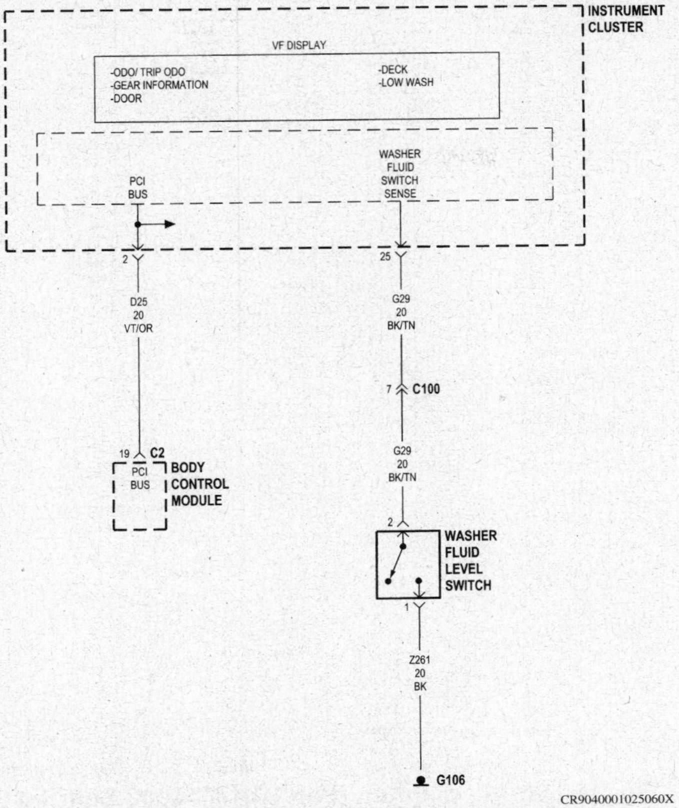

Fig. 10 Wiring diagram (Part 6 of 8). 2001 Sebring Convertible, Sebring Sedan & Stratus Sedan

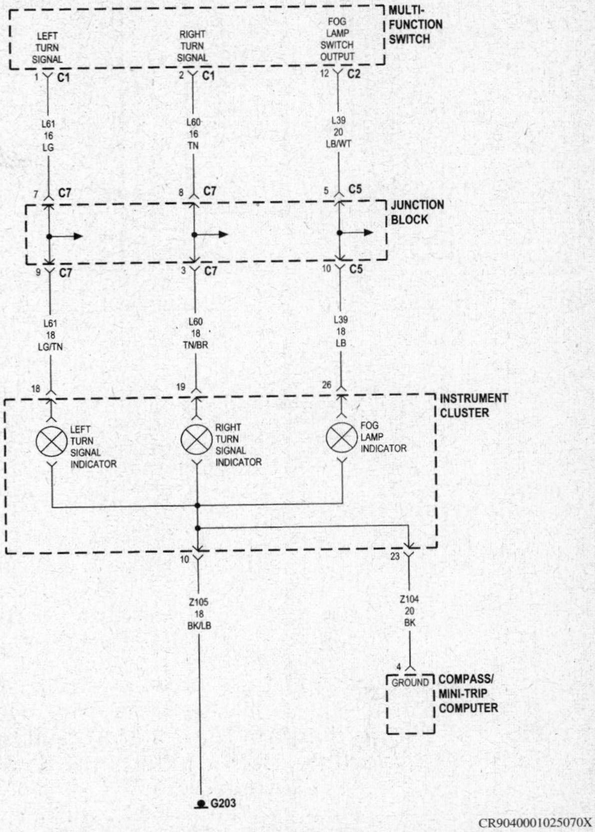

Fig. 10 Wiring diagram (Part 7 of 8). 2001 Sebring Convertible, Sebring Sedan & Stratus Sedan

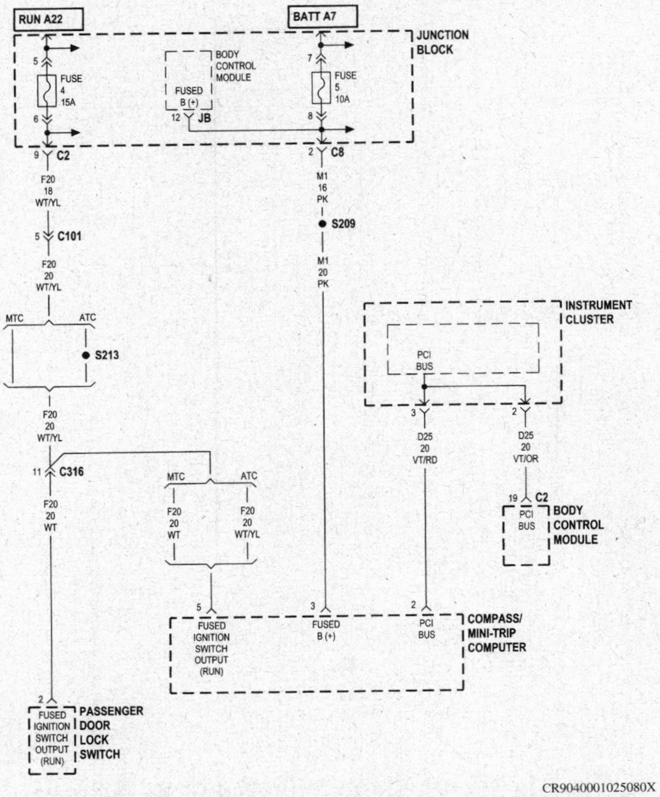

Fig. 10 Wiring diagram (Part 8 of 8). 2001 Sebring Convertible, Sebring Sedan & Stratus Sedan

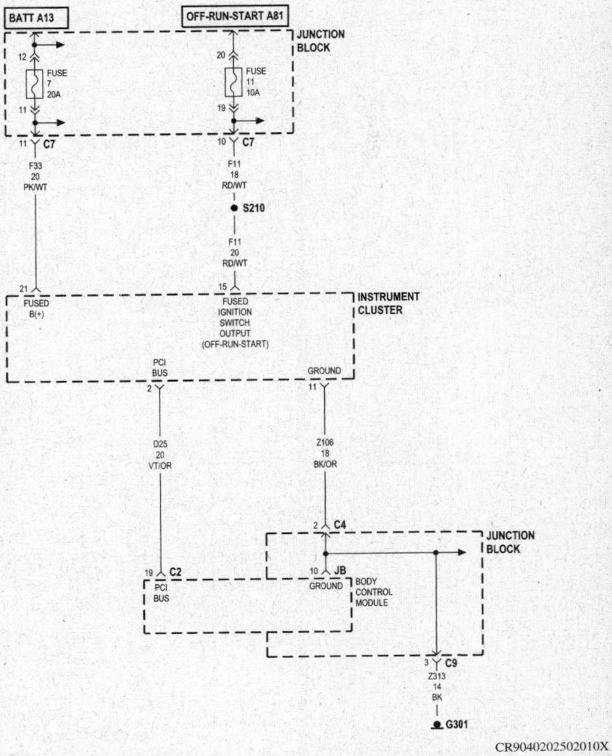

Fig. 11 Wiring diagram (Part 1 of 8). 2002–04 Sebring Convertible, Sebring Sedan & Stratus Sedan

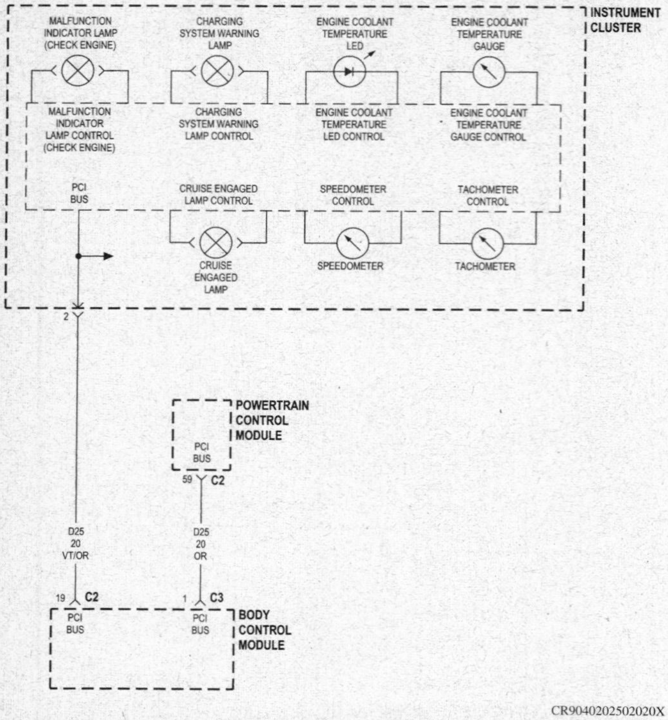

Fig. 11 Wiring diagram (Part 2 of 8). 2002–04 Sebring Convertible, Sebring Sedan & Stratus Sedan

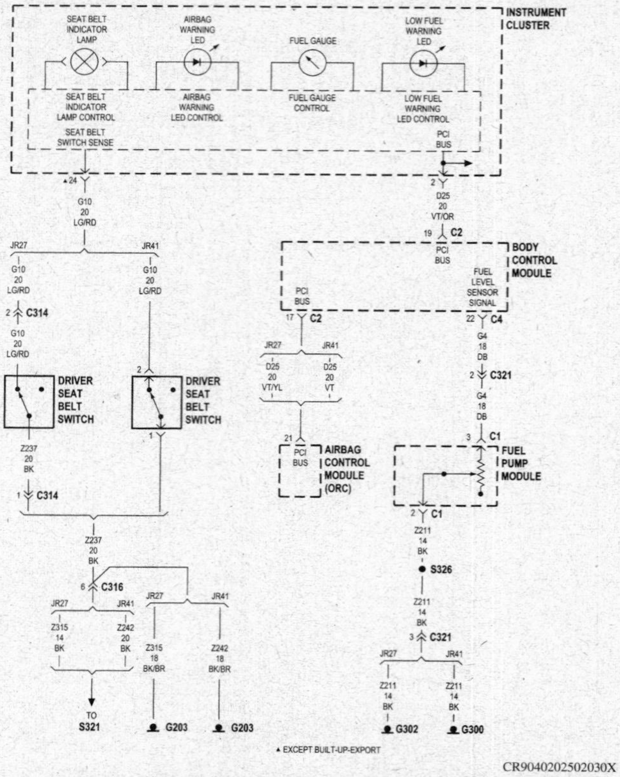

Fig. 11 Wiring diagram (Part 3 of 8). 2002 Sebring Convertible, Sebring Sedan & Stratus Sedan

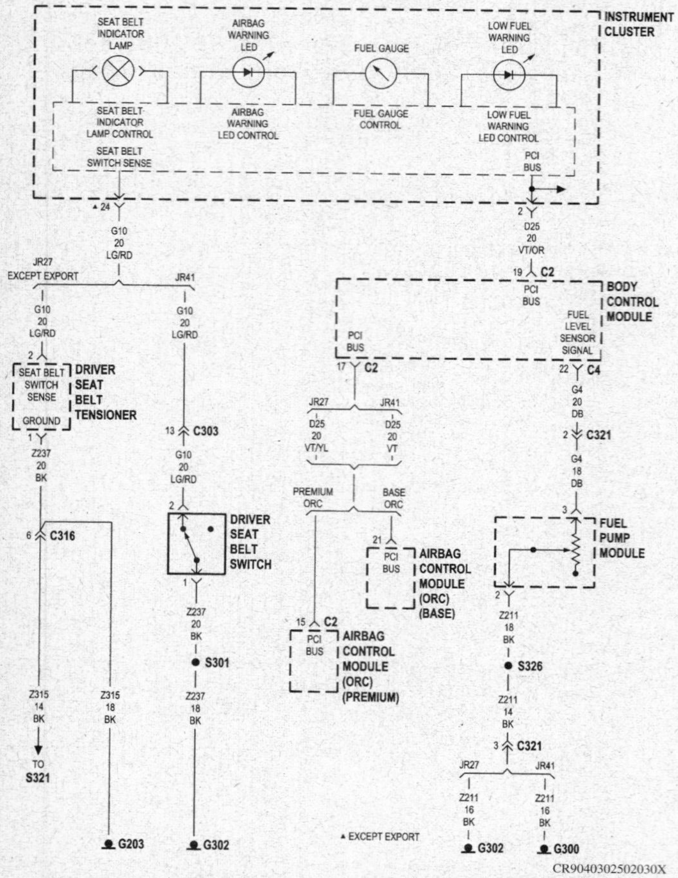

Fig. 11 Wiring diagram (Part 3 of 8). 2003–04 Sebring Convertible, Sebring Sedan & Stratus Sedan

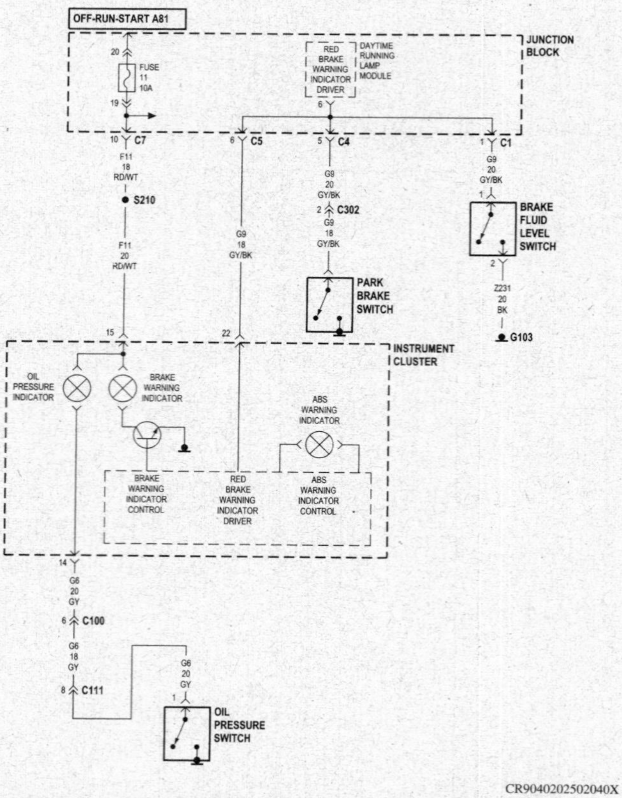

Fig. 11 Wiring diagram (Part 4 of 8). 2002–04 Sebring Convertible, Sebring Sedan & Stratus Sedan

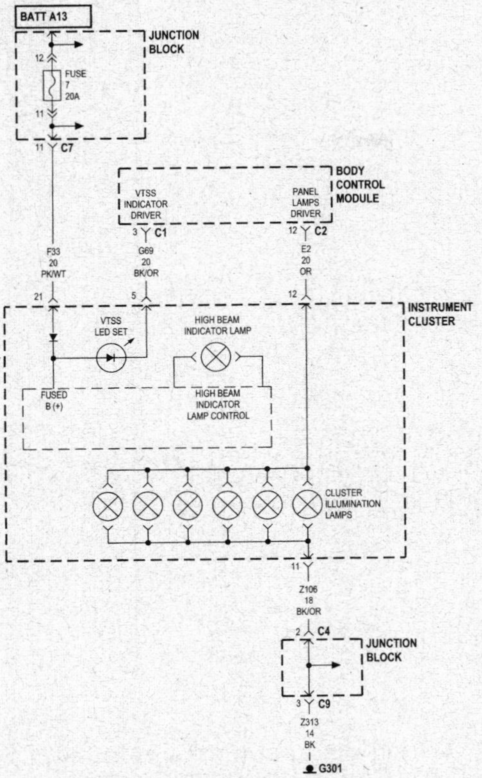

CR9040202502050X

Fig. 11 Wiring diagram (Part 5 of 8). 2002–04 Sebring Convertible, Sebring Sedan & Stratus Sedan

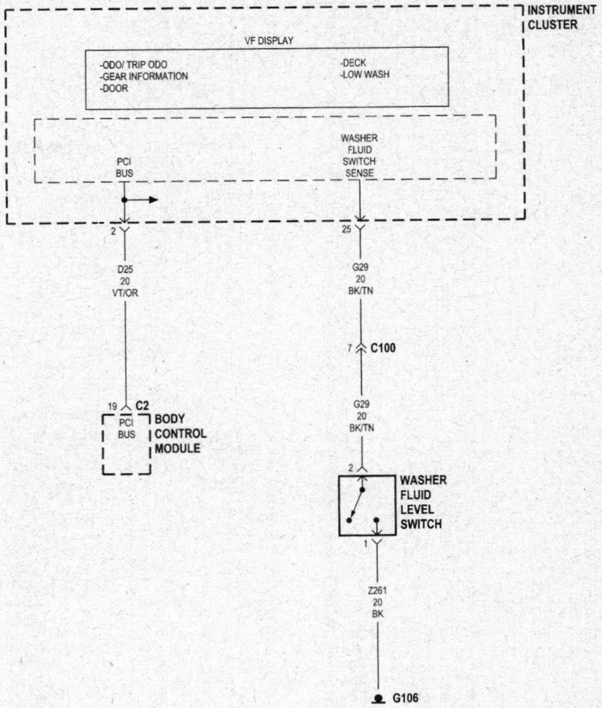

CR9040202502060X

Fig. 11 Wiring diagram (Part 6 of 8). 2002–04 Sebring Convertible, Sebring Sedan & Stratus Sedan

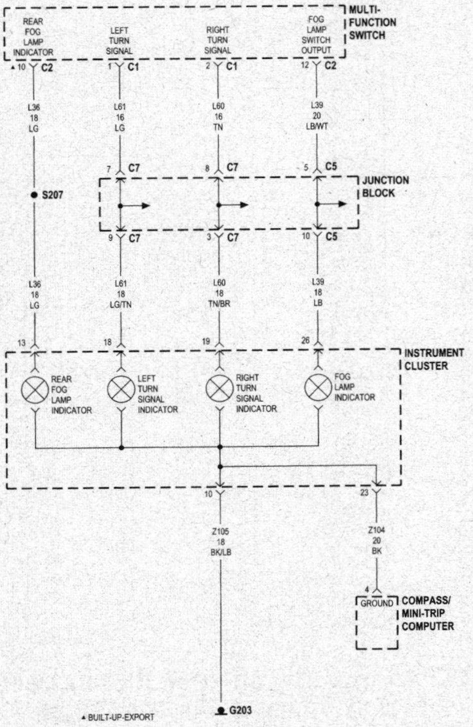

CR9040202502070X

Fig. 11 Wiring diagram (Part 7 of 8). 2002–04 Sebring Convertible, Sebring Sedan & Stratus Sedan

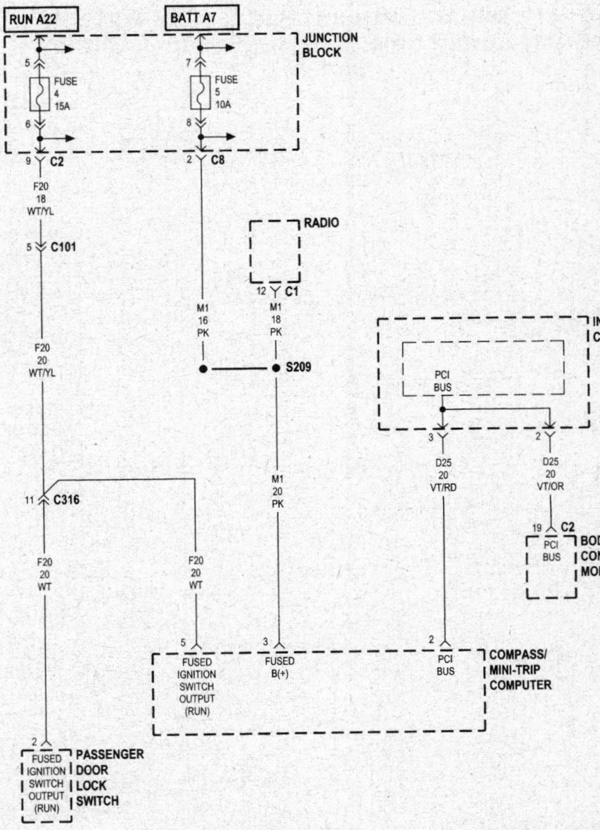

CR9040202502080X

Fig. 11 Wiring diagram (Part 8 of 8). 2002 Sebring Convertible, Sebring Sedan & Stratus Sedan

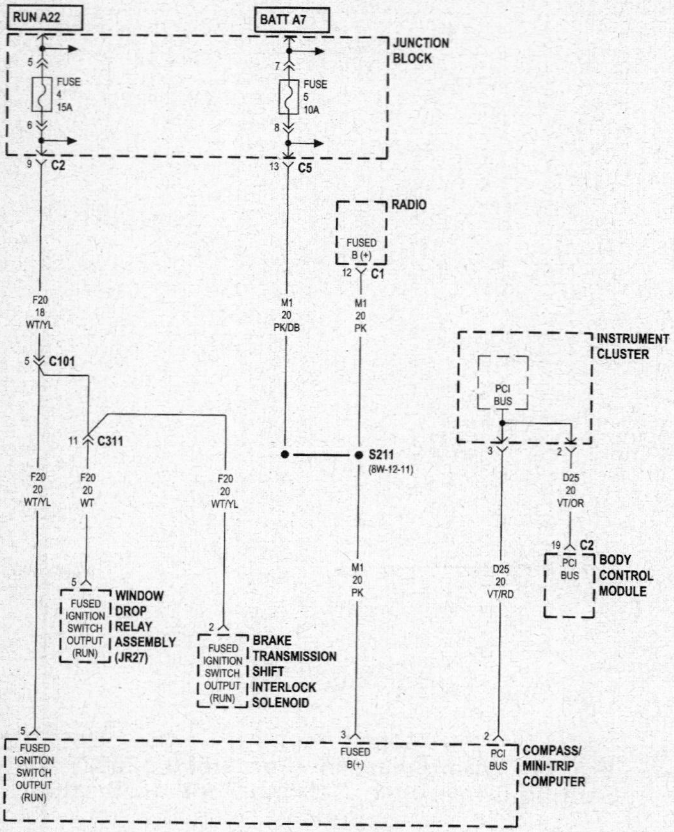

Fig. 11 Wiring diagram (Part 8 of 8). 2003–04 Sebring Convertible, Sebring Sedan & Stratus Sedan

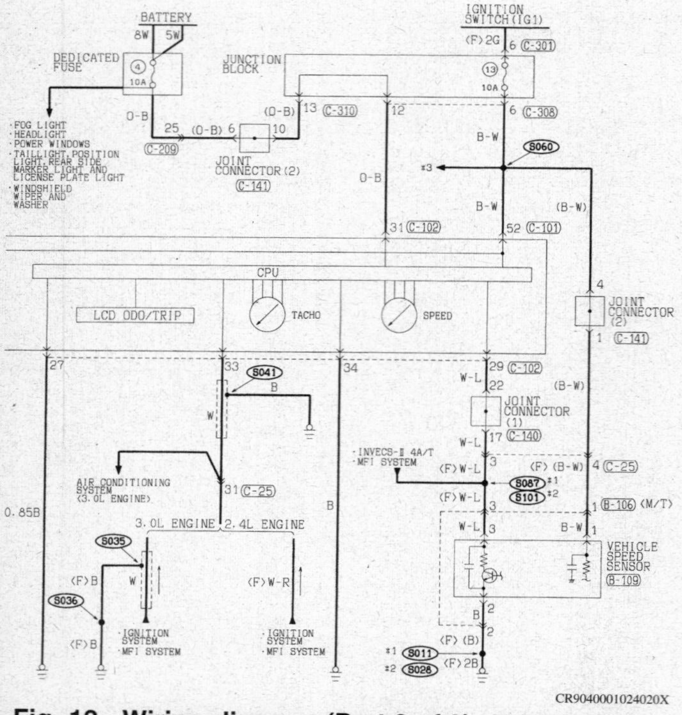

Fig. 12 Wiring diagram (Part 2 of 2). 2001 Sebring Coupe & Stratus Coupe

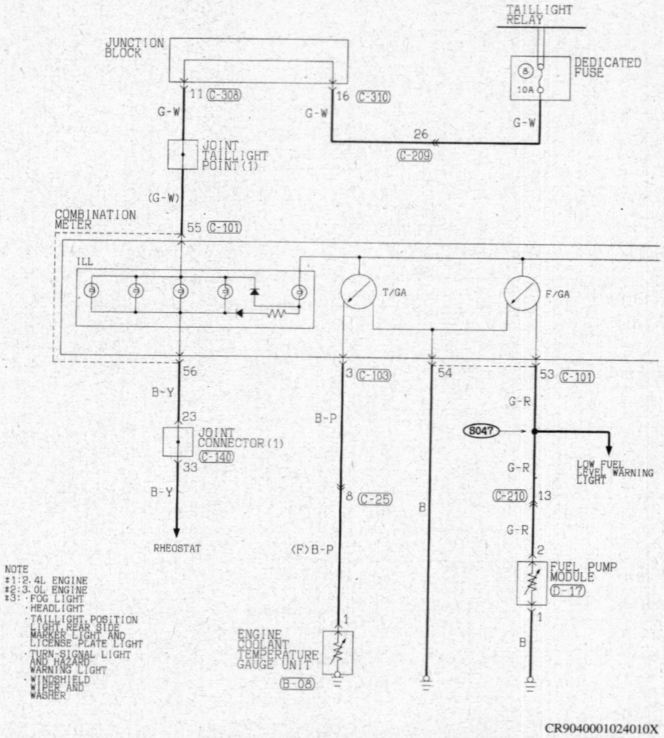

Fig. 12 Wiring diagram (Part 1 of 2). 2001 Sebring Coupe & Stratus Coupe

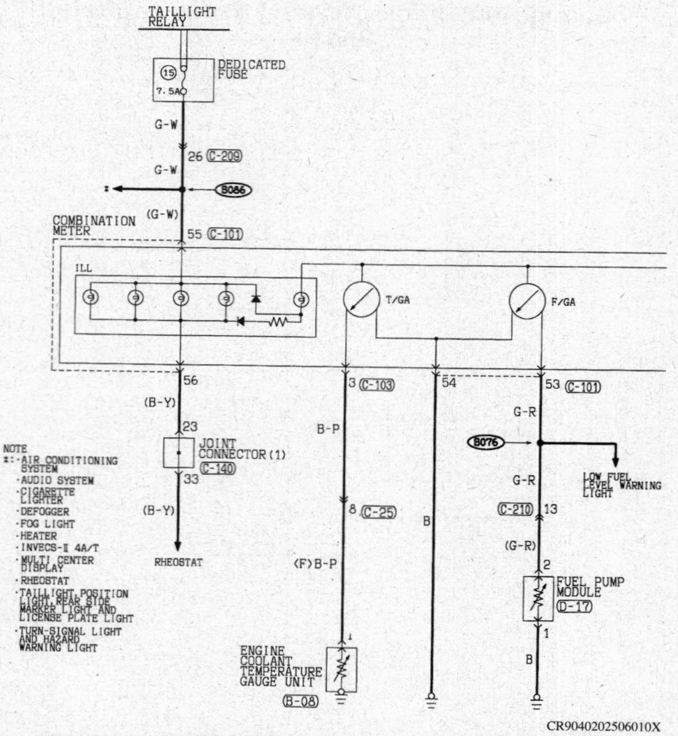

Fig. 13 Wiring diagram (Part 1 of 3). 2002–03 Sebring Coupe & Stratus Coupe

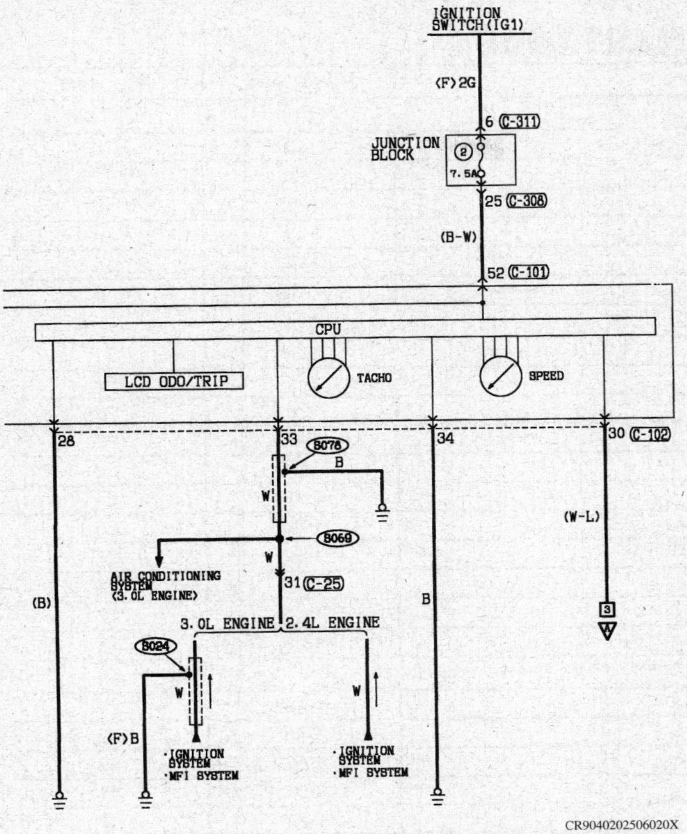

Fig. 13 Wiring diagram (Part 2 of 3). 2002–03 Sebring Coupe & Stratus Coupe

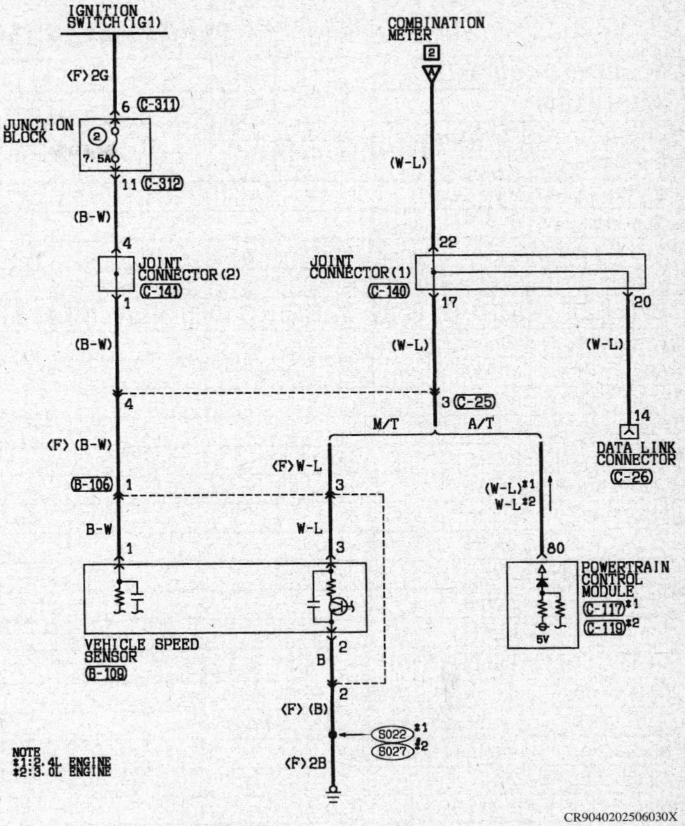

Fig. 13 Wiring diagram (Part 3 of 3). 2002–03 Sebring Coupe & Stratus Coupe

DIAGNOSTIC CHART INDEX

Continued

DIAGNOSTIC CHART INDEX—Continued

Continued

DIAGNOSTIC CHART INDEX—Continued

Test/Description	Page No.	Fig. No.
2002–04 NEON		
Fuel Gauge Inaccurate	1-78	101
Fuel Level Sensor Open	1-73	89
Fuel Level Sensor Short	1-74	90
High Beam Indicator Inoperative	1-78	102
Instrument Cluster Dimming Inoperative	1-79	105
Low Oil Pressure Indicator Always On	1-79	103
Low Oil Pressure Indicator Inoperative	1-79	104
One Gauge Inoperative	1-80	106
Panel Dimmer Open	1-74	91
Powertrain Verification Test VER-2A	1-82	116
PRND Or Autostick Indicator Display Inaccurate Or Inoperative	1-80	107
Rear Fog Lamp Indicator Inoperative	1-80	108
SBEC Message Not Received	1-75	92
Seat Belt Indicator Inoperative	1-81	110
SKIM Message Not Received	1-75	93
SKIS Verification	1-82	117
VF Display Inoperative	1-81	111
2001 SEBRING CONVERTIBLE, SEBRING SEDAN & STRATUS SEDAN		
ABS Lamp Circuit Open	1-83	119
ABS Lamp Circuit Short	1-83	120
Air Bag Lamp Circuit Open	1-83	121
Air Bag Lamp Circuit Short	1-84	122
Body Verification Test VER-1	1-91	143
Brake Warning Indicator Not Operating Properly	1-86	129
Charging System Warning Indicator Not Operating Properly	1-86	130
Cruise Engaged Indicator Not Operating Properly	1-86	131
Engine Coolant Temperature Gauge Inoperative Or Inaccurate	1-87	132
Engine Coolant Temperature Indicator Not Operating Properly	1-87	133
Fuel Gauge Not Operating Properly	1-87	134
Fuel Level Sending Unit Not Operating Properly	1-88	135
High Beam Indicator Not Operating Properly	1-88	136
Low Fuel Warning Indicator Not Operating Properly	1-89	137
Malfunction Indicator Lamp Not Operating Properly	1-89	138
No ABS Bus Messages Received	1-84	123
No BCM Bus Messages Received	1-84	124
No ORC Bus Messages Received	1-84	125
No PCM Bus Messages Received	1-84	126
No TCM Bus Messages Received	1-85	127
Panel Dimming Output Short	1-85	128
Powertrain Verification Test VER-1	1-91	144
Oil Pressure Indicator Not Operating Properly	1-89	139
Seat Belt Indicator Not Operating Properly	1-90	140
SCTM Failure	1-82	118
SKIS Verification Test	1-92	145
Speedometer Not Operating Properly	1-90	141
Tachometer Not Operating Properly	1-91	142
2002–04 SEBRING CONVERTIBLE, SEBRING SEDAN & STRATUS SEDAN		
ABS Lamp Circuit Open	1-92	146
Body Verification Tests	1-99	165
Brake Warning Indicator Always On	1-93	148
Brake Warning Indicator Inoperative	1-93	149
Charging System Warning Indicator Not Operating Properly	1-94	150
Cruise Control Indicator Inoperative	1-94	151
Engine Coolant Temperature Gauge Inoperative Or Inaccurate	1-94	152
Engine Coolant Temperature Indicator Not Operating Properly	1-95	153
Fuel Gauge Not Operating Properly	1-95	154

Continued

DIAGNOSTIC CHART INDEX—Continued

Speedometer does not operate.	Probable cause
[Comment] The cause is probably a defective vehicle speed sensor circuit system or a defective speedometer.	• Malfunction of input speed sensor or output speed sensor • Malfunction of speedometer • Malfunction of harness wire • Malfunction of connector • Malfunction of EATX-ECM • Malfunction of powertrain control module

Disconnect the combination meter connectors C-05 or C-06 and measure at the harness sides.
1. Measure the voltage between terminal (36) and ground when the vehicle is moved forward and backward.
   Ignition switch: ON
   OK: 0 ←→ 4 V (flashing)
2. Voltage between the terminal (10) and ground
   Ignition switch: ON
   OK: Battery positive voltage
3. Continuity between terminal (23) and ground
   OK: Continuity

OK → Check trouble symptom. → NG → Replace the speedometer.

1. NG → Vehicle speed sensor circuit system check

2. NG → **Check the following connectors:** B-41, B-54 and C-06
- NG → **Repair**
- OK → Check trouble symptom. → NG → Check the harness wire between the power supply and combination meter. Repair, if necessary.

3. NG → **Check the following connectors:** C-05, B-54 and B-41
- NG → **Repair**
- OK → Check trouble symptom. → NG → Check the harness wire between the combination meter and ground. Repair, if necessary.

CR9090200200000X

Fig. 14 Speedometer Does Not Operate. Avenger & 2000 Sebring Coupe

Input speed sensor or output speed sensor resistance check
- NG → **Repair**
- OK ↓

Measure at EATX-ECM connector A-75 with the connector connected.
- Measure voltage between terminals (12), (53) and (54)

OK → **Check the following connectors:** A-75, A-87, A-81 and A-29
- NG → **Repair**
- OK → Check trouble symptom. → NG → Check the harness wire between the EATX-ECM and input/output speed sensor.
  - NG → **Repair**
  - OK → Replace the EATX-ECM.

NG ↓

Disconnect the EATX-ECM connector and measure at the harness side.
- Voltage between the terminal (18) and ground.
- Ignition switch: ON

OK: 4.5 V or more

OK → Replace the EATX-ECM.

NG → **Check the following connector:** A-75
- NG → **Repair**
- OK → Check trouble symptom. → NG → Check the harness wire between the EATX-ECM and combination meter. Repair if necessary.

CR9090200202000X

Fig. 16 Vehicle Speed Sensor Circuit System Test. Avenger & 2000 Sebring Coupe

Remove the engine coolant gauge unit connector.
↓
Connect a test light (12 V – 3.4 W) between the harness side connector and the ground.
↓
Turn the ignition switch ON.

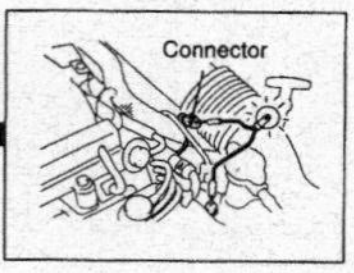

Check the condition of the test light and the gauge.
1. Test light is illuminated (Gauge needle is not moving) → Replace the engine coolant temperature gauge.
2. Test light is illuminated (Gauge needle is moving) → Replace the engine coolant temperature gauge unit.
3. Test light is not illuminated (Gauge needle is not moving) → Repair the harness.

CR9090200204000X

Fig. 18 Engine Coolant Temperature Gauge Test. Avenger & 2000 Sebring Coupe

Tachometer does not operate.	Probable cause
[Comment] There may be no input of ignition signal from engine, a defective meter power supply circuit may exist or a defective meter ground circuit may be present.	• Malfunction of tachometer • Malfunction of harness wire • Malfunction of connector • Malfunction of powertrain control module

SCAN TOOL DIAGNOSTIC TROUBLE CODE
Is diagnostic trouble code 35 output?
- Yes → Troubleshooting.
- No ↓

Disconnect the combination meter connectors C-04, C-05 and C-06. Measure at the harness sides.
1. Voltage between terminal (24) and ground when the vehicle is moved forward and backward.
   Ignition switch: ON
   OK: 4.8 – 5.2 V
2. Voltage between terminal (10) and ground
   Ignition switch: ON
   OK: Battery positive voltage
3. Continuity between terminal (44) and ground
   OK: Continuity

OK → Check trouble symptom. → NG → Replace the tachometer.

1. NG → **Check the following connectors:** A-76, A-78, C-23 and C-05
- NG → **Repair**
- OK → Check trouble symptom. → NG → Check the harness wire between the combination meter and powertrain control module.
  - NG → **Repair**
  - OK → Powertrain control module check

2. NG → **Check the following connectors:** B-41, B-54 and C-06
- NG → **Repair**
- OK → Check trouble symptom. → NG → Check the harness wire between the power supply and combination meter. Repair, if necessary.

3. NG → **Check the following connectors:** C-04, B-54 and B-41
- NG → **Repair**
- OK → Check trouble symptom. → NG → Check the harness wire between combination meter and ground. Repair, if necessary.

CR9090200201000X

Fig. 15 Tachometer Does Not Operate. Avenger & 2000 Sebring Coupe

Remove the fuel gauge unit connector.
↓
Use special tool MB991219 to connect a test light to the harness side connector.
↓
Turn the ignition switch to ON.

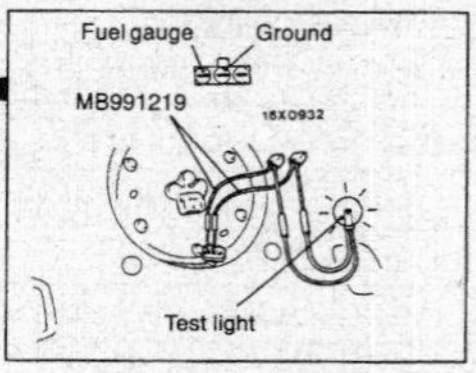

Check the condition of the test light and the gauge.
1. Test light is illuminated (Gauge needle is not moving) → Replace the fuel gauge.
2. Test light is illuminated (Gauge needle is moving) → Replace the fuel gauge unit.
3. Test light is not illuminated (Gauge needle is not moving) → Repair the harness.

CR9090200203000X

Fig. 17 Fuel Gauge Test. Avenger & 2000 Sebring Coupe

Remove the oil pressure gauge unit connector.
↓
Connect a test light (12 V – 3.4 W) between the harness side connector and the ground.
↓
Turn the ignition switch ON.

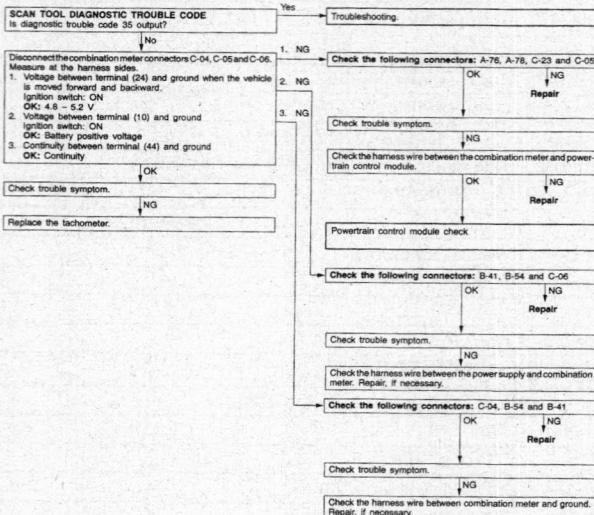

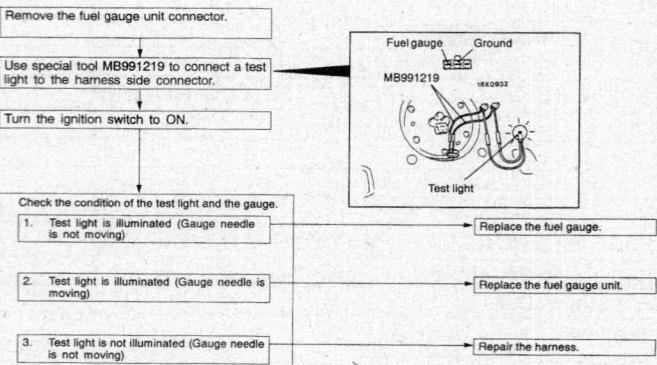

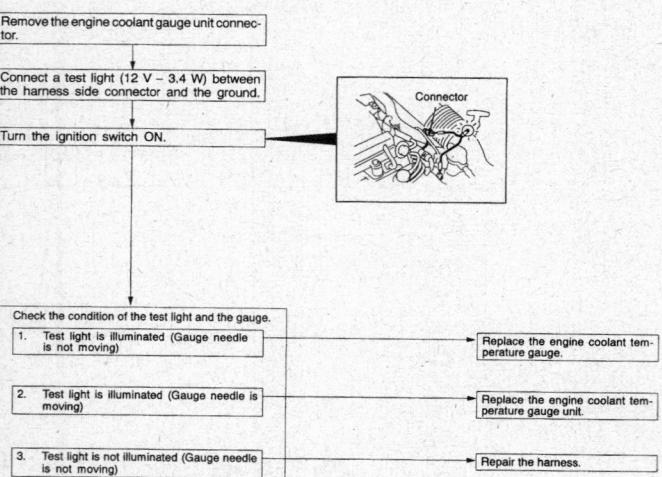

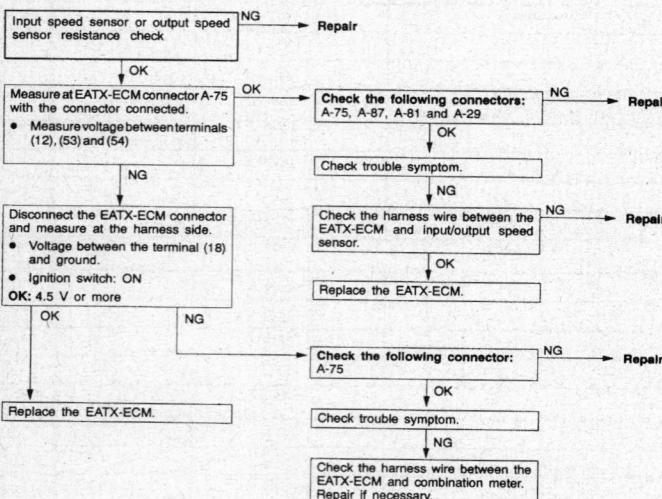

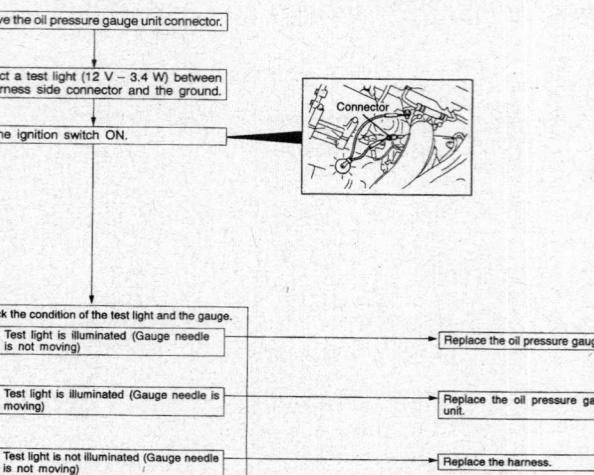

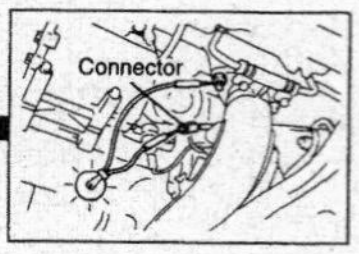

Check the condition of the test light and the gauge.
1. Test light is illuminated (Gauge needle is not moving) → Replace the oil pressure gauge.
2. Test light is illuminated (Gauge needle is moving) → Replace the oil pressure gauge unit.
3. Test light is not illuminated (Gauge needle is not moving) → Replace the harness.

CR9090200205000X

Fig. 19 Oil Pressure Gauge Test. Avenger & 2000 Sebring Coupe

When Monitored and Set Condition:

FUEL LEVEL SENDING CIRCUIT ERROR

When Monitored: With the ignition key on and battery voltage greater than 10 volts.

Set Condition: The voltage at the fuel level sending unit input to the body control module exceeds 95% of battery voltage for over 10 seconds.

POSSIBLE CAUSES
FUEL LEVEL SENSOR GROUND CIRCUIT OPEN
BCM FUEL LEVEL SENSE INPUT CIRCUIT DEFECTIVE
FUEL LEVEL SENSOR SIGNAL SHORT TO GROUND
TANK AND SENDING UNIT DEFECTIVE
DRB DISPLAYS RAM FAULT
DRB SHOWS BUS OPERATIONAL FAILURE
MIC CLUSTER MISMATCH
DEFECTIVE LOW FUEL LAMP BULB
FUEL LEVEL SENDING UNIT DEFECTIVE
FUEL LEVEL SENSOR DEFECTIVE
FUEL LEVEL SENSOR SIGNAL CIRUIT OPEN
FUEL TANK SENDING UNIT DEFECTIVE
OPEN FUEL LEVEL CKT
BCM LOW FUEL LAMP CIRCUIT INPUT DEFECTIVE
DEF BCM LOW FUEL LP CKT INPUT
BCM FUEL LEVEL SENSE SIGNAL INPUT CKT DEFECTIVE
BCM FUEL LEVEL SENSOR INPUT CKT DEF
BCM FUEL LEVEL SENSOR SIGNAL CKT DEFECTIVE
DEFECTIVE CLUSTER CIRCUIT BOARD
FUEL TANK SENDING UNIT DEFECTIVE
SYSTEM OK AT THIS TIME

CR9059900000010X

Fig. 20 Fuel Level Sending Circuit (Part 1 of 5). Breeze, Cirrus, 2000 Sebring Convertible & Stratus

TEST	ACTION
1	Turn Ignition Switch On. With the DRB, select MIC CLUSTER. Does the DRB display BUS OPERATIONAL? Yes → Go To 2 No → Choose appropriate Communication symptom to repair failure. Perform Body Verification TEST VER-1A
2	Turn Ignition Switch On. With the DRB, select MIC CLUSTER. Does the DRB display any of the following problems? NO RESPONSE Refer to symptom * NO RESPONSE INSTRUMENT CLUSTER None of the above Go To 3
3	With the DRB, read MIC DTC'S. Does the DRB show RAM FAULT? Yes → Remove the MIC Cluster and replace the Circuit Board. Perform Body Verification TEST VER-1A No → Go To 4
4	With the DRB, read the MIC Cluster type to verify the correct application (e.g. US or Metric). Does the DRB show the correct MIC Cluster type? Yes → Go To 5 No → Remove the MIC Cluster and replace the Circuit Board. Perform Body Verification TEST VER-1A
5	With the DRB, select BODY COMPUTER Systems Test. Does the DRB show PCM status as INACTIVE ON THE BUS? Yes → Refer to symptom * NO RESPONSE FROM PCM No → Go To 6
6	Is the problem with Fuel Warning Lamp only? Yes → Go To 7 No → Go To 10
7	**The Low Fuel Lamp lights when the Fuel Level is below 1/8 tank approx 940 ohms.** Is the Low Fuel light On when it should be Off? Yes → Replace the Body Control Module. Perform Body Verification TEST VER-1A No → Go To 8

CR9059900000020X

Fig. 20 Fuel Level Sending Circuit (Part 2 of 5). Breeze, Cirrus, 2000 Sebring Convertible & Stratus

TEST	ACTION
8	With the DRB actuate the MIC Bulbs. Did the Low Fuel Lamp light during the test? Yes → Replace the Body Control Module. Perform Body Verification TEST VER-1A No → Go To 9
9	Remove the Cluster and remove and inspect the Low Fuel Bulb. **Check Connectors - Clean / repair as necessary.** Is the Bulb burned out? Yes → Replace Bulb. Perform Body Verification TEST VER-1A No → Replace the Cluster Circuit Board. Perform Body Verification TEST VER-1A
10	Is the problem Gauge accuracy? Yes → Go To 11 No → Go To 13
11	Turn Ignition Off. Disconnect the Fuel Pump Electrical Connector. Remove Fuel Pump Module from Tank. **Check Connectors - Clean / repair as necessary.** Measure the resistance between the Fuel Level Sensor Circuit and ground at the Sending Unit (module). Fuel Tank Level at full, resistance measurement should be between 50 and 90 ohms. Fuel Tank Level at 3/4, resistance measurement should be between 310 and 370 ohms. Fuel Tank Level at 1/2, resistance measurement should be between 520 and 580 ohms. Fuel Tank Level at 1/4, resistance measurement should be between 730 and 790 ohms. Fuel Tank Level at empty, resistance measurement should be between 1020 and 1080 ohms. Does the resistance match the given values? No → Go To 12 Yes → Replace the Body Control Module. Perform Body Verification TEST VER-1A
12	Remove the Fuel Level Sending Unit from the Fuel Tank; observing float attachment. Inspect the Tank for foreign material, and Sending Unit for bent, sticking or binding arm, or defective float. Is the Tank and Sending Unit condition OK? Yes → System operating properly at this time. Perform Body Verification TEST VER-1A No → Repair or Replace as necessary. Perform Body Verification TEST VER-1A
13	Does the Fuel Gauge show Full all the time? Yes → Go To 14 No → Go To 17

CR9059900000030X

Fig. 20 Fuel Level Sending Circuit (Part 3 of 5). Breeze, Cirrus, 2000 Sebring Convertible & Stratus

TEST	ACTION
14	Turn Ignition Off. Disconnect the Fuel Pump Electrical Connector. **Check Connectors - Clean / repair as necessary.** Turn Ignition On (Engine Off). Look at the Fuel Gauge. Does the Fuel Gauge read empty? Yes → Go To 15 No → Go To 16
15	Remove the Fuel Level Sending Unit from the Fuel Tank. Inspect the Tank for foreign material, and Sending Unit for bent, sticking or binding arm. Is the Tank and Sending Unit condition OK? Yes → Replace the Fuel Tank Sending Unit. Perform Body Verification TEST VER-1A No → Repair or replace as necessary. Perform Body Verification TEST VER-1A
16	Key Off. Disconnect the Body 20-Way Connector. **Check Connectors - Clean / repair as necessary.** Using an Ohmmeter, measure the Fuel Level Sensor Signal Circuit to ground. Is the resistance below 5.0 Ohms? Yes → Repair the Fuel Level Sensor Signal for a short to ground. Perform Body Verification TEST VER-1A No → Replace the Body Control Module. Perform Body Verification TEST VER-1A
17	Start the Engine. With the DRB, select BODY COMPUTER, READ DTCs. Does the DRB show FUEL LEVEL SENDING CIRCUIT ERROR? Yes → Go To 18 No → Go To 21
18	Turn Ignition Off. Disconnect the Fuel Pump Electrical Connector. **Check Connectors - Clean / repair as necessary.** Key On. Connect a jumper wire between the Fuel Level Sensor Signal Circuit and the Ground Circuit. With the DRB, Select SENSOR DISPLAY read the FUEL LEVEL VOLTAGE. Is the voltage below 1.0 volt? Yes → Replace the Fuel Level Sensor. Perform Body Verification TEST VER-1A No → Go To 19

CR9059900000040X

Fig. 20 Fuel Level Sending Circuit (Part 4 of 5). Breeze, Cirrus, 2000 Sebring Convertible & Stratus

TEST	ACTION
19	Turn Ignition Off. Disconnect the Fuel Pump Electrical connector. **Check Connectors - Clean / repair as necessary.** Key On. Connect a jumper wire between the Fuel Level Sensor Signal Circuit and Ground. With the DRB, Select SENSOR DISPLAY read the FUEL LEVEL VOLTAGE. Is the Fuel Level voltage below 1.0 volt? Yes → Repair the Open Ground Circuit to the Fuel Level Sensor. Perform Body Verification TEST VER-1A No → Go To 20
20	Key On. Gain access to the BCM 20-way connector but do not disconnect. Backjumper a wire between Fuel Level Sensor Signal Circuit and Ground at BCM. With the DRB, Select SENSOR SIGNAL read the FUEL LEVEL VOLTAGE. Is the Fuel Level voltage below 1.0 volt? Yes → Repair the open Fuel Lvl Sen Sig Ckt between the Sensor and the BCM. Perform Body Verification TEST VER-1A No → Replace the Body Control Module (BCM). Perform Body Verification TEST VER-1A
21	Turn Ignition Off. Disconnect the Fuel Pump Electrical Connector. **Check Connectors - Clean / repair as necessary.** Using a voltmeter measure the Fuel Level Sensor Signal Circuit. Is the voltage above 9.5 volts? Yes → Replace the Fuel Tank Sending Unit. Perform Body Verification TEST VER-1A No → Go To 22
22	Gain access to the Body 20-way Connector (at BCM). **Check Connectors - Clean / repair as necessary.** Using a voltmeter backprobe Fuel Level Sensor Signal (Cav. 15). Is the voltage above 10.0 volts? Yes → Repair the Open Fuel Level Sensor Signal Circuit. Perform Body Verification TEST VER-1A No → Replace the Body Control Module (BCM). Perform Body Verification TEST VER-1A

CR9059900000050X

Fig. 20 Fuel Level Sending Circuit (Part 5 of 5). Breeze, Cirrus, 2000 Sebring Convertible & Stratus

TEST	ACTION
6	Turn Ignition to the Off, (Unlock position). With the DRB select BODY, ELECTRO/ MECH CLUSTER (MIC), ACTUATOR TEST. Actuate all Gauges. Tach Cal Points: #1 (6000), #2 (3000), #3 (3000), #4 (1000) and #5 (0). Speedo Cal Points: #1 (100), #2 (75), #3 (55), #4 (20) and #5 (0). Fuel Cal Points: #1 (FULL), #2 (1/2), #3 (1/2), #4 (EMPTY) and #5 (EMPTY). Temperature Cal Points: #1 (HOT), #2 (1/2), #3 (1/2), #4 (COLD) and #5 (COLD). Do the Gauges move at all? From Low to the Upper Limit? Yes → Go To 7 No → Replace the Instrument Cluster Circuit Board (MIC). Perform Body Verification TEST VER-1A.
7	Turn Ignition On. With the DRB select BODY, BODY COMPUTER, INPUT/ OUTPUT. Read the IGNITION RUN/START status. Does the DRB show Switch CLOSED? Yes → Replace the Body Control Module (BCM). Perform Body Verification TEST VER-1A. No → Refer to symptom * NO RESPONSE FROM BCM (BAT PWR DISCON'D)

CR9059900001020X

Fig. 21 All Gauges Not Operating (Part 2 of 2). Breeze, Cirrus, 2000 Sebring Convertible & Stratus

POSSIBLE CAUSES
BCM IGN RUN/START INPUT CKT DEFECTIVE
INSTRUMENT CLUSTER CKT BOARD OUT OF SPEC
DRB DISPLAYS RAM FAULT
DRB SHOWS BUS OPERATIONAL FAILURE
MIC CLUSTER MISMATCH

TEST	ACTION
1	Turn Ignition Switch On. With the DRB, select MIC CLUSTER. Does the DRB display BUS OPERATIONAL? Yes → Go To 2 No → Choose appropriate Communication symptom to repair failure. Perform Body Verification TEST VER-1A
2	Turn Ignition Switch On. With the DRB, select MIC CLUSTER. Does the DRB display any of the following problems? NO RESPONSE Refer to symptom * NO RESPONSE INSTRUMENT CLUSTER None of the above Go To 3
3	With the DRB, read MIC DTC'S. Does the DRB show RAM FAULT? Yes → Remove the MIC Cluster and replace the Circuit Board. Perform Body Verification TEST VER-1A No → Go To 4
4	With the DRB, read the MIC Cluster type to verify the correct application (e.g. US or Metric). Does the DRB show the correct MIC Cluster type? Yes → Go To 5 No → Remove the MIC Cluster and replace the Circuit Board. Perform Body Verification TEST VER-1A
5	With the DRB, select BODY COMPUTER Systems Test. Does the DRB show PCM status is INACTIVE ON THE BUS? Yes → Refer to symptom * NO RESPONSE FROM PCM No → Go To 6

CR9059900001010X

Fig. 21 All Gauges Not Operating (Part 1 of 2). Breeze, Cirrus, 2000 Sebring Convertible & Stratus

POSSIBLE CAUSES
SEAT BELT LAMP STAYS ON
TURN SIGNAL LAMPS NOT WORKING
EXTERIOR HEAD/FOG LAMPS DEFECTIVE
HIGH BEAM HEADLAMPS NOT LIGHTING
HIGH BEAM INDICATOR LAMP NOT LIGHTING
NOT ABS EQUIPPED VEHICLE
PARK BRAKE OPERATION DEFECTIVE
BCM HIGHBEAM INDICATOR LAMP CKT DEFECTIVE
FUSED IGNITION SWITCH OUTPUT CIRCUIT OPEN
HIGH BEAM INDICATOR BULB DEFECTIVE
LOW FUEL/LAMP BULB DEFECTIVE
LOW OIL PRESSURE
OIL LEVEL LOW
OIL WARNING LAMP/BULB DEFECTIVE
SEATBELT WARNING LAMP/BULB DEFECTIVE
CHECK ENGINE LAMP STATUS ON
CHECK ENGINE LAMP STAYS ON
CRUISE CONTROL LAMP STAYS ON
CRUISE CONTROL LAMP SYS FAILURE
DRB READS CHARGING LIMP IN YES
GENERATOR LAMP NOT LIGHTING
JUNCTION BLOCK DEFECTIVE
ABS WARNING LAMP/BULB DEFECTIVE
BRAKE FLUID LEVEL SWITCH GND CIRCUIT OPEN
BRAKE WARNING LAMP DRIVER CIRCUIT
BRAKE WARNING LAMP GROUND CIRCUIT OPEN
CHECK ENGINE LAMP/BULB DEFECTIVE
COOLANT TEMPERATURE BULB DEFECTIVE
CRUISE CONTROL LAMP/BULB DEFECTIVE
FOG LAMP INDICATOR BULB DEFECTIVE
FOG LAMP SWITCH OUTPUT CIRCUIT DEFECTIVE
GENERATOR LAMP/BULB DEFECTIVE
LEFT TURN SIGNAL CIRCUIT OPEN

CR9059900002010X

Fig. 22 Any Or All Cluster Warning Lamp Problems (Part 1 of 21). Breeze, Cirrus, 2000 Sebring Convertible & Stratus

POSSIBLE CAUSES
OIL PRESS SWITCH SENSE CKT SHORT TO GND
OIL PRESSURE SWITCH SENSE CIRCUIT OPEN
RED BRAKE WARNING LAMP/BULB DEFECTIVE
RIGHT TURN SIGNAL CIRCUIT OPEN
TURN SIGNAL BULBS DEFECTIVE
COOLANT TEMP LAMP NO FUNCTION
COOLANT TEMP LAMP STAYS ON
DRB READS ECT SENSOR LIMP IN YES
ABS WARNING LAMP STAYS ON
AIRBAG WARNING LAMP PROBLEM
BCM SEATBELT WARNING LAMP OUTPUT DEFECTIVE
DEFECTIVE OIL PRESSURE SWITCH
DRB SHOWS DTC'S ARE PRESENT
EATX PRNDL MESSAGE PRESENT
INSTRUMENT CLUSTER CIRCUIT BOARD DEFECTIVE
INSTRUMENT CLUSTER DEFECTIVE
MIC CIRCUIT BOARD DEFECTIVE
BRAKE FLUID LEVEL LOW
BRAKE FLUID RESERVIOR LOW
RED BRAKE WARNING LAMP CIRCUIT SHORT TO GND
BCM CHECK ENGINE LAMP OUTPUT CIRCUIT DEF
BCM COOLANT TEMPERATURE LAMP OUTPUT DEFECT
BCM CRUISE CONTROL LAMP OUTPUT DEFECTIVE
BCM GENERATOR LAMP OUTPUT CIRCUIT DEFECTIVE
BCM LOW FUEL LAMP OUTPUT DEFECTIVE
BRAKE FLUID LEVEL SWITCH DEFECTIVE
DEFECTIVE BCM LOW FUEL LAMP OUTPUT
DEFECTIVE BRAKE FLUID LEVEL SWITCH
DEFECTIVE IGNITION SWITCH
DEFECTIVE PARK BRAKE SWITCH
IGNITION SWITCH DEFECTIVE
INSTRUMENT CLUSTER CIRCUIT BOARD DEFECTIVE
INSTRUMENT CLUSTER CIRCUIT BOARD DEFECTIVE
INSTRUMENT CLUSTER CIRCUIT BOARD FAULTY
INSTRUMENT CLUSTER CIRCUIT BOARD DEFECT
INSTRUMENT CLUSTER DEFECTIVE

CR9059900002020X

Fig. 22 Any Or All Cluster Warning Lamp Problems (Part 2 of 21). Breeze, Cirrus, 2000 Sebring Convertible & Stratus

TEST	ACTION
4	With the DRB, read the MIC Cluster type to verify the correct application (e.g. US or Metric). Does the DRB show the correct MIC Cluster type? Yes → Go To 5 No → Remove the MIC Cluster and replace the Circuit Board. Perform Body Verification TEST VER-1A
5	With the DRB, select BODY COMPUTER Systems Test. Does the DRB show PCM status as INACTIVE ON THE BUS? Yes → Refer to symptom * NO RESPONSE FROM PCM No → Go To 6

CR9059900002040X

Fig. 22 Any Or All Cluster Warning Lamp Problems (Part 4 of 21). Breeze, Cirrus, 2000 Sebring Convertible & Stratus

POSSIBLE CAUSES
MIC CIRCUIT BOARD DEFECTIVE
MIC CIRCUIT BOARD DEFECTIVE
PARK BRAKE SWITCH DEFECTIVE
POWER CONTROL MODULE DEFECTIVE
OPEN RED BRAKE LAMP CIRCUIT
RED BRAKE WARNING LAMP CIRCUIT OPEN
DEFECTIVE MIC CIRCUIT BOARD
ODOMETER/TRIP CHARACTERS NOT LIGHTING
PRND3L CHARACTERS NOT LIGHTING
DRB DISPLAYS RAM FAULT
DRB SHOWS BUS OPERATIONAL FAILURE
INSTRUMENT CLUSTER CIRCUIT BOARD DEFECT
INSTRUMENT CLUSTER CIRCUIT BOARD DEFECTIVE
MIC CIRCUIT BOARD DEFECTIVE
MIC CIRCUIT BOARD DEFECTIVE
MIC CLUSTER MISMATCH
OIL PRESSURE SWITCH DEFECTIVE

TEST	ACTION
1	Turn Ignition Switch On. With the DRB, select MIC CLUSTER. Does the DRB display BUS OPERATIONAL? Yes → Go To 2 No → Choose appropriate Communication symptom to repair failure. Perform Body Verification TEST VER-1A
2	Turn Ignition Switch On. With the DRB, select MIC CLUSTER. Does the DRB display any of the following problems? NO RESPONSE Refer to symptom * NO RESPONSE INSTRUMENT CLUSTER None of the above Go To 3
3	With the DRB, read MIC DTC'S. Does the DRB show RAM FAULT? Yes → Remove the MIC Cluster and replace the Circuit Board. Perform Body Verification TEST VER-1A No → Go To 4

CR9059900002030X

Fig. 22 Any Or All Cluster Warning Lamp Problems (Part 3 of 21). Breeze, Cirrus, 2000 Sebring Convertible & Stratus

TEST	ACTION
6	Note: The Brake Warning Lamp, Fog Lamp Indicator, Oil Warning TRAC off (JX) and Turn Signal Indicator Lamps are hardwired to the Cluster and cannot be actuated with the DRB. The Vacuum Fluorescent Display (VF) located within the Cluster can display DOOR, DECK and LO WASH messages as well as Odometer and Gear position information. The Door, Deck and Lo Wash messages will blank the Odometer reading until these problems are corrected. These messages are not displayed as part of the actuator test, since they are made up from segments of the Odometer Display. Verify the failure or the customer complaint and make sure the vehicle is experiencing the problem at this time. Choose the applicable items from the list below and perform the indicated tests. Which one of the following Warning Lamps is the problem? Vacuum Fluoresent Display Go To 7 Coolant Temperature Lamp Go To 12 Low Fuel Lamp Go To 19 Oil Warning Lamp Go To 22 Seat Belt Lamp Go To 32 Brake Warning Lamp Go To 36 High Beam Indicator Lamp Go To 58 Turn Signal Indicator Lamps Go To 64 Generator Lamp Go To 69 Cruise Control Lamp Go To 74 Check Engine Lamp Go To 79 Fog Lamp Indicator Lamp Go To 84 Amber ABS Warning Lamp Go To 87 Airbag Warning Lamp Refer to Airbag Symptoms. None of the above Test Complete.

CR9059900002050X

Fig. 22 Any Or All Cluster Warning Lamp Problems (Part 5 of 21). Breeze, Cirrus, 2000 Sebring Convertible & Stratus

TEST	ACTION
7	Turn Ignition Key to the Unlock position. NOTE: In the following tests, each character and segment of the VF Display will light. With the DRB select PRND3L LED' S under Electro/Mech Actuators. Do all the PRND3L Characters and Segments light? Yes → Go To 8 No → Replace the VF Display Module and the MIC Circuit Board. Perform Body Verification TEST VER-1A
8	Turn Ignition Key to the unlock position. Stop the PRND3L LED'S VF Display actuate. NOTE: In the following tests, each character and segment of the VF Display will light. With the DRB select ODO/TRIP under Electro/Mech Actuators. Do all the Odometer/Trip Characters and Segments light? Yes → Go To 9 No → Replace the VF Display Module. Perform Body Verification TEST VER-1A
9	Turn Ignition On (Engine Off). With the DRB select BODY COMPUTER, MONITOR DISPLAY, VEHICLE STATUS MONITOR. Is the Transmission type MANUAL? Yes → Go To 10 No → Go To 11
10	The Powertrain Control Module is for a Manual Transmission. Is this a Manual Transmission vehicle? Yes → Test Complete. No → Replace the Powertrain Control Module (PCM). Perform Body Verification TEST VER-1A
11	With the DRB read the Body Control Module DTC'S. Is the DTC EATX PRNDL message present? Yes → Refer to symptom * NO RESPONSE FROM TCM No → The VF Display is operational with no problem found. Perform Body Verification TEST VER-1A
12	Turn Ignition from the Off position to the On (Run) position. Did the Coolant Temperature Lamp light momentarily? Yes → Go To 13 No → Go To 15
13	With the DRB select BODY COMPUTER, MONITOR DISPLAY, LIMP-IN MONITOR. Read the ECT SENSOR LIMP-IN status. Does the DRB read ECT SENSOR LIMP-IN: YES? Yes → Refer to Symptom list for problems related to Powertrain. No → Go To 14

CR9059900002060X

Fig. 22 Any Or All Cluster Warning Lamp Problems (Part 6 of 21). Breeze, Cirrus, 2000 Sebring Convertible & Stratus

TEST	ACTION
14	Does the Coolant Temperature Lamp stay on? Yes → Repair or replace the Mechanical Instrument Cluster Circuit Board as necessary. Perform Body Verification TEST VER-1A No → Temperature Lamp is operational with no problem found.
15	Turn the Ignition Key to the unlock position. With the DRB select ELECTRO/MECH CLUSTER (MIC) actuate ALL LAMPS. Does the Coolant Temperature Lamp light? Yes → Coolant Temperature Lamp is operational with no problems found. No → Go To 16
16	Key Off. Disconnect the Instrument Cluster. **Check Connectors - Clean / repair as necessary.** Remove and Inspect the Coolant Temperature Bulb. **Check Connectors - Clean / repair as necessary.** Is the Bulb defective? Yes → Replace the Coolant Temperature Bulb. Perform Body Verification TEST VER-1A No → Go To 17
17	Key Off. Disconnect the Instrument Cluster. **Check Connectors - Clean / repair as necessary.** Inspect the Instrument Cluster Circuit Board. Is the Cluster Circuit Board defective? Yes → Repair or replace the Mechanical Instrument Cluster Circuit Board as Necessary. Perform Body Verification TEST VER-1A No → Go To 18
18	If there are no potential causes remaining, the BCM is assumed to be defective. View repair options. Repair Replace the Body Control Module (BCM). Perform Body Verification TEST VER-1A
19	Is the Low Fuel Lamp on when it should be off? Yes → Replace the Body Control Module (BCM). Perform Body Verification TEST VER-1A No → Go To 20
20	Turn Ignition to the unlock position. With the DRB actuate ALL LAMPS. Does the Low Fuel Lamp light, and then turn off? Yes → Replace the Body Control Module (BCM). Perform Body Verification TEST VER-1A No → Go To 21

CR9059900002070X

Fig. 22 Any Or All Cluster Warning Lamp Problems (Part 7 of 21). Breeze, Cirrus, 2000 Sebring Convertible & Stratus

TEST	ACTION
21	Disconnect the Instrument Cluster. **Check Connectors - Clean / repair as necessary.** Remove and inspect the Low Fuel Warning Bulb. **Check Connectors - Clean / repair as necessary.** Is the Bulb defective? Yes → Replace the Bulb. Perform Body Verification TEST VER-1A No → Repair or replace the Instrument Cluster Circuit Board. Perform Body Verification TEST VER-1A
22	Key Off, check the Engine Oil level. Is the Oil Level within specification? Yes → Go To 23 No → Adjust as necessary. Perform Body Verification TEST VER-1A
23	Turn Igntion On (Engine Off). Did the Oil Warning Lamp light (Can Indicator)? Yes → Go To 24 No → Go To 28
24	Turn Ignition Off. Remove the Oil Pressure Switch. **Check Connectors - Clean / repair as necessary.** Connect an Oil Pressure Gauge in its place. Start the Engine. Allow the Engine to reach normal operating temperature. Is the Gauge reading 4.0 psi or greater at idle? Yes → Go To 25 No → Refer to the appropriate Service Manual. Perform Body Verification TEST VER-1A
25	Turn Engine Off (Ignition On). Is the Oil Warning Lamp On? Yes → Go To 26 No → Replace the Oil Pressure Switch. Perform Body Verification TEST VER-1A
26	Turn Ignition Off. Disconnect the Instrument Cluster Blue Connector. **Check Connectors - Clean / repair as necessary.** Using an ohmmeter measure the Oil Pressure Switch Sense Circuit to ground. Is the reading below 5.0 ohms? Yes → Repair the Oil Pressure Switch Sense Circuit for a short to ground. Perform Body Verification TEST VER-1A No → Go To 27

CR9059900002080X

Fig. 22 Any Or All Cluster Warning Lamp Problems (Part 8 of 21). Breeze, Cirrus, 2000 Sebring Convertible & Stratus

TEST	ACTION
27	If there are no potential causes remaining, the Instrument Cluster Circuit Board is assumed to be defective. View repair options. Repair Repair or replace the Instrument Cluster Circuit Board as necessary. Perform Body Verification TEST VER-1A
28	Disconnect the Oil Pressure Switch Connector. **Check Connectors - Clean / repair as necessary.** Connect a jumper wire between the Oil Pressure Switch Sense Circuit and Ground. Did the Oil Warning Lamp light (Can Indicator). Yes → Replace the Oil Pressure Switch. Perform Body Verification TEST VER-1A No → Go To 29
29	Disconnect the Oil Pressure Switch Connector. **Check Connectors - Clean / repair as necessary.** Connect a jumper wire between the Oil Pressure Switch Sense Circuit and ground. Disconnect the Instrument Cluster Blue Connector. **Check Connectors - Clean / repair as necessary.** Turn Ignition On (Engine Off). Using a voltmeter measure Fused Ignition Switch Output (Run/Start) (cav. 5). Is the voltage above 10 volts? Yes → Go To 30 No → Repair the open Fused Ignition Switch Output (Run/Start) Circuit. Perform Body Verification TEST VER-1A
30	Key Off. Using an ohmmeter measure the Oil Pressure Switch Sense Circuit (cav. 12) to ground. Is the resistance below 5.0 ohms? Yes → Go To 31 No → Repair the open Oil Pressure Switch Sen Ckt between the Switch and the Instrument Cluster Perform Body Verification TEST VER-1A
31	Remove Oil Warning Lamp (Can Indicator) from Cluster Inspect the Lamp. Is the Lamp open? Yes → Replace the Lamp. Perform Body Verification TEST VER-1A No → Repair or replace the Instrument Cluster as necessary. Perform Body Verification TEST VER-1A
32	Turn Ignition from Off to On (Run) position. Does the Seat Belt Lamp light, and then turn off? Yes → The Seat Belt Warning Lamp is operational with no problems found. Perform Body Verification TEST VER-1A No → Go To 33

CR9059900002090X

Fig. 22 Any Or All Cluster Warning Lamp Problems (Part 9 of 21). Breeze, Cirrus, 2000 Sebring Convertible & Stratus

TEST	ACTION
33	Turn the Ignition Key to the unlock position. With the DRB select ELECTRO/MECH CLUSTER (MIC) actuate ALL LAMPS. Does the Seat Belt Warning Lamp light? Yes → Replace the Body Control Module (BCM). Perform Body Verification TEST No → Go To 34
34	Key Off, disconnect the Instrument Cluster. **Check Connectors - Clean / repair as necessary.** Remove and inspect the Seat Belt Warning Lamp Bulb. Is the Bulb defective? Yes → Replace the Seat Belt Warning Lamp. Perform Body Verification TEST No → Go To 35
35	If there are no potential causes remaining, the MIC Circuit board is assumed to be defective. View repair options. Repair Repair or replace the Mechanical Instrument Cluster Circuit Board as necessary. Perform Body Verification TEST
36	Is the Vehicle Equipped with an Antilock Brake System? (ABS) Yes → Refer to the appropriate Symptom list. No → Go To 37
37	**Make sure the Parking Brake Lever is not applied at this time.** **Make sure the Parking Brake Lever has no binding or interference.** Is there a problem with the Park Brake Pedal operation? Yes → Refer to the appropriate Symptom list. No → Go To 38
38	Turn Ignition On (Engine Off). Is the Brake Warning Lamp on? Yes → Go To 39 No → Go To 45
39	Check the Brake Fluid Level in the Reservoir. Is the Reservoir full? Yes → Go To 40 No → Adjust the Brake Fluid Level as necessary. Perform Body Verification TEST

CR909020025810AX

Fig. 22 Any Or All Cluster Warning Lamp Problems (Part 10 of 21). Breeze, Cirrus & 2000 Stratus

33	Turn the Ignition Key to the unlock position. With the DRB, select ELECTRO/MECH CLUSTER (MIC) actuate ALL LAMPS. Does the Seat Belt Warning Lamp light? Yes → Go To 34 No → Go To 37
34	**NOTE: This path is for a JX Seat Belt Lamp staying on continuously.** Turn Ignition from Off to On (Run) position. Disconnect the Seat Belt Control Timer Module connector. **Check Connectors - Clean / repair as necessary.** Connect a jumper from the Seat Belt Control Timer Module Sense Circuit (CAV.11) to ground (CAV.13). Did the Seat Belt Lamp go out? Yes → Refer to symptom list to repair the Seat Belt Control Timer Module Circuit. Perform Body Verification TEST VER-1A No → Go To 35
35	Disconnect the Seat Belt Control Timer Module connector. **Check Connectors - Clean / repair as necessary.** Connect a jumper from the Seat Belt Control Timer Module Sense Circuit (CAV.11) to ground (CAV.13). Disconnect the IP 22-way connector at the Body Control Module. **Check Connectors - Clean / repair as necessary.** Using an ohmmeter, measure the Seat Belt Control Module Sense to ground. Is the resistance below 5.0 ohms? Yes → Go To 36 No → Repair the open Seat Belt Control Timer Module Sense Circuit. Perform Body Verification TEST VER-1A
36	Disconnect the Seat Belt Control Timer Module connector. **Check Connectors - Clean / repair as necessary.** Disconnect the IP 22-way connector at the Body Control Module. **Check Connectors - Clean / repair as necessary.** Using an ohmmeter, measure the Seat Belt Control Module Sense to ground. Is the resistance below 5.0 ohms? Yes → Repair the Seat Belt Control Timer Module Sense Circuit for a short to ground. Perform Body Verification TEST VER-1A No → Replace the Body control Module. Perform Body Verification TEST VER-1A
37	Key Off, disconnect the Instrument Cluster. **Check Connectors - Clean / repair as necessary.** Remove and inspect the Seat Belt Warning Lamp Bulb. **Check Connectors - Clean / repair as necessary.** Is the Bulb defective? Yes → Replace the Seat Belt Warning Lamp. Perform Body Verification TEST VER-1A No → Repair or replace the Mechanical Instrument Cluster Circuit Board as necessary. Perform Body Verification TEST VER-1A

CR9059900046100X

Fig. 22 Any Or All Cluster Warning Lamp Problems (Part 10 of 21). 2000 Sebring Convertible

38	Is the Vehicle Equipped with an Antilock Brake System? (ABS) Yes → Refer to Chassis Diagnostic Manual. No → Go To 39
39	**Make sure the Parking Brake Lever is not applied at this time.** **Make sure the Parking Brake Lever has no binding or interference.** Is there a problem with the Park Brake operation? Yes → Refer to appropriate Service Manual. No → Go To 40
40	Turn Ignition On (Engine Off). Is the Brake Warning Lamp on? Yes → Go To 41 No → Go To 47
41	Check the Brake Fluid Level in the Reservoir. Is the Reservoir full? Yes → Go To 42 No → Adjust the Brake Fluid Level as necessary. Perform Body Verification TEST VER-1A
42	Turn Ignition On (Engine Off). Disconnect the Brake Fluid Level Switch Connector. **Check Connectors - Clean / repair as necessary.** Did the Brake Warning Lamp go out? Yes → Replace the Brake Fluid Level Switch. Perform Body Verification TEST VER-1A No → Go To 43
43	Turn Ignition On (Engine Off). Disconnect the Parking Brake Lamp Switch Connector. **Check Connectors - Clean / repair as necessary.** Did the Brake Warning Lamp go out? Yes → Replace the Park Brake Switch. Perform Body Verification TEST VER-1A No → Go To 44
44	Turn Ignition Off. Disconnect the Instrument Cluster. **Check Connectors - Clean / repair as necessary.** With the DRB in Ohmmeter Mode, probe the Red Brake Warning Lamp Circuit. Is the resistance below 5.0 ohms? Yes → Go To 45 No → Repair or replace the Instrument Cluster Circuit Board as necessary. Perform Body Verification TEST VER-1A

CR9059900046110X

Fig. 22 Any Or All Cluster Warning Lamp Problems (Part 11 of 21). Breeze, Cirrus, 2000 Sebring Convertible & Stratus

45	Disconnect the Ignition Switch 10-way Connector. **Check Connectors - Clean / repair as necessary.** With the DRB in Ohmmeter Mode, probe the Red Brake Warning Lamp Circuit. Is the resistance below 5.0 ohms? Yes → Repair the Brake Warning Lamp Circuit for a short to Ground. Perform Body Verification TEST VER-1A No → Go To 46
46	If there are no potential causes remaining, the Ignition Switch assumed to be defective. View repair options. Repair Replace the Ignition Switch. Perform Body Verification TEST VER-1A
47	Crank the Engine while monitoring the Brake Warning Lamp. Did the Brake Warning Lamp come on during cranking? Yes → Go To 48 No → Go To 55
48	Turn Ignition On (Engine Off). Apply the Parking Brake Lever. Did the Brake Warning Lamp come on? Yes → Go To 49 No → Go To 53
49	Release the Parking Brake Lever. Are you here because the Brake Fluid Reservoir was empty and the Lamp did not come on? Yes → Go To 50 No → The Brake Warning Lamp is operating properly at this time. Perform Body Verification TEST VER-1A
50	Key Off, disconnect the Low Brake Fluid Level Switch Connector. **Check Connectors - Clean / repair as necessary.** Connect a jumper wire between the Red Brake Warning Lamp and Ground Circuits. Turn Ignition On (Engine Off). Did the Red Brake Warning Lamp come on? Yes → Replace the Brake Fluid Level Switch. Perform Body Verification TEST VER-1A No → Go To 51
51	Key 0ff, disconnect the Low Brake Fluid Level Switch Connector. **Check Connectors - Clean / repair as necessary.** Connect a jumper wire between the Red Brake Warning Lamp circuit and ground. Turn Ignition On (Engine Off). Did the Parking Brake Lamp come on? Yes → Repair the open Ground Circuit to the Brake Fluid Level Switch. Perform Body Verification TEST VER-1A No → Go To 52

CR9059900046120X

Fig. 22 Any Or All Cluster Warning Lamp Problems (Part 12 of 21). Breeze, Cirrus, 2000 Sebring Convertible & Stratus

52	If there are no potential causes remaining, the Brake Warning Lamp Driver Circuit, is assumed to be open. View repair options. Repair Repair the open Brake Warning Lamp Driver Circuit. Perform Body Verification TEST VER-1A
53	Disconnect the Parking Brake Switch Connector. **Check Connectors - Clean / repair as necessary.** Connect a jumper wire between the Red Brake Warning Lamp Circuit and ground. Did the Brake Warning Light come on? Yes → Replace the Parking Brake Switch. Perform Body Verification TEST VER-1A No → Go To 54
54	If there are no potential causes remaining, the Red Brake Warning Lamp Circuit, is assumed to be defective. View repair options. Repair Repair the open Red Brake Warning Lamp Circuit between the Park Brake Switch and Cluster. Perform Body Verification TEST VER-1A
55	Disconnect the Ignition Switch 10-way Connector. **Check Connectors - Clean / repair as necessary.** Turn Ignition Off. Using an ohmmeter measure the Ground Circuit (cav.1). Is the resistance below 5.0 ohms? Yes → Go To 56 No → Repair the open Ground Circuit. Perform Body Verification TEST VER-1A
56	Reconnect the Ignition Switch and turn Ignition Key On (Engine Off). Back jumper a wire between the Red Brake Warning Lamp Circuit and ground. (cav.2) Does the Warning Lamp come on? Yes → Replace the Ignition Switch. Perform Body Verification TEST VER-1A No → Go To 57
57	Back jumper a wire between the Red Brake Warning Lamp Circuit and Ground. (cav.2) Key Off, disconnect the Instrument Cluster Connectors. **Check Connectors - Clean / repair as necessary.** Using an ohmmeter measure the resistance of the Red Brake Warning Lamp Driver Circuit (cav.6) to ground. Is the resistance below 5.0 ohms? Yes → Go To 58 No → Repair the open Red Brake Warning Lamp Circuit. Perform Body Verification TEST VER-1A

CR9059900046130X

Fig. 22 Any Or All Cluster Warning Lamp Problems (Part 13 of 21). Breeze, Cirrus, 2000 Sebring Convertible & Stratus

58	Remove and inspect the Red Brake Warning Lamp. Is the Bulb defective? Yes → Replace the Bulb. Perform Body Verification TEST VER-1A No → Go To 59
59	If there are no potential causes remaining, the Instrument Cluster, is assumed to be defective. View repair options. Repair Replace the Instrument Cluster. Perform Body Verification TEST VER-1A
60	Turn Ignition On (Engine Off). Turn the Headlamps On High Beam. Are the High Beam Headlamps on? Yes → Go To 61 No → Refer to Symptom list for Possible Causes to repair failure.
61	With the DRB select BODY, BODY COMPUTER, INPUT/OUTPUT DISPLAY read the HI BEAM SENSE. Is the Hi Beam Sense On? Yes → Go To 62 No → Go To 64
62	Turn Ignition Key to the unlock position. With the DRB select ELECTOR/MECH CLUSTER (MIC), ACTUATOR TEST, actuate the ALL LAMPS. Does the High Beam Indicator Lamp light? Yes → System is operational with no problem found. No → Go To 63
63	Disconnect the Instrument Cluster. **Check Connectors - Clean / repair as necessary.** Remove and inspect the High Beam Indicator Bulb. Is the Bulb defective? Yes → Replace the High Beam Indicator Bulb. Perform Body Verification TEST VER-1A No → Repair or replace the Instrument Cluster Circuit Board. Perform Body Verification TEST VER-1A
64	Turn Headlamps Off. Turn Ignition Off. Disconnect the Body Controller from the Junction Block. **Check Connectors - Clean / repair as necessary.** Turn the Headlamps On High Beam. Turn Ignition On (Engine Off). Gain access to the Junction Block Internal 12-way Connecter. With the DRB in Voltmeter Mode, probe the Dimmer Switch High Beam output. Is the voltage above 10.0 volts? Yes → Go To 65 No → Replace the Junction Block. Perform Body Verification TEST VER-1A

CR9059900046140X

Fig. 22 Any Or All Cluster Warning Lamp Problems (Part 14 of 21). Breeze, Cirrus, 2000 Sebring Convertible & Stratus

65	If there are no potential causes remaining, the BCM is assumed to be defective. View repair options. Repair Replace the Body Control Module (BCM). Perform Body Verification TEST VER-1A
66	Verify that the Turn Signal Exterior Lamps are working properly. Are the Exterior Turn Signals working properly? Yes → Go To 67 No → Refer to Symptom list for appropriate possible cause.
67	Disconnect the Instrument Cluster. **Check Connectors - Clean / repair as necessary.** Remove and Inspect both Turn Signal Bulbs. Are the Bulbs defective? Yes → Replace the Turn Signal Bulb(s). Perform Body Verification TEST VER-1A No → Go To 68
68	Disconnect the Instrument Cluster. **Check Connectors - Clean / repair as necessary.** Using a voltmeter measure the Right Turn Signal Circuit at the Instrument Cluster C1 Connector. Turn Ignition On. Turn On the Right Turn Signal. Does the voltage ever exceed 10.0 volts? Yes → Go To 69 No → Repair the open Right Turn Signal Circuit. Perform Body Verification TEST VER-1A
69	Disconnect the Instrument Cluster. **Check Connectors - Clean / repair as necessary.** Using a voltmeter measure the Left Turn Signal Circuit at the Instrument Cluster C2 Connector. Turn Ignition On. Turn On the Left Turn Signal. Does the voltage ever exceed 10.0 volts? Yes → Go To 70 No → Repair the open Left Turn Signal Circuit. Perform Body Verification TEST VER-1A
70	If there are no potential causes remaining, the Instrument Cluster Circuit Board, is assumed to be defective. View repair options. Repair Repair or replace the Instrument Cluster Circuit Board. Perform Body Verification TEST VER-1A
71	Start the Engine. With the DRB select BODY, BODY COMPUTER, MONITOR DISPLAY, LIMP-IN MONITER read the CHARGING LIMP-IN status. Does the DRB read CHARGING LIMP-IN YES? Yes → Refer to appropriate Powertrain Diagnostics. No → Go To 72

CR9059900046150X

Fig. 22 Any Or All Cluster Warning Lamp Problems (Part 15 of 21). Breeze, Cirrus, 2000 Sebring Convertible & Stratus

72	Turn Ignition Off. Watch the Generator Lamp while turning the Ignition Key from Off to Run/Start position. Does the Lamp light? Yes → Generator Lamp is operational with no problem found. No → Go To 73
73	Turn Ignition Key to the unlock position. With the DRB actuate the ALL LAMPS. Does the Generator Lamp light? Yes → Replace the Body Control Module (BCM). Perform Body Verification TEST VER-1A No → Go To 74
74	Key Off,disconnect the Instrument Cluster. **Check Connectors - Clean / repair as necessary.** Remove and inspect the Generator Lamp. **Check Connectors - Clean / repair as necessary.** Is the Lamp defective? Yes → Replace the Generator Lamp. Perform Body Verification TEST VER-1A No → Go To 75
75	If there are no potential causes remaining, the MIC Circuit Board is assumed to be defective. View repair options. Repair Repair or replace the Mechanical Instrument Cluster Circuit Board as necessary. Perform Body Verification TEST VER-1A
76	Is the Cruise Control Lamp the only problem with the Cruise Control System? Yes → Go To 77 No → Refer to appropriate Powertrain Diagnostics. Perform Body Verification TEST VER-1A
77	Turn Ignition from the off to the on (run) position. Did the Cruise Control Lamp light and then turn off? Yes → The Cruise Control Lamp is operational with no problems found. Perform Body Verification TEST VER-1A No → Go To 78
78	Turn the Ignition to the unlock position. With the DRB select ELECTRO/MECH CLUSTER (MIC) actuate ALL LAMPS. Did the Cruise Lamp light, and then turn off? Yes → Replace the Body Control Module (BCM). Perform Body Verification TEST VER-1A No → Go To 79

CR9059900046160X

Fig. 22 Any Or All Cluster Warning Lamp Problems (Part 16 of 21). Breeze, Cirrus, 2000 Sebring Convertible & Stratus

79	Disconnect the Instrument Cluster. **Check Connectors - Clean / repair as necessary.** Remove and inspect the Cruise Light Bulb. **Check Connectors - Clean / repair as necessary.** Is the Bulb defective? Yes → Replace the Bulb as necessary. Perform Body Verification TEST VER-1A No → Go To 80
80	If there are no potential causes remaining, the BCM is assumed to be defective. View repair options. Repair Repair or replace the Instrument Cluster Circuit Board. Perform Body Verification TEST VER-1A
81	Start the Engine. With the DRB select BODY, BODY COMPUTER, MONITOR DISPLAY, VEHICLE STATUS MONITOR read the CHECK ENGINE LAMP status. Is the Check Engine Lamp status ON? Yes → Refer to appropriate Powertrain Diagnostics. Perform Body Verification TEST VER-1A No → Go To 82
82	Turn Ignition from off position to the on (run) position. Did the Check Engine Lamp light,and then turn Off? Yes → Check Engine Lamp is operational with no problems found. Perform Body Verification TEST VER-1A No → Go To 83
83	Turn the Ignition Key to the unlock position. With the DRB actuate the ALL LAMPS. Does the Check Engine Lamp light? Yes → Replace the Body Control Module. Perform Body Verification TEST VER-1A No → Go To 84
84	Key off, disconnect the Instrument Cluster. **Check Connectors - Clean / repair as necessary.** Remove and inspect the Check Engine Bulb. **Check Connectors - Clean / repair as necessary.** Is the Bulb defective? Yes → Replace the Check Engine Bulb. Perform Body Verification TEST VER-1A No → Go To 85
85	If there are no potential causes remaining, the MIC Circuit Board, is assumed to be defective. View repair options. Repair Repair or replace the Mechanical Instrument Cluster Circuit Board as necessary. Perform Body Verification TEST VER-1A

CR9059900046170X

Fig. 22 Any Or All Cluster Warning Lamp Problems (Part 17 of 21). Breeze, Cirrus, 2000 Sebring Convertible & Stratus

86	Turn the Headlamps On low beam. Verify that the Low Beam Headlamps are working properly. Turn the Fog Lamps On. Are the Exterior Headlamps and Fog Lamps working properly? Yes → Go To 87 No → Diagnose exterior headlamps & fog lamps.
87	Disconnect the Instrument Cluster. **Check Connectors - Clean / repair as necessary.** Remove and inspect the Fog Lamp Indicator Bulb. Is the Bulb defective? Yes → Replace the Fog Lamp Indicator Bulb. Perform Body Verification TEST VER-1A No → Go To 88
88	Disconnect the Instrument Cluster. **Check Connectors - Clean / repair as necessary.** With the DRB in voltmeter mode, probe the Fog Lamp Switch Output (CAV.1) circuit of the Instrument Cluster C2 Connector. Turn Ignition on. Turn on the Fog Lamps. Is the voltage above 10.0 volts? Yes → Replace the Printed Circuit Board. Perform Body Verification TEST VER-1A No → Repair the Fog Lamp Switch Output Circuit. Perform Body Verification TEST VER-1A
89	**This test covers only the Lamp never coming on even during Bulb check.** Is there a problem with the Lamp not going out when it should? Yes → Refer to Symptom list for problems relating to ABS. No → Go To 90
90	Using the DRB select ANTI-LOCK BRAKES and READ DTC'S. Does the DRB show NO RESPONSE? Yes → Refer to symptom * NO RESP CONTROLLER ANTILOCK BRAKE No → Go To 91
91	Using the DRB select ANTI-LOCK BRAKES and READ DTC'S. Are there any DTC"s present. Yes → Record DTC's and refer to the appropriate Antilock Brake symptoms and failure modes. No → Go To 92
92	Key Off. Remove the Instrument Cluster. Remove and inspect the ABS Bulb. Is the Bulb condition ok? Yes → Go To 93 No → Replace the Bulb. Perform Body Verification TEST VER-1A

CR9059900046180X

Fig. 22 Any Or All Cluster Warning Lamp Problems (Part 18 of 21). Breeze, Cirrus, 2000 Sebring Convertible & Stratus

93	If there are no potential causes remaining, the Instrument Cluster Circuit Board, is assumed to be defective. View repair options. Repair Replace the Printed Circuit Board. Perform Body Verification TEST VER-1A
94	Turn Ignition On (Engine Off). Close both Doors, observe the Odometer area. Does the DECK message appear even though the Deck is closed? Yes → Go To 95 No → Go To 98
95	Ensure the Decklid is adjusted properly. Is the Decklid in proper adjustment? Yes → Go To 96 No → Adjust or repair as necessary. Perform Body Verification TEST VER-1A
96	Open the Decklid and disconnect the single Decklid Ajar Switch Sense wire from the Latch assembly. Turn Ignition On (Engine Off). Did the DECK message disappear? Yes → Replace the Decklid Latch Assembly. Perform Body Verification TEST VER-1A No → Go To 97
97	Disconnect the BCM Engine 14-way Connector. **Check Connectors - Clean / repair as necessary.** Using an ohmmeter measure the Decklid Ajar Switch Sense Circuit (cav. 1). Is the resistance below 100.0 ohms? Yes → Repair the Decklid Ajar Switch Sense Circuit for a short to ground. Perform Body Verification TEST VER-1A No → Replace the Body Control Module. Perform Body Verification TEST VER-1A
98	Turn Ignition On (Engine Off). Open the Decklid. Ensure both Doors are closed. Does the DECK message appear in the Odometer area? Yes → System is operating properly at this time. No → Go To 99
99	Turn Ignition On (Engine Off). Remove the single Latch Ajar wire from the Trunk Latch. **Check Connectors - clean / repair as necessary.** Connect a jumper from this wire to a known good ground. Did the VF Odometer Display change from Miles to Deck? Yes → Replace Trunk Latch assembly. Perform Body Verification TEST VER-1A No → Go To 100

CR9059900046190X

Fig. 22 Any Or All Cluster Warning Lamp Problems (Part 19 of 21). 2000 Sebring Convertible

100	Remove the single Latch Ajar wire from the Trunk Latch. **Check Connectors - clean / repair as necessary.** Disconnect the Body Control Module Engine 14-way connector. **Check Connectors - clean / repair as necessary.** Using an ohmmeter measure the Decklid Ajar Switch Sense Circuit (CAV.1) to ground. Is the Resistance below 5.0 ohms? Yes → Go To 101 No → Repair the open Decklid Ajar Switch Sense Circuit. Perform Body Verification TEST VER-1A
101	Using the DRB select ELECTRO/MECH CLUSTER and actuate PRN3DL LED"S. Did all PRN3DL segments and characters light? Yes → Replace the MIC Cluster Circuit Board. Perform Body Verification TEST VER-1A No → Go To 102
102	If there are no potential causes remaining, the VF PRNDL Display Assembly is assumed to be defective. View repair options. Repair Replace the VF PRNDL Display Assembly. Perform Body Verification TEST VER-1A
103	Disconnect the Low Wash Connector. **Check Connectors - Clean / repair as necessary.** Install a jumper between cavities A and B. Turn Ignition On. Did the Odometer reading change from MILES to LOW WASH? Yes → Replace the Level Sensor inside the Washer Reservoir. Perform Body Verification TEST VER-1A No → Go To 104
104	Disconnect the Low Wash Connector. **Check Connectors - Clean / repair as necessary.** Install a jumper from the Low Washer Sense Circuit (CAV.B) to a known good ground and wait 1 minute. Turn Ignition On. Did the Odometer reading change from MILES to LO WASH? Yes → Repair the Ground Circuit to the Low Wash Level Sensor. Perform Body Verification TEST VER-1A No → Go To 105
105	Disconnect the Low Wash connector. **Check Connectors - Clean / repair as necessary.** Install a jumper from the Low Washer Sense Circuit (CAV.B) to a known good ground. Remove Cluster Red Connecter. Using an ohmmeter measure the Washer Sense Circuit (CAV.8) to Ground. Is the reading below 5.0 ohms? Yes → Go To 106 No → Repair the open in the Low Wash Sense Circuit. Perform Body Verification TEST VER-1A

CR9059900046200X

Fig. 22 Any Or All Cluster Warning Lamp Problems (Part 20 of 21). 2000 Sebring Convertible

106	Using the DRB select ELECTRO/MECH CLUSTER and actuate PRN3DL LED'S. Did all PRN3DL Segments and Characters light? Yes → Replace the MIC Cluster Circuit Board. Perform Body Verification TEST VER-1A No → Go To 107
107	If there are no potential causes remaining, the VF PRNDL Display Assembly, is assumed to be defective. View repair options. Repair Replace the VF PRNDL Display Assembly. Perform Body Verification TEST VER-1A
108	Turn Ignition On (Engine Off). Using the DRB select ELECTRO/MECH CLUSTER, ACTUATOR TESTS actuate ALL LAMPS. Did the Traction Control On Indicator Illuminate? Yes → Check that the vehicle is equipped with the proper CAB and BCM. Perform Body Verification TEST VER-1A No → Go To 109
109	Key Off. Remove the Instrument Cluster. Remove and inspect the Traction Control Indicator Bulb and Socket. Is the Bulb and Socket condition OK? Yes → Go To 110 No → Replace as necessary. Perform Body Verification TEST VER-1A
110	If there are no potential causes remaining, the Printed Circuit Board, is assumed to be defective. View repair options. Repair Replace the Printed Circuit Board as necessary. Perform Body Verification TEST VER-1A

CR9059900046210X

Fig. 22 Any Or All Cluster Warning Lamp Problems (Part 21 of 21). 2000 Sebring Convertible

TEST	ACTION
6	Reinstall the Fuse. Disconnect the Instrument Cluster Red Connector. **Check Connectors - Clean / repair as necessary.** Using a voltmeter, measure the Fused B(+) Circuit (Cav. 5). Is the voltage above 10.0 volts? Yes → Go To 7 No → Repair the Open Fused B+ Circuit as necessary. Perform Body Verification TEST VER-1A
7	If there are no potential causes remaining, the Instrument Cluster is assumed to be defective. View repair options. Repair Replace the Instrument Cluster. Perform Body Verification TEST VER-1A

CR9059900003020X

Fig. 23 Gauges Not Returning To Zero w/Key OFF (Part 2 of 2). Breeze, Cirrus, 2000 Sebring Convertible & Stratus

POSSIBLE CAUSES
DRB SHOWS BUS OPERATIONAL FAILURE
FUSE #7 DEFECTIVE
FUSED B+ CIRCUIT SHORT TO GROUND
OPEN FUSED B+ CIRCUIT
INSTRUMENT CLUSTER DEFECTIVE

TEST	ACTION
1	Turn Ignition Switch On. With the DRB, select MIC CLUSTER. Does the DRB display BUS OPERATIONAL? Yes → Go To 2 No → Repair Bus Message failure. Perform Body Verification TEST VER-1A
2	Turn Ignition Switch On. With the DRB, select MIC CLUSTER. Does the DRB display any of the following problems? NO RESPONSE Refer to symptom * NO RESPONSE INSTRUMENT CLUSTER None of the above Go To 3
3	Turn the Ignition Off. Remove and inspect Fuse #7. Is the Fuse open? Yes → Go To 4 No → Go To 6
4	Using an ohmmeter measure the Fused (B+) Circuit to Ground. Is the resistance below 5.0 ohms? Yes → Repair Fused (B+) Circuit short to Ground. Perform Body Verification TEST VER-1A No → Go To 5
5	If there are no potential causes remaining, the Fuse #7 is assumed to be defective. View repair options. Repair Replace fuse. Perform Body Verification TEST VER-1A

CR9059900003010X

Fig. 23 Gauges Not Returning To Zero w/Key OFF (Part 1 of 2). Breeze, Cirrus, 2000 Sebring Convertible & Stratus

POSSIBLE CAUSES
ODOMETER FAILURE

TEST	ACTION
1	With the DRB, select BODY COMPUTER Systems Test. Does the DRB show PCM status is INACTIVE ON THE BUS? Yes → Refer to symptom * NO RESPONSE FROM PCM No → Replace Odometer. Perform Body Verification TEST VER-1A

CR9059900004000X

Fig. 24 Odometer Problems. Breeze, Cirrus, 2000 Sebring Convertible & Stratus

POSSIBLE CAUSES
ODOMETER/TRIP SWITCH DEFECTIVE

TEST	ACTION
1	Turn Ignition Switch On. With the DRB, read the state of the Trip Reset Button Switch (released/pressed), then depress the button while reading the switch state. Does the switch state change? Yes → Test Complete. No → Replace the MIC Circuit Board. Perform Body Verification TEST VER-1A

CR9059900005000X

Fig. 25 Odometer/Trip Switch. Breeze, Cirrus, 2000 Sebring Convertible & Stratus

POSSIBLE CAUSES
SPEEDOMETER/TACH GAUGE PACK DEFECTIVE
DRB DISPLAYS RAM FAULT
DRB SHOWS BUS OPERATIONAL FAILURE
MIC CLUSTER MISMATCH
VEHICLE SPEED SENSOR DTC'S ARE PRESENT
BCM DEFECTIVE SPEEDOMETER INPUT/OUTPUT
CLUSTER CIRCUIT BOARD DEFECTIVE

TEST	ACTION
1	Turn Ignition Switch On. With the DRB, select MIC CLUSTER. Does the DRB display BUS OPERATIONAL? Yes → Go To 2 No → Choose appropriate Communication symptom to repair failure.
2	Turn Ignition Switch On. With the DRB, select MIC CLUSTER. Does the DRB display any of the following problems? NO RESPONSE Refer to symptom * NO RESPONSE INSTRUMENT CLUSTER None of the above Go To 3
3	With the DRB, read MIC DTC'S. Does the DRB show RAM FAULT? Yes → Remove the MIC Cluster and replace the Circuit Board. No → Go To 4
4	With the DRB, read the MIC Cluster type to verify the correct application (e.g. US or Metric). Does the DRB show the correct MIC Cluster type? Yes → Go To 5 No → Remove the MIC Cluster and replace the Circuit Board.
5	With the DRB, select BODY COMPUTER Systems Test. Does the DRB show PCM status is INACTIVE ON THE BUS? Yes → Refer to symptom * NO RESPONSE FROM PCM No → Go To 6

CR9059900006010X

Fig. 26 Speedometer (Part 1 of 2). Breeze, Cirrus, 2000 Sebring Convertible & Stratus

TEST	ACTION
6	With the DRB read Engine DTC'S. Are there any Vehicle Speed Sensor DTC's displayed? Yes → Refer to Powertrain Diagnostics for repair. No → Go To 7
7	With the DRB actuate the MIC Cluster Gauges. Speedo Cal Points: #1 (100), #2 (75), #3 (55), #4 (20) and #5 (0). Did the Speedometer stop at its calibration points? Yes → Replace BCM. Perform Body Verification TEST VER-1A No → Go To 8
8	Remove the Cluster and access the back of the Gauges. With an ohmmeter measure across pins E5 and E6, E7 and E8. Is the reading across each coil between 200-220 ohms? Yes → Replace the Cluster Circuit Board. Perform Body Verification TEST VER-1A No → Go To 9
9	If there are no potential causes remaining, the Speedometer/Tach Gauge Pack is assumed to be defective. View repair options. Repair Replace the Speedometer/Tachometer Gauge Pack. Perform Body Verification TEST VER-1A

CR9059900006020X

Fig. 26 Speedometer (Part 2 of 2). Breeze, Cirrus, 2000 Sebring Convertible & Stratus

POSSIBLE CAUSES
INSTRUMENT TACHOMETER DEFECTIVE
DRB DISPLAYS RAM FAULT
BCM TACH INPUT/OUTPUT DEFECTIVE
INSTRUMENT CLUSTER CIRCUIT BOARD DEFECTIVE
TACHOMETER/SPEEDOMETER GAUGE PACK
DRB SHOWS BUS OPERATIONAL FAILURE
MIC CLUSTER MISMATCH

TEST	ACTION
1	Turn Ignition Switch On. With the DRB, select MIC CLUSTER. Does the DRB display BUS OPERATIONAL? Yes → Go To 2 No → Choose appropriate Communication symptom to repair failure. Perform Body Verification TEST VER-1A
2	Turn Ignition Switch On. With the DRB, select MIC CLUSTER. Does the DRB display any of the following problems? NO RESPONSE Refer to symptom * NO RESPONSE INSTRUMENT CLUSTER None of the above Go To 3
3	With the DRB, read MIC DTC'S. Does the DRB show RAM FAULT? Yes → Remove the MIC Cluster and replace the Circuit Board. Perform Body Verification TEST VER-1A No → Go To 4
4	With the DRB, read the MIC Cluster type to verify the correct application (e.g. US or Metric). Does the DRB show the correct MIC Cluster type? Yes → Go To 5 No → Remove the MIC Cluster and replace the Circuit Board. Perform Body Verification TEST VER-1A

CR9059900007010X

Fig. 27 Tachometer Problems (Part 1 of 2). Breeze, Cirrus, 2000 Sebring Convertible & Stratus

TEST	ACTION
5	With the DRB, select BODY COMPUTER Systems Test. Does the DRB show PCM status is INACTIVE ON THE BUS? Yes → Refer to symptom * NO RESPONSE FROM PCM No → Go To 6
6	Start Engine. With the DRB select Engine, Sensor Displays, Engine RPM. Is the RPM reading greater than 100? Yes → Go To 7 No → Refer to Powertrain Diagnostics. Perform Body Verification TEST VER-1A
7	With the DRB access the MIC Cluster, actuate the Gauges. Tach Cal Points: #1 (6000), #2 (3000), #3 (3000), #4 (1000) and #5 (0). Did the Tachometer stop at its calibration points? Yes → Replace the Body Control Module (BCM). Perform Body Verification TEST VER-1A No → Go To 8
8	Remove Cluster, gain access to the back of the Tachometer Gauge . With an ohmmeter measure the resistance across E1,E2 and E3,E4 . Are both readings between 200 and 225 ohms? Yes → Go To 9 No → Replace the Tachometer/Speedometer Gauge Pack. Perform Body Verification TEST VER-1A
9	If there are no potential causes remaining, the Instrument Cluster Circuit Board is assumed to be defective. View repair options. Repair Replace Instrument Cluster Circuit Board. Perform Body Verification TEST VER-1A

CR9059900007020X

Fig. 27 Tachometer Problems (Part 2 of 2). Breeze, Cirrus, 2000 Sebring Convertible & Stratus

POSSIBLE CAUSES
DRB DISPLAYS RAM FAULT
MIC CLUSTER MISMATCH
TEMP COOLANT DTC'S PRESENT
BCM TEMPERATURE GAUGE INPUT DEFECTIVE
CLUSTER CIRCUIT BOARD DEFECTIVE
TEMP/FUEL GAUGE PACK DEFECTIVE
DRB SHOWS BUS OPERATIONAL FAILURE

TEST	ACTION
1	Turn Ignition Switch On. With the DRB, select MIC CLUSTER. Does the DRB display BUS OPERATIONAL? Yes → Go To 2 No → Choose appropriate Communication symptom to repair failure. Perform Body Verification TEST VER-1A
2	Turn Ignition Switch On. With the DRB, select MIC CLUSTER. Does the DRB display any of the following problems? NO RESPONSE Refer to symptom * NO RESPONSE INSTRUMENT CLUSTER VF display shows NO BUS Refer to symptom * NO RESPONSE INSTRUMENT CLUSTER VF display is blank Refer to symptom * NO RESPONSE INSTRUMENT CLUSTER false KEY MUST BE IN UNLOCK POSITION Refer to symptom * NO RESPONSE INSTRUMENT CLUSTER None of the above Go To 3
3	With the DRB, read MIC DTC'S. Does the DRB show RAM FAULT? Yes → Remove the MIC Cluster and replace the Circuit Board. Perform Body Verification TEST VER-1A No → Go To 4

CR9059900008010X

Fig. 28 Temperature Gauge (Part 1 of 2). Breeze, Cirrus, 2000 Sebring Convertible & Stratus

TEST	ACTION
4	With the DRB, read the MIC Cluster type to verify the correct application (e.g. US or Metric). Does the DRB show the correct MIC Cluster type? Yes → Go To 5 No → Remove the MIC Cluster and replace the Circuit Board. Perform Body Verification TEST VER-1A
5	With the DRB, select BODY COMPUTER Systems Test. Does the DRB show PCM status is INACTIVE ON THE BUS? Yes → Refer to symptom * NO RESPONSE FROM PCM No → Go To 6
6	With the DRB select Engine, read DTC's. Is the Coolant Temp DTC present? Yes → Refer to Powertrain Diagnostics. Perform Body Verification TEST VER-1A No → Go To 7
7	With the DRB actuate the MIC Cluster Gauges. Temperature Cal Points: #1 (HOT), #2 (1/2), #3 (1/2), #4 (COLD) and #5 (COLD). Did the Coolant Temp Gauge stop at its Cal points? Yes → Replace Body Control Module (BCM). Perform Body Verification TEST VER-1A No → Go To 8
8	Remove the Cluster, access the back of the Coolant Temperature Gauge. Using An ohmmeter measure the resistance across the Temp Gauge Coil pins E9,E10 and E11,E12. Is the resistance between 200 and 225 ohms? Yes → Replace the Cluster Circuit Board. Perform Body Verification TEST VER-1A No → Go To 9
9	If there are no potential causes remaining, the Temp/Fuel Gauge pack is assumed to be defective. View repair options. Repair Replace the Temperature/Fuel Gauge Pack. Perform Body Verification TEST VER-1A

CR9059900008020X

Fig. 28 Temperature Gauge (Part 2 of 2). Breeze, Cirrus, 2000 Sebring Convertible & Stratus

BODY VER-1A
1. Reconnect all previously disconnected components and connectors. 2. If the Sentry Key Immobilizer Module was replaced, obtain the vehicle's unique pin number in step 11. If no replacment was made, continue to next step. 3. If the Body Control Module was replaced you must turn the Ignition On for 15 secs (to learn VIN) or engine will not start. Use the DRB and program all RKE transmitters used with the vehicle. 4. Use the DRB and Recalibrate HVAC doors. 5. Use the DRB and program other options as necessary. If the vehicle is equipped with VTSS, select MISCELLANEOUS and ENABLE VTSS. 6. If any repairs were made to the HVAC system or the Battery was disconnected: Start the Engine and, using the DRB, recalibrate the HVAC doors. 7. Ensure that the Ignition is On, and with the DRB, erase all Diagnostic Trouble Codes. 8. Turn Ignition Off and wait 5 seconds. 9. Turn Ignition On and fully operate the system that was malfunctioning. If the system is operating properly, continue to next step. If not operating properly, select and perform the appropriate test from the symptom list. 10. With the DRB, read Body Control Module Trouble Codes. If no Trouble Codes are present and customer's complaint can not be duplicated, the repair is complete. If any Codes are present, return to Symptom list and follow path specified for that Trouble Code. 11. Obtain the Vehicle's unique PIN number assigned to it's original SKIM module from either the vehicle's invoice number or from Chrysler's Customer Center. 12. With the DRB, select THEFT ALARM, SKIM, MISCELLANEOUS. Select SKIM Module Replaced function and the DRB will prompt you through the following steps. 13. Enter secured access mode using the unique 4 digit PIN number. 14. Program the vehicle's VIN number into the SKIM's memory. 15. Program the country code into the SKIM's memory (US). 16. Transfer the vehicle's unique Secret Key data from the PCM. This process will require the SKIM module to be in secured access mode. The PIN number must be entered into the DRB before the SKIM will enter secured access mode. 17. Once secured access mode is active, the SKIM will remain in that mode for 60 seconds. 18. Program all customer keys into the SKIM's memory. This requires that the SKIM be in secure access mode. The SKIM module will immediatly exit secured access mode after each key is programmed. 19. Note: Secured access mode is not required to query the programmed status of the key. 20. Note: If the PCM is replaced, the unique Secret Key data must be transferred from the SKIM module to the PCM. This procedure requires the SKIM to be placed in secured access mode using the 4-digit PIN code. 21. Note: If three attempts are made to enter secured access mode using an incorrect PIN, secured access mode will be locked out for one hour. To exit this locked out mode, turn the Ignition to the Run position for one Hour. 22. Ensure all accessories are turned off. Also monitor the Battery state and connect a Battery charger if necessary. 23. To program Sentry Keys using the Customer Programming method, which requires two valid smart keys, refer to either the owner's or service manual. 24. Turn the Ignition On, then wait 3 minutes. With the DRB, read the SKIM trouble codes. 25. If no codes are present, the system is operational and the repair is complete. If codes are present, select the appropriate test from the Symptom List.

CR9050000059000X

Fig. 29 Body Verification Test. Breeze, Cirrus, 2000 Sebring Convertible & Stratus

When Monitored and Set Condition:

DIMMING LEVEL SWITCH FAILURE

When Monitored: Continuously.

Set Condition: The BCM detects an open or short circuit condition for 10 seconds on the dimming level switch input.

POSSIBLE CAUSES
BODY CONTROL MODULE
BODY CONTROL MODULE
BODY CONTROL MODULE
OPEN HEADLAMP SWITCH RETURN CIRCUIT
PANEL LAMP DIMMER SIGNAL CIRCUIT SHORTED TO GROUND
CHECK THE PANEL LAMP DIMMER SIGNAL CIRCUIT FOR A SHORT TO VOLTAGE
OPEN PANEL LAMP DIMMER SIGNAL CIRCUIT
PANEL LAMP DIMMER SIGNAL CIRCUIT SHORTED TO THE HEADLAMP SWITCH RETURN CIRCUIT
PANEL LAMP DIMMER SIGNAL CIRCUIT SHORTED TO VOLTAGE
BODY CONTROL MODULE
BODY CONTROL MODULE
WITH THE DRB OBSERVE THE DIMMING LEVEL VOLTAGE WITH HEADLAMP SWITCH DISCONNECTED

TEST	ACTION	APPLICABILITY
1	Turn the ignition on. With the DRB, enter "Body Computer" then "Sensors" and observe the dimming level voltage Is the voltage between 0.2 and 4.0 volts? Yes → Go To 2 No → Go To 3	
2	With the DRB, erase DTC's. Turn the ignition on and rotate the dimming level switch from low to high several times. With the DRB, read DTC's. Did this DTC reset? Yes → If there are no possible causes remaining, replace the BCM. Perform the Body Verification Test - Ver 1. No → Test Complete.	

CR9050000088010X

Fig. 30 Dimming Level Switch Failure (Part 1 of 4). 2000 Concorde, Intrepid, LHS & 300M

TEST	ACTION
3	Turn the ignition on. With the DRB, enter "Body Computer" then "Sensors" and observe the dimming level voltage Is the voltage above 4.8 volts? Yes → Go To 4 No → Go To 10
4	Turn the ignition off. **Note: Make sure all doors are closed and all lamps are turned off.** Disconnect the Headlamp Switch harness connector. Measure the resistance between ground and the Headlamp Switch Return circuit. Is the resistance below 20.0 ohms? Yes → Go To 5 No → Go To 9
5	Turn the ignition off. Disconnect the Headlamp Switch harness connector. Turn the ignition on. Measure the voltage of the Panel Lamp Dimmer Signal circuit. Is the voltage above 10.0 volts? Yes → Go To 6 No → Go To 8
6	Turn the ignition off. Disconnect the Headlamp Switch harness connector. Turn the ignition on. Using a 12-volt Test Light connected to ground, probe the Panel Lamp Dimmer Signal circuit. Is the test light illuminated? Yes → Go To 7 No → Replace the Headlamp Switch. Perform the Body Verification Test - Ver 1.
7	Turn the ignition off. Disconnect the Headlamp Switch harness connector. Disconnect the BCM "C2" harness connector. Turn the ignition on. Using a 12-volt Test Light connected to ground, probe the Panel Lamp Dimmer Signal circuit. Is the test light illuminated? Yes → Repair the Panel Lamp Dimmer Signal circuit for a short to voltage. Perform the Body Verification Test - Ver 1. No → If there are no possible causes remaining, replace the BCM. Perform the Body Verification Test - Ver 1.

CR9050000088020X

Fig. 30 Dimming Level Switch Failure (Part 2 of 4). 2000 Concorde, Intrepid, LHS & 300M

TEST	ACTION
13	View repair options. Repair If there are no possible causes remaining, replace the BCM. Perform the Body Verification Test - Ver 1.

CR9050000088040X

Fig. 30 Dimming Level Switch Failure (Part 4 of 4). 2000 Concorde, Intrepid, LHS & 300M

TEST	ACTION
8	Turn the ignition off. Disconnect the Headlamp Switch harness connector. Disconnect the BCM "C2" harness connector. Measure the resistance of the Panel Lamp Dimmer Signal circuit between the Headlamp Switch connector and the BCM "C2" connector. Is the resistance below 5.0 ohms? Yes → If there are no possible causes remaining, replace the BCM. Perform the Body Verification Test - Ver 1. No → Repair the Panel Lamp Dimmer Signal circuit for an open. Perform the Body Verification Test - Ver 1.
9	Turn the ignition off. Disconnect the Headlamp Switch harness connector. Disconnect the BCM "C2" harness connector. Measure the resistance of the Headlamp Switch Return circuit between the Headlamp Switch connector and the BCM "C2" connector. Is the resistance below 5.0 ohms? Yes → If there are no possible causes remaining, replace the BCM. Perform the Body Verification Test - Ver 1. No → Repair the Headlamp Switch Return circuit for an open. Perform the Body Verification Test - Ver 1.
10	Turn the ignition off. Disconnect the Headlamp Switch harness connector. Disconnect the BCM "C2" harness connector. Measure the resistance between ground and the Panel Lamp Dimmer Signal circuit. Is the resistance below 5.0 ohms? Yes → Repair the Panel Lamp Dimmer Signal circuit for a short to ground. Perform the Body Verification Test - Ver 1. No → Go To 11
11	Turn the ignition off. Disconnect the Headlamp Switch harness connector. Disconnect the BCM "C2" harness connector. Measure the resistance between the Panel Lamp Dimmer Signal circuit and the Headlamp Switch Return circuit. Is the resistance below 5.0 ohms? Yes → Repair the Panel Lamp Dimmer Signal circuit for a short to the Headlamp Switch Return circuit. Perform the Body Verification Test - Ver 1. No → Go To 12
12	Turn the ignition off. Disconnect the Headlamp Switch harness connector. Turn the ignition on. With the DRB, enter "Body Computer" then "Sensors" and observe the dimming level voltage Is the voltage above 5.0 volts? Yes → Replace the Headlamp Switch. Perform the Body Verification Test - Ver 1. No → Go To 13

CR9050000088030X

Fig. 30 Dimming Level Switch Failure (Part 3 of 4). 2000 Concorde, Intrepid, LHS & 300M

When Monitored and Set Condition:

DIMMING LEVEL SWITCH FAILURE

When Monitored: Continuously.

Set Condition: The BCM detects an open or short circuit condition for 10 seconds on the panel lamps dimmer signal circuit.

POSSIBLE CAUSES
CHECKING DIMMING SWITCH POSITIONS
HEADLAMP SWITCH - OPEN
HEADLAMP SWITCH - SHORTED
OPEN HEADLAMP SWITCH RETURN CIRCUIT
PANEL LAMP DIMMER SIGNAL CIRCUIT SHORTED TO GROUND
BCM - HEADLAMP RETURN CIRCUIT OPEN
MEASURE THE VOLTAGE OF THE PANEL LAMP DIMMER SIGNAL CIRCUIT
MEASURE THE VOLTAGE OF THE PANEL LAMP DIMMER SIGNAL CIRCUIT
OPEN PANEL LAMP DIMMER SIGNAL CIRCUIT
PANEL LAMP DIMMER SIGNAL CIRCUIT SHORTED TO THE HEADLAMP SWITCH RETURN CIRCUIT
PANEL LAMP DIMMER SIGNAL CIRCUIT SHORTED TO VOLTAGE

TEST	ACTION
1	Turn the ignition on. With the DRB, select Body Computer then Sensors and observe the dimming level voltage. Is the voltage between 0.4 and 10.2 volts? Yes → Go To 2 No → Go To 3
2	Turn the ignition on. With the DRB, select Body Computer then Sensors. Read the Dimming Level Volts. Set the Panel Dimmer Switch in the Low position then slowly move the switch to the Hi position, then Funeral Mode position, then to the Dome position. **NOTE: The voltage should increase from approximately 0.6 volts in Low to 5.5 volts in Hi.** **NOTE: Funeral mode voltage should be approximately 7.2 volts and Dome mode should be approximately 9.4 volts.** Does the dimmer level volts display correct voltage for the corresponding position as described? Yes → Test Complete. No → Replace the Headlamp Switch. Perform BODY VERIFICATION TEST - VER 1.

CR9050000542010X

Fig. 31 Dimming Level Switch Failure (Part 1 of 3). 2001–04 Concorde, Intrepid, 300M & 2001 LHS

TEST	ACTION
3	Turn the ignition on. With the DRB, select Body Computer then Sensors and observe the dimming level voltage. Is the voltage above 10.2 volts? Yes → Go To 4 No → Go To 9
4	Turn the ignition off. Disconnect the Headlamp Switch harness connector. Disconnect the BCM C2 harness connector. Measure the resistance of the Headlamp Switch Return circuit between the Headlamp Switch connector and the BCM C2 connector. Is the resistance below 5.0 ohms? Yes → Go To 5 No → Repair the Headlamp Switch Return circuit for an open. Perform BODY VERIFICATION TEST - VER 1.
5	Turn the ignition off. Disconnect the Headlamp Switch harness connector. Disconnect the BCM "C2" harness connector. Measure the resistance of the Panel Lamp Dimmer Signal circuit between the Headlamp Switch connector and the BCM "C2" connector. Is the resistance below 5.0 ohms? Yes → Go To 6 No → Repair the Panel Lamp Dimmer Signal circuit for an open. Perform BODY VERIFICATION TEST - VER 1.
6	Turn the ignition off. Disconnect the Headlamp Switch harness connector. Disconnect the BCM "C2" harness connector. Turn the ignition on. Using a 12-volt Test Light connected to ground, probe the Panel Lamp Dimmer Signal circuit. Is the test light illuminated? Yes → Repair the Panel Lamp Dimmer Signal circuit for a short to voltage. Perform BODY VERIFICATION TEST - VER 1. No → Go To 7
7	Turn the ignition off. Disconnect the Headlamp Switch harness connector. Turn the ignition on. Measure the voltage of the Panel Lamp Dimmer Signal circuit. Is the voltage above 10.0 volts? Yes → Go To 8 No → Replace and program the BCM in accordance with the Service Information. Perform BODY VERIFICATION TEST - VER 1.

CR9050000542020X

Fig. 31 Dimming Level Switch Failure (Part 2 of 3). 2001–04 Concorde, Intrepid, 300M & 2001 LHS

When Monitored and Set Condition:

FUEL LEVEL SENDING UNIT FAILURE

When Monitored: With the ignition on.

Set Condition: The BCM detects a high than normal voltage on the fuel level input.

POSSIBLE CAUSES
BODY CONTROL MODULE
BODY CONTROL MODULE
FUEL PUMP MODULE
OPEN GROUND CIRCUIT
MEASURE THE FUEL LEVEL SENSOR SIGNAL CIRCUIT
OPEN FUEL LEVEL SENSOR SIGNAL CIRCUIT

TEST	ACTION	APPLICABILITY
1	Turn the ignition off. Gain access to the body harness C308 connector by removing the rear seat cushion. Disconnect the C308 harness connector. Turn the ignition on. Measure the voltage of the Fuel Level Sensor Signal circuit. Is the voltage above 10.0 volts? Yes → Go To 2 No → Go To 5	
2	Turn the ignition on. Using a 12-volt Test Light connected to ground, probe the fuel level sensor signal circuit at the body harness C308 connector. Is the test light illuminated? Yes → Go To 3 No → Go To 4	
3	Turn the ignition off. Disconnect the BCM "C4" harness connector. Turn the ignition on. Using a 12-volt Test Light connected to ground, probe the fuel level sensor signal circuit at the body harness C308 connector. Is the test light illuminated? Yes → Repair the fuel level sensor signal circuit for a short to voltage. Perform the Body Verification Test - Ver 1. No → If there are no possible causes remaining, replace the BCM. Perform the Body Verification Test - Ver 1.	

CR9050000089010X

Fig. 32 Fuel Level Sending Unit Failure (Part 1 of 2). Concorde, Intrepid & 300M & LHS

TEST	ACTION
8	Turn the ignition off. Disconnect the Headlamp Switch harness connector. Turn the ignition on. Connect a jumper wire between the Panel Lamps Dimmer Signal and the Headlamp Switch Return circuit at the Headlamp Switch harness connector. With the DRB, select Body Computer then Sensors and read the dimming level voltage. Is the voltage below 1.0 volt? Yes → Replace the Headlamp Switch. Perform BODY VERIFICATION TEST - VER 1. No → Replace and program the BCM in accordance with the Service Information. Perform BODY VERIFICATION TEST - VER 1.
9	Turn the ignition off. Disconnect the Headlamp Switch harness connector. Disconnect the BCM "C2" harness connector. Measure the resistance between ground and the Panel Lamp Dimmer Signal circuit. Is the resistance below 1000.0 ohms? Yes → Repair the Panel Lamp Dimmer Signal circuit for a short to ground. Perform BODY VERIFICATION TEST - VER 1. No → Go To 10
10	Turn the ignition off. Disconnect the Headlamp Switch harness connector. Disconnect the BCM "C2" harness connector. Measure the resistance between the Panel Lamp Dimmer Signal circuit and the Headlamp Switch Return circuit. Is the resistance below 1000.0 ohms? Yes → Repair the Panel Lamp Dimmer Signal circuit for a short to the Headlamp Switch Return circuit. Perform BODY VERIFICATION TEST - VER 1. No → Go To 11
11	Turn the ignition off. Disconnect the Headlamp Switch harness connector. Turn the ignition on. Measure the voltage of the Panel Lamp Dimmer Signal circuit. Is the voltage above 10.0 volts? Yes → Replace the Headlamp Switch. Perform BODY VERIFICATION TEST - VER 1. No → Replace and program the BCM in accordance with the Service Information. Perform BODY VERIFICATION TEST - VER 1.

CR9050000542030X

Fig. 31 Dimming Level Switch Failure (Part 3 of 3). 2001–04 Concorde, Intrepid, 300M & 2001 LHS

TEST	ACTION
4	Turn the ignition off. Measure the resistance between ground and the ground circuit. Is the resistance below 5.0 ohms? Yes → If there are no possible causes remaining, replace the Fuel Pump Module. Perform the Body Verification Test - Ver 1. No → Repair the Ground circuit for an open. Perform the Body Verification Test - Ver 1.
5	Turn the ignition on. With the DRB, enter "Body Computer" then "Sensors" and observe the fuel level voltage. Is the voltage above 9.0 volts? Yes → Repair the Fuel Level Sensor Signal circuit for an open. Perform the Body Verification Test - Ver 1. No → If there are no possible causes remaining, replace the BCM. Perform the Body Verification Test - Ver 1.

CR9050000089020X

Fig. 32 Fuel Level Sending Unit Failure (Part 2 of 2). Concorde, Intrepid & 300M & LHS

POSSIBLE CAUSES
AIRBAG TROUBLE CODES
INSTRUMENT CLUSTER
OTHER INSTRUMENT CLUSTER DTC'S
PERFORM INSTRUMENT CLUSTER SELF TEST

TEST	ACTION
1	Turn the ignition on. **Note: The DRB must be able to communicate with the airbag module prior to performing this test.** With the DRB, read airbag DTC's. Are there any airbag DTC's present? Yes → Diagnose Airbag system. Perform the Body Verification Test - Ver 1. No → Go To 2
2	Turn the ignition on. With the DRB, read Instrument Cluster DTC's. Are there any Instrument Cluster DTC's present? Yes → Diagnose Instrument Cluster assembly. Perform the Body Verification Test - Ver 1. No → Go To 3
3	Turn the ignition off then on. This will start the bulb test. Did the airbag warning indicator illuminate for 3 to 10 seconds? Yes → Go To 4 No → Replace the Instrument cluster. Perform the Body Verification Test - Ver 1.
4	View repair options. Repair If there are no possible causes remaining, replace the Instrument Cluster. Perform the Body Verification Test - Ver 1.

CR9050000096000X

Fig. 33 Air Bag Warning Indicator Not Operating Properly. Concorde, Intrepid & 300M & LHS

When Monitored and Set Condition:

NO MESSAGES FROM ABS

When Monitored: With the ignition on.

Set Condition: No ABS messages received for 10 seconds.

POSSIBLE CAUSES
ATTEMPT TO COMMUNICATE WITH THE ANTILOCK BRAKE CONTROL MODULE
INSTRUMENT CLUSTER

TEST	ACTION	APPLICABILITY
1	Turn the ignition on. With the DRB, attempt to communicate with the antilock brake control module. Was the DRB able to I/D or communicate with the antilock brake control module? Yes → Go To 2 No → Check for the related symptom(s). Perform the Body Verification Test - Ver 1.	
2	With the DRB, erase Instrument Cluster DTC's. Turn the ignition on and wait approximately 1 minute. With the DRB, read Instrument Cluster DTC's. Did this DTC reset? Yes → If there are no possible causes remaining, replace the Instrument Cluster. Perform the Body Verification Test - Ver 1. No → Test Complete.	

CR9050000090000X

Fig. 35 No Messages From ABS. Concorde, Intrepid & 300M & LHS

POSSIBLE CAUSES
ANOTHER ABS DIAGNOSTIC TROUBLE CODE SET
INSTRUMENT CLUSTER
OTHER INSTRUMENT CLUSTER DTC'S
PERFORM INSTRUMENT CLUSTER SELF TEST

TEST	ACTION
1	Turn the ignition on. **Note: The DRB must be able to communicate with the CAB prior to performing this test.** With the DRB, read CAB DTC's. Are there any CAB DTC's present? Yes → Check for the related symptom(s). Perform the Body Verification Test - Ver 1. No → Go To 2
2	Turn the ignition on. With the DRB, read Instrument Cluster DTC's. Are there any Instrument Cluster DTC's present? Yes → Diagnose Instrument Cluster assembly. Perform the Body Verification Test - Ver 1. No → Go To 3
3	Turn the ignition off then on. This will start the bulb test. Did ABS warning indicator illuminate for several seconds? Yes → Go To 4 No → Replace the Instrument cluster. Perform the Body Verification Test - Ver 1.
4	View repair options. Repair If there are no possible causes remaining, replace the Instrument Cluster. Perform the Body Verification Test - Ver 1.

CR9050000095000X

Fig. 34 ABS Warning Indicator Not Working Properly. Concorde, Intrepid & 300M & LHS

When Monitored and Set Condition:

NO MESSAGES FROM AECM

When Monitored: With the ignition on.

Set Condition: No airbag messages received for 5 seconds.

POSSIBLE CAUSES
ATTEMPT TO COMMUNICATE WITH THE AIRBAG CONTROL MODULE
INSTRUMENT CLUSTER

TEST	ACTION
1	Turn the ignition on. With the DRB, attempt to communicate with the airbag control module. Was the DRB able to I/D or communicate with the airbag control module? Yes → Go To 2 No → Check for the related symptom(s). Perform the Body Verification Test - Ver 1.
2	With the DRB, erase Instrument Cluster DTC's. Turn the ignition on and wait approximately 1 minute. With the DRB, read Instrument Cluster DTC's. Did this DTC reset? Yes → If there are no possible causes remaining, replace the Instrument Cluster. Perform the Body Verification Test - Ver 1. No → Test Complete.

CR9050000091000X

Fig. 36 No Message From AECM. Concorde, Intrepid & 300M & LHS

When Monitored and Set Condition:

NO MESSAGES FROM BCM

When Monitored: With ignition on.

Set Condition: No BCM messages received for 5 seconds.

POSSIBLE CAUSES
ATTEMPT TO COMMUNICATE WITH THE BCM
INSTRUMENT CLUSTER

TEST	ACTION
1	Turn the ignition on. With the DRB, enter "Body" then "Body Computer". Was the DRB able to I/D or communicate with the BCM? Yes → Go To 2 No → Check for the related symptom(s). Perform the Body Verification Test - Ver 1.
2	With the DRB, erase Instrument Cluster DTC's. Turn the ignition on and wait approximately 1 minute. With the DRB, read Instrument Cluster DTC's. Did this DTC reset? Yes → If there are no possible causes remaining, replace the Instrument Cluster. Perform the Body Verification Test - Ver 1. No → Test Complete.

CR9050000092000X

Fig. 37 No Messages From BCM. Concorde, Intrepid & 300M & LHS

When Monitored and Set Condition:

NO MESSAGES FROM EATX

When Monitored: With the ignition on.

Set Condition: No EATX messages received for 10 seconds.

POSSIBLE CAUSES
ATTEMPT TO COMMUNICATE WITH THE TCM
INSTRUMENT CLUSTER

TEST	ACTION
1	Turn the ignition on. With the DRB, enter "Transmission". Was the DRB able to I/D or communicate with the TCM? Yes → Go To 2 No → Perform the Body Verification Test - Ver 1.
2	With the DRB, erase Instrument Cluster DTC's. Turn the ignition on and wait approximately 1 minute. With the DRB, read Instrument Cluster DTC's. Did this DTC reset? Yes → If there are no possible causes remaining, replace the Instrument Cluster. Perform the Body Verification Test - Ver 1. No → Test Complete.

CR9050000093000X

Fig. 38 No Messages From EATX. Concorde, Intrepid & 300M & LHS

When Monitored and Set Condition:

NO MESSAGES FROM PCM

When Monitored: With the ignition on.

Set Condition: The Instrument Cluster does not receive a PCM message for 20 seconds.

POSSIBLE CAUSES
ATTEMPT TO COMMUNICATE WITH THE POWERTRAIN CONTROL MODULE
INSTRUMENT CLUSTER

TEST	ACTION
1	Attempt to start and idle the engine. Does the engine start and idle? Yes → Go To 2 No → Refer to related symptom(s). Perform BODY VERIFICATION TEST - VER 1.
2	With the DRB, erase the Instrument Cluster DTC's. Start the engine and wait approximately 1 minute. With the DRB, read the Instrument Cluster DTC's. Did this DTC reset? Yes → Replace the Instrument Cluster. Perform BODY VERIFICATION TEST - VER 1. No → Test Complete.

CR9050000543000X

Fig. 39 No Messages From PCM. Concorde, Intrepid & 300M & 2001 LHS

When Monitored and Set Condition:

NO MESSAGES FROM SBEC

When Monitored: With the ignition on.

Set Condition: No SBEC messages received for 20 seconds.

POSSIBLE CAUSES
INSTRUMENT CLUSTER
NO MESSAGES FROM SBEC

TEST	ACTION
1	Attempt to start the vehicle. Does the vehicle start and continue to run? Yes → Go To 2 No → Perform the Body Verification Test - Ver 1.
2	With the DRB, erase Instrument Cluster DTC's. Start the vehicle and continue to run for approximately 1 minute. With the DRB, read Instrument Cluster DTC's. Did this DTC reset? Yes → If there are no possible causes remaining, replace the Instrument Cluster. Perform the Body Verification Test - Ver 1. No → Test Complete.

CR9050000094000X

Fig. 40 No Messages From SBEC. 2000 Concorde, Intrepid, LHS & 300M

POSSIBLE CAUSES
FUSED IGNITION SWITCH OUTPUT CIRCUIT OPEN
CHECK FUSES IN THE JUNCTION BLOCK
FUSED B(+) CIRCUIT OPEN
GROUND CIRCUIT OPEN (C1 CONN)
GROUND CIRCUIT OPEN (C2 CONN)
ATTEMPT TO COMMUNICATE WITH THE BCM
ATTEMPT TO COMMUNICATE WITH THE INSTRUMENT CLUSTER
INSTRUMENT CLUSTER

TEST	ACTION
1	Turn the ignition off. Remove and Inspect Fuse 7 and Fuse 14 from the Junction Block. Is either fuse open? Yes → Diagnose a shorted circuit. Perform the Body Verification Test - Ver 1. No → Go To 2
2	Turn the ignition on. With the DRB, enter "Body" then "Body Computer". Was the DRB able to I/D or communicate with the BCM? Yes → Go To 3 No → Diagnose BCM. Perform the Body Verification Test - Ver 1.
3	Turn the ignition on. With the DRB, enter "Body" then "Electro/Mech Cluster (MIC)". Was the DRB able to I/D or communicate with the Instrument Cluster? Yes → Go To 4 No → Diagnose instrument cluster. Perform the Body Verification Test - Ver 1.
4	Turn the ignition off. Disconnect the Instrument Cluster "C1" harness connector. Measure the resistance between ground and the ground circuit. Is the resistance below 5.0 ohms? Yes → Go To 5 No → Repair the ground circuit for an open. Perform the Body Verification Test - Ver 1.

CR9050000097010X

Fig. 41 All Gauges Not Operating (Part 1 of 2). 2000 Concorde, Intrepid, LHS & 300M

POSSIBLE CAUSES
CHECKING BCM COMMUNICATION
CHECKING I/P FUSES
CHECKING INSTRUMENT CLUSTER COMMUNICATION
FUSED B+ CIRCUIT OPEN
FUSED IGNITION SWITCH OUTPUT CIRCUIT OPEN
GROUND CIRCUIT OPEN
INSTRUMENT CLUSTER

TEST	ACTION
1	Turn the ignition off. Remove and inspect fuse 7 and 14 from the Junction Block. Is either fuse open? Yes → Refer to the (wiring diagrams) for the symptom(s) to diagnose the shorted circuit. Perform BODY VERIFICATION TEST - VER 1. No → Go To 2
2	Turn the ignition on. With the DRB, select Body then Body Computer. Is the DRB able to I/D or communicate with the BCM? Yes → Go To 3 No → Refer to the related symptom(s). Perform BODY VERIFICATION TEST - VER 1.
3	Turn the ignition on. With the DRB, select Body then Electro/Mech Cluster (MIC). Is the DRB able to I/D or communicate with the Instrument Cluster? Yes → Go To 4 No → Refer to the related symptom(s). Perform BODY VERIFICATION TEST - VER 1.
4	Turn the ignition off. Disconnect the Instrument Cluster C1 harness connector. Using a 12-volt test light connected to 12-volts, check the Ground circuit. Does the test light illuminate brightly? Yes → Go To 5 No → Repair the Ground circuit for an open. Perform BODY VERIFICATION TEST - VER 1.

CR9050000544010X

Fig. 42 All Gauges Not Operating (Part 1 of 2). 2001–02 Concorde, Intrepid & 300M & 2001 LHS

TEST	ACTION
5	Turn the ignition off. Disconnect the Instrument Cluster "C2" harness connector. Turn the ignition on. Measure the voltage of the Fused Ignition Switch Output circuit in the Instrument Cluster "C2" connector. Is the voltage above 10.0 volts? Yes → Go To 6 No → Repair the Fused Ignition Switch Output circuit for an open. Perform the Body Verification Test - Ver 1.
6	Turn the ignition off. Disconnect the Instrument Cluster "C2" harness connector. Measure the resistance between ground and the ground circuit. Is the resistance below 5.0 ohms? Yes → Go To 7 No → Repair the ground circuit for an open. Perform the Body Verification Test - Ver 1.
7	Turn the ignition off. Disconnect the Instrument Cluster "C1" harness connector. Measure the voltage of the Fused B+ circuit (cavity 1). Is the voltage above 10.0 volts? Yes → Go To 8 No → Repair the Fused B+ circuit for an open. Perform the Body Verification Test - Ver 1.
8	If there are no possible causes remaining, view "Repair". Repair If there are no possible causes remaining, replace the Instrument Cluster. Perform the Body Verification Test - Ver 1.

CR9050000097020X

Fig. 41 All Gauges Not Operating (Part 2 of 2). 2000 Concorde, Intrepid, LHS & 300M

TEST	ACTION
5	Turn the ignition off. Disconnect the Instrument Cluster C2 harness connector. Turn the ignition on. Using a 12-volt test light connected to ground, check the Fused Ignition Switch Output circuit. Does the test light illuminate brightly? Yes → Go To 6 No → Repair the Fused Ignition Switch Output circuit for an open. Perform BODY VERIFICATION TEST - VER 1.
6	Turn the ignition off. Disconnect the Instrument Cluster C1 harness connector. Using a 12-volt test light connected to ground, check the Fused B+ circuit (cavity 1). Does the test light illuminate brightly? Yes → Replace the Instrument Cluster. Perform BODY VERIFICATION TEST - VER 1. No → Repair the fused B+ circuit for an open. Perform BODY VERIFICATION TEST - VER 1.

CR9050000544020X

Fig. 42 All Gauges Not Operating (Part 2 of 2). 2001–02 Concorde, Intrepid & 300M & 2001 LHS

POSSIBLE CAUSES
FUSED B(+) CIRCUIT OPEN
FUSED IGNITION SWITCH OUTPUT CIRCUIT OPEN
INSTRUMENT CLUSTER GROUND CIRCUIT OPEN
INTERMITTENT CONDITION
INSTRUMENT CLUSTER

TEST	ACTION
1	**NOTE: Diagnose and repair any BCM, PCM, or Communication DTC's before proceeding with this test.** **NOTE: If the cluster does not receive any PCI bus information, all gauge pointers will move to lowest indication and all warning indicators will illuminate.** Turn the ignition off. Perform the Instrument Cluster self-test. Press and hold the Trip Reset button. Turn the ignition on. Observe the cluster during the self-test. All gauge pointers should pause briefly at the calibration points. Did the gauges operate properly during the self-test? Yes → The condition is not present at this time. Monitor DRBIII® parameters while wiggling the related wire harness. Refer to any Technical Service Bulletins (TSB) that may apply. Visually inspect the related wiring harness connectors and terminals. Perform BODY VERIFICATION TEST No → Go To 2
2	Turn the ignition off. Disconnect the Instrument Cluster C1 harness connector. Measure the voltage between the Fused B(+) circuit and ground. Is the voltage above 10.5 volts? Yes → Go To 3 No → Repair the fused B(+) circuit for an open. Perform BODY VERIFICATION TEST
3	Turn the ignition off. Disconnect the Instrument Cluster C1 harness connector. Turn the ignition on. Measure the voltage between the Fused Ignition Switch Output circuit and ground. Is the voltage above 10.5 volts? Yes → Go To 4 No → Repair the Fused Ignition Switch Output circuit for an open. Perform BODY VERIFICATION TEST

CR9090200336010X

Fig. 43 All Gauges Inoperative (Part 1 of 2). 2003–04 Concorde, Intrepid & 300M

POSSIBLE CAUSES
OPEN BRAKE PRESSURE SWITCH (LEVEL SWITCH)
OPEN GROUND CIRCUIT
BRAKE PRESSURE SWITCH (LEVEL SWITCH) SHORTED TO GROUND
CHECK THE BRAKE FLUID LEVEL
CHECK THE PARKING BRAKE LEVER
INSTRUMENT CLUSTER
INSTRUMENT CLUSTER
INSTRUMENT CLUSTER
MONITOR THE BRAKE WARNING INDICATOR WHILE CRANKING ENGINE
OPEN RED BRAKE WARNING INDICATOR DRIVER CIRCUIT
OPEN RED BRAKE WARNING INDICATOR DRIVER CIRCUIT
PARK BRAKE SWITCH OPEN
PARK BRAKE SWITCH SHORTED TO GROUND
RED BRAKE WARNING INDICATOR DRIVER CIRCUIT SHORTED TO GROUND

TEST	ACTION	APPLICABILITY
1	**Note: Make sure the parking brake lever is not engaged at this time.** Check the parking brake lever for any interference or binding linkage. Is there a problem with the parking brake operation. Yes → Inspect parking brake system. Perform the Body Verification Test - Ver 1. No → Go To 2	
2	Are you in this test because the warning indicator did not light with an empty fluid reservoir? Yes → Go To 3 No → Go To 7	
3	Turn the ignition off. Disconnect the brake pressure switch (level switch) harness connector. Turn the ignition on, wait 10 seconds. Connect a jumper wire between the red brake warning indicator driver circuit and the ground circuit. Did the brake warning indicator illuminate with the jumper wire connected? Yes → Replace the brake pressure switch (level switch). Perform the Body Verification Test - Ver 1. No → Go To 4	

CR9050000098010X

Fig. 44 Brake Indicator Not Operating Properly (Part 1 of 4). 2000–02 Concorde, Intrepid & 300M & LHS

TEST	ACTION
4	Turn the ignition off. Disconnect the Instrument Cluster C1 harness connector. Measure the resistance between ground and the Instrument Cluster Ground circuit. Is the resistance below 5.0 ohms? Yes → Replace the Instrument Cluster in accordance with the Service Information. Perform BODY VERIFICATION TEST No → Repair the Instrument Cluster Ground circuit for an open. Perform BODY VERIFICATION TEST

CR9090200336020X

Fig. 43 All Gauges Inoperative (Part 2 of 2). 2003–04 Concorde, Intrepid & 300M

TEST	ACTION
4	Turn the ignition off. Disconnect the brake pressure switch (level switch) harness connector. Turn the ignition on, wait 10 seconds. Connect a jumper wire between the red brake warning indicator driver circuit and chassis ground. Did the brake warning indicator illuminate with the jumper wire connected? Yes → Repair the ground circuit for an open. Perform the Body Verification Test - Ver 1. No → Go To 5
5	Turn the ignition off. Disconnect the brake pressure switch (level switch) harness connector. Disconnect the Instrument Cluster "C2" harness connector. Measure the resistance of the red brake warning indicator driver circuit between the pressure switch connector and the Instrument Cluster "C2" connector. Is the resistance below 5.0 ohms? Yes → Go To 6 No → Repair the red brake warning indicator driver circuit for an open. Perform the Body Verification Test - Ver 1.
6	View repair options. Repair If there are no possible causes remaining, replace the Instrument Cluster. Perform the Body Verification Test - Ver 1.
7	Turn the ignition on. Is the brake warning indicator on after the bulb check? Yes → Go To 8 No → Go To 13
8	Check the brake fluid level in the reservoir. Is the reservoir full? Yes → Go To 9 No → Adjust the brake fluid level as necessary. Perform the Body Verification Test - Ver 1.
9	Disconnect the brake pressure switch (level switch) harness connector. With the key still on, observe the red brake warning indicator. Did the brake warning indicator turn off? Yes → Replace the Brake Pressure Switch (Level Switch). Perform the Body Verification Test - Ver 1. No → Go To 10
10	Disconnect the park brake switch harness connector. With the key still on, observe the red brake warning indicator. Did the brake warning indicator turn off? Yes → Replace the Park Brake Switch. Perform the Body Verification Test - Ver 1. No → Go To 11

CR9050000098020X

Fig. 44 Brake Indicator Not Operating Properly (Part 2 of 4). 2000–02 Concorde, Intrepid & 300M & LHS

TEST	ACTION
11	Turn the ignition off. Disconnect the Instrument Cluster "C2" harness connector. Disconnect the brake pressure switch (level switch) harness connector. Disconnect the park brake switch harness connector. Measure the resistance between ground and the red brake warning indicator driver circuit. Is the resistance below 10.0 ohms? Yes → Repair the red brake warning indicator driver circuit for a short to ground. Perform the Body Verification Test - Ver 1. No → Go To 12
12	View repair options. Repair If there are no possible causes remaining, replace the Instrument Cluster. Perform the Body Verification Test - Ver 1.
13	Turn the ignition on, wait 10 seconds. Engage the parking brake lever. Did the brake warning indicator turn on with the parking brake lever engaged? Yes → Go To 14 No → Go To 15
14	Release the parking brake lever. Crank the engine while observing the brake warning indicator. Did the brake warning indicator turn on while the engine was cranked? Yes → Test Complete. No → Replace the Instrument Cluster. Perform the Body Verification Test - Ver 1.
15	Turn the ignition off. Disconnect the parking brake switch harness connector. Turn the ignition on, wait 10 seconds. Connect a jumper wire between the red brake warning indicator driver circuit and ground. Is the brake warning indicator on? Yes → Replace the park brake switch. Perform the Body Verification Test - Ver 1. No → Go To 16
16	Turn the ignition off. Disconnect the parking brake switch harness connector. Disconnect the Instrument Cluster "C2" harness connector. Measure the resistance of the red brake warning indicator driver circuit between the park brake switch connector and the Instrument Cluster "C2" connector. Is the resistance below 5.0 ohms? Yes → Go To 17 No → Repair the red brake warning indicator driver circuit for an open. Perform the Body Verification Test - Ver 1.

CR9050000098030X

Fig. 44 Brake Indicator Not Operating Properly (Part 3 of 4). 2000–02 Concorde, Intrepid & 300M & LHS

POSSIBLE CAUSES
PARK BRAKE SWITCH
RED BRAKE WARNING INDICATOR DRIVER CIRCUIT OPEN - PARK BRAKE SWITCH TO J/BLOCK
RED BRAKE WARNING INDICATOR DRIVER CIRCUIT OPEN - MIC TO J/BLOCK
BRAKE FLUID LEVEL SWITCH
BRAKE FLUID LEVEL SWITCH GROUND CIRCUIT OPEN
RED BRAKE WARNING INDICATOR CIRCUIT OPEN - BRAKE FLUID LEVEL SWITCH TO J/BLOCK
INTERMITTENT CONDITION
JUNCTION BLOCK
INSTRUMENT CLUSTER

TEST	ACTION
1	Turn the ignition on and observe the BRAKE indicator during the bulb check. Did the BRAKE indicator illuminate during the bulb check? Yes → Go To 2 No → Replace the Instrument Cluster in accordance with the Service Information. Perform BODY VERIFICATION TEST
2	**NOTE: Diagnose and repair any MIC, ABS, or Communication DTC's before proceeding with this test.** Is the Brake Warning Indicator only inoperative while using the Park Brake? Yes → Go To 3 No → Go To 5
3	Disconnect the Park Brake Switch harness connector. Connect a jumper wire between the Red Brake Warning Indicator Driver circuit and ground. Turn the ignition on. Observe the BRAKE indicator. Did the BRAKE indicator illuminate? Yes → Replace the Park Brake Switch in accordance with the Service Information. Perform BODY VERIFICATION TEST No → Go To 4

CR9090200338010X

Fig. 45 Brake Warning Indicator Inoperative (Part 1 of 3). 2003–04 Concorde, Intrepid & 300M

TEST	ACTION
17	View repair options. Repair If there are no possible causes remaining, replace the Instrument Cluster. Perform the Body Verification Test - Ver 1.

CR9050000098040X

Fig. 44 Brake Indicator Not Operating Properly (Part 4 of 4). 2000–02 Concorde, Intrepid & 300M & LHS

TEST	ACTION
4	Turn the ignition off. Disconnect the Park Brake Switch harness connector. Disconnect the Junction Block C7 harness connector. Measure the resistance of the Red Brake Warning Indicator circuit. Is the resistance above 5.0 ohms? Yes → Repair the Red Brake Warning Indicator circuit for an open between the Park Brake Switch and the Junction Block. Perform BODY VERIFICATION TEST No → Go To 8
5	Turn the ignition off. Disconnect the Brake Fluid Level Switch harness connector. Connect a jumper wire between cavity A and cavity B. Turn the ignition on. Did the BRAKE indicator illuminate? Yes → Replace the Brake Fluid Level Switch in accordance with the Service Information. Perform BODY VERIFICATION TEST No → Go To 6
6	Turn the ignition off. Disconnect the Brake Fluid Level Switch harness connector. Measure the resistance between ground and the Brake Fluid Level Switch Ground circuit. Is the resistance above 5.0 ohms? Yes → Repair the Brake Fluid Level Switch Ground circuit for an open. Perform BODY VERIFICATION TEST No → Go To 7
7	Turn the ignition off. Disconnect the Brake Fluid Level Switch harness connector. Disconnect the Junction Block C10 harness connector. Measure the resistance of the Red Brake Warning Indicator circuit between the Switch connector and the Junction Block C10 connector. Is the resistance above 5.0 ohms? Yes → Repair the Red Brake Warning Indicator Switch circuit for an open between the Fluid Level Switch and the Junction Block. Perform BODY VERIFICATION TEST No → Go To 8
8	Turn the ignition off. Disconnect the appropriate Junction Block harness connectors. Using the wiring diagram/schematic as a guide, measure the resistance of the Red Brake Warning Indicator circuit through the Junction Block. Is the resistance above 5 ohms? Yes → Replace the Junction Block in accordance with the Service Information. Perform BODY VERIFICATION TEST No → Go To 9

CR9090200338020X

Fig. 45 Brake Warning Indicator Inoperative (Part 2 of 3). 2003–04 Concorde, Intrepid & 300M

TEST	ACTION
9	Turn the ignition off. Disconnect the Junction Block C3 harness connector. Disconnect the Instrument Cluster C2 harness connector. Measure the resistance of the Red Brake Warning Indicator Driver circuit between the Junction Block C3 harness connector and the Instrument Cluster C2 harness connector. Is the resistance above 5.0 ohms? Yes → Repair the Red Brake Warning Indicator Driver circuit for an open between the Instrument Cluster and the Junction Block. Perform BODY VERIFICATION TEST No → The condition is not present at this time. Monitor DRBIII® parameters while wiggling the related wire harness. Refer to any Technical Service Bulletins (TSB) that may apply. Visually inspect the related wiring harness connectors and terminals. Perform BODY VERIFICATION TEST

CR9090200338030X

Fig. 45 Brake Warning Indicator Inoperative (Part 3 of 3). 2003–04 Concorde, Intrepid & 300M

POSSIBLE CAUSES
ATTEMPT TO COMMUNICATE WITH THE PCM
ENGINE TROUBLE CODES
INSTRUMENT CLUSTER
PERFORM INSTRUMENT CLUSTER SELF TEST

TEST	ACTION
1	Turn the ignition on. With the DRB, enter "Body", "Body Computer", "System Test" then "PCM Monitor". Is the PCM active on the bus? Yes → Go To 2 No → Perform the Body Verification Test - Ver 1.
2	Turn the ignition on. With the DRB, read engine DTC's. Are there any PCM DTC's present? Yes → Diagnose PCM DTC's. Perform the Body Verification Test - Ver 1. No → Go To 3
3	Turn the ignition off then on. This will start the bulb test. Did the check engine (MIL) indicator illuminate for 3 to 10 seconds? Yes → Go To 4 No → Replace the Instrument cluster. Perform the Body Verification Test - Ver 1.
4	View repair options. Repair If there are no possible causes remaining, replace the Instrument Cluster. Perform the Body Verification Test - Ver 1.

CR9050000100000X

Fig. 47 Check Engine Indicator Not Operating Properly. Concorde, Intrepid & 300M & LHS

POSSIBLE CAUSES
CHECK THE CHARGING SYSTEM OPERATION
ENGINE TROUBLE CODES
INSTRUMENT CLUSTER
PERFORM INSTRUMENT CLUSTER SELF TEST

TEST	ACTION
1	Turn the ignition on. With the DRB, read engine DTC's. Are there any PCM DTC's present? Yes → Diagnose the charging system. Perform the Body Verification Test - Ver 1. No → Go To 2
2	Turn the ignition off then on. This will start the bulb test. Did the charging indicator illuminate for 3 to 10 seconds? Yes → Go To 3 No → Replace the Instrument cluster. Perform the Body Verification Test - Ver 1.
3	Check the charging system operation. Follow the service information procedure. Is the charging system operating properly? Yes → Go To 4 No → Diagnose the charging system. Perform the Body Verification Test - Ver 1.
4	View repair options. Repair If there are no possible causes remaining, replace the Instrument Cluster. Perform the Body Verification Test - Ver 1.

CR9050000099000X

Fig. 46 Charging Indicator Not Operating Properly. Concorde, Intrepid & 300M & LHS

POSSIBLE CAUSES
INSTRUMENT CLUSTER
DISCONNECT THE ASH RECEIVER LAMP HARNESS CONNECTOR
DISCONNECT THE ATC MODULE OR THE MTC MODULE HARNESS CONNECTORS
DISCONNECT THE CLOCK HARNESS CONNECTOR (IF EQUIPPED)
DISCONNECT THE HEADLAMP SWITCH HARNESS CONNECTOR
DISCONNECT THE PRND3L ILLUMINATION HARNESS CONNECTOR
DISCONNECT THE RADIO HARNESS CONNECTOR
DISCONNECT THE TRACTION CONTROL SWITCH (IF EQUIPPED)
HEADLAMP SWITCH SHORTED TO VOLTAGE
PANEL LAMP DRIVER CIRCUIT SHORTED TO GROUND
PANEL LAMP DRIVER CIRCUIT SHORTED TO VOLTAGE
OBSERVE THE DIMMING LEVEL VOLTAGE
ATTEMPT TO COMMUNICATE WITH THE INSTRUMENT CLUSTER
CHECK FOR DTCS IN THE INSTRUMENT CLUSTER
CHECK THE PANEL LAMP DRIVER CIRCUIT FOR A SHORT TO GROUND

TEST	ACTION
1	Turn the ignition on. With the DRB, enter "Body" then "Electro/Mech Cluster (MIC)". Was the DRB able to I/D or communicate with the Instrument Cluster? Yes → Go To 2 No → Check for the related symptom(s). Perform the Body Verification Test - Ver 1.

CR9050000101010X

Fig. 48 Cluster & Panel Illumination Problems (Part 1 of 5). 2000 Concorde, Intrepid, LHS & 300M

TEST	ACTION
2	Turn the ignition on. **Note: Check the Instrument Cluster (MIC) for any DTCs.** With the DRB, enter "Body Computer" then "Sensors" and observe the dimming level voltage. Rotate the dimmer switch to the low position, then to the high position and observe the dimming level voltage Does the dimming level voltage change between approximately 0.2 and 3.0 volts? Yes → Go To 3 No → Refer to symptom list for problems related to the Dimming Level Switch Failure DTC. Perform the Body Verification Test - Ver 1.
3	Turn the park lamps on. Rotate the dimmer switch to the low position, then to the high position and observe the panel lamps. Do the panel lamps stay at full intensity with the dimmer switch in any position? Yes → Go To 4 No → Go To 12
4	Turn the park lamps on. Disconnect the Ash Receiver Lamp harness connector. Rotate the dimmer switch to the low position, then to the high position and observe the panel lamps. Did the panel lamps function properly with the dimmer switch? Yes → Repair or replace the Ash Receiver for a short to voltage. Perform the Body Verification Test - Ver 1. No → Go To 5
5	Turn the park lamps on. Disconnect the Clock harness connector (if equipped). Rotate the dimmer switch to the low position, then to the high position and observe the panel lamps. Did the panel lamps function properly with the dimmer switch? Yes → Repair or replace the Clock for a short to voltage. Perform the Body Verification Test - Ver 1. No → Go To 6
6	Turn the park lamps on. Disconnect the PRND3L Illumination harness connector. Rotate the dimmer switch to the low position, then to the high position and observe the panel lamps. Did the panel lamps function properly with the dimmer switch? Yes → Repair or replace the PRND3L for a short to voltage. Perform the Body Verification Test - Ver 1. No → Go To 7

CR9050000101020X

Fig. 48 Cluster & Panel Illumination Problems (Part 2 of 5). 2000 Concorde, Intrepid, LHS & 300M

TEST	ACTION
12	Turn the ignition on. With the DRB, read DTC's in the Instrument Cluster. Is the panel lamps driver output circuit shorted DTC set? Yes → Go To 13 No → Replace the Instrument Cluster. Perform the Body Verification Test - Ver 1.
13	Turn the ignition off. Disconnect the Instrument Cluster "C1" harness connector. Measure the resistance between ground and the Panel Lamps Driver circuit. Is the resistance below 5.0 ohms? Yes → Go To 14 No → Replace the Instrument Cluster. Perform the Body Verification Test - Ver 1.
14	Turn the ignition off. Disconnect the Ash Receiver Lamp harness connector. Measure the resistance between ground and the Panel Lamps Driver circuit in the Instrument Cluster "C1" connector. Is the resistance below 5.0 ohms? Yes → Go To 15 No → Repair or replace the Ash Receiver Lamp for a short to ground. Perform the Body Verification Test - Ver 1.
15	Turn the ignition off. Disconnect the Clock harness connector (if equipped). Measure the resistance between ground and the Panel Lamps Driver circuit in the Instrument Cluster "C1" connector. Is the resistance below 5.0 ohms? Yes → Go To 16 No → Repair or replace the Clock for a short to ground. Perform the Body Verification Test - Ver 1.
16	Turn the ignition off. Disconnect the Headlamp Switch harness connector. Measure the resistance between ground and the Panel Lamps Driver circuit in the Instrument Cluster "C1" connector. Is the resistance below 5.0 ohms? Yes → Go To 17 No → Repair or replace the Headlamp Switch for a short to ground. Perform the Body Verification Test - Ver 1.
17	Turn the ignition off. Disconnect the PRND3L Illumination harness connector. Measure the resistance between ground and the Panel Lamps Driver circuit in the Instrument Cluster "C1" connector. Is the resistance below 5.0 ohms? Yes → Go To 18 No → Repair or replace the PRND3L for a short to ground. Perform the Body Verification Test - Ver 1.

CR9050000101040X

Fig. 48 Cluster & Panel Illumination Problems (Part 4 of 5). 2000 Concorde, Intrepid, LHS & 300M

TEST	ACTION
7	Turn the park lamps on. Disconnect the Radio "C2" harness connector. Rotate the dimmer switch to the low position, then to the high position and observe the panel lamps. Did the panel lamps function properly with the dimmer switch? Yes → Repair or replace the Radio for a short to voltage. Perform the Body Verification Test - Ver 1. No → Go To 8
8	Turn the park lamps on. Disconnect the Traction Control Switch harness connector (if equipped). Rotate the dimmer switch to the low position, then to the high position and observe the panel lamps. Did the panel lamps function properly with the dimmer switch? Yes → Repair or replace the traction control switch for a short to voltage. Perform the Body Verification Test - Ver 1. No → Go To 9
9	Turn the ignition off. Disconnect the Headlamp Switch harness connector. Turn the ignition on. Measure the voltage of the Panel Lamp Driver circuit. Is the voltage above 10.0 volts? Yes → Go To 10 No → Replace the Headlamp Switch. Perform the Body Verification Test - Ver 1.
10	Turn the park lamps on. Disconnect the Automatic Temperature Control Module or the Manual Temperature Control Module harness connectors. Rotate the dimmer switch to the low position, then to the high position and observe the panel lamps. Did the panel lamps function properly with the dimmer switch? Yes → Repair or replace the Temperature Control Module (Automatic or Manual depending what the vehicle is equipped with) for a short to voltage. Perform the Body Verification Test - Ver 1. No → Go To 11
11	Turn the ignition off. Disconnect the Instrument Cluster "C1" harness connector. Turn the ignition on. Measure the voltage of the Panel Lamp Driver circuit in the Instrument Cluster "C1" connector. Is the voltage above 10.0 volts? Yes → Repair the Panel Lamp Driver circuit for a short to voltage. Perform the Body Verification Test - Ver 1. No → If there are no possible causes remaining, replace the Instrument Cluster. Perform the Body Verification Test - Ver 1.

CR9050000101030X

Fig. 48 Cluster & Panel Illumination Problems (Part 3 of 5). 2000 Concorde, Intrepid, LHS & 300M

TEST	ACTION
18	Turn the ignition off. Disconnect the Radio "C2" harness connector. Measure the resistance between ground and the Panel Lamps Driver circuit in the Instrument Cluster "C1" connector. Is the resistance below 5.0 ohms? Yes → Go To 19 No → Repair or replace the Radio for a short to ground. Perform the Body Verification Test - Ver 1.
19	Turn the ignition off. Disconnect the Traction Control Switch harness connector (if equipped). Measure the resistance between ground and the Panel Lamps Driver circuit in the Instrument Cluster "C1" connector. Is the resistance below 5.0 ohms? Yes → Go To 20 No → Repair or replace the traction control switch for a short to ground. Perform the Body Verification Test - Ver 1.
20	Turn the ignition off. Disconnect the Automatic Temperature Control Module or the Manual Temperature Control Module harness connectors. Measure the resistance between ground and the Panel Lamps Driver circuit in the Instrument Cluster "C1" connector. Is the resistance below 5.0 ohms? Yes → Go To 21 No → Repair or replace the Temperature Control Module (Automatic or Manual depending what the vehicle is equipped with) for a short to ground. Perform the Body Verification Test - Ver 1.
21	View repair options. Repair If there are no possible causes remaining, repair the Panel Lamps Driver circuit for a short to ground. Perform the Body Verification Test - Ver 1.

CR9050000101050X

Fig. 48 Cluster & Panel Illumination Problems (Part 5 of 5). 2000 Concorde, Intrepid, LHS & 300M

POSSIBLE CAUSES
CHECKING FOR INSTRUMENT CLUSTER DTC
CHECKING THE PANEL LAMP DRIVER CIRCUIT FOR A SHORT TO GROUND
INSTRUMENT CLUSTER
PANEL LAMP DRIVER CIRCUIT SHORTED TO GROUND
PANEL LAMP DRIVER CIRCUIT SHORTED TO VOLTAGE
CHECKING FOR A SHORT TO GROUND
CHECKING FOR A SHORT TO VOLTAGE
OBSERVE THE DIMMING LEVEL VOLTAGE
ATTEMPT TO COMMUNICATE WITH THE INSTRUMENT CLUSTER

TEST	ACTION
1	Turn the ignition on. With the DRB, select Body then Electro/Mech Cluster (MIC). Was the DRB able to I/D or communicate with the Instrument Cluster? Yes → Go To 2 No → Refer to the related symptom(s). Perform BODY VERIFICATION TEST - VER 1.
2	Turn the ignition on. **Note: Check the Instrument Cluster (MIC) for any DTCs.** With the DRB, select Body Computer then Sensors and observe the dimming level voltage. Rotate the dimmer switch to the low position, then to the high position and observe the dimming level voltage Does the dimming level voltage change between approximately 0.2 and 3.0 volts? Yes → Go To 3 No → Refer to symptom list for problems related to the Dimming Level Switch Failure DTC. Perform BODY VERIFICATION TEST - VER 1.
3	Turn the park lamps on. Rotate the dimmer switch to the low position, then to the high position and observe the panel lamps. Do the panel lamps stay at full intensity with the dimmer switch in any position? Yes → Go To 4 No → Go To 6

CR9050000545010X

Fig. 49 Cluster & Panel Illumination Problems (Part 1 of 3). 2001–04 Concorde, Intrepid & 300M & 2001 LHS

TEST	ACTION
4	Turn the park lamps on. Ensure the ignition key is off while disconnecting the following Modules/Components. Disconnect the following Modules/Components one at a time in an orderly manner (be sure to turn the ignition off before disconnecting any Module). After the disconnection, rotate the dimmer switch to the low position, then to the high position and observe the panel lamps. Disconnect the Ash Receiver Lamp harness connector if equipped. Disconnect the Clock harness connector if equipped. Disconnect the PRND3L Illumination harness connector if equipped. Disconnect the Radio C2 harness connector if equipped. Disconnect the Traction Control Switch harness connector if equipped. Disconnect the Headlamp Switch harness connector. Disconnect the Automatic/Manual Temperature Control Module harness connector. Did the panel lamps function properly after disconnecting any one module/component? Yes → Replace the module/component that was most recently disconnected when the panel lamps functioned properly. Perform BODY VERIFICATION TEST - VER 1. No → Go To 5
5	Turn the ignition off. Disconnect the Instrument Cluster C1 harness connector. Turn the ignition on. Measure the voltage of the Panel Lamp Driver circuit in the Instrument Cluster C1 harness connector. Is the voltage above 10.0 volts? Yes → Repair the Panel Lamp Driver circuit for a short to voltage. Perform BODY VERIFICATION TEST - VER 1. No → Replace the Instrument Cluster. Perform BODY VERIFICATION TEST - VER 1.
6	Turn the ignition on. With the DRB, read Instrument Cluster DTC's. Is the Panel Lamps Driver Output Circuit Shorted DTC set? Yes → Go To 7 No → Replace the Instrument Cluster. Perform BODY VERIFICATION TEST - VER 1.
7	Turn the ignition off. Disconnect the Instrument Cluster C1 harness connector. Measure the resistance between ground and the Panel Lamps Driver circuit Is the resistance below 10.0 ohms? Yes → Go To 8 No → Replace the Instrument Cluster. Perform BODY VERIFICATION TEST - VER 1.

CR9050000545020X

Fig. 49 Cluster & Panel Illumination Problems (Part 2 of 3). 2001–04 Concorde, Intrepid & 300M & 2001 LHS

TEST	ACTION
8	Turn the ignition off. Ensure the ignition key is off while disconnecting the following Modules/Components. Disconnect the following Modules/Components one at a time in an orderly manner (be sure to turn the ignition off before disconnecting any Module). After the disconnection, measure the resistance between ground and the Panel Lamp Driver circuit. Disconnect the Ash Receiver Lamp harness connector if equipped. Disconnect the Clock harness connector if equipped. Disconnect the PRND3L Illumination harness connector if equipped. Disconnect the Radio C2 harness connector if equipped. Disconnect the Traction Control Switch harness connector if equipped. Disconnect the Headlamp Switch harness connector. Disconnect the Automatic/Manual Temperature Control Module harness connector. Did the resistance increase to above 10.0 ohms after disconnecting any one module/component? Yes → Replace the module/component that was most recently disconnected when the resistance increased to above 10.0 ohms. Perform BODY VERIFICATION TEST - VER 1. No → Repair the Panel Lamp Driver circuit for a short to ground. Perform BODY VERIFICATION TEST - VER 1.

CR9050000545030X

Fig. 49 Cluster & Panel Illumination Problems (Part 3 of 3). 2001–04 Concorde, Intrepid & 300M & 2001 LHS

POSSIBLE CAUSES
INSTRUMENT CLUSTER
ATTEMPT TO COMMUNICATE WITH THE PCM
CHECK THE OPERATION OF THE SPEED CONTROL SYSTEM
DEFECTIVE BULB OR SOCKET
ENGINE TROUBLE CODES
INSTRUMENT CLUSTER

TEST	ACTION
1	Turn the ignition off then on. This will start the bulb test. Did the cruise on indicator illuminate for 3 to 10 seconds? Yes → Go To 2 No → Go To 5
2	Turn the ignition on. With the DRB, read engine DTC's. Are there any PCM DTC's present? Yes → Diagnose the speed control system. Perform the Body Verification Test - Ver 1. No → Go To 3
3	Drive vehicle, turn the speed control system on. Does the speed control system operate properly? Yes → Go To 4 No → Diagnose the speed control system. Perform the Body Verification Test - Ver 1.
4	View repair options. Repair If there are no possible causes remaining, replace the Instrument Cluster. Perform the Body Verification Test - Ver 1.
5	Turn the ignition on. With the DRB, enter "Body", "Body Computer", "System Test" then "PCM Monitor". Is the PCM active on the bus? Yes → Go To 6 No → Perform the Body Verification Test - Ver 1.

CR9050000102010X

Fig. 50 Cruise On Indicator Not Operating Properly (Part 1 of 2). Concorde, Intrepid & 300M & LHS

TEST	ACTION
6	Turn the ignition off. Remove and inspect the cruise on bulb and socket. Is there a problem with the bulb or socket? Yes → Repair or replace the defective bulb or socket as needed. Perform the Body Verification Test - Ver 1. No → Replace the Instrument Cluster. Perform the Body Verification Test - Ver 1.

CR9050000102020X

Fig. 50 Cruise On Indicator Not Operating Properly (Part 2 of 2). Concorde, Intrepid & 300M & LHS

TEST	ACTION
5	Open the decklid and observe the decklid ajar indicator. Is the decklid ajar indicator illuminated? Yes → The decklid ajar indicator is operating properly at this time, check for a intermittent wiring condition. Perform the Body Verification Test - Ver 1. No → Go To 6
6	Turn the ignition off. Disconnect the decklid release solenoid/ajar switch harness connector. Connect a jumper wire between the decklid ajar switch sense circuit and ground. With the jumper wire connected to ground, monitor the decklid ajar indicator. Is the decklid ajar indicator illuminated? Yes → Replace the decklid release solenoid/ajar switch. Perform the Body Verification Test - Ver 1. No → Go To 7
7	Turn the ignition off. Disconnect the decklid release solenoid/ajar switch harness connector. Disconnect the Instrument Cluster "C2" harness connector. Measure the resistance of the decklid ajar switch sense circuit between the decklid release solenoid/ajar switch connector and the Instrument Cluster "C2" connector. Is the resistance below 5.0 ohms? Yes → Go To 8 No → Repair the decklid ajar switch sense circuit for an open. Perform the Body Verification Test - Ver 1.
8	Turn the ignition off. Disconnect the Instrument Cluster "C1" harness connector. Measure the voltage of the Fused B+ circuit (cavity 3). Is the voltage above 10.0 volts? Yes → Go To 9 No → Repair the Fused B+ circuit for an open. Perform the Body Verification Test - Ver 1.
9	View repair options. Repair If there are no possible causes remaining, replace the Instrument Cluster. Perform the Body Verification Test - Ver 1.

CR9050000103020X

Fig. 51 Decklid Ajar Indicator Not Operating Properly (Part 2 of 2). Concorde, Intrepid & 300M & LHS

POSSIBLE CAUSES
DECKLID AJAR SWITCH SENSE CIRCUIT SHORTED TO GROUND
DECKLID RELEASE SOLENOID/AJAR SWITCH SHORTED TO GROUND
INSTRUMENT CLUSTER
INSTRUMENT CLUSTER
OPEN DECKLID AJAR SWITCH SENSE CIRCUIT
OPEN DECKLID AND OBSERVE THE DECKLID AJAR INDICATOR
OPEN DECKLID RELEASE SOLENOID/AJAR SWITCH
OPEN FUSED B+ CIRCUIT

TEST	ACTION
1	Ensure the decklid is properly aligned and fully closed. Turn the ignition on. Is the decklid ajar indicator illuminated? Yes → Go To 2 No → Go To 5
2	**Note: Only perform this test if the decklid ajar indicator is on at all times.** Turn the ignition off. Disconnect the decklid release solenoid/ajar switch harness connector. Observe the decklid ajar indicator. Is the decklid ajar indicator illuminated? Yes → Go To 3 No → Replace the decklid release solenoid/ajar switch. Perform the Body Verification Test - Ver 1.
3	**Note: Only perform this test if the decklid ajar indicator is on at all times.** Turn the ignition off. Disconnect the decklid release solenoid/ajar switch harness connector. Disconnect the Instrument Cluster "C2" harness connector. Measure the resistance between ground and the decklid ajar switch sense circuit. Is the resistance below 5.0 ohms? Yes → Repair the decklid ajar switch sense circuit for a short to ground. Perform the Body Verification Test - Ver 1. No → Go To 4
4	View repair options. Repair If there are no possible causes remaining, replace the Instrument Cluster. Perform the Body Verification Test - Ver 1.

CR9050000103010X

Fig. 51 Decklid Ajar Indicator Not Operating Properly (Part 1 of 2). Concorde, Intrepid & 300M & LHS

POSSIBLE CAUSES
INSTRUMENT CLUSTER
CHECK THE DOOR AJAR STATES
INSTRUMENT CLUSTER
PERFORM INSTRUMENT CLUSTER SELF TEST
CHECK THE DOOR AJAR STATES

TEST	ACTION
1	Close all doors. Turn the ignition off then on. This will start the bulb test. Did the door ajar indicator illuminate for 3 to 10 seconds? Yes → Go To 2 No → Replace the Instrument cluster. Perform the Body Verification Test - Ver 1.
2	With all the doors closed, monitor the door ajar indicator. Does the door ajar indicator stay on with all the doors closed? Yes → Go To 3 No → Go To 4
3	Close all doors. With the DRB, enter "Body", "Body Computer" then "Inputs/Outputs" and read both door ajar states. Does the DRB display both door ajar states "Open"? Yes → Replace the Instrument Cluster. Perform the Body Verification Test - Ver 1. No → Inspect the door ajar switches. Perform the Body Verification Test - Ver 1.
4	Open both driver and passenger doors. With the DRB, enter "Body", "Body Computer" then "Inputs/Outputs" and read both door ajar states. Does the DRB display both door ajar states "Closed"? Yes → Go To 5 No → Inspect the door ajar switches. Perform the Body Verification Test - Ver 1.
5	With the doors open, is the door ajar indicator on? Yes → Test Complete. No → Replace the Instrument Cluster. Perform the Body Verification Test - Ver 1.

CR9050000104000X

Fig. 52 Door Ajar Indicator Not Operating Properly. Concorde, Intrepid & 300M & LHS

POSSIBLE CAUSES
CHECK THE ENGINE COOLANT TEMPERATURE GAUGE OPERATION
PERFORM INSTRUMENT CLUSTER SELF TEST

TEST	ACTION
1	Start the engine and allow the engine to reach operating temperature. Does the temperature gauge operate properly? Yes → Go To 2 No → Diagnose engine coolant temperature gauge. Perform the Body Verification Test - Ver 1.
2	Turn the ignition off then on. This will start the bulb test. Did the engine coolant temperature indicator illuminate for 3 to 10 seconds then turn off? Yes → Test Complete. No → Replace the Instrument Cluster. Perform the Body Verification Test - Ver 1.

CR9050000105000X

Fig. 53 Engine Coolant Temperature Indicator Not Operating Properly. Concorde, Intrepid & 300M & LHS

TEST	ACTION
3	**Note: Make sure the fuel tank is not empty before proceeding.** Turn the ignition on. Observe the fuel gauge. What does the fuel gauge display? Empty at all times Go To 4 Between empty and full Go To 5 Full at all times Go To 7
4	Turn the ignition off. Gain access to the body harness connector C308 by removing the rear seat cushion. Disconnect the C308 harness connector. Turn the ignition on. Connect a jumper wire between ground and fuel level sensor signal circuit. With the jumper wire connected to ground, observe the fuel gauge. Does the fuel gauge display FULL? Yes → Remove the fuel pump module from the tank and inspect for a stuck float arm, replace the fuel pump module. Perform the Body Verification Test - Ver 1. No → If there are no possible causes remaining, replace the Instrument Cluster. Perform the Body Verification Test - Ver 1.
5	Turn the ignition off. Disconnect the BCM "C4" harness connector. **Note: To perform this test, add or remove 5 gallons of fuel and take a measurement, then repeat and take another measurement.** Measure the resistance between ground and the Fuel Level Sensor Signal circuit. Match the resistance to these specifications (float arm height in mm): 151.4mm (sensor full stop) - 60+/-10 ohms, 141.0mm (stop on gauge) - 130+/-15 ohms, 105.8mm (3/4 position) - 340+/-30 ohms. Continued: match the resistance to these specifications: 74.5mm (1/2 position) - 550+/-30 ohms, 43.0mm (1/4 position) - 760+/-30 ohms, 11.1mm (empty on gauge) - 920+/-30 ohms, 1.4mm (sensor empty stop) - 1050+/-10 ohms. Does the resistance of the fuel pump module match the resistance specifications both times? Yes → Replace the Instrument Cluster. Perform the Body Verification Test - Ver 1. No → Go To 6
6	Turn the ignition off. Remove the fuel tank from the vehicle. Remove the fuel pump module from the fuel tank. Inspect the fuel pump module for a bent or sticking arm and the fuel tank for any foreign materials. Is the fuel tank and fuel pump module visual condition good? Yes → Replace the Fuel Pump Module. Perform the Body Verification Test - Ver 1. No → Repair or replace as necessary. Perform the Body Verification Test - Ver 1.

CR9050000106020X

Fig. 54 Fuel Gauge Not Operating Properly (Part 2 of 3). Concorde, Intrepid & 300M & LHS

POSSIBLE CAUSES
BODY COTROL MODULE
INSTRUMENT CLUSTER
INSTRUMENT CLUSTER
VISUAL CONDITION NOT GOOD
FUEL GAUGE DISPLAYS EMPTY
INSPECT THE FUEL PUMP MODULE AND THE FUEL TANK
OBSERVE THE FUEL GAUGE
DETERMINE IF FULL GAUGE IS INACCURATE
FUEL LEVEL SENSOR SIGNAL CIRCUIT SHORTED TO GROUND
INSTRUMENT CLUSTER SELF TEST
CHECK FOR ANY BODY CONTROL MODULE DTCS

TEST	ACTION
1	Turn the ignition off. During the self test all gauges should move from their lowest calibration point to their highest calibration point then back down to its lowest. Calibration points for the Fuel Gauge: "E", 1/4, 1/2, "F", 1/2, 1/4, "E". While holding the "trip/reset" button down on the instrument cluster, turn the ignition forward one position (Ulock/Off position) to start the MIC self test, release the button. Did the Fuel Gauge pass the self test? Yes → Go To 2 No → Replace the Instrument Cluster. Perform the Body Verification Test - Ver 1.
2	Turn the ignition on. With the DRB, enter "Body", "Body Computer" then read DTC's. Is the fuel level sending unit failure DTC set? Yes → Diagnose fuel level sending unit failure DTC. Perform the Body Verification Test - Ver 1. No → Go To 3

CR9050000106010X

Fig. 54 Fuel Gauge Not Operating Properly (Part 1 of 3). Concorde, Intrepid & 300M & LHS

TEST	ACTION
7	Turn the ignition off. Gain access to the body harness connector C308 by removing the rear seat cushion. Disconnect the C308 harness connector. Turn the ignition on. With the DRB, enter "Body", "Body Computer" then "Sensors" and observe the fuel level voltage. Is the voltage above 9.0 volts? Yes → Go To 8 No → Go To 9
8	Turn the ignition on. With the C308 harness connector disconnected observe the fuel gauge. Did the fuel gauge drop to empty? Yes → Check the fuel pump module jumper harness between the C308 and the fuel pump module, replace the fuel pump module. Perform the Body Verification Test - Ver 1. No → If there are no possible causes remaining, replace the Instrument Cluster. Perform the Body Verification Test - Ver 1.
9	Turn the ignition off. Disconnect the BCM "C4" harness connector. Measure the resistance between ground and the Fuel Level Sensor Signal circuit. Is the resistance below 5.0 ohms? Yes → Repair the Fuel Level Sensor Signal circuit for a short to ground. Perform the Body Verification Test - Ver 1. No → If there are no possible causes remaining, replace the BCM. Perform the Body Verification Test - Ver 1.

CR9050000106030X

Fig. 54 Fuel Gauge Not Operating Properly (Part 3 of 3). Concorde, Intrepid & 300M & LHS

POSSIBLE CAUSES
CHECK THE FUEL GAUGE OPERATION
PERFORM INSTRUMENT CLUSTER SELF TEST

TEST	ACTION
1	Start the engine and observe the fuel gauge. Does the fuel gauge operate properly? Yes → Go To 2 No → Diagnose the fuel gauge. Perform the Body Verification Test - Ver 1.
2	Turn the ignition off then on. This will start the bulb test. Did the low fuel indicator illuminate for 3 to 10 seconds then turn off? Yes → Test Complete. No → Replace the Instrument Cluster. Perform the Body Verification Test - Ver 1.

CR9050000107000X

Fig. 55 Low Fuel Indicator Not Operating Properly. Concorde, Intrepid & 300M & LHS

TEST	ACTION
5	Turn the ignition off. Disconnect the washer fluid level sensor harness connector. Disconnect the Instrument Cluster "C2" harness connector. Measure the resistance of the washer fluid switch sense circuit between the washer fluid level sensor connector and the Instrument Cluster "C2" connector. Is the resistance below 5.0 ohms? Yes → Go To 6 No → Repair the washer fluid switch sense circuit for an open. Perform the Body Verification Test - Ver 1.
6	Turn the ignition off. Disconnect the washer fluid level sensor harness connector. Turn the ignition on. Connect a jumper wire between the washer fluid switch sense circuit and the ground circuit. With the DRB, enter "Body", "Electro/Mech Cluster (MIC)" then "Inputs/Outputs" and observe the washer fluid switch status. Does the DRB display "Wash Fluid: Closed"? Yes → Replace the washer fluid level sensor. Perform the Body Verification Test - Ver 1. No → Go To 7
7	View repair options. Repair If there are no possible causes remaining, replace the Instrument Cluster. Perform the Body Verification Test - Ver 1.
8	**Note: Perform this test if the low washer fluid indicator is on all the time.** Turn the ignition off. Disconnect the washer fluid level sensor harness connector. Turn the ignition on and wait one minute. Monitor the low washer fluid indicator. Did the low washer fluid indicator turn off. Yes → Replace the washer fluid level sensor. Perform the Body Verification Test - Ver 1. No → Go To 9
9	**Note: Perform this test if the low washer fluid indicator is on all the time.** Turn the ignition off. Disconnect the washer fluid level sensor harness connector. Disconnect the Instrument Cluster "C2" harness connector. Measure the resistance between ground and the washer fluid switch sense circuit. Is the resistance below 5.0 ohms? Yes → Repair the washer fluid switch sense circuit for a short to ground. Perform the Body Verification Test - Ver 1. No → Go To 10

CR9050000108020X

Fig. 56 Low Washer Fluid Indicator Not Operating Properly (Part 2 of 3). Concorde, Intrepid & 300M & LHS

POSSIBLE CAUSES
CHECK THE WASHER FLUID RESERVOIR
INSTRUMENT CLUSTER
INSTRUMENT CLUSTER
OPEN GROUND CIRCUIT
OPEN WASHER FLUID SWITCH SENSE CIRCUIT
PERFORM INSTRUMENT CLUSTER SELF TEST
WASHER FLUID LEVEL SENSOR
WASHER FLUID LEVEL SENSOR
WASHER FLUID SWITCH SENSE CIRCUIT SHORTED TO GROUND

TEST	ACTION
1	Turn the ignition off. Check the level of the washer fluid reservoir. Is the washer fluid reservoir full? Yes → Go To 2 No → Add washer fluid as necessary. Perform the Body Verification Test - Ver 1.
2	Did the low washer fluid indicator fail to turn on when the reservoir was low? Yes → Go To 3 No → Go To 8
3	Turn the ignition off then on. This will start the bulb test. Did the low washer indicator illuminate for 3 to 10 seconds? Yes → Go To 4 No → Replace the Instrument cluster. Perform the Body Verification Test - Ver 1.
4	Turn the ignition off. Disconnect the washer fluid level sensor harness connector. Measure the resistance between ground and the ground circuit. Is the resistance below 10.0 ohms? Yes → Go To 5 No → Repair the ground circuit for an open. Perform the Body Verification Test - Ver 1.

CR9050000108010X

Fig. 56 Low Washer Fluid Indicator Not Operating Properly (Part 1 of 3). Concorde, Intrepid & 300M & LHS

TEST	ACTION
10	View repair options. Repair If there are no possible causes remaining, replace the Instrument Cluster. Perform the Body Verification Test - Ver 1.

CR9050000108030X

Fig. 56 Low Washer Fluid Indicator Not Operating Properly (Part 3 of 3). Concorde, Intrepid, LHS & 300M

POSSIBLE CAUSES
ATTEMPT TO COMMUNICATE WITH THE INSTRUMENT CLUSTER
ATTEMPT TO COMMUNICATE WITH THE TCM
OBSERVE THE INSTRUMENT CLUSTER

TEST	ACTION
1	Turn the ignition on. With the DRB, enter "Body" then "Electro/Mech Cluster (MIC)". Was the DRB able to I/D or communicate with the Instrument Cluster? Yes → Go To 2 No → Diagnose Instrument Cluster assembly. Perform the Body Verification Test - Ver 1.
2	Turn the ignition on. With the DRB, enter "Transmission". Was the DRB able to I/D or communicate with the TCM? Yes → Go To 3 No → Diagnose TCM. Perform the Body Verification Test - Ver 1.
3	Turn the ignition off. While observing the odometer turn the ignition to the run position. Did all odometer segments illuminated? Yes → Test Complete. No → Replace the Instrument Cluster. Perform the Body Verification Test - Ver 1.

CR9050000109000X

Fig. 57 Odometer Not Operating Properly. Concorde, Intrepid & 300M & LHS

TEST	ACTION
4	Turn the ignition off. Remove the oil pressure switch. Install a mechanical pressure gauge where the oil pressure switch was. Start and idle the engine. Allow the engine to reach normal operating temperature. Read the oil pressure gauge. Is the gauge reading 4.0 psi or greater at idle? Yes → Go To 5 No → Diagnose low engine oil pressure. Perform the Body Verification Test - Ver 1.
5	View repair options. Repair If there are no possible causes remaining, replace the oil pressure switch. Perform the Body Verification Test - Ver 1.
6	Turn the ignition off. Disconnect the oil pressure switch harness connector. Disconnect the Instrument Cluster "C2" harness connector. Measure the resistance between ground and the oil pressure switch sense circuit. Is the resistance below 5.0 ohms? Yes → Repair the oil pressure switch sense circuit for a short to ground. Perform the Body Verification Test - Ver 1. No → If there are no possible causes remaining, replace the Instrument Cluster. Perform the Body Verification Test - Ver 1.
7	Turn the ignition off. Disconnect the oil pressure switch harness connector. Connect a jumper wire between ground and the oil pressure switch sense circuit. Turn the ignition on. Is the oil pressure warning indicator on? Yes → Replace the oil pressure switch. Perform the Body Verification Test - Ver 1. No → Go To 8
8	Turn the ignition off. Disconnect the oil pressure switch harness connector. Disconnect the Instrument Cluster "C2" harness connector. Measure the resistance of the oil pressure switch sense circuit between the oil pressure switch connector and the Instrument Cluster "C2" connector. Is the resistance below 5.0 ohms? Yes → Go To 9 No → Inspect the oil pressure switch sensor circuit for an open. Perform the Body Verification Test - Ver 1.

CR9050000110020X

Fig. 58 Oil Pressure Warning Indicator Not Operating Properly (Part 2 of 3). Concorde, Intrepid & 300M & LHS

POSSIBLE CAUSES
INSTRUMENT CLUSTER
INSTRUMENT CLUSTER
LOW ENGINE OIL PRESSURE LESS THAN 4 PSI (COLD)
LOW ENGINE OIL PRESSURE LESS THAN 4 PSI (WARM)
OIL PRESSURE SWITCH
OIL PRESSURE SWITCH SENSE CIRCUIT SHORTED TO GROUND
OPEN OIL PRESSURE SWITCH
OPEN OIL PRESSURE SWITCH SENSE CIRCUIT

TEST	ACTION
1	**Note: Before beginning this test, make sure the oil level is within specifications.** Turn the ignition on. Observe the oil pressure warning indicator. Is the oil pressure warning indicator on? Yes → Go To 2 No → Go To 7
2	Turn the ignition off. Disconnect the oil pressure switch harness connector. Turn the ignition on. Observe the oil pressure warning indicator. Is the oil pressure warning indicator off? Yes → Go To 3 No → Go To 6
3	Turn the ignition off. Remove the oil pressure switch. Install a mechanical pressure gauge where the oil pressure switch was. Start and idle the engine. Read the oil pressure gauge. Is the gauge reading 4.0 psi or greater at idle? Yes → Go To 4 No → Diagnose low engine oil pressure. Perform the Body Verification Test - Ver 1.

CR9050000110010X

Fig. 58 Oil Pressure Warning Indicator Not Operating Properly (Part 1 of 3). Concorde, Intrepid & 300M & LHS

TEST	ACTION
9	View repair options. Repair If there are no possible causes remaining, replace the Instrument Cluster. Perform the Body Verification Test - Ver 1.

CR9050000110030X

Fig. 58 Oil Pressure Warning Indicator Not Operating Properly (Part 3 of 3). Concorde, Intrepid & 300M & LHS

POSSIBLE CAUSES
ATTEMPT TO COMMUNICATE WITH THE INSTRUMENT CLUSTER
INSTRUMENT CLUSTER
MONITOR THE PRND3L INDICATORS WHILE SHIFTING GEARS
OBSERVE THE PRND3L LAMPS WITH THE IGNITION ON

TEST	ACTION
1	Turn the ignition on. With the DRB, enter "Body" then "Electro/Mech Cluster (MIC)". Was the DRB able to I/D or communicate with the Instrument Cluster? Yes → Go To 2 No → Diagnose Instrument Cluster assembly. Perform the Body Verification Test - Ver 1.
2	Observe the PRND3L lamps while cycling the ignition from off to on. **Note: This should turn on all PRND3L indicators at the same time.** Did all the PRND3L indicators illuminate? Yes → Go To 3 No → Replace the Instrument Cluster. Perform the Body Verification Test - Ver 1.
3	Turn the ignition on. With the DRB, enter "Transmission", "Monitor Display", "Shift Lever" then "SLP" and monitor the shift lever status. **Note: Engage the parking brake.** Move the gear shift lever through all the different positions. Does the SLP reading match the state of the transmission gear? Yes → Go To 4 No → Refer to symptom list for problems related to the Transaxle. Perform the Body Verification Test - Ver 1.
4	View repair options. Repair Replace the Instrument Cluster. Perform the Body Verification Test - Ver 1.

CR9050000111000X

Fig. 59 PRND3L Indicator Faults. Concorde, Intrepid & 300M & LHS

TEST	ACTION
5	Unbuckle the driver's seatbelt. With the DRB, enter "Body Computer" then "Inputs/Outputs" and observe the seatbelt switch state. Does the DRB display "seatbelt switch: Closed"? Yes → Replace the Instrument Cluster. Perform the Body Verification Test - Ver 1. No → Go To 6
6	Turn the ignition off. Disconnect the seatbelt switch harness connector. Measure the resistance between ground and the ground circuit. Is the resistance below 5.0 ohms? Yes → Go To 7 No → Repair the ground circuit for an open. Perform the Body Verification Test - Ver 1.
7	Turn the ignition off. Disconnect the seatbelt switch harness connector. Connect a jumper wire between the seatbelt switch sense circuit and the ground circuit. With the DRB, enter "Body Computer" then "Inputs/Outputs" and observe the seatbelt switch state. Does the DRB display "seatbelt switch: Closed"? Yes → Replace the seatbelt switch. Perform the Body Verification Test - Ver 1. No → Go To 8
8	Turn the ignition off. Disconnect the seatbelt switch harness connector. Disconnect the BCM "C4" harness connector. Measure the resistance of the seatbelt switch sense circuit between the seatbelt switch connector and the BCM "C4" connector. Is the resistance below 5.0 ohms? Yes → Go To 9 No → Repair the seatbelt switch sense circuit for an open. Perform the Body Verification Test - Ver 1.
9	View repair options. Repair If there are no possible causes remaining, replace the BCM. Perform the Body Verification Test - Ver 1.
10	Buckle the driver's seatbelt. With the DRB, enter "Body Computer" then "Inputs/Outputs" and observe the seatbelt switch state. Does the DRB display "seatbelt switch: Open"? Yes → Replace the Instrument Cluster. Perform the Body Verification Test - Ver 1. No → Go To 11

CR9050000112020X

Fig. 60 Seat Belt Indicator Not Operating Properly (Part 2 of 3). Concorde, Intrepid & 300M & LHS

POSSIBLE CAUSES
BODY CONTROL MODULE (SEATBELT SWITCH SENSE CIRCUIT SHORTED TO GROUND)
CHECK THE SEATBELT SWITCH STATUS
PERFORM INSTRUMENT CLUSTER SELF TEST
SEATBELT SWITCH SENSE CIRCUIT SHORTED TO GROUND
SEATBELT SWITCH SHORTED TO GROUND
WIRING HARNESS INTERMITTENT DEFECT
BODY CONTROL MODULE (OPEN SEATBELT SWITCH SENSE CIRCUIT)
CHECK THE SEATBELT SWITCH STATUS
OPEN GROUND CIRCUIT
OPEN SEATBELT SWITCH
SEATBELT SWITCH SENSE CIRCUIT OPEN

TEST	ACTION	APPLICABILITY
1	Turn the ignition off then on. This will start the bulb test. Is the seatbelt indicator illuminated? Yes → Go To 2 No → Replace the Instrument cluster. Perform the Body Verification Test - Ver 1.	
2	Turn the ignition on. Buckle the driver's seatbelt and monitor the seatbelt indicator. Did the seatbelt indicator turn off? Yes → Go To 3 No → Go To 10	
3	Turn the ignition on and wait 10 seconds. Unbuckle the seatbelt and observe the seatbelt indicator. Did the seatbelt indicator turn on? Yes → Go To 4 No → Go To 5	
4	Turn the ignition off. **Note: Visually inspect the related wiring harness. Look for any chafed, pierced, pinched, or partially broken wires.** **Note: Visually inspect the related wire harness connectors. Look for broken, bent, pushed out, or corroded terminals.** Were any problems found? Yes → The seatbelt indicator is operational. Check wiring harness/connectors as necessary. Perform the Body Verification Test - Ver 1. No → Test Complete.	

CR9050000112010X

Fig. 60 Seat Belt Indicator Not Operating Properly (Part 1 of 3). Concorde, Intrepid & 300M & LHS

TEST	ACTION
11	Disconnect the seatbelt switch harness connector. With the DRB, enter "Body Computer" then "Inputs/Outputs" and observe the seatbelt switch state. Does the DRB display "seatbelt switch: Open"? Yes → Replace the seatbelt switch. Perform the Body Verification Test - Ver 1. No → Go To 12
12	Turn the ignition off. Disconnect the seatbelt switch harness connector. Disconnect the BCM "C4" harness connector. Measure the resistance between ground and the seatbelt switch sense circuit. Is the resistance below 5.0 ohms? Yes → Repair the seatbelt switch sense circuit for a short to ground. Perform the Body Verification Test - Ver 1. No → Go To 13
13	View repair options. Repair If there are no possible causes remaining, replace the BCM. Perform the Body Verification Test - Ver 1.

CR9050000112030X

Fig. 60 Seat Belt Indicator Not Operating Properly (Part 3 of 3). Concorde, Intrepid & 300M & LHS

POSSIBLE CAUSES
POWERTRAIN CONTROL MODULE
ATTEMPT TO COMMUNICATE WITH THE PCM
ENGINE TROUBLE CODES
INSTRUMENT CLUSTER SELF TEST
OBSERVE THE VEHICLE SPEED DISPLAY IN THE PCM
OBSERVE THE VEHICLE SPEED DISPLAY IN THE INSTRUMENT CLUSTER

TEST	ACTION
1	Turn the ignition on. With the DRB, enter "Body", "Body Computer", "System Test" then "PCM Monitor". Is the PCM active on bus? Yes → Go To 2 No → Check for the related symptom(s). Perform the Body Verification Test - Ver 1.
2	Turn the ignition off. During the self test all gauges should move from their lowest calibration point to their highest calibration point then back down to its lowest. Calibration points for the Speedometer: 0 MPH (0 KM/H), 20 MPH (40 KM/H) , 60 MPH (100 KM/H), 120 MPH (210 KM/H), 60 MPH (100 KM/H), 20 MPH (40 KM/H), 0 MPH (0 KM/H). While holding the "trip/reset" button down on the instrument cluster, turn the ignition forward one position (unlock/off position) to start the MIC self test, release the button. Did the Speedometer pass the self test? Yes → Go To 3 No → Replace the Instrument Cluster. Perform the Body Verification Test - Ver 1.
3	With the DRB read ENGINE DTC's. Are there any engine DTC's present? Yes → Refer to symptom list for problems related to DRIVABILITY. Perform the Body Verification Test - Ver 1. No → Go To 4

CR9050000113010X

Fig. 61 Speedometer Not Operating Properly (Part 1 of 2). Concorde, Intrepid & 300M & LHS

POSSIBLE CAUSES
POWERTRAIN CONTROL MODULE
ATTEMPT TO COMMUNICATE WITH THE PCM
ENGINE TROUBLE CODES
INSTRUMENT CLUSTER SELF TEST
OBSERVE THE RPM DISPLAY IN THE INSTRUMENT CLUSTER
OBSERVE THE RPM DISPLAY IN THE PCM

TEST	ACTION
1	Turn the ignition on. With the DRB, enter "Body", "Body Computer", "System Test" then "PCM Monitor". Is the PCM active on bus? Yes → Go To 2 No → Perform the Body Verification Test - Ver 1.
2	Turn the ignition off. During the self test all gauges should move from their lowest calibration point to their highest calibration point then back down to its lowest. Calibration points for the Tachometer: 0 RPM, 500 RPM, 2000 RPM, 6000 RPM, 2000 RPM, 500 RPM, 0 RPM. While holding the "trip/reset" button down on the instrument cluster, turn the ignition forward one position (unlock/off position) to start the MIC self test, release the button. Did the Tachometer pass the self test? Yes → Go To 3 No → Replace the Instrument Cluster. Perform the Body Verification Test - Ver 1.
3	With the DRB read ENGINE DTC's. Are there any engine DTC's present? Yes → Diagnose any engine DTC's present. Perform the Body Verification Test - Ver 1. No → Go To 4
4	Start the engine. With the DRB, enter "Engine" then "Sensors" and observe the engine RPM display. Does the DRB display engine RPM above 400 RPM? Yes → Go To 5 No → Replace the Powertrain Control Module. Perform the Body Verification Test - Ver 1.

CR9050000114010X

Fig. 62 Tachometer Not Operating Properly (Part 1 of 2). Concorde, Intrepid & 300M & LHS

TEST	ACTION
4	Raise all four wheels off the ground and properly support the vehicle. Start the engine. **Note: If the vehicle is equipped with traction control, the traction control must be disabled.** With the DRB, enter "Engine" then "Sensors" and observe the vehicle speed display. Place the gear shift lever in drive and observe the vehicle speed while accelerating. Does the DRB display vehicle speed increasing proportionally as you accelerate? Yes → Go To 5 No → Check for the related symptom(s) to the vehicle speed sensor. Perform the Body Verification Test - Ver 1.
5	Raise all four wheels off the ground and properly support the vehicle. Start the engine. **Note: If the vehicle is equipped with traction control, the traction control must be disabled.** With the DRB, enter "Body", "Electro/Mech Cluster (MIC)", "Monitor Display" then "Engine Info" and observe the vehicle speed display. Place the gear shift lever in drive and observe the vehicle speed while accelerating. Does the DRB display vehicle speed increasing proportionally as you accelerate? Yes → Replace the Instrument Cluster. Perform the Body Verification Test - Ver 1. No → If there are no possible causes remaining, replace the PCM. Perform the Body Verification Test - Ver 1.

CR9050000113020X

Fig. 61 Speedometer Not Operating Properly (Part 2 of 2). Concorde, Intrepid & 300M & LHS

TEST	ACTION
5	Start the engine. With the DRB, enter "Body", "Electro/Mech Cluster (MIC)", "Monitor Display" then "Engine Info" and observe the engine RPM display. Does the DRB display engine RPM above 400 RPM? Yes → Replace the Instrument Cluster. Perform the Body Verification Test - Ver 1. No → If there are no possible causes remaining, replace the PCM. Perform the Body Verification Test - Ver 1.

CR9050000114020X

Fig. 62 Tachometer Not Operating Properly (Part 2 of 2). Concorde, Intrepid & 300M & LHS

POSSIBLE CAUSES
POWERTRAIN CONTROL MODULE
ATTEMPT TO COMMUNICATE WITH THE PCM
ENGINE TROUBLE CODES
INSTRUMENT CLUSTER SELF TEST
OBSERVE THE TEMPERATURE DISPLAY IN THE INSTRUMENT CLUSTER
OBSERVE THE TEMPERATURE DISPLAY IN THE PCM

TEST	ACTION
1	Turn the ignition on. With the DRB, enter "Body", "Body Computer", "System Test" then "PCM Monitor". Is the PCM active on the bus? Yes → Go To 2 No → Perform the Body Verification Test - Ver 1.
2	Turn the ignition off. During the self test all gauges should move from their lowest calibration point to their highest calibration point then back down to its lowest. Calibration points for the Temperature Gauge: "C", Mid., H Norm., "H", H Norm., Mid., "C". While holding the "trip/reset" button down on the instrument cluster, turn the ignition forward one position (unlock/off position) to start the MIC self test, release the button. Did the Temperature Gauge pass the self test? Yes → Go To 3 No → Replace the Instrument Cluster. Perform the Body Verification Test - Ver 1.
3	With the DRB read ENGINE DTC's. Are there any engine DTC's present? Yes → Diagnose any engine DTC's present. Perform the Body Verification Test - Ver 1. No → Go To 4
4	Start the engine. With the DRB, enter "Engine" then "Sensors" and observe the engine temperature display. Does the DRB display approximately the correct engine temperature? Yes → Go To 5 No → Replace the Powertrain Control Module. Perform the Body Verification Test - Ver 1.

CR9050000115010X

Fig. 63 Temperature Gauge Not Operating Properly (Part 1 of 2). Concorde, Intrepid & 300M & LHS

POSSIBLE CAUSES
INSTRUMENT CLUSTER (TRACTION CONTROL SWITCH SENSE CIRCUIT)
OBSERVE THE TRACTION OFF INDICATOR
OPEN GROUND CIRCUIT
OPEN TRACTION CONTROL SWITCH SENSE CIRCUIT
PERFORM INSTRUMENT CLUSTER SELF TEST
TRACTION CONTROL SWITCH
TRACTION CONTROL SWITCH SENSE CIRCUIT SHORTED TO GROUND
TRACTION CONTROL SWITCH SENSE CIRCUIT SHORTED TO VOLTAGE
WIRING HARNESS INTERMITTENT DEFECT

TEST	ACTION
1	**Note: The DRB must be able to communicate with the CAB module prior to performing this test.** **Note: If any CAB DTC's are present, they must be repaired prior to performing this test.** Turn the ignition off then on. This will start the bulb test. Did the traction off indicator illuminate for several seconds? Yes → Go To 2 No → Replace the Instrument cluster. Perform the Body Verification Test - Ver 1.
2	Cycle the ignition switch from off to on and wait 10 seconds. Is the traction off indicator illuminated? Yes → Replace the Instrument cluster. Perform the Body Verification Test - Ver 1. No → Go To 3
3	Cycle the ignition switch from off to on and wait 10 seconds. Monitor the traction off indicator while pressing and releasing the traction control switch. Does the traction off indicator turn on and off with the traction control switch? Yes → Go To 4 No → Go To 5

CR9050000116010X

Fig. 64 Traction Off Indicator Not Operating Properly (Part 1 of 3). 2000 Concorde, Intrepid, LHS & 300M

TEST	ACTION
5	Start the engine. With the DRB, enter "Body", "Electro/Mech Cluster (MIC)", "Monitor Display" then "Engine Info" and observe the engine temperature display. Does the DRB display approximately the correct engine temperature? Yes → Replace the Instrument Cluster. Perform the Body Verification Test - Ver 1. No → If there are no possible causes remaining, replace the PCM. Perform the Body Verification Test - Ver 1.

CR9050000115020X

Fig. 63 Temperature Gauge Not Operating Properly (Part 2 of 2). Concorde, Intrepid & 300M & LHS

TEST	ACTION
4	Turn the ignition off. **Note: Visually inspect the related wiring harness. Look for any chafed, pierced, pinched, or partially broken wires.** **Note: Visually inspect the related wire harness connectors. Look for broken, bent, pushed out, or corroded terminals.** Were any problems found? Yes → The traction off indicator is operational. Check wiring harness/ connectors as necessary. Perform the Body Verification Test - Ver 1. No → Test Complete.
5	Turn the ignition off Disconnect the traction control switch harness connector. Measure the resistance between ground and the ground circuit. Is the resistance below 5.0 ohms? Yes → Go To 6 No → Repair the ground circuit for an open. Perform the Body Verification Test - Ver 1.
6	Turn the ignition off Disconnect the traction control switch harness connector. Turn the ignition on. Connect a jumper wire between the traction control switch sense circuit and the ground circuit. Monitor the traction off indicator while toggling the jumper wire. Does the traction off indicator turn on and off as the jumper wire is toggled? Yes → Replace the traction control switch. Perform the Body Verification Test - Ver 1. No → Go To 7
7	Turn the ignition off Disconnect the traction control switch harness connector. Disconnect the Instrument Cluster "C2" harness connector. Measure the resistance of the traction control switch sense circuit between the traction control switch connector and the Instrument Cluster "C2" connector. Is the resistance below 5.0 ohms? Yes → Go To 8 No → Repair the traction control switch sense circuit for an open. Perform the Body Verification Test - Ver 1.
8	Turn the ignition off Disconnect the traction control switch harness connector. Disconnect the Instrument Cluster "C2" harness connector. Measure the resistance between ground and the traction control switch sense circuit. Is the resistance below 5.0 ohms? Yes → Repair the traction control switch sense circuit for a short to ground. Perform the Body Verification Test - Ver 1. No → Go To 9

CR9050000116020X

Fig. 64 Traction Off Indicator Not Operating Properly (Part 2 of 3). 2000 Concorde, Intrepid, LHS & 300M

TEST	ACTION
9	Turn the ignition off Disconnect the traction control switch harness connector. Disconnect the Instrument Cluster "C2" harness connector. Turn the ignition on. Measure the voltage of the traction control switch sense circuit. Is the voltage above 1.0 volts? Yes → Repair the traction control switch sense circuit for a short to voltage. Perform the Body Verification Test - Ver 1. No → Go To 10
10	View repair options. Repair If there are no possible causes remaining, replace the Instrument Cluster. Perform the Body Verification Test - Ver 1.

CR9050000116030X

Fig. 64 Traction Off Indicator Not Operating Properly (Part 3 of 3). Concorde, Intrepid, LHS & 300M

BODY VERIFICATION TEST - VER 1	APPLICABILITY
1. Disconnect all jumper wires and reconnect all previously disconnected components and connectors. 2. If the Sentry Key Immobilizer Module (SKIM) or the Powertrain Control Module (PCM) were replaced, proceed to number 6. If the SKIM or PCM were not replaced, continue to the next number. 3. If the Body Control Module was replaced, turn the ignition on for 15 seconds (to learn VIN) or engine may not start (if VTSS equipped). If the vehicle is equipped with VTSS, use the DRB and enable VTSS. 4. Program all other options as needed. 5. If any repairs were made to the HVAC System, disconnect the battery or using the DRBIII, recalibrate the HVAC doors. Proceed to number 13. 6. Obtain the Vehicle's unique PIN number assigned to it's original SKIM module. 7. With the DRBIII, select THEFT ALARM, SKIM, MISCELLANEOUS and select "Skim Module Replaced" function. Enter the 4 digit PIN number to put SKIM in "Access Mode". 8. The DRBIII will prompt you through the following steps. (1) Program the country code into the SKIM's memory. (2) Program the vehicle's VIN number into the SKIM's memory. (3) Transfer the vehicle's Secret Key data from the PCM. 9. Once secured access mode is active, the SKIM will remain in that mode for 60 seconds. 10. Using the DRBIII, program all customer keys into the SKIM's memory. This requires that the SKIM be in secured access mode, using the 4 digit code. 11. Note: If the PCM is replaced, the unique Secret Key data must be transfered from the SKIM to the PCM. This procedure requires the SKIM to be placed in secured access mode using the 4-digit code. 12. Note: If 3 attempts are made to enter secured access mode using an incorrect PIN, secured access mode will be locked out for 1 hour which causes the DRBIII to display "Bus +- Signals Open". To exit this mode, turn ignition to the "Run" pos. for 1 hour. 13. Ensure all accessories are turned off and the battery is fully charged. 14. Ensure that the Ignition is on, and with the DRBIII, record and erase all Diagnostic Trouble Codes from ALL modules. Start the engine and allow it to run for 2 minutes and fully operate the system that was malfunctioning. 15. Turn the ignition off and wait 5 seconds. Turn the ignition on and using the DRBIII, read DTC's from ALL modules. 16. If ANY codes are present select the appropriate symptom from the Symptom List and continue diagnostics. If NO codes are present and the customers complaint cannot be duplicated, the repair is complete.	All

CR9050000424000X

Fig. 66 Body Verification Test. 2000–02 Concorde, Intrepid & 300M & LHS

When Monitored and Set Condition:

ACM MESSAGES NOT RECEIVED BY MIC

When Monitored: Monitored during ignition on.

Set Condition: No ACM messages received for 6 seconds.

POSSIBLE CAUSES
ACM MESSAGES NOT RECEIVED

CR9050000554010X

Fig. 68 ACM Messages Not Received By MIC (Part 1 of 2). 2000 Neon

POSSIBLE CAUSES
INSTRUMENT CLUSTER
INSTRUMENT CLUSTER (INOPERATIVE TRAC ON INDICATOR IN TRACTION CONTROL MODE)
DEFECTIVE BULB OR SOCKET
INSTRUMENT CLUSTER (TRACTION ON INDICATOR ON ALL THE TIME)
TRACTION CONTROL INOPERATIVE

TEST	ACTION
1	**Note: The DRB must be able to communicate with the CAB module prior to performing this test.** **Note: If any CAB DTC's are present, they must be repaired prior to performing this test.** Turn the ignition off then on. This will start the bulb test. Did the traction on indicator illuminate for several seconds? Yes → Go To 2 No → Go To 4
2	Turn the ignition on and wait 10 seconds. Observe the traction on indicator. Is the traction on indicator on all the time? Yes → Replace the Instrument Cluster. Perform the Body Verification Test - Ver 1. No → Go To 3
3	**Note: Perform this test only if the traction on indicator does not illuminate when the vehicle is in a traction control condition.** Drive vehicle to a safe slippery location and stop. Accelerate vehicle to enable the traction control. Can you physically feel the traction control engage while you accelerate in a slippery condition? Yes → Replace the Instrument Cluster. Perform the Body Verification Test - Ver 1. No → Replace the Controller Antilock Brake (CAB) module. Perform the Body Verification Test - Ver 1.
4	Turn the ignition off. Remove and inspect the traction on bulb and socket. Is there a problem with the bulb or socket? Yes → Repair or replace the defective bulb or socket as needed. Perform the Body Verification Test - Ver 1. No → If there are no possible causes remaining, replace the Instrument Cluster. Perform the Body Verification Test - Ver 1.

CR9050000117000X

Fig. 65 Traction On Indicator Not Operating Properly. 2000 Concorde, Intrepid, LHS & 300M

BODY VERIFICATION TEST - VER 1
1. Disconnect all jumper wires and reconnect all previously disconnected components and connectors. **2. NOTE: If the SKIM or PCM was replaced, refer to the service information for proper programming procedures.** 3. If the Body Control Module was replaced, turn the ignition on for 15 seconds (to allow the new BCM to learn VIN) or engine may not start (if VTSS equipped). If the vehicle is equipped with VTSS, use the DRBIII® and enable VTSS. 4. Program all RKE transmitters and other options as necessary. 5. If any repairs were made to the HVAC System, either disconnect the battery or remove JB Fuse #19 for five minutes to calibrate the HVAC doors. 6. Ensure that all accessories are turned off and the battery is fully charged. 7. With the DRBIII®, record and erase all DTC's from ALL modules. Start and run the engine for 2 minutes. Operate all functions of the system that caused the original concern. 8. Turn the ignition off and wait 5 seconds. Turn the ignition on and using the DRBIII®, read DTC's from ALL modules. Are any DTC's present or is the original condition still present? Yes → Repair is not complete, refer to the appropriate symptom. No → Repair is complete.

CR9090200333000X

Fig. 67 Body Verification Test. 2003 Concorde, Intrepid & 300M

TEST	ACTION
132	Turn ignition on. With the DRBIII select: "Passive Restraints" " Airbag" Is there response from the Airbag control module? Yes → NO PROBLEM FOUND AT THIS TIME. Perform the Body Verification test. No → Refer to symptom *NO RESPONSE FROM ACM in the COMMUNICATION category.

CR9050000554020X

Fig. 68 ACM Messages Not Received By MIC (Part 2 of 2). 2000 Neon

When Monitored and Set Condition:

FUEL LEVEL SENSOR OPEN

When Monitored: With Ignition on.

Set Condition: The Instrument Cluster monitors the fuel level sensor signal circuit for a resistance value between approximately 25 ohms to 1100 ohms. If the Cluster senses a resistance greater than 1100 ohms, this code will set.

POSSIBLE CAUSES
SENSOR GROUND CKT OPEN
DEFECTIVE INSTRUMENT CLUSTER - OPEN FUEL LEVEL
FUEL LEVEL SENSOR OPEN
FUEL LEVEL SENSOR SIGNAL CIRCUIT OPEN

CR9050000555010X

Fig. 69 Fuel Level Sensor Open (Part 1 of 2). 2000 Neon

When Monitored and Set Condition:

FUEL LEVEL SENSOR SHORT

When Monitored: When the ignition is on.

Set Condition: The Instrument Cluster monitors the fuel level sensor signal circuit for a resistance value between approximately 25 ohms to 1100 ohms. If the Cluster senses a resistance less than 25 ohms, this code will set.

POSSIBLE CAUSES
DEFECTIVE INSTRUMENT - SHORTED FUEL LEVEL
FUEL LEVEL SENSOR SHORTED
FUEL LEVEL SENSOR SIGNAL WIRE SHORT TO GROUND

CR9050000556010X

Fig. 70 Fuel Level Sensor Short (Part 1 of 2). 2000 Neon

TEST	ACTION
138	Turn ignition off. Disconnect the Instrument Cluster connector. Measure the resistance of the Fuel Level Sensor Signal circuit to ground. Is the resistance below 60 ohms? Yes → Go To 139 No → Go To 139
139	Turn ignition off. Disconnect the Fuel Pump Module connector. Measure the resistance of the Fuel Level Sensor between the Sensor Signal (DB) and the Sensor Ground (BK/LG) circuits (sensor side connector). Is the resistance below 60.0 ohms? Yes → Replace the Fuel Level Sensor. Perform Powertrain Verification Test VER-2A. No → Go To 140
140	Turn ignition off. Disconnect the Instrument Cluster connector. Disconnect the Fuel Pump Module connector. Measure the resistance of the Fuel Level Sensor Signal circuit in the Instrument Cluster connector to ground. Is the resistance below 100.0 ohms? Yes → Repair the Fuel Level Sensor Signal wire for a short to ground Perform Powertrain Verification Test VER-2A. No → Go To 141
141	If there are no potential causes remaining, the Instrument Cluster is assumed to be defective. View repair options. Repair Replace the Instrument Cluster. Perform Powertrain Verification Test VER-2A.

CR9050000556020X

Fig. 70 Fuel Level Sensor Short (Part 2 of 2). 2000 Neon

TEST	ACTION
133	Turn ignition off. Disconnect the Instrument Cluster connector. Measure the resistance of the Fuel Level Sensor Signal circuit to ground. Is the resistance ABOVE 1060.0 ohms? Yes → Go To 134 No → Go To 134
134	Turn ignition off. Disconnect the Fuel Pump Module connector. Measure the resistance of both ground circuis in the fuel pump module connector. Is the resistance below 5.0 ohms in both ground circuits? Yes → Go To 135 No → Repair the open Ground circuit. Perform Powertrain Verification Test VER-2A.
135	Turn ignition off. Disconnect the Fuel Pump Module connector. Measure the resistance of the Fuel Level Sensor between the Sensor Signal (DB) and the Sensor Ground (BK/LG) circuits (sensor side connector). Is the resistance above 160.0 ohms? Yes → Replace the Fuel Level Sensor. Perform Powertrain Verification Test VER-2A. No → Go To 136
136	Turn ignition off. Disconnect the Instrument Cluster connector. Connect a jumper wire between the Fuel Level Sensor Signal circuit and ground. Disconnect the Fuel Pump Module connector. Measure the resistance of the Fuel Level Sensor Signal circuit in the Fuel Pump Module connector to ground. Is the resistance below 5.0 ohms? Yes → Go To 137 No → Repair the open Fuel Level Sensor Signal circuit. Perform Powertrain Verification Test VER-2A.
137	If there are no potential causes remaining, the Instrument Cluster is assumed to be defective. View repair options. Repair Replace the Instrument Cluster. Perform Powertrain Verification Test VER-2A.

CR9050000555020X

Fig. 69 Fuel Level Sensor Open (Part 2 of 2). 2000 Neon

When Monitored and Set Condition:

PANEL DIMMER OPEN

When Monitored: When the ignition is on.

Set Condition: The Instrument Cluster monitors the panel lamps dimmer signal circuit for a resistance value between 0.0 ohms and approximately 3650 ohms. When the cluster senses a value grreater the 3650 ohms, this code will set.

POSSIBLE CAUSES
INSTRUMENT CLUSTER DEFECTIVE - PANEL LAMPS DIMMER OPEN
PANEL LAMPS DIMMER SIGNAL CIRCUIT OPEN
PANEL DIMMER SWITCH OPEN

CR9050000557010X

Fig. 71 Panel Dimmer Open (Part 1 of 2). 2000 Neon

TEST	ACTION
142	Disconnect the Instrument Cluster connector. Measure the resistance of the Panel Lamps Dimmer Signal circuit in the instrument cluster connector to ground. Move the Instrument Panel Dimmer Switch from one extreme to the other and observe the ohmmeter. Did the resistance increment smoothly from approximately 0.0 ohms to approximately 3.5 K ohms? Yes → Replace the Instrument Cluster (not responding to panel lamps dimmer signal). Perform the Body Verification test. No → Go To 143
143	Disconnect the Instrument Cluster connector. Disconnect the Multi-Function switch connector. Measure the resistance of the Panel Lamps Dimmer Signal circuit between the instrument cluster connector and the multi-function switch connector. Is the resistance below 5.0 ohms? Yes → Go To 144 No → Repair the open Panel Lamps Dimmer Signal circuit. Perform the Body Verification test. **Note: Reconnect the Multi-Function Switch connector before proceeding.**
144	Disconnect the Instrument Cluster connector. Measure the resistance of the Panel Lamps Dimmer Signal circuit in the instrument cluster connector to ground. Move the Instrument Panel Dimmer Switch from one extreme to the other and observe the ohmmeter. Did the resistance increment smoothly from approximately O.0 ohms to approximately 3.5 K ohms? Yes → Test Complete. No → Replace the Multi-Function Switch. perform the Body Verification test.

CR9050000557020X

Fig. 71 Panel Dimmer Open (Part 2 of 2). 2000 Neon

TEST	ACTION
145	Turn ignition off. Disconnect the Powertrain Control Module Connector. **Note: Check connectors - Clean/repair as necessary.** Turn the ignition key on. Use a 12 volt test light in the following step. With the 12V test light connected to ground, probe the Fused Ignition in the PCM Connector. Is the test light illuminated and bright? Yes → Go To 146 No → Repair the open or high resistance Fused Ignition Switch Output Circuit between PCM & Ignition Switch. Perform Powertrain Verification Test VER-1A.
146	Turn the Ignition Off. Disconnect the Powertrain Control Module Connector. **Note: Check connectors - Clean/repair as necessary.** Use a 12 volt test light in the following step. Connect the test light to Ground. Probe the B(+) Circuit in the PCM Connector. Is the test light illuminated and bright? No → Repair the fused B+ circuit for High resistance. If open circuit PCM will show "NO RESPONSE" Perform Powertrain Verification Test VER-1A. Yes → Go To 147
147	Turn ignition off. Disconnect the Powertrain Control Module Connector. **Note: Check connectors - Clean/repair as necessary.** Use a 12 volt test light in the following step. Connect 12V test light to B(+). Probe the Ground Circuits, one at a time, in the PCM Connector. Was the light illuminated and bright in each circuit? Yes → Go To 148 No → Repair the ground(s) for an open or high resistance at the Powertrain Control Module. Perform Powertrain Verification Test VER-1A.

CR9050000558020X

Fig. 72 SBEC Messages Not Received By MIC (Part 2 of 3). 2000 Neon

Test Note: All symptoms _ are diagnosed using the same tests. The title for the tests will be SBEC MESSAGES NOT RECEIVED BY MIC.

When Monitored and Set Condition:

SBEC MESSAGES NOT RECEIVED BY MIC

When Monitored: Monitored during ignition on.

Set Condition: No SBEC messages received for 6 seconds.

PCM MESSAGE NOT RECEIVED

When Monitored: Monitored when ignition is on.

Set Condition: No PCM messages received for 6 seconds.

POSSIBLE CAUSES
PCM DEF INTERNAL PCI BUS OPEN
PCM PCI BUS CIRCUIT OPEN
FUSED B(+) CIRCUIT LESS THAN 10.0 VOLTS
FUSED IGNITION SWITCH OUTPUT CIRCUIT OPEN
PCM GROUND CIRCUIT(S) OPEN

CR9050000558010X

Fig. 72 SBEC Messages Not Received By MIC (Part 1 of 3). 2000 Neon

TEST	ACTION
148	With the DRB read PCM Diagnostic Trouble Codes. This is to ensure power and grounds to the PCM are operational. **Note: If the DRB will not read PCM DTC's, follow the "NO RESPONSE TO PCM (SCI only)" symptom path, if vehicle will start. For NO START Conditions follow symptom "NO RESPONSE" in Starting catagory .** Turn ignition off. Disconnect the Powertrain Control Module. Connect the DRBIII to the Data Link connector Use Scope input cable CH7058, Cable to Probe adapter CH7062, and the red and black test probes. Connect the scope input cable to the channel one connector on the DRB. Attach the red and black leads and the cable to probe adapter to the scope input cable. Select DRB Standalone. Select lab scope. Select Live. Select 12 volt square wave. Press F2 for Scope. Press F2 and use the down arrow to set voltage range to 20 volts. Press F2 again when complete. Connect the Black lead to the PCM ground. Connect the Red lead to the PCM PCI Bus circuit Turn the ignition on. Observe the the voltage displayed on the DRB Lab Scope. What is the voltage displayed on the scope? Pulse from 0 to approximately 7.5 volts Go To 149 Steady 0 volts REPAIR OPEN PCI BUS CIRCUIT TO PCM Perform Powertrain Verification Test VER-1A.
149	The Powertrain Control Module has an internal open PCI Bus and must be replaced. The PCM has an internal PCI BUS Open. Repair Replace the Powertrain Control Module. Perform Powertrain Verification Test VER-1A.

CR9050000558030X

Fig. 72 SBEC Messages Not Received By MIC (Part 3 of 3). 2000 Neon

When Monitored and Set Condition:

SKIM MESSAGE NOT RECEIVED BY MIC

When Monitored: Monitored during ignition on.

Set Condition: No SKIM messages received for 6 seconds.

TEST	ACTION
150	Turn ignition on. Connect the DRBIII. Select "THEFT ALARM" then "SKIM". Is there a response from the SKIM module? Yes → Test Complete. No → Refer to symptom *BUS +/- SIGNAL OPEN FROM SKIM

CR9050000559000X

Fig. 73 SKIM Message Not Received By MIC. 2000 Neon

TEST	ACTION	APPLICABILITY
151	Turn ignition off. Remove the Instrument Cluster Remove the non operational LED from the Instrument Cluster. Using a DVOM select "diode mode", connect the leads across the LED. **Note: Ensure that the Red lead is on the "+" of the LED.** Did the LED illuminate? Yes → Replace the Instrument Cluster. Perform the Body Verification test. No → Replace the defective LED. Perform the Body Verification test.	All

CR9050000560020X

Fig. 74 Any Led Indicator Fails Self Test (Part 2 of 2). 2000 Neon

TEST	ACTION
152	Choose from the list below which best describes your problem. Which of the following problems are you experiencing with your gauge(s)? All gauges inoperative Go To 153 Fuel Gauge Inoperative Go To 179 Speedometer Inoperative Go To 180 Tachometer Inoperative Go To 180 Temperture Gauge Inoperative Go To 180 None of the above There are currently no diagnostics to support your problem. Perform the Body Verification test.
153	Remove and inspect the Cluster fuse (#11) in the Fuse Block. Is the fuse open? Yes → Go To 154 No → Go To 160
154	Turn ignition off. Remove the Cluster Fuse from the fuse block. Measure the resistance of the Fused Ignition Switch Output circuit in the instrument cluster connector to ground. Is the resistance below 10.0 ohms? Yes → Go To 155 No → Go To 158
155	Turn ignition off. Remove the Cluster Fuse from the fuse block. Disconnect the Instrument Cluster connector. Measure the resistance of the Fused Ignition Switch Output circuit in the instrument cluster connector to ground. Is the resistance below 10.0 ohms? Yes → Repair Fused Ignition Switch Output wire for a short to ground and replace blown fuse. Perform the Body Verification test. No → Go To 156
156	Turn ignition off. Disconnect the Instrument Cluster connector. Turn ignition on. Measure the Voltage of the Fused Ignition Switch Output circuit in the Instrument Cluster connector. Is the voltage above 10.0 volts? Yes → Go To 157 No → Go To 157

CR9050000561020X

Fig. 75 Any Or All Gauges Inoperative (Part 2 of 8). 2000 Neon

POSSIBLE CAUSES
LED INOPERATIVE
DEFECTIVE INSTRUMENT CLUSTER

CR9050000560010X

Fig. 74 Any Led Indicator Fails Self Test (Part 1 of 2). 2000 Neon

POSSIBLE CAUSES
GROUND CIRCUIT OPEN
DEFECTIVE CLUSTER FUSE
DEFECTIVE FUSE
FUSED IGNITION SWITCH OUTPUT WIRE OPEN
FUSED B(+) WIRE OPEN
FUSED B(+) WIRE SHORT TO GROUND.
PCI BUS CIRCUIT OPEN
GAUGE OR GAUGES NOT OPERATING PROPERLY
BODY DTC'S
ENGINE DTCS
CLUSTER DEFECTIVE - PCI BUS OPEN
INSTRUMENT CLUSTER DEFECT - FUSED B(+) SHORTED
INSTRUMENT CLUSTER DEFECT - FUSED IGNITION SWITCH OUTPUT SHORTED
CLUSTER DEFECTIVE
DEFECTIVE INSTRUMENT CLUSTER
DEFECTIVE INSTRUMENT CLUSTER
FUSED IGNITION SWITCH OUTPUT WIRE SHORT TO GROUND

CR9050000561010X

Fig. 75 Any Or All Gauges Inoperative (Part 1 of 8). 2000 Neon

TEST	ACTION	APPLICABILITY
157	If there are no potential causes remaining, the Instrument Cluster is assumed to be defective. View repair options. Repair Replace the Instrument Cluster. Perform the Body Verification test.	All
158	Turn ignition off. Disconnect the Instrument Cluster connector. Turn ignition on. Measure the Voltage of the Fused Ignition Switch Output circuit in the Instrument Cluster connector. Is the voltage above 10.0 volts? Yes → Go To 159 No → Go To 159	All
159	If there are no potential causes remaining, the fuse is assumed to be defective. View repair options. Repair Replace the defective fuse. Perform the Body Verification test.	All
160	**Note: If this fuse is open the word "Fuse" will flash in the VF display of the cluster (unless the "Cluster" fuse is open also).** Remove and inspect the IOD Fuse in the PDC. Is the fuse open? Yes → Go To 161 No → Go To 168	All
161	Turn ignition off. Remove the IOD fuse in the PDC. Measure the resistance of the fused B(+) circuit in the instrument cluster connector to ground. Is the resistance below 10.0 ohms? Yes → Go To 162 No → Go To 166	All
162	Turn ignition off. Remove the IOD fuse in the PDC. Disconnect the Instrument Cluster connector. Measure the resistance of the fused B(+) circuit in the instrument cluster connector to ground. Is the resistance below 10.0 ohms? Yes → Repair fused B(+) wire for a short to ground and replace blown fuse. Perform the Body Verification test. No → Go To 163	All

CR9050000561030X

Fig. 75 Any Or All Gauges Inoperative (Part 3 of 8). 2000 Neon

TEST	ACTION	APPLICABILITY
163	Turn ignition off. Disconnect the Instrument Cluster connector. Turn ignition on. Measure the Voltage of the Fused Ignition Switch Output circuit in the Instrument Cluster connector. Is the voltage above 10.0 volts? Yes → Go To 165 No → Go To 164	All
164	Turn ignition off. Disconnect the Instrument Cluster connector. Remove Cluster fuse in the Fuse Block. Measure the resistance of the Fused Ignition Switch Output circuit from the instrument cluster connector to the fuse output cavity. Is the resistance below 5.0 ohms? Yes → Go To 165 No → Repair the open Fused Ignition Switch wire. Perform the Body Verification test.	All
165	If there are no potential causes remaining, the Instrument Cluster is assumed to be defective. View repair options. Repair Replace the Instrument Cluster. Perform the Body Verification test.	All
166	Turn ignition off. Disconnect the Instrument Cluster connector. Turn ignition on. Measure the Voltage of the Fused Ignition Switch Output circuit in the Instrument Cluster connector. Is the voltage above 10.0 volts? Yes → Go To 167 No → Go To 167	All
167	If there are no potential causes remaining, the fuse is assumed to be defective. View repair options. Repair Replace the defective fuse. Perform the Body Verification test.	All
168	Turn ignition off. Disconnect the instrument cluster connector. Measure the resistance of the ground circuit in the Instrument Cluster connector. Is the resistance below 5.0 ohms? Yes → Go To 169 No → Repair open instrument cluster ground circuit. Perform the Body Verification test.	All

CR9050000561040X

Fig. 75 Any Or All Gauges Inoperative (Part 4 of 8). 2000 Neon

TEST	ACTION
169	**Note: If this circuit is open the word "Fuse" will flash in the VF display of the cluster.** Turn ignition off. Disconnect the Instrument Cluster connector. Measure the Voltage of the Fused B(+) circuit in the Instrument Cluster connector. Is the voltage above 10.0 volts? Yes → Go To 170 No → Go To 172
170	Turn ignition off. Disconnect the Instrument Cluster connector. Turn ignition on. Measure the Voltage of the Fused Ignition Switch Output circuit in the Instrument Cluster connector. Is the voltage above 10.0 volts? Yes → Go To 171 No → Go To 176
171	**Note: Ensure there is PCI bus communication with other modules. If not, select: "Complete PCI Bus Failure" from the menu and repair as necessary.** Use Scope input cable CH7058, Cable to Probe adapter CH7062, and the red and black test probes. Connect the scope input cable to the channel one connector on the DRB. Attach the red and black leads and the cable to probe adapter to the scope input cable. Select DRB Standalone. Select lab scope. Select Live. Select 12 volt square wave. Press F2 for Scope. Press F2 and use the down arrow to set voltage range to 20 volts. Press F2 again when complete. Disconnect the instrument cluster connector. Connect the Black lead to the chassis ground. Connect the Red lead to the PCI Bus circuit in the instrument cluster C1 connector. Turn the ignition on. Observe the the voltage displayed on the DRB Lab Scope. What is the voltage displayed on the scope? Pulse from 0 to approximately 7.5 volts Go To 178 Steady 0 volts Repair open Instrument Cluster PCI bus circuit. Perform the Body Verification test.
172	Disconnect the Instrument Cluster connector. Remove the IOD (interior lamp) fuse in the PDC. Measure the resistance of the Fused B(+) wire from the Cluster connector to the fuse socket terminal. Is the resistance below 5.0 ohms? Yes → Go To 173 No → Repair the open Fused B(+) wire from the instrument cluster to the fuse. Perform the Body Verification test.

CR9050000561050X

Fig. 75 Any Or All Gauges Inoperative (Part 5 of 8). 2000 Neon

TEST	ACTION
173	Turn ignition off. Disconnect the Instrument Cluster connector. Turn ignition on. Measure the Voltage of the Fused Ignition Switch Output circuit in the Instrument Cluster connector. Is the voltage above 10.0 volts? Yes → Go To 174 No → Go To 176
174	**Note: Ensure there is PCI bus communication with other modules. If not, select: "Complete PCI Bus Failure" from the menu and repair as necessary.** Use Scope input cable CH7058, Cable to Probe adapter CH7062, and the red and black test probes. Connect the scope input cable to the channel one connector on the DRB. Attach the red and black leads and the cable to probe adapter to the scope input cable. Select DRB Standalone. Select lab scope. Select Live. Select 12 volt square wave. Press F2 for Scope. Press F2 and use the down arrow to set voltage range to 20 volts. Press F2 again when complete. Disconnect the instrument cluster connector. Connect the Black lead to the chassis ground. Connect the Red lead to the PCI Bus circuit in the instrument cluster C1 connector. Turn the ignition on. Observe the the voltage displayed on the DRB Lab Scope. What is the voltage displayed on the scope? Pulse from 0 to approximately 7.5 volts Go To 175 Steady 0 volts Repair open Instrument Cluster PCI bus circuit. Perform the Body Verification test.
175	If there are no potential causes remaining, the Instrument Cluster is assumed to be defective. View repair options. Repair Replace the Instrument Cluster. Perform the Body Verification test.

CR9050000561060X

Fig. 75 Any Or All Gauges Inoperative (Part 6 of 8). 2000 Neon

TEST	ACTION
176	**Note: Ensure there is PCI bus communication with other modules. If not, select: "Complete PCI Bus Failure" from the menu and repair as necessary.** Use Scope input cable CH7058, Cable to Probe adapter CH7062, and the red and black test probes. Connect the scope input cable to the channel one connector on the DRB. Attach the red and black leads and the cable to probe adapter to the scope input cable. Select DRB Standalone. Select lab scope. Select Live. Select 12 volt square wave. Press F2 for Scope. Press F2 and use the down arrow to set voltage range to 20 volts. Press F2 again when complete. Disconnect the instrument cluster connector. Connect the Black lead to the chassis ground. Connect the Red lead to the PCI Bus circuit in the instrument cluster C1 connector. Turn the ignition on. Observe the the voltage displayed on the DRB Lab Scope. What is the voltage displayed on the scope? Pulse from 0 to approximately 7.5 volts Go To 177 Steady 0 volts Repair open Instrument Cluster PCI bus circuit. Perform the Body Verification test.
177	Turn ignition off. Disconnect the Instrument Cluster connector. Remove Cluster fuse in the Fuse Block. Measure the resistance of the Fused Ignition Switch Output circuit from the instrument cluster connector to the fuse output cavity. Is the resistance below 5.0 ohms? Yes → Go To 178 No → Repair the open Fused Ignition Switch wire. Perform the Body Verification test.
178	If there are no potential causes remaining, the Instrument Cluster is assumed to be defective. View repair options. Repair Replace the Instrument Cluster. Perform the Body Verification test.
179	Turn ignition on. Using the DRB, read body DTC's. Are there any body DTC's present? Yes → Repair body DTC's as needed. Perform the Body Verification test. No → Replace the Instrument Cluster. Perform the Body Verification test.

CR9050000561070X

Fig. 75 Any Or All Gauges Inoperative (Part 7 of 8). 2000 Neon

TEST	ACTION
180	Turn ignition on. Using the DRB, read engine DTC's. Are there any engine DTC's present? Yes → Repair engine DTC's as needed. Perform the Body Verification test. No → Replace the Instrument Cluster. Perform the Body Verification test.

CR9050000561080X

Fig. 75 Any Or All Gauges Inoperative (Part 8 of 8). 2000 Neon

TEST	ACTION
181	Turn the park lamps on. Rotate the panel dimmer switch from one extreme to the other and observe the Instrument Cluster lamps. Select the proper Cluster Illumination problem. Cluster lamps stay bright. Go To 182 No Cluster Illumination Go To 187 Cluster dims properly. Return to Menu and select another symptom. Perform the Body Verification test.
182	Turn the Panel Dimmer Switch (on multi-function switch) to the lowest setting. With the DRBIII select: "Body", "Mech/Inst Cluster", "Sensors", "Panel Lamps" Does the DRBIII show Panel Lamp voltage GREATER than 2.5 volts? Yes → Go To 183 No → Go To 185
183	Disconnect the Instrument Cluster. Disconnect the Multi-Function Switch connector. Measure the resistance of the Panel Lamps Dimmer Switch Signal circuit in the instrument cluster connector to ground. Is the resistance below 1000.0 ohms? Yes → Repair the Panel Lamps Dimmer Signal wire for a short to ground. Perform the Body Verification test. No → Go To 184
184	If there are no potential causes remaining, the Instrument Cluster is assumed to be defective. View repair options. Repair Replace the Instrument Cluster. Perform the Body Verification test.
185	Disconnect the Instrument Cluster. Disconnect the Multi-Function Switch connector. Measure the resistance of the Panel Lamps Dimmer Switch Signal circuit in the instrument cluster connector to ground. Is the resistance below 1000.0 ohms? Yes → Repair the Panel Lamps Dimmer Signal wire for a short to ground. Perform the Body Verification test. No → Go To 186
186	If there are no potential causes remaining, the Multi-Function Switch is assumed to be defective. View repair options. Repair Replace the Multi- Function Switch. perform the Body Verification test.

CR9050000562020X

Fig. 76 Cluster Illumination Problem (Part 2 of 3). 2000 Neon

POSSIBLE CAUSES
INSTRUMENT CLUSTER DEFECTIVE - COURTESY LAMP STAYS ON
COURTESY LAMP CONTROL WIRE SHORT GROUND
PANEL LAMPS DIMMER SIGNAL WIRE SHORT TO GROUND
PANEL LAMPS DIMMER SWITCH SHORT TO GROUND.
PASSENGER DOOR AJAR/RKE SENSE WIRE SHORT TO GROUND.
DEFECTIVE DRIVER DOOR AJAR SWITCH - SHORTED
INSTRUMENT CLUSTER DEFECTIVE - PASSENGER DOOR AJAR
DRIVER DOOR AJAR SWITCH SENSE WIRE SHORTED
RKE MODULE DEFECTIVE - PASSENGER DOOR AJAR SHORT
INSTRUMENT CLUSTER DEFECTIVE - DRIVER DOOR AJAR SHORT
RKE MODULE DEFECTIVE - DRIVER DOOR AJAR SHORT TO GROUND
LEFT REAR DOOR AJAR SWITCH SHORTED
PASSENGER DOOR AJAR SWITCH SENSE WIRE SHORT TO GROUND.
PASSENGER DOOR AJAR SWITCH SHORTED
RIGHT REAR DOOR AJAR SWITCH SHORTED

CR9050000563010X

Fig. 77 Courtesy Lamps On At All Times (Part 1 of 6). 2000 Neon

POSSIBLE CAUSES
BULBS OPEN
MULTI-FUNCTION SWITCH DEFECTIVE - PANEL LAMPS DIMMER SHORTED
IDENTIFY ILLUMINATION PROBLEM
PANEL LAMPS DIMMER SIGNAL WIRE SHORT TO GROUND
INSTRUMENT CLUSTER DEFECTIVE - PANEL LAMPS SHORTED
INSTRUMENT CLUSTER DEFECTIVE - PANEL LAMPS OPEN

CR9050000562010X

Fig. 76 Cluster Illumination Problem (Part 1 of 3). 2000 Neon

TEST	ACTION
187	With the DRBIII read Electro/Mech Cluster DTC's. Does the DRBIII show the "Panel Dimmer Open" DTC? Yes → Refer to symptom PANEL DIMMER OPEN No → Go To 188
188	Remove the Instrument Cluster. Remove and test some of the Cluster Illumination Bulbs. Are the bulbs Okay? Yes → Go To 189 No → Replace the necessary bulbs Perform the Body Verification test.
189	If there are no potential causes remaining, the Instrument Cluster is assumed to be defective. View repair options. Repair Replace the Instrument Cluster. Perform the Body Verification test.

CR9050000562030X

Fig. 76 Cluster Illumination Problem (Part 3 of 3). 2000 Neon

TEST	ACTION
190	Close all passenger doors. With the DRB III select: "Body" "Electro/Mech Cluster" "Input/Output" Read the "Pas Door Ajar Sw" state. Does the DRBIII Show: "OPEN"? Yes → Go To 191 No → Go To 202
191	Close the driver door. With the DRB III select: "Body" "Electro/Mech Cluster" "Input/Output" Read the "Dvr Door Ajar Sw" state. Does the DRBIII Show: "OPEN"? Yes → Go To 192 No → Go To 197
192	Move the panel lamps dimmer switch to the middle position. Disconnect the Instrument Cluster connector. Measure the resistance of the Panel Lamps Dimmer Signal circuit in the instrument cluster connector. Is the resistance below 100.0 ohms? Yes → Go To 193 No → Go To 195
193	Disconnect the Instrument Cluster connector. Disconnect the Multi-Function switch connector. Measure the resistance of the Panel Lamps Dimmer Signal circuit in the instrument cluster connector. Is the resistance below 100.0 ohms? Yes → Repair the Panel Lamps Dimmer Signal wire for a short to ground. Perform the Body Verification test. No → Go To 194
194	Remove the IOD fuse from the Power Distribution Center. Disconnect the Instrument Cluster connector. Measure the resistance of the Courtesy Lamp Control circuit in the Instrument Cluster connector. Is the resistance below 100.0 ohms? Yes → Repair the Courtesy Lamps Control wire for a short to ground. Perform the Body Verification test. No → Go To 208
195	Remove the IOD fuse from the Power Distribution Center. Disconnect the Instrument Cluster connector. Measure the resistance of the Courtesy Lamp Control circuit in the Instrument Cluster connector. Is the resistance below 100.0 ohms? Yes → Repair the Courtesy Lamps Control wire for a short to ground. Perform the Body Verification test. No → Go To 196

CR9050000563020X

Fig. 77 Courtesy Lamps On At All Times (Part 2 of 6). 2000 Neon

TEST	ACTION
196	If there are no potential causes remaining, the Instrument Cluster is assumed to be defective. View repair options. Repair Replace the Instrument Cluster. Perform the Body Verification test.
197	Turn ignition off. Disconnect the driver door ajar switch connector. Disconnect the Instrument Cluster connector. Disconnect the RKE Module connector. Measure the resistance of the Driver Door Ajar Switch Sense circuit from the door ajar switch connector to ground. Is the resistance below 100.0 ohms? Yes → Repair the Driver Door Ajar Switch Sense wire for a short to ground. Perform the Body Verification test. No → Go To 198
198	Open the Drivers door. Disconnect the Driver Door Ajar Switch connector. With the DRB III select: "Body" "Electro/Mech Cluster" "Input/Output" Read the "Dvr Door Ajar Sw" state. Does the DRBIII show: "Open"? Yes → Replace the defective Door Ajar Switch. Perform the Body Verification test. No → Go To 199
199	Disconnect the RKE Module connector. With the DRB III select: "Body" "Electro/Mech Cluster" "Input/Output" Read the "Dvr Door Ajar Sw" state. Does the DRBIII show "Drv Door Ajar Sw: Open"? Yes → Replace the Remote Keyless Entry Module (driver door ajar shorted). Perform the Body Verification test. No → Go To 200
200	Move the panel lamps dimmer switch to the middle position. Disconnect the Instrument Cluster connector. Measure the resistance of the Panel Lamps Dimmer Signal circuit in the instrument cluster connector. Is the resistance below 100.0 ohms? Yes → Go To 207 No → Go To 201

CR9050000563030X

Fig. 77 Courtesy Lamps On At All Times (Part 3 of 6). 2000 Neon

TEST	ACTION
201	Remove the IOD fuse from the Power Distribution Center. Disconnect the Instrument Cluster connector. Measure the resistance of the Courtesy Lamp Control circuit in the Instrument Cluster connector. Is the resistance below 100.0 ohms? Yes → Repair the Courtesy Lamps Control wire for a short to ground. Perform the Body Verification test. No → Go To 215
202	Close all passenger doors. With the DRB III select: "Body" "Electro/Mech Cluster" "Input/Output" Read the "Pas Door Ajar Sw" state. Remove each passenger door ajar switch and observe the DRBIII. When removing which switch did the DRB change states to read "Pas Door Ajar Sw: Open"? Passenger Door Replace the defective Passenger Door Ajar Switch. Perform the Body Verification test. Left Rear Door Replace the defective Passnger Door Ajar Switch. Perform the Body Verification test. Right Rear Door Replace the Right Rear Door Ajar Switch. Perform the Body Verification test. DRB Did Not Change Go To 203
203	Turn ignition off. Disconnect all passenger door ajar switches. Disconnect the RKE Module connector. Disconnect the Instrument Cluster. Measure the resistance of the Passenger Door Ajar circuit in the Passenger Door Ajar Switch connector. Is the resistance below 100.0 ohms? Yes → Repair the Passenger Door Ajar/RKE Sense wire for a short to ground. Perform the Body Verification test. No → Go To 204
204	Turn ignition off. Disconnect all passenger door ajar switches. Disconnect the RKE Module connector. Disconnect the Instrument Cluster. Measure the resistance of the Passenger Door Ajar circuit in the Passenger Door Ajar Switch connector. Is the resistance below 100.0 ohms? Yes → Repair the Passenger Door Ajar Switch Sense wire for a short to ground. Perform the Body Verification test. No → Go To 205

CR9050000563040X

Fig. 77 Courtesy Lamps On At All Times (Part 4 of 6). 2000 Neon

TEST	ACTION
205	Close the driver door. With the DRB III select: "Body" "Electro/Mech Cluster" "Input/Output" Read the "Dvr Door Ajar Sw" state. Does the DRBIII Show: "OPEN"? Yes → Go To 206 No → Go To 212
206	Move the panel lamps dimmer switch to the middle position. Disconnect the Instrument Cluster connector. Measure the resistance of the Panel Lamps Dimmer Signal circuit in the instrument cluster connector. Is the resistance below 100.0 ohms? Yes → Go To 207 No → Go To 209
207	Disconnect the Instrument Cluster connector. Disconnect the Multi-Function switch connector. Measure the resistance of the Panel Lamps Dimmer Signal circuit in the instrument cluster connector. Is the resistance below 100.0 ohms? Yes → Repair the Panel Lamps Dimmer Signal wire for a short to ground. Perform the Body Verification test. No → Go To 208
208	If there are no potential causes remaining, the Panel Dimmer Switch (Multi-Function Switch) is assumed to be defective. View repair options. Repair Replace the Multi-Function Switch. perform the Body Verification test.
209	Remove the IOD fuse from the Power Distribution Center. Disconnect the Instrument Cluster connector. Measure the resistance of the Courtesy Lamp Control circuit in the Instrument Cluster connector. Is the resistance below 100.0 ohms? Yes → Repair the Courtesy Lamps Control wire for a short to ground. Perform the Body Verification test. No → Go To 210
210	Close all passenger doors. With the DRB III select: "Body" "Electro/Mech Cluster" "Input/Output" Read the "Pas Door Ajar Sw" state. Disconnect the RKE Module connector while observing the DRB.. When the RKE module was disconnected, did the DRB show "Pas Door Ajar Sw: Open"? Yes → Replace the Remote Keyless Entry Module. Perform the Body Verification test. No → Go To 211

CR9050000563050X

Fig. 77 Courtesy Lamps On At All Times (Part 5 of 6). 2000 Neon

TEST	ACTION
211	If there are no potential causes remaining, the Instrument Cluster is assumed to be defective. View repair options. Repair Replace the Instrument Cluster (passenger door ajar malfunction). Perform the Body Verification test.
212	Turn ignition off. Disconnect the driver door ajar switch connector. Disconnect the Instrument Cluster connector. Disconnect the RKE Module connector. Measure the resistance of the Driver Door Ajar Switch Sense circuit from the door ajar switch connector to ground. Is the resistance below 100.0 ohms? Yes → Repair the Driver Door Ajar Switch Sense wire for a short to ground. Perform the Body Verification test. No → Go To 213
213	Open the Drivers door. Disconnect the Driver Door Ajar Switch connector. With the DRB III select: "Body" "Electro/Mech Cluster" "Input/Output" Read the "Dvr Door Ajar Sw" state. Does the DRBIII show: "Open"? Yes → Replace the defective Door Ajar Switch. Perform the Body Verification test. No → Go To 214
214	Disconnect the RKE Module connector. With the DRB III select: "Body" "Electro/Mech Cluster" "Input/Output" Read the "Dvr Door Ajar Sw" state. Does the DRBIII show "Drv Door Ajar Sw: Open"? Yes → Replace the Remote Keyless Entry Module (driver door ajar shorted). Perform the Body Verification test. No → Go To 215
215	If there are no potential causes remaining, the Instrument Cluster is assumed to be defective. View repair options. Repair Replace the Instrument Cluster. Perform the Body Verification test.

CR9050000563060X

Fig. 77 Courtesy Lamps On At All Times (Part 6 of 6). 2000 Neon

POSSIBLE CAUSES
FUSED B(+) CIRCUIT OPEN
INSTRUMENT CLUSTER DEFECTIVE - COURTESY LAMP OPEN
COURTESY LAMP CONTROL CIRCUIT OPEN

CR9050000564010X

Fig. 78 Courtesy Lamps Totally Inoperative (Part 1 of 2). 2000 Neon

POSSIBLE CAUSES
FOG LAMP SWITCH OUTPUT CIRCUIT OPEN
LED INOPERATIVE
INSTRUMENT CLUSTER DEFECTIVE - FOG LAMP INDICATOR OPEN

CR9050000565010X

Fig. 79 Fog Lamp Indicator Inoperative (Part 1 of 2). 2000 Neon

TEST	ACTION
219	Ensure the Fog Lamps are operational before proceeeding. If not, select "Service Information" from the menu and repair as necessary. Disconnect the Instrument Cluster connector. Turn the Fog Lamps on. Measure the voltage between Fog Lamp Switch Output circuit and ground. Is the voltage greater than 10.0 volts? Yes → Go To 220 No → Repair the open Fog Lamp Switch Output circuit. Perform the Body Verification test.
220	Turn ignition off. Remove the Instrument Cluster Remove the Fog Lamp Indicator LED from the Instrument Cluster. Using a DVOM select "diode mode", connect the leads across the LED. **Note: Ensure that the Red lead is on the "+" of the LED.** Did the LED illuminate? Yes → Replace the defective Fog Lamp Indicator LED. Perform the Body Verification test. No → Go To 221
221	If there are no potential causes remaining, the Instrument Cluster is assumed to be defective. View repair options. Repair Replace the Instrument Cluster. Perform the Body Verification test.

CR9050000565020X

Fig. 79 Fog Lamp Indicator Inoperative (Part 2 of 2). 2000 Neon

POSSIBLE CAUSES
BRAKE FLUID LEVEL SWITCH GROUND CIRCUIT OPEN
PARK BRAKE RED BRAKE WARNING INDICATOR DRIVER CIRCUIT OPEN
PARK BRAKE RED BRAKE WARNING INDICATOR DRIVER CIRCUIT SHORTED TO GROUND
DEFECTIVE LED
RED BRAKE WARNING INDICATOR PROBLEM
BRAKE FLUID LEVEL SWITCH RED BRAKE WARNING INDICATOR DRIVER CKT SHORTED TO GND
BRAKE FLUID LEVEL SWITCH OPEN
BRAKE FLUID LEVEL SWITCH SHORTED TO GROUND
PARK BRAKE SWITCH OPEN
PARK BRAKE SWITCH SHORTED TO GROUND
BRAKE FLUID LEVEL SWITCH RED BRAKE WARNING INDICATOR DRIVER CIRCUIT OPEN
PCM TROUBLE CODES
DEFECTIVE CLUSTER
DEFECTIVE CLUSTER

CR9050000566010X

Fig. 80 Red Brake Warning Indicator Not Operating Properly (Part 1 of 4). 2000 Neon

TEST	ACTION
216	Remove the dome lamp lens. Remove and ensure the bulb is good. Measure the voltage of the Fused B(+) circuit in the bulb socket. Is the voltage above 10.0 volts? Yes → Go To 217 No → Repair the open Fused B(+) circuit. Perform the Body Verification test. **Note: Reinstall the dome lamp bulb.**
217	Disconnect the Instrument Cluster connector. Connect a jumper wire between Courtesy lamp Control circuit and ground and observe the dome lamp.. Did the dome lamp illuminate? Yes → Replace the Instrument Cluster. Perform the Body Verification test. No → Go To 218
218	Remove the dome lamp lens. Remove the dome lamp bulb. Disconnect the Instrument Cluster connector. Connect a jumper wire between Courtesy lamp Control circuit in the Instrument Cluster connector and ground. Measure the resistance of the Courtesy Lamp Control circuit in the Dome Lamp Socket. Is the resistance below 5.0 ohms? Yes → Test Complete. No → Repair the open Courtesy Lamp Control Circuit. Perform the Body Verification test.

CR9050000564020X

Fig. 78 Courtesy Lamps Totally Inoperative (Part 2 of 2). 2000 Neon

TEST	ACTION
222	Choose the option below that best describes your problem. Red Brake Warning Indicator has the following problem. Does not illuminate with low brake fluid Go To 223 Does not illuminate with park brake on Go To 227 On all the time Go To 229 Does not illuminate during "key on" Go To 234 None of the above There are currently no diagnostics to support your problem. Perform the Body Verification test.
223	Turn ignition off. Disconnect the Brake Fluid Level Switch connector. Measure the resistance of the Ground circuit in the Brake Fluid Level connector. Is the resistance above 5.0 ohms? Yes → Repair the open Brake Fluid Level Switch Ground circuit. Perform the Body Verification test. No → Go To 224
224	Turn ignition off. Disconnect the Brake Fluid Level Switch connector. Turn ignition on. Place a jumper between cavities 1 and 2 of the Brake Fluid Level connector (harness side). Did the Red Brake Warning indicator illuminate? Yes → Repair the open Brake Fluid Level Switch. Perform the Body Verification test. No → Go To 225
225	Turn ignition off. Disconnect the Brake Fluid Level Switch connector. Disconnect the PCM C2 connector. Measure the resistance of the Red Brake Warning Indicator Driver circuit between the Brake Fluid Level Switch connector (harness side) and the PCM C2 connector. Is the resistance above 5.0 ohms? Yes → Repair the Red Brake Warning Indicator Driver circuit for an open. Perform the Body Verification test. No → Go To 226
226	There are no further possible causes. View repair options. Repair Check for engine DTCs and repair as necessary. Perform the Body Verification test.

CR9050000566020X

Fig. 80 Red Brake Warning Indicator Not Operating Properly (Part 2 of 4). 2000 Neon

TEST	ACTION
227	Turn ignition off. Gain access to and disconnect the Park Brake Switch connector. Remove the Instrument Cluster. Measure the resistance of the Red Brake Warning Indicator Driver circuit between the Instrument Cluster connector and the Park Brake Switch connector. Is the resistance above 5.0 ohms? Yes → Repair the Red Brake Warning Indicator Driver circuit for an open. Perform the Body Verification test. No → Go To 228
228	Turn ignition off. Gain access to and disconnect the Park Brake Switch connector. Ensure that the Parking Brake is engaged. Measure the resistance of the Parking Brake Switch to a known good ground. Is the resistance above 5.0 ohms? Yes → Replace the open Park Brake Switch. Perform the Body Verification test. No → Test Complete.
229	Turn ignition off. Disconnect the Brake Fluid Level Switch connector. Measure the resistance of each cavity of the Brake Fluid Level connector (switch side) to ground. Is the resistance of either wire below 5.0 ohms? Yes → Repair the Brake Fluid Level Switch for a short to ground. Perform the Body Verification test. No → Go To 230
230	Turn ignition off. Gain access to and disconnect the Park Brake Switch connector. Remove the Instrument Cluster. Measure the resistance of the Red Brake Warning Indicator Driver circuit from the Park Brake Switch connector to a know good ground. Is the resistance below 100.0 ohms? Yes → Repair the Red Brake Warning Indicator Driver circuit for an short to ground. Perform the Body Verification test. No → Go To 231
231	Turn ignition off. Gain access to and disconnect the Park Brake Switch connector. Ensure that the Parking Brake is fully released. Measure the resistance of the Parking Brake Switch to a known good ground. Is the resistance below 100.0 ohms? Yes → Repair the Park Brake Switch for a short to ground. Perform the Body Verification test. No → Go To 232

CR9050000566030X

Fig. 80 Red Brake Warning Indicator Not Operating Properly (Part 3 of 4). 2000 Neon

POSSIBLE CAUSES
DEFECTIVE INSTRUMENT CLUSTER

CR9050000567010X

Fig. 81 VF Display Fails Self Test (Part 1 of 2). 2000 Neon

ABS VERIFICATION TEST

1. Turn ignition off.
2. Connect all previously disconnected components and connectors.
3. Turn ignition on.
4. With the DRBIII® erase DTC's.
5. With the DRBIII® read DTC's.
6. If any Diagnostic Trouble Codes are present, return to Symptom list and troubleshoot new or recurring symptom.
7. If there are no DTC's present after turning ignition on, road test the vehicle for at least 5 minutes. Perform several antilock braking stops.
8. **Caution: Ensure braking capability is available before road testing.**
9. Again, with the DRBIII® read DTC's. If any DTC's are present, return to Symptom list.
10. If there are no diagnostic trouble codes present, and the customer's complaint can no longer be duplicated, the repair is complete.

CR9050000909000X

Fig. 82 ABS Verification Test. 2000 Neon

TEST	ACTION
232	Turn ignition off. Disconnect the Brake Fluid Level Switch connector. Disconnect the PCM C2 connector. Measure the resistance of the Red Brake Warning Indicator Driver circuit at the Brake Fluid Level Switch connector (harness side) to a known good ground. Is the resistance below 100.0 ohms? Yes → Repair the Red Brake Warning Indicator Driver circuit for a short to ground. Perform the Body Verification test. No → Go To 233
233	If there are no potential causes remaining, the Instrument Cluster is assumed to be defective. View repair options. Repair Replace the Instrument Cluster. Perform the Body Verification test.
234	Turn ignition off. Remove the Instrument Cluster. Remove the Red Brake Warning Indicator LED from the Instrument Cluster. Using a DVOM select "diode mode", connect the leads across the LED. **Note: Ensure that the Red lead is on the "+" of the LED.** Did the LED illuminate? Yes → Replace the Instrument Cluster. Perform the Body Verification test. No → Replace the defective Red Brake Warning Indicator LED. Perform the Body Verification test.

CR9050000566040X

Fig. 80 Red Brake Warning Indicator Not Operating Properly (Part 4 of 4). 2000 Neon

TEST	ACTION
235	The VF Display is not a repairable or replaceable item. If it has failed the self test, the Instrument Cluster is assumed to be defective. View repair options. Repair Replace the Instrument Cluster. Perform the Body Verification test.

CR9050000567020X

Fig. 81 VF Display Fails Self Test (Part 2 of 2). 2000 Neon

AIRBAG VERIFICATION TEST

1. Remove any special tools or jumper wires and reconnect all previously disconnected components (except the Battery).
2. Turn the Ignition key On and reconnect the Battery.
3. Connect the DRB to the Data Link Connector (use the most current software available).
4. Use the DRB III and erase the stored codes.
5. Turn the Ignition Off,and wait 15 seconds before turning the Ignition On.
6. Wait one minute, and read active codes and if there are none present read the stored codes.
7. If the DRB shows any active or stored codes, return to the Symptom list and follow path specified for that trouble code. If no active or stored codes are present, the repair is complete.

Are any codes present?

YES
Select the appropriate system from the Symptom List and continue diagnostics.

NO
Repair is complete.

CR9050000910000X

Fig. 83 Air Bag Verification Test. 2000 Neon

SKIS VERIFICATION

1. Reconnect all previously disconnected components and connectors.
2. Obtain the vehicle's unique Personal Identification Number (PIN) assigned to it's original SKIM. This number can be obtained from the vehicle's invoice or Chrysler's Customer Center
3. NOTE: When entering PIN, care should be taken because 3 attempts will only be allowed. The SKIM module will then "lock out" the DRB III for 1 hour, which will cause the DRB III to display "Bus +– Signals Open" to SKIM.
4. To exit "lock out" mode, the ignition key needs to remain in the "On" position continually for one hour. Turn off all accessories and connect a battery charger, if necessary.
5. With the DRB III, select "Theft Alarm," "Skim," "Miscellaneous," then select desired procedure and follow the steps displayed.
6. If the SKIM was replaced, ensure all of the vehicles keys are programmed into the new SKIM.

7. Note: Prior to returning vehicle to the customer, perform a module scan to be sure all DTC's are erased. Erase ANY DTC's that are found.

CR9050000911000X

Fig. 84 SKIS Verification Test. 2000 Neon

VERIFICATION TEST - BODY
1. Disconnect all jumper wires and reconnect all previously disconnected components and connectors. 2. If the Sentry Key Immobilizer Module (SKIM) or the Powertrain Control Module (PCM) were replaced, proceed to number 5. If the SKIM or PCM were not replaced, continue to the next number. 3. If the Remote Keyless Entry module was replaced, using the DRBIII® select "Theft Alarm" "VTSS" "Miscellaneous" and "Configure Module". If the vehicle is equipped with VTSS, use the DRB and enable VTSS. Program other options as necessary. 4. Using the DRBIII® program all RKE transmitters used with this vehicle. Proceed to number 12. 5. Obtain the Vehicle's unique PIN number assigned to it's original SKIM module from either the vehicle's invoice or from Chrysler's Customer Center 6. With the DRBIII, select THEFT ALARM, SKIM, MISCELLANEOUS and select "Skim Module Replaced" function. Enter the 4 digit PIN number to put SKIM in "Access Mode". 7. The DRBIII will prompt you through the following steps. (1) Program the country code into the SKIM's memory. (2) Program the vehicle's VIN number into the SKIM's memory. (3) Transfer the vehicle's Secret Key data from the PCM. 8. Once secured access mode is active, the SKIM will remain in that mode for 60 seconds. 9. Using the DRBIII, program all customer keys into the SKIM's memory. This requires that the SKIM be in secured access mode, using the 4 digit code. 10. Note: If the PCM is replaced, the unique Secret Key data must be transfered from the SKIM to the PCM. This procedure requires the SKIM to be placed in secured access mode using the 4-digit code. 11. Note: If 3 attempts are made to enter secured access mode using an incorrect PIN, secured access mode will be locked out for 1 hour which causes the DRBIII to display "Bus +- Signals Open". To exit this mode, turn ignition to the "Run" pos. for 1 hour. 12. Ensure all accessories are turned off and the battery is fully charged. 13. Ensure that the Ignition is on, and with the DRBIII®, erase all Diagnostic Trouble Codes from ALL modules. Start the engine and allow it to run for 2 minutes and fully operate the system that was malfunctioning. 14. Turn the ignition off and wait 5 seconds. Turn the ignition on and using the DRBIII®, read DTC's from ALL modules. 15. If ANY codes are present, select the appropriate symptom from the Symptom List and continue diagnostics. If NO codes are present and the customers complaint cannot be duplicated, the repair is complete.

CR9050000912000X

Fig. 85 Body Verification Test. 2000 Neon

When Monitored and Set Condition:

ABS MESSAGE NOT RECEIVED

When Monitored: With the ignition in the Run/Start position.

Set Condition: The Instrument Cluster detects no PCI Bus message from the CAB module for 12 (twelve) seconds.

POSSIBLE CAUSES
ABS MESSAGE NOT RECEIVED

TEST	ACTION
1	With the DRBIII®, erase DTC's. Cycle the ignition off then on. Wait 30 seconds then with the DRBIII®, read DTC's. Does the DRBIII® display ABS MESSAGE NOT RECEIVED? Yes → perform the appropriate symptom. Perform BODY VERIFICATION TEST - VER 1. No → Test Complete.

CR9050000580000X

Fig. 87 ABS Message Not Received. 2001–04 Neon

VERIFICATION TEST VER-1A
1. Inspect the vehicle to ensure that all engine components are properly installed and connected. Reassemble and reconnect components as necessary. 2. Inspect the engine oil for contamination. If it is contaminated, change the oil and filter. 3. Perform the steps 1 through 6 if the PCM has been replaced. Then proceed with the verification. If the PCM has not been replaced skip those steps and continue verification. 4. If PCM has been changed and correct VIN and mileage have not been programmed a DTC will be set in ABS and Air Bag modules. In addition, if vehicle is equipped with a Sentry Key Immobilizer Module (SKIM), Secret Key data must be updated to enable start. 5. For ABS and Air Bag systems: Enter correct VIN and Mileage in PCM. Erase codes in ABS and Air Bag modules. 6. For SKIM theft alarm: Connect DRB to data link conn. Go to Theft Alarm, SKIM, Misc. and place SKIM in secured access mode, by using the appropriate PIN code for this vehicle. Select Update the Secret Key data. Data will be transferred from SKIM to PCM. 7. Attempt to start the engine. 8. If the engine is unable to start, look for any Technical Service Bulletins that may relate to this condition. Return to Symptom List if necessary. 9. If the engine starts and stays running, the repair is now complete.

CR9050000913000X

Fig. 86 Verification Test VER-1A. 2000 Neon

When Monitored and Set Condition:

ACM MESSAGE NOT RECEIVED

When Monitored: With the ignition in the Run/Start position.

Set Condition: The Instrument Cluster detects no PCI Bus message from the AECM for 5 (five) seconds.

POSSIBLE CAUSES
ACM MESSAGE NOT RECEIVED

TEST	ACTION
1	Turn the ignition on. With the DRBIII®, erase DTC's. Cycle the ignition off then on. Wait 30 seconds then with the DRBIII®, read DTC's. Does the DRBIII® display ACM MESSAGE NOT RECEIVED? Yes → perform the appropriate symptom. Perform BODY VERIFICATION TEST - VER 1. No → Test Complete.

CR9050000581000X

Fig. 88 ACM Message Not Received. 2001–04 Neon

When Monitored and Set Condition:

FUEL LEVEL SENSOR OPEN

When Monitored: With the ignition on. (Customer Complaint: fuel gauge displays empty)

Set Condition: The Instrument Cluster monitors the Fuel Level Sensor Signal circuit resistance. If the Cluster detects a resistance greater than 1100 ohms or less than 25 ohms for 18 seconds, this code will set.

POSSIBLE CAUSES
INTERMITTENT CONDITION
FUEL LEVEL SENSOR SIGNAL CIRCUIT SHORT TO VOLTAGE
FUEL LEVEL SENSOR SIGNAL CIRCUIT OPEN
FUEL PUMP MODULE GROUND CIRCUIT OPEN
FUEL LEVEL SENSOR
INSTRUMENT CLUSTER

TEST	ACTION
1	Turn the ignition on. With the DRBIII®, erase DTC's. Cycle the ignition off and then back on. With the DRBIII®, read DTC's. Does the DRBIII® display "Fuel Level Sensor Open"? No → Test complete. DTC is intermittent. Road test the vehicle and recheck for DTC's. If the code returns, rerun this test. Refer to any Technical Service Bulletins (TSB) that may apply. Inspect related harness and connectors. Perform BODY VERIFICATION TEST - VER 1. Yes → Go To 2
2	Turn the ignition off. Disconnect the Fuel Pump Module harness connector. Check connectors - Clean/repair as necessary. Measure the voltage between the Fuel Level Sensor Signal circuit and ground. Is there any voltage present? Yes → Repair the Fuel Level Sensor Signal circuit for a short to voltage. Perform BODY VERIFICATION TEST - VER 1. No → Go To 3

CR9050000582010X

Fig. 89 Fuel Level Sensor Open (Part 1 of 2). 2001–04 Neon

TEST	ACTION
3	Turn the ignition off. Disconnect the Fuel Pump Module harness connector. Check connectors - Clean/repair as necessary. Connect a jumper wire between the Fuel Level Sensor Signal circuit and ground. Turn the ignition on. With the DRBIII® in Sensors, read the Fuel Sender Volts. Does the DRBIII® display 0 (zero) volts? Yes → Go To 4 No → Repair the Fuel Level Sensor Signal circuit for an open. Perform BODY VERIFICATION TEST - VER 1.
4	Turn the ignition off. Disconnect the Fuel Pump Module harness connector. Check connectors - Clean/repair as necessary. Measure the resistance between ground and the Fuel Level Sensor Ground circuit. Is the resistance below 5.0 ohms? Yes → Go To 5 No → Repair the Fuel Pump Module Ground circuit for an open. Perform BODY VERIFICATION TEST - VER 1.
5	Turn the ignition off. Disconnect the Fuel Pump Module harness connector. Check connectors - Clean/repair as necessary. Measure the resistance of the Fuel Level Sensor between the Sensor Signal circuit pin and the Sensor Ground circuit pin. Is the resistance above 1100 ohms? Yes → Replace the Fuel Level Sender in accordance with the Service Information. Perform BODY VERIFICATION TEST - VER 1. No → Replace the Instrument Cluster in accordance with the Service Information. Perform BODY VERIFICATION TEST - VER 1.

CR9050000582020X

Fig. 89 Fuel Level Sensor Open (Part 2 of 2). 2001–04 Neon

TEST	ACTION
3	Turn the ignition off. Disconnect the Instrument Cluster harness connector. Disconnect the Fuel Pump Module harness connector. Check connectors - Clean/repair as necessary. Measure the resistance of the Fuel Level Sensor Signal circuit to ground. Is the resistance below 10,000 (10 K) ohms? NOTE: it should be infinite. Yes → Repair the Fuel Level Sensor Signal circuit for a short to ground. Perform BODY VERIFICATION TEST - VER 1. No → Replace the Instrument Cluster Perform BODY VERIFICATION TEST - VER 1.

CR9050000583020X

Fig. 90 Fuel Level Sensor Short (Part 2 of 2). 2001–04 Neon

When Monitored and Set Condition:

FUEL LEVEL SENSOR SHORT

When Monitored: When the ignition is on. (Customer Complaint: fuel gauge display empty).

Set Condition: The Instrument Cluster monitors the fuel level sensor signal circuit for resistance value between approximately 25 ohms to 1100 ohms. If the Cluster senses resistance less than 25 ohms, this code will set.

POSSIBLE CAUSES
FUEL LEVEL SENSOR SHORT INTERMITTENT CONDITION
FUEL LEVEL SENSOR
FUEL LEVEL SENSOR SIGNAL CIRCUIT SHORT TO GROUND
INSTRUMENT CLUSTER

TEST	ACTION
1	With the DRBIII®, erase DTC's. Turn the ignition on, wait for one minute. With the DRBIII®, read DTC's. Does the DRBIII® display Fuel Level Sensor Short? No → Test complete. DTC is intermittent. Road test the vehicle and recheck for DTC's. If the code returns, rerun this test. Refer to any Technical Service Bulletins (TSB) that may apply. Inspect related harness and connectors. Perform BODY VERIFICATION TEST - VER 1. Yes → Go To 2
2	Turn the ignition off. Disconnect the Fuel Pump Module harness connector. Check connectors - Clean/repair as necessary. Measure the resistance of the Fuel Level Sensor between the Sensor Signal circuit pin and the Sensor Ground circuit pin (sensor side). Is the resistance below 25.0 ohms? Yes → Replace the Fuel Level Sensor in accordance with the Service Information. Perform BODY VERIFICATION TEST - VER 1. No → Go To 3

CR9050000583010X

Fig. 90 Fuel Level Sensor Short (Part 1 of 2). 2001–04 Neon

When Monitored and Set Condition:

PANEL DIMMER OPEN

When Monitored: When the ignition is on.

Set Condition: The Instrument Cluster monitors the panel lamps dimmer signal circuit for a resistance value between 0.0 ohms and approximately 3,650 ohms. When the cluster senses a value greater than 30,000 ohms for more than 5 seconds, this code will set. When this condition occurs, the cluster illumination will default to full brightness.

POSSIBLE CAUSES
PANEL DIMMER OPEN - INTERMITTENT CONDITION
PANEL LAMPS DIMMER SIGNAL CIRCUIT SHORT TO VOLTAGE
PANEL LAMPS DIMMER SIGNAL CIRCUIT OPEN
PANEL LAMPS DIMMER SWITCH OPEN
PANEL LAMPS DIMMER GROUND CIRCUIT OPEN
INSTRUMENT CLUSTER

TEST	ACTION
1	With the DRBIII®, erase DTC's. Turn the Park Lamps on. Wait 10 (ten) seconds. Rotate the Panel Lamps Dimmer Switch through the full range of adjustment. With the DRBIII®, read DTC's. Does the DRBIII® display Panel Dimmer Open? Yes → Go To 2 No → The condition is not present at this time. Monitor DRBIII® parameters while wiggling the related wire harness. Refer to any Technical Service Bulletins (TSB) that may apply. Visually inspect the related wiring harness and connector terminals. Perform BODY VERIFICATION TEST - VER 1.
2	Turn the ignition off. Disconnect the Instrument Cluster harness connector. Check connectors - Clean/repair as necessary. Measure the voltage between the Panel Lamps Dimmer Signal circuit and ground. Is there any voltage present? Yes → Repair the Panel Lamps Dimmer Signal circuit for a short to voltage. Perform BODY VERIFICATION TEST - VER 1. No → Go To 3

CR9050000584010X

Fig. 91 Panel Dimmer Open (Part 1 of 2). 2001–04 Neon

TEST	ACTION
3	Turn the ignition off. Disconnect the Instrument Cluster harness connector. Disconnect the Multi-Function Switch harness connector. Check connectors - Clean/repair as necessary. Measure the resistance of the Panel Lamps Dimmer Signal circuit. Is the resistance below 5.0 ohms? Yes → Go To 4 No → Repair the open in the Panel Lamps Dimmer Signal circuit. Perform BODY VERIFICATION TEST - VER 1. **NOTE: Reconnect the Multi-Function Switch harness connector before proceeding.**
4	Turn the ignition off. Disconnect the Multi-Function Switch harness connector. Check connectors - Clean/repair as necessary. Measure the resistance of the Panel Lamps Dimmer Ground circuit to a known good ground. Does the resistance measure less than 5.0 ohms? Yes → Go To 5 No → Repair the open in the Panel Lamps Dimmer Ground circuit. Perform BODY VERIFICATION TEST - VER 1.
5	Turn the ignition off. Disconnect the Instrument Cluster harness connector. Ensure the Multi-Function Switch is connected before proceeding. Measure the resistance of the Panel Lamps Dimmer Signal circuit from the Instrument Cluster harness connector to ground. Move the Instrument Panel Dimmer Switch through the entire range of adjustment while observing the ohmmeter. Did the resistance increment smoothly between approximately 0.0 ohms to approximately 3,500 ohms? Yes → Replace the Instrument Cluster Perform BODY VERIFICATION TEST - VER 1. No → Replace the Multi-Function Switch Perform BODY VERIFICATION TEST - VER 1.

CR9050000584020X

Fig. 91 Panel Dimmer Open (Part 2 of 2). 2001–04 Neon

When Monitored and Set Condition:

SKIM MESSAGE NOT RECEIVED

When Monitored: With the ignition in the Run/Start position.

Set Condition: The Instrument Cluster detects no PCI Bus message from the SKIM Module for 20 (twenty) seconds.

POSSIBLE CAUSES
SKIM MESSAGE NOT RECEIVED

TEST	ACTION
1	With the DRBIII®, erase DTC's. Cycle the ignition off then on. Wait 30 seconds then with the DRBIII®, read DTC's. Does the DRBIII® display SKIM MESSAGE NOT RECEIVED? Yes → Refer to the DCI and perform the appropriate symptom. Perform BODY VERIFICATION TEST - VER 1. No → Test Complete.

CR9050000586000X

Fig. 93 SKIM Message Not Received. 2001–04 Neon

When Monitored and Set Condition:

SBEC MESSAGE NOT RECEIVED

When Monitored: With the ignition in the Run/Start position.

Set Condition: The Instrument Cluster detects no PCI Bus message from the SBEC for 20 (twenty) seconds.

POSSIBLE CAUSES
SBEC MESSAGE NOT RECEIVED

TEST	ACTION
1	With the DRBIII®, erase DTC's. Cycle the ignition off then on. Wait 30 seconds then with the DRBIII®, read DTC's. Does the DRBIII® display SBEC MESSAGES NOT RECEIVED? Yes → Refer to the DCI and perform the appropriate symptom. Perform BODY VERIFICATION TEST - VER 1. No → Test Complete.

CR9050000585000X

Fig. 92 SBEC Message Not Received. 2001–04 Neon

POSSIBLE CAUSES
NO RESPONSE - PCI BUS
NO RESPONSE - PCI BUS - POWERTRAIN CONTROL MODULE
NO RESPONSE - PCI BUS - INSTRUMENT CLUSTER
FUSED IGNITION SWITCH OUTPUT CIRCUIT SHORT TO GROUND
FUSED IGNITION SWITCH OUTPUT CIRCUIT OPEN
INSTRUMENT CLUSTER GROUND CIRCUIT OPEN
INSTRUMENT CLUSTER

TEST	ACTION
1	Turn the ignition on. With the DRBIII®, select System Monitors, then J1850 Module Scan. Does the DRBIII® display MIC PRESENT on the BUS? Yes → Go To 2 No → Refer to the DCI and perform the appropriate symptom.
2	Turn the ignition on. With the DRBIII®, select Body, MIC, PCM Monitor. Does the DRBIII® display PCM INACTIVE ON THE BUS? Yes → Refer to the DCI for problems related to *NO RESPONSE FROM THE POWERTRAIN CONTROL MODULE. No → Go To 3
3	Turn the ignition on. With the DRBIII®, select Body, MIC, MODULE DISPLAY. Does the DRBIII® display NO RESPONSE from MIC? Yes → Refer to the DCI for problems related to *NO RESPONSE FROM THE INSTRUMENT CLUSTER. No → Go To 4
4	Turn the ignition off. Inspect the #11 Fuse in the Fuse Block (#10 BUX vehicles). If the fuse is open, replace with proper rated fuse. Turn the ignition on for one minute. Turn the ignition off. Inspect the #11 Fuse in the Fuse Block (#10 BUX vehicles). Is the fuse open? Yes → Repair the Fused Ignition Switch Output circuit for a short to ground. Perform BODY VERIFICATION TEST - VER 1. No → Go To 5

CR9050000587010X

Fig. 94 All Gauges Inoperative (Part 1 of 2). 2001–04 Neon

TEST	ACTION
5	Turn the ignition off. Disconnect the Instrument Cluster harness connector. Turn the ignition on. Measure the voltage between the Fused Ignition Switch Output circuit and ground. Is the voltage above 10.5 volts? Yes → Go To 6 No → Repair the Fused Ignition Switch Output circuit for an open. Perform BODY VERIFICATION TEST - VER 1.
6	Turn the ignition off. Disconnect the Instrument Cluster harness connector. Measure the resistance between ground and the Instrument Cluster Ground circuit. Is the resistance below 5.0 ohms? Yes → Replace the Instrument Cluster Perform BODY VERIFICATION TEST - VER 1. No → Repair the Instrument Cluster Ground circuit for an open. Perform BODY VERIFICATION TEST - VER 1.

CR9050000587020X

Fig. 94 All Gauges Inoperative (Part 2 of 2). 2001–04 Neon

POSSIBLE CAUSES
*LED DEFECTIVE
INSTRUMENT CLUSTER

TEST	ACTION
1	**NOTE: Refer to the Service Information: Diagnosis and Testing - Instrument Cluster Lamps for complete list of Indicators that will illuminate during the Self Test.** **NOTE: Ensure that the Instrument Cluster communicates on the PCI Bus.** **NOTE: Diagnose and repair any PCM, ACM, ABS, RKE, or SKIM DTCs before proceeding with this test.** Turn the ignition off. Remove the Instrument Cluster. Remove the inoperative LED from the Instrument Cluster. Using a DVOM, select "Diode Mode", and connect the leads across the LED. **NOTE: Ensure that the RED lead is on the "+" of the LED.** Did the LED illuminate? Yes → Replace the Instrument Cluster Perform BODY VERIFICATION TEST - VER 1. No → Replace the Indicator LED Perform BODY VERIFICATION TEST - VER 1.

CR9050000588000X

Fig. 95 Any PCI BUS Indicator Inoperative. 2001–04 Neon

POSSIBLE CAUSES
BRAKE WARNING INDICATOR CIRCUIT SHORT TO GROUND
RED BRAKE WARNING INDICATOR DRIVER CIRCUIT SHORT TO GROUND
PARK BRAKE SWITCH
BRAKE FLUID LEVEL SWITCH
INSTRUMENT CLUSTER

TEST	ACTION
1	**NOTE: Ensure that the Brake Fluid is properly filled to the correct level.** Turn the ignition off. Disconnect the Brake Fluid Level Switch harness connector. Turn the ignition on. Is the Brake Warning Indicator illuminated? Yes → Go To 2 No → Replace the Brake Fluid Level Switch in accordance with the Service Information. Perform BODY VERIFICATION TEST - VER 1.
2	Turn the ignition off. Disconnect the Brake Fluid Level Switch harness connector. Disconnect the PCM harness connector. Measure the resistance between ground and the Red Brake Warning Indicator Driver circuit. Is the resistance below 10,00 ohms (should be infinite)? Yes → Repair the Red Brake Warning Indicator Driver circuit for a short to ground (between the Brake Fluid Level Switch and the Instrument Cluster). Perform BODY VERIFICATION TEST - VER 1. No → Go To 3
3	Turn the ignition off. Disconnect the Park Brake Switch harness connector. Measure the resistance between ground and the Park Brake Switch terminal pin. **NOTE: Ensure that the Park Brake is in the released position.** Is the resistance below 100 ohms? Yes → Replace the Park Brake Switch in accordance with the Service Information. Perform BODY VERIFICATION TEST - VER 1. No → Go To 4

CR9050000589010X

Fig. 96 Brake Indicator Always On (Part 1 of 2). 2001 Neon

TEST	ACTION
4	Turn the ignition off. Disconnect the Park Brake Switch harness connector. Disconnect the Instrument Cluster harness connector. Measure the resistance between ground and the Red Brake Warning Indicator Driver circuit. Is the resistance below 10,000 ohms (should be infinite)? Yes → Repair the Brake Warning Indicator circuit for a short to ground (between the Park Brake Switch and the Instrument Cluster). Perform BODY VERIFICATION TEST - VER 1. No → Replace the Instrument Cluster Perform BODY VERIFICATION TEST - VER 1.

CR9050000589020X

Fig. 96 Brake Indicator Always On (Part 2 of 2). 2001 Neon

POSSIBLE CAUSES
BRAKE WARNING INDICATOR CIRCUIT OPEN
INDICATOR LED
BRAKE FLUID LEVEL SWITCH
PARK BRAKE SWITCH
RED BRAKE WARNING INDICATOR DRIVER CIRCUIT OPEN
BRAKE FLUID LEVEL SWITCH GROUND CIRCUIT OPEN
INSTRUMENT CLUSTER

TEST	ACTION
1	**NOTE: The Brake Warning Indicator should illuminate during the bulb check cycle, and will also illuminate using the Self Test.** Observe the Brake Warning Indicator during the bulb check or Instrument Cluster Self Test. Did the indicator illuminate? Yes → Go To 2 No → Go To 6
2	Turn the ignition off. Disconnect the Brake Fluid Level Switch harness connector. Connect a jumper wire between cavity A and cavity B of the Switch harness connector. Turn the ignition on and observe the Brake Warning Indicator. Does the Brake Warning Indicator illuminate? Yes → Replace the Brake Fluid Level Switch Perform BODY VERIFICATION TEST - VER 1. No → Go To 3
3	Turn the ignition off. Disconnect the PCM harness connector. Disconnect the Brake Fluid Level Switch harness connector. Measure the resistance of the Red Brake Warning Indicator Driver circuit. Is the resistance above 5.0 ohms? Yes → Repair the Red Brake Warning Indicator Driver circuit for an open. Perform BODY VERIFICATION TEST - VER 1. No → Go To 4

CR9050000590010X

Fig. 97 Brake Indicator Inoperative (Part 1 of 2). 2001 Neon

TEST	ACTION
4	Turn the ignition off. Disconnect the Brake Fluid Level Switch harness connector. Measure the resistance of the switch ground circuit. Is the resistance above 5.0 ohms? Yes → Repair the Brake Fluid Level Switch Ground circuit for an open. Perform BODY VERIFICATION TEST - VER 1. No → Go To 5
5	Turn the ignition off. Disconnect the Instrument Cluster harness connector. Disconnect the Park Brake Switch harness connector. Measure the resistance of the Brake Warning Indicator circuit. Is the resistance below 5.0 ohms? Yes → Replace the Park Brake Switch Perform BODY VERIFICATION TEST - VER 1. No → Repair the Brake Warning Indicator circuit for an open. Perform BODY VERIFICATION TEST - VER 1.
6	Turn the ignition off. Remove the Instrument Cluster. Remove the inoperative Indicator LED. Using a DVOM, select "Diode Mode", and attach the leads across the LED. **NOTE: Ensure that the RED lead is on the "+" of the LED.** Did the LED illuminate? Yes → Replace the Instrument Cluster Perform BODY VERIFICATION TEST - VER 1. No → Replace the Brake Warning Indicator LED Perform BODY VERIFICATION TEST - VER 1.

CR9050000590020X

Fig. 97 Brake Indicator Inoperative (Part 2 of 2). 2001 Neon

TEST	ACTION
4	Turn the ignition off. Disconnect the Instrument Cluster harness connector. Disconnect the Park Brake Switch harness connector. Measure the resistance of the Brake Warning Indicator circuit. Is the resistance below 5.0 ohms? Yes → Replace the Instrument Cluster Perform BODY VERIFICATION TEST No → Repair the Brake Warning Indicator circuit for an open. Perform BODY VERIFICATION TEST
5	Turn the ignition on. With the DRBIII® in Inputs/Outputs, read the Brake Fluid Level Switch state. Disconnect the Brake Fluid Level Switch harness connector. Connect a jumper wire between cavity A and cavity B of the Brake Fluid Level Switch harness connector. With the DRBIII®, observe the Brake Fluid Level input. Did the Brake Fluid Level input change state? Yes → Replace the Brake Fluid Level Switch Perform BODY VERIFICATION TEST No → Go To 6
6	Turn the ignition off. Disconnect the Brake Fluid Level Switch harness connector. Measure the resistance of the Brake Fluid Level Switch ground circuit. Is the resistance above 5.0 ohms? Yes → Repair the Brake Fluid Level Switch Ground circuit for an open. Perform BODY VERIFICATION TEST No → Go To 7
7	Turn the ignition off. Disconnect the PCM (C2 connector for 2.0L equipped vehicles) harness connector. Disconnect the Brake Fluid Level Switch harness connector. Measure the resistance of the Red Brake Warning Indicator Driver circuit. Is the resistance above 5.0 ohms? Yes → Repair the Red Brake Warning Indicator Driver circuit for an open. Perform BODY VERIFICATION TEST - VER 1. No → Replace the Powertrain Control Module Perform BODY VERIFICATION TEST

CR9090200249020X

Fig. 98 Brake Warning Indicator Inoperative (Part 2 of 3). 2002–04 Neon

POSSIBLE CAUSES
BRAKE WARNING INDICATOR CIRCUIT OPEN
INDICATOR LED
BRAKE FLUID LEVEL SWITCH
PARK BRAKE SWITCH
RED BRAKE WARNING INDICATOR DRIVER CIRCUIT OPEN
BRAKE FLUID LEVEL SWITCH GROUND CIRCUIT OPEN
INSTRUMENT CLUSTER
POWERTRAIN CONTROL MODULE

TEST	ACTION
1	**NOTE: The Brake Warning Indicator should illuminate during the bulb check cycle, and will also illuminate using the Self Test.** Observe the Brake Warning Indicator during the bulb check or Instrument Cluster Self Test. Did the indicator illuminate? Yes → Go To 2 No → Go To 8
2	**NOTE: The Brake Warning Indicator illuminates with the Park Brake engaged or with low Brake Fluid.** Is the Brake Warning Indicator inoperative with the use of the Park brake? Yes → Go To 3 No → Go To 5
3	Turn the ignition off. Disconnect the Park Brake Switch harness connector. Connect a jumper wire between the Brake Warning Indicator circuit and ground. Turn the ignition on and observe the Brake Warning Indicator. Does the Indicator illuminate? Yes → Replace the Park Brake Switch Perform BODY VERIFICATION TEST No → Go To 4

CR9090200249010X

Fig. 98 Brake Warning Indicator Inoperative (Part 1 of 3). 2002–04 Neon

TEST	ACTION
8	Turn the ignition off. Remove the Instrument Cluster. Remove the inoperative Indicator LED. Using a DVOM, select "Diode Mode", and attach the leads across the LED. **NOTE: Ensure that the RED lead is on the "+" of the LED.** Did the LED illuminate? Yes → Replace the Instrument Cluster Perform BODY VERIFICATION TEST No → Replace the Brake Warning Indicator LED Perform BODY VERIFICATION TEST

CR9090200249030X

Fig. 98 Brake Warning Indicator Inoperative (Part 3 of 3). 2002–04 Neon

POSSIBLE CAUSES
FRONT FOG LAMP INDICATOR CIRCUIT OPEN
INDICATOR LED
INSTRUMENT CLUSTER

TEST	ACTION
1	Ensure the Fog Lamps are operational before proceeding. If not, select "Service Information" from the menu and repair as necessary. Disconnect the Instrument Cluster harness connector. Turn the Headlamps on. Turn the Fog Lamps on. **NOTE: Ensure the battery is fully charged.** Measure the voltage between the Fog Lamp Switch Output circuit and ground. Is the voltage greater than 10.0 volts? Yes → Go To 2 No → Repair the open in the Front Fog Lamp Switch Output circuit. Perform BODY VERIFICATION TEST - VER 1.
2	Turn the ignition off. Remove the Instrument Cluster. Remove the inoperative LED. Using a DVOM, select "Diode Mode", and attach the leads across the LED. **NOTE: Ensure that the RED lead is on the "+" of the LED.** Did the indicator illuminate? Yes → Replace the Instrument Cluster Perform BODY VERIFICATION TEST - VER 1. No → Replace the inoperative indicator LED Perform BODY VERIFICATION TEST - VER 1.

CR9050000591000X

Fig. 99 Front Fog Lamp Indicator Inoperative. 2001–04 Neon

POSSIBLE CAUSES
DTC PRESENT
FUEL LEVEL SENSOR
INTERMITTENT CONDITION
INSTRUMENT CLUSTER

TEST	ACTION
1	Turn the ignition on. With the DRBIII®, read DTCs. Does the DRBIII® display Fuel Level Sensor Open or Fuel Level Sensor Short? Yes → Refer to Fuel Level Sensor Open or Fuel Level Sensor Short for the related symptom(s). No → Go To 2
2	Perform the Instrument Cluster Self Test. Turn the ignition off. Press and hold the Trip Reset button. Turn the ignition on. Observe the Fuel Gauge during the Self Test. The Fuel Gauge pointer should pause at each of these following positions: E, 1/2, Full. Did the Fuel Gauge perform the Self Test properly? Yes → Go To 3 No → Replace the Instrument Cluster Perform BODY VERIFICATION TEST

CR9090200250010X

Fig. 101 Fuel Gauge Inaccurate (Part 1 of 2). 2002–04 Neon

TEST	ACTION
3	Turn the ignition off. Remove the Fuel Pump Module from the Fuel Tank. **NOTE: Inspect for physical obstructions in the Fuel Tank. Inspect the Fuel Level Sensor for bent or damaged parts.** Measure the resistance of the Fuel Level Sensor while moving the float arm through the complete range of motion. The Fuel Level Sensor should measure the following resistances: E = 184 - 204 ohms 1/4 = 360 - 410 ohms 1/2 = 565 - 585 ohms 3/4 = 741 - 791 ohms Full = 947 - 967 ohms **NOTE: The Fuel Level Sensor should read resistance through the full range of float arm motion.** Does the Fuel Level Sensor read the proper resistance values through the full range of motion? Yes → The condition is not present at this time. Monitor DRBIII® parameters while wiggling the related wire harness. Refer to any Technical Service Bulletins (TSB) that may apply. Visually inspect the related wiring harness and connector terminals. No → Replace the Fuel Level Sensor Perform BODY VERIFICATION TEST

CR9090200250020X

Fig. 101 Fuel Gauge Inaccurate (Part 2 of 2) 2002–04 Neon

POSSIBLE CAUSES
CHECK FOR DTCS
FUEL LEVEL SENSOR
INTERMITTENT CONDITION
INSTRUMENT CLUSTER

TEST	ACTION
1	Turn the ignition on. With the DRBIII®, read DTCs. Does the DRBIII® display Fuel Level Sensor Open or Fuel Level Sensor Short? Yes → Refer to Fuel Level Sensor Open or Fuel Level Sensor Short for the related symptom(s). No → Go To 2
2	Perform the Instrument Cluster Self Test. Observe the Fuel Gauge during the Self Test. The Fuel Gauge pointer should pause at each of these following positions: E, 1/4, 1/2, 3/4, Full. Did the Fuel Gauge perform the Self Test properly? Yes → Go To 3 No → Replace the Instrument Cluster Perform BODY VERIFICATION TEST - VER 1.
3	Turn the ignition off. Remove the Fuel Pump Module from the Fuel Tank. **NOTE: Inspect for physical obstructions in the Fuel Tank. Inspect the Fuel Level Sensor for bent or damaged parts.** Measure the resistance of the Fuel Level Sensor while moving the float arm through the complete range of motion. The Fuel Level Sensor should measure the following resistance: E = Approximately 65 ohms Full = Approximately 1057 ohms **NOTE: The Fuel Level Sensor should read resistance through the full range of float arm motion.** Does the Fuel Level Sensor read resistance values through the full range of motion? Yes → Test Complete. No → Replace the Fuel Level Sensor Perform BODY VERIFICATION TEST - VER 1.

CR9050000592000X

Fig. 100 Fuel Gauge Inaccurate. 2001 Neon

POSSIBLE CAUSES
HIGH BEAM INDICATOR CIRCUIT OPEN
HIGH BEAM INDICATOR BULB
INSTRUMENT CLUSTER

TEST	ACTION
1	**NOTE: Ensure that the High Beam headlamps operate properly before proceeding with this test.** Turn the ignition off. Disconnect the Instrument Cluster harness connector. Turn on the headlamps and actuate the High Beams. Using a 12-volt test light connected to ground, check the High Beam Indicator circuit. Does the test light illuminate brightly? Yes → Go To 2 No → Repair the High Beam Indicator circuit for an open. Perform BODY VERIFICATION TEST - VER 1.
2	Turn the ignition off. Disconnect the Instrument Cluster harness connector. Remove and inspect the High Beam Indicator bulb. Is the bulb open? Yes → Replace the High Beam Indicator bulb Perform BODY VERIFICATION TEST - VER 1. No → Replace the Instrument Cluster Perform BODY VERIFICATION TEST - VER 1.

CR9050000593000X

Fig. 102 High Beam Indicator Inoperative. 2001–04 Neon

POSSIBLE CAUSES
ENGINE OIL PRESSURE SWITCH
ENGINE OIL PRESSURE SWITCH SENSE CIRCUIT SHORT TO GROUND
POWERTRAIN CONTROL MODULE
INSTRUMENT CLUSTER

TEST	ACTION
1	**NOTE: Ensure that Engine oil pressure is within normal operating range. Refer to the Service Information for specifications.** Allow the engine to idle. With the DRBIII® in Sensors, read the Engine Oil Pressure Switch state. Does the Engine Oil Pressure Switch status read "Closed"? Yes → Go To 2 No → Replace the Instrument Cluster Perform BODY VERIFICATION TEST
2	Turn the ignition off. Disconnect the Engine Oil Pressure Switch harness connector. With the DRBIII® in Sensors, read the Engine Oil Pressure Switch status. Does the Engine Oil Pressure Switch status read "Closed"? Yes → Go To 3 No → Replace the Engine Oil Pressure Switch Perform BODY VERIFICATION TEST
3	Turn the ignition off. Disconnect the Engine Oil Pressure Switch harness connector. Disconnect the PCM (C1 connector on 2.0L equipped vehicles) harness connector. Measure the resistance between ground and the Engine Oil Pressure Switch Sense circuit. Is the resistance below 5.0 ohms? Yes → Repair the Engine Oil Pressure Switch Sense circuit for a short to ground. Perform BODY VERIFICATION TEST No → Replace the Powertrain Control Module Perform POWERTRAIN VERIFICATION TEST

CR9090200251000X

Fig. 103 Low Oil Pressure Indicator Always On. 2002–04 Neon

TEST	ACTION
4	Turn the ignition off. Remove the Instrument Cluster. Remove the Low Oil Pressure indicator LED. Using a DVOM, select "Diode Mode", and attach the leads across the LED. **NOTE: Ensure that the RED lead is on the "+" of the LED.** Did the LED illuminate? Yes → Replace the Instrument Cluster Perform BODY VERIFICATION TEST No → Replace the Low Oil Pressure Indicator LED Perform BODY VERIFICATION TEST

CR9090200252020X

Fig. 104 Low Oil Pressure Indicator Inoperative (Part 2 of 2). 2002–04 Neon

POSSIBLE CAUSES
ENGINE OIL PRESSURE SWITCH
ENGINE OIL PRESSURE SWITCH SENSE CIRCUIT OPEN
INDICATOR LED
POWERTRAIN CONTROL MODULE
INSTRUMENT CLUSTER

TEST	ACTION
1	Turn the ignition off. Perform the Instrument Cluster Self Test. Depress and hold the Trip Odometer reset button while turning the ignition on. Did the Low Oil Pressure Indicator illuminate? Yes → Go To 2 No → Go To 4
2	Turn the ignition on. With the DRBIII® in Sensors, read the Oil Pressure Switch state. Disconnect the Engine Oil Pressure Switch harness connector. With the DRBIII® in Sensors, read the Oil Pressure Switch state. Did the Engine Oil Pressure Switch change states? Yes → Replace the Engine Oil Pressure Switch Perform BODY VERIFICATION TEST No → Go To 3
3	Turn the ignition off. Disconnect the Engine Oil Pressure Switch harness connector. Disconnect the PCM (C1 connector on 2.0L equipped vehicles) harness connector. Measure the resistance of the Engine Oil Pressure Switch Sense circuit. Is the resistance below 5.0 ohms? Yes → Replace the Powertrain Control Module Perform POWERTRAIN VERIFICATION TEST No → Repair the Engine Oil Pressure Switch Sense circuit for an open. Perform BODY VERIFICATION TEST

CR9090200252010X

Fig. 104 Low Oil Pressure Indicator Inoperative (Part 1 of 2). 2002–04 Neon

POSSIBLE CAUSES
CHECK FOR MIC DTC
HEADLAMP SWITCH OUTPUT CIRCUIT OPEN
ILLUMINATION BULB
INSTRUMENT CLUSTER

TEST	ACTION
1	Turn the ignition on. With the DRBIII®, read DTCs. Does the DRBIII® display Panel dimmer Open? Yes → Refer to the Service Information to diagnose "Panel Dimmer Open". Perform BODY VERIFICATION TEST - VER 1. No → Go To 2
2	**NOTE: Ensure that the Park Lamps operate properly before proceeding with this test.** Turn the ignition off. Disconnect the Instrument Cluster harness connector. Turn the Park Lamps on. Using a 12-volt test light connected to ground, check the Headlamp Output circuit. Does the test light illuminate brightly? Yes → Go To 3 No → Repair the Headlamp Switch Output circuit for an open. Perform BODY VERIFICATION TEST - VER 1.
3	Turn the ignition off. Disconnect the Instrument Cluster harness connector. Inspect the Illumination Bulb in question. Is the Illumination Bulb filament open? Yes → Replace the Illumination Bulb Perform BODY VERIFICATION TEST - VER 1. No → Replace the Instrument Cluster Perform BODY VERIFICATION TEST - VER 1.

CR9050000594000X

Fig. 105 Instrument Cluster Dimming Inoperative. 2001–04 Neon

POSSIBLE CAUSES
POWERTRAIN CONTROL MODULE DTCS
INSTRUMENT CLUSTER

TEST	ACTION
1	Turn the ignition off. With the DRBIII®, read DTCs. **NOTE: The PCM will not store any DTCs regarding Oil Pressure concerns.** **NOTE: If Oil Pressure gauge readings are in question and the gauge tests good, a mechanical oil pressure gauge must be attached to the engine.** Does the DRBIII® display any PCM DTCs? Yes → Refer to the DRIVEABILITY category and perform the apropriate symptom. No → Go To 2
2	Turn the ignition off. Perform the Instrument Cluster Self Test. Observe the gauge in question while the Instrument Cluster performs the Self Test. The gauges should position at the following calibration points: Speedometer: 30mph (51km/h BUX), 60mph (102km/h BUX), 90mph (153km/h BUX), 120mph Tachometer: 2000, 4000, 6000, 8000 Fuel: E, 1/2, Full Temperature: Lo, Mid Lo, High Did the gauge in question operate properly? Yes → Test Complete. No → Replace the Instrument Cluster Perform BODY VERIFICATION TEST - VER 1.

CR9050000595000X

Fig. 106 One Gauge Inoperative. 2001–04 Neon

POSSIBLE CAUSES
REAR FOG LAMP INDICATOR CIRCUIT OPEN
INDICATOR LED
INSTRUMENT CLUSTER

TEST	ACTION
1	**NOTE: Ensure that the Rear Fog Lamps operate correctly before proceeding with this test.** Turn the ignition off. Disconnect the Instrument Cluster harness connector. Turn the Rear Fog Lamp switch on. Using a 12-volt test light connected to ground, check the Rear Fog Lamp Indicator circuit. Does the test light illuminate brightly? Yes → Go To 2 No → Repair the Rear Fog Lamp Indicator circuit for an open. Perform BODY VERIFICATION TEST - VER 1.
2	Turn the ignition off. Remove the Instrument Cluster. Remove the inoperative LED. Using a DVOM, select "Diode Mode", and attach the leads across the LED. **NOTE: Ensure that the RED lead is on the "+" of the LED.** Did the LED illuminate? Yes → Replace the Instrument Cluster Perform BODY VERIFICATION TEST - VER 1. No → Replace the Rear Fog Lamp Indicator LED Perform BODY VERIFICATION TEST - VER 1.

CR9050000596000X

Fig. 108 Rear Fog Lamp Indicator Inoperative. 2001–04 Neon

POSSIBLE CAUSES
DTC PRESENT
INTERMITTENT CONDITION
INSTRUMENT CLUSTER

TEST	ACTION
1	**NOTE: Ensure that there is communication between the MIC, PCM, and the TCM before proceeding with this test.** **NOTE: Diagnose and repair any DTCs before proceeding with this test.** **NOTE: Ensure that the TCM passes the Shift Lever Test with the DRBIII® before proceeding with this test.** Turn the ignition on. With the DRBIII®, read DTCs. Does the DRBIII® display any MIC, PCM, or TCM DTCs? Yes → Refer to symptom list for problems related to DTC's. No → Go To 2
2	Perform the Instrument Cluster Self Test. Turn the ignition off. Press and hold the Trip Reset button. Turn the ignition on. Observe the PRND / AutoStick VF display during the Self Test. Did any part of the VF display fail to illuminate? Yes → Replace the Instrument Cluster Perform BODY VERIFICATION TEST No → The condition is not present at this time. Monitor DRBIII® parameters while wiggling the related wire harness. Refer to any Technical Service Bulletins (TSB) that may apply. Visually inspect the related wiring harness and connector terminals.

CR9090200265000X

Fig. 107 PRND Or Autostick Indicator Display Inaccurate Or Inoperative. 2002–04 Neon

POSSIBLE CAUSES
INDICATOR LED
SEAT BELT INDICATOR CIRCUIT OPEN
SEAT BELT SWITCH GROUND OPEN
SEAT BELT SWITCH
INSTRUMENT CLUSTER

TEST	ACTION
1	Turn the ignition off. Perform the Instrument Cluster Self Test. Did the Seat Belt Indicator illuminate? Yes → Go To 2 No → Go To 5
2	Turn the ignition off. Disconnect the Instrument Cluster harness connector. Disconnect the Seat Belt Switch harness connector. Measure the resistance of the Seat Belt Indicator circuit. Is the resistance below 5.0 ohms? Yes → Go To 3 No → Repair the Seat Belt Indicator circuit for an open. Perform BODY VERIFICATION TEST - VER 1.
3	Turn the ignition off. Disconnect the Seat Belt Switch harness connector. Measure the resistance between ground and the Seat Belt Switch Ground circuit. Is the resistance below 5.0 ohms? Yes → Go To 4 No → Repair the Seat Belt Switch Ground circuit for an open. Perform BODY VERIFICATION TEST - VER 1.
4	Turn the ignition off. Disconnect the Seat Belt Switch harness connector. Measure the resistance of the Seat Belt Switch between the Indicator circuit pin and the Ground circuit pin. Is the resistance below 5.0 ohms? Yes → Replace the Instrument Cluster in accordance with the Service Information. Perform BODY VERIFICATION TEST - VER 1. No → Replace the Seat Belt Switch in accordance with the Service Information. Perform BODY VERIFICATION TEST - VER 1.

CR9050000597010X

Fig. 109 Seat Belt Indicator Not Operating Properly (Part 1 of 2). 2001 Neon

TEST	ACTION
5	Turn the ignition off. Remove the Instrument Cluster. Remove the inoperative indicator. Using a DVOM, select "Diode Mode", and attach the leads across the LED. **NOTE: Ensure that the RED lead is on the "+" of the LED.** Did the LED illuminate? Yes → Replace the Instrument Cluster Perform BODY VERIFICATION TEST - VER 1. No → Replace the Seat Belt Indicator LED Perform BODY VERIFICATION TEST - VER 1.

CR9050000597020X

Fig. 109 Seat Belt Indicator Not Operating Properly (Part 2 of 2). 2001 Neon

TEST	ACTION
5	Turn the ignition off. Disconnect the Seat Belt Switch harness connector. Measure the resistance of the Seat Belt Switch between the Indicator circuit pin and the Ground circuit pin. Is the resistance below 5.0 ohms? Yes → Replace the Instrument Cluster Perform BODY VERIFICATION TEST No → Replace the Seat Belt Switch Perform BODY VERIFICATION TEST

CR9090200253020X

Fig. 110 Seat Belt Indicator Inoperative (Part 2 of 2). 2002–04 Neon

ABS VERIFICATION TEST - VER 1
1. Turn the ignition off. 2. Connect all previously disconnected components and connectors. 3. Ensure all accessories are turned off and the battery is fully charged. 4. Ensure that the Ignition is on, and with the DRBIII, erase all Diagnostic Trouble Codes from ALL modules. Start the engine and allow it to run for 2 minutes and fully operate the system that was malfunctioning. 5. Turn the ignition off and wait 5 seconds. Turn the ignition on and using the DRBIII, read DTC's from ALL modules. 6. If any Diagnostic Trouble Codes are present, return to Symptom list and troubleshoot new or recurring symptom. 7. If there are no DTC's present after turning ignition on, road test the vehicle for at least 5 minutes. Perform several antilock braking stops. **8. Caution: Ensure braking capability is available before road testing.** 9. Again, with the DRBIII® read DTC's. If any DTC's are present, return to Symptom list. 10. If there are no Diagnostic Trouble Codes (DTC's) present, and the customer's concern can no longer be duplicated, the repair is complete. Are any DTC's present or is the original concern still present? Yes → Repair is not complete, refer to appropriate symptom. No → Repair is complete.

CR9050000600000X

Fig. 112 ABS Verification Test VER-1. 2001–04 Neon

AIRBAG VERIFICATION TEST - VER 1
1. Remove any special tools or jumper wires and reconnect all previously disconnected components - except the Battery. 2. Turn the Ignition key On and reconnect the Battery. 3. Connect the DRB to the Data Link Connector - use the most current software available. 4. Use the DRB III and erase the stored codes. 5. Turn the Ignition Off, and wait 15 seconds before turning the Ignition On. 6. Wait one minute, and read active codes and if there are none present read the stored codes. 7. Note: If equipped with Passenger Airbag On/Off switch, read the DTC's in all switch positions. 8. If the DRB shows any active or stored codes, return to the Symptom list and follow path specified for that trouble code. If no active or stored codes are present, the repair is complete. Are any codes present? YES Select the appropriate system from the category List and continue diagnostics. NO Repair is complete.

CR9050000601000X

Fig. 113 Air Bag Verification Test VER-1. 2001–04 Neon

POSSIBLE CAUSES
INDICATOR LED
SEAT BELT INDICATOR CIRCUIT OPEN
SEAT BELT SWITCH GROUND OPEN
SEAT BELT SWITCH
INSTRUMENT CLUSTER

TEST	ACTION
1	Turn the ignition off. Perform the Instrument Cluster Self Test. Did the Seat Belt Indicator illuminate? Yes → Go To 3 No → Go To 2
2	Turn the ignition off. Remove the Instrument Cluster. Remove the inoperative indicator. Using a DVOM, select "Diode Mode", and attach the leads across the LED. **NOTE: Ensure that the RED lead is on the "+" of the LED.** Did the LED illuminate? Yes → Go To 3 No → Replace the Seat Belt Indicator LED Perform BODY VERIFICATION TEST
3	Turn the ignition off. Disconnect the Instrument Cluster harness connector. Disconnect the Seat Belt Switch harness connector. Measure the resistance of the Seat Belt Indicator circuit. Is the resistance below 5.0 ohms? Yes → Go To 4 No → Repair the Seat Belt Indicator circuit for an open. Perform BODY VERIFICATION TEST
4	Turn the ignition off. Disconnect the Seat Belt Switch harness connector. Measure the resistance between ground and the Seat Belt Switch Ground circuit. Is the resistance below 5.0 ohms? Yes → Go To 5 No → Repair the Seat Belt Switch Ground circuit for an open. Perform BODY VERIFICATION TEST

CR9090200253010X

Fig. 110 Seat Belt Indicator Inoperative (Part 1 of 2). 2002–04 Neon

POSSIBLE CAUSES
INSTRUMENT CLUSTER

TEST	ACTION
1	Ensure that the Instrument Cluster communicates on the PCI Bus. **NOTE: The Instrument Cluster must be operational for the result of this test to be valid.** The Instrument Cluster Odometer vacuum fluorescent (VF) Display is not a repairable or replaceable item. If there are no possible causes remaining, view repair. Repair Replace the Instrument Cluster Perform BODY VERIFICATION TEST - VER 1.

CR9050000598000X

Fig. 111 VF Display Inoperative. 2001–04 Neon

BODY VERIFICATION TEST - VER 1
1. Disconnect all jumper wires and reconnect all previously disconnected components and connectors. 2. If the Sentry Key Immobilizer Module (SKIM) or the Powertrain Control Module (PCM) were replaced, proceed to number 5. If the SKIM or PCM were not replaced, continue to the next number. 3. If the Remote Keyless Entry module was replaced, using the DRBIII® select "Theft Alarm" "VTSS" "Miscellaneous" and "Configure Module". If the vehicle is equipped with VTSS, use the DRB and enable VTSS. Program other options as necessary. 4. Using the DRBIII® program all RKE transmitters used with this vehicle. Proceed to number 12. 5. Obtain the Vehicle's unique PIN number assigned to it's original SKIM module from either the vehicle's invoice or from Chrysler's Customer Center 6. With the DRBIII, select THEFT ALARM, SKIM, MISCELLANEOUS and select "Skim Module Replaced" function. Enter the 4 digit PIN number to put SKIM in "Access Mode". 7. The DRBIII will prompt you through the following steps. (1) Program the country code into the SKIM's memory. (2) Program the vehicle's VIN number into the SKIM's memory. (3) Transfer the vehicle's Secret Key data from the PCM. 8. Once secured access mode is active, the SKIM will remain in that mode for 60 seconds. 9. Using the DRBIII, program all customer keys into the SKIM's memory. This requires that the SKIM be in secured access mode, using the 4 digit code. 10. Note: If the PCM is replaced, the unique Secret Key data must be transfered from the SKIM to the PCM. This procedure requires the SKIM to be placed in secured access mode using the 4-digit code. 11. Note: If 3 attempts are made to enter secured access mode using an incorrect PIN, secured access mode will be locked out for 1 hour which causes the DRBIII to display "Bus +\- Signals Open". To exit this mode, turn ignition to "Run" position for 1 hour. 12. Ensure all accessories are turned off and the battery is fully charged. 13. Ensure that the Ignition is on, and with the DRBIII®, erase all Diagnostic Trouble Codes from ALL modules. Start the engine and allow it to run for 2 minutes and fully operate the system that was malfunctioning. 14. Turn the ignition off and wait 5 seconds. Turn the ignition on and using the DRBIII®, read DTC's from ALL modules. Are any DTC's present or is the original condition still present? Yes → Repair is not complete, refer to appropriate symptom. No → Repair is complete.

CR9050000602000X

Fig. 114 Body Verification Test VER-1. 2001–04 Neon

POWERTRAIN VERIFICATION TEST VER-1
1. NOTE: If the PCM has been replaced and the correct VIN and mileage have not been programmed, a DTC will be set in the ABS Module, Airbag Module and the SKIM.
2. NOTE: If the vehicle is equipped with a Sentry Key Immobilizer System, Secret Key data must be updated. Refer to the Service Information for the PCM, SKIM and the Transponder (ignition key) for programming information.
3. Inspect the vehicle to ensure that all components related to the repair are connected properly.
4. Inspect the engine oil for fuel contamination. Replace the oil and filter as necessary.
5. Attempt to start the engine.
6. If the No Start condition is still present, refer to the symptom list and perform the diagnostic testing as necessary. refer to and Technical Service Bulletins that may apply.
7. Run the engine for one warm-up cycle to verify operation.
8. With the DRBIII®, confirm that no DTCs or Secondary Indicators are present and that all components are functioning properly.
9. If a DTC is present, refer to the appropriate category and select the corresponding symptom. Are any DTCs present?
Yes → Repair is not complete, refer to appropriate symptom.
No → Repair is complete.

CR9050000603000X

Fig. 115 Powertrain Verification Test VER-1. 2001 Neon

SKIS VERIFICATION
1. Reconnect all previously disconnected components and connectors.
2. Obtain the vehicle's unique Personal Identification Number (PIN) assigned to it's original SKIM. This number can be obtained from the vehicle's invoice or Chrysler's Customer Center
3. NOTE: When entering the PIN, care should be taken because the SKIM will only allow 3 consecutive attempts to enter the correct PIN. If 3 consecutive incorrect PIN's are entered the SKIM will Lock Out the DRB III for 1 hour.
4. To exit Lock Out mode, the ignition key must remain in the Run position continually for 1 hour. Turn off all accessories and connect a battery charger if necessary.
5. With the DRB III, select Theft Alarm, SKIM and Miscellaneous. Then select desired procedure and follow the steps that will be displayed.
6. If the SKIM has been replaced, ensure all of the vehicle ignition keys are programmed to the new SKIM.
7. NOTE: Prior to returning vehicle to the costumer, perform a module scan to be sure that all DTC's are erased. Erase any DTC's that are found.
8. With the DRB III erase all DTC's. Perform 5 ignition key cycles leaving the key on for at least 90 seconds per cycle.
9. With the DRB III, read the SKIM DTC's. Are there any SKIM DTC's?
Yes → Repair is not complete, refer to appropriate symptom.
No → Repair is complete.

CR9050000604000X

Fig. 117 SKIS Verification. 2001–04 Neon

POWERTRAIN VERIFICATION TEST VER - 2
1. NOTE: If the PCM has been replaced and the correct VIN and mileage have not been programmed, a DTC will be set in the ABS Module, Airbag Module and the SKIM.
2. NOTE: If the vehicle is equipped with a Sentry Key Immobilizer System, Secret Key data must be updated. Refer to the Service Information for the PCM, SKIM and the Transponder (ignition key) for programming information.
3. Inspect the vehicle to ensure that all components related to the repair are connected properly.
4. With the DRBIII®, clear DTCs and Reset Memory all engine values.
5. Run the engine for one warm-up cycle to verify proper operation.
6. Road test the vehicle. Use all accessories that may be related to this repair.
7. With the DRBIII®, confirm that no DTC's or Secondary Indicators are present and that all components are functioning properly.
8. If this test is being performed after a No Trouble Code test, verify the symptom is no longer present.
9. If the symptom is still present, or any other symptom or DTC is present refer to the appropriate category and perform the corresponding symptom.
10. Refer to any Technical Service Bulletins that may apply.
11. If there are no DTCs present and all components are functional properly, the repair is complete. Are any DTCs present?
Yes → Repair is not complete, refer to appropriate symptom.
No → Repair is complete.

CR9090200254000X

Fig. 116 Powertrain Verification Test VER-2A. 2002–04 Neon

When Monitored and Set Condition:

SCTM FAILURE

When Monitored: Continuously with ignition on.

Set Condition: BCM sends 12 volt reference signal to seat belt control timer module to monitor SCTM status. If signal is above 10 volts code sets and seat belt light illuminates. Lamp extinguishes once problem is repaired but code stays in memory for 20 key starts.

POSSIBLE CAUSES
JX SEAT BELT WARNING LAMP STAYS ON
SEAT BELT LAMP STAYS ON
DEFECTIVE SEAT BELT WARNING LAMP/BULB
SEAT BELT TIMER MODULE SENSE CIRCUIT OPEN
SEAT BELT TIMER MODULE SENSE CIRCUIT SHORT
DEFECTIVE MIC CIRCUIT BOARD
DEFECTIVE BCM SEAT BELT CIRCUIT

TEST	ACTION
1	Turn Ignition from Off to On (Run) position. Does the Seat Belt Lamp light, and then turn off? Yes → The Seat Belt Warning Lamp is operational with no problems found. Perform Body Verification TEST VER-1A No → Go To 2
2	Turn the Ignition Key to the unlock position. With the DRB, select ELECTRO/MECH CLUSTER (MIC) actuate ALL LAMPS. Does the Seat Belt Warning Lamp light? Yes → Go To 3 No → Go To 6
3	**NOTE: This path is for a JX Seat Belt Lamp staying on continuously.** Turn Ignition from Off to On (Run) position. Disconnect the Seat Belt Control Timer Module connector. **Check Connectors - Clean / repair as necessary.** Connect a jumper from the Seat Belt Control Timer Module Sense Circuit (CAV.11) to ground (CAV.13). Did the Seat Belt Lamp go out? Yes → Refer to symptom list to repair the Seat Belt Control Timer Module Circuit. Perform Body Verification TEST VER-1A No → Go To 4

CR9059900044010X

Fig. 118 SCTM Failure (Part 1 of 2). 2000 Sebring Convertible

TEST	ACTION
4	Disconnect the Seat Belt Control Timer Module connector. **Check Connectors - Clean / repair as necessary.** Connect a jumper from the Seat Belt Control Timer Module Sense Circuit (CAV.11) to ground (CAV.13). Disconnect the IP 22-way connector at the Body Control Module. **Check Connectors - Clean / repair as necessary.** Using an ohmmeter, measure the Seat Belt Control Module Sense to ground. Is the resistance below 5.0 ohms? Yes → Go To 5 No → Repair the open Seat Belt Control Timer Module Sense Circuit. Perform Body Verification TEST VER-1A
5	Disconnect the Seat Belt Control Timer Module connector. **Check Connectors - Clean / repair as necessary.** Disconnect the IP 22-way connector at the Body Control Module. **Check Connectors - Clean / repair as necessary.** Using an ohmmeter, measure the Seat Belt Control Module Sense to ground. Is the resistance below 5.0 ohms? Yes → Repair the Seat Belt Control Timer Module Sense Circuit for a short to ground. Perform Body Verification TEST VER-1A No → Replace the Body control Module. Perform Body Verification TEST VER-1A
6	Key Off, disconnect the Instrument Cluster. **Check Connectors - Clean / repair as necessary.** Remove and inspect the Seat Belt Warning Lamp Bulb. **Check Connectors - Clean / repair as necessary.** Is the Bulb defective? Yes → Replace the Seat Belt Warning Lamp. Perform Body Verification TEST VER-1A No → Repair or replace the Mechanical Instrument Cluster Circuit Board as necessary. Perform Body Verification TEST VER-1A

CR9059900044020X

Fig. 118 SCTM Failure (Part 2 of 2). 2000 Sebring Convertible

When Monitored and Set Condition:

ABS LAMP CIRCUIT SHORT

When Monitored: At power up or when the bulb is requested.

Set Condition: When there is a short detected in the ABS bulb circuit.

POSSIBLE CAUSES
INTERMITTENT WIRING AND CONNECTORS
ABS INDICATOR BULB
EMIC - INTERNAL ERROR

TEST	ACTION
1	Turn the ignition on. With the DRBIII®, record and erase DTC's. Turn the ignition off, wait 15 seconds, then turn the ignition on. With the DRBIII®, read DTCs. Does the DRBIII® display ABS LAMP CIRCUIT SHORT? Yes → Go To 2 No → Go To 4
2	Turn the ignition off to the lock position. **NOTE: Check connectors - Clean/repair as necessary.** Remove and inspect the ABS Indicator Bulb. Does the ABS Indicator Bulb have and internal direct short? Yes → Replace the ABS Indicator Bulb Perform BODY VERIFICATION TEST - VER 1. No → Go To 3
3	If there are no possible causes remaining, view repair. Repair Replace the EMIC. Perform BODY VERIFICATION TEST - VER 1.
4	The conditions necessary to set this DTC are not present at this time. Using the schematics as a guide, inspect the wiring and connectors specific to this circuit. Wiggle the wiring while checking for shorts and open circuits. Were there any problems found? Yes → Repair as necessary. Perform BODY VERIFICATION TEST - VER 1. No → Test Complete.

CR9050000476000X

Fig. 120 ABS Lamp Circuit Short. 2001 Sebring Convertible, Sebring Sedan & Stratus Sedan

When Monitored and Set Condition:

ABS LAMP CIRCUIT OPEN

When Monitored: At power up or when the bulb is requested.

Set Condition: When there is an open detected in the ABS bulb circuit.

POSSIBLE CAUSES
INTERMITTENT WIRING AND CONNECTORS
ABS INDICATOR BULB
EMIC - INTERNAL ERROR

TEST	ACTION
1	Turn the ignition on. With the DRBIII®, record and erase DTC's. Turn the ignition off, wait 15 seconds, then turn the ignition on. With the DRBIII®, read DTCs. Does the DRBIII® display ABS LAMP CIRCUIT OPEN? Yes → Go To 2 No → Go To 4
2	Turn the ignition off to the lock position. **NOTE: Check connectors - Clean/repair as necessary.** Remove and inspect the ABS Indicator Bulb. Is the ABS Indicator Bulb internally open? Yes → Replace the ABS Indicator Bulb Perform BODY VERIFICATION TEST - VER 1. No → Go To 3
3	If there are no possible causes remaining, view repair. Repair Replace the EMIC. Perform BODY VERIFICATION TEST - VER 1.
4	The conditions necessary to set this DTC are not present at this time. Using the schematics as a guide, inspect the wiring and connectors specific to this circuit. Wiggle the wiring while checking for shorts and open circuits. Were there any problems found? Yes → Repair as necessary. Perform BODY VERIFICATION TEST - VER 1. No → Test Complete.

CR9050000475000X

Fig. 119 ABS Lamp Circuit Open. 2001 Sebring Convertible, Sebring Sedan & Stratus Sedan

When Monitored and Set Condition:

AIRBAG LAMP CIRCUIT OPEN

When Monitored: At power up or when the bulb is requested.

Set Condition: When there is an open detected in the Airbag bulb circuit.

POSSIBLE CAUSES
INTERMITTENT WIRING AND CONNECTORS
AIRBAG INDICATOR BULB
EMIC - INTERNAL ERROR

TEST	ACTION
1	Turn the ignition on. With the DRBIII®, record and erase DTC's. Turn the ignition off, wait 15 seconds, then turn the ignition on. With the DRBIII®, read DTCs. Does the DRBIII® display AIRBAG LAMP CIRCUIT OPEN? Yes → Go To 2 No → Go To 4
2	Turn the ignition off to the lock position. **NOTE: Check connectors - Clean/repair as necessary.** Remove and inspect the Airbag Indicator LED. Is the Airbag Indicator Bulb internally open? Yes → Replace the Airbag Indicator Bulb Perform BODY VERIFICATION TEST - VER 1. No → Go To 3
3	If there are no possible causes remaining, view repair. Repair Replace the EMIC. Perform BODY VERIFICATION TEST - VER 1.
4	The conditions necessary to set this DTC are not present at this time. Using the schematics as a guide, inspect the wiring and connectors specific to this circuit. Wiggle the wiring while checking for shorts and open circuits. Were there any problems found? Yes → Repair as necessary. Perform BODY VERIFICATION TEST - VER 1. No → Test Complete.

CR9050000477000X

Fig. 121 Air Bag Lamp Circuit Open. 2001 Sebring Convertible, Sebring Sedan & Stratus Sedan

When Monitored and Set Condition:

AIRBAG LAMP CIRCUIT SHORT

When Monitored: At power up or when the bulb is requested.

Set Condition: When there is a short detected in the Airbag bulb circuit.

POSSIBLE CAUSES
INTERMITTENT WIRING AND CONNECTORS
AIRBAG INDICATOR BULB
EMIC - INTERNAL ERROR

TEST	ACTION	APPLICABILITY
1	Turn the ignition on. With the DRBIII®, record and erase DTC's. Turn the ignition off, wait 15 seconds, then turn the ignition on. With the DRBIII®, read DTCs. Does the DRBIII® display AIRBAG LAMP CIRCUIT SHORT? Yes → Go To 2 No → Go To 4	All
2	Turn the ignition off to the lock position. **NOTE: Check connectors - Clean/repair as necessary.** Remove and inspect the Airbag Indicator Bulb. Does the Airbag Indicator Bulb have and internal direct short? Yes → Replace the Airbag Indicator Bulb Perform BODY VERIFICATION TEST - VER 1. No → Go To 3	All
3	If there are no possible causes remaining, view repair. Repair Replace the EMIC. Perform BODY VERIFICATION TEST - VER 1.	All
4	The conditions necessary to set this DTC are not present at this time. Using the schematics as a guide, inspect the wiring and connectors specific to this circuit. Wiggle the wiring while checking for shorts and open circuits. Were there any problems found? Yes → Repair as necessary. Perform BODY VERIFICATION TEST - VER 1. No → Test Complete.	All

CR9050000478000X

Fig. 122 Air Bag Lamp Circuit Short. 2001 Sebring Convertible, Sebring Sedan & Stratus Sedan

POSSIBLE CAUSES
ATTEMPT TO COMMUNICATE WITH THE BODY CONTROL MODULE
INSTRUMENT CLUSTER

TEST	ACTION
1	Turn the ignition on. With the DRBIII®, attempt to communicate with the BCM. Was the DRBIII® able to I/D or communicate with the BCM? Yes → Go To 2 No → Refer to the related symptom(s). Perform BODY VERIFICATION TEST - VER 1.
2	With the DRBIII®, erase DTC's. Turn the ignition on and wait approximately 1 minute. With the DRBIII®, read DTC's. Did this DTC reset? Yes → Replace the Instrument Cluster. Perform BODY VERIFICATION TEST - VER 1. No → Test Complete.

CR9050000480000X

Fig. 124 No BCM Bus Messages Received. 2001 Sebring Convertible, Sebring Sedan & Stratus Sedan

POSSIBLE CAUSES
ATTEMPT TO COMMUNICATE WITH THE ANTI-LOCK BRAKE SYSTEM MODULE
INSTRUMENT CLUSTER

TEST	ACTION
1	Turn the ignition on. With the DRBIII®, attempt to communicate with the ABS module. Was the DRBIII® able to I/D or communicate with the ABS module? Yes → Go To 2 No → Refer to the related symptom(s). Perform BODY VERIFICATION TEST - VER 1.
2	With the DRBIII®, erase DTC's. Turn the ignition on and wait approximately 1 minute. With the DRBIII®, read DTC's. Did this DTC reset? Yes → Replace the Instrument Cluster. Perform BODY VERIFICATION TEST - VER 1. No → Test Complete.

CR9050000479000X

Fig. 123 No ABS Bus Messages Received. 2001 Sebring Convertible, Sebring Sedan & Stratus Sedan

POSSIBLE CAUSES
ATTEMPT TO COMMUNICATE WITH THE OCCUPANT RESTRAINT CONTROLLER
INSTRUMENT CLUSTER

TEST	ACTION
1	Turn the ignition on. With the DRBIII®, attempt to communicate with the ORC. Was the DRBIII® able to I/D or communicate with the ORC? Yes → Go To 2 No → Refer to the related symptom(s). Perform BODY VERIFICATION TEST - VER 1.
2	With the DRBIII®, erase DTC's. Turn the ignition on and wait approximately 1 minute. With the DRBIII®, read DTC's. Did this DTC reset? Yes → Replace the Instrument Cluster. Perform BODY VERIFICATION TEST - VER 1. No → Test Complete.

CR9050000481000X

Fig. 125 No ORC Bus Messages Received. 2001 Sebring Convertible, Sebring Sedan & Stratus Sedan

POSSIBLE CAUSES
PCM MESSAGE NOT RECEIVED
INSTRUMENT CLUSTER

TEST	ACTION
1	Turn the ignition on. With the DRBIII®, attempt to communicate with the PCM. Was the DRBIII® able to I/D or communicate with the PCM? Yes → Go To 2 No → Refer to the related symptom(s). Perform BODY VERIFICATION TEST - VER 1.
2	With the DRBIII®, erase DTC's. Turn the ignition on and wait approximately 1 minute. With the DRBIII®, read DTC's. Did this DTC reset? Yes → Replace the Instrument Cluster. Perform BODY VERIFICATION TEST - VER 1. No → Test Complete.

CR9050000482000X

Fig. 126 No PCM Bus Messages Received. 2001 Sebring Convertible, Sebring Sedan & Stratus Sedan

POSSIBLE CAUSES
ATTEMPT TO COMMUNICATE WITH THE TCM
INSTRUMENT CLUSTER

TEST	ACTION
1	Turn the ignition on. With the DRBIII® attempt to communicate with the Transmission Control Module. Was the DRBIII® able to I/D or communicate with the TCM? Yes → Go To 2 No → Refer to the related symptom(s). Perform BODY VERIFICATION TEST - VER 1.
2	With the DRBIII® erase DTC's. Turn the ignition on and wait approximately 1 minute. With the DRBIII® read DTC's. Did this DTC reset? Yes → Replace the Instrument Cluster. Perform BODY VERIFICATION TEST - VER 1. No → Test Complete.

CR9050000483000X

Fig. 127 No TCM Bus Messages Received. 2001 Sebring Convertible, Sebring Sedan & Stratus Sedan

TEST	ACTION
3	Turn the ignition on. With the DRBIII®, erase Body Control Module DTCs. Turn the ignition off to the lock position. Disconnect the EMIC harness connector. Turn the ignition on. Turn the Headlamps on. With the DRBIII®, read DTCs. Does the DRBIII® display PANEL DIMMING OUTPUT SHORT? Yes → Go To 4 No → If there are no possible causes remaining, replace the EMIC Perform BODY VERIFICATION TEST - VER 1.
4	Turn the ignition on. With the DRBIII®, erase Body Control Module DTCs. Turn the ignition off to the lock position. Disconnect the PRNDL Lamp harness connector. Turn the ignition on. With the DRBIII®, read DTCs. Does the DRBIII® display PANEL DIMMING OUTPUT SHORT? Yes → Go To 5 No → If there are no possible causes remaining, replace the PRNDL Lamp Perform BODY VERIFICATION TEST - VER 1.
5	Turn the ignition on. With the DRBIII®, erase Body Control Module DTCs. Turn the ignition off to the lock position. Disconnect the HVAC Module harness connector. Turn the ignition on. Turn the Headlamps on. With the DRBIII®, read DTCs. Does the DRBIII® display PANEL DIMMING OUTPUT SHORT? Yes → Go To 6 No → If there are no possible causes remaining, replace the HVAC Module Perform BODY VERIFICATION TEST - VER 1.
6	Turn the ignition on. With the DRBIII®, erase Body Control Module DTCs. Turn the ignition off to the lock position. Disconnect the Radio harness connector. Turn the ignition on. Turn the Headlamps on. With the DRBIII®, read DTCs. Does the DRBIII® display PANEL DIMMING OUTPUT SHORT? Yes → Go To 7 No → If there are no possible causes remaining, replace the Radio Perform BODY VERIFICATION TEST - VER 1.

CR9050000484020X

Fig. 128 Panel Dimming Output Short (Part 2 of 4). 2001 Sebring Convertible, Sebring Sedan & Stratus Sedan

POSSIBLE CAUSES
INTERMITTENT WIRING AND CONNECTORS
ASH RECEIVER LAMP DIMMING CIRCUIT SHORT TO GROUND
EMIC DIMMING CIRCUIT SHORT TO GROUND
HVAC MODULE DIMMING CIRCUIT SHORT TO GROUND
PRNDL LAMP CIRCUIT SHORT TO GROUND
RADIO DIMMING CIRCUIT SHORT TO GROUND
ASH RECEIVER
EMIC
PRNDL LAMP
RADIO
BODY CONTROL MODULE
HVAC MODULE

TEST	ACTION
1	Turn the ignition on. With the DRBIII®, record and erase Body Control Module DTC's. Turn the ignition off, wait 15 seconds, then turn the ignition on. Turn on the Headlamps. With the DRBIII®, read DTCs. Does the DRBIII® display PANEL DIMMING OUTPUT SHORT? Yes → Go To 2 No → Go To 13
2	Turn the ignition on. With the DRBIII®, erase Body Control Module DTCs. Turn the ignition off to the lock position. Disconnect the Ash Receiver Lamp. Turn the ignition on. Turn the Headlamps on. With the DRBIII®, read DTCs. Does the DRBIII® display PANEL DIMMING OUTPUT SHORT? Yes → Go To 3 No → If there are no possible causes remaining, replace the Ash Receiver Lamp Perform BODY VERIFICATION TEST - VER 1.

CR9050000484010X

Fig. 128 Panel Dimming Output Short (Part 1 of 4). 2001 Sebring Convertible, Sebring Sedan & Stratus Sedan

TEST	ACTION
7	Turn the ignition off to the lock position. Disconnect the Body Control Module harness connector. Disconnect the Ash Receiver Lamp. **Note: Check connectors - Clean/repair as necessary.** Measure the resistance between ground and the Ash Receiver Dimming circuit. Is the resistance below 5.0 ohms? Yes → Repair the Ash Receiver Lamp Dimming circuit for a short to ground. Perform BODY VERIFICATION TEST - VER 1. No → Go To 8
8	Turn the ignition off to the lock position. Disconnect the Body Control Module harness connector. Disconnect the EMIC harness connector. **Note: Check connectors - Clean/repair as necessary.** Measure the resistance between ground and the EMIC Dimming circuit. Is the resistance below 5.0 ohms? Yes → Repair the EMIC Dimming circuit for a short to ground. Perform BODY VERIFICATION TEST - VER 1. No → Go To 9
9	Turn the ignition off to the lock position. Disconnect the Body Control Module harness connector. Disconnect the HVAC Module harness connector. **Note: Check connectors - Clean/repair as necessary.** Measure the resistance between ground and the HVAC Module Dimming circuit. Is the resistance below 5.0 ohms? Yes → Repair the HVAC Module Dimming circuit for a short to ground. Perform BODY VERIFICATION TEST - VER 1. No → Go To 10
10	Turn the ignition off to the lock position. Disconnect the Body Control Module harness connector. Disconnect the PRNDL Lamp harness connector. **Note: Check connectors - Clean/repair as necessary.** Measure the resistance between ground and the PRNDL Lamp circuit. Is the resistance below 5.0 ohms? Yes → Repair the PRNDL Lamp circuit for a short to ground. Perform BODY VERIFICATION TEST - VER 1. No → Go To 11
11	Turn the ignition off to the lock position. Disconnect the Body Control Module harness connector. Disconnect the Radio harness connector. **Note: Check connectors - Clean/repair as necessary.** Measure the resistance between ground and the Radio Dimming circuit. Is the resistance below 5.0 ohms? Yes → Repair the Radio Dimming circuit for a short to ground. Perform BODY VERIFICATION TEST - VER 1. No → Go To 12

CR9050000484030X

Fig. 128 Panel Dimming Output Short (Part 3 of 4). 2001 Sebring Convertible, Sebring Sedan & Stratus Sedan

TEST	ACTION
12	If there are no possible causes remaining, view repair. Repair Replace the Body Control Module. Perform BODY VERIFICATION TEST - VER 1.
13	The conditions necessary to set this DTC are not present at this time. Using the schematics as a guide, inspect the wiring and connectors specific to this circuit. Wiggle the wiring while checking for shorts and open circuits. Were there any problems found? Yes → Repair as necessary. Perform BODY VERIFICATION TEST - VER 1. No → Test Complete.

CR9050000484040X

Fig. 128 Panel Dimming Output Short (Part 4 of 4). 2001 Sebring Convertible, Sebring Sedan & Stratus Sedan

TEST	ACTION
4	Turn the ignition off to the lock position. Disconnect the EMIC harness connector. **Note: Check connectors - Clean/repair as necessary.** Ignition on, engine not running. Using a 12-volt test light connected to ground, check the Fused Ignition Switch Output circuit at the EMIC harness connector. **NOTE: The test light must illuminate brightly. Compare the brightness to that of a direct connection to the battery.** Does the test light illuminate brightly? Yes → Go To 5 No → Repair the Fused Ignition Switch Output circuit for an open or high resistance circuit. If the fuse is open make sure to check for a short to ground and repair as necessary. Perform BODY VERIFICATION TEST - VER 1.
5	If there are no possible causes remaining, view repair. Repair Replace the Instrument Cluster Perform BODY VERIFICATION TEST - VER 1.

CR9050000485020X

Fig. 129 Brake Warning Indicator Not Operating Properly (Part 2 of 2). 2001 Sebring Convertible, Sebring Sedan & Stratus Sedan

POSSIBLE CAUSES
CHECK DTCS
DEFECTIVE BULB OR SOCKET
EMIC

TEST	ACTION
1	Ensure there is communication between the PCM, BCM and the Instrument Cluster before proceeding. During the self test all Indicators should illuminate for approximately 4 seconds. While holding the "TRIP/RESET" button, turn the ignition from the "OFF" to the "UNLOCK" position. This will start the MIC self test. Did the Charging System Warning indicator light for approximately 4 seconds then go out? Yes → Go To 2 No → Go To 3
2	Using the DRBIII® read DTC's. Are there any DTC's present? Yes → Refer to symptom list for problems related to the DTC. Perform BODY VERIFICATION TEST - VER 1. No → Go To 3
3	Remove and inspect the Charging System Warning Lamp bulb and socket. Is there a problem with the bulb or socket? Yes → Replace the defective bulb or socket as needed Perform BODY VERIFICATION TEST - VER 1. No → Go To 4
4	If there are no possible causes remaining, view repair. Repair Replace the Instrument Cluster Perform BODY VERIFICATION TEST - VER 1.

CR9050000486000X

Fig. 130 Charging System Warning Indicator Not Operating Properly. 2001 Sebring Convertible, Sebring Sedan & Stratus Sedan

POSSIBLE CAUSES
DEFECTIVE BULB OR SOCKET
FUSED IGNITION SWITCH OUTPUT CIRCUIT OPEN
RED BRAKE WARNING INDICATOR DRIVER
EMIC
EMIC-DRIVER

TEST	ACTION
1	Ensure there is communication between the PCM, BCM and the Instrument Cluster before proceeding. During the self test all Indicators should illuminate for approximately 4 seconds. While holding the "TRIP/RESET" button, turn the ignition from the "OFF" to the "UNLOCK" position. This will start the MIC self test. Did the Brake Warning indicator light for approximately 4 seconds then go out? Yes → Go To 2 No → Go To 3
2	Turn the ignition off to the lock position. Disconnect the EMIC harness connector. Disconnect the Park Brake Switch harness connector. Disconnect the Brake Fluid Level Switch harness connector. Connect a jumper wire between Park Brake Switch circuit and the ground circuit in the Park Brake Switch harness connector. Connect a jumper wire between Brake Fluid Level Switch circuit and the ground circuit in the Brake Fluid Level Switch harness connector. **Note: Check connectors - Clean/repair as necessary.** Ignition on, engine not running. Using a 12-volt test light connected to 12-volts, check the Red Brake Warning Indicator Driver circuit at the EMIC Harness Connector. **NOTE: The test light must illuminate brightly. Compare the brightness to that of a direct connection to the battery.** Does the test light illuminate brightly? Yes → Replace the Instrument Cluster Perform BODY VERIFICATION TEST - VER 1. No → Repair the Red Brake Warning Indicator Driver circuit for an open or high resistance circuit. Perform BODY VERIFICATION TEST - VER 1.
3	Remove and inspect the Brake Warning Indicator Lamp bulb and socket. Is there a problem with the bulb or socket? Yes → Replace the defective bulb or socket as needed Perform BODY VERIFICATION TEST - VER 1. No → Go To 4

CR9050000485010X

Fig. 129 Brake Warning Indicator Not Operating Properly (Part 1 of 2). 2001 Sebring Convertible, Sebring Sedan & Stratus Sedan

POSSIBLE CAUSES
CHECK CRUISE FUNCTION
DEFECTIVE BULB OR SOCKET
EMIC

TEST	ACTION
1	Ensure there is communication between the PCM, BCM and the Instrument Cluster before proceeding. During the self test all Indicators should illuminate for approximately 4 seconds. While holding the "TRIP/RESET" button, turn the ignition from the "OFF" to the "UNLOCK" position. This will start the MIC self test. Did the Cruise indicator light for approximately 4 seconds then go out? Yes → Go To 2 No → Go To 3
2	Start the engine. Drive the vehicle. Activate the cruise system. Does the Cruise system function normally? Yes → Refer to cruise diagnostics for the related symptom(s). Perform BODY VERIFICATION TEST - VER 1. No → Test Complete.
3	Remove and inspect the Cruise Engaged Indicator Lamp bulb and socket. Is there a problem with the bulb or socket? Yes → Replace the defective bulb or socket as needed Perform BODY VERIFICATION TEST - VER 1. No → Go To 4
4	If there are no possible causes remaining, view repair. Repair Replace the Instrument Cluster Perform BODY VERIFICATION TEST - VER 1.

CR9050000487000X

Fig. 131 Cruise Engaged Indicator Not Operating Properly. 2001 Sebring Convertible, Sebring Sedan & Stratus Sedan

POSSIBLE CAUSES
CHECK DTCS
ENGINE COOLANT TEMPERATURE MESSAGE
EMIC

TEST	ACTION	APPLICABILITY
1	Using the DRBIII® read EMIC, PCM and BCM DTC's. Are there any DTC's present? Yes → Before continuing refer to problems related to the DTC and diagnose them first. Perform BODY VERIFICATION TEST - VER 1. No → Go To 2	All
2	Turn the ignition on. With the DRBIII®, read the Engine Coolant Temperature in the PCM, EMIC and the BCM. Do either the EMIC or BCM display a different Engine Coolant Temperature than the PCM? Yes → Refer to problems related to inaccurate Engine Coolant Temperature reading and communications. Perform BODY VERIFICATION TEST - VER 1. No → Go To 3	All
3	During the self test all gauges should move from their minimum point to their maximum point then back down to its minimum. While holding the "TRIP/RESET" button, turn the ignition from the "OFF" to the "UNLOCK" position. This will start the MIC self test. Did the Engine Coolant Temperature gauge pass the self test?? Yes → Go To 4 No → Go To 4	All
4	If there are no possible causes remaining, view repair. Repair Replace the Instrument Cluster in accordance with the Service Information. Perform BODY VERIFICATION TEST - VER 1.	All

CR9050000488000X

Fig. 132 Engine Coolant Temperature Gauge Inoperative Or Inaccurate. 2001 Sebring Convertible, Sebring Sedan & Stratus Sedan

TEST	ACTION
5	If there are no possible causes remaining, view repair. Repair Replace the EMIC. Perform BODY VERIFICATION TEST - VER 1.

CR9050000489020X

Fig. 133 Engine Coolant Temperature Indicator Not Operating Properly (Part 2 of 2). 2001 Sebring Convertible, Sebring Sedan & Stratus Sedan

POSSIBLE CAUSES
CHECK DTCS
ENGINE COOLANT TEMPERATURE WARNING INDICATOR LED
EMIC - INTERNAL ERROR

TEST	ACTION
1	Ensure there is communication between the PCM, BCM and the Instrument Cluster before proceeding. During the self test all Indicators should illuminate for approximately 4 seconds. While holding the "TRIP/RESET" button, turn the ignition from the "OFF" to the "UNLOCK" position. This will start the MIC self test. Did the Engine Coolant Temperature indicator light for approximately 4 seconds then Yes → Go To 2 No → Go To 4
2	Using the DRBIII® read DTC's. Are there any DTC's present? Yes → Refer To problems related to DRIVEABILITY. Perform BODY VERIFICATION TEST - VER 1. No → Go To 3
3	Turn the ignition off to the lock position. **NOTE: Check connectors - Clean/repair as necessary.** Remove and test the Engine Coolant Temperature Warning Indicator LED. Does the Engine Coolant Temperature Warning Indicator LED have an open or internal direct short? Yes → Replace the Engine Coolant Temperature Warning Indicator LED Perform BODY VERIFICATION TEST - VER 1. No → Test Complete.
4	Turn the ignition off to the lock position. **NOTE: Check connectors - Clean/repair as necessary.** Remove and test the Engine Coolant Temperature Warning Indicator LED. Does the Engine Coolant Temperature Warning Indicator LED have an open or internal direct short? Yes → Replace the Engine Coolant Temperature Warning Indicator LED Perform BODY VERIFICATION TEST - VER 1. No → Go To 5

CR9050000489010X

Fig. 133 Engine Coolant Temperature Indicator Not Operating Properly (Part 1 of 2). 2001 Sebring Convertible, Sebring Sedan & Stratus Sedan

POSSIBLE CAUSES
MIC SELF TEST
FUEL LEVEL GAUGE OPERATION
FUEL LEVEL SENDING UNIT OPERATION
FUEL LEVEL SENSOR SIGNAL SHORTED TO GROUND
FUEL LEVEL SIGNAL CIRCUIT SHORT TO GROUND CIRCUIT
BCM

TEST	ACTION
1	Ensure there is communication between the PCM, BCM and the Instrument Cluster before proceeding. During the self test all gauges should move from their minimum position to full scale then back down to minimum again. While holding the "TRIP/RESET" button, turn the ignition from the "OFF" to the "RUN" position. This will start the MIC self test. Did the Fuel Gauge pass the self test? Yes → Go To 2 No → Replace the EMIC Perform BODY VERIFICATION TEST - VER 1.
2	Turn the ignition on. Disconnect the Fuel Tank Module harness connector. Does the Fuel gauge go to Empty? Yes → Replace the Fuel Level Sending Unit Perform BODY VERIFICATION TEST - VER 1. No → Go To 3
3	Turn the ignition on. With the DRBIII® in Body Computer and then Sensors, monitor the Fuel Sensor. Disconnect the Fuel Tank Module harness connector. Does the Fuel Sensor voltage go above 6.0 volts? Yes → Replace the EMIC Perform BODY VERIFICATION TEST - VER 1. No → Go To 4
4	Turn the ignition off. Disconnect the BCM harness connector. Disconnect Fuel Tank Module harness connector. Measure the resistance of the Fuel Level Sensor Signal circuit in the BCM harness connector to ground. Is the resistance below 5.0 ohms? Yes → Repair the Fuel Level Sensor Signal circuit for a short to ground. Perform BODY VERIFICATION TEST - VER 1. No → Go To 5

CR9050000490010X

Fig. 134 Fuel Gauge Not Operating Properly (Part 1 of 2). 2001 Sebring Convertible, Sebring Sedan & Stratus Sedan

TEST	ACTION
5	Turn the ignition off. Disconnect the BCM harness connector. Disconnect Fuel Tank Module harness connector. Measure the resistance between the Fuel Level Sensor Signal circuit and the Fuel level Ground circuit in the BCM harness connector. Is the resistance below 5.0 ohms? Yes → Repair the Fuel Level Sensor Signal circuit for a short to the ground circuit. Perform BODY VERIFICATION TEST - VER 1. No → Go To 6
6	If there are no possible causes remaining, view repair. Repair Replace the Body Control Module. Perform BODY VERIFICATION TEST - VER 1.

CR9050000490020X

Fig. 134 Fuel Gauge Not Operating Properly (Part 2 of 2). 2001 Sebring Convertible, Sebring Sedan & Stratus Sedan

TEST	ACTION
4	Turn the ignition off. Disconnect the Fuel Tank Module harness connector. Turn the ignition on. With the DRBIII® in Body Computer then Sensors, monitor the Fuel Sensor. Using a jumper wire, jumper the Fuel Level Sensor Signal circuit to the ground circuit in the Fuel Tank Module harness connector. Does the DRB display below 0.5 volt? Yes → Replace the Fuel Level Sending Unit. Perform BODY VERIFICATION TEST - VER 1. No → Go To 5
5	Turn the ignition off. Disconnect the Fuel Tank Module harness connector. Disconnect the BCM harness connector. Measure the resistance of the Fuel Level Sensor Signal circuit between the Fuel Tank Module harness connector and the BCM harness connector. Is the resistance below 5.0 ohms? Yes → Go To 6 No → Repair the Fuel Level Sensor Signal for an open. Perform BODY VERIFICATION TEST - VER 1.
6	If there are no possible causes remaining, view repair. Repair Replace the Body Control Module. Perform BODY VERIFICATION TEST - VER 1.
7	The conditions necessary to set this DTC are not present at this time. Using the schematics as a guide, inspect the wiring and connectors specific to this circuit. Wiggle the wiring while checking for shorts and open circuits. Were there any problems found? Yes → Repair as necessary. Perform BODY VERIFICATION TEST - VER 1. No → Test Complete.

CR9050000491020X

Fig. 135 Fuel Level Sending Unit Not Operating Properly (Part 2 of 2). 2001 Sebring Convertible, Sebring Sedan & Stratus Sedan

POSSIBLE CAUSES
FUEL LEVEL SENSOR SIGNAL SHORTED TO B+
GROUND CIRCUIT OPEN
INTERMITTENT WIRING AND CONNECTORS
FUEL LEVEL SENDING UNIT OPERATION
FUEL LEVEL SENSOR SIGNAL CIRCUIT OPEN
BCM

TEST	ACTION
1	Turn the ignition on. With the DRBIII®, erase DTCs. Cycle the ignition off and on, leaving ignition key on for at least 15 seconds. With the DRBIII® in Body Computer, read DTCs. Does the DTC reset? Yes → Go To 2 No → Go To 7
2	Turn the ignition off. Disconnect the Fuel Tank Module harness connector. Turn the ignition on. **NOTE: The BCM sends out a low current 12 volt signal on the Fuel Level Sensor Signal circuit. This low current should not illuminate a 12 volt test light.** Using a 12-volt test light connected to ground, probe the Fuel Level Sensor Signal circuit in the Fuel Tank Module harness connector. Does the test light illuminate? Yes → Repair the Fuel Level Sensor Signal circuit shorted to battery voltage. Perform BODY VERIFICATION TEST - VER 1. No → Go To 3
3	Turn the ignition on. Disconnect the Fuel Tank Module harness connector. Measure the resistance of the Ground circuits in the Fuel Tank Module harness connector. Is the resistance below 5.0 ohms for both measurements? Yes → Go To 4 No → Repair the Ground circuit for an open. Perform BODY VERIFICATION TEST - VER 1.

CR9050000491010X

Fig. 135 Fuel Level Sending Unit Not Operating Properly (Part 1 of 2). 2001 Sebring Convertible, Sebring Sedan & Stratus Sedan

POSSIBLE CAUSES
CHECK HIGH BEAM FUNCTION
HIGH BEAM SENSE CIRCUIT OPEN
DEFECTIVE BULB OR SOCKET
EMIC

TEST	ACTION
1	Ensure there is communication between the PCM, BCM and the Instrument Cluster before proceeding. During the self test all Indicators should illuminate for approximately 4 seconds. While holding the "TRIP/RESET" button, turn the ignition from the "OFF" to the "UNLOCK" position. This will start the MIC self test. Did the High Beam indicator light for approximately 4 seconds then go out? Yes → Go To 2 No → Go To 4
2	Turn the ignition on. Turn the Headlamps ON. Activate the High Beams. Do the High Beams function normally? Yes → Go To 3 No → Refer to exterior lighting diagnostics for the related symptom(s). Perform BODY VERIFICATION TEST - VER 1.
3	Turn the ignition off to the lock position. Disconnect the EMIC harness connector. Disconnect the Multifunction Switch harness connector. **Note: Check connectors - Clean/repair as necessary.** Measure the resistance of the High Beam Sense circuit between the EMIC harness connector and the Multifunction Switch harness connector. Is the resistance above 5.0 ohms? Yes → Repair the High Beam Sense circuit for an open or high resistance circuit. Perform BODY VERIFICATION TEST - VER 1. No → Go To 5
4	Remove and inspect the High Beam Indicator Lamp bulb and socket. Is there a problem with the bulb or socket? Yes → Replace the defective bulb or socket as needed Perform BODY VERIFICATION TEST - VER 1. No → Go To 5

CR9050000492010X

Fig. 136 High Beam Indicator Not Operating Properly (Part 1 of 2). 2001 Sebring Convertible, Sebring Sedan & Stratus Sedan

TEST	ACTION
5	If there are no possible causes remaining, view repair. Repair Replace the Instrument Cluster Perform BODY VERIFICATION TEST - VER 1.

CR9050000492020X

Fig. 136 High Beam Indicator Not Operating Properly (Part 2 of 2). 2001 Sebring Convertible, Sebring Sedan & Stratus Sedan

POSSIBLE CAUSES
CHECK DTCS
DEFECTIVE BULB OR SOCKET
EMIC

TEST	ACTION
1	Ensure there is communication between the PCM, BCM and the Instrument Cluster before proceeding. During the self test all Indicators should illuminate for approximately 4 seconds. While holding the "TRIP/RESET" button, turn the ignition from the "OFF" to the "UNLOCK" position. This will start the MIC self test. Did the Malfunction Indicator Lamp indicator light for approximately 4 seconds then go out? Yes → Go To 2 No → Go To 3
2	Using the DRBIII® read DTC's. Are there any DTC's present? Yes → Refer to problems related to the DTC. Perform BODY VERIFICATION TEST - VER 1. No → Go To 3
3	Remove and inspect the Malfunction Indicator Lamp bulb and socket. Is there a problem with the bulb or socket? Yes → Replace the defective bulb or socket as needed Perform BODY VERIFICATION TEST - VER 1. No → Go To 4
4	If there are no possible causes remaining, view repair. Repair Replace the Instrument Cluster Perform BODY VERIFICATION TEST - VER 1.

CR9050000494000X

Fig. 138 Malfunction Indicator Lamp Not Operating Properly. 2001 Sebring Convertible, Sebring Sedan & Stratus Sedan

POSSIBLE CAUSES
OIL PRESSURE INDICATOR STUCK ON TEST
DEFECTIVE BULB OR SOCKET
FUSED IGNITION SWITCH OUTPUT CIRCUIT OPEN
OIL PRESSURE SWITCH CIRCUIT OPEN
OIL PRESSURE SWITCH CIRCUIT SHORT TO GROUND
EMIC

TEST	ACTION
1	Without starting the engine, turn the ignition on. Does the Oil Pressure Indicator illuminate? Yes → Go To 2 No → Go To 4
2	Start the engine. Does the Oil Pressure Indicator go out? Yes → Test Complete. Perform BODY VERIFICATION TEST - VER 1. No → Go To 3
3	Turn the ignition off to the lock position. Disconnect the EMIC harness connector. **Note: Check connectors - Clean/repair as necessary.** Using a 12-volt test light connected to 12-volts, check the Oil Pressure Switch circuit. **NOTE: The test light must illuminate brightly. Compare the brightness to that of a direct connection to the battery.** Does the test light illuminate brightly? Yes → Repair the Oil Pressure Switch circuit or Sensor for a short to ground. Perform BODY VERIFICATION TEST - VER 1. No → Go To 7
4	Remove and inspect the Oil Pressure Warning Indicator Lamp bulb and socket. Is there a problem with the bulb or socket? Yes → Replace the defective bulb or socket as needed Perform BODY VERIFICATION TEST - VER 1. No → Go To 5

CR9050000495010X

Fig. 139 Oil Pressure Indicator Not Operating Properly (Part 1 of 2). 2001 Sebring Convertible, Sebring Sedan & Stratus Sedan

POSSIBLE CAUSES
CHECK DTCS
LOW FUEL WARNING INDICATOR LED
EMIC - INTERNAL ERROR

TEST	ACTION
1	Ensure there is communication between the PCM, BCM and the Instrument Cluster before proceeding. During the self test all Indicators should illuminate for approximately 4 seconds. While holding the "TRIP/RESET" button, turn the ignition from the "OFF" to the "UNLOCK" position. This will start the MIC self test. Did the Low Fuel Warning indicator light for approximately 4 seconds then go out? Yes → Go To 2 No → Go To 3
2	Using the DRBIII® read DTC's. Is the DTC FUEL LEVEL SENDING UNIT INOP present? Yes → Refer to diagnosis of that DTC. Perform BODY VERIFICATION TEST - VER 1. No → Go To 3
3	Turn the ignition off to the lock position. **NOTE: Check connectors - Clean/repair as necessary.** Remove and test the Low Fuel Warning Indicator LED. Does the Low Fuel Warning Indicator LED have an open or internal direct short? Yes → Replace the Low Fuel Warning Indicator LED Perform BODY VERIFICATION TEST - VER 1. No → Go To 4
4	If there are no possible causes remaining, view repair. Repair Replace the EMIC. Perform BODY VERIFICATION TEST - VER 1.

CR9050000493000X

Fig. 137 Low Fuel Warning Indicator Not Operating Properly. 2001 Sebring Convertible, Sebring Sedan & Stratus Sedan

TEST	ACTION
5	Turn the ignition off to the lock position. Disconnect the EMIC harness connector. **Note: Check connectors - Clean/repair as necessary.** Ignition on, engine not running. Using a 12-volt test light connected to ground, check the Fused Ignition Switch Output circuit. **NOTE: The test light must illuminate brightly. Compare the brightness to that of a direct connection to the battery.** Does the test light illuminate brightly? Yes → Go To 6 No → Repair the Fused Ignition Switch Output circuit for an open or high resistance circuit. If the fuse is open make sure to check for a short to ground and repair as necessary. Perform BODY VERIFICATION TEST - VER 1.
6	Turn the ignition off to the lock position. Disconnect the EMIC harness connector. **Note: Check connectors - Clean/repair as necessary.** Start the engine. Using a 12-volt test light connected to 12-volts, check the Oil Pressure Switch circuit. **NOTE: The test light must illuminate brightly. Compare the brightness to that of a direct connection to the battery.** Does the test light illuminate brightly? Yes → Repair the Oil Pressure Switch circuit or sender for an open or high resistance circuit. Perform BODY VERIFICATION TEST - VER 1. No → Go To 7
7	If there are no possible causes remaining, view repair. Repair Replace the Instrument Cluster Perform BODY VERIFICATION TEST - VER 1.

CR9050000495020X

Fig. 139 Oil Pressure Indicator Not Operating Properly (Part 2 of 2). 2001 Sebring Convertible, Sebring Sedan & Stratus Sedan

POSSIBLE CAUSES
SEAT BELT SWITCH SENSE CIRCUIT OPEN
SEAT BELT SWITCH GROUND CIRCUIT OPEN
SEAT BELT SWITCH OPEN
SEAT BELT SWITCH SENSE CIRCUIT SHORT TO GROUND
SEAT BELT SWITCH SHORT
SEAT BELT INDICATOR
INSTRUMENT CLUSTER
SEAT BELT SWITCH

TEST	ACTION
1	Turn the ignition on. While observing the Seat Belt Indicator, buckle and unbuckle the drivers seatbelt. What was the Status of the Indicator? Indicator always ON Go To 2 Indicator always OFF Go To 5
2	Ensure there is communication between the PCM, BCM and the Instrument Cluster before proceeding. During the self test all Indicators should illuminate for approximately 4 seconds. While holding the "TRIP/RESET" button, turn the ignition from the "OFF" to the "UNLOCK" position. This will start the MIC self test. Did the Seat Belt indicator light for approximately 4 seconds then go out? Yes → Go To 3 No → If there are no possible causes remaining, replace the Instrument Cluster Perform BODY VERIFICATION TEST - VER 1.
3	Turn the ignition off to the lock position. Disconnect the EMIC harness connector. **Note: Check connectors - Clean/repair as necessary.** Measure the resistance between ground and the Seat Belt Switch Sense circuit. Is the resistance above 5.0 ohms? Yes → Repair the Seat Belt Switch Sense circuit for a short to ground. Perform BODY VERIFICATION TEST - VER 1. No → Go To 4

CR9050000496010X

Fig. 140 Seat Belt Indicator Not Operating Properly (Part 1 of 3). 2001 Sebring Convertible, Sebring Sedan & Stratus Sedan

TEST	ACTION
8	Turn the ignition off to the lock position. Disconnect the Seat Belt Switch harness connector. **Note: Check connectors - Clean/repair as necessary.** Buckle the Seat Belt. Measure the resistance of the Switch. Is the resistance above 5.0 ohms? Yes → If there are no possible causes remaining, replace the Seat Belt Switch Perform BODY VERIFICATION TEST - VER 1. No → If there are no possible causes remaining, replace the Instrument Cluster Perform BODY VERIFICATION TEST - VER 1.
9	Turn the ignition off to the lock position. **NOTE: Check connectors - Clean/repair as necessary.** Remove and test the Seat Belt Indicator LED. Does the Seat Belt Indicator LED have an open or internal direct short? Yes → Replace the Seat Belt Indicator LED Perform BODY VERIFICATION TEST - VER 1. No → If there are no possible causes remaining, replace the Instrument Cluster Perform BODY VERIFICATION TEST - VER 1.

CR9050000496030X

Fig. 140 Seat Belt Indicator Not Operating Properly (Part 3 of 3). 2001 Sebring Convertible, Sebring Sedan & Stratus Sedan

TEST	ACTION
4	Turn the ignition off to the lock position. Disconnect the EMIC harness connector. Disconnect the Seat Belt Switch harness connector. **Note: Check connectors - Clean/repair as necessary.** Measure the resistance between ground and the Seat Belt Switch Sense circuit. Is the resistance below 5.0 ohms? Yes → Repair the Seat Belt Switch Sense circuit for a short to ground. Perform BODY VERIFICATION TEST - VER 1. No → If there are no possible causes remaining, replace the Seat Belt Switch Perform BODY VERIFICATION TEST - VER 1.
5	Ensure there is communication between the PCM, BCM and the Instrument Cluster before proceeding. During the self test all Indicators should illuminate for approximately 4 seconds. While holding the "TRIP/RESET" button, turn the ignition from the "OFF" to the "UNLOCK" position. This will start the MIC self test. Did the Seat Belt indicator light for approximately 4 seconds then go out? Yes → Go To 6 No → Go To 9
6	Turn the ignition off to the lock position. Disconnect the EMIC harness connector. Disconnect the Seat belt Switch harness connector. **Note: Check connectors - Clean/repair as necessary.** Measure the resistance of the Seat Belt Switch Sense circuit between the EMIC harness connector and the Seat Belt Switch harness connector. Is the resistance above 5.0 ohms? Yes → Repair the Seat Belt Switch Sense circuit for an open. Perform BODY VERIFICATION TEST - VER 1. No → Go To 7
7	Turn the ignition off to the lock position. Disconnect the Seat Belt Switch harness connector. **Note: Check connectors - Clean/repair as necessary.** Measure the resistance between ground and the Seat Belt Switch Ground circuit. Is the resistance above 5.0 ohms? Yes → Repair the Seat Belt Switch Ground circuit for an open. Perform BODY VERIFICATION TEST - VER 1. No → Go To 8

CR9050000496020X

Fig. 140 Seat Belt Indicator Not Operating Properly (Part 2 of 3). 2001 Sebring Convertible, Sebring Sedan & Stratus Sedan

POSSIBLE CAUSES
CHECK DTCS
INSTRUMENT CLUSTER SELF TEST
MISSING OR INCORRECT PINION FACTOR
VEHICLE SPEED MESSAGE
EMIC

TEST	ACTION
1	Using the DRBIII® read EMIC, PCM, ABS and BCM DTC's. Are there any DTC's present? Yes → Before continuing refer to problems related to the DTC and diagnose them first. Perform BODY VERIFICATION TEST - VER 1. No → Go To 2
2	During the self test all gauges should move from their minimum point to their maximum point then back down to its minimum. While holding the "TRIP/RESET" button, turn the ignition from the "OFF" to the "UNLOCK" position. This will start the MIC self test. Did the Speedometer gauge pass the self test?? Yes → Go To 3 No → Replace the Instrument Cluster Perform BODY VERIFICATION TEST - VER 1.
3	With the DRBIII®, verify that the pinion factor is correctly programmed. Is the pinion factor programmed correctly? Yes → Go To 4 No → Using the Diagnostic (Transmission, or Chassis)/Service Manual Information as a guide, program the correct pinion factor, and then verify that the Speedometer is working. Perform BODY VERIFICATION TEST - VER 1.
4	Turn the ignition on. Drive the vehicle With the DRBIII®, read the Vehicle Speed in the EMIC, BCM and the ABS Module Wheel Speed. Do either the EMIC or BCM display a different Vehicle Speed than the ABS Module Wheel Speed? Yes → Refer to problems related to inaccurate Vehicle Speed and communications. Perform BODY VERIFICATION TEST - VER 1. No → Go To 5

CR9050000497010X

Fig. 141 Speedometer Not Operating Properly (Part 1 of 2). 2001 Sebring Convertible, Sebring Sedan & Stratus Sedan

TEST	ACTION
5	If there are no possible causes remaining, view repair. Repair Replace the Instrument Cluster Perform BODY VERIFICATION TEST - VER 1.

CR9050000497020X

Fig. 141 Speedometer Not Operating Properly (Part 2 of 2). 2001 Sebring Convertible, Sebring Sedan & Stratus Sedan

TEST	ACTION
5	If there are no possible causes remaining, view repair. Repair Replace the Instrument Cluster Perform BODY VERIFICATION TEST - VER 1.

CR9050000498020X

Fig. 142 Tachometer Not Operating Properly (Part 2 of 2). 2001 Sebring Convertible, Sebring Sedan & Stratus Sedan

BODY VERIFICATION TEST - VER 1
1. Disconnect all jumper wires and reconnect all previously disconnected components and connectors. 2. If the Sentry Key Immobilizer Module (SKIM) or the Powertrain Control Module (PCM) was replaced, proceed to number 6. If the SKIM or PCM was not replaced, continue to the next number. 3. If the Body Control Module was replaced, turn the ignition on for 15 seconds (to allow the new BCM to learn VIN) or engine may not start (if VTSS equipped). If the vehicle is equipped with VTSS, use the DRBIII® and enable VTSS. 4. Program all other options as needed. 5. If any repairs were made to the HVAC System, disconnect the battery or, using the DRBIII®, recalibrate the HVAC doors. Proceed to number 13. 6. Obtain the Vehicle's unique PIN assigned to it's original SKIM from either the vehicle's invoice or from Chrysler's Customer Assistance Center 7. NOTE: Once Secured Access Mode is active, the SKIM will remain in that mode for 60 seconds. 8. With the DRBIII®, select THEFT ALARM, SKIM, MISCELLANEOUS and select SKIM REPLACED. Enter the 4 digit PIN to put the SKIM in Secured Access Mode. 9. The DRBIII® will prompt for the following steps. (1) Program the country code into the SKIM's memory. (2) Program the vehicle's VIN into the SKIM memory. (3) Transfer the vehicle's Secret Key data from the PCM. 10. Using the DRBIII®, program all customer keys into the SKIM memory. This requires that the SKIM be in Secured Access Mode, using the 4 digit PIN. 11. Note: If the PCM is replaced, the VIN and the unique Secret Key data must be transferred from the SKIM to the PCM. This procedure requires the SKIM to be placed in Secured Access Mode using the 4-digit PIN. 12. Note: After 3 attempts at entering Secured Access Mode with an incorrect PIN, Secured Access Mode will be locked out for 1 hour and the DRBIII® will display "Bus +\- Signals Open" or "No Response". To exit this mode, turn ignition to Run for 1 hour. 13. Ensure that all accessories are turned off and the battery is fully charged. 14. Ensure that the Ignition is on. 15. With the DRBIII®, record and erase all DTCs from ALL modules. Start and run the engine for 2 minutes. Operate all functions of the system that caused the original concern. 16. Turn the ignition off and wait 5 seconds. Turn the ignition on and using the DRBIII®, read DTCs from ALL modules. Are any DTC's present or is the original condition still present? Yes → Repair is not complete, refer to appropriate symptom. No → Repair is complete.

CR9050000502000X

Fig. 143 Body Verification Test VER-1. 2001 Sebring Convertible, Sebring Sedan & Stratus Sedan

POSSIBLE CAUSES
CHECK DTCS
INSTRUMENT CLUSTER SELF TEST
NO ENGINE RPM
ENGINE RPM MESSAGE
EMIC

TEST	ACTION
1	Using the DRBIII® read EMIC, PCM and BCM DTC's. Are there any DTC's present? Yes → Before continuing refer to problems related to the DTC and diagnose them first. Perform BODY VERIFICATION TEST - VER 1. No → Go To 2
2	During the self test all gauges should move from their minimum point to their maximum point then back down to its minimum. While holding the "TRIP/RESET" button, turn the ignition from the "OFF" to the "UNLOCK" position. This will start the MIC self test. Did the Speedometer gauge pass the self test?? Yes → Go To 3 No → Replace the Instrument Cluster Perform BODY VERIFICATION TEST - VER 1.
3	Start the engine. With the DRBIII®, read the Engine RPM in the PCM. Does the PCM display an accurate Engine RPM? Yes → Refer to symptom list for problems related to inaccurate or no Engine RPM. Perform BODY VERIFICATION TEST - VER 1. No → Go To 4
4	Start the engine. With the DRBIII®, read the Engine RPM in the PCM, EMIC and the BCM. Do either the EMIC or BCM display a different Engine RPM than the PCM? Yes → Refer to problems related to inaccurate Engine RPM and communications. Perform BODY VERIFICATION TEST - VER 1. No → Go To 5

CR9050000498010X

Fig. 142 Tachometer Not Operating Properly (Part 1 of 2). 2001 Sebring Convertible, Sebring Sedan & Stratus Sedan

POWERTRAIN VERIFICATION TEST VER-1
1. NOTE: If the PCM has been replaced and the correct VIN and mileage have not been programmed, a DTC will be set in the ABS Module, Airbag Module and the SKIM. **2. NOTE: If the vehicle is equipped with a Sentry Key Immobilizer System, Secret Key data must be updated.** 3. Inspect the vehicle to ensure that all components related to the repair are connected properly. 4. Inspect the engine oil for fuel contamination. Replace the oil and filter as necessary. 5. Attempt to start the engine. 6. If the No Start condition is still present, refer to and perform the diagnostic testing as necessary. refer to and Technical Service Bulletins that may apply. 7. Run the engine for one warm-up cycle to verify operation. 8. With the DRBIII®, confirm that no DTCs or Secondary Indicators are present and that all components are functioning properly. 9. If a DTC is present, refer to the appropriate category and select the corresponding symptom. Are any DTCs present? Yes → Repair is not complete, refer to appropriate symptom. No → Repair is complete.

CR9050000503000X

Fig. 144 Powertrain Verification Test VER-1. 2001 Sebring Convertible, Sebring Sedan & Stratus Sedan

SKIS VERIFICATION
1. Reconnect all previously disconnected components and connectors. 2. Obtain the vehicle's unique Personal Identification Number (PIN) assigned to it's original SKIM. This number can be obtained from the vehicle's invoice or Chrysler's Customer Center (1-800-992-1997). **3. NOTE: When entering the PIN, care should be taken because the SKIM will only allow 3 consecutive attempts to enter the correct PIN. If 3 consecutive incorrect PIN's are entered the SKIM will Lock Out the DRB III for 1 hour.** 4. To exit Lock Out mode, the ignition key must remain in the Run position continually for 1 hour. Turn off all accessories and connect a battery charger if necessary. 5. With the DRB III, select Theft Alarm, SKIM and Miscellaneous. Then select desired procedure and follow the steps that will be displayed. 6. If the SKIM has been replaced, ensure all of the vehicle ignition keys are programmed to the new SKIM. **7. NOTE: Prior to returning vehicle to the costumer, perform a module scan to be sure that all DTC's are erased. Erase any DTC's that are found.** 8. With the DRB III erase all DTC's. Perform 5 ignition key cycles leaving the key on for at least 90 seconds per cycle. 9. With the DRB III, read the SKIM DTC's. Are there any SKIM DTC's? Yes → Repair is not complete, refer to appropriate symptom. No → Repair is complete.

CR9050000504000X

Fig. 145 SKIS Verification Test. 2001 Sebring Convertible, Sebring Sedan & Stratus Sedan

TEST	ACTION
1	**NOTE: Ensure that the Junction Block Fuse #11 is not open. If the fuse is open make sure to check for a short to ground.** Turn the ignition on. With the DRBIII®, record and erase DTC's. Turn the ignition off, wait 15 seconds, then turn the ignition on. With the DRBIII®, read DTCs. Did the Indicator Lamp Open or Short DTC reset? Yes → Go To 2 No → Test Complete.
2	Turn the ignition off. Remove and inspect the Indicator Bulb in question. Is the Indicator Bulb in question defective? Yes → Replace the Indicator Bulb Perform BODY VERIFICATION TEST No → Replace the Instrument Cluster Perform BODY VERIFICATION TEST

CR9090200286020X

Fig. 146 ABS Lamp Circuit Open (Part 2 of 2). 2002–04 Sebring Convertible, Sebring Sedan & Stratus Sedan

Test Note: All symptoms listed above are diagnosed using the same tests. The title for the tests will be ABS LAMP CIRCUIT OPEN.

When Monitored and Set Condition:

ABS LAMP CIRCUIT OPEN

When Monitored: The Instrument Cluster performs an internal diagnostic of the indicator circuit at power up and when the bulb is requested.

Set Condition: When the Instrument Cluster detects a fault in the ABS bulb circuit.

ABS LAMP CIRCUIT SHORT

When Monitored: The Instrument Cluster performs an internal diagnostic at power up and when the bulb is requested.

Set Condition: When the Instrument Clusteris detects a fault in the ABS bulb circuit.

AIRBAG LAMP CIRCUIT OPEN

When Monitored: The Instrument Cluster performs an internal diagnostic of the circuit at power up and when the bulb is requested.

Set Condition: When the Instrument Cluster is detects a fault in the Airbag bulb circuit.

AIRBAG LAMP CIRCUIT SHORT

When Monitored: The Instrument Cluster performs an internal diagnostic at power up and when the bulb is requested.

Set Condition: When the Instrument Cluster detects a fault in the Airbag bulb circuit.

POSSIBLE CAUSES
INDICATOR BULB
INSTRUMENT CLUSTER

CR9090200286010X

Fig. 146 ABS Lamp Circuit Open (Part 1 of 2). 2002–04 Sebring Convertible, Sebring Sedan & Stratus Sedan

When Monitored and Set Condition:

FUEL LEVEL SENDING UNIT FAILURE

When Monitored: With the ignition on.

Set Condition: The BCM detects an out of range, open or short circuit on the Fuel Level Sensor Signal circuit.

POSSIBLE CAUSES
FUEL LEVEL SENSOR SIGNAL CIRCUIT SHORTED TO VOLTAGE
FUEL LEVEL SENSOR SIGNAL CIRCUIT OPEN
FUEL LEVEL SENSOR GROUND CIRCUIT OPEN
FUEL LEVEL SENSOR SIGNAL CIRCUIT SHORT TO SENSOR GROUND CIRCUIT
FUEL LEVEL SENSOR SIGNAL CIRCUIT SHORT TO GROUND
FUEL LEVEL SENSOR
INTERMITTENT CONDITION
BODY CONTROL MODULE

TEST	ACTION
1	Turn the ignition on. With the DRBIII®, erase DTCs. Cycle the ignition. Wait approximately 1 minute. With the DRBIII® in Body Computer, read DTCs. Does the DTC reset? Yes → Go To 2 No → The condition is not present at this time. Monitor DRBIII® parameters while wiggling the related wire harness. Refer to any Technical Service Bulletins (TSB) that may apply. Visually inspect the related wiring harness and connector terminals. Perform BODY VERIFICATION TEST

CR9090200287010X

Fig. 147 Fuel Level Sending Unit Failure (Part 1 of 3). 2002–04 Sebring Convertible, Sebring Sedan & Stratus Sedan

TEST	ACTION
2	Turn the ignition off. Disconnect the Fuel Tank Module harness connector. Turn the ignition on. **NOTE: The BCM sends out a low current 12 volt signal on the Fuel Level Sensor Signal circuit. This low current should not illuminate a 12 volt test light.** Using a 12-volt test light connected to ground, probe the Fuel Level Sensor Signal circuit in the Fuel Tank Module harness connector. Does the test light illuminate? Yes → Repair the Fuel Level Sensor Signal circuit for a short to voltage. Perform BODY VERIFICATION TEST No → Go To 3
3	Turn the ignition off. Disconnect the Fuel Tank Module harness connector. Measure the resistance of the Fuel Level Sensor Ground circuit in the Fuel Tank Module harness connector. Is the resistance below 5.0 ohms? Yes → Go To 4 No → Repair the Fuel Level Sensor Ground circuit for an open. Perform BODY VERIFICATION TEST
4	Turn the ignition off. Disconnect the BCM harness connector. Disconnect the Fuel Tank Module harness connector. Measure the resistance between the Fuel Level Sensor Signal circuit and the Sensor Ground circuit in the BCM connector. Is the resistance below 5.0 ohms? Yes → Repair the Fuel Level Sensor Signal circuit for a short to the Sensor Ground circuit. Perform BODY VERIFICATION TEST No → Go To 5
5	Turn the ignition off. Disconnect the BCM harness connector. Disconnect the Fuel Tank Module harness connector. Measure the resistance between ground and the Fuel Level Sensor Signal circuit. Is the resistance below 5.0 ohms? Yes → Repair the Fuel Level Sensor Signal circuit for a short to ground. Perform BODY VERIFICATION TEST No → Go To 6
6	Turn the ignition off. Disconnect the Fuel Tank Module harness connector. Disconnect the BCM harness connector. Measure the resistance of the Fuel Level Sensor Signal circuit between the Fuel Tank Module harness connector and the BCM harness connector. Is the resistance below 5.0 ohms? Yes → Go To 7 No → Repair the Fuel Level Sensor Signal circuit for an open. Perform BODY VERIFICATION TEST

CR9090200287020X

Fig. 147 Fuel Level Sending Unit Failure (Part 2 of 3). 2002–04 Sebring Convertible, Sebring Sedan & Stratus Sedan

POSSIBLE CAUSES
BRAKE FLUID LEVEL SWITCH
PARK BRAKE SWITCH
RED BRAKE WARNING INDICATOR DRIVER CIRCUIT SHORT TO GROUND
INSTRUMENT CLUSTER

TEST	ACTION
1	**NOTE: If vehicle is equipped with ABS, diagnose and repair any ABS Lamp or Communication DTCs before proceeding with this test.** **NOTE: If vehicle is NOT equipped with ABS, ensure that the Instrument Cluster is not configured for ABS.** **NOTE: Ensure that the Brake Fluid is correctly filled and that the Base Brakes are operating properly before proceeding with this test.** Turn the ignition off. Disconnect the Brake Fluid Level Switch harness connector. Turn the ignition on. Observe the Brake Warning Indicator. Is the Brake Warning Indicator illuminated? Yes → Go To 2 No → Replace the Brake Fluid Level Switch Perform BODY VERIFICATION TEST
2	Turn the ignition off. Disconnect the Park Brake Switch harness connector. Turn the ignition on. Observe the Brake Warning Indicator. Is the Brake Warning Indicator illuminated? Yes → Go To 3 No → Replace the Park Brake Switch Perform BODY VERIFICATION TEST
3	Turn the ignition off. Disconnect the Brake Fluid Level Switch harness connector. Disconnect the Park Brake Switch harness connector. Disconnect the Instrument Cluster harness connector. Measure the resistance between ground and the Red Brake Warning Indicator circuit. Is the resistance below 5.0 ohms? Yes → Repair the Red Brake Warning Indicator Driver circuit for a short to ground. Perform BODY VERIFICATION TEST No → Replace the Instrument Cluster Perform BODY VERIFICATION TEST

CR9090200288000X

Fig. 148 Brake Warning Indicator Always On. 2002–04 Sebring Convertible, Sebring Sedan & Stratus Sedan

TEST	ACTION
7	Turn the ignition off. Disconnect the Fuel Tank Module harness connector. Measure the resistance of the Fuel Level Sensor. The Fuel Level Sensor resistance must be within the following values: Full = Approximately 130 Ohms 3/4 = Approximately 340 Ohms 1/2 = Approximately 550 Ohms 1/4 = Approximately 760 Ohms Empty = Approximately 940 Ohms Does the Fuel Level Sensor resistance measure within specifications? Yes → Replace the Body Control Module Perform BODY VERIFICATION TEST No → Replace the Fuel Level Sensor Perform BODY VERIFICATION TEST

CR9090200287030X

Fig. 147 Fuel Level Sending Unit Failure (Part 3 of 3). 2002–04 Sebring Convertible, Sebring Sedan & Stratus Sedan

POSSIBLE CAUSES
INDICATOR BULB
PARK BRAKE SWITCH
PARK BRAKE SWITCH RED BRAKE WARNING INDICATOR DRIVER CIRCUIT OPEN
BRAKE FLUID LEVEL SWITCH
BRAKE FLUID LEVEL SWITCH GROUND CIRCUIT OPEN
BRAKE FLUID LEVEL SWITCH RED BRAKE WARNING INDICATOR DRIVER CIRCUIT OPEN
INSTRUMENT CLUSTER

TEST	ACTION
1	Perform the Instrument Cluster Self Test. Turn the ignition off. Press and hold the Trip Reset button. Turn the ignition to the Unlock position. Release the Trip Reset button when the Self Test begins. Observe the Brake Warning Indicator during the Self Test. Did the Brake Warning Indicator illuminate for approximately 4 seconds and turn off? Yes → Go To 2 No → Remove and inspect the Brake Warning Indicator bulb and socket, if found to be defective, replace as necessary. If the bulb and socket check OK, replace the Instrument Cluster Perform BODY VERIFICATION TEST
2	Is the fault condition related to the Park Brake? Yes → Go To 3 No → Go To 5
3	Turn the ignition off. Disconnect the Park Brake Switch harness connector. Connect a jumper wire between the Red Brake Warning Indicator circuit and ground. Turn the ignition on. Observe the Brake Warning Indicator. Did the Brake Warning Indicator illuminate? Yes → Replace the Park Brake Switch Perform BODY VERIFICATION TEST No → Go To 4

CR9090200289010X

Fig. 149 Brake Warning Indicator Inoperative (Part 1 of 2). 2002–04 Sebring Convertible, Sebring Sedan & Stratus Sedan

TEST	ACTION
4	Turn the ignition off. Disconnect the Park Brake Switch harness connector. Disconnect the Instrument Cluster harness connector. Measure the resistance of the Red Brake Warning Indicator circuit between the Park Brake Switch connector and the Instrument Cluster connector. Is the resistance above 5.0 ohms? Yes → Repair the Red Brake Warning Indicator Driver circuit between the Park Brake Switch and the Instrument Cluster for an open. Perform BODY VERIFICATION TEST No → Replace the Instrument Cluster Perform BODY VERIFICATION TEST
5	Turn the ignition off. Disconnect the Brake Fluid Level Switch harness connector. Connect a jumper wire between cavity 1 and cavity 2. Turn the ignition on. Observe the Brake Warning Indicator. Did the Brake Warning Indicator illuminate? Yes → Replace the Brake Fluid Level Switch Perform BODY VERIFICATION TEST No → Go To 6
6	Turn the ignition off. Disconnect the Brake Fluid Level Switch harness connector. Measure the resistance between ground and the Brake Fluid Level Switch Ground circuit. Is the resistance below 5.0 ohms? Yes → Go To 7 No → Repair the Brake Fluid Level Switch Ground circuit for an open. Perform BODY VERIFICATION TEST - VER 1.
7	Turn the ignition off. Disconnect the Brake Fluid Level Switch harness connector. Disconnect the Instrument Cluster harness connector. Measure the resistance of the Red Brake Warning Indicator Driver circuit between the Brake Fluid Level Switch connector and the Instrument Cluster connector. Is the resistance below 5.0 ohms? Yes → Replace the Instrument Cluster Perform BODY VERIFICATION TEST No → Repair the Red Brake Warning Indicator Driver circuit between the Brake Fluid Level Switch and the Instrument Cluster for an open. Perform BODY VERIFICATION TEST

CR9090200289020X

Fig. 149 Brake Warning Indicator Inoperative (Part 2 of 2). 2002–04 Sebring Convertible, Sebring Sedan & Stratus Sedan

POSSIBLE CAUSES
NO CRUISE OPERATION
INDICATOR BULB
INSTRUMENT CLUSTER

TEST	ACTION
1	**NOTE: Ensure that the Junction Block Fuse #11 is not open. If the fuse is open make sure to check for a short to ground.** **NOTE: Ensure that there is communication between the PCM, BCM, and the Instrument Cluster before proceeding with this test.** Perform the Instrument Cluster Self Test. Turn the ignition off. Press and hold the Trip Reset button. Turn the ignition to the Unlock position. Release the Trip Reset button when the Self Test begins. Observe the Cruise Indicator during the Self Test. Did the Cruise indicator illuminate for approximately 4 seconds and then turn off? Yes → Go To 2 No → Go To 3
2	Start the engine. Drive the vehicle. Activate the Cruise system. Does the Cruise system operate properly? Yes → Test Complete. No → Refer to Cruise diagnostics for the related symptom(s). Perform BODY VERIFICATION TEST
3	Remove and inspect the Cruise Engaged Indicator Lamp bulb and socket. Is the bulb or socket defective? Yes → Replace the Cruise Indicator bulb or socket as necessary Perform BODY VERIFICATION TEST No → Replace the Instrument Cluster Perform BODY VERIFICATION TEST

CR9090200291000X

Fig. 151 Cruise Control Indicator Inoperative. 2002–04 Sebring Convertible, Sebring Sedan & Stratus Sedan

POSSIBLE CAUSES
DTC PRESENT
INTERMITTENT CONDITION
INDICATOR BULB
INSTRUMENT CLUSTER

TEST	ACTION
1	**NOTE: Ensure that the Junction Block Fuse #11 is not open. If the fuse is open make sure to check for a short to ground.** **NOTE: Ensure that there is communication between the PCM, BCM, and the Instrument Cluster before proceeding with this test.** Perform the Instrument Cluster Self Test. Turn the ignition off. Press and hold the Trip Reset button. Turn the ignition to the Unlock position. Release the Trip Reset button when the Self Check begins. Observe the Charging System Warning Indicator during the Self Test. Did the Charging System Warning Indicator illuminate for approximately 4 seconds and then turn off? Yes → Go To 2 No → Go To 3
2	Using the DRBIII®, read DTC's. Are there any DTC's present? Yes → Refer to symptom list for problems related to the DTC. Perform BODY VERIFICATION TEST No → The condition is not present at this time. Monitor DRBIII® parameters while wiggling the related wire harness. Refer to any Technical Service Bulletins (TSB) that may apply. Visually inspect the related wiring harness and connector terminals. Perform BODY VERIFICATION TEST
3	Remove and inspect the Charging System Warning Indicator bulb and socket. Is the indicator bulb or socket defective? Yes → Replace the Indicator bulb or socket as necessary Perform BODY VERIFICATION TEST No → Replace the Instrument Cluster Perform BODY VERIFICATION TEST

CR9090200290000X

Fig. 150 Charging System Warning Indicator Not Operating Properly. 2002–04 Sebring Convertible, Sebring Sedan & Stratus Sedan

POSSIBLE CAUSES
DTC PRESENT
ENGINE COOLANT TEMPERATURE BUS MESSAGE
INSTRUMENT CLUSTER

TEST	ACTION
1	Using the DRBIII® read EMIC, PCM, and BCM DTC's. Are there any DTC's present? Yes → Refer to DRIVEABILITY information for the related symptom(s). Perform BODY VERIFICATION TEST - VER 1. No → Go To 2
2	Perform the Instrument Cluster Self Test. Turn the ignition off. Press and hold the Trip Reset button. Turn the ignition to the Unlock position. Observe the Engine Coolant Temperature gauge during the Self Test. The gauge will position the indicator needle at the following calibration points: C, H, 1/2, C Did the Engine Coolant Temperature Gauge position the needle correctly? Yes → Go To 3 No → Replace the Instrument Cluster Perform BODY VERIFICATION TEST
3	Turn the ignition on. With the DRBIII®, read the Engine Coolant Temperature in the PCM, EMIC and the BCM. Does either the EMIC or BCM display a different Engine Coolant Temperature than the PCM? Yes → Refer to symptom list for problems related to inaccurate Engine Coolant Temperature reading and communications. Perform BODY VERIFICATION TEST No → Replace the Instrument Cluster Perform BODY VERIFICATION TEST

CR9090200292000X

Fig. 152 Engine Coolant Temperature Gauge Inoperative Or Inaccurate. 2002–04 Sebring Convertible, Sebring Sedan & Stratus Sedan

POSSIBLE CAUSES
DTC PRESENT
ENGINE COOLANT TEMPERATURE WARNING INDICATOR LED
INSTRUMENT CLUSTER

TEST	ACTION
1	**NOTE: Ensure that there is communication between the PCM, BCM, and the Instrument Cluster before proceeding with this test.** Perform the Instrument Cluster Self Test. Turn the ignition off. **NOTE: The Instrument Cluster will illuminate the Engine Coolant Temperature indicator at 124°C (255°F). The indicator will turn off at 121°C (250°F).** Press and hold the Trip Reset button. Turn the ignition to the Unlock position. Release the Trip Reset button when the Self Test begins. Observe the Engine Coolant Temperature Warning indicator during the Self Test. Did the Engine Coolant Temperature indicator illuminate for approximately 4 seconds and then turn of Yes → Go To 2 No → Go To 3
2	Turn the ignition on. Using the DRBIII® read DTC's. Are there any DTC's present? Yes → Refer to symptom list for problems related to DRIVEABILITY. Perform BODY VERIFICATION TEST No → Go To 3
3	Turn the ignition off. Remove the Engine Coolant Temperature Warning Indicator LED. Using a DVOM, select "Diode Mode" and connect the leads across the LED. **CAUTION: Ensure that the RED lead is on the "+" of the LED.** Did the Engine Coolant Temperature Warning Indicator LED illuminate? Yes → Replace the Instrument Cluster Perform BODY VERIFICATION TEST No → Replace the Engine Coolant Temperature Warning Indicator LED Perform BODY VERIFICATION TEST

CR9090200293000X

Fig. 153 Engine Coolant Temperature Indicator Not Operating Properly. 2002–04 Sebring Convertible, Sebring Sedan & Stratus Sedan

POSSIBLE CAUSES
DIMMER SWITCH HIGH BEAM OUTPUT CIRCUIT SHORT TO VOLTAGE
JUNCTION BLOCK SHORT TO VOLTAGE
MULTI- FUNCTION SWITCH
BODY CONTROL MODULE
INSTRUMENT CLUSTER

TEST	ACTION
1	Turn the ignition on. With the DRBIII® in Body Control Inputs/Outputs, read the Hi Beams state. Does the DRBIII® Inputs/Outputs, display On? Yes → Go To 2 No → Replace the Instrument Cluster Perform BODY VERIFICATION TEST
2	Turn the ignition off. Disconnect the Multi- Function Switch harness connector. Turn the ignition on. With the DRBIII® in Body Control Inputs/Outputs, read the Hi Beams state. Does the DRBIII® display On? Yes → Go To 3 No → Replace the Multi- Function Switch Perform BODY VERIFICATION TEST
3	Turn the ignition off. Disconnect the Multi- Function Switch harness connector. Disconnect the Junction Block C6 harness connector. Turn the ignition on. Measure the voltage between the Dimmer Switch High Beam Output circuit and ground. Is there any voltage present? Yes → Repair the Dimmer Switch High Beam Output circuit between the Multi- Function Switch and the Junction Block for a short to voltage. Perform BODY VERIFICATION TEST No → Go To 4

CR9090200295010X

Fig. 155 High Beam Indicator Always On (Part 1 of 2). 2002–04 Sebring Convertible, Sebring Sedan & Stratus Sedan

POSSIBLE CAUSES
INTERMITTENT CONDITION
FUEL LEVEL SENSOR
INSTRUMENT CLUSTER

TEST	ACTION
1	**NOTE: Ensure that there is communication between the PCM, BCM, and the Instrument Cluster before proceeding with this test.** Perform the Instrument Cluster Self Test. Turn the ignition off. Press and hold the Trip/Reset button. Turn the ignition to the Unlock position. Observe the Fuel Gauge during the Self Test. The Fuel Gauge should position the indicator needle at the following calibration points: E, F, 1/2, E Did the Fuel Gauge position the needle correctly? Yes → Go To 2 No → Replace the Instrument Cluster Perform BODY VERIFICATION TEST
2	Turn the ignition off. Disconnect the Fuel Pump Module harness connector. Measure the resistance of the Fuel Level Sensor. The Fuel Level Sensor resistance must be within the following values: Full = Approximately 130 Ohms 3/4 = Approximately 340 Ohms 1/2 = Approximately 550 Ohms 1/4 = Approximately 760 Ohms Empty = Approximately 940 Ohms Does the Fuel Level Sensor resistance measure within specifications? Yes → The condition is not present at this time. Monitor DRBIII® parameters while wiggling the related wire harness. Refer to any Technical Service Bulletins (TSB) that may apply. Visually inspect the related wiring harness and connector terminals. Perform BODY VERIFICATION TEST No → Replace the Fuel Level Sensor Perform BODY VERIFICATION TEST

CR9090200294000X

Fig. 154 Fuel Gauge Not Operating Properly. 2002–04 Sebring Convertible, Sebring Sedan & Stratus Sedan

TEST	ACTION
4	Turn the ignition off. Disconnect the Junction Block C6 harness connector. Turn the ignition on. Measure the voltage between the #3 Fuse in the Junction Block and ground. Is there any voltage present? Yes → Replace the Junction Block Perform BODY VERIFICATION TEST No → Replace the Body Control Module Perform BODY VERIFICATION TEST

CR9090200295020X

Fig. 155 High Beam Indicator Always On (Part 2 of 2). 2002–04 Sebring Convertible, Sebring Sedan & Stratus Sedan

POSSIBLE CAUSES
INDICATOR BULB
DIMMER SWITCH HIGH BEAM OUTPUT CIRCUIT OPEN
BODY CONTROL MODULE
JUNCTION BLOCK
MULTI- FUNCTION SWITCH OPEN
INSTRUMENT CLUSTER

TEST	ACTION
1	**NOTE: Ensure that the Junction Block Fuse #11 is not open. If the fuse is open make sure to check for a short to ground.** **NOTE: Ensure that the Exterior High Beam Headlamps operate properly before proceeding with this test.** Turn the ignition on. With the DRBIII® in MIC Actuators, actuate the Hi Beam Lamp. Did the High Beam Indicator illuminate? Yes → Go To 2 No → Go To 6
2	Turn the ignition on. With the DRBIII® in Body Control Inputs/Outputs, read the Hi Beams state while actuating the High Beam Headlamps. Does the DRBIII® Inputs/Outputs display On? Yes → Replace the Instrument Cluster Perform BODY VERIFICATION TEST No → Go To 3
3	Turn the ignition off. Disconnect the Junction Block C6 harness connector. Actuate the High Beam Headlamps. Measure the voltage between the Dimmer Switch High Beam Output circuit and ground at the Junction Block C6 harness connector. Is the voltage above 10.5 volts? Yes → Go To 4 No → Go To 5

CR9090200296010X

Fig. 156 High Beam Indicator Inoperative (Part 1 of 2). 2002–04 Sebring Convertible, Sebring Sedan & Stratus Sedan

TEST	ACTION
4	Turn the ignition off. Disconnect and isolate the Negative Battery cable. Disconnect the Junction Block C6 harness connector. Disconnect the BCM from the Junction Block. Using the Wiring Diagrams as a guide, measure the resistance of the Dimmer Switch High Beam Output circuit through the Junction Block. Is the resistance above 10 ohms? Yes → Replace the Junction Block in accordance with the Service Information. Perform BODY VERIFICATION TEST No → Replace the Body Control Module Perform BODY VERIFICATION TEST
5	Turn the ignition off. Disconnect the Junction Block C6 harness connector. Disconnect the Multi- Function Switch harness connector. Measure the resistance of the Dimmer Switch High Beam Output circuit. Is the resistance above 5.0 ohms? Yes → Repair the Dimmer Switch High Beam Output circuit between the Multi- Function Switch and the Junction Block for an open. Perform BODY VERIFICATION TEST No → Replace the Multi- Function Switch Perform BODY VERIFICATION TEST
6	Turn the ignition off. Remove and inspect the High Beam Indicator bulb and socket. Is the bulb or socket defective? Yes → Replace the High Beam Indicator Bulb or socket Perform BODY VERIFICATION TEST No → Replace the Instrument Cluster Perform BODY VERIFICATION TEST

CR9090200296020X

Fig. 156 High Beam Indicator Inoperative (Part 2 of 2). 2002–04 Sebring Convertible, Sebring Sedan & Stratus Sedan

POSSIBLE CAUSES
DTC PRESENT
INTERMITTENT CONDITION
INDICATOR LED
INSTRUMENT CLUSTER

TEST	ACTION
1	**NOTE: Ensure that the Junction Block Fuse #11 is not open. If the fuse is open make sure to check for a short to ground.** **NOTE: Ensure that there is communication between the PCM, BCM, and the Instrument Cluster before proceeding with this test.** Perform the Instrument Cluster Self Test. Turn the ignition off. Press and hold the Trip/Reset button. Turn the ignition to the Unlock position. During the Self Test all of the Indicators should illuminate for approximately 4 seconds. Observe the Low Fuel Warning Indicator during the Self Test. Did the Low Fuel Warning Indicator illuminate for approximately 4 seconds then turn off? Yes → Go To 2 No → Go To 3
2	Using the DRBIII® read DTC's. Is the DTC FUEL LEVEL SENDING UNIT INOP present? Yes → Refer to symptom list for diagnosis of the DTC. Perform BODY VERIFICATION TEST No → The condition is not present at this time. Monitor DRBIII® parameters while wiggling the related wire harness. Refer to any Technical Service Bulletins (TSB) that may apply. Visually inspect the related wiring harness connector terminals. Perform BODY VERIFICATION TEST
3	Turn the ignition off. Remove and test the Low Fuel Warning Indicator LED. Using a DVOM, select "Diode Mode" and connect the leads across the LED. **NOTE: Ensure that the RED lead is on the "+" of the LED.** Did the Low Fuel Warning Indicator LED illuminate? Yes → Replace the Instrument Cluster Perform BODY VERIFICATION TEST No → Replace the Low Fuel Warning Indicator LED Perform BODY VERIFICATION TEST

CR9090200297000X

Fig. 157 Low Fuel Warning Indicator Not Operating Properly. 2002–04 Sebring Convertible, Sebring Sedan & Stratus Sedan

POSSIBLE CAUSES
DTC PRESENT
INTERMITTENT CONDITION
INDICATOR BULB OR SOCKET
INSTRUMENT CLUSTER

TEST	ACTION
1	**NOTE: Ensure that there is communication between the PCM, BCM, and the Instrument Cluster before proceeding with this test.** Perform the Instrument Cluster Self Test. Turn the ignition off. Press and hold the Trip/Reset button. Turn the ignition to the Unlock position. During the self test all Indicators should illuminate for approximately 4 seconds. Observe the Malfunction Indicator Lamp during the Self Test. Did the Malfunction Indicator Lamp Indicator illuminate for approximately 4 seconds then turn off? Yes → Go To 2 No → Go To 3
2	Using the DRBIII® read DTC's. Are there any DTC's present? Yes → Refer to symptom list for problems related to the DTC. Perform BODY VERIFICATION TEST No → The condition is not present at this time. Monitor DRBIII® parameters while wiggling the related wire harness. Refer to any Technical Service Bulletins (TSB) that may apply. Visually inspect the related wiring harness and connector terminals. Perform BODY VERIFICATION TEST
3	Remove and inspect the Malfunction Indicator Lamp bulb and socket. Is there a problem with the bulb or socket? Yes → Replace the Indicator bulb or socket as necessary Perform BODY VERIFICATION TEST No → Replace the Instrument Cluster Perform BODY VERIFICATION TEST

CR9090200298000X

Fig. 158 Malfunction Indicator Lamp Not Operating Properly. 2002–04 Sebring Convertible, Sebring Sedan & Stratus Sedan

POSSIBLE CAUSES
INTERMITTENT CONDITION
OIL PRESSURE INDICATOR CIRCUIT SHORT TO GROUND
OIL PRESSURE SWITCH ALWAYS CLOSED
OIL PRESSURE SWITCH ALWAYS OPEN
OIL PRESSURE WARNING LAMP INDICATOR BULB OR SOCKET
OIL PRESSURE INDICATOR CIRCUIT SHORT TO VOLTAGE
FUSED IGNITION SWITCH OUTPUT CIRCUIT OPEN
OIL PRESSURE INDICATOR CIRCUIT OPEN
INSTRUMENT CLUSTER

TEST	ACTION
1	**NOTE: Ensure that the engine has normal operating oil pressure before proceeding with test. Refer to the Service Manual for specifications.** Without starting the engine, turn the ignition on. Does the Oil Pressure Indicator illuminate? Yes → Go To 2 No → Go To 4
2	Start the engine. Does the Oil Pressure Indicator turn off? Yes → The condition is not present at this time. Monitor DRBIII® parameters while wiggling the related wire harness. Refer to any Technical Service Bulletins (TSB) that may apply. Visually inspect the related wiring harness and connector terminals. Perform BODY VERIFICATION TEST No → Go To 3
3	Turn the ignition off. Disconnect the Instrument Cluster harness connector. Disconnect the Oil Pressure Switch harness connector. Measure the resistance between ground and the Oil Pressure Switch circuit. Is the resistance below 5.0 ohms? Yes → Repair the Oil Pressure Indicator circuit for a short to ground. Perform BODY VERIFICATION TEST No → Replace the Oil Pressure Switch Perform BODY VERIFICATION TEST

CR9090200299010X

Fig. 159 Oil Pressure Indicator Not Operating Properly (Part 1 of 2). 2002–04 Sebring Convertible, Sebring Sedan & Stratus Sedan

POSSIBLE CAUSES
DTC PRESENT
INTERMITTENT CONDITION
INSTRUMENT CLUSTER

TEST	ACTION
1	**NOTE: Ensure that the correct Instrument Cluster is installed and is correctly configured for the vehicle.** **NOTE: Ensure that there is communication between the MIC, PCM, and the TCM before proceeding with this test.** **NOTE: Diagnose and repair any DTCs before proceeding with this test.** **NOTE: Ensure that the TCM passes the Shift Lever Test with the DRBIII® before proceeding with this test.** Turn the ignition on. With the DRBIII®, read DTCs. Does the DRBIII® display any MIC, PCM, or TCM DTCs? Yes → Refer to symptom list for problems related to DTC's. Perform BODY VERIFICATION TEST No → Go To 2
2	Perform the Instrument Cluster Self Test. Turn the ignition off. Press and hold the Trip Reset button. Turn the ignition on. Observe the PRND / AutoStick VF display during the Self Test. Did any part of the VF display fail to illuminate? Yes → Replace the Instrument Cluster Perform BODY VERIFICATION TEST No → The condition is not present at this time. Monitor DRBIII® parameters while wiggling the related wire harness. Refer to any Technical Service Bulletins (TSB) that may apply. Visually inspect the related wiring harness and connector terminals. Perform BODY VERIFICATION TEST

CR9090200300000X

Fig. 160 PRND Or Autostick Indicator Inaccurate Or Inoperative. 2002–04 Sebring Convertible, Sebring Sedan & Stratus Sedan

TEST	ACTION
4	Remove and inspect the Oil Pressure Warning Indicator Lamp bulb and socket. Is there a problem with the bulb or socket? Yes → Replace the Indicator bulb or socket as necessary in accordance with the Service Information. Perform BODY VERIFICATION TEST No → Go To 5
5	Turn the ignition off. Disconnect the Instrument Cluster harness connector. Disconnect the Oil Pressure Switch harness connector. Turn the ignition on. Measure the voltage between the Oil Pressure Indicator circuit and ground. Is there any voltage present? Yes → Repair the Oil Pressure Indicator circuit for a short to voltage. Perform BODY VERIFICATION TEST No → Go To 6
6	Turn the ignition off. Disconnect the Instrument Cluster harness connector. Turn the ignition on. Using a 12-volt test light connected to ground, check the Fused Ignition Switch Output circuit. Does the test light illuminate brightly? Yes → Go To 7 No → Repair the Fused Ignition Switch Output circuit for an open or high resistance circuit. If the fuse is open make sure to check for a short to ground and repair as necessarv. Perform BODY VERIFICATION TEST
7	Turn the ignition off. Disconnect the Oil Pressure Switch harness connector. Turn the ignition on. Using a 12-volt test light connected to ground, check the Oil Pressure Indicator circuit. Does the test light illuminate brightly? Yes → Go To 8 No → Repair the Oil Pressure Indicator circuit for an open. Perform BODY VERIFICATION TEST
8	Turn the ignition off. Disconnect the Oil Pressure Switch harness connector. Measure the resistance between the Oil Pressure Switch terminal pin and ground. **NOTE: With the engine not running the Oil Pressure Switch should be closed to ground.** Does the Oil Pressure Switch terminal pin have continuity to ground? Yes → Replace the Instrument Cluster in accordance with the Service Information. Perform BODY VERIFICATION TEST No → Replace the Oil Pressure Switch Perform BODY VERIFICATION TEST

CR9090200299020X

Fig. 159 Oil Pressure Indicator Not Operating Properly (Part 2 of 2). 2002–04 Sebring Convertible, Sebring Sedan & Stratus Sedan

POSSIBLE CAUSES
SEAT BELT SWITCH
SEAT BELT SWITCH GROUND CIRCUIT OPEN
SEAT BELT SWITCH SENSE CIRCUIT OPEN
INSTRUMENT CLUSTER

TEST	ACTION
1	Turn the ignition off. Disconnect the Seat Belt Switch harness connector. Connect a jumper wire between cavity 1 and cavity 2. **NOTE: For vehicles equipped with Seat Belt Pre- Tensioner, use the Wiring Diagrams as a guide to ensure proper terminal selection.** Turn the ignition on. Observe the Seat Belt Indicator. Did the Seat Belt Indicator illuminate for approximately 4 seconds and turn off? Yes → Replace the Seat Belt Buckle Perform BODY VERIFICATION TEST No → Go To 2
2	Turn the ignition off. Disconnect the Seat Belt Switch harness connector. Measure the resistance between ground and the Seat Belt Switch Ground circuit. Is the resistance above 5.0 ohms? Yes → Repair the Seat Belt Switch Ground circuit for an open. Perform BODY VERIFICATION TEST No → Go To 3
3	Turn the ignition off. Disconnect the Seat Belt Switch harness connector. Disconnect the Instrument Cluster harness connector. Measure the resistance of the Seat Belt Switch Sense circuit between the Seat Belt Switch connector and the Instrument Cluster connector. Is the resistance above 5.0 ohms? Yes → Repair the Seat Belt Switch Sense circuit for an open. Perform BODY VERIFICATION TEST No → Replace the Instrument Cluster Perform BODY VERIFICATION TEST

CR9090200301000X

Fig. 161 Seat Belt Indicator Always On. 2002–04 Sebring Convertible, Sebring Sedan & Stratus Sedan

POSSIBLE CAUSES
SEAT BELT SWITCH
SEAT BELT SWITCH SENSE CIRCUIT SHORT TO GROUND
SEAT BELT INDICATOR LED
INSTRUMENT CLUSTER

TEST	ACTION
1	**NOTE: Ensure that the Junction Block Fuse #11 is not open. If the fuse is open make sure to check for a short to ground.** **NOTE: Ensure that the Instrument Cluster is configured with the correct code.** Perform the Instrument Cluster Self Test. Turn the ignition off. Press and hold the Trip/Reset button. Turn the ignition to the Unlock position. Observe the Seat Belt Indicator during the Self Test. Did the Seat Belt indicator illuminate for approximately 4 seconds then turn off? Yes → Go To 2 No → Go To 4
2	Turn the ignition off. Disconnect the Seat Belt Switch harness connector. **NOTE: Performing this test on vehicles equipped with Pre- Tensioners will set a DTC in the ACM. Clear codes after repairs are complete.** Turn the ignition on. Observe the Seat Belt Indicator Did the Seat Belt indicator illuminate? Yes → Replace the Seat Belt Buckle Perform BODY VERIFICATION TEST No → Go To 3
3	Turn the ignition off. Disconnect the Instrument Cluster harness connector. Disconnect the Seat Belt Switch harness connector. Measure the resistance between ground and the Seat Belt Switch Sense circuit. Is the resistance below 5.0 ohms? Yes → Repair the Seat Belt Switch Sense circuit for a short to ground. Perform BODY VERIFICATION TEST No → Replace the Instrument Cluster Perform BODY VERIFICATION TEST

CR9090200302010X

Fig. 162 Seat Belt Indicator Inoperative (Part 1 of 2). 2002–04 Sebring Convertible, Sebring Sedan & Stratus Sedan

POSSIBLE CAUSES
DTC PRESENT
INTERMITTENT CONDITION
MISSING OR INCORRECT PINION FACTOR
VEHICLE SPEED MESSAGE
INSTRUMENT CLUSTER

TEST	ACTION
1	Using the DRBIII® read EMIC, PCM, ABS and BCM DTC's. Are there any DTC's present? Yes → Refer to the symptom list for problems related to the DTC. Perform BODY VERIFICATION TEST No → Go To 2
2	Perform the Instrument Cluster Self Test. Turn the ignition off. Press and hold the Trip/Reset button. Turn the ignition to the Unlock position. Observe the Speedometer during the Self Test. The Speedometer should position the indicator needle at the following calibration points: 0, 100, 75, 55, 20, 0 (MPH) Did the Speedometer needle position correctly? Yes → Go To 3 No → Replace the Instrument Cluster Perform BODY VERIFICATION TEST
3	With the DRBIII®, verify that the pinion factor is correctly programmed. Is the pinion factor programmed correctly? Yes → Go To 4 No → Using the Diagnostic (Transmission, or Chassis)/Service Manual Information as a guide, program the correct Pinion Factor. Perform BODY VERIFICATION TEST

CR9090200303010X

Fig. 163 Speedometer Not Operating Properly (Part 1 of 2). 2002–04 Sebring Convertible, Sebring Sedan & Stratus Sedan

TEST	ACTION
4	Turn the ignition off. Remove and test the Seat Belt Indicator LED. Using a DVOM, select "Diode Mode" and connect the leads across the LED. **NOTE: Ensure that the RED lead is on the "+" of the LED.** Did the Seat Belt Indicator illuminate? Yes → Replace the Instrument Cluster Perform BODY VERIFICATION TEST No → Replace the Seat Belt Indicator LED Perform BODY VERIFICATION TEST

CR9090200302020X

Fig. 162 Seat Belt Indicator Inoperative (Part 2 of 2). 2002–04 Sebring Convertible, Sebring Sedan & Stratus Sedan

TEST	ACTION
4	Turn the ignition on. Drive the vehicle With the DRBIII® in Monitors, read the Vehicle Speed in the EMIC, BCM and the PCM. Does the EMIC or BCM Monitor display a different Vehicle Speed than the PCM Wheel Speed? Yes → Refer to symptom list for problems related to inaccurate Vehicle Speed and communications. Perform BODY VERIFICATION TEST No → The condition is not present at this time. Monitor DRBIII® parameters while wiggling the related wire harness. Refer to any Technical Service Bulletins (TSB) that may apply. Visually inspect the related wiring harness and connector terminals. Perform BODY VERIFICATION TEST

CR9090200303020X

Fig. 163 Speedometer Not Operating Properly (Part 2 of 2). 2002–04 Sebring Convertible, Sebring Sedan & Stratus Sedan

POSSIBLE CAUSES
DTC PRESENT
INTERMITTENT CONDITION
INSTRUMENT CLUSTER

TEST	ACTION
1	Using the DRBIII® read EMIC, PCM and BCM DTC's. Are there any DTC's present? Yes → Refer to symptom list for problems related to the DTC. Perform BODY VERIFICATION TEST - VER 1. No → Go To 2
2	Perform the Instrument Cluster Self Test. Turn the ignition off. Press and hold the Trip/Reset button. Turn the ignition to the Unlock position. Observe the Tachometer during the Self Test. The Tachometer should position the indicator needle at the following calibration points: 0, 6000, 3000, 1000, 0 Did the Tachometer needle position correctly? Yes → The condition is not present at this time. Monitor DRBIII® parameters while wiggling the related wire harness. Refer to any Technical Service Bulletins (TSB) that may apply. Visually inspect the related wiring harness and connector terminals. Perform BODY VERIFICATION TEST No → Replace the Instrument Cluster Perform BODY VERIFICATION TEST

CR9090200304000X

Fig. 164 Tachometer Not Operating Properly. 2002–04 Sebring Convertible, Sebring Sedan & Stratus Sedan

BODY VERIFICATION TEST - VER 1

1. Disconnect all jumper wires and reconnect all previously disconnected components and connectors.
2. If the Sentry Key Immobilizer Module (SKIM) or the Powertrain Control Module (PCM) was replaced, proceed to number 6. If the SKIM or PCM was not replaced, continue to the next number.
3. If the Body Control Module was replaced, turn the ignition on for 15 seconds (to allow the new BCM to learn VIN) or engine may not start (if VTSS equipped). If the vehicle is equipped with VTSS, use the DRBIII® and enable VTSS.
4. Program all other options as needed.
5. If any repairs were made to the HVAC System, disconnect the battery or, using the DRBIII®, recalibrate the HVAC doors. Proceed to number 13.
6. Obtain the Vehicle's unique PIN assigned to it's original SKIM from either the vehicle's invoice or from Chrysler's Customer Assistance Center (1-800-992-1997).
7. NOTE: Once Secured Access Mode is active, the SKIM will remain in that mode for 60 seconds.
8. With the DRBIII®, select THEFT ALARM, SKIM, MISCELLANEOUS and select SKIM REPLACED. Enter the 4 digit PIN to put the SKIM in Secured Access Mode.
9. The DRBIII® will prompt for the following steps. (1) Program the country code into the SKIM's memory. (2) Program the vehicle's VIN into the SKIM memory. (3) Transfer the vehicle's Secret Key data from the PCM.
10. Using the DRBIII®, program all customer keys into the SKIM memory. This requires that the SKIM be in Secured Access Mode, using the 4 digit PIN.
11. Note: If the PCM is replaced, the VIN and the unique Secret Key data must be transferred from the SKIM to the PCM. This procedure requires the SKIM to be placed in Secured Access Mode using the 4-digit PIN.
12. Note: After 3 attempts at entering Secured Access Mode with an incorrect PIN, Secured Access Mode will be locked out for 1 hour and the DRBIII® will display "Bus +\- Signals Open" or "No Response". To exit this mode, turn ignition to Run for 1 hour.
13. Ensure that all accessories are turned off and the battery is fully charged.
14. Ensure that the Ignition is on.
15. With the DRBIII®, record and erase all DTCs from ALL modules. Start and run the engine for 2 minutes. Operate all functions of the system that caused the original concern.
16. Turn the ignition off and wait 5 seconds. Turn the ignition on and using the DRBIII®, read DTCs from ALL modules.

Are any DTC's present or is the original condition still present?

Yes → Repair is not complete, refer to appropriate symptom.

No → Repair is complete.

CR9090200285000X

Fig. 165 Body Verification Tests. 2002–04 Sebring Convertible, Sebring Sedan & Stratus Sedan

TECHNICAL DESCRIPTION (COMMENT)

The cause may be a faulty vehicle speed sensor circuit system or a faulty speedometer. Vehicle speed sensor is also used by the engine control module (ECM) <M/T> or powertrain control module (PCM) <A/T>, auto-cruise control-ECU.

TROUBLESHOOTING HINTS

- Malfunction of the vehicle speed sensor
- Malfunction of the combination meter (printed-circuit board or speedometer and tachometer)
- Malfunction of the ECM <M/T> or PCM <A/T>
- Malfunction of the auto-cruise control-ECU
- Damaged harness wires or connectors

DIAGNOSIS

Required Special Tools:

- MB991223: Harness Set
- MB991502: Scan Tool (MUT-II)

⚠ CAUTION

To prevent damage to scan tool always turn the ignition switch to "LOCK" (OFF) position before connecting or disconnecting scan tool.

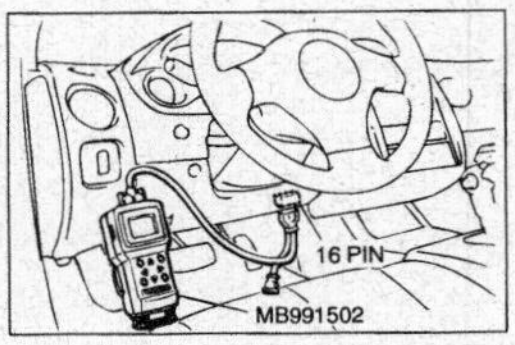

STEP 1. Check the vehicle speed sensor

(1) Connect scan tool MB991502 to the data link connector.
(2) Turn the ignition switch to "ON" position.
(3) Read the MFI system diagnostic trouble code.

Q: Is MFI system DTC P0500 output?

YES : Go to Step 12 .
NO : Go to Step 2 .

STEP 2. Check the odometer and trip odometer operation.

Q: Do the odometer and trip odometer work correctly?

YES : Go to Step 9 .
NO : Go to Step 3 .

STEP 3. Check the combination meter power supply circuit at the combination meter connector C-101.

(1) Disconnect the combination meter connector C-101.
(2) Turn the ignition switch to "ON" position.
(3) Measure the voltage between terminal 52 and ground.

Q: Is the voltage 12 volts (battery positive voltage) between terminal 52 and ground?

YES : Go to Step 6 .
NO : Go to Step 4 .

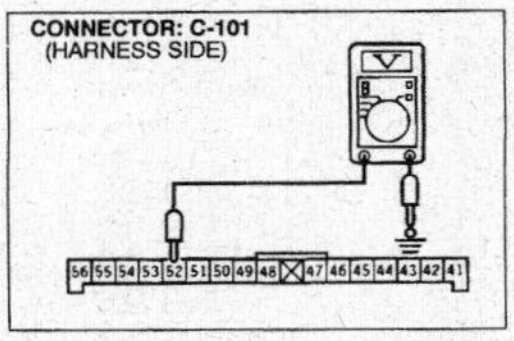

CR9090200210020X

Fig. 166 Speedometer Does Not Work (Part 2 of 14). 2001 Sebring Coupe & Stratus Coupe

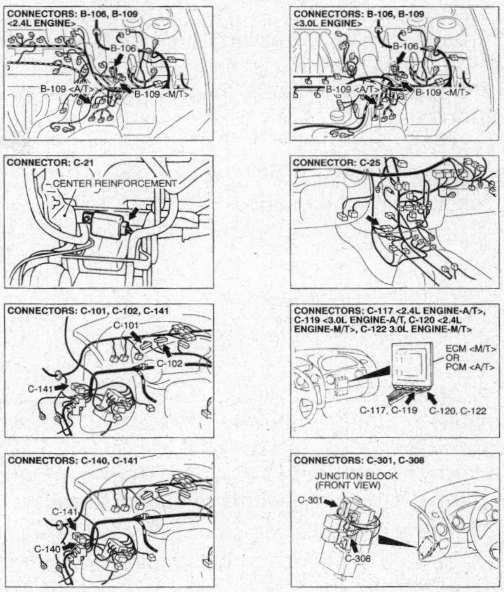

CIRCUIT OPERATION

- The ignition switch (IG1) circuit is the power source for the speedometer and vehicle speed sensor.
- The vehicle speed sensor is installed on the transaxle. Four pulses are generated with one turn of the vehicle speed sensor shaft. These pulse signals are sent into the speedometer. The speedometer calculates the pulse signals, and operates the indicator. At the same time, the travel distance is calculated.

CR9090200210010X

Fig. 166 Speedometer Does Not Work (Part 1 of 14). 2001 Sebring Coupe & Stratus Coupe

STEP 4. Check the combination meter connector C-101 for damage.

Q: Is combination meter connector C-101 in good condition?

YES : Go to Step 5 .
NO : Repair or replace it. The speedometer should work normally.

STEP 5. Check the harness wires between combination meter connector C-101 and ignition switch (IG1).

NOTE: After checking junction block connectors C-301 and C-308, check the wires. If junction block connectors C-301 and C-308 are damaged, repair or replace them.

Q: Is the harness wires between combination meter connector C-101 and ignition switch (IG1) in good condition?

YES : There is no action to be taken.
NO : Repair them. The speedometer should work normally.

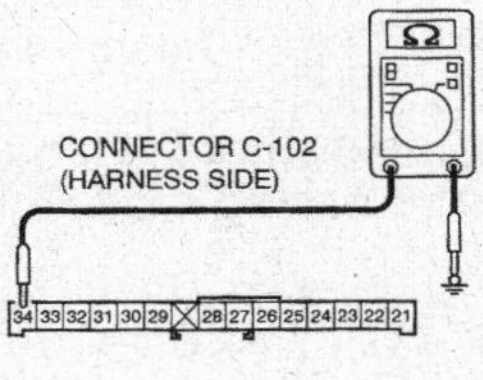

STEP 6. Check the combination meter (speedometer) ground circuit at the combination meter connector C-102.

(1) Disconnect the combination meter connector C-102.
(2) Measure the resistance between terminal 34 and ground.

Q: Is the resistance value less than 2 ohm?

YES : Repair or repair the combination meter (printed-circuit board or speedometer and tachometer). The speedometer should work normally.
NO : Go to Step 7 .

CR9090200210030X

Fig. 166 Speedometer Does Not Work (Part 3 of 14). 2001 Sebring Coupe & Stratus Coupe

STEP 7. Check the combination meter connector C-102 for damage.

Q: Is combination meter connector C-102 in good condition?

YES : Go to Step 8 .

NO : Repair or replace it. The speedometer should work normally.

STEP 8. Check the harness wire between combination meter connector C-102 and ground.

Q: Is the harness wire between combination meter connector C-102 and ground in good condition?

YES : There is no action to be taken.

NO : Repair it. The speedometer should work normally.

CR9090200210040X

Fig. 166 Speedometer Does Not Work (Part 4 of 14). 2001 Sebring Coupe & Stratus Coupe

STEP 11. Check the harness wires between combination meter connector C-102 and vehicle speed sensor connector B-109.

NOTE: After checking intermediate connector B-106<M/T>, C-25, and joint connector C-140, check the wires. If intermediate connector C-25 and joint connector-140 are damaged, repair or replace them.

Q: Are the harness wires between combination meter connector C-102 and vehicle speed sensor connector B-109 in good condition?

YES : There is no action to be taken.

NO : repair them. The speedometer should work normally.

CR9090200210060X

Fig. 166 Speedometer Does Not Work (Part 6 of 14). 2001 Sebring Coupe & Stratus Coupe

STEP 9. Check the combination meter vehicle speed sensor input signal circuit at the combination meter connector C-102.

(1) Disconnect the vehicle speed sensor connector B-109.
(2) Disconnect the combination meter connector C-102.
(3) Turn the ignition switch to "ON" position.

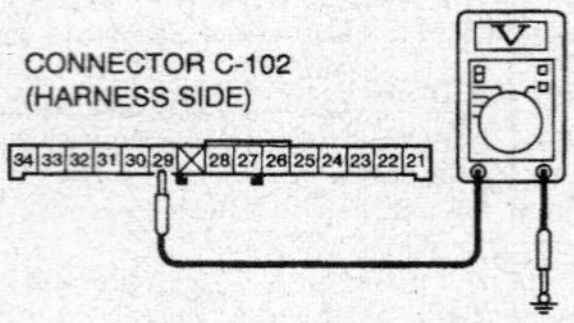

(4) Measure the voltage between terminal 29 and ground.

Q: Is the voltage approximately 5 volts?

YES : Repair or repair the combination meter (printed-circuit board or speedometer and tachometer). The speedometer should work normally.

NO : Go to Step 10 .

STEP 10. Check the combination meter connector C-102 for damage.

Q: Is combination meter connector C-102 in good condition?

YES : Go to Step 11.

NO : Repair or replace it. The speedometer should work normally.

CR9090200210050X

Fig. 166 Speedometer Does Not Work (Part 5 of 14). 2001 Sebring Coupe & Stratus Coupe

STEP 12. Check the vehicle speed sensor power supply circuit at the vehicle speed meter connector B-109.

(1) Disconnect the vehicle speed sensor connector B-109.
(2) Turn the ignition switch to "ON" position.
(3) Measure the voltage between terminal 1 and ground.

Q: Is the voltage approximately 12 volts (battery positive voltage)?

YES : Go to Step 15 .

NO : Go to Step 13 .

STEP 13. Check the vehicle speed sensor connector B-109 damage.

Q: Is vehicle speed sensor connector B-109 in good condition?

YES : Go to Step 14 .

NO : Repair or replace it. The speedometer should work normally.

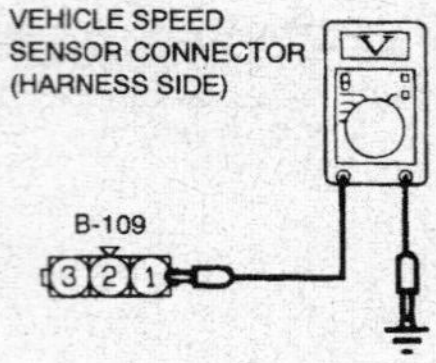

CR9090200210070X

Fig. 166 Speedometer Does Not Work (Part 7 of 14). 2001 Sebring Coupe & Stratus Coupe

STEP 14. Check the harness wires between vehicle speed sensor connector B-109 and ignition switch (IG1).
NOTE: After checking junction block connectors C-301 and C-308, joint connector B-106<M/T>,C-141 and intermediate connector C-25, check the wires. If junction block connectors C-301 and C-308, joint connector C-141 and intermediate connector B-106<M/T>, C-25 are damaged, repair or replace them.

Q: Are the harness wires between vehicle speed sensor connector C-08 and ignition switch (IG1) in good condition?

YES : There is no action to be taken.
NO : Repair them. The speedometer should work normally.

CR9090200210080X

Fig. 166 Speedometer Does Not Work (Part 8 of 14). 2001 Sebring Coupe & Stratus Coupe

STEP 17. Check the harness wire between vehicle speed sensor connector B-109 and ground.

Q: Is the harness wire between vehicle speed sensor connector B-109 and ground in good condition?

YES : There is no action to be taken.
NO : Repair it. The speedometer should work normally.

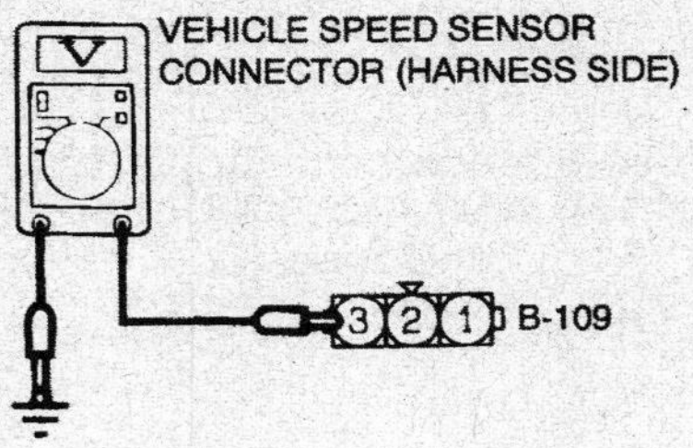

STEP 18. Check the vehicle speed sensor signal circuit at the vehicle speed sensor connector B-109.
(1) Disconnect the vehicle speed sensor connector B-109.
(2) Turn the ignition switch to "ON"
(3) Measure the voltage between terminal 3 and ground.

Q: Is the voltage approximately 9 volts or more?

More than approximately 9 volts : Replace the vehicle speed sensor. The speedometer should work normally.
Approximately 9 volts : Go to Step 19 .

CR9090200210100X

Fig. 166 Speedometer Does Not Work (Part 10 of 14). 2001 Sebring Coupe & Stratus Coupe

STEP 15. Check the vehicle speed sensor ground circuit at the vehicle speed sensor connector B-109.
(1) Disconnect the vehicle speed sensor connector B-109.
(2) Measure the resistance between terminal 2 and ground.

Q: Is the resistance less than 2 ohms?

YES : Go to Step 18 .
NO : Go to Step 16 .

STEP 16. Check the vehicle speed sensor connector B-109 for damage.

Q: Is vehicle speed connector B-109 in good condition?

YES : Go to Step 17.
NO : Repair or replace it. The speedometer should work normally.

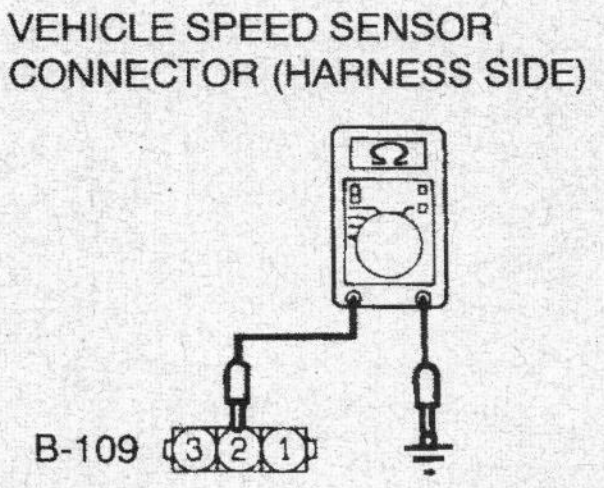

CR9090200210090X

Fig. 166 Speedometer Does Not Work (Part 9 of 14). 2001 Sebring Coupe & Stratus Coupe

STEP 19. Check the vehicle speed sensor connector B-109, auto-cruise control-ECU connector C-21, ECM <M/T> connector C-120 <2.4L-M/T>, C-122 <3.0L-M/T> or PCM <A/T> connector C-117 <2.4L-A/T>, C-119 <3.0L-A/T> and combination meter connector C-102.

CR9090200210110X

Fig. 166 Speedometer Does Not Work (Part 11 of 14). 2001 Sebring Coupe & Stratus Coupe

Q: Are vehicle speed sensor connector B-109, auto-cruise control-ECU connector C-21 ECM <M/T> connector C-120 <2.4L-M/T>, C-122 <3.0L-M/T> or PCM <A/T> connector C-117 <2.4L-A/T>, C-119 <3.0L-A/T> and combination meter connector C-102 in good condition?

YES : Go to Step 20.
NO : Repair or replace it. The speedometer should work normally.

CR9090200210120X

Fig. 166 Speedometer Does Not Work (Part 12 of 14). 2001 Sebring Coupe & Stratus Coupe

STEP 20. Check the harness wires from vehicle speed sensor connector B-109 to auto-cruise control-ECU connector C-21, ECM <M/T> connector C-120 <2.4L-M/T>, C-122 <3.0L-M/T> or PCM <A/T> connector C-117 <2.4L-A/T>, C-119 <3.0L-A/T> and combination meter connector C-102.

NOTE: After checking joint connector C-140 and intermediate connector C-25,check the wires. If joint connector C-140 and intermediate connector C-25 are damaged, repair or replace them.

Q: Are the harness wires from vehicle speed sensor connector B-109 to auto-cruise control-ECU connector C-21, ECM <M/T> connector C-120 <2.4L-M/T>, C-122 <3.0L-M/T> or PCM <A/T> connector C-117 <2.4L-A/T>, C-119 <3.0L-A/T> and combination meter connector C-102 in good condition?

YES : Go to Step 21 .

NO : Repair them. The speedometer should work normally.

CR9090200210130X

Fig. 166 Speedometer Does Not Work (Part 13 of 14). 2001 Sebring Coupe & Stratus Coupe

STEP 21. Check each equipment.
Disconnect auto-cruise control-ECU connector C-21 and combination meter connector C-102 in that order one by one. Then check that MFI system DTC P0500 does not reset under any conditions.

⚠ CAUTION

To prevent damage to scan tool MB991502, always turn the ignition switch to "LOCK" (OFF) position before connecting or disconnecting scan tool MB991502.

(1) Connect scan tool to the data link connector.
(2) Turn the ignition switch to "ON" position.
(3) Read the MFI system diagnostic trouble code.

Q: Does MFI system DTC P0500 reset when one of auto-cruise control-ECU or combination meter, ECM <M/T> or PCM <A/T> is disconnected?

YES : Go to Step 22 .

NO : Replace the auto -cruise control-ECU, combination meter or ECM <M/T> or PCM <A/T> where applicable.The speedometer should work normally.

STEP 22. Recheck for malfunction.

Q: Is a malfunction eliminated?

YES : This diagnosis is complete.(If no malfunctions are not found in all steps, an intermittent malfunction is suspected.

NO : Replace the speedometer

CR9090200210140X

Fig. 166 Speedometer Does Not Work (Part 14 of 14). 2001 Sebring Coupe & Stratus Coupe

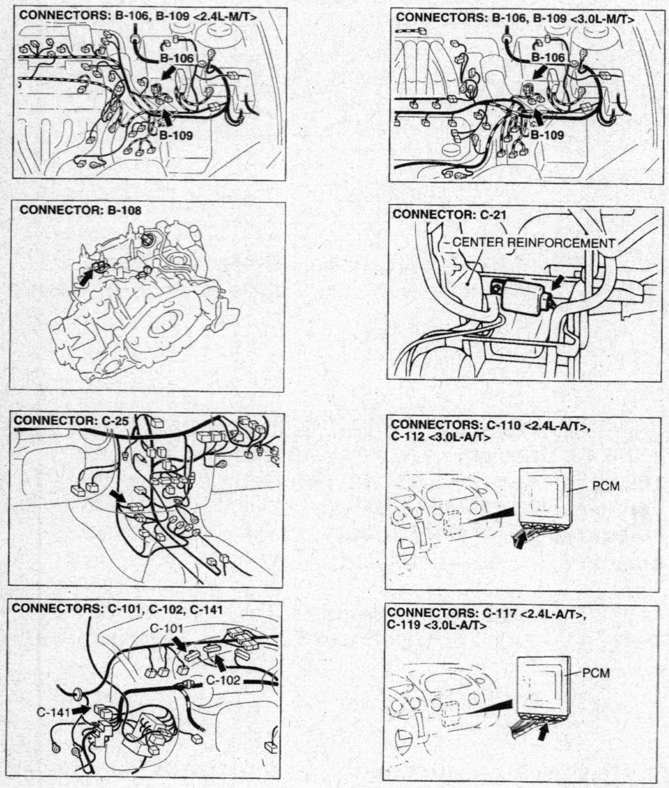

CR9090200217010X

Fig. 167 Speedometer Does Not Work (Part 1 of 28). 2002 Sebring Coupe & Stratus Coupe

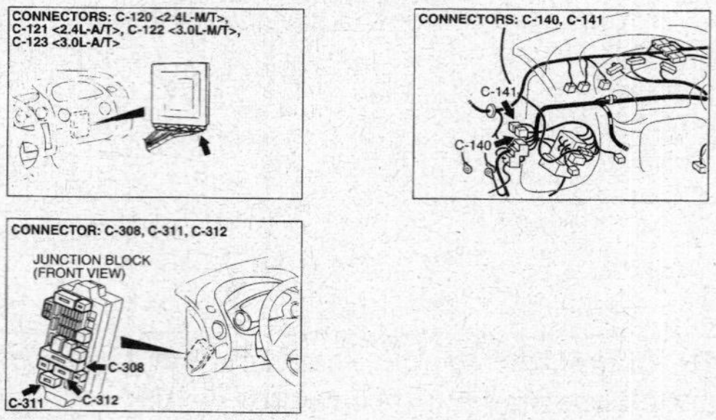

CIRCUIT OPERATION
- The ignition switch (IG1) circuit is the power source for the speedometer and vehicle speed sensor <M/T> or output shaft speed sensor <A/T>.
- The vehicle speed sensor <M/T> or outputshaft speed sensor <A/T> are installed on the transaxle. Four pulses are generated with one turn of the vehicle speed sensor shaft. In case of M/T, these pulse signals are sent into the speedometer. and in case of A/T, these pulse signals are sent into the PCM and sent into the speedometer. The speedometer calculates the pulse signals, and operates the indicator. At the same time, the travel distance is calculated.

TECHNICAL DESCRIPTION (COMMENT)
The cause may be a faulty vehicle speed sensor circuit system or a faulty speedometer. Vehicle speed sensor is also used by the engine control module (ECM) <M/T> or powertrain control module (PCM) <A/T>, auto-cruise control-ECU.

TROUBLESHOOTING HINTS
- Malfunction of the vehicle speed sensor <M/T> or output shaft speed sensor <A/T>
- Malfunction of the combination meter (printed-circuit board or speedometer and tachometer)
- Malfunction of the ECM <M/T> or PCM <A/T>
- Malfunction of the auto-cruise control-ECU
- Damaged harness wires or connectors

DIAGNOSIS

Required Special Tools:
- MB991223: Harness Set
- MB991502: Scan Tool (MUT-II)

CR9090200217020X

Fig. 167 Speedometer Does Not Work (Part 2 of 28). 2002 Sebring Coupe & Stratus Coupe

⚠ CAUTION
To prevent damage to scan tool always turn the ignition switch to "LOCK" (OFF) position before connecting or disconnecting scan tool.

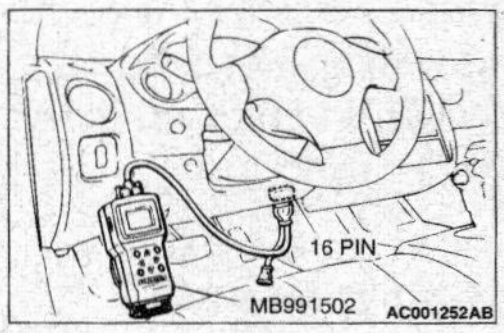

STEP 1. Check the speedometer.

1. Connect scan tool MB991502 to the data link connector.
2. Use scan tool MB991502 to enter a simulated vehicle speed.

Q: Dose the speedometer correspond with the simulated vehicle speed?

YES : Go to Step 2.
NO : Go to Step 4.

STEP 2. Check the vehicle speed sensor

(1) Turn the ignition switch to "ON" position.
(2) Read the MFI system diagnostic trouble code.

Q: Is MFI system DTC P0500 output?

YES :
- For M/T, Go to Step 13.
- For A/T, Go to Step22.

NO : Go to Step 3.

STEP 3. Check the odometer and trip odometer operation.

Q: Do the odometer and trip odometer work correctly?

YES : Go to Step 10.
NO : Go to Step 4.

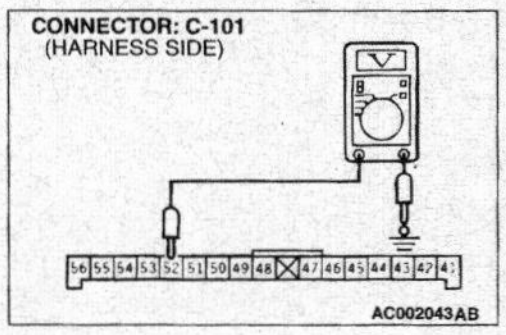

STEP 4. Check the combination meter power supply circuit at the combination meter connector C-101.

(1) Disconnect the combination meter connector C-101.
(2) Turn the ignition switch to "ON" position.
(3) Measure the voltage between terminal 52 and ground.

Q: Is the voltage 12 volts (battery positive voltage) between terminal 52 and ground?

YES : Go to Step 7.
NO : Go to Step 5.

CR9090200217030X

Fig. 167 Speedometer Does Not Work (Part 3 of 28). 2002 Sebring Coupe & Stratus Coupe

STEP 5. Check the combination meter connector C-101 for damage.

Q: Is combination meter connector C-101 in good condition?

YES : Go to Step 6.
NO : Repair or replace it. The speedometer should work normally.

STEP 6. Check the harness wires between combination meter connector C-101 and ignition switch (IG1).

NOTE: After checking junction block connectors C-311 and C-308, check the wires. If junction block connectors C-311 and C-308 are damaged, repair or replace them.

Q: Is the harness wires between combination meter connector C-101 and ignition switch (IG1) in good condition?

YES : There is no action to be taken.
NO : Repair them. The speedometer should work normally.

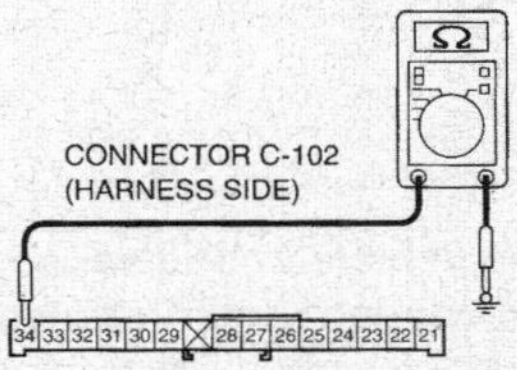

STEP 7. Check the combination meter (speedometer) ground circuit at the combination meter connector C-102.

(1) Disconnect the combination meter connector C-102.
(2) Measure the resistance between terminal 34 and ground.

Q: Is the resistance value less than 2 ohm?

YES : Repair or replace the combination meter (printed-circuit board or speedometer and tachometer). The speedometer should work normally.
NO : Go to Step 8.

CR9090200217040X

Fig. 167 Speedometer Does Not Work (Part 4 of 28). 2002 Sebring Coupe & Stratus Coupe

STEP 8. Check the combination meter connector C-102 for damage.

Q: Is combination meter connector C-102 in good condition?

YES : Go to Step 9.
NO : Repair or replace it. The speedometer should work normally.

STEP 9. Check the harness wire between combination meter connector C-102 and ground.

Q: Is the harness wire between combination meter connector C-102 and ground in good condition?

YES : There is no action to be taken.
NO : Repair it. The speedometer should work normally.

CR9090200217050X

Fig. 167 Speedometer Does Not Work (Part 5 of 28). 2002 Sebring Coupe & Stratus Coupe

STEP 10. Check the combination meter vehicle speed sensor input signal circuit at the combination meter connector C-102.

(1) Disconnect the vehicle speed sensor connector B-109 <MT>.
(2) Disconnect the combination meter connector C-102.
(3) Turn the ignition switch to "ON" position.

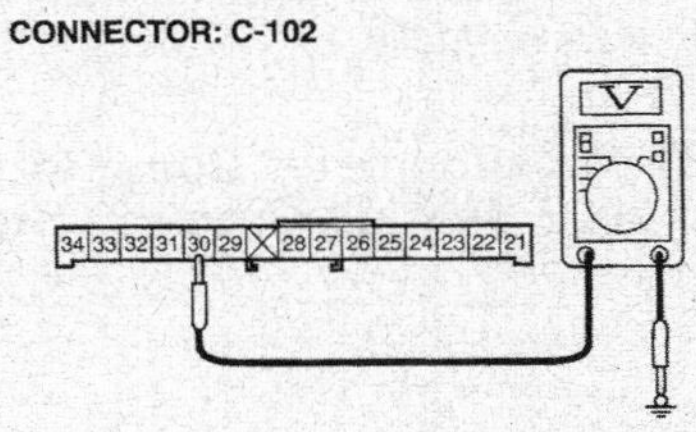

(4) Measure the voltage between terminal 30 and ground.

Q: Is the voltage approximately 5 volts?

YES : Repair or replace the combination meter (printed-circuit board or speedometer and tachometer). The speedometer should work normally.
NO : Go to Step 11.

CR9090200217060X

Fig. 167 Speedometer Does Not Work (Part 6 of 28). 2002 Sebring Coupe & Stratus Coupe

STEP 11. Check the combination meter connector C-102 for damage.

Q: Is combination meter connector C-102 in good condition?

YES : For M/T go to Step 12.
For A/T go to Step 22.

NO : Repair or replace it. The speedometer should work normally.

CR9090200217070X

Fig. 167 Speedometer Does Not Work (Part 7 of 28). 2002 Sebring Coupe & Stratus Coupe

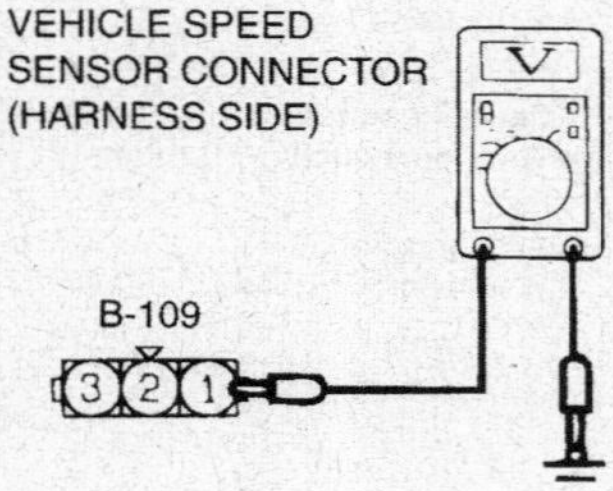

STEP 13. Check the vehicle speed sensor power supply circuit at the vehicle speed meter connector B-109 <M/T>.

(1) Disconnect the vehicle speed sensor connector B-109 <M/T>.
(2) Turn the ignition switch to "ON" position.
(3) Measure the voltage between terminal 1 and ground.

Q: Is the voltage approximately 12 volts (battery positive voltage)?

YES : Go to Step 16.

NO : Go to Step 14.

STEP 14. Check the vehicle speed sensor connector B-109 <M/T> damage.

Q: Is vehicle speed sensor connector B-109 <M/T> in good condition?

YES : Go to Step 15.

NO : Repair or replace it. The speedometer should work normally.

CR9090200217090X

Fig. 167 Speedometer Does Not Work (Part 9 of 28). 2002 Sebring Coupe & Stratus Coupe

STEP 12. Check the harness wires between combination meter connector C-102 and vehicle speed sensor connector B-109 <M/T>.

NOTE: After checking intermediate connector B-106 <M/T>, C-25, and joint connector C-140, check the wires. If intermediate connector C-25 and joint connector C-140 are damaged, repair or replace them.

Q: Are the harness wires between combination meter connector C-102 and vehicle speed sensor connector B-109 in good condition?

YES : There is no action to be taken.

NO : Repair them. The speedometer should work normally.

CR9090200217080X

Fig. 167 Speedometer Does Not Work (Part 8 of 28). 2002 Sebring Coupe & Stratus Coupe

STEP 15. Check the harness wires between vehicle speed sensor connector B-109 <M/T> and ignition switch (IG1).

NOTE: After checking junction block connectors C-311 and C-312, joint connector C-141 and intermediate connector B-106 <M/T>, C-25, check the wires. If junction block connectors C-311 and C-312, joint connector C-141 and intermediate connector B-106 <M/T>, C-25 are damaged, repair or replace them.

Q: Are the harness wires between vehicle speed sensor connector C-08 and ignition switch (IG1) in good condition?

YES : There is no action to be taken.

NO : Repair them. The speedometer should work normally.

CR9090200217100X

Fig. 167 Speedometer Does Not Work (Part 10 of 28). 2002 Sebring Coupe & Stratus Coupe

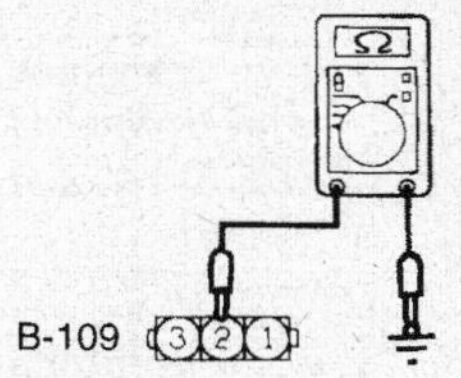

STEP 16. Check the vehicle speed sensor ground circuit at the vehicle speed sensor connector B-109 <M/T>.

(1) Disconnect the vehicle speed sensor connector B-109 <M/T>.

(2) Measure the resistance between terminal 2 and ground.

Q: Is the resistance less than 2 ohm?

YES : Go to Step 19.

NO : Go to Step 17.

STEP 17. Check the vehicle speed sensor connector B-109 <M/T> for damage.

Q: Is vehicle speed connector B-109 <M/T> in good condition?

YES : Go to Step 18.

NO : Repair or replace it. The speedometer should work normally.

CR9090200217110X

Fig. 167 Speedometer Does Not Work (Part 11 of 28). 2002 Sebring Coupe & Stratus Coupe

STEP 18. Check the harness wire between vehicle speed sensor connector B-109 and ground.

NOTE: After checking intermediate connector B-106 <M/T>, check the wires. If jintermediate connector B-106 <M/T> is damaged, repair or replace it.

Q: Is the harness wire between vehicle speed sensor connector B-109 <M/T> and ground in good condition?

YES : There is no action to be taken.

NO : Repair it. The speedometer should work normally.

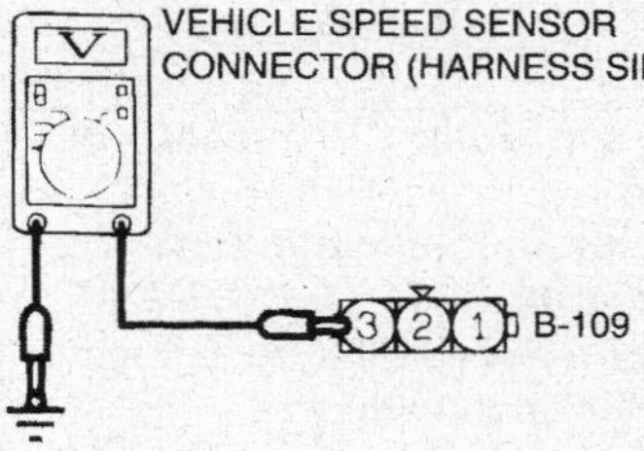

STEP 19. Check the vehicle speed sensor signal circuit at the vehicle speed sensor connector B-109.

(1) Disconnect the vehicle speed sensor connector B-109.

(2) Turn the ignition switch to "ON"

(3) Measure the voltage between terminal 3 and ground.

Q: Is the voltage approximately 9 volts or more?

More than approximately 9 volts : Replace the vehicle speed sensor. The speedometer should work normally.

Approximately 9 volts : Go to Step 20.

CR9090200217120X

Fig. 167 Speedometer Does Not Work (Part 12 of 28). 2002 Sebring Coupe & Stratus Coupe

STEP 20. Check the vehicle speed sensor connector B-109 <M/T>, auto-cruise control-ECU connector C-21, ECM <M/T> connector C-120 <2.4L-M/T>, C-122 <3.0L-M/T> and combination meter connector C-102.

Q: Are vehicle speed sensor connector B-109, auto-cruise control-ECU connector C-21 ECM <M/T> connector C-120 <2.4L-M/T>, C-122 <3.0L-M/T> and combination meter connector C-102 in good condition?

YES : Go to Step 21.

NO : Repair or replace it. The speedometer should work normally.

CR9090200217130X

Fig. 167 Speedometer Does Not Work (Part 13 of 28). 2002 Sebring Coupe & Stratus Coupe

STEP 21. Check the harness wires from vehicle speed sensor connector B-109 <M/T> to auto-cruise control-ECU connector C-21, ECM <M/T> connector C-120 <2.4L-M/T>, C-122 <3.0L-M/T> and combination meter connector C-102.

NOTE: After checking joint connector C-140 and intermediate connector C-25,check the wires. If joint connector C-140 and intermediate connector C-25 are damaged, repair or replace them.

Q: Are the harness wires from vehicle speed sensor connector B-109 to auto-cruise control-ECU connector C-21, ECM <M/T> connector C-120 <2.4L-M/T>, C-122 <3.0L-M/T> and combination meter connector C-102 in good condition?

YES : Go to Step 43.

NO : Repair them. The speedometer should work normally.

CR9090200217140X

Fig. 167 Speedometer Does Not Work (Part 14 of 28). 2002 Sebring Coupe & Stratus Coupe

STEP 22. Using scan tool MB991502, read the A/T diagnostic trouble code.

⚠ CAUTION

To prevent damage to scan tool MB991502, always turn the ignition switch to "LOCK" (OFF) position before connecting or disconnecting scan tool MB991502.

(1) Connect scan tool MB991502 to the data link connector.
(2) Turn the ignition switch to "ON" position.
(3) Read the A/T diagnostic trouble code.
(4) Turn the ignition switch to "LOCK" (OFF) position.

Q: Is A/T diagnostic trouble code number "23" output?

YES : Go to Step 29.
NO : Go to Step 23.

CR9090200217150X

Fig. 167 Speedometer Does Not Work (Part 15 of 28). 2002 Sebring Coupe & Stratus Coupe

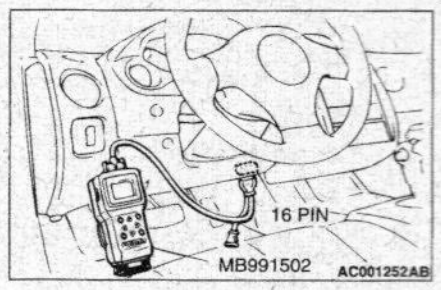

STEP 23. Using scan tool MB991502, check data list item 29: Vehicle Speed Signal.

(1) Start the engine.
(2) Set scan tool MB991502 to data reading mode for item 29: Vehicle Speed Signal.
- Check that the speedometer and scan tool display speed match when driving at a vehicle speed of 40 km/h (25 mph).

(3) Turn the ignition switch to "LOCK" (OFF) position.

Q: Is the sensor operating properly?

YES : This malfunction is intermittent.

NO : Go to Step 24.

STEP 24. Using the oscilloscope, check the waveform at PCM connector C-117 <2.4L> or C-119 <3.0L>.

(1) Do not disconnect connector C-117 <2.4L> or C-119 <3.0L>.

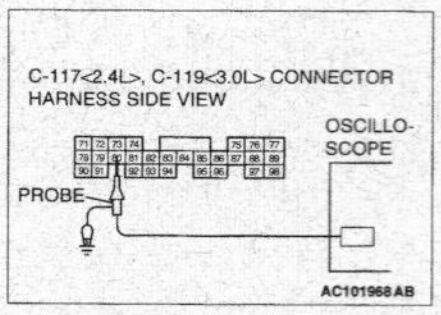

(2) Connect an oscilloscope probe to PCM connector C-117 <2.4L> or C-119 <3.0L> terminal 80 by backprobing.
(3) Start the engine.

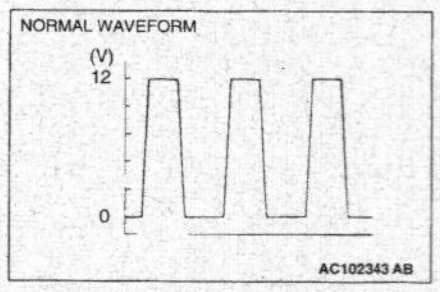

(4) Check the waveform.
- The waveform should show a pattern similar to the illustration when running the vehicle.

(5) Turn the ignition switch to "LOCK" (OFF) position.

Q: Is the waveform normal?

YES : Go to Step 25.
NO : Go to Step 26.

CR9090200217160X

Fig. 167 Speedometer Does Not Work (Part 16 of 28). 2002 Sebring Coupe & Stratus Coupe

STEP 25. Check connector C-117 <2.4L> or C-119 <3.0L> at PCM for damage.

Q: Is the connector in good condition?

YES : Go to Step 28.
NO : Repair or replace it. The speedometer should work normally.

STEP 26. Check the connector C-102 at combination meter for damage.

Q: Are the harness wires in good condition?

YES : Go to Step 27.
NO : Repair or replace it.

CR9090200217170X

Fig. 167 Speedometer Does Not Work (Part 17 of 28). 2002 Sebring Coupe & Stratus Coupe

STEP 27. Check harness wires between combination meter connector C-102 and PCM connector C-117 <2.4L> or 119 <3.0L>.

NOTE: After checking, joint connector C-140 and intermediate connector C-25, check the wires. If joint connector C-140 and intermediate connector C-25 are damaged, repair or replace them.

Q: Is the harness wire in good condition?

YES : Go to Step 28.
NO : Repair it.

CR9090200217180X

Fig. 167 Speedometer Does Not Work (Part 18 of 28). 2002 Sebring Coupe & Stratus Coupe

STEP 28. Using scan tool MB991502, check data list item 29: Vehicle Speed Signal.

⚠ CAUTION

To prevent damage to scan tool MB991502, always turn the ignition switch to "LOCK" (OFF) position before connecting or disconnecting scan tool MB991502.

(1) Connect scan tool MB991502 to the data link connector.
(2) Start the engine.
(3) Set scan tool MB991502 to data reading mode for item 29, Vehicle Speed Signal.
- Check that the speedometer and scan tool display speed match when driving at a vehicle speed of 40 km/h (25 mph).

(4) Turn the ignition switch to "LOCK" (OFF) position.

Q: Is the sensor operating properly?

YES : This malfunction is intermittent.

NO : Replace the PCM.

STEP 29. Using scan tool MB991502, check data list item 23: Output Shaft Speed Sensor.

(1) Set scan tool MB991502 to data reading mode for item 23: Output Shaft Speed Sensor.
- When driving at constant speed of 50km/h (31mph), the display should be "1,600 – 1,900 r/min." <2.4L Engine>, "1,300 – 1,600 r/min." <3.0L Engine> (Gear range: 3rd gear)

(2) Turn the ignition switch to "LOCK" (OFF) position.

Q: Is the sensor operating properly?

YES : This malfunction is intermittent.

NO : Go to Step 30.

CR9090200217190X

Fig. 167 Speedometer Does Not Work (Part 19 of 28). 2002 Sebring Coupe & Stratus Coupe

STEP 30. Check the ground voltage at PCM connector C-110 <2.4L> or C-112 <3.0L> by backprobing.

(1) Do not disconnect connector C-110 <2.4L> or C-112 <3.0L>.
(2) Turn the ignition switch to the "ON" position.
(3) Measure the voltage between terminal 16 and ground by backprobing.
   - Voltage should be 0.5 volt or less.
(4) Turn the ignition switch to the "LOCK" (OFF) position.

Q: Is the voltage normal?

YES : Go to Step 32.
NO : Go to Step 31.

STEP 31. Check connector C-110 <2.4L> or C-112 <3.0L> at PCM for damage.

Q: Is the connector in good condition?

YES : Go to Step 32.
NO : Repair or replace it.

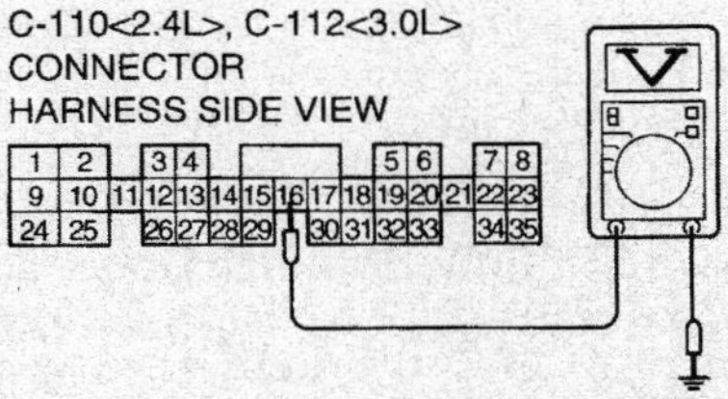

CR9090200217200X

Fig. 167 Speedometer Does Not Work (Part 20 of 28). 2002 Sebring Coupe & Stratus Coupe

STEP 32. Check the sensor output voltage at PCM connector C-121 <2.4L> or C-123 <3.0L> by backprobing.

(1) Do not disconnect connector C-121 <2.4L> or C-123 <3.0L>.
(2) Disconnect connector B-108 at the output shaft speed sensor.
(3) Turn the ignition switch to "ON" position.
(4) Measure the voltage between terminal 104 and ground by backprobing.
   - Voltage should be between 4.9 and 5.1 volts.
(5) Turn the ignition switch to "LOCK" (OFF) position.

Q: Is the voltage normal?

YES : Go to Step 35.
NO : Go to Step 33.

STEP 33. Check connectors C-121 <2.4L> or C-123 <3.0L> at PCM and B-108 at output shaft speed sensor for damage.

Q: Are the connectors in good condition?

YES : Go to Step 34.
NO : Repair or replace it.

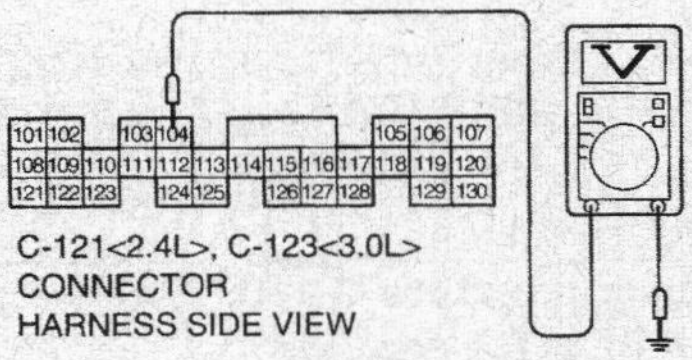

CR9090200217210X

Fig. 167 Speedometer Does Not Work (Part 21 of 28). 2002 Sebring Coupe & Stratus Coupe

STEP 34. Check harness for short circuit to ground between PCM connector C-121 <2.4L> or C-123 <3.0L> terminal 104 and output shaft speed sensor connector B-37 terminal 2.

Q: Is the harness wire in good condition?

YES : Go to Step 35.
NO : Repair it.

CR9090200217220X

Fig. 167 Speedometer Does Not Work (Part 22 of 28). 2002 Sebring Coupe & Stratus Coupe

STEP 35. Using the oscilloscope, check the waveform at PCM connectors C-110, C-121 <2.4L> or C-112, C-123 <3.0L> by backprobing.

(1) Do not disconnect connectors C-110, C-121 <2.4L> or C-112, C-123<3.0L>.

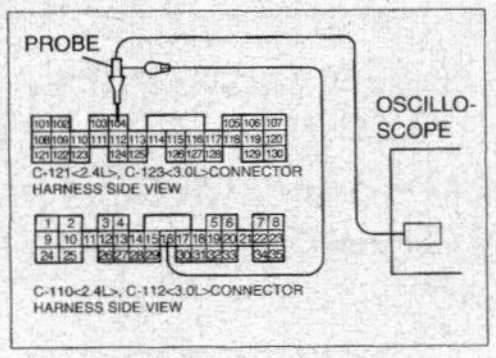

(2) Connect an oscilloscope probe to PCM connector C-110 <2.4L> or C-112 <3.0L> terminal 16 and to PCM connector C-121 <2.4L> or C-123 <3.0L> terminal 104 by backprobing.
(3) Start the engine and run at constant speed of 50km/h (31mph). (Gear range: 3rd gear)

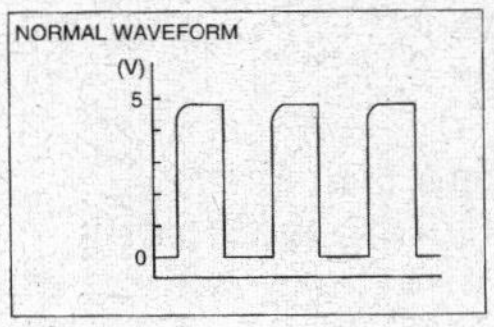

(4) Check the waveform.
   - The waveform should show a pattern similar to the illustration. The maximum value should be 4.8 volts and more and the minimum value 0.8 volts and less. The output waveform should not contain the noise.
(5) Turn the ignition switch to "LOCK" (OFF) position.

Q: Is the waveform normal?

YES : Go to Step 36.
NO : Go to Step 37.

STEP 36. Check connectors C-110, C-121 <2.4L> or C-112, C-123 <3.0L> at PCM for damage.

Q: Are the connectors in good condition?

YES : Go to Step 24.
NO : Repair or replace it.

CR9090200217230X

Fig. 167 Speedometer Does Not Work (Part 23 of 28). 2002 Sebring Coupe & Stratus Coupe

STEP 37. Check connectors C-110, C-121 <2.4L> or C-112, C-123 <3.0L> at PCM and B-108 at output shaft speed sensor for damage.

Q: Are the connectors in good condition?

YES : Go to Step 38.
NO : Repair or replace it.

STEP 38. Check the continuity at output shaft speed sensor connector B-108.

(1) Disconnect connector B108 and measure at the harness side.

HARNESS
CONNECTOR: B-108

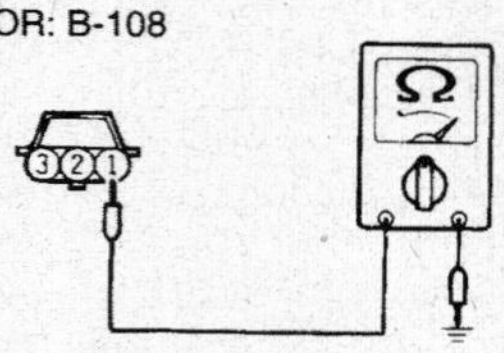

(2) Check for the continuity between terminal 1 and ground.
- Should be less than 2 ohm.

Q: Is the continuity normal?

YES : Go to Step 39.
NO : Go to Step 41.

CR9090200217240X

Fig. 167 Speedometer Does Not Work (Part 24 of 28). 2002 Sebring Coupe & Stratus Coupe

STEP 41. Check connectors C-110, C-121 <2.4L> or C-112, C-123 <3.0L> at PCM for damage.

Q: Are the connectors in good condition?

YES : Go to Step 42.
NO : Repair or replace it.

CR9090200217260X

Fig. 167 Speedometer Does Not Work (Part 26 of 28). 2002 Sebring Coupe & Stratus Coupe

STEP 42. Check harness wires between PCM connectors C-110, C-121 <2.4L> or C-112, C-123 <3.0L> and junction block connector C-311.

Q: Are harness wires between the PCM connectors C-110, C-121 <2.4L> or C-112, C-123 <3.0L> and junction block connector C-311 in good condition?

YES : Go to Step 43.
NO : Repair or replace it.

CR9090200217270X

Fig. 167 Speedometer Does Not Work (Part 27 of 28). 2002 Sebring Coupe & Stratus Coupe

STEP 39. Check the sensor output voltage at output shaft speed sensor connector B-108.

(1) Disconnect connector B-108 and measure at the harness side.
(2) Turn the ignition switch to "ON" position.
(3) Measure the voltage between terminal 2 and ground.
- Voltage should be between 4.9 and 5.1 volts.

(4) Turn the ignition switch to "LOCK" (OFF) position.

Q: Is the voltage normal?

YES : Go to Step 40.
NO : Repair it because of harness open circuit between output shaft speed sensor connector B-37 terminal 2 and PCM connector C-42 terminal 104.

STEP 40. Check the power supply voltage at output shaft speed sensor connector B-108.

(1) Disconnect connector B-108 and measure at the harness side.
(2) Turn the ignition switch to "ON" position.

HARNESS
CONNECTOR: B-108

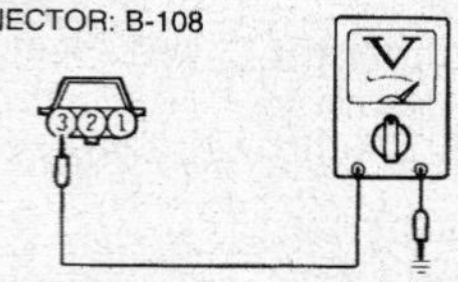

(3) Measure the voltage between terminal 3 and ground.
- Voltage should be battery positive voltage.

(4) Turn the ignition switch to "LOCK" (OFF) position.

Q: Is the voltage normal?

YES : Go to Step 43.
NO : Go to Step 41.

CR9090200217250X

Fig. 167 Speedometer Does Not Work (Part 25 of 28). 2002 Sebring Coupe & Stratus Coupe

STEP 43. Check each equipment.

Disconnect auto-cruise control-ECU connector C-21 and combination meter connector C-102 in that order one by one. Then check that MFI system DTC P0500 does not reset under any conditions.

⚠ CAUTION

To prevent damage to scan tool MB991502, always turn the ignition switch to "LOCK" (OFF) position before connecting or disconnecting scan tool MB991502.

(1) Connect scan tool to the data link connector.
(2) Turn the ignition switch to "ON" position.
(3) Read the MFI system diagnostic trouble code.

Q: Does MFI system DTC P0500 reset when one of auto-cruise control-ECU or combination meter, ECM <M/T> or PCM <A/T> is disconnected?

YES : Go to Step 44.
NO : Replace the auto -cruise control-ECU, combination meter or ECM <M/T> or PCM <A/T> where applicable. The speedometer should work normally.

STEP 44. Recheck for malfunction.

Q: Is a malfunction eliminated?

YES : This diagnosis is complete.(If no malfunctions are not found in all steps, an intermittent malfunction is suspected.
NO : Replace the speedometer.

CR9090200217280X

Fig. 167 Speedometer Does Not Work (Part 28 of 28). 2002 Sebring Coupe & Stratus Coupe

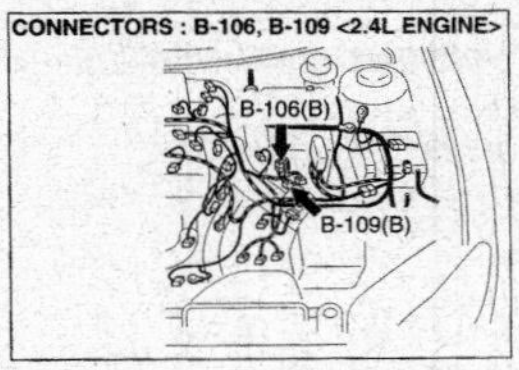

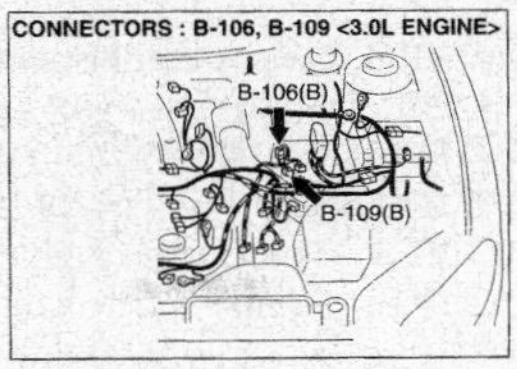

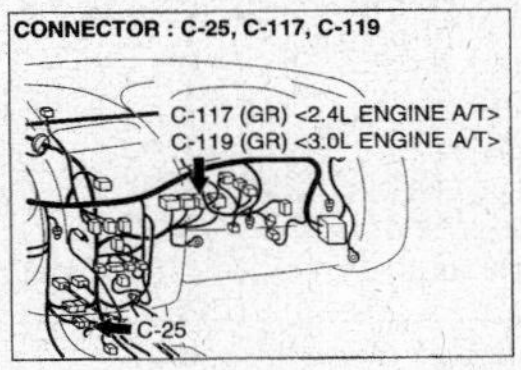

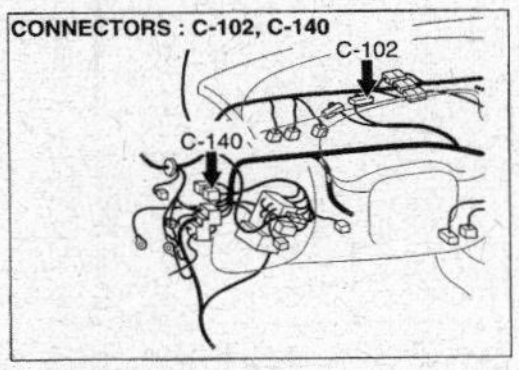

CIRCUIT OPERATION

- The ignition switch (IG1) circuit is the power source for the speedometer and vehicle speed sensor <M/T> or output shaft speed sensor <A/T>.
- The vehicle speed sensor <M/T> or outputs haft speed sensor <A/T> are installed on the transaxle. Four pulses are generated with one turn of the vehicle speed sensor shaft. In case of M/T, these pulse signals are sent into the speedometer, and in case of A/T, these pulse signals are sent into the PCM and sent into the speedometer. The speedometer calculates the pulse signals, and operates the indicator. At the same time, the travel distance is calculated.

TECHNICAL DESCRIPTION (COMMENT)

The cause may be a faulty vehicle speed sensor circuit system or a faulty speedometer. The vehicle speed sensor is also used by the engine control module (ECM) <M/T> or the powertrain control module (PCM) <A/T> or the auto-cruise control-ECU.

TROUBLESHOOTING HINTS

- Malfunction of the vehicle speed sensor <M/T> or output shaft speed sensor <A/T>
- Malfunction of the combination meter (printed-circuit board or speedometer and tachometer)
- Malfunction of the ECM <M/T> or PCM <A/T>
- Malfunction of the auto-cruise control-ECU
- Damaged harness wires or connectors

DIAGNOSIS

Required Special Tools:

- MB991223: Harness Set
- MB991502: Scan Tool (MUT-II)

STEP 1. Check the speedometer by observing the other meters.

Check to see that the tachometer, fuel gauge and water thermometer are operating normally.

Q: Do all other meters operate?

YES <other meters all operate.> : Go to Step 2.
NO <one of the meters do not operate.>

CR9090200219010X

Fig. 168 Speedometer Does Not Work (Part 1 of 4). 2003 Sebring Coupe & Stratus Coupe

STEP 2. Using scan tool MB991502, read the diagnostic trouble code (DTC).

⚠ CAUTION

To prevent damage to the scan tool, always turn the ignition switch to "LOCK" (OFF) position before connecting or disconnecting the scan tool.

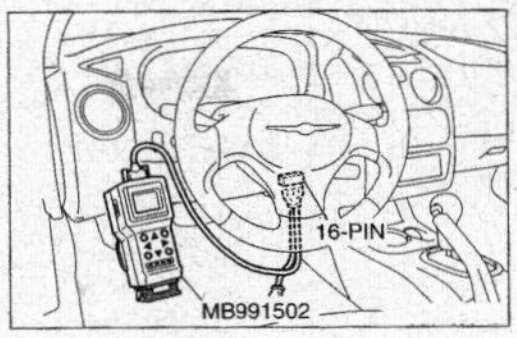

1. Connect scan tool MB991502 to the data link connector.
2. Turn the ignition switch to the "ON" position.
3. Read the MFI system diagnostic trouble code.

Q: Is DTC P0500 set?

YES : Refer to MOTOR's "Domestic Engine Performance & Driveability Manual".
NO : Go to Step 3.

STEP 3. Check combination meter connector C-102, PCM connector C-117 <A/T-2.4 L>, C-119 <A/T-3.0 L> and vehicle speed sensor connector B-109 <M/T> for damage.

Q: Are combination meter connector C-102, PCM connector C-117 <A/T-2.4 L>, C-119 <A/T-3.0 L> and vehicle speed sensor connector B-109 <M/T> in good condition?

YES : Go to Step 4.
NO : Repair or replace the connector(s). The speedometer should work normally.

CR9090200219020X

Fig. 168 Speedometer Does Not Work (Part 2 of 4). 2003 Sebring Coupe & Stratus Coupe

STEP 5. Check the speedometer by operating the auto-cruise control system.

Q: Does auto-cruise control work?

YES : Replace the combination meter. The speedometer should work normally.
NO : Replace the vehicle speed sensor <M/T> or PCM <A/T>. The speedometer should work normally.

CR9090200219040X

Fig. 168 Speedometer Does Not Work (Part 4 of 4). 2003 Sebring Coupe & Stratus Coupe

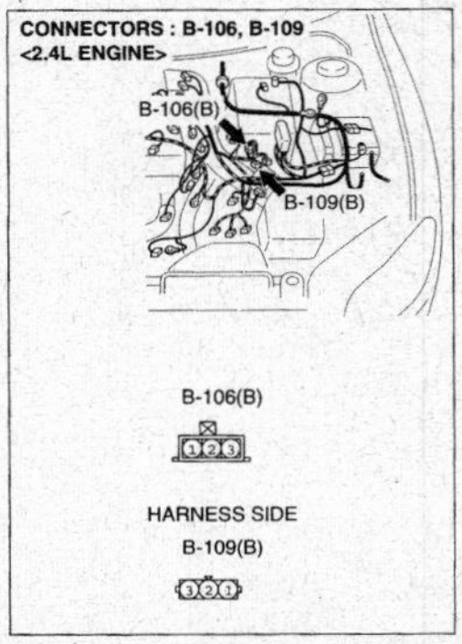

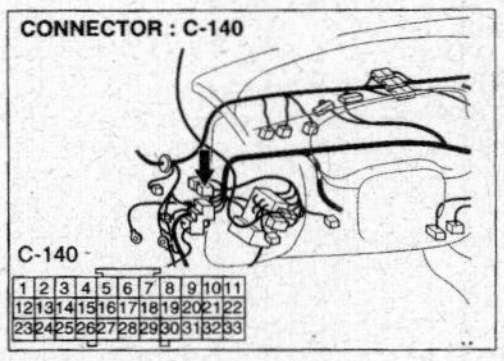

STEP 4. Check the wiring harnesses between combination meter connector C-102 (terminal 44) and PCM connector C-117 <A/T-2.4 L> (terminal 80), C-119 <A/T-3.0 L> (terminal 80) or vehicle speed sensor connector B-109 <M/T> (terminal 3).

NOTE: Also check intermediate connectors B-106 <M/T>, C-25 and joint connector C-140. If intermediate connectors B-106 <M/T>, C-25 or joint connector C-140 are damaged, repair or replace the connector

Q: Are the wiring harnesses between combination meter connector C-102 (terminal 44) and PCM connector C-117 <A/T-2.4 L> (terminal 80), C-119 <A/T-3.0 L> (terminal 80) or vehicle speed sensor connector B-109 <M/T> (terminal 3) in good condition?

YES : Go to Step 5.
NO : Repair the wiring harness(es). The speedometer should work normally.

CR9090200219030X

Fig. 168 Speedometer Does Not Work (Part 3 of 4). 2003 Sebring Coupe & Stratus Coupe

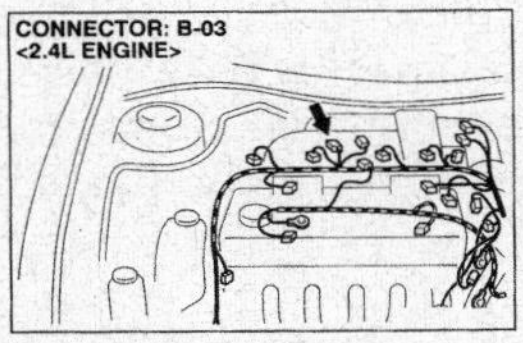

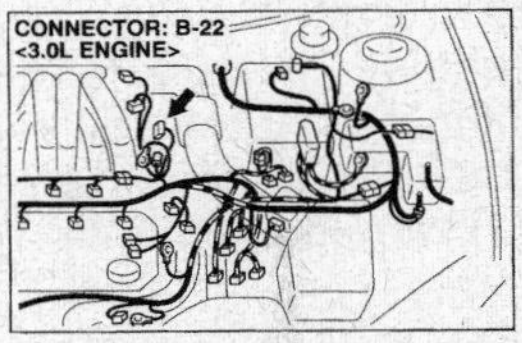

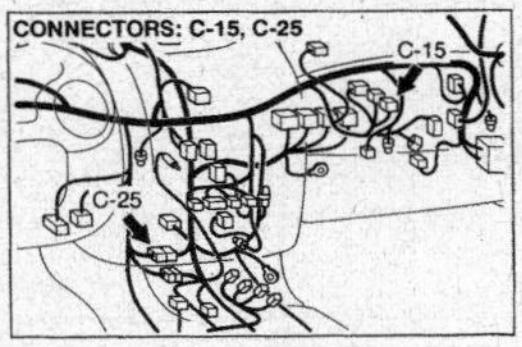

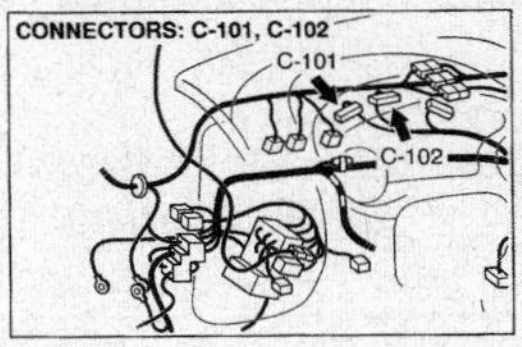

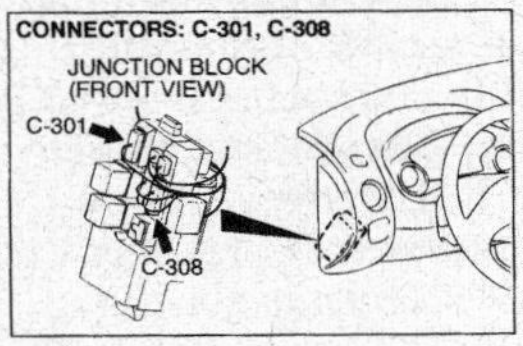

CIRCUIT OPERATION

- The tachometer power is supplied from the ignition switch (IG) circuit.
- For vehicles with 2.4L engine, the tachometer detects the ignition signal by the engine control module via the ignition failure sensor.
- For vehicles with 3.0L engine, the tachometer detects the ignition signal control via the distributor assembly.

TECHNICAL DESCRIPTION (COMMENT)

The ignition signal may not be sent from the engine, or there may be a malfunction in the power supply or ground circuit.

TROUBLESHOOTING HINTS

- Malfunction of the combination meter (printed circuit board or speedometer and tachometer)
- Damaged harness wires or connectors

DIAGNOSIS

Required Special Tools:

- MB991223: Harness Set
- MB991502: Scan Tool (MUT-II)

CR9090200211010X

Fig. 169 Tachometer Does Not Work (Part 1 of 5). 2001 Sebring Coupe & Stratus Coupe

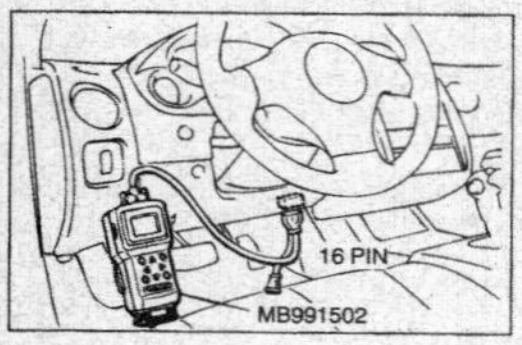

⚠ CAUTION
To prevent damage to scan tool MB991502, always turn the ignition switch to "LOCK" (OFF) position before connecting or disconnecting scan tool.

STEP 1. Check the vehicle speed sensor
(1) Connect scan tool MB991502 to the data link connector.
(2) Turn the ignition switch to "ON" position.
(3) Read the MFI system diagnostic trouble code.

Q: Is MFI system DTC P0300 output?
YES : Refer to MOTOR's "Domestic Engine Performance & Driveability Manual".
NO : Go to Step 2 .

STEP 2. Check the speedometer operation.
Q: Does the speedometer work normally?
YES : Inspect speedometer.
NO : Go to Step 3 .

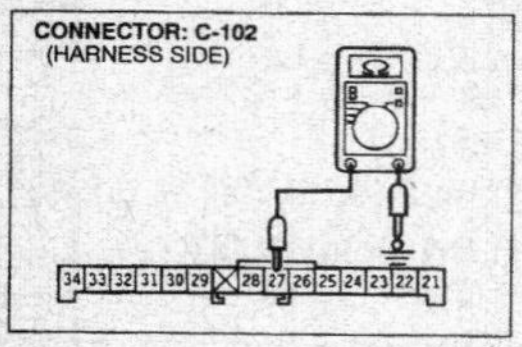

STEP 3. Check the combination meter (tachometer) ground circuit at the combination meter connector C-102.
(1) Disconnect the combination meter connector C-102.
(2) Measure the resistance between terminal 27 and ground.

Q: Is the resistance less than 2 ohms?
YES : Go to Step 6 .
NO : Go to Step 4 .

STEP 4. Check the combination meter connector C-102 for damage.
Q: Is combination meter connector C-102 in good condition?
YES : Go to Step 5.
NO : Repair or replace it. The tachometer should work normally.

STEP 5. Check the harness wires between combination meter connector C-102 and ground.
Q: Is the harness wires between combination meter connector C-102 and ground in good condition?
YES : There is no action to be taken.
NO : Repair it. The tachometer should work normally.

CR9090200211020X

Fig. 169 Tachometer Does Not Work (Part 2 of 5). 2001 Sebring Coupe & Stratus Coupe

STEP 6. Check the ignition signal input circuit at the combination meter connector C-102.
(1) Disconnect the combination meter connector C-102.
(2) Start the engine and run at idle.
(3) Measure the voltage between terminal 33 and ground.

Q: Is the voltage approximately 10 volts?
YES : Repair or repair the combination meter (printed-circuit board or speedometer and tachometer).
NO : Go to Step 7 .

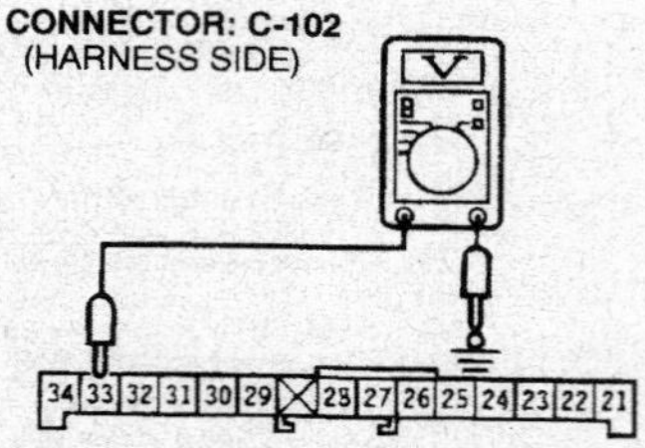

CR9090200211030X

Fig. 169 Tachometer Does Not Work (Part 3 of 5). 2001 Sebring Coupe & Stratus Coupe

STEP 7. Check the ignition failure sensor connector B-03 <2.4L engine>, distributor assembly connector B-22 <3.0L engine>, automatic compressor controller connector C-15 <3.0L engine> and combination meter connector C-102 for damage.

Q: Are ignition failure sensor connector B-03 <2.4L engine>, distributor assembly connector B-22 <3.0L engine>, automatic compressor controller connector C-15 <3.0L engine> and combination meter connector C-102 in good condition?
YES : Go to Step 8 .
NO : Repair or replace it. The tachometer should work normally.

CR9090200211040X

Fig. 169 Tachometer Does Not Work (Part 4 of 5). 2001 Sebring Coupe & Stratus Coupe

STEP 8. Check the harness wires from combination meter connector C-102 to ignition failure sensor connector B-03 <2.4L engine>, distributor assembly connector B-22 <3.0L engine> and automatic compressor controller connector C-15 <3.0L engine>.
NOTE: After checking intermediate connector C-25, check the wires. If intermediate connector C-25 is damaged, repair or replace it.

Q: Are the harness wires from combination meter connector C-102 to ignition failure sensor connector B-03 <2.4L engine>, distributor assembly connector B-22 <3.0L engine> and automatic compressor controller connector C-15 <3.0L engine> in good condition?
YES : There is no action to be taken.
NO : Repair it. The tachometer should work normally.

CR9090200211050X

Fig. 169 Tachometer Does Not Work (Part 5 of 5). 2001 Sebring Coupe & Stratus Coupe

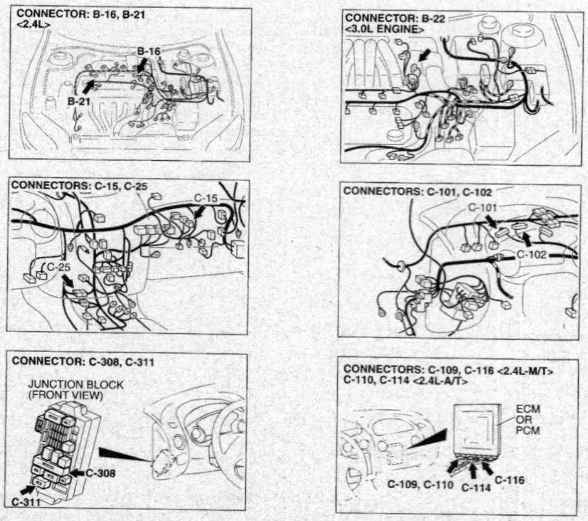

CIRCUIT OPERATION
- The tachometer power is supplied from the ignition switch (IG) circuit.
- For vehicles with 2.4L engine, the tachometer detects the ignition signal by the engine control module via the ignition coils.
- For vehicles with 3.0L engine, the tachometer detects the ignition signal control via the distributor assembly.

TECHNICAL DESCRIPTION (COMMENT)
The ignition signal may not be sent from the engine, or there may be a malfunction in the power supply or ground circuit.

TROUBLESHOOTING HINTS
- Malfunction of the combination meter (printed circuit board or speedometer and tachometer)
- Damaged harness wires or connectors
- Malfunction of the ECM <M/T> or PCM <A/T>

DIAGNOSIS
Required Special Tools:
- MB991223: Harness Set
- MB991502: Scan Tool (MUT-II)

CR9090200218010X

Fig. 170 Tachometer Does Not Work (Part 1 of 10). 2002 Sebring Coupe & Stratus Coupe

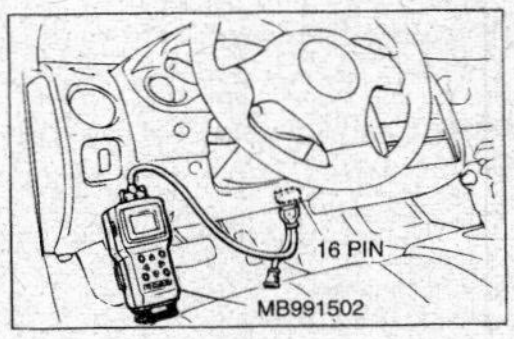

STEP 1. Check the MFI system

⚠ **CAUTION**

To prevent damage to scan tool MB991502, always turn the ignition switch to "LOCK" (OFF) position before connecting or disconnecting scan tool.

(1) Connect scan tool MB991502 to the data link connector.
(2) Turn the ignition switch to "ON" position.
(3) Read the MFI system diagnostic trouble code.

Q: Is MFI system DTC P0300 output?
YES : Check the MFI system, Go to Step 9.
NO : Go to Step 2.

STEP 2. Check the speedometer operation.

Q: Does the speedometer work normally?
YES : Inspect speedometer.
NO : Go to Step 3.

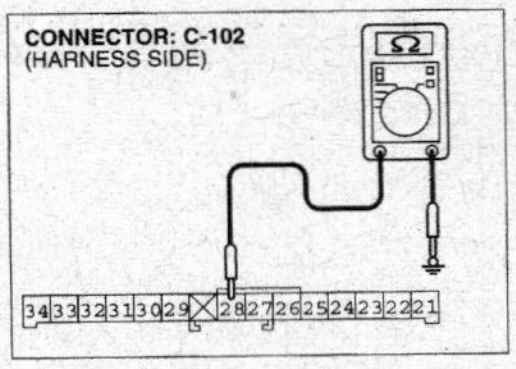

STEP 3. Check the combination meter (tachometer) ground circuit at the combination meter connector C-102.

(1) Disconnect the combination meter connector C-102.
(2) Measure the resistance between terminal 28 and ground.

Q: Is the resistance less than 2 ohm?
YES : Go to Step 6.
NO : Go to Step 4.

STEP 4. Check the combination meter connector C-102 for damage.

Q: Is combination meter connector C-102 in good condition?
YES : Go to Step 5.
NO : Repair or replace it. The tachometer should work normally.

CR9090200218020X

Fig. 170 Tachometer Does Not Work (Part 2 of 10). 2002 Sebring Coupe & Stratus Coupe

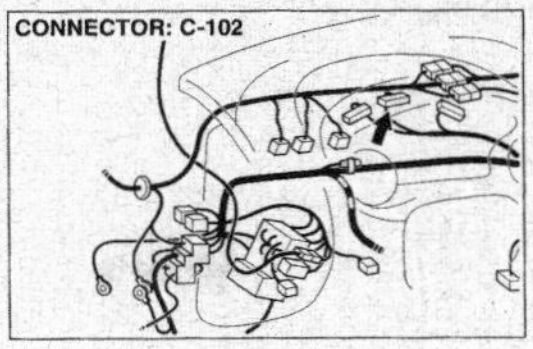

STEP 5. Check the harness wires between combination meter connector C-102 and ground.

Q: Is the harness wires between combination meter connector C-102 and ground in good condition?
YES : There is no action to be taken.
NO : Repair it. The tachometer should work normally.

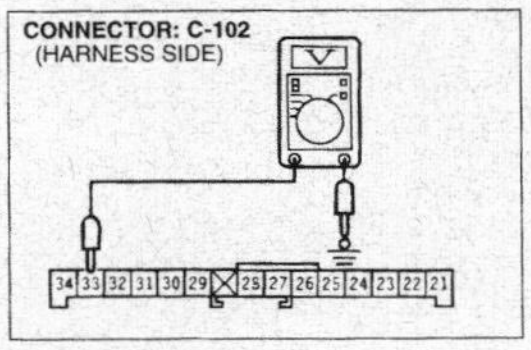

STEP 6. Check the ignition signal input circuit at the combination meter connector C-102.

(1) Disconnect the combination meter connector C-102.
(2) Start the engine and run at idle.
(3) Measure the voltage between terminal 33 and ground.

Q: Is the voltage approximately 10 volts?
YES : Repair or replace the combination meter. (printed-circuit board or speedometer and tachometer)
NO : Go to Step 7.

CR9090200218030X

Fig. 170 Tachometer Does Not Work (Part 3 of 10). 2002 Sebring Coupe & Stratus Coupe

STEP 7. Check the ECM connector C-116 <2.4L M/T> or PCM connector C-114 <2.4L A/T>, distributor assembly connector B-22 <3.0L engine>, automatic compressor controller connector C-15 <3.0L engine> and combination meter connector C-102 for damage.

Q: Are ECM connector C-116 <2.4L M/T> or PCM connector C-114 <2.4L A/T>, distributor assembly connector B-22 <3.0L engine>, automatic compressor controller connector C-15 <3.0L engine> and combination meter connector C-102 in good condition?
YES : Go to Step 8.
NO : Repair or replace them. The tachometer should work normally.

CR9090200218040X

Fig. 170 Tachometer Does Not Work (Part 4 of 10). 2002 Sebring Coupe & Stratus Coupe

STEP 8. Check the harness wires from combination meter connector C-102 to ECM connector C-116 <2.4L M/T> or PCM connector C-114 <2.4L A/T>, distributor assembly connector B-22 <3.0L engine> and automatic compressor controller connector C-15 <3.0L engine>.

NOTE: After checking intermediate connector C-25, check the wires. If intermediate connector C-25 is damaged, repair or replace it.

Q: Are the harness wires from combination meter connector C-102 to ignition failure sensor connector B-03 <2.4L engine>, distributor assembly connector B-22 <3.0L engine> and automatic compressor controller connector C-15 <3.0L engine> in good condition?
YES : There is no action to be taken.
NO : Repair it. The tachometer should work normally.

CR9090200218050X

Fig. 170 Tachometer Does Not Work (Part 5 of 10). 2002 Sebring Coupe & Stratus Coupe

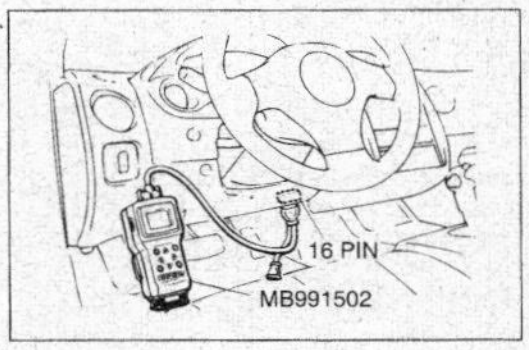

STEP 9. Using scan tool MB991502, check data list item 22: Crankshaft Position Sensor.

(1) Start the engine and run at idle.
(2) Set scan tool MB991502 to the data reading mode for item 22, Crankshaft Position Sensor.
(3) Check the waveform of the crankshaft position sensor while keeping the engine speed constant.
- The pulse width should be constant.
(4) Turn the ignition switch to the "LOCK" (OFF) position.

Q: Is the sensor operating properly?
YES : Go to Step 10.
NO : Refer to MOTOR's "Domestic Engine Performance & Driveability Manual".

STEP 10. Using scan tool MB991502, check data list item 81: Long - Term Fuel Compensation (trim).

(1) Start the engine and run at idle.
(2) Set scan tool MB991502 to the data reading mode for item 81, Long – Term Fuel Compensation (trim).
- The fuel trim should be between -12.5 and +12.5 when the load is 2,500 r/min (during closed loop) after the engine is warmed.
(3) Turn the ignition switch to the "LOCK" (OFF) position.

Q: Is the specification normal?
YES : Go to Step 11.
NO : Refer to MOTOR's "Domestic Engine Performance & Driveability Manual".

CR9090200218060X

Fig. 170 Tachometer Does Not Work (Part 6 of 10). 2002 Sebring Coupe & Stratus Coupe

STEP 11. Using scan tool MB991502, check data list item 82: Short - Term Fuel Compensation (trim).
(1) Start the engine and run at idle.
(2) Set scan tool MB991502 to the data reading mode for item 82, Short – Term Fuel Compensation (trim).
- The fuel trim should be between -25 and +16.8 when the load is 2,500 r/min (during closed loop) after the engine is warmed.

(3) Turn the ignition switch to the "LOCK" (OFF) position.

Q: Is the specification normal?
YES : Go to Step 12.
NO : Refer to MOTOR's "Domestic Engine Performance & Driveability Manual".

STEP 12. Check the ignition coil spark
(1) Check each ignition coil spark.
(2) Remove the intake manifold.
(3) Remove the spark plug and connect to the spark plug cable.
(4) Ground the spark plug side electrode securely.
- When the engine is cranked, the spark plug should spark.

Q: Did it spark?
YES : Go to Step 15.
NO : Go to Step 13.

STEP 13. Check the spark plugs.

⚠ CAUTION
Do not attempt to adjust the gap of the platinum plug. Cleaning of the platinum plug may result in damage to the platinum tips. Therefore, if carbon deposits must be removed, use a plug cleaner and complete cleaning within 20 seconds to protect the electrode. Do not use a wire brush.
(1) Check the plug gap and replace if the limit is exceeded.
Standard value: 1.0 – 1.1 mm (0.039 – 0.043 inch)
Limit: 1.3 mm (0.051 inch)

Q: Is the plug gap at the standard value?
YES : Go to Step 14.
NO : Replace the faulty spark plug. Then go to Step 1.

CR9090200218070X

Fig. 170 Tachometer Does Not Work (Part 7 of 10). 2002 Sebring Coupe & Stratus Coupe

STEP 17. Check connector C-109 at ECM <M/T> or connector C-110 at PCM <A/T> and ignition coil connector B-16 and B-21 for damage <2.4L engine>.
Q: Is the connector in good condition?
YES : Go to Step 18.
NO : Refer to MOTOR's "Domestic Engine Performance & Driveability Manual".

STEP 18. Check for harness damage between ignition coil B-16, B-21 and ECM connector C-109 <M/T> or PCM connector C-110<A/T>.
Q: Is the harness wire in good condition?
YES : Go to Step 19.
NO : Repair it. Then go to Step 1.

CR9090200218090X

Fig. 170 Tachometer Does Not Work (Part 9 of 10). 2002 Sebring Coupe & Stratus Coupe

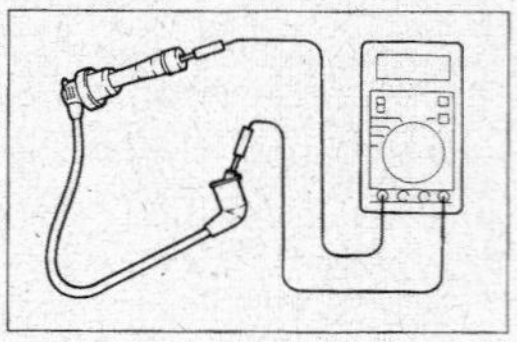

STEP 14. Check the spark plug cable.
(1) Check the cap and coating for cracks.
(2) Measure the resistance.
Limit: maximum 22 kΩ
Q: Is the resistance normal?
YES : Refer to MOTOR's "Domestic Engine Performance & Driveability Manual".
NO : Replace the faulty spark plug cable. Then go to Step 1.

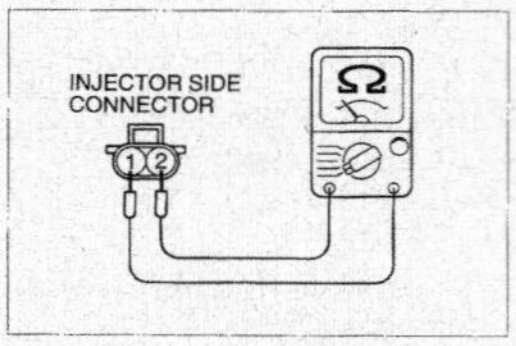

STEP 15. Check the injector.
(1) Disconnect the injector connector.
(2) Measure the resistance between each injector side connector terminal 1 and 2.
Standard value: 13 – 16 ohm [at 20° C (68° F)]
Q: Is the resistance standard value?
YES : Go to Step 16.
NO : Replace the faulty injector. Then go to Step 1.

STEP 16. Check connector at injector for damage.
Q: Is the connector in good condition?
YES :
- Go to Step 17 <2.4L engine>.
- Go to Step 20 <3.0L engine>.

NO : Repair or replace the faulty injector. Then go to Step 21.

CR9090200218080X

Fig. 170 Tachometer Does Not Work (Part 8 of 10). 2002 Sebring Coupe & Stratus Coupe

STEP 19. Check the following items.
(1) Check the following items, and repair or replace the defective component.
a. Check for skipped timing belt teeth.
b. Check compression.
c. EGR valve failed.

Q: Are there any abnormalities?
YES : Go to Step 20.
NO : Repair or replace it. Then go to Step 1.

STEP 20. Replace the injector.
(1) Replace the injector.
(2) Carry out a test drive with the drive cycle pattern.
(3) Check the diagnostic trouble code (DTC).

Q: Is the DTC P0300 is output?
YES : Replace the ECM or PCM. Then go to Step 1.
NO : The inspection is complete.

CR9090200218100X

Fig. 170 Tachometer Does Not Work (Part 10 of 10). 2002 Sebring Coupe & Stratus Coupe

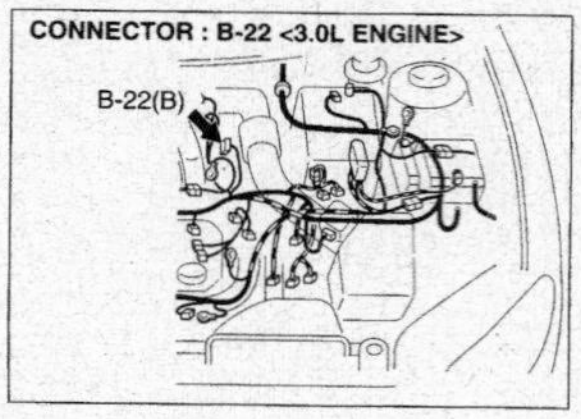

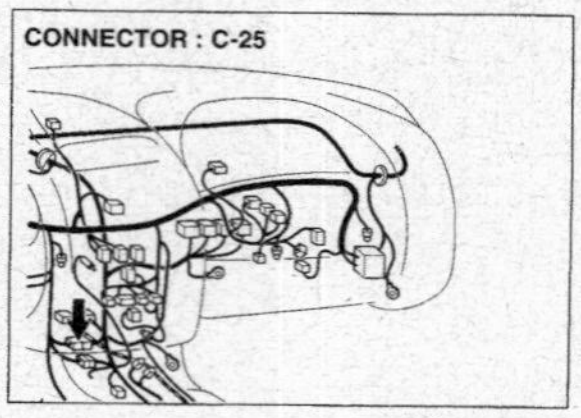

CR9090200220010X

Fig. 171 Tachometer Does Not Work (Part 1 of 5). 2003 Sebring Coupe & Stratus Coupe

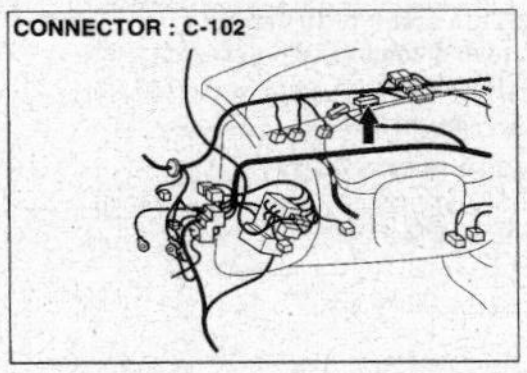

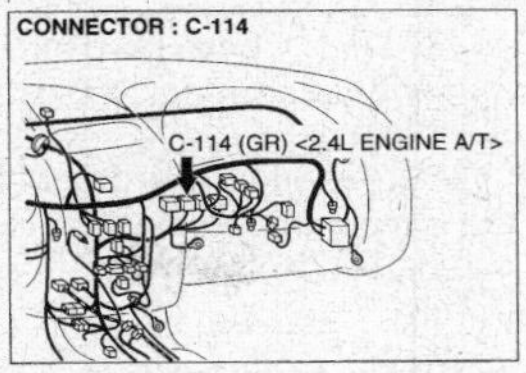

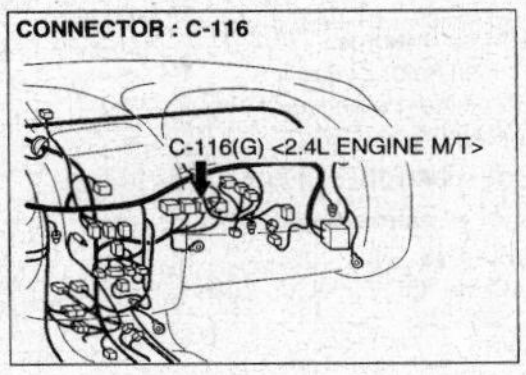

CIRCUIT OPERATION

- The tachometer power is supplied from the ignition switch (IG) circuit.
- For vehicles with 2.4L engine, the tachometer detects the ignition signal by the engine control module <M/T> or power control module <A/T> via the ignition coils.
- For vehicles with 3.0L engine, the tachometer detects the ignition signal control via the distributor assembly.

TECHNICAL DESCRIPTION (COMMENT)

The cause is thought to be because vehicle speed sensor <M/T> or PCM <A/T> signals are not transmitted or due to combination meter error.

TROUBLESHOOTING HINTS

- Malfunction of the combination meter (printed circuit board or speedometer and tachometer)
- Malfunction of the ECM <2.4L engine - M/T>
- Malfunction of the PCM <2.4L engine - A/T>
- Malfunction of the distributor <3.0L engine>
- Damaged wiring harness or connectors

DIAGNOSIS

Required Special Tools:

- MB991223: Harness Set
- MB991502: Scan Tool (MUT-II)

STEP 1. Check the tachometer by observing the other meters.

Check to see that the speedometer, fuel gauge and water thermometer operate normally.

Q: Do all other meters operate?

YES <other meters all operate> : Go to Step 2.
NO <one of the meters does not operate>

CR9090200220020X

Fig. 171 Tachometer Does Not Work (Part 2 of 5). 2003 Sebring Coupe & Stratus Coupe

STEP 2. Using scan tool MB991502, read the diagnostic trouble code (DTC).

⚠ CAUTION

To prevent damage to scan tool MB991502, always turn the ignition switch to "LOCK" (OFF) position before connecting or disconnecting scan tool.

(1) Connect scan tool MB991502 to the data link connector.
(2) Turn the ignition switch to "ON" position.
(3) Read the MFI system diagnostic trouble code.

Q: Are MFI system - related DTC(s) set?

YES : Refer to MOTOR's "Domestic Engine Performance & Driveability Manual".

NO : Go to Step 3.

STEP 3. Check combination meter connector C-102, ECM connector C-116 <M/T-2.4 L>, PCM connector C-114 <A/T-2.4 L> and distributor assembly connector B-22 <3.0 L> for damage.

Q: Are combination meter connector C-102, ECM connector C-116 <M/T-2.4 L>, PCM connector C-117 <A/T-2.4 L>, C-119 <A/T-3.0 L> and distributor assembly connector B-22 <3.0 L> in good condition?

YES : Go to Step 4.

NO : Repair or replace the connector(s). The speedometer should work normally.

CR9090200220030X

Fig. 171 Tachometer Does Not Work (Part 3 of 5). 2003 Sebring Coupe & Stratus Coupe

STEP 4. Check wiring harnesses between combination meter connector C-102 (terminal 40) and ECM connector C-116 <M/T-2.4 L> (terminal 58), PCM connector C-114 <A/T-2.4 L> (terminal 43) or distributor assembly connector B-22 <3.0 L> (terminal 2).

NOTE: Also check intermediate connectors C-25. If intermediate connectors C-25 is damaged, repair or replace the connector

CR9090200220040X

Fig. 171 Tachometer Does Not Work (Part 4 of 5). 2003 Sebring Coupe & Stratus Coupe

Q: Are the wiring harnesses between combination meter connector C-102 (terminal 40) and ECM connector C-116 <M/T-2.4 L> (terminal 58), PCM connector C-114 <A/T-2.4 L> (terminal 43) or distributor assembly connector B-22 <3.0 L> (terminal 2) in good condition?

YES : Go to Step 5.

NO : Repair the wiring harness(es). The speedometer should work normally.

STEP 5. Replace and check the combination meter.

Q: Does the tachometer operate?

YES : There is no action to be taken.

NO : Replace the vehicle speed sensor <M/T> or PCM <A/T>. The tachometer should work normally.

CR9090200220050X

Fig. 171 Tachometer Does Not Work (Part 5 of 5). 2003 Sebring Coupe & Stratus Coupe

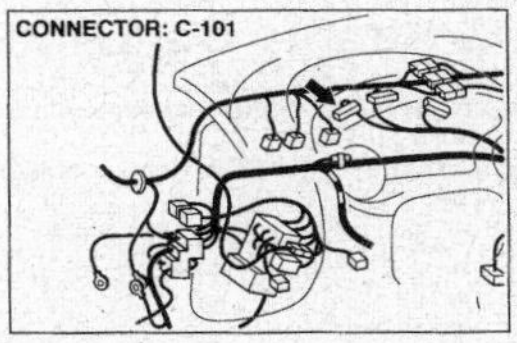

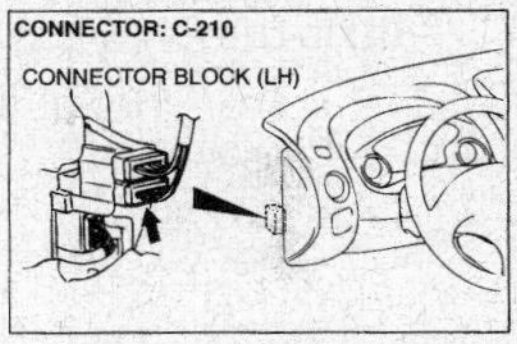

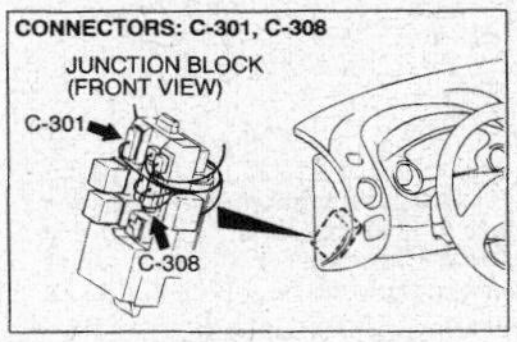

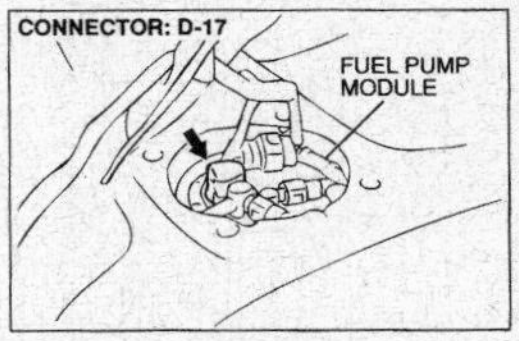

CIRCUIT OPERATION

- The ignition switch (IG1) circuit is the power source for the fuel gauge.
- The resistance value fluctuates causing the circuit current to fluctuate when the fuel gauge unit the float moves up and down.
- The fuel gauge moves the needle by the circuit current.

TECHNICAL DESCRIPTION (COMMENT)

If the ignition switch (IG1) circuit is open, the gauge needle will not move at all. If the ground circuit is open, the gauge needle will move up to its extreme position.

TROUBLESHOOTING

- Malfunction of the fuel pump module (fuel gauge unit)
- Malfunction of the combination meter (printed-circuit board or fuel gauge assembly)

DIAGNOSIS

Required Special Tool:
MB991223: Harness Set

STEP 1. Check the speedometer operation.

Q: Does the speedometer work normally?

YES : Go to Step 2 .
NO : Inspect speedometer.

CR9090200212010X

Fig. 172 Fuel Gauge Does Not Work (Part 1 of 4). 2001–03 Sebring Coupe & Stratus Coupe

STEP 2. Check the fuel pump module signal circuit at the fuel pump module connector D-17 by backprobing.

(1) Do not disconnect the fuel pump module connector D-17.
(2) Turn the ignition switch to "ON" position.
(3) Measure the voltage between terminal 2 and ground by backprobing.

Q: Is the voltage approximately 5 volts or more?

YES : Go to Step 5 .
NO : Go to Step 3 .

STEP 3. Check the fuel pump module connector D-17 and combination meter connector C-101 for damage.

Q: Are fuel pump module connector D-17 and combination meter connector C-101 in good condition?

YES : Go to Step 4 .
NO : Repair or replace it. The fuel gauge should work normally.

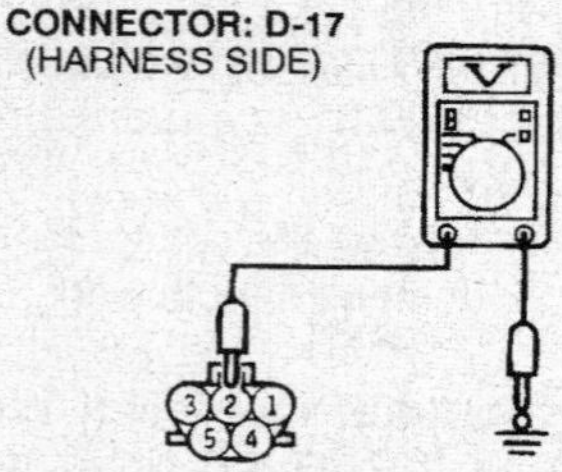

CR9090200212020X

Fig. 172 Fuel Gauge Does Not Work (Part 2 of 4). 2001–03 Sebring Coupe & Stratus Coupe

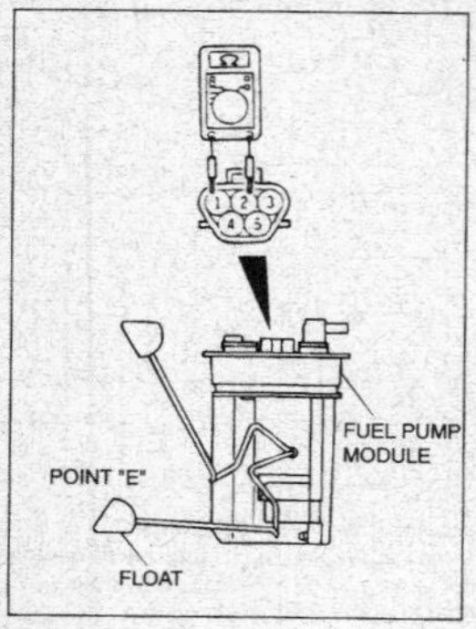

STEP 6. Check the fuel pump module connector D-17 for damage.

Q: Is fuel gauge unit connector D-17 in good condition?

YES : Go to Step 7 .
NO : Repair or replace it. The fuel gauge should work normally.

STEP 7. Check the harness wire between fuel pump module connector D-17 and ground.

Q: Is the harness wire between fuel pump module connector D-17 and ground in good condition?

YES : There is no action to be taken.
NO : Repair them. The fuel gauge should work normally.

STEP 8. Check the fuel gauge unit.

(1) Remove the fuel pump module from the fuel tank. (Refer to GROUP 14C, Fuel Tank P.23C-14 .
(2) Check resistance value between terminals 2 and 1 is at standard value when the fuel gauge unit float is at point "F" (highest) and point "E" (lowest).
(3) Check that the resistance value changes smoothly when the float moves slowly between point "F" (highest) and "E" (lowest).

Q: Is the resistance 3 - 5 ohms (at point "F") and 110 - 112 ohms (at point "E")?

YES : Repair or replace the combination meter (printed-circuit board or fuel gauge assembly). The fuel gauge should work normally.
NO : Replace the fuel gauge unit. The fuel gauge should work normally.

CR9090200212040X

Fig. 172 Fuel Gauge Does Not Work (Part 4 of 4). 2001–03 Sebring Coupe & Stratus Coupe

STEP 4. Check the harness wires between fuel pump module connector D-17 and combination meter connector C-101.

NOTE: After checking intermediate connector C-210, check the wire. If intermediate connector C-210 is damaged, repair or replace it.

Q: Are the harness wires between fuel pump module connector D-17 and combination meter connector C-101 in good condition?

YES : Repair or replace the combination meter (printed-circuit board or fuel gauge assembly). The fuel gauge should work normally.
NO : Repair them. The fuel gauge should work normally.

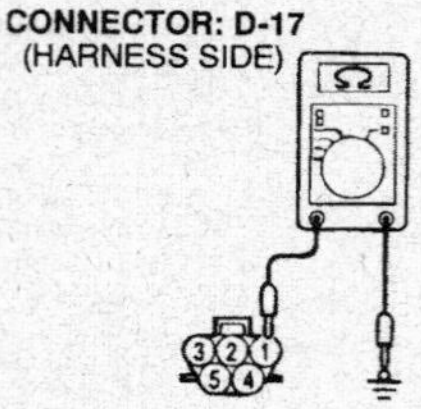

STEP 5. Check the fuel pump module ground circuit at the fuel pump module connector D-17 by backprobing.

(1) Do not disconnect the fuel gauge unit connector D-17.
(2) Measure the resistance between terminal 1 and ground by backprobing.

Q: Is the resistance less than 2 ohms?

YES : Go to Step 8 .
NO : Go to Step 6 .

CR9090200212030X

Fig. 172 Fuel Gauge Does Not Work (Part 3 of 4). 2001–03 Sebring Coupe & Stratus Coupe

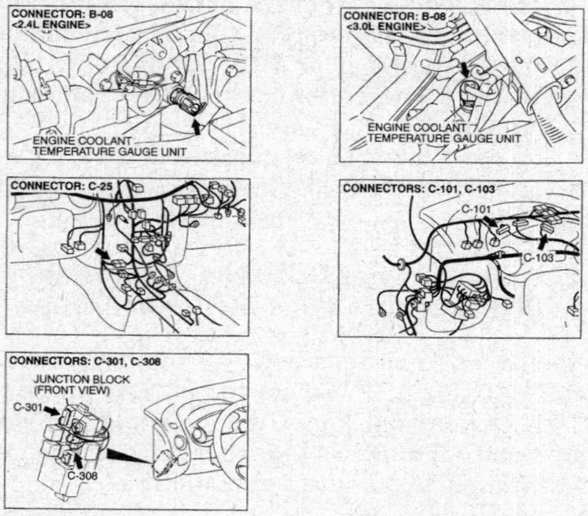

CIRCUIT OPERATION

- The ignition switch (IG1) circuit is the power source for the engine coolant temperature gauge.
- Resistance value, which the engine coolant temperature gauge unit sends to the combination meter, is dependent on temperature of the engine coolant. This causes circuit current to fluctuate.
- The engine coolant temperature gauge moves the needle according to the circuit current.

TECHNICAL DESCRIPTION (COMMENT)

If the ignition switch (IG1) circuit is open, the gauge needle will not move at all. If the ground circuit is open, the gauge needle will move up to its extreme position.

TROUBLESHOOTING

- Malfunction of the engine coolant temperature gauge unit
- Malfunction of the combination meter (printed-circuit board or engine coolant temperature gauge assembly)
- Damaged harness wires or connectors

DIAGNOSIS

Required Special Tool:
MB991223: Harness Set

CR9090200213010X

Fig. 173 Engine Coolant Temperature Gauge Does Not Work (Part 1 of 5). 2001–03 Sebring Coupe & Stratus Coupe

STEP 1. Check the speedometer operation.

Q: Does the speedometer work normally?

YES : Go to Step 2 .
NO : Inspect speedometer.

STEP 2. Check the engine coolant temperature sensor signal circuit at the engine coolant temperature sensor connector B-08 by backprobing.

(1) Do not disconnect the engine coolant temperature sensor connector B-08.
(2) Turn the ignition switch to "ON" position.
(3) Measure the voltage between terminal 1 and ground by backprobing.

Q: Is the voltage approximately 9 volts or more?

YES : Go to Step 5.
NO : Go to Step 3.

CONNECTOR: B-08
(HARNESS SIDE)

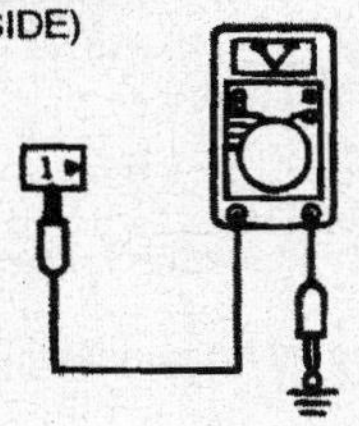

CR9090200213020X

Fig. 173 Engine Coolant Temperature Gauge Does Not Work (Part 2 of 5). 2001–03 Sebring Coupe & Stratus Coupe

STEP 4. Check the harness wires between engine coolant temperature sensor connector B-08 and combination meter connector C-103.

NOTE: After checking intermediate connector C-25, check the wire. If intermediate connector C-25 is damaged, repair or replace it.

Q: Are the harness wires between engine coolant temperature sensor connector B-08 and combination meter connector C-103 in good condition?

YES : Repair or replace the combination meter (printed-circuit board or engine coolant temperature gauge assembly). The engine coolant temperature gauge should work normally.
NO : Repair them. The engine coolant temperature gauge should work normally.

CR9090200213040X

Fig. 173 Engine Coolant Temperature Gauge Does Not Work (Part 4 of 5). 2001–03 Sebring Coupe & Stratus Coupe

STEP 3. Check the engine coolant temperature sensor connector B-08 and combination meter connector C-103 for damage.

Q: Are engine coolant temperature sensor connector B-08 and combination meter connector C-103 in good condition?

YES : Go to Step 4 .
NO : Repair or replace it. The engine coolant temperature gauge should work normally.

CR9090200213030X

Fig. 173 Engine Coolant Temperature Gauge Does Not Work (Part 3 of 5). 2001–03 Sebring Coupe & Stratus Coupe

STEP 5. Check the engine coolant temperature gauge unit.

(1) Drain the engine coolant.
(2) Remove the engine coolant temperature gauge unit.
(3) Immerse the unit in 78°X (150° F) water to measure the resistance.

Q: Is the resistance 104 ±13.5 ohms?

YES : Repair or replace the combination meter (printed-circuit board or engine coolant temperature gauge assembly). The engine coolant temperature gauge should work normally.
NO : Replace the engine coolant temperature gauge unit. The engine coolant temperature gauge should work normally.

CR9090200213050X

Fig. 173 Engine Coolant Temperature Gauge Does Not Work (Part 5 of 5). 2001–03 Sebring Coupe & Stratus Coupe

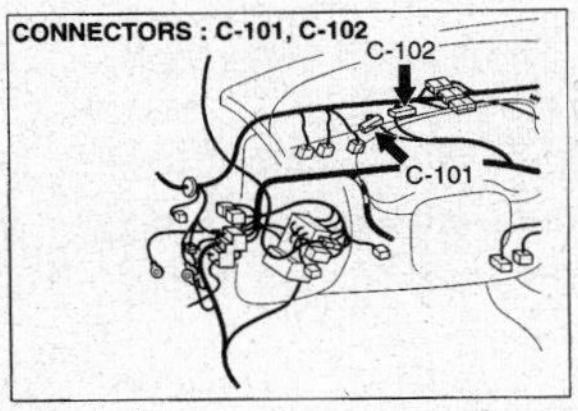

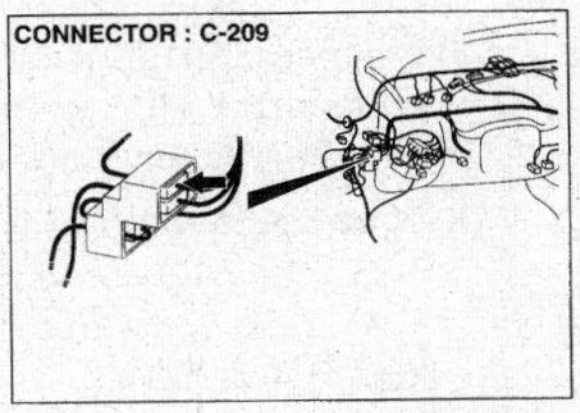

CR9090200221010X

Fig. 174 Instrument Cluster Does Not Work (Part 1 of 7). 2003 Sebring Coupe & Stratus Coupe

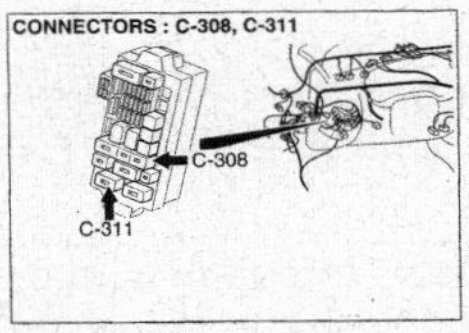

CIRCUIT OPERATION
The combination meter is powered by the ignition switch (IG1) and the battery.

TECHNICAL DESCRIPTION (COMMENT)
The cause is thought to be malfunction of the power, ground circuitry of the combination meter.

TROUBLESHOOTING HINTS
- Malfunction of the combination meter (printed-circuit board or speedometer and tachometer)
- Damaged wiring harness or connectors

DIAGNOSIS

Required Special Tools:
- MB991223: Harness Set

STEP 1. Measure at combination meter connector C-102 in order to check the battery circuit of power supply system to the combination meter.

(1) Disconnect combination meter connector C-102, and measure at the wiring harness side.

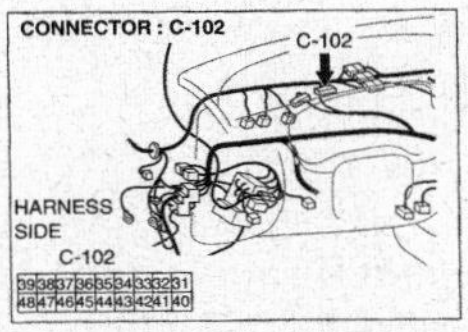

(2) Measure the voltage between terminal 31 and ground.
- The measured value should be approximately 12 volts (battery positive voltage).

Q: Does the measured voltage correspond with this range?

YES : Go to Step 4.
NO : Go to Step 2.

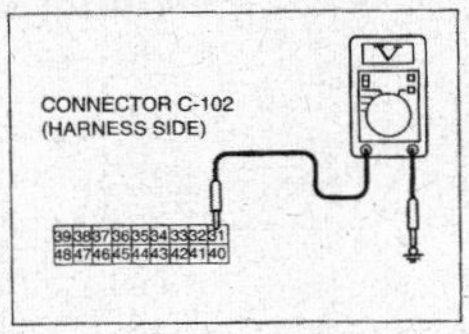

CR9090200221020X

Fig. 174 Instrument Cluster Does Not Work (Part 2 of 7). 2003 Sebring Coupe & Stratus Coupe

STEP 2. Check combination meter connector C-102 for damage.

Q: Is combination meter connector C-102 in good condition?

YES : Go to Step 3.

NO : Repair or replace the connector. Check to see that all meters operate.

STEP 3. Check the wiring harnesses between combination meter connector C-102 (terminal 31) and the battery.

NOTE: Also check intermediate connector C-209. If intermediate connectors C-209 are damaged, repair or replace the connector

Q: Are the wiring harnesses between combination meter connector C-102 (terminal 31) and the battery in good condition?

YES : There is no action to be taken.

NO : Repair the wiring harness(es). Check to see that all meters operate.

CR9090200221030X

Fig. 174 Instrument Cluster Does Not Work (Part 3 of 7). 2003 Sebring Coupe & Stratus Coupe

STEP 6. Check the wiring harnesses between combination meter connector C-101 (terminal 12) and ignition switch (IG1).

NOTE: Also check junction connectors C-308 and C-311. If junction connectors C-308 or C-311 are damaged, repair or replace the connector

Q: Are the wiring harness between combination meter connector C-101 (terminal 12) and ignition switch (IG1) in good condition?

YES : There is no action to be taken.

NO : Repair the wiring harness(es). Check to see that all meters operate.

CR9090200221050X

Fig. 174 Instrument Cluster Does Not Work (Part 5 of 7). 2003 Sebring Coupe & Stratus Coupe

STEP 4. Measure at combination meter connector C-101 in order to check the battery circuit of power supply system to the combination meter.

(1) Disconnect combination meter connector C-101, and measure at the wiring harness side.

(2) Turn the ignition switch to "ON" position.

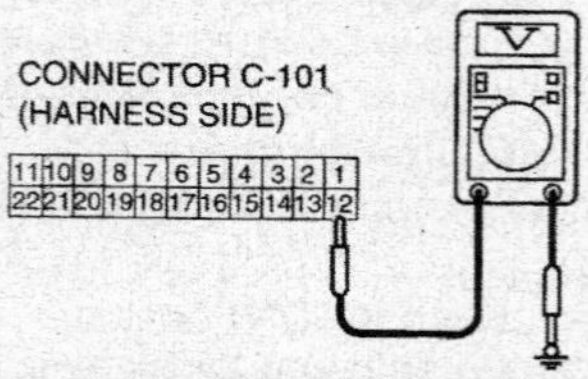

(3) Measure the voltage between terminal 12 and ground.

- The measured value should be approximately 12 volts (battery positive voltage).

Q: Does the measured voltage correspond with this range?

YES : Go to Step 7.

NO : Go to Step 5.

STEP 5. Check combination meter connector C-101 for damage.

Q: Is combination meter connector C-101 in good condition?

YES : Go to Step 6.

NO : Repair or replace the connector. Check to see that all meters operate.

CR9090200221040X

Fig. 174 Instrument Cluster Does Not Work (Part 4 of 7). 2003 Sebring Coupe & Stratus Coupe

STEP 7. Measure at combination meter connector C-101 and C-102 in order to check the ground circuit to the combination meter.

(1) Disconnect combination meter connector C-101 and C-102, and measure at the wiring harness side.

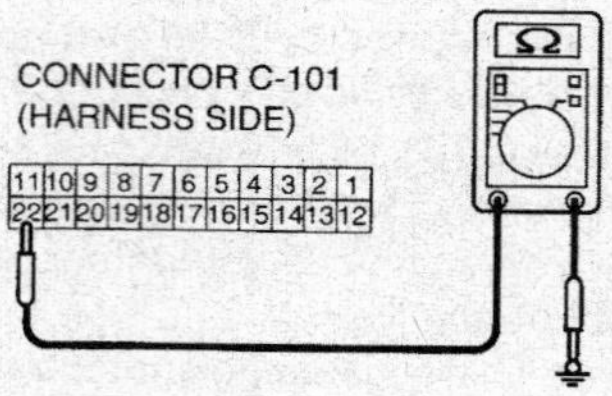

(2) Measure the resistance between combination meter connector C-101 terminal 22 and ground.

- The measured value should be 2 ohms or less.

(3) Measure the resistance between combination meter connector C-102 terminal 48 and ground.

- The measured value should be 2 ohms or less.

Q: Does the measured voltage correspond with this range?

YES : Repair the combination meter. Check to see that all meters operate.

NO : Go to Step 8.

CR9090200221060X

Fig. 174 Instrument Cluster Does Not Work (Part 6 of 7). 2003 Sebring Coupe & Stratus Coupe

STEP 8. Check combination meter connector C-101 and C-102 for damage.

Q: Are combination meter connector C-101 and C-102 in good condition?

YES : Go to Step 9.

NO : Repair or replace the connector(s). Check to see that all meters operate.

STEP 9. Check the wiring harness between combination meter connector C-101 (terminal 22), C-102 (terminal 48) and ground.

Q: Is the wiring harness between combination meter connector C-101 (terminal 22), C-102 (terminal 48) and ground in good condition?

YES : There is no action to be taken.

NO : Repair the wiring harness. Check to see that all meters operate.

CR9090200221070X

Fig. 174 Instrument Cluster Does Not Work (Part 7 of 7). 2003 Sebring Coupe & Stratus Coupe

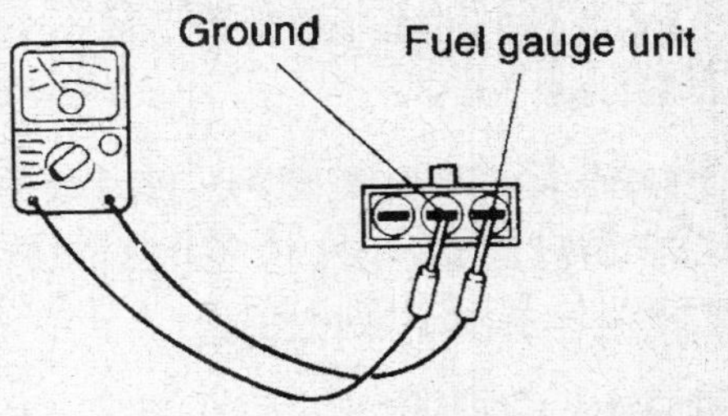

CR9090200207000X

Fig. 175 Fuel gauge sending unit resistance measurement. Avenger & 2000 Sebring Coupe

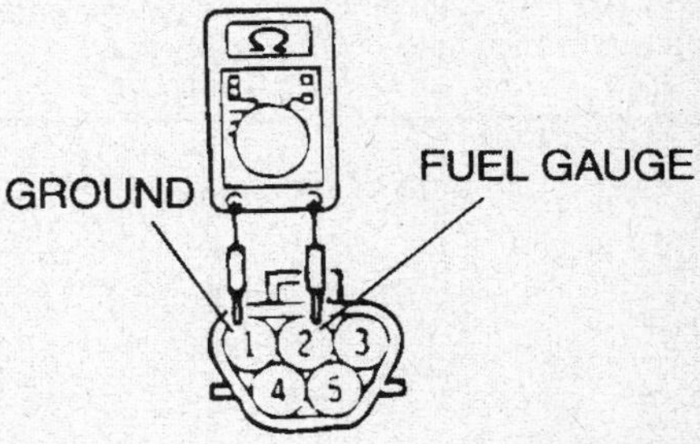

CR9090200214000X

Fig. 178 Fuel gauge sending unit resistance measurement. 2001–03 Sebring Coupe & Stratus Coupe

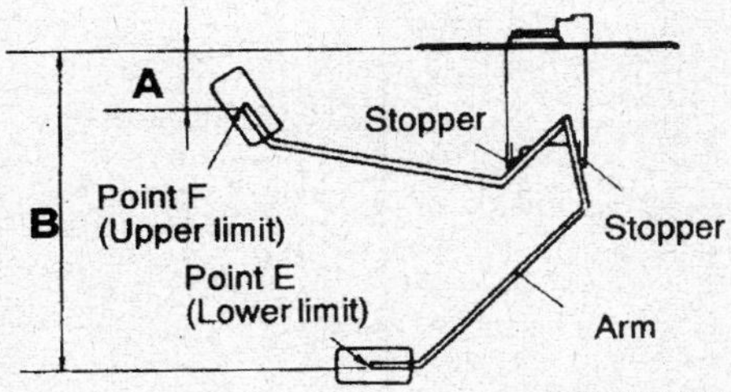

CR9090200206000X

Fig. 176 Fuel gauge float measurement. Avenger & 2000 Sebring Coupe

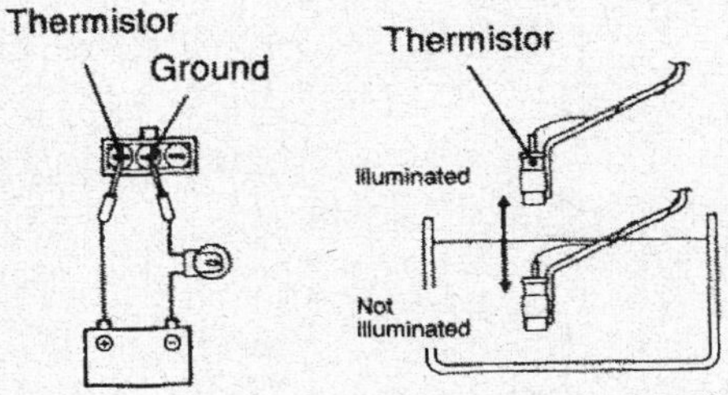

CR9090200208000X

Fig. 177 Thermistor test. Avenger & 2000 Sebring Coupe

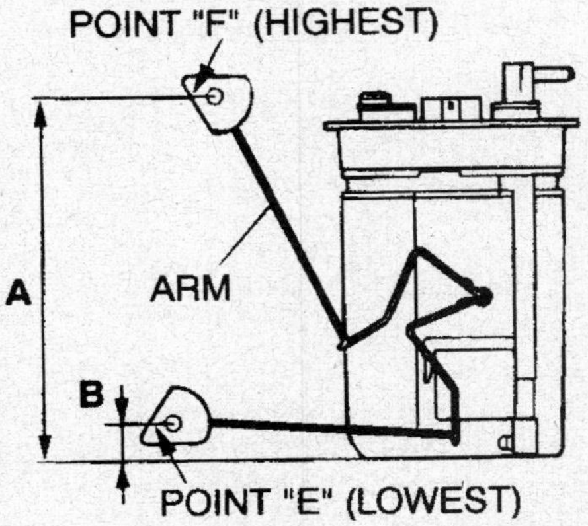

CR9090200215000X

Fig. 179 Fuel gauge float measurement. 2001–03 Sebring Coupe & Stratus Coupe

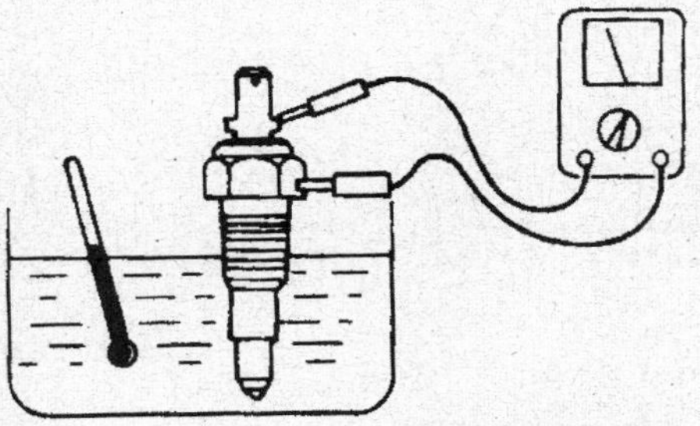

CR9090200209000X

Fig. 180 ECT sending unit measurement. Avenger

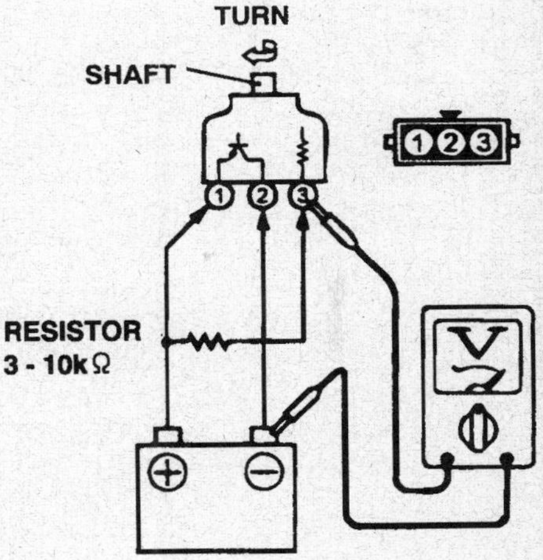

CR9090200216000X

Fig. 181 Vehicle speed sensor test. 2001–03 Sebring Coupe & Stratus Coupe

TECHNICAL SERVICE BULLETINS

Fuel Gauge Drops to E Or Instrument Cluster Goes Full Bright

2001 CONCORDE, INTREPID, LHS OR 300M

On some of these models the fuel gauge may drop to E, the low fuel indicator illuminate and/or the instrument cluster illumination goes to full bright for a few seconds before returning to normal operation.

This condition may be caused by the Body Control Module (BCM) programming.

To correct this condition, flash the BCM with the latest software.

Gauge Pointer On Wrong Side Of Stop

2000 BREEZE, CIRRUS, NEON, SEBRING CONVERTIBLE & STRATUS SEDAN

On some of these models the instrument cluster gauge points may be on the wrong side of stops.

To correct this condition, conduct cluster self test as follows:

1. Press and hold trip-reset button.
2. Turn ignition switch On without cranking engine.
3. Instrument cluster indicators should illuminate except for turns signals, high beam and fog lamp.
4. Gauge points should then step through scales and sweep back to proper position.

SPEED CONTROL SYSTEMS

NOTE: On Air Bag Equipped Models, Refer To "Air Bag System Precautions" Located In The Front Of This Manual For System Disarming & Arming Procedures.

NOTE: Refer To "Computer Relearn Procedures" Located In The Front Of This Manual When Battery Power To The Computer Has Been Interrupted.

NOTE: "Electrical Symbol & Wire Color Code Identification" Located In The Front Of This Manual May Be Used As An Aid When Using Wiring Circuits Found In This Section.

INDEX

DESCRIPTION

This speed control system is electrically controlled and vacuum operated. The electronic control is integrated into the Powertrain Control Module (PCM) on most models.

PRECAUTIONS

Air Bag Systems

Refer to "Air Bag System Precautions" in the front of this manual for system disarming and arming procedures.

Battery Ground Cable

Prior to service, disconnect battery ground cable and isolate as required.

ADJUSTMENTS

Avenger & 2000 Sebring Coupe

1. Remove link protector, **Fig. 1.**
2. Inspect accelerator, cruse control and throttle inner cables for slack. If slack is excessive or there is no play, proceed to next step.
3. Loosen adjusting bolts and nuts. **Do not remove bolts or nuts.**
4. **On models equipped with automatic transaxle,** adjust accelerate cable adjusting nut so link hits stopper and inner play is .08–.12 inch, **Figs. 2 and 3.**
5. **On models equipped with manual transaxle,** adjust accelerate adjusting nut so link hits stopper and accelerate inner cable play is .00–.04 inch, **Figs. 2 and 3.**
6. **On all models,** adjust throttle cable adjusting nut so lever hits link and inner cable play is .04–.08 inch, **Figs. 4 and 5.**
7. Hold link in place at lever and speed control cable, **Figs. 6 and 7.**

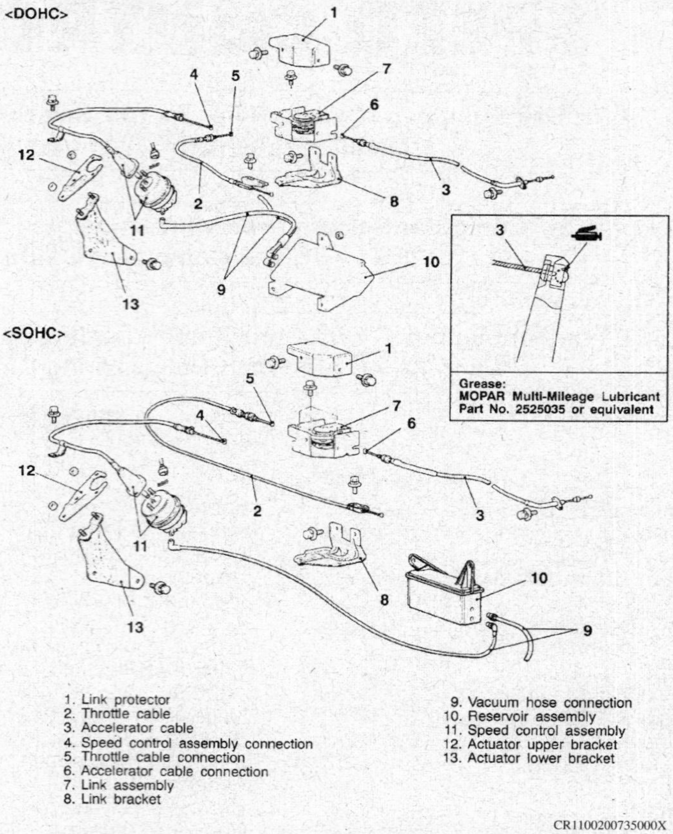

Fig. 1 Cruise control replacement

SYSTEM DIAGNOSIS & TESTING

Accessing Diagnostic Trouble Codes

WITH SCAN TOOL

Connect suitably program scan tool to Data Link Connector (DLC), and follow manufacturer's instructions.

LESS SCAN TOOL

AVENGER

1. Cycle ignition switch On-Off-On-Off-On within five seconds.
2. Check engine/Malfunction Indicator Lamp (MIL) will flash codes.
3. There is slight pause between flashes with longer pause to separate digits.

SEBRING & STRATUS COUPE

2000

Refer to "Avenger" for DTC accessing procedure less scan tool.

2001-03

1. Turn ignition switch to On position while holding cruse control switch in SET position.
2. Move cruise control switch to RES position within one second.
3. Instrument cluster cruise control indicator lamp will flash codes as follows:
   a. Three second pause.
   b. One second flash for ten digit.
   c. Two second pause between digits.
   d. Half second flash, half second pause to first digit.
4. The indicator lamp with flash off and on in half second intervals with there are no codes.

Diagnostic Trouble Codes Interpretation

AVENGER

Refer to **Fig. 8,** for Diagnostic Trouble Code (DTC) interpretation.

BREEZE & CIRRUS

Refer to **Fig. 9,** for Diagnostic Trouble Code (DTC) interpretation.

CONCORDE, INTREPID, LHS & 300M

2000-01

Refer to **Fig. 9,** for Diagnostic Trouble Code (DTC) interpretation.

2002-04

Refer to **Fig. 10,** for Diagnostic Trouble Code (DTC) interpretation.

NEON

2000-02

Refer to **Fig. 9,** for Diagnostic Trouble Code (DTC) interpretation.

2003-04

Refer to **Fig. 10,** for Diagnostic Trouble Code (DTC) interpretation.

SEBRING & STRATUS

CONVERTIBLE & SEDAN

2000-02

Refer to **Fig. 9,** for Diagnostic Trouble Code (DTC) interpretation.

2003-04

Refer to **Fig. 10,** for Diagnostic Trouble Code (DTC) interpretation.

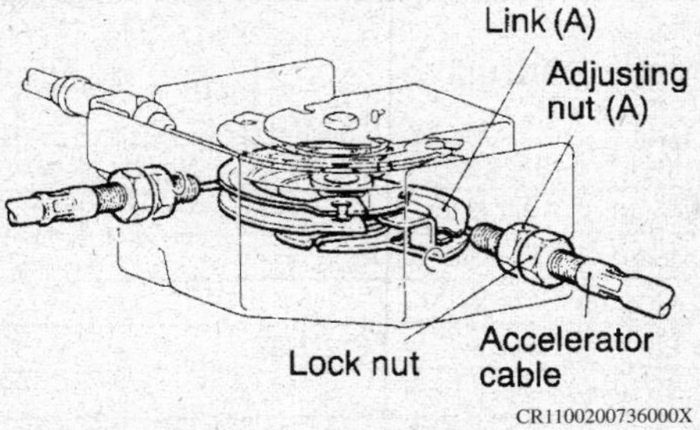

Fig. 2 Accelerator cable adjustment. Avenger & 2000 Sebring Coupe w/DOHC engine

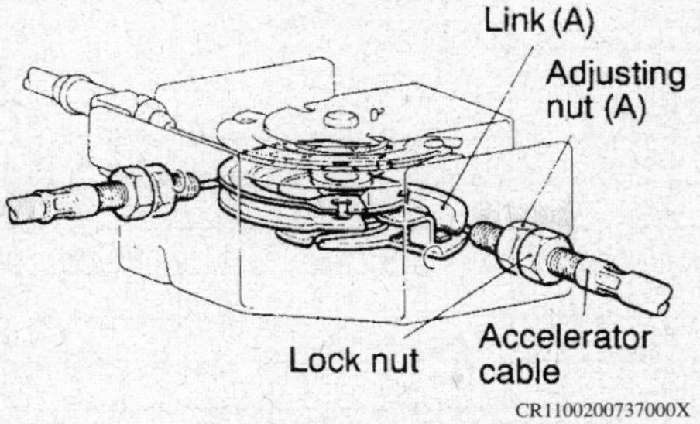

Fig. 3 Accelerator cable adjustment. Avenger & 2000 Sebring Coupe w/SOHC engine

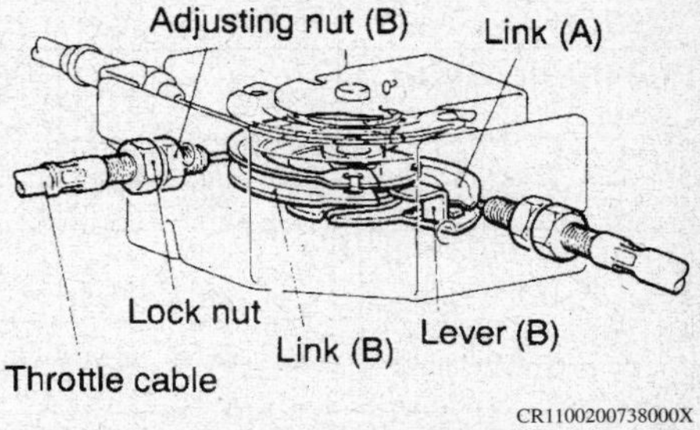

Fig. 4 Throttle cable adjustment. Avenger & 2000 Sebring Coupe w/DOHC engine

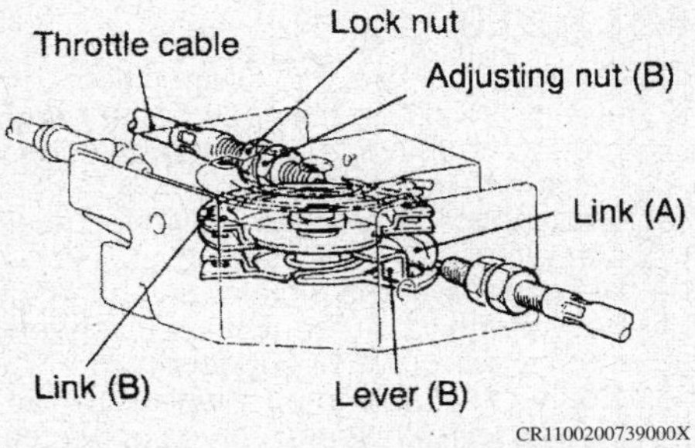

Fig. 5 Throttle cable adjustment. Avenger & 2000 Sebring Coupe w/SOHC engine

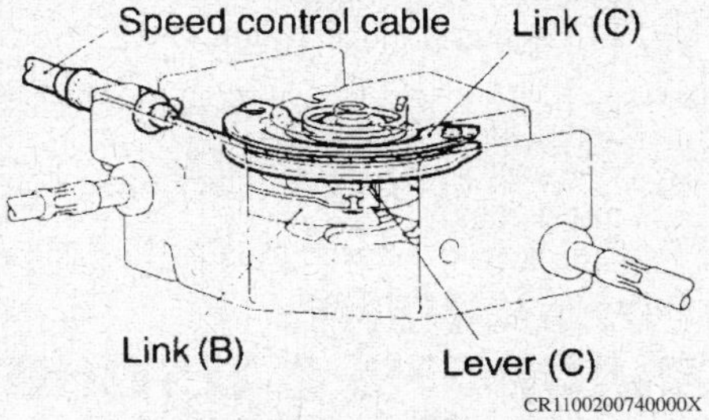

Fig. 6 Speed control cable adjustment. Avenger & 2000 Sebring Coupe w/DOHC engine

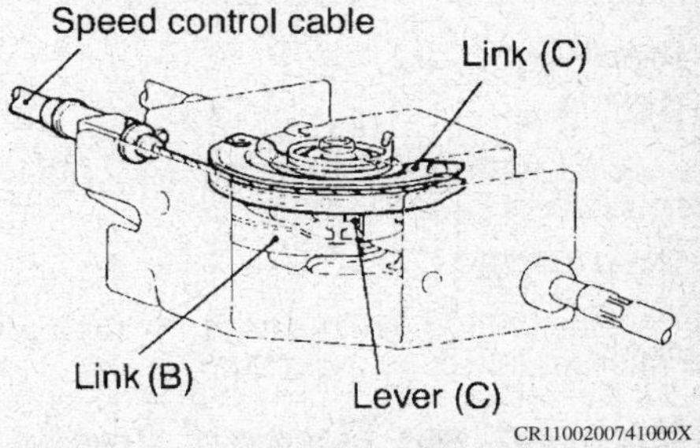

Fig. 7 Speed control cable adjustment. Avenger & 2000 Sebring Coupe w/SOHC engine

COUPE

2000

Refer to **Fig. 9,** for Diagnostic Trouble Code (DTC) interpretation.

2001-03

Refer to **Fig. 11,** for Diagnostic Trouble Code (DTC) interpretation.

Wiring Diagrams

AVENGER

Refer to **Figs. 12 and 13,** for wiring diagrams.

BREEZE & CIRRUS

Refer to **Fig. 14,** for wiring diagrams.

CONCORDE, INTREPID, LHS & 300M

Refer to **Figs. 15 through 17,** for wiring diagrams.

CROSSFIRE

Refer to **Fig. 18,** for wiring diagrams.

NEON

Refer to **Figs. 19 through 21,** for wiring diagrams.

SEBRING

CONVERTIBLE

Refer to **Figs. 22 and 23,** for wiring diagrams.

COUPE

2000

Refer to **Figs. 12 and 13,** for wiring diagrams.

2001-03

Refer to **Figs. 24 through 31,** for wiring diagrams.

SEDAN

Refer to **Fig. 23,** for wiring diagrams.

STRATUS

COUPE

Refer to **Figs. 24 through 31,** for wiring diagrams.

SEDAN

2000

Refer to **Fig. 14,** for wiring diagrams.

2001-04

Refer to **Fig. 23,** for wiring diagrams.

Diagnostic Tests

AVENGER

Refer to **Figs. 32 through 37,** for diagnostic tests.

BREEZE & CIRRUS

Refer to **Figs. 38 through 45,** for diagnostic tests.

CONCORDE, INTREPID, LHS & 300M

2000

Refer to **Figs. 46 through 49,** for diagnostic tests.

2001

Refer to **Figs. 50 through 52,** for diagnostic tests.

2002-04

Refer to **Figs. 53 through 60,** for diagnostic tests.

NEON

2000

Refer to **Figs. 61 through 63,** for diagnostic tests.

2001-02

Refer to **Figs. 50 through 52,** for diagnostic tests.

2003-04

Refer to **Figs. 53 through 60,** for diagnostic tests.

SEBRING & STRATUS

CONVERTIBLE & SEDAN

2000

Refer to **Figs. 38 through 44,** for diagnostic tests.

2001-02

Refer to **Figs. 50 through 52,** for diagnostic tests.

Code			Interpretation
Generic Scan Tool	Lamp Flash	MUT-II Scan Tool	
P0500	15	35	Vehicle Speed Signal System
P0605	53	02	Powertrain Control Module
—		15	Speed Control Servo Solenoid Valve
	34	86	Cruise Control Switch
		87	Cruise Control Switch
—	77	82	Cruse Control Relay

Fig. 8 DTC interpretation. Avenger & 2000 Sebring Coupe

2003-04

Refer to **Figs. 53 through 60,** for diagnostic tests.

COUPE

2000

Refer to **Figs. 32 through 37,** for diagnostic tests.

2001-03

Refer to **Figs. 64 through 69,** for diagnostic trouble code procedures.

Symptom Based Tests

AVENGER

Refer to **Figs. 70 through 79,** for symptom based tests.

SEBRING & STRATUS COUPE

2000

Refer to **Figs. 70 through 79,** for symptom based tests.

2001-03

Refer to **Figs. 80 through 87,** for symptom procedures.

Clearing Diagnostic Trouble Codes

WITH SCAN TOOL

Connect a suitably programmed scan tool to Data Link Connector (DLC), and follow manufacturer's instructions.

LESS SCAN TOOL

AVENGER

1. Remove battery ground cable for 10 seconds or more.
2. Connect cable.
3. Start and idle engine for approximately 15 minutes.

2000 SEBRING COUPE

Refer to "Avenger" for DTC clearing procedure less scan tool.

2001-03 SEBRING & STRATUS COUPE

1. Turn ignition switch to ON position while holding cruise control switch in SET position.
2. Move cruise control switch to RES position within one second.
3. Ensure instrument panel cruise indicator lamp is flashing.
4. Put cruise control switch in SET position.
5. Depress brake pedal and hold for five seconds or more.
6. Release brake pedal and cruise control switch.
7. Turn ignition switch to LOCK position.

COMPONENT DIAGNOSIS & TESTING

Stop Lamp Switch

AVENGER

Refer to **Fig. 88,** for stop lamp switch continuity test.

BREEZE & CIRRUS

1. Remove stop lamp switch and disconnect connector, **Fig. 89.**
2. Inspect continuity between switch terminal Nos. 5 and 6. When plunger is depressed, there should be continuity between terminal Nos. 1 and 2, and Nos. 3 and 4.
3. If continuity is not as specified, adjusted switch by pulling out plunger to end of travel which is approximately ¾ inch.
4. If continuity is still not as specified, replace switch.

CONCORDE, INTREPID, LHS & 300M

Refer to "Breeze & Cirrus" for stop lamp switch continuity test.

NEON

Refer to "Breeze & Cirrus" for stop lamp switch continuity test.

SEBRING & STRATUS

CONVERTIBLE & SEDAN

Refer to "Breeze & Cirrus" for stop lamp switch continuity test.

COUPE

2000

Refer to **Fig. 88,** for stop lamp switch continuity test.

2001-03

Refer to **Fig. 90,** for stop lamp switch continuity test.

Speed Control Servo

AVENGER

1. Turn ignition switch to ON position.
2. Measure voltage between battery and ground negative lead with speed control switch in On position.
3. Disconnect servo four-way electrical connector.
4. Measure harness pin No. 3 voltage, If no voltage is present inspect speed control servo power supply circuit.
5. Connect suitable jumper wire between harness pin No. 2 and servo connector pin No. 3.
6. Measure voltage at pins Nos. 1, 2 and 4. If no voltage is present replace servo.
7. Inspect four-way servo connector pin No. 4 to ground for continuity. If there is no continuity, repair ground circuit.
8. Disconnect speed control cable at throttle body.
9. Disconnect four-way electrical connector and vacuum lines at servo.
10. Connect battery voltage to servo pin No. 3.
11. Ground servo connector pins Nos. 1, 2 and 4.
12. Apply 10–15 inches of vacuum to servo using suitable hand held vacuum pump.
13. Ensure throttle cable pulls in and holds as long as vacuum pump is connected.
14. After one minute, ensure cable is still holding. If cable does not hold, replace servo.

BREEZE & CIRRUS

1. Turn ignition switch to ON position without starting engine.
2. Activate speed control ON switch.
3. Disconnect four-way electrical connector and vacuum harness at servo.
4. Connect suitable jumper wire between from servo and wire connector pins No. 3.
5. Ground servo pins Nos. 2 and 4. **Do not connect pin No. 1**
6. Apply 10–15 inches of vacuum to servo vacuum nipple using suitable hand held vacuum pump.
7. If servo pulls cable, replace servo.
8. Ground pin No. 1.
9. Ensure throttle cable pulls in and holds as long as vacuum pump is connected.
10. After one minute, ensure cable is still holding. If cable does not hold, replace servo.

Code	Interpretation
P1595	Speed Control Solenoid Circuits
P1596	Speed Control Switch Always High
P1597	Speed Control Switch Always Low
P1683	Speed Control Power Relay Circuit

Fig. 9 DTC interpretation. Breeze, Cirrus, LHS, 2000 Stratus, 2000–02 Neon, Sebring Convertible, Sebring Sedan, Stratus Sedan, 2001 Concorde, Intrepid & 300M

11. Disconnect pin No. 3 jumper. If cable does not return, replace servo.

CONCORDE, INTREPID, LHS & 300M

Refer to "Breeze & Cirrus" for speed control servo test procedure

NEON

Refer to "Breeze & Cirrus" for speed control servo test procedure

SEBRING & STRATUS

CONVERTIBLE & SEDAN

Refer to "Breeze & Cirrus" for speed control servo procedure

COUPE

2000

Refer to "Avenger" for speed control servo test procedure.

2001–03

1. Disconnect cruise control vacuum pump hose and connect suitable vacuum gauge.
2. Disconnect vacuum pump electrical connector.
3. Connect battery positive to pump connector terminal No. 1 and negative to terminals Nos. 2, 3 and 4. Vacuum should be 8 inches.
4. Disconnect terminal No. 4 and vacuum should be 8 inches.
5. Disconnect terminal No. 2 and vacuum should be zero inches.
6. Connect terminal No. 2 and disconnect terminal No. 3. Vacuum should be zero inches.

Vacuum Supply

1. Disconnect servo vacuum hose and install suitable vacuum gauge, **Fig. 91.**
2. Start and idle engine. There should be at least 10 inches of vacuum.
3. Shut off engine and ensure vacuum holds.
4. If vacuum is not within specifications, inspect for leaks in vacuum lines, check valve, vacuum reservoir or poor engine performance

Speed Control Relay

AVENGER & 2000 SEBRING COUPE

Refer to **Fig. 92,** to speed control relay continuity.

Speed Control Main Switch

AVENGER & 2000 SEBRING COUPE

1. Operate On/Off switch and inspect for continuity, **Fig. 93.**
2. Connect battery positive voltage to terminal No. 1 and negative to No. 4.
3. Turn main switch to On position and ensure there is battery voltage between terminal No. 5 and ground.
4. to ground, then place On/Off switch in On position.
5. Place switch in Off position and ensure there is zero volts between terminal No. 5 and ground.

Speed Control Switch

AVENGER

Refer to **Fig. 94,** to speed control switch continuity test.

Code	Interpretation
P0579	Speed Control Switch No. 1 Performance
P0580	Speed Control Switch No. 1 Low
P0581	Speed Control Switch No. 1 High
P0582	Speed Control Vacuum Solenoid Circuit
P0586	Speed Control Vent Solenoid Circuit
P0594	Speed Control Servo Power Circuit

Fig. 10 DTC interpretation. 2002–04 Concorde, Intrepid, 300M, 2003–04 Neon, Sebring Convertible, Sebring Sedan & Stratus Sedan

Code	Interpretation
11	Cruise Vacuum Pump Drive
12	Vehicle Speed Sensor
14	Stop Lamp Switch
15	Cruise Control Switch
16	Cruise Control-ECU
17	Throttle Position Sensor

Fig. 11 DTC interpretation. 2001–03 Sebring Coupe & Stratus Coupe

SEBRING & STRATUS COUPE

2000

Refer to **Fig. 94,** to speed control switch continuity test.

2001–03

Refer to **Fig. 95,** for speed control switch resistance test.

Vacuum Actuator

2001–03 SEBRING & STRATUS COUPE

1. Disconnect vacuum actuator hose.
2. Connect suitable vacuum hand pump to actuator, **Fig. 96.**
3. Ensure throttle lever operates when applying vacuum and vacuum is maintained.

Clutch Pedal Position Switch

2001–03 SEBRING & STRATUS COUPE

Refer to **Fig. 97,** for clutch pedal position switch continuity test.

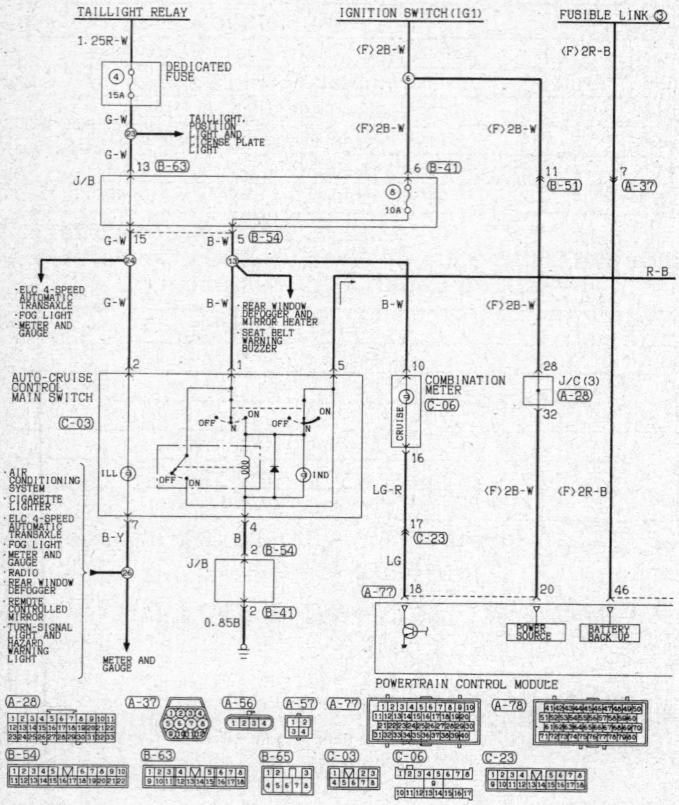

Fig. 12 Wiring diagram (Part 1 of 6). Avenger & 2000 Sebring Coupe w/DOHC engine

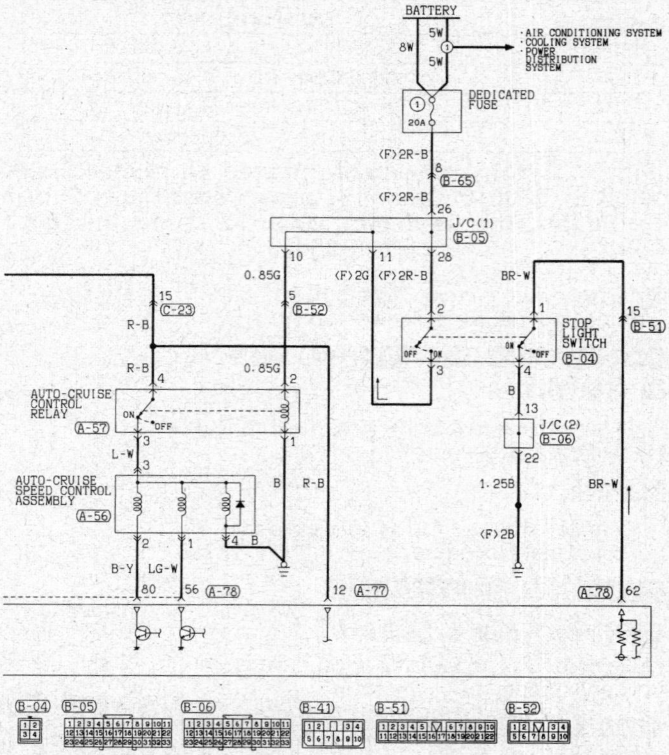

Fig. 12 Wiring diagram (Part 2 of 6). Avenger & 2000 Sebring Coupe w/DOHC engine

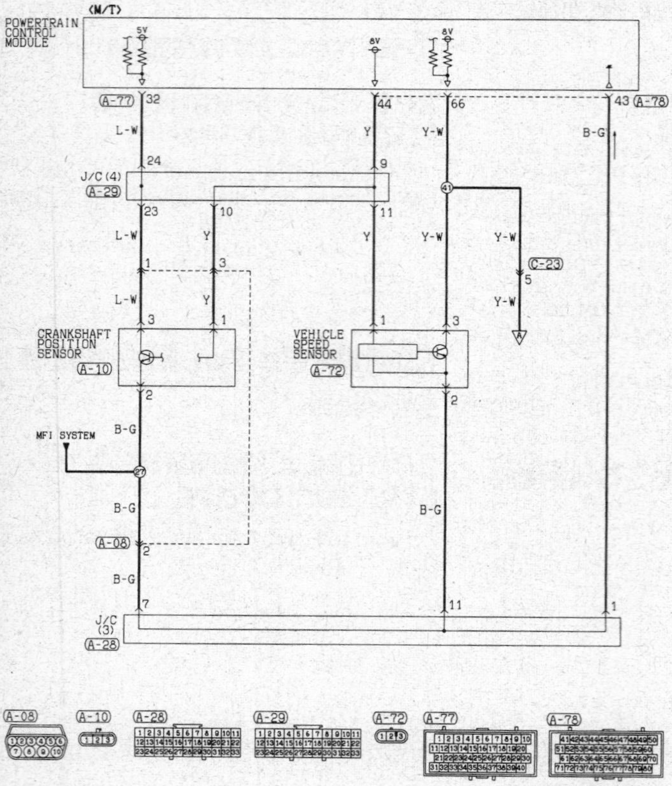

Fig. 12 Wiring diagram (Part 3 of 6). Avenger & 2000 Sebring Coupe w/DOHC engine

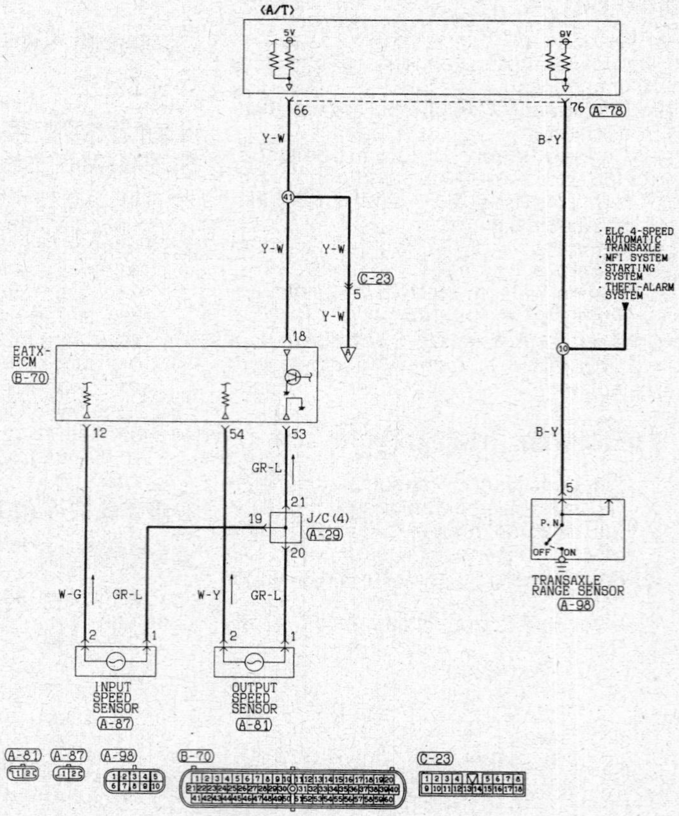

Fig. 12 Wiring diagram (Part 4 of 6). Avenger & 2000 Sebring Coupe w/DOHC engine

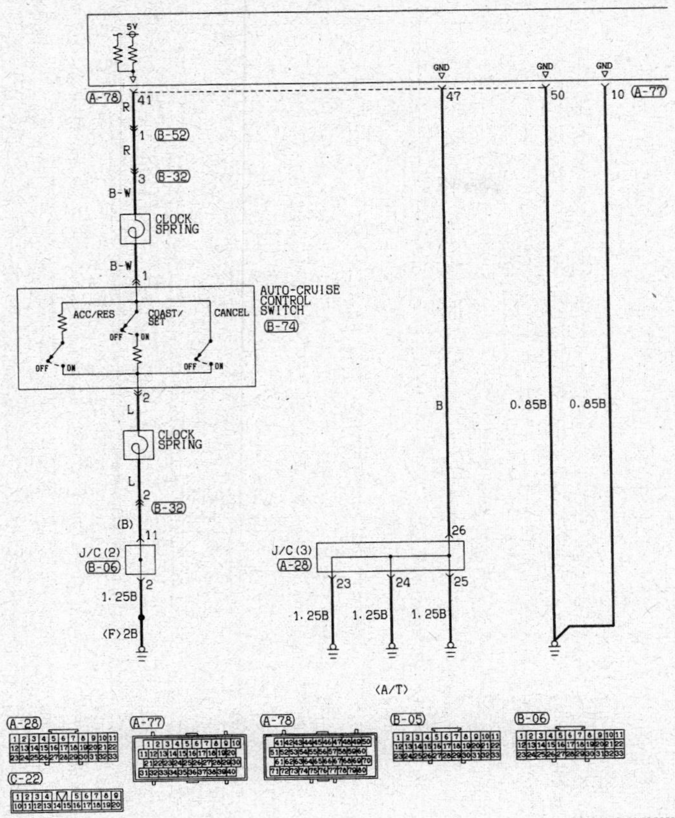

CR1109800536050X

Fig. 12 Wiring diagram (Part 5 of 6). Avenger & 2000 Sebring Coupe w/DOHC engine

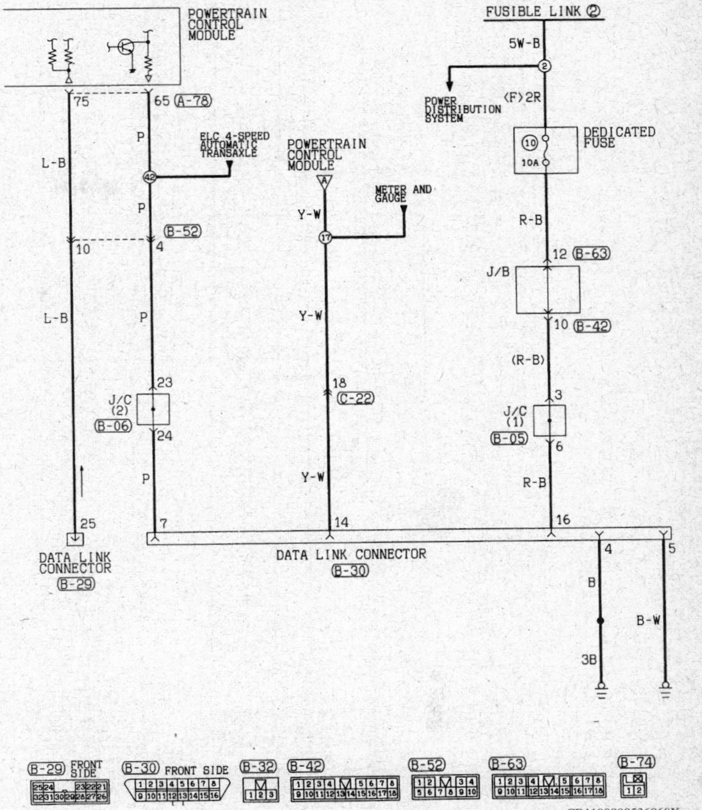

CR1109800536060X

Fig. 12 Wiring diagram (Part 6 of 6). Avenger & 2000 Sebring Coupe w/DOHC engine

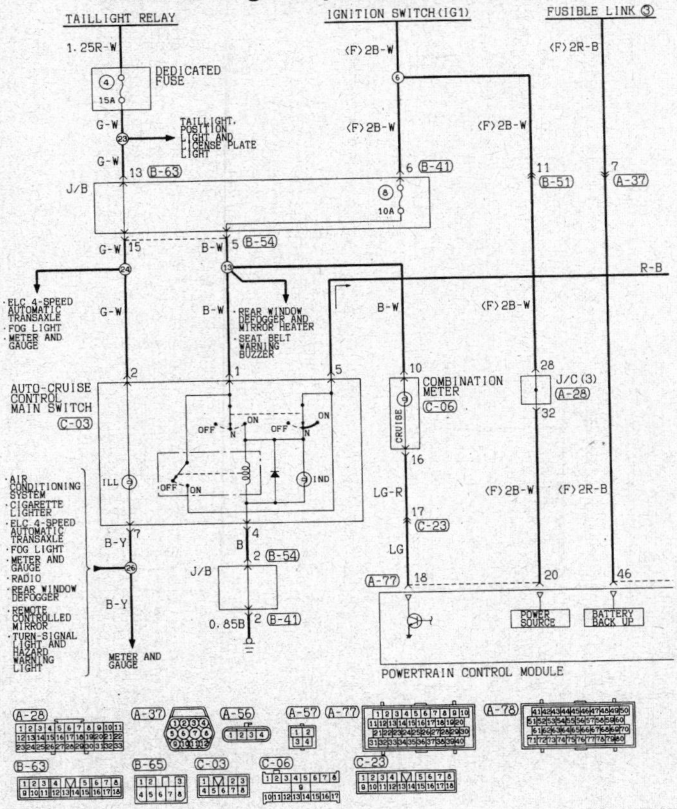

CR1109800537010X

Fig. 13 Wiring diagram (Part 1 of 4). Avenger & 2000 Sebring Coupe w/SOHC engine

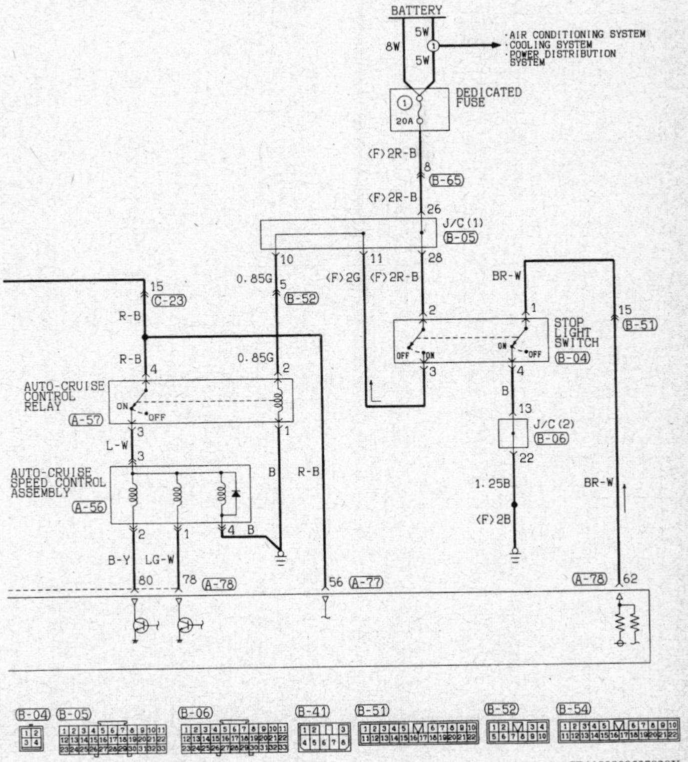

CR1109800537020X

Fig. 13 Wiring diagram (Part 2 of 4). Avenger & 2000 Sebring Coupe w/SOHC engine

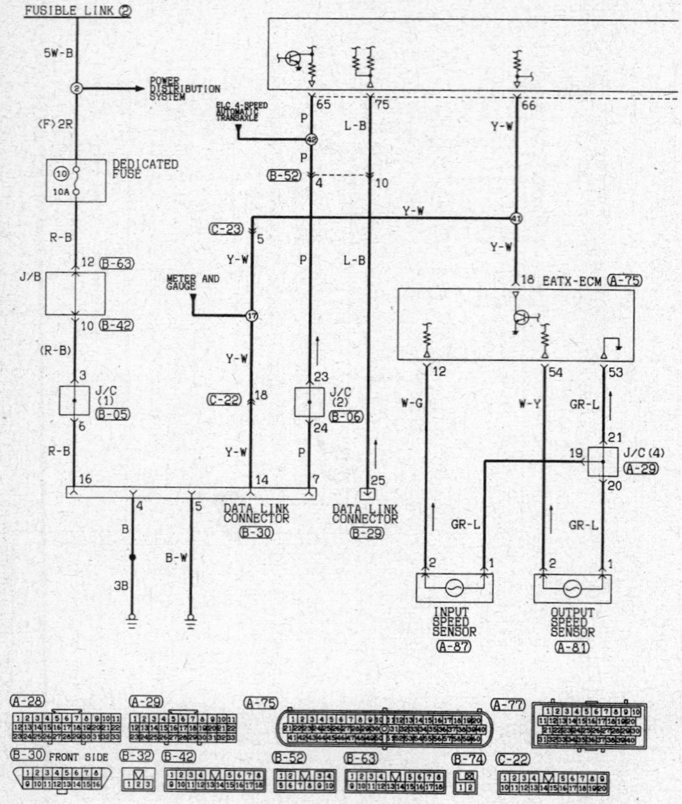

Fig. 13 Wiring diagram (Part 3 of 4). Avenger & 2000 Sebring Coupe w/SOHC engine

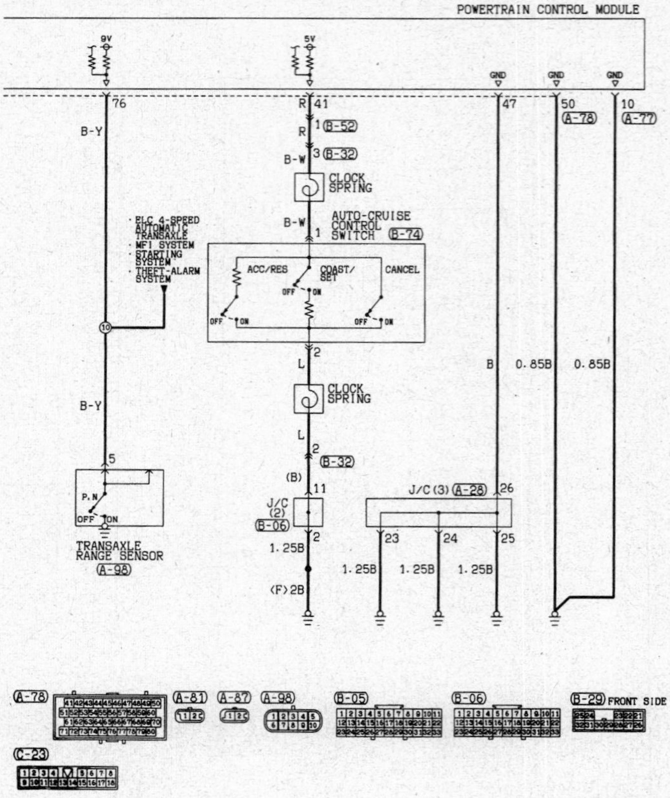

Fig. 13 Wiring diagram (Part 4 of 4). Avenger & 2000 Sebring Coupe w/SOHC engine

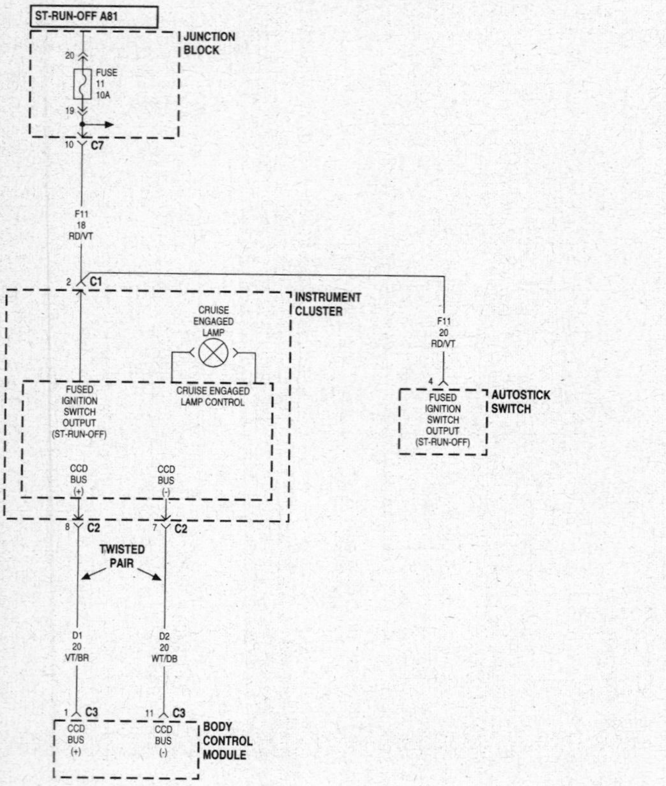

Fig. 14 Wiring diagram (Part 1 of 2). Breeze, Cirrus & 2000 Stratus

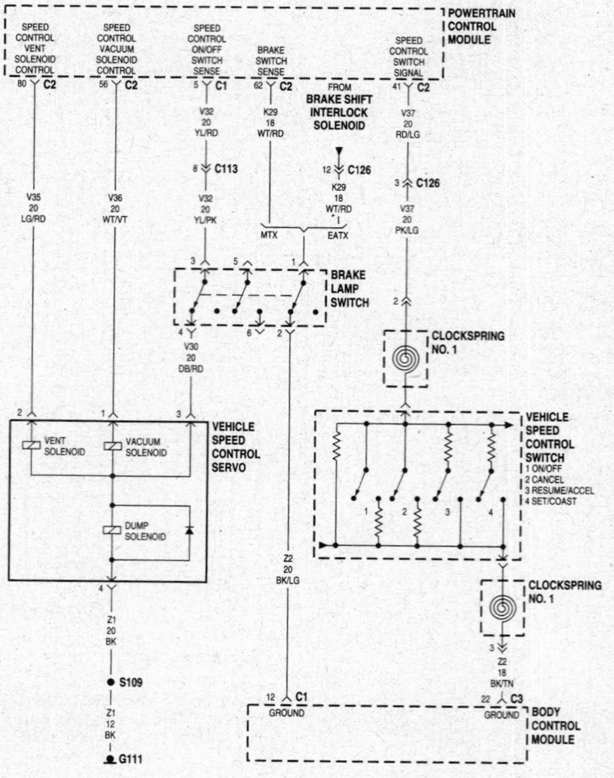

Fig. 14 Wiring diagram (Part 2 of 2). Breeze, Cirrus & 2000 Stratus

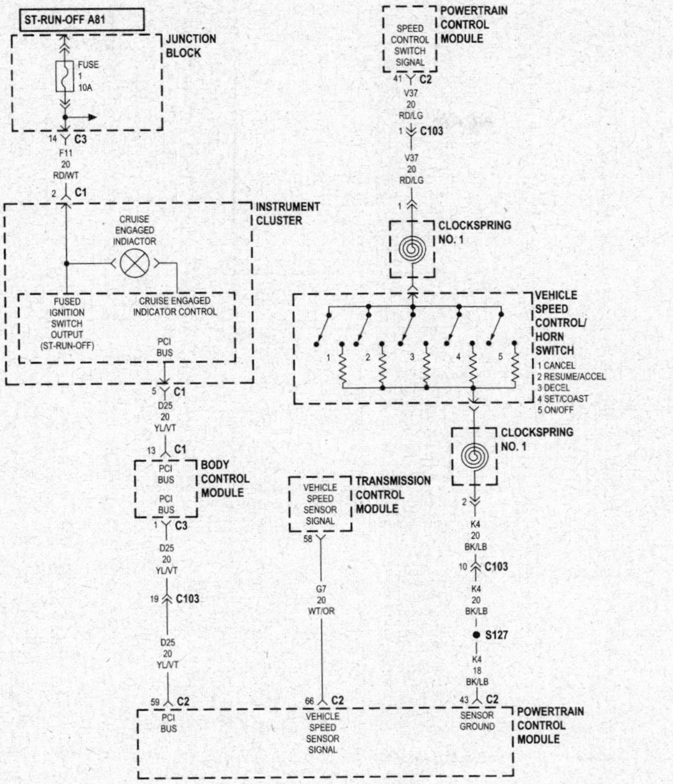

CR1100000640010X

Fig. 15 Wiring diagram (Part 1 of 2). 2000 Concorde, Intrepid, LHS & 300M

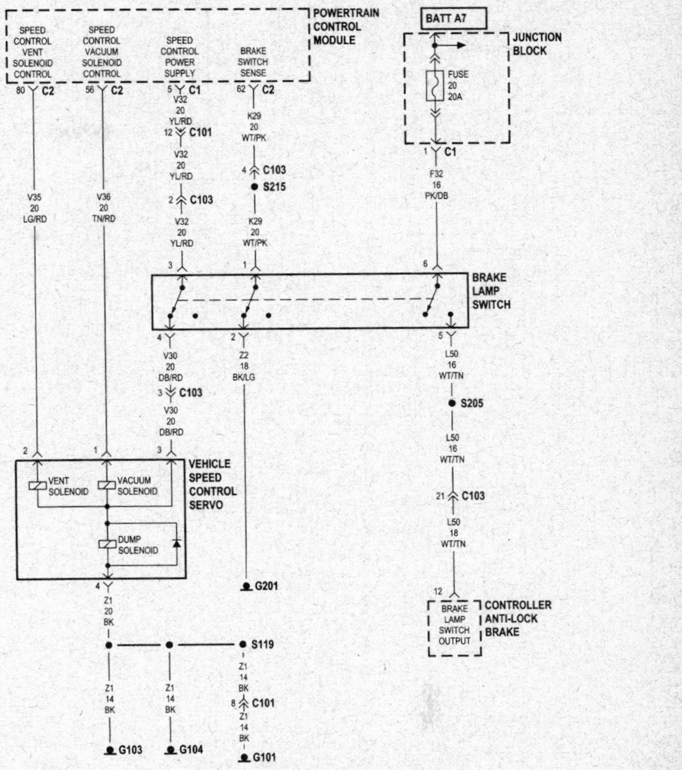

CR1100000640020X

Fig. 15 Wiring diagram (Part 2 of 2). 2000 Concorde, Intrepid, LHS & 300M

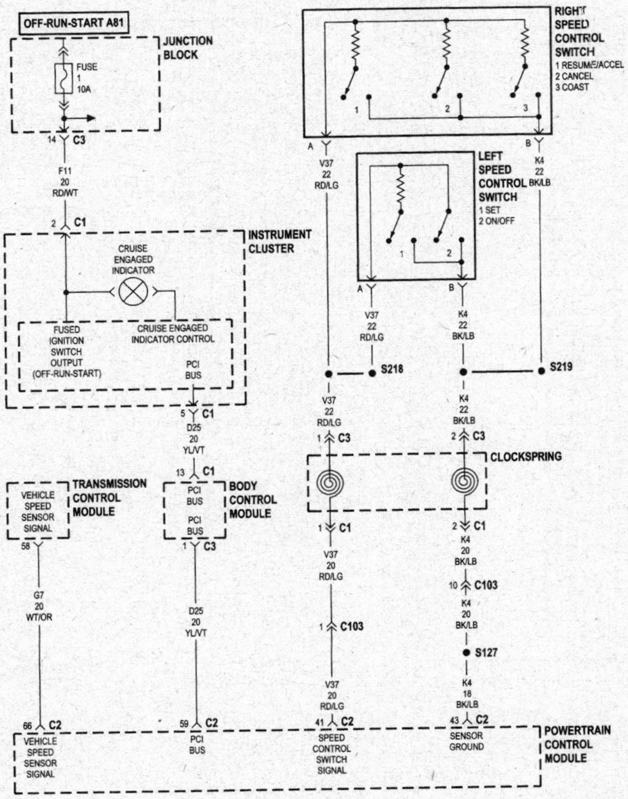

CR1100000665010X

Fig. 16 Wiring diagram (Part 1 of 2). 2001 Concorde, Intrepid, LHS & 300M

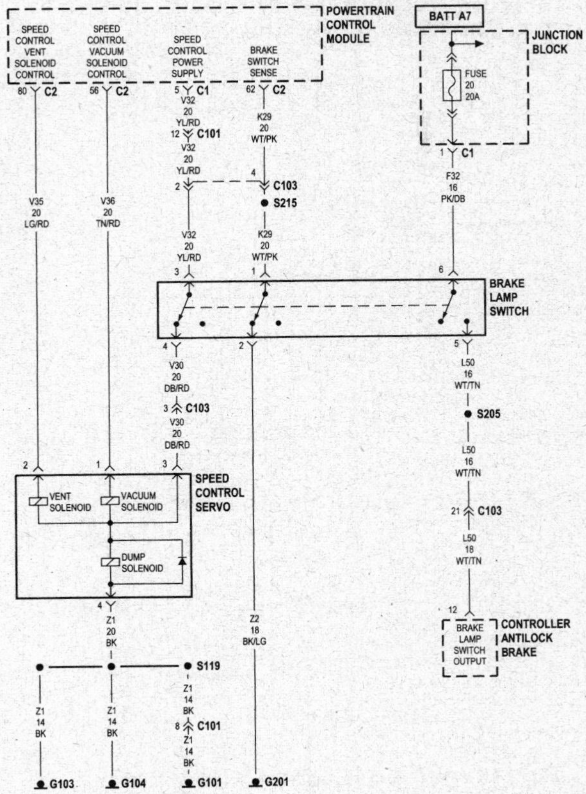

CR1100000665020X

Fig. 16 Wiring diagram (Part 2 of 2). 2001 Concorde, Intrepid, LHS & 300M

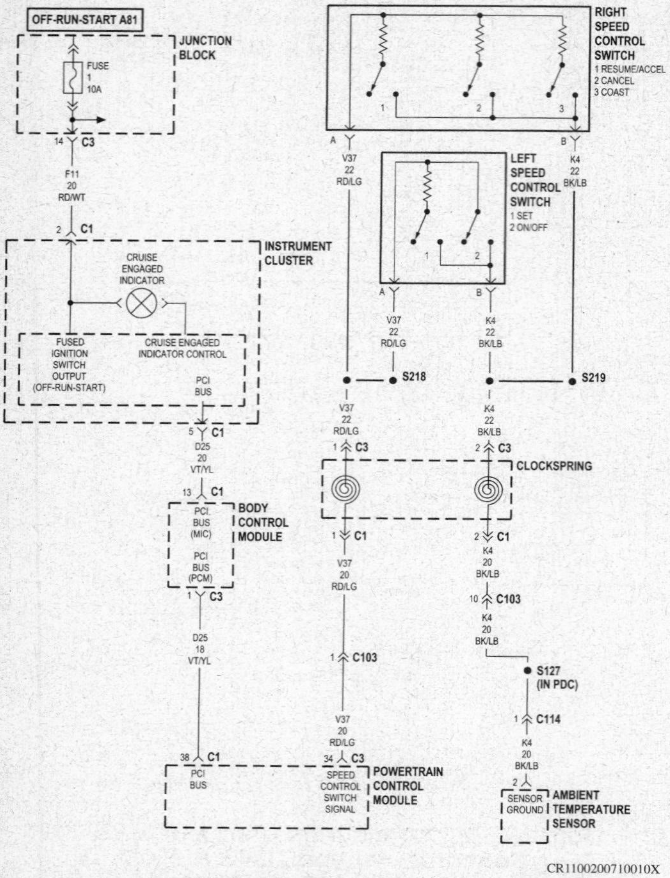

Fig. 17 Wiring diagram (Part 1 of 2). 2002–04 Concorde, Intrepid & 300M

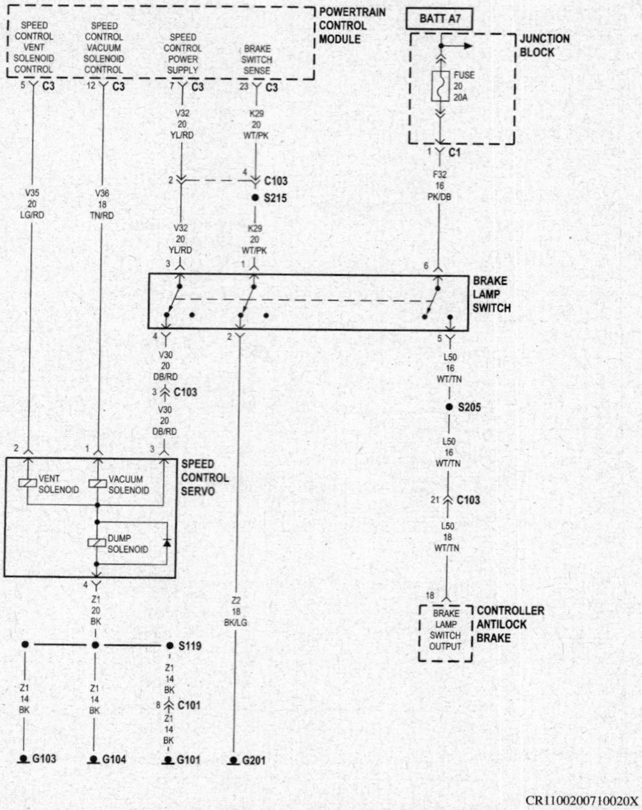

Fig. 17 Wiring diagram (Part 2 of 2). 2002–04 Concorde, Intrepid & 300M

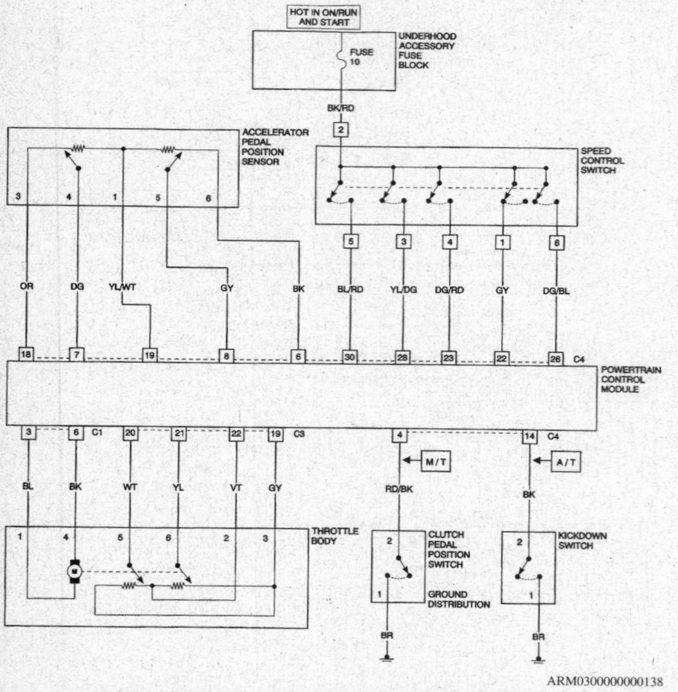

Fig. 18 Wiring diagram. Crossfire

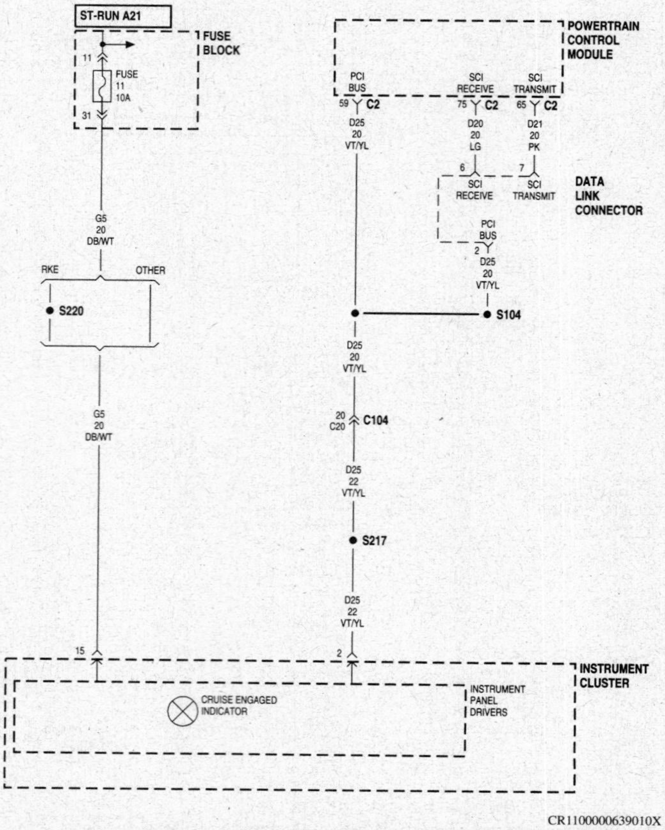

Fig. 19 Wiring diagram (Part 1 of 2). 2000 Neon

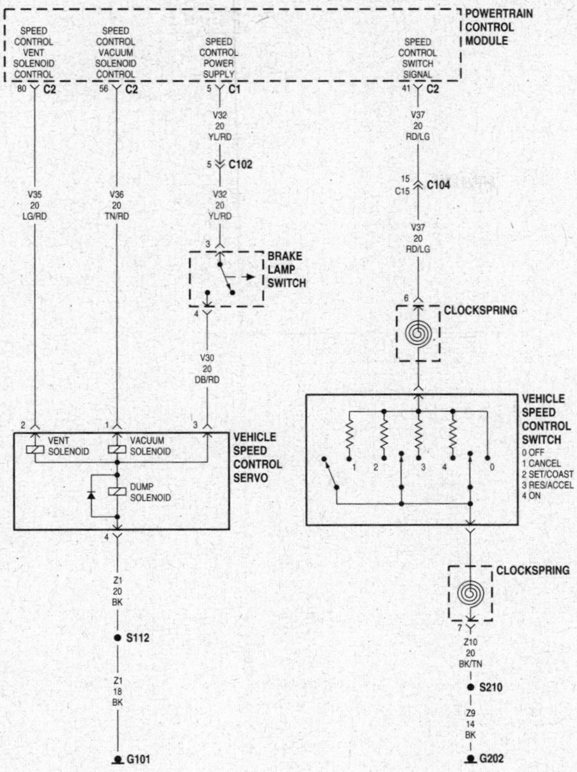

CR1100000639020X

Fig. 19 Wiring diagram (Part 2 of 2). 2000 Neon

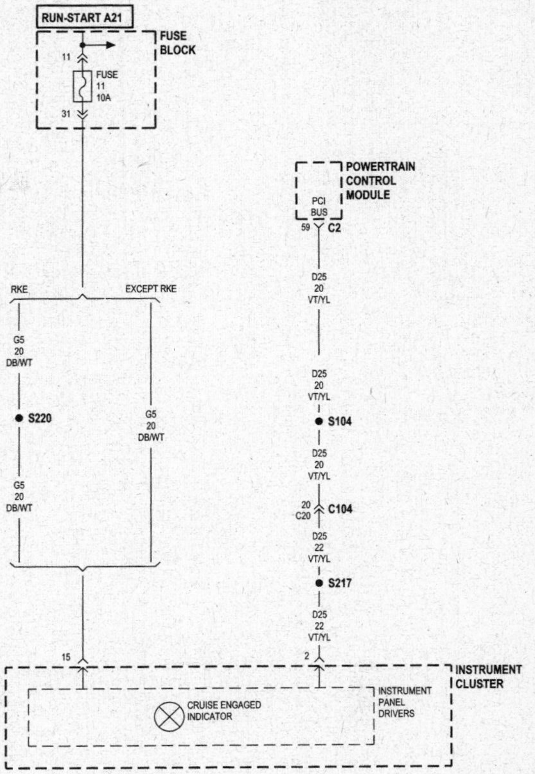

CR1100100715010X

Fig. 20 Wiring diagram (Part 1 of 3). 2001 Neon

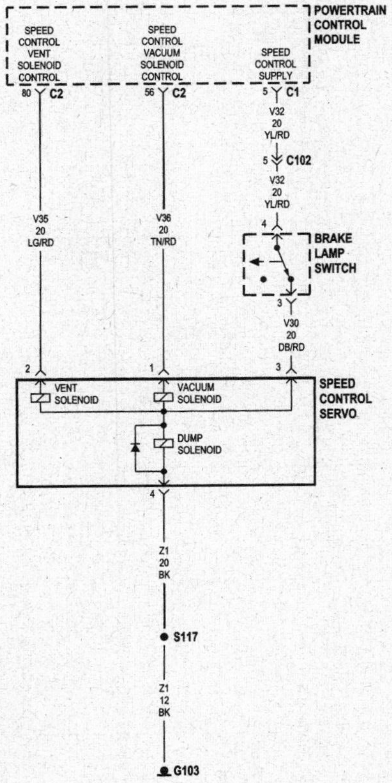

CR1100100715020X

Fig. 20 Wiring diagram (Part 2 of 3). 2001 Neon

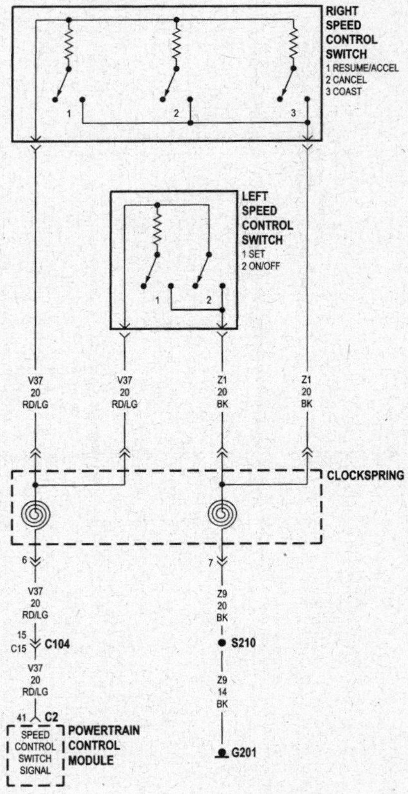

CR1100100715030X

Fig. 20 Wiring diagram (Part 3 of 3). 2001 Neon

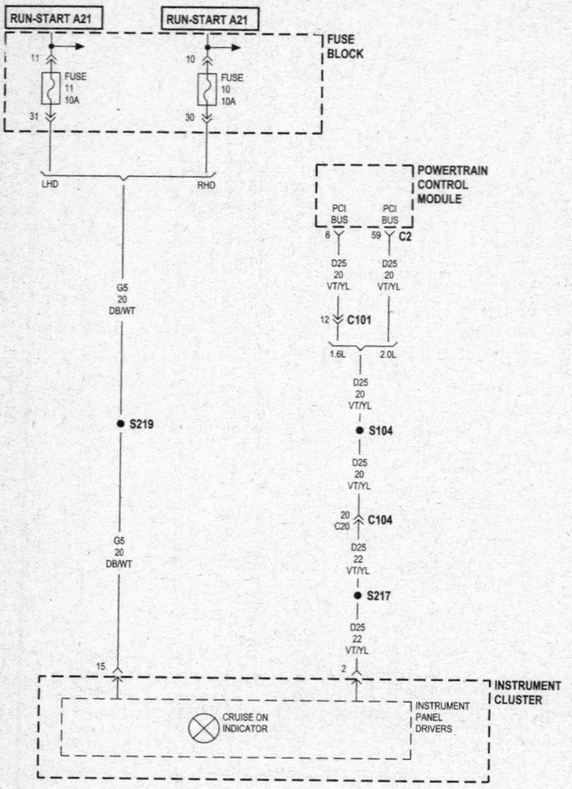

Fig. 21 Wiring diagram (Part 1 of 3). 2002–04 Neon

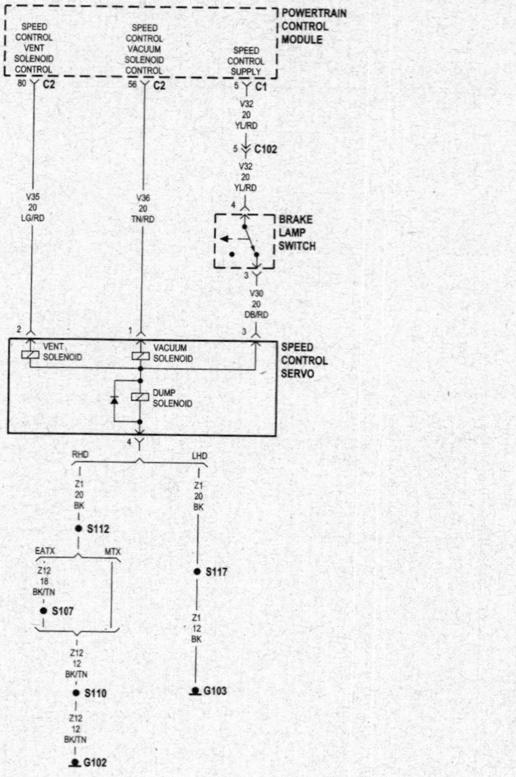

Fig. 21 Wiring diagram (Part 2 of 3). 2002–04 Neon

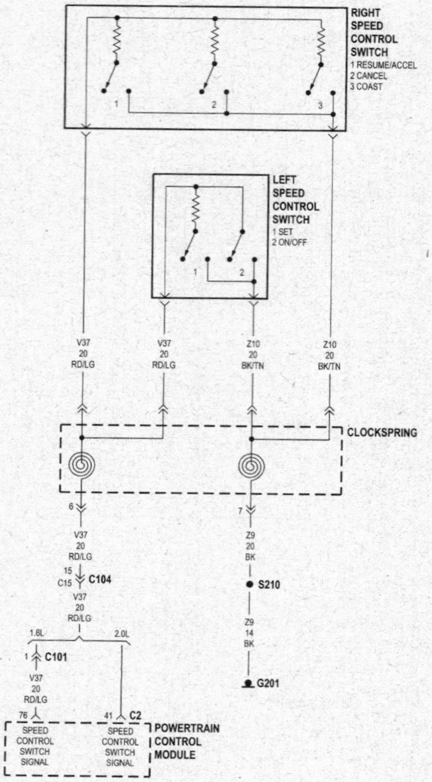

Fig. 21 Wiring diagram (Part 3 of 3). 2002–04 Neon

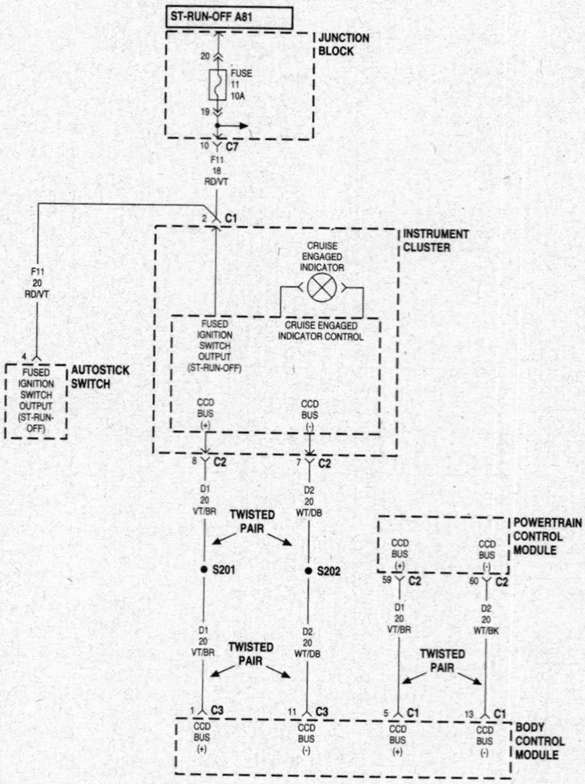

Fig. 22 Wiring diagram (Part 1 of 2). 2000 Sebring Convertible

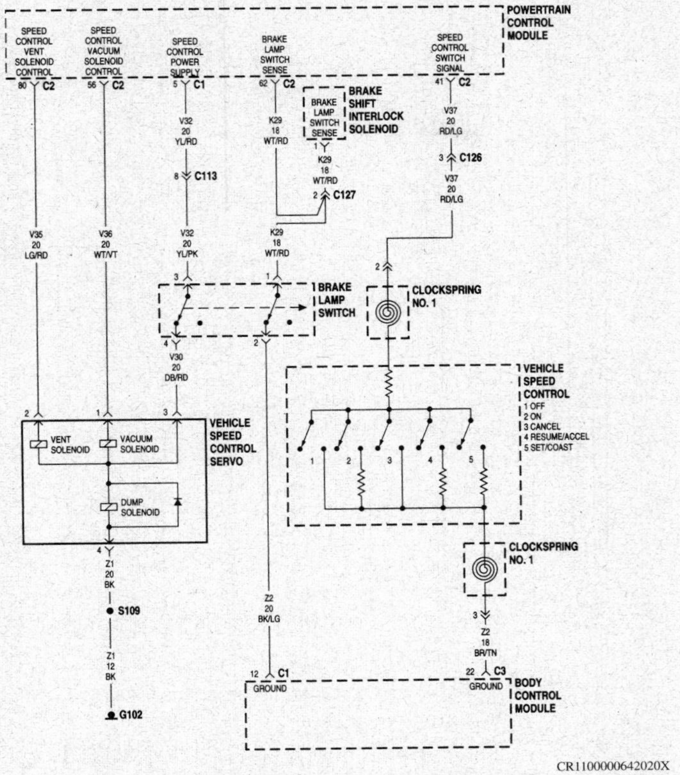

Fig. 22 Wiring diagram (Part 2 of 2). 2000 Sebring Convertible

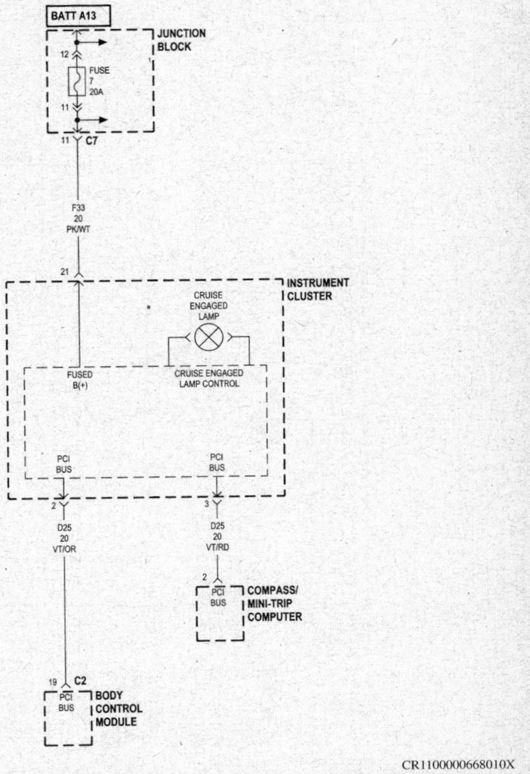

Fig. 23 Wiring diagram (Part 1 of 3). 2001–04 Sebring Convertible, Sebring Sedan & Stratus Sedan

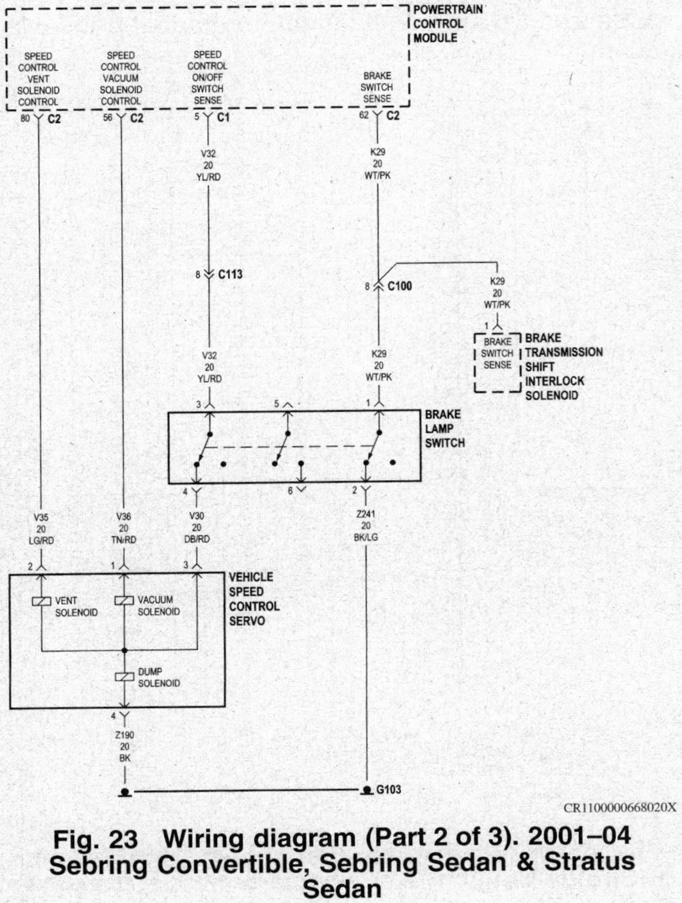

Fig. 23 Wiring diagram (Part 2 of 3). 2001–04 Sebring Convertible, Sebring Sedan & Stratus Sedan

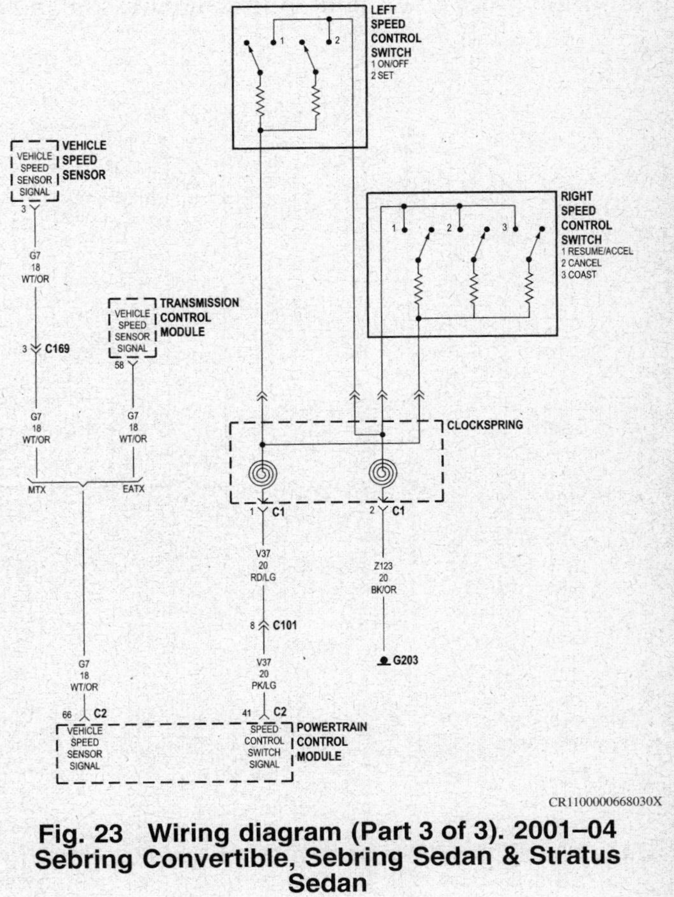

Fig. 23 Wiring diagram (Part 3 of 3). 2001–04 Sebring Convertible, Sebring Sedan & Stratus Sedan

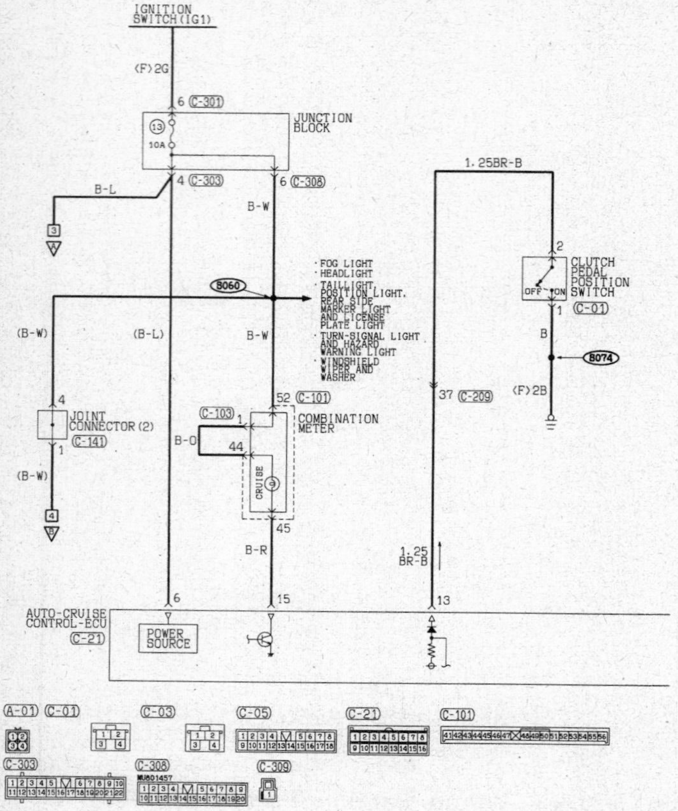

CR1100000683010X

Fig. 24 Wiring diagram (Part 1 of 4). 2001 Sebring & Stratus Coupe w/2.4L engine & manual transaxle

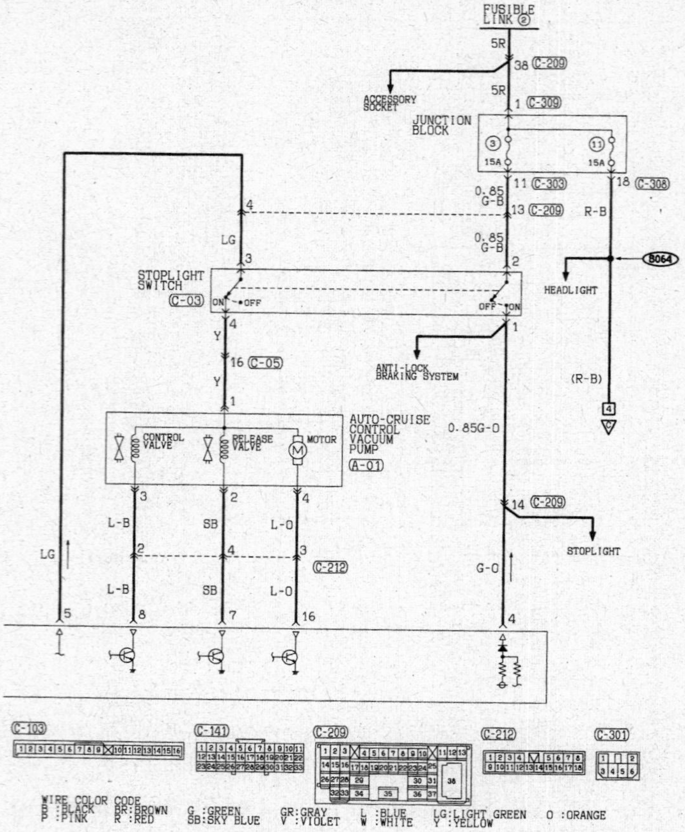

CR1100000683020X

Fig. 24 Wiring diagram (Part 2 of 4). 2001 Sebring & Stratus Coupe w/2.4L engine & manual transaxle

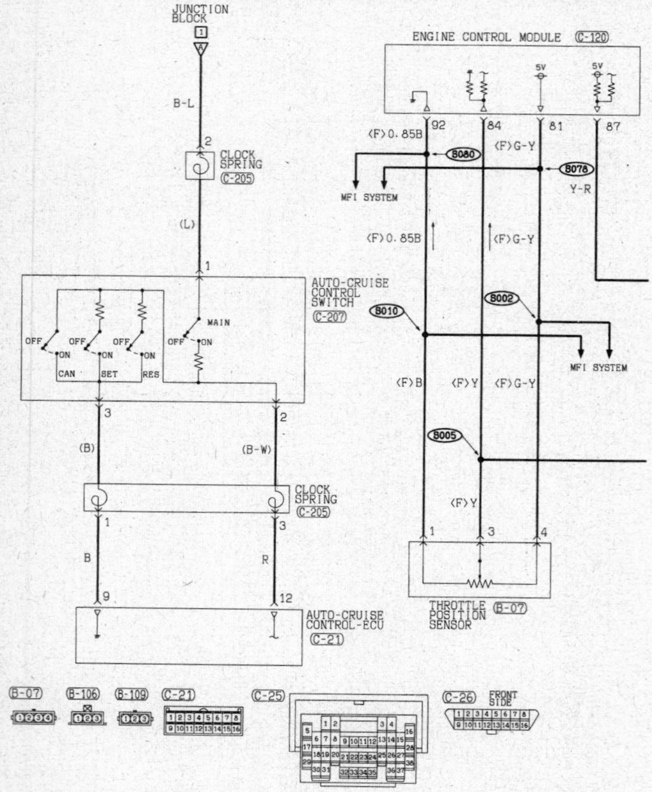

CR1100000683030X

Fig. 24 Wiring diagram (Part 3 of 4). 2001 Sebring & Stratus Coupe w/2.4L engine & manual transaxle

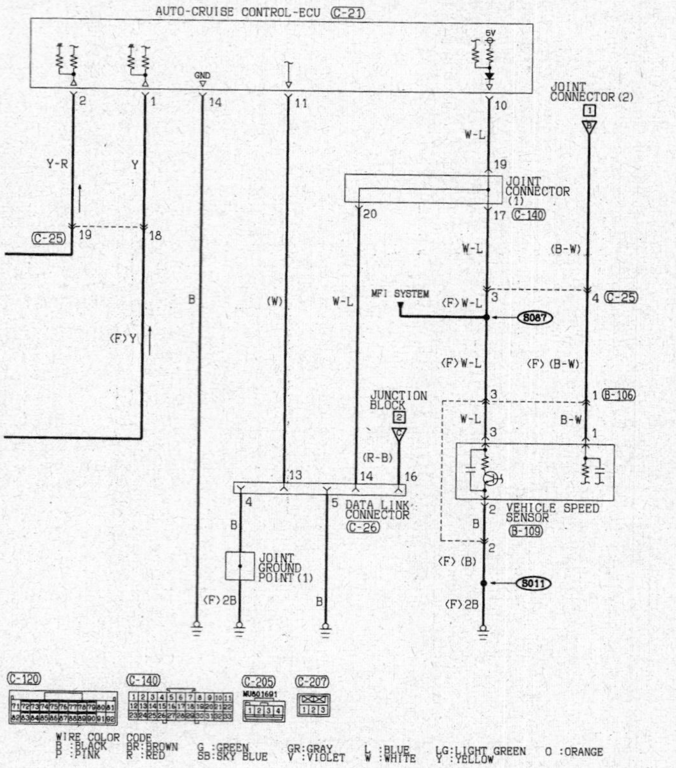

CR1100000683040X

Fig. 24 Wiring diagram (Part 4 of 4). 2001 Sebring & Stratus Coupe w/2.4L engine & manual transaxle

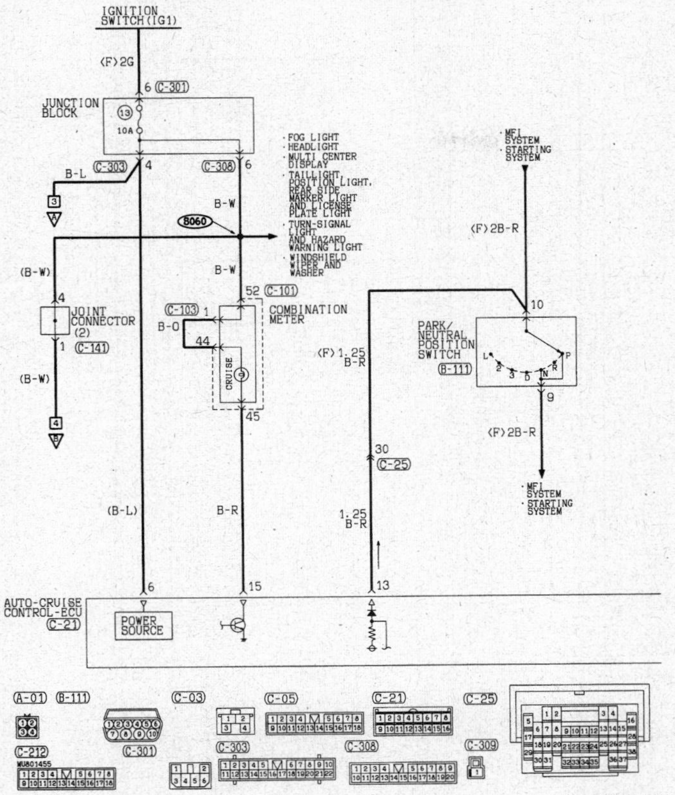

CR1100000684010X

Fig. 25 Wiring diagram (Part 1 of 4). 2001 Sebring & Stratus Coupe w/2.4L engine & automatic transaxle

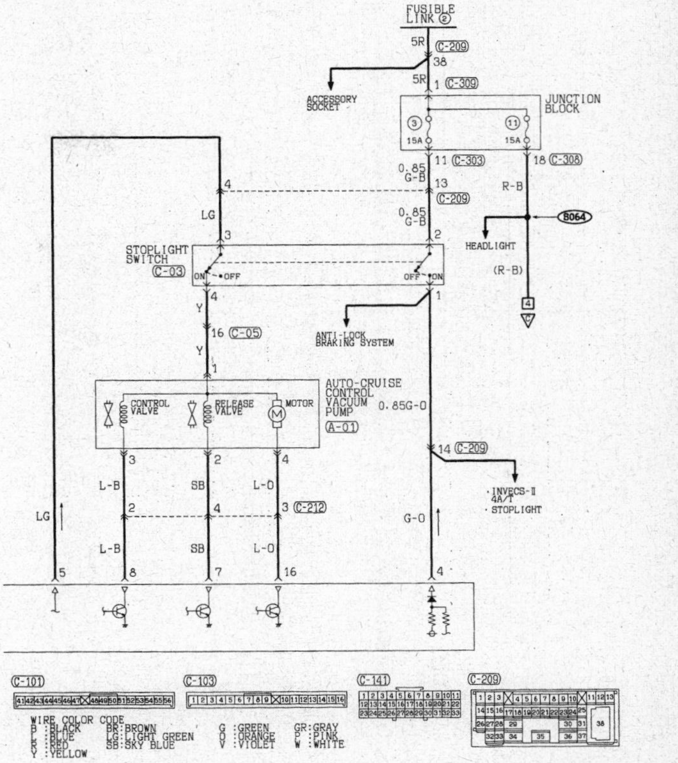

CR1100000684020X

Fig. 25 Wiring diagram (Part 2 of 4). 2001 Sebring & Stratus Coupe w/2.4L engine & automatic transaxle

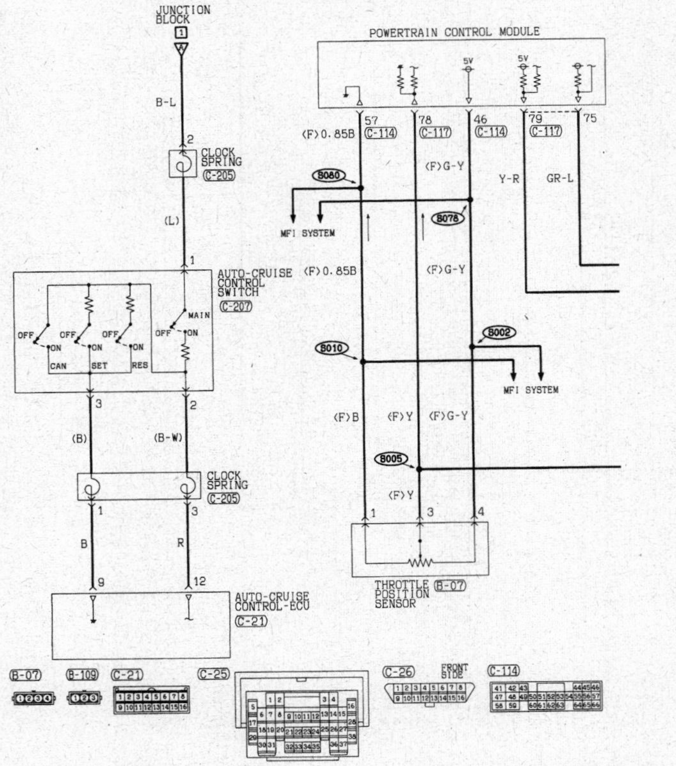

CR1100000684030X

Fig. 25 Wiring diagram (Part 3 of 4). 2001 Sebring & Stratus Coupe w/2.4L engine & automatic transaxle

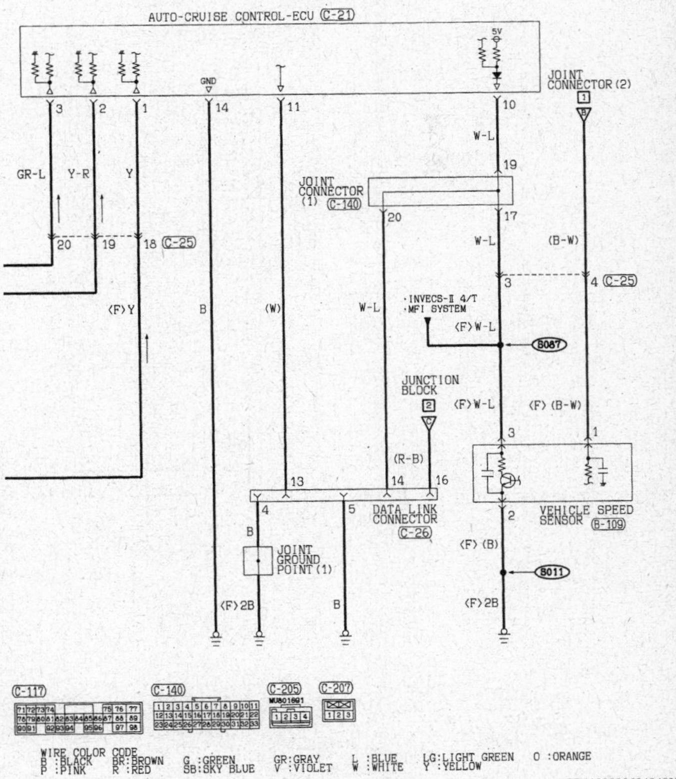

CR1100000684040X

Fig. 25 Wiring diagram (Part 4 of 4). 2001 Sebring & Stratus Coupe w/2.4L engine & automatic transaxle

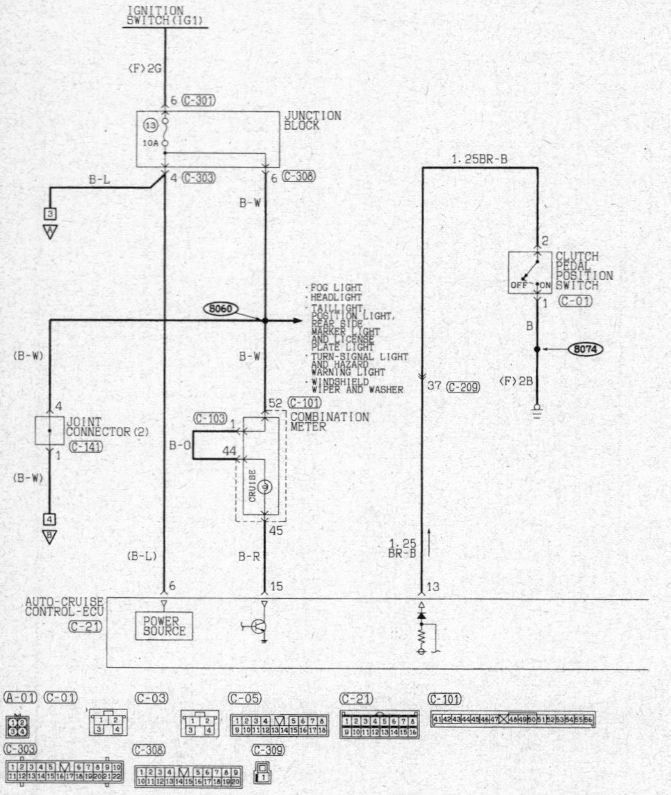

CR1100000685010X

Fig. 26 Wiring diagram (Part 1 of 4). 2001 Sebring & Stratus Coupe w/3.0L engine & manual transaxle

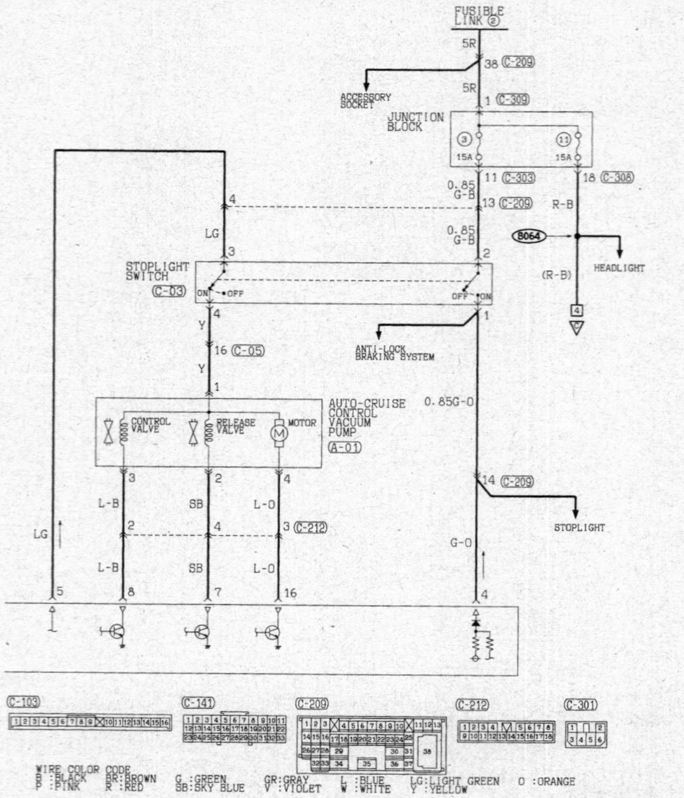

CR1100000685020X

Fig. 26 Wiring diagram (Part 2 of 4). 2001 Sebring & Stratus Coupe w/3.0L engine & manual transaxle

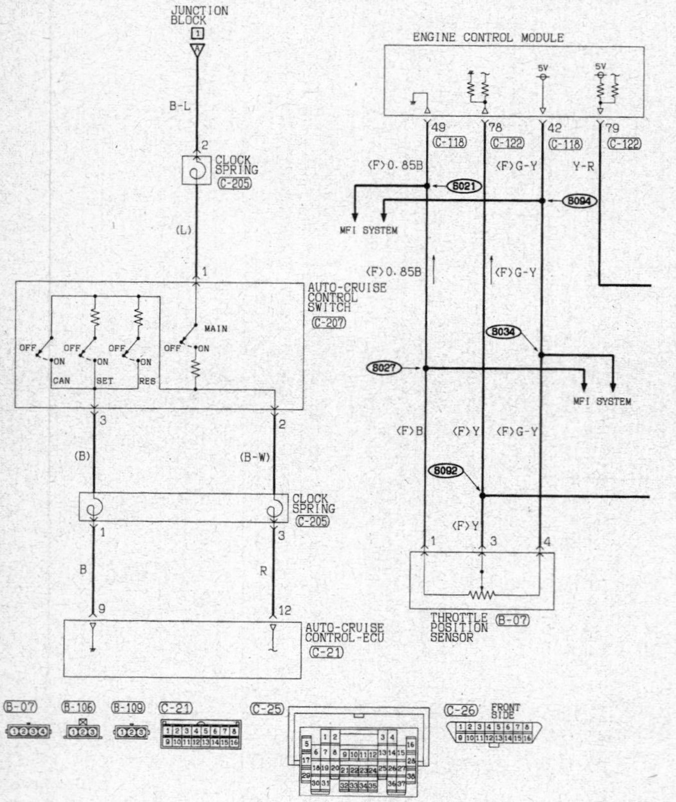

CR1100000685030X

Fig. 26 Wiring diagram (Part 3 of 4). 2001 Sebring & Stratus Coupe w/3.0L engine & manual transaxle

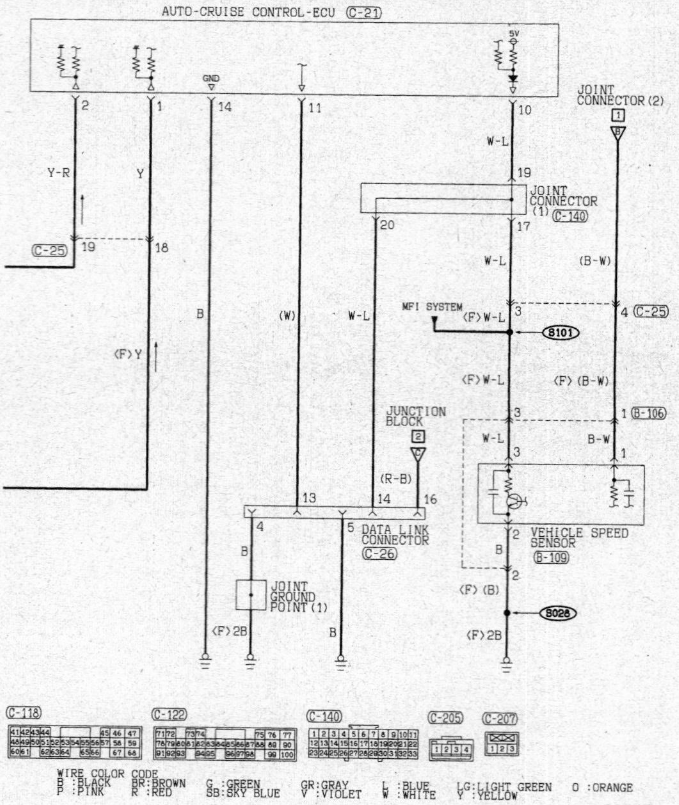

CR1100000685040X

Fig. 26 Wiring diagram (Part 4 of 4). 2001 Sebring & Stratus Coupe w/3.0L engine & manual transaxle

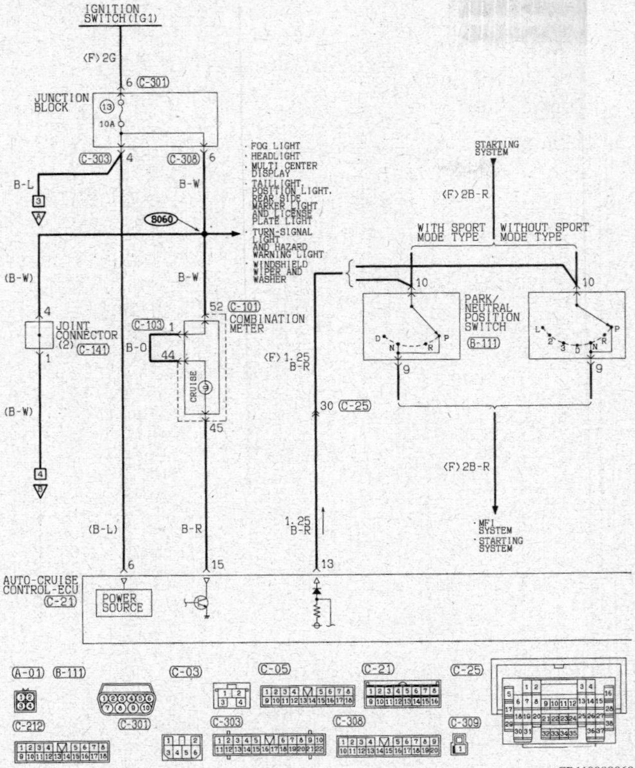

CR1100000686010X

Fig. 27 Wiring diagram (Part 1 of 4). 2001 Sebring & Stratus Coupe w/3.0L engine & automatic transaxle

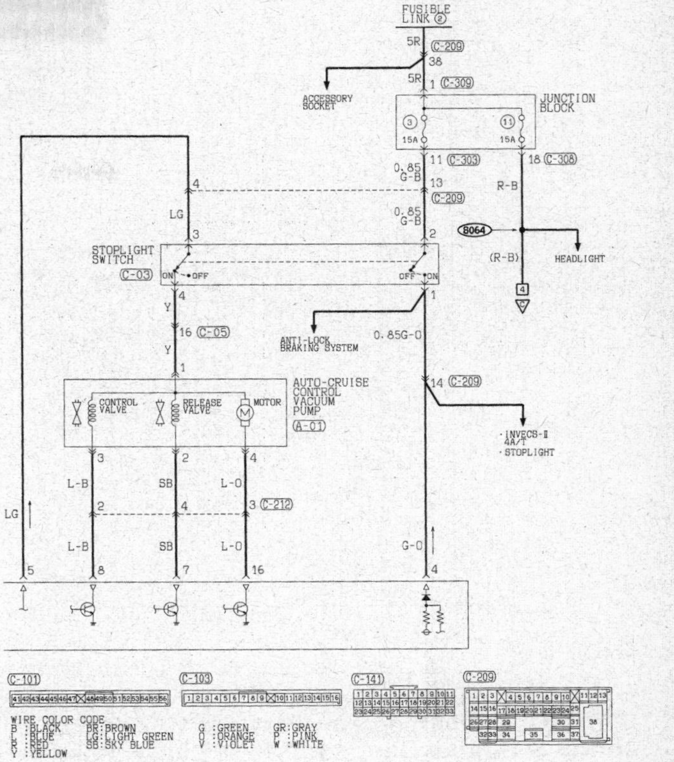

CR1100000686020X

Fig. 27 Wiring diagram (Part 2 of 4). 2001 Sebring & Stratus Coupe w/3.0L engine & automatic transaxle

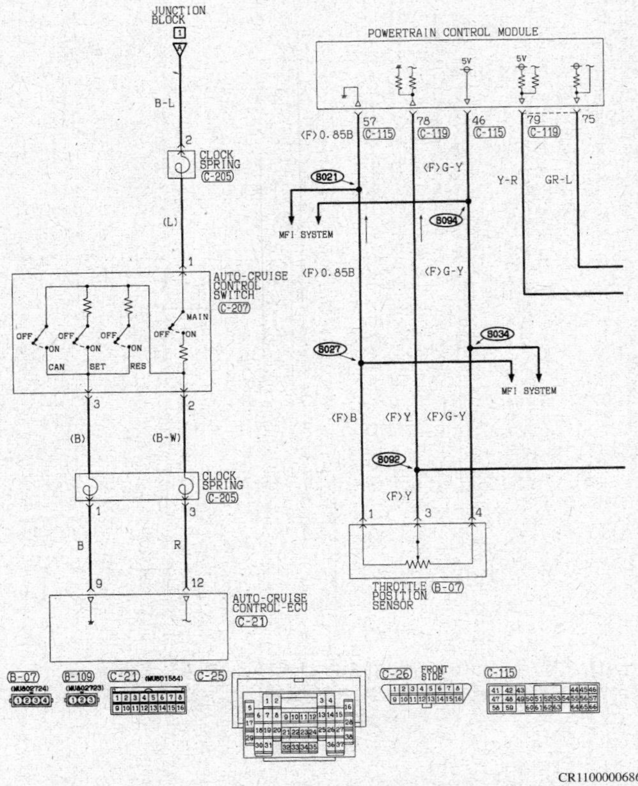

CR1100000686030X

Fig. 27 Wiring diagram (Part 3 of 4). 2001 Sebring & Stratus Coupe w/3.0L engine & automatic transaxle

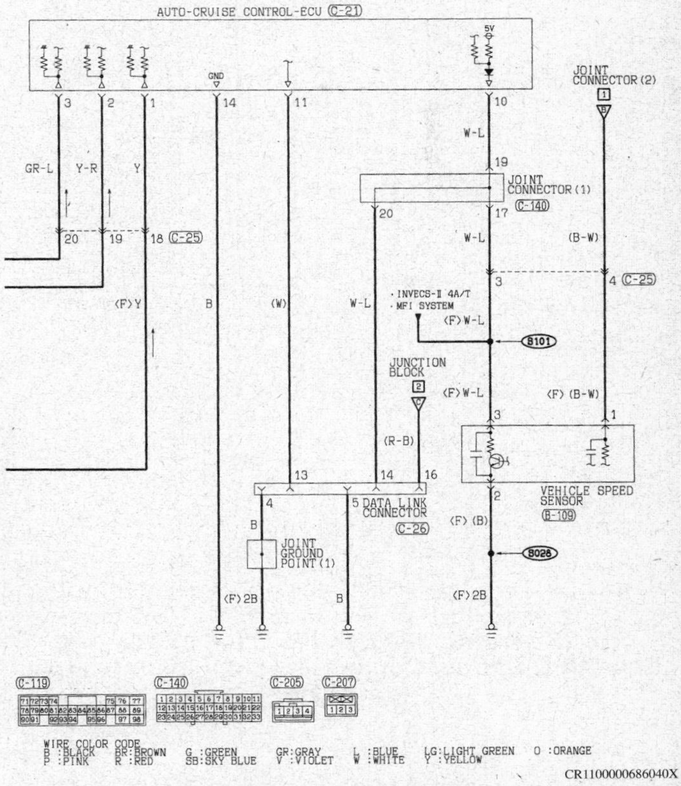

CR1100000686040X

Fig. 27 Wiring diagram (Part 4 of 4). 2001 Sebring & Stratus Coupe w/3.0L engine & automatic transaxle

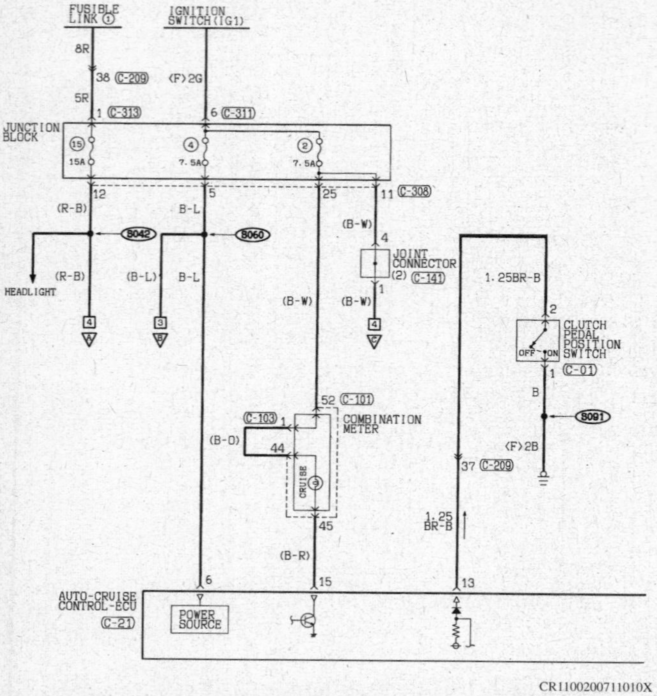

Fig. 28 Wiring diagram (Part 1 of 4). 2002–03 Sebring & Stratus Coupe w/2.4L engine & manual transaxle

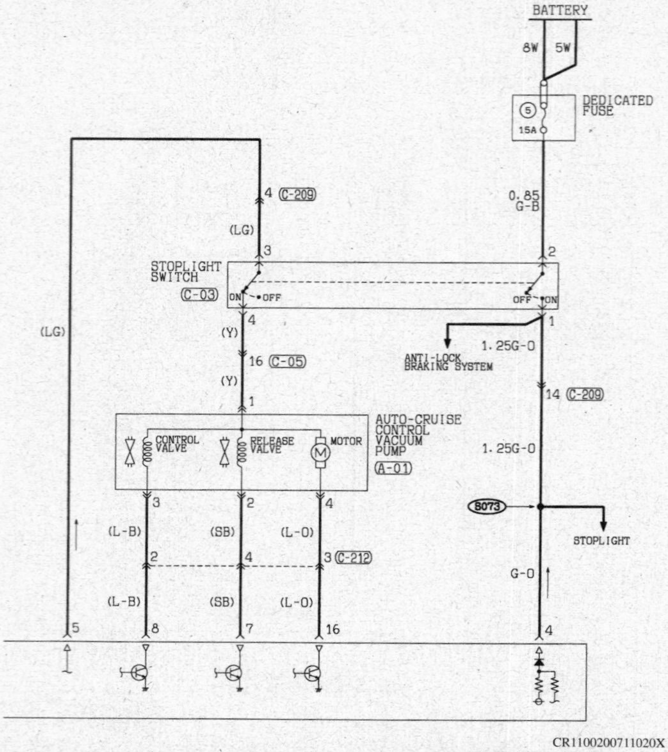

Fig. 28 Wiring diagram (Part 2 of 4). 2002–03 Sebring & Stratus Coupe w/2.4L engine & manual transaxle

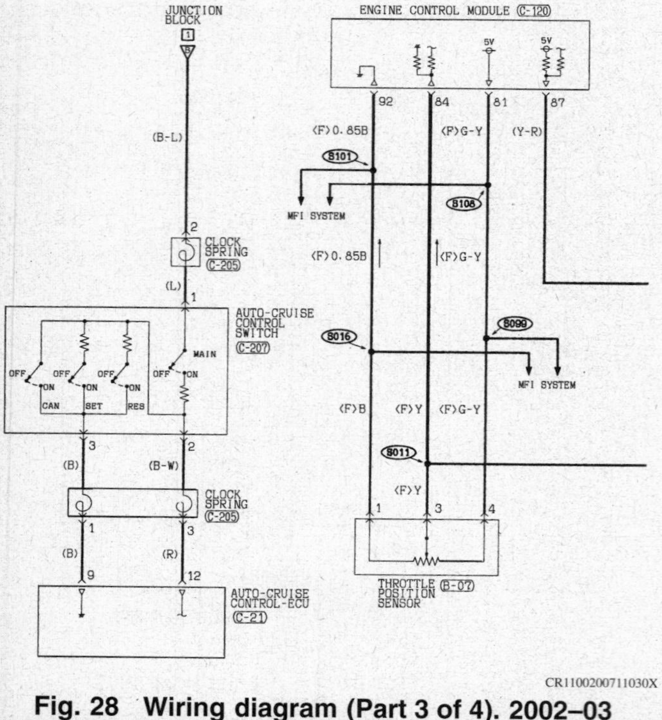

Fig. 28 Wiring diagram (Part 3 of 4). 2002–03 Sebring & Stratus Coupe w/2.4L engine & manual transaxle

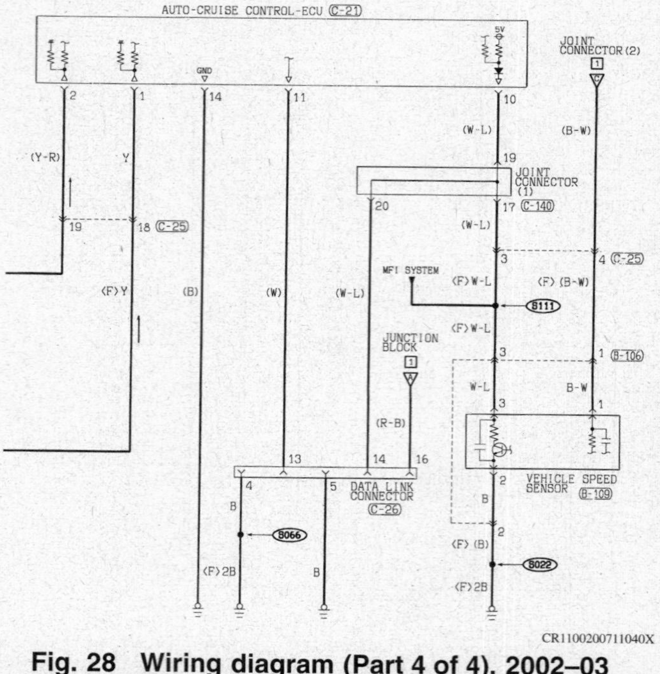

Fig. 28 Wiring diagram (Part 4 of 4). 2002–03 Sebring & Stratus Coupe w/2.4L engine & manual transaxle

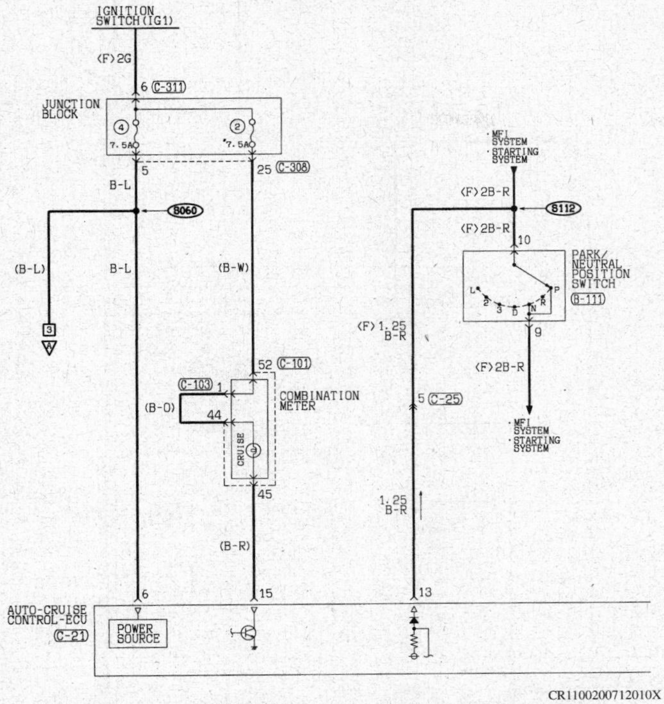

Fig. 29 Wiring diagram (Part 1 of 4). 2002–03 Sebring & Stratus Coupe w/2.4L engine & automatic transaxle

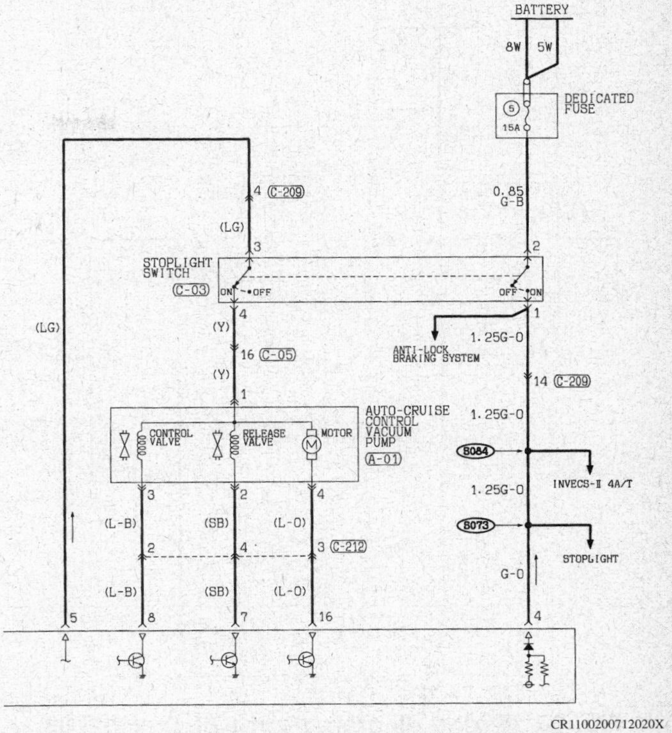

Fig. 29 Wiring diagram (Part 2 of 4). 2002–03 Sebring & Stratus Coupe w/2.4L engine & automatic transaxle

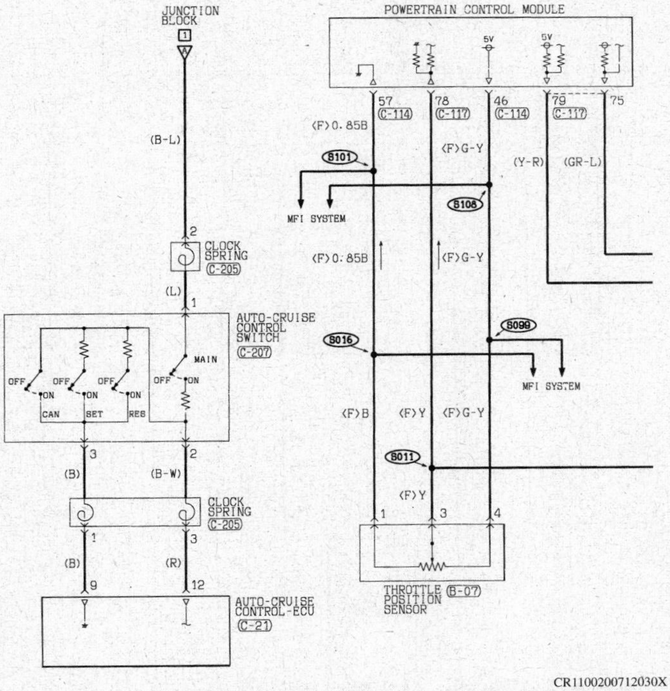

Fig. 29 Wiring diagram (Part 3 of 4). 2002–03 Sebring & Stratus Coupe w/2.4L engine & automatic transaxle

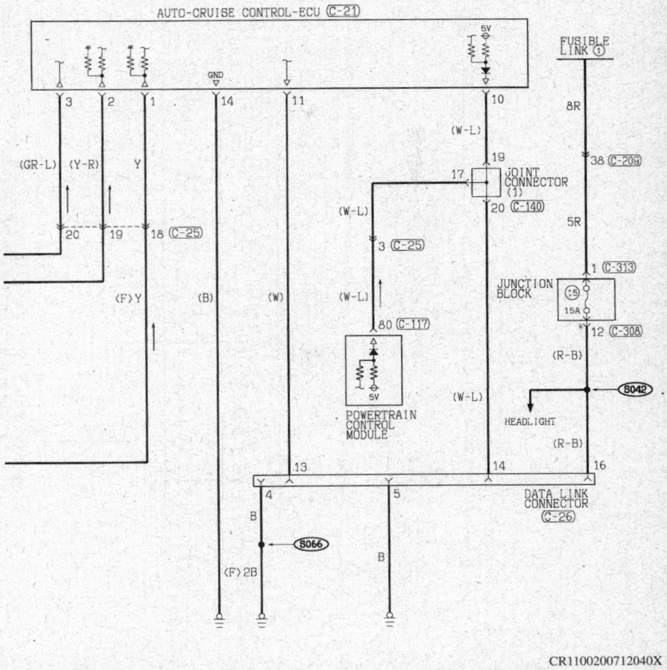

Fig. 29 Wiring diagram (Part 4 of 4). 2002–03 Sebring & Stratus Coupe w/2.4L engine & automatic transaxle

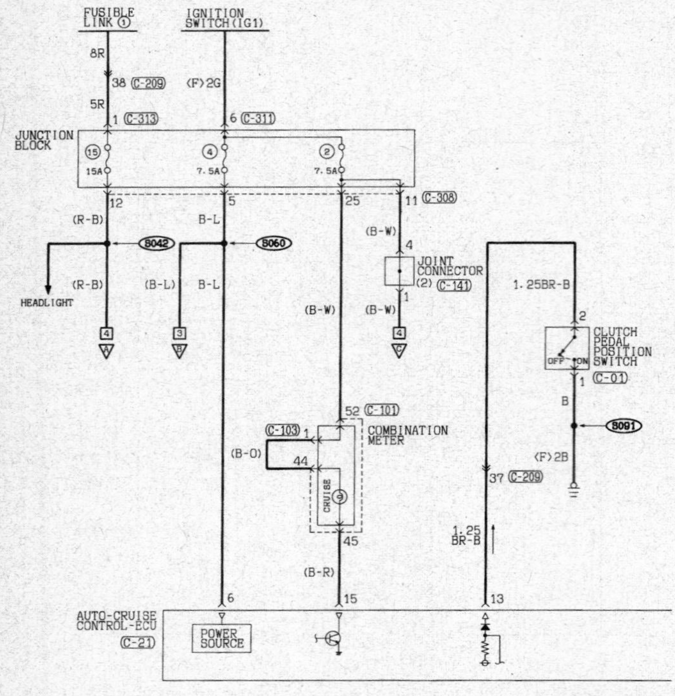

Fig. 30 Wiring diagram (Part 1 of 4). 2002–03 Sebring & Stratus Coupe w/3.0L engine & manual transaxle

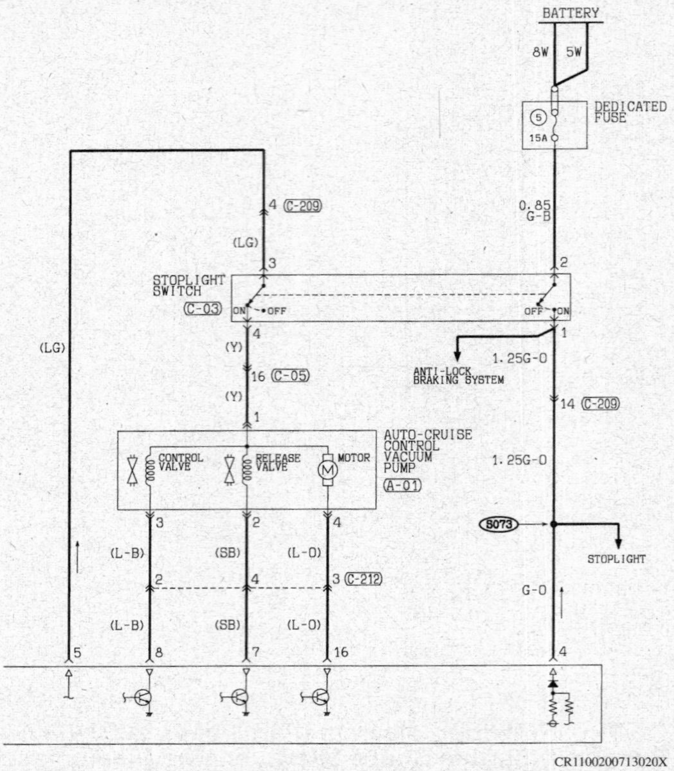

Fig. 30 Wiring diagram (Part 2 of 4). 2002–03 Sebring & Stratus Coupe w/3.0L engine & manual transaxle

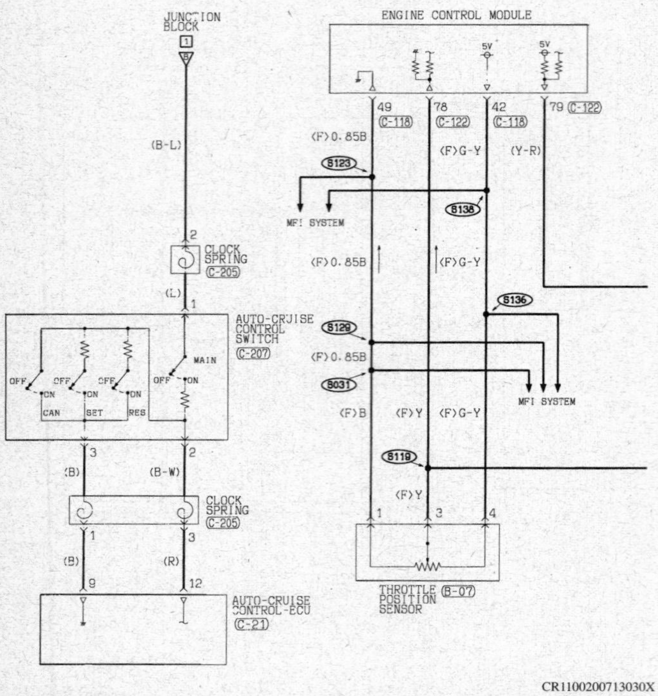

Fig. 30 Wiring diagram (Part 3 of 4). 2002–03 Sebring & Stratus Coupe w/3.0L engine & manual transaxle

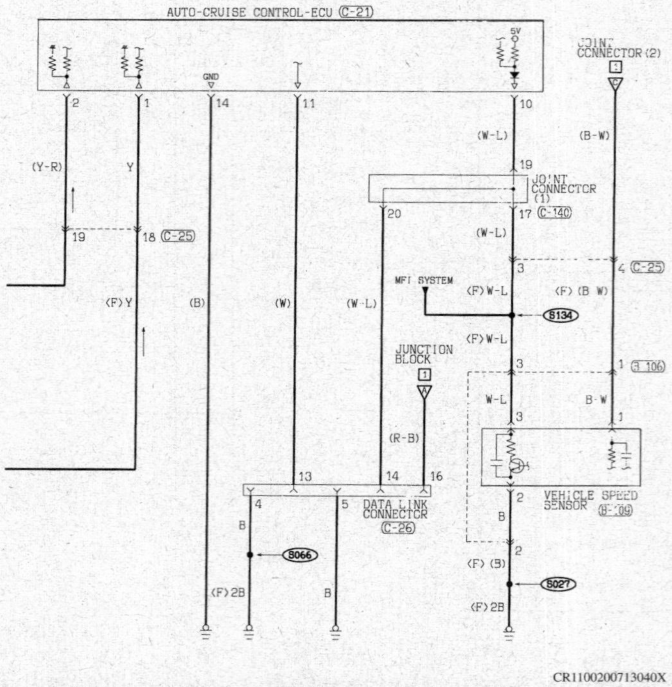

Fig. 30 Wiring diagram (Part 4 of 4). 2002–03 Sebring & Stratus Coupe w/3.0L engine & manual transaxle

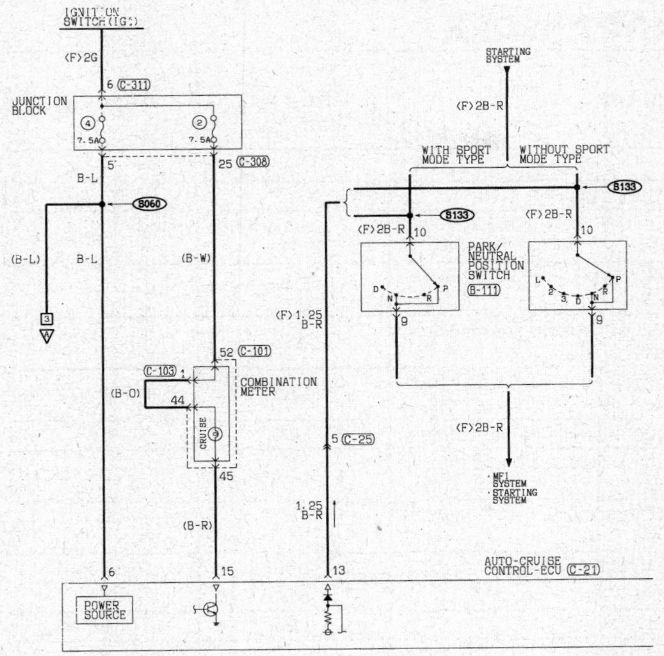

CR1100200714010X

Fig. 31 Wiring diagram (Part 1 of 4). 2002–03 Sebring & Stratus Coupe w/3.0L engine & automatic transaxle

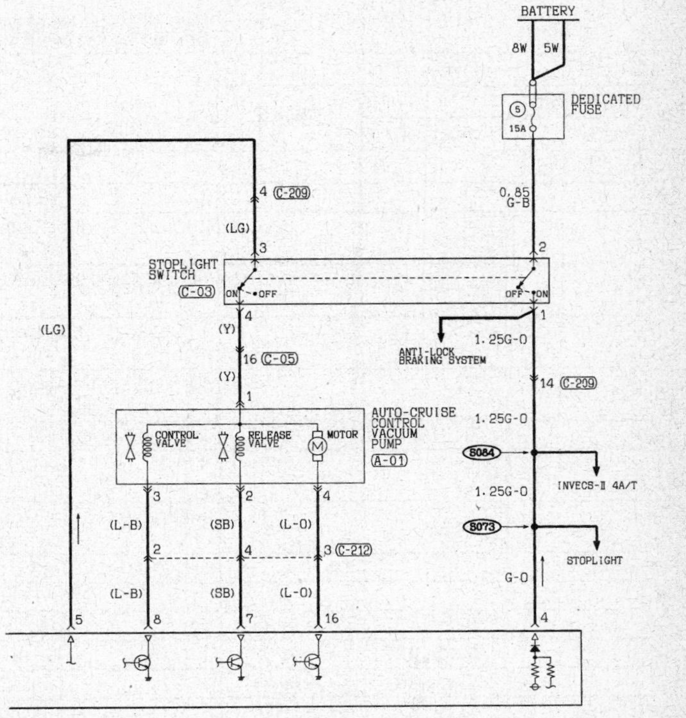

CR1100200714020X

Fig. 31 Wiring diagram (Part 2 of 4). 2002–03 Sebring & Stratus Coupe w/3.0L engine & automatic transaxle

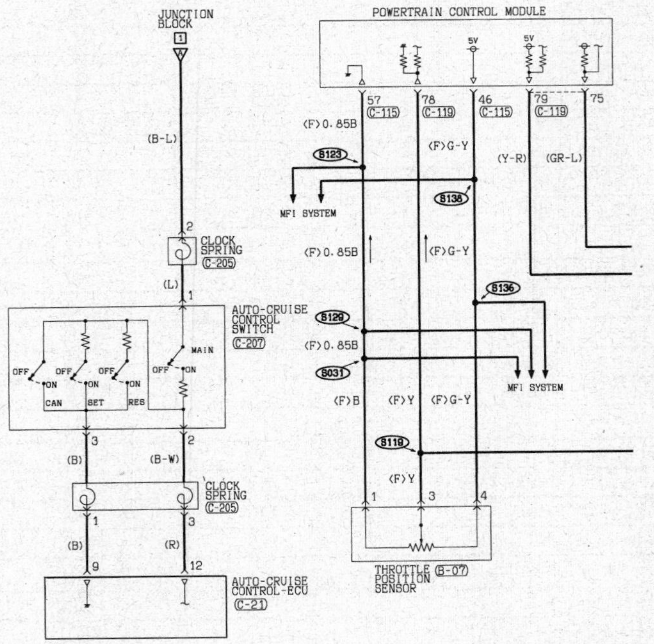

CR1100200714030X

Fig. 31 Wiring diagram (Part 3 of 4). 2002–03 Sebring & Stratus Coupe w/3.0L engine & automatic transaxle

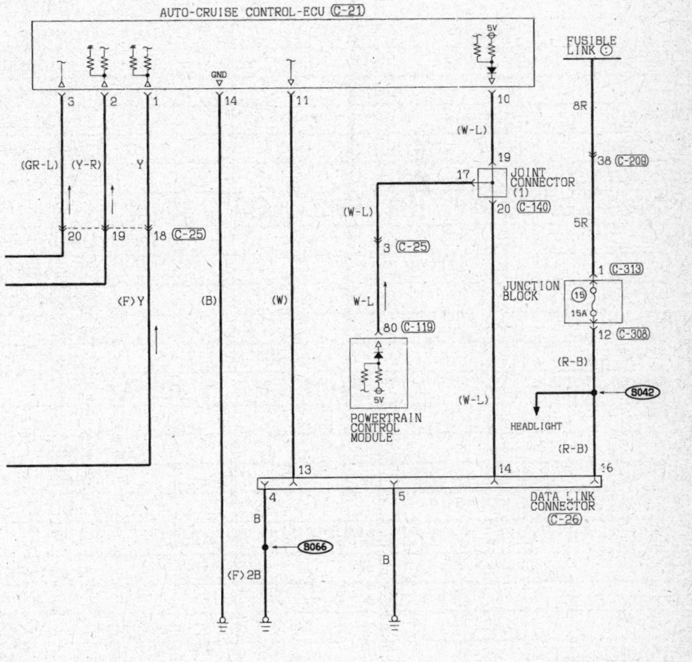

CR1100200714040X

Fig. 31 Wiring diagram (Part 4 of 4). 2002–03 Sebring & Stratus Coupe w/3.0L engine & automatic transaxle

DIAGNOSTIC CHART INDEX

Code Scan Tool Generic	Code Scan Tool MUT-II	Flash	Description	Page No.	Fig. No.
AVENGER					
—	—	—	Cruise Control Cannot Be Set	2-53	75
—	—	—	Cruise Control Does Not Cancel When Brake Pedal Is Depressed	2-53	72
—	—	—	Cruise Control Does Not Cancel When CANCEL Switch Is ON	2-53	74
—	—	—	Cruise Control Does Not Cancel When Engine Speed Rises Suddenly	2-53	71
—	—	—	Cruise Control Does Not Cancel When Selector Set To N Position	2-53	73
—	—	—	Cruise Control Main Switch Lamp Does Not Illuminate	2-54	78
—	—	—	Instrument Cluster Cruise Control Indicator Lamp Does Not Illuminate	2-54	79
—	—	—	Instrument Panel Cruise Control Indicator Lamp Does Not Illuminate	2-54	77
—	—	—	Scan Tool Communications Not Possible	2-53	70
—	—	—	Speed Hunts w/Cruise Control Set	2-54	76
—	Code 15	Code 34	Speed Control Servo Solenoid	2-25	34
—	Code 82	Code 77	Cruise Control Relay	2-25	37
—	Code 86	Code 34	Cruise Control Switch	2-25	35
—	Code 87	Code 34	Cruise Control Switch	2-25	36
P0500	Code 35	Code 15	Vehicle Speed Signal	2-25	32
P0605	Code 02	Code 53	Powertrain Control Module	2-25	33
2000 BREEZE & CIRRUS					
—	—	—	Brake Switch Sense	2-25	38
—	—	—	Park/Neutral Position Switch	2-29	42
—	—	—	Speed Control Denied Message	2-29	43
—	—	—	Speed Control Operation	2-29	44
—	—	—	Verification Test VER-4A	2-31	45
P1595	—	—	Speed Control Solenoid Circuits	2-26	39
P1596	—	—	Speed Control Switch Always High	2-28	40
P1597	—	—	Speed Control Switch Always Low	2-28	41
2000 CONCORDE, INTREPID, LHS & 300M					
—	—	—	Speed Control System With No DTCs Present	2-34	48
—	—	—	Powertrain Verification Test VER-4	2-36	49
P1595	—	—	Speed Control Solenoid Circuits	2-31	46
P1597	—	—	Speed Control Switch Always Low	2-33	47
P1683	—	—	Speed Control Solenoid Circuits	2-31	46
2001 CONCORDE, INTREPID, LHS, & 300M					
—	—	—	Verification Test VER-4	2-38	52
P1595	—	—	Speed Control Solenoid Circuits	2-36	50
P1683	—	—	Speed Control Solenoid Circuits	2-36	50
P1597	—	—	Speed Control Switch Always Low	2-37	51
2002–04 CONCORDE, INTREPID & 300M					
—	—	—	Verification Test VER-4	2-42	59
—	—	—	Verification Test VER-5	2-42	60
P0579	—	—	Speed Control Switch No. 1 Performance	2-38	53
P0580	—	—	Speed Control Switch No. 1 Low	2-39	54
P0581	—	—	Speed Control Switch No. 1 High	2-39	55
P0582	—	—	Speed Control Vacuum Solenoid Circuit	2-40	56
P0586	—	—	Speed Control Vent Solenoid Circuit	2-40	57
P0594	—	—	Speed Control Servo Power Circuit	2-41	58
2000 NEON					
—	—	—	Verification Test 4A	2-46	63
P1595	—	—	Speed Control Solenoid & Power Relay Circuits	2-42	61

Continued

DIAGNOSTIC CHART INDEX—Continued

Code Scan Tool Generic	MUT-II	Flash	Description	Page No.	Fig. No.
2000 NEON					
P1693	—	—	Speed Control Solenoid & Power Relay Circuits	2-42	61
—	—	—	Speed Control Operation With No DTCs Present	2-44	62
2001–02 NEON					
—	—	—	Verification Test VER-4	2-38	52
P1595	—	—	Speed Control Solenoid Circuits	2-36	50
P1683	—	—	Speed Control Solenoid Circuits	2-36	50
P1597	—	—	Speed Control Switch Always Low	2-37	51
2003–04 NEON					
—	—	—	Verification Test VER-4	2-42	59
—	—	—	Verification Test VER-5	2-42	60
P0579	—	—	Speed Control Switch No. 1 Performance	2-38	53
P0580	—	—	Speed Control Switch No. 1 Low	2-39	54
P0581	—	—	Speed Control Switch No. 1 High	2-39	55
P0582	—	—	Speed Control Vacuum Solenoid Circuit	2-40	56
P0586	—	—	Speed Control Vent Solenoid Circuit	2-40	57
P0594	—	—	Speed Control Servo Power Circuit	2-41	58
2000 SEBRING CONVERTIBLE					
—	—	—	Brake Switch Sense	2-25	38
—	—	—	Park/Neutral Position Switch	2-29	42
—	—	—	Speed Control Denied Message	2-29	43
—	—	—	Speed Control Operation	2-29	44
—	—	—	Verification Test VER-4A	2-31	45
P1595	—	—	Speed Control Solenoid Circuits	2-26	39
P1596	—	—	Speed Control Switch Always High	2-28	40
P1597	—	—	Speed Control Switch Always Low	2-28	41
2001–02 SEBRING CONVERTIBLE					
—	—	—	Verification Test VER-4	2-38	52
P1595	—	—	Speed Control Solenoid Circuits	2-36	50
P1683	—	—	Speed Control Solenoid Circuits	2-36	50
P1597	—	—	Speed Control Switch Always Low	2-37	51
2003–04 SEBRING CONVERTIBLE					
—	—	—	Verification Test VER-4	2-42	59
—	—	—	Verification Test VER-5	2-42	60
P0579	—	—	Speed Control Switch No. 1 Performance	2-38	53
P0580	—	—	Speed Control Switch No. 1 Low	2-39	54
P0581	—	—	Speed Control Switch No. 1 High	2-39	55
P0582	—	—	Speed Control Vacuum Solenoid Circuit	2-40	56
P0586	—	—	Speed Control Vent Solenoid Circuit	2-40	57
P0594	—	—	Speed Control Servo Power Circuit	2-41	58
2000 SEBRING COUPE					
—	—	—	Cruise Control Cannot Be Set	2-53	75
—	—	—	Cruise Control Does Not Cancel When Brake Pedal Is Depressed	2-53	72
—	—	—	Cruise Control Does Not Cancel When CANCEL Switch Is ON	2-53	74
—	—	—	Cruise Control Does Not Cancel When Engine Speed Rises Suddenly	2-53	71
—	—	—	Cruise Control Does Not Cancel When Selector Set To N Position	2-53	73
—	—	—	Cruise Control Main Switch Lamp Does Not Illuminate	2-54	78
—	—	—	Instrument Cluster Cruise Control Indicator Lamp Does Not Illuminate	2-54	79
—	—	—	Instrument Panel Cruise Control Indicator Lamp Does Not Illuminate	2-54	77

Continued

DIAGNOSTIC CHART INDEX—Continued

Code Scan Tool Generic	Code Scan Tool MUT-II	Flash	Description	Page No.	Fig. No.
2000 SEBRING COUPE					
—	—	—	Scan Tool Communications Not Possible	2-53	70
—	—	—	Speed Hunts W/Cruise Control Set	2-54	76
—	Code 15	Code 34	Speed Control Servo Solenoid	2-25	34
—	Code 82	Code 77	Cruise Control Relay	2-25	37
—	Code 86	Code 34	Cruise Control Switch	2-25	35
—	Code 87	Code 34	Cruise Control Switch	2-25	36
P0500	Code 35	Code 15	Vehicle Speed Signal	2-25	32
P0605	Code 02	Code 53	Powertrain Control Module	2-25	33
2001–03 SEBRING & STRATUS COUPE					
—	—	—	Cruise Control Cannot Be Set	2-59	85
—	—	—	Cruise Control Does Not Cancel When Brakes Are Applied	2-56	81
—	—	—	Cruise Control Does Not Cancel When CANCEL Switch Is Set To On	2-59	84
—	—	—	Cruise Control Does Not Cancel When Clutch Pedal Depressed	2-57	82
—	—	—	Cruise Control Does Not Cancel When Selector Moved To N Position	2-58	83
—	—	—	Cruise Control Indicator Does Not Illuminate	2-60	87
—	—	—	Hunting At Set Speed	2-59	86
—	—	—	Scan Tool Communication Not Possible	2-54	80
—	—	Code 11	Cruise Vacuum Pump Drive	2-46	64
—	—	Code 12	Vehicle Speed Sensor	2-48	65
—	—	Code 14	Stop Lamp Switch	2-48	66
—	—	Code 15	Cruise Control Switch	2-50	67
—	—	Code 16	Cruise Control-ECU	2-51	68
—	—	Code 17	Throttle Position Sensor	2-52	69
2000 STRATUS					
—	—	—	Brake Switch Sense	2-25	38
—	—	—	Park/Neutral Position Switch	2-29	42
—	—	—	Speed Control Denied Message	2-29	43
—	—	—	Speed Control Operation	2-29	44
—	—	—	Verification Test VER-4A	2-31	45
P1595	—	—	Speed Control Solenoid Circuits	2-26	39
P1596	—	—	Speed Control Switch Always High	2-28	40
P1597	—	—	Speed Control Switch Always Low	2-28	41
2001–02 SEBRING SEDAN, STRATUS SEDAN					
—	—	—	Verification Test VER-4	2-38	52
P1595	—	—	Speed Control Solenoid Circuits	2-36	50
P1683	—	—	Speed Control Solenoid Circuits	2-36	50
P1597	—	—	Speed Control Switch Always Low	2-37	51
2003–04 SEBRING & STRATUS SEDAN					
—	—	—	Verification Test VER-4	2-42	59
—	—	—	Verification Test VER-5	2-42	60
P0579	—	—	Speed Control Switch No. 1 Performance	2-38	53
P0580	—	—	Speed Control Switch No. 1 Low	2-39	54
P0581	—	—	Speed Control Switch No. 1 High	2-39	55
P0582	—	—	Speed Control Vacuum Solenoid Circuit	2-40	56
P0586	—	—	Speed Control Vent Solenoid Circuit	2-40	57
P0594	—	—	Speed Control Servo Power Circuit	2-41	58

Code No.	Scan tool 23 (35) General scan tool P0500 MIL 15	No Vehicle Speed Sensor Signal	Probable cause
[Comment] Background • The vehicle speed sensor serves as a PCM input switching voltage between 0 and 5 volts. • Once the vehicle is in motion and the throttle is open, information from the sensor is sampled every 11 milliseconds and compared to a minimum threshold equal to 1 mph. • If the sensors output voltage indicates a speed higher than this threshold, the sensor is considered to be operating normally. • Failure of the sensor would be quite noticeable because the speedometer would fail to operate. • Diagnostic features that depend on the speed sensor may never execute if this component fails. Range of Check • Engine coolant temperature: 83°C (180°F) or more • Transaxle: Other than N or P range (A/T only). • 31 seconds after starting engine • Brakes not applied • Throttle valve: Open • Engine: 1,800 r/min or more • Difference between the atmospheric pressure and intake manifold pressure: 34 kPa (10 in.Hg) or more Set Condition • Vehicle speed: Less than 1mph for 11 seconds			• Open or shorted signal circuit • Speedometer pinion damaged • Open 9-volt supply circuit • Open sensor ground circuit • Vehicle speed sensor failed • PCM failed

<M/T>

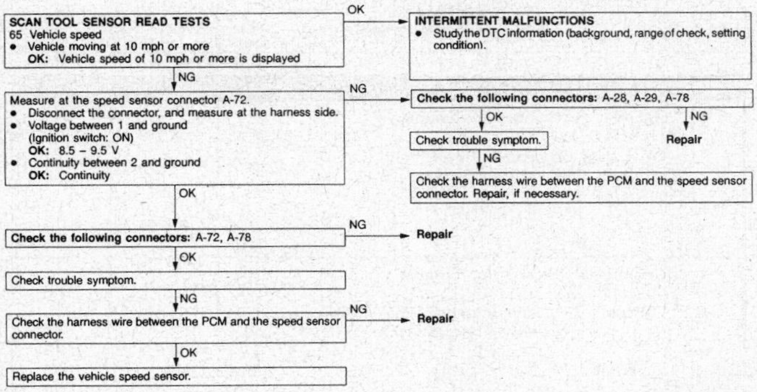

CR1029909140000X

Fig. 32 Code P0500/35/15: Vehicle Speed Signal. Avenger & 2000 Sebring Coupe

Replace the cruise control switch.

CR1100200722000X

Fig. 36 Code —/87/34: Cruise Control Switch. Avenger & 2000 Sebring Coupe

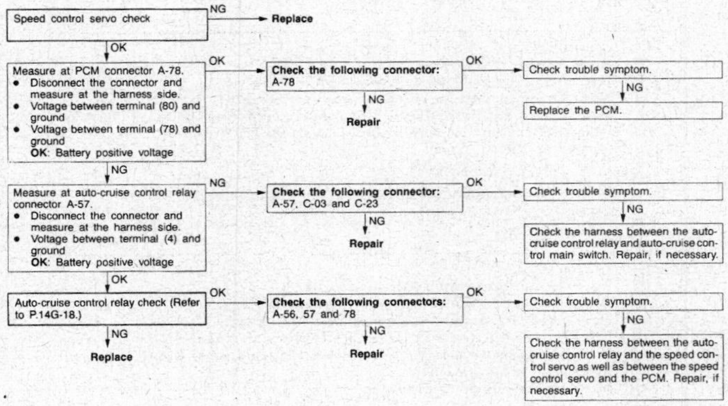

CR1100200724000X

Fig. 37 Code —/82/77: Cruise Control Relay. Avenger & 2000 Sebring Coupe

Replace the powertrain control module.

CR1100200720000X

Fig. 33 Code P0605/02/53: Powertrain Control Module. Avenger & 2000 Sebring Coupe

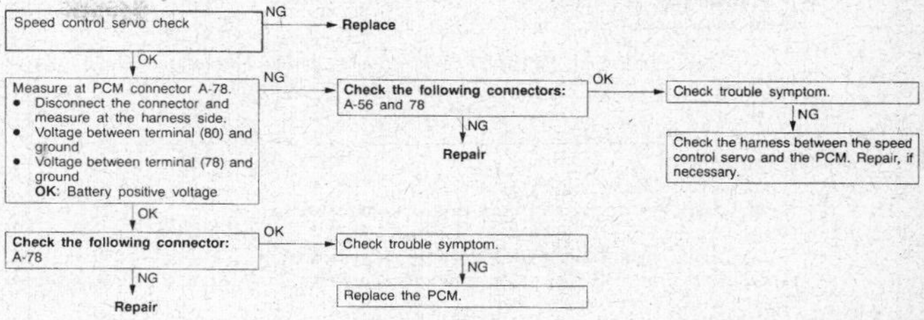

CR1100200721000X

Fig. 34 Code —/15/34: Speed Control Servo Solenoid. Avenger & 2000 Sebring Coupe

Replace the cruise control switch.

CR1100200723000X

Fig. 35 Code —/86/34: Cruise Control Switch. Avenger & 2000 Sebring Coupe

POSSIBLE CAUSES
GROUND CIRCUIT OPEN
PCM CONNECTOR TERMINAL OBSERVABLE DEFECT
BRAKE SWITCH DEFECTIVE
BRAKE SWITCH SENSE CIRCUIT OPEN
BRAKE SWITCH SENSE CIRCUIT SHORTED TO GROUND
PCM DEFECTIVE (BRAKE SWITCH SENSE)

TEST	ACTION
1	Ignition Off Disconnect the Brake Switch Connector. **Note: Check connectors - Clean/repair as necessary.** Key on. Using a Voltmeter, measure the voltage of the Brake Switch Sense Circuit at the Brake Switch Connector. Is the voltage above 10.0 volts? Yes → Go To 2 No → Go To 4
2	Disconnect the Brake Switch Connector. **Note: Check connectors - Clean/repair as necessary.** Connect a Jumper between the Brake Switch Sense and ground. Ignition On, Engine Not Running. With the DRB, read the Brake Switch input status. Does the DRB show Brake Switch "released"? Yes → Go To 3 No → Repair the open Ground Circuit.
3	If there are no potential causes remaining. View repair options. Repair Replace the Brake Switch.
4	Ignition Off Disconnect the Powertrain Control Module. **Note: Check connectors - Clean/repair as necessary.** Is any Terminal damaged, pushed out or miswired? Yes → Repair as necessary. No → Go To 5

CR1100000626010X

Fig. 38 Brake Switch Sense (Part 1 of 2). Breeze, Cirrus & 2000 Sebring Convertible & Stratus

TEST	ACTION
5	Ignition Off Disconnect the Brake Switch Connector. **Note: Check connectors - Clean/repair as necessary.** Disconnect the Powertrain Control Module. **Note: Check connectors - Clean/repair as necessary.** Using an Ohmmeter, measure the resistance of the Brake Switch Sense Circuit at PCM Connector to ground. Is the resistance below 5.0 ohms? Yes → Repair the Brake Switch Sense Circuit shorted to ground. No → Go To 6
6	Ignition Off Disconnect the Brake Switch Connector. **Note: Check connectors - Clean/repair as necessary.** Disconnect the Powertrain Control Module. **Note: Check connectors - Clean/repair as necessary.** Using an Ohmmeter, measure the Brake Switch Sense Circuit from the PCM to the Brake Switch. Is the resistance below 5.0 ohms? Yes → Go To 7 No → Repair the open Brake Switch Sense Circuit, Brake Switch to PCM.
7	If there are no potential causes remaining. View repair options. Repair Replace the PCM.

CR1100000626020X

Fig. 38 Brake Switch Sense (Part 2 of 2). Breeze, Cirrus & 2000 Sebring Convertible & Stratus

TEST	ACTION
3	Ignition Off. Using the Schematics as a guide, inspect the Wiring and Connectors. Were any problems found? Yes → Repair as necessary. No → Go To 4
4	Ignition On, Engine Not Running. Turn S/C on. With the DRB actuate the S/C Vent Solenoid. Wiggle the Wiring Harness from S/C Servo and Brake Switch to Powertrain Control Module. Did the wiggling interrupt the S/C Servo actuation? Yes → Repair as necessary where wiggling caused the actuation to be interrupted. No → Go To 5
5	Ignition On, Engine Not Running. Turn S/C on. With the DRB actuate the S/C Vacuum Solenoid. Wiggle the Wiring Harness from S/C Servo and Brake Switch to Powertrain Control Module. Did the wiggling interrupt the S/C actuation? Yes → Repair as necessary where wiggling caused the actuation to be interrupted. No → Test Complete.
6	Ignition Off. Disconnect the Speed Control Servo 4-Way Connector. **Note: Check connectors - Clean/repair as necessary.** **Note: Ensure the Brake Pedal is not depressed during the following steps.** Key on, Engine off. Turn S/C Switch on. Using a Voltmeter measure the S/C Brake Switch Output Circuit at 4-Way Connector. Is the voltage above 10.0 volts? Yes → Go To 14 No → Go To 7
7	Ignition Off Disconnect the Brake Switch Connector. **Note: Check connectors - Clean/repair as necessary.** **Note: Ensure the Brake Pedal is not depressed during the following steps.** Turn key on, engine off. Using a Voltmeter, measure voltage of the S/C Power Supply Circuit at the Brake Switch Connector. Is the voltage above 10.0 volts? Yes → Go To 8 No → Go To 10

CR1100000627020X

Fig. 39 Code P1595: Speed Control Solenoid Circuits (Part 2 of 7). Breeze, Cirrus, 2000 Sebring Convertible & Stratus

POSSIBLE CAUSES
GROUND CIRCUIT OPEN
S/C BRAKE SWITCH OUTPUT CIRCUIT OPEN
S/C POWER SUPPLY CIRCUIT OPEN
SWITCHED S/C POWER SUPPLY CIRCUIT SHORTED TO GROUND
S/C SERVO DEFECTIVE (12V DRIVER CIRCUIT)
S/C VACUUM SOLENOID CONTROL CIRCUIT OPEN
S/C VACUUM SOLENOID CONTROL CKT SHORT TO GROUND
S/C VENT SOLENOID CONTROL CIRCUIT OPEN
S/C VENT SOLENOID CONTROL CKT SHORT TO GROUND
S/C WIRING HARNESS INTERMITTENT DEFECT (S/C VENT SOL AC)
BRAKE SWITCH DEFECTIVE
PCM DEFECTIVE (12V DRIVER CIRCUIT)
S/C WIRING HARNESS INTERMITTENT DEFECT (S/C VAC SOL AC)
S/C WIRING HARNESS OBSERVABLE DEFECT

TEST	ACTION
1	Ignition On, Engine Not Running. Turn S/C On. With the DRB actuate the S/C Vent Solenoid. Does the Speed Control Servo click? Yes → Go To 2 No → Go To 13
2	Ignition On, Engine Not Running. Turn S/C on. With the DRB, actuate the S/C Vacuum Solenoid. Does the Speed Control Servo click? Yes → Go To 3 No → Go To 6

CR1100000627010X

Fig. 39 Code P1595: Speed Control Solenoid Circuits (Part 1 of 7). Breeze, Cirrus, 2000 Sebring Convertible & Stratus

TEST	ACTION
8	Ignition Off Using Service Manual procedure, check Brake Switch. Was Brake Switch OK? Yes → Go To 9 No → Replace Brake Switch.
9	Ignition Off. Disconnect the Brake Switch Connector. Disconnect the Speed Control Servo 4-Way Connector. **Note: Check connectors - Clean/repair as necessary.** **Note: Ensure the Brake Pedal is not depressed during the following steps.** Using an Ohmmeter measure the resistance of the S/C Brake Switch Output Ckt from Servo Conn to ground. Is the resistance below 5.0 ohms? Yes → Repair Switched S/C Power Circuit shorted to Ground. No → Go To 23
10	Ignition Off. Disconnect the Brake Switch Connector. Disconnect the Speed Control Servo 4-Way Connector. **Note: Check connectors - Clean/repair as necessary.** **Note: Ensure the Brake Pedal is not depressed during the following steps.** Using an Ohmmeter measure the resistance of the S/C Brake Switch Output Ckt from Servo Conn to ground. Is the resistance below 5.0 ohms? Yes → Repair Switched S/C Power Circuit shorted to Ground. No → Go To 11
11	Ignition Off. Disconnect the Brake Switch Connector. **Note: Check connectors - Clean/repair as necessary.** Disconnect the Powertrain Control Module **Note: Check connectors - Clean/repair as necessary.** Using an Ohmmeter measure resistance of S/C Power Supply Circuit, PCM to Brake Switch Connector. Is the resistance below 5.0 ohms? Yes → Go To 12 No → Repair the open S/C Power Supply Circuit.

CR1100000627030X

Fig. 39 Code P1595: Speed Control Solenoid Circuits (Part 3 of 7). Breeze, Cirrus, 2000 Sebring Convertible & Stratus

TEST	ACTION
12	Ignition On, Engine Not Running. Turn S/C on. With the DRB actuate the S/C Vent Solenoid. Wiggle the Wiring Harness from S/C Servo and Brake Switch to Powertrain Control Module. Did the wiggling interrupt the S/C Servo actuation? Yes → Repair as necessary where wiggling caused the actuation to be interrupted. No → Go To 27
13	Ignition Off. Disconnect the Speed Control Servo 4-Way Connector. **Note: Check connectors - Clean/repair as necessary.** **Note: Ensure the Brake Pedal is not depressed during the following steps.** Key on, Engine off. Turn S/C Switch on. Using a Voltmeter measure the S/C Brake Switch Output Circuit at 4-Way Connector. Is the voltage above 10.0 volts? Yes → Go To 14 No → Go To 20
14	Ignition Off. Disconnect the Speed Control Servo 4-Way Connector. **Note: Check connectors - Clean/repair as necessary.** Using an Ohmmeter, measure resistance of Ground Circuit at Servo Conn to Ground. Is the resistance below 5.0 ohms? Yes → Go To 15 No → Repair open Ground Circuit.
15	Ignition Off. Disconnect the Speed Control Servo 4-Way Connector. **Note: Check connectors - Clean/repair as necessary.** Disconnect Powertrain Control Module Connectors. **Note: Check connectors - Clean/repair as necessary.** With an Ohmmeter measure the resistance of the S/C Vacuum Solenoid Control Circuit from the PCM to the Servo Connector. Is the resistance below 5.0 ohms? Yes → Go To 16 No → Repair the open S/C Vacuum Solenoid Control Circuit.

CR1100000627040X

Fig. 39 Code P1595: Speed Control Solenoid Circuits (Part 4 of 7). Breeze, Cirrus, 2000 Sebring Convertible & Stratus

TEST	ACTION
16	Ignition Off. Disconnect the Speed Control Servo 4-Way Connector. **Note: Check connectors - Clean/repair as necessary.** Disconnect Powertrain Control Module Connectors. **Note: Check connectors - Clean/repair as necessary.** With an Ohmmeter measure the resistance of the S/C Vacuum Solenoid Control Circuit from the Servo Connector to a good ground. Is the resistance below 5.0 ohms? Yes → Repair the short to ground in the S/C Vacuum Solenoid Control Circuit. No → Go To 17
17	Ignition Off. Disconnect the Speed Control Servo 4-Way Connector. **Note: Check connectors - Clean/repair as necessary.** Disconnect Powertrain Control Module Connectors. **Note: Check connectors - Clean/repair as necessary.** With an Ohmmeter measure the resistance of the S/C Vent Solenoid Control Circuit from the PCM to the Servo Connector. Is the resistance below 5.0 ohms? Yes → Go To 18 No → Repair the open S/C Vent Solenoid Control Circuit.
18	Ignition Off. Disconnect the S/C Servo 4-Way Connector. **Note: Check connectors - Clean/repair as necessary.** Disconnect Powertrain Control Module Connectors. **Note: Check connectors - Clean/repair as necessary.** With an Ohmmeter, measure the resistance of the S/C Vent Solenoid Control Circuit from the Servo Connector to a good Ground. Is the resistance below 5.0 ohms? Yes → Repair the short to ground in the S/C Vent Solenoid Control Circuit. No → Go To 19
19	There are no potential causes remaining. View repair options. Repair Replace the S/C Servo.

CR1100000627050X

Fig. 39 Code P1595: Speed Control Solenoid Circuits (Part 5 of 7). Breeze, Cirrus, 2000 Sebring Convertible & Stratus

TEST	ACTION
20	Ignition Off Disconnect the Brake Switch Connector. **Note: Check connectors - Clean/repair as necessary.** **Note: Ensure the Brake Pedal is not depressed during the following steps.** Turn key on, engine off. Using a Voltmeter, measure voltage of the S/C Power Supply Circuit at the Brake Switch Connector. Is the voltage above 10.0 volts? Yes → Go To 21 No → Go To 25
21	Ignition Off. Disconnect the Brake Switch Connector. Disconnect the Speed Control Servo 4-Way Connector. **Note: Check connectors - Clean/repair as necessary.** **Note: Ensure the Brake Pedal is not depressed during the following steps.** Using an Ohmmeter measure the resistance of the S/C Brake Switch Output Ckt from Servo Conn to ground. Is the resistance below 5.0 ohms? Yes → Repair Switched S/C Power Circuit shorted to Ground. No → Go To 22
22	Ignition Off Using Service Manual procedure, check Brake Switch. Was Brake Switch OK? Yes → Go To 23 No → Replace Brake Switch.
23	Ignition Off Disconnect the S/C Servo 4-Way Connector. **Note: Check connectors - Clean/repair as necessary.** Disconnect the Brake Switch Connector. **Note: Check connectors - Clean/repair as necessary.** With an Ohmmeter, test the resistance of the S/C Brake Switch Output Circuit from the Brake Switch Connector to Servo Connector. Is the resistance above 5.0 ohms? Yes → Repair the open S/C Brake Switch Output Circuit. No → Go To 24
24	If there are no potential causes remaining. View repair options. Repair Replace the Brake Switch.

CR1100000627060X

Fig. 39 Code P1595: Speed Control Solenoid Circuits (Part 6 of 7). Breeze, Cirrus, 2000 Sebring Convertible & Stratus

TEST	ACTION
25	Ignition Off. Disconnect the Brake Switch Connector. Disconnect the Speed Control Servo 4-Way Connector. **Note: Check connectors - Clean/repair as necessary.** **Note: Ensure the Brake Pedal is not depressed during the following steps.** Using an Ohmmeter measure the resistance of the S/C Brake Switch Output Ckt from Servo Conn to ground. Is the resistance below 5.0 ohms? Yes → Repair Switched S/C Power Circuit shorted to Ground. No → Go To 26
26	Ignition Off. Disconnect the Brake Switch Connector. **Note: Check connectors - Clean/repair as necessary.** Disconnect the Powertrain Control Module **Note: Check connectors - Clean/repair as necessary.** Using an Ohmmeter measure resistance of S/C Power Supply Circuit, PCM to Brake Switch Connector. Is the resistance below 5.0 ohms? Yes → Go To 27 No → Repair the open S/C Power Supply Circuit.
27	There are no potential causes remaining. View repair options. Repair Replace the Powertrain Control Module.

CR1100000627070X

Fig. 39 Code P1595: Speed Control Solenoid Circuits (Part 7 of 7). Breeze, Cirrus, 2000 Sebring Convertible & Stratus

POSSIBLE CAUSES
S/C WIRING HARNESS INTERMITTENT DEFECT
SPEED CONTROL ON/OFF SWITCH DEFECTIVE
SPEED CONTROL SWITCH GROUND CIRCUIT OPEN
POWERTRAIN CONTROL MODULE DEFECTIVE
SPEED CONTROL SWITCH SIGNAL CKT SHORTED TO VOLTAGE
SPEED CONTROL SWITCH SIGNAL CKT OPEN PCM TO CLOCK SPRING
SPEED CONTROL SWITCH SIGNAL CKT OPEN AT CLOCK SPRING

TEST	ACTION
1	Ignition On, Engine Not Running With the DRB under I/O's, read the Speed Control inputs. Watch the DRB and push the Speed Control On/Off Switch several times, leave on. Did the DRB show Speed Control Switch off and on? Yes → Go To 2 No → Go To 3
2	Ignition On, Engine Not Running With the DRB, monitor switch voltage while wiggling wiring, PCM to Speed Control On/Off Switch. Was voltage above 4.9 volts at any time while wiggling? Yes → Repair the Wiring at the point where voltage fluctuates when Harness is wiggled. No → Test Complete.
3	Ignition Off Disconnect the Speed Control On/Off Switch 2-Way Connector only. **Note: Check connectors - Clean/repair as necessary.** Using an Ohmmeter, measure the S/C Switch Ground Circuit at the On/Off Switch 2-Way Conn. Is the resistance below 5.0 ohms? Yes → Go To 4 No → Repair open ground circuit to Speed Control Switch.

CR1100000628010X

Fig. 40 Code P1596: Speed Control Switch Always High (Part 1 of 3). Breeze, Cirrus & 2000 Sebring Convertible & Stratus

TEST	ACTION
4	Ignition Off Disconnect the Speed Control On/Off Switch 2-Way Connector only. **Note: Check connectors - Clean/repair as necessary.** Measure the S/C Sw Signal Ckt for voltage at the On/Off Switch 2-Way Conn. Is the voltage above 4.8 volts? Yes → Repair the Speed Control Switch Signal Circuit for a short to voltage. No → Go To 5
5	Ignition Off Disconnect the Speed Control On/Off Switch 2-Way Connector only. Disconnect the Powertrain Control Module. **Note: Check connectors - Clean/repair as necessary.** Using an Ohmmeter, measure the Speed Control Switch Signal Circuit resistance from PCM to Speed Control On/Off Switch Connector. Is the resistance below 5.0 ohms? Yes → Go To 6 No → Go To 8
6	Ignition Off Disconnect the Speed Control On/Off Switch 2-Way Connector only. **Note: Check connectors - Clean/repair as necessary.** Using an Ohmmeter, measure the resistance across the S/C On/Off Switch. Is the resistance below 25.0 K-ohms? Yes → Go To 7 No → Replace the On/Off Switch.
7	Turn Ignition off. There are no potential causes remaining. View repair options. Repair Replace Powertrain Control Module.
8	Ignition Off Disconnect the Clock Spring Connector. **Note: Check connectors - Clean/repair as necessary.** Using an Ohmmeter, measure resistance of S/C Switch Signal Circuit from PCM to Clock Spring Connector. Is the resistance below 5.0 ohms? Yes → Go To 9 No → Repair open Speed Control Switch Signal Circuit PCM to Clock Spring.

CR1100000628020X

Fig. 40 Code P1596: Speed Control Switch Always High (Part 2 of 3). Breeze, Cirrus & 2000 Sebring Convertible & Stratus

TEST	ACTION
9	Ignition Off If there are no potential causes remaining, replace the Speed Control Switch Signal Circuit is assumed to be open at Clockspring. Is the resistance below 5.0 ohms? Yes → Repair open Speed Control Switch Signal Circuit at Clock Spring. No → Test Complete.

CR1100000628030X

Fig. 40 Code P1596: Speed Control Switch Always High (Part 3 of 3). Breeze, Cirrus & 2000 Sebring Convertible & Stratus

POSSIBLE CAUSES
S/C SWITCH SIGNAL CIRCUIT SHORTED TO GROUND
S/C SIGNAL CIRCUIT SHORTED TO SENSOR GROUND
PCM DEFECTIVE
S/C SWITCH DEFECTIVE

TEST	ACTION
1	Ignition On, Engine Not Running Record all DTC's and freeze frame data, now erase codes before proceeding. With DRB, read the S/C Switch volts in Sensors. Is the S/C Switch voltage below 1.0 volt? Yes → Go To 2 No → Test Complete.
2	Ignition Off Disconnect the S/C Switch. **Note: Check connectors - Clean/repair as necessary.** Using an Ohmmeter, measure the resistance between the S/C Signal Circuit and the Sensor Ground Circuit. Is the resistance below 5.0 ohms? Yes → Repair S/C Signal Circuit shorted to Sensor Ground. No → Go To 3
3	Ignition Off Disconnect the S/C Switch. **Note: Check connectors - Clean/repair as necessary.** Turn ignition on, with engine not running. With the DRB, read the S/C Switch volts in Sensors. Did the S/C Switch volts change to 5.0 volts? Yes → Replace the S/C Switch. No → Go To 4

CR1100000629010X

Fig. 41 Code P1597: Speed Control Switch Always Low (Part 1 of 2). Breeze, Cirrus & 2000 Sebring Convertible & Stratus

TEST	ACTION
4	Ignition Off Disconnect the S/C Switch. **Note: Check connectors - Clean/repair as necessary.** Disconnect the Powertrain Control Module. **Note: Check connectors - Clean/repair as necessary.** With an Ohmmeter, measure resistance of S/C Switch Signal Circuit to ground at the PCM Connector. Is the resistance below 5.0 ohms? Yes → Repair S/C Switch Signal Circuit for a short to ground. No → Go To 5
5	There are no potential causes remaining. View repair options. Repair Replace the Powertrain Control Module.

CR1100000629020X

Fig. 41 Code P1597: Speed Control Switch Always Low (Part 2 of 2). Breeze, Cirrus & 2000 Sebring Convertible & Stratus

TEST	ACTION
1	At this time the Speed Control switch and servo functions appear to operate properly. Using the DRB, monitor the speed control "output" status. Road test the vehicle at speeds over 35 MPH and attempt to set the speed control. The following items will not allow the speed control to set. The last or most recent cause for speed control not to set is indicated by the "Denied" status. If ON/OFF Denied message is indicated, the PCM does not see an "ON" signal from the switch at cavity 41. If SPEED Denied message is indicated, the vehicle speed as seen by the PCM at cavity 66 is not greater than 30 MPH. If RPM Denied message is indicated, the engine RPM is excessively high. If BRAKE Denied message is indicated, the brake switch sense circuit is open indicating to the PCM that the brakes are applied. The sense circuit, cavity 62 of the PCM, is grounded through the brake pedal switch when the brakes are released. If P/N Denied message is indicated, park/neutral switch sense circuit is grounded indicating to PCM that transmission is not in gear. The sense circuit, cavity 76 of PCM, is grounded through the park/neutral switch when transmission is in park or neutral. If RPM/SPD Denied message is indicated, the PCM senses excessive engine RPM for a given vehicle speed. If SOL FLT Denied message is indicated, the PCM senses a servo solenoid circuit trouble code that is maturing or set in memory. Have the previous instructions been completed? Test Complete.

CR1100000631000X

Fig. 43 Speed Control Denied Message. Breeze, Cirrus & 2000 Sebring Convertible & Stratus

POSSIBLE CAUSES
PARK/NEUTRAL POSITION SENSE CKT SHORTED TO GND
PARK/NEUTRAL POSITION SWITCH DEFECTIVE
PCM DEFECTIVE

TEST	ACTION
1	Ignition Off Disconnect the PCM. **Note: Check connectors - Clean/repair as necessary.** Disconnect the Park/Neutral or TRS Switch. **Note: Check connectors - Clean/repair as necessary.** Using an Ohmmeter, measure the P/N Switch Sense Circuit to ground at PCM Connector. Is the resistance below 5.0 ohms? Yes → Repair the Park/Neutral Position Switch Sense Circuit shorted to ground. No → Go To 2
2	Ignition Off Disconnect the PCM. **Note: Check connectors - Clean/repair as necessary.** **Note: The gear selector should still be in Drive.** Using an Ohmmeter, measure the P/N Switch Sense Circuit to Ground at PCM Connector. Is the resistance below 5.0 ohms? Yes → Go To 3 No → Replace the PCM.
3	If there are no potential causes remaining. View repair options. Repair Replace the Park/Neutral or TRS Switch.

CR1100000630000X

Fig. 42 Park/Neutral Position Switch. Breeze, Cirrus & 2000 Sebring Convertible & Stratus

POSSIBLE CAUSES
GROUND CIRCUIT OPEN
S/C BRAKE SWITCH OUTPUT CIRCUIT SHORTED TO GROUND
S/C POWER SUPPLY CIRCUIT (PCM TO BRK SWITCH) OPEN
CANCEL SWITCH DEFECTIVE
SET/RESUME SWITCH DEFECTIVE
BRAKE SWITCH DEFECTIVE
BRAKE SWITCH CONNECTOR OBSERVABLE DEFECT
PCM (SPEED CONTROL) DEFECTIVE
S/C SERVO CONNECTOR TERMINAL OBSERVABLE DEFECT
VACUUM RESERVOIR DEFECTIVE
VACUUM SUPPLY LEAK OR RESTRICTION
THROTTLE CABLE DEFECTIVE

TEST	ACTION
1	**Note: Use this test only when there are no speed control codes set.** Ignition On, Engine Not Running. With the DRB, monitor the Speed Control Switch inputs. While observing display, press the Speed Control "ON" Switch. Does the DRB show Speed Control Switch "ON"? Yes → Go To 2 No → Refer to symptom SPEED CONTROL ON/OFF SWITCH
2	Ignition On, Engine Not Running. With the DRB, monitor the Speed Control Switch inputs. While observing the display, press the Set Switch several times. Does the DRB show Set Switch "pressed" or "released"? Yes → Go To 3 No → Refer to symptom SPEED CONTROL SET/RESUME SWITCH
3	Ignition On, Engine Not Running. With the DRB, monitor the Speed Control Switch inputs. While observing the display, press the Brake Pedal several times. Does the DRB show Brake Switch "pressed" or "released"? Yes → Go To 4 No → Refer to symptom BRAKE SWITCH SENSE

CR1100000632010X

Fig. 44 Speed Control Operation (Part 1 of 6). Breeze, Cirrus, 2000 Sebring Convertible & Stratus

TEST	ACTION
4	Ignition On, Engine Not Running. With the DRB, monitor the Speed Control Switch inputs. While observing the display, move the Gear Selector to DRIVE. Does the DRB show P/N switch "D/R"? Yes → Go To 5 No → Refer to symptom PARK/NEUTRAL POS SWITCH
5	Ignition On, Engine Not Running. With the DRB, monitor the Speed Control Switch inputs. While observing the display, press the Cancel Switch several times. Does the DRB show Cancel Switch "pressed" or "released"? Yes → Go To 6 No → Replace the Cancel Switch.
6	Ignition On, Engine Not Running. With the DRB, monitor the Speed Control Switch inputs. While observing the display, press the Resume Switch several times. Does the DRB show resume switch "pressed" or "released"? Yes → Go To 8 No → Replace the Set/Resume Switch.
7	Ignition Off. Disconnect the S/C Servo Connector. **Note: Check connectors - Clean/repair as necessary.** Inspect Connector. Is any terminal damaged, pushed out or miswired? Yes → Repair as necessary. No → Go To 8
8	Ignition Off. Disconnect the S/C Servo Connector. **Note: Check connectors - Clean/repair as necessary.** Ignition On, Engine Not Running. With the DRB, actuate the S/C Vent Solenoid. Using a Voltmeter, measure the S/C Brake Switch Circuit at S/C Connector. Is the voltage above 10.0 volts? Yes → Go To 9 No → Go To 18
9	Start Engine. Allow to idle 1 minute. Ignition On, Engine Not Running. With the DRB, actuate the S/C Servo Solenoids. Does the Throttle open and close? Yes → Refer to symptom SPEED CONTROL DENIED MESSAGE No → Go To 10

CR1100000632020X

Fig. 44 Speed Control Operation (Part 2 of 6). Breeze, Cirrus, 2000 Sebring Convertible & Stratus

TEST	ACTION
10	Ignition Off. Disconnect the S/C Servo Connector. **Note: Check connectors - Clean/repair as necessary.** Using an Ohmmeter, measure the resistance of the Ground Circuit to ground. Is the resistance below 5.0 ohms? Yes → Go To 11 No → Repair the open Ground Circuit.
11	Ignition Off. Disconnect the Vacuum Supply from the S/C Servo. **Note: Check connectors - Clean/repair as necessary.** Attach Vacuum Gauge to the disconnected hose. Start engine. Does the Vacuum Gauge read Manifold Vacuum? Yes → Go To 12 No → Repair the Vacuum Supply for a leak or restriction.
12	Ignition Off. Disconnect the Vacuum Supply to the S/C Servo. **Note: Check connectors - Clean/repair as necessary.** Attach a Vacuum Gauge to the disconnected hose. Start Engine. Turn engine off, observe Vacuum Gauge for 10 seconds. Does the vacuum hold for at least 10 seconds? Yes → Go To 11 No → Replace the Vacuum Reservoir.
13	Ignition Off. Measure the S/C Brake Switch Output Circuit to ground at Servo Connector. Is the resistance below 5.0 ohms? Yes → Repair the short to ground S/C Brake Switch Output Circuit. No → Go To 14
14	Ignition Off. Disconnect the Brake Switch Connector. **Note: Check connectors - Clean/repair as necessary.** Ignition On, Engine Not Running. With the DRB, actuate the S/C Vent Solenoid. Measure the S/C Power Supply Circuit Voltage at Brake Switch Connector. Is the voltage above 10.0 volts? Yes → Go To 15 No → Go To 17

CR1100000632030X

Fig. 44 Speed Control Operation (Part 3 of 6). Breeze, Cirrus, 2000 Sebring Convertible & Stratus

TEST	ACTION
15	Ignition Off. Using the Service Manual procedure, check the Brake Switch. Was the Brake Switch adjustment okay? Yes → Go To 16 No → Replace Brake Switch.
16	Ignition Off. Disconnect the Brake Switch Connector. **Note: Check connectors - Clean/repair as necessary.** Inspect Connector. Is any Terminal damaged, pushed out, or miswired? Yes → Repair as necessary. No → Go To 24
17	Ignition Off. Disconnect the Brake Switch Connector. **Note: Check connectors - Clean/repair as necessary.** Inspect Connector. Is any Terminal damaged, pushed out, or miswired? Yes → Repair as necessary. No → Go To 27
18	Ignition Off. Using an Ohmmeter, measure the S/C Brake Switch Output Circuit to ground at Servo Connector. Is the resistance below 5.0 ohms? Yes → Repair the short to ground S/C Brake Switch Output Circuit. No → Go To 19
19	Ignition Off. Disconnect the S/C Servo Connector. **Note: Check connectors - Clean/repair as necessary.** Using an Ohmmeter, measure the resistance of the Ground Circuit to ground. Is the resistance below 5.0 ohms? Yes → Go To 20 No → Repair the open Ground Circuit.

CR1100000632040X

Fig. 44 Speed Control Operation (Part 4 of 6). Breeze, Cirrus, 2000 Sebring Convertible & Stratus

TEST	ACTION
20	Ignition Off. Disconnect the Brake Switch Connector. **Note: Check connectors - Clean/repair as necessary.** Ignition On, Engine Not Running. With the DRB, actuate the S/C Vent Solenoid. Using a Voltmeter, measure the S/C Power Supply Circuit Voltage at Brake Switch Connector. Is the voltage above 10.0 volts? Yes → Go To 21 No → Go To 25
21	Ignition Off. Using the Service Manual procedure, check the Brake Switch. Was the Brake Switch okay? Yes → Go To 22 No → Replace Brake Switch.
22	Ignition Off. Disconnect the Brake Switch Connector. **Note: Check connectors - Clean/repair as necessary.** Inspect Connector. Is any Terminal damaged, pushed out, or miswired? Yes → Repair as necessary. No → Go To 23
23	Ignition Off. Disconnect the S/C Servo Connector. **Note: Check connectors - Clean/repair as necessary.** Inspect Connector. Is any terminal damaged, pushed out or miswired? Yes → Repair as necessary. No → Go To 24
24	If there are no potential causes remaining, replace the Brake Switch. View repair options. Repair Replace the Brake Switch.
25	Ignition Off. Disconnect the Brake Switch Connector. **Note: Check connectors - Clean/repair as necessary.** Inspect Connector. Is any Terminal damaged, pushed out, or miswired? Yes → Repair as necessary. No → Go To 26

CR1100000632050X

Fig. 44 Speed Control Operation (Part 5 of 6). Breeze, Cirrus, 2000 Sebring Convertible & Stratus

TEST	ACTION
26	Ignition Off. Disconnect the S/C Servo Connector. **Note: Check connectors - Clean/repair as necessary.** Inspect Connector. Is any terminal damaged, pushed out or miswired? Yes → Repair as necessary. No → Go To 27
27	Ignition Off. Disconnect the Brake Switch Connector. Disconnect the PCM. **Note: Check connectors - Clean/repair as necessary.** Test the resistance of the S/C Power Supply Circuit, PCM to Brake Switch. Is the resistance below 5.0 ohms? Yes → Go To 28 No → Repair the open S/C Power Supply Circuit PCM to Brake Switch.
28	If there are no potential causes remaining, replace the PCM. View repair options. Repair Replace the PCM.

CR1100000632060X

Fig. 44 Speed Control Operation (Part 6 of 6). Breeze, Cirrus, 2000 Sebring Convertible & Stratus

P1595-SPEED CONTROL SOLENOID CIRCUITS

When Monitored: With the ignition key on, the speed control switched on, the SET switch pressed and the vehicle in drive gear moving above 35 MPH.

Set Condition: The powertrain control module actuates the vacuum and vent solenoids but they do not respond.

P1683-SPD CTRL PWR RELAY; OR S/C 12V DRIVER CKT

When Monitored: With the ignition key on and the speed control switched on.

Set Condition: The speed control power supply circuit is either open or shorted to ground.

POSSIBLE CAUSES
GROUND CIRCUIT AT S/C SERVO CONNECTOR OPEN
S/C WIRING HARNESS INTERMITTENT PROBLEM (S/C VAC SOL AC)
S/C VACUUM SOLENOID CONTROL CIRCUIT OPEN
S/C VACUUM SOLENOID CONTROL CKT SHORT TO GROUND
S/C VENT SOLENOID CONTROL CIRCUIT OPEN
S/C VENT SOLENOID CONTROL CKT SHORT TO GROUND
S/C WIRING HARNESS INTERMITTENT PROBLEM (S/C VENT SOL AC)
S/C WIRING HARNESS OBSERVABLE PROBLEM
S/C POWER SUPPLY CIRCUIT OPEN
S/C POWER SUPPLY CIRCUIT SHORTED TO GROUND
S/C SERVO (12V DRIVER CIRCUIT)
S/C SERVO (12V DRIVER CIRCUIT)
BRAKE SWITCH
BRAKE SWITCH OUT OF ADJUSTMENT
S/C BRAKE SWITCH OUTPUT CIRCUIT OPEN
S/C BRAKE SWITCH OUTPUT CIRCUIT SHORTED TO GROUND
PCM DEFECTIVE

CR1100000623010X

Fig. 46 Codes P1595 & P1683: Speed Control Solenoid Circuits (Part 1 of 7). 2000 Concorde, Intrepid, LHS & 300M

VERIFICATION TEST VER-4A
1. Speed Control Verification **2. Note: If the PCM has been changed and the correct VIN and mileage have not been programmed, a DTC will be set in the ABS and Air Bag modules. In addition, if the vehicle is equipped with a SKIM, Secret Key data must be updated to enable starting.** 3. For ABS and Air Bag Systems: ACTION: Enter correct VIN and mileage in PCM. Erase codes in ABS and Air Bag modules. 4. For SKIM Theft Alarm: ACTION: 5. Connect DRB to Data Link Connector. 6. Go to Theft Alarm, SKIM, misc and place SKIM in secured access mode, by using appropriate PIN code for vehicle. 7. 3 Select Update Secret Key data. Data will be transferred from SKIM to PCM. 8. Inspect the vehicle to ensure that all engine components are connected. Reassemble and reconnect all components as necessary. 9. Connect the DRB to the PCM Data Link Connector and erase the codes. **10. Note: Ensure no other speed control problems remain by doing the following:** 11. Road test the vehicle at a speed above 30 MPH. 12. Turn the S/C ON/OFF Switch to the ON position. 13. Depress and release the SET Switch. If the S/C did not engage, the repair is not complete. **14. Note: Check for Technical Service Bulletins that pertain to S/C problems and then, if necessary, return to the symptom list and restart diagnostic testing for that symptom.** 15. Quickly depress and release the RESUME/ACCEL Switch. If vehicle speed did not increase by 2 MPH, the repair is not complete. 16. Press and HOLD Coast Switch, vehicle speed should decrease, if no decrease, the repair is not complete. 17. Using caution, depress and release the brake pedal. If the S/C did not disengage, the repair is not complete. 18. Bring the vehicle speed back up to 25 MPH. 19. Depress the RESUME/ACCEL Switch. If the S/C did not resume the previously set speed, the repair is not complete. 20. Hold down the SET Switch. If vehicle did not decelerate, the repair is not complete. 21. Ensure vehicle speed is greater than 30 MPH and release the SET Switch. If vehicle did not adjust and set a new vehicle speed, the repair is not complete. 22. Depress and release the Cancel Switch. If the S/C did not disengage, the repair is not complete. 23. Bring the vehicle back up above 35 and engage S/C. 24. Turn the ON/OFF Switch to OFF position. If S/C did not disengage, the repair is not complete. 25. If the vehicle successfully passed all of the previous tests, the S/C System is now functioning as designed. The repair is now complete. Repair is not complete, refer to appropriate symptom.

CR1100200752000X

Fig. 45 Verification Test VER-4A. Breeze, Cirrus, 2000 Sebring Convertible & Stratus

POSSIBLE CAUSES
PCM DEFECTIVE (12V DRIVER CIRCUIT)
PCM DEFEFECTIVE

TEST	ACTION
1	Ignition On, Engine Not Running. With the DRB actuate the S/C Vent Solenoid. Does the Speed Control Servo click? Yes → Go To 2 No → Go To 13
2	Ignition On, Engine Not Running. With the DRB, actuate the S/C Vacuum Solenoid. Does the Speed Control Servo click? Yes → Go To 3 No → Go To 6
3	Turn ignition off. Using the Schematics as a guide, inspect the Wiring and Connectors. Were any problems found? Yes → Repair as necessary. Perform the Powertrain Verification Test - Ver 4 No → Go To 4
4	Ignition On, Engine Not Running. With the DRB actuate the S/C Vent Solenoid. Wiggle the Wiring Harness from S/C Servo and Brake Switch to Powertrain Control Module. Did the wiggling interrupt the S/C Servo actuation? Yes → Repair as necessary where wiggling caused the actuation to be interrupted. Perform the Powertrain Verification Test - Ver 4 No → Go To 5
5	Ignition On, Engine Not Running. With the DRB actuate the S/C Vacuum Solenoid. Wiggle the Wiring Harness from S/C Servo and Brake Switch to Powertrain Control Module. Did the wiggling interrupt the S/C actuation? Yes → Repair as necessary where wiggling caused the actuation to be interrupted. Perform the Powertrain Verification Test - Ver 4 No → Test Complete.

CR1100000623020X

Fig. 46 Codes P1595 & P1683: Speed Control Solenoid Circuits (Part 2 of 7). 2000 Concorde, Intrepid, LHS & 300M

TEST	ACTION
6	Ignition On, Engine Not Running. With the DRB actuate the S/C Vent Solenoid. Wiggle the Wiring Harness from S/C Servo and Brake Switch to Powertrain Control Module. Did the wiggling interrupt the S/C Servo actuation? Yes → Repair as necessary where wiggling caused the actuation to be interrupted. No → Go To 7
7	Turn ignition off. Disconnect the Speed Control Servo 4-Way Connector. **Note: Check connectors - Clean/repair as necessary.** **Note: Ensure the Brake Pedal is not depressed during the following steps.** Key on, Engine off. Turn S/C Switch on. With the DRB, actuate the S/C Vacuum Solenoid. Using a 12-Volt Test Light, check the S/C Brake Switch Output Circuit at the Servo connector. Is the light illuminated and bright? Yes → Go To 8 No → Go To 19
8	Turn ignition off. Disconnect the Speed Control Servo Connector. **Note: Check connectors - Clean/repair as necessary.** Using an Ohmmeter, measure the resistance of the Ground Circuit at the Servo Connector to ground. Is the resistance below 5.0 ohms? Yes → Go To 9 No → Repair open Ground Circuit at S/C Servo Connector.
9	Turn ignition off. Disconnect the Speed Control Servo Connector. Disconnect Powertrain Control Module Connectors. **Note: Check connectors - Clean/repair as necessary.** With an Ohmmeter, measure the resistance of the S/C Vacuum Solenoid Control Circuit from the PCM to the Servo Connector. Is the resistance below 5.0 ohms? Yes → Go To 10 No → Repair the open S/C Vacuum Solenoid Control Circuit.

CR1100000623030X

Fig. 46 Codes P1595 & P1683: Speed Control Solenoid Circuits (Part 3 of 7). 2000 Concorde, Intrepid, LHS & 300M

TEST	ACTION
10	Turn ignition off. Disconnect the Speed Control Servo Connector. Disconnect Powertrain Control Module Connectors. **Note: Check connectors - Clean/repair as necessary.** With an Ohmmeter, measure the resistance of the S/C Vacuum Solenoid Control Circuit from the Servo Connector to a good ground. Is the resistance below 5.0 ohms? Yes → Repair the short to ground in the S/C Vacuum Solenoid Control Circuit. No → Go To 11
11	Turn ignition off. Disconnect the S/C Servo. Using the DRB, actuate the S/C Vacuum solenoid. Using a 12 Volt Test Light connected to B(+), probe the S/C Vacuum Solenoid Control Circuit. Does the test light blink on and off? Yes → Replace the S/C Servo. No → Go To 12
12	If there are no possible causes remaining, replace the PCM. View repair options. Repair Replace the Powertrain Control Module.
13	Turn ignition off. Disconnect the Speed Control Servo 4-Way Connector. **Note: Check connectors - Clean/repair as necessary.** **Note: Ensure the Brake Pedal is not depressed during the following steps.** Key on, Engine off. Turn S/C Switch on. With the DRB, actuate the S/C Vacuum Solenoid. Using a 12-Volt Test Light, check the S/C Brake Switch Output Circuit at the Servo connector. Is the light illuminated and bright? Yes → Go To 14 No → Go To 19
14	Turn ignition off. Disconnect the Speed Control Servo Connector. **Note: Check connectors - Clean/repair as necessary.** Using an Ohmmeter, measure the resistance of the Ground Circuit at the Servo Connector to ground. Is the resistance below 5.0 ohms? Yes → Go To 15 No → Repair open Ground Circuit at S/C Servo Connector.

CR1100000623040X

Fig. 46 Codes P1595 & P1683: Speed Control Solenoid Circuits (Part 4 of 7). 2000 Concorde, Intrepid, LHS & 300M

TEST	ACTION
15	Turn ignition off. Disconnect the Speed Control Servo Connector. Disconnect Powertrain Control Module Connectors. **Note: Check connectors - Clean/repair as necessary.** With an Ohmmeter, measure the resistance of the S/C Vent Solenoid Control Circuit from the PCM to the Servo Connector. Is the resistance below 5.0 ohms? Yes → Go To 16 No → Repair the open S/C Vent Solenoid Control Circuit.
16	Turn ignition off. Disconnect the S/C Servo Connector. Disconnect Powertrain Control Module Connectors. **Note: Check connectors - Clean/repair as necessary.** With an Ohmmeter, measure the resistance of the S/C Vent Solenoid Control Circuit from the Servo Connector to a good Ground. Is the resistance below 5.0 ohms? Yes → Repair the short to ground in the S/C Vent Solenoid Control Circuit. No → Go To 17
17	Turn ignition off. Disconnect the S/C Servo. Using the DRB, actuate the S/C Vent solenoid. Using a 12 Volt Test Light connected to B(+), probe the S/C Vent Solenoid Control Circuit. Does the test light blink on and off? Yes → Replace the S/C Servo. No → Go To 18
18	If there are no possible causes remaining, replace the PCM. View repair options. Repair Replace the Powertrain Control Module.
19	Turn ignition off. Using Service Procedure, check Brake Switch adjustment. Was Brake Switch adjustment OK? Yes → Go To 20 No → Adjust Brake Switch.

CR1100000623050X

Fig. 46 Codes P1595 & P1683: Speed Control Solenoid Circuits (Part 5 of 7). 2000 Concorde, Intrepid, LHS & 300M

TEST	ACTION
20	Turn ignition off. Disconnect the Brake Switch Connector. **Note: Check connectors - Clean/repair as necessary.** Be sure the brake pedal is not depressed during the next step. Using an ohmmeter, measure the resistance between the S/C power supply circuit and the S/C brake switch output circuit (measurement taken across switch). Is the resistance below 5.0 ohms? Yes → Go To 21 No → Replace the Brake Switch.
21	Turn ignition off. Disconnect the Brake Switch connector. Disconnect the Powertrain Control Module. **Note: Check connectors - Clean/repair as necessary.** Using an Ohmmeter, measure the resistance between the S/C Power Supply Circuit and ground at the Brake Switch connector. Is the resistance below 5.0 ohms? Yes → Repair S/C Power Supply Circuit shorted to ground. No → Go To 22
22	Turn ignition off. Disconnect the Brake Switch Connector. Disconnect the Powertrain Control Module **Note: Check connectors - Clean/repair as necessary.** Using an Ohmmeter, measure the resistance of the S/C Power Supply Circuit from the PCM to the Brake Switch Connector. Is the resistance below 5.0 ohms? Yes → Go To 23 No → Repair the open S/C Power Supply Circuit.
23	Turn ignition off. Disconnect the Speed Control Servo 4-Way Connector. Disconnect the brake switch connector. **Note: Check connectors - Clean/repair as necessary.** Using an Ohmmeter, measure the resistance of the S/C Brake Switch Output circuit from Servo Connector to ground. Is the resistance below 5.0 ohms? Yes → Repair Switched S/C Brake Switch Output circuit shorted to ground. No → Go To 24

CR1100000623060X

Fig. 46 Codes P1595 & P1683: Speed Control Solenoid Circuits (Part 6 of 7). 2000 Concorde, Intrepid, LHS & 300M

TEST	ACTION
24	Turn ignition off. Disconnect the S/C Servo Connector. Disconnect the Brake Switch Connector. **Note: Check connectors - Clean/repair as necessary.** With an Ohmmeter, measure the resistance of the S/C Brake Switch Output Circuit from the Brake Switch Connector to the Servo Connector. Is the resistance above 5.0 ohms? Yes → Repair the open S/C Brake Switch Output Circuit. No → Go To 25
25	If there are no possible causes remaining, replace the Powertrain Control Module. View repair options. Repair Replace the Powertrain Control Module.

CR1100000623070X

Fig. 46 Codes P1595 & P1683: Speed Control Solenoid Circuits (Part 7 of 7). 2000 Concorde, Intrepid, LHS & 300M

TEST	ACTION
3	Turn ignition off. Disconnect the S/C RESUME/ACCEL Switch. **Note: Check connectors - Clean/repair as necessary.** Turn ignition on, with engine not running. With the DRB, read the S/C Switch volts in Sensors. Did the S/C Switch volts go above 4.0 volts? Yes → Replace the Resume/Accel Switch. No → Go To 4
4	Disconnect the clockspring connector (instrument panel wiring side). Turn ignition on, with engine not running. With the DRB, read the S/C Switch volts in Sensors. Did the S/C Switch volts change to 5.0 volts? Yes → Replace the Clockspring. No → Go To 5
5	Turn ignition off. Disconnect the S/C ON/OFF Switch. Disconnect the Powertrain Control Module. **Note: Check connectors - Clean/repair as necessary.** Using an Ohmmeter, measure the resistance between the S/C Signal Circuit and the Sensor Ground Circuit at the ON/OFF switch connector. Is the resistance below 5.0 ohms? Yes → Repair S/C Signal Circuit shorted to Sensor Ground. No → Go To 6
6	Turn ignition off. Disconnect the S/C ON/OFF Switch. Disconnect the Powertrain Control Module. **Note: Check connectors - Clean/repair as necessary.** With an Ohmmeter, measure resistance of S/C Switch Signal Circuit to ground at the PCM Connector. Is the resistance below 5.0 ohms? Yes → Repair S/C Switch Signal Circuit for a short to ground. No → Go To 7
7	If there are no possible causes remaining, replace the Powertrain Control Module. View repair options. Repair Replace the Powertrain Control Module.
8	Turn ignition off. Using the Schematics as a guide, inspect the Wiring and Connectors. Were any problems found? Yes → Repair as necessary. No → Go To 9

CR1100000624020X

Fig. 47 Code P1597: Speed Control Switch Always Low (Part 2 of 3). 2000 Concorde, Intrepid, LHS & 300M

P1597-SPEED CONTROL SWITCH ALWAYS LOW

When Monitored: With the ignition key on and battery voltage above 10.4 volts.

Set Condition: When switch voltage is less than 0.39 volts for 2 minutes.

POSSIBLE CAUSES
CLOCKSPRING SHORTED TO GROUND
S/C WIRING HARNESS OBSERVABLE PROBLEM
S/C SWITCH (ON/OFF)
S/C SWITCH (RESUME/ACCEL)
S/C SIGNAL CIRCUIT SHORTED TO SENSOR GROUND
S/C SWITCH SIGNAL CIRCUIT SHORTED TO GROUND
SPEED CONTROL ON/OFF SWITCH STUCK
SPEED CONTROL RESUME/ACCEL SWITCH STUCK
PCM

TEST	ACTION
1	Ignition On, Engine Not Running With DRB, read the S/C Switch volts in Sensors. Is the S/C Switch voltage below 1.0 volt? Yes → Go To 2 No → Go To 8
2	Turn ignition off. Disconnect the S/C ON/OFF Switch. **Note: Check connectors - Clean/repair as necessary.** Turn ignition on, with engine not running. With the DRB, read the S/C Switch volts in Sensors. Did the S/C Switch volts change to 5.0 volts? Yes → Replace the S/C ON/OFF Switch. No → Go To 3

CR1100000624010X

Fig. 47 Code P1597: Speed Control Switch Always Low (Part 1 of 3). 2000 Concorde, Intrepid, LHS & 300M

TEST	ACTION
9	Disconnect the Speed Control On/Off Switch. With the DRB, read the Speed Control Switch Voltage. Did the DRB show Speed Control Switch Voltage go from below 4.0 Volts to above 4.0 Volts? Yes → Replace the Left Speed Control Switch. No → Go To 10
10	Disconnect the Speed Control Resume/Accel Switch. With the DRB, read the Speed Control Switch Voltage. Did the DRB show Speed Control Switch Voltage go from below 4.0 Volts to above 4.0 Volts? Yes → Replace the Right Speed Control Switch. No → Test Complete.

CR1100000624030X

Fig. 47 Code P1597: Speed Control Switch Always Low (Part 3 of 3). 2000 Concorde, Intrepid, LHS & 300M

POSSIBLE CAUSES
GROUND CIRCUIT AT S/C SERVO CONNECTOR OPEN
GROUND CIRCUIT TO S/C RESUME/ACCEL SWITCH CONNECTOR OPEN
S/C SW SIGNAL CKT TO CLOCKSPRING CONN OPEN
SPEED CONTROL SWITCH GROUND CIRCUIT OPEN CLOCKSPRING TO S/C SWITCH
SPEED CONTROL SWITCH GROUND CIRCUIT OPEN PCM TO CLOCKSPRING
CLOCKSPRING SHORTED TO GROUND
DRB DOES NOT SHOW SET SWITCH "PRESSED" OR RELEASED
S/C WIRING HARNESS OBSERVABLE PROBLEM
CANCEL SWITCH
COAST SWITCH
THROTTLE CABLE OBSERVABLE PROBLEM
THROTTLE OPENS AND CLOSES
S/C SWITCH (ON/OFF)
S/C SWITCH (RESUME/ACCEL)
S/C SIGNAL CIRCUIT SHORTED TO SENSOR GROUND
S/C SWITCH SIGNAL CIRCUIT SHORTED TO GROUND
SPEED CONTROL ON/OFF SWITCH
SPEED CONTROL ON/OFF SWITCH STUCK
SPEED CONTROL RESUME/ACCEL SWITCH
SPEED CONTROL RESUME/ACCEL SWITCH STUCK
SPEED CONTROL SW SIG CKT OPEN PCM TO CLOCK SPRING
SPEED CONTROL SW SIG CKT OPEN CLOCKSPRING TO S/C SWITCH
SPEED CONTROL SWITCH SIGNAL CKT SHORTED TO VOLTAGE
PCM
POWERTRAIN CONTROL MODULE

TEST	ACTION
1	Ignition on, with engine not running. With the DRB, monitor the Speed Control Switch inputs. While observing the display, press the Brake Pedal several times. Does the DRB show Brake Switch "pressed" and "released"? Yes → Go To 2 No → Refer to symptom *BRAKE SWITCH SENSE STATUS DOES NOT CHANGE ON DRB in the SPEED CONTROL category.

CR1100000625010X

Fig. 48 Speed Control System With No DTCs Present (Part 1 of 9). 2000 Concorde, Intrepid, LHS & 300M

TEST	ACTION
2	Turn ignition off. Using the Schematics as a guide, inspect the Wiring and Connectors. Were any problems found? Yes → Repair as necessary. No → Go To 3
3	Ignition on, with engine running. With the DRB, monitor the Speed Control Switch inputs. While observing the display, press the On/Off Switch several times. Does the DRB show On/Off Switch "pressed" and "released"? Yes → Go To 4 No → Go To 16
4	Turn ignition off. Disconnect the Speed Control Servo Connector. **Note: Check connectors - Clean/repair as necessary.** Using an Ohmmeter, measure the resistance of the Ground Circuit at the Servo Connector to ground. Is the resistance below 5.0 ohms? Yes → Go To 5 No → Repair open Ground Circuit at S/C Servo Connector.
5	Ignition on, with engine not running. With the DRB, monitor the P/N Switch inputs. While observing the display, move the Gear Selector to DRIVE. Does the DRB show P/N switch "D/R"? Yes → Go To 6 No → Refer to MOTOR'S DOMESTIC TRANSMISSION MANUAL
6	Inspect the throttle cable and linkage for any binding or damage. Is the cable or linkage disconnected or damaged? Yes → Repair as necessary. No → Go To 7
7	Ignition on, with engine running. With the DRB, monitor the Speed Control Switch inputs. While observing the display, press the Set Switch several times. Does the DRBIII show the Set Switch status change appropriately from Pressed to Released? Yes → Go To 8 No → Replace the Left S/C Switch.

CR1100000625020X

Fig. 48 Speed Control System With No DTCs Present (Part 2 of 9). 2000 Concorde, Intrepid, LHS & 300M

TEST	ACTION
8	Ignition On, Engine Running. With the DRB, monitor the Speed Control Switch inputs. While observing the display, press the Resume Switch several times. Does the DRBIII show the Resume Switch status change appropriately from Pressed to Released? Yes → Go To 9 No → Go To 12
9	Ignition on, with engine not running. With the DRB III read DTC's. Are any Vehicle Speed Signal codes set? Yes → Refer to symptom P0500 in MOTOR'S AUTO ENGINE PERFORMANCE AND DRIVEABILITY MANUAL No → Go To 10
10	Ignition On, Engine Running. With the DRB, monitor the Speed Control Switch inputs. While observing the display, press the Cancel Switch several times. Does the DRBIII show the Cancel Switch status change appropriately from Pressed to Released? Yes → Go To 11 No → Replace the Right S/C Switch.
11	Ignition On, Engine Running. With the DRB, monitor the Speed Control Switch inputs. While observing the display, press the Coast Switch several times. Does the DRBIII show the Coast Switch status change appropriately from Pressed to Released? Yes → Go To 41 No → Replace the Right S/C Switch.
12	Ignition on, with engine not running. With the DRB III read DTC's. Are any Vehicle Speed Signal codes set? Yes → Refer to symptom P0500 in MOTOR'S AUTO ENGINE PERFORMANCE AND DRIVEABILITY MANUAL No → Go To 13
13	Turn ignition off. Disconnect the Speed Control Resume/Accel Switch. **Note: Check connectors - Clean/repair as necessary.** Using an Ohmmeter, measure the resistance of the Sensor Ground Circuit from the S/C Resume/Accel Connector to a good Ground. Is the resistance below 5.0 ohms? Yes → Go To 14 No → Repair the open sensor ground circuit, right S/C switch connector to the clockspring connector.

CR1100000625030X

Fig. 48 Speed Control System With No DTCs Present (Part 3 of 9). 2000 Concorde, Intrepid, LHS & 300M

TEST	ACTION
14	Turn ignition off. Disconnect both Speed Control Switches. **Note: Check connectors - Clean/repair as necessary.** Using an Ohmmeter, measure the resistance of the Speed Control Switch Signal Circuit and Sensor Ground Circuit from the On/Off Switch connector to the Resume/Accel connector. Is resistance below 5.0 ohms for both circuits? Yes → Go To 15 No → Replace the Clockspring.
15	Turn ignition off. Disconnect the Speed Control Resume/Accel Switch. **Note: Check connectors - Clean/repair as necessary.** Connect a Jumper between the S/C Switch Signal and Sensor Ground at the switch connector. Ignition On, Engine Not Running. With the DRB, read the S/C Switch voltage. Does the DRB show S/C Switch is less than 1.0 volt? Yes → Replace the right Speed Control Switch. No → Go To 41
16	Turn ignition off. Disconnect the Speed Control Servo Connector. **Note: Check connectors - Clean/repair as necessary.** Using an Ohmmeter, measure the resistance of the Ground Circuit at the Servo Connector to ground. Is the resistance below 5.0 ohms? Yes → Go To 17 No → Repair open Ground Circuit at S/C Servo Connector.
17	Inspect the throttle cable and linkage for any binding or damage. Is the cable or linkage disconnected or damaged? Yes → Repair as necessary. No → Go To 18
18	Ignition On, Engine Running. With the DRB, read the Speed Control Switch voltage. Does the DRB show Speed Control Switch voltage above 4.0 volts? Yes → Go To 19 No → Go To 29

CR1100000625040X

Fig. 48 Speed Control System With No DTCs Present (Part 4 of 9). 2000 Concorde, Intrepid, LHS & 300M

TEST	ACTION
19	Ignition on, with engine not running. With the DRB, monitor the P/N Switch inputs. While observing the display, move the Gear Selector to DRIVE. Does the DRB show P/N switch "D/R"? Yes → Go To 20 No → Refer to MOTOR'S DOMESTIC TRANSMISSION MANUAL
20	Turn ignition off. Disconnect both Speed Control Switches. **Note: Check connectors - Clean/repair as necessary.** Using an Ohmmeter, measure the resistance of the Speed Control Switch Signal Circuit and Sensor Ground Circuit from the On/Off Switch connector to the Resume/Accel connector. Is resistance below 5.0 ohms for both circuits? Yes → Go To 21 No → Replace the Clockspring.
21	Turn ignition off. Disconnect the Speed Control On/Off Switch 2-Way Connector. Disconnect the clockspring connector. **Note: Check connectors - Clean/repair as necessary.** Using an Ohmmeter, measure the resistance of the S/C Switch Sensor Ground Circuit from the On/Off Switch 2-Way Connector to the clockspring connector. Is the resistance below 5.0 ohms? Yes → Go To 22 No → Replace the Clockspring.
22	Turn ignition off. Disconnect the clockspring connector (instrument panel harness side). Disconnect the PCM. **Note: Check connectors - Clean/repair as necessary.** Using an Ohmmeter, measure the resistance of the S/C Switch Sensor Ground Circuit from the PCM to the clockspring connector. Is the resistance below 5.0 ohms? Yes → Go To 23 No → Repair open ground circuit from PCM to clockspring.
23	Turn ignition off. Disconnect the Speed Control On/Off Switch 2-Way Connector only. **Note: Check connectors - Clean/repair as necessary.** Using an Ohmmeter, measure the resistance across the S/C On/Off Switch then press and release the On/Off button. Did the resistance go from below 5.0 ohms when pressed to an open circuit when released? Yes → Go To 24 No → Replace the On/Off Switch.

CR1100000625050X

Fig. 48 Speed Control System With No DTCs Present (Part 5 of 9). 2000 Concorde, Intrepid, LHS & 300M

TEST	ACTION
24	Ignition on, with engine not running. With the DRB III read DTC's. Are any Vehicle Speed Signal codes set? Yes → Refer to symptom P0500 in MOTOR'S AUTO ENGINE PERFORMANCE AND DRIVEABILITY MANUAL No → Go To 25
25	Turn ignition off. Disconnect the Speed Control On/Off Switch 2-Way Connector only. **Note: Check connectors - Clean/repair as necessary.** Turn ignition on. Using a voltmeter, measure the S/C Switch Signal Circuit for voltage at the On/Off Switch 2-Way Connector. Is the voltage above 6.0 volts? Yes → Repair the Speed Control Switch Signal Circuit for a short to voltage. No → Go To 26
26	Turn ignition off. Disconnect the Clockspring connector (instrument panel harness side). Disconnect the PCM. **Note: Check connectors - Clean/repair as necessary.** Using an Ohmmeter, measure the resistance of the S/C Switch Signal Circuit from the PCM to the Clockspring Connector. Is the resistance below 5.0 ohms? Yes → Go To 27 No → Repair open Speed Control Switch Signal Circuit PCM to Clockspring.
27	Turn ignition off. Disconnect the Clockspring Connector. Disconnect the On/Off switch 2-way connector. **Note: Check connectors - Clean/repair as necessary.** Using an Ohmmeter, measure the resistance of the S/C Switch Signal Circuit from the clockspring to the On/Off switch connector. Is the resistance below 5.0 ohms? Yes → Go To 28 No → Replace the Clockspring.
28	If there are no possible causes remaining, replace the Powertrain Control Module. View repair options. Repair Replace Powertrain Control Module.

CR1100000625060X

Fig. 48 Speed Control System With No DTCs Present (Part 6 of 9). 2000 Concorde, Intrepid, LHS & 300M

TEST	ACTION
29	Ignition on, with engine not running. With the DRB, monitor the P/N Switch inputs. While observing the display, move the Gear Selector to DRIVE. Does the DRB show P/N switch "D/R"? Yes → Go To 30 No → Refer to MOTOR'S DOMESTIC TRANSMISSION MANUAL
30	Ignition On, Engine Not Running With DRB, read the S/C Switch volts in Sensors. Is the S/C Switch voltage below 1.0 volt? Yes → Go To 31 No → Go To 38
31	Ignition on, with engine not running. With the DRB III read DTC's. Are any Vehicle Speed Signal codes set? Yes → Refer to symptom P0500 in MOTOR'S AUTO ENGINE PERFORMANCE AND DRIVEABILITY MANUAL No → Go To 32
32	Turn ignition off. Disconnect the S/C ON/OFF Switch. **Note: Check connectors - Clean/repair as necessary.** Turn ignition on, with engine not running. With the DRB, read the S/C Switch volts in Sensors. Did the S/C Switch volts change to 5.0 volts? Yes → Replace the S/C ON/OFF Switch. No → Go To 33
33	Turn ignition off. Disconnect the S/C RESUME/ACCEL Switch. **Note: Check connectors - Clean/repair as necessary.** Turn ignition on, with engine not running. With the DRB, read the S/C Switch volts in Sensors. Did the S/C Switch volts go above 4.0 volts? Yes → Replace the Resume/Accel Switch. No → Go To 34
34	Disconnect the clockspring connector (instrument panel wiring side). Turn ignition on, with engine not running. With the DRB, read the S/C Switch volts in Sensors. Did the S/C Switch volts change to 5.0 volts? Yes → Replace the Clockspring. No → Go To 35

CR1100000625070X

Fig. 48 Speed Control System With No DTCs Present (Part 7 of 9). 2000 Concorde, Intrepid, LHS & 300M

TEST	ACTION
35	Turn ignition off. Disconnect the S/C ON/OFF Switch. Disconnect the Powertrain Control Module. **Note: Check connectors - Clean/repair as necessary.** Using an Ohmmeter, measure the resistance between the S/C Signal Circuit and the Sensor Ground Circuit at the ON/OFF switch connector. Is the resistance below 5.0 ohms? Yes → Repair S/C Signal Circuit shorted to Sensor Ground. No → Go To 36
36	Turn ignition off. Disconnect the S/C ON/OFF Switch. Disconnect the Powertrain Control Module. **Note: Check connectors - Clean/repair as necessary.** With an Ohmmeter, measure resistance of S/C Switch Signal Circuit to ground at the PCM Connector. Is the resistance below 5.0 ohms? Yes → Repair S/C Switch Signal Circuit for a short to ground. No → Go To 37
37	If there are no possible causes remaining, replace the Powertrain Control Module. View repair options. Repair Replace the Powertrain Control Module. Perform the Powertrain Verification Test - Ver 4
38	Ignition on, with engine not running. With the DRB III read DTC's. Are any Vehicle Speed Signal codes set? Yes → Refer to symptom P0500 in MOTOR'S AUTO ENGINE PERFORMANCE AND DRIVEABILITY MANUAL No → Go To 39
39	Disconnect the Speed Control On/Off Switch. With the DRB, read the Speed Control Switch Voltage. Did the DRB show Speed Control Switch Voltage go from below 4.0 Volts to above 4.0 Volts? Yes → Replace the Left Speed Control Switch. No → Go To 40
40	Disconnect the Speed Control Resume/Accel Switch. With the DRB, read the Speed Control Switch Voltage. Did the DRB show Speed Control Switch Voltage go from below 4.0 Volts to above 4.0 Volts? Yes → Replace the Right Speed Control Switch. No → Go To 41

CR1100000625080X

Fig. 48 Speed Control System With No DTCs Present (Part 8 of 9). 2000 Concorde, Intrepid, LHS & 300M

TEST	ACTION
41	Start Engine. Allow engine to idle for 1 minute. Turn engine off, then ignition on, engine not running. With the DRB, actuate the Speed Control Servo Solenoids. Does the Throttle open and close? Yes → Go To 42 No → Perform Speed Control Vacuum Supply Test per appropriate service procedure.
42	At this time the Speed Control Switch and Servo functions appear to operate properly. Using the DRB, monitor the Speed Control OUTPUT status. Road test the Vehicle at speeds over 35 MPH (55kmh) and attempt to set the Speed Control. The following items will not allow the Speed Control to set. The last or most recent cause for Speed Control not to set is indicated by the DENIED status. If ON/OFF Denied message is indicated, the Powertrain Control Module does not see an ON signal from the Switch. If SPEED Denied message is indicated, the Vehicle Speed as seen by the Powertrain Control Module is not greater than 36 MPH. If RPM Denied message is indicated, the Engine RPM is excessively high. If BRAKE Denied message is indicated, the Brake Switch Sense Circuit is open indicating to the PCM that the Brakes are applied. The Sense Circuit is grounded through the Brake Pedal Switch when the brakes are released. If P/N Denied message is indicated, Park/Neutral Switch Sense Circuit is grounded indicating to PCM that Transmission is not in gear. The Sense Circuit is grounded through the P/N Switch when Transmission is in Park or Neutral. If RPM/SPD Denied message is indicated, the PCM senses excessive Engine RPM for a given Vehicle speed. If SOL FLT Denied message is indicated, the Powertrain Control Module senses a Servo Solenoid Circuit trouble code that is maturing or set in memory. Continue if the previous instructions have been completed. Repair Test Complete.

CR1100000625090X

Fig. 48 Speed Control System With No DTCs Present (Part 9 of 9). 2000 Concorde, Intrepid, LHS & 300M

POWERTRAIN VERIFICATION TEST VER - 4
1. Inspect the vehicle to ensure that all engine components are properly installed and connected. Reassemble and reconnect components as necessary. 2. Connect the DRB to the data link connector and erase all codes. 3. If the PCM has been replaced, perform steps 4 through 6, then continue with the verification. 4. If PCM has been changed and correct VIN and mileage have not been programmed, a DTC will be set in ABS and Air bag modules. In addition, if vehicle is equipped with a Sentry Key Immobilizer Module (SKIM), Secret Key data must be updated to enable start. 5. For ABS and Air Bag systems: Enter correct VIN and Mileage in PCM. Erase codes in ABS and Air Bag modules. 6. For SKIM theft alarm: Connect DRB to data link conn. Go to Theft Alarm, SKIM, Misc. and place SKIM in secured access mode, by using the appropriate PIN code for this vehicle. Select Update the Secret Key data. Data will be transferred from SKIM to PCM. 7. Turn the speed control ON (if equipped, cruise light will be on). 8. Depress and release the SET Switch. If the speed control did not engage, the repair is not complete. Check for TSBs that pertain to speed control problem and then, if necessary, return to Symptom List. 9. Depress and hold the RESUME/ACCEL Switch. If the vehicle speed did not increase by at least 2 mph, the repair is not complete. Check for TSBs that pertain to speed control problem and then, if necessary, return to Symptom List. 10. Press and hold the COAST switch. The vehicle speed should decrease. If it did not decrease, the repair is not complete. Check for TSBs that pertain to speed control problem and then, if necessary, return to Symptom List. 11. Using caution, depress and release the brake pedal. If the speed control did not disengage, the repair is not complete. Check for TSBs that pertain to speed control problem and then, if necessary, return to Symptom List. 12. Bring the vehicle speed back up to 35 MPH. 13. Depress the RESUME/ACCEL switch. If the speed control did not resume the previously set speed, the repair is not complete. Check for TSBs that pertain to speed control problem and then, if necessary, return to Symptom List. 14. Hold down the SET switch. If the vehicle did not decelerate, the repair is not complete. Check for TSBs that pertain to speed control problem and then, if necessary, return to Symptom List. 15. Ensure vehicle speed is greater than 35 mph and release the SET Switch. If vehicle did not adjust and set a new vehicle speed, the repair is not complete. Check for TSBs that pertain to speed control problem and then, if necessary, return to Symptom List. 16. Depress and release the CANCEL switch. If the speed control did not disengage, the repair is not complete. Check for TSBs that pertain to speed control problem and then, if necessary, return to Symptom List. 17. Bring the vehicle speed back up above 35 mph and engage speed control. 18. Depress the OFF switch to turn OFF, (Cruise light will be off). If the speed control did not disengage, the repair is not complete. Check for TSBs that pertain to speed control problem and then, if necessary, return to Symptom List. 19. If the vehicle successfully passed all of the previous tests, the speed control system is now functioning as designed. The repair is now complete. Repair is not complete, refer to appropriate symptom.

CR1029910766000X

Fig. 49 Powertrain Verification Test VER-4. 2000 Concorde, Intrepid, LHS & 300M

When Monitored and Set Condition:

P1595-SPEED CONTROL SOLENOID CIRCUITS

When Monitored: With the ignition on. Battery voltage greater than 10 volts. Speed Control Switched on.

Set Condition: The Powertrain Control Module actuates the vacuum and vent solenoids but they do not respond.

P1683-SPD CTRL PWR RELAY; OR S/C 12V DRIVER CKT

When Monitored: With the ignition key on. The speed control switched on.

Set Condition: The speed control power supply circuit is either open or shorted to ground.

POSSIBLE CAUSES
GROUND CIRCUIT OPEN
INTERMITTENT CONDITION
S/C BRAKE SWITCH OUTPUT CIRCUIT
SPEED CONTROL SWITCH OUTPUT OPEN
BRAKE LAMP SWITCH
SPEED CONTROL POWER SUPPLY CIRCUIT
PCM (S/C POWER SUPPLY)
SPEED CONTROL VACUUM SOLENOID
SPEED CONTROL VACUUM SOLENOID CONTROL CIRCUIT OPEN
PCM (VACUUM SOLENOID)
SPEED CONTROL VACUUM SOLENOID CONTROL CIRCUIT SHORTED TO GROUND
SPEED CONTROL VENT SOLENOID
SPEED CONTROL VENT SOLENOID CONTROL CIRCUIT OPEN
SPEED CONTROL VENT SOLENOID CONTROL CIRCUIT SHORTED TO GROUND
PCM (VENT SOLENOID)

CR1100000662010X

Fig. 50 Codes P1595 & P1683: Speed Control Solenoid Circuits (Part 1 of 5). 2001–02 Neon, Sebring Convertible, Sebring Sedan, Stratus Sedan, 2001 Concorde, Intrepid, LHS, & 300M

TEST	ACTION
1	Turn the ignition on. **NOTE: In the below step you will need to actuate both S/C solenoids separately. Note the operation of the each solenoid when actuated.** With the DRBIII®, actuate the Speed Control Vacuum Solenoid and note operation. With the DRBIII®, actuate the Speed Control Vent Solenoid and note operation. Choose the conclusion that best matches the solenoids operation? Vacuum Solenoid not operating Go To 2 Vent Solenoid not operating Go To 6 Both S/C Solenoids not operating Go To 10 Both S/C Solenoids operating Go To 15
2	Turn the ignition off. Disconnect the Speed Control Servo harness connector. Turn the ignition on. With the DRBIII®, actuate the Speed Control Vacuum Solenoid. Using a 12-volt test light connected to 12-volts, probe the Speed Control Vacuum Solenoid Control circuit. Does the test light illuminate brightly and flash? Yes → Replace the Speed Control Servo. Perform POWERTRAIN VERIFICATION TEST VER - 4. No → Go To 3
3	Turn the ignition off. Disconnect the S/C Servo harness connector. Disconnect the PCM harness connector. Measure the resistance of the Speed Control Vacuum Solenoid Control circuit between the PCM harness connector and Speed Control Servo harness connector. Is the resistance below 5.0 ohms? Yes → Go To 4 No → Repair the Speed Control Vacuum Solenoid Control circuit for an open. Perform POWERTRAIN VERIFICATION TEST VER - 4.
4	Turn the ignition off. Disconnect the S/C Servo harness connector. Disconnect the PCM harness connector. Measure the resistance of the Speed Control Vacuum Solenoid Control circuit in the PCM harness connector to ground. Is the resistance below 5.0 ohms? Yes → Repair the Speed Control Vacuum Solenoid Control circuit for a short to ground. Perform POWERTRAIN VERIFICATION TEST VER - 4. No → Go To 5

CR1100000662020X

Fig. 50 Codes P1595 & P1683: Speed Control Solenoid Circuits (Part 2 of 5). 2001–02 Neon, Sebring Convertible, Sebring Sedan, Stratus Sedan, 2001 Concorde, Intrepid, LHS, & 300M

TEST	ACTION
5	If the there are no possible causes remaining, view repair. Repair Replace and program the Powertrain Control Module Module in accordance with the Service Information. Perform POWERTRAIN VERIFICATION TEST VER - 4.
6	Turn the ignition off. Disconnect the Speed Control Servo harness connector. Turn the ignition on. With the DRBIII®, actuate the Speed Control Vent Solenoid. Using a 12-volt test light connected to 12-volts, probe the Speed Control Vent Solenoid Control circuit in the Speed Control Servo harness connector. Does the test light illuminate brightly and flash? Yes → Replace the Speed Control Servo. Perform POWERTRAIN VERIFICATION TEST VER - 4. No → Go To 7
7	Turn the ignition off. Disconnect the S/C Servo harness connector. Disconnect the PCM harness connector. Measure the resistance of the Speed Control Vent Solenoid Control circuit between the PCM harness connector and Speed Control Servo harness connector. Is the resistance below 5.0 ohms? Yes → Go To 8 No → Repair the Speed Control Vacuum Solenoid Control circuit for an open. Perform POWERTRAIN VERIFICATION TEST VER - 4.
8	Turn the ignition off. Disconnect the S/C Servo harness connector. Disconnect the PCM harness connector. Measure the resistance of the Speed Control Vent Solenoid Control circuit in the PCM harness connector to ground. Is the resistance below 5.0 ohms? Yes → Repair the Speed Control Vacuum Solenoid Control circuit for a short to ground. Perform POWERTRAIN VERIFICATION TEST VER - 4. No → Go To 9
9	If the there are no possible causes remaining, view repair. Repair Replace and program the Powertrain Control Module Module in accordance with the Service Information. Perform POWERTRAIN VERIFICATION TEST VER - 4.

CR1100000662030X

Fig. 50 Codes P1595 & P1683: Speed Control Solenoid Circuits (Part 3 of 5). 2001–02 Neon, Sebring Convertible, Sebring Sedan, Stratus Sedan, 2001 Concorde, Intrepid, LHS, & 300M

TEST	ACTION
15	Turn the ignition off. Disconnect the S/C Servo harness connector. Using a 12-volt test light connected to 12-volts, probe the ground circuit in the S/C Servo harness connector. Does the test light illuminate brightly? Yes → Go To 16 No → Repair the ground circuit for an open. Perform POWERTRAIN VERIFICATION TEST VER - 4.
16	**WARNING: WHEN THE ENGINE IS OPERATING, DO NOT STAND IN A DIRECT LINE WITH THE FAN. DO NOT PUT YOUR HANDS NEAR THE PULLEYS, BELTS OR FAN. DO NOT WEAR LOOSE CLOTHING.** **NOTE: The conditions that set the DTC are not present at this time. The following list may help in identifying the intermittent condition.** With the engine running at normal operating temperature, monitor the DRB parameters related to the DTC while wiggling the wiring harness. Look for parameter values to change and/or a DTC to set. Review the DRB Freeze Frame information. If possible, try to duplicate the conditions under which the DTC was set. Refer to any Technical Service Bulletins (TSB) that may apply. Visually inspect the related wiring harness. Look for any chafed, pierced, pinched, or partially broken wires. Visually inspect the related wiring harness connectors. Look for broken, bent, pushed out, or corroded terminals. Were any of the above conditions present? Yes → Repair as necessary Perform POWERTRAIN VERIFICATION TEST VER - 4. No → Test Complete.

CR1100000662050X

Fig. 50 Codes P1595 & P1683: Speed Control Solenoid Circuits (Part 5 of 5). 2001–02 Neon, Sebring Convertible, Sebring Sedan, Stratus Sedan, 2001 Concorde, Intrepid, LHS, & 300M

TEST	ACTION
10	Turn the ignition off. Disconnect the S/C Servo harness connector. Turn the ignition on. Using a 12-volt test light connected to ground, probe the S/C Brake Switch Output circuit in the S/C Servo harness connector. Does the test light illuminate brightly? Yes → Replace the Speed Control Servo. Perform POWERTRAIN VERIFICATION TEST VER - 4. No → Go To 11
11	Turn the ignition off. Disconnect the Speed Control Servo harness connector. Disconnect the Brake Lamp Switch harness connector. Measure the resistance of the Speed Control Brake Switch Output circuit between the Speed Control Servo harness connector and Brake Lamp Switch harness connector. Is the resistance below 5.0 ohms? Yes → Go To 12 No → Repair the Speed Control Brake Switch Output circuit for an open. Perform POWERTRAIN VERIFICATION TEST VER - 4.
12	Disconnect the Brake Lamp Switch harness connector. Turn the ignition on. Using a 12-volt test light connected to ground, probe the Speed Control Power Supply circuit in the Brake Lamp Switch harness connector. Does the test light illuminate brightly? Yes → Replace the Brake Lamp Switch. Perform POWERTRAIN VERIFICATION TEST VER - 4. No → Go To 13
13	Turn the ignition off. Disconnect the PCM harness connector. Disconnect the Brake Lamp Switch harness connector. Measure the resistance of the Speed Control Power Supply circuit between the PCM harness connector and the Brake Lamp Switch harness connector. Is the resistance below 5.0 ohms? Yes → Go To 14 No → Repair the Speed Control Supply circuit for an open. Perform POWERTRAIN VERIFICATION TEST VER - 4.
14	If there are no possible causes remaining, view repair. Repair Replace and program the Powertrain Control Module Module in accordance with the Service Information. Perform POWERTRAIN VERIFICATION TEST VER - 4.

CR1100000662040X

Fig. 50 Codes P1595 & P1683: Speed Control Solenoid Circuits (Part 4 of 5). 2001–02 Neon, Sebring Convertible, Sebring Sedan, Stratus Sedan, 2001 Concorde, Intrepid, LHS, & 300M

When Monitored and Set Condition:

P1597-SPEED CONTROL SWITCH ALWAYS LOW

When Monitored: With the ignition key on. Battery voltage above 10 volts.

Set Condition: When switch voltage is less than 0.43 volts for 2 minutes.

POSSIBLE CAUSES
INTERMITTENT CONDITION
SPEED CONTROL ON/OFF SWITCH
SPEED CONTROL RESUME/ACCEL SWITCH
SPEED CONTROL SWITCH SIGNAL CIRCUIT SHORTED TO SENSOR GROUND
SPEED CONTROL SWITCH SIGNAL CIRCUIT SHORTED TO GROUND
PCM

TEST	ACTION
1	Turn the ignition on. With the DRBIII®, read the Speed Control voltage. Is the Speed Control voltage below 1.0 volts? Yes → Go To 2 No → Go To 7
2	Turn the ignition on. With the DRBIII®, monitor the Speed Control Switch voltage. Disconnect the Speed Control On/Off Switch harness connector. Did the volt change to above 4.7 volts? Yes → Replace the Speed Control On/Off Switch. Perform POWERTRAIN VERIFICATION TEST VER - 4. No → Go To 3
3	Turn the ignition on. With the DRBIII®, monitor the Speed Control Switch voltage. Disconnect the Speed Control Resume/Accel Switch harness connector. Did the volt change to above 4.7 volts? Yes → Replace the Speed Control Resume/Accel Switch. Perform POWERTRAIN VERIFICATION TEST VER - 4. No → Go To 4

CR1100000663010X

Fig. 51 Code P1597: Speed Control Switch Always Low (Part 1 of 2). 2001–02 Neon, Sebring Convertible, Sebring Sedan, Stratus Sedan, 2001 Concorde, Intrepid, LHS, & 300M

TEST	ACTION
4	Turn the ignition off. Disconnect the Speed Control On/Off Switch harness connector. Disconnect the Speed Control Resume/Accel Switch harness connector. Disconnect the PCM harness connector. Measure the resistance between the Speed Control Switch Signal circuit and the Sensor ground circuit in the PCM harness connector. Is the resistance below 5.0 ohms? Yes → Repair the Speed Control Switch Signal circuit shorted to Sensor ground circuit. Perform POWERTRAIN VERIFICATION TEST VER - 4. No → Go To 5
5	Turn the ignition off. Disconnect the Speed Control On/Off Switch harness connector. Disconnect the Speed Control Resume/Accel Switch harness connector. Disconnect the PCM harness connector. Measure the resistance of the Speed Control Switch Signal circuit in PCM harness connector to ground. Is the resistance below 5.0 ohms? Yes → Repair the Speed Control Switch Signal circuit shorted to ground. Perform POWERTRAIN VERIFICATION TEST VER - 4. No → Go To 6
6	If there are no possible causes remaining, view repair. Repair Replace and program the Powertrain Control Module in accordance with the Service Information. Perform POWERTRAIN VERIFICATION TEST VER - 4.
7	**WARNING: WHEN THE ENGINE IS OPERATING, DO NOT STAND IN A DIRECT LINE WITH THE FAN. DO NOT PUT YOUR HANDS NEAR THE PULLEYS, BELTS OR FAN. DO NOT WEAR LOOSE CLOTHING.** **NOTE: The conditions that set the DTC are not present at this time. The following list may help in identifying the intermittent condition.** With the engine running at normal operating temperature, monitor the DRB parameters related to the DTC while wiggling the wiring harness. Look for parameter values to change and/or a DTC to set. Review the DRB Freeze Frame information. If possible, try to duplicate the conditions under which the DTC was set. Refer to any Technical Service Bulletins (TSB) that may apply. Visually inspect the related wiring harness. Look for any chafed, pierced, pinched, or partially broken wires. Visually inspect the related wiring harness connectors. Look for broken, bent, pushed out, or corroded terminals. Were any of the above conditions present? Yes → Repair as necessary Perform POWERTRAIN VERIFICATION TEST VER - 4. No → Test Complete.

CR1100000663020X

Fig. 51 Code P1597: Speed Control Switch Always Low (Part 2 of 2). 2001–02 Neon, Sebring Convertible, Sebring Sedan, Stratus Sedan, 2001 Concorde, Intrepid, LHS, & 300M

POWERTRAIN VERIFICATION TEST VER - 4
1. NOTE: If the PCM has been replaced and the correct VIN and mileage have not been programmed, a DTC will be set in the ABS Module, Airbag Module and the SKIM. **2. NOTE: If the vehicle is equipped with a Sentry Key Immobilizer System, Secret Key data must be updated. Refer to the Service Information for the PCM, SKIM and the Transponder (ignition key) for programming information.** 3. Inspect the vehicle to ensure that all engine components are properly installed and connected. 4. Connect the DRB to the data link connector and erase all codes. 5. Turn the speed control ON (if equipped, cruise light will be on). 6. Depress and release the SET Switch. If the speed control did not engage, the repair is not complete. Check for TSBs that pertain to speed control problem and then, if necessary, return to Symptom List. 7. Depress and hold the RESUME/ACCEL Switch. If the vehicle speed did not increase by at least 2 mph, the repair is not complete. Check for TSBs that pertain to speed control problem and then, if necessary, return to Symptom List. 8. Press and hold the COAST switch. The vehicle speed should decrease. If it did not decrease, the repair is not complete. Check for TSBs that pertain to speed control problem and then, if necessary, return to Symptom List. 9. Using caution, depress and release the brake pedal. If the speed control did not disengage, the repair is not complete. Check for TSBs that pertain to speed control problem and then, if necessary, return to Symptom List. 10. Bring the vehicle speed back up to 35 MPH. 11. Depress the RESUME/ACCEL switch. If the speed control did not resume the previously set speed, the repair is not complete. Check for TSBs that pertain to speed control problem and then, if necessary, return to Symptom List. 12. Hold down the SET switch. If the vehicle did not decelerate, the repair is not complete. Check for TSBs that pertain to speed control problem and then, if necessary, return to Symptom List. 13. Ensure vehicle speed is greater than 35 mph and release the SET Switch. If vehicle did not adjust and set a new vehicle speed, the repair is not complete. Check for TSBs that pertain to speed control problem and then, if necessary, return to Symptom List. 14. Depress and release the CANCEL switch. If the speed control did not disengage, the repair is not complete. Check for TSBs that pertain to speed control problem and then, if necessary, return to Symptom List. 15. Bring the vehicle speed back up above 35 mph and engage speed control. 16. Depress the OFF switch to turn OFF, (Cruise light will be off). If the speed control did not disengage, the repair is not complete. Check for TSBs that pertain to speed control problem and then, if necessary, return to Symptom List. 17. If the vehicle successfully passed all of the previous tests, the speed control system is now functioning as designed. The repair is now complete. Did the Speed Control pass the above test? Yes → Repair is complete. No → Repair is not complete, refer to appropriate symptom.

CR1100000664000X

Fig. 52 Verification Test VER-4. 2001–02 Neon, Sebring Convertible, Sebring Sedan, Stratus Sedan, 2001 Concorde, Intrepid, LHS, & 300M

POSSIBLE CAUSES
SPEED CONTROL SWITCH STATUS
SPEED CONTROL SWITCHES
(V37) S/C SWITCH SIGNAL CIRCUIT SHORTED TO SENSOR GROUND
(V37) S/C SWITCH SIGNAL CIRCUIT SHORTED TO GROUND
(V37) S/C SWITCH SIGNAL CIRCUIT SHORTED TO BATTERY VOLTAGE
(V37) S/C SWITCH SIGNAL CIRCUIT OPEN
(K4) SENSOR GROUND OPEN
PCM

TEST	ACTION
1	Ignition on, engine not running. With the DRBIII®, monitor each switch function for the Speed Control Switches. Press and release each Speed Control Button. - Resume/Accel - Cancel - Decel (Coast) - On/Off - Set Does each switch function change status when pressing and then depressing each switch? Yes → Refer to the INTERMITTENT CONDITION symptom in the Driveability category. Perform POWERTRAIN VERIFICATION TEST VER - 4 No → Go To 2
2	Turn the ignition off. Remove the Speed Control Switches from the steering wheel. Measure the resistance across each Switch Control Switch. Monitor the ohmmeter while pressing each function button on each switch. Resume/Accel - 15,400 ohms Cancel - 909 +/- 9 ohms Decel (Coast) - 2940 +/- 30 ohms On/Off - 0 ohms Set - 6650 +/- 66 ohms Does the function on the Speed Control Switches have the correct ohm value? Yes → Go To 3 No → Replace the Speed Control Switch that had the incorrect resistance value. Perform POWERTRAIN VERIFICATION TEST VER - 4

CR1100200753010X

Fig. 53 Code P0579: Speed Control Switch No. 1 Performance (Part 1 of 3). 2002–04 Concorde, Intrepid, 300M, 2003–04 Neon, Sebring Convertible & Sebring & Stratus Sedan

TEST	ACTION
3	Turn the ignition off. Disconnect the Speed Control On/Off Switch harness connector. Disconnect the Speed Control Resume/Accel Switch harness connector. Disconnect the PCM harness connector. Measure the resistance between the (V37) S/C Switch Signal circuit and the (K4) Sensor ground circuit in the Speed Control harness connector. Is the resistance below 5.0 ohms? Yes → Repair the (V37) S/C Switch Signal circuit shorted to the (K4) Sensor Ground circuit. Perform POWERTRAIN VERIFICATION TEST VER - 4 No → Go To 4
4	Turn the ignition off. Disconnect the Speed Control On/Off Switch harness connector. Disconnect the Speed Control Resume/Accel Switch harness connector. Disconnect the PCM harness connector. Measure the voltage of the (V37) Speed Control Switch Signal circuit at the Speed Control harness connector. Is the is the voltage above 5.0 volts? Yes → Repair the (V37) S/C Switch Signal circuit shorted to the battery voltage. Perform POWERTRAIN VERIFICATION TEST VER - 4 No → Go To 5
5	Turn the ignition off. Disconnect the Speed Control On/Off Switch harness connector. Disconnect the Speed Control Resume/Accel Switch harness connector. Disconnect the PCM harness connector. Measure the resistance between ground and the (V37) S/C Switch Signal circuit at the Speed Control harness connector. Is the resistance below 100 ohms? Yes → Repair the (V37) Speed Control Switch Signal circuit shorted to the ground. Perform POWERTRAIN VERIFICATION TEST VER - 4 No → Go To 6
6	**NOTE: The measurement must be taken from both Speed Control Switch harness connectors.** Turn the ignition off. Disconnect the Speed Control On/Off Switch harness connector. Disconnect the Speed Control Resume/Accel Switch harness connector. Disconnect the PCM harness connector. **CAUTION: DO NOT PROBE THE PCM HARNESS CONNECTORS. PROBING THE PCM HARNESS CONNECTORS WILL DAMAGE THE PCM TERMINALS RESULTING IN POOR TERMINAL TO PIN CONNECTION. INSTALL MILLER SPECIAL TOOL #8815 TO PERFORM DIAGNOSIS.** Measure the resistance of the (V37) S/C Switch Signal circuit from the Speed Control harness connector to the appropriate terminal of special tool #8815. Is the resistance below 5.0 ohms for both measurements? Yes → Go To 7 No → Repair the (V37) Speed Control Switch Signal circuit for an open. Perform POWERTRAIN VERIFICATION TEST VER - 4

CR1100200753020X

Fig. 53 Code P0579: Speed Control Switch No. 1 Performance (Part 2 of 3). 2002–04 Concorde, Intrepid, 300M, 2003–04 Neon, Sebring Convertible & Sebring & Stratus Sedan

TEST	ACTION
7	**NOTE: The measurement must be taken from both Speed Control Switch harness connector.** Turn the ignition off. Disconnect the Speed Control On/Off Switch harness connector. Disconnect the Speed Control Resume/Accel Switch harness connector. Disconnect the PCM harness connector. **CAUTION: DO NOT PROBE THE PCM HARNESS CONNECTORS. PROBING THE PCM HARNESS CONNECTORS WILL DAMAGE THE PCM TERMINALS RESULTING IN POOR TERMINAL TO PIN CONNECTION. INSTALL MILLER SPECIAL TOOL #8815 TO PERFORM DIAGNOSIS.** Measure the resistance of the (K4) Sensor Ground circuit from the Speed Control harness connector to the appropriate terminal of special tool #8815. Is the resistance below 5.0 ohms for both measurement? Yes → Go To 8 No → Repair the (K4) Sensor Ground circuit for an open. Perform POWERTRAIN VERIFICATION TEST VER - 4
8	**NOTE: Before continuing, check the PCM harness connector terminals for corrosion, damage or terminal push out. Repair as necessary.** If there are no possible causes remaining, view repair. Repair Replace and program the Powertrain Control Module in accordance with the Service Information. Perform POWERTRAIN VERIFICATION TEST VER - 4

CR1100200753030X

Fig. 53 Code P0579: Speed Control Switch No. 1 Performance (Part 3 of 3). 2002–04 Concorde, Intrepid, 300M, 2003–04 Neon, Sebring Convertible & Sebring & Stratus Sedan

TEST	ACTION
4	Turn the ignition off. Disconnect the Speed Control On/Off Switch harness connector. Disconnect the Speed Control Resume/Accel Switch harness connector. Disconnect the PCM harness connector. **CAUTION: DO NOT PROBE THE PCM HARNESS CONNECTORS. PROBING THE PCM HARNESS CONNECTORS WILL DAMAGE THE PCM TERMINALS RESULTING IN POOR TERMINAL TO PIN CONNECTION. INSTALL MILLER SPECIAL TOOL #8815 TO PERFORM DIAGNOSIS.** Measure the resistance between the (K4) Sensor ground circuit and the (V37) S/C Switch Signal circuit at the Speed Control Switch. Is the resistance below 5.0 ohms? Yes → Repair the (V37) S/C Switch Signal circuit short to (K4) Sensor ground circuit. Perform POWERTRAIN VERIFICATION TEST VER - 4 No → Go To 5
5	Turn the ignition off. Disconnect the Speed Control On/Off Switch harness connector. Disconnect the Speed Control Resume/Accel Switch harness connector. Disconnect the PCM harness connector. **CAUTION: DO NOT PROBE THE PCM HARNESS CONNECTORS. PROBING THE PCM HARNESS CONNECTORS WILL DAMAGE THE PCM TERMINALS RESULTING IN POOR TERMINAL TO PIN CONNECTION. INSTALL MILLER SPECIAL TOOL #8815 TO PERFORM DIAGNOSIS.** Measure the resistance between ground and the (V37) S/C Switch Signal circuit to the appropriate terminal of special tool #8815. Is the resistance below 5.0 ohms? Yes → Repair the short to ground in the (V37) S/C Switch Signal circuit. Perform POWERTRAIN VERIFICATION TEST VER - 4 No → Go To 6
6	**NOTE: Before continuing, disconnect the PCM harness connector and check the related wiring terminals for corrosion, damage or terminal push out. Repair as necessary.** If there are no possible causes remaining, view repair. Repair Replace and program the Powertrain Control Module in accordance with the Service Information. Perform POWERTRAIN VERIFICATION TEST VER - 4

CR1100200754020X

Fig. 54 Code P0580: Speed Control Switch No. 1 Low (Part 2 of 2). 2002–04 Concorde, Intrepid, 300M, 2003–04 Neon, Sebring Convertible & Sebring & Stratus Sedan

POSSIBLE CAUSES
SPEED CONTROL SWITCH VOLTAGE LOW
SPEED CONTROL ON/OFF SWITCH
SPEED CONTROL RESUME/ACCEL SWITCH
(V37) S/C SWITCH SIGNAL CIRCUIT SHORTED TO (K4) SENSOR GROUND
(V37) S/C SWITCH SIGNAL CIRCUIT SHORTED TO GROUND
PCM

TEST	ACTION
1	**NOTE: Do not press any of the Speed Control Switch buttons.** Ignition on, engine not running. With the DRBIII®, read the Speed Control voltage. Is the Speed Control voltage below 1.0 volt? Yes → Go To 2 No → Refer to the INTERMITTENT CONDITION symptom in the Driveability category. Perform POWERTRAIN VERIFICATION TEST VER - 4
2	Ignition on, engine not running. With the DRBIII®, monitor the Speed Control Switch voltage. Disconnect the Speed Control On/Off Switch harness connector. Did the voltage change to above 4.7 volts? Yes → Replace the Speed Control On/Off Switch. Perform POWERTRAIN VERIFICATION TEST VER - 4 No → Go To 3
3	Ignition on, engine not running. With the DRBIII®, monitor the Speed Control Switch voltage. Disconnect the Speed Control Resume/Accel Switch harness connector. Did the volt change to above 4.7 volts? Yes → Replace the Speed Control Resume/Accel Switch. Perform POWERTRAIN VERIFICATION TEST VER - 4 No → Go To 4

CR1100200754010X

Fig. 54 Code P0580: Speed Control Switch No. 1 Low (Part 1 of 2). 2002–04 Concorde, Intrepid, 300M, 2003–04 Neon, Sebring Convertible & Sebring & Stratus Sedan

POSSIBLE CAUSES
SPEED CONTROL SWITCH VOLTAGE HIGH
SPEED CONTROL SWITCHES
(V37) S/C SWITCH SIGNAL CIRCUIT SHORTED TO BATTERY VOLTAGE
(K4) SENSOR GROUND OPEN
PCM

TEST	ACTION
1	**NOTE: Do not press any of the Speed Control Switch buttons.** Ignition on, engine not running. With the DRBIII®, read the Speed Control voltage. Is the Speed Control voltage above 4.8 volt? Yes → Go To 2 No → Refer to the INTERMITTENT CONDITION symptom in the Driveability category. Perform POWERTRAIN VERIFICATION TEST VER - 4
2	Turn the ignition off. Remove the Speed Control Switches from the steering wheel. Measure the resistance across each Speed Control Switch. Monitor the ohmmeter while pressing each function button on each switch. Resume/Accel - 15,400 ohms Cancel - 909 +/- 9 ohms Decel (Coast) - 2940 +/- 30 ohms On/Off - 0 ohms Set - 6650 +/- 66 ohms Does the function on the Speed Control Switches have the correct ohm value? Yes → Go To 3 No → Replace the Speed Control Switch that had the incorrect resistance value. Perform POWERTRAIN VERIFICATION TEST VER - 4

CR1100200755010X

Fig. 55 Code P0581: Speed Control Switch No. 1 High (Part 1 of 2). 2002–04 Concorde, Intrepid, 300M, 2003–04 Neon, Sebring Convertible & Sebring & Stratus Sedan

TEST	ACTION
3	Turn the ignition off. Disconnect the Speed Control On/Off Switch harness connector. Disconnect the Speed Control Resume/Accel Switch harness connector. Disconnect the PCM harness connector. Measure the voltage of the (V37) S/C Switch Signal circuit at the Speed Control harness connector. Is the is the voltage above 5.0 volts? Yes → Repair the (V37) S/C Switch Signal circuit shorted to the battery voltage. Perform POWERTRAIN VERIFICATION TEST VER - 4 No → Go To 4
4	**NOTE: The measurement must be taken from both Speed Control Switch harness connector.** Turn the ignition off. Disconnect the Speed Control On/Off Switch harness connector. Disconnect the Speed Control Resume/Accel Switch harness connector. Disconnect the PCM harness connector. **CAUTION: DO NOT PROBE THE PCM HARNESS CONNECTORS. PROBING THE PCM HARNESS CONNECTORS WILL DAMAGE THE PCM TERMINALS RESULTING IN POOR TERMINAL TO PIN CONNECTION. INSTALL MILLER SPECIAL TOOL #8815 TO PERFORM DIAGNOSIS.** Measure the resistance of the (K4) Sensor Ground circuit from the Speed Control harness connector to the appropriate terminal of special tool #8815. Is the resistance below 5.0 ohms for both measurement? Yes → NOTE: Before continuing, check the PCM harness connector terminals for corrosion, damage or terminal push out. Repair as necessary. Replace and program the Powertrain Control Module in accordance with the Service Information. Perform POWERTRAIN VERIFICATION TEST VER - 4 No → Repair the (K4) Sensor Ground circuit for an open. Perform POWERTRAIN VERIFICATION TEST VER - 4

CR1100200755020X

Fig. 55 Code P0581: Speed Control Switch No. 1 High (Part 2 of 2). 2002–04 Concorde, Intrepid, 300M, 2003–04 Neon, Sebring Convertible & Sebring & Stratus Sedan

TEST	ACTION
3	Turn the ignition off. Disconnect the S/C Servo harness connector. Disconnect the PCM harness connector. **CAUTION: DO NOT PROBE THE PCM HARNESS CONNECTORS. PROBING THE PCM HARNESS CONNECTORS WILL DAMAGE THE PCM TERMINALS RESULTING IN POOR TERMINAL TO PIN CONNECTION. INSTALL MILLER SPECIAL TOOL #8815 TO PERFORM DIAGNOSIS.** Measure the resistance of the (V36) S/C Vacuum Sol Control circuit from the Speed Control Servo harness connector to the appropriate terminal of special tool # 8815. Is the resistance below 5.0 ohms? Yes → Go To 4 No → Repair the open/high resistance in the (V36) S/C Vacuum Sol Control circuit. Perform POWERTRAIN VERIFICATION TEST VER - 4
4	Turn the ignition off. Disconnect the S/C Servo harness connector. Disconnect the PCM harness connector. Measure the resistance between ground and the (V36) S/C Vacuum Solenoid Control circuit at the Speed Control Servo harness connector. Is the resistance below 100 ohms? Yes → Repair the short to ground in the (V36) S/C Vacuum Sol Control circuit. Perform POWERTRAIN VERIFICATION TEST VER - 4 No → Go To 5
5	**NOTE: Before continuing, check the PCM harness connector terminals for corrosion, damage, or terminal push out. Repair as necessary.** If the there are no possible causes remaining, view repair. Repair Replace and program the Powertrain Control Module in accordance with the Service Information. Perform POWERTRAIN VERIFICATION TEST VER - 4

CR1100200756020X

Fig. 56 Code P0582: Speed Control Vacuum Solenoid Circuit (Part 2 of 2). 2002–04 Concorde, Intrepid, 300M, 2003–04 Neon, Sebring Convertible & Sebring & Stratus Sedan

POSSIBLE CAUSES
SPEED CONTROL SOLENOID OPERATION
SPEED CONTROL VACUUM SOLENOID
(V36) S/C VACUUM SOL CONTROL CIRCUIT SHORTED TO GROUND
(V36) S/C VACUUM SOL CONTROL CIRCUIT OPEN
PCM (VACUUM SOLENOID)

TEST	ACTION
1	Ignition on, engine not running. With the DRBIII®, read DTCs and record the related Freeze Frame data. With the DRBIII®, actuate the Speed Control Vacuum Solenoid and note operation. Does the Speed Control Vacuum Solenoid actuate properly? Yes → Refer to the INTERMITTENT CONDITION symptom in the Driveability category. Perform POWERTRAIN VERIFICATION TEST VER - 4 No → Go To 2
2	Turn the ignition off. Disconnect the Speed Control Servo harness connector. Ignition on, engine not running. With the DRBIII®, actuate the Speed Control Vacuum Solenoid. Using a 12-volt test light connected to ground, probe the S/C Vacuum Control circuit. Does the test light illuminate brightly and flash? Yes → Replace the Speed Control Servo. Perform POWERTRAIN VERIFICATION TEST VER - 4 No → Go To 3

CR1100200756010X

Fig. 56 Code P0582: Speed Control Vacuum Solenoid Circuit (Part 1 of 2). 2002–04 Concorde, Intrepid, 300M, 2003–04 Neon, Sebring Convertible & Sebring & Stratus Sedan

POSSIBLE CAUSES
SPEED CONTROL SOLENOID OPERATION
SPEED CONTROL VENT SOLENOID
(V35) S/C VENT SOL CONTROL CIRCUIT OPEN
(V35) S/C VENT SOL CONTROL CIRCUIT SHORTED TO GROUND
PCM (VENT SOLENOID)

TEST	ACTION
1	Ignition on, engine not running. With the DRBIII®, read DTCs and record the related Freeze Frame data. With the DRBIII®, actuate the Speed Control Vent Solenoid and note operation. Does the Speed Control Vent Solenoid acutate properly? Yes → Refer to the INTERMITTENT CONDITION symptom in the Driveability category. Perform POWERTRAIN VERIFICATION TEST VER - 4 No → Go To 2
2	Turn the ignition off. Disconnect the Speed Control Servo harness connector. Ignition on, engine not running. With the DRBIII®, actuate the Speed Control Vent Solenoid. Using a 12-volt test light connected to ground, probe the (V35) Speed Control Vent Solenoid Control circuit in the Speed Control Servo harness connector. Does the test light illuminate brightly and flash? Yes → Replace the Speed Control Servo. Perform POWERTRAIN VERIFICATION TEST VER - 4 No → Go To 3

CR1100200757010X

Fig. 57 Code P0586: Speed Control Vent Solenoid Circuit (Part 1 of 2). 2002–04 Concorde, Intrepid, 300M, 2003–04 Neon, Sebring Convertible & Sebring & Stratus Sedan

TEST	ACTION
3	Turn the ignition off. Disconnect the S/C Servo harness connector. Disconnect the PCM harness connector. **CAUTION: DO NOT PROBE THE PCM HARNESS CONNECTORS. PROBING THE PCM HARNESS CONNECTORS WILL DAMAGE THE PCM TERMINALS RESULTING IN POOR TERMINAL TO PIN CONNECTION. INSTALL MILLER SPECIAL TOOL #8815 TO PERFORM DIAGNOSIS.** Measure the resistance of the (V35) S/C Vent Sol Control circuit from the Speed Control Servo harness connector to the appropriate terminal of special tool #8815. Is the resistance below 5.0 ohms? Yes → Go To 4 No → Repair the open/high resistance in the (V35) S/C Vent Sol Control circuit. Perform POWERTRAIN VERIFICATION TEST VER - 4
4	Turn the ignition off. Disconnect the S/C Servo harness connector. Disconnect the PCM harness connector. Measure the resistance between ground and the (V35) S/C Vent Sol Control circuit at the Speed Control Servo harness connector. Is the resistance below 100 ohms? Yes → Repair the short to ground in the (V35) Speed Control Vent Solenoid Control circuit. Perform POWERTRAIN VERIFICATION TEST VER - 4 No → Go To 5
5	**NOTE: Before continuing, check the PCM harness connector terminals for corrosion, damage, or terminal push out. Repair as necessary.** If the there are no possible causes remaining, view repair. Repair Replace and program the Powertrain Control Module in accordance with the Service Information. Perform POWERTRAIN VERIFICATION TEST VER - 4

CR1100200757020X

Fig. 57 Code P0586: Speed Control Vent Solenoid Circuit (Part 2 of 2). 2002–04 Concorde, Intrepid, 300M, 2003–04 Neon, Sebring Convertible & Sebring & Stratus Sedan

TEST	ACTION
2	Turn the ignition off. Disconnect the PCM harness connector. Disconnect the Brake Lamp Switch harness connector. **CAUTION: DO NOT PROBE THE PCM HARNESS CONNECTORS. PROBING THE PCM HARNESS CONNECTORS WILL DAMAGE THE PCM TERMINALS RESULTING IN POOR TERMINAL TO PIN CONNECTION. INSTALL MILLER SPECIAL TOOL #8815 TO PERFORM DIAGNOSIS.** Measure the resistance of the (V32) S/C Power Supply circuit from the Brake Lamp Switch harness connector to the appropriate terminal of special tool #8815. Is the resistance below 5.0 ohms? Yes → Go To 3 No → Repair the open/high resistance in the (V32) S/C Power Supply circuit between the PCM and Brake Switch. Perform POWERTRAIN VERIFICATION TEST VER - 5
3	Turn the ignition off. Disconnect the PCM harness connector. Disconnect the Brake Switch harness connector. Measure the resistance between ground and the (V32) S/C Power Supply circuit in the Brake Switch harness connector. Is the resistance below 100 ohms? Yes → Go To 4 No → Repair the short to ground in the (V32) S/C Power Supply circuit. Perform POWERTRAIN VERIFICATION TEST VER - 5
4	Turn the ignition off. Disconnect the S/C Servo harness connector. Disconnect the Brake Switch harness connector. Measure the resistance of the (V40) S/C Brake Switch Output circuit from the Brake Switch harness connector to the S/C Servo harness connector. Is the resistance below 5.0 ohms? Yes → Go To 5 No → Repair the open/high resistance in the (V40) S/C Brake Switch Output circuit. Perform POWERTRAIN VERIFICATION TEST VER - 5
5	Turn the ignition off. Disconnect the Speed Control Servo harness connector. Disconnect the Brake Switch harness connector. Measure the resistance between ground and the (V40) S/C Brake Switch Output circuit at the Speed Control Servo harness connector. Is the resistance below 100 ohms? Yes → Repair the short to ground in the (V40) S/C Brake Switch Output circuit. Perform POWERTRAIN VERIFICATION TEST VER - 5 No → Go To 6

CR1100200758020X

Fig. 58 Code P0594: Speed Control Servo Power Circuit (Part 2 of 3). 2002–04 Concorde, Intrepid, 300M, 2003–04 Neon, Sebring Convertible & Sebring & Stratus Sedan

POSSIBLE CAUSES
(V40) S/C BRAKE SWITCH OUTPUT CIRCUIT
(V32) S/C POWER SUPPLY CIRCUIT
(V32) S/C POWER SUPPLY CIRCUIT SHORTED TO GROUND
(V40) S/C BRAKE SWITCH OUTPUT CIRCUIT SHORTEDTO GROUND
(V40) S/C BRAKE SWITCH OUTPUT CIRCUIT OPEN
BRAKE LAMP SWITCH
PCM (S/C SOURCE CIRCUIT)

TEST	ACTION
1	Turn the ignition off. Disconnect the Speed Control Servo harness connector. Ignition on, engine not running. **NOTE: It is necessary to PRESS and HOLD the Speed Control Switch in the ON position while checking for voltage.** Using a 12-volt test light connected to ground, probe the (V40) S/C Brake Switch Output terminal in the Servo Harness connector. Does the test light illuminate brightly? Yes → Refer to the INTERMITTENT CONDITION symptom in the Driveability category. Perform POWERTRAIN VERIFICATION TEST VER - 5 No → Go To 2

CR1100200758010X

Fig. 58 Code P0594: Speed Control Servo Power Circuit (Part 1 of 3). 2002–04 Concorde, Intrepid, 300M, 2003–04 Neon, Sebring Convertible & Sebring & Stratus Sedan

TEST	ACTION
6	Disconnect the Brake Lamp Switch harness connector. Ignition on, engine not running. Using a 12-volt test light connected to ground, probe the (V32) Speed Control Power Supply circuit in the Brake Lamp Switch harness connector. **NOTE: It is necessary to HOLD the Cruise Control Switch in the ON position to get an accurate reading.** Does the test light illuminate brightly? Yes → Replace the Brake Lamp Switch. Perform POWERTRAIN VERIFICATION TEST VER - 5 No → Go To 7
7	**NOTE: Before continuing, check the PCM harness connector terminals for corrosion, damage, or terminal push out. Repair as necessary.** If there are no possible causes remaining, view repair. Repair Replace and program the Powertrain Control Module in accordance with the Service Information. Perform POWERTRAIN VERIFICATION TEST VER - 5

CR1100200758030X

Fig. 58 Code P0594: Speed Control Servo Power Circuit (Part 3 of 3). 2002–04 Concorde, Intrepid, 300M, 2003–04 Neon, Sebring Convertible & Sebring & Stratus Sedan

POWERTRAIN VERIFICATION TEST VER - 4 - NGC
1. NOTE: After completing the Powertrain Verification Test the Transmission Verification Test must be performed.
2. NOTE: If the PCM has been replaced and the correct VIN and mileage have not been programmed, a DTC will be set in the ABS Module, Airbag Module and the SKIM.
3. NOTE: If the vehicle is equipped with a Sentry Key Immobilizer System, Secret Key data must be updated. Refer to the Service Information for the PCM, SKIM and the Transponder (ignition key) for programming information.
4. Inspect the vehicle to ensure that all engine components are properly installed and connected.
5. Connect the DRBIII® to the data link connector and erase all codes.
6. Turn the speed control ON (if equipped, cruise light will be on).
7. Press and release the SET Switch. If the speed control did not engage, the repair is not complete. Check for TSBs that pertain to speed control problem and then, if necessary, return to Symptom List.
8. Press and hold the RESUME/ACCEL Switch. If the vehicle speed did not increase by at least 2 mph, the repair is not complete. Check for TSBs that pertain to speed control problem and then, if necessary, return to Symptom List.
9. Press and hold the COAST switch. The vehicle speed should decrease. If it did not decrease, the repair is not complete. Check for TSBs that pertain to speed control problem and then, if necessary, return to Symptom List.
10. Using caution, press and release the brake pedal. If the speed control did not disengage, the repair is not complete. Check for TSBs that pertain to speed control problem and then, if necessary, return to Symptom List.
11. Bring the vehicle speed back up to 35 MPH.
12. Press the RESUME/ACCEL switch. If the speed control did not resume the previously set speed, the repair is not complete. Check for TSBs that pertain to speed control problem and then, if necessary, return to Symptom List.
13. Hold down the SET switch. If the vehicle did not decelerate, the repair is not complete. Check for TSBs that pertain to speed control problem and then, if necessary, return to Symptom List.
14. Ensure vehicle speed is greater than 35 mph and release the SET Switch. If vehicle did not adjust and set a new vehicle speed, the repair is not complete. Check for TSBs that pertain to speed control problem and then, if necessary, return to Symptom List.
15. Press and release the CANCEL switch. If the speed control did not disengage, the repair is not complete. Check for TSBs that pertain to speed control problem and then, if necessary, return to Symptom List.
16. Bring the vehicle speed back up above 35 mph and engage speed control.
17. Turn the Speed Control Off. (Cruise light will be off). If the speed control did not disengage, the repair is not complete. Check for TSBs that pertain to speed control problem and then, if necessary, return to Symptom List.
18. If the vehicle successfully passed all of the previous tests, the speed control system is now functioning as designed. The repair is now complete.
Did the Speed Control pass the above test?
Yes → Repair is complete.
No → Repair is not complete, refer to appropriate symptom.

CR1100200759000X

Fig. 59 Verification Test VER-4. 2002–04 Concorde, Intrepid, 300M, 2003–04 Neon, Sebring Convertible & Sebring & Stratus Sedan

P1595-SPEED CONTROL SOLENOID CIRCUITS

When Monitored: With the ignition key on, the speed control switched on, the SET switch pressed and the vehicle in drive gear moving between 30-100 mph (45-165 kmh).

Set Condition: The powertrain control module actuates the vacuum and vent solenoids but they do not respond.

P1683-SPD CTRL PWR RELAY; OR S/C 12V DRIVER CKT

When Monitored: With the ignition key on and the speed control switched on.

Set Condition: The speed control power supply circuit is either open or shorted to ground.

POSSIBLE CAUSES
SPEED CONTROL

CR1100000633010X

Fig. 61 Codes P1595 & P1693: Speed Control Solenoid & Power Relay Circuits (Part 1 of 7). 2000 Neon

POWERTRAIN VERIFICATION TEST VER - 5 - NGC
1. NOTE: After completing the Powertrain Verification Test the Transmission Verification Test must be performed.
2. NOTE: If the PCM has been replaced and the correct VIN and mileage have not been programmed, a DTC will be set in the ABS Module, Airbag Module and the SKIM.
3. NOTE: If the vehicle is equipped with a Sentry Key Immobilizer System, Secret Key data must be updated. Refer to the Service Information for the PCM, SKIM and the Transponder (ignition key) for programming information.
4. Inspect the vehicle to ensure that all engine components are properly installed and connected. Reassemble and reconnect components as necessary.
5. Connect the DRBIII® to the data link connector.
6. Ensure the fuel tank has at least a quarter tank of fuel. Turn off all accessories.
7. If a Comprehensive Component DTC was repaired, perform steps 5 - 8. If a Major OBDII Monitor DTC was repaired skip those steps and continue verification.
8. After the ignition has been off for at least 10 seconds, restart the vehicle and run 2 minutes.
9. If the Good Trip counter changed to one or more and there are no new DTC's, the repair was successful and is now complete. Erase DTC's and disconnect the DRBIII®.
10. If the repaired DTC has reset, the repair is not complete. Check for any related TSB's or flash updates and return to the Symptom list.
11. If another DTC has set, return to the Symptom List and follow the path specified for that DTC.
12. With the DRBIII®, monitor the appropriate pre-test enabling conditions until all conditions have been met. Once the conditions have been met, switch screen to the appropriate OBDII monitor, (Audible beeps when the monitor is running).
13. If the monitor ran, and the Good Trip counter changed to one or more, the repair was successful and is now complete. Erase DTC's and disconnect the DRBIII®.
14. If the repaired OBDII trouble code has reset or was seen in the monitor while on the road test, the repair is not complete. Check for any related technical service bulletins or flash updates and return to Symptom List.
15. If another DTC has set, return to the Symptom List and follow the path specified for that DTC.
Are any DTCs present?
Yes → Repair is not complete, refer to appropriate symptom.
No → Repair is complete.

CR1100200760000X

Fig. 60 Verification Test VER-5. 2002–04 Concorde, Intrepid, 300M, 2003–04 Neon, Sebring Convertible & Sebring & Stratus Sedan

POSSIBLE CAUSES
GROUND CIRCUIT AT S/C SERVO CONNECTOR OPEN
S/C WIRING HARNESS INTER DEFECT (S/C VAC SOL AC)
S/C VACUUM SOLENOID CONTROL CIRCUIT OPEN
S/C VACUUM SOLENOID CONTROL CKT SHORT TO GROUND
S/C VENT SOLENOID CONTROL CIRCUIT OPEN
S/C VENT SOLENOID CONTROL CKT SHORT TO GROUND
S/C WIRING HARNESS INTER DEFECT (S/C VENT SOL AC)
S/C WIRING HARNESS OBSERVABLE DEFECT
S/C SERVO DEFECTIVE (12V DRIVER CIRCUIT)
S/C SERVO DEFECTIVE (12V DRIVER CIRCUIT)
S/C POWER SUPPLY CIRCUIT OPEN
S/C POWER SUPPLY CIRCUIT SHORTED TO GROUND
BRAKE SWITCH DEFECTIVE
BRAKE SWITCH OUT OF ADJUSTMENT
S/C BRAKE SWITCH OUTPUT CIRCUIT OPEN
S/C BRAKE SWITCH OUTPUT CIRCUIT SHORTED TO GROUND
PCM DEFECTIVE
PCM DEFECTIVE (12V DRIVER CIRCUIT)
PCM DEFEFECTIVE

CR1100000633020X

Fig. 61 Codes P1595 & P1693: Speed Control Solenoid & Power Relay Circuits (Part 2 of 7). 2000 Neon

TEST	ACTION
686	Ignition On, Engine Not Running. With the DRB actuate the S/C Vent Solenoid. Does the Speed Control Servo click? Yes → Go To 687 No → Go To 698
687	Ignition On, Engine Not Running. With the DRB, actuate the S/C Vacuum Solenoid. Does the Speed Control Servo click? Yes → Go To 688 No → Go To 691
688	Turn ignition off. Using the Schematics as a guide, inspect the Wiring and Connectors. Were any problems found? Yes → Repair as necessary. No → Go To 689
689	Ignition On, Engine Not Running. With the DRB actuate the S/C Vent Solenoid. Wiggle the Wiring Harness from S/C Servo and Brake Switch to Powertrain Control Module. Did the wiggling interrupt the S/C Servo actuation? Yes → Repair as necessary where wiggling caused the actuation to be interrupted. No → Go To 690
690	Ignition On, Engine Not Running. With the DRB actuate the S/C Vacuum Solenoid. Wiggle the Wiring Harness from S/C Servo and Brake Switch to Powertrain Control Module. Did the wiggling interrupt the S/C actuation? Yes → Repair as necessary where wiggling caused the actuation to be interrupted. No → Test Complete.
691	Ignition On, Engine Not Running. With the DRB actuate the S/C Vent Solenoid. Wiggle the Wiring Harness from S/C Servo and Brake Switch to Powertrain Control Module. Did the wiggling interrupt the S/C Servo actuation? Yes → Repair as necessary where wiggling caused the actuation to be interrupted. No → Go To 692

CR1100000633030X

Fig. 61 Codes P1595 & P1693: Speed Control Solenoid & Power Relay Circuits (Part 3 of 7). 2000 Neon

TEST	ACTION
692	Turn ignition off. Disconnect the Speed Control Servo 4-Way Connector. **Note: Check connectors - Clean/repair as necessary.** **Note: Ensure the Brake Pedal is not depressed during the following steps.** Key on, Engine off. Turn S/C Switch on. With the DRB, actuate the S/C Vacuum Solenoid. Using a 12-Volt Test Light, check the S/C Brake Switch Output Circuit at the Servo connector. Is the light illuminated and bright? Yes → Go To 693 No → Go To 704
693	Turn ignition off. Disconnect the Speed Control Servo Connector. **Note: Check connectors - Clean/repair as necessary.** Using an Ohmmeter, measure the resistance of the Ground Circuit at the Servo Connector to ground. Is the resistance below 5.0 ohms? Yes → Go To 694 No → Repair open Ground Circuit at S/C Servo Connector.
694	Turn ignition off. Disconnect the Speed Control Servo Connector. Disconnect Powertrain Control Module Connectors. **Note: Check connectors - Clean/repair as necessary.** With an Ohmmeter, measure the resistance of the S/C Vacuum Solenoid Control Circuit from the PCM to the Servo Connector. Is the resistance below 5.0 ohms? Yes → Go To 695 No → Repair the open S/C Vacuum Solenoid Control Circuit.
695	Turn ignition off. Disconnect the Speed Control Servo Connector. Disconnect Powertrain Control Module Connectors. **Note: Check connectors - Clean/repair as necessary.** With an Ohmmeter, measure the resistance of the S/C Vacuum Solenoid Control Circuit from the Servo Connector to a good ground. Is the resistance below 5.0 ohms? Yes → Repair the short to ground in the S/C Vacuum Solenoid Control Circuit. No → Go To 696

CR1100000633040X

Fig. 61 Codes P1595 & P1693: Speed Control Solenoid & Power Relay Circuits (Part 4 of 7). 2000 Neon

TEST	ACTION
696	Turn ignition off. Disconnect the S/C Servo. Using the DRB, actuate the S/C Vacuum solenoid. Using a 12 Volt Test Light connected to B(+), probe the S/C Vacuum Solenoid Control Circuit. Does the test light blink on and off? Yes → Replace the S/C Servo. No → Go To 697
697	If there are no potential causes remaining, the PCM is assumed to be defective. View repair options. Repair Replace the Powertrain Control Module.
698	Turn ignition off. Disconnect the Speed Control Servo 4-Way Connector. **Note: Check connectors - Clean/repair as necessary.** **Note: Ensure the Brake Pedal is not depressed during the following steps.** Key on, Engine off. Turn S/C Switch on. With the DRB, actuate the S/C Vacuum Solenoid. Using a 12-Volt Test Light, check the S/C Brake Switch Output Circuit at the Servo connector. Is the light illuminated and bright? Yes → Go To 699 No → Go To 704
699	Turn ignition off. Disconnect the Speed Control Servo Connector. **Note: Check connectors - Clean/repair as necessary.** Using an Ohmmeter, measure the resistance of the Ground Circuit at the Servo Connector to ground. Is the resistance below 5.0 ohms? Yes → Go To 700 No → Repair open Ground Circuit at S/C Servo Connector.
700	Turn ignition off. Disconnect the Speed Control Servo Connector. Disconnect Powertrain Control Module Connectors. **Note: Check connectors - Clean/repair as necessary.** With an Ohmmeter, measure the resistance of the S/C Vent Solenoid Control Circuit from the PCM to the Servo Connector. Is the resistance below 5.0 ohms? Yes → Go To 701 No → Repair the open S/C Vent Solenoid Control Circuit.

CR1100000633050X

Fig. 61 Codes P1595 & P1693: Speed Control Solenoid & Power Relay Circuits (Part 5 of 7). 2000 Neon

TEST	ACTION
701	Turn ignition off. Disconnect the S/C Servo Connector. Disconnect Powertrain Control Module Connectors. **Note: Check connectors - Clean/repair as necessary.** With an Ohmmeter, measure the resistance of the S/C Vent Solenoid Control Circuit from the Servo Connector to a good Ground. Is the resistance below 5.0 ohms? Yes → Repair the short to ground in the S/C Vent Solenoid Control Circuit. No → Go To 702
702	Turn ignition off. Disconnect the S/C Servo. Using the DRB, actuate the S/C Vent solenoid. Using a 12 Volt Test Light connected to B(+), probe the S/C Vent Solenoid Control Circuit. Does the test light blink on and off? Yes → Replace the S/C Servo. No → Go To 703
703	If there are no potential causes remaining, the PCM is assumed to be defective. View repair options. Repair Replace the Powertrain Control Module.
704	Turn ignition off. Using Service Procedure, check Brake Switch adjustment. Was Brake Switch adjustment OK? Yes → Go To 705 No → Adjust Brake Switch.
705	Turn ignition off. Disconnect the Brake Switch Connector. **Note: Check connectors - Clean/repair as necessary.** Be sure the brake pedal is not depressed during the next step. Using an ohmmeter, measure the resistance between the S/C power supply circuit and the S/C brake switch output circuit (measurement taken across switch). Is the resistance below 5.0 ohms? Yes → Go To 706 No → Replace the Brake Switch.

CR1100000633060X

Fig. 61 Codes P1595 & P1693: Speed Control Solenoid & Power Relay Circuits (Part 6 of 7). 2000 Neon

TEST	ACTION
706	Turn ignition off. Disconnect the Brake Switch connector. Disconnect the Powertrain Control Module. **Note: Check connectors - Clean/repair as necessary.** Using an Ohmmeter, measure the resistance between the S/C Power Supply Circuit and ground at the Brake Switch connector. Is the resistance below 5.0 ohms? Yes → Repair S/C Power Supply Circuit shorted to ground. No → Go To 707
707	Turn ignition off. Disconnect the Brake Switch Connector. Disconnect the Powertrain Control Module **Note: Check connectors - Clean/repair as necessary.** Using an Ohmmeter, measure the resistance of the S/C Power Supply Circuit from the PCM to the Brake Switch Connector. Is the resistance below 5.0 ohms? Yes → Go To 708 No → Repair the open S/C Power Supply Circuit.
708	Turn ignition off. Disconnect the Speed Control Servo 4-Way Connector. Disconnect the brake switch connector. **Note: Check connectors - Clean/repair as necessary.** Using an Ohmmeter, measure the resistance of the S/C Brake Switch Output circuit from Servo Connector to ground. Is the resistance below 5.0 ohms? Yes → Repair Switched S/C Brake Switch Output circuit shorted to ground. No → Go To 709
709	Turn ignition off. Disconnect the S/C Servo Connector. Disconnect the Brake Switch Connector. **Note: Check connectors - Clean/repair as necessary.** With an Ohmmeter, measure the resistance of the S/C Brake Switch Output Circuit from the Brake Switch Connector to the Servo Connector. Is the resistance above 5.0 ohms? Yes → Repair the open S/C Brake Switch Output Circuit. No → Go To 710
710	If there are no potential causes remaining, the Powertrain Control Module is assumed to be defective. View repair options. Repair Replace the Powertrain Control Module.

CR1100000633070X

Fig. 61 Codes P1595 & P1693: Speed Control Solenoid & Power Relay Circuits (Part 7 of 7). 2000 Neon

TEST	ACTION
711	Ignition on, with engine not running. With the DRB, monitor the Speed Control Switch inputs. While observing the display, press the Brake Pedal several times. Does the DRB show Brake Switch "pressed" and "released"? Yes → Go To 712 No → Refer to symptom *BRAKE SWITCH SENSE STATUS DOES NOT CHANGE ON DRB
712	Turn ignition off. Disconnect the Speed Control Servo Connector. **Note: Check connectors - Clean/repair as necessary.** Using an Ohmmeter, measure the resistance of the Ground Circuit at the Servo Connector to ground. Is the resistance below 5.0 ohms? Yes → Go To 713 No → Repair open Ground Circuit at S/C Servo Connector.
713	Ignition on, with engine running. While observing the display, press the On/Off Switch several times. With the DRB, monitor the Speed Control Switch inputs. Does the DRB show On/Off Switch "pressed" and "released"? Yes → Go To 714 No → Go To 726
714	Turn ignition off. Using the Schematics as a guide, inspect the Wiring and Connectors. Were any problems found? Yes → Repair as necessary. No → Go To 715
715	Ignition on, with engine not running. With the DRB, monitor the P/N Switch inputs. While observing the display, move the Gear Selector to DRIVE. Does the DRB show P/N switch "D/R"? Yes → Go To 716 No → Refer to **MOTOR'S DOMESTIC TRANSMISSION MANUAL**
716	Inspect the throttle cable and linkage for any binding or damage. Is the cable or linkage disconnected or damaged? Yes → Repair as necessary. No → Go To 717

CR1100000634020X

Fig. 62 Speed Control Operation With No DTCs Present (Part 2 of 9). 2000 Neon

POSSIBLE CAUSES
GROUND CIRCUIT AT S/C SERVO CONNECTOR OPEN
GROUND CIRCUIT TO S/C RESUME/ACCEL SWITCH CONNECTOR OPEN
S/C SW SIGNAL CKT TO CLOCKSPRING CONN OPEN
SPEED CONTROL SWITCH GROUND CIRCUIT OPEN CLOCKSPRING TO S/C SWITCH
SPEED CONTROL SWITCH GROUND CIRCUIT OPEN PCM TO CLOCKSPRING
CLOCKSPRING DEFECTIVE
DRB DOES NOT SHOW SET SWITCH "PRESSED" OR RELEASED
S/C WIRING HARNESS OBSERVABLE DEFECT
CANCEL SWITCH DEFECTIVE
COAST SWITCH DEFECTIVE
THROTTLE CABLE OBSERVABLE DEFECT
THROTTLE OPENS AND CLOSES
S/C SWITCH DEFECTIVE (ON/OFF)
S/C SWITCH DEFECTIVE (RESUME/ACCEL)
SPEED CONTROL ON/OFF SWITCH DEFECTIVE
SPEED CONTROL ON/OFF SWITCH STUCK
SPEED CONTROL RESUME/ACCEL SWITCH DEFECTIVE
SPEED CONTROL RESUME/ACCEL SWITCH STUCK
S/C SIGNAL CIRCUIT SHORTED TO SENSOR GROUND
S/C SWITCH SIGNAL CIRCUIT SHORTED TO GROUND
SPEED CONTROL SW SIG CKT OPEN PCM TO CLOCK SPRING
SPEED CONTROL SW SIG CKT OPEN CLOCKSPRING TO S/C SWITCH
SPEED CONTROL SWITCH SIGNAL CKT SHORTED TO VOLTAGE
PCM DEFECTIVE
POWERTRAIN CONTROL MODULE DEFECTIVE

CR1100000634010X

Fig. 62 Speed Control Operation With No DTCs Present (Part 1 of 9). 2000 Neon

TEST	ACTION
717	Ignition on, with engine running. With the DRB, monitor the Speed Control Switch inputs. While observing the display, press the Set Switch several times. Does the DRBIII show the Set Switch status change appropriately from Pressed to Released? Yes → Go To 718 No → Replace the Left S/C Switch.
718	Ignition On, Engine Running. With the DRB, monitor the Speed Control Switch inputs. While observing the display, press the Resume Switch several times. Does the DRBIII show the Resume Switch status change appropriately from Pressed to Released? Yes → Go To 719 No → Go To 722
719	Ignition on, with engine not running. With the DRB III read DTC's. Are any Vehicle Speed Signal codes set? Yes → Refer to symptom P0500 **in MOTOR'S AUTO ENGINE PERFORMANCE AND DRIVEBILITY MANUAL** No → Go To 720
720	Ignition On, Engine Running. With the DRB, monitor the Speed Control Switch inputs. While observing the display, press the Cancel Switch several times. Does the DRBIII show the Cancel Switch status change appropriately from Pressed to Released? Yes → Go To 721 No → Replace the Right S/C Switch.
721	Ignition On, Engine Running. With the DRB, monitor the Speed Control Switch inputs. While observing the display, press the Coast Switch several times. Does the DRBIII show the Coast Switch status change appropriately from Pressed to Released? Yes → Go To 752 No → Replace the Right S/C Switch.
722	Ignition on, with engine not running. With the DRB III read DTC's. Are any Vehicle Speed Signal codes set? Yes → Refer to symptom P0500 **in MOTOR'S AUTO ENGINE PERFORMANCE AND DRIVEBILITY MANUAL** No → Go To 723

CR1100000634030X

Fig. 62 Speed Control Operation With No DTCs Present (Part 3 of 9). 2000 Neon

TEST	ACTION
723	Turn ignition off. Disconnect the Speed Control Resume/Accel Switch. **Note: Check connectors - Clean/repair as necessary.** Using an Ohmmeter, measure the resistance of the Sensor Ground Circuit from the S/C Resume/Accel Connector to a good Ground. Is the resistance below 5.0 ohms? Yes → Go To 724 No → Repair the open sensor ground circuit, right S/C switch connector to the clockspring connector.
724	Turn ignition off. Disconnect both Speed Control Switches. **Note: Check connectors - Clean/repair as necessary.** Using an Ohmmeter, measure the resistance of the Speed Control Switch Signal Circuit and Sensor Ground Circuit from the On/Off Switch connector to the Resume/Accel connector. Is resistance below 5.0 ohms for both circuits? Yes → Go To 725 No → Replace the Clockspring.
725	Turn ignition off. Disconnect the Speed Control Resume/Accel Switch. **Note: Check connectors - Clean/repair as necessary.** Connect a Jumper between the S/C Switch Signal and Sensor Ground at the switch connector. Ignition On, Engine Not Running. With the DRB, read the S/C Switch voltage. Does the DRB show S/C Switch is less than 1.0 volt? Yes → Replace the right Speed Control Switch. No → Go To 752
726	Turn ignition off. Using the Schematics as a guide, inspect the Wiring and Connectors. Were any problems found? Yes → Repair as necessary. No → Go To 727
727	Ignition On, Engine Running. With the DRB, read the Speed Control Switch voltage. Does the DRB show Speed Control Switch voltage above 4.0 volts? Yes → Go To 728 No → Go To 739

CR1100000634040X

Fig. 62 Speed Control Operation With No DTCs Present (Part 4 of 9). 2000 Neon

TEST	ACTION
728	Ignition on, with engine not running. With the DRB, monitor the P/N Switch inputs. While observing the display, move the Gear Selector to DRIVE. Does the DRB show P/N switch "D/R"? Yes → Go To 729 No → Refer to MOTOR'S DOMESTIC TRANSMISSION MANUAL
729	Inspect the throttle cable and linkage for any binding or damage. Is the cable or linkage disconnected or damaged? Yes → Repair as necessary. No → Go To 730
730	Turn ignition off. Disconnect both Speed Control Switches. **Note: Check connectors - Clean/repair as necessary.** Using an Ohmmeter, measure the resistance of the Speed Control Switch Signal Circuit and Sensor Ground Circuit from the On/Off Switch connector to the Resume/Accel connector. Is resistance below 5.0 ohms for both circuits? Yes → Go To 731 No → Replace the Clockspring.
731	Turn ignition off. Disconnect the Speed Control On/Off Switch 2-Way Connector. Disconnect the clockspring connector. **Note: Check connectors - Clean/repair as necessary.** Using an Ohmmeter, measure the resistance of the S/C Switch Sensor Ground Circuit from the On/Off Switch 2-Way Connector to the clockspring connector. Is the resistance below 5.0 ohms? Yes → Go To 732 No → Replace the Clockspring.
732	Turn ignition off. Disconnect the clockspring connector (instrument panel harness side). Disconnect the PCM. **Note: Check connectors - Clean/repair as necessary.** Using an Ohmmeter, measure the resistance of the S/C Switch Sensor Ground Circuit from the PCM to the clockspring connector. Is the resistance below 5.0 ohms? Yes → Go To 733 No → Repair open ground circuit from PCM to clockspring.

CR1100000634050X

Fig. 62 Speed Control Operation With No DTCs Present (Part 5 of 9). 2000 Neon

TEST	ACTION
733	Turn ignition off. Disconnect the Speed Control On/Off Switch 2-Way Connector only. **Note: Check connectors - Clean/repair as necessary.** Using an Ohmmeter, measure the resistance across the S/C On/Off Switch then press and release the On/Off button. Did the resistance go from below 5.0 ohms when pressed to an open circuit when released? Yes → Go To 734 No → Replace the On/Off Switch.
734	Turn ignition off. Disconnect the Speed Control On/Off Switch 2-Way Connector only. **Note: Check connectors - Clean/repair as necessary.** Turn ignition on. Using a voltmeter, measure the S/C Switch Signal Circuit for voltage at the On/Off Switch 2-Way Connector. Is the voltage above 6.0 volts? Yes → Repair the Speed Control Switch Signal Circuit for a short to voltage. No → Go To 735
735	Ignition on, with engine not running. With the DRB III read DTC's. Are any Vehicle Speed Signal codes set? Yes → Refer to symptom P0500 in MOTOR'S AUTO ENGINE PERFORMANCE AND DRIVEABILITY MANUAL No → Go To 736
736	Turn ignition off. Disconnect the Clockspring connector (instrument panel harness side). Disconnect the PCM. **Note: Check connectors - Clean/repair as necessary.** Using an Ohmmeter, measure the resistance of the S/C Switch Signal Circuit from the PCM to the Clockspring Connector. Is the resistance below 5.0 ohms? Yes → Go To 737 No → Repair open Speed Control Switch Signal Circuit PCM to Clockspring.
737	Turn ignition off. Disconnect the Clockspring Connector. Disconnect the On/Off switch 2-way connector. **Note: Check connectors - Clean/repair as necessary.** Using an Ohmmeter, measure the resistance of the S/C Switch Signal Circuit from the clockspring to the On/Off switch connector. Is the resistance below 5.0 ohms? Yes → Go To 738 No → Replace the Clockspring.

CR1100000634060X

Fig. 62 Speed Control Operation With No DTCs Present (Part 6 of 9). 2000 Neon

TEST	ACTION
738	If there are no potential causes remaining, the PCM is assumed to be defective. View repair options. Repair Replace Powertrain Control Module.
739	Ignition on, with engine not running. With the DRB, monitor the P/N Switch inputs. While observing the display, move the Gear Selector to DRIVE. Does the DRB show P/N switch "D/R"? Yes → Go To 740 No → Refer to MOTOR'S DOMESTIC TRANSMISSION MANUAL
740	Inspect the throttle cable and linkage for any binding or damage. Is the cable or linkage disconnected or damaged? Yes → Repair as necessary. No → Go To 741
741	Ignition On, Engine Not Running With DRB, read the S/C Switch volts in Sensors. Is the S/C Switch voltage below 1.0 volt? Yes → Go To 742 No → Go To 749
742	Ignition on, with engine not running. With the DRB III read DTC's. Are any Vehicle Speed Signal codes set? Yes → Refer to symptom P0500 in MOTOR'S AUTO ENGINE PERFORMANCE AND DRIVEABILITY MANUAL No → Go To 743
743	Turn ignition off. Disconnect the S/C ON/OFF Switch. **Note: Check connectors - Clean/repair as necessary.** Turn ignition on, with engine not running. With the DRB, read the S/C Switch volts in Sensors. Did the S/C Switch volts change to 5.0 volts? Yes → Replace the S/C ON/OFF Switch. No → Go To 744

CR1100000634070X

Fig. 62 Speed Control Operation With No DTCs Present (Part 7 of 9). 2000 Neon

TEST	ACTION
744	Turn ignition off. Disconnect the S/C RESUME/ACCEL Switch. **Note: Check connectors - Clean/repair as necessary.** Turn ignition on, with engine not running. With the DRB, read the S/C Switch volts in Sensors. Did the S/C Switch volts go above 4.0 volts? Yes → Replace the Resume/Accel Switch. No → Go To 745
745	Disconnect the clockspring connector (instrument panel wiring side). Turn ignition on, with engine not running. With the DRB, read the S/C Switch volts in Sensors. Did the S/C Switch volts change to 5.0 volts? Yes → Replace the Clockspring. No → Go To 746
746	Turn ignition off. Disconnect the S/C ON/OFF Switch. Disconnect the Powertrain Control Module. **Note: Check connectors - Clean/repair as necessary.** Using an Ohmmeter, measure the resistance between the S/C Signal Circuit and the Sensor Ground Circuit at the ON/OFF switch connector. Is the resistance below 5.0 ohms? Yes → Repair S/C Signal Circuit shorted to Sensor Ground. No → Go To 747
747	Turn ignition off. Disconnect the S/C ON/OFF Switch. Disconnect the Powertrain Control Module. **Note: Check connectors - Clean/repair as necessary.** With an Ohmmeter, measure resistance of S/C Switch Signal Circuit to ground at the PCM Connector. Is the resistance below 5.0 ohms? Yes → Repair S/C Switch Signal Circuit for a short to ground. No → Go To 748
748	If there are no potential causes remaining, the PCM is assumed to be defective. View repair options. Repair Replace the Powertrain Control Module. Perform Powertrain Test Verification VER-4A.
749	Ignition on, with engine not running. With the DRB III read DTC's. Are any Vehicle Speed Signal codes set? Yes → Refer to symptom P0500 in MOTOR'S AUTO ENGINE PERFORMANCE AND DRIVEABILITY MANUAL No → Go To 750

CR1100000634080X

Fig. 62 Speed Control Operation With No DTCs Present (Part 8 of 9). 2000 Neon

VERIFICATION TEST VER-4A
1. Inspect the vehicle to ensure that all engine components are properly installed and connected. Reassemble and reconnect components as necessary. 2. Connect the DRB to the data link connector and erase all codes. 3. If the PCM has been replaced, perform steps 4 through 6, then continue with the verification. 4. If PCM has been changed and correct VIN and mileage have not been programmed, a DTC will be set in ABS and Air bag modules. In addition, if vehicle is equipped with a Sentry Key Immobilizer Module (SKIM), Secret Key data must be updated to enable start. 5. For ABS and Air Bag systems: Enter correct VIN and Mileage in PCM. Erase codes in ABS and Air Bag modules. 6. For SKIM theft alarm: Connect DRB to data link conn. Go to Theft Alarm, SKIM, Misc. and place SKIM in secured access mode, by using the appropriate PIN code for this vehicle. Select Update the Secret Key data. Data will be transferred from SKIM to PCM. 7. Turn the speed control ON (if equipped, cruise light will be on). 8. Depress and release the SET Switch. If the speed control did not engage, the repair is not complete. Check for TSBs that pertain to speed control problem and then, if necessary, return to Symptom List. 9. Depress and hold the RESUME/ACCEL Switch. If the vehicle speed did not increase by at least 2 mph, the repair is not complete. Check for TSBs that pertain to speed control problem and then, if necessary, return to Symptom List. 10. Press and hold the COAST switch. The vehicle speed should decrease. If it did not decrease, the repair is not complete. Check for TSBs that pertain to speed control problem and then, if necessary, return to Symptom List. 11. Using caution, depress and release the brake pedal. If the speed control did not disengage, the repair is not complete. Check for TSBs that pertain to speed control problem and then, if necessary, return to Symptom List. 12. Bring the vehicle speed back up to 35 MPH. 13. Depress the RESUME/ACCEL switch. If the speed control did not resume the previously set speed, the repair is not complete. Check for TSBs that pertain to speed control problem and then, if necessary, return to Symptom List. 14. Hold down the SET switch. If the vehicle did not decelerate, the repair is not complete. Check for TSBs that pertain to speed control problem and then, if necessary, return to Symptom List. 15. Ensure vehicle speed is greater than 35 mph and release the SET Switch. If vehicle did not adjust and set a new vehicle speed, the repair is not complete. Check for TSBs that pertain to speed control problem and then, if necessary, return to Symptom List. 16. Depress and release the CANCEL switch. If the speed control did not disengage, the repair is not complete. Check for TSBs that pertain to speed control problem and then, if necessary, return to Symptom List. 17. Bring the vehicle speed back up above 35 mph and engage speed control. 18. Depress the OFF switch to turn OFF, (Cruise light will be off). If the speed control did not disengage, the repair is not complete. Check for TSBs that pertain to speed control problem and then, if necessary, return to Symptom List. 19. If the vehicle successfully passed all of the previous tests, the speed control system is now functioning as designed. The repair is now complete.

CR1029910374000X

Fig. 63 Verification Test VER-4A. 2000 Neon

TEST	ACTION
750	Disconnect the Speed Control On/Off Switch. With the DRB, read the Speed Control Switch Voltage. Did the DRB show Speed Control Switch Voltage go from below 4.0 Volts to above 4.0 Volts? Yes → Replace the Left Speed Control Switch. No → Go To 751
751	Disconnect the Speed Control Resume/Accel Switch. With the DRB, read the Speed Control Switch Voltage. Did the DRB show Speed Control Switch Voltage go from below 4.0 Volts to above 4.0 Volts? Yes → Replace the Right Speed Control Switch. No → Go To 752
752	Start Engine. Allow engine to idle for 1 minute. Turn engine off, then ignition on, engine not running. With the DRB, actuate the Speed Control Servo Solenoids. Does the Throttle open and close? Yes → Go To 753 No → Perform Speed Control Vacuum Supply Test
753	At this time the Speed Control Switch and Servo functions appear to operate properly. Using the DRB, monitor the Speed Control OUTPUT status. Road test the Vehicle at speeds over 35 MPH (55kmh) and attempt to set the Speed Control. The following items will not allow the Speed Control to set. The last or most recent cause for Speed Control not to set is indicated by the DENIED status. If ON/OFF Denied message is indicated, the Powertrain Control Module does not see an ON signal from the Switch. If SPEED Denied message is indicated, the Vehicle Speed as seen by the Powertrain Control Module is not greater than 36 MPH. If RPM Denied message is indicated, the Engine RPM is excessively high. If BRAKE Denied message is indicated, the Brake Switch Sense Circuit is open indicating to the PCM that the Brakes are applied. The Sense Circuit is grounded through the Brake Pedal Switch when the brakes are released. If P/N Denied message is indicated, Park/Neutral Switch Sense Circuit is grounded indicating to PCM that Transmission is not in gear. The Sense Circuit is grounded through the P/N Switch when Transmission is in Park or Neutral. If RPM/SPD Denied message is indicated, the PCM senses excessive Engine RPM for a given Vehicle speed. If SOL FLT Denied message is indicated, the Powertrain Control Module senses a Servo Solenoid Circuit trouble code that is maturing or set in memory. Press Continue if the previous instructions have been completed. Repair Test Complete.

CR1100000634090X

Fig. 62 Speed Control Operation With No DTCs Present (Part 9 of 9). 2000 Neon

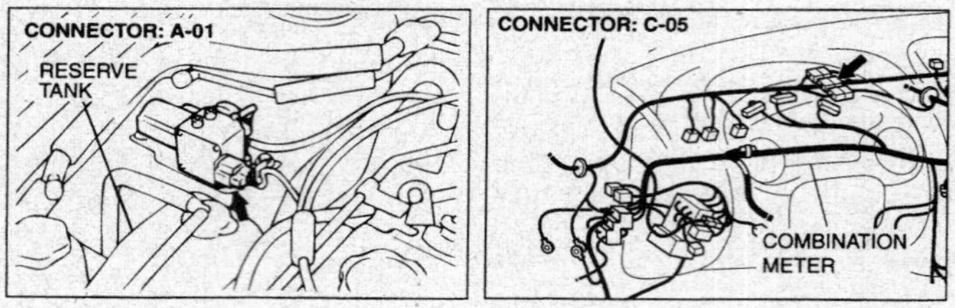

CR1100000670010X

Fig. 64 Code 11: Cruise Vacuum Pump Drive (Part 1 of 5). 2001–03 Sebring & Stratus Coupe

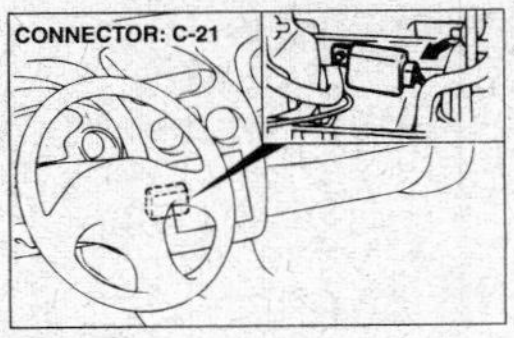

CIRCUIT OPERATION

This circuit activates the vacuum pump used to accelerate/decelerate, set, and cancel the vehicle speed.

The auto-cruise control-ECU controls the control valve, release valve, and motor by turning the transistor in the ECU on and off.

DTC SET CONDITIONS

Any drive signal for the release valve, control valve or motor is not input to the auto-cruise control-ECU.

TROUBLESHOOTING HINTS

The most likely causes for this code to be set are:

- Malfunction of the auto-cruise vacuum pump.
- Damaged harness or connector.
- Malfunction of the auto-cruise control-ECU.

DIAGNOSIS

Required Special Tool:

- MB991223: Harness Set

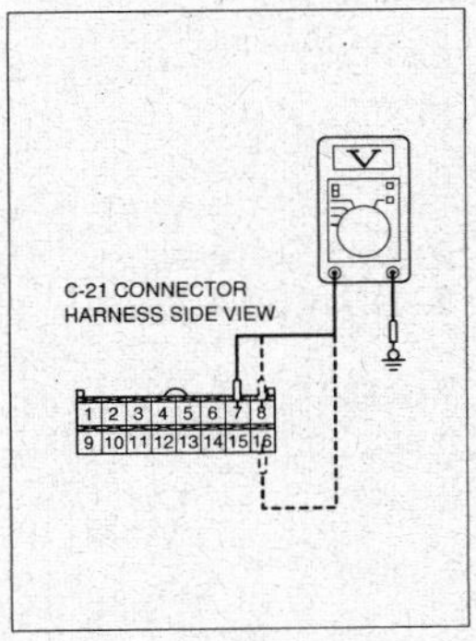

STEP 1. Check the output circuit voltage at auto-cruise control-ECU connector C-21 by backprobing.

(1) Do not disconnect auto-cruise control-ECU connector C-21.
(2) Turn the ignition switch to "ON" position and the auto-cruise control main switch to "ON" position.
(3) Measure the voltage between terminal 7 and ground by backprobing.
- Voltage should be battery positive voltage. [When decelerating with the "SET" switch while driving at constant speed (Release valve open).]

(4) Measure the voltage between terminal 8 and ground by backprobing.
- Voltage should be battery positive voltage. [When decelerating with the "SET" switch while driving at constant speed. (Control valve open).]

(5) Measure the voltage between terminal 16 and ground by backprobing.
- Voltage should be battery positive voltage. (When the motor is stopped during a constant road speed.)

(6) Turn the ignition switch to "LOCK" (OFF) position.

Q: Are all of the above values satisfied?

YES : Check that diagnostic trouble code 11 is not output. If diagnostic trouble code 11 is output, replace the auto-cruise control-ECU. Then check that diagnostic trouble code 11 is not.

NO : Go to Step 2.

CR1100000670020X

Fig. 64 Code 11: Cruise Vacuum Pump Drive (Part 2 of 5). 2001–03 Sebring & Stratus Coupe

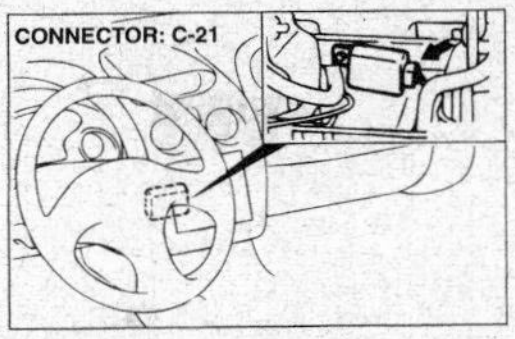

STEP 2. Check auto-cruise control-ECU connector C-21 and intermediate connector C-212.

Q: Is the connector damaged?

YES : Repair or replace connector. Then check that diagnostic trouble code 11 is not output.

NO : Go to Step 3.

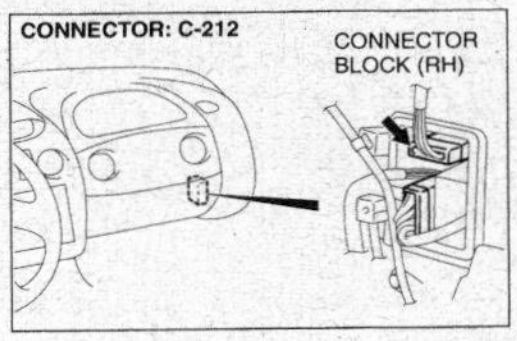

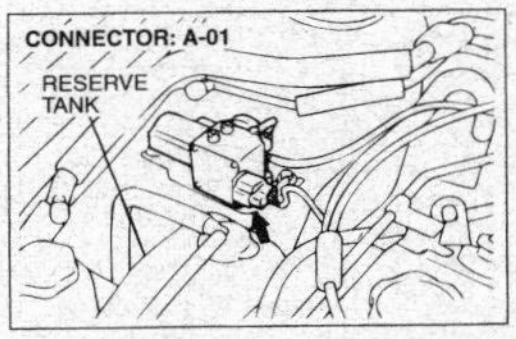

STEP 3. Check auto-cruise control vacuum pump connector A-01.

Q: Is the connector damaged?

YES : Repair or replace connector. Then check that diagnostic trouble code 11 is not output.

NO : Go to Step 4.

CR1100000670030X

Fig. 64 Code 11: Cruise Vacuum Pump Drive (Part 3 of 5). 2001–03 Sebring & Stratus Coupe

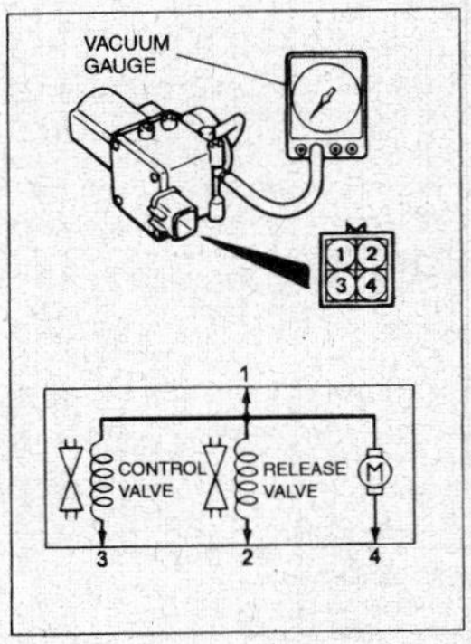

STEP 4. Check the auto-cruise vacuum pump.

(1) Disconnect the vacuum hose from the auto-cruise vacuum pump and connect a vacuum gauge to the vacuum pump.
(2) Disconnect the vacuum pump connector.
(3) Check the auto-cruise vacuum pump and valves according to the following procedure:
- Connect the positive battery terminal to auto-cruise vacuum pump connector terminal 1, and the negative battery terminal to terminals 2, 3, and 4. The vacuum gauge should read 27 kPa (8.0 in Hg) or more.
- The vacuum should be maintained when terminal 4 is disconnected from the negative battery terminal while terminals 1, 2, and 3 remain connected. Then the vacuum gauge should read 0 kPa (0 in Hg) when terminal 2 is disconnected from the negative battery terminal while terminals 1, and 3 remain connected.
- The vacuum should be maintained when terminal 4 is disconnected from the negative battery terminal while terminals 1, 2, and 3 remain connected. Then the vacuum gauge should read 0 kPa (0 in Hg) when terminal 3 is disconnected from the negative battery terminal while terminals 1, and 2 remain connected.

Q: Are all of the above values satisfied?

YES : Go to Step 5.

No : Replace the auto-cruise vacuum pump. Then check that diagnostic trouble code 11 is not output.

CR1100000670040X

Fig. 64 Code 11: Cruise Vacuum Pump Drive (Part 4 of 5). 2001–03 Sebring & Stratus Coupe

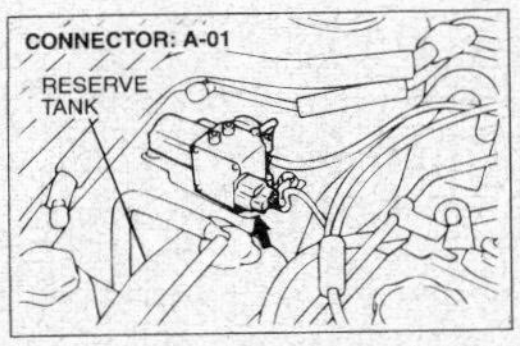

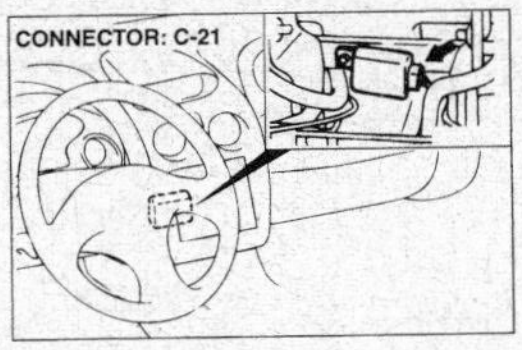

STEP 5. Check the harness wire between auto-cruise control vacuum pump connector A-01 and auto-cruise control-ECU connector C-21.

Q: Is any harness wire between auto-cruise control vacuum pump connector A-01 and auto-cruise control-ECU connector C-21 damaged?

YES : Repair the harness wire and then check that diagnostic trouble code 11 is not output.

NO : Check that diagnostic trouble code 11 is not output. If diagnostic trouble code 11 is output, replace the auto-cruise control-ECU. Then check that diagnostic trouble code 11 is not output.

CR1100000670050X

Fig. 64 Code 11: Cruise Vacuum Pump Drive (Part 5 of 5). 2001–03 Sebring & Stratus Coupe

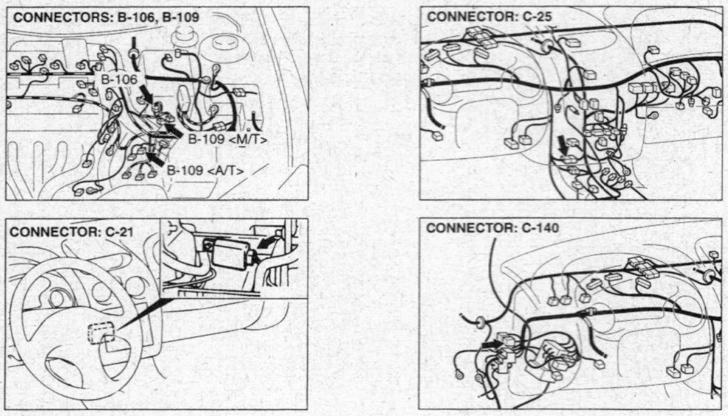

CIRCUIT OPERATION

This circuit checks the operation of the vehicle speed sensor.
When the vehicle moves forward and reverses, the sensor turns ON and OFF repeatedly.

DTC SET CONDITIONS

The vehicle speed signals from the vehicle speed sensor are not input to the auto-cruise control-ECU when the vehicle speed is 40 km/h (25 mph) or more.

TROUBLESHOOTING HINTS

The most likely causes for this code to be set are:
- Malfunction of the vehicle speed sensor.
- Damaged harness or connector.
- Malfunction of the auto-cruise control-ECU.

DIAGNOSIS

Required Special Tool:
- MB991223: Harness Set

STEP 1. Check the speedometer.

Q: Does the speedometer work normally?

YES : Go to Step 2.

No : Check the speedometer circuit and repair or replace as required.

CR1100000671010X

Fig. 65 Code 12: Vehicle Speed Sensor (Part 1 of 2). 2001–03 Sebring & Stratus Coupe

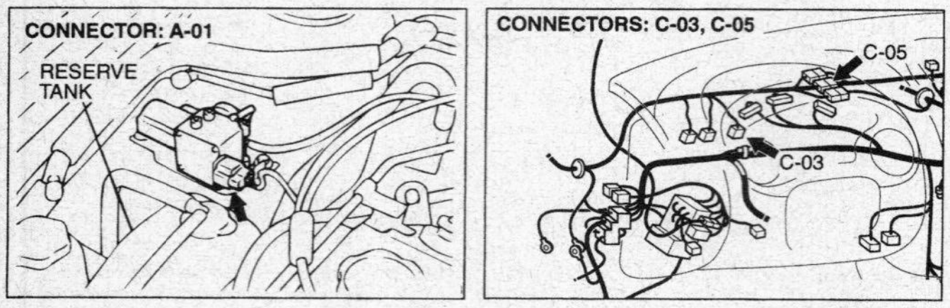

CR1100000672010X

Fig. 66 Code 14: Stop Lamp Switch (Part 1 of 9). 2001–03 Sebring & Stratus Coupe

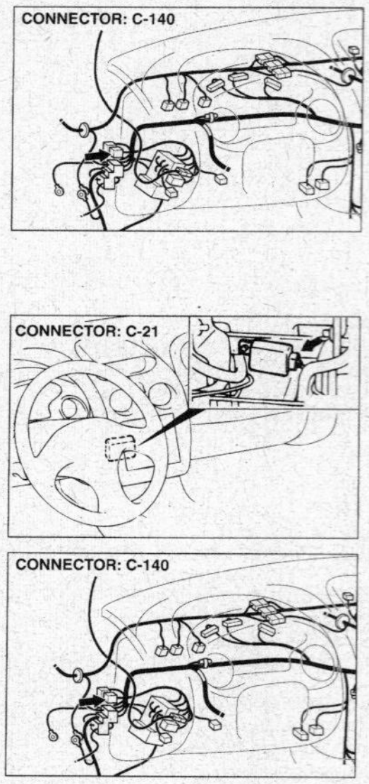

STEP 2. Check joint connector (1) C-140.

Q: Is the connector damaged?

YES : Repair or replace connector. Then check that diagnostic trouble code 12 is not output.

NO : Go to Step 3

STEP 3. Check the harness wire between auto-cruise control-ECU connector C-21 and joint connector (1) C-140.

Q: Is any harness wire between auto-cruise control-ECU connector C-21 and joint connector (4) C-140 damaged?

YES : Repair the harness wire and then check that diagnostic trouble code 12 is not output.

NO : Check that diagnostic trouble code 12 is not output. If diagnostic trouble code 12 is output, replace the auto-cruise control-ECU. Then check that diagnostic trouble code 12 is not output.

CR1100000671020X

Fig. 65 Code 12: Vehicle Speed Sensor (Part 2 of 2). 2001–03 Sebring & Stratus Coupe

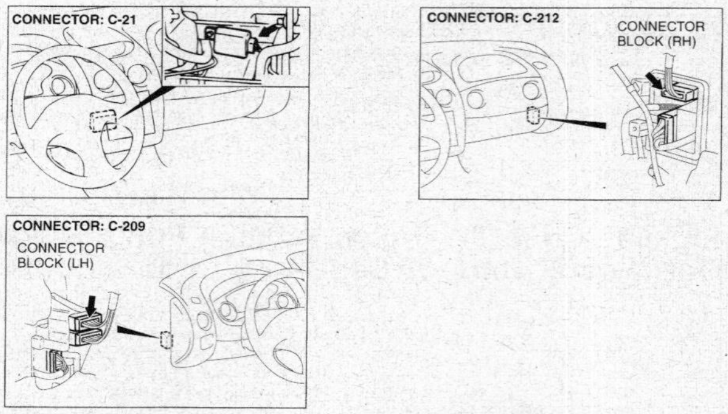

CIRCUIT OPERATION

This circuit supplies the power to the vacuum pump. The battery positive voltage is supplied to the auto-cruise control vacuum pump by turning on the transistor at terminal number 16 of the auto-cruise control-ECU.
The conditions for turning on the transistor at terminal number 16 of the auto-cruise control-ECU are as follows.
- Ignition switch "ON"
- Auto-cruise control main switch "ON"
- Stoplight switch ON

DTC SET CONDITIONS

None of the drive signals from release valve, control valve and motor of the auto-cruise vacuum pump are input to the auto-cruise control-ECU.

TROUBLESHOOTING HINTS

The most likely causes for this code to be set are:
- Malfunction of the stoplight switch
- Malfunction of the auto-cruise vacuum pump
- Damaged harness or connector.
- Malfunction of the auto-cruise control-ECU

DIAGNOSIS

Required Special Tool:
- MB991223: Harness Set

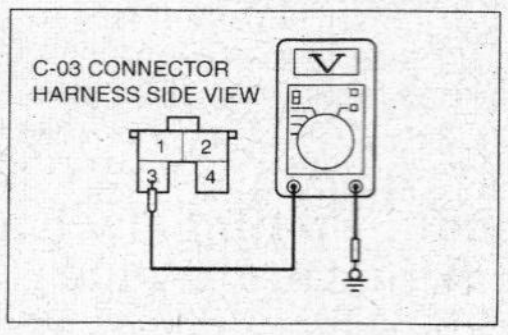

STEP 1. Check the output circuit voltage at stoplight switch connector C-03 by backprobing.

(1) Do not disconnect stoplight switch connector C-03.
(2) Turn the ignition switch to "ON" position.
(3) Measure the voltage between terminal 3 and ground by backprobing.
(4) Turn the ignition switch to "LOCK" (OFF) position.

Q: Is the voltage approximately battery positive voltage?

YES : Go to Step 3.

NO : Go to Step 2.

CR1100000672020X

Fig. 66 Code 14: Stop Lamp Switch (Part 2 of 9). 2001–03 Sebring & Stratus Coupe

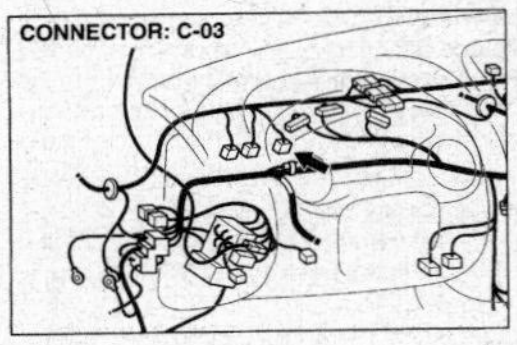

STEP 2. Check stoplight switch connector C-03.
Q: Is the connector damaged?

YES : Repair or replace connector.
Then check that diagnostic trouble code 14 is not output.

NO : Go to Step 13.

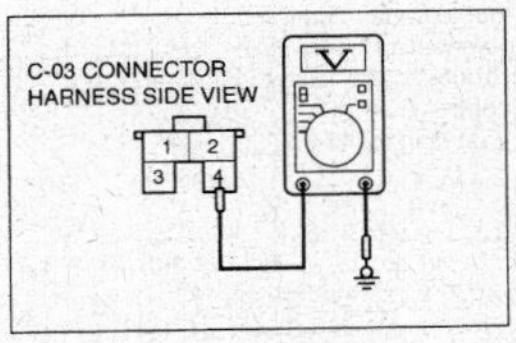

STEP 3. Check the output circuit voltage at stoplight switch connector C-03 by backprobing.
(1) Do not disconnect stoplight switch connector C-03.
(2) Turn the ignition switch to "ON" position and the auto-cruise control main switch to "ON" position.
(3) Measure the voltage between terminal 4 and ground by backprobing.
(4) Turn the ignition switch to "LOCK" (OFF) position.

Q: Is the voltage approximately battery positive voltage?

YES : Go to Step 6.

NO : Go to Step 4.

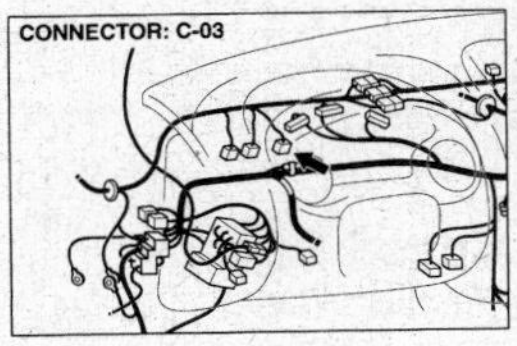

STEP 4. Check stoplight switch connector C-03.
Q: Is the connector damaged?

YES : Repair or replace connector.
Then check that diagnostic trouble code 14 is not output.

NO : Go to Step 5.

CR1100000672030X

Fig. 66 Code 14: Stop Lamp Switch (Part 3 of 9). 2001–03 Sebring & Stratus Coupe

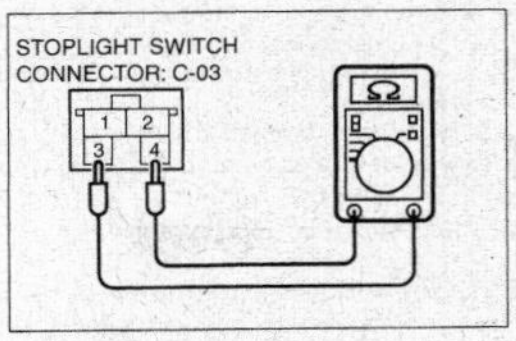

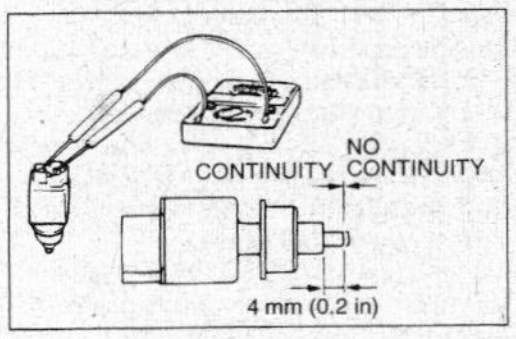

STEP 5. Check the stoplight switch.
(1) Disconnect stoplight switch connector C-03.
(2) Connect an ohmmeter to the stoplight switch between terminals 3 and 4, and check whether there is continuity when the plunger of the stoplight switch is pushed in and an open circuit when it is released.
(3) The stoplight switch is in good condition if the circuit is open when the plunger is pushed in to a depth of within 4 mm (0.2 inch) from the outer case edge surface, and if there is continuity when it is released.

Q: Is the circuit is open?

YES : Replace the stoplight switch.
Then check that a diagnostic trouble code 14 is not output.

NO : Check that diagnostic trouble code 14 is not output.
If diagnostic trouble code 14 is output, replace the auto-cruise control-ECU.
Then check that diagnostic trouble code 14 is not output.

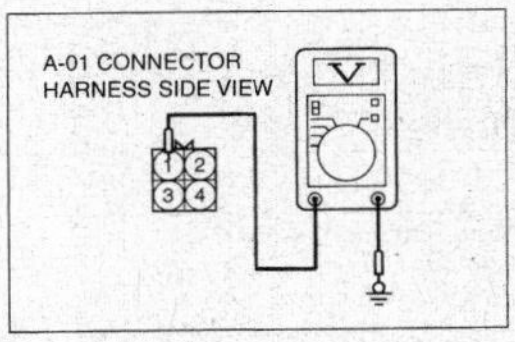

STEP 6. Check the output circuit voltage at auto-cruise control vacuum pump connector A-01 by backprobing.
(1) Do not disconnect auto-cruise control vacuum pump connector A-01.
(2) Turn the ignition switch to "ON" position and the auto-cruise control main switch to "ON" position.
(3) Measure the voltage between terminal 1 and ground by backprobing.
(4) Turn the ignition switch to "LOCK" (OFF) position.

Q: Is the voltage approximately battery positive voltage?

YES : Go to Step 8.

NO : Go to Step 7.

CR1100000672040X

Fig. 66 Code 14: Stop Lamp Switch (Part 4 of 9). 2001–03 Sebring & Stratus Coupe

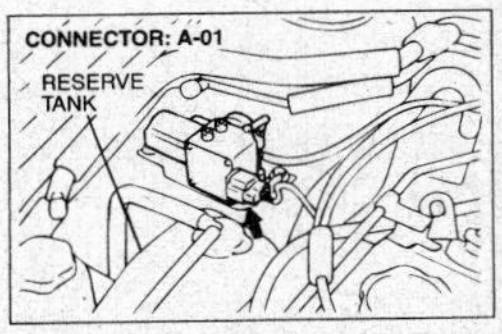

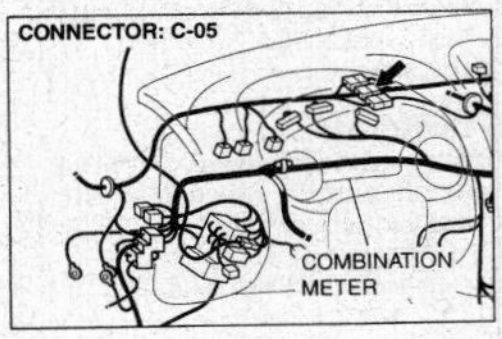

STEP 7. Check auto-cruise control vacuum pump connector A-01 and intermediate connector C-05.
Q: Is any connector damaged?

YES : Repair or replace connector.
Then check that diagnostic trouble code 14 is not output.

NO : Check the harness wire between stoplight switch connector C-03 and auto-cruise control vacuum pump connector A-01 for open circuit or damage.
Then repair if necessary.
Then check that diagnostic trouble code 14 is not output.

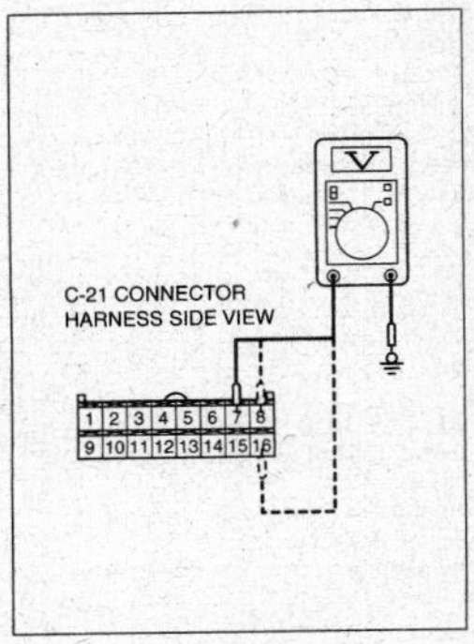

STEP 8. Check the output circuit voltage at auto-cruise control-ECU connector C-21 by backprobing.
(1) Do not disconnect auto-cruise control-ECU connector C-21.
(2) Turn the ignition switch to "ON" position and the auto-cruise control main switch to "ON" position.
(3) Measure the voltage between terminal 7 and ground by backprobing.
- Voltage should be battery positive voltage.
[When decelerating with the "SET" switch while driving at constant speed (Release valve open).]

(4) Measure the voltage between terminal 8 and ground by backprobing.
- Voltage should be battery positive voltage.
[When decelerating with the "SET" switch while driving at constant speed. (Control valve open).]

(5) Measure the voltage between terminal 16 and ground by backprobing.
- Voltage should be battery positive voltage.
(When the motor is stopped during a constant road speed.)

(6) Turn the ignition switch to "LOCK" (OFF) position.

Q: Are all of the above values satisfied?

YES : Check that diagnostic trouble code 14 is not output.
If diagnostic trouble code 14 is output, replace the auto-cruise control-ECU.
Then check that diagnostic trouble code 14 is not.

NO : Go to Step 9.

CR1100000672050X

Fig. 66 Code 14: Stop Lamp Switch (Part 5 of 9). 2001–03 Sebring & Stratus Coupe

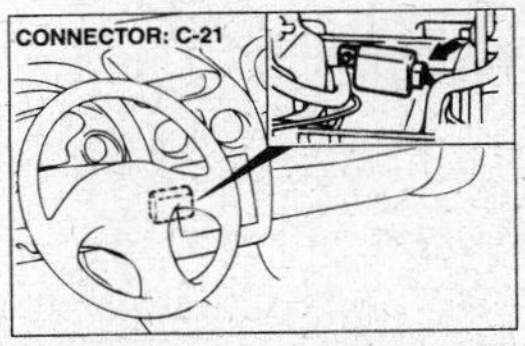

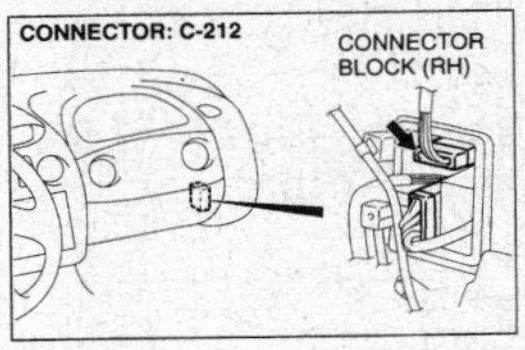

STEP 9. Check auto-cruise control-ECU connector C-21 and intermediate connector C-212.
Q: Is the connector damaged?

YES : Repair or replace connector.
Then check that diagnostic trouble code 14 is not output.

NO : Go to Step 10.

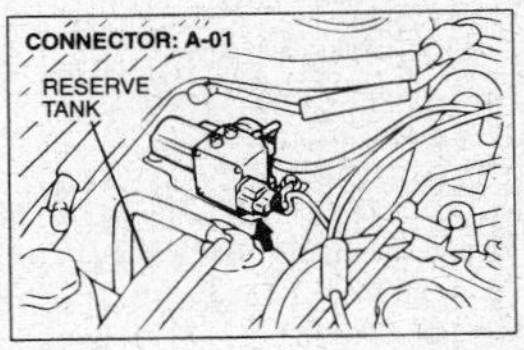

STEP 10. Check auto-cruise control vacuum pump connector A-01.
Q: Is the connector damaged?

YES : Repair or replace connector.
Then check that diagnostic trouble code 14 is not output.

NO : Go to Step 11.

CR1100000672060X

Fig. 66 Code 14: Stop Lamp Switch (Part 6 of 9). 2001–03 Sebring & Stratus Coupe

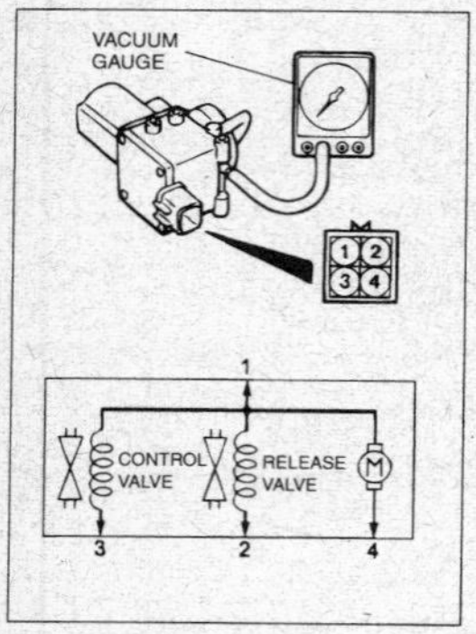

STEP 11. Check the auto-cruise vacuum pump.

(1) Disconnect the vacuum hose from the auto-cruise vacuum pump and connect a vacuum gauge to the vacuum pump.
(2) Disconnect the vacuum pump connector.
(3) Check the auto-cruise vacuum pump and valves according to the following procedure:

- Connect the positive battery terminal to auto-cruise vacuum pump connector terminal 1, and the negative battery terminal to terminals 2, 3, and 4.
  The vacuum gauge should read 27 kPa (8.0 in Hg) or more.
- The vacuum should be maintained when terminal 4 is disconnected from the negative battery terminal while terminals 1, 2, and 3 remain connected.
  Then the vacuum gauge should read 0 kPa (0 in Hg) when terminal 2 is disconnected from the negative battery terminal while terminals 1, and 3 remain connected.
- The vacuum should be maintained when terminal 4 is disconnected from the negative battery terminal while terminals 1, 2, and 3 remain connected.
  Then the vacuum gauge should read 0 kPa (0 in Hg) when terminal 3 is disconnected from the negative battery terminal while terminals 1, and 2 remain connected.

Q: Are all of the above values satisfied?

YES : Go to Step 12.
No : Replace the auto-cruise vacuum pump.
Then check that diagnostic trouble code 14 is not output.

CR1100000672070X

Fig. 66 Code 14: Stop Lamp Switch (Part 7 of 9). 2001–03 Sebring & Stratus Coupe

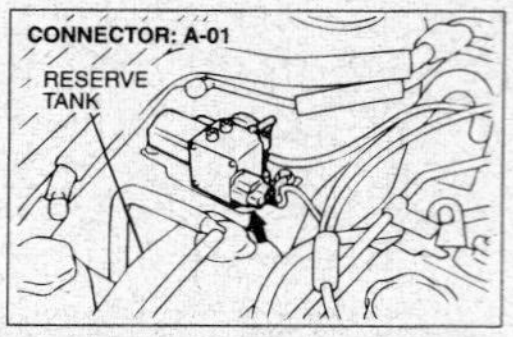

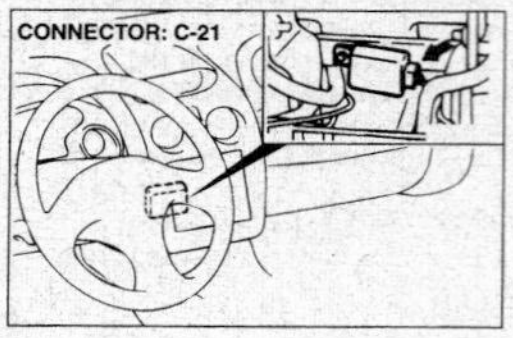

STEP 12. Check the harness wire between auto-cruise control vacuum pump connector A-01 and auto-cruise control-ECU connector C-21.

Q: Is any harness wire between auto-cruise control vacuum pump connector A-01 and auto-cruise control-ECU connector C-21 damaged?

YES : Repair harness wire and then check that diagnostic trouble code 14 is not output.
NO : Check that diagnostic trouble code 14 is not output. If diagnostic trouble code 14 is output, replace the auto-cruise control-ECU.
Then check that diagnostic trouble code 14 is not output.

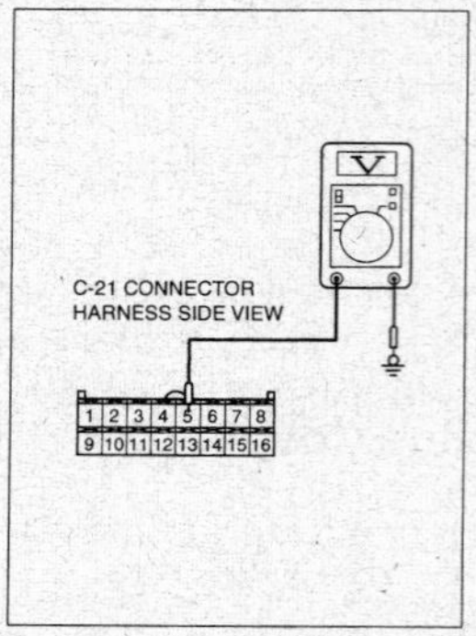

STEP 13. Check the output circuit voltage at auto-cruise control-ECU connector C-21 by backprobing.

(1) Do not disconnect auto-cruise control-ECU connector C-21.
(2) Turn the ignition switch to "ON" position and the auto-cruise control main switch to "ON" position.
(3) Measure the voltage between terminal 5 and ground by backprobing.
(4) Turn the ignition switch to "LOCK" (OFF) position.

Q: Is the voltage approximately battery positive voltage?

YES : Go to Step 14.
NO : Go to Step 15.

CR1100000672080X

Fig. 66 Code 14: Stop Lamp Switch (Part 8 of 9). 2001–03 Sebring & Stratus Coupe

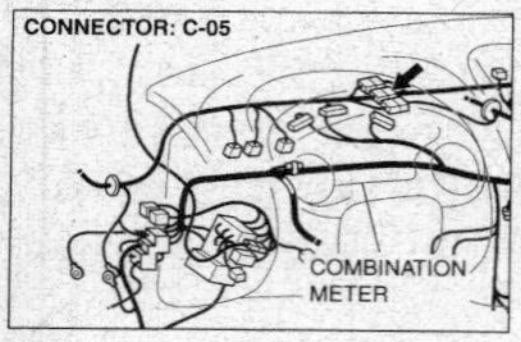

STEP 14. Check intermediate connector C-05.

Q: Is any connector damaged?

YES : Repair or replace connector.
Then check that diagnostic trouble code 14 is not output.
NO : Check the harness wire between auto-cruise control-ECU connector C-21 and stoplight switch connector C-03 for open circuit or damage.
Then repair if necessary.
Then check that diagnostic trouble code 14 is not output.

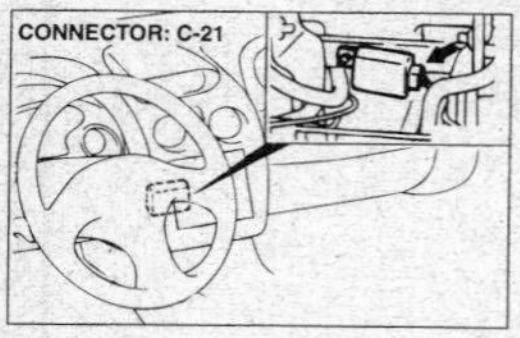

STEP 15. Check auto-cruise control-ECU connector C-21.

Q: Is the connector damaged?

YES : Repair or replace connector.
Then check that diagnostic trouble code 14 is not output.
NO : Check that diagnostic trouble code 14 is not output.
If diagnostic trouble code 14 is output, replace the auto-cruise control-ECU.
Then check that diagnostic trouble code 14 is not output.

CR1100000672090X

Fig. 66 Code 14: Stop Lamp Switch (Part 9 of 9). 2001–03 Sebring & Stratus Coupe

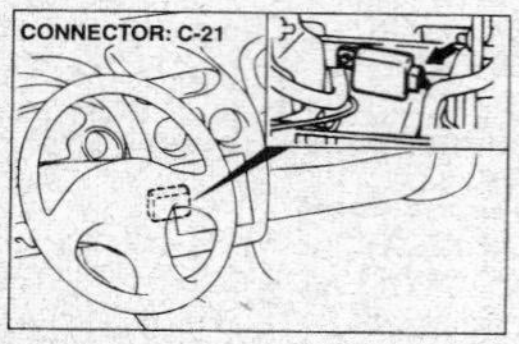

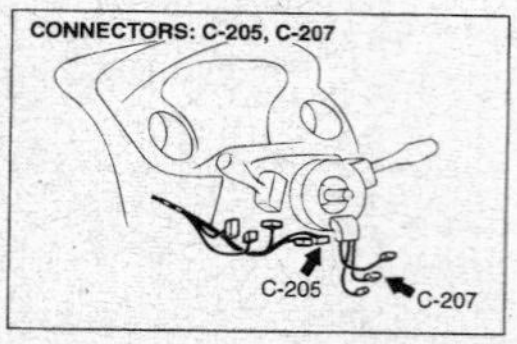

CIRCUIT OPERATION

This circuit judges the signals of each switch ("OFF," "SET," "RESUME," "CANCEL" and "MAIN") of the auto-cruise control switch.
The auto-cruise control-ECU detects the state of the auto-cruise control switch by sensing the voltages shown below.

- When all switches are OFF, the ECU detects 3.5 - 5.0 volts.

CR1100000673010X

Fig. 67 Code 15: Cruise Control Switch (Part 1 of 6). 2001–03 Sebring & Stratus Coupe

- When the "SET" switch is ON, the ECU detects 0.4 - 2.3 volts.
- When the "RESUME" switch is ON, the ECU detects 2.3 - 3.5 volts.
- When the "CANCEL" switch is ON, the ECU detects 0.4 volts or less.
- When the main switch is ON, the ECU detects 7.0 volts.

DTC SET CONDITIONS

This code is output when the auto-cruise control switch "RESUME" switch, "SET" switch or "CANCEL" switch stays ON.

TROUBLESHOOTING HINTS

The most likely causes for this code to be set are:

- Malfunction of the auto-cruise control switch.
- Malfunction of the clock spring.
- Damaged harness or connector.
- Malfunction of the auto-cruise control-ECU

DIAGNOSIS

Required Special Tool:

- MB991223: Harness Set

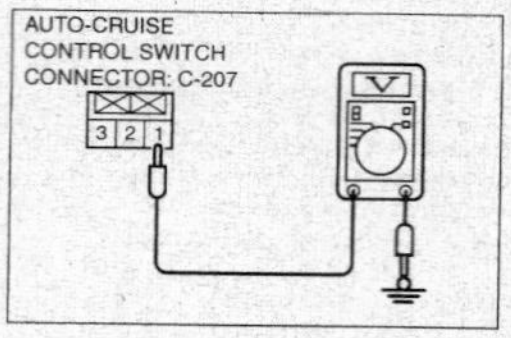

STEP 1. Check the 12-Volt supply circuit voltage at auto-cruise control switch connector C-207.

(1) Disconnect auto-cruise control switch connector C-207 and measure at the harness side.
(2) Turn the ignition switch to "ON" position.
(3) Measure the voltage between terminal 1 and ground.
(4) Turn the ignition switch to "LOCK" (OFF) position.

Q: Is the voltage approximately battery positive voltage?

YES : Go to Step 5.
NO : Go to Step 2.

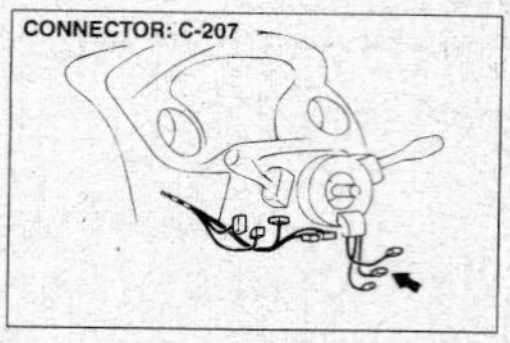

STEP 2. Check auto-cruise control switch connector C-207.

Q: Is the connector damaged?

YES : Repair or replace connector.
Then check that diagnostic trouble code 15 is not output.
NO : Go to Step 3.

CR1100000673020X

Fig. 67 Code 15: Cruise Control Switch (Part 2 of 6). 2001–03 Sebring & Stratus Coupe

STEP 3. Check the clock spring.

Q: Is the clock spring damaged?

YES : Replace the clock spring.
Then check that diagnostic trouble code 15 is not output.

NO : Go to Step 4.

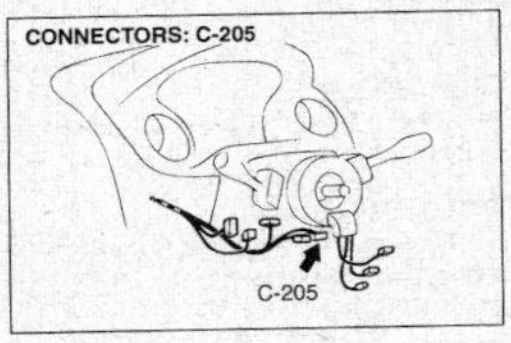

STEP 4. Check clock spring connector C-205.

Q: Is any connector damaged?

YES : Repair or replace connector.
Then check that diagnostic trouble code 15 is not output.

NO : Check the harness wire between multi-purpose fuse No.13 and auto-cruise control switch connector C-207 for open circuit or damage.
Then repair if necessary.
Then check that diagnostic trouble code 15 is not output.

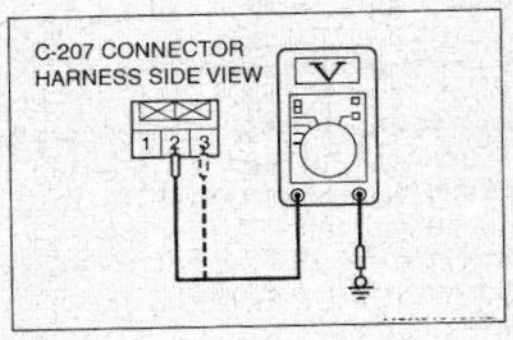

STEP 5. Check the output circuit voltage at auto-cruise control switch connector C-207 by backprobing.

(1) Do not disconnect auto-cruise control switch connector C-207.
(2) Turn the ignition switch to "ON" position.
(3) Measure the voltage between terminal 2 and ground by backprobing.
- Voltage should be battery positive voltage. (MAIN switch is at the "ON" position.)

(4) Measure the voltage between terminal 3 and ground by backprobing.
- Voltage should be between 6.8 and 7.2 volts. (MAIN switch is at the "ON" position.)
- Voltage should be between 3.5 and 5.0 volts. (All switches are at the "OFF" position.)
- Voltage should be between 0.4 and 2.3 volts. ("SET" switch is at the "ON" position)
- Voltage should be between 2.3 and 3.5 volts. ("RESUME" switch is at the "ON" position.)
- Voltage should be between 1 volt or less. ("CANCEL" switch is at the "ON" position.)

(5) Turn the ignition switch to "LOCK" (OFF) position.

Q: Is the voltage within specifications?

YES : Go to Step 8.

NO : Go to Step 6.

CR1100000673030X

Fig. 67 Code 15: Cruise Control Switch (Part 3 of 6). 2001–03 Sebring & Stratus Coupe

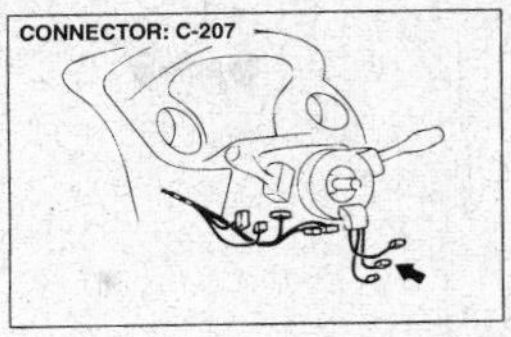

STEP 6. Check auto-cruise control switch connector C-207.

Q: Is the connector damaged?

YES : Repair or replace connector.
Then check that diagnostic trouble code 15 is not output.

NO : Go to Step 7.

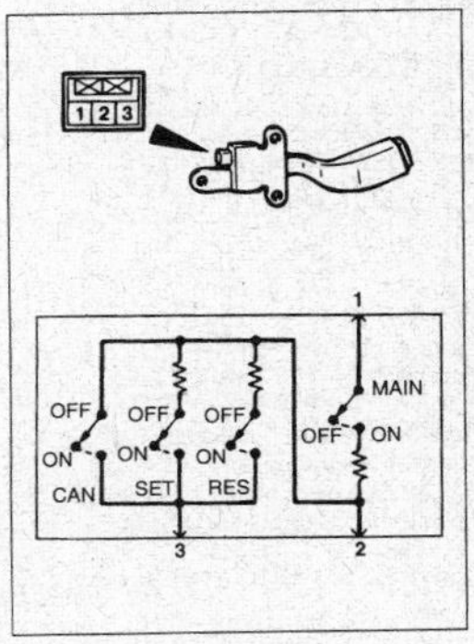

STEP 7. Check the auto-cruise control switch.

(1) Disconnect auto-cruise control switch.
(2) Measure the resistance between the terminals when each of the "SET", "RESUME", "CANCEL" and MAIN switch is pressed.

SWITCH POSITION	RESISTANCE BETWEEN TERMINALS	
MAIN switch "OFF"	Terminal 1 and 2	Less than 2 ohm
MAIN switch "ON"	Terminal 1 and 2	Approximately 3.9 kΩ
"CANCEL" switch "ON"	Terminal 2 and 3	Approximately 0 Ω
"RESUME" switch "ON"	Terminal 2 and 3	Approximately 910 Ω
"SET" switch "ON"	Terminal 2 and 3	Approximately 220 Ω

Q: Is the values measured correspond to those in the table below?

YES : Check that diagnostic trouble code 15 is not output.
If diagnostic trouble code 15 is output, replace the auto-cruise control-ECU.
Then check that diagnostic trouble code 15 is not output.

NO : Replace the auto-cruise control switch.
Then check that diagnostic trouble code 15 is not output.

CR1100000673040X

Fig. 67 Code 15: Cruise Control Switch (Part 4 of 6). 2001–03 Sebring & Stratus Coupe

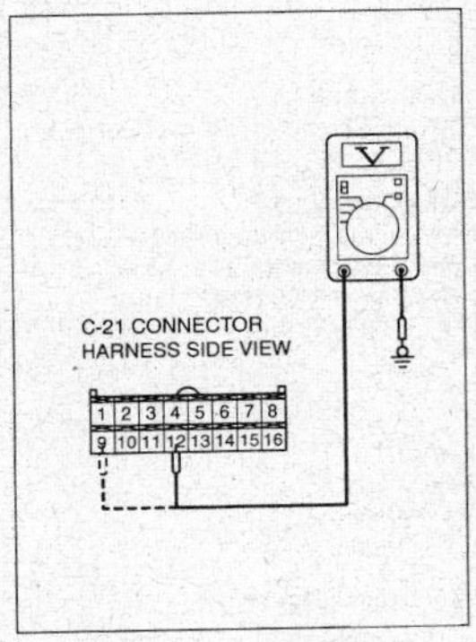

STEP 8. Check the output circuit voltage at auto-cruise control-ECU connector C-21 by backprobing.

(1) Do not disconnect auto-cruise control-ECU connector C-21.
(2) Turn the ignition switch to "ON" position.
(3) Measure the voltage between terminal 12 and ground by backprobing.
- Voltage should be battery positive voltage. (The MAIN switch is at the "ON" position.)

(4) Measure the voltage between terminal 9 and ground by backprobing.
- Voltage should be between 6.8 and 7.2 volts. (MAIN switch is at the "ON" position.)
- Voltage should be between 3.5 and 5.0 volts. (All switches are at the "OFF" position.)
- Voltage should be between 0.4 and 2.3 volts. ("SET" switch is at the "ON" position.)
- Voltage should be between 2.3 and 3.5 volts. ("RESUME" switch is at the "ON" position.)
- Voltage should be between 1 volt or less. ("CANCEL" switch is at the "ON" position.)

(5) Turn the ignition switch to "LOCK" (OFF) position.

Q: Is the voltage within specifications?

YES : Check that diagnostic trouble code 15 is not output.
If diagnostic trouble code 15 is output, replace the auto-cruise control-ECU.
Then check that diagnostic trouble code 15 is not output.

NO : Go to Step 9.

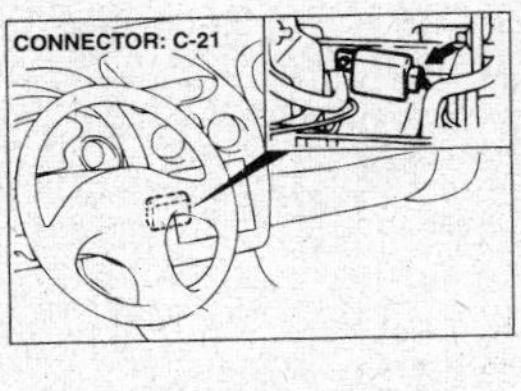

STEP 9. Check auto-cruise control-ECU connector C-21.

Q: Is the connector damaged?

YES : Repair or replace connector.
Then check that diagnostic trouble code 15 is not output.

NO : Go to Step 10.

STEP 10. Check the clock spring.

Q: Is the clock spring damaged?

YES : Replace the clock spring.
Then check that diagnostic trouble code 15 is not output.

NO : Go to Step 11.

CR1100000673050X

Fig. 67 Code 15: Cruise Control Switch (Part 5 of 6). 2001–03 Sebring & Stratus Coupe

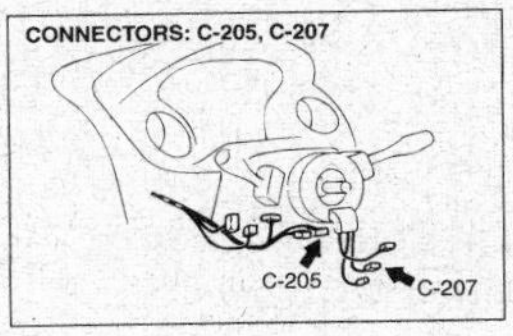

STEP 11. Check auto-cruise control switch connector C-207, clock spring connector C-205.

Q: Is any connector damaged?

YES : Repair or replace connector.
Then check that diagnostic trouble code 15 is not output.

NO : Go to Step 12.

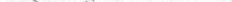

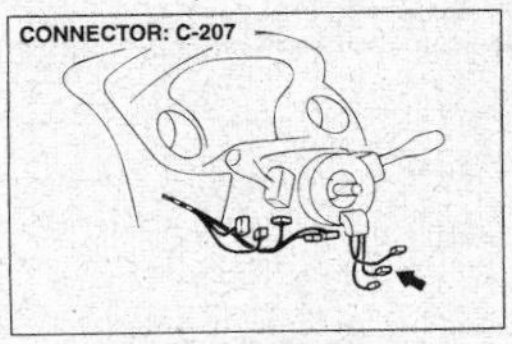

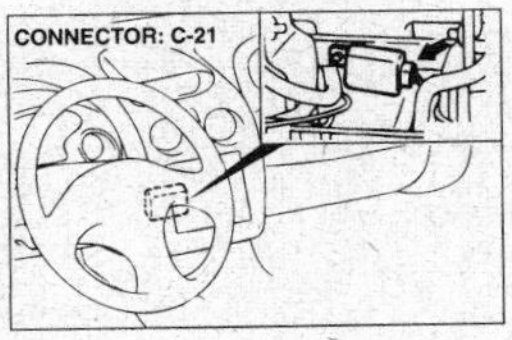

STEP 12. Check the harness wire between auto-cruise control switch connector C-207 and auto-cruise control-ECU connector C-21.

Q: Is any harness wire between auto-cruise control switch connector C-207 and auto-cruise control-ECU connector C-21 damaged?

YES : Repair harness wire and then check that diagnostic trouble code 15 is not output.

NO : Check that diagnostic trouble code 15 is not output.
If diagnostic trouble code 15 is output, replace the auto-cruise control-ECU.
Then check that diagnostic trouble code 15 is not output.

CR1100000673060X

Fig. 67 Code 15: Cruise Control Switch (Part 6 of 6). 2001–03 Sebring & Stratus Coupe

DTC 16: Auto-cruise Control-ECU

DTC SET CONDITIONS

This code is output when a problem is found on the cancel status hold circuit or microcomputer operation monitor circuit, which is incorporated in the auto-cruise control-ECU.

TROUBLESHOOTING HINTS

Malfunction of the auto-cruise control-ECU.

DIAGNOSIS

Replace the auto-cruise control-ECU.
Check that diagnostic trouble code 16 is not output.

CR1100000674010X

Fig. 68 Code 16: Cruise Control-ECU (Part 1 of 5). 2001–03 Sebring & Stratus Coupe

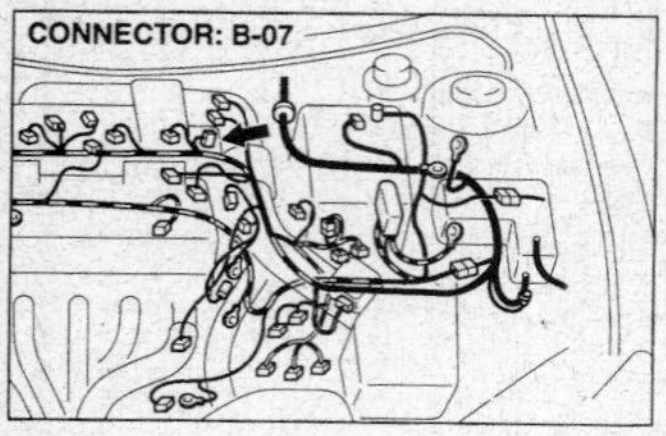

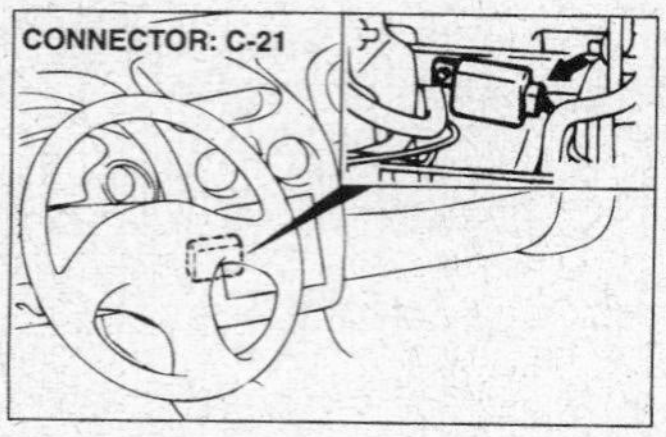

CR1100000674020X

Fig. 68 Code 16: Cruise Control-ECU (Part 2 of 5). 2001–03 Sebring & Stratus Coupe

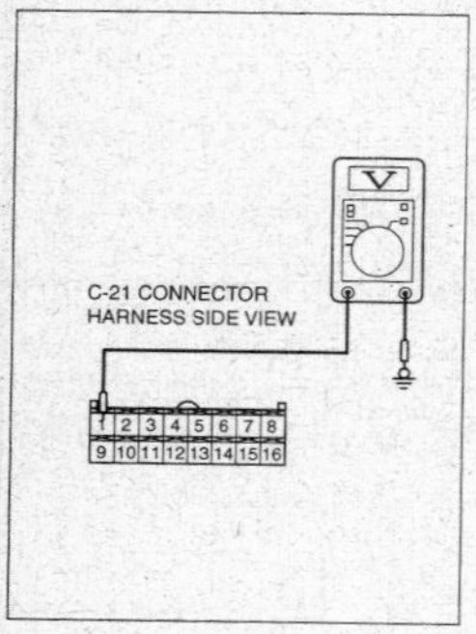

STEP 2. Check the output circuit voltage at auto-cruise control-ECU connector C-21 by backprobing.

(1) Do not disconnect auto-cruise control-ECU connector C-21.
(2) Turn the ignition switch to "ON" position and the auto-cruise control main switch to "ON" position.
(3) Measure the voltage between terminal 1 and ground by backprobing.
- Voltage should be between 4.0 and 5.5 volts. (When accelerator pedal is fully depressed.)]
- Voltage should be between 0.4 and 1.0 volts. (When accelerator pedal is released.)

(4) Turn the ignition switch to "LOCK" (OFF) position.

Q: Are the voltage within specifications?

YES : Check that diagnostic trouble code 17 is not output. If diagnostic trouble code 17 is output, replace the auto-cruise control-ECU. Then check that diagnostic trouble code 17 is not.

NO : Go to Step 3.

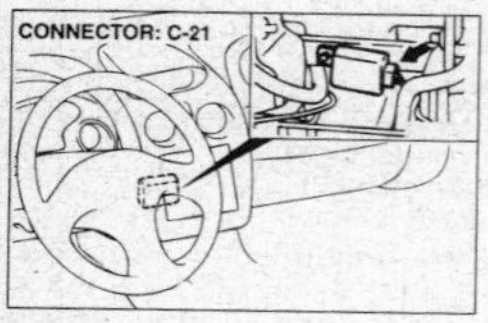

STEP 3. Check auto-cruise control-ECU connector C-21.

Q: Is the connector damaged?

YES : Repair or replace connector. Then check that diagnostic trouble code 17 is not output.

NO : Go to Step 4.

CR1100000674040X

Fig. 68 Code 16: Cruise Control-ECU (Part 4 of 5). 2001–03 Sebring & Stratus Coupe

STEP 4. Check the harness wire between throttle position sensor connector B-07 and auto-cruise control-ECU connector C-21.

Q: Is the harness wire between throttle position sensor connector B-07 and auto-cruise control-ECU connector C-21 damaged?

YES : Repair harness wire and then check that diagnostic trouble code 17 is not output.

NO : Check that diagnostic trouble code 17 is not output. If diagnostic trouble code 17 is output, replace the auto-cruise control-ECU. Then check that diagnostic trouble code 17 is not output.

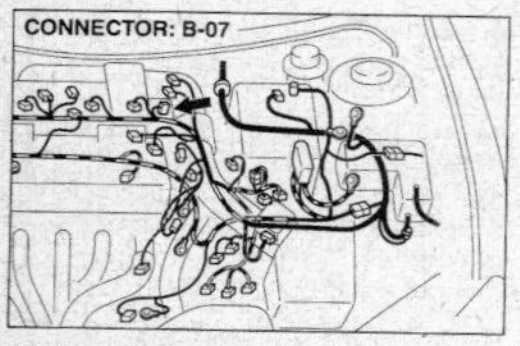

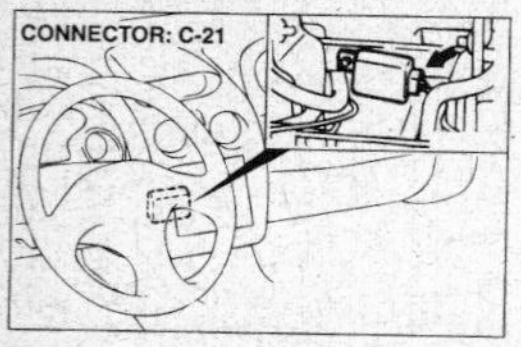

CR1100000674050X

Fig. 68 Code 16: Cruise Control-ECU (Part 5 of 5). 2001–03 Sebring & Stratus Coupe

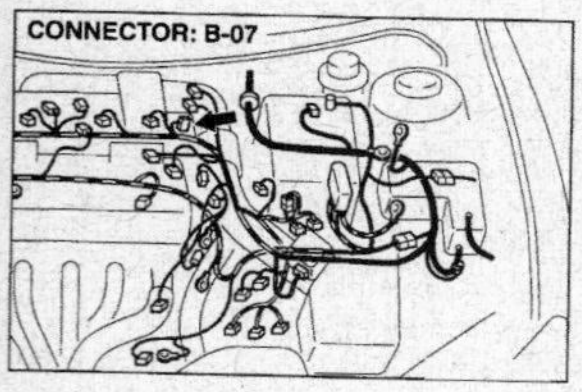

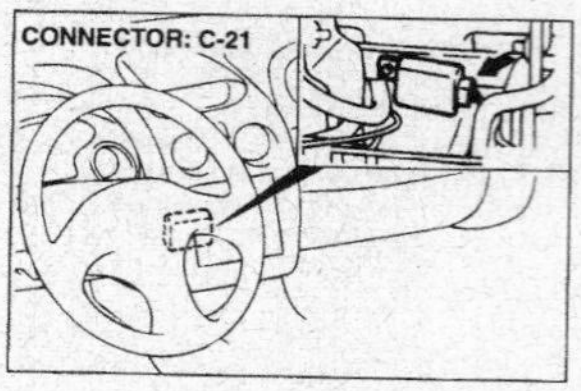

CR1100200749010X

Fig. 69 Code 17: Throttle Position Sensor (Part 1 of 4). 2001–03 Sebring & Stratus Coupe

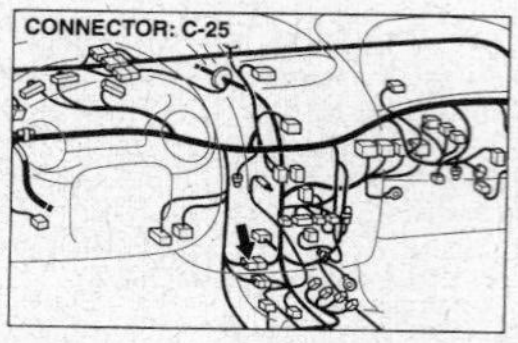

CIRCUIT OPERATION

The throttle position sensor signal is sent to the auto-cruise control-ECU through this circuit.
The auto-cruise control-ECU receives a signal from the throttle position sensor at terminal 3.
The signal is OFF when the accelerator pedal is depressed, and ON when the accelerator pedal is released.
The throttle position sensor sends a voltage signal to terminal 1 of the auto-cruise control-ECU.
The voltage depends on throttle opening angle.

DTC SET CONDITIONS

If 2.5 volts or more 0.2 volts or less is output for four seconds or more.

TROUBLESHOOTING HINTS

The most likely causes for this code to be set are:
- Malfunction of the throttle position sensor.
- Damaged harness or connector.
- Malfunction of the auto-cruise control-ECU.

DIAGNOSIS

Required Special Tools:
MB991502: Scan Tool (MUT-II)
MB991223: Harness Set

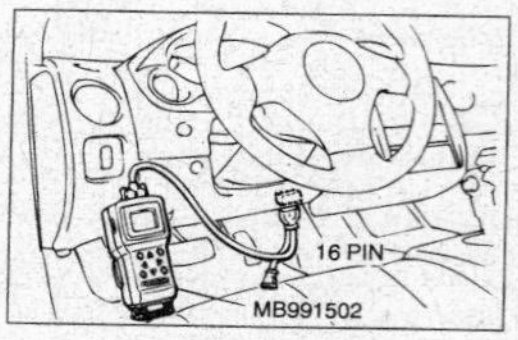

STEP 1. Check the throttle position sensor.

⚠ CAUTION

To prevent damage to scan tool MB991502, always turn the ignition switch to "LOCK"(OFF) position before connecting or disconnecting scan tool MB991502.

(1) Using scan tool MB991502.
(2) Connect scan tool MB991502 to the data link connector.
(3) Turn the ignition switch to "ON" position.
(4) Read the MFI-DTC.
(5) Turn the ignition switch to "LOCK"(OFF) position.

Q: Is the MFI-DTC P0120 is output?

YES : For 2.4L Engine
For 3.0L Engine

NO : Go to Step 2.

CR1100000674030X

Fig. 68 Code 16: Cruise Control-ECU (Part 3 of 5). 2001–03 Sebring & Stratus Coupe

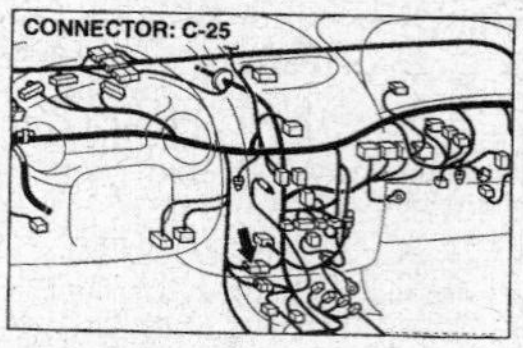

CIRCUIT OPERATION

The throttle position sensor signal is sent to the auto-cruise control-ECU through this circuit.
The auto-cruise control-ECU receives a signal from the throttle position sensor at terminal 3.
The signal is OFF when the accelerator pedal is depressed, and ON when the accelerator pedal is released.
The throttle position sensor sends a voltage signal to terminal 1 of the auto-cruise control-ECU.
The voltage depends on throttle opening angle.

DTC SET CONDITIONS

If 2.5 volts or more 0.2 volts or less is output for four seconds or more.

TROUBLESHOOTING HINTS

The most likely causes for this code to be set are:
- Malfunction of the throttle position sensor.
- Damaged harness or connector.
- Malfunction of the auto-cruise control-ECU.

DIAGNOSIS

Required Special Tools:
MB991502: Scan Tool (MUT-II)
MB991223: Harness Set

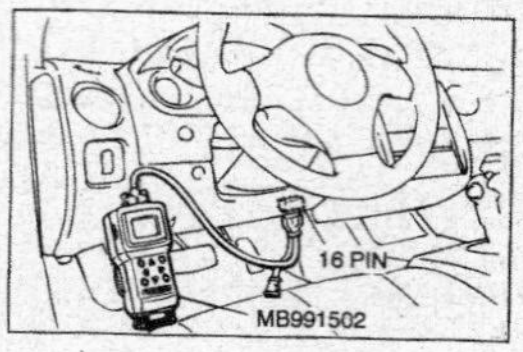

STEP 1. Check the throttle position sensor.

⚠ CAUTION

To prevent damage to scan tool MB991502, always turn the ignition switch to "LOCK"(OFF) position before connecting or disconnecting scan tool MB991502.

(1) Using scan tool MB991502.
(2) Connect scan tool MB991502 to the data link connector.
(3) Turn the ignition switch to "ON" position.
(4) Read the MFI-DTC.
(5) Turn the ignition switch to "LOCK"(OFF) position.

Q: Is the MFI-DTC P0120 is output?

YES : Refer to MOTOR's "Domestic Engine Performnce & Driveability Manual".

NO : Go to Step 2.

CR1100200749020X

Fig. 69 Code 17: Throttle Position Sensor (Part 2 of 4). 2001–03 Sebring & Stratus Coupe

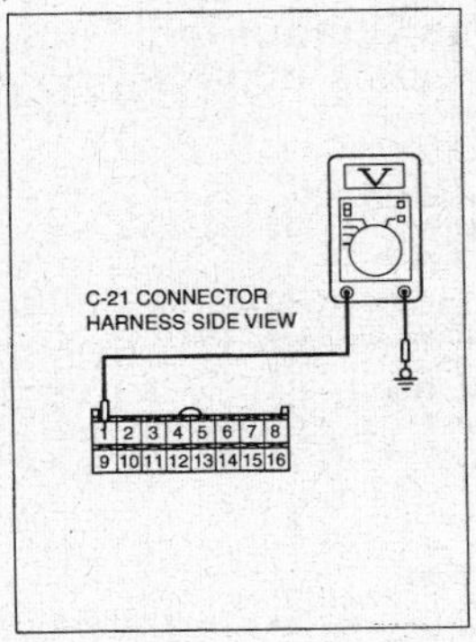

STEP 2. Check the output circuit voltage at auto-cruise control-ECU connector C-21 by backprobing.

(1) Do not disconnect auto-cruise control-ECU connector C-21.
(2) Turn the ignition switch to "ON" position and the auto-cruise control main switch to "ON" position.
(3) Measure the voltage between terminal 1 and ground by backprobing.
- Voltage should be between 4.0 and 5.5 volts. (When accelerator pedal is fully depressed.)]
- Voltage should be between 0.4 and 1.0 volts. (When accelerator pedal is released.)

(4) Turn the ignition switch to "LOCK" (OFF) position.

Q: Are the voltage within specifications?

YES : Check that diagnostic trouble code 17 is not output. If diagnostic trouble code 17 is output, replace the auto-cruise control-ECU. Then check that diagnostic trouble code 17 is not.

NO : Go to Step 3.

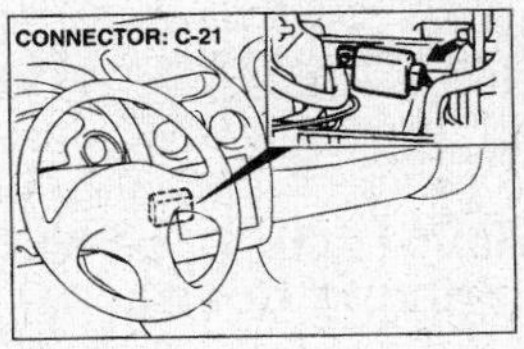

STEP 3. Check auto-cruise control-ECU connector C-21.

Q: Is the connector damaged?

YES : Repair or replace connector.

Then check that diagnostic trouble code 17 is not output.

NO : Go to Step 4.

CR1100200749030X

Fig. 69 Code 17: Throttle Position Sensor (Part 3 of 4). 2001–03 Sebring & Stratus Coupe

Refer to MOTOR's "Domestic Engine Performance & Driveability Manual"

CR1100200725000X

Fig. 70 Scan Tool Communications Not Possible. Avenger & 2000 Sebring Coupe

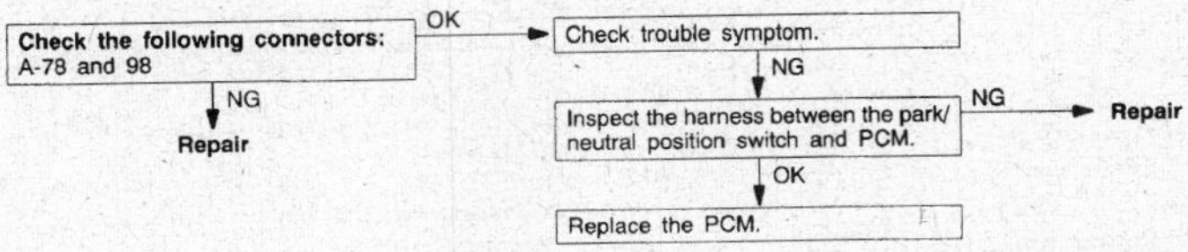

CR1100200728000X

Fig. 73 Cruise Control Does Not Cancel When Selector Set To N Position. Avenger & 2000 Sebring Coupe w/automatic transaxle

Replace the auto-cruise control switch.

CR1100200729000X

Fig. 74 Cruise Control Does Not Cancel When CANCEL Switch Is ON. Avenger & 2000 Sebring Coupe

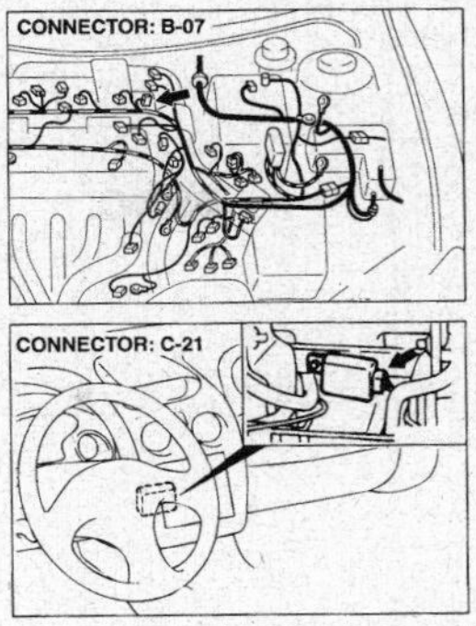

STEP 4. Check the harness wire between throttle position sensor connector B-07 and auto-cruise control-ECU connector C-21.

Q: Is the harness wire between throttle position sensor connector B-07 and auto-cruise control-ECU connector C-21 damaged?

YES : Repair harness wire and then check that diagnostic trouble code 17 is not output.

NO : Check that diagnostic trouble code 17 is not output. If diagnostic trouble code 17 is output, replace the auto-cruise control-ECU. Then check that diagnostic trouble code 17 is not output.

CR1100200749040X

Fig. 69 Code 17: Throttle Position Sensor (Part 4 of 4). 2001–03 Sebring & Stratus Coupe

Replace the powertrain control module.

CR1100200726000X

Fig. 71 Cruise Control Does Not Cancel When Engine Speed Rises Suddenly. Avenger & 2000 Sebring Coupe

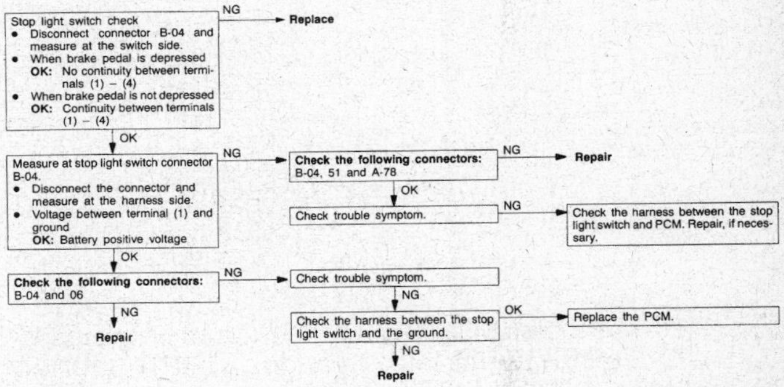

CR1100200727000X

Fig. 72 Cruise Control Does Not Cancel When Brake Pedal Is Depressed. Avenger & 2000 Sebring Coupe

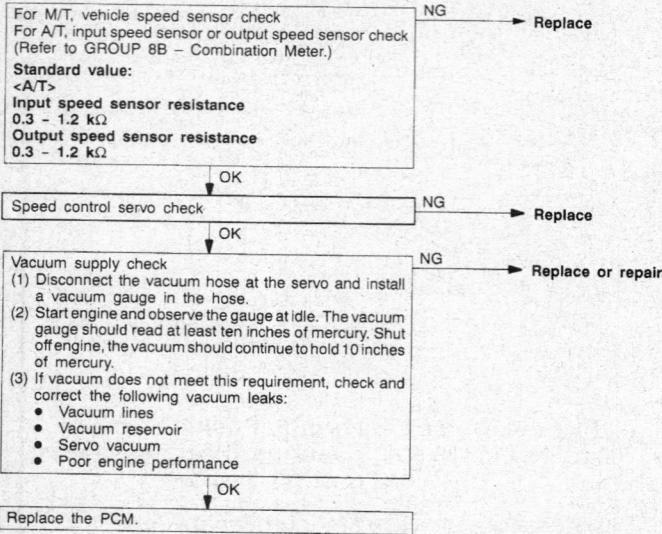

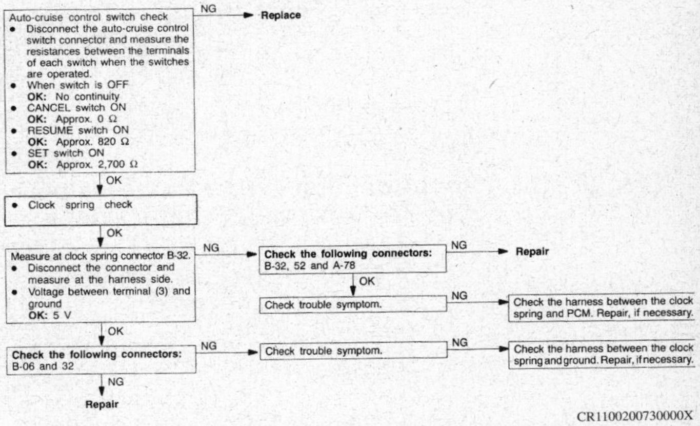

CR1100200730000X

Fig. 75 Cruise Control Cannot Be Set. Avenger & 2000 Sebring Coupe

For M/T, vehicle speed sensor check
For A/T, input speed sensor or output speed sensor check
(Refer to GROUP 8B – Combination Meter.)
Standard value:
<A/T>
Input speed sensor resistance
0.3 – 1.2 kΩ
Output speed sensor resistance
0.3 – 1.2 kΩ
— NG → **Replace**
↓ OK

Speed control servo check — NG → **Replace**
↓ OK

Vacuum supply check
(1) Disconnect the vacuum hose at the servo and install a vacuum gauge in the hose.
(2) Start engine and observe the gauge at idle. The vacuum gauge should read at least ten inches of mercury. Shut off engine, the vacuum should continue to hold 10 inches of mercury.
(3) If vacuum does not meet this requirement, check and correct the following vacuum leaks:
- Vacuum lines
- Vacuum reservoir
- Servo vacuum
- Poor engine performance

— NG → **Replace or repair**
↓ OK

Replace the PCM.

CR1100200731000X

Fig. 76 Speed Hunts W/Cruise Control Set. Avenger & 2000 Sebring Coupe

Indicator continuity check
- Remove the combination meter
- Continuity between terminals (10) – (16)
OK: Continuity

— NG → **Replace**
↓ OK

Does the indicator illuminates when terminal No. 22 of PCM harness-side connector A-77 is grounded?
— No → **Check the following connectors:** A-77, C-06 and C-23 — NG → **Repair**
↓ OK
Check trouble symptom.
↓ NG
Check the harness between the combination meter and PCM. Repair, if necessary.

↓ Yes
Replace the PCM.

CR1100200734000X

Fig. 79 Instrument Cluster Cruise Control Indicator Lamp Does Not Illuminate. Avenger & 2000 Sebring Coupe

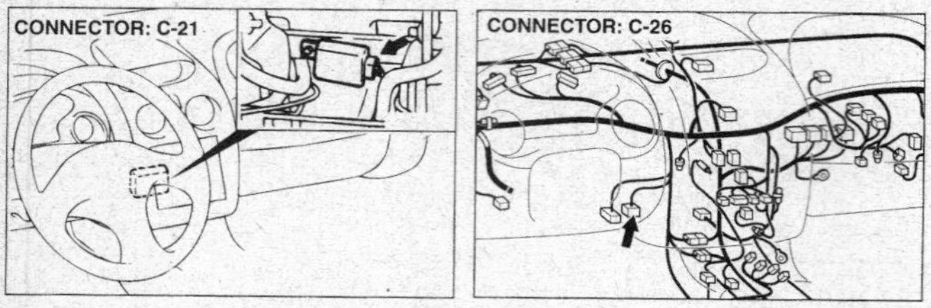

CR1100000676010X

Fig. 80 Scan Tool Communication Not Possible (Part 1 of 7). 2001–03 Sebring & Stratus Coupe

Replace the cruise control main switch.

CR1100200732000X

Fig. 77 Instrument Panel Cruise Control Indicator Lamp Does Not Illuminate. Avenger & 2000 Sebring Coupe

Auto-cruise control main switch check — NG → **Replace**
↓ OK

Measure at auto-cruise control main switch connector C-03.
- Disconnect the connector and measure at the harness side.
- Voltage between terminal (2) and ground
OK: Battery positive voltage

— NG → **Check the following connectors:** B-54 and 63 — NG → **Repair**
↓ OK
Check trouble symptom.
↓ NG
Check the harness between the auto-cruise control main switch and power supply. Repair, if necessary.

↓ OK
Check the following connector: C-03 — NG → **Repair**
↓ OK
Check trouble symptom.
↓ NG
Check the harness between the auto-cruise control main switch and rheostat. Repair, if necessary.

CR1100200733000X

Fig. 78 Cruise Control Main Switch Lamp Does Not Illuminate. Avenger & 2000 Sebring Coupe

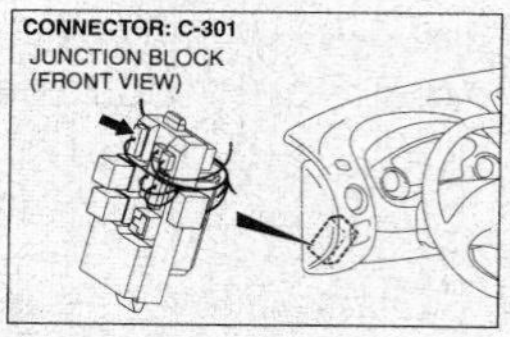

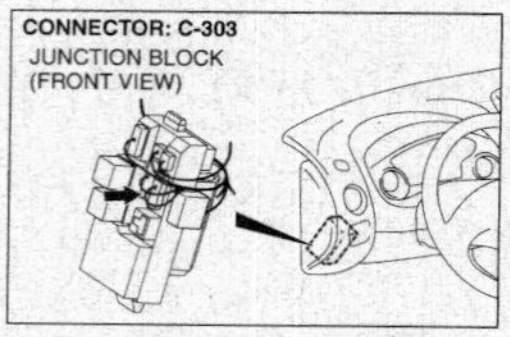

CIRCUIT OPERATION

Power of the auto-cruise control-ECU is transmitted from the ignition switch (IG1) to the auto-cruise control-ECU through multi-purpose fuse 13 in the junction block.

TECHNICAL DESCRIPTION (COMMENT)

The cause is probably a malfunction of the auto-cruise control-ECU power supply circuit or the auto-cruise control-ECU ground circuit.

TROUBLESHOOTING HINTS

- Damaged harness or connector.
- Malfunction of the auto-cruise control-ECU.

DIAGNOSIS

Required Special Tool:

- MB991223: Harness Set

STEP 1. Check the output circuit voltage at auto-cruise control-ECU connector C-21 by backprobing.

(1) Do not disconnect auto-cruise control switch connector C-21.
(2) Turn the ignition switch to "ON" position.
(3) Measure the voltage between terminal 6 and ground by backprobing.
(4) Turn the ignition switch to "LOCK" (OFF) position.

Q: Is the voltage approximately battery positive voltage?

YES : Go to Step 5.
NO : Go to Step 2.

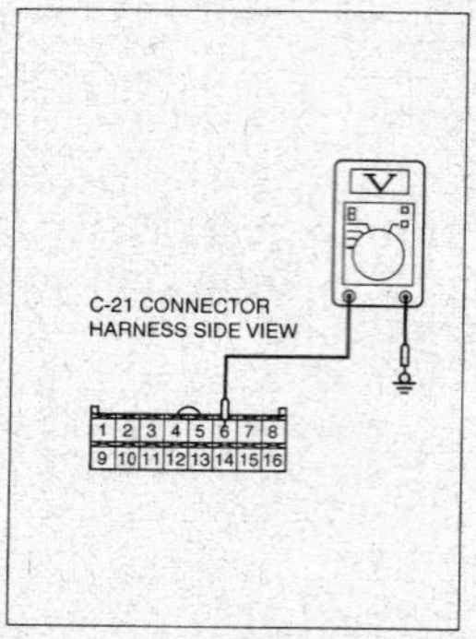

CR1100000676020X

Fig. 80 Scan Tool Communication Not Possible (Part 2 of 7). 2001–03 Sebring & Stratus Coupe

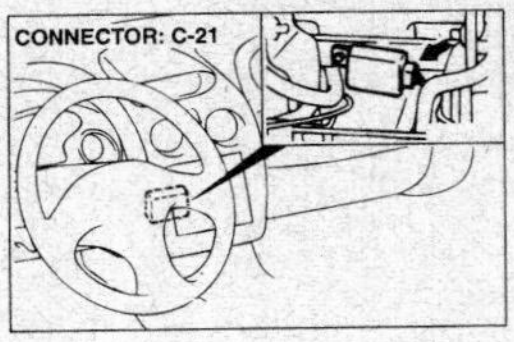

STEP 2. Check auto-cruise control-ECU connector C-21.
Q: Is the connector damaged?
- **YES :** Repair or replace connector. Then check that the malfunction is eliminated.
- **NO :** Go to Step 3.

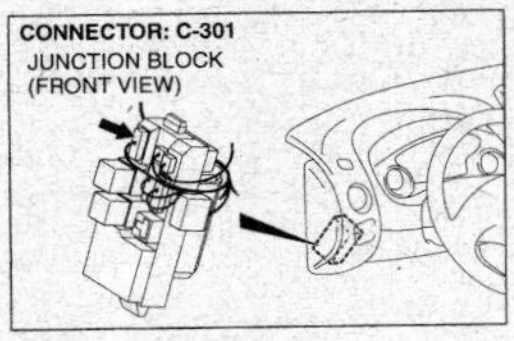

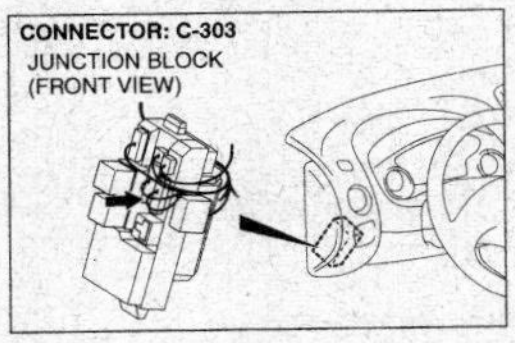

STEP 3. Check junction block connector C-301 and C-303.
Q: Is any connector damaged?
- **YES :** Repair or replace connector. Then check that the malfunction is eliminated.
- **NO :** Go to Step 4.

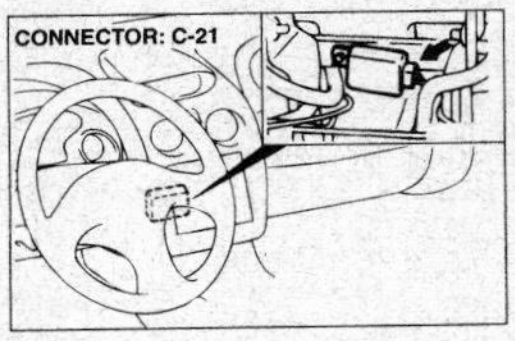

STEP 4. Check the harness wire between ignition switch and auto-cruise control-ECU connector C-21.
Q: Is any harness wire between ignition switch and auto-cruise control-ECU connector C-21 damaged?
- **YES :** Repair the harness wire and then check that the malfunction is eliminated.
- **NO :** Check that the malfunction is eliminated. If the malfunction is eliminated, replace the auto-cruise control-ECU. Then check that the malfunction is eliminated.

CR1100000676030X

Fig. 80 Scan Tool Communication Not Possible (Part 3 of 7). 2001–03 Sebring & Stratus Coupe

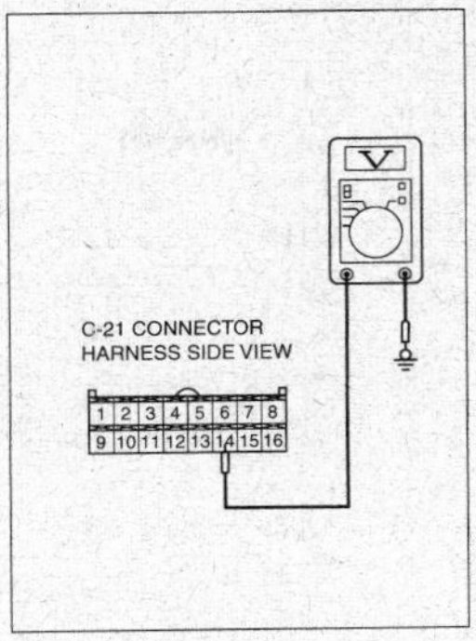

STEP 5. Check the ground circuit voltage at auto-cruise control-ECU connector C-21 by backprobing.
(1) Do not disconnect auto-cruise control switch connector C-21.
(2) Turn the ignition switch to "ON" position.
(3) Measure the voltage between terminal 14 and ground by backprobing.
(4) Turn the ignition switch to "LOCK" (OFF) position.

Q: Is the voltage approximately 0.5 volts or less?
- **YES :** Go to Step 8.
- **NO :** Go to Step 6.

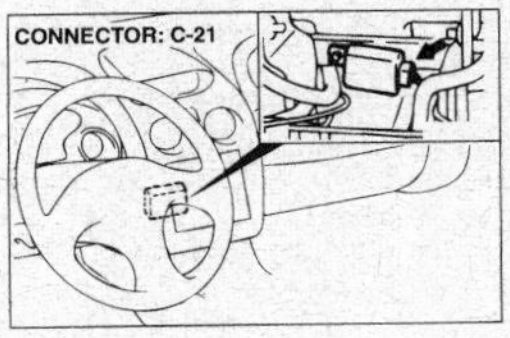

STEP 6. Check auto-cruise control-ECU connector C-21.
Q: Is the connector damaged?
- **YES :** Repair or replace connector. Then check that the malfunction is eliminated.
- **NO :** Go to Step 7.

CR1100000676040X

Fig. 80 Scan Tool Communication Not Possible (Part 4 of 7). 2001–03 Sebring & Stratus Coupe

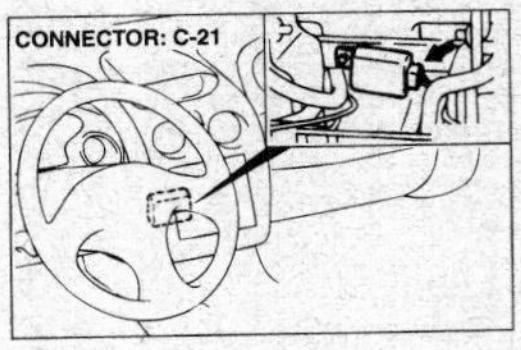

STEP 7. Check the harness wire between auto-cruise control-ECU connector C-21 and ground.
Q: Is any harness wire between auto-cruise control-ECU connector C-21 and ground damaged?
- **YES :** Repair the harness wire and then check that the malfunction is eliminated.
- **NO :** Check that the malfunction is eliminated. If the malfunction is eliminated, replace the auto-cruise control-ECU. Then check that the malfunction is eliminated.

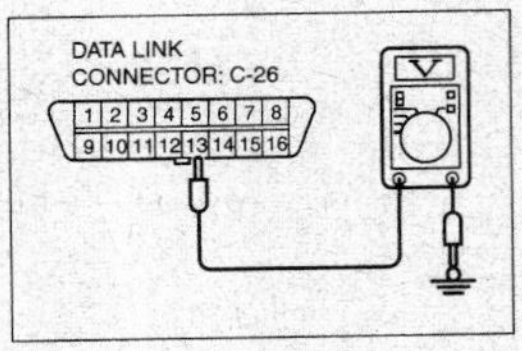

STEP 8. Check the output circuit voltage at data link connector C-26.
(1) Turn the ignition switch to "ON" position.
(2) Measure the voltage between terminal 13 and ground.
(3) Turn the ignition switch to "LOCK" (OFF) position.

Q: Is the voltage approximately 4 volts or more?
- **YES :** Check that the malfunction is eliminated. If the malfunction is eliminated, replace the auto-cruise control-ECU. Then check that the malfunction is eliminated.
- **NO :** Go to Step 9.

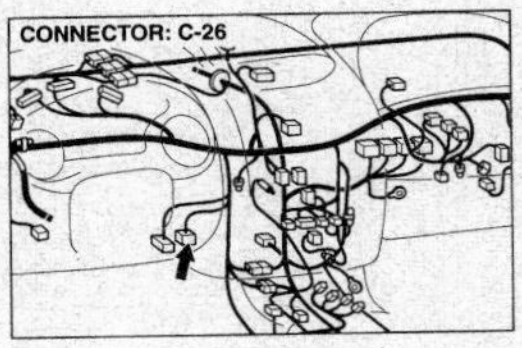

STEP 9. Check data link connector C-26.
Q: Is the connector damaged?
- **YES :** Repair or replace connector. Then check that the malfunction is eliminated.
- **NO :** Go to Step 10.

CR1100000676050X

Fig. 80 Scan Tool Communication Not Possible (Part 5 of 7). 2001–03 Sebring & Stratus Coupe

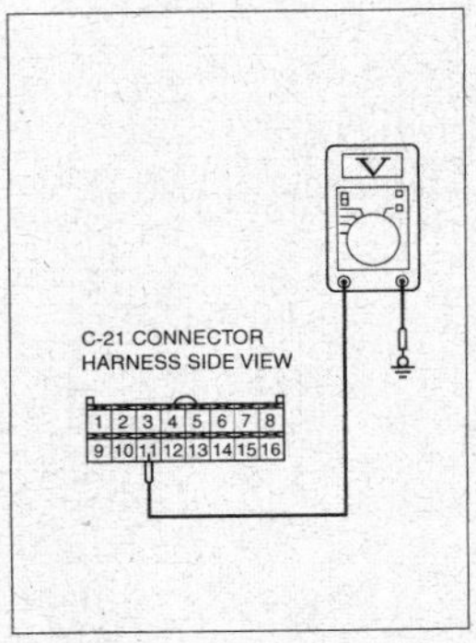

STEP10. Check the output circuit voltage at auto-cruise control-ECU connector C-21 by backprobing.
(1) Do not disconnect auto-cruise control switch connector C-21.
(2) Turn the ignition switch to "ON" position.
(3) Measure the voltage between terminal 11 and ground by backprobing.
(4) Turn the ignition switch to "LOCK" (OFF) position.

Q: Is the voltage approximately 4 volts or more?
- **YES :** Go to Step 11.
- **NO :** Go to Step 12.

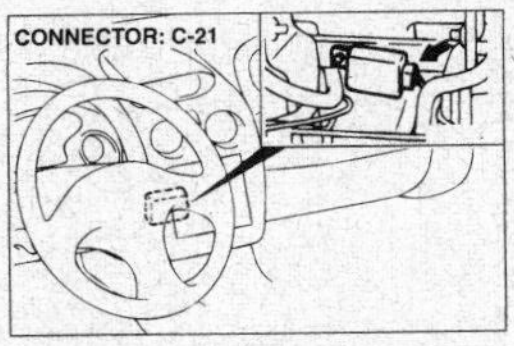

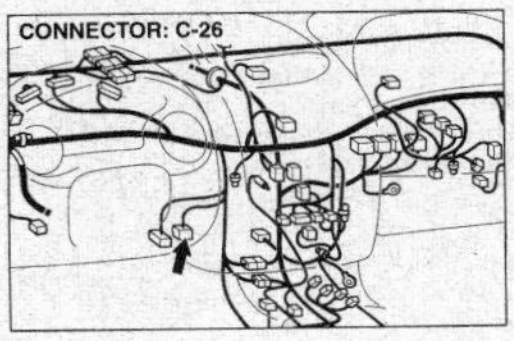

STEP 11. Check the harness wire between auto-cruise control-ECU connector C-21 and data link connector C-26.
Q: Is any harness wire between auto-cruise control-ECU connector C-21 and data link connector C-26 damaged?
- **YES :** Repair the harness wire and then check that the malfunction is eliminated.
- **NO :** Check that the malfunction is eliminated. If the malfunction is eliminated, replace the auto-cruise control-ECU. Then check that the malfunction is eliminated.

CR1100000676060X

Fig. 80 Scan Tool Communication Not Possible (Part 6 of 7). 2001–03 Sebring & Stratus Coupe

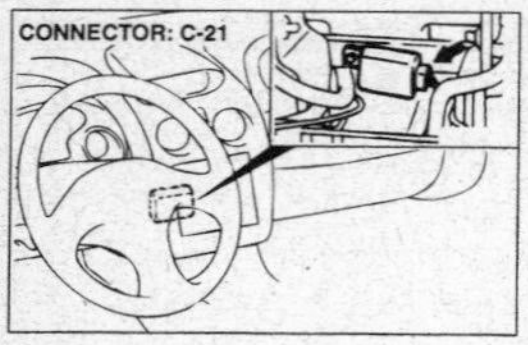

STEP 12. Check auto-cruise control-ECU connector C-21.
Q: Is the connector damaged?
YES : Repair or replace connector.
Then check that the malfunction is eliminated.
NO : Check that the malfunction is eliminated.
If the malfunction is eliminated, replace the auto-cruise control-ECU.
Then check that the malfunction is eliminated.

CR1100000676070X

Fig. 80 Scan Tool Communication Not Possible (Part 7 of 7). 2001–03 Sebring & Stratus Coupe

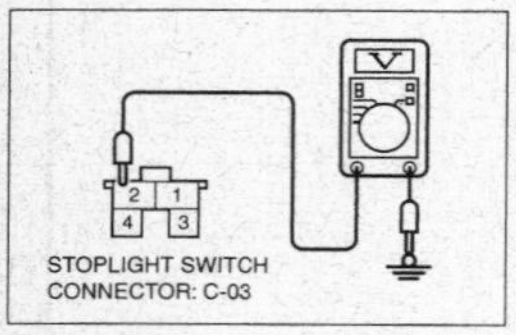

STEP 2. Check the 12-Volt supply circuit voltage at stoplight switch connector C-03.
(1) Disconnect stoplight switch connector C-03 and measure at the harness side.
(2) Measure the voltage between terminal 2 and ground.
Q: Is the voltage approximately battery positive voltage?
YES : Go to Step 6.
NO : Go to Step 3.

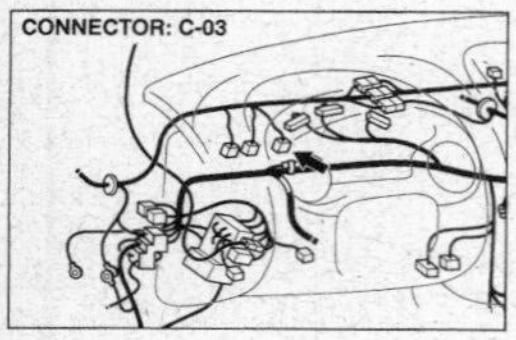

STEP 3. Check stoplight switch connector C-03.
Q: Is the connector damaged?
YES : Repair or replace connector.
Then check that the malfunction is eliminated.
NO : Go to Step 4.

CR1100000677020X

Fig. 81 Cruise Control Does Not Cancel When Brakes Are Applied (Part 2 of 6). 2001–03 Sebring & Stratus Coupe

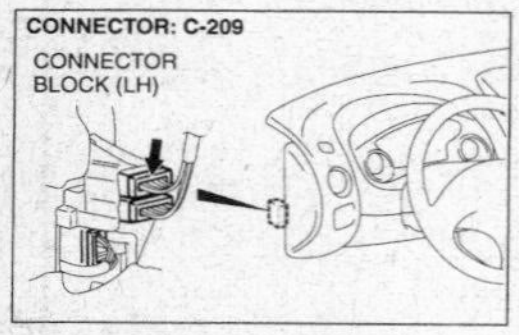

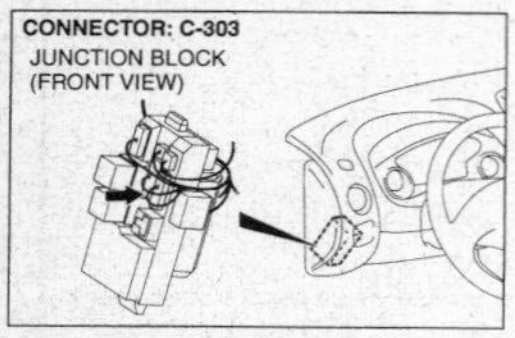

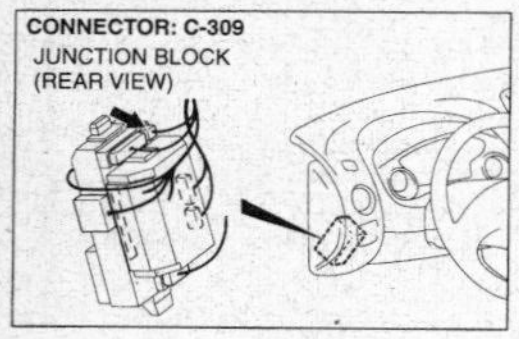

STEP 4. Check intermediate connector C-209 and junction connector C-303 and C-309.
Q: Is any connectors damaged?
YES : Repair or replace connector.
Then check that the malfunction is eliminated.
NO : Go to Step 5.

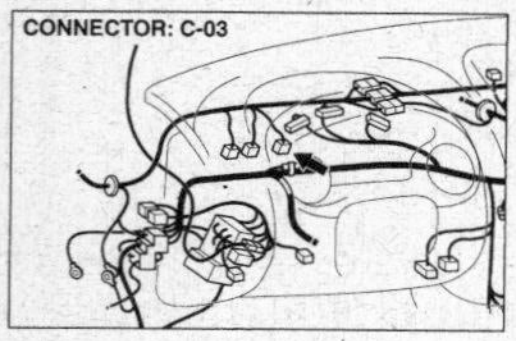

STEP 5. Check the harness wire between fusible link No.2 and stoplight switch connector C-03.
Q: Is any harness wire between fusible link No.2 and stoplight switch connector C-03 damaged?
YES : Repair the harness wire and then check that the malfunction is eliminated.
NO : Check that the malfunction is eliminated.
If the malfunction is eliminated, replace the auto-cruise control-ECU.
Then check that the malfunction is eliminated.

CR1100000677030X

Fig. 81 Cruise Control Does Not Cancel When Brakes Are Applied (Part 3 of 6). 2001–03 Sebring & Stratus Coupe

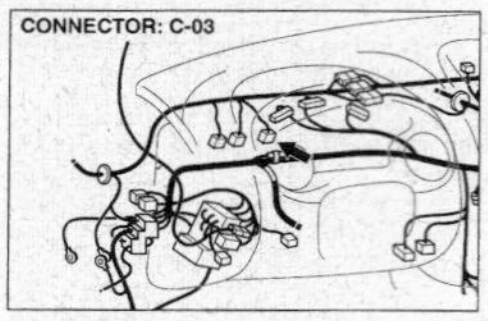

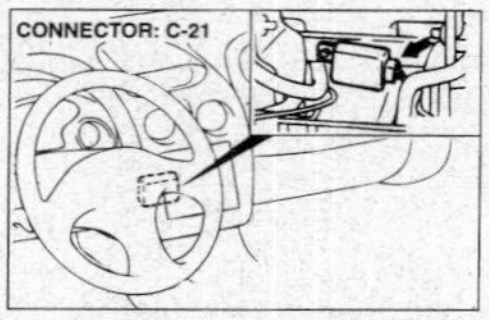

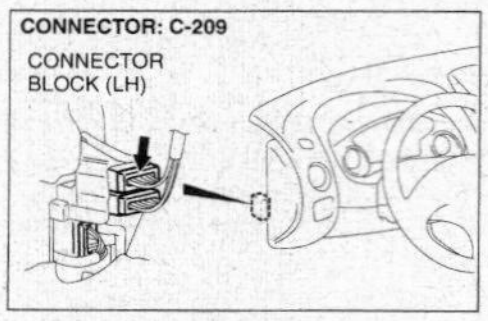

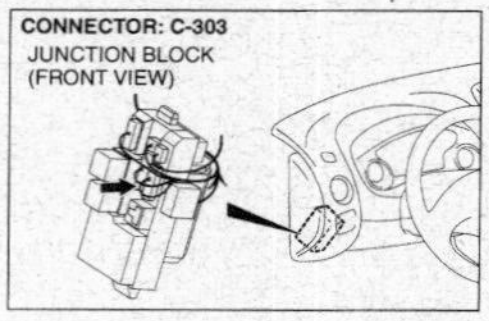

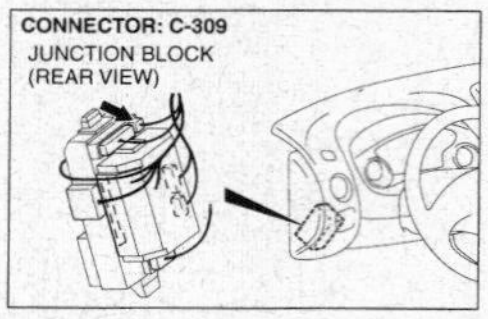

CIRCUIT OPERATION
This is the stoplight switch input signal circuit.
The signal is sent to the stoplight switch from multi-purpose fuse 3, and is then sent to the auto-cruise control-ECU.

TECHNICAL DESCRIPTION (COMMENT)
The cause is probably a malfunction of the stoplight switch circuit.

TROUBLESHOOTING HINTS
- Malfunction of the stoplight switch.
- Damaged harness or connector.
- Malfunction of the auto-cruise control-ECU.

DIAGNOSIS

Required Special Tool:
- MB991223: Harness Set

STEP 1. Check if the stoplight illuminates.
Q: Is the stoplight illuminated?
YES : Go to Step 9.
NO : Go to Step 2.

CR1100000677010X

Fig. 81 Cruise Control Does Not Cancel When Brakes Are Applied (Part 1 of 6). 2001–03 Sebring & Stratus Coupe

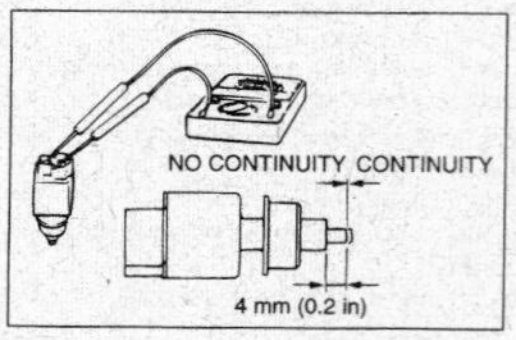

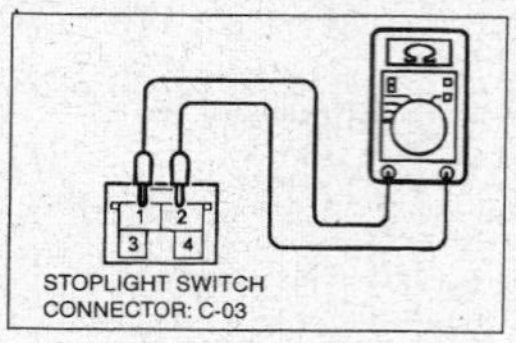

STEP 6. Check the stoplight switch.
(1) Disconnect harness connector C-03 at the stoplight switch.
(2) Connect an ohmmeter to the stoplight switch, and check continuity when the plunger of the stoplight switch is pushed in and when it is released.
(3) The stoplight switch is in good condition if the circuit is open when the plunger is pushed in to a depth of within 4 mm (0.2 inch) from the outer case edge surface, and if the resistance value is less than 2 ohm when it is released.
(4) The check for continuity should be made at terminals 1 and 2 of the stoplight switch.
Q: Is the circuit open?
YES : Replace the stoplight switch.
Then check that the malfunction is eliminated.
NO : Go to Step 7.

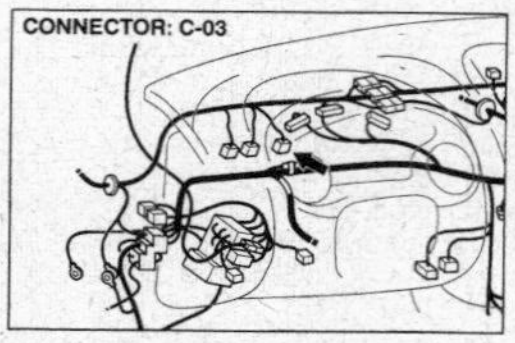

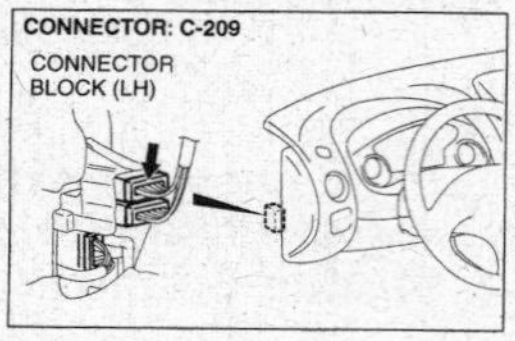

STEP 7. Check stoplight switch connector C-03 and intermediate connector C-209.
Q: Is any connector damaged?
YES : Repair or replace connector.
Then check that the malfunction is eliminated.
NO : Go to Step 8.

CR1100000677040X

Fig. 81 Cruise Control Does Not Cancel When Brakes Are Applied (Part 4 of 6). 2001–03 Sebring & Stratus Coupe

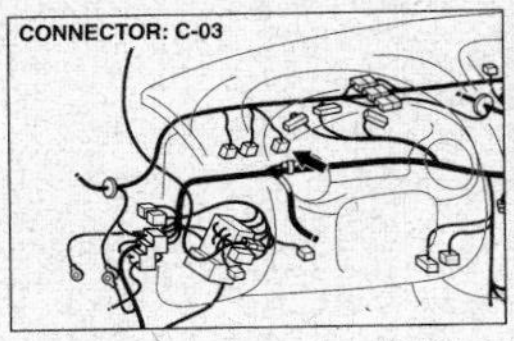

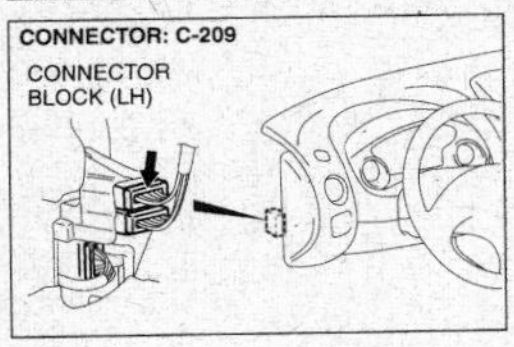

STEP 8. Check the harness wire between stoplight switch connector C-03 and intermediate connector C-209.

Q: Is any harness wire between stoplight switch connector C-03 and intermediate connector C-209 damaged?

YES : Repair the harness wire and then check that the malfunction is eliminated.

NO : Check that the malfunction is eliminated.
If the malfunction is eliminated, replace the auto-cruise control-ECU.
Then check that the malfunction is eliminated.

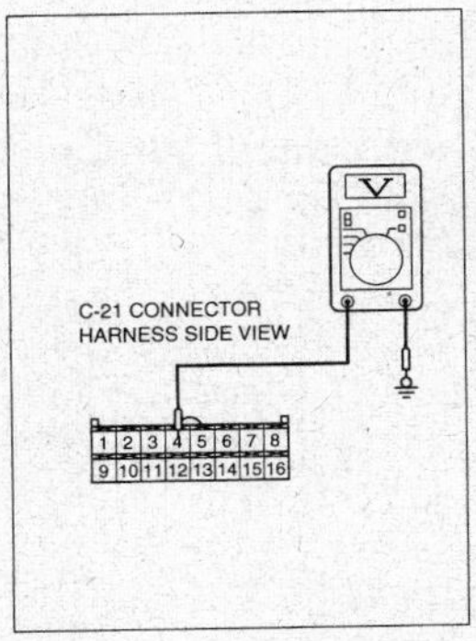

STEP 9. Check the output circuit voltage at auto-cruise control-ECU connector C-21 by backprobing.

(1) Do not disconnect auto-cruise control switch connector C-21.
(2) Turn the ignition switch to "ON" position.
(3) Measure the voltage between terminal 4 and ground by backprobing.
- Voltage should be battery positive volts. (When brake pedal is depressed.)
- Voltage should be 0.5 volts or less. (When brake pedal is not depressed.)

(4) Turn the ignition switch to "LOCK" (OFF) position.

Q: Is the voltage within specifications?

YES : Check that the malfunction is eliminated.
If the malfunction is eliminated, replace the auto-cruise control-ECU.
Then check that the malfunction is eliminated.

NO : Go to Step 10.

CR1100000677050X

Fig. 81 Cruise Control Does Not Cancel When Brakes Are Applied (Part 5 of 6). 2001–03 Sebring & Stratus Coupe

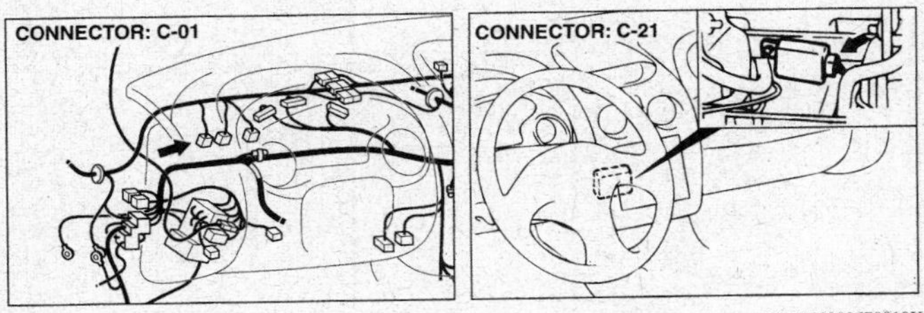

CR1100000678010X

Fig. 82 Cruise Control Does Not Cancel When Clutch Pedal Depressed (Part 1 of 5). 2001–03 Sebring & Stratus Coupe

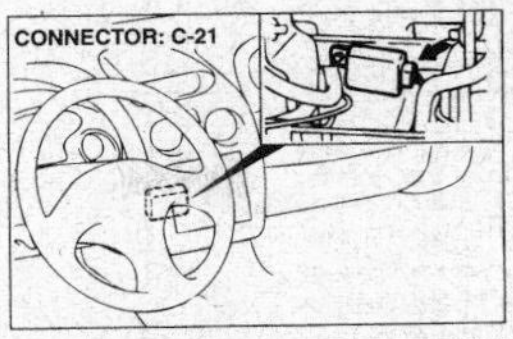

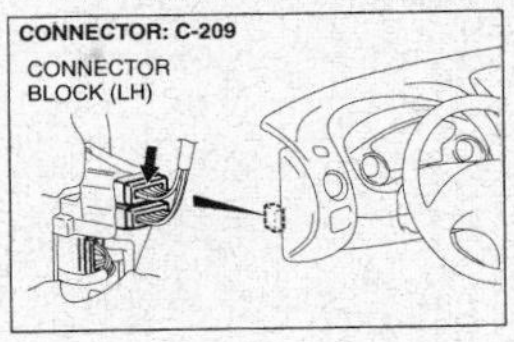

STEP 10. Check auto-cruise control-ECU connector C-21 and intermediate connector C-209.

Q: Is the connector damaged?

YES : Repair or replace connector.
Then check that the malfunction is eliminated.

NO : Go to Step 11.

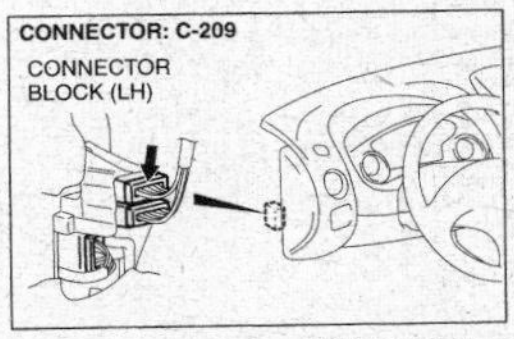

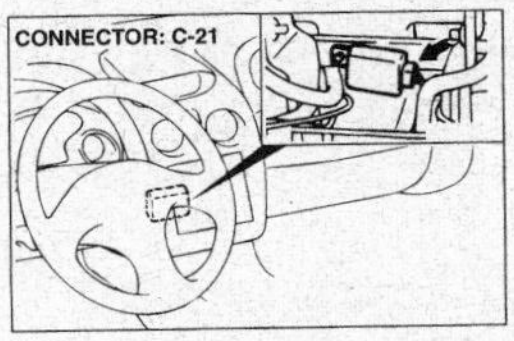

STEP 11. Check the harness wire between intermediate connector C-209 and auto-cruise control-ECU connector C-21.

Q: Is any harness wire between intermediate connector C-209 and auto-cruise control-ECU connector C-21 damaged?

YES : Repair the harness wire and then check that the malfunction is eliminated.

NO : Check that the malfunction is eliminated.
If the malfunction is eliminated, replace the auto-cruise control-ECU
Then check that the malfunction is eliminated.

CR1100000677060X

Fig. 81 Cruise Control Does Not Cancel When Brakes Are Applied (Part 6 of 6). 2001–03 Sebring & Stratus Coupe

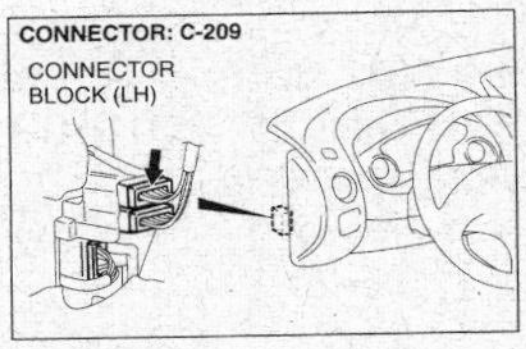

CIRCUIT OPERATION

This circuit indicates the operation status of the clutch pedal position switch. When the clutch pedal position switch is ON (clutch pedal is depressed), the voltage of auto-cruise control-ECU terminal number 13 will indicate 0 volt.

TECHNICAL DESCRIPTION (COMMENT)

The cause is probably a malfunction of the clutch pedal position switch circuit.

TROUBLESHOOTING HINTS

- Malfunction of the clutch pedal position switch.
- Damaged harness or connector.
- Malfunction of the auto-cruise control-ECU.

DIAGNOSIS

STEP 1. Check the clutch pedal position switch.

1.Disconnect clutch pedal position switch connector C-01.
2.Measure the continuity between the terminals.

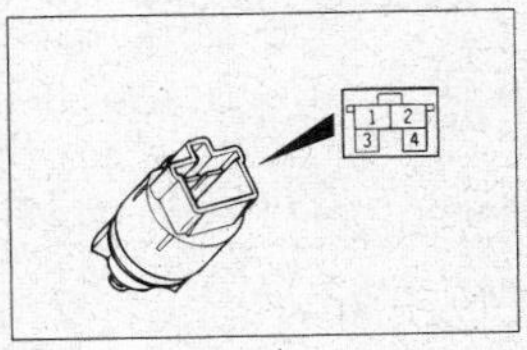

MEASUREMENT CONDITIONS	TERMINAL CONNECTOR OF TESTER	SPECIFIED CONDITION
When clutch pedal is depressed.	1 - 2	Continuity
When clutch pedal is not depressed.	1 - 2	No continuity

Q: Is the continuity meet the table above?

Yes : Go to Step 2.

No : Replace the clutch pedal position switch.
Then check that the malfunction is eliminated.

CR1100000678020X

Fig. 82 Cruise Control Does Not Cancel When Clutch Pedal Depressed (Part 2 of 5). 2001–03 Sebring & Stratus Coupe

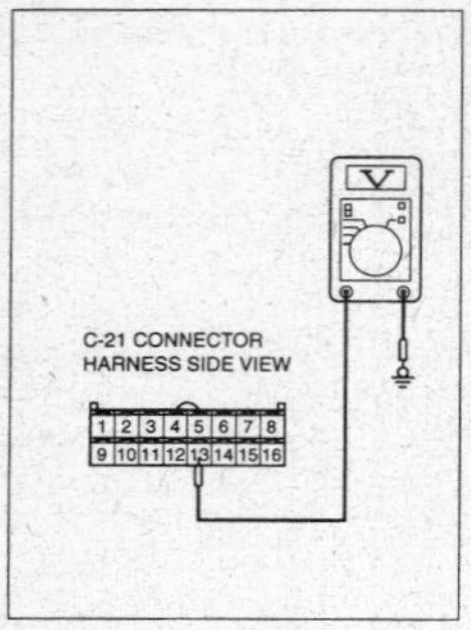

STEP 2. Check the output circuit voltage at auto-cruise control-ECU connector C-21 by backprobing.

(1) Do not disconnect auto-cruise control switch connector C-21.
(2) Turn the ignition switch to "ON" position.
(3) Measure the voltage between terminal 13 and ground by backprobing.
- Voltage should be 0.5 volts or less. (When clutch pedal is depressed.)
- Voltage should be battery positive voltage. (When clutch pedal is not depressed.)

Q: Is the voltage within specifications?

YES : Check that the malfunction is eliminated. If the malfunction is eliminated, replace the auto-cruise control-ECU. Then check that the malfunction is eliminated.

NO : Go to Step 3.

CR1100000678030X

Fig. 82 Cruise Control Does Not Cancel When Clutch Pedal Depressed (Part 3 of 5). 2001–03 Sebring & Stratus Coupe

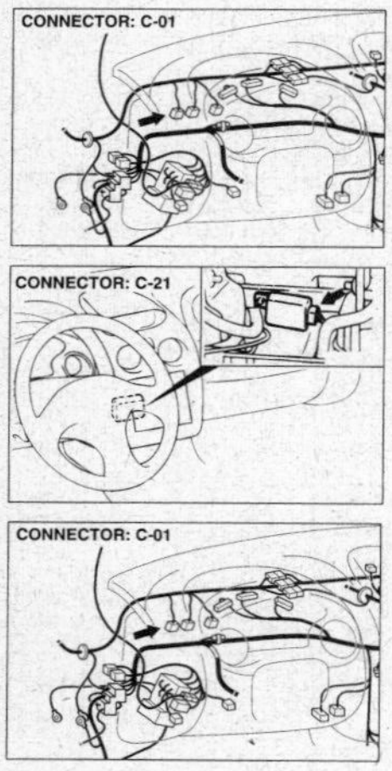

STEP 4. Check the harness wire between clutch pedal position switch connector C-01 and auto-cruise control-ECU connector C-21.

Q: Is any harness wire between clutch pedal position switch connector C-01 and auto-cruise control-ECU connector C-21 damaged?

YES : Repair the harness wire and then check that the malfunction is eliminated.

NO : Go to Step 5.

STEP 5. Check the harness wire between clutch pedal position switch connector C-01 and ground wire.

Q: Is any harness wire between clutch pedal position switch connector C-01 and ground wire damaged?

YES : Repair the harness wire and then check that the malfunction is eliminated.

NO : Check that the malfunction is eliminated. If the malfunction is eliminated, replace the auto-cruise control-ECU. Then check that the malfunction is eliminated.

CR1100000678050A

Fig. 82 Cruise Control Does Not Cancel When Clutch Pedal Depressed (Part 5 of 5). 2001–03 Sebring & Stratus Coupe

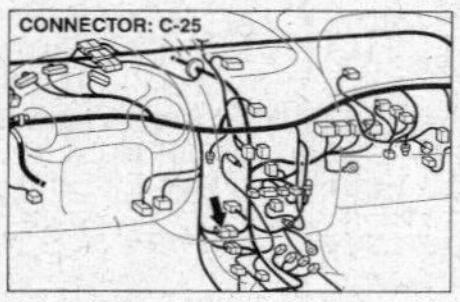

CIRCUIT OPERATION

This circuit transmits the "N" or "P" position signal of the park/neutral position switch to the auto-cruise control-ECU.
When the park/neutral position switch is at the "N" or "P" position, auto-cruise control-ECU terminal number 13 will receives 0 volt.

TECHNICAL DESCRIPTION (COMMENT)

The cause is probably an open-circuit in the output signal circuit in "N" range.

TROUBLESHOOTING HINTS

- Malfunction of the park/neutral position switch.
- Damaged harness or connector.
- Malfunction of the auto-cruise control-ECU.

DIAGNOSIS

Required Special Tool:

- MB991223: Harness Set

STEP 1. Check the output circuit voltage at park/neutral position switch connector B-111 by backprobing.

(1) Do not disconnect park/neutral position switch connector B-111.
(2) Turn the ignition switch to "ON" position.
(3) Measure the voltage between terminal 10 and ground by backprobing.
- Voltage should be battery positive voltage. (When select lever is in a position other than "N" range.)
- Voltage should be 0.5 volts or less. (When select lever is in "N" range.)

(4) Turn the ignition switch to "LOCK" (OFF) position.

Q: Is the voltage within specifications?

YES : Check that the malfunction is eliminated. If the malfunction is eliminated, replace the auto-cruise control-ECU. Then check that the malfunction is eliminated.

NO : Go to Step 2.

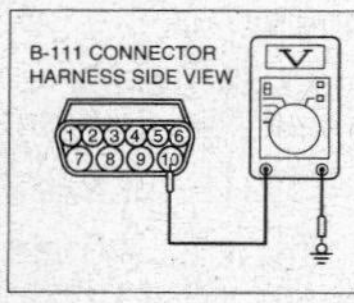

CR1100000679020X

Fig. 83 Cruise Control Does Not Cancel When Selector Moved To N Position (Part 2 of 5). 2001–03 Sebring & Stratus Coupe

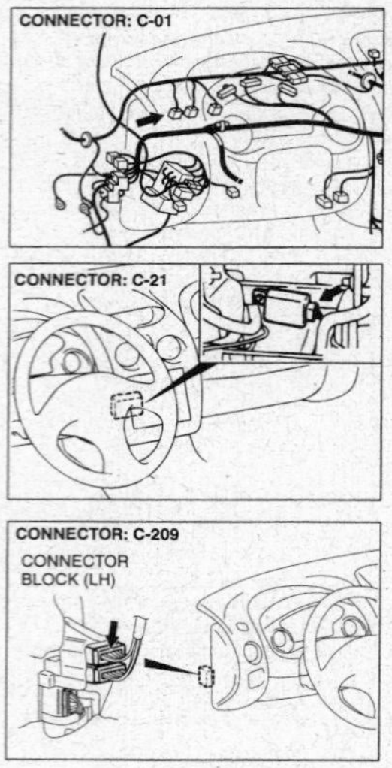

STEP 3. Check clutch pedal position switch connector C-01 and auto-cruise control-ECU connector C-21 and intermediate connector C-209.

Q: Is any connector damaged?

YES : Repair or replace connector. Then check that the malfunction is eliminated.

NO : Go to Step 4.

CR1100000678040X

Fig. 82 Cruise Control Does Not Cancel When Clutch Pedal Depressed (Part 4 of 5). 2001–03 Sebring & Stratus Coupe

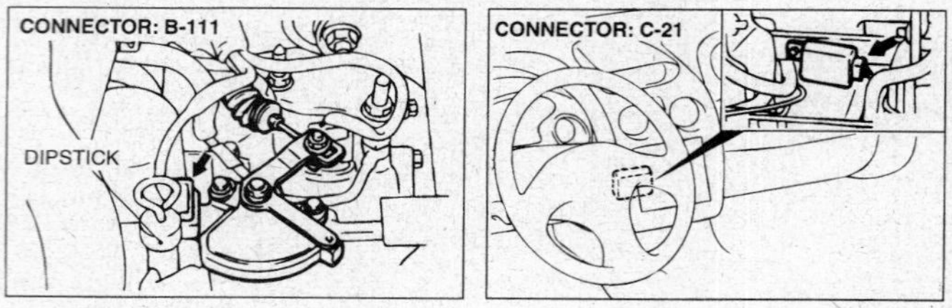

CR1100000679010X

Fig. 83 Cruise Control Does Not Cancel When Selector Moved To N Position (Part 1 of 5). 2001–03 Sebring & Stratus Coupe

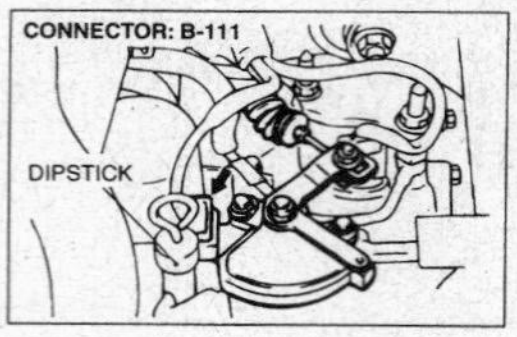

STEP 2. park/neutral position switch connector B-111.

Q: Is the connector damaged?

YES : Repair or replace connector. Then check that the malfunction is eliminated.

NO : Go to Step 3.

STEP 3. Check the circuit at the park/neutral position switch.

(1) Disconnect the park/neutral position switch connector B-111.
(2) Measure the continuity park/neutral position switch connector terminals.

ITEMS	TERMINAL CONNECTOR OF TESTER	SPECIFIED CONDITION
P	3 - 8, 9 - 10	Less than 2 ohm.
N	4 - 8, 9 - 10	

Q: Is the continuity meet the table above?

YES : Go to Step 4.

NO : Replace the park/neutral position switch. Then check that the malfunction is eliminated.

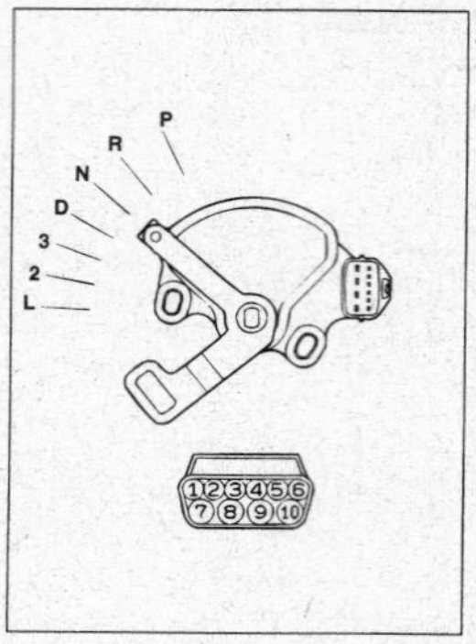

CR1100000679030X

Fig. 83 Cruise Control Does Not Cancel When Selector Moved To N Position (Part 3 of 5). 2001–03 Sebring & Stratus Coupe

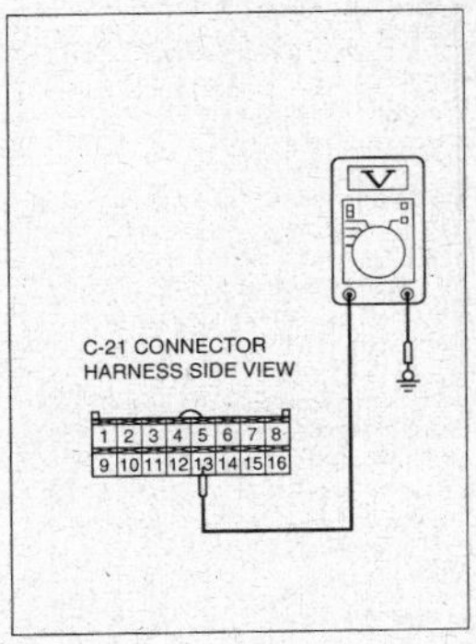

STEP 4. Check the output circuit voltage at auto-cruise control-ECU connector C-21 by backprobing.

(1) Do not disconnect auto-cruise control switch connector C-21.
(2) Turn the ignition switch to "ON" position.
(3) Measure the voltage between terminal 13 and ground by backprobing.
- Voltage should be battery positive voltage. (When select lever is in a position other than "N" range.)
- Voltage should be 0.5 volts or less. (When select lever is in "N" range.)

(4) Turn the ignition switch to "LOCK" (OFF) position.

Q: Is the voltage within specifications?

YES : Check that the malfunction is eliminated. If the malfunction is eliminated, replace the auto-cruise control-ECU. Then check that the malfunction is eliminated.

NO : Go to Step 5.

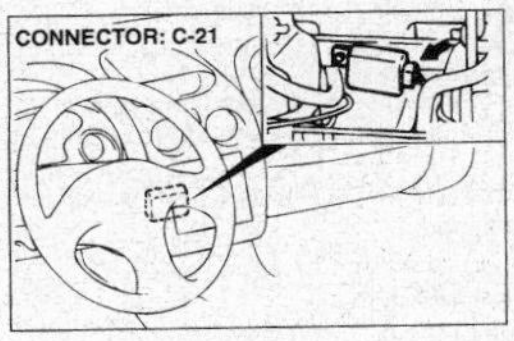

STEP 5. Check auto-cruise control-ECU connector C-21.

Q: Is the connector damaged?

YES : Repair or replace connector. Then check that the malfunction is eliminated.

NO : Go to Step 6.

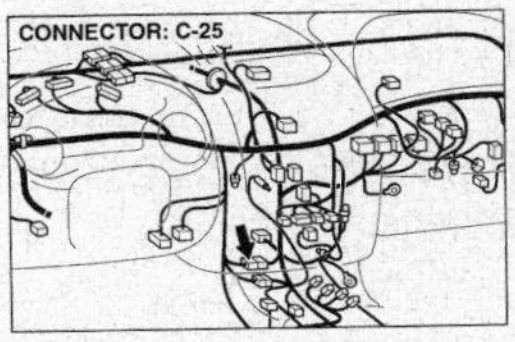

STEP 6. Check intermediate connector C-25.

Q: Is the connector damaged?

YES : Repair or replace connector. Then check that the malfunction is eliminated.

NO : Go to Step 7.

CR1100000679040X

Fig. 83 Cruise Control Does Not Cancel When Selector Moved To N Position (Part 4 of 5). 2001–03 Sebring & Stratus Coupe

TECHNICAL DESCRIPTION (COMMENT)

The fail-safe function is probably cancelling auto-cruise control.
In this case, scan tool MB991502 can be used to check the trouble symptoms in each system by checking the diagnostic trouble codes.
The scan tool can also be used to check if the circuits of each input switch are normal or not by checking the input switch codes.

TROUBLESHOOTING HINTS

- Malfunction of the auto-cruise control switch.
- Malfunction of the auto-cruise control-ECU.
- Malfunction of the auto-cruise control switch.
- Malfunction of the auto-cruise control-ECU.

CR1100000680010A

Fig. 85 Cruise Control Cannot Be Set (Part 1 of 3). 2001–03 Sebring & Stratus Coupe

DIAGNOSIS

Required Special Tools:
MB991502: Scan Tool (MUT-II)
MB991223: Harness Set

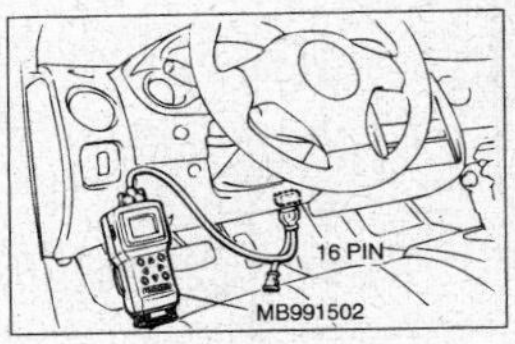

STEP 1. Can the auto-cruise control-ECU communicate with scan tool MB991502?

⚠ CAUTION

To prevent damage to scan tool MB991502, always turn the ignition switch to "LOCK"(OFF) position before connecting or disconnecting scan tool MB991502.

(1) Using scan tool MB991502.
(2) Connect scan tool MB991502 to the data link connector.
(3) Turn the ignition switch to "ON" position.

Q: Can the auto-cruise control-ECU communicate with the scan tool?

YES : Go to Step 2.

NO : Inspect each trouble symptom.

STEP 2. Is any diagnostic trouble code output?

Q: Is any diagnostic trouble code output?

YES : Diagnostic trouble code number 11, 12, 14, 15, 16 or 17 is output, refer to the following. Then check that the malfunction is eliminated.

NO : Go to Step 3.

CR1100000680020A

Fig. 85 Cruise Control Cannot Be Set (Part 2 of 3). 2001–03 Sebring & Stratus Coupe

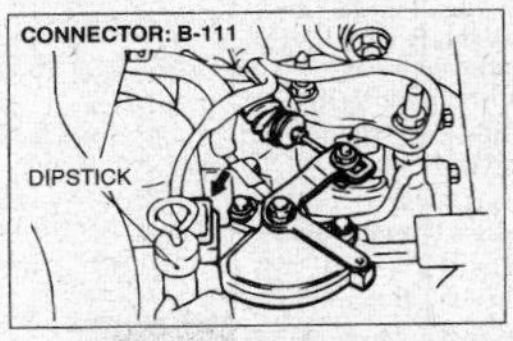

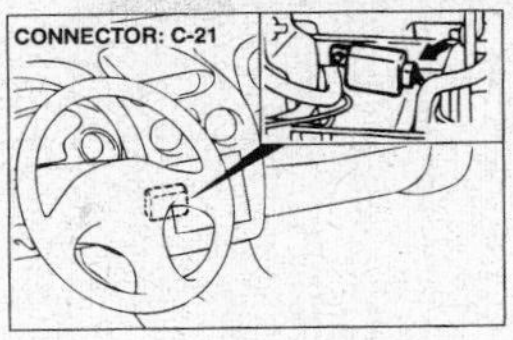

STEP 7. Check the harness wire between park/neutral position switch connector B-111 and auto-cruise control-ECU connector C-21.

Q: Is any harness wire between park/neutral position switch connector B-111 and auto-cruise control-ECU connector C-21 damaged?

YES : Repair the harness wire and then check that the malfunction is eliminated.

NO : Check that the malfunction is eliminated. If the malfunction is eliminated, replace the auto-cruise control-ECU. Then check that the malfunction is eliminated.

CR1100000679050X

Fig. 83 Cruise Control Does Not Cancel When Selector Moved To N Position (Part 5 of 5). 2001–03 Sebring & Stratus Coupe

TECHNICAL DESCRIPTION (COMMENT)

The cause is probably an open-circuit in the output in the circuit inside the "CANCEL" switch.

TROUBLESHOOTING HINTS

- Malfunction of the auto-cruise control switch.

DIAGNOSIS

Replace the auto-cruise control switch.
Then check the malfunction is eliminated.

CR1100000680010X

Fig. 84 Cruise Control Does Not Cancel When CANCEL Switch Is Set To On. 2001–03 Sebring & Stratus Coupe

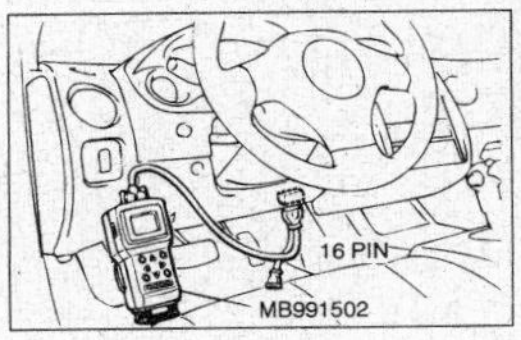

STEP 3.Using scan tool MB991502, check data list.

⚠ CAUTION

To prevent damage to scan tool MB991502, always turn the ignition switch to "LOCK"(OFF) position before connecting or disconnecting scan tool MB991502.

(1) Using scan tool MB991502.
(2) Connect scan tool MB991502 to the data link connector.
(3) Check the following items in the data list.
- Item 04: Auto-cruise control "CANCEL" switch.
- Item 05: Stoplight switch.
- Item 14: Clutch pedal position switch <M/T>.
- Item 14: Park/neutral position switch <A/T>.

(4) Turn the ignition switch to "ON" position.

Q: Is the check above meet the specifications?

YES : Check that the malfunction is eliminated. If the malfunction is eliminated, replace the auto-cruise control-ECU. Then that the malfunction is eliminated.

NO : Follow the diagnostic trouble code procedures and the symptom procedures below.

CR1100000680030A

Fig. 85 Cruise Control Cannot Be Set (Part 3 of 3). 2001–03 Sebring & Stratus Coupe

TECHNICAL DESCRIPTION (COMMENT)

The cause is probably the malfunction of the vehicle speed sensor or incorrect vacuum in the auto-cruise control vacuum pump or actuator.

TROUBLESHOOTING HINTS

- Malfunction of the vehicle speed sensor.
- Malfunction of the auto-cruise control vacuum pump.
- Malfunction of the actuator.
- Malfunction of the auto-cruise control-ECU.

DIAGNOSIS

Required Special Tool:
- MB991223: Harness Set

CR1100000681010X

Fig. 86 Hunting At Set Speed (Part 1 of 3). 2001–03 Sebring & Stratus Coupe

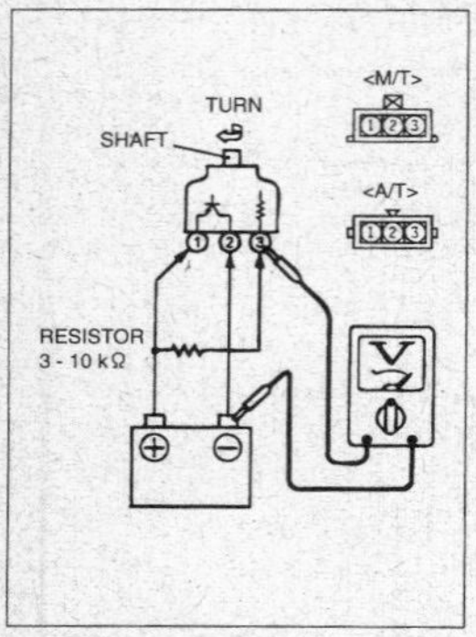

STEP 1. Check the vehicle speed sensor.

(1) Remove the vehicle speed sensor and connect a 3 - 10-kΩ resistor as shown in the illustration.

(2) Turn the shaft of the vehicle speed sensor and check that there is voltage between terminals 2 - 3. (one turn = four pulses)

Q: Is the voltage within specifications?

YES : Go to Step 2.

NO : Replace the vehicle speed sensor. Then check that the malfunction is eliminated.

CR1100000681020X

Fig. 86 Hunting At Set Speed (Part 2 of 3). 2001–03 Sebring & Stratus Coupe

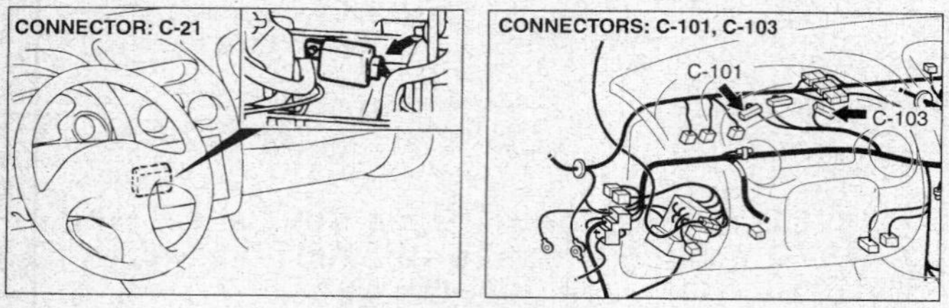

CR1100000682010X

Fig. 87 Cruise Control Indicator Does Not Illuminate (Part 1 of 7). 2001–03 Sebring & Stratus Coupe

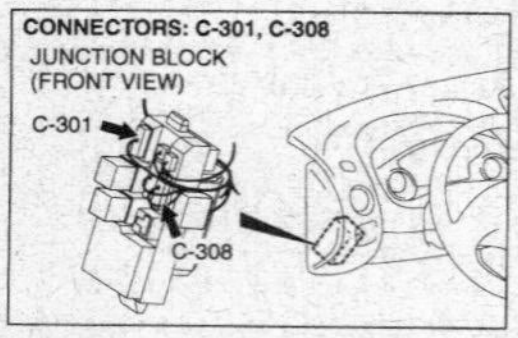

CIRCUIT OPERATION

The power for the auto-cruise indicator in the combination meter is supplied from the ignition switch (IG1).

When the auto-cruise control system is operating, the transistor inside the auto-cruise control-ECU illuminates the auto-cruise indicator through ECU terminal number 15.

TECHNICAL DESCRIPTION (COMMENT)

The cause is probably the malfunction of the indicator bulb or the malfunction of the connector or harness.

TROUBLESHOOTING HINTS

- Malfunction of the indicator bulb.
- Damaged harness or connector.
- Malfunction of the auto-cruise control-ECU.

DIAGNOSIS

Required Special Tool:

- MB991223: Harness Set

STEP 1. Check the auto-cruise control indicator bulb.

(1) Remove the combination meter.

(2) Check the auto-cruise control indicator bulb.

Q: Is the bulb blown?

YES : Replace the bulb. Then check that the malfunction is eliminated.

No : Go to Step 2.

CR1100000682020X

Fig. 87 Cruise Control Indicator Does Not Illuminate (Part 2 of 7). 2001–03 Sebring & Stratus Coupe

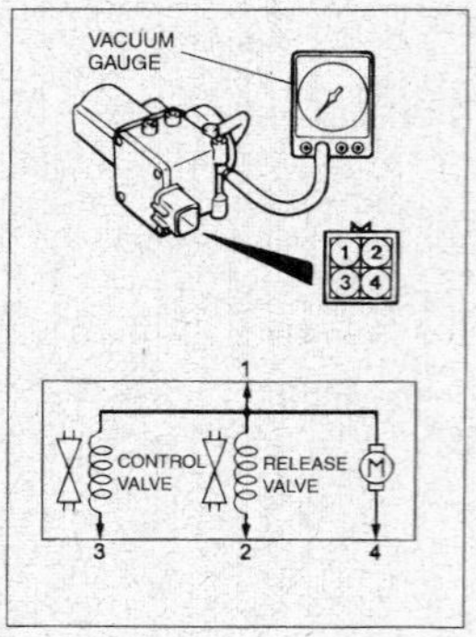

STEP2. Check the auto-cruise vacuum pump.

(1) Disconnect the vacuum hose from the auto-cruise vacuum pump and connect a vacuum gauge to the vacuum pump.

(2) Disconnect the vacuum pump connector.

(3) Check the auto-cruise vacuum pump and valves according to the following procedure:

- Connect the positive battery terminal to auto-cruise vacuum pump connector terminal 1, and the negative battery terminal to terminals 2, 3, and 4.
  Then the vacuum gauge should read 27 kPa (8.0 in Hg) or more.
- The vacuum should be maintained when terminal 4 is disconnected from the negative battery terminal while terminals 1, 2, and 3 remain connected.
  Then the vacuum gauge should read 0 kPa (0 in Hg) when terminal 2 is disconnected from the negative battery terminal while terminals 1, and 3 remain connected.
- The vacuum should be maintained when terminal 4 is disconnected from the negative battery terminal while terminals 1, 2, and 3 remain connected.
  Then check the vacuum gauge should read 0 kPa (0 in Hg) when terminal 3 is disconnected from the negative battery terminal while terminals 1, and 2 remain connected.

Q: Are all of the above values satisfied?

Yes : Go to Step 3.

No : Replace the auto-cruise vacuum pump. Then that the malfunction is eliminated.

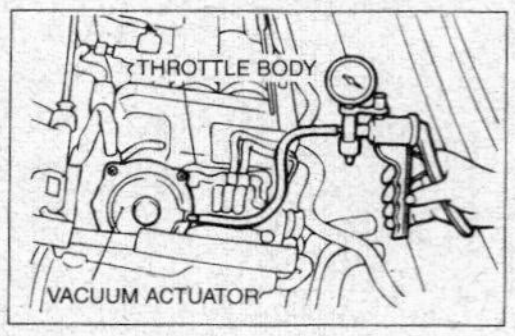

STEP 3. Check the vacuum actuator.

(1) Disconnect the vacuum hose from the vacuum actuator, and then connect a hand vacuum pump to the vacuum actuator.

(2) Apply a vacuum and check that the throttle lever moves and the vacuum is maintained.

Q: Is the vacuum actuator damaged?

YES : Replace the vacuum actuator. Then check that the malfunction is eliminated.

NO : Check that the malfunction is eliminated. If the malfunction is eliminated, replace the auto-cruise control-ECU. Then check that the malfunction is eliminated.

CR1100000681030X

Fig. 86 Hunting At Set Speed (Part 3 of 3). 2001–03 Sebring & Stratus Coupe

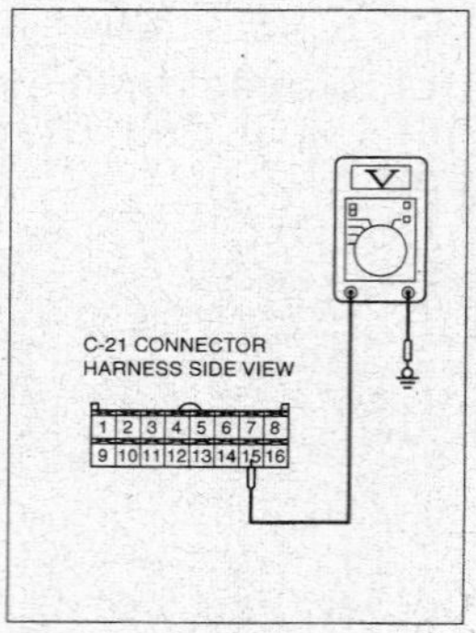

STEP 2. Check the output circuit voltage at auto-cruise control-ECU connector C-21 by backprobing.

(1) Do not disconnect auto-cruise control switch connector C-21.

(2) Turn the ignition switch to "ON" position.

(3) Measure the voltage between terminal 15 and ground by backprobing.

(4) Turn the ignition switch to "LOCK" (OFF) position.

Q: Is the voltage approximately battery positive voltage?

YES : Check that the malfunction is eliminated. If the malfunction is eliminated, replace the auto-cruise control-ECU. Then check that the malfunction is eliminated.

NO : Go to Step 3.

CR1100000682030X

Fig. 87 Cruise Control Indicator Does Not Illuminate (Part 3 of 7). 2001–03 Sebring & Stratus Coupe

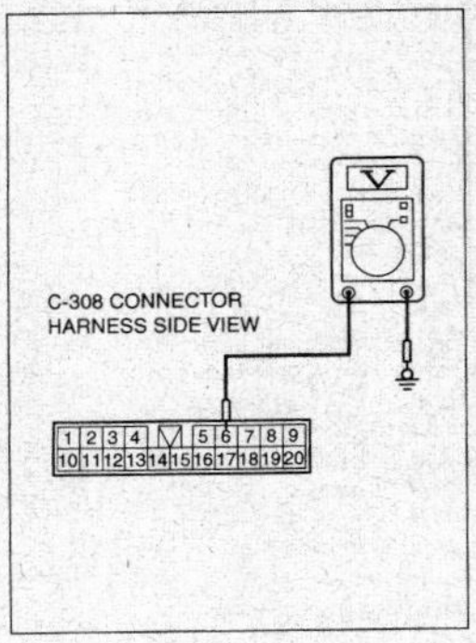

STEP 3. Check the output circuit voltage at junction block connector C-308 by backprobing.

(1) Do not disconnect auto-cruise control switch connector C-308.
(2) Turn the ignition switch to "ON" position.
(3) Measure the voltage between terminal 6 and ground by backprobing.
(4) Turn the ignition switch to "LOCK" (OFF) position.

Q: Is the voltage approximately battery positive voltage?

YES : Go to Step 5.
NO : Go to Step 4.

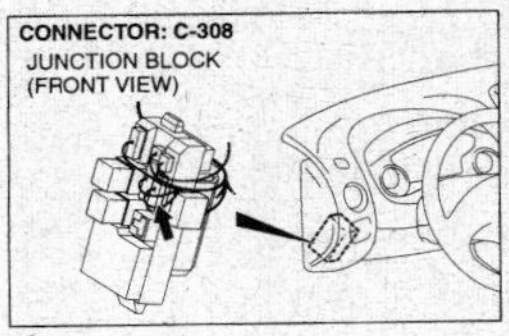

STEP 4. Check junction block connector C-308.

Q: Is the connector damaged?

YES : Repair or replace connector.
Then check that the malfunction is eliminated.
NO : Replace the junction block.
Then check that the malfunction is eliminated.

CR1100000682040X

Fig. 87 Cruise Control Indicator Does Not Illuminate (Part 4 of 7). 2001–03 Sebring & Stratus Coupe

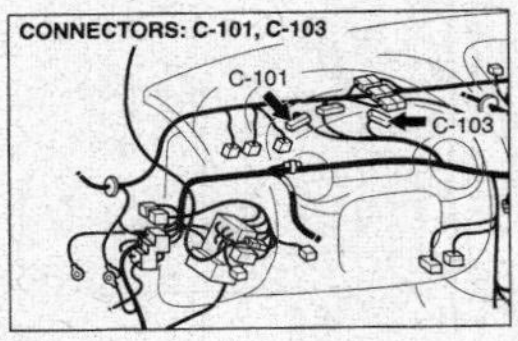

STEP 5. Check combination meter connector C-101 and C-103.

Q: Is any connector damaged?

YES : Repair or replace connector.
Then check that the malfunction is eliminated.
NO : Go to Step 6.

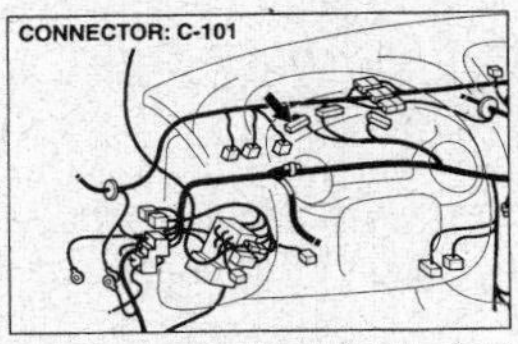

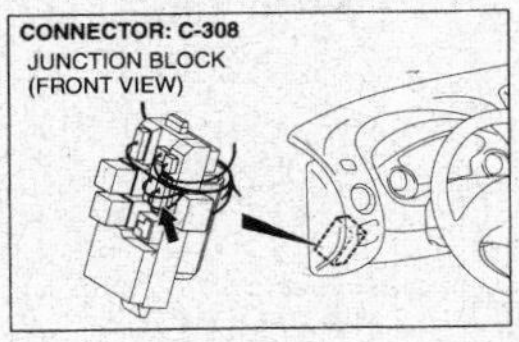

STEP 6. Check the harness wire between combination meter connector C-101 and junction block connector C-308.

Q: Is any harness wire between combination meter connector C-101 and junction block connector C-308 damaged?

YES : Repair the harness wire and then check that the malfunction is eliminated.
NO : Go to Step 7.

CR1100000682050X

Fig. 87 Cruise Control Indicator Does Not Illuminate (Part 5 of 7). 2001–03 Sebring & Stratus Coupe

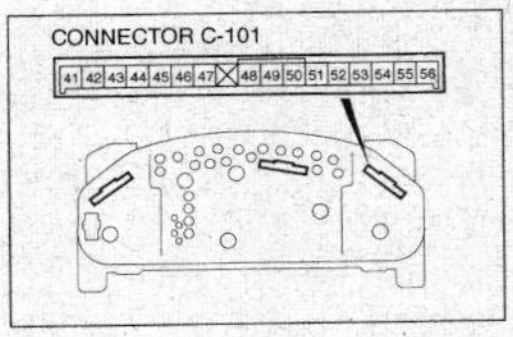

STEP 7. Check the combination meter.

(1) Remove the combination meter and measure at the combination meter side
(2) Measure the continuity between terminal 44 and 45 at conductor C-101.

Q: Is the continuity less than 2 ohm?

YES : Go to Step 8.)
NO : Replace the combination meter.
Then check that the malfunction is eliminated.

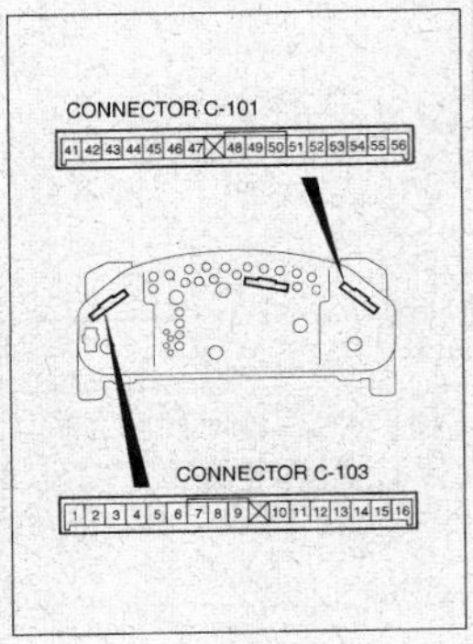

STEP 8. Check the combination meter.

(1) Remove the combination meter and measure at the combination meter side.
(2) Measure the continuity between terminal 52 at conductor C-101 and terminal 1 at conductor C-103.

Q: Is the continuity less than 2 ohm?

YES : Go to Step 9.)
NO : Replace the combination meter.
Then check that the malfunction is eliminated.

CR1100000682060X

Fig. 87 Cruise Control Indicator Does Not Illuminate (Part 6 of 7). 2001–03 Sebring & Stratus Coupe

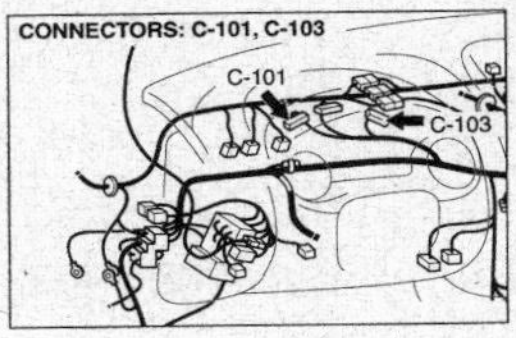

STEP 9. Check the harness wire between combination meter connector C-101 and C-103.

Q: Is any harness wire between combination meter connector C-101 and C-103 damaged?

YES : Repair the harness wire and then check that the malfunction is eliminated.
NO : Go to Step 10.

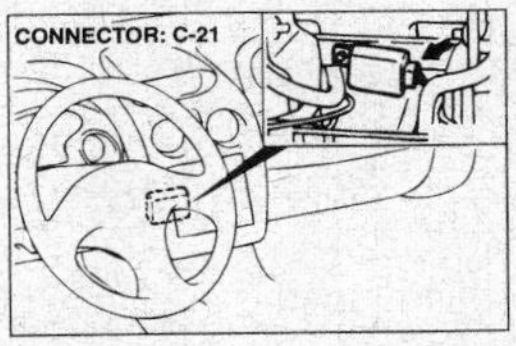

STEP 10. Check auto-cruise control-ECU connector C-21.

Q: Is the connector damaged?

YES : Repair or replace connector.
Then check that the malfunction is eliminated.
NO : Go to Step 11.

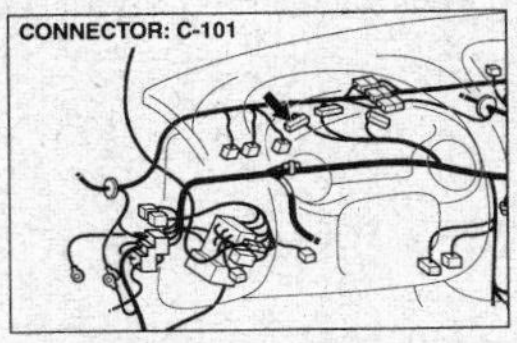

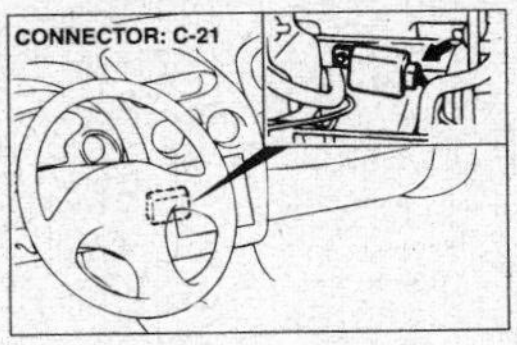

STEP 11. Check the harness wire between combination meter connector C-101 and auto-cruise control-ECU connector C-21.

Q: Is any harness wire between combination meter connector C-101 and auto-cruise control-ECU connector C-21 damaged?

YES : Repair the harness wire and then check that the malfunction is eliminated.
NO : Check that the malfunction is eliminated.
If the malfunction is eliminated, replace the auto-cruise control-ECU.
Then check that the malfunction is eliminated.

CR1100000682070X

Fig. 87 Cruise Control Indicator Does Not Illuminate (Part 7 of 7). 2001–03 Sebring & Stratus Coupe

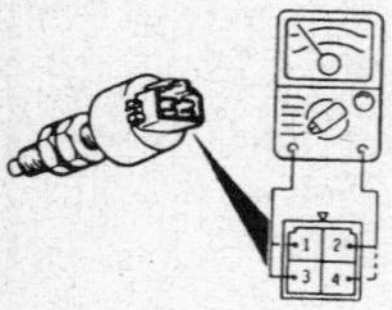

Measurement conditions	For stop light circuit terminal		For auto-cruise control circuit terminal	
	2	3	1	4
When brake pedal depressed.	O—	—O		
When brake pedal not depressed.			O—	—O

NOTE
O—O indicates that there is continuity between the terminals.

CR1109500411000X

Fig. 88 Stop lamp switch continuity inspection. Avenger & 2000 Sebring Coupe

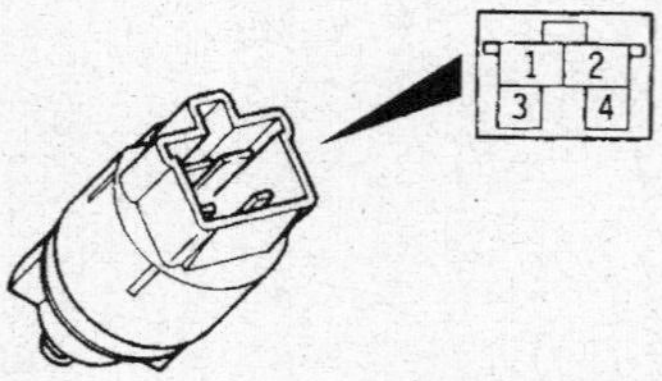

MEASUREMENT CONDITIONS	TERMINAL CONNECTOR OF TESTER	SPECIFIED CONDITION
When brake pedal is depressed. (for stoplight circuit)	1 - 2	Continuity
	3 - 4	No continuity
When brake pedal is not depressed. (for auto-cruise control circuit)	1 - 2	No continuity
	3 - 4	Continuity

CR1100200750000X

Fig. 90 Stop lamp switch continuity test. 2001–03 Sebring & Stratus Coupe

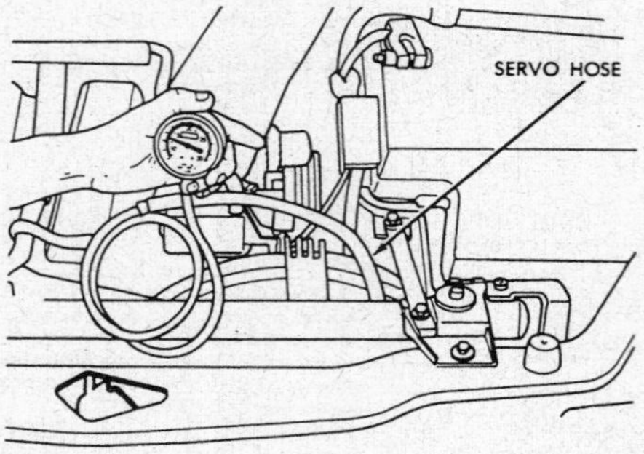

CR1109500347000X

Fig. 91 Vacuum supply test

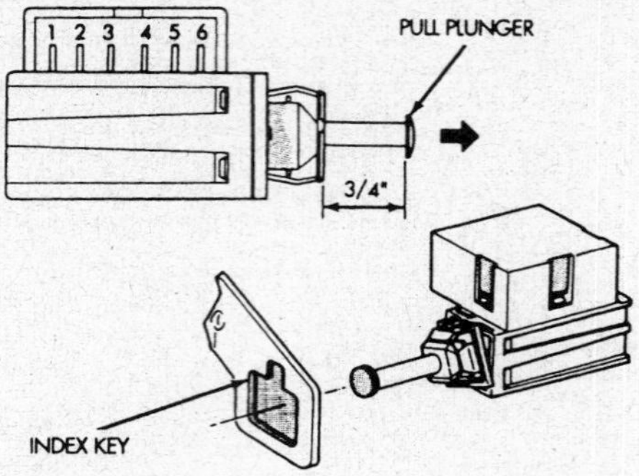

CR1109500346000X

Fig. 89 Stop lamp switch replacement. Breeze, Cirrus, Concorde, Intrepid, LHS, Neon, Sebring Convertible, Sebring Sedan, Stratus Sedan & 300M

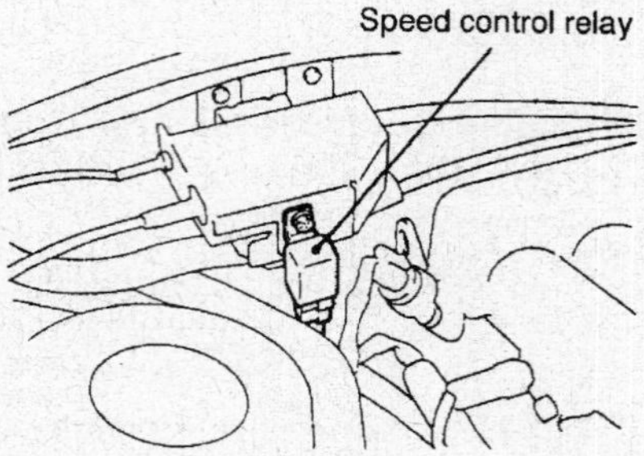

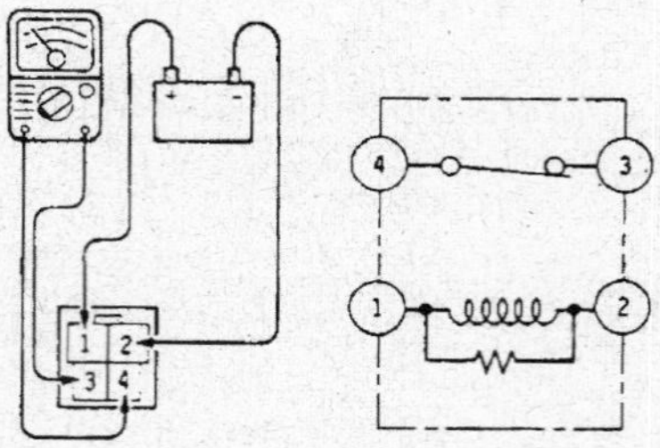

Battery voltage	Terminal No.			
	1	2	3	4
Power is not supplied	O—	—O	O—	—O
Power is supplied	⊕—	—⊖		

CR1100200742000X

Fig. 92 Speed control relay continuity test. Avenger & 2000 Sebring Coupe

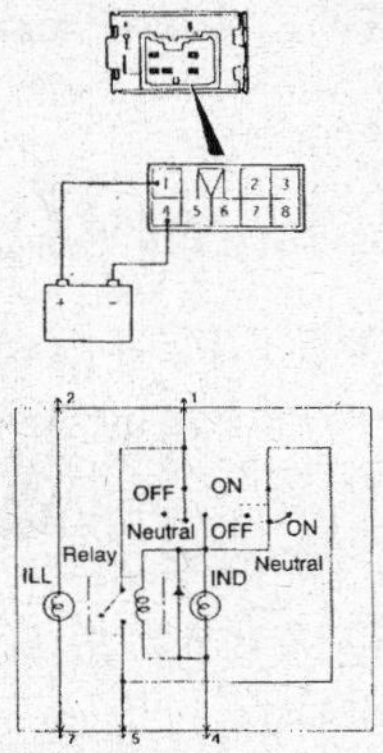

Switch position	Terminal No. 1	IND	4	5	2	ILL	7
OFF	⊕ —	—	⊖		○ —	(lamp)	— ○
Neutral	⊕ —	—	⊖ ○ —	— ○	○ —	(lamp)	— ○
ON	⊕ — ○ —	— (lamp)	⊖ — ○	○	○ —	(lamp)	— ○

CR1100200743000X

Fig. 93 On/Off Switch continuity inspection. Avenger & 2000 Sebring Coupe

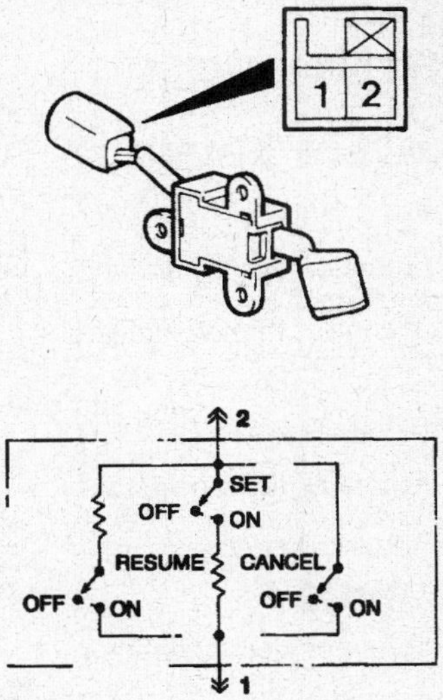

Switch position	Resistance between terminals
Switch OFF	No continuity
CANCEL switch ON	Approx. 0 Ω
RESUME switch ON	Approx. 820 Ω
SET switch ON	Approx. 2,700 Ω

CR1100200744000X

Fig. 94 Speed control switch continuity test. Avenger & 2000 Sebring Coupe

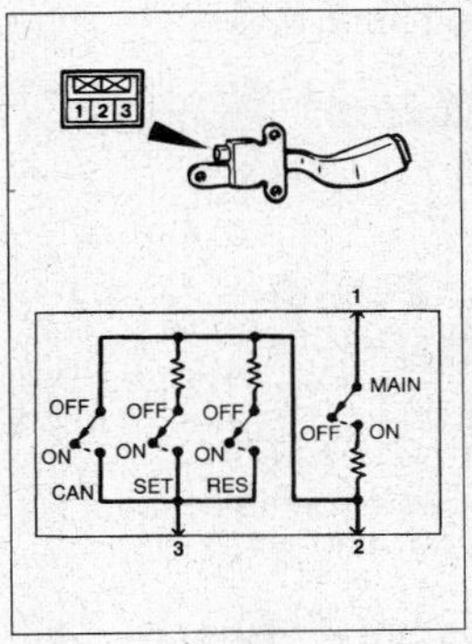

SWITCH POSITION	RESISTANCE BETWEEN TERMINALS	
"MAIN" switch "OFF"	Terminals 1 and 2	Less than 2 ohm
"MAIN" switch "ON"	Terminals 1 and 2	Approximately 3.9 kΩ
"CANCEL" switch ON	Terminals 2 and 3	Approximately 0 Ω
"RESUME" switch ON	Terminals 2 and 3	Approximately 910 Ω
"SET" switch ON	Terminals 2 and 3	Approximately 220 Ω

CR1100000690000X

Fig. 95 Speed control resistance test. 2001–03 Sebring & Stratus Coupe

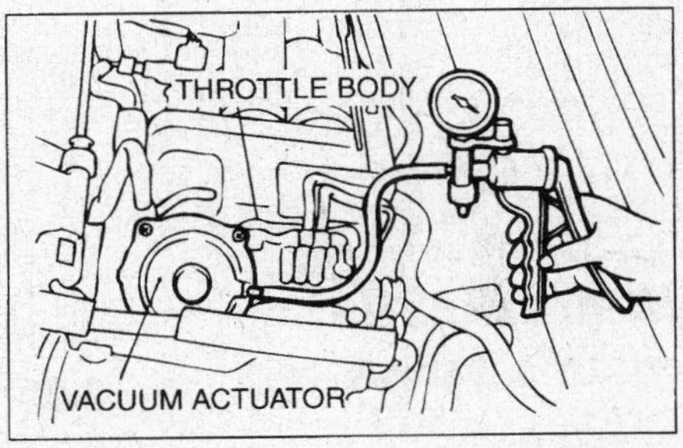

CR1100000689000X

Fig. 96 Actuator vacuum test. 2001–03 Sebring & Stratus Coupe

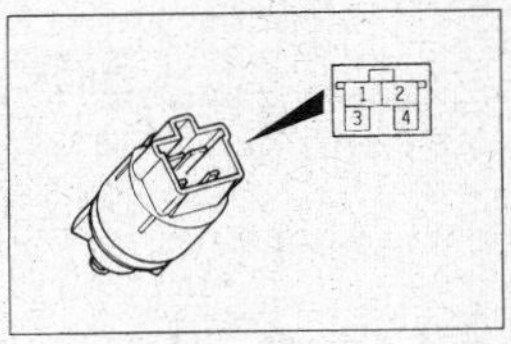

MEASUREMENT CONDITIONS	TERMINAL CONNECTOR OF TESTER	SPECIFIED CONDITION
When clutch pedal is depressed.	1 - 2	Continuity
When clutch pedal is not depressed.	1 - 2	No continuity

CR1100000688000X

Fig. 97 Clutch pedal position switch continuity test. 2001–03 Sebring & Stratus Coupe

COMPONENT REPLACEMENT

Speed Control Servo

AVENGER

1. Remove link protector, throttle and accelerator cables, **Fig. 1.**
2. Remove speed control, throttle and accelerator cable connections.
3. Remove link and bracket.
4. Remove vacuum hose connection.
5. Remove reservoir.
6. Remove speed control, then the actuator upper and lower brackets.
7. Reverse procedure to install.

BREEZE & CIRRUS

1. Disconnect servo electrical connector and hose.
2. Remove two cable mounting nuts.
3. Remove cable to servo hair pin.
4. Remove servo.
5. Reverse procedure to install.

CONCORDE, INTREPID, LHS & 300M

1. Remove three servo bracket mounting bolts.
2. Disconnect electrical connections and vacuum hose.
3. Remove two speed control cable and mounting bracket to servo nuts.
4. Remove servo mounting bracket.
5. Remove cable to servo clip, then the mounting bracket.
6. Reverse procedure to install.

NEON

Refer to "Breeze & Cirrus" for speed control servo replacement procedure.

SEBRING & STRATUS

CONVERTIBLE & SEDAN

2000

Refer to "Breeze & Cirrus" for speed control servo replacement procedure.

2001–04

1. Remove nuts servo bracket to shock tower mounting nuts.
2. Disconnect electrical connectors and vacuum hoses.
3. Remove speed control cable and mounting bracket mounting nuts.
4. Remove cable to servo clip, then the mounting bracket, **Fig. 98.**
5. Reverse procedure to install.

COUPE

2000

Refer to "Avenger" for speed control servo replacement procedure.

2001–03

1. Disconnect vacuum hose and pipe, then the electrical connector, **Fig. 99.**
2. Remove vacuum pump, spacer, rubber mount and bracket.
3. Reverse procedure to install.

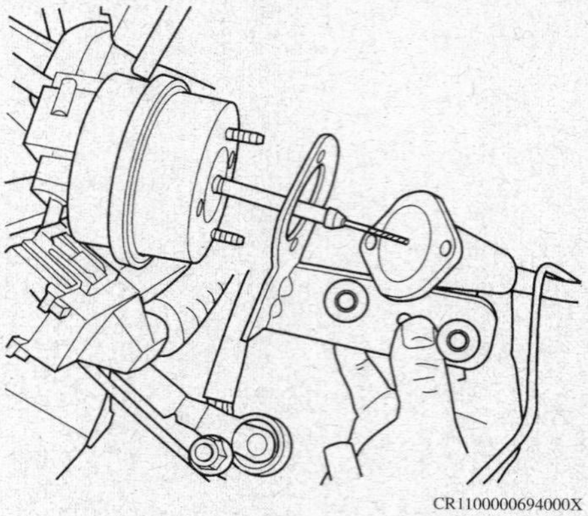

Fig. 98 Speed control servo replacement. 2001–04 Sebring & Stratus Sedan

Speed Control Servo Cable

AVENGER

1. Remove link protector, throttle and accelerator cables, **Fig. 1.**
2. Remove speed control, throttle and accelerator cable connections.
3. Reverse procedure to install.

BREEZE & CIRRUS

1. Remove throttle cable cover.
2. Remove throttle body cable clasp.
3. Remove speed control cable from throttle lever by sliding clasp out of hole.
4. Lift tabs and cables out of bracket.
5. Disconnect servo electrical connector and hose.
6. Remove two bracket mounting nuts.
7. Push cable housing nuts to servo.
8. Remove clip and cable.
9. Reverse procedure to install.

CONCORDE, INTREPID, LHS & 300M

1. **On models equipped with 3.2L and 3.5L engines,** remove intake manifold throttle cable bracket
2. **On all models,** remove speed control cable from throttle lever by sliding clasp out of hole.
3. Lift tabs and cables out of bracket.
4. Remove two mounting nuts and one bolt from servo bracket.
5. Disconnect servo electrical connector and hose.
6. Remove two servo speed control cable and mounting bracket nuts.
7. Remove cable to servo clip and servo mounting bracket.
8. Reverse procedure to install.

NEON

Refer to "Breeze & Cirrus" for cable replacement procedure.

SEBRING & STRATUS

CONVERTIBLE & SEDAN

Refer to "Breeze & Cirrus" for cable replacement procedure.

2000 COUPE

Refer to "Avenger" for cable replacement procedure.

Control Module

AVENGER

1. Remove air cleaner.
2. Remove Powertrain Control Module (PCM), **Fig. 100.**
3. Reverse procedure to install.

SEBRING & STRATUS COUPE

2000

Refer to "Avenger" for control module replacement procedure.

2001–03

1. Remove steering wheel as outlined under "Electrical" in appropriate chassis chapter of **MOTOR's "Auto Repair Manual."**
2. Remove cruise control switch, **Fig. 101.**
3. Remove center panel as outlined in "Dash Panel Service" chapter.
4. Remove cruise control module.
5. Reverse procedure to install.

Speed Control Main Switch

AVENGER & 2000 SEBRING COUPE

1. Remove instrument panel switch, **Fig. 102.**
2. Remove speed control main switch.
3. Reverse procedure to install.

Speed Control Switch

AVENGER

1. Remove driver's air bag module as outlined in "Passive Restraints Systems" chapter, **Fig. 103.**
2. Remove cruise control switch.
3. Reverse procedure to install.

BREEZE & CIRRUS

1. Turn ignition switch to OFF position.
2. Remove mounting screws and switches with rocking motion, **Fig. 104.**
3. Disconnect two-way electrical connector.
4. Remove switch.
5. Reverse procedure to install.

CONCORDE, INTREPID, LHS & 300M

Refer to "Breeze & Cirrus" for speed control switch replacement procedure.

NEON

2000–01

Refer to "Breeze & Cirrus" for speed control switch replacement procedure.

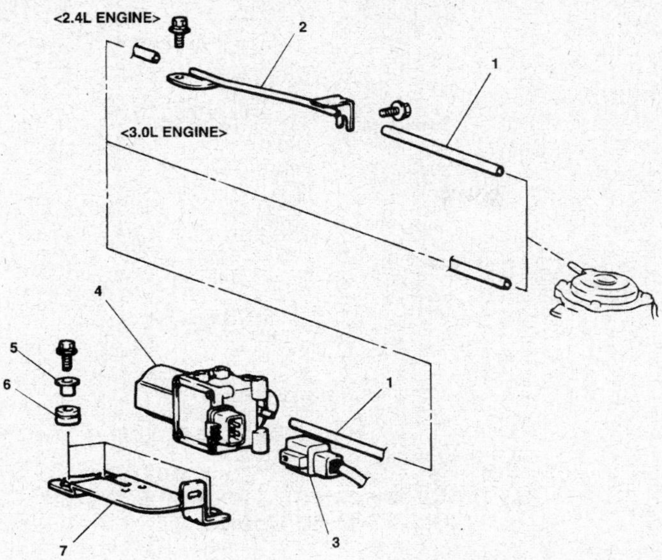

1. VACUUM HOSE
2. VACUUM PIPE
3. WIRING CONNECTOR
4. VACUUM PUMP ASSEMBLY
5. SPACER
6. RUBBER MOUNT
7. PUMP BRACKET

CR1100000692000A

Fig. 99 Speed control actuator replacement. 2001–03 Sebring & Stratus Coupe

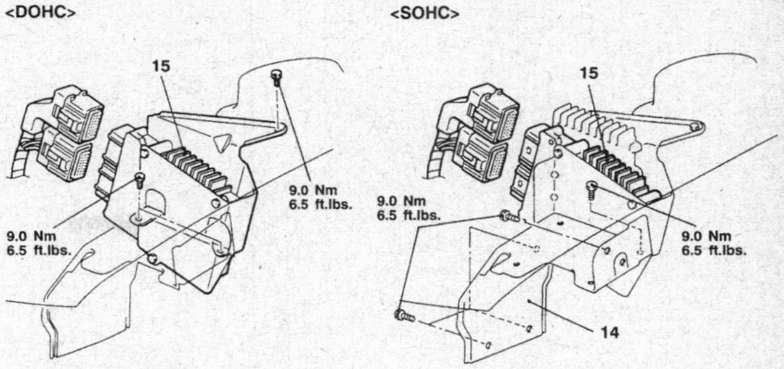

- Air cleaner
14. Powertrain control module bracket <SOHC>
15. Powertrain control module

CR1100200745000X

Fig. 100 PCM replacement. Avenger & 2000 Sebring Coupe

2002–04

1. Remove air cleaner lid, then disconnect air temperature sensor inlet and air hose.
2. Turn ignition switch to OFF position.
3. Remove driver's air bag module as outlined in "Passive Restraints Systems" chapter.
4. Remove speed control switch top mounting bolt.
5. Turn steering wheel so switch is at 6 o'clock position.
6. Remove two mounting screws from switch back.
7. Disconnect electrical connector and remove switch.
8. Reverse procedure to install.

SEBRING & STRATUS

CONVERTIBLE & SEDAN

Refer to "Breeze & Cirrus" for speed control switch replacement procedure.

COUPE

2000

Refer to "Avenger" for speed control switch replacement procedure.

2001–03

1. Remove steering wheel as outlined under "Electrical" in appropriate chassis chapter of **MOTOR's "Auto Repair Manual."**
2. Remove cruise control switch, **Fig. 101.**
3. Reverse procedure to install.

Speed Sensor

AVENGER

AUTOMATIC TRANSAXLE

1. Remove transaxle range sensor, **Fig. 105.**
2. Remove stop lamp switch.
3. Remove input and out speed sensors.
4. Reverse procedure to install.

MANUAL TRANSAXLE

1. Remove stop lamp switch, **Fig. 105.**
2. Remove vehicle speed sensor.
3. Reverse procedure to install.

SEBRING & STRATUS COUPE

2000

Refer to "Avenger" for speed sensor replacement procedure.

2001–03

1. Remove throttle position sensor, **Fig. 106.**
2. Remove stop lamp switch.
3. **On models equipped with manual transaxle,** remove clutch pedal position switch.
4. **On all models,** remove Park/Neutral Position (PNP) switch.
5. Remove vehicle speed sensor.
6. Reverse procedure to install.

Vacuum Reservoir

CONCORDE, INTREPID, LHS & 300M

1. Disconnect PCM electrical connectors.
2. Remove PCM mounting bolts and PCM.
3. Remove and reposition coolant reservoir without disconnecting hoses.
4. Remove PDC and bracket.
5. Remove vacuum reservoir.
6. Disconnect vacuum hose.
7. Reverse procedure to install.

NEON

2000

1. Raise and support vehicle.
2. Remove vacuum reservoir top mounting bolt.
3. Disconnect vacuum hoses.
4. Remove reservoir.
5. Reverse procedure to install.

2001–04

1. Remove passenger side cowl screen.
2. Remove mounting nuts and vacuum reservoir.
3. Reverse procedure to install.

Stop Lamp Switch

NEON

1. Depress brake pedal while rotating switch in a counterclockwise direction approximately 30°.
2. Pull switch out of bracket and disconnect wiring harness connector.
3. Reverse procedure to install, noting the following:
   a. Pull switch plunger out to full length of travel.
   b. Align switch index key with bracket slot.

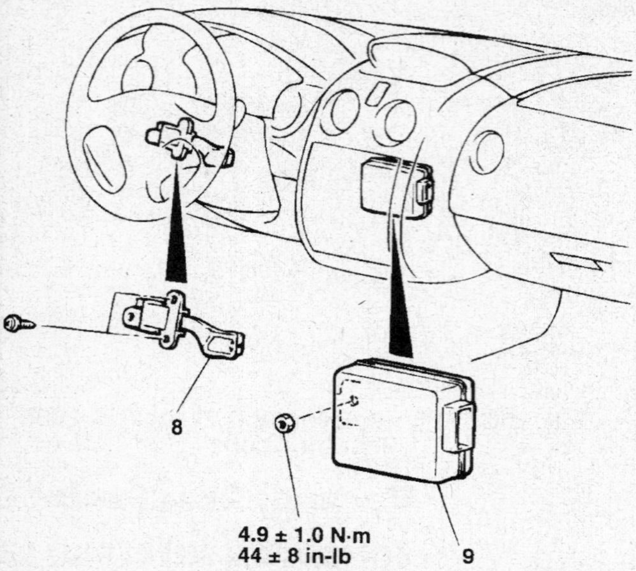

Fig. 101 Speed control switch, control unit & sensor replacement. 2001–03 Sebring & Stratus Coupe

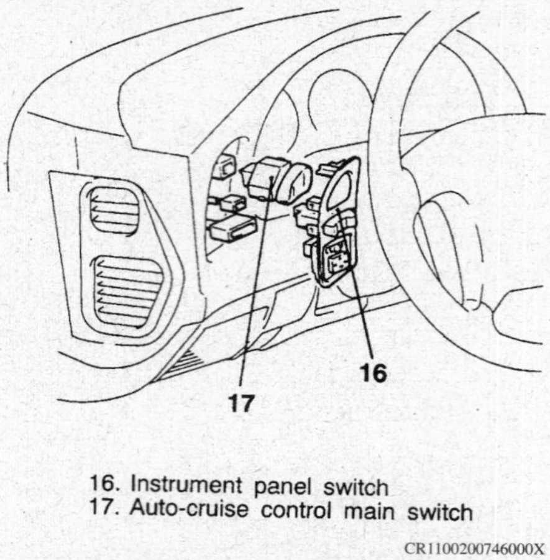

Fig. 102 Speed control main switch replacement. Avenger & 2000 Sebring Coupe

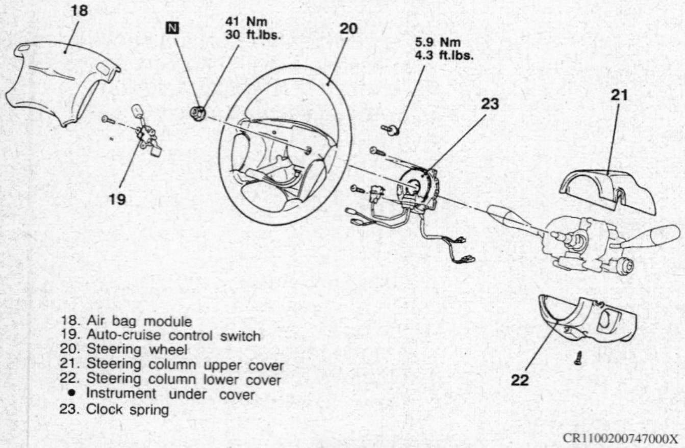

Fig. 103 Speed control switch replacement. Avenger & 2000 Sebring Coupe

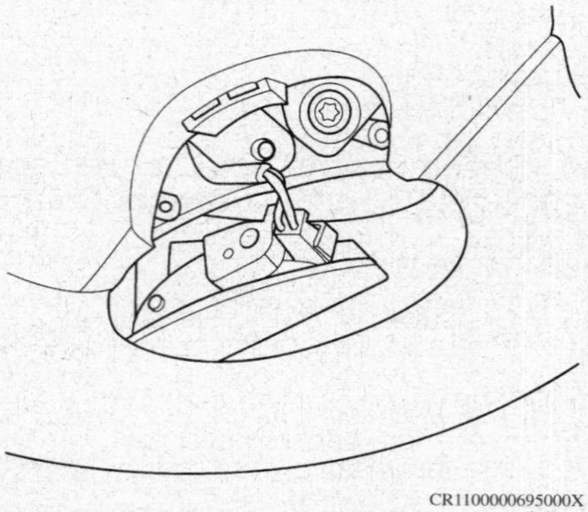

Fig. 104 Speed control switch replacement. Breeze, Cirrus, Concorde, Intrepid, LHS, Sebring Convertible, Sebring Sedan, Stratus Sedan, 300M & 2000–01 Neon

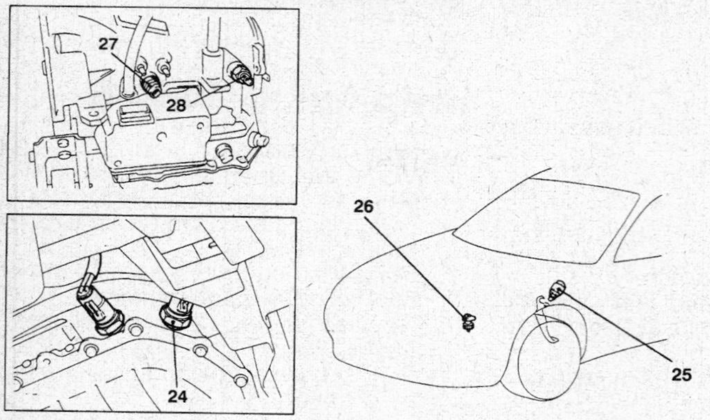

Fig. 105 Speed sensor replacement. Avenger & 2000 Sebring Coupe

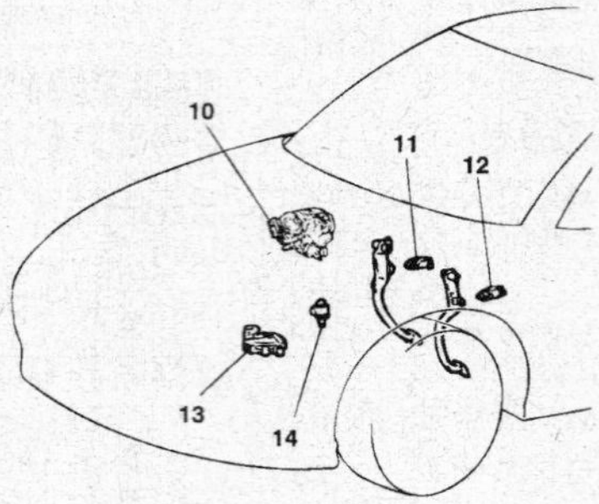

Fig. 106 Sensor replacement. 2001–03 Sebring & Stratus Coupe

WIPER SYSTEMS

NOTE: On Air Bag Equipped Models, Refer To "Air Bag System Precautions" Located In The Front Of This Manual For System Disarming & Arming Procedures.

NOTE: Refer To "Computer Relearn Procedures" Located In The Front Of This Manual When Battery Power To The Computer Has Been Interrupted.

NOTE: "Electrical Symbol & Wire Color Code Identification" Located In The Front Of This Manual May Be Used As An Aid When Using Wiring Circuits Found In This Section.

INDEX

PRECAUTIONS

Air Bag Systems

Refer to "Air Bag System Precautions" in the front of this manual for system disarming and arming procedures.

Battery Ground Cable

Prior to service, disconnect battery ground cable and isolate as required.

DESCRIPTION

The wiper system operates only when the ignition switch is On or in the Accessory position. The wiper motor has permanent magnet fields. HI and Low speeds are determined by current flow to the appropriate set of brushes.

Except Neon

The intermittent wiper system in addition to HI and Low speeds, has a delay mode. The delay mode is done by a variable resistor in the wiper switch and Body Control Module (BCM). The BCM controls timing for the wiper On/Off, as well as the wiper HI/LO relay.

Neon

The intermittent wiper system, in addition to Hi and Low speeds, has a Delay Mode and a Pulse Mode. The Delay Mode, with a delay range of 1–15 seconds, is controlled by a variable resistor in the wiper switch and two relays. One relay turns the wipers On/Off and the other changes the speed. The Pulse mode allows one or two sweeps of the wiper system at the drivers command. With the switch in either Off or Delay position, a momentary movement of the switch into Wash position will activate Pulse Mode.

TROUBLESHOOTING

Avenger

WIPERS DO NOT OPERATE

1. Inspect for blown multi-purpose fuse No. 9.
2. Inspect ground connection.

WIPERS DO NOT OPERATE AT LOW OR HIGH SPEED

1. Inspect wiper switch.

WIPERS DO NOT STOP

1. Inspect wiper motor.
2. Inspect intermittent wiper relay.
3. Inspect wiper switch.

WIPERS DO NOT OPERATE IN INTERMITTENT MODE

1. Inspect voltage of steering column switch terminal No. 7 with intermittent wiper relay energized.
2. If voltage is 0 volts, inspect intermittent wiper relay or wiper switch.
3. If voltage is 12 volts, inspect intermittent wiper relay.
4. If voltage is alternating between 0–12 volts, system is satisfactory.

INTERVAL PERIOD WILL NOT ADJUST

1. Inspect variable intermittent wiper control switch.
2. Inspect intermittent wiper relay.

WIPER OPERATION NOT COORDINATED w/WASHER

1. Inspect intermittent wiper relay.

WASHER/WIPER IS INOPERATIVE

1. Inspect washer motor.
2. Inspect washer switch.

Breeze & Cirrus

MOTOR WILL NOT RUN IN ANY SWITCH POSITION

1. Inspect for blown fuse No. 15 in junction block and No. 8 in power distribution center.
2. Replace faulty fuses, then inspect motor operation in all switch positions. If motor is still inoperative and fuse does not blow, proceed to next step. If replacement fuse blows. proceed as follows:
   a. Disconnect motor connector.
   b. Replace fuse No. 15 from junction block.
   c. If fuse does not blow, proceed to next step.
   d. If fuse blows, wiper control circuitry is at fault.
3. Disconnect motor wire connector.
4. Inspect motor low speed operation by connecting jumper wire between battery positive terminal and motor connector pin B, then connect other jumper wire to battery ground and motor connector pin C.
5. Inspect high speed operation by connecting battery positive jumper to motor connector pin A and battery ground to motor connector pin C.
6. If motor has no high or low speed, inspect motor wiring harness connector pin C for good ground. If ground is satisfactory, replace motor. If ground is not satisfactory, repair circuit.
7. If motor runs, inspect for battery voltage at distribution center intermittent relay terminal No. 29. If there is no voltage inspect fuse 18. If there is battery voltage, proceed to next step.
8. Inspect hi-lo wiper relay terminal No. 28 motor to wiring harness connector pin A for continuity.
9. Inspect hi-lo wiper relay terminal No. 11 to motor wiring harness connector pin B for continuity. If satisfactory proceed to next step. If not, repair circuit.
10. Inspect continuity between hi-lo wiper relay terminal 36 to intermittent wiper relay terminal No. 37. If satisfactory inspect for faulty relays. If not, repair circuit.
11. Disconnect J3 14-way connector from body controller.
12. Inspect for continuity between J3 14-way connector terminal No. 7 to intermittent wiper relay terminal No. 13 If satisfactory proceed to next step. If not, repair circuit.
13. With wiper switch connected, connect suitable voltmeter positive lead to BCM J1 22-way connector terminal No. 10.
14. Turn ignition switch to On position.
15. Move wiper switch from Off position to High position. If voltage increases from zero to 10 volts in High position, replace BCM. If no voltage is present, inspect continuity from wiper switch terminal No. 2 to BCM J3 22-way connector terminal No. 10.

MOTOR RUNS SLOWLY AT ALL SPEEDS

1. Remove wiper arms and blades, then disconnect wiper motor connector. Drive link from motor.
2. Connect suitable ammeter between battery ground terminal and motor connector pin C. Connect battery positive to motor connector pin B.
3. If motor runs and average ammeter reading is more than 6 amps, replace motor.
4. If motor runs and average ammeter reading is less than 6 amps, inspect wiper linkage or pivots are binding.

MOTOR WILL RUN AT HIGH SPEED, BUT NOT AT LOW SPEED

1. Disconnect motor connector.
2. Connect jumper wire between battery positive terminal and motor connector pin A.
3. Connect second jumper wire between ground and motor connector pin C.
4. If motor does not run, replace motor. If motor runs proceed to next step,
5. Inspect for continuity between hi-lo wiper relay terminal No. 28 and wiper motor wire harness connector pin A. If satisfactory, proceed to next step. If not satisfactory, repair circuit.
6. Inspect for faulty hi-lo wiper relay.

MOTOR WILL RUN AT LOW SPEED, BUT NOT AT HIGH SPEED

1. Disconnect motor connector.
2. Connect jumper wire between battery positive and motor connector pin B.
3. Connect second jumper between battery ground and motor connector pin C.
4. If motor does not run, replace motor. If motor runs proceed to next step.
5. Inspect continuity between hi-lo wiper relay terminal No. 11 and wiper motor wire harness connector pin B. If satisfactory proceed to next step. If continuity is not satisfactory, repair circuit.
6. Inspect for faulty hi-lo wiper relay.

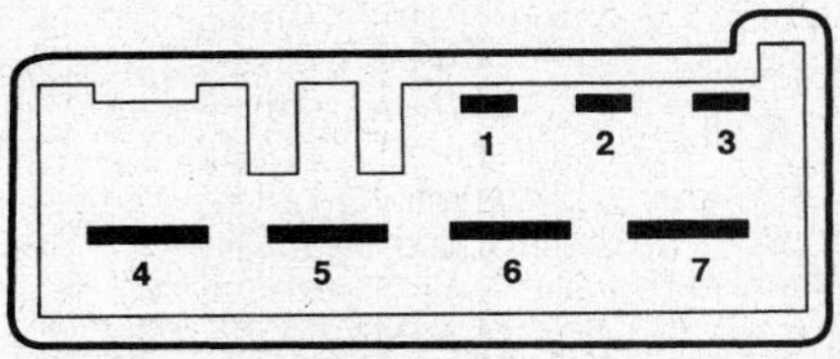

SWITCH POSITION		TERMINALS	RESISTANCE VALUE
OFF		PINS 1 T0 3	OPEN 300 K OHMS
DELAY LEVEL	1	PINS 1 TO 3	9.72 K OHMS
	2	PINS 1 TO 3	8.22 K OHMS
	3	PINS 1 TO 3	6.61 K OHMS
	4	PINS 1 TO 3	5.12K OHMS
	5	PINS 1 TO 3	3.67K OHMS
	6	PINS 1 TO 3	2.22K OHMS
LOW		PINS 1 TO 3	1.02 K OHMS
HIGH		PINS 1 TO 3	0.51K OHMS
WASH		PINS 1 TO 2	0 OHMS

CR9029900330000X

Fig. 1 Ammeter to wiper motor connection. Concorde, Intrepid, LHS & 300M

WIPERS RUN AT HIGH SPEED w/SWITCH IN LOW SPEED & WIPERS OPERATE IN INTERMITTENT MODE, BUT EACH WIPE IS AT HIGH SPEED

1. Disconnect motor connector.
2. Connect suitable jumper wire between battery positive and motor wiring harness connector pin B.
3. Connect second lead between battery ground and motor wiring harness connector pin C.
4. If motor runs at low speed, then inspect for faulty hi-lo wiper relay or for crossed wires in harness from hi-lo relay motor.
5. If motor runs at high speed, replace motor.
6. Inspect for short to ground by disconnecting body controller J3 14-way connector pin No. 8, then remove intermittent wiper relay.
7. If none of previous conditions are present, replace body controller.

WIPERS RUN AT LOW SPEED w/SWITCH IN HIGH SPEED POSITION

1. Inspect for faulty hi-lo wiper relay.
2. Inspect for open circuit between hi-lo wiper relay terminal No. 12 and body controller J3 14-way connector terminal No. 8. If satisfactory, inspect wiper switch. If not satisfactory, repair circuit.

MOTOR RUNS w/SWITCH IN OFF POSITION

1. Inspect BCM J3 14-way connector pin No. 8 for continuity to ground with wipers in park position.
2. If no ground signal, test wiper motor. If ground is received test multi-function switch.
3. If multi-function switch test good, replace BCM.

WIPER RUN CONTINUOUSLY w/SWITCH IN INTERMITTENT POSITION

1. Inspect for ground at wiper motor wire connector pin D.
2. With wiper motor in PARK position, inspect for continuity between motor connector pins C and D . If satisfactory, proceed to next step. If not satisfactory, replace motor.
3. Inspect for continuity between motor wire harness connector pin D and body controller J3 14-way connector terminal No. 2.
4. Inspect for short circuit to battery or ignition feed in circuit.

WHEN COLUMN SWITCH IS TURNED OFF WIPERS STOP WITHOUT RETURNING TO PARK POSITION

Refer to "Wiper Run Continuously w/Switch In Intermittent Position."

WIPERS DO NOT RUN WHEN WASHER MOTOR IS ENGAGED

1. Disconnect body controller J3 14-way connector.
2. Connect suitable voltmeter positive lead to 14-way connector terminal No. 10 and negative lead to ground.
3. Engage washer switch so that washer motor runs continuously.
4. If voltage is zero, inspect wiring between washer motor and body controller.
5. Ensure 14-way connector is disconnected and inspect pin No. 10 to ensure 12 volts. If no voltage is present, replace BCM. If voltage is present, inspect for wiring short.

Concorde, Intrepid, LHS & 300M

MOTOR WILL NOT RUN IN ANY SWITCH POSITION

1. Inspect for blown fuse No. 5 in junction block and fuse M in power distribution center.
2. If fuses are faulty, replace, then inspect motor operation in all switch positions. If motor is still inoperative and fuse does not blow, continue to next step. If replacement fuse blows, proceed as follows:
   a. Disconnect motor connector and replace fuse 5 from Junction Block.
   b. If fuse does not blow, proceed to next step 2.
   c. If fuse blows, wiper control circuitry is at fault.
3. Disconnect motor wire connector.
4. Connect suitable jumper wire between battery positive terminal and wiper motor connector pin No. 2 .

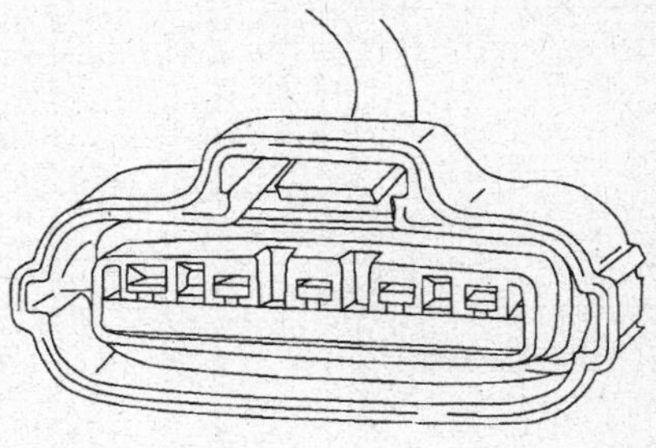

CAV	COLOR	FUNCTION
1	RD/YL	WIPER SWITCH HIGH SPEED OUTPUT
2	BR/WT	WIPER SWITCH LOW SPEED OUTPUT
4	TN/RD	WIPER PARK SWITCH SENSE
5	BK	GROUND

CR9029900331000X

Fig. 2 Wiper motor connector. Concorde, Intrepid, LHS & 300M

5. Connect another jumper wire to ground and wiper motor connector pin No. 5.
6. If motor does not run, replace motor. If motor runs, proceed to next step.
7. Connect suitable wire between battery positive terminal and wiper motor connector pin No. 1. Connect another jumper wire to ground and wiper motor connector pin No. 5.
8. If motor does not run, replace motor. If motor runs, proceed to next step.
9. Inspect wiper motor wire harness connector for good ground at pin No. 5. If satisfactory proceed to next step. If not satisfactory, repair ground circuit.
10. Place wiper switch to On position and connect to terminals D and A of the intermittent wiper relay at Power Distribution Center. If battery voltage is present proceed to next step, If not, repair circuit.
11. Inspect hi-lo wiper relay terminal D to motor wire connector. pin No. 1 for continuity. If satisfactory proceed to next step. If not satisfactory, repair circuit.
12. Inspect terminal E of hi-lo wiper relay to motor wire connector pin No. 2 for continuity. If satisfactory proceed to next step, if not repair as required.
13. Inspect continuity between HI-LO wiper relay terminal B to intermittent wiper relay terminal B. If satisfactory inspect for faulty relays, if not repair circuit.
14. Disconnect BCM C3 bone 12-way connector.
15. Inspect continuity from BCM C3 24-way connector terminal No. 4 to intermittent wiper relay terminal C. If satisfactory, proceed to next step, If not satisfactory, repair circuit.
16. Connect voltmeter positive lead to BCM C2 24-way connector terminal No. 8 and negative lead to ground.
17. Turn ignition switch On and slowly move wiper switch from Off position through each position to High.
18. If voltage increases from zero to volts in High position, replace BCM. If no voltage is present proceed to next step.
19. Inspect continuity from wiper switch connector terminal No. 3 to BCM C2

CONDITION	POSSIBLE CAUSES	CORRECTION
WIPER ARM(S) CHATTER ON WINDSHIELD.	1. Permanent set of blade element edge.	1. Inspect rubber element for permanent set. If not OK, replace rubber element.
	2. Bent or damaged blade structure.	2. Inspect blade. If not OK, replace blade.
	3. Bent or damaged arm.	3. Inspect arm. If not OK, adjust blade to arm clearance. See procedure in this section. Reinspect, if not OK, replace arm.
DRIVER AND/OR PASSENGER ARM WILL NOT CYCLE (OPERATE).	1. Loose arm to pivot shaft.	1. Check arm to pivot shaft connection for looseness. Torque attachment nut to specification.
	2. Stripped arm to pivot shaft.	2. Check arm to pivot shaft for stripping. Torque nut to specification. If not OK, replace arm, pivot shaft or both.
DRIVER AND/OR PASSENGER ARM OR BLADE HITS COWL GRILLE OR WINDSHIELD MOLDINGS.	1. Arm(s) out of position.	1. Remove arm off pivot shaft, cycle module to park. Reposition arm/blade to location marks on windshield. Secure arm to pivot shaft and torque to specification. recheck wiper arm travel.
WIPER BLADE(S) STREAK.	1. Contamination on blade element or windshield.	1. Clean blade element edge with mild soap or alcohol and water. Clean windshield with mild soap or non-abrasive cleanser and water. Check for proper wipe quality. If not OK, replace blade element.
	2. Blade element damaged.	2. Replace blade element.

ARM0300000000139

Fig. 3 Troubleshooting procedures (Part 1 of 2). Crossfire

CONDITION	POSSIBLE CAUSES	CORRECTION
COWL GRILLE NOZZLE WILL NOT FLOW.	1. Frozen nozzle.	1. De-ice nozzle by allowing time for underhood engine heat to thaw nozzle. If not OK, move vehicle into heated area. Ensure washer fluid is properly blended for ambient outside temperatures.
	2. Nozzle hose not flowing.	2. Ensure nozzle hose is not pinched, loose, broken, or disconnected. If not OK, properly route or repair nozzle hose.
	3. Nozzle or nozzle hose plugged by contamination.	3. Clean nozzle hose of contamination. Determine source of contamination; inspect reservoir and clean system as required.
WASHER FLUID OUTPUT IS LOW.	1. Partially pinched hose.	1. Ensure washer hose is not partially pinched. If not OK, properly route hose.
	2. Reverse polarity to pump.	2. Check for crossed circuity to pump. If not OK, repair circuit.
	3. Nozzle or nozzle hose plugged by contamination.	3. Clean nozzle hose of contamination. Determine source of contamination; inspect reservoir and clean system as required.
COWL GRILLE NOZZLE STREAM OVERSHOOTS WINDSHIELD.	1. Nozzle not seated in cowl grille properly	1. Ensure nozzle is aligned and snapped in place properly.
	2. Nozzle jet(s) out of adjustment.	2. Adjust nozzle jets using a safety pin.

ARM0300000000140

Fig. 3 Troubleshooting procedures (Part 2 of 2). Crossfire

24-way connector terminal No. 8 of . If there is no continuity, repair circuit.

20. Connect voltmeter positive lead to wiper switch connector terminal No. 1. If ignition voltage is present replace wiper switch. If there is no voltage, inspect continuity from fuse 5 to wiper switch connector terminal No. 1.

MOTOR RUNS SLOWLY AT ALL SPEEDS

1. Disconnect motor wire harness, then remove wiper arms and blades.
2. Disconnect motor drive link.
3. Connect suitable ammeter between battery ground jump start terminal and wiper motor connector pin No. 5, **Fig. 1.**
4. Connect battery positive wire to wiper motor connector pin No. 2.
5. If reading is more than 10 amps with hot motor and dry windshield, replace wiper motor. If ammeter is less than 10 amps, repeat procedure.
6. Ensure wiper linkage or pivots are not binding.

MOTOR WILL RUN AT HIGH SPEED, BUT NOT MOVE AT LOW SPEED

1. Disconnect motor connector.
2. Connect suitable jumper wire between battery positive terminal and wiper motor connector pin No. 2.
3. Connect second wire between ground and wiper motor wire harness connector pin No. 5, **Fig. 2.**
4. If wiper motor runs proceed to next step. If motor does not run, replace motor.
5. Inspect hi/lo wiper relay terminal E to wiper motor harness connector pin No. 2 for open circuit.
6. If satisfactory proceed to next step, If not satisfactory, repair circuit.
7. Inspect for faulty hi/lo wiper relay.

MOTOR WILL RUN AT LOW SPEED, BUT NOT MOVE HIGH SPEED

1. Disconnect motor connector.
2. Connect suitable jumper wire between battery positive terminal and wiper motor connector pin No. 1.
3. Connect second wire between ground and wiper motor connector pin No. 5.
4. If motor runs proceed to next step. If motor does not run, replace motor.
5. Inspect hi/lo wiper relay terminal D to wiper motor wire harness connector pin No. 2 for open circuit.
6. If satisfactory proceed to next step, If not satisfactory, repair circuit.
7. Inspect for faulty HI/LO wiper relay.

WIPERS RUN AT HIGH SPEED w/SWITCH IN LOW SPEED & WIPERS OPERATE IN INTERMITTENT MODE, BUT EACH WIPE IS AT HIGH SPEED

1. Disconnect motor connector.
2. Connect suitable jumper wire between battery positive start terminal and wiper motor connector pin No. 2.
3. Connect second lead between ground and wiper motor connector pin No. 5.
4. If motor runs at low speed proceed to next step, If motor runs at high speed, replace motor.
5. Inspect for faulty hi/lo wiper relay.
6. Disconnect BCM C3 bone 12-way connector and remove hi/lo wiper relay.
7. Inspect C3 bone 12-way connector terminal No. 12 for short to ground. If there is continuity, repair circuit. If there is no continuity to ground, replace BCM.

WIPERS RUN AT LOW SPEED w/SWITCH IN HIGH SPEED POSITION

1. Inspect for faulty hi-lo wiper relay.
2. Inspect for open circuit between hi/lo wiper relay terminal C and BCM 33 bone 12-way connector terminal No. 12 .
3. If satisfactory, inspect wiper switch. If not satisfactory, repair circuit.

MOTOR RUNS w/SWITCH IN OFF POSITION

1. Inspect wiper motor wiring harness for shorts between low speed motor feed terminal No. 2 or high speed motor feed terminal No. 1 and battery or ignition.
2. Inspect for faulty wiper on/off or hi/lo relay.
3. Inspect circuit from on/off relay terminal C to hi/lo relay terminal B for short to battery or ignition.
4. Disconnect BCM C3 bone 12-way connector. Inspect circuit from C3 bone 12-way connector terminal No. 4 to on/off wiper relay terminal C for short to ground.
5. Inspect circuit from C2 24-way connector terminal No. 3 to wiper motor harness connector pin No. 4. If open circuit, repair.
6. Connect voltmeter positive lead to C2 24-way connector terminal No. 8 and negative lead to ground. If measurement is more than zero volts, inspect wiper switch and wiring.
7. Connect voltmeter positive lead to C3 12-way connector terminal No. 8. If measurement is 10–15 volts, inspect circuit for short to battery or ignition. If measurement is zero volts, replace BCM.

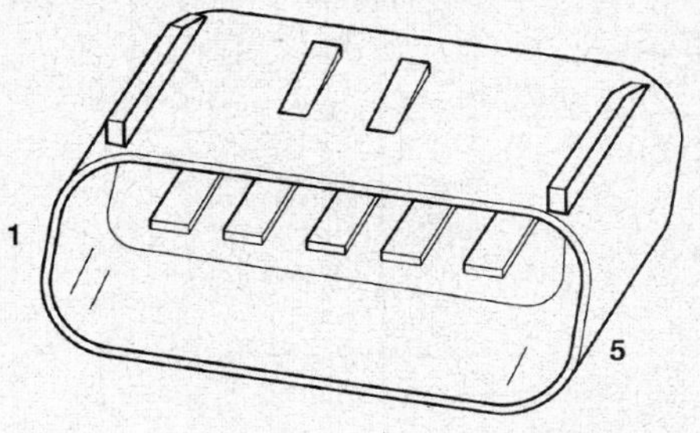

Fig. 4 Wiper motor connector. Neon

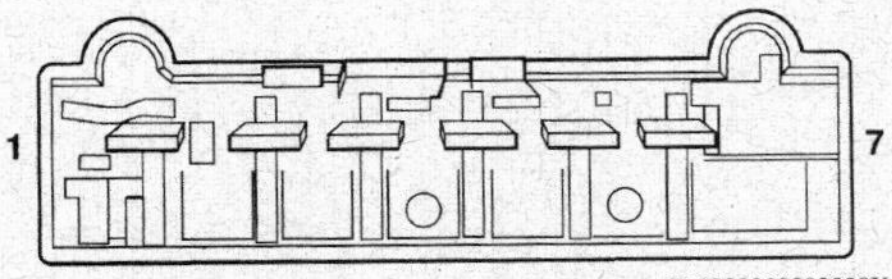

Fig. 5 Wiper switch connector. Neon

WIPER WILL RUN CONTINUOUSLY w/SWITCH IN INTERMITTENT POSITION

1. Inspect for ground at wiper motor wire connector pin No. 4. If grounded, replace motor.
2. With wiper motor in PARK position, inspect for continuity between wiper motor connector pins Nos. 4 and 5. If there is continuity proceed to next step, If there is not continuity , replace motor.
3. Disconnect wiper motor wire harness connector and BCM C3 12-way connector.
4. Inspect for continuity between wiper motor wire harness connector pin No. 1 and BCM C3 12-way connector terminal No. 3.

WHEN COLUMN SWITCH IS TURNED OFF WIPERS STOP WITHOUT RETURNING TO PARK POSITION

Refer to "Wiper Will Run Continuously w/Switch In Intermittent Position."

WIPERS DO NOT RUN WHEN WASHER MOTOR IS ENGAGED

1. Disconnect BCM C2 24-way connector.
2. Connect voltmeter positive lead to 24-way connector terminal No. 7.
3. Engage washer switch so that washer motor runs continuously.
4. If voltage is zero, inspect wiring between washer switch terminal No. 2 and BCM.
5. If battery voltage is present, replace BCM.

CONDITION	POSSIBLE CAUSES	CORRECTION
WIPER BLADES DO NOT PARK PROPERLY.	(1) WIPER ARMS IMPROPERLY PARKED. (2) WIPER ARMS ARE LOOSE ON PIVOT SHAFT. (3) MOTOR CRANK LOOSE AT OUTPUT SHAFT.	(1) REMOVE WIPER ARMS AND REPARK. REFER TO WIPER ARM REMOVAL AND INSTALLATION. (2) REMOVE WIPER ARM AND REPARK. REFER TO WIPER ARM REMOVAL AND INSTALLATION. (3) REMOVE WIPER ARM, RUN WIPER MOTOR TO PARK POSITION AND REMOVE THE MODULE. WITHOUT ROTATING THE MOTOR OUTPUT SHAFT, REMOVE THE CRANK AND CLEAN ANY FOREIGN MATTER FROM THE MOTOR SHAFT. INSTALL THE MOTOR CRANK IN ITS ORIGINAL POSITION.
MOTOR STOPS IN ANY POSITION WHEN THE SWITCH IS TURNED OFF.	(1) OPEN PARK CIRCUIT.	(1) CHECK PARK SWITCH BY DISCONNECTING THE WIRE CONNECTOR AND APPLY BATTERY VOLTAGE TO PIN 4. PLACE A JUMPER WIRE FROM PIN 2 TO PIN 3 AND THEN TO AN EXTERNAL GROUND. REPLACE MOTOR IF IT DOES NOT PARK.
MOTOR WILL NOT STOP WHEN THE SWITCH IS TURNED OFF.	(1) FAULTY SWITCH. (2) LOCK OF DYNAMIC BRAKE ON WET GLASS.	(1) CHECK SWITCH IN LOW, HIGH AND INTERMITTENT POSITION. (2) ENSURE PARK SWITCH HAS CLEAN GROUND.
WIPER BLADES SLAP AGAINST COWL SCREEN OR WINDOW MOLDINGS.	(1) WIPER ARMS ARE PARKED INCORRECTLY.	(1) PARK WIPER ARMS.
BLADES CHATTER.	(1) FOREIGN SUBSTANCE SUCH AS POLISH ON GLASS OR BLADES. (2) ARMS TWISTED, BLADE AT WRONG ANGLE ON GLASS. (3) BLADE STRUCTURE BENT. (4) BLADE ELEMENT HAS PERMANENT SET.	(1) CLEAN GLASS AND BLADE ELEMENT WITH NON-ABRASIVE CLEANER. (2) REPLACE ARM. (3) REPLACE BLADE. (4) REPLACE BLADE ELEMENT.
WIPER KNOCK AT REVERSAL.	(1) LINKAGE BUSHINGS WORN. (2) ARMATURE ENDPLAY IN MOTOR.	(1) REPLACE WORN LINK. REFER TO WIPER LINKAGE REMOVAL AND INSTALLATION. (2) REPLACE WIPER MOTOR.
WIPER MOTOR WILL NOT RUN.	(1) BLOWN FUSE. (2) NEW FUSE BLOWS. (3) NEW FUSE BLOWS. (4) NO VOLTAGE AT MOTOR. (5) POOR GROUND.	(1) REPLACE FUSE, AND RUN SYSTEM. (2) CHECK FOR SHORT IN WIRING OR SWITCH. (3) REPLACE FUSE, REMOVE MOTOR CONNECTOR, TURN SWITCH ON, FUSE DOES NOT BLOW, REPLACE MOTOR. (4) CHECK SWITCH AND WIRING HARNESS. (5) REPAIR GROUND WIRE CONNECTION AS NECESSARY.

CR9029900393000X

Fig. 6 Wiper motor test. Neon

Crossfire

Refer to **Fig. 3,** for troubleshooting procedures.

Neon

MOTOR WILL NOT OPERATE IN SOME OR ALL SWITCH POSITIONS

1. Inspect fuse No. 1 in fuse block.
   a. If fuse is satisfactory, proceed to next step.
   b. If fuse is faulty, replace and inspect wiper functions in all switch positions.
   c. If motor inoperative and fuse does not blow, proceed to next step.
2. Disconnect motor harness connector, **Fig. 4.**
   a. Connect jumper wire between battery positive terminal and terminal 4 of motor connector.
   b. Connect jumper wire to battery ground terminal and motor ground strap.
   c. Connect positive jumper wire to terminal 5 of motor connector, negative jumper wire to motor ground strap to inspect high speed motor.
   d. If motor is inoperative, proceed to next step. If motor is satisfactory, proceed to step 4.
3. Inspect ground at motor ground strap. If satisfactory replace motor, if not repair ground circuit as required.
4. Inspect terminal 2 wiper switch connector for proper continuity to ground, repair as required.

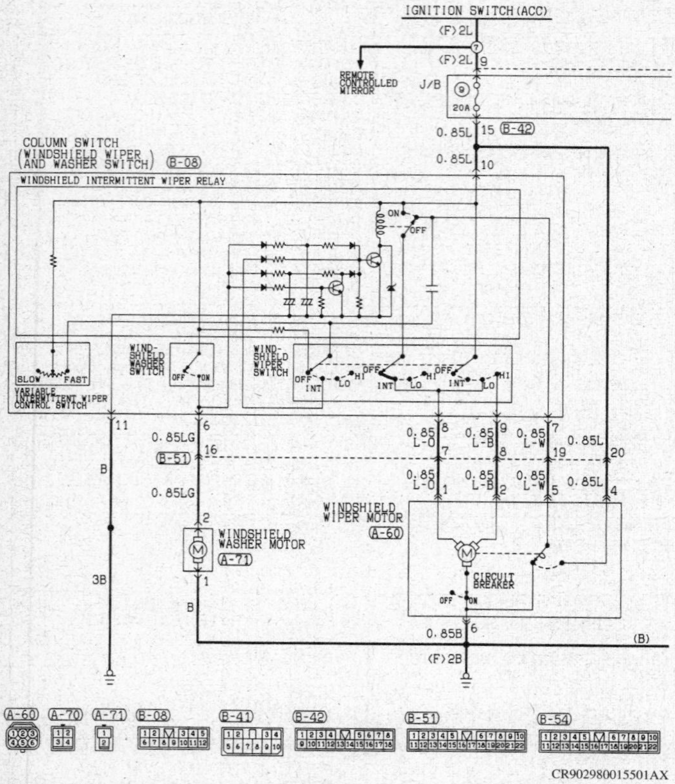

Fig. 7 Wiring diagram (Part 1 of 2). Avenger & 2000 Sebring Coupe

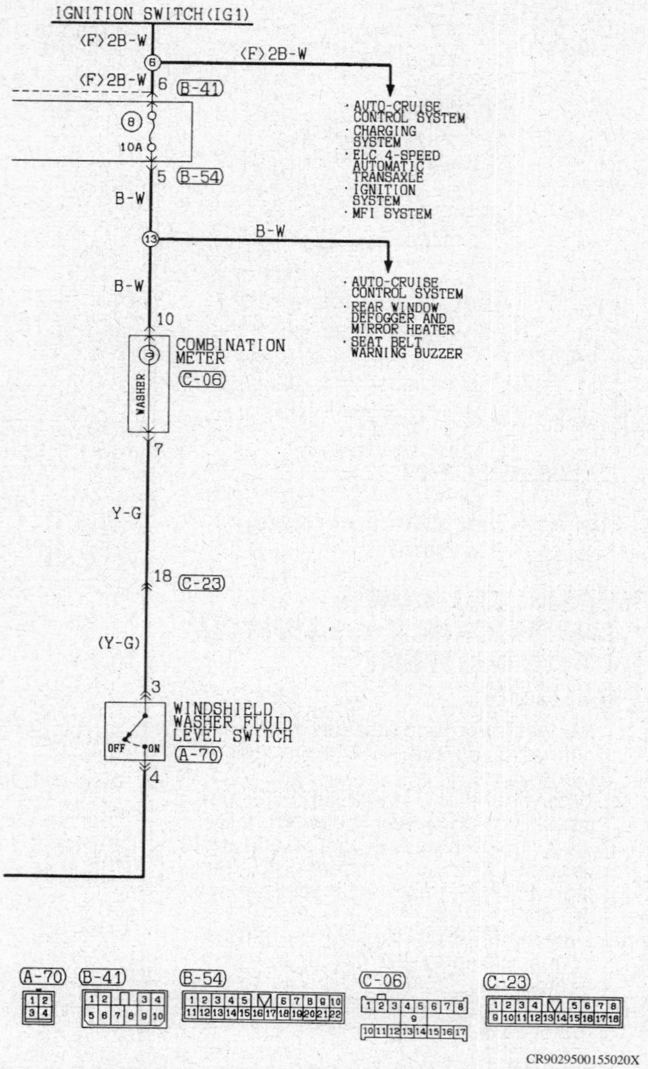

Fig. 7 Wiring diagram (Part 2 of 2). Avenger & 2000 Sebring Coupe

5. 1With wiper switch connected:
   a. Connect positive lead to terminal 4 of wiper switch connector, **Fig. 5.**
   b. If no voltage, repair wiring as required. If satisfactory, proceed to next step.
   c. Connect positive lead to terminal 6 of wiper switch connector. Move switch to LOW position, if no voltage, replace switch.
   d. Connect positive lead to terminal 5 of wiper switch connector. Move switch to HIGH position, if no voltage, replace switch.
6. Disconnect motor connector and replace fuse No. 1 in fuse block.
   a. If fuse does not blow, replace motor.
   b. If fuse blows, disconnect wiper switch and replace fuse.
   c. If fuse does not blow, replace switch.
   d. If fuse blows, repair wiring as required.

MOTOR OPERATES SLOWLY AT ALL SPEEDS

1. Disconnect motor linkage from motor, connect ammeter between battery positive terminal and terminal 4 of motor connector.
   a. If motor operates and ammeter is more than 6 amps proceed to next step.
   b. If less than 6 amps, proceed to step 3.
2. Inspect high and low circuits for short to ground.
3. Inspect wiper linkage and pivots for binding or caught points.

WIPERS RUN AT HIGH SPEED w/SWITCH IN LOW SPEED POSITION OR WIPERS RUN AT LOW SPEED w/SWITCH IN HIGH SPEED POSITION

1. Inspect for crossed wires in motor pigtail wire connector.
2. Inspect for crossed wires in harness connector from wiper switch to motor.
3. If satisfactory, replace wiper switch.

WIPERS WILL OPERATE CONTINUOUSLY w/THE SWITCH IN THE INTERMITTENT POSITION-WHEN WIPER SWITCH IS TURNED OFF, WIPERS STOP WITHOUT RETURNING TO PARK POSITION

1. Ensure good ground connection at motor ground.

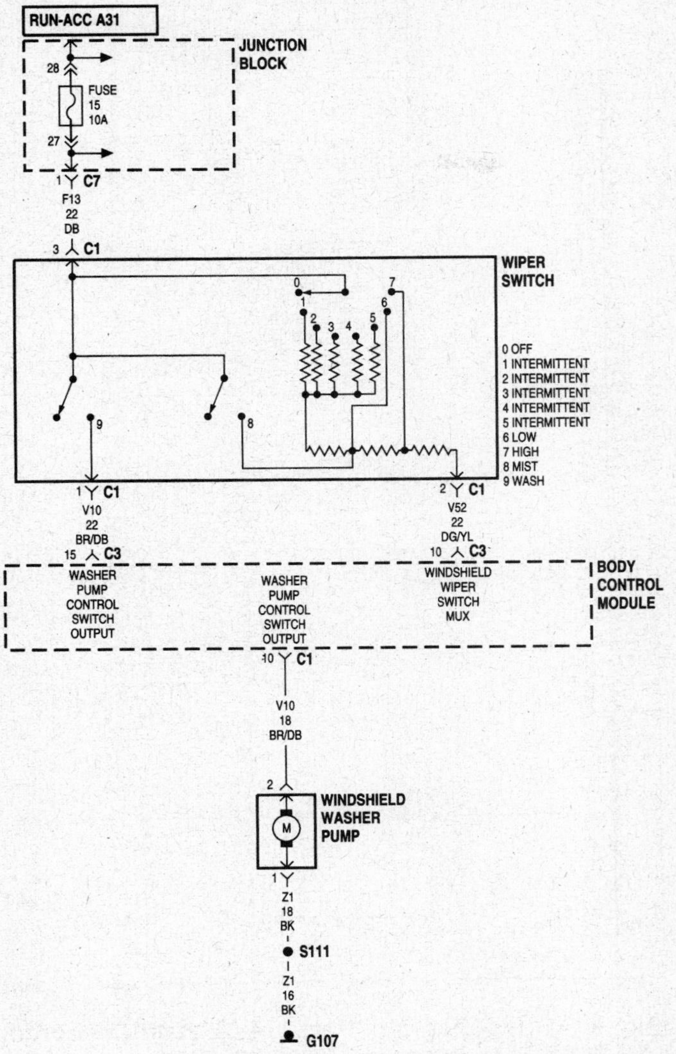

CR9029700216010X

Fig. 8 Wiring diagram (Part 1 of 2). Breeze, Cirrus & 2000 Stratus

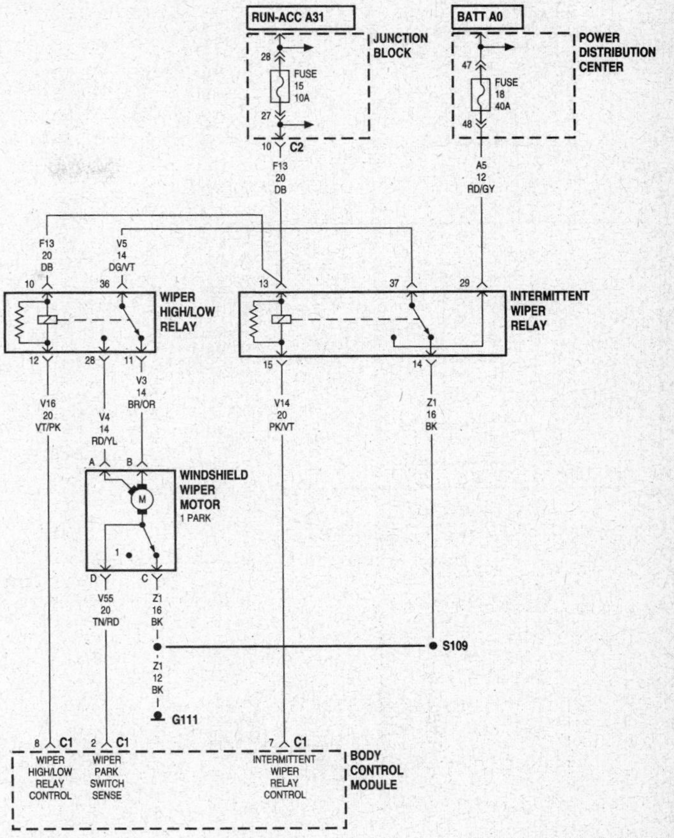

CR9029700216020X

Fig. 8 Wiring diagram (Part 2 of 2). Breeze, Cirrus & 2000 Stratus

2. Turn ignition OFF, disconnect wiper switch harness connector.
3. Motor in park position, inspect continuity between terminal 2 of wiper switch connector and ground strap.
4. If continuity exists, replace wiper switch, if no continuity, repair wiring as required.

WIPERS DO NOT OPERATE WHEN WASHER MOTOR IS ENGAGED OR WIPERS DO OPERATE IN INTERMITTENT POSITION

Inspect for ground at motor ground strap and wiper switch terminal 2. If satisfactory replace wiper switch, if not, repair wiring.

Refer to **Fig. 6,** for further wiper motor testing and diagnosis.

Sebring & Stratus

CONVERTIBLE & SEDAN

Refer to "Breeze & Cirrus" for troubleshooting procedure.

COUPE

Refer to "Avenger" for troubleshooting procedure.

SYSTEM DIAGNOSIS & TESTING

Wiring Diagrams

AVENGER

Refer to **Fig. 7,** for wiring diagram.

BREEZE & CIRRUS

Refer to **Fig. 8,** for wiring diagram.

CONCORDE, INTREPID, LHS & 300M

Refer to **Figs. 9 and 10,** for wiring diagrams.

CROSSFIRE

Refer to **Fig. 11,** for wiring diagrams.

NEON

Refer to **Figs. 12 and 13,** for wiring diagrams.

SEBRING & STRATUS

CONVERTIBLE

Refer to **Figs. 14 and 15,** for wiring diagrams.

COUPE

2000

Refer to **Fig. 7,** for wiring diagram.

2001–03

Refer to **Figs. 16 and 17,** for wiring diagrams.

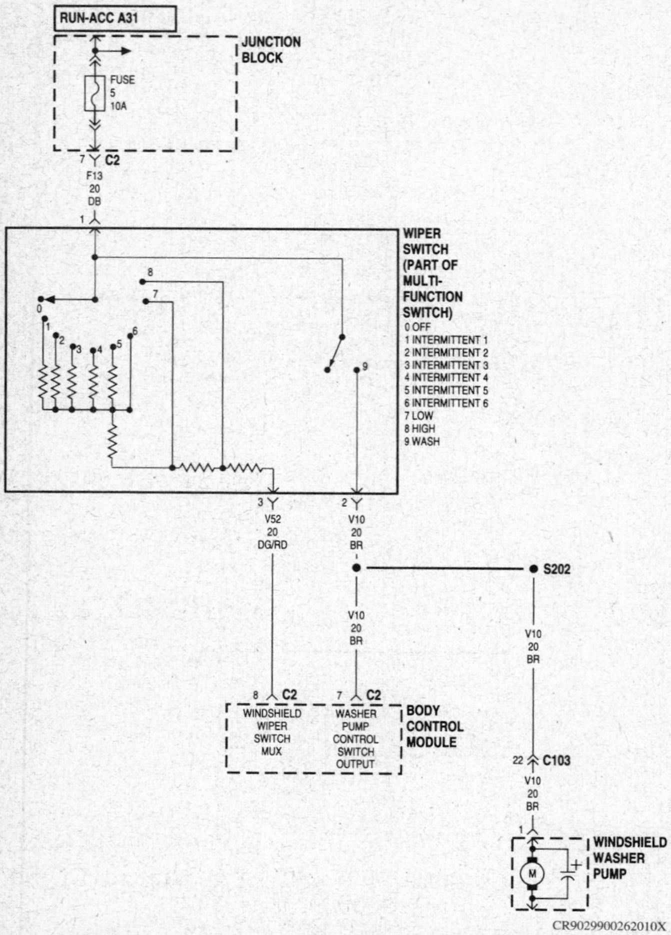

Fig. 9 Wiring diagram (Part 1 of 3). 2000 Concorde, Intrepid, LHS & 300M

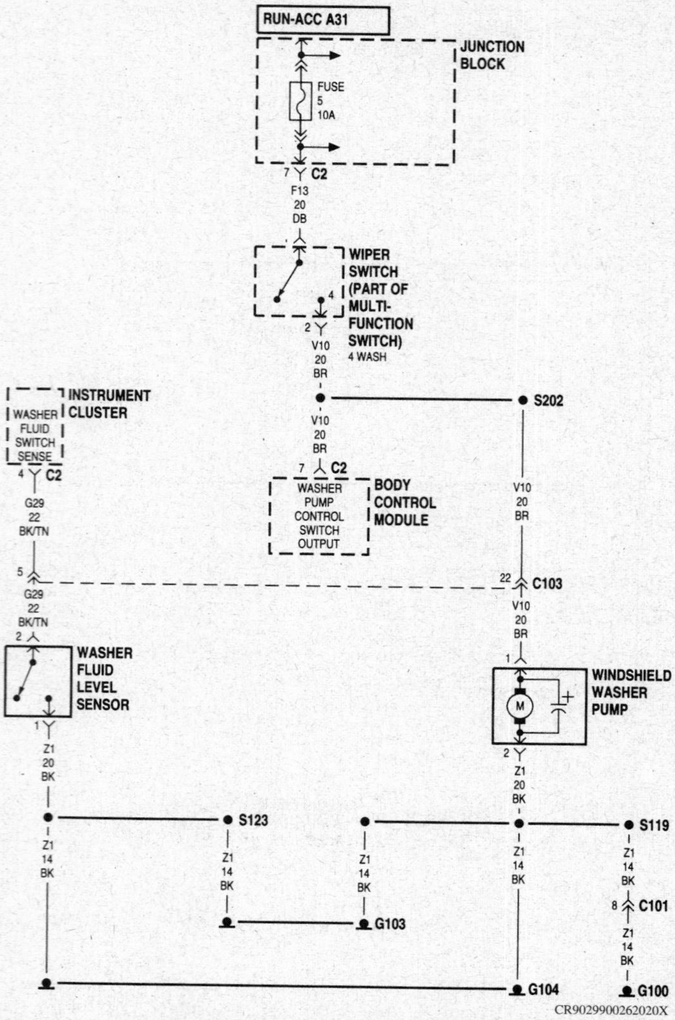

Fig. 9 Wiring diagram (Part 2 of 3). 2000 Concorde, Intrepid, LHS & 300M

SEDAN

2000

Refer to **Fig. 8,** for wiring diagrams.

2001-03

Refer to **Fig. 15,** for wiring diagrams.

Symptom Base Diagnostic Tests

AVENGER

Refer to "Component Diagnosis & Testing."

BREEZE & CIRRUS

Refer to **Figs. 18 through 27,** for diagnosis and testing procedures.

CONCORDE, INTREPID, LHS & 300M

2000

Refer to **Fig. 28 through 37,** for diagnosis and testing procedures.

2001-04

Refer to **Figs. 38 through 48,** for diagnosis and testing procedures.

CROSSFIRE

Refer to **Figs. 49 through 57,** for diagnosis and testing procedures.

NEON

Refer to "Troubleshooting" and "Component Diagnosis & Testing" for diagnosis and testing procedures.

SEBRING & STRATUS

CONVERTIBLE & SEDAN

2000

Refer to **Figs. 18 through 27,** for diagnosis and testing procedures.

2001-04

Refer to **Figs. 58 through 61,** for diagnostic procedures.

COUPE

2000

Refer to "Component Diagnosis & Testing."

2001-03

Refer to **Figs. 62 through 68,** for diagnostic procedures.

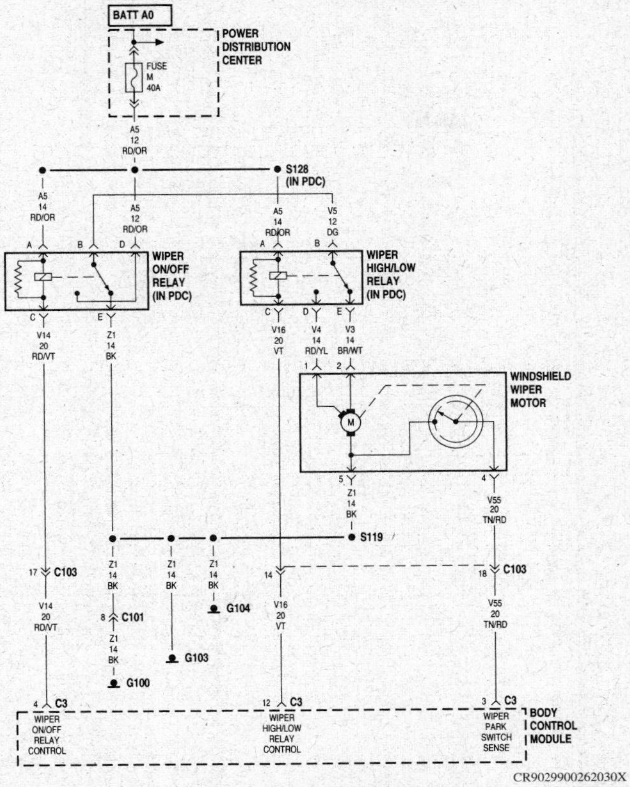

Fig. 9 Wiring diagram (Part 3 of 3). 2000 Concorde, Intrepid, LHS & 300M

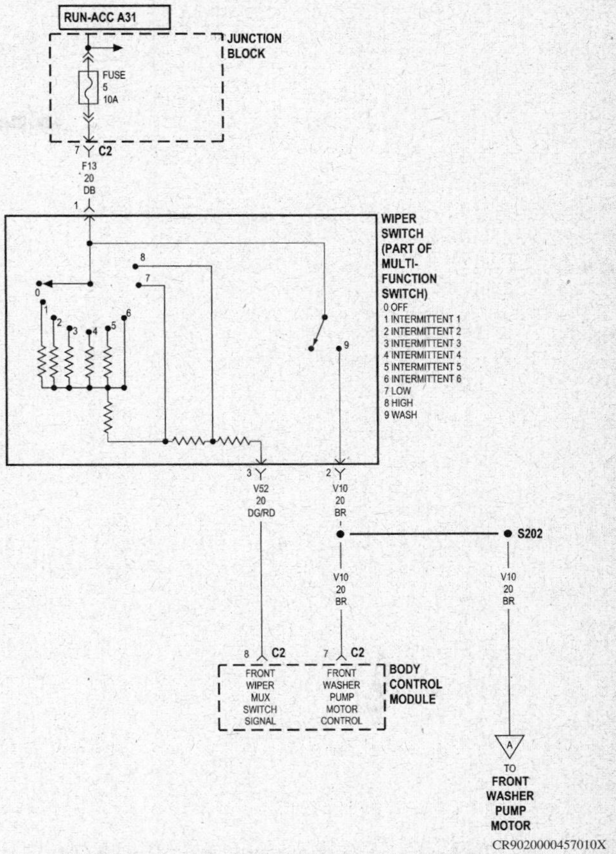

Fig. 10 Wiring diagram (Part 1 of 3). 2001–04 Concorde, Intrepid & 300M & 2001 LHS

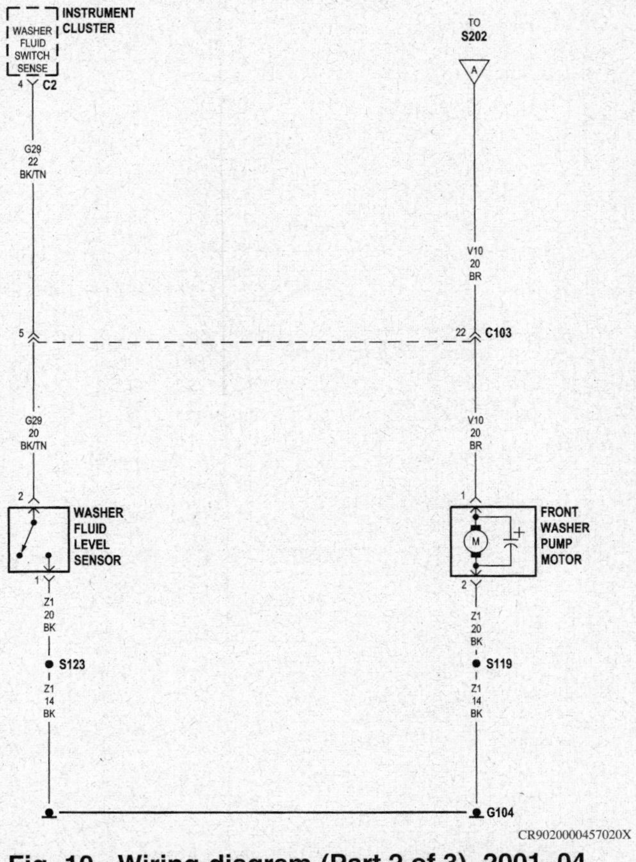

Fig. 10 Wiring diagram (Part 2 of 3). 2001–04 Concorde, Intrepid & 300M & 2001 LHS

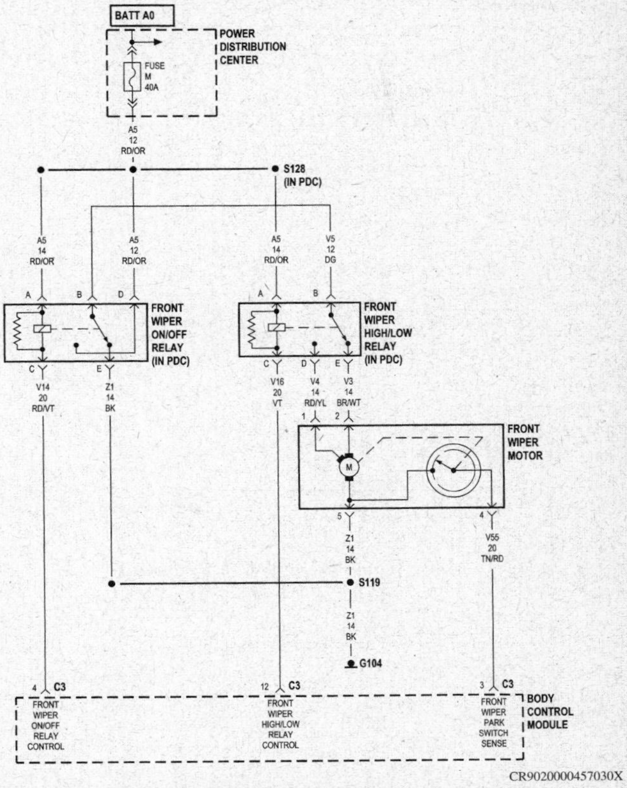

Fig. 10 Wiring diagram (Part 3 of 3). 2001–04 Concorde, Intrepid & 300M & 2001 LHS

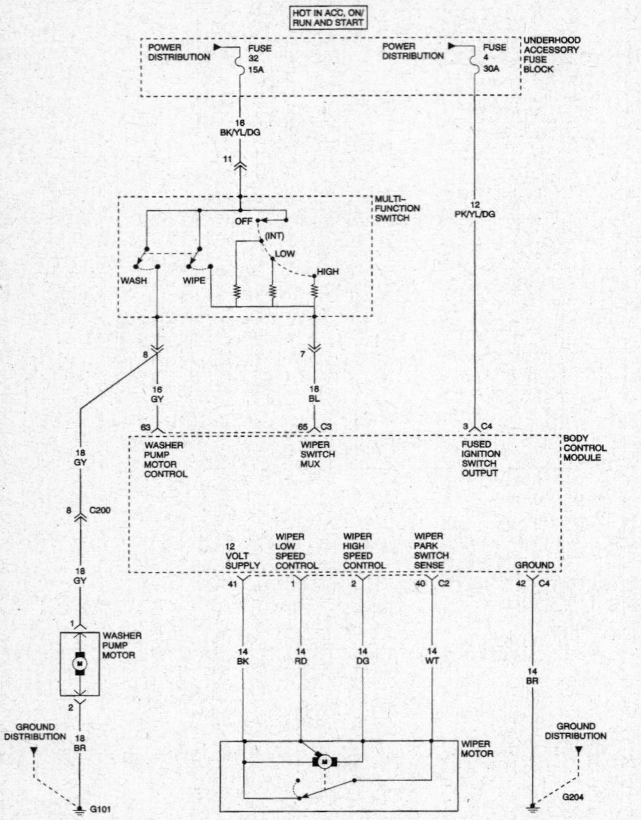

ARM0300000000141

Fig. 11 Wiring diagram. Crossfire

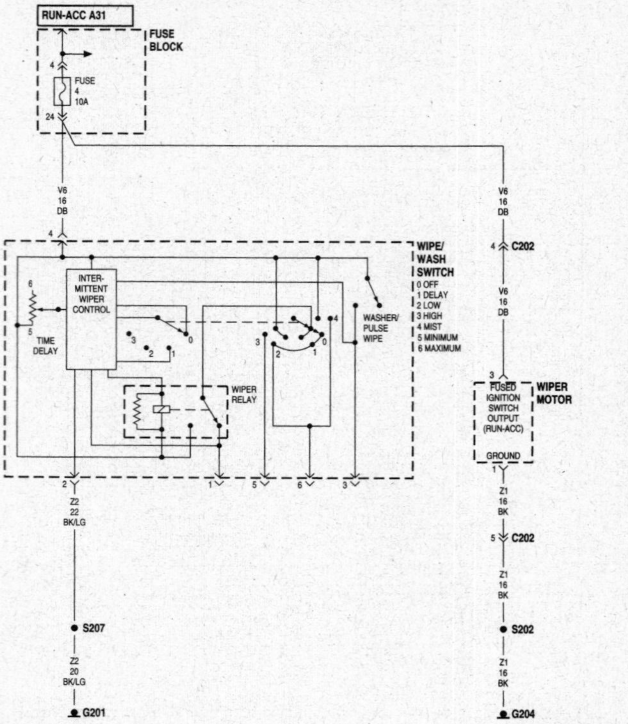

CR9029900388000X

Fig. 12 Wiring diagram (Part 1 of 2). 2000 Neon

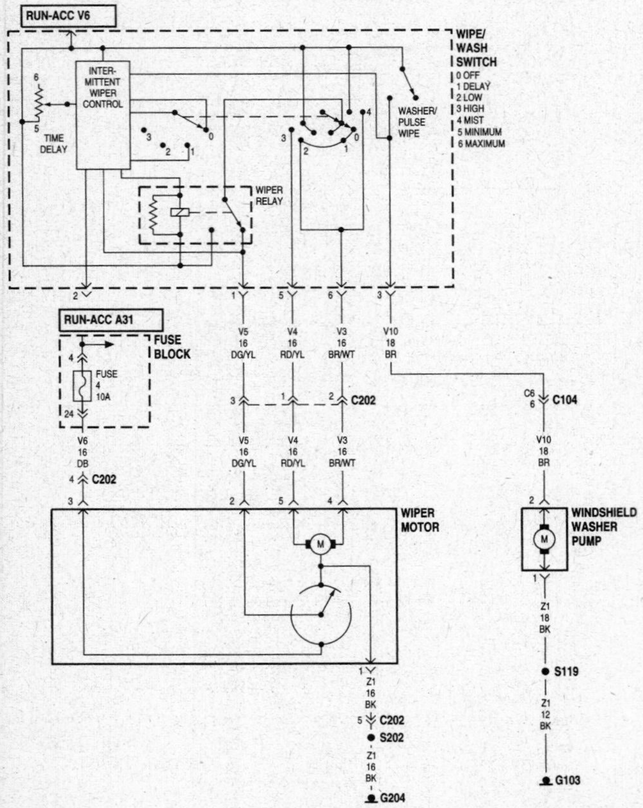

CR9029900389000X

Fig. 12 Wiring diagram (Part 2 of 2). 2000 Neon

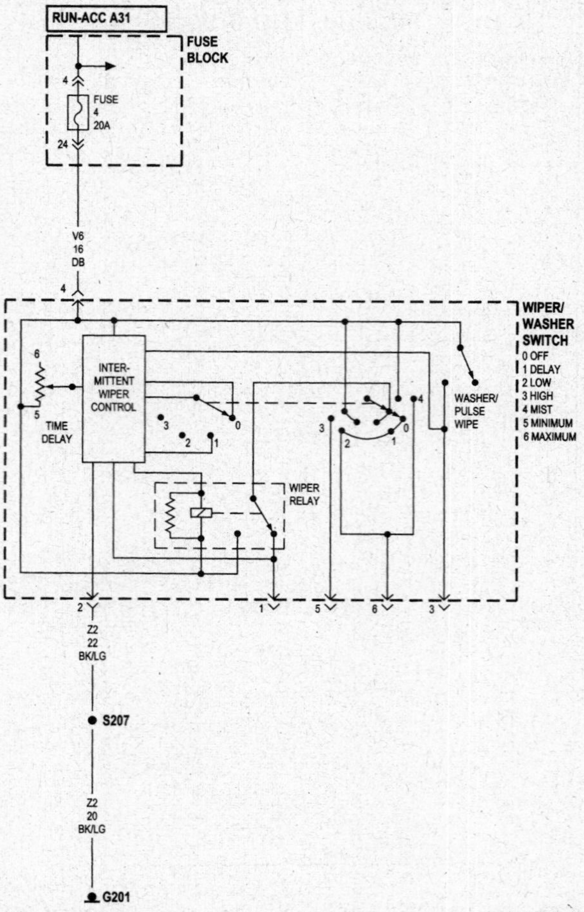

CR9020200517010X

Fig. 13 Wiring diagram (Part 1 of 2). 2001–04 Neon

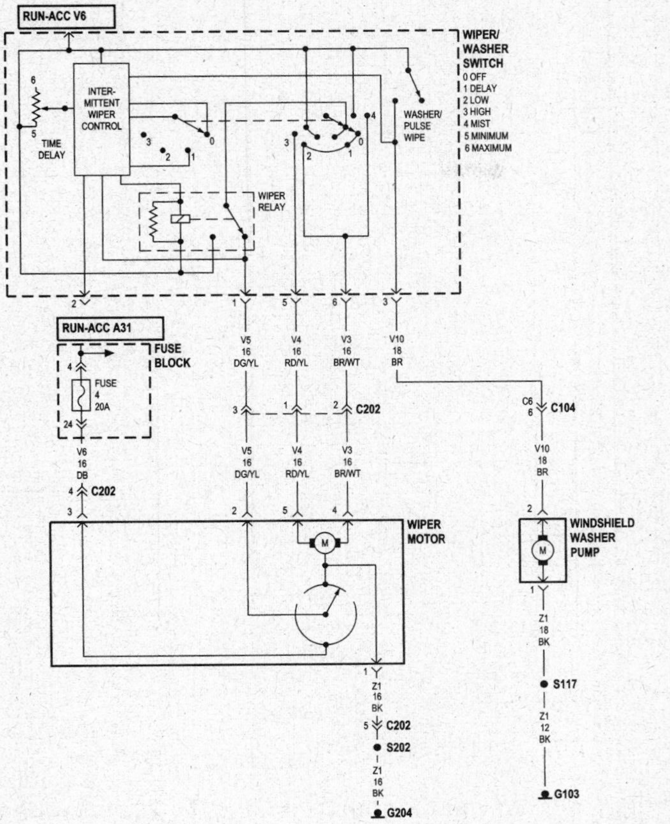

Fig. 13 Wiring diagram (Part 2 of 2). 2001–04 Neon

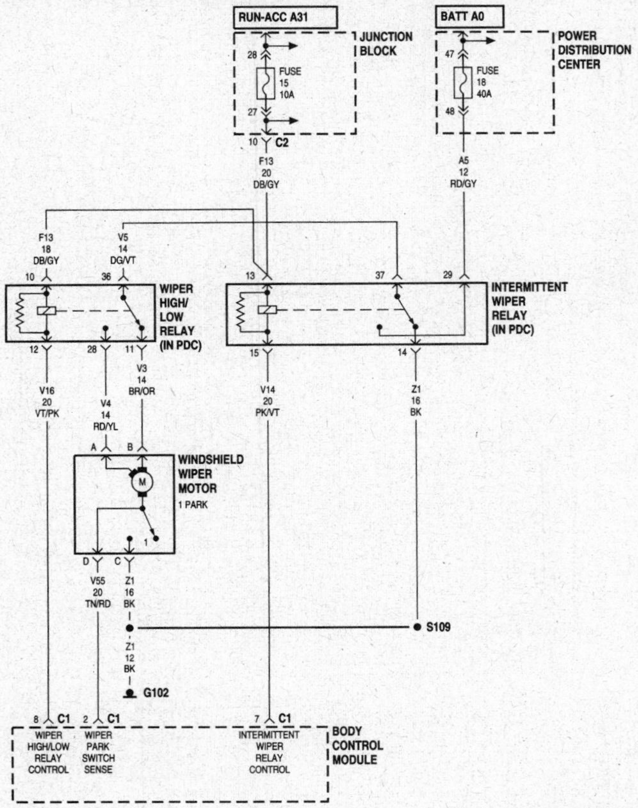

Fig. 14 Wiring diagram (Part 2 of 2). 2000 Sebring Convertible

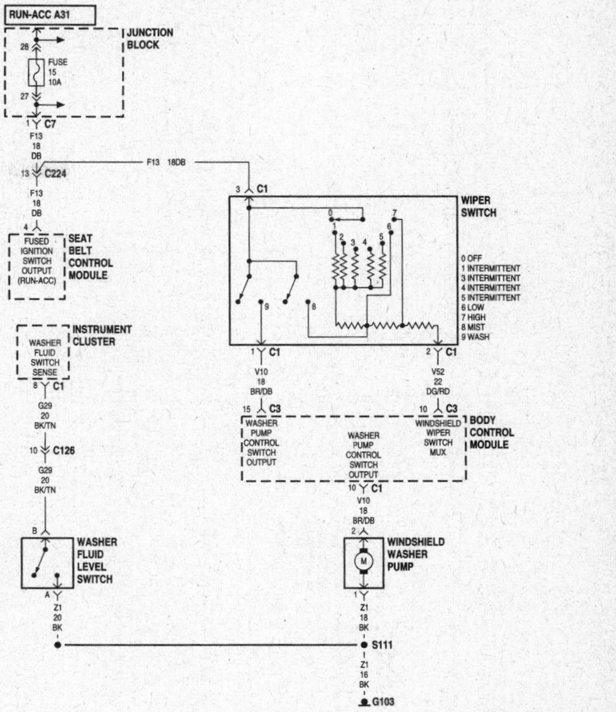

Fig. 14 Wiring diagram (Part 1 of 2). 2000 Sebring Convertible

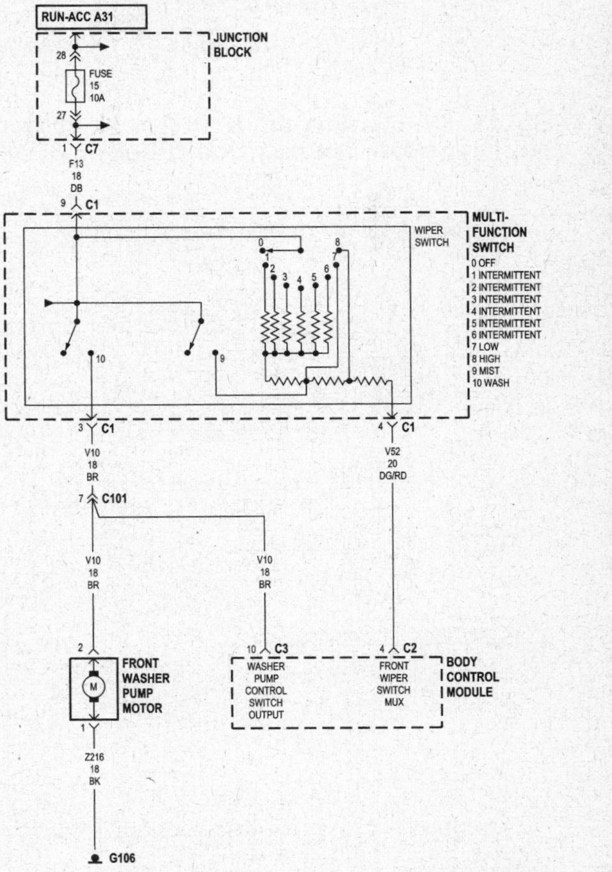

Fig. 15 Wiring diagram (Part 1 of 2). 2001–04 Sebring Sedan, Sebring Convertible & Stratus Sedan

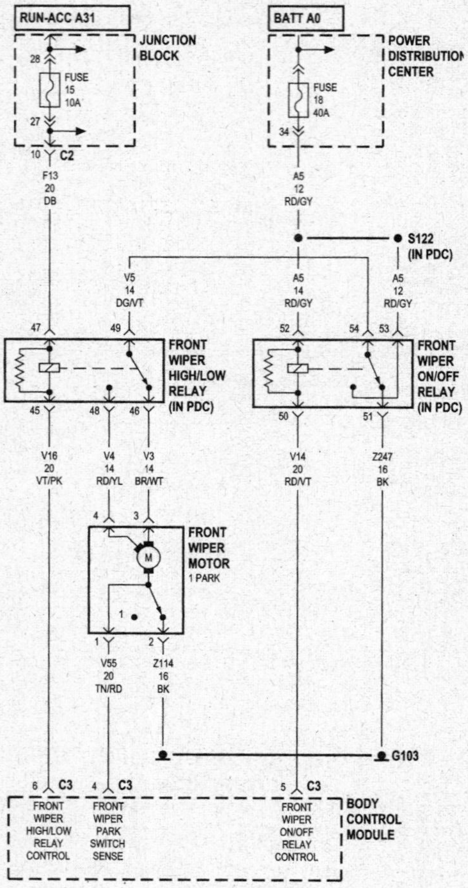

CR9020200518020X

Fig. 15 Wiring diagram (Part 2 of 2). 2001–04 Sebring Sedan, Sebring Convertible & Stratus Sedan

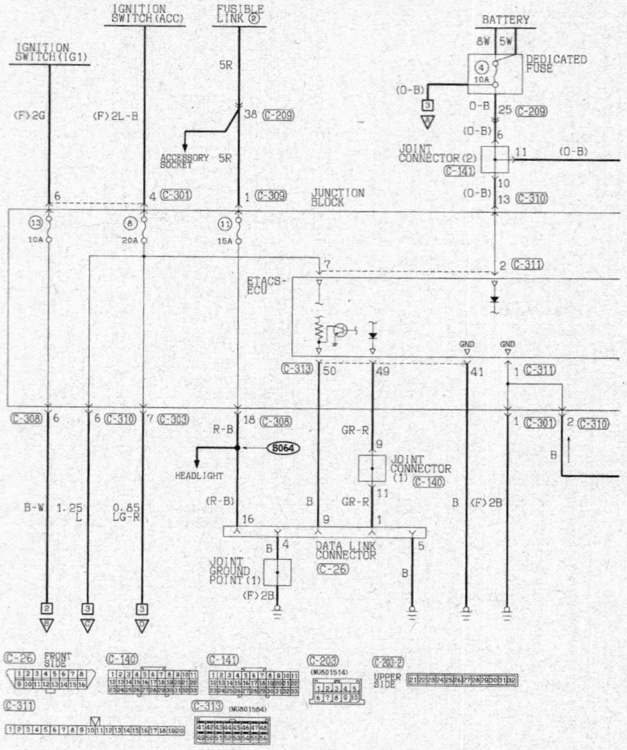

CR9020000463010X

Fig. 16 Wiring diagram (Part 1 of 4). 2001 Sebring & Stratus Coupe

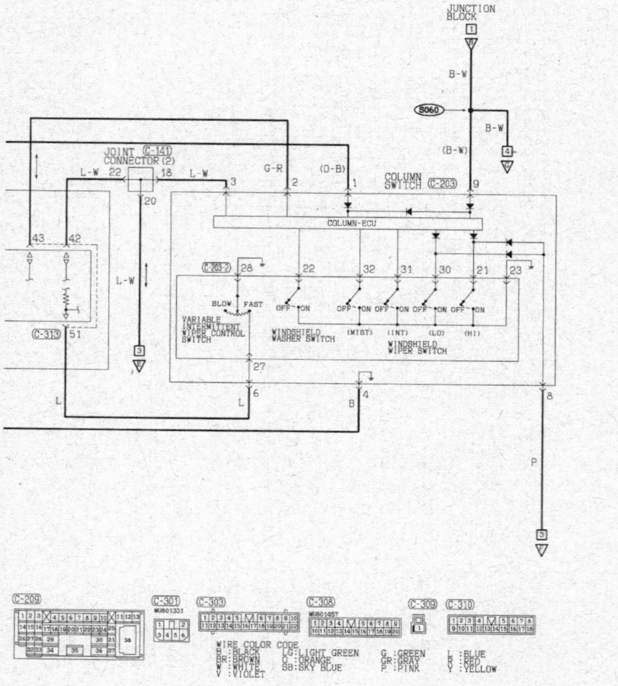

CR9020000463020X

Fig. 16 Wiring diagram (Part 2 of 4). 2001 Sebring & Stratus Coupe

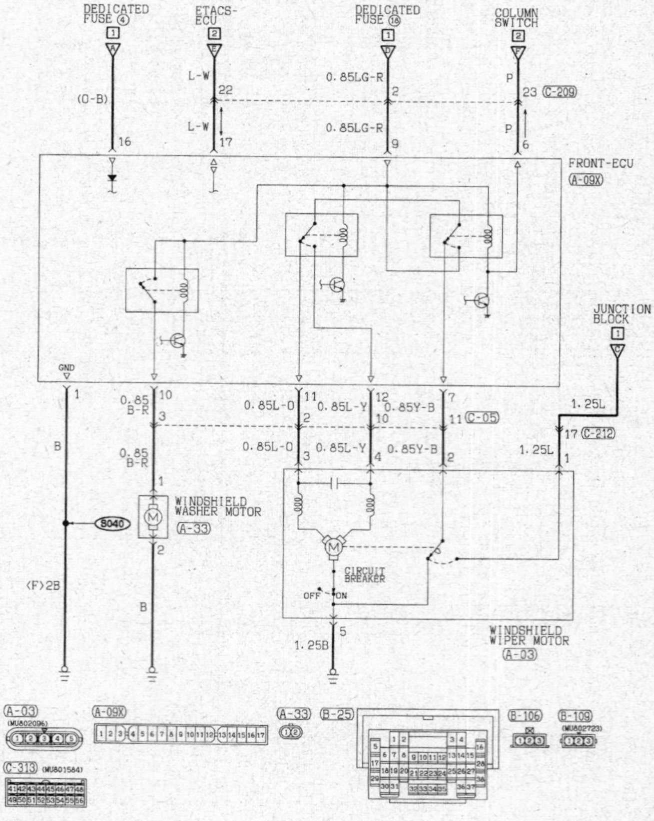

CR9020000463030X

Fig. 16 Wiring diagram (Part 3 of 4). 2001 Sebring & Stratus Coupe

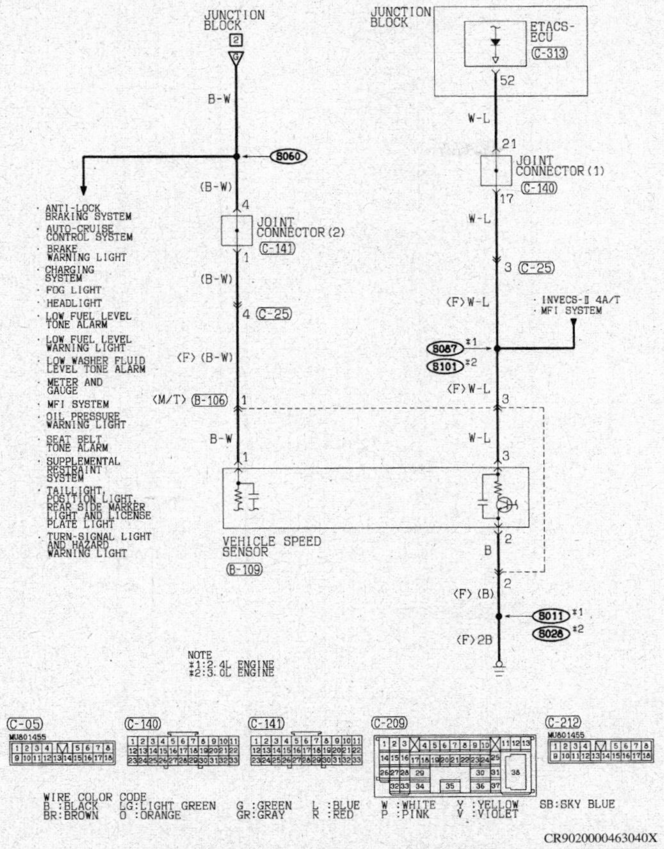

Fig. 16 Wiring diagram (Part 4 of 4). 2001 Sebring & Stratus Coupe

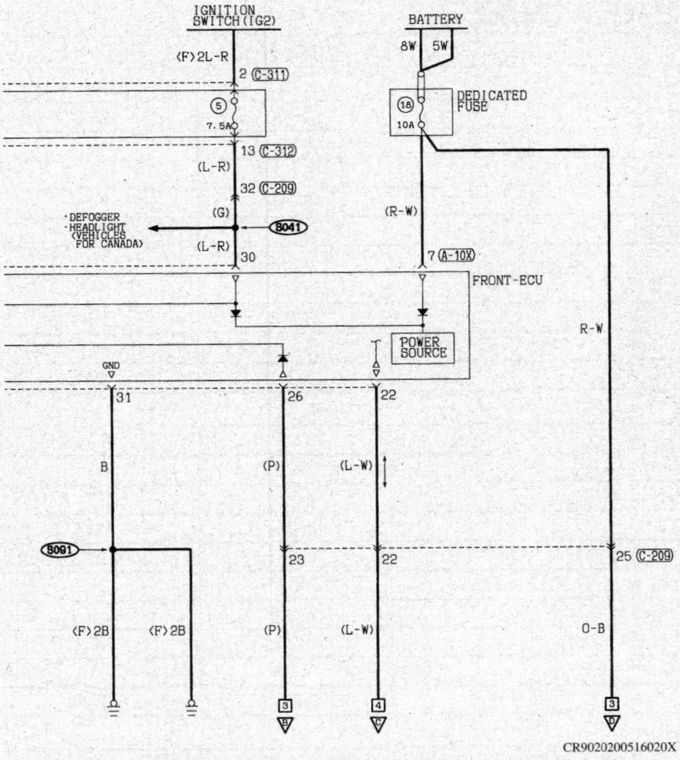

Fig. 17 Wiring diagram (Part 2 of 5). 2002–03 Sebring & Stratus Coupe

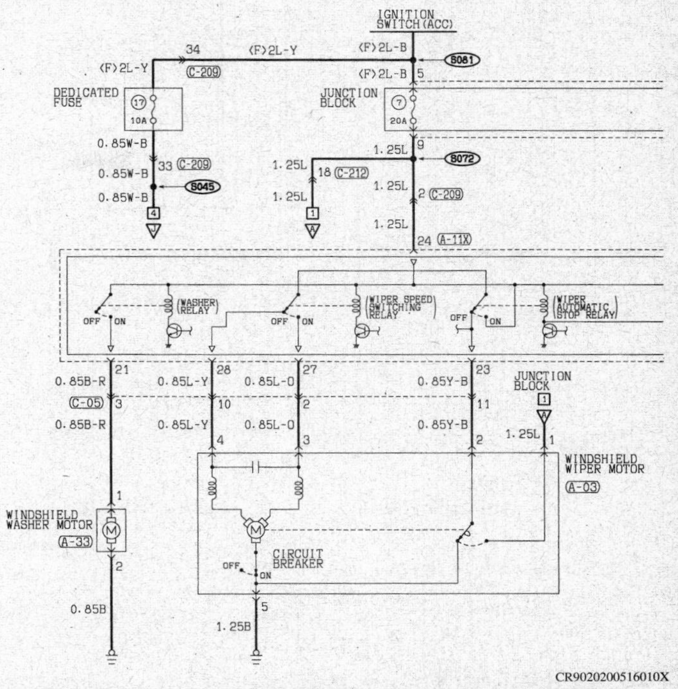

Fig. 17 Wiring diagram (Part 1 of 5). 2002–03 Sebring & Stratus Coupe

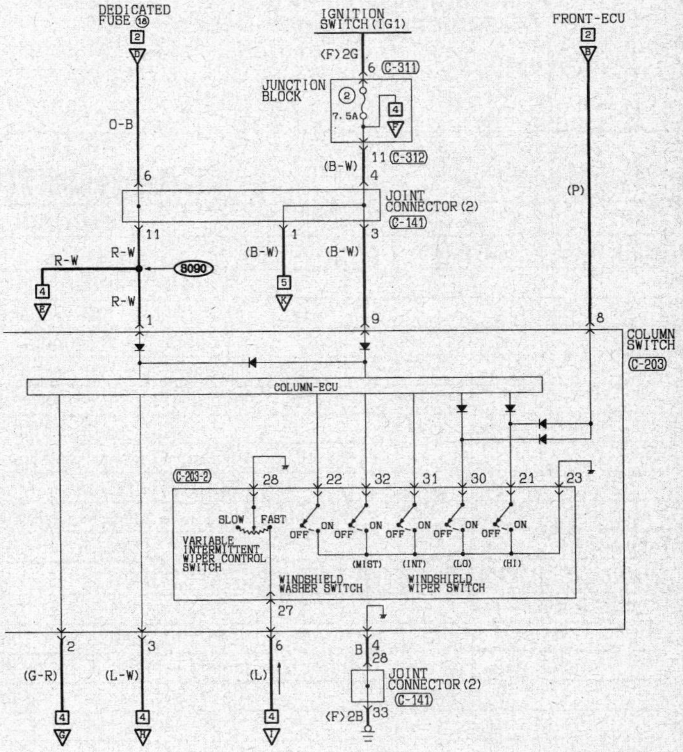

Fig. 17 Wiring diagram (Part 3 of 5). 2002–03 Sebring & Stratus Coupe

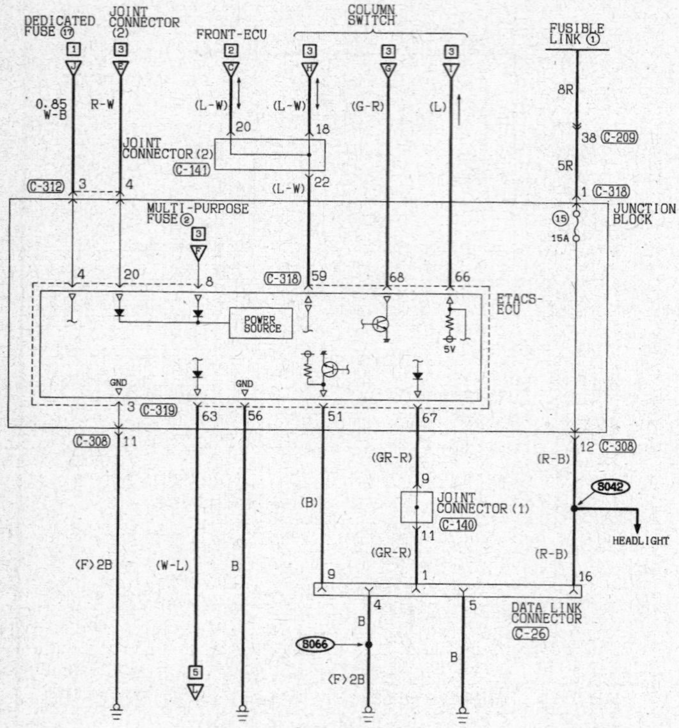

Fig. 17 Wiring diagram (Part 4 of 5). 2002–03 Sebring & Stratus Coupe

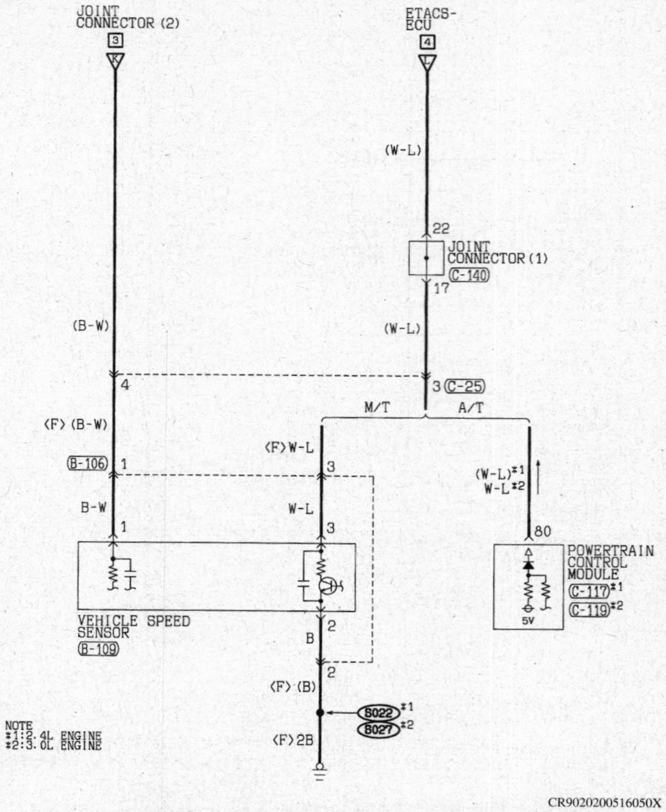

Fig. 17 Wiring diagram (Part 5 of 5). 2002–03 Sebring & Stratus Coupe

DIAGNOSTIC CHART INDEX

Test	Description	Page No.	Fig. No.
BREEZE & CIRRUS			
—	Wipers Not Parking In Off Position	3-19	21
—	Wipers Not Working At All	3-16	19
—	Wipers Not Working At High Speed	3-19	23
—	Wipers Not Working At Low Speed	3-20	24
—	Wipers Not Working Properly/Intermittent	3-19	22
—	Wiper Park Switch Failure	3-16	18
—	Wipers Operate On High Speed Only	3-20	25
—	Wipers Run Constantly w/Ignition On	3-21	26
—	Wiper Washer Function Not Working	3-18	20
Test VER 1A	Verification Test	3-21	27
2000 CONCORDE, INTREPID, LHS & 300M			
Test VER 1-A	Verification Test	3-27	37
—	Windshield Washer Inoperative	3-22	29
—	Windshield Washer Runs All Time w/Ignition On	3-23	30
—	Wipers Do Not Wipe After Wash	3-24	33
—	Wipers Not Working At All	3-24	34
—	Wipers Not Working At High Speed	3-26	35
—	Wipers Not Working At Low Speed	3-23	31
—	Wipers Operation Erratic In Intermittent Speeds	3-24	32
—	Wiper Park Switch Failure/Wipers Run Continuously	3-22	28
—	Wipers Run All Time w/Ignition On	3-26	36
2001–04 CONCORDE, INTREPID & 300M & 2001 LHS			
Test VER1	Body Verification Test	3-33	48
—	Headlamp Washers Not Operating Properly	3-28	39

Continued

DIAGNOSTIC CHART INDEX—Continued

Test	Description	Page No.	Fig. No.
2001–04 CONCORDE, INTREPID & 300M & 2001 LHS			
—	Washer Inoperative	3-28	40
—	Washer Runs All Times w/Ignition On	3-29	41
—	Wipers Do Not Wiper After Wash	3-30	44
—	Wiper Erratic Operation In Intermittent Speeds	3-30	43
—	Wiper Not Working At All	3-31	45
—	Wiper Not Working In High Speed	3-32	46
—	Wiper Not Working At Low Speed	3-29	42
—	Wiper Park Switch Failure/Wipers Run Continuously	3-27	38
—	Wiper Runs All Times With Ignition On	3-33	47
CROSSFIRE			
—	Voltage Supply Open	3-33	49
—	Washers Inoperative	3-34	50
—	Washers Run Continuously w/Ignition On	3-34	51
—	Wipers Inoperative	3-34	52
—	Wipers Highspeed Inoperative	3-35	53
—	Wipers Low Speed Inoperative	3-35	54
—	Wipers Intermittent Speed Inoperative	3-35	55
—	Wipers Run Continuously w/Ignition On	3-35	56
—	Body Verification Test	3-36	57
2001–03 SEBRING & STRATUS COUPE			
Test G-1	Windshield Wiper Does Not Operate	3-37	62
Test G-2	Any Wiper Switch Position Inoperative	3-39	63
Test G-3	Wiper Does Not Park	3-40	64
Test G-4	Intermittent Wiper Interval Cannot Be Adjusted	3-42	65
Test G-5	Windshield Washer Does Not Work	3-43	66
Test G-6	Low Washer Fluid Level Warning Light Does Not Work Normally (2001)	3-45	67
	Low Washer Fluid Level Warning Light Does Not Work Normally (2002–03)	3-48	68
2000 SEBRING CONVERTIBLE			
—	Wipers Not Parking In Off Position	3-19	21
—	Wipers Not Working At All	3-16	19
—	Wipers Not Working At High Speed	3-19	23
—	Wipers Not Working At Low Speed	3-20	24
—	Wipers Not Working Properly/Intermittent	3-19	22
—	Wiper Park Switch Failure	3-16	18
—	Wipers Operate On High Speed Only	3-20	25
—	Wipers Run Constantly w/Ignition On	3-21	26
—	Wiper Washer Function Not Working	3-18	20
Test VER 1A	Verification Test	3-21	27
2001–04 SEBRING CONVERTIBLE, SEBRING SEDAN & STRATUS SEDAN			
—	Wiper On/Off Relay Output Shorted High	3-36	58
—	Wiper On/Off Relay Output Shorted Low	3-36	59
—	Wiper Park Switch Open Circuit	3-37	60
—	Wiper Park Switch Shorted To Ground	3-37	61
2000 STRATUS			
—	Wipers Not Parking In Off Position	3-19	21
—	Wipers Not Working At All	3-16	19
—	Wipers Not Working At High Speed	3-19	23
—	Wipers Not Working At Low Speed	3-20	24
—	Wipers Not Working Properly/Intermittent	3-19	22
—	Wiper Park Switch Failure	3-16	18
—	Wipers Operate On High Speed Only	3-20	25
—	Wipers Run Constantly w/Ignition On	3-21	26
—	Wiper Washer Function Not Working	3-18	20
Test VER 1A	Verification Test	3-21	27

When Monitored: With the Ignition key on, wipers operating in the Intermittent mode, and battery voltage greater than 10 volts.

Set Condition: The wiper switch is in the Intermittent position and the park switch input does not go to 0 volts within 18 seconds.

POSSIBLE CAUSES
WIPER PARK SWITCH TOGGLE CLOSED/OPEN
OPEN WIPER PARK SWITCH SENSE CIRCUIT
WIPER MOTOR/WIPER PARK CONNECTOR
BCM/WIPER PARK SWITCH DEFAULT

TEST	ACTION
1	Turn Ignition On. Operate the Wipers in the Intermittent mode. With the DRB, select MONITOR DISPLAY, WIPER SYSTEM. Monitor the Wiper Park Switch. Does the Wiper Park Switch toggle from Closed to Open? Yes → System is operating properly. Clear any Trouble Codes and try to reproduce fault. Perform Body Verification TEST VER-1A. No → Go To 2

CR9029900378010X

Fig. 18 Wiper Park Switch Failure (Part 1 of 2). Breeze, Cirrus & 2000 Sebring Convertible & Stratus

TEST	ACTION
2	Turn the Wipers Off. Disconnect the Wiper Motor Connector. **Check connectors. Clean/repair as necessary.** With the DRB, select MONITOR DISPLAY, WIPER SYSTEM. Monitor the Wiper Park Switch. **Note: The DRB must still be monitoring the Wiper Park Switch for the next step.** Connect a jumper wire between Wiper Park Switch Sense Circuit (Cav D) and ground. Does the Wiper Park Switch show CLOSED? Yes → Replace the Wiper Motor. Perform Body Verification TEST VER-1A. No → Go To 3
3	Gain access to the Engine 14-Way Connector.(at BCM) Backprobe a jumper wire between the Wiper Park Switch Sense Ckt. and ground. Does the Wiper Park Switch show CLOSED? Yes → Repair the open Wiper Park Switch Sense Circuit. Perform Body Verification TEST VER-1A. No → Go To 4
4	If there are no potential causes remaining, the Body Control Module is assumed to be defective. View repair options. Repair Replace the Body Control Module. Perform Body Verification TEST VER-1A.

CR9029900378020X

Fig. 18 Wiper Park Switch Failure (Part 2 of 2). Breeze, Cirrus & 2000 Sebring Convertible & Stratus

POSSIBLE CAUSES
SCI/PCI COMM FAILURE- BUS OPERATIONAL
OPEN B (+) CIRCUIT- BATTERY/WIPER FUSE
OPEN IGNITION SWITCH OUTPUT CIRCUIT
INTERMITTENT WIPER RELAY
INTERMITTENT WIPER RELAY/RLY COIL
FUSED B (+) CIRCUIT SHORT/GND
HI/LO WIPER RELAY HI SPEED OUTPUT CIRCUIT- SHORT/GND
OPEN FUSED B(+) CIRCUIT-BETWEEN FUSE/INTERMITTENT RELAY
OPEN GROUND CIRCUIT
OPEN INTERMITTENT WIPER RELAY CONTROL CIRCUIT
OPEN WIPER RELAY COMMON CIRCUIT BETWEEN INTMITTENT-HI/LO RELAY
WIPER RELAY COMMON CKT SHORT/GND
HI/LO WIPER RELAY LO SPEED OUTPUT CIRCUIT- SHORT/GND
OPEN HI/LO WIPER LO SPEED OUTPUT CIRCUIT BETWEEN H/L RLY
OPEN WWIPER SWITCH SIGNAL CIRCUIT BETWEEN SW/BCM
WWIPER SWITCH SIGNAL CKT SHORT/GROUND
FUSED IGNITION SWITCH OUTPUT CKT SHORT/GND
OPEN FUSED IGNITION SWITCH OUTPUT CIRCUIT
OPEN FUSED IGNITION SWITCH OUTPUT CIRCUIT- SWITCH/FUSE #15
HI/LO WIPER RELAY- WIPER MOTOR
HI/LO WIPER RELAY-RELAY COIL
MULTI-FUNCTION SWITCH/BCM
MULTI-FUNCTION SWITCH/FUSED IGNITION SWITCH OUTPUT CKT
WIPER MOTOR/GROUND CKT
WIPER MOTOR/H/L RELAY DEFAULT
BCM DEFAULT
BCM/WIPER MOTOR OPERATE
BCM/WIPER MOTOR ACTUATION

CR9029900379010X

Fig. 19 Wipers Not Working At All (Part 1 of 8). Breeze, Cirrus & 2000 Sebring Convertible & Stratus

TEST	ACTION
1	Turn the Ignition On (Engine Off). With the DRB, select BODY, BODY COMPUTER. What message does the DRB display? A. BUS OPERATIONAL Choose appropriate Bus Failure from the Communications Symptom category of symptoms and diagnose the Communications problem first. Perform Verification TEST VER-1A. B. NO RESPONSE Refer to symptom * NO RESPONSE FROM BCM (BAT PWR DISCON'D) D. NONE OF THE ABOVE Go To 2
2	Turn Ignition On (Engine Off). With the DRB, actuate the Wipers in Low Speed mode. Does the Wiper Motor operate in the Low Speed mode? Yes → Go To 4 No → Go To 3
3	Stop the Wiper Motor actuation. With the DRB, actuate the Wipers in the High Speed mode. Does the Wiper Motor operate in the High Speed mode? Yes → Go To 4 No → Go To 10
4	Stop the Wiper Motor actuation. Turn the Ignition On. With the DRB, read the Intermittent Wipe Sensor. While monitoring the DRB, gradually move the Wiper Switch from the Off to Hi position. Does the DRB show any reading above INTRMT WIPE : 0V? Yes → Replace the Body Control Module. Perform Body Verification TEST VER-1A. No → Go To 5
5	Disconnect the Multi-Function Switch C1 Connector. **Check connectors. Clean/repair as necessary.** Turn Ignition On. Using a voltmeter, measure the Fused Ignition Switch Output Circuit (Cav 3). Is the voltage above 10.0 volts? Yes → Go To 6 No → Repair the open Fused Ignition Switch Output Circuit between the Switch and Fuse #15. Perform Body Verification TEST VER-1A.

CR9029900379020X

Fig. 19 Wipers Not Working At All (Part 2 of 8). Breeze, Cirrus & 2000 Sebring Convertible & Stratus

TEST	ACTION
6	Turn Ignition Off. Disconnect the Body Control Module I/P 22-Way Connector. **Check connectors. Clean/repair as necessary.** Using a ohmmeter, measure the Windshield Wiper Sw Signal Ckt. (Cav 10). Is the resistance below 100.0 ohms? Yes → Repair the Windshield Wiper Switch Signal Circuit for a short to ground. Perform Body Verification TEST VER-1A. No → Go To 7
7	Turn Ignition Off. Disconnect the Body Control Module I/P 22-Way Connector. Disconnect Multi/Functional Switch C1 Connector. **Check connectors. Clean/repair as necessary.** Using a ohmmeter in the following step. Measure the Windshield Wiper Switch Signal Circuit. Is the resistance below 5.0 ohms? Yes → Go To 8 No → Repair the open Windshield Wiper Switch Signal Circuit between the Switch and the Body Control Module. Perform Body Verification TEST VER-1A.
8	Reconnect the Multi-Function Switch. Turn the Wiper Switch to the Low or Hi position. Turn Ignition On. Using a voltmeter, measure the Windshield Wiper Switch Signal Circuit. (Cav 10) Is the voltage above 10.0 volts? Yes → Go To 9 No → Replace the Multi-Function Switch. Perform Body Verification TEST VER-1A.
9	If there are no potential causes remaining, the Body Control Module is assumed defective. View repair options. Repair Replace the Body Control Module. Perform Body Verification TEST VER-1A.
10	Stop the Wiper Motor actuation. With the DRB, read the Intermittent Wiper Sensor. While monitoring the DRB, gradually move the Wiper Switch from the Off to Hi position. Does the DRB show any reading above INTRM WIPE: 0.0V? Yes → Go To 11 No → Go To 26
11	Gain access to the PDC. Remove and inspect the Wiper Fuse. Is the Fuse open? Yes → Go To 12 No → Go To 17

CR9029900379030X

Fig. 19 Wipers Not Working At All (Part 3 of 8). Breeze, Cirrus & 2000 Sebring Convertible & Stratus

TEST	ACTION
16	If there are no potential causes remaining, the Wiper Motor is assumed to be defective. View repair options. Repair Replace the Wiper Motor. Perform Body Verification TEST VER-1A. **Replace the Wiper Fuse.**
17	Ignition On. Using a voltmeter, measure the B (+) Circuit. Is the voltage above 10.0 volts? Yes → Go To 18 No → Repair the open B (+) Circuit fron the Battery to the Wiper Fuse. Perform Body Verification TEST VER-1A.
18	Ignition On. Reinstall the Wiper Fuse. Disconnect the Intermittent Wiper Relay. **Check connectors. Clean/repair as necessary.** Using a voltmeter, measure Fused B(+) (Cav 29) in Inter Wiper Rly Conn. Is the voltage above 10.0 volts? Yes → Go To 19 No → Repair the open Fused B(+) Circuit between the Fuse and Intermittent Relay. Perform Body Verification TEST VER-1A.
19	Turn Ignition On. Connect a jumper wire between Cavity 37 and Cavity 29 of the Intermittent Relay. Does the Wiper Motor operate? Yes → Go To 26 No → Go To 20
20	Remove the Hi/Lo Wiper Motor Relay. **Check connectors. Clean/repair as necessary.** **Note: Make sure the jumper wire is still connected between Cav 37 and Cav 29 of the Inter Relay. NOTE: MAKE SURE THE JUMPER WIRE IS STILL CONNECTED BETWEEN CAVS "37" AND "29" OF THE INTER RELAY.** Turn Ignition On. Using a voltmeter, measure the Wiper Relay Common Circuit (Cavity 36) in the Hi/Lo Relay Connector. Is the voltage above 10.0 volts? Yes → Go To 21 No → Repair the open Wiper Relay Common Circuit between the Intermittent and Hi/Lo Relays. Perform Body Verification TEST VER-1A.
21	Disconnect a jumper wire in the Intermittent Relay Connector. Turn the Ignition On. Connect a jumper wire between Intermittent Relay Cav 29 and Hi/Lo Relay Cav 11. Does the Wiper Motor Operate in the Low Speed mode? Yes → Go To 22 No → Go To 23

CR9029900379050X

Fig. 19 Wipers Not Working At All (Part 5 of 8). Breeze, Cirrus & 2000 Sebring Convertible & Stratus

TEST	ACTION
12	Remove the Intermittent Wiper Relay. **Check connectors. Clean/repair as necessary.** Remove the Hi/Lo Wiper Relay. **Check connectors. Clean/repair as necessary.** Turn Ignition Off. Using an ohmmeter, measure the Fused B (+) Ckt. (Cav 29) in the Inter. Relay Conn. Is the resistance below 10.0 ohms? Yes → Repair the Fused B (+) Circuit for a short to ground, and replace the Wiper Fuse. Perform Body Verification TEST VER-1A. No → Go To 13 **Replace the Wiper Fuse.**
13	Remove the Intermittent Wiper Relay. **Check connectors. Clean/repair as necessary.** Remove the Hi/Lo Wiper Relay. **Check connectors. Clean/repair as necessary.** Turn Ignition Off. Using the ohmmeter, measure the Wiper Relay Common Ckt (Cav 37) in the Intermittent Relay Connector. Is the resistance below 10.0 ohms? Yes → Repair the Wiper Relay Common Circuit for a short to ground, and replace the Wiper Fuse. Perform Body Verification TEST VER-1A. No → Go To 14 **Replace the Wiper Fuse.**
14	Disconnect the Wiper Motor Connector. **Check connectors. Clean/repair as necessary.** Turn Ignition Off. Using an ohmmeter, measure Cavity 11 in the Hi/Lo Relay Conn. to ground. Is the resistance below 100.0 ohms? Yes → Repair the Hi/Lo Wiper Relay Low Speed Output Circuit for a short to ground, and replace the Wiper Fuse. Perform Body Verification TEST VER-1A. No → Go To 15 **Replace the Wiper Fuse.**
15	Disconnect the Wiper Motor Connector. **Check connectors. Clean/repair as necessary.** Turn Ignition Off. Using an ohmmeter, measure Cavity 28 in the Hi/Lo Relay Connector to ground. Is the resistance below 100.0 ohms? Yes → Repair the Hi/Lo Wiper Relay High Speed Output Circuit for a short to ground, and replace the Wiper Fuse. Perform Body Verification TEST VER-1A. No → Go To 16 **Replace the Wiper Fuse.**

CR9029900379040X

Fig. 19 Wipers Not Working At All (Part 4 of 8). Breeze, Cirrus & 2000 Sebring Convertible & Stratus

TEST	ACTION
22	Disconnect the jumper wire in the Intermittent Relay Connector. Turn the Ignition On. Connect a jumper wire between the Intermittent Relay Cav 29 and Hi/Lo Relay Cav 11. Does the Wiper Motor operate in the Low Speed mode? Yes → Replace the Hi/Lo Wiper Relay. Perform Body Verification TEST VER-1A. No → Test Complete.
23	Disconnect the Wiper Motor Connector. **Check connectors. Clean/repair as necessary.** Connect a jumper wire between Intermittent Relay Cav 29 and Hi/Lo Relay Cav 11. Turn Ignition On. **NOTE: Make sure the jumper wire is still connected between the two relay connectors.** Using a voltmeter, measure the Hi/Lo Wiper Rly Low Speed Output Ckt (Cav B). Is the voltage above 10.0 volts? Yes → Go To 24 No → Repair the open Hi/Lo Wiper Relay Low Speed Output Circuit between the Hi/Lo Relay and Wiper Motor. Perform Body Verification TEST VER-1A.
24	Disconnect the Wiper Motor Connector. **Check connectors. Clean/repair as necessary.** Key Off. Using an ohmmeter, measure the Ground Circuit (Cav C) in the Wiper Motor Connector. Is the resistance below 5.0 ohms? Yes → Go To 25 No → Repair the open Ground Circuit. Perform Body Verification TEST VER-1A.
25	If there are no potential causes remaining, the Wiper Motor is assumed to be defective. View repair options. Repair Replace the Wiper Motor. Perform Body Verification TEST VER-1A.
26	Remove the Intermittent Wiper Relay. (if connected) **Check connector. Clean/repair as necessary.** With a voltmeter, measure the Fused Ign Sw Output (Cav 13) in the Intermittent Relay. Ensure Ignition is On. Is the voltage above 10.0 volts? Yes → Go To 27 No → Go To 30

CR9029900379060X

Fig. 19 Wipers Not Working At All (Part 6 of 8). Breeze, Cirrus & 2000 Sebring Convertible & Stratus

TEST	ACTION
27	Reinstall the Intermittent Wiper Relay. Gain access to the Body Control Module but do not disconnect. Backprobe a jumper wire between the Inter Wiper Relay Control Ckt and ground. Does the Wiper Motor operate? Yes → Replace the Body Control Module. Perform Body Verification TEST VER-1A. No → Go To 28
28	Again, remove the Intermittent Wiper Relay. **Check connectors. Clean/repair as necessary.** **Note: The jumper wire must still be connected between the BCM and ground.** Turn Ignition Off. Use an ohmmeter in the following step. Measure the Intermittent Wiper Relay Control Ckt. Is the resistance below 15.0 ohms? Yes → Replace the Intermittent Wiper Relay. Perform Body Verification TEST VER-1A. No → Go To 29
29	Again, remove the Intermittent Wiper Relay. **Check connectors. Clean/repair as necessary.** **Note: The jumper wire must still be connected between the BCM and ground.** Turn Ignition OFF. Use an ohmmeter in the following step. Measure the Intermittent Wiper Relay Control Ckt. Is the resistance below 15.0 ohms? Yes → Test Complete. No → Repair the open Intermittent Wiper Relay Control Circuit between the Body Control Module and Intermittent Relay. Perform Body Verification TEST VER-1A.
30	Turn Ignition Off. Remove and inspect Fuse #15 in the Junction Block. Is the Fuse open? Yes → Go To 31 No → Go To 35
31	Remove the Hi/Lo Wiper Relay. **Check connectors. Clean/repair as necessary.** Turn Ignition Off. Use an ohmmeter in the following step. Measure the Hi/Lo Wiper Relay Coil (Terminals 1 & 2). Is the resistance between 65 and 90 ohms? Yes → Go To 32 No → Replace the Hi/Lo Wiper Relay, and replace Fuse #15. Perform Body Verification TEST VER-1A. **Replace Fuse # 15.**

CR9029900379070X

Fig. 19 Wipers Not Working At All (Part 7 of 8). Breeze, Cirrus & 2000 Sebring Convertible & Stratus

TEST	ACTION
32	Remove the Intermittent Wiper Relay. **Check connectors. Clean/repair as necessary.** Turn Ignition Off. Using an ohmmeter in the following step. Measure the Intermitent Wiper Relay Coil (Terminal 1 & 2). Is the resistance between 65 and 90 ohms? Yes → Go To 33 No → Replace the Intermittent Wiper Relay, and replace Fuse #15. Perform Body Verification TEST VER-1A. **Replace Fuse # 15.**
33	Disconnect the Multi-Function Switch C1 Connector. **Check connectors. Clean/repair as necessary.** Turn Ignition Off. Using an ohmmeter, measure the Fused Ignition Switch Output Circuit (Cavity 3) to ground (Cavity 5). Is the resistance below 5.0 ohms? Yes → Repair the Fused Ignition Switch Output Circuit for a short to ground, and replace Fuse #15. Perform Body Verification TEST VER-1A. No → Go To 34 **Replace Fuse # 15.**
34	Disconnect the Multi-Function Switch Right Connector. **Check connectors. Clean/repair as necessary.** Turn Ignition Off. Using an ohmmeter, measure the Fused Ignition Switch Output Circuit (Cavity 3) to ground (Cavity 5). Is the resistance below 5.0 ohms? Yes → Test Complete. No → Replace the Multi-Function Switch, and replace Fuse #15. Perform Body Verification TEST VER-1A. **Replace Fuse # 15.**
35	Turn Ignition On. Using a voltmeter, measure the Ignition Switch Output Circuit . Is the voltage above 10.0 volts? Yes → Repair the open Fused Ignition Switch Output Circuit. Perform Body Verification TEST VER-1A. No → Go To 36
36	Turn Ignition On. Using a voltmeter, measure the Ignition Switch Output Circuit . Is the voltage above 10.0 volts? Yes → Test Complete. No → Repair the open Ignition Switch Output Circuit. Perform Body Verification TEST VER-1A.

CR9029900379080X

Fig. 19 Wipers Not Working At All (Part 8 of 8). Breeze, Cirrus & 2000 Sebring Convertible & Stratus

POSSIBLE CAUSES
DO WIPERS OPERATE
OPEN WASHER PUMP CONTROL CIRCUIT
OPEN WASHER PUMP CONTROL SWITCH OUTPUT CKT
OPEN GROUND CIRCUIT/WASHER PUMP CONNECTOR
DEFECTIVE WASHER PUMP
MULTI-FUNCTION SW/WASHER SW
BCM/WASHER SWITCH
BCM/WIPER OPERATES
DEFAULT BCM/10 VOLTS
BCM/WASHER PUMP CONTROL CKT.

TEST	ACTION
1	**Note: Make sure the Washer Fluid Jar is full before proceeding.** Turn Ignition On. Momentarily pull and then release the Wash Button on the Stalk Switch. Did the Washer Pump operate? Yes → Go To 2 No → Go To 4
2	**Note: Make sure the Washer Fluid Jar is full before proceeding.** Momentarily pull and then release the Wash Button on the Stalk Switch. Turn Ignition On. Did the Wipers operate? Yes → System is operating properly. Perform Verification TEST VER-1A. No → Replace the Body Control Module. Perform Body Verification TEST VER-1A.
3	**Note: Make sure the Washer Jar is full before proceeding.** Turn Ignition On. Momentarily pull and then release the Wash Button on the Stalk Switch. Did the Wipers operate?
4	Turn Ignition On. Did the Wipers operate? Yes → Go To 5 No → Go To 9

CR9029900380010X

Fig. 20 Wiper Washer Function Not Working (Part 1 of 3). Breeze, Cirrus & 2000 Sebring Convertible & Stratus

TEST	ACTION
5	Disconnect the Washer Pump Connector. Turn Ignition Off. Using an ohmmeter, measure the Ground Circuit at the Connector. Is the resistance below 5.0 ohms? Yes → Go To 6 No → Repair the open Ground Circuit to the Washer Pump Connector. Perform Body Verification TEST VER-1A.
6	Turn Ignition On. Disconnect the Washer Pump Connector. **Check connector. Clean/repair as necessary.** Activate the Washer Switch during the following step. Using a voltmeter, measure the Washer Pump Cntrl Ckt (Cav B) while activating the Switch. Is the voltage above 10.0 volts? Yes → Replace the Washer Pump. Perform Body Verification TEST VER-1A. No → Go To 7
7	Gain access to the BCM Engine 14- Way Connector but do not disconnect. Activate the Washer Switch during the following step. Turn Ignition On. Using a voltmeter, backprobe and measure the Washer Pump Control Circuit (Cav 10) while activating the Switch. Is the voltage above 10.0 volts? Yes → Repair the open Washer Pump Control Circuit between the BCM and Washer Pump. Perform Body Verification TEST VER-1A. No → Go To 8
8	Gain access to the BCM Engine 14-Way Connector but do not disconnect. Activate the Washer Switch during the following step. Using a voltmeter, measure the Washer Pump Control Ckt. (Cavity 10) while activating Switch. Is the voltage above 10.0 volts? Yes → Test Complete. No → Replace the Body Control Module. Perform Body Verification TEST VER-1A.
9	Turn Ignition On. With the DRB, read the WASHER SWITCH status while pulling the Stalk Switch. Does the DRB show WASHER SW : CLOSED? Yes → Replace the Body Conrtol Module. Perform Body Verification TEST VER-1A. No → Go To 10

CR9029900380020X

Fig. 20 Wiper Washer Function Not Working (Part 2 of 3). Breeze, Cirrus & 2000 Sebring Convertible & Stratus

TEST	ACTION
10	Disconnect the Right Multi-Function Switch C1 Connector. **Note: Check connectors. Clean/repair as necessary.** Turn Ignition On. Connect a jumper wire between the Fused Ign Switch Output Circuit (Cav 3) and the Washer Pump Control Switch Output Ckt. (Cav 1). With the DRB, read the WASHER SWITCH status with the jumper connected. Does the DRB show WASHER SW: CLOSED? Yes → Replace the Multi-Function Switch. Perform Body Verification TEST VER-1A. No → Go To 11
11	Disconnect the Body Control Module I/P 22-Way Connector. **check connectors. Clean/repair as necessary.** Connect a jumper wire between the Fused Ign Switch Output Circuit (Cav 3) and the Washer Pump Control Switch Output Ckt. (Cav 1). Turn Ignition On. **Note: Ensure the jumper in the Multi-Function Switch is still connected.** Using a voltmeter, measure the Washer Pump Control Switch Output (Cav 15). Is the voltage above 10.0 volts? Yes → Go To 12 No → Repair the open Washer Pump Control Switch Output Circuit. Perform Body Verification TEST VER-1A.
12	Gain access to the BCM Engine 14-Way Connector but do not disconnect. Activate the Washer Switch during the following step. Turn Ignition On. Using a voltmeter, backprobe and measure the Washer Pump Control Circuit (Cav 10) while activating the Switch. Is the voltage above 10.0 volts? Yes → Repair the open Washer Pump Control Circuit between the BCM and Washer Pump. Perform Body Verification TEST VER-1A. No → Go To 13
13	If there are no potential causes remaining, the Body Control Module is assumed to be defective. View repair options. Repair Replace the Body Control Module. Perform Body Verification TEST VER-1A.

CR9029900380030X

Fig. 20 Wiper Washer Function Not Working (Part 3 of 3). Breeze, Cirrus & 2000 Sebring Convertible & Stratus

POSSIBLE CAUSES
MULTI-FUNCTION SWITCH/STALK SWITCH
BCM/WIPER STALK SWICH

TEST	ACTION
1	Turn the ignition on (Engine off). With the DRB, select Body Control Module. Does the DRB display NO RESPONSE? Yes → Refer to symptom * NO RESPONSE FROM BCM (BAT PWR DISCON'D) No → Go to 2
2	Turn the ignition On. With the DRB, monitor the wiper voltage, while moving the Wiper Stalk Switch through all six Intermittent Wiper Positions. Did the voltage change proportionally as the switch was moved through the different positions? Yes → Replace the BOdy Control Module Perform Body verification TEST VER-1A No → Replace the Multi-Function Switch. Perform Body Verification TEST VER 1-A.

CR9029900382010X

Fig. 22 Wipers Not Working Properly/Intermittent. Breeze, Cirrus & 2000 Sebring Convertible & Stratus

TEST	ACTION
889	Turn the Ignition On (Engine Off). Record and erase the trouble codes in the BCM. Operate the Wiper System in the following modes: High Speed , Low Speed, all Intermittent Switch, and Wash Mode (with the Wiper Off). Are there trouble codes present? Yes → Go To 890 No → Test Complete.
890	Turn Ignition On. Operate the Wipers in the Intermittent mode. With the DRB, select MONITOR DISPLAY, WIPER SYSTEM. Monitor the Wiper Park Switch. Does the Wiper Park Switch toggle from Closed to Open? Yes → System is operating properly. Clear any Trouble Codes and try to reproduce fault. Perform Body Verification TEST VER-1A. No → Go To 891
891	Turn the Wipers Off. Disconnect the Wiper Motor Connector. **Check connectors. Clean/repair as necessary.** With the DRB, select MONITOR DISPLAY, WIPER SYSTEM. Monitor the Wiper Park Switch. **Note: The DRB must still be monitoring the Wiper Park Switch for the next step.** Connect a jumper wire between Wiper Park Switch Sense Circuit (Cav D) and ground. Does the Wiper Park Switch show CLOSED? Yes → Replace the Wiper Motor. Perform Body Verification TEST VER-1A. No → Go To 892
892	Gain access to the Engine 14-Way Connector.(at BCM) Backprobe a jumper wire between the Wiper Park Switch Sense Ckt. and ground. Does the Wiper Park Switch show CLOSED? Yes → Repair the open Wiper Park Switch Sense Circuit. Perform Body Verification TEST VER-1A. No → Go To 893
893	If there are no potential causes remaining, the Body Control Module is assumed to be defective. View repair options. Repair Replace the Body Control Module. Perform Body Verification TEST VER-1A.

CR9029900381000X

Fig. 21 Wipers Not Parking In Off Position. Breeze, Cirrus & 2000 Sebring Convertible & Stratus

POSSIBLE CAUSES
OPEN HI/LO WIPER RELAY CONTROL CIRCUIT
OPEN HI/LO WIPER RELAY HI SPEED OUTPUT CIRCUIT
OPEN FUSED IGNITION OUTPUT CIRCUIT- HI/LO WIPER RELAY
HI/LO WIPER RLY-ACTUATION
MULTI-FUNCT SW/INTERM VOLTAGE
WIPER MOTOR/H-L WIPER RLY HI SPEED
BCM-HI/LO WIPER DEFAULT
DEF BCM/MULTI-FUNCTION SWITCH

TEST	ACTION
1	Turn Ignition On. With the DRB, actuate the Wipers in the High Speed mode. Does the Wiper Motor operate in the High Speed mode? Yes → Go To 2 No → Go To 3
2	Turn Ignition On. Stop the High Speed Wiper Motor actuation. With the DRB, read the Intermittent Wipe Sensor voltage While monitoring the DRB, move the Wiper Switch to the High position. Is the Intermittent Wiper voltage above 6.5 volts? Yes → Go To 3 No → Replace the Multi-Function Switch. Perform Body Verification TEST VER-1A.
3	Stop the High Speed Wiper Motor actuation. **Note: Ensure Ignition is On.** Remove the Hi/Lo Wiper Relay. **Check connectors. Clean/repair as necessary.** Use a voltmeter in the following step. Measure the Fused Ign Sw Output (Cav 10) in the Hi/Lo Relay Connector. Is the voltage above 10.0 volts? Yes → Go To 4 No → Repair the open Fused Ignition Switch Output Circuit. Perform Body Verification TEST VER-1A.

CR9029900383010X

Fig. 23 Wipers Not Working At High Speed (Part 1 of 3). Breeze, Cirrus & 2000 Sebring Convertible & Stratus

TEST	ACTION
4	Stop the High Speed Wiper Motor actuation. Remove the Hi/Lo Wiper Relay. **Check connectors. Clean/repair as necessary.** Connect a jumper between the Fused Ign Switch Output (Cav 10) and Wiper Hi/Lo Rly Hi Spd Out (Cav 28) in the Hi/Lo Relay Connector. Does the Wiper Motor operate in the High Speed mode? Yes → Go To 5 No → Go To 7
5	**WARNING: Disconnect the jumper wire then disconnect the Wiper Motor Connector.** **Check connectors. Clean/repair as necessary.** Reconnect jumper wire as in previous step. Use a test light in the following step. Connect the test light between the Hi/Lo Wiper Relay Control Ckt. and ground. Turn Ignition On. With the DRB, actuate the Wipers in the High Speed mode. During the actuation, observe the test light. Does the test light come on and off during actuation? Yes → Replace the Hi/Lo Wiper Relay. Perform Body Verification TEST VER-1A. No → Go To 6
6	Key Off. Stop the Wiper actuation. Disconnect the Body Control Module Engine 14-Way Connector. **Check connectors. Clean/repair as necessary.** Connect a jumper wire from Hi/Lo Wiper Relay Control (Cav 8) to ground. Connect a test light between Fused Ignition Switch Output (Cav 10) and Hi/Lo Wiper Relay Control (Cav12). Turn Ignition On (Engine Off). Is the test light on? Yes → Go To 7 No → Repair the open Hi/Lo Wiper Relay Control Circuit. Perform Body Verification TEST VER-1A.
7	Connect a jumper between Fused Ign Switch Output (Cav 10) and Wiper Hi/Lo Rly Hi Spd Out (Cav 28) in the Hi/Lo Relay Connector. **Check connectors. Clean/repair as necessary.** **WARNING: Disconnect the jumper wire then disconnect the Wiper Motor Connector.** Reconnect jumper wire as in previous step. Turn Ignition On. Using a voltmeter, measure the Hi/Lo Wiper Relay Hi Speed Output Ckt.(Cav A). Is the voltage above 10.0 volts? Yes → Go To 8 No → Repair the open Hi/Lo Wiper Relay Hi Speed Output Circuit. Perform Body Verification TEST VER-1A.

CR9029900383020X

Fig. 23 Wipers Not Working At High Speed (Part 2 of 3). Breeze, Cirrus & 2000 Sebring Convertible & Stratus

TEST	ACTION
909	Turn the Ignition On. With the DRB, actuate the Wiper Motor in Low Speed. Does the Wiper Motor operate in the Low Speed mode? Yes → Go To 910 No → Go To 911
910	Stop the Low Speed Wiper Motor actuation. Turn Ignition On. With the DRB, read the Intermittent Wipe Sensor voltage. While monitoring the DRB, move the Wiper Switch to the Low Speed position. Is the Intermittent Wiper voltage approx. 5.5 volts? Yes → Replace the Body Control Module. Perform Body Verification TEST VER-1A. No → Replace the Multi-Function Switch. Perform Body Verification TEST VER-1A.
911	Turn Ignition On (Engine Off). Remove the Wiper Hi/Lo Relay. Connect a jumper wire between Fused Ign Switch Output (Cav 10) and Hi/Lo Wiper Relay Lo Spd Output (Cav 11) in Wiper Hi/Lo Relay Connector. Does the Wiper Motor operate in Low Speed? Yes → Replace the Hi/Lo Wiper Relay. Perform Body Verification TEST VER-1A. No → Go To 912
912	Remove the Wiper Hi/Lo Relay. **WARNING: Disconnect the jumper wire then disconnect the Wiper Motor Connector.** **Check connectors. Clean/repair as necessary.** Connect a jumper wire between Fused Ign Switch Output (cav 10) and Hi/Lo Wiper Relay Lo Spd Output (cav 11) in Wiper Hi/Lo Relay Connector. Turn Ignition On. Using a voltmeter, measure Hi/Lo Wiper Relay Lo Speed Output Ckt. (Cav B) Is the voltage above 10.0 volts? Yes → Replace the Wiper Motor. Perform Body Verification TEST VER-1A. No → Repair the open Hi/Lo Wiper Relay Lo Speed Output Circuit. Perform Body Verification TEST VER-1A.

CR9029900384000X

Fig. 24 Wipers Not Working At Low Speed (Part 1 of 2) . Breeze, Cirrus & 2000 Sebring Convertible & Stratus

TEST	ACTION
8	Connect a jumper between Fused Ign Switch Output (Cav 10) and Wiper Hi/Lo Rly Hi Spd Out (Cav 28) in the Hi/Lo Relay Connector. **WARNING: Disconnect the jumper wire then disconnect the Wiper Motor Connector.** **Check connectors. Clean/repair as necessary.** Reconnect jumper wire as in previous step. Turn Ignition On. Using a voltmeter, measure the Hi/Lo Wiper Relay Hi Speed Output Ckt.(Cav A). Is the voltage above 10.0 volts? Yes → Replace the Wiper Motor. Perform Body Verification TEST VER-1A. No → Test Complete.

CR9029900383030X

Fig. 23 Wipers Not Working At High Speed (Part 3 of 3). Breeze, Cirrus & 2000 Sebring Convertible & Stratus

TEST	ACTION
5	**WARNING: Disconnect the jumper wire then disconnect the Wiper Motor Connector.** Turn Ignition On. Connect a jumper wire between Fused Ign Switch Output (cav 10) and Hi/Lo Wiper Relay Lo Spd Output (cav 11) in Wiper Hi/Lo Relay Connector. Using a voltmeter, measure Hi/Lo Wiper Relay Lo Speed Output Ckt. (Cav B) Is the voltage above 10.0 volts? Yes → Replace the Wiper Motor. Perform Body Verification TEST VER-1A. No → Test Complete.

CR9029900384020X

Fig. 24 Wipers Not Working At Low Speed (Part 2 of 2). Breeze, Cirrus & 2000 Sebring Convertible & Stratus

POSSIBLE CAUSES
HI/LO WIPER RELAY CONTROL CKT SHORT/GND
HI/LO WIPER RELAY
BCM/HI-LO WIPER RELAY

TEST	ACTION
1	Remove the Hi/Lo Wiper Relay. Replace the original Hi/Lo Wiper Relay with a known good relay. Turn Ignition On. Turn the Wipers On and observe the operation. Do the Wipers now operate properly in the Low and High Speed mode? Yes → Replace the Hi/Lo Wiper Relay. Perform Body Verification TEST VER-1A. No → Go To 2
2	Key Off. Disconnect the Body Control Module Engine 14- Way Connector. **Check connectors. Clean/repair as necessary.** Remove the substitute Hi/Lo Relay. Using an ohmmeter, measure the Hi/Lo Wiper Relay Control Circuit (Cavity 8) to ground (Cavity 12). Is the resistance below 100.0 ohms? Yes → Repair the Hi/Lo Wiper Relay Control Circuit for a short to ground. Perform Body Verification TEST VER-1A. No → Go To 3
3	If there are no potential causes remaining, the Body Control Module is assumed to be defective. View repair options. Repair Replace the Body Control Module. Perform Body Verification TEST VER-1A.

CR9029900385000X

Fig. 25 Wipers Operate On High Speed Only. Breeze, Cirrus & 2000 Sebring Convertible & Stratus

POSSIBLE CAUSES
INTERM WIPER RELAY CONTROL CKT SH/GND
INTERM WIPER RLY
W/WIPER SW SIGNAL CKT-SHORT/VOLTS
WIPER PARK SWITCH SENSE CIRCUIT - SHORT TO GROUND
WIPER PARK SWITCH SENSE CIRCUIT OPEN
MULTI-FUNCTION SW/SW CONN
DEFECTIVE WIPER MOTOR/WIPERS RUN CONSTANTLY
BCM/WWIPERS SW SIG CKT
DEFECTIVE BCM- WIPERS RUN CONSTANTLY
DEFECTIVE WIPER MOTOR-RUNS CONSTANTLY

TEST	ACTION
1	**Note: The Ignition must be On and the Wiper Switch must be Off before proceeding.** With the DRB, read the Intermittent Wiper voltage. Does the DRB show Intermittent Wiper voltage above 0.5 volts? Yes → Go To 2 No → Go To 5
2	Key Off. Disconnect the Body Control Module I/P 22-Way Connector. **Check connectors. Clean/repair as necessary.** Turn Ignition On (Engine Off). Using a voltmeter, measure the Windshield Wiper Switch Signal Ckt (Cavity 10) to the Chassis Ground. Is the voltage above 0.5 volts? Yes → Go To 3 No → Replace the Body Control Module. Perform Body Verification TEST VER-1A.
3	Key Off. Disconnect the Right Multi-Function Switch C1 Connector. **Check connectors. Clean/repair as necessary.** Turn Ignition On (Engine Off). **Note: The Voltmeter must still be connected from a previous step.** Using a voltmeter, measure the Windshield Wiper Switch Signal Ckt (Cavity 10) to the Chassis Ground. Is the voltage above 0.5 volts? Yes → Repair the W/Wiper Switch Signal Circuit for a Short to Voltage. Perform Body Verification TEST VER-1A. No → Go To 4

CR9029900386010X

Fig. 26 Wipers Run Constantly w/Ignition On (Part 1 of 3). Breeze, Cirrus & 2000 Sebring Convertible & Stratus

TEST	ACTION
4	Key Off. Disconnect the Multi-Function Switch C1 Connector. **Check connectors. Clean/repair as necessary.** Turn Ignition On (Engine Off). **NOTE: The Voltmeter must still be connected from a previous step.** Using a voltmeter, measure the Windshield Wiper Switch Signal Ckt (Cavity 10) to the Chassis Ground. Is the voltage above 0.5 volts? Yes → Replace the Multi-Function Switch. Perform Body Verification TEST VER-1A. No → Test Complete.
5	Key Off. Remove the Intermittent Wiper Relay. Replace the original Intermittent Wiper Relay with a known good one. Turn Ignition On. Do the Wipers still operate constantly? Yes → Go To 6 No → Replace the Intermittent Wiper Relay. Perform Body Verification TEST VER-1A.
6	Turn the Ignition Off when the Wipers are not in the park position. Disconnect the Body Control Module Engine 14-Way Connector. **Check connectors - Clean/repair as necessary.** Using an ohmmeter, measure the Wiper Park Switch Sense Ckt (Cav 2). Is the resistance below 100.0 ohms? Yes → Go To 7 No → Go To 8
7	Disconnect the Wiper Motor Connector. **Note: Check connectors - Clean/repair as necessary.** Using an ohmmeter, measure the Wiper Park Switch Sense Circuit. Is the resistance below 100.0 ohms? Yes → Repair the Wiper Park Switch Sense Circuit for a short to ground. Perform Body Verification TEST VER-1A. No → Replace the Wiper Motor. Perform Body Verification TEST VER-1A.
8	Key Off. Remove the substitute Intermittent Wiper Relay. Disconnect the Body Control Module Engine 14- Way Connector. **Check connectors. Clean/repair as necessary.** Using an ohmmeter, measure the Inter Wiper Rly Control Ckt (Cav7). Is the resistance below 100.0 ohms? Yes → Repair the Intermittent Wiper Relay Control Circuit for a Short to Ground. Perform Body Verification TEST VER-1A. No → Go To 9

CR9029900386020X

Fig. 26 Wipers Run Constantly w/Ignition On (Part 2 of 3). Breeze, Cirrus & 2000 Sebring Convertible & Stratus

TEST	ACTION
9	Turn the Ignition Off. Disconnect the Wiper Motor Connector. **Check connectors - Clean/repair as necessary.** Using the DRB select, MOINTOR DISPLAY, WIPER SYSTEM and monitor the Wiper Park Switch. Connect a jumper wire between the Wiper Park Switch Sense and the ground circuits in the Wiper Motor Connector. Turn the Ignition On (Engine Off). Does the Wiper Park Switch show CLOSED? Yes → Replace the Wiper Motor. Perform Body Verification TEST VER-1A. No → Go To 10
10	Gain access to the BCM C1 (Engine 14-Way) Connector but do not disconnect. Backprobe a jumper wire between the Wiper Park Switch Sense Circuit and ground. Does the Wiper Park Switch show CLOSED? Yes → Repair the open Wiper Park Switch Sense Ckt. Perform Body Verification TEST VER-1A. No → Replace the Body Control Module. Perform Body Verification TEST VER-1A.

CR9029900386030X

Fig. 26 Wipers Run Constantly w/Ignition On (Part 3 of 3). Breeze, Cirrus & 2000 Sebring Convertible & Stratus

1. Reconnect all previously disconnected components and connectors.
2. If the Sentry Key Immoblizer Module was replaced, obtain the vehicle's unique pin number in step 9. If no replacment was made, continue to next step.
3. If the Body Control Module was replaced you must turn the Ignition On for 15 secs (to learn VIN) or engine will not start. Use the DRB and program all RKE transmitters used with the vehicle.
4. Use the DRB and Recalibrate HVAC doors.
5. Use the DRB and program other options as necessary. If the vehiocle is equipped with VTSS, select MISCELLANEOUS and ENABLE VTSS.
6. If any repairs were made to the HVAC system or the Battery was disconnected: Start the Engine and, using the DRB, recalibrate the HVAC doors.
7. Ensure that the Ignition is On, and with the DRB, erase all Diagnostic Trouble Codes.
8. Turn Ignition Off and wait 5 seconds.
9. Turn Ignition On and fully operate the system that was malfunctioning. If the system is operating properly, continue to next step. If not operating properly, select and perform the appropriate test from the symptom list.
10. With the DRB, read Body Control Module Trouble Codes. If no Trouble Codes are present and customer's complaint can not be duplicated, the repair is complete. If any Codes are present, return to Symptom list and follow path specified for that Trouble Code.
11. Obtain the Vehicle's unique PIN number assigned to it's original SKIM module from either the vehicle's invoice number or from Chrysler's Customer Center.
12. With the DRB, select THEFT ALARM, SKIM, MISCELLANEOUS. Select SKIM Module Replaced function and the DRB will prompt you through the following steps.
13. Enter secured access mode using the unique 4 digit PIN number.
14. Program the vehicle's VIN number into the SKIM's memory.
15. Program the country code into the SKIM's memory (US).
16. Transfer the vehicle's unique Secret Key data from the PCM. This process will require the SKIM module to be in secured access mode. The PIN number must be entered into the DRB before the SKIM will enter secured access mode.
17. Once secured access mode is active, the SKIM will remain in that mode for 60 seconds.
18. Program all customer keys into the SKIM's memory. This requires that the SKIM be in secure access mode. The SKIM module will immediatly exit secured access mode after each key is programmed.
19. Note: Secured access mode is not required to query the programmed status of the key.
20. Note: If the PCM is replaced, the unique Secret Key data must be transferred from the SKIM module to the PCM. This procedure requires the SKIM to be placed in secured access mode using the 4-digit PIN code.
21. Note: If three attempts are made to enter secured access mode using an incorrect PIN, secured access mode will be locked out for one hour. To exit this locked out mode, turn the Ignition to the Run position for one Hour.
22. Ensure all accessories are turned off. Also monitor the Battery state and connect a Battery charger if necessary.
23. To program Sentry Keys using the Customer Programming method, which requires two valid smart keys, refer to either the owner's or service manual.
24. Turn the Ignition On, then wait 3 minutes. With the DRB, read the SKIM trouble codes.
25. If no codes are present, the system is operational and the repair is complete. If codes are present, select the appropriate test from the Symptom List.

CR9029900387000X

Fig. 27 Test VER 1A: Verification Test. Breeze, Cirrus & 2000 Sebring Convertible & Stratus

TEST	ACTION
1	Turn the ignition on. With the DRBIII®, erase BCM DTC's. Turn the ignition off, then turn the ignition on. Turn the windshield wiper switch to each intermittent position, then low and high speed positions. Turn the windshield wiper switch to the off position. With the DRBIII®, read BCM DTC's. Does the DRB display "WIPER PARK SWITCH FAILURE"? Yes → Go To 2 No → Test Complete, code not present at this time.
2	Turn the ignition off. Disconnect the windshield wiper motor harness connector. Disconnect the BCM C3 harness connector. Measure the resistance of the wiper park switch sense circuit between the BCM C3 harness connector and the wiper motor harness connector. Is the resistance below 5.0 ohms? Yes → Go To 3 No → Repair the wiper park switch sense circuit for an open. Perform BODY VERIFICATION TEST

CR9029900367010X

Fig. 28 Wiper Park Switch Failure/Wipers Run Continuously (Part 1 of 2). 2000 Concorde, Intrepid, LHS & 300M

TEST	ACTION
3	Turn the ignition off. Disconnect the windshield wiper motor harness connector. Disconnect the BCM C3 harness connector. Measure the resistance between ground and the wiper park switch sense circuit. Is the resistance below 100.0 ohms? Yes → Repair the wiper park switch sense circuit for a short to ground. Perform BODY VERIFICATION TEST No → Go To 4
4	Turn the ignition off. Disconnect the windshield wiper motor harness connector. Disconnect the BCM C3 harness connector. Turn the ignition on. Measure the voltage of the wiper park switch sense circuit. Is there any voltage present? Yes → Repair the wiper park switch sense circuit for a short to voltage. Perform BODY VERIFICATION TEST No → Go To 5
5	Turn the ignition off. Disconnect the windshield wiper motor harness connector. **Note: Check connectors - Clean/repair as necessary.** **Note: Ensure the ignition, all lights and accessories are turned off.** Using a 12-volt test light connected to 12-volts, check the ground circuit at the windsheild wiper motor harness connector. Is the test light on? Yes → Go To 6 No → Repair the open Wiper Motor Ground Circuit. Perform BODY VERIFICATION TEST
6	Turn the ignition off. Disconnect the windshield wiper motor harness connector. Turn the ignition on. With the DRBIII® in Inputs/Outputs, read the wiper park switch state. Connnect one end of a jumper wire to the wiper park switch sense circuit at the windshield wiper motor harness connector. While observing the DRB III, connect the other end of the jumper wire to ground for several seconds, then disconnect the jumper wire from ground. Did wiper park switch input change state when connected to ground then disconnected from ground? Yes → Go To 7 No → Replace the Body Control Module. Perform BODY VERIFICATION TEST.
7	If there are no possible causes remaining, view repair. Repair Replace the Wiper Motor. Perform BODY VERIFICATION TEST

CR9029900367020X

Fig. 28 Wiper Park Switch Failure/Wipers Run Continuously (Part 2 of 2). 2000 Concorde, Intrepid, LHS & 300M

TEST	ACTION
1	Turn the ignition on. Using a 12-volt test light connected to ground, check the ignition switch output ACC/RUN circuit at the junction block fuse #5 connector. Is the test light on? Yes → Go To 2 No → Repair the open ignition switch output Run/Acc circuit . Perform BODY VERIFICATION TEST
2	Turn the ignition off. Remove and inspect junction block fuse #5. Is the fuse open? Yes → Go To 3 No → Go To 7 **Note: Reinstall the fuse if it is not open.**
3	Turn the ignition off. Disconnect the multi-function switch harness connector. Remove junction block fuse #5. Measure the resistance between ground and the fused ignition switch output ACC/RUN circuit. Is the resistance below 100.0 ohms? Yes → Repair the Fused Ignition Switch Output Run/ACC circuit shorted to ground.. Perform BODY VERIFICATION TEST No → Go To 4

CR9029900368010X

Fig. 29 Windshield Washer Inoperative (Part 1 of 3). 2000 Concorde, Intrepid, LHS & 300M

TEST	ACTION
4	Turn the ignition off. Disconnect the multi-function switch harness connector and remove the multi-function switch from the steering column. Ensure that the washer switch is in the off position. **Note: Check connectors - Clean/repair as necessary.** Measure the resistance of the multi-function switch between terminal #1 and each of the remaining six terminals in the 7-way connector (component side). Is the resistance below 100.0 ohms for any of the measurements? Yes → Replace the Right Multi-Function Switch. Perform BODY VERIFICATION TEST No → Go To 5
5	Turn the ignition off. Disconnect the washer pump harness connector. Disconnect the BCM C2 harness connector. Disconnect the multi-function switch harness connector. **Note: Check connectors - Clean/repair as necessary.** Measure the resistance between ground and the washer pump control switch output circuit. Is the resistance below 100.0 ohms? Yes → Repair Washer Pump Control Switch Output circuit shorted to ground. Perform BODY VERIFICATION TEST No → Go To 6
6	If there are no possible causes remaining, view repair. Repair Test Complete.
7	Turn the ignition off. Disconnect the washer pump harness connector. **Note: Check connectors - Clean/repair as necessary** Using a 12-volt test light connected to 12-volts, check the washer pump ground circuit. Is the test light on? Yes → Go To 8 No → Repair open ground circuit. Perform BODY VERIFICATION TEST
8	Turn the ignition off. Disconnect the multi-function switch harness connector. Turn the ignition on. Using a 12-volt test light connected to ground, check the fused ignition switch output circuit. Is the test light on? Yes → Go To 9 No → Repair the open Fused Ignition Switch Output Run/Acc. Perform BODY VERIFICATION TEST

CR9029900368020X

Fig. 29 Windshield Washer Inoperative (Part 2 of 3). 2000 Concorde, Intrepid, LHS & 300M

TEST	ACTION
9	Turn the ignition off. Disconnect the multi-function switch harness connector and remove the multi-function switch from the steering column. **Note: Check connectors - Clean/repair as necessary.** Measure the resistance of the multi-function switch between terminals #1 and #2. Monitor the ohmmeter while pushing and releasing the washer switch. **Note: The resistance reading should change from above 100.0 ohms when the washer switch is released to below 5.0 ohms when the switch is pressed.** Did the resistance readings change from above 100.0 ohms to below 5.0 ohms as described in Note? Yes → Go To 10 No → Replace the multi-function swtich. Perform BODY VERIFICATION TEST
10	Turn the ignition off. Disconnect the windshield washer pump motor harness connector. **Note: Check connectors - Clean/repair as necessary.** Turn the ignition on. Using a 12-volt test light connected to ground, check the washer pump motor control output circuit at the windshield washer pump motor harness connector. Monitor the test light while pressing and releasing the washer switch. does the test light turn on and off while pressing and releasing the washer switch? Yes → Go To 11 No → Repair the open washer pump motor control output circuit. Perform BODY VERIFICATION TEST
11	Disconnect the washer pump harness connector. **Note: Check connectors - Clean/repair as necessary.** Using a 12-volt test light connected to ground, check the washer pump control switch output circuit at the windshield wiper motor harness connector. Monitor the test light while pressing and releasing the washer switch. Does the test light turn on and off when pressing and releasing the washer switch? Yes → Replace the Winshield Washer Pump/Motor. Perform BODY VERIFICATION TEST. No → Test Complete.

CR9029900368030X

Fig. 29 Windshield Washer Inoperative (Part 3 of 3). 2000 Concorde, Intrepid, LHS & 300M

TEST	ACTION
1	Remove the wiper high/low relay. Connect a jumper wire between the fused B(+) circuit at cavity A and the wiper low speed output circuit at cavity E. Observe windshield wiper operation. Are the windshield wipers operating at low speed? Yes → Go To 2 No → Go To 6
2	Turn the ignition off. Install a known good relay in place of the wiper high/low relay. Turn the ignition on. Turn the multi-function switch to the low wiper setting, then to the high wiper setting. Observe wiper operation for each setting. Do the low speed and high speed wipers operate correctly? Yes → Replace the defective Wiper HIGH/LOW Relay. Perform BODY VERIFICATION TEST No → Go To 3
3	Turn the ignition off. Disconnect the multi-function switch harness connector and remove the multi-function switch from the steering column. Set the multi-function switch to the low speed position. Measure the resistance between terminals #1 and #3 of the multi-function switch connector (component side). Is the resistance between 980.0 and 1060.0 ohms? Yes → Go To 4 No → Replace the multi-function switch. Perform BODY VERIFICATION TEST

CR9029900371010X

Fig. 31 Wipers Not Working At Low Speed (Part 1 of 2). 2000 Concorde, Intrepid, LHS & 300M

TEST	ACTION
1	Ensure that the washer switch is in the off position. Turn the ignition on. Disconnect the multi-function switch harness connector. Does the wiper and washers stop working when the multi-function switch is disconnected? Yes → Go To 2 No → Repair washer pump motor control output circuit short to voltage. Perform BODY VERIFICATION TEST
2	Ensure that the windshield washer switch is in the off position. Turn the ignition on. Disconnect the multi-function switch harness connector. Did the wiper and washers stop working when the multi-function switch is disconnected? Yes → Replace the multi-function switch. Perform BODY VERIFICATION TEST No → Test Complete.

CR9029900370000X

Fig. 30 Windshield Washer Runs All Time w/Ignition On. 2000 Concorde, Intrepid, LHS & 300M

TEST	ACTION
4	Turn the ignition off. Remove the wiper high/low relay from the PDC. Disconnect the BCM C3 harness connector. **Note: Check connectors - Clean/repair as necessary.** Measure the resistance between ground and the wiper high/low relay control circuit. Is the resistance below 100.0 ohms? Yes → Repair the Wiper High/Low Relay Control circuit shorted to ground. Perform BODY VERIFICATION TEST No → Go To 5
5	If there are no possible causes, view repair Repair Replace the Body Control Module. Perform BODY VERIFICATION TEST.
6	Remove the wiper high/low relay from the PDC. Using a 12-volt test light connected to ground, check the fused B(+) circuit. Is the test light on? Yes → Go To 7 No → Repair the fused B(+) circuit for an open. Perform the Body Verification Test - Ver 1.
7	Turn the ignition off. Remove the wiper high/low relay from the PDC.. Disconnect the wiper motor harness connector. **Note: Check connectors - Clean/repair as necessary.** Measure the resistance of the low speed output circuit between the wiper motor and the PDC high/low relay connector (cavity E). Is the resistance below 5.0 ohms? Yes → Go To 8 No → Repair the open Low Speed Output circuit between the High/Low Relay in the Power Distribution Center and the Wiper Motor connector. Perform BODY VERIFICATION TEST
8	If there are no possible causes, view repair Repair Replace the Wiper Motor. Perform BODY VERIFICATION TEST.

CR9029900371020X

Fig. 31 Wipers Not Working At Low Speed (Part 2 of 2). 2000 Concorde, Intrepid, LHS & 300M

TEST	ACTION
1	Substitute the wiper on/off relay with a known good relay. Turn the ignition on. Turn the wipers on. Does the system now operate correctly? Yes → Replace the Wiper On/Off Relay. Perform BODY VERIFICATION TEST. No → Go To 2
2	Turn the ignition off. Disconnect the windshield wiper motor harness connector. Disconnect the BCM C3 harness connector. Measure the resistance of the wiper park switch sense circuit between the BCM C3 harness connector and the wiper motor harness connector. Is the resistance below 5.0 ohms? Yes → Go To 3 No → Repair the wiper park switch sense circuit for an open. Perform BODY VERIFICATION TEST
3	Turn the ignition off. Disconnect the windshield wiper motor harness connector. Disconnect the BCM C3 harness connector. Measure the resistance between ground and the wiper park switch sense circuit. Is the resistance below 100.0 ohms? Yes → Repair the wiper park switch sense circuit for a short to ground. Perform BODY VERIFICATION TEST No → Go To 4

CR9029900372010X

Fig. 32 Wipers Operation Erratic In Intermittent Speeds (Part 1 of 2). 2000 Concorde, Intrepid, LHS & 300M

TEST	ACTION
1	Turn the ignition on. Turn the wiper switch to each intermittent position, then to the low speed and high speed positions. **Note: Observe wiper operation when selecting each speed of operation.** Do the wipers operate correctly at all selected speeds? Yes → Go To 2 No → Refer to symptom list for problems related to wiper operation.
2	Turn the ignition off. Disconnect the body control module C2 harness connector. **Note: Check connectors - Clean/repair as necessary.** Turn the ignition on. Using a 12-volt test light connected to ground, check the washer pump control switch output circuit at the body control module C2 harness connector. Monitor the test light while pressing and releasing the washer switch. Does the test light flash on and off while pressing and releasing the washer switch? Yes → Go To 3 No → Repair the open washer pump control switch output circuit at the body control module C2 harness connector. Perform BODY VERIFICATION TEST
3	If there are no possible causes remaining, replace the BCM. View repair options Replace the BCM. Perform BODY VERIFICATION TEST.

CR9029900373000X

Fig. 33 Wipers Do Not Wipe After Wash. 2000 Concorde, Intrepid, LHS & 300M

TEST	ACTION
4	Turn the ignition off. Disconnect the windsheild wiper motor harness connector. Turn the ignition on. With the DRBIII® in Inputs/Outputs, read the wiper park switch state. Connnect one end of a jumper wire to the wiper park switch sense circuit at the windsheild wiper motor harness connector. While observing the DRB III, connect the other end of the jumper wire to ground for several seconds, then disconnect the jumper wire from ground. Did wiper park switch input change state when connected to ground then disconnected from ground? Yes → Replace the wiper motor. Perform BODY VERIFICATION TEST No → Replace the Body Control Module. Perform BODY VERIFICATION TEST.

CR9029900372020X

Fig. 32 Wipers Operation Erratic In Intermittent Speeds (Part 2 of 2). 2000 Concorde, Intrepid, LHS & 300M

TEST	ACTION
1	Turn the ignition off. Remove the wiper on/off relay. Connect a jumper wire between cavity D (87) and cavity B (30) of the wiper on/off relay connector in the PDC. Observe windshield wiper operation. Do the wipers operate with the jumper wire connected? Yes → Go To 2 No → Go To 14
2	With the DRBIII®, read the intermittent wiper switch status while slowly turning the wiper switch from the off position to the high speed position. **Note: The switch voltage displayed on the DRB III should increase from approximately 0.0 volts to 8.5 volts as the switch is turned from the off position to the high speed position.** Did the switch voltage change from aprroximately 0.0 volts to 8.5 volts as described? Yes → Go To 3 No → Go To 8
3	Remove the wiper on/off relay from the PDC. Using a 12-volt test light connected to ground, check both fused B(+) circuits at the wiper on/off relay connector in the PDC. Is the test light on when checking each circuit? Yes → Go To 4 No → Repair the open fused B(+) circuit(s). Perform the Body Verification Test - Ver 1.

CR9029900374010X

Fig. 34 Wipers Not Working At All (Part 1 of 5). 2000 Concorde, Intrepid, LHS & 300M

TEST	ACTION
4	Substitute the wiper on/off relay with a known good relay. Turn the ignition on. Turn the wipers on. Does the system now operate correctly? Yes → Replace the Wiper On/Off Relay. Perform BODY VERIFICATION TEST. No → Go To 5
5	Turn the ignition off. Remove the wiper on/off relay from the PDC. Disconnect the BCM C3 harness connector. **Note: Check connectors - Clean/repair as necessary.** Connect a jumper wire between the wiper on/off relay control circuit at the BCM C3 harness connector and ground. Measure the resistance bewteen ground and the wiper on/off relay control circuit at the PDC. Is the resistance below 5.0 ohms? Yes → Go To 6 No → Repair the open Wiper On/Off Relay Control circuit. Perform BODY VERIFICATION TEST
6	Turn the ignition off. Remove the wiper on/off relay from the PDC. Disconnect the BCM C3 harness connector. **Note: Check connectors - Clean/repair as necessary.** Turn the ignition on. Measure the voltage of the wiper on/off relay control circuit at the BCM C3 harness connector. Is the voltage above 1.0 volt? Yes → Repair the Wiper On/Off Relay Control circuit shorted to battery. Perform BODY VERIFICATION TEST No → Go To 7
7	Remove the wiper on/off relay from the PDC. Using a 12-volt test light connected to 12-volts, probe the wiper on/off relay control circuit at the wiper on/off relay connector in the PDC. With the DRBIII®, actuate the wiper on/off relay. Observe the test light. Does the test light turn on and off during actuation? Yes → Test Complete. No → Replace the Body Control Module. Perform BODY VERIFICATION TEST.
8	Turn the ignition off. Disconnect the multi-function switch harness connector. Disconnect the BCM C3 harness connector. Turn the ignition on. Measure the voltage of the wiper mux switch signal circuit. Is the voltage above 1.0 volt? Yes → Repair the Wiper Mux Switch Signal Circuit for a short to voltage. Perform BODY VERIFICATION TEST. No → Go To 9

CR9029900374020X

Fig. 34 Wipers Not Working At All (Part 2 of 5). 2000 Concorde, Intrepid, LHS & 300M

TEST	ACTION
14	Remove the wiper on/off relay from the PDC. Using a 12-volt test light connected to ground, check both fused B(+) circuits at the wiper on/off relay connector in the PDC. Is the test light on when checking each circuit? Yes → Go To 15 No → Repair the open fused B(+) circuit(s). Perform the Body Verification Test - Ver 1.
15	Turn the ignition off. Install a known good relay in place of the wiper high/low relay. Turn the ignition on. Turn the multi-function switch to the low wiper setting, then to the high wiper setting. Observe wiper operation for each setting. Do the low speed and high speed wipers operate correctly? Yes → Replace the defective Wiper HIGH/LOW Relay. Perform BODY VERIFICATION TEST No → Go To 16
16	Turn the ignition off. Disconnect the windshield wiper motor harness connector. **Note: Check connectors - Clean/repair as necessary.** **Note: Ensure the ignition, all lights and accessories are turned off.** Using a 12-volt test light connected to 12-volts, check the ground circuit at the windsheild wiper motor harness connector. Is the test light on? Yes → Go To 17 No → Repair the open Wiper Motor Ground Circuit. Perform BODY VERIFICATION TEST
17	Turn the ignition off. Remove the wiper high/low and on/off relays from the PDC. **Note: Check connectors - Clean/repair as necessary.** Measure the resistance of the common circuit between the high/low relay connector (in PDC) and the on/off relay (in PDC). Is the resistance below 10.0 ohms? Yes → Go To 18 No → Repair the open Common Circuit between the High/Low and On/Off Relays in the Power Distribution Center. Perform BODY VERIFICATION TEST
18	Turn the ignition off. Remove the wiper high/low and on/off relays from the PDC. **Note: Check connectors - Clean/repair as necessary.** Measure the resistance of the common circuit between ground and the high/low relay connector (in PDC). Is the resistance below 10.0 ohms? Yes → Repair the Common Circuit shorted to ground at the Power Distribution Center. Perform BODY VERIFICATION TEST No → Go To 19

CR9029900374040X

Fig. 34 Wipers Not Working At All (Part 4 of 5). 2000 Concorde, Intrepid, LHS & 300M

TEST	ACTION
9	Turn the ignition off. Disconnect the multi-function switch harness connector. Turn the ignition on. Using a 12-volt test light connected to ground, check the fused ignition switch output circuit. Is the test light on? Yes → Go To 10 No → Repair the open Fused Ignition Switch Output Run/Acc. Perform BODY VERIFICATION TEST
10	Turn the ignition off. Disconnect the multi-function switch harness connector. Disconnect the BCM C2 harness connector. Measure the resistance of the windshield wiper switch mux circuit between the BCM C2 harness connector and the right multi-function harness connector. Is the resistance below 5.0 ohms? Yes → Go To 11 No → Repair the open Windshield Wiper Switch Mux circuit. Perform BODY VERIFICATION TEST
11	Turn the ignition off. Disconnect the multi-function switch harness connector. Disconnect the BCM C2 harness connector. Measure the resistance of the wiper mux switch signal circuit between the BCM C2 harness connector and ground. Is the resistance below 100.0 ohms? Yes → Repair the Windshield Wiper Switch Mux circuit shorted to ground. Perform BODY VERIFICATION TEST No → Go To 12
12	Turn the ignition off. Disconnect the multi-function switch harness connector. Turn the ignition on. With the DRBIII, read the intermittent wiper switch volts. Using a 12-volt test light connected to 12-volts, momentarily connect and disconnect the test light to the wiper mux switch signal circuit at the multi-function switch harness connector. Does the DRBIII show intermittent wiper switch volts change from 0.0 volts to above 10.0 volts? Yes → Go To 13 No → Replace the Body Control Module. Perform BODY VERIFICATION TEST.
13	If there are no other possible causes, view repair. Repair Test Complete.

CR9029900374030X

Fig. 34 Wipers Not Working At All (Part 3 of 5). 2000 Concorde, Intrepid, LHS & 300M

TEST	ACTION
19	Turn the ignition on. Disconnect the windshield wiper motor harness connector. Turn the wiper switch to the low speed position. Using a 12-volt test light connected to ground, check the low speed output circuit at the wiper motor harness connector. Turn the wiper switch to the high speed position. Using a 12-volt test light connected to ground, check the high speed output circuit at the wiper motor harness connector. Is the test light on for each circuit? Yes → Replace the Wiper Motor. Perform BODY VERIFICATION TEST. No → Test Complete.

CR9029900374050X

Fig. 34 Wipers Not Working At All (Part 5 of 5). 2000 Concorde, Intrepid, LHS & 300M

TEST	ACTION
1	Remove the wiper high/low relay. Connect a jumper wire between the fused B(+) circuit at cavity A and the wiper high speed output circuit at cavity D. Observe windshield wiper operation. Are the windshield wipers operating at high speed? Yes → Go To 2 No → Go To 7
2	Turn the ignition off. Install a known good relay in place of the wiper high/low relay. Turn the ignition on. Turn the multi-function switch to the low wiper setting, then to the high wiper setting. Observe wiper operation for each setting. Do the low speed and high speed wipers operate correctly? Yes → Replace the defective Wiper HIGH/LOW Relay. Perform BODY VERIFICATION TEST No → Go To 3
3	Turn the ignition off. Disconnect the multi-function switch harness connector and remove the multi-function switch from the steering column. Set the multi-function switch to the high speed position. Measure the resistance between terminals #1 and #3 of the multi-function switch connector (component side). Is the resistance between 480.0 and 540.0 ohms? Yes → Go To 4 No → Replace the multi-function switch. Perform BODY VERIFICATION TEST

CR9029900375010X

Fig. 35 Wipers Not Working At High Speed (Part 1 of 3). 2000 Concorde, Intrepid, LHS & 300M

TEST	ACTION
4	Turn the ignition off. Remove the wiper high/low relay from the PDC. Disconnect the BCM C3 harness connector. Turn the ignition on. Measure the voltage of the wiper high/low relay control circuit. Is there any voltage present? Yes → Repair the wiper high/low relay control circuit for a short to voltage. Perform BODY VERIFICATION TEST No → Go To 5
5	Turn the ignition off. Remove the wiper high/low relay from the PDC. Disconnect the BCM C3 harness connector. **Note: Check connectors - Clean/repair as necessary.** Measure the resistance of the wiper high/low relay control circuit between the PDC connector and the BCM C3 harness connector. Is the resistance below 5.0 ohms? Yes → Go To 6 No → Repair the open Wiper High/Low Relay Control circuit. Perform BODY VERIFICATION TEST
6	If there are no possible causes, view repair Repair Replace the Body Control Module. Perform BODY VERIFICATION TEST.
7	Remove the wiper high/low relay from the PDC. Using a 12-volt test light connected to ground, check the fused B(+) circuit. Is the test light on? Yes → Go To 8 No → Repair the fused B(+) circuit for an open. Perform the Body Verification Test - Ver 1.
8	Turn the ignition off. Remove the wiper high/low relay. Disconnect the wiper motor harness connector. **Note: Check connectors - Clean/repair as necessary.** Connect a jumper wire between the wiper high speed output circuit at the wiper harness connector and ground. Using a 12-volt test light connected to 12-volts, check the high speed output circuit at the wiper high/low relay connector in the PDC. Is the test light on? Yes → Go To 9 No → Repair the open High Speed Output circuit between the High/Low Relay in the Power Distribution Center and the Wiper Motor connector. Perform BODY VERIFICATION TEST

CR9029900375020X

Fig. 35 Wipers Not Working At High Speed (Part 2 of 3). 2000 Concorde, Intrepid, LHS & 300M

TEST	ACTION
9	Turn the ignition off. Remove the wiper high/low relay. Disconnect the wiper motor harness connector. **Note: Check connectors - Clean/repair as necessary.** Measure the resistance between ground and the wiper high speed output circuit. Is the resistance below 100.0 ohms? Yes → Repair the High Speed Output circuit shorted to ground. Perform BODY VERIFICATION TEST No → Go To 10
10	Turn the ignition off. Remove the wiper high/low relay from the PDC. Disconnect the wiper motor harness connector. **Note: Check connectors - Clean/repair as necessary.** Turn the ignition on. Measure the voltage of the wiper high speed output circuit at the PDC high/low relay connector (cavity 87). Is there any voltage present? Yes → Repair the High Speed Output circuit shorted to battery. Perform BODY VERIFICATION TEST No → Go To 11
11	If there are no possible causes remaining, view repair. Repair Replace the Wiper Motor. Perform BODY VERIFICATION TEST.

CR9029900375030X

Fig. 35 Wipers Not Working At High Speed (Part 3 of 3). 2000 Concorde, Intrepid, LHS & 300M

TEST	ACTION
1	Install a known good relay in place of the wiper on/off relay. Does the system now operate correctly? Yes → Replace the Wiper On/Off Relay. Perform BODY VERIFICATION TEST. No → Go To 2
2	Turn the ignition off. Remove the wiper on/off and high/low relays. **Note: Check connectors - Clean/repair as necessary.** Turn the ignition on. Measure the voltage of the common circuit at the wiper high/low relay connector in the PDC. Is the voltage above 10.0 volts? Yes → Repair the Common Circuit shorted to battery at the Power Distribution Center. Perform BODY VERIFICATION TEST No → Go To 3
3	Turn the ignition off. Remove the wiper high/low relay from the PDC. Disconnect the wiper motor harness connector. **Note: Check connectors - Clean/repair as necessary.** Turn the ignition on. Measure the voltage of the wiper high speed output circuit at the PDC high/low relay connector (cavity 87). Is there any voltage present? Yes → Repair the High Speed Output circuit shorted to battery. Perform BODY VERIFICATION TEST No → Go To 4

CR9029900376010X

Fig. 36 Wipers Run All Time w/Ignition On (Part 1 of 2). 2000 Concorde, Intrepid, LHS & 300M

TEST	ACTION
4	Turn the ignition off. Remove the wiper high/low relay. Disconnect the wiper motor harness connector. **Note: Check connectors - Clean/repair as necessary.** Turn the ignition on. Measure the voltage of the low speed output circuit at the PDC. Is there any voltage present? Yes → Repair the Low Speed Output circuit shorted to battery. Perform BODY VERIFICATION TEST No → Go To 5
5	Turn the ignition off. Remove the wiper on/off relay from the PDC. Disconnect the BCM C3 harness connector. **Note: Check connectors - Clean/repair as necessary.** Measure the resistance between ground and the wiper on/off relay control circuit. Is the resistance below 100.0 ohms? Yes → Repair the Wiper On/Off Relay Control circuit shorted to ground. Perform BODY VERIFICATION TEST No → Go To 6
6	If there are no possible causes remaining, view repair Repair Replace the Body Control Module. Perform BODY VERIFICATION TEST.

CR9029900376020X

Fig. 36 Wipers Run All Times w/Ignition On (Part 2 of 2). 2000 Concorde, Intrepid, LHS & 300M

When Monitored and Set Condition:

WIPER PARK SWITCH FAILURE/WIPERS RUN CONTINUOUSLY

When Monitored: The ignition must be in the run position and battery voltage supplied to the BCM on the Fused B(+) circuit.

Set Condition: The code will set if the BCM does not detect a low to high voltage transition on the Wiper Park Switch Sense circuit within 8 seconds after energizing the wiper relay On/Off relay.

POSSIBLE CAUSES
WIPER PARK SWITCH OPERATION
WIPER PARK SWITCH SENSE CIRCUIT SHORT TO VOLTAGE
WIPER PARK SWITCH SENSE CIRCUIT OPEN
WIPER PARK SWITCH SENSE CIRCUIT SHORT TO GROUND
GROUND CIRCUIT OPEN
WIPER MOTOR OPERATION
BCM

TEST	ACTION
1	Turn the ignition on. With the DRBIII®, erase BCM DTC's. Cycle the ignition off and then on. Turn the windshield wiper switch to each intermittent position, then low and high speed positions. Turn the windshield wiper switch to the off position. With the DRBIII®, read BCM DTC's. Does the DRB display WIPER PARK SWITCH FAILURE? Yes → Go To 2 No → At this time the condition to set the code is not present. Inspect the related wiring harness and connectors, repair as necessary. Perform BODY VERIFICATION TEST - VER 1.
2	Turn the ignition off. Disconnect the Windshield Wiper Motor harness connector. Disconnect the BCM C3 harness connector. Turn the ignition on. Measure the voltage of the Wiper Park Switch Sense circuit in the Windshield Wiper Motor harness connector. Is there any voltage present? Yes → Repair the Wiper Park Switch Sense circuit for a short to voltage. Perform BODY VERIFICATION TEST - VER 1. No → Go To 3

CR9020000446010X

Fig. 38 Wiper Park Switch Failure/Wipers Run Continuously (Part 1 of 2). 2001–04 Concorde, Intrepid & 300M & 2001 LHS

BODY VERIFICATION TEST - VER 1
1. Disconnect all jumper wires and reconnect all previously disconnected components and connectors. 2. If the Sentry Key Immobilizer Module (SKIM) or the Powertrain Control Module (PCM) were replaced, proceed to number 6. If the SKIM or PCM were not replaced, continue to the next number. 3. If the Body Control Module was replaced, turn the ignition on for 15 seconds (to learn VIN) or engine may not start (if VTSS equipped). If the vehicle is equipped with VTSS, use the DRB and enable VTSS. 4. Program all other options as needed. 5. If any repairs were made to the HVAC System, disconnect the battery or using the DRBIII, recalibrate the HVAC doors. Proceed to number 13. 6. Obtain the Vehicle's unique PIN number assigned to it's original SKIM module 7. With the DRBIII, select THEFT ALARM, SKIM, MISCELLANEOUS and select "Skim Module Replaced" function. Enter the 4 digit PIN number to put SKIM in "Access Mode". 8. The DRBIII will prompt you through the following steps. (1) Program the country code into the SKIM's memory. (2) Program the vehicle's VIN number into the SKIM's memory. (3) Transfer the vehicle's Secret Key data from the PCM. 9. Once secured access mode is active, the SKIM will remain in that mode for 60 seconds. 10. Using the DRBIII, program all customer keys into the SKIM's memory. This requires that the SKIM be in secured access mode, using the 4 digit code. 11. Note: If the PCM is replaced, the unique Secret Key data must be transfered from the SKIM to the PCM. This procedure requires the SKIM to be placed in secured access mode using the 4-digit code. 12. Note: If 3 attempts are made to enter secured access mode using an incorrect PIN, secured access mode will be locked out for 1 hour which causes the DRBIII to display "Bus +- Signals Open". To exit this mode, turn ignition to the "Run" pos. for 1 hour. 13. Ensure all accessories are turned off and the battery is fully charged. 14. Ensure that the Ignition is on, and with the DRBIII, record and erase all Diagnostic Trouble Codes from ALL modules. Start the engine and allow it to run for 2 minutes and fully operate the system that was malfunctioning. 15. Turn the ignition off and wait 5 seconds. Turn the ignition on and using the DRBIII, read DTC's from ALL modules. 16. If ANY codes are present select the appropriate symptom from the Symptom List and continue diagnostics. If NO codes are present and the customers complaint cannot be duplicated, the repair is complete.

CR9029900377000X

Fig. 37 Test VER 1-A: Verification Test. 2000 Concorde, Intrepid, LHS & 300M

TEST	ACTION
3	Turn the ignition off. Disconnect the Windshield Wiper Motor harness connector. Disconnect the BCM C3 harness connector. Measure the resistance of the Wiper Park Switch Sense circuit between the BCM C3 harness connector and the Wiper Motor harness connector. Is the resistance below 5.0 ohms? Yes → Go To 4 No → Repair the Wiper Park Switch Sense circuit for an open. Perform BODY VERIFICATION TEST - VER 1.
4	Turn the ignition off. Disconnect the Windshield Wiper Motor harness connector. Disconnect the BCM C3 harness connector. Measure the resistance between ground and the Wiper Park Switch Sense circuit in the BCM C3 harness connector. Is the resistance below 100.0 ohms? Yes → Repair the Wiper Park Switch Sense circuit for a short to ground. Perform BODY VERIFICATION TEST - VER 1. No → Go To 5
5	Turn the ignition off. Disconnect the Windshield Wiper Motor harness connector. **NOTE: Ensure the ignition switch, all lights and accessories are turned off.** Using a 12-volt test light connected to 12-volts, probe the Ground circuit in the Windshield Wiper Motor harness connector. Does the test light illuminate brightly? Yes → Go To 6 No → Repair the Wiper Motor Ground circuit for an open. Perform BODY VERIFICATION TEST - VER 1.
6	Turn the ignition off. Disconnect the Windshield Wiper Motor harness connector. Turn the ignition on. With the DRBIII® in Inputs/Outputs, read the wiper park switch state. Connect one end of a jumper wire to the wiper park switch sense circuit at the windshield wiper motor harness connector. While observing the DRBIII®, connect the other end of the jumper wire to ground for several seconds, then disconnect the jumper wire from ground. Did the wiper park switch input change state when connected to ground then disconnected from ground? Yes → Replace the Wiper Motor. Perform BODY VERIFICATION TEST - VER 1. No → Replace the Body Control Module. Perform BODY VERIFICATION TEST - VER 1.

CR9020000446020X

Fig. 38 Wiper Park Switch Failure/Wipers Run Continuously (Part 2 of 2). 2001–04 Concorde, Intrepid & 300M & 2001 LHS

POSSIBLE CAUSES
EXTERIOR LIGHTING SYSTEM NOT OPERATING PROPERLY
WINDSHIELD WIPER/WASHER SYSTEM NOT OPERATING PROPERLY
FUSED B+ CIRCUIT(S) OPEN
HEADLAMP WASHER RELAY
HEADLAMP WASHER PUMP MOTOR
HEADLAMP WASHER RELAY OUTPUT CIRCUIT SHORTED TO VOLTAGE
HEADLAMP WASHER RELAY OUTPUT CIRCUIT SHORTED TO GROUND
HEADLAMP WASHER RELAY OUTPUT CIRCUIT OPEN
HEADLAMP WASHER PUMP MOTOR GROUND CIRCUIT OPEN
HEADLAMP WASHER RELAY CONTROL CIRCUIT SHORTED TO VOLTAGE
HEADLAMP WASHER RELAY CONTROL CIRCUIT SHORTED TO GROUND
HEADLAMP WASHER RELAY CONTROL CIRCUIT OPEN
BCM - RELAY CONTROL OPEN

TEST	ACTION
1	**NOTE: The exterior lighting must be working properly for the Headlamp Washer Pump Motor to operate properly.** Turn the ignition on. Turn on the park lamps, fog lamps, low beam headlamps and high beam headlamps and note the operation of the appropriate lamps when selected. Do the appropriate lamps operate properly when turned on? Yes → Go To 2 No → Perform BODY VERIFICATION TEST - VER 1.
2	Turn the ignition on. Turn the low speed windshield wipers on. Push and release the wash button on the Multi-function Switch. Did the windshield wipers and washers operate properly? Yes → Go To 3 No → Perform BODY VERIFICATION TEST - VER 1.
3	Turn the ignition off. Remove the Headlamp Washer Relay from the PDC. Using a 12-volt test light connected to ground, check both Fused B(+) circuits in the Headlamp Washer Relay connector. Is the test light on for both circuits? Yes → Go To 4 No → Repair the Fused B(+) circuit(s) for an open. Perform BODY VERIFICATION TEST - VER 1.

CR9020000447010X

Fig. 39 Headlamp Washers Not Operating Properly (Part 1 of 3). 2001–04 Concorde, Intrepid & 300M & 2001 LHS

TEST	ACTION
9	Turn the ignition off. Disconnect the Headlamp Washer Pump Motor harness connector. Using a 12-volt test light connected to 12-volts, check the Ground circuit in the Headlamp Washer Pump Motor harness connector. Is the test light on? Yes → Go To 10 No → Repair the Headlamp Washer Pump Motor Ground circuit for an open. Perform BODY VERIFICATION TEST - VER 1.
10	Turn the ignition off. Remove the Headlamp Washer Relay from the PDC. Disconnect the BCM C3 harness connector. Turn the ignition on. Measure the voltage of the Headlamp Washer Relay Control circuit. Is the voltage above 1.0 volt? Yes → Repair the Headlamp Washer Relay Control circuit for a short to voltage. Perform BODY VERIFICATION TEST - VER 1. No → Go To 11
11	Turn the ignition off. Remove the Headlamp Washer Relay from the PDC. Disconnect the BCM C3 harness connector. Measure the resistance between ground and the Headlamp Washer Relay Control circuit. Is the resistance above 100 kohms? Yes → Go To 12 No → Repair the Headlamp Washer Relay Control circuit for a short to ground. Perform BODY VERIFICATION TEST - VER 1.
12	Turn the ignition off. Remove the Headlamp Washer Relay from the PDC. Disconnect the BCM C3 harness connector. Measure the resistance of the Headlamp Washer Relay Control circuit between the BCM C3 harness connector and the Headlamp Washer Relay connector. Is the resistance below 5.0 ohms? Yes → Go To 13 No → Repair the Headlamp Washer Relay Control circuit for an open. Perform BODY VERIFICATION TEST - VER 1.
13	If there are no possible causes remaining, view repair. Repair Replace the Body Control Module (BCM). Perform BODY VERIFICATION TEST - VER 1.

CR9020000447030X

Fig. 39 Headlamp Washers Not Operating Properly (Part 3 of 3). 2001–04 Concorde, Intrepid & 300M & 2001 LHS

TEST	ACTION
4	Turn the ignition off. Install a substitute relay in place of the Headlamp Washer Relay. Turn the ignition on. With the DRBIII®, actuate the Headlamp Washer Relay. Did the Headlamp Washers operate? Yes → Replace the Headlamp Washer Relay. Perform BODY VERIFICATION TEST - VER 1. No → Go To 5
5	Turn the ignition off. Disconnect the Headlamp Washer Pump Motor harness connector. Connect a 12-volt test light between the Headlamp Washer Pump Motor harness connector cavities. With the DRBIII®, actuate the Headlamp Washer Relay. Does the test light cycle on and off during actuation? Yes → Replace the Headlamp Washer Pump Motor. Perform BODY VERIFICATION TEST - VER 1. No → Go To 6
6	Turn the ignition off. Remove the Headlamp Washer Relay from the PDC. Turn the ignition on. Measure the voltage of the Headlamp Washer Relay Output circuit in the Headlamp Washer Relay connector. Is the voltage above 1.0 volt? Yes → Repair the Headlamp Washer Relay Output circuit for a short to voltage. Perform BODY VERIFICATION TEST - VER 1. No → Go To 7
7	Turn the ignition off. Remove the Headlamp Washer Relay from the PDC. Disconnect the Headlamp Washer Pump Motor harness connector. Measure the resistance between ground and the Headlamp Washer Relay Output circuit. Is the resistance above 100 kohms? Yes → Go To 8 No → Repair the Headlamp Washer Relay Output circuit for a short to ground. Perform BODY VERIFICATION TEST - VER 1.
8	Turn the ignition off. Remove the Headlamp Washer Relay from the PDC. Disconnect the Headlamp Washer Pump Motor harness connector. Measure the resistance of the Headlamp Washer Relay Output circuit. Is the resistance below 5.0 ohms? Yes → Go To 9 No → Repair the Headlamp Washer Relay Output circuit for an open. Perform BODY VERIFICATION TEST - VER 1.

CR9020000447020X

Fig. 39 Headlamp Washers Not Operating Properly (Part 2 of 3). 2001–04 Concorde, Intrepid & 300M & 2001 LHS

POSSIBLE CAUSES
IGNITION SWITCH OUTPUT RUN/ACC CIRCUIT OPEN
FUSED IGNITION SWITCH OUTPUT RUN/ACC SHORT TO GROUND
WASHER PUMP MOTOR CONTROL CIRCUIT SHORT TO GROUND
WASHER PUMP SWITCH INTERNALLY SHORTED
WASHER PUMP SHORTED
FUSED IGNITION SWITCH OUTPUT RUN/ACC CIRCUIT OPEN
GROUND CIRCUIT OPEN
WASHER PUMP CONTROL SWITCH OUTPUT CIRCUIT OPEN
WASHER PUMP SWITCH OPEN

TEST	ACTION
1	Turn the ignition on. Using a 12-volt test light connected to ground, probe the Ignition Switch Output ACC/RUN circuit in the junction block fuse #5 connector. Does the test light illuminate brightly? Yes → Go To 2 No → Repair the open Ignition Switch Output Run/Acc circuit . Perform BODY VERIFICATION TEST - VER 1.
2	Turn the ignition off. Remove and inspect junction block fuse #5. Is the fuse open? Yes → Go To 3 No → Go To 7 **Note: Reinstall the fuse if it is not open.**
3	Turn the ignition off. Disconnect the Multi-Function Switch harness connector. Remove junction block fuse #5. Measure the resistance between ground and the fused ignition switch output ACC/RUN circuit. Is the resistance below 100.0 ohms? Yes → Repair the Fused Ignition Switch Output Run/ACC circuit shorted to ground. Perform BODY VERIFICATION TEST - VER 1. No → Go To 4

CR9020000448010X

Fig. 40 Washer Inoperative (Part 1 of 3). 2001–03 Concorde, Intrepid & 300M & 2001 LHS

TEST	ACTION
4	Turn the ignition off. Disconnect the Washer Pump harness connector. Disconnect the BCM C2 harness connector. Disconnect the Multi-Function Switch harness connector. Measure the resistance between ground and the Washer Pump Control Switch Output circuit. Is the resistance below 100.0 ohms? Yes → Repair Washer Pump Control Switch Output circuit shorted to ground. Perform BODY VERIFICATION TEST - VER 1. No → Go To 5
5	Turn the ignition off. Disconnect the Multi-Function Switch harness connector. Remove the Multi-Function Switch from the Steering Column. Ensure that the washer switch is in the off position. Measure the resistance of the Multi-Function Switch between terminal 1 and each of the remaining six terminals in the 7-way connector (component side). Is the resistance below 100.0 ohms for any of the measurements? Yes → Replace the Right Multi-Function Switch. Perform BODY VERIFICATION TEST - VER 1. No → Go To 6
6	If there are no possible causes remaining, view repair. Repair Replace the Windshield Washer Pump Motor. Perform BODY VERIFICATION TEST - VER 1.
7	Turn the ignition off. Disconnect the Multi-Function Switch harness connector. Turn the ignition on. Using a 12-volt test light connected to ground, probe the fused ignition switch output circuit. Does the test light illuminate? Yes → Go To 8 No → Repair the Fused Ignition Switch Output Run/Acc for an open. Perform BODY VERIFICATION TEST - VER 1.
8	Turn the ignition off. Disconnect the Washer Pump harness connector. Using a 12-volt test light connected to 12-volts, probe the washer pump ground circuit. Does the test light illuminate brightly? Yes → Go To 9 No → Repair Ground circuit for an open. Perform BODY VERIFICATION TEST - VER 1.

CR9020000448020X

Fig. 40 Washer Inoperative (Part 2 of 3). 2001–03 Concorde, Intrepid & 300M & 2001 LHS

POSSIBLE CAUSES
WASHER PUMP MOTOR CONTROL OUTPUT CIRCUIT SHORTED TO VOLTAGE
WASHER PUMP SWITCH SHORT TO VOLTAGE

TEST	ACTION
1	Ensure that the washer switch is in the off position. Turn the ignition on. Disconnect the Multi-Function Switch harness connector. Does the wiper and washers stop working when the multi-function switch is disconnected? Yes → Go To 2 No → Repair Washer Pump Motor Control Output circuit short to voltage. Perform BODY VERIFICATION TEST - VER 1.
2	Ensure that the windshield washer switch is in the off position. Turn the ignition on. Disconnect the Multi-Function Switch harness connector. Did the wiper and washers stop working when the multi-function switch is disconnected? Yes → Replace the Multi-Function Switch. Perform BODY VERIFICATION TEST - VER 1. No → Test Complete.

CR9020000449000X

Fig. 41 Washer Runs All Times w/Ignition On. 2001–04 Concorde, Intrepid & 300M & 2001 LHS

TEST	ACTION
9	Turn the ignition off. Disconnect the Windshield Washer Pump Motor harness connector. Turn the ignition on. Using a 12-volt test light connected to ground, probe the Washer Pump Motor Control Output circuit at the Windshield Washer Pump Motor harness connector. Monitor the test light while pressing and releasing the washer switch. Does the test light turn on and off while pressing and releasing the washer switch? Yes → Go To 10 No → Repair the Washer Pump Motor Control Output circuit for an open. Perform BODY VERIFICATION TEST - VER 1.
10	Turn the ignition off. Disconnect the Multi-Function Switch harness connector. Remove the Multi-Function Switch from the steering column. Measure the resistance of the Multi-Function Switch between terminals 1 and 2. Monitor the ohmmeter while pushing and releasing the washer switch. **Note: The resistance reading should change from above 100.0 ohms when the washer switch is released to below 5.0 ohms when the switch is pressed.** Did the resistance readings change from above 100.0 ohms to below 5.0 ohms as described in Note? Yes → Test Complete. No → Replace the Multi-Function Swtich. Perform BODY VERIFICATION TEST - VER 1.

CR9020000448030X

Fig. 40 Washer Inoperative (Part 3 of 3). 2001–03 Concorde, Intrepid & 300M & 2001 LHS

POSSIBLE CAUSES
WIPER HIGH/LOW RELAY
WIPER HIGH/LOW RELAY CONTROL CIRCUIT SHORTED TO GROUND
MULTI-FUNCTION SWITCH LOW SWITCH OPEN
FUSED B(+) CIRCUIT OPEN
LOW SPEED OUTPUT CIRCUIT OPEN
WIPER MOTOR
BCM

TEST	ACTION
1	Remove the Wiper High/Low Relay. Connect a jumper wire between the Fused B(+) circuit and the Wiper Low Speed Output circuit. Observe windshield wiper operation. Are the windshield wipers operating at low speed? Yes → Go To 2 No → Go To 6
2	Turn the ignition off. Install a substitute relay in place of the Wiper High/Low Relay. Turn the ignition on. Turn the Multi-Function Switch to the low wiper setting, then to the high wiper setting. Observe wiper operation for each setting. Do the low speed and high speed wipers operate correctly? Yes → Replace the Wiper HIGH/LOW Relay. Perform BODY VERIFICATION TEST - VER 1. No → Go To 3
3	Turn the ignition off. Disconnect the Multi-Function Switch harness connector and remove the Multi-Function Switch from the steering column. Set the multi-function switch to the low speed position. Measure the resistance between terminals 1 and 3 of the Multi-Function Switch connector (component side). Is the resistance between 980.0 and 1060.0 ohms? Yes → Go To 4 No → Replace the Multi-Function Switch. Perform BODY VERIFICATION TEST - VER 1.

CR9020000450010X

Fig. 42 Wiper Not Working At Low Speed (Part 1 of 2). 2001–04 Concorde, Intrepid & 300M & 2001 LHS

TEST	ACTION
4	Turn the ignition off. Remove the Wiper High/Low Relay from the PDC. Disconnect the BCM C3 harness connector. Measure the resistance between ground and the Wiper High/Low Relay Control circuit. Is the resistance below 100.0 ohms? Yes → Repair the Wiper High/Low Relay Control circuit shorted to ground. Perform BODY VERIFICATION TEST - VER 1. No → Go To 5
5	If there are no possible causes, view repair Repair Replace the Body Control Module. Perform BODY VERIFICATION TEST - VER 1.
6	Remove the Wiper High/Low Relay from the PDC. Using a 12-volt test light connected to ground, probe the Fused B(+) circuit. Does the test light illuminate? Yes → Go To 7 No → Repair the Fused B(+) circuit for an open. Perform BODY VERIFICATION TEST - VER 1.
7	Turn the ignition off. Remove the Wiper High/Low Relay from the PDC. Disconnect the Wiper Motor harness connector. Measure the resistance of the Low Speed Output circuit between the wiper motor and the PDC High/Low Relay connector. Is the resistance below 5.0 ohms? Yes → Go To 8 No → Repair the Low Speed Output circuit for an open. Perform BODY VERIFICATION TEST - VER 1.
8	If there are no possible causes, view repair Repair Replace the Wiper Motor. Perform BODY VERIFICATION TEST - VER 1.

CR9020000450020X

Fig. 42 Wiper Not Working At Low Speed (Part 2 of 2). 2001–04 Concorde, Intrepid & 300M & 2001 LHS

TEST	ACTION
4	Turn the ignition off. Disconnect the Windshield Wiper Motor harness connector. Turn the ignition on. With the DRBIII® in Inputs/Outputs, monitor the wiper park switch state. Connect one end of a jumper wire to the Wiper Park Switch Sense circuit at the Windshield Wiper Motor harness connector. While observing the DRBIII®, hold the other end to ground for several seconds. Did wiper park switch input change state when connected to ground then disconnected from ground? Yes → Replace the Wiper Motor. Perform BODY VERIFICATION TEST - VER 1. No → Replace the Body Control Module. Perform BODY VERIFICATION TEST - VER 1.

CR9020000451020X

Fig. 43 Wiper Erratic Operation In Intermittent Speeds (Part 2 of 2). 2001–04 Concorde, Intrepid & 300M & 2001 LHS

POSSIBLE CAUSES
WIPER ON/OFF RELAY
WIPER PARK SWITCH SENSE CIRCUIT OPEN
WIPER PARK SWITCH SENSE CIRCUIT SHORT TO GROUND
WIPER MOTOR
BCM

TEST	ACTION
1	Install a substitute relay in place of the Wiper On/Off Relay Turn the ignition on. Turn the wipers on. Does the system operate correctly? Yes → Replace the Wiper On/Off Relay. Perform BODY VERIFICATION TEST - VER 1. No → Go To 2
2	Turn the ignition off. Disconnect the Windshield Wiper Motor harness connector. Disconnect the BCM C3 harness connector. Measure the resistance of the Wiper Park Switch Sense circuit between the BCM C3 harness connector and the Wiper Motor harness connector. Is the resistance below 5.0 ohms? Yes → Go To 3 No → Repair the Wiper Park Switch Sense circuit for an open. Perform BODY VERIFICATION TEST - VER 1.
3	Turn the ignition off. Disconnect the Windshield Wiper Motor harness connector. Disconnect the BCM C3 harness connector. Measure the resistance between ground and the Wiper Park Switch Sense circuit. Is the resistance below 100.0 ohms? Yes → Repair the Wiper Park Switch Sense circuit for a short to ground. Perform BODY VERIFICATION TEST - VER 1. No → Go To 4

CR9020000451010X

Fig. 43 Wiper Erratic Operation In Intermittent Speeds (Part 1 of 2). 2001–04 Concorde, Intrepid & 300M & 2001 LHS

POSSIBLE CAUSES
WIPER OPERATION
WASHER PUMP CONTROL SWITCH OUTPUT CIRCUIT OPEN
BCM

TEST	ACTION
1	Turn the ignition on. Turn the wiper switch to each intermittent position, then to the low speed and high speed positions. **NOTE: Observe wiper operation when selecting each speed of operation.** Do the wipers operate correctly at all selected speeds? Yes → Go To 2 No → Refer to the Wiper category and perform the appropriate symptom. Perform BODY VERIFICATION TEST - VER 1.
2	Turn the ignition off. Disconnect the BCM C2 harness connector. Turn the ignition on. Using a 12-volt test light connected to ground, probe the Washer Pump Control Switch Output circuit at the BCM C2 harness connector. Monitor the test light while pressing and releasing the washer switch. Does the test light flash on and off while pressing and releasing the washer switch? Yes → Go To 3 No → Repair the Washer Pump Control Switch Output circuit for an open. Perform BODY VERIFICATION TEST - VER 1.
3	If there are no possible causes remaining, view repair Repair Replace the BCM. Perform BODY VERIFICATION TEST - VER 1.

CR9020000452000X

Fig. 44 Wipers Do Not Wiper After Wash. 2001–04 Concorde, Intrepid & 300M & 2001 LHS

POSSIBLE CAUSES
WIPER MUX CIRCUIT SHORTED TO VOLTAGE
FUSED B(+) CIRCUIT
FUSED B(+) CIRCUIT OPEN
GROUND CIRCUIT OPEN
WIPER HIGH/LOW RELAY
COMMON CIRCUIT SHORTED TO GROUND
OPEN COMMON CIRCUIT OPEN
WIPER ON/OFF RELAY
WIPER ON/OFF RELAY CONTROL CIRCUIT OPEN
WIPER ON/OFF RELAY CONTROL CIRCUIT SHORTED TO VOLTAGE
FUSED IGNITION SWITCH OUTPUTCIRCUIT OPEN
WINDSHIELD WIPER SWITCH MUX CIRCUIT OPEN
WINDSHIELD WIPER SWITCH MUX CIRCUIT SHORTED TO GROUND
WIPER MOTOR
BCM-ON/OFF RELAY DRIVER
BCM WIPER MUX CIRCUIT OPEN
MULTI-FUNCTION SWITCH

TEST	ACTION
1	Turn the ignition off. Remove the Wiper On/Off Relay. Connect a jumper wire between the Fused B+ circuit and Front Wiper relay Common in the PDC. Observe windshield wiper operation. Do the wipers operate with the jumper wire connected? Yes → Go To 2 No → Go To 14
2	With the DRBIII®, read the intermittent wiper switch status while slowly turning the wiper switch from the off position to the high speed position. **NOTE: The switch voltage displayed on the DRBIII® should increase from approximately 0.0 volts to 8.5 volts as the switch is turned from the off position to the high speed position.** Did the switch voltage change from aprroximately 0.0 volts to 8.5 volts as described? Yes → Go To 3 No → Go To 9

CR9020000453010X

Fig. 45 Wiper Not Working At All (Part 1 of 5). 2001–04 Concorde, Intrepid & 300M & 2001 LHS

TEST	ACTION
3	Remove the Wiper On/Off Relay from the PDC. Using a 12-volt test light connected to ground, probe both Fused B(+) circuits in the PDC. Does the test light illuminate brightly at each terminal? Yes → Go To 4 No → Repair the Fused B(+) circuit(s) for an open. Perform BODY VERIFICATION TEST - VER 1.
4	Install a substitute relay in place of the Wiper On/Off Relay. Turn the ignition on. Turn the wipers on. Does the system operate correctly? Yes → Replace the Wiper On/Off Relay. Perform BODY VERIFICATION TEST - VER 1. No → Go To 5
5	Turn the ignition off. Remove the Wiper On/Off Relay from the PDC. Disconnect the BCM C3 harness connector. Connect a jumper wire between the Wiper On/Off Relay Control circuit at the BCM C3 harness connector to ground. Measure the resistance between ground and the Wiper On/Off Relay Control circuit in the PDC. Is the resistance below 5.0 ohms? Yes → Go To 6 No → Repair the Wiper On/Off Relay Control circuit for an open. Perform BODY VERIFICATION TEST - VER 1.
6	Turn the ignition off. Remove the Wiper On/Off Relay from the PDC. Disconnect the BCM C3 harness connector. Turn the ignition on. Measure the voltage of the Wiper On/Off Relay Control circuit at the BCM C3 harness connector. Is the voltage above 1.0 volt? Yes → Repair the Wiper On/Off Relay Control circuit shorted to battery. Perform BODY VERIFICATION TEST - VER 1. No → Go To 7
7	Turn the ignition off. Disconnect the Multi-Function Switch harness connector. Turn the ignition on. Using a 12-volt test light connected to ground, probe the Fused Ignition Switch Output circuit. Does the test light illuminate brightly? Yes → Go To 8 No → Repair the Fused Ignition Switch Output circuit. Perform BODY VERIFICATION TEST - VER 1.

CR9020000453020X

Fig. 45 Wiper Not Working At All (Part 2 of 5). 2001–04 Concorde, Intrepid & 300M & 2001 LHS

TEST	ACTION
8	Remove the Wiper On/Off Relay from the PDC. Using a 12-volt test light connected to 12-volts, probe the wiper on/off relay control circuit at the Wiper On/Off Relay connector in the PDC. With the DRBIII®, actuate the wiper on/off relay. Observe the test light. Does the test light turn on and off during actuation? Yes → Test Complete. No → Replace the Body Control Module. Perform BODY VERIFICATION TEST - VER 1.
9	Turn the ignition off. Disconnect the Multi-Function Switch harness connector. Turn the ignition on. Using a 12-volt test light connected to ground, probe the Fused Ignition Switch Output circuit. Does the test light illuminate brightly? Yes → Go To 10 No → Repair the Fused Ignition Switch Output circuit. Perform BODY VERIFICATION TEST - VER 1.
10	Turn the ignition off. Disconnect the Multi-Function Switch harness connector. Disconnect the BCM C3 harness connector. Turn the ignition on. Measure the voltage of the Wiper MUX Switch Signal circuit. Is the voltage above 1.0 volt? Yes → Repair the wiper switch mux signal circuit for a short to voltage. Perform BODY VERIFICATION TEST - VER 1. No → Go To 11
11	Turn the ignition off. Disconnect the Multi-Function Switch harness connector. Disconnect the BCM C2 harness connector. Measure the resistance of the Windshield Wiper Switch MUX circuit between the BCM C2 harness connector and the Multi-Function harness connector. Is the resistance below 5.0 ohms? Yes → Go To 12 No → Repair the Windshield Wiper Switch MUX circuit for an open. Perform BODY VERIFICATION TEST - VER 1.
12	Turn the ignition off. Disconnect the Multi-Function Switch harness connector. Disconnect the BCM C2 harness connector. Measure the resistance of the Wiper MUX Switch Signal circuit between the BCM C2 harness connector and ground. Is the resistance below 100.0 ohms? Yes → Repair the Windshield Wiper Switch MUX circuit shorted to ground. Perform BODY VERIFICATION TEST - VER 1. No → Go To 13

CR9020000453030X

Fig. 45 Wiper Not Working At All (Part 3 of 5). 2001–04 Concorde, Intrepid & 300M & 2001 LHS

TEST	ACTION
13	Turn the ignition off. Disconnect the multi-function switch harness connector. Turn the ignition on. With the DRBIII®, read the intermittent wiper switch volts. Using a 12-volt test light connected to 12-volts, momentarily connect and disconnect the test light to the wiper mux switch signal circuit at the multi-function switch harness connector. Does the DRBIII® show intermittent wiper switch volts change from 0.0 volts to above 10.0 volts? Yes → Replace the Multi-Function Switch. Perform BODY VERIFICATION TEST - VER 1. No → Replace the Body Control Module. Perform BODY VERIFICATION TEST - VER 1.
14	Remove the Wiper On/Off Relay from the PDC. Using a 12-volt test light connected to ground, probe both Fused B(+) circuits in the PDC. Does the test light illuminate brightly at each terminal? Yes → Go To 15 No → Repair the Fused B(+) circuit(s) for an open. Perform BODY VERIFICATION TEST - VER 1.
15	Turn the ignition off. Disconnect the Windshield Wiper Motor harness connector. **NOTE: Ensure the ignition, all lights and accessories are turned off for at least 30 seconds.** Using a 12-volt test light connected to 12-volts, probe the Ground circuit at the windshield wiper motor harness connector. Does the test light illuminate brightly? Yes → Go To 16 No → Repair the Ground circuit for an open. Perform BODY VERIFICATION TEST - VER 1.
16	Turn the ignition off. Install a substitute relay in place of the Wiper High/Low Relay Turn the ignition on. Turn the Multi-Function Switch to the low wiper setting, then to the high wiper setting. Observe wiper operation for each setting. Do the low speed and high speed wipers operate correctly? Yes → Replace the Wiper High/Low Relay. Perform BODY VERIFICATION TEST - VER 1. No → Go To 17
17	Turn the ignition off. Remove the Wiper High/Low Relay from the PDC. Remove the Wiper On/Off Relay from the PDC. Measure the resistance of the Common circuit between ground in the PDC. Is the resistance below 10.0 ohms? Yes → Repair the Common Circuit for a shorted to ground. Perform BODY VERIFICATION TEST - VER 1. No → Go To 18

CR9020000453040X

Fig. 45 Wiper Not Working At All (Part 4 of 5). 2001–04 Concorde, Intrepid & 300M & 2001 LHS

TEST	ACTION
18	Turn the ignition off. Remove the wiper High/Low Relay from the PDC. Remove the wiper On/Off Relay from the PDC. Measure the resistance of the Common circuit between the High/Low Relay and the On/Off relay in the PDC. Is the resistance below 10.0 ohms? Yes → Go To 19 No → Repair the Common circuit for an open. Perform BODY VERIFICATION TEST - VER 1.
19	Turn the ignition on. Disconnect the Windshield Wiper Motor harness connector. Turn the wiper switch to the low speed position. Using a 12-volt test light connected to ground, probe the low speed output circuit at the wiper motor harness connector. Does the test light illuminate brightly? Yes → Replace the Wiper Motor. Perform BODY VERIFICATION TEST - VER 1. No → Test Complete.

CR9020000453050X

Fig. 45 Wiper Not Working At All (Part 5 of 5). 2001–04 Concorde, Intrepid & 300M & 2001 LHS

TEST	ACTION
4	Turn the ignition off. Remove the Wiper High/Low Relay from the PDC. Disconnect the BCM C3 harness connector. Turn the ignition on. Measure the voltage of the Wiper High/Low Relay Control circuit. Is there any voltage present? Yes → Repair the Wiper High/Low Relay Control circuit for a short to voltage. Perform BODY VERIFICATION TEST - VER 1. No → Go To 5
5	Turn the ignition off. Remove the Wiper High/Low Relay from the PDC. Disconnect the BCM C3 harness connector. Measure the resistance of the Wiper High/Low Relay Control circuit between the PDC connector and the BCM C3 harness connector. Is the resistance below 5.0 ohms? Yes → Go To 6 No → Repair the Wiper High/Low Relay Control circuit for an open. Perform BODY VERIFICATION TEST - VER 1.
6	If there are no possible causes, view repair Repair Replace the Body Control Module. Perform BODY VERIFICATION TEST - VER 1.
7	Remove the Wiper High/Low Relay from the PDC. Using a 12-volt test light connected to ground, probe the fused B(+) circuit in the PDC. Does the test light illuminate brightly? Yes → Go To 8 No → Repair the Fused B(+) circuit for an open. Perform BODY VERIFICATION TEST - VER 1.
8	Turn the ignition off. Remove the Wiper High/Low Relay. Disconnect the Wiper Motor harness connector. Connect a jumper wire between the Wiper High Speed Output circuit at the wiper harness connector and ground. Using a 12-volt test light connected to 12-volts, probe the High Speed Output circuit at the Wiper High/Low Relay connector. Does the test light illuminate brightly? Yes → Go To 9 No → Repair the High Speed Output circuit for an open. Perform BODY VERIFICATION TEST - VER 1.

CR9020000454020X

Fig. 46 Wiper Not Working In High Speed (Part 2 of 3). 2001–04 Concorde, Intrepid & 300M & 2001 LHS

POSSIBLE CAUSES
WIPER HIGH/LOW RELAY
MULTI-FUNCTION SWITCH HIGH SWITCH OPEN
WIPER HIGH/LOW RELAY CONTROL CKT SHORT TO VOLTAGE
WIPER HIGH/LOW RELAY CONTROL CIRCUIT OPEN
FUSED B(+) CKT OPEN
HIGH SPEED OUTPUT CIRCUIT OPEN
HIGH SPEED OUTPUT SHORTED TO GROUND
BCM
WIPER MOTOR--HI SPEED RELAY

TEST	ACTION
1	Remove the Wiper High/Low Relay. Connect a jumper wire between the Fused B(+) circuit and the Wiper High Speed output circuit. Observe windshield wiper operation. Are the windshield wipers operating at high speed? Yes → Go To 2 No → Go To 7
2	Turn the ignition off. Install a substitute relay in place of the Wiper High/Low Relay. Turn the ignition on. Turn the multi-function switch to the low wiper setting, then to the high wiper setting. Observe wiper operation for each setting. Do the low speed and high speed wipers operate correctly? Yes → Replace the Wiper High/Low Relay. Perform BODY VERIFICATION TEST - VER 1. No → Go To 3
3	Turn the ignition off. Disconnect the Multi-Function Switch harness connector and remove the Multi-Function Switch from the steering column. Set the Multi-Function Switch to the high speed position. Measure the resistance between terminals 1 and 3 in the Multi-Function Switch connector (component side). Is the resistance between 480.0 and 540.0 ohms? Yes → Go To 4 No → Replace the Multi-Function Switch. Perform BODY VERIFICATION TEST - VER 1.

CR9020000454010X

Fig. 46 Wiper Not Working In High Speed (Part 1 of 3). 2001–04 Concorde, Intrepid & 300M & 2001 LHS

TEST	ACTION
9	Turn the ignition off. Remove the Wiper High/Low Relay. Disconnect the Wiper Motor harness connector. Measure the resistance between ground and the Wiper High Speed Output circuit. Is the resistance below 100.0 ohms? Yes → Repair the High Speed Output circuit shorted to ground. Perform BODY VERIFICATION TEST - VER 1. No → Go To 10
10	If there are no possible causes remaining, view repair. Repair Replace the Wiper Motor. Perform BODY VERIFICATION TEST - VER 1.

CR9020000454030X

Fig. 46 Wiper Not Working In High Speed (Part 3 of 3). 2001–04 Concorde, Intrepid & 300M & 2001 LHS

POSSIBLE CAUSES
WIPER ON/OFF RELAY
WIPER ON/OFF RELAY CONTROL CIRCUIT SHORTED TO GROUND
LOW SPEED OUTPUT CIRCUIT SHORTED TO VOLTAGE
HIGH SPEED OUTPUT CIRCUIT SHORTED TO VOLTAGE
COMMON CIRCUIT SHORTED TO VOLTAGE
BCM

TEST	ACTION
1	Install a substitute relay in place of the Wiper On/Off Relay. Do the Wipers operate correctly? Yes → Replace the Wiper On/Off Relay. Perform BODY VERIFICATION TEST - VER 1. No → Go To 2
2	Turn the ignition off. Remove the Wiper On/Off Relay from the PDC. Disconnect the BCM C3 harness connector. Measure the resistance between ground and the Wiper On/Off Relay Control circuit. Is the resistance below 100.0 ohms? Yes → Repair the Wiper On/Off Relay Control circuit for a shorted to ground. Perform BODY VERIFICATION TEST - VER 1. No → Go To 3
3	Turn the ignition off. Remove the Wiper High/Low Relay. Disconnect the Wiper Motor harness connector. Turn the ignition on. Measure the voltage of the Low Speed Output circuit at the PDC. Is there any voltage present? Yes → Repair the Low Speed Output circuit for a shorted to battery. Perform BODY VERIFICATION TEST - VER 1. No → Go To 4
4	Turn the ignition off. Remove the Wiper High/Low Relay from the PDC. Disconnect the Wiper Motor harness connector. Turn the ignition on. Measure the voltage of the Wiper High Speed Output circuit at the PDC High/Low Relay connector. Is there any voltage present? Yes → Repair the High Speed Output circuit for a shorted to battery. Perform BODY VERIFICATION TEST - VER 1. No → Go To 5

CR9020000455010X

Fig. 47 Wiper Runs All Times With Ignition On (Part 1 of 2). 2001–04 Concorde, Intrepid & 300M & 2001 LHS

BODY VERIFICATION TEST - VER 1
1. Disconnect all jumper wires and reconnect all previously disconnected components and connectors. 2. If the Sentry Key Immobilizer Module (SKIM) or the Powertrain Control Module (PCM) was replaced, proceed to number 6. If the SKIM or PCM was not replaced, continue to the next number. 3. If the Body Control Module was replaced, turn the ignition on for 15 seconds (to allow the new BCM to learn VIN) or engine may not start (if VTSS equipped). If the vehicle is equipped with VTSS, use the DRBIII® and enable VTSS. 4. Program all other options as needed. 5. If any repairs were made to the HVAC System, disconnect the battery or, using the DRBIII®, recalibrate the HVAC doors. Proceed to number 13. 6. Obtain the Vehicle's unique PIN assigned to it's original SKIM 7. NOTE: Once Secured Access Mode is active, the SKIM will remain in that mode for 60 seconds. 8. With the DRBIII®, select THEFT ALARM, SKIM, MISCELLANEOUS and select SKIM REPLACED. Enter the 4 digit PIN to put the SKIM in Secured Access Mode. 9. The DRBIII® will prompt for the following steps. (1) Program the country code into the SKIM's memory. (2) Program the vehicle's VIN into the SKIM memory. (3) Transfer the vehicle's Secret Key data from the PCM. 10. Using the DRBIII®, program all customer keys into the SKIM memory. This requires that the SKIM be in Secured Access Mode, using the 4 digit PIN. 11. Note: If the PCM is replaced, the VIN and the unique Secret Key data must be transferred from the SKIM to the PCM. This procedure requires the SKIM to be placed in Secured Access Mode using the 4-digit PIN. 12. Note: If 3 attempts are made to enter Secured Access Mode using an incorrect PIN, Secured Access Mode will be locked out for 1 hour which causes the DRBIII® to display "Bus +\- Signals Open". To exit this mode, turn ignition to Run for 1 hour. 13. Ensure that all accessories are turned off and the battery is fully charged. 14. Ensure that the Ignition is on. 15. With the DRBIII®, record and erase all DTCs from ALL modules. Start and run the engine for 2 minutes. Operate all functions of the system that caused the original concern. 16. Turn the ignition off and wait 5 seconds. Turn the ignition on and using the DRBIII®, read DTCs from ALL modules. Are any DTC's present or is the original condition still present? Yes → Repair is not complete, refer to appropriate symptom. No → Repair is complete.

CR9020000456000X

Fig. 48 Test VER1: Body Verification Test. 2001–04 Concorde, Intrepid, Sebring Convertible, Sebring Sedan, Stratus Sedan & 300M & 2001 LHS

TEST	ACTION
5	Turn the ignition off. Remove the Wiper On/Off and High/Low Relays. Turn the ignition on. Measure the voltage of the Common circuit at the Wiper High/Low Relay connector in the PDC. Is the voltage above 10.0 volts? Yes → Repair the Common Circuit shorted to battery voltage. Perform BODY VERIFICATION TEST - VER 1. No → Go To 6
6	If there are no possible causes remaining, view repair Repair Replace the Body Control Module. Perform BODY VERIFICATION TEST - VER 1.

CR9020000455020X

Fig. 47 Wiper Runs All Times With Ignition On (Part 2 of 2). 2001–04 Concorde, Intrepid & 300M & 2001 LHS

1. MEASURE THE VOLTAGE OF THE FUSED IGNITON SWITCH OUTPUT CIRCUIT

Note: Inspect Fuse 4 located in the Underhood Accessory Fuse Block. If the fuse is open, repair the cause of the open fuse before continuing.

Turn the ignition on.

Disconnect the BCM harness connector.

Note: Check connectors - Clean/repair as necessary.

Measure the voltage of the Fused Ignition Switch Output circuit at the BCM C4 harness connector.

Is the voltage between 12 and 16 volts?

Yes >> Replace the Body Control Module.
Perform BODY VERIFICATION TEST.

No >> Repair the Fused Ignition Switch Output circuit for an open.
Perform BODY VERIFICATION TEST.

ARM0300000000142

Fig. 49 Voltage Supply Open. Crossfire

1. MEASURE WASHER PUMP MOTOR CIRCUIT RESISTANCE

Note: If any BCM DTCs are set, diagnose them first before continuing.
Turn the ignition off.
Disconnect the Multi-Function Switch harness connector.
Disconnect the Washer Pump Motor harness connector.
Note: Check connectors - Clean/repair as necessary.
Connect a jumper wire between cavity 1 and cavity 2 of the Washer Pump Motor harness connector.
Measure the resistance between ground and the Washer Pump Motor Control circuit at cavity 8 of the Multi-Function Switch harness connector.

Is the resistance below 5.0 ohms?

Yes >> Go to 2
No >> Repair the Washer Pump Motor Control circuit for an open.
Perform BODY VERIFICATION TEST.

2. MEASURE MULTI-FUNCTION SWITCH VOLTAGE

Disconnect the jumper wire.
Connect the Multi-Function Switch harness connector.
Turn the ignition on.
Depress the washer switch, and measure the voltage of the Washer Pump Motor Control circuit at the Washer Pump Motor Connector.

Is the voltage above 10 volts?

Yes >> Replace the Washer Pump Motor.
Perform BODY VERIFICATION TEST.
No >> Replace the Multi-Function Switch.
Perform BODY VERIFICATION TEST.

ARM0300000000143

Fig. 50 Washers Inoperative. Crossfire

1. MEASURE MULTI-FUNCTION SWITCH VOLTAGE

Note: If any BCM DTCs are set, diagnose them first before continuing.
Turn the ignition off.
Disconnect the Multi-Function Switch harness connector.
Note: Check connectors - Clean/repair as necessary.
Connect a fused jumper wire from B(+) to cavity 11 of the Multi-Function Switch.
Measure the voltage of the Washer Pump Motor Control circuit at the Multi-Function Switch harness connector.

Is voltage present?

Yes >> Replace the Multi-Function Switch.
Perform BODY VERIFICATION TEST.
No >> Go to 2

2. MEASURE WASHER PUMP MOTOR CIRCUIT VOLTAGE

Disconnect the Washer Pump Motor harness connector.
Disconnect the BCM harness connector.
Note: Check connectors - Clean/repair as necessary.
Turn the ignition on.
Measure the voltage of the Washer Pump Motor Control circuit at cavity 8 of the Multi-Function Switch harness connector.

Is voltage present?

Yes >> Repair the Washer Pump Motor Control circuit for a short to voltage.
Perform BODY VERIFICATION TEST.
No >> Replace the Body Control Module.
Perform BODY VERIFICATION TEST.

ARM0300000000144

Fig. 51 Washers Run Continuously w/Ignition On. Crossfire

1. MEASURE WIPER/WASHER FUSED B(+) CIRCUIT VOLTAGE

Note: If any BCM DTCs are set, diagnose them first before continuing.
Note: Inspect Fuse 32 located in the Underhood Accessory Fuse Block. If the fuse is open, repair the cause of the open fuse before continuing.
Turn the ignition off.
Disconnect the Multi-Function Switch harness connector.
Note: Check connectors - Clean/repair as necessary.
Turn the ignition on.
Measure the voltage of the Fused B(+) circuit at the Multi-Function Switch harness connector.

Is the voltage above 10 volts?

Yes >> Go to 2
No >> Repair the Fused B(+) circuit for an open.
Perform BODY VERIFICATION TEST.

2. TEST THE WIPER MOTOR

Turn the ignition off.
Disconnect the Body Control Module (BCM) C2 harness connector.
Note: Check connectors - Clean/repair as necessary.
Connect a jumper wire between cavity 1 of the BCM C2 harness connector and B(+).
Connect a jumper wire between cavity 41 of the BCM C2 harness connector and ground.

With the jumper wires connected, does the Wiper Motor move?

Yes >> Go to 3
No >> Replace the Wiper Motor.
Perform BODY VERIFICATION TEST.

ARM0300000000145

Fig. 52 Wipers Inoperative (Part 1 of 2). Crossfire

3. MEASURE WIPER SWITCH MUX CIRCUIT RESISTANCE

Measure the resistance of the Wiper Switch Mux circuit from the Multi-Function Switch harness connector to the BCM harness connector.

Is the resistance below 5.0 ohms?

Yes >> Go to 4
No >> Repair the Wiper Switch Mux circuit for an open.
Perform BODY VERIFICATION TEST.

4. MEASURE WIPER SWITCH MUX CIRCUIT VOLTAGE

Connect the Multi-Function Switch harness connector.
Turn the ignition on.
Measure the voltage of the Wiper Switch Mux circuit at the BCM C3 connector cavity 65 with the Wiper Switch in the High position.

Is the voltage approximately 12 volts?

Yes >> Replace the Body Control Module.
Perform BODY VERIFICATION TEST.
No >> Replace the Multi-Function Switch.
Perform BODY VERIFICATION TEST.

ARM0300000000146

Fig. 52 Wipers Inoperative (Part 2 of 2). Crossfire

1. TEST THE WIPER MOTOR

Note: If any BCM DTCs are set, diagnose them first before continuing.

Turn the ignition off.

Disconnect the Body Control Module (BCM) C2 harness connector.

Note: Check connectors - Clean/repair as necessary.

Connect a jumper wire between cavity 1 of the BCM C2 harness connector and B(+).

Connect a jumper wire between cavity 41 of the BCM C2 harness connector and ground.

With the jumper wires connected, does the Wiper Motor move?

Yes >> Go to 2

No >> Replace the Wiper Motor.
Perform BODY VERIFICATION TEST.

2. MEASURE WIPER SWITCH MUX CIRCUIT VOLTAGE

Connect the BCM harness connector.

Turn the ignition on.

Backprobe the BCM C3 harness connector cavity 65 for voltage with the Wiper Switch in the High position.

Is the voltage approximately 12 volts?

Yes >> Replace the Body Control Module.
Perform BODY VERIFICATION TEST.

No >> Replace the Multi-Function Switch.

Perform BODY VERIFICATION TEST.

ARM0300000000147

Fig. 53 Wipers Highspeed Inoperative. Crossfire

1. MEASURE WIPER SWITCH MUX CIRCUIT VOLTAGE

Note: If any BCM DTCs are set, diagnose them first before continuing.

Turn the ignition on.

Backprobe the Body Control Module (BCM) C3 harness connector cavity 65 for voltage with the Wiper Switch in the Intermittent position.

Is the voltage approximately 3 to 4 volts?

Yes >> Replace the Body Control Module.
Perform BODY VERIFICATION TEST.

No >> Replace the Multi-Function Switch.

Perform BODY VERIFICATION TEST.

ARM0300000000149

Fig. 55 Wipers Intermittent Speed Inoperative. Crossfire

1. TEST THE WIPER MOTOR

Note: If any BCM DTCs are set, diagnose them first before continuing.

Turn the ignition off.

Disconnect the Body Control Module (BCM) C2 harness connector.

Note: Check connectors - Clean/repair as necessary.

Connect a jumper wire between cavity 2 of the BCM C2 harness connector and B(+).

Connect a jumper wire between cavity 41 of the BCM C2 harness connector and ground.

With the jumper wires connected, does the Wiper Motor move?

Yes >> Go to 2

No >> Replace the Wiper Motor.
Perform BODY VERIFICATION TEST.

2. MEASURE WIPER SWITCH MUX CIRCUIT VOLTAGE

Disconnect the jumper wires.

Connect the BCM harness connector.

Turn the ignition on.

Backprobe the BCM C3 harness connector cavity 65 for voltage with the Wiper Switch in the Low position.

Is the voltage approximately 7 to 8 volts?

Yes >> Replace the Body Control Module.
Perform BODY VERIFICATION TEST.

No >> Replace the Multi-Function Switch.

Perform BODY VERIFICATION TEST.

ARM0300000000148

Fig. 54 Wipers Low Speed Inoperative. Crossfire

1. MEASURE MULTI-FUNCTION SWITCH VOLTAGE

Note: If any BCM DTCs are set, diagnose them first before continuing.

Turn the ignition off.

Disconnect the Multi-Function Switch harness connector.

Note: Check connectors - Clean/repair as necessary.

Connect a fused jumper wire from B(+) to cavity 11 of the Multi-Function Switch.

Measure the voltage of the Wiper Switch Mux circuit at cavity 7 of the Multi-Function Switch harness connector.

Is voltage present?

Yes >> Replace the Multi-Function Switch.
Perform BODY VERIFICATION TEST.

No >> Go to 2

2. MEASURE WIPER SWITCH MUX CIRCUIT VOLTAGE

Disconnect the jumper wire.

Disconnect the BCM harness connector.

Note: Check connectors - Clean/repair as necessary.

Turn the ignition on.

Measure the voltage of the Wiper Switch Mux circuit at cavity 7 of the Multi-Function Switch harness connector.

Is voltage present?

Yes >> Repair the Wiper Switch Mux circuit for a short to voltage.
Perform BODY VERIFICATION TEST.

No >> Replace the Body Control Module.

Perform BODY VERIFICATION TEST.

ARM0300000000150

Fig. 56 Wipers Run Continuously w/Ignition On. Crossfire

1.

Turn the ignition off.

Disconnect all jumper wires and reconnect all previously disconnected components and connectors.

Note: If the SKREEM or the PCM was replaced, refer to the service information for proper programming procedures.

If the Body Control Module was replaced, turn the ignition on for 15 seconds (to allow the new BCM to learn VIN) or engine may not start.

Program all RKE transmitters and other options as necessary.

With the DRB III®, erase all Diagnostic Trouble Codes (DTCs) from ALL modules. Start the engine and allow it to run for 2 minutes. Operate all functions of the system that caused the original complaint.

Ensure that all accessories are turned off and the battery is fully charged.

Turn the ignition off and wait 5 seconds. Turn the ignition on and using the DRB III®, read DTCs from ALL modules.

Are any DTCs present or is the original complaint still present?

Are any DTCs present?

YES >> Repair is not complete, refer to appropriate symptom.

NO >> Repair is complete.

ARM0300000000151

Fig. 57 Body Verification Test. Crossfire

When Monitored: Continuously.

Set Condition: BCM detects a low (ground) signal on the wiper on/off relay output.

POSSIBLE CAUSES
INTERMITTENT CONDITION
OPEN CIRCUIT
SHORT TO GROUND
HI/LO WIPER RELAY
BODY CONTROL MODULE

TEST	ACTION
1	Turn the ignition on. With the DRBIII®, clear all BCM DTC's. Actuate the Wipers. With the DRBIII®, read the DTC information. Does the DRBIII® read: Wiper On/Off Relay Output Shorted Low? Yes → Go To 2 No → The condition that caused the symptom is currently not present. Inspect the related wiring for a possible intermittent condition. Look for any chafed, pierced, pinched, or partially broken wires. Perform BODY VERIFICATION TEST - VER 1.
2	Disconnect the BCM from the junction block. Connect a jumper wire between the HI/LO Wiper Relay Control Circuit and ground. With the DRBIII®, monitor the wiper relay. Does the Wiper Relay show CLOSED? Yes → Repair the HI/LO Wiper Relay Control Circuit for an open condition. Perform BODY VERIFICATION TEST - VER 1. No → Go To 3
3	Turn the ignition off. Remove the HI/LO Wiper Relay. Disconnect the BCM from the junction block. Measure the resistance of the HI/LO Wiper Relay Output Circuit. Is the resistance below 5.0 ohms? Yes → Repair the HI/LO Wiper Relay Output Circuit for a short to ground condition. Perform BODY VERIFICATION TEST - VER 1. No → Go To 4

CR9020100527010X

Fig. 59 Wiper On/Off Relay Output Shorted Low (Part 1 of 2) . 2001–04 Sebring Convertible, Sebring Sedan & Stratus Sedan

When Monitored: Continuoulsy.

Set Condition: BCM detects a high level on the wiper on/off relay output when it is attempting to turn on the wipers.

POSSIBLE CAUSES
INTERMITTENT CONDITION
SHORT TO BATTERY
HI/LO WIPER RELAY
BODY CONTROL MODULE

TEST	ACTION
1	Turn the ignition on. With the DRBIII®, clear all BCM DTC's. Actuate the Wipers. With the DRBIII®, read the DTC information. Does the DRBIII® read: Wiper On/Off Relay Output Shorted High? Yes → Go To 2 No → The condition that caused the symptom is currently not present. Inspect the related wiring for a possible intermittent condition. Look for any chafed, pierced, pinched, or partially broken wires. Perform BODY VERIFICATION TEST - VER 1.
2	Turn the ignition off. Disconnect the HI/LO Wiper Relay. Disconnect the BCM from the junction block. Measure the voltage of the HI/LO Wiper Relay Control Circuit. Is the voltage below 5.0 volts? Yes → Repair the Wiper HI/LO Relay Control Circuit for a short to battery. Perform BODY VERIFICATION TEST - VER 1. No → Go To 3
3	Turn the ignition off. Install a known good relay in place of the HI/LO Wiper Relay. Turn the Wipers on. Do the Wipers operate normally? Yes → Replace the HI/LO Wiper Relay. Perform BODY VERIFICATION TEST - VER 1. No → Replace the Body Control Module. Perform BODY VERIFICATION TEST - VER 1.

CR9020100526000X

Fig. 58 Wiper On/Off Relay Output Shorted High. 2001–04 Sebring Convertible, Sebring Sedan & Stratus Sedan

TEST	ACTION
4	Turn the ignition off. Install a known good relay in place of the HI/LO Wiper Relay. Turn the wipers on. Do the Wipers operate normally? Yes → Replace the Wiper HI/LO Relay. Perform BODY VERIFICATION TEST - VER 1. No → Replace the Body Control Module. Perform BODY VERIFICATION TEST - VER 1.

CR9020100527020X

Fig. 59 Wiper On/Off Relay Output Shorted Low (Part 2 of 2). 2001–04 Sebring Convertible, Sebring Sedan & Stratus Sedan

When Monitored: With the wipers on (any speed).

Set Condition: BCM fails to detect a park signal from the wiper motor for 18 consecutive seconds.

POSSIBLE CAUSES
INTERMITTENT CONDITION
OPEN WIPER PARK SWITCH SENSE CIRCUIT
SHORT TO BATTERY
WIPER MOTOR
BODY CONTROL MODULE

TEST	ACTION
1	Turn the ignition on. With the DRBIII®, clear all BCM DTC's. Actuate the Wipers. With the DRBIII®, read the DTC information. Does the DRBIII® read: Wiper Park Switch Open Circuit? Yes → Go To 2 No → The condition that caused the symptom is currently not present. Inspect the related wiring for a possible intermittent condition. Look for any chafed, pierced, pinched, or partially broken wires. Perform BODY VERIFICATION TEST - VER 1.
2	Disconnect the BCM C3 harness connector. Connect a jumper wire between the Wiper Park Switch Sense Circuit and ground. With the DRBIII®, monitor the Wiper Park Switch. Does the Wiper Park Switch show CLOSED? Yes → Repair the Wiper Park Switch Sense Circuit for an open condition. Perform BODY VERIFICATION TEST - VER 1. No → Go To 3

CR9020100528010X

Fig. 60 Wiper Park Switch Open Circuit (Part 1 of 2). 2001–04 Sebring Convertible, Sebring Sedan & Stratus Sedan

When Monitored: With the wipers on (any speed).

Set Condition: BCM fails to detect a park signal from the wiper motor.

POSSIBLE CAUSES
INTERMITTENT CONDITION
SHORT TO GROUND
WIPER SWITCH
BODY CONTROL MODULE

TEST	ACTION
1	Turn the ignition on. With the DRBIII®, clear all BCM DTC's. Actuate the Wipers. With the DRBIII®, read the DTC information. Does the DRBIII® read: Wiper Park Switch Shorted to Ground? Yes → Go To 2 No → The condition that caused the symptom is currently not present. Inspect the related wiring for a possible intermittent condition. Look for any chafed, pierced, pinched, or partially broken wires. Perform BODY VERIFICATION TEST - VER 1.
2	Turn the ignition off. Disconnect the Junction Block Harness Connector from the front of the junction block. Disconnect the Wiper Park Switch harness connector. Remove the Body Control Module from the junction block. Using a 12-volt test light connected to ground, check the Wiper Park Switch Sense circuit. Does the test light illuminate brightly? Yes → Go To 3 No → Repair the Wiper Park Switch Sense Circuit for a short to ground condition. Perform BODY VERIFICATION TEST - VER 1.

CR9020100529010X

Fig. 61 Wiper Park Switch Shorted To Ground (Part 1 of 2). 2001–04 Sebring Convertible, Sebring Sedan & Stratus Sedan

TEST	ACTION
3	Turn the ignition off. Disconnect the Wiper Park Switch. Disconnect the BCM from the junction block. Measure the voltage of the Wiper Relay Control Circuit. Is the voltage below 5.0 volts? Yes → Go To 4 No → Repair the HI/LO Wiper Relay Control Circuit for a short to voltage. Perform BODY VERIFICATION TEST - VER 1.
4	Turn the Wipers off. Disconnect the Wiper Motor Connector. With the DRBIII®, monitor the Wiper Park Switch. Connect a jumper wire between the Wiper Park Switch Sense Circuit and ground. Does the Wiper Park Switch show CLOSED? Yes → Replace the Wiper Motor. Perform BODY VERIFICATION TEST - VER 1. No → Replace the Body Control Module. Perform BODY VERIFICATION TEST - VER 1.

CR9020100528020X

Fig. 60 Wiper Park Switch Open Circuit (Part 2 of 2). 2001–04 Sebring Convertible, Sebring Sedan & Stratus Sedan

TEST	ACTION
3	Disconnect the Junction Block harness connector. Disconnect the Wiper Switch connector. Measure the resistance of the Wiper Switch MUX Circuit. Is the resistance below 5.0 ohms? Yes → Replace the Wiper Switch. Perform BODY VERIFICATION TEST - VER 1. No → Replace the Body Control Module. Perform BODY VERIFICATION TEST - VER 1.

CR9020100529020X

Fig. 61 Wiper Park Switch Shorted To Ground (Part 2 of 2). 2001–04 Sebring Convertible, Sebring Sedan & Stratus Sedan

TROUBLESHOOTING HINTS

- Malfunction of the wiper motor
- Malfunction of the column switch (windshield wiper and washer switch)
- Malfunction of the front-ECU
- Damaged harness wires and connectors

DIAGNOSIS

Required Special Tools:

- MB991223: Test Harness Set
- MB991502: Scan Tool (MUT-II)
- MB991529: Diagnostic Trouble Code Check Harness

STEP 1. Check method of the input signal

Q: Which is to be used, the scan tool or the voltmeter to check the input signal?

Scan tool MB991502 : Go to Step 2.

Voltmeter : Go to Step 3.

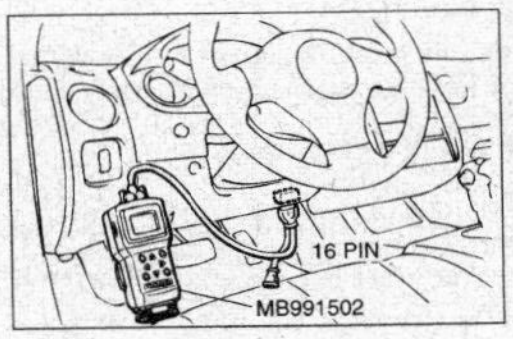

STEP 2. Check the input signal (by using scan tool MB991502).

Check the input signals from the windshield wiper switches.

⚠ CAUTION

To prevent damage to scan tool MB991502, always turn the ignition switch to the "LOCK" (OFF) position before connecting or disconnecting scan tool MB991502.

(1) Connect scan tool MB991502 to the data link connector.

(2) Check that the tone alarm of scan tool MB991502 sounds when the input signal enters.

Q: Does the tone alarm of scan tool MB991502 sounds when the input signal enters?

YES : Go to Step 4.

NO : Check the windshield wiper switch input circuit.

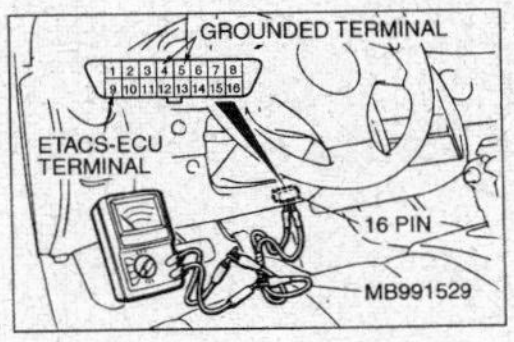

STEP 3. Check the input signal (by using a voltmeter).

Check the input signals from the windshield wiper switches.

(1) Use special tool MB991529 to connect a voltmeter between ground terminal 4 or 5 and ETACS-ECU terminal 9 of the data link connector.

(2) Check that the voltmeter indicator deflects once when the input signal enters.

Q: Does the voltmeter indicator deflect?

YES : Go to Step 4.

NO : Check the windshield wiper switch input circuit.

CR9020000464010X

Fig. 62 Test G-1: Windshield Wiper Does Not Operate (Part 1 of 4). 2001–03 Sebring & Stratus Coupe

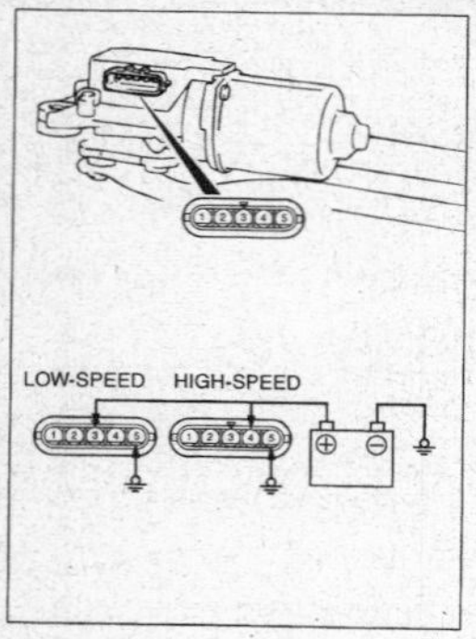

STPE 4. Check the windshield wiper motor.
(1) Disconnect the wiper motor connector A-03.
(2) Connect a battery to the wiper motor as shown in the illustration and check motor operation at low-speed and high-speed.

Q: Is the wiper motor in good condition?
YES : Go to Step 5.
NO : Replace the wiper motor. The windshield wiper should work normally.

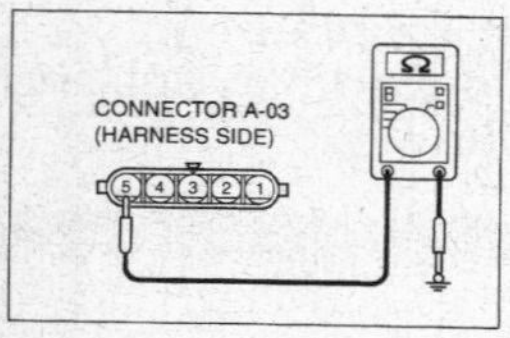

STEP 5. Check the wiper motor ground circuit at wiper motor connector A-03.
(1) Disconnect wiper motor connector A-03 and measure at the harness side.
(2) Measure the resistance between terminal 5 and ground.

Q: Is the resistance less than 2 ohm?
YES : Go to Step 8.
NO : Go to Step 6.

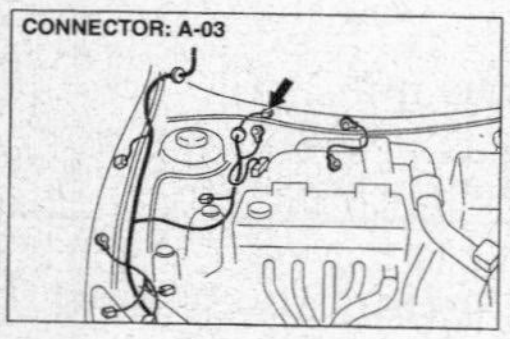

STEP 6. Check wiper motor connector A-03 for damage.
Q: Is wiper motor connector A-03 in good condition?
YES : Go to Step 7.
NO : Repair or replace it. The windshield wiper should work normally.

CR9020000464020X

Fig. 62 Test G-1: Windshield Wiper Does Not Operate (Part 2 of 4). 2001–03 Sebring & Stratus Coupe

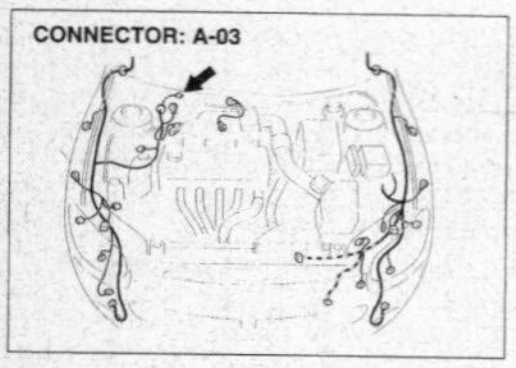

STEP 7. Check the harness wire between wiper motor connector A-03 and ground.
Q: Is the harness wire between wiper motor connector A-03 and ground in good condition?
YES : There is no action to be taken.
NO : Repair it. The windshield wiper should work normally.

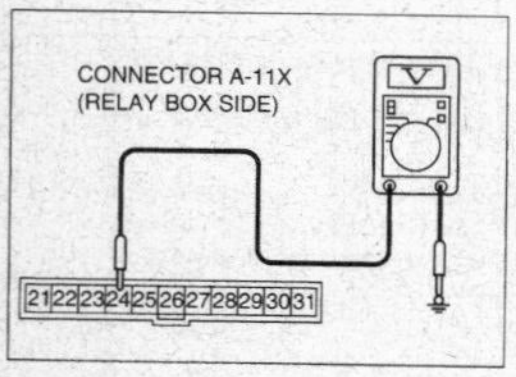

STEP 8. Check the front-ECU power supply circuit [ignition switch (ACC)] at the front-ECU connector A-11X.
(1) Disconnect the front-ECU connector A-11X and measure at the relay box side.
(2) Turn the ignition switch to "ACC" position.
(3) Measure the voltage between terminal 24 and ground.
- The measured value should be approximately 12 volts (battery positive voltage).

Q: Does the measured voltage correspond with this range?
YES : Replace the front-ECU. The windshield wiper should work normally.
NO : Go to Step 9.

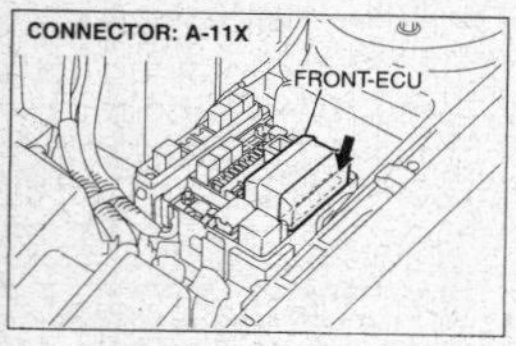

STEP 9. Check front-ECU connector A-11X for damage.
Q: Is front-ECU connector A-11X in good condition?
YES : Go to Step 10.
NO : Repair or replace it. The windshield wiper should work normally.

CR9020200464050X

Fig. 62 Test G-1: Windshield Wiper Does Not Operate (Part 3 of 4). 2002–03 Sebring & Stratus Coupe

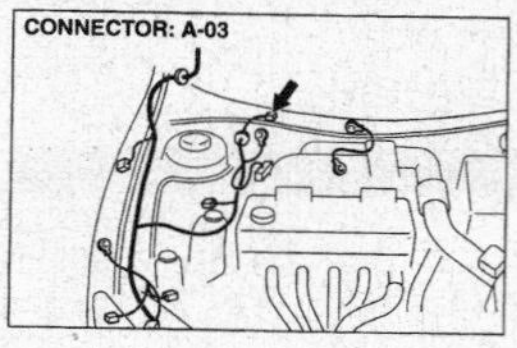

STEP 7. Check the harness wire between wiper motor connector A-03 and ground.
Q: Is the harness wire between wiper motor connector A-03 and ground in good condition?
YES : There is no action to be taken.
NO : Repair it. The windshield wiper should work normally.

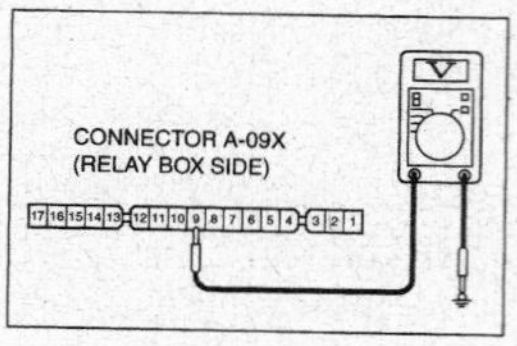

STEP 8. Check the front-ECU power supply circuit [ignition switch (ACC)] at the front-ECU connector A-09X.
(1) Disconnect the front-ECU connector A-09X and measure at the relay box side.
(2) Turn the ignition switch to "ACC" position.
(3) Measure the voltage between terminal 9 and ground.

Q: Is the voltage approximately 12 volts (battery positive voltage)?
YES : Replace the front-ECU. The windshield wiper should work normally.
NO : Go to Step 9.

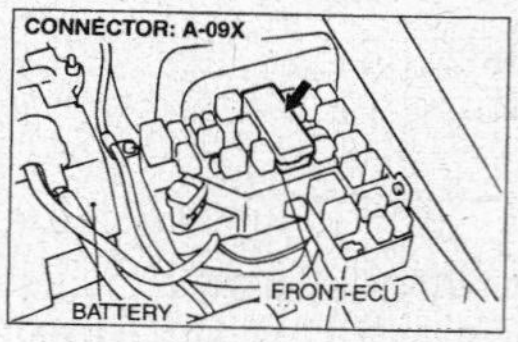

STEP 9. Check front-ECU connector A-09X for damage.
Q: Is front-ECU connector A-09X in good condition?
YES : Go to Step 10.
NO : Repair or replace it. The windshield wiper should work normally.

CR9020000464030X

Fig. 62 Test G-1: Windshield Wiper Does Not Operate (Part 3 of 4). 2001 Sebring & Stratus Coupe

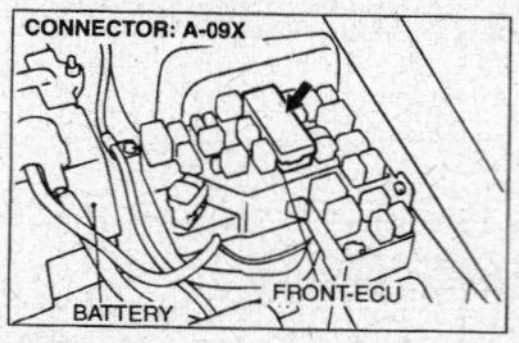

STEP 10. Check the harness wires between front-ECU connector A-09X and ignition switch (ACC).

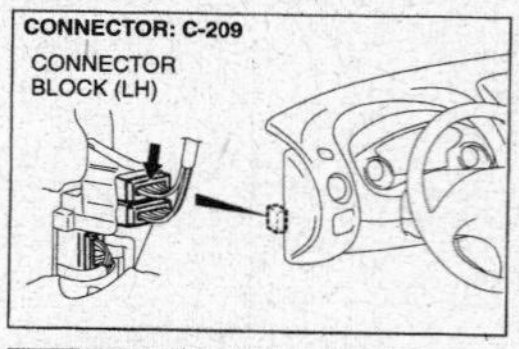

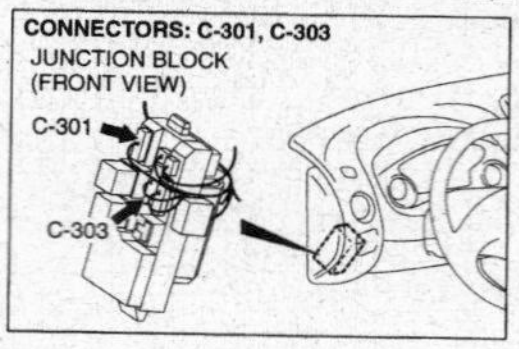

NOTE: After checking intermediate connector C-209 and junction block connectors C-303 and C-301, check the wires. If intermediate connector C-209 and junction block connectors C-303 and C-301 are damaged, repair or replace them.

Q: Are the harness wires between front-ECU connector A-09X and ignition switch (ACC) in good condition?
YES : There is no action to be taken.
NO : Repair them. The windshield wiper should work normally.

CR9020000464040X

Fig. 62 Test G-1: Windshield Wiper Does Not Operate (Part 4 of 4). 2001 Sebring & Stratus Coupe

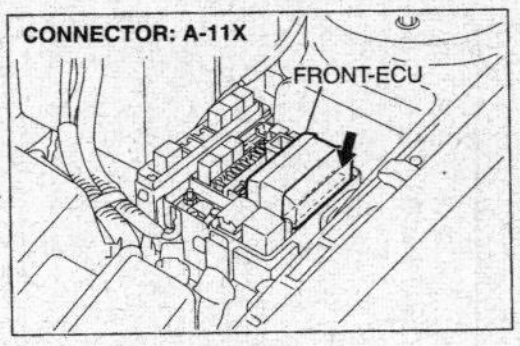

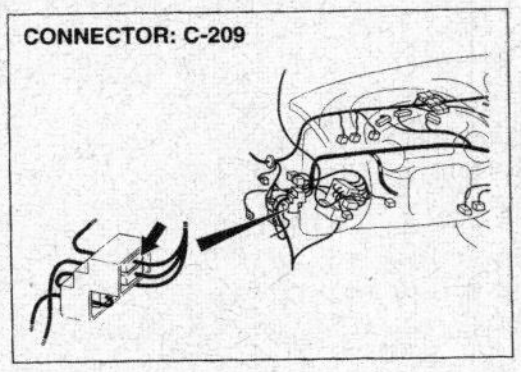

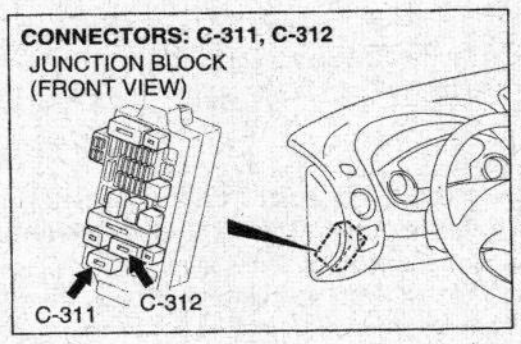

STEP 10. Check the harness wires between front-ECU connector A-11X and ignition switch (ACC).

Q: Are the harness wires between front-ECU connector A-11X and ignition switch (ACC) in good condition?

YES : There is no action to be taken.

NO : Repair them. The windshield wiper should work normally.

CR9020200464060X

Fig. 62 Test G-1: Windshield Wiper Does Not Operate (Part 4 of 4). 2002–03 Sebring & Stratus Coupe

Windshield Wiper Motor Drive Circuit

CIRCUIT OPERATION

A signal from the windshield wiper switch is sent through the column-ECU inside the column switch to the front-ECU. The signal turns on the relay inside the front-ECU to operate the wiper motor.

TECHNICAL DESCRIPTION (COMMENT)

The wiper motor, column switch (windshield wiper and washer switch) or the front-ECU may be defective.

TROUBLESHOOTING HINTS

- Malfunction of the wiper motor
- Malfunction of the column switch (windshield wiper and washer switch)
- Malfunction of the front-ECU
- Damaged harness wires and connectors

CR9020000465010X

Fig. 63 Test G-2: Any Wiper Switch Position Inoperative (Part 1 of 4). 2001–03 Sebring & Stratus Coupe

DIAGNOSIS

Required Special Tools:

- MB991223: Test Harness Set
- MB991502: Scan Tool (MUT-II)
- MB991529: Diagnostic Trouble Code Check Harness

STEP 1. Check method of the input signal

Q: Which is to be used, the scan tool or the voltmeter to check the input signal?

Scan tool MB991502 : Go to Step 2.

Voltmeter : Go to Step 3.

STEP 2. Check the input signal (by using scan tool MB991502).

Check the input signals from the windshield wiper switches.

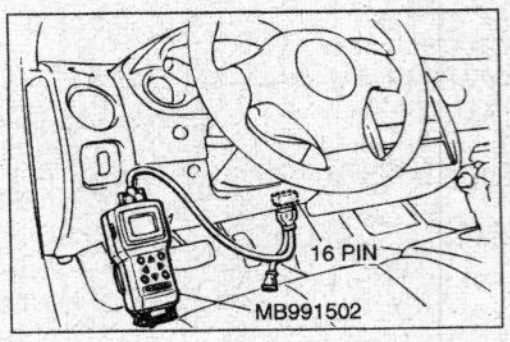

⚠ CAUTION

To prevent damage to scan tool MB991502, always turn the ignition switch to the "LOCK" (OFF) position before connecting or disconnecting scan tool MB991502.

(1) Connect scan tool MB991502 to the data link connector.

(2) Check that the tone alarm of scan tool MB991502 sounds when the input signal enters.

Q: Does the tone alarm of scan tool MB991502 sound when the input signal enters?

YES : Go to Step 4.

NO : Check the windshield wiper switch input circuit.

STEP 3. Check the input signal (by using a voltmeter).

Check the input signals from the windshield wiper switches.

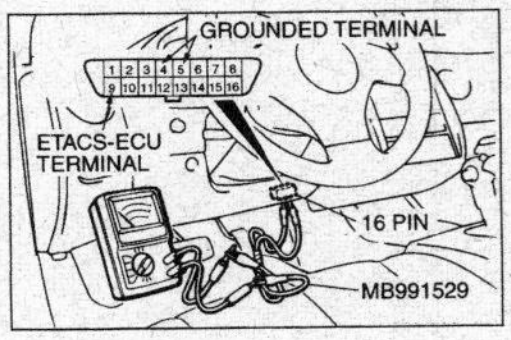

(1) Use special tool MB991529 to connect a voltmeter between ground terminal 4 or 5 and ETACS-ECU terminal 9 of the data link connector.

(2) Check that the voltmeter indicator deflects once when the input signal enters.

Q: Does the voltmeter indicator deflect?

YES : Go to Step 4.

NO : Check the windshield wiper switch input circuit.

CR9020000465020X

Fig. 63 Test G-2: Any Wiper Switch Position Inoperative (Part 2 of 4). 2001–03 Sebring & Stratus Coupe

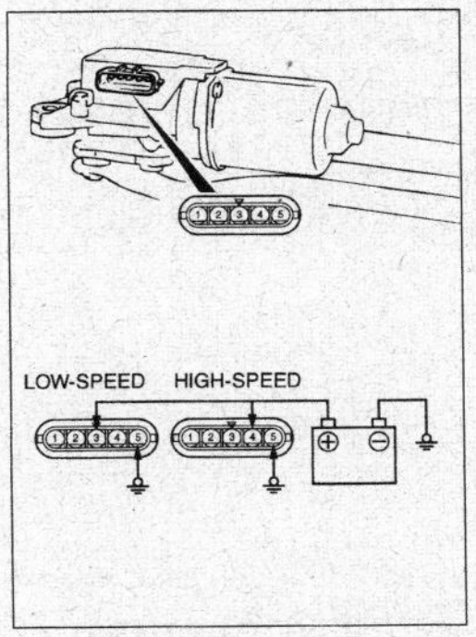

STPE 4. Check the windshield wiper motor.

(1) Disconnect the wiper motor connector A-03.

(2) Connect a battery to the wiper motor as shown in the illustration and check motor operation at low-speed and high-speed.

Q: Is the wiper motor in good condition?

YES : Go to Step 5.

NO : Replace the wiper motor. The windshield wiper should work normally when the windshield wiper switch is set to all positions.

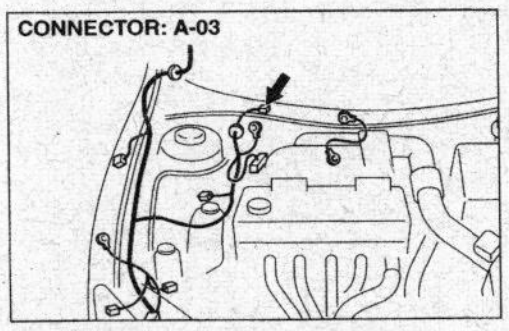

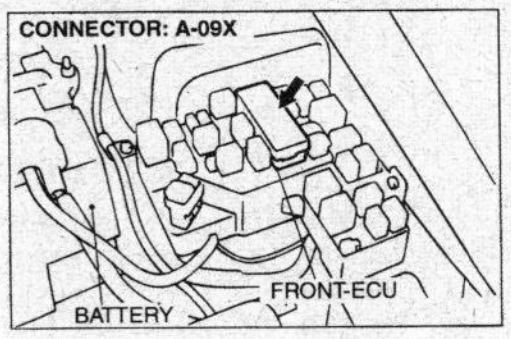

STEP 5. Check the wiper motor connector A-03 and front-ECU connector A-09X for damage.

Q: Are wiper motor connector A-03 and front-ECU connector A-09X in good condition?

YES : Go to Step 6.

NO : Repair or replace them. The windshield wiper should work normally when the windshield wiper switch is set to all positions.

CR9020000465030X

Fig. 63 Test G-2: Any Wiper Switch Position Inoperative (Part 3 of 4). 2001 Sebring & Stratus Coupe

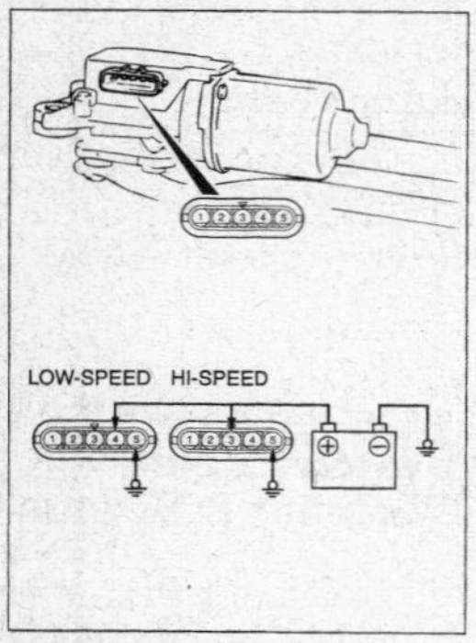

STEP 4. Check the windshield wiper motor.
(1) Disconnect the wiper motor connector A-03.
(2) Connect a battery to the wiper motor as shown in the illustration and check motor operation at low-speed and high-speed.

Q: Is the wiper motor in good condition?
YES : Go to Step 5.
NO : Replace the wiper motor. The windshield wiper should work normally when the windshield wiper switch is set to all positions.

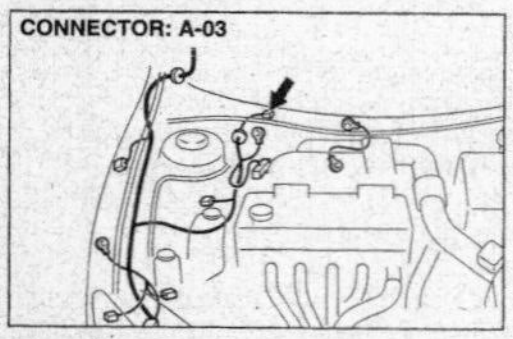

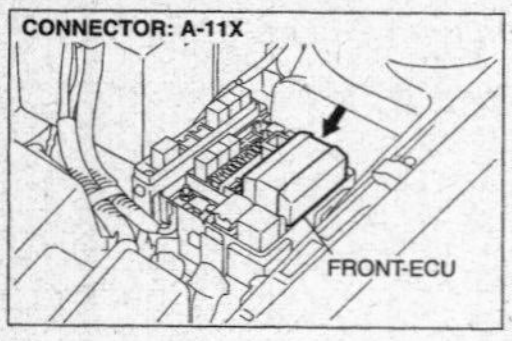

STEP 5. Check the wiper motor connector A-03 and front-ECU connector A-11X for damage.
Q: Are wiper motor connector A-03 and front-ECU connector A-11X in good condition?
YES : Go to Step 6.
NO : Repair or replace them.
The windshield wiper should work normally when the windshield wiper switch is set to all positions.

CR9020200465050X

Fig. 63 Test G-2: Any Wiper Switch Position Inoperative (Part 3 of 4). 2002–03 Sebring & Stratus Coupe

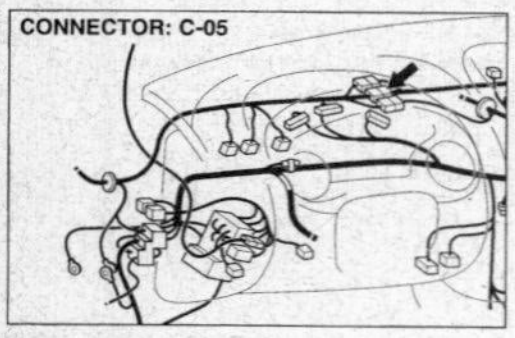

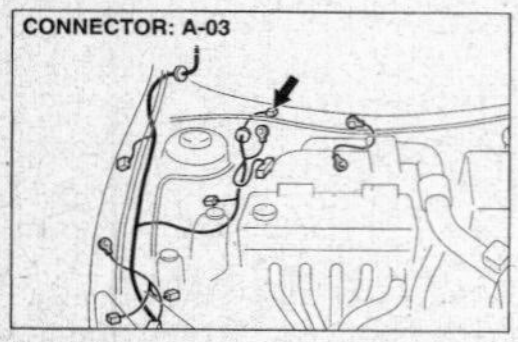

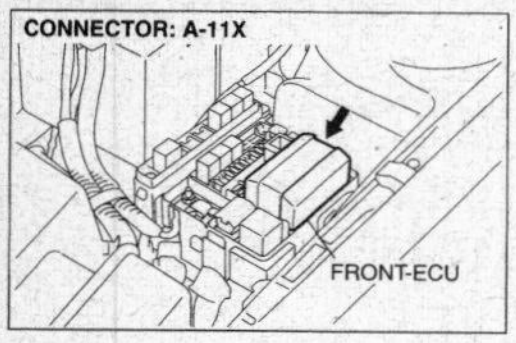

STEP 6. Check the harness wires between wiper motor connector A-03 and front-ECU connector A-11X.
NOTE: After checking intermediate connector C-05, check the wires. If intermediate connector C-05 is damaged, repair or replace it.

Q: Are the harness wires between wiper motor connector A-03 and front-ECU connector A-11X in good condition?
YES : There is no action to be taken.
NO : Repair them. The windshield wiper should work normally when the windshield wiper switch is set to all positions.

CR9020200465060X

Fig. 63 Test G-2: Any Wiper Switch Position Inoperative (Part 4 of 4). 2002–03 Sebring & Stratus Coupe

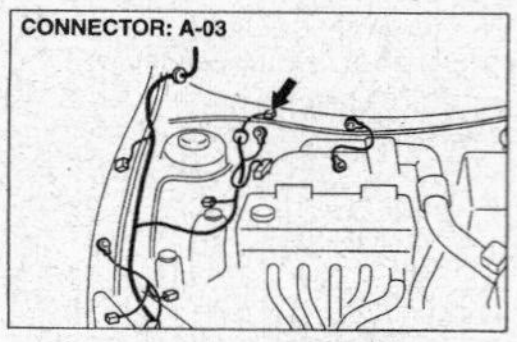

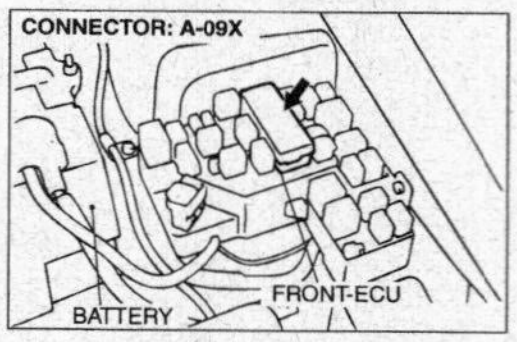

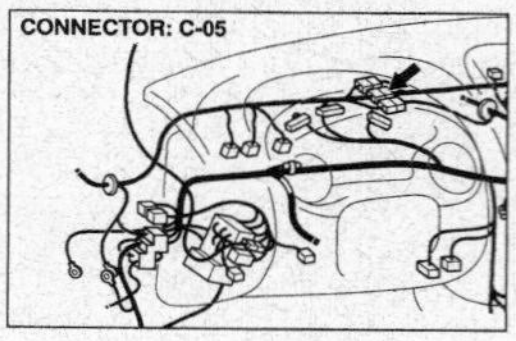

STEP 6. Check the harness wires between wiper motor connector A-03 and front-ECU connector A-09X.

NOTE: After checking intermediate connector C-05, check the wires. If intermediate connector C-05 is damaged, repair or replace it.

Q: Are the harness wires between wiper motor connector A-03 and front-ECU connector A-09X in good condition?
YES : There is no action to be taken.
NO : Repair them. The windshield wiper should work normally when the windshield wiper switch is set to all positions.

CR9020000465040X

Fig. 63 Test G-2: Any Wiper Switch Position Inoperative (Part 4 of 4). 2001 Sebring & Stratus Coupe

Windshield Wiper Motor Drive Circuit

CIRCUIT OPERATION
A signal from the windshield wiper switch is sent through the column-ECU inside the column switch to the front-ECU. The signal turns on the relay inside the front-ECU to operate the wiper motor.

TECHNICAL DESCRIPTION (COMMENT)
The wiper motor or the front-ECU may be defective.

TROUBLESHOOTING HINTS
- Malfunction of the wiper motor
- Malfunction of the front-ECU
- Damaged harness wires and connectors

CR9020000466010X

Fig. 64 Test G-3: Wiper Does Not Park (Part 1 of 5). 2001–03 Sebring & Stratus Coupe

DIAGNOSIS

Required Special Tool:
- MB991223: Test Harness Set

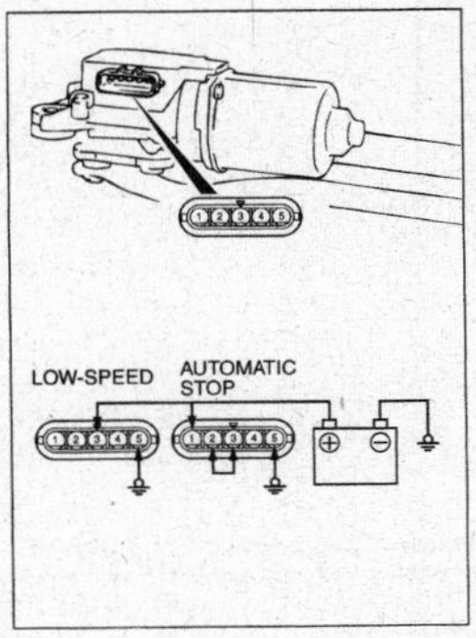

STEP 1. Check the windshield wiper motor
(1) Disconnect the wiper motor connector A-03.
(2) Run the wiper motor at low-speed, disconnect the battery, and stop the motor.
(3) Reconnect the battery as shown in the illustration, and confirm that after the motor starts turning at low-speed, and stops at the automatic stop position.

Q: Is the wiper motor in good condition?
YES : Go to Step 2.
NO : Replace the wiper motor. The windshield wiper should stop at the predetermined park position.

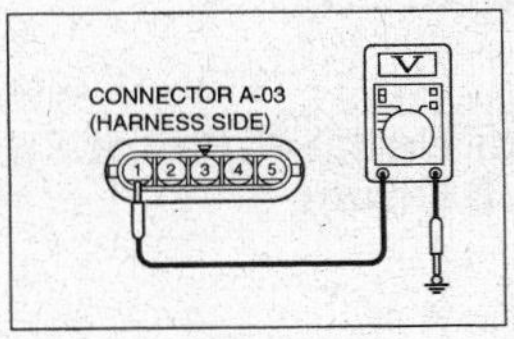

STEP 2. Check the wiper motor power supply circuit at the wiper motor connector A-03 by backprobing.
(1) Do not disconnect the wiper motor connector A-03.
(2) Turn the ignition switch to "ACC" position.
(3) Measure the voltage between terminal 1 and ground by backprobing.

Q: Is the voltage approximately 12 volts (battery positive voltage)?
YES : Go to Step 5.
NO : Go to Step 3.

CR9020000466020X

Fig. 64 Test G-3: Wiper Does Not Park (Part 2 of 5). 2001–03 Sebring & Stratus Coupe

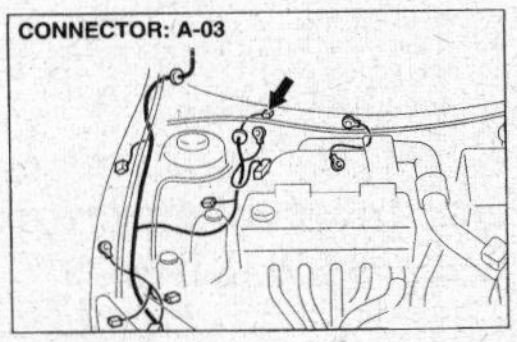

STEP 3. Check wiper motor connector A-03 for damage.
Q: Is wiper motor connector A-03 in good condition?
YES : Go to Step 4.
NO : Repair or replace it. The windshield wiper should stop at the predetermined park position.

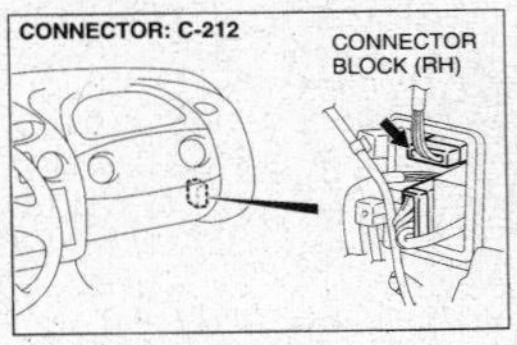

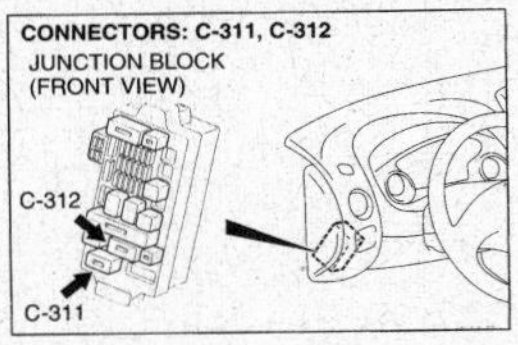

STEP 4. Check the harness wires between wiper motor connector A-03 and ignition switch (ACC).
NOTE: After checking intermediate connector C-212 and junction block connectors C-311 and C-312, check the wires. If intermediate connector C-212 or junction block connectors C-311 or C-312 are damaged, repair or replace them.

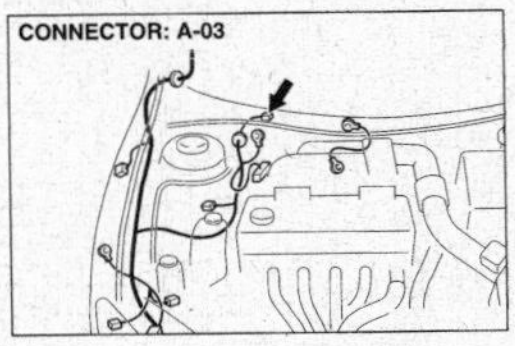

Q: Are the harness wires between wiper motor connector A-03 and ignition switch (ACC) in good condition?
YES : Go to Step 5.
NO : Repair or replace them. The windshield wiper should stop at the predetermined park position.

CR9020200466060X

Fig. 64 Test G-3: Wiper Does Not Park (Part 3 of 5). 2002–03 Sebring & Stratus Coupe

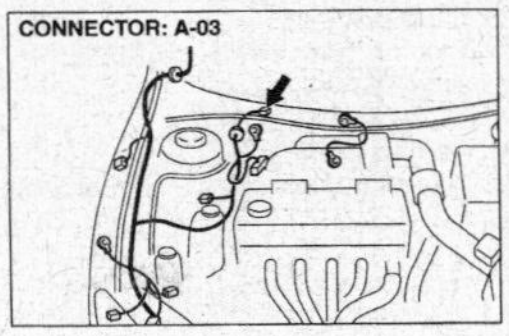

STEP 3. Check wiper motor connector A-03 for damage.
Q: Is wiper motor connector A-03 in good condition?
YES : Go to Step 4.
NO : Repair or replace it. The windshield wiper should stop at the predetermined park position.

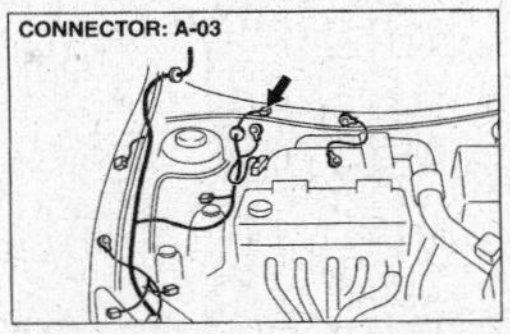

STEP 4. Check the harness wires between wiper motor connector A-03 and ignition switch (ACC).

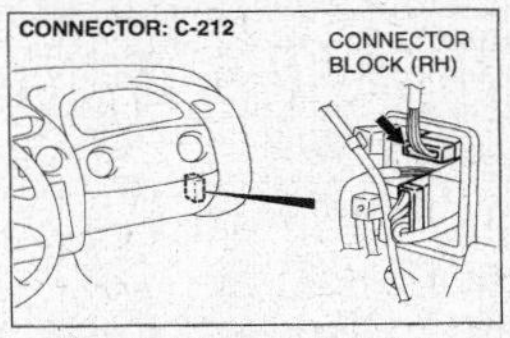

NOTE: After checking intermediate connector C-212 and junction block connectors C-310 and C-301, check the wires. If intermediate connector C-212 and junction block connectors C-310 and C-301 are damaged, repair or replace them.

Q: Are the harness wires between wiper motor connector A-03 and ignition switch (ACC) in good condition?
YES : There is no action to be taken.
NO : Repair or replace them. The windshield wiper should stop at the predetermined park position.

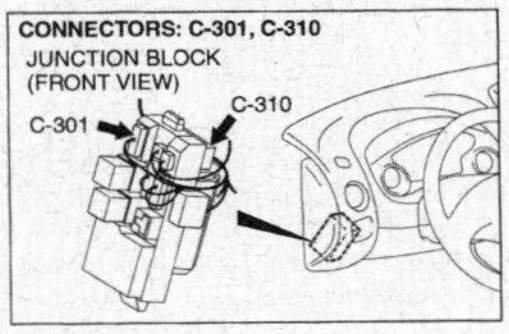

CR9020000466030X

Fig. 64 Test G-3: Wiper Does Not Park (Part 3 of 5). 2001 Sebring & Stratus Coupe

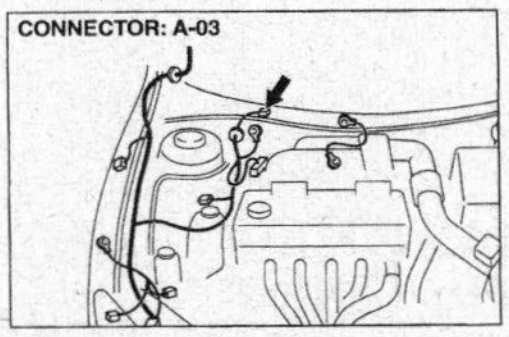

STEP 5. Check the wiper motor connector A-03 and front-ECU connector A-09X for damage.
Q: Are wiper motor connector A-03 and front-ECU connector A-09X in good condition?
YES : Go to Step 6.
NO : Repair or replace them. The windshield wiper should stop at the predetermined park position.

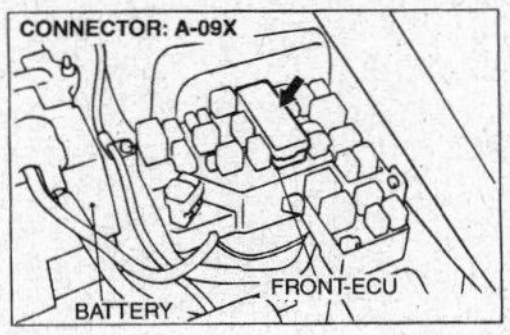

CR9020000466040X

Fig. 64 Test G-3: Wiper Does Not Park (Part 4 of 5). 2001 Sebring & Stratus Coupe

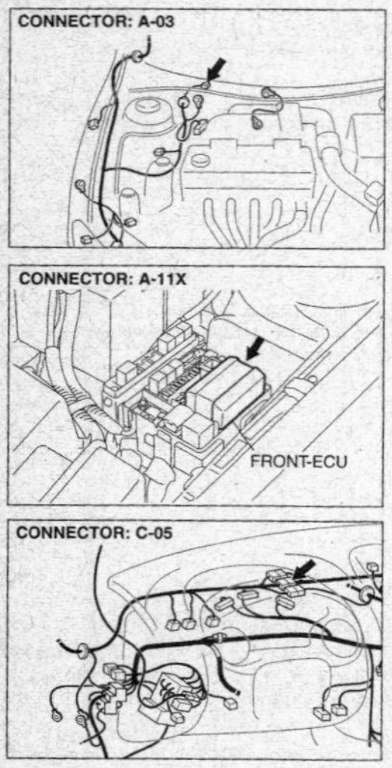

STEP 5. Check the wiper motor connector A-03 and front-ECU connector A-11X for damage.

Q: Are wiper motor connector A-03 and front-ECU connector A-11X in good condition?

YES : Go to Step 6.

NO : Repair or replace them. The windshield wiper should stop at the predetermined park position.

STEP 6. Check the harness wires between wiper motor connector A-03 and front-ECU connector A-11X.

NOTE: After checking intermediate connector C-05, check the wires. If intermediate connector C-05 is damaged, repair or replace it.

CR9020200466070X

Fig. 64 Test G-3: Wiper Does Not Park (Part 4 of 5). 2002–03 Sebring & Stratus Coupe

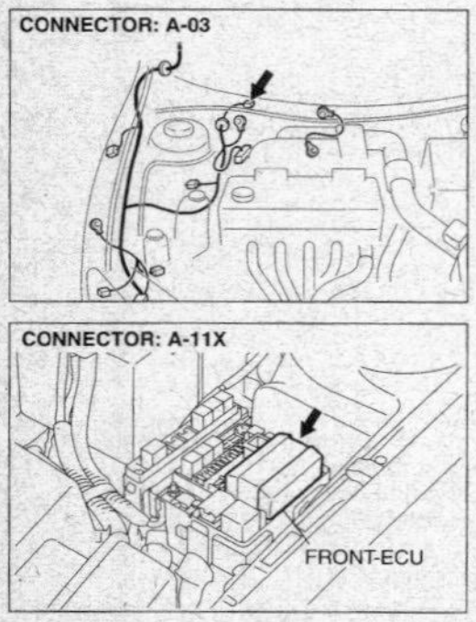

Q: Is the harness wires between wiper motor connector A-03 and front-ECU connector A-11X in good condition?

YES : No action to be taken.

NO : Repair them. The windshield wiper should stop at the predetermined park position.

CR9020200466080X

Fig. 64 Test G-3: Wiper Does Not Park (Part 5 of 5). 2002–03 Sebring & Stratus Coupe

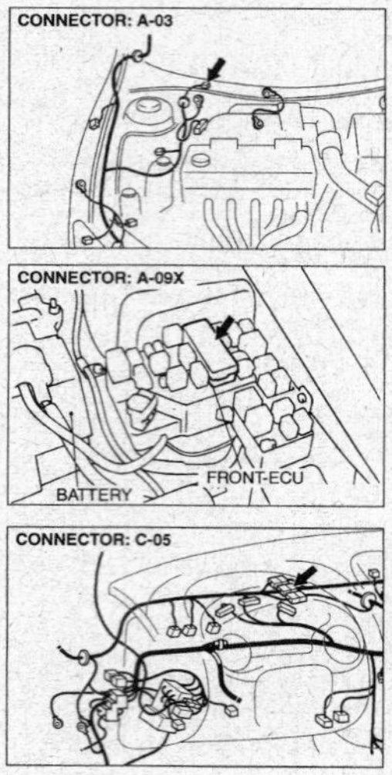

STEP 6. Check the harness wires between wiper motor connector A-03 and front-ECU connector A-09X.

NOTE: After checking intermediate connector C-05, check the wires. If intermediate connector C-05 is damaged, repair or replace it.

Q: Is the harness wires between wiper motor connector A-03 and front-ECU connector A-09X in good condition?

YES : There is no action to be taken.

NO : Repair them. The windshield wiper should stop at the predetermined park position.

CR9020000466050X

Fig. 64 Test G-3: Wiper Does Not Park (Part 5 of 5). 2001 Sebring & Stratus Coupe

TECHNICAL DESCRIPTION (COMMENT)

The ETACS-ECU calculates the intermittent wiper interval from the following input signals, and sends a signal to the front-ECU through the SWS communication line.

- Speed sensor
- Windshield intermittent wiper interval adjusting knob

If the signal is defective, the front-ECU will ignore the signal and set the intermittent wiper interval to four seconds.

TROUBLESHOOTING HINTS

- Malfunction of speed sensor
- Malfunction of the column switch (windshield wiper and washer switch)
- Malfunction of the ETACS-ECU
- Malfunction of the front-ECU
- Damaged harness wires or connectors

CR9020000467010X

Fig. 65 Test G-4: Intermittent Wiper Interval Cannot Be Adjusted (Part 1 of 3). 2001 Sebring & Stratus Coupe

TECHNICAL DESCRIPTION (COMMENT)
The ETACS-ECU calculates the intermittent wiper interval from the following input signals, and sends a signal to the front-ECU through the SWS communication line.
If the signal is defective, the front-ECU will ignore the signal and set the intermittent wiper interval to four seconds.

TROUBLESHOOTING HINTS
- Malfunction of the column switch (windshield wiper and washer switch)
- Malfunction of the ETACS-ECU
- Malfunction of the front-ECU
- Damaged harness wires or connectors

DIAGNOSIS

Required Special Tools:
- MB991223: Test Harness Set
- MB991502: Scan Tool (MUT-II)
- MB991529: Diagnostic Trouble Code Check Harness

STEP 1. Check method of the input signal

Q: Which is to be used, the scan tool or the voltmeter to check the input signal?
Scan tool MB991502 : Go to Step 2.
Voltmeter : Go to Step 3.

CR9020200467040X

Fig. 65 Test G-4: Intermittent Wiper Interval Cannot Be Adjusted (Part 1 of 3). 2002–03 Sebring & Stratus Coupe

DIAGNOSIS

Required Special Tools:
- MB991223: Test Harness Set
- MB991502: Scan Tool (MUT-II)
- MB991529: Diagnostic Trouble Code Check Harness

STEP 1. Check method of the input signal

Q: Which is to be used, the scan tool or the voltmeter to check the input signal?
Scan tool MB991502 : Go to Step 2.
Voltmeter : Go to Step 3.

STEP 2. Check the input signal (by using scan tool MB991502).
Check the input signals from the following switches.
- Speed sensor
- Windshield intermittent wiper interval adjusting knob

NOTE: If the windshield intermittent wiper interval adjusting knob is rotated from "FAST" to "SLOW" when the ignition switch is at the "ON" position, the ETACS-ECU will send a signal around the medium knob position.

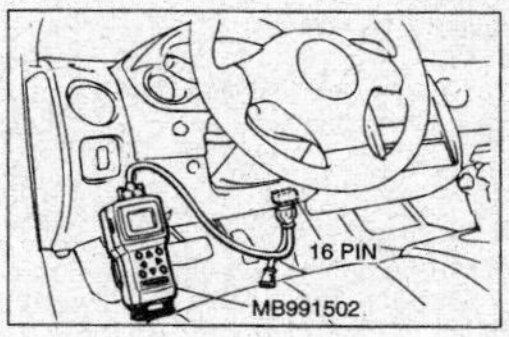

⚠ CAUTION
To prevent damage to scan tool MB991502, always turn the ignition switch to the "LOCK" (OFF) position before connecting or disconnecting scan tool MB991502.
(1) Connect scan tool MB991502 to the data link connector.
(2) Check that the tone alarm of scan tool MB991502 sounds when the input signal enters.

Q: Does the tone alarm of scan tool MB991502 sound when the input signal enters?
YES : Go to Step 4.
NO : Check the relevant input circuit.

CR9020000467020X

Fig. 65 Test G-4: Intermittent Wiper Interval Cannot Be Adjusted (Part 2 of 3). 2001–03 Sebring & Stratus Coupe

STEP 3. Check the input signal (by using a voltmeter).
Check the input signals from the following switches.
- Speed sensor
- Windshield intermittent wiper interval adjusting knob

NOTE: If the windshield intermittent wiper interval adjusting knob is rotated from "FAST" to "SLOW" when the ignition switch is at the "ON" position, the ETACS-ECU will send a signal around the medium knob position.

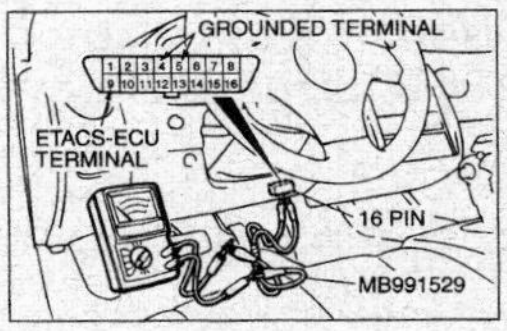

(1) Use special tool MB991529 to connect a voltmeter between ground terminal 4 or 5 and ETACS-ECU terminal 9 of the data link connector.
(2) Check that the voltmeter indicator deflects once when the input signal enters.

Q: Does the voltmeter indicator deflect?
YES : Go o Step 4.
NO : Check the relevant input circuit.

STEP 4. Replacement of ECU
(1) Replace the front-ECU.
(2) The windshield intermittent wiper interval should be changed.

Q: Is it possible to adjust the windshield intermittent wiper interval?
YES : There is no action to be taken.
NO : Replace the ETACS-ECU. The windshield intermittent wiper interval should be changed.

CR9020000467030X

Fig. 65 Test G-4: Intermittent Wiper Interval Cannot Be Adjusted (Part 3 of 3). 2001–03 Sebring & Stratus Coupe

CIRCUIT OPERATION
A signal from the windshield washer switch is sent through the column-ECU inside the column switch to the front-ECU. The signal turns on the relay inside the front-ECU to operate the washer motor.

TECHNICAL DESCRIPTION (COMMENT)
The washer motor, the column switch (windshield wiper and washer switch) or the front-ECU may be defective.

TROUBLESHOOTING HINTS
- Malfunction of the washer motor
- Malfunction of the column switch (windshield wiper and washer switch)
- Malfunction of the front-ECU
- Damaged harness wires and connectors

DIAGNOSIS

Required Special Tools:
- MB991223: Test Harness Set
- MB991502: Scan Tool (MUT-II)
- MB991529: Diagnostic Trouble Code Check Harness

STEP 1. Check the windshield wiper operation.

Q: Does the windshield wiper work normally?
YES : Go to Step 2 <when using scan tool MB991502> or 3 <when using a voltmeter>.
NO : Solve the problem first.

CR9020000468010X

Fig. 66 Test G-5: Windshield Washer Does Not Work (Part 1 of 5). 2001–03 Sebring & Stratus Coupe

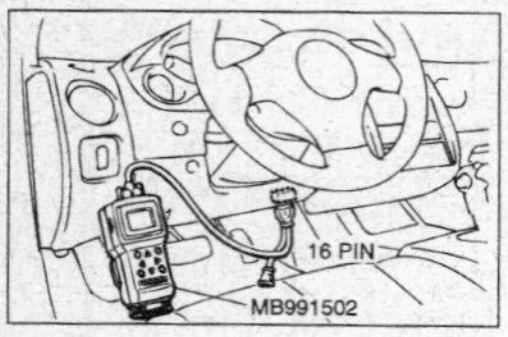

STEP 2. Check the input signal (by using scan tool MB991502).
Check the input signal from the windshield washer switch.

⚠ CAUTION
To prevent damage to scan tool MB991502, always turn the ignition switch to the "LOCK" (OFF) position before connecting or disconnecting scan tool MB991502.

(1) Connect scan tool MB991502 to the data link connector.
(2) Check that the tone alarm of scan tool MB991502 sounds when the input signal enters.

Q: Does the tone alarm of scan tool MB991502 sound when the input signal enters?
YES : Go to Step 4.
NO : Check the input signal circuit from the windshield washer switch.

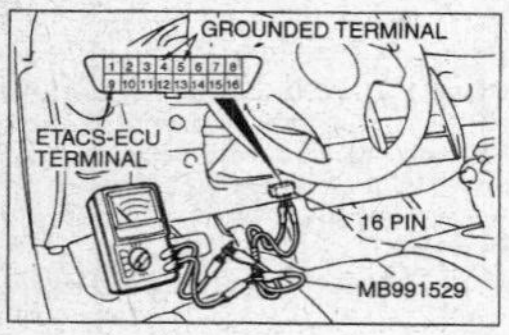

STEP 3. Check the input signal (by using a voltmeter).
Check the input signal from the windshield washer switch.
(1) Use special tool MB991529 to connect a voltmeter between ground terminal 4 or 5 and ETACS-ECU terminal 9 of the data link connector.
(2) Check that the voltmeter indicator deflects once when the input signal enters.

Q: Does the voltmeter indicator deflect?
YES : Go to Step 4.
NO : Check the input signal circuit from the windshield washer switch.

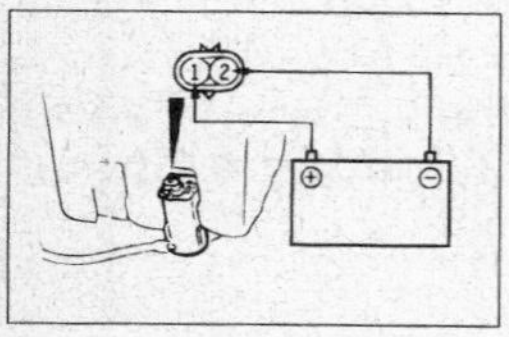

STEP 4. Check the washer motor.
(1) Disconnect the washer motor connector A-33.
(2) Fill the washer tank with water.
(3) Check that the water squirts out strongly when battery positive voltage is applied to terminals 1 and 2.

Q: Is the washer motor in good condition?
YES : Go to Step 5.
NO : Replace it. The windshield washer should work normally.

CR9020000468020X

Fig. 66 Test G-5: Windshield Washer Does Not Work (Part 2 of 5). 2001–03 Sebring & Stratus Coupe

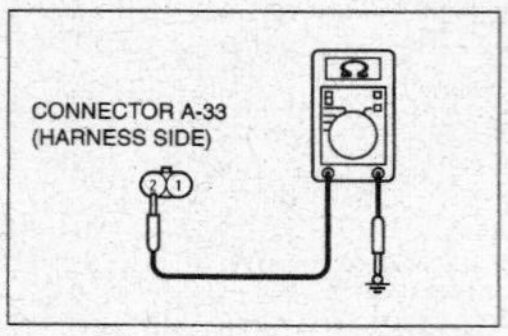

STEP 5. Check the washer motor ground circuit at the washer motor connector A-33.
(1) Disconnect the washer motor connector A-33 and measure at the harness side.
(2) Measure the resistance between terminal 2 and ground.

Q: Is the resistance between terminal 2 and ground less than 2 ohm?
YES : Go to Step 8.
NO : Go to Step 6.

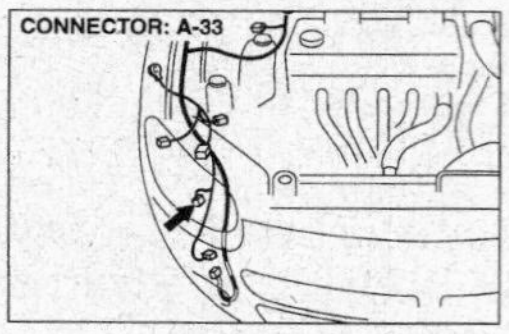

STEP 6. Check washer motor connector A-33 for damage.
Q: Is washer motor connector A-33 in good condition?
YES : Go to Step 7.
NO : Repair or replace it. The windshield washer should work normally.

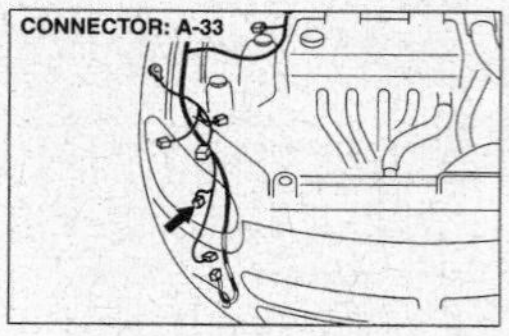

STEP 7. Check the harness wire between washer motor connector A-33 and ground.
Q: Is the harness wire between washer motor connector A-33 and ground in good condition?
YES : There is no action to be taken.
NO : Repair it. The windshield washer should work normally.

CR9020000468030X

Fig. 66 Test G-5: Windshield Washer Does Not Work (Part 3 of 5). 2001–03 Sebring & Stratus Coupe

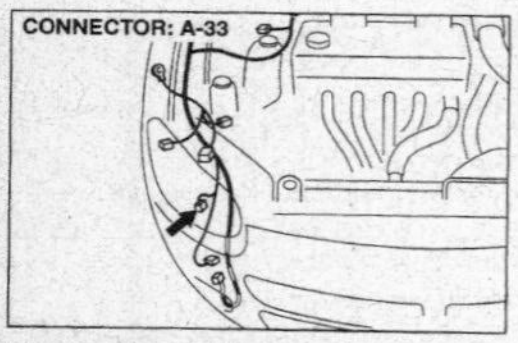

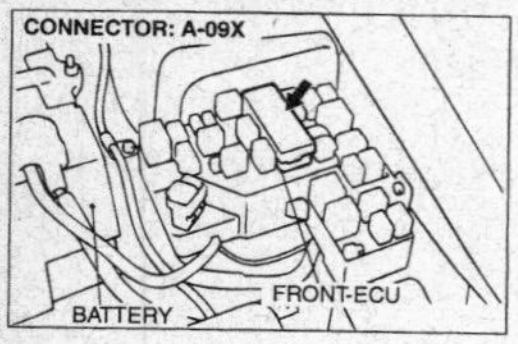

STEP 8. Check washer motor connector A-33 and front-ECU connector A-09X for damage.
Q: Are washer motor connector A-33 and front-ECU connector A-09X in good condition?
YES : Go to Step 9.
NO : Repair or replace them. The windshield washer should work normally.

CR9020000468040X

Fig. 66 Test G-5: Windshield Washer Does Not Work (Part 4 of 5). 2001 Sebring & Stratus Coupe

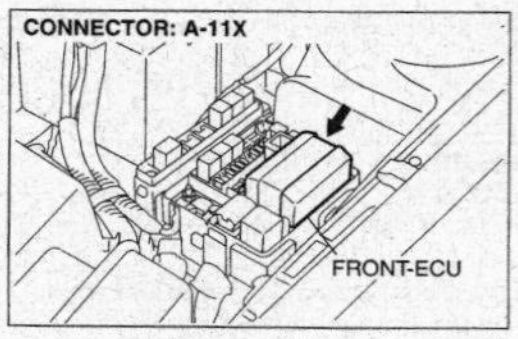

STEP 8. Check washer motor connector A-33 and front-ECU connector A-11X for damage.
Q: Are washer motor connector A-33 and front-ECU connector A-11X in good condition?
YES : Go to Step 9.
NO : Repair or replace them. The windshield washer should work normally.

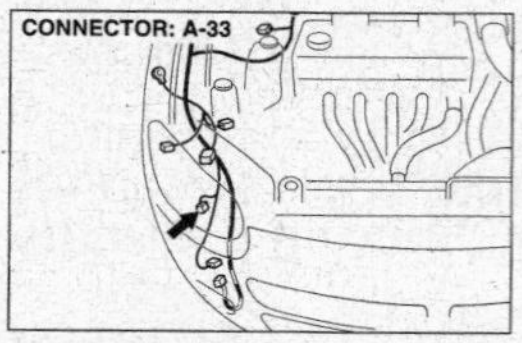

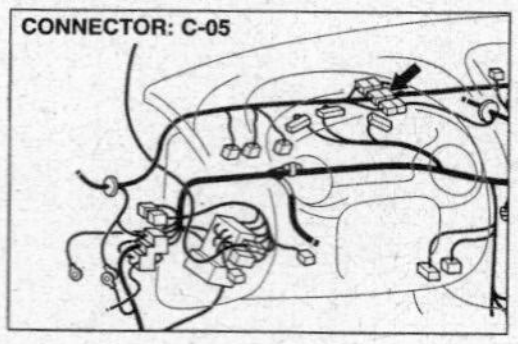

STEP 9. Check the harness wires between washer motor connector A-33 and front-ECU connector A-11X.
NOTE: After checking intermediate connector C-05, check the wires. If intermediate connector C-05 is damaged, repair or replace it.

CR9020200468060X

Fig. 66 Test G-5: Windshield Washer Does Not Work (Part 4 of 5). 2002–03 Sebring & Stratus Coupe

STEP 9. Check the harness wires between washer motor connector A-33 and front-ECU connector A-09X.

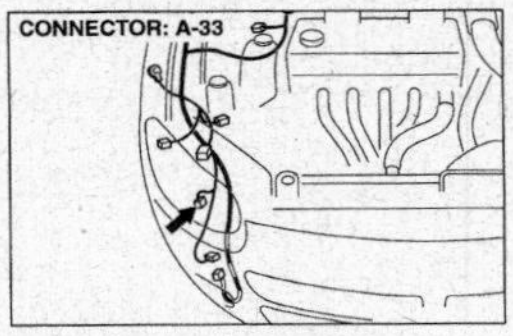

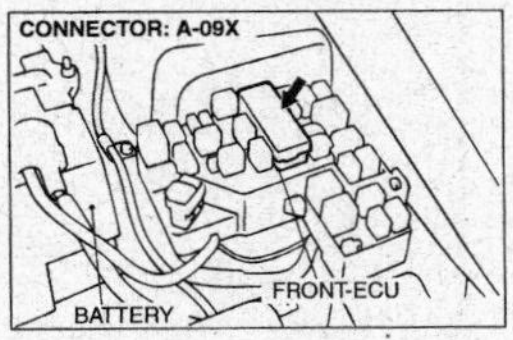

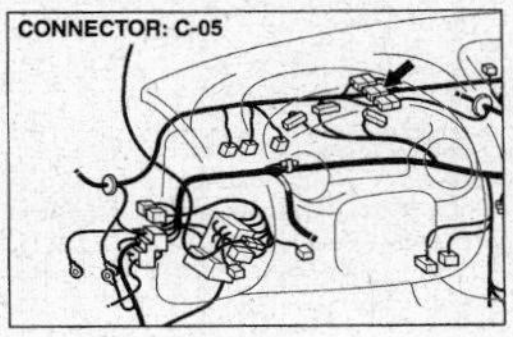

NOTE: After checking intermediate connector C-05, check the wires. If intermediate connector C-05 is damaged, repair or replace it.

Q: Are the harness wires between washer motor connector A-33 and front-ECU connector A-09X in good condition?

YES : There is no action to be taken.

NO : Repair them. The windshield washer should work normally.

CR9020000468050X

Fig. 66 Test G-5: Windshield Washer Does Not Work (Part 5 of 5). 2001 Sebring & Stratus Coupe

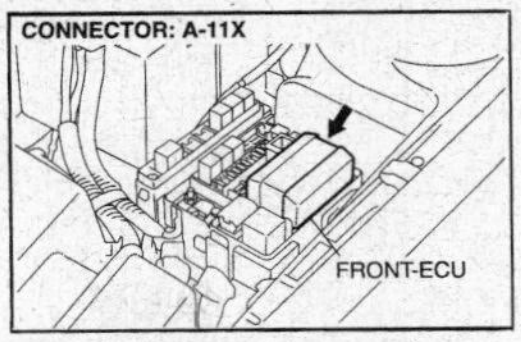

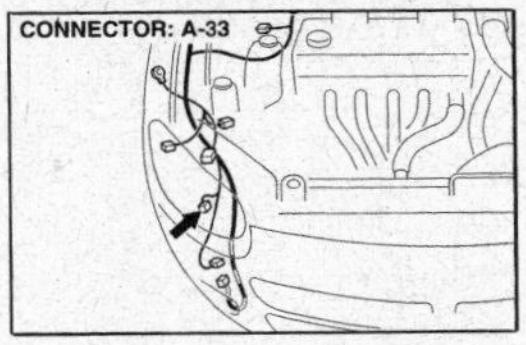

Q: Are the harness wires between washer motor connector A-33 and front-ECU connector A-11X in good condition?

YES : No action to be taken.

NO : Repair them. The windshield washer should work normally.

CR9020200468070X

Fig. 66 Test G-5: Windshield Washer Does Not Work (Part 5 of 5). 2002–03 Sebring & Stratus Coupe

CIRCUIT OPERATION

The ETACS-ECU illuminates the low washer fluid level warning light when the washer fluid level gets lower.

TECHNICAL DESCRIPTION (COMMENT)

The ETACS-ECU illuminates the low washer fluid level warning light according to the input signals from the following switches:

- Ignition switch (IG1)
- Washer fluid level switch

If the low washer fluid level warning light does not illuminate, the relevant input signal circuit, the combination meter (low washer fluid level warning light bulb or printed-circuit board) or the ETACS-ECU may be defective.

TROUBLESHOOTING HINTS

- Malfunction of the washer fluid level switch
- Malfunction of the combination meter (low washer fluid level warning light bulb or printed-circuit board)
- Malfunction of the ETACS-ECU
- Damaged harness wires or connectors

DIAGNOSIS

Required Special Tools:

- MB991223: Test Harness Set
- MB991502: Scan Tool (MUT-II)
- MB991529: Diagnostic Trouble Code Check Harness

STEP 1. Check method of the input signal

Q: Which is to be used, the scan tool or the voltmeter to check the input signal?

Scan tool MB991502 : Go to Step 2.

Voltmeter : Go to Step 3.

CR9020000469010X

Fig. 67 Test G-6: Low Washer Fluid Level Warning Light Does Not Work Normally (Part 1 of 6). 2001 Sebring & Stratus Coupe

STEP 2. Check the input signal (by using scan tool MB991502).

Check the input signals from the following switches:

- Ignition switch (IG1)
- Washer fluid level switch

⚠ CAUTION

To prevent damage to scan tool MB991502, always turn the ignition switch to the "LOCK" (OFF) position before connecting or disconnecting scan tool MB991502.

(1) Connect scan tool MB991502 to the data link connector.

(2) Check that the tone alarm of scan tool MB991502 sounds when the input signal enters.

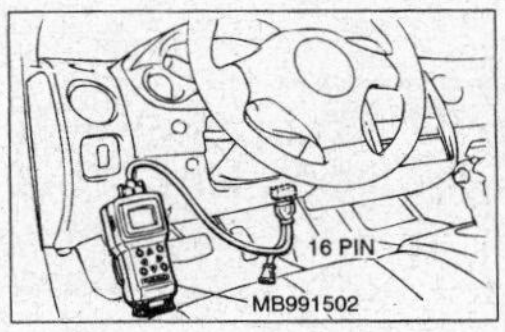

Q: Does the tone alarm of scan tool MB991502 sound when the input signal enters?

YES : Go to Step 4.

NO : Check the relevant input signal circuit.

STEP 3. Check the input signal (by using a voltmeter).

Check the input signals from the following switches:

- Ignition switch (IG1)
- Washer fluid level switch

(1) Use special tool MB991529 to connect a voltmeter between ground terminal 4 or 5 and ETACS-ECU terminal 9 of the data link connector.

(2) Check that the voltmeter indicator deflects once when the input signal enters.

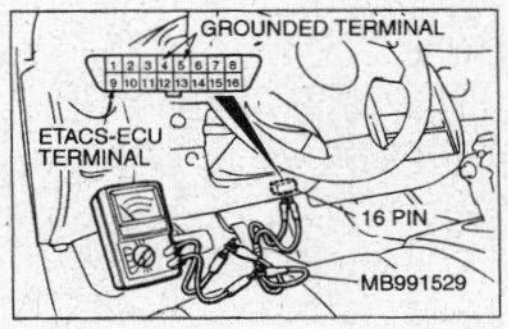

Q: Does the voltmeter indicator deflect?

YES : Go to Step 4.

NO : Check the relevant input signal circuit.

STEP 4. Check the low washer fluid level warning light circuit at the ETACS-ECU connector C-313.

(1) Disconnect the ETACS-ECU connector C-312 and measure at the harness side.

(2) Turn the ignition switch to the "ON" position.

(3) Connect terminal 37 to the ground.

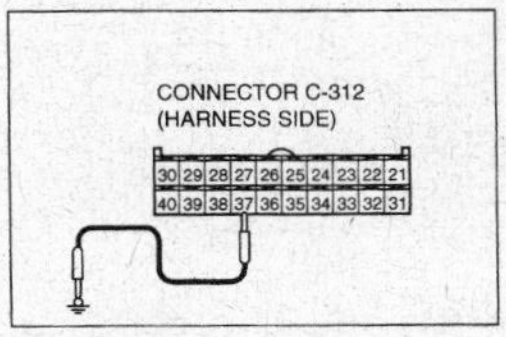

Q: Does the low washer fluid level warning light illuminate?

YES : Replace the ETACS-ECU. The low washer fluid level warning light should work normally.

NO : Go to Step 5.

CR9020000469020X

Fig. 67 Test G-6: Low Washer Fluid Level Warning Light Does Not Work Normally (Part 2 of 6). 2001 Sebring & Stratus Coupe

STEP 5. Check the low washer fluid level warning light bulb.

Q: Is the low washer fluid level warning light bulb in good condition?

YES : Go to Step 6.
NO : Replace it. The low washer fluid level warning light should work normally.

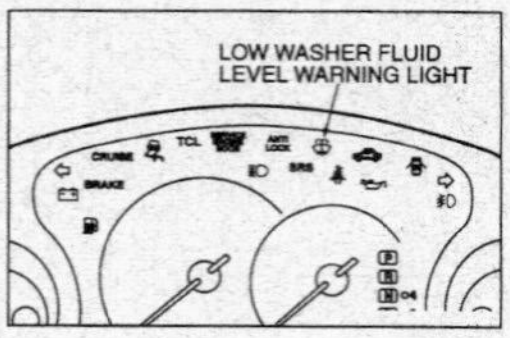

STEP 6. Check the combination meter (printed-circuit board).

(1) Remove the combination meter.
(2) Remove the low washer fluid level warning light bulb. Then measure the resistance between the bulb terminals.
(3) Install the bulb to the combination meter, and then measure the resistance between connector C-101 terminal 51 and connector C-103 terminal 16. The resistance reading at this time should be much the same as the resistance measured at Step (2).

Q: Are the two resistance values extremely different each other?

YES : Repair or replace the combination meter (printed circuit board). The low washer fluid level warning light should work normally.
NO (much the same) : Go to Step 7.

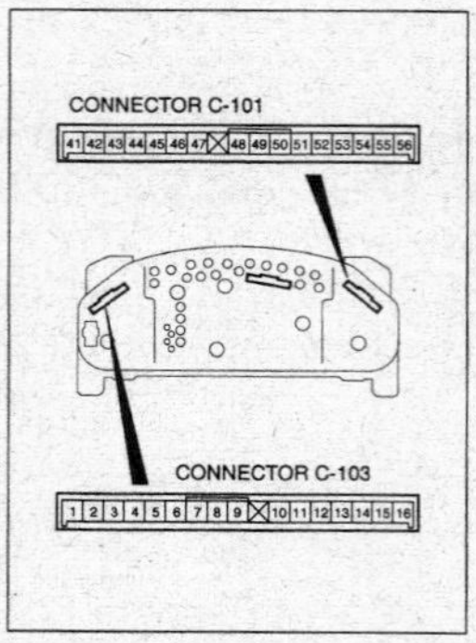

CR9020000469030X

Fig. 67 Test G-6: Low Washer Fluid Level Warning Light Does Not Work Normally (Part 3 of 6). 2001 Sebring & Stratus Coupe

STEP 7. Check the combination meter power supply circuit at the combination meter connector C-101.

(1) Disconnect the combination meter connector C-101 and measure at the harness side.
(2) Turn the ignition switch to the "ON" position.
(3) Measure the voltage between terminal 52 and ground.

Q: Is the voltage approximately 12 volts (battery positive voltage)?

YES : Go to Step 10.
NO : Go to Step 8.

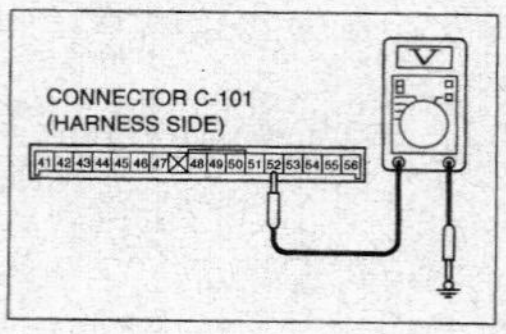

STEP 8. Check combination meter connector C-101 for damage.

Q: Is combination meter connector C-101 in good condition?

YES : Go to Step 9.
NO : Repair or replace it. The low washer fluid level warning light should work normally.

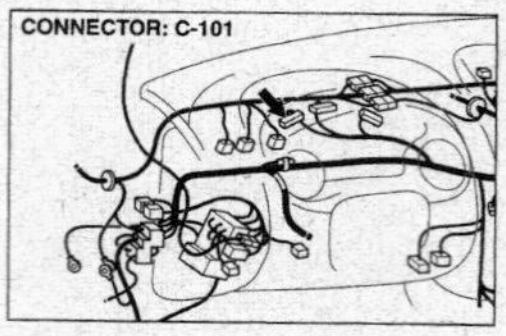

CR9020000469040X

Fig. 67 Test G-6: Low Washer Fluid Level Warning Light Does Not Work Normally (Part 4 of 6). 2001 Sebring & Stratus Coupe

STEP 9. Check the harness wires between combination meter connector C-101 and ignition switch (IG1).

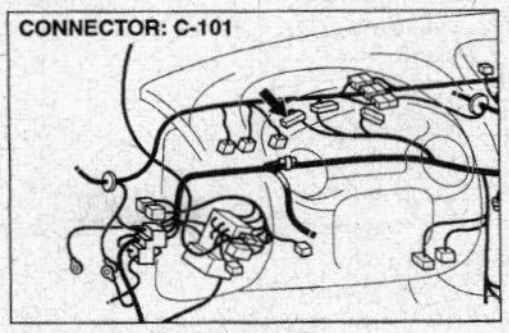

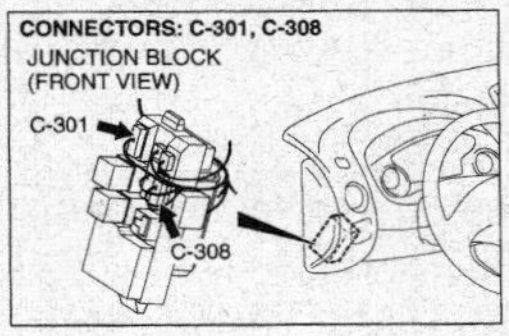

NOTE: After checking junction block connectors C-308 and C-301, check the wires. If junction block connectors C-308 and C-301 are damaged, repair or replace them.

Q: Are the harness wires between combination meter connector C-101 and ignition switch (IG1) in good condition?

YES : There is no action to be taken.
NO : Repair or replace them. The low washer fluid level warning light should work normally.

STEP 10. Check combination meter connector C-103 and ETACS-ECU connector C-312 for damage.
Q: Are combination meter connector C-103 and ETACS-ECU connector C-312 in good condition?

YES : Go to Step 11.
NO : Repair or replace them. The low washer fluid level warning light should work normally.

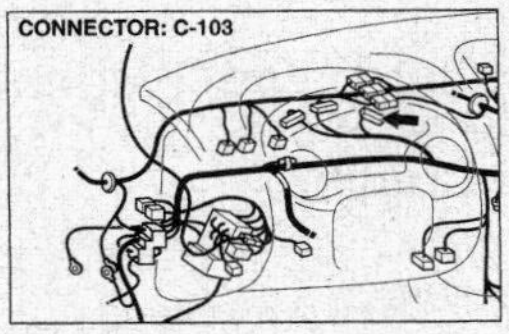

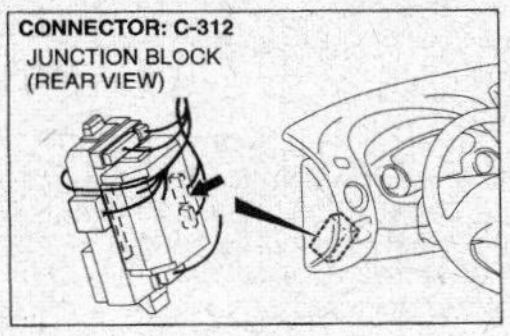

CR9020000469050X

Fig. 67 Test G-6: Low Washer Fluid Level Warning Light Does Not Work Normally (Part 5 of 6). 2001 Sebring & Stratus Coupe

STEP 11. Check the harness wire between combination meter connector C-103 and ETACS-ECU connector C-312.
Q: Is the harness wire between combination meter connector C-102 and ETACS-ECU connector C-312 in good condition?

YES : There is no action to be taken.
NO : Repair it. The low washer fluid level warning light should work normally.

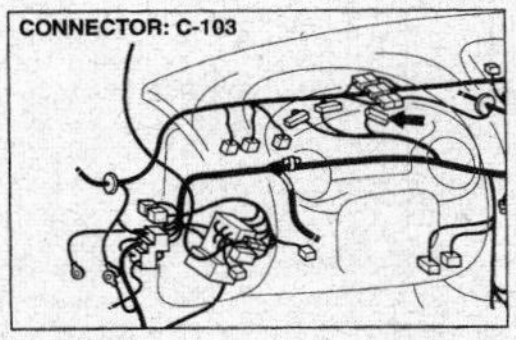

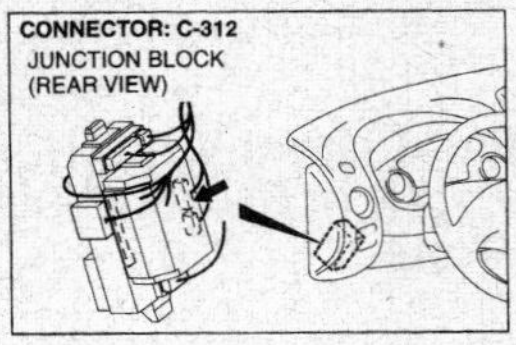

CR9020000469060X

Fig. 67 Test G-6: Low Washer Fluid Level Warning Light Does Not Work Normally (Part 6 of 6). 2001 Sebring & Stratus Coupe

CIRCUIT OPERATION
The ETACS-ECU illuminates the low washer fluid level warning light when the washer fluid level gets lower.

TECHNICAL DESCRIPTION (COMMENT)
The ETACS-ECU illuminates the low washer fluid level warning light according to the input signals from the following switches:
- Ignition switch (IG1)
- Washer fluid level switch

If the low washer fluid level warning light does not illuminate, the relevant input signal circuit, the combination meter (low washer fluid level warning light bulb or printed-circuit board) or the ETACS-ECU may be defective.

TROUBLESHOOTING HINTS
- Malfunction of the washer fluid level switch
- Malfunction of the combination meter (low washer fluid level warning light bulb or printed-circuit board)
- Malfunction of the ETACS-ECU
- Damaged harness wires or connectors

DIAGNOSIS

Required Special Tools:
- MB991223: Test Harness Set
- MB991502: Scan Tool (MUT-II)
- MB991529: Diagnostic Trouble Code Check Harness

STEP 1. Check method of the input signal

Q: Which is to be used, the scan tool or the voltmeter to check the input signal?
Scan tool MB991502 : Go to Step 2.
Voltmeter : Go to Step 3.

CR9020200519010X

Fig. 68 Test G-6: Low Washer Fluid Level Warning Light Does Not Work Normally (Part 1 of 6). 2002–03 Sebring & Stratus Coupe

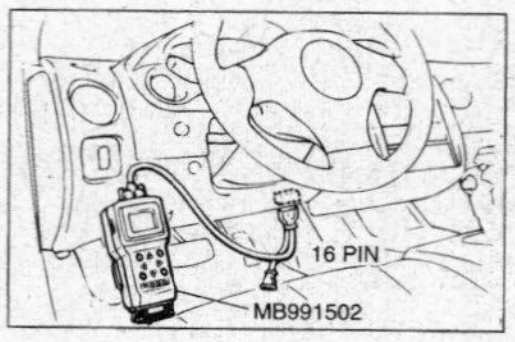

STEP 2. Check the input signal (by using scan tool MB991502).
Check the input signals from the following switches:
- Ignition switch (IG1)
- Washer fluid level switch

⚠ CAUTION
To prevent damage to scan tool MB991502, always turn the ignition switch to the "LOCK" (OFF) position before connecting or disconnecting scan tool MB991502.
(1) Connect scan tool MB991502 to the data link connector.
(2) Check that the tone alarm of scan tool MB991502 sounds when the input signal enters.

Q: Does the tone alarm of scan tool MB991502 sound when the input signal enters?
YES : Go to Step 4.
NO : Check the ignition switch (IG1) input signal circuit. Check the washer fluid level switch input signal circuit.

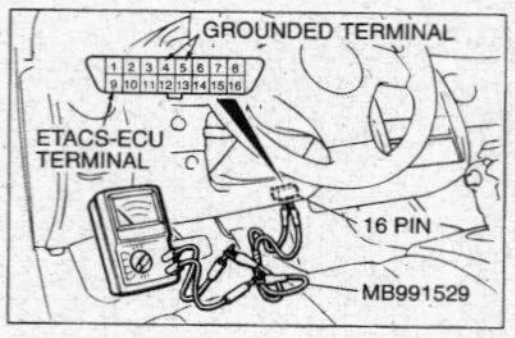

STEP 3. Check the input signal (by using a voltmeter).
Check the input signals from the following switches:
- Ignition switch (IG1)
- Washer fluid level switch

(1) Use special tool MB991529 to connect a voltmeter between ground terminal 4 or 5 and ETACS-ECU terminal 9 of the data link connector.
(2) Check that the voltmeter indicator deflects once when the input signal enters.

Q: Does the voltmeter indicator deflect?
YES : Go to Step 4.
NO : Check the ignition switch (IG1) input signal circuit. Check the washer fluid level switch input signal circuit.

CR9020200519020X

Fig. 68 Test G-6: Low Washer Fluid Level Warning Light Does Not Work Normally (Part 2 of 6). 2002–03 Sebring & Stratus Coupe

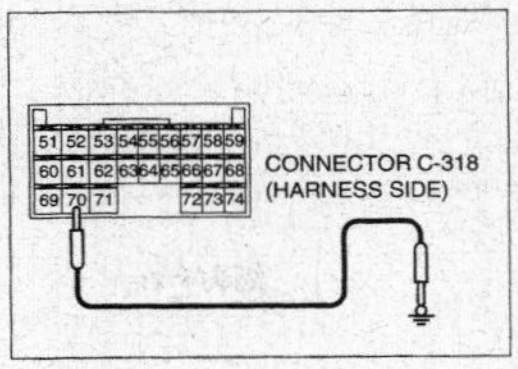

STEP 4. Check the low washer fluid level warning light circuit at the ETACS-ECU connector C-318.

(1) Disconnect the ETACS-ECU connector C-318 and measure at the harness side.
(2) Turn the ignition switch to the "ON" position.
(3) Connect terminal 73 to the ground.

Q: Does the low washer fluid level warning light illuminate?

YES : Replace the ETACS-ECU. The low washer fluid level warning light should work normally.
NO : Go to Step 5.

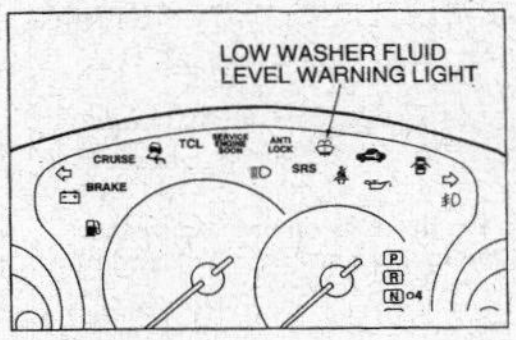

STEP 5. Check the low washer fluid level warning light bulb.

Q: Is the low washer fluid level warning light bulb in good condition?

YES : Go to Step 6.
NO : Replace it. The low washer fluid level warning light should work normally.

CR9020200519030X

Fig. 68 Test G-6: Low Washer Fluid Level Warning Light Does Not Work Normally (Part 3 of 6). 2002–03 Sebring & Stratus Coupe

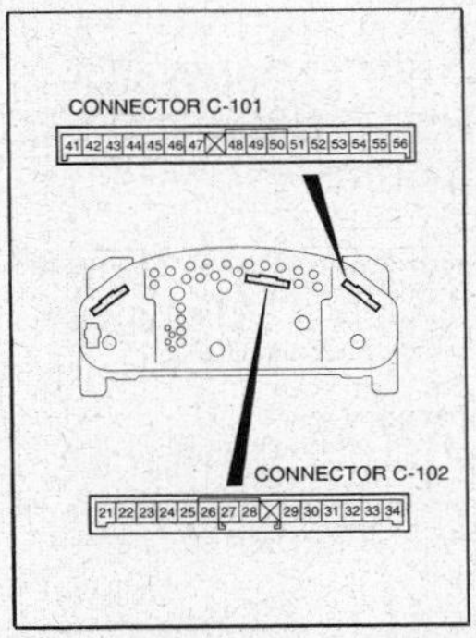

STEP 6. Check the combination meter (printed-circuit board).

(1) Remove the combination meter.
(2) Remove the low washer fluid level warning light bulb. Then measure the resistance between the bulb terminals.
(3) Install the bulb to the combination meter, and then measure the resistance between connector C-101 terminal 52 and connector C-102 terminal 27. The resistance reading at this time should be much the same as the resistance measured at Step (2).

Q: Are the two resistance values extremely different each other?

YES : Repair or replace the combination meter (printed circuit board). The low washer fluid level warning light should work normally.
NO (much the same) : Go to Step 7.

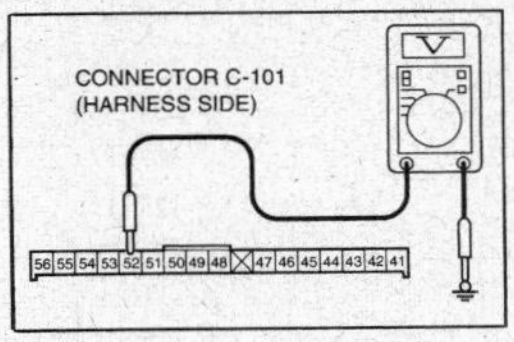

STEP 7. Check the combination meter power supply circuit at the combination meter connector C-101.

(1) Disconnect the combination meter connector C-101 and measure at the harness side.
(2) Turn the ignition switch to the "ON" position.
(3) Measure the voltage between terminal 52 and ground.
- The measured value should be approximately 12 volts (battery positive voltage).

Q: Does the measured voltage correspond with this range?

YES : Go to Step 10.
NO : Go to Step 8.

CR9020200519040X

Fig. 68 Test G-6: Low Washer Fluid Level Warning Light Does Not Work Normally (Part 4 of 6). 2002–03 Sebring & Stratus Coupe

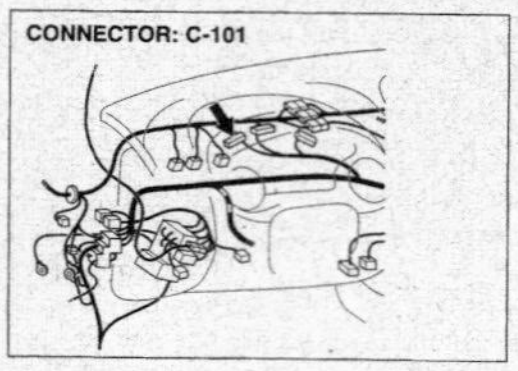

STEP 8. Check combination meter connector C-101 for damage.

Q: Is combination meter connector C-101 in good condition?

YES : Go to Step 9.

NO : Repair or replace it. The low washer fluid level warning light should work normally.

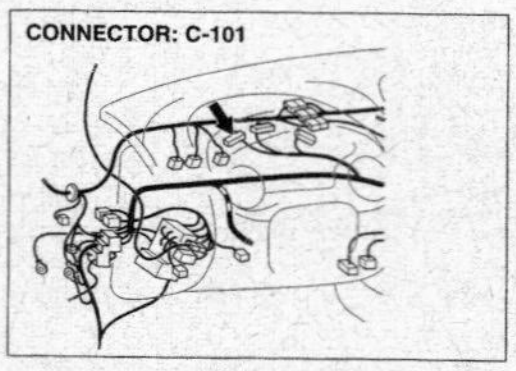

STEP 9. Check the harness wires between combination meter connector C-101 and ignition switch (IG1).

NOTE: After checking junction block connectors C-308 and C-311, check the wires. If junction block connectors C-308 or C-311 are damaged, repair or replace them.

Q: Are the harness wires between combination meter connector C-101 and ignition switch (IG1) in good condition?

YES : Go to Step 10.

NO : Repair or replace them. The low washer fluid level warning light should work normally.

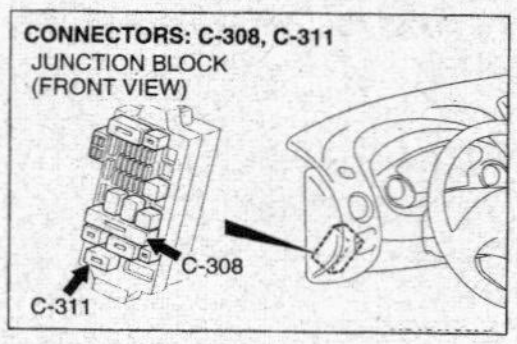

CR9020200519050X

Fig. 68 Test G-6: Low Washer Fluid Level Warning Light Does Not Work Normally (Part 5 of 6). 2002–03 Sebring & Stratus Coupe

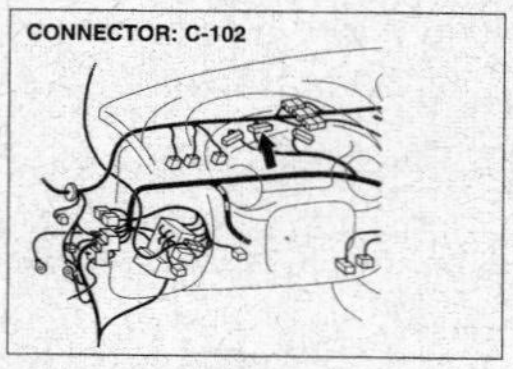

STEP 10. Check combination meter connector C-102 and ETACS-ECU connector C-318 for damage.

Q: Are combination meter connector C-102 and ETACS-ECU connector C-318 in good condition?

YES : Go to Step 11.

NO : Repair or replace them. The low washer fluid level warning light should work normally.

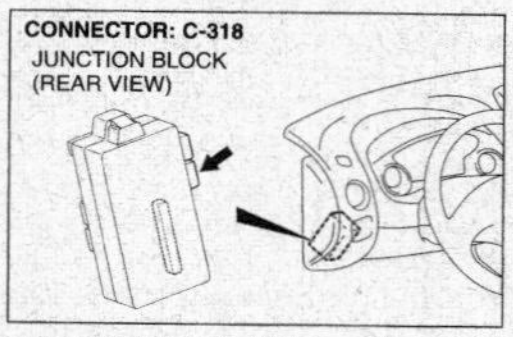

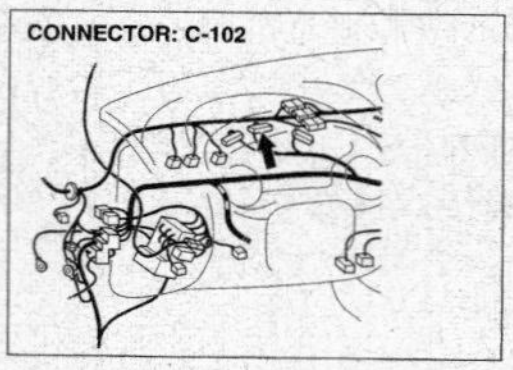

STEP 11. Check the harness wire between combination meter connector C-102 and ETACS-ECU connector C-318.

Q: Is the harness wire between combination meter connector C-102 and ETACS-ECU connector C-318 in good condition?

YES : No action to be taken.

NO : Repair it. The low washer fluid level warning light should work normally.

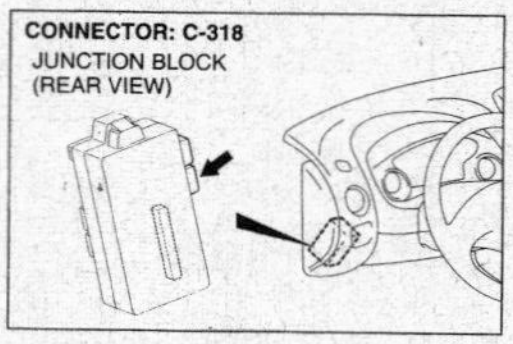

CR9020200519060X

Fig. 68 Test G-6: Low Washer Fluid Level Warning Light Does Not Work Normally (Part 6 of 6). 2002–03 Sebring & Stratus Coupe

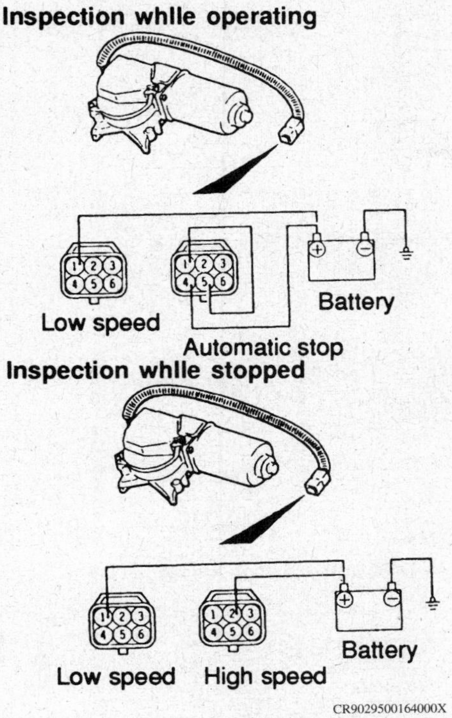

Fig. 69 Front wiper motor inspection. Avenger & 2000 Sebring Coupe

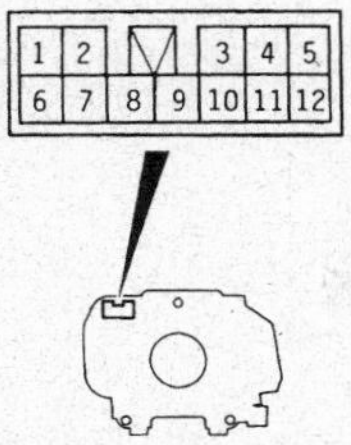

Switch position		Terminal No. 6	7	8	9	10
Wiper switch	OFF		O	O		
	INT		O	O		
	1 (LO)			O	—	O
	2 (HI)				O	O
Washer switch	ON	O	—	—	—	O

CR9029800257000X

Fig. 70 Front wiper switch inspection. Avenger & 2000 Sebring Coupe

COMPONENT DIAGNOSIS & TESTING

Avenger

FRONT

WIPER MOTOR LOW OR HIGH SPEED

Connect battery voltage to wiper motor and ensure normal operation at low and high speeds, **Fig. 69.**

WIPER MOTOR STOP CIRCUIT

1. Operate wiper motor at low speed and intermediately disconnect battery to allow wiper motor to stop.
2. Connect terminals and ensure wiper motor stops at automatically stopped position following low speed operation, **Fig. 69.**

WIPER & WASHER SWITCH

1. Inspect continuity between terminals, **Fig. 70.**
2. If continuity is not as specified, replace switch.

WIPER RELAY

1. Connect wiper switch electrical connector, then place ignition switch in ACC position.
2. Inspect intermittent operation time when wiper switch is turned to INT position. Wipers should operate every three seconds for fast operation and every 12 seconds for slow operation.

REAR

WIPER MOTOR LOW OR HIGH SPEED

Connect battery voltage to wiper motor and ensure normal operation at low and high speeds, **Fig. 71.**

WIPER MOTOR STOP CIRCUIT

1. Operate wiper motor at low speed and intermediately disconnect battery to allow wiper motor to stop.
2. Connect terminals and ensure wiper motor stops at automatically stopped position following low speed operation, **Fig. 71.**

WIPER & WASHER SWITCH

1. Inspect continuity between terminals, **Fig. 72.**
2. If continuity is not as specified, replace switch.

Breeze & Cirrus,

Refer to "Troubleshooting" for wiper motor tests.

Concorde, Intrepid & LHS

WIPER MOTOR

Refer to "Troubleshooting" for wiper motor tests.

INTERMITTENT WIPER SWITCH

1. Disconnect switch wires from body wiring in steering column.
2. Test for continuity between terminals of switch, **Fig. 73.**
3. When testing switch first position is Off, the next six are delay wipe. Low is next detent and high is full counterclockwise detent position.

Crossfire

Refer to "Symptom Base Diagnostic Tests" for component diagnosis and testing.

Neon

WIPER SWITCH

1. Disconnect wiper switch wiring from main wiring at steering column
2. Test continuity between connector pins.

WIPER MOTOR RUNS SLOW

1. Remove wiper arms and cowl panel.
2. Disconnect wiper linkage and wiring connector from motor.
3. Connect suitable ammeter between motor and battery positive terminal, **Fig. 74.**
4. With motor running, if current draw is more than 6 amps, inspect for binding in shafts and linkage.
5. With motor running, if current draw is less than 6 amps, inspect wiper circuits for short to ground.

Sebring & Stratus

CONVERTIBLE & SEDAN

Refer to "Breeze & Cirrus" for component diagnosis and testing.

2000 COUPE

Refer to "Avenger" for component diagnosis and testing.

2001-03 COUPE

WIPER MOTOR

1. Connect battery voltage to wiper motor, then inspect low speed and high speed operation, **Fig. 75.**
2. Run wiper motor at low speed, then disconnect battery to stop motor.
3. Reconnect battery and confirm motor starts running in low speed, then stops at automatic stop position.

WASHER MOTOR

Ensure washer motor sprays when battery voltage is applied to terminal 1 and terminal 2 is grounded, **Fig. 76.**

WASHER FLUID LEVEL SWITCH

1. Connect suitable circuit tester to level sensor connector, **Fig. 77.**
2. Ensure when float is moved down, circuit is closed and when float is moved up, circuit is open.

WIPER & WASHER SWITCH

1. Measure resistance of intermittent wiper interval adjusting knob between terminal Nos. 27 and 28, **Figs. 78 and 79.**
2. . Resistance should rise smoothly from zero ohms at FAST position to 1 kohm at SLOW position.

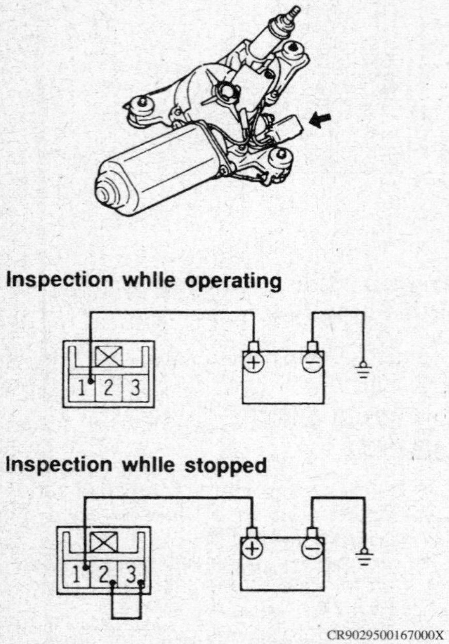
Inspection while operating
1 2 3
Inspection while stopped
1 2 3
CR9029500167000X

Fig. 71 Rear wiper motor inspection. Avenger & 2000 Sebring Coupe

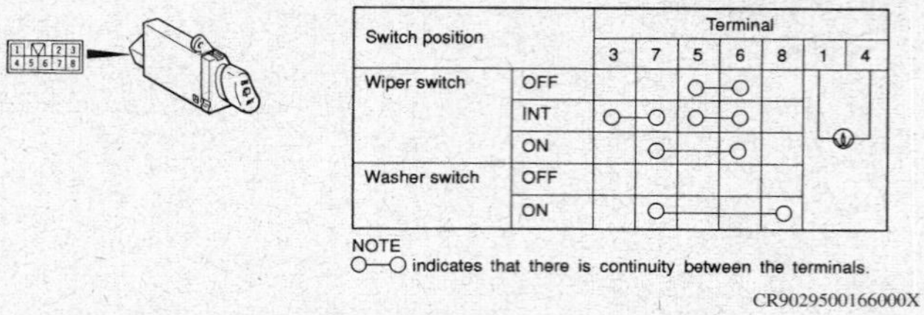
Switch position
Terminal
3 7 5 6 8 1 4
Wiper switch
OFF
INT
ON
Washer switch
OFF
ON
NOTE
O—O indicates that there is continuity between the terminals.
CR9029500166000X

Fig. 72 Rear wiper switch inspection. Avenger & 2000 Sebring Coupe

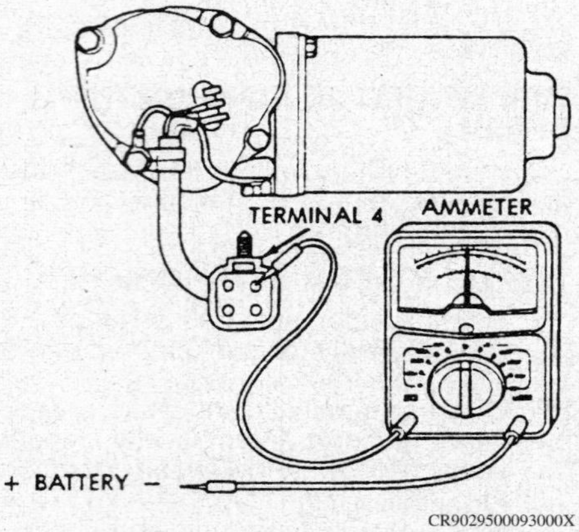

Fig. 74 Wiper motor current test. Neon

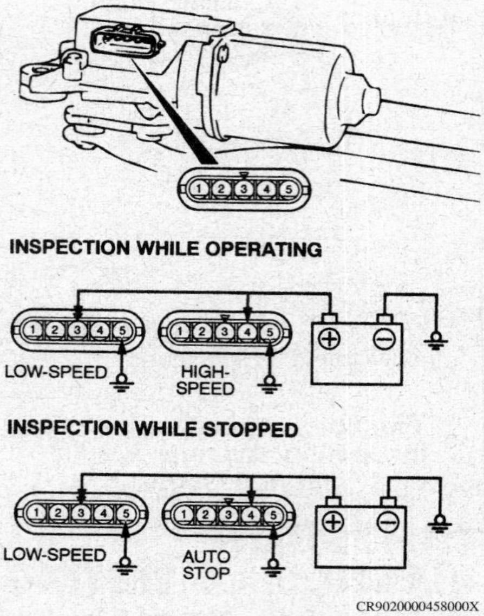

Fig. 75 Wiper motor inspection. 2001–03 Sebring & Stratus Coupe

SWITCH POSITION		TERMINALS	RESISTANCE VALUE
OFF		PINS 1 T0 3	OPEN > 300 K OHMS
DELAY LEVEL	1	PINS 1 TO 3	9.72 K OHMS
	2	PINS 1 TO 3	8.22 K OHMS
	3	PINS 1 TO 3	6.61 K OHMS
	4	PINS 1 TO 3	5.12K OHMS
	5	PINS 1 TO 3	3.67K OHMS
	6	PINS 1 TO 3	2.22K OHMS
LOW		PINS 1 TO 3	1.02 K OHMS
HIGH		PINS 1 TO 3	0.51K OHMS
WASH		PINS 1 TO 2	0 OHMS

CR9029900332000X

Fig. 73 Intermittent wiper switch test. Concorde, Intrepid, LHS & 300M

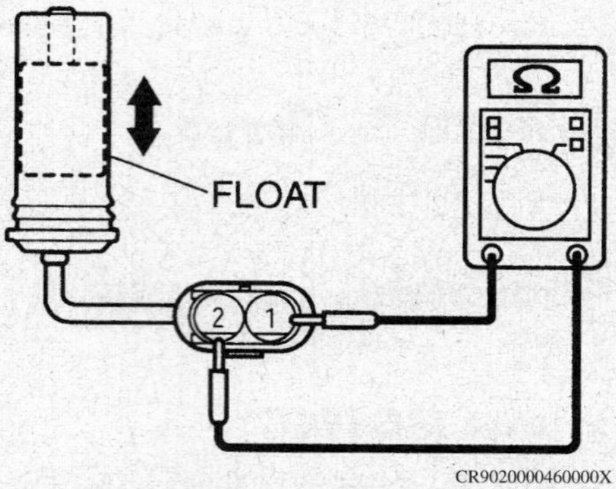

Fig. 77 Washer fluid level switch inspection. 2001–03 Sebring & Stratus Coupe

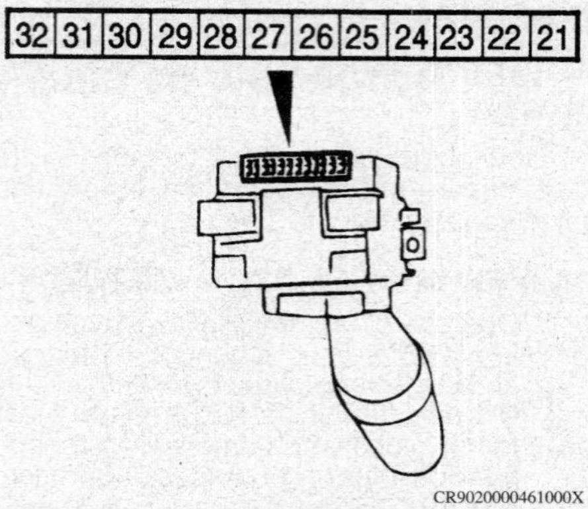
32 31 30 29 28 27 26 25 24 23 22 21
CR9020000461000X

Fig. 78 Wiper switch connector end view. 2001–03 Sebring & Stratus Coupe

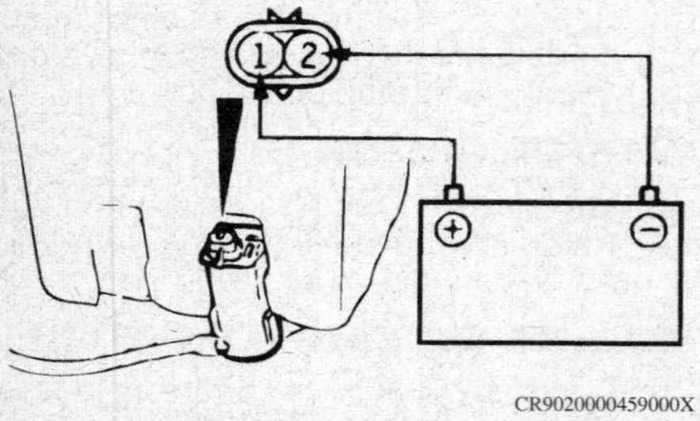
CR9020000459000X

Fig. 76 Washer motor inspection. 2001–03 Sebring & Stratus Coupe

SWITCH POSITION	TESTER CONNECTION	SPECIFIED CONDITION
OFF	–	No continuity
Windshield mist wiper switch	23 – 32	Continuity
Windshield intermittent wiper switch	23 – 31	Continuity
Windshield low-speed wiper switch	23 – 30	Continuity
Windshield high-speed wiper switch	21 – 23	Continuity
Windshield washer switch	22 – 23	Continuity

CR9020000462000X

Fig. 79 Wiper & washer switch inspection. 2001–03 Sebring & Stratus Coupe

PASSIVE RESTRAINT SYSTEMS
Air Bag System

NOTE: Refer To "Computer Relearn Procedures" Located In The Front Of This Manual When Battery Power To The Computer Has Been Interrupted.

NOTE: Refer To "Diagnosis & Testing" In MOTOR's "Air Bag Manual" Or "Air Bag Diagnosis CD" For Information Not Covered In This Section.

INDEX

AIR BAG SYSTEM DISARMING & ARMING

Disarming

It may be required to access and record all Diagnostic Trouble Codes (DTCs) prior to disarming the air bag system.

1. Place ignition switch in Lock position.
2. **On Neon, Sebring and Stratus models,** disconnect and isolate battery ground cable.
3. **On Concorde, Intrepid, LHS and 300M models,** disconnect and isolate battery ground cable remote terminal at remote battery post, **Fig. 1.**
4. **On all models except Sebring and Stratus Coupe, wait at least two minutes after disconnection before doing any further work on vehicle. The air bag system is designed to retain enough voltage to deploy air bags for a short time even after battery has been disconnected.**
5. **On Sebring and Stratus Coupe, wait at least sixty seconds after disconnection before doing any further work on vehicle. The air bag system**

is designed to retain enough voltage to deploy air bags for a short time even after battery has been disconnected.

Arming

1. **Ensure no one is inside vehicle and ignition switch is in Lock position.**
2. Connect battery ground or negative remote cable or terminal.
3. Turn ignition On **from a safe position below or at the sides of the air bag modules.**
4. The SRS lamp should light for seven to ten seconds, then remain off for at least 45 seconds to indicate SRS is functioning properly.

DESCRIPTION & OPERATION

The Supplemental Restraint System (SRS) is designed to supplement the driver's and passenger's seat belts to help reduce risk or severity of injury to front seat occupants by activating and deploying a driver's and passenger's air bag modules in certain types of side or frontal collisions.

PRECAUTIONS

Battery Ground Cable

Prior to service, disconnect battery ground cable and isolate as required.

General Safety Precautions

The fasteners, screws and bolts used for air bag components have special coatings and are specifically designed for air bag systems. They must not be replaced with substitutes. If fastener replacement is required, use proper fasteners provided in service package.

Always wear safety glasses when servicing an air bag equipped vehicle or when handling an air bag module.

This system is a sensitive, complex electromechanical unit. Before attempting to diagnose, remove, or install any air bag system component, the air bag system must be disarmed. Refer to "Air Bag System Disarming & Arming."

Avoid working in front of air bag modules. It is safer to approach them from the side or below.

Ensure no one is inside vehicle when air bag system is being armed. Refer to "Air Bag System Disarming & Arming."

Handling & Storage Of Live Module

At no time should any source of electricity be permitted near the inflator on back of module. When carrying a live module, trim cover of air bag module should be pointed away from body to minimize injury in event of an accidental deployment.

When handling a steering column with an air bag module attached, never place column on floor or other surface with steering wheel or module facing down. When handling a passenger's air bag module, never place it on a surface with paper-like tyvek cover face down and saddle brackets pointing up.

Clean Up Procedure

Wear safety glasses, rubber gloves, particle dust mask and protective clothing with long sleeves. Place tape over exhaust vents in air bag so that no additional powder will escape into vehicle. Roll or fold passenger's air bag toward instrument panel surface and close cover over folded air bag. Tape cover closed. Remove driver's air bag module from vehicle then passenger's air bag module.

Use a vacuum cleaner to remove any residual powder from vehicle interior, working from outside to center of vehicle. Vacuum heater and A/C ducts as well. Run blower motor on low speed and vacuum any powder expelled from plenum. It may be required to vacuum interior of vehicle a second time to ensure all powder is recovered.

Vehicle Scrapping

Prior to scrapping a vehicle, the air bag modules must be deployed. Refer to "Air Bag Module Disposal" as outlined under "Component Service."

Air Bag Disposal Procedure

Refer to "Air Bag Module Disposal" as outlined under "Component Service."

SCHEDULED MAINTENANCE

Refer to "Vehicle Maintenance Schedules" located in the front of this manual for air bag system schedule maintenance.

WIRING & CIRCUIT DIAGRAMS

Refer to "Diagnosis & Testing" in **MOTOR's "Air Bag Manual" or "Air Bag Diagnosis CD"** for wiring and circuit diagrams.

WIRE HARNESS & CONNECTOR REPAIR

Never attempt to repair wiring harness or connectors of SRS. If wiring harness or connectors are diagnosed as faulty, replace entire wiring harness.

COMPONENT LOCATIONS

Refer to "Diagnosis & Testing" in **MOTOR's "Air Bag Manual" or "Air Bag Diagnosis CD"** for component locations.

DIAGNOSIS & TESTING

Refer to "Diagnosis & Testing" in **MOTOR's "Air Bag Manual" or "Air Bag Diagnosis CD"** for additional air bag system diagnosis and testing procedures.

COLLISION INSPECTION

On vehicles which have experienced an air bag system deployment, certain SRS components must be replaced.

Avenger, Sebring Coupe & Stratus Coupe

WHEN FRONT AIR BAGS DEPLOY

1. Replace air bag modules and control module.
2. Inspect clockspring as outlined under "When Air Bags Do Not Deploy."
3. Inspect steering wheel wiring harness and connectors for damage and terminal deformation.
4. Install driver's air bag module, then inspect fit and alignment with steering wheel.
5. Inspect steering wheel for noise, binds or difficult operation and excessive play.
6. Inspect wiring harness for binding.
7. Inspect wiring harness connectors for damage, poor connections and deformed terminals.

WHEN SIDE AIR BAGS DEPLOY

1. Replace front seatback assemblies, side impact sensors and control module.
2. Inspect wiring harness for binding.
3. Inspect wiring harness connectors for damage, poor connections and deformed terminals.

WHEN AIR BAGS DO NOT DEPLOY

Inspect and replace air bag system components if there any visible signs of damage, dents, cracks or deformation.

CONTROL MODULE

1. Inspect control unit case and brackets for dents, cracks or deformities.
2. Inspect connectors and lock lever for damage.
3. Inspect terminals for deformities.

AIR BAG MODULES

1. Inspect pad cover for dents, cracks or deformities.
2. Inspect connectors for damage, terminals for deformities and harness for binding.
3. Inspect air bag inflator case for dents, cracks or deformities.
4. Install driver's air bag module, then inspect fit and alignment with steering wheel.
5. Install passenger's air bag module and inspect fit and alignment with instrument panel and crossmember.

FRONT SEATBACK ASSEMBLY

1. Inspect for abnormalities in seat air bag module deployment section.
2. Inspect for connector damage, terminal bents and harness clamping.

CLOCKSPRING

1. Inspect clockspring connectors and protective tube for damage.
2. Inspect terminals for deformities.
3. Inspect case for damage.

SIDE IMPACT SENSOR

1. Inspect center pillar for bending or corrosion.
2. Inspect side impact sensors for dents, breaks or bends.
3. Inspect harness for clamping, connectors for damage and terminals for bents.

STEERING WHEEL, COLUMN & SHAFT

1. Inspect steering wheel wiring harness and connectors for damage.
2. Inspect wiring harness terminals for deformities.
3. Install driver's air bag module, then inspect fit and alignment with steering wheel.
4. Inspect steering wheel for noise, binds, difficult operation and excessive freeplay.

Breeze, Cirrus, Concorde, Crossfire, Intrepid, LHS, Neon, Sebring Convertible, Sebring Sedan, Stratus Sedan & 300M

On Concorde, Intrepid, LHS and 300M models, if the driver's air bag module has deployed in a collision, it must be replaced, along with the clockspring assembly, steering wheel and the complete steering column assembly with shrouds and lower column coupler. If the passenger's air bag module has deployed, it must be replaced, along with the instrument panel and pad assembly. In cases of side air bag module deployment, the entire seatback and all damaged components must be replaced. After roof panel air bags have been deployed, the roof panel aie bag module, headliner, A, B and C pillar trim panels as required.

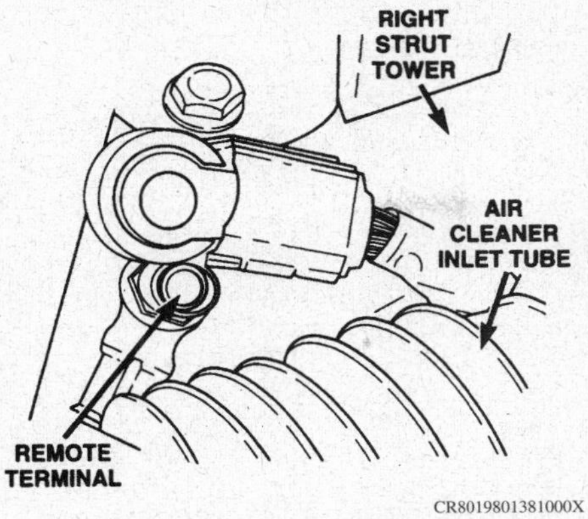

Fig. 1 Battery ground remote terminal. Concorde, Intrepid, LHS & 300M

On Neon models, if the driver's air bag module has deployed in a collision, it must be replaced, along with the clockspring assembly and the steering column assembly with lower column coupler. If the passenger's air bag module has deployed, it must be replaced, along with the instrument panel righthand trim bezel. Also inspect the instrument panel lower knee blocker and top cover, replacing these and any other suspect components as required.

On Crossfire, Sebring Sedan and Stratus Sedan models, if the driver's air bag module has deployed in a collision it must be replaced, along with the clockspring assembly. The instrument panel and pad will require replacement if the passenger's air bag module has deployed. If a roof panel air bag module has deployed, replace the headliner since crease lines will have occurred during deployment.

After all collisions, minor or major, perform a complete system inspection, as follows:

SRS WARNING LAMP INSPECTION

When the ignition is turned On or engine is started, the SRS warning lamp will light for approximately seven seconds, then go off. If the lamp operates as specified, the system is functioning properly. If the lamp stays lit more than seven seconds or lights when driving, a system malfunction or condition is indicated. Refer to "Diagnosis & Testing."

CONTROL MODULE

1. Inspect case and brackets for dents, cracks, deformities, or rust. **SRS may not deploy properly if SRS-ECU is improperly installed.**
2. Inspect SRS-ECU connectors for damaged or deformed terminals.
3. Inspect lock lever for damage or rust.

AIR BAG MODULE

DRIVER'S

1. Remove module as outlined under "Component Service."
2. Inspect pad cover for dents, cracks or deformities.
3. Inspect hooks and connector for deformities and binding harness.
4. Inspect air bag inflator case for damage.
5. Install air bag module to steering wheel to inspect fit and alignment.

PASSENGER'S

1. Remove module as outlined under "Component Service."
2. Inspect cover for dents, cracks and deformities.
3. Inspect connector for deformed terminal and binding harness.
4. Inspect inflator case for damage.

SIDE IMPACT

1. Remove module as outlined under "Component Service."
2. Inspect covers for dents, cracks and deformities.
3. Inspect electrical connector for deformed terminals.

ROOF PANEL

1. Remove module as outlined under "Component Service."
2. Inspect inflator pan (quarter trim upper support at C-pillar).
3. **On models equipped with sunroof,** inspect sunroof drain and replace if cracked.
4. **On all models,** replace headliner, upper A, B and C pillar trim panels if roof panel air bag module has deployed.

CLOCKSPRING

1. Remove clockspring as outlined under "Component Service."
2. Inspect connectors, protective tube and terminals for damage and deformities.
3. Visually inspect case and gears for damage.

STEERING WHEEL, COLUMN & INTERMEDIATE JOINT

1. Inspect wiring harness, connectors and terminals for damage and deformities.
2. Install air bag module to inspect fit and alignment.
3. Inspect steering wheel for noise, binding, difficult operation or excessive freeplay.

FRONT WIRING HARNESS & BODY WIRING HARNESS

1. Inspect harness connectors for damaged or deformed terminals.
2. Inspect harness for any crimps or binding.
3. Inspect harness wiring for any fraying or damage.
4. Replace harness or connectors if they show any signs of damage.

COMPONENT SERVICE

Prior to performing service procedure, disarm air bag system as described under "Air Bag System

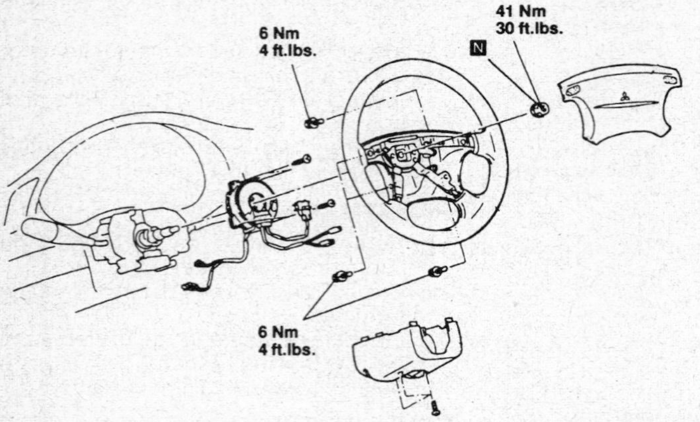

Fig. 2 Air bag module & clockspring removal. Avenger & 2000 Sebring Coupe

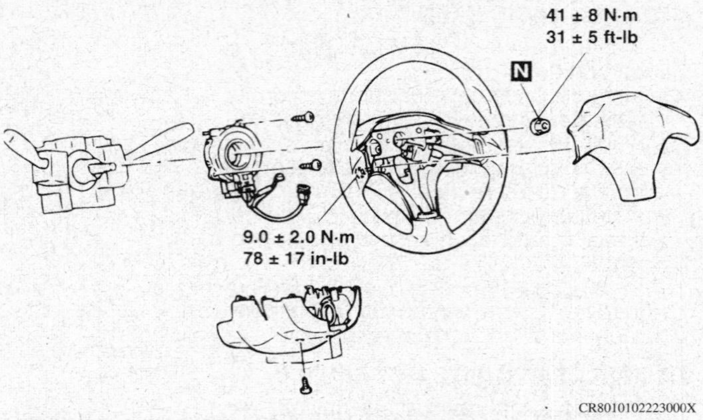

Fig. 3 Air bag module & clockspring removal. Stratus Coupe & 2001–03 Sebring Coupe

Disarming & Arming." Failure to disarm air bag system could result in system deployment and personal injury.

Pre-Installation Inspection

Prior to installation of an air bag module or the clockspring, the following pre-installation inspection should be performed:

1. Ensure disconnected air bag module or clockspring connector are not in contact with any vehicle components.
2. Connect suitably programmed scan tool to DLC. **Ensure ignition is Off when connecting or disconnecting scan tool.**
3. Connect battery ground cable, then turn ignition On.
4. Only DTCs that should be present are those for removed air bag module or clockspring.
5. Turn ignition Off, then disconnect scan tool.
6. Disarm SRS as outlined under "Air Bag System Disarming & Arming."
7. Any DTCs indicated, other than those for removed air bag module or clockspring, must have indicated component or circuit repaired or replaced prior to air bag module or clockspring installation.

Driver's Side Air Bag Module, Replace

AVENGER, SEBRING COUPE & STRATUS COUPE

1. Disarm air bag as described under "Air Bag System Disarming & Arming."
2. Remove mounting screws from rear of steering wheel and air bag module, **Figs. 2 and 3.**
3. Reverse procedure to install.

BREEZE, CIRRUS, SEBRING CONVERTIBLE, SEBRING SEDAN & STRATUS SEDAN

1. Disarm air bag system as outlined under "Air Bag System Disarming & Arming."
2. Remove speed control switch or covers from steering wheel, then disconnect electrical connectors.
3. Remove air bag module mounting bolts from steering wheel.
4. Lift module and disconnect wire connector by lifting secondary latch and using finger grips. **Do not use metallic tool to pry connector off.**
5. Disconnect horn wire.
6. **On Breeze, Cirrus, Sebring Sedan and Stratus Sedan models,** remove speed control wires from under brackets and from wire guides.
7. **On all models,** remove driver's air bag module.
8. Reverse procedure to install.

CONCORDE, INTREPID, LHS & 300M

1. Disarm air bag system as outlined under "Air Bag System Disarming & Arming."
2. Remove speed control switches or covers from steering wheel and disconnect wiring.
3. Remove air bag module mounting bolts.
4. Lift module, then disconnect air bag and horn wiring connectors. Remove connector lock from air bag module by pulling it straight out. **Do not twist connector lock.**
5. Remove air bag module from steering wheel.
6. Reverse procedure to install.

CROSSFIRE

1. Disarm air bag system as outlined under "Air Bag System Disarming & Arming."
2. Remove two attaching screws from behind steering wheel, **Fig. 4.**
3. Remove driver's side air bag module from column, then disconnect electrical connectors.
4. Disconnect clockspring electrical connector.
5. Remove driver's side air bag module.
6. Reverse procedure to install.

NEON

1. Disarm air bag system as outlined under "Air Bag System Disarming & Arming."
2. Remove speed control switches or covers from steering wheel armature and disconnect electrical connectors.
3. Remove module mounting bolts, nuts or screws from steering wheel sides.
4. Lift module, then disconnect air bag squib wire and horn electrical connectors.
5. Remove driver's air bag module.
6. Reverse procedure to install.

Passenger's Side Air Bag Module, Replace

AVENGER, SEBRING COUPE & STRATUS COUPE

1. Disarm air bag system as outlined under "Air Bag System Disarming & Arming."
2. Remove glove compartment.
3. Remove air bag module mounting screws and disconnect air bag module electrical connector.
4. Remove passenger's air bag module.
5. Reverse procedure to install.

BREEZE, CIRRUS, SEBRING CONVERTIBLE, SEBRING SEDAN & STRATUS SEDAN

2000

Deployed

1. Disarm air bag system as outlined under "Air Bag System Disarming & Arming."
2. Remove instrument panel as outlined in "Dash Panel Service" chapter.
3. Disconnect passenger's air bag electrical connector.
4. Remove mounting bolts, nuts and passenger's air bag module.
5. Reverse procedure to instal.

Non-Deployed

1. Disarm air bag system as outlined under "Air Bag System Disarming & Arming."

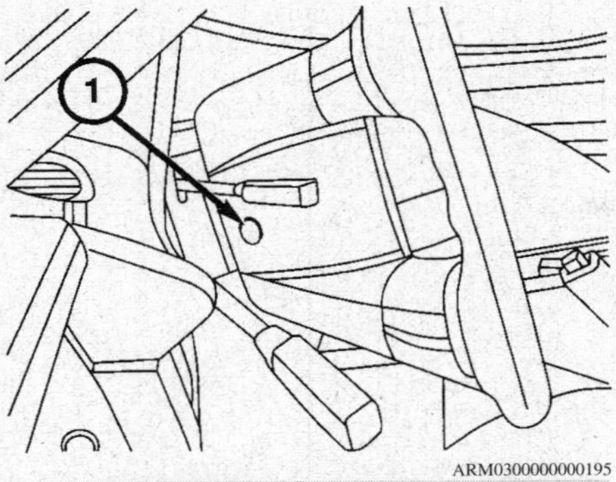

Fig. 4 Driver's side air bag module removal. Crossfire

2. Remove Air Bag fuse.
3. Open and fully lower glove compartment.
4. Disconnect air bag module electrical connector.
5. Remove mounting screws, nuts and passenger's air bag module.
6. Reverse procedure to install.

2001-03

1. Disarm air bag system as outlined under "Air Bag System Disarming & Arming."
2. Open and lower glove compartment.
3. Disconnect passenger's air bag module electrical connector.
4. Remove mounting screws, nuts and air bag module.
5. Reverse procedure to install.

CONCORDE, INTREPID, LHS & 300M

2000

Deployed

1. Disarm air bag system as outlined under "Air Bag System Disarming & Arming."
2. Roll or fold air bag toward instrument panel.
3. Tuck air bag into instrument panel air bag module opening.
4. Close ripped instrument panel pad over folded bag and tape pad closed.
5. Remove passenger's air bag module as outlined under "Passenger's Air Bag Module, Deployed."
6. Reverse procedure to install.

Non-Deployed

1. Disarm air bag as described under "Air Bag System Disarming & Arming."
2. Remove instrument panel as outlined in "Dash Panel Service" chapter.
3. Remove four glove compartment door screws.
4. **On six-passenger models,** proceed as follows:
   a. Unsnap ashtray receiver door.
   b. Remove four screws at chin bezel and release two clips by gently pulling rearward to disconnect.
   c. Gently pry out center bezel using trim stick tool.
   d. Disconnect harness connectors at

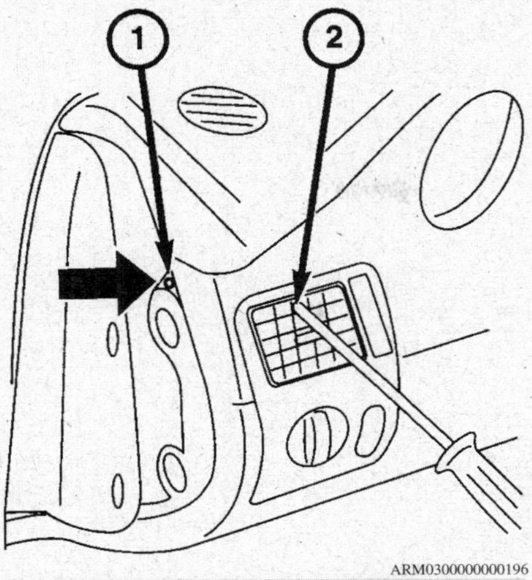

Fig. 5 Vent screw removal. Crossfire

power outlet and temperature control.

5. **On all models,** remove eight glove compartment closeout mounting screws
6. Disconnect glove compartment lamp switch.
7. Rotate instrument panel to access rear side.
8. Remove three rod and boot mounting screws.
9. Remove five left and righthand demister duct mounting screws .
10. Remove five center and righthand distribution duct mounting screws.
11. Disconnect air bag module yellow wire harness connector and three fasteners.
12. Remove two screws at left and righthand pencil struts.
13. Remove nine mounting screws and air bag module.
14. Remove four reinforcement brace mounting screws.
15. Reverse procedure to install.

2001-02

Non-Deployed

1. Disarm air bag as described under "Air Bag System Disarming & Arming."
2. Remove mounting screws and glove compartment door.
3. Remove instrument panel righthand end cap.
4. **On models equipped with center console,** proceed as follows:
   a. Remove setscrew and transaxle range selector lever handle.
   b. Remove console shifter bezel.
   c. Remove console righthand side trim panel.
5. **On all models,** remove five glove compartment closeout screws through door opening.
6. Remove left and righthand A-pillar trim moldings.
7. Remove instrument panel lefthand end cap.
8. Disconnect hood release cable.

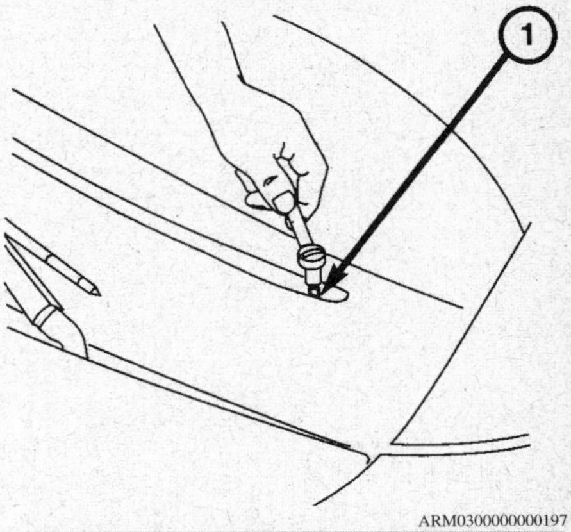

Fig. 6 Defroster grille bolt removal. Crossfire

9. Disconnect trunk lid release switch electrical connector.
10. Remove instrument panel lefthand lower trim cover.
11. Remove lefthand knee blocker.
12. Remove instrument panel center bezel, then disconnect HVAC control head and traction control switch. electrical connectors.
13. **On models equipped with console,** remove instrument panel lefthand side cover.
14. **On all models,** remove center instrument panel floor bin.
15. Remove two center instrument panel lower mounting nuts.
16. Remove driver's side air distribution ducts.
17. Disconnect brake switch electrical connector.
18. Remove bulkhead electrical connector mounting screw. **Connector does not have to be disconnected.**
19. Disconnect Occupant Restraint Controller (ORC) electrical connector.
20. Disconnect two center instrument panel ground eyelets on lefthand side of floor tunnel.
21. Remove four steering column nuts and lower column to floor.
22. Remove three lower lefthand and upper lefthand instrument panel mounting bolts.
23. Disconnect instrument panel to body harness electrical connector.
24. Remove three lower righthand and upper righthand instrument panel mounting bolts.
25. Pull instrument panel righthand side back and set it on righthand seat.
26. Remove four righthand demister duct mounting screws.
27. Remove two righthand distribution duct mounting screws.
28. Disconnect passenger's air bag module electrical connector and its tree fasteners.
29. Remove left and righthand pencil strut to passenger's air bag module screws.
30. Disconnect instrument panel wiring harness from air bag module reinforcement bracket.

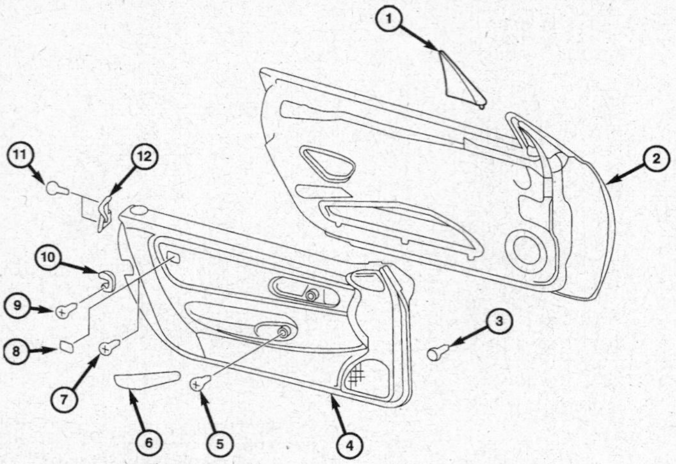

1 - ESCUTCHEON COVER
2 - DOOR
3 - SHEET METAL CLIP NUTS
4 - DOOR TRIM PANEL
5 - SCREW
6 - PULL HANDLE COVER
7 - SCREW
8 - SRS COVER
9 - SCREW
10 - CLIP
11 - SCREWS
12 - CHROME DOOR END COVER

ARM0300000000198

Fig. 7 Door trim panel removal. Crossfire

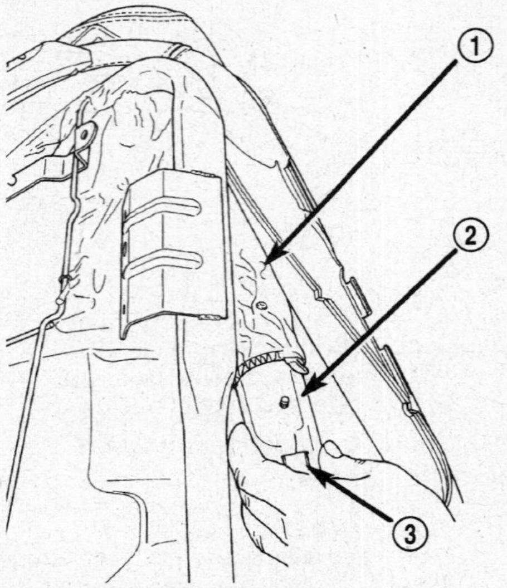

1 - SEAT AIRBAG NYLON SLEEVE
2 - SEAT AIRBAG
3 - SEAT AIRBAG ELECTRICAL CONNECTOR

CR8010102563000X

Fig. 8 Side air bag electrical connector. Neon

31. Remove four deployment door reinforcement mounting screws.
32. Remove five passenger's air bag module retainer mounting screws.
33. Remove passenger's air bag module.
34. Remove four passenger's air bag module reinforcement brace screws.
35. Reverse procedure to install.

Deployed

1. Disarm air bag system as outlined under "Air Bag System Disarming & Arming."
2. Remove instrument panel as outlined in "Dash Panel Service" chapter.
3. Remove mounting screws and passenger air bag module
4. Reverse procedure to install.

CROSSFIRE

1. Disarm air bag system as outlined under "Air Bag System Disarming & Arming."
2. Remove A-pillar trim panel.
3. Remove lefthand and righthand fuse covers.
4. Remove attaching screw located within the lefthand and righthand air vents, **Fig. 5.**
5. Remove attaching screw from insde of fuse panel covers.
6. Remove attaching screws from center console to top on instrument panel.
7. Remove attaching screws from inside glove compartment.
8. Remove defroster grille screws, then the defroster outwards.
9. Remove bolts from lefthand and righthand side under defroster grille, **Fig. 6.**
10. Remove sheet metal clips from both A-pillars.
11. Remove top panel of instrument panel.
12. Disconnect passenger's side air bag module electrical connector from air bag module.
13. Remove four attaching bolts to instrument panel duct.
14. Remove passenger's side air bag module.
15. Reverse procedure to install, tighten to specifications.

NEON

2000-03

1. Disarm air bag system as outlined under "Air Bag System Disarming & Arming."
2. Remove instrument panel top cover.
3. Remove three screws to glove compartment door and remove door.
4. Remove three passenger air bag screws attaching cover to top of instrument panel and two screws attaching lower panel.
5. Disconnect electrical connector and remove passenger's air bag module.
6. Reverse procedure to install.

Side Impact Air Bag Module, Replace

CONCORDE, INTREPID, LHS & 300M

REMOVAL

Do not replace a deployed side air bag module. The complete seatback and all damaged components must be replaced.

1. Move front seat into full forward position.
2. Disarm air bag as described under "Air Bag System Disarming & Arming."
3. Remove plastic back panel from seatback and discard push pins.
4. Place seatback onto suitable clean bench.
5. Disconnect seatback trim cover J-strap from upper, lower and air bag sides of seat.
6. Disconnect side air bag module electrical connector.
7. Push two retaining tabs in using two fingers and pull connector straight from module.
8. Remove side air bag module mounting nuts.
9. Grasp upper air bag side of seatback trim cover, then pull trim cover and cushion over top of seatback frame.
10. Carefully work between seatback trim cover cushion and frame to unhook air bag module studs from nylon sleeve, then slide module out of sleeve. **Avoid tearing sleeve since this will affect module's functioning. Replace seatback trim cover if sleeve tears.**

INSTALLATION

1. Carefully slide air bag module, with its electrical connector facing downward toward seat cushion, into nylon sleeve until mounting studs align with holes in sleeve. **Avoid tearing sleeve since this will affect module's functioning. Replace seatback trim cover if sleeve tears.**
2. **Ensure air bag module is inside nylon sleeve before installing mounting nuts.**
3. Pull air bag module and sleeve assembly up to align mounting studs with seatback frame mounting holes.
4. Install and tighten air bag module mounting nuts.
5. Position seatback upper trim cover and cushion over seatback frame.
6. Connect air bag module electrical connector.
7. **Ensure yellow locking tab is in upper, LOCKED position and that connector cannot be removed after tab is positioned.**
8. Install seatback plastic panel with new push pins.

CROSSFIRE

1. Disarm air bag as described under "Air

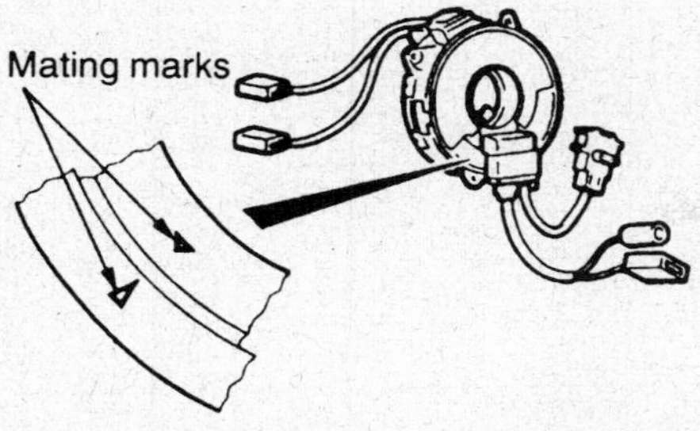

Fig. 9 Clockspring alignment marks. Avenger, Sebring Coupe & Stratus Coupe

Bag System Disarming & Arming."
2. Remove ignition key.
3. Remove door trim panel in numbered sequence, **Fig. 7.**
4. Disconnect electrical connector(s).
5. Drill out mounting rivets attaching side impact air bag module.
6. Remove side impact air bag module.
7. Reverse procedure to install.

NEON

1. Move front seat into full forward position.
2. Disarm air bag as described under "Air Bag System Disarming & Arming."
3. Remove front seat from vehicle.
4. Grasp seat back panel at upper corners and pull rearward on panel until panel disconnects on both side of upper portion.
5. Remove two lower mounting screws.
6. Disconnect seatback trim cover J-strap from upper, lower and air bag sides of seat.
7. Disconnect seat belt electrical connector by sliding yellow locking tab down to unlock, then push in side retaining tabs and pull apart connector, **Fig. 8.**
8. Remove seat air bag mounting nuts.
9. Grab upper air bag side of seat back trim cover, then pull cover and cushion over top of seat back frame.
10. Unhook seat air bag studs from nylon sleeve and slide air bag from sleeve.
11. Reverse procedure to install.

SEBRING COUPE & STRATUS COUPE

Do not replace a deployed side air bag module. The complete seatback and all damaged components must be replaced.

1. Disarm air bag as described under "Air Bag System Disarming & Arming."
2. Disconnect harness connector.
3. Remove seat anchor cover.
4. Remove mounting bolts, nuts and front seat.
5. Disconnect reclining adjuster knob.
6. **On driver's seat,** remove clip and height adjuster knob.
7. **On all models,** remove shield covers and inner seat belt.
8. Remove hog ring, then the seat cushion cover, pad and frame.
9. Remove seat back.
10. Reverse procedure to install seat back with side impact air bag module.

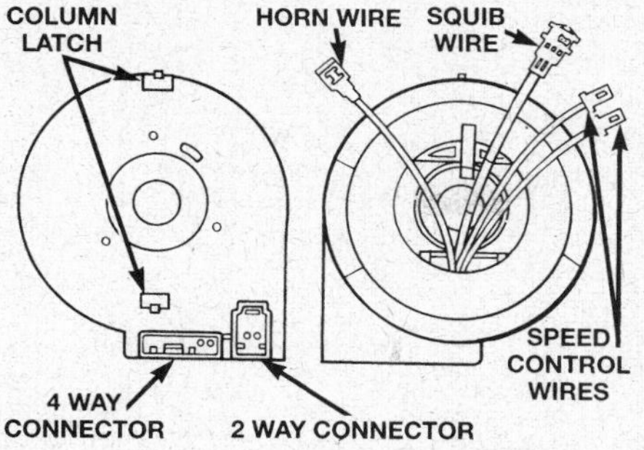

Fig. 10 Clockspring replacement. Breeze, Cirrus, Sebring Convertible, Sebring Sedan & Stratus Sedan

Roof Panel Air Bag Module, Replace

SEBRING SEDAN & STRATUS SEDAN

If the roof panel air bag module is being replaced because of deployment, the headliner must be replaced.

1. Disarm air bag as described under "Air Bag System Disarming & Arming."
2. Remove door sill plates and weatherstrips.
3. Remove instrument panel end cap/ fuse cover.
4. Remove mounting screws, sun visors and supports.
5. Disconnect clips and remove A-pillar trim.
6. Pry shoulder belt knob off using trim stick tool.
7. Remove cover, then the mounting bolt and seat belt turning loop.
8. Remove lower seat belt anchor bolt.
9. Disconnect clips and remove B-pillar trim.
10. Remove front/rear assist handles and/ or coat hooks.
11. Remove rear seat cushion and stopper, then the rear seatback and side.
12. Remove mounting screws and scuff plate, then the front pillar trim.
13. Remove seat belt sash guide cover, then the mounting bolt and front seat belt anchor.
14. Remove mounting screws and upper quarter trim panel.
15. Disconnect headline electrical connectors from instrument panel bracket and fuse panel.
16. Pull map lamp and roof switch down at rear to disconnect clips.
17. Disconnect headliner rear locating clips above rear window using suitable trim stick tool.
18. Pull headline down and disconnect clips around sunroof.
19. Disconnect sunroof module electrical connector.
20. Recline front seats and tilt seat wheel fully up.
21. Move shifter fully rearward and remove headliner.
22. Remove front tether mounting bolt at

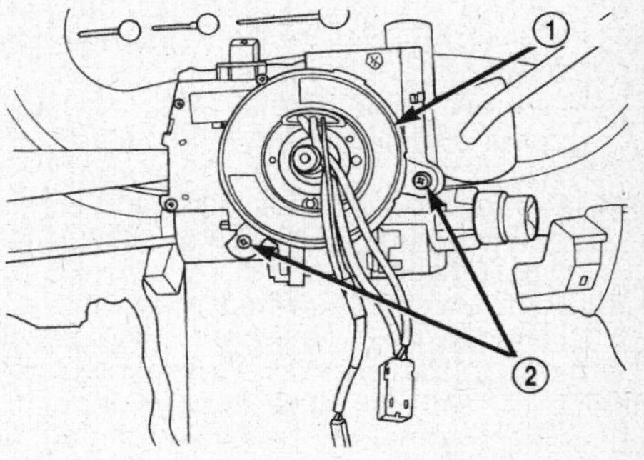

1 – CLOCKSPRING
2 – MOUNTING SCREWS

CR8019802225000X

Fig. 11 Clockspring replacement. Concorde, LHS, Intrepid & 300M

instrument panel on A-pillar.
23. Remove five short mounting bolts along roof line.
24. Remove four long mounting bolts to rear along roof line and at C-pillar.
25. Remove and discard all push fasteners. **Ensure all are completely removed.**
26. Disconnect wiring harness electrical connector from rear of roof panel module.
27. Remove roof panel air bag module from vehicle.
28. Reverse procedure to install.

Clockspring, Replace

AVENGER, SEBRING COUPE & STRATUS COUPE

1. Ensure front wheels are in straight-ahead position, then remove key from ignition.
2. Disarm air bag system as outlined under "Air Bag System Disarming & Arming."
3. Remove air bag module as outlined under "Driver's Air Bag Module, Replace."
4. Remove steering wheel using puller tool No. MB990803, or equivalent. **Do not hammer on wheel.**
5. Remove steering column lower cover.
6. Remove mounting screws and clockspring. Disconnect electrical connector.
7. Reverse procedure to install, noting the following:
   a. Align clockspring by turning fully clockwise, then turning counterclockwise approximately 3–3⅛ turn to align mating marks, **Fig. 9.**
   b. Ensure front wheels are still in straight-ahead position, then mount clockspring into position.
   c. Ensure all wiring and connectors are properly routed to avoid pinching.

BREEZE, CIRRUS, SEBRING CONVERTIBLE, SEBRING SEDAN & STRATUS SEDAN

1. Ensure front wheels are in straight-ahead position.

2. Disarm air bag system as outlined under "Air Bag System Disarming & Arming."
3. Remove mounting screws, then the upper and lower steering column covers.
4. Remove driver's air bag module as outlined under "Driver's Air Bag Module, Replace."
5. Remove steering wheel mounting nut.
6. Remove steering wheel using puller tool No. CJ2001P, or equivalent. Carefully feed all wires through steering wheel armature to avoid damaging wires.
7. Remove steering column shrouds.
8. Remove three mounting screws and multi-function switch, then disconnect electrical connectors from rear side of clockspring, **Fig. 10.**
9. Remove clockspring by lifting top locking tab up slightly to guide it over lock housing.
10. Reverse procedure to install, noting the following:
    a. Ensure wheels are in straight-ahead position.
    b. **On 2000 models,** center clockspring by rotating rotor until yellow indicator centers in centering window. Arrow on rotor will be pointing at window if clockspring is properly centered.
    c. **On 2001–03 models,** depress plastic drive pin, rotate rotor clockwise until it stops, then rotate counterclockwise three turns and release drive pin. Wires should end up on top.

CONCORDE, INTREPID, LHS & 300M

REMOVAL

1. Ensure front wheels are in straight ahead position.
2. Rotate steering wheel clockwise 180° to right and lock in place using ignition lock cylinder. Remove key.
3. Disarm air bag as described under "Air Bag System Disarming & Arming."
4. Remove driver's air bag module as describe under "Driver's Air Bag Module, Replace."
5. Remove steering wheel using suitable puller tool.
6. Remove tilt wheel release lever.
7. Remove steering column upper and lower shrouds, then disconnect connectors between clockspring and instrument panel wiring harness at base of steering column, **Fig. 11.**
8. Remove halo lamp wire from clockspring side clip.
9. Remove mounting screws and pull clockspring from steering shaft.

CENTERING

1. Depress clockspring plastic locking pin to disconnect locking mechanism.
2. Keep locking mechanism disconnected, then slowly and gently rotate clockspring rotor until yellow dot appears in centering window and black arrow aligns with drive pin.
3. Install steering wheel upside down with wheels rotated 180° clockwise.

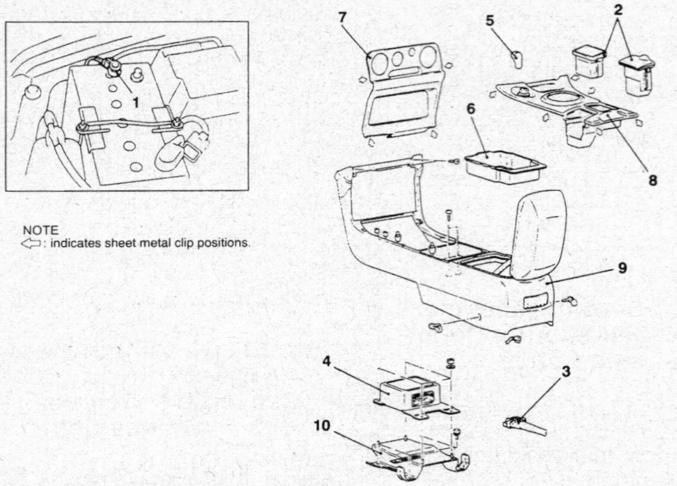

Removal steps
1. Negative (–) battery cable connection
2. Inner box
3. SRS-ECU and harness connector connection
4. SRS-ECU
5. Shift lever knob <M/T>
6. Ashtray or accessory box
7. Center console panel
8. Floor console panel assembly
9. Floor console assembly
10. Bracket

CR8019801374000X

Fig. 12 SRS-ECU removal. Avenger & 2000 Sebring Coupe

INSTALLATION

1. Ensure steering wheel is still positioned clockwise 180° to right and locked in place with ignition lock cylinder.
2. Locate clockspring on steering shaft and push down on rotor until clockspring is fully seated on column.
3. Install clockspring mounting screws and tighten.
4. Connect clockspring to instrument panel harness, ensuring wiring is properly routed and not pinched. Electrical connectors and locking tabs must be securely connected.
5. Install steering column shrouds with wiring securely inside them.
6. Install tilt steering release lever.
7. Install steering wheel. Ensuring hub flats align with clockspring.
8. Route clockspring wiring through large hub opening area of steering wheel. Ensuring it does not pinch.
9. Turn ignition key to unlock column and position steering wheel in straight-ahead position.
10. Route speed control wiring under and behind air bag module mounting tabs.
11. Connect horn and air bag module electrical connectors.
12. Install air bag module and tighten mounting bolts.
13. Connect speed control electrical connectors to switches.

CROSSFIRE

The clockspring can not be repaired. It must be replaced if faulty or damaged, or if driver air bag module has been deployed.

1. Ensure front wheels are in straight ahead position.
2. Remove driver's side air bag module as outlined in "Driver's Side Air Bag Module, Replace."
3. Remove steering wheel countersunk screw from steering column using suitable long hex tool.
4. Remove screws that secure clockspring case to multi-function switch mounting plate.
5. Remove clockspring.
6. Reverse procedure to install, noting the following:
    a. If removed clockspring is to be reused, ensure to secure the clockspring rotor to clockspring case to maintain clockspring centering until unit is installed on steering column.
    b. Ensure front wheels are in straight ahead position.
    c. Hold clockspring case in one hand so that it is oriented as it would be on steering column.
    d. With other hand, rotate clockspring rotor clockwise to end its travel.
    e. Rotate rotor two and a half more turns counterclockwise, until arrows on clockspring rotor label and clockspring case are aligned. The uppermost pin on the lower surface of clockspring rotor should now be in oblong pin.
    f. Clockspring is now centered, tighten to specifications to clockspring case to maintain centering until installed on steering column.

NEON

REMOVAL

1. Ensure wheels are in straight-ahead position.
2. Rotate steering wheel 180° to right and lock column with ignition lock cylinder. Remove key.

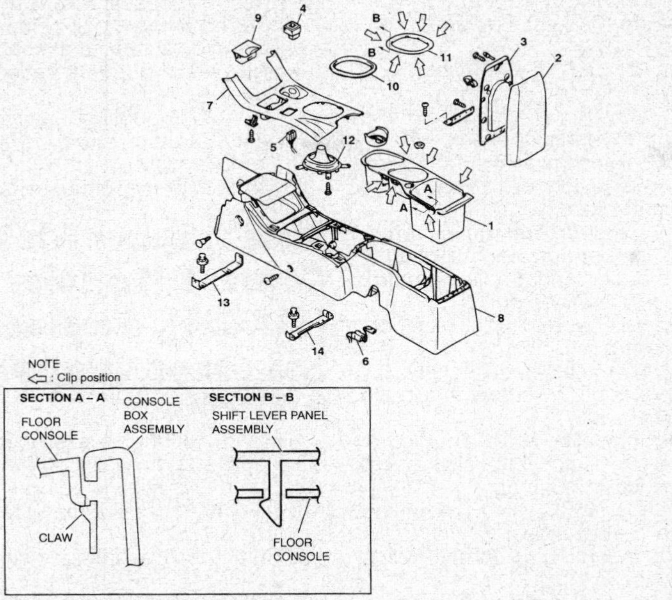

1. CONSOLE BOX ASSEMBLY
2. CONSOLE LID
3. CONSOLE LID COVER
4. DOOR MIRROR CONTROL SWITCH
5. DOOR MIRROR CONTROL SWITCH HARNESS
6. ACCCESSARY SOCKET HARNESS
7. FLOOR CONSOLE INDICATOR PANEL
8. FLOOR CONSOLE
9. ASHTRAY
10. SHIFT LEVER PANEL ASSEMBLY <M/T>
11. GARNISH <A/T>
12. SHIFT LEVER BOOT <M/T>
13. FLOOR CONSOLE BRACKET A
14. FLOOR CONSOLE BRACKET B

CR8010102224000X

Fig. 13 SRS-ECU removal. Stratus Coupe & 2001–03 Sebring Coupe

3. Disarm air bag system as outlined under “Air Bag System Disarming & Arming.”
4. Remove speed control switches or covers and disconnect electrical connectors.
5. Remove air bag module as outlined under “Driver's Air Bag Module, Replace.”
6. Remove steering wheel using puller tool No. CJ2001P, or equivalent.
7. Remove upper and lower steering column shrouds.
8. Disconnect clockspring wiring connectors.
9. Unlatch and remove clockspring assembly from steering shaft.
10. Rotate clockspring rotor clockwise 180° counterclockwise, then lock clockspring rotor in center position using paper clip wire through hole in rotor 10 o'clock position.

CENTERING

1. Keeping locking mechanism disconnected, rotate clockspring rotor clockwise to end of its travel. **Do not apply excessive force.**
2. From end of travel, rotate rotor 2½ turns counterclockwise. **At this position, horn wire and squib wire should end up at bottom. If not, turn rotor counterclockwise until wires are properly positioned, but not more than 180°.**
3. Engage clockspring locking mechanism.

INSTALLATION

1. Ensure steering wheel is 180° clockwise and locked with ignition lock cylinder.
2. Ensure directional signal stalk is in neutral position.
3. When installing original clockspring, remove locking wire and rotate rotor 180° clockwise.
4. When installing a new clockspring, remove grenade pin and rotate rotor 180° clockwise.
5. Locate properly centered clockspring on steering shaft, then push down on rotor until clockspring is fully seated.
6. Connect clockspring electrical connectors, ensuring wiring is properly routed. Connectors, locking tabs and halo lamp wire must also be properly positioned.
7. Install steering column shrouds, ensuring all wiring is inside them.
8. Install steering wheel with flats on hub aligned with clockspring.
9. Pull horn, air bag and speed control leads through larger slot. Ensure they do not pinch under wheel.
10. Route speed control wiring under and behind air bag module mounting tabs.
11. Connect horn lead wire and air bag leads to air bag module.
12. Install air bag module,

Air Bag Control Module (ACM), Replace

The ACM/Air Bag System Diagnostic Module (ASDM), Occupant Restraint Controller (ORC), Seat Belt Control Timer Module (SCTM), SRS Diagnosis Unit (SDU) and SRS Air Bag Electronic Control Unit (SRS-ECU) contain sensitive sensors which enable the systems to deploy the air bags or seat belt retractor solenoids. **To avoid accidental deployment, never connect these units to the electrical system unless they are bolted to the vehicle.**

AVENGER, SEBRING COUPE & STRATUS COUPE

1. Disarm air bag system as outlined under “Air Bag System Disarming & Arming.”
2. Remove floor console trim, **Figs. 12 and 13.**
3. Disconnect SRS-ECU electrical connectors.
4. Mark for installation, then remove mounting bolts and control module.
5. Reverse procedure to install, noting the following:
   a. **On Stratus Coupe and 2001–02 Sebring Coupe models,** ensure ground bolt (identified by letter E) on head) is installed original position.
   b. **On all models,** ensure SRS-ECU is securely mounted before connecting electrical connector.
   c. Ensure wiring and electrical connectors are not pinched.
   d. Connect battery ground cable and ensure SRS warning lamp operates properly.

BREEZE, CIRRUS, SEBRING CONVERTIBLE, SEBRING SEDAN & STRATUS SEDAN

1. Disarm air bag system as outlined under “Air Bag System Disarming & Arming.”
2. Raise parking brake lever as high as possible.
3. **On models equipped with manual transaxle,** remove shift lever knob and boot.
4. **On models equipped with automatic transaxle,** remove shifter lever knob and unclip shift indicator bezel.
5. **On all models,** remove floor console mounting screws and floor shifter mounting nuts.
6. Disconnect console electrical connectors at floor pan.
7. Remove console.
8. Remove parking brake lever assembly if required.

9. Disconnect module electrical connector.
10. Remove mounting screws and control module.
11. Reverse procedure to install.

CONCORDE, INTREPID, LHS & 300M

FIVE-PASSENGER MODELS

1. Disarm air bag system as outlined under "Air Bag System Disarming & Arming."
2. **On Concorde models,** remove instrument panel as outlined under "Dash Panel Service."
3. **On Intrepid, LHS & 300M models,** proceed as follows:
   a. Remove one shift knob hex mounting screw.
   b. Remove two screws at shifter bezel.
   c. Disconnect power outlet electrical connector and remove bezel.
   d. Remove instrument panel lefthand end cap covering junction block.
   e. Remove two screws to steering column cover, then pull rearward to disconnect clips.
   f. Open glove compartment door and continue to pull until compartment drops and screws in upper and lower lefthand corners of bin are visible.
   g. Pull off console righthand side panel.
   h. Remove two screws and console lefthand side panel.
4. **On all models,** slide red tab out, push down on locking latch, then disconnect ORC electrical connector.
5. Remove two ORC side mounting screws on driver's side.
6. Loosen top mounting screw on driver's side.
7. Lift ORC up and remove. **If module cannot be lifted out, loosen passenger's side screw .**
8. Reverse procedure to install, noting the following:
   a. Ensure module arrow is pointing forward.
   b. Module must be securely located in its bracket, with module mounting bosses properly positioned.

SIX-PASSENGER MODELS

1. Disarm air bag system as outlined under "Air Bag System Disarming & Arming."
2. Open glove compartment door and continue to pull until compartment drops and screws in upper and lower lefthand corners of bin are visible.
3. **On Concorde models,** remove instrument panel as outlined under "Passenger's Air Bag Module, Replace," non-deployed.
4. **On Intrepid, LHS & 300M models,** proceed as follows:
   a. Remove instrument panel lefthand end cap covering junction block.
   b. Remove two screws to steering column cover, then pull rearward to disconnect clips.
   c. Remove instrument panel center bezel. Temperature control module, power outlet and traction control switch will also pop out.
   d. Disconnect center bezel electrical connectors.
   e. Remove four chin bezel screws.
   f. Remove floor bin screw and push fastener.
5. **On all models,** slide red tab out, push down on locking latch, then disconnect ORC electrical connector.
6. Remove two ORC side mounting screws on driver's side.
7. Loosen top mounting screw on driver's side.
8. Lift ORC up and remove. **If module cannot be lifted out, loosen passenger's side screw .**
9. Reverse procedure to install, noting the following:
   a. Ensure module arrow is pointing forward.
   b. Module must be securely located in its bracket, with module mounting bosses properly positioned.

CROSSFIRE

1. Disarm air bag as described under "Air Bag System Disarming & Arming."
2. Remove center console as outlined in "Dash Panel Service" chapter.
3. Disconnect electrical connector to OCR.
4. Remove attaching bolts from OCR to transmission tunnel.
5. Remove OCR from vehicle.
6. Reverse procedure to install.

NEON

The parking brake lever's auto adjusting feature contains a clockspring loaded to approximately 20 pounds of force. Do not release the adjuster lockout device before installing cables into the equalizer. Keep hands out of the adjuster sector and pawl area.

1. Disarm air bag system as outlined under "Air Bag System Disarming & Arming."
2. **On models equipped with manual transaxle,** remove shift knob fastener and knob.
3. **On all models,** remove rear console mounting screws at console bracket.
4. Remove console mounting screws located in forward cup holders.
5. Remove center floor console at rear and guide it out from under instrument panel.
6. Remove mounting nuts and disconnect ACM connectors.
7. Remove ACM.
8. Reverse procedure to install.

Side Impact Air Bag Control Module (SIACM), Replace

CONCORDE, INTREPID, LHS & 300M

1. Disarm air bag as described under "Air Bag System Disarming & Arming."
2. Remove B-pillar lower trim.
3. Disconnect SIACM electrical connector.
4. Remove mounting screws and SIACM.
5. Reverse procedure to install.

NEON

1. Disarm air bag as described under "Air Bag System Disarming & Arming."
2. Remove lower seat trim, then disconnect harness side of seat air bag connector.
3. Remove lower B-pillar trim.
4. Remove seat belt retractor.
5. Remove mounting nuts, ground and SIACM. Disconnect electrical connector.
6. Reverse procedure to install.

SEBRING SEDAN & STRATUS SEDAN

1. Disarm air bag as described under "Air Bag System Disarming & Arming."
2. Remove scuff plates and door weatherstrip.
3. Pry shoulder belt knob off using suitable trim stick.
4. Remove cover, mounting bolt and seat belt turning loop.
5. Remove lower seat belt anchor mounting bolt.
6. Disconnect clips and remove upper B-pillar trim panel.
7. Disconnect seat belt access panel clips.
8. Remove B-pillar trim mounting screws and disconnect clips.
9. Route seat belt through access hole and remove lower B-pillar trim panel.
10. Disconnect SIACM electrical connector.
11. Remove mounting screws and SIACM.
12. Reverse procedure to install.

Side Impact Sensor

CROSSFIRE

1. Disarm air bag as described under "Air Bag System Disarming & Arming."
2. Remove ignition key.
3. Remove door sill trim plates.
4. Remove seat track covers, then the front seat bolts.
5. Remove rear seat bolts.
6. Remove seat bolt, then the seat from vehicle.
7. Remove carpet as required to access side impact sensor.
8. Disconnet electrical connector to side impact sensor.
9. Remove side impact sensor attaching screws, then the side impact sensor from vehicle.
10. Reverse procedure to install, tighten to specifications.

SEBRING COUPE & STRATUS COUPE

1. Disarm air bag system as outlined under "Air Bag System Disarming & Arming."
2. Remove rear seat cushion and stopper, then the rear seatback and side.
3. Remove mounting screws and scuff plate, then the front pillar trim.
4. Remove seat belt sash guide cover, then the mounting bolt and front seat belt anchor.
5. Remove mounting screws and upper quarter trim panel.
6. Disconnect rear personal lamp.
7. Remove lower mounting bolts and rear seat belt anchor.
8. Remove mounting screws and lower quarter trim panel.
9. Remove mounting nuts and side impact sensor.
10. Reverse procedure to install.

Air Bag Module Disposal

After deployment, air bag modules should be placed in a plastic bag and disposed of in the same manner as any other scrap parts, except that the following points should be carefully noted during disposal:

1. **Inflator will be quite hot immediately after deployment. Wait 30 minutes to allow air bag to cool.**
2. **When handling a deployed air bag module, a face shield and rubber gloves should be worn.**
3. There may be material adhered to air bag module that could irritate eyes and/or skin. **If any irritation develops, seek medical attention.** Note following:
   a. If sinus or throat irritation is encountered during air bag removal, exit vehicle and breath fresh air.
   b. If material does come in contact with eyes and/or skin, immediately rinse affected area with a large amount of cool, clean water.
   c. If sinus, throat, skin or any other type of irritation continues, consult a physician.
4. After handling a deployed air bag module, wash hands and rinse thoroughly with water.
5. Do not put water or oil on air bag after deployment.
6. Put deployed air bag in a hermetically sealed container and discard it.
7. Use a vacuum cleaner to remove any residual powder from vehicle interior as follows:
   a. Work from outside to center of vehicle.
   b. Vacuum A/C, vent, defroster and heater ducts.
   c. Run blower motor on low speed and vacuum any powder expelled from plenum.
   d. It may be required to vacuum interior of vehicle a second time to ensure all powder is recovered.
8. An air bag that has been deployed should be removed as outlined under "Driver's Air Bag Module, Replace," "Passenger's Air Bag Module, Replace," "Side Impact Air Bag Module, Replace," or "Roof Panel Air Bag Module, Replace"
9. Prior to removing deployed air bag module place tape over air bag exhaust vents.
10. Before disposing of a vehicle equipped with air bag(s), or prior to disposing of air bag module, the module must be deployed as follows:
    a. If vehicle is to be scrapped, deploy air bag(s) inside vehicle.
    b. If vehicle is to continue in service, air bags must be removed and deployed outside vehicle.

AVENGER, SEBRING COUPE & STRATUS COUPE

Before deploying air bag, ensure there are no people, animals or objects in or near vehicle.

Do not perform deployment outside if a strong wind is blowing or if there is even a slight breeze. Air bag should be deployed downwind from battery.

Wear safety glasses and suitable ear protection.

Inflator will be quite hot immediately after deployment. Wait 30 minutes to allow air bag to cool.

Do not inhale gas from air bag.

DEPLOYMENT INSIDE VEHICLE

1. Park vehicle in an isolated location with 30 feet of open area on all sides.
2. Open all windows and doors of vehicle.
3. Disconnect and remove vehicle battery from vehicle. **Wait at least two minutes after disconnecting battery cable before doing any further work. The SRS is designed to retain enough voltage to deploy air bags for a short time even after battery has been disconnected.**
4. Remove steering column lower cover and disconnect clockspring red two-pin connector from body wiring connector.
5. Open glove compartment and disconnect passenger's air bag module red two-pin connector from body wiring harness.
6. **On models equipped with side impact air bag modules,** disconnect red two-pin connector from floor wiring harness.
7. **On all models,** connect two wires, each at least 20 feet in length, to two leads of special SRS air bag adapter harness tool No. MB686560, or equivalent. Cover connections with tape. **Other ends of two wires should be connected to each other to prevent unwanted air bag deployment.**
8. **If deploying driver's air bag module,** connect SRS air bag adapter harness to clockspring red two-pin connector, then pass deployment wires out of vehicle.
9. **If deploying passenger's air bag module,** connect SRS air bag adapter harness to passenger air bag module red two-pin connector, then pass deployment wires out of vehicle.
10. **If deploying side impact air bag module,** connect SRS air bag adapter harness to side impact air bag module red two-pin connector, then pass deployment wires out of vehicle.
11. **On all models,** cover vehicle with suitable car cover.
12. From as far away as possible, separate two connected wires and connect them to fully charged 12-volt battery. Air bag modules should deploy.
13. If deployment does not occur, contact DaimlerChrysler for further instructions.

DEPLOYMENT OUTSIDE VEHICLE

1. Disconnect and remove vehicle battery . **Wait at least two minutes after disconnecting battery cable before doing any further work. The SRS is designed to retain enough voltage to deploy air bags for a short time even after battery has been disconnected.**
2. Remove air bag module(s) as outlined under "Driver's Air Bag Module, Replace," "Passenger's Air Bag Module, Replace," "Side Impact Air Bag Module, Replace" and "Roof Panel Air Bag Module, Replace."
3. Locate flat, spacious outside area at least 30 feet away from any people, animals, equipment or other objects.
4. **If deploying side impact air bag module,** place seatback with its back contacting ground.
5. **On all models,** connect two wires, 20 feet in length, to two leads of special SRS air bag adapter harness tool No. MB686560, or equivalent, and cover connections with tape. **Other ends of two wires should be connected to each other to prevent unwanted air bag deployment.**
6. **If deploying driver's or passenger's air bag module,** proceed as follows:
   a. Mount air bag module with suitable thick wire to discarded tire and wheel assembly.
   b. Ensure module is facing upward.
   c. Route deployment wiring under tire and wheel assembly. **Leave some slack to prevent damage to adapter harness.**
   d. Stack three more discarded tires without wheels on top of tire where air bag module has been secured.
   e. Lash all four tires and wheel together with suitable rope at four locations.
7. **On all models,** from as far away as possible, separate two connected wires from each other and connect them to fully charged 12-volt battery. Air bag modules should now deploy.
8. If deployment does not occur, contact DaimlerChrysler for further instructions.

BREEZE, CIRRUS, CONCORDE, CROSSFIRE, INTREPID, LHS, NEON, SEBRING CONVERTIBLE, SEBRING SEDAN, STRATUS SEDAN & 300M

Consult DaimlerChrysler Corporation for proper deployment procedures.

TIGHTENING SPECIFICATIONS

Year	Component	Torque/Ft. Lbs.
AVENGER		
2000	Driver's Side Air Bag Module	48①
	Steering Wheel	30
BREEZE, CIRRUS, SEBRING CONVERTIBLE, SEBRING SEDAN & STRATUS SEDAN		
2000	Air Bag Control Module	10–13
	Driver's Side Air Bag Module, Bolt (Except Sebring Convertible)	81–90①
	Driver's Side Air Bag Module, Bolt (Sebring Convertible)	90–100①
	Driver's Side Air Bag Module, Nut	100①
	Multi-Function Switch	14–22①
	Passenger's Side Air Bag Module, Bolt	20①
	Passenger's Side Air Bag Module, Nut	100①
	Speed Control Switch	6–24①
	Steering Wheel, Bolt	40
	Steering Wheel, Nut	45
2001–04	Air Bag Control Module	84–120①
	Driver's Side Air Bag Module, Bolt (Sebring Convertible)	90–100①
	Driver's Side Air Bag Module, Bolt (Sebring Sedan & Stratus Sedan)	75–85①
	Driver's Side Air Bag Module, Nut	100①
	Front Seat Track To Floor	45
	Multi-Function Switch	14–22①
	Passenger's Side Air Bag Module, Bolt	66①
	Passenger's Side Air Bag Module, Nut	100①
	Roof Panel Air Bag Module, Long Bolt	87–107①
	Roof Panel Air Bag Module, Short Bolt	43–63①
	Speed Control Switch	6–24①
	Steering Column Support Bracket	13
	Steering Wheel, Bolt	40
	Steering Wheel, Nut	45
CONCORDE, INTREPID, LHS & 300M		
2000–2004	Clockspring	24①
	Driver's Side Air Bag Module (2000)	96①
	Driver's Side Air Bag Module (2001–03)	65–85①
	Impact Sensor	25–46①
	Occupant Restraint Controller (ORC)	84–120①
	Passenger's Side Air Bag Module (2000)	45①
	Passenger's Side Air Bag Module (2001–03)	20①
	Passenger's Side Air Bag Module Deployment Door Reinforcement	75①
	Pencil Strut To Passenger's Side Air Bag Module	45①
	Side Impact Air Bag Module	95①
	Speed Control Switch	13①
	Steering Column Flex Coupler Pinch Bolt	20
	Steering Column Support Bracket	105①
	Steering Wheel	45

Continued

TIGHTENING SPECIFICATIONS—Continued

Year	Component	Torque/Ft. Lbs.
CROSSFIRE		
2004	Air Bag Module To Steering Wheel Screw	71①
	Driver's Side Air Bag Module Screw	71①
	OCR Bolt To Floor	26
	Passenger's Air Bag To Instrument Panel Duct	26
	Rear Seat Belt Bolts	37
	Seat Belt Buckle Bolt	26
	Seat Belt End Fitting Bolt	71①
	Seat Belt Guide Fitting Bolt	26
	Seat Belt Tensioner To B-Pillar Bolt	88①
NEON		
2000–2004	Air Bag Control Module	108–120①
	Driver's Side Air Bag Module	90–100①
	Lower Seat Back Panel	9①
	Parking Brake Lever Assembly To Console Bracket	21
	Passenger's Side Air Bag Module, Nut	17–25
	Passenger's Side Air Bag Module, Screw	20①
	Side Air Bag Module	95①
	Steering Wheel	45
SEBRING COUPE & STRATUS COUPE		
2000	Driver's Side Air Bag Module	48①
	Steering Wheel	30
2001–03	Clockspring	5–7①
	Driver's Side Air Bag Module	61–95①
	Rear Seat Belt Anchor	26–40
	Side Impact Sensor	35–51①
	SRS-ECU	35–51①
	Steering Wheel	26–36

① — Inch lbs.

DASH PANEL SERVICE

NOTE: Refer To The "Dash Gauges" Chapter For Related Information.

NOTE: On Air Bag Equipped Models, Refer To "Air Bag System Precautions" Located In The Front Of This Manual For System Disarming & Arming Procedures.

NOTE: Refer To "Computer Relearn Procedures" Located In The Front Of This Manual When Battery Power To The Computer Has Been Interrupted.

NOTE: Prior To Performing Any Service Operations Listed In This Section, Consult The "Technical Service Bulletins" Section For Related Information.

INDEX

PRECAUTIONS

Air Bag Systems

Refer to "Air Bag System Precautions" in the front of this manual for system disarming and arming procedures.

Battery Ground Cable

Prior to service, disconnect battery ground cable and isolate as required.

DASH PANEL

REPLACE

Avenger

1. Remove floor console in numbered sequence, **Fig. 1.**
2. Remove instrument panel in numbered sequence, **Fig. 2,** noting the following:
   a. Push stopper in direction of arrow to unlock, **Fig. 3.**
   b. Push lever pin to disconnect air outlet changeover damper cable and remove heater control assembly, **Fig. 4.**
3. Reverse numbered sequence to install, **Figs. 1 and 2.** Noting the following:
   a. Set temperature control knob on heater control assembly and air mix damper lever to MAX HOT position, push outer cable in direction of arrow, **Fig. 5,** and secure with clip. Cable should have not have any slack.
   b. Set knob for air outlet changeover and air outlet changeover damper lever to defrost position, push outer cable in direction of arrow, **Fig. 6,** and secure with clip. Cable should have not have any slack.
   c. Set lever for inside/outside air changeover and inside/outside air changeover damper lever to inside air recirculation position.
   d. With inside/outside air changeover damper lever touching blower case stopper, install cable to lever pin, push outer cable in direction of arrow and secure with clip, **Fig. 7.** Cable should have not have any slack.
   e. Turn cool air bypass lever of center air outlet fully downward, pull cool air bypass damper lever fully toward you and install cable to lever pin.
   f. Push outer cable in direction of arrow and secure with clip, **Fig. 8.** Cable should have not have any slack.
   g. Ensure all connectors are securely connected and wiring harnesses are not pinched.

Breeze & Cirrus

1. Open both front doors and remove instrument panel end covers, **Fig. 9.**
2. Remove transaxle range indicator bezel from floor console, floor center console mounting screws and floor center console.
3. Disconnect air bag control module.
4. Remove two screws adjacent to radio and screw below HVAC control in center bezel.
5. Remove screw at lefthand end of panel, pull on hood to disconnect eight clips and remove hood.
6. Remove mounting screws and cubby bin, then the mounting screws and knee bolster.
7. Open glove compartment door and press side walls inward to lower access panel.
8. Remove mounting screws and push pin from forward floor console.
9. Carefully remove floor console from vehicle.
10. Remove center instrument panel trim bezel using trim stick tool No. C-4755 or equivalent.
11. Pull driver's side underpanel silencer off of distribution duct.
12. Remove instrument panel top cover mounting screw from passenger side and lift righthand rear edge to disconnect clips along rear edge.
13. Lift rear edge and slid top cover rearward to remove.
14. Remove HVAC control mounting screws and radio.
15. Remove HVAC mounting screws from duct and HVAC mounting bolts from cross-vehicle beam.
16. Close glove compartment door and remove screws attaching panel retainer to plenum.
17. Remove steering column retaining

nuts, then lower the column to floor.
18. Disconnect engine and body wiring harness from junction block.
19. Remove one push pin to righthand underpanel silencer.
20. Remove following instrument panel fasteners:
    a. Four at lefthand end of cross-vehicle beam.
    b. Three at righthand end of cross-vehicle beam.
    c. Two at steering column plenum.
    d. One at glove compartment hinge to A-pillar.
    e. Two at center support to floor pan bracket.
21. Remove HVAC screws at bottom of dash panel and instrument panel fasteners.
22. Lift and pull reward to remove instrument panel.
23. Reverse procedure to install, noting the following:
    a. Install steering column onto support bracket studs with retaining nuts loosely installed.
    b. Tighten two lower retaining nuts to hold column in place.
    c. Ensure both breakaway capsules are still fully seated in upper column mounting bracket slots and mounting studs are centered in capsules, **Fig. 10.**
    d. Tighten both mounting nuts equally until upper column mounting bracket is seated against support bracket.
    e. **Torque** four bracket nuts to 106 inch lbs.

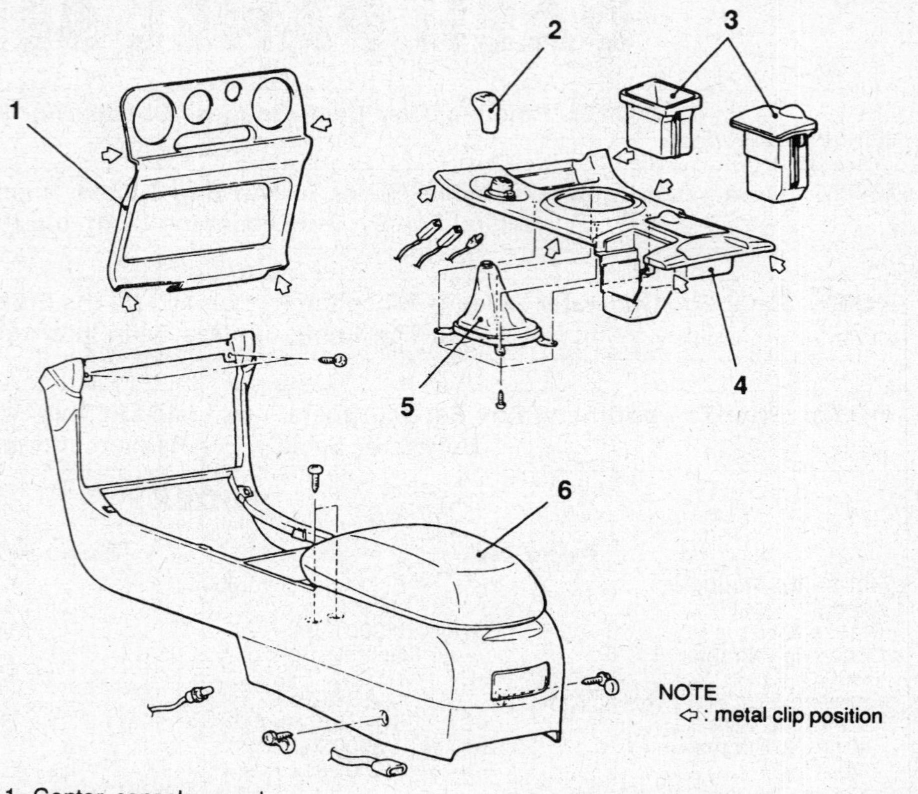

Fig. 1 Floor console replacement. 2000 Avenger & Sebring Coupe

Concorde, Intrepid, LHS & 300M

1. Ensure front wheels are pointed in straight-ahead position.
2. Remove transaxle range selector lever hex retaining screw.
3. Remove instrument panel lefthand and righthand end covers, **Figs. 11 through 13.**
4. **On 300M models,** remove center bezel.
5. **On all models,** remove shifter bezel using trim stick tool No. C-4755, or equivalent, disconnect all electrical connectors.
6. Remove two screws from lower instrument panel cover (outside end).
7. Disconnect luggage compartment release switch electrical connector.
8. Pull rearward on lower instrument panel cover to release clips.
9. Disconnect cable at brake release handle.
10. Pull rearward and remove lower instrument panel cover.
11. **On models equipped for six passenger seating,** proceed as follows:
    a. Remove one screw and one push pin mounting center floor storage bin to instrument panel.
    b. Remove lower floor storage bin from vehicle.
12. **On models equipped with floor console,** proceed as follows:
    a. Remove center bezel using trim stick tool No. C-4755, or equivalent.
    b. Disconnect electrical connectors at heater, A/C controls and traction control switch.
    c. Remove console lefthand side cover retaining screws, then pull outward to remove.
    d. Lower the glove compartment door.
    e. Remove console righthand side cover retaining screws, then pull console outward.
    f. Remove two front bracket screws and two screws inside console bin, then the console.
13. **On all models,** remove center lower instrument panel retaining nuts.
14. Remove four bolts to steel reinforcement from lower side of lower instrument panel cover.
15. Disconnect DLC from reinforcement.
16. Remove steering column from vehicle as outlined in "Steering Columns" chapter.
17. Remove lefthand floor duct silencer pad.
18. Disconnect heater, A/C housing and Air Bag Control Module (ACM) electrical connectors, then the ground eyelets near floor tunnel at firewall.
19. Gently pry out on lefthand and righthand A-pillar moldings.
20. Gently pry up on instrument panel top cover and remove toward rear of vehicle.
21. Remove righthand and lefthand cowl trim panels.
22. Remove righthand underdash silencer pad.
23. Disconnect two righthand side electrical connectors at radio antenna and amplifier cable.
24. Disconnect lefthand side electrical connectors at junction block and Body Control Module (BCM).
25. Disconnect front wiper defrost grid wire electrical connector.
26. Remove one instrument panel retaining screw behind glove compartment.
27. Remove remaining instrument panel retaining screws.
28. Pull rearward on instrument panel, ensuring all electrical connectors and wiring are free and clear.
29. Remove instrument panel from vehicle and place on a clean suitable workbench.
30. Reverse procedure to install.

Crossfire

1. Remove top panel of dash panel as outlined in "Passenger's Side Air Bag Module, Replace" in "Passive Restraint Systems" chapter.
2. Remove air nozzles.
3. Remove steering column undercover attaching screw, then the cover.
4. Remove fuse panel cover.
5. Remove lower instrument attaching

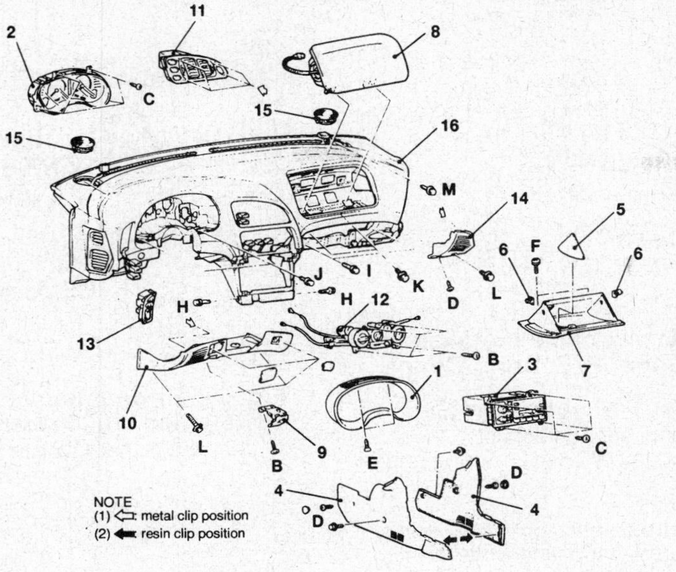

1. Meter bezel
2. Combination meter
3. Radio and tape player
4. Console side cover
5. Sunglasses holder
6. Stopper
7. Glove box
8. Passenger's side air bag module assembly
9. Hood lock release handle
10. Instrument under cover L.H.
11. Center air outlet assembly
12. Heater control assembly
13. Instrument panel switch
14. Instrument under cover R.H.
15. Front speaker
16. Instrument panel assembly

CR9149700069000X

Fig. 2 Instrument panel replacement. 2000 Avenger & Sebring Coupe

screws from illumination control module, side of instrument panel and support bar, **Fig. 14.**

6. Remove illumination control module.
7. Remove underside cover screws from cover, **Fig. 15.**
8. Remove lower instrument cover from upper instrument cover.
9. Remove hood latch release handle to lower instrument panel, guiding handle through lower cover, **Fig. 16.**
10. Remove lower panel from upper panel, then the lower instrument panel, **Fig. 17.**
11. Remove carpeting from righthand side passenger area.
12. Remove lower instrument panel attaching screws to glove compartment, **Fig. 18.**
13. Pull lower instrument panel from compartment.
14. Reverse procedure to install.

Neon

1. Move front seats as far rearward as possible.
2. Ensure front wheels are locked in straight-ahead position, to prevent clockspring damage.
3. Remove A-pillar trim using trim stick tool No. C-4755, or equivalent.
4. Remove instrument panel top cover, **Fig. 19.**
5. Remove instrument cluster bezel.
6. Remove lefthand lower instrument panel cover by gently pulling rearward.
7. Remove steering column lower cover.
8. **On models equipped with speed control,** remove speed control switches from steering wheel.
9. **On all models,** remove driver's side air bag module to steering wheel mounting screws.
10. Disconnect air bag module electrical connectors, then remove module from steering wheel.
11. Hold steering wheel firmly in place, then remove steering wheel retaining nut.
12. **On models equipped with steering wheel damper weight,** remove weight from steering wheel.
13. **On all models,** remove steering wheel from steering column using a suitable steering wheel puller tool. **Do not pound on shaft.**
14. Remove key from ignition.
15. Remove steering column lower and upper shrouds.
16. Remove steering column coupler retaining pin.
17. Loosen pinch bolt nut, then remove coupling pinch bolt.
18. Separate upper and lower steering column couplings.
19. **On models equipped with automatic transaxle,** disconnect transaxle ignition interlock cable from column. Depress tab on top of cable connector and remove cable from rear side of ignition cylinder housing.
20. **On all models,** remove two column to instrument panel lower mounting nuts.
21. Remove two column to instrument panel upper mounting nuts.

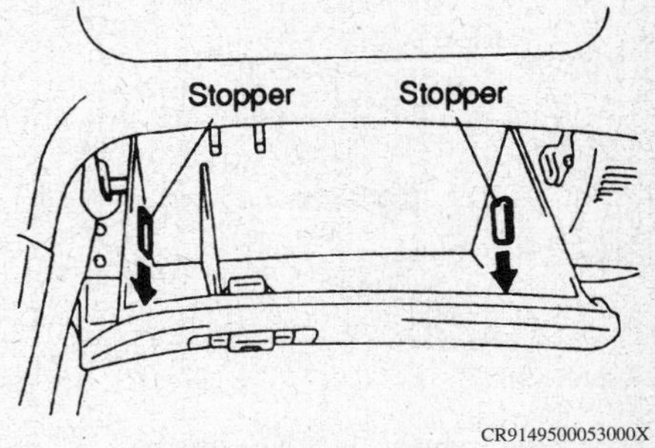

Fig. 3 Stopper removal. 2000 Avenger & Sebring Coupe

22. Lower steering column away from instrument panel.
23. Disconnect air bag clockspring electrical connector.
24. Disconnect electrical connectors at multi-function, windshield wiper, ignition and Sentry Key Immobilizer Module (SKIM) switches.
25. Carefully remove steering column from vehicle.
26. Remove instrument panel lefthand and righthand end covers.
27. Remove lefthand and righthand cowl side panels.
28. Apply parking brake, then remove floor center console, **Fig. 20.**
29. Remove Data Link Connector (DLC) from instrument panel by depressing side tabs.
30. Remove four instrument panel to firewall retaining bolts.
31. Remove two bolts on top of brake pedal support bracket.
32. Remove two center support bolts.
33. Remove lefthand and righthand A-pillar mounting bolts.
34. Disconnect vanity and rearview mirror electrical connector at top lefthand side of instrument panel.
35. Disconnect two harness connectors to heater HVAC at top righthand of instrument panel.
36. Remove both A/C outlet barrels.
37. Remove heater and A/C control knobs.
38. Gently pry outward on center bezel and remove from instrument panel.
39. Remove two heater and A/C control head retaining screws.
40. Disconnect electrical and vacuum connectors at heater and A/C control head.
41. Pull heater and A/C control head out of instrument panel, twist 90° and push back through opening. **Leave control cables in place.**
42. Disconnect electrical connectors at Air Bag Control Module (ACM), parking brake warning lamp switch and PRNDL lamp.
43. Remove two bolts at top of brake pedal bracket, then carefully remove instrument panel from vehicle.
44. Reverse procedure to install, noting the following:
    a. Feed HVAC control into opening at back of panel. Align 75–way electrical connector and carefully guide panel into position. The use of two ½ inch drift pins or bolts will ensure

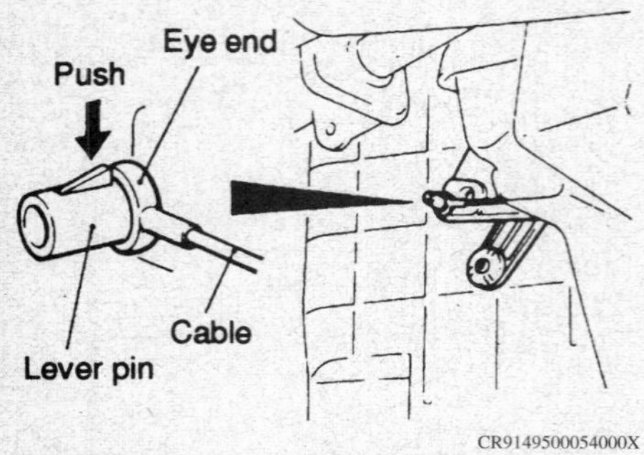

Fig. 4 Heater control assembly removal. 2000 Avenger & Sebring Coupe

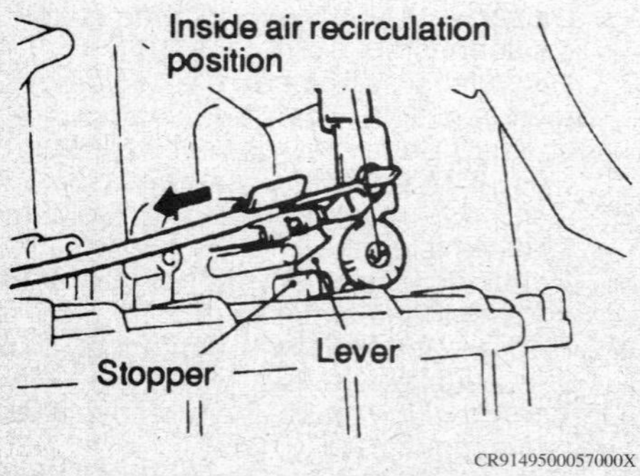

Fig. 7 Air recirculation cable installation. 2000 Avenger & Sebring Coupe

proper vertical position on panel.

b. **On models equipped with tilt steering,** do not release tilt lever from locked position until after steering column has been securely installed on instrument panel.
c. **On all models,** install two steering column lower mounting nuts, then the upper nuts, **torque** to 12 ft. lbs.
d. **Torque** column pinch bolt to 21 ft. lbs.
e. **Torque** steering wheel retaining nut to 45 ft. lbs.
f. **Torque** driver's air bag module to steering wheel bolts to 90 inch lbs.

Sebring Convertible

2000

Refer to "Breeze & Cirrus" for instrument panel replacement procedure.

2001–04

The instrument panel and HVAC assemblies are removed as an assembly. If service is required to an individual unit, separation will be required.

1. Recover A/C refrigerant as outlined in "Air Conditioning" chapter.
2. Drain engine coolant into a suitable container.
3. Remove mounting bolt attaching A/C lines to strut tower, then the A/C lines from evaporator.
4. Remove heater hoses from heater core.
5. Remove two top HVAC housing retaining nuts in engine compartment.

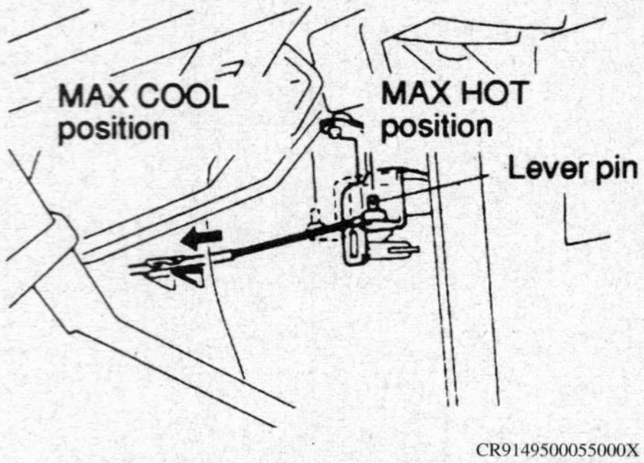

Fig. 5 Air mix cable installation. 2000 Avenger & Sebring Coupe

6. Raise and support vehicle, then remove two lower HVAC housing retaining nuts.
7. Lower vehicle.
8. Position front seats forward to gain access to rear mounting bolts on floor, then remove bolts.
9. Position front seats rearward and remove front floor mounting bolts.
10. Disconnect wire harness and electrical connectors, then remove seats from vehicle. **Do not handle seat by adjuster release bar when removing spring loaded seats.**
11. Remove retaining screw to shift knob range indicator bezel.
12. Remove floor console mounting screws, then the floor console.
13. Remove audio amplifier mounting screws and disconnect electrical connector, then the audio amplifier.
14. Remove mounting screws from lefthand and righthand cowl kick panels, then the panels.
15. Remove lefthand and righthand rear floor heat ducts using trim stick tool No. C-4755, or equivalent.
16. Remove lefthand and righthand sill plates, instrument panel end covers and A pillar trim using trim stick tool No. C-4755, or equivalent.
17. Disconnect door harness electrical connectors located in A pillars.
18. Open glove compartment, pinch in on both sides, then pull down to disengage hinges.
19. Remove four lefthand and righthand A pillar to instrument panel mounting bolts, then the silencers.
20. Remove lefthand and righthand center instrument panel support bolts.
21. Remove lefthand support strut mounting bolt.
22. Disconnect junction block wire connectors.
23. Remove two screws, then the steering column shrouds.
24. Disconnect transaxle shift interlock wire connector.
25. Remove four steering column mounting bolts, then lower steering column to floor.
26. Pry up on rear of instrument panel cover using trim stick tool No. C4755, or equivalent, then remove instrument panel cover, **Fig. 21.**
27. Remove seven bolts and five screws mounting instrument panel to cowl supports, then lift instrument panel up and move rearward to separate from cowl mountings, **Fig. 22.**

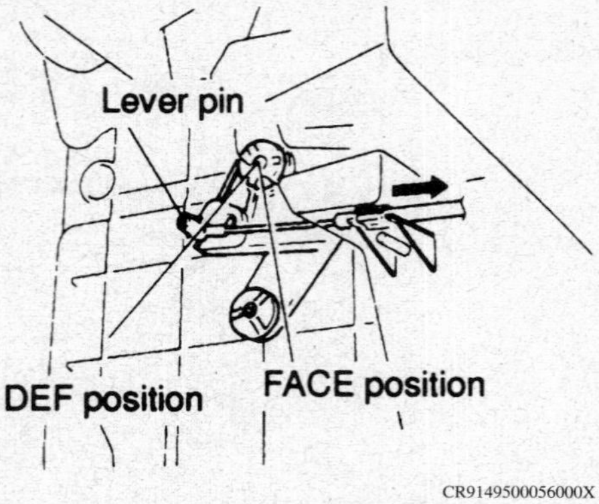

Fig. 6 Air changeover cable installation. 2000 Avenger & Sebring Coupe

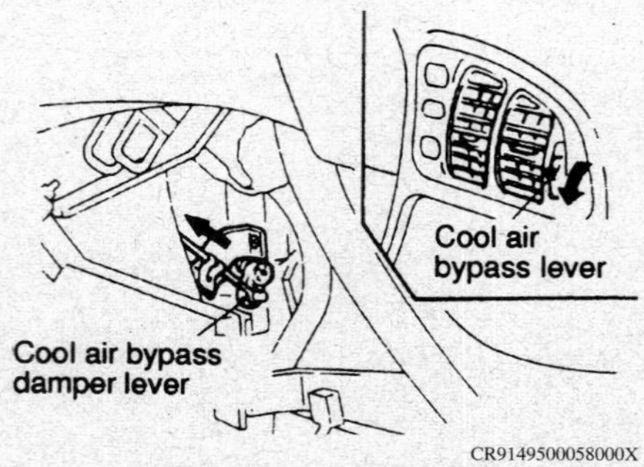

Fig. 8 Center air outlet installation. 2000 Avenger, Sebring Coupe

28. Tilt instrument panel rearward to prevent coolant from leaking, then remove instrument panel from vehicle.
29. Reverse procedure to install.

Sebring & Stratus Coupe

2001–03

1. Remove floor console in numbered sequence, **Fig. 23.**
2. Remove steering wheel and column in sequence, **Fig. 24. Do not hammer on steering wheel to remove,** use removal tool No. MB990803, or equivalent.
3. Remove instrument panel in numbered sequence, **Figs. 25 and 26.**
4. Reverse procedure to install.

Sebring Sedan

2000

Refer to "Breeze & Cirrus" for instrument panel replacement procedure.

2001–04

Refer to "2001–04" in "Sebring Convertible" for instrument panel replacement procedure.

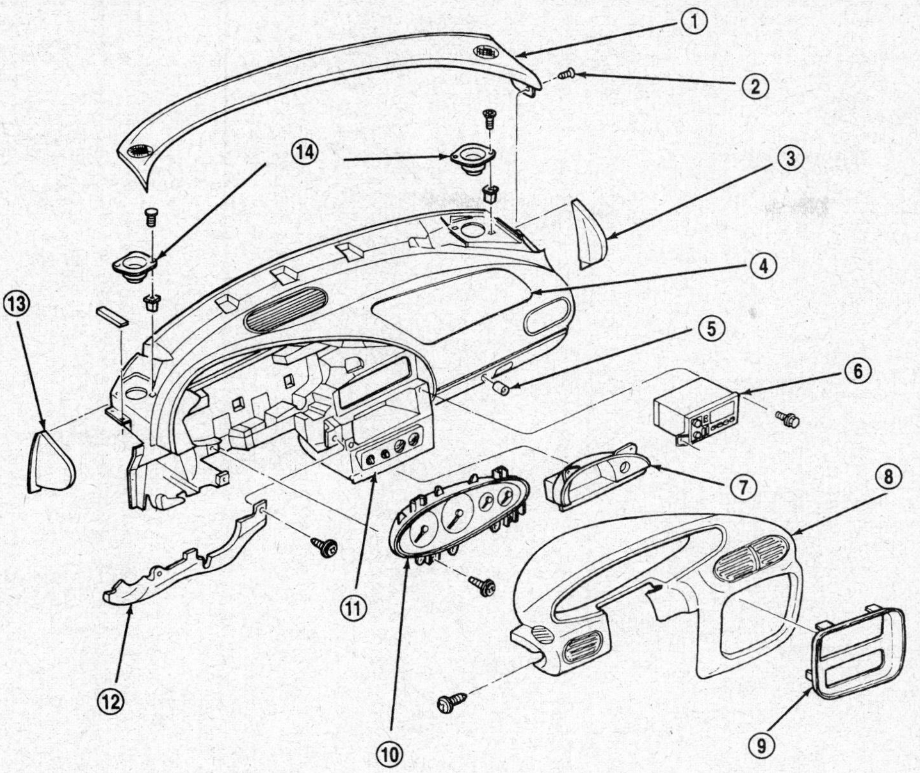

1 – TOP COVER
2 – SCREW
3 – END COVER
4 – PASSENGER AIRBAG MODULE
5 – GLOVE BOX LOCK CYLINDER
6 – RADIO
7 – CUBBY BIN
8 – INSTRUMENT CLUSTER HOOD
9 – CENTER BEZEL
10 – INSTRUMENT CLUSTER
11 – HVAC
12 – KNEE BOLSTER
13 – END COVER
14 – SPEAKERS

CR9149700068000X

Fig. 9 Dash panel replacement. 2000 Breeze, Cirrus, Sebring Convertible, Sebring Sedan & Stratus Sedan

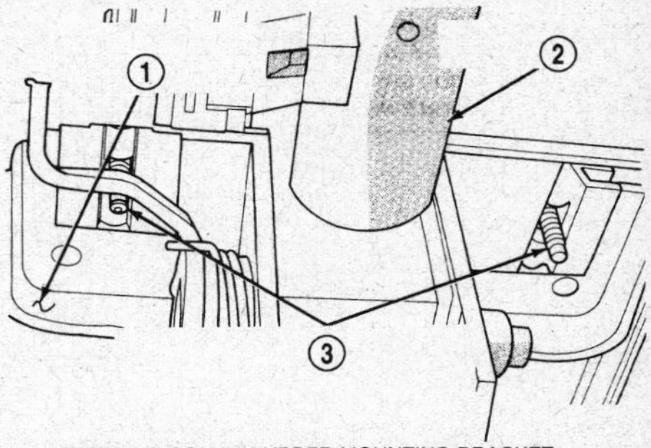

1 – STEERING COLUMN UPPER MOUNTING BRACKET
2 – STEERING COLUMN ASSEMBLY
3 – THESE 2 MOUNTING STUDS MUST BE IN THE CENTER OF THE MOUNTING CAPSULES AS SHOWN BEFORE TIGHTENING AND TORQUING THE UPPER MOUNT NUTS.

CR6040000148000X

Fig. 10 Steering column mounting stud positioning. 2000 Breeze, Cirrus, Sebring Convertible, Sebring Sedan & Stratus Sedan

Stratus Sedan

2000

Refer to "Breeze & Cirrus" for instrument panel replacement procedure.

2001–04

Refer to "2001–04" in "Sebring Convertible" for instrument panel replacement procedure.

TECHNICAL SERVICE BULLETINS

Glove Compartment Door Latch Rattles

2001 SEBRING & STRATUS COUPE

On some these models the glove compartment may exhibit a rattling condition or loose lock cylinder.

This condition may be caused by fatigue of the cylinder retaining tab or crush ribs during cylinder installation.

To correct this condition a revised latch (P/N MR791347), that incorporates a plastic slider to reduce vibration must be installed. Confirm condition originates from glove compartment latch and not items stored in the glove compartment, then inspect slider for material type, **Fig. 27.** If material is plastic, further diagnosis will be required, if material is metal proceed as follows:

1. Insert ignition key into lock and rotate cylinder to the unlocked position.
2. Insert a small screwdriver or pick into lock tumbler opening, then rotate key/lock cylinder counter clockwise 90°. **Lock retaining tab is the furthest tab from opening.**
3. Pull key cylinder from lock assembly.
4. Ensure key cylinder is in the unlocked position and insert key cylinder with key into revised latch assembly.
5. Confirm latch operation prior to installing latch assembly in glove compartment door.
6. Instal latch assembly into glove compartment door and confirm operation.

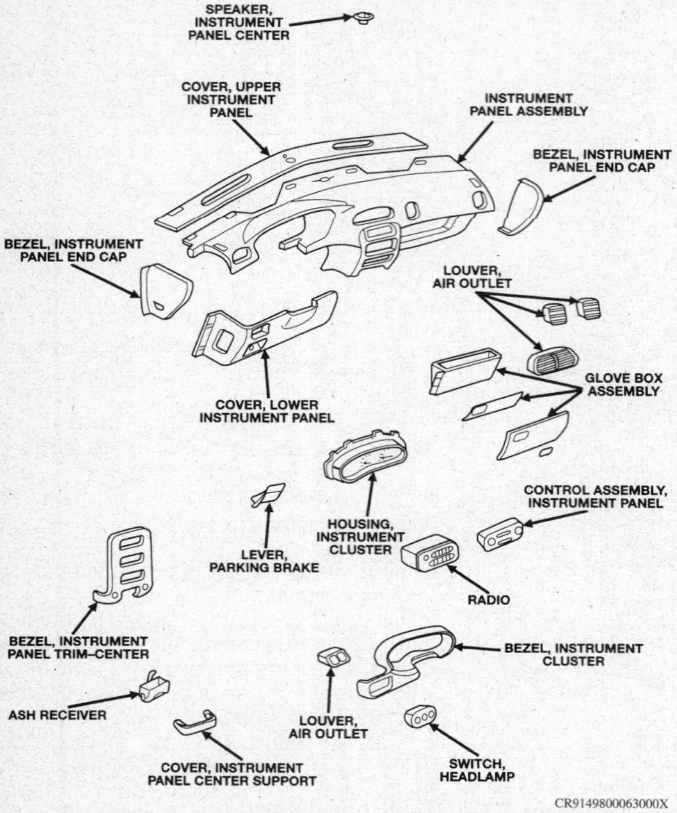

Fig. 11 Exploded view of instrument panel. Concorde

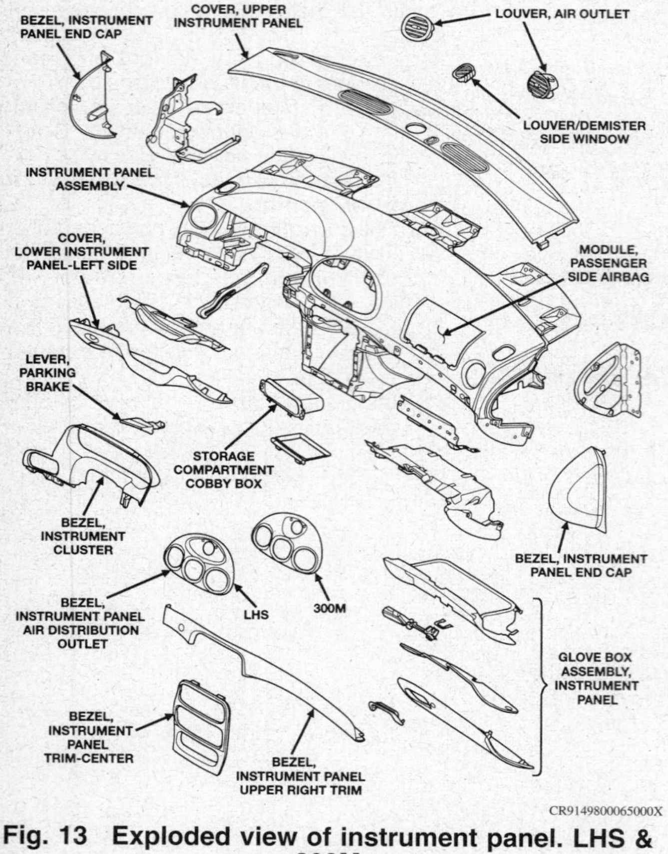

Fig. 13 Exploded view of instrument panel. LHS & 300M

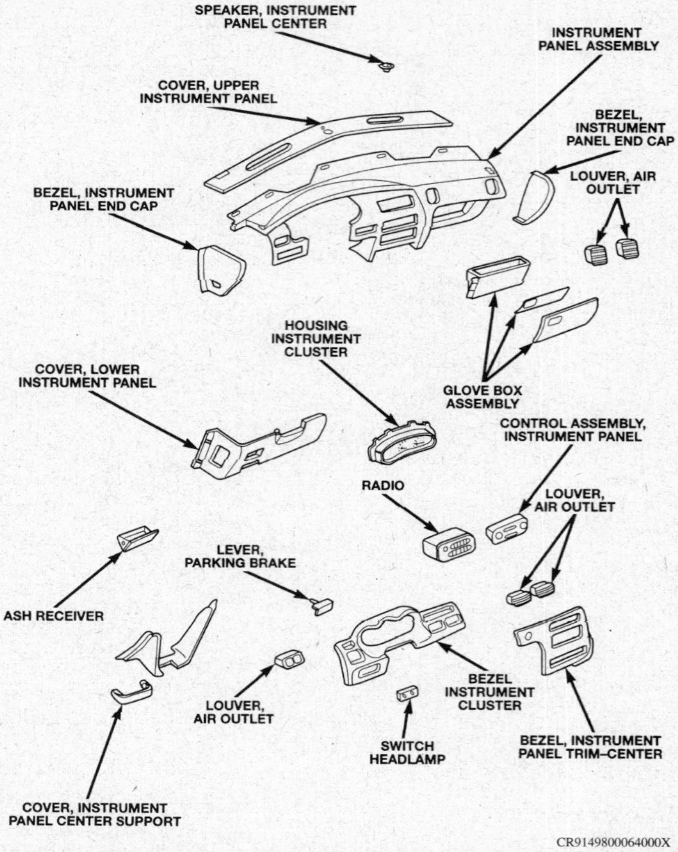

Fig. 12 Exploded view of instrument panel. Intrepid

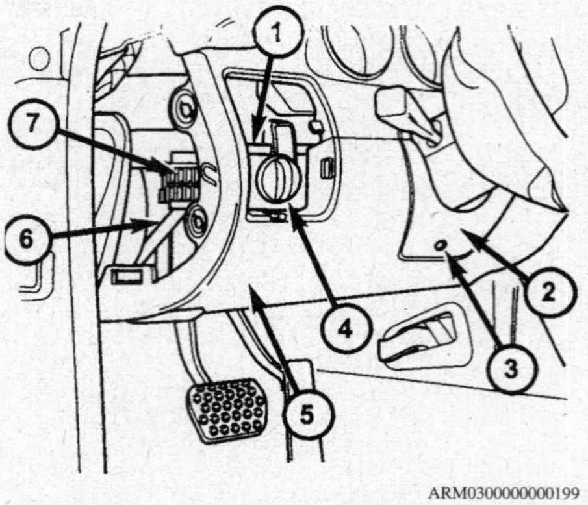

Fig. 14 Illumination control module removal. Crossfire

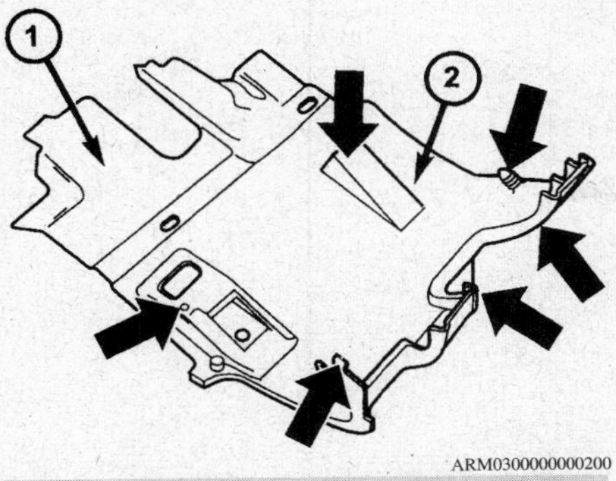

Fig. 15 Underside cover screw removal. Crossfire

Fig. 16 Hood latch release removal. Crossfire

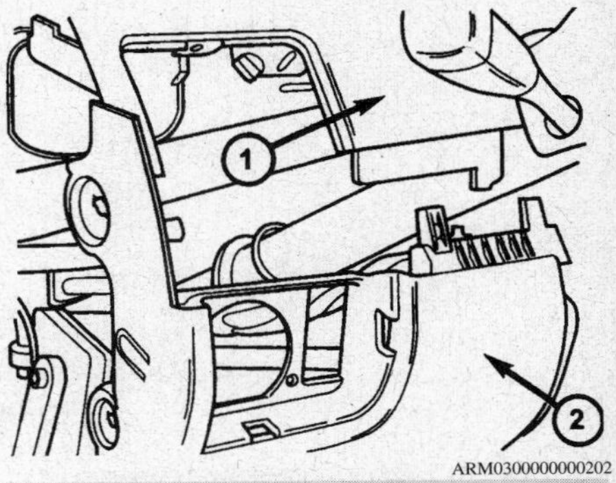

Fig. 17 Lower instrument panel removal. Crossfire

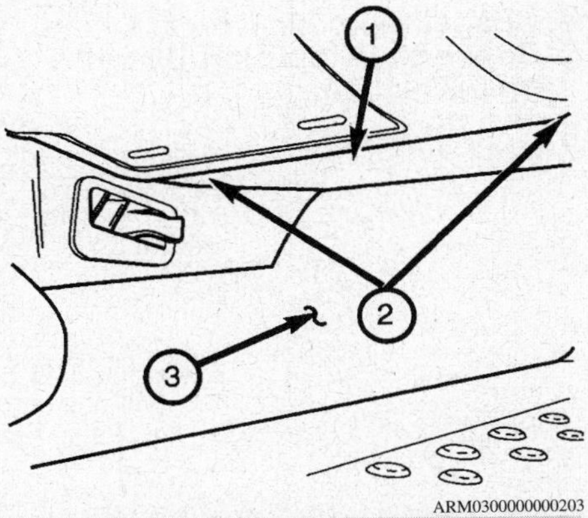

Fig. 18 Lower instrument panel removal. Crossfire

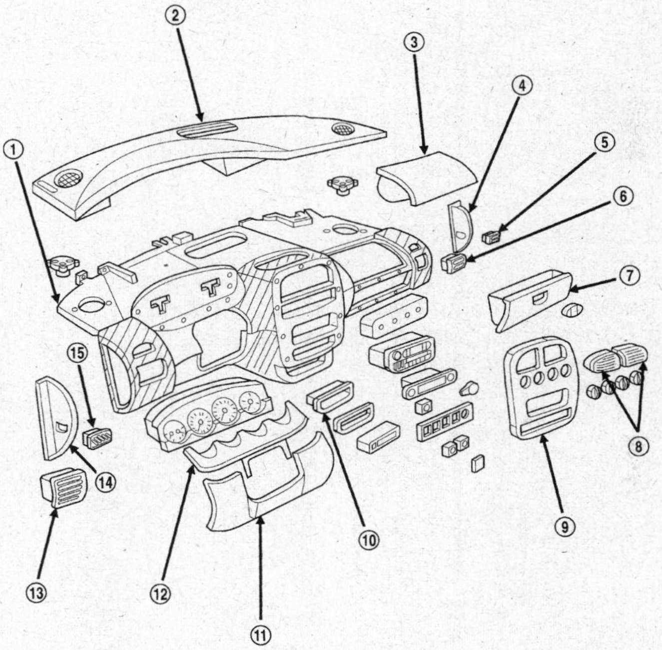

Fig. 19 Exploded view of instrument panel. Neon

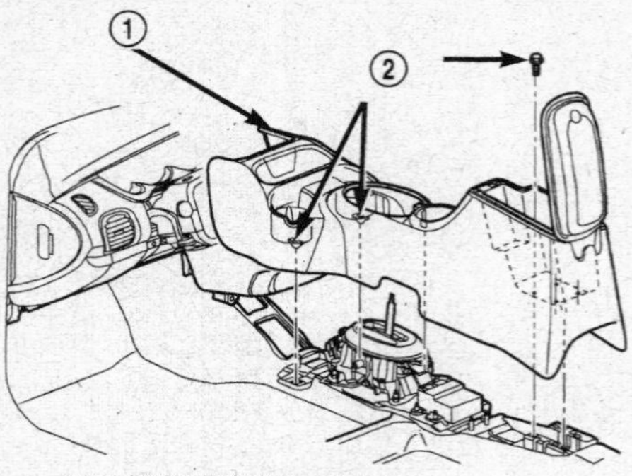

1 - FLOOR CONSOLE WITH ARMREST
2 - ATTACHING SCREWS

CR9140100079000X

Fig. 20 Floor center console. Neon

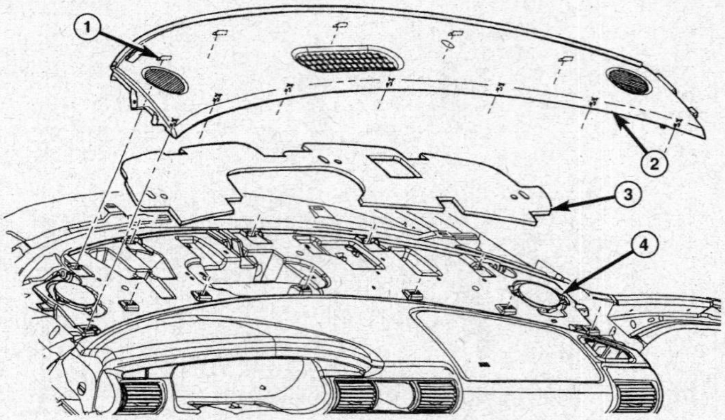

1 - CLIPS
2 - INSTRUMENT PANEL TOP COVER
3 - INSTRUMENT PANEL PAD
4 - INSTRUMENT PANEL ASSEMBLY

CR9140100080000X

Fig. 21 Instrument panel top cover replacement. 2001–04 Sebring Convertible, Sebring Sedan & Stratus Sedan

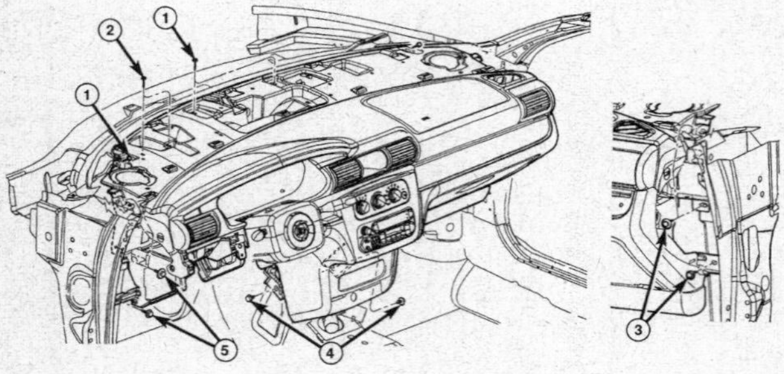

1 - INSTRUMENT PANEL TO PLENUM SCREW
2 - INSTRUMENT PANEL STEERING COLUMN TO COWL PLENUM SCREW
3 - RIGHT COWL SIDE BOLTS
4 - INSTRUMENT PANEL CENTER BRACE TO FLOOR
5 - LEFT COWL SIDE BOLTS

CR9140100081000X

Fig. 22 Instrument panel replacement. 2001–04 Sebring Convertible, Sebring Sedan & Stratus Sedan

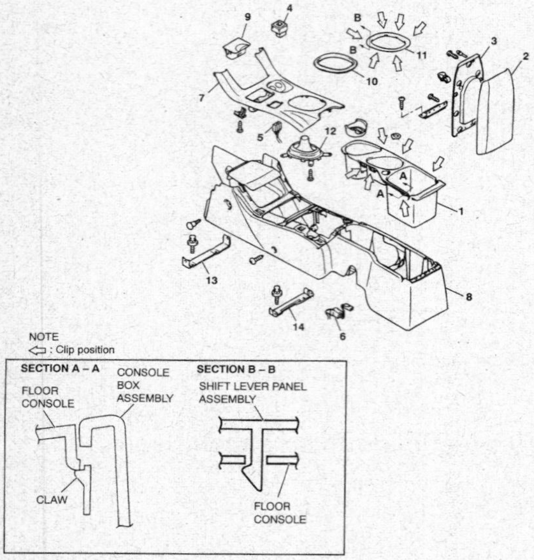

REMOVAL STEPS
1. CONSOLE BOX ASSEMBLY
2. CONSOLE LID
3. CONSOLE LID COVER
4. DOOR MIRROR CONTROL SWITCH
5. DOOR MIRROR CONTROL SWITCH HARNESS
6. ACCCESSARY SOCKET HARNESS
7. FLOOR CONSOLE INDICATOR PANEL

REMOVAL STEPS (Continued)
8. FLOOR CONSOLE
9. ASHTRAY
10. SHIFT LEVER PANEL ASSEMBLY <M/T>
11. GARNISH <A/T>
12. SHIFT LEVER BOOT <M/T>
13. FLOOR CONSOLE BRACKET A
14. FLOOR CONSOLE BRACKET B

CR9140000072000X

Fig. 23 Floor console replacement. 2001–03 Sebring Coupe & Stratus Coupe

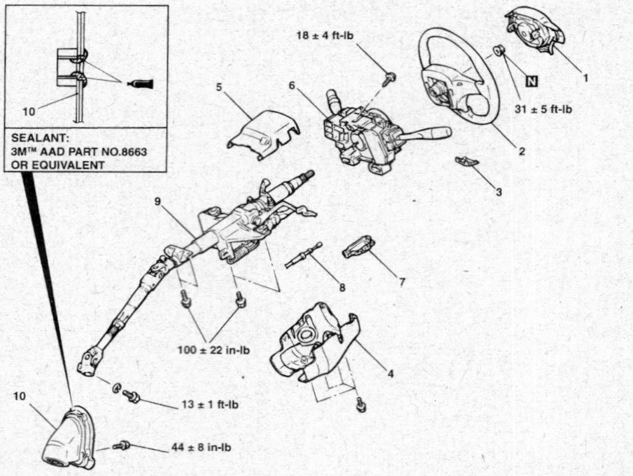

REMOVAL STEPS
1. AIR BAG MODULE
2. STEERING WHEEL
3. COVER
• INSTRUMENT PANEL UNDER COVER
4. LOWER COLUMN COVER
5. UPPER COLUMN COVER

REMOVAL STEPS (Continued)
6. CLOCK SPRING AND COLUMN SWITCH ASSEMBLY
7. COVER <A/T>
8. KEY INTERLOCK CABLE <A/T>
9. STEERING SHAFT ASSEMBLY
10. STEERING COVER ASSEMBLY

CR9140000073000X

Fig. 24 Exploded view of steering column & wheel assembly. 2001–03 Sebring Coupe & Stratus Coupe

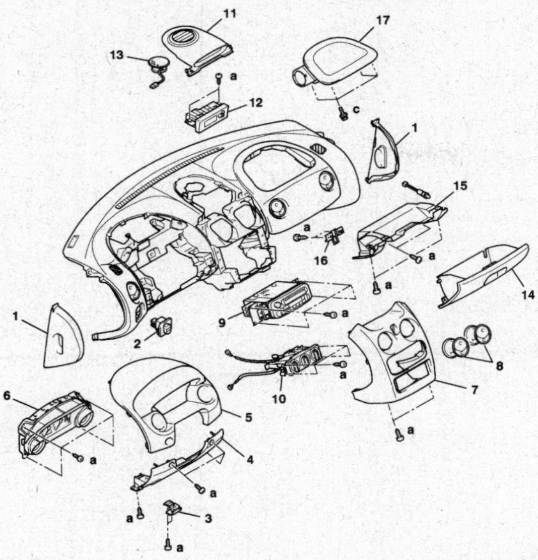

REMOVAL STEPS
1. INSTRUMENT PANEL SIDE COVER
2. FOG LAMP SWITCH ASSEMBLY
3. HOOD LOCK RELEASE HANDLE
4. INSTRUMENT PANEL UNDER COVER
5. METER BEZEL ASSEMBLY
6. COMVINATION METER
7. CENTER PANEL ASSEMBLY
8. AIR OUTLET (CENTER SIDE)
9. RADIO AND TAPE PLAYER ASSEMBLY
10. HEATER CONTROL ASSEMBLY

REMOVAL STEPS (Continued)
11. CENTER HOOD
12. MULTI CENTER DISPLAY
13. CENTER SPEAKER
14. GLOVE BOX, OUTER
15. GLOVE BOX, INNER
16. GLOVE BOX STRIKER
17. AIR BAG MODULE (PASSENGER'S SIDE)

CR9140000074010X

Fig. 25 Instrument panel replacement (Part 1 of 2). 2001–02 Sebring Coupe & Stratus Coupe

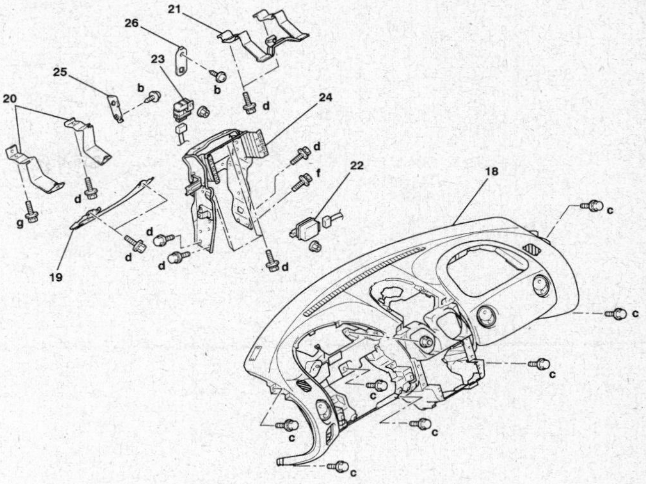

REMOVAL STEPS
18. INSTEUMENT PANEL ASSEMBLY
19. INSTEUMENT PANEL REINFORCEMENT
20. KNEE ABSORBER (DRIVER'S SIDE)
21. KNEE ABSORBER (PASSENGER'S SIDE)
22. AUTO-CRUISE CONTROL-ECU

REMOVAL STEPS (Continued)
23. IMMOBILIZER-ECU
24. INSTURMENT PANEL CENTER REINFORCEMENT
25. FOOT LAMP BRACKET A
26. FOOT LAMP BRACKET B

CR9140000074020X

Fig. 25 Instrument panel replacement (Part 2 of 2). 2001–02 Sebring Coupe & Stratus Coupe

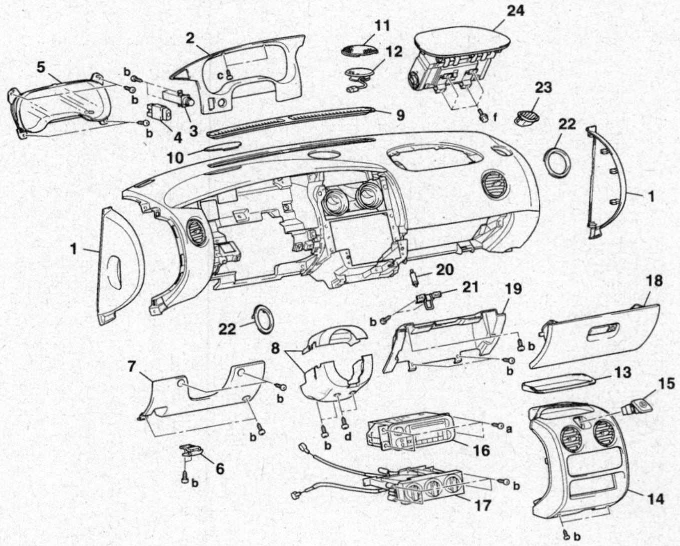

1. INSTRUMENT PANEL SIDE COVER
2. METER BEZEL
3. RHEOSTAT SWITCH
4. FRONT FOG LIGHT SWITCH
5. COMBINATION METER
6. FOOD LOCK RELEASE HANDLE
7. DRIVER'S SIDE UNDER COVER
8. COLUMN COVER
9. DEFROSTER GARNISH
10. INSTRUMENT PANEL UPPER PLUG
11. SPEAKER GARNISH
12. SPEAKER
13. RUBBER MAT
14. CENTER PANEL ASSEMBLY
15. HAZARD SWITCH
16. RADIO AND TAPE PLAYER ASSEMBLY
17. HEATER CONTROL ASSEMBLY
18. GLOVE BOX ASSEMBLY
19. GLOVE BOX CASE
20. GLOVE BOX LIGHT SWITCH ASSEMBLY
21. GLOVE BOX STRIKER
22. AIR OUTLET BEZEL
23. SIDE DEFROSTER GRILLE RH
24. PASSENGER'S SIDE AIR BAG MODULE ASSEMBLY

CR9140200083010X

Fig. 26 Instrument panel replacement (Part 1 of 2). 2003 Sebring Coupe & Stratus Coupe

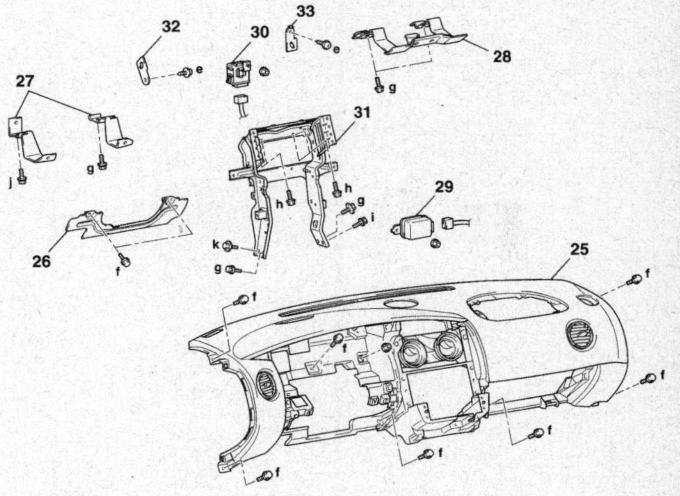

25. INSTRUMENT PANEL ASSEMBLY
26. INSTRUMENT PANEL REINFORCEMENT
27. KNEE ABSORBER (DRIVER'S SIDE)
28. KNEE ABSORBER (PASSENGER'S SIDE)
29. AUTO-CRUISE CONTROL-ECU
30. IMMOBILIZER-ECU
31. INSTRUMENT PANEL CENTER REINFORCEMENT
32. FOOT LAMP BRACKET A
33. FOOT LAMP BRACKET B

CR9140200083020X

Fig. 26 Instrument panel replacement (Part 2 of 2). 2003 Sebring Coupe & Stratus Coupe

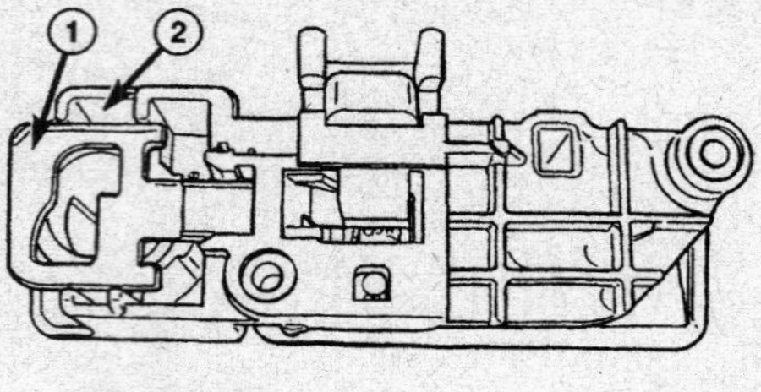

1 - Slider - Plastic
2 - Lock Tumbler Opening

CR9140100077000X

Fig. 27 Glove compartment slider

ANTI-LOCK BRAKES

TABLE OF CONTENTS

Application Chart

Year	Model	System Type
2000	Avenger	Bosch
	Breeze	Teves
	Cirrus	Teves
	Concorde	Teves
	Intrepid	Teves
	LHS	Teves
	Neon	Teves
	Sebring Convertible	Teves
	Sebring Coupe	Bosch
	Stratus	Teves
	300M	Teves
2001	Concorde	Teves
	Intrepid	Teves
	LHS	Teves
	Neon	Teves
	Sebring Convertible	Teves
	Sebring Coupe	Bosch
	Sebring Sedan	Teves
	Stratus Coupe	Bosch
	Stratus Sedan	Teves
	300M	Teves
2002–03	Concorde	Teves
	Intrepid	Teves
	Neon	Teves
	Sebring Convertible	Teves
	Sebring Coupe	Bosch
	Sebring Sedan	Teves
	Stratus Coupe	Bosch
	Stratus Sedan	Teves
2004	Concorde	Teves
	Crossfire	Bosch
	Intrepid	Teves
	Neon	Teves
	Sebring Convertible	Teves
	Sebring Sedan	Teves
	Stratus Sedan	Teves
	300M	Teves

Bosch Anti-Lock Braking System

NOTE: On Air Bag Equipped Models, Refer To "Air Bag System Precautions" Located In The Front Of This Manual For System Disarming & Arming Procedures.

NOTE: Refer To "Computer Relearn Procedures" Located In The Front Of This Manual When Battery Power To The Computer Has Been Interrupted.

NOTE: "Electrical Symbol & Wire Color Code Identification" Located In The Front Of This Manual May Be Used As An Aid When Using Wiring Circuits Found In This Section.

INDEX

PRECAUTIONS

Air Bag Systems

Refer to "Air Bag System Precautions" in the front of this manual for system disarming and arming procedures.

Battery Ground Cable

Prior to service, disconnect battery ground cable and isolate as required.

DESCRIPTION

The Bosch Anti-Lock Braking System (ABS) prevents the wheels from locking up when braking, regardless of the surface conditions. This allows the vehicleto stop in a shorter distance and allows the driver to maintain directional control of the vehicle during heavy braking.

During normal braking conditions, the ABS operates like a conventional diagonally split, hydraulic power assist system. During heavy braking, however, each wheel's braking pressure is modulated according to its speed. To maintain vehicle stability, both rear wheels receive the same signal.

Refer to **Figs. 1 through 3,** for ABS component locations.

TROUBLESHOOTING

Refer to flow charts in "Symptom Based Diagnosis" in "Diagnosis & Testing" when troubleshooting the anti-lock brake system.

DIAGNOSIS & TESTING

Accessing Diagnostic Trouble Codes

WITH SCAN TOOL

1. Connect scan tool MB991502, or equivalently programmed scan tool, to Data Link Connector (DLC) located under lefthand side of instrument panel, **Fig. 4.**
2. Turn ignition switch to On position.
3. Access Diagnostic Trouble Codes (DTCs) following tool manufacturer's instructions.

LESS SCAN TOOL

1. Ground Data Link Connector (DLC) terminal No. 1 using Diagnostic Trouble Code (DTC) check harness tool or equivalent, **Fig. 5.**
2. Turn ignition switch to On position.
3. ABS warning lamp will begin flash any stored DTCs, **Fig. 6.**

Diagnostic Trouble Code Interpretation

Refer to **Fig. 7,** for diagnostic trouble code interpretation.

Wiring Diagrams

Refer to **Figs. 8 through 13,** for Anti-Lock Brake System (ABS) wiring diagrams.

Connector Pin Identification

Refer to **Figs. 14 through 18,** for ABS connector terminal identification.

Diagnostic Tests

2000

Refer to **Figs. 19 through 25,** for ABS diagnostic tests.

2001–02

Refer to **Figs. 26 through 29,** for ABS diagnostic tests.

2003

Refer to **Figs. 30 through 33,** for ABS diagnostic tests.

Symptom Based Diagnosis

2000

Refer to **Figs. 34 through 37,** for symptom based diagnosis.

2001-02

Refer to **Figs. 38 through 40,** for symptom based diagnosis.

2003

Refer to **Figs. 41 through 43,** for symptom based diagnosis.

2004

CROSSFIRE

ABS

Refer to **Figs. 44 through 60,** for ABS diagnostic tests.

BAS

Refer to **Figs. 61 through 71,** for BAS diagnostic tests.

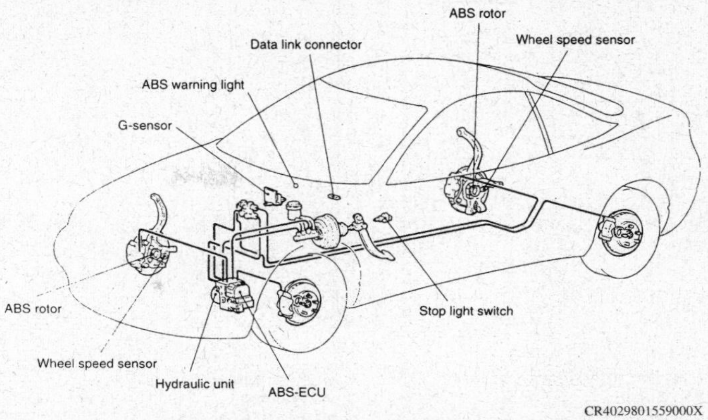

Fig. 1 ABS component locations. Avenger & 2000 Sebring Coupe

Clearing Diagnostic Trouble Codes

WITH SCAN TOOL

1. Connect scan tool No. MB991502, or equivalently programmed scan tool, to Data Link Connector (DLC) located under lefthand side of instrument panel, **Fig. 4.**
2. Turn ignition switch to On position.
3. Erase Diagnostic Trouble Codes (DTCs) following tool manufacturer's instructions.

LESS SCAN TOOL

If ABS-ECU functions have stopped because of the fail-safe function, the diagnostic trouble codes cannot be erased.

2000

1. Activate stop lamp switch.
2. Turn ignition switch to On position.
3. Stop lamp will operate 10 times in succession, **Fig. 72.**
4. Trouble codes should now be erased.
5. If ABS lamp remains illuminated, refer to "Diagnosis & Testing."

2001-03

1. Ground Data Link Connector (DLC) terminal No. 1 using Diagnostic Trouble Code (DTC) check harness tool or equivalent, **Fig. 5.**
2. Depress and hold brake pedal.
3. Turn ignition switch to On position.
4. Within three seconds of turning ignition switch to On position release brake pedal.
5. Press and release brake pedal at least 10 continuous times.
6. Turn ignition switch to LOCK position.

Component Tests

ABS ECU

TERMINAL VOLTAGE

1. Measure voltage between ground terminals Nos. 16 and 19 and respective terminals.
2. Compare result, **Figs. 14 and 15.**
3. If voltage varies from standard value, inspect corresponding sensor, actuator and related wiring.

HARNESS-SIDE TERMINAL RESISTANCE & CONTINUITY

1. Turn ignition switch to OFF position and disconnect ABS-ECU connectors.
2. Measure resistance between terminals, **Figs. 16 and 17.**
3. If resistance varies from standard value, inspect corresponding sensor, actuator and related wiring.

WHEEL SPEED SENSOR

1. Raise and support vehicle, release parking brake.
2. Disconnect ABS-ECU harness connector.
3. Rotate wheel ½–1 turn per second and measure voltage between terminals, **Fig. 73.**
4. **On 2000 models,** reading should be 70 mvolts. or more
5. **On 2001–03 models,** reading should be 42–300 mvolts.
6. **On all models,** if voltage is low, inspect for too great clearance between sensor pole and ABS rotor. Although not adjustable, distance between sensor and rotor's toothed surface should be 1.11–1.12 inches.
7. Ensure no metallic foreign material had adhered to speed sensor tip.
8. Ensure speed senor pole is not damaged.
9. Measure resistance between speed sensor terminals, noting the following:
   a. **On 2000 models,** if resistance is not 1 –1.5 kohms, replace sensor.
   b. **On 2001–03 models,** if resistance is not 1.28–1.92 kohms, replace sensor.
10. **On all models,** disconnect all speed sensor connectors.
11. Measure resistance between connector terminals Nos. 1 and 2 to speed sensor body. If circuit is not open, replace sensor.

HYDRAULIC UNIT

1. Raise and support vehicle.
2. Release parking brake and feel drag force on each wheel.
3. Turn ignition key to LOCK position and Connect scan tool No. MB991502, or equivalently programmed scan tool, to Data Link Connector (DLC) located under lefthand side of the instrument panel, **Fig. 4.**
4. Ensure shift lever is in Neutral position.
5. Force-drive ABS actuator using scan tool.
6. Turn wheel by hand and inspect change in braking force when brake pedal is depressed.
7. Compare brake system operation, **Fig. 74.**
8. Ensure actuator force-driven braking is 176–220 lbs., at front wheels and 132–175 lbs., are rear wheels.
9. If brakes do not operate as specified, refer to **Fig. 75,** for diagnosis and repair.

SYSTEM SERVICE

Brake System Bleed

Refer to "Hydraulic Brake Systems" chapter in Volume 1 for brake bleeding procedures.

Component Replacement

HYDRAULIC CONTROL UNIT (HCU)

The hydraulic unit must not be disassembled, its nuts and bolts must not be loosened. Do not drop or subject the hydraulic unit to any impact shocks. Do not turn hydraulic unit upside down or lay unit on its side.

2000

1. Drain brake fluid into suitable container.
2. Remove lefthand fender inner splash shield.
3. Remove lefthand headlamp assembly.
4. **On models equipped with non-turbocharged engine,** remove air cleaner assembly, ECM and relay box bracket.
5. **On models equipped with turbocharged engine,** remove power steering oil reservoir mounting bolts, then

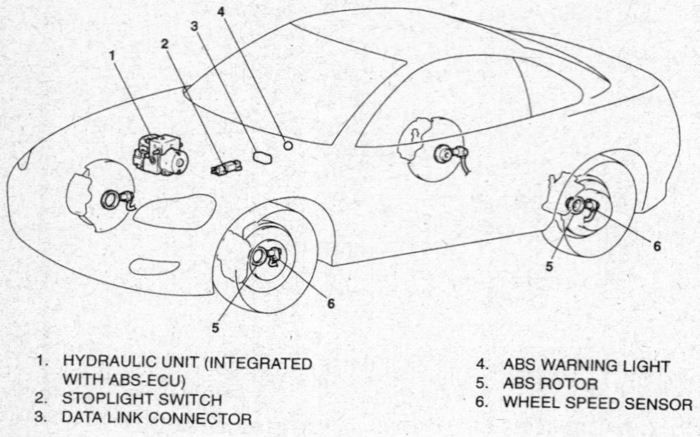

Fig. 2 ABS component locations. 2001–03 Stratus Coupe & Sebring Coupe

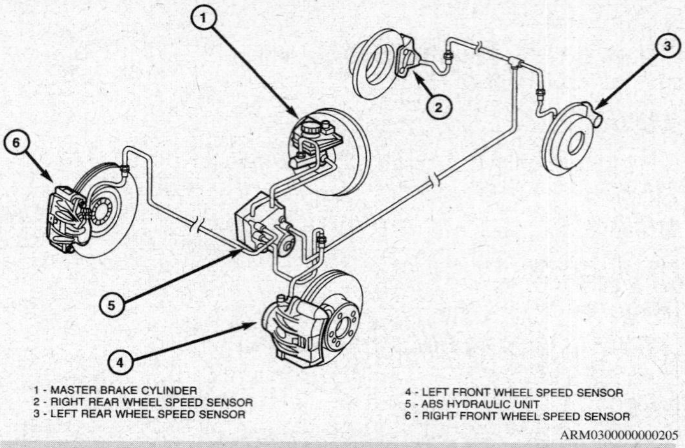

Fig. 3 ABS component locations Crossfire

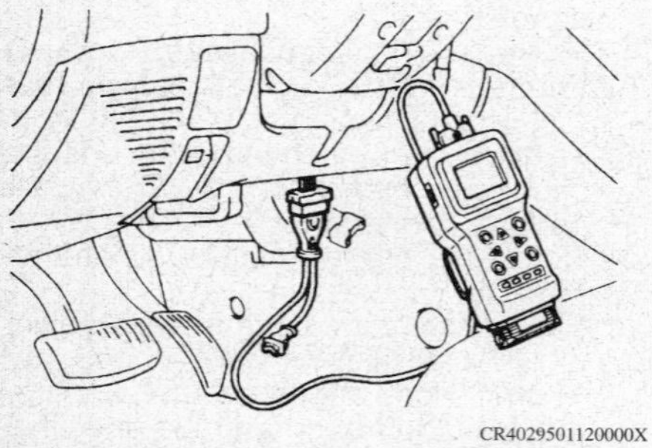

Fig. 4 Data Link Connector (DLC) location

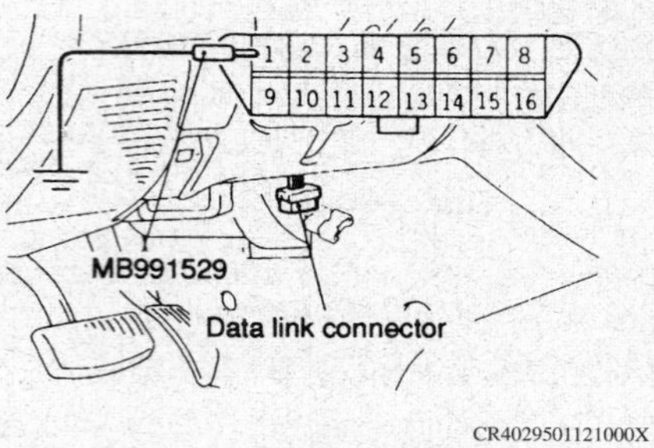

Fig. 5 DLC grounding

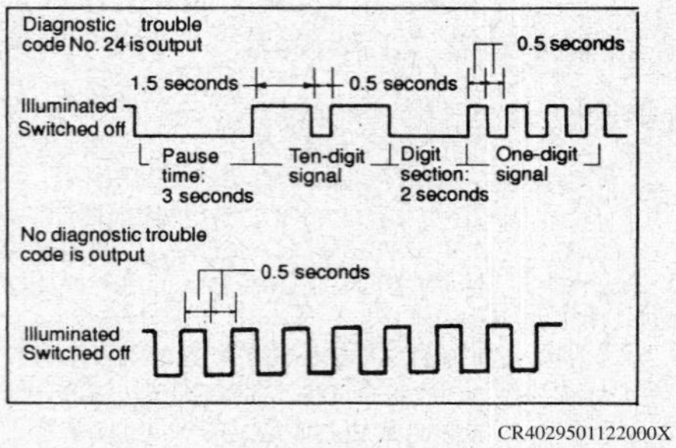

Fig. 6 ABS warning lamp operation

power steering pressure and return pipe clamp mounting bolts.

6. **On all models,** disconnect harness connector. **Fig. 76.**
7. Mark brake lines for installation alignment, then remove them.
8. Remove mounting nuts and HCU.
9. Remove mounting bolts and bracket.
10. Reverse procedure to install. **Torque** hydraulic brake line fittings to 11 ft. lbs.

2001-03

1. Remove mounting bolts, nuts and strut tower bar.
2. Drain brake fluid into suitable container, **Fig. 77.**
3. Mark brake lines for installation alignment, then remove them.
4. Remove mounting nuts and HCU.
5. Remove mounting bolts and bracket.
6. Reverse procedure to install, noting the following:
   a. **Torque** bracket mounting bolts to 18–26 ft. lbs.
   b. **Torque** brake line fittings to 10–12 ft. lbs.

2004

1. Clean HCU, ensure that debris is cleared away from brake lines.
2. Drain brake fluid into suitable container.
3. Mark brake lines for installation alignment, then remove them.
4. Remove mounting nuts and HCU.
5. Remove mounting bolts and bracket.
6. Reverse procedure to install.

WHEEL SPEED SENSORS

EXCEPT CROSSFIRE

Refer to **Figs. 78 and 79,** when replacing wheel speed sensors.

CROSSFIRE

Front

1. Remove flange to steering knuckle attaching bolts.
2. Remove wheel speed sensor from steering knuckle.
3. Disconnect wheel speed brake wear indicator electrical harness from body connector.
4. Reverse procedure to install.

Rear

1. Remove rear wheel speed sensor to rear knuckle attaching bolt.
2. Remove rear wheel speed sensor from knuckle.
3. Remove rubber grommet from body, unhook wheel speed sensor wire harness from mount.
4. Disconnect electrical harness connector.
5. Reverse procedure to install.

ABS ECU

The ABS ECU is incorporated with the Hydraulic Control Unit (HCU). Refer to "Hydraulic Control Unit" for ABS ECU replacement procedures.

Code	Description
AVENGER & 2000 SEBRING COUPE	
11	Wheel Speed Sensor Circuit Open
12	Wheel Speed Sensor Circuit Open
13	Wheel Speed Sensor Circuit Open
14	Wheel Speed Sensor Circuit Open
15	Wheel Speed Sensor System
16	Power Supply System
21	Front Righthand Wheel Speed Sensor Short Circuit
22	Front Lefthand Wheel Speed Sensor Short Circuit
23	Rear Righthand Wheel Speed Sensor Short Circuit
24	Rear Lefthand Wheel Speed Sensor Short Circuit
38	Stop Lamp Switch System
41	Front Righthand Inlet Solenoid Valve
42	Front Lefthand Inlet Solenoid Valve
43	Rear Righthand Inlet Solenoid Valve
44	Rear Lefthand Inlet Solenoid Valve
45	Front Righthand Outlet Solenoid Valve
46	Front Lefthand Outlet Solenoid Valve
47	Rear Righthand Outlet Solenoid Valve
48	Rear Lefthand Outlet Solenoid Valve
51	Valve Power Supply
53	Pump Motor
63	ABS-ECU
2001–03 STRATUS COUPE & SEBRING COUPE	
11	Wheel Speed Sensor Open Or Short Circuit
12	Wheel Speed Sensor Open Or Short Circuit
13	Wheel Speed Sensor Open Or Short Circuit
14	Wheel Speed Sensor Open Or Short Circuit
15	Wheel Speed Sensor Abnormal Output Signal
16	Power Supply
21	Front Righthand Wheel Speed Sensor
22	Front Lefthand Wheel Speed Sensor
23	Rear Righthand Wheel Speed Sensor
24	Rear Lefthand Wheel Speed Sensor
31	Traction Control Front Lefthand Inlet Solenoid Valve
32	Traction Control Front Lefthand Outlet Solenoid Valve
33	Traction Control Front Righthand Inlet Solenoid Valve
34	Traction Control Front Righthand Outlet Solenoid Valve
38	Stop Lamp Switch System
41	ABS Front Righthand Inlet Solenoid Valve
42	ABS Front Lefthand Inlet Solenoid Valve
43	ABS Rear Righthand Inlet Solenoid Valve
44	ABS Rear Lefthand Inlet Solenoid Valve
45	ABS Front Righthand Outlet Solenoid Valve
46	ABS Front Lefthand Outlet Solenoid Valve
47	ABS Rear Righthand Outlet Solenoid Valve
48	ABS Rear Lefthand Outlet Solenoid Valve
51	Valve Power Supply
53	Pump Power
63	ABS-ECU

Fig. 7 DTC interpretation

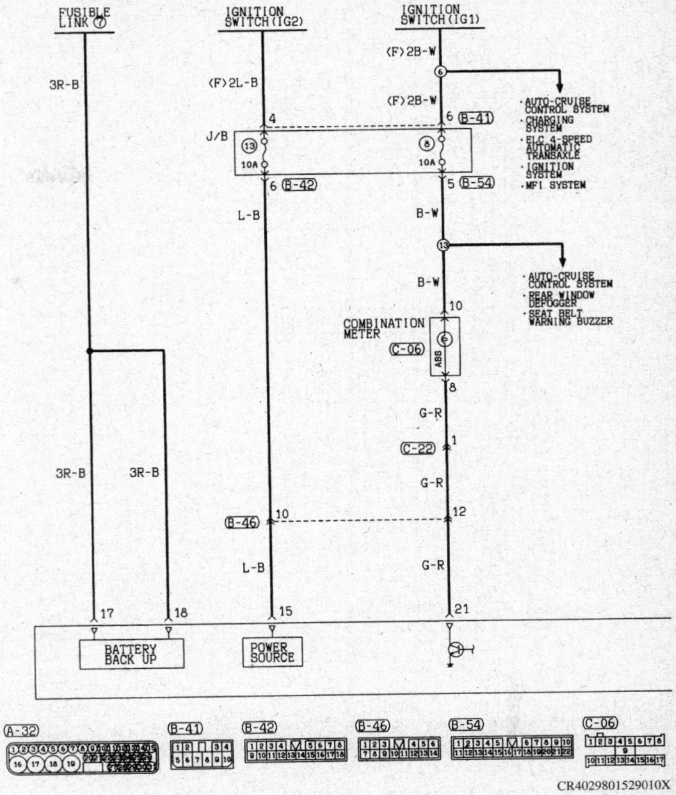

Fig. 8 Wiring diagram (Part 1 of 5). Avenger & 2000 Sebring Coupe

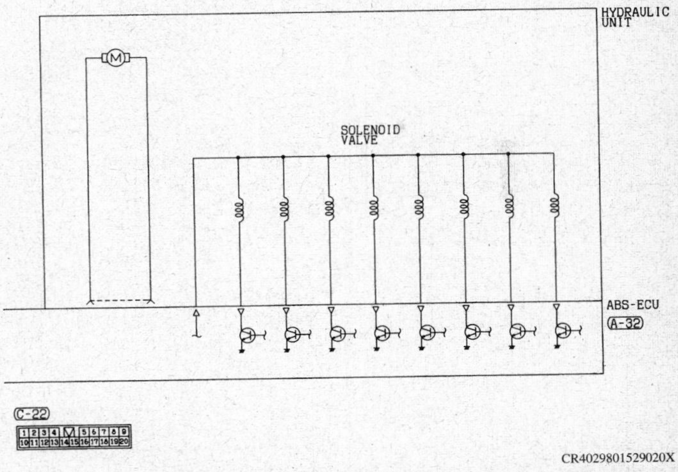

Fig. 8 Wiring diagram (Part 2 of 5). Avenger & 2000 Sebring Coupe

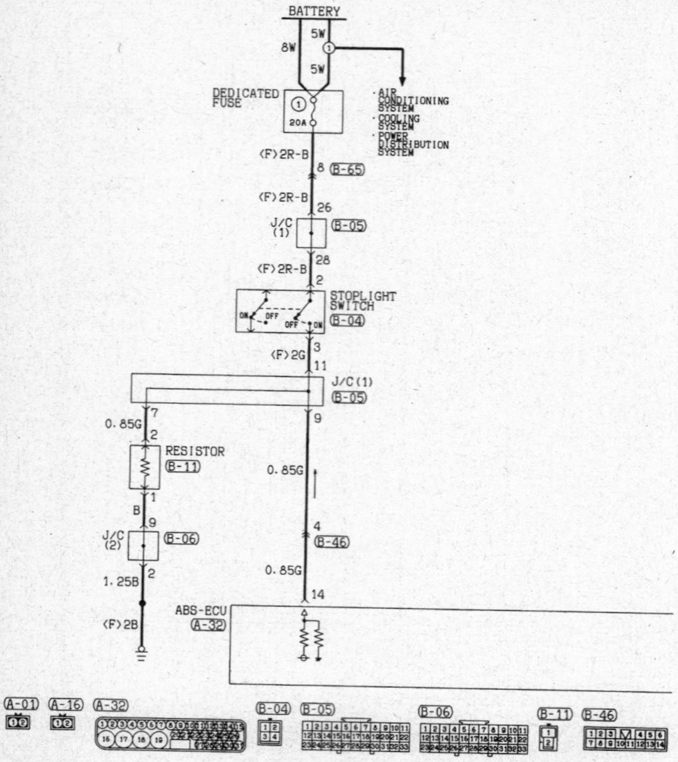

Fig. 8 Wiring diagram (Part 3 of 5). Avenger & 2000 Sebring Coupe

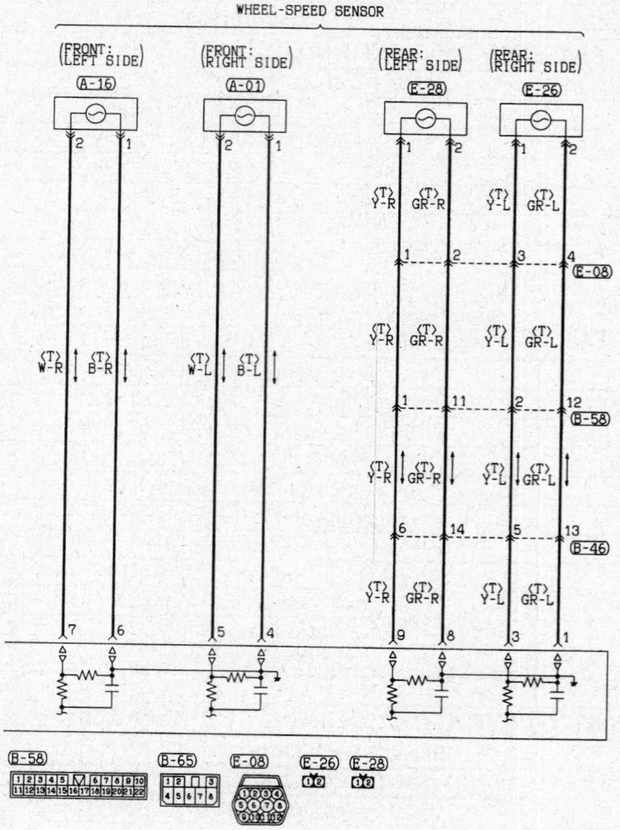

Fig. 8 Wiring diagram (Part 4 of 5). Avenger & 2000 Sebring Coupe

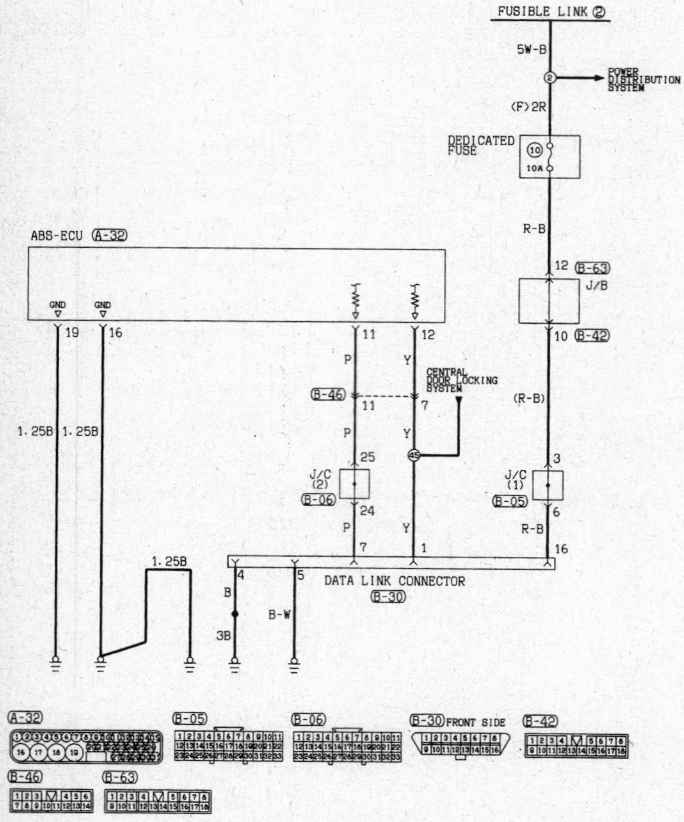

Fig. 8 Wiring diagram (Part 5 of 5). Avenger & 2000 Sebring Coupe

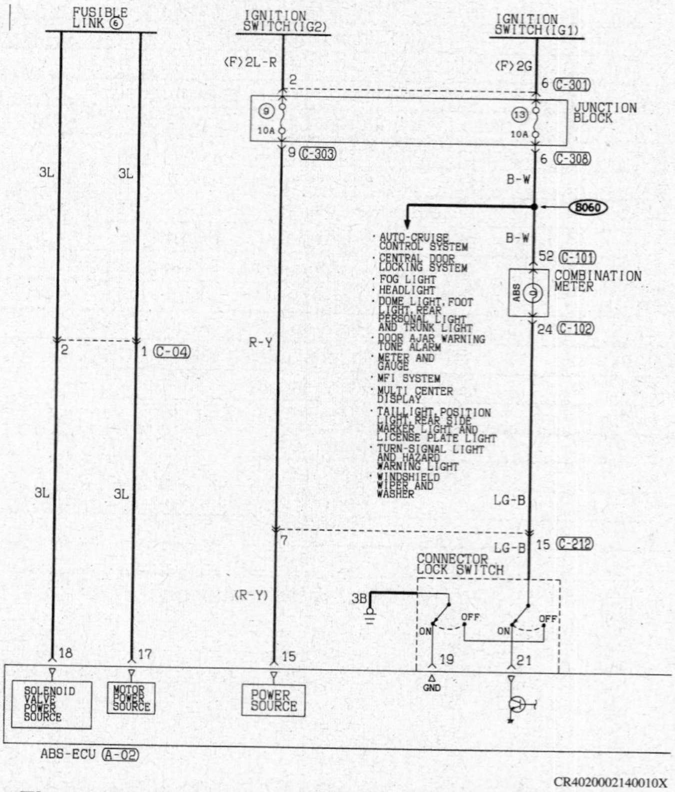

Fig. 9 Wiring diagram (Part 1 of 4). 2001 Sebring Coupe & Stratus Coupe less traction control

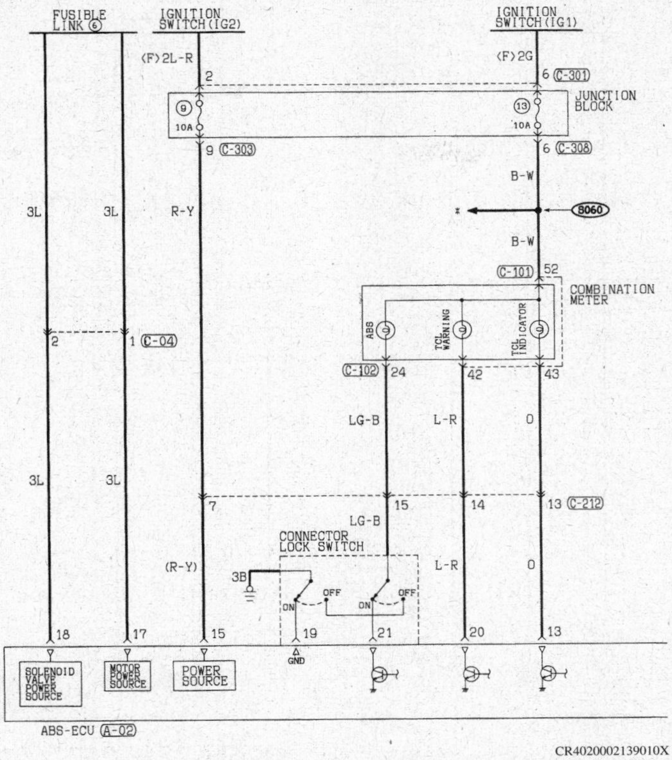

Fig. 9 Wiring diagram (Part 1 of 4). 2001 Sebring Coupe & Stratus Coupe w/traction control system

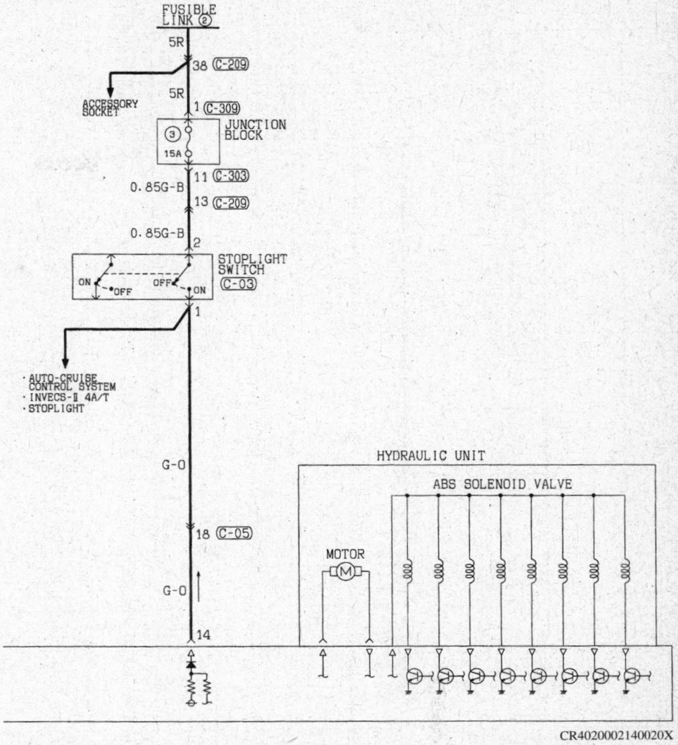

Fig. 9 Wiring diagram (Part 2 of 4). 2001 Sebring Coupe & Stratus Coupe

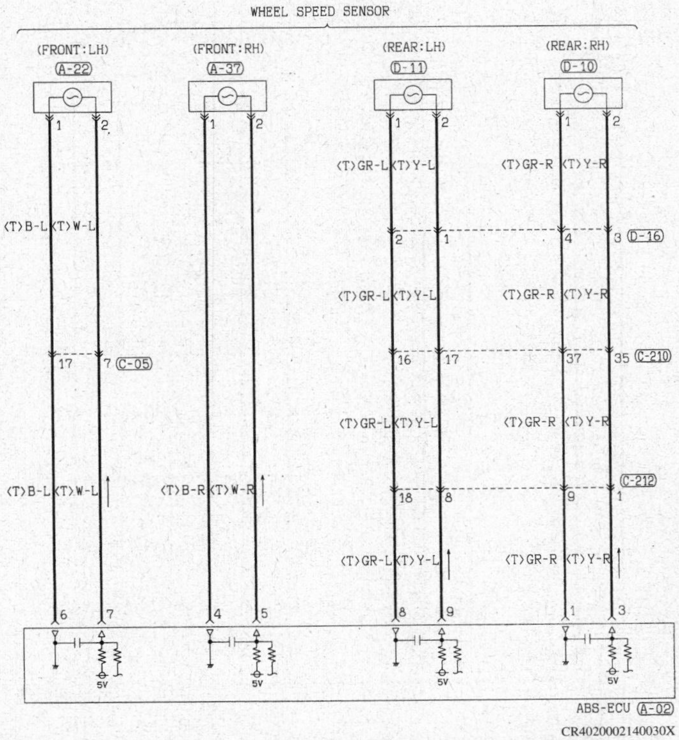

Fig. 9 Wiring diagram (Part 3 of 4). 2001 Sebring Coupe & Stratus Coupe

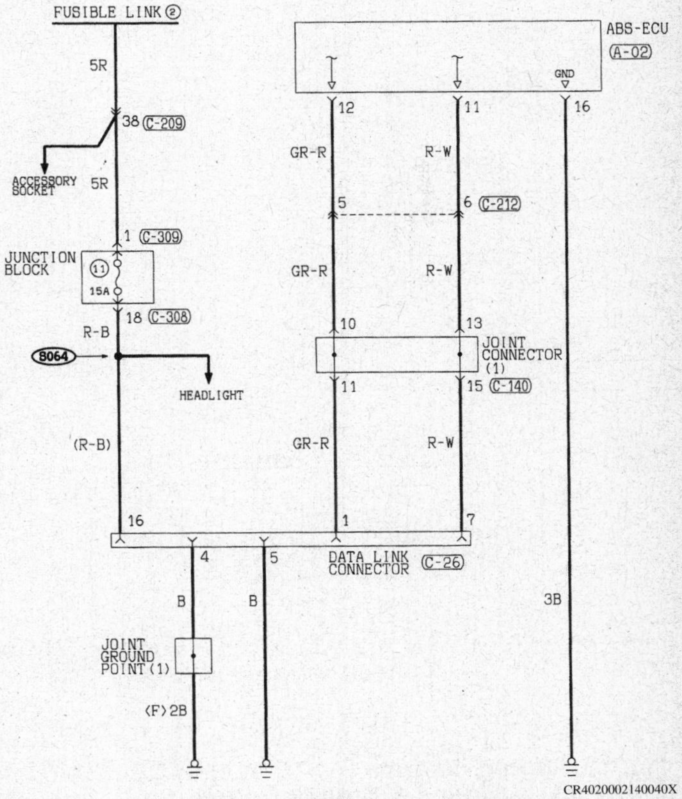

Fig. 9 Wiring diagram (Part 4 of 4). 2001 Sebring Coupe & Stratus Coupe

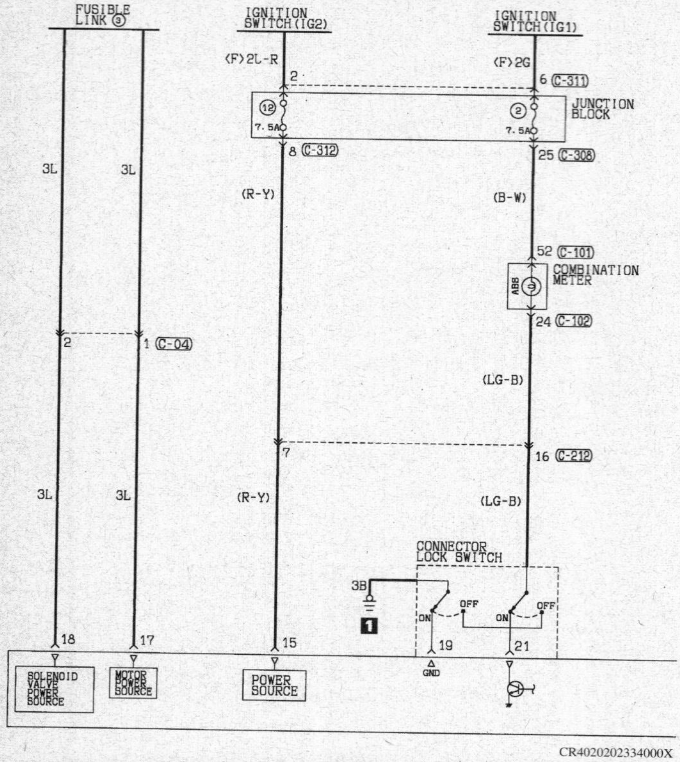

Fig. 10 Wiring diagram (Part 1 of 4). 2002 Sebring Coupe & Stratus Coupe less traction control

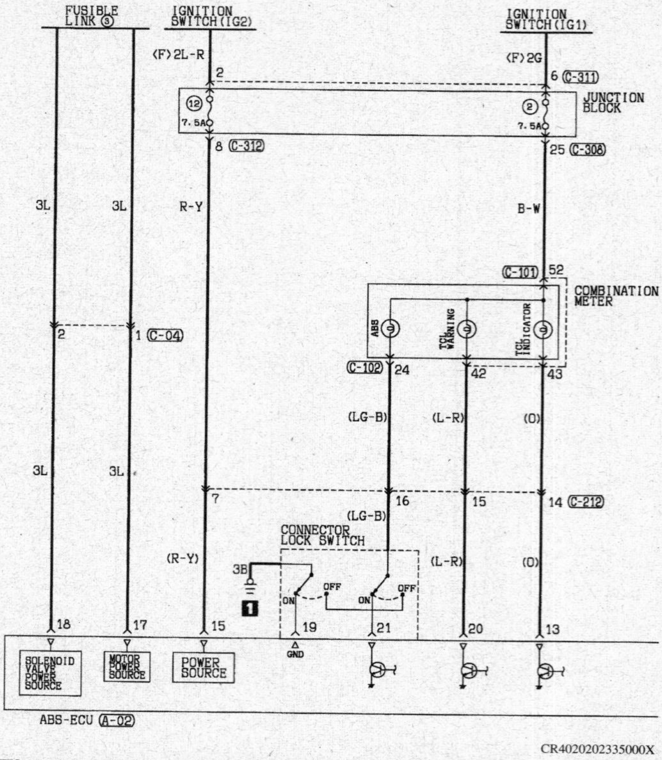

Fig. 10 Wiring diagram (Part 1 of 4). 2002 Sebring Coupe & Stratus Coupe w/traction control

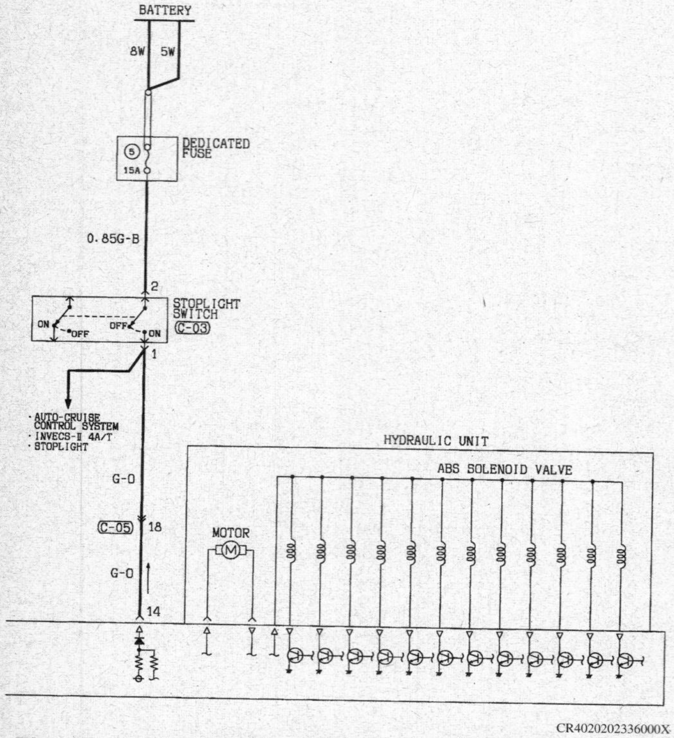

Fig. 10 Wiring diagram (Part 2 of 4). 2002 Sebring Coupe & Stratus Coupe

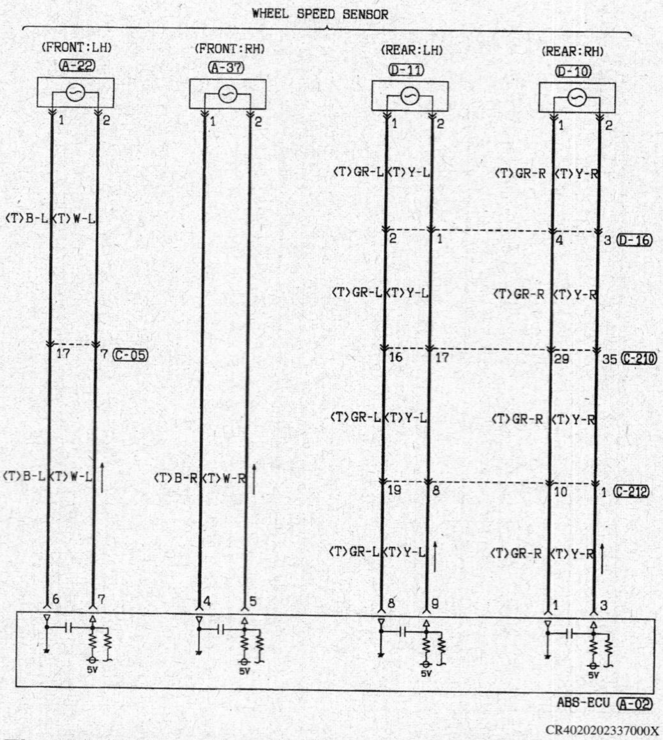

Fig. 10 Wiring diagram (Part 3 of 4). 2002 Sebring Coupe & Stratus Coupe

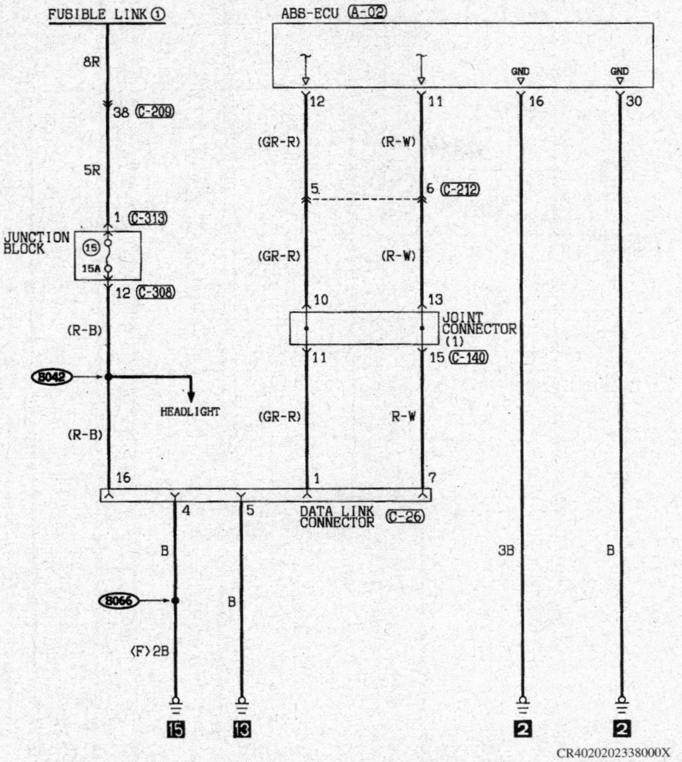

Fig. 10 Wiring diagram (Part 4 of 4). 2002 Sebring Coupe & Stratus Coupe

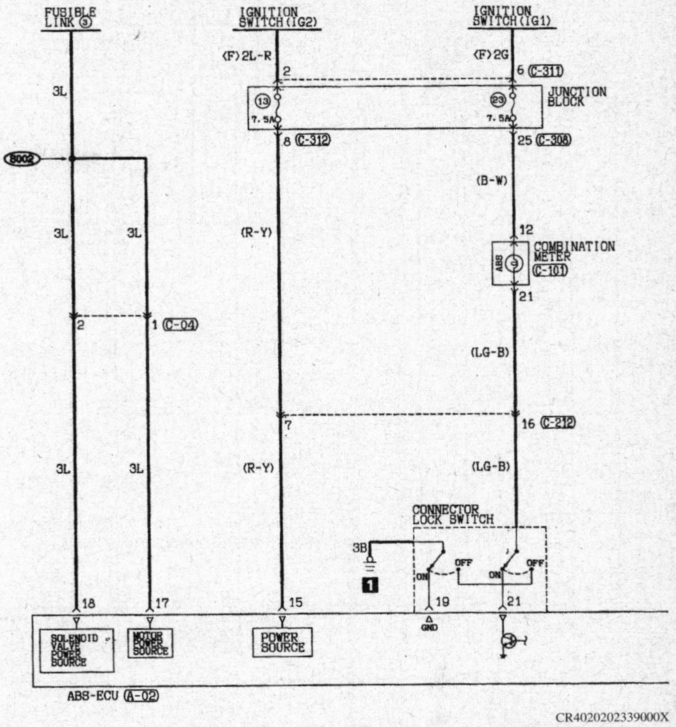

Fig. 11 Wiring diagram (Part 1 of 4). 2003 Sebring Coupe & Stratus Coupe less traction control

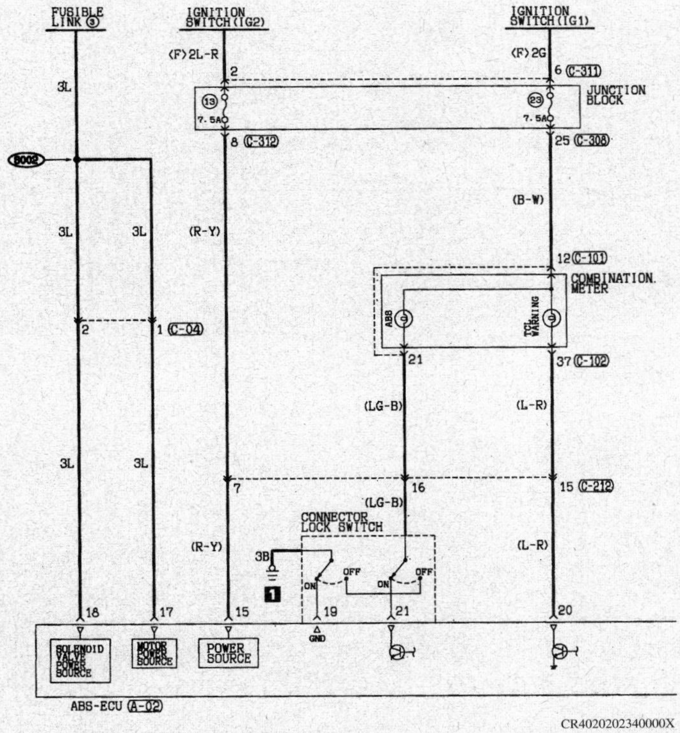

Fig. 11 Wiring diagram (Part 1 of 4). 2003 Sebring Coupe & Stratus Coupe w/traction control

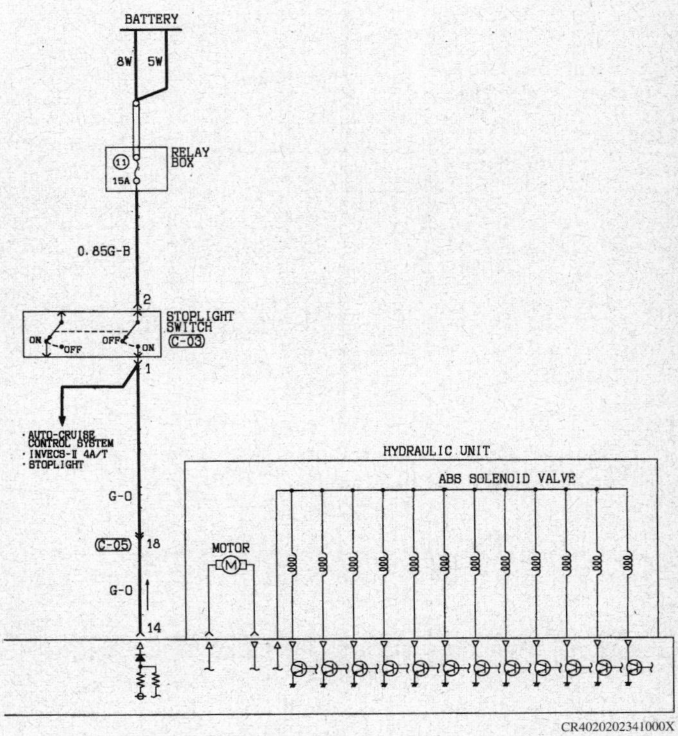

Fig. 11 Wiring diagram (Part 2 of 4). 2003 Sebring Coupe & Stratus Coupe

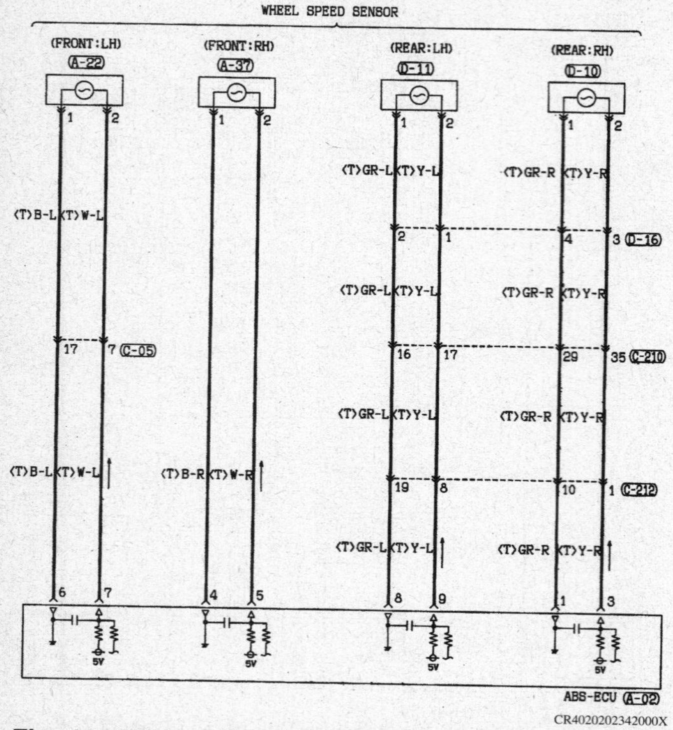

Fig. 11 Wiring diagram (Part 3 of 4). 2003 Sebring Coupe & Stratus Coupe

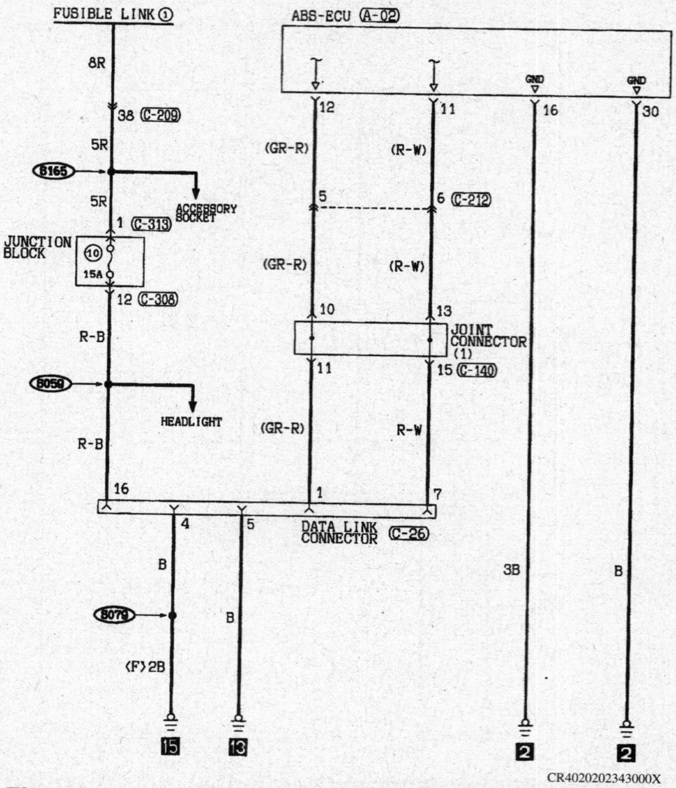

Fig. 11 Wiring diagram (Part 4 of 4). 2003 Sebring Coupe & Stratus Coupe

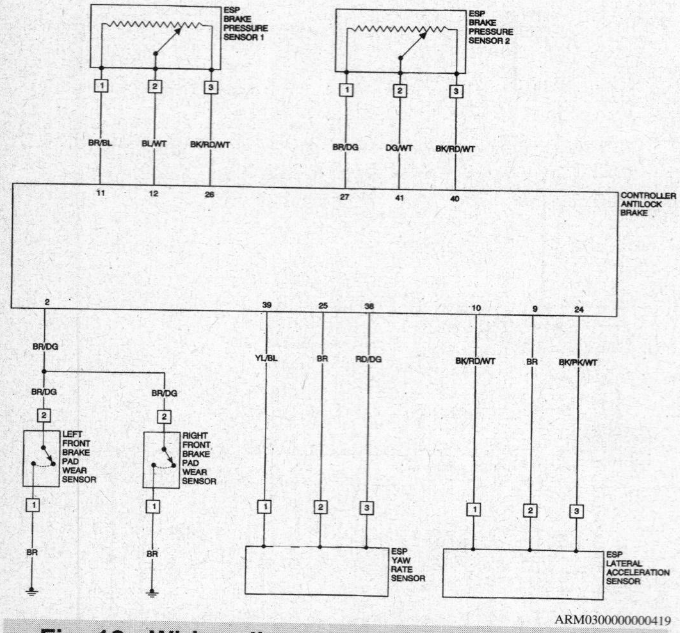

Fig. 12 Wiring diagram (Part 1 of 3). Crossfire w/ABS

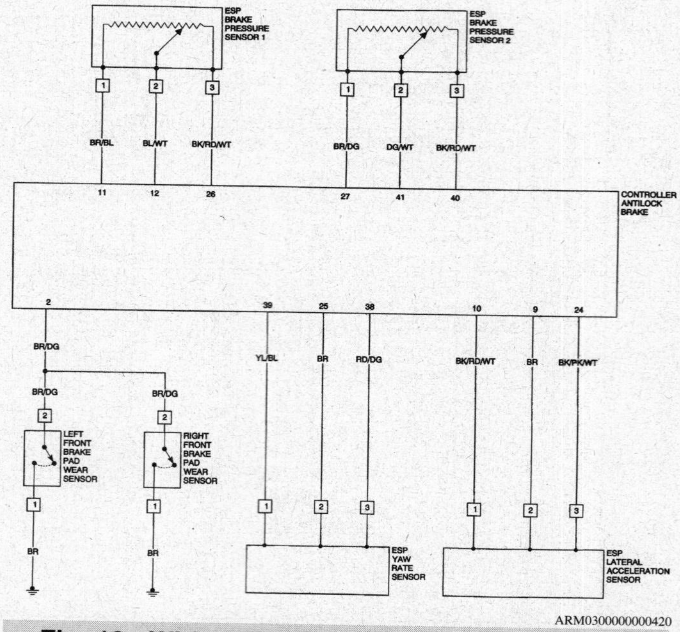

Fig. 12 Wiring diagram (Part 2 of 3). Crossfire w/ABS

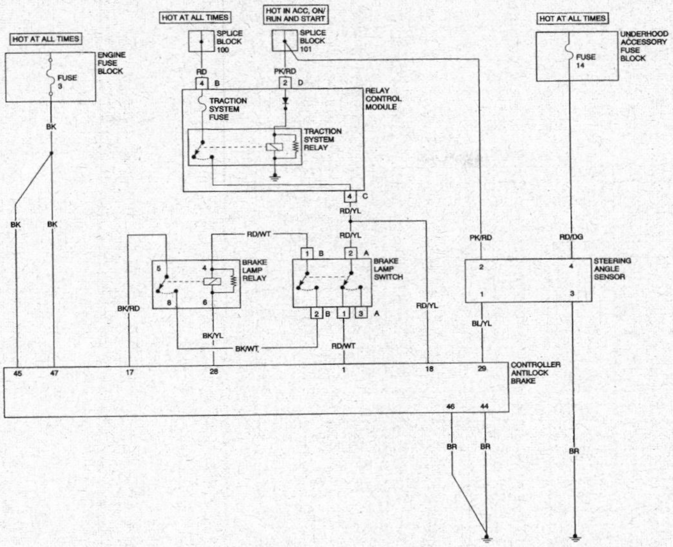

ARM0300000000421

Fig. 12 Wiring diagram (Part 3 of 3). Crossfire w/ABS

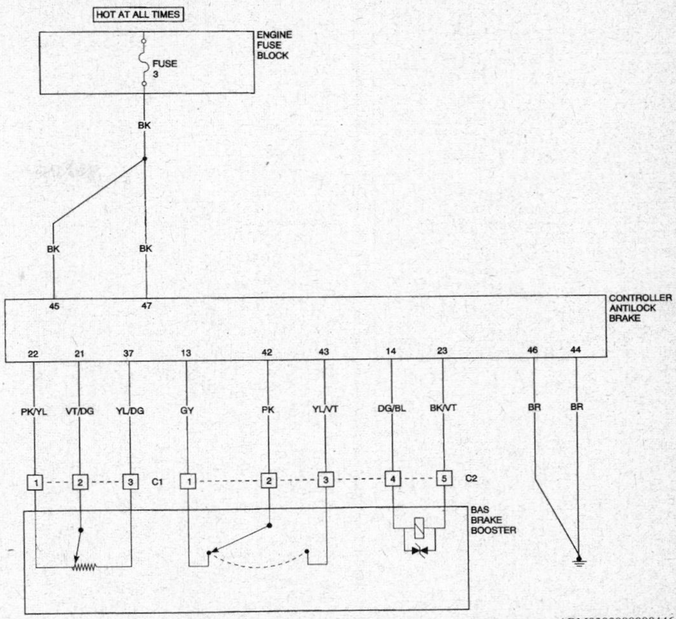

ARM0300000000446

Fig. 13 Wiring diagram. Crossfire w/BAS

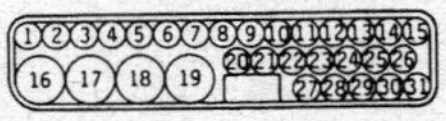

Connector terminal No.	Signal	Checking requirements		Normal condition
11	Scan tool	Connect the scan tool		Serial communication with the scan tool
		Do not connect the scan tool		1 V or less
12	Input from diagnosis indication selection	Connect the scan tool		0 V
		Do not connect the scan tool		Approx. 12 V
14	Input from stop light switch	Ignition switch: ON	Stop light switch: ON	System voltage
			Stop light switch: OFF	1 V or less
15	ABS-ECU power supply	Ignition switch: ON		System voltage
		Ignition switch: START		0 V
17	Pump motor power supply	Always		System voltage
18	Solenoid valve power supply	Always		System voltage
21	Output to ABS warning light	Ignition switch: ON	The light is switched off.	System voltage
			The light is illuminated.	0 – 2 V

CR4029801528010X

Fig. 14 Connector pin identification. Avenger & 2000 Sebring Coupe

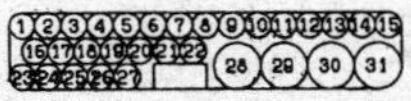

Connector terminal No.	Signal	Normal condition
1 – 3	Rear-right wheel speed sensor	1.0 – 1.5 kΩ
4 – 5	Front-right wheel speed sensor	1.0 – 1.5 kΩ
6 – 7	Front-left wheel speed sensor	1.0 – 1.5 kΩ
8 – 9	Rear-left wheel speed sensor	1.0 – 1.5 kΩ
16 – Body ground	ABS-ECU ground	Continuity
19 – Body ground		

CR4029801528020X

Fig. 15 Connector pin identification. Avenger & 2000 Sebring Coupe

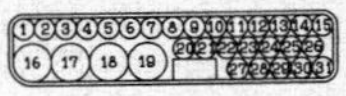

CONNECTOR TERMINAL NO	SIGNAL	CHECKING REQUIREMENT	NORMAL CONDITION
14	Input from stoplight switch	Stoplight switch: ON	Battery positive voltage
		Stoplight switch: OFF	Approximately 0 V
15	ABS-ECU power supply	Ignition switch: ON	Battery positive voltage
17	Motor power supply	Always	Battery positive voltage
18	Solenoid valve power supply	Always	Battery positive voltage

RESISTANCE AND CONTINUITY BETWEEN HARNESS-SIDE CONNECTOR TERMINALS

1. Turn the ignition switch to the "LOCK" (OFF) position and disconnect the ABS-ECU connectors before checking resistance and continuity.
2. Check between the terminals indicated in the table below.
3. The terminal layouts are shown in the illustration below.

CR4020002152010X

Fig. 16 Connector pin identification. 2001–03 Stratus Coupe & Sebring Coupe

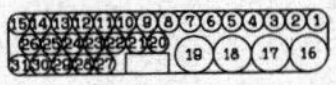

CONNECTOR TERMINAL NO.	SIGNAL	NORMAL CONDITION
6 - 7	Front-left wheel speed sensor	1.28 - 1.92 kΩ
1 - 3	Rear-right wheel speed sensor	1.28 - 1.92 kΩ
4 - 5	Front-right wheel speed sensor	1.28 - 1.92 kΩ
8 - 9	Rear-left wheel speed sensor	1.28 - 1.92 kΩ
16 - body ground	Solenoid valve ground	Less than 2 ohms
19 - body ground	Motor ground	Less than 2 ohms

CR4020002152020X

Fig. 17 Connector pin identification. 2001–03 Stratus Coupe & Sebring Coupe

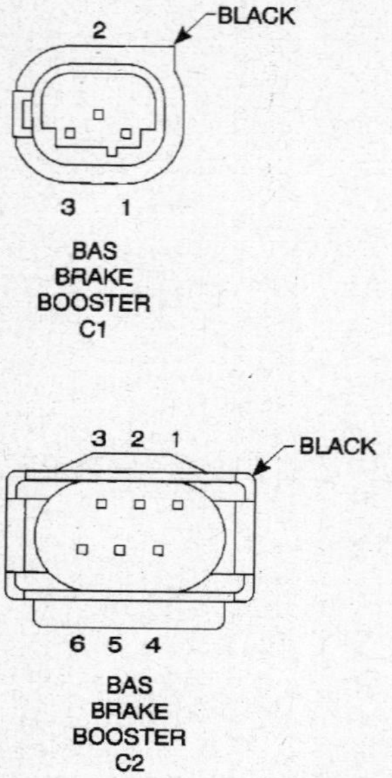

ARM0300000000447

Fig. 18 Connector pin identification (Part 1 of 4). Crossfire

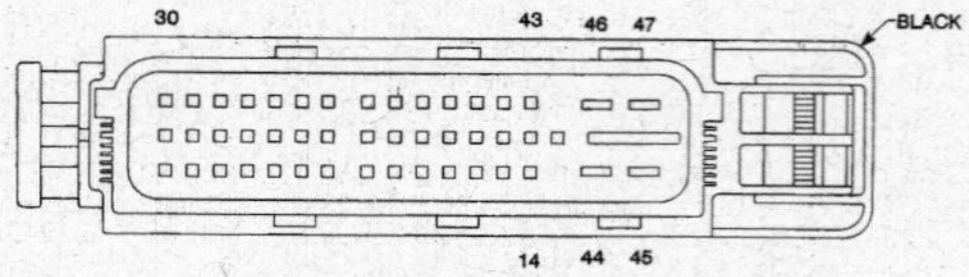

CONTROLLER ANTILOCK BRAKE — BLACK 47 WAY

CAVITY	COLOR	GAUGE	FUNCTION
1	RD/WT	20	BRAKE LAMP SWITCH OUTPUT
2	BR/DG	18	BRAKE PAD WEAR INDICATOR DRIVER
3	BR	18	LEFT FRONT WHEEL SPEED SENSOR SIGNAL
4	DG	18	LEFT FRONT WHEEL SPEED SENSOR 12V SUPPLY
5	DG/WT	20	WHEEL SPEED SENSOR OUTPUT
6	BR	20	LEFT REAR WHEEL SPEED SENSOR SIGNAL
7	BL	20	LEFT REAR WHEEL SPEED SENSOR 12 VOLT SUPPLY
8	YL/BL	20	SCI TRANSMIT
9	BR	20	SENSOR GROUND
10	BK/RD/WT	20	ESP LATERAL ACCELERATION SENSOR SIGNAL
11	BR/BL	20	SENSOR GROUND
12	BL/WT	20	ESP BRAKE PRESSURE SENSOR 1 SIGNAL
13	GY	20	BAS RELEASE SWITCH SENSOR (RELEASED)
14	DG/BL	18	5 VOLT SUPPLY
15	DG	20	CAN HIGH
16	WT	20	CAN LOW
17	BK/RD	20	BRAKE LAMP RELAY OUTPUT
18	RD/YL	18	TRACTION SYSTEM RELAY OUTPUT
19	BL/DG	20	WHEEL SPEED SENSOR OUTPUT
20	—	—	—
21	VT/DG	20	BAS TRAVEL SENSOR SIGNAL
22	PK/YL	20	5 VOLT SUPPLY
23	BK/VT	20	BAS CONTROL
24	BK/PK/WT	20	5 VOLT SUPPLY
25	BR	20	SENSOR GROUND
26	BK/RD/WT	20	5 VOLT SUPPLY
27	BR/DG	20	SENSOR GROUND
28	BK/YL	20	BRAKE LAMP RELAY CONTROL
29	BL/YL	20	STEERING ANGLE SENSOR SIGNAL
30	YL	20	ESP OFF SWITCH SENSE
31	DG/VT	20	PARK BRAKE SWITCH SENSE
32	BR	18	RIGHT FRONT WHEEL SPEED SENSOR SIGNAL
33	WT	18	RIGHT FRONT WHEEL SPEED SENSOR 12V SUPPLY
34	—	—	—
35	BR	20	RIGHT REAR WHEEL SPEED SENSOR SIGNAL
36	YL	20	RIGHT REAR WHEEL SPEED SENSOR 12V SUPPLY
37	YL/DG	20	SENSOR GROUND
38	RD/DG	20	5 VOLT SUPPLY
39	YL/BL	20	ESP YAW RATE SENSOR SIGNAL
40	BK/RD/WT	20	5 VOLT SUPPLY
41	DG/WT	20	ESP BRAKE PRESSURE SENSOR 2 SIGNAL
42	PK	20	12 VOLT SUPPLY
43	YL/VT	18	BAS RELEASE SWITCH SENSOR (APPLIED)
44	BR	12	GROUND
45	BK	14	FUSED B(+)
46	BR	10	GROUND
47	BK	10	FUSED B(+)

ARM0300000000448

Fig. 18 Connector pin identification (Part 2 of 4). Crossfire

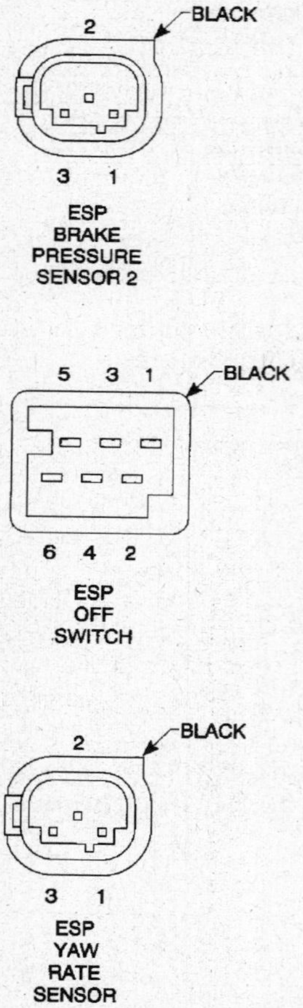

ARM0300000000449

Fig. 18 Connector pin identification (Part 3 of 4). Crossfire

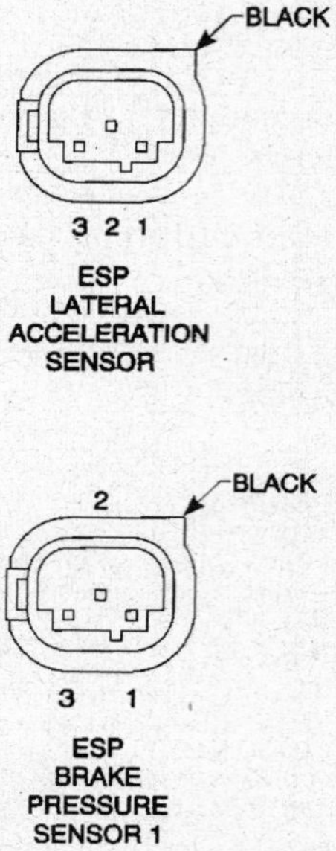

ARM0300000000450

Fig. 18 Connector pin identification (Part 4 of 4). Crossfire

DIAGNOSTIC CHART INDEX

Code	Description	Page No.	Fig. No.
AVENGER & 2000 SEBRING COUPE			
—	ABS Warning Lamp Does Not Illuminate w/Key On	6-25	35
—	ABS Warning Lamp Remains Illuminated w/Engine Running	6-25	36
—	Brake Operation Irregular	6-25	37
—	Communication w/Scan Tool Not Possible	6-24	34
11	Wheel Speed Sensor Circuit Open	6-15	19
12	Wheel Speed Sensor Circuit Open	6-15	19
13	Wheel Speed Sensor Circuit Open	6-15	19
14	Wheel Speed Sensor Circuit Open	6-15	19
15	Wheel Speed Sensor System	6-15	20
16	Power Supply System	6-15	21
21	Wheel Speed Sensor Excessive Gap Or Short Circuit	6-15	22
22	Wheel Speed Sensor Excessive Gap Or Short Circuit	6-15	22
23	Wheel Speed Sensor Excessive Gap Or Short Circuit	6-15	22
24	Wheel Speed Sensor Excessive Gap Or Short Circuit	6-15	22
38	Stop Lamp Switch System	6-15	23
51	Valve Power Supply	6-15	24
53	Pump Motor	6-16	25
2001–02 SEBRING COUPE & STRATUS COUPE			
—	ABS Warning Lamp Remains Illuminated After Engine Is Started	6-27	40
—	Communication w/Scan Tool Is Not Possible	6-25	38
—	When Ignition Switch In ON Position, ABS Warning Lamp Does Not Illuminate	6-26	39
11	Wheel Speed Sensor	6-16	26
12	Wheel Speed Sensor	6-16	26
13	Wheel Speed Sensor	6-16	26
14	Wheel Speed Sensor	6-16	26
15	Wheel Speed Sensor Abnormal Output Signal	6-17	27
21	Wheel Speed Sensor	6-16	26
22	Wheel Speed Sensor	6-16	26
23	Wheel Speed Sensor	6-16	26
24	Wheel Speed Sensor	6-16	26
38	Stop Lamp Switch System	6-18	28
41	ABS Solenoid Valve Inside Hydraulic Unit, Valve Power Supply Or Pump Motor	6-19	29
42	ABS Solenoid Valve Inside Hydraulic Unit, Valve Power Supply Or Pump Motor	6-19	29
43	ABS Solenoid Valve Inside Hydraulic Unit, Valve Power Supply Or Pump Motor	6-19	29
44	ABS Solenoid Valve Inside Hydraulic Unit, Valve Power Supply Or Pump Motor	6-19	29
45	ABS Solenoid Valve Inside Hydraulic Unit, Valve Power Supply Or Pump Motor	6-19	29
46	ABS Solenoid Valve Inside Hydraulic Unit, Valve Power Supply Or Pump Motor	6-19	29
47	ABS Solenoid Valve Inside Hydraulic Unit, Valve Power Supply Or Pump Motor	6-19	29
48	ABS Solenoid Valve Inside Hydraulic Unit, Valve Power Supply Or Pump Motor	6-19	29
51	ABS Solenoid Valve Inside Hydraulic Unit, Valve Power Supply Or Pump Motor	6-19	29
53	ABS Solenoid Valve Inside Hydraulic Unit, Valve Power Supply Or Pump Motor	6-19	29
2003 SEBRING COUPE & STRATUS COUPE			
—	ABS Warning Lamp Does Not Illuminate When Ignition Key is In ON Position	6-28	42
—	ABS Warning Lamp Remains Illuminated After Engine Is Started	6-29	43
—	Communications Between Scan Tool & ABS-ECU Is Not Possible	6-27	41
11	Wheel Speed Sensor	6-19	30
12	Wheel Speed Sensor	6-19	30
13	Wheel Speed Sensor	6-19	30
14	Wheel Speed Sensor	6-19	30
15	Wheel Speed Sensor Abnormal Output Signal	6-21	31
21	Wheel Speed Sensor	6-19	30
22	Wheel Speed Sensor	6-19	30
23	Wheel Speed Sensor	6-19	30
24	Wheel Speed Sensor	6-19	30
38	Stop Lamp Switch System	6-23	32
41	ABS Solenoid Valve Inside Hydraulic Unit	6-24	33

Continued

DIAGNOSTIC CHART INDEX—Continued

Code	Description	Page No.	Fig. No.
2003 SEBRING COUPE & STRATUS COUPE			
42	ABS Solenoid Valve Inside Hydraulic Unit	6-24	33
43	ABS Solenoid Valve Inside Hydraulic Unit	6-24	33
44	ABS Solenoid Valve Inside Hydraulic Unit	6-24	33
45	ABS Solenoid Valve Inside Hydraulic Unit	6-24	33
46	ABS Solenoid Valve Inside Hydraulic Unit	6-24	33
47	ABS Solenoid Valve Inside Hydraulic Unit	6-24	33
48	ABS Solenoid Valve Inside Hydraulic Unit	6-24	33
51	Valve Power Supply	6-24	33
53	Pump Motor	6-24	33
CROSSFIRE w/ABS			
—	CAB Internal Failure	6-30	44
—	CAB System Undervoltage	6-30	45
—	CAB System Overvoltage	6-31	46
—	CAB BUS Comminication Fault	6-31	47
—	No CAN Communications w/PCM	6-32	48
—	No CAN Coomunications w/TCM	6-32	49
—	Lefthand Front Wheel Speed Sensor Fault	6-32	50
—	Righthand Front Wheel Speed Sensor Fault	6-33	51
—	Lefthand Rear Wheel Speed Sensor Fault	6-35	52
—	Righthand Rear Wheel Speed Sensor Fault	6-36	53
—	ESP Yaw Rate Sensor Fault	6-37	54
—	Steering Angle Sensor Fault	6-38	55
—	ESP Brake Pressure Sensor 1 Fault	6-38	56
—	ESP Brake Pressure Sensor 2 Fault	6-39	57
—	ESP Lateral Acceleration Sensor Fault	6-40	58
—	Brake Lamp Switch Fault	6-41	59
—	ABS Verification Test	6-42	60
CROSSFIRE w/BAS			
—	CAB Internal Failure	6-43	61
—	CAB System Undervoltage	6-43	62
—	CAB System Overvoltage	6-43	63
—	PCM Not Identified Or Incorrect	6-43	64
—	CAN BUS Communication General Fault	6-44	65
—	No CAN Communications w/PCM	6-44	66
—	Release Switch Fault	6-44	67
—	BAS Travel Sensor Fault	6-45	68
—	Brake Lamp Switch Fault	6-46	69
—	BAS Solenoid Valve Fault	6-47	70
—	Verification Test	6-48	71

	Probable cause
The ABS-ECU detects breaks in the wheel speed sensor wire.	• Malfunction of wheel speed sensor • Malfunction of wiring harness or connector • Malfunction of ABS rotor • Malfunction of ABS-ECU

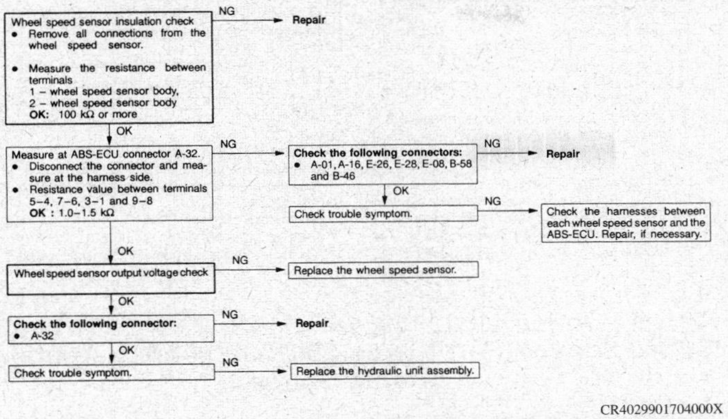

Fig. 19 Codes 11, 12, 13 & 14: Wheel Speed Sensor Circuit Open. Avenger & 2000 Sebring Coupe

	Probable cause
This diagnostic trouble code is output when the ABS-ECU power voltage is outside the standard value. Furthermore, if the voltage returns to normal, this diagnostic trouble code will not be output.	• Malfunction of wiring harness or connector. • Malfunction of battery or generator • Malfunction of ABS-ECU

Caution

If the battery voltage drops during check, this code will be output as a current problem, and correct diagnostic of the problem cannot be made.

Before carrying out the following check, check the battery condition, and recharge it if necessary.

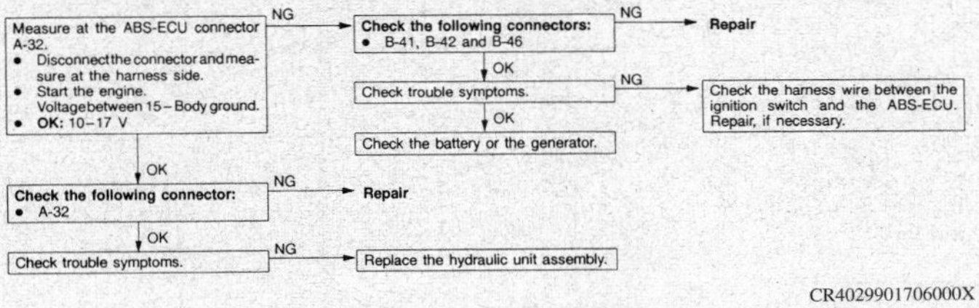

Fig. 21 Code 16: Power Supply System. Avenger & 2000 Sebring Coupe

	Probable cause
The ABS-ECU outputs this diagnostic trouble code in the following cases. • Stop light switch remains on for more than 15 minutes while the ABS is not functioning. • The harness wire for the stop light switch may be open-circuited. If the stop light operates normally, there is an open circuit in the harness for the stop light switch input circuit or there is a malfunction in the ABS-ECU.	• Malfunction of stop light switch • Malfunction of harness or connector • Malfunction of ABS-ECU

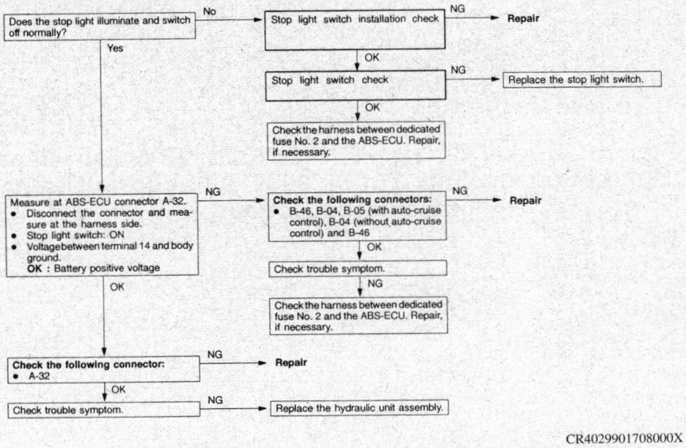

Fig. 23 Code 38: Stop Lamp Switch System. Avenger & 2000 Sebring Coupe

Code No. 15 Wheel speed sensor system	Probable cause
This diagnostic trouble code is output when there is a malfunction (other than broken wire or short circuit) in any of the wheel speed sensor output signals while driving. The following can be considered as the cause of the wheel speed sensor output malfunction. • Distortion of ABS rotor, teeth missing. • Low frequency noise interference when sensor harness wire is broken. • Noise interference in sensor signal. • Sensor output signal is below the standard value or amplitude modulation is over the standard value. Using an oscilloscope to measure the wave shape of the wheel speed sensor output signal is very effective. • Broken sensor harness. • Poor connection of connector.	• Malfunction of wheel speed sensor • Malfunction of wiring harness • Malfunction of ABS rotor • Malfunction of wheel bearing • Malfunction of ABS-ECU

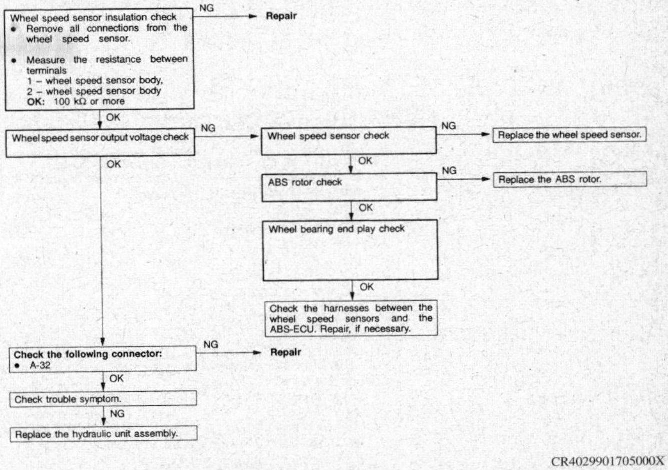

Fig. 20 Code 15: Wheel Speed Sensor System. Avenger & 2000 Sebring Coupe

	Probable cause
[Comment] These diagnostic trouble codes are output when the detection speed of the wheel speed sensors is below the standard value.	• Improper installation of wheel speed sensor • Malfunction of wheel speed sensor (intermittent open circuit or short circuit) • Malfunction of ABS rotor (chipped tooth or rotor not installed) • Noise interference in wheel speed sensor • Malfunction of ABS-ECU

NOTE

1. Momentary interruptions within approximately 100 ms are not detected.
2. To inspect the twisted pair wires in the wheel speed sensor, check if there is any damage to the cables, and flex the cables to check for any open circuits.

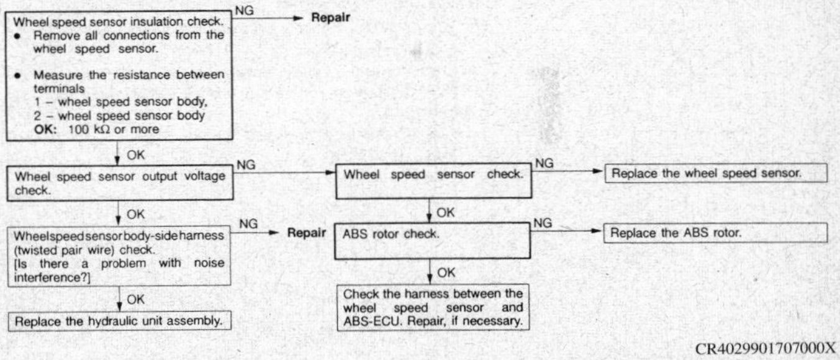

Fig. 22 Codes 21, 22, 23 & 24: Wheel Speed Sensor Excessive Gap Or Short Circuit. Avenger & 2000 Sebring Coupe

	Probable cause
This code is output when there is an abnormality in the solenoid valve power supply system.	• Malfunction of wiring harness or connecter • Malfunction of ABS-ECU • Blown fuse

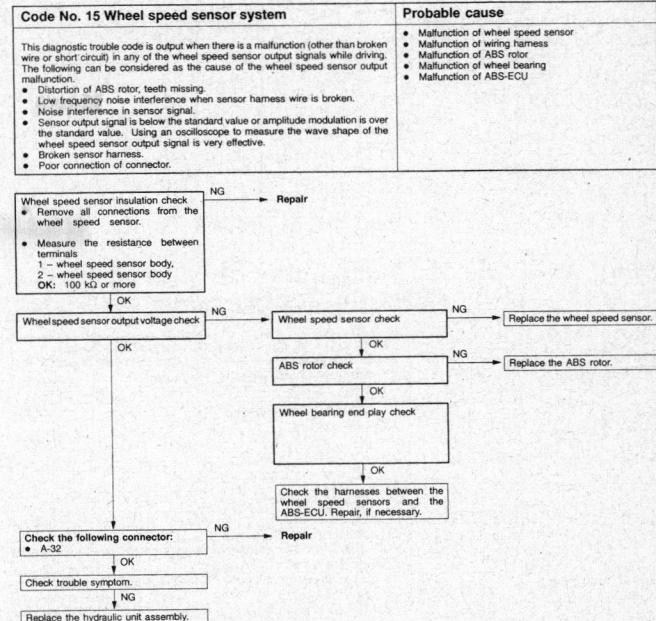

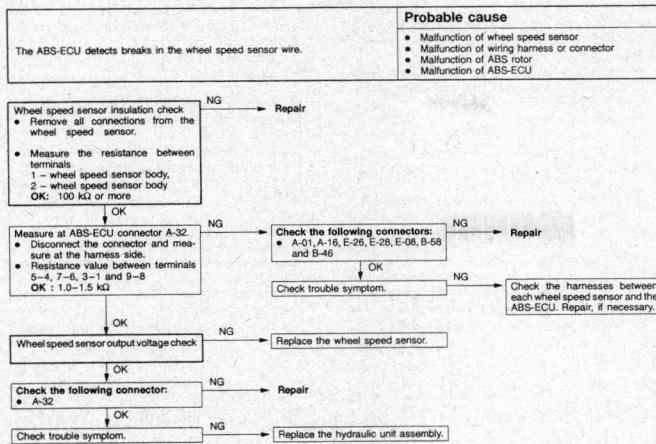

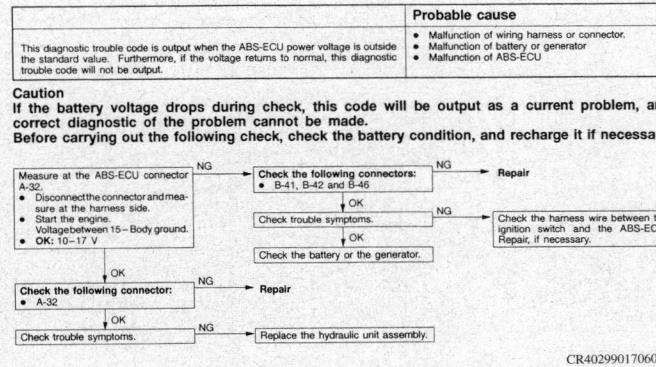

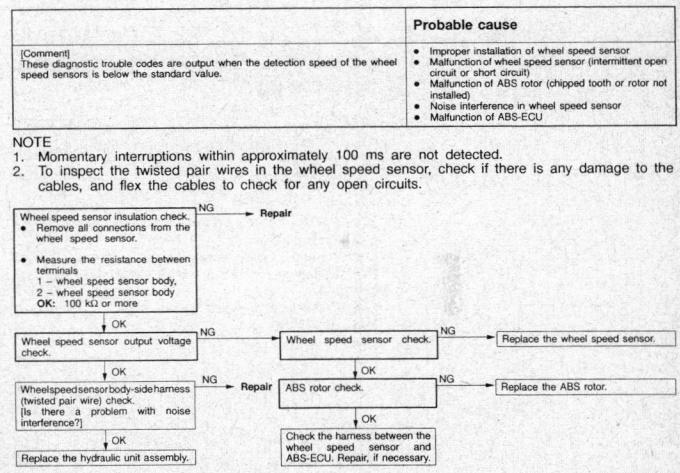

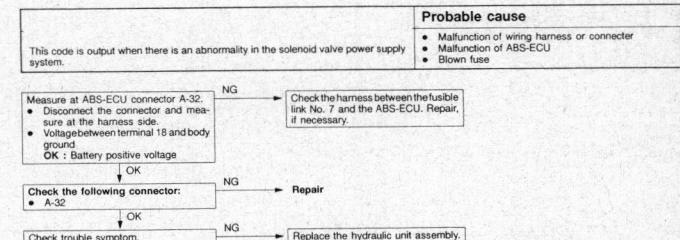

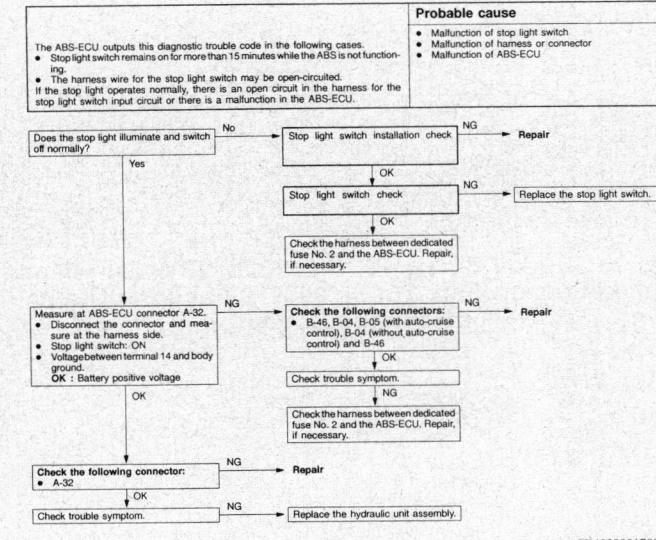

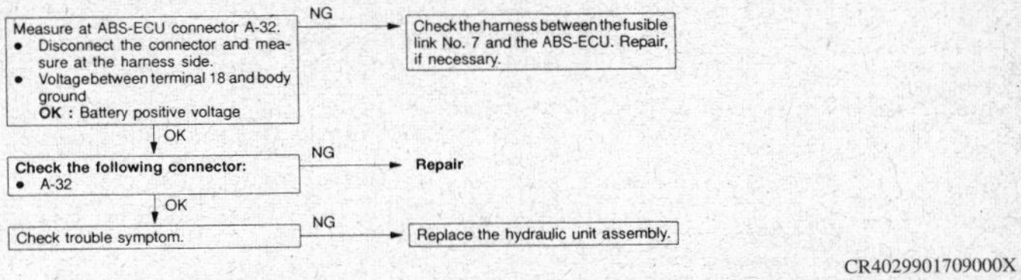

Fig. 24 Code 51: Valve Power Supply. Avenger & 2000 Sebring Coupe

	Probable cause
This code is output when there is an abnormality in the pump motor system.	• Malfunction of wiring harness or connector • Malfunction of hydraulic unit • Malfunction of ABS-ECU

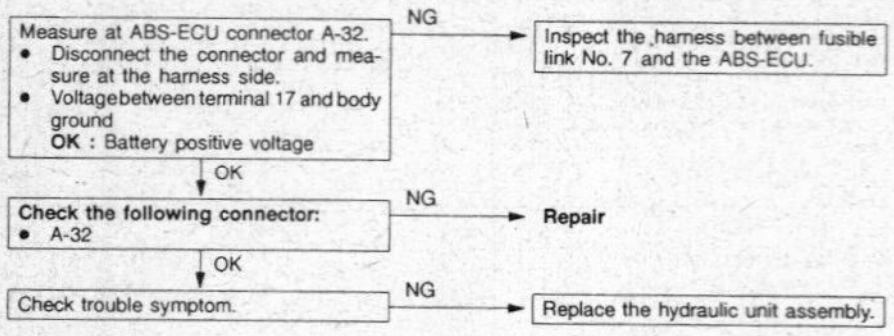

CR4029901710000X

Fig. 25 Code 53: Pump Motor. Avenger & 2000 Sebring Coupe

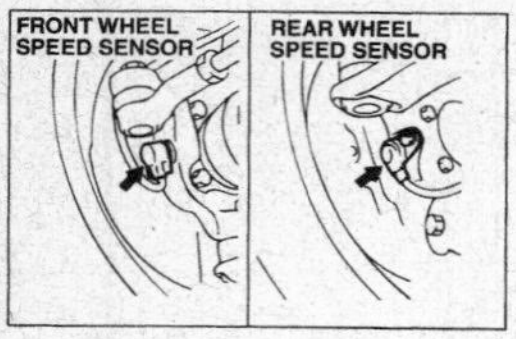

STEP 1. Check the wheel speed sensor installation.

Q: Is the wheel speed sensor bolted securely in place at the front knuckle or the rear knuckle?

YES : Go to Step 2.
NO : Install it properly.

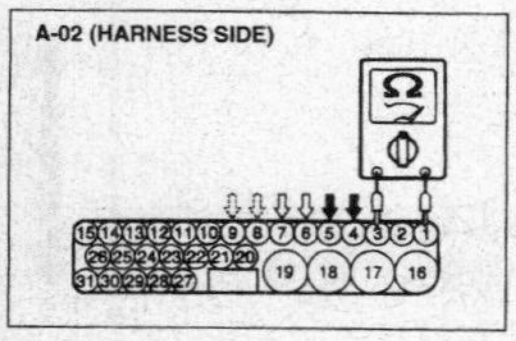

STEP 2. Check wheel speed sensor circuit at the ABS-ECU connector A-02.

(1) Disconnect connector A-02 and measure at the harness side.
(2) Measure the resistance between the ABS-ECU connector terminals 1 and 3, 4 and 5, 6 and 7, 8 and 9.

Standard Value: 1.28 - 1.92 kΩ

Q: Is the resistance between terminals 1 and 3, 4 and 5, 6 and 7, 8 and 9 within the standard value?

YES : Go to Step 6.
NO : Go to Step 3. or 4. or 5.

CR4020002141020X

Fig. 26 Codes 11, 12, 13, 14, 21, 22, 23 & 24: Wheel Speed Sensor (Part 2 of 5). 2001–02 Sebring Coupe & Stratus Coupe

STEP 3. Check the harness wires between ABS-ECU connector A-02 and wheel speed sensor <front: LH> connector A-22.

NOTE: After inspecting intermediate connector C-05, inspect the wire. If intermediate connector C-05 is damaged, repair or replace it.

If the connector has been repaired or replaced, go to Step 9.

Q: Are any harness wires between ABS-ECU connector A-02 and wheel speed sensor <front: LH> connector A-22 damaged?

YES : Repair them and go to Step 9.
NO : Go to Step 7.

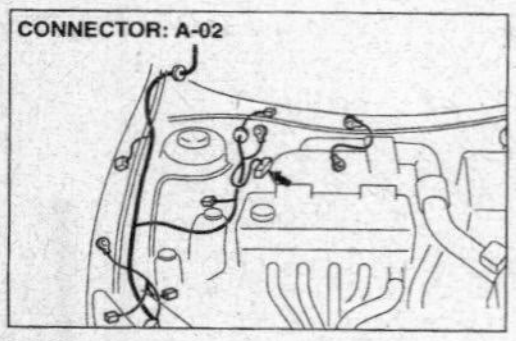

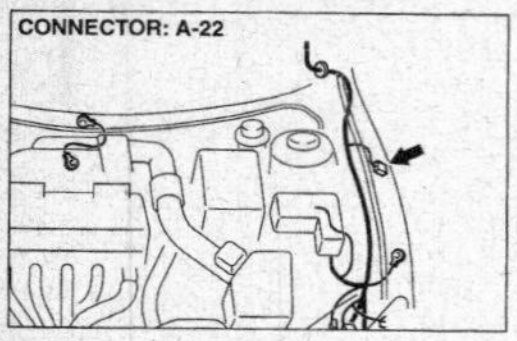

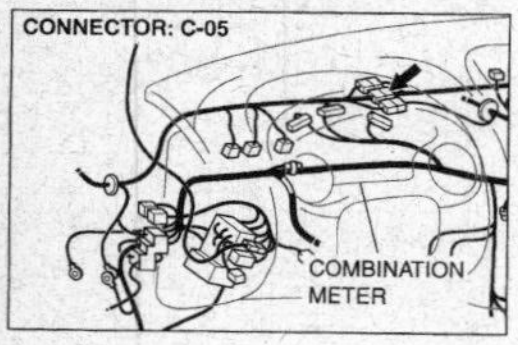

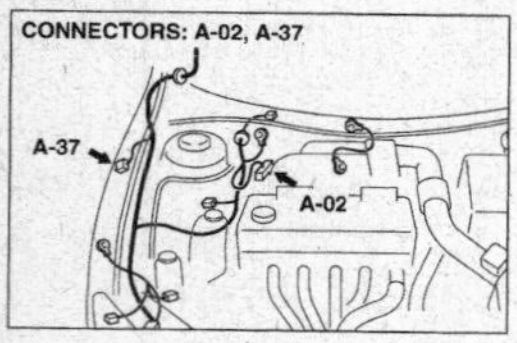

STEP 4. Check the harness wires between ABS-ECU connector A-02 and wheel speed sensor <front: RH> connector A-37.

Q: Are any harness wires between ABS-ECU connector A-02 and wheel speed sensor <front: RH> connector A-37 damaged?

YES : Repair them and then go to Step 9.
NO : Go to Step 7.

CR4020002141030X

Fig. 26 Codes 11, 12, 13, 14, 21, 22, 23 & 24: Wheel Speed Sensor (Part 3 of 5). 2001–02 Sebring Coupe & Stratus Coupe

CIRCUIT OPERATION

- A toothed ABS rotor generates a voltage pulse as it moves across the pickup field of each wheel speed sensor.
- The amount of voltage generated at each wheel is determined by the clearance between the ABS rotor teeth and the wheel speed sensor, and by the speed of rotation.
- The wheel speed sensors transmit the frequency of the voltage pulses and the amount of voltage generated by each pulse to the ABS electronic control unit (ABS-ECU).
- The ABS hydraulic unit modulates the amount of braking force individually applied to each wheel cylinder.

ABS DTC SET CONDITIONS

- DTCs 11, 12, 13, 14 are output when signal is not input due to breakage of the (+) or (-) wire of one or more of the four wheel-speed sensors. DTCs 21, 22, 23, 24 are output in the following cases:
- Open circuit is not found but no input is received by one or more of the four wheel-speed sensors at 10 km/h (6 mph) or more.
- Sensor output drops due to a malfunctioning sensor or warped ABS rotor.

TROUBLESHOOTING HINTS (The most likely causes for these DTCs to set are:)

DTC 11, 12, 13, 14
- Malfunction of the wheel speed sensor
- Damaged wiring harness or connector
- Malfunction of the hydraulic unit (Integrated with ABS-ECU)

DTC 21, 22, 23, 24
- Malfunction of the wheel speed sensor
- Damaged wiring harness and connector
- Malfunction of the hydraulic unit (Integrated with ABS-ECU)
- Malfunction of the ABS rotor
- Malfunction of the wheel bearing
- Excessive clearance between the sensor and ABS rotor

CR4020002141010X

Fig. 26 Codes 11, 12, 13, 14, 21, 22, 23 & 24: Wheel Speed Sensor (Part 1 of 5). 2001–02 Sebring Coupe & Stratus Coupe

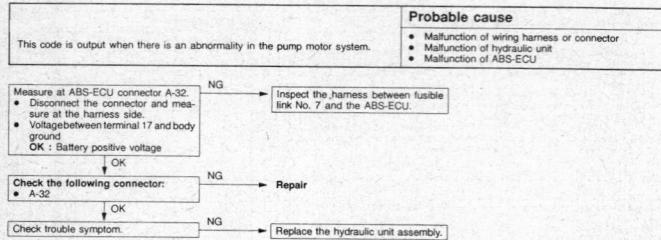

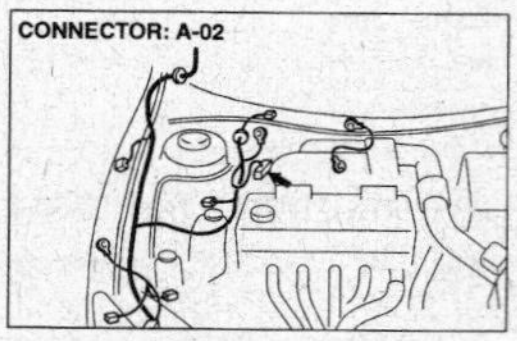

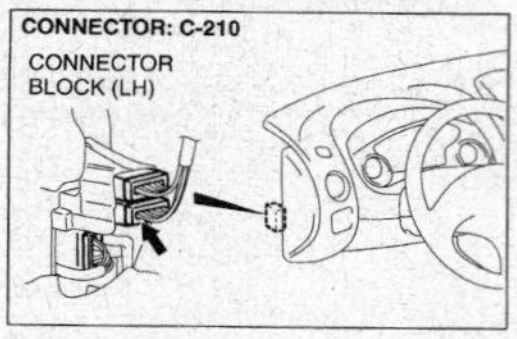

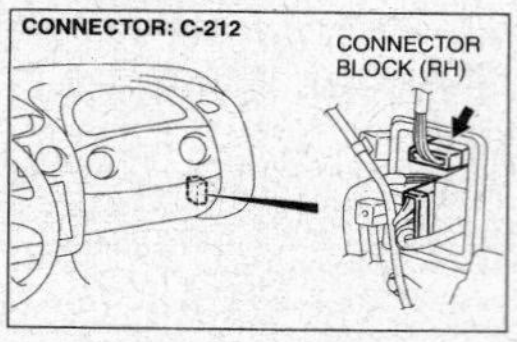

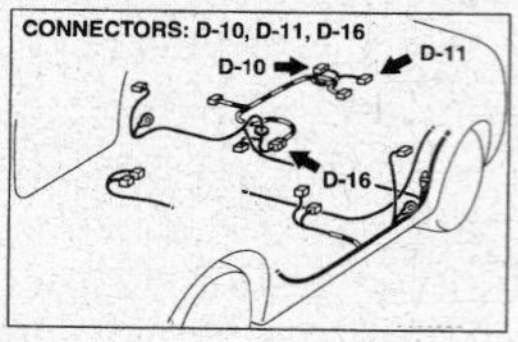

STEP 5. Check the harness wires between ABS-ECU connector A-02 and wheel speed sensor connector D-11 <rear: LH> or D-10 <rear RH>.

NOTE: After inspecting intermediate connector C-212,C-210 or D-16, inspect the wire. If intermediate connector C-212,C-210 or D-16 is damaged, repair or replace it.

If the connector has been repaired or replaced, go to Step 9 .

Q: Are any harness wires between ABS-ECU connector A-02 and wheel speed sensor connector D-11 <rear: LH> or D-10 <rear RH> damaged?

YES : Repair them and then go to Step 9.
NO : Go to Step 7.

CR4020002141040X

Fig. 26 Codes 11, 12, 13, 14, 21, 22, 23 & 24: Wheel Speed Sensor (Part 4 of 5). 2001–02 Sebring Coupe & Stratus Coupe

STEP 6. Check the wheel speed sensor output voltage.

Output Voltage:

- When measured with a voltmeter: 42 mV or more
- When measured with oscilloscope (maximum voltage): 200 mV or more

Q: Does the voltage meet the specification?

YES : Replace the hydraulic unit (integrated with ABS-ECU) and then go to Step 9.

NO : Go to Step 7.

STEP 7. Check the wheel speed sensor or ABS rotor.
Refer to P.5B-49.If there is damage in any of the check items, replace the wheel speed sensor.

- Check items:
- Wheel speed sensor internal resistance

Standard value: 1.28 - 1.92 kΩ

- Insulation between the Wheel speed sensor body and connector terminals
- Toothed ABS rotor check

Q: Is the wheel speed sensor or ABS rotor damaged?

YES : Replace it and then go to Step 9.

NO : Go to Step 8.

STEP 8. Check the wheel bearing.

Q: Is the wheel bearing damaged?

YES : Replace it and then go to Step 9.

NO : Go to Step 9.

STEP 9. Check the diagnostic trouble codes.

Q: Do the diagnostic trouble codes 11, 12, 13, 14, 21, 22, 23 and 24 reset?

YES : Go to Step 1.

NO : This diagnosis is complete.

CR4020202344000X

Fig. 26 Codes 11, 12, 13, 14, 21, 22, 23 & 24: Wheel Speed Sensor (Part 5 of 5). 2001–02 Sebring Coupe & Stratus Coupe

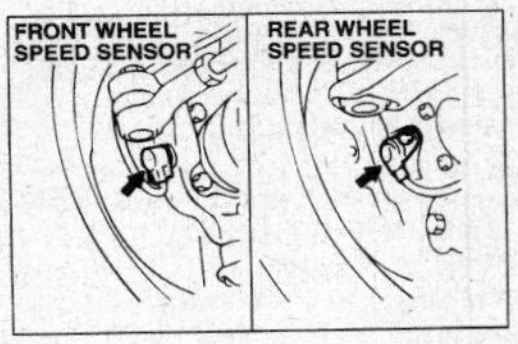

STEP 1. Check the wheel speed sensor installation.

Q: Is the wheel speed sensor bolted securely in place at the front knuckle or the rear knuckle?

YES : Go to Step 2.

No : Install it properly. Then go to Step 8.

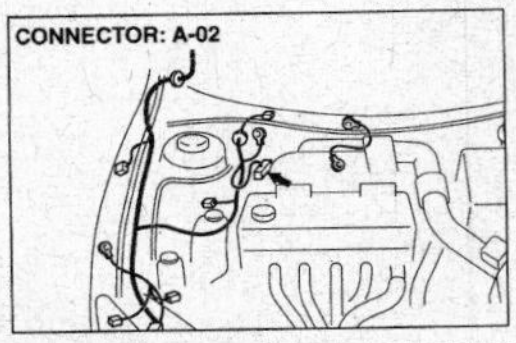

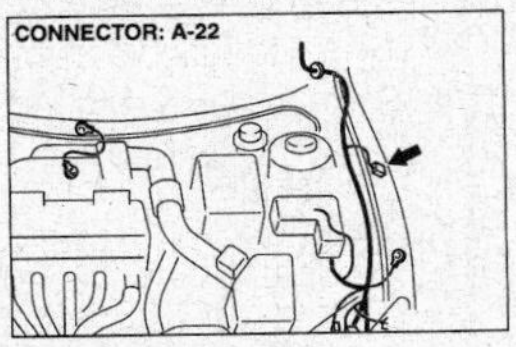

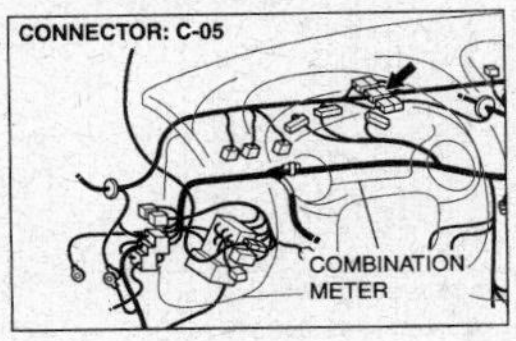

STEP 2. Check the harness wires between ABS-ECU connector A-02 and wheel speed sensor <front: LH> connector A-22.

NOTE: After inspecting intermediate connector C-05, inspect the wire. If intermediate connector C-05 is damaged, repair or replace it. If the connector has been repaired or replaced, go to Step 8.

Q: Are any harness wires between ABS-ECU connector A-02 and wheel speed sensor <front: LH> connector A-22 damaged?

YES : Repair them and go to Step 8.

NO : Go to Step 6.

CR4020002142020X

Fig. 27 Code 15: Wheel Speed Sensor Abnormal Output Signal (Part 2 of 5). 2001–02 Sebring Coupe & Stratus Coupe

WHEEL SPEED SENSOR CIRCUIT

CIRCUIT OPERATION

ABS DTC SET CONDITIONS

- DTC 15 is output when output signal produced by any of wheel-speed sensor is abnormal (excluding short and open-circuits).

TROUBLESHOOTING HINTS (The most likely causes for these DTC to set is:)

- Improper installation of the wheel speed sensor
- Malfunction of the wheel speed sensor
- Damaged wiring harness or connector
- Malfunction of the ABS rotor
- Malfunction of the wheel bearing

CR4020002142010X

Fig. 27 Code 15: Wheel Speed Sensor Abnormal Output Signal (Part 1 of 5). 2001–02 Sebring Coupe & Stratus Coupe

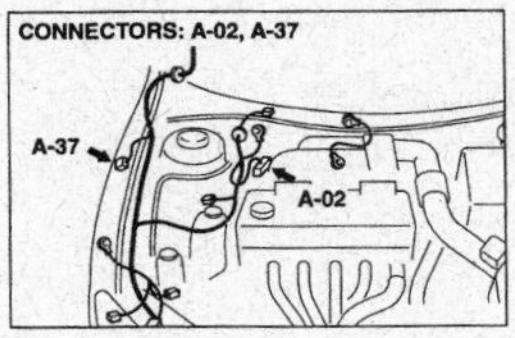

STEP 3. Check the harness wires between ABS-ECU connector A-02 and wheel speed sensor <front: RH> connector A-37.

Q: Are any harness wires between ABS-ECU connector A-02 and wheel speed sensor <front: RH> connector A-37 damaged?

YES : Repair them and then go to Step 8.

NO : Go to Step 6.

CR4020002142030X

Fig. 27 Code 15: Wheel Speed Sensor Abnormal Output Signal (Part 3 of 5). 2001–02 Sebring Coupe & Stratus Coupe

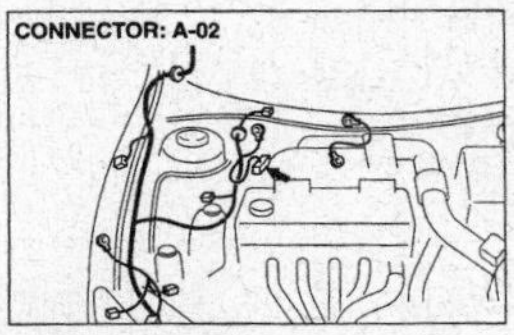

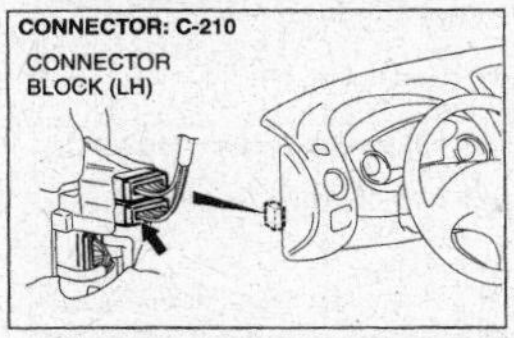

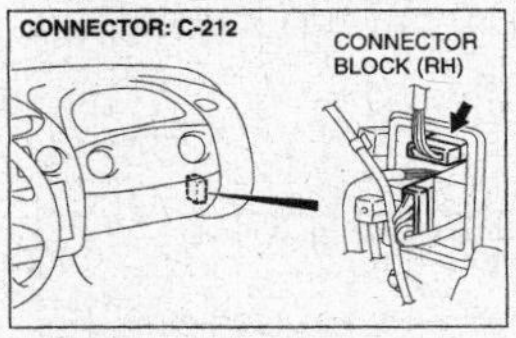

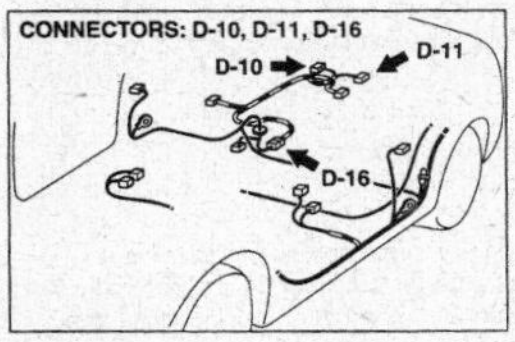

STEP 4. Check the harness wires between ABS-ECU connector A-02 and wheel speed sensor connector D-11 <rear: LH> or D-10 <rear RH>.

NOTE: After inspecting intermediate connector C-212,C-210 or D-16, inspect the wire. If intermediate connector C-212,C-210 or D-16 is damaged, repair or replace it. If the connector has been repaired or replaced, go to Step 8.

Q: Are any harness wires between ABS-ECU connector A-02 and wheel speed sensor connector D-11 <rear: LH> or D-10 <rear RH> damaged?

YES : Repair them and then go to Step 8.

NO : Go to Step 6.

CR4020002142040X

Fig. 27 Code 15: Wheel Speed Sensor Abnormal Output Signal (Part 4 of 5). 2001–02 Sebring Coupe & Stratus Coupe

STEP 5. Check the wheel speed sensor output voltage.

Output Voltage:

- When measured with a voltmeter: 42 mV or more
- When measured with oscilloscope (maximum voltage): 200 mV or more

Q: Does the voltage meet the specification?

YES : Replace the hydraulic unit (integrated with ABS-ECU) and then go to Step 8.
NO : Go to Step 6.

STEP 6. Check the wheel speed sensor or ABS rotor.
If there is damage in any of the check items, replace the wheel speed sensor.

- Check items:
- Wheel speed sensor internal resistance

Standard value: 1.28 - 1.92 kΩ

- Insulation between the wheel speed sensor body and the connector terminals
- Toothed ABS rotor check

Q: Is the wheel speed sensor or ABS rotor damaged?

YES : Replace it and then go to Step 8.
NO : Go to Step 7.

STEP 7. Check the wheel bearing.

Q: Is the wheel bearing damaged?

YES : Replace it and then go to Step 8.
NO : Go to Step 8.

STEP 8. Check the diagnostic trouble codes.

Q: Do the diagnostic trouble code 15 reset?

YES : Go to Step 1.
NO : This diagnosis is complete.

CR4020002142050X

Fig. 27 Code 15: Wheel Speed Sensor Abnormal Output Signal (Part 5 of 5). 2001–02 Sebring Coupe & Stratus Coupe

CIRCUIT OPERATION

- The ON signal when the brake pedal is pressed or the OFF signal when the brake pedal is released is input to the ABS-ECU (terminal 14).

ABS DTC SET CONDITION
Output is provided in the following cases:

- Stoplight switch is not operating properly and remains in ON state for more than 15 minutes.
- Stoplight switch system harness is damaged and no signal is input to ABS-ECU.

TROUBLESHOOTING HINTS
The most likely causes for DTC is to set are:

- Malfunction of the stoplight switch
- Damaged wiring harness and connector
- Malfunction of the hydraulic unit (Integrated with ABS-ECU)

STEP 1. Check the stoplight operation.

Q: Does the stoplight light or go out correctly?

YES : Go to Step 3.
NO : Go to Step 2.

CR4020002143010X

Fig. 28 Code 38: Stop Lamp Switch System (Part 1 of 4). 2001–02 Sebring Coupe & Stratus Coupe

STEP 2. Check the stoplight switch installation condition.

Q: Is the stoplight switch installed properly?

YES : Go to Step 4.
NO : Repair it and then go to Step 7.

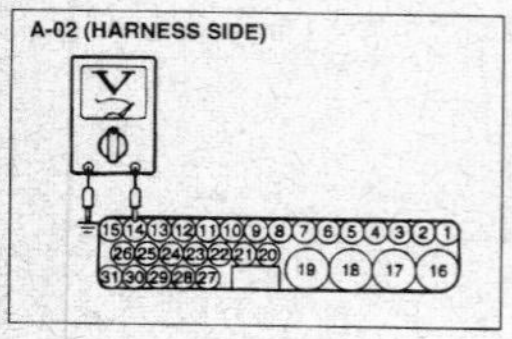

STEP 3. Check the stoplight switch circuit at ABS-ECU connector A-02.

(1) Disconnect connector A-02 and measure at the harness side.
(2) Turn the stoplight switch ON.
(3) Measure the voltage between terminal 14 and ground.

Q: Is the battery positive voltage approximately 12volts?

YES : Replace the hydraulic unit and then go to Step 7.
NO : Go to Step 5.

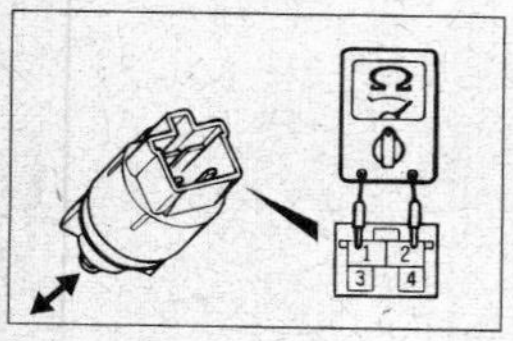

STEP 4. Check the stoplight switch continuity.

(1) Remove the stoplight switch.
(2) Connect an ohmmeter to the stoplight switch terminals 1 and 2, and check whether there is continuity when the plunger of the stoplight switch is pushed in and when it is released.

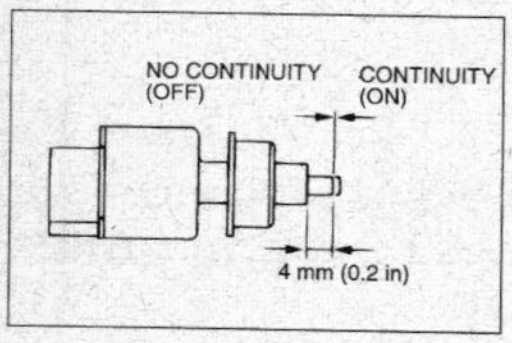

(3) The stoplight switch is in good condition if there is no continuity when the plunger is pushed in to a depth of within 4 mm (0.2 inch) from the outer case edge surface, and if there is continuity when it is released.

Q: Is the stoplight switch damaged?

YES : Replace it and then go to Step 7.
NO : Go to Step 6.

CR4020002143020X

Fig. 28 Code 38: Stop Lamp Switch System (Part 2 of 4). 2001–02 Sebring Coupe & Stratus Coupe

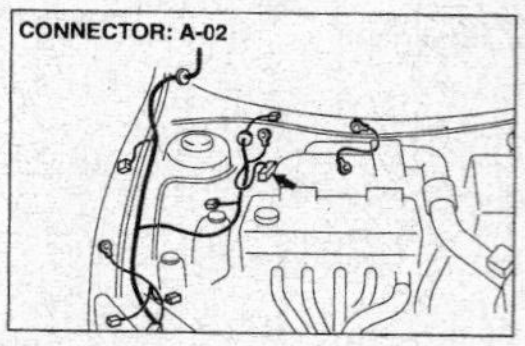

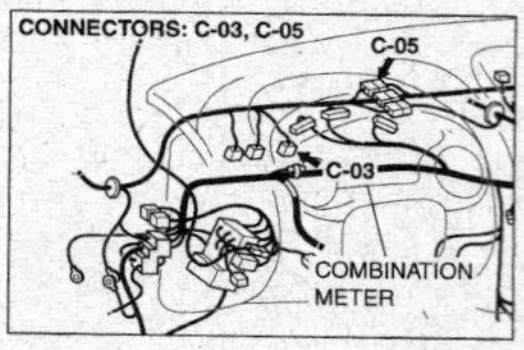

STEP 5. Check the harness wire between ABS-ECU connector A-02 and stoplight switch connector C-03.
NOTE: After inspecting intermediate connector C-05, inspect the wire. If intermediate connector C-05 is damaged, repair or replace it. If the connector has been repaired or replaced, go to Step 7.

Q: Is any harness wire between ABS-ECU connector A-02 and stoplight switch connector C-03 damaged?

YES : Repair it and then go to Step 7.
NO : No action is to be taken.

CR4020002143030X

Fig. 28 Code 38: Stop Lamp Switch System (Part 3 of 4). 2001–02 Sebring Coupe & Stratus Coupe

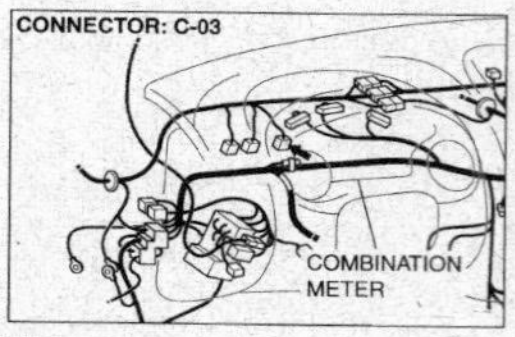

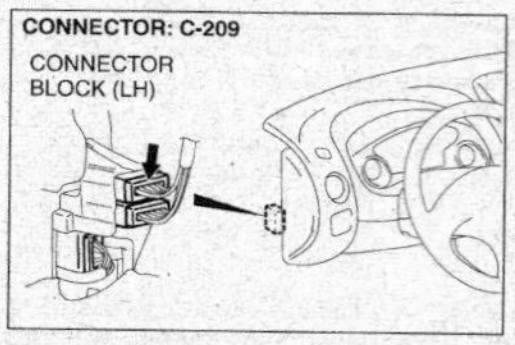

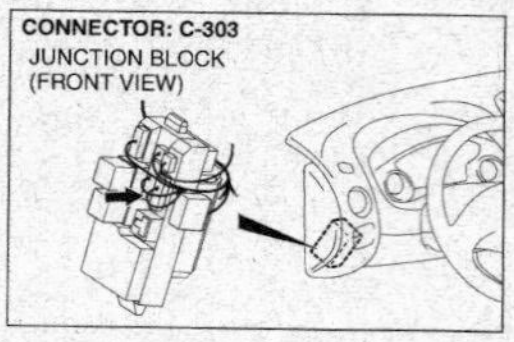

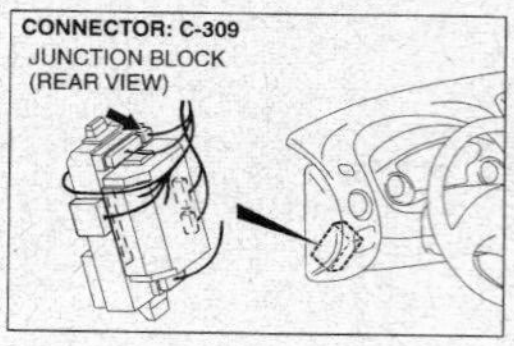

STEP 6. Check the harness wire between fusible link number 2 and stoplight switch connector C-03.
NOTE: After inspecting intermediate connector C-209, C-303, or C-309, inspect the wire. If intermediate connector C-209, C-303, or C-309 is damaged, repair or replace it. If the connector has been repaired or replaced, go to Step 7.

Q: Is any harness wire between fusible link number 2 and stoplight switch connector C-03 damaged?

YES : Repair it and then go to Step 7.
NO : Check and repair the harness wire between stoplight switch and stoplight. Then go to Step7.

STEP 7. Check the diagnostic trouble codes.

Q: Does the diagnostic trouble code 38 reset?

YES : Return to Step 1.
NO : This diagnosis is complete.

CR4020002143040X

Fig. 28 Code 38: Stop Lamp Switch System (Part 4 of 4). 2001–02 Sebring Coupe & Stratus Coupe

CIRCUIT OPERATION

Power is continuously supplied to the ABS-ECU through fusible link number 6 to operate the solenoid valve and motor.

ABS DTC SET CONDITIONS

These codes are displayed if the power supply circuit of solenoid valve or motor is open or shorted.

CR4020002144010X

Fig. 29 Codes 41, 42, 43, 44, 45, 46, 47, 48, 51, & 53: ABS Solenoid Valve Inside Hydraulic Unit, Valve Power Supply Or Pump Motor (Part 1 of 2). 2001–02 Sebring Coupe & Stratus Coupe

CIRCUIT OPERATION

- A toothed ABS rotor generates a voltage pulse as it moves across the pickup field of each wheel speed sensor.
- The amount of voltage generated at each wheel is determined by the clearance between the ABS rotor teeth and the wheel speed sensor, and by the speed of rotation.
- The wheel speed sensors transmit the frequency of the voltage pulses and the amount of voltage generated by each pulse to the ABS electronic control unit (ABS-ECU).
- The ABS hydraulic unit modulates the amount of braking force individually applied to each wheel cylinder.

ABS DTC SET CONDITIONS

- DTCs 11, 12, 13, 14 are output when signal is not input due to breakage of the (+) or (–) wire of one or more of the four wheel-speed sensors. DTCs 21, 22, 23, 24 are output in the following cases:
- Open circuit is not found but no input is received by one or more of the four wheel-speed sensors at 10 km/h (6 mph) or more.
- Sensor output drops due to a malfunctioning sensor or warped ABS rotor.

TROUBLESHOOTING HINTS (The most likely causes for these DTCs to set are:)

DTC 11, 12, 13, 14
- Malfunction of the wheel speed sensor
- Damaged wiring harness or connector
- Malfunction of the hydraulic unit (Integrated with ABS-ECU)

DTC 21, 22, 23, 24
- Malfunction of the wheel speed sensor
- Damaged wiring harness and connector
- Malfunction of the hydraulic unit (Integrated with ABS-ECU)
- Malfunction of the ABS rotor
- Malfunction of the wheel bearing
- Excessive clearance between the sensor and ABS rotor

CR4020202356000X

Fig. 30 Codes 11, 12, 13, 14, 21, 22, 23 & 24: Wheel Speed Sensor (Part 1 of 9). 2003 Sebring Coupe & Stratus Coupe

DIAGNOSIS

Required Special Tool:
- MB991223: Harness Set

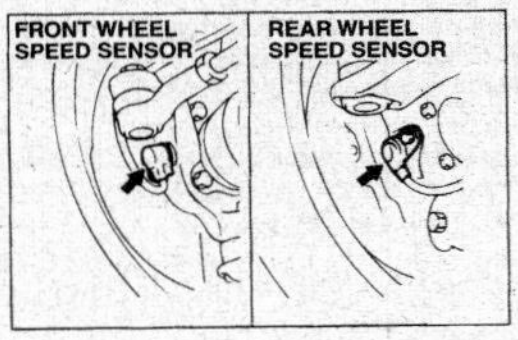

STEP 1. Check the wheel speed sensor installation.

Q: Is the wheel speed sensor bolted securely in place at the front knuckle or the rear knuckle?

YES : Go to Step 2.
NO : Install it properly Then go to Step 10.

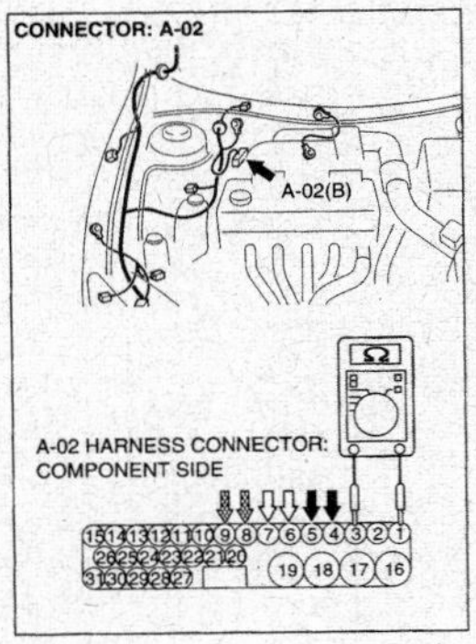

STEP 2. Check the wheel speed sensor circuit at ABS-ECU connector A-02.

(1) Disconnect connector A-02 and measure at the harness side.
(2) Measure the resistance between the ABS-ECU connector terminals 1 and 3, 4 and 5, 6 and 7, 8 and 9.

Standard Value: 1.28 – 1.92 kΩ

Q: Is the resistance between terminals 1 and 3, 4 and 5, 6 and 7, 8 and 9 within the standard value?

YES : Go to Step 7.
NO : Go to Step 3, 4, 5 or 6.

CR4020202357000X

Fig. 30 Codes 11, 12, 13, 14, 21, 22, 23 & 24: Wheel Speed Sensor (Part 2 of 9). 2003 Sebring Coupe & Stratus Coupe

TROUBLESHOOTING HINTS
- Damaged wiring harness or connector
- Malfunction of the hydraulic unit (integrated with ABS-ECU)

DIAGNOSIS

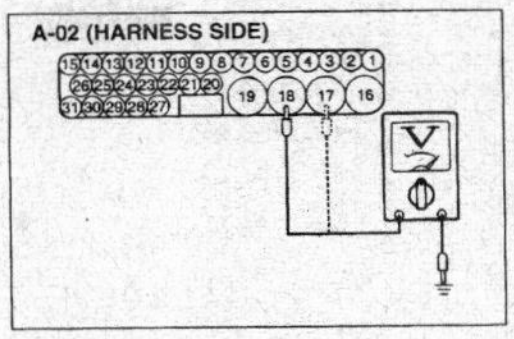

STEP 1. Check the solenoid valve or motor power supply circuit at ABS-ECU connector A-02.

(1) Disconnect connector A-02 and measure at the harness side.
(2) Measure the voltage between terminal 18 and ground or 17 and ground.

Q: Is battery positive voltage approximately 12 volts?

YES : Replace the hydraulic unit (integrated with ABS-ECU) and then go to Step 3.
NO : Go to Step 2.

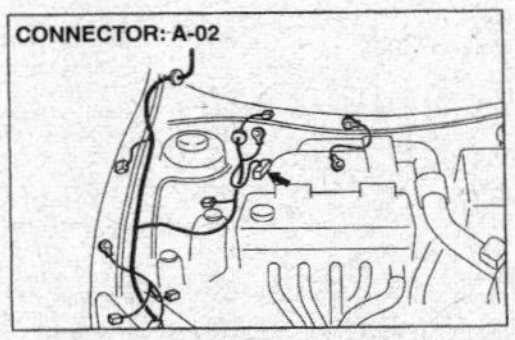

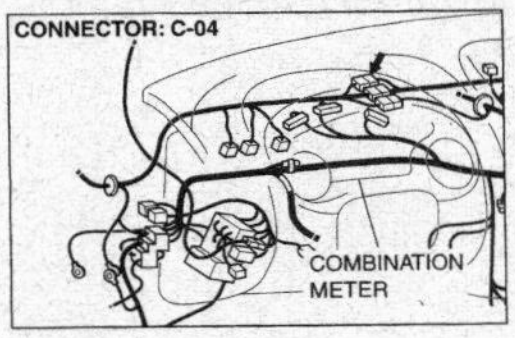

STEP 2. Check the harness wire between fusible link number 6 and ABS-ECU connector A-02.

Q: Is any harness wire between fusible link number 6 and ABS-ECU connector A-02 damaged?

YES : Repair it and after inspecting intermediate connector C-04, inspect the wire. If intermediate connector C-04 is damaged, repair or replace it then go to Step 3.
NO : Go to Step 3.

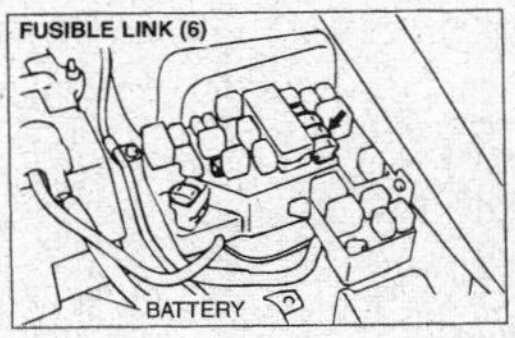

STEP 3. Check the diagnostic trouble codes.

Q: Do the diagnostic trouble codes 41, 42, 43, 44, 45, 46, 47, 48, 51 and 53 reset?

YES : Go to Step 1.
NO : This diagnosis is complete.

CR4020002144020X

Fig. 29 Codes 41, 42, 43, 44, 45, 46, 47, 48, 51, & 53: ABS Solenoid Valve Inside Hydraulic Unit, Valve Power Supply Or Pump Motor (Part 2 of 2). 2001–02 Sebring Coupe & Stratus Coupe

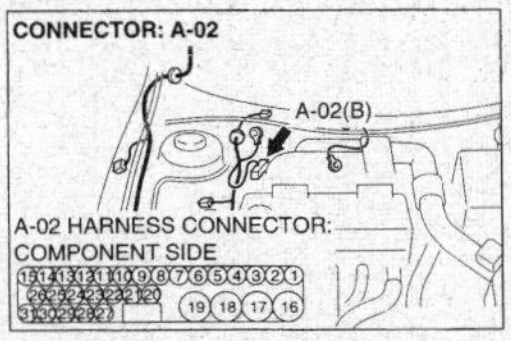

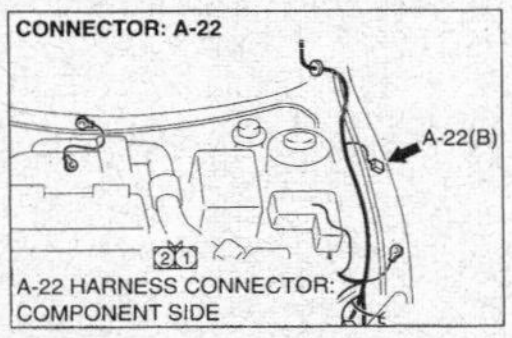

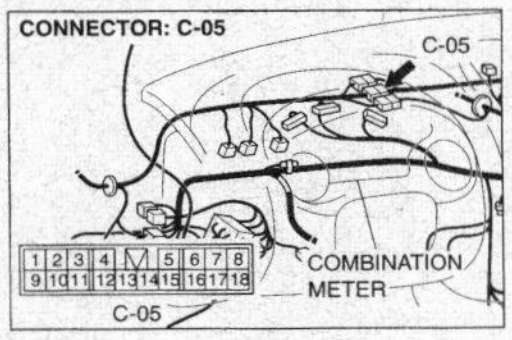

STEP 3. Check the harness wires between ABS-ECU connector A-02 terminal 6 and wheel speed sensor <front: LH> connector A-22 terminal 1 or ABS-ECU connector A-02 terminal 7 and wheel speed sensor <front: LH> connector A-22 terminal 2.

NOTE: After inspecting intermediate connector C-05, inspect the wire. If intermediate connector C-05 is damaged, repair or replace it. If the connector has been repaired or replaced, go to Step 10.

Q: Are any harness wires between ABS-ECU connector A-02 terminal 6 and wheel speed sensor <front: LH> connector A-22 terminal 1 or ABS-ECU connector A-02 terminal 7 and wheel speed sensor <front: LH> connector A-22 terminal 2 damaged?

YES : Repair them and go to Step 10.
NO : Go to Step 8.

CR4020202358000X

Fig. 30 Codes 11, 12, 13, 14, 21, 22, 23 & 24: Wheel Speed Sensor (Part 3 of 9). 2003 Sebring Coupe & Stratus Coupe

STEP 4. Check the harness wires between ABS-ECU connector A-02 terminal 4 and wheel speed sensor <front: RH> connector A-37 terminal 1 or ABS-ECU connector A-02 terminal 5 and wheel speed sensor <front: RH> connector A-37 terminal 2.

Q: Are any harness wires between ABS-ECU connector A-02 terminal 4 and wheel speed sensor <front: RH> connector A-37 terminal 1 or ABS-ECU connector A-02 terminal 5 and wheel speed sensor <front: RH> connector A-37 terminal 2 damaged?

YES : Repair them and then go to Step 10.
NO : Go to Step 8.

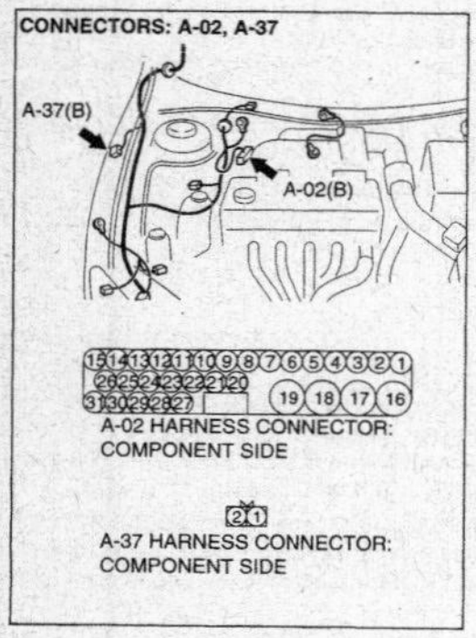

CR4020202359000X

Fig. 30 Codes 11, 12, 13, 14, 21, 22, 23 & 24: Wheel Speed Sensor (Part 4 of 9). 2003 Sebring Coupe & Stratus Coupe

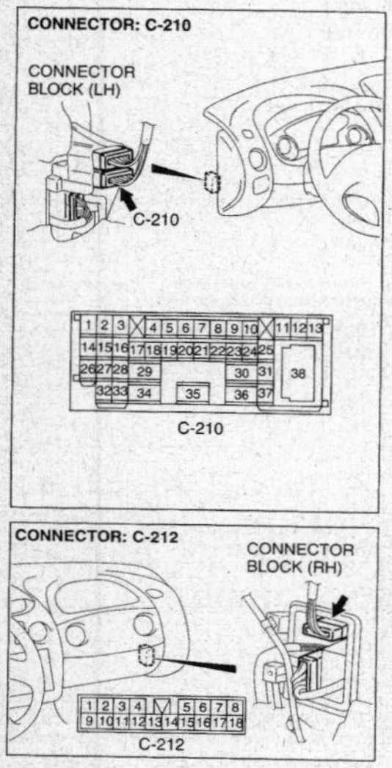

Q: Are any harness wires between ABS-ECU connector A-02 terminal 1 and wheel speed sensor <rear: LH> connector D-11 terminal 1 or ABS-ECU connector A-02 terminal 3 and wheel speed sensor <rear: LH> connector D-11 terminal 2 damaged?

YES : Repair them and then go to Step 10.
NO : Go to Step 8.

CR4020202361000X

Fig. 30 Codes 11, 12, 13, 14, 21, 22, 23 & 24: Wheel Speed Sensor (Part 6 of 9). 2003 Sebring Coupe & Stratus Coupe

STEP 5. Check the harness wires between ABS-ECU connector A-02 terminal 1 and wheel speed sensor <rear: LH> connector D-11 terminal 1 or ABS-ECU connector A-02 terminal 3 and wheel speed sensor <rear: LH> connector D-11 terminal 2.

NOTE: After inspecting intermediate connectors C-212, C-210 and D-16, inspect the wire. If intermediate connector C-212, C-210 or D-16 is damaged, repair or replace it. If the connector has been repaired or replaced, go to Step 10.

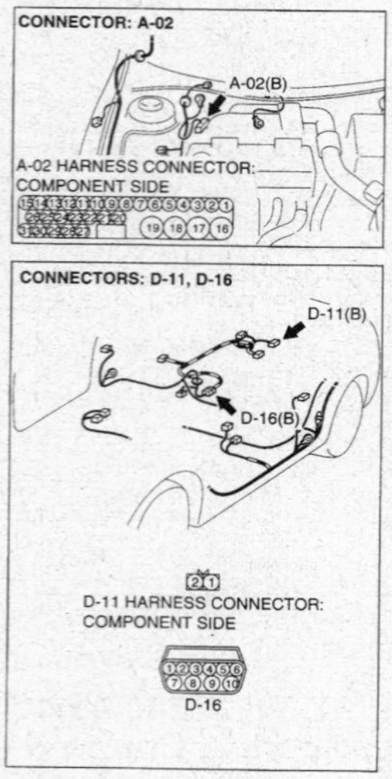

CR4020202360000X

Fig. 30 Codes 11, 12, 13, 14, 21, 22, 23 & 24: Wheel Speed Sensor (Part 5 of 9). 2003 Sebring Coupe & Stratus Coupe

STEP 6. Check the harness wires between ABS-ECU connector A-02 terminal 8 and wheel speed sensor <rear RH> connector D-10 terminal 1 or ABS-ECU connector A-02 terminal 9 and wheel speed sensor <rear RH> connector D-10 terminal 2.

NOTE: After inspecting intermediate connectors C-212, C-210 and D-16, inspect the wire. If intermediate connector C-212, C-210 or D-16 is damaged, repair or replace it. If the connector has been repaired or replaced, go to Step 10.

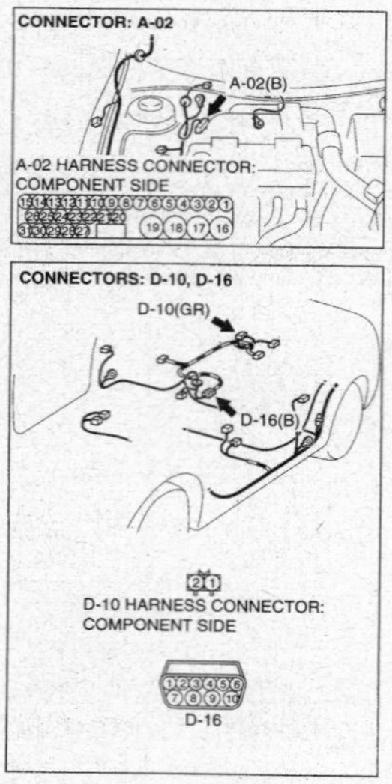

CR4020202362000X

Fig. 30 Codes 11, 12, 13, 14, 21, 22, 23 & 24: Wheel Speed Sensor (Part 7 of 9). 2003 Sebring Coupe & Stratus Coupe

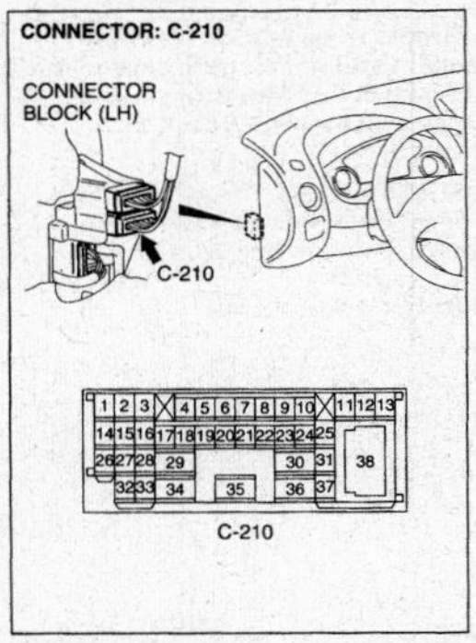

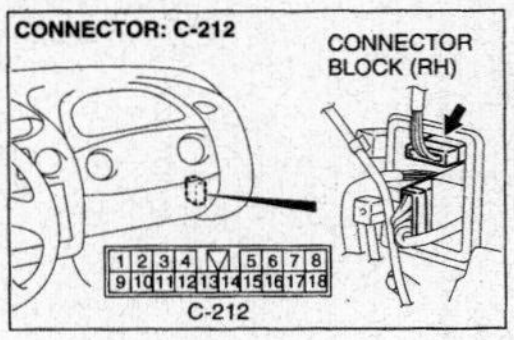

Q: Are any harness wires between ABS-ECU connector A-02 terminal 8 and wheel speed sensor <rear RH> connector D-10 terminal 1 or ABS-ECU connector A-02 terminal 9 and wheel speed sensor <rear RH> connector D-10 terminal 2 damaged?

YES : Repair them and then go to Step 10.
NO : Go to Step 8.

STEP 7. Check the wheel speed sensor output voltage.

Output Voltage:

- When measured with a voltmeter: 42 mV or more
- When measured with an oscilloscope (maximum voltage): 200 mV or more

Q: Does the voltage meet the specification?

YES : Replace the hydraulic unit (integrated with ABS-ECU) and then go to Step 10.
NO : Go to Step 8.

CR4020202363000X

Fig. 30 Codes 11, 12, 13, 14, 21, 22, 23 & 24: Wheel Speed Sensor (Part 8 of 9). 2003 Sebring Coupe & Stratus Coupe

STEP 8. Check the wheel speed sensor or ABS rotor.
If there is damage in any of the check items, replace the wheel speed sensor.

Check items:

- Wheel speed sensor internal resistance
  Standard value: 1.28 – 1.92 kΩ
- Insulation between the Wheel speed sensor body and connector terminals
- Toothed ABS rotor check

Q: Is the wheel speed sensor or ABS rotor damaged?

YES : Replace it and then go to Step 10.
NO : Go to Step 9.

STEP 9. Check the wheel bearing.
Front Hub Assembly
Rear Axle Hub

Q: Is the wheel bearing damaged?

YES : Replace it and then go to Step 10.
NO : Go to Step 10.

STEP 10. Check the diagnostic trouble code.

Q: Are diagnostic trouble codes 11, 12, 13, 14, 21, 22, 23 and 24 reset?

YES : Go to Step 1.
NO : The procedure is complete.

CR4020202364000X

Fig. 30 Codes 11, 12, 13, 14, 21, 22, 23 & 24: Wheel Speed Sensor (Part 9 of 9). 2003 Sebring Coupe & Stratus Coupe

WHEEL SPEED SENSOR CIRCUIT

CIRCUIT OPERATION

ABS DTC SET CONDITIONS

- DTC 15 is output when output signal produced by any of wheel-speed sensor is abnormal (excluding short and open-circuits).

TROUBLESHOOTING HINTS (The most likely causes for this DTC to set are:)

- Improper installation of the wheel speed sensor
- Malfunction of the wheel speed sensor
- Damaged wiring harness or connector
- Malfunction of the ABS rotor
- Malfunction of the wheel bearing

DIAGNOSIS

Required Special Tool:

- **MB1223: HARNESS SET**

CR4020202365000X

Fig. 31 Code 15: Wheel Speed Sensor Abnormal Output Signal (Part 1 of 8). 2003 Sebring Coupe & Stratus Coupe

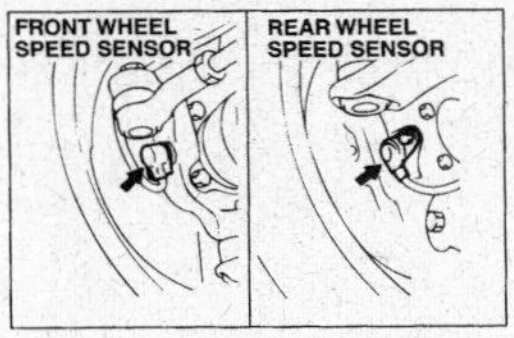

STEP 1. Check the wheel speed sensor installation.

Q: Is the wheel speed sensor bolted securely in place at the front knuckle or the rear knuckle?

YES : Go to Step 2.
No : Install it properly. Then go to Step 9.

STEP 2. Check the harness wires between ABS-ECU connector A-02 terminal 6 and wheel speed sensor <front: LH> connector A-22 terminal 1 or ABS-ECU connector A-02 terminal 7 and wheel speed sensor <front: LH> connector A-22 terminal 2.

NOTE: After inspecting intermediate connector C-05, inspect the wires. If intermediate connector C-05 is damaged, repair or replace it. If the connector has been repaired or replaced, go to Step 9.

Q: Are any harness wires between ABS-ECU connector A-02 terminal 6 and wheel speed sensor <front: LH> connector A-22 terminal 1 or ABS-ECU connector A-02 terminal 7 and wheel speed sensor <front: LH> connector A-22 terminal 2 damaged?

YES : Repair them and go to Step 9.
NO : Go to Step 7.

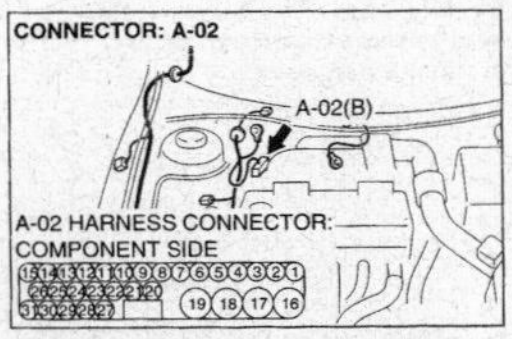

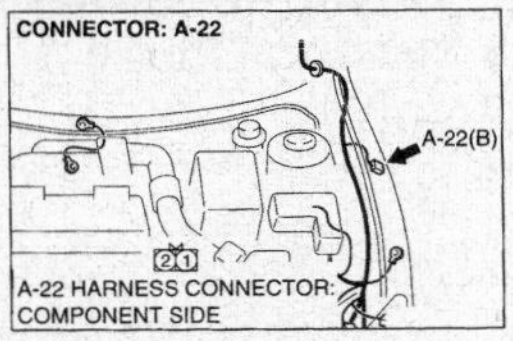

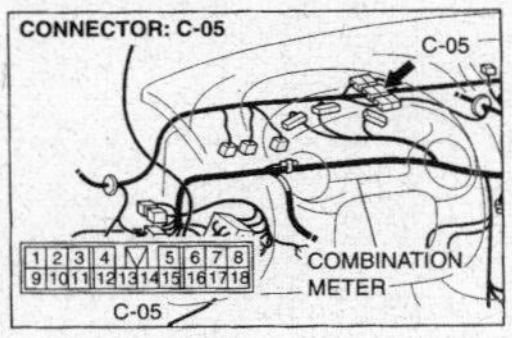

CR4020202366000X

Fig. 31 Code 15: Wheel Speed Sensor Abnormal Output Signal (Part 2 of 8). 2003 Sebring Coupe & Stratus Coupe

STEP 3. Check the harness wires between ABS-ECU connector A-02 terminal 4 and wheel speed sensor <front: RH> connector A-37 terminal 1 or ABS-ECU connector A-02 terminal 5 and wheel speed sensor <front: RH> connector A-37 terminal 2.

Q: Are any harness wires between ABS-ECU connector A-02 terminal 4 and wheel speed sensor <front: RH> connector A-37 terminal 1 or ABS-ECU connector A-02 terminal 5 and wheel speed sensor <front: RH> connector A-37 terminal 2 damaged?

YES : Repair them and then go to Step 9.

NO : Go to Step 7.

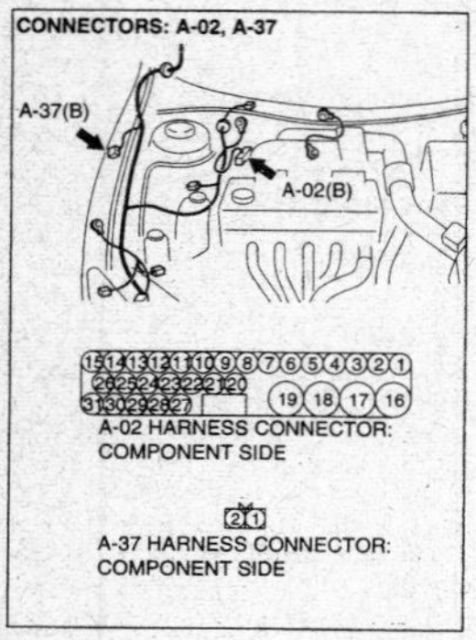

CR4020202367000X

Fig. 31 Code 15: Wheel Speed Sensor Abnormal Output Signal (Part 3 of 8). 2003 Sebring Coupe & Stratus Coupe

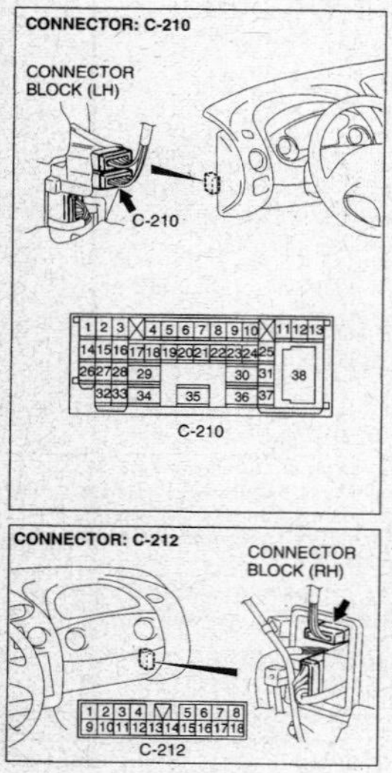

Q: Are any harness wires between ABS-ECU connector A-02 terminal 1 and wheel speed sensor <rear: LH> connector D-11 terminal 1 or ABS-ECU connector A-02 terminal 3 and wheel speed sensor <rear: LH> connector D-11 terminal 2 damaged?

YES : Repair them and then go to Step 9.

NO : Go to Step 7.

CR4020202369000X

Fig. 31 Code 15: Wheel Speed Sensor Abnormal Output Signal (Part 5 of 8). 2003 Sebring Coupe & Stratus Coupe

STEP 4. Check the harness wires between ABS-ECU connector A-02 terminal 1 and wheel speed sensor <rear: LH> connector D-11 terminal 1 or ABS-ECU connector A-02 terminal 3 and wheel speed sensor <rear: LH> connector D-11 terminal 2.

NOTE: After inspecting intermediate connectors C-212,C-210 and D-16, inspect the wire. If intermediate connector C-212,C-210 or D-16 is damaged, repair or replace it.

If the connector has been repaired or replaced, go to Step 9.

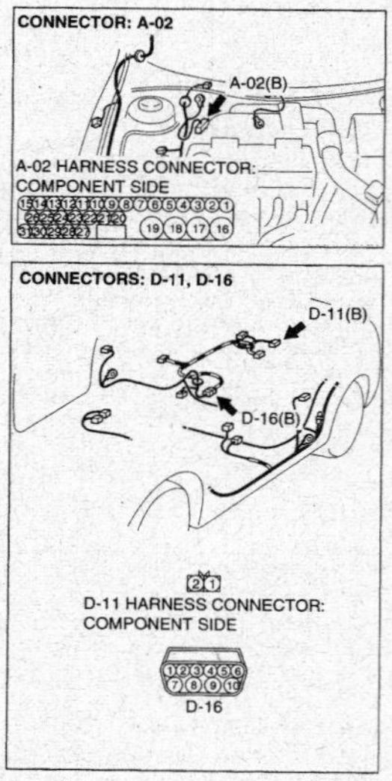

CR4020202368000X

Fig. 31 Code 15: Wheel Speed Sensor Abnormal Output Signal (Part 4 of 8). 2003 Sebring Coupe & Stratus Coupe

STEP 5. Check the harness wires between ABS-ECU connector A-02 terminal 8 and wheel speed sensor <rear RH> connector D-10 terminal 1 or ABS-ECU connector A-02 terminal 9 and wheel speed sensor <rear RH> connector D-10 terminal 2.

NOTE: After inspecting intermediate connectors C-212,C-210 and D-16, inspect the wire. If intermediate connector C-212,C-210 or D-16 is damaged, repair or replace it.

If the connector has been repaired or replaced, go to Step 9.

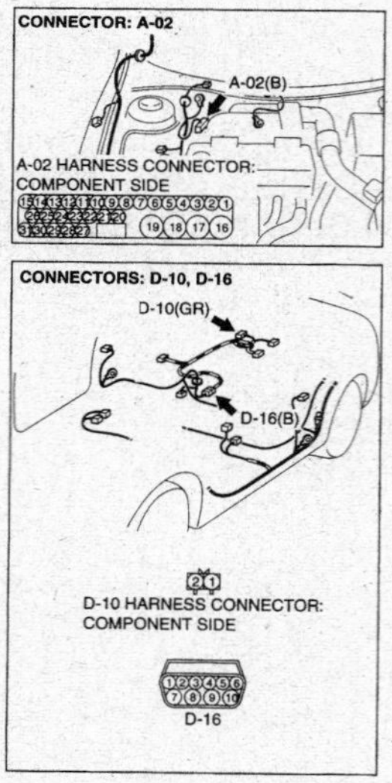

CR4020202370000X

Fig. 31 Code 15: Wheel Speed Sensor Abnormal Output Signal (Part 6 of 8). 2003 Sebring Coupe & Stratus Coupe

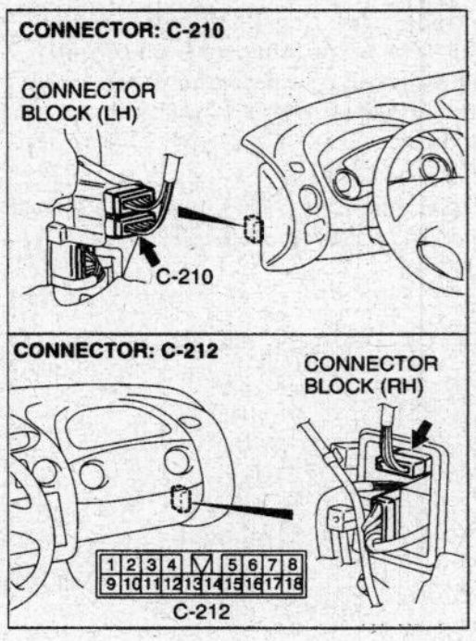

Q: Are any harness wires between ABS-ECU connector A-02 terminal 8 and wheel speed sensor <rear RH> connector D-10 terminal 1 or ABS-ECU connector A-02 terminal 9 and wheel speed sensor <rear RH> connector D-10 terminal 2 damaged?

YES : Repair them and then go to Step 9S9.
NO : Go to Step 7.

STEP 6. Check the wheel speed sensor output voltage.

Output Voltage:
- When measured with a voltmeter: 42 mV or more
- When measured with an oscilloscope (maximum voltage): 200 mV or more

Q: Does the voltage meet the specification?

YES : Replace the hydraulic unit (integrated with ABS-ECU) and then go to Step 9.
NO : Go to Step 7.

STEP 7. Check the wheel speed sensor or ABS rotor.
If there is damage in any of the check items, replace the wheel speed sensor.

Check items:
- Wheel speed sensor internal resistance

  Standard value: 1.28 – 1.92 kΩ
- Insulation between the wheel speed sensor body and the connector terminals
- Toothed ABS rotor check

Q: Is the wheel speed sensor or ABS rotor damaged?

YES : Replace it and then go to Step 9.
NO : Go to Step 8.

CR4020202371000X

Fig. 31 Code 15: Wheel Speed Sensor Abnormal Output Signal (Part 7 of 8). 2003 Sebring Coupe & Stratus Coupe

STEP 8. Check the wheel bearing.
Front Hub Assembly
Rear Axle Hub

Q: Is the wheel bearing damaged?

YES : Replace it and then go to Step 9.
NO : Go to Step 9.

STEP 9. Check the diagnostic trouble code.

Q: Do the diagnostic trouble code 15 reset?

YES : Go to Step 1.
NO : The procedure is complete.

CR4020202372000X

Fig. 31 Code 15: Wheel Speed Sensor Abnormal Output Signal (Part 8 of 8). 2003 Sebring Coupe & Stratus Coupe

CIRCUIT OPERATION
- The ON signal when the brake pedal is pressed or the OFF signal when the brake pedal is released is input to the ABS-ECU (terminal 14).

ABS DTC SET CONDITION
Output is provided in the following cases:
- Stoplight switch is not operating properly and remains in ON state for more than 15 minutes.
- Stoplight switch system harness is damaged and no signal is input to ABS-ECU.

TROUBLESHOOTING HINTS
The most likely causes for DTC is to set are:
- Malfunction of the stoplight switch
- Damaged wiring harness and connector
- Malfunction of the hydraulic unit (Integrated with ABS-ECU)

DIAGNOSIS

Required Special Tool:
- MB991223: Harness Set

STEP 1. Check the stoplight operation.

Q: Does the stoplight light or go out correctly?

YES : Go to Step 3.
NO : Go to Step 2.

STEP 2. Check the stoplight switch installation condition.

Q: Is the stoplight switch installed properly?

YES : Go to Step 4.
NO : Repair it and then go to Step 7.

CR4020202373000X

Fig. 32 Code 38: Stop Lamp Switch System (Part 1 of 4). 2003 Sebring Coupe & Stratus Coupe

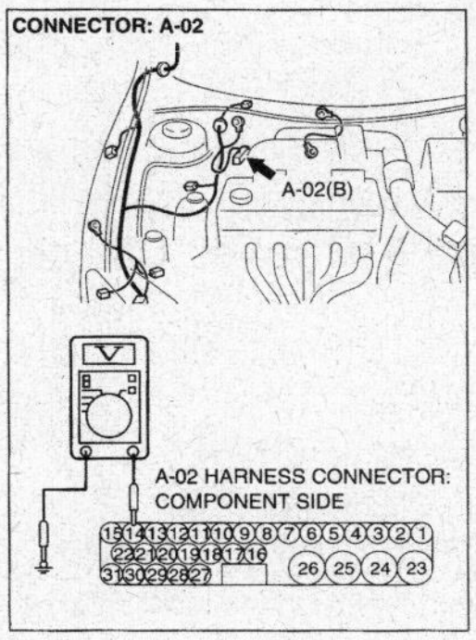

STEP 3. Check the stoplight switch circuit at ABS-ECU connector A-02.
(1) Disconnect connector A-02 and measure at the harness side.
(2) Turn the stoplight switch ON.
(3) Measure the voltage between terminal 14 and ground.

Q: Is battery positive voltage (approximately 12 volts) present?

YES : Replace the hydraulic unit and then go to Step 7.
NO : Go to Step 5.

STEP 4. Check the stoplight switch continuity.
(1) Remove the stoplight switch

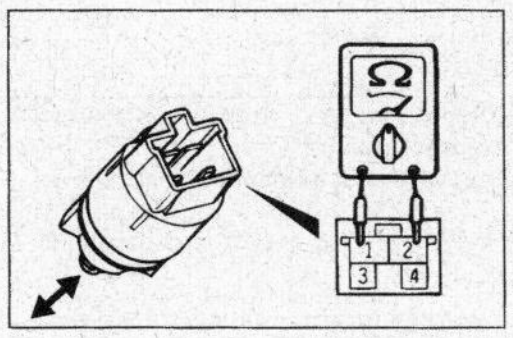

(2) Connect an ohmmeter to stoplight switch terminals 1 and 2, and check whether there is continuity when the plunger of the stoplight switch is pushed in and when it is released.

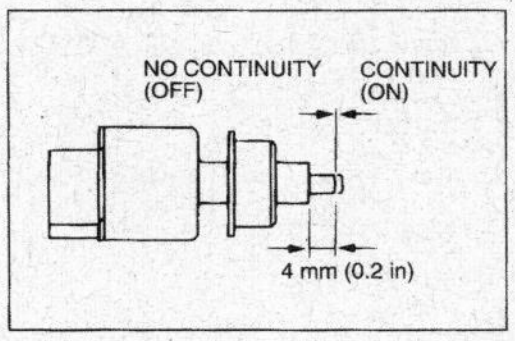

(3) The stoplight switch is in good condition if there is no continuity when the plunger is pushed in to a depth of within 4 mm (0.2 inch) from the outer case edge surface, and if there is continuity when it is released.

Q: Is the stoplight switch damaged?

YES : Replace it and then go to Step 7.
NO : Go to Step 6.

CR4020202374000X

Fig. 32 Code 38: Stop Lamp Switch System (Part 2 of 4). 2003 Sebring Coupe & Stratus Coupe

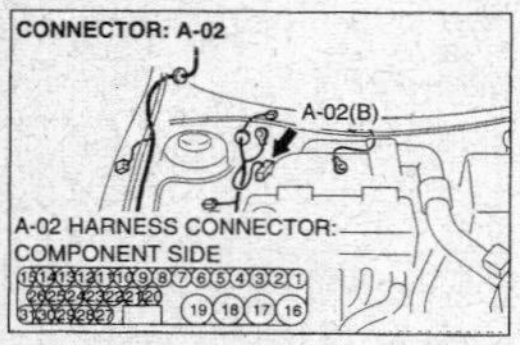

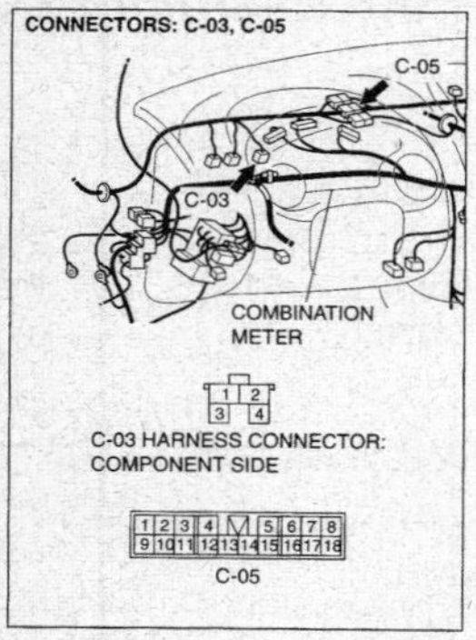

STEP 5. Check the harness wire between ABS-ECU connector A-02 terminal 14 and stoplight switch connector C-03 terminal 1.

NOTE: After inspecting intermediate connector C-05, inspect the wire. If intermediate connector C-05 is damaged, repair or replace it.

If the connector has been repaired or replaced, go to Step 7.

Q: Is any harness wire between ABS-ECU connector A-02 terminal 14 and stoplight switch connector C-03 terminal 1 damaged?

YES : Repair it and then go to Step 7.
NO : No action is to be taken.

CR4020202376000X

Fig. 32 Code 38: Stop Lamp Switch System (Part 3 of 4). 2003 Sebring Coupe & Stratus Coupe

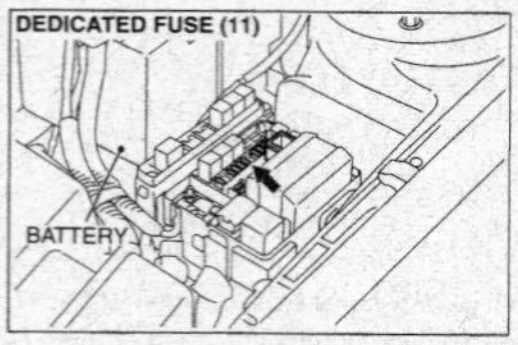

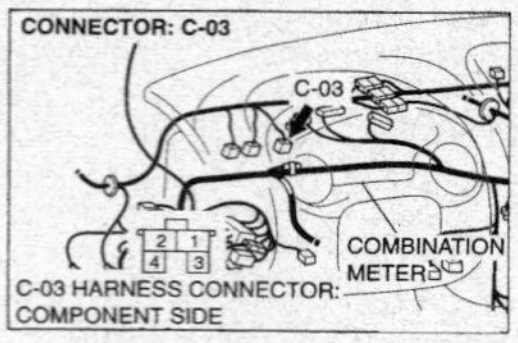

STEP 6. Check the harness wire between dedicated fuse number 11 and stoplight switch connector C-03 terminal 2.

Q: Is the harness wire between dedicated fuse number 11 and stoplight switch connector C-03 terminal 2 damaged?

YES : Repair it and then go to Step 7.
NO : Check and repair the harness wire between stoplight switch and stoplight. Then go to Step7.

STEP 7. Check the diagnostic trouble code.

Q: Does the diagnostic trouble code 38 reset?

YES : Return to Step 1.
NO : The procedure is complete.

CR4020202375000X

Fig. 32 Code 38: Stop Lamp Switch System (Part 4 of 4). 2003 Sebring Coupe & Stratus Coupe

CIRCUIT OPERATION

Power is continuously supplied to the ABS-ECU through fusible link number 3 to operate the solenoid valve and motor.

ABS DTC SET CONDITIONS

These codes are displayed if the power supply circuit of solenoid valve or motor is open or shorted.

TROUBLESHOOTING HINTS

- Damaged wiring harness or connector
- Malfunction of the hydraulic unit (integrated with ABS-ECU)

DIAGNOSIS

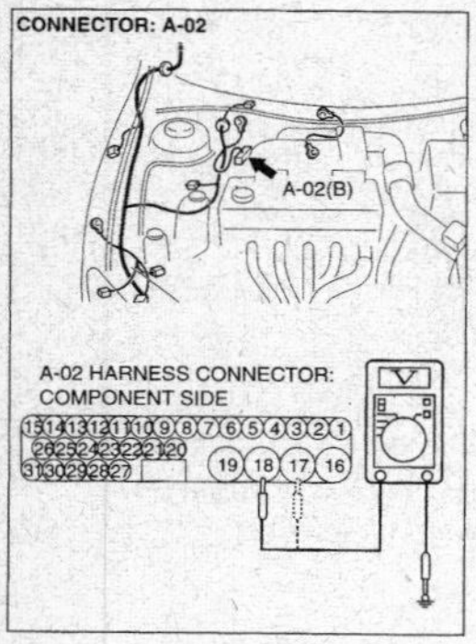

STEP 1. Check the solenoid valve or motor power supply circuit at ABS-ECU connector A-02.

(1) Disconnect connector A-02 and measure at the harness side.
(2) Measure the voltage between terminal 18 and ground or 17 and ground.

Q: Is battery positive voltage (approximately 12 volts) present?

YES : Replace the hydraulic unit (integrated with ABS-ECU) and then go to Step 3.
NO : Go to Step 2.

CR4020202377000X

Fig. 33 Codes 41, 42, 43, 44, 45, 46, 47, 48, 51 & 53: ABS Solenoid Valve Inside Hydraulic Unit (Part 1 of 2). 2003 Sebring Coupe & Stratus Coupe

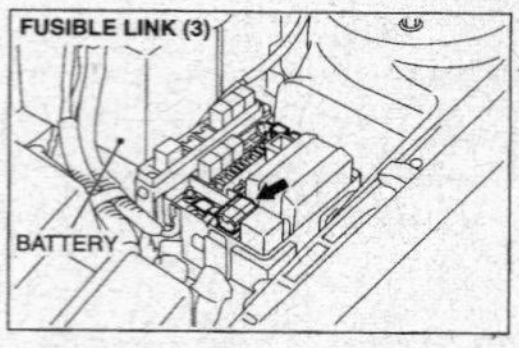

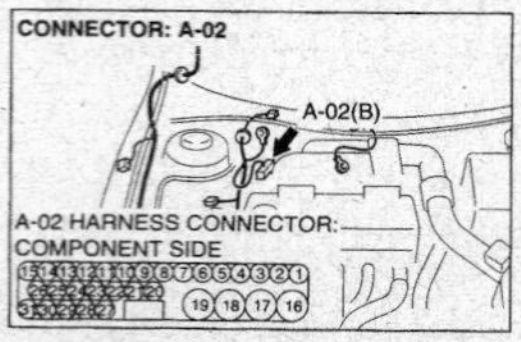

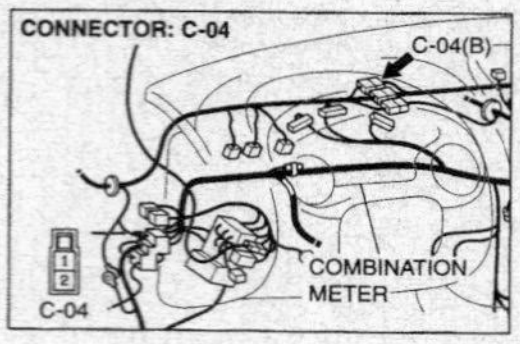

STEP 2. Check the harness wire between fusible link number 3 and ABS-ECU connector A-02 terminal 17 or terminal 18.

NOTE: After inspecting intermediate connector C-04, inspect the wires. If intermediate connector C-04 is damaged, repair or replace it.

If the connector has been repaired or replaced, go to Step 3.

Q: Is any harness wire between fusible link number 3 and ABS-ECU connector A-02 terminal 17 or terminal 18 damaged?

YES : Repair it then go to Step 3.
NO : Go to Step 3.

STEP 3. Check the diagnostic trouble code.

Q: Do the diagnostic trouble codes 41, 42, 43, 44, 45, 46, 47, 48, 51 or 53 reset?

YES : Go to Step 1.
NO : The procedure is complete.

CR4020202378000X

Fig. 33 Codes 41, 42, 43, 44, 45, 46, 47, 48, 51 & 53: ABS Solenoid Valve Inside Hydraulic Unit (Part 2 of 2). 2003 Sebring Coupe & Stratus Coupe

Communication with scan tool is not possible. (Communication with all systems is not possible.)	Probable cause
[Comment] The reason is probably a defect in the power supply system (including ground) for the diagnostic line.	• Malfunction of connector • Malfunction of harness

Refer to Diagnostic Tests

CR4029901711000X

Fig. 34 Communication w/Scan Tool Not Possible (Part 1 of 2). Avenger & 2000 Sebring Coupe

Communication with scan tool is not possible. (Communication with ABS only is not possible.)	Probable cause
[Comment] When communication with the scan tool is not possible, the cause is probably an open circuit in the ABS-ECU power circuit or an open circuit in the diagnostic output circuit.	• Blown fuse • Malfunction of wiring harness or connector • Malfunction of ABS-ECU

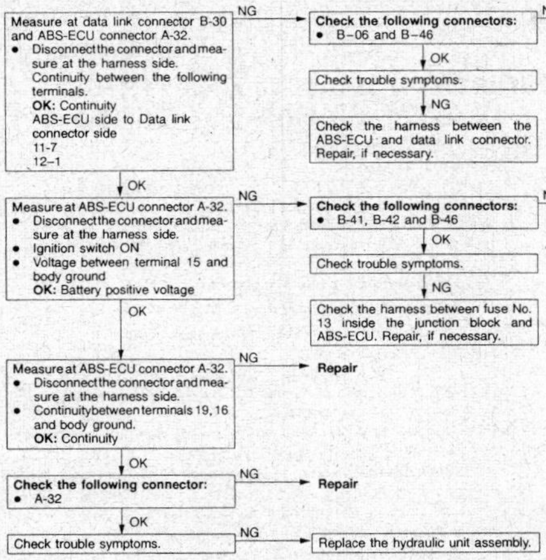

CR4029901712000X

Fig. 34 Communication w/Scan Tool Not Possible (Part 2 of 2). Avenger & 2000 Sebring Coupe

Even after the engine is started, the ABS warning light remains illuminated.	Probable cause
[Comment] There is probably a short in the ABS warning light illumination circuit.	• Malfunction of combination meter • Malfunction of ABS-ECU • Malfunction of wiring

NOTE
This trouble symptom is limited to cases where communication with the scan tool is possible (ABS-ECU power supply is normal) and the diagnostic trouble code is a normal diagnostic trouble code.

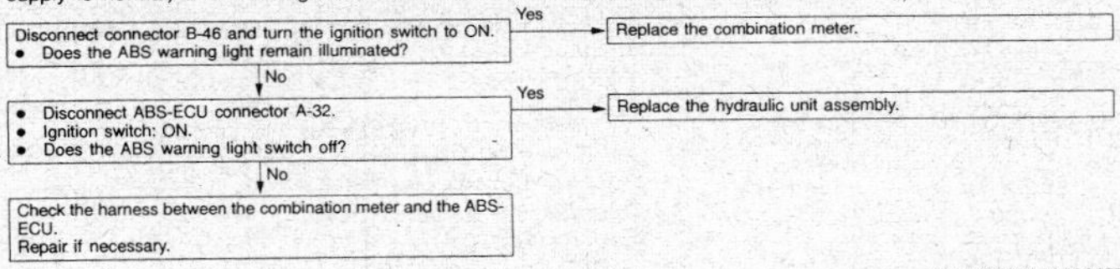

CR4029901714000X

Fig. 36 ABS Warning Lamp Remains Illuminated w/Engine Running. Avenger & 2000 Sebring Coupe

When ignition key is turned to "ON" (engine stopped), ABS warning light does not illuminate.	Probable cause
[Comment] When power is supplied to the ABS-ECU, the valve relay changes from ON to OFF → ON by the initial check, and thus even if there is a problem with the circuit between ABS warning light and ABS-ECU, the light will illuminate once when the valve relay is OFF. Accordingly, the cause of the light not illuminating is probably an open circuit in the light power circuit, a blown light bulb, or an open circuit in both the circuit between the ABS warning light and the ABS-ECU and the circuit between the ABS warning light and the ABS valve relay. When other warning lights also do not illuminate, the cause is probably a blown fuse.	• Blown fuse • Burnt out ABS warning light bulb • Malfunction of wiring harness or connector

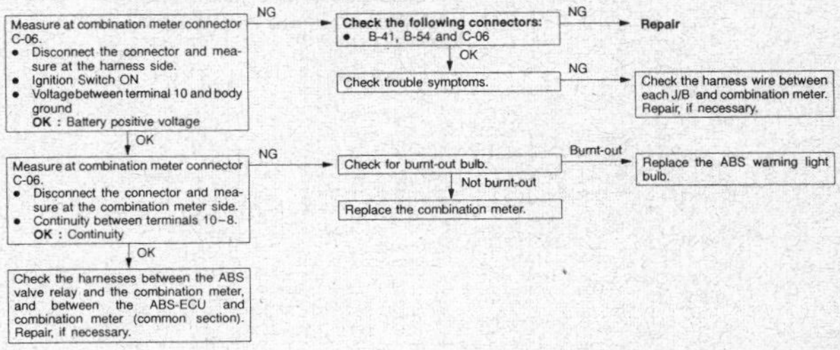

CR4029901713000X

Fig. 35 ABS Warning Lamp Does Not Illuminate w/Key On. Avenger & 2000 Sebring Coupe

Break operation is irregular.	Probable cause
This varies depending on the driving conditions and the road surface conditions, so problemdiagnosis is difficult. However, if a normal diagnostic trouble code is displayed, carry out the following inspection.	• Improper installation of wheel speed sensor • Incorrect sensor harness contact • Foreign material adhering to wheel speed sensor • Malfunction of wheel speed sensor • Malfunction of ABS rotor • Malfunction of wheel bearing • Malfunction of hydraulic unit • Malfunction of ABS-ECU

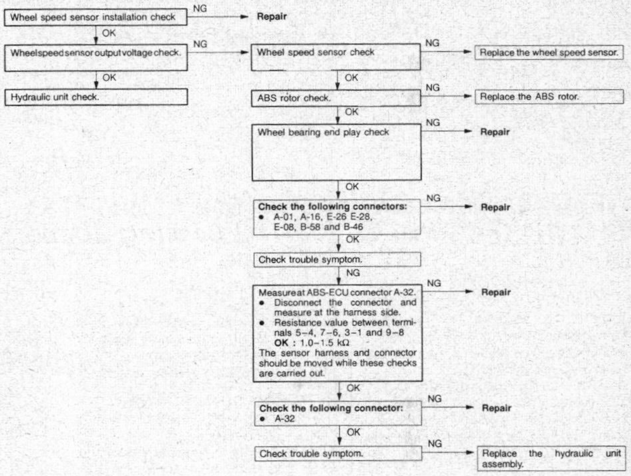

CR4029901715000X

Fig. 37 Brake Operation Irregular. Avenger & 2000 Sebring Coupe

CIRCUIT OPERATION

- The diagnostic output is made from the ABS-ECU (terminal 11) to the diagnostic output terminal (terminal 7) of the data link connector.
- When the data link connector's diagnostic test mode control terminal (terminal 1) is grounded, the ABS-ECU (terminal 12) will go into diagnostic mode.

TECHNICAL DESCRIPTION (COMMENT)
When communication with the scan tool is not possible, the cause is probably an open circuit in the ABS-ECU power circuit or an open circuit in the diagnostic output circuit.

TROUBLESHOOTING HINTS (The most likely causes for this case:)

- Blown fuse
- Damaged wiring harness and connector
- Malfunction of the hydraulic unit (Integrated with ABS-ECU)

DIAGNOSIS

Required Special Tool:

- MB991223: Harness Set

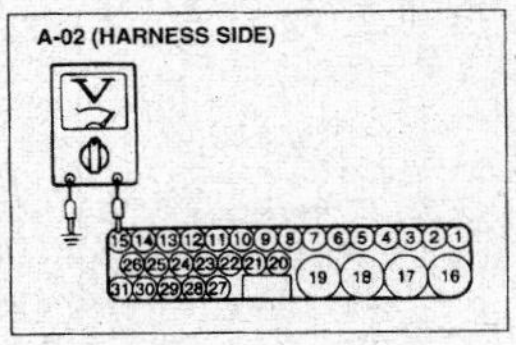

STEP 1. Check the power supply circuit at ABS-ECU connector A-02.
(1) Disconnect connector A-02 and measure at the harness side.
(2) Start the engine.
(3) Measure the voltage between terminal 15 and ground.

Q: Is voltage approximately 12 volts?
YES : Go to Step 3.
NO : Go to Step 2.

CR4020202345000X

Fig. 38 Communication w/Scan Tool Is Not Possible (Part 1 of 4). 2001–02 Sebring Coupe & Stratus Coupe

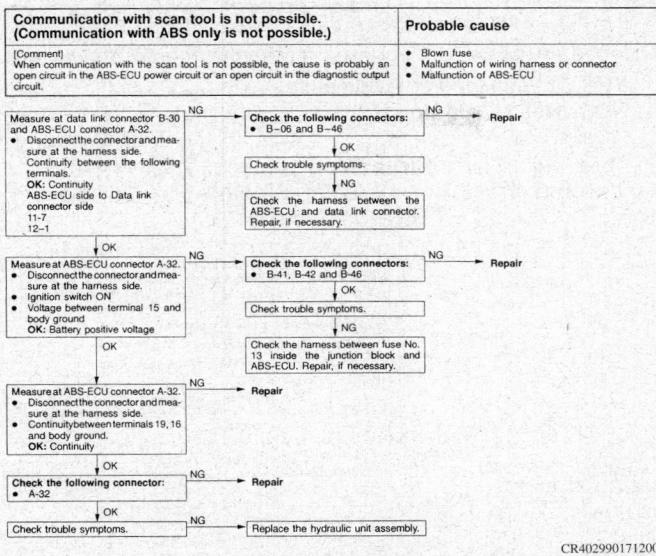

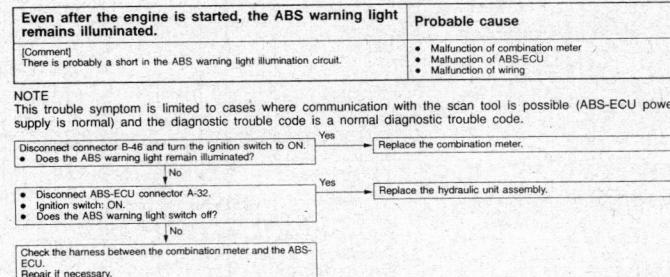

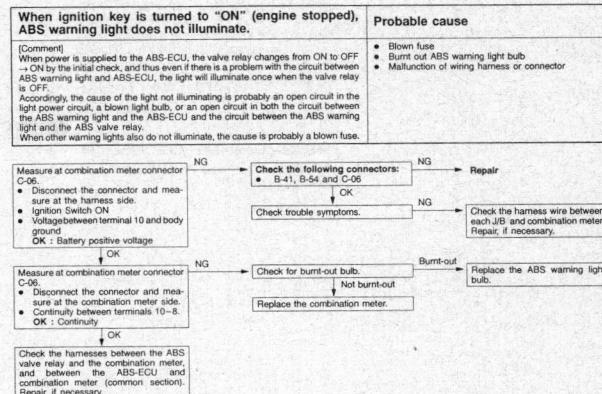

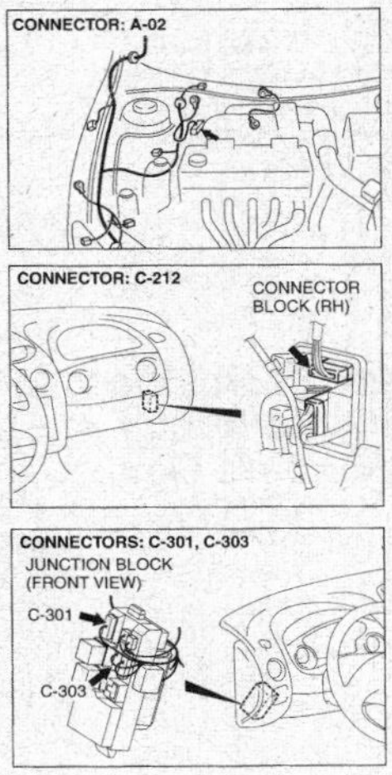

STEP 2. Check the harness wire between ignition switch (IG2) and ABS-ECU connector A-02
NOTE: After inspecting intermediate connector C-212, C-301, or C-303, inspect the wire. If intermediate connector C-212, C-301, or C-303 is damaged, repair or replace it. Refer to GROUP 8W1, Harness Connector InspectionP.8W1-2. If the connector has been repaired or replaced, go to Step 3 .

Q: Is any harness wire between ignition switch (IG2) and ABS-ECU connector A-02 damaged?
YES : Repair them and go to Step 5.
NO : Go to Step 3.

CR4020202346000X

Fig. 38 Communication w/Scan Tool Is Not Possible (Part 2 of 4). 2001–02 Sebring Coupe & Stratus Coupe

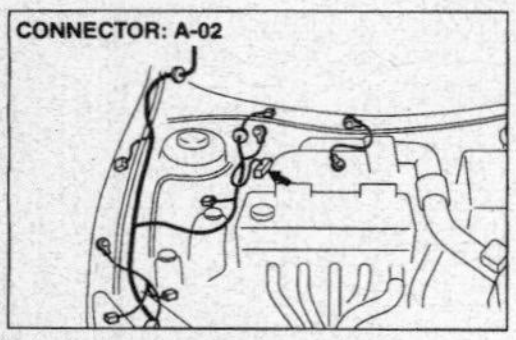

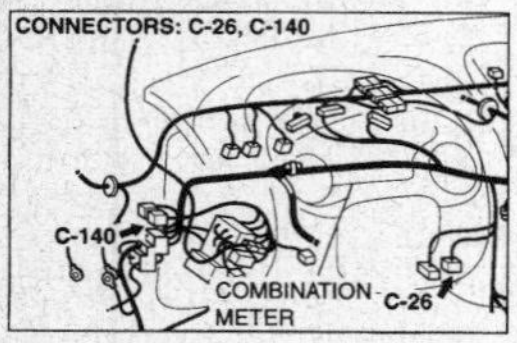

STEP 3. Check the harness wire between ABS-ECU connector A-02 and data link connector C-26.
NOTE: After inspecting intermediate connector C-140 or C-212, inspect the wire. If intermediate connector C-140 or C-212 is damaged, repair or replace it. If the connector has been repaired or replaced, go to Step 4.

Q: Is any harness wire between ABS-ECU connector A-02 and data link connector C-26 damaged?
- **YES :** Repair them and go to Step 5.
- **NO :** Go to Step 4.

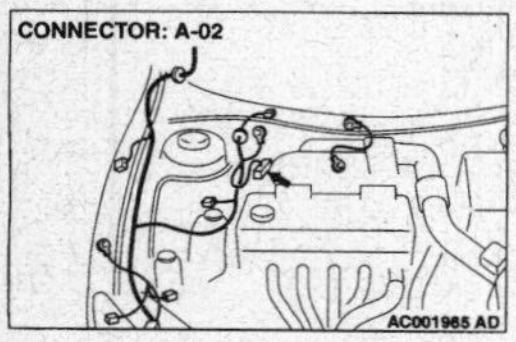

STEP 4. Check the harness wires between ABS-ECU connector A-02 and ground.

Q: Are any harness wires between ABS-ECU connector A-02 and ground damaged?
- **YES :** Repair them and then go to Step 5.
- **NO :** Go to Step 5.

CR4020202347000X

Fig. 38 Communication w/Scan Tool Is Not Possible (Part 3 of 4). 2001–02 Sebring Coupe & Stratus Coupe

STEP 5. Check symptoms

Q: Does the scan tool communicate with the ABS system?
- **YES :** This diagnosis is complete.
- **NO :** Return to Step 1.

CR4020202348000X

Fig. 38 Communication w/Scan Tool Is Not Possible (Part 4 of 4). 2001–02 Sebring Coupe & Stratus Coupe

CIRCUIT OPERATION
- The ABS warning light power is supplied from the ignition switch. The ABS-ECU grounds the circuit to illuminate the light.
- The ABS-ECU illuminates the ABS warning light for 3 seconds while running self-check. This light can be illuminated for 3 seconds upon start-up or ignition switch to the "ON" position, engine stopped.

TECHNICAL DESCRIPTION (COMMENT)
The cause may be: an open circuit in the ABS warning light power supply circuit, a blown ABS warning light bulb, or malfunction of the ABS-ECU.

TROUBLESHOOTING HINTS
The most likely causes for this case:
- Blown fuse
- Damaged wiring harness or connector
- Burnt out ABS warning light bulb
- Malfunction of the ABS-ECU

DIAGNOSIS

Required Special Tool:
- MB991223: Harness Set

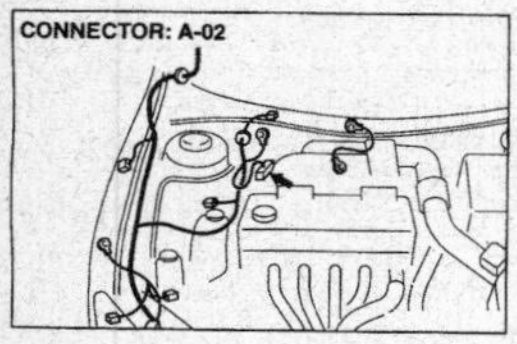

STEP 1. Check the ABS warning light circuit at ABS-ECU connector A-02.
(1) Disconnect ABS-ECU connector A-02.
(2) Turn the ignition switch to the "ON" position.

Q: Does the ABS warning light illuminate?
- **YES :** Replace the hydraulic unit (integrated with ABS-ECU) and then go to Step 9.
- **NO :** Go to Step 2.

CR4020202349000X

Fig. 39 When Ignition Switch In ON Position, ABS Warning Lamp Does Not Illuminate (Part 1 of 5). 2001–02 Sebring Coupe & Stratus Coupe

STEP 2 Check the ABS warning light bulb.
(1) Remove the combination meter
(2) Check the ABS warning light bulb.

Q: Is the bulb burned out?
- **YES :** Replace the bulb and then go to Step 9.
- **NO :** Go to Step 3.

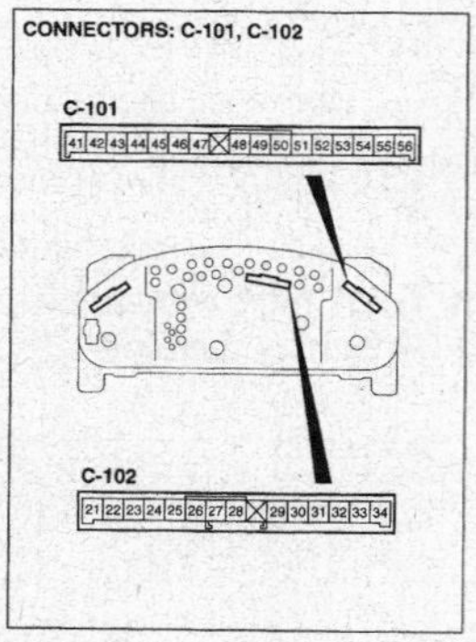

STEP 3. Check the combination meter for continuity.
(1) Remove the combination meter.
(2) Remove the ABS warning light bulb. Then measure the resistance between the bulb terminals.
(3) Install the ABS warning light bulb to the combination meter, and then measure the resistance between connector C-101 terminal 52 and connector C-102 terminal 24. The resistance reading at this time should be much the same as the resistance measured at step (2).

Q: Are the two resistance values extremely different each other?
- **YES :** Replace the combination meter (printed circuit board).
- **NO :** Go to Step 4.

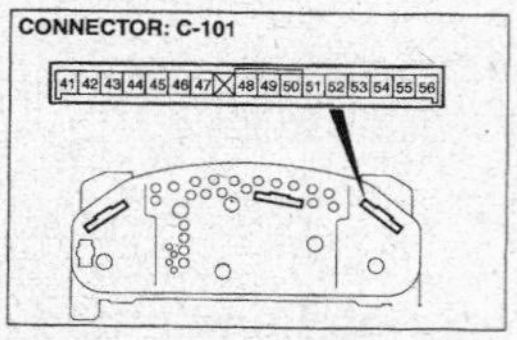

STEP 4. Check the combination meter power supply circuit.
(1) Disconnect connector C-101, and check at the harness side.
(2) Turn the ignition switch to the "ON" position.
(3) Measure the voltage between terminal 52 and ground. It should be approximately 12 V (battery positive voltage.)

Q: Is the voltage approximately 12 V?
- **YES :** Go to Step 5.
- **NO :** Go to Step 7.

CR4020202350000X

Fig. 39 When Ignition Switch In ON Position, ABS Warning Lamp Does Not Illuminate (Part 2 of 5). 2001–02 Sebring Coupe & Stratus Coupe

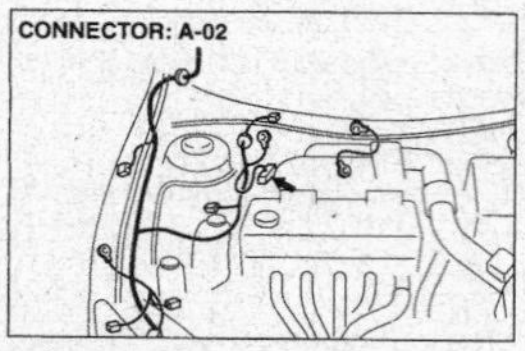

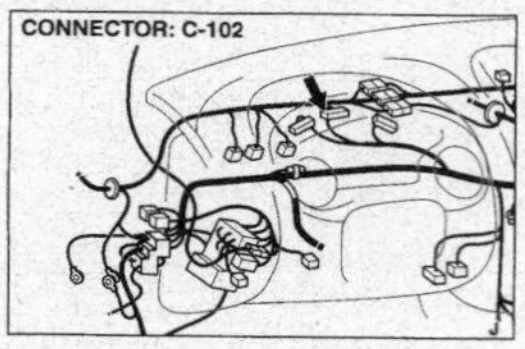

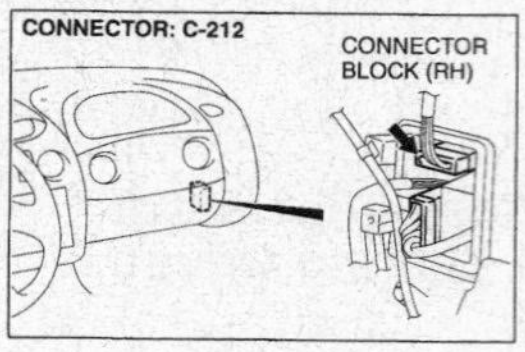

STEP 5. Check connectors C-102, C-212, and A-02.
Check connectors C-102, C-212, and A-02. (Refer to GROUP 8W1, Harness Connector Inspection P.8W1-2.)

Q: Is any of the connectors damaged?
- **YES :** Repair it and then go to Step 9.
- **NO :** Go to Step 6.

CR4020202351000X

Fig. 39 When Ignition Switch In ON Position, ABS Warning Lamp Does Not Illuminate (Part 3 of 5). 2001–02 Sebring Coupe & Stratus Coupe

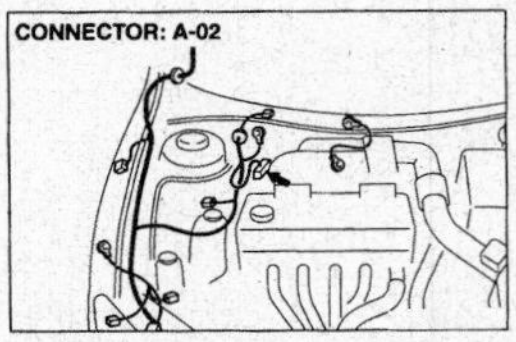

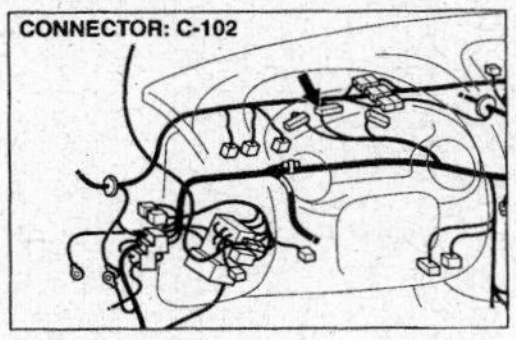

STEP 6. Check the continuity between the combination meter and the ABS-ECU.
Check the continuity between combination meter connector C-102 and ABS-ECU connector A-02.

Q: Is there the continuity between combination meter connector C-102 and ABS-ECU connector A-02?

YES : Go to Step 9.
NO : Repair the harness wire and then go to Step 9.

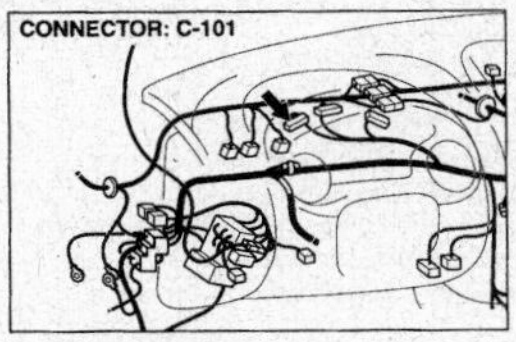

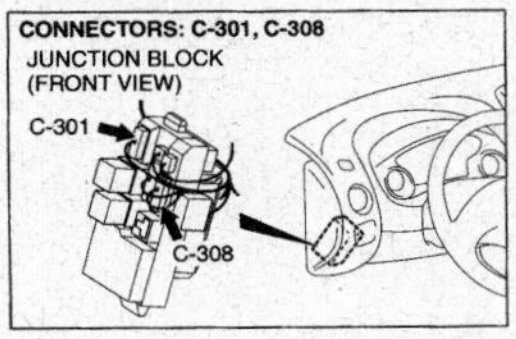

STEP 7. Check connectors C-101, C-308, and C-301.
Check connectors C-101, C-308, and C-301.

Q: Are any of the connectors damaged?

YES : Repair it and then go to Step 9.
NO : Go to Step 8.

CR4020202352000X

Fig. 39 When Ignition Switch In ON Position, ABS Warning Lamp Does Not Illuminate (Part 4 of 5). 2001–02 Sebring Coupe & Stratus Coupe

CIRCUIT OPERATION

- The ABS-ECU controls the illumination of the ABS warning light by turning the power transistor in the control unit ON and OFF
- The ABS-ECU illuminates the ABS warning light on start-up. It turns the light off after 3 seconds when the ABS-ECU completes the self-check.

TECHNICAL DESCRIPTION (COMMENT)

The cause is probably the ABS-ECU and hydraulic unit assembly malfunction.

TROUBLESHOOTING HINTS (The most likely causes for this condition:)

- Damaged wiring harness
- Malfunction of the hydraulic unit (integrated with ABS-ECU)

DIAGNOSIS

Required Special Tool:

- MB991223: Harness Set

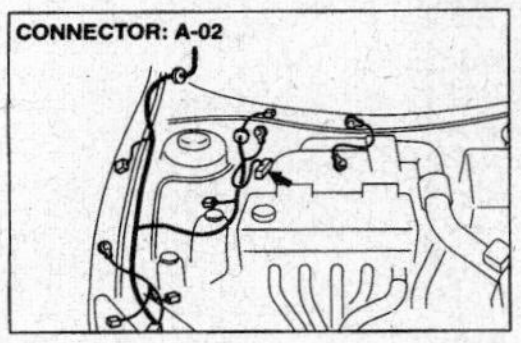

STEP 1. Check the ABS warning light circuit at ABS-ECU connector A-02.
(1) Disconnect ABS-ECU connector A-02.
(2) Turn the ignition switch to the "ON" position.

Q: Is the ABS warning light illuminate?

YES : Go to Step 2.
NO : Replace the ABS-ECU and then go to Step 3.

CR4020202354000X

Fig. 40 ABS Warning Lamp Remains Illuminated After Engine Is Started (Part 1 of 2). 2001–02 Sebring Coupe & Stratus Coupe

CIRCUIT OPERATION

- The diagnostic output is made from the ABS-ECU (terminal 11) to the diagnostic output terminal (terminal 7) of the data link connector.
- When the data link connector's diagnostic test mode control terminal (terminal 1) is grounded, the ABS-ECU (terminal 12) will go into diagnostic mode.

TECHNICAL DESCRIPTION (COMMENT)

When communication with the scan tool is not possible, the cause is probably an open circuit in the ABS-ECU power circuit or an open circuit in the diagnostic output circuit.

TROUBLESHOOTING HINTS (The most likely causes for this case:)

- Blown fuse
- Damaged wiring harness and connector
- Malfunction of the hydraulic unit (Integrated with ABS-ECU)

CR4020202379000X

Fig. 41 Communications Between Scan Tool & ABS-ECU Is Not Possible (Part 1 of 6). 2003 Sebring Coupe & Stratus Coupe

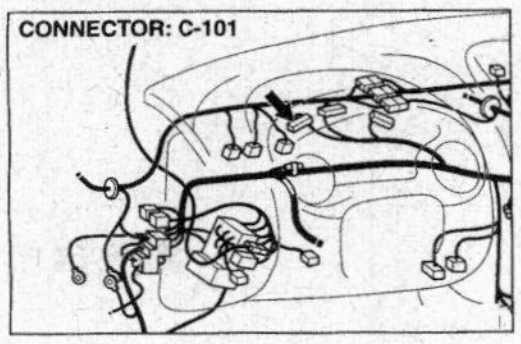

STEP 8. Check the continuity between the ignition switch (IG1) and the combination meter.

Q: Is there any continuity (less than 2 ohm) between the ignition switch (IG1) and combination meter connector C-101?

YES : Go to Step 9.
NO : Repair the harness wire and then go to Step 9.

STEP 9. Check symptoms

Q: Does the ABS warning light illuminate for 3 seconds when the ignition switch is turned to the "ON" position with engine stopped or upon start-up?

YES : This diagnosis is complete.
NO : Return to Step 1.

CR4020202353000X

Fig. 39 When Ignition Switch In ON Position, ABS Warning Lamp Does Not Illuminate (Part 5 of 5). 2001–02 Sebring Coupe & Stratus Coupe

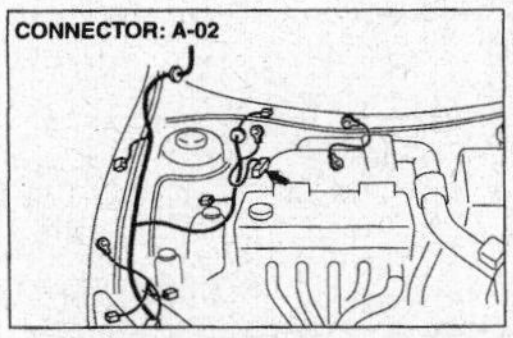

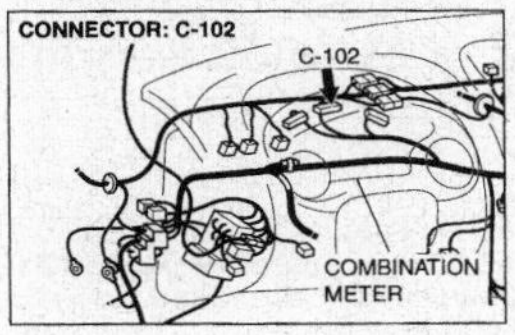

STEP 2. Check the harness wires between ABS-ECU connector A-02 and ABS warning light connector C-102.

Q: Are any harness wires between ABS-ECU connector A-02 and ABS warning light connector C-102 damaged?

YES : Repair them and then go to Step 3.
NO : Go to Step 3.

STEP 3. Check symptoms

Q: Does the ABS warning light turn off 3 seconds after start-up?

YES : This diagnosis is complete.
NO : Return to Step 1.

CR4020202355000X

Fig. 40 ABS Warning Lamp Remains Illuminated After Engine Is Started (Part 2 of 2). 2001–02 Sebring Coupe & Stratus Coupe

DIAGNOSIS

Required Special Tool:

- MB991223: Harness Set

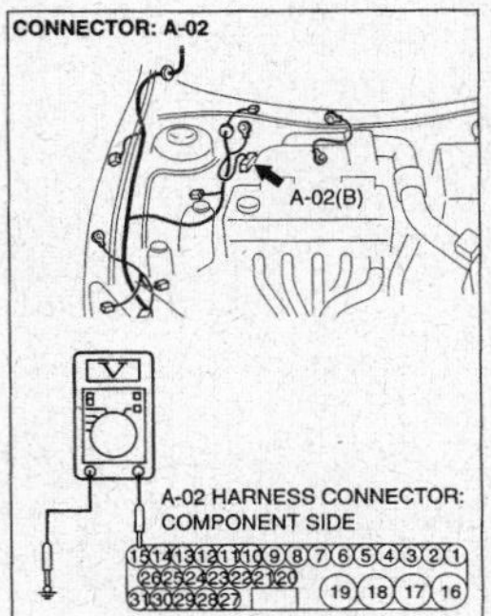

STEP 1. Check the power supply circuit at ABS-ECU connector A-02.
(1) Disconnect connector A-02 and measure at the harness side.
(2) Start the engine.
(3) Measure the voltage between terminal 15 and ground.

Q: Is battery positive voltage (approximately 12 volts) present?

YES : Go to Step 3.
NO : Go to Step 2.

CR4020202380000X

Fig. 41 Communications Between Scan Tool & ABS-ECU Is Not Possible (Part 2 of 6). 2003 Sebring Coupe & Stratus Coupe

STEP 2. Check the harness wire between ignition switch (IG2) connector C-202 terminal 4 and ABS-ECU connector A-02 terminal 15.

NOTE: After inspecting intermediate connectors C-212, C-311, and C-312, inspect the wire. If intermediate connector C-212, C-311, or C-312 is damaged, repair or replace it.

If the connector has been repaired or replaced, go to Step 3.

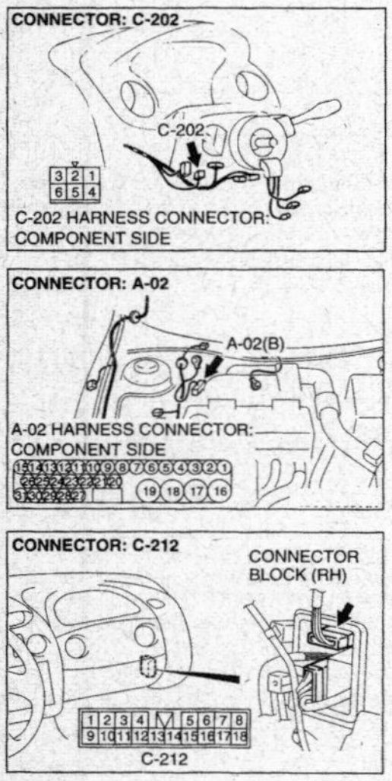

CR4020202381000X

Fig. 41 Communications Between Scan Tool & ABS-ECU Is Not Possible (Part 3 of 6). 2003 Sebring Coupe & Stratus Coupe

STEP 3. Check the harness wire between ABS-ECU connector A-02 terminal 11 and data link connector C-26 terminal 7 or ABS-ECU connector A-02 terminal 12 and data link connector C-26 terminal 1.

NOTE: After inspecting intermediate connectors C-140 and C-212, inspect the wire. If intermediate connector C-140 or C-212 is damaged, repair or replace it.

If the connector has been repaired or replaced, go to Step 4.

Q: Is any harness wire between ABS-ECU connector A-02 terminal 11 and data link connector C-26 terminal 7 or ABS-ECU connector A-02 terminal 12 and data link connector C-26 terminal 1 damaged?

YES : Repair them and go to Step 5.

NO : Go to Step 4.

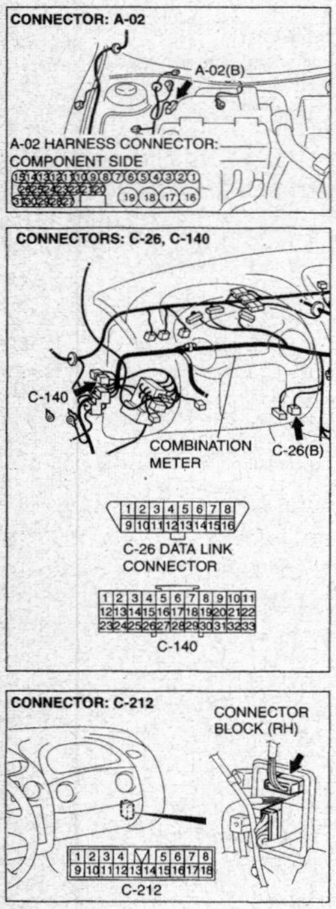

CR4020202383000X

Fig. 41 Communications Between Scan Tool & ABS-ECU Is Not Possible (Part 5 of 6). 2003 Sebring Coupe & Stratus Coupe

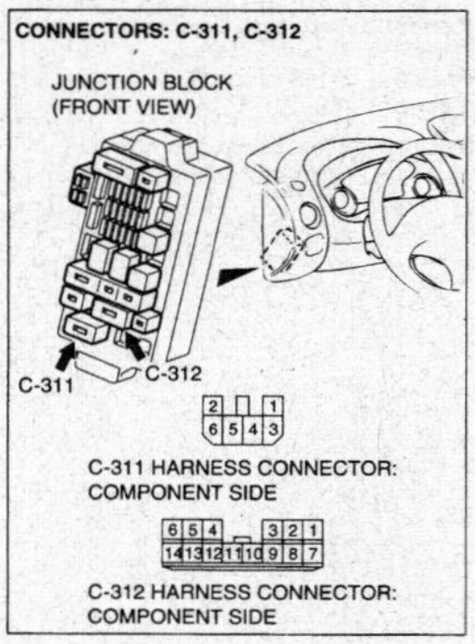

Q: Is any harness wire between ignition switch (IG2) connector C-202 terminal 4 and ABS-ECU connector A-02 terminal 15 damaged?

YES : Repair them and go to Step 5.

NO : Go to Step 3.

CR4020202382000X

Fig. 41 Communications Between Scan Tool & ABS-ECU Is Not Possible (Part 4 of 6). 2003 Sebring Coupe & Stratus Coupe

STEP 4. Check the harness wires between ABS-ECU connector A-02 terminal 19 and ground.

Q: Are any harness wires between ABS-ECU connector A-02 terminal 19 and ground damaged?

YES : Repair them and then go to Step 5.

NO : Go to Step 5.

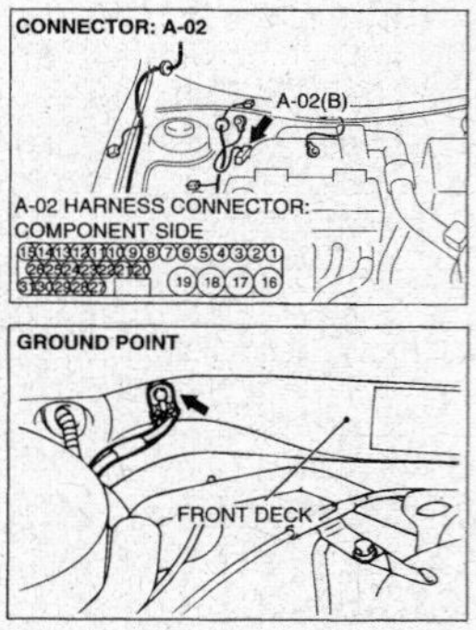

STEP 5. Check symptom.

Q: Does the scan tool communicate with the ABS system?

YES : The procedure is complete.

NO : Return to Step 1.

CR4020202384000X

Fig. 41 Communications Between Scan Tool & ABS-ECU Is Not Possible (Part 6 of 6). 2003 Sebring Coupe & Stratus Coupe

CIRCUIT OPERATION

- The ABS warning light power is supplied from the ignition switch. The ABS-ECU grounds the circuit to illuminate the light.
- The ABS-ECU illuminates the ABS warning light for 3 seconds while running self-check. This light can be illuminated for 3 seconds upon start-up or ignition switch to the "ON" position, engine stopped.

TECHNICAL DESCRIPTION (COMMENT)

The cause may be: an open circuit in the ABS warning light power supply circuit, a blown ABS warning light bulb, or malfunction of the ABS-ECU.

TROUBLESHOOTING HINTS

The most likely causes for this case:

- Blown fuse
- Damaged wiring harness or connector
- Burnt out ABS warning light bulb
- Malfunction of the ABS-ECU

DIAGNOSIS

Required Special Tool:

- MB991223: Harness Set

STEP 1. Check the ABS warning light circuit at ABS-ECU connector A-02.

(1) Disconnect ABS-ECU connector A-02.
(2) Turn the ignition switch to the "ON" position.

Q: Does the ABS warning light illuminate?

YES : Replace the hydraulic unit (integrated with ABS-ECU) and then go to Step 7.

NO : Go to Step 2.

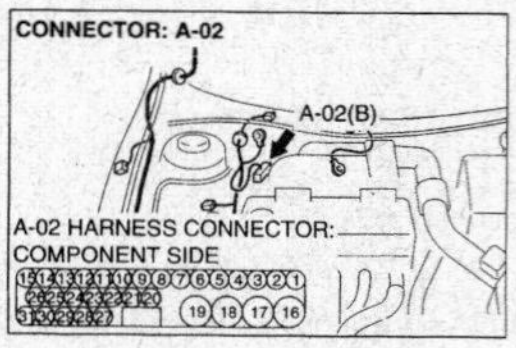

CR4020202385000X

Fig. 42 ABS Warning Lamp Does Not Illuminate When Ignition Key is In ON Position (Part 1 of 6). 2003 Sebring Coupe & Stratus Coupe

STEP 2 Check the ABS warning light bulb.
(1) Remove the combination meter
(2) Check the ABS warning light bulb.

Q: Is the bulb burned out?
YES : Replace the bulb and then go to Step 7.
NO : Go to Step 3.

STEP 3. Check the combination meter for continuity.
(1) Remove the combination meter.
(2) Remove the ABS warning light bulb. Then measure the resistance between the bulb terminals.
(3) Install the ABS warning light bulb to the combination meter, and then measure the resistance between connector C-101 terminal 12 and terminal 21. The resistance reading at this time should be much the same as the resistance measured at step (2).

Q: Are the two resistance values extremely different each other?
YES : Replace the combination meter (printed circuit board) and then go to Step 7.
NO : Go to Step 4.

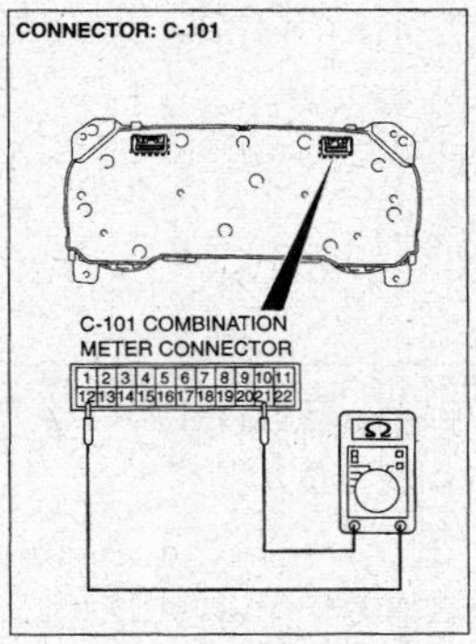

CR4020202386000X

Fig. 42 ABS Warning Lamp Does Not Illuminate When Ignition Key is In ON Position (Part 2 of 6). 2003 Sebring Coupe & Stratus Coupe

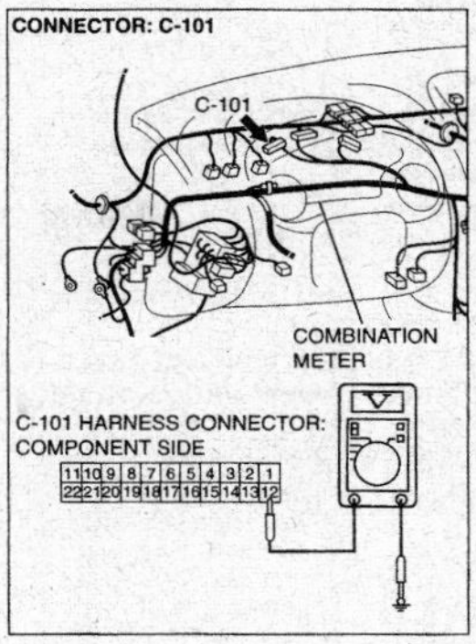

STEP 4. Check the combination meter power supply circuit.
(1) Disconnect connector C-101, and check at the harness side.
(2) Turn the ignition switch to the "ON" position.
(3) Measure the voltage between terminal 12 and ground. It should be battery positive voltage (approximately 12 volts).

Q: Is battery positive voltage (approximately 12 volts) present?
YES : Go to Step 5.
NO : Go to Step 6.

CR4020202387000X

Fig. 42 ABS Warning Lamp Does Not Illuminate When Ignition Key is In ON Position (Part 3 of 6). 2003 Sebring Coupe & Stratus Coupe

STEP 5. Check the harness wire between the combination meter connector C-101 terminal 21 and the ABS-ECU A-02 terminal 21.

NOTE: After inspecting intermediate connector C-212 inspect the wire. If intermediate connector C-212 is damaged, repair or replace it. If the connector has been repaired or replaced, go to Step 7.

Q: Is any harness wire between combination meter connector C-101 terminal 21 and ABS-ECU connector A-02 terminal 21 damaged?
YES : Repair it and then go to Step 7.
NO : Go to Step 7.

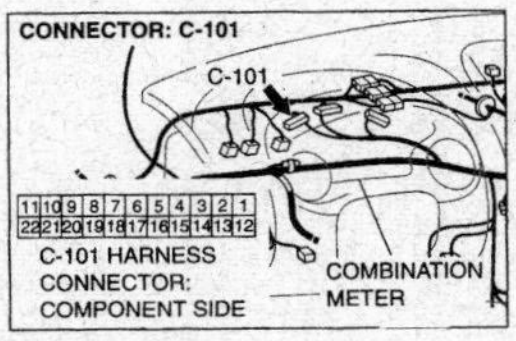

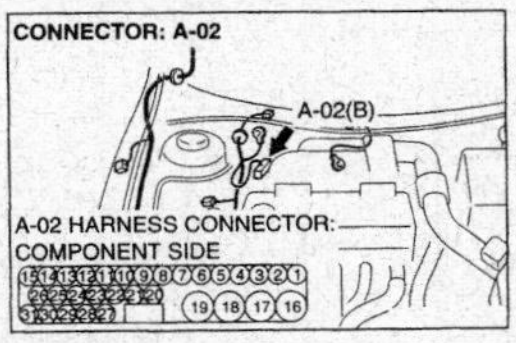

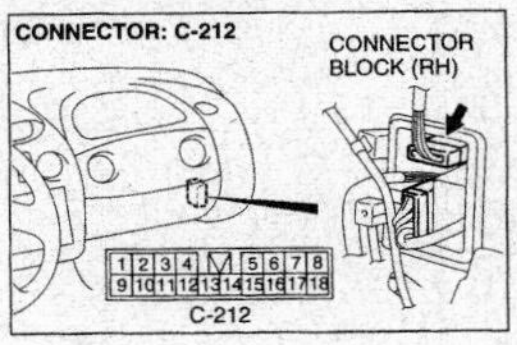

CR4020202388000X

Fig. 42 ABS Warning Lamp Does Not Illuminate When Ignition Key is In ON Position (Part 4 of 6). 2003 Sebring Coupe & Stratus Coupe

STEP 6. Check the harness wire between ignition switch (IG1) connector C-202 terminal 2 and combination meter connector C-101 terminal 12.

NOTE: After inspecting intermediate connectors C-308 and C-311, inspect the wires. If intermediate connector C-308 or C-311 is damaged, repair or replace it. If the connector has been repaired or replaced, go to Step 7.

Q: Is any harness wire between the ignition switch (IG1) connector C-202 terminal 2 and the combination meter connector C-101 terminal 12 damaged?
YES : Repair it and then go to Step 7.
NO : Go to Step 7.

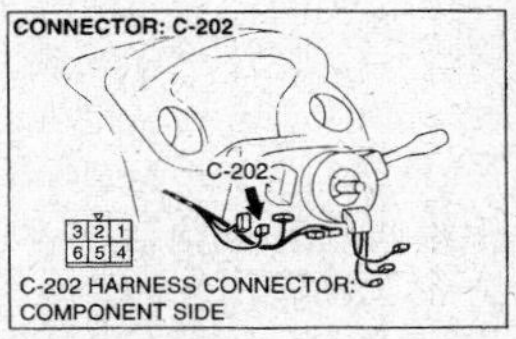

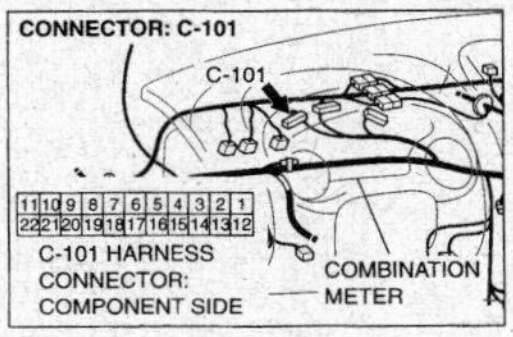

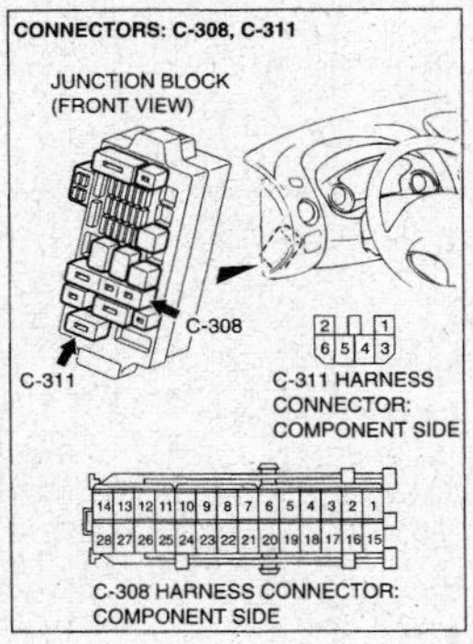

CR4020202389000X

Fig. 42 ABS Warning Lamp Does Not Illuminate When Ignition Key is In ON Position (Part 5 of 6). 2003 Sebring Coupe & Stratus Coupe

STEP 7. Check symptom.

Q: Does the ABS warning light illuminate for 3 seconds when the ignition switch is turned to the "ON" position with engine stopped or upon start-up?
YES : The procedure is complete.
NO : Return to Step 1.

CR4020202390000X

Fig. 42 ABS Warning Lamp Does Not Illuminate When Ignition Key is In ON Position (Part 6 of 6). 2003 Sebring Coupe & Stratus Coupe

CIRCUIT OPERATION

- The ABS-ECU controls the illumination of the ABS warning light by turning the power transistor in the control unit ON and OFF
- The ABS-ECU illuminates the ABS warning light on start-up. It turns the light off after 3 seconds when the ABS-ECU completes the self-check.

TECHNICAL DESCRIPTION (COMMENT)
The cause is probably the ABS-ECU and hydraulic unit assembly malfunction.

TROUBLESHOOTING HINTS (The most likely causes for this condition:)

- Damaged wiring harness
- Malfunction of the hydraulic unit (integrated with ABS-ECU)

CR4020202391000X

Fig. 43 ABS Warning Lamp Remains Illuminated After Engine Is Started (Part 1 of 3). 2003 Sebring Coupe & Stratus Coupe

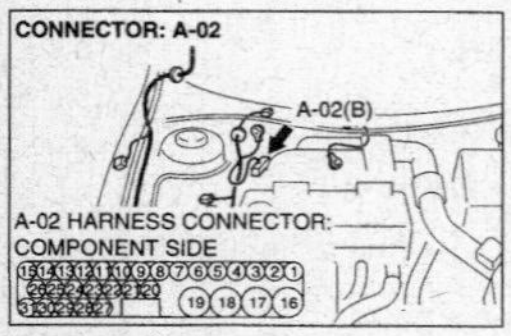

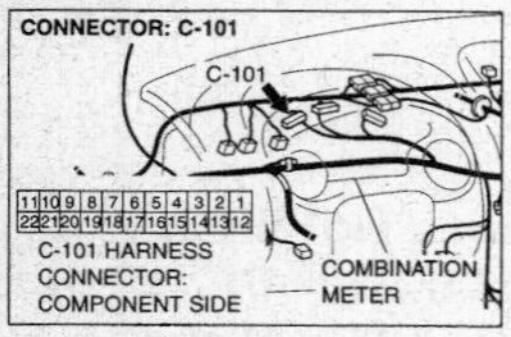

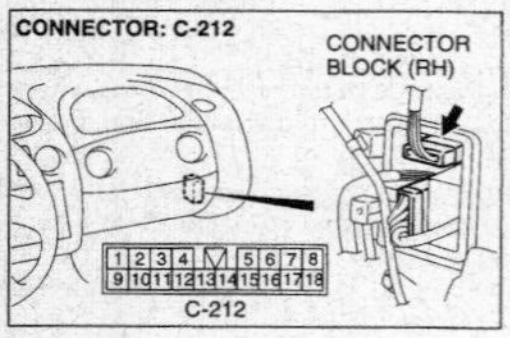

DIAGNOSIS

Required Special Tool:

- MB991223: Harness Set

STEP 1. Check the harness wires between ABS-ECU connector A-02 terminal 21 and combination meter connector C-101 terminal 21.

NOTE: After inspecting intermediate connector C-212 inspect the wire. If intermediate connector C-212 is damaged, repair or replace it. If the connector has been repaired or replaced, go to Step 3.

Q: Is any harness wire between ABS-ECU connector A-02 terminal 21 and combination meter connector C-101 terminal 21 damaged?

YES : Repair it and then go to Step 3.
NO : Go to Step 2.

CR4020202392000X

Fig. 43 ABS Warning Lamp Remains Illuminated After Engine Is Started (Part 2 of 3). 2003 Sebring Coupe & Stratus Coupe

1. MEASURE THE VOLTAGE OF THE CAB FUSED B(+) CIRCUIT

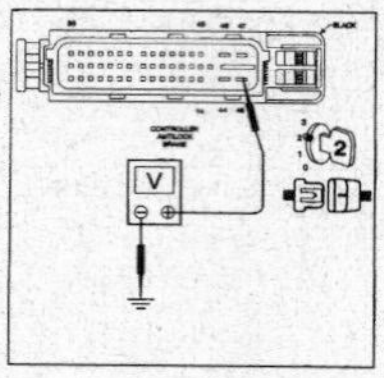

Turn the ignition off.
Disconnect the CAB harness connector.
Note: Check connectors - Clean/repair as necessary.
Turn the ignition on.
Measure the voltage of the Fused B(+) circuit at cavity 45 of the CAB harness connector.

Is the voltage between 12 and 16 volts?

Yes >> Go to 2
No >> System voltage must be between 12 and 16 volts. Repair the voltage concern as necessary.
Perform ABS VERIFICATION TEST.

2. MEASURE THE VOLTAGE OF THE CAB FUSED B(+) CIRCUIT

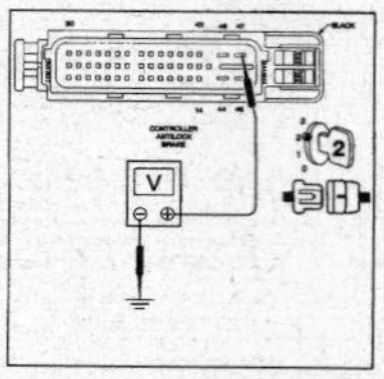

With the ignition on.
Measure the voltage of the Fused B(+) circuit at cavity 47 of the CAB harness connector.

Is the voltage between 12 and 16 volts?

Yes >> Replace the Controller Antilock Brake.
Perform ABS VERIFICATION TEST.
No >> System voltage must be between 12 and 16 volts. Repair the voltage concern as necessary.
Perform ABS VERIFICATION TEST.

ARM0300000000206

Fig. 44 CAB Internal Failure. ABS

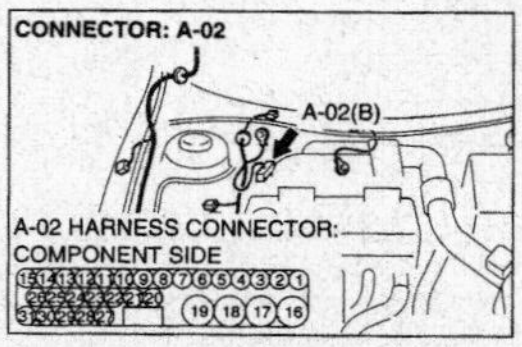

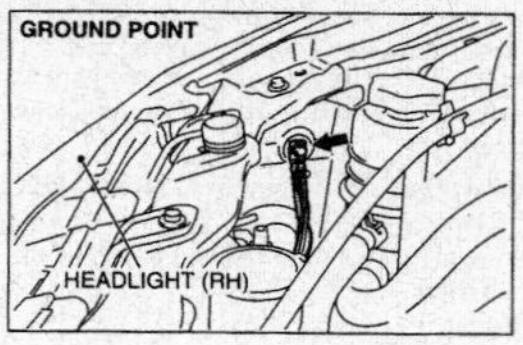

STEP 2. Check the harness wires between ABS-ECU connector A-02 terminal 19 and ground.

Q: Is the harness wire between ABS-ECU connector A-02 terminal 19 and ground damaged?

YES : Repair it and then go to Step 3.
NO : Replace the ABS-ECU and then go to Step 3.

STEP 3. Check symptom.

Q: Does the ABS warning light turn off 3 seconds after start-up?

YES : The procedure is complete.
NO : Return to Step 1.

CR4020202393000X

Fig. 43 ABS Warning Lamp Remains Illuminated After Engine Is Started (Part 3 of 3). 2003 Sebring Coupe & Stratus Coupe

1. WITH THE DRB III®, READ DTCs

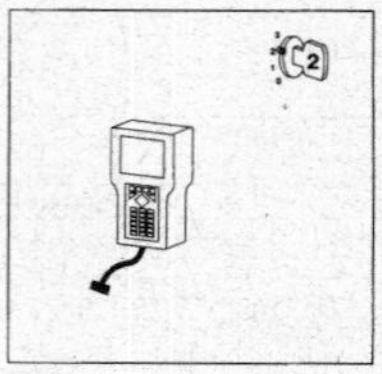

Turn the ignition on.
With the DRB III®, erase DTCs.
Turn the ignition off.
Turn the ignition on.
Start the engine.
Drive the vehicle above 10 MPH for at least 20 seconds.
Stop the vehicle.
With the DRB III®, read DTCs.

Does the DRB III® display a System Undervoltage DTC?

Yes >> Go to 2
No >> The condition that caused this DTC to set is currently not present. Inspect the related wiring harness for a possible intermittent condition.

2. MEASURE THE BATTERY VOLTAGE

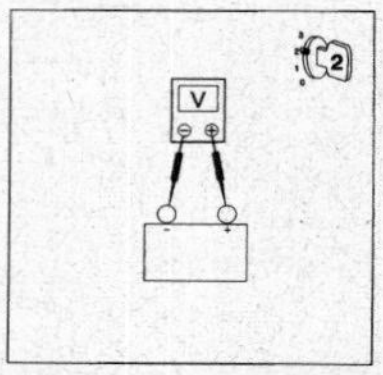

Start the engine.
Measure the battery voltage with the engine running.

Is the battery voltage below 10 volts?

Yes >> Refer to the appropriate service information for charging system testing and repair.
Perform ABS VERIFICATION TEST.
No >> Go to 3

ARM0300000000207

Fig. 45 CAB System Undervoltage (Part 1 of 2). ABS

3. MEASURE THE VOLTAGE OF THE FUSED B(+) CIRCUIT

Turn the ignition off.
Disconnect the CAB harness connector.
Note: Check connectors - Clean/repair as necessary.
Turn the ignition on.
Measure the voltage of the Fused B(+) circuit at cavity 45 of the CAB harness connector.

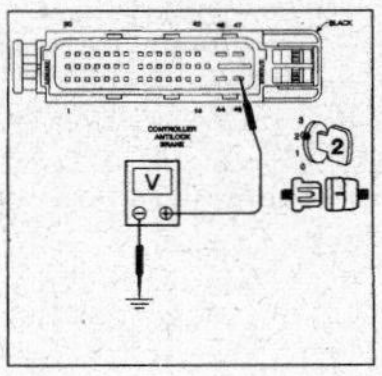

Is the voltage above 10 volts?

Yes >> Go to 4

No >> Repair the Fused B(+) circuit for an open.
Perform ABS VERIFICATION TEST.

4. MEASURE THE VOLTAGE OF THE FUSED B(+) CIRCUIT

With the ignition on.
Measure the voltage of the Fused B(+) circuit at cavity 47 of the CAB harness connector.

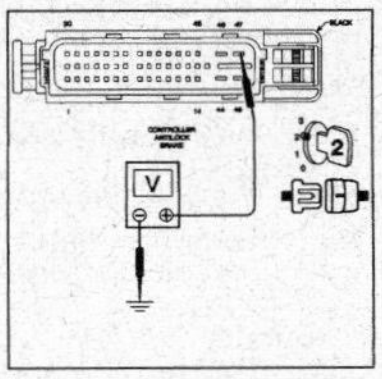

Is the voltage above 10 volts?

Yes >> Replace the Controller Antilock Brake.
Perform ABS VERIFICATION TEST.

No >> Repair the Fused B(+) circuit for an open.
Perform ABS VERIFICATION TEST.

ARM0300000000208

Fig. 45 CAB System Undervoltage (Part 2 of 2). ABS

3. MEASURE THE RESISTANCE OF THE GROUND CIRCUIT

Turn the ignition off.
Disconnect the CAB connector.
Note: Check connectors - Clean/repair as necessary.
Measure the resistance between ground and the Ground circuit at cavity 46 of the CAB harness connector.

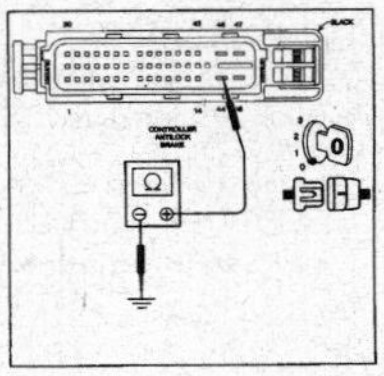

Is the resistance below 5.0 ohms?

Yes >> Go to 4

No >> Repair the Ground circuit for an open.
Perform ABS VERIFICATION TEST.

4. MEASURE THE RESISTANCE OF THE GROUND CIRCUIT

With the ignition off.
Measure the resistance between ground and the Ground circuit at cavity 44 of the CAB harness connector.

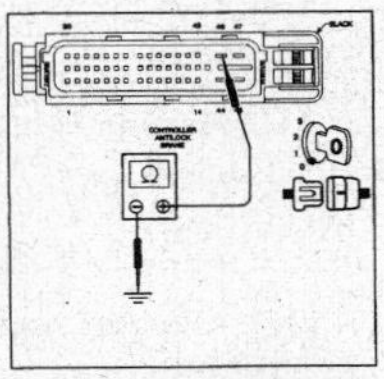

Is the resistance below 5.0 ohms?

Yes >> Replace the Controller Antilock Brake.
Perform ABS VERIFICATION TEST.

No >> Repair the Ground circuit for an open.
Perform ABS VERIFICATION TEST.

ARM0300000000210

Fig. 46 CAB System Overvoltage (Part 2 of 2). ABS

1. WITH THE DRB III®, READ DTCs

Turn the ignition on.
With the DRB III®, erase DTCs.
Turn the ignition off.
Turn the ignition on.
Start the engine.
With the DRB III®, read DTCs.

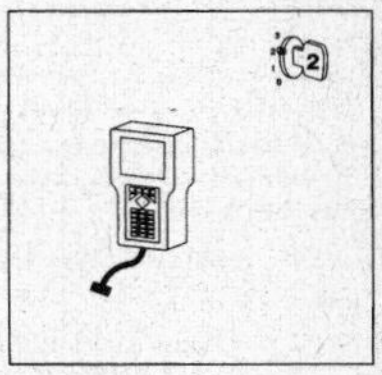

Does the DRB III® display a System Overvoltage DTC?

Yes >> Go to 2

No >> The condition that caused this DTC to set is currently not present. Inspect the related wiring harness for a possible intermittent condition.

2. MEASURE THE BATTERY VOLTAGE

Start the engine.
Raise engine speed above 1,800 RPM.
Measure the battery voltage.

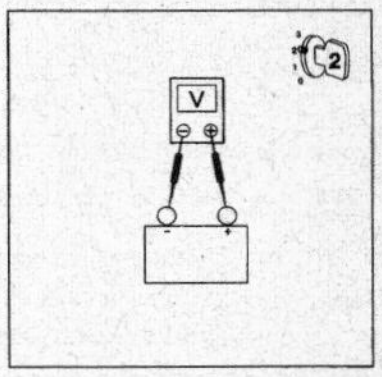

Is the voltage above 16 volts?

Yes >> Refer to the appropriate service information for charging system testing and repair.
Perform ABS VERIFICATION TEST.

No >> Go to 3

ARM0300000000209

Fig. 46 CAB System Overvoltage (Part 1 of 2). ABS

1. MEASURE THE RESISTANCE OF THE CAN C BUS (+) CIRCUIT

Turn the ignition off.
Disconnect the CAB harness connector.
Disconnect the harness connectors of the other modules on the CAN Bus network.
Note: Check connectors - Clean/repair as necessary.
Measure the resistance of the CAN C Bus (+) circuit from the CAB harness connector to the harness connectors of the other modules on the CAN Bus network.

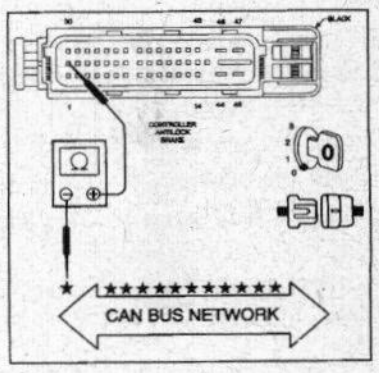

Is the resistance below 1.0 ohm?

Yes >> Go to 2

No >> Repair the CAN C Bus (+) circuit for an open.
Perform ABS VERIFICATION TEST.

2. MEASURE THE RESISTANCE OF THE CAN C BUS (-) CIRCUIT

With the ignition off.
Measure the resistance of the CAN C Bus (-) circuit from the CAB harness connector to the harness connectors of the other modules on the CAN Bus network.

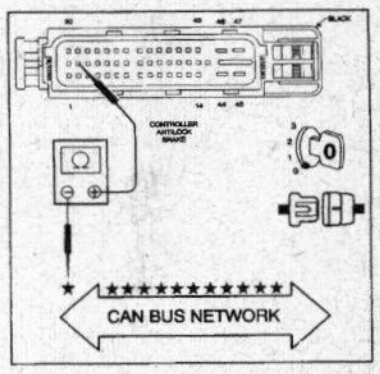

Is the resistance below 1.0 ohm?

Yes >> Replace the Controller Antilock Brake.
Perform ABS VERIFICATION TEST.

No >> Repair the CAN C Bus (-) circuit for an open.
Perform ABS VERIFICATION TEST.

ARM0300000000211

Fig. 47 CAB BUS Comminication Fault. ABS

Diagnostic Test

1. **MEASURE THE RESISTANCE OF THE CAN C BUS (+) CIRCUIT**

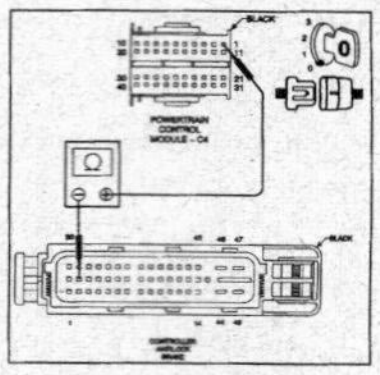

Turn the ignition off.
Disconnect the CAB harness connector.
Disconnect the PCM harness connector.
Note: Check connectors - Clean/repair as necessary.
Measure the resistance of the CAN C Bus (+) circuit from the CAB harness connector to the PCM harness connector.

Is the resistance below 1.0 ohm?

Yes >> Go to 2

No >> Repair the CAN C Bus (+) circuit for an open.
Perform ABS VERIFICATION TEST.

2. **MEASURE THE RESISTANCE OF THE CAN C BUS (-) CIRCUIT**

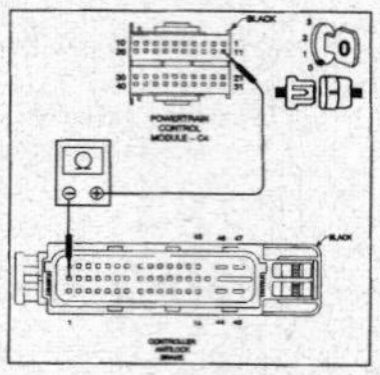

With the ignition off.
Measure the resistance of the CAN C Bus (-) circuit from the CAB harness connector to the PCM harness connector.

Is the resistance below 1.0 ohm?

Yes >> Replace the Controller Antilock Brake.
Perform ABS VERIFICATION TEST.

No >> Repair the CAN C Bus (-) circuit for an open.
Perform ABS VERIFICATION TEST.

ARM0300000000212

Fig. 48 No CAN Communications w/PCM. ABS

1. **WITH THE DRB III®, READ DTCs**

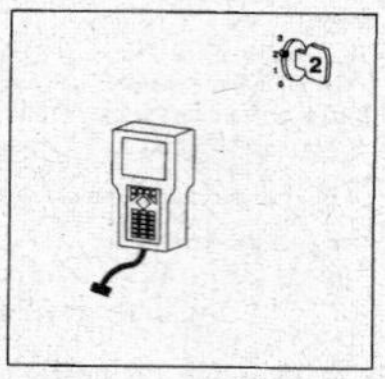

Turn the ignition on.
With the DRB III®, erase DTCs.
Turn the ignition off.
Turn the ignition on.
Start the engine.
CAUTION: Ensure braking capability is available before road testing.
Drive the vehicle above 10 MPH for at least 20 seconds.
Stop the vehicle.
With the DRB III®, read DTCs.

Does the DRB III® display a PCM Not Identified or Incorrect DTC?

Yes >> Replace the Controller Antilock Brake.
Perform ABS VERIFICATION TEST.

No >> The condition that caused this DTC to set is currently not present.
Perform ABS VERIFICATION TEST.

ARM0300000000214

Fig. 49 No CAN Coomunications w/TCM (Part 2 of 2). ABS

1. **WITH THE DRB III®, READ DTCs**

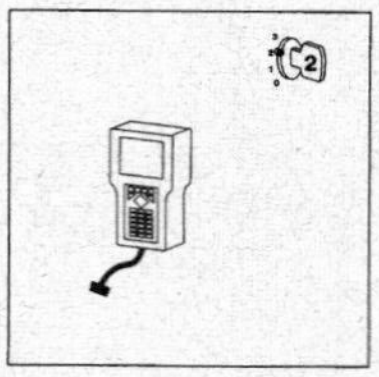

Turn the ignition on.
With the DRB III®, record and erase DTCs.
Turn the ignition off.
Turn the ignition on.
With the DRB III®, read DTCs.

Does the DRB III® display a Left Front Wheel Speed Sensor Circuit Failure DTC?

Yes >> Go to 2

No >> Go to 12

2. **INSPECT THE LEFT FRONT WHEEL SPEED SENSOR**

Turn the ignition off.
Inspect the Left Front Wheel Speed Sensor and connector.

Is the Sensor or Connector damaged?

Yes >> Repair as necessary.
Perform ABS VERIFICATION TEST.

No >> Go to 3

ARM0300000000215

Fig. 50 Lefthand Front Wheel Speed Sensor Fault (Part 1 of 5). ABS

1. **MEASURE THE RESISTANCE OF THE CAN C BUS (+) CIRCUIT**

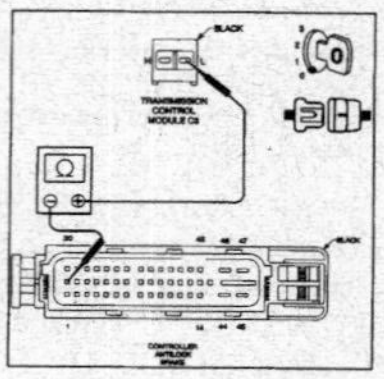

Turn the ignition off.
Disconnect the CAB harness connector.
Disconnect the TCM harness connector.
Note: Check connectors - Clean/repair as necessary.
Measure the resistance of the CAN C Bus (+) circuit from the CAB harness connector to the TCM harness connector.

Is the resistance below 1.0 ohm?

Yes >> Go to 2

No >> Repair the CAN C Bus (+) circuit for an open.
Perform ABS VERIFICATION TEST.

2. **MEASURE THE RESISTANCE OF THE CAN C BUS (-) CIRCUIT**

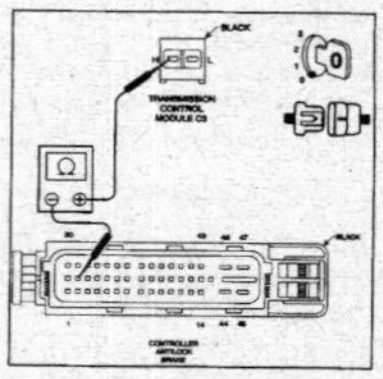

With the ignition off.
Measure the resistance of the CAN C Bus (-) circuit from the CAB harness connector to the TCM harness connector.

Is the resistance below 1.0 ohm?

Yes >> Replace the Controller Antilock Brake.
Perform ABS VERIFICATION TEST.

No >> Repair the CAN C Bus (-) circuit for an open.
Perform ABS VERIFICATION TEST.

ARM0300000000213

Fig. 49 No CAN Coomunications w/TCM (Part 1 of 2). ABS

3. **MEASURE THE VOLTAGE OF THE LEFT FRONT WHEEL SPEED SENSOR 12 VOLT SUPPLY CIRCUIT**

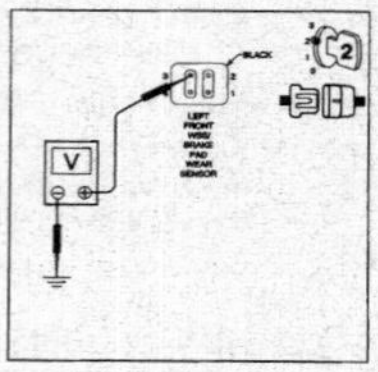

With the ignition off.
Disconnect the Left Front Wheel Speed Sensor harness connector.
Note: Check connectors - Clean/repair as necessary.
Turn the ignition on.
Measure the voltage of the Left Front Wheel Speed Sensor 12 Volt Supply circuit at the Left Front Wheel Speed Sensor harness connector.

Is the voltage approximately 12 volts?

Yes >> Go to 7

No >> Go to 4

4. **MEASURE THE VOLTAGE OF THE LEFT FRONT WHEEL SPEED SENSOR 12 VOLT SUPPLY CIRCUIT**

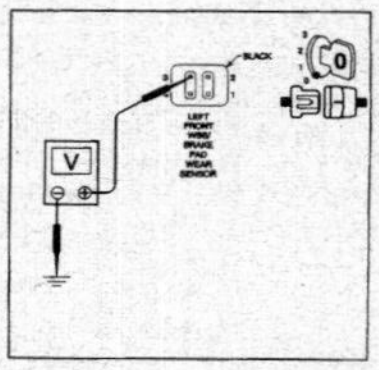

Turn the ignition off.
Measure the voltage of the Left Front Wheel Speed Sensor 12 Volt Supply circuit at the Left Front Wheel Speed Sensor harness connector.

Is the voltage 0 volts?

Yes >> Go to 5

No >> Replace the Controller Antilock Brake.
Perform ABS VERIFICATION TEST.

5. **MEASURE THE RESISTANCE BETWEEN GROUND AND THE LEFT FRONT WHEEL SPEED SENSOR 12 VOLT SUPPLY CIRCUIT**

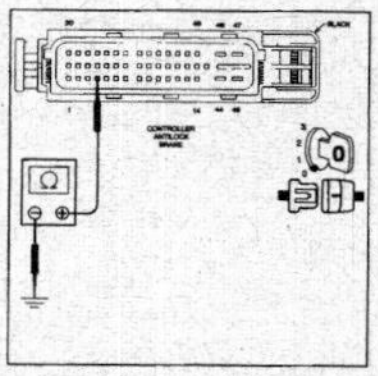

With the ignition off.
Disconnect the CAB harness connector.
Note: Check connectors - Clean/repair as necessary.
Measure the resistance between ground and the Left Front Wheel Speed Sensor 12 Volt Supply circuit at the CAB harness connector.

Is the resistance below 15k ohms?

Yes >> Repair the Left Front Wheel Speed Sensor 12 Volt Supply circuit for a short to ground.
Perform ABS VERIFICATION TEST.

No >> Go to 6

ARM0300000000216

Fig. 50 Lefthand Front Wheel Speed Sensor Fault (Part 2 of 5). ABS

6. MEASURE THE RESISTANCE OF THE LEFT FRONT WHEEL SPEED SENSOR 12 VOLT SUPPLY CIRCUIT

With the ignition off.
Measure the resistance of the Left Front Wheel Speed Sensor 12 Volt Supply circuit from the CAB harness connector to the Left Front Wheel Speed Sensor harness connector.

Is the resistance below 5.0 ohms?

Yes >> Go to 7

No >> Repair the Left Front Wheel Speed Sensor 12 Volt Supply circuit for an open.
Perform ABS VERIFICATION TEST.

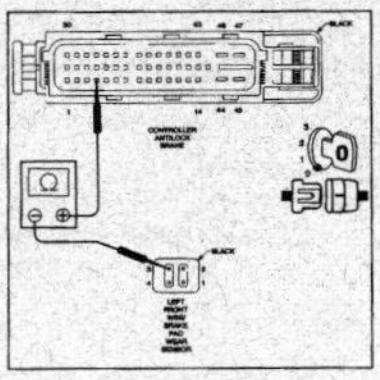

7. MEASURE THE RESISTANCE OF THE LEFT FRONT WHEEL SPEED SENSOR SIGNAL CIRCUIT

With the ignition off.
Reconnect the CAB harness connector.
Measure the resistance between ground and the Left Front Wheel Speed Sensor Signal circuit.

Is the resistance less than 100 ohms?

Yes >> Go to 10

No >> Go to 8

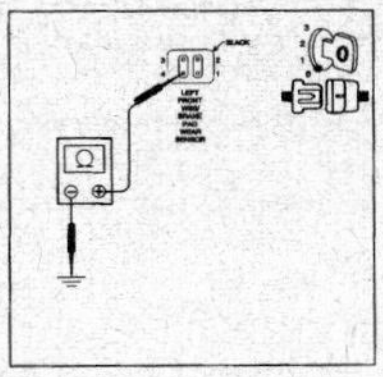

8. MEASURE THE RESISTANCE OF THE LEFT FRONT WHEEL SPEED SENSOR SIGNAL CIRCUIT

With the ignition off.
Measure the resistance between ground and the Left Front Wheel Speed Sensor Signal circuit.

Is the resistance greater than 300 ohms?

Yes >> Go to 9

No >> Replace the Left Front Wheel Speed Sensor.

Perform ABS VERIFICATION TEST.

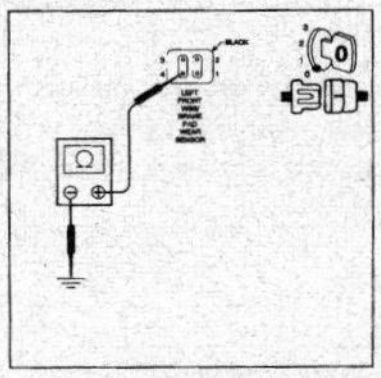

ARM0300000000217

Fig. 50 Lefthand Front Wheel Speed Sensor Fault (Part 3 of 5). ABS

9. MEASURE THE RESISTANCE OF THE LEFT FRONT WHEEL SPEED SENSOR SIGNAL CIRCUIT

With the ignition off.
Disconnect the CAB harness connector.
Note: Check connectors - Clean/repair as necessary.
Measure the resistance of the Left Front Wheel Speed Sensor Signal circuit from the CAB harness connector to the Left Front Wheel Speed Sensor harness connector.

Is the resistance below 5.0 ohms?

Yes >> Go to 11

No >> Repair the Left Front Wheel Speed Sensor Signal circuit for an open.
Perform ABS VERIFICATION TEST.

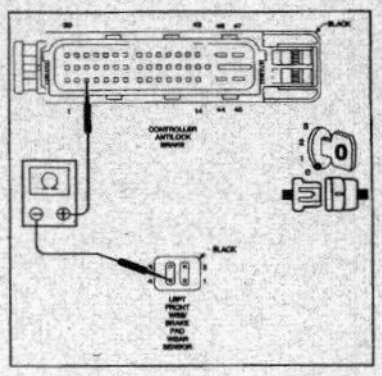

10. MEASURE THE RESISTANCE BETWEEN GROUND AND THE LEFT FRONT WHEEL SPEED SENSOR SIGNAL CIRCUIT

With the ignition off.
Measure the resistance between ground and the Left Front Wheel Speed Sensor Signal circuit at the CAB harness connector.

Is the resistance below 15k ohms?

Yes >> Repair the Left Front Wheel Speed Sensor Signal circuit for a short to ground.
Perform ABS VERIFICATION TEST.

No >> Go to 11

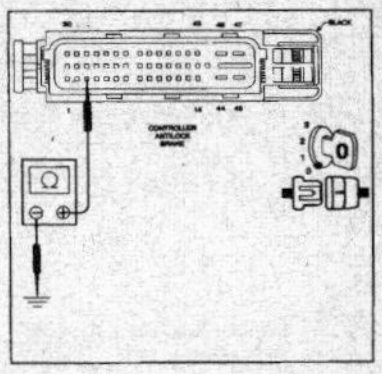

11. MEASURE THE RESISTANCE BETWEEN THE LEFT FRONT WHEEL SPEED SENSOR 12 VOLT SUPPLY CIRCUIT AND THE SENSOR SIGNAL CIRCUIT

With the ignition off.
Measure the resistance between the Left Front Wheel Speed Sensor 12 Volt Supply circuit and the Left Front Wheel Speed Sensor Signal circuit at the CAB harness connector.

Is the resistance below 1000.0 ohms?

Yes >> Repair the Left Front Wheel Speed Sensor 12 Volt Supply circuit for a short to the Left Front Wheel Speed Sensor Signal circuit.
Perform ABS VERIFICATION TEST.

No >> Replace the Controller Antilock Brake.

Perform ABS VERIFICATION TEST.

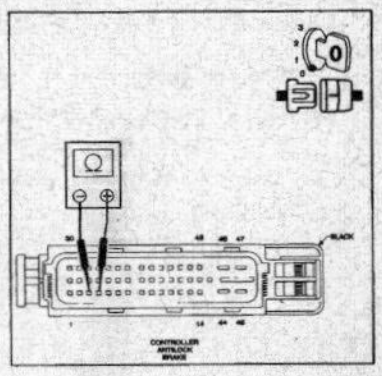

ARM0300000000218

Fig. 50 Lefthand Front Wheel Speed Sensor Fault (Part 4 of 5). ABS

12. VISUALLY INSPECT COMPONENTS FOR DAMAGE AND CORRECT INSTALLATION

Visually inspect the related wiring harness and connectors. Look for any chafed, pierced, pinched, or partially broken wires. Look for broken, bent, pushed out, or corroded terminals.
Visually inspect the Left Front Wheel Speed Sensor, connector and tone wheel for damage and correct installation.

Are there any visible Sensor, connector or tone wheel concerns?

Yes >> Correct the sensor, connector or tone wheel concerns as necessary.
Perform ABS VERIFICATION TEST.

No >> Go to 13

13. MONITOR ALL WHEEL SPEED SENSORS WITH THE DRB III®

With the DRB III®, erase DTCs.
Start the engine.
With an assistant to drive, use the DRB III® to monitor all wheel speed sensors. Slowly accelerate as straight as possible from a stop to 15 MPH.

Is the Left Front Wheel Speed Sensor Signal 0 or differing from others by more than 3 MPH?

Yes >> Replace the Left Front Wheel Speed Sensor.

Perform ABS VERIFICATION TEST.

No >> Inspect and repair the related wiring harness for a possible intermittent condition.
Perform ABS VERIFICATION TEST.

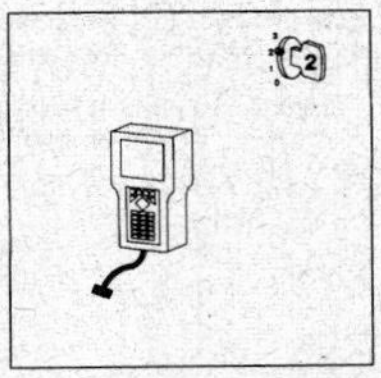

ARM0300000000219

Fig. 50 Lefthand Front Wheel Speed Sensor Fault (Part 5 of 5). ABS

1. WITH THE DRB III®, READ DTCs

Turn the ignition on.
With the DRB III®, record and erase DTCs.
Turn the ignition off.
Turn the ignition on.
With the DRB III®, read DTCs.

Does the DRB III® display a Right Front Wheel Speed Sensor Circuit Failure DTC?

Yes >> Go to 2

No >> Go to 12

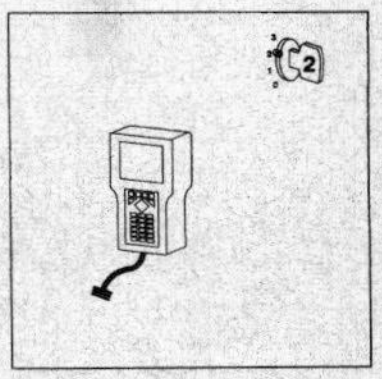

2. INSPECT THE RIGHT FRONT WHEEL SPEED SENSOR

Turn the ignition off.
Inspect the Right Front Wheel Speed Sensor and connector.

Is the Sensor or Connector damaged?

Yes >> Repair as necessary.
Perform ABS VERIFICATION TEST.

No >> Go to 3

ARM0300000000220

Fig. 51 Righthand Front Wheel Speed Sensor Fault (Part 1 of 5). ABS

3. MEASURE THE VOLTAGE OF THE RIGHT FRONT WHEEL SPEED SENSOR 12 VOLT SUPPLY CIRCUIT

With the ignition off.
Disconnect the Right Front Wheel Speed Sensor harness connector.
Note: Check connectors - Clean/repair as necessary.
Turn the ignition on.
Measure the voltage of the Right Front Wheel Speed Sensor 12 Volt Supply circuit at the Right Front Wheel Speed Sensor harness connector.

Is the voltage approximately 12 volts?

Yes >> Go to 7
No >> Go to 4

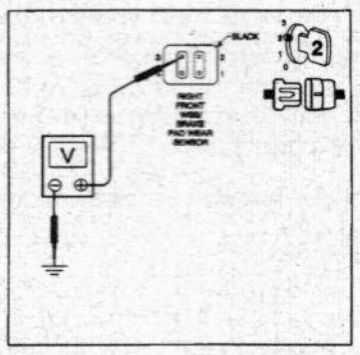

4. MEASURE THE VOLTAGE OF THE RIGHT FRONT WHEEL SPEED SENSOR 12 VOLT SUPPLY CIRCUIT

Turn the ignition off.
Measure the voltage of the Right Front Wheel Speed Sensor 12 Volt Supply circuit at the Right Front Wheel Speed Sensor harness connector.

Is the voltage 0 volts?

Yes >> Go to 5
No >> Replace the Controller Antilock Brake.

Perform ABS VERIFICATION TEST.

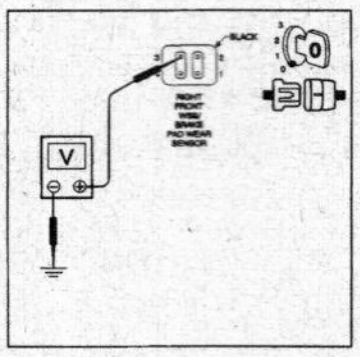

5. MEASURE THE RESISTANCE BETWEEN GROUND AND THE RIGHT FRONT WHEEL SPEED SENSOR 12 VOLT SUPPLY CIRCUIT

With the ignition off.
Disconnect the CAB harness connector.
Note: Check connectors - Clean/repair as necessary.
Measure the resistance between ground and the Right Front Wheel Speed Sensor 12 Volt Supply circuit at the CAB harness connector.

Is the resistance below 15k ohms?

Yes >> Repair the Right Front Wheel Speed Sensor 12 Volt Supply circuit for a short to ground.
Perform ABS VERIFICATION TEST.
No >> Go to 6

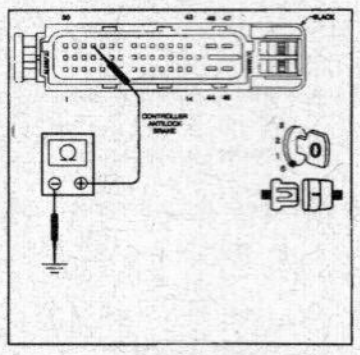

ARM0300000000221

Fig. 51 Righthand Front Wheel Speed Sensor Fault (Part 2 of 5). ABS

6. MEASURE THE RESISTANCE OF THE RIGHT FRONT WHEEL SPEED SENSOR 12 VOLT SUPPLY CIRCUIT

With the ignition off.
Measure the resistance of the Right Front Wheel Speed Sensor 12 Volt Supply circuit from the CAB harness connector to the Right Front Wheel Speed Sensor harness connector.

Is the resistance below 5.0 ohms?

Yes >> Go to 7
No >> Repair the Right Front Wheel Speed Sensor 12 Volt Supply circuit for an open.
Perform ABS VERIFICATION TEST.

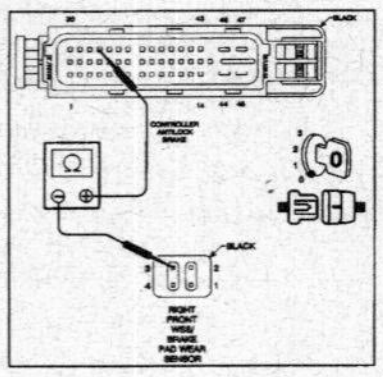

7. MEASURE THE RESISTANCE OF THE RIGHT FRONT WHEEL SPEED SENSOR SIGNAL CIRCUIT

With the ignition off.
Reconnect the CAB harness connector.
Measure the resistance between ground and the Right Front Wheel Speed Sensor Signal circuit.

Is the resistance less than 100 ohms?

Yes >> Go to 10
No >> Go to 8

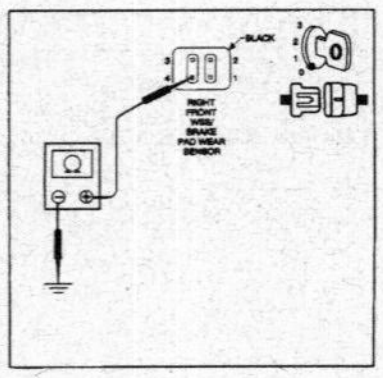

8. MEASURE THE RESISTANCE OF THE RIGHT FRONT WHEEL SPEED SENSOR SIGNAL CIRCUIT

With the ignition off.
Measure the resistance between ground and the Right Front Wheel Speed Sensor Signal circuit.

Is the resistance greater than 300 ohms?

Yes >> Go to 9
No >> Replace the Right Front Wheel Speed Sensor.

Perform ABS VERIFICATION TEST.

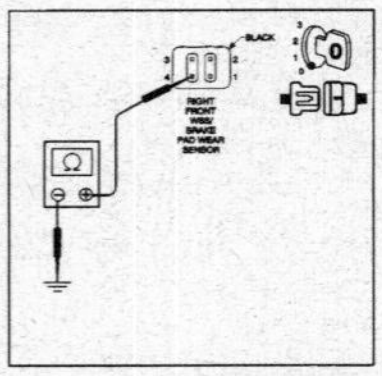

ARM0300000000222

Fig. 51 Righthand Front Wheel Speed Sensor Fault (Part 3 of 5). ABS

9. MEASURE THE RESISTANCE OF THE RIGHT FRONT WHEEL SPEED SENSOR SIGNAL CIRCUIT

With the ignition off.
Disconnect the CAB harness connector.
Note: Check connectors - Clean/repair as necessary.
Measure the resistance of the Right Front Wheel Speed Sensor Signal circuit from the CAB harness connector to the Right Front Wheel Speed Sensor harness connector.

Is the resistance below 5.0 ohms?

Yes >> Go to 11
No >> Repair the Right Front Wheel Speed Sensor Signal circuit for an open.
Perform ABS VERIFICATION TEST.

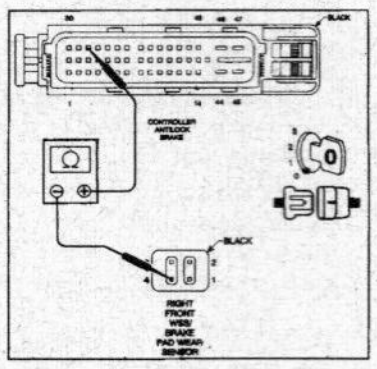

10. MEASURE THE RESISTANCE BETWEEN GROUND AND THE RIGHT FRONT WHEEL SPEED SENSOR SIGNAL CIRCUIT

With the ignition off.
Measure the resistance between ground and the Right Front Wheel Speed Sensor Signal circuit at the CAB harness connector.

Is the resistance below 15k ohms?

Yes >> Repair the Right Front Wheel Speed Sensor signal circuit for a short to ground.
Perform ABS VERIFICATION TEST.
No >> Go to 11

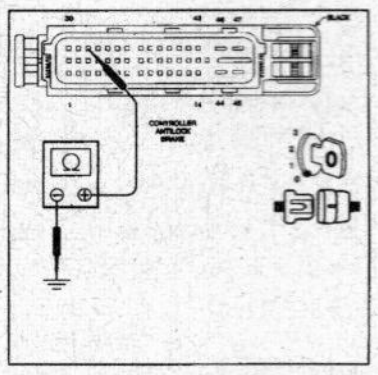

11. MEASURE THE RESISTANCE BETWEEN THE RIGHT FRONT WHEEL SPEED SENSOR 12 VOLT SUPPLY CIRCUIT AND THE SENSOR SIGNAL CIRCUIT

With the ignition off.
Measure the resistance between the Right Front Wheel Speed Sensor 12 Volt Supply circuit and the Right Front Wheel Speed Sensor Signal circuit at the CAB harness connector.

Is the resistance below 1000.0 ohms?

Yes >> Repair the Right Front Wheel Speed Sensor 12 Volt Supply circuit for a short to the Right Front Wheel Speed Sensor Signal circuit.
Perform ABS VERIFICATION TEST.
No >> Replace the Controller Antilock Brake.

Perform ABS VERIFICATION TEST.

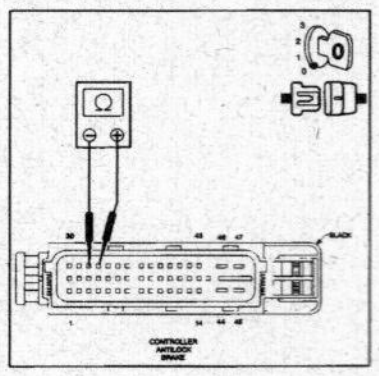

ARM0300000000223

Fig. 51 Righthand Front Wheel Speed Sensor Fault (Part 4 of 5). ABS

12. VISUALLY INSPECT COMPONENTS FOR DAMAGE AND CORRECT INSTALLATION

Visually inspect the related wiring harness and connectors. Look for any chafed, pierced, pinched, or partially broken wires. Look for broken, bent, pushed out, or corroded terminals.
Visually inspect the Right Front Wheel Speed Sensor, connector and tone wheel for damage and correct installation.

Are there any visible Sensor, connector or tone wheel concerns?

Yes >> Correct the sensor, connector or tone wheel concerns as necessary.
Perform ABS VERIFICATION TEST.
No >> Go to 13

13. MONITOR ALL WHEEL SPEED SENSORS WITH THE DRB III®

With the DRB III®, erase DTCs.
Start the engine.
With an assistant to drive, use the DRB III® to monitor all wheel speed sensors. Slowly accelerate as straight as possible from a stop to 15 MPH.

Is the Right Front Wheel Speed Sensor Signal 0 or differing from others by more than 3 MPH?

Yes >> Replace the Right Front Wheel Speed Sensor.

Perform ABS VERIFICATION TEST.
No >> Inspect and repair the related wiring harness for a possible intermittent condition.
Perform ABS VERIFICATION TEST.

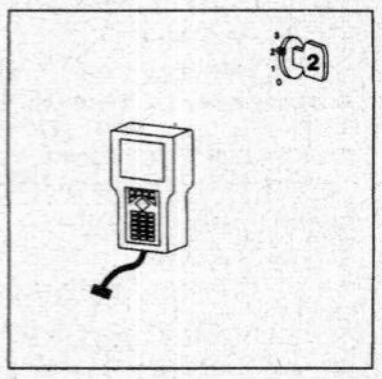

ARM0300000000224

Fig. 51 Righthand Front Wheel Speed Sensor Fault (Part 5 of 5). ABS

1. WITH THE DRB III®, READ DTCs

Turn the ignition on.
With the DRB III®, record and erase DTCs.
Turn the ignition off.
Turn the ignition on.
With the DRB III®, read DTCs.

Does the DRB III® display a Left Rear Wheel Speed Sensor Circuit Failure DTC?

Yes >> Go to 2
No >> Go to 12

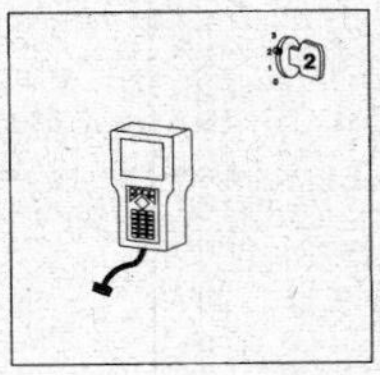

2. INSPECT THE LEFT REAR WHEEL SPEED SENSOR

Turn the ignition off.
Inspect the Left Rear Wheel Speed Sensor and connector.

Is the Sensor or Connector damaged?

Yes >> Repair as necessary.
Perform ABS VERIFICATION TEST.
No >> Go to 3

ARM0300000000225

Fig. 52 Lefthand Rear Wheel Speed Sensor Fault (Part 1 of 5). ABS

3. MEASURE THE VOLTAGE OF THE LEFT REAR WHEEL SPEED SENSOR 12 VOLT SUPPLY CIRCUIT

With the ignition off.
Disconnect the Left Rear Wheel Speed Sensor harness connector.
Note: Check connectors - Clean/repair as necessary.
Turn the ignition on.
Measure the voltage of the Left Rear Wheel Speed Sensor 12 Volt Supply circuit at the Left Rear Wheel Speed Sensor harness connector.

Is the voltage approximately 12 volts?

Yes >> Go to 7
No >> Go to 4

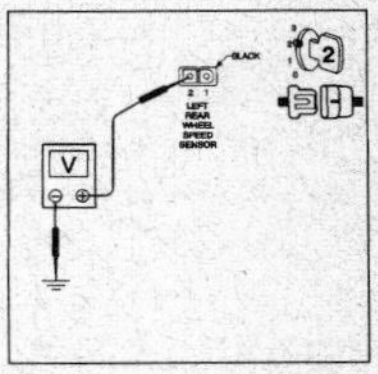

4. MEASURE THE VOLTAGE OF THE LEFT REAR WHEEL SPEED SENSOR 12 VOLT SUPPLY CIRCUIT

Turn the ignition off.
Measure the voltage of the Left Rear Wheel Speed Sensor 12 Volt Supply circuit at the Left Rear Wheel Speed Sensor harness connector.

Is the voltage 0 volts?

Yes >> Go to 5
No >> Replace the Controller Antilock Brake.
Perform ABS VERIFICATION TEST.

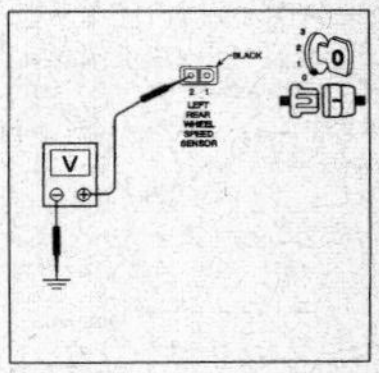

5. MEASURE THE RESISTANCE BETWEEN GROUND AND THE LEFT REAR WHEEL SPEED SENSOR 12 VOLT SUPPLY CIRCUIT

With the ignition off.
Disconnect the CAB harness connector.
Note: Check connectors - Clean/repair as necessary.
Measure the resistance between ground and the Left Rear Wheel Speed Sensor 12 Volt Supply circuit at the CAB harness connector.

Is the resistance below 15k ohms?

Yes >> Repair the Left Rear Wheel Speed Sensor 12 Volt Supply circuit for a short to ground.
Perform ABS VERIFICATION TEST.
No >> Go to 6

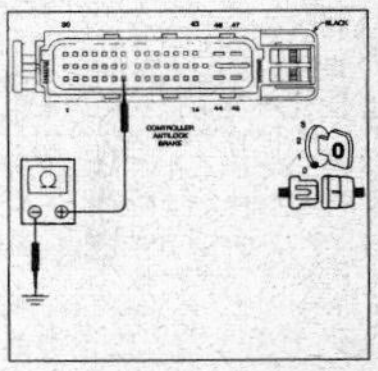

ARM0300000000226

Fig. 52 Lefthand Rear Wheel Speed Sensor Fault (Part 2 of 5). ABS

6. MEASURE THE RESISTANCE OF THE LEFT REAR WHEEL SPEED SENSOR 12 VOLT SUPPLY CIRCUIT

With the ignition off.
Measure the resistance of the Left Rear Wheel Speed Sensor 12 Volt Supply circuit from the CAB harness connector to the Left Rear Wheel Speed Sensor harness connector.

Is the resistance below 5.0 ohms?

Yes >> Go to 7
No >> Repair the Left Rear Wheel Speed Sensor 12 Volt Supply circuit for an open.
Perform ABS VERIFICATION TEST.

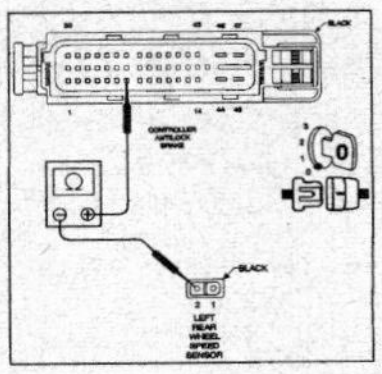

7. MEASURE THE RESISTANCE OF THE LEFT REAR WHEEL SPEED SENSOR SIGNAL CIRCUIT

With the ignition off.
Reconnect the CAB harness connector.
Measure the resistance between ground and the Left Rear Wheel Speed Sensor Signal circuit.

Is the resistance less than 100 ohms?

Yes >> Go to 10
No >> Go to 8

8. MEASURE THE RESISTANCE OF THE LEFT REAR WHEEL SPEED SENSOR SIGNAL CIRCUIT

With the ignition off.
Measure the resistance between ground and the Left Rear Wheel Speed Sensor Signal circuit.

Is the resistance greater than 300 ohms?

Yes >> Go to 9
No >> Replace the Left Rear Wheel Speed Sensor.
Perform ABS VERIFICATION TEST.

ARM0300000000227

Fig. 52 Lefthand Rear Wheel Speed Sensor Fault (Part 3 of 5). ABS

9. MEASURE THE RESISTANCE OF THE LEFT REAR WHEEL SPEED SENSOR SIGNAL CIRCUIT

With the ignition off.
Disconnect the CAB harness connector.
Note: Check connectors - Clean/repair as necessary.
Measure the resistance of the Left Rear Wheel Speed Sensor Signal circuit from the CAB harness connector to the Left Rear Wheel Speed Sensor harness connector.

Is the resistance below 5.0 ohms?

Yes >> Go to 11
No >> Repair the Left Rear Wheel Speed Sensor Signal circuit for an open.
Perform ABS VERIFICATION TEST.

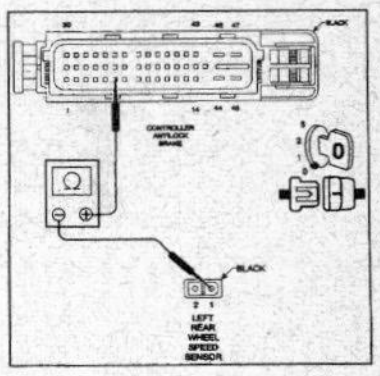

10. MEASURE THE RESISTANCE BETWEEN GROUND AND THE LEFT REAR WHEEL SPEED SENSOR SIGNAL CIRCUIT

With the ignition off.
Measure the resistance between ground and the Left Rear Wheel Speed Sensor Signal circuit at the CAB harness connector.

Is the resistance below 15k ohms?

Yes >> Repair the Left Rear Wheel Speed Sensor Signal circuit for a short to ground.
Perform ABS VERIFICATION TEST.
No >> Go to 11

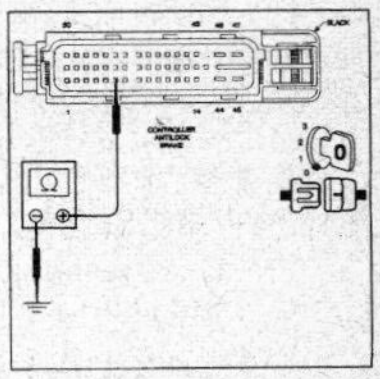

11. MEASURE THE RESISTANCE BETWEEN THE LEFT REAR WHEEL SPEED SENSOR 12 VOLT SUPPLY CIRCUIT AND THE SENSOR SIGNAL CIRCUIT

With the ignition off.
Measure the resistance between the Left Rear Wheel Speed Sensor 12 Volt Supply circuit and the Left Rear Wheel Speed Sensor Signal circuit at the CAB harness connector.

Is the resistance below 1000.0 ohms?

Yes >> Repair the Left Rear Wheel Speed Sensor 12 Volt Supply circuit for a short to the Left Rear Wheel Speed Sensor Signal circuit.
Perform ABS VERIFICATION TEST.
No >> Replace the Controller Antilock Brake.
Perform ABS VERIFICATION TEST.

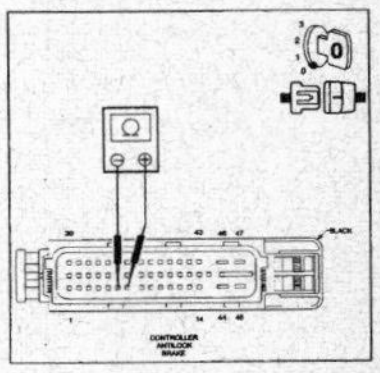

ARM0300000000228

Fig. 52 Lefthand Rear Wheel Speed Sensor Fault (Part 4 of 5). ABS

12. VISUALLY INSPECT COMPONENTS FOR DAMAGE AND CORRECT INSTALLATION

Visually inspect the related wiring harness and connectors. Look for any chafed, pierced, pinched, or partially broken wires. Look for broken, bent, pushed out, or corroded terminals.
Visually inspect the Left Rear Wheel Speed Sensor, connector and tone wheel for damage and correct installation.

Are there any visible Sensor, connector or tone wheel concerns?

Yes >> Correct the sensor, connector or tone wheel concerns as necessary.
Perform ABS VERIFICATION TEST.

No >> Go to 13

13. MONITOR ALL WHEEL SPEED SENSORS WITH THE DRB III®

With the DRB III®, erase DTCs.
Start the engine.
With an assistant to drive, use the DRB III® to monitor all wheel speed sensors. Slowly accelerate as straight as possible from a stop to 15 MPH.

Is the Left Rear Wheel Speed Sensor Signal 0 or differing from others by more than 3 MPH?

Yes >> Replace the Left Rear Wheel Speed Sensor.
Perform ABS VERIFICATION TEST.

No >> Inspect and repair the related wiring harness for a possible intermittent condition.
Perform ABS VERIFICATION TEST.

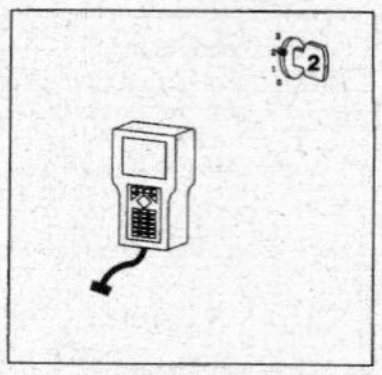

ARM0300000000229

Fig. 52 Lefthand Rear Wheel Speed Sensor Fault (Part 5 of 5). ABS

3. MEASURE THE VOLTAGE OF THE RIGHT REAR WHEEL SPEED SENSOR 12 VOLT SUPPLY CIRCUIT

With the ignition off.
Disconnect the Right Rear Wheel Speed Sensor connector.
Note: Check connectors - Clean/repair as necessary.
Turn the ignition on.
Measure the voltage of the Right Rear Wheel Speed Sensor 12 Volt Supply circuit at the Right Rear Wheel Speed Sensor harness connector.

Is the voltage approximately 12 volts?

Yes >> Go to 7

No >> Go to 4

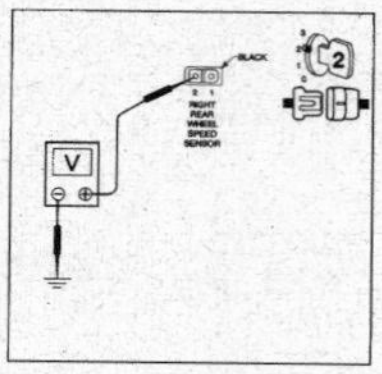

4. MEASURE THE VOLTAGE OF THE RIGHT REAR WHEEL SPEED SENSOR 12 VOLT SUPPLY CIRCUIT

Turn the ignition off.
Measure the voltage of the Right Rear Wheel Speed Sensor 12 Volt Supply circuit at the Right Rear Wheel Speed Sensor harness connector.

Is the voltage 0 volts?

Yes >> Go to 5

No >> Replace the Controller Antilock Brake.
Perform ABS VERIFICATION TEST.

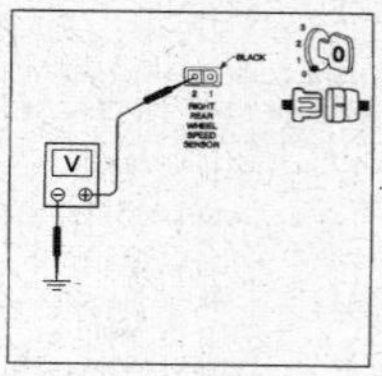

5. MEASURE THE RESISTANCE BETWEEN GROUND AND THE RIGHT REAR WHEEL SPEED SENSOR 12 VOLT SUPPLY CIRCUIT

Turn the ignition off.
Disconnect the CAB harness connector.
Note: Check connectors - Clean/repair as necessary.
Measure the resistance between ground and the Right Rear Wheel Speed Sensor 12 Volt Supply circuit at the CAB harness connector.

Is the resistance below 15k ohms?

Yes >> Repair the Right Rear Wheel Speed Sensor 12 Volt Supply circuit for a short to ground.
Perform ABS VERIFICATION TEST.

No >> Go to 6

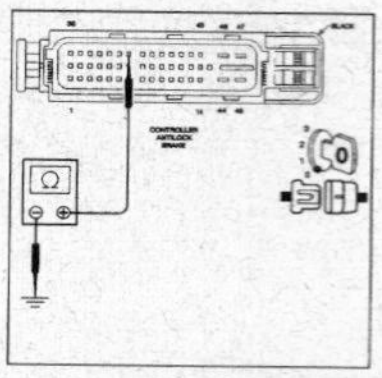

ARM0300000000231

Fig. 53 Righthand Rear Wheel Speed Sensor Fault (Part 2 of 5). ABS

1. WITH THE DRB III®, READ DTCs

Turn the ignition on.
With the DRB III®, record and erase DTCs.
Turn the ignition off.
Turn the ignition on.
With the DRB III®, read DTCs.

Does the DRB III® display a Right Rear Wheel Speed Sensor Circuit Failure DTC?

Yes >> Go to 2

No >> Go to 12

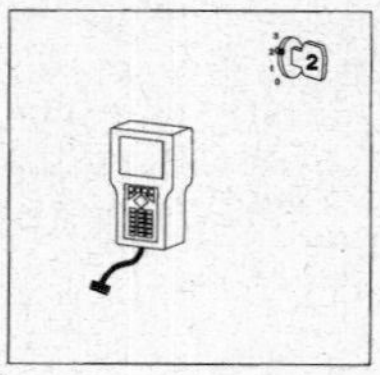

2. INSPECT THE RIGHT REAR WHEEL SPEED SENSOR

Turn the ignition off.
Inspect the Right Rear Wheel Speed Sensor and connector.

Is the Sensor or Connector damaged?

Yes >> Repair as necessary.
Perform ABS VERIFICATION TEST.

No >> Go to 3

ARM0300000000230

Fig. 53 Righthand Rear Wheel Speed Sensor Fault (Part 1 of 5). ABS

6. MEASURE THE RESISTANCE OF THE RIGHT REAR WHEEL SPEED SENSOR 12 VOLT SUPPLY CIRCUIT

With the ignition off.
Measure the resistance of the Right Rear Wheel Speed Sensor 12 Volt Supply circuit from the CAB harness connector to the Right Rear Wheel Speed Sensor harness connector.

Is the resistance below 5.0 ohms?

Yes >> Go to 7

No >> Repair the Right Rear Wheel Speed Sensor 12 volt supply circuit for an open.
Perform ABS VERIFICATION TEST.

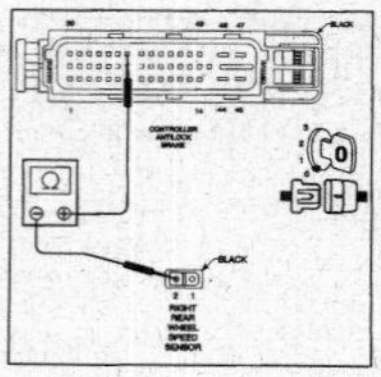

7. MEASURE THE RESISTANCE OF THE RIGHT REAR WHEEL SPEED SENSOR SIGNAL CIRCUIT

With the ignition off.
Reconnect the CAB harness connector.
Measure the resistance between ground and the Right Rear Wheel Speed Sensor Signal circuit.

Is the resistance less than 100 ohms?

Yes >> Go to 10

No >> Go to 8

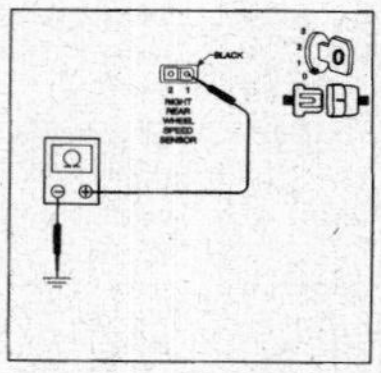

8. MEASURE THE RESISTANCE OF THE RIGHT REAR WHEEL SPEED SENSOR SIGNAL CIRCUIT

With the ignition off.
Measure the resistance between ground and the Right Rear Wheel Speed Sensor Signal circuit.

Is the resistance greater than 300 ohms?

Yes >> Go to 9

No >> Replace the Right Rear Wheel Speed Sensor.
Perform ABS VERIFICATION TEST.

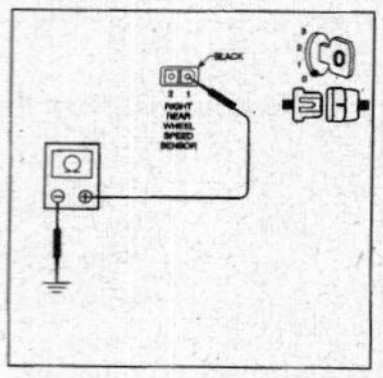

ARM0300000000232

Fig. 53 Righthand Rear Wheel Speed Sensor Fault (Part 3 of 5). ABS

9. MEASURE THE RESISTANCE OF THE RIGHT REAR WHEEL SPEED SENSOR SIGNAL CIRCUIT

With the ignition off.
Disconnect the CAB harness connector.

Note: Check connectors - Clean/repair as necessary.

Measure the resistance of the Right Rear Wheel Speed Sensor Signal circuit from the CAB harness connector to the Right Rear Wheel Speed Sensor harness connector.

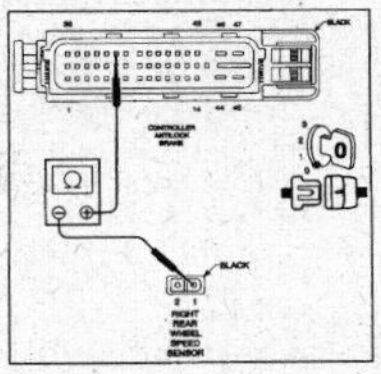

Is the resistance below 5.0 ohms?

Yes >> Go to 11

No >> Repair the Right Rear Wheel Speed Sensor Signal circuit for an open.
Perform ABS VERIFICATION TEST.

10. MEASURE THE RESISTANCE BETWEEN GROUND AND THE RIGHT REAR WHEEL SPEED SENSOR SIGNAL CIRCUIT

With the ignition off.
Measure the resistance between ground and the Right Rear Wheel Speed Sensor Signal circuit at the CAB harness connector.

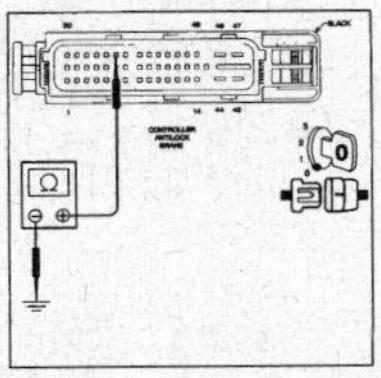

Is the resistance below 15k ohms?

Yes >> Repair the Right Rear Wheel Speed Sensor Signal circuit for a short to ground.
Perform ABS VERIFICATION TEST.

No >> Go to 11

11. MEASURE THE RESISTANCE BETWEEN THE RIGHT REAR WHEEL SPEED SENSOR 12 VOLT SUPPLY CIRCUIT AND THE SENSOR SIGNAL CIRCUIT

With the ignition off.
Measure the resistance between the Right Rear Wheel Speed Sensor 12 Volt Supply circuit and the Right Rear Wheel Speed Sensor Signal circuit at the CAB harness connector.

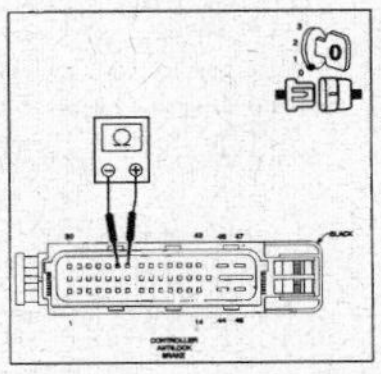

Is the resistance below 1000.0 ohms?

Yes >> Repair the Right Rear Wheel Speed Sensor 12 Volt Supply circuit for a short to the Right Rear Wheel Speed Sensor Signal circuit.
Perform ABS VERIFICATION TEST.

No >> Replace the Controller Antilock Brake.
Perform ABS VERIFICATION TEST.

ARM0300000000233

Fig. 53 Righthand Rear Wheel Speed Sensor Fault (Part 4 of 5). ABS

12. VISUALLY INSPECT COMPONENTS FOR DAMAGE AND CORRECT INSTALLATION

Visually inspect the related wiring harness and connectors. Look for any chafed, pierced, pinched, or partially broken wires. Look for broken, bent, pushed out, or corroded terminals.
Visually inspect the Right Rear Wheel Speed Sensor, connector and tone wheel for damage and correct installation.

Are there any visible Sensor, connector or tone wheel concerns?

Yes >> Correct the sensor, connector or tone wheel concerns as necessary.
Perform ABS VERIFICATION TEST.

No >> Go to 13

13. MONITOR ALL WHEEL SPEED SENSORS WITH THE DRB III®

With the DRB III®, erase DTCs.
Start the engine.
With an assistant to drive, use the DRB III® to monitor all wheel speed sensors. Slowly accelerate as straight as possible from a stop to 15 MPH.

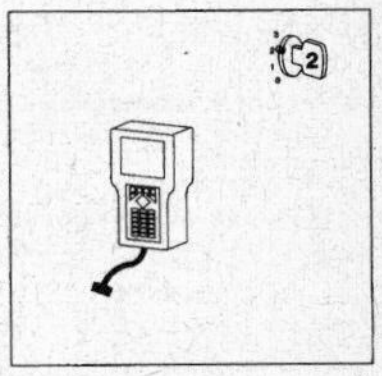

Is the Right Rear Wheel Speed Sensor Signal 0 or differing from others by more than 3 MPH?

Yes >> Replace the Right Rear Wheel Speed Sensor.
Perform ABS VERIFICATION TEST.

No >> Inspect and repair the related wiring harness for a possible intermittent condition.
Perform ABS VERIFICATION TEST.

ARM0300000000234

Fig. 53 Righthand Rear Wheel Speed Sensor Fault (Part 5 of 5). ABS

1. MEASURE THE VOLTAGE OF THE ESP YAW RATE SENSOR SIGNAL CIRCUIT

Turn the ignition off.
Disconnect the CAB harness connector.
Disconnect the ESP Yaw Rate Sensor harness connector.

Note: Check connectors - Clean/repair as necessary.

Turn the ignition on.
Measure the voltage of the ESP Yaw Rate Sensor Signal circuit at the ESP Yaw Rate Sensor harness connector.

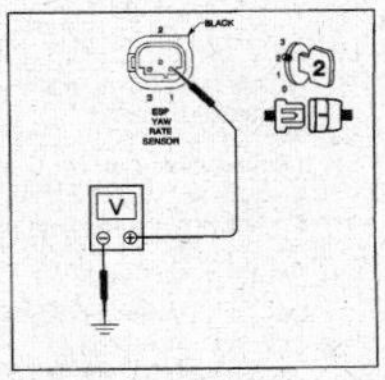

Is voltage present?

Yes >> Repair the ESP Yaw Rate Sensor Signal circuit for a short to voltage.
Perform ABS VERIFICATION TEST.

No >> Go to 2

ARM0300000000235

Fig. 54 ESP Yaw Rate Sensor Fault (Part 1 of 4). ABS

2. MEASURE THE RESISTANCE BETWEEN THE ESP YAW RATE SIGNAL CIRCUIT AND THE 5-VOLT SUPPLY CIRCUIT

With the ignition off.
Measure the resistance between the ESP Yaw Rate Sensor Signal circuit and the 5-Volt Supply circuit in the ESP Yaw Rate Sensor harness connector.

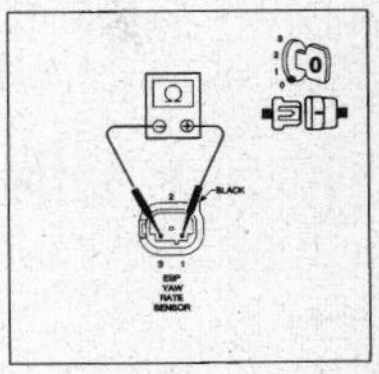

Is the resistance below 10K ohms?

Yes >> Repair the ESP Yaw Rate Sensor Signal circuit for a short to the 5-Volt Supply circuit.
Perform ABS VERIFICATION TEST.

No >> Go to 3

3. MEASURE THE RESISTANCE OF THE ESP YAW RATE SENSOR SIGNAL CIRCUIT

With the ignition off.
Measure the resistance of the ESP Yaw Rate Sensor Signal circuit from the CAB harness connector to the ESP Yaw Rate Sensor harness connector.

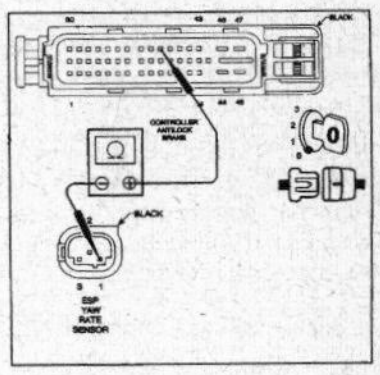

Is the resistance below 5.0 ohms?

Yes >> Go to 4

No >> Repair the ESP Yaw Rate Sensor Signal circuit for an open.
Perform ABS VERIFICATION TEST.

4. MEASURE THE RESISTANCE BETWEEN GROUND AND THE ESP YAW RATE SENSOR GROUND CIRCUIT

With the ignition off.
Measure the resistance between ground and the Sensor Ground circuit.

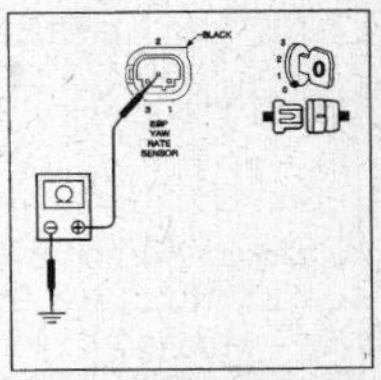

Is the resistance below 10K ohms?

Yes >> Repair the Sensor Ground circuit for a short to ground.
Perform ABS VERIFICATION TEST.

No >> Go to 5

ARM0300000000236

Fig. 54 ESP Yaw Rate Sensor Fault (Part 2 of 4). ABS

5. MEASURE THE VOLTAGE OF THE 5-VOLT SUPPLY CIRCUIT

With the ignition off.
Reconnect the CAB harness connector.
Turn the ignition on.
Measure the voltage of the 5-Volt Supply circuit at the ESP Yaw Rate Sensor harness connector.

Is the voltage between 4.5 and 5.0 volts?

Yes >> Go to 6
No >> Go to 8

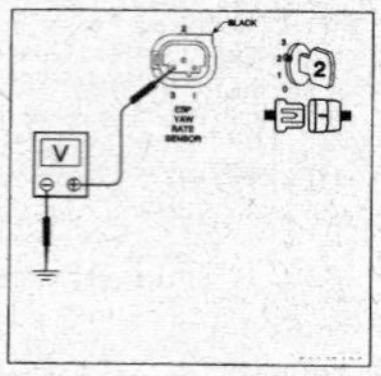

6. MEASURE THE RESISTANCE BETWEEN GROUND AND THE ESP YAW RATE SENSOR SIGNAL CIRCUIT

Turn the ignition off.
Disconnect the CAB harness connector.
Note: Check connectors - Clean/repair as necessary.
Measure the resistance between ground and the ESP Yaw Rate Sensor Signal circuit.

Is the resistance below 10K ohms?

Yes >> Repair the ESP Yaw Rate Sensor Signal circuit for a short to ground.
Perform ABS VERIFICATION TEST.
No >> Go to 7

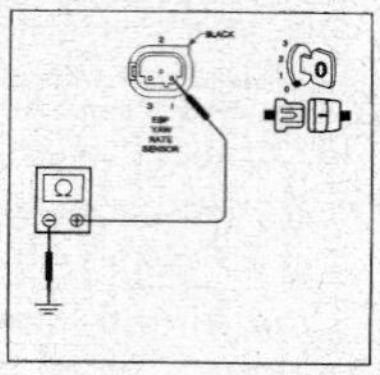

7. MEASURE THE RESISTANCE BETWEEN THE ESP YAW RATE SENSOR SIGNAL CIRCUIT AND THE SENSOR GROUND CIRCUIT

With the ignition off.
Measure the resistance between the ESP Yaw Rate Sensor Signal circuit and the Sensor Ground circuit in the ESP Yaw Rate Sensor harness connector.

Is the resistance below 10K ohms?

Yes >> Repair the ESP Yaw Rate Sensor Signal circuit for a short to the Sensor Ground circuit.
Perform ABS VERIFICATION TEST.
No >> Replace the ESP Yaw Rate Sensor.
Perform ABS VERIFICATION TEST.

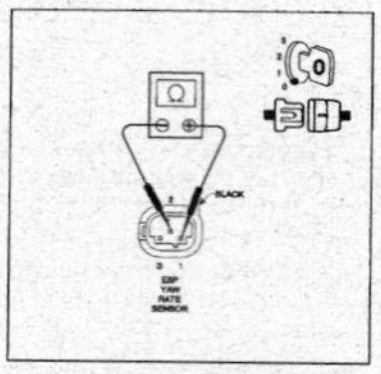

ARM0300000000237

Fig. 54 ESP Yaw Rate Sensor Fault (Part 3 of 4). ABS

1. MEASURE STEERING ANGLE SENSOR FUSED B(+) CIRCUIT VOLTAGE

Note: Inspect Fuse 14 located in the Underhood Accessory Fuse Block. If the fuse is open, repair the cause of the open fuse before continuing.
Turn the ignition off.
Disconnect the Steering Angle Sensor harness connector.
Note: Check connectors - Clean/repair as necessary.
Turn the ignition on.
Measure the voltage of the Fused B(+) circuit at the Steering Angle Sensor harness connector.

Is the voltage above 10 volts?

Yes >> Go to 2
No >> Repair the Steering Angle Sensor Fused B(+) circuit.
Perform ABS VERIFICATION TEST.

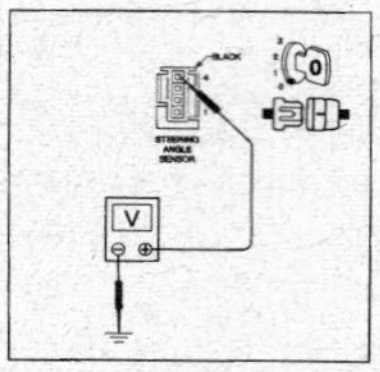

ARM0300000000239

Fig. 55 Steering Angle Sensor Fault (Part 1 of 3). ABS

5. MEASURE THE STEERING ANGLE SENSOR GROUND CIRCUIT RESISTANCE

Turn the ignition off.
Measure the resistance between ground and the Sensor Ground circuit.

Is the resistance below 5.0 ohms?

Yes >> Replace the Steering Angle Sensor.
Perform ABS VERIFICATION TEST.
No >> Repair the Sensor Ground circuit for an open.
Perform ABS VERIFICATION TEST.

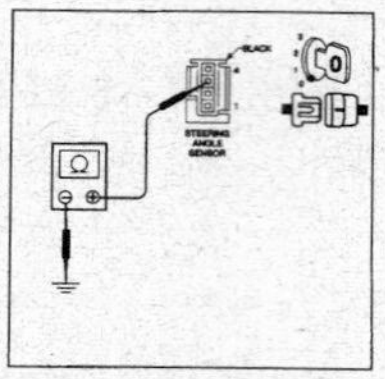

ARM0300000000241

Fig. 55 Steering Angle Sensor Fault (Part 3 of 3). ABS

8. MEASURE THE RESISTANCE BETWEEN GROUND AND THE ESP YAW RATE SENSOR 5-VOLT SUPPLY CIRCUIT

Turn the ignition off.
Disconnect the CAB harness connector.
Note: Check connectors - Clean/repair as necessary.
Measure the resistance between ground and the 5-Volt Supply circuit.

Is the resistance below 10K ohms?

Yes >> Repair the 5-Volt Supply circuit for a short to ground.
Perform ABS VERIFICATION TEST.
No >> Go to 9

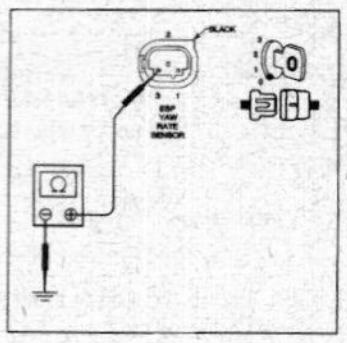

9. MEASURE THE RESISTANCE OF THE ESP YAW RATE SENSOR 5-VOLT SUPPLY CIRCUIT

With the ignition off.
Measure the resistance of the 5-Volt Supply circuit from the ESP Yaw Rate Sensor harness connector to the CAB harness connector.

Is the resistance below 5.0 ohms?

Yes >> Replace the Controller Antilock Brake.
Perform ABS VERIFICATION TEST.
No >> Repair the ESP Yaw Rate Sensor 5-Volt Supply circuit for an open.
Perform ABS VERIFICATION TEST.

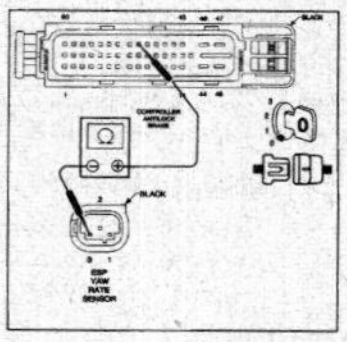

ARM0300000000238

Fig. 54 ESP Yaw Rate Sensor Fault (Part 4 of 4). ABS

2. MEASURE THE STEERING ANGLE SENSOR SIGNAL CIRCUIT RESISTANCE

Turn the ignition off.
Disconnect the CAB harness connector.
Note: Check connectors - Clean/repair as necessary.
Measure the resistance of the Steering Angle Sensor Signal circuit from the CAB harness connector to the Steering Angle Sensor harness connector.

Is the resistance below 5.0 ohms?

Yes >> Go to 3
No >> Repair the Steering Angle Sensor Signal circuit for an open.
Perform ABS VERIFICATION TEST.

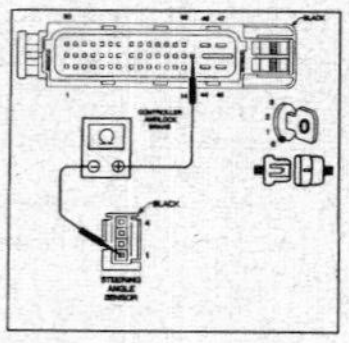

3. MEASURE THE STEERING ANGLE SENSOR SIGNAL CIRCUIT RESISTANCE

With the ignition off.
Measure the resistance between ground and the Steering Angle Sensor Signal circuit.

Is the resistance below 10K ohms?

Yes >> Repair the Steering Angle Sensor Signal circuit for a short to ground.
Perform ABS VERIFICATION TEST.
No >> Go to 4

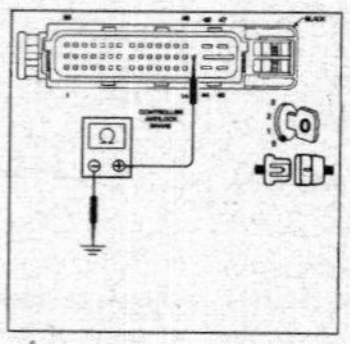

4. MEASURE THE VOLTAGE OF THE STEERING ANGLE SENSOR SIGNAL CIRCUIT

Turn the ignition on.
Measure the voltage of the Steering Angle Sensor Signal circuit at the Steering Angle Sensor harness connector.

Is voltage present?

Yes >> Repair the Steering Angle Sensor Signal circuit for a short to voltage.
Perform ABS VERIFICATION TEST.
No >> Go to 5

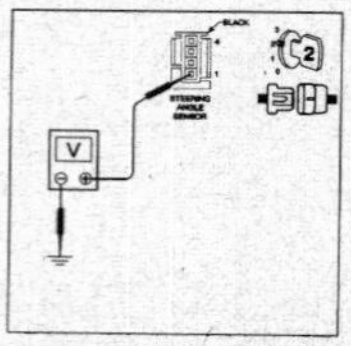

ARM0300000000240

Fig. 55 Steering Angle Sensor Fault (Part 2 of 3). ABS

1. MEASURE THE VOLTAGE OF THE ESP BRAKE PRESSURE SENSOR 1 SIGNAL CIRCUIT

Turn the ignition off.
Disconnect the CAB harness connector.
Disconnect the ESP Brake Pressure Sensor 1 harness connector.
Note: Check connectors - Clean/repair as necessary.
Turn the ignition on.
Measure the voltage of the ESP Brake Pressure Sensor 1 Signal circuit at the ESP Brake Pressure Sensor 1 harness connector.

Is voltage present?

Yes >> Repair the ESP Brake Pressure Sensor 1 Signal circuit for a short to voltage.
Perform ABS VERIFICATION TEST.
No >> Go to 2

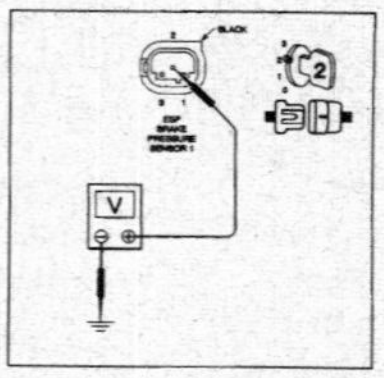

ARM0300000000402

Fig. 56 ESP Brake Pressure Sensor 1 Fault (Part 1 of 4). ABS

2. **MEASURE THE RESISTANCE BETWEEN THE ESP BRAKE PRESSURE 1 SIGNAL CIRCUIT AND THE 5-VOLT SUPPLY CIRCUIT**

Turn the ignition off.
Measure the resistance between the ESP Brake Pressure Sensor 1 Signal circuit and the 5-Volt Supply circuit in the ESP Brake Pressure Sensor 1 harness connector.

Is the resistance below 10K ohms?

Yes >> Repair the ESP Brake Pressure Sensor 1 Signal circuit for a short to the 5-Volt Supply circuit.
Perform ABS VERIFICATION TEST.

No >> Go to 3

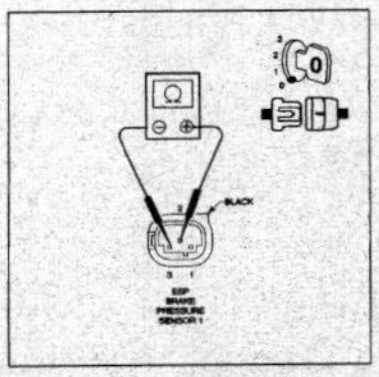

3. **MEASURE THE RESISTANCE OF THE ESP BRAKE PRESSURE SENSOR 1 SIGNAL CIRCUIT**

With the ignition off.
Measure the resistance of the ESP Brake Pressure Sensor 1 Signal circuit from the CAB harness connector to the ESP Brake Pressure Sensor 1 harness connector.

Is the resistance below 5.0 ohms?

Yes >> Go to 4

No >> Repair the ESP Brake Pressure Sensor 1 Signal circuit for an open.
Perform ABS VERIFICATION TEST.

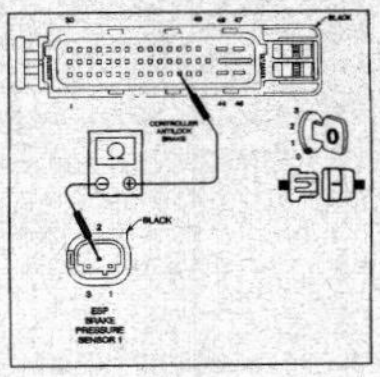

4. **MEASURE THE RESISTANCE BETWEEN GROUND AND THE ESP BRAKE PRESSURE SENSOR 1 GROUND CIRCUIT**

With the ignition off.
Measure the resistance between ground and the Sensor Ground circuit.

Is the resistance below 10K ohms?

Yes >> Repair the Sensor Ground circuit for a short to ground.
Perform ABS VERIFICATION TEST.

No >> Go to 5

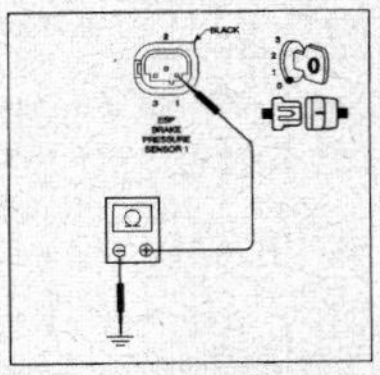

ARM0300000000403

Fig. 56 ESP Brake Pressure Sensor 1 Fault (Part 2 of 4). ABS

5. **MEASURE THE VOLTAGE OF THE 5-VOLT SUPPLY CIRCUIT**

With the ignition off.
Reconnect the CAB harness connector.
Turn the ignition on.
Measure the voltage of the 5-Volt Supply circuit at the ESP Brake Pressure Sensor 1 harness connector.

Is the voltage between 4.5 and 5.0 volts?

Yes >> Go to 6

No >> Go to 8

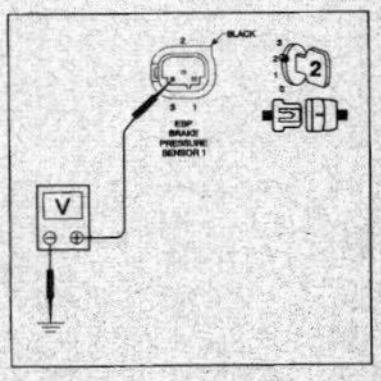

6. **MEASURE THE RESISTANCE BETWEEN GROUND AND THE ESP BRAKE PRESSURE SENSOR 1 SIGNAL CIRCUIT**

Turn the ignition off.
Disconnect the CAB harness connector.
Note: Check connectors - Clean/repair as necessary.
Measure the resistance between ground and the ESP Brake Pressure Sensor 1 Signal circuit.

Is the resistance below 10K ohms?

Yes >> Repair the ESP Brake Pressure Sensor 1 Signal circuit for a short to ground.
Perform ABS VERIFICATION TEST.

No >> Go to 7

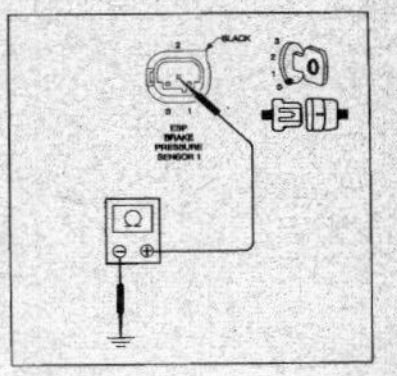

7. **MEASURE THE RESISTANCE BETWEEN THE ESP BRAKE PRESSURE SENSOR 1 SIGNAL CIRCUIT AND THE SENSOR GROUND CIRCUIT**

With the ignition off.
Measure the resistance between the ESP Brake Pressure Sensor 1 Signal circuit and the Sensor Ground circuit in the ESP Brake Pressure Sensor 1 harness connector.

Is the resistance below 10K ohms?

Yes >> Repair the ESP Brake Pressure Sensor 1 Signal circuit for a short to the Sensor Ground circuit.
Perform ABS VERIFICATION TEST.

No >> Replace the ESP Brake Pressure Sensor 1.
Perform ABS VERIFICATION TEST.

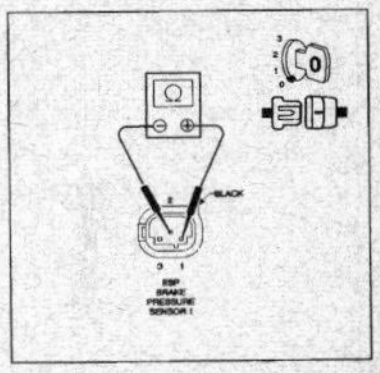

ARM0300000000404

Fig. 56 ESP Brake Pressure Sensor 1 Fault (Part 3 of 4). ABS

8. **MEASURE THE RESISTANCE BETWEEN GROUND AND THE ESP BRAKE PRESSURE SENSOR 5-VOLT SUPPLY CIRCUIT**

Turn the ignition off.
Disconnect the CAB harness connector.
Note: Check connectors - Clean/repair as necessary.
Measure the resistance between ground and the 5-Volt Supply circuit.

Is the resistance below 10K ohms?

Yes >> Repair the 5-Volt Supply circuit for a short to ground.
Perform ABS VERIFICATION TEST.

No >> Go to 9

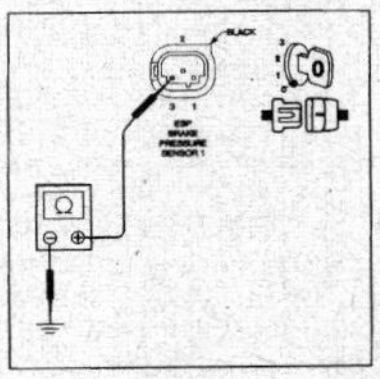

9. **MEASURE THE RESISTANCE OF THE ESP BRAKE PRESSURE SENSOR 5-VOLT SUPPLY CIRCUIT**

With the ignition off.
Measure the resistance of the 5-Volt Supply circuit from the ESP Brake Pressure Sensor 1 harness connector to the CAB harness connector.

Is the resistance below 5.0 ohms?

Yes >> Replace the Controller Antilock Brake.
Perform ABS VERIFICATION TEST.

No >> Repair the ESP Brake Pressure Sensor 5-Volt Supply circuit for an open.
Perform ABS VERIFICATION TEST.

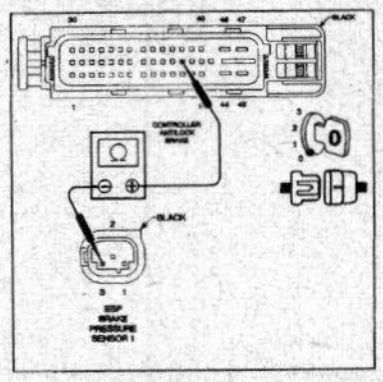

ARM0300000000405

Fig. 56 ESP Brake Pressure Sensor 1 Fault (Part 4 of 4). ABS

1. **MEASURE THE VOLTAGE OF THE ESP BRAKE PRESSURE SENSOR 2 SIGNAL CIRCUIT**

Turn the ignition off.
Disconnect the CAB harness connector.
Disconnect the ESP Brake Pressure Sensor 2 harness connector.
Note: Check connectors - Clean/repair as necessary.
Turn the ignition on.
Measure the voltage of the ESP Brake Pressure Sensor 2 Signal circuit at the ESP Brake Pressure Sensor 2 harness connector.

Is voltage present?

Yes >> Repair the ESP Brake Pressure Sensor 2 Signal circuit for a short to voltage.
Perform ABS VERIFICATION TEST.

No >> Go to 2

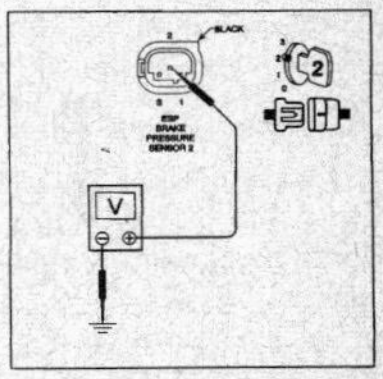

ARM0300000000406

Fig. 57 ESP Brake Pressure Sensor 2 Fault (Part 1 of 4). ABS

2. MEASURE THE RESISTANCE BETWEEN THE ESP BRAKE PRESSURE 2 SIGNAL CIRCUIT AND THE 5-VOLT SUPPLY CIRCUIT

Turn the ignition off.
Measure the resistance between the ESP Brake Pressure Sensor 2 Signal circuit and the 5-Volt Supply circuit in the ESP Brake Pressure Sensor 2 harness connector.

Is the resistance below 10K ohms?

Yes >> Repair the ESP Brake Pressure Sensor 2 Signal circuit for a short to the 5-Volt Supply circuit.
Perform ABS VERIFICATION TEST.

No >> Go to 3

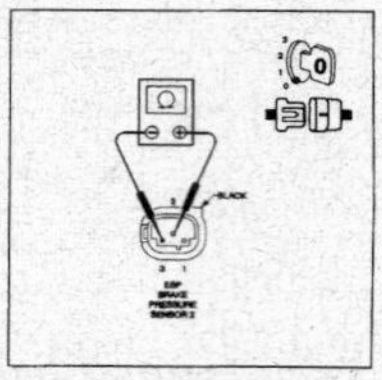

3. MEASURE THE RESISTANCE OF THE ESP BRAKE PRESSURE SENSOR 2 SIGNAL CIRCUIT

With the ignition off.
Measure the resistance of the ESP Brake Pressure Sensor 2 Signal circuit from the CAB harness connector to the ESP Brake Pressure Sensor 2 harness connector.

Is the resistance below 5.0 ohms?

Yes >> Go to 4

No >> Repair the ESP Brake Pressure Sensor 2 Signal circuit for an open.
Perform ABS VERIFICATION TEST.

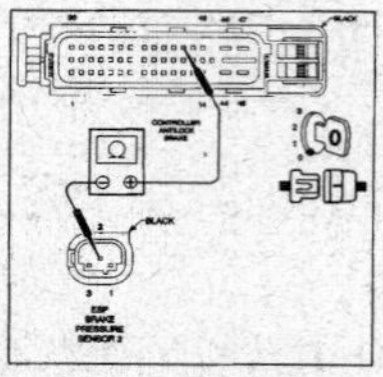

4. MEASURE THE RESISTANCE BETWEEN GROUND AND THE ESP BRAKE PRESSURE SENSOR 2 GROUND CIRCUIT

With the ignition off.
Measure the resistance between ground and the Sensor Ground circuit.

Is the resistance below 10K ohms?

Yes >> Repair the Sensor Ground circuit for a short to ground.
Perform ABS VERIFICATION TEST.

No >> Go to 5

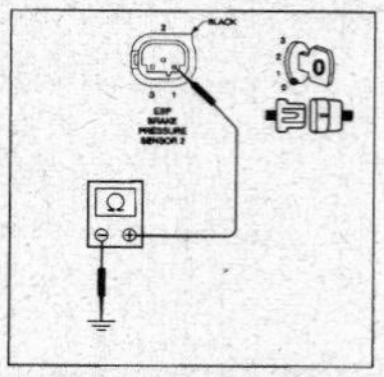

ARM0300000000407

Fig. 57 ESP Brake Pressure Sensor 2 Fault (Part 2 of 4). ABS

5. MEASURE THE VOLTAGE OF THE 5-VOLT SUPPLY CIRCUIT

With the ignition off.
Reconnect the CAB harness connector.
Turn the ignition on.
Measure the voltage of the 5-Volt Supply circuit at the ESP Brake Pressure Sensor 2 harness connector.

Is the voltage between 4.5 and 5.0 volts?

Yes >> Go to 6

No >> Go to 8

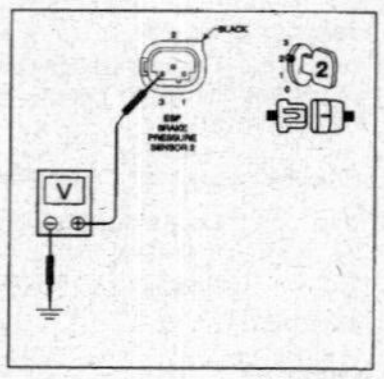

6. MEASURE THE RESISTANCE BETWEEN GROUND AND THE ESP BRAKE PRESSURE SENSOR 2 SIGNAL CIRCUIT

Turn the ignition off.
Disconnect the CAB harness connector.
Note: Check connectors - Clean/repair as necessary.
Measure the resistance between ground and the ESP Brake Pressure Sensor 2 Signal circuit.

Is the resistance below 10K ohms?

Yes >> Repair the ESP Brake Pressure Sensor 2 Signal circuit for a short to ground.
Perform ABS VERIFICATION TEST.

No >> Go to 7

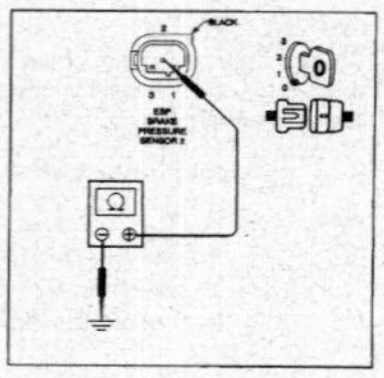

7. MEASURE THE RESISTANCE BETWEEN THE ESP BRAKE PRESSURE SENSOR 2 SIGNAL CIRCUIT AND THE SENSOR GROUND CIRCUIT

With the ignition off.
Measure the resistance between the ESP Brake Pressure Sensor 2 Signal circuit and the Sensor Ground circuit in the ESP Brake Pressure Sensor 2 harness connector.

Is the resistance below 10K ohms?

Yes >> Repair the ESP Brake Pressure Sensor 2 Signal circuit for a short to the Sensor Ground circuit.
Perform ABS VERIFICATION TEST.

No >> Replace the ESP Brake Pressure Sensor 2.

Perform ABS VERIFICATION TEST.

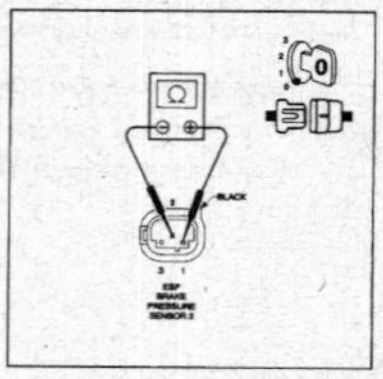

ARM0300000000408

Fig. 57 ESP Brake Pressure Sensor 2 Fault (Part 3 of 4). ABS

8. MEASURE THE RESISTANCE BETWEEN GROUND AND THE ESP BRAKE PRESSURE SENSOR 5-VOLT SUPPLY CIRCUIT

Turn the ignition off.
Disconnect the CAB harness connector.
Note: Check connectors - Clean/repair as necessary.
Measure the resistance between ground and the 5-Volt Supply circuit.

Is the resistance below 10K ohms?

Yes >> Repair the 5-Volt Supply circuit for a short to ground.
Perform ABS VERIFICATION TEST.

No >> Go to 9

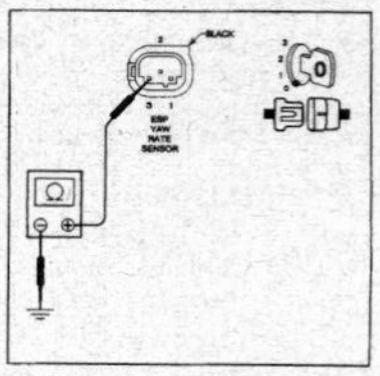

9. MEASURE THE RESISTANCE OF THE ESP BRAKE PRESSURE SENSOR 5-VOLT SUPPLY CIRCUIT

With the ignition off.
Measure the resistance of the 5-Volt Supply circuit from the ESP Brake Pressure Sensor 2 harness connector to the CAB harness connector.

Is the resistance below 5.0 ohms?

Yes >> Replace the Controller Antilock Brake.

Perform ABS VERIFICATION TEST.

No >> Repair the ESP Brake Pressure Sensor 5-Volt Supply circuit for an open.
Perform ABS VERIFICATION TEST.

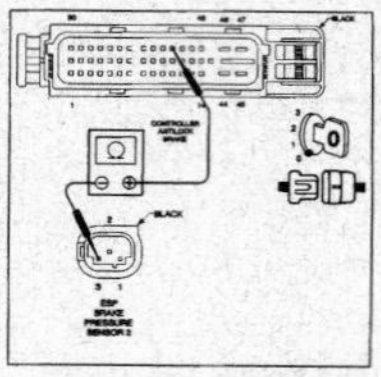

ARM0300000000409

Fig. 57 ESP Brake Pressure Sensor 2 Fault (Part 4 of 4). ABS

1. MEASURE THE VOLTAGE OF THE ESP LATERAL ACCELERATION SENSOR SIGNAL CIRCUIT

Turn the ignition off.
Disconnect the CAB harness connector.
Disconnect the ESP Lateral Acceleration Sensor harness connector.
Note: Check connectors - Clean/repair as necessary.
Turn the ignition on.
Measure the voltage of the ESP Lateral Acceleration Sensor Signal circuit at the ESP Lateral Acceleration Sensor harness connector.

Is voltage present?

Yes >> Repair the ESP Lateral Acceleration Sensor Signal circuit for a short to voltage.
Perform ABS VERIFICATION TEST.

No >> Go to 2

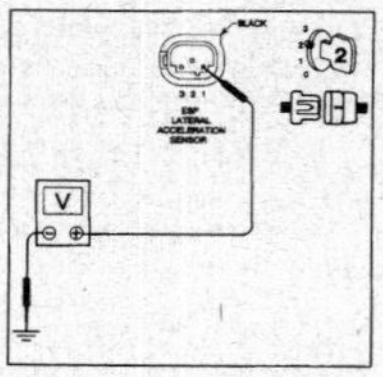

ARM0300000000410

Fig. 58 ESP Lateral Acceleration Sensor Fault (Part 1 of 4). ABS

2. MEASURE THE RESISTANCE BETWEEN THE ESP LATERAL ACCELERATION SIGNAL CIRCUIT AND THE 5-VOLT SUPPLY CIRCUIT

With the ignition off.
Measure the resistance between the ESP Lateral Acceleration Sensor Signal circuit and the 5-Volt Supply circuit in the ESP Lateral Acceleration Sensor harness connector.

Is the resistance below 10K ohms?

Yes >> Repair the ESP Lateral Acceleration Sensor Signal circuit for a short to the 5-Volt Supply circuit.
Perform ABS VERIFICATION TEST.

No >> Go to 3

3. MEASURE THE RESISTANCE OF THE ESP LATERAL ACCELERATION SENSOR SIGNAL CIRCUIT

With the ignition off.
Measure the resistance of the ESP Lateral Acceleration Sensor Signal circuit from the CAB harness connector to the ESP Lateral Acceleration Sensor harness connector.

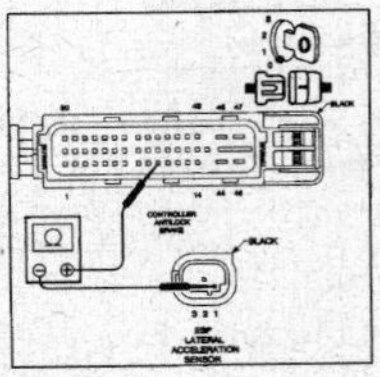

Is the resistance below 5.0 ohms?

Yes >> Go to 4

No >> Repair the ESP Lateral Acceleration Sensor Signal circuit for an open.
Perform ABS VERIFICATION TEST.

4. MEASURE THE RESISTANCE BETWEEN GROUND AND THE ESP LATERAL ACCELERATION SENSOR GROUND CIRCUIT

With the ignition off.
Measure the resistance between ground and the Sensor Ground circuit.

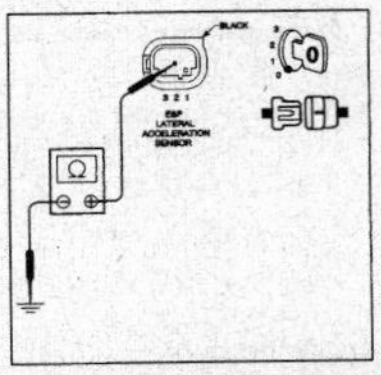

Is the resistance below 10K ohms?

Yes >> Repair the Sensor Ground circuit for a short to ground.
Perform ABS VERIFICATION TEST.

No >> Go to 5

ARM0300000000411

Fig. 58 ESP Lateral Acceleration Sensor Fault (Part 2 of 4). ABS

5. MEASURE THE VOLTAGE OF THE 5-VOLT SUPPLY CIRCUIT

With the ignition off.
Reconnect the CAB harness connector.
Turn the ignition on.
Measure the voltage of the 5-Volt Supply circuit in the ESP Lateral Acceleration Sensor harness connector.

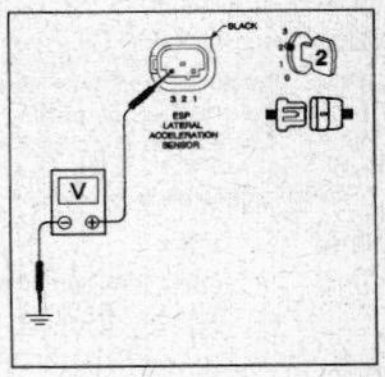

Is the voltage between 4.5 and 5.0 volts?

Yes >> Go to 6

No >> Go to 8

6. MEASURE THE RESISTANCE BETWEEN GROUND AND THE ESP LATERAL ACCELERATION SENSOR SIGNAL CIRCUIT

Turn the ignition off.
Disconnect the CAB harness connector.
Note: Check connectors - Clean/repair as necessary.
Measure the resistance between ground and the ESP Lateral Acceleration Sensor Signal circuit.

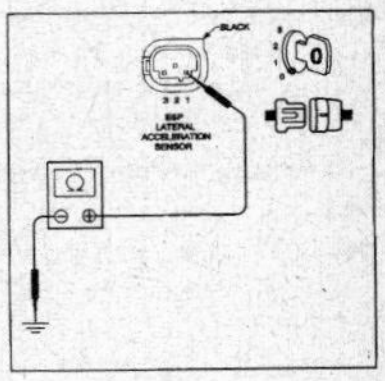

Is the resistance below 10K ohms?

Yes >> Repair the ESP Lateral Acceleration Sensor Signal circuit for a short to ground.
Perform ABS VERIFICATION TEST.

No >> Go to 7

7. MEASURE THE RESISTANCE BETWEEN THE ESP LATERAL ACCELERATION SENSOR SIGNAL CIRCUIT AND THE SENSOR GROUND CIRCUIT

With the ignition off.
Measure the resistance between the ESP Lateral Acceleration Sensor Signal circuit and the Sensor Ground circuit in the ESP Lateral Acceleration Sensor harness connector.

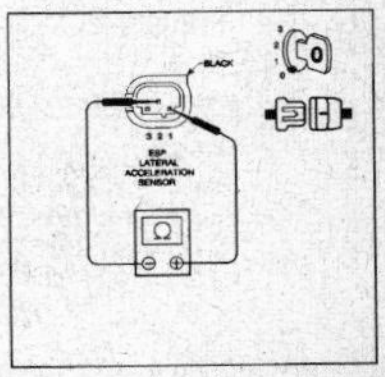

Is the resistance below 10K ohms?

Yes >> Repair the ESP Lateral Acceleration Sensor Signal circuit for a short to the Sensor Ground circuit.
Perform ABS VERIFICATION TEST.

No >> Replace the ESP Lateral Acceleration Sensor.

Perform ABS VERIFICATION TEST.

ARM0300000000412

Fig. 58 ESP Lateral Acceleration Sensor Fault (Part 3 of 4). ABS

8. MEASURE THE RESISTANCE BETWEEN GROUND AND THE ESP LATERAL ACCELERATION SENSOR 5-VOLT SUPPLY CIRCUIT

Turn the ignition off.
Disconnect the CAB harness connector.
Note: Check connectors - Clean/repair as necessary.
Measure the resistance between ground and the 5-Volt Supply circuit.

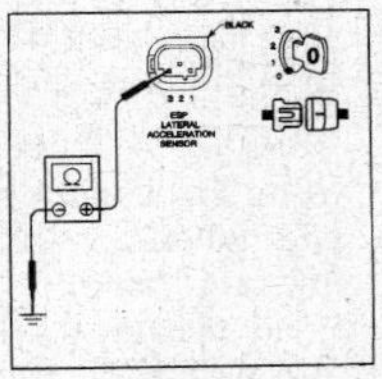

Is the resistance below 10K ohms?

Yes >> Repair the 5-Volt Supply circuit for a short to ground.
Perform ABS VERIFICATION TEST.

No >> Go to 9

9. MEASURE THE RESISTANCE OF THE ESP LATERAL ACCELERATION SENSOR 5-VOLT SUPPLY CIRCUIT

With the ignition off.
Measure the resistance of the 5-Volt Supply circuit from the ESP Lateral Acceleration Sensor harness connector to the CAB harness connector.

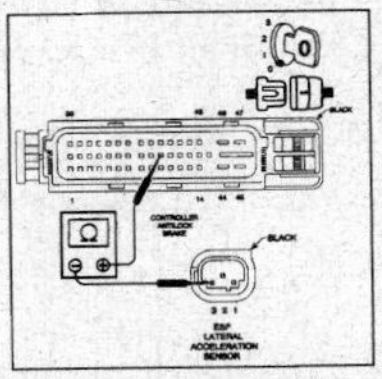

Is the resistance below 5.0 ohms?

Yes >> Replace the Controller Antilock Brake.

Perform ABS VERIFICATION TEST.

No >> Repair the ESP Lateral Acceleration Sensor 5-Volt Supply circuit for an open.
Perform ABS VERIFICATION TEST.

ARM0300000000413

Fig. 58 ESP Lateral Acceleration Sensor Fault (Part 4 of 4). ABS

1. MEASURE BRAKE LAMP SWITCH VOLTAGE

Note: Inspect Fuse 2 located in the Illumination Control Module/IP Fuse Block. If the fuse is open, repair the cause of the open fuse before continuing.
Turn the ignition off.
Disconnect the Brake Lamp Switch harness connector.
Note: Check connectors - Clean/repair as necessary.
Turn the ignition on.
Measure the voltage of the Fused Ignition Switch Output circuit at the Brake Lamp Switch harness connector.

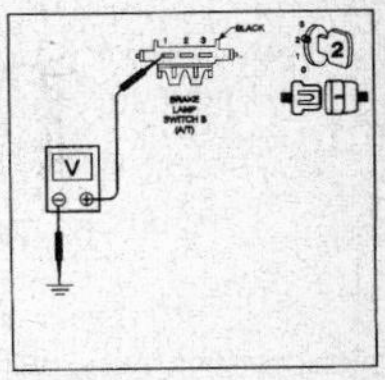

Is the voltage above 10 volts?

Yes >> Go to 2

No >> Repair the Fused Ignition Switch Output circuit for an open.
Perform ABS VERIFICATION TEST.

2. MEASURE THE RESISTANCE BETWEEN THE BRAKE LAMP SWITCH AND THE BRAKE LAMP RELAY

With the ignition off.
Remove the Brake Lamp Relay.
Note: Check connectors - Clean/repair as necessary.
Measure the resistance of the circuit from the Brake Lamp Switch harness connector B cavity 2 to the Brake Lamp Relay harness connector cavity 8.

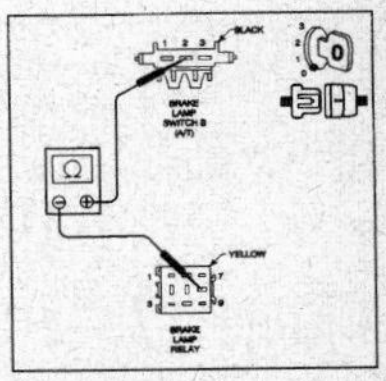

Is the resistance below 5.0 ohms?

Yes >> Go to 3

No >> Repair the circuit for an open.
Perform ABS VERIFICATION TEST.

ARM0300000000414

Fig. 59 Brake Lamp Switch Fault (Part 1 of 4). ABS

3. MEASURE THE RESISTANCE BETWEEN THE BRAKE LAMP SWITCH AND THE CAB

With the ignition off.
Disconnect the CAB harness connector.

Note: Check connectors - Clean/repair as necessary.

Measure the resistance of the Brake Lamp Switch Output circuit from the Brake Lamp Switch harness connector to the CAB harness connector.

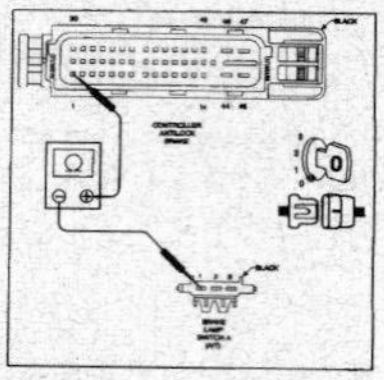

Is the resistance below 5.0 ohms?

Yes >> Go to 4

No >> Repair the Brake Lamp Switch Output circuit for an open.
Perform ABS VERIFICATION TEST.

4. MEASURE BRAKE LAMP RELAY VOLTAGE

With the ignition off.
Reconnect the Brake Lamp Switch harness connector.
Turn the ignition on.
Have an assistant depress the brake pedal while measuring the voltage at the Brake Lamp Relay harness connector cavity 8.

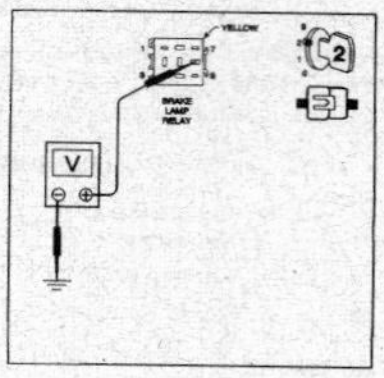

Is the voltage above 10 volts?

Yes >> Go to 5

No >> Replace the Brake Lamp Switch.
Perform ABS VERIFICATION TEST.

5. MEASURE THE RESISTANCE BETWEEN THE BRAKE LAMP RELAY AND THE CAB

Turn the ignition off.
Measure the resistance of the Brake Lamp Relay Control circuit between the Brake Lamp Relay harness connector and the CAB harness connector.

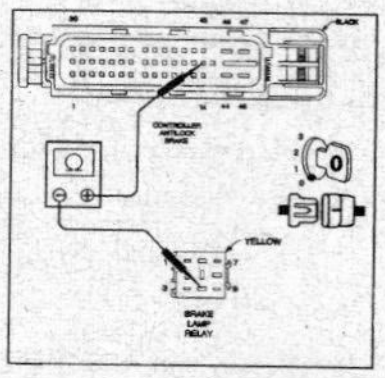

Is the resistance below 5.0 ohms?

Yes >> Go to 6

No >> Repair the Brake Lamp Relay control circuit between the Brake Lamp Relay and the CAB for an open.
Perform ABS VERIFICATION TEST.

ARM0300000000415

Fig. 59 Brake Lamp Switch Fault (Part 2 of 4). ABS

6. MEASURE BRAKE LAMP RELAY CONTROL CIRCUIT VOLTAGE

Turn the ignition on.
Measure the voltage of the Brake Lamp Relay Control circuit at the CAB harness connector.

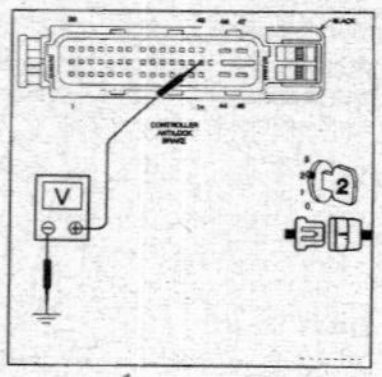

Is voltage present?

Yes >> Repair the Brake Lamp Relay Control circuit for a short to voltage.
Perform ABS VERIFICATION TEST.

No >> Go to 7

7. MEASURE BRAKE LAMP RELAY CONTROL CIRCUIT VOLTAGE

Turn the ignition off.
Install a jumper wire between cavities 4 and 6 of the Brake Lamp Relay harness connector.
Turn the ignition on.
Measure the voltage of the Brake Lamp Relay Control circuit at the CAB harness connector.

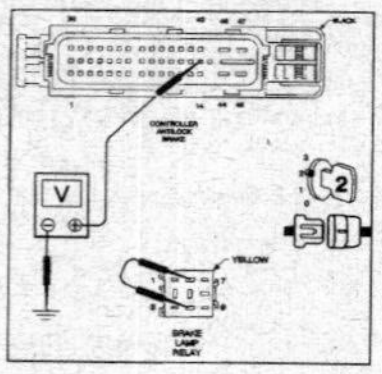

Is the voltage above 10 volts?

Yes >> Go to 8

No >> Repair the Brake Lamp Relay Control circuit for an open.
Perform ABS VERIFICATION TEST.

8. MEASURE BRAKE LAMP RELAY OUTPUT CIRCUIT RESISTANCE

With the ignition off and the jumper wire removed from the Brake Lamp Relay harness connector.
Measure the resistance of the Brake Lamp Relay Output circuit from the Brake Lamp Relay harness connector to the CAB harness connector.

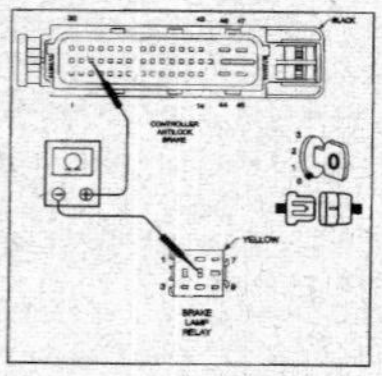

Is the resistance below 5.0 ohms?

Yes >> Go to 9

No >> Repair the Brake Lamp Relay Output circuit for an open.
Perform ABS VERIFICATION TEST.

ARM0300000000416

Fig. 59 Brake Lamp Switch Fault (Part 3 of 4). ABS

9. MEASURE BRAKE LAMP RELAY OUTPUT CIRCUIT VOLTAGE

Turn the ignition on.
Measure the voltage of the Brake Lamp Relay Output circuit at the CAB harness connector.

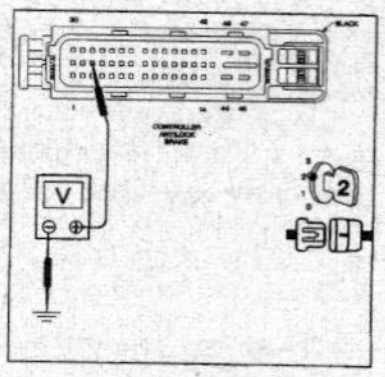

Is voltage present?

Yes >> Repair the Brake Lamp Relay Output circuit for a short to voltage.
Perform ABS VERIFICATION TEST.

No >> Go to 10

10. MEASURE BRAKE LAMP RELAY OUTPUT CIRCUIT VOLTAGE

Turn the ignition off.
Install a jumper wire between cavities 8 and 5 of the Brake Lamp Relay harness connector.
Turn the ignition on.
Have an assistant depress the brake pedal while measuring the voltage of the Brake Lamp Relay Output circuit at the CAB harness connector.

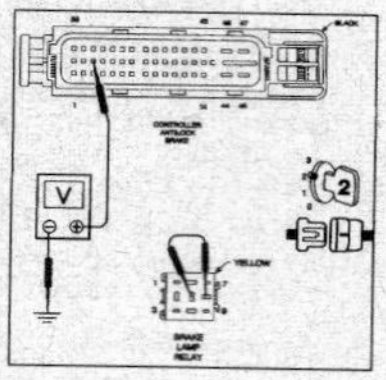

Is the voltage above 10 volts?

Yes >> Replace the Controller Antilock Brake.
Perform ABS VERIFICATION TEST.

No >> Replace the Brake Lamp Relay.
Perform ABS VERIFICATION TEST.

ARM0300000000417

Fig. 59 Brake Lamp Switch Fault (Part 4 of 4). ABS

1.

Turn the ignition off.

Disconnect all jumper wires and reconnect all previously disconnected components and connectors.

With the DRB III®, erase all Diagnostic Trouble Codes (DTCs) from ALL modules. Start the engine and allow it to run for 2 minutes.

Turn the ignition off and wait 5 seconds. Turn the ignition on and using the DRB III®, read DTCs from ALL modules.

CAUTION: Ensure braking capability is available before road testing.

Note: For sensor signal and pump motor faults, the CAB must sense all 4 wheels at 25 km/h (15 MPH) before the CAB will extinguish the indicator lamp.

Road test the vehicle for a minimum of 5 minutes. Perform several antilock braking stops.

Again, with the DRB III®, confirm that no DTCs are present and that all components are functioning properly.

If there are no DTCs present and all components are functioning properly, the repair is complete.

Are any DTCs present?

YES >> Repair is not complete, refer to appropriate symptom.

NO >> Repair is complete.

ARM0300000000418

Fig. 60 ABS Verification Test. ABS

1. MEASURE THE VOLTAGE OF THE CAB FUSED B(+) CIRCUIT

Turn the ignition off.
Disconnect the CAB harness connector.
Note: Check connectors - Clean/repair as necessary.
Turn the ignition on.
Measure the voltage of the Fused B(+) circuit at cavity 45 of the CAB harness connector.

Is the voltage between 12 and 16 volts?

Yes >> Go to 2

No >> System voltage must be between 12 and 16 volts. Repair the voltage concern as necessary.
Perform ABS VERIFICATION TEST.

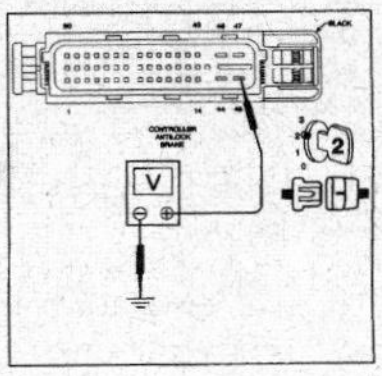

2. MEASURE THE VOLTAGE OF THE CAB FUSED B(+) CIRCUIT

With the ignition on.
Measure the voltage of the Fused B(+) circuit at cavity 47 of the CAB harness connector.

Is the voltage between 12 and 16 volts?

Yes >> Replace the Controller Antilock Brake.
Perform ABS VERIFICATION TEST.

No >> System voltage must be between 12 and 16 volts. Repair the voltage concern as necessary.
Perform ABS VERIFICATION TEST.

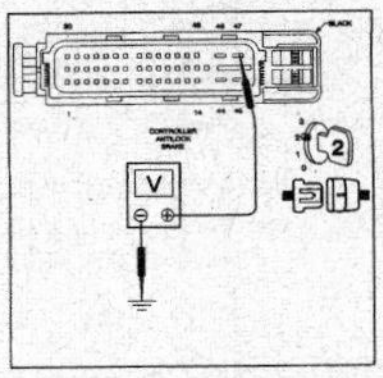

ARM0300000000422

Fig. 61 CAB Internal Failure. BAS

3. MEASURE THE VOLTAGE OF THE FUSED B(+) CIRCUIT

Turn the ignition off.
Disconnect the CAB harness connector.
Note: Check connectors - Clean/repair as necessary.
Turn the ignition on.
Measure the voltage of the Fused B(+) circuit at cavity 45 of the CAB harness connector.

Is the voltage above 10 volts?

Yes >> Go to 4

No >> Repair the Fused B(+) circuit for an open.
Perform ABS VERIFICATION TEST.

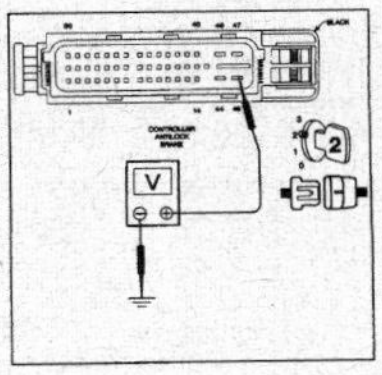

4. MEASURE THE VOLTAGE OF THE FUSED B(+) CIRCUIT

With the ignition on.
Measure the voltage of the Fused B(+) circuit at cavity 47 of the CAB harness connector.

Is the voltage above 10 volts?

Yes >> Replace the Controller Antilock Brake.
Perform ABS VERIFICATION TEST.

No >> Repair the Fused B(+) circuit for an open.
Perform ABS VERIFICATION TEST.

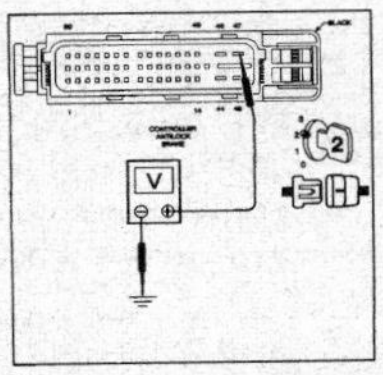

ARM0300000000424

Fig. 62 CAB System Undervoltage (Part 2 of 2). BAS

3. MEASURE THE RESISTANCE OF THE GROUND CIRCUIT

Turn the ignition off.
Disconnect the CAB connector.
Note: Check connector - Clean/repair as necessary.
Measure the resistance between ground and the Ground circuit at cavity 46 of the CAB harness connector.

Is the resistance below 5.0 ohms?

Yes >> Go to 4

No >> Repair the Ground circuit for an open.
Perform ABS VERIFICATION TEST.

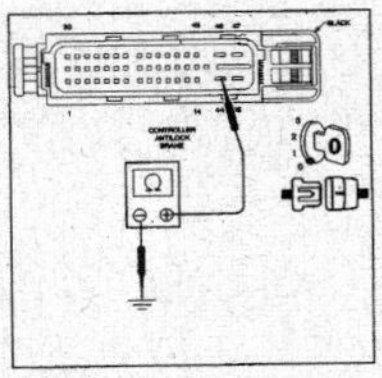

4. MEASURE THE RESISTANCE OF THE GROUND CIRCUIT

With the ignition off.
Measure the resistance between ground and the Ground circuit at cavity 44 of the CAB harness connector.

Is the resistance below 5.0 ohms?

Yes >> Replace the Controller Antilock Brake.
Perform ABS VERIFICATION TEST.

No >> Repair the Ground circuit for an open.
Perform ABS VERIFICATION TEST.

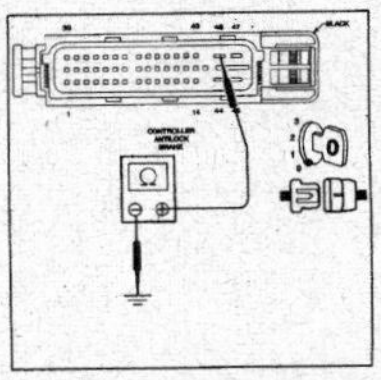

ARM0300000000426

Fig. 63 CAB System Overvoltage (Part 2 of 2). BAS

1. WITH THE DRB III®, READ DTCs

Turn the ignition on.
With the DRB III®, erase DTCs.
Turn the ignition off.
Turn the ignition on.
Start the engine.
Drive the vehicle above 10 MPH for at least 20 seconds.
Stop the vehicle.
With the DRB III®, read DTCs.

Does the DRB III® display a System Undervoltage DTC?

Yes >> Go to 2

No >> The condition that caused this DTC to set is currently not present. Inspect the related wiring harness for a possible intermittent condition.

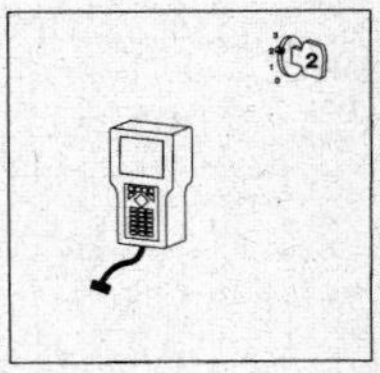

2. MEASURE THE BATTERY VOLTAGE

Start the engine.
Measure the battery voltage with the engine running.

Is the battery voltage below 10 volts?

Yes >> Refer to the appropriate service information for charging system testing and repair.
Perform ABS VERIFICATION TEST.

No >> Go to 3

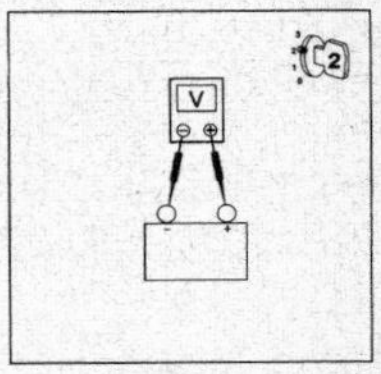

ARM0300000000423

Fig. 62 CAB System Undervoltage (Part 1 of 2). BAS

1. WITH THE DRB III®, READ DTCs

Turn the ignition on.
With the DRB III®, erase DTCs.
Turn the ignition off.
Turn the ignition on.
Start the engine.
With the DRB III®, read DTCs.

Does the DRB III® display a System Overvoltage DTC?

Yes >> Go to 2

No >> The condition that caused this DTC to set is currently not present. Inspect the related wiring harness for a possible intermittent condition.

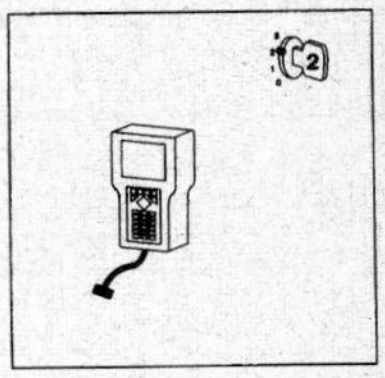

2. MEASURE THE BATTERY VOLTAGE

Start the engine.
Raise engine speed above 1,800 RPM.
Measure the battery voltage.

Is the voltage above 16 volts?

Yes >> Refer to the appropriate service information for charging system testing and repair.
Perform ABS VERIFICATION TEST.

No >> Go to 3

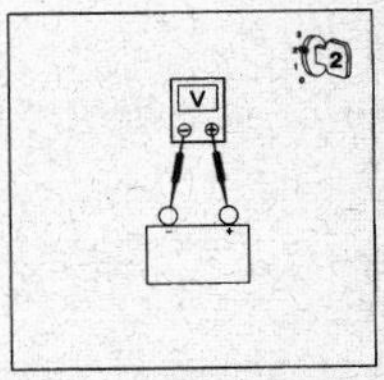

ARM0300000000425

Fig. 63 CAB System Overvoltage (Part 1 of 2). BAS

1. WITH THE DRB III®, READ DTCs

Turn the ignition on.
With the DRB III®, erase DTCs.
Turn the ignition off.
Turn the ignition on.
Start the engine.
CAUTION: Ensure braking capability is available before road testing.
Drive the vehicle above 10 MPH for at least 20 seconds.
Stop the vehicle.
With the DRB III®, read DTCs.

Does the DRB III® display a PCM Not Identified or Incorrect DTC?

Yes >> Replace the Controller Antilock Brake.
Perform ABS VERIFICATION TEST.

No >> The condition that caused this DTC to set is currently not present.
Perform ABS VERIFICATION TEST.

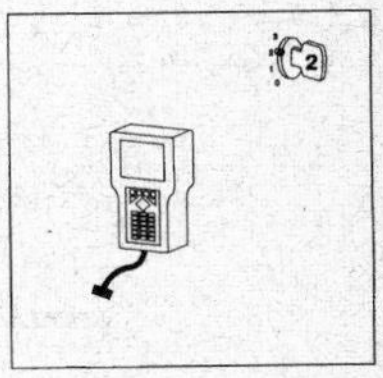

ARM0300000000427

Fig. 64 PCM Not Identified Or Incorrect. BAS

1. **MEASURE THE RESISTANCE OF THE CAN C BUS (+) CIRCUIT**

Turn the ignition off.
Disconnect the CAB harness connector.
Disconnect the harness connectors of the other modules on the CAN Bus network.
Note: Check connectors - Clean/repair as necessary.
Measure the resistance of the CAN C Bus (+) circuit from the CAB harness connector to the harness connectors of the other modules on the CAN Bus network.

Is the resistance below 1.0 ohm?

Yes >> Go to 2
No >> Repair the CAN C Bus (+) circuit for an open.
Perform ABS VERIFICATION TEST.

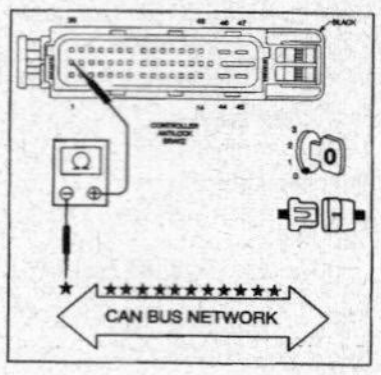

2. **MEASURE THE RESISTANCE OF THE CAN C (-) BUS CIRCUIT**

With the ignition off.
Measure the resistance of the CAN C Bus (-) circuit from the CAB harness connector to the harness connectors of the other modules on the CAN Bus network.

Is the resistance below 1.0 ohm?

Yes >> Replace the Controller Antilock Brake.
Perform ABS VERIFICATION TEST.
No >> Repair the CAN C Bus (-) circuit for an open.
Perform ABS VERIFICATION TEST.

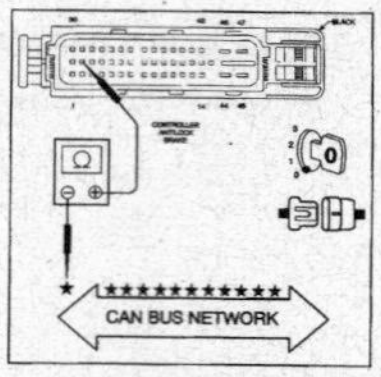

ARM0300000000428

Fig. 65 CAN BUS Communication General Fault. BAS

1. **MEASURE THE VOLTAGE OF THE BAS RELEASE SWITCH SENSE (APPLIED) CIRCUIT**

Turn the ignition off.
Disconnect the BAS Brake Booster harness connector.
Note: Check connectors - Clean/repair as necessary.
Turn the ignition on.
Measure the voltage of the BAS Release Switch Sense (Applied) circuit at the BAS Brake Booster harness connector.

Is the voltage above 5.0 volts?

Yes >> Repair the BAS Release Switch Sense (Applied) circuit for a short to voltage.
Perform ABS VERIFICATION TEST.
No >> Go to 2

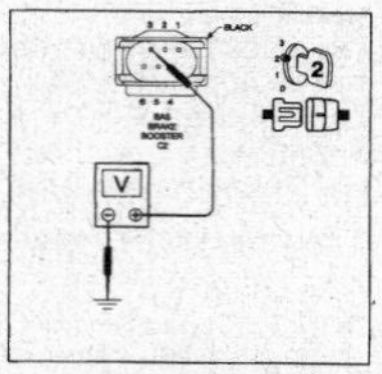

ARM0300000000430

Fig. 67 Release Switch Fault (Part 1 of 4). BAS

2. **MEASURE THE RESISTANCE BETWEEN THE BAS RELEASE SWITCH SENSE (APPLIED) CIRCUIT AND THE SENSE (REFERENCE) CIRCUIT**

With the ignition off.
Disconnect the CAB harness connector.
Note: Check connectors - Clean/repair as necessary.
Measure the resistance between the BAS Release Switch Sense (Applied) circuit and the Sense (Reference) circuit in the BAS Brake Booster harness connector.

Is the resistance below 5.0 ohms?

Yes >> Repair the BAS Release Switch Sense (Applied) circuit for a short to the Sense (Reference) circuit.
Perform ABS VERIFICATION TEST.
No >> Go to 3

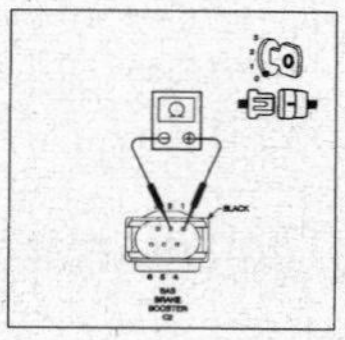

3. **MEASURE THE RESISTANCE OF THE BAS RELEASE SWITCH SENSE (APPLIED) CIRCUIT**

With the ignition off.
Measure the resistance of the BAS Release Switch Sense (Applied) circuit from the CAB harness connector to the BAS Brake Booster harness connector.

Is the resistance below 5.0 ohms?

Yes >> Go to 4
No >> Repair the BAS Release Switch Sense (Applied) circuit for an open.
Perform ABS VERIFICATION TEST.

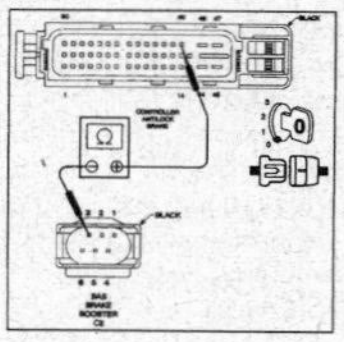

4. **MEASURE THE RESISTANCE BETWEEN GROUND AND THE BAS RELEASE SWITCH 12 VOLT SUPPLY CIRCUIT**

With the ignition off.
Measure the resistance between ground and the BAS Release Switch 12 Volt Supply circuit.

Is the resistance below 100 ohms?

Yes >> Repair the BAS Release Switch 12 Volt Supply circuit for a short to ground.
Perform ABS VERIFICATION TEST.
No >> Go to 5

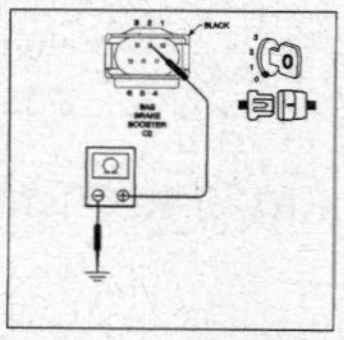

ARM0300000000431

Fig. 67 Release Switch Fault (Part 2 of 4). BAS

1. **MEASURE THE RESISTANCE OF THE CAN C BUS (+) CIRCUIT**

Turn the ignition off.
Disconnect the CAB harness connector.
Disconnect the PCM harness connector.
Note: Check connectors - Clean/repair as necessary.
Measure the resistance of the CAN C Bus (+) circuit from the CAB harness connector to the PCM harness connector.

Is the resistance below 1.0 ohm?

Yes >> Go to 2
No >> Repair the CAN C Bus (+) circuit for an open.
Perform ABS VERIFICATION TEST.

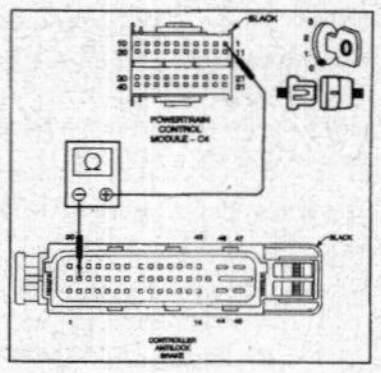

2. **MEASURE THE RESISTANCE OF THE CAN C BUS (-) CIRCUIT**

With the ignition off.
Measure the resistance of the CAN C Bus (-) circuit from the CAB harness connector to the PCM harness connector.

Is the resistance below 1.0 ohm?

Yes >> Replace the Controller Antilock Brake.
Perform ABS VERIFICATION TEST.
No >> Repair the CAN C Bus (-) circuit for an open.
Perform ABS VERIFICATION TEST.

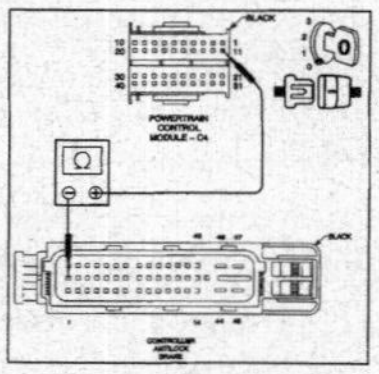

ARM0300000000429

Fig. 66 No CAN Communications w/PCM. BAS

5. **MEASURE THE VOLTAGE OF THE SENSE (REFERENCE) CIRCUIT**

With the ignition off.
Reconnect the CAB harness connector.
Turn the ignition on.
Measure the voltage of the BAS Release Switch Sense (Reference) circuit at the BAS Brake Booster harness connector.

Is the voltage between 10 and 12 volts?

Yes >> Go to 6
No >> Go to 8

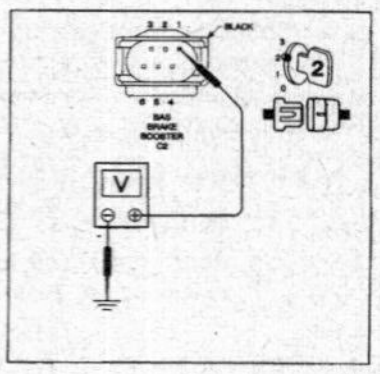

6. **MEASURE THE RESISTANCE BETWEEN GROUND AND THE BAS RELEASE SWITCH SENSE (APPLIED) CIRCUIT**

Turn the ignition off.
Disconnect the CAB harness connector.
Note: Check connectors - Clean/repair as necessary.
Measure the resistance between ground and the BAS Release Switch Sense (Applied) circuit.

Is the resistance below 100 ohms?

Yes >> Repair the BAS Release Switch Sense (Applied) circuit for a short to ground.
Perform ABS VERIFICATION TEST.
No >> Go to 7

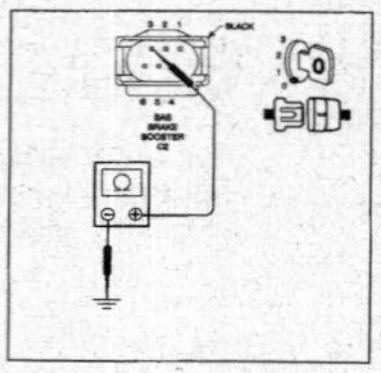

7. **MEASURE THE RESISTANCE BETWEEN THE BAS RELEASE SWITCH SENSE (APPLIED) CIRCUIT AND THE 12 VOLT SUPPLY CIRCUIT**

With the ignition off.
Measure the resistance between the BAS Release Switch Sense (Applied) circuit and the BAS Release Switch 12 Volt Supply circuit in the BAS Brake Booster harness connector.

Is the resistance below 100 ohms?

Yes >> Repair the BAS Release Switch Sense (Applied) circuit for a short to the BAS Release Switch 12 Volt Supply circuit.
Perform ABS VERIFICATION TEST.
No >> Replace the BAS Brake Booster.
Perform ABS VERIFICATION TEST.

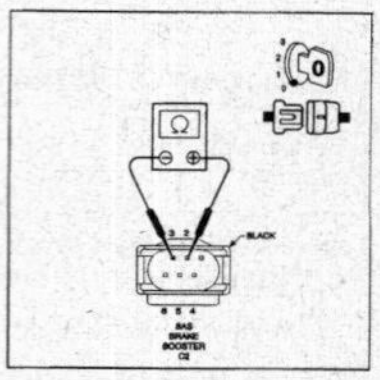

ARM0300000000432

Fig. 67 Release Switch Fault (Part 3 of 4). BAS

8. MEASURE THE RESISTANCE BETWEEN GROUND AND THE BAS RELEASE SWITCH SENSOR (RELEASED) CIRCUIT

Turn the ignition off.
Disconnect the CAB harness connector.
Note: Check connectors - Clean/repair as necessary.
Measure the resistance between ground and the BAS Release Switch Sensor (Released) circuit at the BAS Brake Booster harness connector.

Is the resistance below 100 ohms?

Yes >> Repair the BAS Release Switch Sensor (Released) circuit for a short to ground.
Perform ABS VERIFICATION TEST.

No >> Go to 9

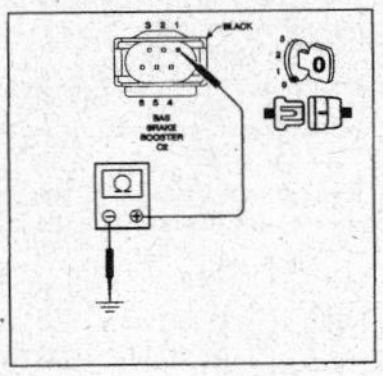

9. MEASURE THE RESISTANCE OF THE BAS RELEASE SWITCH SENSE (RELEASED) CIRCUIT

With the ignition off.
Measure the resistance of the BAS Release Switch Sensor (Released) circuit at the BAS Brake Booster harness connector and the CAB harness connector.

Is the resistance below 5.0 ohms?

Yes >> Replace the Controller Antilock Brake.
Perform ABS VERIFICATION TEST.

No >> Repair the BAS Release Switch Sensor (Released) circuit for an open.
Perform ABS VERIFICATION TEST.

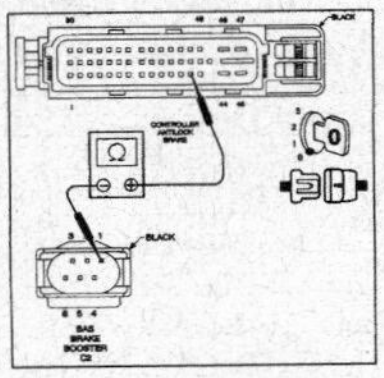

ARM0300000000433

Fig. 67 Release Switch Fault (Part 4 of 4). BAS

2. MEASURE THE RESISTANCE BETWEEN THE BAS TRAVEL SENSOR SIGNAL CIRCUIT AND THE 5-VOLT SUPPLY CIRCUIT

With the ignition off.
Disconnect the CAB harness connector.
Note: Check connectors - Clean/repair as necessary.
Measure the resistance between the BAS Travel Sensor Signal circuit and the 5-Volt supply circuit in the BAS Brake Booster harness connector.

Is the resistance below 5.0 ohms?

Yes >> Repair the BAS Travel Sensor Signal circuit for a short to the 5-Volt Supply circuit.
Perform ABS VERIFICATION TEST.

No >> Go to 3

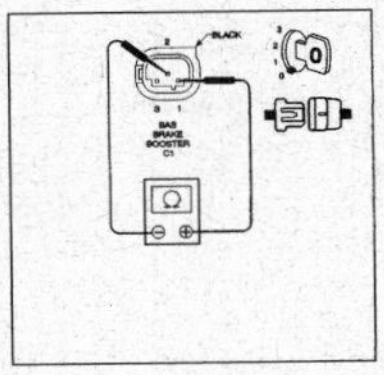

3. MEASURE THE RESISTANCE OF THE BAS TRAVEL SENSOR SIGNAL CIRCUIT

With the ignition off.
Measure the resistance of the BAS Travel Sensor Signal circuit from the CAB harness connector to the BAS Brake Booster harness connector.

Is the resistance below 5.0 ohms?

Yes >> Go to 4

No >> Repair the BAS Travel Sensor Signal circuit for an open.
Perform ABS VERIFICATION TEST.

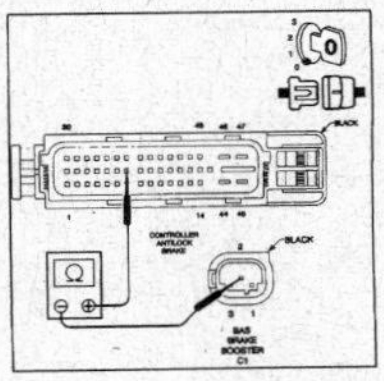

4. MEASURE THE RESISTANCE BETWEEN GROUND AND THE BAS TRAVEL SENSOR GROUND CIRCUIT

With the ignition off.
Measure the resistance between ground and the BAS Travel Sensor Ground circuit.

Is the resistance below 100 ohms?

Yes >> Repair the BAS Travel Sensor Ground circuit for a short to ground.
Perform ABS VERIFICATION TEST.

No >> Go to 5

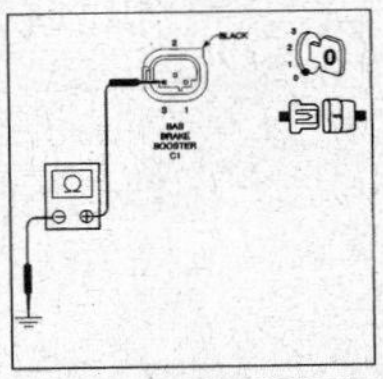

ARM0300000000435

Fig. 68 BAS Travel Sensor Fault (Part 2 of 4). BAS

1. MEASURE THE VOLTAGE OF THE BAS TRAVEL SENSOR SIGNAL CIRCUIT

Turn the ignition off.
Disconnect the BAS Brake Booster harness connector.
Note: Check connectors - Clean/repair as necessary.
Turn the ignition on.
Measure the voltage of the BAS Travel Sensor Signal circuit at the BAS Brake Booster harness connector.

Is the voltage above 5.0 volts?

Yes >> Repair the BAS Travel Sensor Signal circuit for a short to voltage.
Perform ABS VERIFICATION TEST.

No >> Go to 2

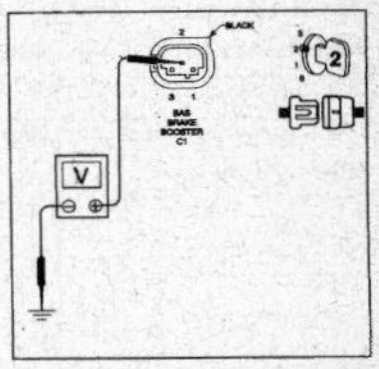

ARM0300000000434

Fig. 68 BAS Travel Sensor Fault (Part 1 of 4). BAS

5. MEASURE THE VOLTAGE OF THE 5-VOLT SUPPLY CIRCUIT

With the ignition off.
Reconnect the CAB harness connector.
Turn the ignition on.
Measure the voltage of the BAS Travel Sensor 5-Volt Supply circuit at the BAS Brake Booster harness connector.

Is the voltage between 4.5 and 5.0 volts?

Yes >> Go to 6

No >> Go to 8

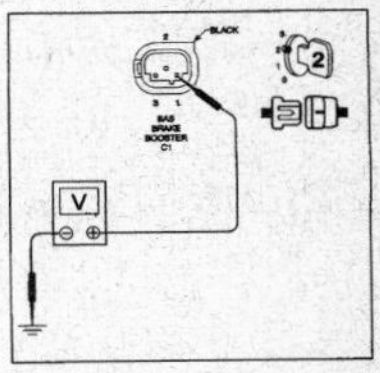

6. MEASURE THE RESISTANCE BETWEEN GROUND AND THE BAS TRAVEL SENSOR SIGNAL CIRCUIT

Turn the ignition off.
Disconnect the CAB harness connector.
Note: Check connectors - Clean/repair as necessary.
Measure the resistance between ground and the BAS Travel Sensor Signal circuit.

Is the resistance below 100 ohms?

Yes >> Repair the BAS Travel Sensor Signal circuit for a short to ground.
Perform ABS VERIFICATION TEST.

No >> Go to 7

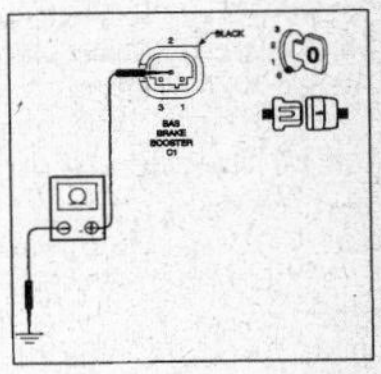

7. MEASURE THE RESISTANCE BETWEEN THE BAS TRAVEL SENSOR SIGNAL CIRCUIT AND THE GROUND CIRCUIT

With the ignition off.
Measure the resistance between the BAS Travel Sensor Signal circuit and the BAS Travel Sensor Ground circuit in the BAS Brake Booster harness connector.

Is the resistance below 100 ohms?

Yes >> Repair the BAS Travel Sensor Signal circuit for a short to the BAS Travel Sensor Ground circuit.
Perform ABS VERIFICATION TEST.

No >> Replace the BAS Brake Booster.
Perform ABS VERIFICATION TEST.

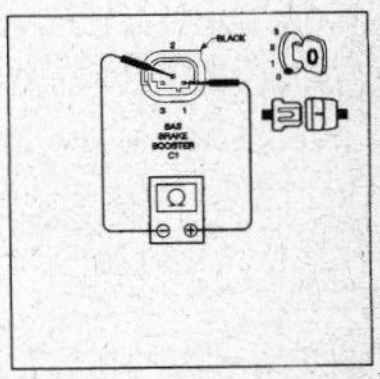

ARM0300000000436

Fig. 68 BAS Travel Sensor Fault (Part 3 of 4). BAS

8. MEASURE THE RESISTANCE BETWEEN GROUND AND THE BAS TRAVEL SENSOR 5-VOLT SUPPLY CIRCUIT

Turn the ignition off.
Disconnect the CAB harness connector.
Note: Check connectors - Clean/repair as necessary.
Measure the resistance between ground and the 5-Volt Supply circuit.

Is the resistance below 100 ohms?

Yes >> Repair the 5-Volt Supply circuit for a short to ground.
Perform ABS VERIFICATION TEST.

No >> Go to 9

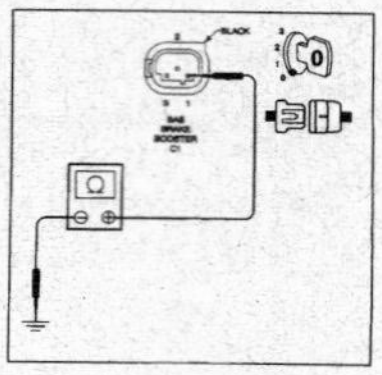

9. MEASURE THE RESISTANCE OF THE BAS TRAVEL SENSOR 5-VOLT SUPPLY CIRCUIT

With the ignition off.
Measure the resistance of the 5-Volt Supply circuit from the BAS Brake Booster harness connector to the CAB harness connector.

Is the resistance below 5.0 ohms?

Yes >> Replace the Controller Antilock Brake.
Perform ABS VERIFICATION TEST.

No >> Repair the BAS Travel Sensor 5-Volt Supply circuit for an open.
Perform ABS VERIFICATION TEST.

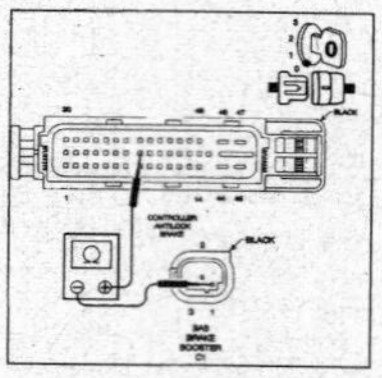

ARM0300000000437

Fig. 68 BAS Travel Sensor Fault (Part 4 of 4). BAS

1. MEASURE BRAKE LAMP SWITCH VOLTAGE

Note: Inspect Fuse 2 located in the Illumination Control Module/IP Fuse Block. If the fuse is open, repair the cause of the open fuse before continuing.
Turn the ignition off.
Disconnect the Brake Lamp Switch harness connector.
Note: Check connectors - Clean/repair as necessary.
Turn the ignition on.
Measure the voltage of the Fused Ignition Switch Output circuit at the Brake Lamp Switch harness connector.

Is the voltage above 10 volts?

Yes >> Go to 2

No >> Repair the Fused Ignition Switch Output circuit for an open.
Perform ABS VERIFICATION TEST.

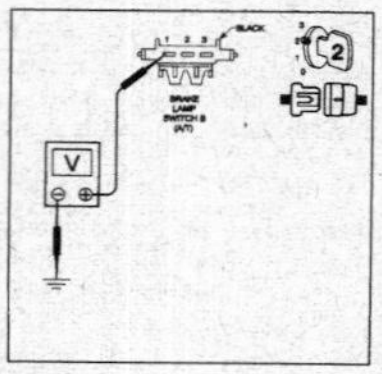

2. MEASURE THE RESISTANCE BETWEEN THE BRAKE LAMP SWITCH AND THE BRAKE LAMP RELAY

With the ignition off.
Remove the Brake Lamp Relay.
Note: Check connectors - Clean/repair as necessary.
Measure the resistance of the circuit from the Brake Lamp Switch harness connector B cavity 2 to the Brake Lamp Relay harness connector cavity 8.

Is the resistance below 5.0 ohms?

Yes >> Go to 3

No >> Repair the circuit for an open.
Perform ABS VERIFICATION TEST.

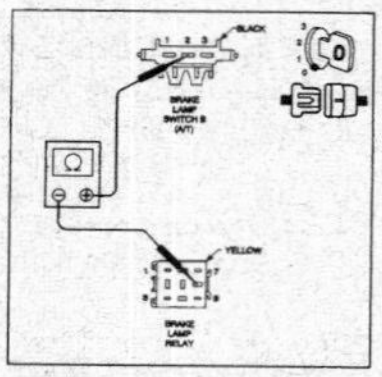

ARM0300000000438

Fig. 69 Brake Lamp Switch Fault (Part 1 of 4). BAS

3. MEASURE THE RESISTANCE BETWEEN THE BRAKE LAMP SWITCH AND THE CAB

With the ignition off.
Disconnect the CAB harness connector.
Note: Check connectors - Clean/repair as necessary.
Measure the resistance of the Brake Lamp Switch Output circuit from the Brake Lamp Switch harness connector to the CAB harness connector.

Is the resistance below 5.0 ohms?

Yes >> Go to 4

No >> Repair the Brake Lamp Switch Output circuit for an open.
Perform ABS VERIFICATION TEST.

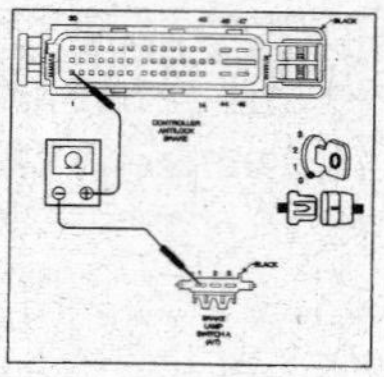

4. MEASURE BRAKE LAMP RELAY VOLTAGE

With the ignition off.
Reconnect the Brake Lamp Switch harness connector.
Turn the ignition on.
Have an assistant depress the brake pedal while measuring the voltage at the Brake Lamp Relay harness connector cavity 8.

Is the voltage above 10 volts?

Yes >> Go to 5

No >> Replace the Brake Lamp Switch.
Perform ABS VERIFICATION TEST.

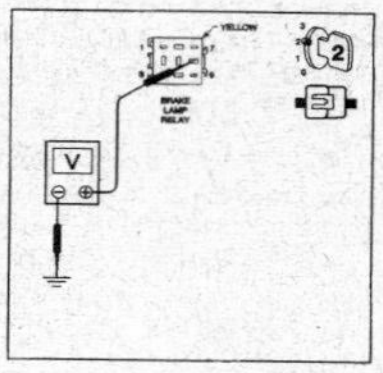

5. MEASURE THE RESISTANCE BETWEEN THE BRAKE LAMP RELAY AND THE CAB

Turn the ignition off.
Measure the resistance of the Brake Lamp Relay Control circuit between the Brake Lamp Relay harness connector and the CAB harness connector.

Is the resistance below 5.0 ohms?

Yes >> Go to 6

No >> Repair the Brake Lamp Relay control circuit between the Brake Lamp Relay and the CAB for an open.
Perform ABS VERIFICATION TEST.

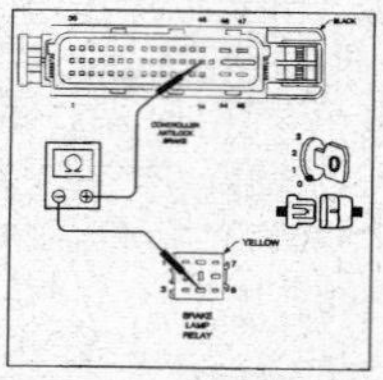

ARM0300000000439

Fig. 69 Brake Lamp Switch Fault (Part 2 of 4). BAS

6. MEASURE BRAKE LAMP RELAY CONTROL CIRCUIT VOLTAGE

Turn the ignition on.
Measure the voltage of the Brake Lamp Relay Control circuit at the CAB harness connector.

Is voltage present?

Yes >> Repair the Brake Lamp Relay Control circuit for a short to voltage.
Perform ABS VERIFICATION TEST.

No >> Go to 7

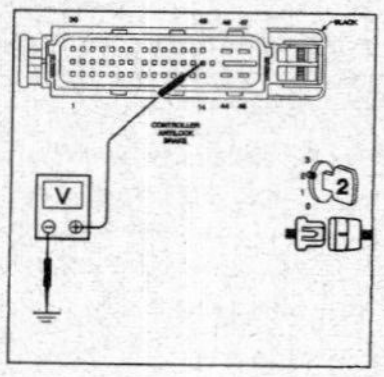

7. MEASURE BRAKE LAMP RELAY CONTROL CIRCUIT VOLTAGE

Turn the ignition off.
Install a jumper wire between cavities 4 and 6 of the Brake Lamp Relay harness connector.
Turn the ignition on.
Measure the voltage of the Brake Lamp Relay Control circuit at the CAB harness connector.

Is the voltage above 10 volts?

Yes >> Go to 8

No >> Repair the Brake Lamp Relay Control circuit for an open.
Perform ABS VERIFICATION TEST.

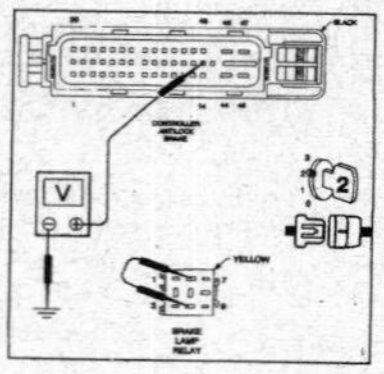

8. MEASURE BRAKE LAMP RELAY OUTPUT CIRCUIT RESISTANCE

With the ignition off and the jumper wire removed from the Brake Lamp Relay harness connector.
Measure the resistance of the Brake Lamp Relay Output circuit from the Brake Lamp Relay harness connector to the CAB harness connector.

Is the resistance below 5.0 ohms?

Yes >> Go to 9

No >> Repair the Brake Lamp Relay Output circuit for an open.
Perform ABS VERIFICATION TEST.

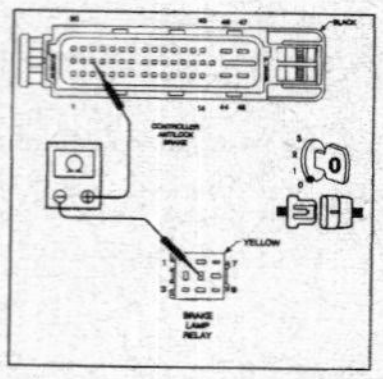

ARM0300000000440

Fig. 69 Brake Lamp Switch Fault (Part 3 of 4). BAS

9. MEASURE BRAKE LAMP RELAY OUTPUT CIRCUIT VOLTAGE

Turn the ignition on.
Measure the voltage of the Brake Lamp Relay Output circuit at the CAB harness connector.

Is voltage present?

Yes >> Repair the Brake Lamp Relay Output circuit for a short to voltage.
Perform ABS VERIFICATION TEST.

No >> Go to 10

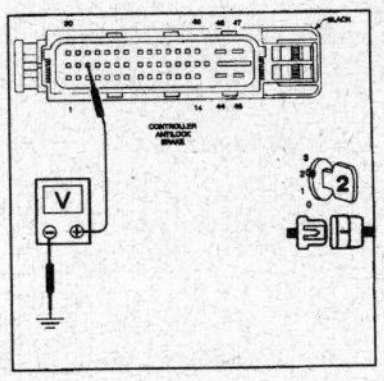

10. MEASURE BRAKE LAMP RELAY OUTPUT CIRCUIT VOLTAGE

Turn the ignition off.
Install a jumper wire between cavities 8 and 5 of the Brake Lamp Relay harness connector.
Turn the ignition on.
Have an assistant depress the brake pedal while measuring the voltage of the Brake Lamp Relay Output circuit at the CAB harness connector.

Is the voltage above 10 volts?

Yes >> Replace the Controller Antilock Brake.
Perform ABS VERIFICATION TEST.

No >> Replace the Brake Lamp Relay.
Perform ABS VERIFICATION TEST.

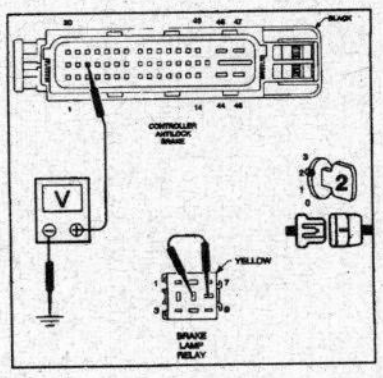

ARM0300000000441

Fig. 69 Brake Lamp Switch Fault (Part 4 of 4). BAS

2. MEASURE THE RESISTANCE OF THE BAS SOLENOID VALVE CONTROL CIRCUIT

With the ignition off.
Measure the resistance of the BAS Solenoid Valve Control circuit from the CAB harness connector to the BAS Brake Booster harness connector.

Is the resistance below 5.0 ohms?

Yes >> Go to 3

No >> Repair the BAS Solenoid Valve Control circuit for an open.
Perform ABS VERIFICATION TEST.

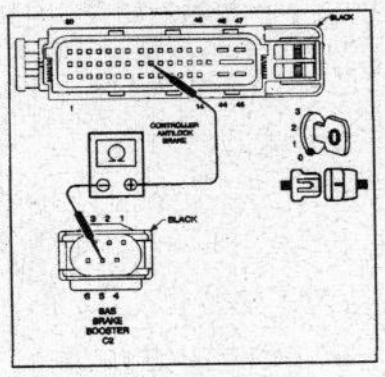

3. MEASURE THE RESISTANCE OF THE BAS SOLENOID VALVE CIRCUITS

With the ignition off.
Measure the resistance between the BAS Solenoid Valve circuits at the BAS Brake Booster harness connector.

Is the resistance below 10K ohms?

Yes >> Repair the BAS Solenoid Valve circuits for a short to each other.
Perform ABS VERIFICATION TEST.

No >> Go to 4

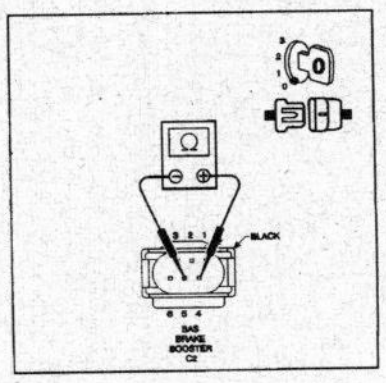

4. MEASURE THE VOLTAGE OF THE BAS SOLENOID VALVE 5-VOLT SUPPLY CIRCUIT

Turn the ignition on.
Measure the voltage of the BAS Solenoid Valve 5-Volt Supply circuit at the BAS Brake Booster harness connector.

Is voltage present?

Yes >> Repair the BAS Solenoid Valve 5-Volt Supply circuit for a short to voltage.
Perform ABS VERIFICATION TEST.

No >> Go to 5

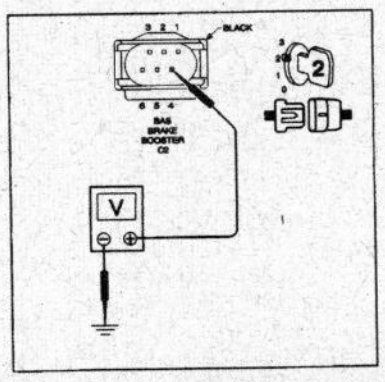

ARM0300000000443

Fig. 70 BAS Solenoid Valve Fault (Part 2 of 3). BAS

1. MEASURE THE RESISTANCE OF THE BAS SOLENOID VALVE 5-VOLT SUPPLY CIRCUIT

Turn the ignition off.
Disconnect the CAB harness connector.
Disconnect the BAS Brake Booster harness connector.
Note: Check connectors - Clean/repair as necessary.
Measure the resistance of the BAS Solenoid Valve 5-Volt Supply circuit from the CAB harness connector to the BAS Brake Booster harness connector.

Is the resistance below 5.0 ohms?

Yes >> Go to 2

No >> Repair the BAS Solenoid Valve 5-Volt Supply circuit for an open.
Perform ABS VERIFICATION TEST.

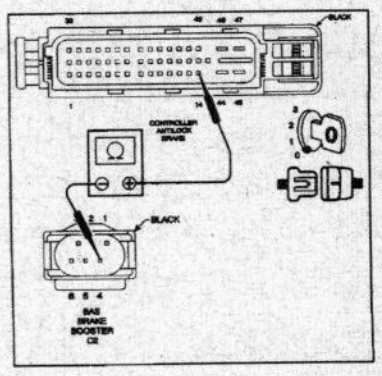

ARM0300000000442

Fig. 70 BAS Solenoid Valve Fault (Part 1 of 3). BAS

5. MEASURE THE VOLTAGE OF THE BAS SOLENOID VALVE CONTROL CIRCUIT

With the ignition on.
Measure the voltage of the BAS Solenoid Valve Control circuit at the BAS Brake Booster harness connector.

Is voltage present?

Yes >> Repair the BAS Solenoid Valve Control circuit for a short to voltage.
Perform ABS VERIFICATION TEST.

No >> Go to 6

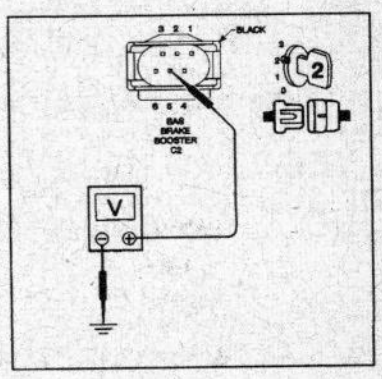

6. MEASURE THE RESISTANCE OF THE BAS SOLENOID VALVE 5-VOLT SUPPLY CIRCUIT

Turn the ignition off.
Measure the resistance between ground and the BAS Solenoid Valve 5-Volt Supply circuit.

Is the resistance below 10K ohms?

Yes >> Repair the BAS Solenoid Valve 5-Volt Supply circuit for a short to ground.
Perform ABS VERIFICATION TEST.

No >> Go to 7

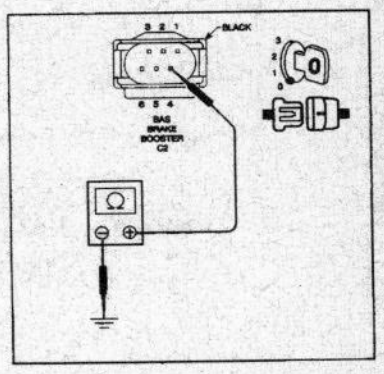

7. MEASURE THE RESISTANCE OF THE BAS SOLENOID VALVE CONTROL CIRCUIT

With the ignition off.
Measure the resistance between ground and the BAS Solenoid Valve Control circuit.

Is the resistance below 10K ohms?

Yes >> Repair the BAS Solenoid Valve Control circuit for a short to ground.
Perform ABS VERIFICATION TEST.

No >> Replace the BAS Brake Booster.
Perform ABS VERIFICATION TEST.

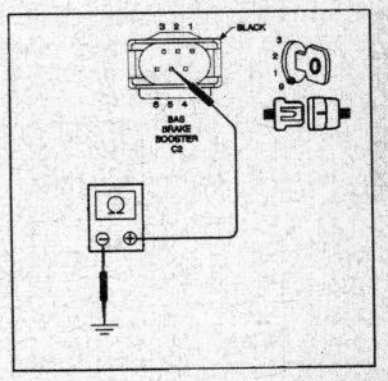

ARM0300000000444

Fig. 70 BAS Solenoid Valve Fault (Part 3 of 3). BAS

1.

Turn the ignition off.

Disconnect all jumper wires and reconnect all previously disconnected components and connectors.

With the DRB III®, erase all Diagnostic Trouble Codes (DTCs) from ALL modules. Start the engine and allow it to run for 2 minutes.

Turn the ignition off and wait 5 seconds. Turn the ignition on and using the DRB III®, read DTCs from ALL modules.

CAUTION: Ensure braking capability is available before road testing.

Note: For sensor signal and pump motor faults, the CAB must sense all 4 wheels at 25 km/h (15 MPH) before the CAB will extinguish the indicator lamp.

Road test the vehicle for a minimum of 5 minutes. Perform several antilock braking stops.

Again, with the DRB III®, confirm that no DTCs are present and that all components are functioning properly.

If there are no DTCs present and all components are functioning properly, the repair is complete.

Are any DTCs present?

YES >> Repair is not complete, refer to appropriate symptom.

NO >> Repair is complete.

ARM0300000000445

Fig. 71 Verification Test. BAS

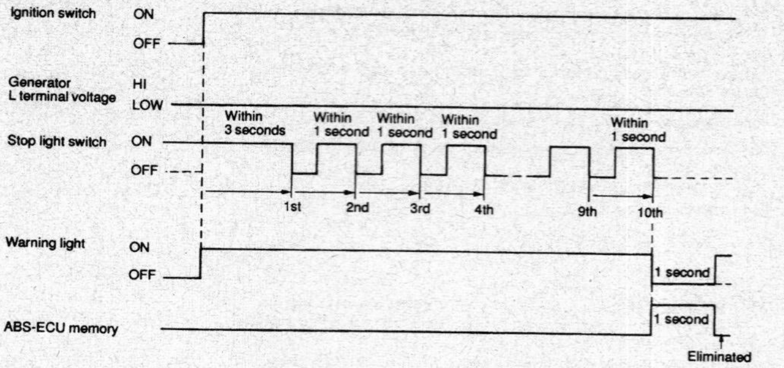

CR4029501185000X

Fig. 72 Clearing DTCs

Wheels	Front left	Front right	Rear left	Rear right
Terminal No.	6	4	8	1
	7	5	9	3

CR4029801555000X

Fig. 73 Wheel speed sensor voltage inspection

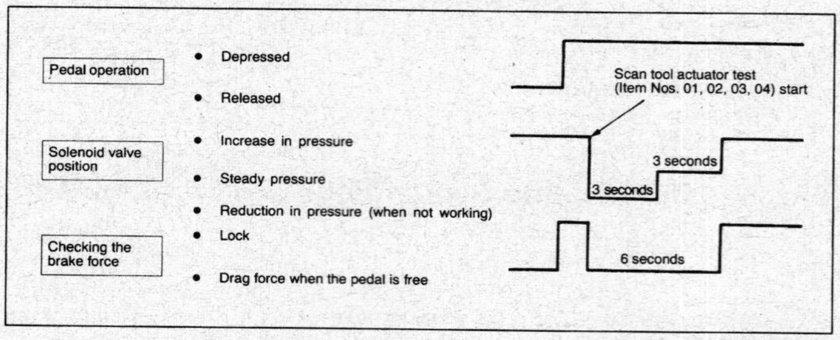

CR4029801556000X

Fig. 74 Hydraulic control unit inspection

No.	Operation	Judgement - Normal	Judgement - Abnormal	Probable cause	Remedy
01	(1) Depress brake pedal to lock wheel. (2) Using the scan tool, select the wheel to be checked and force the actuator to operate. (3) Turn the selected wheel manually to check the change of brake force.	Brake force released for 6 seconds after locking.	Wheel does not lock when brake pedal is depressed.	Clogged brake line other than hydraulic unit	Check and clean brake line
02				Clogged hydraulic circuit in hydraulic unit	Replace hydraulic unit assembly
03			Brake force is not released	Incorrect hydraulic unit brake tube connection	Connect correctly
04				Hydraulic unit solenoid valve not functioning correctly	Replace hydraulic unit assembly

CR4029801557000X

Fig. 75 Hydraulic control unit diagnosis table

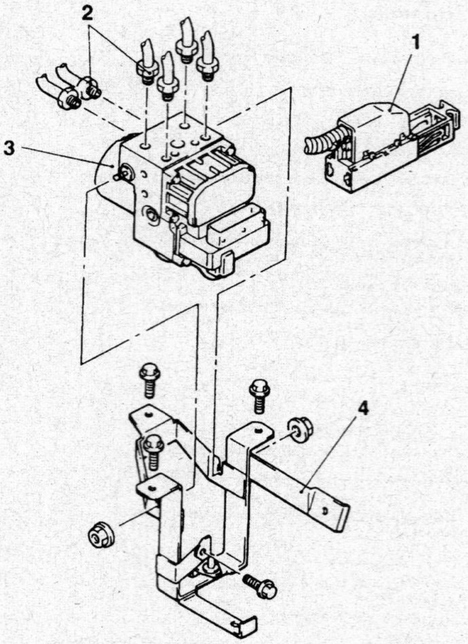

1. Harness connector
2. Brake pipe connection
3. Hydraulic unit and ABS-ECU
4. Hydraulic unit bracket assembly

CR4029801558000X

Fig. 76 HCU replacement. Avenger & 2000 Sebring Coupe

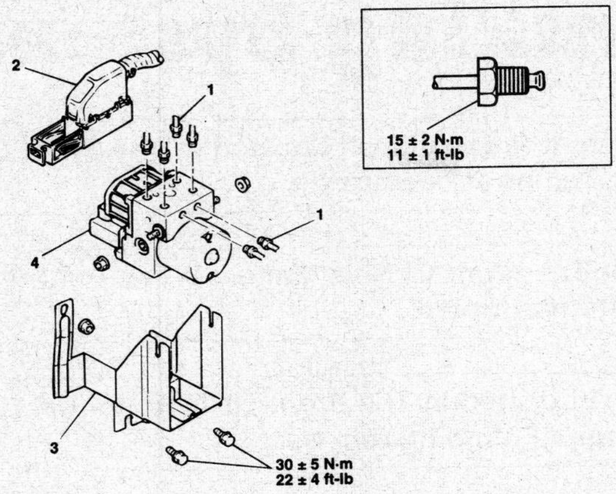

1 BRAKE TUBE
2 HARNESS CONNECTOR
3 BRACKET ASSEMBLY
4 HYDRAULIC UNIT

CR4020002151000X

Fig. 77 HCU replacement. 2001–03 Stratus Coupe & Sebring Coupe

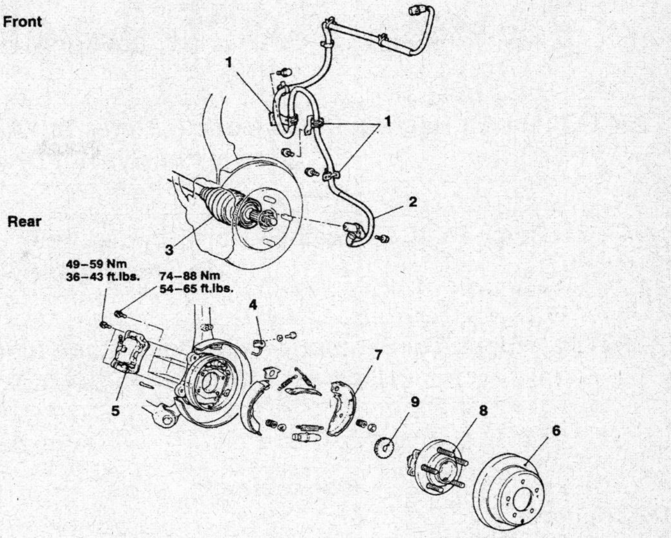

1. Clip
2. Front wheel speed sensor
3. Drive shaft
4. Rear wheel speed sensor
5. Caliper assembly
6. Brake disc
7. Shoe and lining assembly
8. Rear hub assembly
9. Rear ABS rotor

CR4020202394000X

Fig. 78 Wheel speed sensor replacement. Avenger & 2000 Sebring Coupe

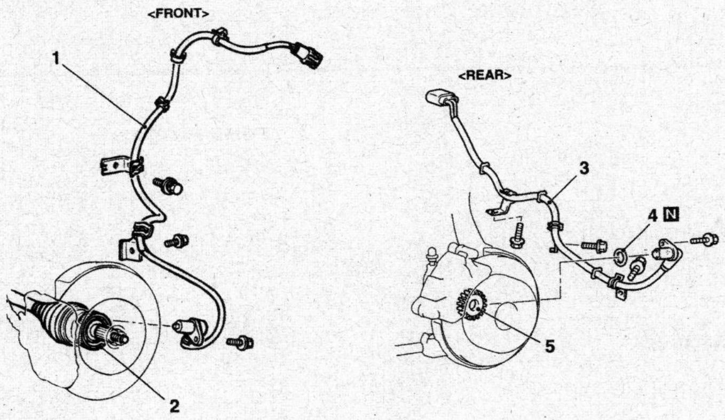

1. FRONT SPEED SENSOR
2. FRONT ABS ROTOR WITH DRIVESHAFT
3. REAR SPEED SENSOR
4. O-RING
5. REAR ABS ROTOR

CR4020202395000X

Fig. 79 Wheel speed sensor replacement. 2001–03 Stratus Coupe & Sebring Coupe

Teves Anti-Lock Braking System

NOTE: On Air Bag Equipped Models, Refer To "Air Bag System Precautions" Located In The Front Of This Manual For System Disarming & Arming Procedures.

NOTE: Refer To "Computer Relearn Procedures" Located In The Front Of This Manual When Battery Power To The Computer Has Been Interrupted.

NOTE: "Electrical Symbol & Wire Color Code Identification" Located In The Front Of This Manual May Be Used As An Aid When Using Wiring Circuits Found In This Section.

INDEX

PRECAUTIONS

Air Bag Systems

Refer to "Air Bag System Precautions" in the front of this manual for system disarming and arming procedures.

Battery Ground Cable

Prior to service, disconnect battery ground cable and isolate as required.

DESCRIPTION

The Teves Mark 20e Anti-Lock Braking System (ABS) prevents the wheels from locking up during hard braking, regardless of the surface conditions. This allows the vehicleto stop in a shorter distance, and allows the driver to maintain directional control of the vehicle during heavy braking conditions.

The Teves Mark 20e system combines the Controller Anti-Lock Brake (CAB) and the Hydraulic Control Unit (HCU) into a one piece assembly called the Integrated Control Unit (ICU). Refer to **Figs. 1 through 5,** for system components and locations.

TROUBLESHOOTING

Refer to flow charts in "Symptom Based Diagnosis" in "Diagnosis & Testing" when troubleshooting the anti-lock brake system.

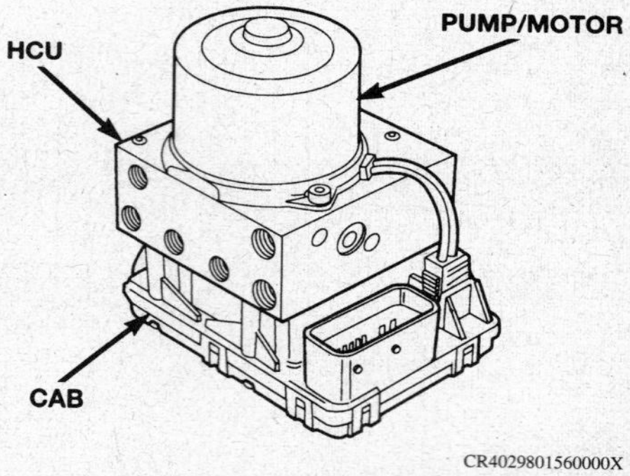

Fig. 1 ICU assembly

DIAGNOSIS & TESTING

Accessing Diagnostic Trouble Codes

1. Connect programmed scan tool, to Data Link Connector (DLC) located under lefthand side of instrument panel.
2. Turn ignition switch to On position.
3. Access Diagnostic Trouble Codes (DTCs) following tool manufacturer's instructions.

Diagnostic Trouble Code Interpretation

Refer to the DRB II or III scan tool for Diagnostic Trouble Code (DTC) interpretation.

Wiring Diagrams

BREEZE, CIRRUS & 2000 STRATUS

Refer to **Fig. 6,** for wiring diagrams.

CONCORDE, INTREPID, LHS & 300M

Refer to **Fig. 7,** for wiring diagram.

NEON

Refer to **Figs. 8 and 9,** for wiring diagrams.

SEBRING CONVERTIBLE, SEBRING SEDAN & STRATUS SEDAN

Refer to **Figs. 10 and 11,** for wiring diagrams.

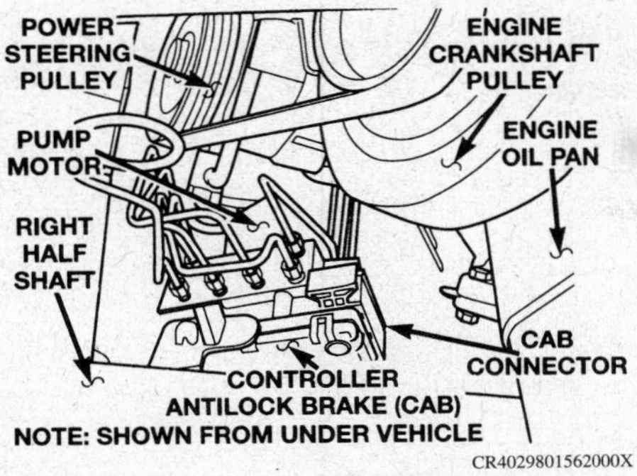

Fig. 2 ICU assembly location. Breeze, Cirrus, 2000 Sebring Convertible & Stratus

Symptom Based Diagnosis

BREEZE, CIRRUS & 2000 STRATUS

2000-03

Refer to **Figs. 12 through 30,** for symptom based diagnosis.

CONCORDE, INTREPID, LHS & 300M

2000

Refer to **Figs. 31 through 53,** for symptom based diagnosis.

2001-02

Refer to **Figs. 54 through 74,** for symptom based diagnosis.

2003-04

Refer to **Figs. 75 through 89,** for symptom based diagnosis.

NEON

2000

Refer to **Figs. 90 through 107,** for symptom based diagnosis.

2001-02

Refer to **Figs. 108 through 123,** for symptom based diagnosis.

2003-04

Refer to **Figs. 124 through 136,** for symptom based diagnosis.

SEBRING CONVERTIBLE, SEBRING SEDAN & STRATUS SEDAN

2000

Refer to **Figs. 137 through 157,** for symptom based diagnosis.

2001-02

Refer to **Figs. 158 through 172,** for symptom based diagnosis.

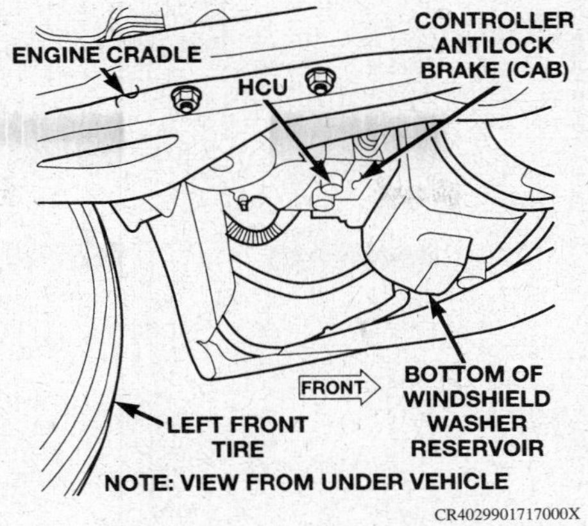

Fig. 3 ICU assembly location. Concorde, Intrepid, LHS & 300M

TERMINAL NO.			
Front left	Rear right	Front right	Rear left
6	1	4	8
7	3	5	9

CR4020102329000X

Fig. 5 ICU assembly location. 2001–04 Sebring Convertible, Sebring Sedan & Stratus Sedan

2003-04

Refer to **Figs. 173 through 186,** for symptom based diagnosis.

Clearing Diagnostic Trouble Codes

Refer to scan tool manufacturer's instructions when clearing stored codes.

SYSTEM SERVICE

Brake System Bleed

The TEVES Mark 20e anti-lock brake system must be bled as two independent braking systems. The non-ABS portion of the brake system should be bled the same as any non-ABS system. The ABS portion of the system requires the use of a DRB, or equivalently programmed scan tool.

1. To bleed non-ABS portion of system, refer to "Hydraulic Brakes" chapter in Volume 1.
2. To bleed the ABS portion of the system, connect DRB scan tool to vehicle diagnostics connector, located under the lefthand side of instrument panel.
3. Set can tool to Bleed ABS routine.
4. Apply brake pedal firmly and initiate Bleed ABS cycle, then release brake pedal.
5. Repeat previous step until brake fluid flows clear and free of bubbles. **Inspect brake fluid level frequently during bleed procedure to prevent reservoir from running low.**
6. Test drive vehicle to ensure brakes are operating correctly.

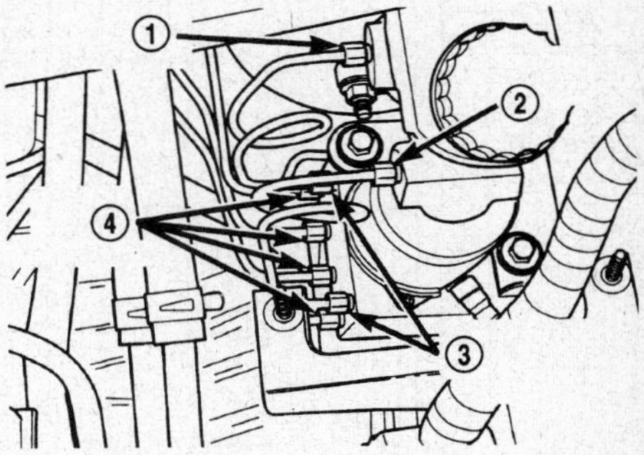

1 – PRIMARY BRAKE TUBE
2 – SECONDARY BRAKE TUBE
3 – BRAKE TUBES FROM MASTER CYLINDER
4 – BRAKE TUBES TO BRAKES

CR4020002022000X

Fig. 4 ICU assembly location. Neon

Component Replacement

INTEGRATED CONTROL UNIT (ICU)

The TEVES Mark 20 anti-lock brake system incorporates the Controller Anti-Lock Brake (CAB) and Hydraulic Control Unit (HCU) as an assembly called the Integrated Control Unit (ICU). The CAB cannot be removed separately. The ICU must be serviced as an assembly.

BREEZE & CIRRUS

1. Isolate master cylinder reservoir from brake hydraulic system by depress brake pedal past its first inch of travel and hold it position using suitable brake pedal positioning tool.
2. Raise and support vehicle.
3. Remove engine compartment right-hand splash shield.
4. Disconnect oxygen sensor harness from vehicle wiring harness.
5. Remove muffler bracket. ground strap.
6. Remove exhaust manifold exhaust pipe mounting bolts, **Fig. 187.**
7. Remove all support isolators from exhaust system. Leave them attached to vehicle.
8. Lower complete exhaust system away from underbody.
9. Remove ICU heat shield from mounting bracket.
10. Clean ICU surfaces and brake tube connections using suitable brake cleaner.
11. Remove four chassis brake tubes from ICU outlet ports, then the primary and secondary brake tubes from master cylinder and ICU inlet ports.
12. Remove ICU mounting bracket front leg to front suspension crossmember bolt.
13. Remove two ICU mounting bracket to front suspension crossmember bolts.
14. Remove ICU side to mounting bracket bolt.
15. Remove two ICU top to mounting

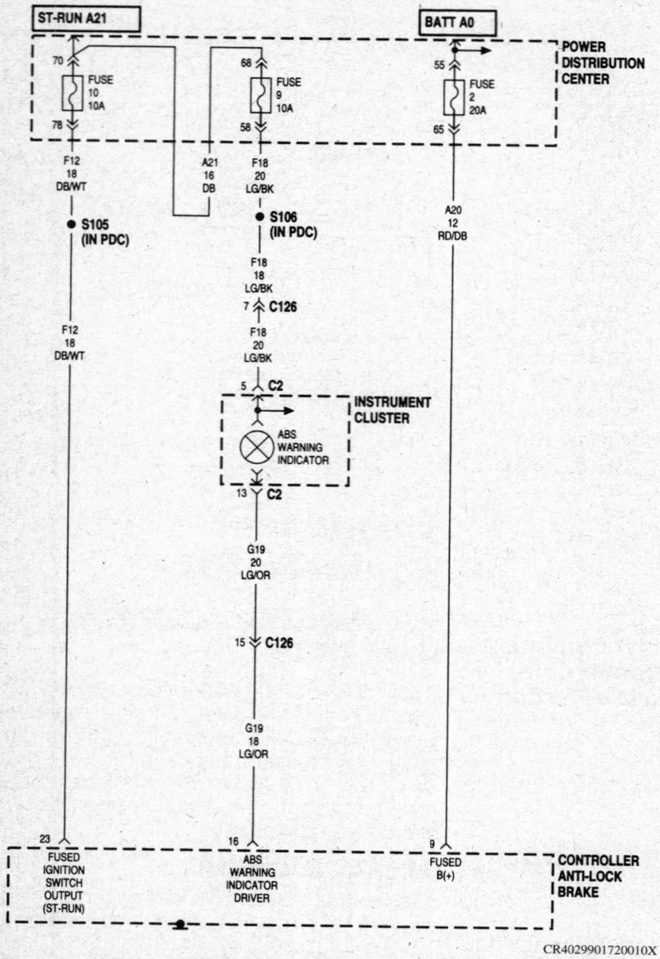

Fig. 6 Wiring diagram (Part 1 of 4). Breeze, Cirrus & 2000 Stratus

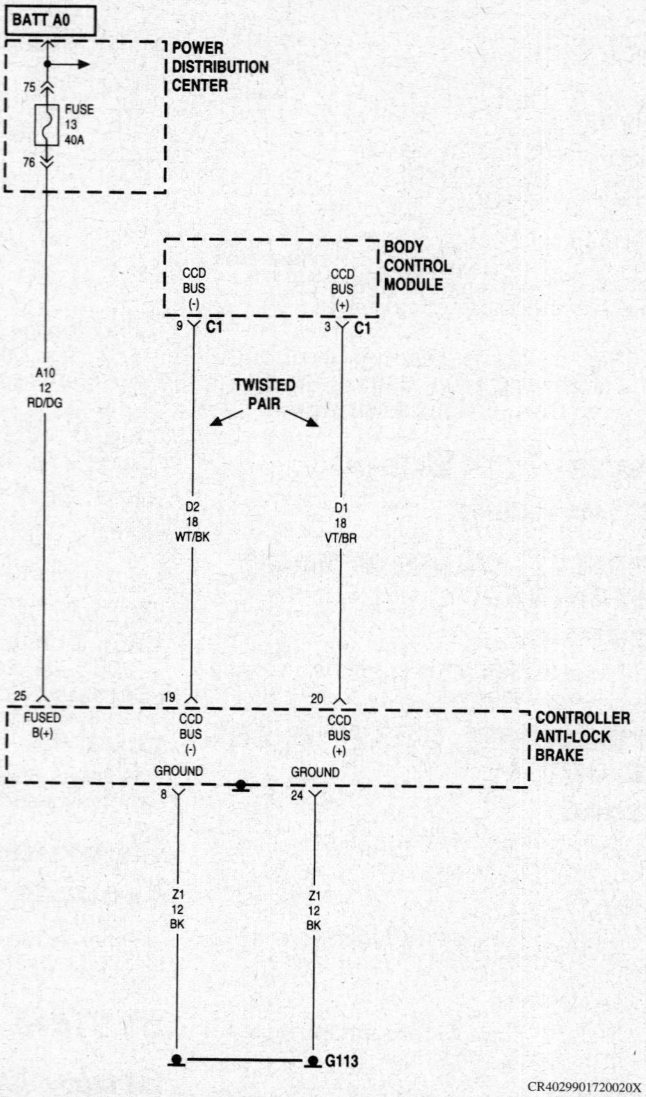

Fig. 6 Wiring diagram (Part 2 of 4). Breeze, Cirrus & 2000 Stratus

bracket bolts.
16. Disconnect CAB 25-way wiring harness connector.
17. Remove ICU by pulling it out through area between righthand driveshaft and frame rail.
18. Reverse procedure to install, noting the following:
    a. **Torque** three ICU to mounting bracket bolts to 97 inch lbs.
    b. **Torque** three ICU mounting bracket to crossmember bolts to 20 ft. lbs.

NEON

1. Depress brake pedal past first one inch of travel and secure in position using suitable brake pedal holder tool.
2. Remove battery.
3. Remove air cleaner box mounting bolt and nut, then disconnect air inlet sensor electrical connector.
4. Lift air cleaner box upward and forward.
5. Remove mounting bolts and battery tray.
6. Disconnect master cylinder primary and secondary brake lines. Install plugs or caps on lines and openings.
7. Disconnect CAB 25-way connector.
8. Mark brake lines from master cylinder for installation alignment.
9. Disconnect HCU primary and secondary brake lines.
10. Disconnect remaining HCU brake lines.
11. Remove three mounting bolts and ICU.
12. Place ICU in suitable vise with CAB facing upward.
13. Remove mounting screws and CAB.
14. Reverse procedure to install, noting the following:
    a. **Torque** ICU mounting bolts to 97 inch lbs.
    b. **Torque** brake lines to 12 ft. lbs., using suitable crow foot torque wrench.
    c. **Torque** battery tray mounting bolts and nuts to 11 ft. lbs.

CONCORDE, INTREPID, LHS & 300M

1. Depress brake pedal past first one inch of travel and secure in position using suitable brake pedal holder tool.
2. Remove speed control servo mounting bolt and nuts, then disconnect electrical connector.
3. Position speed control servo aside with cable attached.
4. Remove mounting screw and position washer bottle filler neck aside without loosening.
5. Remove mounting nut and bolt, then lift up and position transmission controller and bracket aside.
6. Thoroughly clean ICU surfaces using suitable brake components cleaner.
7. Remove ICU primary and secondary brake tubes.
8. Disconnect ICU harness connector.
9. Raise and support vehicle, then remove lefthand front tire and wheel assembly.
10. Remove mounting bolts and position lefthand inner splash shield aside.
11. Remove three mounting bolts and ICU by pulling around lefthand side mounting bracket and through wheelwell.
12. Remove ICU from mounting bracket.
13. Reverse procedure to install. **Torque**

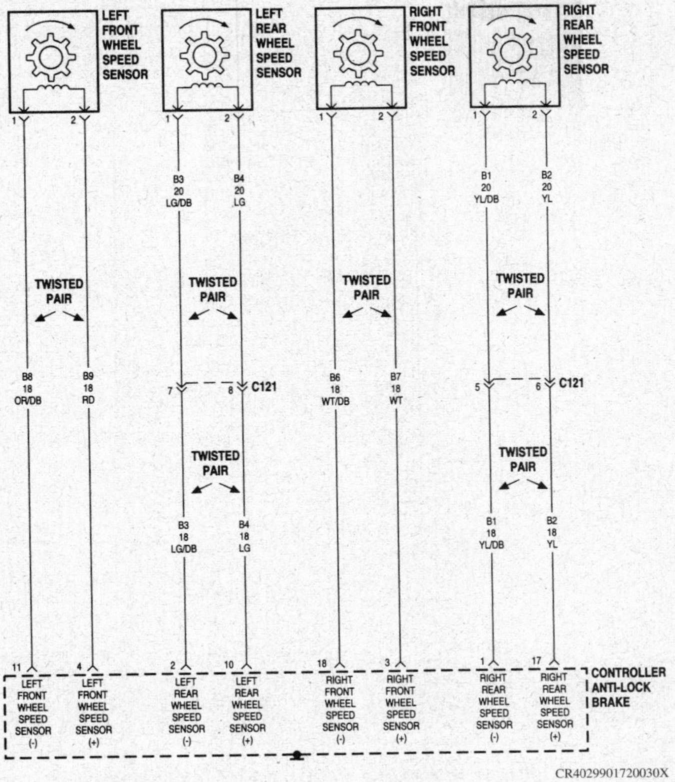

Fig. 6 Wiring diagram (Part 3 of 4). Breeze, Cirrus & 2000 Stratus

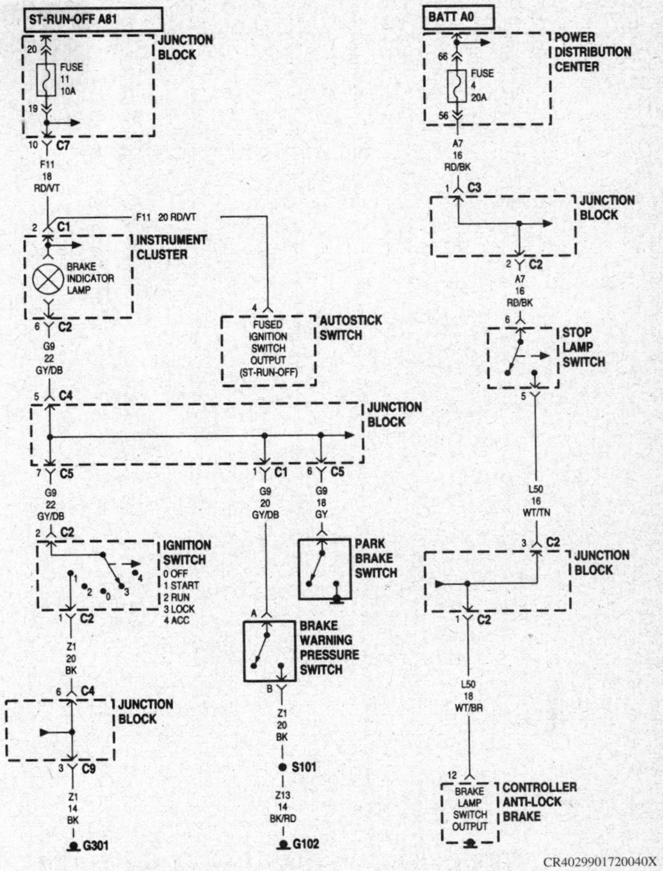

Fig. 6 Wiring diagram (Part 4 of 4). Breeze, Cirrus & 2000 Stratus

brake lines to 12 ft. lbs.

SEBRING CONVERTIBLE, SEBRING SEDAN & STRATUS SEDAN

2000

Refer to "Breeze & Cirrus" for integrate control unit replacement procedure.

2001-04

1. Depress brake pedal past first one inch of travel and secure in position using suitable brake pedal holder tool.
2. Remove air cleaner housing.
3. Remove ICU master cylinder primary and secondary brake tubes.
4. Remove four ICU junction block top chassis brake tubes.
5. Disconnect CAB 24-way wiring harness.
6. Remove three mounting bolts and ICU.
7. Reverse procedure to install, noting the following:
   a. **Torque** ICU mounting bolts to 97 inch lbs.
   b. **Torque** brake tubes to 12 ft. lbs.

WHEEL SPEED SENSOR

Inspect tone wheel for missing or broken teeth, ensure tone wheel has not made contact with wheel speed sensor. Replace tone wheel if runout exceeds .010 inch.

BREEZE & CIRRUS

Front

1. Raise and support vehicle, then remove tire and wheel assembly.
2. Remove grommet retaining clip mounting screw and pull sensor assembly from fender shield grommet.
3. Disconnect speed sensor connector from vehicle wiring harness connector, then remove speed sensor cable routing bracket from front strut.
4. Remove mounting screw and sensor from steering knuckle. **Do not use pliers.** If sensor is seized in knuckle, remove as follows:
   a. Remove brake caliper and rotor.
   b. Gently tap sensor until it is free from knuckle using suitable punch and hammer.
5. Reverse procedure to install, noting the following:
   a. Coat sensor head with suitable high temperature multi-purpose E.P. grease.
   b. **Torque** speed sensor head to 60 inch lbs.
   c. **Torque** wheel lug nuts to 95 ft. lbs., in two steps.

Rear

1. Unplug speed sensor cable connector from vehicle wiring harness in luggage compartment.
2. Raise and support vehicle, then remove tire and wheel assembly.
3. Remove speed sensor cable sealing grommet retainer from rear frame rail.
4. Remove speed sensor sealing grommet and cable body.
5. Remove speed sensor routing clips from upper control arm and brake flex hose routing bracket.
6. Remove rear speed sensor head from rear brake support plate. **Do not use pliers on sensor head.** If sensor is hard to remove, proceed as follows:
   a. Tap sensor ear edge using suitable hammer and punch.
   b. Rock sensor side to side until free.
7. Reverse procedure to install. **Torque** speed sensor mounting bolt to 55 inch lbs.

CONCORDE, INTREPID, LHS & 300M

Front

Refer to "Breeze & Cirrus" for front wheel speed sensor replacement procedure.

Rear

1. Remove rear seat back and cushion,

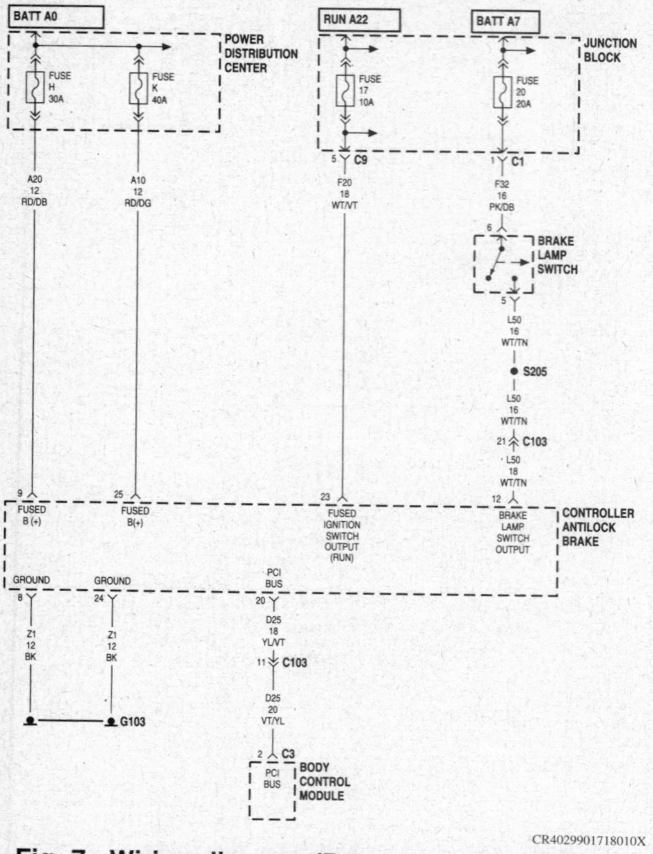

Fig. 7 Wiring diagram (Part 1 of 2). Concorde, Intrepid, LHS & 300M

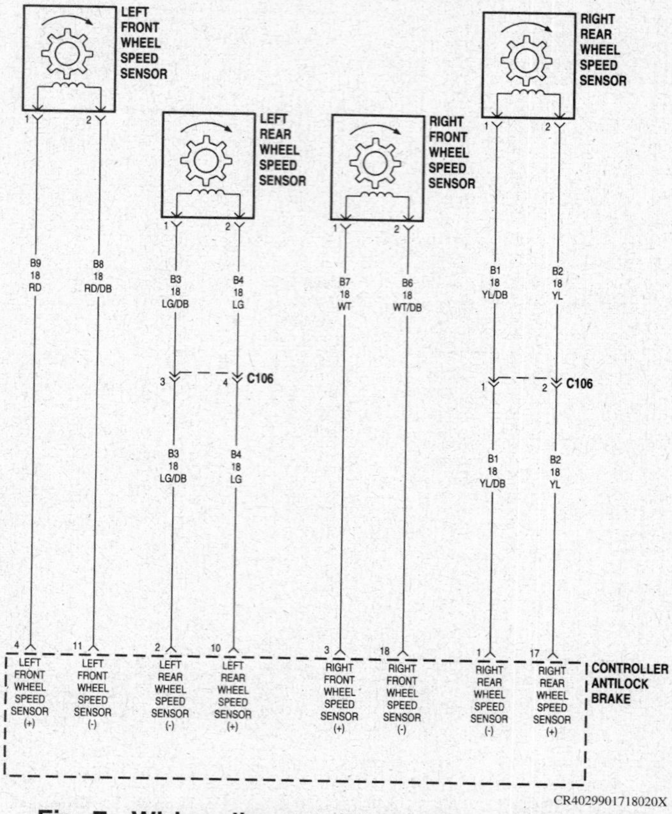

Fig. 7 Wiring diagram (Part 2 of 2). Concorde, Intrepid, LHS & 300M

then disconnect speed sensor connector.
2. Raise and support vehicle, then remove tire and wheel assembly.
3. Remove grommet from floor pan and wire harness cable end.
4. Remove sensor cable from strut tower flange routing bracket.
5. Remove wheel speed sensor head and routing bracket from caliper adapter.
6. Reverse procedure to install. **Torque** speed sensor mounting bolt to 60 inch lbs.

NEON

Front

1. Raise and support vehicle, then disconnect speed sensor electrical connector.
2. Remove speed sensor cable grommet from outside frame rail brake hose bracket.
3. Remove mounting bolt and speed sensor from steering knuckle.
4. Remove speed sensor mounting screws from rear of strut.
5. Reverse procedure to install.

Rear

1. Raise and support vehicle.
2. Remove rear tire and wheel assembly.
3. Remove clip attaching speed sensor cable connector to body and disconnect speed sensor cable connector from wiring harness.
4. Remove speed sensor cable routing bracket from rear brake flex hose mounting bracket.
5. Remove speed sensor cable from routing clips on rear brake flex hose and chassis brake tube.
6. Remove speed sensor mounting bolt from drum brake support or disc brake adapter.
7. Remove speed sensor cable routing bracket mounting bolt from rear strut assembly.
8. Remove sensor head from support plate or adapter. **Do not use pliers on sensor head.** If sensor is hard to remove, proceed as follows:
   a. Tap sensor ear edge using suitable hammer and punch.
   b. Rock sensor side to side until free.
9. Reverse procedure to install. **Torque** speed sensor mounting bolt to 105 inch lbs.

2000 SEBRING CONVERTIBLE & STRATUS

Refer to "Breeze & Cirrus" for front and rear wheel speed sensor replacement procedures.

2001–04 SEBRING CONVERTIBLE, SEBRING SEDAN & STRATUS SEDAN

Front

Refer to "Breeze & Cirrus" for front wheel speed sensor replacement procedure.

Rear

1. Fold down rear seat back and disconnect speed sensor connector from wiring harness at lower outside corner of seat back.
2. Raise and support vehicle, then remove tire and wheel assembly.
3. Remove harness sealing grommet and speed sensor routing clip for upper control arm.
4. Remove mounting bolt and speed sensor.
5. Reverse procedure to install. **Torque** speed sensor mounting bolt to 75 inch lbs.

CONTROLLER ANTI-LOCK BRAKE (CAB)

The TEVES Mark 20e anti-lock brake system incorporates the Controller Anti-Lock Brake (CAB) and Hydraulic Control Unit (HCU) as an assembly called the Integrated Control Unit (ICU). The CAB cannot be removed separately. The ICU must be serviced as an assembly. Refer to "Integrated Control Unit (ICU)" for CAB replacement procedures.

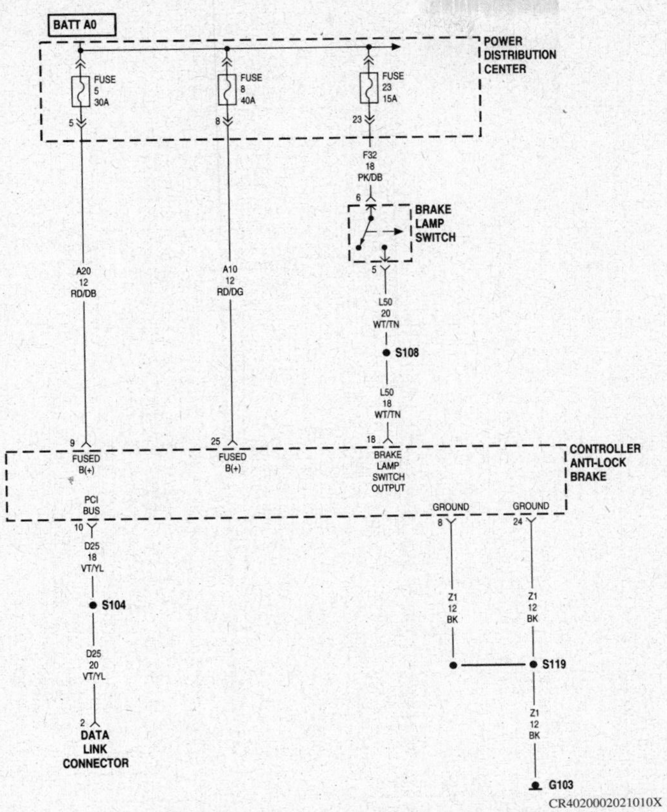

Fig. 8 Wiring diagram (Part 1 of 3). 2000–01 Neon

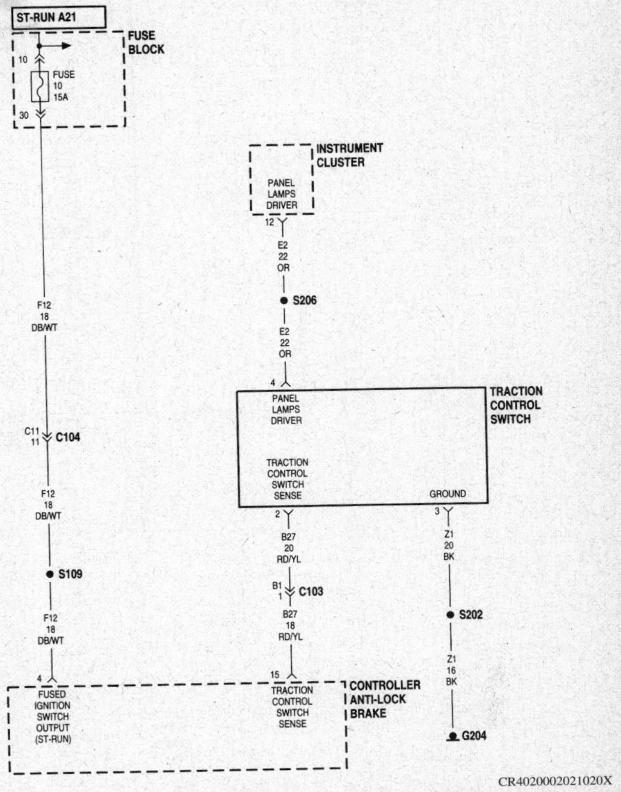

Fig. 8 Wiring diagram (Part 2 of 3). 2000–01 Neon

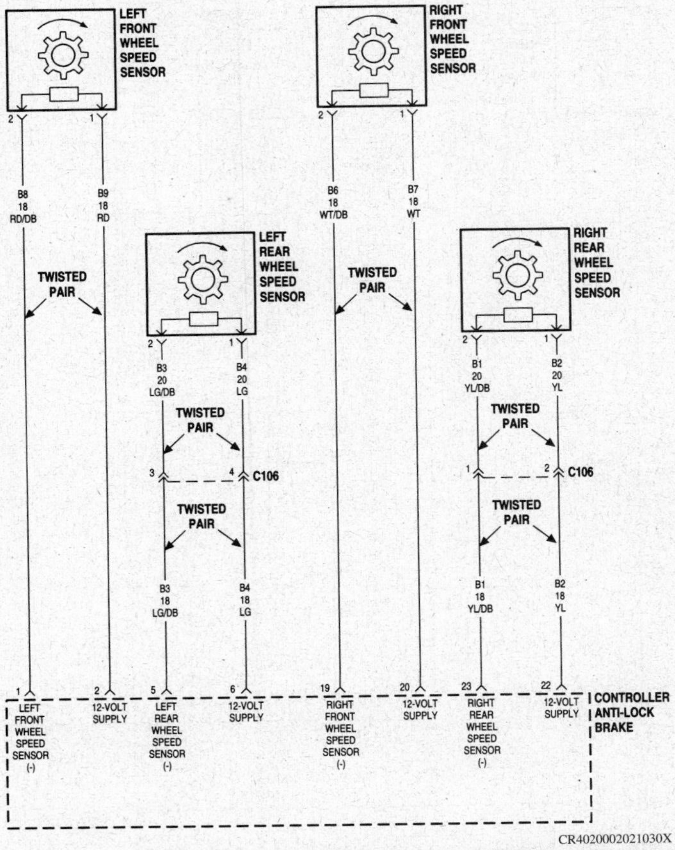

Fig. 8 Wiring diagram (Part 3 of 3). 2000–01 Neon

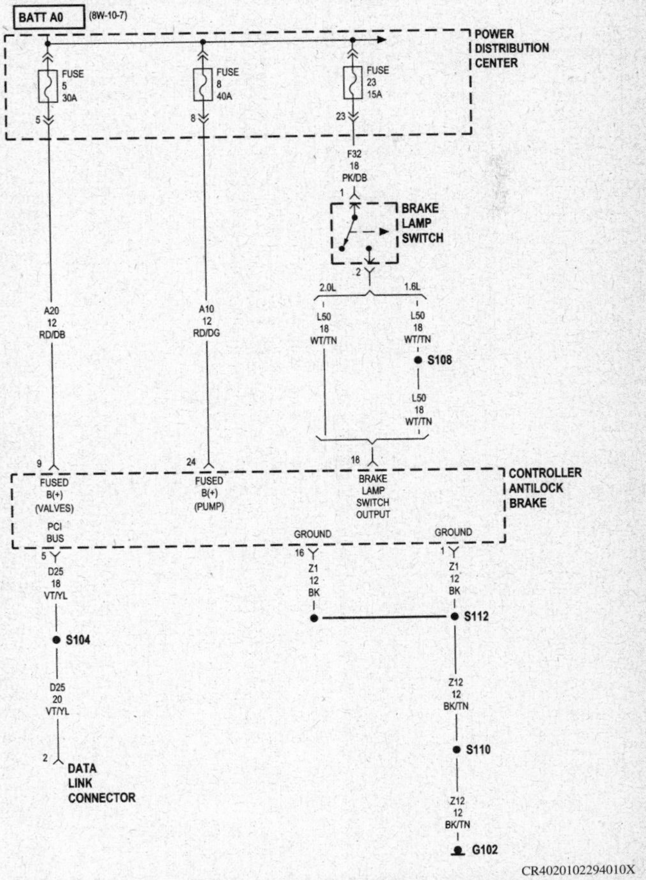

Fig. 9 Wiring diagram (Part 1 of 3). 2002–04 Neon

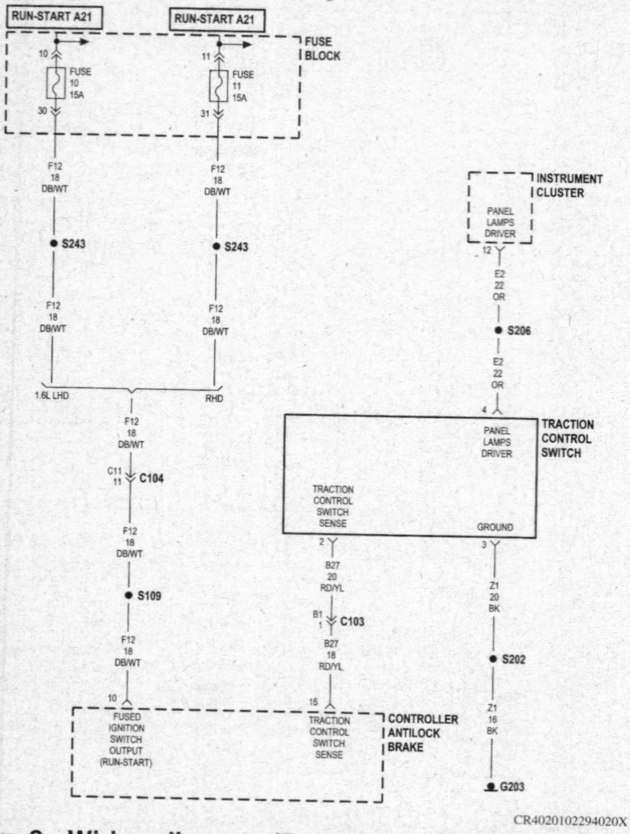

Fig. 9 Wiring diagram (Part 2 of 3). 2002–04 Neon

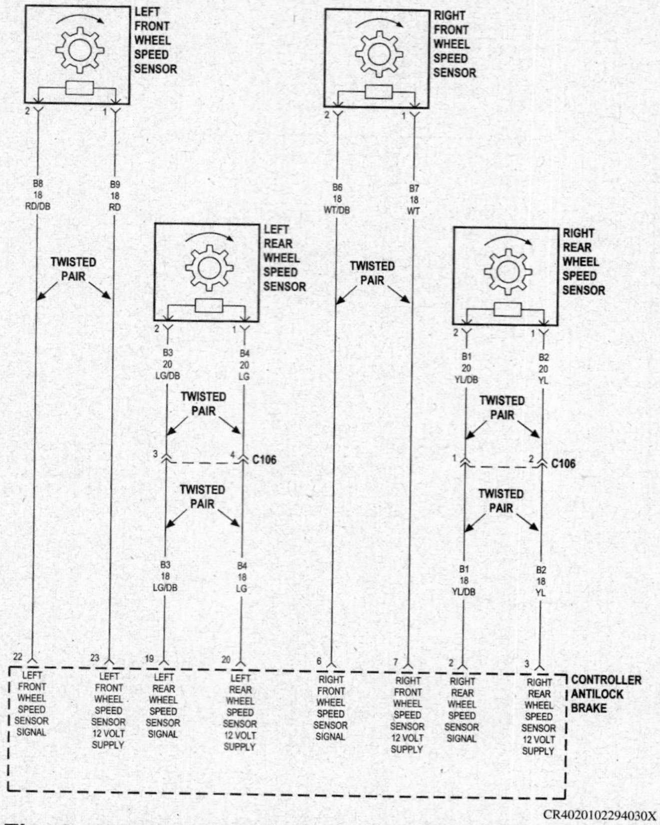

Fig. 9 Wiring diagram (Part 3 of 3). 2002–04 Neon

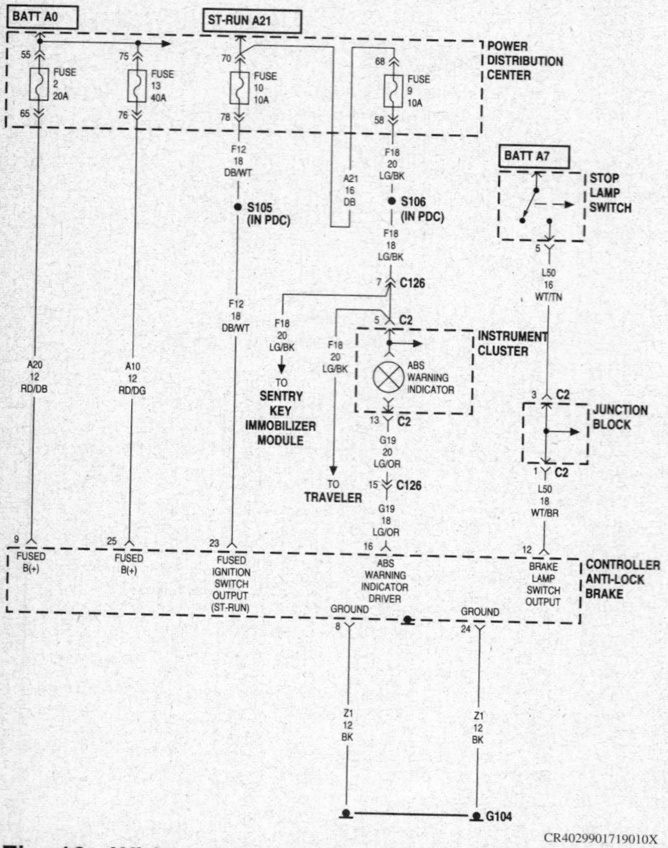

Fig. 10 Wiring diagram (Part 1 of 5). 2000 Sebring Convertible

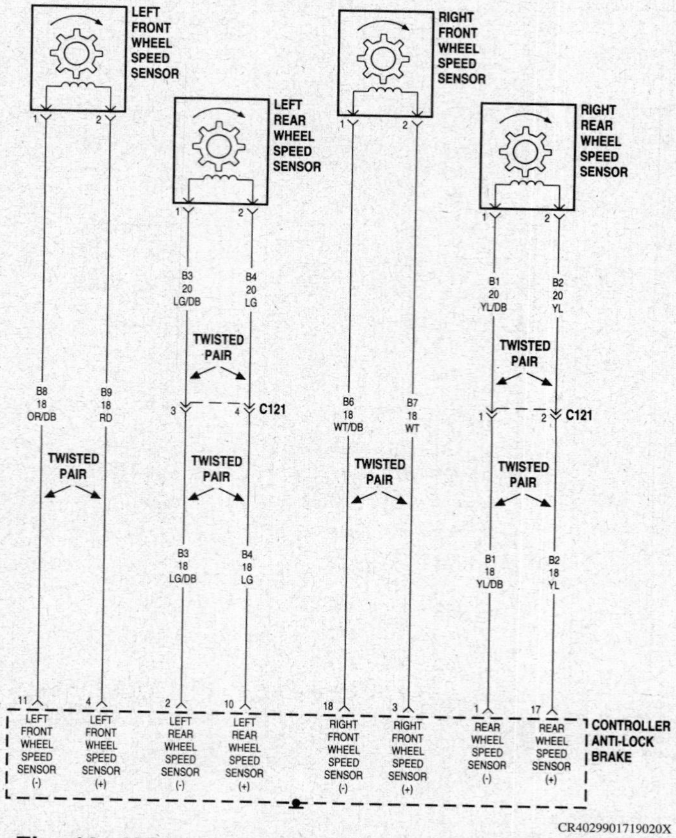

Fig. 10 Wiring diagram (Part 2 of 5). 2000 Sebring Convertible

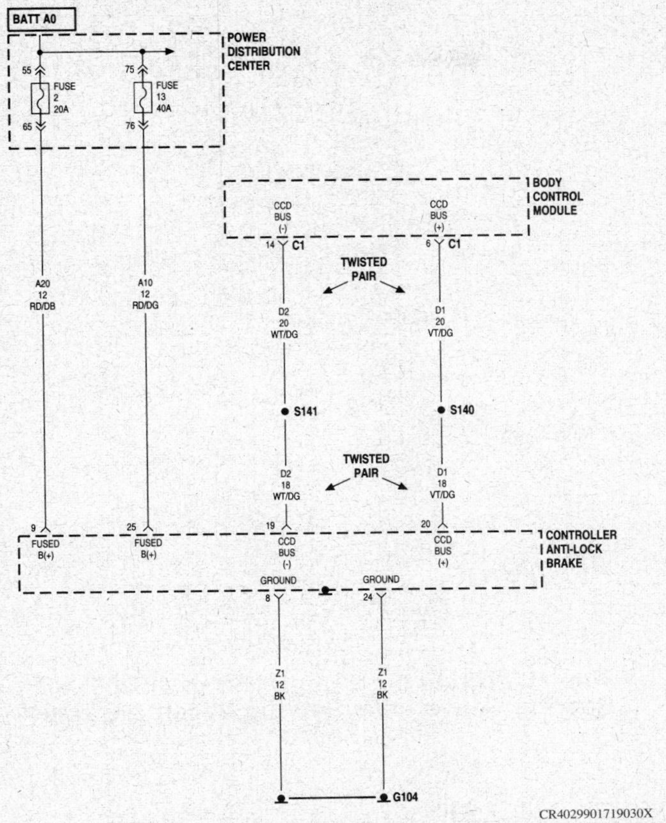

Fig. 10 Wiring diagram (Part 3 of 5). 2000 Sebring Convertible

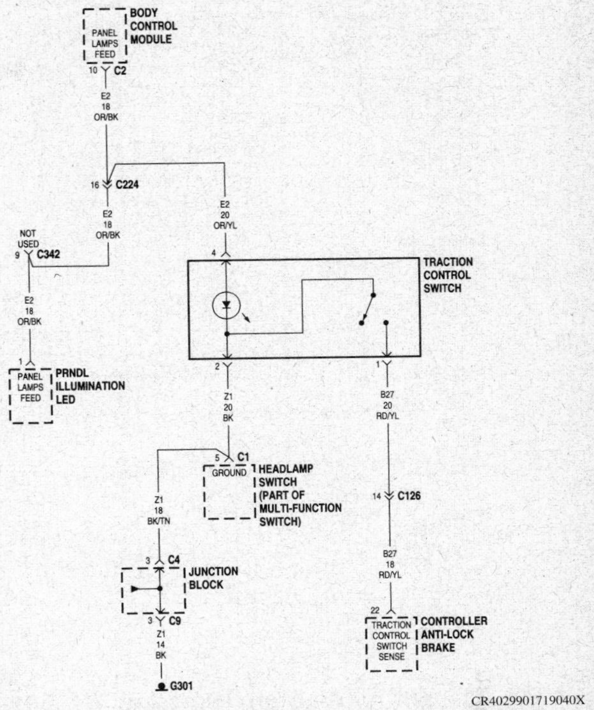

Fig. 10 Wiring diagram (Part 4 of 5). 2000 Sebring Convertible

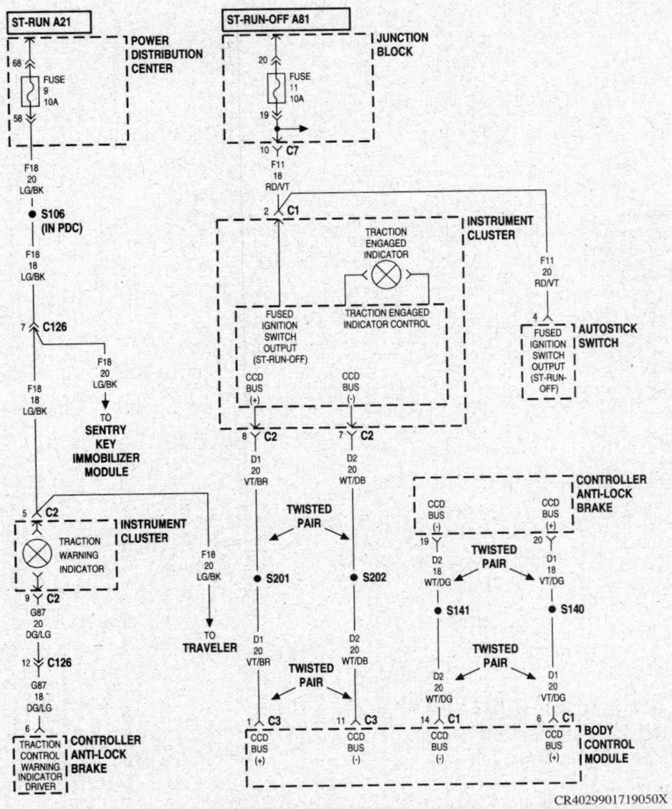

Fig. 10 Wiring diagram (Part 5 of 5). 2000 Sebring Convertible

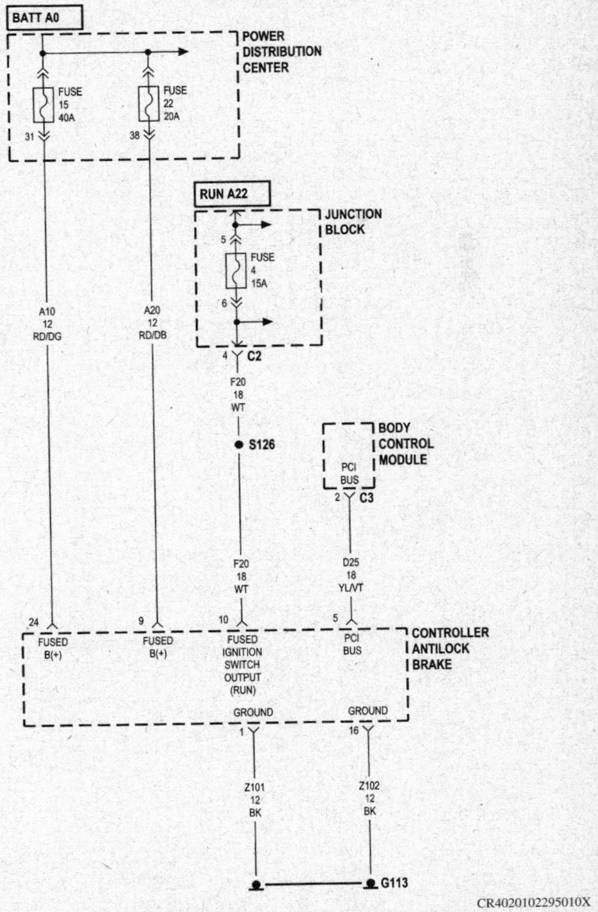

Fig. 11 Wiring diagram (Part 1 of 4). 2001–04 Sebring Convertible, Sebring Sedan & Stratus Sedan

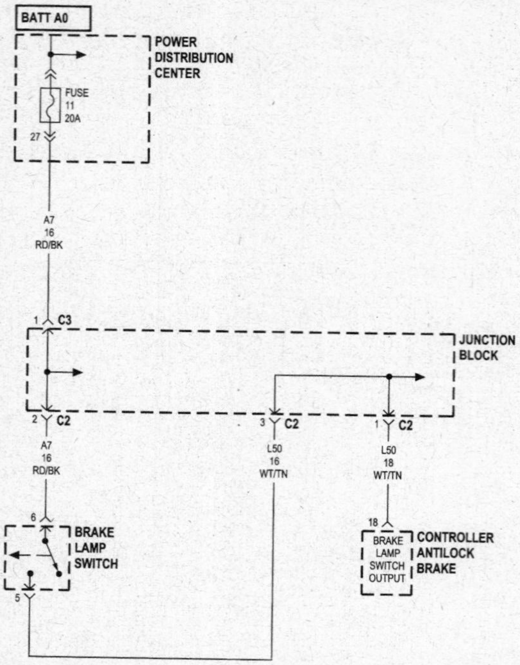

CR4020102295020X

Fig. 11 Wiring diagram (Part 2 of 4). 2001–04 Sebring Convertible, Sebring Sedan & Stratus Sedan

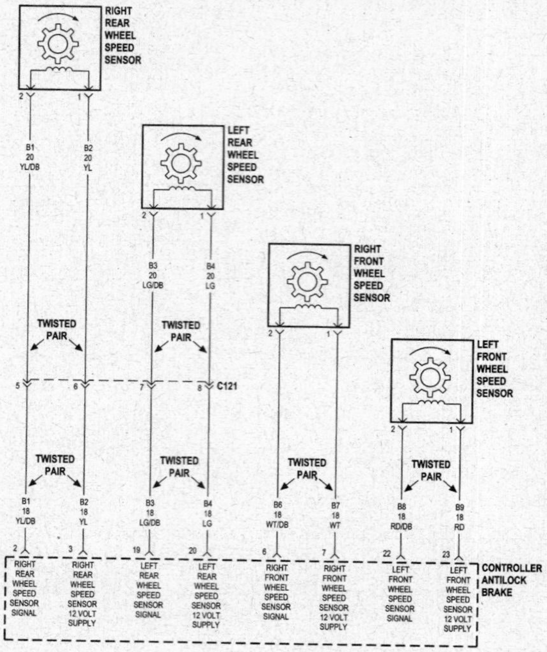

CR4020102295030X

Fig. 11 Wiring diagram (Part 3 of 4). 2001–04 Sebring Convertible, Sebring Sedan & Stratus Sedan

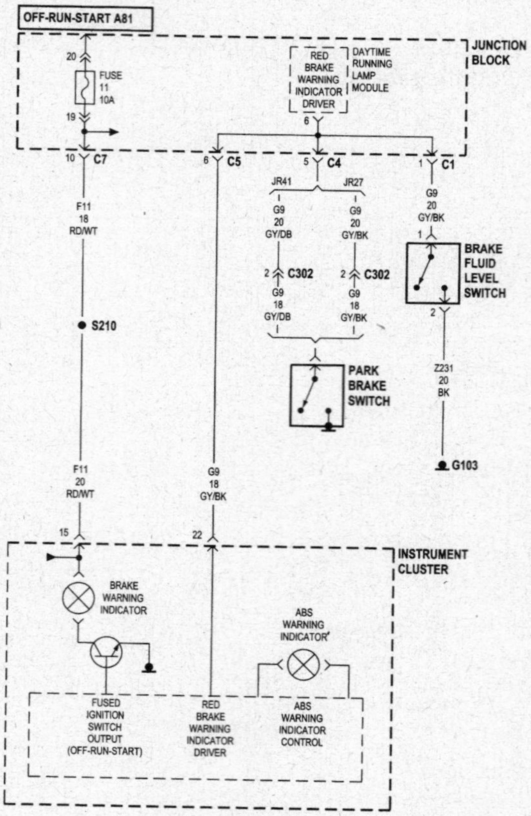

CR4020102295040X

Fig. 11 Wiring diagram (Part 4 of 4). 2001–04 Sebring Convertible, Sebring Sedan & Stratus Sedan

DIAGNOSTIC CHART INDEX

Test	Description	Page No.	Fig. No.
2000 CONCORDE, INTREPID, LHS & 300M			
—	ABS Warning Lamp	6-74	31
—	ABS Verification Test	6-89	51
—	Body Verification Test	6-89	52
—	Brake Lamp Switch	6-86	46
—	CAB Power Feed Circuit	6-75	32
—	Controller Failure	6-75	33
—	Lefthand Front Sensor Circuit Failure	6-76	34
—	Lefthand Front Sensor Signal Failure	6-77	35
—	Lefthand Rear Sensor Circuit Failure	6-78	36
—	Lefthand Rear Sensor Signal Failure	6-79	37
—	PCI Bus Communication	6-80	38
—	Powertrain Verification Test	6-89	53
—	Pump Motor Not Working Properly	6-80	39
—	Righthand Front Sensor Circuit Failure	6-81	40
—	Righthand Front Sensor Signal Failure	6-82	41
—	Righthand Rear Sensor Circuit Failure	6-83	42
—	Righthand Rear Sensor Signal Failure	6-84	43
—	Scan Tool No Response From CAB	6-88	50
—	System Overvoltage	6-85	44
—	System Undervoltage	6-85	45
—	Traction Control ON Indicator Illuminated	6-86	47
—	Traction Control Switch	6-87	48
—	Traction Control OFF Indicator Illuminated	6-87	49
2001 CONCORDE, INTREPID, LHS & 300M			
—	ABS Verification Test VER 1	6-102	74
—	ABS Warning Indicator	6-90	54
—	Brake Lamp Switch	6-101	71
—	CAB Power Feed Circuit	6-90	55
—	Controller Failure	6-91	56
—	Lefthand Front Sensor Circuit Failure	6-91	57
—	Lefthand Front Sensor Signal Failure	6-92	58
—	Lefthand Rear Sensor Circuit Failure	6-93	59
—	Lefthand Rear Sensor Signal Failure	6-94	60
—	PCI Bus Communication	6-96	63
—	Pump Motor Not Working Properly	6-96	64
—	Righthand Front Sensor Circuit Failure	6-97	65
—	Righthand Front Sensor Signal Failure	6-98	66
—	Righthand Rear Sensor Circuit Failure	6-99	67
—	Righthand Rear Sensor Signal Failure	6-100	68
—	System Overvoltage	6-100	69
—	System Undervoltage	6-101	70
—	TRAC Off Indicator Never/Always On	6-102	72
—	TRAC On Indicator Always/Never On	6-102	73
2002 CONCORDE, INTREPID & 300M			
—	ABS Verification Test VER 1	6-102	74
—	ABS Warning Indicator	6-90	54
—	Brake Lamp Switch	6-101	71
—	CAB Power Feed Circuit	6-90	55
—	Controller Failure	6-91	56
—	Lefthand Front, Lefthand Rear, Righthand Front & Righthand Rear Sensor Circuit Failure	6-94	61
—	Lefthand Front, Lefthand Rear, Righthand Front & Righthand Rear Sensor Signal Failure	6-95	62
—	PCI Bus Communication	6-96	63
—	Pump Motor Not Working Properly	6-96	64
—	System Overvoltage	6-100	69

Continued

DIAGNOSTIC CHART INDEX—Continued

Test	Description	Page No.	Fig. No.
2002 CONCORDE, INTREPID & 300M			
—	System Undervoltage	6-101	70
—	TRAC Off Indicator Never/Always On	6-102	72
—	TRAC On Indicator Always/Never On	6-102	73
2003 CONCORDE, INTREPID & 300M			
—	ABS Verification Test	6-110	89
—	Brake Lamp Switch Inoperative	6-109	85
—	BUS System Communication Failure	6-102	75
—	CAB Internal Failure	6-103	76
—	Cluster Lamp Failure	6-103	77
—	Incorrect Tone Wheel Failure	6-104	78
—	Lefthand Front, Lefthand Rear, Righthand Front & Righthand Rear Sensor Circuit Failure	6-104	79
—	Lefthand Front, Lefthand Rear, Righthand Front & Righthand Rear Wheel Speed Signal Failure	6-105	80
—	No Response From Controller Anti-Lock Brake	6-110	88
—	Pump Circuit Failure	6-106	81
—	System Overvoltage	6-107	82
—	System Undervoltage	6-107	83
—	Valve Power Feed Failure	6-108	84
—	TRAC OFF Indicator Never/Always On	6-109	86
—	TRAC ON Indicator Never/Always ON	6-109	87
2000 NEON			
—	ABS Verification Test	6-123	107
—	CAB Power Feed Circuit	6-111	90
—	Cluster Fault	6-111	91
—	Controller Failure	6-112	92
—	Lefthand Front Sensor Circuit Failure	6-112	93
—	Lefthand Front Sensor Signal Failure	6-113	94
—	Lefthand Rear Sensor Circuit Failure	6-114	95
—	Lefthand Rear Sensor Signal Failure	6-115	96
—	PCI Bus Communication	6-116	97
—	Pump Motor Not Working Properly	6-116	98
—	Righthand Front Sensor Circuit Failure	6-117	99
—	Righthand Front Sensor Signal Failure	6-118	100
—	Righthand Rear Sensor Circuit Failure	6-119	101
—	Righthand Rear Sensor Signal Failure	6-120	102
—	Scan Tool No Response From CAB Controller	6-123	106
—	System Overvoltage	6-121	103
—	System Undervoltage	6-122	104
—	Traction Control Switch	6-122	105
2001–02 NEON			
—	CAB Power Feed	6-123	108
—	Cluster Failure	6-124	109
—	Controller Failure	6-124	110
—	Lefthand Front Sensor Circuit Failure	6-125	111
—	Lefthand Front Wheel Speed Signal Failure	6-125	112
—	Lefthand Rear Sensor Circuit Failure	6-126	113
—	Lefthand Rear Wheel Speed Signal Circuit	6-126	114
—	PCI BUS Communication	6-127	115
—	Pump Motor Not Working Properly	6-127	116
—	Righthand Front Sensor Circuit Failure	6-128	117
—	Righthand Front Wheel Speed Signal Failure	6-129	118
—	Righthand Rear Sensor Circuit Failure	6-129	119
—	Righthand Rear Wheel Speed Signal Failure	6-130	120
—	System Overvoltage	6-130	121
—	System Undervoltage	6-131	122

Continued

DIAGNOSTIC CHART INDEX—Continued

Test	Description	Page No.	Fig. No.
2001–02 NEON			
—	Verification Test VER 1	6-131	123
2003 NEON			
—	ABS Verification Test	6-139	136
—	Brake Lamp Switch Inoperative	6-138	134
—	CAB Power Feed	6-132	124
—	Cluster Failure	6-132	125
—	Controller Failure	6-133	126
—	Incorrect Tone Wheel Failure	6-133	127
—	Lefthand Front, Lefthand Rear, Righthand Front & Righthand Rear Sensor Circuit Failure	6-134	128
—	Lefthand Front, Lefthand Rear, Righthand Front & Righthand Rear Wheel Speed/ Signal Failure	6-135	129
—	No Response From Controller Anti-Lock Brake	6-139	135
—	PCI BUS Communications	6-136	130
—	Pump Motor Not Working Properly	6-136	131
—	System Over Voltage	6-137	132
—	System Under Voltage	6-138	133
2000 SEBRING CONVERTIBLE			
—	ABS Verification Test	6-151	157
—	ABS Warning Lamp	6-139	137
—	Brake Switch	6-148	153
—	CAB Power Feed Circuit	6-140	138
—	CCD Communication	6-141	139
—	Controller Failure	6-141	140
—	Incorrect Tone Wheel	6-141	141
—	Lefthand Front Sensor Circuit Failure	6-142	142
—	Lefthand Front Sensor Signal Failure	6-142	143
—	Lefthand Rear Sensor Circuit Failure	6-143	144
—	Lefthand Rear Sensor Signal Failure	6-144	145
—	Pump Motor Circuit Not Working Properly	6-144	146
—	Righthand Front Sensor Circuit Failure	6-145	147
—	Righthand Front Sensor Signal Failure	6-146	148
—	Righthand Rear Sensor Circuit failure	6-146	149
—	Righthand Rear Sensor Signal Failure	6-147	150
—	Scan Tool No Response Message	6-149	154
—	System Overvoltage	6-148	151
—	System Undervoltage	6-148	152
—	Traction Control Switch	6-149	155
—	Traction Control Warning Lamp Illuminated	6-150	156
2001 SEBRING CONVERTIBLE & SEBRING SEDAN			
—	Brake Lamp Failure	6-156	170
—	BUS System Communications Failure	6-151	158
—	CAB Internal Failure	6-151	160
—	Cluster Lamp Failure	6-151	161
—	Incorrect Tone Wheel Failure	6-152	163
—	Front & Rear Sensor Circuit Failure	6-152	164
—	Front & Rear Wheel Speed Signal Failure	6-153	165
—	Pump Circuit Failure	6-153	166
—	System Overvoltage	6-154	167
—	System Undervoltage	6-155	168
—	Valve Power Feed Failure	6-155	169
—	Verification Test VER 1	6-156	172
2002 SEBRING CONVERTIBLE & SEBRING SEDAN			
—	Brake Lamp Failure	6-156	171
—	BUS System Communications Failure	6-151	159
—	CAB Internal Failure	6-151	160

Continued

DIAGNOSTIC CHART INDEX—Continued

Test	Description	Page No.	Fig. No.
2002 SEBRING CONVERTIBLE & SEBRING SEDAN			
—	Cluster Lamp Failure	6-152	162
—	Incorrect Tone Wheel Failure	6-152	163
—	Front & Rear Sensor Circuit Failure	6-152	164
—	Front & Rear Wheel Speed Signal Failure	6-153	165
—	Pump Circuit Failure	6-153	166
—	System Overvoltage	6-154	167
—	System Undervoltage	6-155	168
—	Valve Power Feed Failure	6-155	169
—	Verification Test VER 1	6-156	172
2003 SEBRING CONVERTIBLE & SEBRING SEDAN			
—	ABS Lamp Flashing After CAB Replacement	6-163	183
—	ABS Verification Test	6-164	186
—	Brake Lamp Switch Inoperative	6-163	184
—	BUS System Communication Failure	6-156	173
—	CAB Internal Failure	6-157	174
—	Cluster Lamp Failure	6-157	175
—	Incorrect Tone Wheel Failure	6-158	176
—	Lefthand Front, Lefthand Rear, Righthand Front & Righthand Rear Sensor Circuit Failure	6-158	177
—	Lefthand Front, Lefthand Rear, Righthand Front & Righthand Rear Wheel Speed Signal Failure	6-159	178
—	No Response From Controller Anti-Lock Brake	6-164	185
—	Pump Circuit Failure	6-160	179
—	System Overvoltage	6-161	180
—	System Undervoltage	6-162	181
—	Valve Power Feed Failure	6-162	182
BREEZE, CIRRUS & 2000 STRATUS			
—	ABS Warning Lamp	6-64	12
—	Brake Lamp Switch	6-73	28
—	CAB Power Feed Circuit	6-64	13
—	CCD Communication	6-65	14
—	Controller Failure	6-65	15
—	Incorrect Tone Wheel	6-66	16
—	Lefthand Front Sensor Circuit Failure	6-66	17
—	Lefthand Front Sensor Signal Failure	6-67	18
—	Lefthand Rear Sensor Circuit Failure	6-67	19
—	Lefthand Rear Sensor Signal Failure	6-68	20
—	Pump Motor Circuit Not Working Properly	6-69	21
—	Righthand Front Sensor Circuit Failure	6-70	22
—	Righthand Front Sensor Signal Failure	6-70	23
—	Righthand Front Sensor Circuit Failure	6-71	24
—	Righthand Rear Sensor Signal Failure	6-72	25
—	System Overvoltage	6-72	26
—	Scan Tool No Response Message	6-74	29
—	System Undervoltage	6-73	27
—	Brake Lamp Switch	6-73	28
—	Verification Test	6-74	30
2001 STRATUS SEDAN			
—	Brake Lamp Failure	6-156	170
—	BUS System Communications Failure	6-151	158
—	CAB Internal Failure	6-151	160
—	Cluster Lamp Failure	6-151	161
—	Incorrect Tone Wheel Failure	6-152	163
—	Front & Rear Sensor Circuit Failure	6-152	164
—	Front & Rear Wheel Speed Signal Failure	6-153	165
—	Pump Circuit Failure	6-153	166

Continued

DIAGNOSTIC CHART INDEX—Continued

When Monitored: 1. Ignition on. 2. Checked every 7 milliseconds.

Set Condition: When the ABS warning lamp driver circuit voltage does not match the CAB commands, the Diagnostic Trouble Code (DTC) is set.

POSSIBLE CAUSES
ABS WARNING LAMP DEFECTIVE
ABS WARNING LAMP DRIVER CIRCUIT OPEN
ABS WARNING LAMP DRIVER CIRCUIT SHORTED TO GROUND
CAB CONNECTOR OBSERVABLE DEFECT
INSTRUMENT CLUSTER DEFECTIVE
FUSED IGNITION SWITCH OUTPUT CIRCUIT OPEN
CAB DEFECTIVE

TEST	ACTION
1	**Note: If any Diagnostic Trouble Codes are present, they must be repaired prior to performing this test.** Turn the Ignition off. Turn the Ignition on. Observe the ABS Warning Lamp in the Instrument Cluster. Does the ABS Warning Lamp stay on for several seconds then go out? Yes → The ABS Warning Lamp Circuit is operating properly at this time. Perform ABS Verification Test VER-1A. No → Go To 2
2	**Note: If any Diagnostic Trouble Codes are present, they must be repaired prior to performing this test.** Turn the Ignition off. Turn the Ignition on. Observe the ABS Warning Lamp in the Instrument Cluster. Is the ABS Warning Lamp on steady? Yes → Go To 3 No → Go To 6

CR4020001963010X

Fig. 12 ABS Warning Lamp (Part 1 of 3). Breeze, Cirrus & 2000 Stratus

TEST	ACTION
3	Turn the Ignition off. Disconnect the CAB. **Note: Check connectors - Clean/repair as necessary.** Inspect all Terminals. Is any Terminal damaged, pushed out or miswired? Yes → Repair as necessary. Perform ABS Verification Test VER-1A. No → Go To 4
4	Turn the Ignition off. Disconnect the CAB. **Note: Check connectors - Clean/repair as necessary.** Disconnect the Instrument Cluster Connector. **Note: Check connectors - Clean/repair as necessary.** Turn the Ignition on. Using a test light connected to 12 volts, probe the ABS Warning Lamp Driver Circuit. Is the test light on? Yes → Repair the ABS Warning Lamp Driver Circuit for a short to ground. Perform ABS Verification Test VER-1A. No → Go To 5
5	If there are no potential causes remaining, the CAB is assumed to be defective. View repair options. Repair Replace the CAB. Perform ABS Verification Test VER-1A.
6	Turn the Ignition on. Set the Parking Brake. Is the Red Brake Warning Lamp on? Yes → Go To 7 No → Repair the open Fused Ignition Switch Output Circuit to the Lamps. Perform ABS Verification Test VER-1A.
7	Turn the Ignition off. Gain access to the ABS Warning Lamp Bulb. Is the Bulb okay? Yes → Go To 8 No → Replace the Bulb. Perform ABS Verification Test VER-1A.
8	**The Instrument Cluster and Bulb must be installed to perform this test.** Use a voltmeter to backprobe the ABS Warning Lamp Driver Circuit at the Instrument Cluster. Turn the Ignition on. Is the voltage above 10 volts? Yes → Go To 9 No → Replace the Instrument Cluster Printed Circuit Board. Perform ABS Verification Test VER-1A.

CR4020001963020X

Fig. 12 ABS Warning Lamp (Part 2 of 3). Breeze, Cirrus & 2000 Stratus

TEST	ACTION
9	Turn the Ignition off. Disconnect the CAB Connector. **Note: Check connectors - Clean/repair as necessary.** Turn the Ignition on. Using a voltmeter, measure the ABS Warning Lamp Driver Circuit. Is the voltage above 10 volts? Yes → Go To 10 No → Repair the open ABS Warning Lamp Driver Circuit. Perform ABS Verification Test VER-1A.
10	If there are no potential causes remaining, replace the CAB. View repair options. Yes → Replace the CAB. Perform ABS Verification Test VER-1A.

CR4020001963030X

Fig. 12 ABS Warning Lamp (Part 3 of 3). Breeze, Cirrus & 2000 Stratus

When Monitored: 1. With ignition on. 2. The CAB monitors the Fused B(+) circuit at cavity 9 at all times for proper system voltage.

Set Condition: If the Voltage is missing when the CAB detects that an internal main driver is not on, then the Diagnostic Trouble Code (DTC) is set.

POSSIBLE CAUSES
ABS/SYSTEM FUSE #2 DEFECTIVE
FUSED B(+) CIRCUIT OPEN
FUSED B(+) CIRCUIT INTERMITTENTLY SHORTED TO GROUND
FUSED B(+) CIRCUIT SHORTED TO GROUND
CAB CONNECTOR OBSERVABLE DEFECT
HCU/PUMP DEFECTIVE
CAB DEFECTIVE

TEST	ACTION
1	Ignition On, Engine Not Running With the DRB, erase DTC's. Turn the Ignition off. Turn the Ignition on. With the DRB, read DTC's. Is the "Cab Power Feed Circuit Failure" code set right now? Yes → Go To 2 No → Go To 9
2	Turn the Ignition off. Remove and inspect the ABS Fuse #2 from the Power Distribution Center (PDC). Is the ABS Fuse #2 okay? Yes → Go To 3 No → Go To 6
3	Turn the Ignition off. Disconnect the CAB Connector. **Note: Check connectors - Clean/repair as necessary.** Inspect all Terminals. Is any Terminal damaged, pushed out or miswired? Yes → Repair as necessary. Perform ABS Verification Test VER-1A. No → Go To 4

CR4020001964010X

Fig. 13 CAB Power Feed Circuit (Part 1 of 2). Breeze, Cirrus & 2000 Stratus

TEST	ACTION
4	Turn the Ignition off. Disconnect CAB Connector. **Note: Check connectors - Clean/repair as necessary.** Turn Ignition on, with engine not running. Using a Voltmeter, measure the Fused B(+) Circuit, CAB Cavity 9. Is the voltage above 10.0 volts? Yes → Go To 5 No → Repair the open Fused B(+) Circuit. Perform ABS Verification Test VER-1A.
5	If there are no potential causes remaining, replace the CAB. View repair options. Repair Replace the CAB. Perform ABS Verification Test VER-1A.
6	Turn the Ignition off. Inspect the Fused B(+) Circuit for signs of an intermittent short to ground. Is the Wiring Harness okay? Yes → Go To 7 No → Repair the Fused B(+) circuit short to ground and replace the ABS Fuse. Perform ABS Verification Test VER-1A.
7	Turn the Ignition off. Remove the ABS Fuse #2 from the Power Distribution Center (PDC). Using an Ohmmeter, measure the resistance between the Fused B(+) Circuit and ground. Is the resistance below 10 ohms? Yes → Go To 8 No → Replace the faulty ABS Fuse. Perform ABS Verification Test VER-1A.
8	Turn the Ignition off. Remove the ABS Fuse #2 in the Power Distribution Center (PDC). Using an ohmmeter, measure the resistance between the Fused B(+) circuit and ground at the Power Distribution Center (PDC). Disconnect the CAB connector. Is the resistance below 10,000 ohms? Yes → Repair Fused B(+) circuit shorted to ground. No → Replace the HCU/Pump and replace the ABS fuse. Perform ABS Verification Test VER-1A.
9	Turn the Ignition off. Using the schematic as a guide, inspect the Wiring and Connectors. Were any problems found? Yes → Repair as necessary. Perform ABS Verification Test VER-1A. No → Test Complete.

CR4020001964020X

Fig. 13 CAB Power Feed Circuit (Part 2 of 2). Breeze, Cirrus & 2000 Stratus

TEST	ACTION
3	Turn the Ignition off. Disconnect the Controller Antilock Brake Connector. **Note: Check connectors - Clean/repair as necessary.** Connect a jumper wire between CCD Bus (+) and CCD Bus (-) Circuit, CAB Cavity 20 and 19. Ignition on, with engine not running. With the DRB, perform the CCD Bus Test. Does the DRB display, "Bus shorted together"? Yes → Check other Modules on this Bus for this DTC. If no other Modules have a DTC, replace the Controller Antilock Brake (CAB). Perform ABS Verification Test VER-1A. No → Go To 4
4	Turn the Ignition off. Disconnect the Controller Antilock Brake Connector. **Note: Check connectors - Clean/repair as necessary.** Connect a jumper wire between CCD Bus (+) and CAB Ground, CAB Cavity 20 and 8. Ignition on, with engine not running. With the DRB, perform the CCD Bus Test. Does the DRB show "Bus shorted to ground"? Yes → Go To 5 No → Repair the open CCD Bus (+) Circuit. Perform ABS Verification Test VER-1A.
5	Turn the Ignition off. Disconnect the Controller Antilock Brake Connector. **Note: Check connectors - Clean/repair as necessary.** Connect a jumper wire between CCD Bus (-) and CAB Ground, CAB Cavity 19 and 8. Ignition on, with engine not running. With the DRB, perform the CCD Bus Test. Does the DRB show "Bus shorted to ground"? Yes → Go To 6 No → Repair the open CCD Bus (-) Circuit. Perform ABS Verification Test VER-1A.
6	Turn the Ignition off. Using the schematic as a guide, inspect the Wiring and Connections. Were any problems found? Yes → Repair as necessary. Perform ABS Verification Test VER-1A. No → Test Complete.

CR4020001965020X

Fig. 14 CCD Communication (Part 2 of 2). Breeze, Cirrus & 2000 Stratus

When Monitored: Ignition on.

Set Condition: The Diagnostic Trouble Code (DTC) is set when the CAB cannot transmit the ABS status message for 15 seconds.

POSSIBLE CAUSES
CAB CONNECTOR OBSERVABLE DEFECT
CCD BUS (+) CIRCUIT OPEN
CCD BUS (-) CIRCUIT OPEN
OTHER MODULES
CAB DEFECTIVE

TEST	ACTION
1	Ignition On, Engine Not Running With the DRB, erase DTC's. Turn the Ignition off. Turn the Ignition on. With the DRB, read the DTC's. Did the "CCD Communication" DTC set right now? Yes → Go To 2 No → Go To 6
2	Turn the Ignition off. Disconnect the Controller Antilock Brake Connector. **Note: Check connectors - Clean/repair as necessary.** Inspect all Terminals. Is any Terminal damaged, pushed out or miswired? Yes → Repair as necessary. Perform ABS Verification Test VER-1A. No → Go To 3

CR4020001965010X

Fig. 14 CCD Communication (Part 1 of 2). Breeze, Cirrus & 2000 Stratus

When Monitored: 1. Ignition on. 2. The CAB monitors its own internal microprocessors for proper operation.

Set Condition: If an error occurs within the microprocessor, the Diagnostic Trouble Code (DTC) is set.

POSSIBLE CAUSES
CAB CONNECTOR OBSERVABLE DEFECT
CAB GROUND CIRCUIT(S) OPEN
VEHICLE ACCESSORIES CONNECTIONS OBSERVABLE DEFECT
CAB DEFECTIVE

TEST	ACTION
1	Turn the Ignition off. Inspect the vehicle for any accessories that have been installed. Inspect for proper power and ground connections and/or Antenna Cable routing. Were any problems found? Yes → Repair as necessary. Perform ABS Verification Test VER-1A. No → Go To 2
2	Turn the Ignition off. Disconnect the CAB. **Note: Check connectors - Clean/repair as necessary.** Inspect the Ground Circuits in CAB, Cavities 8 and 24. Is any Terminal damaged, pushed out, or miswired? Yes → Repair as necessary. Perform ABS Verification Test VER-1A. No → Go To 3
3	Turn the Ignition off. Disconnect the CAB Connector. **Note: Check connectors - Clean/repair as necessary.** Using an Ohmmeter, measure the resistance between the CAB Ground Circuits and ground, CAB Cavities 8 and 24 and Battery Ground. Is the resistance below 1.0 ohms? Yes → Go To 4 No → Repair the open Ground Circuit(s). Perform ABS Verification Test VER-1A.

CR4020001966010X

Fig. 15 Controller Failure (Part 1 of 2). Breeze, Cirrus & 2000 Stratus

TEST	ACTION
4	Turn the Ignition off. Disconnect the CAB Connector. **Note: Check connectors - Clean/repair as necessary.** Turn ignition on, turn on all accessories. Using a Voltmeter, measure the Ground Circuits in Cavity 8 or 24. Is the voltage above 1.0 volt? Yes → Repair the open Ground Circuit(s). Perform ABS Verification Test VER-1A. No → Go To 5
5	If there are no potential causes remaining, replace the CAB. View repair options. Repair Replace the CAB. Perform ABS Verification Test VER-1A.

CR4020001966020X

Fig. 15 Controller Failure (Part 2 of 2). Breeze, Cirrus & 2000 Stratus

When Monitored: 1. Ignition on. 2. The CAB monitors the wheel speed sensor circuit continuity at all times.

Set Condition: If the CAB detects an open or shorted wheel speed sensor circuit, the Diagnostic Trouble Code (DTC) will set.

POSSIBLE CAUSES
WIRING & CONNECTORS OBSERVABLE DEFECT
LEFT FRONT WHEEL SPEED SENSOR (+) CIRCUIT OPEN
LEFT FRONT WHEEL SPEED SENSOR (+) CIRCUIT SHORTED TO GROUND
LEFT FRONT WHEEL SPEED SENSOR (-) CIRCUIT OPEN
LEFT FRONT WHEEL SPEED SENSOR (-) CIRCUIT SHORTED TO GROUND
LEFT FRONT WHEEL SPEED SENSOR CONNECTOR OBSERVABLE DAMAGE
LEFT FRONT WHEEL SPEED SENSOR DAMAGED OR CONNECTOR DISCONNECTED
LEFT FRONT WHEEL SPEED SENSOR DEFECTIVE (SHORT TO GROUND CHECK)
LEFT FRONT WHEEL SPEED SENSOR DEFECTIVE (RESISTANCE CHECK)
CAB DEFECTIVE

TEST	ACTION
1	Ignition On, Engine Not Running With the DRB, read DTC's. With the DRB, erase DTC's. Turn the Ignition off. Turn the Ignition on. With the DRB, read DTC's. Did the DTC set again right now? Yes → Go To 2 No → Go To 11
2	Turn the Ignition off. Inspect the Left Front Wheel Speed Sensor and Connector. Is the Sensor damaged or Connector disconnected? Yes → Repair as necessary. Perform ABS Verification Test VER-1A. No → Go To 3

CR4020001968010X

Fig. 17 Lefthand Front Sensor Circuit Failure (Part 1 of 3). Breeze, Cirrus & 2000 Stratus Coupe

When Monitored: 1. Ignition on. 2. Vehicle speed above 40 km/h (24 mph) on all our wheels for more than 2 minutes.

Set Condition: The CAB counts the number of pulses from the wheel speed sensors and compares the values. If the CAB determines that one or both of the front wheel speed sensor signals are significantly different then the rear speed signals, the Diagnostic Trouble Code (DTC) is set.

POSSIBLE CAUSES
INCORRECT TONE WHEEL

TEST	ACTION
1	An incorrect Tone Wheel was installed on the vehicle. View repair options Yes → Replace Tone Wheel

CR4020001967000X

Fig. 16 Incorrect Tone Wheel. Breeze, Cirrus & 2000 Stratus Coupe

TEST	ACTION
3	Turn the Ignition off. Disconnect the Left Front Wheel Speed Sensor Connector. **Note: Check connectors - Clean/repair as necessary.** Inspect all Terminals. Is any Terminal damaged, pushed out or miswired? Yes → Repair as necessary. Perform ABS Verification Test VER-1A. No → Go To 4
4	Turn the Ignition off. Disconnect the Left Front Wheel Speed Sensor Connector. **Note: Check connectors - Clean/repair as necessary.** Disconnect the CAB Connector. **Note: Check connectors - Clean/repair as necessary.** Connect a Jumper Wire between the Left Front Wheel Speed Sensor (+) Circuit and ground. Using an Ohmmeter, measure the resistance between the Left Front Wheel Speed Sensor (+) Circuit and ground, CAB Cavities 4 and 8. Is the resistance below 10 ohms? Yes → Go To 5 No → Repair the open Left Front Wheel Speed Sensor (+) Circuit. Perform ABS Verification Test VER-1A.
5	Turn the Ignition off. Disconnect the Left Front Wheel Speed Sensor Connector. **Note: Check connectors - Clean/repair as necessary.** Disconnect the CAB Connector. **Note: Check connectors - Clean/repair as necessary.** Using an Ohmmeter, measure the resistance between the Wheel Speed Sensor (+) Circuit and ground. Is the resistance below 15,000 ohms? Yes → Repair the Left Front Wheel Speed Sensor (+) Circuit shorted to ground. Perform ABS Verification Test VER-1A. No → Go To 6
6	Turn the Ignition off. Disconnect the Left Front Wheel Speed Sensor Connector. **Note: Check connectors - Clean/repair as necessary.** Using an Ohmmeter, measure the resistance between either one of the Left Front Wheel Speed Sensor pins and ground. Is the resistance below 15,000 ohms? Yes → Replace the Left Front Wheel Speed Sensor. Perform ABS Verification Test VER-1A. No → Go To 7

CR4020001968020X

Fig. 17 Lefthand Front Sensor Circuit Failure (Part 2 of 3). Breeze, Cirrus & 2000 Stratus Coupe

TEST	ACTION
7	Turn the Ignition off. Disconnect the Left Front Wheel Speed Sensor Connector. **Note: Check connectors - Clean/repair as necessary.** Disconnect the CAB Connector. **Note: Check connectors - Clean/repair as necessary.** Connect a Jumper Wire between the Left Front Wheel Speed Sensor (-) and ground. Using an Ohmmeter, measure the resistance between the Left Front Wheel Speed Sensor (-) Circuit and ground, CAB Cavities 11 and 8. Is the resistance below 10 ohms? Yes → Go To 8 No → Repair the open Left Front Wheel Speed Sensor (-) Circuit. Perform ABS Verification Test VER-1A.
8	Turn the Ignition off. Disconnect the Left Front Wheel Speed Sensor Connector. **Note: Check connectors - Clean/repair as necessary.** Disconnect the CAB Connector. **Note: Check connectors - Clean/repair as necessary.** Using an Ohmmeter, measure the resistance between the Left Front Wheel Speed Sensor (-) Circuit and ground. Is the resistance below 15,000 ohms? Yes → Repair the Left Front Wheel Speed Sensor (-) Circuit shorted to ground. Perform ABS Verification Test VER-1A. No → Go To 9
9	Turn the Ignition off. Disconnect the Left Front Wheel Speed Sensor Connector. **Note: Check connectors - Clean/repair as necessary.** Using an Ohmmeter, measure the resistance of the Left Front Wheel Speed Sensor. Is the resistance between 2,160 and 2,640 ohms? Yes → Go To 10 No → Replace the Left Front Wheel Speed Sensor. Perform ABS Verification Test VER-1A.
10	If there are no potential causes remaining, replace the CAB. View repair options. Repair Replace the CAB. Perform ABS Verification Test VER-1A.
11	Turn the Ignition off. Using the schematic as a guide, inspect the Wiring and Connections. Were any problems found? Yes → Repair as necessary. Perform ABS Verification Test VER-1A. No → Test Complete.

CR4020001968030X

Fig. 17 Lefthand Front Sensor Circuit Failure (Part 3 of 3). Breeze, Cirrus & 2000 Stratus Coupe

TEST	ACTION
3	Turn the Ignition off. Inspect the Left Front Wheel Speed Sensor. Is the Left Front Wheel Speed Sensor loose or damaged? Yes → Repair as necessary. Perform ABS Verification Test VER-1A. No → Go To 4
4	Turn the Ignition off. Inspect the Tone Wheel for damaged or missing teeth. **Note: The teeth should be perfectly square, not bent or nicked.** Is the Tone Wheel okay? Yes → Go To 5 No → Replace the Tone Wheel. Perform ABS Verification Test VER-1A.
5	Turn the Ignition off. Using a Feeler Gauge, measure the Sensor Air Gap. **Note: The Air Gap should be checked at least in four places on the Tone Wheel.** Is the Air Gap within 0.17 to 1.80 mm (0.007" to 0.071")? Yes → Go To 6 No → Repair as necessary. Perform ABS Verification Test VER-1A.
6	Turn the Ignition off. Inspect the Wheel Bearings for excessive runout or clearance. **Refer to service information if necessary for procedures or specifications.** Is the Bearing clearance okay? Yes → Go To 7 No → Repair as necessary. Perform ABS Verification Test VER-1A.
7	Turn the Ignition off. Disconnect the CAB Connector. **Note: Check connectors - Clean/repair as necessary.** Inspect all Terminals. Is any Terminal damaged, pushed out or miswired? Yes → Repair as necessary. Perform ABS Verification Test VER-1A. No → Go To 8
8	Turn the Ignition off. Disconnect the CAB Connector. **Note: Check connectors - Clean/repair as necessary.** Using an Ohmmeter, measure the resistance of the Left Front Wheel Speed Sensor Circuit, CAB Cavities 4 and 11. Is the resistance below 200 ohms? Yes → Repair the Left Front Wheel Speed Sensor Circuits shorted together. Perform ABS Verification Test VER-1A. No → Go To 9

CR4020001969020X

Fig. 18 Lefthand Front Sensor Signal Failure (Part 2 of 3). Breeze, Cirrus & 2000 Stratus Coupe

When Monitored: The CAB monitors the wheel speed sensor signal at all times. 1. Comparison is checked at drive off or every 7 milliseconds. 2. Continuity is checked continuously. 3. Phase length supervision is checked every 7 milliseconds.

Set Condition: If the sensor signal is missing, as soon as vehicle speed exceeds 19 km/h (12 mph) the Diagnostic Trouble Code (DTC) will set. If during an ABS stop, the CAB commands any valve solenoid on for an extended length of time, and does not see a corresponding wheel speed change, the DTC is set.

POSSIBLE CAUSES
CAB CONNECTOR OBSERVABLE DEFECT
LEFT FRONT WHEEL SPEED SENSOR AIR GAP OUT OF SPECIFICATION
LEFT FRONT WHEEL SPEED SENSOR CIRCUITS SHORTED TOGETHER
LEFT FRONT WHEEL SPEED SENSOR DEFECTIVE
LEFT FRONT WHEEL SPEED SENSOR OBSERVABLE DEFECT
LEFT FRONT TONE WHEEL DEFECTIVE
LEFT FRONT WHEEL BEARING CLEARANCE OUT OF SPECIFICATION

TEST	ACTION
1	Ignition On, Engine Not Running With the DRB, read DTC's. Is the Left Front Sensor Circuit Failure DTC present right now? Yes → Refer to symptom LEFT FRONT SENSOR CIRCUIT FAILURE. No → Go To 2
2	Have an assistant drive the vehicle while you monitor the Left Front Wheel Speed Sensor. Slowly accelerate as straight as possible from a stop to 24 km/h (15 mph). Did the Left Front Wheel Speed Sensor Signal show 0 km/h (0 mph) or lag behind the other sensors more than 5 km/j (3 mph)? Yes → Go To 3 No → At this time, the Wheel Speed Sensor is OK. The DTC may have been set by attempting to stop on very slick road surfaces or brakes locking up due to lining contamination or overheating. If any of these conditions are present, repair as necessary. Test Complete. Perform ABS Verification Test VER-1A.

CR4020001969010X

Fig. 18 Lefthand Front Sensor Signal Failure (Part 1 of 3). Breeze, Cirrus & 2000 Stratus Coupe

TEST	ACTION
9	If there are no potential causes remaining, replace the Left Front Wheel Speed Sensor. View repair options. Repair Replace the Left Front Wheel Speed Sensor. Perform ABS Verification Test VER-1A.

CR4020001969030X

Fig. 18 Lefthand Front Sensor Signal Failure (Part 3 of 3). Breeze, Cirrus & 2000 Stratus Coupe

When Monitored: 1. Ignition on. 2. The CAB monitors the wheel speed sensor circuit continuity at all times.

Set Condition: If the CAB detects an open or shorted wheel speed sensor circuit, the Diagnostic Trouble Code (DTC) is set.

POSSIBLE CAUSES
WIRING AND CONNECTORS OBSERVABLE DEFECT
LEFT REAR WHEEL SPEED SENSOR (+) CIRCUIT OPEN
LEFT REAR WHEEL SPEED SENSOR (-) CIRCUIT OPEN
LEFT REAR WHEEL SPEED SENSOR (+) CIRCUIT SHORTED TO GROUND
LEFT REAR WHEEL SPEED SENSOR (-) CIRCUIT SHORTED TO GROUND
LEFT REAR WHEEL SPEED SENSOR CONNECTOR OBSERVABLE DAMAGE
LEFT REAR WHEEL SPEED SENSOR DAMAGED OR CONNECTOR DISCONNECTED
LEFT REAR WHEEL SPEED SENSOR DEFECTIVE (SHORTED TO GROUND CHECK)
LEFT REAR WHEEL SPEED SENSOR DEFECTIVE (RESISTANCE CHECK)
CAB DEFECTIVE

TEST	ACTION
1	Ignition On, Engine Not Running With the DRB, read DTC's. With the DRB, erase DTC's. Turn the Ignition off. Turn the Ignition on. With the DRB, read DTC's. Did the DTC's set again right now? Yes → Go To 2 No → Go To 11
2	Turn the Ignition off. Inspect the Left Rear Wheel Speed Sensor and Connector. Is the Wheel Speed Sensor damaged or Connector disconnected? Yes → Repair as necessary. Perform ABS Verification Test VER-1A. No → Go To 3

CR4020001970010X

Fig. 19 Lefthand Rear Sensor Circuit Failure (Part 1 of 3). Breeze, Cirrus & 2000 Stratus Coupe

TEST	ACTION
3	Turn the Ignition off. Disconnect the Left Rear Wheel Speed Sensor Connector. **Note: Check connectors - Clean/repair as necessary.** Inspect all Terminals. Is any Terminal damaged, pushed out, or miswired? Yes → Repair as necessary. Perform ABS Verification Test VER-1A. No → Go To 4
4	Turn the Ignition off. Disconnect the Left Rear Wheel Speed Sensor Connector. **Note: Check connectors - Clean/repair as necessary.** Disconnect the CAB Connector. **Note: Check connectors - Clean/repair as necessary.** Connect a jumper wire between the Left Rear Wheel Speed Sensor (+) and ground. Using an Ohmmeter, measure the resistance between the Left Rear Wheel Speed Sensor (+) Circuit and ground, CAB Cavity 10 and 8. Is the resistance below 10 ohms? Yes → Go To 5 No → Repair the open Left Rear Wheel Speed Sensor (+) Circuit. Perform ABS Verification Test VER-1A.
5	Turn the Ignition off. Disconnect the Left Rear Wheel Speed Sensor Connector. **Note: Check connectors - Clean/repair as necessary.** Disconnect the CAB Connector. **Note: Check connectors - Clean/repair as necessary.** Using an Ohmmeter, measure the resistance between the Left Rear Wheel Speed Sensor (+) Circuit and ground. Is the resistance below 15,000 ohms? Yes → Repair the Left Rear Wheel Speed Sensor (+) Circuit shorted to ground. Perform ABS Verification Test VER-1A. No → Go To 6
6	Turn the Ignition off. Disconnect the Left Rear Wheel Speed Sensor Connector. **Note: Check connectors - Clean/repair as necessary.** Disconnect the CAB Connector. **Note: Check connectors - Clean/repair as necessary.** Connect a jumper wire between the Left Rear Wheel Speed Sensor (-) and ground. Using an Ohmmeter, measure the resistance between the Left Rear Wheel Speed Sensor (-) Circuit and ground, CAB Cavity 2 and 8. Is the resistance below 10 ohms? Yes → Go To 7 No → Repair the open Left Rear Wheel Speed Sensor (-) Circuit. Perform ABS Verification Test VER-1A.

CR4020001970020X

Fig. 19 Lefthand Rear Sensor Circuit Failure (Part 2 of 3). Breeze, Cirrus & 2000 Stratus Coupe

TEST	ACTION
7	Turn the Ignition off. Disconnect the Left Rear Wheel Speed Sensor Connector. **Note: Check connectors - Clean/repair as necessary.** Disconnect the CAB Connector. **Note: Check connectors - Clean/repair as necessary.** Using an Ohmmeter, measure the resistance between the Left Rear Wheel Speed Sensor (-) Circuit and ground. Is the resistance below 15,000 ohms? Yes → Repair the Left Rear Wheel Speed Sensor (-) Circuit shorted to ground. Perform ABS Verification Test VER-1A. No → Go To 8
8	Turn the Ignition off. Disconnect the Left Rear Wheel Speed Sensor Connector. **Note: Check connectors - Clean/repair as necessary.** Using an Ohmmeter, measure the resistance of the Left Rear Wheel Speed Sensor. Is the resistance between 2,160 and 2,640 ohms? Yes → Go To 9 No → Replace the Left Rear Wheel Speed Sensor. Perform ABS Verification Test VER-1A.
9	Turn the Ignition off. Disconnect the Left Rear Wheel Speed Sensor Connector. **Note: Check connectors - Clean/repair as necessary.** Using an Ohmmeter, measure the resistance between either one of the Wheel Speed Sensor pins and ground. Is the resistance below 15,000 ohms? Yes → Replace the Wheel Speed Sensor. Perform ABS Verification Test VER-1A. No → Go To 10
10	If there are no potential causes remaining, replace the CAB. View repair options. Repair Replace the CAB. Perform ABS Verification Test VER-1A.
11	Turn the Ignition off. Using a schematic as a guide, inspect the Wiring and Connections. Were any problems found? Yes → Repair as necessary. Perform ABS Verification Test VER-1A. No → Test Complete.

CR4020001970030X

Fig. 19 Lefthand Rear Sensor Circuit Failure (Part 3 of 3). Breeze, Cirrus & 2000 Stratus Coupe

When Monitored: 1. Ignition on. 2. The CAB monitors the wheel speed signals at all times.

Set Condition: If the sensor signal is missing, as soon as vehicle speed exceeds 19 km/h (12 mph) the Diagnostic Trouble Code (DTC) will set. If during an ABS stop, the CAB commands any valve solenoid on for an extended length of time, and does not see a corresponding wheel speed change, the DTC is set.

POSSIBLE CAUSES
CAB CONNECTOR OBSERVABLE DEFECT
LEFT REAR WHEEL SPEED SENSOR AIR GAP OUT OF SPECIFICATION
LEFT REAR WHEEL SPEED SENSOR CIRCUITS SHORTED TOGETHER
LEFT REAR WHEEL SPEED SENSOR DEFECTIVE
LEFT REAR WHEEL SPEED SENSOR OBSERVABLE DEFECT
LEFT REAR TONE WHEEL DEFECTIVE
LEFT REAR WHEEL BEARING CLEARANCE OUT OF SPEC

TEST	ACTION
1	Ignition On, Engine Not Running With DRB, read DTC's. Is the Left Rear Sensor Circuit failure DTC present right now? Yes → Refer to symptom LEFT REAR SENSOR CIRCUIT FAILURE. No → Go To 2
2	Engine Running Have an assistant drive the vehicle while you monitor the Left Rear Wheel Speed Sensor. Slowly accelerate as straight as possible from a stop to 24 km/h (15 mph). Did the Left Rear Wheel Speed Sensor Signal show 0 km/h (0 mph) or lag behind the other sensors more than 5 km/h (3 mph)? Yes → Go To 3 No → At this time, the Wheel Speed Sensor is OK. The DTC may have been set by attempting to stop on very slick road surfaces or brakes locking up due to lining contamination or overheating. If any of these conditions are present, repair as necessary. Test Complete. Perform ABS Verfication Test VER-1A.

CR4020001971010X

Fig. 20 Lefthand Rear Sensor Signal Failure (Part 1 of 3). Breeze, Cirrus & 2000 Stratus Coupe

TEST	ACTION
3	Turn the Ignition off. Inspect the Left Rear Wheel Speed Sensor. Is the Left Rear Wheel Speed Sensor loose or damaged? Yes → Repair as necessary. Perform ABS Verification Test VER-1A. No → Go To 4
4	Turn the Ignition off. Inspect the Tone Wheel for damaged or missing teeth. **Note: The teeth should be perfectly square, not bent or nicked.** Is the Tone Wheel okay? Yes → Go To 5 No → Replace the Tone Wheel. Perform ABS Verification Test VER-1A.
5	Turn the Ignition off. Using a Feeler Gauge, measure the Sensor Air Gap. **Note: The Air Gap should be checked in at least four places on the Tone Wheel.** Is the Air Gap within 0.37 to 1.50 mm (0.14" to 0.059")? Yes → Go To 6 No → Repair as necessary. Perform ABS Verification Test VER-1A.
6	Turn the Ignition off. Inspect the Wheel Bearings for excessive runout or clearance. **Refer to service information if necessary for procedures or specifications.** Is the Bearing clearance okay? Yes → Go To 7 No → Repair as necessary. Perform ABS Verification Test VER-1A.
7	Turn the Ignition off. Disconnect the CAB Connector. **Note: Check connectors - Clean/repair as necessary.** Inspect all Terminals. Is any Terminal damaged, pushed out, or miswired? Yes → Repair as necessary. Perform ABS Verification Test VER-1A. No → Go To 8
8	Turn the Ignition off. Disconnect the CAB Connector. **Note: Check connectors - Clean/repair as necessary.** Using an Ohmmeter, measure the resistance of the Left Rear Wheel Speed Sensor Circuit, CAB Cavities 2 and 10. Is the resistance below 200 ohms? Yes → Repair the Left Rear Wheel Speed Sensor Circuits shorted together. Perform ABS Verification Test VER-1A. No → Go To 9

CR4020001971020X

Fig. 20 Lefthand Rear Sensor Signal Failure (Part 2 of 3). Breeze, Cirrus & 2000 Stratus Coupe

TEST	ACTION
9	If there are no potential causes remaining, replace the Left Rear Wheel Speed Sensor. View repair options. Repair Replace the Left Rear Wheel Speed Sensor. Perform ABS Verification Test VER-1A.

CR4020001971030X

Fig. 20 Lefthand Rear Sensor Signal Failure (Part 3 of 3). Breeze, Cirrus & 2000 Stratus Coupe

TEST	ACTION
3	Turn the Ignition on. Is the Pump/Motor running continuously? Yes → Replace the CAB. Perform ABS Verification Test VER-1A. No → Go To 4
4	Turn the Ignition off. Check the ABS Pump Fuse #13 in the PDC. Is the Fuse okay? Yes → Go To 5 No → Check for a short to ground in Fused B+ Circuit. If no short is found, replace faulty ABS fuse. Perform ABS Verification Test VER-1A.
5	Turn the Ignition off. Disconnect the CAB Connector. **Note: Check connectors - Clean/repair as necessary.** Inspect all Terminals. Is any Terminal damaged, pushed out or miswired? Yes → Repair as necessary. Perform ABS Verification Test VER-1A. No → Go To 6
6	Turn the Ignition off. Disconnect the CAB Connector. **Note: Check connectors - Clean/repair as necessary.** Using a 12 volt test light connected to ground, probe the Fused B(+) Circuit, CAB Cavity 25. Is the test light on? Yes → Go To 7 No → Repair the open Fused B+ Circuit. Perform ABS Verification Test VER-1A.
7	Turn the Ignition off. Disconnect the CAB Connector. **Note: Check connectors - Clean/repair as necessary.** Using an Ohmmeter, connect probes between the CAB Ground Circuits and ground, CAB Cavities 8 and 24, and Battery ground. Is the resistance below 1.0 ohms? Yes → Go To 8 No → Repair the open Ground Circuit. Perform ABS Verification Test VER-1A.
8	Turn the Ignition off. Disconnect the Pump Motor Two Terminal Connector from CAB. **Note: Check connectors - Clean/repair as necessary.** Inspect all Terminals. Is any Terminal damaged, pushed out or miswired? Yes → Repair as necessary. Perform ABS Verification Test VER-1A. No → Go To 9

CR4020001972020X

Fig. 21 Pump Motor Circuit Not Working Properly (Part 2 of 3). Breeze, Cirrus & 2000 Stratus Coupe

When Monitored: Ignition on. The CAB monitors the pump at all times. The CAB commands the pump on at 19 km/h (12 mph) to check its operation, provided the brake is not applied. If the driver has their foot on the brake, the test will run at 39 km/h (24 mph).

Set Condition: The Diagnostic Trouble Code (DTC) is stored when the CAB detects that the pump cannot run when commanded on OR is running erroneously. If the pump is off at the end of an ABS stop when the pump is commanded on, or if the pump is on when the pump is commanded off, the DTC is set.

POSSIBLE CAUSES
ABS PUMP FUSE #13 DEFECTIVE
FUSED B+ CIRCUIT OPEN
CAB GROUND CIRCUIT(S) OPEN
PUMP MOTOR TERMINAL CONNECTOR OBSERVABLE DEFECT
PUMP MOTOR WIRING HARNESS OBSERVABLE DEFECT
PUMP MOTOR/HCU DEFECTIVE
CAB CONNECTOR OBSERVABLE DEFECT
CAB DEFECTIVE

TEST	ACTION
1	Ignition On, Engine Not Running With the DRB, read DTC's. Is the CAB Power Feed Circuit code present? Yes → Refer to symptom CAB POWER FEED CIRCUIT. No → Go To 2
2	Ignition On, Engine Not Running With the DRB, erase DTC's. Turn the Ignition off. Turn the Ignition on. With the DRB, under "System Test" perform "Pump Test." Did pump motor work properly? Yes → Go To 11 No → Go To 3

CR4020001972010X

Fig. 21 Pump Motor Circuit Not Working Properly (Part 1 of 3). Breeze, Cirrus & 2000 Stratus Coupe

TEST	ACTION
9	Turn the Ignition off. Disconnect the CAB Connector. **Note: Check connectors - Clean/repair as necessary.** Disconnect Pump Motor Connector. **Note: Check connectors - Clean/repair as necessary.** Connect a jumper wire between CAB Cav. 25 and Pump Motor (+) Terminal. Connect another jumper wire between the Pump Motor (-) Terminal and ground. Is the Pump Motor operating properly? Yes → Replace the CAB. Perform ABS Verification Test VER-1A. No → Go To 10
10	If there are no potential causes remaining, the Pump Motor/HCU is assumed to be defective. View repair options. Repair Replace the Pump Motor/HCU. Perform ABS Verification Test VER-1A.
11	Turn the Ignition off. Using the schematic as a guide, inspect the Wiring and Connections. Were any problems found? Yes → Repair as necessary. Perform ABS Verification Test VER-1A. No → Test Complete.

CR4020001972030X

Fig. 21 Pump Motor Circuit Not Working Properly (Part 3 of 3). Breeze, Cirrus & 2000 Stratus Coupe

When Monitored: 1. Ignition on. 2. The CAB monitors the wheel speed circuit continuity at all times.

Set Condition: If the CAB detects an open or shorted wheel speed sensor circuit, the Diagnostic Trouble Code (DTC) will set.

POSSIBLE CAUSES
WIRING AND CONNECTORS OBSERVABLE DEFECT
RIGHT FRONT WHEEL SPEED SENSOR CONNECTOR OBSERVABLE DAMAGE
RIGHT FRONT WHEEL SPEED SENSOR DAMAGED OR CONNECTOR DISCONNECTED
RIGHT FRONT WHEEL SPEED SENSOR (+) CIRCUIT OPEN
RIGHT FRONT WHEEL SPEED SENSOR (+) CIRCUIT SHORTED TO GROUND
RIGHT FRONT WHEEL SPEED SENSOR (-) CIRCUIT OPEN
RIGHT FRONT WHEEL SPEED SENSOR (-) CIRCUIT SHORTED TO GROUND
RIGHT FRONT WHEEL SPEED SENSOR DEFECTIVE (SHORT TO GROUND CHECK)
RIGHT FRONT WHEEL SPEED SENSOR DEFECTIVE (RESISTANCE CHECK)
CAB DEFECTIVE

TEST	ACTION
1	Ignition On, Engine Not Running With the DRB, read the DTC's. With the DRB, erase the DTC's. Turn the Ignition off. Turn the Ignition on. Did the DTC set again right now? Yes → Go To 2 No → Go To 11
2	Turn the Ignition off. Inspect the Right Front Wheel Speed Sensor and Connector. Is the Sensor damaged or Connector disconnected? Yes → Repair as necessary. Perform ABS Verification Test VER-1A. No → Go To 3

CR4020001973010X

Fig. 22 Righthand Front Sensor Circuit Failure (Part 1 of 3). Breeze, Cirrus & 2000 Stratus Coupe

TEST	ACTION
3	Turn the Ignition off. Disconnect the Right Front Wheel Speed Sensor Connector. **Note: Check connectors - Clean/repair as necessary.** Inspect all Terminals. Is any Terminal damaged, pushed out or miswired? Yes → Repair as necessary. Perform ABS Verification Test VER-1A. No → Go To 4
4	Turn the Ignition off. Disconnect the Right Front Wheel Speed Sensor Connector. **Note: Check connectors - Clean/repair as necessary.** Disconnect the CAB Connector. **Note: Check connectors - Clean/repair as necessary.** Connect a jumper wire between the Right Front Wheel Speed Sensor (+) and ground. Using an Ohmmeter, measure the resistance between the Right Front Wheel Speed Sensor (+) Circuit and ground, CAB Cavities 3 and 8. Is the resistance below 10 ohms? Yes → Go To 5 No → Repair the open Right Front Wheel Speed Sensor (+) Circuit. Perform ABS Verification Test VER-1A.
5	Turn the Ignition off. Disconnect the Right Front Wheel Speed Sensor Connector. **Note: Check connectors - Clean/repair as necessary.** Disconnect the CAB Connector. **Note: Check connectors - Clean/repair as necessary.** Using an Ohmmeter, measure the resistance between the Right Front Wheel Speed Sensor (+) Circuit and ground. Is the resistance below 15,000 ohms? Yes → Repair the Right Front Wheel Speed Sensor (+) Circuit shorted to ground. Perform ABS Verification Test VER-1A. No → Go To 6
6	Turn the Ignition off. Disconnect the Right Front Wheel Speed Sensor Connector. **Note: Check connectors - Clean/repair as necessary.** Using an Ohmmeter, measure the resistance between either one of the Right Front Wheel Speed Sensor pins and ground. Is the resistance below 15,000 ohms? Yes → Replace the Right Front Wheel Speed Sensor. Perform ABS Verification Test VER-1A. No → Go To 7

CR4020001973020X

Fig. 22 Righthand Front Sensor Circuit Failure (Part 2 of 3). Breeze, Cirrus & 2000 Stratus Coupe

TEST	ACTION
7	Turn the Ignition off. Disconnect the Right Front Wheel Speed Sensor Connector. **Note: Check connectors - Clean/repair as necessary.** Disconnect the CAB Connector. **Note: Check connectors - Clean/repair as necessary.** Connect a jumper wire between the Right Front Wheel Speed Sensor (-) and ground. Using an Ohmmeter, measure the resistance between the Right Front Wheel Speed Sensor (-) Circuit and ground, CAB Cavities 18 and 8. Is the resistance below 10 ohms? Yes → Go To 8 No → Repair the open Right Front Wheel Speed Sensor (-) Circuit. Perform ABS Verification Test VER-1A.
8	Turn the Ignition off. Disconnect the Right Front Wheel Speed Sensor Connector. **Note: Check connectors - Clean/repair as necessary.** Disconnect the CAB Connector. **Note: Check connectors - Clean/repair as necessary.** Using an Ohmmeter, measure the resistance between the Right Front Wheel Speed Sensor (-) Circuit and ground. Is the resistance below 15,000 ohms? Yes → Repair the Right Front Wheel Speed Sensor (-) Circuit shorted to ground. Perform ABS Verification Test VER-1A. No → Go To 9
9	Turn the Ignition off. Disconnect the Right Front Wheel Speed Sensor Connector. **Note: Check connectors - Clean/repair as necessary.** Using an Ohmmeter, measure the resistance of the Right Front Wheel Speed Sensor. Is the resistance between 2,160 and 2,640 ohms? Yes → Go To 10 No → Replace the Right Front Wheel Speed Sensor. Perform ABS Verification Test VER-1A.
10	If there are no potential causes remaining, replace the CAB. View repair options. Repair Replace the Controller Antilock Brake. Perform ABS Verification Test VER-1A.
11	Turn the Ignition off. Using the schematic as a guide, inspect the Wiring and Connections. Were any problems found? Yes → Repair as necessary. Perform ABS Verification Test VER-1A. No → Test Complete.

CR4020001973030X

Fig. 22 Righthand Front Sensor Circuit Failure (Part 3 of 3). Breeze, Cirrus & 2000 Stratus Coupe

When Monitored: 1. Ignition on. 2. The CAB monitors the wheel speed signals at all times.

Set Condition: If the sensor signal is missing, as soon as vehicle speed exceeds 19 km/h (12 mph) the Diagnostic Trouble Code (DTC) will set. If during an ABS stop, the CAB commands any valve solenoid on for an extended length of time, and does not see a corresponding wheel speed change, the DTC is set.

POSSIBLE CAUSES
CAB CONNECTOR OBSERVABLE DEFECT
RIGHT FRONT WHEEL SPEED SENSORAIR GAP OUT OF SPECIFICATION
RIGHT FRONT SHEEL SPEED SENSOR CIRCUITS SHORTED TOGETHER
RIGHT FRONT WHEEL SPEED SENSOR DEFECTIVE
RIGHT FRONT WHEEL SPEED SENSOR OBSERVABLE DEFECT
RIGHT FRONT TONE WHEEL DEFECTIVE
RIGHT FRONT WHEEL BEARING CLEARANCE OUT OF SPECIFICATION

TEST	ACTION
1	Ignition On, Engine Not Running With the DRB, read DTC's. Is the Right Front Sensor Circuit Failure DTC present right now? Yes → Refer to symptom RIGHT FRONT SENSOR CIRCUIT FAILURE. No → Go To 2
2	Turn the Ignition off. Inspect the Right Front Wheel Speed Sensor. Is the Right Front Wheel Speed Sensor loose or damaged? Yes → Repair as necessary. Perform ABS Verification Test VER-1A. No → Go To 3

CR4020001974010X

Fig. 23 Righthand Front Sensor Signal Failure (Part 1 of 3). Breeze, Cirrus & 2000 Stratus Coupe

TEST	ACTION
3	Have an assistant drive the vehicle while you monitor the Right Front Wheel Speed Sensor. Slowly accelerate as straight as possible from a stop to 24 km/h (15 mph). Did the Right Front Wheel Speed Sensor Signal show 0 km/h (0 mph) or lag behind the other sensors more than 5 km/h (3 mph)? Yes → Go To 4 No → At this time, the Wheel Speed Sensor is OK. The DTC may have been set by attempting to stop on very slick Road surfaces or Brakes locking up due to Lining contamination or overheating. If any of these conditions are present, repair as necessary. Test Complete. Perform ABS Verfication Test VER-1A.
4	Turn the Ignition off. Inspect the Tone Wheel for damaged or missing teeth. **Note: The teeth should be perfectly square, not bent or nicked.** Is the Tone Wheel okay? Yes → Go To 5 No → Replace the Tone Wheel. Perform ABS Verification Test VER-1A.
5	Turn the Ignition off. Using a Feeler Gauge, measure the Sensor Air Gap. **Note: The Air Gap should be checked at least in four places on the Tone Wheel.** Is the Air Gap within 0.17 to 1.80 mm (0.007" to 0.071")? Yes → Go To 6 No → Repair as necessary. Perform ABS Verification Test VER-1A.
6	Turn the Ignition off. Inspect the Wheel Bearings for excessive runout or clearance. **Refer to service information if necessary for procedures or specifications.** Is the Bearing clearance okay? Yes → Go To 7 No → Repair as necessary. Perform ABS Verification Test VER-1A.
7	Turn the Ignition off. Disconnect the CAB Connector. **Note: Check connectors - Clean/repair as necessary.** Inspect all Terminals. Is any Terminal damaged, pushed out or miswired? Yes → Repair as necessary. Perform ABS Verification Test VER-1A. No → Go To 8

CR4020001974020X

Fig. 23 Righthand Front Sensor Signal Failure (Part 2 of 3). Breeze, Cirrus & 2000 Stratus Coupe

When Monitored: 1. Ignition on. 2. The CAB monitors the wheel speed circuit continuity at all times.

Set Condition: If the CAB detects an open or shorted wheel speed sensor circuit, the Diagnostic Trouble Code (DTC) will set.

POSSIBLE CAUSES
WIRING AND CONNECTORS OBSERVABLE DEFECT
RIGHT REAR WHEEL SPEED SENSOR CONNECTOR OBSERVABLE DEFECT
RIGHT REAR WHEEL SPEED SENSOR DAMAGED OR CONNECTOR DISCONNECTED
RIGHT REAR WHEEL SPEED SENSOR (+) CIRCUIT OPEN
RIGHT REAR WHEEL SPEED SENSOR (-) CIRCUIT OPEN
RIGHT REAR WHEEL SPEED SENSOR(+) CIRCUIT SHORTED TO GROUND
RIGHT REAR WHEEL SPEED SENSOR (-) CIRCUIT SHORTED TO GROUND
RIGHT REAR WHEEL SPEED SENSOR DEFECTIVE (SHORT TO GROUND CHECK)
RIGHT REAR WHEEL SPEED SENSOR DEFECTIVE (RESISTANCE CHECK)
CAB DEFECTIVE

TEST	ACTION
1	Ignition On, Engine Not Running With the DRB, read DTC's. With the DRB, erase DTC's. Turn the Ignition off. Turn the Ignition on. With the DRB, read DTC's. Did the DTC set again right now? Yes → Go To 2 No → Go To 11
2	Turn the Ignition off. Disconnect the Right Rear Wheel Speed Sensor Connector. **Note: Check connectors - Clean/repair as necessary.** Inspect all Terminals. Is any Terminal damaged, pushed out or miswired? Yes → Repair as necessary. Perform ABS Verification Test VER-1A. No → Go To 3

CR4020001975010X

Fig. 24 Righthand Front Sensor Circuit Failure (Part 1 of 3). Breeze, Cirrus & 2000 Stratus Coupe

TEST	ACTION
8	Turn the Ignition off. Disconnect the CAB Connector. **Note: Check connectors - Clean/repair as necessary.** Using an Ohmmeter, measure the resistance of the Right Front Wheel Speed Sensor Circuit, CAB Cavities 3 and 18. Is the resistance below 200 ohms? Yes → Repair the Right Front Wheel Speed Sensor Circuits shorted together. Perform ABS Verification Test VER-1A. No → Go To 9
9	If there are no potential causes remaining, replace the Right Front Wheel Speed Sensor. View repair options. Repair Replace the Right Front Wheel Speed Sensor. Perform ABS Verification Test VER-1A.

CR4020001974030X

Fig. 23 Righthand Front Sensor Signal Failure (Part 3 of 3). Breeze, Cirrus & 2000 Stratus Coupe

TEST	ACTION
3	Turn the Ignition off. Inspect the Right Rear Wheel Speed Sensor and Connector. Is the Sensor damaged or Connector disconnected? Yes → Repair as necessary. Perform ABS Verification Test VER-1A. No → Go To 4
4	Turn the Ignition off. Disconnect the Right Rear Wheel Speed Sensor Connector. **Note: Check connectors - Clean/repair as necessary.** Disconnect the CAB Connector. **Note: Check connectors - Clean/repair as necessary.** Connect a jumper wire between the Right Rear Wheel Speed Sensor (+) Circuit and ground. Using an Ohmmeter, measure the resistance between the Right Rear Wheel Speed Sensor (+) Circuit and ground, CAB Cavity 17 and 8. Is the resistance below 10 ohms? Yes → Go To 5 No → Repair the open Right Rear Wheel Speed Sensor (+) Circuit. Perform ABS Verification Test VER-1A.
5	Turn the Ignition off. Disconnect the Right Rear Wheel Speed Sensor Connector. **Note: Check connectors - Clean/repair as necessary.** Disconnect the CAB Connector. **Note: Check connectors - Clean/repair as necessary.** Using an Ohmmeter, measure the resistance between the Right Rear Wheel Speed Sensor (+) Circuit and ground. Is the resistance below 15,000 ohms? Yes → Repair the Right Rear Wheel Speed Sensor (+) Circuit Shorted to Ground. Perform ABS Verification Test VER-1A. No → Go To 6
6	Turn the Ignition off. Disconnect the Right Rear Wheel Speed Sensor Connector. **Note: Check connectors - Clean/repair as necessary.** Disconnect the CAB Connector. **Note: Check connectors - Clean/repair as necessary.** Connect a jumper wire between the Right Rear Wheel Speed Sensor (-) and ground. Using an Ohmmeter, measure the resistance between the Right Rear Wheel Speed Sensor (-) Circuit and ground, CAB Cavity 1 and 8. Is the resistance below 10 ohms? Yes → Go To 7 No → Repair the open Right Rear Wheel Speed Sensor (-) Circuit. Perform ABS Verification Test VER-1A.

CR4020001975020X

Fig. 24 Righthand Front Sensor Circuit Failure (Part 2 of 3). Breeze, Cirrus & 2000 Stratus Coupe

TEST	ACTION
7	Turn the Ignition off. Disconnect the Right Rear Wheel Speed Sensor Connector. **Note: Check connectors - Clean/repair as necessary.** Disconnect the CAB Connector. **Note: Check connectors - Clean/repair as necessary.** Using an Ohmmeter, measure the resistance between the Right Rear Wheel Speed Sensor (-) Circuit and ground. Is the resistance below 15,000 ohms? Yes → Repair the Right Rear Wheel Speed Sensor (-) Circuit Shorted to ground. Perform ABS Verification Test VER-1A. No → Go To 8
8	Turn the Ignition off. Disconnect the Right Rear Wheel Speed Sensor Connector. **Note: Check connectors - Clean/repair as necessary.** Using an Ohmmeter, measure the resistance between either one of the Right Rear Wheel Speed Sensor pins and ground. Is the resistance below 15,000 ohms? Yes → Replace the Right Rear Wheel Speed Sensor. Perform ABS Verification Test VER-1A. No → Go To 9
9	Turn the Ignition off. Disconnect the Right Rear Wheel Speed Sensor Connector. **Note: Check connectors - Clean/repair as necessary.** Using an Ohmmeter, measure the resistance of the Right Rear Wheel Speed Sensor. Is the resistance between 2,160 and 2,640 ohms? Yes → Go To 10 No → Replace the Right Rear Wheel Speed Sensor. Perform ABS Verification Test VER-1A.
10	If there are no potential causes remaining, replace the CAB. View repair options. Repair Replace the CAB. Perform ABS Verification Test VER-1A.
11	Turn the Ignition off. Using the schematic as a guide, inspect the Wiring and Connections. Were any problems found? Yes → Repair as necessary. Perform ABS Verification Test VER-1A. No → Test Complete.

CR4020001975030X

Fig. 24 Righthand Front Sensor Circuit Failure (Part 3 of 3). Breeze, Cirrus & 2000 Stratus Coupe

TEST	ACTION
3	Turn the Ignition off. Inspect the Right Rear Wheel Speed Sensor. Is the Right Rear Wheel Speed Sensor loose or damaged? Yes → Repair as necessary. Perform ABS Verification Test VER-1A. No → Go To 4
4	Turn the Ignition off. Inspect the Tone Wheel for damaged or missing teeth. **Note: The teeth should be perfectly square, not bent or nicked.** Is the Tone Wheel okay? Yes → Go To 5 No → Replace the Tone Wheel. Perform ABS Verification Test VER-1A.
5	Turn the Ignition off. Using a Feeler Gauge measure the Sensor Air Gap. **Note: The Air Gap should be checked at least in four places on the Tone Wheel.** Is the Air Gap within: 0.37 to 1.50mm (0.014" to 0.059")? Yes → Go To 6 No → Repair as necessary. Perform ABS Verification Test VER-1A.
6	Turn the Ignition off. Inspect the Wheel Bearings for excessive runout or clearance Refer to appropriate service information if necessary for procedures or specifications. Is the Bearing clearance okay? Yes → Go To 7 No → Repair as necessary. Perform ABS Verification Test VER-1A.
7	Turn the Ignition off. Disconnect the CAB Connector. **Note: Check connectors - Clean/repair as necessary.** Inspect all Terminals. Is any Terminal damaged, pushed out or miswired? Yes → Repair as necessary. Perform ABS Verification Test VER-1A. No → Go To 8
8	Turn the Ignition off. Disconnect the CAB Connector. **Note: Check connectors - Clean/repair as necessary.** Using an Ohmmeter, measure the resistance of the Right Rear Wheel Speed Sensor Circuit, CAB Cavities 1 and 17. Is the resistance below 200 ohms? Yes → Repair the Right Rear Wheel Speed Sensor Circuits shorted together. Perform ABS Verification Test VER-1A. No → Go To 9

CR4020001976020X

Fig. 25 Righthand Rear Sensor Signal Failure (Part 2 of 3). Breeze, Cirrus & 2000 Stratus Coupe

When Monitored: Ignition on. The CAB monitors the wheel speed signals at all times.

Set Condition: If the sensor signal is missing, as soon as vehicle speed exceeds 19 km/h (12 mph) the Diagnostic Trouble Code (DTC) will set. If during an ABS stop, the CAB commands any valve solenoid on for an extended length of time, and does not see a corresponding wheel speed change, the DTC is set.

POSSIBLE CAUSES
CAB CONNECTOR OBSERVABLE DEFECT
RIGHT REAR WHEEL SPEED SENSOR CIRCUITS SHORTED TOGETHER
RIGHT REAR WHEEL SPEED SENSOR AIR GAP OUT OF SPECIFICATION
RIGHT REAR WHEEL SPEED SENSOR DEFECTIVE
RIGHT REAR WHEEL SPEED SENSOR OBSERVABLE DEFECT
TONE WHEEL DEFECTIVE
RIGHT REAR WHEEL BEARING CLEARANCE OUT OF SPECIFICATION

TEST	ACTION
1	Ignition On, Engine Not Running With DRB, read DTC's. Is the Right Rear Sensor Circuit failure DTC present right now? Yes → Refer to symptom RIGHT REAR SENSOR CIRCUIT FAILURE. No → Go To 2
2	Have an assistant drive the vehicle while you monitor the Right Rear Wheel Speed Sensor. Slowly accelerate as straight as possible from a stop to 24 km/h (15 mph). Did the Right Rear Wheel Speed Sensor Signal show 0 km/h (0 mph) or lag behind the other sensors more than 5 km/h (3 mph)? Yes → Go To 3 No → At this time, the Right Rear Wheel Speed Sensor is OK. The DTC may have been set by attempting to stop on very slick road surfaces or brakes locking up due to lining contamination or overheating. If any of these conditions are present, repair as necessary. Test Complete. Perform ABS Verfication Test VER-1A.

CR4020001976010X

Fig. 25 Righthand Rear Sensor Signal Failure (Part 1 of 3). Breeze, Cirrus & 2000 Stratus Coupe

TEST	ACTION
9	If there are no potential causes remaining, replace the Right Rear Wheel Speed Sensor. View repair options. Repair Replace the Right Rear Wheel Speed Sensor. Perform ABS Verification Test VER-1A.

CR4020001976030X

Fig. 25 Righthand Rear Sensor Signal Failure (Part 3 of 3). Breeze, Cirrus & 2000 Stratus Coupe

When Monitored: 1. Ignition on. 2. The CAB monitors the Fused B+ Circuit at all times for proper system voltage.

Set Condition: If the voltage is above 19 volts at the CAB, the Diagnostic Trouble Code (DTC) is set.

POSSIBLE CAUSES
BATTERY CHARGER CONNECTED
CHARGING SYSTEM DEFECTIVE
CAB DEFECTIVE

TEST	ACTION
1	Is a battery charger connected to the vehicle? Yes → Charge Battery to proper level, disconnect the charger and clear Diagnostic trouble codes. Perform ABS Verification Test VER-1A. No → Go To 2
2	Ignition On, Engine Not Running With the DRB, select sensors, read the ignition voltage. Does the DRB show above 16 volts? Yes → Go To 3 No → Test Complete.
3	Turn the Ignition off. Disconnect the CAB Connector. **Note: Check connectors - Clean/repair as necessary.** Inspect all Terminals. Engine Running. Is any Terminal damaged, pushed out or miswired? Yes → Repair as necessary. Perform ABS Verification Test VER-1A. No → Go To 4

CR4020001977010X

Fig. 26 System Overvoltage (Part 1 of 2). Breeze, Cirrus & 2000 Stratus Coupe

TEST	ACTION
4	Turn the Ignition off. Disconnect the CAB Connector. **Note: Check connectors - Clean/repair as necessary.** Engine Running. Raise the RPM's to above 1,800. Using an Voltmeter, measure the Fused Ignition Switch Output Circuit, CAB Cavity 23. Is the voltage above 16 volts? Yes → Refer to appropriate service instruction for Charging System testing and repair. Perform ABS Verification Test VER-1A. No → Go To 5
5	Turn the Ignition on. Using the DRB, erase the DTC's. Start engine. Did the DTC reset? Yes → Replace the CAB. Perform ABS Verification Test VER-1A. No → Test Complete.

CR4020001977020X

Fig. 26 System Overvoltage (Part 2 of 2). Breeze, Cirrus & 2000 Stratus Coupe

POSSIBLE CAUSES
BRAKE LAMP SWITCH CONNECTOR OBSERVABLY DEFECTIVE
CAB CONNECTOR OBSERVABLY DEFECTIVE
BRAKE LAMP SWITCH DEFECTIVE
BRAKE LAMP SWITCH OUTPUT CIRCUIT OPEN
BRAKE LAMP SWITCH OUTPUT CIRCUIT SHORT TO VOLTAGE
CAB DEFECTIVE

TEST	ACTION
1	Turn the Ignition off. Disconnect the Controller Antilock Brake Connector. **Note: Check connectors - Clean/repair as necessary.** Inspect all Terminals. Is any Terminal damaged, pushed out or miswired? Yes → Repair as necessary. Perform ABS Verification Test VER-1A. No → Go To 2
2	Turn the Ignition off. Disconnect the Controller Antilock Brake Connector. **Note: Check connectors - Clean/repair as necessary.** **Note: Make sure the Brake Pedal is released.** Turn ignition on. Using a Voltmeter, measure the Brake Lamp Switch Output Circuit, CAB Cavity 12. Is the voltage above 8 volts? Yes → Go To 3 No → Go To 6
3	Turn the Ignition off. Disconnect the Brake Lamp Switch Connector. **Note: Check connectors - Clean/repair as necessary.** Inspect all Terminals. Is any Terminal damaged, pushed out or miswired? Yes → Repair as necessary. Perform ABS Verification Test VER-1A. No → Go To 4

CR4020001979010X

Fig. 28 Brake Lamp Switch (Part 1 of 2). Breeze, Cirrus & 2000 Stratus Coupe

When Monitored: 1. Ignition on. 2. The CAB monitors the voltage at the Fused Ignition Switch Output Circuit at all times above 10 km/h (6 mph) for proper system voltage.

Set Condition: If the voltage is below 9 volts on the Fused Ignition Switch Output Circuit at the CAB, the Diagnostic Trouble Code (DTC) is set.

POSSIBLE CAUSES
FUSED IGNITION SWITCH OUTPUT CIRCUIT RESISTANCE HIGH
BATTERY VOLTAGE BELOW 13.0 VOLTS
CAB DEFECTIVE

TEST	ACTION
1	Engine Running Raise RPM's above 1,800. Using a Voltmeter, measure the battery voltage. Is the voltage below 13.0 volts? Yes → Refer to the appropriate service information for Charging System Testing and Repair. No → Go To 2
2	Engine Running Raise RPM's above 1,800. With the DRB, select sensors, read the ignition voltage. Using a Voltmeter, measure the voltage at the battery. Does the DRB show "ignition voltage" within 1 volt of the battery volts? Yes → Test Complete. No → Repair the Fused Ignition Switch Output Circuit for high resistance. Perform ABS Verification Test VER-1A.

CR4020001978000X

Fig. 27 System Undervoltage. Breeze, Cirrus & 2000 Stratus Coupe

TEST	ACTION
4	Turn the Ignition off. Disconnect the Brake Lamp Switch Connector. **Note: Check connectors - Clean/repair as necessary.** Disconnect the Controller Antilock Brake Connector. **Note: Check connectors - Clean/repair as necessary.** Ignition on, engine not running. Using a Voltmeter, measure the Brake Lamp Switch Output Circuit. Is the voltage above 8 volts? Yes → Repair the Brake Switch Output Circuit for a short to voltage. Perform ABS Verification Test VER-1A. No → Go To 5
5	If there are no potential causes remaining, the Brake Lamp Switch is assumed to be defective. View repair options. Repair Adjust or replace the Brake Switch. Perform ABS Verification Test VER-1A.
6	Turn the Ignition off. Disconnect the Controller Antilock Brake Connector. **Note: Check connectors - Clean/repair as necessary.** **Note: Make sure the Brake Pedal is released.** Turn ignition on. Using a Voltmeter, measure the Brake Lamp Switch Output Circuit. While still probing the Brake Lamp Switch Output Circuit depress the Brake Pedal. Is the voltage above 8 volts? Yes → Go To 7 No → Repair the open Brake Switch Output Circuit. Perform ABS Verification Test VER-1A.
7	If there are no potential causes remaining, replace the CAB. View repair options. Repair Replace the CAB. Perform ABS Verification Test VER-1A.

CR4020001979020X

Fig. 28 Brake Lamp Switch (Part 2 of 2). Breeze, Cirrus & 2000 Stratus Coupe

POSSIBLE CAUSES
PCM, ABS FUSE #10 DEFECTIVE
CAB GROUND CIRCUIT(S) OPEN
FUSED IGNITION SWITCH OUTPUT CIRCUIT OPEN
FUSED IGNITION SWITCH OUTPUT CIRCUIT SHORT TO GROUND
CCD BUS (+) CIRCUIT OPEN
CCD BUS (-) CIRCUIT OPEN
CAB CONNECTOR OBSERVABLE DEFECT
CAB DEFECTIVE

TEST	ACTION
1	Turn the Ignition off. Disconnect the Controller Antilock Brake Connector. **Note: Check connectors - Clean/repair as necessary.** Is any Terminal damaged, pushed out or miswired? Yes → Repair as necessary. Peform ABS Verfication Test Ver-1A. No → Go to 2
2	Turn the Ignition off. Disconnect the Controller Antilock Brake Connector. **Note: Check connectors - Clean/repair as necessary.** Using an Ohmmeter, measure the resistance between CAB Ground Circuits and Ground, CAB Cavities 8 and 24 and Battery Ground. Is the resistance below 1.0 ohms? Yes → Go To 3 No → Repair the open Ground Circuit(s). Perform ABS Verification Test VER-1A.
3	Turn the Ignition off. Disconnect the Controller Antilock Brake Connector. **Note: Check connectors - Clean/repair as necessary.** Ignition on, engine not running. Using a Voltmeter, measure the Fused Ignition Switch Output Circuit, CAB Cavity 23. Is the voltage above 10.0 volts? Yes → Go To 4 No → Go To 7

CR4020001980010X

Fig. 29 Scan Tool No Response Message (Part 1 of 3). Breeze, Cirrus & 2000 Stratus Coupe

TEST	ACTION
9	If there are no potential causes remaining, replace the ABS Fuse. View repair options. Repair Replace faulty Fuse. Perform ABS Verification Test VER-1A.

CR4020001980030X

Fig. 29 Scan Tool No Response Message (Part 3 of 3). Breeze, Cirrus & 2000 Stratus Coupe

ABS VERIFICATION TEST VER-1A
Connect all previously disconnected components and connectors. With the DRBIII®, erase all DTCs. Turn the ignition on. With the DRBIII®, read DTC's. If any diagnostic trouble codes are present, return to Main Menu and troubleshoot new or recurring symptom. If there are no codes present upon key up, road test the vehicle for at least 5 minutes. Perform several antilock braking stops and traction control starts if equipped. **Caution: Ensure braking capability is available before road testing.** Again, with the DRBIII®, read diagnostic trouble codes. If any codes are present, return to Main Menu and troubleshoot new or recurring symptom. If there are no diagnostic trouble codes present and the customer's complaint can no longer be duplicated, the repair is complete. Return to Symptom List and troubleshoot new or recurring symptom. Repair Repair is not complete, refer to appropriate symptom.

CR4020001981000X

Fig. 30 Verification Test. Breeze, Cirrus & 2000 Stratus Coupe

TEST	ACTION
4	Turn the Ignition off. Disconnect the Controller Antilock Brake Connector. **Note: Check connectors - Clean/repair as necessary.** Connect a jumper wire between CCD Bus (+) and CCD Bus (-) Circuit, CAB Cavities 20 and 19. Ignition on, engine not running. With the DRB, perform the CCD Bus Test. Does the DRB display "Bus Shorted Together"? Yes → Replace the Controller Antilock Brake (CAB). Perform ABS Verification Test VER-1A. No → Go To 5
5	Turn the Ignition off. Disconnect the Controller Antilock Brake Connector. **Note: Check connectors - Clean/repair as necessary.** Connect a jumper from the CCD Bus (+) and the CAB Ground, CAB Cavities 20 and 8. Ignition on, engine not running. With the DRB, perform the CCD Bus Test. Does the DRB display "Bus Shorted To Ground"? Yes → Go To 6 No → Repair the open CCD Bus (+) Circuit. Perform ABS Verification Test VER-1A.
6	Turn the Ignition off. Disconnect the Controller Antilock Brake Connector. **Note: Check connectors - Clean/repair as necessary.** Connect a jumper from the CCD Bus (+) and the CAB Ground. Ignition on, engine not running. With the DRB, perform the CCD Bus Test. Does the DRB display "Bus Shorted To Ground"? Yes → Test complete Repair the open CCD Bus (-) Circuit. Perform ABS Verification Test VER-1A.
7	Turn the Ignition off. Inspect the PCM, ABS Fuse #10 in the Power Distribution Center Is the Fuse okay? Yes → Repair the open Fused Ignition Switch Output Circuit. Perform ABS Verification Test VER-1A. No → Go To 8
8	Turn the Ignition off. Disconnect the Controller Antilock Brake Connector. **Note: Check connectors - Clean/repair as necessary.** Using an Ohmmeter, measure between the Fused Ignition Switch Output Circuit CAB Cavity 23, and the Battery Ground. Is the resistance below 10 ohms? Yes → Repair the Fused Ignition Switch Output Circuit for a short to ground. Perform ABS Verification Test VER-1A. No → Go To 9

CR4020001980020X

Fig. 29 Scan Tool No Response Message (Part 2 of 3). Breeze, Cirrus & 2000 Stratus Coupe

When Monitored: Ignition on. The CAB will periodically send a status message of the ABS warning indicator to the Mechanical Instrument Cluster (MIC) via the PCI BUS. The CAB monitors the message that is received from the instrument cluster for the proper state.

Set Condition: If the MIC determines that the ABS warning indicator can not be turned on, or does not match the CAB commanded ABS warning indicator status, the MIC will send a message to the CAB and the CAB will set this Diagnostic Trouble Code (DTC).

POSSIBLE CAUSES
ANOTHER ABS DIAGNOSTIC TROUBLE CODE SET
INSTRUMENT CLUSTER
OTHER INSTRUMENT CLUSTER DTC'S
PERFORM INSTRUMENT CLUSTER SELF TEST

TEST	ACTION
1	Turn the ignition on. With the DRB, read Instrument Cluster DTC's. Are there any Instrument Cluster DTC's present? Yes → Inspect instrument cluster. Perform the Body Verification Test - Ver 1. No → Go To 2
2	Turn the ignition off then on. This will start the bulb test. Did ABS warning indicator illuminate for several seconds? Yes → Go To 3 No → Replace the Instrument cluster. Perform the Body Verification Test - Ver 1.
3	Turn the ignition on. **Note: The DRB must be able to communicate with the CAB prior to performing this test.** With the DRB, read CAB DTC's. Are there any CAB DTC's present? Yes → Refer to the Brakes (CAB) category for the related symptom(s). Perform the Body Verification Test - Ver 1. No → Go To 4

CR4020001940010X

Fig. 31 ABS Warning Lamp (Part 1 of 2). 2000 Concorde, Intrepid, LHS & 300M

TEST	ACTION
4	View repair options. Repair If there are no possible causes remaining, replace the Instrument Cluster. Perform the Body Verification Test - Ver 1.

CR4020001940020X

Fig. 31 ABS Warning Lamp (Part 2 of 2). 2000 Concorde, Intrepid, LHS & 300M

TEST	ACTION
4	Turn the ignition off. Disconnect the ABS Fuse H from the PDC. Disconnect the CAB connector. **Note: Check connector - Clean/repair as necessary.** Using a test light connected to 12 volts, probe the Fused B(+) Circuit. Is the test light on? Yes → Repair the Fused B(+) Circuit Shorted to Ground. Perform ABS VERIFICATION TEST. No → Go To 5
5	Turn the ignition off. Disconnect the ABS Fuse H from the Power Distribution Center (PDC). Disconnect the CAB connector. **Note: Check connector - Clean/repair as necessary.** Measure the resistance of the Fused B(+) circuit between the PDC Fuse terminal and the CAB connector. Is the resistance below 5 ohms? Yes → Go To 6 No → Repair Fused B(+) Circuit Open. Perform ABS VERIFICATION TEST.
6	Turn the ignition off. Disconnect the Fuse H from the PDC. The CAB must be connected for the results of this test to be valid. Using a test light connected to 12 volts, probe the Fused B(+) Circuit. Is the test light on? Yes → Replace the CAB. Perform ABS VERIFICATION TEST. No → Go To 7
7	Turn the ignition off. If there are no potential causes remaining, replace the Fuse. View repair options. Repair Replace the Fuse. Perform ABS VERIFICATION TEST.
8	Turn the ignition off. Disconnect the ABS Fuse H from the Power Distribution Center (PDC). Disconnect the CAB connector. **Note: Check connector - Clean/repair as necessary.** Measure the resistance of the Fused B(+) circuit between the PDC Fuse terminal and the CAB connector. Is the resistance below 5 ohms? Yes → Go To 9 No → Repair Fused B(+) Circuit Open. Perform ABS VERIFICATION TEST.

CR4020001941020X

Fig. 32 CAB Power Feed Circuit (Part 2 of 3). 2000 Concorde, Intrepid, LHS & 300M

TEST	ACTION
9	If there are no potential causes remaining, replace the CAB. View repair options. Repair Replace the CAB. Perform ABS VERIFICATION TEST.
10	Turn the ignition off. Visually inspect the related wiring harness. Look for any chafed, pierced, pinched, or partially broken wires. Visually inspect the related wire harness connectors. Look for broken, bent, pushed out, or corroded terminals. Refer to any Technical Service Bulletins that may apply. Were any problems found? Yes → Repair as necessary. Perform the ABS Verification Test - Ver 1. No → Test Complete.

CR4020001941030X

Fig. 32 CAB Power Feed Circuit (Part 3 of 3). 2000 Concorde, Intrepid, LHS & 300M

When Monitored: Ignition on. The CAB monitors the Fused B(+) circuit at all times for proper system voltage.

Set Condition: If the Fused B(+) voltage is missing when the CAB detects that an internal main driver is not "on", the Diagnostic Trouble Code (DTC) is set.

POSSIBLE CAUSES
INTERMITTENT DTC
FUSE BLOWN - FUSED B(+) CIRCUIT
FUSED B(+) CIRCUIT OPEN
FUSED B(+) CIRCUIT SHORTED TO GROUND
FUSED B(+) CIRCUIT INTERMITTENTLY SHORTED TO GROUND
CAB DEFECTIVE - FUSED B(+) CIRCUIT OPEN
CAB DEFECTIVE - FUSED B(+) CIRCUIT SHORTED TO GROUND

TEST	ACTION
1	Turn the ignition on. With the DRBIII®, erase DTC's. Turn the ignition off. Turn the ignition on. Drive the vehicle above 25 km/h (15 mph) for at least 10 seconds. Stop the vehicle. With the DRBIII®, read DTC's. Is the "CAB Power Feed Circuit" DTC present right now? Yes → Go To 2 No → Go To 10
2	Turn the ignition off. Remove and Inspect the ABS Fuse H in the Power Distribution Center (PDC). Is the Fuse blown? Yes → Go To 3 No → Go To 8
3	Turn the ignition off. Visually inspect the Fused B(+) Circuit in the wiring harness from the PDC to the CAB. Look for any sign of an intermittent short to ground. Is the wiring harness OK? Yes → Go To 4 No → Repair the Fused B(+) Circuit Shorted to Ground. Perform ABS VERIFICATION TEST.

CR4020001941010X

Fig. 32 CAB Power Feed Circuit (Part 1 of 3). 2000 Concorde, Intrepid, LHS & 300M

When Monitored: Ignition on. Two microprocessors, internal to the CAB, calculate the wheel speed independently of each other then compare the results.

Set Condition: If the values that each microprocessor calculate for wheel speed differ by more than 1.5% for more than 70 milliseconds (MS), the Diagnostic Trouble Code (DTC) is set.

POSSIBLE CAUSES
GROUND CIRCUIT CONNECTION POOR
GROUND CIRCUIT OPEN
CAB DEFECTIVE - GROUND CIRCUIT OPEN
GROUND CIRCUIT RADIO FREQUENCY INTERFERENCE

TEST	ACTION
1	Turn the ignition on. With the DRBIII®, actuate the pump motor. Measure the voltage drop across the CAB ground circuit connection at body ground with the pump motor running. Is the voltage above 0.10 volts? Yes → Repair Ground Circuit Poor Connection. Perform ABS VERIFICATION TEST. No → Go To 2
2	Turn the ignition off. Disconnect the CAB connector. **Note: Check connector - Clean/repair as necessary.** Measure the resistance of the ground circuits. Is the resistance below 1.0 ohm? Yes → Go To 3 No → Repair Ground Circuit Open. Perform ABS VERIFICATION TEST.

CR4020001942010X

Fig. 33 Controller Failure (Part 1 of 2). 2000 Concorde, Intrepid, LHS & 300M

TEST	ACTION
3	Turn the ignition off. Disconnect the CAB connector. **Note: Check connector - Clean/repair as necessary.** Turn the ignition on. Turn on all accessories. Measure the voltage of the ground circuit. Is the voltage below 1.0 volts? Yes → Go To 4 No → Repair as necessary. Unsplice any accessories connected to the CAB ground circuit. Reroute and shield any high voltage cables away from the CAB ground circuit. Perform ABS VERIFICATION TEST.
4	If there are no potential causes remaining, replace the CAB. View repair options. Repair Replace the CAB. Perform ABS VERIFICATION TEST.

CR4020001942020X

Fig. 33 Controller Failure (Part 2 of 2). 2000 Concorde, Intrepid, LHS & 300M

TEST	ACTION
2	Turn the ignition off. Inspect the Left Front Wheel Speed Sensor and Connector. Is the Sensor or Connector Damaged? Yes → Repair as necessary. Perform ABS VERIFICATION TEST. No → Go To 3
3	Turn the ignition off. Disconnect the CAB connector. **Note: Check connector - Clean/repair as necessary.** Measure the resistance across the Left Front Wheel Speed Sensor (+) circuit and the Left Front Wheel Speed Sensor (-) circuit at the CAB connector. Is the resistance between 900 and 1,300 ohms? Yes → Go To 4 No → Go To 8
4	Turn the ignition off. Disconnect the Left Front Wheel Speed Sensor Connector. **Note: Check connector - Clean/repair as necessary.** Disconnect the CAB Connector. **Note: Check connector - Clean/repair as necessary.** Measure the resistance between the Left Front Wheel Speed Sensor (+) Circuit and ground. Is the resistance below 15,000 ohms? Yes → Repair the Left Front Wheel Speed Sensor (+) Circuit Shorted to Ground. Perform ABS VERIFICATION TEST. No → Go To 5
5	Turn the ignition off. Disconnect the Left Front Wheel Speed Sensor Connector. **Note: Check connector - Clean/repair as necessary.** Disconnect the CAB Connector. **Note: Check connector - Clean/repair as necessary.** Measure the resistance between the Left Front Wheel Speed Sensor (-) Circuit and ground. Is the resistance below 15,000 ohms? Yes → Repair the Left Front Wheel Speed Sensor (-) Circuit Shorted to Ground. Perform ABS VERIFICATION TEST. No → Go To 6
6	Turn the ignition off. Disconnect the Left Front Wheel Speed Sensor Connector. **Note: Check connector - Clean/repair as necessary.** Measure the resistance between both of the Left Front Wheel Speed Sensor Terminals and ground. Is the resistance below 15,000 ohms? Yes → Replace the Left Front Wheel Speed Sensor. Perform ABS VERIFICATION TEST. No → Go To 7

CR4020001943020X

Fig. 34 Lefthand Front Sensor Circuit Failure (Part 2 of 5). 2000 Concorde, Intrepid, LHS & 300M

When Monitored: Ignition on. The CAB monitors the wheel speed circuit every 7 milliseconds (ms).

Set Condition: If the CAB detects an open or shorted wheel speed sensor circuit, the Diagnostic Trouble Code (DTC) will set.

POSSIBLE CAUSES
LEFT FRONT WHEEL SPEED SENSOR (+) CIRCUIT OPEN
LEFT FRONT WHEEL SPEED SENSOR (-) CIRCUIT OPEN
LEFT FRONT WHEEL SPEED SENSOR (+) CIRCUIT SHORTED TO GROUND
LEFT FRONT WHEEL SPEED SENSOR (-) CIRCUIT SHORTED TO GROUND
LEFT FRONT WHEEL SPEED SENSOR (+) CIRCUIT SHORTED TO VOLTAGE
LEFT FRONT WHEEL SPEED SENSOR (-) CIRCUIT SHORTED TO VOLTAGE
INTERMITTENT CIRCUIT DTC
LEFT FRONT WHEEL SPEED SENSOR RESISTANCE OUT OF SPECIFICATION
LEFT FRONT WHEEL SPEED SENSOR DEFECTIVE - SHORTED TO GROUND
CAB DEFECTIVE - LEFT FRONT WHEEL SPEED SENSOR (+) CIRCUIT OPEN
CAB DEFECTIVE - LEFT FRONT WHEEL SPEED SENSOR (-) CIRCUIT OPEN
CAB DEFECTIVE - LEFT FRONT WHEEL SPEED SENSOR (+) CIRCUIT SHORTED TO GROUND
LEFT FRONT WHEEL SPEED SENSOR OR CONNECTOR DAMAGE

TEST	ACTION
1	Turn the ignition on. With the DRBIII®, read DTC's. With the DRBIII®, erase DTC's. Turn the ignition off. Turn the ignition on. With the DRBIII®, read DTC's. Does the DRBIII® display "Left Front Wheel Speed Sensor Circuit Failure" DTC present right now? Yes → Go To 2 No → Go To 16

CR4020001943010X

Fig. 34 Lefthand Front Sensor Circuit Failure (Part 1 of 5). 2000 Concorde, Intrepid, LHS & 300M

TEST	ACTION
7	If there are no possible causes remaining, replace the CAB. View repair options. Repair Replace the CAB. Perform ABS VERIFICATION TEST.
8	Turn the ignition off. Disconnect the Left Front Wheel Speed Sensor Connector. **Note: Check connector - Clean/repair as necessary.** Connect a jumper wire between the Left Front Wheel Speed Sensor (+) Circuit and ground. Disconnect the CAB Connector. **Note: Check connector - Clean/repair as necessary.** Measure the resistance between the Left Front Wheel Speed Sensor (+) Circuit and ground. Is the resistance below 5 ohms? Yes → Go To 9 No → Repair the Left Front Wheel Speed Sensor (+) Circuit Open. Perform ABS VERIFICATION TEST.
9	Turn the ignition off. Disconnect the Left Front Wheel Speed Sensor Connector. **Note: Check connector - Clean/repair as necessary.** Connect a jumper wire between the Left Front Wheel Speed Sensor (-) Circuit and ground. Disconnect the CAB Connector. **Note: Check connector - Clean/repair as necessary.** Measure the resistance between the Left Front Wheel Speed Sensor (-) Circuit and ground at the CAB connector. Is the resistance below 5 ohms? Yes → Go To 10 No → Repair the Left Front Wheel Speed Sensor (-) Circuit Open. Perform ABS VERIFICATION TEST.
10	Turn the ignition off. Disconnect the Left Front Wheel Speed Sensor Connector. **Note: Check connector - Clean/repair as necessary.** Disconnect the CAB Connector. **Note: Check connector - Clean/repair as necessary.** Measure the resistance between the Left Front Wheel Speed Sensor (+) Circuit and ground. Is the resistance below 15,000 ohms? Yes → Repair the Left Front Wheel Speed Sensor (+) Circuit Shorted to Ground. Perform ABS VERIFICATION TEST. No → Go To 11

CR4020001943030X

Fig. 34 Lefthand Front Sensor Circuit Failure (Part 3 of 5). 2000 Concorde, Intrepid, LHS & 300M

TEST	ACTION
11	Turn the ignition off. Disconnect the Left Front Wheel Speed Sensor Connector. **Note: Check connector - Clean/repair as necessary.** Disconnect the CAB Connector. **Note: Check connector - Clean/repair as necessary.** Measure the resistance between the Left Front Wheel Speed Sensor (-) Circuit and ground. Is the resistance below 15,000 ohms? Yes → Repair the Left Front Wheel Speed Sensor (-) Circuit Shorted to Ground. Perform ABS VERIFICATION TEST. No → Go To 12
12	Turn the ignition off. Disconnect the Left Front Wheel Speed Sensor connector. **Note: Check connector - Clean/repair as necessary.** Disconnect the CAB connector. **Note: Check connector - Clean/repair as necessary.** Turn the ignition on. Measure the voltage of the Left Front Wheel Speed Sensor (+) Circuit. Is the voltage above 1 volt? Yes → Repair Left Front Wheel Speed Sensor (+) Circuit Shorted to Voltage. Perform ABS VERIFICATION TEST. No → Go To 13
13	Turn the ignition off. Disconnect the Left Rear Wheel Speed Sensor connector. **Note: Check connector - Clean/repair as necessary.** Disconnect the CAB connector. **Note: Check connector - Clean/repair as necessary.** Turn the ignition on. Measure the voltage of the Left Front Wheel Speed Sensor (-) Circuit. Is the voltage above 1 volt? Yes → Repair Left Front Wheel Speed Sensor (-) Circuit Shorted to Voltage. Perform ABS VERIFICATION TEST. No → Go To 14
14	Turn the ignition off. Disconnect the Left Front Wheel Speed Sensor Connector. **Note: Check connector - Clean/repair as necessary.** Measure the resistance of the the Left Front Wheel Speed Sensor. Is the resistance between 900 and 1,300 ohms? Yes → Go To 15 No → Replace the Left Front Wheel Speed Sensor. Perform ABS VERIFICATION TEST.

CR4020001943040X

Fig. 34 Lefthand Front Sensor Circuit Failure (Part 4 of 5). 2000 Concorde, Intrepid, LHS & 300M

When Monitored: Wheel speed comparison is checked at drive off or every 7 milliseconds (ms). Wheel speed continuity is checked every 7 milliseconds. Wheel speed phase length supervision is checked every 7 milliseconds.

Set Condition: If, during an ABS stop, the CAB commands any valve solenoid on for an extended length of time, and does not see a corresponding wheel speed change, the Diagnostic Trouble Code (DTC) is set. The DTC can also set if the signal is missing or erratic.

POSSIBLE CAUSES
TONE WHEEL DEFECTIVE
LEFT FRONT WHEEL SPEED SENSOR FUNCTIONAL TEST
INTERMITTENT SIGNAL DTC
LEFT FRONT WHEEL SPEED SENSOR CIRCUITS SHORTED TOGETHER
CAB DEFECTIVE - UNABLE TO READ LEFT FRONT WHEEL SPEED SENSOR SIGNAL
LEFT FRONT WHEEL BEARING OUT OF SPECIFICATION
LEFT FRONT WHEEL SPEED SENSOR AIR GAP OUT OF SPECIFICATION
LEFT FRONT WHEEL SPEED SENSOR OR CONNECTOR DAMAGED

TEST	ACTION
1	Turn the ignition on. With the DRBIII®, read DTC's. Are the "Left Front Sensor Signal Failure" and "Left Front Sensor Circuit Failure" DTC's present? Yes → Refer to symptom LEFT FRONT SENSOR CIRCUIT FAILURE No → Go To 2
2	Turn the ignition on. Have an assistant drive the vehicle while you monitor the Left Front Wheel Speed Sensor Signal, using the DRBIII®. Slowly accelerate as straight as possible from a stop to 24 Km/h (15 Mph). With the DRBIII®, monitor all wheel speed sensor signals. Did Left Front WSS Signal show 0 Km/h (0 Mph) or lag the other sensors by more than 5 km/h (3 mph)? Yes → Go To 3 No → Go To 11

CR4020001944010X

Fig. 35 Lefthand Front Sensor Signal Failure (Part 1 of 3). 2000 Concorde, Intrepid, LHS & 300M

TEST	ACTION
15	Turn the ignition off. Disconnect the Left Front Wheel Speed Sensor Connector. **Note: Check connector - Clean/repair as necessary.** Measure the resistance between both of the Left Front Wheel Speed Sensor Terminals and ground. Is the resistance below 15,000 ohms? Yes → Replace the Left Front Wheel Speed Sensor. Perform ABS VERIFICATION TEST. No → Test Complete.
16	Turn the ignition off. Visually inspect the related wiring harness. Look for any chafed, pierced, pinched, or partially broken wires. Visually inspect the related wire harness connectors. Look for broken, bent, pushed out, or corroded terminals. Refer to any Technical Service Bulletins that may apply. Were any problems found? Yes → Repair as necessary. Perform the ABS Verification Test - Ver 1. No → Test Complete.

CR4020001943050X

Fig. 34 Lefthand Front Sensor Circuit Failure (Part 5 of 5). 2000 Concorde, Intrepid, LHS & 300M

TEST	ACTION
3	Turn the ignition off. Inspect the Tone Wheel for damaged or missing teeth, cracks, or looseness. **Note: The Tone Wheel Teeth should be perfectly square, not bent or nicked.** Is the Tone Wheel OK? Yes → Go To 4 No → Replace the Tone Wheel. Perform the ABS Verification Test - Ver 1.
4	Turn the ignition off. Inspect the Left Front Wheel Speed Sensor and Connector. Is the Sensor or Connector Damaged? Yes → Repair as necessary. Perform ABS VERIFICATION TEST. No → Go To 5
5	Turn the ignition off. Inspect the wheel bearings for excessive runout or clearance. **Note: Refer to the appropriate service information, if necessary, for procedures or specifications.** Is the bearing clearance OK ? Yes → Go To 6 No → Repair as necessary. Perform ABS VERIFICATION TEST.
6	Turn the ignition off. Using a Feeler Gauge, measure the Wheel Speed Sensor Air Gap. **Note: The Air Gap should be checked in at least four places on the Tone Wheel.** Is the Air Gap between 0.42 mm - 1.71 mm (0.017" - 0.068") ? Yes → Go To 7 No → Repair as necessary. Perform ABS VERIFICATION TEST.
7	Turn the ignition off. Disconnect the Left Front Wheel Speed Sensor Connector. **Note: Check connector - Clean/repair as necessary.** Raise the left front wheel off the ground. Using a voltmeter in Alternating Current (AC) mode, probe the Left Front Wheel Speed Sensor (+) Circuit and Left Front Wheel Speed Sensor (-) Circuit at the Left Front Wheel Speed Sensor connector. Quickly rotate the wheel by hand while observing voltmeter reading. Does the voltage go above 650 milivolts as the wheel is rotated? Yes → Go To 8 No → Replace the Left Front Wheel Speed Sensor. Perform ABS VERIFICATION TEST.

CR4020001944020X

Fig. 35 Lefthand Front Sensor Signal Failure (Part 2 of 3). 2000 Concorde, Intrepid, LHS & 300M

TEST	ACTION
8	Turn the ignition off. Disconnect the CAB Connector. **Note: Check connector - Clean/repair as necessary.** Measure the resistance of the Left Front Wheel Speed Sensor Circuits. Is the resistance below 200 ohms? Yes → Repair the Left Front Wheel Speed Sensor Circuits Shorted Together. Perform ABS VERIFICATION TEST. No → Go To 9
9	Turn the ignition off. Disconnect the CAB connector. **Note: Check connector - Clean/repair as necessary.** Using a voltmeter in Alternating Current (AC) mode, measure the Left Front Wheel Speed Sensor (+) Signal Circuit and Left Front Wheel Speed Sensor (-) Circuit at the CAB connector. Quickly rotate the wheel by spinning the tire by hand. Measure the Alternating Current (AC) voltage of the Left Front Wheel Speed Sensor Circuit. Is the voltage above 650 millivolts? Yes → Go To 10 No → Go To 10
10	If there are no potential causes remaining, replace the CAB. View repair options. Repair Replace the CAB. Perform ABS VERIFICATION TEST.
11	Turn the ignition off. Visually Inspect Wheel Speed Sensor. Visually Inspect Tone Wheel. Visually Inspect Wiring Harness. Visually inspect brakes for locking up due to lining contamination or overheating. Inspect all Components for defects which may cause a Signal DTC to set. Is any Component Damaged? Yes → Repair as necessary. Perform the ABS Verification Test - Ver 1. No → Test Complete.

CR4020001944030X

Fig. 35 Lefthand Front Sensor Signal Failure (Part 3 of 3). 2000 Concorde, Intrepid, LHS & 300M

TEST	ACTION
2	Turn the ignition off. Inspect the Left Rear Wheel Speed Sensor and Connector. Is the Sensor or Connector Damaged? Yes → Repair as necessary. Perform ABS VERIFICATION TEST. No → Go To 3
3	Turn the ignition off. Disconnect the CAB connector. **Note: Check connector - Clean/repair as necessary.** Measure the resistance across the Left Rear Wheel Speed Sensor (+) Circuit and the Left Rear Wheel Speed Sensor (-) Circuit in the CAB connector. Is the resistance between 900 and 1,300 ohms? Yes → Go To 4 No → Go To 8
4	Turn the ignition off. Disconnect the Left Rear Wheel Speed Sensor Connector. **Note: Check connector - Clean/repair as necessary.** Measure the resistance between either one of the Left Rear Wheel Speed Sensor terminals and ground. Is the resistance below 15,000 ohms? Yes → Replace the Left Rear Wheel Speed Sensor. Perform ABS VERIFICATION TEST. No → Go To 5
5	Turn the ignition off. Disconnect the Left Rear Wheel Speed Sensor Connector. **Note: Check connector - Clean/repair as necessary.** Disconnect the CAB Connector. **Note: Check connector - Clean/repair as necessary.** Measure the resistance between the Left Rear Wheel Speed Sensor (+) Circuit and ground. Is the resistance below 15,000 ohms? Yes → Repair the Left Rear Wheel Speed Sensor (+) Circuit Shorted to Ground. Perform ABS VERIFICATION TEST. No → Go To 6
6	Turn the ignition off. Disconnect the Left Rear Wheel Speed Sensor Connector. **Note: Check connector - Clean/repair as necessary.** Disconnect the CAB Connector. **Note: Check connector - Clean/repair as necessary.** Measure the resistance between the Left Rear Wheel Speed Sensor (-) Circuit and ground. Is the resistance below 15,000 ohms? Yes → Repair the Left Rear Wheel Speed Sensor (-) Circuit Shorted to Ground. Perform ABS VERIFICATION TEST. No → Go To 7

CR4020001945020X

Fig. 36 Lefthand Rear Sensor Circuit Failure (Part 2 of 5). 2000 Concorde, Intrepid, LHS & 300M

When Monitored: Ignition on. The CAB monitors the wheel speed circuit every 7 milliseconds (ms).

Set Condition: If the CAB detects an open or shorted wheel speed sensor circuit, the Diagnostic Trouble Code (DTC) will set.

POSSIBLE CAUSES
LEFT REAR WHEEL SPEED SENSOR (+) CIRCUIT OPEN
LEFT REAR WHEEL SPEED SENSOR (-) CIRCUIT OPEN
LEFT REAR WHEEL SPEED SENSOR (+) CIRCUIT SHORTED TO GROUND
LEFT REAR WHEEL SPEED SENSOR (-) CIRCUIT SHORTED TO GROUND
LEFT REAR WHEEL SPEED SENSOR (+) CIRCUIT SHORTED TO VOLTAGE
LEFT REAR WHEEL SPEED SENSOR (-) CIRCUIT SHORTED TO VOLTAGE
INTERMITTENT CIRCUIT DTC
LEFT REAR WHEEL SPEED SENSOR RESISTANCE OUT OF SPECIFICATION
LEFT REAR WHEEL SPEED SENSOR DEFECTIVE - SHORTED TO GROUND
CAB DEFECTIVE - LEFT REAR WHEEL SPEED SENSOR (+) CIRCUIT OPEN
CAB DEFECTIVE - LEFT REAR WHEEL SPEED SENSOR (-) CIRCUIT OPEN
CAB DEFECTIVE - LEFT REAR WHEEL SPEED SENSOR (+) CIRCUIT SHORTED TO GROUND
LEFT REAR WHEEL SPEED SENSOR OR CONNECTOR DAMAGE

TEST	ACTION
1	Turn the ignition on. With the DRBIII®, read DTC's. With the DRBIII®, erase DTC's. Turn the ignition off. Turn the ignition on. With the DRBIII®, read DTC's. Does the DRBIII® display the "Left Rear Wheel Speed Sensor Circuit Failure" DTC present right now? Yes → Go To 2 No → Go To 16

CR4020001945010X

Fig. 36 Lefthand Rear Sensor Circuit Failure (Part 1 of 5). 2000 Concorde, Intrepid, LHS & 300M

TEST	ACTION
7	If there are no possible causes remaining, replace the CAB. View repair options. Repair Replace the CAB. Perform ABS VERIFICATION TEST.
8	Turn the ignition off. Disconnect the Left Rear Wheel Speed Sensor Connector. **Note: Check connector - Clean/repair as necessary.** Connect a jumper wire between the Left Rear Wheel Speed Sensor (+) Circuit and ground. Disconnect the CAB Connector. **Note: Check connector - Clean/repair as necessary.** Measure the resistance between the Left Rear Wheel Speed Sensor (+) Circuit and ground at the CAB connector. Is the resistance below 5 ohms? Yes → Go To 9 No → Repair the Left Rear Wheel Speed Sensor (+) Circuit Open. Perform ABS VERIFICATION TEST.
9	Turn the ignition off. Disconnect the Left Rear Wheel Speed Sensor Connector. **Note: Check connector - Clean/repair as necessary.** Connect a jumper wire between the Left Rear Wheel Speed Sensor (-) Circuit and ground. Disconnect the CAB Connector. **Note: Check connector - Clean/repair as necessary.** Measure the resistance between the Left Rear Wheel Speed Sensor (-) Circuit and ground at the CAB connector. Is the resistance below 5 ohms? Yes → Go To 10 No → Repair the Left Rear Wheel Speed Sensor (-) Circuit Open. Perform ABS VERIFICATION TEST.
10	Turn the ignition off. Disconnect the Left Rear Wheel Speed Sensor Connector. **Note: Check connector - Clean/repair as necessary.** Disconnect the CAB Connector. **Note: Check connector - Clean/repair as necessary.** Measure the resistance between the Left Rear Wheel Speed Sensor (+) Circuit and ground. Is the resistance below 15,000 ohms? Yes → Repair the Left Rear Wheel Speed Sensor (+) Circuit Shorted to Ground. Perform ABS VERIFICATION TEST. No → Go To 11

CR4020001945030X

Fig. 36 Lefthand Rear Sensor Circuit Failure (Part 3 of 5). 2000 Concorde, Intrepid, LHS & 300M

TEST	ACTION
11	Turn the ignition off. Disconnect the Left Rear Wheel Speed Sensor Connector. **Note: Check connector - Clean/repair as necessary.** Disconnect the CAB Connector. **Note: Check connector - Clean/repair as necessary.** Measure the resistance between the Left Rear Wheel Speed Sensor (-) Circuit and ground. Is the resistance below 15,000 ohms? Yes → Repair the Left Rear Wheel Speed Sensor (-) Circuit Shorted to Ground. Perform ABS VERIFICATION TEST. No → Go To 12
12	Turn the ignition off. Disconnect the Left Rear Wheel Speed Sensor connector. Disconnect the CAB connector. **Note: Check connector - Clean/repair as necessary.** Turn the ignition on. Measure the voltage of the Left Rear Wheel Speed Sensor (+) Circuit. Is the voltage above 1 volt? Yes → Repair Left Rear Wheel Speed Sensor (+) Circuit Shorted to Voltage. Perform ABS VERIFICATION TEST. No → Go To 13
13	Turn the ignition off. Disconnect the Left Rear Wheel Speed Sensor Connector. **Note: Check connector - Clean/repair as necessary.** Disconnect the CAB Connector. **Note: Check connector - Clean/repair as necessary.** Turn the ignition on. Measure the voltage of the Left Rear Wheel Speed Sensor (-) Circuit. Is the voltage above 1 volt? Yes → Repair Left Rear Wheel Speed Sensor (-) Circuit Shorted to Voltage. Perform ABS VERIFICATION TEST. No → Go To 14
14	Turn the ignition off. Disconnect the Left Rear Wheel Speed Sensor Connector. **Note: Check connector - Clean/repair as necessary.** Measure the resistance between either one of the Left Rear Wheel Speed Sensor terminals and ground. Is the resistance below 15,000 ohms? Yes → Replace the Left Rear Wheel Speed Sensor. Perform ABS VERIFICATION TEST. No → Go To 15

CR4020001945040X

Fig. 36 Lefthand Rear Sensor Circuit Failure (Part 4 of 5). 2000 Concorde, Intrepid, LHS & 300M

When Monitored: Wheel speed comparison is checked at drive off or every 7 milliseconds (ms). Wheel speed continuity is checked every 7 milliseconds. Wheel speed phase length supervision is checked every 7 milliseconds.

Set Condition: If, during an ABS stop, the CAB commands any valve solenoid on for an extended length of time, and does not see a corresponding wheel speed change, the Diagnostic Trouble Code (DTC) is set. The DTC can also set if the signal is missing or erratic.

POSSIBLE CAUSES
TONE WHEEL DEFECTIVE
LEFT REAR WHEEL SPEED SENSOR FUNCTIONAL TEST
INTERMITTENT SIGNAL DTC
LEFT REAR WHEEL SPEED SENSOR CIRCUITS SHORTED TOGETHER
CAB DEFECTIVE - UNABLE TO READ LEFT REAR WHEEL SPEED SENSOR SIGNAL
LEFT REAR WHEEL BEARING OUT OF SPECIFICATION
LEFT REAR WHEEL SPEED SENSOR AIR GAP OUT OF SPECIFICATION
LEFT REAR WHEEL SPEED SENSOR OR CONNECTOR DAMAGED

TEST	ACTION
1	Turn the ignition on. With the DRBIII®, read DTC's. Are the "Left Rear Sensor Signal Failure" and "Left Rear Sensor Circuit Failure" DTC's present now? Yes → Refer to symptom LEFT REAR SENSOR CIRCUIT FAILURE No → Go To 2
2	Turn the ignition on. Have an assistant drive the vehicle while you monitor the Left Rear Wheel Speed Sensor Signal, using the DRBIII®. Slowly accelerate as straight as possible from a stop to 24 Km/h (15 Mph). With the DRBIII®, monitor all wheel speed sensor signals. Did Left Rear WSS Signal show 0 Km/h (0 Mph) or lag the other sensors by more than 5 km/h (3 mph)? Yes → Go To 3 No → Go To 11

CR4020001946010X

Fig. 37 Lefthand Rear Sensor Signal Failure (Part 1 of 3). 2000 Concorde, Intrepid, LHS & 300M

TEST	ACTION
15	Turn the ignition off. Disconnect the Left Rear Wheel Speed Sensor Connector. **Note: Check connector - Clean/repair as necessary.** Measure the resistance of the the Left Rear Wheel Speed Sensor. Is the resistance between 900 and 1,300 ohms? Yes → Test Complete. No → Replace the Left Front Wheel Speed Sensor. Perform ABS VERIFICATION TEST.
16	Turn the ignition off. Visually inspect the related wiring harness. Look for any chafed, pierced, pinched, or partially broken wires. Visually inspect the related wire harness connectors. Look for broken, bent, pushed out, or corroded terminals. Refer to any Technical Service Bulletins that may apply. Were any problems found? Yes → Repair as necessary. Perform the ABS Verification Test - Ver 1. No → Test Complete.

CR4020001945050X

Fig. 36 Lefthand Rear Sensor Circuit Failure (Part 5 of 5). 2000 Concorde, Intrepid, LHS & 300M

TEST	ACTION
3	Turn the ignition off. Inspect the Tone Wheel for damaged or missing teeth, cracks, or looseness. **Note: The Tone Wheel Teeth should be perfectly square, not bent or nicked.** Is the Tone Wheel OK? Yes → Go To 4 No → Replace the Tone Wheel. Perform the ABS Verification Test - Ver 1.
4	Turn the ignition off. Inspect the Left Rear Wheel Speed Sensor and Connector. Is the Sensor or Connector Damaged? Yes → Repair as necessary. Perform ABS VERIFICATION TEST. No → Go To 5
5	Turn the ignition off. Inspect the wheel bearings for excessive runout or clearance. **Note: Refer to the appropriate service information, if necessary, for procedures or specifications.** Is the bearing clearance OK? Yes → Go To 6 No → Repair as necessary. Perform ABS VERIFICATION TEST.
6	Turn the ignition off. Using a Feeler Gauge measure the Wheel Speed Sensor Air Gap. **Note: The Air Gap should be checked in at least Four places on the Tone Wheel.** Is the Air Gap between 0.38 mm - 1.31 mm (0.015" - 0.052")? Yes → Go To 7 No → Repair as necessary. Perform ABS VERIFICATION TEST.
7	Turn the ignition off. Disconnect the Left Rear Wheel Speed Sensor Connector. **Note: Check connector - Clean/repair as necessary.** Raise the left rear wheel off the ground. Using a voltmeter in Alternating Current (AC) mode, measure the Left Rear Wheel Speed Sensor (+) circuit and the Left Rear Wheel Speed Sensor (-) circuit at Left Rear Wheel Speed Sensor connector. Quickly rotate the wheel by hand while observing voltmeter reading. Does the voltage go above 650 millivolts as the wheel is rotated? Yes → Go To 8 No → Replace the Left Rear Wheel Speed Sensor. Perform ABS VERIFICATION TEST.

CR4020001946020X

Fig. 37 Lefthand Rear Sensor Signal Failure (Part 2 of 3). 2000 Concorde, Intrepid, LHS & 300M

TEST	ACTION
8	Turn the ignition off. Disconnect the CAB Connector. **Note: Check connector - Clean/repair as necessary.** Measure the resistance of the Left Rear Wheel Speed Sensor Circuits. Is the resistance below 200 ohms? Yes → Repair the Left Rear Wheel Speed Sensor Circuits shorted together. Perform ABS VERIFICATION TEST. No → Go To 9
9	Turn the ignition off. Disconnect the CAB connector. **Note: Check connector - Clean/repair as necessary.** Using a voltmeter in Alternating Current (AC) mode, measure the Left Rear Wheel Speed Sensor circuits at the CAB conector. Quicky rotate the wheel by spinning the tire by hand. Measure the Alternating Current (AC) voltage of the Left Rear Wheel Speed Sensor Circuit. Is the voltage above 650 millivolts? Yes → Go To 10 No → Go To 10
10	If there are no potential causes remaining, replace the CAB. View repair options. Repair Replace the CAB. Perform ABS VERIFICATION TEST.
11	Turn the ignition off. Visually Inspect Wheel Speed Sensor. Visually Inspect Tone Wheel. Visually Inspect Wiring Harness. Visually inspect brakes for locking up due to lining contamination or overheating. Inspect all Components for defects which may cause a Signal DTC to set. Is any Component Damaged? Yes → Repair as necessary. Perform the ABS Verification Test - Ver 1. No → Test Complete.

CR4020001946030X

Fig. 37 Lefthand Rear Sensor Signal Failure (Part 3 of 3). 2000 Concorde, Intrepid, LHS & 300M

TEST	ACTION
3	Turn the ignition off. Disconnect the CAB connector. **Note: Check connector - Clean/repair as necessary.** Disconnect BCM connector. **Note: Check connectors - Clean/repair as necessary.** Measure the resistance of the PCI Bus Circuit between the CAB connector and the BCM connector. Is the resistance below 5 ohms? Yes → Go To 4 No → Repair the PCI Bus Circuit Open. Perform ABS VERIFICATION TEST. **Note: Reconnect the BCM harness connector.**
4	Turn the ignition off. Disconnect the CAB connector. **Note: Check connector - Clean/repair as necessary** Make sure that the BCM is connected. Turn the ignition on. Using the DRBIII® Lab Scope, measure the voltage of the PCI BUS circuit. Is the voltage above 0.4 volts? Yes → Go To 5 No → Replace the BCM. Perform ABS VERIFICATION TEST.
5	If there are no potential causes remaining, replace the CAB. Replace the CAB. Repair Replace the CAB. Perform ABS VERIFICATION TEST.
6	Turn the ignition off. Visually inspect the related wiring harness. Look for any chafed, pierced, pinched, or partially broken wires. Visually inspect the related wire harness connectors. Look for broken, bent, pushed out, or corroded terminals. Refer to any Technical Service Bulletins that may apply. Were any problems found? Yes → Repair as necessary. Perform the ABS Verification Test - Ver 1. No → Test Complete.

CR4020001947020X

Fig. 38 PCI Bus Communication (Part 2 of 2). 2000 Concorde, Intrepid, LHS & 300M

When Monitored: Ignition on, every 7 milliseconds (ms).

Set Condition: This Diagnostic Trouble Code (DTC) is set when the CAB cannot transmit the ABS warning lamp status message for 5 seconds. This DTC can also be set if the CAB does not receive a message from the instrument cluster for 10 seconds.

POSSIBLE CAUSES
INTERMITTENT DTC
PCI BUS OPEN TO CAB
PCI BUS CIRCUIT VOLTAGE TEST
CAB DEFECTIVE - PCI CIRCUIT OPEN

TEST	ACTION
1	Turn the ignition on. With the DRBIII®, erase DTC's. Turn the ignition off. Turn the ignition on. Wait 20 seconds. With the DRBIII®, read ABS Diagnostic Trouble Codes (DTC's). Does the DRBIII® display "PCI Bus Communication" DTC present right now? Yes → Go To 2 No → Go To 6
2	Turn the ignition on. With the DRBIII®, read Mechanical Instrument Cluster (MIC) Diagnostic Trouble Codes (DTC's). Does the MIC have the "ABS Message Not Received by MIC" DTC set? Yes → Refer to symptom NO MESSAGES FROM ABS No → Go To 3

CR4020001947010X

Fig. 38 PCI Bus Communication (Part 1 of 2). 2000 Concorde, Intrepid, LHS & 300M

When Monitored: Ignition on. The CAB commands the pump on at 20 km/h (12 mph) to check its operation, if the brake switch is not applied. If the driver has their foot on the brake, the test will run at 40 km/h (25 mph). The CAB monitors pump voltage every 7 milliseconds.

Set Condition: The DTC is stored when the CAB detects: 1) Improper voltage decay after the pump was turned off. 2) Pump not energized by the CAB, but voltage is present for 3.5 seconds. 3) Pump is turned on by the CAB, but their is insufficient voltage to operate it.

POSSIBLE CAUSES
FUSE BLOWN - PUMP MOTOR CIRCUIT
GROUND CIRCUIT POOR CONNECTION
FUSED B(+) CIRCUIT OPEN
CAB DEFECTIVE - FUSED B(+) CIRCUIT OPEN
ABS PUMP MOTOR DOES NOT ROTATE
CAB DEFECTIVE - FUSED B(+) CIRCUIT SHORTED TO GROUND
FUSED B(+) CIRCUIT INTERMITTENTLY SHORTED TO GROUND
FUSED B(+) CIRCUIT SHORTED TO GROUND
CAB DEFECTIVE - PUMP MOTOR RUNNING CONTINUOUSLY

TEST	ACTION
1	Turn the ignition on. With the DRBIII®, read DTC's. Is the "CAB Power Feed Circuit" DTC present now? Yes → Refer to symptom CAB POWER FEED CIRCUIT No → Go To 2
2	Turn the ignition off. Remove and Inspect ABS PUMP Fuse K in the PDC. Is the Fuse blown? Yes → Go To 3 No → Go To 7

CR4020001948010X

Fig. 39 Pump Motor Not Working Properly (Part 1 of 3). 2000 Concorde, Intrepid, LHS & 300M

TEST	ACTION
3	Turn the ignition off. Visually inspect the Fused B(+) Circuit in the wiring harness from the PDC to the CAB. Look for any sign of an Intermittent Short to Ground. Is the wiring harness OK? Yes → Go To 4 No → Repair the Fused B (+) Circuit shorted to ground. Perform ABS VERIFICATION TEST.
4	Turn the ignition off. Disconnect the ABS PUMP Fuse K from the PDC. Disconnect the CAB connector. **Note: Check connector - Clean/repair as necessary.** Using a test light connected to 12 volts, probe the Fused B (+) Circuit. Is the test light on? Yes → Repair the Fused B (+) Circuit Shorted to Ground. Perform ABS VERIFICATION TEST. No → Go To 5
5	Turn the ignition off. Disconnect the ABS PUMP Fuse K from the PDC. The CAB must be connected for the results of this test to be valid. Using a test light connected to 12 volts, probe the Fused B (+) circuit. Is the test light on? Yes → Replace the CAB. Perform ABS VERIFICATION TEST. No → Go To 6
6	Turn the ignition off. If there are no potential causes remaining, replace the Fuse. View repair options Repair Replace the ABS Pump Motor Fuse. Perform ABS VERIFICATION TEST.
7	Turn the ignition on. With the DRBIII®, actuate the pump motor. Measure the voltage drop across the ABS ground circuit connection, with the pump motor running. Is the voltage below 0.1 volt? Yes → Go To 8 No → Repair the poor ground circuit. Perform ABS VERIFICATION TEST.

CR4020001948020X

Fig. 39 Pump Motor Not Working Properly (Part 2 of 3). 2000 Concorde, Intrepid, LHS & 300M

TEST	ACTION
8	Turn the ignition off. Disconnect the ABS PUMP Fuse K from the Power Distribution Center (PDC). Disconnect the CAB connector. **Note: Check connector - Clean/repair as necessary.** Measure the resistance of the Fused B (+) circuit between the PDC Fuse Terminal and the CAB connector. Is the resistance below 10 ohms? Yes → Go To 9 No → Repair Fused B (+) Circuit Open. Perform ABS VERIFICATION TEST.
9	Turn the ignition off. Disconnect Pump Motor Connector. Connect a 10 gauge jumper wire between pump motor Fused B (+) circuit and a known good Fused B (+) circuit capable of providing 40 amps. Connect a 10 gauge jumper wire between pump motor ground circuit and a known good body ground. Monitor Pump Motor operation. Is the pump motor running? Yes → Go To 10 No → Replace the ABS Pump Motor. Perform ABS VERIFICATION TEST.
10	Turn the ignition off. Reconnect all connectors. Turn the ignition on. Monitor the pump motor for continuous operation. Is the pump motor running continuously? Yes → Replace the CAB. Perform ABS VERIFICATION TEST. No → Go To 11
11	If there are no potential causes remaining, replace the CAB. View repair options. Repair Replace the CAB Perform ABS VERIFICATION TEST.

CR4020001948030X

Fig. 39 Pump Motor Not Working Properly (Part 3 of 3). 2000 Concorde, Intrepid, LHS & 300M

When Monitored: Ignition on. The CAB monitors the wheel speed circuit every 7 milliseconds (ms).

Set Condition: If the CAB detects an open or shorted wheel speed sensor circuit, the Diagnostic Trouble Code (DTC) will set.

POSSIBLE CAUSES
RIGHT FRONT WHEEL SPEED SENSOR (+) CIRCUIT OPEN
RIGHT FRONT WHEEL SPEED SENSOR (-) CIRCUIT OPEN
RIGHT FRONT WHEEL SPEED SENSOR (+) CIRCUIT SHORTED TO GROUND
RIGHT FRONT WHEEL SPEED SENSOR (-) CIRCUIT SHORTED TO GROUND
RIGHT FRONT WHEEL SPEED SENSOR (+) CIRCUIT SHORTED TO VOLTAGE
RIGHT FRONT WHEEL SPEED SENSOR (-) CIRCUIT SHORTED TO VOLTAGE
INTERMITTENT CIRCUIT DTC
RIGHT FRONT WHEEL SPEED SENSOR RESISTANCE OUT OF SPECIFICATION
RIGHT FRONT WHEEL SPEED SENSOR DEFECTIVE - SHORTED TO GROUND
CAB DEFECTIVE - RIGHT FRONT WHEEL SPEED SENSOR (+) CIRCUIT OPEN
CAB DEFECTIVE - RIGHT FRONT WHEEL SPEED SENSOR (-) CIRCUIT OPEN
CAB DEFECTIVE - RIGHT FRONT WHEEL SPEED SENSOR (+) CIRCUIT SHORTED TO GROUND
RIGHT FRONT WHEEL SPEED SENSOR OR CONNECTOR DAMAGE

TEST	ACTION
1	Turn the ignition on. With the DRBIII®, read DTC's. With the DRBIII®, erase DTC's. Turn the ignition off. Turn the ignition on. With the DRBIII®, read DTC's. Does the DRBIII® display "Right Front Wheel Speed Sensor Circuit Failure" DTC present right now? Yes → Go To 2 No → Go To 16

CR4020001949010X

Fig. 40 Righthand Front Sensor Circuit Failure (Part 1 of 5). 2000 Concorde, Intrepid, LHS & 300M

TEST	ACTION
2	Turn the ignition off. Inspect the Right Front Wheel Speed Sensor and Connector. Is the Sensor or Connector Damaged? Yes → Repair as necessary. Perform ABS VERIFICATION TEST. No → Go To 3
3	Turn the ignition off. Disconnect the CAB connector. **Note: Check connector - Clean/repair as necessary.** Measure the voltage across the Right Front Wheel Speed Sensor (+) circuit and the Right Front Wheel Speed Sensor (-) Circuit in the CAB connector. Is the resistance between 900 and 1,300 ohms? Yes → Go To 4 No → Go To 8
4	Turn the ignition off. Disconnect the Right Front Wheel Speed Sensor connector. **Note: Check connector - Clean/repair as necessary.** Disconnect the CAB Connector. **Note: Check connector - Clean/repair as necessary.** Measure the resistance between the Right Front Wheel Speed Sensor (+) Circuit and ground. Is the resistance below 15,000 ohms? Yes → Repair the Right Front Wheel Speed Sensor (+) Circuit Shorted to Ground. Perform ABS VERIFICATION TEST. No → Go To 5
5	Turn the ignition off. Disconnect the Right Front Wheel Speed Sensor connector. **Note: Check connector - Clean/repair as necessary.** Disconnect the CAB Connector. **Note: Check connector - Clean/repair as necessary.** Measure the resistance between the Right Front Wheel Speed Sensor (-) Circuit and ground. Is the resistance below 15,000 ohms? Yes → Repair the Right Front Wheel Speed Sensor (-) Circuit Shorted to Ground. Perform ABS VERIFICATION TEST. No → Go To 6
6	Turn the ignition off. Disconnect the Right Front Wheel Speed Sensor connector. **Note: Check connector - Clean/repair as necessary.** Measure the resistance between either one of the Right Front Wheel Speed Sensor terminals and ground. Is the resistance below 15,000 ohms? Yes → Replace the Right Front Wheel Speed Sensor. Perform ABS VERIFICATION TEST. No → Go To 7

CR4020001949020X

Fig. 40 Righthand Front Sensor Circuit Failure (Part 2 of 5). 2000 Concorde, Intrepid, LHS & 300M

TEST	ACTION
7	If there are no possible causes remaining, replace the CAB. View repair options. Repair Replace the CAB. Perform ABS VERIFICATION TEST.
8	Turn the ignition off. Disconnect the Right Front Wheel Speed Sensor connector. **Note: Check connector - Clean/repair as necessary.** Connect a jumper wire between the Right Front Wheel Speed Sensor (+) Circuit and ground. Disconnect the CAB Connector. **Note: Check connector - Clean/repair as necessary.** Measure the resistance between the Right Front Wheel Speed Sensor (+) Circuit and ground at the CAB connector. Is the resistance below 5 ohms? Yes → Go To 9 No → Repair the Right Front Wheel Speed Sensor (+) Circuit Open. Perform ABS VERIFICATION TEST.
9	Turn the ignition off. Disconnect the Right Front Wheel Speed Sensor connector. **Note: Check connector - Clean/repair as necessary.** Connect a jumper wire between the Right Front Wheel Speed Sensor (-) Circuit and ground. Disconnect the CAB Connector. **Note: Check connector - Clean/repair as necessary.** Measure the resistance between the Right Front Wheel Speed Sensor (-) Circuit and ground at the CAB connector. Is the resistance below 5 ohms? Yes → Go To 10 No → Repair the Right Front Wheel Speed Sensor (-) Circuit Open. Perform ABS VERIFICATION TEST.
10	Turn the ignition off. Disconnect the Right Front Wheel Speed Sensor connector. **Note: Check connector - Clean/repair as necessary.** Disconnect the CAB Connector. **Note: Check connector - Clean/repair as necessary.** Measure the resistance between the Right Front Wheel Speed Sensor (+) Circuit and ground. Is the resistance below 15,000 ohms? Yes → Repair the Right Front Wheel Speed Sensor (+) Circuit Shorted to Ground. Perform ABS VERIFICATION TEST. No → Go To 11

CR4020001949030X

Fig. 40 Righthand Front Sensor Circuit Failure (Part 3 of 5). 2000 Concorde, Intrepid, LHS & 300M

TEST	ACTION
11	Turn the ignition off. Disconnect the Right Front Wheel Speed Sensor connector. **Note: Check connector - Clean/repair as necessary.** Disconnect the CAB Connector. **Note: Check connector - Clean/repair as necessary.** Measure the resistance between the Right Front Wheel Speed Sensor (-) Circuit and ground. Is the resistance below 15,000 ohms? Yes → Repair the Right Front Wheel Speed Sensor (-) Circuit Shorted to Ground. Perform ABS VERIFICATION TEST. No → Go To 12
12	Turn the ignition off. Disconnect the Right Rear Wheel Speed Sensor connector. **Note: Check connector - Clean/repair as necessary.** Disconnect the CAB connector. **Note: Check connector - Clean/repair as necessary.** Turn the ignition on. Measure the voltage of the Right Front Wheel Speed Sensor (+) Circuit. Is the voltage above 1 volt? Yes → Repair Right Front Wheel Speed Sensor (+) Circuit Shorted to Voltage. Perform ABS VERIFICATION TEST. No → Go To 13
13	Turn the ignition off. Disconnect the Right Front Wheel Speed Sensor connector. **Note: Check connector - Clean/repair as necessary.** Disconnect the CAB Connector. **Note: Check connector - Clean/repair as necessary.** Turn the ignition on. Measure the voltage of the Right Front Wheel Speed Sensor (-) circuit. Is the voltage above 1 volt? Yes → Repair Right Front Wheel Speed Sensor (-) Circuit Shorted to Voltage. Perform ABS VERIFICATION TEST. No → Go To 14
14	Turn the ignition off. Disconnect the Right Front Wheel Speed Sensor Connector. **Note: Check connector - Clean/repair as necessary.** Measure the resistance of the the Right Front Wheel Speed Sensor. Is the resistance between 900 and 1,300 ohms? Yes → Go To 15 No → Replace the Right Front Wheel Speed Sensor. Perform ABS VERIFICATION TEST.

CR4020001949040X

Fig. 40 Righthand Front Sensor Circuit Failure (Part 4 of 5). 2000 Concorde, Intrepid, LHS & 300M

TEST	ACTION
15	Turn the ignition off. Disconnect the Right Front Wheel Speed Sensor connector. **Note: Check connector - Clean/repair as necessary.** Measure the resistance between either one of the Right Front Wheel Speed Sensor terminals and ground. Is the resistance below 15,000 ohms? Yes → Replace the Right Front Wheel Speed Sensor. Perform ABS VERIFICATION TEST. No → Test Complete.
16	Turn the ignition off. Visually inspect the related wiring harness. Look for any chafed, pierced, pinched, or partially broken wires. Visually inspect the related wire harness connectors. Look for broken, bent, pushed out, or corroded terminals. Refer to any Technical Service Bulletins that may apply. Were any problems found? Yes → Repair as necessary. Perform the ABS Verification Test - Ver 1. No → Test Complete.

CR4020001949050X

Fig. 40 Righthand Front Sensor Circuit Failure (Part 5 of 5). 2000 Concorde, Intrepid, LHS & 300M

When Monitored: Wheel speed comparison is checked at drive off or every 7 milliseconds (ms). Wheel speed continuity is checked every 7 milliseconds. Wheel speed phase length supervision is checked every 7 milliseconds.

Set Condition: If, during an ABS stop, the CAB commands any valve solenoid on for an extended length of time, and does not see a corresponding wheel speed change, the Diagnostic Trouble Code (DTC) is set. The DTC can also set if the signal is missing or erratic.

POSSIBLE CAUSES
TONE WHEEL DEFECTIVE
RIGHT FRONT WHEEL SPEED SENSOR FUNCTIONAL TEST
INTERMITTENT SIGNAL DTC
RIGHT FRONT WHEEL SPEED SENSOR CIRCUITS SHORTED TOGETHER
CAB DEFECTIVE - UNABLE TO READ RIGHT FRONT WHEEL SPEED SENSOR SIGNAL
RIGHT FRONT WHEEL BEARING OUT OF SPECIFICATION
RIGHT FRONT WHEEL SPEED SENSOR AIR GAP OUT OF SPECIFICATION
RIGHT FRONT WHEEL SPEED SENSOR OR CONNECTOR DAMAGED

TEST	ACTION
1	Turn the ignition on. With the DRBIII®, read DTC's. Are "Right Front Sensor Signal Failure" and "Right Front Sensor Circuit Failure" DTC's present now? Yes → Refer to symptom RIGHT FRONT SENSOR CIRCUIT FAILURE No → Go To 2
2	Turn the ignition on. Have an assistant drive the vehicle while you monitor the Right Front Wheel Speed Sensor Signal, using the DRBIII®. Slowly accelerate as straight as possible from a stop to 24 Km/h (15 Mph). With the DRBIII®, monitor all wheel speed sensor signals. Did RFWSS Signal show 0 Km/h (0 Mph) or lag behind the other sensors more than 5 km/h (3 mph)? Yes → Go To 3 No → Go To 11

CR4020001950010X

Fig. 41 Righthand Front Sensor Signal Failure (Part 1 of 3). 2000 Concorde, Intrepid, LHS & 300M

TEST	ACTION
3	Turn the ignition off. Inspect the Tone Wheel for damaged or missing teeth, cracks, or looseness. **Note: The Tone Wheel Teeth should be perfectly square, not bent or nicked.** Is the Tone Wheel OK? Yes → Go To 4 No → Replace the Tone Wheel. Perform the ABS Verification Test - Ver 1.
4	Turn the ignition off. Inspect the Right Front Wheel Speed Sensor and Connector. Is the Sensor or Connector Damaged? Yes → Repair as necessary. Perform ABS VERIFICATION TEST. No → Go To 5
5	Turn the ignition off. Inspect the wheel bearings for excessive runout or clearance. **Note: Refer to the appropriate service information, if necessary, for procedures or specifications.** Is the bearing clearance OK? Yes → Go To 6 No → Repair as necessary. Perform ABS VERIFICATION TEST.
6	Turn the ignition off. Using a Feeler Gauge measure the Wheel Speed Sensor Air Gap. **Note: The Air Gap should be checked in at least four places on the Tone Wheel.** Is the Air Gap between 0.42 mm - 1.71 mm (0.017" - 0.068")? Yes → Go To 7 No → Repair as necessary. Perform ABS VERIFICATION TEST.
7	Turn the ignition off. Disconnect the Right Front Wheel Speed Sensor connector. **Note: Check connector - Clean/repair as necessary.** Raise the right front wheel off the ground. Using a voltmeter in Alternating Current (AC) mode, probe the Right Front Wheel Speed Sensor (+) circuit and the Right Front Wheel Speed Sensor (-) circuit at the Right Front Wheel Speed Sensor connector. Quickly rotate the wheel by hand while observing voltmeter reading. Does the voltage go above 650 millivolts as the wheel is rotated? Yes → Go To 8 No → Replace the Right Front Wheel Speed Sensor. Perform ABS VERIFICATION TEST.

CR4020001950020X

Fig. 41 Righthand Front Sensor Signal Failure (Part 2 of 3). 2000 Concorde, Intrepid, LHS & 300M

TEST	ACTION
8	Turn the ignition off. Disconnect the CAB Connector. **Note: Check connector - Clean/repair as necessary.** Measure the resistance of the Right Front Wheel Speed Sensor Circuits. Is the resistance below 200 ohms? Yes → Repair the Right Front Wheel Speed Sensor Circuits Shorted Together. Perform ABS VERIFICATION TEST. No → Go To 9
9	Turn the ignition off. Disconnect the CAB connector. **Note: Check connector - Clean/repair as necessary.** Using a voltmeter in Alternating Current (AC) mode, measure the Right Front Wheel Speed Sensor circuits at the CAB connector. Quickly rotate the wheel by spinning the tire by hand. Measure the Alternating Current (AC) voltage of the Right Front Wheel Speed Sensor Circuit. Is the voltage above 650 millivolts? Yes → Go To 10 No → Go To 10
10	If there are no potential causes remaining, replace the CAB. View repair options. Repair Replace the CAB. Perform ABS VERIFICATION TEST.
11	Turn the ignition off. Visually Inspect Wheel Speed Sensor. Visually Inspect Tone Wheel. Visually Inspect Wiring Harness. Visually inspect brakes for locking up due to lining contamination or overheating. Inspect all Components for defects which may cause a Signal DTC to set. Is any Component Damaged? Yes → Repair as necessary. Perform the ABS Verification Test - Ver 1. No → Test Complete.

CR4020001950030X

Fig. 41 Righthand Front Sensor Signal Failure (Part 3 of 3). 2000 Concorde, Intrepid, LHS & 300M

When Monitored: Ignition on. The CAB monitors the wheel speed circuit every 7 milliseconds (ms).

Set Condition: If the CAB detects an open or shorted wheel speed sensor circuit, the Diagnostic Trouble Code (DTC) will set.

POSSIBLE CAUSES
RIGHT REAR WHEEL SPEED SENSOR (+) CIRCUIT OPEN
RIGHT REAR WHEEL SPEED SENSOR (-) CIRCUIT OPEN
RIGHT REAR WHEEL SPEED SENSOR (+) CIRCUIT SHORTED TO GROUND
RIGHT REAR WHEEL SPEED SENSOR (-) CIRCUIT SHORTED TO GROUND
RIGHT REAR WHEEL SPEED SENSOR (+) CIRCUIT SHORTED TO VOLTAGE
RIGHT REAR WHEEL SPEED SENSOR (-) CIRCUIT SHORTED TO VOLTAGE
INTERMITTENT CIRCUIT DTC
RIGHT REAR WHEEL SPEED SENSOR RESISTANCE OUT OF SPECIFICATION
RIGHT REAR WHEEL SPEED SENSOR DEFECTIVE - SHORTED TO GROUND
CAB DEFECTIVE- RIGHT REAR WHEEL SPEED SENSOR (+) CIRCUIT OPEN
CAB DEFECTIVE-RIGHT REAR WHEEL SPEED SENSOR (-) CIRCUIT OPEN
CAB DEFECTIVE - RIGHT REAR WHEEL SPEED SENSOR (+) CIRCUIT SHORTED TO GROUND
RIGHT REAR WHEEL SPEED SENSOR OR CONNECTOR DAMAGE

TEST	ACTION
1	Turn the ignition on. With the DRBIII®, read DTC's. With the DRBIII®, erase DTC's. Turn the ignition off. Turn the ignition on. With the DRBIII®, read DTC's. Does the DRBIII® display "Right Rear Wheel Speed Sensor Circuit Failure" DTC present right now? Yes → Go To 2 No → Go To 16

CR4020001951010X

Fig. 42 Righthand Rear Sensor Circuit Failure (Part 1 of 5). 2000 Concorde, Intrepid, LHS & 300M

TEST	ACTION
2	Turn the ignition off. Inspect the Right Rear Wheel Speed Sensor and Connector. Is the Sensor or Connector Damaged? Yes → Repair as necessary. Perform ABS VERIFICATION TEST. No → Go To 3
3	Turn the ignition off. Disconnect the CAB connector. **Note: Check connector - Clean/repair as necessary.** Turn the ignition on. Measure the voltage across the Right Rear Wheel Speed Sensor (+) circuit and the Right Rear Wheel Speed Sensor (-) Circuit in the CAB connector. Is the resistance between 900 and 1,300 ohms? Yes → Go To 4 No → Go To 8
4	Turn the ignition off. Disconnect the Right Rear Wheel Speed Sensor Connector. **Note: Check connector - Clean/repair as necessary.** Disconnect the CAB Connector. **Note: Check connector - Clean/repair as necessary.** Measure the resistance between the Right Rear Wheel Speed Sensor (+) Circuit and ground. Is the resistance below 15,000 ohms? Yes → Repair the Right Rear Wheel Speed Sensor (+) Circuit Shorted to Ground. Perform ABS VERIFICATION TEST. No → Go To 5
5	Turn the ignition off. Disconnect the Right Rear Wheel Speed Sensor connector. **Note: Check connector - Clean/repair as necessary.** Disconnect the CAB Connector. **Note: Check connector - Clean/repair as necessary.** Measure the resistance between the Right Rear Wheel Speed Sensor (-) Circuit and ground. Is the resistance below 15,000 ohms? Yes → Repair the Right Rear Wheel Speed (-) Circuit Shorted to Ground. Perform ABS VERIFICATION TEST. No → Go To 6
6	Turn the ignition off. Disconnect the Right Rear Wheel Speed Sensor connector. **Note: Check connector - Clean/repair as necessary.** Measure the resistance between either one of the Right Rear Wheel Speed Sensor terminals and ground. Is the resistance below 15,000 ohms? Yes → Replace the Right Rear Wheel Speed Sensor. Perform ABS VERIFICATION TEST. No → Go To 7

CR4020001951020X

Fig. 42 Righthand Rear Sensor Circuit Failure (Part 2 of 5). 2000 Concorde, Intrepid, LHS & 300M

TEST	ACTION
7	If there are no possible causes remaining, replace the CAB. View repair options. Repair Replace the CAB. Perform ABS VERIFICATION TEST.
8	Turn the ignition off. Disconnect the Right Rear Wheel Speed Sensor connector. **Note: Check connector - Clean/repair as necessary.** Connect a jumper wire between the Right Rear Wheel Speed Sensor (+) Circuit and ground. Disconnect the CAB Connector. **Note: Check connector - Clean/repair as necessary.** Measure the resistance between the Right Rear Wheel Speed Sensor (+) Circuit and ground at the CAB connector. Is the resistance below 5 ohms? Yes → Go To 9 No → Repair the Right Rear Wheel Speed Sensor (+) Circuit Open. Perform ABS VERIFICATION TEST.
9	Turn the ignition off. Disconnect the Right Rear Wheel Speed Sensor Connector. **Note: Check connector - Clean/repair as necessary.** Connect a jumper wire between the Right Rear Wheel Speed Sensor (-) Circuit and ground. Disconnect the CAB Connector. **Note: Check connector - Clean/repair as necessary.** Measure the resistance between the Right Rear Wheel Speed Sensor (-) Circuit and ground at the CAB connector. Is the resistance below 5 ohms? Yes → Go To 10 No → Repair the Right Rear Wheel Speed Sensor (-) Circuit Open. Perform ABS VERIFICATION TEST.
10	Turn the ignition off. Disconnect the Right Rear Wheel Speed Sensor Connector. **Note: Check connector - Clean/repair as necessary.** Disconnect the CAB Connector. **Note: Check connector - Clean/repair as necessary.** Measure the resistance between the Right Rear Wheel Speed Sensor (+) Circuit and ground. Is the resistance below 15,000 ohms? Yes → Repair the Right Rear Wheel Speed Sensor (+) Circuit Shorted to Ground. Perform ABS VERIFICATION TEST. No → Go To 11

CR4020001951030X

Fig. 42 Righthand Rear Sensor Circuit Failure (Part 3 of 5). 2000 Concorde, Intrepid, LHS & 300M

TEST	ACTION
11	Turn the ignition off. Disconnect the Right Rear Wheel Speed Sensor connector. **Note: Check connector - Clean/repair as necessary.** Disconnect the CAB Connector. **Note: Check connector - Clean/repair as necessary.** Measure the resistance between the Right Rear Wheel Speed Sensor (-) Circuit and ground. Is the resistance below 15,000 ohms? Yes → Repair the Right Rear Wheel Speed (-) Circuit Shorted to Ground. Perform ABS VERIFICATION TEST. No → Go To 12
12	Turn the ignition off. Disconnect the Right Rear Wheel Speed Sensor connector. **Note: Check connector - Clean/repair as necessary.** Turn the ignition on. Measure the voltage of the Right Rear Wheel Speed Sensor (+) Circuit. Is the voltage above 1 volt? Yes → Repair Right Rear Wheel Speed Sensor (+) Circuit Shorted to Voltage. Perform ABS VERIFICATION TEST. No → Go To 13
13	Turn the ignition off. Disconnect the Right Rear Wheel Speed Sensor connector. **Note: Check connector - Clean/repair as necessary.** Disconnect the CAB Connector. **Note: Check connector - Clean/repair as necessary.** Turn the ignition on. Measure the voltage of the Right Rear Wheel Speed Sensor (-) Circuit. Is the voltage above 1 volt? Yes → Repair Right Rear Wheel Speed Sensor (-) Circuit Shorted to Voltage. Perform ABS VERIFICATION TEST. No → Go To 14
14	Turn the ignition off. Disconnect the Right Rear Wheel Speed Sensor Connector. **Note: Check connector - Clean/repair as necessary.** Measure the resistance of the the Right Rear Wheel Speed Sensor. Is the resistance between 900 and 1,300 ohms? Yes → Go To 15 No → Replace the Right Front Wheel Speed Sensor. Perform ABS VERIFICATION TEST.

CR4020001951040X

Fig. 42 Righthand Rear Sensor Circuit Failure (Part 4 of 5). 2000 Concorde, Intrepid, LHS & 300M

TEST	ACTION
15	Turn the ignition off. Disconnect the Right Rear Wheel Speed Sensor connector. **Note: Check connector - Clean/repair as necessary.** Measure the resistance between either one of the Right Rear Wheel Speed Sensor terminals and ground. Is the resistance below 15,000 ohms? Yes → Replace the Right Rear Wheel Speed Sensor. Perform ABS VERIFICATION TEST. No → Test Complete.
16	Turn the ignition off. Visually inspect the related wiring harness. Look for any chafed, pierced, pinched, or partially broken wires. Visually inspect the related wire harness connectors. Look for broken, bent, pushed out, or corroded terminals. Refer to any Technical Service Bulletins that may apply. Were any problems found? Yes → Repair as necessary. Perform the ABS Verification Test - Ver 1. No → Test Complete.

CR4020001951050X

Fig. 42 Righthand Rear Sensor Circuit Failure (Part 5 of 5). 2000 Concorde, Intrepid, LHS & 300M

When Monitored: Wheel speed comparison is checked at drive off or every 7 milliseconds (ms). Wheel speed continuity is checked every 7 milliseconds. Wheel speed phase length supervision is checked every 7 milliseconds.

Set Condition: If, during an ABS stop, the CAB commands any valve solenoid on for an extended length of time, and does not see a corresponding wheel speed change, the Diagnostic Trouble Code (DTC) is set. The DTC can also set if the signal is missing or erratic.

POSSIBLE CAUSES
TONE WHEEL DEFECTIVE
RIGHT REAR WHEEL SPEED SENSOR FUNCTIONAL TEST
INTERMITTENT SIGNAL DTC
RIGHT REAR WHEEL SPEED SENSOR CIRCUITS SHORTED TOGETHER
CAB DEFECTIVE - UNABLE TO READ RIGHT REAR WHEEL SPEED SENSOR SIGNAL
RIGHT REAR WHEEL BEARING OUT OF SPECIFICATION
RIGHT REAR WHEEL SPEED SENSOR AIR GAP OUT OF SPECIFICATION
RIGHT REAR WHEEL SPEED SENSOR OR CONNECTOR DAMAGED

TEST	ACTION
1	Turn the ignition on. With the DRBIII®, read DTC's. Are "Right Rear Sensor Signal Failure" and "Right Rear Sensor Circuit Failure" DTC's present now? Yes → Refer to symptom RIGHT REAR SENSOR CIRCUIT FAILURE No → Go To 2
2	Turn the ignition on. Have an assistant drive the vehicle while you monitor the Right Rear Wheel Speed Sensor Signal, using the DRBIII®. Slowly accelerate as straight as possible from a stop to 24 Km/h (15 Mph). With the DRBIII®, monitor all wheel speed sensor signals. Did the RRWSS Signal show 0 Km/h (0 Mph) or lag behind the other sensors more than 5 km/h (3 mph)? Yes → Go To 3 No → Go To 11

CR4020001952010X

Fig. 43 Righthand Rear Sensor Signal Failure (Part 1 of 3). 2000 Concorde, Intrepid, LHS & 300M

TEST	ACTION
3	Turn the ignition off. Inspect the Tone Wheel for damaged or missing teeth, cracks, or looseness. **Note: The Tone Wheel Teeth should be perfectly square, not bent or nicked.** Is the Tone Wheel OK? Yes → Go To 4 No → Replace the Tone Wheel. Perform the ABS Verification Test - Ver 1.
4	Turn the ignition off. Inspect the Right Rear Wheel Speed Sensor and Connector. Is the Sensor or Connector Damaged? Yes → Repair as necessary. Perform ABS VERIFICATION TEST. No → Go To 5
5	Turn the ignition off. Inspect the wheel bearings for excessive runout or clearance. **Note: Refer to the appropriate service information, if necessary, for procedures or specifications.** Is the bearing clearance OK? Yes → Go To 6 No → Repair as necessary. Perform ABS VERIFICATION TEST.
6	Turn the ignition off. Using a Feeler Gauge, measure the Wheel Speed Sensor Air Gap. **Note: The Air Gap should be checked in at least Four places on the Tone Wheel.** Is the Air Gap between 0.38 mm - 1.31 mm (0.015″ - 0.052″)? Yes → Go To 7 No → Repair as necessary. Perform ABS VERIFICATION TEST.
7	Turn the ignition off. Disconnect the Right Rear Wheel Speed Sensor Connector. **Note: Check connector - Clean/repair as necessary.** Raise the right rear wheel off the ground. Using a voltmeter in Alternating Current (AC) mode, probe the Right Rear Wheel Speed Sensor (+) circuit and the Right Rear Wheel Speed Sensor (-) circuit at the Right Rear Wheel Speed Sensor connector. Quickly rotate the wheel by hand while observing voltmeter reading. Does the voltage go above 650 millivolts as the wheel is rotated? Yes → Go To 8 No → Replace the Right Rear Wheel Speed Sensor. Perform ABS VERIFICATION TEST.

CR4020001952020X

Fig. 43 Righthand Rear Sensor Signal Failure (Part 2 of 3). 2000 Concorde, Intrepid, LHS & 300M

When Monitored: Ignition on. The CAB monitors the Fused B(+) circuit at all times for proper system voltage.

Set Condition: If the voltage is between 17 and 19 volts for greater than 420 milliseconds (ms), the Diagnostic Trouble Code (DTC) is set.

POSSIBLE CAUSES
INTERMITTENT DTC
BATTERY OVERCHARGED
FUSED IGNITION SWITCH OUTPUT CIRCUIT OVERVOLTAGE

TEST	ACTION
1	Turn the ignition on. With the DRBIII®, erase DTC's. Turn the ignition off. Turn the ignition on. Start the engine. With the DRBIII®, read DTC's. Is the System Overvoltage DTC present right now? Yes → Go To 2 No → Go To 4
2	Turn the ignition off. Inspect for battery charger connected to battery. Is a battery charger connected to the battery? Yes → Charge battery to proper level. Disconnect the battery charger. Clear DTC's. Perform ABS VERIFICATION TEST. No → Go To 3
3	Turn the ignition off. Disconnect the CAB connector. **Note: Check connector - Clean/repair as necessary.** Start the engine. Raise engine RPM's above 1800. Measure the voltage of the Fused B(+) (Valves) Circuit. Is the voltage above 16.5 volts ? Yes → Refer to appropriate service information for charging system testing and repair. Perform ABS VERIFICATION TEST. No → Test Complete.

CR4020001953010X

Fig. 44 System Overvoltage (Part 1 of 2). 2000 Concorde, Intrepid, LHS & 300M

TEST	ACTION
8	Turn the ignition off. Disconnect the CAB Connector. **Note: Check connector - Clean/repair as necessary.** Measure the resistance of the Right Rear Wheel Speed Sensor Circuits. Is the resistance below 200 ohms? Yes → Repair the Right Rear Wheel Speed Sensor Circuits Shorted Together. Perform ABS VERIFICATION TEST. No → Go To 9
9	Turn the ignition off. Disconnect the CAB connector. **Note: Check connector - Clean/repair as necessary.** Using a voltmeter in Alternating Current (AC) mode, measure the Right Rear Wheel Speed Sensor circuits at the CAB connector. Quickly rotate the wheel by spinning the tire by hand. Measure the Alternating Current (AC) voltage of the Right Rear Wheel Speed Sensor Circuit. Is the voltage above 650 millivolts? Yes → Go To 10 No → Go To 10
10	If there are no potential causes remaining, replace the CAB. View repair options. Repair Replace the CAB. Perform ABS VERIFICATION TEST.
11	Turn the ignition off. Visually Inspect Wheel Speed Sensor. Visually Inspect Tone Wheel. Visually Inspect Wiring Harness. Visually inspect brakes for locking up due to lining contamination or overheating. Inspect all Components for defects which may cause a Signal DTC to set. Is any Component Damaged? Yes → Repair as necessary. Perform the ABS Verification Test - Ver 1. No → Test Complete.

CR4020001952030X

Fig. 43 Righthand Rear Sensor Signal Failure (Part 3 of 3). 2000 Concorde, Intrepid, LHS & 300M

TEST	ACTION
4	Turn the ignition off. Visually inspect the related wiring harness. Look for any chafed, pierced, pinched, or partially broken wires. Visually inspect the related wire harness connectors. Look for broken, bent, pushed out, or corroded terminals. Refer to any Technical Service Bulletins that may apply. Were any problems found? Yes → Repair as necessary. Perform the ABS Verification Test - Ver 1. No → Test Complete.

CR4020001953020X

Fig. 44 System Overvoltage (Part 2 of 2). 2000 Concorde, Intrepid, LHS & 300M

When Monitored: Ignition on. The CAB monitors the Fused Ignition Switch Output circuit voltage above 10 km/h (6 mph) every 7 milliseconds for proper system voltage.

Set Condition: If the voltage is below 9.5 volts, the Diagnostic Trouble Code (DTC) is set.

POSSIBLE CAUSES
INTERMITTENT DTC
FUSED IGNITION SWITCH OUTPUT CIRCUIT HIGH RESISTANCE
FUSED IGNITION SWITCH OUTPUT CIRCUIT UNDERVOLTAGE

TEST	ACTION
1	Turn the ignition on. With the DRBIII®, erase DTC's. Turn the ignition off. Turn the ignition on. Start the engine. Drive the vehicle above 16 Kh/m (10 mph) for at least 20 seconds. Stop the vehicle With the DRBIII®, read DTC's. Is the "System Undervoltage" DTC present right now? Yes → Go To 2 No → Go To 4
2	Turn the ignition on. With the DRBIII®, select Sensors. With the DRBIII®, read the "Ignition Voltage" status and record. Measure the voltage at the battery and record. Compare voltage measurements. Does the DRBIII® display ignition voltage within one volt of the battery voltage? Yes → Go To 3 No → Repair the Fused Ignition Switch Output Circuit for high resistance Perform ABS VERIFICATION TEST.

CR4020001954010X

Fig. 45 System Undervoltage (Part 1 of 2). 2000 Concorde, Intrepid, LHS & 300M

TEST	ACTION
3	Turn the ignition off. Disconnect the CAB connector. **Note: Check connector - Clean/repair as necessary.** Start the engine. Raise engine RPM's above 1800. Measure the voltage of the Fused Ignition Switch Output circuit. Is the voltage below 9.5 volts ? Yes → Refer to appropriate service information for charging system testing and repair. Perform ABS VERIFICATION TEST. No → Test Complete.
4	Turn the ignition off. Visually inspect the related wiring harness. Look for any chafed, pierced, pinched, or partially broken wires. Visually inspect the related wire harness connectors. Look for broken, bent, pushed out, or corroded terminals. Refer to any Technical Service Bulletins that may apply. Were any problems found? Yes → Repair as necessary. Perform the ABS Verification Test - Ver 1. No → Test Complete.

CR4020001954020X

Fig. 45 System Undervoltage (Part 2 of 2). 2000 Concorde, Intrepid, LHS & 300M

TEST	ACTION
4	Turn the ignition off. Disconnect the Brake Lamp Switch Connector. **Note: Check connectors - Clean/repair as necessary.** Using an ohmmeter, measure the resistance between the Brake Lamp Switch Sense terminal and the Ground terminal (measurement taken across switch). Apply and release the Brake Pedal while monitoring the ohmmeter. Does the resistance change from below 5.0 ohms to open circuit? Yes → Go To 5 No → Replace the Brake Switch. Perform the Powertrain Verification Test - Ver 4
5	Turn the ignition off. Disconnect the Brake Lamp Switch harness connector. Disconnect the CAB harness connector. Using an ohmmeter, measure the resistance of the Brake Lamp Switch Sense Circuit at the Brake Lamp Switch Connector to a good ground. Is the resistance below 5.0 ohms? Yes → Repair the Brake Lamp Switch Sense Circuit for a short to ground. Perform the Powertrain Verification Test - Ver 4 No → Go To 6
6	Turn ignition off. Disconnect the Brake Switch Connector. Using an ohmmeter, measure the resistance between the Brake Switch Ground circuit and ground (B-). Is the resistance below 5.0 ohms? Yes → Go To 7 No → Repair the open Brake Switch Ground Circuit. Perform the Powertrain Verification Test - Ver 4
7	Turn ignition off. Disconnect the Brake Switch Connector. **Note: Check connectors - Clean/repair as necessary.** Using an ohmmeter, measure the resistance between the Brake Switch Sense terminal and the Ground terminal (measurement taken across switch). Apply and release the Brake Pedal while monitoring the ohmmeter. Does the resistance change from below 5.0 ohms to open circuit? Yes → Go To 8 No → Replace the Brake Switch. Perform the Powertrain Verification Test - Ver 4
8	If there are no possible causes remaining, replace the CAB. View repair options. Repair Replace the CAB.

CR4020001955020X

Fig. 46 Brake Lamp Switch (Part 2 of 2). 2000 Concorde, Intrepid, LHS & 300M

POSSIBLE CAUSES
BRAKE SWITCH (SENSE CIRCUIT)
BRAKE SWITCH GROUND CIRCUIT OPEN
DRB DOES NOT SHOW BRAKE SW PRESSED OR RELEASED
BRAKE SWITCH GROUND CIRCUIT OPEN
BRAKE SWITCH SENSE CIRCUIT OPEN
CAB DEFECTIVE - BRAKE LAMP SWITCH SENSE
BRAKE SWITCH (SENSE CIRCUIT)
BRAKE LAMP SWITCH SENSE CIRCUIT SHORT TO GROUND

TEST	ACTION
1	Ignition on, with engine not running. With the DRBIII® in Inputs/Outputs, monitor the Brake Lamp Switch state. While observing the display, press the Brake Pedal several times. Does the DRBIII® show Brake Switch "pressed" and "released"? Yes → The Brake Lamp Switch is operating properly at this time. Perform the Appropriate Verification Test. No → Go To 2
2	Turn the ignition off. Disconnect the Brake Lamp Switch Connector. Using an ohmmeter, measure the resistance between the Brake Lamp Switch Ground circuit and ground (B-). Is the resistance below 5.0 ohms? Yes → Go To 3 No → Repair the open Brake Switch Ground Circuit. Perform the Powertrain Verification Test - Ver 4
3	Turn the ignition off. Disconnect the Brake Lamp Switch Connector. Disconnect the CAB connector. Using an ohmmeter, measure the resistance of the Brake Lamp Switch Sense Circuit between the Brake Lamp Switch and the CAB. Is the resistance below 5.0 ohms? Yes → Go To 4 No → Repair the open Brake Lamp Switch Sense Circuit. Perform the Powertrain Verification Test - Ver 4

CR4020001955010X

Fig. 46 Brake Lamp Switch (Part 1 of 2). 2000 Concorde, Intrepid, LHS & 300M

POSSIBLE CAUSES
INSTRUMENT CLUSTER
INSTRUMENT CLUSTER (INOPERATIVE TRAC ON INDICATOR IN TRACTION CONTROL MODE)
DEFECTIVE BULB OR SOCKET
INSTRUMENT CLUSTER (TRACTION ON INDICATOR ON ALL THE TIME)
TRACTION CONTROL INOPERATIVE

TEST	ACTION
1	**Note: The DRB must be able to communicate with the CAB module prior to performing this test.** **Note: If any CAB DTC's are present, they must be repaired prior to performing this test.** Turn the ignition off then on. This will start the bulb test. Did the traction on indicator illuminate for several seconds? Yes → Go To 2 No → Go To 4
2	Turn the ignition on and wait 10 seconds. Observe the traction on indicator. Is the traction on indicator on all the time? Yes → Replace the Instrument Cluster. Perform the Body Verification Test - Ver 1. No → Go To 3
3	**Note: Perform this test only if the traction on indicator does not illuminate when the vehicle is in a traction control condition.** Drive vehicle to a safe slippery location and stop. Accelerate vehicle to enable the traction control. Can you physically feel the traction control engage while you accelerate in a slippery condition? Yes → Replace the Instrument Cluster. Perform the Body Verification Test - Ver 1. No → Replace the Controller Antilock Brake (CAB) module. Perform the Body Verification Test - Ver 1.
4	Turn the ignition off. Remove and inspect the traction on bulb and socket. Is there a problem with the bulb or socket? Yes → Repair or replace the defective bulb or socket as needed. Perform the Body Verification Test - Ver 1. No → If there are no possible causes remaining, replace the Instrument Cluster. Perform the Body Verification Test - Ver 1.

CR4020001956000X

Fig. 47 Traction Control ON Indicator Illuminated. 2000 Concorde, Intrepid, LHS & 300M

POSSIBLE CAUSES
TRACTION CONTROL SWITCH NOT OPERATIONAL
TRACTION CONTROL SWITCH GROUND CIRCUIT OPEN
TRACTION CONTROL SWITCH SENSE CIRCUIT OPEN
TRACTION CONTROL SWITCH STUCK OPEN
INSTRUMENT CLUSTER DEFECTIVE - TRACTION CONTROL SWITCH SENSE CIRCUIT OPEN
INSTRUMENT CLUSTER "TRAC OFF" INDICATOR OPERATIONAL
INSTRUMENT CLUSTER DEFECTIVE - TRACTION CONTROL SWITCH CIRCUIT SHORTED TO GROUND
TRACTION CONTROL SWITCH SENSE CIRCUIT SHORTED TO GROUND
TRACTION CONTROL SWITCH STUCK CLOSED
TRACTION CONTROL SWITCH SENSE CIRCUIT SHORTED TO VOLTAGE

TEST	ACTION
1	Turn the ignition on. Depress the Traction Control Switch on dash several times while watching the "TRAC OFF" Indicator in the Instrument Cluster. Does the Indicator change from nothing to "TRAC OFF"? Yes → The Traction Control Switch is operating properly at this time. Perform the ABS Verification Test - Ver 1. No → Go To 2
2	Turn the ignition off. Turn the ignition on. **Note: If any DTC's are present, they must be repaired prior to performing this test.** Observe the "TRAC OFF" indicator immediately after the ignition is turned on. Did the "TRAC OFF" indicator come on for several seconds then go out? Yes → Go To 3 No → Replace the Instrument Cluster.
3	Turn the ignition off. Disconnect the Traction Control Switch. **Note: Check connector - Clean/repair as necessary.** Turn the ignition on. Momentarily connect a jumper wire between the traction control switch sense circuit and the ground circuit in the traction control switch connector. Did the "TRAC OFF" indicator come on? Yes → Go To 4 No → Go To 6

CR4020001957010X

Fig. 48 Traction Control Switch (Part 1 of 3). 2000 Concorde, Intrepid, LHS & 300M

TEST	ACTION
9	Turn the ignition off. Disconnect the Instrument Cluster harness connector. **Note: Check connector - Clean/repair as necessary.** Disconnect the Traction Control Switch Connector. **Note: Check connector - Clean/repair as necessary.** Turn the ignition on. Using a test light connected to ground, probe the Traction Control Switch Sense circuit. Is the test light on? Yes → Repair the Traction Control Switch Sense circuit for a short to voltage. No → Go To 10
10	If there are no potential causes remaining, replace the Instrument Cluster. View repair options. Repair Replace the Instrument Cluster.

CR4020001957030X

Fig. 48 Traction Control Switch (Part 3 of 3). 2000 Concorde, Intrepid, LHS & 300M

TEST	ACTION
4	Turn the ignition off. Disconnect the Traction Connector Switch Connector. **Note: Check connector - Clean/repair as necessary.** Measure across the Traction Control Switch Sense circuit and Ground circuit, on Switch. Depress the Traction Control Switch. Using an ohmmeter, take measurement while depressing the Traction Control Switch. Is the resistance below 2.0 ohms across switch when the switch is depressed? Yes → Go To 5 No → Replace the Traction Control Switch.
5	Turn the ignition off. Disconnect the Traction Connector Switch Connector. **Note: Check connector - Clean/repair as necessary.** Measure across the Traction Control Switch Sense circuit and Ground circuit, on Switch. Measure resistance of the Traction Control Switch. Is the resistance below 2.0 ohms across switch? Yes → Replace the Traction Control Switch. No → Test Complete.
6	Turn the ignition off. Disconnect the Traction Control Switch harness connector. **Note: Check connector - Clean/repair as necessary.** Using a test light connected to 12 volts, probe the Traction Control Switch Ground Circuit. Is the test light on? Yes → Go To 7 No → Repair the Ground Circuit Open.
7	Turn the ignition off. Disconnect the Instrument Cluster harness connector C2. **Note: Check connector - Clean/repair as necessary.** Disconnect the Traction Control Switch Connector. **Note: Check connector - Clean/repair as necessary.** Measure the resistance of the Traction Control Switch Sense Circuit. Is the resistance below 5.0 ohms? Yes → Go To 8 No → Repair the Traction Control Switch Sense Circuit Open.
8	Turn the ignition off. Disconnect the Instrument Cluster harness connector. **Note: Check connector - Clean/repair as necessary.** Disconnect the Traction Control Switch Connector. **Note: Check connector - Clean/repair as necessary.** Using a test light connected to 12 volts, probe the Traction Control Switch Sense circuit. Is the test light on? Yes → Repair the Traction Control Switch Sense Circuit Shorted to Ground. No → Go To 9

CR4020001957020X

Fig. 48 Traction Control Switch (Part 2 of 3). 2000 Concorde, Intrepid, LHS & 300M

POSSIBLE CAUSES
INSTRUMENT CLUSTER (TRACTION CONTROL SWITCH SENSE CIRCUIT)
OBSERVE THE TRACTION OFF INDICATOR
OPEN GROUND CIRCUIT
OPEN TRACTION CONTROL SWITCH SENSE CIRCUIT
PERFORM INSTRUMENT CLUSTER SELF TEST
TRACTION CONTROL SWITCH
TRACTION CONTROL SWITCH SENSE CIRCUIT SHORTED TO GROUND
TRACTION CONTROL SWITCH SENSE CIRCUIT SHORTED TO VOLTAGE
WIRING HARNESS INTERMITTENT DEFECT

TEST	ACTION
1	**Note: The DRB must be able to communicate with the CAB module prior to performing this test.** **Note: If any CAB DTC's are present, they must be repaired prior to performing this test.** Turn the ignition off then on. This will start the bulb test. Did the traction off indicator illuminate for several seconds? Yes → Go To 2 No → Replace the Instrument cluster. Perform the Body Verification Test - Ver 1.
2	Cycle the ignition switch from off to on and wait 10 seconds. Is the traction off indicator illuminated? Yes → Replace the Instrument cluster. Perform the Body Verification Test - Ver 1. No → Go To 3
3	Cycle the ignition switch from off to on and wait 10 seconds. Monitor the traction off indicator while pressing and releasing the traction control switch. Does the traction off indicator turn on and off with the traction control switch? Yes → Go To 4 No → Go To 5

CR4020001958010X

Fig. 49 Traction Control OFF Indicator Illuminated (Part 1 of 3). 2000 Concorde, Intrepid, LHS & 300M

TEST	ACTION
4	Turn the ignition off. **Note: Visually inspect the related wiring harness. Look for any chafed, pierced, pinched, or partially broken wires.** **Note: Visually inspect the related wire harness connectors. Look for broken, bent, pushed out, or corroded terminals.** Were any problems found? Yes → The traction off indicator is operational. Check wiring harness/ connectors as necessary. Perform the Body Verification Test - Ver 1. No → Test Complete.
5	Turn the ignition off Disconnect the traction control switch harness connector. Measure the resistance between ground and the ground circuit. Is the resistance below 5.0 ohms? Yes → Go To 6 No → Repair the ground circuit for an open. Perform the Body Verification Test - Ver 1.
6	Turn the ignition off Disconnect the traction control switch harness connector. Turn the ignition on. Connect a jumper wire between the traction control switch sense circuit and the ground circuit. Monitor the traction off indicator while toggling the jumper wire. Does the traction off indicator turn on and off as the jumper wire is toggled? Yes → Replace the traction control switch. Perform the Body Verification Test - Ver 1. No → Go To 7
7	Turn the ignition off Disconnect the traction control switch harness connector. Disconnect the Instrument Cluster "C2" harness connector. Measure the resistance of the traction control switch sense circuit between the traction control switch connector and the Instrument Cluster "C2" connector. Is the resistance below 5.0 ohms? Yes → Go To 8 No → Repair the traction control switch sense circuit for an open. Perform the Body Verification Test - Ver 1.
8	Turn the ignition off Disconnect the traction control switch harness connector. Disconnect the Instrument Cluster "C2" harness connector. Measure the resistance between ground and the traction control switch sense circuit. Is the resistance below 5.0 ohms? Yes → Repair the traction control switch sense circuit for a short to ground. Perform the Body Verification Test - Ver 1. No → Go To 9

CR4020001958020X

Fig. 49 Traction Control OFF Indicator Illuminated (Part 2 of 3). 2000 Concorde, Intrepid, LHS & 300M

POSSIBLE CAUSES
PCI BUS OPEN TO CAB
FUSED IGNITION SWITCH OUTPUT CIRCUIT INTERMITTENTLY SHORTED TO GROUND
FUSED IGNITION SWITCH OUTPUT CIRCUIT OPEN
FUSED IGNITION SWITCH OUTPUT CIRCUIT SHORTED TO GROUND
GROUND CIRCUIT OPEN
CAB DEFECTIVE - FUSED IGNITION SWITCH OUTPUT SHORTED TO GROUND
CAB DEFECTIVE - CAN NOT COMMUNICATE

TEST	ACTION
1	Turn the ignition on. **Note: As soon as one or more module communicates with the DRBIII®, answer the question.** With the DRBIII®, select PASSIVE RESTRAINTS, then select AIRBAG. With the DRBIII®, select BODY, then select BODY CONTROL MODULE. Were you able to establish communication with any of the modules? Yes → Go To 2 No → Refer to symptom PCI BUS COMMUNICATION FAILURE
2	Turn the ignition off. Remove and Inspect Fuse #17 in the Junction Block. Is the Fuse blown? Yes → Go To 3 No → Go To 7
3	Turn the ignition off. Visually inspect the Fused Ignition Switch Output Circuit in the wiring harness from the Junction Block to the CAB. Look for any sign of an intermittent short to ground. Is the wiring harness OK? Yes → Go To 4 No → Repair the Fused Ignition Switch Output Circuit for a short to ground Perform ABS VERIFICATION TEST.

CR4020001959010X

Fig. 50 Scan Tool No Response From CAB (Part 1 of 3). 2000 Concorde, Intrepid, LHS & 300M

TEST	ACTION
9	Turn the ignition off Disconnect the traction control switch harness connector. Disconnect the Instrument Cluster "C2" harness connector. Turn the ignition on. Measure the voltage of the traction control switch sense circuit. Is the voltage above 1.0 volts? Yes → Repair the traction control switch sense circuit for a short to voltage. Perform the Body Verification Test - Ver 1. No → Go To 10
10	View repair options. Repair If there are no possible causes remaining, replace the Instrument Cluster. Perform the Body Verification Test - Ver 1.

CR4020001958030X

Fig. 49 Traction Control OFF Indicator Illuminated (Part 3 of 3). 2000 Concorde, Intrepid, LHS & 300M

TEST	ACTION
4	Turn the ignition off. Disconnect the Fuse #17 from the Junction Block. Disconnect the CAB connector. **Note: Check connector - Clean/repair as necessary.** Using a test light connected to 12 volts, probe the Fused Ignition Switch Output Circuit. Is the test light on? Yes → Repair Fused Ignition Switch Output Circuit Shorted to Ground Perform ABS VERIFICATION TEST. No → Go To 5
5	Turn the ignition off. Disconnect the Fuse #17 from the Junction Block. The CAB must be connected for the results of this test to be valid. Using a test light connected to 12 volts, probe the Fused Ignition Switch Output Circuit. Is the test light on? Yes → Replace the CAB. Perform ABS VERIFICATION TEST. No → Go To 6
6	Turn the ignition off. If there are no potential causes remaining, replace the Fuse. View repair options. Repair Test Complete.
7	Turn the ignition off. Disconnect the CAB connector. **Note: Check connector - Clean/repair as necessary.** Disconnect BCM connector. **Note: Check connectors - Clean/repair as necessary.** Measure the resistance of the PCI Bus Circuit between the CAB connector and the BCM connector. Is the resistance below 5 ohms? Yes → Go To 8 No → Repair the PCI Bus Circuit Open. Perform ABS VERIFICATION TEST. **Note: Reconnect the BCM harness connector.**
8	Turn the ignition off. Disconnect the Fuse #17 in the Junction Block. Disconnect the CAB connector. **Note: Check connector - Clean/repair as necessary.** Measure the resistance of the Fused Ignition Switch Output circuit between the Junction Block Fuse Terminal and the CAB connector. Is the resistance below 5 ohms? Yes → Go To 9 No → Repair Fused Ignition Switch Output Circuit Open Perform ABS VERIFICATION TEST.

CR4020001959020X

Fig. 50 Scan Tool No Response From CAB (Part 2 of 3). 2000 Concorde, Intrepid, LHS & 300M

TEST	ACTION
9	Turn the ignition off. Disconnect the CAB connector. **Note: Check connector - Clean/repair as necessary.** Measure the resistance of the ground circuits. Is the resistance below 1.0 ohm? Yes → Go To 10 No → Repair Ground Circuit Open. Perform ABS VERIFICATION TEST.
10	If there are no potential causes remaining, replace the CAB. View repair options. Repair Replace the CAB. Perform ABS VERIFICATION TEST.

CR4020001959030X

Fig. 50 Scan Tool No Response From CAB (Part 3 of 3). 2000 Concorde, Intrepid, LHS & 300M

ABS VERIFICATION TEST - VER 1.
1. Turn the ignition off. 2. Connect all previously disconnected components and connectors. 3. Turn the ignition on. 4. With the DRBIII®, erase DTC's. 5. With the DRBIII®, read DTC's. 6. If any Diagnostic Trouble Codes are present, return to Symptom list and troubleshoot new or recurring symptom. 7. If there are no DTC's present after turning ignition on, road test the vehicle for at least 5 minutes. Perform several antilock braking stops. **8. Caution: Ensure braking capability is available before road testing.** 9. Again, with the DRBIII® read DTC's. If any DTC's are present, return to Symptom list. 10. If there are no Diagnostic Trouble Codes (DTC's) present, and the customer's complaint can no longer be duplicated, the repair is complete.

CR4020001960000X

Fig. 51 ABS Verification Test. 2000 Concorde, Intrepid, LHS & 300M

BODY VERIFICATION TEST - VER 1
1. Disconnect all jumper wires and reconnect all previously disconnected components and connectors. 2. If the Sentry Key Immobilizer Module (SKIM) or the Powertrain Control Module (PCM) were replaced, proceed to number 6. If the SKIM or PCM were not replaced, continue to the next number. 3. If the Body Control Module was replaced, turn the ignition on for 15 seconds (to learn VIN) or engine may not start (if VTSS equipped). If the vehicle is equipped with VTSS, use the DRB and enable VTSS. 4. Program all other options as needed. 5. If any repairs were made to the HVAC System, disconnect the battery or using the DRBIII, recalibrate the HVAC doors. Proceed to number 13. 6. Obtain the Vehicle's unique PIN number assigned to it's original SKIM module from the vehicle's invoice 7. With the DRBIII, select THEFT ALARM, SKIM, MISCELLANEOUS and select "Skim Module Replaced" function. Enter the 4 digit PIN number to put SKIM in "Access Mode". 8. The DRBIII will prompt you through the following steps. (1) Program the country code into the SKIM's memory. (2) Program the vehicle's VIN number into the SKIM's memory. (3) Transfer the vehicle's Secret Key data from the PCM. 9. Once secured access mode is active, the SKIM will remain in that mode for 60 seconds. 10. Using the DRBIII, program all customer keys into the SKIM's memory. This requires that the SKIM be in secured access mode, using the 4 digit code. 11. Note: If the PCM is replaced, the unique Secret Key data must be transfered from the SKIM to the PCM. This procedure requires the SKIM to be placed in secured access mode using the 4-digit code. 12. Note: If 3 attempts are made to enter secured access mode using an incorrect PIN, secured access mode will be locked out for 1 hour which causes the DRBIII to display "Bus +- Signals Open". To exit this mode, turn ignition to the "Run" pos. for 1 hour. 13. Ensure all accessories are turned off and the battery is fully charged. 14. Ensure that the Ignition is on, and with the DRBIII, record and erase all Diagnostic Trouble Codes from ALL modules. Start the engine and allow it to run for 2 minutes and fully operate the system that was malfunctioning. 15. Turn the ignition off and wait 5 seconds. Turn the ignition on and using the DRBIII, read DTC's from ALL modules. 16. If ANY codes are present select the appropriate symptom from the Symptom List and continue diagnostics. If NO codes are present and the customers complaint cannot be duplicated, the repair is complete.

CR4020001961000X

Fig. 52 Body Verification Test. 2000 Concorde, Intrepid, LHS & 300M

POWERTRAIN VERIFICATION TEST VER - 4
1. Inspect the vehicle to ensure that all engine components are properly installed and connected. Reassemble and reconnect components as necessary. 2. Connect the DRB to the data link connector and erase all codes. 3. If the PCM has been replaced, perform steps 4 through 6, then continue with the verification. 4. If PCM has been changed and correct VIN and mileage have not been programmed, a DTC will be set in ABS and Air bag modules. In addition, if vehicle is equipped with a Sentry Key Immobilizer Module (SKIM), Secret Key data must be updated to enable start. 5. For ABS and Air Bag systems: Enter correct VIN and Mileage in PCM. Erase codes in ABS and Air Bag modules. 6. For SKIM theft alarm: Connect DRB to data link conn. Go to Theft Alarm, SKIM, Misc. and place SKIM in secured access mode, by using the appropriate PIN code for this vehicle. Select Update the Secret Key data. Data will be transferred from SKIM to PCM. 7. Turn the speed control ON (if equipped, cruise light will be on). 8. Depress and release the SET Switch. If the speed control did not engage, the repair is not complete. Check for TSBs that pertain to speed control problem and then, if necessary, return to Symptom List. 9. Depress and hold the RESUME/ACCEL Switch. If the vehicle speed did not increase by at least 2 mph, the repair is not complete. Check for TSBs that pertain to speed control problem and then, if necessary, return to Symptom List. 10. Press and hold the COAST switch. The vehicle speed should decrease. If it did not decrease, the repair is not complete. Check for TSBs that pertain to speed control problem and then, if necessary, return to Symptom List. 11. Using caution, depress and release the brake pedal. If the speed control did not disengage, the repair is not complete. Check for TSBs that pertain to speed control problem and then, if necessary, return to Symptom List. 12. Bring the vehicle speed back up to 35 MPH. 13. Depress the RESUME/ACCEL switch. If the speed control did not resume the previously set speed, the repair is not complete. Check for TSBs that pertain to speed control problem and then, if necessary, return to Symptom List. 14. Hold down the SET switch. If the vehicle did not decelerate, the repair is not complete. Check for TSBs that pertain to speed control problem and then, if necessary, return to Symptom List. 15. Ensure vehicle speed is greater than 35 mph and release the SET Switch. If vehicle did not adjust and set a new vehicle speed, the repair is not complete. Check for TSBs that pertain to speed control problem and then, if necessary, return to Symptom List. 16. Depress and release the CANCEL switch. If the speed control did not disengage, the repair is not complete. Check for TSBs that pertain to speed control problem and then, if necessary, return to Symptom List. 17. Bring the vehicle speed back up above 35 mph and engage speed control. 18. Depress the OFF switch to turn OFF, (Cruise light will be off). If the speed control did not disengage, the repair is not complete. Check for TSBs that pertain to speed control problem and then, if necessary, return to Symptom List. 19. If the vehicle successfully passed all of the previous tests, the speed control system is now functioning as designed. The repair is now complete.

CR4020001962000X

Fig. 53 Powertrain Verification Test. 2000 Concorde, Intrepid, LHS & 300M

CLUSTER DTC PRESENT
INSTRUMENT CLUSTER BULB CONCERN
CAB DTC PRESENT
INSTRUMENT CLUSTER INTERNAL CONCERN

TEST	ACTION
1	Turn the ignition on. With the DRBIII®, read DTCs. Are there any Instrument Cluster DTCs present? Yes → Refer to the INSTRUMENT CLUSTER category for the related symptom(s). Perform ABS VERIFICATION TEST - VER 1. No → Go To 2
2	Turn the ignition off. Observe the instrument cluster indicators. Turn the ignition on. Did the ABS Indicator illuminate for several seconds? Yes → Go To 3 No → Replace the Instrument Cluster in accordance with the Service Information. Perform ABS VERIFICATION TEST - VER 1.
3	Turn the ignition on. **NOTE: The DRBIII® communication with the CAB must be operational for the result of this test to be valid.** With the DRBIII®, read DTCs. Are there any CAB DTCs present? Yes → Refer to BRAKES category for the related symptom(s). After repair of the CAB DTC, perform the ABS Verification Test. Perform ABS VERIFICATION TEST - VER 1. No → Go To 4
4	If there are no possible causes remaining, view repair. Repair Replace the Instrument Cluster in accordance with the Service Information. Perform ABS VERIFICATION TEST - VER 1.

CR4020002153000X

Fig. 54 ABS Warning Indicator. 2001–02 Concorde, Intrepid, 300M & 2001 LHS

TEST	ACTION
3	Turn the ignition off. Visually inspect the Fused B(+) Circuit in the wiring harness from the Junction Block to the CAB. Look for any sign of an intermittent short to ground. Is the wiring harness OK? Yes → Go To 4 No → Repair the Fused B(+) Circuit Shorted to Ground. Perform ABS VERIFICATION TEST - VER 1.
4	Turn the ignition off. Remove the ABS Fuse 17 from the Junction Block. Disconnect the CAB harness connector. **Note: Check connector - Clean/repair as necessary.** Using a test light connected to 12 volts, probe the Fused B(+) Circuit. Is the test light on? Yes → Repair the Fused B(+) Circuit Shorted to Ground. Perform ABS VERIFICATION TEST - VER 1. No → Go To 5
5	Turn the ignition off. Remove the ABS Fuse 17 from the Junction Block. The CAB must be connected for the results of this test to be valid. Using a test light connected to 12 volts, probe the Fused B(+) Circuit at the Junction Block fuse terminal. Is the test light on? Yes → Replace the CAB. Perform ABS VERIFICATION TEST - VER 1. No → Go To 6
6	Turn the ignition off. If there are no potential causes remaining, view repair. Repair Replace the Fuse. Perform ABS VERIFICATION TEST - VER 1.
7	Remove the ABS Fuse 17 from the Junction Block. Turn the ignition on. Measure the voltage of the Fused B+ supply to Fuse 17 in the Junction Block. Is the voltage above 10 volts? Yes → Go To 8 No → Repair the B+ Supply circuit for an open. Perform ABS VERIFICATION TEST - VER 1.
8	Turn the ignition off. Remove the ABS Fuse 17 from the Junction Block. Disconnect the CAB harness connector. **Note: Check connector - Clean/repair as necessary.** Measure the resistance of the Fused B(+) circuit between the Junction Block Fuse terminal 17 and the CAB connector. Is the resistance below 5 ohms? Yes → Go To 9 No → Repair Fused B(+) Circuit Open. Perform ABS VERIFICATION TEST - VER 1.

CR4020002154020X

Fig. 55 CAB Power Feed Circuit (Part 2 of 3). 2001–02 Concorde, Intrepid, 300M & 2001 LHS

When Monitored and Set Condition:

CAB POWER FEED CIRCUIT

When Monitored: Ignition on. The CAB monitors the Fused B(+) circuit at all times for proper system voltage.

Set Condition: If the Fused B(+) voltage is missing when the CAB detects that an internal main driver is not "on", the Diagnostic Trouble Code (DTC) is set.

INTERMITTENT DTC
BLOWN FUSE - FUSED B(+) CIRCUIT
NO B+ SUPPLY TO FUSE
FUSED B(+) CIRCUIT OPEN
FUSED B(+) CIRCUIT INTERMITTENTLY SHORTED TO GROUND
FUSED B(+) CIRCUIT SHORTED TO GROUND
CAB - FUSED B(+) CIRCUIT OPEN
CAB - FUSED B(+) CIRCUIT SHORTED TO GROUND

TEST	ACTION
1	Turn the ignition on. With the DRBIII®, erase DTC's. Turn the ignition off. Turn the ignition on. Drive the vehicle above 25 km/h (15 mph) for at least 10 seconds. Stop the vehicle. With the DRBIII®, read DTC's. Does the DRBIII® display CAB Power Feed Circuit DTC present right now? Yes → Go To 2 No → Go To 10
2	Turn the ignition off. Remove and Inspect the ABS Fuse 17 in the Junction Block. Is the Fuse blown? Yes → Go To 3 No → Go To 7

CR4020002154010X

Fig. 55 CAB Power Feed Circuit (Part 1 of 3). 2001–02 Concorde, Intrepid, 300M & 2001 LHS

TEST	ACTION
9	If there are no potential causes remaining, view repair. Repair Replace the CAB. Perform ABS VERIFICATION TEST - VER 1.
10	Turn the ignition off. Visually inspect the related wiring harness. Look for any chafed, pierced, pinched, or partially broken wires. Visually inspect the related wire harness connectors. Look for broken, bent, pushed out, or corroded terminals. Refer to any Hotline letters or Technical Service Bulletins that may apply. Were any problems found? Yes → Repair as necessary. Perform ABS VERIFICATION TEST - VER 1. No → Test Complete.

CR4020002154030X

Fig. 55 CAB Power Feed Circuit (Part 3 of 3). 2001–02 Concorde, Intrepid, 300M & 2001 LHS

When Monitored and Set Condition:

CONTROLLER FAILURE

When Monitored: Ignition on. The CAB monitors its internal microprocessors for correct operation.

Set Condition: If the CAB detects an internal fault, the DTC is set.

GROUND AND POWER CONNECTIONS
GROUND CIRCUIT HIGH RESISTANCE
GROUND CIRCUIT INTERFERENCE
CAB - INTERNAL FAILURE

TEST	ACTION
1	Inspect for non-factory wiring that may interfere with CAB power or ground circuits. Disconnect the CAB harness connector. Inspect the CAB wiring harness for incorrect routing and damage. Inspect the CAB harness and component connectors for corrosion and damage. Were any concerns found? Yes → Repair as necessary. Perform ABS VERIFICATION TEST - VER 1. No → Go To 2
2	Turn the ignition off. Disconnect the CAB harness connector. **Note: Check connector - Clean/repair as necessary.** Measure the resistance of the CAB ground circuits to body ground. Is the resistance below 1.0 ohm? Yes → Go To 3 No → Repair the Ground circuit high resistance. Perform ABS VERIFICATION TEST - VER 1.
3	Turn the ignition off. Disconnect the CAB harness connector. **Note: Check connector - Clean/repair as necessary.** Turn the ignition on. Turn on all accessories. Measure the voltage of the Ground circuit. Is the voltage below 1.0 volts? Yes → Go To 4 No → Repair as necessary. Unsplice any accessories connected to the CAB ground circuit. Reroute and shield any high voltage cables away from the CAB ground circuit. Perform ABS VERIFICATION TEST - VER 1.

CR4020002155010X

Fig. 56 Controller Failure (Part 1 of 2). 2001–02 Concorde, Intrepid, 300M & 2001 LHS

When Monitored and Set Condition:

LEFT FRONT SENSOR CIRCUIT FAILURE

When Monitored: Ignition on. The CAB monitors the wheel speed circuit every 7 milliseconds (ms).

Set Condition: If the CAB detects an open or shorted wheel speed sensor circuit, the Diagnostic Trouble Code (DTC) will set.

LEFT FRONT WHEEL SPEED SENSOR OR CONNECTOR DAMAGE
INTERMITTENT DTC
LEFT FRONT WHEEL SPEED SENSOR (+) CIRCUIT SHORTED TO GROUND
LEFT FRONT WHEEL SPEED SENSOR (-) CIRCUIT SHORTED TO GROUND
LEFT FRONT WHEEL SPEED SENSOR SHORTED TO GROUND
CAB - INTERNAL SHORT OR OPEN
LEFT FRONT WHEEL SPEED SENSOR (+) CIRCUIT OPEN
LEFT FRONT WHEEL SPEED SENSOR (-) CIRCUIT OPEN
LEFT FRONT WHEEL SPEED SENSOR (+) CIRCUIT SHORTED TO VOLTAGE
LEFT FRONT WHEEL SPEED SENSOR (-) CIRCUIT SHORTED TO VOLTAGE
LEFT FRONT WHEEL SPEED SENSOR CIRCUITS SHORT TOGETHER
LEFT FRONT WHEEL SPEED SENSOR RESISTANCE OUT OF SPECIFICATION

TEST	ACTION
1	Turn the ignition on. With the DRBIII®, read DTC's. With the DRBIII®, erase DTC's. Turn the ignition off. Turn the ignition on. With the DRBIII®, read DTC's. Does the DRBIII® display "Left Front Wheel Speed Sensor Circuit Failure" DTC present right now? Yes → Go To 2 No → Go To 14
2	Turn the ignition off. Inspect the Left Front Wheel Speed Sensor and Connector. Is the Sensor or Connector Damaged? Yes → Repair as necessary. Perform ABS VERIFICATION TEST - VER 1. No → Go To 3

CR4020002156010X

Fig. 57 Lefthand Front Sensor Circuit Failure (Part 1 of 4). 2001 Concorde, Intrepid, LHS & 300M

TEST	ACTION
4	If there are no potential causes remaining, view repair. Repair Replace the CAB. Perform ABS VERIFICATION TEST - VER 1.

CR4020002155020X

Fig. 56 Controller Failure (Part 2 of 2). 2001–02 Concorde, Intrepid, 300M & 2001 LHS

TEST	ACTION
3	Turn the ignition off. Disconnect the CAB connector. **Note: Check connector - Clean/repair as necessary.** Measure the resistance across the Left Front Wheel Speed Sensor (+) circuit and the Left Front Wheel Speed Sensor (-) circuit at the CAB connector. Is the resistance between 900 and 1,300 ohms? Yes → Go To 4 No → Go To 8
4	Turn the ignition off. Disconnect the Left Front Wheel Speed Sensor Connector. Disconnect the CAB Connector. Measure the resistance between the Left Front Wheel Speed Sensor (+) Circuit and ground. Is the resistance below 15,000 ohms? Yes → Repair the Left Front Wheel Speed Sensor (+) Circuit Short to Ground. Perform ABS VERIFICATION TEST - VER 1. No → Go To 5
5	Turn the ignition off. Disconnect the Left Front Wheel Speed Sensor Connector. **Note: Check connector - Clean/repair as necessary.** Disconnect the CAB Connector. **Note: Check connector - Clean/repair as necessary.** Measure the resistance between the Left Front Wheel Speed Sensor (-) Circuit and ground. Is the resistance below 15,000 ohms? Yes → Repair the Left Front Wheel Speed Sensor (-) Circuit Short to Ground. Perform ABS VERIFICATION TEST - VER 1. No → Go To 6
6	Turn the ignition off. Disconnect the Left Front Wheel Speed Sensor Connector. **Note: Check connector - Clean/repair as necessary.** On the component, measure the resistance between both of the Left Front Wheel Speed Sensor Terminals and ground. Is the resistance below 15,000 ohms? Yes → Replace the Left Front Wheel Speed Sensor. Perform ABS VERIFICATION TEST - VER 1. No → Go To 7
7	If there are no possible causes remaining, view repair. Repair Replace the CAB. Perform ABS VERIFICATION TEST - VER 1.

CR4020002156020X

Fig. 57 Lefthand Front Sensor Circuit Failure (Part 2 of 4). 2001 Concorde, Intrepid, LHS & 300M

TEST	ACTION
8	Turn the ignition off. Disconnect the Left Front Wheel Speed Sensor Connector. **Note: Check connector - Clean/repair as necessary.** Disconnect the CAB Connector. **Note: Check connector - Clean/repair as necessary.** Measure the resistance of the wheel speed sensor (+) circuit. Is the resistance below 5 ohms? Yes → Go To 9 No → Repair the Left Front Wheel Speed Sensor (+) Circuit Open. Perform ABS VERIFICATION TEST - VER 1.
9	Turn the ignition off. Disconnect the Left Front Wheel Speed Sensor Connector. **Note: Check connector - Clean/repair as necessary.** Disconnect the CAB Connector. **Note: Check connector - Clean/repair as necessary.** Measure the resistance of the Left Front Wheel Speed Sensor (-) circuit. Is the resistance below 5 ohms? Yes → Go To 10 No → Repair the Left Front Wheel Speed Sensor (-) Circuit Open. Perform ABS VERIFICATION TEST - VER 1.
10	Turn the ignition off. Disconnect the Left Front Wheel Speed Sensor connector. **Note: Check connector - Clean/repair as necessary.** Disconnect the CAB connector. **Note: Check connector - Clean/repair as necessary.** Turn the ignition on. Measure the voltage of the Left Front Wheel Speed Sensor (+) Circuit. Is the voltage above 1 volt? Yes → Repair Left Front Wheel Speed Sensor (+) Circuit Shorted to Voltage. Perform ABS VERIFICATION TEST - VER 1. No → Go To 11
11	Turn the ignition off. Disconnect the Left Front Wheel Speed Sensor connector. **Note: Check connector - Clean/repair as necessary.** Disconnect the CAB connector. **Note: Check connector - Clean/repair as necessary.** Turn the ignition on. Measure the voltage of the Left Front Wheel Speed Sensor (-) Circuit. Is the voltage above 1 volt? Yes → Repair Left Front Wheel Speed Sensor (-) Circuit Short to Voltage. Perform ABS VERIFICATION TEST - VER 1. No → Go To 12

CR4020002156030X

Fig. 57 Lefthand Front Sensor Circuit Failure (Part 3 of 4). 2001 Concorde, Intrepid, LHS & 300M

When Monitored and Set Condition:

LEFT FRONT SENSOR SIGNAL FAILURE

When Monitored: Wheel speed comparison is checked at drive off or every 7 milliseconds (ms). Sensor circuit continuity is checked every 7 milliseconds. Wheel speed phase length supervision is checked every 7 milliseconds.

Set Condition: If, during an ABS stop, the CAB commands any valve solenoid on for an extended length of time, and does not see a corresponding wheel speed change, the Diagnostic Trouble Code (DTC) is set. The DTC can also set if the signal is missing or erratic.

LEFT FRONT WHEEL SPEED SENSOR OR CONNECTOR DAMAGED
TONE WHEEL DAMAGED
LEFT FRONT WHEEL SPEED SENSOR AIR GAP OUT OF SPECIFICATION
LEFT FRONT WHEEL BEARING OUT OF SPECIFICATION
INTERMITTENT SIGNAL DTC

TEST	ACTION
1	Turn the ignition on. Using the DRBIII®, monitor the Left Front Wheel Speed Sensor while an assistant drives the vehicle. Slowly accelerate as straight as possible from a stop to 24 km/h (15 mph). With the DRBIII®, monitor all wheel speed sensors. Is Left Front WSS Signal 0 km/h (0 mph) or differing from others by more than 5 km/h (3 mph)? Yes → Go To 2 No → Go To 6
2	Turn the ignition off. Inspect the Left Front Wheel Speed Sensor and Connector. Is the Sensor or Connector Damaged? Yes → Repair as necessary. The vehicle must be driven at 24 km/h (15 mph) to extinguish ABS and TRAC ON indicators. Perform ABS VERIFICATION TEST - VER 1. No → Go To 3

CR4020002157010X

Fig. 58 Lefthand Front Sensor Signal Failure (Part 1 of 2). 2001 Concorde, Intrepid, LHS & 300M

TEST	ACTION
12	Turn the ignition off. Disconnect the CAB Connector. Disconnect the left front wheel speed sensor harness connector. Measure the resistance through the Wheel Speed Sensor (+) and (-) circuits at the CAB harness connector. Is the resistance below 200 ohms? Yes → Repair the Left Front Wheel Speed Sensor Circuits Shorted together. Perform ABS VERIFICATION TEST - VER 1. No → Go To 13
13	If there are no possible causes remaining, view repair. Repair Replace the Left Front Wheel Speed Sensor. Perform ABS VERIFICATION TEST - VER 1.
14	Turn the ignition off. Visually inspect the related wiring harness. Look for any chafed, pierced, pinched, or partially broken wires. Visually inspect the related wire harness component and in-line connectors. Look for broken, bent, pushed out, or corroded terminals. Refer to any Hotline letters or Technical Service Bulletins that may apply. Were any problems found? Yes → Repair as necessary. Perform ABS VERIFICATION TEST - VER 1. No → Test Complete.

CR4020002156040X

Fig. 57 Lefthand Front Sensor Circuit Failure (Part 4 of 4). 2001 Concorde, Intrepid, LHS & 300M

TEST	ACTION
3	Turn the ignition off. Inspect the Tone Wheel for damaged or missing teeth, cracks, or looseness. **Note: The Tone Wheel Teeth should be perfectly square, not bent or nicked.** Is the Tone Wheel OK? Yes → Go To 4 No → Replace the Tone Wheel. The vehicle must be driven at 24 km/h (15 mph) to extinguish ABS and TRAC ON indicators. Perform ABS VERIFICATION TEST - VER 1.
4	Turn the ignition off. Using a Feeler Gauge, measure the Wheel Speed Sensor Air Gap. **NOTE: The Air Gap should be checked in at least four places on the Tone Wheel.** Is the Air Gap between 0.42 mm - 1.71 mm (0.017" - 0.068")? Yes → Go To 5 No → Repair as necessary. The vehicle must be driven at 24 km/h (15 mph) to extinguish ABS and TRAC ON indicators. Perform ABS VERIFICATION TEST - VER 1.
5	Turn the ignition off. Inspect the wheel bearings for excessive runout or clearance. **Note: Refer to the appropriate service information, if necessary, for procedures or specifications.** Is the bearing clearance OK ? Yes → Test Complete. No → Repair as necessary. The vehicle must be driven at 24 km/h (15 mph) to extinguish ABS and TRAC ON indicators. Perform ABS VERIFICATION TEST - VER 1.
6	Turn the ignition off. Visually inspect wheel speed sensor. Visually inspect tone wheel. Visually inspect wiring harness. Visually inspect brakes for locking up due to lining contamination or overheating. Inspect all Components for defects which may cause a Signal DTC to set. Is any Component Damaged? Yes → Repair as necessary. The vehicle must be driven at 24 km/h (15 mph) to extinguish ABS and TRAC ON indicators. Perform ABS VERIFICATION TEST - VER 1. No → Test Complete.

CR4020002157020X

Fig. 58 Lefthand Front Sensor Signal Failure (Part 2 of 2). 2001 Concorde, Intrepid, LHS & 300M

When Monitored and Set Condition:

LEFT REAR SENSOR CIRCUIT FAILURE

When Monitored: Ignition on. The CAB monitors the wheel speed circuit every 7 milliseconds (ms).

Set Condition: If the CAB detects an open or shorted wheel speed sensor circuit, the Diagnostic Trouble Code (DTC) will set.

LEFT REAR WHEEL SPEED SENSOR OR CONNECTOR DAMAGE
LEFT REAR WHEEL SPEED SENSOR (+) CIRCUIT SHORTED TO GROUND
LEFT REAR WHEEL SPEED SENSOR (-) CIRCUIT SHORTED TO GROUND
LEFT REAR WHEEL SPEED SENSOR - SHORT TO GROUND
CAB - INTERNAL SHORT OR OPEN
LEFT REAR WHEEL SPEED SENSOR (+) CIRCUIT OPEN
LEFT REAR WHEEL SPEED SENSOR (-) CIRCUIT OPEN
LEFT REAR WHEEL SPEED SENSOR (+) CIRCUIT SHORTED TO VOLTAGE
LEFT REAR WHEEL SPEED SENSOR (-) CIRCUIT SHORTED TO VOLTAGE
LEFT REAR WHEEL SPEED SENSOR CIRCUITS SHORT TOGETHER
LEFT REAR WHEEL SPEED SENSOR RESISTANCE OUT OF SPECIFICATION
INTERMITTENT CIRCUIT DTC

TEST	ACTION
1	Turn the ignition on. With the DRBIII®, read DTC's. With the DRBIII®, erase DTC's. Turn the ignition off. Turn the ignition on. With the DRBIII®, read DTC's. Does the DRBIII® display LR Wheel Speed Sensor Circuit Failure DTC? Yes → Go To 2 No → Go To 14
2	Turn the ignition off. Inspect the Left Rear Wheel Speed Sensor and Connector. Is the Sensor or Connector Damaged? Yes → Repair as necessary. Perform ABS VERIFICATION TEST - VER 1. No → Go To 3

CR4020002158010X

Fig. 59 Lefthand Rear Sensor Circuit Failure (Part 1 of 4). 2001 Concorde, Intrepid, LHS & 300M

TEST	ACTION
8	Turn the ignition off. Disconnect the Left Rear Wheel Speed Sensor Connector. **Note: Check connector - Clean/repair as necessary.** Disconnect the CAB Connector. **Note: Check connector - Clean/repair as necessary.** Measure the resistance of the wheel speed sensor (+) circuit. Is the resistance below 5 ohms? Yes → Go To 9 No → Repair the Left Rear Wheel Speed Sensor (+) Circuit Open. Perform ABS VERIFICATION TEST - VER 1.
9	Turn the ignition off. Disconnect the Left Rear Wheel Speed Sensor Connector. **Note: Check connector - Clean/repair as necessary.** Disconnect the CAB Connector. **Note: Check connector - Clean/repair as necessary.** Measure the resistance of the Left Rear Wheel Speed Sensor (-) circuit. Is the resistance below 5 ohms? Yes → Go To 10 No → Repair the Left Rear Wheel Speed Sensor (-) Circuit Open. Perform ABS VERIFICATION TEST - VER 1.
10	Turn the ignition off. Disconnect the Left Rear Wheel Speed Sensor connector. **Note: Check connector - Clean/repair as necessary.** Disconnect the CAB connector. **Note: Check connector - Clean/repair as necessary.** Turn the ignition on. Measure the voltage of the Left Rear Wheel Speed Sensor (+) Circuit. Is the voltage above 1 volt? Yes → Repair Left Rear Wheel Speed Sensor (+) Circuit Shorted to Voltage. Perform ABS VERIFICATION TEST - VER 1. No → Go To 11
11	Turn the ignition off. Disconnect the Left Rear Wheel Speed Sensor connector. **Note: Check connector - Clean/repair as necessary.** Disconnect the CAB connector. **Note: Check connector - Clean/repair as necessary.** Turn the ignition on. Measure the voltage of the Left Rear Wheel Speed Sensor (-) Circuit. Is the voltage above 1 volt? Yes → Repair Left Rear Wheel Speed Sensor (-) Circuit Short to Voltage. Perform ABS VERIFICATION TEST - VER 1. No → Go To 12

CR4020002158030X

Fig. 59 Lefthand Rear Sensor Circuit Failure (Part 3 of 4). 2001 Concorde, Intrepid, LHS & 300M

TEST	ACTION
3	Turn the ignition off. Disconnect the CAB connector. **Note: Check connector - Clean/repair as necessary.** Measure the resistance across the Left Rear Wheel Speed Sensor (+) and (-) circuits at the CAB connector. Is the resistance between 900 and 1,300 ohms? Yes → Go To 4 No → Go To 8
4	Turn the ignition off. Disconnect the Left Rear Wheel Speed Sensor Connector. Disconnect the CAB Connector. Measure the resistance between the Left Rear Wheel Speed Sensor (+) Circuit and ground. Is the resistance below 15,000 ohms? Yes → Repair the Left Rear Wheel Speed Sensor (+) circuit Short to Ground. Perform ABS VERIFICATION TEST - VER 1. No → Go To 5
5	Turn the ignition off. Disconnect the Left Rear Wheel Speed Sensor Connector. **Note: Check connector - Clean/repair as necessary.** Disconnect the CAB Connector. **Note: Check connector - Clean/repair as necessary.** Measure the resistance between the Left Rear Wheel Speed Sensor (-) circuit and ground. Is the resistance below 15,000 ohms? Yes → Repair the Left Rear Wheel Speed Sensor (-) Circuit Short to Ground. Perform ABS VERIFICATION TEST - VER 1. No → Go To 6
6	Turn the ignition off. Disconnect the Left Rear Wheel Speed Sensor Connector. **Note: Check connector - Clean/repair as necessary.** Measure the resistance between ground and each of the Left Rear Wheel Speed Sensor circuits. Is the resistance below 15,000 ohms? Yes → Replace the Left Rear Wheel Speed Sensor. Perform ABS VERIFICATION TEST - VER 1. No → Go To 7
7	If there are no possible causes remaining, view repair. Repair Replace the CAB. Perform ABS VERIFICATION TEST - VER 1.

CR4020002158020X

Fig. 59 Lefthand Rear Sensor Circuit Failure (Part 2 of 4). 2001 Concorde, Intrepid, LHS & 300M

TEST	ACTION
12	Turn the ignition off. Disconnect the CAB Connector. Disconnect the Left Rear Wheel Speed Sensor harness connector. Measure the resistance through the Wheel Speed Sensor (+) and (-) circuits at the CAB harness connector. Is the resistance below 200 ohms? Yes → Repair the Left Rear Wheel Speed Sensor Circuits Shorted together. Perform ABS VERIFICATION TEST - VER 1. No → Go To 13
13	If there are no possible causes remaining, view repair. Repair Replace the Left Rear Wheel Speed Sensor. Perform ABS VERIFICATION TEST - VER 1.
14	Turn the ignition off. Visually inspect the related wiring harness. Look for any chafed, pierced, pinched, or partially broken wires. Visually inspect the related wire harness component and in-line connectors. Look for broken, bent, pushed out, or corroded terminals. Refer to any Hotline letters or Technical Service Bulletins that may apply. Were any problems found? Yes → Repair as necessary. Perform ABS VERIFICATION TEST - VER 1. No → Test Complete.

CR4020002158040X

Fig. 59 Lefthand Rear Sensor Circuit Failure (Part 4 of 4). 2001 Concorde, Intrepid, LHS & 300M

When Monitored and Set Condition:

LEFT REAR SENSOR SIGNAL FAILURE

When Monitored: Wheel speed comparison is checked at drive off or every 7 milliseconds (ms). Wheel speed circuit continuity is checked every 7 milliseconds. Wheel speed phase length supervision is checked every 7 milliseconds.

Set Condition: If, during an ABS stop, the CAB commands any valve solenoid on for an extended length of time, and does not see a corresponding wheel speed change, the Diagnostic Trouble Code (DTC) is set. The DTC can also set if the signal is missing or erratic.

LEFT REAR WHEEL SPEED SENSOR OR CONNECTOR DAMAGED
TONE WHEEL DAMAGED
LEFT REAR WHEEL SPEED SENSOR AIR GAP OUT OF SPECIFICATION
LEFT REAR WHEEL BEARING OUT OF SPECIFICATION
LEFT REAR WHEEL SPEED SENSOR INOPERATIVE
CAB - WON'T RESPOND TO LEFT REAR WHEEL SPEED SENSOR SIGNAL
INTERMITTENT SIGNAL DTC

TEST	ACTION
1	While an assistant drives the vehicle, monitor the Wheel Speed Sensors using the DRBIII®. Slowly accelerate as straight as possible from a stop to 24 km/h (15 mph). Is the Left Rear WSS Signal 0 km/h (0 mph) or differing from others by more than 5 km/h (3 mph)? Yes → Go To 2 No → Go To 7
2	Turn the ignition off. Inspect the Left Rear Wheel Speed Sensor and Connector. Is the Sensor or Connector Damaged? Yes → Repair as necessary. The vehicle must be driven at 24 km/h (15 mph) to extinguish ABS and TRAC ON indicators. Perform ABS VERIFICATION TEST - VER 1. No → Go To 3

CR4020002159010X

Fig. 60 Lefthand Rear Sensor Signal Failure (Part 1 of 3). 2001 Concorde, Intrepid, LHS & 300M

TEST	ACTION
7	Turn the ignition off. Visually inspect wheel speed sensor. Visually inspect tone wheel. Visually inspect wiring harness. Visually inspect brakes for locking up due to lining contamination or overheating. Inspect all Components for defects which may cause a Signal DTC to set. Is any Component Damaged? Yes → Repair as necessary. The vehicle must be driven at 24 km/h (15 mph) to extinguish ABS and TRAC ON indicators. Perform ABS VERIFICATION TEST - VER 1. No → Test Complete.

CR4020002159030X

Fig. 60 Lefthand Rear Sensor Signal Failure (Part 3 of 3). 2001 Concorde, Intrepid, LHS & 300M

TEST	ACTION
3	Turn the ignition off. Inspect the Tone Wheel for damaged or missing teeth, cracks, or looseness. **Note: The Tone Wheel Teeth should be perfectly square, not bent or nicked.** Is the Tone Wheel OK? Yes → Go To 4 No → Replace the Tone Wheel. The vehicle must be driven at 24 km/h (15 mph) to extinguish ABS and TRAC ON indicators. Perform ABS VERIFICATION TEST - VER 1.
4	Turn the ignition off. Using a Feeler Gauge, measure the Wheel Speed Sensor Air Gap. **NOTE: The Air Gap should be checked in at least four places on the Tone Wheel.** Is the Air Gap between 0.42 mm - 1.71 mm (0.017" - 0.068") ? Yes → Go To 5 No → Repair as necessary. The vehicle must be driven at 24 km/h (15 mph) to extinguish ABS and TRAC ON indicators. Perform ABS VERIFICATION TEST - VER 1.
5	Turn the ignition off. Inspect the wheel bearings for excessive runout or clearance. **Note: Refer to the appropriate service information, if necessary, for procedures or specifications.** Is the bearing clearance OK ? Yes → Go To 6 No → Repair as necessary. The vehicle must be driven at 24 km/h (15 mph) to extinguish ABS and TRAC ON indicators. Perform ABS VERIFICATION TEST - VER 1.
6	Turn the ignition off. Disconnect the CAB connector. Set up a voltmeter to measure AC voltage on the Left Rear Wheel Speed Sensor Signal Circuits at the CAB connector. Raise the left rear wheel off the ground. Quickly rotate the wheel by spinning the tire by hand. Measure the AC voltage on the Left Rear Wheel Speed Sensor (+) and (-) Signal Circuits. Does the voltage go above 650 millivolts as the wheel is rotated? Yes → Replace the CAB. The vehicle must be driven at 24 km/h (15 mph) to extinguish ABS and TRAC ON indicators. Perform ABS VERIFICATION TEST - VER 1. No → Replace the Left Rear Wheel Speed Sensor. The vehicle must be driven at 24 km/h (15 mph) to extinguish ABS and TRAC ON indicators. Perform ABS VERIFICATION TEST - VER 1.

CR4020002159020X

Fig. 60 Lefthand Rear Sensor Signal Failure (Part 2 of 3). 2001 Concorde, Intrepid, LHS & 300M

When Monitored and Set Condition:

LEFT FRONT SENSOR CIRCUIT FAILURE

When Monitored: Ignition on. The CAB monitors the wheel speed circuit every 7 milliseconds (ms).

Set Condition: If the CAB detects an open or shorted wheel speed sensor circuit, the Diagnostic Trouble Code (DTC) will set.

LEFT REAR SENSOR CIRCUIT FAILURE

When Monitored: Ignition on. The CAB monitors the wheel speed circuit every 7 milliseconds (ms).

Set Condition: If the CAB detects an open or shorted wheel speed sensor circuit, the Diagnostic Trouble Code (DTC) will set.

RIGHT FRONT SENSOR CIRCUIT FAILURE

When Monitored: Ignition on. The CAB monitors the wheel speed circuit every 7 milliseconds (ms).

Set Condition: If the CAB detects an open or shorted wheel speed sensor circuit, the Diagnostic Trouble Code (DTC) will set.

RIGHT REAR SENSOR CIRCUIT FAILURE

When Monitored: Ignition on. The CAB monitors the wheel speed circuit every 7 milliseconds (ms).

Set Condition: If the CAB detects an open or shorted wheel speed sensor circuit, the Diagnostic Trouble Code (DTC) will set.

POSSIBLE CAUSES
SENSOR OR CONNECTOR DAMAGE
WHEEL SPEED SENSOR FAULT
SENSOR CIRCUITS SHORTED OR OPEN

CR4020102292010X

Fig. 61 Lefthand Front, Lefthand Rear, Righthand Front & Righthand Rear Sensor Circuit Failure (Part 1 of 3). 2002 Concorde, Intrepid & 300M

POSSIBLE CAUSES
CAB - INTERNAL FAULT
INTERMITTENT CIRCUIT DTC

TEST	ACTION
1	Turn the ignition on. With the DRBIII®, record and erase DTC's. Turn the ignition off. Turn the ignition on. With the DRBIII®, read DTC's. Does the DRBIII® display a Wheel Speed Sensor Circuit Failure DTC? Yes → Go To 2 No → Go To 5
2	Turn the ignition off. Inspect the affected Wheel Speed Sensor and Connector. Is the Sensor or Connector Damaged? Yes → Repair as necessary. Perform ABS VERIFICATION TEST - VER 1. No → Go To 3
3	Turn the ignition off. Disconnect the affected Wheel Speed Sensor connector. **Note: Check connector - Clean/repair as necessary.** Turn the ignition on. Using a 12-volt test light connected to ground, check the Sensor 12 volt Supply circuit. Measure the resistance between ground and the Sensor Signal circuit. Was the test light bright and the resistance between 100 and 300 ohms? Yes → Replace the Wheel Speed Sensor Perform ABS VERIFICATION TEST - VER 1. No → Go To 4
4	Turn the ignition off. Disconnect the affected Wheel Speed Sensor connector. **Note: Check connector - Clean/repair as necessary.** Disconnect the CAB connector. **Note: Check connector - Clean/repair as necessary.** Turn the ignition on. Check the Wheel Speed Sensor 12 volt Supply and Signal circuits for a short to battery, ground, to each other and for an open. For the purposes of this test, a short to ground must be below 15k ohms. Was any circuit short or open found? Yes → Repair the Wheel Speed Sensor circuit short or open. Perform ABS VERIFICATION TEST - VER 1. No → Replace the Controller Antilock Brake Perform ABS VERIFICATION TEST - VER 1.

CR4020102292020X

Fig. 61 Lefthand Front, Lefthand Rear, Righthand Front & Righthand Rear Sensor Circuit Failure (Part 2 of 3). 2002 Concorde, Intrepid & 300M

When Monitored and Set Condition:

LEFT FRONT SENSOR SIGNAL FAILURE

When Monitored: Wheel speed comparison is checked at drive off or every 7 milliseconds (ms). Sensor signal continuity is checked every 7 milliseconds. Wheel speed phase length supervision is checked every 7 milliseconds.

Set Condition: If, during an ABS stop, the CAB commands any valve solenoid on for an extended length of time, and does not see a corresponding wheel speed change, the Diagnostic Trouble Code (DTC) is set. The DTC can also set if the signal is missing or erratic.

LEFT REAR SENSOR SIGNAL FAILURE

When Monitored: Wheel speed comparison is checked at drive off or every 7 milliseconds (ms). Wheel speed circuit continuity is checked every 7 milliseconds. Wheel speed phase length supervision is checked every 7 milliseconds.

Set Condition: If, during an ABS stop, the CAB commands any valve solenoid on for an extended length of time, and does not see a corresponding wheel speed change, the Diagnostic Trouble Code (DTC) is set. The DTC can also set if the signal is missing or erratic.

RIGHT FRONT SENSOR SIGNAL FAILURE

When Monitored: Wheel speed comparison is checked at drive off or every 7 milliseconds (ms). Wheel speed continuity is checked every 7 milliseconds. Wheel speed phase length supervision is checked every 7 milliseconds.

Set Condition: If, during an ABS stop, the CAB commands any valve solenoid on for an extended length of time, and does not see a corresponding wheel speed change, the Diagnostic Trouble Code (DTC) is set. The DTC can also set if the signal is missing or erratic.

CR4020102293010X

Fig. 62 Lefthand Front, Lefthand Rear, Righthand Front & Righthand Rear Sensor Signal Failure (Part 1 of 3). 2002 Concorde, Intrepid & 300M

TEST	ACTION
5	Turn the ignition off. Visually inspect the related wiring harness. Look for any chafed, pierced, pinched, or partially broken wires. Visually inspect the related wire harness connectors. Look for broken, bent, pushed out, or corroded terminals. Were any problems found? Yes → Repair as necessary. Perform ABS VERIFICATION TEST - VER 1. No → Test Complete.

CR4020102292030X

Fig. 61 Lefthand Front, Lefthand Rear, Righthand Front & Righthand Rear Sensor Circuit Failure (Part 3 of 3). 2002 Concorde, Intrepid & 300M

RIGHT REAR SENSOR SIGNAL FAILURE

When Monitored: Wheel speed comparison is checked at drive off or every 7 milliseconds (ms). Wheel speed circuit continuity is checked every 7 milliseconds. Wheel speed phase length supervision is checked every 7 milliseconds.

Set Condition: If, during an ABS stop, the CAB commands any valve solenoid on for an extended length of time, and does not see a corresponding wheel speed change, the Diagnostic Trouble Code (DTC) is set. The DTC can also set if the signal is missing or erratic.

POSSIBLE CAUSES
SENSOR OR TONE WHEEL CONCERN
SENSOR OUTPUT INTERMITTENT OR OPEN
CAB SETTING FALSE DTC
WHEEL SPEED SENSOR INOPERATIVE
INTERMITTENT SIGNAL DTC

TEST	ACTION
1	With the DRBIII®, erase DTCs. Turn the ignition off. Start the engine. With an assistant, drive the vehicle as straight as possible and maintain a steady speed above 24 km/h (15 mph). With the DRBIII®, monitor all wheel speed sensors. Note whether the speed of the affected wheel is zero. Note whether the speed of the affected wheel differs from others by 5 km/h (3 mph) or more. Is the affected wheel speed zero or differing from others? Yes → Go To 2 No → Go To 3
2	Inspect the Wheel Speed Sensor, Connector and Tone Wheel at the affected wheel. **NOTE: Inspect components for damage, correct installation and sensor/tone wheel air gap.** Are there any visible Sensor, Connector or Tone Wheel concerns? Yes → Correct the sensor, connector or tone wheel concern as necessary. The vehicle must be driven at 24 km/h (15 mph) to extinguish ABS and TRAC OFF indicators. Perform ABS VERIFICATION TEST - VER 1. No → Replace the Wheel Speed Sensor The vehicle must be driven at 24 km/h (15 mph) to extinguish ABS and TRAC OFF indicators. Perform ABS VERIFICATION TEST - VER 1.

CR4020102293020X

Fig. 62 Lefthand Front, Lefthand Rear, Righthand Front & Righthand Rear Sensor Signal Failure (Part 2 of 3). 2002 Concorde, Intrepid & 300M

TEST	ACTION
3	With the DRBIII®, read DTCs. Did the DTC reoccur? Yes → Replace the Controller Antilock Brake The vehicle must be driven at 24 km/h (15 mph) to extinguish ABS and TRAC OFF indicators. Perform ABS VERIFICATION TEST - VER 1. No → Go To 4
4	Turn the ignition off. Visually inspect wheel speed sensor. Visually inspect tone wheel. Visually inspect wiring harness. Visually inspect brakes for locking up due to lining contamination or overheating. Inspect all Components for defects which may cause a Signal DTC to set. Is any Component Damaged? Yes → Repair as necessary. The vehicle must be driven at 24 km/h (15 mph) to extinguish ABS and TRAC OFF indicators. Perform ABS VERIFICATION TEST - VER 1. No → Test Complete.

CR4020102293030X

Fig. 62 Lefthand Front, Lefthand Rear, Righthand Front & Righthand Rear Sensor Signal Failure (Part 3 of 3). 2002 Concorde, Intrepid & 300M

When Monitored and Set Condition:

PUMP MOTOR NOT WORKING PROPERLY

When Monitored: Ignition on. The CAB commands the pump on at 20 km/h (12 mph) to check its operation, if the brake switch is not applied. If the brake is applied, the test will run at 40 km/h (25 mph). The CAB monitors pump voltage every 7 milliseconds.

Set Condition: The DTC is stored when the CAB detects: 1) Improper voltage decay after the pump was turned off. 2) Pump not energized by the CAB, but voltage is present for 3.5 seconds. 3) Pump is turned on by the CAB, but without sufficient voltage to operate it.

CAB - PUMP MOTOR RUNNING CONTINUOUSLY
ABS PUMP MOTOR INTERMITTENT DTC
FUSED B(+) CIRCUIT INTERMITTENTLY SHORTED TO GROUND
FUSED B(+) CIRCUIT SHORTED TO GROUND
CAB - FUSED B(+) CIRCUIT SHORTED TO GROUND
FUSE BLOWN - PUMP MOTOR CIRCUIT
NO B+ SUPPLY TO FUSE
ABS PUMP MOTOR INOPERATIVE
FUSED B(+) CIRCUIT OPEN
GROUND CIRCUIT OPEN
GROUND CIRCUIT HIGH RESISTANCE
CAB - INTERNAL FAULT

TEST	ACTION
1	Turn the ignition off. Turn the ignition on. Monitor the pump motor for continuous operation. Is the pump motor running continuously? Yes → Replace the Controller Anti-Lock Brake in accordance with the Service Information. Perform ABS VERIFICATION TEST - VER 1. No → Go To 2

CR4020002161010X

Fig. 64 Pump Motor Not Working Properly (Part 1 of 4). 2001–02 Concorde, Intrepid, 300M & 2001 LHS

When Monitored and Set Condition:

PCI BUS COMMUNICATION

When Monitored: Ignition ON, every 7 ms.

Set Condition: When the CAB does not receive a message from the instrument cluster for 10 seconds.

CHECK COMMUNICATION TO MIC
CAB-- INTERNAL FAULT

TEST	ACTION
1	Turn the ignition on. With the DRBIII®, attempt to communicate with the MIC Was the DRB able to I/D or communicate with the MIC? Yes → Go To 2 No → Refer to the Communication category and perform the symptom Bus +/- Signals Open from the Controller Anti-Lock Brake. Perform ABS VERIFICATION TEST - VER 1.
2	With the DRB, erase DTC's. Turn the ignition on and wait approximately 1 minute. With the DRB, read DTC's. Did this DTC reset? Yes → Replace the Controller Anti-Lock Brake in accordance with the Service Information. Perform ABS VERIFICATION TEST - VER 1. No → Test Complete.

CR4020002160000X

Fig. 63 PCI Bus Communication. 2001–02 Concorde, Intrepid, 300M & 2001 LHS

TEST	ACTION
2	Turn the ignition on. With the DRBIII®, read DTC's. With the DRBIII®, erase DTC's. Turn the ignition off. Turn the ignition on. With the DRBIII®, actuate the ABS pump motor. Did the Pump Motor operate when actuated? No → Go To 3 Yes → Go To 14
3	Turn the ignition off. Remove and inspect the ABS Pump fuse K in the PDC. Is the Fuse blown? Yes → Go To 4 No → Go To 8
4	Turn the ignition off. Visually inspect the Fused B(+) Circuit in the wiring harness from the PDC to the CAB. Look for any sign of an Intermittent Short to Ground. Is the wiring harness OK? Yes → Go To 5 No → Repair the Fused B(+) Circuit shorted to ground. Perform ABS VERIFICATION TEST - VER 1.
5	Turn the ignition off. Remove the ABS PUMP Fuse K from the Power Distribution Center (PDC). Disconnect the CAB connector. **Note: Check connector - Clean/repair as necessary.** Using a test light connected to 12 volts, probe the Fused B (+) Circuit. Is the test light on? Yes → Repair the Fused B(+) circuit short to ground. Perform ABS VERIFICATION TEST - VER 1. No → Go To 6
6	Turn the ignition off. Remove the ABS PUMP Fuse K from the PDC. The CAB must be connected for the results of this test to be valid. Using a test light connected to 12 volts, probe the Fused B (+) circuit in the PDC. Is the test light on? Yes → Replace the Controller Anti-Lock Brake in accordance with the Service Information. Perform ABS VERIFICATION TEST - VER 1. No → Go To 7
7	Turn the ignition off. If there are no potential causes remaining, replace the Fuse. View repair options Repair Replace the ABS Pump Motor Fuse. Perform ABS VERIFICATION TEST - VER 1.

CR4020002161020X

Fig. 64 Pump Motor Not Working Properly (Part 2 of 4). 2001–02 Concorde, Intrepid, 300M & 2001 LHS

TEST	ACTION
8	Turn the ignition on. Using a 12-volt test light connected to ground, check the B+ supply to Fuse K in the PDC. Is the B+ supply OK? Yes → Go To 9 No → Repair the B+ supply for an open. Perform ABS VERIFICATION TEST - VER 1.
9	Turn the ignition off. Disconnect Pump Motor Connector. Connect a 10 gauge jumper wire between pump motor Fused B (+) circuit and a 40 Amp Fused B (+) circuit. Connect a 10 gauge jumper wire between pump motor ground circuit and a known good body ground. Monitor Pump Motor operation. Is the pump motor running? Yes → Go To 10 No → Replace the ABS Pump Motor/Hydraulic Control Unit assembly. Perform ABS VERIFICATION TEST - VER 1.
10	Turn the ignition off. Remove the ABS PUMP Fuse K from the Power Distribution Center (PDC). Disconnect the CAB connector. **Note: Check connector - Clean/repair as necessary.** Measure the resistance of the Fused B (+) circuit between the PDC Fuse Terminal and the CAB connector. Is the resistance below 10 ohms? Yes → Go To 11 No → Repair the Fused B(+) circuit for an open. Perform ABS VERIFICATION TEST - VER 1.
11	Turn the ignition off. Disconnect CAB Connector. **Note: Check connector - Clean/repair as necessary.** Measure the resistance of the CAB ground circuits. Is the resistance below 1.0 ohms? Yes → Go To 12 No → Repair the ground circuit circuit for an open. Perform ABS VERIFICATION TEST - VER 1.
12	Turn the ignition on. With the DRBIII®, enable pump motor actuation. **NOTE: Pump motor will not operate, but voltage will be applied.** Measure the voltage drop across the ABS ground circuit connection, with pump motor actuation enabled. Is the voltage below 0.1 volt? Yes → Go To 13 No → Repair the Ground circuit for an open. Perform ABS VERIFICATION TEST - VER 1.

CR4020002161030X

Fig. 64 Pump Motor Not Working Properly (Part 3 of 4). 2001–02 Concorde, Intrepid, 300M & 2001 LHS

When Monitored and Set Condition:

RIGHT FRONT SENSOR CIRCUIT FAILURE

When Monitored: Ignition on. The CAB monitors the wheel speed circuit every 7 milliseconds (ms).

Set Condition: If the CAB detects an open or shorted wheel speed sensor circuit, the Diagnostic Trouble Code (DTC) will set.

RIGHT FRONT WHEEL SPEED SENSOR OR CONNECTOR DAMAGE
INTERMITTENT DTC
RIGHT FRONT WHEEL SPEED SENSOR (+) CIRCUIT SHORTED TO GROUND
RIGHT FRONT WHEEL SPEED SENSOR (-) CIRCUIT SHORTED TO GROUND
RIGHT FRONT WHEEL SPEED SENSOR - SHORT TO GROUND
CAB - INTERNAL SHORT OR OPEN
RIGHT FRONT WHEEL SPEED SENSOR (+) CIRCUIT OPEN
RIGHT FRONT WHEEL SPEED SENSOR (-) CIRCUIT OPEN
RIGHT FRONT WHEEL SPEED SENSOR (+) CIRCUIT SHORTED TO VOLTAGE
RIGHT FRONT WHEEL SPEED SENSOR (-) CIRCUIT SHORTED TO VOLTAGE
RIGHT FRONT WHEEL SPEED SENSOR CIRCUITS SHORT TOGETHER
RIGHT FRONT WHEEL SPEED SENSOR RESISTANCE OUT OF SPECIFICATION

TEST	ACTION
1	Turn the ignition on. With the DRBIII®, read DTC's. With the DRBIII®, erase DTC's. Turn the ignition off. Turn the ignition on. With the DRBIII®, read DTC's. Does the DRBIII® display RF Wheel Speed Sensor Circuit Failure DTC? Yes → Go To 2 No → Go To 14
2	Turn the ignition off. Inspect the Right Front Wheel Speed Sensor and Connector. Is the Sensor or Connector Damaged? Yes → Repair as necessary. Perform ABS VERIFICATION TEST - VER 1. No → Go To 3

CR4020002162010X

Fig. 65 Righthand Front Sensor Circuit Failure (Part 1 of 4). 2001 Concorde, Intrepid & 300M

TEST	ACTION
13	If there are no potential causes remaining, view repair. Repair Replace the Controller Anti-Lock Brake in accordance with the Service Information. Perform ABS VERIFICATION TEST - VER 1.
14	Turn the ignition off. Visually inspect the related wiring harness. Look for any chafed, pierced, pinched, or partially broken wires. Visually inspect the related wire harness connectors. Look for broken, bent, pushed out, or corroded terminals. Refer to any Hotline letters or Technical Service Bulletins that may apply. Were any problems found? Yes → Repair as necessary. Perform ABS VERIFICATION TEST - VER 1. No → Test Complete.

CR4020002161040X

Fig. 64 Pump Motor Not Working Properly (Part 4 of 4). 2001–02 Concorde, Intrepid, 300M & 2001 LHS

TEST	ACTION
3	Turn the ignition off. Disconnect the CAB connector. **Note: Check connector - Clean/repair as necessary.** Measure the resistance across the Right Front Wheel Speed Sensor (+) and (-) circuits at the CAB connector. Is the resistance between 900 and 1,300 ohms? Yes → Go To 4 No → Go To 8
4	Turn the ignition off. Disconnect the Right Front Wheel Speed Sensor Connector. Disconnect the CAB Connector. Measure the resistance between the Right Front Wheel Speed Sensor (+) Circuit and ground. Is the resistance below 15,000 ohms? Yes → Repair the Right Front Wheel Speed Sensor (+) circuit Short to Ground. Perform ABS VERIFICATION TEST - VER 1. No → Go To 5
5	Turn the ignition off. Disconnect the Right Front Wheel Speed Sensor harness connector. **Note: Check connector - Clean/repair as necessary.** Disconnect the CAB Connector. **Note: Check connector - Clean/repair as necessary.** Measure the resistance between the Right Front Wheel Speed Sensor (-) circuit and ground. Is the resistance below 15,000 ohms? Yes → Repair the Right Front Wheel Speed Sensor (-) Circuit Short to Ground. Perform ABS VERIFICATION TEST - VER 1. No → Go To 6
6	Turn the ignition off. Disconnect the Right Front Wheel Speed Sensor harness connector. **Note: Check connector - Clean/repair as necessary.** On the sensor, measure the resistance between ground and both of the Right Front Wheel Speed Sensor terminals. Is the resistance below 15,000 ohms? Yes → Replace the Right Front Wheel Speed Sensor. Perform ABS VERIFICATION TEST - VER 1. No → Go To 7
7	If there are no possible causes remaining, view repair. Repair Replace the CAB. Perform ABS VERIFICATION TEST - VER 1.

CR4020002162020X

Fig. 65 Righthand Front Sensor Circuit Failure (Part 2 of 4). 2001 Concorde, Intrepid & 300M

TEST	ACTION
8	Turn the ignition off. Disconnect the Right Front Wheel Speed Sensor Connector. **Note: Check connector - Clean/repair as necessary.** Disconnect the CAB Connector. **Note: Check connector - Clean/repair as necessary.** Measure the resistance of the wheel speed sensor (+) circuit. Is the resistance below 5 ohms? Yes → Go To 9 No → Repair the Right Front Wheel Speed Sensor (+) Circuit Open. Perform ABS VERIFICATION TEST - VER 1.
9	Turn the ignition off. Disconnect the Right Front Wheel Speed Sensor Connector. **Note: Check connector - Clean/repair as necessary.** Disconnect the CAB harness connector C2. **Note: Check connector - Clean/repair as necessary.** Measure the resistance of the Right Front Wheel Speed Sensor (-) circuit. Is the resistance below 5 ohms? Yes → Go To 10 No → Repair the Right Front Wheel Speed Sensor (-) Circuit Open. Perform ABS VERIFICATION TEST - VER 1.
10	Turn the ignition off. Disconnect the Right Front Wheel Speed Sensor harness connector. **Note: Check connector - Clean/repair as necessary.** Disconnect the CAB harness connector C2. **Note: Check connector - Clean/repair as necessary.** Turn the ignition on. Measure the voltage of the Right Front Wheel Speed Sensor (+) Circuit. Is the voltage above 1 volt? Yes → Repair Right Front Wheel Speed Sensor (+) Circuit Shorted to Voltage. Perform ABS VERIFICATION TEST - VER 1. No → Go To 11
11	Turn the ignition off. Disconnect the Right Front Wheel Speed Sensor harness connector. **Note: Check connector - Clean/repair as necessary.** Disconnect the CAB harness connector C2. **Note: Check connector - Clean/repair as necessary.** Turn the ignition on. Measure the voltage of the Right Front Wheel Speed Sensor (-) Circuit. Is the voltage above 1 volt? Yes → Repair Right Front Wheel Speed Sensor (-) Circuit Short to Voltage. Perform ABS VERIFICATION TEST - VER 1. No → Go To 12

CR4020002162030X

Fig. 65 Righthand Front Sensor Circuit Failure (Part 3 of 4). 2001 Concorde, Intrepid & 300M

When Monitored and Set Condition:

RIGHT FRONT SENSOR SIGNAL FAILURE

When Monitored: Wheel speed comparison is checked at drive off or every 7 milliseconds (ms). Wheel speed continuity is checked every 7 milliseconds. Wheel speed phase length supervision is checked every 7 milliseconds.

Set Condition: If, during an ABS stop, the CAB commands any valve solenoid on for an extended length of time, and does not see a corresponding wheel speed change, the Diagnostic Trouble Code (DTC) is set. The DTC can also set if the signal is missing or erratic.

RIGHT FRONT WHEEL SPEED SENSOR OR CONNECTOR DAMAGED
TONE WHEEL DAMAGED
RIGHT FRONT WHEEL SPEED SENSOR AIR GAP OUT OF SPECIFICATION
RIGHT FRONT WHEEL BEARING OUT OF SPECIFICATION
RIGHT FRONT WHEEL SPEED SENSOR INOPERATIVE
CAB - WON'T RESPOND TO RIGHT FRONT WHEEL SPEED SENSOR SIGNAL
INTERMITTENT SIGNAL DTC

TEST	ACTION
1	While an assistant drives the vehicle, monitor the Wheel Speed Sensors using the DRBIII®. Slowly accelerate as straight as possible from a stop to 24 km/h (15 mph). Is the Right Front WSS Signal 0 km/h (0 mph) or differing from others by more than 5 km/h (3 mph)? Yes → Go To 2 No → Go To 7
2	Turn the ignition off. Inspect the Right Front Wheel Speed Sensor and Connector. Is the Sensor or Connector Damaged? Yes → Repair as necessary. The vehicle must be driven at 24 km/h (15 mph) to extinguish ABS and TRAC ON indicators. Perform ABS VERIFICATION TEST - VER 1. No → Go To 3

CR4020002163010X

Fig. 66 Righthand Front Sensor Signal Failure (Part 1 of 3). 2001 Concorde, Intrepid & 300M

TEST	ACTION
12	Turn the ignition off. Disconnect the CAB Connector. Disconnect the Right Front Wheel Speed Sensor harness connector. Measure the resistance through the Wheel Speed Sensor (+) and (-) circuits at the CAB harness connector. Is the resistance below 200 ohms? Yes → Repair the Right Front Wheel Speed Sensor Circuits Shorted together. Perform ABS VERIFICATION TEST - VER 1. No → Go To 13
13	If there are no possible causes remaining, view repair. Repair Replace the Right Front Wheel Speed Sensor. Perform ABS VERIFICATION TEST - VER 1.
14	Turn the ignition off. Visually inspect the related wiring harness. Look for any chafed, pierced, pinched, or partially broken wires. Visually inspect the related wire harness component and in-line connectors. Look for broken, bent, pushed out, or corroded terminals. Refer to any Hotline letters or Technical Service Bulletins that may apply. Were any problems found? Yes → Repair as necessary. Perform ABS VERIFICATION TEST - VER 1. No → Test Complete.

CR4020002162040X

Fig. 65 Righthand Front Sensor Circuit Failure (Part 4 of 4). 2001 Concorde, Intrepid & 300M

TEST	ACTION
3	Turn the ignition off. Inspect the Tone Wheel for damaged or missing teeth, cracks, or looseness. **Note: The Tone Wheel Teeth should be perfectly square, not bent or nicked.** Is the Tone Wheel OK? Yes → Go To 4 No → Replace the Tone Wheel. The vehicle must be driven at 24 km/h (15 mph) to extinguish ABS and TRAC ON indicators. Perform ABS VERIFICATION TEST - VER 1.
4	Turn the ignition off. Using a Feeler Gauge, measure the Wheel Speed Sensor Air Gap. **NOTE: The Air Gap should be checked in at least four places on the Tone Wheel.** Is the Air Gap between 0.42 mm - 1.71 mm (0.017" - 0.068")? Yes → Go To 5 No → Repair as necessary. The vehicle must be driven at 24 km/h (15 mph) to extinguish ABS and TRAC ON indicators. Perform ABS VERIFICATION TEST - VER 1.
5	Turn the ignition off. Inspect the wheel bearings for excessive runout or clearance. **Note: Refer to the appropriate service information, if necessary, for procedures or specifications.** Is the bearing clearance OK ? Yes → Go To 6 No → Repair as necessary. The vehicle must be driven at 24 km/h (15 mph) to extinguish ABS and TRAC ON indicators. Perform ABS VERIFICATION TEST - VER 1.
6	Turn the ignition off. Disconnect the CAB harness connector C2. Set up a voltmeter to measure AC voltage on the Right Front Wheel Speed Sensor Signal Circuits at the CAB connector. Raise the right front wheel off the ground. Quickly rotate the wheel by spinning the tire by hand. Measure the AC voltage on the Right Front Wheel Speed Sensor (+) and (-) Signal Circuits. Does the voltage go above 650 millivolts as the wheel is rotated? Yes → Replace the CAB. The vehicle must be driven at 24 km/h (15 mph) to extinguish ABS and TRAC ON indicators. Perform ABS VERIFICATION TEST - VER 1. No → Replace the Right Front Wheel Speed Sensor. The vehicle must be driven at 24 km/h (15 mph) to extinguish ABS and TRAC ON indicators. Perform ABS VERIFICATION TEST - VER 1.

CR4020002163020X

Fig. 66 Righthand Front Sensor Signal Failure (Part 2 of 3). 2001 Concorde, Intrepid & 300M

TEST	ACTION
7	Turn the ignition off. Visually inspect wheel speed sensor. Visually inspect tone wheel. Visually inspect wiring harness. Visually inspect brakes for locking up due to lining contamination or overheating. Inspect all Components for defects which may cause a Signal DTC to set. Is any Component Damaged? Yes → Repair as necessary. The vehicle must be driven at 24 km/h (15 mph) to extinguish ABS and TRAC ON indicators. Perform ABS VERIFICATION TEST - VER 1. No → Test Complete.

CR4020002163030X

Fig. 66 Righthand Front Sensor Signal Failure (Part 3 of 3). 2001 Concorde, Intrepid & 300M

TEST	ACTION
3	Turn the ignition off. Disconnect the CAB connector. **Note: Check connector - Clean/repair as necessary.** Measure the resistance across the Right Rear Wheel Speed Sensor (+) and (-) circuits at the CAB connector. Is the resistance between 900 and 1,300 ohms? Yes → Go To 4 No → Go To 8
4	Turn the ignition off. Disconnect the Right Rear Wheel Speed Sensor Connector. Disconnect the CAB Connector. Measure the resistance between the Right Rear Wheel Speed Sensor (+) Circuit and ground. Is the resistance below 15,000 ohms? Yes → Repair the Right Rear Wheel Speed Sensor (+) circuit Short to Ground. Perform ABS VERIFICATION TEST - VER 1. No → Go To 5
5	Turn the ignition off. Disconnect the Right Rear Wheel Speed Sensor Connector. **Note: Check connector - Clean/repair as necessary.** Disconnect the CAB Connector. **Note: Check connector - Clean/repair as necessary.** Measure the resistance between the Right Rear Wheel Speed Sensor (-) circuit and ground. Is the resistance below 15,000 ohms? Yes → Repair the Right Rear Wheel Speed Sensor (-) Circuit Short to Ground. Perform ABS VERIFICATION TEST - VER 1. No → Go To 6
6	Turn the ignition off. Disconnect the Right Rear Wheel Speed Sensor Connector. **Note: Check connector - Clean/repair as necessary.** Measure the resistance between ground and both of the Right Rear Wheel Speed Sensor circuits. Is the resistance below 15,000 ohms? Yes → Replace the Right Rear Wheel Speed Sensor. Perform ABS VERIFICATION TEST - VER 1. No → Go To 7
7	If there are no possible causes remaining, view repair. Repair Replace the CAB. Perform ABS VERIFICATION TEST - VER 1.

CR4020002164020X

Fig. 67 Righthand Rear Sensor Circuit Failure (Part 2 of 4). 2001 Concorde, Intrepid & 300M

When Monitored and Set Condition:

RIGHT REAR SENSOR CIRCUIT FAILURE

When Monitored: Ignition on. The CAB monitors the wheel speed circuit every 7 milliseconds (ms).

Set Condition: If the CAB detects an open or shorted wheel speed sensor circuit, the Diagnostic Trouble Code (DTC) will set.

RIGHT REAR WHEEL SPEED SENSOR OR CONNECTOR DAMAGE
INTERMITTENT DTC
RIGHT REAR WHEEL SPEED SENSOR (+) CIRCUIT SHORTED TO GROUND
RIGHT REAR WHEEL SPEED SENSOR (-) CIRCUIT SHORTED TO GROUND
RIGHT REAR WHEEL SPEED SENSOR - SHORT TO GROUND
CAB - INTERNAL SHORT OR OPEN
RIGHT REAR WHEEL SPEED SENSOR (+) CIRCUIT OPEN
RIGHT REAR WHEEL SPEED SENSOR (-) CIRCUIT OPEN
RIGHT REAR WHEEL SPEED SENSOR (+) CIRCUIT SHORTED TO VOLTAGE
RIGHT REAR WHEEL SPEED SENSOR (-) CIRCUIT SHORTED TO VOLTAGE
RIGHT REAR WHEEL SPEED SENSOR CIRCUITS SHORT TOGETHER
RIGHT REAR WHEEL SPEED SENSOR RESISTANCE OUT OF SPECIFICATION

TEST	ACTION
1	Turn the ignition on. With the DRBIII®, read DTC's. With the DRBIII®, erase DTC's. Turn the ignition off. Turn the ignition on. With the DRBIII®, read DTC's. Does the DRBIII® display RR Wheel Speed Sensor Circuit Failure DTC? Yes → Go To 2 No → Go To 14
2	Turn the ignition off. Inspect the Right Rear Wheel Speed Sensor and Connector. Is the Sensor or Connector Damaged? Yes → Repair as necessary. Perform ABS VERIFICATION TEST - VER 1. No → Go To 3

CR4020002164010X

Fig. 67 Righthand Rear Sensor Circuit Failure (Part 1 of 4). 2001 Concorde, Intrepid & 300M

TEST	ACTION
8	Turn the ignition off. Disconnect the Right Rear Wheel Speed Sensor Connector. **Note: Check connector - Clean/repair as necessary.** Disconnect the CAB Connector. **Note: Check connector - Clean/repair as necessary.** Measure the resistance of the wheel speed sensor (+) circuit. Is the resistance below 5 ohms? Yes → Go To 9 No → Repair the Right Rear Wheel Speed Sensor (+) Circuit Open. Perform ABS VERIFICATION TEST - VER 1.
9	Turn the ignition off. Disconnect the Right Rear Wheel Speed Sensor Connector. **Note: Check connector - Clean/repair as necessary.** Disconnect the CAB Connector. **Note: Check connector - Clean/repair as necessary.** Measure the resistance of the Right Rear Wheel Speed Sensor (-) circuit. Is the resistance below 5 ohms? Yes → Go To 10 No → Repair the Right Rear Wheel Speed Sensor (-) Circuit Open. Perform ABS VERIFICATION TEST - VER 1.
10	Turn the ignition off. Disconnect the Right Rear Wheel Speed Sensor connector. **Note: Check connector - Clean/repair as necessary.** Disconnect the CAB connector. **Note: Check connector - Clean/repair as necessary.** Turn the ignition on. Measure the voltage of the Right Rear Wheel Speed Sensor (+) Circuit. Is the voltage above 1 volt? Yes → Repair Right Rear Wheel Speed Sensor (+) Circuit Shorted to Voltage. Perform ABS VERIFICATION TEST - VER 1. No → Go To 11
11	Turn the ignition off. Disconnect the Right Rear Wheel Speed Sensor connector. **Note: Check connector - Clean/repair as necessary.** Disconnect the CAB connector. **Note: Check connector - Clean/repair as necessary.** Turn the ignition on. Measure the voltage of the Right Rear Wheel Speed Sensor (-) Circuit. Is the voltage above 1 volt? Yes → Repair Right Rear Wheel Speed Sensor (-) Circuit Short to Voltage. Perform ABS VERIFICATION TEST - VER 1. No → Go To 12

CR4020002164030X

Fig. 67 Righthand Rear Sensor Circuit Failure (Part 3 of 4). 2001 Concorde, Intrepid & 300M

TEST	ACTION
12	Turn the ignition off. Disconnect the CAB Connector. Disconnect the Right Rear Wheel Speed Sensor harness connector. Measure the resistance through the Wheel Speed Sensor (+) and (-) circuits at the CAB harness connector. Is the resistance below 200 ohms? Yes → Repair the Right Rear Wheel Speed Sensor Circuits Shorted together. Perform ABS VERIFICATION TEST - VER 1. No → Go To 13
13	If there are no possible causes remaining, view repair. Repair Replace the Right Rear Wheel Speed Sensor. Perform ABS VERIFICATION TEST - VER 1.
14	Turn the ignition off. Visually inspect the related wiring harness. Look for any chafed, pierced, pinched, or partially broken wires. Visually inspect the related wire harness component and in-line connectors. Look for broken, bent, pushed out, or corroded terminals. Refer to any Hotline letters or Technical Service Bulletins that may apply. Were any problems found? Yes → Repair as necessary. Perform ABS VERIFICATION TEST - VER 1. No → Test Complete.

CR4020002164040X

Fig. 67 Righthand Rear Sensor Circuit Failure (Part 4 of 4). 2001 Concorde, Intrepid & 300M

TEST	ACTION
3	Turn the ignition off. Inspect the Tone Wheel for damaged or missing teeth, cracks, or looseness. **Note: The Tone Wheel Teeth should be perfectly square, not bent or nicked.** Is the Tone Wheel OK? Yes → Go To 4 No → Replace the Tone Wheel. The vehicle must be driven at 24 km/h (15 mph) to extinguish ABS and TRAC ON indicators. Perform ABS VERIFICATION TEST - VER 1.
4	Turn the ignition off. Using a Feeler Gauge, measure the Wheel Speed Sensor Air Gap. **NOTE: The Air Gap should be checked in at least four places on the Tone Wheel.** Is the Air Gap between 0.42 mm - 1.71 mm (0.017" - 0.068") ? Yes → Go To 5 No → Repair as necessary. The vehicle must be driven at 24 km/h (15 mph) to extinguish ABS and TRAC ON indicators. Perform ABS VERIFICATION TEST - VER 1.
5	Turn the ignition off. Inspect the wheel bearings for excessive runout or clearance. **Note: Refer to the appropriate service information, if necessary, for procedures or specifications.** Is the bearing clearance OK ? Yes → Go To 6 No → Repair as necessary. The vehicle must be driven at 24 km/h (15 mph) to extinguish ABS and TRAC ON indicators. Perform ABS VERIFICATION TEST - VER 1.
6	Turn the ignition off. Disconnect the CAB connector. Set up a voltmeter to measure AC voltage on the Right Rear Wheel Speed Sensor Signal Circuits at the CAB connector. Raise the right rear wheel off the ground. Quickly rotate the wheel by spinning the tire by hand. Measure the AC voltage on the Right Rear Wheel Speed Sensor (+) and (-) Signal Circuits. Does the voltage go above 650 millivolts as the wheel is rotated? Yes → Replace the CAB. The vehicle must be driven at 24 km/h (15 mph) to extinguish ABS and TRAC ON indicators. Perform ABS VERIFICATION TEST - VER 1. No → Replace the Right Rear Wheel Speed Sensor. The vehicle must be driven at 24 km/h (15 mph) to extinguish ABS and TRAC ON indicators. Perform ABS VERIFICATION TEST - VER 1.

CR4020002165020X

Fig. 68 Righthand Rear Sensor Signal Failure (Part 2 of 3). 2001 Concorde, Intrepid & 300M

When Monitored and Set Condition:

RIGHT REAR SENSOR SIGNAL FAILURE

When Monitored: Wheel speed comparison is checked at drive off or every 7 milliseconds (ms). Wheel speed circuit continuity is checked every 7 milliseconds. Wheel speed phase length supervision is checked every 7 milliseconds.

Set Condition: If, during an ABS stop, the CAB commands any valve solenoid on for an extended length of time, and does not see a corresponding wheel speed change, the Diagnostic Trouble Code (DTC) is set. The DTC can also set if the signal is missing or erratic.

RIGHT REAR WHEEL SPEED SENSOR OR CONNECTOR DAMAGED
TONE WHEEL DAMAGED
RIGHT REAR WHEEL SPEED SENSOR AIR GAP OUT OF SPECIFICATION
RIGHT REAR WHEEL BEARING OUT OF SPECIFICATION
RIGHT REAR WHEEL SPEED SENSOR INOPERATIVE
CAB - WON'T RESPOND TO RIGHT REAR WHEEL SPEED SENSOR SIGNAL
INTERMITTENT SIGNAL DTC

TEST	ACTION
1	While an assistant drives the vehicle, monitor the Wheel Speed Sensors using the DRBIII®. Slowly accelerate as straight as possible from a stop to 24 km/h (15 mph). Is the Right Rear WSS Signal 0 km/h (0 mph) or differing from others by more than 5 km/h (3 mph)? Yes → Go To 2 No → Go To 7
2	Turn the ignition off. Inspect the Right Rear Wheel Speed Sensor and Connector. Is the Sensor or Connector Damaged? Yes → Repair as necessary. The vehicle must be driven at 24 km/h (15 mph) to extinguish ABS and TRAC ON indicators. Perform ABS VERIFICATION TEST - VER 1. No → Go To 3

CR4020002165010X

Fig. 68 Righthand Rear Sensor Signal Failure (Part 1 of 3). 2001 Concorde, Intrepid & 300M

TEST	ACTION	APPLICABILITY
7	Turn the ignition off. Visually inspect wheel speed sensor. Visually inspect tone wheel. Visually inspect wiring harness. Visually inspect brakes for locking up due to lining contamination or overheating. Inspect all Components for defects which may cause a Signal DTC to set. Is any Component Damaged? Yes → Repair as necessary. Perform ABS VERIFICATION TEST - VER 1. No → Test Complete.	All

CR4020002165030X

Fig. 68 Righthand Rear Sensor Signal Failure (Part 3 of 3). 2001 Concorde, Intrepid & 300M

When Monitored and Set Condition:

SYSTEM OVERVOLTAGE

When Monitored: Ignition on. The CAB monitors the Fused B(+) circuit at all times for proper system voltage.

Set Condition: If the voltage is above 16.5 volts for greater than 420 milliseconds (ms), the Diagnostic Trouble Code (DTC) is set.

BATTERY OVERCHARGED
FUSED IGNITION SWITCH OUTPUT HIGH
GROUND CIRCUIT OPEN
CAB - INTERNAL FAULT
INTERMITTENT DTC

TEST	ACTION
1	Turn the ignition on. With the DRBIII®, erase DTC's. Turn the ignition off. Turn the ignition on. Start the engine. With the DRBIII®, read DTC's. Does the DRBIII® display System Overvoltage DTC present right now? Yes → Go To 2 No → Go To 6
2	Turn the ignition off. Inspect for battery charger connected to battery. Is a battery charger connected to the battery? Yes → Charge battery to proper level. Disconnect the battery charger. Clear DTC's. Perform ABS VERIFICATION TEST - VER 1. No → Go To 3

CR4020002166010X

Fig. 69 System Overvoltage (Part 1 of 2). 2001–02 Concorde, Intrepid, 300M & 2001 LHS

TEST	ACTION	APPLICABILITY
3	Turn the ignition off. Disconnect the CAB connector. **Note: Check connector - Clean/repair as necessary.** Start the engine. Raise engine speed above 1,800 RPM. Measure the battery voltage. Is the voltage above 16.5 volts ? Yes → Refer to appropriate service information for charging system testing and repair. Perform ABS VERIFICATION TEST - VER 1. No → Go To 4	All
4	Turn the ignition off. Disconnect the CAB connector. **Note: Check connector - Clean/repair as necessary.** Measure the resistance of the ground circuits. Is the resistance below 1.0 ohm? Yes → Go To 5 No → Repair the Ground circuit for an open. Perform ABS VERIFICATION TEST - VER 1.	All
5	If there are no potential causes remaining, view repair. Repair Replace the Controller Antilock Brake. Perform ABS VERIFICATION TEST - VER 1.	All
6	Turn the ignition off. Visually inspect the related wiring harness. Look for any chafed, pierced, pinched, or partially broken wires. Visually inspect the related wire harness connectors. Look for broken, bent, pushed out, or corroded terminals. Refer to any Hotline letters or Technical Service Bulletins that may apply. Were any problems found? Yes → Repair as necessary. Perform ABS VERIFICATION TEST - VER 1. No → Test Complete.	All

CR4020002166020X

Fig. 69 System Overvoltage (Part 2 of 2). 2001–02 Concorde, Intrepid, 300M & 2001 LHS

TEST	ACTION
4	Disconnect the CAB harness connector. Turn the ignition on. Measure the voltage of the Fused Ignition Switch circuit. Is the voltage above 10 volts? Yes → Go To 5 No → Repair the Fused Ignition Switch Output Circuit for high resistance Perform ABS VERIFICATION TEST - VER 1.
5	If there are no potential causes remaining, view repair. Repair Replace the Controller Antilock Brake. Perform ABS VERIFICATION TEST - VER 1.
6	Turn the ignition off. Visually inspect the related wiring harness. Look for any chafed, pierced, pinched, or partially broken wires. Visually inspect the related wire harness connectors. Look for broken, bent, pushed out, or corroded terminals. Refer to any Hotline letters or Technical Service Bulletins that may apply. Were any problems found? Yes → Repair as necessary. Perform ABS VERIFICATION TEST - VER 1. No → Test Complete.

CR4020002167020X

Fig. 70 System Undervoltage (Part 2 of 2). 2001–02 Concorde, Intrepid, 300M & 2001 LHS

When Monitored and Set Condition:

SYSTEM UNDERVOLTAGE

When Monitored: Ignition on. The CAB monitors the Fused Ignition Switch Output circuit voltage above 10 km/h (6 mph) every 7 milliseconds for proper system voltage.

Set Condition: If the voltage is below 9.5 volts, the Diagnostic Trouble Code (DTC) is set.

BATTERY VOLTAGE LOW
INTERMITTENT DTC
FUSED IGNITION SWITCH OUTPUT CIRCUIT HIGH RESISTANCE
GROUND CIRCUIT OPEN
CAB - INTERNAL FAULT

TEST	ACTION
1	Turn the ignition on. With the DRBIII®, erase DTC's. Turn the ignition off. Turn the ignition on. Start the engine. Drive the vehicle above 16 Km/h (10 mph) for at least 20 seconds. Stop the vehicle With the DRBIII®, read DTC's. Does the DRBIII® display System Undervoltage DTC present right now? Yes → Go To 2 No → Go To 6
2	Engine Running. Measure the battery voltage. Is the battery voltage below 10 volts? Yes → Refer to appropriate service information for charging system testing and repair. Perform ABS VERIFICATION TEST - VER 1. No → Go To 3
3	Turn the ignition off. Disconnect the CAB connector. **Note: Check connector - Clean/repair as necessary.** Measure the resistance of the ground circuits. Is the resistance below 1.0 ohm? Yes → Go To 4 No → Repair the Ground circuit for an open. Perform ABS VERIFICATION TEST - VER 1.

CR4020002167010X

Fig. 70 System Undervoltage (Part 1 of 2). 2001–02 Concorde, Intrepid, 300M & 2001 LHS

CHECK BRAKE LAMP SWITCH OUTPUT
BRAKE LAMP SWITCH B+ OPEN
BRAKE LAMP SWITCH OUTPUT CIRCUIT SHORT OR OPEN
BRAKE LAMP SWITCH OPEN
CAB -- INTERNAL OPEN

TEST	ACTION
1	With the DRBIII® in Inputs/Outputs, read the Brake Lamp Switch state. Press and release the brake pedal. Does the DRBIII® display PRESSED and RELEASED? Yes → The Brake Lamp Switch is OK. Perform ABS VERIFICATION TEST - VER 1. No → Go To 2
2	Disconnect the Brake Lamp Switch harness connector. Using a 12-volt test light connected to ground, check the Brake Lamp Switch Fused B+ circuit. Does the test light illuminate brightly ? Yes → Go To 3 No → Repair the Brake Lamp Switch Fused B+ circuit for an open. Perform ABS VERIFICATION TEST - VER 1.
3	Disconnect the Brake Lamp Switch harness connector. Connect a jumper wire between the Brake Lamp Switch B+ and Output circuits. With the DRBIII® in Inputs/Outputs, read the Brake Lamp Switch state. Does the DRBIII® display PRESSED? Yes → Replace the Brake Lamp Switch in accordance with the Service Information. Perform ABS VERIFICATION TEST - VER 1. No → Go To 4
4	Disconnect the CAB harness connector. Disconnect the Brake Lamp Switch harness connector. Check the Brake Lamp Switch Output circuit for a short to voltage and an open. Is the Brake Lamp Switch Output circuit shorted or open? Yes → Repair the Brake Lamp Switch Output circuit for a short to voltage or an open. Perform ABS VERIFICATION TEST - VER 1. No → Replace the Controller Anti-Lock Brake in accordance with the Service Information. Perform ABS VERIFICATION TEST - VER 1.

CR4020002168000X

Fig. 71 Brake Lamp Switch. 2001–02 Concorde, Intrepid, 300M & 2001 LHS

INSTRUMENT CLUSTER FAILS BULB CHECK
TRAC OFF SWITCH GROUND OPEN
TRAC OFF SWITCH INOPERATIVE
CHECK TRAC OFF SWITCH
TRAC OFF SWITCH SENSE CIRCUIT SHORT TO B+, GROUND OR OPEN
INSTRUMENT CLUSTER INTERNAL FAULT

TEST	ACTION
1	**Note: If any DTC's are present, they must be repaired prior to performing this test.** Turn the ignition off. Turn the ignition on. Observe the TRAC OFF indicator. Did the TRAC OFF indicator come on for several seconds then go out? Yes → Go To 2 No → Replace the Instrument Cluster in accordance with the Service Information. Perform ABS VERIFICATION TEST - VER 1.
2	Turn the headlamps ON. Depress the TRAC OFF switch. Does the TRAC OFF switch button illuminate? Yes → Go To 3 No → Go To 5
3	Turn the ignition off. Disconnect the TRAC OFF Switch harness connector. Turn the ignition on. Connect and disconnect a jumper wire between TRAC OFF Switch Ground and TRAC OFF Switch Sense circuits. Does the TRAC OFF Indicator light and then go out? Yes → Replace the TRAC OFF switch. Perform ABS VERIFICATION TEST - VER 1. No → Go To 4

CR4020002169010X

Fig. 72 TRAC Off Indicator Never/Always On (Part 1 of 2). 2001–02 Concorde, Intrepid, 300M & 2001 LHS

PERFORM INSTRUMENT CLUSTER SELF TEST
CHECK TRACTION CONTROL OPERATION
RECHECK TRAC ON INDICATOR
CAB - NO TRAC ON INDICATOR

TEST	ACTION
1	**Note: The DRB must be able to communicate with the CAB module prior to performing this test.** **Note: If any CAB DTC's are present, they must be repaired prior to performing this test.** Perform the KEY-ON bulb test. Did the Trac On indicator illuminate and then go out? Yes → Go To 2 No → Refer to INSTRUMENT CLUSTER for the related symptom(s). Perform ABS VERIFICATION TEST - VER 1.
2	Make sure the Traction Control system has not been deactivated with the TRAC OFF switch. **NOTE: The purpose of this test is to determine if the Traction Control system is operating.** With the DRBIII® in Inputs/Outputs, read the ABS Pump Motor voltage state. Accelerate sufficient to cause drive wheel slip. Does the DRBIII® display approximately 9 volts? Yes → Go To 3 No → Replace the Controller Anti-Lock Brake Perform ABS VERIFICATION TEST - VER 1.
3	Replace the Instrument Cluster in accordance with the Service Information. Make sure the Traction Control system has not been deactivated with the TRAC OFF switch. **NOTE: The purpose of this test is to determine if replacing the Instrument Cluster has corrected the problem.** Accelerate sufficient to cause drive wheel slip. Does the TRAC ON indicator illuminate during Traction Control activation? Yes → Repair is complete. Perform ABS VERIFICATION TEST - VER 1. No → Replace the Controller Anti-Lock Brake Perform ABS VERIFICATION TEST - VER 1.

CR4020002170000X

Fig. 73 TRAC On Indicator Always/Never On. 2001–02 Concorde, Intrepid, 300M & 2001 LHS

TEST	ACTION
4	Turn the ignition off. Disconnect the TRAC OFF Switch harness connector. Disconnect the CAB harness connector. Check the TRAC OFF Switch Sense circuit for short to B+ or ground and for an open. Is the Sense circuit shorted or open? Yes → Repair the TRAC OFF Switch Sense circuit for a short to battery, ground or for an open. Perform ABS VERIFICATION TEST - VER 1. No → Replace the Instrument Cluster in accordance with the Service Information. Perform ABS VERIFICATION TEST - VER 1.
5	Disconnect the TRAC OFF switch harness connector. Using a 12-volt test light connected to 12-volts, check the TRAC OFF Switch Ground circuit. Does the test light illuminate? Yes → Replace the TRAC OFF Switch. Perform ABS VERIFICATION TEST - VER 1. No → Repair the TRAC OFF Switch Ground circuit for an open. Perform ABS VERIFICATION TEST - VER 1.

CR4020002169020X

Fig. 72 TRAC Off Indicator Never/Always On (Part 2 of 2). 2001–02 Concorde, Intrepid, 300M & 2001 LHS

ABS VERIFICATION TEST - VER 1
1. Turn the ignition off. 2. Connect all previously disconnected components and connectors. 3. Ensure all accessories are turned off and the battery is fully charged. 4. Ensure that the Ignition is on, and with the DRBIII, erase all Diagnostic Trouble Codes from ALL modules. Start the engine and allow it to run for 2 minutes and fully operate the system that was malfunctioning. 5. Turn the ignition off and wait 5 seconds. Turn the ignition on and using the DRBIII, read DTC's from ALL modules. 6. If any Diagnostic Trouble Codes are present, return to Symptom list and troubleshoot new or recurring symptom. 7. If there are no DTC's present after turning ignition on, road test the vehicle for at least 5 minutes. Perform several antilock braking stops. **8. Caution: Ensure braking capability is available before road testing.** 9. Again, with the DRBIII® read DTC's. If any DTC's are present, return to Symptom list. 10. If there are no Diagnostic Trouble Codes (DTC's) present, and the customer's concern can no longer be duplicated, the repair is complete. Are any DTC's present or is the original concern still present? Yes → Repair is not complete, refer to appropriate symptom. No → Repair is complete.

CR4020002171000X

Fig. 74 ABS Verification Test VER 1. 2001–02 Concorde, Intrepid, 300M & 2001 LHS

POSSIBLE CAUSES
INTERMITTENT CONDITION
ELECTRO-MECHANICAL INSTRUMENT CLUSTER DTC PRESENT
BUS CIRCUIT OPEN
CAB - INTERNAL FAILURE

TEST	ACTION
1	Turn the ignition on. With the DRBIII®, read DTCs. With the DRBIII®, read Freeze Frame information. With the DRBIII®, erase DTCs. Turn the ignition off. Turn the ignition on. With the DRBIII®, read DTCs. Does the DRBIII® display BUS SYSTEM COMMUNICATION FAILURE? Yes → Go To 2 No → Go To 4
2	Turn the ignition on. With the DRBIII®, read EMIC DTCs. Does the DRBIII® display NO MESSAGES FROM ABS? Yes → Refer to symptom NO MESSAGES FROM ABS Perform ABS VERIFICATION TEST No → Go To 3

CR4020202396000X

Fig. 75 BUS System Communication Failure (Part 1 of 2). 2003–04 Concorde, Intrepid & 300M

TEST	ACTION
3	Turn the ignition off. Disconnect the negative (-) battery cable. Disconnect the CAB harness connector. **NOTE: check connector - Clean/repair as necessary.** Measure the resistance of the Bus circuit between the CAB connector and the Data Link Connector (DLC). Is the resistance below 5.0 ohms? Yes → Replace the Controller Antilock Brake in accordance with the Service Information. Perform ABS VERIFICATION TEST No → Repair the Bus circuit for an open. Perform ABS VERIFICATION TEST
4	Turn the ignition off. Visually inspect the related wiring harness. Look for any chafed, pierced, pinched, or partially broken wires. Visually inspect the related wire harness connectors. Look for broken, bent, pushed out, or corroded terminals. Were any problems found? Yes → Repair as necessary. Perform ABS VERIFICATION TEST No → Test Complete.

CR4020202397000X

Fig. 75 BUS System Communication Failure (Part 2 of 2). 2003–04 Concorde, Intrepid & 300M

TEST	ACTION
3	Turn the ignition off. Disconnect the CAB harness connector. Using a 12-volt test light connected to 12-volts, probe the CAB harness connector ground circuits. Did the test light illuminate? Yes → Go To 4 No → Repair the CAB Ground circuit for an open. Perform ABS VERIFICATION TEST
4	Turn the ignition off. Using a 12-volt test light connected to ground, probe the ABS Valve Fused B(+) circuit at the CAB harness connector. Did the test light illuminate? Yes → Go To 5 No → Repair the ABS Valve Fused B(+) circuit for an open. Perform ABS VERIFICATION TEST
5	Turn the ignition off. Using a 12-volt test light connected to ground, probe the ABS Pump Fused B(+) circuit at the CAB harness connector. Did the test light illuminate? Yes → Replace the Controller Antilock Brake in accordance with the Service Information. Perform ABS VERIFICATION TEST No → Repair the ABS Pump Fused B(+) circuit for an open. Perform ABS VERIFICATION TEST
6	Turn the ignition off. Visually inspect the related wiring harness. Look for any chafed, pierced, pinched, or partially broken wires. Visually inspect the related wire harness connectors. Look for broken, bent, pushed out, or corroded terminals. Refer to any Technical Service Bulletins that may apply. Were any problems found? Yes → Repair as necessary. Perform ABS VERIFICATION TEST No → Test Complete.

CR4020202399000X

Fig. 76 CAB Internal Failure (Part 2 of 2). 2003–04 Concorde, Intrepid & 300M

POSSIBLE CAUSES
INTERMITTENT DTC
DAMAGED CAB/CAB HARNESS CONNECTOR
CAB - GROUND CIRCUIT OPEN
ABS VALVE FUSED B(+) CIRCUIT OPEN
ABS PUMP FUSED B(+) CIRCUIT OPEN
CAB - INTERNAL FAULT

TEST	ACTION
1	Turn the ignition on. With the DRBIII®, read DTCs. With the DRBIII®, erase DTCs. Turn the ignition off. Turn the ignition on. With the DRBIII®, read DTCs. Does the DRBIII® display CAB INTERNAL FAILURE? Yes → Go To 2 No → Go To 6
2	Turn the ignition off. Disconnect the CAB harness connector. Inspect the CAB/CAB harness connector for damage. Is ther any broken, bent, pushed out, corroded or spread terminals? Yes → Repair as necessary. Perform ABS VERIFICATION TEST - VER 1. No → Go To 3

CR4020202398000X

Fig. 76 CAB Internal Failure (Part 1 of 2). 2003–04 Concorde, Intrepid & 300M

POSSIBLE CAUSES
INSTRUMENT CLUSTER OR ABS DTC PRESENT
INSTRUMENT CLUSTER
CAB--NO DTC SIGNAL TO THE INSTRUMENT CLUSTER
CAB -- PERMANENT FAULT SIGNAL
CAB--NO KEY-ON BULB CHECK SIGNAL

TEST	ACTION
1	Turn the ignition on. With the DRBIII®, read DTCs. Are there any Instrument Cluster or ABS DTCs present? Yes → Refer to the appropriate category for the related symptom(s). Perform ABS VERIFICATION TEST No → Go To 2
2	Turn the ignition off. Perform the Key-on Bulb Check. Does the ABS Warning Indicator light and then go out after a few seconds? Yes → Go To 3 No. Light remains after bulb check. Replace the Controller Antilock Brake Perform ABS VERIFICATION TEST No. Indicator never comes on. Go To 4

CR4020202400000X

Fig. 77 Cluster Lamp Failure (Part 1 of 2). 2003–04 Concorde, Intrepid & 300M

TEST	ACTION
3	**NOTE: The DRBIII® communication with the CAB must be operational for the result of this test to be valid.** Turn the ignition off. Remove ABS Valve fuse. Perform the Key-on Bulb Check. Does the ABS Indicator remain on after the bulb check? Yes → Test Complete. No → Replace the Controller Antilock Brake Perform ABS VERIFICATION TEST
4	**NOTE: The following steps will initiate the Instrument Cluster self test.** Turn the ignition off. Press and hold the odometer reset button. Turn the ignition to RUN. Observe the Instrument Cluster indicators. Release the odometer reset button. Did the ABS Indicator illuminate during the Instrument Cluster self test? Yes → Replace the Controller Antilock Brake in accordance with the Service Information. Perform ABS VERIFICATION TEST No → Replace the Instrument Cluster Perform ABS VERIFICATION TEST

CR4020202401000X

Fig. 77 Cluster Lamp Failure (Part 2 of 2). 2003–04 Concorde, Intrepid & 300M

POSSIBLE CAUSES
INCORRECT TIRES ON VEHICLE
INCORRECT TONE WHEEL ON VEHICLE

TEST	ACTION
1	Inspect the tire sizes on the vehicle. Is a smaller than production tire, mini spare, or two mini spares installed on both front wheels? Yes → Replace the incorrect tire(s) size with production size tire(s). Perform ABS VERIFICATION TEST No → Go To 2
2	Count the number of tone wheel teeth on both of the front driveshafts. Does one or both tone wheel(s) have (56 or 40) teeth? Yes → Replace the front driveshaft(s) with the incorrect number of tone wheel teeth. Perform ABS VERIFICATION TEST No → Test Complete.

CR4020202402000X

Fig. 78 Incorrect Tone Wheel Failure. 2003–04 Concorde, Intrepid & 300M

POSSIBLE CAUSES
CAB - 12 VOLT SUPPLY CIRCUIT FAULT
CAB - SIGNAL CIRCUIT FAULT
WHEEL SPEED SENSOR 12 VOLT SUPPLY SHORT TO GROUND
WHEEL SPEED SENSOR SIGNAL CIRCUIT INOPERATIVE

TEST	ACTION
1	Turn the ignition on. With the DRBIII®, read DTCs. With the DRBIII®, read the Freeze Frame information. With the DRBIII®, erase DTCs. Turn the ignition off. Turn the ignition on. With the DRBIII®, read DTCs. **NOTE: The CAB must sense all four wheels at 25km/h (15 mph) before it will extinguish the ABS indicators.** Does the DRBIII® display SENSOR CIRCUIT FAILURE? Yes → Go To 2 No → Go To 13
2	Turn the ignition off. Inspect the CAB connector, affected Wheel Speed Sensor, and affected Wheel Speed Sensor connector. Is the affected Wheel Speed Sensor or any of the connectors damaged? Yes → Repair as necessary. Perform ABS VERIFICATION TEST No → Go To 3
3	Turn the ignition off. Disconnect the affected Wheel Speed Sensor connector. **Note: Check connector - Clean/repair as necessary.** Turn the ignition on. Measure the voltage between affected Wheel Speed Sensor 12 Volt Supply circuit and ground. Is the voltage above 10 volts? Yes → Go To 6 No → Go To 4
4	Turn the ignition off. Disconnect the CAB harness connector. Disconnect the affected Wheel Speed Sensor connector. Using a 12-volt test light connected to 12-volts, probe the affected Wheel Speed Sensor 12 Volt Supply circuit. Does the test light illuminate? Yes → Repair the affected Wheel Speed Sensor 12 Volt Supply circuit for a short to ground. Perform ABS VERIFICATION TEST No → Go To 5

CR4020202404000X

Fig. 79 Lefthand Front, Lefthand Rear, Righthand Front & Righthand Rear Sensor Circuit Failure (Part 2 of 5). 2003–04 Concorde, Intrepid & 300M

Test Note: All symptoms listed above are diagnosed using the same tests. The title for the tests will be LEFT FRONT SENSOR CIRCUIT FAILURE.

When Monitored and Set Condition:

LEFT FRONT SENSOR CIRCUIT FAILURE

When Monitored: Ignition on. The CAB monitors the wheel speed circuit continuously.

Set Condition: If the CAB detects an open or shorted wheel speed sensor circuit, the Diagnostic Trouble Code (DTC) will set.

LEFT REAR SENSOR CIRCUIT FAILURE

When Monitored: Ignition on. The CAB monitors the wheel speed circuit continuously.

Set Condition: If the CAB detects an open or shorted wheel speed sensor circuit, the Diagnostic Trouble Code (DTC) will set.

RIGHT FRONT SENSOR CIRCUIT FAILURE

When Monitored: Ignition on. The CAB monitors the wheel speed circuit continuously.

Set Condition: If the CAB detects an open or shorted wheel speed sensor circuit, the Diagnostic Trouble Code (DTC) will set.

RIGHT REAR SENSOR CIRCUIT FAILURE

When Monitored: Ignition on. The CAB monitors the wheel speed circuit continuously.

Set Condition: If the CAB detects an open or shorted wheel speed sensor circuit, the Diagnostic Trouble Code (DTC) will set.

POSSIBLE CAUSES
INTERMITTENT CONDITION
WHEEL SPEED SENSOR OR CONNECTOR DAMAGE
WHEEL SPEED SENSOR SIGNAL CIRCUIT FAULT
WHEEL SPEED SENSOR 12 VOLT SUPPLY CIRCUIT SHORT TO GROUND
WHEEL SPEED SENSOR 12 VOLT SUPPLY CIRCUIT OPEN
WHEEL SPEED SENSOR SIGNAL CIRCUIT SHORT TO GROUND
WHEEL SPEED SENSOR SIGNAL CIRCUIT OPEN

CR4020202403000X

Fig. 79 Lefthand Front, Lefthand Rear, Righthand Front & Righthand Rear Sensor Circuit Failure (Part 1 of 5). 2003–04 Concorde, Intrepid & 300M

TEST	ACTION
5	Turn the ignition off. Disconnect the CAB harness connector. Disconnect the affected Wheel Speed Sensor connector. Connect a jumper wire between affected Wheel Speed Sensor 12 Volt Supply circuit and ground. Using a 12-volt test light connected to 12-volts, probe the affected Wheel Speed Sensor 12 Volt Supply circuit. Does the test light illuminate? Yes → Go To 6 No → Repair the affected Wheel Speed Sensor 12 Volt Supply circuit for an open. Perform ABS VERIFICATION TEST
6	Turn the ignition off. Disconnect the affected Wheel Speed Sensor connector. **NOTE: Check connector - Clean/repair as necessary.** Turn the ignition on. Measure the voltage between affected Wheel Speed Sensor Signal circuit and ground. Is the voltage above 1 volt? Yes → Repair the affected Wheel Speed Sensor Signal circuit for a short to voltage. Perform ABS VERIFICATION TEST No → Go To 7
7	Turn the ignition off. Disconnect the CAB harness connector. Disconnect the affected Wheel Speed Sensor connector. Using a 12-volt test light connected to 12-volts, probe the affected Wheel Speed Sensor Signal circuit. Does the test light illuminate? Yes → Repair the affected Wheel Speed Sensor Signal circuit for a short to ground. Perform ABS VERIFICATION TEST No → Go To 8
8	Turn the ignition off. Disconnect the CAB harness connector. Disconnect the affected Wheel Speed Sensor connector. Connect a jumper wire between affected Wheel Speed Sensor Signal circuit and ground. Using a 12-volt test light connected to 12-volts, probe the affected Wheel Speed Sensor Signal circuit. Does the test light illuminate? Yes → Go To 9 No → Repair the affected Wheel Speed Sensor Signal circuit for an open. Perform ABS VERIFICATION TEST

CR4020202405000X

Fig. 79 Lefthand Front, Lefthand Rear, Righthand Front & Righthand Rear Sensor Circuit Failure (Part 3 of 5). 2003–04 Concorde, Intrepid & 300M

TEST	ACTION
9	Turn the ignition off. Remove the CAB harness strain relief to access wires. Reconnect the CAB harness connector. Turn the ignition on. Measure the voltage between affected Wheel Speed Sensor 12 Volt Supply circuit and ground. Is the voltage above 10 volts? Yes → Go To 10 No → Replace the Controller Antilock Brake Perform ABS VERIFICATION TEST
10	Turn the ignition off. Remove the CAB harness strain relief to access wires. Reconnect the CAB harness connector. Turn the ignition on. Measure the voltage between affected Wheel Speed Sensor 12 Volt Supply circuit and affected Wheel Speed Sensor Signal circuit. Is the voltage above 10 volts? Yes → Go To 11 No → Replace the Controller Antilock Brake Perform ABS VERIFICATION TEST
11	Turn the ignition off. Reconnect ALL affected Wheel Speed Sensor circuit connectors. Disconnect the affected Wheel Speed Sensor connector. Turn the ignition on. Measure the voltage of the affected Wheel Speed Sensor 12 Volt Supply circuit in the affected Wheel Speed Sensor connector while reconnecting the sensor connector. Did the affected Wheel Speed Sensor 12 Volt Supply circuit drop voltage to 0 DC volts? Yes → Replace the affected Wheel Speed Sensor Perform ABS VERIFICATION TEST No → Go To 12
12	Turn the ignition off. Reconnect ALL affected Wheel Speed Sensor circuit connectors. Turn the ignition on. Measure the DC voltage of the Wheel Speed Sensor Signal circuit in the affected Wheel Speed Sensor connector. Slowly rotate the wheel. Does the DC voltage toggle between 1.6 volts to .8 volts? Yes → Go To 13 No → Replace the affected Wheel Speed Sensor Perform ABS VERIFICATION TEST

CR4020202406000X

Fig. 79 Lefthand Front, Lefthand Rear, Righthand Front & Righthand Rear Sensor Circuit Failure (Part 4 of 5). 2003–04 Concorde, Intrepid & 300M

Test Note: All symptoms listed above are diagnosed using the same tests. The title for the tests will be LEFT FRONT WHEEL SPEED SIGNAL FAILURE.

When Monitored and Set Condition:

LEFT FRONT WHEEL SPEED SIGNAL FAILURE

When Monitored: Wheel speed comparison is checked and verified at drive off and continuously thereafter.

Set Condition: If, during an ABS stop, the CAB commands any valve solenoid on for an extended length of time, and does not see a corresponding wheel speed change, the Diagnostic Trouble Code (DTC) is set. The DTC can also set if the signal is missing or erratic.

LEFT REAR WHEEL SPEED SIGNAL FAILURE

When Monitored: Wheel speed comparison is checked and verified at drive off and continuously thereafter.

Set Condition: If, during an ABS stop, the CAB commands any valve solenoid on for an extended length of time, and does not see a corresponding wheel speed change, the Diagnostic Trouble Code (DTC) is set. The DTC can also set if the signal is missing or erratic.

RIGHT FRONT WHEEL SPEED SIGNAL FAILURE

When Monitored: Wheel speed comparison is checked and verified at drive off and continuously thereafter.

Set Condition: If, during an ABS stop, the CAB commands any valve solenoid on for an extended length of time, and does not see a corresponding wheel speed change, the Diagnostic Trouble Code (DTC) is set. The DTC can also set if the signal is missing or erratic.

RIGHT REAR WHEEL SPEED SIGNAL FAILURE

When Monitored: Wheel speed comparison is checked and verified at drive off and continuously thereafter.

Set Condition: If, during an ABS stop, the CAB commands any valve solenoid on for an extended length of time, and does not see a corresponding wheel speed change, the Diagnostic Trouble Code (DTC) is set. The DTC can also set if the signal is missing or erratic.

CR4020202408000X

Fig. 80 Lefthand Front, Lefthand Rear, Righthand Front & Righthand Rear Wheel Speed Signal Failure (Part 1 of 3). 2003–04 Concorde, Intrepid & 300M

TEST	ACTION
13	Turn the ignition off. Visually inspect the related wiring harness. Look for any chafed, pierced, pinched, or partially broken wires. Visually inspect the related wire harness connectors. Look for broken, bent, pushed out, or corroded terminals. Refer to any Technical Service Bulletins that may apply. Were any problems found? Yes → Repair as necessary. Perform ABS VERIFICATION TEST No → Test Complete.

CR4020202407000X

Fig. 79 Lefthand Front, Lefthand Rear, Righthand Front & Righthand Rear Sensor Circuit Failure (Part 5 of 5). 2003–04 Concorde, Intrepid & 300M

POSSIBLE CAUSES
WHEEL SPEED SIGNAL FAILURE DTC PRESENT
AFFECTED WHEEL SPEED SENSOR SIGNAL INOPERATIVE
AFFECTED WHEEL SPEED SENSOR CONNECTOR DAMAGED
AFFECTED WHEEL SPEED SENSOR TONE WHEEL DAMAGED
AFFECTED WHEEL SPEED SENSOR AIR GAP FAULT
WHEEL BEARING FAULT
BRAKE LINING FAULT
AFFECTED WHEEL SPEED SENSOR CIRCUIT ELECTRICAL FAULT

TEST	ACTION
1	Turn the ignition on. With the DRBIII®, read DTCs. With the DRBIII®, read Freeze Frame information. **NOTE: The CAB must sense ALL 4 wheels at 25 km/h (15 mph) before it will extinguish the ABS indicators.** Does the DRBIII® display WHEEL SPEED/SIGNAL FAILURE and SENSOR CIRCUIT FAILURE? Yes → Refer to the affected Wheel Speed SENSOR CIRCUIT FAILURE for the related symptom(s). Perform ABS VERIFICATION TEST - VER 1. No → Go To 2
2	Turn the ignition on. With the DRBIII® in Sensors, monitor ALL the Wheel Speed Sensor Signals while an assistant drives the vehicle. Slowly accelerate as straight as possible from a stop to 24 km/h (15 mph). Is the affected Wheel Speed Signal showing 0 km/h (0 mph)? Yes → Go To 3 No → The condition is not present at this time. Monitor DRBIII® parameters while wiggling the related wiring harness. Refer to any Technical Service Bulletins(TSB) that may apply. Visually inspect the related wiring harness and connector terminals. Perform ABS VERIFICATION TEST
3	Turn the ignition off. Inspect the CAB connector, affected Wheel Speed Sensor, and affected Wheel Speed Sensor connector. Is the Wheel Speed Sensor or any connector damaged? Yes → Repair as necessary. Perform ABS VERIFICATION TEST No → Go To 4

CR4020202409000X

Fig. 80 Lefthand Front, Lefthand Rear, Righthand Front & Righthand Rear Wheel Speed Signal Failure (Part 2 of 3). 2003–04 Concorde, Intrepid & 300M

TEST	ACTION
4	Turn ignition off. Inspect the affected Tone Wheel for damaged, missing teeth, cracks, or looseness **NOTE: The Tone Wheel teeth should be perfectly square, not bent, or nicked.** Is the affected Tone Wheel OK? Yes → Go To 5 No → Replace the Tone Wheel Perform ABS VERIFICATION TEST
5	Turn the ignition off. Using a Feeler Gauge, measure the affected Wheel Speed Sensor Air Gap. **NOTE: Refer to the appropriate service information, if necessary, for procedures or specifications.** Is the Air Gap OK? Yes → Go To 6 No → Repair as necessary. Perform ABS VERIFICATION TEST
6	Turn the ignition off. Inspect the wheel bearings for excessive runout or clearance. **NOTE: Refer to the appropriate service information, if necessary, for procedures or specifications.** Is the bearing clearance OK ? Yes → Go To 7 No → Repair as necessary. Perform ABS VERIFICATION TEST
7	Turn the ignition off. Visually inspect brakes for locking up due to lining contamination or overheating. Inspect all Components for defects which may cause a Signal DTC to set. Is any Component Damaged? Yes → Repair as necessary. Perform ABS VERIFICATION TEST No → Refer to symptom SENSOR CIRCUIT FAILURE for further diagnostics. Perform ABS VERIFICATION TEST

CR4020202410000X

Fig. 80 Lefthand Front, Lefthand Rear, Righthand Front & Righthand Rear Wheel Speed Signal Failure (Part 3 of 3). 2003–04 Concorde, Intrepid & 300M

TEST	ACTION
2	Turn the ignition off. Turn the ignition on. With the DRBIII®, read DTCs. With the DRBIII®, erase DTCs. Turn the ignition off. Turn the ignition on. With the DRBIII®, actuate the ABS Pump Motor. Did the ABS Pump Motor operate? Yes → Go To 3 No → Go To 4
3	Turn the ignition off. Visually inspect the related wiring harness. Look for any chafed, pierced, pinched, or partially broken wires. Make sure the Pump Motor connecter is secure. Visually inspect the related wire harness connectors. Look for broken, bent, pushed out, or corroded terminals. Refer to any or Technical Service Bulletins that may apply. Were any problems found? Yes → Repair as necessary. Perform ABS VERIFICATION TEST No → Test Complete.
4	Turn the ignition off. Remove and inspect the ABS Pump fuse. Is the ABS Pump fuse open? Yes → Go To 5 No → Go To 8
5	Turn the ignition off. Visually inspect the ABS Pump Fused B(+) circuit in the wiring harness. Look for any sign of an intermittent short to ground. Is the wiring harness OK? Yes → Go To 6 No → Repair the ABS Pump Fused B(+) circuit for a short to ground. Perform ABS VERIFICATION TEST
6	Turn the ignition off. Disconnect the CAB harness connector. Check connectors - Clean/repair as necessary. Using a 12-volt test light connected to 12-volts, probe the ABS Pump Fused B(+) circuit fuse terminal. Does the test light illuminate? Yes → Repair the ABS Pump Fused B(+) circuit for a short to ground. Perform ABS VERIFICATION TEST No → Go To 7

CR4020202412000X

Fig. 81 Pump Circuit Failure (Part 2 of 4). 2003–04 Concorde, Intrepid & 300M

POSSIBLE CAUSES
CAB - PUMP MOTOR RUNNING CONTINUOUSLY
ABS PUMP FUSE
ABS PUMP MOTOR INTERMITTENT DTC
DAMAGED CAB/CAB HARNESS CONNECTOR
ABS PUMP FUSED B(+) CIRCUIT INTERMITTENT SHORT TO GROUND
ABS PUMP FUSED B(+) CIRCUIT SHORT TO GROUND
CAB - INTERNAL FAULT
ABS PUMP MOTOR INOPERATIVE
ABS PUMP MOTOR OPEN
ABS PUMP MOTOR B(+) CIRCUIT OPEN
ABS PUMP MOTOR GROUND CIRCUIT OPEN
CAB - INTERNAL FAULT

TEST	ACTION
1	Turn the ignition off. Turn the ignition on. Monitor the ABS Pump Motor for continuous operation. **NOTE: The CAB must sense ALL wheels at 25 km/h (15 mph) before it will extinguish the ABS indicators.** Is the ABS Pump Motor running continuously? Yes → Replace the Controller Antilock Brake Perform ABS VERIFICATION TEST No → Go To 2

CR4020202411000X

Fig. 81 Pump Circuit Failure (Part 1 of 4). 2003–04 Concorde, Intrepid & 300M

TEST	ACTION
7	Turn the ignition off. Reconnect the CAB harness connector. Using a 12-volt test light connected to 12-volts, probe the ABS Pump Fused B(+) circuit fuse terminal. Does the test light illuminate? Yes → Replace the Controller Antilock Brake Perform ABS VERIFICATION TEST No → Replace the ABS Pump fuse. If the fuse is open make sure to check for a short to ground. Perform ABS VERIFICATION TEST
8	Turn the ignition off. Disconnect the CAB harness connector. Inspect the CAB and CAB harness connector for damage. Is there any broken, bent, pushed out, corroded, or spread terminals? Yes → Repair as necessary. Perform ABS VERIFICATION TEST No → Go To 9
9	Turn the ignition off. Reinstall the ABS Pump fuse. Disconnect the ABS Pump Motor connector. Check connectors - Clean/repair as necessary. Connect a 10 gauge 40 amp fused jumper wire between the ABS Pump Fused B(+) terminal in the CAB harness connector to the ABS Pump Motor connector RED wired terminal. Connect a 10 gauge jumper wire between the Ground circuit terminal in the CAB harness connector to the ABS Pump Motor connector BLACK wired terminal. Did the ABS Pump Motor operate? Yes → Replace the Controller Antilock Brake Perform ABS VERIFICATION TEST No → Go To 10
10	Turn the ignition off. Disconnect the ABS Pump Motor connector. Check connectors - Clean/repair as necessary. Connect a 10 gauge 40 amp fused jumper wire between the ABS Pump Motor connector RED wired terminal and an alternate 40 amp capable B(+) source. Connect a 10 gauge jumper wire between the ABS Pump Motor connector BLACK wired terminal and ground Did the ABS Pump Motor operate? Yes → Go To 11 No → Replace the Hydraulic Control Unit Perform ABS VERIFICATION TEST

CR4020202413000X

Fig. 81 Pump Circuit Failure (Part 3 of 4). 2003–04 Concorde, Intrepid & 300M

TEST	ACTION
11	Turn the ignition off. Disconnect the ABS Pump Motor connector. Check connectors - Clean/repair as necessary. Connect a 10 gauge 40 amp fused jumper wire between the ABS Pump Fused B(+) terminal in the CAB harness connector to the ABS Pump Motor connector RED wired terminal. Connect a 10 gauge jumper wire between the ABS Pump Motor connector BLACK wired terminal and ground. Did the ABS Pump Motor operate? Yes → Repair the ABS Pump Motor Fused B(+) circuit for an open. Perform ABS VERIFICATION TEST No → Repair the ABS Pump Motor Ground circuit for an open. Perform ABS VERIFICATION TEST

CR4020202414000X

Fig. 81 Pump Circuit Failure (Part 4 of 4). 2003–04 Concorde, Intrepid & 300M

TEST	ACTION
3	Turn the ignition off. Disconnect the CAB connector. **Note: Check connector - Clean/repair as necessary.** Start the engine. Raise engine speed above 1,800 RPM's Measure the voltage between Fused Ignition Switch Output (RUN) circuit and ground. Is the voltage above 16.5 volts ? Yes → Refer to appropriate service information for Charging System testing and repair. Perform ABS VERIFICATION TEST No → Go To 4
4	Turn the ignition off. Disconnect the CAB connector. **Note: Check connector - Clean/repair as necessary.** Inspect the CAB and CAB harness connector for damage. Is there any broken, bent, pushed out, corroded, or spread terminals? Yes → Repair as necessary. Perform ABS VERIFICATION TEST No → Go To 5
5	Turn the ignition off. Disconnect the CAB connector. **Note: Check connector - Clean/repair as necessary.** Using a 12-volt test light connected to 12-volts, probe the Ground circuits. Does the test light illuminate? Yes → Go To 6 No → Repair the Ground circuit for an open. Perform ABS VERIFICATION TEST
6	Turn the ignition off. Reconnect the CAB harness connector. Turn the ignition on. With the DRBIII® in Sensors, read the ignition voltage. Does the DRBIII® display ignition voltage above 16 volts? Yes → Replace the Controller Antilock Brake Perform ABS VERIFICATION TEST No → Go To 7

CR4020202416000X

Fig. 82 System Overvoltage (Part 2 of 3). 2003–04 Concorde, Intrepid & 300M

POSSIBLE CAUSES
INTERMITTENT DTC
BATTERY CHARGER CONNECTED
FUSED IGNITION SWITCH OUTPUT (RUN) CIRCUIT HIGH
DAMAGED CAB/CAB HARNESS CONNECTOR
CAB - GROUND CIRCUIT OPEN
CAB - INTERNAL FAULT

TEST	ACTION
1	Turn the ignition on. With the DRBIII®, read DTC's. With the DRBIII®, erase DTC's. Turn the ignition off. Turn the ignition on. Start the engine. With the DRBIII®, read DTC's. Does the DRBIII® display SYSTEM OVER VOLTAGE? Yes → Go To 2 No → Go To 7
2	Is a battery charger connected to the vehicle? Yes → Ensure the battery is fully charged. Perform ABS VERIFICATION TEST No → Go To 3

CR4020202415000X

Fig. 82 System Overvoltage (Part 1 of 3). 2003–04 Concorde, Intrepid & 300M

TEST	ACTION
7	Turn the ignition off. Visually inspect the related wiring harness. Look for any chafed, pierced, pinched, or partially broken wires. Visually inspect the related wire harness connectors. Look for broken, bent, pushed out, or corroded terminals. Refer to any or Technical Service Bulletins that may apply. Ensure the battery is fully charged. Inspect the vehicle for aftermarket accessories that may exceed the Generator System output. Using the wiring diagram/schematic as a guide, inspect the wiring and connectors. Were any problems found? Yes → Repair as necessary. Perform ABS VERIFICATION TEST No → Test Complete.

CR4020202417000X

Fig. 82 System Overvoltage (Part 3 of 3). 2003–04 Concorde, Intrepid & 300M

POSSIBLE CAUSES
INTERMITTENT DTC
DAMAGED CAB/CAB HARNESS CONNECTOR
RUNNING BATTERY VOLTAGE LOW
CAB - GROUND CIRCUIT OPEN
FUSED IGNITION SWITCH OUTPUT (RUN) CIRCUIT OPEN
CAB - INTERNAL FAULT

TEST	ACTION
1	Turn the ignition on. With the DRBIII®, read DTC's. With the DRBIII®, erase DTC's. Turn the ignition off. Turn the ignition on. Start the engine. Drive the vehicle above 16 km/h (10 mph) for at least 20 seconds. Stop the vehicle With the DRBIII®, read DTC's. Does the DRBIII® display SYSTEM UNDER VOLTAGE ? Yes → Go To 2 No → Go To 6
2	Engine Running. Measure the battery voltage. Is the battery voltage below 10 volts? Yes → Refer to appropriate service information for charging system testing and repair. Perform ABS VERIFICATION TEST No → Go To 3

CR4020202418000X

Fig. 83 System Undervoltage (Part 1 of 2). 2003–04 Concorde, Intrepid & 300M

TEST	ACTION
3	Turn the ignition off. Disconnect the CAB harness connector. Inspect the CAB and CAB harness connector for damage. Is there any broken, bent, pushed out, corroded, or spread terminals? Yes → Repair as necessary. Perform ABS VERIFICATION TEST No → Go To 4
4	Turn the ignition off. Disconnect the CAB harness connector. Using a 12-volt test light connected to 12-volts, probe the Ground circuits. Does the test light illuminate? Yes → Go To 5 No → Repair the Ground circuit for an open. Perform ABS VERIFICATION TEST
5	Turn the ignition on. Using a 12-volt test light connected to ground, probe the Fused Ignition Switch Output (RUN) circuit. Does the test light illuminate? Yes → Replace the Controller Antilock Brake Perform ABS VERIFICATION TEST No → Repair the Fused Ignition Switch Output (RUN) circuit for an open. Perform ABS VERIFICATION TEST
6	Turn the ignition off. Visually inspect the related wiring harness. Look for any chafed, pierced, pinched, or partially broken wires. Visually inspect the related wire harness connectors. Look for broken, bent, pushed out, or corroded terminals. Refer to any Technical Service Bulletins that may apply. Ensure the battery is fully charged. Inspect the vehicle for aftermarket accessories that may exceed the Generator System output. Using the wiring diagram/schematic as a guide, inspect the wiring and connectors. Were any problems found? Yes → Repair as necessary. Perform ABS VERIFICATION TEST No → Test Complete.

CR4020202419000X

Fig. 83 System Undervoltage (Part 2 of 2). 2003–04 Concorde, Intrepid & 300M

TEST	ACTION
3	Turn the ignition off. Visually inspect the ABS Valve Fused B(+) circuit in the wiring harness. Look for any sign of an intermittent short to ground. Is the wiring harness OK? Yes → Go To 4 No → Repair the ABS Valve Fused B(+) circuit for a short to ground. Perform ABS VERIFICATION TEST
4	Turn the ignition off. Disconnect the CAB harness connector. **Note: Check connector - Clean/repair as necessary.** Using a test light connected to 12 volts, probe the ABS Valve Fused B(+) circuit fuse terminal. Did the test light illuminate? Yes → Repair the ABS Valve Fused B(+) circuit for a short to ground. Perform ABS VERIFICATION TEST No → Go To 5
5	Turn the ignition off. Reconnect the CAB harness connector. **NOTE: The CAB harness connector must be reconnected for the results of this test to be valid.** Using a test light connected to 12 volts, probe the ABS Valve Fused B(+) circuit fuse terminal. Did the test light illuminate? Yes → Replace the Controller Antilock Brake Perform ABS VERIFICATION TEST No → Replace the ABS Valve Fused B(+) fuse. If the fuse is open make sure to check for a short to ground. Perform ABS VERIFICATION TEST
6	Turn the ignition off. Disconnect the CAB harness connector. Inspect the CAB and CAB harness connector for damage. Is there any broken, bent, pushed out, corroded or spread terminals? Yes → Repair as necessary. Perform ABS VERIFICATION TEST No → Go To 7
7	Turn the ignition off. Using a 12-volt test light connected to ground, probe the B(+) supply at the ABS Valve fuse terminal. Did the test light illuminate? Yes → Go To 8 No → Repair the ABS Valve Fused B(+) supply circuit for an open. Perform ABS VERIFICATION TEST

CR4020202421000X

Fig. 84 Valve Power Feed Failure (Part 2 of 3). 2003–04 Concorde, Intrepid & 300M

POSSIBLE CAUSES
INTERMITTENT DTC
ABS VALVE FUSE
ABS VALVE FUSED B(+) SUPPLY CIRCUIT OPEN
ABS VALVE FUSED B(+) CIRCUIT OPEN
ABS VALVE FUSED B(+) CIRCUIT INTERMITTENT SHORT TO GROUND
ABS VALVE FUSED B(+) CIRCUIT SHORT TO GROUND
DAMAGED CAB/CAB HARNESS CONNECTOR
CAB - GROUND CIRCUIT OPEN
CAB - INTERNAL FAULT

TEST	ACTION
1	Turn the ignition on. With the DRBIII®, read DTC's. With the DRBIII®, erase DTC's. Turn the ignition off. Turn the ignition on. With the DRBIII®, read DTC's. Does the DRBIII® display VALVE POWER FEED FAILURE? Yes → Go To 2 No → Go To 10
2	Turn the ignition off. Remove and Inspect the ABS Valve fuse. Is the ABS Valve fuse open? Yes → Go To 3 No → Go To 6

CR4020202420000X

Fig. 84 Valve Power Feed Failure (Part 1 of 3). 2003–04 Concorde, Intrepid & 300M

TEST	ACTION
8	Reinstall the ABS Valve fuse. Disconnect the CAB harness connector. Using a 12-volt test light connected to ground, probe the ABS Valve Fused B(+) circuit at the CAB harness connector. Did the test light illuminate? Yes → Go To 9 No → Repair the ABS Valve Fused B(+) circuit for an open. Perform ABS VERIFICATION TEST
9	Turn the ignition off. Using a 12-volt test light connected to 12-volts, probe the ground circuits at the CAB harness connector. Did the test light illuminate? Yes → Replace the Controller Antilock Brake Perform ABS VERIFICATION TEST No → Repair the CAB Ground circuit for an open. Perform ABS VERIFICATION TEST
10	Turn the ignition off. Visually inspect the related wiring harness. Look for any chafed, pierced, pinched, or partially broken wires. Visually inspect the related wire harness connectors. Look for broken, bent, pushed out, or corroded terminals. Refer to any Technical Service Bulletins that may apply. Were any problems found? Yes → Repair as necessary. Perform ABS VERIFICATION TEST No → Test Complete.

CR4020202422000X

Fig. 84 Valve Power Feed Failure (Part 3 of 3). 2003–04 Concorde, Intrepid & 300M

POSSIBLE CAUSES
CHECK BRAKE LAMP SWITCH OUTPUT
BRAKE LAMP SWITCH B+ OPEN
BRAKE LAMP SWITCH OPEN
BRAKE LAMP SWITCH OUTPUT CIRCUIT SHORT OR OPEN
CAB – INTERNAL OPEN

TEST	ACTION
1	With the DRBIII® in Inputs/Outputs, read the Brake Lamp Switch state. Press and release the brake pedal. Does the DRBIII® display PRESSED and RELEASED? Yes → The Brake Lamp Switch is OK. Perform ABS VERIFICATION TEST No → Go To 2
2	Disconnect the Brake Lamp Switch harness connector. Using a 12-volt test light connected to ground, check the Brake Lamp Switch Fused B+ circuit. Does the test light illuminate brightly ? Yes → Go To 3 No → Repair the Brake Lamp Switch Fused B+ circuit for an open. Perform ABS VERIFICATION TEST
3	Disconnect the Brake Lamp Switch harness connector. Connect a jumper wire between the Brake Lamp Switch B+ and Brake Lamp Switch Output circuits. With the DRBIII® in Inputs/Outputs, read the Brake Lamp Switch state. Does the DRBIII® display PRESSED? Yes → Replace the Brake Lamp Switch Perform ABS VERIFICATION TEST No → Go To 4
4	Disconnect the CAB harness connector. Disconnect the Brake Lamp Switch harness connector. Check the Brake Lamp Switch Output circuit for a short to voltage and for an open. Is the Brake Lamp Switch Output circuit shorted or open? Yes → Repair the Brake Lamp Switch Output circuit for a short to voltage or an open. Perform ABS VERIFICATION TEST No → Replace the Controller Antilock Brake Perform ABS VERIFICATION TEST

CR4020202423000X

Fig. 85 Brake Lamp Switch Inoperative. 2003–04 Concorde, Intrepid & 300M

TEST	ACTION
4	Turn the ignition off. Disconnect the TRAC OFF Switch harness connector. Disconnect the CAB harness connector. Check the TRAC OFF Switch Sense circuit for short to B+ or ground and for an open. Is the Sense circuit shorted or open? Yes → Repair the TRAC OFF Switch Sense circuit for a short to battery, ground or for an open. Perform ABS VERIFICATION TEST No → Replace the Instrument Cluster Perform ABS VERIFICATION TEST
5	Disconnect the TRAC OFF switch harness connector. Using a 12-volt test light connected to 12-volts, check the TRAC OFF Switch Ground circuit. Does the test light illuminate? Yes → Replace the TRAC OFF Switch. Perform ABS VERIFICATION TEST No → Repair the TRAC OFF Switch Ground circuit for an open. Perform ABS VERIFICATION TEST

CR4020202425000X

Fig. 86 TRAC OFF Indicator Never/Always On (Part 2 of 2). 2003–04 Concorde, Intrepid & 300M

POSSIBLE CAUSES
INSTRUMENT CLUSTER FAILS BULB CHECK
TRAC OFF SWITCH GROUND OPEN
TRAC OFF SWITCH INOPERATIVE
CHECK TRAC OFF SWITCH
TRAC OFF SWITCH SENSE CIRCUIT SHORT TO B+, GROUND OR OPEN
INSTRUMENT CLUSTER INTERNAL FAULT

TEST	ACTION
1	**Note: If any DTC's are present, they must be repaired prior to performing this test.** Turn the ignition off. Turn the ignition on. Observe the TRAC OFF indicator. Did the TRAC OFF indicator come on for several seconds then go out? Yes → Go To 2 No → Replace the Instrument Cluster Perform ABS VERIFICATION TEST
2	Turn the headlamps ON. Depress the TRAC OFF switch. Does the TRAC OFF switch button illuminate? Yes → Go To 3 No → Go To 5
3	Turn the ignition off. Disconnect the TRAC OFF Switch harness connector. Turn the ignition on. Connect and disconnect a jumper wire between TRAC OFF Switch Ground and TRAC OFF Switch Sense circuits. Does the TRAC OFF Indicator light and then go out? Yes → Replace the TRAC OFF switch. Perform ABS VERIFICATION TEST No → Go To 4

CR4020202424000X

Fig. 86 TRAC OFF Indicator Never/Always On (Part 1 of 2). 2003–04 Concorde, Intrepid & 300M

POSSIBLE CAUSES
FAILS KEY-ON BULB TEST
CHECK TRACTION CONTROL OPERATION
RECHECK TRAC ON INDICATOR
CAB - NO TRAC ON INDICATOR

TEST	ACTION
1	**NOTE: The DRBIII® must be able to communicate with the CAB prior to performing this test.** **Note: If any CAB DTC's are present, they must be repaired prior to performing this test.** Perform the KEY-ON bulb test. Did the Trac On indicator illuminate and then go out? Yes → Go To 2 No → Refer to INSTRUMENT CLUSTER for the related symptom(s). Perform ABS VERIFICATION TEST
2	Make sure the Traction Control system has not been deactivated with the TRAC OFF switch. **NOTE: The purpose of this test is to determine if the Traction Control system is operating.** With the DRBIII® in Inputs/Outputs, read the ABS Pump Motor voltage state. Accelerate sufficient to cause drive wheel slip. Does the DRBIII® display approximately 9 volts? Yes → Go To 3 No → Replace the Controller Anti-Lock Brake Perform ABS VERIFICATION TEST
3	Replace the Instrument Cluster Make sure the Traction Control system has not been deactivated with the TRAC OFF switch. **NOTE: The purpose of this test is to determine if replacing the Instrument Cluster has corrected the problem.** Accelerate sufficient to cause drive wheel slip. Does the TRAC ON indicator illuminate during Traction Control activation? Yes → Repair is complete. Perform ABS VERIFICATION TEST No → Replace the Controller Anti-Lock Brake Perform ABS VERIFICATION TEST

CR4020202426000X

Fig. 87 TRAC ON Indicator Never/Always ON. 2003–04 Concorde, Intrepid & 300M

POSSIBLE CAUSES
NO RESPONSE FROM CAB
REPLACE FUSE #17
FUSED IGNITION SWITCH OUTPUT CIRCUIT SHORTED TO GROUND
GROUND CIRCUIT OPEN
OPEN FUSED IGNITION SWITCH OUTPUT CIRCUIT
CONTROLLER ANTILOCK BRAKE (CAB) MODULE
PCI BUS CIRCUIT OPEN
BODY CONTROL MODULE

TEST	ACTION
1	Turn the ignition on. **Note: As soon as one or more module communicates with the DRB, answer the question.** With the DRB, attempt to communicate with the Airbag Control Module. With the DRB, attempt to communicate with the Body Control Module (BCM). Was the DRB able to I/D or establish communications with either of the modules? Yes → Go To 2 No → Refer to the Communications category and perform the symptom PCI Bus Communication Failure. Perform ABS VERIFICATION TEST
2	Turn the ignition off. Remove and inspect fuse #17 in the junction block. Is the fuse open? Yes → Go To 3 No → Go To 4
3	Turn the ignition off. Replace Fuse #17 in the junction block. Turn the ignition on. Remove and inspect fuse #17 in the junction block. Is the fuse open? Yes → Repair the Fused Ignition Switch Output circuit for a short to ground. Perform ABS VERIFICATION TEST No → Check the Fused Ignition Switch Output circuit for an intermittent short to ground. Perform ABS VERIFICATION TEST

CR4020202427000X

Fig. 88 No Response From Controller Anti-Lock Brake (Part 1 of 3). 2003–04 Concorde, Intrepid & 300M

TEST	ACTION
4	Turn the ignition off. Disconnect the CAB harness connector. Using a 12-volt test light connected to 12-volts, probe both ground circuits. Is the test light illuminated for both circuits? Yes → Go To 5 No → Repair the ground circuit(s) for an open. Perform ABS VERIFICATION TEST
5	Turn the ignition off. **NOTE: Ensure fuse #17 is installed in the junction block.** Disconnect the CAB harness connector. Turn the ignition on. Using a 12-volt test light connected to ground, probe the Fused Ignition Switch Output circuit. Is the test light illuminated? Yes → Go To 6 No → Repair the Fused Ignition Switch Output circuit for an open. Perform ABS VERIFICATION TEST
6	**Note: Ensure there is PCI Bus communication with other modules on the vehicle before proceeding. If not, refer to the symptom list from the menu and repair as necessary.** Disconnect the CAB harness connector. Use Scope input cable CH7058, Cable to Probe adapter CH7062, and the red and black test probes. Connect the scope input cable to the channel one connector on the DRB. Attach the red and black leads and the cable to probe adapter to the scope input cable. With the DRBIII® select Pep Module Tools. Select lab scope. Select Live Data. Select 12 volt square wave. Press F2 for Scope. Press F2 and use the down arrow to set voltage range to 20 volts. Set Probe to x10. Press F2 again when complete. Connect the Black lead to the chassis ground. Connect the Red lead to the PCI Bus circuit in the CAB connector. Turn the ignition on. Observe the voltage display on the DRB Lab Scope. Does the voltage pulse from 0 to approximately 7.5 volts? Yes → Replace the Controller Antilock Brake (CAB) Perform ABS VERIFICATION TEST No → Go To 7

CR4020202428000X

Fig. 88 No Response From Controller Anti-Lock Brake (Part 2 of 3). 2003–04 Concorde, Intrepid & 300M

TEST	ACTION
7	Turn the ignition off. Disconnect the CAB harness connector. Disconnect the BCM C3 harness connector. Measure the resistance of the PCI bus circuit between the CAB connector and the BCM C3 connector. Is the resistance below 5.0 ohms? Yes → Replace the Body Control Module Perform ABS VERIFICATION TEST No → Repair the PCI Bus circuit for an open. Perform ABS VERIFICATION TEST

CR4020202429000X

Fig. 88 No Response From Controller Anti-Lock Brake (Part 3 of 3). 2003–04 Concorde, Intrepid & 300M

ABS VERIFICATION TEST - VER 1
1. Turn the ignition off. 2. Connect all previously disconnected components and connectors. 3. Ensure all accessories are turned off and the battery is fully charged. 4. Ensure that the Ignition is on, and with the DRBIII, erase all Diagnostic Trouble Codes from ALL modules. Start the engine and allow it to run for 2 minutes and fully operate the system that was malfunctioning. 5. Turn the ignition off and wait 5 seconds. Turn the ignition on and using the DRBIII, read DTC's from ALL modules. 6. If any Diagnostic Trouble Codes are present, return to Symptom list and troubleshoot new or recurring symptom. **7. NOTE: For Sensor Signal and Pump Motor faults, the CAB must sense all 4 wheels at 25 km/h (15 mph) before it will extinguish the ABS Indicator.** 8. If there are no DTC's present after turning ignition on, road test the vehicle for at least 5 minutes. Perform several antilock braking stops. **9. Caution: Ensure braking capability is available before road testing.** 10. Again, with the DRBIII® read DTC's. If any DTC's are present, return to Symptom list. 11. If there are no Diagnostic Trouble Codes (DTC's) present, and the customer's concern can no longer be duplicated, the repair is complete. Are any DTC's present or is the original concern still present? Yes → Repair is not complete, refer to appropriate symptom. No → Repair is complete.

CR4020202430000X

Fig. 89 ABS Verification Test. 2003–04 Concorde, Intrepid & 300M

When Monitored: Ignition on. The CAB monitors the Fused B+ circuit at all times for proper system voltage.

Set Condition: If the Fused B+ voltage is missing when the CAB detects that an internal main driver is not "on", the Diagnostic Trouble Code (DTC) is set.

POSSIBLE CAUSES
INTERMITTENT DTC
FUSE BLOWN - FUSED B(+) CIRCUIT
FUSED B(+) CIRCUIT OPEN
FUSED B(+) CIRCUIT SHORTED TO GROUND
FUSED B(+) CIRCUIT INTERMITTENTLY SHORTED TO GROUND
CAB DEFECTIVE - FUSED B(+) CIRCUIT OPEN
CAB DEFECTIVE - FUSED B(+) CIRCUIT SHORTED TO GROUND

CR4020001982010X

Fig. 90 CAB Power Feed Circuit (Part 1 of 3). 2000 Neon

TEST	ACTION
1	Turn ignition on. With the DRBIII® erase DTC's. Turn ignition off. Turn ignition on. With the DRBIII® read DTC's. Is the CAB Power Feed Circuit DTC present? Yes → Go To 2 No → Go To 10
2	Turn ignition off. Remove and Inspect Fuse #5 in the PDC. Is the Fuse blown? Yes → Go To 3 No → Go To 8
3	Turn ignition off. Visually inspect the Fused B(+) Circuit in the wiring harness from the PDC to the CAB. Look for any sign of an intermittent short to ground. Is the wiring harness OK? Yes → Go To 4 No → Repair the Fused B(+) Circuit Shorted to Ground. Perform ABS VERIFICATION TEST.
4	Turn ignition off. Disconnect the #5 Fuse from the PDC. Disconnect the CAB connector. **Note: Check connector - Clean/repair as necessary.** Using a test light connected to 12 volts, probe the Fused B(+) Circuit. Is the test light on? Yes → Repair the Fused B(+) Circuit Shorted to Ground. Perform ABS VERIFICATION TEST. No → Go To 5
5	Turn ignition off. Disconnect the #5 Fuse from the PDC. Disconnect the CAB connector. **Note: Check connector - Clean/repair as necessary.** Measure the resistance of the Fused B(+) circuit. Is the resistance below 5 ohms? Yes → Go To 6 No → Repair Fused B(+) Circuit Open. Perform ABS VERIFICATION TEST.
6	Turn ignition off. Disconnect the #5 Fuse from the PDC. Using a test light connected to 12 volts, probe the Fused B(+) Circuit. Is the test light on? Yes → Replace the CAB. Perform ABS VERIFICATION TEST. No → Go To 7

CR4020001982020X

Fig. 90 CAB Power Feed Circuit (Part 2 of 3). 2000 Neon

TEST	ACTION
7	Turn ignition off. If there are no potential causes remaining, the Fuse is assumed to be defective. View repair options. Repair Replace the Fuse. Perform ABS VERIFICATION TEST.
8	Turn ignition off. Disconnect the #5 Fuse from the PDC. Disconnect the CAB connector. **Note: Check connector - Clean/repair as necessary.** Measure the resistance of the Fused B(+) circuit. Is the resistance below 5 ohms? Yes → Go To 9 No → Repair Fused B(+) Circuit Open. Perform ABS VERIFICATION TEST.
9	If there are no potential causes remaining, the CAB is assumed to be defective. View repair options. Repair Replace the CAB. Perform ABS VERIFICATION TEST.
10	Turn ignition off. Visually inspect the related wiring harness. Look for any chafed, pierced, pinched, or partially broken wires. Visually inspect the related wire harness connectors. Look for broken, bent, pushed out, or corroded terminals. Refer to Technical Service Bulletins that may apply. Were any problems found? Yes → Repair as necessary. Perform ABS VERIFICATION TEST. No → Test Complete.

CR4020001982030X

Fig. 90 CAB Power Feed Circuit (Part 3 of 3). 2000 Neon

When Monitored: Ignition on, every time a message is sent from the instrument cluster.

Set Condition: This DTC will be set when the message from the instrument cluster, via PCI Bus, informs the CAB that it can not turn on the ABS Warning Indicator or the Red Brake Warning Indicator.

POSSIBLE CAUSES
INTERMITTENT DTC

CR4020001983010X

Fig. 91 Cluster Fault (Part 1 of 2). 2000 Neon

TEST	ACTION
11	Turn ignition on. With the DRBIII®, try to communicate with the Mechanical Instrument Cluster (MIC), not the CAB module. Does the DRBIII® display "Bus +/- Signal Open? Yes → Refer to symptom BUS +/- SIGNALS OPEN FROM INSTRUMENT CLUSTER No → Go To 12
12	Turn ignition off. Visually inspect the related wiring harness. Look for any chafed, pierced, pinched, or partially broken wires. Visually inspect the related wire harness connectors. Look for broken, bent, pushed out, or corroded terminals. Refer to any Technical Service Bulletins that may apply. Were any problems found? Yes → Repair as necessary. Perform ABS VERIFICATION TEST. No → Test Complete.

CR4020001983020X

Fig. 91 Cluster Fault (Part 2 of 2). 2000 Neon

When Monitored: Ignition on. Two microprocessors, internal to the CAB, calculate the wheel speed independently of each other then compare the results.

Set Condition: If the values that each microprocessor calculate for wheel speed differ by more than 1.5% for more than 70 milliseconds (MS), the Diagnostic Trouble Code (DTC) is set.

POSSIBLE CAUSES
GROUND CIRCUIT CONNECTION POOR
GROUND CIRCUIT OPEN
CAB DEFECTIVE - GROUND CIRCUIT OPEN
GROUND CIRCUIT RADIO FREQUENCY INTERFERENCE

CR4020001984010X

Fig. 92 Controller Failure (Part 1 of 2). 2000 Neon

TEST	ACTION
13	Turn ignition on. With the DRBIII®, actuate the pump motor. Measure the voltage drop across the CAB ground circuit connection with the pump motor running. Is the voltage above 0.10 volts? Yes → Repair Ground Circuit Poor Connection. Perform ABS VERIFICATION TEST. No → Go To 14
14	Turn ignition off. Disconnect the CAB connector. **Note: Check connector - Clean/repair as necessary.** Measure the resistance of the ground circuits. Is the resistance below 1.0 ohm? Yes → Go To 15 No → Repair Ground Circuit Open. Perform ABS VERIFICATION TEST.
15	Turn ignition off. Disconnect the CAB connector. **Note: Check connector - Clean/repair as necessary.** Turn ignition on. Turn on all accessories. Measure the voltage of the ground circuit. Is the voltage below 1.0 volts? Yes → Go To 16 No → Repair as necessary. Perform ABS VERIFICATION TEST.
16	If there are no potential causes remaining, the CAB is assumed to be defective. View repair options. Repair Replace the CAB. Perform ABS VERIFICATION TEST.

CR4020001984020X

Fig. 92 Controller Failure (Part 2 of 2). 2000 Neon

When Monitored: Ignition on. The CAB monitors the wheel speed circuit every 7 milliseconds (ms).

Set Condition: If the CAB detects an open or shorted wheel speed sensor circuit, the Diagnostic Trouble Code (DTC) will set.

POSSIBLE CAUSES
LEFT FRONT WHEEL SPEED SENSOR 12 VOLT SUPPLY CIRCUIT OPEN
LEFT FRONT WHEEL SPEED SENSOR SIGNAL
LEFT FRONT WHEEL SPEED SENSOR SIGNAL CIRCUIT OPEN
LEFT FRONT WHEEL SPEED SENSOR 12 VOLT SUPPLY CIRCUIT SHORTED TO GROUND
LEFT FRONT WHEEL SPEED SENSOR DEFECTIVE - SHORTED TO GROUND
LEFT FRONT WHEEL SPEED SENSOR OR CONNECTOR DAMAGED
CAB DEFECTIVE - LEFT FRONT WHEEL SPEED SENSOR 12 VOLT SUPPLY OPEN
CAB DEFECTIVE - LEFT FRONT WHEEL SPEED SENSOR SIGNAL CIRCUIT OPEN
CAB DEFECTIVE - LEFT FRONT WHEEL SPEED SENSOR 12 VOLT SUPPLY SHORTED TO GROUND
CAB DEFECTIVE - LEFT FRONT WHEEL SPEED SIGNAL CIRCUIT SHORTED TO GROUND
CAB DEFECTIVE - UNABLE TO READ LEFT FRONT WHEEL SPEED SENSOR SIGNAL
LEFT FRONT WHEEL SPEED SENSOR SIGNAL CIRCUIT SHORTED TO GROUND
LEFT FRONT WHEEL SPEED SENSOR CIRCUITS SHORTED TOGETHER
LEFT FRONT WHEEL SPEED SENSOR SIGNAL SHORTED TO B(+)

CR4020001985010X

Fig. 93 Lefthand Front Sensor Circuit Failure (Part 1 of 5). 2000 Neon

TEST	ACTION
17	Turn ignition on. With the DRBIII®, read DTC's. With the DRBIII® erase DTC's. Turn ignition off. Turn ignition on. With the DRBIII® read DTC's. Is the Left Front Wheel Speed Sensor Circuit Failure DTC present? Yes → Go To 18 No → Go To 33
18	Turn ignition off. Disconnect the Left Front Wheel Speed Sensor connector. **Note: Check connector - Clean/repair as necessary.** Turn ignition on. Measure the voltage across the Left Front Wheel Speed Sensor 12 Volt Supply circuit and the Left Front Wheel Speed Sensor Signal circuit in the Left Front Wheel Speed Sensor connector. Is the voltage above 10 volts? Yes → Go To 19 No → Go To 23
19	Turn ignition off. Inspect the Left Front Wheel Speed Sensor and Connector. Is the Sensor or Connector Damaged? Yes → Repair as necessary. Perform ABS VERIFICATION TEST. No → Go To 20
20	Turn ignition off. Disconnect the CAB Connector. **Note: Check connector - Clean/repair as necessary.** Remove harness strain relief to access wires in CAB connector for backprobing. Using a voltmeter in Direct Current (DC) mode, and special tool 6801, backprobe the Left Front Wheel Speed Sensor Signal circuit at CAB. Reconnect the CAB connector. Turn ignition on. Slowly rotate the wheel while observing voltmeter reading. Does the voltage change from approximately 1.6 volts to 0.8 volts as the wheel is rotated? Yes → Go To 21 No → Replace the Left Front Wheel Speed Sensor. Perform ABS VERIFICATION TEST.
21	Turn ignition off. Disconnect the Left Front Wheel Speed Sensor Connector. **Note: Check connector - Clean/repair as necessary.** Measure the resistance between both of the Left Front Wheel Speed Sensor Terminals and ground. Is the resistance below 15,000 ohms? Yes → Replace the Left Front Wheel Speed Sensor. Perform ABS VERIFICATION TEST. No → Go To 22

CR4020001985020X

Fig. 93 Lefthand Front Sensor Circuit Failure (Part 2 of 5). 2000 Neon

TEST	ACTION
22	If there are no potential causes remaining, the CAB is assumed to be defective. View repair options. Repair Replace the CAB. Perform ABS VERIFICATION TEST.
23	Turn ignition off. Disconnect the Left Front Wheel Speed Sensor Connector. **Note: Check connector - Clean/repair as necessary.** Disconnect the CAB Connector. **Note: Check connector - Clean/repair as necessary.** Connect a jumper wire between the Left Front Wheel Speed Sensor 12 Volt Supply Circuit and ground. Measure the resistance between the Left Front Wheel Speed Sensor 12 Volt Supply Circuit and ground. Is the resistance below 5 ohms? Yes → Go To 24 No → Repair the Left Front Wheel Speed Sensor 12 Volt Supply Circuit Open. Perform ABS VERIFICATION TEST.
24	Turn ignition off Disconnect the Left Front Wheel Speed Sensor Connector. **Note: Check connector - Clean/repair as necessary.** Disconnect the CAB Connector. **Note: Check connector - Clean/repair as necessary.** Connect a jumper wire between the Left Front Wheel Speed Sensor Signal Circuit and ground. Measure the resistance between the Left Front Wheel Speed Sensor Signal Circuit and ground. Is the resistance below 5 ohms? Yes → Go To 25 No → Repair the Left Front Wheel Speed Sensor Signal Circuit Open. Perform ABS VERIFICATION TEST.
25	Turn ignition off Disconnect the Left Front Wheel Speed Sensor Connector. **Note: Check connector - Clean/repair as necessary.** Disconnect the CAB Connector. **Note: Check connector - Clean/repair as necessary.** Measure the resistance between the Left Front Wheel Speed Sensor 12 Volt Supply Circuit and ground. Is the resistance below 15,000 ohms? Yes → Repair the Left Front Wheel Speed Sensor 12 Volt Supply Circuit Shorted to Ground. Perform ABS VERIFICATION TEST. No → Go To 26

CR4020001985030X

Fig. 93 Lefthand Front Sensor Circuit Failure (Part 3 of 5). 2000 Neon

TEST	ACTION
26	Turn ignition off Disconnect the Left Front Wheel Speed Sensor Connector. **Note: Check connector - Clean/repair as necessary.** Disconnect the CAB Connector. **Note: Check connector - Clean/repair as necessary.** Measure the resistance between the Left Front Wheel Speed Sensor Signal Circuit and ground. Is the resistance below 15,000 ohms? Yes → Repair the Left Front Wheel Speed Sensor Signal Circuit Shorted to Ground. Perform ABS VERIFICATION TEST. No → Go To 27
27	Turn ignition off Disconnect the CAB Connector. **Note: Check connector - Clean/repair as necessary.** Measure the resistance of the Left Front Wheel Speed Sensor Circuits. Is the resistance below 200 ohms? Yes → Repair the Left Front Wheel Speed Sensor Circuits Shorted Together and Replace the Left Front Wheel Speed Sensor. Perform ABS VERIFICATION TEST. No → Go To 28
28	Turn ignition off. Disconnect the Left Rear Wheel Speed Sensor connector. **Note: Check connector - Clean/repair as necessary.** Disconnect the CAB connector. **Note: Check connector - Clean/repair as necessary.** Turn ignition on. Measure the voltage of the Left Front Wheel Speed Sensor Signal Circuit. Is the voltage above 1 volt? Yes → Repair Left Front Wheel Speed Sensor Signal Cricuit Shorted to Voltage and Replace Left Front Wheel Speed Sensor Perform ABS VERIFICATION TEST. No → Go To 29
29	Turn ignition off. Disconnect the Left Front Wheel Speed Sensor connector. **Note: Check connector - Clean/repair as necessary.** Turn ignition on. Measure the voltage of the Left Front Wheel Speed Sensor 12 Volt Supply Circuit. Is the voltage above 10 volts? Yes → Go To 30 No → Replace the CAB. Perform ABS VERIFICATION TEST.

CR4020001985040X

Fig. 93 Lefthand Front Sensor Circuit Failure (Part 4 of 5). 2000 Neon

When Monitored: Wheel speed comparison is checked at drive off or every 7 milliseconds (ms). Wheel speed continuity is checked every 7 milliseconds. Wheel speed phase length supervision is checked every 7 milliseconds.

Set Condition: If, during an ABS stop, the CAB commands any valve solenoid on for an extended length of time, and does not see a corresponding wheel speed change, the Diagnostic Trouble Code (DTC) is set. The DTC can also set if the signal is missing or erratic.

POSSIBLE CAUSES
TONE WHEEL DEFECTIVE
LEFT FRONT WHEEL SPEED SENSOR SIGNAL
INTERMITTENT SIGNAL DTC
LEFT FRONT WHEEL SPEED SENSOR OR CONNECTOR DAMAGED
LEFT FRONT WHEEL BEARING OUT OF SPECIFICATION
LEFT FRONT WHEEL SPEED SENSOR FUNCTIONAL TEST
LEFT FRONT WHEEL SPEED SENSOR AIR GAP OUT OF SPECIFICATION
CAB DEFECTIVE - UNABLE TO READ LEFT FRONT WHEEL SPEED SENSOR SIGNAL

CR4020001986010X

Fig. 94 Lefthand Front Sensor Signal Failure (Part 1 of 3). 2000 Neon

TEST	ACTION
30	Turn ignition off. Disconnect the Left Front Wheel Speed Sensor connector. **Note: Check connector - Clean/repair as necessary.** Turn ignition on. Using a test light connected to 12 volts, probe the Left Front Wheel Speed Sensor Signal Circuit. Is the test light on? Yes → Go To 31 No → Replace the CAB. Perform ABS VERIFICATION TEST.
31	Turn ignition off. Disconnect the Left Front Wheel Speed Sensor connector. **Note: Check connector - Clean/repair as necessary.** Turn ignition on. Using a test light connected to 12 volts, probe the Left Front Wheel Speed Sensor 12 Volt Supply Circuit. Is the test light on? Yes → Replace the CAB. Perform ABS VERIFICATION TEST. No → Go To 32
32	Turn ignition off. Disconnect the Left Front Wheel Speed Sensor connector. **Note: Check connector - Clean/repair as necessary.** Turn ignition on. Using a test light connected to 12 volts, probe the Left Front Wheel Speed Sensor Signal Circuit. Is the test light on? Yes → Replace the CAB. Perform ABS VERIFICATION TEST. No → Test Complete.
33	Turn ignition off. Visually inspect the related wiring harness. Look for any chafed, pierced, pinched, or partially broken wires. Visually inspect the related wire harness connectors. Look for broken, bent, pushed out, or corroded terminals. Refer to any Technical Service Bulletins that may apply. Were any problems found? Yes → Test Complete. No → Test Complete.

CR4020001985050X

Fig. 93 Lefthand Front Sensor Circuit Failure (Part 5 of 5). 2000 Neon

TEST	ACTION
34	Turn ignition on. With the DRBIII® read DTC's. Are the Left Front Sensor Signal Failure and Left Front Sensor Circuit Failure DTC's present? Yes → Refer to symptom LEFT FRONT SENSOR CIRCUIT FAILURE No → Go To 35
35	Turn ignition on. Have an assistant drive the vehicle while you monitor the Left Front Wheel Speed Sensor Signal, using the DRBIII®. Slowly accelerate as straight as possible from a stop to 24 Km/h (15 Mph). With the DRBIII®, monitor all wheel speed sensor signals. Did the Left Front Wheel Speed Sensor Signal show 0 Km/h (0 Mph)? Yes → Go To 36 No → Go To 43
36	Turn ignition off. Inspect the Tone Wheel for damaged or missing teeth. **Note: The Tone Wheel Teeth should be perfectly square, not bent or nicked.** Is the Tone Wheel OK? Yes → Go To 37 No → Replace the Tone Wheel. Perform ABS VERIFICATION TEST.
37	Turn ignition off. Inspect the Left Front Wheel Speed Sensor and Connector. Is the Sensor or Connector Damaged? Yes → Repair as necessary. Perform ABS VERIFICATION TEST. No → Go To 38
38	Turn ignition off. Inspect the wheel bearings for excessive runout or clearance. **Note: Refer to the appropriate service information, if necessary, for procedures or specifications.** Is the bearing clearance OK ? Yes → Go To 39 No → Repair as necassary. Perform ABS VERIFICATION TEST.
39	Turn ignition off. Using a Feeler Gauge, measure the Sensor Air Gap. **Note: The Air Gap should be checked in at least four places on the Tone Wheel.** Is the Air Gap between 0.25 mm - 1.39 mm (0.010" - 0.056"), preferred 0.82 mm (0.033")? Yes → Go To 40 No → Repair as necessary. Perform ABS VERIFICATION TEST.

CR4020001986020X

Fig. 94 Lefthand Front Sensor Signal Failure (Part 2 of 3). 2000 Neon

TEST	ACTION
40	Turn ignition off. Disconnect the CAB Connector. **Note: Check connector - Clean/repair as necessary.** Remove harness strain relief to access wires in CAB connector for backprobing. Using a voltmeter in Direct Current (DC) mode, and special tool 6801, backprobe the Left Front Wheel Speed Sensor Signal circuit at CAB. Reconnect the CAB connector. Turn ignition on. Slowly rotate the wheel while observing voltmeter reading. Does the voltage change from approximately 1.6 volts to 0.8 volts as the wheel is rotated? Yes → Go To 41 No → Replace the Left Front Wheel Speed Sensor. Perform ABS VERIFICATION TEST.
41	Turn ignition off. Disconnect the Left Front Wheel Speed Sensor Connector. **Note: Check connector - Clean/repair as necessary.** Connect a single jumper wire from the harness side of Left Front Wheel Speed Sensor 12 Volt Supply circuit into the Left Front Wheel Speed Sensor connector mating terminal. Using a voltmeter in Direct Current (DC) mode, probe the Left Front Wheel Speed Sensor Signal Circuit at Left Front Wheel Speed Sensor connector. Turn ignition on. Slowly rotate the wheel while observing voltmeter reading. Does the voltage change from approximately 1.6 volts to 0.8 volts as the wheel is rotated? Yes → Go To 42 No → Replace the Left Front Wheel Speed Sensor. Perform ABS VERIFICATION TEST.
42	If there are no potential causes remaining, the CAB is assumed to be defective. View repair options. Repair Replace the CAB. Perform ABS VERIFICATION TEST.
43	Turn ignition off. Visually Inspect Wheel Speed Sensor. Visually Inspect Tone Wheel. Visually Inspect Wiring Harness. Visually inspect brakes for locking up due to lining contamination or overheating. Inspect all Components for defects which may cause a Signal DTC to set. Is any Component Damaged? Yes → Repair as necessary. Perform ABS VERIFICATION TEST. No → Test Complete.

CR4020001986030X

Fig. 94 Lefthand Front Sensor Signal Failure (Part 3 of 3). 2000 Neon

TEST	ACTION
44	Turn ignition on. With the DRBIII® read DTC's. With the DRBIII® erase DTC's. Turn ignition off. Turn ignition on. With the DRBIII® read DTC's. Is the Left Rear Wheel Speed Sensor Circuit Failure DTC present? Yes → Go To 45 No → Go To 60
45	Turn ignition off. Disconnect the Left Rear Wheel Speed Sensor connector. **Note: Check connector - Clean/repair as necessary.** Turn ignition on. Measure the voltage across the Left Rear Wheel Speed Sensor 12 Volt Supply circuit and the Left Rear Wheel Speed Sensor Signal Circuit in the Left Rear Wheel Speed Sensor connector. Is the voltage above 10 volts? Yes → Go To 46 No → Go To 50
46	Turn ignition off Inspect the Left Rear Wheel Speed Sensor and Connector. Is the Sensor or Connector Damaged? Yes → Repair as necessary. Perform ABS VERIFICATION TEST. No → Go To 47
47	Turn ignition off. Disconnect the Left Rear Wheel Speed Sensor Connector. **Note: Check connector - Clean/repair as necessary.** Measure the resistance between either one of the Left Rear Wheel Speed Sensor terminals and ground. Is the resistance below 15,000 ohms? Yes → Replace the Left Rear Wheel Speed Sensor. Perform ABS VERIFICATION TEST. No → Go To 48
48	Turn ignition off. Disconnect the CAB connector. **Note: Check connector - Clean/repair as necessary.** Remove harness strain relief to access wires in CAB connector for backprobing. Using a voltmeter in Direct Current (DC) mode, and special tool 6801, backprobe the Left Rear Wheel Speed Sensor Signal Circuit at CAB. Reconnect the CAB connector. Turn ignition on. Slowly rotate the wheel while observing voltmeter reading. Does the voltage change from approximately 1.6 volts to 0.8 volts as the wheel is rotated? Yes → Go To 49 No → Replace the Left Rear Wheel Speed Sensor. Perform ABS VERIFICATION TEST.

CR4020001987020X

Fig. 95 Lefthand Rear Sensor Circuit Failure (Part 2 of 5). 2000 Neon

When Monitored: Ignition on. The CAB monitors the wheel speed circuit every 7 milliseconds (ms).

Set Condition: If the CAB detects an open or shorted wheel speed sensor circuit, the Diagnostic Trouble Code (DTC) will set.

POSSIBLE CAUSES
LEFT REAR WHEEL SPEED SENSOR 12 VOLT SUPPLY CIRCUIT OPEN
LEFT REAR WHEEL SPEED SENSOR SIGNAL
LEFT REAR WHEEL SPEED SENSOR SIGNAL CIRCUIT OPEN
LEFT REAR WHEEL SPEED SENSOR 12 SUPPLY CIRCUIT SHORTED TO GROUND
LEFT REAR WHEEL SPEED SENSOR DEFECTIVE - SHORTED TO GROUND
LEFT REAR WHEEL SPEED SENSOR OR CONNECTOR DAMAGED
CAB DEFECTIVE - LEFT REAR WHEEL SPEED SENSOR 12 VOLT SUPPLY OPEN
CAB DEFECTIVE - LEFT REAR WHEEL SPEED SENSOR SIGNAL CIRCUIT OPEN
CAB DEFECTIVE - LEFT REAR WHEEL SPEED SENSOR 12 VOLT SUPPLY SHORTED TO GROUND
CAB DEFECTIVE - LEFT REAR WHEEL SPEED SENSOR SIGNAL CIRCUIT SHORTED TO GROUND
CAB DEFECTIVE - UNABLE TO READ LEFT REAR WHEEL SPEED SENSOR SIGNAL
LEFT REAR WHEEL SPEED SENSOR SIGNAL CIRCUIT SHORTED TO GROUND
LEFT REAR WHEEL SPEED SENSOR CIRCUITS SHORTED TOGETHER
LEFT REAR WHEEL SPEED SENSOR SIGNAL SHORTED TO B(+)

CR4020001987010X

Fig. 95 Lefthand Rear Sensor Circuit Failure (Part 1 of 5). 2000 Neon

TEST	ACTION
49	If there are no potential causes remaining, the CAB is assumed to be defective. View repair options. Repair Replace the CAB. Perform ABS VERIFICATION TEST.
50	Turn ignition off. Disconnect the Left Rear Wheel Speed Sensor Connector. **Note: Check connector - Clean/repair as necessary.** Disconnect the CAB Connector. **Note: Check connector - Clean/repair as necessary.** Connect a jumper wire between the Left Rear Wheel Speed Sensor 12 Volt Supply Circuit and ground. Measure the resistance between the Left Rear Wheel Speed Sensor 12 Volt Supply Circuit and ground. Is the resistance below 5 ohms? Yes → Go To 51 No → Repair the Left Rear Wheel Speed Sensor 12 Volt Supply Circuit Open. Perform ABS VERIFICATION TEST.
51	Turn ignition off. Disconnect the Left Rear Wheel Speed Sensor Connector. **Note: Check connector - Clean/repair as necessary.** Disconnect the CAB Connector. **Note: Check connector - Clean/repair as necessary.** Connect a jumper wire between the Left Rear Wheel Speed Sensor Signal Circuit and ground. Measure the resistance between the Left Rear Wheel Speed Sensor Signal Circuit and ground. Is the resistance below 5 ohms? Yes → Go To 52 No → Repair the Left Rear Wheel Speed Sensor Signal Circuit Open. Perform ABS VERIFICATION TEST.
52	Turn ignition off. Disconnect the Left Rear Wheel Speed Sensor Connector. **Note: Check connector - Clean/repair as necessary.** Disconnect the CAB Connector. **Note: Check connector - Clean/repair as necessary.** Measure the resistance between the Left Rear Wheel Speed Sensor 12 Volt Supply Circuit and ground. Is the resistance below 15,000 ohms? Yes → Repair the Left Rear Wheel Speed Sensor 12 Volt Supply Circuit Shorted to Ground. Perform ABS VERIFICATION TEST. No → Go To 53

CR4020001987030X

Fig. 95 Lefthand Rear Sensor Circuit Failure (Part 3 of 5). 2000 Neon

TEST	ACTION
53	Turn ignition off Disconnect the CAB Connector. **Note: Check connector - Clean/repair as necessary.** Measure the resistance of the Left Rear Wheel Speed Sensor Circuits. Is the resistance below 200 ohms? Yes → Repair the Left Rear Wheel Speed Sensor Circuits shorted together and Replace the Left Front Wheel Speed Sensor. Perform ABS VERIFICATION TEST. No → Go To 54
54	Turn ignition off. Disconnect the Left Rear Wheel Speed Sensor Connector. **Note: Check connector - Clean/repair as necessary.** Disconnect the CAB Connector. **Note: Check connector - Clean/repair as necessary.** Measure the resistance between the Left Rear Wheel Speed Sensor Signal Circuit and ground. Is the resistance below 15,000 ohms? Yes → Repair the Left Rear Wheel Speed Sensor Signal Circuit Shorted to Ground. Perform ABS VERIFICATION TEST. No → Go To 55
55	Turn ignition off. Disconnect the Left Rear Wheel Speed Sensor Connector. **Note: Check connector - Clean/repair as necessary.** Disconnect the CAB Connector. **Note: Check connector - Clean/repair as necessary.** Turn ignition on. Measure the voltage of the Left Rear Wheel Speed Sensor Signal Circuit. Is the voltage above 1 volt? Yes → Repair Left Rear Wheel Speed Sensor Signal Circuit Shorted to Voltage and Replace Left Rear Wheel Speed Sensor. Perform ABS VERIFICATION TEST. No → Go To 56
56	Turn ignition off. Disconnect the Left Rear Wheel Speed Sensor connector. **Note: Check connector - Clean/repair as necessary.** Turn ignition on. Measure the voltage of the Left Rear Wheel Speed Sensor 12 Volt Supply Circuit. Is the test light on? Yes → Go To 57 No → Replace the CAB. Perform ABS VERIFICATION TEST.

CR4020001987040X

Fig. 95 Lefthand Rear Sensor Circuit Failure (Part 4 of 5). 2000 Neon

When Monitored: Wheel speed comparison is checked at drive off or every 7 milliseconds (ms). Wheel speed continuity is checked every 7 milliseconds. Wheel speed phase length supervision is checked every 7 milliseconds.

Set Condition: If, during an ABS stop, the CAB commands any valve solenoid on for an extended length of time, and does not see a corresponding wheel speed change, the Diagnostic Trouble Code (DTC) is set. The DTC can also set if the signal is missing or erratic.

POSSIBLE CAUSES
TONE WHEEL DEFECTIVE
LEFT REAR WHEEL SPEED SENSOR SIGNAL
INTERMITTENT SIGNAL DTC
LEFT REAR WHEEL SPEED SENSOR OR CONNECTOR DAMAGED
LEFT REAR WHEEL BEARING OUT OF SPECIFICATION
LEFT REAR WHEEL SPEED SENSOR FUNCTIONAL TEST
LEFT REAR WHEEL SPEED SENSOR AIR GAP OUT OF SPECIFICATION
CAB DEFECTIVE - UNABLE TO READ LEFT REAR WHEEL SPEED SENSOR SIGNAL

CR4020001988010X

Fig. 96 Lefthand Rear Sensor Signal Failure (Part 1 of 3). 2000 Neon

TEST	ACTION
57	Turn ignition off. Disconnect the Left Rear Wheel Speed Sensor connector. **Note: Check connector - Clean/repair as necessary.** Turn ignition on. Using a test light connected to 12 volts, probe the Left Rear Wheel Speed Sensor Signal Circuit. Is the test light on? Yes → Go To 58 No → Replace CAB. Perform ABS VERIFICATION TEST.
58	Turn ignition off. Disconnect the Left Rear Wheel Speed Sensor connector. **Note: Check connector - Clean/repair as necessary.** Turn ignition on. Using a test light connected to 12 volts, probe the Left Rear Wheel Speed Sensor 12 Volt Supply Circuit. Is the test light on? Yes → Replace the CAB. Perform ABS VERIFICATION TEST. No → Go To 59
59	Turn ignition off. Disconnect the Left Rear Wheel Speed Sensor connector. **Note: Check connector - Clean/repair as necessary.** Turn ignition on. Using a test light connected to 12 volts, probe the Left Rear Wheel Speed Sensor Signal Circuit. Is the test light on? Yes → Replace the CAB. Perform ABS VERIFICATION TEST. No → Test Complete.
60	Turn ignition off. Visually inspect the related wiring harness. Look for any chafed, pierced, pinched, or partially broken wires. Visually inspect the related wire harness connectors. Look for broken, bent, pushed out, or corroded terminals. Refer to any Technical Service Bulletins that may apply. Were any problems found? Yes → Test Complete. No → Test Complete.

CR4020001987050X

Fig. 95 Lefthand Rear Sensor Circuit Failure (Part 5 of 5). 2000 Neon

TEST	ACTION
61	Turn ignition on. With the DRBIII® read DTC's. Are the Left Rear Sensor Signal Failure and Left Rear Sensor Circuit Failure DTC's present? Yes → Refer to symptom LEFT REAR SENSOR CIRCUIT FAILURE No → Go To 62
62	Turn ignition on. Have an assistant drive the vehicle while you monitor the Left Rear Wheel Speed Sensor Signal, using the DRBIII®. Slowly accelerate as straight as possible from a stop to 24 Km/h (15 Mph). With the DRBIII®, monitor all wheel speed sensor signals. Did the Left Rear Wheel Speed Sensor Signal show 0 Km/h (0 Mph)? Yes → Go To 63 No → Go To 70
63	Turn ignition off. Inspect the Tone Wheel for damaged or missing teeth. **Note: The Tone Wheel Teeth should be perfectly square, not bent or nicked.** Is the Tone Wheel OK? Yes → Go To 64 No → Replace the Tone Wheel. Perform ABS VERIFICATION TEST.
64	Turn ignition off Inspect the Left Rear Wheel Speed Sensor and Connector. Is the Sensor or Connector Damaged? Yes → Repair as necessary. Perform ABS VERIFICATION TEST. No → Go To 65
65	Turn ignition off. Inspect the Wheel Bearings for excessive runout or clearance. **Note: Refer to the appropriate service information, if necessary, for procedures or specifications.** Is the Bearing Clearance OK? Yes → Go To 66 No → Repair as necassary. Perform ABS VERIFICATION TEST.
66	Turn ignition off. Using a Feeler Gauge measure the Wheel Speed Sensor Air Gap. **Note: The Air Gap should be checked in at least Four places on the Tone Wheel.** Is the Air Gap between 0.37 mm - 1.42 mm (0.015" - 0.057"), preferred 0.90 mm (0.036")? Yes → Go To 67 No → Repair as necessary. Perform ABS VERIFICATION TEST.

CR4020001988020X

Fig. 96 Lefthand Rear Sensor Signal Failure (Part 2 of 3). 2000 Neon

TEST	ACTION
67	Turn ignition off. Disconnect the CAB connector. **Note: Check connector - Clean/repair as necessary.** Remove harness strain relief to access wires in CAB connector for backprobing. Using a voltmeter in Direct Current (DC) mode, and special tool 6801, backprobe the Left Rear Wheel Speed Sensor Signal Circuit at CAB. Reconnect the CAB connector. Turn ignition on. Slowly rotate the wheel while observing voltmeter reading. Does the voltage change from approximately 1.6 volts to 0.8 volts as the wheel is rotated? Yes → Go To 68 No → Replace the Left Rear Wheel Speed Sensor. Perform ABS VERIFICATION TEST.
68	Turn ignition off. Disconnect the Left Rear Wheel Speed Sensor Connector. **Note: Check connector - Clean/repair as necessary.** Connect a single jumper wire from the harness side of Left Rear Wheel Speed Sensor 12 Volt Supply Circuit into the Left Rear Wheel Speed Sensor connector mating terminal. Using a voltmeter in Direct Current (DC) mode, measure the Left Rear Wheel Speed Sensor Signal Circuit at Left Rear Wheel Speed Sensor conector. Turn ignition on. Slowly rotate the wheel while observing voltmeter reading. Does the voltage change from approximately 1.6 volts to 0.8 volts as the wheel is rotated? Yes → Go To 69 No → Replace the Left Rear Wheel Speed Sensor. Perform ABS VERIFICATION TEST.
69	If there are no potential causes remaining, the CAB is assumed to be defective. View repair options. Repair Replace the CAB. Perform ABS VERIFICATION TEST.
70	Turn ignition off. Visually Inspect Wheel Speed Sensor. Visually Inspect Tone Wheel. Visually Inspect Wiring Harness. Visually inspect brakes for locking up due to lining contamination or overheating. Inspect all Components for defects which may cause a Signal DTC to set. Is any Component Damaged? Yes → Repair as necessary. Perform ABS VERIFICATION TEST. No → Test Complete.

CR4020001988030X

Fig. 96 Lefthand Rear Sensor Signal Failure (Part 3 of 3). 2000 Neon

TEST	ACTION
71	Turn ignition on. With the DRBIII® erase DTC's. Turn ignition off. Turn ignition on. Wait 20 seconds. With the DRBIII®, read ABS Diagnostic Trouble Codes (DTC's). Is the PCI Bus Communication DTC present? Yes → Go To 72 No → Go To 76
72	Turn ignition on. With the DRBIII®, read DTC's in Mechanical Instrument Cluster (MIC). Does the MIC have the "ABS Message Not Received by MIC" DTC set? Yes → Repair as required. No → Go To 73
73	Turn ignition off. Disconnect the CAB connector. **Note: Check connector - Clean/repair as necessary.** Measure the resistance of the PCI Bus Circuit between the CAB connector and the Data Link Connector (DLC) . Is the resistance below 5 ohms? Yes → Go To 74 No → Repair the PCI Bus Circuit Open. Perform ABS VERIFICATION TEST.
74	Turn ignition off. Disconnect the CAB connector. **Note: Check connector - Clean/repair as necessary** Turn ignition on. Using the DRBIII® Lab Scope, measure the voltage of the PCI BUS circuit. Is the voltage above 0.4 volts? Yes → Go To 75 No → Go To 75
75	If there are no potential causes remaining, the CAB is assumed defective. Replace the CAB. Repair Replace the CAB. Perform ABS VERIFICATION TEST.
76	Turn ignition off. Visually inspect the related wiring harness. Look for any chafed, pierced, pinched, or partially broken wires. Visually inspect the related wire harness connectors. Look for broken, bent, pushed out, or corroded terminals. Refer to any Technical Service Bulletins that may apply. Were any problems found? Yes → Repair as necessary. Perform ABS VERIFICATION TEST. No → Test Complete.

CR4020001989020X

Fig. 97 PCI Bus Communication (Part 2 of 2). 2000 Neon

When Monitored: Ignition on, every 7 milliseconds (ms).

Set Condition: This DTC will be set when the CAB does not recieve a message from the instrument cluster for 10 seconds.

POSSIBLE CAUSES
INTERMITTENT DTC
PCI BUS OPEN TO CAB
CAB DEFECTIVE - PCI CIRCUIT OPEN

CR4020001989010X

Fig. 97 PCI Bus Communication (Part 1 of 2). 2000 Neon

When Monitored: Ignition on. The CAB commands the pump on at 25 km/h (15 mph) to check its operation, if the brake switch is not applied. If the driver has their foot on the brake, the test will run at 40 km/h (25 mph). The CAB monitors pump voltage every 7 milliseconds.

Set Condition: The DTC is stored when the CAB detects: 1) Improper voltage decay after the pump was turned off. 2) Pump not energized by the CAB, but voltage is present for 3.5 seconds. 3) Pump is turned on by the CAB, but their is insufficient voltage to operate it.

POSSIBLE CAUSES
FUSE BLOWN - PUMP MOTOR CIRCUIT
GROUND CIRCUIT POOR CONNECTION
FUSED B(+) CIRCUIT OPEN
CAB DEFECTIVE - FUSED B(+) CIRCUIT OPEN
ABS PUMP MOTOR DOES NOT ROTATE
CAB DEFECTIVE - FUSED B(+) CIRCUIT SHORTED TO GROUND
FUSED B(+) CIRCUIT INTERMITTENTLY SHORTED TO GROUND
FUSED B(+) CIRCUIT SHORTED TO GROUND
CAB DEFECTIVE - PUMP MOTOR RUNNING CONTINUOUSLY

CR4020001990010X

Fig. 98 Pump Motor Not Working Properly (Part 1 of 4). 2000 Neon

TEST	ACTION
77	Turn ignition on. With the DRBIII® read DTC's. Is the CAB Power Feed Circuit DTC present? Yes → Refer to symptom CAB POWER FEED CIRCUIT No → Go To 78
78	Turn ignition on. With the DRBIII® read DTC's. With the DRBIII® erase DTC's. Turn ignition off. Turn ignition on. With the DRBIII® actuator the pump motor. Did the Pump Motor operate as commanded by the DRBIII®? No → Go To 79 Yes → Go To 89
79	Turn ignition off. Remove and Inspect Fuse #8 in the PDC. Is the Fuse blown? Yes → Go To 80 No → Go To 84
80	Turn ignition off. Visually inspect the Fused B(+) Circuit in the wiring harness from the PDC to the CAB. Look for any sign of an Intermittent Short to Ground. Is the wiring harness OK? Yes → Go To 81 No → Repair the Fused B(+) Circuit shorted to ground. Perform ABS VERIFICATION TEST.
81	Turn ignition off. Disconnect the Fuse #8 from the PDC. Disconnect the CAB connector. **Check connector - Clean/repair as necessary.** Using a test light connected to 12 volts, probe the Fused B(+) Circuit. Is the test light on? Yes → Repair the Fused B(+) Circuit Shorted to Ground. Perform ABS VERIFICATION TEST. No → Go To 82
82	Turn ignition off. Disconnect the Fuse #8 from the PDC. Using a test light connected to 12 volts, probe the Fused B(+) circuit. Monitor the test light. Is the test light on? Yes → Replace the CAB. Perform ABS VERIFICATION TEST. No → Go To 83

CR4020001990020X

Fig. 98 Pump Motor Not Working Properly (Part 2 of 4). 2000 Neon

TEST	ACTION
83	Turn ignition off. If there are no potential causes remaining, the Fuse is assumed to be defective. View repair options Repair Replace the ABS Pump Motor Fuse. Perform ABS VERIFICATION TEST.
84	Turn ignition on. With the DRBIII®, actuate the pump motor. Measure the voltage drop across the ABS ground circuit connection, with the pump motor running. Is the voltage below 0.1 volt? Yes → Go To 85 No → Repair the poor ground circuit. Perform ABS VERIFICATION TEST.
85	Turn ignition off. Disconnect the Fuse #8 from the PDC. Disconnect the CAB connector. **Check connector - Clean/repair as necessary.** Measure the resistance of the Fused B(+) circuit. Is the resistance below 10 ohms? Yes → Go To 86 No → Repair Fused B(+) Circuit Open. Perform ABS VERIFICATION TEST.
86	Turn ignition off. Disconnect Pump Motor Connector. Connect a 10 gauge jumper wire between pump motor ground circuit and a known good body ground. Connect a 10 gauge jumper wire between pump motor Fused B(+) circuit and known good Fused B(+) circuit capable of providing 40 amps. Monitor Pump Motor operation. Is the pump motor running? Yes → Go To 87 No → Replace the ABS Pump Motor. Perform ABS VERIFICATION TEST.
87	Turn ignition off. Reconnect all connectors. Turn ignition on. Monitor the pump motor for continuous operation. Is the pump motor running continuously? Yes → Replace the CAB. Perform ABS VERIFICATION TEST. No → Go To 88
88	If there are no potential causes remaining, the CAB is assumed to be defective. View repair options. Repair Replace the CAB Perform ABS VERIFICATION TEST.

CR4020001990030X

Fig. 98 Pump Motor Not Working Properly (Part 3 of 4). 2000 Neon

When Monitored: Ignition on. The CAB monitors the wheel speed circuit every 7 milliseconds (ms).

Set Condition: If the CAB detects an open or shorted wheel speed sensor circuit, the Diagnostic Trouble Code (DTC) will set.

POSSIBLE CAUSES
RIGHT FRONT WHEEL SPEED SENSOR 12 VOLT SUPPLY CIRCUIT OPEN
RIGHT FRONT WHEEL SPEED SENSOR SIGNAL
RIGHT FRONT WHEEL SPEED SENSOR SIGNAL CIRCUIT OPEN
RIGHT FRONT WHEEL SPEED SENSOR 12 VOLT SUPPLY CIRCUIT SHORTED TO GROUND
RIGHT FRONT WHEEL SPEED SENSOR DEFECTIVE - SHORTED TO GROUND
RIGHT FRONT WHEEL SPEED SENSOR OR CONNECTOR DAMAGED
CAB DEFECTIVE - RIGHT FRONT WHEEL SPEED SENSOR 12 VOLT SUPPLY OPEN
CAB DEFECTIVE - RIGHT FRONT WHEEL SPEED SENSOR SIGNAL CIRCUIT OPEN
CAB DEFECTIVE - RIGHT FRONT WHEEL SPEED SENSOR 12 VOLT SUPPLY SHORTED TO GROUND
CAB DEFECTIVE - RIGHT FRONT WHEEL SPEED SENSOR SIGNAL CIRCUIT SHORTED TO GROUND
CAB DEFECTIVE - UNABLE TO READ RIGHT FRONT WHEEL SPEED SENSOR SIGNAL
RIGHT FRONT WHEEL SPEED SENSOR SIGNAL CIRCUIT SHORTED TO GROUND
RIGHT FRONT WHEEL SPEED SENSOR CIRCUITS SHORTED TOGETHER
RIGHT FRONT WHEEL SPEED SENSOR SIGNAL SHORTED TO B(+)

CR4020001991010X

Fig. 99 Righthand Front Sensor Circuit Failure (Part 1 of 5). 2000 Neon

TEST	ACTION
89	Turn ignition off. Visually inspect the related wiring harness. Look for any chafed, pierced, pinched, or partially broken wires. Visually inspect the related wire harness connectors. Look for broken, bent, pushed out, or corroded terminals. Refer to any Technical Service Bulletins that may apply. Were any problems found? Yes → Test Complete. No → Test Complete.

CR4020001990040X

Fig. 98 Pump Motor Not Working Properly (Part 4 of 4). 2000 Neon

TEST	ACTION
90	Turn ignition on. With the DRBIII® read DTC's. With the DRBIII® erase DTC's. Turn ignition off. Turn ignition on. With the DRBIII® read DTC's. Did the Right Front Wheel Speed Sensor Circuit Failure DTC set again? Yes → Go To 91 No → Go To 106
91	Turn ignition off. Disconnect the Right Front Wheel Speed Sensor connector. **Note: Check connector - Clean/repair as necessary.** Turn ignition on. Measure the voltage across the Right Front Wheel Speed Sensor 12 Volt Supply circuit and the Right Front Wheel Speed Sensor Signal Circuit in the Right Front Wheel Speed Sensor connector. Is the voltage above 10 volts? Yes → Go To 92 No → Go To 96
92	Turn ignition off. Inspect the Right Front Wheel Speed Sensor and Connector. Is the Sensor or Connector Damaged? Yes → Repair as necessary. Perform ABS VERIFICATION TEST. No → Go To 93
93	Turn ignition off. Disconnect the CAB Connector. **Note: Check connector - Clean/repair as necessary.** Remove harness strain relief to access wires in CAB connector for backprobing. Using a voltmeter in Direct Current (DC) mode, and special tool 6801, backprobe the Right Front Wheel Speed Sensor Signal Circuit at CAB. Reconnect the CAB connector. Turn ignition on. Slowly rotate the wheel while observing voltmeter reading. Does the voltage change from approximately 1.6 volts to 0.8 volts as the wheel is rotated? Yes → Go To 94 No → Replace the Right Front Wheel Speed Sensor. Perform ABS VERIFICATION TEST.
94	Turn ignition off. Disconnect the Right Front Wheel Speed Sensor connector. **Note: Check connector - Clean/repair as necessary.** Measure the resistance between either one of the Right Front Wheel Speed Sensor terminals and ground. Is the resistance below 15,000 ohms? Yes → Replace the Right Front Wheel Speed Sensor. Perform ABS VERIFICATION TEST. No → Go To 95

CR4020001991020X

Fig. 99 Righthand Front Sensor Circuit Failure (Part 2 of 5). 2000 Neon

TEST	ACTION
95	If there are no potential causes remaining, the CAB is assumed to be defective. View repair options. Repair Replace the CAB. Perform ABS VERIFICATION TEST.
96	Turn ignition off. Disconnect the Right Front Wheel Speed Sensor connector. **Note: Check connector - Clean/repair as necessary.** Disconnect the CAB Connector. **Note: Check connector - Clean/repair as necessary.** Connect a jumper wire between the Right Front Wheel Speed Sensor 12 Volt Supply Circuit and ground. Measure the resistance between the Right Front Wheel Speed Sensor 12 Volt Supply Circuit and ground. Is the resistance below 5 ohms? Yes → Go To 97 No → Repair the Right Front Wheel Speed Sensor 12 Volt Supply Circuit Open. Perform ABS VERIFICATION TEST.
97	Turn ignition off. Disconnect the Right Front Wheel Speed Sensor connector. **Note: Check connector - Clean/repair as necessary.** Disconnect the CAB Connector. **Note: Check connector - Clean/repair as necessary.** Connect a jumper wire between the Right Front Wheel Speed Sensor Signal Circuit and ground. Measure the resistance between the Right Front Wheel Speed Sensor Signal Circuit and ground. Is the resistance below 5 ohms? Yes → Go To 98 No → Repair the Right Front Wheel Speed Sensor Signal Circuit Open. Perform ABS VERIFICATION TEST.
98	Turn ignition off. Disconnect the Right Front Wheel Speed Sensor connector. **Note: Check connector - Clean/repair as necessary.** Disconnect the CAB Connector. **Note: Check connector - Clean/repair as necessary.** Measure the resistance between the Right Front Wheel Speed Sensor 12 Volt Circuit and ground. Is the resistance below 15,000 ohms? Yes → Repair the Right Front Wheel Speed Sensor 12 Volt Supply Circuit Shorted to Ground. Perform ABS VERIFICATION TEST. No → Go To 99

CR4020001991030X

Fig. 99 Righthand Front Sensor Circuit Failure (Part 3 of 5). 2000 Neon

TEST	ACTION
103	Turn ignition off. Disconnect the Right Front Wheel Speed Sensor connector. **Note: Check connector - Clean/repair as necessary.** Turn ignition on. Using a test light connected to 12 volts, probe the Right Front Wheel Speed Sensor Signal Circuit. Is the test light on? Yes → Go To 104 No → Replace CAB. Perform ABS VERIFICATION TEST.
104	Turn ignition off. Disconnect the Right Front Wheel Speed Sensor connector. **Note: Check connector - Clean/repair as necessary.** Turn ignition on. Using a test light connected to 12 volts, probe the Right Front Wheel Speed Sensor 12 Volt Supply Circuit. Is the test light on? Yes → Replace the CAB. Perform ABS VERIFICATION TEST. No → Go To 105
105	Turn ignition off. Disconnect the Right Front Wheel Speed Sensor connector. **Note: Check connector - Clean/repair as necessary.** Turn ignition on. Using a test light connected to 12 volts, probe the Right Front Wheel Speed Sensor Signal Circuit. Is the test light on? Yes → Replace the CAB. Perform ABS VERIFICATION TEST. No → Test Complete.
106	Turn Ignition Off. Visually inspect the related wiring harness. Look for any chafed, pierced, pinched, or partially broken wires. Visually inspect the related wire harness connectors. Look for broken, bent, pushed out, or corroded terminals. Refer to any Technical Service Bulletins that may apply. Were any problems found? Yes → Test Complete. No → Test Complete.

CR4020001991050X

Fig. 99 Righthand Front Sensor Circuit Failure (Part 5 of 5). 2000 Neon

TEST	ACTION
99	Turn ignition off. Disconnect the Right Front Wheel Speed Sensor connector. **Note: Check connector - Clean/repair as necessary.** Disconnect the CAB Connector. **Note: Check connector - Clean/repair as necessary.** Measure the resistance between the Right Front Wheel Speed Sensor Signal Circuit and ground. Is the resistance below 15,000 ohms? Yes → Repair the Right Front Wheel Speed Sensor Signal Circuit Shorted to Ground. Perform ABS VERIFICATION TEST. No → Go To 100
100	Turn ignition off. Disconnect the CAB Connector. **Note: Check connector - Clean/repair as necessary.** Measure the resistance of the Right Front Wheel Speed Sensor Circuits. Is the resistance below 200 ohms? Yes → Repair the Right Front Wheel Speed Sensor Circuits Shorted Together and Replace the Right Front Wheel Speed Sensor. Perform ABS VERIFICATION TEST. No → Go To 101
101	Turn ignition off. Disconnect the Right Front Wheel Speed Sensor connector. **Note: Check connector - Clean/repair as necessary.** Disconnect the CAB Connector. **Note: Check connector - Clean/repair as necessary.** Turn ignition on. Measure the voltage of the Right Front Wheel Speed Sensor Signal circuit. Is the voltage above 1 volt? Yes → Repair Right Front Wheel Speed Sensor Signal Cricuit Shorted to Voltage and Replace Right Front Wheel Speed Sensor. Perform ABS VERIFICATION TEST. No → Go To 102
102	Turn ignition off. Disconnect the Right Front Wheel Speed Sensor connector. **Note: Check connector - Clean/repair as necessary.** Turn ignition on. Measure the voltage of the Right Front Wheel Speed Sensor 12 Volt Supply Circuit. Is the voltage above 10 volts? Yes → Go To 103 No → Replace the CAB. Perform ABS VERIFICATION TEST.

CR4020001991040X

Fig. 99 Righthand Front Sensor Circuit Failure (Part 4 of 5). 2000 Neon

When Monitored: Wheel speed comparison is checked at drive off or every 7 milliseconds (ms). Wheel speed continuity is checked every 7 milliseconds. Wheel speed phase length supervision is checked every 7 milliseconds.

Set Condition: If, during an ABS stop, the CAB commands any valve solenoid on for an extended length of time, and does not see a corresponding wheel speed change, the Diagnostic Trouble Code (DTC) is set. The DTC can also set if the signal is missing or erratic.

POSSIBLE CAUSES
TONE WHEEL DEFECTIVE
RIGHT FRONT WHEEL SPEED SENSOR SIGNAL
INTERMITTENT SIGNAL DTC
RIGHT FRONT WHEEL SPEED SENSOR OR CONNECTOR DAMAGED
RIGHT FRONT WHEEL BEARING OUT OF SPECIFICATION
RIGHT FRONT WHEEL SPEED SENSOR FUNCTIONAL TEST
RIGHT FRONT WHEEL SPEED SENSOR AIR GAP OUT OF SPECIFICATION
CAB DEFECTIVE - UNABLE TO READ RIGHT FRONT WHEEL SPEED SENSOR SIGNAL

CR4020001992010X

Fig. 100 Righthand Front Sensor Signal Failure (Part 1 of 3). 2000 Neon

TEST	ACTION
107	Turn ignition on. With the DRBIII® read DTC's. Are the Right Front Sensor Signal Failure and Right Front Sensor Circuit Failure DTC's present? Yes → Refer to symptom RIGHT FRONT SENSOR CIRCUIT FAILURE No → Go To 108
108	Turn ignition on. Have an assistant drive the vehicle while you monitor the Right Front Wheel Speed Sensor Signal, using the DRBIII®. Slowly accelerate as straight as possible from a stop to 24 Km/h (15 Mph). With the DRBIII®, monitor all wheel speed sensor signals. Did Right Front Wheel Speed Sensor Signal show 0 Km/h (0 Mph)? Yes → Go To 109 No → Go To 116
109	Turn ignition off. Inspect the Tone Wheel for damaged or missing teeth. **Note: The Tone Wheel Teeth should be perfectly square, not bent or nicked.** Is the Tone Wheel OK? Yes → Go To 110 No → Replace the Tone Wheel. Perform ABS VERIFICATION TEST.
110	Turn ignition off. Inspect the Right Front Wheel Speed Sensor and Connector. Is the Sensor or Connector Damaged? Yes → Repair as necessary. Perform ABS VERIFICATION TEST. No → Go To 111
111	Turn ignition off. Inspect the wheel bearings for excessive runout or clearance. **Note: Refer to the appropriate service information, if necessary, for procedures or specifications.** Is the bearing clearance OK? Yes → Go To 112 No → Repair as necassary. Perform ABS VERIFICATION TEST.
112	Turn ignition off. Using a Feeler Gauge measure the Wheel Speed Sensor Air Gap. **Note: The Air Gap should be checked in at least four places on the Tone Wheel.** Is the Air Gap between 0.25 mm - 1.39 mm (0.010" - 0.056"), preferred 0.82 mm (0.033")? Yes → Go To 113 No → Repair as necessary. Perform ABS VERIFICATION TEST.

CR4020001992020X

Fig. 100 Righthand Front Sensor Signal Failure (Part 2 of 3). 2000 Neon

When Monitored: Ignition on. The CAB monitors the wheel speed circuit every 7 milliseconds (ms).

Set Condition: If the CAB detects an open or shorted wheel speed sensor circuit, the Diagnostic Trouble Code (DTC) will set.

POSSIBLE CAUSES
RIGHT REAR WHEEL SPEED SENSOR 12 VOLT SUPPLY CIRCUIT OPEN
RIGHT REAR WHEEL SPEED SENSOR SIGNAL
RIGHT REAR WHEEL SPEED SENSOR SIGNAL CIRCUIT OPEN
RIGHT REAR WHEEL SPEED SENSOR 12 VOLT SUPPLY CIRCUIT SHORTED TO GROUND
RIGHT REAR WHEEL SPEED SENSOR DEFECTIVE - SHORTED TO GROUND
RIGHT REAR WHEEL SPEED SENSOR OR CONNECTOR DAMAGED
CAB DEFECTIVE-RIGHT REAR WHEEL SPEED SENSOR 12 VOLT SUPPLY CIRCUIT OPEN
CAB DEFECTIVE - RIGHT REAR WHEEL SPEED SENSOR 12 VOLT SUPPLY SHORTED TO GROUND
CAB DEFECTIVE-RIGHT REAR WHEEL SPEED SENSOR SIGNAL CIRCUIT OPEN
CAB DEFECTIVE - RIGHT REAR WHEEL SPEED SENSOR SIGNAL CIRCUIT SHORTED TO GROUND
CAB DEFECTIVE - UNABLE TO READ RIGHT REAR WHEEL SPEED SENSOR SIGNAL
RIGHT REAR WHEEL SPEED SENSOR SIGNAL CIRCUIT SHORTED TO GROUND
RIGHT REAR WHEEL SPEED SENSOR CIRCUITS SHORTED TOGETHER
RIGHT REAR WHEEL SPEED SENSOR SIGNAL SHORTED TO B(+)

CR4020001993010X

Fig. 101 Righthand Rear Sensor Circuit Failure (Part 1 of 6). 2000 Neon

TEST	ACTION
113	Turn ignition off. Disconnect the CAB Connector. **Note: Check connector - Clean/repair as necessary.** Remove harness strain relief to access wires in CAB connector for backprobing. Using a voltmeter in Direct Current (DC) mode, and special tool 6801, backprobe the Right Front Wheel Speed Sensor Signal Circuit at CAB. Reconnect the CAB connector. Turn ignition on. Slowly rotate the wheel while observing voltmeter reading. Does the voltage change from approximately 1.6 volts to 0.8 volts as the wheel is rotated? Yes → Go To 114 No → Replace the Right Front Wheel Speed Sensor. Perform ABS VERIFICATION TEST.
114	Turn ignition off. Disconnect the Right Front Wheel Speed Sensor connector. **Note: Check connector - Clean/repair as necessary.** Connect a single jumper wire from the harness side of Right Front Wheel Speed Sensor 12 Volt Supply Circuit into the Right Front Wheel Speed Sensor connector mating terminal. Using a voltmeter in Direct Current (DC) mode, probe the Right Front Wheel Speed Sensor signal circuit at Right Front Wheel Speed Sensor connector. Turn ignition on. Slowly rotate the wheel while observing voltmeter reading. Does the voltage change from approximately 1.6 volts to 0.8 volts as the wheel is rotated? Yes → Go To 115 No → Replace the Right Front Wheel Speed Sensor. Perform ABS VERIFICATION TEST.
115	If there are no potential causes remaining, the CAB is assumed to be defective. View repair options. Repair Replace the CAB. Perform ABS VERIFICATION TEST.
116	Turn ignition off. Visually Inspect Wheel Speed Sensor. Visually Inspect Tone Wheel. Visually Inspect Wiring Harness. Visually inspect brakes for locking up due to lining contamination or overheating. Inspect all Components for defects which may cause a Signal DTC to set. Is any Component Damaged? Yes → Repair as necessary. Perform ABS VERIFICATION TEST. No → Test Complete.

CR4020001992030X

Fig. 100 Righthand Front Sensor Signal Failure (Part 3 of 3). 2000 Neon

TEST	ACTION
117	Turn ignition on. With the DRBIII® read DTC's. With the DRBIII® erase DTC's. Turn ignition off. Turn ignition on. With the DRBIII® read DTC's. Did the Right Rear Wheel Speed Sensor Circuit Failure DTC set again? Yes → Go To 118 No → Go To 134
118	Turn ignition off. Disconnect the Right Rear Wheel Speed Sensor connector. **Note: Check connector - Clean/repair as necessary.** Turn ignition on. Measure the voltage across the Right Rear Wheel Speed Sensor 12 Volt Supply circuit and the Right Rear Wheel Speed Sensor Signal Circuit in the Right Rear Wheel Speed Sensor connector. Is the voltage above 10 volts? Yes → Go To 119 No → Go To 122
119	Turn ignition off. Inspect the Right Rear Wheel Speed Sensor and Connector. Is the Sensor or Connector Damaged? Yes → Repair as necessary. Perform ABS VERIFICATION TEST. No → Go To 120
120	Turn ignition off. Disconnect the CAB Connector. **Note: Check connector - Clean/repair as necessary.** Remove harness strain relief to access wires in CAB connector for backprobing. Using a voltmeter in Direct Current (DC) mode, and special tool 6801, backprobe the Right Rear Wheel Speed Sensor Signal Circuit at CAB. Reconnect the CAB connector. Turn ignition on. Slowly rotate the wheel while observing voltmeter reading. Does the voltage change from approximately 1.6 volts to 0.8 volts as the wheel is rotated? Yes → Go To 121 No → Replace the Right Rear Wheel Speed Sensor. Perform ABS VERIFICATION TEST.
121	Turn ignition off. Disconnect the Right Rear Wheel Speed Sensor connector. **Note: Check connector - Clean/repair as necessary.** Measure the resistance between either one of the Right Rear Wheel Speed Sensor terminals and ground. Is the resistance below 15,000 ohms? Yes → Replace the Right Rear Wheel Speed Sensor. Perform ABS VERIFICATION TEST. No → Go To 133

CR4020001993020X

Fig. 101 Righthand Rear Sensor Circuit Failure (Part 2 of 6). 2000 Neon

TEST	ACTION
122	Turn ignition off. Disconnect the Right Rear Wheel Speed Sensor connector. **Note: Check connector - Clean/repair as necessary.** Disconnect the CAB Connector. **Note: Check connector - Clean/repair as necessary.** Connect a jumper wire between the Right Rear Wheel Speed Sensor 12 Volt Supply Circuit and ground. Measure the resistance between the Right Rear Wheel Speed Sensor 12 Volt Supply Circuit and ground. Is the resistance below 5 ohms? Yes → Go To 123 No → Repair the Right Rear Wheel Speed Sensor 12 Volt Supply Circuit Open. Perform ABS VERIFICATION TEST.
123	Turn ignition off. Disconnect the Right Rear Wheel Speed Sensor Connector. **Note: Check connector - Clean/repair as necessary.** Disconnect the CAB Connector. **Note: Check connector - Clean/repair as necessary.** Connect a jumper wire between the Right Rear Wheel Speed Sensor Signal Circuit and ground. Measure the resistance between the Right Rear Wheel Speed Sensor Signal Circuit and ground. Is the resistance below 5 ohms? Yes → Go To 124 No → Repair the Right Rear Wheel Speed Sensor Signal Circuit Open. Perform ABS VERIFICATION TEST.
124	Turn ignition off. Disconnect the Right Rear Wheel Speed Sensor Connector. **Note: Check connector - Clean/repair as necessary.** Disconnect the CAB Connector. **Note: Check connector - Clean/repair as necessary.** Measure the resistance between the Right Rear Wheel Speed Sensor 12 Volt Supply Circuit and ground. Is the resistance below 15,000 ohms? Yes → Repair the Right Rear Wheel Speed Sensor 12 Volt Supply Circuit Shorted to Ground. Perform ABS VERIFICATION TEST. No → Go To 125

CR4020001993030X

Fig. 101 Righthand Rear Sensor Circuit Failure (Part 3 of 6). 2000 Neon

TEST	ACTION
129	Turn ignition off. Disconnect the Right Rear Wheel Speed Sensor connector. **Note: Check connector - Clean/repair as necessary.** Turn ignition on. Using a test light connected to 12 volts, probe the Right Rear Wheel Speed Sensor 12 Volt Supply Circuit. Is the test light on? Yes → Replace the CAB. Perform ABS VERIFICATION TEST. No → Go To 130
130	Turn ignition off. Disconnect the Right Rear Wheel Speed Sensor connector. **Note: Check connector - Clean/repair as necessary.** Turn ignition on. Using a test light connected to 12 volts, probe the Right Rear Wheel Speed Sensor Signal Circuit. Is the test light on? Yes → Replace the CAB. Perform ABS VERIFICATION TEST. No → Go To 131
131	Turn ignition off. Disconnect the Right Rear Wheel Speed Sensor connector. **Note: Check connector - Clean/repair as necessary.** Turn ignition on. Using a test light connected to 12 volts, probe the Right Rear Wheel Speed Sensor Signal Circuit. Is the test light on? Yes → Replace the CAB. Perform ABS VERIFICATION TEST. No → Go To 132
132	Turn ignition off. Disconnect the CAB Connector. **Note: Check connector - Clean/repair as necessary.** Remove harness strain relief to access wires in CAB connector for backprobing. Using a voltmeter in Direct Current (DC) mode, and special tool 6801, backprobe the Right Rear Wheel Speed Sensor Signal Circuit at CAB. Reconnect the CAB connector. Turn ignition on. Slowly rotate the wheel while observing voltmeter reading. Does the voltage change from approximately 1.6 volts to 0.8 volts as the wheel is rotated? Yes → Go To 133 No → Replace the Right Rear Wheel Speed Sensor. Perform ABS VERIFICATION TEST.
133	If there are no potential causes remaining, the CAB is assumed to be defective. View repair options. Repair Replace the CAB. Perform ABS VERIFICATION TEST.

CR4020001993050X

Fig. 101 Righthand Rear Sensor Circuit Failure (Part 5 of 6). 2000 Neon

TEST	ACTION
125	Turn ignition off. Disconnect the Right Rear Wheel Speed Sensor connector. **Note: Check connector - Clean/repair as necessary.** Disconnect the CAB Connector. **Note: Check connector - Clean/repair as necessary.** Measure the resistance between the Right Rear Wheel Speed Sensor Signal Circuit and ground. Is the resistance below 15,000 ohms? Yes → Repair the Right Rear Wheel Speed Signal Circuit Shorted to Ground. Perform ABS VERIFICATION TEST. No → Go To 126
126	Turn ignition off. Disconnect the CAB Connector. **Note: Check connector - Clean/repair as necessary.** Measure the resistance of the Right Rear Wheel Speed Sensor Circuits. Is the resistance below 200 ohms? Yes → Repair the Right Rear Wheel Speed Sensor Circuits Shorted Together and Replace the Right Rear Wheel Speed Sensor. Perform ABS VERIFICATION TEST. No → Go To 127
127	Turn ignition off. Disconnect the Right Rear Wheel Speed Sensor connector. **Note: Check connector - Clean/repair as necessary.** Disconnect the CAB Connector. **Note: Check connector - Clean/repair as necessary.** Turn ignition on. Measure the voltage of the Right Rear Wheel Speed Sensor Signal Circuit. Is the voltage above 1 volt? Yes → Repair Right Rear Wheel Speed Sensor Signal Circuit Shorted to Voltage and Replace Right Rear Wheel Speed Sensor. Perform ABS VERIFICATION TEST. No → Go To 128
128	Turn ignition off. Disconnect the Right Rear Wheel Speed Sensor connector. **Note: Check connector - Clean/repair as necessary.** Turn ignition on. Measure the voltage of the Right Rear Wheel Speed Sensor 12 Volt Supply Circuit. Is the voltage above 10 volts? Yes → Go To 129 No → Replace the CAB. Perform ABS VERIFICATION TEST.

CR4020001993040X

Fig. 101 Righthand Rear Sensor Circuit Failure (Part 4 of 6). 2000 Neon

TEST	ACTION
134	Turn ignition off. Visually inspect the related wiring harness. Look for any chafed, pierced, pinched, or partially broken wires. Visually inspect the related wire harness connectors. Look for broken, bent, pushed out, or corroded terminals. Refer to any Technical Service Bulletins that may apply. Were any problems found? Yes → Test Complete. No → Test Complete.

CR4020001993060X

Fig. 101 Righthand Rear Sensor Circuit Failure (Part 6 of 6). 2000 Neon

When Monitored: Wheel speed comparison is checked at drive off or every 7 milliseconds (ms). Wheel speed continuity is checked every 7 milliseconds. Wheel speed phase length supervision is checked every 7 milliseconds.

Set Condition: If, during an ABS stop, the CAB commands any valve solenoid on for an extended length of time, and does not see a corresponding wheel speed change, the Diagnostic Trouble Code (DTC) is set. The DTC can also set if the signal is missing or erratic.

POSSIBLE CAUSES
TONE WHEEL DEFECTIVE
RIGHT REAR WHEEL SPEED SENSOR SIGNAL
INTERMITTENT SIGNAL DTC
RIGHT REAR WHEEL SPEED SENSOR OR CONNECTOR DAMAGED
RIGHT REAR WHEEL BEARING OUT OF SPECIFICATION
RIGHT REAR WHEEL SPEED SENSOR FUNCTIONAL TEST
RIGHT REAR WHEEL SPEED SENSOR AIR GAP OUT OF SPECIFICATION
CAB DEFECTIVE - UNABLE TO READ RIGHT REAR WHEEL SPEED SENSOR SIGNAL

CR4020001994010X

Fig. 102 Righthand Rear Sensor Signal Failure (Part 1 of 3). 2000 Neon

TEST	ACTION
135	Turn ignition on. With the DRBIII® read DTC's. Are the Right Rear Sensor Signal Failure and Right Rear Sensor Circuit Failure DTC's present? Yes → Refer to symptom RIGHT REAR SENSOR CIRCUIT FAILURE No → Go To 136
136	Turn ignition on. Have an assistant drive the vehicle while you monitor the Right Rear Wheel Speed Sensor Signal, using the DRBIII®. Slowly accelerate as straight as possible from a stop to 24 Km/h (15 Mph). With the DRBIII®, monitor all wheel speed sensor signals. Did the Right Rear Wheel Speed Sensor Signal show 0 Km/h (0 Mph)? Yes → Go To 137 No → Go To 144
137	Turn ignition off. Inspect the Tone Wheel for damaged or missing teeth. **Note: The Tone Wheel Teeth should be perfectly square, not bent or nicked.** Is the Tone Wheel OK? Yes → Go To 138 No → Replace the Tone Wheel. Perform ABS VERIFICATION TEST.
138	Turn ignition off. Inspect the Right Rear Wheel Speed Sensor and Connector. Is the Sensor or Connector Damaged? Yes → Repair as necessary. Perform ABS VERIFICATION TEST. No → Go To 139
139	Turn ignition off. Inspect the wheel bearings for excessive runout or clearance. **Note: Refer to the appropriate service information, if necessary, for procedures or specifications.** Is the bearing clearance OK? Yes → Go To 140 No → Repair as necessary. Perform ABS VERIFICATION TEST.
140	Turn ignition off. Using a Feeler Gauge measure the Sensor Air Gap. **Note: The Air Gap should be checked in at least Four places on the Tone Wheel.** Is the Air Gap between 0.37 mm - 1.42 mm (0.015" - 0.057"), preferred 0.90 mm (0.036")? Yes → Go To 141 No → Repair as necessary. Perform ABS VERIFICATION TEST.

CR4020001994020X

Fig. 102 Righthand Rear Sensor Signal Failure (Part 2 of 3). 2000 Neon

When Monitored: Ignition on. The CAB monitors the Fused Ignition Switched Output circuit at all times for proper system voltage.

Set Condition: If the voltage is between 17 and 19 volts for greater than 420 milliseconds (ms), the Diagnostic Trouble Code (DTC) is set.

POSSIBLE CAUSES
INTERMITTENT DTC
BATTERY OVERCHARGED
FUSED IGNITION SWITCH OUTPUT CIRCUIT OVERVOLTAGE

CR4020001995010X

Fig. 103 System Overvoltage (Part 1 of 2). 2000 Neon

TEST	ACTION
141	Turn ignition off. Disconnect the CAB Connector. **Note: Check connector - Clean/repair as necessary.** Remove harness strain relief to access wires in CAB connector for backprobing. Using a voltmeter in Direct Current (DC) mode, and special tool 6801, backprobe the Right Rear Wheel Speed Sensor Signal Circuit at CAB. Reconnect the CAB connector. Turn ignition on. Slowly rotate the wheel while observing voltmeter reading. Does the voltage change from approximately 1.6 volts to 0.8 volts as the wheel is rotated? Yes → Go To 142 No → Replace the Right Rear Wheel Speed Sensor. Perform ABS VERIFICATION TEST.
142	Turn ignition off. Disconnect the Right Rear Wheel Speed Sensor Connector. **Note: Check connector - Clean/repair as necessary.** Connect a single jumper wire from the harness side of Right Rear Wheel Speed Sensor 12 Volt Supply circuit into the Right Rear Wheel Speed Sensor connector mating terminal. Using a voltmeter in Direct Current (DC) mode, probe the Right Rear Wheel Speed Sensor Signal circuit at Right Rear Wheel Speed Sensor connector. Turn ignition on. Slowly rotate the wheel while observing voltmeter reading. Does the voltage change from approximately 1.6 volts to 0.8 volts as the wheel is rotated? Yes → Go To 143 No → Replace the Right Rear Wheel Speed Sensor. Perform ABS VERIFICATION TEST.
143	If there are no potential causes remaining, the CAB is assumed to be defective. View repair options. Repair Replace the CAB. Perform ABS VERIFICATION TEST.
144	Visually Inspect Wheel Speed Sensor. Visually Inspect Tone Wheel. Visually Inspect Wiring Harness. Visually inspect brakes for locking up due to lining contamination or overheating. Inspect all Components for defects which may cause a Signal DTC to set. Is any Component Damaged? Yes → Repair as necessary. Perform ABS VERIFICATION TEST. No → Test Complete.

CR4020001994030X

Fig. 102 Righthand Rear Sensor Signal Failure (Part 3 of 3). 2000 Neon

TEST	ACTION
145	Turn ignition on. With the DRBIII® erase DTC's. Turn ignition off. Turn ignition on. With the DRBIII® read DTC's. Is the System Overvoltage DTC present? Yes → Go To 146 No → Go To 148
146	Turn ignition off. Inspect for battery charger connected to battery. Is a battery charger connected to the battery? Yes → Charge battery to proper level. Disconnect the battery charger. Clear DTC's. Perform ABS VERIFICATION TEST. No → Go To 147
147	Turn ignition off. Disconnect the CAB connector. **Note: Check connector - Clean/repair as necessary.** Start engine. Raise engine RPM's above 1800. Measure the voltage of the Fused Ignition Switch Output Circuit. Is the voltage above 16.5 volts ? Yes → Refer to appropriate service information for charging system testing and repair. Perform ABS VERIFICATION TEST. No → Test Complete.
148	Turn ignition off. Visually inspect the related wiring harness. Look for any chafed, pierced, pinched, or partially broken wires. Visually inspect the related wire harness connectors. Look for broken, bent, pushed out, or corroded terminals. Refer to any Technical Service Bulletins that may apply. Were any problems found? Yes → Repair as necessary. Perform ABS VERIFICATION TEST. No → Test Complete.

CR4020001995020X

Fig. 103 System Overvoltage (Part 2 of 2). 2000 Neon

When Monitored: Ignition on. The CAB monitors the Fused Ignition Switch Output circuit voltage every 7 milliseconds for proper system voltage.

Set Condition: If the voltage is below 8 volts, the Diagnostic Trouble Code (DTC) is set.

POSSIBLE CAUSES
INTERMITTENT DTC
FUSED IGNITION SWITCH OUTPUT CIRCUIT HIGH RESISTANCE
FUSED IGNITION SWITCH OUTPUT CIRCUIT UNDERVOLTAGE

CR4020001996010X

Fig. 104 System Undervoltage (Part 1 of 2). 2000 Neon

TEST	ACTION
149	Turn ignition on. With the DRBIII® erase DTC's. Turn ignition off. With the DRBIII® read DTC's. Is the System Undervoltage DTC present? Yes → Go To 150 No → Go To 152
150	Turn ignition on. With the DRBIII®, select Sensors. Read the "Ignition Voltage" and record. Measure the voltage at the battery and record. Compare voltage measurements. Does the DRBIII® show ignition voltage within one volt of the battery voltage? Yes → Go To 151 No → Repair the Fused Ignition Switch Output Circuit for high resistance Perform ABS VERIFICATION TEST.
151	Turn ignition off. Disconnect the CAB connector. **Note: Check connector - Clean/repair as necessary.** Start engine. Raise engine RPM's above 1800. Measure the voltage of the Fused Ignition Switch Output circuit. Is the voltage below 13 volts ? Yes → Refer to appropriate service information for charging system testing and repair. Perform ABS VERIFICATION TEST. No → Test Complete.
152	Turn ignition off. Visually inspect the related wiring harness. Look for any chafed, pierced, pinched, or partially broken wires. Visually inspect the related wire harness connectors. Look for broken, bent, pushed out, or corroded terminals. Refer to any Technical Service Bulletins that may apply. Were any problems found? Yes → Repair as necessary. Perform ABS VERIFICATION TEST. No → Test Complete.

CR4020001996020X

Fig. 104 System Undervoltage (Part 2 of 2). 2000 Neon

POSSIBLE CAUSES
CAB DEFECTIVE-TRACTION CONTROL SWITCH CIRCUIT SHORTED TO GROUND
CAB DEFECTIVE-TRACTION CONTROL SWITCH SENSE CIRCUIT OPEN
TRACTION CONTROL SWITCH GROUND CIRCUIT OPEN
TRACTION CONTROL SWITCH SENSE CIRCUIT OPEN
TRACTION CONTROL SWITCH SENSE CIRCUIT SHORTED TO GROUND
TRACTION CONTROL SWITCH STUCK CLOSED
TRACTION CONTROL SWITCH STUCK OPEN

CR4020001997010X

Fig. 105 Traction Control Switch (Part 1 of 3). 2000 Neon

TEST	ACTION
153	Turn ignition on. Depress the Traction Control Switch on dash several times while watching the "Trac Off" Lamp in the Instrument Cluster. Does Lamp change from "Trac Off" to nothing? Yes → Test Complete. No → Go To 154
154	Turn ignition on. Depress the Traction Control Switch on dash several times while watching the "Trac Off" Lamp in the Instrument Cluster. Does the Instrument Cluster display "Trac Off" all the time? Yes → Go To 155 No → Go To 158
155	Turn ignition off. Disconnect the CAB Connector. **Note: Check connector - Clean/repair as necessary.** Disconnect the Traction Control Switch Connector. **Note: Check connector - Clean/repair as necessary.** Measure the resistance of the Traction Control Switch Sense circuit and ground. Is the resistance below 5.0 ohms? Yes → Repair the Traction Control Switch Sense Circuit Shorted to Ground. No → Go To 156
156	Turn ignition off. Disconnect the Traction Connector Switch Connector. **Note: Check connector - Clean/repair as necessary.** Measure across the Traction Control Switch Sense circuit and Ground circuit, on Switch. Measure resistance of the Traction Control Switch. Is the resistance below 2.0 ohms across switch? Yes → Replace the Traction Control Switch. No → Go To 157
157	If there are no potential causes remaining, the CAB is assumed to be defective. View repair options. Repair Replace the CAB.
158	Turn ignition off. Disconnect the Traction Control Switch Connector. **Note: Check connector - Clean/repair as necessary.** Turn ignition on. Measure the voltage of the Traction Control Switch Sensor Circuit in the vehicle harness. Is the voltage above 9 volts. Yes → Go To 159 No → Go To 161

CR4020001997020X

Fig. 105 Traction Control Switch (Part 2 of 3). 2000 Neon

TEST	ACTION
159	Turn ignition off Disconnect the Traction Control Switch Connector. **Note: Check connector - Clean/repair as necessary.** Measure the resistance of the Ground Circuit in the vehicle harness. Is the resistance below 5 ohms? Yes → Go To 160 No → Repair the Ground Circuit Open.
160	Turn ignition off. Disconnect the Traction Connector Switch Connector. **Note: Check connector - Clean/repair as necessary.** Measure across the Traction Control Switch Sense circuit and Ground circuit, on Switch. Depress the Traction Control Switch. Measure resistance while depressing the Traction Control Switch. Is the resistance below 2.0 ohms across switch when the switch is depressed? Yes → Test Complete. No → Replace the Traction Control Switch.
161	Turn ignition off. Disconnect the CAB Connector. **Note: Check connector - Clean/repair as necessary.** Disconnect the Traction Control Switch Connector. **Note: Check connector - Clean/repair as necessary.** Measure the resistance of the Traction Control Switch Sense Circuit. Is the resistance below 5.0 ohms? Yes → Go To 162 No → Repair the Traction Control Switch Sense Circuit Open.
162	Turn ignition off. Disconnect the Traction Connector Switch Connector. **Note: Check connector - Clean/repair as necessary.** Measure across the Traction Control Switch Sense circuit and Ground circuit, on Switch. Depress the Traction Control Switch. Measure resistance while depressing the Traction Control Switch. Is the resistance below 2.0 ohms across switch when the switch is depressed? Yes → Go To 163 No → Replace the Traction Control Switch.
163	If there are no potential causes remaining, the CAB is assumed to be defective. View repair options. Repair Replace the CAB.

CR4020001997030X

Fig. 105 Traction Control Switch (Part 3 of 3). 2000 Neon

POSSIBLE CAUSES
PCI BUS OPEN TO CAB
FUSED IGNITION SWITCH OUTPUT CIRCUIT INTERMITTENTLY SHORTED TO GROUND
FUSED IGNITION SWITCH OUTPUT CIRCUIT OPEN
FUSED IGNITION SWITCH OUTPUT CIRCUIT SHORTED TO GROUND
GROUND CIRCUIT OPEN
CAB DEFECTIVE - FUSED IGNITION SWITCH OUTPUT SHORTED TO GROUND
CAB DEFECTIVE - NO RESPONSE

CR4020001998010X

Fig. 106 Scan Tool No Response From CAB Controller (Part 1 of 3). 2000 Neon

TEST	ACTION
170	Turn ignition off. Disconnect the CAB connector. **Note: Check connector - Clean/repair as necessary.** Measure the resistance of the PCI Bus Circuit between the CAB connector and the Data Link Connector (DLC) . Is the resistance below 5 ohms? Yes → Go To 171 No → Repair the PCI Bus Circuit Open. Perform ABS VERIFICATION TEST.
171	Turn ignition off. Disconnect the #10 Fuse in the Fuse Block. Disconnect the CAB connector. **Note: Check connector - Clean/repair as necessary.** Measure the resistance of the Fused Ignition Switch Output circuit. Is the resistance below 5 ohms? Yes → Go To 172 No → Repair Fused Ignition Switch Output Circuit Open Perform ABS VERIFICATION TEST.
172	Turn ignition off. Disconnect the CAB connector. **Note: Check connector - Clean/repair as necessary.** Measure the resistance of the ground circuits. Is the resistance below 1.0 ohm? Yes → Go To 173 No → Repair Ground Circuit Open. Perform ABS VERIFICATION TEST.
173	If there are no potential causes remaining, the CAB is assumed to be defective. View repair options. Repair Replace the CAB. Perform ABS VERIFICATION TEST.

CR4020001998030X

Fig. 106 Scan Tool No Response From CAB Controller (Part 3 of 3). 2000 Neon

ABS VERIFICATION TEST
1. Turn ignition off. 2. Connect all previously disconnected components and connectors. 3. Turn ignition on. 4. With the DRBIII® erase DTC's. 5. With the DRBIII® read DTC's. 6. If any Diagnostic Trouble Codes are present, return to Symptom list and troubleshoot new or recurring symptom. 7. If there are no DTC's present after turning ignition on, road test the vehicle for at least 5 minutes. Perform several antilock braking stops. **8. Caution: Ensure braking capability is available before road testing.** 9. Again, with the DRBIII® read DTC's. If any DTC's are present, return to Symptom list. 10. If there are no diagnostic trouble codes present, and the customer's complaint can no longer be duplicated, the repair is complete.

CR4020001999000X

Fig. 107 ABS Verification Test. 2000 Neon

TEST	ACTION
164	Turn ignition on. **As soon as one or more module communicates with the DRBIII®, answer the question.** With the DRBIII®, select PASSIVE RESTRAINTS, then select AIRBAG. With the DRBIII®, select MECHANICAL INSTRUMENT CLUSTER. Were you able to establish communication with any of the modules? Yes → Go To 165 No → Refer to symptom COMPLETE PCI BUS FAILURE
165	Turn ignition off. Remove and Inspect Fuse #10 in the Fuse Block. Is the Fuse blown? Yes → Go To 166 No → Go To 170
166	Turn ignition off. Visually inspect the Fused Ignition Switch Output Circuit in the wiring harness from the Fuse Block to the CAB. Look for any sign of an intermittent short to ground. Is the wiring harness OK? Yes → Go To 167 No → Repair the Fused Ignition Switch Output Circuit Shorted to Ground Perform ABS VERIFICATION TEST.
167	Turn ignition off. Disconnect the #10 Fuse from the Fuse Block. Disconnect the CAB connector. **Note: Check connector - Clean/repair as necessary.** Using a test light connected to 12 volts, probe the Fused Ignition Switch Output Circuit. Is the test light on? Yes → Repair Fused Ignition Switch Output Circuit Shorted to Ground Perform ABS VERIFICATION TEST. No → Go To 168
168	Turn ignition off. Disconnect the #10 Fuse from the Fuse Block. Using a test light connected to 12 volts, probe the Fused Ignition Switch Output Circuit. Is the test light on? Yes → Replace the CAB. Perform ABS VERIFICATION TEST. No → Go To 169
169	Turn ignition off. If there are no potential causes remaining, the Fuse is assumed to be defective. View repair options. Repair Test Complete.

CR4020001998020X

Fig. 106 Scan Tool No Response From CAB Controller (Part 2 of 3). 2000 Neon

When Monitored and Set Condition:

CAB POWER FEED

When Monitored: Ignition on. The CAB monitors the Fused B(+) circuit at all times for proper system voltage.

Set Condition: If the Fused B(+) voltage is missing when the CAB detects that an internal main driver is not "on", the Diagnostic Trouble Code (DTC) is set.

POSSIBLE CAUSES
INTERMITTENT DTC
BLOWN FUSE - FUSED B(+) CIRCUIT
NO B+ SUPPLY TO FUSE
FUSED B(+) CIRCUIT OPEN
FUSED B(+) CIRCUIT INTERMITTENTLY SHORTED TO GROUND
FUSED B(+) CIRCUIT SHORTED TO GROUND
CAB - FUSED B(+) CIRCUIT OPEN
CAB - FUSED B(+) CIRCUIT SHORTED TO GROUND

TEST	ACTION
1	Turn the ignition on. With the DRBIII®, erase DTC's. Turn the ignition off. Turn the ignition on. Drive the vehicle above 25 km/h (15 mph) for at least 10 seconds. Stop the vehicle. With the DRBIII®, read DTC's. Does the DRBIII® display CAB Power Feed? Yes → Go To 2 No → Go To 10
2	Turn the ignition off. Remove and Inspect the ABS Fuse 10 in the Fuse Block. Is the Fuse blown? Yes → Go To 3 No → Go To 7

CR4020102296010X

Fig. 108 CAB Power Feed (Part 1 of 3). 2001–02 Neon

TEST	ACTION
3	Turn the ignition off. Visually inspect the Fused B(+) Circuit in the wiring harness from the Fuse Block to the CAB. Look for any sign of an intermittent short to ground. Is the wiring harness OK? Yes → Go To 4 No → Repair the Fused B(+) Circuit Shorted to Ground. Perform ABS VERIFICATION TEST - VER 1.
4	Turn the ignition off. Remove the ABS Fuse 10 from the Fuse Block. Disconnect the CAB harness connector. **Note: Check connector - Clean/repair as necessary.** Using a test light connected to 12 volts, probe the Fused B(+) Circuit. Is the test light on? Yes → Repair the Fused B(+) Circuit Shorted to Ground. Perform ABS VERIFICATION TEST - VER 1. No → Go To 5
5	Turn the ignition off. Remove the ABS Fuse 19 from the Junction Block. The CAB must be connected for the results of this test to be valid. Using a test light connected to 12 volts, probe the Fused B(+) Circuit at the Junction Block fuse terminal. Is the test light on? Yes → Replace the CAB. Perform ABS VERIFICATION TEST - VER 1. No → Go To 6
6	Turn the ignition off. If there are no potential causes remaining, view repair. Repair Replace the Fuse. Perform ABS VERIFICATION TEST - VER 1.
7	Remove the ABS Fuse 10 from the Fuse Block. Turn the ignition on. Measure the voltage of the Fused B+ supply to Fuse 10 in the Fuse Block. Is the voltage above 10 volts? Yes → Go To 8 No → Repair the B+ Supply circuit for an open. Perform ABS VERIFICATION TEST - VER 1.
8	Turn the ignition off. Remove the ABS Fuse 10 from the Fuse Block. Disconnect the CAB harness connector. **Note: Check connector - Clean/repair as necessary.** Measure the resistance of the Fused B(+) circuit between the Fuse Block Fuse terminal 10 and the CAB connector. Is the resistance below 5 ohms? Yes → Go To 9 No → Repair Fused B(+) Circuit Open. Perform ABS VERIFICATION TEST - VER 1.

CR4020102296020X

Fig. 108 CAB Power Feed (Part 2 of 3). 2001–02 Neon

When Monitored and Set Condition:

CLUSTER FAILURE

When Monitored: Ignition on, every time a message is sent from the instrument cluster.

Set Condition: When the message from the instrument cluster, via the PCI Bus, informs the CAB that it cannot turn on the ABS Warning Indicator or the Red Brake Warning Indicator.

POSSIBLE CAUSES
CLUSTER FAILURE DTC PRESENT
INTERMITTENT DTC

TEST	ACTION
1	With the DRBIII®, erase DTCs. With the DRBIII®, read DTCs. Does the DRBIII® display Cluster Failure? Yes → Replace the Instrument Cluster Perform ABS VERIFICATION TEST - VER 1. No → Go To 2
2	Turn the ignition off. Visually inspect the related wiring harness. Look for any chafed, pierced, pinched, or partially broken wires. Visually inspect the related wire harness connectors. Look for broken, bent, pushed out, or corroded terminals. Were any problems found? Yes → Repair as necessary. Perform ABS VERIFICATION TEST - VER 1. No → Test Complete.

CR4020102297000X

Fig. 109 Cluster Failure. 2001–02 Neon

TEST	ACTION
9	If there are no potential causes remaining, view repair. Repair Replace the CAB. Perform ABS VERIFICATION TEST - VER 1.
10	Turn the ignition off. Visually inspect the related wiring harness. Look for any chafed, pierced, pinched, or partially broken wires. Visually inspect the related wire harness connectors. Look for broken, bent, pushed out, or corroded terminals. Were any problems found? Yes → Repair as necessary. Perform ABS VERIFICATION TEST - VER 1. No → Test Complete.

CR4020102296030X

Fig. 108 CAB Power Feed (Part 3 of 3). 2001–02 Neon

When Monitored and Set Condition:

CONTROLLER FAILURE

When Monitored: Ignition on. The CAB monitors its internal microprocessors for correct operation.

Set Condition: If the CAB detects an internal fault, the DTC is set.

POSSIBLE CAUSES
GROUND AND POWER CONNECTIONS
GROUND CIRCUIT HIGH RESISTANCE
GROUND CIRCUIT INTERFERENCE
CAB - INTERNAL FAILURE

TEST	ACTION
1	Inspect for non-factory wiring that may interfere with CAB power or ground circuits. Disconnect the CAB harness connector. Inspect the CAB wiring harness for incorrect routing and damage. Inspect the CAB harness and component connectors for corrosion and damage. Were any concerns found? Yes → Repair as necessary. Perform ABS VERIFICATION TEST - VER 1. No → Go To 2
2	Turn the ignition off. Disconnect the CAB harness connector. **Note: Check connector - Clean/repair as necessary.** Measure the resistance of the CAB ground circuits to body ground. Is the resistance below 1.0 ohm? Yes → Go To 3 No → Repair the Ground circuit high resistance. Perform ABS VERIFICATION TEST - VER 1.
3	Turn the ignition off. Disconnect the CAB harness connector. **Note: Check connector - Clean/repair as necessary.** Turn the ignition on. Turn on all accessories. Measure the voltage of the Ground circuit. Is the voltage below 1.0 volts? Yes → Go To 4 No → Repair as necessary. Unsplice any accessories connected to the CAB ground circuit. Reroute and shield any high voltage cables away from the CAB ground circuit. Perform ABS VERIFICATION TEST - VER 1.

CR4020102298010X

Fig. 110 Controller Failure (Part 1 of 2). 2001–02 Neon

TEST	ACTION
4	If there are no potential causes remaining, view repair. Repair Replace the CAB. Perform ABS VERIFICATION TEST - VER 1.

CR4020102298020X

Fig. 110 Controller Failure (Part 2 of 2). 2001–02 Neon

When Monitored and Set Condition:

LF SENSOR CIRCUIT FAILURE

When Monitored: Ignition on. The CAB monitors the wheel speed circuit every 7 milliseconds (ms).

Set Condition: If the CAB detects an open or shorted wheel speed sensor circuit, the Diagnostic Trouble Code (DTC) will set.

POSSIBLE CAUSES
LEFT FRONT WHEEL SPEED SENSOR OR CONNECTOR DAMAGE
LEFT FRONT WHEEL SPEED SENSOR CIRCUITS SHORTED OR OPEN
CAB--NO OUTPUT
INTERMITTENT CIRCUIT DTC
LEFT FRONT WHEEL SPEED SENSOR -- NO OUTPUT
CAB - UNABLE TO READ LEFT FRONT WHEEL SPEED SENSOR SIGNAL

TEST	ACTION
1	Turn the ignition on. With the DRBIII®, record and erase DTC's. Turn the ignition off. Turn the ignition on. With the DRBIII®, read DTC's. Does the DRBIII® display LF Sensor Circuit Failure? Yes → Go To 2 No → Go To 6
2	Turn the ignition off. Inspect the Left Front Wheel Speed Sensor and Connector.' Is the Sensor or Connector Damaged? Yes → Repair as necessary. Perform ABS VERIFICATION TEST - VER 1. No → Go To 3

CR4020102299010X

Fig. 111 Lefthand Front Sensor Circuit Failure (Part 1 of 2). 2001–02 Neon

TEST	ACTION
3	Turn the ignition off. Disconnect the Left Front Wheel Speed Sensor connector. **Note: Check connector - Clean/repair as necessary.** Disconnect the CAB connector. **Note: Check connector - Clean/repair as necessary.** Turn the ignition on. Check the Left Front Wheel Speed Sensor 12 volt Supply and Signal circuits for a short to battery, ground, to each other and for open. For the purposes of this test, a short to ground must be below 15k ohms. Was any circuit short or open found? Yes → Repair Left Front Wheel Speed Sensor circuit short or open. Perform ABS VERIFICATION TEST - VER 1. No → Go To 4
4	Turn ignition off. Make sure the CAB is not disconnected. Disconnect the Left Front Wheel Speed Sensor connector. **Note: Check connector - Clean/repair as necessary.** Turn ignition on. Measure the voltage across the Left Front Wheel Speed Sensor 12 Volt Supply and Signal circuits at the Left Front Wheel Speed Sensor connector. Is the voltage above 10 volts? Yes → Go To 5 No → Replace the Controller Antilock Brake Perform ABS VERIFICATION TEST - VER 1.
5	Turn ignition off. Disconnect the CAB harness connector. Remove the harness strain relief to access the wires in the CAB connector. Using a DC voltmeter and special tool 6801, backprobe the Wheel Speed Sensor 12 volt Supply and Signal circuits at the CAB. Reconnect the CAB. Turn ignition on. Slowly rotate the left front wheel while observing voltmeter reading. Does the voltage change from approximately 1.6 volts to 0.8 volts as the wheel is rotated? Yes → Replace the CAB. Perform ABS VERIFICATION TEST - VER 1. No → Replace the Left Front Wheel Speed Sensor. Perform ABS VERIFICATION TEST - VER 1.
6	Turn the ignition off. Visually inspect the related wiring harness. Look for any chafed, pierced, pinched, or partially broken wires. Visually inspect the related wire harness connectors. Look for broken, bent, pushed out, or corroded terminals. Were any problems found? Yes → Repair as necessary. Perform ABS VERIFICATION TEST - VER 1. No → Test Complete.

CR4020102299020X

Fig. 111 Lefthand Front Sensor Circuit Failure (Part 2 of 2). 2001–02 Neon

When Monitored and Set Condition:

LF WHEEL SPEED/ SIGNAL FAILURE

When Monitored: Wheel speed comparison is checked at drive off or every 7 milliseconds (ms). Sensor circuit continuity is checked every 7 milliseconds. Wheel speed phase length supervision is checked every 7 milliseconds.

Set Condition: If, during an ABS stop, the CAB commands any valve solenoid on for an extended length of time, and does not see a corresponding wheel speed change, the Diagnostic Trouble Code (DTC) is set. The DTC can also set if the signal is missing or erratic.

POSSIBLE CAUSES
LEFT FRONT WHEEL SPEED SENSOR OR CONNECTOR DAMAGED
TONE WHEEL DAMAGED
LEFT FRONT WHEEL SPEED SENSOR AIR GAP OUT OF SPECIFICATION
LEFT FRONT WHEEL BEARING OUT OF SPECIFICATION
LEFT FRONT WHEEL SPEED SENSOR INOPERATIVE
CAB - WON'T RESPOND TO LEFT FRONT WHEEL SPEED SENSOR SIGNAL
INTERMITTENT SIGNAL DTC

TEST	ACTION
1	Turn the ignition on. Using the DRBIII®, monitor the Left Front Wheel Speed Sensor while an assistant drives the vehicle. Slowly accelerate as straight as possible from a stop to 24 km/h (15 mph). With the DRBIII®, monitor all wheel speed sensors. Is Left Front WSS Signal 0 km/h (0 mph) or differing from others by more than 5 km/h (3 mph)? Yes → Go To 2 No → Go To 7
2	Turn the ignition off. Inspect the Left Front Wheel Speed Sensor and Connector. Is the Sensor or Connector Damaged? Yes → Repair as necessary. Perform ABS VERIFICATION TEST - VER 1. No → Go To 3

CR4020102300010X

Fig. 112 Lefthand Front Wheel Speed Signal Failure (Part 1 of 3). 2001–02 Neon

TEST	ACTION
3	Turn the ignition off. Inspect the Tone Wheel for damaged or missing teeth, cracks, or looseness. **Note: The Tone Wheel Teeth should be perfectly square, not bent or nicked.** Is the Tone Wheel OK? Yes → Go To 4 No → Replace the Tone Wheel. Perform ABS VERIFICATION TEST - VER 1.
4	Turn the ignition off. Using a Feeler Gauge, measure the Wheel Speed Sensor Air Gap. **NOTE: The Air Gap should be checked in at least four places on the Tone Wheel.** Is the Air Gap between 0.42 mm - 1.71 mm (0.017" - 0.068") ? Yes → Go To 5 No → Repair as necessary. Perform ABS VERIFICATION TEST - VER 1.
5	Turn the ignition off. Inspect the wheel bearings for excessive runout or clearance. Is the bearing clearance OK ? Yes → Go To 6 No → Repair as necessary. Perform ABS VERIFICATION TEST - VER 1.
6	Turn ignition off. Disconnect the CAB harness connector. Remove the harness strain relief to access the wires in the CAB connector. Using a DC voltmeter and special tool 6801, backprobe the Wheel Speed Sensor 12 volt Supply and Signal circuits at the CAB. Reconnect the CAB. Turn the ignition on. Slowly rotate the left front wheel while observing voltmeter reading. Does the voltage change from approximately 1.6 volts to 0.8 volts as the wheel is rotated? Yes → Replace the Controller Antilock Brake Perform ABS VERIFICATION TEST - VER 1. No → Replace the Left Front Wheel Speed Sensor Perform ABS VERIFICATION TEST - VER 1.

CR4020102300020X

Fig. 112 Lefthand Front Wheel Speed Signal Failure (Part 2 of 3). 2001–02 Neon

TEST	ACTION
7	Turn the ignition off. Visually inspect wheel speed sensor. Visually inspect tone wheel. Visually inspect wiring harness. Visually inspect brakes for locking up due to lining contamination or overheating. Inspect all Components for defects which may cause a Signal DTC to set. Is any Component Damaged? Yes → Repair as necessary. Perform ABS VERIFICATION TEST - VER 1. No → Test Complete.

CR4020102300030X

Fig. 112 Lefthand Front Wheel Speed Signal Failure (Part 3 of 3). 2001–02 Neon

TEST	ACTION
3	Turn the ignition off. Disconnect the Left Rear Wheel Speed Sensor connector. **Note: Check connector - Clean/repair as necessary.** Disconnect the CAB connector. **Note: Check connector - Clean/repair as necessary.** Turn the ignition on. Check the Left Rear Wheel Speed Sensor 12 volt Supply and Signal circuits for a short to battery, ground, to each other and for open. For the purposes of this test, a short to ground must be below 15k ohms. Was any circuit short or open found? Yes → Repair Left Rear Wheel Speed Sensor circuit short or open. Perform ABS VERIFICATION TEST - VER 1. No → Go To 4
4	Turn ignition off. Disconnect the Left Rear Wheel Speed Sensor connector. Turn ignition on. Measure the voltage across the Left Rear Wheel Speed Sensor 12 Volt Supply and Signal circuits at the Left Rear Wheel Speed Sensor connector. Is the voltage above 10 volts? Yes → Go To 5 No → Replace the Controller Antilock Brake Perform ABS VERIFICATION TEST - VER 1.
5	Turn ignition off. Disconnect the CAB harness connector. Remove the harness strain relief to access the wires in the CAB connector. Using a DC voltmeter and special tool 6801, backprobe the Wheel Speed Sensor 12 volt Supply and Signal circuits at the CAB. Reconnect the CAB. Turn ignition on. Slowly rotate the left rear wheel while observing voltmeter reading. Does the voltage change from approximately 1.6 volts to 0.8 volts as the wheel is rotated? Yes → Replace the Controller Anti-Lock Brake Perform ABS VERIFICATION TEST - VER 1. No → Replace the Left Rear Wheel Speed Sensor. Perform ABS VERIFICATION TEST - VER 1.
6	Turn the ignition off. Visually inspect the related wiring harness. Look for any chafed, pierced, pinched, or partially broken wires. Visually inspect the related wire harness connectors. Look for broken, bent, pushed out, or corroded terminals. Were any problems found? Yes → Repair as necessary. Perform ABS VERIFICATION TEST - VER 1. No → Test Complete.

CR4020102301020X

Fig. 113 Lefthand Rear Sensor Circuit Failure (Part 2 of 2). 2001–02 Neon

When Monitored and Set Condition:

LR SENSOR CIRCUIT FAILURE

When Monitored: Ignition on. The CAB monitors the wheel speed circuit every 7 milliseconds (ms).

Set Condition: If the CAB detects an open or shorted wheel speed sensor circuit, the Diagnostic Trouble Code (DTC) will set.

POSSIBLE CAUSES
LEFT REAR WHEEL SPEED SENSOR OR CONNECTOR DAMAGE
LEFT REAR WHEEL SPEED SENSOR CIRCUITS SHORTED OR OPEN
CAB-NO OUTPUT
LEFT REAR WHEEL SPEED SENSOR -- NO OUTPUT
CAB - UNABLE TO READ LEFT REAR WHEEL SPEED SENSOR SIGNAL
INTERMITTENT CIRCUIT DTC

TEST	ACTION
1	Turn the ignition on. With the DRBIII®, record and erase DTC's. Turn the ignition off. Turn the ignition on. With the DRBIII®, read DTC's. Does the DRBIII® display LR Sensor Circuit Failure? Yes → Go To 2 No → Go To 6
2	Turn the ignition off. Inspect the Left Rear Wheel Speed Sensor and Connector. Is the Sensor or Connector Damaged? Yes → Repair as necessary. Perform ABS VERIFICATION TEST - VER 1. No → Go To 3

CR4020102301010X

Fig. 113 Lefthand Rear Sensor Circuit Failure (Part 1 of 2). 2001–02 Neon

When Monitored and Set Condition:

LR WHEEL SPEED/ SIGNAL FAILURE

When Monitored: Wheel speed comparison is checked at drive off or every 7 milliseconds (ms). Wheel speed circuit continuity is checked every 7 milliseconds. Wheel speed phase length supervision is checked every 7 milliseconds.

Set Condition: If, during an ABS stop, the CAB commands any valve solenoid on for an extended length of time, and does not see a corresponding wheel speed change, the Diagnostic Trouble Code (DTC) is set. The DTC can also set if the signal is missing or erratic.

POSSIBLE CAUSES
LEFT REAR WHEEL SPEED SENSOR OR CONNECTOR DAMAGED
TONE WHEEL DAMAGED
LEFT REAR WHEEL SPEED SENSOR AIR GAP OUT OF SPECIFICATION
WHEEL BEARINGS OUT OF SPECIFICATION
INTERMITTENT SIGNAL DTC

TEST	ACTION
1	Turn the ignition on. While an assistant drives, use the DRBIII® to monitor all Wheel Speed Sensors. Slowly accelerate as straight as possible from a stop to 24 Km/h (15 Mph). With the DRBIII®, monitor all wheel speed sensors. Is Left Rear WSS Signal 0 km/h (0 mph) or differing from others by more than 5 km/h (3 mph)? Yes → Go To 2 No → Go To 6
2	Turn the ignition off. Inspect the Left Rear Wheel Speed Sensor and Connector. Is the Sensor or Connector damaged? Yes → Repair as necessary. Perform ABS VERIFICATION TEST - VER 1. No → Go To 3
3	Turn the ignition off. Inspect the Tone Wheel for damaged or missing teeth, cracks, or looseness. **Note: The Tone Wheel Teeth should be perfectly square, not bent or nicked.** Is the Tone Wheel OK? Yes → Go To 4 No → Replace the Tone Wheel. Perform ABS VERIFICATION TEST - VER 1.

CR4020102302010X

Fig. 114 Lefthand Rear Wheel Speed Signal Circuit (Part 1 of 2). 2001–02 Neon

TEST	ACTION
4	Turn the ignition off. Using a Feeler Gauge, measure the Wheel Speed Sensor Air Gap. **NOTE: The Air Gap should be checked in at least four places on the Tone Wheel.** Is the Air Gap between 0.42 mm - 1.71 mm (0.017" - 0.068") ? Yes → Go To 5 No → Repair as necessary. Perform ABS VERIFICATION TEST - VER 1.
5	Turn the ignition off. Inspect the wheel bearings at the affected wheel for excessive runout or clearance. Is the bearing clearance OK ? Yes → Test Complete. No → Repair as necessary. Perform ABS VERIFICATION TEST - VER 1.
6	Turn the ignition off. Visually inspect wheel speed sensor. Visually inspect tone wheel. Visually inspect wiring harness. Visually inspect brakes for locking up due to lining contamination or overheating. Inspect all Components for defects which may cause a Signal DTC to set. Is any Component Damaged? Yes → Repair as necessary. Perform ABS VERIFICATION TEST - VER 1. No → Test Complete.

CR4020102302020X

Fig. 114 Lefthand Rear Wheel Speed Signal Circuit (Part 2 of 2). 2001–02 Neon

When Monitored and Set Condition:

PUMP MOTOR NOT WORKING PROPERLY

When Monitored: Ignition on. The CAB commands the pump on at 20 km/h (12 mph) to check its operation, if the brake switch is not applied. If the brake is applied, the test will run at 40 km/h (25 mph). The CAB monitors pump voltage every 7 milliseconds.

Set Condition: The DTC is stored when the CAB detects: 1) Improper voltage decay after the pump was turned off. 2) Pump not energized by the CAB, but voltage is present for 3.5 seconds. 3) Pump is turned on by the CAB, but without sufficient voltage to operate it.

POSSIBLE CAUSES
CAB - PUMP MOTOR RUNNING CONTINUOUSLY
ABS PUMP MOTOR INTERMITTENT DTC
FUSED B(+) CIRCUIT INTERMITTENTLY SHORTED TO GROUND
FUSED B(+) CIRCUIT SHORTED TO GROUND
CAB - FUSED B(+) CIRCUIT SHORTED TO GROUND
FUSE BLOWN - PUMP MOTOR CIRCUIT
NO B+ SUPPLY TO FUSE
ABS PUMP MOTOR INOPERATIVE
FUSED B(+) CIRCUIT OPEN
GROUND CIRCUIT OPEN
GROUND CIRCUIT HIGH RESISTANCE
CAB - INTERNAL FAULT

TEST	ACTION
1	Turn the ignition off. Reconnect all connectors. Turn the ignition on. Monitor the pump motor for continuous operation. Is the pump motor running continuously? Yes → Replace the Controller Anti-Lock Brake Perform ABS VERIFICATION TEST - VER 1. No → Go To 2

CR4020102304010X

Fig. 116 Pump Motor Not Working Properly (Part 1 of 4). 2001–02 Neon

When Monitored and Set Condition:

PCI BUS COMMUNICATION

When Monitored: Ignition ON, every 7 ms.

Set Condition: When the CAB does not receive a message from the instrument cluster for 10 seconds.

POSSIBLE CAUSES
CHECK COMMUNICATION TO MIC
CAB-- INTERNAL FAULT

TEST	ACTION
1	Turn the ignition on. With the DRBIII®, attempt to communicate with the MIC Was the DRB able to I/D or communicate with the MIC? Yes → Go To 2 No → Refer to the Communication category and perform the symptom Bus +/- Signals Open from the Controller Anti-Lock Brake. Perform ABS VERIFICATION TEST - VER 1.
2	With the DRB, erase DTC's. Turn the ignition on and wait approximately 1 minute. With the DRB, read DTC's. Did this DTC reset? Yes → Replace the Controller Anti-Lock Brake Perform ABS VERIFICATION TEST - VER 1. No → Test Complete.

CR4020102303000X

Fig. 115 PCI BUS Communication. 2001–02 Neon

TEST	ACTION
2	Turn the ignition on. With the DRBIII®, read DTC's. With the DRBIII®, erase DTC's. Turn the ignition off. Turn the ignition on. With the DRBIII®, actuate the ABS pump motor. Did the Pump Motor operate when actuated? No → Go To 3 Yes → Go To 14
3	Turn the ignition off. Remove and inspect the ABS Pump fuse #8 in the PDC. Is the Fuse blown? Yes → Go To 4 No → Go To 8
4	Turn the ignition off. Visually inspect the Fused B(+) Circuit in the wiring harness from the PDC to the CAB. Look for any sign of an Intermittent Short to Ground. Is the wiring harness OK? Yes → Go To 5 No → Repair the Fused B(+) Circuit shorted to ground. Perform ABS VERIFICATION TEST - VER 1.
5	Turn the ignition off. Remove the ABS PUMP Fuse # 8 from the Power Distribution Center (PDC). Disconnect the CAB connector. **Note: Check connector - Clean/repair as necessary.** Using a test light connected to 12 volts, probe the Fused B (+) Circuit. Is the test light on? Yes → Repair the Fused B(+) circuit short to ground. Perform ABS VERIFICATION TEST - VER 1. No → Go To 6
6	Turn the ignition off. Remove the ABS PUMP Fuse 8 from the PDC. The CAB must be connected for the results of this test to be valid. Using a test light connected to 12 volts, probe the Fused B (+) circuit in the PDC. Is the test light on? Yes → Replace the Controller Anti-Lock Brake Perform ABS VERIFICATION TEST - VER 1. No → Go To 7
7	Turn the ignition off. If there are no potential causes remaining, replace the Fuse. If there are no possible causes remaining, view repair. Repair Replace the ABS Pump Motor Fuse. Perform ABS VERIFICATION TEST - VER 1.

CR4020102304020X

Fig. 116 Pump Motor Not Working Properly (Part 2 of 4). 2001–02 Neon

TEST	ACTION
8	Turn the ignition on. Using a 12-volt test light connected to ground, check the B+ supply to Fuse 8 in the PDC. Is the B+ supply OK? Yes → Go To 9 No → Repair the B+ supply for an open. Perform ABS VERIFICATION TEST - VER 1.
9	Turn the ignition off. Disconnect Pump Motor Connector. Connect a 10 gauge jumper wire between pump motor Fused B (+) circuit and a 40 Amp Fused B (+) circuit. Connect a 10 gauge jumper wire between pump motor ground circuit and a known good body ground. Monitor Pump Motor operation. Is the pump motor running? Yes → Go To 10 No → Replace the ABS Pump Motor/Hydraulic Control Unit assembly. Perform ABS VERIFICATION TEST - VER 1.
10	Turn the ignition off. Remove the ABS PUMP Fuse 8 from the Power Distribution Center (PDC). Disconnect the CAB connector. **Note: Check connector - Clean/repair as necessary.** Measure the resistance of the Fused B (+) circuit between the PDC Fuse Terminal and the CAB connector. Is the resistance below 10 ohms? Yes → Go To 11 No → Repair the Fused B(+) circuit for an open. Perform ABS VERIFICATION TEST - VER 1.
11	Turn the ignition off. Disconnect CAB Connector. **Note: Check connector - Clean/repair as necessary.** Measure the resistance of the CAB ground circuits. Is the resistance below 1.0 ohm? Yes → Go To 12 No → Repair the ground circuit circuit for an open. Perform ABS VERIFICATION TEST - VER 1.
12	Turn the ignition on. With the DRBIII®, enable pump motor actuation. **NOTE: Pump motor will not operate, but voltage will be applied.** Measure the voltage drop across the ABS ground circuit connection, with pump motor actuation enabled. Is the voltage below 0.1 volt? Yes → Go To 13 No → Repair the Ground circuit for an open. Perform ABS VERIFICATION TEST - VER 1.

CR4020102304030X

Fig. 116 Pump Motor Not Working Properly (Part 3 of 4). 2001–02 Neon

When Monitored and Set Condition:

RF SENSOR CIRCUIT FAILURE

When Monitored: Ignition on. The CAB monitors the wheel speed circuit every 7 milliseconds.

Set Condition: If the CAB detects an open or shorted wheel speed sensor circuit, the Diagnostic Trouble Code (DTC) will set.

POSSIBLE CAUSES
RIGHT FRONT WHEEL SPEED SENSOR OR CONNECTOR DAMAGE
RIGHT FRONT WHEEL SPEED SENSOR CIRCUITS SHORTED OR OPEN
CAB-NO OUTPUT
RIGHT FRONT WHEEL SPEED SENSOR -- NO OUTPUT
CAB - UNABLE TO READ RIGHT FRONT WHEEL SPEED SENSOR SIGNAL
INTERMITTENT CIRCUIT DTC

TEST	ACTION
1	Turn the ignition on. With the DRBIII®, record and erase DTC's. Turn the ignition off. Turn the ignition on. With the DRBIII®, read DTC's. Does the DRBIII® display RF Sensor Circuit Failure? Yes → Go To 2 No → Go To 6
2	Turn the ignition off. Inspect the Right Front Wheel Speed Sensor and Connector. Is the Sensor or Connector Damaged? Yes → Repair as necessary. Perform ABS VERIFICATION TEST - VER 1. No → Go To 3

CR4020102305010X

Fig. 117 Righthand Front Sensor Circuit Failure (Part 1 of 2). 2001–02 Neon

TEST	ACTION
13	If there are no potential causes remaining, view repair. Repair Replace the Controller Anti-Lock Brake Perform ABS VERIFICATION TEST - VER 1.
14	Turn the ignition off. Visually inspect the related wiring harness. Look for any chafed, pierced, pinched, or partially broken wires. Visually inspect the related wire harness connectors. Look for broken, bent, pushed out, or corroded terminals. Were any problems found? Yes → Repair as necessary. Perform ABS VERIFICATION TEST - VER 1. No → Test Complete.

CR4020102304040X

Fig. 116 Pump Motor Not Working Properly (Part 4 of 4). 2001–02 Neon

TEST	ACTION
3	Turn the ignition off. Disconnect the Right Front Wheel Speed Sensor connector. **Note: Check connector - Clean/repair as necessary.** Disconnect the CAB connector. **Note: Check connector - Clean/repair as necessary.** Turn the ignition on. Check the Right Front Wheel Speed Sensor 12 volt Supply and Signal circuits for a short to battery, ground, to each other and for open. For the purposes of this test, a short to ground must be below 15k ohms. Was any circuit short or open found? Yes → Repair Right Front Wheel Speed Sensor circuit short or open. Perform ABS VERIFICATION TEST - VER 1. No → Go To 4
4	Turn ignition off. Make sure the CAB is not disconnected. Disconnect the Left Front Wheel Speed Sensor connector. Turn ignition on. Measure the voltage across the Right Front Wheel Speed Sensor 12 Volt Supply and Signal circuits at the Right Front Wheel Speed Sensor connector. Is the voltage above 10 volts? Yes → Go To 5 No → Replace the Controller Antilock Brake Perform ABS VERIFICATION TEST - VER 1.
5	Turn ignition off. Disconnect the CAB harness connector. Remove the harness strain relief to access the wires in the CAB connector. Using a DC voltmeter and special tool 6801, backprobe the Wheel Speed Sensor 12 volt Supply and Signal circuits at the CAB. Reconnect the CAB. Turn ignition on. Slowly rotate the right front wheel while observing voltmeter reading. Does the voltage change from approximately 1.6 volts to 0.8 volts as the wheel is rotated? Yes → Replace the CAB. Perform ABS VERIFICATION TEST - VER 1. No → Replace the Right Front Wheel Speed Sensor. Perform ABS VERIFICATION TEST - VER 1.
6	Turn the ignition off. Visually inspect the related wiring harness. Look for any chafed, pierced, pinched, or partially broken wires. Visually inspect the related wire harness connectors. Look for broken, bent, pushed out, or corroded terminals. Were any problems found? Yes → Repair as necessary. Perform ABS VERIFICATION TEST - VER 1. No → Test Complete.

CR4020102305020X

Fig. 117 Righthand Front Sensor Circuit Failure (Part 2 of 2). 2001–02 Neon

When Monitored and Set Condition:

RF WHEEL SPEED/ SIGNAL FAILURE

When Monitored: Wheel speed comparison is checked at drive off or every 7 milliseconds (ms). Wheel speed continuity is checked every 7 milliseconds. Wheel speed phase length supervision is checked every 7 milliseconds.

Set Condition: If, during an ABS stop, the CAB commands any valve solenoid on for an extended length of time, and does not see a corresponding wheel speed change, the Diagnostic Trouble Code (DTC) is set. The DTC can also set if the signal is missing or erratic.

POSSIBLE CAUSES
RIGHT FRONT WHEEL SPEED SENSOR OR CONNECTOR DAMAGED
TONE WHEEL DAMAGED
RIGHT FRONT WHEEL SPEED SENSOR AIR GAP OUT OF SPECIFICATION
WHEEL BEARINGS OUT OF SPECIFICATION
INTERMITTENT SIGNAL DTC

TEST	ACTION
1	Turn the ignition on. While an assistant drives, use the DRBIII® to monitor all Wheel Speed Sensors. Slowly accelerate as straight as possible from a stop to 24 Km/h (15 Mph). With the DRBIII®, monitor all wheel speed sensors. Is Right Front WSS Signal 0 km/h (0 mph) or differing from others by more than 5 km/h (3 mph)? Yes → Go To 2 No → Go To 6
2	Turn the ignition off. Inspect the Right Front Wheel Speed Sensor and Connector. Is the Sensor or Connector damaged? Yes → Repair as necessary. Perform ABS VERIFICATION TEST - VER 1. No → Go To 3
3	Turn the ignition off. Inspect the Tone Wheel for damaged or missing teeth, cracks, or looseness. **Note: The Tone Wheel Teeth should be perfectly square, not bent or nicked.** Is the Tone Wheel OK? Yes → Go To 4 No → Replace the Tone Wheel. Perform ABS VERIFICATION TEST - VER 1.

CR4020102306010X

Fig. 118 Righthand Front Wheel Speed Signal Failure (Part 1 of 2). 2001–02 Neon

RR SENSOR CIRCUIT FAILURE

When Monitored: Ignition on. The CAB monitors the wheel speed circuit every 7 milliseconds (ms).

Set Condition: If the CAB detects an open or shorted wheel speed sensor circuit, the Diagnostic Trouble Code (DTC) will set.

POSSIBLE CAUSES
RIGHT REAR WHEEL SPEED SENSOR OR CONNECTOR DAMAGE
RIGHT REAR WHEEL SPEED SENSOR CIRCUITS SHORTED OR OPEN
CAB-NO OUTPUT
RIGHT REAR WHEEL SPEED SENSOR -- NO OUTPUT
CAB - UNABLE TO READ RIGHT REAR WHEEL SPEED SENSOR SIGNAL
INTERMITTENT CIRCUIT DTC

TEST	ACTION
1	Turn the ignition on. With the DRBIII®, read DTC's. With the DRBIII®, erase DTC's. Turn the ignition off. Turn the ignition on. With the DRBIII®, read DTC's. Does the DRBIII® display RR Sensor Circuit Failure? Yes → Go To 2 No → Go To 6
2	Turn the ignition off. Inspect the Right Rear Wheel Speed Sensor and Connector. Is the Sensor or Connector Damaged? Yes → Repair as necessary. Perform ABS VERIFICATION TEST - VER 1. No → Go To 3

CR4020102307010X

Fig. 119 Righthand Rear Sensor Circuit Failure (Part 1 of 2). 2001–02 Neon

TEST	ACTION
4	Turn the ignition off. Using a Feeler Gauge, measure the Wheel Speed Sensor Air Gap. **NOTE: The Air Gap should be checked in at least four places on the Tone Wheel.** Is the Air Gap between 0.42 mm - 1.71 mm (0.017" - 0.068") ? Yes → Go To 5 No → Repair as necessary. Perform ABS VERIFICATION TEST - VER 1.
5	Turn the ignition off. Inspect the wheel bearings at the affected wheel for excessive runout or clearance. Is the bearing clearance OK ? Yes → Test Complete. No → Repair as necessary. Perform ABS VERIFICATION TEST - VER 1.
6	Turn the ignition off. Visually inspect wheel speed sensor. Visually inspect tone wheel. Visually inspect wiring harness. Visually inspect brakes for locking up due to lining contamination or overheating. Inspect all Components for defects which may cause a Signal DTC to set. Is any Component Damaged? Yes → Repair as necessary. Perform ABS VERIFICATION TEST - VER 1. No → Test Complete.

CR4020102306020X

Fig. 118 Righthand Front Wheel Speed Signal Failure (Part 2 of 2). 2001–02 Neon

TEST	ACTION
3	Turn the ignition off. Disconnect the Right Rear Wheel Speed Sensor connector. **Note: Check connector - Clean/repair as necessary.** Disconnect the CAB connector. **Note: Check connector - Clean/repair as necessary.** Turn the ignition on. Check the Right Rear Wheel Speed Sensor 12 volt Supply and Signal circuits for a short to battery, ground, to each other and for open. For the purposes of this test, a short to ground must be below 15k ohms. Was any circuit short or open found? Yes → Repair Right Rear Wheel Speed Sensor circuit short or open. Perform ABS VERIFICATION TEST - VER 1. No → Go To 4
4	Turn ignition off. Make sure the CAB is not disconnected. Disconnect the Right Rear Wheel Speed Sensor connector. Turn ignition on. Measure the voltage across the Right Rear Wheel Speed Sensor 12 Volt Supply and Signal circuits at the Right Rear Wheel Speed Sensor connector. Is the voltage above 10 volts? Yes → Go To 5 No → Replace the Controller Antilock Brake Perform ABS VERIFICATION TEST - VER 1.
5	Turn ignition off. Disconnect the CAB harness connector. Remove the harness strain relief to access the wires in the CAB connector. Using a DC voltmeter and special tool 6801, backprobe the Wheel Speed Sensor 12 volt Supply and Signal circuits at the CAB. Reconnect the CAB. Turn ignition on. Slowly rotate the right rear wheel while observing voltmeter reading. Does the voltage change from approximately 1.6 volts to 0.8 volts as the wheel is rotated? Yes → Replace the Controller Anti-Lock Brake Perform ABS VERIFICATION TEST - VER 1. No → Replace the Right Rear Wheel Speed Sensor. Perform ABS VERIFICATION TEST - VER 1.
6	Turn the ignition off. Visually inspect the related wiring harness. Look for any chafed, pierced, pinched, or partially broken wires. Visually inspect the related wire harness connectors. Look for broken, bent, pushed out, or corroded terminals. Were any problems found? Yes → Repair as necessary. Perform ABS VERIFICATION TEST - VER 1. No → Test Complete.

CR4020102307020X

Fig. 119 Righthand Rear Sensor Circuit Failure (Part 2 of 2). 2001–02 Neon

RR WHEEL SPEED/ SIGNAL FAILURE

When Monitored: Wheel speed comparison is checked at drive off or every 7 milliseconds (ms). Wheel speed circuit continuity is checked every 7 milliseconds. Wheel speed phase length supervision is checked every 7 milliseconds.

Set Condition: If, during an ABS stop, the CAB commands any valve solenoid on for an extended length of time, and does not see a corresponding wheel speed change, the Diagnostic Trouble Code (DTC) is set. The DTC can also set if the signal is missing or erratic.

POSSIBLE CAUSES
RIGHT REAR WHEEL SPEED SENSOR OR CONNECTOR DAMAGED
TONE WHEEL DAMAGED
RIGHT REAR WHEEL SPEED SENSOR AIR GAP OUT OF SPECIFICATION
WHEEL BEARINGS OUT OF SPECIFICATION
RIGHT REAR WHEEL SPEED SENSOR INOPERATIVE
CAB - WON'T RESPOND TO WHEEL SPEED SENSOR SIGNAL
INTERMITTENT SIGNAL DTC

TEST	ACTION
1	Turn the ignition on. While an assistant drives, use the DRBIII® to monitor all Wheel Speed Sensors. Slowly accelerate as straight as possible from a stop to 24 Km/h (15 Mph). With the DRBIII®, monitor all wheel speed sensors. Is Right Rear WSS Signal 0 Km/h (0 Mph) or differing from others by more than 5kmh (3mph)? Yes → Go To 2 No → Go To 7
2	Turn the ignition off. Inspect the Right Rear Wheel Speed Sensor and Connector. Is the Sensor or Connector damaged? Yes → Repair as necessary. Perform ABS VERIFICATION TEST - VER 1. No → Go To 3

CR4020102308010X

Fig. 120 Righthand Rear Wheel Speed Signal Failure (Part 1 of 3). 2001–02 Neon

TEST	ACTION
3	Turn the ignition off. Inspect the Tone Wheel for damaged or missing teeth, cracks, or looseness. **Note: The Tone Wheel Teeth should be perfectly square, not bent or nicked.** Is the Tone Wheel OK? Yes → Go To 4 No → Replace the Tone Wheel Perform ABS VERIFICATION TEST - VER 1.
4	Turn the ignition off. Using a Feeler Gauge, measure the Wheel Speed Sensor Air Gap. **NOTE: The Air Gap should be checked in at least four places on the Tone Wheel.** Is the Air Gap between 0.42 mm - 1.71 mm (0.017" - 0.068") ? Yes → Go To 5 No → Repair as necessary. Perform ABS VERIFICATION TEST - VER 1.
5	Turn the ignition off. Inspect the wheel bearings at the affected wheel for excessive runout or clearance. Is the bearing clearance OK ? Yes → Go To 6 No → Repair as necessary. Perform ABS VERIFICATION TEST - VER 1.
6	Turn ignition off. Disconnect the CAB harness connector. Remove the harness strain relief to access the wires in the CAB connector. With a voltmeter and special tool 6801, backprobe the Wheel Speed Sensor 12 volt Supply and Signal circuits for the affected wheel at the CAB. Reconnect the CAB. Turn the ignition on. Slowly rotate the right rear wheel while observing the voltmeter reading. Does the voltage change from approximately 1.6 volts to 0.8 volts as the wheel is rotated? Yes → Replace the Controller Antilock Brake Perform ABS VERIFICATION TEST - VER 1. No → Replace the Right Rear Wheel Speed Sensor Perform ABS VERIFICATION TEST - VER 1.

CR4020102308020X

Fig. 120 Righthand Rear Wheel Speed Signal Failure (Part 2 of 3). 2001–02 Neon

TEST	ACTION
7	Turn the ignition off. Visually inspect wheel speed sensor. Visually inspect tone wheel. Visually inspect wiring harness. Visually inspect brakes for locking up due to lining contamination or overheating. Inspect all Components for defects which may cause a Signal DTC to set. Is any Component Damaged? Yes → Repair as necessary. Perform ABS VERIFICATION TEST - VER 1. No → Test Complete.

CR4020102308030X

Fig. 120 Righthand Rear Wheel Speed Signal Failure (Part 3 of 3). 2001–02 Neon

When Monitored and Set Condition:

SYSTEM OVERVOLTAGE

When Monitored: Ignition on. The CAB monitors the Fused B(+) circuit at all times for proper system voltage.

Set Condition: If the voltage is above 16.5 volts for greater than 420 milliseconds (ms), the Diagnostic Trouble Code (DTC) is set.

POSSIBLE CAUSES
BATTERY OVERCHARGED
INTERMITTENT DTC
FUSED IGNITION SWITCH OUTPUT HIGH
GROUND CIRCUIT OPEN
CAB - INTERNAL FAULT

TEST	ACTION
1	Turn the ignition on. With the DRBIII®, erase DTC's. Turn the ignition off. Turn the ignition on. Start the engine. With the DRBIII®, read DTC's. Does the DRBIII® display System Overvoltage DTC? Yes → Go To 2 No → Go To 6
2	Turn the ignition off. Inspect for battery charger connected to battery. Is a battery charger connected to the battery? Yes → Charge battery to proper level. Disconnect the battery charger. Clear DTC's. Perform ABS VERIFICATION TEST - VER 1. No → Go To 3

CR4020102309010X

Fig. 121 System Overvoltage (Part 1 of 2). 2001–02 Neon

TEST	ACTION
3	Turn the ignition off. Disconnect the CAB connector. **Note: Check connector - Clean/repair as necessary.** Start the engine. Raise engine speed above 1,800 RPM. Measure the battery voltage. Is the voltage above 16.5 volts ? Yes → Repair charging system Perform ABS VERIFICATION TEST - VER 1. No → Go To 4
4	Turn the ignition off. Disconnect the CAB connector. **Note: Check connector - Clean/repair as necessary.** Measure the resistance of the ground circuits. Is the resistance below 1.0 ohm? Yes → Go To 5 No → Repair the Ground circuit for an open. Perform ABS VERIFICATION TEST - VER 1.
5	If there are no potential causes remaining, view repair. Repair Replace the Controller Anti-Lock Brake Perform ABS VERIFICATION TEST - VER 1.
6	Turn the ignition off. Visually inspect the related wiring harness. Look for any chafed, pierced, pinched, or partially broken wires. Visually inspect the related wire harness connectors. Look for broken, bent, pushed out, or corroded terminals. Were any problems found? Yes → Repair as necessary. Perform ABS VERIFICATION TEST - VER 1. No → Test Complete.

CR4020102309020X

Fig. 121 System Overvoltage (Part 2 of 2). 2001–02 Neon

TEST	ACTION
4	Disconnect the CAB harness connector. Turn the ignition on. Measure the voltage of the Fused Ignition Switch circuit. Is the voltage above 10 volts? Yes → Go To 5 No → Repair the Fused Ignition Switch Output Circuit for high resistance Perform ABS VERIFICATION TEST - VER 1.
5	If there are no potential causes remaining, view repair. Repair Replace the Controller Antilock Brake. Perform ABS VERIFICATION TEST - VER 1.
6	Turn the ignition off. Visually inspect the related wiring harness. Look for any chafed, pierced, pinched, or partially broken wires. Visually inspect the related wire harness connectors. Look for broken, bent, pushed out, or corroded terminals. Were any problems found? Yes → Repair as necessary. Perform ABS VERIFICATION TEST - VER 1. No → Test Complete.

CR4020102310020X

Fig. 122 System Undervoltage (Part 2 of 2). 2001–02 Neon

When Monitored and Set Condition:

SYSTEM UNDERVOLTAGE

When Monitored: Ignition on. The CAB monitors the Fused Ignition Switch Output circuit voltage above 10 km/h (6 mph) every 7 milliseconds for proper system voltage.

Set Condition: If the voltage is below 9.5 volts, the Diagnostic Trouble Code (DTC) is set.

POSSIBLE CAUSES
BATTERY VOLTAGE LOW
INTERMITTENT DTC
FUSED IGNITION SWITCH OUTPUT CIRCUIT HIGH RESISTANCE
GROUND CIRCUIT OPEN
CAB - INTERNAL FAULT

TEST	ACTION
1	Turn the ignition on. With the DRBIII®, erase DTC's. Turn the ignition off. Turn the ignition on. Start the engine. Drive the vehicle above 16 km/h (10 mph) for at least 20 seconds. Stop the vehicle With the DRBIII®, read DTC's. Does the DRBIII® display System Undervoltage DTC? Yes → Go To 2 No → Go To 6
2	Engine Running. Measure the battery voltage. Is the battery voltage below 10 volts? Yes → Repair charging system Perform ABS VERIFICATION TEST - VER 1. No → Go To 3
3	Turn the ignition off. Disconnect the CAB connector. **Note: Check connector - Clean/repair as necessary.** Measure the resistance of the ground circuits. Is the resistance below 1.0 ohm? Yes → Go To 4 No → Repair the Ground circuit for an open. Perform ABS VERIFICATION TEST - VER 1.

CR4020102310010X

Fig. 122 System Undervoltage (Part 1 of 2). 2001–02 Neon

ABS VERIFICATION TEST - VER 1
1. Turn the ignition off. 2. Connect all previously disconnected components and connectors. 3. Ensure all accessories are turned off and the battery is fully charged. 4. Ensure that the Ignition is on, and with the DRBIII, erase all Diagnostic Trouble Codes from ALL modules. Start the engine and allow it to run for 2 minutes and fully operate the system that was malfunctioning. 5. Turn the ignition off and wait 5 seconds. Turn the ignition on and using the DRBIII, read DTC's from ALL modules. 6. If any Diagnostic Trouble Codes are present, return to Symptom list and troubleshoot new or recurring symptom. 7. If there are no DTC's present after turning ignition on, road test the vehicle for at least 5 minutes. Perform several antilock braking stops. **8. Caution: Ensure braking capability is available before road testing.** 9. Again, with the DRBIII® read DTC's. If any DTC's are present, return to Symptom list. 10. If there are no Diagnostic Trouble Codes (DTC's) present, and the customer's concern can no longer be duplicated, the repair is complete. Are any DTC's present or is the original concern still present? Yes → Repair is not complete, refer to appropriate symptom. No → Repair is complete.

CR4020102311000X

Fig. 123 Verification Test VER 1. 2001–02 Neon

When Monitored and Set Condition:

CAB POWER FEED

When Monitored: Ignition on. The CAB monitors the ABS Valve Fused B(+) circuit at all times for proper system voltage.

Set Condition: If the ABS Valve Fused B(+) voltage is missing, the Diagnostic Trouble Code (DTC) is set.

POSSIBLE CAUSES
INTERMITTENT DTC
ABS VALVE FUSE
ABS VALVE FUSED B(+) SUPPLY CIRCUIT OPEN
ABS VALVE FUSED B(+) CIRCUIT OPEN
ABS VALVE FUSED B(+) CIRCUIT INTERMITTENT SHORT TO GROUND
ABS VALVE FUSED B(+) CIRCUIT SHORT TO GROUND
DAMAGED CAB/CAB HARNESS CONNECTOR
CAB - GROUND CIRCUIT OPEN
CAB - INTERNAL FAULT

TEST	ACTION
1	Turn the ignition on. With the DRBIII®, read DTC's. With the DRBIII®, erase DTC's. Turn the ignition off. Turn the ignition on. With the DRBIII®, read DTC's. Does the DRBIII® display CAB POWER FEED? Yes → Go To 2 No → Go To 10
2	Turn the ignition off. Remove and Inspect the ABS Valve fuse. Is the ABS Valve fuse open? Yes → Go To 3 No → Go To 6

ARM66CR000000002

Fig. 124 CAB Power Feed (Part 1 of 3). 2003–04 Neon

TEST	ACTION
8	Reinstall the ABS Valve fuse. Disconnect the CAB harness connector. Using a 12-volt test light connected to ground, probe the ABS Valve Fused B(+) circuit at the CAB harness connector. Did the test light illuminate? Yes → Go To 9 No → Repair the ABS Valve Fused B(+) circuit for an open. Perform ABS VERIFICATION TEST
9	Turn the ignition off. Using a 12-volt test light connected to 12-volts, probe the ground circuits at the CAB harness connector. Did the test light illuminate? Yes → Replace the Controller Antilock Brake Perform ABS VERIFICATION TEST No → Repair the CAB Ground circuit for an open. Perform ABS VERIFICATION TEST
10	Turn the ignition off. Visually inspect the related wiring harness. Look for any chafed, pierced, pinched, or partially broken wires. Visually inspect the related wire harness connectors. Look for broken, bent, pushed out, or corroded terminals. Refer to any Hotline letters or Technical Service Bulletins that may apply. Were any problems found? Yes → Repair as necessary. Perform ABS VERIFICATION TEST No → Test Complete.

ARM66CR000000004

Fig. 124 CAB Power Feed (Part 3 of 3). 2003–04 Neon

TEST	ACTION
3	Turn the ignition off. Visually inspect the ABS Valve Fused B(+) circuit in the wiring harness. Look for any sign of an intermittent short to ground. Is the wiring harness OK? Yes → Go To 4 No → Repair the ABS Valve Fused B(+) circuit for a short to ground. Perform ABS VERIFICATION TEST - VER 1.
4	Turn the ignition off. Disconnect the CAB harness connector. **Note: Check connector - Clean/repair as necessary.** Using a test light connected to 12 volts, probe the ABS Valve Fused B(+) circuit fuse terminal. Did the test light illuminate? Yes → Repair the ABS Valve Fused B(+) circuit for a short to ground. Perform ABS VERIFICATION TEST No → Go To 5
5	Turn the ignition off. Reconnect the CAB harness connector. **NOTE: The CAB harness connector must be reconnected for the results of this test to be valid.** Using a test light connected to 12 volts, probe the ABS Valve Fused B(+) circuit fuse terminal. Did the test light illuminate? Yes → Replace the Controller Antilock Brake Perform ABS VERIFICATION TEST No → Replace the ABS Valve Fused B(+) fuse. If the fuse is open make sure to check for a short to ground. Perform ABS VERIFICATION TEST
6	Turn the ignition off. Disconnect the CAB harness connector. Inspect the CAB and CAB harness connector for damage. Is there any broken, bent, pushed out, corroded or spread terminals? Yes → Repair as necessary. Perform ABS VERIFICATION TEST No → Go To 7
7	Turn the ignition off. Using a 12-volt test light connected to ground, probe the B(+) supply at the ABS Valve fuse terminal. Did the test light illuminate? Yes → Go To 8 No → Repair the ABS Valve Fused B(+) supply circuit for an open. Perform ABS VERIFICATION TEST

ARM66CR000000003

Fig. 124 CAB Power Feed (Part 2 of 3). 2003–04 Neon

When Monitored and Set Condition:

CLUSTER FAILURE

When Monitored: Ignition on, every time a message is sent from the instrument cluster.

Set Condition: When the message from the instrument cluster, via the PCI Bus, informs the CAB that it cannot turn on the ABS Warning Indicator or the Red Brake Warning Indicator.

POSSIBLE CAUSES
INSTRUMENT CLUSTER OR ABS DTC PRESENT
INSTRUMENT CLUSTER
CAB--NO DTC SIGNAL TO THE INSTRUMENT CLUSTER
CAB -- PERMANENT FAULT SIGNAL
CAB--NO KEY-ON BULB CHECK SIGNAL

TEST	ACTION
1	Turn the ignition on. With the DRBIII®, read DTCs. Are there any Instrument Cluster or ABS DTCs present? Yes → Refer to the appropriate category for the related symptom(s). Perform ABS VERIFICATION TEST No → Go To 2
2	Turn the ignition off. Perform the Key-on Bulb Check. Does the ABS Warning Indicator light and then go out after a few seconds? Yes → Go To 3 No. Light remains after bulb check. Replace the Controller Antilock Brake Perform ABS VERIFICATION TEST No. Indicator never comes on. Go To 4

ARM66CR000000005

Fig. 125 Cluster Failure (Part 1 of 2). 2003–04 Neon

TEST	ACTION
3	**NOTE: The DRBIII® communication with the CAB must be operational for the result of this test to be valid.** Turn the ignition off. Remove ABS Valve fuse. Perform the Key-on Bulb Check. Does the ABS Indicator remain on after the bulb check? Yes → Test Complete. No → Replace the Controller Antilock Brake Perform ABS VERIFICATION TEST
4	**NOTE: The following steps will initiate the Instrument Cluster self test.** Turn the ignition off. Press and hold the odometer reset button. Turn the ignition to RUN. Observe the Instrument Cluster indicators. Release the odometer reset button. Did the ABS Indicator illuminate during the Instrument Cluster self test? Yes → Replace the Controller Antilock Brake in accordance with the Service Information. Perform ABS VERIFICATION TEST No → Replace the Instrument Cluster Perform ABS VERIFICATION TEST

ARM66CR000000006

Fig. 125 Cluster Failure (Part 2 of 2). 2003–04 Neon

TEST	ACTION
4	Turn the ignition off. Using a 12-volt test light connected to ground, probe the ABS Valve Fused B(+) circuit at the CAB harness connector. Did the test light illuminate? Yes → Go To 5 No → Repair the ABS Valve Fused B(+) circuit for an open. Perform ABS VERIFICATION TEST
5	Turn the ignition off. Using a 12-volt test light connected to ground, probe the ABS Pump Fused B(+) circuit at the CAB harness connector. Did the test light illuminate? Yes → Replace the Controller Antilock Brake Perform ABS VERIFICATION TEST No → Repair the ABS Pump Fused B(+) circuit for an open. Perform ABS VERIFICATION TEST
6	Turn the ignition off. Visually inspect the related wiring harness. Look for any chafed, pierced, pinched, or partially broken wires. Visually inspect the related wire harness connectors. Look for broken, bent, pushed out, or corroded terminals. Refer to any Hotline letters or Technical Service Bulletins that may apply. Were any problems found? Yes → Repair as necessary. Perform ABS VERIFICATION TEST No → Test Complete.

ARM66CR000000008

Fig. 126 Controller Failure (Part 2 of 2). 2003–04 Neon

When Monitored and Set Condition:

CONTROLLER FAILURE

When Monitored: Ignition on. The CAB monitors its internal microprocessors for correct operation.

Set Condition: If the CAB detects an internal fault, the DTC is set.

POSSIBLE CAUSES
INTERMITTENT DTC
DAMAGED CAB/CAB HARNESS CONNECTOR
CAB - GROUND CIRCUIT OPEN
ABS VALVE FUSED B(+) CIRCUIT OPEN
ABS PUMP FUSED B(+) CIRCUIT OPEN
CAB - INTERNAL FAULT

TEST	ACTION
1	Turn the ignition on. With the DRBIII®, read DTCs. With the DRBIII®, erase DTCs. Turn the ignition off. Turn the ignition on. With the DRBIII®, read DTCs. Does the DRBIII® display CONTROLLER FAILURE? Yes → Go To 2 No → Go To 6
2	Turn the ignition off. Disconnect the CAB harness connector. Inspect the CAB/CAB harness connector for damage. Is ther any broken, bent, pushed out, corroded or spread terminals? Yes → Repair as necessary. Perform ABS VERIFICATION TEST No → Go To 3
3	Turn the ignition off. Disconnect the CAB harness connector. Using a 12-volt test light connected to 12-volts, probe the CAB harness connector ground circuits. Did the test light illuminate? Yes → Go To 4 No → Repair the CAB Ground circuit for an open. Perform ABS VERIFICATION TEST

ARM66CR000000007

Fig. 126 Controller Failure (Part 1 of 2). 2003–04 Neon

When Monitored and Set Condition:

INCORRECT TONE WHEEL FAILURE

When Monitored: Ignition on. Checks continuously.

Set Condition: Requires 2 minutes to detect when all wheels are above 40 km/h (24 mph).

POSSIBLE CAUSES
INCORRECT TIRES ON VEHICLE
INCORRECT TONE WHEEL ON VEHICLE

TEST	ACTION
1	Inspect the tire sizes on the vehicle. Is a smaller than production tire, mini spare, or two mini spares installed on both front wheels? Yes → Replace the incorrect tire(s) size with production size tire(s). Perform ABS VERIFICATION TEST No → Go To 2
2	Count the number of tone wheel teeth on both of the front driveshafts. Does one or both tone wheel(s) have (56 or 40) teeth? Yes → Replace the front driveshaft(s) with the incorrect number of tone wheel teeth. Perform ABS VERIFICATION TEST No → Test Complete.

ARM66CR000000009

Fig. 127 Incorrect Tone Wheel Failure. 2003–04 Neon

Test Note: **All symptoms listed above are diagnosed using the same tests. The title for the tests will be LEFT FRONT SENSOR CIRCUIT FAILURE.**

When Monitored and Set Condition:

LEFT FRONT SENSOR CIRCUIT FAILURE

When Monitored: Ignition on. The CAB monitors the wheel speed circuit continuously.

Set Condition: If the CAB detects an open or shorted wheel speed sensor circuit, the Diagnostic Trouble Code (DTC) will set.

LEFT REAR SENSOR CIRCUIT FAILURE

When Monitored: Ignition on. The CAB monitors the wheel speed circuit continuously.

Set Condition: If the CAB detects an open or shorted wheel speed sensor circuit, the Diagnostic Trouble Code (DTC) will set.

RIGHT FRONT SENSOR CIRCUIT FAILURE

When Monitored: Ignition on. The CAB monitors the wheel speed circuit continuously.

Set Condition: If the CAB detects an open or shorted wheel speed sensor circuit, the Diagnostic Trouble Code (DTC) will set.

RIGHT REAR SENSOR CIRCUIT FAILURE

When Monitored: Ignition on. The CAB monitors the wheel speed circuit continuously.

Set Condition: If the CAB detects an open or shorted wheel speed sensor circuit, the Diagnostic Trouble Code (DTC) will set.

POSSIBLE CAUSES
INTERMITTENT CONDITION
WHEEL SPEED SENSOR OR CONNECTOR DAMAGE
WHEEL SPEED SENSOR SIGNAL CIRCUIT FAULT
WHEEL SPEED SENSOR 12 VOLT SUPPLY CIRCUIT SHORT TO GROUND
WHEEL SPEED SENSOR 12 VOLT SUPPLY CIRCUIT OPEN
WHEEL SPEED SENSOR SIGNAL CIRCUIT SHORT TO GROUND
WHEEL SPEED SENSOR SIGNAL CIRCUIT OPEN

ARM66CR000000010

Fig. 128 Lefthand Front, Lefthand Rear, Righthand Front & Righthand Rear Sensor Circuit Failure (Part 1 of 5). 2003–04 Neon

POSSIBLE CAUSES
CAB - 12 VOLT SUPPLY CIRCUIT FAULT
CAB - SIGNAL CIRCUIT FAULT
WHEEL SPEED SENSOR 12 VOLT SUPPLY SHORT TO GROUND
WHEEL SPEED SENSOR SIGNAL CIRCUIT INOPERATIVE

TEST	ACTION
1	Turn the ignition on. With the DRBIII®, read DTCs. With the DRBIII®, read the Freeze Frame information. With the DRBIII®, erase DTCs. Turn the ignition off. Turn the ignition on. With the DRBIII®, read DTCs. **NOTE: The CAB must sense all four wheels at 25km/h (15 mph) before it will extinguish the ABS indicators.** Does the DRBIII® display SENSOR CIRCUIT FAILURE? Yes → Go To 2 No → Go To 13
2	Turn the ignition off. Inspect the CAB connector, affected Wheel Speed Sensor, and affected Wheel Speed Sensor connector. Is the affected Wheel Speed Sensor or any of the connectors damaged? Yes → Repair as necessary. Perform ABS VERIFICATION TEST No → Go To 3
3	Turn the ignition off. Disconnect the affected Wheel Speed Sensor connector. **Note: Check connector - Clean/repair as necessary.** Turn the ignition on. Measure the voltage between affected Wheel Speed Sensor 12 Volt Supply circuit and ground. Is the voltage above 10 volts? Yes → Gó To 6 No → Go To 4
4	Turn the ignition off. Disconnect the CAB harness connector. Disconnect the affected Wheel Speed Sensor connector. Using a 12-volt test light connected to 12-volts, probe the affected Wheel Speed Sensor 12 Volt Supply circuit. Does the test light illuminate? Yes → Repair the affected Wheel Speed Sensor 12 Volt Supply circuit for a short to ground. Perform ABS VERIFICATION TEST No → Go To 5

ARM66CR000000011

Fig. 128 Lefthand Front, Lefthand Rear, Righthand Front & Righthand Rear Sensor Circuit Failure (Part 2 of 5). 2003–04 Neon

TEST	ACTION
5	Turn the ignition off. Disconnect the CAB harness connector. Disconnect the affected Wheel Speed Sensor connector. Connect a jumper wire between affected Wheel Speed Sensor 12 Volt Supply circuit and ground. Using a 12-volt test light connected to 12-volts, probe the affected Wheel Speed Sensor 12 Volt Supply circuit. Does the test light illuminate? Yes → Go To 6 No → Repair the affected Wheel Speed Sensor 12 Volt Supply circuit for an open. Perform ABS VERIFICATION TEST
6	Turn the ignition off. Disconnect the affected Wheel Speed Sensor connector. **NOTE: Check connector - Clean/repair as necessary.** Turn the ignition on. Measure the voltage between affected Wheel Speed Sensor Signal circuit and ground. Is the voltage above 1 volt? Yes → Repair the affected Wheel Speed Sensor Signal circuit for a short to voltage. Perform ABS VERIFICATION TEST No → Go To 7
7	Turn the ignition off. Disconnect the CAB harness connector. Disconnect the affected Wheel Speed Sensor connector. Using a 12-volt test light connected to 12-volts, probe the affected Wheel Speed Sensor Signal circuit. Does the test light illuminate? Yes → Repair the affected Wheel Speed Sensor Signal circuit for a short to ground. Perform ABS VERIFICATION TEST No → Go To 8
8	Turn the ignition off. Disconnect the CAB harness connector. Disconnect the affected Wheel Speed Sensor connector. Connect a jumper wire between affected Wheel Speed Sensor Signal circuit and ground. Using a 12-volt test light connected to 12-volts, probe the affected Wheel Speed Sensor Signal circuit. Does the test light illuminate? Yes → Go To 9 No → Repair the affected Wheel Speed Sensor Signal circuit for an open. Perform ABS VERIFICATION TEST

ARM66CR000000012

Fig. 128 Lefthand Front, Lefthand Rear, Righthand Front & Righthand Rear Sensor Circuit Failure (Part 3 of 5). 2003–04 Neon

TEST	ACTION
9	Turn the ignition off. Remove the CAB harness strain relief to access wires. Reconnect the CAB harness connector. Turn the ignition on. Measure the voltage between affected Wheel Speed Sensor 12 Volt Supply circuit and ground. Is the voltage above 10 volts? Yes → Go To 10 No → Replace the Controller Antilock Brake Perform ABS VERIFICATION TEST
10	Turn the ignition off. Remove the CAB harness strain relief to access wires. Reconnect the CAB harness connector. Turn the ignition on. Measure the voltage between affected Wheel Speed Sensor 12 Volt Supply circuit and affected Wheel Speed Sensor Signal circuit. Is the voltage above 10 volts? Yes → Go To 11 No → Replace the Controller Antilock Brake Perform ABS VERIFICATION TEST
11	Turn the ignition off. Reconnect ALL affected Wheel Speed Sensor circuit connectors. Disconnect the affected Wheel Speed Sensor connector. Turn the ignition on. Measure the voltage of the affected Wheel Speed Sensor 12 Volt Supply circuit in the affected Wheel Speed Sensor connector while reconnecting the sensor connector. Did the affected Wheel Speed Sensor 12 Volt Supply circuit drop voltage to 0 DC volts? Yes → Replace the affected Wheel Speed Sensor Perform ABS VERIFICATION TEST No → Go To 12
12	Turn the ignition off. Reconnect ALL affected Wheel Speed Sensor circuit connectors. Turn the ignition on. Measure the DC voltage of the Wheel Speed Sensor Signal circuit in the affected Wheel Speed Sensor connector. Slowly rotate the wheel. Does the DC voltage toggle between 1.6 volts to .8 volts? Yes → Go To 13 No → Replace the affected Wheel Speed Sensor Perform ABS VERIFICATION TEST

ARM66CR000000013

Fig. 128 Lefthand Front, Lefthand Rear, Righthand Front & Righthand Rear Sensor Circuit Failure (Part 4 of 5). 2003–04 Neon

TEST	ACTION
13	Turn the ignition off. Visually inspect the related wiring harness. Look for any chafed, pierced, pinched, or partially broken wires. Visually inspect the related wire harness connectors. Look for broken, bent, pushed out, or corroded terminals. Refer to any Hotline letters or Technical Service Bulletins that may apply. Were any problems found? Yes → Repair as necessary. Perform ABS VERIFICATION TEST No → Test Complete.

ARM66CR000000014

Fig. 128 Lefthand Front, Lefthand Rear, Righthand Front & Righthand Rear Sensor Circuit Failure (Part 5 of 5). 2003–04 Neon

POSSIBLE CAUSES
WHEEL SPEED SIGNAL FAILURE DTC PRESENT
AFFECTED WHEEL SPEED SENSOR SIGNAL INOPERATIVE
AFFECTED WHEEL SPEED SENSOR CONNECTOR DAMAGED
AFFECTED WHEEL SPEED SENSOR TONE WHEEL DAMAGED
AFFECTED WHEEL SPEED SENSOR AIR GAP FAULT
WHEEL BEARING FAULT
BRAKE LINING FAULT
AFFECTED WHEEL SPEED SENSOR CIRCUIT ELECTRICAL FAULT

TEST	ACTION
1	Turn the ignition on. With the DRBIII®, read DTCs. With the DRBIII®, read Freeze Frame information. **NOTE: The CAB must sense ALL 4 wheels at 25 km/h (15 mph) before it will extinguish the ABS indicators.** Does the DRBIII® display WHEEL SPEED/SIGNAL FAILURE and SENSOR CIRCUIT FAILURE? Yes → Refer to the affected Wheel Speed SENSOR CIRCUIT FAILURE for the related symptom(s). Perform ABS VERIFICATION TEST No → Go To 2
2	Turn the ignition on. With the DRBIII® in Sensors, monitor ALL the Wheel Speed Sensor Signals while an assistant drives the vehicle. Slowly accelerate as straight as possible from a stop to 24 km/h (15 mph). Is the affected Wheel Speed Signal showing 0 km/h (0 mph)? Yes → Go To 3 No → The condition is not present at this time. Monitor DRBIII® parameters while wiggling the related wiring harness. Refer to any Technical Service Bulletins(TSB) that may apply. Visually inspect the related wiring harness and connector terminals. Perform ABS VERIFICATION TEST
3	Turn the ignition off. Inspect the CAB connector, affected Wheel Speed Sensor, and affected Wheel Speed Sensor connector. Is the Wheel Speed Sensor or any connector damaged? Yes → Repair as necessary. Perform ABS VERIFICATION TEST No → Go To 4

ARM66CR000000016

Fig. 129 Lefthand Front, Lefthand Rear, Righthand Front & Righthand Rear Wheel Speed/Signal Failure (Part 2 of 3). 2003–04 Neon

Test Note: **All symptoms listed above are diagnosed using the same tests. The title for the tests will be LEFT FRONT WHEEL SPEED/ SIGNAL FAILURE.**

When Monitored and Set Condition:

LEFT FRONT WHEEL SPEED/ SIGNAL FAILURE

When Monitored: Ignition on. Wheel speed is checked and verified at drive off and continuously thereafter.

Set Condition: If, during an ABS stop, the CAB commands any valve solenoid on for an extended length of time, and does not see a corresponding wheel speed change, the Diagnostic Trouble Code (DTC) is set. The DTC can also set if the signal is missing or erratic.

LEFT REAR WHEEL SPEED/ SIGNAL FAILURE

When Monitored: Ignition on. Wheel speed is checked and verified at drive off and continuously thereafter.

Set Condition: If, during an ABS stop, the CAB commands any valve solenoid on for an extended length of time, and does not see a corresponding wheel speed change, the Diagnostic Trouble Code (DTC) is set. The DTC can also set if the signal is missing or erratic.

RIGHT FRONT WHEEL SPEED/ SIGNAL FAILURE

When Monitored: Ignition on. Wheel speed is checked and verified at drive off and continuously thereafter.

Set Condition: If, during an ABS stop, the CAB commands any valve solenoid on for an extended length of time, and does not see a corresponding wheel speed change, the Diagnostic Trouble Code (DTC) is set. The DTC can also set if the signal is missing or erratic.

RIGHT REAR WHEEL SPEED/ SIGNAL FAILURE

When Monitored: Ignition on. Wheel speed is checked and verified at drive off and continuously thereafter.

Set Condition: If, during an ABS stop, the CAB commands any valve solenoid on for an extended length of time, and does not see a corresponding wheel speed change, the Diagnostic Trouble Code (DTC) is set. The DTC can also set if the signal is missing or erratic.

ARM66CR000000015

Fig. 129 Lefthand Front, Lefthand Rear, Righthand Front & Righthand Rear Wheel Speed/Signal Failure (Part 1 of 3). 2003–04 Neon

TEST	ACTION
4	Turn ignition off. Inspect the affected Tone Wheel for damaged, missing teeth, cracks, or looseness. **NOTE: The Tone Wheel teeth should be perfectly square, not bent, or nicked.** Is the affected Tone Wheel OK? Yes → Go To 5 No → Replace the Tone Wheel Perform ABS VERIFICATION TEST
5	Turn the ignition off. Using a Feeler Gauge, measure the affected Wheel Speed Sensor Air Gap. **NOTE: Refer to the appropriate service information, if necessary, for procedures or specifications.** Is the Air Gap OK? Yes → Go To 6 No → Repair as necessary. Perform ABS VERIFICATION TEST
6	Turn the ignition off. Inspect the wheel bearings for excessive runout or clearance. **NOTE: Refer to the appropriate service information, if necessary, for procedures or specifications.** Is the bearing clearance OK ? Yes → Go To 7 No → Repair as necessary. Perform ABS VERIFICATION TEST
7	Turn the ignition off. Visually inspect brakes for locking up due to lining contamination or overheating. Inspect all Components for defects which may cause a Signal DTC to set. Is any Component Damaged? Yes → Repair as necessary. Perform ABS VERIFICATION TEST No → Refer to symptom SENSOR CIRCUIT FAILURE for further diagnostics. Perform ABS VERIFICATION TEST

ARM66CR000000017

Fig. 129 Lefthand Front, Lefthand Rear, Righthand Front & Righthand Rear Wheel Speed/Signal Failure (Part 3 of 3). 2003–04 Neon

When Monitored and Set Condition:

PCI BUS COMMUNICATION

When Monitored: Ignition on.

Set Condition: When the CAB does not receive a message from the instrument cluster for 10 seconds.

POSSIBLE CAUSES
INTERMITTENT CONDITION
ELECTRO-MECHANICAL INSTRUMENT CLUSTER DTC PRESENT
PCI BUS CIRCUIT OPEN
CAB - INTERNAL FAILURE

TEST	ACTION
1	Turn the ignition on. With the DRBIII®, read DTCs. With the DRBIII®, read Freeze Frame information. With the DRBIII®, erase DTCs. Turn the ignition off. Turn the ignition on. With the DRBIII®, read DTCs. Does the DRBIII® display PCI BUS COMMUNICATION? Yes → Go To 2 No → Go To 4
2	Turn the ignition on. With the DRBIII®, read EMIC DTCs. Does the DRBIII® display ABS MESSAGE NOT RECEIVED? Yes → Refer to symptom ABS MESSAGE NOT RECEIVED Perform ABS VERIFICATION TEST No → Go To 3

ARM66CR000000018

Fig. 130 PCI BUS Communications (Part 1 of 2). 2003–04 Neon

TEST	ACTION
3	Turn the ignition off. Disconnect the negative (-) battery cable. Disconnect the CAB harness connector. **NOTE: check connector - Clean/repair as necessary.** Measure the resistance of the PCI Bus circuit between the CAB connector and the Data Link Connector (DLC). Is the resistance below 5.0 ohms? Yes → Replace the Controller Antilock Brake Perform ABS VERIFICATION TEST No → Repair the PCI Bus circuit for an open. Perform ABS VERIFICATION TEST
4	Turn the ignition off. Visually inspect the related wiring harness. Look for any chafed, pierced, pinched, or partially broken wires. Visually inspect the related wire harness connectors. Look for broken, bent, pushed out, or corroded terminals. Were any problems found? Yes → Repair as necessary. Perform ABS VERIFICATION TEST No → Test Complete.

ARM66CR000000019

Fig. 130 PCI BUS Communications (Part 2 of 2). 2003–04 Neon

When Monitored and Set Condition:

PUMP MOTOR NOT WORKING PROPERLY

When Monitored: Ignition on. The CAB commands the pump on at 20 km/h (12 mph) to check its operation, if the brake switch is not applied. If the brake is applied, the test will run at 40 km/h (25 mph).

Set Condition: The DTC is stored when the CAB detects: 1) Improper voltage decay after the pump was turned off. 2) Pump not energized by the CAB, but voltage is present for 3.5 seconds. 3) Pump is turned on by the CAB, but without sufficient voltage to operate it.

POSSIBLE CAUSES
CAB - PUMP MOTOR RUNNING CONTINUOUSLY
ABS PUMP FUSE
ABS PUMP MOTOR INTERMITTENT DTC
DAMAGED CAB/CAB HARNESS CONNECTOR
ABS PUMP FUSED B(+) CIRCUIT INTERMITTENT SHORT TO GROUND
ABS PUMP FUSED B(+) CIRCUIT SHORT TO GROUND
CAB - INTERNAL FAULT
ABS PUMP MOTOR INOPERATIVE
ABS PUMP MOTOR OPEN
ABS PUMP MOTOR B(+) CIRCUIT OPEN
ABS PUMP MOTOR GROUND CIRCUIT OPEN
CAB - INTERNAL FAULT

TEST	ACTION
1	Turn the ignition off. Turn the ignition on. Monitor the ABS Pump Motor for continuous operation. **NOTE: The CAB must sense ALL wheels at 25 km/h (15 mph) before it will extinguish the ABS indicators.** Is the ABS Pump Motor running continuously? Yes → Replace the Controller Antilock Brake Perform ABS VERIFICATION TEST No → Go To 2

ARM66CR000000020

Fig. 131 Pump Motor Not Working Properly (Part 1 of 4). 2003–04 Neon

TEST	ACTION
2	Turn the ignition off. Turn the ignition on. With the DRBIII®, read DTCs. With the DRBIII®, erase DTCs. Turn the ignition off. Turn the ignition on. With the DRBIII®, actuate the ABS Pump Motor. Did the ABS Pump Motor operate? Yes → Go To 3 No → Go To 4
3	Turn the ignition off. Visually inspect the related wiring harness. Look for any chafed, pierced, pinched, or partially broken wires. Make sure the Pump Motor connecter is secure. Visually inspect the related wire harness connectors. Look for broken, bent, pushed out, or corroded terminals. Refer to any Technical Service Bulletins that may apply. Were any problems found? Yes → Repair as necessary. Perform ABS VERIFICATION TEST No → Test Complete.
4	Turn the ignition off. Remove and inspect the ABS Pump fuse. Is the ABS Pump fuse open? Yes → Go To 5 No → Go To 8
5	Turn the ignition off. Visually inspect the ABS Pump Fused B(+) circuit in the wiring harness. Look for any sign of an intermittent short to ground. Is the wiring harness OK? Yes → Go To 6 No → Repair the ABS Pump Fused B(+) circuit for a short to ground. Perform ABS VERIFICATION TEST
6	Turn the ignition off. Disconnect the CAB harness connector. Check connectors - Clean/repair as necessary. Using a 12-volt test light connected to 12-volts, probe the ABS Pump Fused B(+) circuit fuse terminal. Does the test light illuminate? Yes → Repair the ABS Pump Fused B(+) circuit for a short to ground. Perform ABS VERIFICATION TEST No → Go To 7

ARM66CR000000021

Fig. 131 Pump Motor Not Working Properly (Part 2 of 4). 2003–04 Neon

TEST	ACTION
7	Turn the ignition off. Reconnect the CAB harness connector. Using a 12-volt test light connected to 12-volts, probe the ABS Pump Fused B(+) circuit fuse terminal. Does the test light illuminate? Yes → Replace the Controller Antilock Brake Perform ABS VERIFICATION TEST No → Replace the ABS Pump fuse. If the fuse is open make sure to check for a short to ground. Perform ABS VERIFICATION TEST
8	Turn the ignition off. Disconnect the CAB harness connector. Inspect the CAB and CAB harness connector for damage. Is there any broken, bent, pushed out, corroded, or spread terminals? Yes → Repair as necessary. Perform ABS VERIFICATION TEST No → Go To 9
9	Turn the ignition off. Reinstall the ABS Pump fuse. Disconnect the ABS Pump Motor connector. Check connectors - Clean/repair as necessary. Connect a 10 gauge 40 amp fused jumper wire between the ABS Pump Fused B(+) terminal in the CAB harness connector to the ABS Pump Motor connector RED wired terminal. Connect a 10 gauge jumper wire between the Ground circuit terminal in the CAB harness connector to the ABS Pump Motor connector BLACK wired terminal. Did the ABS Pump Motor operate? Yes → Replace the Controller Antilock Brake Service Information. Perform ABS VERIFICATION TEST No → Go To 10
10	Turn the ignition off. Disconnect the ABS Pump Motor connector. Check connectors - Clean/repair as necessary. Connect a 10 gauge 40 amp fused jumper wire between the ABS Pump Motor connector RED wired terminal and an alternate 40 amp capable B(+) source. Connect a 10 gauge jumper wire between the ABS Pump Motor connector BLACK wired terminal and ground Did the ABS Pump Motor operate? Yes → Go To 11 No → Replace the Hydraulic Control Unit Perform ABS VERIFICATION TEST

ARM66CR000000022

Fig. 131 Pump Motor Not Working Properly (Part 3 of 4). 2003–04 Neon

When Monitored and Set Condition:

SYSTEM OVER VOLTAGE

When Monitored: Ignition on. The CAB monitors the Fused B(+) circuit at all times for proper system voltage.

Set Condition: If the voltage is above 16.5 volts, the Diagnostic Trouble Code (DTC) is set.

POSSIBLE CAUSES
INTERMITTENT DTC
BATTERY CHARGER CONNECTED
FUSED IGNITION SWITCH OUTPUT (RUN) CIRCUIT HIGH
DAMAGED CAB/CAB HARNESS CONNECTOR
CAB - GROUND CIRCUIT OPEN
CAB - INTERNAL FAULT

TEST	ACTION
1	Turn the ignition on. With the DRBIII®, read DTC's. With the DRBIII®, erase DTC's. Turn the ignition off. Turn the ignition on. Start the engine. With the DRBIII®, read DTC's. Does the DRBIII® display SYSTEM OVER VOLTAGE? Yes → Go To 2 No → Go To 7
2	Is a battery charger connected to the vehicle? Yes → Ensure the battery is fully charged. Perform ABS VERIFICATION TEST No → Go To 3

ARM66CR000000024

Fig. 132 System Over Voltage (Part 1 of 3). 2003–04 Neon

TEST	ACTION
11	Turn the ignition off. Disconnect the ABS Pump Motor connector. Check connectors - Clean/repair as necessary. Connect a 10 gauge 40 amp fused jumper wire between the ABS Pump Fused B(+) terminal in the CAB harness connector to the ABS Pump Motor connector RED wired terminal. Connect a 10 gauge jumper wire between the ABS Pump Motor connector BLACK wired terminal and ground. Did the ABS Pump Motor operate? Yes → Repair the ABS Pump Motor Fused B(+) circuit for an open. Perform ABS VERIFICATION TEST No → Repair the ABS Pump Motor Ground circuit for an open. Perform ABS VERIFICATION TEST

ARM66CR000000023

Fig. 131 Pump Motor Not Working Properly (Part 4 of 4). 2003–04 Neon

TEST	ACTION
3	Turn the ignition off. Disconnect the CAB connector. **Note: Check connector - Clean/repair as necessary.** Start the engine. Raise engine speed above 1,800 RPM's Measure the voltage between Fused Ignition Switch Output (RUN) circuit and ground. Is the voltage above 16.5 volts ? Yes → Refer to appropriate service information for Charging System testing and repair. Perform ABS VERIFICATION TEST No → Go To 4
4	Turn the ignition off. Disconnect the CAB connector. **Note: Check connector - Clean/repair as necessary.** Inspect the CAB and CAB harness connector for damage. Is there any broken, bent, pushed out, corroded, or spread terminals? Yes → Repair as necessary. Perform ABS VERIFICATION TEST No → Go To 5
5	Turn the ignition off. Disconnect the CAB connector. **Note: Check connector - Clean/repair as necessary.** Using a 12-volt test light connected to 12-volts, probe the Ground circuits. Does the test light illuminate? Yes → Go To 6 No → Repair the Ground circuit for an open. Perform ABS VERIFICATION TEST
6	Turn the ignition off. Reconnect the CAB harness connector. Turn the ignition on. With the DRBIII® in Sensors, read the ignition voltage. Does the DRBIII® display ignition voltage above 16 volts? Yes → Replace the Controller Antilock Brake Perform ABS VERIFICATION TEST No → Go To 7

ARM66CR000000025

Fig. 132 System Over Voltage (Part 2 of 3). 2003–04 Neon

TEST	ACTION
7	Turn the ignition off. Visually inspect the related wiring harness. Look for any chafed, pierced, pinched, or partially broken wires. Visually inspect the related wire harness connectors. Look for broken, bent, pushed out, or corroded terminals. Refer to any Technical Service Bulletins that may apply. Ensure the battery is fully charged. Inspect the vehicle for aftermarket accessories that may exceed the Generator System output. Using the wiring diagram/schematic as a guide, inspect the wiring and connectors. Were any problems found? Yes → Repair as necessary. Perform ABS VERIFICATION TEST No → Test Complete.

ARM66CR000000026

Fig. 132 System Over Voltage (Part 3 of 3). 2003–04 Neon

TEST	ACTION
3	Turn the ignition off. Disconnect the CAB harness connector. Inspect the CAB and CAB harness connector for damage. Is there any broken, bent, pushed out, corroded, or spread terminals? Yes → Repair as necessary. Perform ABS VERIFICATION TEST No → Go To 4
4	Turn the ignition off. Disconnect the CAB harness connector. Using a 12-volt test light connected to 12-volts, probe the Ground circuits. Does the test light illuminate? Yes → Go To 5 No → Repair the Ground circuit for an open. Perform ABS VERIFICATION TEST
5	Turn the ignition on. Using a 12-volt test light connected to ground, probe the Fused Ignition Switch Output (RUN) circuit. Does the test light illuminate? Yes → Replace the Controller Antilock Brake Perform ABS VERIFICATION TEST No → Repair the Fused Ignition Switch Output (RUN) circuit for an open. Perform ABS VERIFICATION TEST
6	Turn the ignition off. Visually inspect the related wiring harness. Look for any chafed, pierced, pinched, or partially broken wires. Visually inspect the related wire harness connectors. Look for broken, bent, pushed out, or corroded terminals. Refer to any Technical Service Bulletins that may apply. Ensure the battery is fully charged. Inspect the vehicle for aftermarket accessories that may exceed the Generator System output. Using the wiring diagram/schematic as a guide, inspect the wiring and connectors. Were any problems found? Yes → Repair as necessary. Perform ABS VERIFICATION TEST No → Test Complete.

ARM66CR000000028

Fig. 133 System Under Voltage (Part 2 of 2). 2003–04 Neon

When Monitored and Set Condition:

SYSTEM UNDER VOLTAGE

When Monitored: Ignition on. The CAB monitors the Fused Ignition Switch Output for proper system voltage.

Set Condition: If the voltage is below 9.5 volts, the Diagnostic Trouble Code (DTC) is set.

POSSIBLE CAUSES
INTERMITTENT DTC
DAMAGED CAB/CAB HARNESS CONNECTOR
RUNNING BATTERY VOLTAGE LOW
CAB - GROUND CIRCUIT OPEN
FUSED IGNITION SWITCH OUTPUT (RUN) CIRCUIT OPEN
CAB - INTERNAL FAULT

TEST	ACTION
1	Turn the ignition on. With the DRBIII®, read DTC's. With the DRBIII®, erase DTC's. Turn the ignition off. Turn the ignition on. Start the engine. Drive the vehicle above 16 km/h (10 mph) for at least 20 seconds. Stop the vehicle With the DRBIII®, read DTC's. Does the DRBIII® display SYSTEM UNDER VOLTAGE ? Yes → Go To 2 No → Go To 6
2	Engine Running. Measure the battery voltage. Is the battery voltage below 10 volts? Yes → Refer to appropriate service information for charging system testing and repair. Perform ABS VERIFICATION TEST - VER 1. No → Go To 3

ARM66CR000000027

Fig. 133 System Under Voltage (Part 1 of 2). 2003–04 Neon

POSSIBLE CAUSES
CHECK BRAKE LAMP SWITCH OUTPUT
BRAKE LAMP SWITCH B+ OPEN
BRAKE LAMP SWITCH OPEN
BRAKE LAMP SWITCH OUTPUT CIRCUIT SHORT OR OPEN
CAB -- INTERNAL OPEN

TEST	ACTION
1	With the DRBIII® in Inputs/Outputs, read the Brake Lamp Switch state. Press and release the brake pedal. Does the DRBIII® display PRESSED and RELEASED? Yes → The Brake Lamp Switch is OK. Perform ABS VERIFICATION TEST No → Go To 2
2	Disconnect the Brake Lamp Switch harness connector. Using a 12-volt test light connected to ground, check the Brake Lamp Switch Fused B+ circuit. Does the test light illuminate brightly ? Yes → Go To 3 No → Repair the Brake Lamp Switch Fused B+ circuit for an open. Perform ABS VERIFICATION TEST
3	Disconnect the Brake Lamp Switch harness connector. Connect a jumper wire between the Brake Lamp Switch B+ and Brake Lamp Switch Output circuits. With the DRBIII® in Inputs/Outputs, read the Brake Lamp Switch state. Does the DRBIII® display PRESSED? Yes → Replace the Brake Lamp Switch Perform ABS VERIFICATION TEST No → Go To 4
4	Disconnect the CAB harness connector. Disconnect the Brake Lamp Switch harness connector. Check the Brake Lamp Switch Output circuit for a short to voltage and for an open. Is the Brake Lamp Switch Output circuit shorted or open? Yes → Repair the Brake Lamp Switch Output circuit for a short to voltage or an open. Perform ABS VERIFICATION TEST No → Replace the Controller Antilock Brake Perform ABS VERIFICATION TEST

ARM66CR000000029

Fig. 134 Brake Lamp Switch Inoperative. 2003–04 Neon

POSSIBLE CAUSES
NO RESPONSE FROM CAB
GROUND CIRCUIT OPEN
OPEN FUSED IGNITION SWITCH OUTPUT CIRCUIT
OPEN PCI BUS CIRCUIT
CONTROLLER ANTILOCK BRAKE

TEST	ACTION
1	Turn the ignition on. **Note: As soon as one or more module communicates with the DRB, answer the question.** With the DRB, attempt to communicate with the Airbag Control Module (ACM). With the DRB, attempt to communicate with the Instrument Cluster (MIC). Was the DRB able to I/D or establish communications with either of the modules? Yes → Go To 2 No → Refer to the Communications category and perform the symptom PCI Bus Communication Failure. Perform ABS VERIFICATION TEST
2	Turn the ignition off. Disconnect the CAB harness connector. Using a 12-volt test light connected to 12-volts, probe both ground circuits. Is the test light illuminated for both circuits? Yes → Go To 3 No → Repair the ground circuit(s) for an open. Perform ABS VERIFICATION TEST
3	Turn the ignition off. Disconnect the CAB harness connector. Turn the ignition on. Using a 12-volt test light connected to ground, probe the Fused Ignition Switch Output circuit. Is the test light illuminated? Yes → Go To 4 No → Repair the Fused Ignition Switch Output circuit for an open. Perform ABS VERIFICATION TEST

ARM66CR000000030

Fig. 135 No Response From Controller Anti-Lock Brake (Part 1 of 2). 2003–04 Neon

TEST	ACTION
4	**Note: Ensure there is PCI Bus communication with other modules on the vehicle before proceeding. If not, refer to the symptom list from the menu and repair as necessary.** Disconnect the CAB harness connector. Use Scope input cable CH7058, Cable to Probe adapter CH7062, and the red and black test probes. Connect the scope input cable to the channel one connector on the DRB. Attach the red and black leads and the cable to probe adapter to the scope input cable. With the DRBIII® select Pep Module Tools. Select lab scope. Select Live Data. Select 12 volt square wave. Press F2 for Scope. Press F2 and use the down arrow to set voltage range to 20 volts. Set Probe to x10. Press F2 again when complete. Connect the Black lead to the chassis ground. Connect the Red lead to the PCI Bus circuit in the CAB connector. Turn the ignition on. Observe the voltage display on the DRB Lab Scope. Does the voltage pulse from 0 to approximately 7.5 volts? Yes → Go To 5 No → Repair the PCI Bus circuit for an open. Perform ABS VERIFICATION TEST
5	If there are no possible causes remaining, view repair. Repair Replace the Controller Antilock Brake Perform ABS VERIFICATION TEST

ARM66CR000000031

Fig. 135 No Response From Controller Anti-Lock Brake (Part 2 of 2). 2003–04 Neon

ABS VERIFICATION TEST - VER 1
1. Turn the ignition off. 2. Connect all previously disconnected components and connectors. 3. Ensure all accessories are turned off and the battery is fully charged. 4. Ensure that the Ignition is on, and with the DRBIII, erase all Diagnostic Trouble Codes from ALL modules. Start the engine and allow it to run for 2 minutes and fully operate the system that was malfunctioning. 5. Turn the ignition off and wait 5 seconds. Turn the ignition on and using the DRBIII, read DTC's from ALL modules. 6. If any Diagnostic Trouble Codes are present, return to Symptom list and troubleshoot new or recurring symptom. **7. NOTE: For Sensor Signal and Pump Motor faults, the CAB must sense all 4 wheels at 25 km/h (15 mph) before it will extinguish the ABS Indicator.** 8. If there are no DTC's present after turning ignition on, road test the vehicle for at least 5 minutes. Perform several antilock braking stops. **9. Caution: Ensure braking capability is available before road testing.** 10. Again, with the DRBIII® read DTC's. If any DTC's are present, return to Symptom list. 11. If there are no Diagnostic Trouble Codes (DTC's) present, and the customer's concern can no longer be duplicated, the repair is complete. Are any DTC's present or is the original concern still present? Yes → Repair is not complete, refer to appropriate symptom. No → Repair is complete.

ARM66CR000000032

Fig. 136 ABS Verification Test. 2003–04 Neon

When Monitored: 1. Ignition on. 2. Checked every 7 milliseconds.

Set Condition: When the ABS warning lamp driver circuit voltage does not match the CAB commands, the Diagnostic Trouble Code (DTC) is set.

POSSIBLE CAUSES
ABS WARNING LAMP DEFECTIVE
ABS WARNING LAMP DRIVER CIRCUIT OPEN
ABS WARNING LAMP DRIVER CIRCUIT SHORTED TO GROUND
CAB CONNECTOR OBSERVABLE DEFECT
FUSED IGNITION SWITCH OUTPUT CIRCUIT OPEN
INSTRUMENT CLUSTER DEFECTIVE
CAB DEFECTIVE

TEST	ACTION
1	**Note: If any Diagnostic Trouble Codes are present, they must be repaired prior to performing this test.** Ignition off, then turn ignition on. Observe the ABS Warning Lamp in the Instrument Cluster. Does the ABS Warning Lamp stay on for several seconds then go out? Yes → The ABS Warning Lamp Circuit is operating properly at this time. Perform ABS Verification Test VER-1A. No → Go To 2
2	**Note: If any Diagnostic Trouble Codes are present, they must be repaired prior to performing this test.** Turn the ignition Off. Turn ignition on. Observe the ABS Warning Lamp in the Instrument Cluster. Is the ABS Warning Lamp on steady? Yes → Go To 3 No → Go To 6

CR4020002000010X

Fig. 137 ABS Warning Lamp (Part 1 of 3). 2000 Sebring Convertible

TEST	ACTION
3	Turn the ignition Off. Disconnect the CAB. Note: Check connectors - Clean/repair as necessary. Inspect all Terminals. Is any Terminal damaged, pushed out or miswired? Yes → Repair as necessary. Perform ABS Verification Test VER-1A. No → Go To 4
4	Turn the ignition Off. Disconnect the CAB. Disconnect the instrument cluster connector. Note: Check connectors - Clean/repair as necessary. Turn ignition on. Using a test light connected to 12 volts, probe the Warning Lamp Driver Circuit. Is the test light on? Yes → Repair the ABS Warning Lamp Driver Circuit for a short to ground. Perform ABS Verification Test VER-1A. No → Go To 5
5	If there are no potential causes remaining, replace the CAB. View repair options. Repair Replace the CAB. Perform ABS Verification Test VER-1A.
6	Ignition On, Engine Not Running Set the Parking Brake. Is the Red Brake Warning Lamp on? Yes → Go To 7 No → Repair the open Fused Ignition Switch Output Circuit to the Lamps. Perform ABS Verification Test VER-1A.
7	Turn the ignition Off. Gain access to the Warning Lamp Bulb. Is the Bulb okay? Yes → Go To 8 No → Replace the Bulb. Perform ABS Verification Test VER-1A.
8	The Instrument Cluster and bulb must be installed to perform this test. Use a voltmeter to backprobe the ABS Warning Lamp Driver Circuit at the Instrument Cluster. Turn the ignition on. Is the voltage above 10 volts? Yes → Go To 9 No → Replace the Instrument Cluster Printed Circuit Board. Perform ABS Verification Test VER-1A.

CR4020002000020X

Fig. 137 ABS Warning Lamp (Part 2 of 3). 2000 Sebring Convertible

When Monitored: 1. With ignition on. 2. The CAB monitors the Fused B(+) circuit at cavity 9 at all times for proper system voltage.

Set Condition: If the Fused B(+) voltage is missing when the CAB detects that an internal main driver is not on, then the Diagnostic Trouble Code (DTC) is set.

POSSIBLE CAUSES

ABS/SYSTEM FUSE #2 DEFECT
CAB POWER FEED CIRCUIT OBSERVABLE DEFECT
SHORTED TO GROUND
FUSED B(+) CIRCUIT INTERMITTENT CY
FUSED B(+) CIRCUIT SHORTED TO GROUND
FUSED B(+) CIRCUIT OPEN SHORTED TO GROUND
CAB CONNECTOR OBSERVABLE DEFECT
HCU/PUMP DEFECTIVE
CAB DEFECTIVE

TEST	ACTION
1	Ignition On, Engine Not Running With the DRB, erase DTC's. Turn the ignition off. Turn the ignition on. With the DRB, read DTC's. Is the "Cab Power Feed Circuit Failure" code set right now? Yes → Go To 2 No → Go To 9
2	Turn the ignition Off. Remove and inspect the ABS Fuse #2 from the Power Distribution Center (PDC). Is the ABS Fuse #2 okay? Yes → Go To 3 No → Go To 6

CR4020002001010X

Fig. 138 CAB Power Feed Circuit (Part 1 of 3). 2000 Sebring Convertible

TEST	ACTION
9	Turn the ignition Off. Disconnect the CAB Connector. Note: Check connectors - Clean/repair as necessary. Turn the ignition on. Using a voltmeter, measure the ABS Warning Lamp Driver Circuit. Is the voltage above 10 volts? Yes → Go To 10 No → Repair the open ABS Warning Lamp Driver Circuit. Perform ABS Verification Test VER-1A.
10	If there are no potential causes remaining, replace the CAB. View repair options. Yes → Replace the CAB. Perform ABS Verification Test VER-1A.

CR4020002000030X

Fig. 137 ABS Warning Lamp (Part 3 of 3). 2000 Sebring Convertible

TEST	ACTION
3	Turn the ignition Off. Disconnect the CAB Connector. Note: Check connectors - Clean/repair as necessary. Inspect all Terminals. Is any Terminal damaged, pushed out or miswired? Yes → Repair as necessary. Perform ABS Verification Test VER-1A. No → Go To 4
4	Turn the ignition Off. Disconnect CAB Connector. Note: Check connectors - Clean/repair as necessary. Turn Ignition on, with engine not running. Using a Voltmeter, measure the Fused B(+) Circuit, CAB Cavity 9. Is the voltage above 10.0 volts? Yes → Go To 5 No → Repair the open Fused B(+) Circuit. Perform ABS Verification Test VER-1A.
5	If there are no potential causes remaining, the CAB is assumed to be defective. View repair options. Repair Replace the CAB. Perform ABS Verification Test VER-1A.
6	Turn the ignition Off. Remove the ABS Fuse #2 from the Power Distribution Center (PDC). Inspect the Fused B(+) Circuit for signs of an intermittent short to ground. Is the Wiring Harness okay? Yes → Go To 7 No → Repair the Fused B(+) Circuit shorted to ground and replace the ABS Fuse. Perform ABS Verification Test VER-1A.
7	Turn the ignition Off. Remove the ABS Fuse #2 from the Power Distribution Center (PDC). Using an Ohmmeter, measure the resistance between the Fused B (+) Circuit and ground. Is the resistance below 10 ohms? Yes → Go To 8 No → Perform ABS Verification Test VER-1A.
8	Turn the ignition Off. Remove the ABS Fuse #2 in the PDC. Using an ohmmeter, measure the resistance between the Fused B(+) circuit and the ground at the PDC. Disconnect the CAB connector. Is the resistance below 10,000 ohms? Yes → Repair Fused B(+) circuit shorted to ground. No → Replace the HCU/Pump and replace the ABS fuse. Perform ABS Verification Test VER-1A.

CR4020002001020X

Fig. 138 CAB Power Feed Circuit (Part 2 of 3). 2000 Sebring Convertible

TEST	ACTION
9	Turn the ignition Off. Using the schematic as a guide, inspect the Wiring and Connectors. Were any problems found? Yes → Repair as necessary. Perform ABS Verification Test VER-1A. No → Test Complete.

CR4020002001030X

Fig. 138 CAB Power Feed Circuit (Part 3 of 3). 2000 Sebring Convertible

TEST	ACTION
3	Turn the ignition Off. Disconnect the Controller Antilock Brake Connector. **Note: Check connectors - Clean/repair as necessary.** Connect a jumper wire between CCD Bus (+) and CCD Bus (-) Circuit. Ignition on, with engine not running. With the DRB, perform the CCD Bus Test. Does the DRB display, "Bus shorted together"? Yes → Test Complete. No → Check other Modules on this Bus for this DTC. If no other Modules have a DTC, replace the Controller Antilock Brake (CAB). Perform ABS Verification Test VER-1A.
4	Turn the ignition Off. Disconnect the Controller Antilock Brake Connector. **Note: Check connectors - Clean/repair as necessary.** Connect a jumper wire between CCD Bus (+) and CAB Ground. Ignition on, with engine not running. With the DRB, perform the CCD Bus Test. Does the DRB show "Bus shorted to ground"? Yes → Go To 4 No → Repair the open CCD Bus (+) Circuit. Perform ABS Verification Test VER-1A.
5	Turn the ignition Off. Disconnect the Controller Antilock Brake Connector. **Note: Check connectors - Clean/repair as necessary.** Connect a jumper wire between CCD Bus (-) and CAB Ground. Ignition on, with engine not running. With the DRB, perform the CCD Bus Test. Does the DRB show "Bus shorted to ground"? Yes → Go To 5 No → Repair the open CCD Bus (-) Circuit. Perform ABS Verification Test VER-1A.
6	Turn the ignition Off. Using the schematic as a guide, inspect the Wiring and Connections. Were any problems found? Yes → Repair as necessary. Perform ABS Verification Test VER-1A. No → Test Complete.

CR4020002002020X

Fig. 139 CCD Communication (Part 2 of 2). 2000 Sebring Convertible

TEST	ACTION
4	Turn the ignition Off. Disconnect the CAB Connector. **Note: Check connectors - Clean/repair as necessary.** Turn the ignition on. Turn on all accessories. Using a Voltmeter, measure the Ground Circuits in Cavity 8 or 24. Is the voltage above 1.0 volt? Yes → Repair the open Ground Circuits. Perform ABS Verification Test VER-1A. No → Go To 5
5	If there are no potential causes remaining, repalce the CAB. View repair options. Repair Replace the CAB. Perform ABS Verification Test VER-1A.

CR4020002003020X

Fig. 140 Controller Failure (Part 2 of 2). 2000 Sebring Convertible

When Monitored: Ignition on.

Set Condition: The Diagnostic Trouble Code (DTC) is set when the CAB cannot transmit the ABS status message for 15 seconds.

POSSIBLE CAUSES
CAB CONNECTOR OBSERVABLE DEFECT
WIRING AND CONNECTIONS OBSERVABLE DEFECT
CCD BUS (+) CIRCUIT OPEN
CCD BUS (-) CIRCUIT OPEN
OTHER MODULES DTC
CAB DEFECTIVE

TEST	ACTION
1	Ignition On, Engine Not Running. With the DRB, erase DTC's. Turn the ignition off. Turn the ignition on. With the DRB, read the DTC's. Did the "CCD Communication" DTC set right now? Yes → Go To 2 No → Go To 6
2	Turn the ignition Off. Disconnect the Controller Antilock Brake Connector. **Note: Check connectors - Clean/repair as necessary.** Inspect all Terminals. Is any Terminal damaged, pushed out or miswired? Yes → Repair as necessary. Perform ABS Verification Test VER-1A. No → Go To 3

CR4020002002010X

Fig. 139 CCD Communication (Part 1 of 2). 2000 Sebring Convertible

When Monitored: 1. Ignition on. 2. The CAB monitors its own internal microprocessors for proper operation.

Set Condition: If an error occurs within the microprocessor, the Diagnostic Trouble Code (DTC) is set.

POSSIBLE CAUSES
CAB CONNECTOR OBSERVABLE DEFECT
CAB GROUND CIRCUIT(S) OPEN
VEHICLE ACCESSORIES CONNECTIONS OBSERVABLE DEFECT
CAB DEFECTIVE

TEST	ACTION
1	Turn the ignition Off. Inspect the vehicle for any accessories that have been installed. Inspect for proper power and ground connections and/or Antenna Cable routing. Were any problems found? Yes → Repair as necessary. Perform ABS Verification Test VER-1A. No → Go To 2
2	Turn the ignition Off. Disconnect the CAB. **Note: Check connectors - Clean/repair as necessary.** Inspect the Ground Circuits in CAB, cavities 8 and 24. Is any Terminal damaged, pushed out, or miswired? Yes → Repair as necessary. Perform ABS Verification Test VER-1A. No → Go To 3
3	Turn the ignition Off. Disconnect the CAB Connector. **Note: Check connectors - Clean/repair as necessary.** Using an Ohmmeter, measure the resistance between the CAB Ground Circuits and ground, Cavity 8 and 24 and Battery ground. Is the resistance below 1.0 ohms? Yes → Go To 4 No → Repair the open Ground Circuit(s). Perform ABS Verification Test VER-1A.

CR4020002003010X

Fig. 140 Controller Failure (Part 1 of 2). 2000 Sebring Convertible

When Monitored: 1. Ignition on. 2. Vehicle speed above 40 km/h (24 mph) on all our wheels for more than 2 minutes.

Set Condition: The CAB counts the number of pulses from the wheel speed sensors and compares the values. If the CAB determines that one or both of the front wheel speed sensor signals are significantly different then the rear speed signals, the Diagnostic Trouble Code (DTC) is set.

POSSIBLE CAUSES
INCORRECT TONE WHEEL

TEST	ACTION
1	An incorrect Tone Wheel was installed on the vehicle. View repair options Yes → Replace Tone Wheel

CR4020002004000X

Fig. 141 Incorrect Tone Wheel. 2000 Sebring Convertible

When Monitored: 1. Ignition on. 2. The CAB monitors the wheel speed sensor circuit continuity at all times.

Set Condition: If the CAB detects an open or shorted wheel speed sensor circuit, the Diagnostic Trouble Code (DTC) will set.

POSSIBLE CAUSES
WIRING & CONNECTORS OBSERVABLE DEFECT
LEFT FRONT WHEEL SPEED SENSOR CONNECTOR OBSERVABLE DAMAGE
LEFT FRONT WHEEL SPEED SENSOR DAMAGED OR CONNECTOR DISCONNECTED
LEFT FRONT WHEEL SPEED SENSOR (+) CIRCUIT OPEN
LEFT FRONT WHEEL SPEED SENSOR (+) CIRCUIT SHORTED TO GROUND
LEFT FRONT WHEEL SPEED SENSOR (-) CIRCUIT OPEN
LEFT FRONT WHEEL SPEED SENSOR (-) CIRCUIT SHORTED TO GROUND
LEFT FRONT WHEEL SPEED SENSOR DEFECTIVE (SHORT TO GROUND CHECK)
LEFT FRONT WHEEL SPEED SENSOR DEFECTIVE (RESISTANCE CHECK)
CAB DEFECTIVE

TEST	ACTION
1	Ignition On, Engine Not Running. With the DRB, read DTC's. With the DRB erase DTC's. Turn ignition off, turn ignition on. With the DRB, read DTC's. Did the DTC set again right now? Yes → Go To 2 No → Go To 11
2	Turn the ignition Off. Disconnect the Left Front Wheel Speed Sensor Connector. **Note: Check connectors - Clean/repair as necessary.** Inspect all Terminals. Is any Terminal damaged, pushed out or miswired? Yes → Repair as necessary. Perform ABS Verification Test VER-1A. No → Go To 3

CR4020002005010X

Fig. 142 Lefthand Front Sensor Circuit Failure (Part 1 of 3). 2000 Sebring Convertible

TEST	ACTION
3	Turn the ignition Off. Inspect the Left Front Wheel Speed Sensor and Connector. Is the Left Front Sensor damaged or Connector disconnected? Yes → Repair as necessary. Perform ABS Verification Test VER-1A. No → Go To 4
4	Turn the ignition Off. Disconnect the Left Front Wheel Speed Sensor Connector. **Note: Check connectors - Clean/repair as necessary.** Disconnect the CAB Connector. **Note: Check connectors - Clean/repair as necessary.** Connect a Jumper Wire between the Left Front Wheel Speed Sensor (+) Circuit and ground. Using an Ohmmeter, measure the resistance between the Left Front Wheel Speed Sensor (+) Circuit and ground, CAB Cavities 4 and 8. Is the resistance below 10 ohms? Yes → Go To 5 No → Repair the open Left Front Wheel Speed Sensor (+) Circuit. Perform ABS Verification Test VER-1A.
5	Turn the ignition Off. Disconnect the Left Front Wheel Speed Sensor Connector. **Note: Check connectors - Clean/repair as necessary.** Disconnect the CAB Connector. **Note: Check connectors - Clean/repair as necessary.** Using an Ohmmeter, measure the resistance between the Left Front Wheel Speed Sensor (+) Circuit and ground. Is the resistance below 15,000 ohms? Yes → Repair the Left Front Wheel Speed Sensor (+) Circuit shorted to ground. Perform ABS Verification Test VER-1A. No → Go To 6
6	Turn the ignition Off. Disconnect the Left Front Wheel Speed Sensor Connector. **Note: Check connectors - Clean/repair as necessary.** Using an Ohmmeter, measure the resistance between either one of the Left Front Wheel Speed Sensor pins and ground. Is the resistance below 15,000 ohms? Yes → Replace the Left Front Wheel Speed Sensor. Perform ABS Verification Test VER-1A. No → Go To 7

CR4020002005020X

Fig. 142 Lefthand Front Sensor Circuit Failure (Part 2 of 3). 2000 Sebring Convertible

TEST	ACTION
7	Turn the ignition Off. Disconnect the Left Front Wheel Speed Sensor Connector. **Note: Check connectors - Clean/repair as necessary.** Disconnect the CAB Connector. **Note: Check connectors - Clean/repair as necessary.** Connect a Jumper Wire between the Left Front Wheel Speed Sensor (-) and ground. Using an Ohmmeter, measure the resistance between the Left Front Wheel Speed Sensor (-) Circuit and ground, CAB Cavities 11 and 8. Is the resistance below 10 ohms? Yes → Go To 8 No → Repair the open Left Front Wheel Speed Sensor (-) Circuit. Perform ABS Verification Test VER-1A.
8	Turn the ignition Off. Disconnect the Left Front Wheel Speed Sensor Connector. **Note: Check connectors - Clean/repair as necessary.** Disconnect the CAB Connector. **Note: Check connectors - Clean/repair as necessary.** Using an Ohmmeter, measure the resistance between the Left Front Wheel Speed Sensor (-) Circuit and ground. Is the resistance below 15,000 ohms? Yes → Repair the Left Front Wheel Speed Sensor (-) Circuit shorted to ground. Perform ABS Verification Test VER-1A. No → Go To 9
9	Turn the ignition Off. Disconnect the Left Front Wheel Speed Sensor Connector. **Note: Check connectors - Clean/repair as necessary.** Using an Ohmmeter, measure the resistance of the Left Front Wheel Speed Sensor. Is the resistance between 2,160 and 2,640 ohms? Yes → Go To 10 No → Replace the Left Front Wheel Speed Sensor. Perform ABS Verification Test VER-1A.
10	If there are no potential causes remaining, replace the CAB. View repair options. Repair Replace the CAB. Perform ABS Verification Test VER-1A.
11	Turn the ignition Off. Using the schematic as a guide, inspect the Wiring and Connections. Were any problems found? Yes → Repair as necessary. Perform ABS Verification Test VER-1A. No → Test Complete.

CR4020002005030X

Fig. 142 Lefthand Front Sensor Circuit Failure (Part 3 of 3). 2000 Sebring Convertible

When Monitored: The CAB monitors the wheel speed sensor signal at all times. 1. Comparison is checked at drive off or every 7 milliseconds. 2. Continuity is checked continuously. 3. Phase length supervision is checked every 7 milliseconds.

Set Condition: If the sensor signal is missing, as soon as vehicle speed exceeds 19 Km/h (12 mph) the Diagnostic Trouble Code (DTC) will set. If during an ABS stop, the CAB commands any valve solenoid on for an extended length of time, and does not see a corresponding wheel speed change, the DTC is set.

POSSIBLE CAUSES
CAB CONNECTOR OBSERVABLE DEFECT
LEFT FRONT WHEEL SPEED SENSOR CIRCUITS SHORTED TOGETHER
LEFT FRONT TONE WHEEL DEFECTIVE
LEFT FRONT WHEEL SPEED SENSOR AIR GAP OUT OF SPECIFICATION
LEFT FRONT WHEEL BEARING CLEARANCE OUT OF SPECIFICATION
LEFT FRONT WHEEL SPEED SENSOR DEFECTIVE
LEFT FRONT WHEEL SPEED SENSOR OBSERVABLE DEFECT

TEST	ACTION
1	Ignition On, Engine Not Running With the DRB, read DTC. Is the Left Front Sensor Circuit failure DTC present right now? Yes → Refer to symptom LEFT FRONT SENSOR CIRCUIT FAILURE. No → Go To 2
2	Have an assistant drive the vehicle while you monitor the Left Front Wheel Speed Sensor. Slowly accelerate as straight as possible from a stop to 24 Km/h (15 MPH). Did the Left Front Wheel Speed Sensor Signal show 0 Km/h (0 MPH) or lag behind the other sensors more than 5 Km/h (3 MPH)? Yes → Go To 3 No → At this time, the Wheel Speed Sensor is OK. The DTC may have been set by attempting to stop on very slick road surfaces or brakes locking up due to lining contamination or overheating. If any of these conditions are present, repair as necessary. Test Complete. Perform ABS Verification Test VER-1A

CR4020002006010X

Fig. 143 Lefthand Front Sensor Signal Failure (Part 1 of 3). 2000 Sebring Convertible

TEST	ACTION
3	Turn the ignition Off. Inspect the Left Front Wheel Speed Sensor. Is the Left Front Wheel Speed Sensor loose or damaged? Yes → Repair as necessary. Perform ABS Verification Test VER-1A. No → Go To 4
4	Turn the ignition Off. Inspect the Tone Wheel for damaged or missing teeth. **Note: The teeth should be perfectly square, not bent or nicked.** Is the Tone Wheel okay? Yes → Go To 5 No → Replace the Tone Wheel. Perform ABS Verification Test VER-1A.
5	Turn the ignition Off. Using a Feeler Gauge, measure the Sensor Air Gap. **Note: The Air Gap should be checked at least in four places on the Tone Wheel.** Is the Air Gap within 0.17 to 1.80 mm (0.007″ to 0.071″)? Yes → Go To 6 No → Repair as necessary. Perform ABS Verification Test VER-1A.
6	Turn the ignition Off. Inspect the Wheel Bearings for excessive runout or clearance. **Refer to service information if necessary for procedures or specifications.** Is the Bearing clearance okay? Yes → Go To 7 No → Repair as necessary. Perform ABS Verification Test VER-1A.
7	Turn the ignition Off. Disconnect the CAB Connector. **Note: Check connectors - Clean/repair as necessary.** Inspect all Terminals. Is any Terminal damaged, pushed out or miswired? Yes → Repair as necessary. Perform ABS Verification Test VER-1A. No → Go To 8
8	Turn the ignition Off. Disconnect the CAB Connector. **Note: Check connectors - Clean/repair as necessary.** Using an Ohmmeter, measure the resistance of the Left Front Wheel Speed Sensor Circuit, CAB Cavities 4 and 11. Is the resistance below 200 ohms? Yes → Repair the Left Front Wheel Speed Sensor Circuits shorted together. Perform ABS Verification Test VER-1A. No → Go To 9

CR4020002006020X

Fig. 143 Lefthand Front Sensor Signal Failure (Part 2 of 3). 2000 Sebring Convertible

When Monitored: 1. Ignition on. 2. The CAB monitors the wheel speed circuit continuity at all times.

Set Condition: If the CAB detects an open or shorted wheel speed sensor circuit, the Diagnostic Trouble Code (DTC) is set.

POSSIBLE CAUSES
WIRING AND CONNECTORS OBSERVABLE DEFECT
LEFT REAR WHEEL SPEED SENSOR CONNECTOR OBSERVABLE DAMAGE
LEFT REAR WHEEL SPEED SENSOR DAMAGED OR CONNECTOR DISCONNECTED
LEFT REAR WHEEL SPEED SENSOR (+) CIRCUIT OPEN
LEFT REAR WHEEL SPEED SENSOR (+) CIRCUIT SHORTED TO GROUND
LEFT REAR WHEEL SPEED SENSOR (-) CIRCUIT OPEN
LEFT REAR WHEEL SPEED SENSOR (-) CIRCUIT SHORTED TO GROUND
LEFT REAR WHEEL SPEED SENSOR DEFECTIVE (SHORT TO GROUND CHECK)
LEFT REAR WHEEL SPEED SENSOR DEFECTIVE (RESISTANCE CHECK)
CAB DEFECTIVE

TEST	ACTION
1	Ignition On, Engine Not Running. With the DRB, read DTC's. With the DRB, erase DTC's Turn the ignition off. Turn the ignition on. With the DRB, read DTC's. Did the DTC's set again right now? Yes → Go To 2 No → Go To 11
2	Turn the ignition Off. Inspect the Left Rear Wheel Speed Sensor and Connector. Is the Left Rear Wheel Speed Sensor damaged or Connector disconnected? Yes → Repair as necessary. Perform ABS Verification Test VER-1A. No → Go To 3

CR4020002007010X

Fig. 144 Lefthand Rear Sensor Circuit Failure (Part 1 of 3). 2000 Sebring Convertible

TEST	ACTION
9	If there are no potential causes remaining, the Left Front Wheel Speed Sensor is assumed to be defective. View repair options. Repair Replace the Left Front Wheel Speed Sensor. Perform ABS Verification Test VER-1A.

CR4020002006030X

Fig. 143 Lefthand Front Sensor Signal Failure (Part 3 of 3). 2000 Sebring Convertible

TEST	ACTION
3	Turn the ignition Off. Disconnect the Left Rear Wheel Speed Sensor Connector. **Note: Check connectors - Clean/repair as necessary.** Inspect all Terminals. Is any Terminal damaged, pushed out, or miswired? Yes → Repair as necessary. Perform ABS Verification Test VER-1A. No → Go To 4
4	Turn the ignition Off. Disconnect the Left Rear Wheel Speed Sensor Connector. **Note: Check connectors - Clean/repair as necessary.** Disconnect the CAB Connector. **Note: Check connectors - Clean/repair as necessary.** Connect a jumper wire between the Left Rear Wheel Speed Sensor (+) Circuit and ground. Using an Ohmmeter, measure the resistance between the Left Rear Wheel Speed Sensor (+) Circuit and ground, CAB Cavity 10 and 8. Is the resistance below 10 ohms? Yes → Go To 5 No → Repair the open Left Rear Wheel Speed Sensor (+) Circuit. Perform ABS Verification Test VER-1A.
5	Turn the ignition Off. Disconnect the Left Rear Wheel Speed Sensor Connector. **Note: Check connectors - Clean/repair as necessary.** Disconnect the CAB Connector. **Note: Check connectors - Clean/repair as necessary.** Using an Ohmmeter, measure the resistance between the Left Rear Wheel Speed Sensor (+) Circuit and ground. Is the resistance below 15,000 ohms? Yes → Repair the Left Rear Wheel Speed Sensor (+) Circuit shorted to ground. Perform ABS Verification Test VER-1A. No → Go To 6
6	Turn the ignition Off. Disconnect the Left Rear Wheel Speed Sensor Connector. **Note: Check connectors - Clean/repair as necessary.** Using an Ohmmeter, measure the resistance between either one of the WSS pins and ground. Is the resistance below 15,000 ohms? Yes → Replace the Wheel Speed Sensor. Perform ABS Verification Test VER-1A. No → Go To 7

CR4020002007020X

Fig. 144 Lefthand Rear Sensor Circuit Failure (Part 2 of 3). 2000 Sebring Convertible

TEST	ACTION
7	Turn the ignition Off. Disconnect the Left Rear Wheel Speed Sensor Connector. **Note: Check connectors - Clean/repair as necessary.** Disconnect the CAB Connector. **Note: Check connectors - Clean/repair as necessary.** Connect a jumper wire between the Left Rear Wheel Speed Sensor (-) and ground. Using an Ohmmeter, measure the resistance between the Left Rear Wheel Speed Sensor (-) Circuit and ground, CAB Cavity 2 and 8. Is the resistance below 10 ohms? Yes → Go To 8 No → Repair the open Left Rear Wheel Speed Sensor (-) Circuit. Perform ABS Verification Test VER-1A.
8	Turn the ignition Off. Disconnect the Left Rear Wheel Speed Sensor Connector. **Note: Check connectors - Clean/repair as necessary.** Disconnect the CAB Connector. **Note: Check connectors - Clean/repair as necessary.** Using an Ohmmeter, measure the resistance between the Left Rear Wheel Speed Sensor (-) Circuit and ground. Is the resistance below 15,000 ohms? Yes → Repair the Left Rear Wheel Speed Sensor (-) Circuit shorted to ground. Perform ABS Verification Test VER-1A. No → Go To 9
9	Turn the ignition Off. Disconnect the Left Rear Wheel Speed Sensor Connector. **Note: Check connectors - Clean/repair as necessary.** Using an Ohmmeter, measure the resistance of the Left Rear Wheel Speed Sensor. Is the resistance between 2,160 and 2,640 ohms? Yes → Go To 10 No → Replace the Wheel Speed Sensor. Perform ABS Verification Test VER-1A.
10	If there are no potential causes remaining, replace the CAB. View repair options. Repair Replace the CAB. Perform ABS Verification Test VER-1A.
11	Turn the ignition Off. Using a schematic as a guide, inspect the Wiring and Connections. Were any problems found? Yes → Repair as necessary. Perform ABS Verification Test VER-1A. No → Test Complete.

CR4020002007030X

Fig. 144 Lefthand Rear Sensor Circuit Failure (Part 3 of 3). 2000 Sebring Convertible

TEST	ACTION
3	Turn the ignition Off. Inspect the Left Rear Wheel Speed Sensor. Is the Left Rear Wheel Speed Sensor loose or damaged? Yes → Repair as necessary. Perform ABS Verification Test VER-1A. No → Go To 4
4	Turn the ignition Off. Inspect the Tone Wheel for damaged or missing teeth. **Note: The teeth should be perfectly square, not bent or nicked.** Is the Tone Wheel okay? Yes → Go To 5 No → Replace the Tone Wheel. Perform ABS Verification Test VER-1A.
5	Turn the ignition Off. Using a Feeler Gauge, measure the Sensor Air Gap. **Note: The Air Gap should be checked in at least four places on the Tone Wheel.** Is the Air Gap within 0.37 to 1.50 mm (0.015" to 0.059")? Yes → Go To 6 No → Repair as necessary. Perform ABS Verification Test VER-1A.
6	Turn the ignition Off. Inspect the Wheel Bearings for excessive runout or clearance. **Refer to service information if necessary for procedures or specifications.** Is the Bearing clearance okay? Yes → Go To 7 No → Repair as necessary. Perform ABS Verification Test VER-1A.
7	Turn the ignition Off. Disconnect the CAB Connector. **Note: Check connectors - Clean/repair as necessary.** Inspect all Terminals. Is any Terminal damaged, pushed out, or miswired? Yes → Repair as necessary. Perform ABS Verification Test VER-1A. No → Go To 8
8	Turn the ignition Off. Disconnect the CAB Connector. **Note: Check connectors - Clean/repair as necessary.** Using an Ohmmeter, measure the resistance of the Left Rear Wheel Speed Sensor Circuit, CAB Cavities 2 and 10. Is the resistance below 200 ohms? Yes → Repair the Left Rear Wheel Speed Sensor Circuits shorted together. Perform ABS Verification Test VER-1A. No → Go To 9

CR4020002008020X

Fig. 145 Lefthand Rear Sensor Signal Failure (Part 2 of 3). 2000 Sebring Convertible

When Monitored: 1. Ignition on. 2. The CAB monitors the wheel speed signals at all times.

Set Condition: If the sensor signal is missing, as soon as vehicle speed exceeds 19 Km/h (12 mph) the Diagnostic Trouble Code will set. If during an ABS stop, the CAB commands any valve solenoid on for an extended length of time, and does not see a corresponding wheel speed change, the DTC is set.

POSSIBLE CAUSES
CAB CONNECTOR OBSERVABLE DEFECT
LEFT REAR WSS AIR GAP OUT OF SPECIFICATION
LEFT REAR WSS CIRCUITS SHORTED TOGETHER
LEFT REAR WSS SENSOR DEFECTIVE
LEFT REAR WSS SENSOR OBSERVABLE DEFECT
LEFT REAR TONE WHEEL DEFECTIVE
LEFT REAR WHEEL BEARING CLEARANCE OUT OF SPEC

TEST	ACTION
1	Ignition On, Engine Not Running With DRB, read DTC's. Is the Left Rear Sensor Circuit failure DTC present right now? Yes → Refer to symptom LEFT REAR SENSOR CIRCUIT FAILURE. No → Go To 2
2	Engine Running Have an assistant drive the vehicle while you monitor the Left Rear Wheel Speed Sensor. Slowly accelerate as straight as possible from a stop to 24 Km/h (15 MPH). Did the Left Rear Wheel Speed Sensor Signal show 0 Km/h (0 MPH) or lag behind the other sensors more than 5 Km/h (3 MPH)? Yes → Go To 3 No → At this time, the WSS is OK. The TC may have been set by attempting to stop on very slick Road surfaces or Brakes locking up due to Lining contamination or overheating. If any of these conditions are present, repair as necessary. Test Complete. Perform ABS Verification Test VER-1A

CR4020002008010X

Fig. 145 Lefthand Rear Sensor Signal Failure (Part 1 of 3). 2000 Sebring Convertible

TEST	ACTION
9	If there are no potential causes remaining, replace the Left Rear Wheel Speed Sensor. View repair options. Repair Replace the Left Rear Wheel Speed Sensor. Perform ABS Verification Test VER-1A.

CR4020002008030X

Fig. 145 Lefthand Rear Sensor Signal Failure (Part 3 of 3). 2000 Sebring Convertible

When Monitored: Ignition on. The CAB monitors the pump at all times. The CAB commands the pump on at 19 Km/h (12 mph) to check its operation, provided the brake is not applied. If the driver has their foot on the brake, the test will run at 39 Km/h (24 mph).

Set Condition: The DTC is stored when the CAB detects that the pump cannot run when commanded on OR is running erroneously. If the pump is off at the end of an ABS stop when the pump is commanded on, or if the pump is on when the pump is commanded off, the DTC is set.

POSSIBLE CAUSES
ABS PUMP FUSE #13 DEFECTIVE
CAB CONNECTOR OBSERVABLE DEFECT
FUSED B+ CIRCUIT OPEN
CAB GROUND CIRCUITS OPEN
PUMP MOTOR TERMINAL CONNECTOR OBSERVABLE DEFECT
PUMP MOTOR WIRING HARNESS OBSERVABLE DEFECT
PUMP MOTOR/HCU DEFECTIVE
CAB DEFECTIVE

TEST	ACTION
1	Ignition On, Engine Not Running With the DRB read DTC's. Is the CAB Power Feed Circuit code present right now? Yes → Refer to symptom CAB POWER FEED CIRCUIT. No → Go To 2
2	Ignition On, Engine Not Running With the DRB, erase DTC's. Turn the ignition off. Turn ignition on. With the DRB, under "System Test" perform "Pump Test." Did pump motor work properly? Yes → Go To 11 No → Go To 3

CR4020002009010X

Fig. 146 Pump Motor Circuit Not Working Properly (Part 1 of 3). 2000 Sebring Convertible

TEST	ACTION
3	Turn the ignition On. Is the Pump/Motor running continuously? Yes → Replace the CAB. Perform ABS Verification Test VER-1A. No → Go To 4
4	Turn the ignition Off. Check the ABS Pump Fuse #13 in the PDC. Is the Fuse okay? Yes → Go To 5 No → Check for a short to ground in Fused B+ Circuit. If no short is found, replace faulty ABS fuse. Perform ABS Verification Test VER-1A.
5	Turn the ignition Off. Disconnect the CAB Connector. **Note: Check connectors - Clean/repair as necessary.** Inspect all Terminals. Is any Terminal damaged, pushed out or miswired? Yes → Repair as necessary. Perform ABS Verification Test VER-1A. No → Go To 6
6	Turn the ignition Off. Disconnect the CAB Connector. **Note: Check connectors - Clean/repair as necessary.** Using a 12 Volt test light connected to ground, probe the Fused B+ Circuit, CAB Cavity 25. Is the test light on? Yes → Go To 7 No → Repair the open Fused B+ Circuit. Perform ABS Verification Test VER-1A.
7	Turn the ignition Off. Disconnect the CAB Connector. **Note: Check connectors - Clean/repair as necessary.** Using an Ohmmeter, connect probes between the CAB Ground Circuits and ground, CAB Cavities 8 and 24, and Battery ground. Is the resistance below 1.0 ohms? Yes → Go To 8 No → Repair the open Ground Circuit. Perform ABS Verification Test VER-1A.
8	Turn the ignition Off. Disconnect the Pump Motor Two Terminal Connector from CAB. **Note: Check connectors - Clean/repair as necessary.** Inspect all Terminals. Is any Terminal damaged, pushed out or miswired? Yes → Repair as necessary. Perform ABS Verification Test VER-1A. No → Go To 9

CR4020002009020X

Fig. 146 Pump Motor Circuit Not Working Properly (Part 2 of 3). 2000 Sebring Convertible

When Monitored: 1. Ignition on. 2. The CAB monitors the wheel speed circuit continuity at all times.

Set Condition: If the CAB detects an open or shorted wheel speed sensor circuit, the Diagnostic Trouble Code (DTC) will set.

POSSIBLE CAUSES
WIRING AND CONNECTORS OBSERVABLE DEFECT
RIGHT FRONT WHEEL SPEED SENSOR CONNECTOR OBSERVABLE DAMAGE
RIGHT FRONT WHEEL SPEED SENSOR DAMAGED OR CONNECTOR DISCONNECTED
RIGHT FRONT WHEEL SPEED SENSOR (+) CIRCUIT OPEN
RIGHT FRONT WHEEL SPEED SENSOR (+) CIRCUIT SHORTED TO GROUND
RIGHT FRONT WHEEL SPEED SENSOR (-) CIRCUIT OPEN
RIGHT FRONT WHEEL SPEED SENSOR (-) CIRCUIT SHORTED TO GROUND
RIGHT FRONT WHEEL SPEED SENSOR DEFECTIVE (SHORT TO GROUND CHECK)
RIGHT FRONT WHEEL SPEED SENSOR DEFECTIVE (RESISTANCE CHECK)
CAB DEFECTIVE

TEST	ACTION
1	Ignition On, Engine Not Running With the DRB, read the DTC's. With the DRB, erase DTC's. Turn the ignition Off. Turn ignition on. With the DRB, read DTC's. Did the DTC set again right now? Yes → Go To 2 No → Go To 11
2	Turn the ignition Off. Disconnect the Right Front Wheel Speed Sensor Connector. **Note: Check connectors - Clean/repair as necessary.** Inspect all Terminals. Is any Terminal damaged, pushed out or miswired? Yes → Repair as necessary. Perform ABS Verification Test VER-1A. No → Go To 3

CR4020002010010X

Fig. 147 Righthand Front Sensor Circuit Failure (Part 1 of 3). 2000 Sebring Convertible

TEST	ACTION
9	Turn the ignition Off. Disconnect the CAB Connector. **Note: Check connectors - Clean/repair as necessary.** Disconnect Pump Motor Connector. **Note: Check connectors - Clean/repair as necessary.** Connect a jumper wire between CAB Cav. 25 and Pump Motor (+) Terminal. Connect another jumper wire between the Pump Motor (-) Terminal and ground. Is the Pump Motor operating properly? Yes → Replace the CAB. Perform ABS Verification Test VER-1A. No → Go To 10
10	If there are no potential causes remaining, replace the Pump Motor/HCU. View repair options. Repair Replace the Pump Motor/HCU. Perform ABS Verification Test VER-1A.
11	Turn the ignition Off. Using the schematic as a guide, inspect the Wiring and Connections. Were any problems found? Yes → Repair as necessary. Perform ABS Verification Test VER-1A. No → Test Complete.

CR4020002009030X

Fig. 146 Pump Motor Circuit Not Working Properly (Part 3 of 3). 2000 Sebring Convertible

TEST	ACTION
3	Turn the ignition Off. Inspect the Right Front Wheel Speed Sensor and Connector. Is the Sensor damaged or Connector disconnected? Yes → Repair as necessary. Perform ABS Verification Test VER-1A. No → Go To 4
4	Turn the ignition Off. Disconnect the Right Front Wheel Speed Sensor Connector. **Note: Check connectors - Clean/repair as necessary.** Disconnect the CAB Connector. **Note: Check connectors - Clean/repair as necessary.** Connect a jumper wire between the Right Front Wheel Speed Sensor (+) and ground. Using an Ohmmeter, measure the resistance between the Right Front Wheel Speed Sensor (+) Circuit and ground, CAB Cavities 3 and 8. Is the resistance below 10 ohms? Yes → Go To 5 No → Repair the open Right Front Wheel Speed Sensor (+) Circuit. Perform ABS Verification Test VER-1A.
5	Turn the ignition Off. Disconnect the Right Front Wheel Speed Sensor Connector. **Note: Check connectors - Clean/repair as necessary.** Disconnect the CAB Connector. **Note: Check connectors - Clean/repair as necessary.** Using an Ohmmeter, measure the resistance between the Wheel Speed Sensor (+) Circuit and ground. Is the resistance below 15,000 ohms? Yes → Repair the Wheel Speed Sensor (+) Circuit shorted to ground. Perform ABS Verification Test VER-1A. No → Go To 6
6	Turn the ignition Off. Disconnect the Right Front Wheel Speed Sensor Connector. **Note: Check connectors - Clean/repair as necessary.** Using an Ohmmeter, measure the resistance between either one of the Right Front Wheel Speed Sensor pins and ground. Is the resistance below 15,000 ohms? Yes → Replace the Wheel Speed Sensor. Perform ABS Verification Test VER-1A. No → Go To 7

CR4020002010020X

Fig. 147 Righthand Front Sensor Circuit Failure (Part 2 of 3). 2000 Sebring Convertible

TEST	ACTION
7	Turn the ignition Off. Disconnect the Right Front Wheel Speed Sensor Connector. **Note: Check connectors - Clean/repair as necessary.** Disconnect the CAB Connector. **Note: Check connectors - Clean/repair as necessary.** Connect a jumper wire between the Right Front Wheel Speed Sensor (-) and ground. Using an Ohmmeter, measure the resistance between the Right Front Wheel Speed Sensor (-) Circuit and ground, CAB Cavities 18 and 8. Is the resistance below 10 ohms? Yes → Go To 8 No → Repair the open Right Front Wheel Speed Sensor (-) Circuit. Perform ABS Verification Test VER-1A.
8	Turn the ignition Off. Disconnect the Right Front Wheel Speed Sensor Connector. **Note: Check connectors - Clean/repair as necessary.** Disconnect the CAB Connector. **Note: Check connectors - Clean/repair as necessary.** Using an Ohmmeter, measure the resistance between the Right Front Wheel Speed Sensor (-) Circuit and ground. Is the resistance below 15,000 ohms? Yes → Repair the Right Front Wheel Speed Sensor (-) Circuit shorted to ground. Perform ABS Verification Test VER-1A. No → Go To 9
9	Turn the ignition Off. Disconnect the Right Front Wheel Speed Sensor Connector. **Note: Check connectors - Clean/repair as necessary.** Using an Ohmmeter, measure the resistance of the Right Front Wheel Speed Sensor. Is the resistance between 2,160 and 2,640 ohms? Yes → Go To 10 No → Replace the Right Front Wheel Speed Sensor. Perform ABS Verification Test VER-1A.
10	If there are no potential causes remaining, replace the CAB. View repair options. Repair Replace the Controller Antilock Brake. Perform ABS Verification Test VER-1A.
11	Turn the ignition Off. Using the schematic as a guide, inspect the Wiring and Connections. Were any problems found? Yes → Repair as necessary. Perform ABS Verification Test VER-1A. No → Test Complete.

CR4020002010030X

Fig. 147 Righthand Front Sensor Circuit Failure (Part 3 of 3). 2000 Sebring Convertible

TEST	ACTION
3	Turn the ignition Off. Inspect the Right Front Wheel Speed Sensor. Is the Right Front Wheel Speed Sensor loose or damaged? Yes → Repair as necessary. Perform ABS Verification Test VER-1A. No → Go To 4
4	Turn the ignition Off. Inspect the Tone Wheel for damaged or missing teeth. **Note: The teeth should be perfectly square, not bent or nicked.** Is the Tone Wheel okay? Yes → Go To 5 No → Replace the Tone Wheel. Perform ABS Verification Test VER-1A.
5	Turn the ignition Off. Using a Feeler Gauge, measure the Sensor Air Gap. **Note: The Air Gap should be checked at least in four places on the Tone Wheel.** Is the Air Gap within 0.17 to 1.80 mm (0.007" to 0.071")? Yes → Go To 6 No → Repair as necessary. Perform ABS Verification Test VER-1A.
6	Turn the ignition Off. Inspect the Wheel Bearings for excessive runout or clearance. **Refer to service information if necessary for procedures or specifications.** Is the Bearing clearance okay? Yes → Go To 7 No → Repair as necessary. Perform ABS Verification Test VER-1A.
7	Turn the ignition Off. Disconnect the CAB Connector. **Note: Check connectors - Clean/repair as necessary.** Inspect all Terminals. Is any Terminal damaged, pushed out or miswired? Yes → Repair as necessary. Perform ABS Verification Test VER-1A. No → Go To 8
8	Turn the ignition Off. Disconnect the CAB Connector. **Note: Check connectors - Clean/repair as necessary.** Using an Ohmmeter, measure the resistance of the Right Front Wheel Speed Sensor Circuit, CAB Cavities 3 and 18. Is the resistance below 200 ohms? Yes → Repair the Right Front Wheel Speed Sensor Circuits shorted together. Perform ABS Verification Test VER-1A. No → Go To 9

CR4020002011020X

Fig. 148 Righthand Front Sensor Signal Failure (Part 2 of 3). 2000 Sebring Convertible

When Monitored: 1. Ignition on. 2. The CAB monitors the wheel speed signals at all times.

Set Condition: If the sensor signal is missing, as soon as vehicle speed exceeds 19 Km/h (12 mph) the Diagnostic Trouble Code (DTC) will set. If during an ABS stop, the CAB commands any valve solenoid on for an extended length of time, and does not see a corresponding wheel speed change, the DTC is set.

POSSIBLE CAUSES
CAB CONNECTOR OBSERVABLE DEFECT
RIGHT FRONT WHEEL SPEED SENSOR CIRCUITS SHORTED TOGETHER
RIGHT FRONT WHEEL SPEED SENSOR AIR GAP OUT OF SPECIFICATION
RIGHT FRONT WHEEL SPEED SENSOR DEFECTIVE
RIGHT FRONT WHEEL SPEED SENSOR OBSERVABLE DEFECT
RIGHT FRONT TONE WHEEL DEFECTIVE
WHEEL BEARING CLEARANCE OUT OF SPECIFICATION

TEST	ACTION
1	Ignition On, Engine Not Running With the DRB, read DTC. Is the Right Front Sensor Circuit failure DTC present right now? Yes → Refer to symptom RIGHT FRONT SENSOR CIRCUIT FAILURE. No → Go To 2
2	Have an assistant drive the vehicle while you monitor the Right Front Wheel Speed Sensor. Slowly accelerate as straight as possible from a stop to 24 Km/h (15 MPH). Did the Right Front Wheel Speed Sensor Signal show 0 Km/h (0 MPH) or lag behind the other sensors more than 5 Km/h (3 MPH)? Yes → Go To 3 No → At this time, the Wheel Speed Sensor is OK. The Wheel Speed Sensor may have been set by attempting to stop on very slick Road surfaces or Brakes locking up due to Lining contamination or overheating. If any of these conditions are present, repair as necessary. Test Complete. Perform ABS Verification Test VER-1A

CR4020002011010X

Fig. 148 Righthand Front Sensor Signal Failure (Part 1 of 3). 2000 Sebring Convertible

TEST	ACTION
9	If there are no potential causes remaining, replace the Right Front Wheel Speed Sensor. View repair options. Repair Replace the Right Front WSS. Perform ABS Verification Test VER-1A.

CR4020002011030X

Fig. 148 Righthand Front Sensor Signal Failure (Part 3 of 3). 2000 Sebring Convertible

When Monitored: 1. Ignition on. 2. The CAB monitors the wheel speed circuit continuity at all times.

Set Condition: If the CAB detects an open or shorted wheel speed sensor circuit, the Diagnostic Trouble Code (DTC) will set.

POSSIBLE CAUSES
WIRING AND CONNECTORS OBSERVABLE DEFECT
RIGHT REAR WHEEL SPEED SENSOR (+) CIRCUIT OPEN
RIGHT REAR WHEEL SPEED SENSOR (+) CIRCUIT SHORTED TO GROUND
RIGHT REAR WHEEL SPEED SENSOR (-) CIRCUIT OPEN
RIGHT REAR WHEEL SPEED SENSOR (-) CIRCUIT SHORTED TO GROUND
RIGHT REAR WHEEL SPEED SENSOR CONNECTOR OBSERVABLE DAMAGE
RIGHT REAR WHEEL SPEED SENSOR DAMAGED OR CONNECTOR DISCONNECTED
RIGHT REAR WHEEL SPEED SENSOR DEFECTIVE (SHORT TO GROUND CHECK)
RIGHT REAR WHEEL SPEED SENSOR DEFECTIVE (RESISTANCE CHECK)
CAB DEFECTIVE

TEST	ACTION
1	Ignition On, Engine Not Running With the DRB, read DTC's. With the DRB, erase DTC's. Turn the ignition off. Turn the ignition on. With the DRB, read DTC's. Did the DTC set again right now? Yes → Go To 2 No → Go To 11
2	Turn the ignition Off. Disconnect the Right Rear Wheel Speed Sensor Connector. **Note: Check connectors - Clean/repair as necessary.** Inspect all Terminals. Is any Terminal damaged, pushed out or miswired? Yes → Repair as necessary. Perform ABS Verification Test VER-1A. No → Go To 3

CR4020002012010X

Fig. 149 Righthand Rear Sensor Circuit failure (Part 1 of 3). 2000 Sebring Convertible

TEST	ACTION
3	Turn the ignition Off. Inspect the Right Rear Wheel Speed Sensor and Connector. Is the Sensor damaged or Connector disconnected? Yes → Repair as necessary. Perform ABS Verification Test VER-1A. No → Go To 4
4	Turn the ignition Off. Disconnect the Right Rear Wheel Speed Sensor Connector. **Note: Check connectors - Clean/repair as necessary.** Disconnect the CAB Connector. **Note: Check connectors - Clean/repair as necessary.** Connect a jumper wire between the Right Rear Wheel Speed Sensor (+) Circuit and ground. Using an Ohmmeter, measure the resistance between the Right Rear Wheel Speed Sensor (+) Circuit and ground, CAB Cavity 17 and 8. Is the resistance below 10 ohms? Yes → Go To 5 No → Repair the open Right Rear Wheel Speed Sensor (+) Circuit. Perform ABS Verification Test VER-1A.
5	Turn the ignition Off. Disconnect the Right Rear Wheel Speed Sensor Connector. **Note: Check connectors - Clean/repair as necessary.** Disconnect the CAB Connector. **Note: Check connectors - Clean/repair as necessary.** Using an Ohmmeter, measure the resistance between the Right Rear Wheel Speed Sensor (+) Circuit and ground. Is the resistance below 15,000 ohms? Yes → Repair the Right Rear Wheel Speed Sensor (+) Circuit shorted to Ground. Perform ABS Verification Test VER-1A. No → Go To 6
6	Turn the ignition Off. Disconnect the Right Rear Wheel Speed Sensor Connector. **Note: Check connectors - Clean/repair as necessary.** Disconnect the CAB Connector. **Note: Check connectors - Clean/repair as necessary.** Connect a jumper wire between the Right Rear Wheel Speed Sensor (-) and ground. Using an Ohmmeter, measure the resistance between the Right Rear Wheel Speed Sensor (-) Circuit and ground, CAB Cavity 1 and 8. Is the resistance below 10 ohms? Yes → Go To 7 No → Repair the open Right Rear Wheel Speed Sensor (-) Circuit. Perform ABS Verification Test VER-1A.

CR4020002012020X

Fig. 149 Righthand Rear Sensor Circuit failure (Part 2 of 3). 2000 Sebring Convertible

When Monitored: Ignition on. The CAB monitors the wheel speed signals at all times.

Set Condition: If the sensor signal is missing, as soon as vehicle speed exceeds 19 Km/h (12 mph) the Diagnostic Trouble Code (DTC) will set. If during an ABS stop, the CAB commands any valve solenoid on for an extended length of time, and does not see a corresponding wheel speed change, the DTC is set.

POSSIBLE CAUSES
CAB CONNECTOR OBSERVABLE DEFECT
RIGHT REAR WHEEL SPEED SENSOR CIRCUITS SHORTED TOGETHER
RIGHT REAR WHEEL SPEED SENSOR AIR GAP OUT OF SPECIFICATION
RIGHT REAR WHEEL SPEED SENSOR DEFECTIVE
RIGHT REAR WHEEL SPEED SENSOR OBSERVABLE DEFECT
RIGHT REAR TONE WHEEL DEFECTIVE
RIGHT REAR WHEEL BEARING CLEARANCE OUT OF SPECIFICATION

TEST	ACTION
1	Ignition On, Engine Not Running With DRB, read DTC's. Is the Right Rear Sensor Circuit failure DTC present right now? Yes → Refer to symptom RIGHT REAR SENSOR CIRCUIT FAILURE. No → Go To 2
2	Have an assistant drive the vehicle while you monitor the Right Rear Wheel Speed Sensor. Slowly accelerate as straight as possible from a stop to 24 Km/h (15 MPH). Did the Right Rear Wheel Speed Sensor Signal show 0 Km/h (0 MPH) or lag behind the other sensors more than 5 Km/h (3 MPH)? Yes → Go To 3 No → At this time, the Wheel Speed Sensor is OK. The TC may have been set by attempting to stop on very slick road surfaces or brakes locking up due to lining contamination or overheating. If any of these conditions are present, repair as necessary. Test Complete. Perform ABS Verification Test VER-1A.

CR4020002013010X

Fig. 150 Righthand Rear Sensor Signal Failure (Part 1 of 3). 2000 Sebring Convertible

TEST	ACTION
7	Turn the ignition Off. Disconnect the Right Rear Wheel Speed Sensor Connector. **Note: Check connectors - Clean/repair as necessary.** Disconnect the CAB Connector. **Note: Check connectors - Clean/repair as necessary.** Using an Ohmmeter, measure the resistance between the Right Rear Wheel Speed Sensor (-) Circuit and ground. Is the resistance below 15,000 ohms? Yes → Repair the Right Rear Wheel Speed Sensor (-) Circuit shorted to ground. Perform ABS Verification Test VER-1A. No → Go To 8
8	Turn the ignition Off. Disconnect the Right Rear Wheel Speed Sensor Connector. **Note: Check connectors - Clean/repair as necessary.** Using an Ohmmeter, measure the resistance between either one of the Right Rear Wheel Speed Sensor pins and ground. Is the resistance below 15,000 ohms? Yes → Replace the Right Rear Wheel Speed Sensor. Perform ABS Verification Test VER-1A. No → Go To 9
9	Turn the ignition Off. Disconnect the Right Rear Wheel Speed Sensor Connector. **Note: Check connectors - Clean/repair as necessary.** Using an Ohmmeter, measure the resistance of the Right Rear Wheel Speed Sensor. Is the resistance between 2,160 and 2,640 ohms? Yes → Go To 10 No → Replace the Right Rear Wheel Speed Sensor. Perform ABS Verification Test VER-1A.
10	If there are no potential causes remaining, replace the CAB. View repair options. Repair Replace the CAB. Perform ABS Verification Test VER-1A.
11	Turn the ignition Off. Using the schematic as a guide, inspect the Wiring and Connections. Were any problems found? Yes → Repair as necessary. Perform ABS Verification Test VER-1A. No → Test Complete.

CR4020002012030X

Fig. 149 Righthand Rear Sensor Circuit failure (Part 3 of 3). 2000 Sebring Convertible

TEST	ACTION
3	Turn the ignition Off. Inspect the Tone Wheel for damaged or missing teeth. **Note: The teeth should be perfectly square, not bent or nicked.** Is the Tone Wheel okay? Yes → Go To 4 No → Replace the Tone Wheel. Perform ABS Verification Test VER-1A.
4	Turn the ignition Off. Using a Feeler Gauge measure the Sensor Air Gap. **Note: The Air Gap should be checked at least in four places on the Tone Wheel.** Is the Air Gap within: 0.37 to 1.50mm (0.015'' to 0.059'')? Yes → Go To 5 No → Repair as necessary. Perform ABS Verification Test VER-1A.
5	Turn the ignition Off. Inspect the Wheel Bearings for excessive runout or clearance. Refer to appropriate service information if necessary for procedures or specifications. Is the Bearing clearance okay? Yes → Go To 6 No → Repair as necessary. Perform ABS Verification Test VER-1A.
6	Turn the ignition Off. Disconnect the CAB Connector. **Note: Check connectors - Clean/repair as necessary.** Inspect all Terminals. Is any Terminal damaged, pushed out or miswired? Yes → Repair as necessary. Perform ABS Verification Test VER-1A. No → Go To 7
7	Turn the ignition Off. Inspect the Right Rear Wheel Speed Sensor. Is the Right Rear Wheel Speed Sensor loose or damaged? Yes → Repair as necessary. Perform ABS Verification Test VER-1A. No → Go To 8
8	Turn the ignition Off. Disconnect the CAB Connector. **Note: Check connectors - Clean/repair as necessary.** Using an Ohmmeter, measure the resistance of the Right Rear Wheel Speed Sensor Circuit, CAB Cavities 1 and 17. Is the resistance below 200 ohms? Yes → Repair the Right Rear Wheel Speed Sensor Circuits shorted together. Perform ABS Verification Test VER-1A. No → Go To 9

CR4020002013020X

Fig. 150 Righthand Rear Sensor Signal Failure (Part 2 of 3). 2000 Sebring Convertible

TEST	ACTION
9	If there are no potential causes remaining, replace the Right Rear Wheel Speed Sensor. View repair options. Repair Replace the Right Rear WSS. Perform ABS Verification Test VER-1A.

CR4020002013030X

Fig. 150 Righthand Rear Sensor Signal Failure (Part 3 of 3). 2000 Sebring Convertible

TEST	ACTION
4	Turn the ignition Off. Disconnect the CAB Connector. **Note: Check connectors-Clean/repair as necessary.** Engine running. Raise the RPM's to above 1,800. Using a Voltmeter, measure the Fused Ignition Switch Output Circuit, CAB Cavity 23. Is the voltage above 16 volts? Yes → Refer to appropriate service instructions for Charging System testing and repair. Perform ABS Verification Test VER-1A. No → Go To 5
5	Using the DRB, erase the DTC's. Engine running. Did the DTC reset? Yes → Replace the CAB. Perform ABS Verification Test VER-1A. No → Test Complete.

CR4020002014020X

Fig. 151 System Overvoltage (Part 2 of 2). 2000 Sebring Convertible

When Monitored: 1. Ignition on. 2. The CAB monitors the voltage at the Fused Ignition Switch Output Circuit at all times above 10 km/h (6 mph) for proper system voltage.

Set Condition: If the voltage is below 9 volts on the Fused Ignition Switch Output Circuit at the CAB, the Diagnostic Trouble Code (DTC) is set.

POSSIBLE CAUSES
ABS SYSTEM VOLTAGE BELOW 13.0 VOLTS
FUSED IGNITION SWITCH OUTPUT CIRCUIT RESISTANCE HIGH
CAB DEFECTIVE

TEST	ACTION
1	Engine Running Raise RPM's above 1800. Using a Voltmeter, measure the battery voltage. Is the voltage below 13.0 volts? Yes → Refer to the appropriate service information for Charging System Testing and Repair. No → Go To 2
2	Engine Running With the DRB, select sensors, read the ignition voltage. Using a Voltmeter, measure the voltage at the battery. Does the DRB show "ignition voltage" within 1 volt of the battery volts? Yes → Test Complete. No → Repair the Fused Ignition Switch Output Circuit for high resistance. Perform ABS Verification Test VER-1A.

CR4020002015000X

Fig. 152 System Undervoltage. 2000 Sebring Convertible

When Monitored: 1. Ignition on. 2. The CAB monitors the Fused B+ Circuit at all times for proper system voltage.

Set Condition: If the voltage is above 19 volts at the CAB, the Diagnostic Trouble Code (DTC) is set.

POSSIBLE CAUSES
BATTERY CHARGER CONNECTED
CHARGING SYSTEM DEFECTIVE
CAB DEFECTIVE

TEST	ACTION
1	Is a battery charger connected to the vehicle? Yes → Charge Battery to proper level, disconnect the charger and clear diagnostic trouble codes. Perform ABS Verification Test VER-1A. No → Go To 2
2	Ignition On, Engine Not Running With the DRB, select sensors, read the ignition voltage. Does the DRB show above 16 volts? Yes → Go To 3 No → Test Complete.
3	Turn the ignition Off. Disconnect the CAB Connector. **Note: Check connectors-Clean/repair as necessary.** Inspect all Terminals. Is any Terminal damaged, pushed out or miswired? Yes → Repair as necessary. Perform ABS Verification Test VER-1A. No → Go To 4

CR4020002014010X

Fig. 151 System Overvoltage (Part 1 of 2). 2000 Sebring Convertible

POSSIBLE CAUSES
BRAKE SWITCH CONN OBSERVABLE DEFECT
BRAKE SWITCH DEFECTIVE
BRAKE SWITCH OUTPUT CIRCUIT OPEN
BRAKE SWITCH OUTPUT CIRCUIT SHORT TO VOLTAGE
CAB CONNECTOR OBSERVABLE DEFECT
CAB DEFECT

TEST	ACTION
1	Turn the ignition Off. Disconnect the Controller Antilock Brake Connector. **Note: Check connectors - Clean/repair as necessary.** Inspect all Terminals. Is any Terminal damaged, pushed out or miswired? Yes → Repair as necessary. Perform ABS Verification Test VER-1A. No → Go To 2
2	Turn the ignition Off. Disconnect the Controller Antilock Brake Connector. **Note: Check connectors - Clean/repair as necessary.** **Note: Make sure the Brake Pedal is released.** Turn ignition on. Using a Voltmeter, measure the Brake Lamp Switch Output Circuit, CAB Cavity 12. Is the voltage above 8 volts? Yes → Go To 3 No → Go To 6
3	Turn the ignition Off. Disconnect the Brake Lamp Switch Connector. **Note: Check connectors - Clean/repair as necessary.** Inspect all Terminals. Is any Terminal damaged, pushed out or miswired? Yes → Repair as necessary. Perform ABS Verification Test VER-1A. No → Go To 4

CR4020002016010X

Fig. 153 Brake Switch (Part 1 of 2). 2000 Sebring Convertible

TEST	ACTION
4	Turn the ignition Off. Disconnect the Brake Lamp Switch Connector. **Note: Check connectors - Clean/repair as necessary.** Disconnect the Controller Antilock Brake Connector. **Note: Check connectors - Clean/repair as necessary.** Ignition on, engine not running. Using a Voltmeter, measure the Brake Lamp Switch Output Circuit. Is the voltage above 8 volts? Yes → Repair the Brake Switch Output Circuit for a short to voltage. Perform ABS Verification Test VER-1A. No → Go To 5
5	If there are no potential causes remaining, replace the Brake Lamp Switch. View repair options. Repair Adjust or replace the Brake Switch. Perform ABS Verification Test VER-1A.
6	Turn the ignition Off. Disconnect the Controller Antilock Brake Connector. **Note: Check connectors - Clean/repair as necessary.** **Note: Make sure the Brake Pedal is released.** Turn ignition on. Using a Voltmeter, measure the Brake Lamp Switch Output Circuit. While still probing the Brake Lamp Switch Output Circuit depress the Brake Pedal. Is the voltage above 8 volts? Yes → Go To 7 No → Repair the open Brake Switch Output Circuit. Perform ABS Verification Test VER-1A.
7	If there are no potential causes remaining, replace the CAB. View repair options. Repair Replace the CAB. Perform ABS Verification Test VER-1A.

CR4020002016020X

Fig. 153 Brake Switch (Part 2 of 2). 2000 Sebring Convertible

TEST	ACTION
4	Turn the ignition Off. Disconnect the Controller Antilock Brake Connector. **Note: Check connectors - Clean/repair as necessary.** Connect a jumper wire between CCD Bus (+) and CCD Bus (-) Circuit, CAB Cavities 20 and 19. Ignition on, engine not running. With the DRB, perform the CCD Bus Test. Does the DRB display "Bus Shorted Together"? Yes → Replace the Controller Antilock Brake (CAB). Perform ABS Verification Test VER-1A. No → Go To 5
5	Turn the ignition Off. Disconnect the Controller Antilock Brake Connector. **Note: Check connectors - Clean/repair as necessary.** Connect a jumper from the CCD Bus (+) and the CAB Ground. Ignition on, engine not running. With the DRB, perform the CCD Bus Test. Does the DRB display "Bus Shorted To Ground"? Yes → Go To 6 No → Repair the open CCD Bus (+) Circuit. Perform ABS Verification Test VER-1A.
6	Turn the ignition Off. Disconnect the Controller Antilock Brake Connector. **Note: Check connectors - Clean/repair as necessary.** Connect a jumper from the CCD Bus (-) and the CAB Ground. Ignition on, engine not running. With the DRB, perform the CCD Bus Test. Does the DRB display "Bus Shorted To Ground"? Yes → Test complete No → Repair the open CCD Bus (-) Circuit. Perform ABS Verification Test VER-1A.
7	Turn the ignition Off. Inspect the PCM, ABS Fuse in the Power Distribution Center. Is the Fuse okay? Yes → Repair the open Fused Ignition Switch Output Circuit. Perform ABS Verification Test VER-1A. No → Go To 8
8	Turn the ignition Off. Disconnect the Controller Antilock Brake Connector. **Note: Check connectors - Clean/repair as necessary.** Using an Ohmmeter, measure between the Fused Ignition Switch Output Circuit CAB Cavity 23, and the Battery Ground. Is the resistance below 10 ohms? Yes → Repair the Fused Ignition Switch Output Circuit for a short to ground. Perform ABS Verification Test VER-1A. No → Go To 9

CR4020002017020X

Fig. 154 Scan Tool No Response Message (Part 2 of 3). 2000 Sebring Convertible

POSSIBLE CAUSES
PCM, ABS FUSE #10 DEFECTIVE
CAB GROUND CIRCUIT(S) OPEN
FUSED IGNITION SWITCH OUTPUT CIRCUIT OPEN
FUSED IGNITION SWITCH OUTPUT CIRCUIT SHORT TO GROUND
CCD BUS(+) CIRCUIT OPEN
CCD BUS(-) CIRCUIT OPEN
CAB CONNECTOR OBSERVABLE DEFECT
CAB DEFECTIVE

TEST	ACTION
1	Turn the ignition Off. Disconnect the Controller Antilock Brake Connector. **Note: Check connectors - Clean/repair as necessary.** Is any Terminal damaged, pushed out or miswired? Yes → Repair as necessary. Perform ABS Verification Test VER-1A. No → Go To 2
2	Turn the ignition Off. Disconnect the Controller Antilock Brake Connector. **Note: Check connectors - Clean/repair as necessary.** Using an Ohmmeter, measure the resistance between CAB Ground Circuits and Ground, CAB Cavities 8 and 24 and Battery Ground. Is the resistance below 1.0 ohms? Yes → Go To 3 No → Repair the open Ground Circuit(s). Perform ABS Verification Test VER-1A.
3	Turn the ignition Off. Disconnect the Controller Antilock Brake Connector. **Note: Check connectors - Clean/repair as necessary.** Ignition on, engine not running. Using a Voltmeter, measure the Fused Ignition Switch Output Circuit, CAB Cavity 23. Is the voltage above 10.0 volts? Yes → Go To 4 No → Go To 7

CR4020002017010X

Fig. 154 Scan Tool No Response Message (Part 1 of 3). 2000 Sebring Convertible

TEST	ACTION
9	If there are no potential causes remaining, replace the ABS Fuse. View repair options. Repair Replace faulty Fuse. Perform ABS Verification Test VER-1A.

CR4020002017030X

Fig. 154 Scan Tool No Response Message (Part 3 of 3). 2000 Sebring Convertible

POSSIBLE CAUSES
TRACTION CONTROL SWITCH OPERATING PROPERLY
CAB CONNECTOR OBSERVABLE DEF
TRACTION CONTROL SWITCH GROUND CIRCUIT OPEN
TRACTION CONTROL SWITCH DEFECTIVE
TRACTION CONTROL SWITCH SENSOR CIRCUIT OPEN
TRACTION CONTROL SWITCH SENSOR CIRCUIT SHORT TO GND
TRACTION CONTROL SWITCH SENSOR CIRCUIT SHORT TO B+
CAB DEFECTIVE

TEST	ACTION
1	Ignition On, Engine Not Running. Depress the Traction Control Switch on dash several times while watching the "Trac Off" Lamp in the Instrument Cluster. Does Lamp change from "Trac Off" to nothing? Yes → Traction Control Switch is operating properly at this time. Perform ABS Verification Test VER-1A. No → Go To 2
2	Ignition On, Engine Not Running. Depress the Traction Control Switch on dash several times while watching the "Trac Off" Lamp in the Instrument Cluster. Does the Instrument Cluster display "Trac Off" all the time? Yes → Repair Traction Control Switch Sensor Circuit short to ground. If OK, Refer to Traction Control Warning Lamp "TRAC OFF". Perform ABS Verification Test VER-1A. No → Go To 3
3	Turn the ignition Off. Disconnect the Traction Control Switch Connector. **Note: Check connectors - Clean/repair as necessary.** Using an Ohmmeter, measure the Traction Control Switch Sense Circuit and Ground Circuit. Depress the Traction Control Switch. Does the Ohmmeter read continuity (near 0 ohms) across switch when the switch is depressed? Yes → Go To 4 No → Replace the Traction Control Switch. Perform ABS Verification Test VER-1A.

CR4020002018010X

Fig. 155 Traction Control Switch (Part 1 of 3). 2000 Sebring Convertible

TEST	ACTION
4	Turn the ignition Off. Disconnect the Traction Control Switch Connector. **Note: Check connectors - Clean/repair as necessary.** Turn Ignition On. Using a Voltmeter, measure the Traction Control Switch Sense Circuit in the Vehicle Harness. Is the voltage above 9 volts. Yes → Go To 5 No → Go To 7
5	Turn the ignition Off. Disconnect the Traction Control Switch Connector. **Note: Check connectors - Clean/repair as necessary.** Ignition On, Engine Not Running. Using an Voltmeter, measure across the Traction Control Switch Sense Circuit and the Ground Circuit in the vehicle harness. Is the voltage above 9 volts? Yes → Go To 6 No → Repair the open Ground Circuit. Perform ABS Verification Test VER-1A.
6	If there are no potential causes remaining, replace the CAB. View repair options. Repair Replace the CAB. Perform ABS Verification Test VER-1A.
7	Turn the ignition Off. Disconnect the CAB Connector. **Note: Check connectors - Clean/repair as necessary.** Is any terminal damaged, pushed out or miswired? Yes → Repair as necessary. Perform ABS Verification Test VER-1A. No → Go To 8
8	Turn the ignition Off. Disconnect the CAB Connector. **Note: Check connectors - Clean/repair as necessary.** Disconnect the Traction Control Switch Connector. **Note: Check connectors - Clean/repair as necessary.** Ignition On. Using a Voltmeter, measure the Traction Control Switch Sense Circuit. Is the voltage above 1.0 volts? Yes → Repair the Traction Control Switch Sensor Circuit short to voltage. Perform ABS Verification Test VER-1A. No → Go To 9

CR4020002018020X

Fig. 155 Traction Control Switch (Part 2 of 3). 2000 Sebring Convertible

POSSIBLE CAUSES
CAB CONNECTOR TERMINALS OBSERVABLE DEFECTIVE
TRAC OFF LAMP BULB DEFECTIVE
TRACTION CONTROL WARNING LAMP DRIVER CIRCUIT OPEN
TRACTION CONTROL WARNING LAMP DRIVER CIRCUIT SHORTED TO GROUND
FUSED IGNITION SWITCH OUTPUT CIRCUIT OPEN
CAB DEFECTIVE

TEST	ACTION
1	Turn the ignition Off. **Note: If any Diagnostic Trouble Codes are present, they must be repaired prior to performing this test.** Turn Ignition On. Observe the Traction Control Warning Lamp "TRAC OFF" in the Information Center. Does the "TRAC OFF" Lamp stay on for several seconds then go out? Yes → "TRAC OFF" lamp is operating properly at this time. Perform ABS verification Test Ver-1A. No → Go To 2
2	Turn the ignition Off. Turn Ignition On. Observe the Traction Control Warning Lamp "TRAC OFF" in the instrument cluster. Is the "TRAC OFF" Lamp on steady? Yes → Go To 8 No → Go To 3
3	Ignition On, Engine Not Running. Set the Parking Brake. Is the Red Brake Warning Lamp on? Yes → Go To 4 No → Repair the open Fused Ignition Switch Output Circuit to the lamps. Perform ABS Verification Test Ver-1A.
4	Turn the ignition Off. Gain access to the "TRAC OFF" Lamp Bulb. Is the bulb okay? Yes → Go To 5 No → Replace the bulb. Perform ABS Verification Test VER-1A.

CR4020002019010X

Fig. 156 Traction Control Warning Lamp Illuminated (Part 1 of 2). 2000 Sebring Convertible

TEST	ACTION
9	Turn the ignition Off. Disconnect the CAB Connector. **Note: Check connectors - Clean/repair as necessary.** Disconnect the Traction Control Switch Connector. **Note: Check connectors - Clean/repair as necessary.** Using an Ohmmeter, measure the Traction Control Switch Sense Circuit for continuity between the Traction Control Switch and the CAB. Is the resistance below 5.0 ohms? Yes → Go To 10 No → Repair the open Traction Control Switch Sensor Circuit. Perform ABS Verification Test VER-1A.
10	If there are no potential causes remaining, replace the CAB. View repair options. Repair Replace the CAB. Perform ABS Verification Test VER-1A.

CR4020002018030X

Fig. 155 Traction Control Switch (Part 3 of 3). 2000 Sebring Convertible

TEST	ACTION
5	Turn the ignition Off. Disconnect the CAB. **Note: Check connectors - Clean/repair as necessary.** Inspect all Terminals. Is any Terminal damaged, pushed out or miswired? Yes → Repair as necessary. Perform ABS Verification Test VER-1A. No → Go To 6
6	Turn the ignition Off. Disconnect the CAB **Note: Check connector. Clean/repair as necessary.** Disconnect the Instrument cluster **Note: Check connector. Clean/repair as necessary.** Using an ohmmeter measure the resistance of the Traction Control Warning Lamp Driver Circuit. Is the resistance below 10 ohms? Yes → Repair the open Traction Control Warning Lamp Driver Circuit. Perform ABS Verification Test VER-1A. No → Go To 7
7	If there are no potential causes remaining, repalce the CAB. View repair options. Repair Replace the CAB. Perform ABS Verification Test VER-1A.
8	Turn the ignition Off. Disconnect the CAB Connector **Note: Check connector. Clean/repair as necessary.** Is any terminal damaged, pushed out, or miswired? Yes → Repair as necessary. No → Go To 10
9	Turn the ignition On. Is the "TRAC OFF" Lamp on? Yes → Repair the Traction Control Warning Lamp Driver Circuit for a short to ground. No → Go To 10
10	If there are no potential causes remaining, replace the CAB. View repair options. Repair Replace the CAB. Perform ABS Verification Test VER-1A.

CR4020002019020X

Fig. 156 Traction Control Warning Lamp Illuminated (Part 2 of 2). 2000 Sebring Convertible

ABS VERIFICATION TEST VER-1
Connect all previously disconnected components and connectors. With the DRBIII®, erase all DTCs. Turn the ignition on. With the DRBIII®, read diagnostic trouble codes. If any diagnostic trouble codes are present, return to Main Menu and troubleshoot new or recurring symptom. If there are no codes present upon key up, road test the vehicle for at least 5 minutes. Perform several antilock braking stops and traction control starts if equipped. **Caution: Ensure braking capability is available before road testing.** Again, with the DRBIII®, read diagnostic trouble codes. If any codes are present, return to Main Menu and troubleshoot new or recurring symptom. If there are no diagnostic trouble codes present and the customer's complaint can no longer be duplicated, the repair is complete. Return to Symptom List and troubleshoot new or recurring symptom.

CR4020002020000X

Fig. 157 ABS Verification Test. 2000 Sebring Convertible

When Monitored and Set Condition:

BUS SYSTEM COMMUNICATION FAILURE

When Monitored: Ignition ON, every 7 ms.

Set Condition: When the CAB does not receive a message from the instrument cluster for 10 seconds.

POSSIBLE CAUSES
CHECK COMMUNICATION TO MIC
INTERMITTENT DTC
CAB-- INTERNAL FAULT

TEST	ACTION
1	Turn the ignition on. With the DRBIII®, attempt to communicate with the MIC Was the DRB able to I/D or communicate with the MIC? Yes → Go To 2 No → Communication category and perform the symptom Bus +/- Signals Open from the Controller Anti-Lock Brake. Perform ABS VERIFICATION TEST - VER 1.
2	With the DRB, erase DTC's. Turn the ignition on and wait approximately 1 minute. With the DRB, read DTC's. Did this DTC reappear? Yes → Replace the Controller Anti-Lock Brake Perform ABS VERIFICATION TEST - VER 1. No → Go To 3
3	Turn the ignition off. Visually inspect the related wiring harness. Look for any chafed, pierced, pinched, or partially broken wires. Visually inspect the related wire harness connectors. Look for broken, bent, pushed out, or corroded terminals. Were any problems found? Yes → Repair as necessary. Perform ABS VERIFICATION TEST - VER 1. No → Test Complete.

CR4020102324000X

Fig. 159 BUS System Communications Failure. 2002 Sebring Convertible, Sebring Sedan & Stratus Sedan

When Monitored and Set Condition:

CAB INTERNAL FAILURE

When Monitored: Ignition on. The CAB monitors its internal microprocessors for correct operation.

Set Condition: If the CAB detects an internal fault, the DTC is set.

POSSIBLE CAUSES
CAB - INTERNAL CONCERN

TEST	ACTION
1	The only possible cause is a CAB internal concern. If there are no possible causes remaining, view repair. View repair. Replace the Controller Antilock Brake Perform ABS VERIFICATION TEST - VER 1.

CR4020102313000X

Fig. 160 CAB Internal Failure. 2001–02 Sebring Convertible, Sebring Sedan & Stratus Sedan

When Monitored and Set Condition:

BUS SYSTEM COMMUNICATION FAILURE

When Monitored: Ignition ON, every 7 ms.

Set Condition: When the CAB does not receive a message from the instrument cluster for 10 seconds.

POSSIBLE CAUSES
CHECK COMMUNICATION TO MIC
CAB-- INTERNAL FAULT

TEST	ACTION
1	Turn the ignition on. With the DRBIII®, attempt to communicate with the MIC Was the DRB able to I/D or communicate with the MIC? Yes → Go To 2 No → Communication category and perform the symptom Bus +/- Signals Open from the Controller Anti-Lock Brake. Perform ABS VERIFICATION TEST - VER 1.
2	With the DRB, erase DTC's. Turn the ignition on and wait approximately 1 minute. With the DRB, read DTC's. Did this DTC reappear? Yes → Replace the Controller Anti-Lock Brake Perform ABS VERIFICATION TEST - VER 1. No → Test Complete.

CR4020102312000X

Fig. 158 BUS System Communications Failure. 2001 Sebring Convertible, Sebring Sedan & Stratus Sedan

When Monitored and Set Condition:

CLUSTER LAMP FAILURE

When Monitored: Key ON. After Key-ON bulb check.

Set Condition: When the instrument cluster informs the CAB that the cluster cannot turn on the ABS Lamp.

POSSIBLE CAUSES
CLUSTER DTC PRESENT
CLUSTER INTERNAL FAULT
CAB -- NO ABS INDICATOR MESSAGE
CAB -- ABS INDICATOR FAULT

TEST	ACTION
1	Turn the ignition on. With the DRBIII®, read DTCs. Are there any Instrument Cluster DTCs present? Yes → Repair the INSTRUMENT CLUSTER Perform ABS VERIFICATION TEST - VER 1. No → Go To 2
2	Turn the ignition off. Observe the instrument cluster indicators. Turn the ignition on. Did the ABS Indicator illuminate for several seconds and then go out? Yes → Go To 3 No → Go To 4
3	**NOTE: The DRBIII® communication with the CAB must be operational for the result of this test to be valid.** Turn the ignition off. Remove Fuse 21 (ABS valve power) from the IPM. Perform the Key-on Bulb Check. Does the ABS Indicator remain on after the bulb check? Yes → Test Complete. No → Replace the Controller Antilock Brake Perform ABS VERIFICATION TEST - VER 1.

CR4020102314010X

Fig. 161 Cluster Lamp Failure (Part 1 of 2). 2001 Sebring Convertible, Sebring Sedan & Stratus Sedan

TEST	ACTION
4	**NOTE: The purpose of this test is to perform the Instrument Cluster self test.** Turn the ignition off. Depress and hold the Odometer Reset Button. Turn the Key from OFF to ON. Release the Odometer Reset Button. Do the Instrument Cluster Indicators and Gauges activate and deactivate? Yes → Replace the Controller Antilock Brake Perform ABS VERIFICATION TEST - VER 1. No → Replace the Instrument Cluster Perform ABS VERIFICATION TEST - VER 1.

CR4020102314020X

Fig. 161 Cluster Lamp Failure (Part 2 of 2). 2001 Sebring Convertible, Sebring Sedan & Stratus Sedan

When Monitored and Set Condition:

INCORRECT TONE WHEEL FAILURE

When Monitored: Key ON. Vehicle speed above 40 km/h (25mph) for 2 minutes.

Set Condition: When the CAB detects an unexpected wheel speed condition caused by a tire size that does not meet vehicle specification.

POSSIBLE CAUSES
CAB - SETTING FALSE CODE
TIRES NOT TO SPECIFICATION

TEST	ACTION
1	Inspect the tires. Do the tires meet vehicle specification? Yes → Replace the Controller Antilock Brake Perform ABS VERIFICATION TEST - VER 1. No → Replace the tires not meeting vehicle specification. Perform ABS VERIFICATION TEST - VER 1.

CR4020102315000X

Fig. 163 Incorrect Tone Wheel Failure. 2001–02 Sebring Convertible, Sebring Sedan & Stratus Sedan

When Monitored and Set Condition:

LEFT FRONT SENSOR CIRCUIT FAILURE

When Monitored: Ignition on. The CAB monitors the wheel speed circuit every 7 milliseconds (ms).

Set Condition: If the CAB detects an open or shorted wheel speed sensor circuit, the Diagnostic Trouble Code (DTC) will set.

LEFT REAR SENSOR CIRCUIT FAILURE

When Monitored: Ignition on. The CAB monitors the wheel speed circuit every 7 milliseconds (ms).

Set Condition: If the CAB detects an open or shorted wheel speed sensor circuit, the Diagnostic Trouble Code (DTC) will set.

RIGHT FRONT SENSOR CIRCUIT FAILURE

When Monitored: Ignition on. The CAB monitors the wheel speed circuit every 7 milliseconds (ms).

Set Condition: If the CAB detects an open or shorted wheel speed sensor circuit, the Diagnostic Trouble Code (DTC) will set.

RIGHT REAR SENSOR CIRCUIT FAILURE

When Monitored: Ignition on. The CAB monitors the wheel speed circuit every 7 milliseconds (ms).

Set Condition: If the CAB detects an open or shorted wheel speed sensor circuit, the Diagnostic Trouble Code (DTC) will set.

POSSIBLE CAUSES
SENSOR OR CONNECTOR DAMAGE
WHEEL SPEED SENSOR FAULT
SENSOR CIRCUITS SHORTED OR OPEN

CR4020102316010X

Fig. 164 Front & Rear Sensor Circuit Failure (Part 1 of 3). 2001–02 Sebring Convertible, Sebring Sedan & Stratus Sedan

When Monitored and Set Condition:

CLUSTER LAMP FAILURE

When Monitored: Key ON. After Key-ON bulb check.

Set Condition: When the instrument cluster informs the CAB that the cluster cannot turn on the ABS Lamp.

POSSIBLE CAUSES
CLUSTER DTC PRESENT
CLUSTER INTERNAL FAULT
CAB -- NO ABS INDICATOR MESSAGE

TEST	ACTION
1	Turn the ignition on. With the DRBIII®, read DTCs. Are there any Instrument Cluster DTCs present? Yes → Repair the INSTRUMENT CLUSTER Perform ABS VERIFICATION TEST - VER 1. No → Go To 2
2	Turn the ignition off. Observe the instrument cluster indicators. Turn the ignition on. Did the ABS Indicator illuminate for several seconds and then go out? Yes → Go To 3 No → Go To 3
3	**NOTE: The DRBIII® communication with the CAB must be operational for the result of this test to be valid.** Turn the ignition off. Remove Fuse 21 (ABS valve power) from the IPM. Perform the Key-on Bulb Check. Does the ABS Indicator remain on after the bulb check? Yes → Replace the Instrument Cluster in accordance with the Service Information. Perform ABS VERIFICATION TEST - VER 1. No → Replace the Controller Antilock Brake in accordance with the Service Information. Perform ABS VERIFICATION TEST - VER 1.

CR4020102325000X

Fig. 162 Cluster Lamp Failure. 2002 Sebring Convertible, Sebring Sedan & Stratus Sedan

POSSIBLE CAUSES
CAB - INTERNAL FAULT
INTERMITTENT CIRCUIT DTC

TEST	ACTION
1	Turn the ignition on. With the DRBIII®, record and erase DTC's. Turn the ignition off. Turn the ignition on. With the DRBIII®, read DTC's. Does the DRBIII® display a Wheel Speed Sensor Circuit Failure DTC? Yes → Go To 2 No → Go To 5
2	Turn the ignition off. Inspect the affected Wheel Speed Sensor and Connector. Is the Sensor or Connector Damaged? Yes → Repair as necessary. Perform ABS VERIFICATION TEST - VER 1. No → Go To 3
3	Turn the ignition off. Disconnect the affected Wheel Speed Sensor connector. **Note: Check connector - Clean/repair as necessary.** Turn the ignition on. Using a 12-volt test light connected to ground, check the Sensor 12 volt Supply circuit. Measure the resistance between ground and the Sensor Signal circuit. Was the test light bright and the resistance between 100 and 300 ohms? Yes → Replace the Wheel Speed Sensor Perform ABS VERIFICATION TEST - VER 1. No → Go To 4
4	Turn the ignition off. Disconnect the affected Wheel Speed Sensor connector. **Note: Check connector - Clean/repair as necessary. .** Disconnect the CAB connector. **Note: Check connector - Clean/repair as necessary.** Turn the ignition on. Check the Wheel Speed Sensor 12 volt Supply and Signal circuits for a short to battery, ground, to each other and for an open. For the purposes of this test, a short to ground must be below 15k ohms. Was any circuit short or open found? Yes → Repair the Wheel Speed Sensor circuit short or open. Perform ABS VERIFICATION TEST - VER 1. No → Replace the Controller Antilock Brake Perform ABS VERIFICATION TEST - VER 1.

CR4020102316020X

Fig. 164 Front & Rear Sensor Circuit Failure (Part 2 of 3). 2001–02 Sebring Convertible, Sebring Sedan & Stratus Sedan

TEST	ACTION
5	Turn the ignition off. Visually inspect the related wiring harness. Look for any chafed, pierced, pinched, or partially broken wires. Visually inspect the related wire harness connectors. Look for broken, bent, pushed out, or corroded terminals. Were any problems found? Yes → Repair as necessary. Perform ABS VERIFICATION TEST - VER 1. No → Test Complete.

CR4020102316030X

Fig. 164 Front & Rear Sensor Circuit Failure (Part 3 of 3). 2001–02 Sebring Convertible, Sebring Sedan & Stratus Sedan

RIGHT REAR WHEEL SPEED SIGNAL FAILURE

When Monitored: Wheel speed comparison is checked at drive off or every 7 milliseconds (ms). Wheel speed circuit continuity is checked every 7 milliseconds. Wheel speed phase length supervision is checked every 7 milliseconds.

Set Condition: If, during an ABS stop, the CAB commands any valve solenoid on for an extended length of time, and does not see a corresponding wheel speed change, the Diagnostic Trouble Code (DTC) is set. The DTC can also set if the signal is missing or erratic.

POSSIBLE CAUSES
SENSOR OR TONE WHEEL CONCERN
SENSOR OUTPUT INTERMITTENT OR OPEN
WHEEL SPEED SENSOR INOPERATIVE
INTERMITTENT SIGNAL DTC

TEST	ACTION
1	With the DRBIII®, erase DTCs. Turn the ignition off. Start the engine. With an assistant, drive the vehicle as straight as possible and maintain a steady speed above 24 km/h (15 mph). With the DRBIII®, monitor all wheel speed sensors. Note whether the speed of the affected wheel is zero. Note whether the speed of the affected wheel differs from others by 5 km/h (3 mph) or more. Is the affected wheel speed zero or differing from others? Yes → Go To 2 No → Go To 3
2	Inspect the Wheel Speed Sensor, Connector and Tone Wheel at the affected wheel. **NOTE: Inspect components for damage and correct installation.** Are there any visible Sensor, Connector or Tone Wheel concerns? Yes → Correct the sensor, connector or tone wheel concern as necessary. The vehicle must be driven at 25 km/h (15 mph) to extinguish the ABS indicator. Perform ABS VERIFICATION TEST - VER 1. No → Replace the Wheel Speed Sensor The vehicle must be driven at 25 km/h (15 mph) to extinguish the ABS indicator. Perform ABS VERIFICATION TEST - VER 1.

CR4020102317020X

Fig. 165 Front & Rear Wheel Speed Signal Failure (Part 2 of 3). 2001–02 Sebring Convertible, Sebring Sedan & Stratus Sedan

TEST	ACTION
3	With the DRBIII®, read DTCs. Did the DTC reoccur? Yes → Replace the Wheel Speed Sensor in accordance with the Service Information. The vehicle must be driven at 25 km/h (15 mph) to extinguish the ABS indicator. Perform ABS VERIFICATION TEST - VER 1. No → Go To 4
4	Turn the ignition off. Visually inspect wheel speed sensor. Visually inspect tone wheel. Visually inspect wiring harness. Visually inspect brakes for locking up due to lining contamination or overheating. Inspect all Components for defects which may cause a Signal DTC to set. Is any Component Damaged? Yes → Repair as necessary. The vehicle must be driven at 25 km/h (15 mph) to extinguish the ABS indicator. Perform ABS VERIFICATION TEST - VER 1. No → Test Complete.

CR4020102317030X

Fig. 165 Front & Rear Wheel Speed Signal Failure (Part 3 of 3). 2001–02 Sebring Convertible, Sebring Sedan & Stratus Sedan

When Monitored and Set Condition:

LEFT FRONT WHEEL SPEED SIGNAL FAILURE

When Monitored: Wheel speed comparison is checked at drive off or every 7 milliseconds (ms). Sensor signal continuity is checked every 7 milliseconds. Wheel speed phase length supervision is checked every 7 milliseconds.

Set Condition: If, during an ABS stop, the CAB commands any valve solenoid on for an extended length of time, and does not see a corresponding wheel speed change, the Diagnostic Trouble Code (DTC) is set. The DTC can also set if the signal is missing or erratic.

LEFT REAR WHEEL SPEED SIGNAL FAILURE

When Monitored: Wheel speed comparison is checked at drive off or every 7 milliseconds (ms). Wheel speed circuit continuity is checked every 7 milliseconds. Wheel speed phase length supervision is checked every 7 milliseconds.

Set Condition: If, during an ABS stop, the CAB commands any valve solenoid on for an extended length of time, and does not see a corresponding wheel speed change, the Diagnostic Trouble Code (DTC) is set. The DTC can also set if the signal is missing or erratic.

RIGHT FRONT WHEEL SPEED SIGNAL FAILURE

When Monitored: Wheel speed comparison is checked at drive off or every 7 milliseconds (ms). Wheel speed continuity is checked every 7 milliseconds. Wheel speed phase length supervision is checked every 7 milliseconds.

Set Condition: If, during an ABS stop, the CAB commands any valve solenoid on for an extended length of time, and does not see a corresponding wheel speed change, the Diagnostic Trouble Code (DTC) is set. The DTC can also set if the signal is missing or erratic.

CR4020102317010X

Fig. 165 Front & Rear Wheel Speed Signal Failure (Part 1 of 3). 2001–02 Sebring Convertible, Sebring Sedan & Stratus Sedan

When Monitored and Set Condition:

PUMP CIRCUIT FAILURE

When Monitored: Ignition on. The CAB commands the pump on at 20 km/h (12 mph) to check its operation, if the brake switch is not applied. If the brake is applied, the test will run at 40 km/h (25 mph). The CAB monitors pump voltage every 7 milliseconds.

Set Condition: The DTC is stored when the CAB detects: 1) Improper voltage decay after the pump was turned off. 2) Pump not energized by the CAB, but voltage is present for 3.5 seconds. 3) Pump is turned on by the CAB, but without sufficient voltage to operate it.

POSSIBLE CAUSES
CAB - PUMP MOTOR RUNNING CONTINUOUSLY
PUMP HARNESS DISCONNECTED
ABS PUMP MOTOR INTERMITTENT DTC
GROUND CIRCUIT HIGH RESISTANCE
FUSED B(+) CIRCUIT OPEN
GROUND CIRCUIT OPEN
CAB - INTERNAL FAULT
CAB - SETTING FALSE CODE

TEST	ACTION
1	Turn the ignition off. Turn the ignition on. Monitor the pump motor for continuous operation. Is the pump motor running continuously? Yes → Replace the Controller Anti-Lock Brake The vehicle must be driven at 25 km/h (15 mph) to extinguish the ABS indicator. Perform ABS VERIFICATION TEST - VER 1. No → Go To 2
2	Turn the ignition on. With the DRBIII®, read DTC's. With the DRBIII®, erase DTC's. Turn the ignition off. Turn the ignition on. With the DRBIII®, actuate the ABS pump motor. Did the Pump Motor operate when actuated? Yes → Go To 3 No → Go To 4

CR4020102318010X

Fig. 166 Pump Circuit Failure (Part 1 of 3). 2001–02 Sebring Convertible, Sebring Sedan & Stratus Sedan

TEST	ACTION
3	Turn the ignition off. Visually inspect the related wiring harness. Look for any chafed, pierced, pinched, or partially broken wires. Visually inspect the related wire harness connectors. Look for broken, bent, pushed out, or corroded terminals. Were any problems found? Yes → Repair as necessary. The vehicle must be driven at 25 km/h (15 mph) to extinguish the ABS indicator. Perform ABS VERIFICATION TEST - VER 1. No → Replace the Controller Anti-Lock Brake The vehicle must be driven at 25 km/h (15 mph) to extinguish the ABS indicator. Perform ABS VERIFICATION TEST - VER 1.
4	Check the short Wiring Harness between the ABS Pump and the CAB. Check for disconnect and damage. Is the harness disconnected or damaged? Yes → Reconnect or repair the Pump Harness as necessary. Perform ABS VERIFICATION TEST - VER 1. No → Go To 5
5	Turn the ignition on. With the DRBIII®, enable pump motor actuation. **NOTE: Pump motor will not operate, but voltage will be applied.** Measure the voltage drop across the ABS ground circuit connection, with pump motor actuation enabled. Is the voltage below 0.1 volt? Yes → Go To 6 No → Repair the Ground circuit for high resistance. The vehicle must be driven at 25 km/h (15 mph) to extinguish the ABS indicator. Perform ABS VERIFICATION TEST - VER 1.
6	Turn the ignition off. Disconnect the CAB connector. **Note: Check connector - Clean/repair as necessary.** Turn the ignition on. Using a 12-volt test light connected to ground, check the Pump Motor Fused B+ circuit. Does the test light illuminate brightly? Yes → Go To 7 No → Repair the Fused B(+) circuit for an open. The vehicle must be driven at 25 km/h (15 mph) to extinguish the ABS indicator. Perform ABS VERIFICATION TEST - VER 1.

CR4020102318020X

Fig. 166 Pump Circuit Failure (Part 2 of 3). 2001–02 Sebring Convertible, Sebring Sedan & Stratus Sedan

When Monitored and Set Condition:

SYSTEM OVERVOLTAGE

When Monitored: Ignition on. The CAB monitors the Fused B(+) circuit at all times for proper system voltage.

Set Condition: If the voltage is above 16.5 volts for greater than 420 milliseconds (ms), the Diagnostic Trouble Code (DTC) is set.

POSSIBLE CAUSES
BATTERY OVERCHARGED
FUSED IGNITION SWITCH OUTPUT HIGH
GROUND CIRCUIT OPEN
CAB - INTERNAL FAULT
INTERMITTENT DTC

TEST	ACTION
1	Turn the ignition on. With the DRBIII®, erase DTC's. Turn the ignition off. Turn the ignition on. Start the engine. With the DRBIII®, read DTC's. Does the DRBIII® display System Overvoltage DTC? Yes → Go To 2 No → Go To 6
2	Turn the ignition off. Inspect for battery charger connected to battery. Is a battery charger connected to the battery? Yes → Charge battery to proper level. Disconnect the battery charger. Clear DTC's. Perform ABS VERIFICATION TEST - VER 1. No → Go To 3

CR4020102319010X

Fig. 167 System Overvoltage (Part 1 of 2). 2001–02 Sebring Convertible, Sebring Sedan & Stratus Sedan

TEST	ACTION
7	Turn the ignition off. Disconnect CAB Connector. **Note: Check connector - Clean/repair as necessary.** Measure the resistance of the CAB ground circuits. Is the resistance below 1.0 ohm? Yes → Go To 8 No → Repair the ground circuit for an open. The vehicle must be driven at 25 km/h (15 mph) to extinguish the ABS indicator. Perform ABS VERIFICATION TEST - VER 1.
8	If there are no possible causes remaining, view repair. Repair Replace the Controller Anti-Lock Brake The vehicle must be driven at 25 km/h (15 mph) to extinguish the ABS indicator. Perform ABS VERIFICATION TEST - VER 1.

CR4020102318030X

Fig. 166 Pump Circuit Failure (Part 3 of 3). 2001–02 Sebring Convertible, Sebring Sedan & Stratus Sedan

TEST	ACTION
3	Turn the ignition off. Disconnect the CAB connector. **Note: Check connector - Clean/repair as necessary.** Start the engine. Raise engine speed above 1,800 RPM. Measure the battery voltage. Is the voltage above 16.5 volts ? Yes → Repair charging system Perform ABS VERIFICATION TEST - VER 1. No → Go To 4
4	Turn the ignition off. Disconnect the CAB connector. **Note: Check connector - Clean/repair as necessary.** Measure the resistance of the ground circuits. Is the resistance below 1.0 ohm? Yes → Go To 5 No → Repair the Ground circuit for an open. Perform ABS VERIFICATION TEST - VER 1.
5	If there are no potential causes remaining, view repair. Repair Replace the Controller Antilock Brake. Perform ABS VERIFICATION TEST - VER 1.
6	Turn the ignition off. Visually inspect the related wiring harness. Look for any chafed, pierced, pinched, or partially broken wires. Visually inspect the related wire harness connectors. Look for broken, bent, pushed out, or corroded terminals. Were any problems found? Yes → Repair as necessary. Perform ABS VERIFICATION TEST - VER 1. No → Test Complete.

CR4020102319020X

Fig. 167 System Overvoltage (Part 2 of 2). 2001–02 Sebring Convertible, Sebring Sedan & Stratus Sedan

When Monitored and Set Condition:

SYSTEM UNDERVOLTAGE

When Monitored: Ignition on. The CAB monitors the Fused Ignition Switch Output circuit voltage above 10 km/h (6 mph) every 7 milliseconds for proper system voltage.

Set Condition: If the voltage is below 9.5 volts, the Diagnostic Trouble Code (DTC) is set.

POSSIBLE CAUSES
BATTERY VOLTAGE LOW
INTERMITTENT DTC
FUSED IGNITION SWITCH OUTPUT CIRCUIT HIGH RESISTANCE
CAB - INTERNAL FAULT

TEST	ACTION
1	Turn the ignition on. With the DRBIII®, erase DTC's. Turn the ignition off. Turn the ignition on. Start the engine. Drive the vehicle above 16 km/h (10 mph) for at least 20 seconds. Stop the vehicle With the DRBIII®, read DTC's. Does the DRBIII® display System Undervoltage DTC? Yes → Go To 2 No → Go To 5
2	Engine Running. Measure the battery voltage. Is the battery voltage below 10 volts? Yes → Repair charging system Perform ABS VERIFICATION TEST - VER 1. No → Go To 3
3	Disconnect the CAB harness connector. Turn the ignition on. Measure the voltage of the Fused Ignition Switch circuit. Is the voltage above 10 volts? Yes → Go To 4 No → Repair the Fused Ignition Switch Output Circuit for high resistance Perform ABS VERIFICATION TEST - VER 1.

CR4020102320010X

Fig. 168 System Undervoltage (Part 1 of 2). 2001–02 Sebring Convertible, Sebring Sedan & Stratus Sedan

TEST	ACTION
4	If there are no potential causes remaining, view repair. Repair Replace the Controller Antilock Brake. Perform ABS VERIFICATION TEST - VER 1.
5	Turn the ignition off. Visually inspect the related wiring harness. Look for any chafed, pierced, pinched, or partially broken wires. Visually inspect the related wire harness connectors. Look for broken, bent, pushed out, or corroded terminals. Were any problems found? Yes → Repair as necessary. Perform ABS VERIFICATION TEST - VER 1. No → Test Complete.

CR4020102320020X

Fig. 168 System Undervoltage (Part 2 of 2). 2001–02 Sebring Convertible, Sebring Sedan & Stratus Sedan

When Monitored and Set Condition:

VALVE POWER FEED FAILURE

When Monitored: Ignition ON for at least 3.5 seconds. ABS Power Relay closed. Valve command for a particular solenoid not present.

Set Condition: Low feedback voltage from the low side of all the solenoids for over 20 consecutive controller checks spaced 5 ms apart.

POSSIBLE CAUSES
INTERMITTENT DTC
BLOWN FUSE - FUSED B(+) CIRCUIT
NO B+ SUPPLY TO FUSE
FUSED B(+) CIRCUIT OPEN
B(+) CIRCUIT SHORTED TO GROUND
CAB - FUSED B(+) CIRCUIT OPEN
CAB - FUSED B(+) CIRCUIT SHORTED TO GROUND

TEST	ACTION
1	Turn the ignition on. With the DRBIII®, erase DTC's. Turn the ignition off. Turn the ignition on. Drive the vehicle above 25 km/h (15 mph) for at least 10 seconds. Stop the vehicle. With the DRBIII®, read DTC's. Does the DRBIII® display Valve Power Feed Circuit DTC present right now? Yes → Go To 2 No → Go To 9
2	Turn the ignition off. Remove and Inspect the ABS Fuse 22 in the PDC. Is the Fuse blown? Yes → Go To 3 No → Go To 6

CR4020102321010X

Fig. 169 Valve Power Feed Failure (Part 1 of 3). 2001–02 Sebring Convertible, Sebring Sedan & Stratus Sedan

TEST	ACTION
3	Turn the ignition off. Remove the ABS Fuse 22 from the PDC. Disconnect the CAB harness connector. **Note: Check connector - Clean/repair as necessary.** Using a test light connected to 12 volts, probe the Fused B(+) Circuit. Does the test light illuminate brightly? Yes → Repair the Fused B(+) Circuit short to ground. Perform ABS VERIFICATION TEST - VER 1. No → Go To 4
4	Turn the ignition off. Remove the ABS Fuse 22 from the PDC. The CAB must be connected for the results of this test to be valid. Using a test light connected to 12 volts, probe the Fused B(+) Circuit at the PDC fuse terminal. Does the test light illuminate brightly? Yes → Replace the Controller Antilock Brake Perform ABS VERIFICATION TEST - VER 1. No → Go To 5
5	Turn the ignition off. If there are no potential causes remaining, view repair. Repair Replace the Fuse. Perform ABS VERIFICATION TEST - VER 1.
6	Remove the ABS Fuse 22 from the PDC. Turn the ignition on. Measure the voltage of the Fused B+ supply to Fuse 22 in the PDC. Is the voltage above 10 volts? Yes → Go To 7 No → Repair the B+ Supply circuit for an open. Perform ABS VERIFICATION TEST - VER 1.
7	Turn the ignition off. Remove the ABS Fuse 22 from the PDC. Disconnect the CAB harness connector. **Note: Check connector - Clean/repair as necessary.** Measure the resistance of the Fused B(+) circuit between PDC Fuse terminal 22 and the CAB connector. Is the resistance below 5 ohms? Yes → Go To 8 No → Repair the Fuse B+ circuit for an open. Perform ABS VERIFICATION TEST - VER 1.
8	If there are no possible causes remaining, view repair. Repair Replace the Controller Antilock Brake in accordance with the Service Information. Perform ABS VERIFICATION TEST - VER 1.

CR4020102321020X

Fig. 169 Valve Power Feed Failure (Part 2 of 3). 2001–02 Sebring Convertible, Sebring Sedan & Stratus Sedan

TEST	ACTION
9	Turn the ignition off. Visually inspect the related wiring harness. Look for any chafed, pierced, pinched, or partially broken wires. Visually inspect the related wire harness connectors. Look for broken, bent, pushed out, or corroded terminals. Were any problems found? Yes → Repair as necessary. Perform ABS VERIFICATION TEST - VER 1. No → Test Complete.

CR4020102321030X

Fig. 169 Valve Power Feed Failure (Part 3 of 3). 2001–02 Sebring Convertible, Sebring Sedan & Stratus Sedan

POSSIBLE CAUSES
CHECK BRAKE LAMP SWITCH OUTPUT
BRAKE LAMP SWITCH B+ OPEN
BRAKE LAMP SWITCH OUTPUT CIRCUIT SHORT OR OPEN
BRAKE LAMP SWITCH OPEN
CAB -- INTERNAL OPEN

TEST	ACTION
1	With the DRBIII® in Inputs/Outputs, read the Brake Lamp Switch state. Press and release the brake pedal. Does the DRBIII® display PRESSED and RELEASED? Yes → The Brake Lamp Switch is OK. Perform ABS VERIFICATION TEST - VER 1. No → Go To 2
2	Disconnect the Brake Lamp Switch harness connector. Using a 12-volt test light connected to ground, check the Brake Lamp Switch Fused B+ circuit. Does the test light illuminate brightly ? Yes → Go To 3 No → Repair the Brake Lamp Switch Fused B+ circuit for an open. Perform ABS VERIFICATION TEST - VER 1.
3	Disconnect the Brake Lamp Switch harness connector. Connect a jumper wire between the Brake Lamp Switch B+ and Output circuits. With the DRBIII® in Inputs/Outputs, read the Brake Lamp Switch state. Does the DRBIII® display PRESSED? Yes → Replace the Brake Lamp Switch Perform ABS VERIFICATION TEST - VER 1. No → Go To 4
4	Disconnect the CAB harness connector. Disconnect the Brake Lamp Switch harness connector. Check the Brake Lamp Switch Output circuit for a short to voltage and for an open. Is the Brake Lamp Switch Output circuit shorted or open? Yes → Repair the Brake Lamp Switch Output circuit for a short to voltage or an open. Perform ABS VERIFICATION TEST - VER 1. No → Replace the Controller Anti-Lock Brake Perform ABS VERIFICATION TEST - VER 1.

CR4020102322000X

Fig. 170 Brake Lamp Failure. 2001 Sebring Convertible, Sebring Sedan & Stratus Sedan

TEST	ACTION
5	Disconnect the CAB harness connector. Disconnect the Brake Lamp Switch harness connector. Check the Brake Lamp Switch Output circuit for a short to voltage, short to ground and for an open. Is the Brake Lamp Switch Output circuit shorted or open? Yes → Repair the Brake Lamp Switch Output circuit for a short to voltage or an open. Perform ABS VERIFICATION TEST - VER 1. No → Replace the Controller Anti-Lock Brake Perform ABS VERIFICATION TEST - VER 1.

CR4020102326020X

Fig. 171 Brake Lamp Failure (Part 2 of 2). 2002 Sebring Convertible, Sebring Sedan & Stratus Sedan

ABS VERIFICATION TEST - VER 1
1. Turn the ignition off. 2. Connect all previously disconnected components and connectors. 3. Ensure all accessories are turned off and the battery is fully charged. 4. Ensure that the Ignition is on, and with the DRBIII, erase all Diagnostic Trouble Codes from ALL modules. Start the engine and allow it to run for 2 minutes and fully operate the system that was malfunctioning. 5. Turn the ignition off and wait 5 seconds. Turn the ignition on and using the DRBIII, read DTC's from ALL modules. 6. If any Diagnostic Trouble Codes are present, return to Symptom list and troubleshoot new or recurring symptom. 7. If there are no DTC's present after turning ignition on, road test the vehicle for at least 5 minutes. Perform several antilock braking stops. **8. Caution: Ensure braking capability is available before road testing.** 9. Again, with the DRBIII® read DTC's. If any DTC's are present, return to Symptom list. 10. If there are no Diagnostic Trouble Codes (DTC's) present, and the customer's concern can no longer be duplicated, the repair is complete. Are any DTC's present or is the original concern still present? Yes → Repair is not complete, refer to appropriate symptom. No → Repair is complete.

CR4020102323000X

Fig. 172 Verification Test VER 1. 2001–02 Sebring Convertible, Sebring Sedan & Stratus Sedan

POSSIBLE CAUSES
CHECK BRAKE LAMP SWITCH OUTPUT
BRAKE LAMP SWITCH B+ OPEN
BRAKE LAMP SWITCH OUTPUT CIRCUIT SHORT OR OPEN
BRAKE LAMP SWITCH OUTPUT CIRCUIT SHORT TO GROUND OR BATTERY
BRAKE LAMP SWITCH OPEN
CAB -- INTERNAL OPEN

TEST	ACTION
1	With the DRBIII® in Inputs/Outputs, read the Brake Lamp Switch state. Press and release the brake pedal. Does the DRBIII® display CLOSED and OPEN? Yes → The Brake Lamp Switch is OK. Perform ABS VERIFICATION TEST - VER 1. No → Go To 2
2	Disconnect the Brake Lamp Switch harness connector. Disconnect the CAB harness connector. Using a 12-volt test light connected to ground, check the Brake Lamp Switch Output circuit. Using a 12-volt test light connected to battery, check the Brake Lamp Switch Output circuit. Does the test light illuminate brightly for either check? Yes → Repair the Brake Lamp Switch Output circuit for a short to battery or ground. Perform ABS VERIFICATION TEST - VER 1. No → Go To 3
3	Disconnect the Brake Lamp Switch harness connector. Using a 12-volt test light connected to ground, check the Brake Lamp Switch Fused B+ circuit. Does the test light illuminate brightly ? Yes → Go To 4 No → Repair the Brake Lamp Switch Fused B+ circuit for an open. Perform ABS VERIFICATION TEST - VER 1.
4	Disconnect the Brake Lamp Switch harness connector. Connect a jumper wire between the Brake Lamp Switch B+ and Output circuits. With the DRBIII® in Inputs/Outputs, read the Brake Lamp Switch state. Does the DRBIII® display CLOSED? Yes → Replace the Brake Lamp Switch Perform ABS VERIFICATION TEST - VER 1. No → Go To 5

CR4020102326010X

Fig. 171 Brake Lamp Failure (Part 1 of 2). 2002 Sebring Convertible, Sebring Sedan & Stratus Sedan

When Monitored and Set Condition:

BUS SYSTEM COMMUNICATION FAILURE

When Monitored: Ignition ON, continuously.

Set Condition: When the CAB does not receive a message from the instrument cluster for 10 seconds.

POSSIBLE CAUSES
INTERMITTENT CONDITION
ELECTRO-MECHANICAL INSTRUMENT CLUSTER DTC PRESENT
BUS CIRCUIT OPEN
CAB - INTERNAL FAILURE

TEST	ACTION
1	Turn the ignition on. With the DRBIII®, read DTCs. With the DRBIII®, read Freeze Frame information. With the DRBIII®, erase DTCs. Turn the ignition off. Turn the ignition on. With the DRBIII®, read DTCs. Does the DRBIII® display BUS SYSTEM COMMUNICATION FAILURE? Yes → Go To 2 No → Go To 4
2	Turn the ignition on. With the DRBIII®, read EMIC DTCs. Does the DRBIII® display ABS MESSAGES NOT RECEIVED? Yes → Refer to symptom ABS MESSAGES NOT RECEIVED Perform ABS VERIFICATION TEST No → Go To 3

ARM66CR000000033

Fig. 173 BUS System Communication Failure (Part 1 of 2). 2003–04 Sebring Convertible, Sebring Sedan & Stratus Sedan

TEST	ACTION
3	Turn the ignition off. Disconnect the negative (-) battery cable. Disconnect the CAB harness connector. **NOTE: check connector - Clean/repair as necessary.** Measure the resistance of the Bus circuit between the CAB connector and the Data Link Connector (DLC). Is the resistance below 5.0 ohms? Yes → Replace the Controller Antilock Brake Perform ABS VERIFICATION TEST No → Repair the Bus circuit for an open. Perform ABS VERIFICATION TEST
4	Turn the ignition off. Visually inspect the related wiring harness. Look for any chafed, pierced, pinched, or partially broken wires. Visually inspect the related wire harness connectors. Look for broken, bent, pushed out, or corroded terminals. Were any problems found? Yes → Repair as necessary. Perform ABS VERIFICATION TEST No → Test Complete.

ARM66CR000000034

Fig. 173 BUS System Communication Failure (Part 2 of 2). 2003–04 Sebring Convertible, Sebring Sedan & Stratus Sedan

TEST	ACTION
4	Turn the ignition off. Using a 12-volt test light connected to ground, probe the ABS Valve Fused B(+) circuit at the CAB harness connector. Did the test light illuminate? Yes → Go To 5 No → Repair the ABS Valve Fused B(+) circuit for an open. Perform ABS VERIFICATION TEST
5	Turn the ignition off. Using a 12-volt test light connected to ground, probe the ABS Pump Fused B(+) circuit at the CAB harness connector. Did the test light illuminate? Yes → Replace the Controller Antilock Brake Perform ABS VERIFICATION TEST No → Repair the ABS Pump Fused B(+) circuit for an open. Perform ABS VERIFICATION TEST
6	Turn the ignition off. Visually inspect the related wiring harness. Look for any chafed, pierced, pinched, or partially broken wires. Visually inspect the related wire harness connectors. Look for broken, bent, pushed out, or corroded terminals. Refer to any Technical Service Bulletins that may apply. Were any problems found? Yes → Repair as necessary. Perform ABS VERIFICATION TEST No → Test Complete.

ARM66CR000000036

Fig. 174 CAB Internal Failure (Part 2 of 2). 2003–04 Sebring Convertible, Sebring Sedan & Stratus Sedan

When Monitored and Set Condition:

CAB INTERNAL FAILURE

When Monitored: Ignition on. The CAB monitors its internal microprocessors for correct operation.

Set Condition: If the CAB detects an internal fault, the DTC is set.

POSSIBLE CAUSES
INTERMITTENT DTC
DAMAGED CAB/CAB HARNESS CONNECTOR
CAB - GROUND CIRCUIT OPEN
ABS VALVE FUSED B(+) CIRCUIT OPEN
ABS PUMP FUSED B(+) CIRCUIT OPEN
CAB - INTERNAL FAULT

TEST	ACTION
1	Turn the ignition on. With the DRBIII®, read DTCs. With the DRBIII®, erase DTCs. Turn the ignition off. Turn the ignition on. With the DRBIII®, read DTCs. Does the DRBIII® display CAB INTERNAL FAILURE? Yes → Go To 2 No → Go To 6
2	Turn the ignition off. Disconnect the CAB harness connector. Inspect the CAB/CAB harness connector for damage. Is ther any broken, bent, pushed out, corroded or spread terminals? Yes → Repair as necessary. Perform ABS VERIFICATION TEST No → Go To 3
3	Turn the ignition off. Disconnect the CAB harness connector. Using a 12-volt test light connected to 12-volts, probe the CAB harness connector ground circuits. Did the test light illuminate? Yes → Go To 4 No → Repair the CAB Ground circuit for an open. Perform ABS VERIFICATION TEST

ARM66CR000000035

Fig. 174 CAB Internal Failure (Part 1 of 2). 2003–04 Sebring Convertible, Sebring Sedan & Stratus Sedan

When Monitored and Set Condition:

CLUSTER LAMP FAILURE

When Monitored: Key ON. After Key-ON bulb check.

Set Condition: When the instrument cluster informs the CAB that the cluster cannot turn on the ABS Lamp.

POSSIBLE CAUSES
INSTRUMENT CLUSTER OR ABS DTC PRESENT
INSTRUMENT CLUSTER
CAB--NO DTC SIGNAL TO THE INSTRUMENT CLUSTER
CAB -- PERMANENT FAULT SIGNAL
CAB--NO KEY-ON BULB CHECK SIGNAL

TEST	ACTION
1	Turn the ignition on. With the DRBIII®, read DTCs. Are there any Instrument Cluster or ABS DTCs present? Yes → Refer to the appropriate category for the related symptom(s). Perform ABS VERIFICATION TEST No → Go To 2
2	Turn the ignition off. Perform the Key-on Bulb Check. Does the ABS Warning Indicator light and then go out after a few seconds? Yes → Go To 3 No. Light remains after bulb check. Replace the Controller Antilock Brake Perform ABS VERIFICATION TEST No. Indicator never comes on. Go To 4

ARM66CR000000037

Fig. 175 Cluster Lamp Failure (Part 1 of 2). 2003–04 Sebring Convertible, Sebring Sedan & Stratus Sedan

TEST	ACTION
3	**NOTE: The DRBIII® communication with the CAB must be operational for the result of this test to be valid.** Turn the ignition off. Remove ABS Valve fuse. Perform the Key-on Bulb Check. Does the ABS Indicator remain on after the bulb check? Yes → Test Complete. No → Replace the Controller Antilock Brake Perform ABS VERIFICATION TEST
4	**NOTE: The following steps will initiate the Instrument Cluster self test.** Turn the ignition off. Press and hold the odometer reset button. Turn the ignition to RUN. Observe the Instrument Cluster indicators. Release the odometer reset button. Did the ABS Indicator illuminate during the Instrument Cluster self test? Yes → Replace the Controller Antilock Brake Perform ABS VERIFICATION TEST No → Replace the Instrument Cluster Perform ABS VERIFICATION TEST

ARM66CR000000038

Fig. 175 Cluster Lamp Failure (Part 2 of 2). 2003–04 Sebring Convertible, Sebring Sedan & Stratus Sedan

When Monitored and Set Condition:

INCORRECT TONE WHEEL FAILURE

When Monitored: Ignition ON. Vehicle speed above 40 km/h (25mph) for 2 minutes.

Set Condition: When the CAB detects an unexpected wheel speed condition caused by a tire size that does not meet vehicle specification.

POSSIBLE CAUSES
INCORRECT TIRES ON VEHICLE
INCORRECT TONE WHEEL ON VEHICLE

TEST	ACTION
1	Inspect the tire sizes on the vehicle. Is a smaller than production tire, mini spare, or two mini spares installed on both front wheels? Yes → Replace the incorrect tire(s) size with production size tire(s). Perform ABS VERIFICATION TEST No → Go To 2
2	Count the number of tone wheel teeth on both of the front driveshafts. Does one or both tone wheel(s) have (56 or 40) teeth? Yes → Replace the front driveshaft(s) with the incorrect number of tone wheel teeth. Perform ABS VERIFICATION TEST No → Test Complete.

ARM66CR000000039

Fig. 176 Incorrect Tone Wheel Failure. 2003–04 Sebring Convertible, Sebring Sedan & Stratus Sedan

Test Note: All symptoms listed above are diagnosed using the same tests. The title for the tests will be LEFT FRONT SENSOR CIRCUIT FAILURE.

When Monitored and Set Condition:

LEFT FRONT SENSOR CIRCUIT FAILURE

When Monitored: Ignition on. The CAB monitors the wheel speed circuit continuously.

Set Condition: If the CAB detects an open or shorted wheel speed sensor circuit, the Diagnostic Trouble Code (DTC) will set.

LEFT REAR SENSOR CIRCUIT FAILURE

When Monitored: Ignition on. The CAB monitors the wheel speed circuit continuously.

Set Condition: If the CAB detects an open or shorted wheel speed sensor circuit, the Diagnostic Trouble Code (DTC) will set.

RIGHT FRONT SENSOR CIRCUIT FAILURE

When Monitored: Ignition on. The CAB monitors the wheel speed circuit continuously.

Set Condition: If the CAB detects an open or shorted wheel speed sensor circuit, the Diagnostic Trouble Code (DTC) will set.

RIGHT REAR SENSOR CIRCUIT FAILURE

When Monitored: Ignition on. The CAB monitors the wheel speed circuit continuously.

Set Condition: If the CAB detects an open or shorted wheel speed sensor circuit, the Diagnostic Trouble Code (DTC) will set.

POSSIBLE CAUSES
INTERMITTENT CONDITION
WHEEL SPEED SENSOR OR CONNECTOR DAMAGE
WHEEL SPEED SENSOR SIGNAL CIRCUIT FAULT
WHEEL SPEED SENSOR 12 VOLT SUPPLY CIRCUIT SHORT TO GROUND
WHEEL SPEED SENSOR 12 VOLT SUPPLY CIRCUIT OPEN
WHEEL SPEED SENSOR SIGNAL CIRCUIT SHORT TO GROUND
WHEEL SPEED SENSOR SIGNAL CIRCUIT OPEN

ARM66CR000000040

Fig. 177 Lefthand Front, Lefthand Rear, Righthand Front & Righthand Rear Sensor Circuit Failure (Part 1 of 5). 2003–04 Sebring Convertible, Sebring Sedan & Stratus Sedan

POSSIBLE CAUSES
CAB - 12 VOLT SUPPLY CIRCUIT FAULT
CAB - SIGNAL CIRCUIT FAULT
WHEEL SPEED SENSOR 12 VOLT SUPPLY SHORT TO GROUND
WHEEL SPEED SENSOR SIGNAL CIRCUIT INOPERATIVE

TEST	ACTION
1	Turn the ignition on. With the DRBIII®, read DTCs. With the DRBIII®, read the Freeze Frame information. With the DRBIII®, erase DTCs. Turn the ignition off. Turn the ignition on. With the DRBIII®, read DTCs. **NOTE: The CAB must sense all four wheels at 25km/h (15 mph) before it will extinguish the ABS indicators.** Does the DRBIII® display SENSOR CIRCUIT FAILURE? Yes → Go To 2 No → Go To 13
2	Turn the ignition off. Inspect the CAB connector, affected Wheel Speed Sensor, and affected Wheel Speed Sensor connector. Is the affected Wheel Speed Sensor or any of the connectors damaged? Yes → Repair as necessary. Perform ABS VERIFICATION TEST No → Go To 3
3	Turn the ignition off. Disconnect the affected Wheel Speed Sensor connector. **Note: Check connector - Clean/repair as necessary.** Turn the ignition on. Measure the voltage between affected Wheel Speed Sensor 12 Volt Supply circuit and ground. Is the voltage above 10 volts? Yes → Go To 6 No → Go To 4
4	Turn the ignition off. Disconnect the CAB harness connector. Disconnect the affected Wheel Speed Sensor connector. Using a 12-volt test light connected to 12-volts, probe the affected Wheel Speed Sensor 12 Volt Supply circuit. Does the test light illuminate? Yes → Repair the affected Wheel Speed Sensor 12 Volt Supply circuit for a short to ground. Perform ABS VERIFICATION TEST No → Go To 5

ARM66CR000000041

Fig. 177 Lefthand Front, Lefthand Rear, Righthand Front & Righthand Rear Sensor Circuit Failure (Part 2 of 5). 2003–04 Sebring Convertible, Sebring Sedan & Stratus Sedan

TEST	ACTION
5	Turn the ignition off. Disconnect the CAB harness connector. Disconnect the affected Wheel Speed Sensor connector. Connect a jumper wire between affected Wheel Speed Sensor 12 Volt Supply circuit and ground. Using a 12-volt test light connected to 12-volts, probe the affected Wheel Speed Sensor 12 Volt Supply circuit. Does the test light illuminate? Yes → Go To 6 No → Repair the affected Wheel Speed Sensor 12 Volt Supply circuit for an open. Perform ABS VERIFICATION TEST
6	Turn the ignition off. Disconnect the affected Wheel Speed Sensor connector. **NOTE: Check connector - Clean/repair as necessary.** Turn the ignition on. Measure the voltage between affected Wheel Speed Sensor Signal circuit and ground. Is the voltage above 1 volt? Yes → Repair the affected Wheel Speed Sensor Signal circuit for a short to voltage. Perform ABS VERIFICATION TEST No → Go To 7
7	Turn the ignition off. Disconnect the CAB harness connector. Disconnect the affected Wheel Speed Sensor connector. Using a 12-volt test light connected to 12-volts, probe the affected Wheel Speed Sensor Signal circuit. Does the test light illuminate? Yes → Repair the affected Wheel Speed Sensor Signal circuit for a short to ground. Perform ABS VERIFICATION TEST No → Go To 8
8	Turn the ignition off. Disconnect the CAB harness connector. Disconnect the affected Wheel Speed Sensor connector. Connect a jumper wire between affected Wheel Speed Sensor Signal circuit and ground. Using a 12-volt test light connected to 12-volts, probe the affected Wheel Speed Sensor Signal circuit. Does the test light illuminate? Yes → Go To 9 No → Repair the affected Wheel Speed Sensor Signal circuit for an open. Perform ABS VERIFICATION TEST

ARM66CR000000042

Fig. 177 Lefthand Front, Lefthand Rear, Righthand Front & Righthand Rear Sensor Circuit Failure (Part 3 of 5). 2003–04 Sebring Convertible, Sebring Sedan & Stratus Sedan

TEST	ACTION
13	Turn the ignition off. Visually inspect the related wiring harness. Look for any chafed, pierced, pinched, or partially broken wires. Visually inspect the related wire harness connectors. Look for broken, bent, pushed out, or corroded terminals. Refer to any Hotline letters or Technical Service Bulletins that may apply. Were any problems found? Yes → Repair as necessary. Perform ABS VERIFICATION TEST No → Test Complete.

ARM66CR000000044

Fig. 177 Lefthand Front, Lefthand Rear, Righthand Front & Righthand Rear Sensor Circuit Failure (Part 5 of 5). 2003–04 Sebring Convertible, Sebring Sedan & Stratus Sedan

TEST	ACTION
9	Turn the ignition off. Remove the CAB harness strain relief to access wires. Reconnect the CAB harness connector. Turn the ignition on. Measure the voltage between affected Wheel Speed Sensor 12 Volt Supply circuit and ground. Is the voltage above 10 volts? Yes → Go To 10 No → Replace the Controller Antilock Brake Perform ABS VERIFICATION TEST
10	Turn the ignition off. Remove the CAB harness strain relief to access wires. Reconnect the CAB harness connector. Turn the ignition on. Measure the voltage between affected Wheel Speed Sensor 12 Volt Supply circuit and affected Wheel Speed Sensor Signal circuit. Is the voltage above 10 volts? Yes → Go To 11 No → Replace the Controller Antilock Brake Perform ABS VERIFICATION TEST
11	Turn the ignition off. Reconnect ALL affected Wheel Speed Sensor circuit connectors. Disconnect the affected Wheel Speed Sensor connector. Turn the ignition on. Measure the voltage of the affected Wheel Speed Sensor 12 Volt Supply circuit in the affected Wheel Speed Sensor connector while reconnecting the sensor connector. Did the affected Wheel Speed Sensor 12 Volt Supply circuit drop voltage to 0 DC volts? Yes → Replace the affected Wheel Speed Sensor Perform ABS VERIFICATION TEST No → Go To 12
12	Turn the ignition off. Reconnect ALL affected Wheel Speed Sensor circuit connectors. Turn the ignition on. Measure the DC voltage of the Wheel Speed Sensor Signal circuit in the affected Wheel Speed Sensor connector. Slowly rotate the wheel. Does the DC voltage toggle between 1.6 volts to .8 volts? Yes → Go To 13 No → Replace the affected Wheel Speed Sensor Perform ABS VERIFICATION TEST

ARM66CR000000043

Fig. 177 Lefthand Front, Lefthand Rear, Righthand Front & Righthand Rear Sensor Circuit Failure (Part 4 of 5). 2003–04 Sebring Convertible, Sebring Sedan & Stratus Sedan

Test Note: All symptoms listed above are diagnosed using the same tests. The title for the tests will be LEFT FRONT WHEEL SPEED SIGNAL FAILURE.

When Monitored and Set Condition:

LEFT FRONT WHEEL SPEED SIGNAL FAILURE

When Monitored: Wheel speed comparison is checked and verified at drive off and continuously thereafter.

Set Condition: If, during an ABS stop, the CAB commands any valve solenoid on for an extended length of time, and does not see a corresponding wheel speed change, the Diagnostic Trouble Code (DTC) is set. The DTC can also set if the signal is missing or erratic.

LEFT REAR WHEEL SPEED SIGNAL FAILURE

When Monitored: Wheel speed comparison is checked and verified at drive off and continuously thereafter.

Set Condition: If, during an ABS stop, the CAB commands any valve solenoid on for an extended length of time, and does not see a corresponding wheel speed change, the Diagnostic Trouble Code (DTC) is set. The DTC can also set if the signal is missing or erratic.

RIGHT FRONT WHEEL SPEED SIGNAL FAILURE

When Monitored: Wheel speed comparison is checked and verified at drive off and continuously thereafter.

Set Condition: If, during an ABS stop, the CAB commands any valve solenoid on for an extended length of time, and does not see a corresponding wheel speed change, the Diagnostic Trouble Code (DTC) is set. The DTC can also set if the signal is missing or erratic.

RIGHT REAR WHEEL SPEED SIGNAL FAILURE

When Monitored: Wheel speed comparison is checked and verified at drive off and continuously thereafter.

Set Condition: If, during an ABS stop, the CAB commands any valve solenoid on for an extended length of time, and does not see a corresponding wheel speed change, the Diagnostic Trouble Code (DTC) is set. The DTC can also set if the signal is missing or erratic.

ARM66CR000000045

Fig. 178 Lefthand Front, Lefthand Rear, Righthand Front & Righthand Rear Wheel Speed Signal Failure (Part 1 of 3). 2003–04 Sebring Convertible, Sebring Sedan & Stratus Sedan

POSSIBLE CAUSES
WHEEL SPEED SIGNAL FAILURE DTC PRESENT
AFFECTED WHEEL SPEED SENSOR SIGNAL INOPERATIVE
AFFECTED WHEEL SPEED SENSOR CONNECTOR DAMAGED
AFFECTED WHEEL SPEED SENSOR TONE WHEEL DAMAGED
AFFECTED WHEEL SPEED SENSOR AIR GAP FAULT
WHEEL BEARING FAULT
BRAKE LINING FAULT
AFFECTED WHEEL SPEED SENSOR CIRCUIT ELECTRICAL FAULT

TEST	ACTION
1	Turn the ignition on. With the DRBIII®, read DTCs. With the DRBIII®, read Freeze Frame information. **NOTE: The CAB must sense ALL 4 wheels at 25 km/h (15 mph) before it will extinguish the ABS indicators.** Does the DRBIII® display WHEEL SPEED/SIGNAL FAILURE and SENSOR CIRCUIT FAILURE? Yes → Refer to the affected Wheel Speed SENSOR CIRCUIT FAILURE for the related symptom(s). Perform ABS VERIFICATION TEST No → Go To 2
2	Turn the ignition on. With the DRBIII® in Sensors, monitor ALL the Wheel Speed Sensor Signals while an assistant drives the vehicle. Slowly accelerate as straight as possible from a stop to 24 km/h (15 mph). Is the affected Wheel Speed Signal showing 0 km/h (0 mph)? Yes → Go To 3 No → The condition is not present at this time. Monitor DRBIII® parameters while wiggling the related wiring harness. Refer to any Technical Service Bulletins(TSB) that may apply. Visually inspect the related wiring harness and connector terminals. Perform ABS VERIFICATION TEST
3	Turn the ignition off. Inspect the CAB connector, affected Wheel Speed Sensor, and affected Wheel Speed Sensor connector. Is the Wheel Speed Sensor or any connector damaged? Yes → Repair as necessary. Perform ABS VERIFICATION TEST No → Go To 4

ARM66CR000000046

Fig. 178 Lefthand Front, Lefthand Rear, Righthand Front & Righthand Rear Wheel Speed Signal Failure (Part 2 of 3). 2003–04 Sebring Convertible, Sebring Sedan & Stratus Sedan

TEST	ACTION
4	Turn ignition off. Inspect the affected Tone Wheel for damaged, missing teeth, cracks, or looseness **NOTE: The Tone Wheel teeth should be perfectly square, not bend, or nicked.** Is the affected Tone Wheel OK? Yes → Go To 5 No → Replace the Tone Wheel Perform ABS VERIFICATION TEST
5	Turn the ignition off. Using a Feeler Gauge, measure the affected Wheel Speed Sensor Air Gap. **NOTE: Refer to the appropriate service information, if necessary, for procedures or specifications.** Is the Air Gap OK? Yes → Go To 6 No → Repair as necessary. Perform ABS VERIFICATION TEST
6	Turn the ignition off. Inspect the wheel bearings for excessive runout or clearance. **NOTE: Refer to the appropriate service information, if necessary, for procedures or specifications.** Is the bearing clearance OK ? Yes → Go To 7 No → Repair as necessary. Perform ABS VERIFICATION TEST
7	Turn the ignition off. Visually inspect brakes for locking up due to lining contamination or overheating. Inspect all Components for defects which may cause a Signal DTC to set. Is any Component Damaged? Yes → Repair as necessary. Perform ABS VERIFICATION TEST No → Refer to symptom SENSOR CIRCUIT FAILURE for further diagnostics. Perform ABS VERIFICATION TEST

ARM66CR000000047

Fig. 178 Lefthand Front, Lefthand Rear, Righthand Front & Righthand Rear Wheel Speed Signal Failure (Part 3 of 3). 2003–04 Sebring Convertible, Sebring Sedan & Stratus Sedan

When Monitored and Set Condition:

PUMP CIRCUIT FAILURE

When Monitored: Ignition on. The CAB commands the pump on at 20 km/h (12 mph) to check its operation, if the brake switch is not applied. If the brake is applied, the test will run at 40 km/h (25 mph).

Set Condition: The DTC is stored when the CAB detects: 1) Improper voltage decay after the pump was turned off. 2) Pump not energized by the CAB, but voltage is present for 3.5 seconds. 3) Pump is turned on by the CAB, but without sufficient voltage to operate it.

POSSIBLE CAUSES
CAB - PUMP MOTOR RUNNING CONTINUOUSLY
ABS PUMP FUSE
ABS PUMP MOTOR INTERMITTENT DTC
DAMAGED CAB/CAB HARNESS CONNECTOR
ABS PUMP FUSED B(+) CIRCUIT INTERMITTENT SHORT TO GROUND
ABS PUMP FUSED B(+) CIRCUIT SHORT TO GROUND
CAB - INTERNAL FAULT
ABS PUMP MOTOR INOPERATIVE
ABS PUMP MOTOR OPEN
ABS PUMP MOTOR B(+) CIRCUIT OPEN
ABS PUMP MOTOR GROUND CIRCUIT OPEN
CAB - INTERNAL FAULT

TEST	ACTION
1	Turn the ignition off. Turn the ignition on. Monitor the ABS Pump Motor for continuous operation. **NOTE: The CAB must sense ALL wheels at 25 km/h (15 mph) before it will extinguish the ABS indicators.** Is the ABS Pump Motor running continuously? Yes → Replace the Controller Antilock Brake Perform ABS VERIFICATION TEST No → Go To 2

ARM66CR000000048

Fig. 179 Pump Circuit Failure (Part 1 of 4). 2003–04 Sebring Convertible, Sebring Sedan & Stratus Sedan

TEST	ACTION
2	Turn the ignition off. Turn the ignition on. With the DRBIII®, read DTCs. With the DRBIII®, erase DTCs. Turn the ignition off. Turn the ignition on. With the DRBIII®, actuate the ABS Pump Motor. Did the ABS Pump Motor operate? Yes → Go To 3 No → Go To 4
3	Turn the ignition off. Visually inspect the related wiring harness. Look for any chafed, pierced, pinched, or partially broken wires. Make sure the Pump Motor connecter is secure. Visually inspect the related wire harness connectors. Look for broken, bent, pushed out, or corroded terminals. Refer to any Hotline letters or Technical Service Bulletins that may apply. Were any problems found? Yes → Repair as necessary. Perform ABS VERIFICATION TEST No → Test Complete.
4	Turn the ignition off. Remove and inspect the ABS Pump fuse. Is the ABS Pump fuse open? Yes → Go To 5 No → Go To 8
5	Turn the ignition off. Visually inspect the ABS Pump Fused B(+) circuit in the wiring harness. Look for any sign of an intermittent short to ground. Is the wiring harness OK? Yes → Go To 6 No → Repair the ABS Pump Fused B(+) circuit for a short to ground. Perform ABS VERIFICATION TEST
6	Turn the ignition off. Disconnect the CAB harness connector. Check connectors - Clean/repair as necessary. Using a 12-volt test light connected to 12-volts, probe the ABS Pump Fused B(+) circuit fuse terminal. Does the test light illuminate? Yes → Repair the ABS Pump Fused B(+) circuit for a short to ground. Perform ABS VERIFICATION TEST No → Go To 7

ARM66CR000000049

Fig. 179 Pump Circuit Failure (Part 2 of 4). 2003–04 Sebring Convertible, Sebring Sedan & Stratus Sedan

TEST	ACTION
7	Turn the ignition off. Reconnect the CAB harness connector. Using a 12-volt test light connected to 12-volts, probe the ABS Pump Fused B(+) circuit fuse terminal. Does the test light illuminate? Yes → Replace the Controller Antilock Brake Perform ABS VERIFICATION TEST No → Replace the ABS Pump fuse. If the fuse is open make sure to check for a short to ground. Perform ABS VERIFICATION TEST
8	Turn the ignition off. Disconnect the CAB harness connector. Inspect the CAB and CAB harness connector for damage. Is there any broken, bent, pushed out, corroded, or spread terminals? Yes → Repair as necessary. Perform ABS VERIFICATION TEST No → Go To 9
9	Turn the ignition off. Reinstall the ABS Pump fuse. Disconnect the ABS Pump Motor connector. Check connectors - Clean/repair as necessary. Connect a 10 gauge 40 amp fused jumper wire between the ABS Pump Fused B(+) terminal in the CAB harness connector to the ABS Pump Motor connector RED wired terminal. Connect a 10 gauge jumper wire between the Ground circuit terminal in the CAB harness connector to the ABS Pump Motor connector BLACK wired terminal. Did the ABS Pump Motor operate? Yes → Replace the Controller Antilock Brake Perform ABS VERIFICATION TEST No → Go To 10
10	Turn the ignition off. Disconnect the ABS Pump Motor connector. Check connectors - Clean/repair as necessary. Connect a 10 gauge 40 amp fused jumper wire between the ABS Pump Motor connector RED wired terminal and an alternate 40 amp capable B(+) source. Connect a 10 gauge jumper wire between the ABS Pump Motor connector BLACK wired terminal and ground Did the ABS Pump Motor operate? Yes → Go To 11 No → Replace the Hydraulic Control Unit Perform ABS VERIFICATION TEST

ARM66CR000000050

Fig. 179 Pump Circuit Failure (Part 3 of 4). 2003–04 Sebring Convertible, Sebring Sedan & Stratus Sedan

When Monitored and Set Condition:

SYSTEM OVER VOLTAGE

When Monitored: Ignition on. The CAB monitors the Fused B(+) circuit at all times for proper system voltage.

Set Condition: If the voltage is above 16.5 volts, the Diagnostic Trouble Code (DTC) is set.

POSSIBLE CAUSES
INTERMITTENT DTC
BATTERY CHARGER CONNECTED
FUSED IGNITION SWITCH OUTPUT (RUN) CIRCUIT HIGH
DAMAGED CAB/CAB HARNESS CONNECTOR
CAB - GROUND CIRCUIT OPEN
CAB - INTERNAL FAULT

TEST	ACTION
1	Turn the ignition on. With the DRBIII®, read DTC's. With the DRBIII®, erase DTC's. Turn the ignition off. Turn the ignition on. Start the engine. With the DRBIII®, read DTC's. Does the DRBIII® display SYSTEM OVER VOLTAGE? Yes → Go To 2 No → Go To 7
2	Is a battery charger connected to the vehicle? Yes → Ensure the battery is fully charged. Perform ABS VERIFICATION TEST No → Go To 3

ARM66CR000000052

Fig. 180 System Overvoltage (Part 1 of 3). 2003–04 Sebring Convertible, Sebring Sedan & Stratus Sedan

TEST	ACTION
11	Turn the ignition off. Disconnect the ABS Pump Motor connector. Check connectors - Clean/repair as necessary. Connect a 10 gauge 40 amp fused jumper wire between the ABS Pump Fused B(+) terminal in the CAB harness connector to the ABS Pump Motor connector RED wired terminal. Connect a 10 gauge jumper wire between the ABS Pump Motor connector BLACK wired terminal and ground. Did the ABS Pump Motor operate? Yes → Repair the ABS Pump Motor Fused B(+) circuit for an open. Perform ABS VERIFICATION TEST No → Repair the ABS Pump Motor Ground circuit for an open. Perform ABS VERIFICATION TEST

ARM66CR000000051

Fig. 179 Pump Circuit Failure (Part 4 of 4). 2003–04 Sebring Convertible, Sebring Sedan & Stratus Sedan

TEST	ACTION
3	Turn the ignition off. Disconnect the CAB connector. **Note: Check connector - Clean/repair as necessary.** Start the engine. Raise engine speed above 1,800 RPM's Measure the voltage between Fused Ignition Switch Output (RUN) circuit and ground. Is the voltage above 16.5 volts ? Yes → Refer to appropriate service information for Charging System testing and repair. Perform ABS VERIFICATION TEST No → Go To 4
4	Turn the ignition off. Disconnect the CAB connector. **Note: Check connector - Clean/repair as necessary.** Inspect the CAB and CAB harness connector for damage. Is there any broken, bent, pushed out, corroded, or spread terminals? Yes → Repair as necessary. Perform ABS VERIFICATION TEST No → Go To 5
5	Turn the ignition off. Disconnect the CAB connector. **Note: Check connector - Clean/repair as necessary.** Using a 12-volt test light connected to 12-volts, probe the Ground circuits. Does the test light illuminate? Yes → Go To 6 No → Repair the Ground circuit for an open. Perform ABS VERIFICATION TEST
6	Turn the ignition off. Reconnect the CAB harness connector. Turn the ignition on. With the DRBIII® in Sensors, read the ignition voltage. Does the DRBIII® display ignition voltage above 16 volts? Yes → Replace the Controller Antilock Brake Perform ABS VERIFICATION TEST No → Go To 7

ARM66CR000000053

Fig. 180 System Overvoltage (Part 2 of 3). 2003–04 Sebring Convertible, Sebring Sedan & Stratus Sedan

TEST	ACTION
7	Turn the ignition off. Visually inspect the related wiring harness. Look for any chafed, pierced, pinched, or partially broken wires. Visually inspect the related wire harness connectors. Look for broken, bent, pushed out, or corroded terminals. Refer to any Hotline letters or Technical Service Bulletins that may apply. Ensure the battery is fully charged. Inspect the vehicle for aftermarket accessories that may exceed the Generator System output. Using the wiring diagram/schematic as a guide, inspect the wiring and connectors. Were any problems found? Yes → Repair as necessary. Perform ABS VERIFICATION TEST No → Test Complete.

ARM66CR000000054

Fig. 180 System Overvoltage (Part 3 of 3). 2003–04 Sebring Convertible, Sebring Sedan & Stratus Sedan

TEST	ACTION
3	Turn the ignition off. Disconnect the CAB harness connector. Inspect the CAB and CAB harness connector for damage. Is there any broken, bent, pushed out, corroded, or spread terminals? Yes → Repair as necessary. Perform ABS VERIFICATION TEST No → Go To 4
4	Turn the ignition off. Disconnect the CAB harness connector. Using a 12-volt test light connected to 12-volts, probe the Ground circuits. Does the test light illuminate? Yes → Go To 5 No → Repair the Ground circuit for an open. Perform ABS VERIFICATION TEST
5	Turn the ignition on. Using a 12-volt test light connected to ground, probe the Fused Ignition Switch Output (RUN) circuit. Does the test light illuminate? Yes → Replace the Controller Antilock Brake Perform ABS VERIFICATION TEST No → Repair the Fused Ignition Switch Output (RUN) circuit for an open. Perform ABS VERIFICATION TEST
6	Turn the ignition off. Visually inspect the related wiring harness. Look for any chafed, pierced, pinched, or partially broken wires. Visually inspect the related wire harness connectors. Look for broken, bent, pushed out, or corroded terminals. Refer to any Hotline letters or Technical Service Bulletins that may apply. Ensure the battery is fully charged. Inspect the vehicle for aftermarket accessories that may exceed the Generator System output. Using the wiring diagram/schematic as a guide, inspect the wiring and connectors. Were any problems found? Yes → Repair as necessary. Perform ABS VERIFICATION TEST No → Test Complete.

ARM66CR000000056

Fig. 181 System Undervoltage (Part 2 of 2). 2003–04 Sebring Convertible, Sebring Sedan & Stratus Sedan

When Monitored and Set Condition:

SYSTEM UNDER VOLTAGE

When Monitored: Ignition on. The CAB monitors the Fused Ignition Switch Output circuit voltage above 10 km/h (6 mph) for proper system voltage.

Set Condition: If the voltage is below 9.5 volts, the Diagnostic Trouble Code (DTC) is set.

POSSIBLE CAUSES
INTERMITTENT DTC
DAMAGED CAB/CAB HARNESS CONNECTOR
RUNNING BATTERY VOLTAGE LOW
CAB - GROUND CIRCUIT OPEN
FUSED IGNITION SWITCH OUTPUT (RUN) CIRCUIT OPEN
CAB - INTERNAL FAULT

TEST	ACTION
1	Turn the ignition on. With the DRBIII®, read DTC's. With the DRBIII®, erase DTC's. Turn the ignition off. Turn the ignition on. Start the engine. Drive the vehicle above 16 km/h (10 mph) for at least 20 seconds. Stop the vehicle With the DRBIII®, read DTC's. Does the DRBIII® display SYSTEM UNDER VOLTAGE ? Yes → Go To 2 No → Go To 6
2	Engine Running. Measure the battery voltage. Is the battery voltage below 10 volts? Yes → Refer to appropriate service information for charging system testing and repair. Perform ABS VERIFICATION TEST No → Go To 3

ARM66CR000000055

Fig. 181 System Undervoltage (Part 1 of 2). 2003–04 Sebring Convertible, Sebring Sedan & Stratus Sedan

When Monitored and Set Condition:

VALVE POWER FEED FAILURE

When Monitored: Ignition ON. The CAB checks it's microprocessors for correct operation continuously.

Set Condition: If the CAB detects an internal fault, the DTC is set.

POSSIBLE CAUSES
INTERMITTENT DTC
ABS VALVE FUSE
ABS VALVE FUSED B(+) SUPPLY CIRCUIT OPEN
ABS VALVE FUSED B(+) CIRCUIT OPEN
ABS VALVE FUSED B(+) CIRCUIT INTERMITTENT SHORT TO GROUND
ABS VALVE FUSED B(+) CIRCUIT SHORT TO GROUND
DAMAGED CAB/CAB HARNESS CONNECTOR
CAB - GROUND CIRCUIT OPEN
CAB - INTERNAL FAULT

TEST	ACTION
1	Turn the ignition on. With the DRBIII®, read DTC's. With the DRBIII®, erase DTC's. Turn the ignition off. Turn the ignition on. With the DRBIII®, read DTC's. Does the DRBIII® display VALVE POWER FEED FAILURE? Yes → Go To 2 No → Go To 10
2	Turn the ignition off. Remove and Inspect the ABS Valve fuse. Is the ABS Valve fuse open? Yes → Go To 3 No → Go To 6

ARM66CR000000057

Fig. 182 Valve Power Feed Failure (Part 1 of 3). 2003–04 Sebring Convertible, Sebring Sedan & Stratus Sedan

TEST	ACTION
3	Turn the ignition off. Visually inspect the ABS Valve Fused B(+) circuit in the wiring harness. Look for any sign of an intermittent short to ground. Is the wiring harness OK? Yes → Go To 4 No → Repair the ABS Valve Fused B(+) circuit for a short to ground. Perform ABS VERIFICATION TEST - VER 1.
4	Turn the ignition off. Disconnect the CAB harness connector. **Note: Check connector - Clean/repair as necessary.** Using a test light connected to 12 volts, probe the ABS Valve Fused B(+) circuit fuse terminal. Did the test light illuminate? Yes → Repair the ABS Valve Fused B(+) circuit for a short to ground. Perform ABS VERIFICATION TEST No → Go To 5
5	Turn the ignition off. Reconnect the CAB harness connector. **NOTE: The CAB harness connector must be reconnected for the results of this test to be valid.** Using a test light connected to 12 volts, probe the ABS Valve Fused B(+) circuit fuse terminal. Did the test light illuminate? Yes → Replace the Controller Antilock Brake Perform ABS VERIFICATION TEST No → Replace the ABS Valve Fused B(+) fuse. If the fuse is open make sure to check for a short to ground. Perform ABS VERIFICATION TEST
6	Turn the ignition off. Disconnect the CAB harness connector. Inspect the CAB and CAB harness connector for damage. Is there any broken, bent, pushed out, corroded or spread terminals? Yes → Repair as necessary. Perform ABS VERIFICATION TEST No → Go To 7
7	Turn the ignition off. Using a 12-volt test light connected to ground, probe the B(+) supply at the ABS Valve fuse terminal. Did the test light illuminate? Yes → Go To 8 No → Repair the ABS Valve Fused B(+) supply circuit for an open. Perform ABS VERIFICATION TEST

ARM66CR000000058

Fig. 182 Valve Power Feed Failure (Part 2 of 3). 2003–04 Sebring Convertible, Sebring Sedan & Stratus Sedan

POSSIBLE CAUSES
IMPROPERLY CONFIGURED CAB

TEST	ACTION
1	Turn the ignition on. Connect the DRBIII® to the Data Link Connector. Select Anti - lock Brakes from the DRBIII® main menu. **NOTE: If DRBIII® is unable to I/D or communicate with CAB, refer to NO RESPONSE test.** Select Miscellaneous from menu. Select Set Pinion Factor from menu. Does the vehicle have unknown tires and unknown rear axle? Press Enter, to change will be displayed. Press Enter. Select the tire size that is installed on the vehicle. Press Enter. Select correct axle. Press Enter. The tire size and axle selected will be displayed. Press Enter to accept these values. Programming Successful! will be displayed. Does the DRBIII® display PROGRAMMING SUCCESSFUL? Yes → Test Complete. No → Ensure DRBIII® software is current and retry on a known good vehicle. Communicate with other modules, refer to symptom(s). Perform ABS VERIFICATION TEST - VER 1.

ARM66CR000000060

Fig. 183 ABS Lamp Flashing After CAB Replacement. 2003–04 Sebring Convertible, Sebring Sedan & Stratus Sedan

TEST	ACTION
8	Reinstall the ABS Valve fuse. Disconnect the CAB harness connector. Using a 12-volt test light connected to ground, probe the ABS Valve Fused B(+) circuit at the CAB harness connector. Did the test light illuminate? Yes → Go To 9 No → Repair the ABS Valve Fused B(+) circuit for an open. Perform ABS VERIFICATION TEST
9	Turn the ignition off. Using a 12-volt test light connected to 12-volts, probe the ground circuits at the CAB harness connector. Did the test light illuminate? Yes → Replace the Controller Antilock Brake Perform ABS VERIFICATION TEST No → Repair the CAB Ground circuit for an open. Perform ABS VERIFICATION TEST
10	Turn the ignition off. Visually inspect the related wiring harness. Look for any chafed, pierced, pinched, or partially broken wires. Visually inspect the related wire harness connectors. Look for broken, bent, pushed out, or corroded terminals. Refer to any Hotline letters or Technical Service Bulletins that may apply. Were any problems found? Yes → Repair as necessary. Perform ABS VERIFICATION TEST No → Test Complete.

ARM66CR000000059

Fig. 182 Valve Power Feed Failure (Part 3 of 3). 2003–04 Sebring Convertible, Sebring Sedan & Stratus Sedan

POSSIBLE CAUSES
CHECK BRAKE LAMP SWITCH OUTPUT
BRAKE LAMP SWITCH B+ OPEN
BRAKE LAMP SWITCH OPEN
BRAKE LAMP SWITCH OUTPUT CIRCUIT SHORT OR OPEN
CAB -- INTERNAL OPEN

TEST	ACTION
1	With the DRBIII® in Inputs/Outputs, read the Brake Lamp Switch state. Press and release the brake pedal. Does the DRBIII® display PRESSED and RELEASED? Yes → The Brake Lamp Switch is OK. Perform ABS VERIFICATION TEST No → Go To 2
2	Disconnect the Brake Lamp Switch harness connector. Using a 12-volt test light connected to ground, check the Brake Lamp Switch Fused B+ circuit. Does the test light illuminate brightly ? Yes → Go To 3 No → Repair the Brake Lamp Switch Fused B+ circuit for an open. Perform ABS VERIFICATION TEST
3	Disconnect the Brake Lamp Switch harness connector. Connect a jumper wire between the Brake Lamp Switch B+ and Brake Lamp Switch Output circuits. With the DRBIII® in Inputs/Outputs, read the Brake Lamp Switch state. Does the DRBIII® display PRESSED? Yes → Replace the Brake Lamp Switch Perform ABS VERIFICATION TEST No → Go To 4
4	Disconnect the CAB harness connector. Disconnect the Brake Lamp Switch harness connector. Check the Brake Lamp Switch Output circuit for a short to voltage and for an open. Is the Brake Lamp Switch Output circuit shorted or open? Yes → Repair the Brake Lamp Switch Output circuit for a short to voltage or an open. Perform ABS VERIFICATION TEST No → Replace the Controller Antilock Brake Perform ABS VERIFICATION TEST

ARM66CR000000061

Fig. 184 Brake Lamp Switch Inoperative. 2003–04 Sebring Convertible, Sebring Sedan & Stratus Sedan

POSSIBLE CAUSES
NO RESPONSE FROM CAB
CHECK JUNCTION BLOCK FUSE
GROUND CIRCUIT OPEN
OPEN FUSED IGNITION SWITCH OUTPUT CIRCUIT
CONTROLLER ANTILOCK BRAKE (CAB) MODULE
PCI BUS CIRCUIT OPEN
BODY CONTROL MODULE

TEST	ACTION
1	Turn the ignition on. **Note: As soon as one or more module communicates with the DRB, answer the question.** With the DRB, attempt to communicate with the Airbag Control Module. With the DRB, attempt to communicate with the Body Control Module (BCM). Was the DRB able to I/D or establish communications with either of the modules? Yes → Go To 2 No → Refer to the Communications category and perform the symptom PCI Bus Communication Failure. Perform ABS VERIFICATION TEST
2	Turn the ignition off. Remove and inspect fuse #4 in the junction block. Is the fuse open? Yes → Check the Fused Ignition Switch Output circuit for a short to ground. Replace Fuse #4. Perform ABS VERIFICATION TEST No → Go To 3
3	Turn the ignition off. Disconnect the CAB harness connector. Using a 12-volt test light connected to 12-volts, probe both ground circuits. Is the test light illuminated for both circuits? Yes → Go To 4 No → Repair the ground circuit(s) for an open. Perform ABS VERIFICATION TEST

ARM66CR000000062

Fig. 185 No Response From Controller Anti-Lock Brake (Part 1 of 2). 2003–04 Sebring Convertible, Sebring Sedan & Stratus Sedan

ABS VERIFICATION TEST - VER 1
1. Turn the ignition off. 2. Connect all previously disconnected components and connectors. 3. Ensure all accessories are turned off and the battery is fully charged. 4. Ensure that the Ignition is on, and with the DRBIII, erase all Diagnostic Trouble Codes from ALL modules. Start the engine and allow it to run for 2 minutes and fully operate the system that was malfunctioning. 5. Turn the ignition off and wait 5 seconds. Turn the ignition on and using the DRBIII, read DTC's from ALL modules. 6. If any Diagnostic Trouble Codes are present, return to Symptom list and troubleshoot new or recurring symptom. **7. NOTE: For Sensor Signal and Pump Motor faults, the CAB must sense all 4 wheels at 25 km/h (15 mph) before it will extinguish the ABS Indicator.** 8. If there are no DTC's present after turning ignition on, road test the vehicle for at least 5 minutes. Perform several antilock braking stops. **9. Caution: Ensure braking capability is available before road testing.** 10. Again, with the DRBIII® read DTC's. If any DTC's are present, return to Symptom list. 11. If there are no Diagnostic Trouble Codes (DTC's) present, and the customer's concern can no longer be duplicated, the repair is complete. Are any DTC's present or is the original concern still present? Yes → Repair is not complete, refer to appropriate symptom. No → Repair is complete.

ARM66CR000000064

Fig. 186 ABS Verification Test. 2003–04 Sebring Convertible, Sebring Sedan & Stratus Sedan

TEST	ACTION
4	Turn the ignition off. **NOTE: Ensure fuse #4 is installed in the junction block.** Disconnect the CAB harness connector. Turn the ignition on. Using a 12-volt test light connected to ground, probe the Fused Ignition Switch Output circuit. Is the test light illuminated? Yes → Go To 5 No → Repair the Fused Ignition Switch Output circuit for an open. Perform ABS VERIFICATION TEST
5	**Note: Ensure there is PCI Bus communication with other modules on the vehicle before proceeding. If not, refer to the symptom list from the menu and repair as necessary.** Disconnect the CAB harness connector. Use Scope input cable CH7058, Cable to Probe adapter CH7062, and the red and black test probes. Connect the scope input cable to the channel one connector on the DRB. Attach the red and black leads and the cable to probe adapter to the scope input cable. With the DRBIII®, select Pep Module Tools. Select lab scope. Select Live Data. Select 12 volt square wave. Press F2 for Scope. Press F2 and use the down arrow to set voltage range to 20 volts. Set Probe to x10. Press F2 again when complete. Connect the Black lead to the chassis ground. Connect the Red lead to the PCI Bus circuit in the CAB connector. Turn the ignition on. Observe the voltage display on the DRB Lab Scope. Does the voltage pulse from 0 to approximately 7.5 volts? Yes → Replace the Controller Antilock Brake (CAB) Perform ABS VERIFICATION TEST No → Go To 6
6	Turn the ignition off. Disconnect the CAB harness connector. Disconnect the BCM C3 harness connector. Measure the resistance of the PCI bus circuit between the CAB connector and the BCM C3 connector. Is the resistance below 5.0 ohms? Yes → Replace the Body Control Module Perform ABS VERIFICATION TEST No → Repair the PCI Bus circuit for an open. Perform ABS VERIFICATION TEST

ARM66CR000000063

Fig. 185 No Response From Controller Anti-Lock Brake (Part 2 of 2). 2003–04 Sebring Convertible, Sebring Sedan & Stratus Sedan

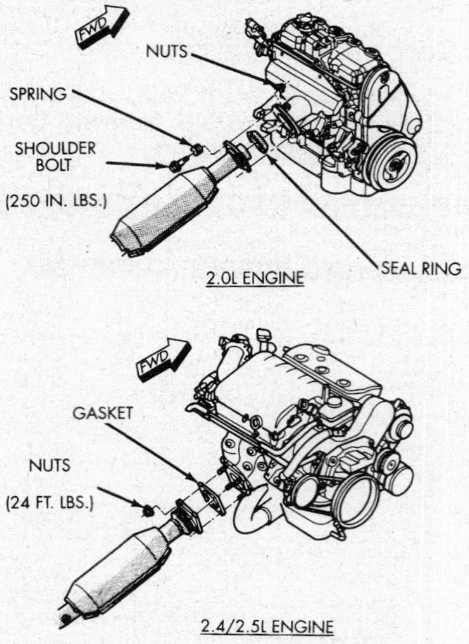

CR40298015650000X

Fig. 187 Exhaust replacement. Breeze, Cirrus, 2000 Sebring Convertible & Stratus

TIRE PRESSURE MONITORING SYSTEM

INDEX

PRECAUTIONS

Air Bag Systems

Refer to "Air Bag System Precautions" in the front of this manual for system disarming and arming procedures.

Battery Ground Cable

Prior to service, disconnect battery ground cable and isolate as required.

DESCRIPTION

The Tire Pressure Monitoring (TPM) system monitors air pressure in all five tires including full-size spare. Sensors mounted in each wheels valve stem transmit tire pressure readings to a receiver locate din the overhead console. These transmission occur once ever minute at speed more than 20 mph. The TPM system remains active even if not displayed.

If a road time pressure exceeds the low or high pressure threshold, **Fig. 1**, the TPM system will display a message and sound a chime. The EVIC will then go into tire pressure display screen and flash the pressure value on the tire that is low or high for the rest of the ignition cycle or until either the C/T, MEMO, STEP or RESET button is pressed.

If a road tire is replace by the spare, the RPM system will display SPARE SWAP DETECTED along with a chime. This could take up to 10 minutes at 20 mph.

Description	Pressure, psi		
	Crossfire	300M	300M Special
High Pressure Threshold	—	45	45
Placard Pressure (Cold)	—	30	34
Low Pressure Threshold	26	24	28

Fig. 1 TPM threshold pressures

DIAGNOSIS & TESTING

Accessing Diagnostic Trouble Codes

Connect a suitably programmed DRB scan tool to Data Link Connector (DLC), and follow manufacturer's instructions.

Wiring Diagrams

Refer to **Fig. 2**, for wiring diagrams.

Diagnostic Tests

CROSSFIRE

Refer to **Figs. 3 through 18,** for diagnostic testing.

300M

Refer to **Figs. 19 and 20,** for diagnostic testing.

Clearing Diagnostic Trouble Codes

Connect a suitably programmed DRB scan tool to Data Link Connector (DLC), and follow manufacturer's instructions.

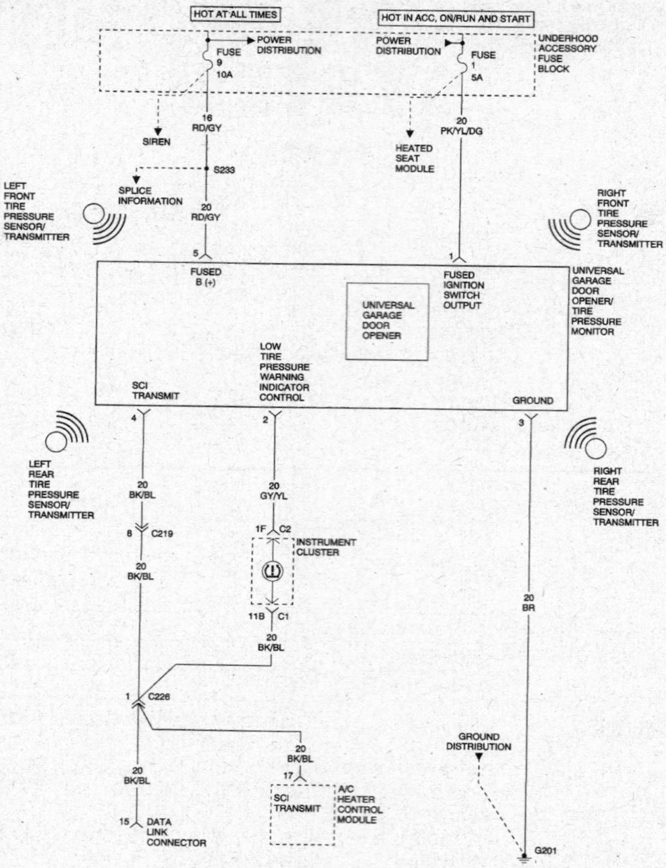

ARM0300000000451

Fig. 2 Wiring diagram. Crossfire

DIAGNOSTIC CHART INDEX

Code	Description	Page No.	Fig. No.
CROSSFIRE			
—	Initialization Fault	7-3	3
—	Tire Pressure Monitor Module Fault	7-3	4
—	Tire Pressure Sensor Transmitter Signal Fault	7-3	5
—	Signal Jammed	7-3	6
—	Lefthand Front Tire Pressure Sensor Transmitter Signal Jammed	7-4	7
—	Lefthand Rear Tire Pressure Sensor Transmitter Signal Jammed	7-4	8
—	Righthand Front Tire Pressure Sensor Transmitter Signal Jammed	7-4	9
—	Righthand Rear Tire Pressure Sensor Transmitter Signal Jammed	7-4	10
—	Tire Pressure Sensor Transmitter Inop	7-5	11
—	Transmitter Failure	7-5	12
—	Lefthand Front Tire Pressure Sensor Transmitter	7-5	13
—	Lefthand Rear Tire Pressure Sensor Transmitter	7-5	14
—	Righthand Front Tire Pressure Sensor Transmitter	7-6	15
—	Righthand Rear Tire Pressure Sensor Transmitter	7-6	16
—	Tire Pressure Sensor Transmitter Low Battery	7-6	17
—	Tire Pressure Verification Test	7-6	18
300M			
—	TPM Diagnosis & Testing	7-6	19
—	Tire Pressure Verification Test	7-7	20

1. **PROGRAMMING TIRE PRESSURE MONITOR**

Turn the ignition on.
With the DRB III® and a calibration magnet, program the Tire Pressure Monitor module for all four tire pressure sensor/transmitters.
Disconnect the DRB III® and prepare the vehicle for a road test.
Road test the vehicle above 33 km/h (20 MPH) for a minimum of two minutes.
With the DRB III® read the last 32 transmissions received by the Tire Pressure Monitor.

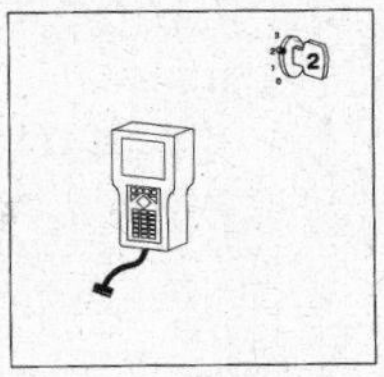

Does the DRB III® display any of the tire pressure transmitter IDs in the last 32 transmissions?

Yes >> Repair is complete.
Perform TIRE PRESSURE MONITOR VERIFICATION TEST.

No >> Replace and program the Tire Pressure Monitor module.
Perform TIRE PRESSURE MONITOR VERIFICATION TEST.

ARM0300000000452

Fig. 3 Initialization Fault. Crossfire

When Monitored and Set Condition

LEFT FRONT TIRE PRESSURE SENSOR/TRANSMITTER SIGNAL JAMMED

- When Monitored: With the ignition on, the Tire Pressure Monitor (TPM) monitors the tire pressure sensor/transmitters approximately once a minute (60 – 68 seconds) when the vehicle speed is above 33 km/h (20 MPH).
- Set Condition: If the Tire Pressure Monitor (TPM) module receives an undetectable frequency transmission from the left front tire pressure sensor/transmitter, the DTC will be set.

LEFT REAR TIRE PRESSURE SENSOR/TRANSMITTER SIGNAL JAMMED

- When Monitored: With the ignition on, the Tire Pressure Monitor (TPM) monitors the tire pressure sensor/transmitters approximately once a minute (60 – 68 seconds) when the vehicle speed is above 33 km/h (20 MPH).
- Set Condition: If the Tire Pressure Monitor (TPM) module receives an undetectable frequency transmission from the left front tire pressure sensor/transmitter, the DTC will be set.

RIGHT FRONT TIRE PRESSURE SENSOR/TRANSMITTER SIGNAL JAMMED

- When Monitored: With the ignition on, the Tire Pressure Monitor (TPM) monitors the tire pressure sensor/transmitters approximately once a minute (60 – 68 seconds) when the vehicle speed is above 33 km/h (20 MPH).
- Set Condition: If the Tire Pressure Monitor (TPM) module receives an undetectable frequency transmission from the left front tire pressure sensor/transmitter, the DTC will be set.

RIGHT REAR TIRE PRESSURE SENSOR/TRANSMITTER SIGNAL JAMMED

- When Monitored: With the ignition on, the Tire Pressure Monitor (TPM) monitors the tire pressure sensor/transmitters approximately once a minute (60 – 68 seconds) when the vehicle speed is above 33 km/h (20 MPH).
- Set Condition: If the Tire Pressure Monitor (TPM) module receives an undetectable frequency transmission from the left front tire pressure sensor/transmitter, the DTC will be set.

SIGNAL JAMMED

- When Monitored: With the ignition on, the Tire Pressure Monitor (TPM) monitors the tire pressure sensor/transmitters approximately once a minute (60 – 68 seconds) when the vehicle speed is above 33 km/h (20 MPH).
- Set Condition: If the Tire Pressure Monitor (TPM) module receives an undetectable frequency transmission from a tire pressure sensor/transmitter, the DTC will be set.

POSSIBLE CAUSES
OUTSIDE RADIO FREQUENCY INTERFERENCE

ARM0300000000454

Fig. 5 Tire Pressure Sensor Transmitter Signal Fault (Part 1 of 2). Crossfire

1. **INSPECT TIRE PRESSURE SENSOR/TRANSMITTERS**

Turn the ignition off.
Inspect all four vehicle wheels for the Tire Pressure Sensor/Transmitters being present.

Do all the wheels have tire pressure sensor/transmitters?

Yes >> Go to 2

No >> Install the Tire Pressure Sensor/Transmitters and program module.
Perform TIRE PRESSURE MONITOR VERIFICATION TEST.

2. **PROGRAMMING TIRE PRESSURE MONITOR**

Turn the ignition on.
With the DRB III® and a calibration magnet, program the Tire Pressure Monitor module for all four sensor/transmitters.
Disconnect the DRB III® and prepare the vehicle for a road test.
Road test the vehicle above 33 km/h (20 MPH) for a minimum of two minutes.
With the DRB III® read the last 32 transmissions received by the Tire Pressure Monitor.

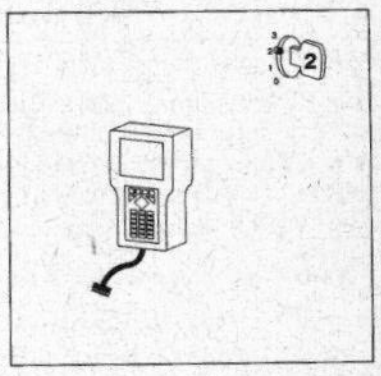

Does the DRB III® display any of the tire pressure transmitter IDs in the last 32 transmissions?

Yes >> Repair is complete.
Perform TIRE PRESSURE MONITOR VERIFICATION TEST.

No >> Replace and program the Tire Pressure Monitor module.
Perform TIRE PRESSURE MONITOR VERIFICATION TEST.

ARM0300000000453

Fig. 4 Tire Pressure Monitor Module Fault. Crossfire

1. **INSPECT TIRE PRESSURE SENSOR/TRANSMITTERS**

Turn the ignition on.
With the DRB III®, read DTCs.

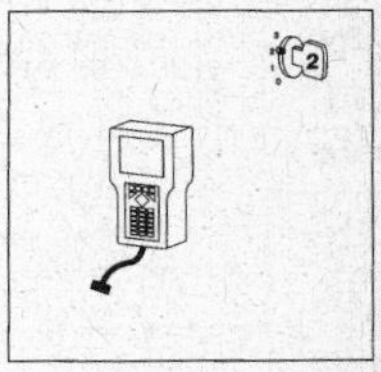

Does the DRB III® display a Sensor/Transmitter Signal Jammed DTC?

Yes >> Replace the Tire Pressure Sensor/Transmitter at the affected wheel.
Perform TIRE PRESSURE MONITOR VERIFICATION TEST.

No >> The condition that caused this DTC is currently not present. Inspect the related wiring harness for a possible intermittent condition.
Perform TIRE PRESSURE MONITOR VERIFICATION TEST.

ARM0300000000455

Fig. 5 Tire Pressure Sensor Transmitter Signal Fault (Part 2 of 2). Crossfire

1. **CHECK FOR CURRENT DTC**

Turn the ignition on.
With the DRB III®, read the TPM DTCs.

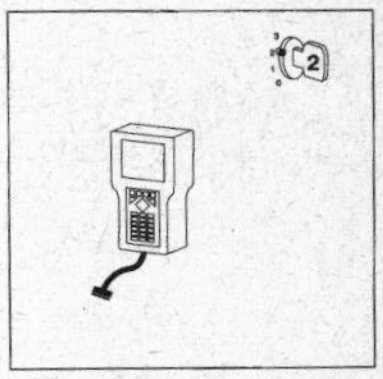

Is this DTC preset?

Yes >> For complete diagnosis of this DTC, refer to TIRE PRESSURE SENSOR/TRANSMITTER SIGNAL JAMMED.

No >> Go To 2

2. **INTERMITTENT WIRING AND CONNECTORS**

The conditions necessary to set this DTC are not present at this time.

Note: Check connectors — Clean/repair as necessary. Poor pin to terminal connections can set DTCs.Using the wiring diagram/schematic as a guide, inspect the wiring and connectors specific to this DTC. Wiggle the wires while checking for shorts and open circuits.

Note: Check for any Technical Service Bulletins that may apply.

Were there any problems found?

Yes >> Repair as necessary.
Perform TIRE PRESSURE VERIFICATION TEST.

No >> The condition that caused this DTC to set is currently not present. Inspect the related wiring harness for a possible intermittent condition.

ARM0300000000456

Fig. 6 Signal Jammed. Crossfire

1. **CHECK FOR CURRENT DTC**

Turn the ignition on.
With the DRB III®, read the TPM DTCs.

Is this DTC preset?

Yes >> For complete diagnosis of this DTC, refer to TIRE PRESSURE SENSOR/TRANSMITTER SIGNAL JAMMED.

No >> Go To 2

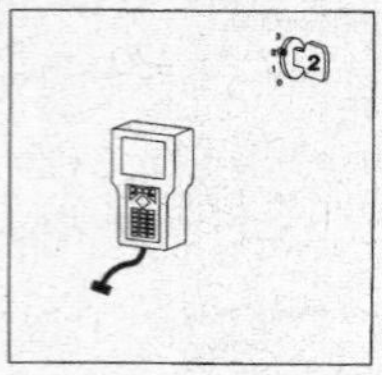

2. **INTERMITTENT WIRING AND CONNECTORS**

The conditions necessary to set this DTC are not present at this time.

Note: Check connectors — Clean/repair as necessary. Poor pin to terminal connections can set DTCs.Using the wiring diagram/schematic as a guide, inspect the wiring and connectors specific to this DTC. Wiggle the wires while checking for shorts and open circuits.

Note: Check for any Technical Service Bulletins that may apply.

Were there any problems found?

Yes >> Repair as necessary.
Perform TIRE PRESSURE VERIFICATION TEST.

No >> The condition that caused this DTC to set is currently not present. Inspect the related wiring harness for a possible intermittent condition.

ARM0300000000457

Fig. 7 Lefthand Front Tire Pressure Sensor Transmitter Signal Jammed. Crossfire

1. **CHECK FOR CURRENT DTC**

Turn the ignition on.
With the DRB III®, read the TPM DTCs.

Is this DTC preset?

Yes >> For complete diagnosis of this DTC, refer to TIRE PRESSURE SENSOR/TRANSMITTER SIGNAL JAMMED.

No >> Go To 2

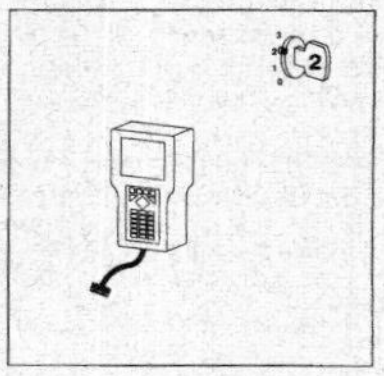

2. **INTERMITTENT WIRING AND CONNECTORS**

The conditions necessary to set this DTC are not present at this time.

Note: Check connectors — Clean/repair as necessary. Poor pin to terminal connections can set DTCs.Using the wiring diagram/schematic as a guide, inspect the wiring and connectors specific to this DTC. Wiggle the wires while checking for shorts and open circuits.

Note: Check for any Technical Service Bulletins that may apply.

Were there any problems found?

Yes >> Repair as necessary.
Perform TIRE PRESSURE VERIFICATION TEST.

No >> The condition that caused this DTC to set is currently not present. Inspect the related wiring harness for a possible intermittent condition.

ARM0300000000458

Fig. 8 Lefthand Rear Tire Pressure Sensor Transmitter Signal Jammed. Crossfire

1. **CHECK FOR CURRENT DTC**

Turn the ignition on.
With the DRB III®, read the TPM DTCs.

Is this DTC preset?

Yes >> For complete diagnosis of this DTC, refer to TIRE PRESSURE SENSOR/TRANSMITTER SIGNAL JAMMED.

No >> Go To 2

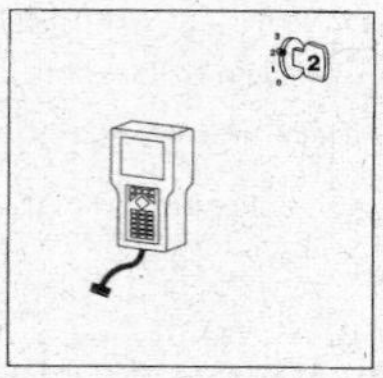

2. **INTERMITTENT WIRING AND CONNECTORS**

The conditions necessary to set this DTC are not present at this time.

Note: Check connectors — Clean/repair as necessary. Poor pin to terminal connections can set DTCs.Using the wiring diagram/schematic as a guide, inspect the wiring and connectors specific to this DTC. Wiggle the wires while checking for shorts and open circuits.

Note: Check for any Technical Service Bulletins that may apply.

Were there any problems found?

Yes >> Repair as necessary.
Perform TIRE PRESSURE VERIFICATION TEST.

No >> The condition that caused this DTC to set is currently not present. Inspect the related wiring harness for a possible intermittent condition.

ARM0300000000459

Fig. 9 Righthand Front Tire Pressure Sensor Transmitter Signal Jammed. Crossfire

1. **CHECK FOR CURRENT DTC**

Turn the ignition on.
With the DRB III®, read the TPM DTCs.

Is this DTC preset?

Yes >> For complete diagnosis of this DTC, refer to TIRE PRESSURE SENSOR/TRANSMITTER SIGNAL JAMMED.

No >> Go To 2

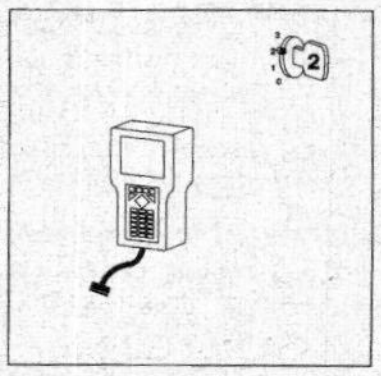

2. **INTERMITTENT WIRING AND CONNECTORS**

The conditions necessary to set this DTC are not present at this time.

Note: Check connectors — Clean/repair as necessary. Poor pin to terminal connections can set DTCs.Using the wiring diagram/schematic as a guide, inspect the wiring and connectors specific to this DTC. Wiggle the wires while checking for shorts and open circuits.

Note: Check for any Technical Service Bulletins that may apply.

Were there any problems found?

Yes >> Repair as necessary.
Perform TIRE PRESSURE VERIFICATION TEST.

No >> The condition that caused this DTC to set is currently not present. Inspect the related wiring harness for a possible intermittent condition.

ARM0300000000460

Fig. 10 Righthand Rear Tire Pressure Sensor Transmitter Signal Jammed. Crossfire

When Monitored and Set Condition

LEFT FRONT TIRE PRESSURE SENSOR/TRANSMITTER

- When Monitored: With the ignition on, the Tire Pressure Monitor (TPM) monitors the tire pressure sensor/transmitters approximately once a minute (60 – 68 seconds) when the vehicle speed is above 33 km/h (20 MPH).
- Set Condition: If the Tire Pressure Monitor (TPM) module receives a transmission from the left front tire pressure sensor/transmitter that the battery is low, the DTC will be set.

LEFT REAR TIRE PRESSURE SENSOR/TRANSMITTER

- When Monitored: With the ignition on, the Tire Pressure Monitor (TPM) monitors the tire pressure sensor/transmitters approximately once a minute (60 – 68 seconds) when the vehicle speed is above 33 km/h (20 MPH).
- Set Condition: If the Tire Pressure Monitor (TPM) module receives a transmission from the left rear tire pressure sensor/transmitter that the battery is low, the DTC will be set.

RIGHT FRONT TIRE PRESSURE SENSOR/TRANSMITTER

- When Monitored: With the ignition on, the Tire Pressure Monitor (TPM) monitors the tire pressure sensor/transmitters approximately once a minute (60 – 68 seconds) when the vehicle speed is above 33 km/h (20 MPH).
- Set Condition: If the Tire Pressure Monitor (TPM) module receives a transmission from the right front tire pressure sensor/transmitter that the battery is low, the DTC will be set.

RIGHT REAR TIRE PRESSURE SENSOR/TRANSMITTER

- When Monitored: With the ignition on, the Tire Pressure Monitor (TPM) monitors the tire pressure sensor/transmitters approximately once a minute (60 – 68 seconds) when the vehicle speed is above 33 km/h (20 MPH).
- Set Condition: If the Tire Pressure Monitor (TPM) module receives a transmission from the right rear tire pressure sensor/transmitter that the battery is low, the DTC will be set.

TRANSMITTER FAILURE

- When Monitored: With the ignition on, the Tire Pressure Monitor (TPM) monitors the tire pressure sensor/transmitters approximately once a minute (60 – 68 seconds) when the vehicle speed is above 33 km/h (20 MPH).
- Set Condition: If the Tire Pressure Monitor (TPM) module receives a transmission from a tire pressure sensor/transmitter that the battery is low, the DTC will be set.

POSSIBLE CAUSES
TIRE PRESSURE SENSOR/TRANSMITTER

ARM0300000000461

Fig. 11 Tire Pressure Sensor Transmitter Inop (Part 1 of 2). Crossfire

1. **INSPECT TIRE PRESSURE SENSOR/TRANSMITTERS**

Turn the ignition on.
With the DRB III®, read DTCs.

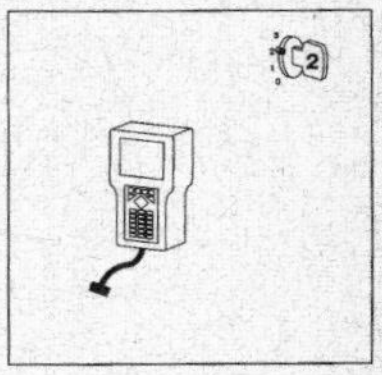

Does the DRB III® display a Tire Pressure Sensor/Transmitter DTC?

Yes >> Replace the Tire Pressure Sensor/Transmitter at the affected wheel.
Perform TIRE PRESSURE MONITOR VERIFICATION TEST.

No >> The condition that caused this DTC is currently not present. Inspect the related wiring harness for a possible intermittent condition.
Perform TIRE PRESSURE MONITOR VERIFICATION TEST.

ARM0300000000462

Fig. 11 Tire Pressure Sensor Transmitter Inop (Part 2 of 2). Crossfire

1. **CHECK FOR CURRENT DTC**

Turn the ignition on.
With the DRB III®, read the TCM DTCs.

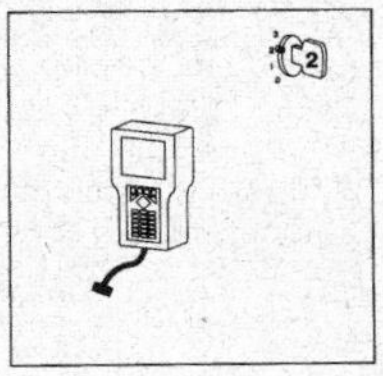

Is this DTC preset?

Yes >> For complete diagnosis of this DTC, refer to TIRE PRESSURE SENSOR/TRANSMITTER.

No >> Go To 2

2. **INTERMITTENT WIRING AND CONNECTORS**

The conditions necessary to set this DTC are not present at this time.

Note: Check connectors — Clean/repair as necessary. Poor pin to terminal connections can set DTCs.Using the wiring diagram/schematic as a guide, inspect the wiring and connectors specific to this DTC. Wiggle the wires while checking for shorts and open circuits.

Note: Check for any Technical Service Bulletins that may apply.

Were there any problems found?

Yes >> Repair as necessary.
Perform TIRE PRESSURE VERIFICATION TEST.

No >> The condition that caused this DTC to set is currently not present. Inspect the related wiring harness for a possible intermittent condition.

ARM0300000000463

Fig. 12 Transmitter Failure. Crossfire

1. **CHECK FOR CURRENT DTC**

Turn the ignition on.
With the DRB III®, read the TCM DTCs.

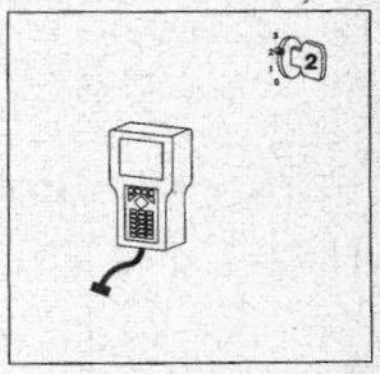

Is this DTC preset?

Yes >> For complete diagnosis of this DTC, refer to TIRE PRESSURE SENSOR/TRANSMITTER.

No >> Go To 2

2. **INTERMITTENT WIRING AND CONNECTORS**

The conditions necessary to set this DTC are not present at this time.

Note: Check connectors — Clean/repair as necessary. Poor pin to terminal connections can set DTCs.Using the wiring diagram/schematic as a guide, inspect the wiring and connectors specific to this DTC. Wiggle the wires while checking for shorts and open circuits.

Note: Check for any Technical Service Bulletins that may apply.

Were there any problems found?

Yes >> Repair as necessary.
Perform TIRE PRESSURE VERIFICATION TEST.

No >> The condition that caused this DTC to set is currently not present. Inspect the related wiring harness for a possible intermittent condition.

ARM0300000000464

Fig. 13 Lefthand Front Tire Pressure Sensor Transmitter. Crossfire

1. **CHECK FOR CURRENT DTC**

Turn the ignition on.
With the DRB III®, read the TCM DTCs.

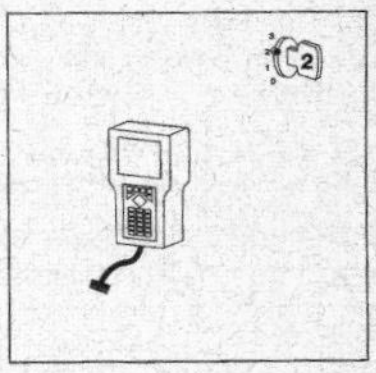

Is this DTC preset?

Yes >> For complete diagnosis of this DTC, refer to TIRE PRESSURE SENSOR/TRANSMITTER.

No >> Go To 2

2. **INTERMITTENT WIRING AND CONNECTORS**

The conditions necessary to set this DTC are not present at this time.

Note: Check connectors — Clean/repair as necessary. Poor pin to terminal connections can set DTCs.Using the wiring diagram/schematic as a guide, inspect the wiring and connectors specific to this DTC. Wiggle the wires while checking for shorts and open circuits.

Note: Check for any Technical Service Bulletins that may apply.

Were there any problems found?

Yes >> Repair as necessary.
Perform TIRE PRESSURE VERIFICATION TEST.

No >> The condition that caused this DTC to set is currently not present. Inspect the related wiring harness for a possible intermittent condition.

ARM0300000000465

Fig. 14 Lefthand Rear Tire Pressure Sensor Transmitter. Crossfire

1. CHECK FOR CURRENT DTC

Turn the ignition on.
With the DRB III®, read the TCM DTCs.

Is this DTC preset?

Yes >> For complete diagnosis of this DTC, refer to TIRE PRESSURE SENSOR/TRANSMITTER.

No >> Go To 2

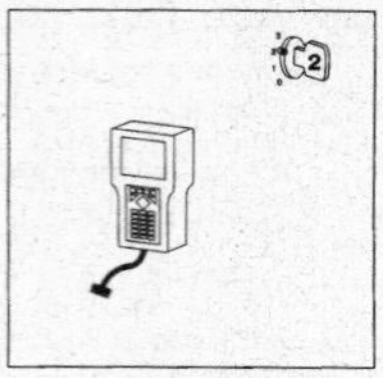

2. INTERMITTENT WIRING AND CONNECTORS

The conditions necessary to set this DTC are not present at this time.

Note: Check connectors — Clean/repair as necessary. Poor pin to terminal connections can set DTCs.Using the wiring diagram/schematic as a guide, inspect the wiring and connectors specific to this DTC. Wiggle the wires while checking for shorts and open circuits.

Note: Check for any Technical Service Bulletins that may apply.

Were there any problems found?

Yes >> Repair as necessary.
Perform TIRE PRESSURE VERIFICATION TEST.

No >> The condition that caused this DTC to set is currently not present. Inspect the related wiring harness for a possible intermittent condition.

ARM0300000000466

Fig. 15 Righthand Front Tire Pressure Sensor Transmitter. Crossfire

When Monitored And Set Condition

LEFT FRONT TIRE PRESSURE SENSOR/TRANSMITTER LOW BATTERY

- When Monitored: With the ignition on, the Tire Pressure Monitor (TPM) monitors the tire pressure sensor/transmitters approximately once a minute (60 – 68 seconds) when the vehicle speed is above 33 km/h (20 MPH).
- Set Condition: If the Tire Pressure Monitor (TPM) module receives a transmission from the left front tire pressure sensor/transmitter that the battery is low, the DTC will be set.

LEFT REAR TIRE PRESSURE SENSOR/TRANSMITTER LOW BATTERY

- When Monitored: With the ignition on, the Tire Pressure Monitor (TPM) monitors the tire pressure sensor/transmitters approximately once a minute (60 – 68 seconds) when the vehicle speed is above 33 km/h (20 MPH).
- Set Condition: If the Tire Pressure Monitor (TPM) module receives a transmission from the left rear tire pressure sensor/transmitter that the battery is low, the DTC will be set.

RIGHT FRONT TIRE PRESSURE SENSOR/TRANSMITTER LOW BATTERY

- When Monitored: With the ignition on, the Tire Pressure Monitor (TPM) monitors the tire pressure sensor/transmitters approximately once a minute (60 – 68 seconds) when the vehicle speed is above 33 km/h (20 MPH).
- Set Condition: If the Tire Pressure Monitor (TPM) module receives a transmission from the right front tire pressure sensor/transmitter that the battery is low, the DTC will be set.

RIGHT REAR TIRE PRESSURE SENSOR/TRANSMITTER LOW BATTERY

- When Monitored: With the ignition on, the Tire Pressure Monitor (TPM) monitors the tire pressure sensor/transmitters approximately once a minute (60 – 68 seconds) when the vehicle speed is above 33 km/h (20 MPH).
- Set Condition: If the Tire Pressure Monitor (TPM) module receives a transmission from the right rear tire pressure sensor/transmitter that the battery is low, the DTC will be set.

LOW BATTERY

- When Monitored: With the ignition on, the Tire Pressure Monitor (TPM) monitors the tire pressure sensor/transmitters approximately once a minute (60 – 68 seconds) when the vehicle speed is above 33 km/h (20 MPH).
- Set Condition: If the Tire Pressure Monitor (TPM) module receives a transmission from a tire pressure sensor/transmitter that the battery is low, the DTC will be set.

POSSIBLE CAUSES
TIRE PRESSURE SENSOR/TRANSMITTER LOW BATTERY

ARM0300000000468

Fig. 17 Tire Pressure Sensor Transmitter Low Battery (Part 1 of 2). Crossfire

1. Check for current DTC

Disconnect all jumper wires and reconnect all previously disconnected components and connectors.

Drive the vehicle at 40 km/h (25 MPH) for at least 2 minutes.

With the DRB III®, confirm that no DTCs are present and that all components are functioning properly.

If a DTC is present, refer to the appropriate category and select the corresponding symptom.

Are any DTCs present?

YES >> Repair is not complete, refer to appropriate symptom.

NO >> Repair is complete.

ARM0300000000470

Fig. 18 Tire Pressure Verification Test. Crossfire

1. CHECK FOR CURRENT DTC

Turn the ignition on.
With the DRB III®, read the TCM DTCs.

Is this DTC preset?

Yes >> For complete diagnosis of this DTC, refer to TIRE PRESSURE SENSOR/TRANSMITTER.

No >> Go To 2

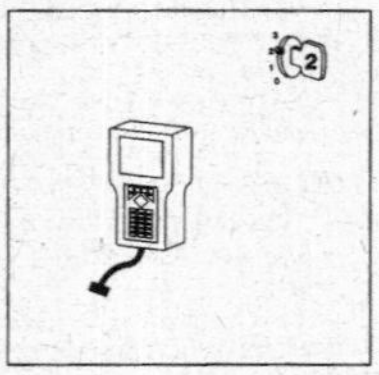

2. INTERMITTENT WIRING AND CONNECTORS

The conditions necessary to set this DTC are not present at this time.

Note: Check connectors — Clean/repair as necessary. Poor pin to terminal connections can set DTCs.Using the wiring diagram/schematic as a guide, inspect the wiring and connectors specific to this DTC. Wiggle the wires while checking for shorts and open circuits.

Note: Check for any Technical Service Bulletins that may apply.

Were there any problems found?

Yes >> Repair as necessary.
Perform TIRE PRESSURE VERIFICATION TEST.

No >> The condition that caused this DTC to set is currently not present. Inspect the related wiring harness for a possible intermittent condition.

ARM0300000000467

Fig. 16 Righthand Rear Tire Pressure Sensor Transmitter. Crossfire

1. INSPECT TIRE PRESSURE SENSOR/TRANSMITTERS

Turn the ignition on.
With the DRB III®, read DTCs.

Does the DRB III® display a Sensor/Transmitter Low Battery DTC?

Yes >> Replace the Tire Pressure Sensor/Transmitter at the affected wheel
Perform TIRE PRESSURE MONITOR VERIFICATION TEST.

No >> The condition that caused this DTC is currently not present. Inspect the related wiring harness for a possible intermittent condition.
Perform TIRE PRESSURE MONITOR VERIFICATION TEST.

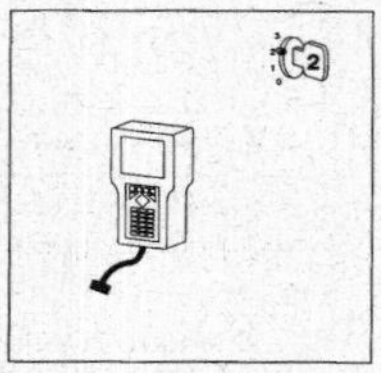

ARM0300000000469

Fig. 17 Tire Pressure Sensor Transmitter Low Battery (Part 2 of 2). Crossfire

Test Note: All symptoms listed above are diagnosed using the same tests. The title for the tests will be LF SENSOR BATTERY LOW.

When Monitored and Set Condition:

LF SENSOR BATTERY LOW

When Monitored: Key ON.

Set Condition: When the EVIC detects a low battery condition from the LF Sensor/Transmitter.

LF TIRE PRESSURE SENSOR FAILURE

When Monitored: Key ON.

Set Condition: When the EVIC detects a no-transmit condition from the LF Sensor/Transmitter.

LR SENSOR BATTERY LOW

When Monitored: Key ON.

Set Condition: When the EVIC detects a low battery condition from the LR Sensor/Transmitter.

LR TIRE PRESSURE SENSOR FAILURE

When Monitored: Key ON.

Set Condition: When the EVIC detects a no-transmit condition from the LR Sensor/Transmitter.

RF SENSOR BATTERY LOW

When Monitored: Key ON.

Set Condition: When the EVIC detects a low battery condition from the RF Sensor/Transmitter.

ARM66CR000000066

Fig. 19 TPM diagnosis & testing (Part 1 of 3). 300M

RF TIRE PRESSURE SENSOR FAILURE

When Monitored: Key ON.

Set Condition: When the EVIC detects a no-transmit condition from the RF Sensor/Transmitter.

RR SENSOR BATTERY LOW

When Monitored: Key ON.

Set Condition: When the EVIC detects a low battery condition from the RR Sensor/Transmitter.

RR TIRE PRESSURE SENSOR FAILURE

When Monitored: Key ON.

Set Condition: When the EVIC detects a no-transmit condition from the RR Sensor/Transmitter.

SPARE TIRE PRESSURE SENSOR FAILURE

When Monitored: Key ON.

Set Condition: When the EVIC detects a no-transmit condition from the Spare Tire Sensor/Transmitter.

SPARE TIRE SENSOR BATTERY LOW

When Monitored: Key ON.

Set Condition: When the EVIC detects a low battery condition from the Spare Tire Sensor/Transmitter.

POSSIBLE CAUSES
EVIC INTERNAL FAULT
SENSOR/TRANSMITTER INTERNAL FAULT

TEST	ACTION
1	Using the procedure in the System Description, retrain the EVIC With the DRBIII®, record and erase DTC's. Drive the vehicle for 10 minutes at 32 km/h (20 mph). With the DRBIII®, read DTCs. Does the DRBIII® display a Sensor Failure or Sensor Low Battery message? Yes → Replace the indicated Tire Pressure Sensor/Transmitter. Perform TIRE PRESSURE VERIFICATION TEST. No → Go To 2

ARM66CR000000067

Fig. 19 TPM diagnosis & testing (Part 2 of 3). 300M

TEST	ACTION
2	Turn the ignition on. Observe the EVIC display. Does the EVIC display SERVICE TIRE PRESS. SYSTEM? Yes → Replace the EVIC Perform TIRE PRESSURE VERIFICATION TEST. No → Test Complete.

ARM66CR000000068

Fig. 19 TPM diagnosis & testing (Part 3 of 3). 300M

TIRE PRESSURE VERIFICATION TEST
1. Perform the EVIC training as instructed in the System Description. 2. Using the DRBIII® or the EVIC RESET button, set the EVIC to Diagnostics mode (blank screen). **3. NOTE: Set the EVIC as follows:** 4. Press and hold the EVIC RESET button for five seconds (EVIC will beep). 5. Set the EVIC to display BLOCK COUNTERS. **6. NOTE: A vehicle graphic will display showing counters at wheel locations.** 7. Drive the vehicle at 40 km/h (25 mph) for at least 2 minutes. 8. Observe that the counters increment at least 3 sensor/transmitter receptions for each wheel. Can the EVIC be trained and do the counters show Sensor/Transmitter receptions? Yes → Repair is complete. No → Refer to Diagnosing System Faults in the Description and Operation for this system.

ARM66CR000000069

Fig. 20 Tire pressure verification test. 300M

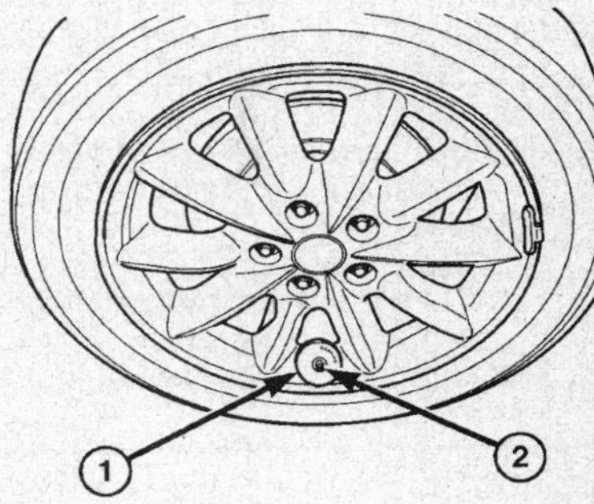

1 - RE-LEARN MAGNET
2 - VALVE STEM

ARM66CR000000072

Fig. 21 Pressure moitior sensor programming. 300M

COMPONENT SERVICE

Pressure Monitor Sensor Programming

CROSSFIRE

The vehicle's tires must not have been rotated above 5 mph in the last two minutes prior to programming.

1. Connect a suitably programmed DRB scan tool to Data Link Connector (DLC).
2. Access CHASSIS SYSTEMS.
3. Select TIRE PRESSURE MONITOR.
4. Select appropriate function from menu.
5. Place a magnet special tool No. 8821 at valve stem of required wheel.
6. DRB scan tool will display PROGRAM TRANSMITTER COMPLETE or direct you to next wheel.
7. Remove magnet, unless programming entire module, then proceed to next wheel.
8. Exit function once programming complete.
9. Verify module programming as indicated by sensor id's in SENSOR DISPLAY.

300M

To train the EVIC to recognize the source locations of pressure sensor signals, proceed as follows:

1. Locate RETAIN TIRE SENSORS — NO on EVIC menu. Press STEP button to select YES.
2. EVIC display will prompt: TRAIN LEFT FRONT TIRE .
3. Position relearn magnet special tool No. 8821, or equivalent magnet, over lefthand front valve stem for at least five seconds, **Fig. 21.**
4. When EVIC has received transmitted message from Remote Tire Pressure Monitor (RTPM), it will chirp horn and display next train request.
5. There is a 60-second timer for learning the first tire location and 30 seconds between remaining tires. If timer expires, EVIC will abort training procedure and display TRAINING ABORTED. Any IDs learned during current session will be discarded.
6. EVIC will request initiation of training sequence for each tire, one-by-one in clockwise direction

COMPONENT REPLACEMENT

Pressure Monitor Sensor, Replace

CROSSFIRE

1. Remove tire and wheel assembly from vehicle.
2. Remove balancing weights from wheel.
3. Remove valve cap, then the valve stem using suitable tool.
4. Remove valve stem nut attaching sensor to wheel.
5. Break down upper and bottom bead on tire, then dismount upper bead.
6. Remove tire pressure sensor transmitter from tire.
7. Reverse procedure to install, noting the following:
   a. When tightening tire pressure sensor, hold sensor in position.
   b. **Torque** sensor nut to 35 inch lbs.

300M

The valve stem cap contains an O-ring seal. **Do not substitute a regular valve stem cap.**

The valve stem is made of aluminum with a nickel plated brass core. **Do not substitute a valve stem core made of a different material.**

REMOVAL

1. Raise and support vehicle, then remove tire and wheel assembly.

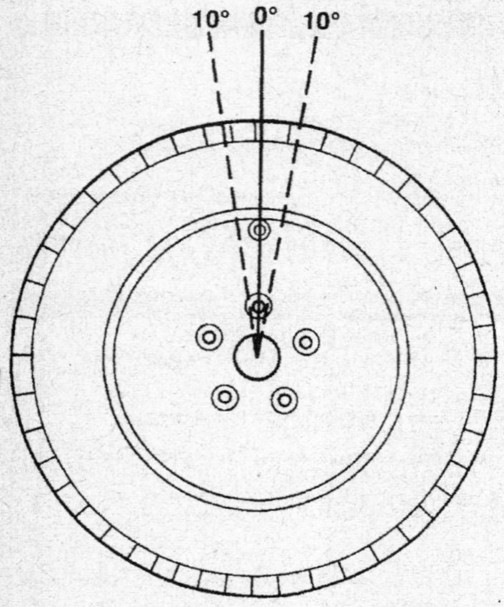

ARM66CR000000070

Fig. 22 Tire dismount tool location

2. Dismount tire following tire changer manufacturer's instructions, noting the following:
   a. Avoid breaking tire bead from rim in sensor area on both front and back sides.
   b. When dismounting tire, inset mount/dismount tool at within 10° of valve stem, **Fig. 22.**
3. Remove sensor to wheel nut using

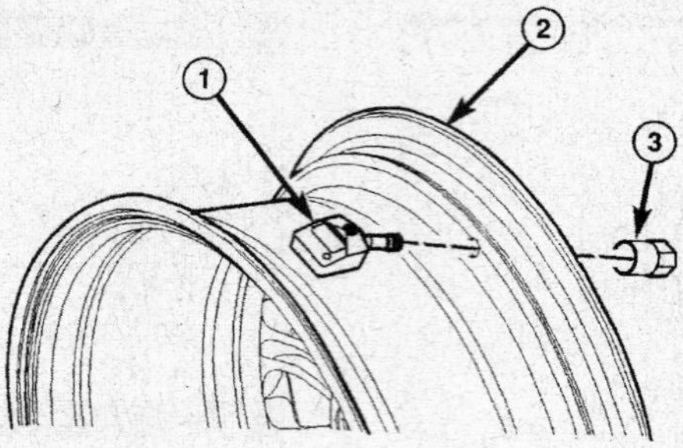

1 - TIRE PRESSURE SENSOR
2 - WHEEL
3 - NUT

ARM66CR000000071

Fig. 23 Pressure monitor sensor replacement

suitable thin wall socket, then the sensor.

INSTALLATION

1. Clean contact area and install new valve stem sealing grommet.
2. Install sensor, **Fig. 23.**
3. Mount tire following tire changer manufacturer's instructions, noting the following:
   a. Mount wheel on changer with valve stem 210° clockwise from tool or changer head.
   b. Ensure sensor is clear on lower bead breaker area.
   c. **On changers that rotate wheel,**

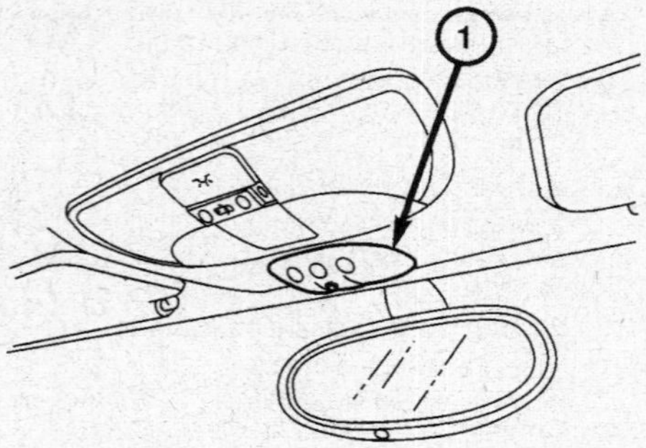

ARM0300000000471

Fig. 24 Tire pressure module removal. Crossfire

rotate wheel clockwise.
   d. **On changers that rotate tool,** rotate tool counterclockwise.
4. Install tire and wheel assembly, then lower vehicle.
5. Retrain tire pressure sensors as outlined under "Pressure Monitor Sensor Programming."

Tire Pressure Module

CROSSFIRE

1. Remove module using suitable plastic wedge in between headliner and TPM, **Fig. 24.**
2. Reverse procedure to install.

DASH GAUGES & WARNING INDICATORS

NOTE: On Air Bag Equipped Models, Refer To "Air Bag System Precautions" Located In The Front Of This Manual For System Disarming & Arming Procedures.

NOTE: Refer To "Computer Relearn Procedures" Located In The Front Of This Manual When Battery Power To The Computer Has Been Interrupted.

NOTE: "Electrical Symbol & Wire Color Code Identification" Located In The Front Of This Manual May Be Used As An Aid When Using Wiring Circuits Found In This Section.

NOTE: Refer To The "Dash Panel Service" Section For Dash Panel Removal Procedures.

NOTE: Refer To The "Electronic Instrumentation" Section In MOTOR's "Domestic Engine Performance & Driveability Manual" For Information Related To Electronic Instrumentation.

INDEX

PRECAUTIONS

Air Bag Systems

Refer to "Air Bag System Precautions" in front of this manual for system disarming and arming procedures.

Battery Ground Cable

Prior to service, disconnect battery ground cable and isolate as required.

TROUBLESHOOTING

Air Bag Warning Lamp

Air bag warning lamp illuminates when there is an air bag system concern.

Refer to **MOTOR's "Air Bag Manual" or "Air Bag Diagnostics CD."**

Anti-Lock Brake Warning Lamp

The Anti-lock brake warning lamp will illuminate if the system controller detects any fault in the anti-lock brake system. Normal brake system operation will remain operational, but wheels could lock during panic stop.

Refer to "Anti-Lock Brake" chapter.

Brake Warning Lamp

1. Brake fluid level switch.
2. Low brake fluid level.
3. Parking brake system.
4. Instrument cluster and circuit.
5. Ignition switch and ABS module.
6. Miniature bulb and brake check relay.

Charging System Warning Lamp

1. Wiring circuits and bulb.
2. Instrument cluster and battery.
3. Alternator.
4. Inspect fuse and voltage regulator.
5. Inspect for corroded terminals.
6. Inspect Powertrain Control Module (PCM).

Check Engine Warning Lamp

Check engine or Malfunction Indicator Lamp (MIL) indicator is illuminated by Powertrain Control Module (PCM). Refer to

MOTOR's "Air Bag Manual" or "Air Bag Diagnostics CD."

Low Coolant Warning Lamp

1. Wiring circuits and bulb.
2. Low coolant level switch.
3. Instrument cluster.
4. Generic electronic module.

Low Fuel Level Warning Lamp

1. Fuel gauge and fuel indicator module.
2. Instrument cluster circuit.
3. Miniature bulb.
4. Fuel sender and Rear Electronic Module (REM).

Low Oil Level Warning Lamp

1. Wiring Circuits and bulb.
2. Oil pressure switch.
3. Low engine oil.
4. Instrument cluster.

Low Oil Pressure Warning Lamp

1. Wiring Circuits and bulb.
2. Oil pressure switch.
3. Low engine oil pressure.
4. Low engine oil.
5. Instrument cluster.

Low Tire Pressure Warning Lamp

1. Low tire pressure.
2. Low tire pressure sensor and bulb.
3. Low tire pressure module.
4. Wiring circuits and fuse.

Low Washer Fluid Warning Lamp

1. Wiring circuits and bulb.
2. Windshield washer low fluid switch.
3. Instrument cluster.
4. Low washer fluid level.
5. Indicator lamp module and sensor.

Safety Belt Warning Lamp

1. Wiring circuits and bulb.
2. Safety belt switch and fuse.
3. Instrument cluster.
4. Generic electronic module.

WIRING DIAGRAMS

Continental

Refer to **Figs. 1 and 2,** for instrument cluster wiring diagrams.

Contour & Mystique

Refer to **Fig. 3,** for instrument cluster wiring diagram.

Cougar

Refer to **Figs. 4 and 5,** for instrument cluster wiring diagrams.

Crown Victoria & Grand Marquis

Refer to **Figs. 6 through 10,** for instrument cluster wiring diagrams.

Escort & ZX2

Refer to **Figs. 11 and 12,** for instrument cluster wiring diagrams.

Focus

Refer to **Figs. 13 through 15,** for instrument cluster wiring diagrams.

LS

Refer to **Figs. 16 and 17,** for instrument cluster wiring diagrams.

Marauder

Refer to **Fig. 18,** for instrument cluster wiring diagram.

Mustang

Refer to **Figs. 19 and 20,** for instrument cluster wiring diagrams.

Sable & Taurus

Refer to **Figs. 21 through 24,** for instrument cluster wiring diagrams for gasoline and Flex Fuel Vehicles (FFV).

Thunderbird

Refer to **Fig. 25,** for instrument cluster wiring diagram.

Town Car

Refer to **Figs. 26 through 28,** for instrument cluster wiring diagrams.

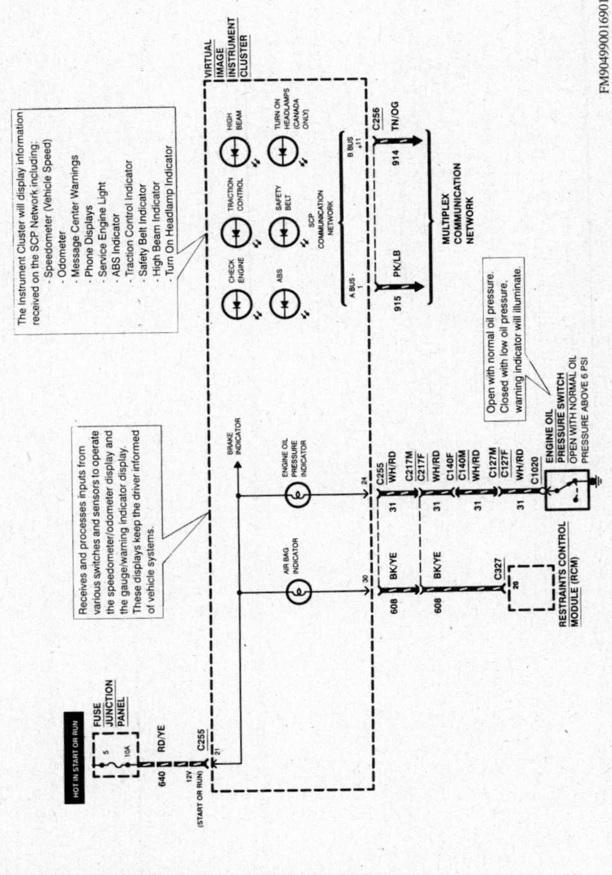

Fig. 1 Instrument cluster wiring diagram (Part 1 of 5). 2000–01 Continental

FM9049900169010X

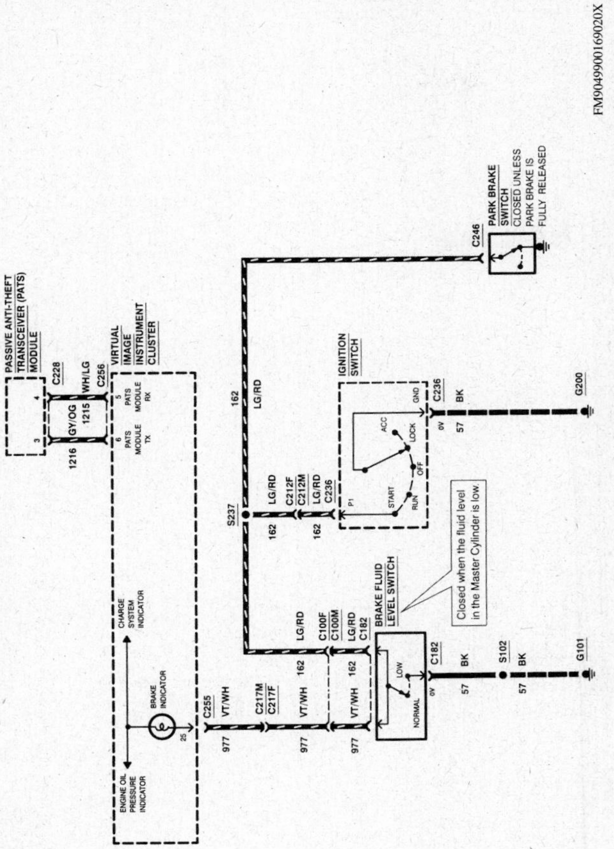

Fig. 1 Instrument cluster wiring diagram (Part 2 of 5). 2000–01 Continental

FM9049900169020X

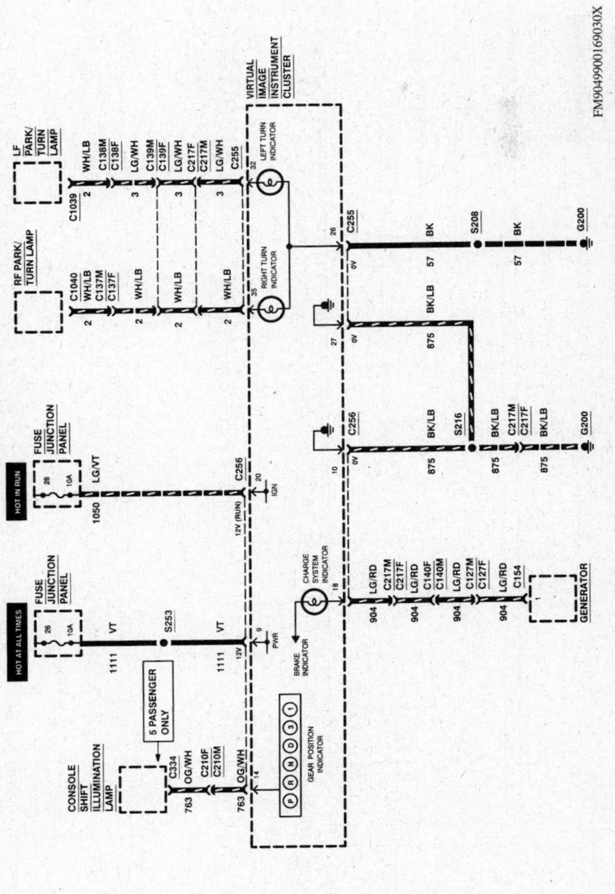

Fig. 1 Instrument cluster wiring diagram (Part 3 of 5). 2000–01 Continental

FM9049900169030X

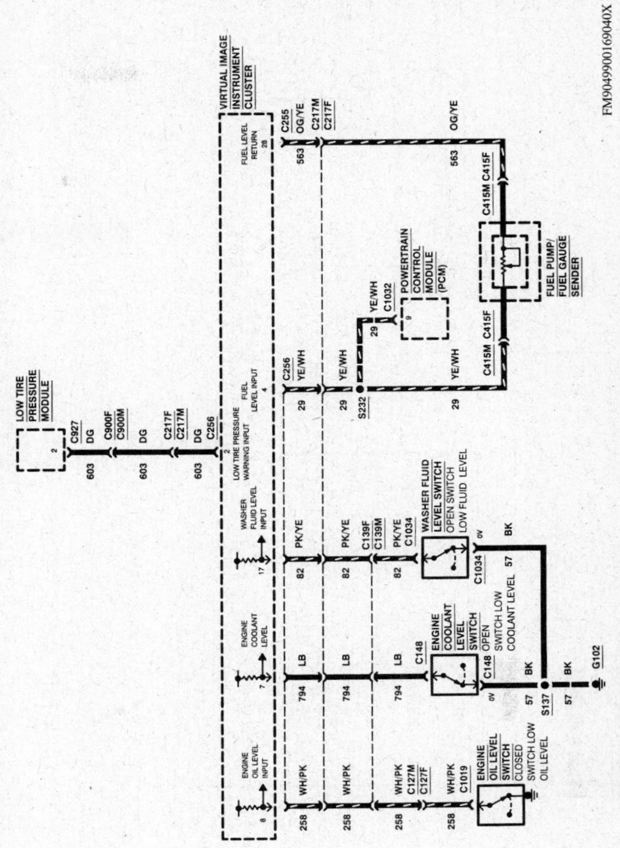

Fig. 1 Instrument cluster wiring diagram (Part 4 of 5). 2000–01 Continental

FM9049900169040X

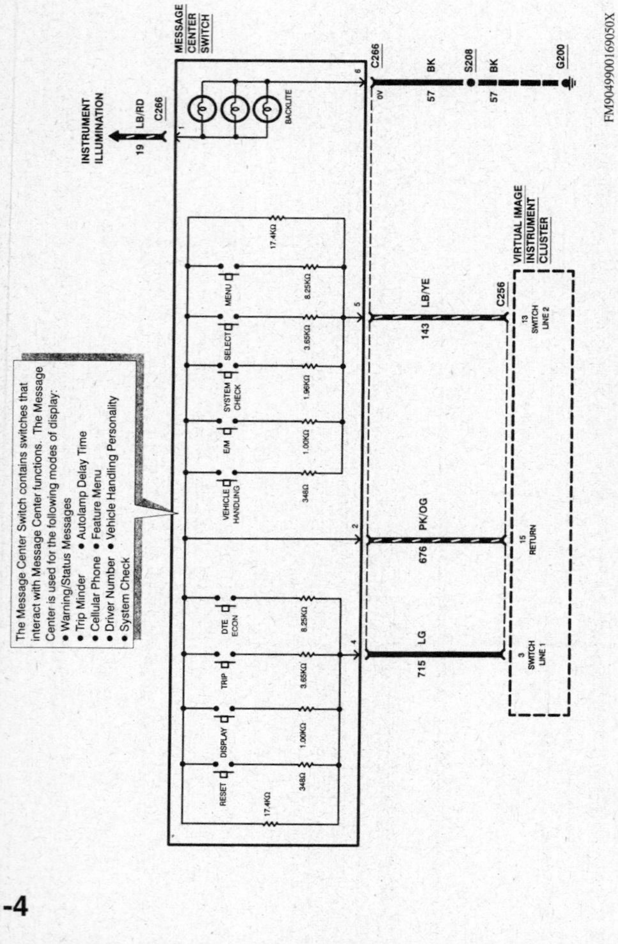

The Message Center Switch contains switches that interact with Message Center functions. The Message Center is used for the following modes of display:
• Warning/Status Messages
• Trip Minder • Autolamp Delay Time
• Cellular Phone • Feature Menu
• Driver Number • Vehicle Handling Personality
• System Check
INSTRUMENT ILLUMINATION
MESSAGE CENTER SWITCH
VIRTUAL IMAGE INSTRUMENT CLUSTER
BACKLITE
FM9049900169050X

Fig. 1 Instrument cluster wiring diagram (Part 5 of 5). 2000–01 Continental

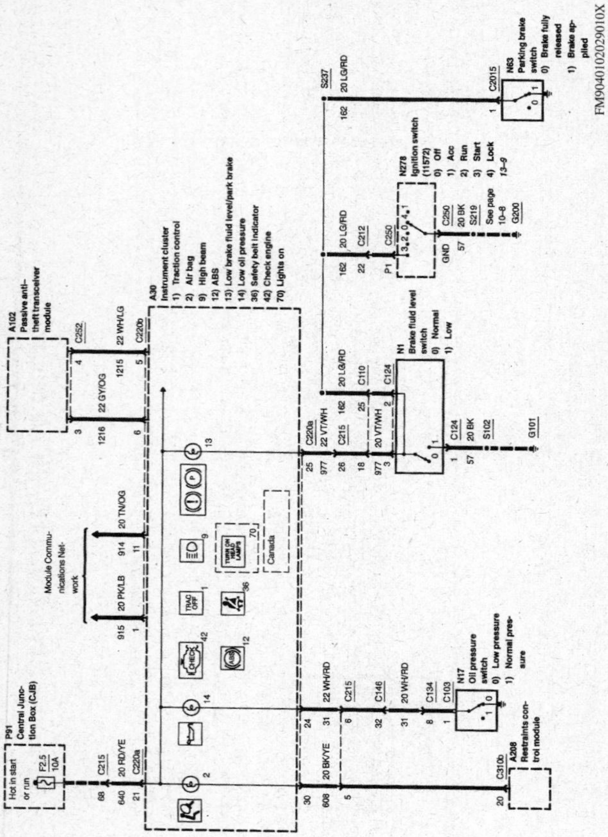

Fig. 2 Instrument cluster wiring diagram (Part 1 of 4). 2002–04 Continental

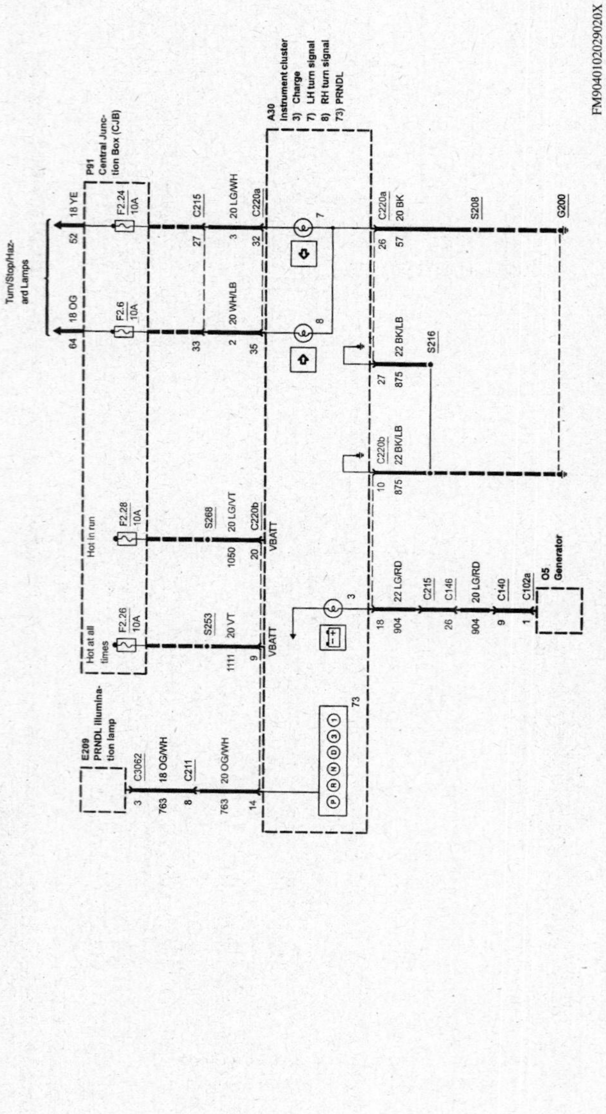

Fig. 2 Instrument cluster wiring diagram (Part 2 of 4). 2002–04 Continental

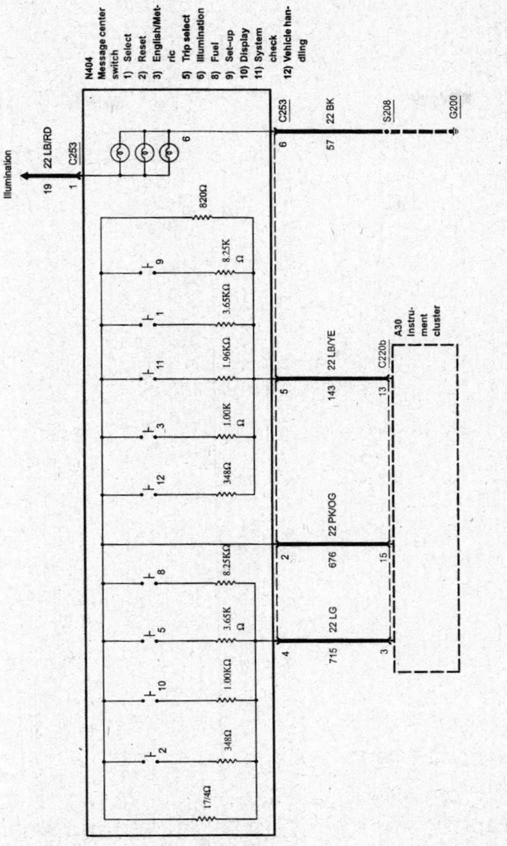

FM9040102029040X

Fig. 2 Instrument cluster wiring diagram (Part 4 of 4). 2002–04 Continental

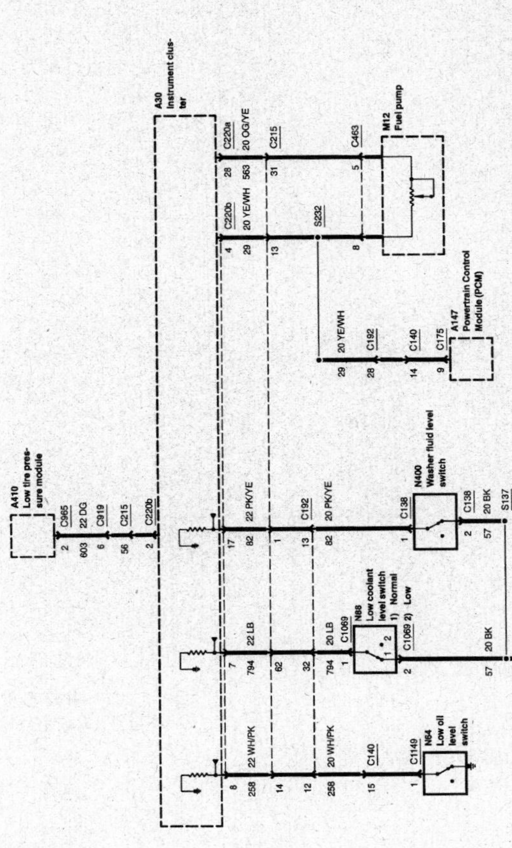

FM9040102029030X

Fig. 2 Instrument cluster wiring diagram (Part 3 of 4). 2002–04 Continental

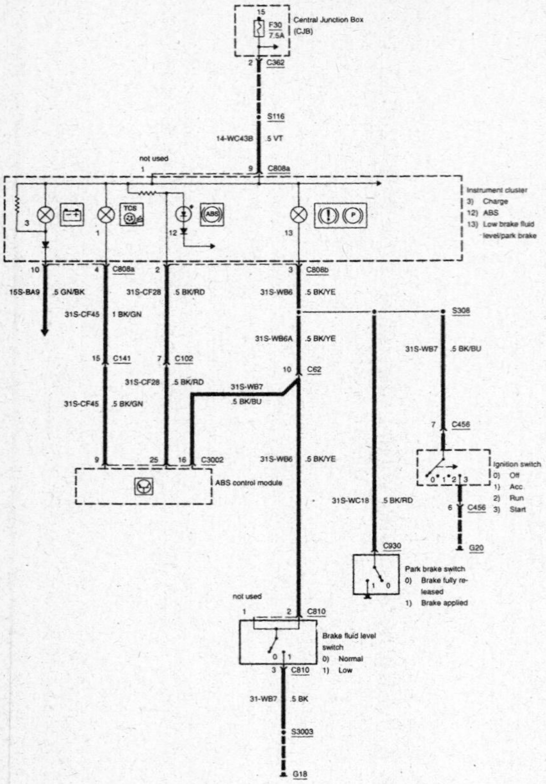

FM1049900437010X

Fig. 3 Instrument cluster wiring diagram (Part 1 of 5). Contour & Mystique w/ABS

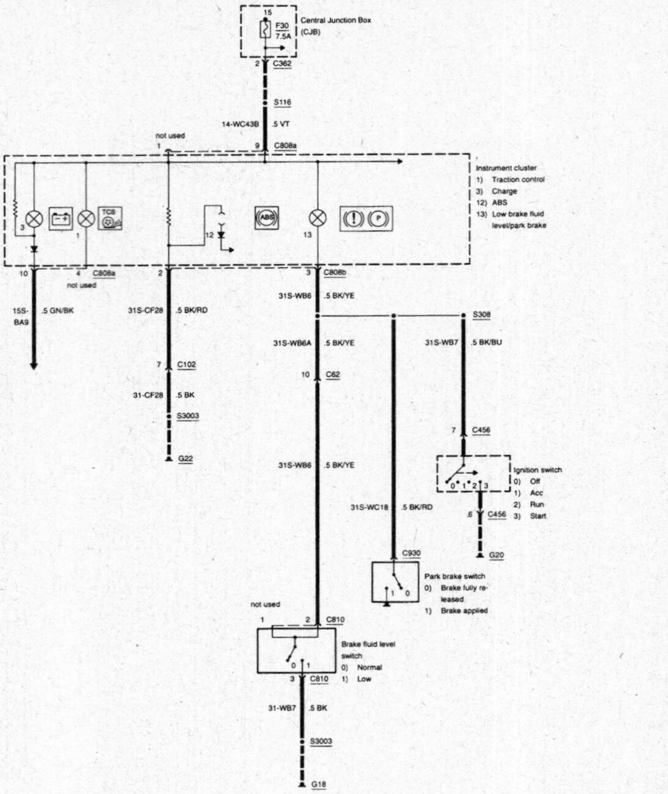

FM1049900437020X

Fig. 3 Instrument cluster wiring diagram (Part 1 of 5). Contour & Mystique less ABS

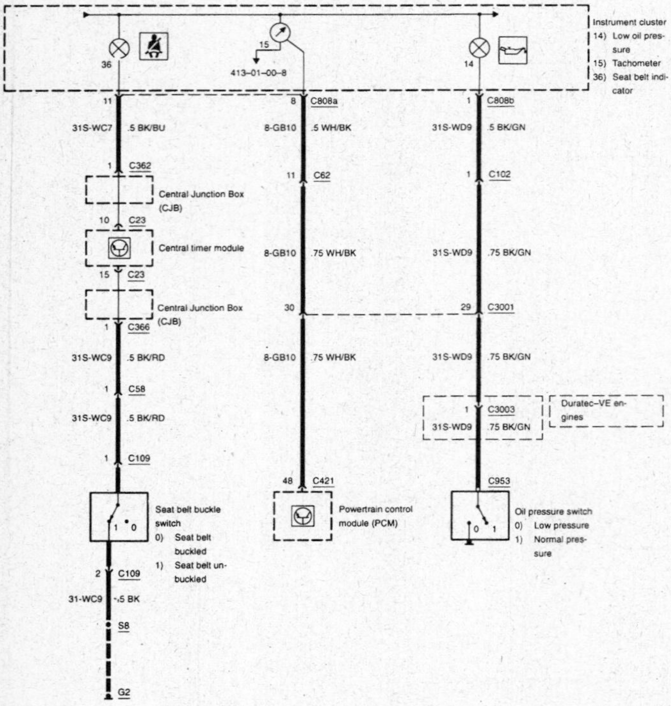

FM1049900437030X

Fig. 3 Instrument cluster wiring diagram (Part 2 of 5). Contour & Mystique w/tachometer

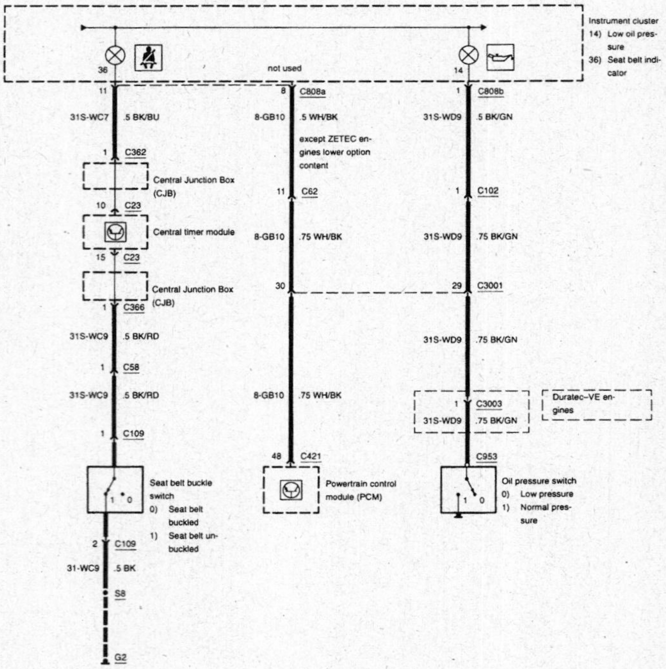

FM1049900437040X

Fig. 3 Instrument cluster wiring diagram (Part 2 of 5). Contour & Mystique less tachometer

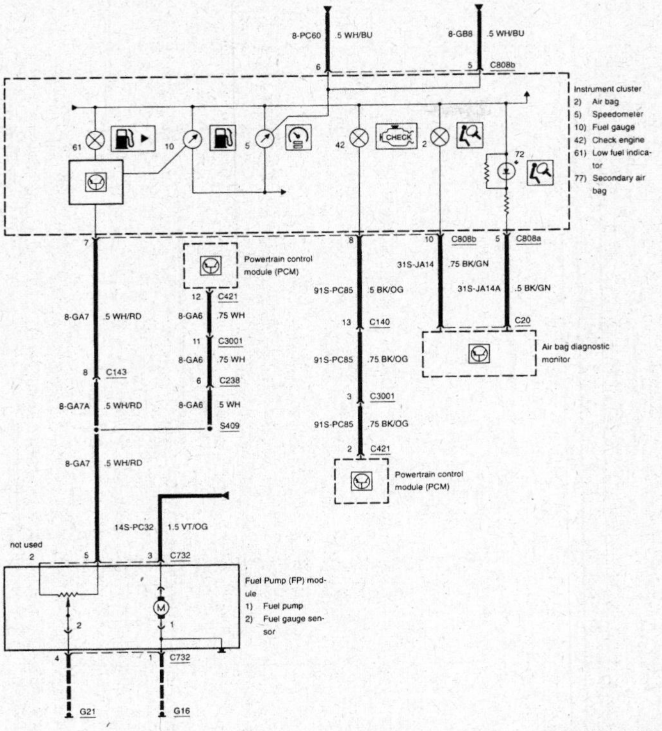

FM1049900437050X

Fig. 3 Instrument cluster wiring diagram (Part 3 of 5). Contour & Mystique w/automatic transmission

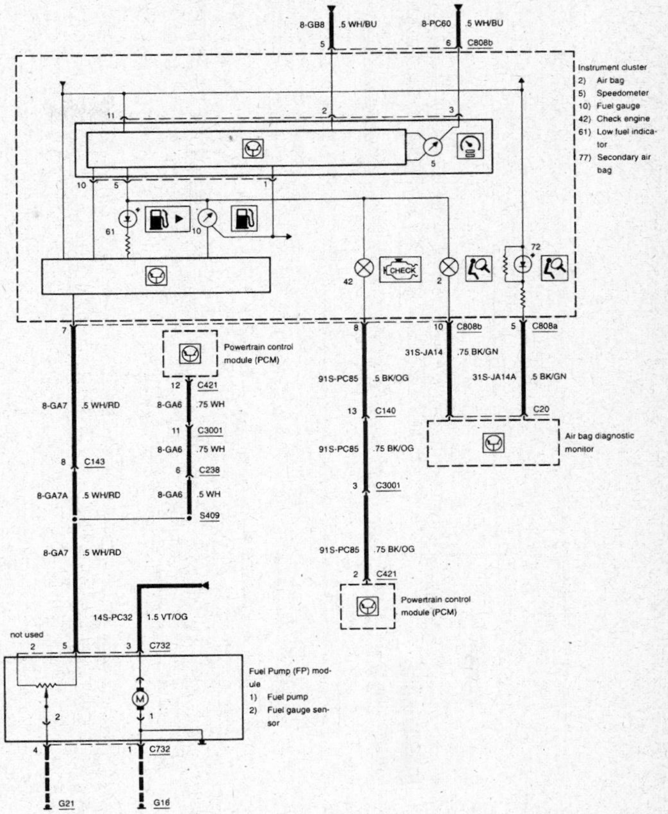

FM1049900437060X

Fig. 3 Instrument cluster wiring diagram (Part 3 of 5). Contour & Mystique w/manual transmission

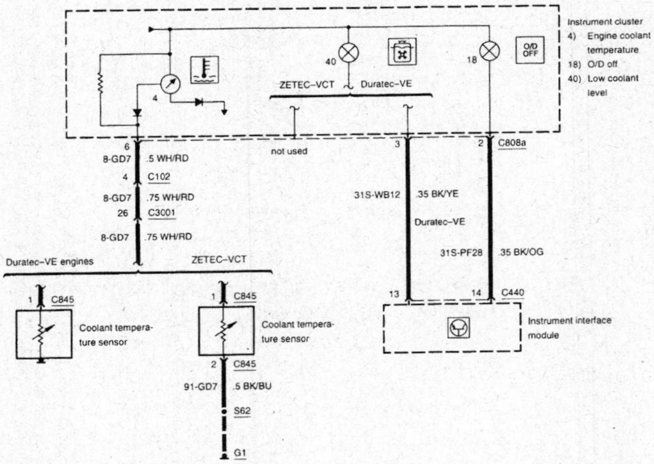

FM1049900437070X

Fig. 3 Instrument cluster wiring diagram (Part 4 of 5). Contour & Mystique

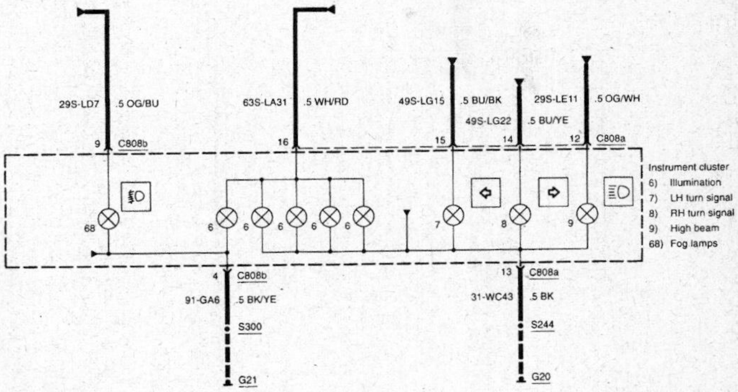

FM1049900437080X

Fig. 3 Instrument cluster wiring diagram (Part 5 of 5). Contour & Mystique

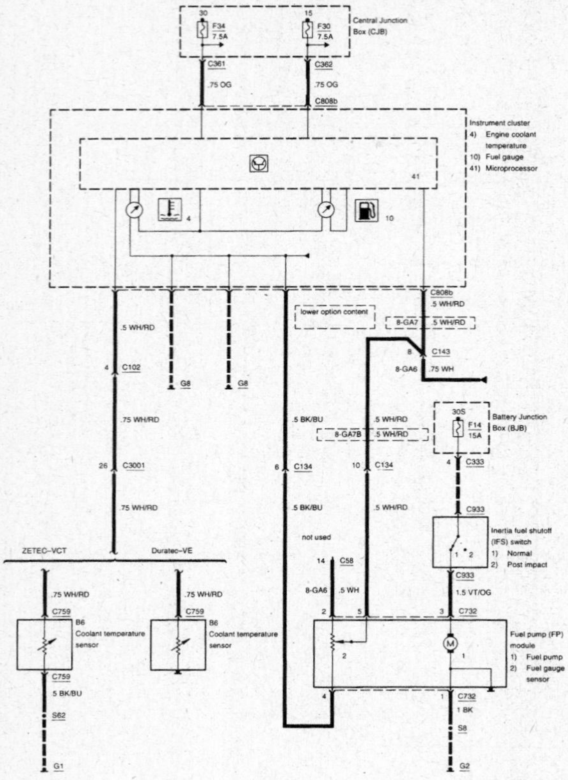

FM1049900365010X

Fig. 4 Instrument cluster wiring diagram (Part 1 of 7). 2000–01 Cougar

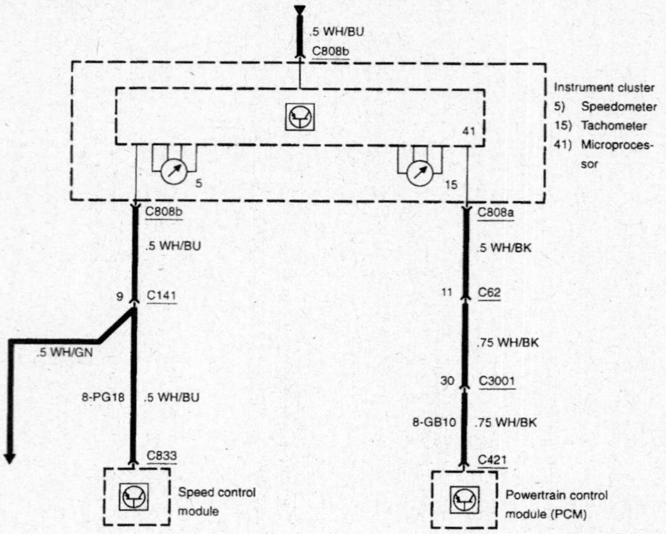

FM1049900365020X

Fig. 4 Instrument cluster wiring diagram (Part 2 of 7). 2000–01 Cougar

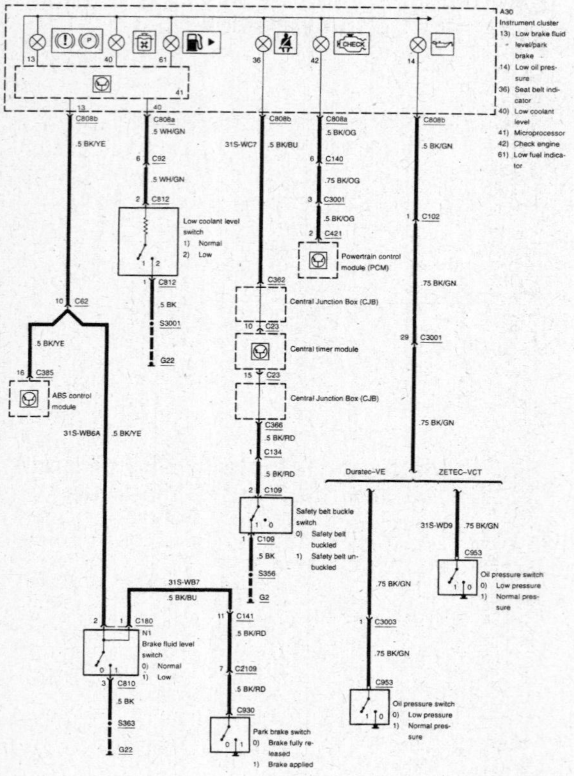

FM1049900365030X

Fig. 4 Instrument cluster wiring diagram (Part 3 of 7). 2000–01 Cougar

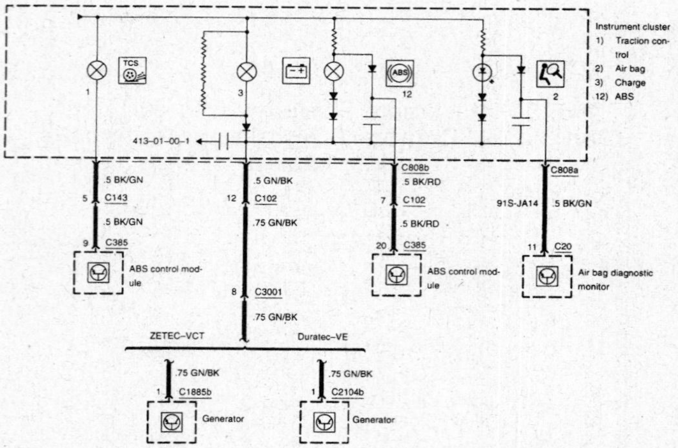

FM1049900365040X

Fig. 4 Instrument cluster wiring diagram (Part 4 of 7). 2000–01 Cougar

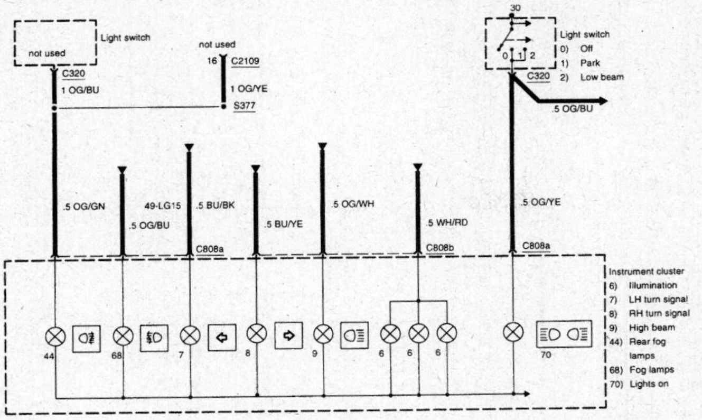

FM1049900365050X

Fig. 4 Instrument cluster wiring diagram (Part 5 of 7). 2000–01 Cougar

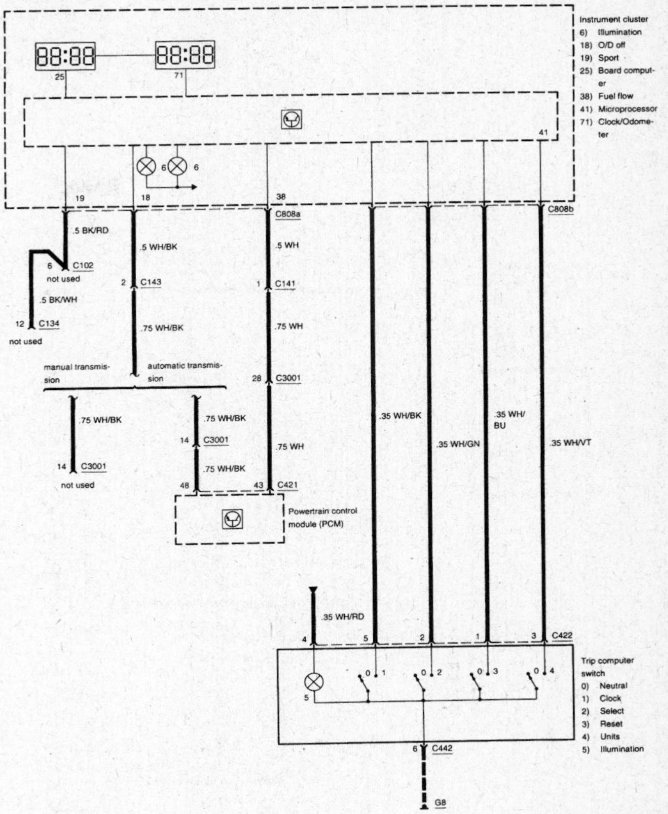

FM1049900365060X

Fig. 4 Instrument cluster wiring diagram (Part 6 of 7). 2000–01 Cougar

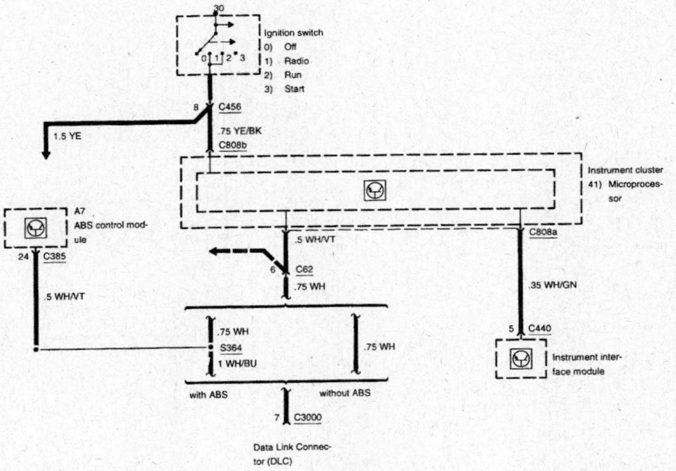

FM1049900365070X

Fig. 4 Instrument cluster wiring diagram (Part 7 of 7). 2000–01 Cougar

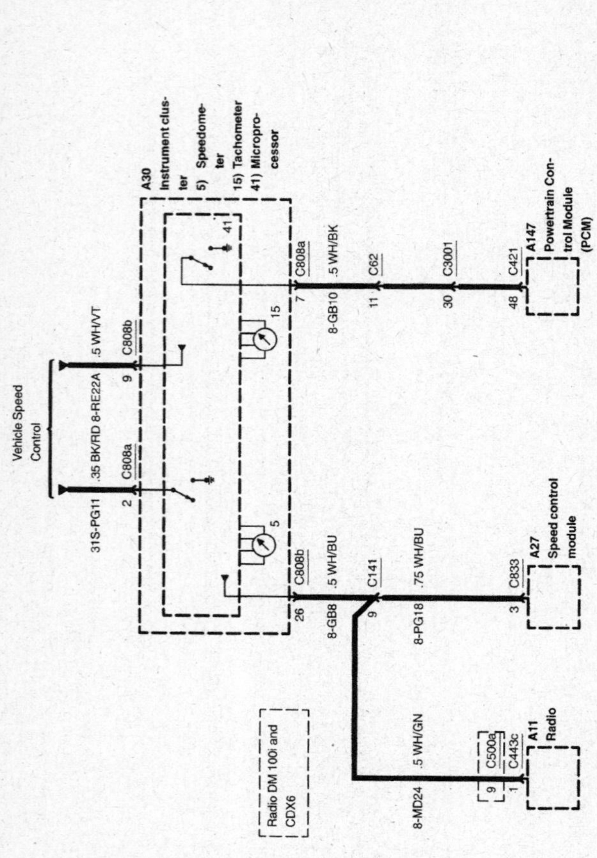

FM9090201355020X

Fig. 5 Instrument cluster wiring diagram (Part 2 of 10). 2002 Cougar

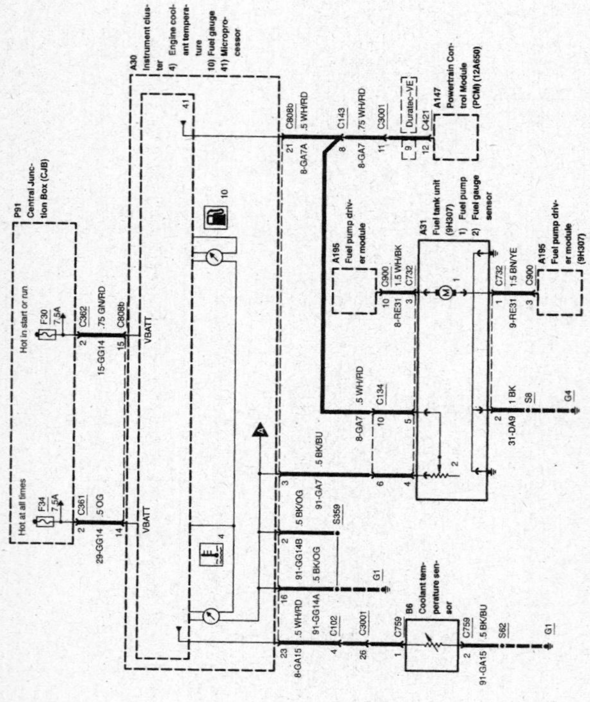

FM9090201355010X

Fig. 5 Instrument cluster wiring diagram (Part 1 of 10). 2002 Cougar

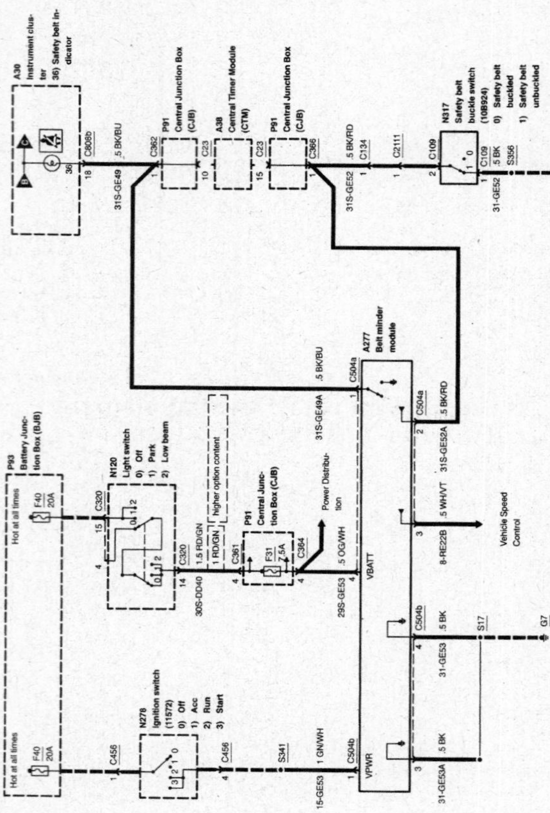

FM9090201355040X

Fig. 5 Instrument cluster wiring diagram (Part 4 of 10). 2002 Cougar

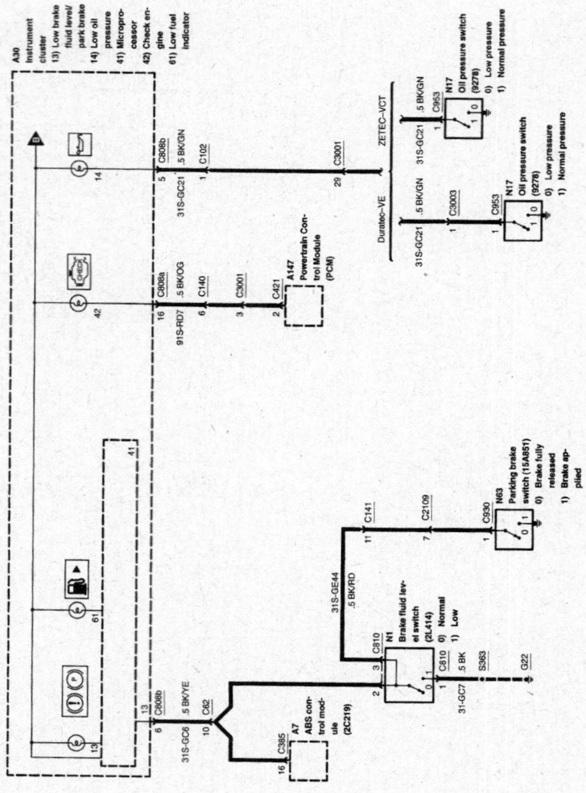

FM9090201355030X

Fig. 5 Instrument cluster wiring diagram (Part 3 of 10). 2002 Cougar

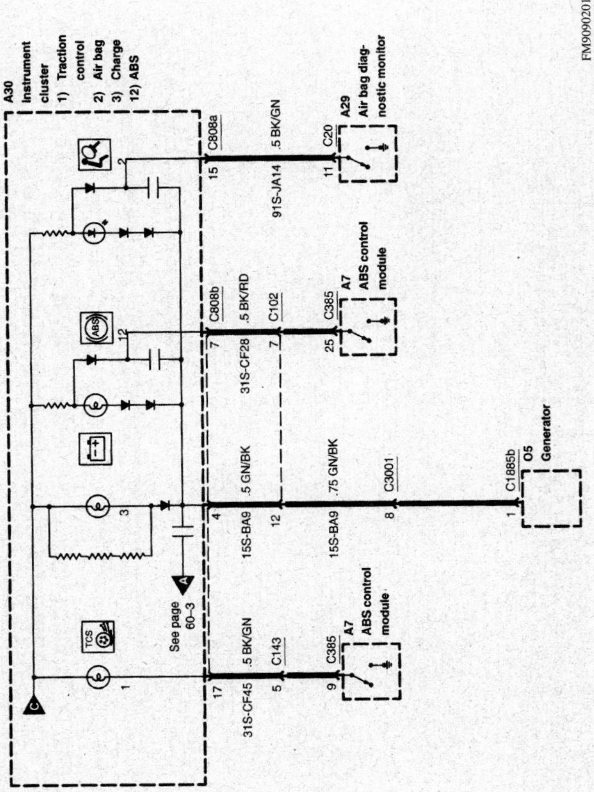

FM9090201355050X

Fig. 5 Instrument cluster wiring diagram (Part 5 of 10). 2002 Cougar

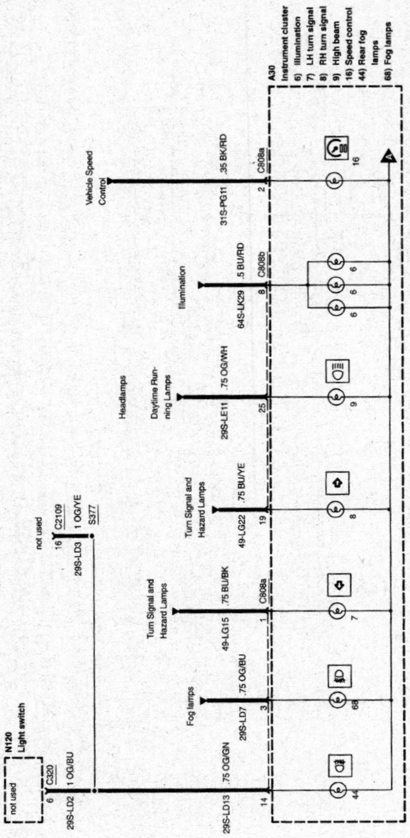

FM9090201355060X

Fig. 5 Instrument cluster wiring diagram (Part 6 of 10). 2002 Cougar

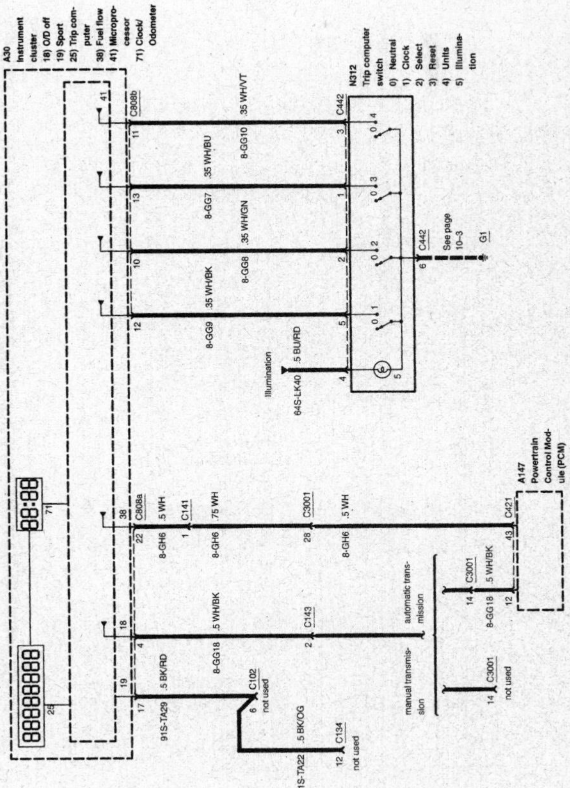

FM9090201355070X

Fig. 5 Instrument cluster wiring diagram (Part 7 of 10). 2002 Cougar

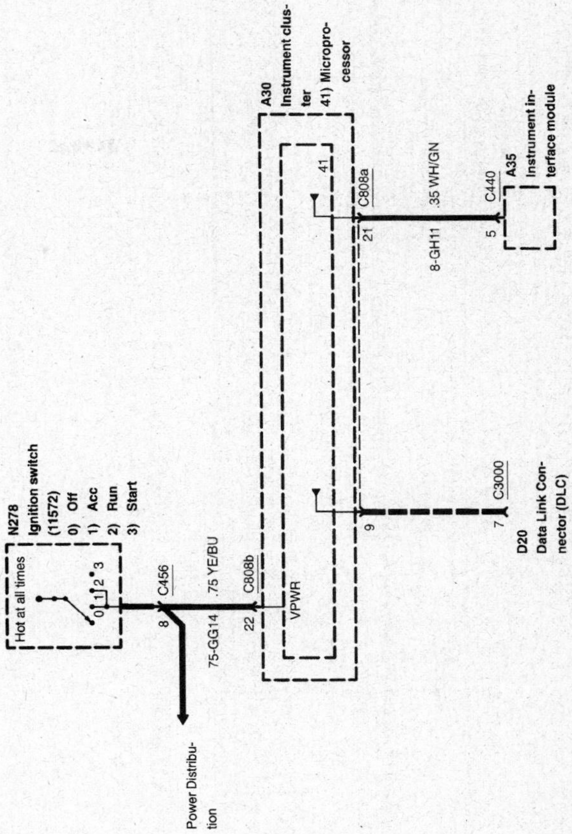

FM9090201355080X

Fig. 5 Instrument cluster wiring diagram (Part 8 of 10). 2002 Cougar

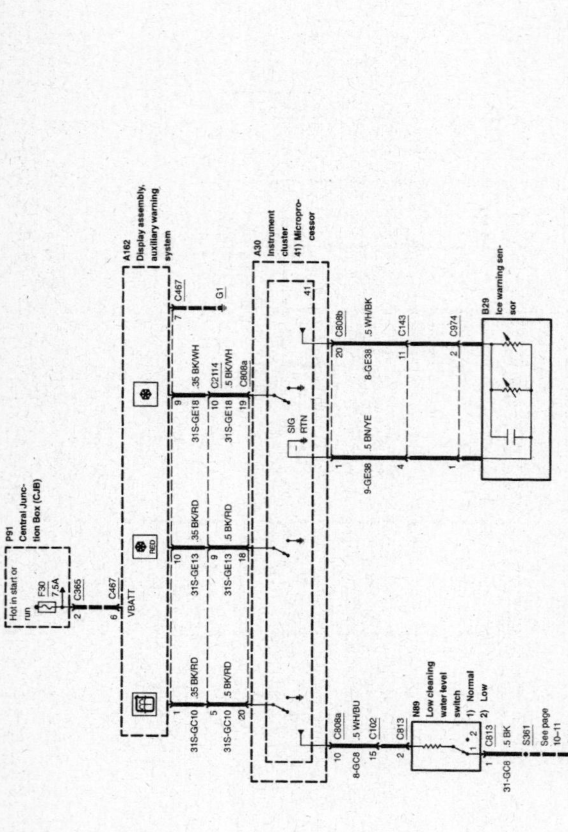

Fig. 5 Instrument cluster wiring diagram (Part 9 of 10). 2002 Cougar

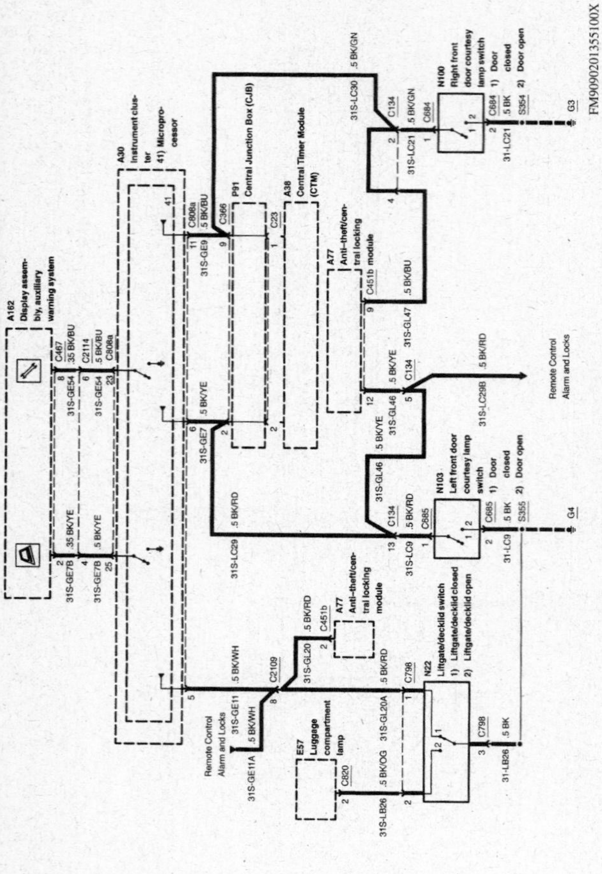

Fig. 5 Instrument cluster wiring diagram (Part 10 of 10). 2002 Cougar

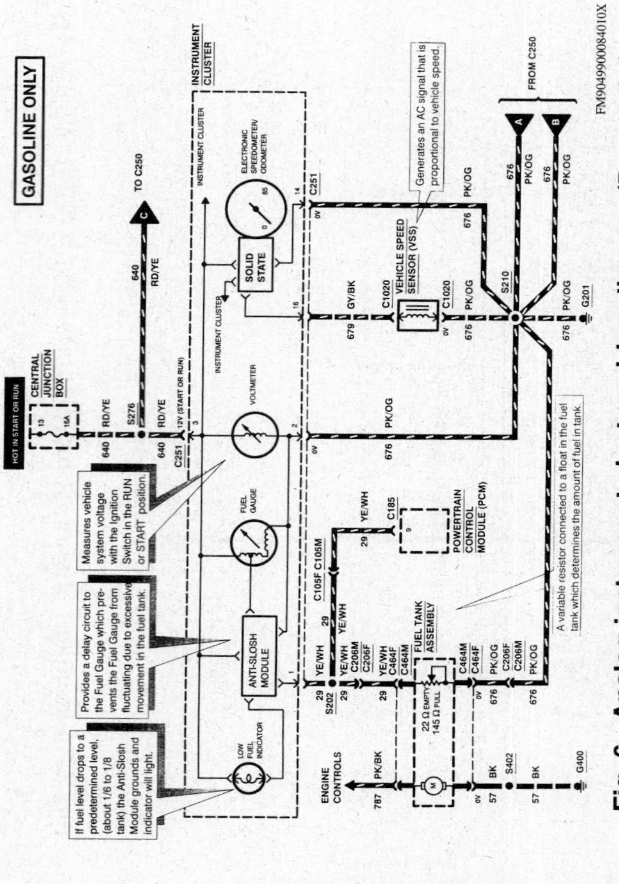

Fig. 6 Analog instrument cluster wiring diagram (Part 1 of 7). 2000–01 Crown Victoria & Grand Marquis

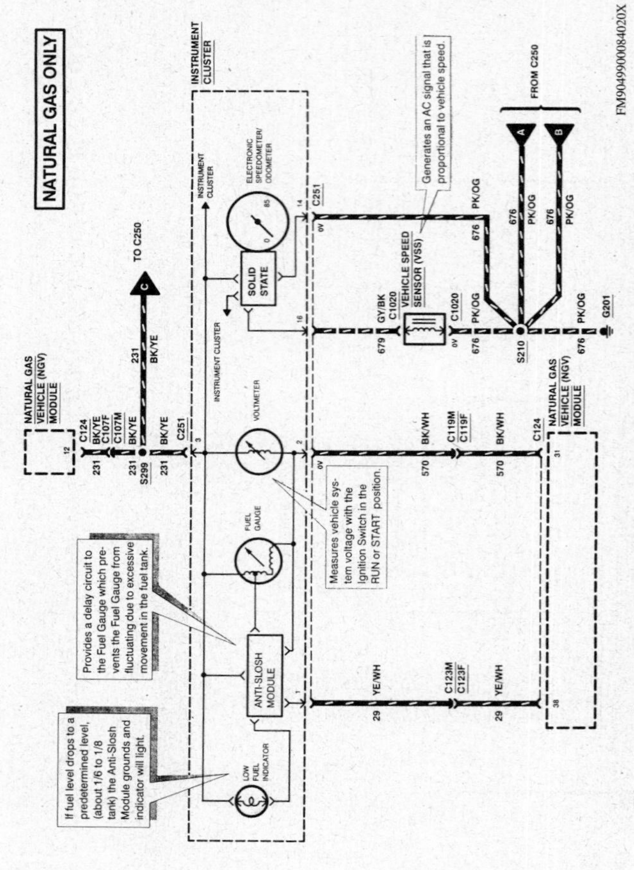

Fig. 6 Analog instrument cluster wiring diagram (Part 2 of 7). 2000–01 Crown Victoria & Grand Marquis

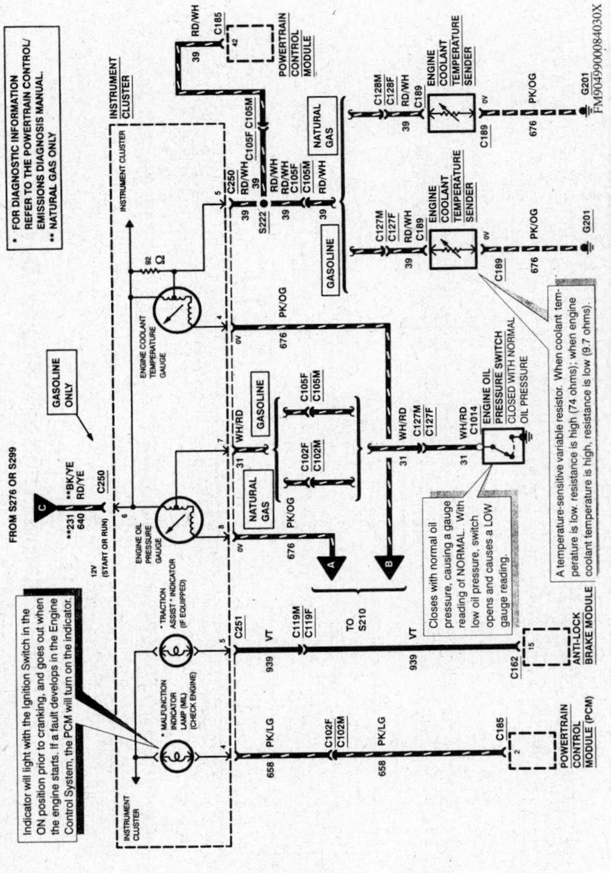

FM9049900084030X

Fig. 6 Analog instrument cluster wiring diagram (Part 3 of 7). 2000–01 Crown Victoria & Grand Marquis

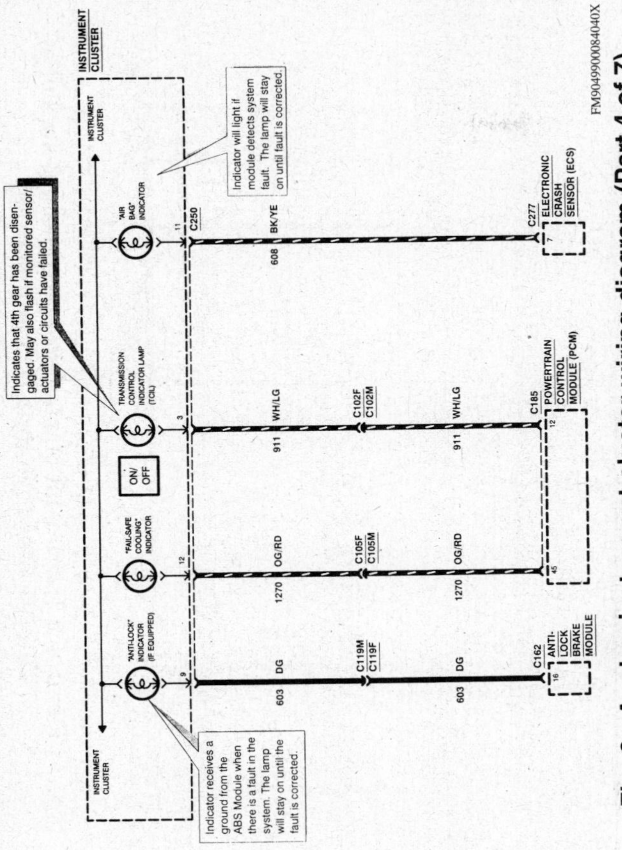

FM9049900084040X

Fig. 6 Analog instrument cluster wiring diagram (Part 4 of 7). 2000–01 Crown Victoria & Grand Marquis

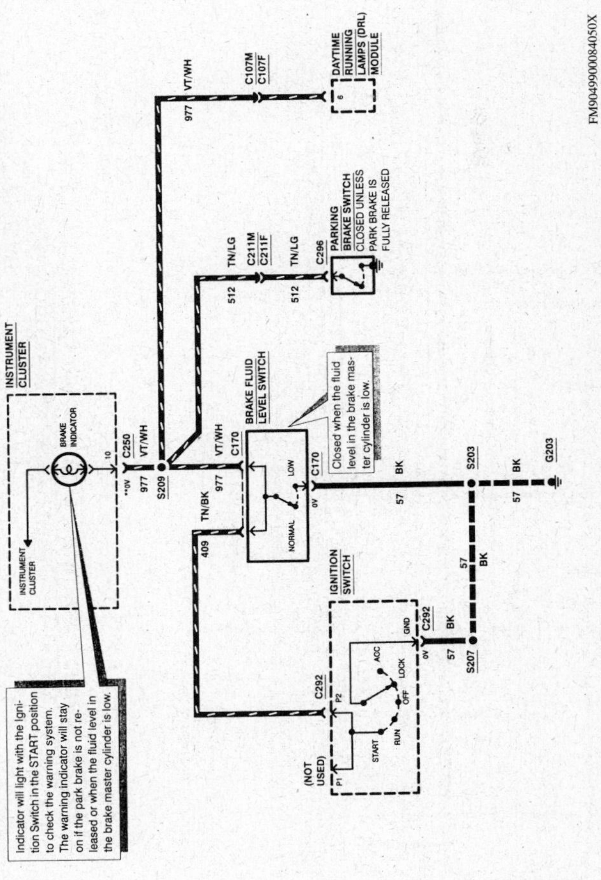

FM9049900084050X

Fig. 6 Analog instrument cluster wiring diagram (Part 5 of 7). 2000–01 Crown Victoria & Grand Marquis

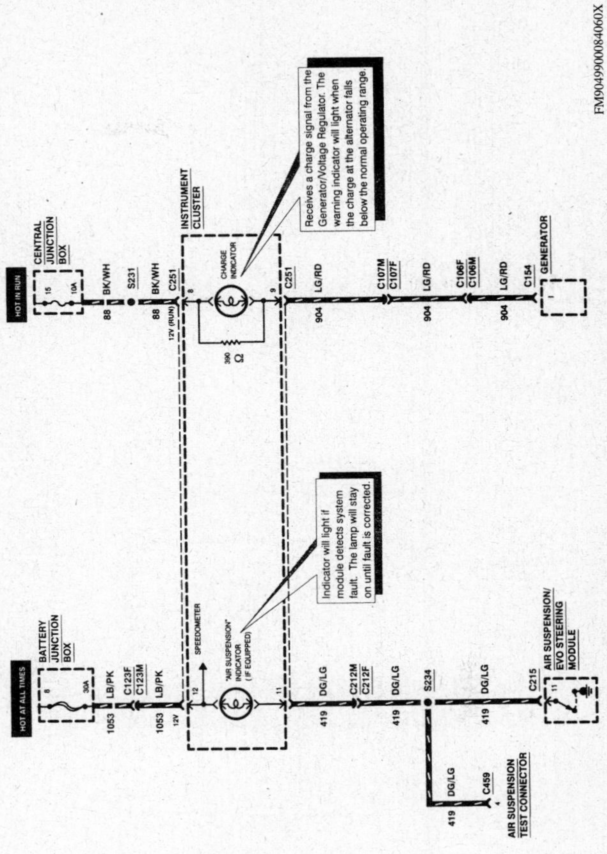

FM9049900084060X

Fig. 6 Analog instrument cluster wiring diagram (Part 6 of 7). 2000–01 Crown Victoria & Grand Marquis

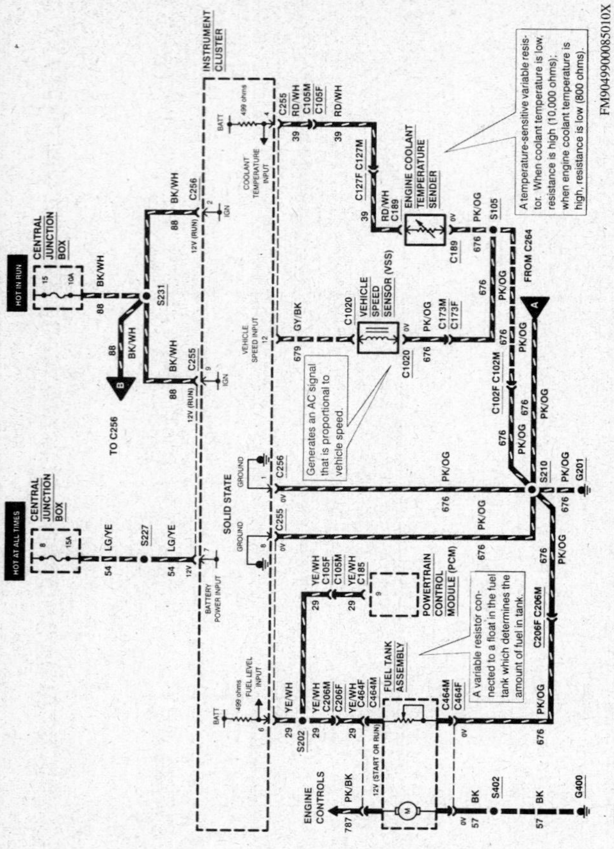

Fig. 7 Electronic instrument cluster wiring diagram (Part 1 of 4). 2000–01 Crown Victoria & Grand Marquis

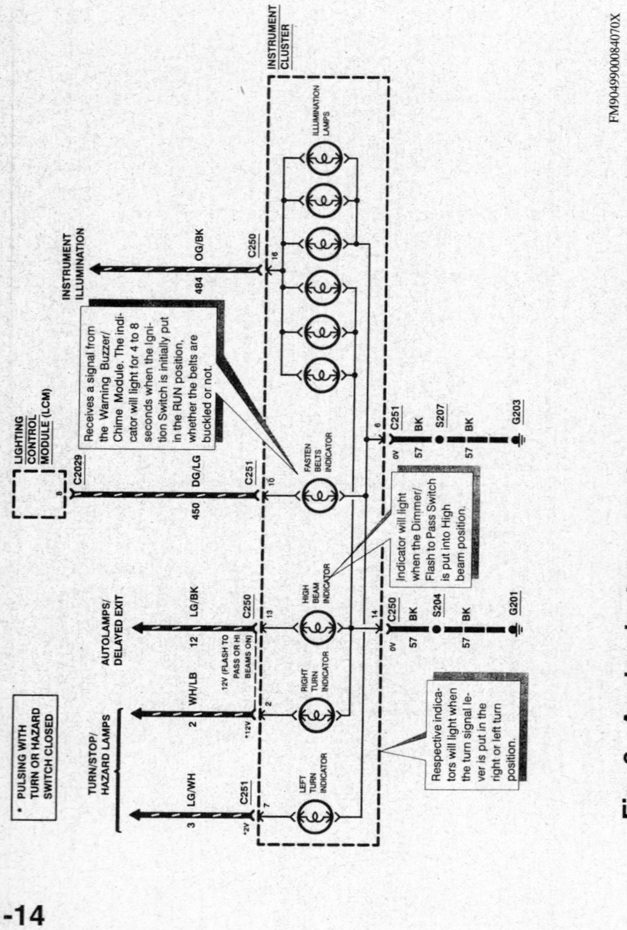

Fig. 6 Analog instrument cluster wiring diagram (Part 7 of 7). 2000–01 Crown Victoria & Grand Marquis

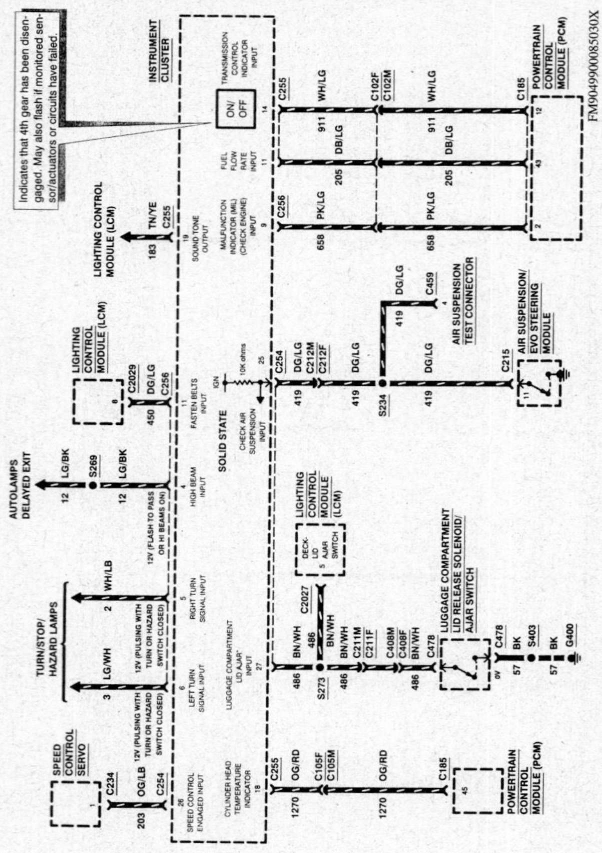

Fig. 7 Electronic instrument cluster wiring diagram (Part 3 of 4). 2000–01 Crown Victoria & Grand Marquis

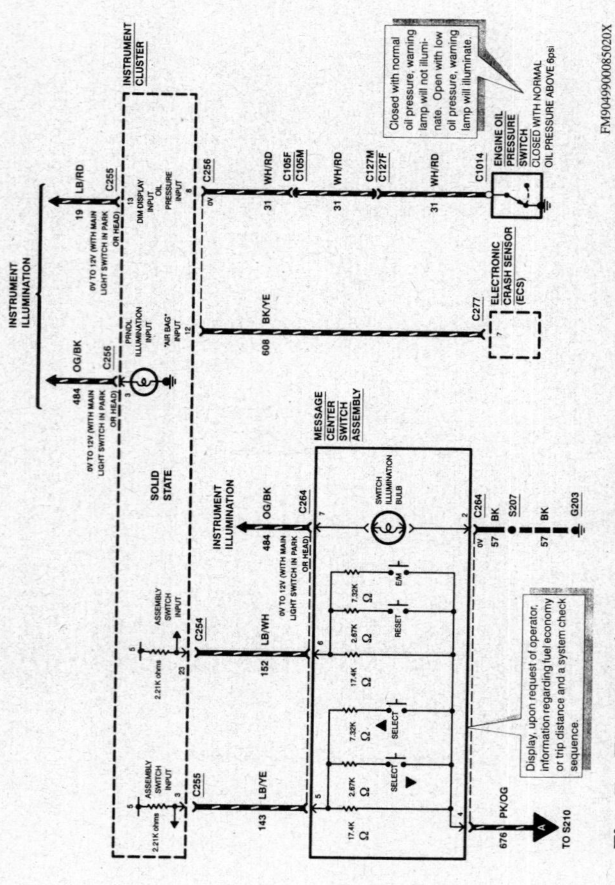

Fig. 7 Electronic instrument cluster wiring diagram (Part 2 of 4). 2000–01 Crown Victoria & Grand Marquis

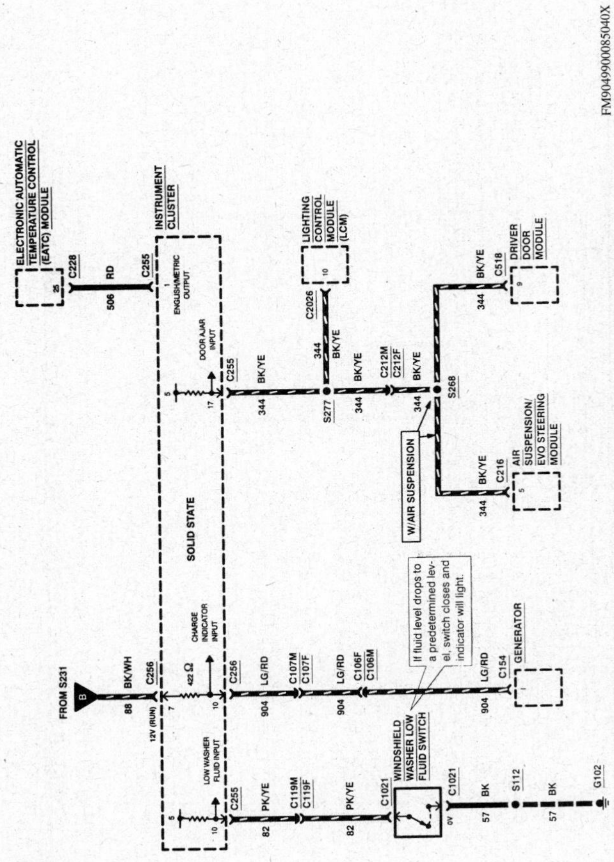

Fig. 7 Electronic instrument cluster wiring diagram (Part 4 of 4). 2000–01 Crown Victoria & Grand Marquis

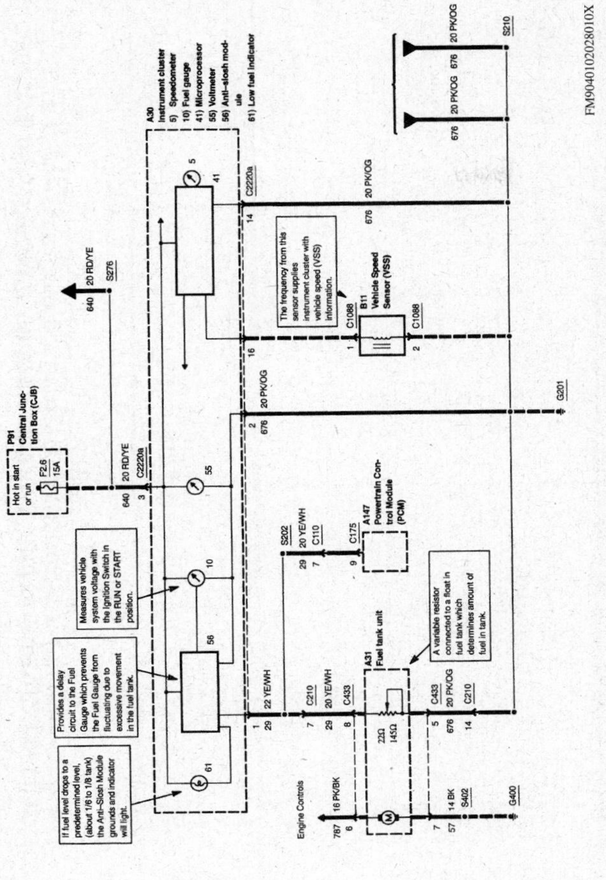

Fig. 8 Analog instrument cluster wiring diagram (Part 1 of 5). 2002 Crown Victoria & Grand Marquis

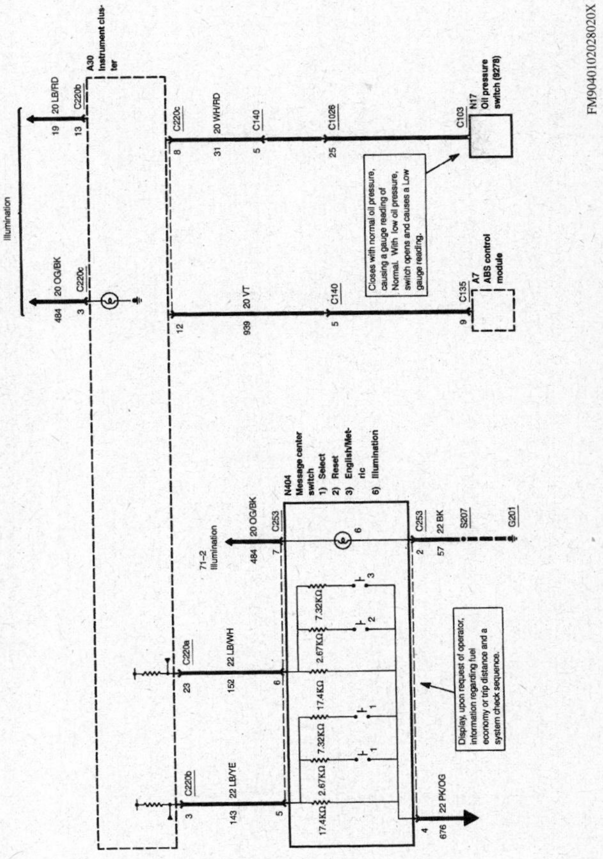

Fig. 8 Digital instrument cluster wiring diagram (Part 2 of 5). 2002 Crown Victoria & Grand Marquis

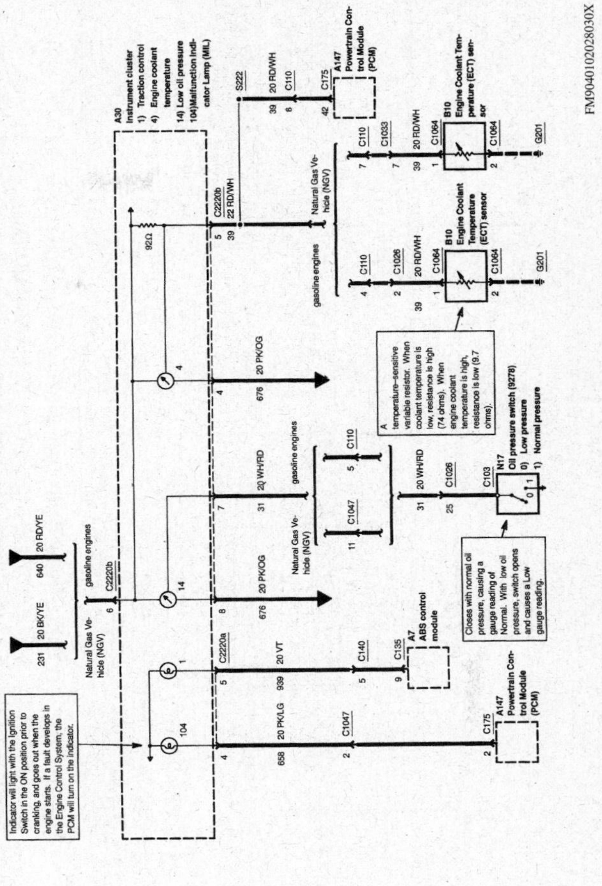

Fig. 8 Analog instrument cluster wiring diagram (Part 3 of 5). 2002 Crown Victoria & Grand Marquis

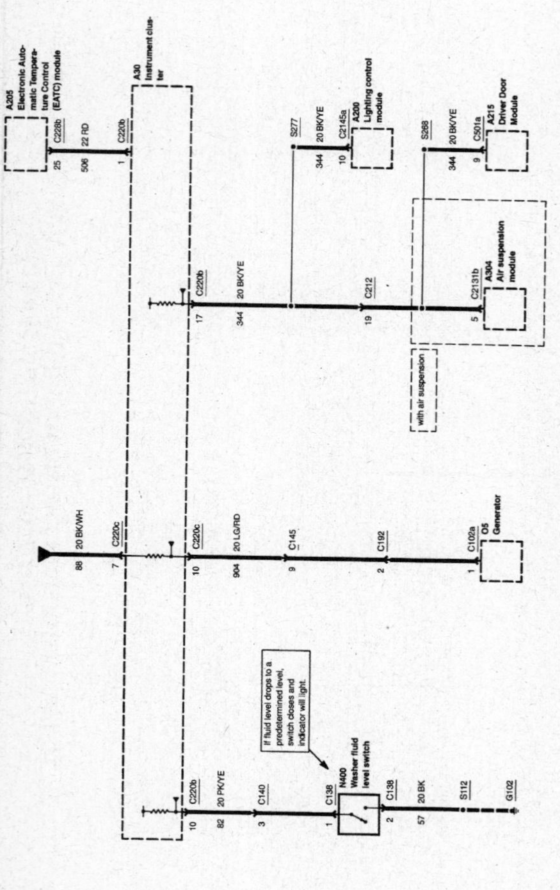

FM9040102028040X

Fig. 8 Digital instrument cluster wiring diagram (Part 4 of 5). 2002 Crown Victoria & Grand Marquis

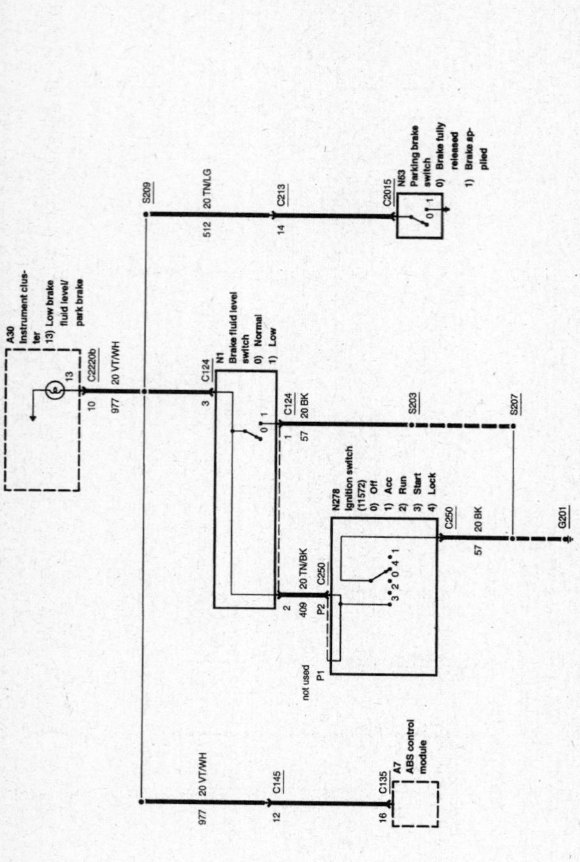

FM9040102028050X

Fig. 8 Analog instrument cluster wiring diagram (Part 5 of 5). 2002 Crown Victoria & Grand Marquis

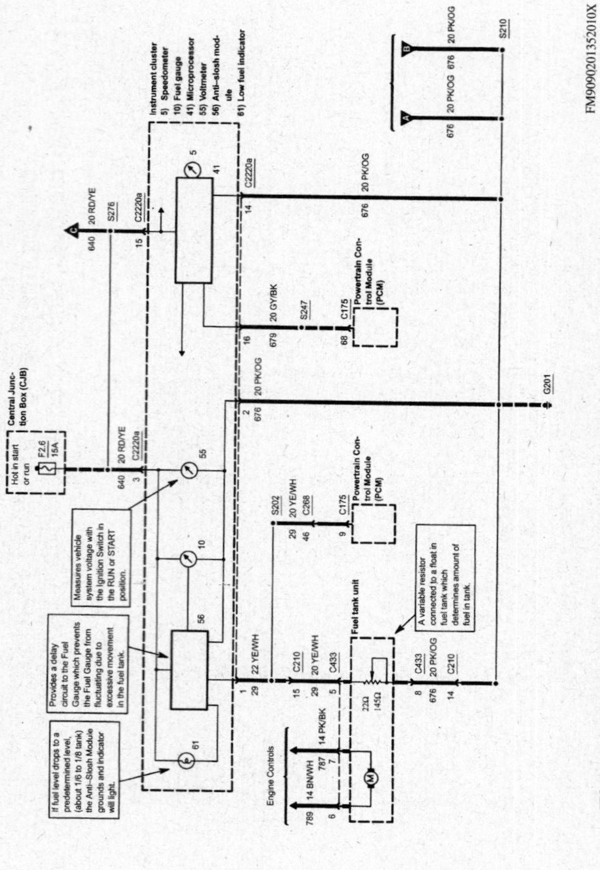

FM9090201352010X

Fig. 9 Analog instrument cluster wiring diagram (Part 1 of 6). 2003–04 Crown Victoria & Grand Marquis w/gasoline engine

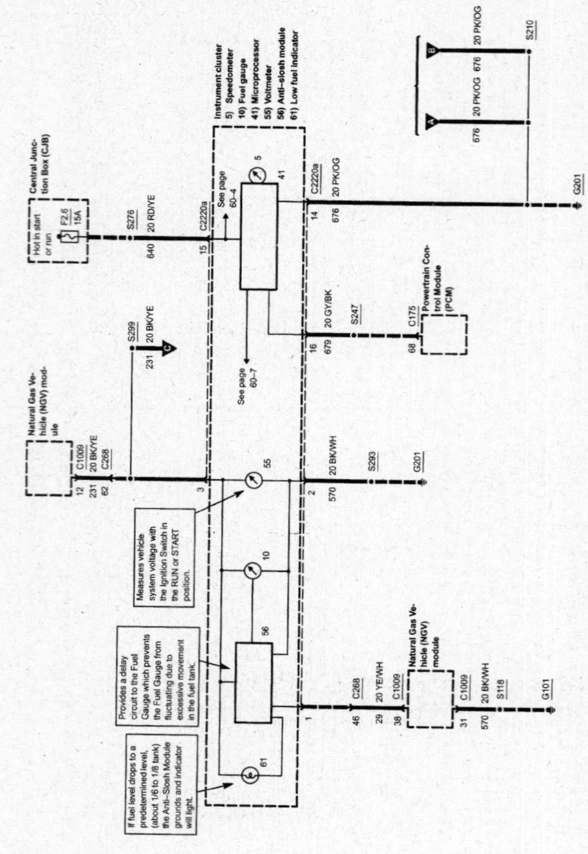

FM9090201352020X

Fig. 9 Analog instrument cluster wiring diagram (Part 1 of 6). 2003–04 Crown Victoria & Grand Marquis w/natural gas engine

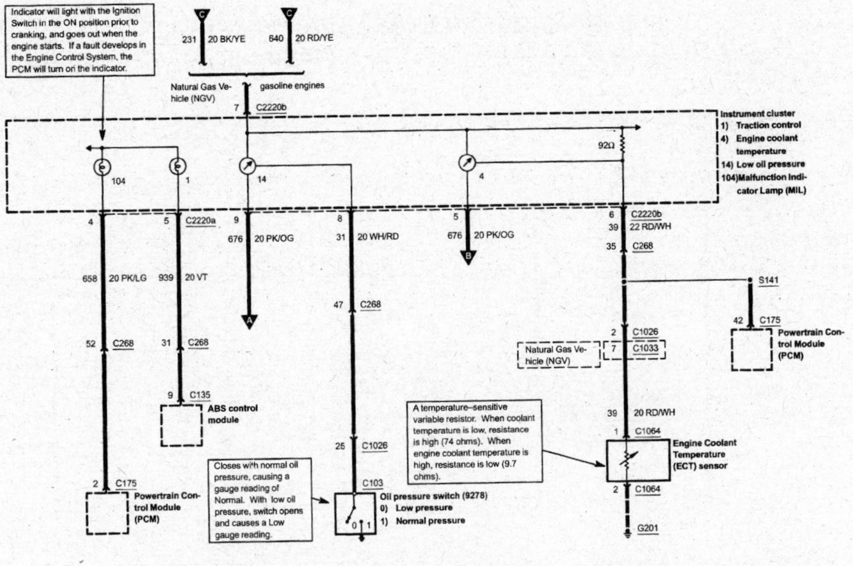

FM9090201352030X

Fig. 9 Analog instrument cluster wiring diagram (Part 2 of 6). 2003–04 Crown Victoria & Grand Marquis

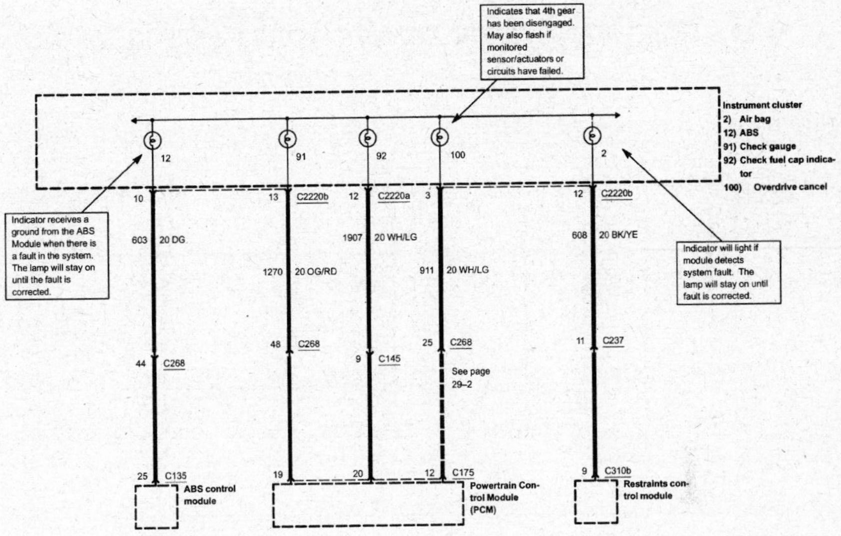

FM9090201352040X

Fig. 9 Analog instrument cluster wiring diagram (Part 3 of 6). 2003–04 Crown Victoria & Grand Marquis

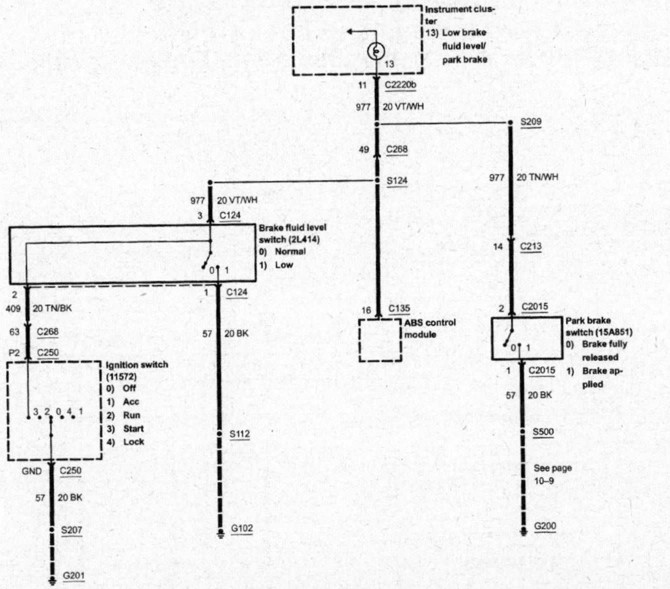

FM9090201352050X

Fig. 9 Analog instrument cluster wiring diagram (Part 4 of 6). 2003–04 Crown Victoria & Grand Marquis

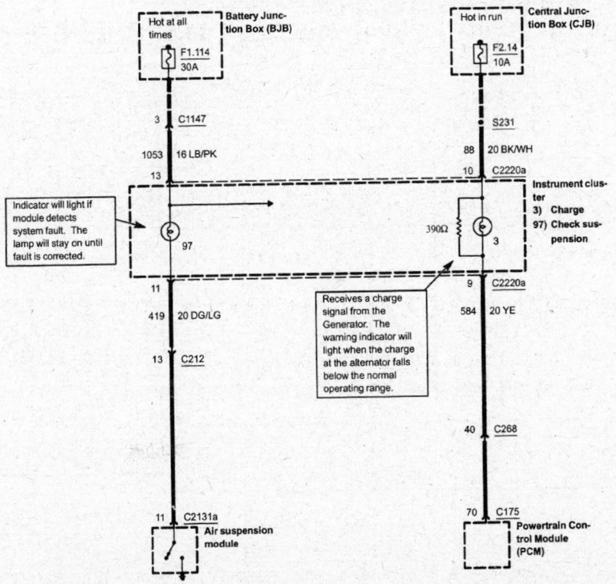

FM9090201352060X

Fig. 9 Analog instrument cluster wiring diagram (Part 5 of 6). 2003–04 Crown Victoria & Grand Marquis

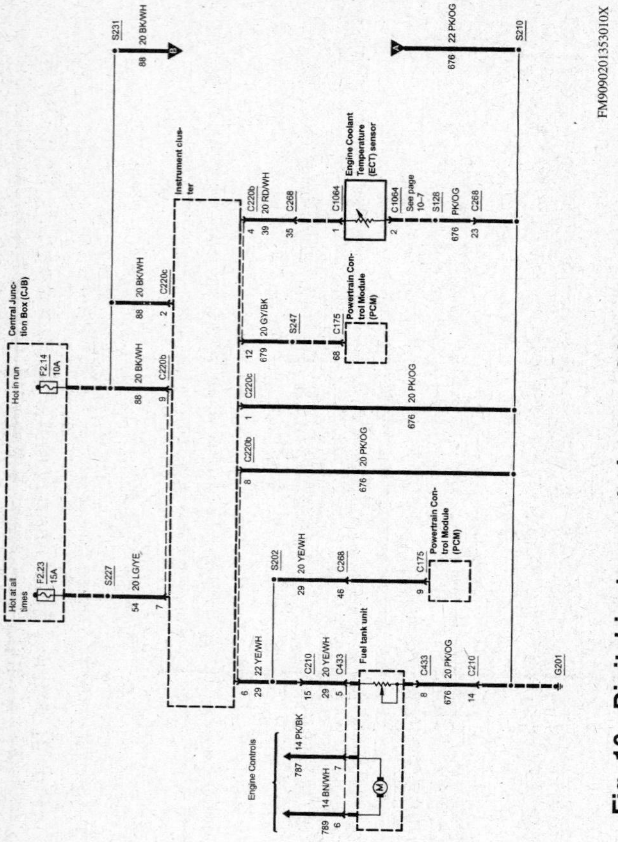

Fig. 10 Digital instrument cluster wiring diagram (Part 1 of 4). 2003–04 Crown Victoria & Grand Marquis

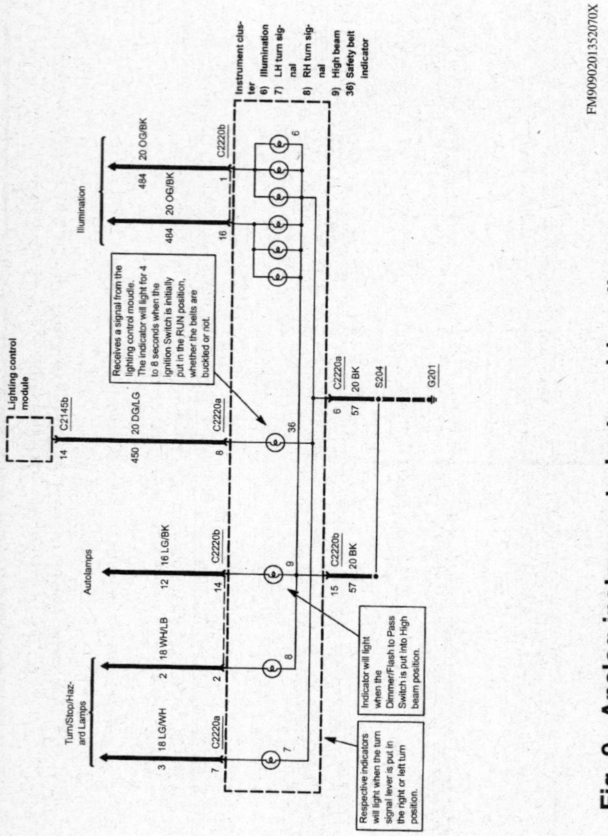

Fig. 9 Analog instrument cluster wiring diagram (Part 6 of 6). 2003–04 Crown Victoria & Grand Marquis

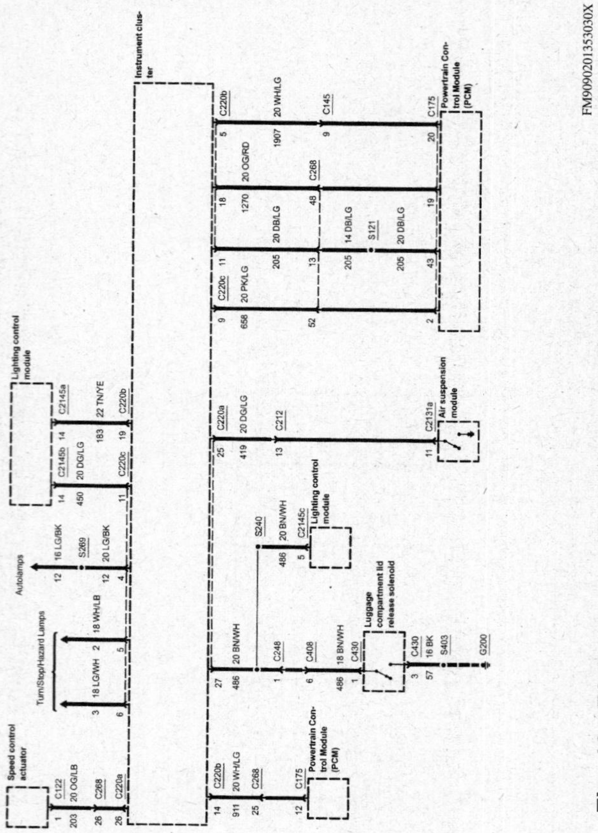

Fig. 10 Digital instrument cluster wiring diagram (Part 3 of 4). 2003–04 Crown Victoria & Grand Marquis

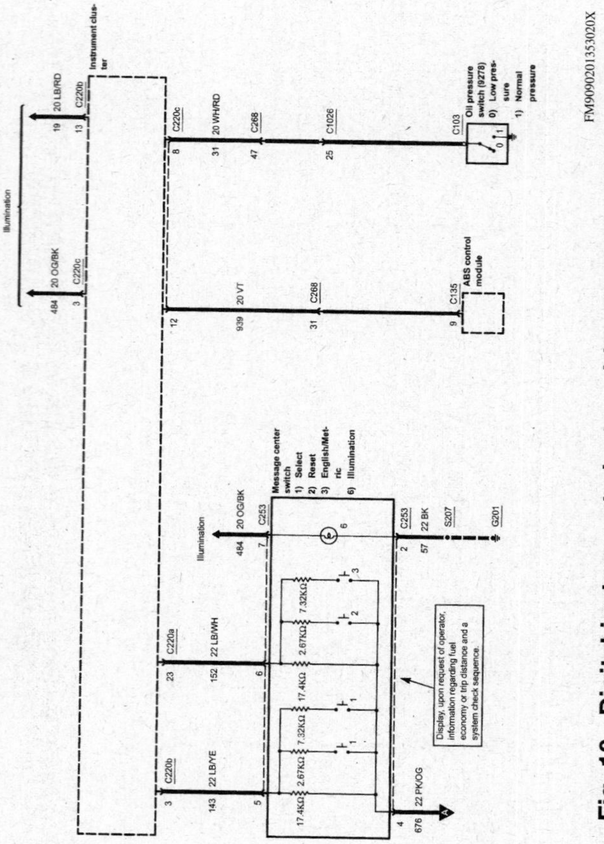

Fig. 10 Digital instrument cluster wiring diagram (Part 2 of 4). 2003–04 Crown Victoria & Grand Marquis

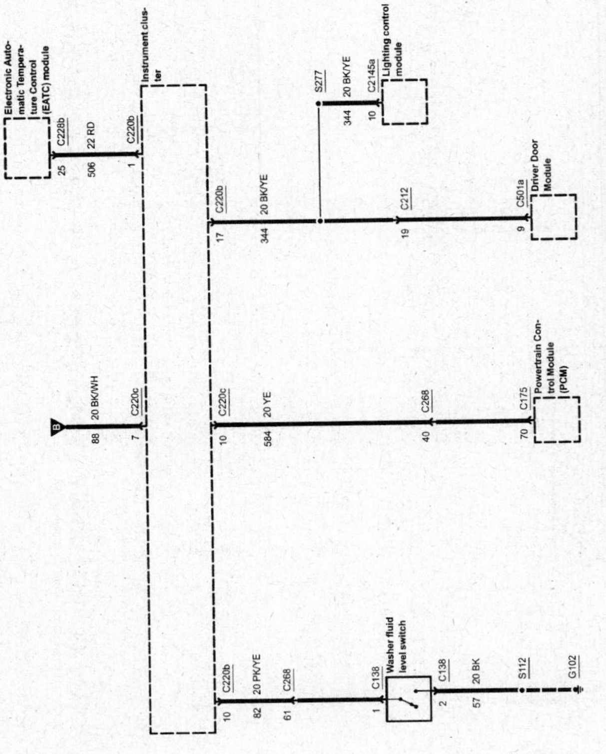

Fig. 10 Digital instrument cluster wiring diagram (Part 4 of 4). 2003–04 Crown Victoria & Grand Marquis

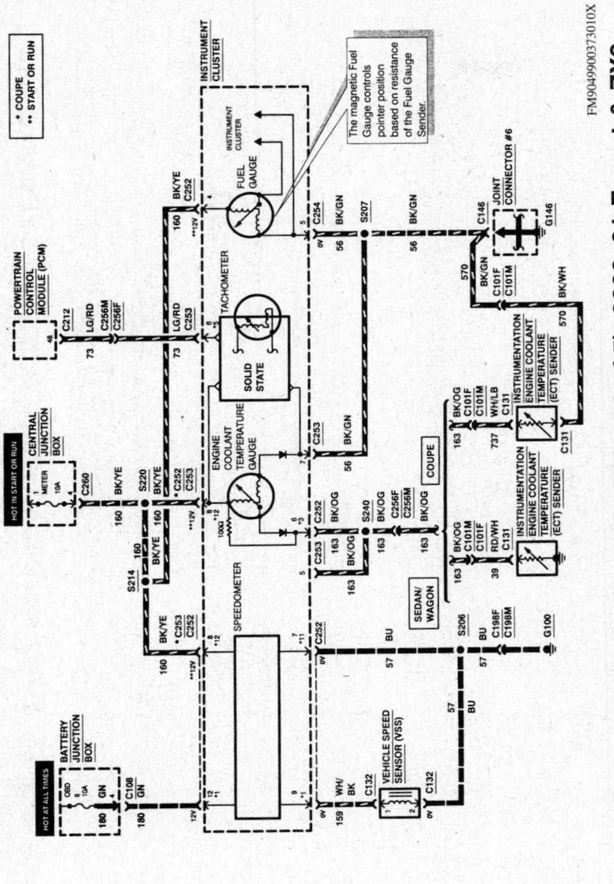

Fig. 11 Instrument cluster (Part 1 of 5). 2000–01 Escort & ZX2

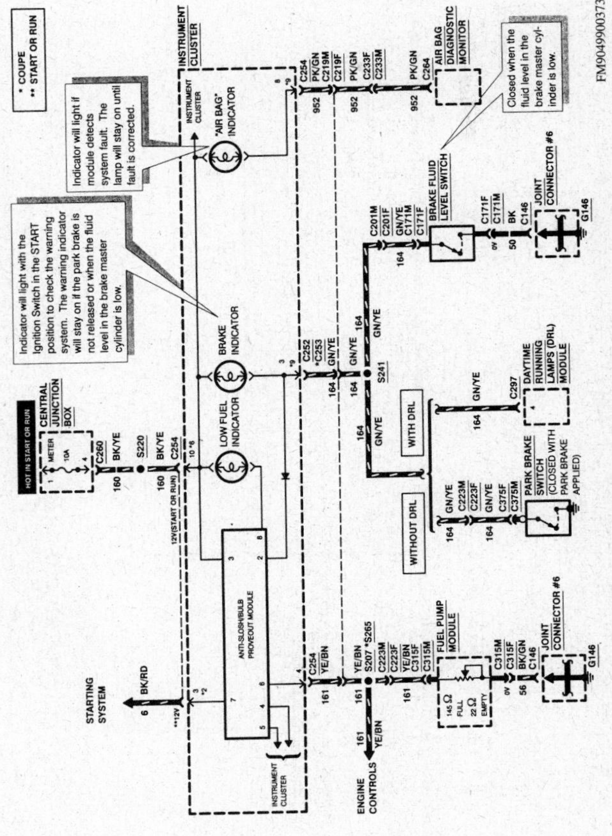

Fig. 11 Instrument cluster (Part 2 of 5). 2000–01 Escort & ZX2

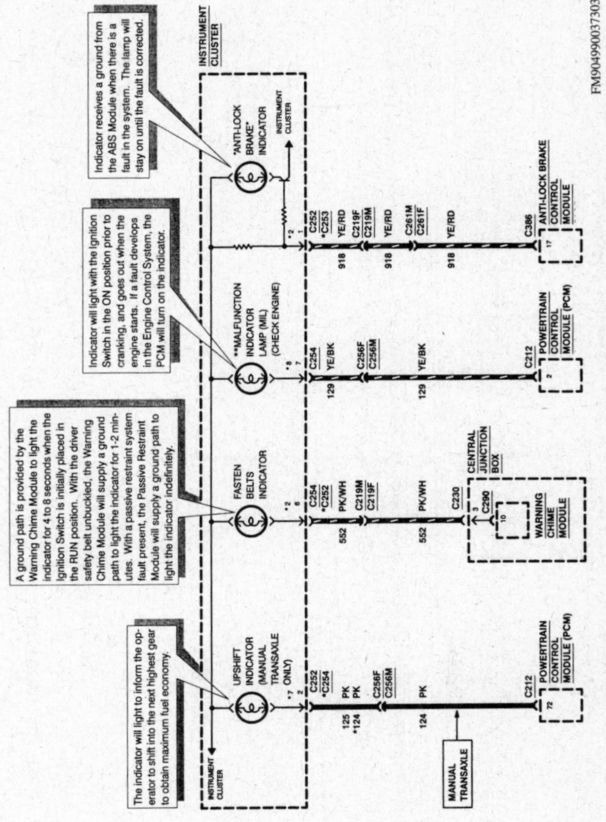

Fig. 11 Instrument cluster (Part 3 of 5). 2000–01 Escort & ZX2

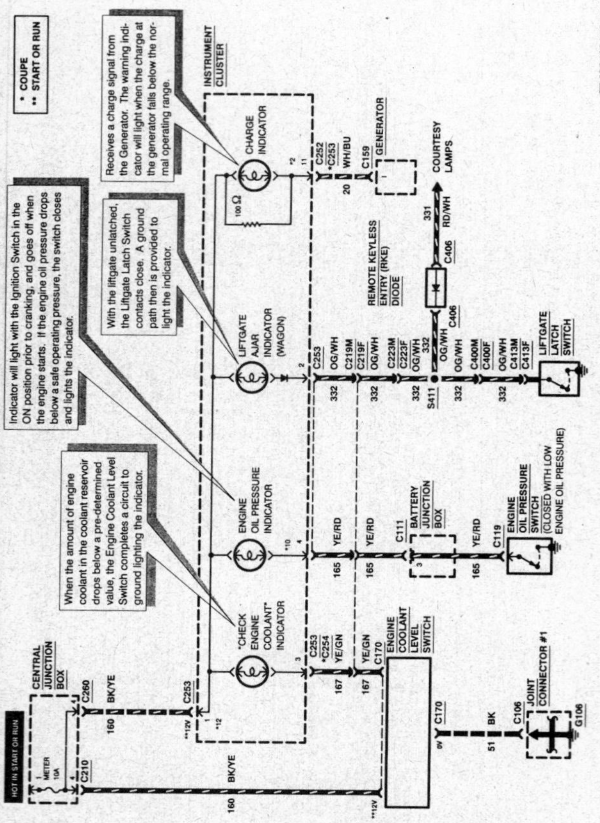

Fig. 11 Instrument cluster (Part 4 of 5). 2000–01 Escort & ZX2

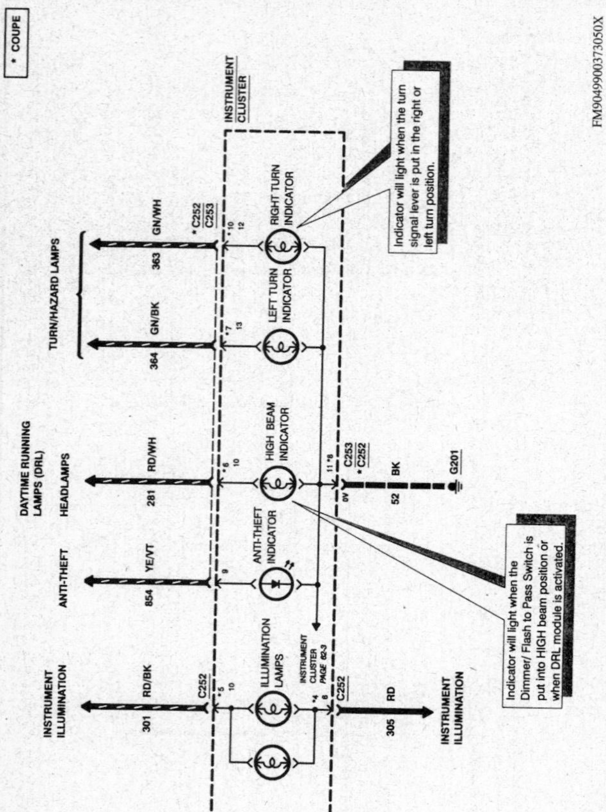

Fig. 11 Instrument cluster (Part 5 of 5). 2000–01 Escort & ZX2

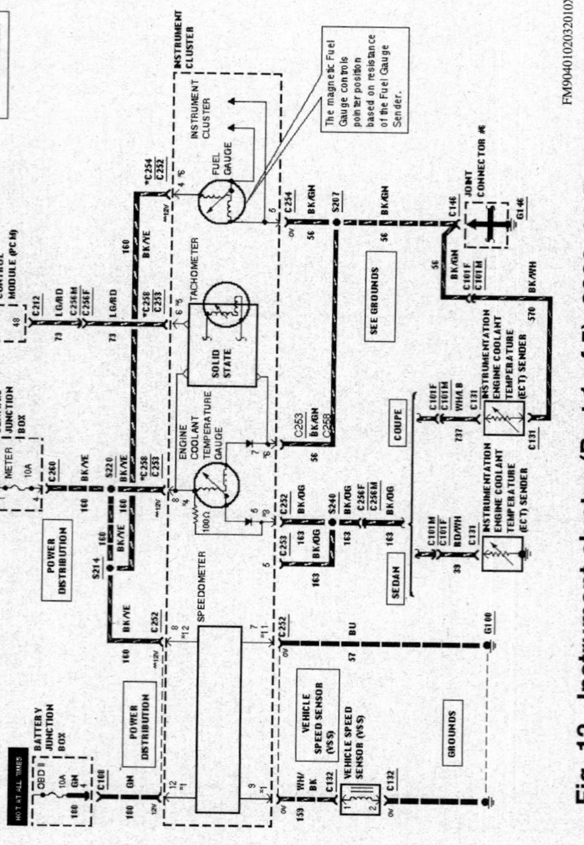

Fig. 12 Instrument cluster (Part 1 of 5). 2002–04 Escort & ZX2

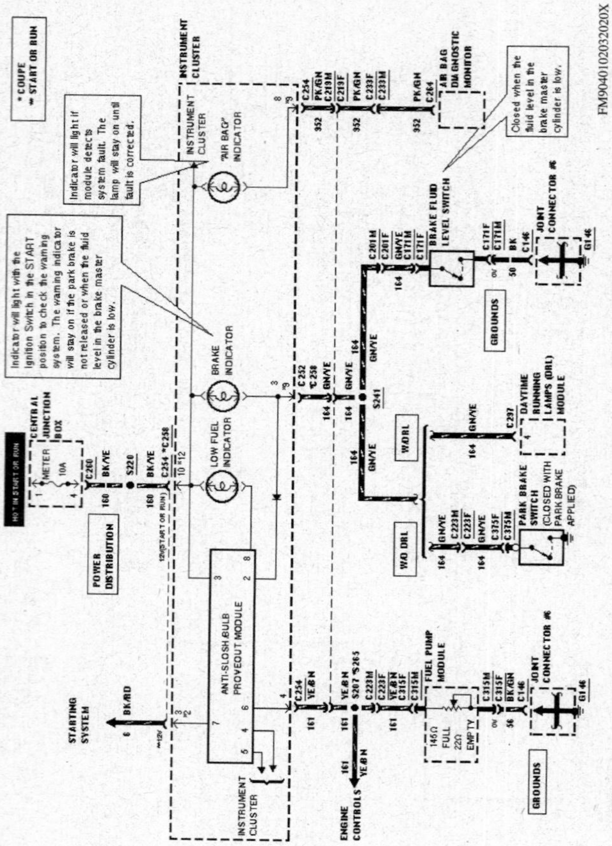

Fig. 12 Instrument cluster (Part 2 of 5). 2002–04 Escort & ZX2

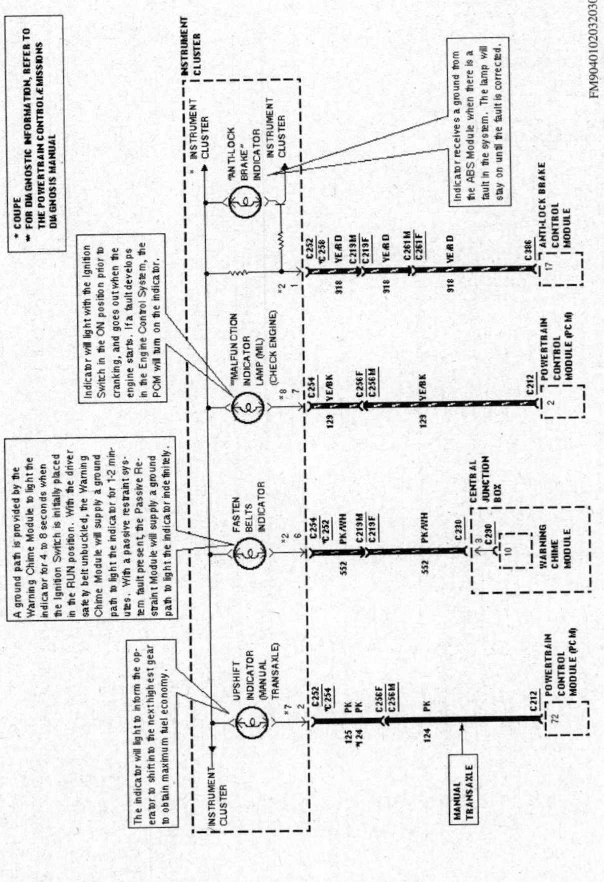

Fig. 12 Instrument cluster (Part 3 of 5). 2002–04 Escort & ZX2

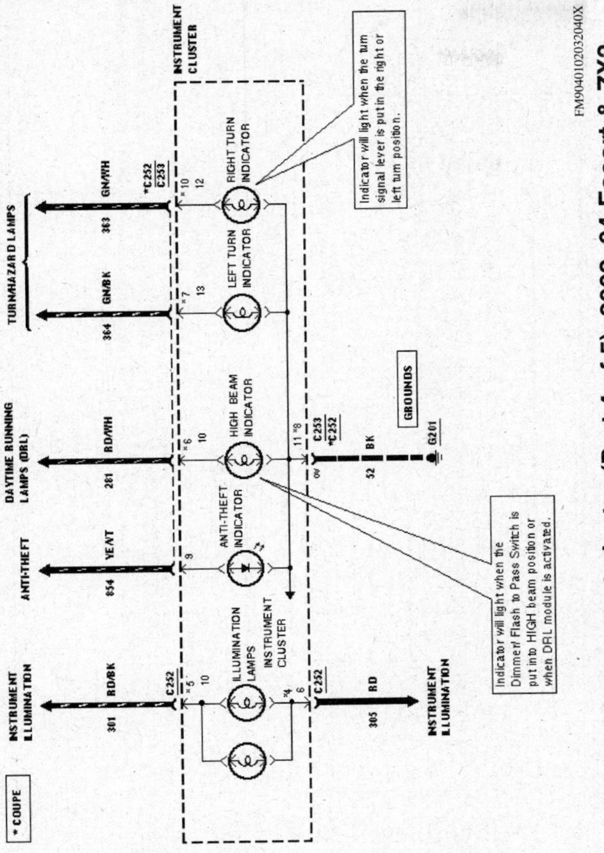

Fig. 12 Instrument cluster (Part 4 of 5). 2002–04 Escort & ZX2

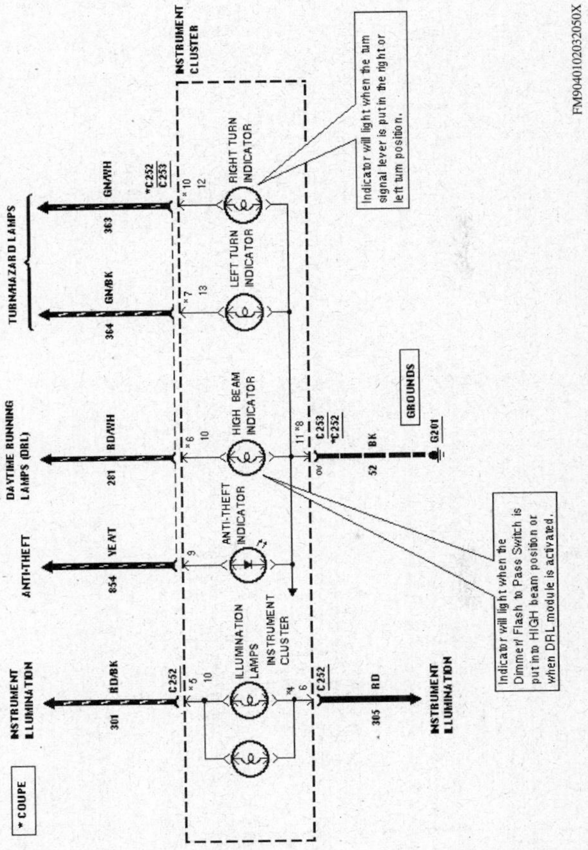

Fig. 12 Instrument cluster (Part 5 of 5). 2002–04 Escort & ZX2

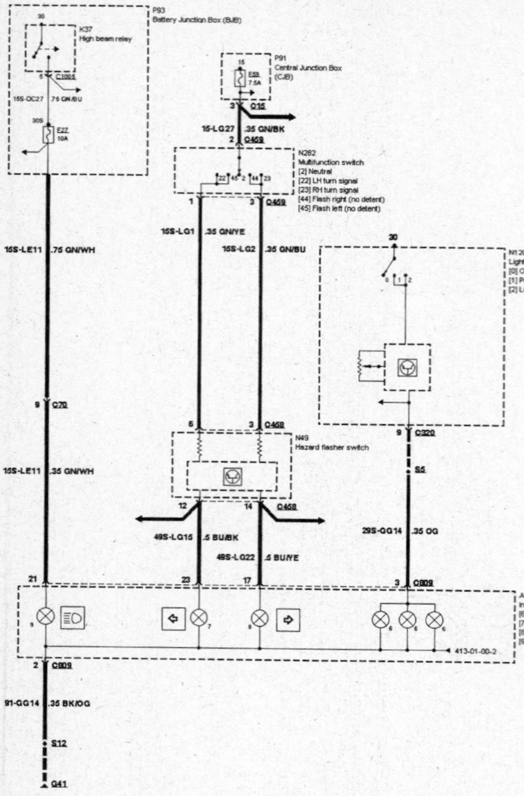

FM9090001288010X

Fig. 13 Instrument cluster wiring diagram (Part 1 of 5). 2000–01 Focus

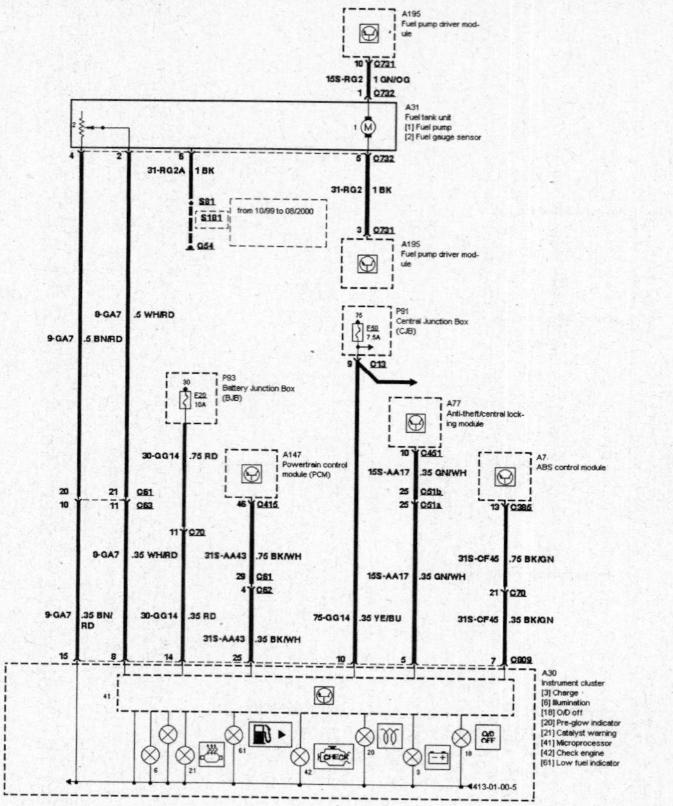

FM9090001288020X

Fig. 13 Instrument cluster wiring diagram (Part 2 of 5). 2000–01 Focus

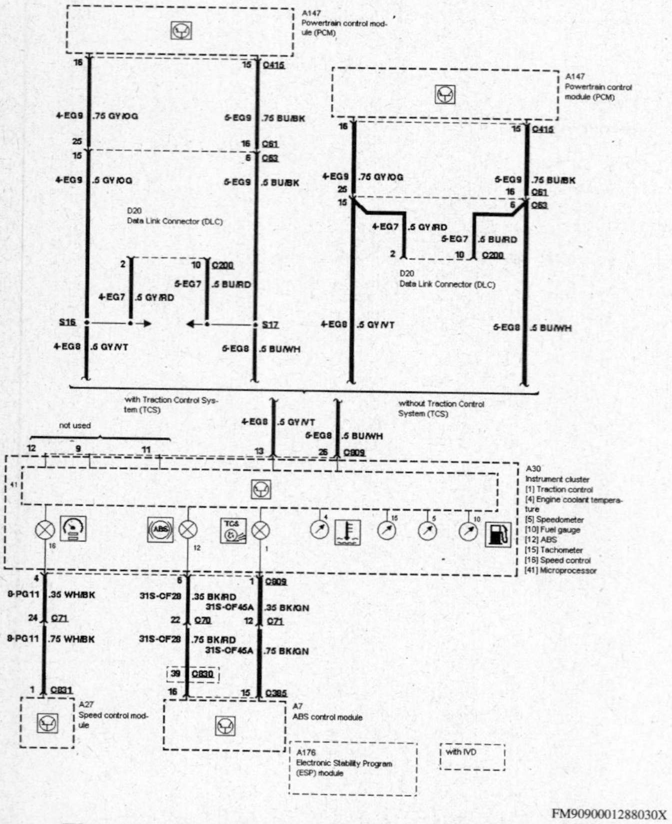

FM9090001288030X

Fig. 13 Instrument cluster wiring diagram (Part 3 of 5). 2000–01 Focus

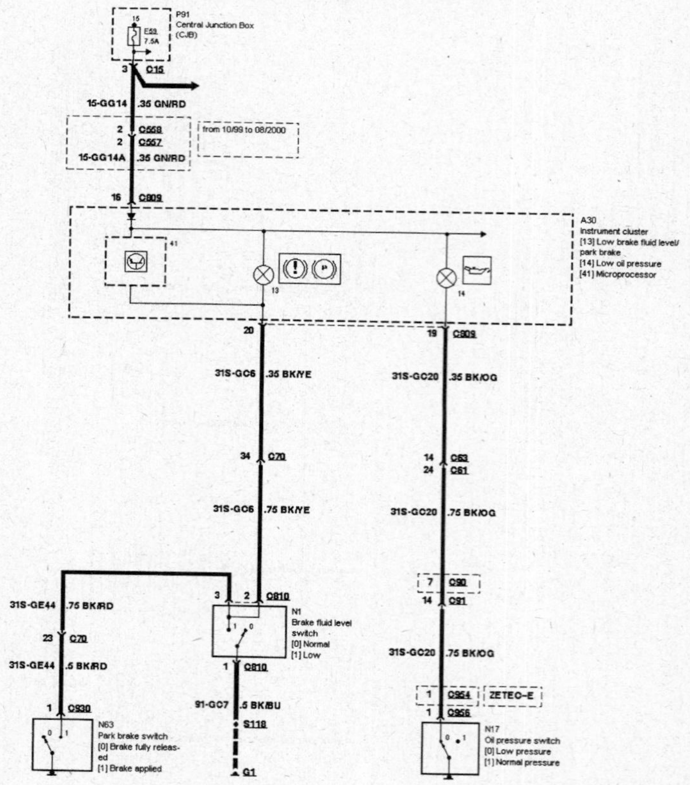

FM9090001288040X

Fig. 13 Instrument cluster wiring diagram (Part 4 of 5). 2000–01 Focus

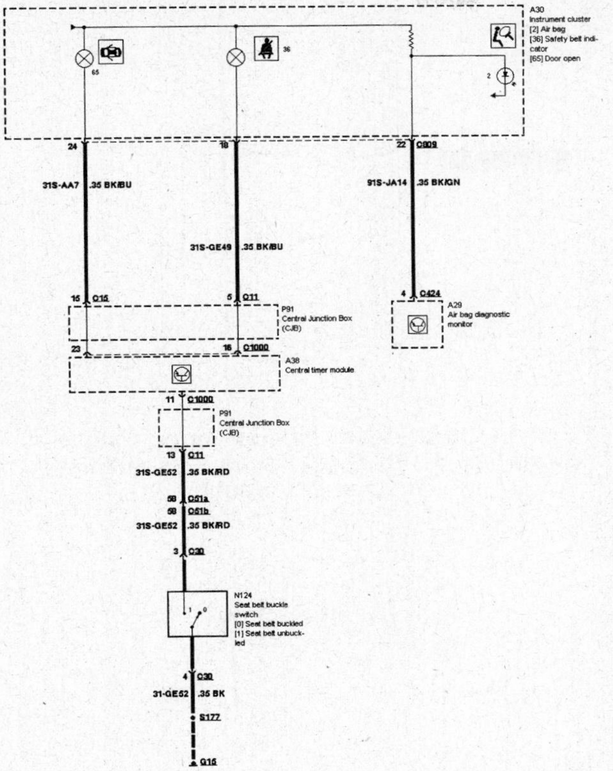

FM9090001288050X

Fig. 13 Instrument cluster wiring diagram (Part 5 of 5). 2000–01 Focus

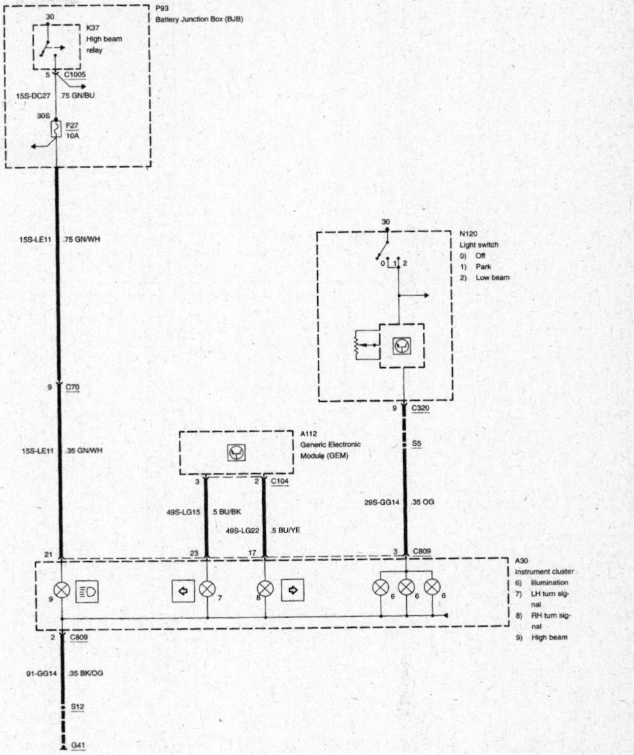

FM9090201356010X

Fig. 14 Instrument cluster wiring diagram (Part 1 of 5). 2002–04 Focus less auxiliary instrument cluster

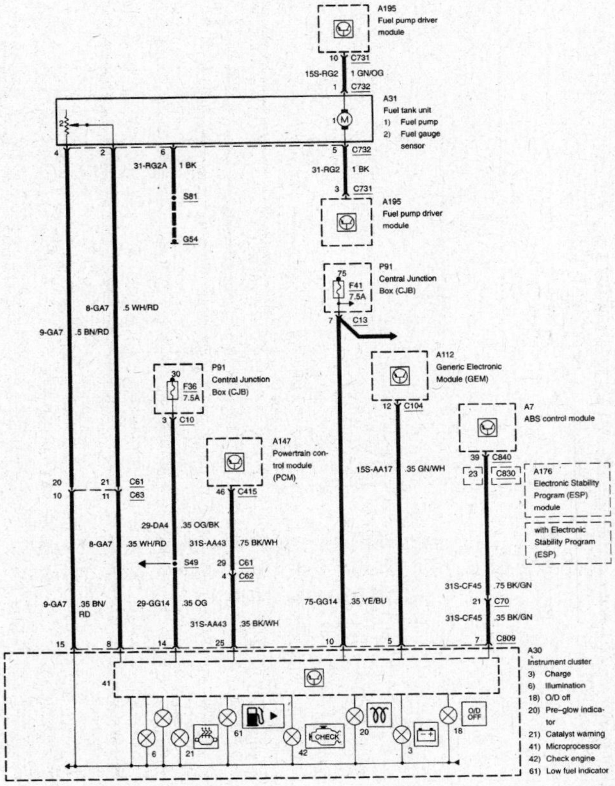

FM9090201356020X

Fig. 14 Instrument cluster wiring diagram (Part 2 of 5). 2002–04 Focus less auxiliary instrument cluster

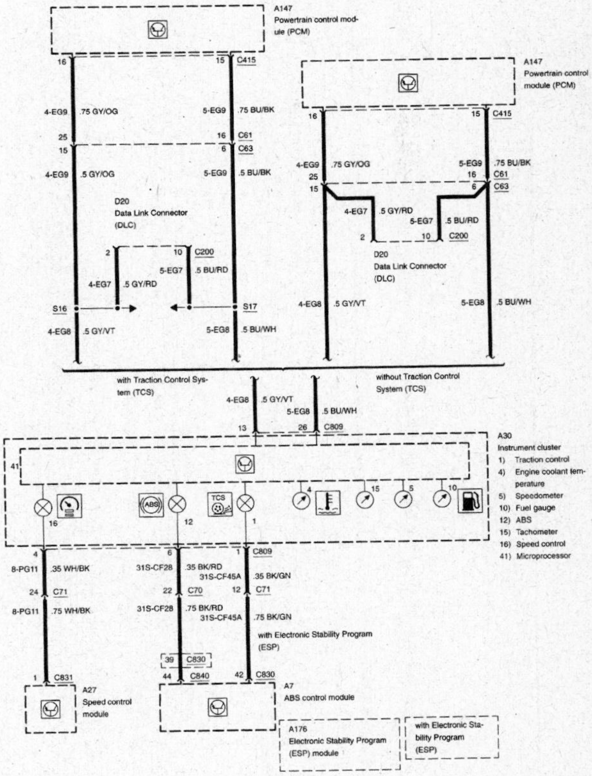

FM9090201356030X

Fig. 14 Instrument cluster wiring diagram (Part 3 of 5). 2002–04 Focus less auxiliary instrument cluster

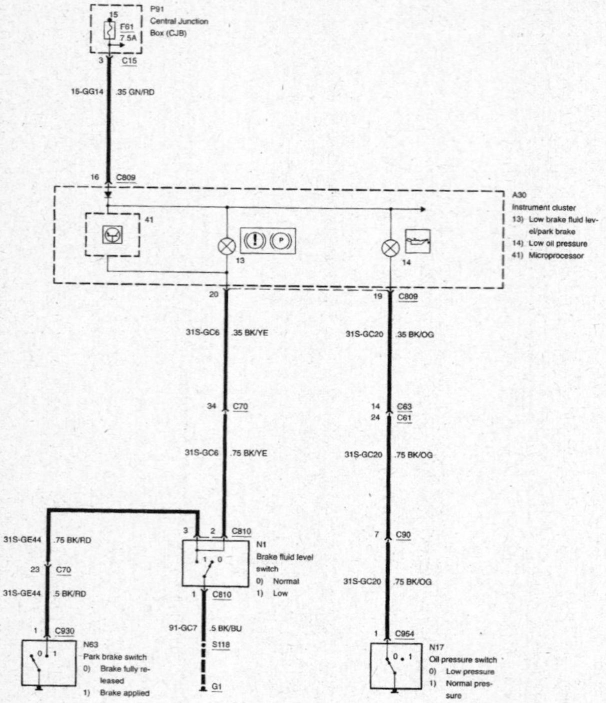

FM9090201356040X

Fig. 14 Instrument cluster wiring diagram (Part 4 of 5). 2002–04 Focus less auxiliary instrument cluster

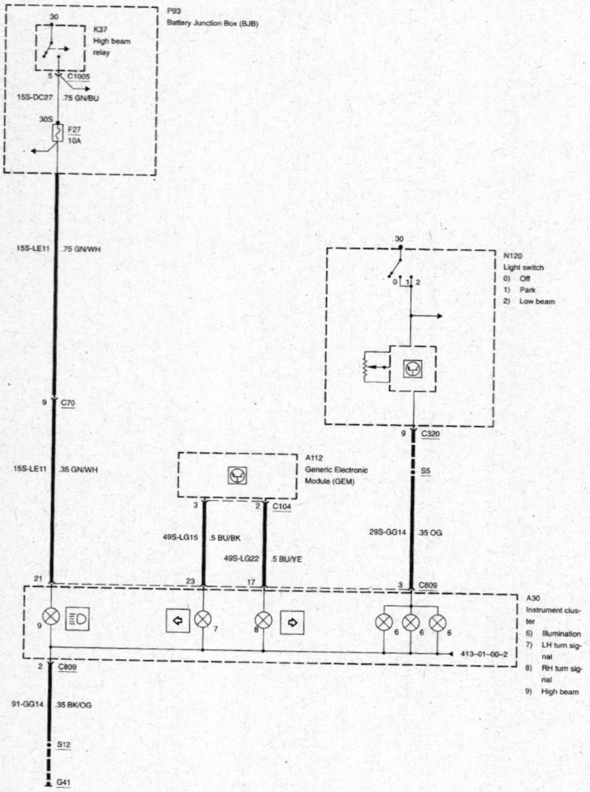

FM9090201357010X

Fig. 15 Instrument cluster wiring diagram (Part 1 of 6). 2002–04 Focus 3-door w/auxiliary instrument cluster

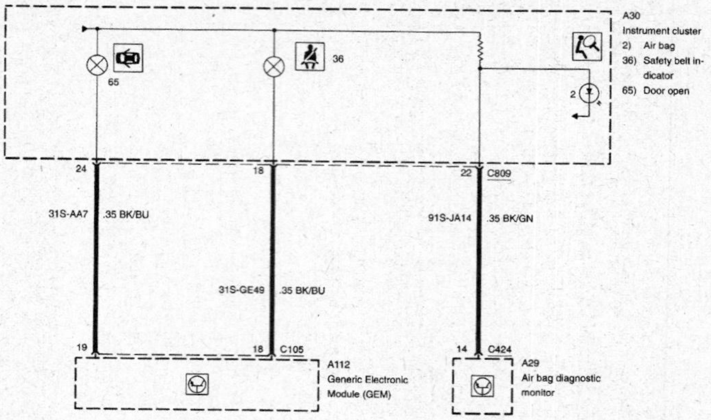

FM9090201356050X

Fig. 14 Instrument cluster wiring diagram (Part 5 of 5). 2002–04 Focus less auxiliary instrument cluster

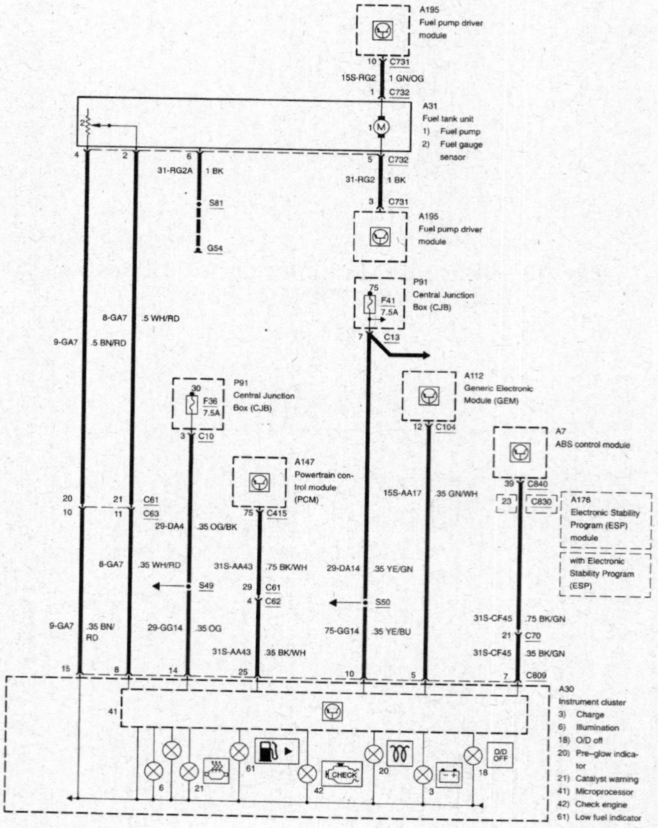

FM9090201357020X

Fig. 15 Instrument cluster wiring diagram (Part 2 of 6). 2002–04 Focus 3-door w/auxiliary instrument cluster

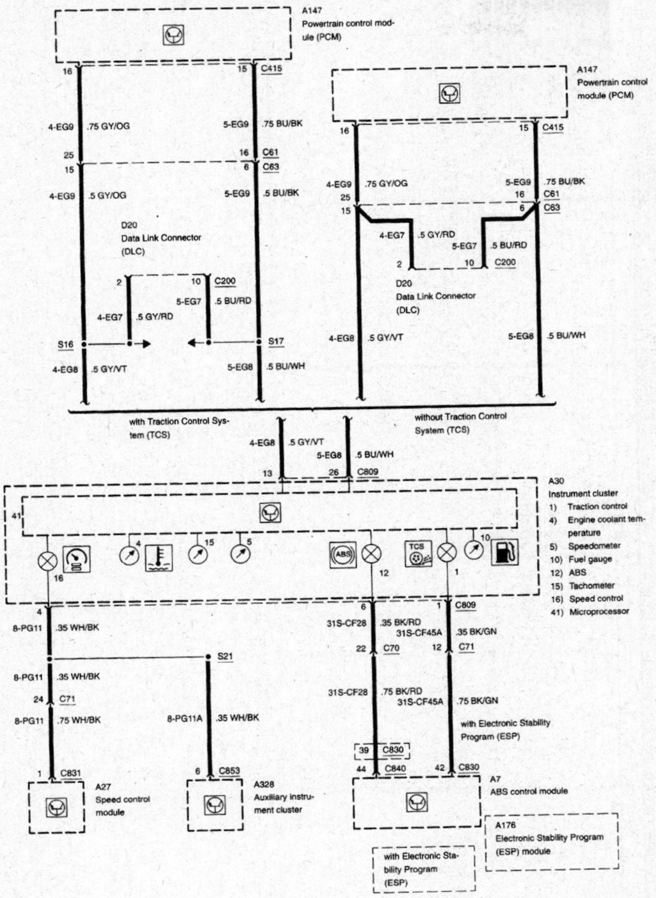

FM9090201357030X

Fig. 15 Instrument cluster wiring diagram (Part 3 of 6). 2002–04 Focus 3-door w/auxiliary instrument cluster

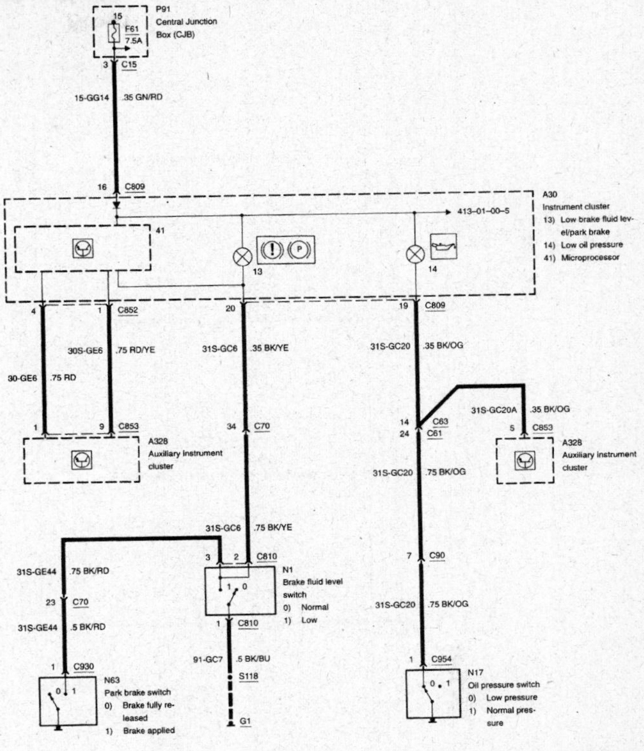

FM9090201357040X

Fig. 15 Instrument cluster wiring diagram (Part 4 of 6). 2002–04 Focus 3-door w/auxiliary instrument cluster

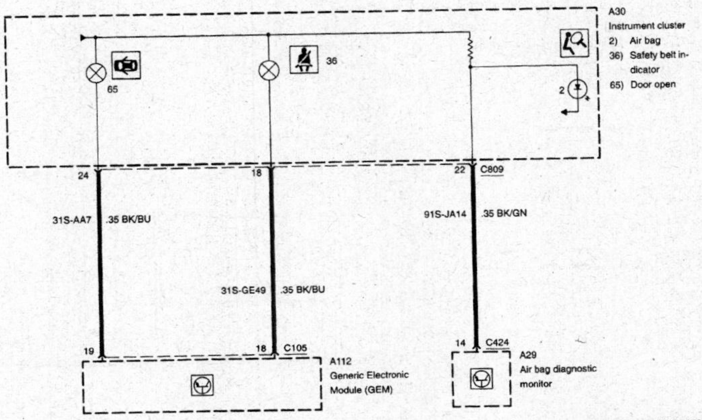

FM9090201357050X

Fig. 15 Instrument cluster wiring diagram (Part 5 of 6). 2002–04 Focus 3-door w/auxiliary instrument cluster

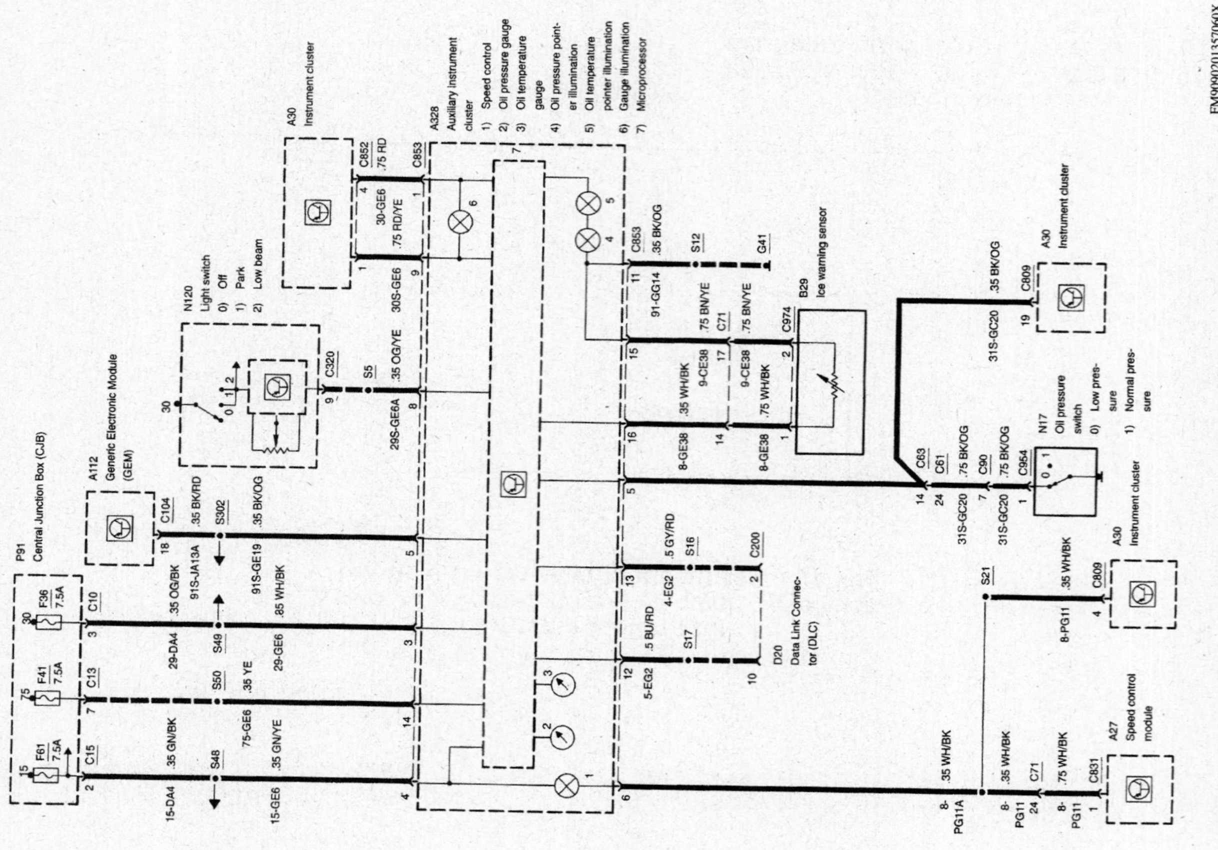

Fig. 15 Instrument cluster wiring diagram (Part 6 of 6). 2002–04 Focus 3-door w/auxiliary instrument cluster

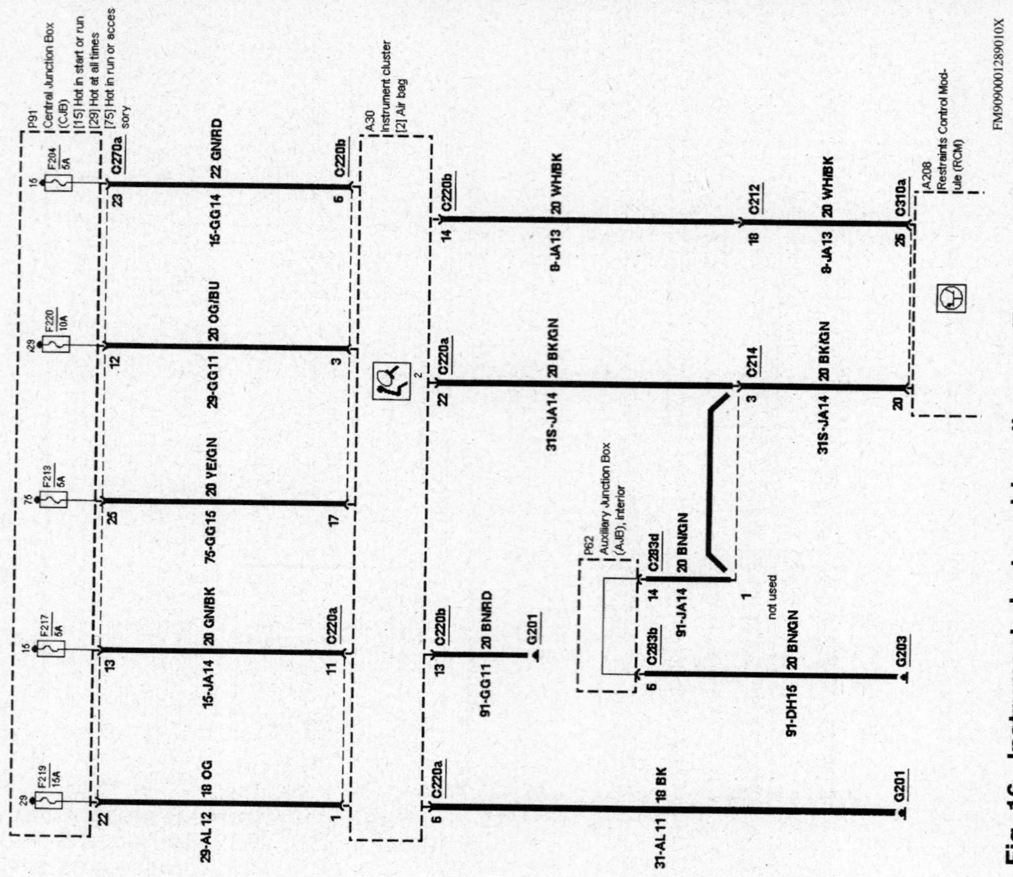

Fig. 16 Instrument cluster wiring diagram (Part 1 of 5). 2000–01 LS

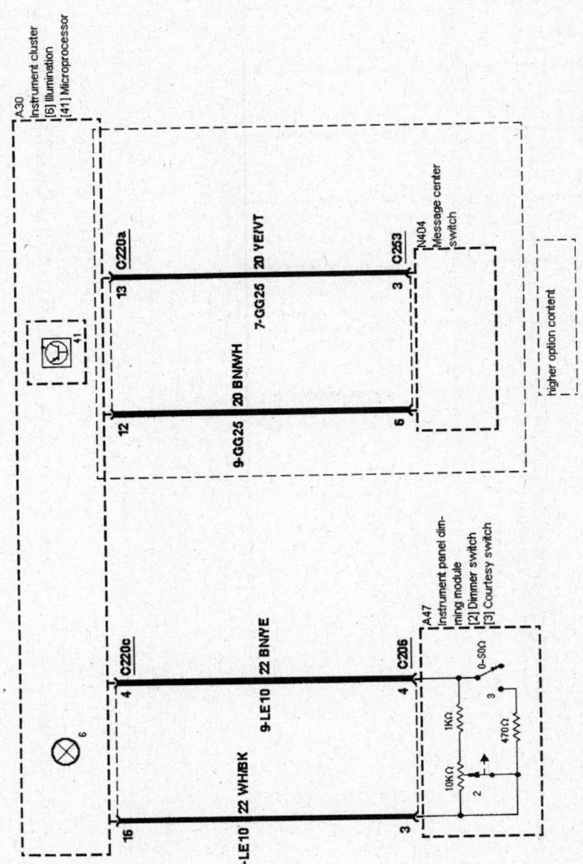

Fig. 16 Instrument cluster wiring diagram (Part 2 of 5). 2000–01 LS

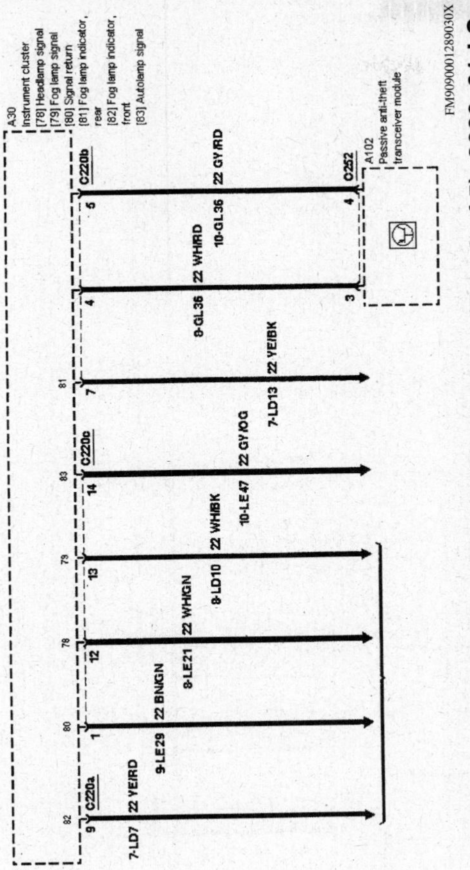

Fig. 16 Instrument cluster wiring diagram (Part 3 of 5). 2000–01 LS

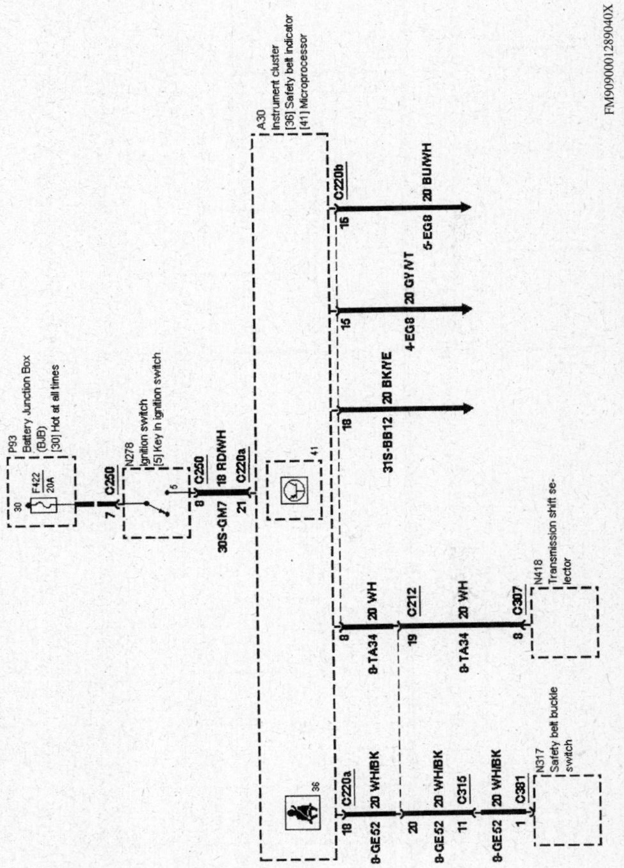

Fig. 16 Instrument cluster wiring diagram (Part 4 of 5). 2000–01 LS

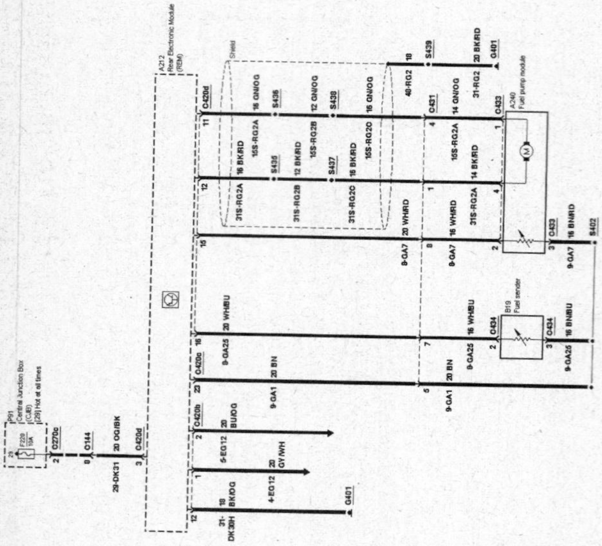

FM9090001289050X

Fig. 16 Instrument cluster wiring diagram (Part 5 of 5). 2000–01 LS

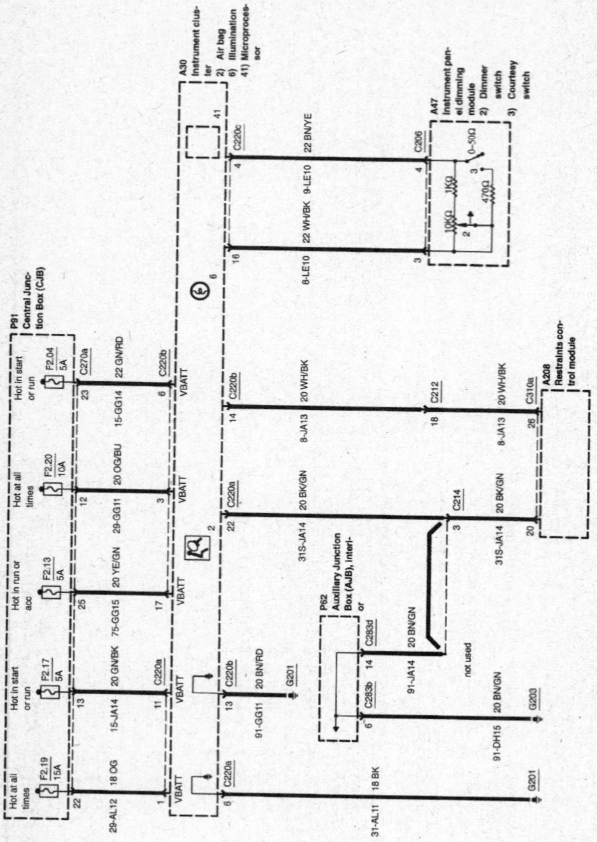

FM9040102027010X

Fig. 17 Instrument cluster wiring diagram (Part 1 of 5). 2002–04 LS

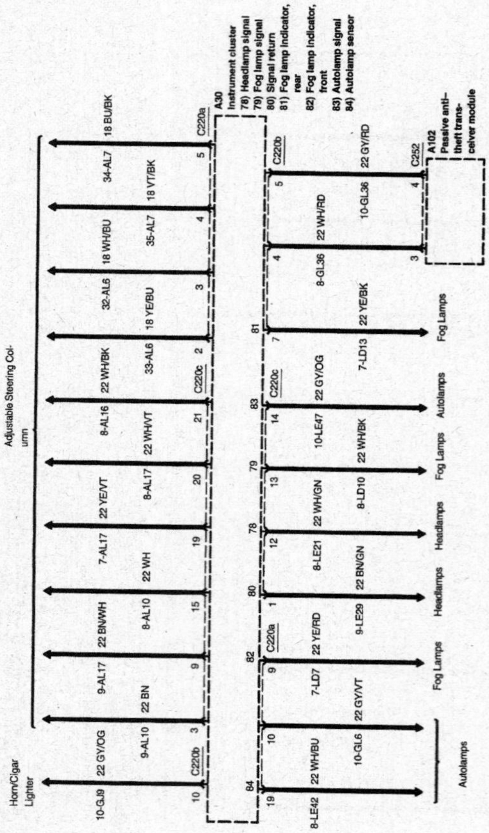

FM9040102027020X

Fig. 17 Instrument cluster wiring diagram (Part 2 of 5). 2002–04 LS

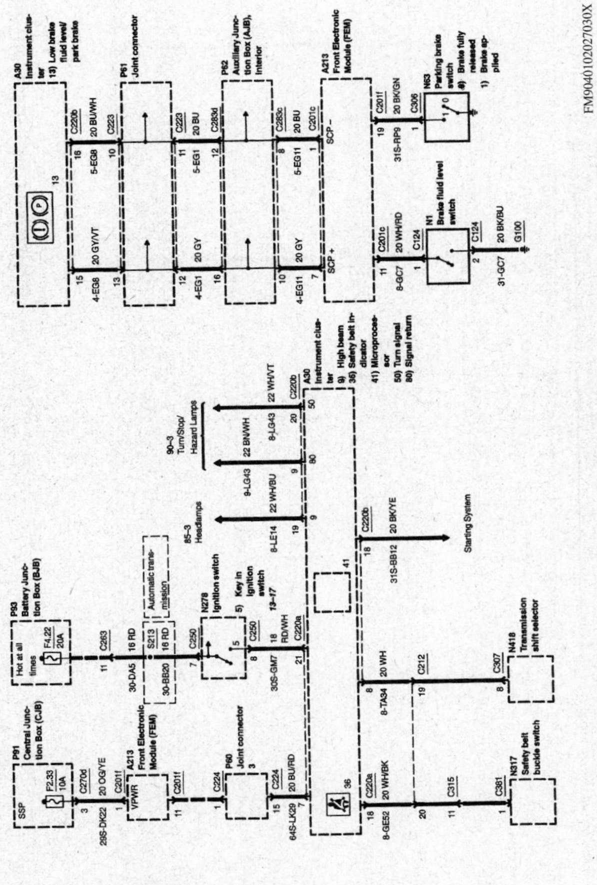

Fig. 17 Instrument cluster wiring diagram (Part 3 of 5). 2002–04 LS

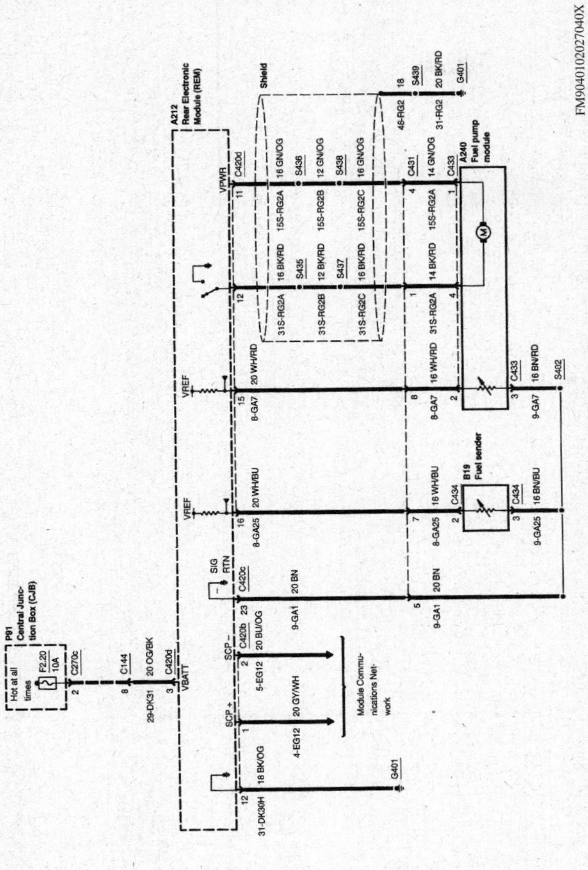

Fig. 17 Instrument cluster wiring diagram (Part 4 of 5). 2002–04 LS

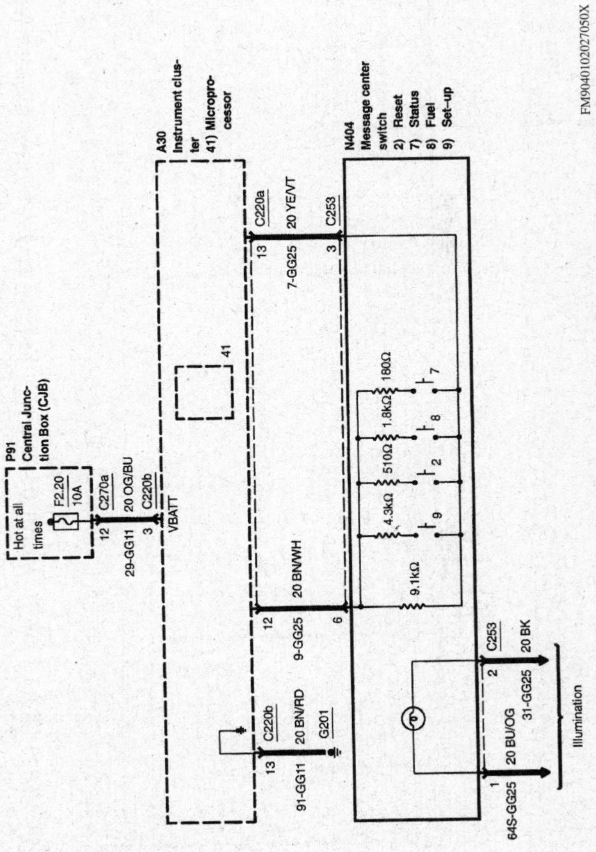

Fig. 17 Instrument cluster wiring diagram (Part 5 of 5). 2002–04 LS

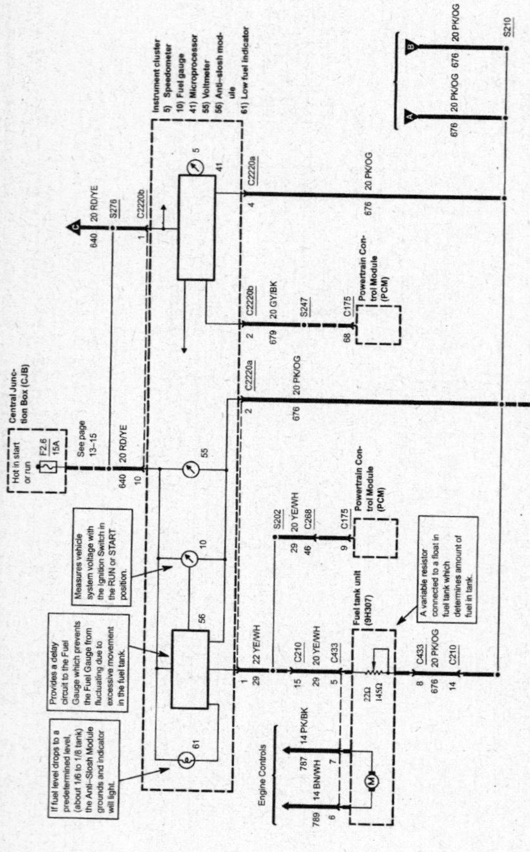

FM909020135401 0X

Fig. 18 Instrument cluster wiring diagram (Part 1 of 6). Marauder

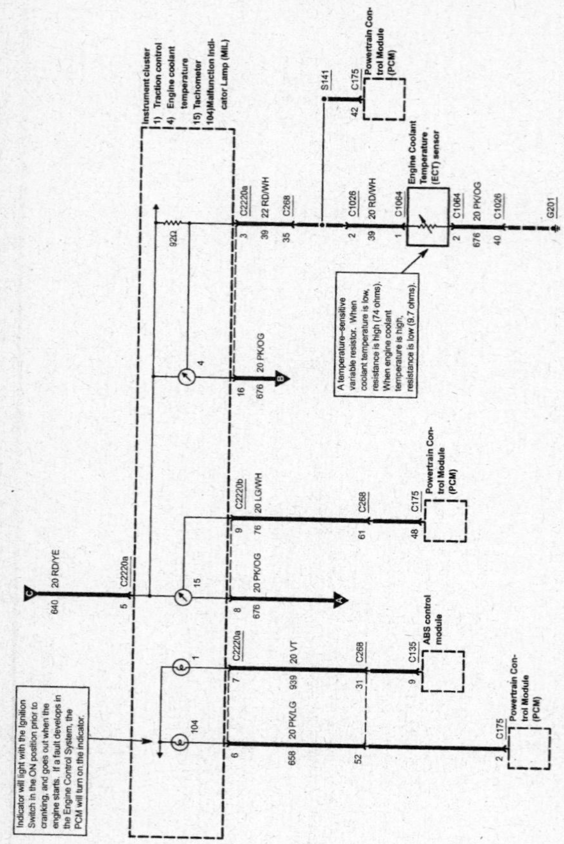

FM909020135402 0X

Fig. 18 Instrument cluster wiring diagram (Part 2 of 6). Marauder

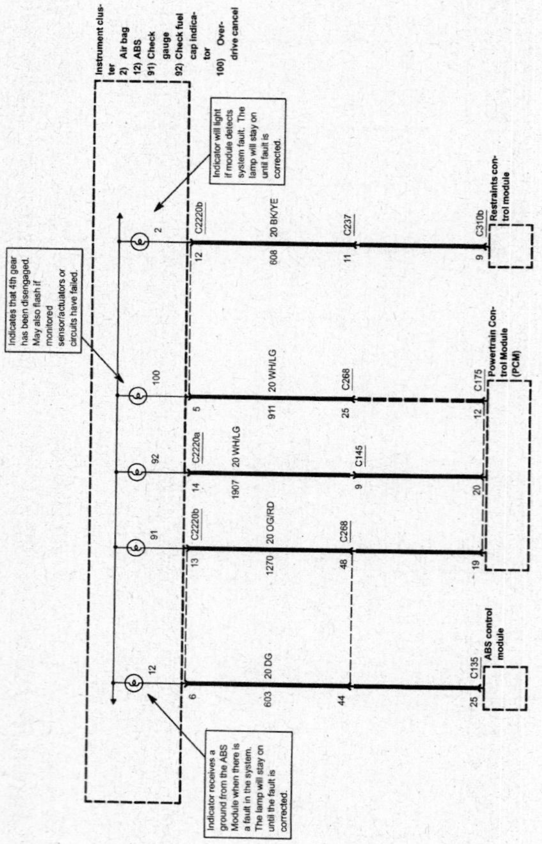

FM909020135403 0X

Fig. 18 Instrument cluster wiring diagram (Part 3 of 6). Marauder

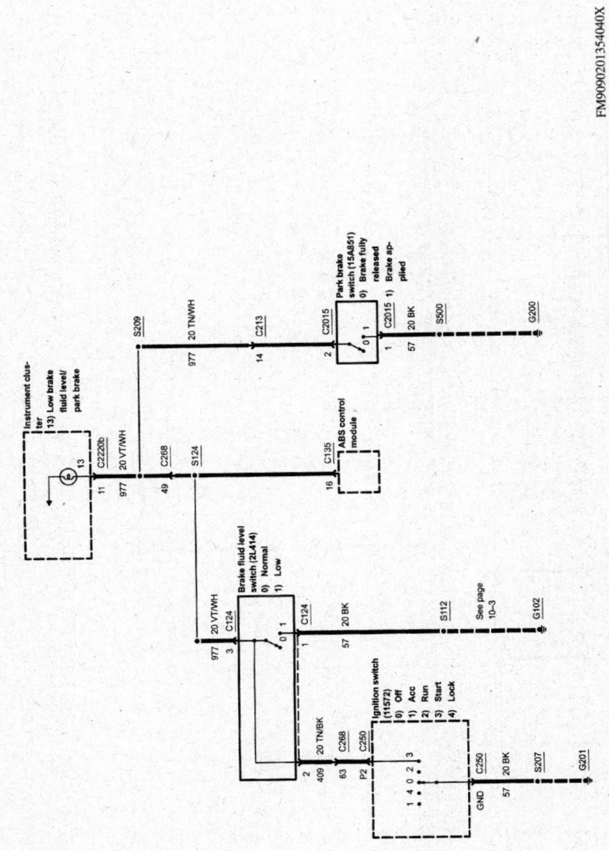

FM9090201354040X

Fig. 18 Instrument cluster wiring diagram (Part 4 of 6). Marauder

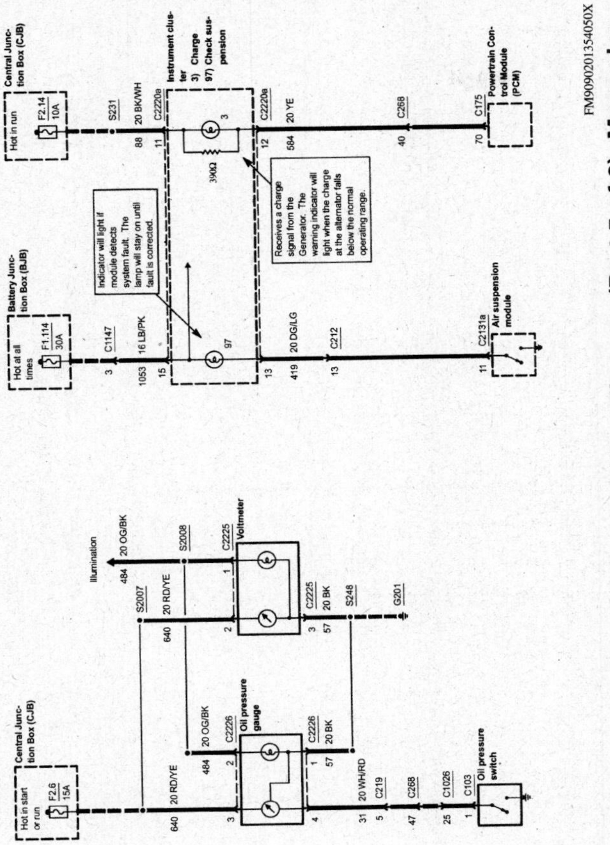

FM9090201354050X

Fig. 18 Instrument cluster wiring diagram (Part 5 of 6). Marauder

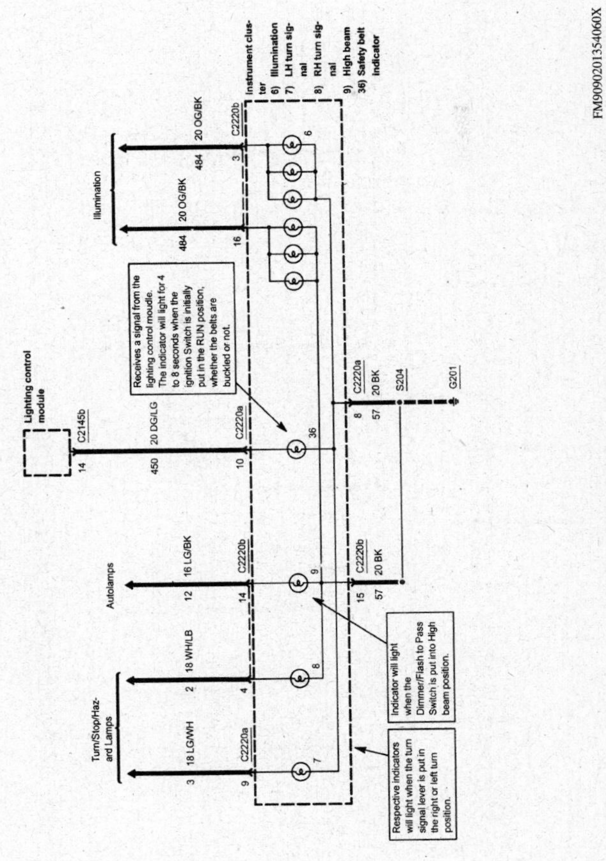

FM9090201354060X

Fig. 18 Instrument cluster wiring diagram (Part 6 of 6). Marauder

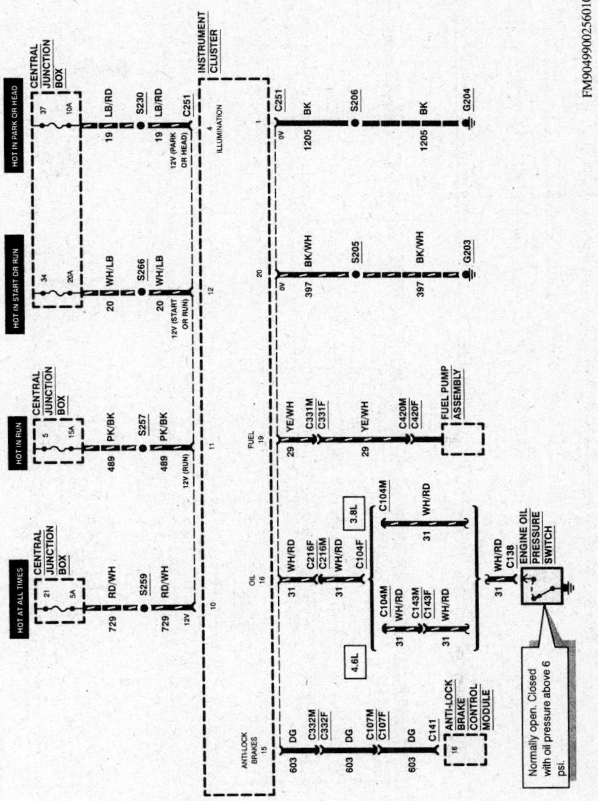

FM9049900256010X

Fig. 19 Instrument cluster wiring (Part 1 of 2). 2000–01 Mustang

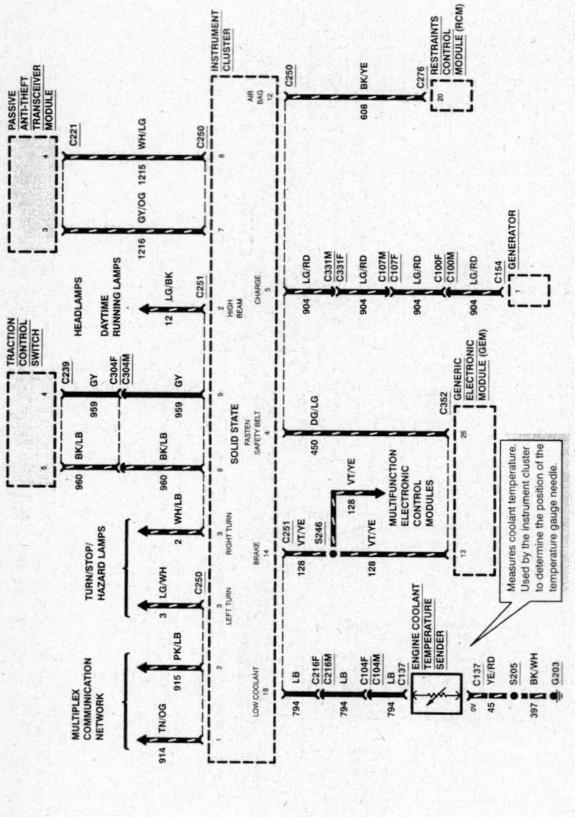

FM9049900256020X

Fig. 19 Instrument cluster wiring (Part 2 of 2). 2000–01 Mustang

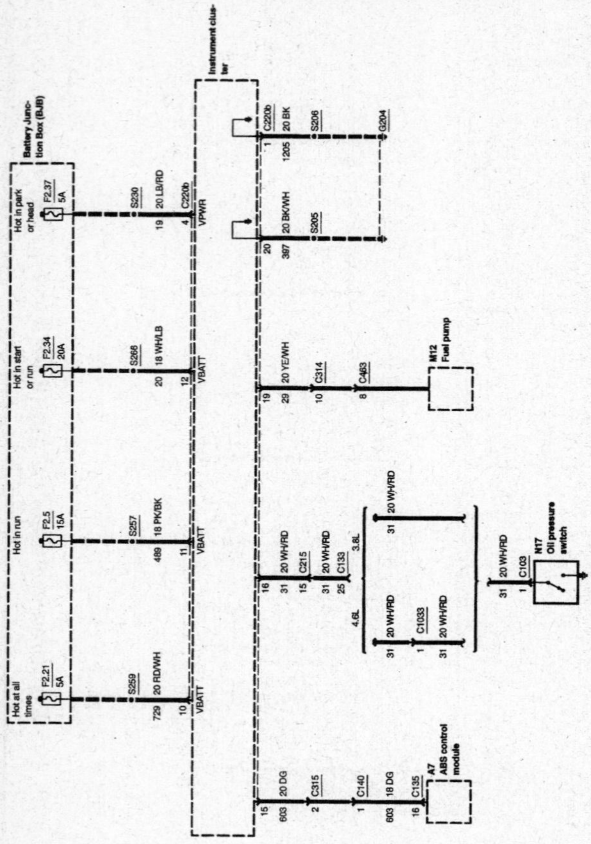

FM9040102024010X

Fig. 20 Instrument cluster wiring (Part 1 of 2). 2002–04 Mustang

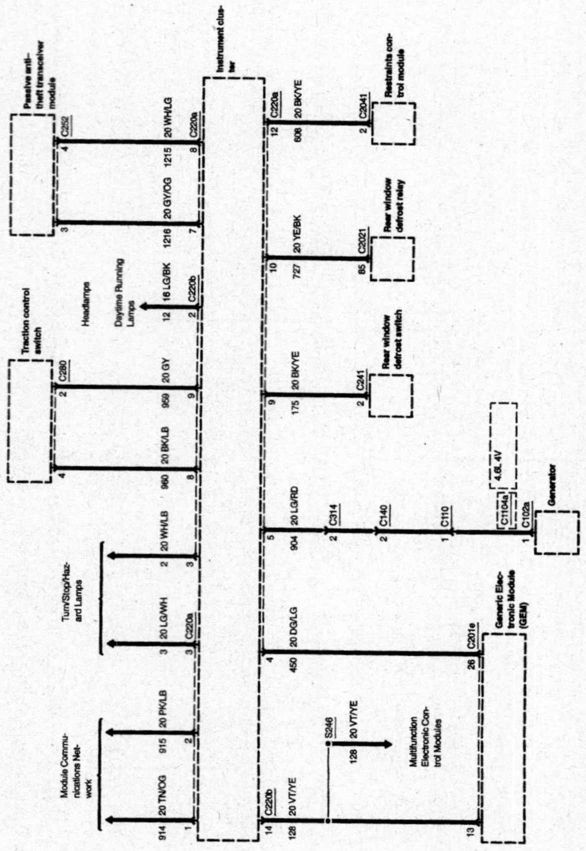

FM9040102024020X

Fig. 20 Instrument cluster wiring (Part 2 of 2). 2002–04 Mustang

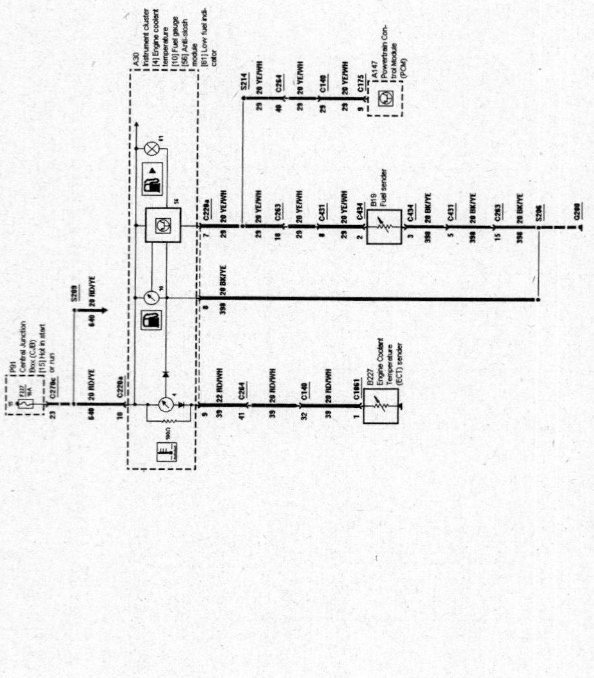

FM9090001291010X

Fig. 21 Instrument cluster wiring diagram (Part 1 of 6). 2000 Sable & Taurus less FFV

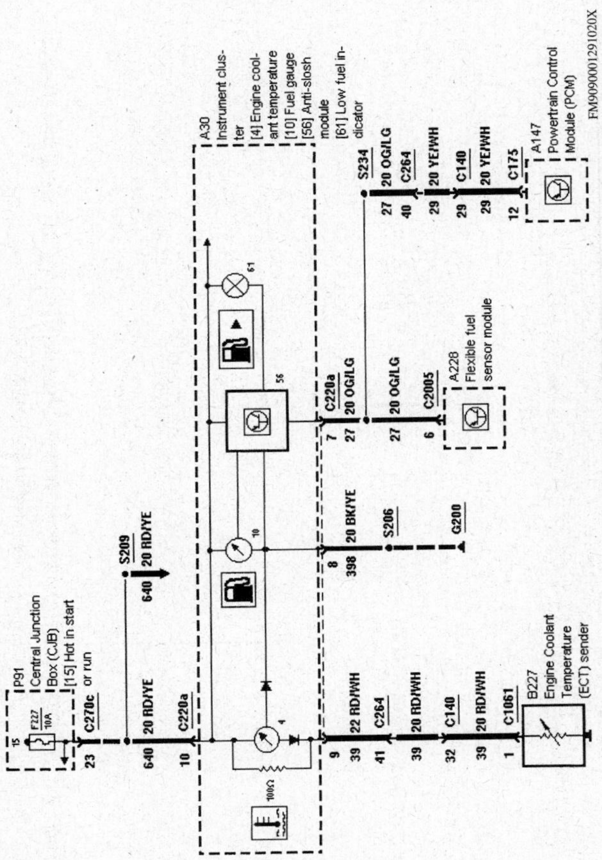

Fig. 21 Instrument cluster wiring diagram (Part 1 of 6). 2000 Sable & Taurus w/FFV

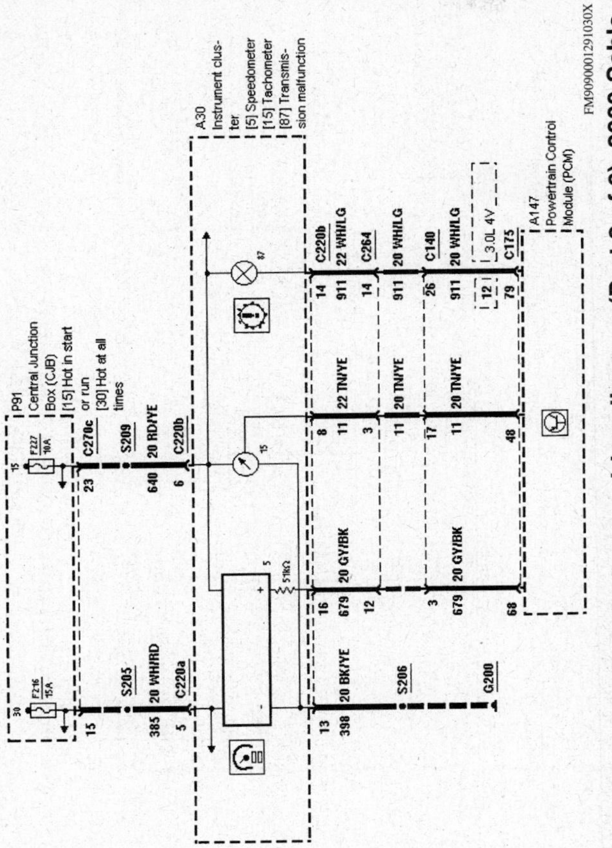

Fig. 21 Instrument cluster wiring diagram (Part 2 of 6). 2000 Sable & Taurus

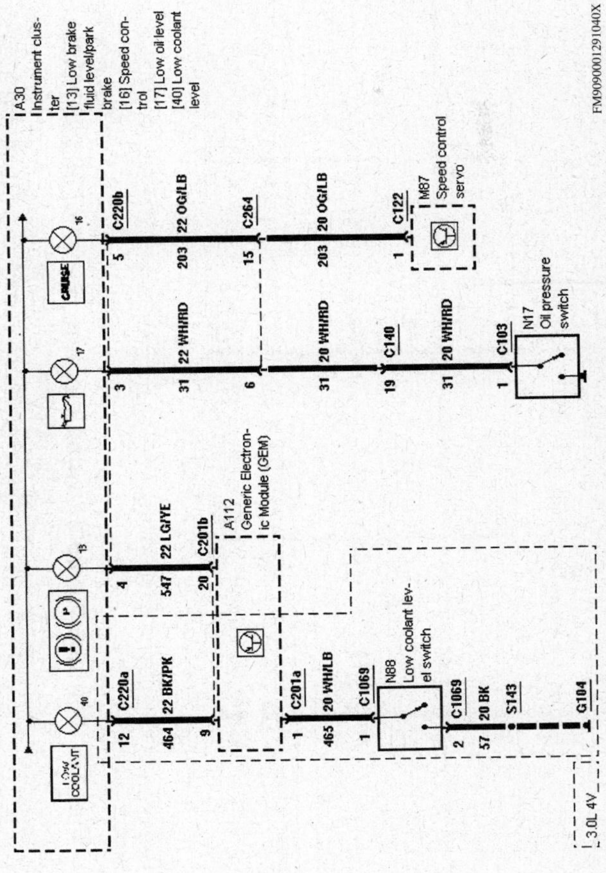

Fig. 21 Instrument cluster wiring diagram (Part 3 of 6). 2000 Sable & Taurus

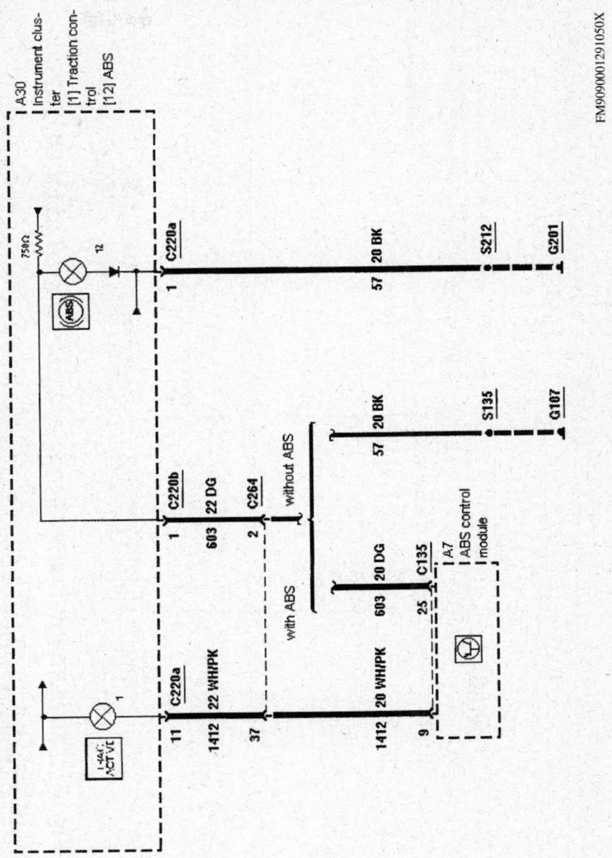

Fig. 21 Instrument cluster wiring diagram (Part 4 of 6). 2000 Sable & Taurus

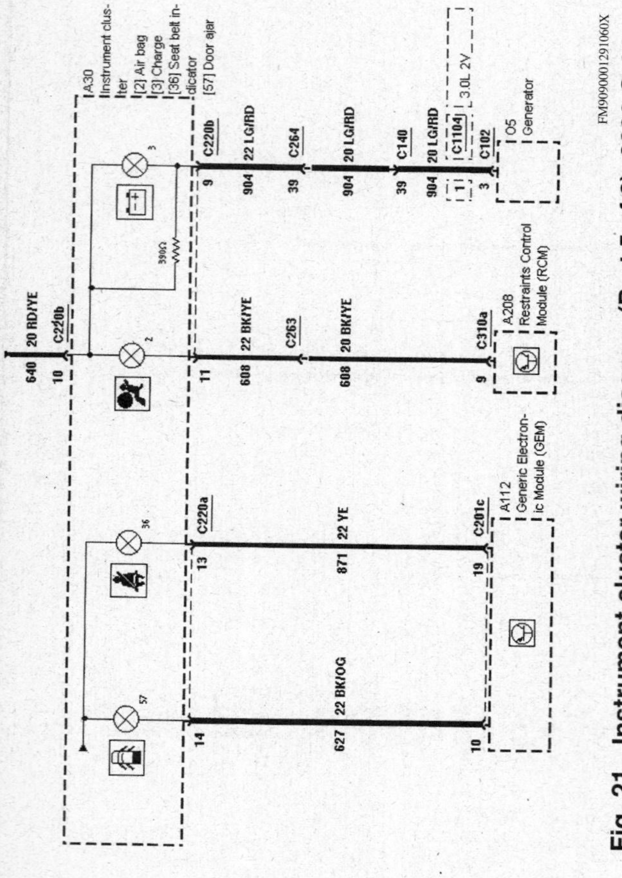

FM9090001291060X

Fig. 21 Instrument cluster wiring diagram (Part 5 of 6). 2000 Sable & Taurus

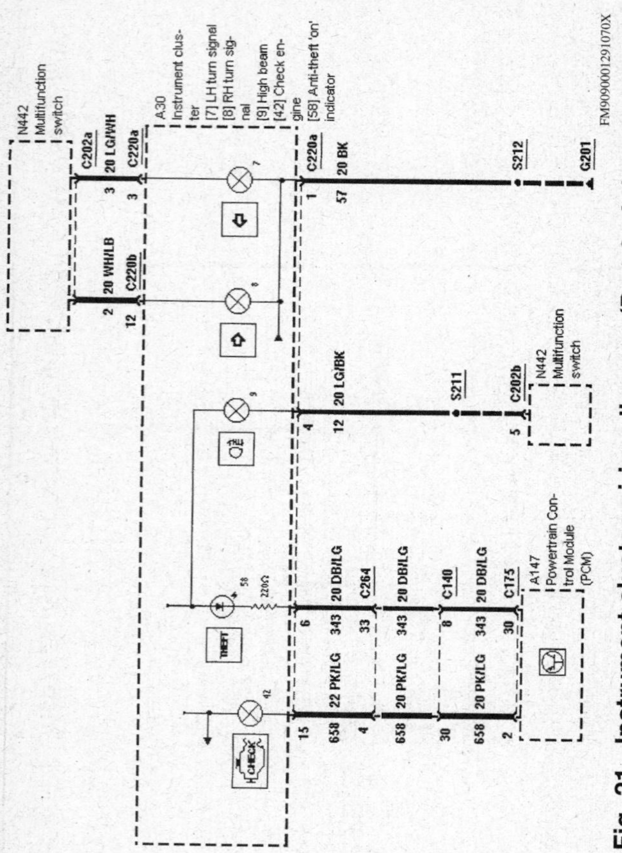

FM9090001291070X

Fig. 21 Instrument cluster wiring diagram (Part 6 of 6). 2000 Sable & Taurus

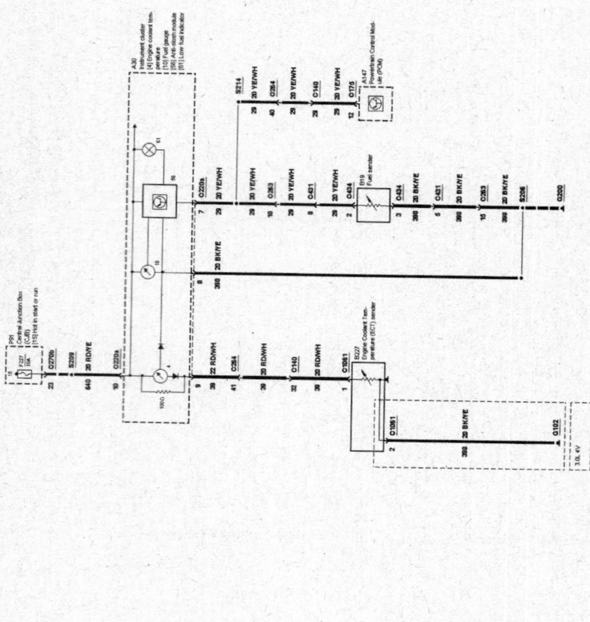

FM9090001292010X

Fig. 22 Instrument cluster wiring diagram (Part 1 of 8). 2001 Sable & Taurus less FFV

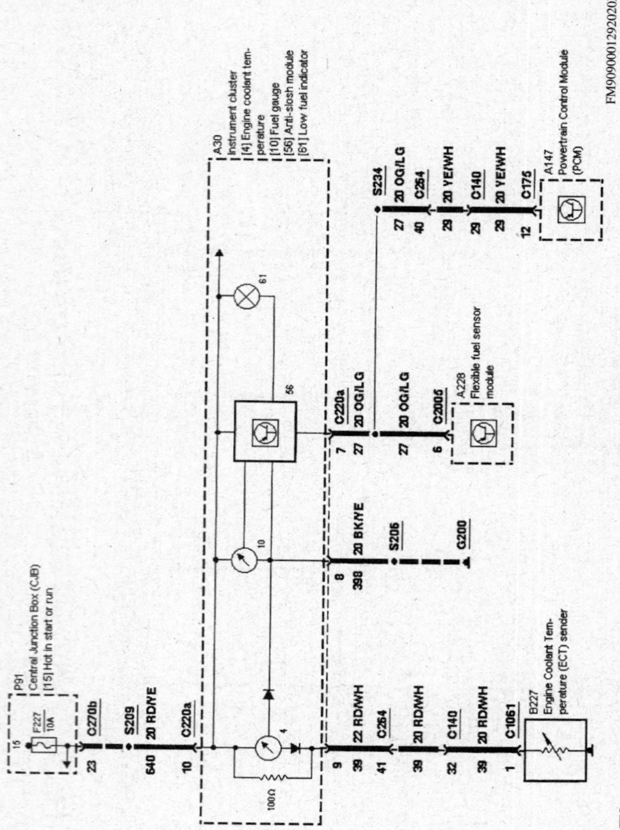

FM9090001292020X

Fig. 22 Instrument cluster wiring diagram (Part 2 of 8). 2001 Sable & Taurus w/FFV

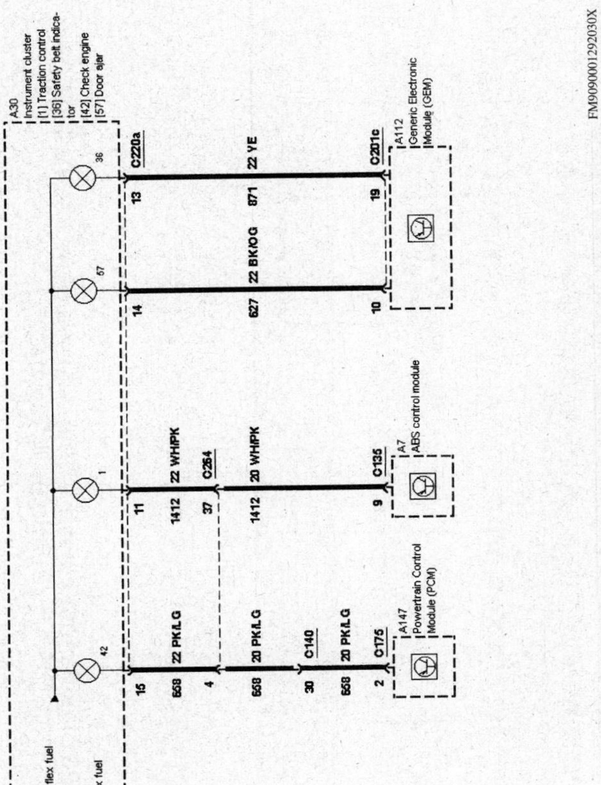

Fig. 22 Instrument cluster wiring diagram (Part 3 of 8). 2001 Sable & Taurus

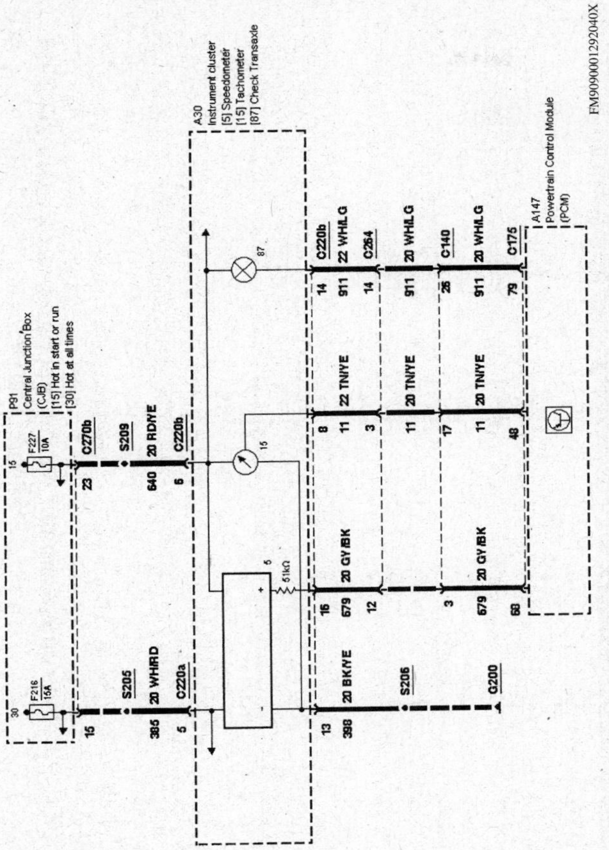

Fig. 22 Instrument cluster wiring diagram (Part 4 of 8). 2001 Sable & Taurus less FFV

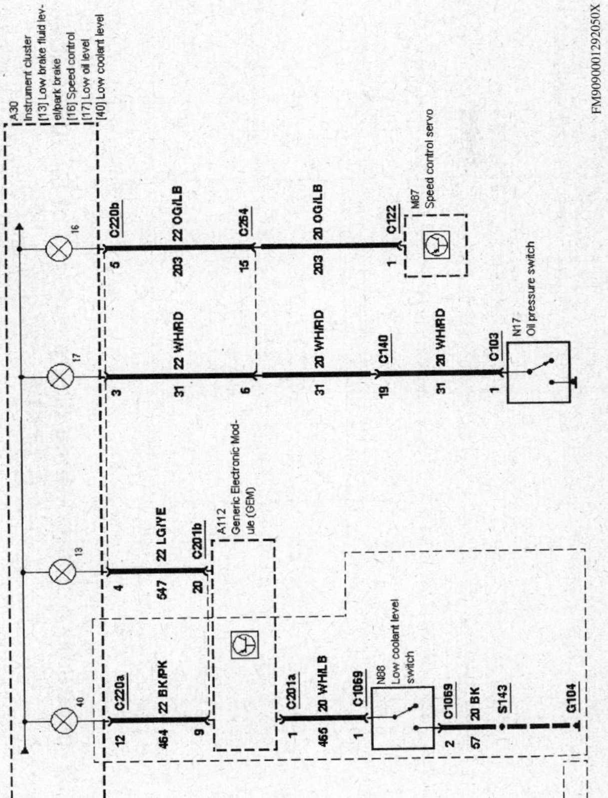

Fig. 22 Instrument cluster wiring diagram (Part 5 of 8). 2001 Sable & Taurus

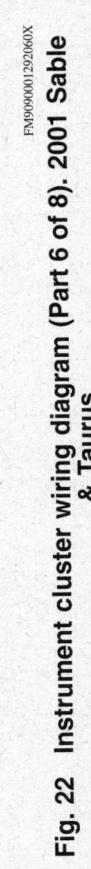

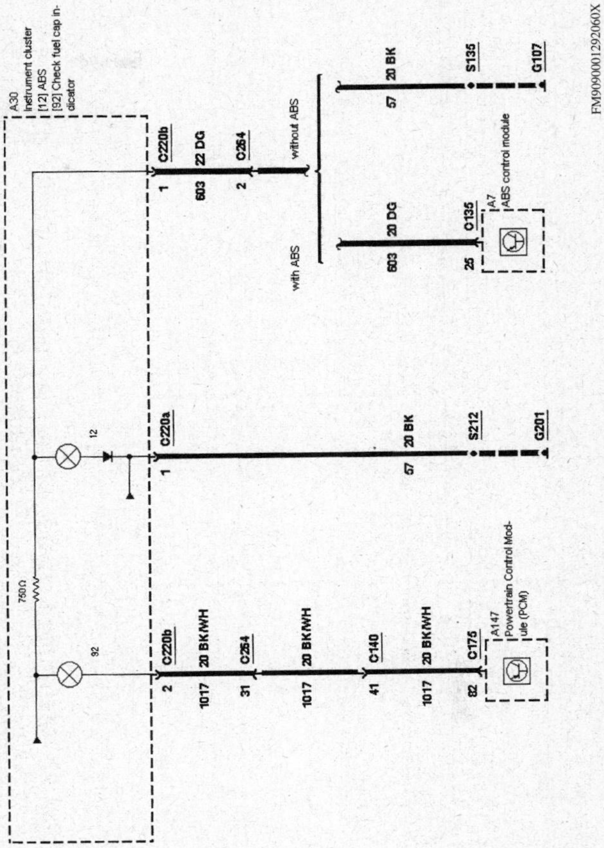

Fig. 22 Instrument cluster wiring diagram (Part 6 of 8). 2001 Sable & Taurus

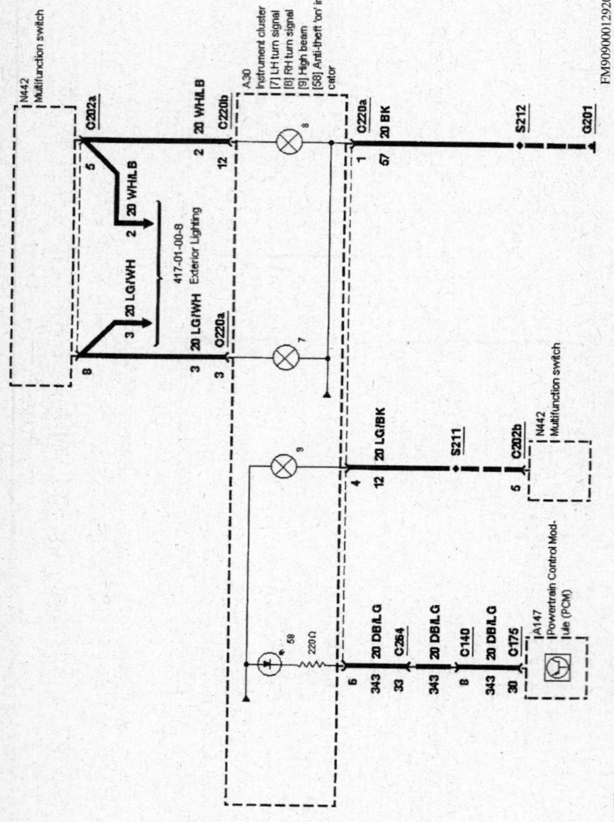

FM9090001292070X

Fig. 22 Instrument cluster wiring diagram (Part 7 of 8). 2001 Sable & Taurus

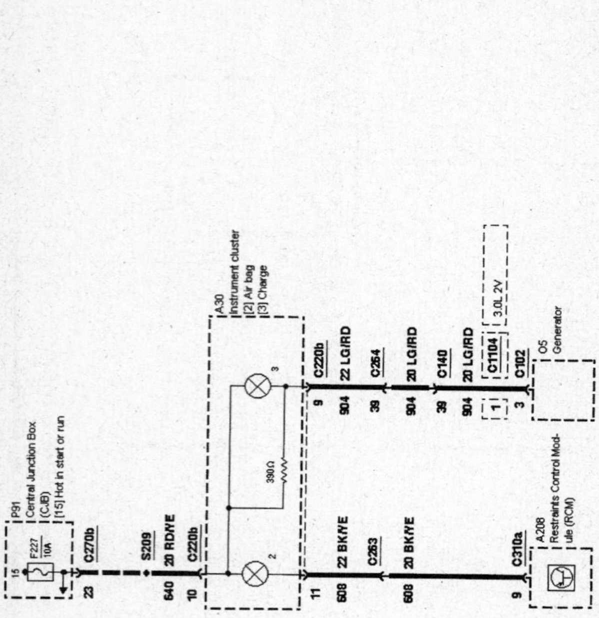

FM9090001292080X

Fig. 22 Instrument cluster wiring diagram (Part 8 of 8). 2001 Sable & Taurus

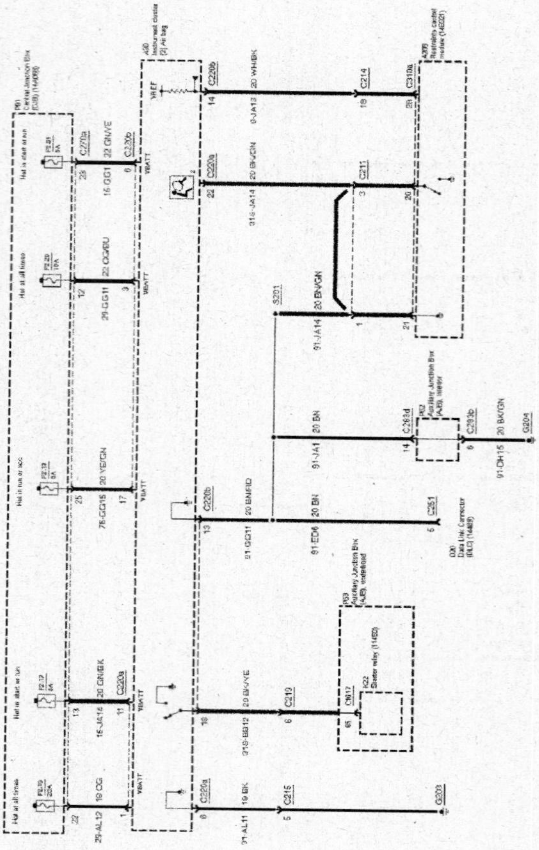

FM9040102031010X

Fig. 23 Instrument cluster wiring diagram (Part 1 of 4). 2002–04 Sable & Taurus

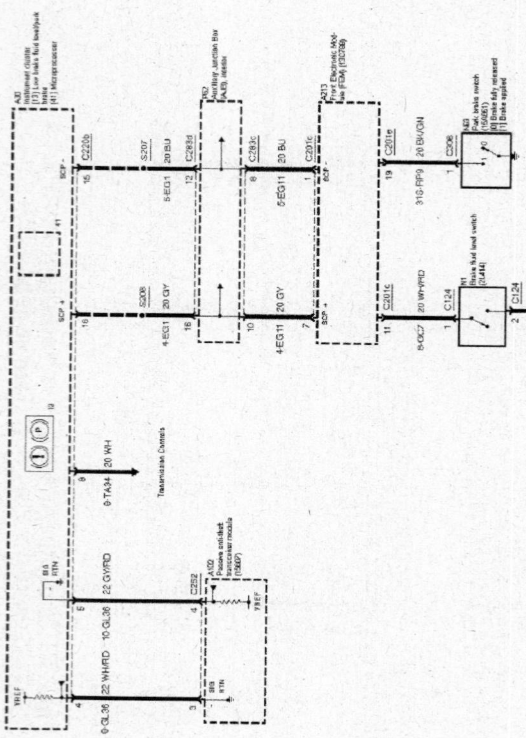

FM9040102031020X

Fig. 23 Instrument cluster wiring diagram (Part 2 of 4). 2002–04 Sable & Taurus

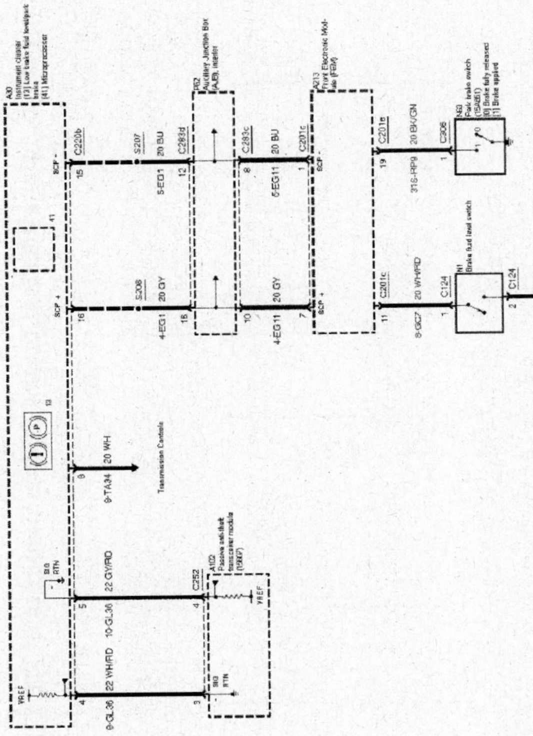

FM9040102031030X

Fig. 23 Instrument cluster wiring diagram (Part 3 of 4). 2002–04 Sable & Taurus

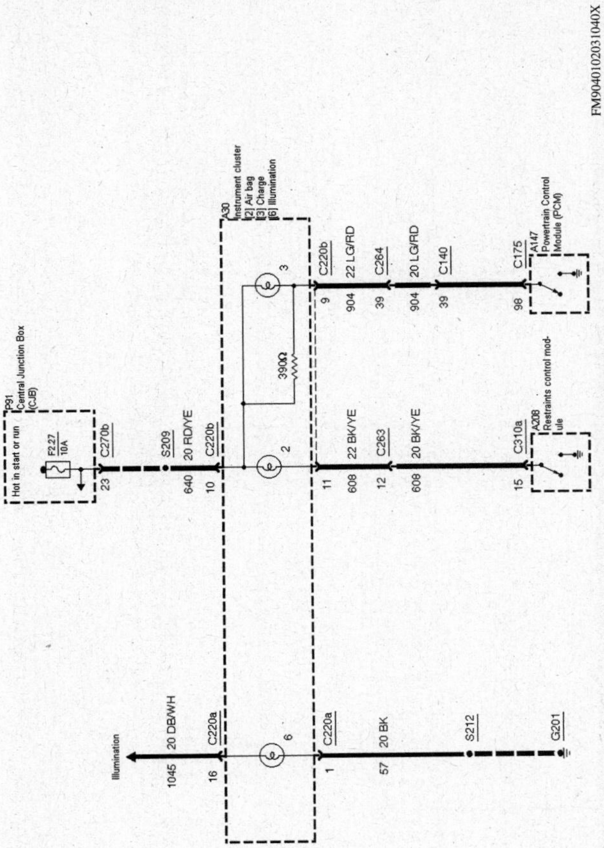

FM9040102031040X

Fig. 23 Instrument cluster wiring diagram (Part 4 of 4). 2002–04 Sable & Taurus

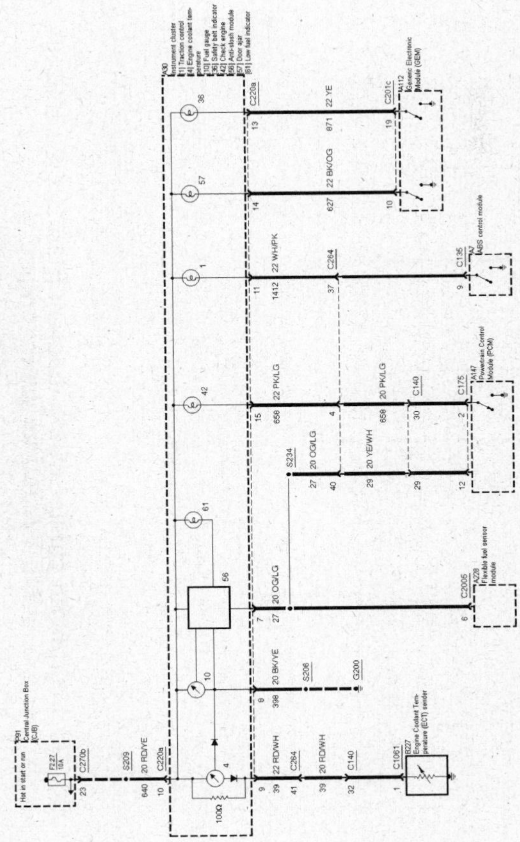

FM9040102033010X

Fig. 24 Instrument cluster wiring diagram (Part 1 of 4). 2002–04 Sable & Taurus w/FFV engine

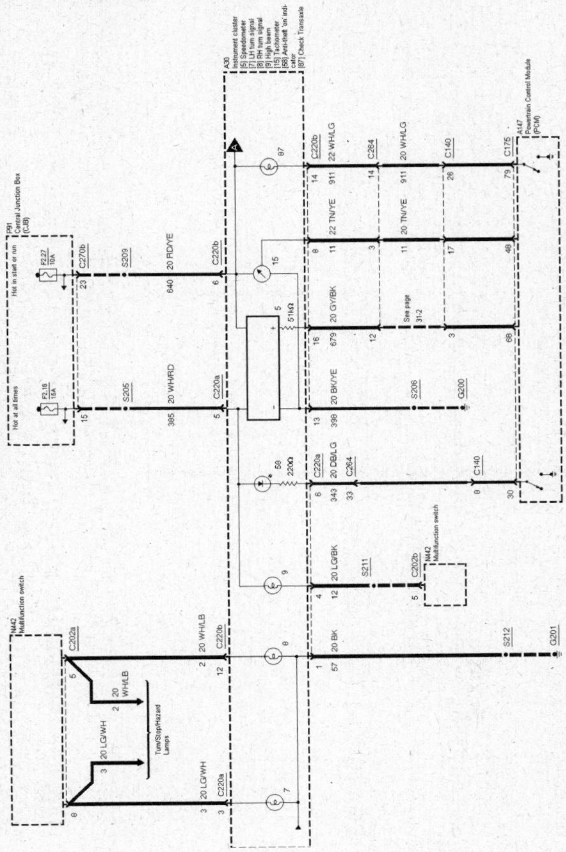

FM9040102033020X

Fig. 24 Instrument cluster wiring diagram (Part 2 of 4). 2002–04 Sable & Taurus w/FFV engine

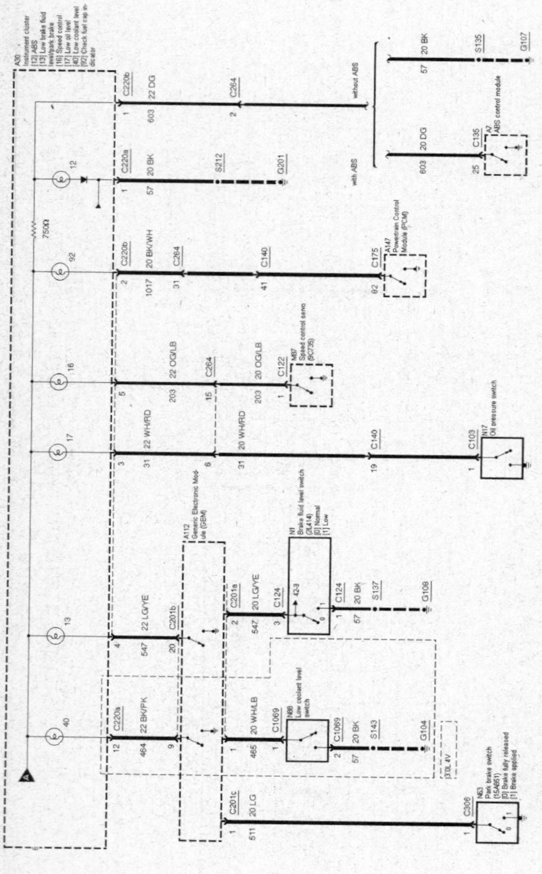

FM9040102033030X

Fig. 24 Instrument cluster wiring diagram (Part 3 of 4). 2002–04 Sable & Taurus w/FFV engine

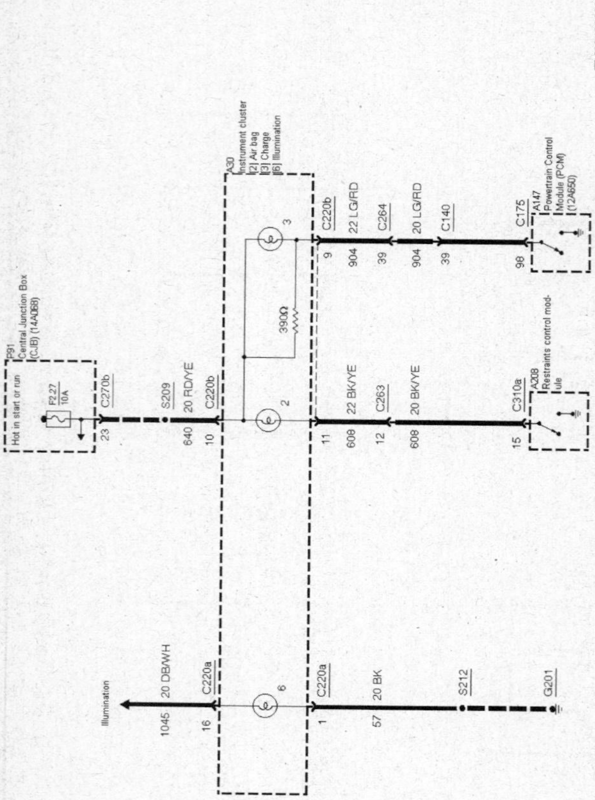

FM9040102033040X

Fig. 24 Instrument cluster wiring diagram (Part 4 of 4). 2002–04 Sable & Taurus w/FFV engine

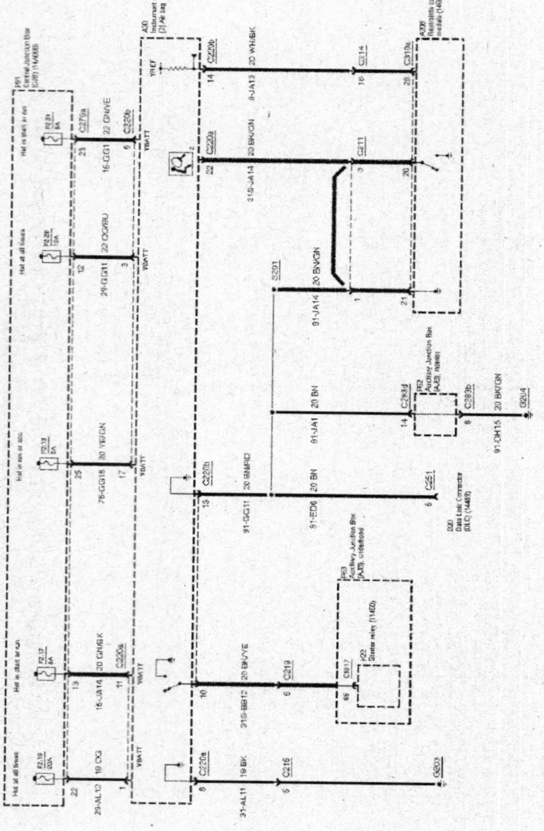

FM9040102030010X

Fig. 25 Instrument cluster wiring diagram (Part 1 of 4). Thunderbird

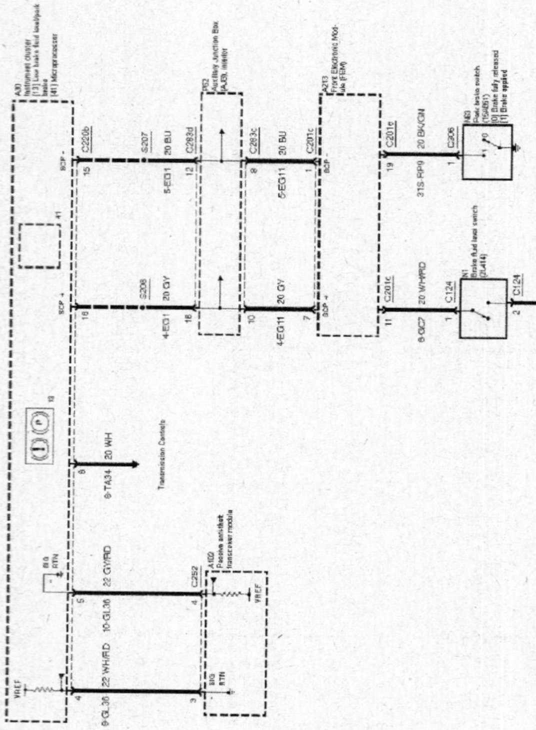

FM9040102030020X

Fig. 25 Instrument cluster wiring diagram (Part 2 of 4). Thunderbird

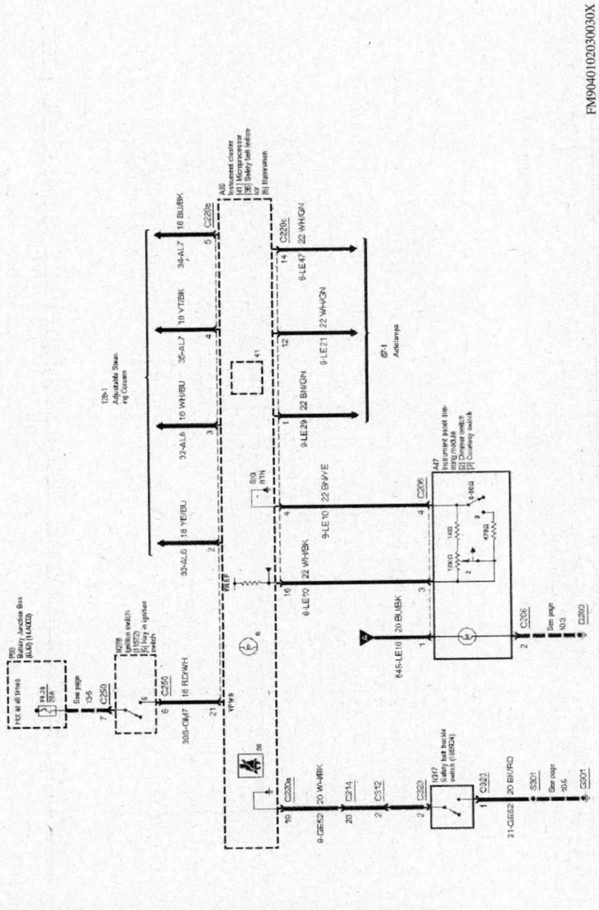

Fig. 25 Instrument cluster wiring diagram (Part 3 of 4). Thunderbird

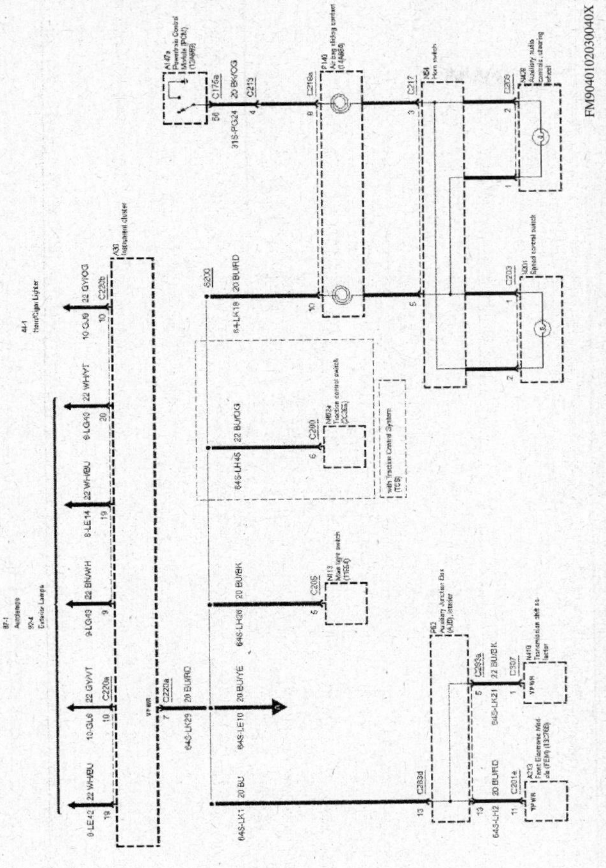

Fig. 25 Instrument cluster wiring diagram (Part 4 of 4). Thunderbird

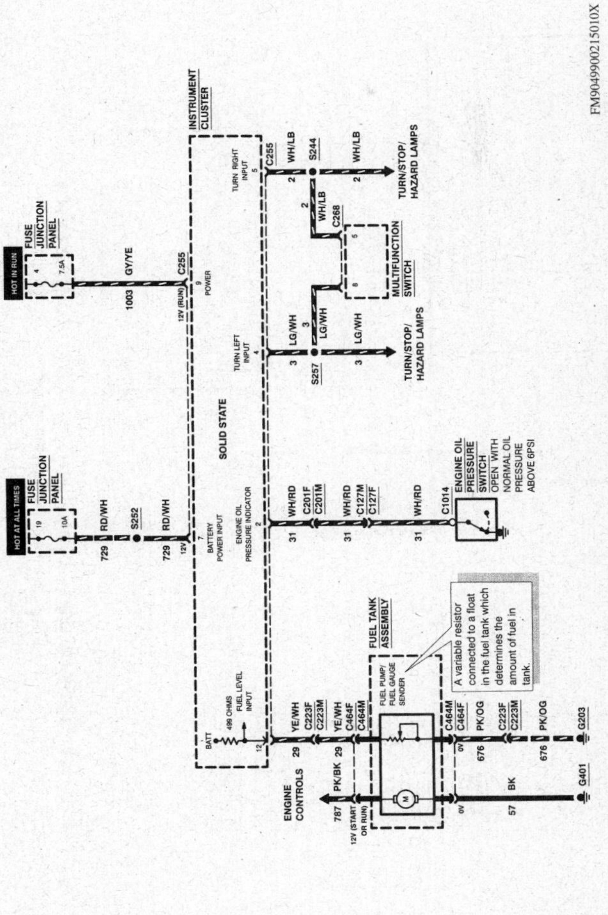

Fig. 26 Instrument cluster wiring diagram (Part 1 of 4). 2000–01 Town Car

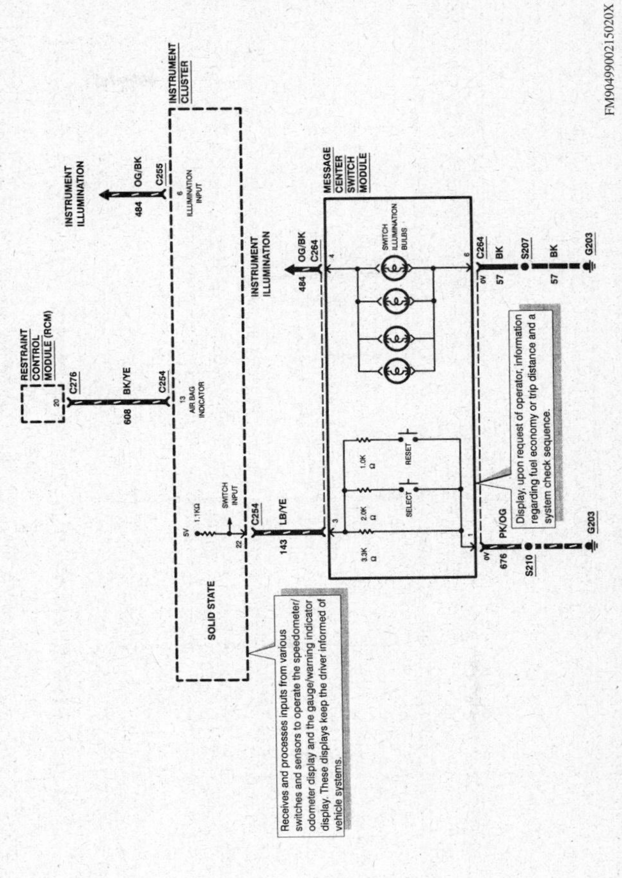

Fig. 26 Instrument cluster wiring diagram (Part 2 of 4). 2000–01 Town Car

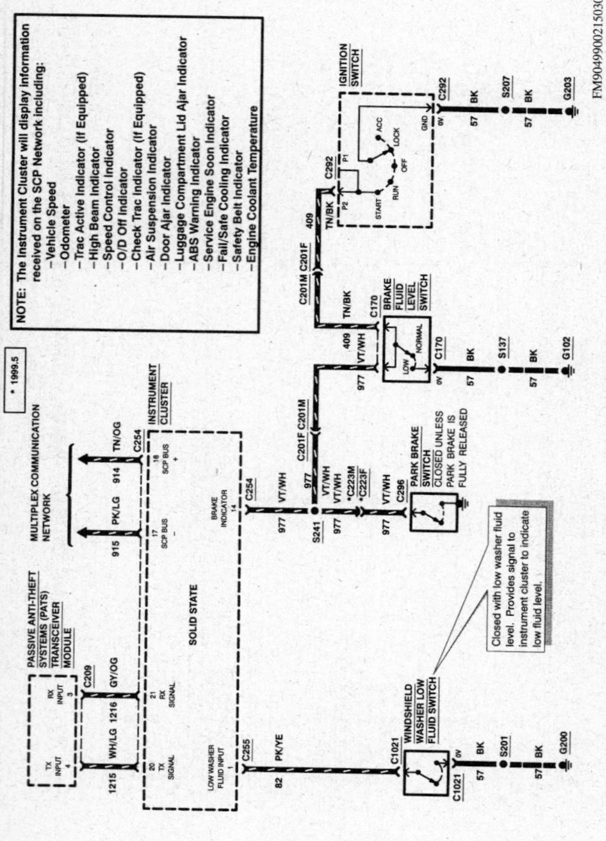

Fig. 26 Instrument cluster wiring diagram (Part 3 of 4). 2000–01 Town Car

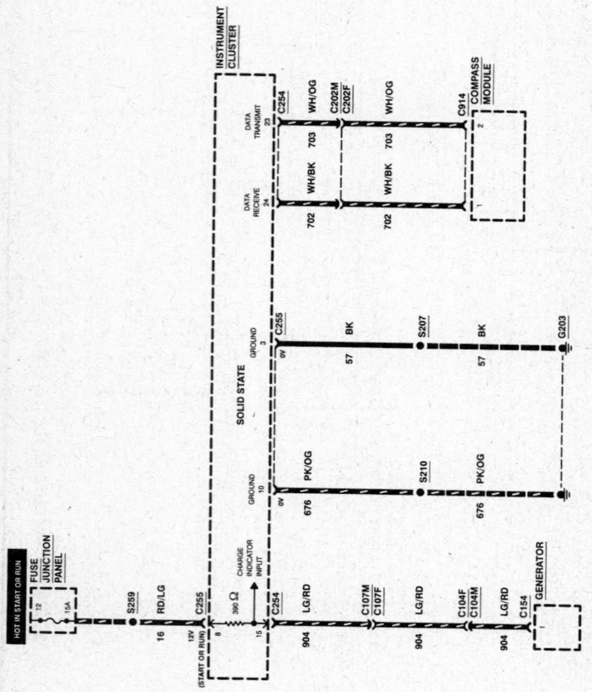

Fig. 26 Instrument cluster wiring diagram (Part 4 of 4). 2000–01 Town Car

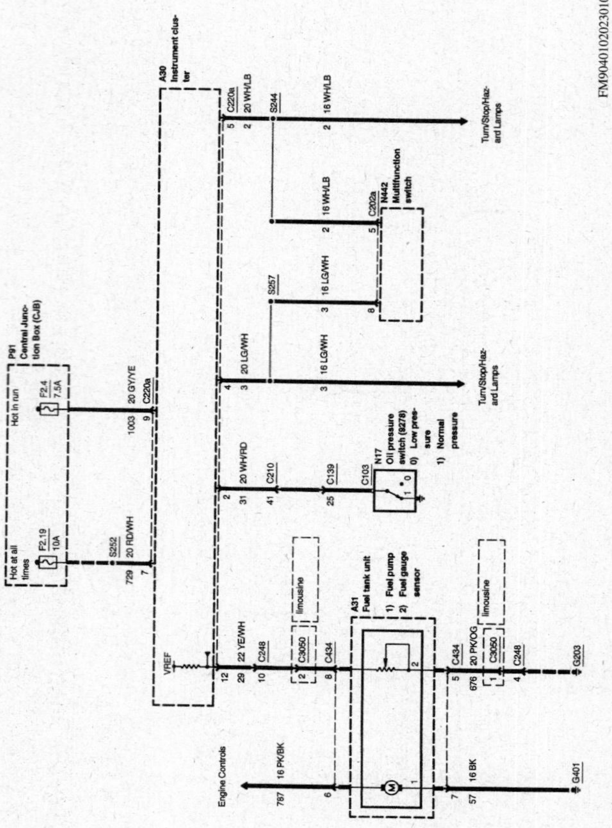

Fig. 27 Instrument cluster wiring diagram (Part 1 of 4). 2002 Town Car

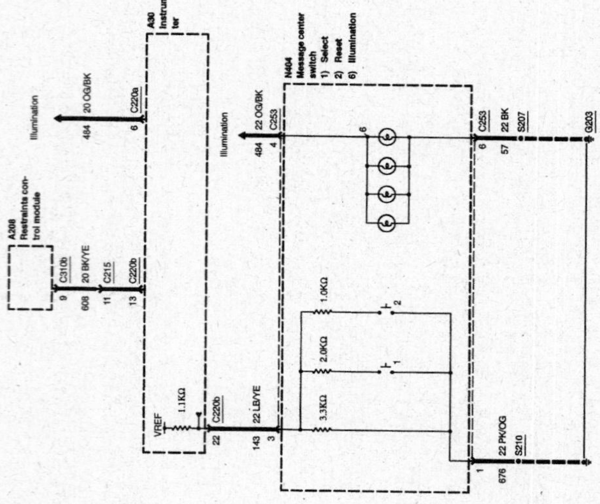

Fig. 27 Instrument cluster wiring diagram (Part 2 of 4). 2002 Town Car

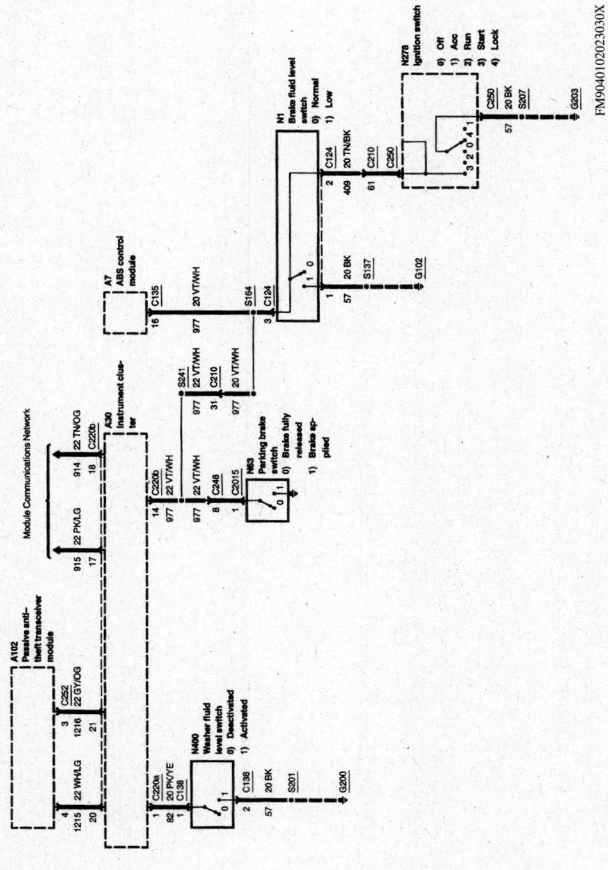

FM9040102023030X

Fig. 27 Instrument cluster wiring diagram (Part 3 of 4). 2002 Town Car

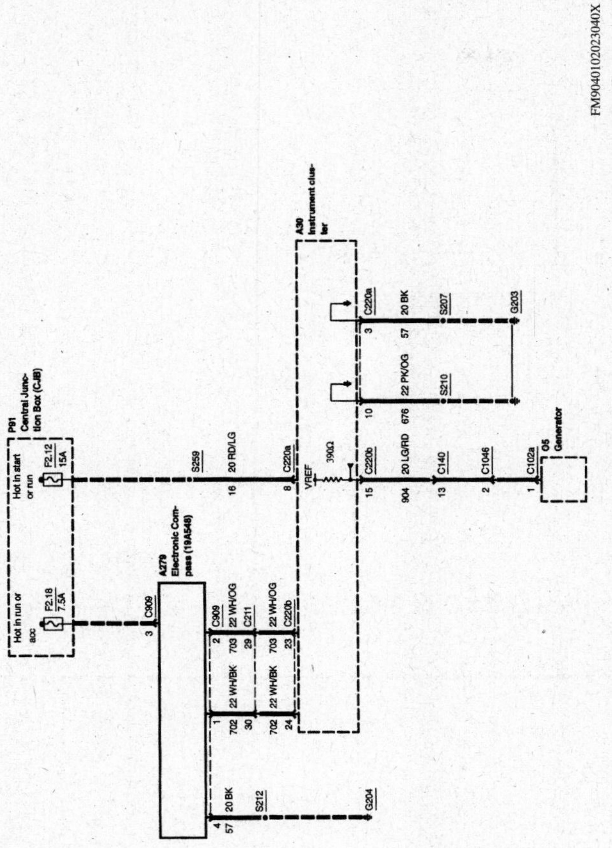

FM9040102023040X

Fig. 27 Instrument cluster wiring diagram (Part 4 of 4). 2002 Town Car

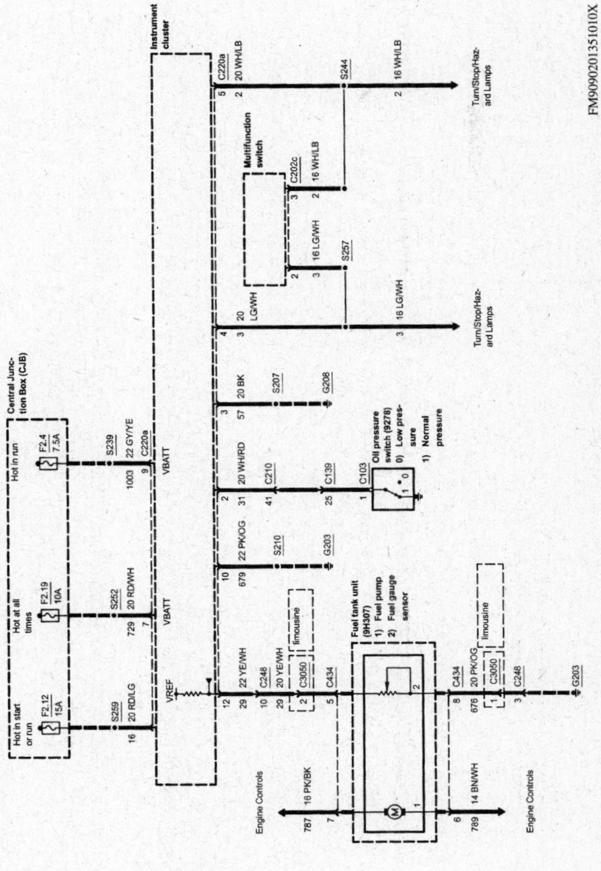

FM9090201351010X

Fig. 28 Instrument cluster wiring diagram (Part 1 of 3). 2003–04 Town Car

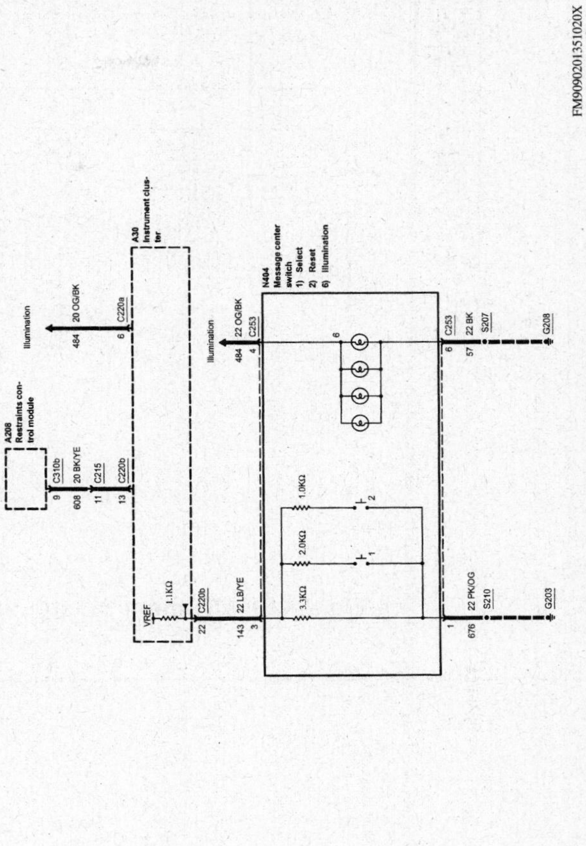

FM9090201351020X

Fig. 28 Instrument cluster wiring diagram (Part 2 of 3). 2003–04 Town Car

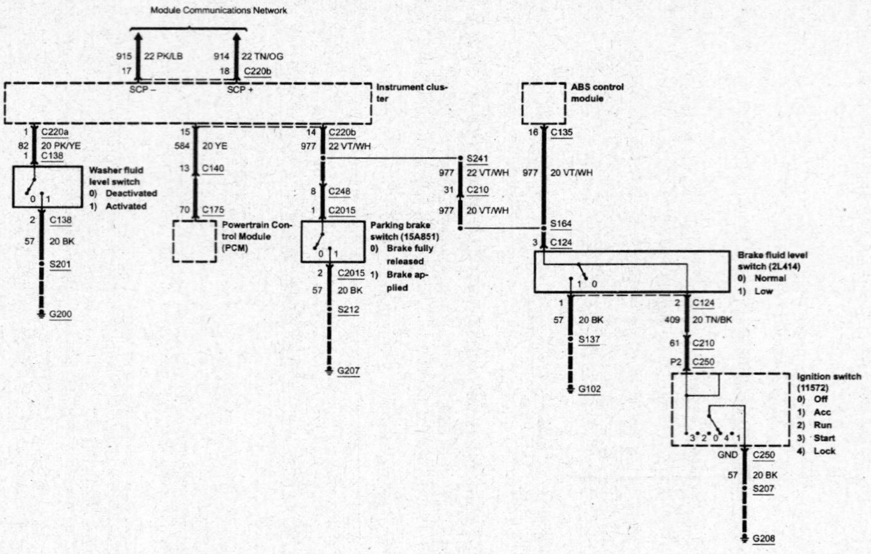

FM9090201351030X

Fig. 28 Instrument cluster wiring diagram (Part 3 of 3). 2003–04 Town Car

SPEED CONTROL SYSTEMS

NOTE: On Air Bag Equipped Models, Refer To "Air Bag System Precautions" Located In The Front Of This Manual For System Disarming & Arming Procedures.

NOTE: Refer To "Computer Relearn Procedures" Located In The Front Of This Manual When Battery Power To The Computer Has Been Interrupted.

NOTE: "Electrical Symbol & Wire Color Code Identification" Located In The Front Of This Manual May Be Used As An Aid When Using Wiring Circuits Found In This Section.

INDEX

DESCRIPTION

Continental, Contour, Crown Victoria, Grand Marquis, Marauder, Mystique & Town Car

The speed control system consists of a speed control servo, speed control actuator, Vehicle Speed Sensor (VSS) horn relay, stop lamp switch and deactivator switch, anti-lock brake control module, message center display and speed control cable.

The system operates independently of engine vacuum, so there are no vacuum lines.

To operate the speed control system, vehicle speed must exceed 30 mph. When ON-OFF switch is activated, the system is ready to accept a set speed signal. When vehicle speed stabilizes and ON switch is engaged, operator may depress or release SET/ACCEL button. This set speed will be maintained until a new set speed has been selected, brake pedal has been depressed or system is turned Off.

Vehicle set speed may be increased manually by pressing accelerator until higher speed is reached, then depressing and releasing SET/ACCEL button. Set speed can also be increased by depressing and holding SET/ACCEL button. When set speed increases to desired level, release SET/ACCEL button or momentarily tap SET/ACCEL switch and the vehicle will accelerate 1 mph for each tap.

Cougar

The speed control system is operated by means of five switches on the steering wheel. The speed control unit provides signals to the stepper motor housed in the actuator. The stepper motor moves the throttle body cam by means of an internal gear train and a cable linkage. The vehicle speed sensor generates the reference signal that the control unit compares to the speed setting selected by the driver. If a discrepancy exists, the stepper motor will adjust the throttle body cam setting, correcting the vehicle speed.

Any of the switches operated by the brake or clutch pedal will interrupt the speed control operation by releasing the speed control actuator cable and returning the throttle body cam to the position set by the throttle pedal.

The speed control actuator is mounted on the lefthand inner fender behind the suspension unit top mount. The speed control actuator incorporates the following components, electronic speed control unit, stepper motor and gear train, electromagnetic coupling and reduction gearing.

The speed control unit evaluates incoming signals from the system sensors and switches. It actuates a stepper motor and cable linkage to adjust the throttle body cam, maintaining a constant vehicle road speed.

When the speed control system is activated, the windings in the stepper motor are energized by the speed control actuator which ensures accurate positioning of the throttle body cam. The vehicle road speed then settles to the speed selected by the driver.

Escort, Mustang, Sable, Taurus & ZX2

The speed control system consists of a speed control servo, actuator, Output Shaft Speed (OSS) or Vehicle Speed (VSS) sensor, horn relay and bracket, speed control actuator switches, stop lamp switch, and deactivator switch.

Additional components required for vehicles equipped with traction assist system include a speed control cutout relay located in power distribution box, traction assist disable switch mounted on instrument panel.

Manual transaxle vehicles with or without traction assist require a clutch pedal position switch mounted on pedal bracket.

The system operates independently of engine vacuum. No vacuum lines are required.

To operate speed control system, vehicle speed must exceed 25–30 mph. When ON-OFF switch is actuated, system is ready to accept a set speed signal. When vehicle speed stabilizes (above 30 mph), and ON switch is engaged, operator may depress or release SET/ACCEL button. This set speed will be maintained until a new speed has been set, brake pedal has been depressed, or system is turned off.

Vehicle speed may be reduced by applying brake or clutch pedal and then resetting speed using method outlined above or by depressing COAST switch. When vehicle has slowed to desired speed, COAST switch is released and new speed is set automatically or momentarily tap COAST switch and the vehicle speed will decrease 1 mph from each tap. If vehicle speed is reduced below 30 mph, operator must manually increase speed and reset system.

Vehicle set speed may be increased manually by pressing accelerator until higher speed is reached, then depressing and releasing SET/ACCEL button. Set speed can also be increased by depressing and holding SET/ACCEL button. When set speed increases to desired level, release SET/ACCEL button or momentarily tap SET/ACCEL switch and the vehicle will accelerate 1 mph for each tap.

Focus

On these models, the speed control module provides signals to the actuator, which moves the throttle by means of an internal gear train and an actuator cable. The Vehicle Speed Sensor (VSS) generates the reference signal for the servo to compare to the set speed chosen by the driver. Should a mismatch exist, the stepper servo will adjust the throttle and correct the vehicle speed.

Any of the switches operated by the brake or clutch pedal will deactivate the speed control servo by closing the throttle.

The speed control servo is mounted on the bulkhead and contains an electronic module, a stepper motor and gear train electromagnetic coupling and reduction gearing.

The speed control servo evaluates the incoming speed signal from the speed sensor and switch inputs and adjusts the throttle to maintain a steady vehicle speed. If the clutch pedal or the brake pedal are depressed, the speed control servo deactivates the speed control. The servo then enters a standby mode.

When the steering wheel ON switch is pressed while the vehicle is traveling at a speed greater than 30 mph, the speed control actuator will accept speed inputs.

The + (SET/ACC) switch is used to set or accelerate the vehicle at speeds above 30 mph. The switch can be used in three ways: 1.) Accelerate vehicle to required speed with accelerator pedal, then press and release + (SET/ACC) switch. Vehicle will then maintain required speed. 2.) Press + (SET/ACC) switch and hold it down until vehicle reaches required speed. When released, speed is stored in memory and used to maintain vehicle speed. 3.) Press + (SET/ACC) switch repeatedly in order to increase vehicle speed by 1 mph increments.

The – (COAST) switch is for reducing vehicle speed and can be used in two ways: 1.) Press and hold – (COAST) switch down until vehicle reaches required speed. When switch is released, the speed is stored in memory and used to maintain vehicle speed. 2.) Press – (COAST) switch repeatedly to reduce vehicle road speed by 1 mph increments.

Pressing the = (RESUME) switch returns the vehicle to the set speed when speed control is in its standby mode. Pressing and releasing the = (RESUME) switch at any speed greater than 30 mph will return the vehicle to the previous set speed.

Pressing the OFF switch deactivates the speed control system. The speed setting stored in the memory will be deleted.

If the brake pedal is lightly tapped when the speed control system is active, the servo receives an input from the stop lamp switch. This will command the speed control servo to close the throttle at a controlled rate. The system is put in standby mode.

If the brake pedal is rapidly depressed when the speed control system is active, the servo receives a command from the deactivator switch. This causes the electromagnetic actuated coupling to disconnect from the stepper motor and deactivate, letting the cable and throttle close under throttle return spring control. The system is put in standby mode.

If the clutch pedal is depressed when the speed control system is active, the servo receives a command from the Clutch Pedal Position (CPP) switch. This causes the servo to deactivate and close the throttle at a controlled rate. The system is put in a standby mode.

LS & Thunderbird

The speed control system consists of the Powertrain Control Module (PCM), speed control servo, speed control set telltale, actuator switches, deactivator switch, Brake Pedal Position (BPP) switch, Clutch Pedal Position (CPP) switch (manual transmission), Digital Transmission range (DTR) sensor (automatic transmission) and speed control actuator cable.

The electronic stepper motor is controlled by turning the three phases of the motor ON and OFF in sequence. The sequence determines the motor direction based on vehicle speed. The speed control module is fully integrated into the PCM. the PCM strategy uses engine control to accelerate smoothly. In instances where the vehicle tends to want to exceed set speed, the PCM will invoke an engine braking strategy to help maintain the desired vehicle speed.

Whenever the system is engaged and active, a speed control set indicator will be illuminated in the instrument cluster.

The BPP switch is a normally open switch. When the brake pedal is applied with the speed control system engaged, the BPP switch closes, putting the vehicle speed control in standby mode.

PRECAUTIONS

Air Bag Systems

Refer to "Air Bag System Precautions" in front of this manual for system disarming and arming procedures.

Battery Ground Cable

Prior to service, disconnect battery ground cable and isolate as required.

ADJUSTMENTS

Actuator Cable

CONTINENTAL, CROWN VICTORIA, GRAND MARQUIS, MARAUDER & TOWN CAR

1. Remove retaining clip from actuator cable adjuster at throttle, **Fig. 1.**
2. Ensure throttle is in fully closed position.
3. Pull on actuator cable to take up slack, then loosen at least one notch so there is approximately .118 inch (3 mm) of slack in cable.
4. Insert cable clip and snap into place.
5. Ensure throttle linkage operates freely and smoothly.

ESCORT & ZX2

1. Remove speed control cable adjuster clip from cable adjuster.
2. Adjust control cable freeplay to .04–.12 inch.
3. Install servo control cable adjuster clip into cable adjuster.

SABLE & TAURUS

1. Remove retaining clip from actuator cable adjuster at throttle.
2. Ensure throttle is in fully closed position.
3. Pull on actuator cable to take up slack, then loosen at least one notch so there is approximately .118 inch (3 mm) of slack in cable.
4. Insert cable clip and snap into place.
5. Ensure throttle linkage operates freely and smoothly.

Deactivator Switch

CONTOUR, COUGAR, FOCUS & MYSTIQUE

1. Pull switch plunger out to its full extent.
2. Fully depress brake pedal.
3. Install the switch.
4. Slowly release brake pedal.

MUSTANG, SABLE & TAURUS

The deactivator switch is located at the pedal bracket above stop lamp switch.

1. Disconnect deactivator switch hook from plastic pedal stem.
2. Fully depress deactivator switch hook and plunger assembly. Ensure hook is against switch body and locking tab snaps into place in switch hook.
3. Fully depress brake pedal and attach switch hook.
4. Release brake pedal and allow pedal to return to normal position.

SYSTEM DIAGNOSIS & TESTING

Wiring Diagrams

CONTINENTAL

Refer to system wiring circuit diagram, **Figs. 2 through 4,** when performing system diagnosis and testing.

CONTOUR & MYSTIQUE

Refer to system wiring circuit diagrams, **Figs. 5 and 6,** when performing system diagnosis and testing.

COUGAR

Refer to system wiring circuit diagrams, **Figs. 7 through 9,** when performing system diagnosis and testing.

CROWN VICTORIA, GRAND MARQUIS & MARAUDER

Refer to system wiring circuit diagrams, **Figs. 10 and 11,** when performing system diagnosis and testing.

ESCORT & ZX2

Refer to system wiring circuit diagrams, **Figs. 12 and 13,** when performing system diagnosis and testing.

FOCUS

Refer to system wiring circuit diagrams, **Figs. 14 and 15,** when performing system diagnosis and testing.

LS

Refer to system wiring circuit diagrams, **Figs. 16 and 17,** when performing system diagnosis and testing.

MUSTANG

Refer to system wiring circuit diagram, **Figs. 18 and 19,** when performing system diagnosis and testing.

SABLE & TAURUS

Refer to system wiring circuit diagrams, **Figs. 20 and 21,** when performing system diagnosis and testing.

TOWN CAR

Refer to system wiring circuit diagrams, **Figs. 22 through 24,** when performing system diagnosis and testing.

THUNDERBIRD

Refer to system wiring circuit diagram, **Fig. 25,** when performing system diagnosis and testing.

Diagnostic Procedures

CONTINENTAL

2000

Refer to **Fig. 26,** for symptom chart and **Figs. 27 through 38,** for diagnostic pinpoint test procedures.

2001–04

Refer to **Fig. 39,** for symptom chart and **Figs. 40 through 52,** for diagnostic pinpoint test procedures.

CONTOUR & MYSTIQUE

Refer to speed control symptom chart, **Fig. 53,** when performing system diagnosis and testing. Refer to **Figs. 54 through 61,** for pinpoint tests.

COUGAR

Refer to **Fig. 62** for symptom chart and **Figs. 63 through 68** for pinpoint tests.

CROWN VICTORIA, GRAND MARQUIS & MARAUDER

Refer to **Fig. 69,** for symptom chart and to **Figs. 70 through 80,** for pinpoint tests.

ESCORT & ZX2

2000

Refer to **Fig. 81,** for diagnostic symptom chart and **Figs. 82 through 88,** for diagnostic pinpoint tests.

2001–04

Refer to **Fig. 89,** for diagnostic symptom chart and **Figs. 90 through 97,** for diagnostic pinpoint tests.

FOCUS

Diagnostic and troubleshooting procedures consist of a series of pinpoint tests designed to locate faults to be serviced in the speed control system, which can be diagnosed using Rotunda Speed Control Tester tool No. 007-00013, or equivalent.

Refer to **Fig. 98,** for diagnostic symptom chart and to **Figs. 99 through 103,** for diagnostic pinpoint tests.

LS & THUNDERBIRD

Refer to **Fig. 104,** for symptom chart and **Figs. 105 through 112,** for pinpoint tests.

MUSTANG

Refer to **Fig. 113,** for diagnostic symptom chart and **Figs. 114 through 121,** for diagnostic pinpoint tests.

SABLE & TAURUS

Perform Self-Test Diagnostics to access trouble codes as follows:

This is a Key On Engine Off (KOEO) test that is conducted in Park only with parking brake fully applied.

1. Enter Self-Diagnostics by depressing speed control OFF switch while turning ignition On, ensuring engine does not start and is not running. The speed control indicator on instrument panel will flash once to indicate that speed control module entered diagnostic mode. Five additional flashes at this point indicate a faulty speed control servo. Release OFF switch.
2. If ON switch is not pressed within five seconds after entering diagnostic mode, then module times out and procedure must be started over. Press remaining switches in sequence: ON, RSM, CST and SET/ACCEL.
3. Speed control indicator will flash as each switch is pressed. Press each switch in sequence immediately after lamp goes out for previous switch.
4. After all five speed control switches complete sequence, speed control indicator will flash to indicate a pass or fail.
5. 1 flash–Test passed (with dynamic throttle pull).
6. 2 flashes–Brake pedal position (BPP) switch is faulty, circuit is faulty, or brake pedal is applied.
7. 3 flashes–Brake deactivation switch is open or circuit is faulty.
8. 4 flashes–Vehicle speed signal is out of range or not connected.
9. Immediately after static test has passed, the speed control servo will perform a dynamic test automatically by actuating throttle lever from 1 MM–10 MM of travel from idle position.
10. During dynamic throttle pull, observe throttle movement to witness any binding or sticking of actuator cable, proper connection of throttle actuator cable to throttle lever, and ensure throttle returns back to idle position. If improper connection and or binding or sticking of actuator is observed, go to symptom chart.
11. Turn ignition Off and proceed to symptom chart.

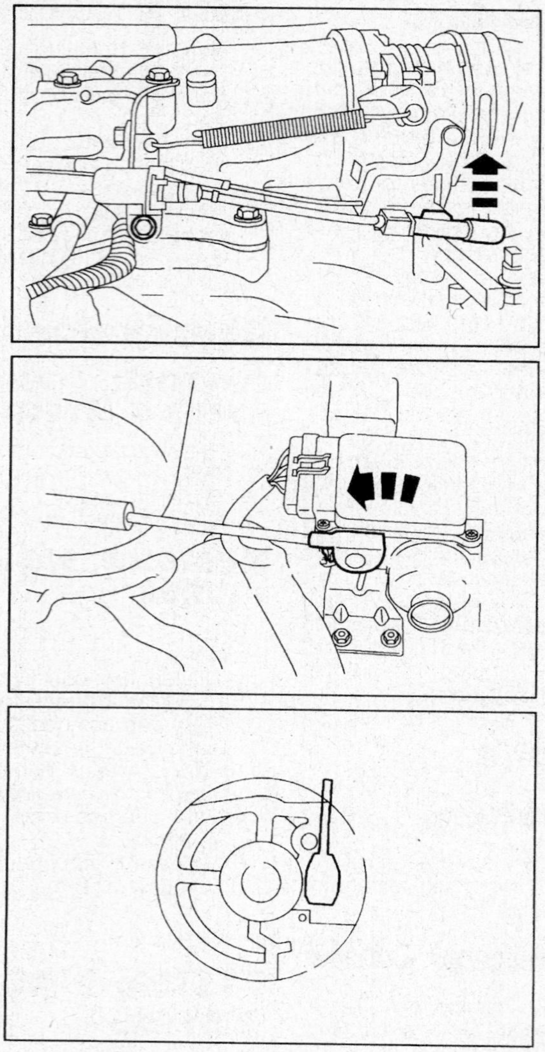

FM1109900673000X

Fig. 1 Actuator cable. Continental, Crown Victoria, Grand Marquis, Marauder & Town Car

PINPOINT TEST INSTRUCTIONS

1. Do not run any of following Pinpoint Tests unless you are so instructed by Quick Test. Each Pinpoint Test assumes that a fault has been detected in system with direction to enter a specific service routine. Performing any Pinpoint Test without direction from Quick Test may produce improper results and cause replacement of satisfactory components.
2. Do not replace any component unless test result indicates that it should be replaced.
3. When more than one diagnostic trouble code is received, always start service with first code received.
4. Do not measure voltage or resistance at ECA or connect any test lamps to it unless otherwise specified.
5. Isolate both ends of a circuit, and turn ignition Off whenever inspecting it for shorts or continuity, unless otherwise specified.
6. Disconnect solenoids and switches from harness before measuring for continuity, resistance or energizing by way of 12 volt source, unless otherwise instructed.
7. In using Pinpoint Tests, follow each step in order, starting from first step in appropriate test. Follow each step until fault is found.
8. An open is defined as any resistance reading greater than 5 ohms, unless otherwise specified.
9. A short is defined as any resistance reading less than 10,000 ohms to ground, unless otherwise specified. Refer to Pinpoint Tests.

PINPOINT TESTS

2000

Refer to **Fig. 122,** for symptom chart and **Figs. 123 through 134,** for pinpoint tests.

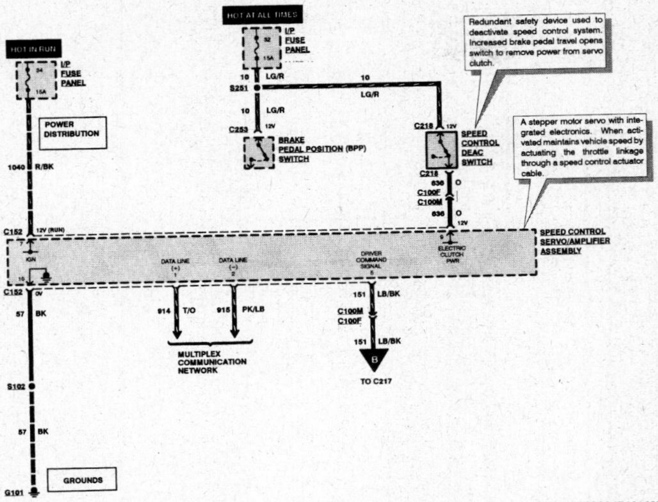

FM1109800474010X

Fig. 2 Wiring diagram (Part 1 of 2). 2000 Continental

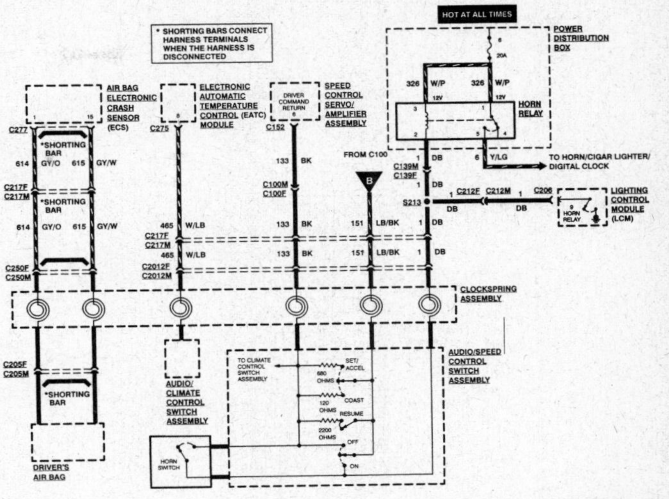

FM1109800474020X

Fig. 2 Wiring diagram (Part 2 of 2). 2000 Continental

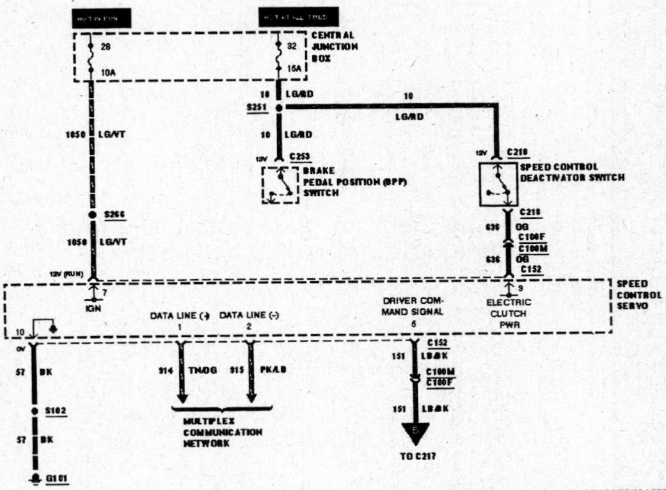

FM1100100726010X

Fig. 3 Wiring diagram (Part 1 of 2). 2001 Continental

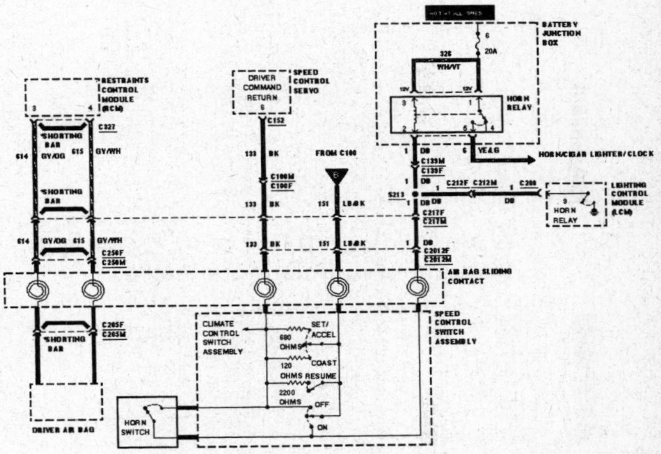

FM1100100726020X

Fig. 3 Wiring diagram (Part 2 of 2). 2001 Continental

2001–04

Refer to **Fig. 135,** for symptom chart and **Figs. 136 through 143,** for pinpoint tests.

TOWN CAR

Refer to **Figs. 144 and 145,** for symptom charts and **Figs. 146 through 157,** for pinpoint tests.

COMPONENT DIAGNOSIS & TESTING

For Procedures Not Found In This Section, Refer To Specific Pinpoint Tests in "System Diagnosis & Testing."

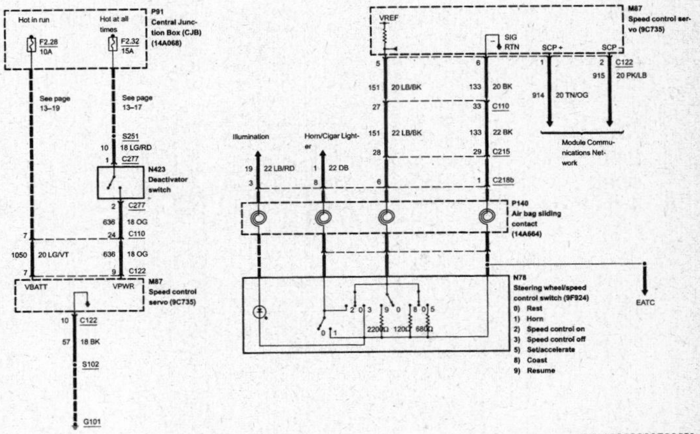

FM1100100827000X

Fig. 4 Wiring diagram. 2002–04 Continental

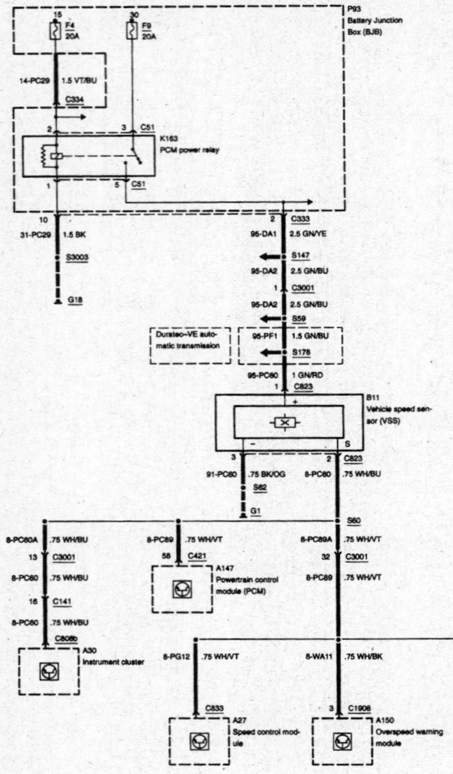

FM1109800491010X

Fig. 5 Wiring diagram (Part 1 of 2). Contour & Mystique w/automatic transaxle

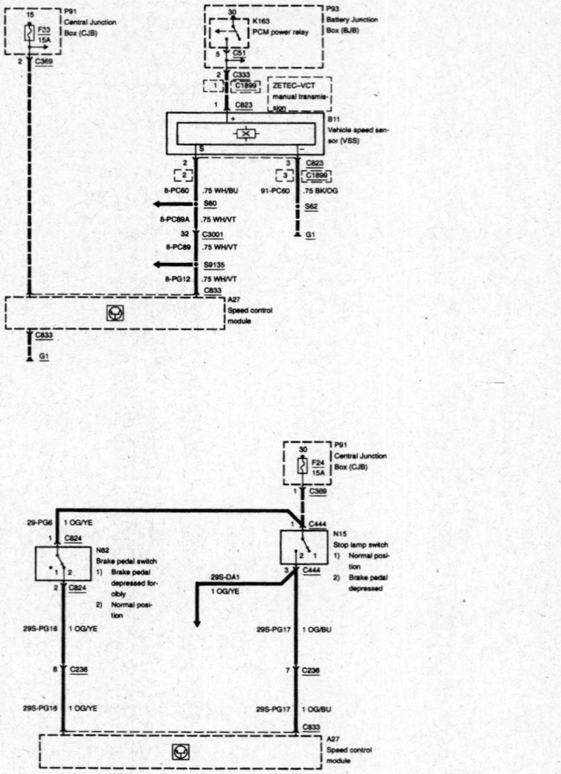

FM1109800491020X

Fig. 5 Wiring diagram (Part 2 of 2). Contour & Mystique w/automatic transaxle

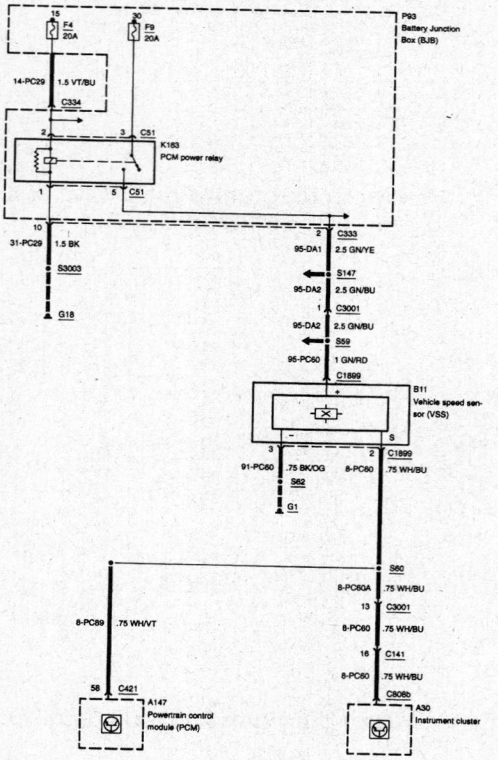

FM1109800490010X

Fig. 6 Wiring diagram (Part 1 of 2). Contour & Mystique w/manual transaxle

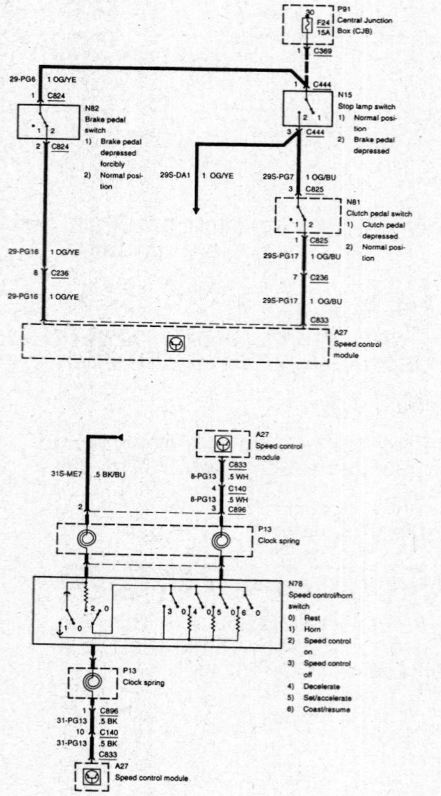

FM1109800490020X

Fig. 6 Wiring diagram (Part 2 of 2). Contour & Mystique w/manual transaxle

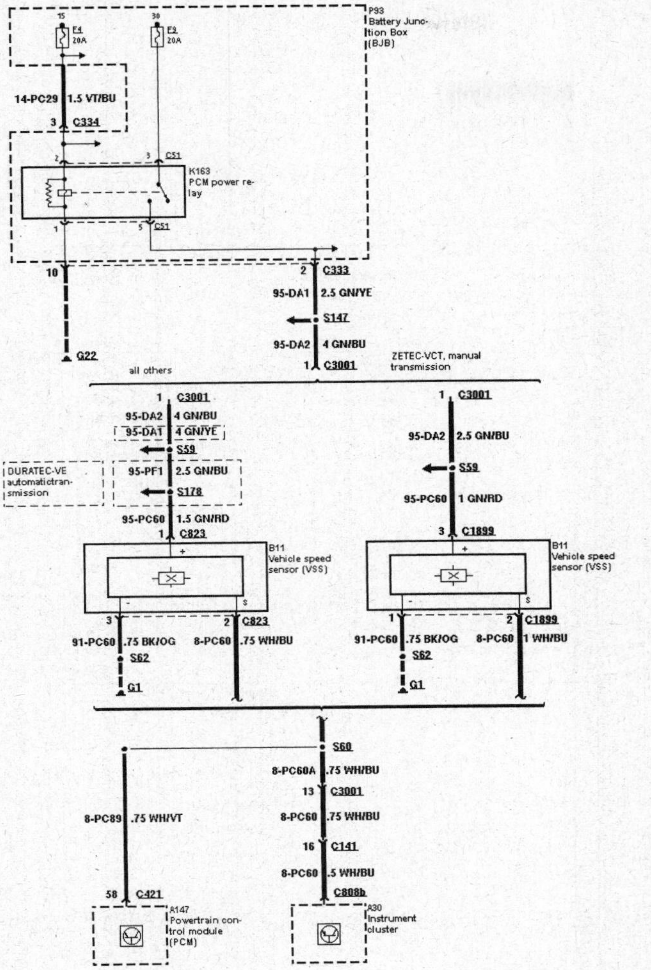

FM1109800571010X

Fig. 7 Wiring diagram (Part 1 of 4). 2000 Cougar

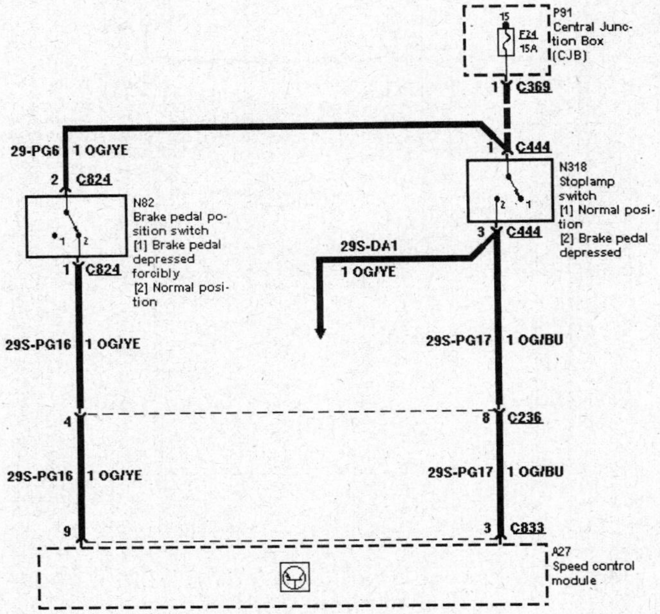

FM1109800571030X

Fig. 7 Wiring diagram (Part 2 of 4). 2000 Cougar w/manual transaxle

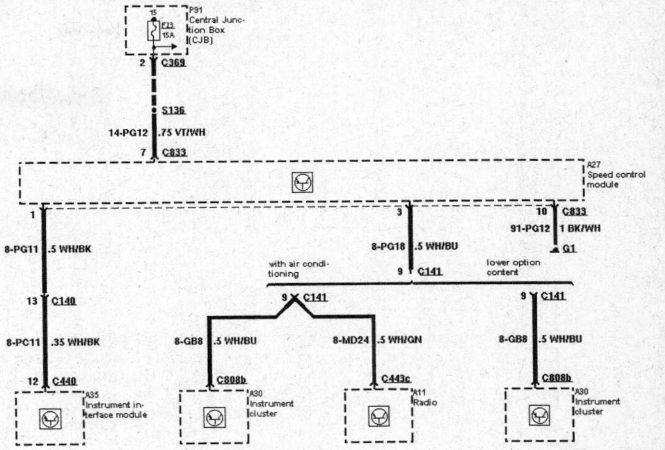

FM1109800571020X

Fig. 7 Wiring diagram (Part 2 of 4). 2000 Cougar w/automatic transaxle

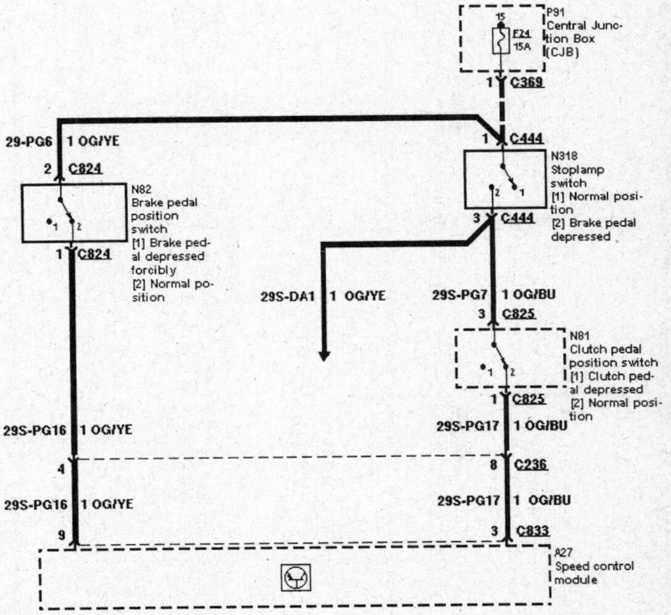

FM1109800571040X

Fig. 7 Wiring diagram (Part 3 of 4). 2000 Cougar

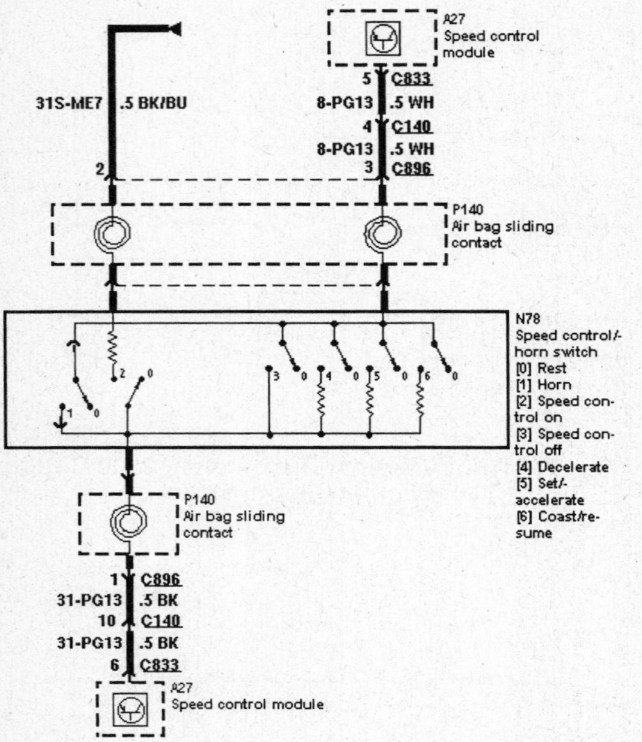

FM1109800571050X

Fig. 7 Wiring diagram (Part 4 of 4). 2000 Cougar

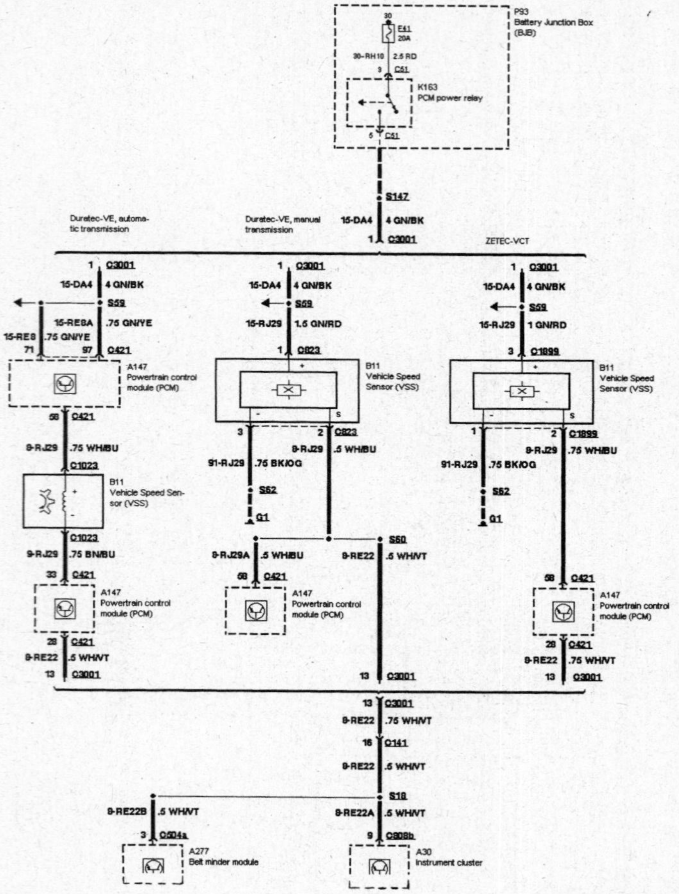

FM1100100723010X

Fig. 8 Wiring diagram (Part 1 of 4). 2001 Cougar

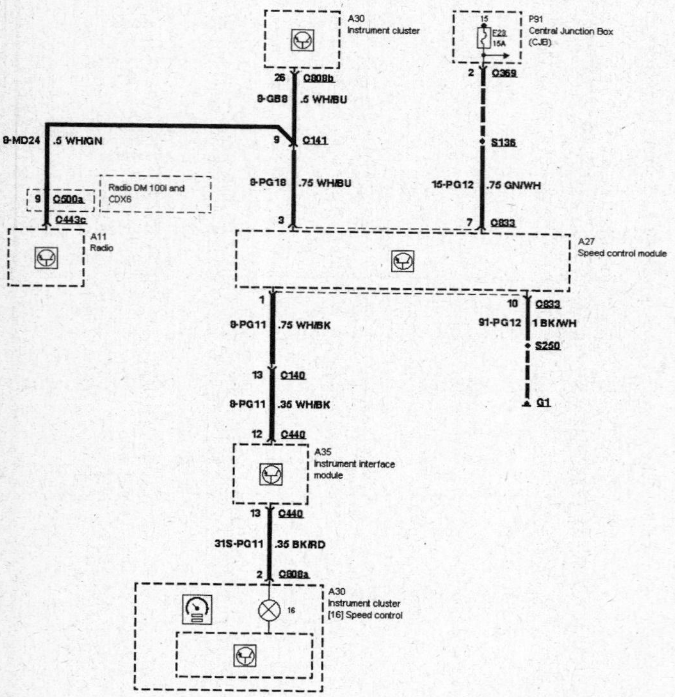

FM1100100723020X

Fig. 8 Wiring diagram (Part 2 of 4). 2001 Cougar

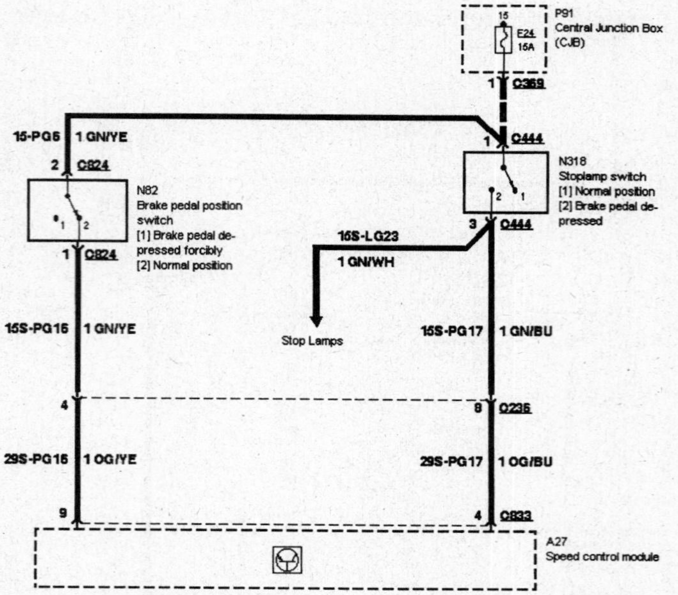

FM1100100723030X

Fig. 8 Wiring diagram (Part 3 of 4). 2001 Cougar w/automatic transaxle

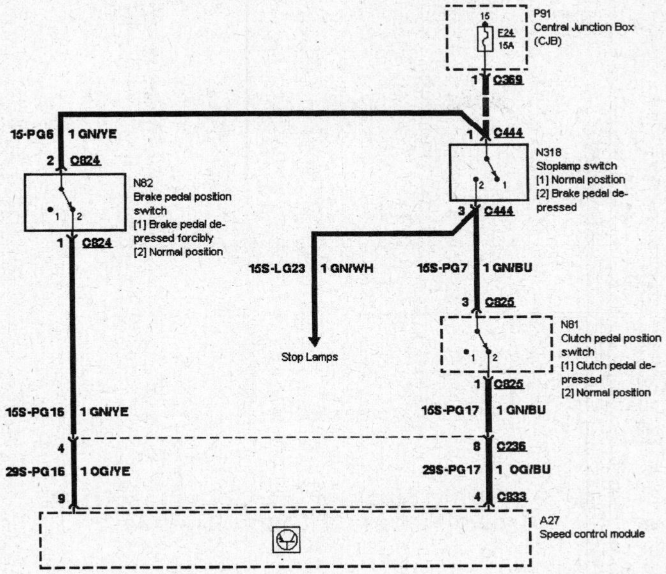

FM1100100723040X

Fig. 8 Wiring diagram (Part 3 of 4). 2001 Cougar w/manual transaxle

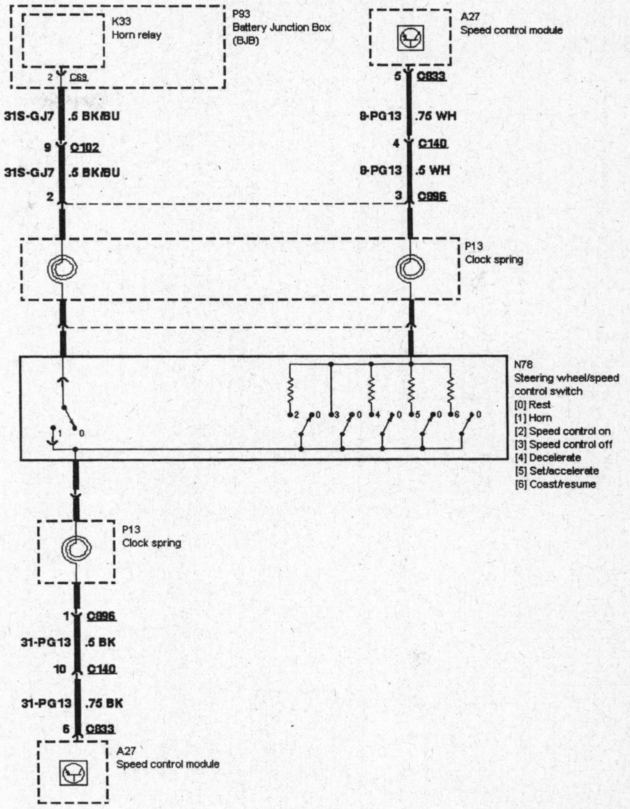

FM1100100723050X

Fig. 8 Wiring diagram (Part 4 of 4). 2001 Cougar

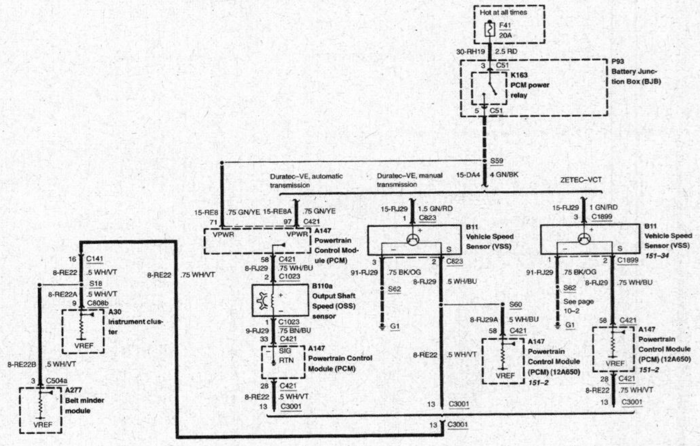

FM1100200833010X

Fig. 9 Wiring diagram (Part 1 of 3). 2002 Cougar

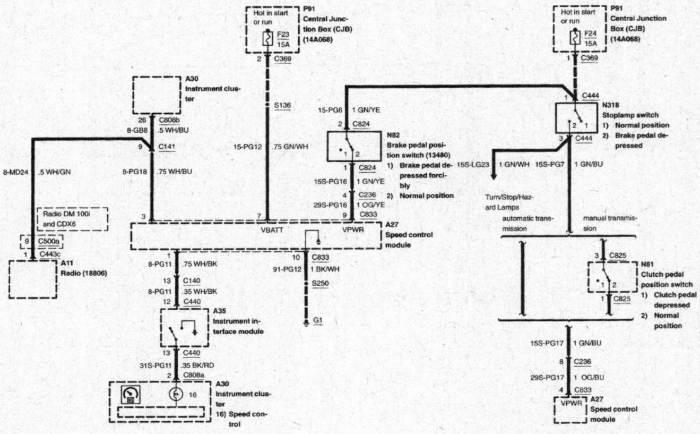

FM1100200833020X

Fig. 9 Wiring diagram (Part 2 of 3). 2002 Cougar

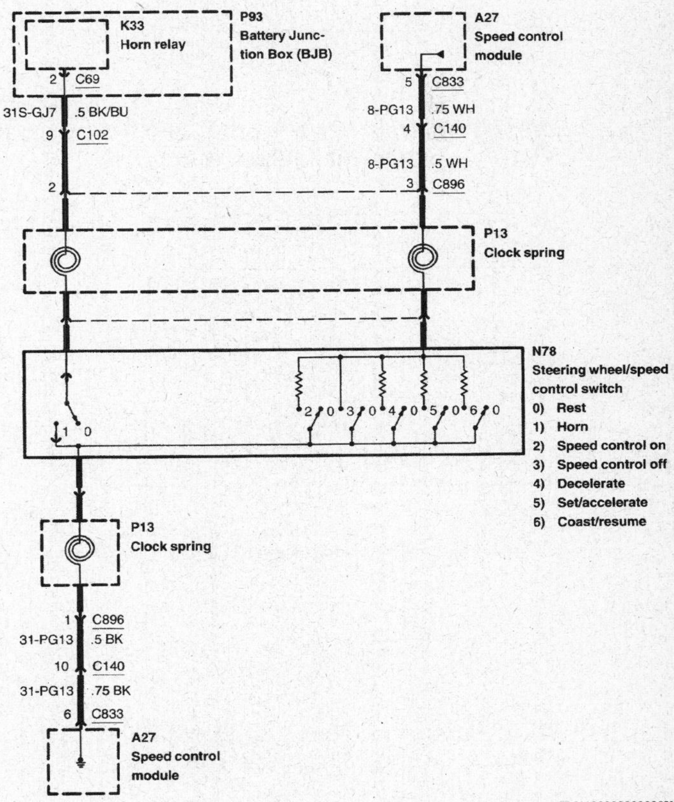

FM1100200833030X

Fig. 9 Wiring diagram (Part 3 of 3). 2002 Cougar

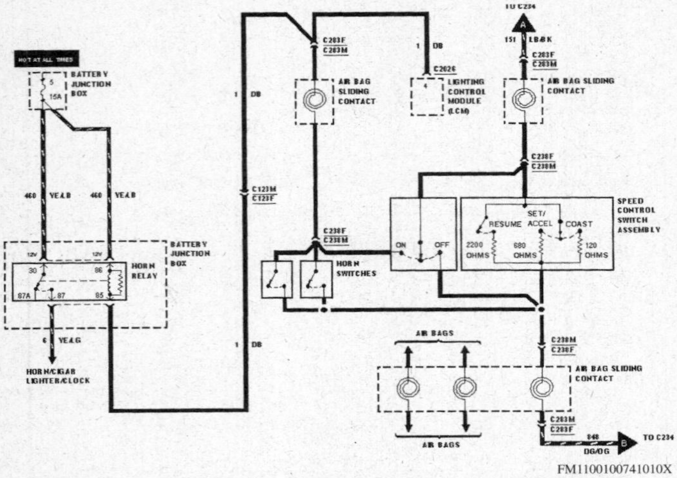

Fig. 10 Wiring diagram (Part 1 of 2). 2000–02 Crown Victoria & Grand Marquis

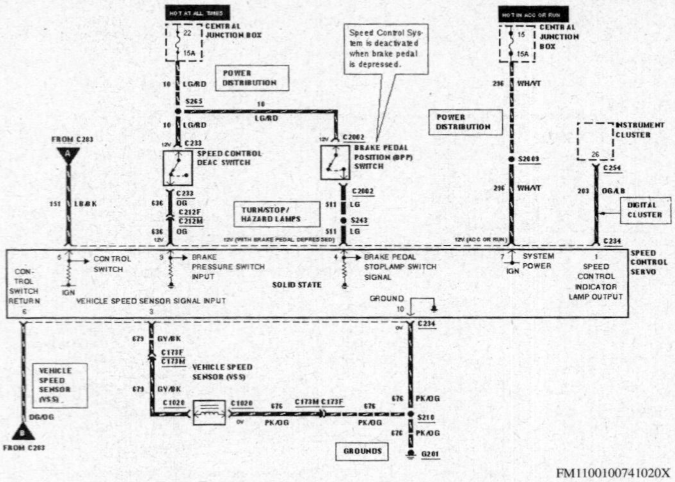

Fig. 10 Wiring diagram (Part 2 of 2). 2000–02 Crown Victoria & Grand Marquis

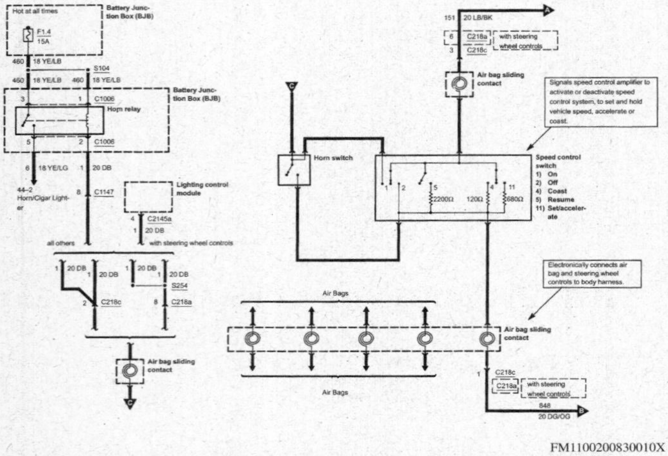

Fig. 11 Wiring diagram (Part 1 of 2). 2003–04 Crown Victoria, Grand Marquis & Marauder

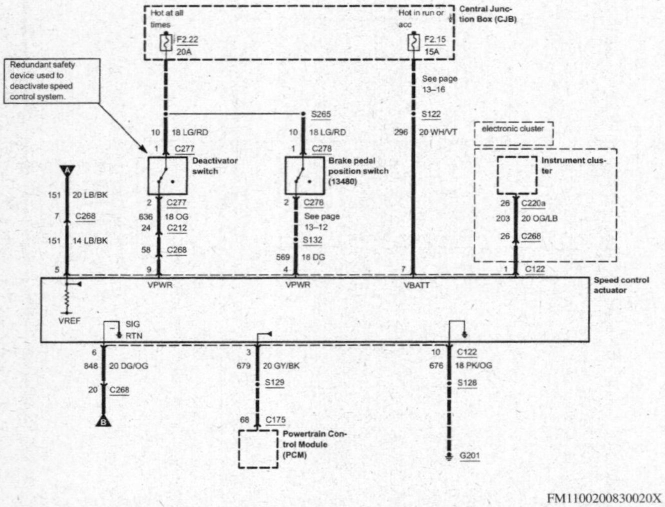

Fig. 11 Wiring diagram (Part 2 of 2). 2003–04 Crown Victoria, Grand Marquis & Marauder

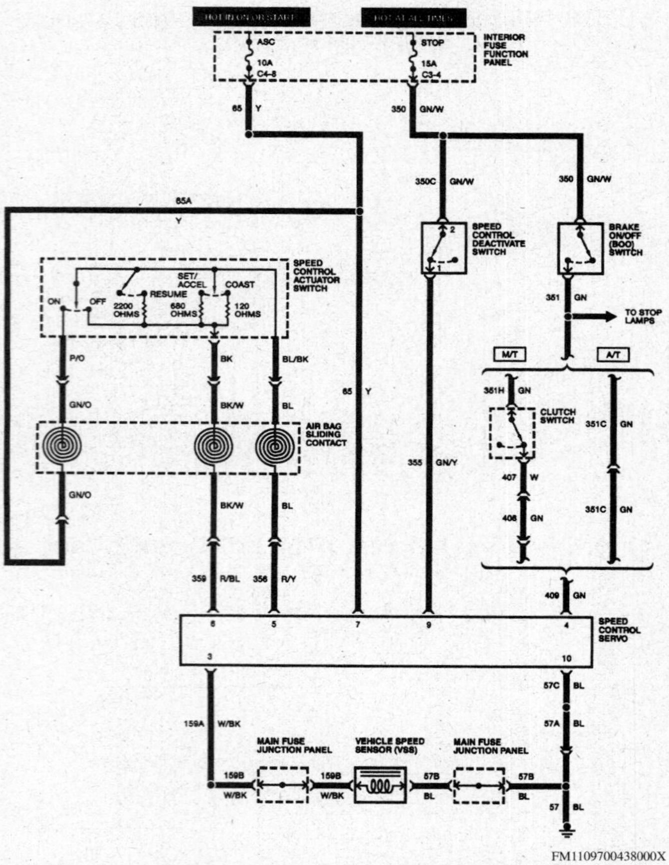

Fig. 12 Wiring diagram. 2000 Escort & ZX2

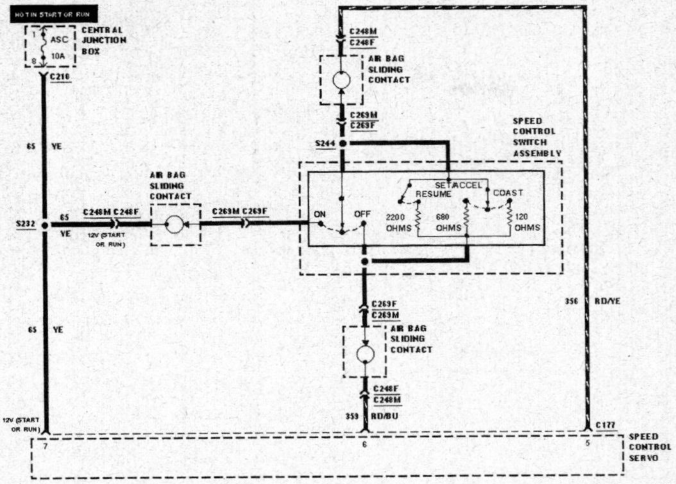

FM1100100701010X

Fig. 13 Wiring diagram (Part 1 of 2). 2001–04 Escort & ZX2

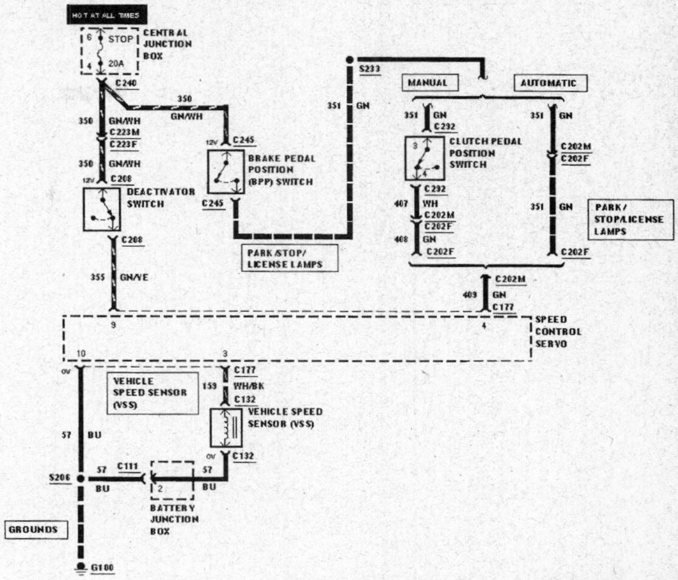

FM1100100701020X

Fig. 13 Wiring diagram (Part 2 of 2). 2001–04 Escort & ZX2

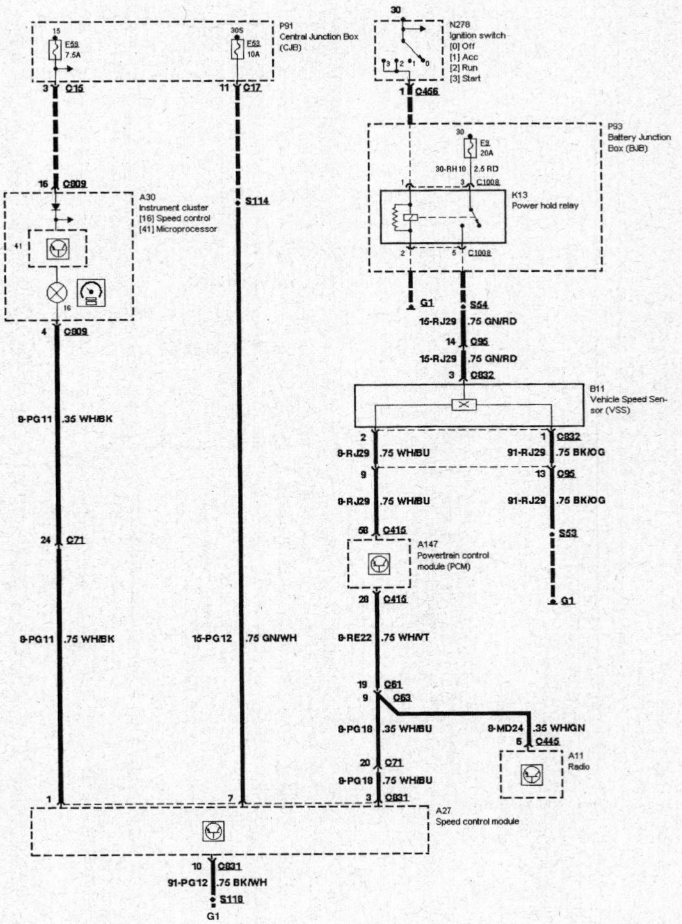

FM1100100763010X

Fig. 14 Wiring diagram (Part 1 of 2). Focus w/manual transaxle

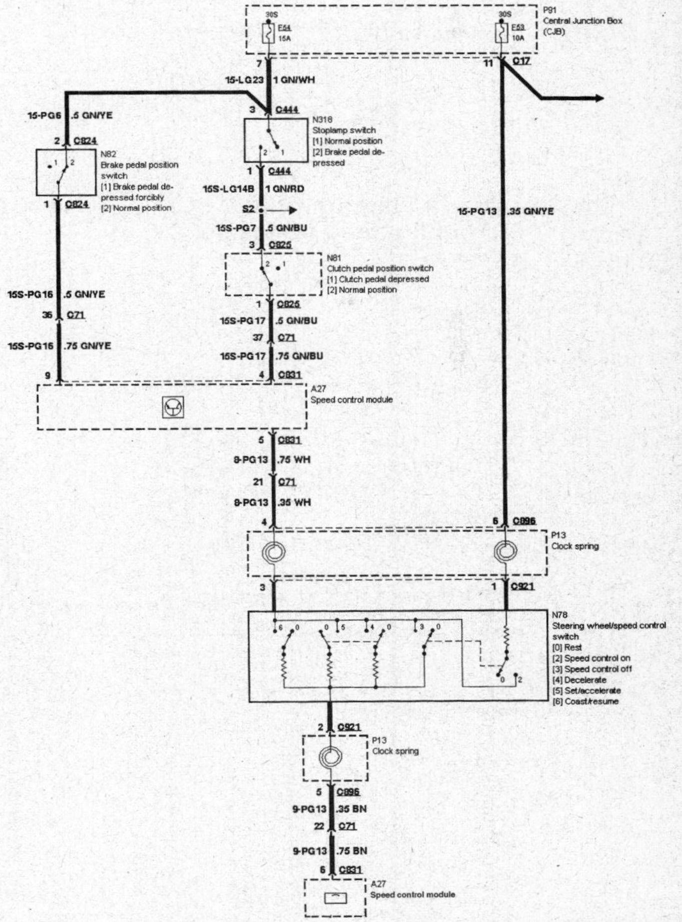

FM1100100763020X

Fig. 14 Wiring diagram (Part 2 of 2). Focus w/manual transaxle

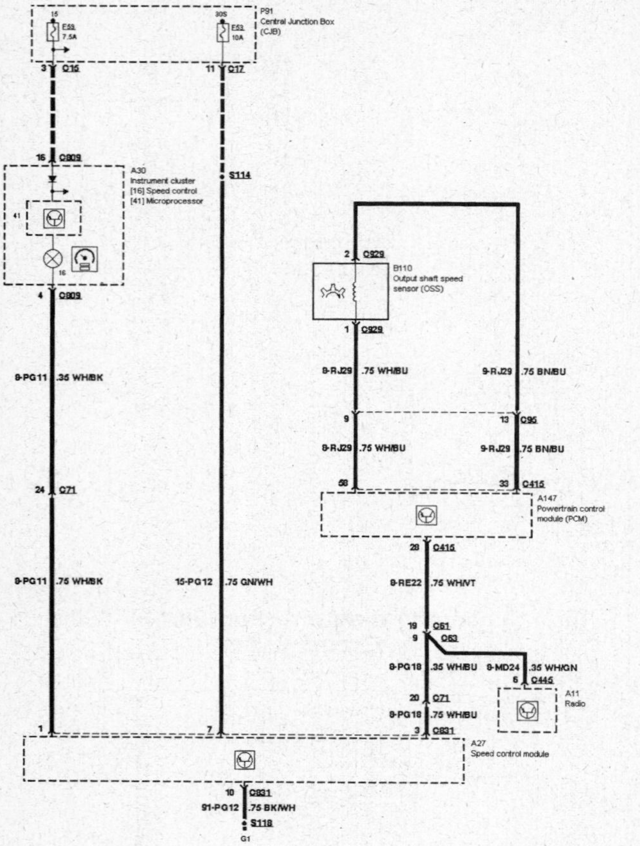

FM1100100764010X

Fig. 15 Wiring diagram (Part 1 of 2). Focus w/automatic transaxle

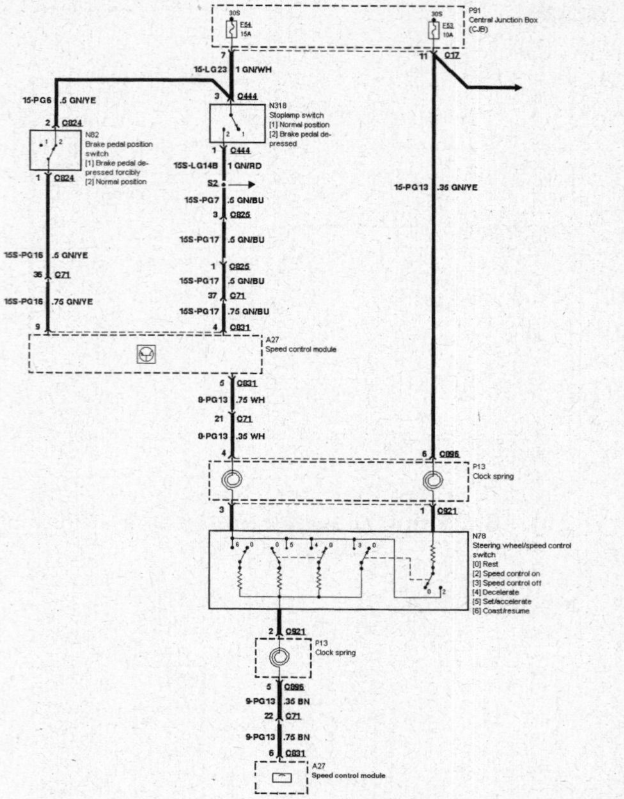

FM1100100764020X

Fig. 15 Wiring diagram (Part 2 of 2). Focus w/automatic transaxle

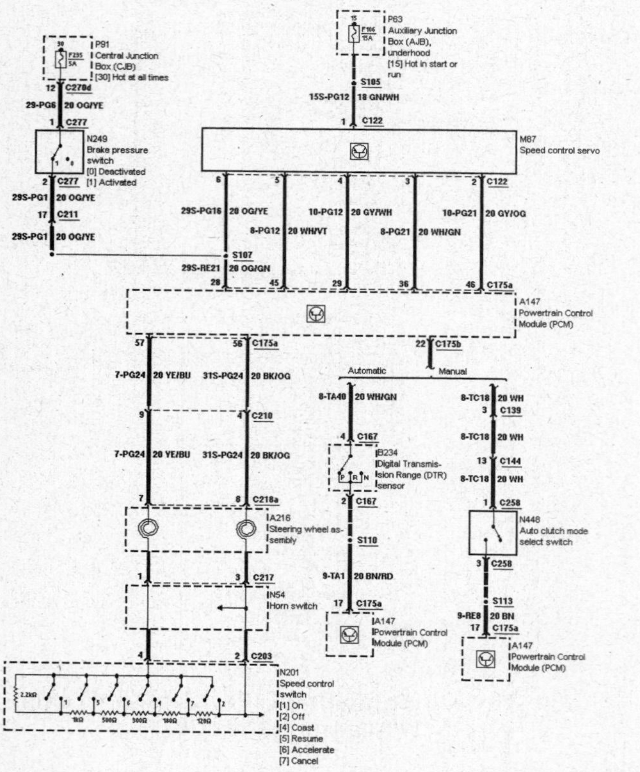

FM1109900685000X

Fig. 16 Wiring diagram. 2000 LS

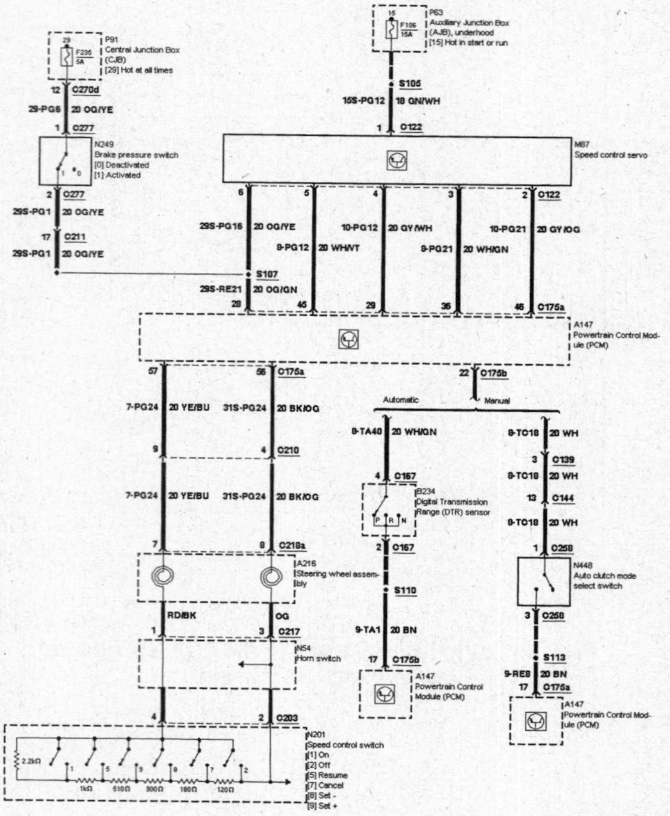

FM1100100754000X

Fig. 17 Wiring diagram. 2001–04 LS

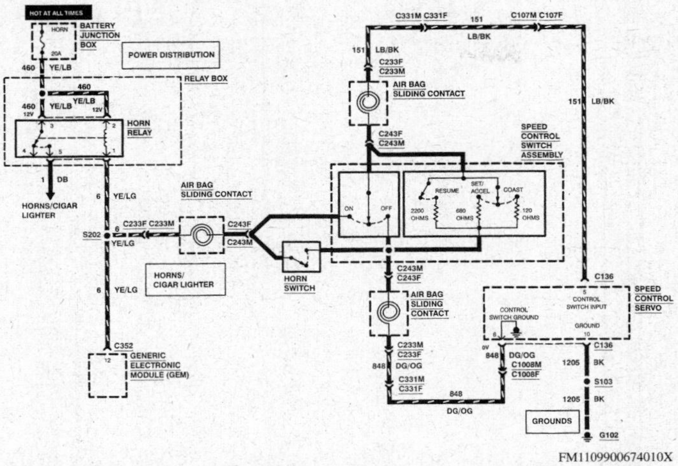

Fig. 18 Wiring Diagram (Part 1 of 2). 2000–02 Mustang

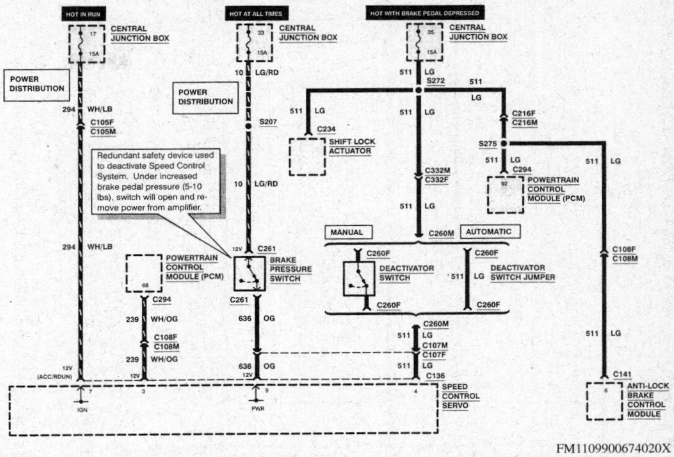

Fig. 18 Wiring Diagram (Part 2 of 2). 2000–02 Mustang

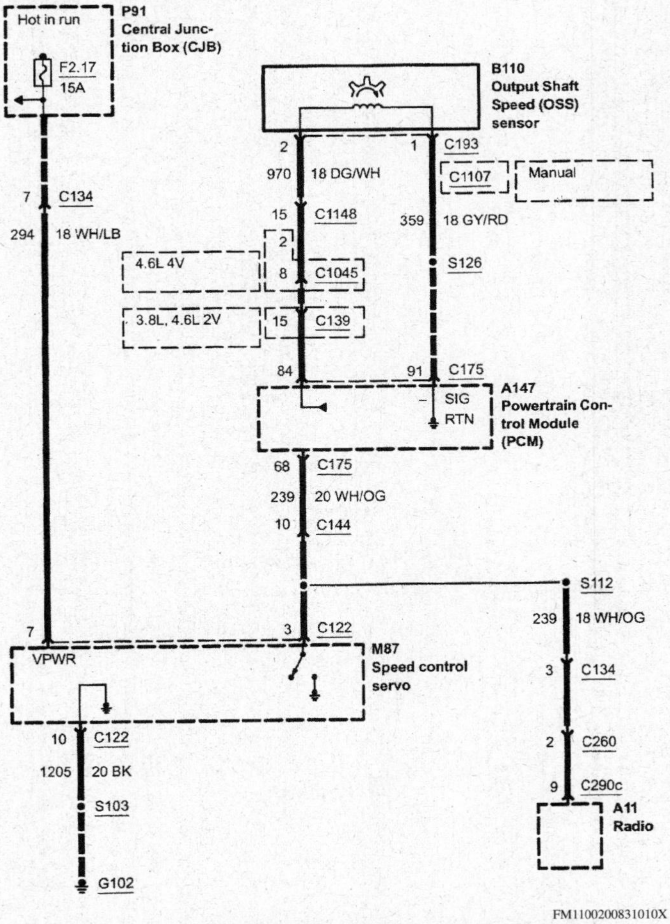

Fig. 19 Wiring diagram (Part 1 of 3). 2003–04 Mustang

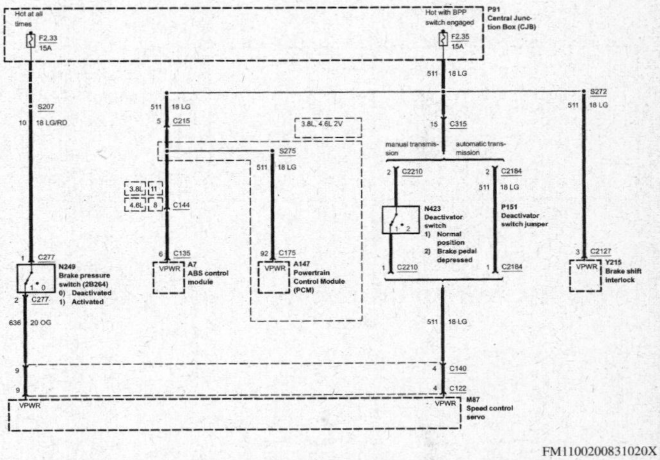

Fig. 19 Wiring diagram (Part 2 of 3). 2003–04 Mustang

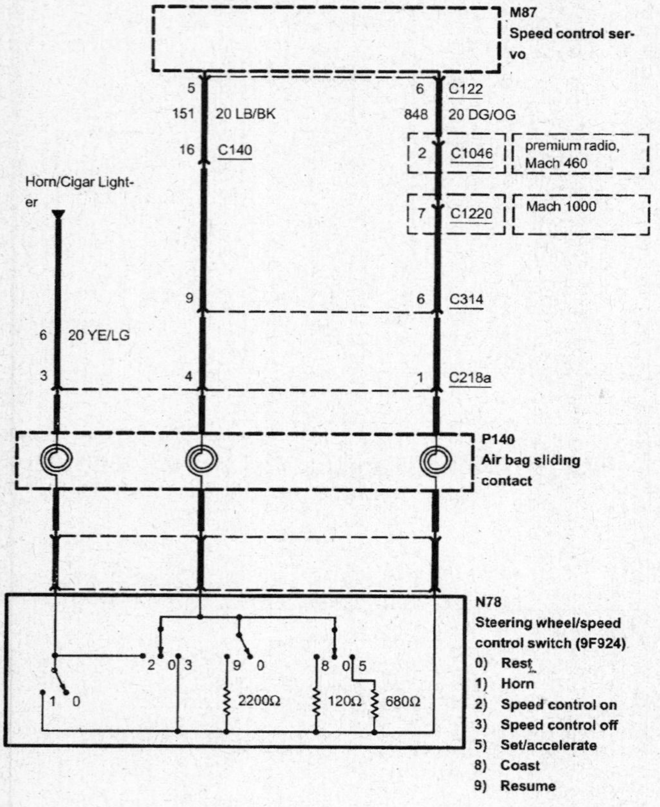

FM1100200831030X

Fig. 19 Wiring diagram (Part 3 of 3). 2003–04 Mustang

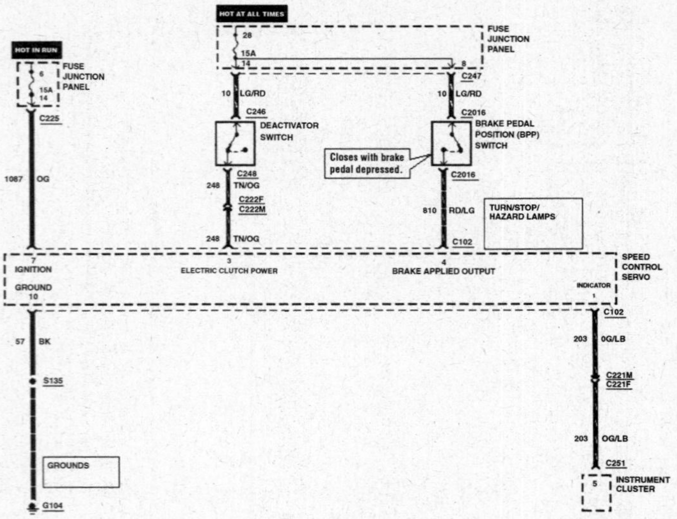

FM1109800572010X

Fig. 20 Wiring diagram (Part 1 of 2). 2000 Sable & Taurus

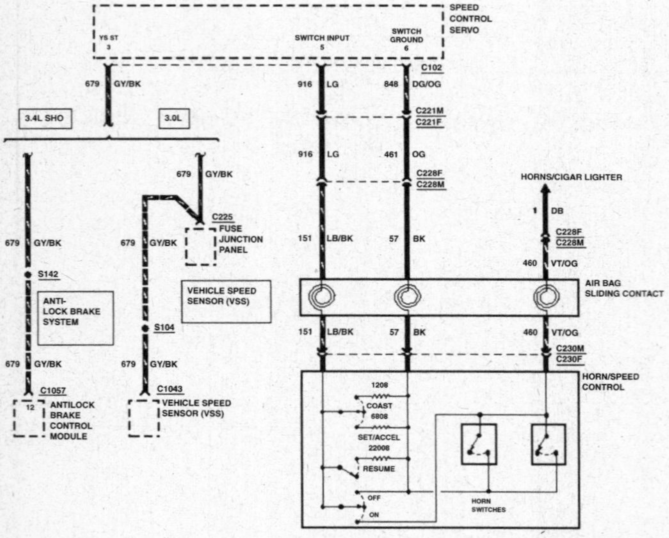

FM1109800572020X

Fig. 20 Wiring diagram (Part 2 of 2). 2000 Sable & Taurus

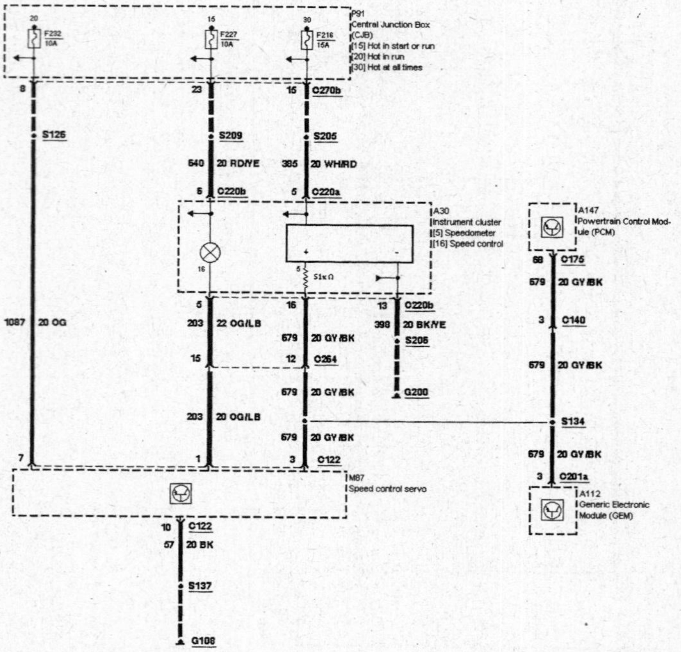

FM1100100711010X

Fig. 21 Wiring diagram (Part 1 of 3). 2001–04 Sable & Taurus

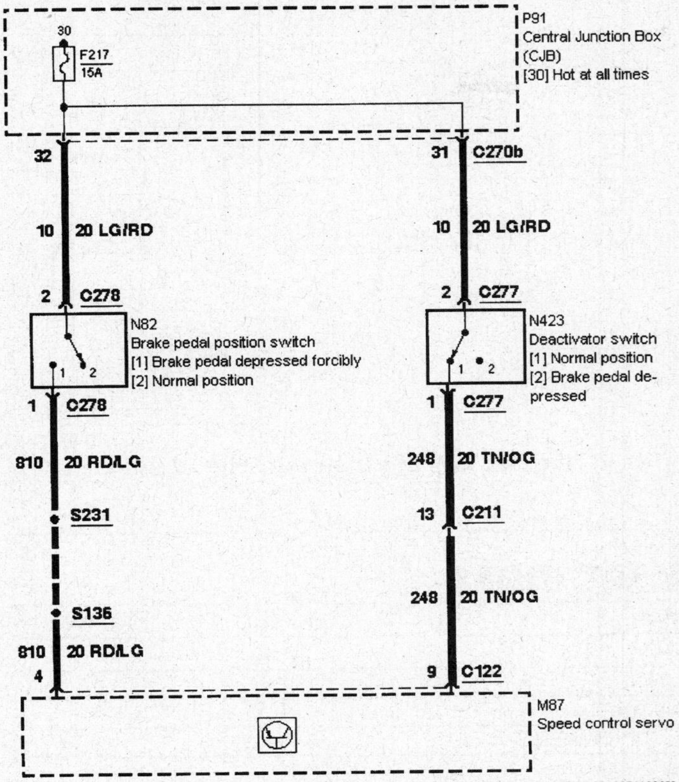

FM1100100711020X

Fig. 21 Wiring diagram (Part 2 of 3). 2001–04 Sable & Taurus

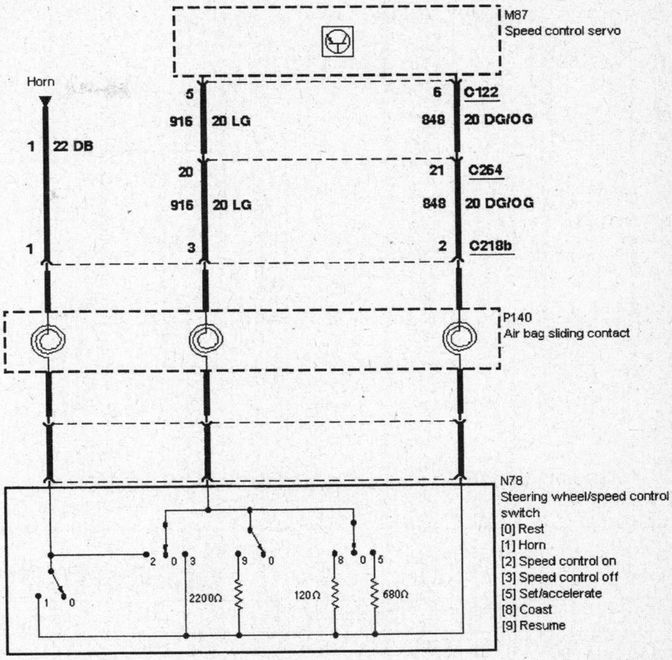

FM1100100711030X

Fig. 21 Wiring diagram (Part 3 of 3). 2001–04 Sable & Taurus

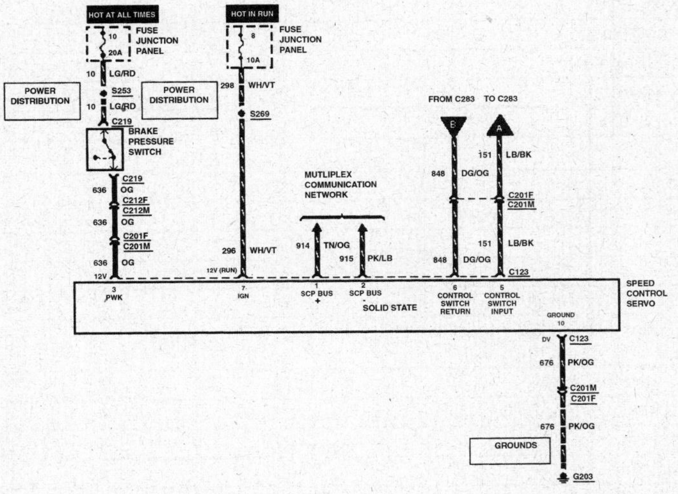

FM1109800583010X

Fig. 22 Wiring diagram (Part 1 of 2). 2000–01 Town Car

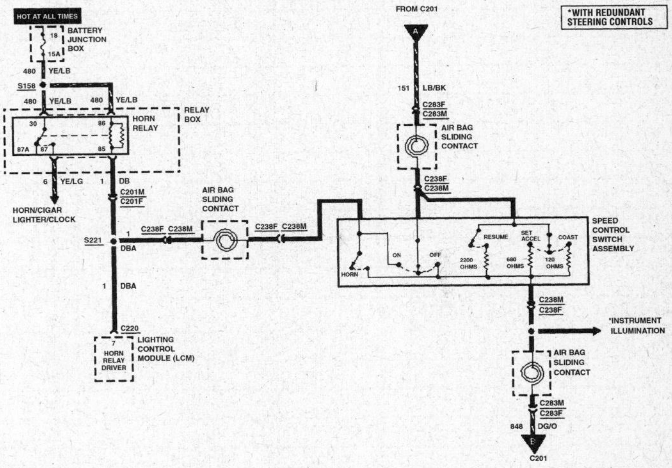

FM1109800583020X

Fig. 22 Wiring diagram (Part 2 of 2). 2000–01 Town Car

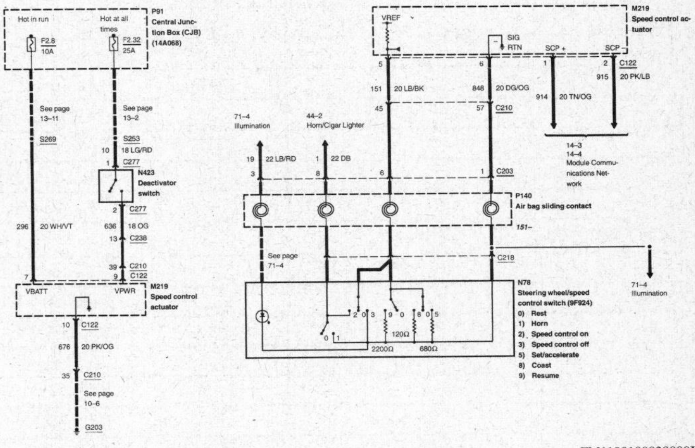

FM1100100828000X

Fig. 23 Wiring diagram. 2002 Town Car

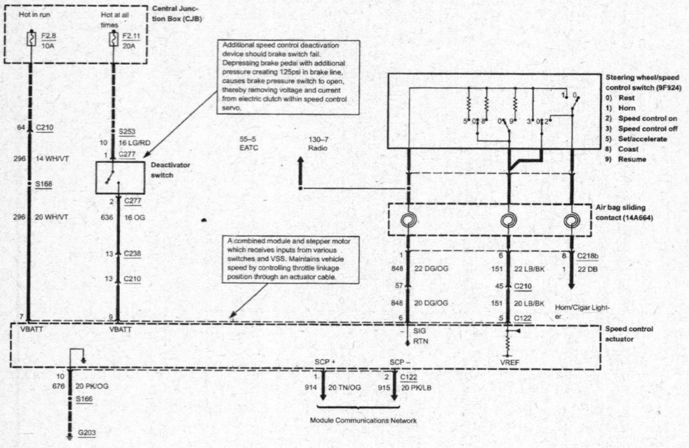

FM1100200832000X

Fig. 24 Wiring diagram. 2003–04 Town Car

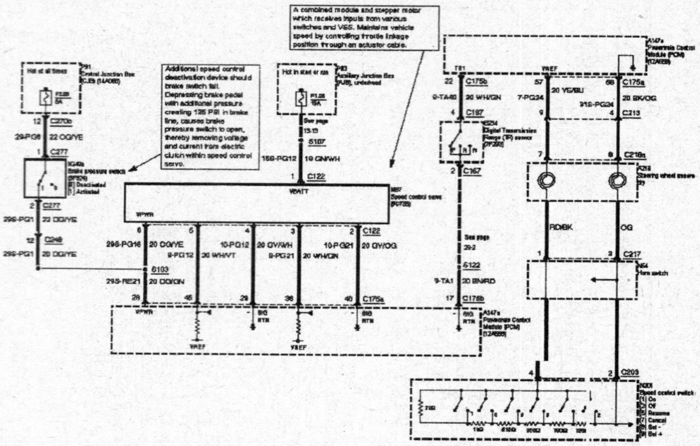

FM1100100829000X

Fig. 25 Wiring diagram. Thunderbird

DIAGNOSTIC CHART INDEX

Test	Code	Description	Page No.	Fig. No.
2000 CONTINENTAL				
—	—	Symptom Chart	2-19	26
A	B1318	Battery Voltage Low	2-19	27
B	C1109	Throttle Position Did Not Return To Idle After Self-Test	2-19	28
C	C1126	Speed Control Actuator Stuck For Two Minutes Or Longer	2-19	29
D	C1127	Deactivator Switch Circuit Failure	2-20	30
E	C1179	Speed Control Cable Slack Failure	2-20	31
F	—	No Communication With Speed Control Servo Module	2-21	32
G	—	Speed Control Inoperative	2-21	33
H	—	Set Speed Fluctuates	2-22	34
J	—	COAST Switch Inoperative	2-22	35
K	—	SET/ACCEL Switch Inoperative	2-22	36
L	—	RESUME Switch Inoperative	2-23	37
M	—	OFF Switch Inoperative	2-23	38
2001–04 CONTINENTAL				
—	—	Diagnostic Trouble Code Index	2-23	39
A	—	No Communication w/Module, Speed Control Servo	2-23	40
B	—	Unable To Enter Self-Test	2-24	41
C	B1318	Battery Voltage Low	2-24	42
D	C1109	Throttle Position Did Not Return To Idle After Self-Test	2-24	43
E	C1126	Speed Control Actuator Switch Stuck For Two Minutes Or Longer	2-25	44
F	C1127	Deactivator Switch Circuit Failure	2-26	45
G	C1179	Speed Control Cable Slack Failure	2-27	46
H	—	Speed Control Inoperative, No DTCs	2-27	47
I	—	Set Speed Fluctuates	2-29	48
J	—	COAST Switch Inoperative	2-29	49
K	—	SET/ACCEL Switch Inoperative	2-29	50
L	—	RESUME Switch Inoperative	2-30	51
M	—	OFF Switch Inoperative	2-30	52
CONTOUR & MYSTIQUE				
—	—	Symptom Chart	2-31	53
A	—	Speed Control Inoperative	2-31	54
B	—	Speed Control Does Not Disengage When Brakes are Applied	2-34	55
C	—	OFF Switch Inoperative	2-35	56
D	—	Coast Switch Inoperative	2-35	57
E	—	SET/ACCEL Switch Inoperative	2-35	58
F	—	Resume Switch Inoperative	2-36	59

Continued

DIAGNOSTIC CHART INDEX—Continued

Test	Code	Description	Page No.	Fig. No.
CONTOUR & MYSTIQUE				
G	—	Set Speed Fluctuates	2-36	60
H	—	Speed Control Does Not Disengage When Clutch Is Applied	2-36	61
COUGAR				
—	—	Speed Control Symptom Chart	2-36	62
A	—	Speed Control Inoperative	2-37	63
B	—	System Does Not Disengage When Brakes Are Applied	2-39	64
C	—	Coast Switch Inoperative	2-40	65
D	—	Resume Switch Inoperative	2-40	66
E	—	Speed Control Does Not Deactivate When Clutch Is Depressed	2-40	67
F	—	Set Speed Fluctuates	2-40	68
CROWN VICTORIA, GRAND MARQUIS & MARAUDER				
—	—	Symptom Chart	2-41	69
A	—	Speed Control Inoperative	2-42	70
B	—	Set Speed Fluctuates	2-45	71
C	—	Speed Control Does Not Disengage When Brakes Are Applied	2-46	72
D	—	COAST Switch Inoperative	2-47	73
E	—	SET/ACCEL Switch Inoperative	2-47	74
F	—	RESUME Switch Inoperative	2-48	75
G	—	OFF Switch Inoperative	2-48	76
H	—	Flash w/Last Switch Pressed, But No Dynamic Pull Occurs At Throttle & Speed Control Inoperative	2-48	77
I	—	Flash Code 2, BPP Switch Failure	2-49	78
J	—	Flash Code 3, Deactivator Switch Circuit Failure	2-49	79
K	—	Flash w/Last Switch Pressed, Dynamic Pull Occurs At Throttle & Speed Control Inoperative	2-51	80
2000 ESCORT & ZX2				
—	—	Symptom Chart	2-51	81
A	—	Speed Control Inoperative	2-51	82
B	—	Set Speed Fluctuates	2-53	83
C	—	Speed Control Does Not Disengage When Brakes Are Applied	2-54	84
D	—	Coast Switch Inoperative	2-54	85
E	—	SET/ACCEL Switch Inoperative	2-55	86
F	—	Resume Switch Inoperative	2-55	87
G	—	Off Switch Inoperative	2-56	88
2001–04 ESCORT & ZX2				
—	—	Symptom Chart	2-56	89
A	—	Speed Control Inoperative	2-57	90
B	—	Set Speed Fluctuates	2-62	91
C	—	Speed Control Does Not Disengage When Brakes Are Applied	2-63	92
D	—	Speed Control Does Not Disengage When Clutch Is Applied	2-64	93
E	—	Coast Switch Inoperative	2-64	94
F	—	SET/ACCEL Switch Inoperative	2-65	95
G	—	Resume Switch Inoperative	2-65	96
H	—	Off Switch Inoperative	2-65	97
FOCUS				
—	—	Symptom Chart	2-66	98
A	—	Speed Control Inoperative	2-66	99
B	—	System Does Not Disengage When Brakes Are Applied	2-70	100
C	—	COAST Switch Inoperative	2-71	101
D	—	RESUME Switch Inoperative	2-72	102
E	—	Speed Control Does Not Deactivate When Clutch Is Depressed	2-72	103
LS & THUNDERBIRD				
—	—	Symptom Chart	2-73	104
A	—	No Communication w/PCM	2-73	105
B	—	Unable To Enter Self-Test	2-73	106
C	P1565	Speed Control Command Switches High/Out Of Range	2-74	107

Continued

DIAGNOSTIC CHART INDEX—Continued

Test	Code	Description	Page No.	Fig. No.
LS & THUNDERBIRD				
D	P1566	Speed Control Command Switches Low/Out Of Range	2-75	108
E	P1567	NGSC Driver Fault	2-77	109
F	P1568	NGSC Servo Self-Test Failure	2-80	110
G	P1572/P0703	Brake On/Off Failure	2-82	111
H	—	Speed Control Inoperative	2-83	112
MUSTANG				
—	—	Symptom Chart	2-86	113
A	—	Speed Control Inoperative	2-86	114
B	—	Set Speed Fluctuates	2-88	115
C	—	Speed Control Does Not Disengage When Brakes Are Applied	2-89	116
D	—	Speed Control Does Not Disengage When Clutch Is Applied	2-89	117
E	—	Speed Control Switch Is Inoperative, Coast	2-89	118
F	—	Speed Control Switch Is Inoperative, SET/ACCEL	2-89	119
G	—	Speed Control Switch Is Inoperative, Resume	2-89	120
H	—	Speed Control Switch Is Inoperative, Off	2-90	121
2000 SABLE & TAURUS				
—	—	Symptom Chart	2-90	122
A	—	Flash Code 1, No Dynamic Pull At Speed Control Servo	2-90	123
B	—	Flash Code 2, Brake Pedal Position Switch Circuity	2-90	124
C	—	Flash Code 3, Deactivator Switch Circuitry	2-90	125
D	—	Flash Code 4, Vehicle Speed Signal Input Circuitry	2-90	126
E	—	No Flash Codes, Speed Control Inoperative	2-91	127
F	—	Speed Control Indicator Does Not Turn On	2-91	128
G	—	Speed Control Indicator Does Not Turn Off	2-91	129
H	—	Coast Switch Inoperative	2-91	130
J	—	SET/ACCEL Switch Inoperative	2-91	131
K	—	Resume Switch Inoperative	2-91	132
L	—	Off Switch Inoperative	2-91	133
M	—	Set Speed Fluctuates	2-92	134
2001–04 SABLE & TAURUS				
—	—	Symptom Chart	2-92	135
A	—	With Last Switch Depressed & No Dynamic Pull Occurs At Throttle	2-92	136
B	—	BPP Switch Or Circuit Failure	2-93	137
C	—	Deactivator Switch Or Circuit Failure	2-94	138
D	—	Dynamic Pull Occurs At Throttle & Speed Control Inoperative	2-94	139
E	—	Speed Control Inoperative, No Flash Codes	2-95	140
F	—	Speed Control Switch Inoperative	2-98	141
G	—	Speed Control Indicator Lamp Always On	2-98	142
H	—	Set Speed Fluctuates	2-99	143
TOWN CAR				
—	—	Symptom Chart	2-99	144
—	—	Diagnostic Trouble Code Interpretation	2-99	145
A	1318	Battery Voltage Low	2-99	146
B	C1109	Throttle Position Did Not Return To Idle After Self-Test	2-100	147
C	C1126	Speed Control Actuator Switch Stuck For Two Minutes Or Longer	2-100	148
D	C1127	Deactivator Switch Circuit Failure	2-100	149
E	C1179	Speed Control Cable Slack Failure	2-101	150
F	—	No Communication w/Module, Speed Control Servo	2-101	151
G	—	Speed Control Inoperative, No DTCs	2-102	152
H	—	Set Speed Fluctuates	2-102	153
J	—	Coast Switch Inoperative	2-102	154
K	—	SET/ACCEL Switch Inoperative	2-103	155
L	—	Resume Switch Inoperative	2-103	156
M	—	OFF Switch Inoperative	2-103	157

DTCS	DTC Caused By	Description	Action
B1318	Speed Control Servo	Battery Voltage Low	GO to Pinpoint Test A.
B1342	Speed Control Servo	ECU is Defective	REPLACE the speed control servo. TEST the system for normal operation.
C1109	Speed Control Servo	Throttle Position Did Not Return To Idle After Self-Test	GO to Pinpoint Test B.
C1126	Speed Control Servo	Speed Control Actuator Switch Stuck for Two Minutes or Longer	GO to Pinpoint Test C.
C1127	Speed Control Servo	Deactivator Switch Circuit Failure	GO to Pinpoint Test D.
C1179	Speed Control Servo	Speed Control Cable Slack Failure	GO to Pinpoint Test E.
U1027	PCM	SCP Invalid or Missing Data for Engine RPM	PERFORM the PCM Self-Test.
U1041	Anti-Lock Brake Control Module	SCP Invalid or Missing Data for Vehicle Speed	PERFORM the Anti-Lock Brake Control Module Self-Test.

FM1109800477010X

Fig. 26 Speed control symptom chart (Part 1 of 2). 2000 Continental

TEST CONDITIONS	TEST DETAILS/RESULTS/ACTIONS
A1 CHECK CIRCUIT 57 (BK) FOR AN OPEN	
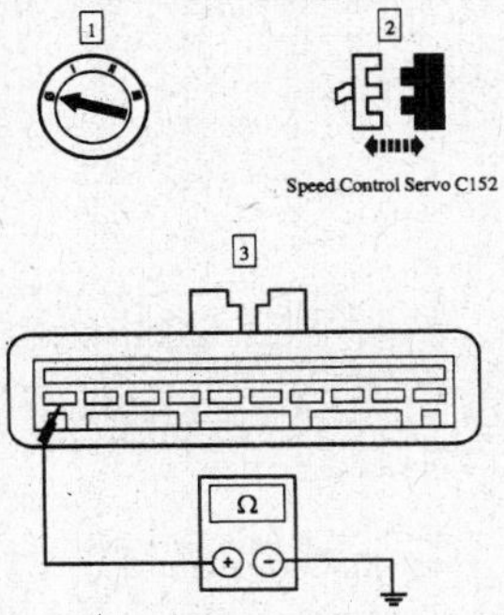	3 Measure the resistance between speed control servo C152-10, circuit 57 (BK), and ground. • Is the resistance less than 5 ohms? → **Yes** **Diagnose Charging System** → **No** REPAIR circuit 57 (BK). CLEAR the DTCs. TEST the system for normal operation.

FM1109800478000X

Fig. 27 Test A: Code B1318, Battery Voltage Low. 2000 Continental

TEST CONDITIONS	TEST DETAILS/RESULTS/ACTIONS
B2 CHECK THE THROTTLE LEVER	
	1 Check the throttle lever for sticking or binding. • Is the throttle lever OK? → **Yes** GO to **B3**. → **No** REPAIR and/or REPLACE as necessary. CLEAR the DTCs. TEST the system for normal operation.
B3 CHECK THE SPEED CONTROL ACTUATOR CABLE ADJUSTMENT	
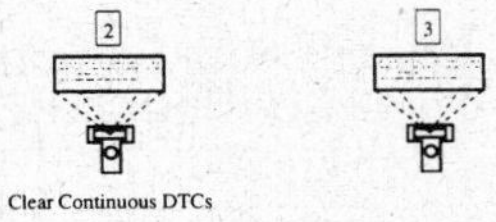	1 Perform the speed control actuator cable adjustment. 3 Retrieve and Document DTCs. • Is DTC C1109 retrieved? → **Yes** REPLACE the speed control servo. TEST the system for normal operation. → **No** System is OK.

FM1109800479020X

Fig. 28 Test B: Code C1109, Throttle Position Did Not Return To Idle After Self-Test (Part 2 of 2). 2000 Continental

Condition	Possible Source	Action
• No Communication With The Module — Speed Control Servo	• Fuse(s). • Circuitry. • Speed control servo.	• GO to Pinpoint Test F.
• The Speed Control Is Inoperative — No DTCs	• Circuitry. • Speed control actuator switch. • Speed control servo.	• GO to Pinpoint Test G.
• The Set Speed Fluctuates	• Speed control actuator cable. • Throttle lever. • Speed control servo.	• GO to Pinpoint Test H.
• The Coast Switch Is Inoperative	• Speed control actuator switch. • Speed control servo.	• GO to Pinpoint Test J.
• The SET/ACCEL Switch Is Inoperative	• Speed control actuator switch. • Speed control servo.	• GO to Pinpoint Test K.
• The Resume Switch Is Inoperative	• Speed control actuator switch. • Speed control servo.	• GO to Pinpoint Test L.
• The OFF Switch Is Inoperative	• Speed control actuator switch. • Speed control servo.	• GO to Pinpoint Test M.
• One or More Speed Control Message(s) Are Not Displayed On The Message Center	• Speed control servo. • Virtual image cluster (VIC).	
• No Speed Control Messages Are Displayed On The Message Center	• Speed control servo. • Virtual image cluster (VIC).	

FM1109800477020X

Fig. 26 Speed control symptom chart (Part 2 of 2). 2000 Continental

TEST CONDITIONS	TEST DETAILS/RESULTS/ACTIONS
B1 CHECK THE SPEED CONTROL ACTUATOR CABLE	
	1 Check the speed control actuator cable for sticking or binding. • Is the speed control actuator cable OK? → **Yes** GO to **B2**. → **No** REPLACE the speed control actuator cable. CLEAR the DTCs. TEST the system for normal operation.

FM1109800479010X

Fig. 28 Test B: Code C1109, Throttle Position Did Not Return To Idle After Self-Test (Part 1 of 2). 2000 Continental

TEST CONDITIONS	TEST DETAILS/RESULTS/ACTIONS
C1 CHECK THE SPEED CONTROL ACTUATOR SWITCH	
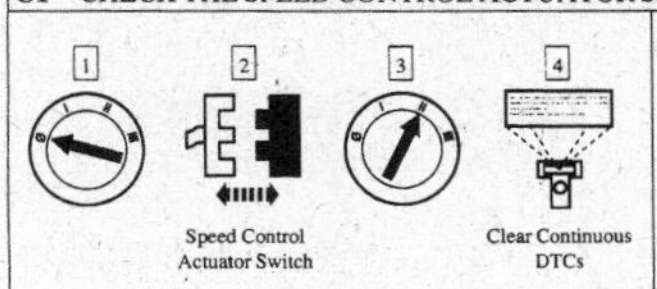	5 Wait three minutes.

FM1109800480010X

Fig. 29 Test C: Code C1126, Speed Control Actuator Stuck For Two Minutes Or Longer (Part 1 of 3). 2000 Continental

TEST CONDITIONS	TEST DETAILS/RESULTS/ACTIONS
C1 CHECK THE SPEED CONTROL ACTUATOR SWITCH	
6 	6 Retrieve and document continuous DTCs. • Is DTC C1126 retrieved? → **Yes** GO to **C2**. → **No** REPLACE the speed control actuator switch;
C2 CHECK CIRCUIT 151 (LB/BK) FOR SHORT TO GROUND	
1 2 3 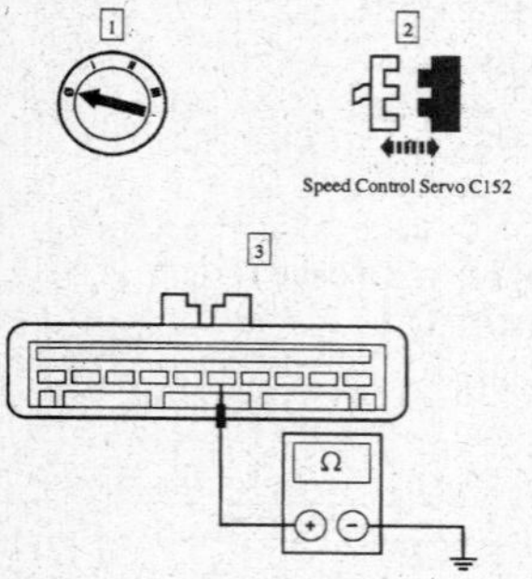	3 Measure the resistance between speed control servo C152-5, circuit 151 (LB/BK), and ground. • Is the resistance greater than 10,000 ohms? → **Yes** REPLACE the speed control servo. TEST the system for normal operation. → **No** GO to **C3**.

FM1109800480020X

Fig. 29 Test C: Code C1126, Speed Control Actuator Stuck For Two Minutes Or Longer (Part 2 of 3). 2000 Continental

TEST CONDITIONS	TEST DETAILS/RESULTS/ACTIONS
D1 CHECK FUSE JUNCTION PANEL FUSE 32 (15A)	
1 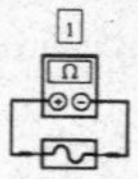	• Is the fuse OK? → **Yes** GO to **D2**. → **No** REPLACE the fuse. TEST the system for normal operation. If the fuse fails again, CHECK for short to ground. REPAIR as necessary. CLEAR the DTCs. TEST the system for normal operation.

FM1109800481010X

Fig. 30 Test D: Code C1127, Deactivator Switch Circuit Failure (Part 1 of 3). 2000 Continental

TEST CONDITIONS	TEST DETAILS/RESULTS/ACTIONS
D4 CHECK CIRCUIT 636 (O) FOR AN OPEN	
1 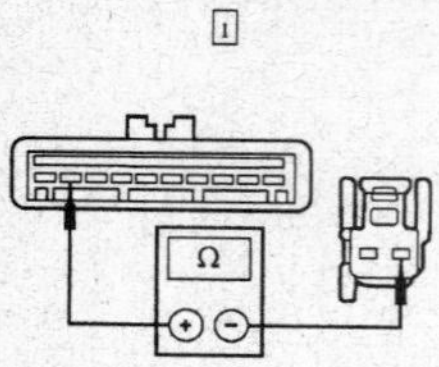	1 Measure the resistance between speed control servo C152-9, circuit 636 (O), and deactivator switch C218, circuit 636 (O). • Is the resistance less than 5 ohms? → **Yes** REPLACE the deactivator switch CLEAR the DTCs. TEST the system for normal operation. → **No** REPAIR circuit 636 (O). CLEAR the DTCs. TEST the system for normal operation.

FM1109800481030X

Fig. 30 Test D: Code C1127, Deactivator Switch Circuit Failure (Part 3 of 3). 2000 Continental

TEST CONDITIONS	TEST DETAILS/RESULTS/ACTIONS
C3 CHECK THE AIR BAG SLIDING CONTACT	
1 2 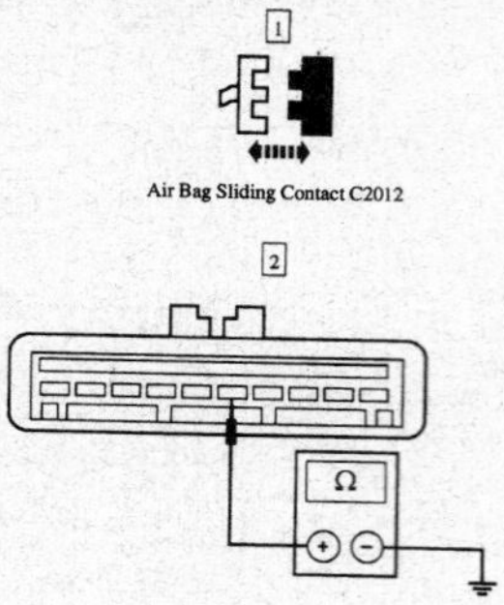	2 Measure the resistance between speed control servo C152-5, circuit 151 (LB/BK), and ground. • Is the resistance greater than 10,000 ohms? → **Yes** REPLACE the air bag sliding contact. CLEAR the DTCs. TEST the system for normal operation. → **No** REPAIR circuit 151 (LB/BK). CLEAR the DTCs. TEST the system for normal operation.

FM1109800480030X

Fig. 29 Test C: Code C1126, Speed Control Actuator Stuck For Two Minutes Or Longer (Part 3 of 3). 2000 Continental

TEST CONDITIONS	TEST DETAILS/RESULTS/ACTIONS
D2 CHECK THE SPEED CONTROL SERVO	
1 2 3 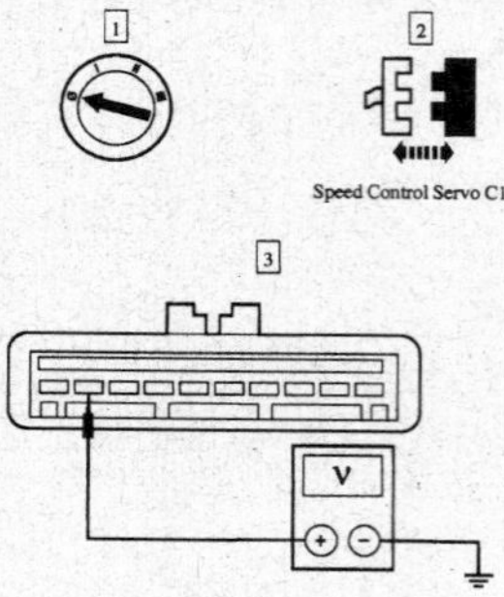	3 Measure the voltage between speed control servo C152-9, circuit 636 (O), and ground, while firmly applying and releasing the brake pedal. • Is the voltage greater than 10 volts with the brake pedal released and zero volts with the brake pedal applied? → **Yes** REPLACE the speed control servo. TEST the system for normal operation. → **No** GO to **D3**.
D3 CHECK CIRCUIT 10 (LG/R) FOR AN OPEN	
1 2 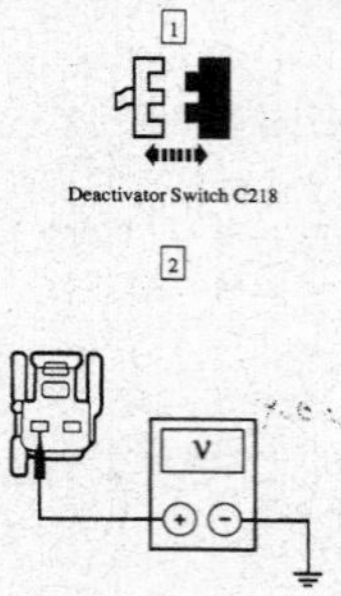	2 Measure the voltage between deactivator switch C218, circuit 10 (LG/R), and ground. • Is the voltage greater than 10 volts? → **Yes** GO to **D4**. → **No** REPAIR circuit 10 (LG/R). CLEAR the DTCs. TEST the system for normal operation.

FM1109800481020X

Fig. 30 Test D: Code C1127, Deactivator Switch Circuit Failure (Part 2 of 3). 2000 Continental

TEST CONDITIONS	TEST DETAILS/RESULTS/ACTIONS
E1 CHECK THE SPEED CONTROL ACTUATOR CABLE ADJUSTMENT	
2 3 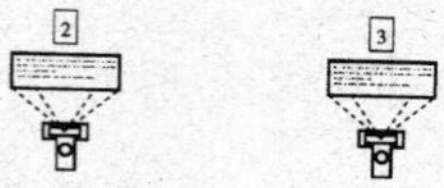	1 Perform the speed control actuator cable adjustment. 3 Retrieve and document DTCs. • Is DTC C1179 retrieved? → **Yes** REPLACE the speed control servo. TEST the system for normal operation. → **No** System is OK.

FM1109800482000X

Fig. 31 Test E: Code C1179, Speed Control Cable Slack Failure. 2000 Continental

TEST CONDITIONS	TEST DETAILS/RESULTS/ACTIONS
F1 CHECK THE FUSE JUNCTION PANEL FUSE 34 (15A)	
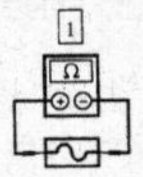 Fuse Junction Panel Fuse 34 (15A)	• Is the fuse OK? → **Yes** GO to **F2**. → **No** REPLACE the fuse. TEST the system for normal operation. If the fuse fails again, CHECK for short to ground. REPAIR as necessary. TEST the system for normal operation.
F2 CHECK CIRCUIT 1040 (R/LB) FOR AN OPEN	
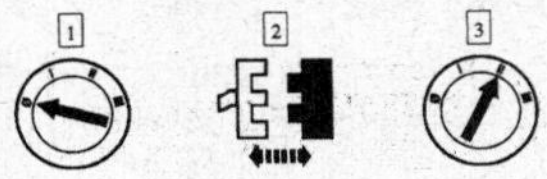 Speed Control Servo C152 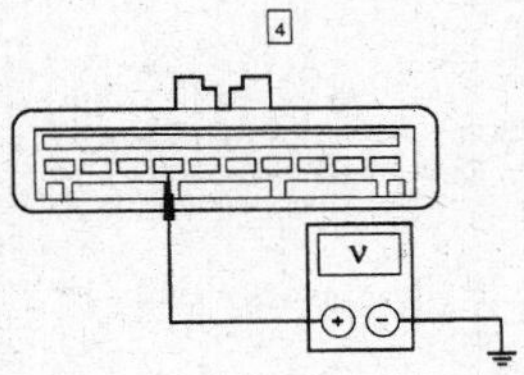	4 Measure the voltage between speed control servo C152-7, circuit 1040 (R/LB), and ground. • Is the voltage greater than 10 volts? → **Yes** GO to **F3**. → **No** REPAIR circuit 1040 (R/LB). TEST the system for normal operation.

FM1109800483010X

Fig. 32 Test F: No Communication With Speed Control Servo Module (Part 1 of 2). 2000 Continental

TEST CONDITIONS	TEST DETAILS/RESULTS/ACTIONS
F3 CHECK CIRCUIT 57 (BK) FOR AN OPEN	
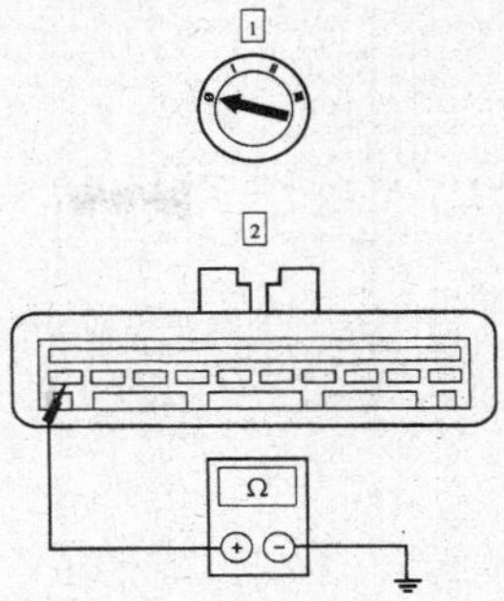	2 Measure the resistance between speed control servo C152-10, circuit 57 (BK), and ground. • Is the resistance less than 5 ohms? → **Yes** Diagnose module communications. → **No** REPAIR circuit 57 (BK). TEST the system for normal operation.

FM1109800483020X

Fig. 32 Test F: No Communication With Speed Control Servo Module (Part 2 of 2). 2000 Continental

TEST CONDITIONS	TEST DETAILS/RESULTS/ACTIONS
G1 CHECK THE HORN SYSTEM	
	1 Verify the horn system operates by pressing the horn switch. • Does the horn system operate properly? → **Yes** GO to **G2**. → **No** Diagnose Horn

FM1109800484010X

Fig. 33 Test G: Speed Control Inoperative (Part 1 of 5). 2000 Continental

TEST CONDITIONS	TEST DETAILS/RESULTS/ACTIONS
G2 CHECK THE SPEED CONTROL ACTUATOR SWITCH ON	
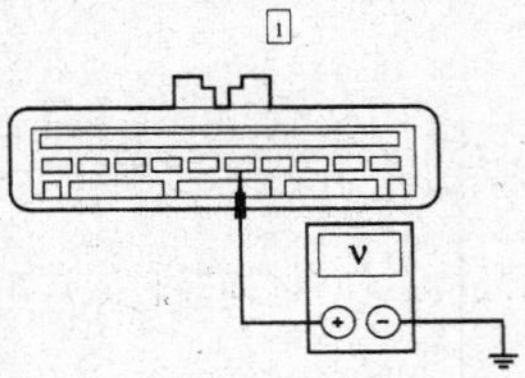	1 Measure the voltage between speed control servo C152-5, circuit 151 (LB/BK), and ground while pressing the speed control actuator switch ON. • Is the voltage greater than 10 volts? → **Yes** GO to **G3**. → **No** GO to **G4**.
G3 CHECK THE SPEED CONTROL ACTUATOR SWITCH SET/ACCEL	
 Speed Control Servo C152 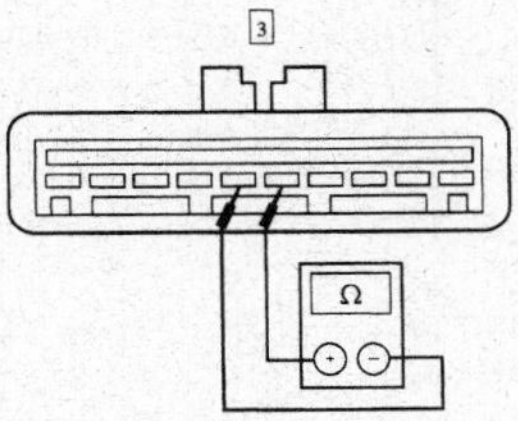	3 Measure the resistance between speed control servo C152-5, circuit 151 (LB/BK), and speed control servo C152-6, circuit 133 (BK), while pressing the speed control actuator switch SET/ACCEL. • Is the resistance between 612-748 ohms with the switch pressed and greater than 10,000 ohms with the switch released? → **Yes** REPLACE the speed control servo . TEST the system for normal operation. → **No** REPLACE the speed control actuator switch TEST the system for normal operation.

FM1109800484020X

Fig. 33 Test G: Speed Control Inoperative (Part 2 of 5). 2000 Continental

TEST CONDITIONS	TEST DETAILS/RESULTS/ACTIONS
G4 CHECK CIRCUIT 151 (LB/BK) FOR AN OPEN	
 Air Bag Sliding Contact C2012 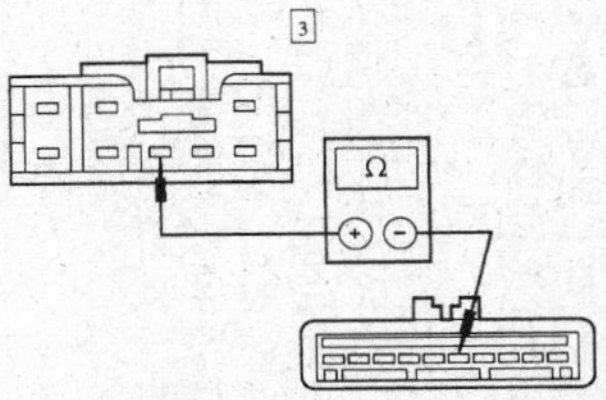	3 Measure the resistance between air bag sliding contact C2012F-6, circuit 151 (LB/BK), and speed control servo C152-5, circuit 151 (LB/BK). • Is the resistance less than 5 ohms? → **Yes** GO to **G5**. → **No** REPAIR circuit 151 (LB/BK). TEST the system for normal operation.
G5 CHECK THE AIR BAG SLIDING CONTACT	
	1 Remove the driver side air bag.

FM1109800484030X

Fig. 33 Test G: Speed Control Inoperative (Part 3 of 5). 2000 Continental

TEST CONDITIONS	TEST DETAILS/RESULTS/ACTIONS
G5 CHECK THE AIR BAG SLIDING CONTACT	
2 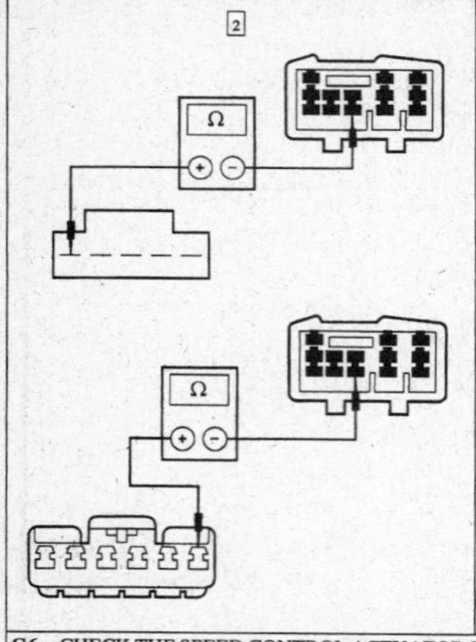	2 If not equipped with remote audio/climate controls, measure the resistance between top of air bag sliding contact terminal 1, and air bag sliding contact C2012M-6. If equipped with remote audio/climate controls, measure the resistance between top of air bag sliding contact terminal 6, and air bag sliding contact C2012M-6. • Is the resistance less than 1 ohm? → **Yes** If not equipped with remote audio/climate controls, REPLACE the speed control actuator switch. TEST the system for normal operation. If equipped with remote audio/climate controls, GO to **G6**. → **No** REPLACE the air bag sliding contact TEST the system for normal operation.
G6 CHECK THE SPEED CONTROL ACTUATOR SWITCH WIRE HARNESS	
1 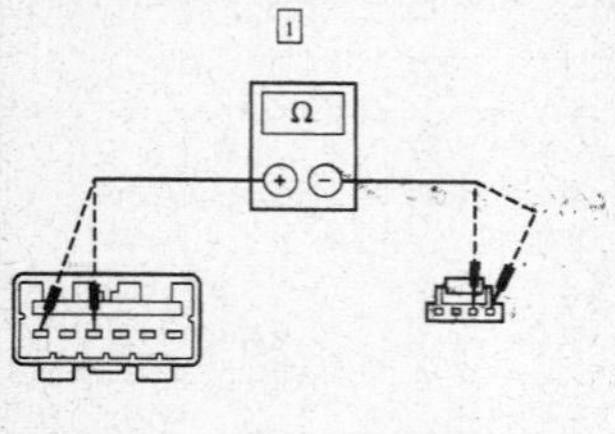	1 Measure the resistance between top of air bag sliding contact connector, and speed control actuator switch connector as follows:

Top of Air Bag Sliding Contact Connector	Speed Control Actuator Switch Connector
Pin 6	Pin 1
Pin 4	Pin 2

FM1109800484040X

Fig. 33 Test G: Speed Control Inoperative (Part 4 of 5). 2000 Continental

TEST CONDITIONS	TEST DETAILS/RESULTS/ACTIONS
J1 CHECK THE SPEED CONTROL ACTUATOR SWITCH COAST	
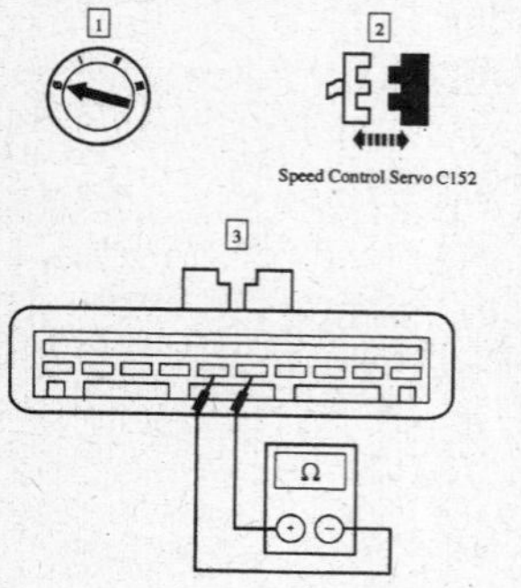	3 Measure the resistance between speed control servo C152-5, circuit 151 (LB/BK), and speed control servo C152-6, circuit 133 (BK), while pressing the speed control actuator switch COAST. • Is the resistance between 105-135 ohms with the COAST pressed and greater than 10,000 ohms with the COAST released? → **Yes** REPLACE the speed control servo. TEST the system for normal operation. → **No** REPLACE the speed control actuator switch; TEST the system for normal operation.

FM1109800486000X

Fig. 35 Test J: COAST Switch Inoperative. 2000 Continental

TEST CONDITIONS	TEST DETAILS/RESULTS/ACTIONS
G6 CHECK THE SPEED CONTROL ACTUATOR SWITCH WIRE HARNESS	
	• Are the resistances less than 5 ohms? → **Yes** REPLACE the speed control actuator switch TEST the system for normal operation. → **No** REPLACE the speed control actuator switch wire harness. TEST the system for normal operation.

FM1109800484050X

Fig. 33 Test G: Speed Control Inoperative (Part 5 of 5). 2000 Continental

TEST CONDITIONS	TEST DETAILS/RESULTS/ACTIONS
H1 CHECK THE SPEED CONTROL ACTUATOR CABLE	
	1 Check the throttle lever and speed control actuator cable for proper operation, while performing the speed control servo Slack test on NGS Tester. • Does the throttle lever operate properly? → **Yes** REPLACE the speed control servo. TEST the system for normal operation. → **No** REPAIR and/or REPLACE as necessary. TEST the system for normal operation.

FM1109800485000X

Fig. 34 Test H: Set Speed Fluctuates. 2000 Continental

TEST CONDITIONS	TEST DETAILS/RESULTS/ACTIONS
K1 CHECK THE SPEED CONTROL ACTUATOR SWITCH COAST	
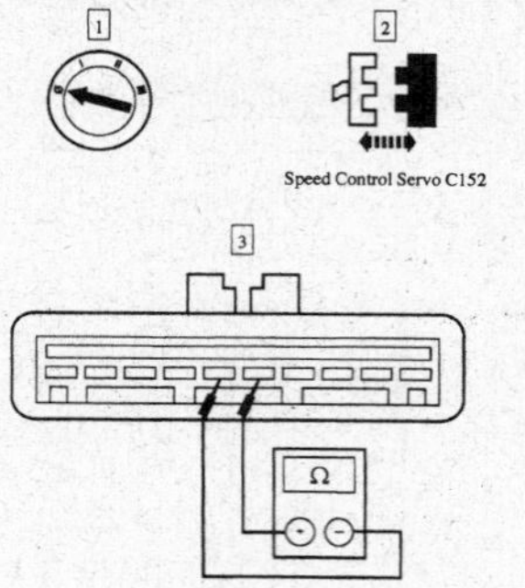	3 Measure the resistance between speed control servo C152-5, circuit 151 (LB/BK), and speed control servo C152-6, circuit 133 (BK), while pressing the speed control actuator switch SET/ACCEL. Is the resistance between 610-750 ohms with the SET/ACCEL pressed and greater than 10,000 ohms with the SET/ACCEL released? → **Yes** REPLACE the speed control servo. TEST the system for normal operation. → **No** REPLACE the speed control actuator switch TEST the system for normal operation.

FM1109800487000X

Fig. 36 Test K: SET/ACCEL Switch Inoperative. 2000 Continental

TEST CONDITIONS	TEST DETAILS/RESULTS/ACTIONS
L1 CHECK THE SPEED CONTROL ACTUATOR SWITCH RESUME	
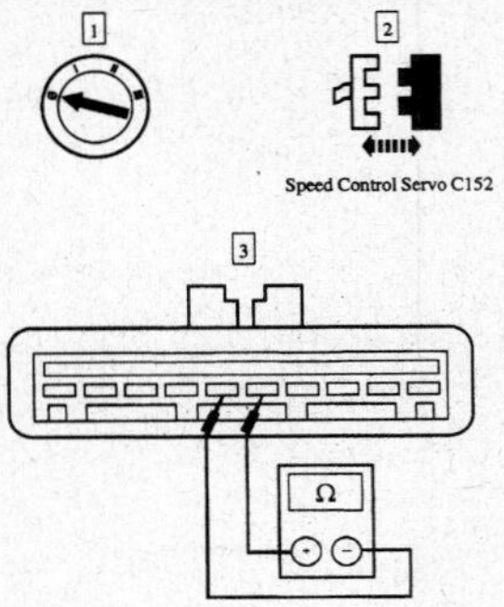	3 Measure the resistance between speed control servo C152-5, circuit 151 (LB/BK), and speed control servo C152-6, circuit 133 (BK), while pressing the speed control actuator switch RESUME. • Is the resistance between 1980-2420 ohms with the RESUME pressed and greater than 10,000 ohms with the RESUME released? → **Yes** REPLACE the speed control servo. TEST the system for normal operation. → **No** REPLACE the speed control actuator switch; TEST the system for normal operation.

FM1109800488000X

Fig. 37 Test L: RESUME Switch Inoperative. 2000 Continental

DTCS	Description	Source	Action
B1318	Battery Voltage Low	Speed Control Servo	GO to Pinpoint Test C.
B1342	ECU is Defective	Speed Control Servo	INSTALL a new speed control servo. TEST the system for normal operation.
C1109	Throttle Position Did Not Return to Idle After Self -Test	Speed Control Servo	GO to Pinpoint Test D.
C1126	Speed Control Actuator Switch Stuck for Two Minutes or Longer	Speed Control Servo	GO to Pinpoint Test E.
C1127	Deactivator Switch Circuit Failure	Speed Control Servo	GO to Pinpoint Test F.
C1179	Speed Control Cable Slack Failure	Speed Control Servo	GO to Pinpoint Test G.
U1027	SCP Invalid or Missing Data for Engine RPM	PCM	CARRY OUT the PCM Self -Test.
U1041	SCP Invalid or Missing Data for Vehicle Speed	Anti-Lock Brake Control Module	CARRY OUT the Anti-Lock Brake Control Module Self -Test.
U1051	SCP Invalid or Missing Data for Brakes	LCM	CARRY OUT the LCM Self -Test.
U1059	SCP Invalid or Missing Data for Transmission /Trans-axle/PRNDL	PCM	CARRY OUT the PCM Self -Test.

FM1100100727010X

Fig. 39 Diagnostic trouble code index. 2001–04 Continental

TEST CONDITIONS	TEST DETAILS/RESULTS/ACTIONS
M1 CHECK THE SPEED CONTROL ACTUATOR SWITCH OFF	
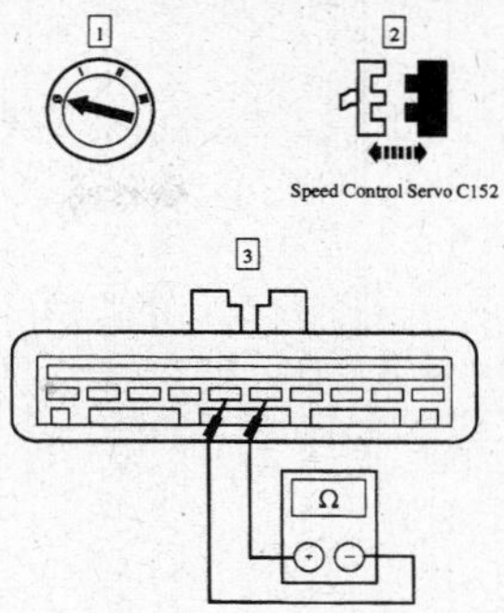	3 Measure the resistance between speed control servo C152-5, circuit 151 (LB/BK), and speed control servo C152-6, circuit 133 (BK), while pressing the speed control actuator switch OFF. • Is the resistance less than 5 ohms with the OFF pressed and greater than 10,000 ohms with the OFF released? → **Yes** REPLACE the speed control servo. TEST the system for normal operation. → **No** REPLACE the speed control actuator switch; TEST the system for normal operation.

FM1109800489000X

Fig. 38 Test M: OFF Switch Inoperative. 2000 Continental

A1 CHECK CIRCUIT 1050 (RD/LB) FOR AN OPEN

FM1100100728010X

Fig. 40 Test A: No Communication w/Module, Speed Control Servo (Part 1 of 3). 2001–04 Continental

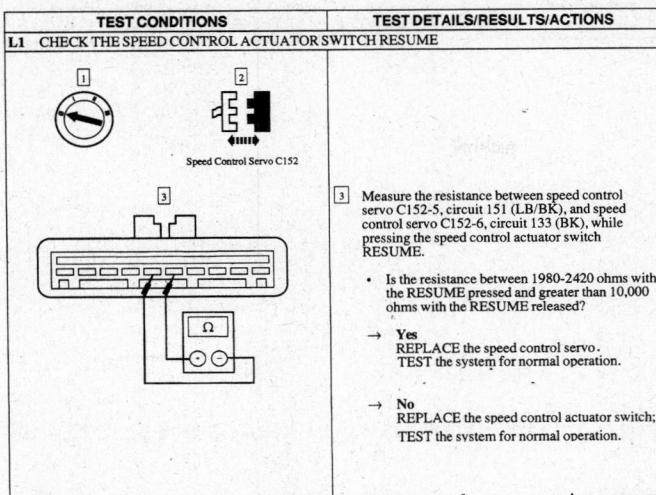

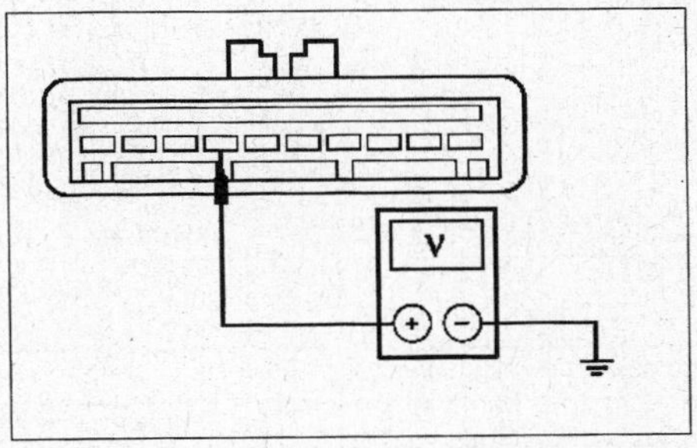

4

Measure the voltage between speed control servo C152 Pin 7, Circuit 1050 (RD/LB), harness side and ground.

- **Is the voltage greater than 10 volts?**

→ **Yes**

Go to «A2».

→ **No**

REPAIR the circuit. TEST the system for normal operation.

FM1100100728020X

Fig. 40 Test A: No Communication w/Module, Speed Control Servo (Part 2 of 3). 2001–04 Continental

A2 CHECK CIRCUIT 57 (BK) FOR AN OPEN

1

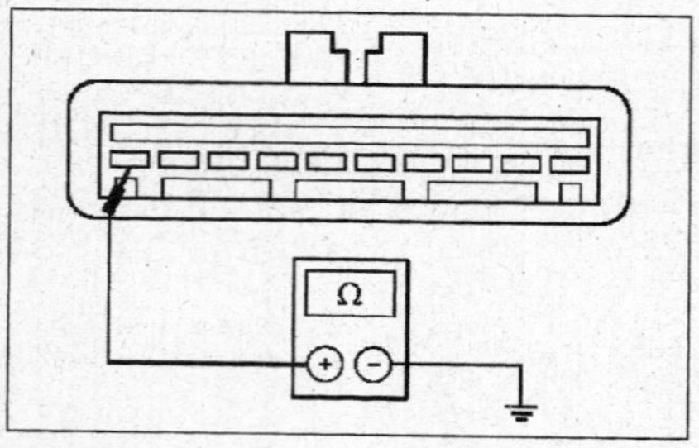

2

Measure the resistance between speed control servo C152 Pin 10, Circuit 57 (BK), harness side and ground.

- **Is the resistance less than 5 ohms?**

➔ **Yes**

Diagnose module communication network fault condition.

➔ **No**

Repair the circuit. Test for normal operation.

FM1100100728030X

Fig. 40 Test A: No Communication w/Module, Speed Control Servo (Part 3 of 3). 2001–04 Continental

C1 CHECK CIRCUIT 1050 (RD/LB) LOW VOLTAGE

1

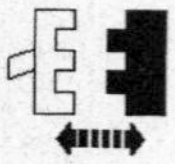

2 *Speed Control Servo C152*

3

FM1100100730010X

Fig. 42 Test C: DTC B1318, Battery Voltage Low (Part 1 of 2). 2001–04 Continental

D1 CHECK THE SPEED CONTROL ACTUATOR CABLE

1 Check the speed control actuator cable for sticking or binding.

- **Is the speed control actuator cable OK?**

➔ **Yes**

Go to «D2».

➔ **No**

INSTALL a new speed control actuator cable; CLEAR the DTCs. TEST the system for normal operation.

FM1100100731010X

Fig. 43 Test D: DTC C1109, Throttle Position Did Not Return To Idle After Self-Test (Part 1 of 3). 2001–04 Continental

B1 CHECK THE COMMUNICATIONS TO THE SPEED CONTROL SERVO

1

Check the communication to the speed control servo.

- **Does scan tool communicate with the speed control servo?**

➔ **Yes**

INSTALL a new speed control servo.

➔ **No**

GO to «Pinpoint Test A».

FM1100100729000X

Fig. 41 Test B: Unable To Enter Self-Test. 2001–04 Continental

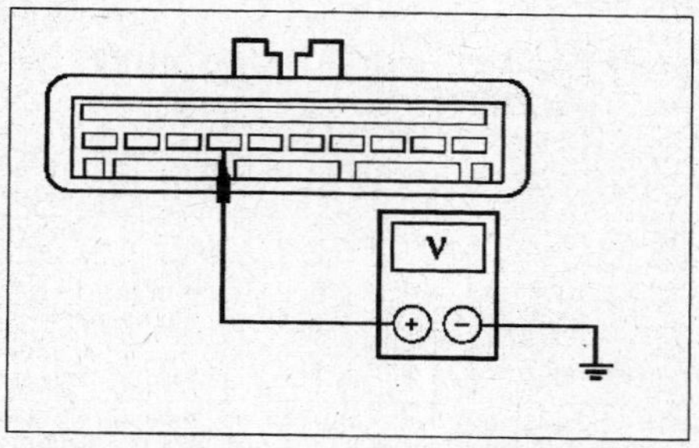

4

Measure the voltage between speed control servo C152 Pin 7, Circuit 1050 (RD/LB), harness side and ground.

- **Is the voltage greater than 10 volts?**

➔ **Yes**

CLEAR the DTC's. REPEAT the self-test.

➔ **No**

Diagnose charging system or electrical system fault condition.

FM1100100730020X

Fig. 42 Test C: DTC B1318, Battery Voltage Low (Part 2 of 2). 2001–04 Continental

D2 CHECK THE THROTTLE LEVER

1 Check the throttle lever for sticking or binding.

- **Is the throttle lever OK?**

➔ **Yes**

Go to «D3».

➔ **No**

REPAIR as necessary. CLEAR the DTCs. TEST the system for normal operation.

FM1100100731020X

Fig. 43 Test D: DTC C1109, Throttle Position Did Not Return To Idle After Self-Test (Part 2 of 3). 2001–04 Continental

D3 CHECK THE SPEED CONTROL ACTUATOR CABLE ADJUSTMENT

1 Carry out the speed control actuator cable adjustment.

2 CLEAR the DTCs. REPEAT the self-test.

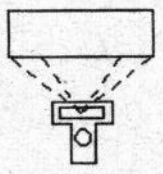

3

Retrieve and document DTCs.

- **Is DTC C1109 retrieved?**

→ **Yes**

INSTALL a new speed control servo; TEST the system for normal operation.

→ **No**

System is OK.

FM1100100731030X

Fig. 43 Test D: DTC C1109, Throttle Position Did Not Return To Idle After Self-Test (Part 3 of 3). 2001–04 Continental

5 Wait three minutes.

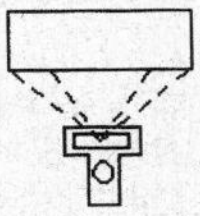

6

Retrieve and document continuous DTCs.

- **Is DTC C1126 retrieved?**

→ **Yes**

Go to «E2».

→ **No**

INSTALL a new speed control actuator switch; TEST the system for normal operation.

FM1100100732020X

Fig. 44 Test E: DTC C1126, Speed Control Actuator Switch Stuck For Two Minutes Or Longer (Part 2 of 5). 2001–04 Continental

E1 CHECK THE SPEED CONTROL ACTUATOR SWITCH

1

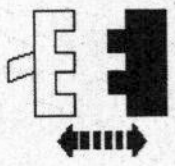

2 *Speed Control Actuator Switch*

3

4 *Clear Continuous DTCs*

FM1100100732010X

Fig. 44 Test E: DTC C1126, Speed Control Actuator Switch Stuck For Two Minutes Or Longer (Part 1 of 5). 2001–04 Continental

E2 CHECK CIRCUIT 151 (LB/BK) FOR SHORT TO GROUND

1

2 *Speed Control Servo C152*

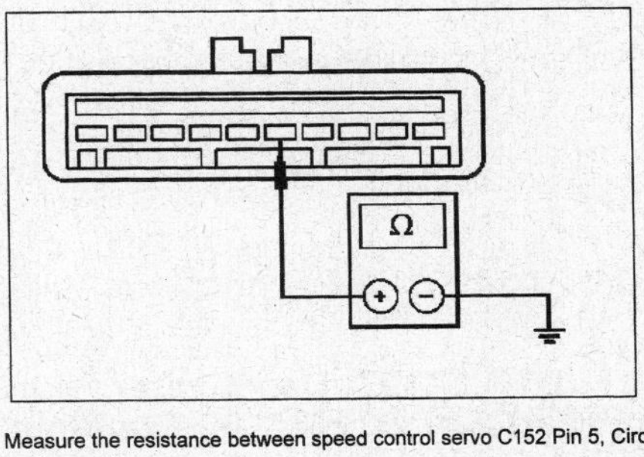

3

Measure the resistance between speed control servo C152 Pin 5, Circuit 151 (LB/BK), harness side and ground.

FM1100100732030X

Fig. 44 Test E: DTC C1126, Speed Control Actuator Switch Stuck For Two Minutes Or Longer (Part 3 of 5). 2001–04 Continental

- **Is the resistance greater than 10,000 ohms?**

➔ **Yes**

INSTALL a new speed control servo; TEST the system for normal operation.

➔ **No**

Go to «E3».

FM1100100732040X

Fig. 44 Test E: DTC C1126, Speed Control Actuator Switch Stuck For Two Minutes Or Longer (Part 4 of 5). 2001–04 Continental

F1	CHECK THE SPEED CONTROL SERVO

1

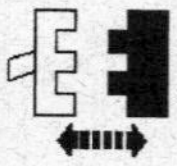

2

Speed Control Servo C152

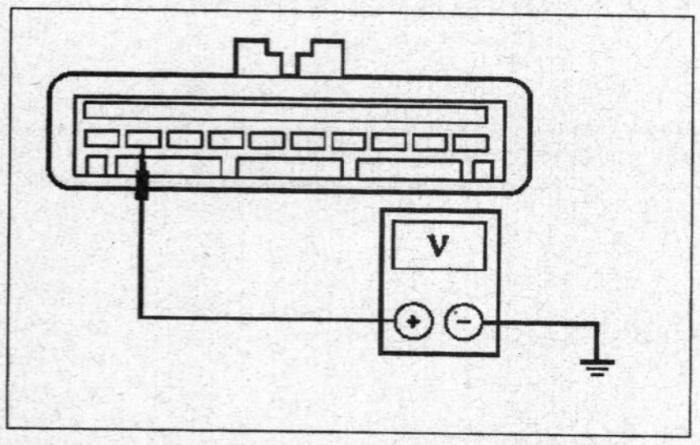

3

Measure the voltage between speed control servo C152 Pin 9, Circuit 636 (OG), harness side and ground, while firmly applying and releasing the brake pedal.

FM1100100733010X

Fig. 45 Test F: DTC C1127, Deactivator Switch Circuit Failure (Part 1 of 4). 2001–04 Continental

- **Is the voltage greater than 10 volts with the brake pedal released and zero volts with the brake pedal applied?**

➔ **Yes**

INSTALL a new speed control servo; TEST the system for normal operation.

➔ **No**

Go to «F2».

FM1100100733020X

Fig. 45 Test F: DTC C1127, Deactivator Switch Circuit Failure (Part 2 of 4). 2001–04 Continental

E3	CHECK THE AIR BAG SLIDING CONTACT

1

Air Bag Sliding Contact C2012

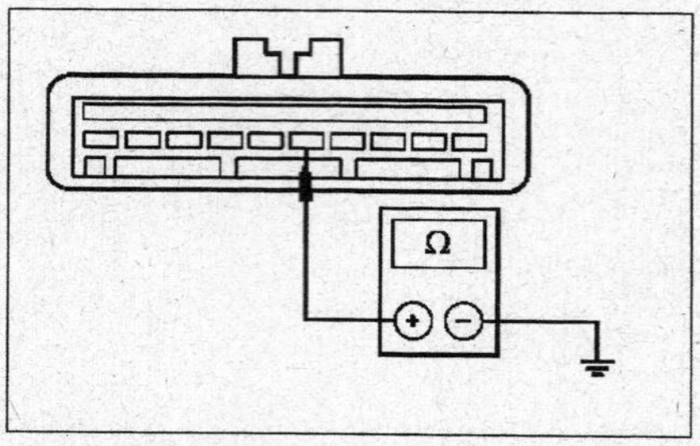

2

Measure the resistance between speed control servo C152 Pin 5, Circuit 151 (LB/BK), harness side and ground.

- **Is the resistance greater than 10,000 ohms?**

➔ **Yes**

INSTALL a new air bag sliding contact; CLEAR the DTCs. TEST the system for normal operation.

➔ **No**

REPAIR the circuit. CLEAR the DTCs. TEST the system for normal operation.

FM1100100732050X

Fig. 44 Test E: DTC C1126, Speed Control Actuator Switch Stuck For Two Minutes Or Longer (Part 5 of 5). 2001–04 Continental

F2	CHECK CIRCUIT 10 (LG/RD) FOR AN OPEN

1

Deactivator Switch C218

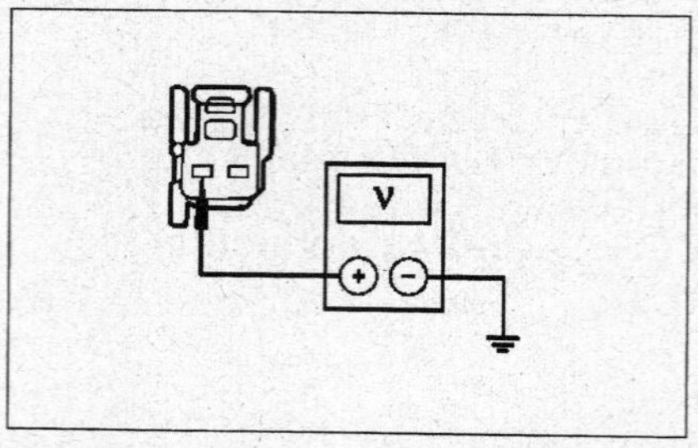

2

Measure the voltage between deactivator switch C218, Circuit 10 (LG/RD), harness side and ground.

- **Is the voltage greater than 10 volts?**

➔ **Yes**

Go to «F3».

➔ **No**

REPAIR the circuit. CLEAR the DTCs. TEST the system for normal operation.

FM1100100733030X

Fig. 45 Test F: DTC C1127, Deactivator Switch Circuit Failure (Part 3 of 4). 2001–04 Continental

F3 CHECK CIRCUIT 636 (OG) FOR AN OPEN

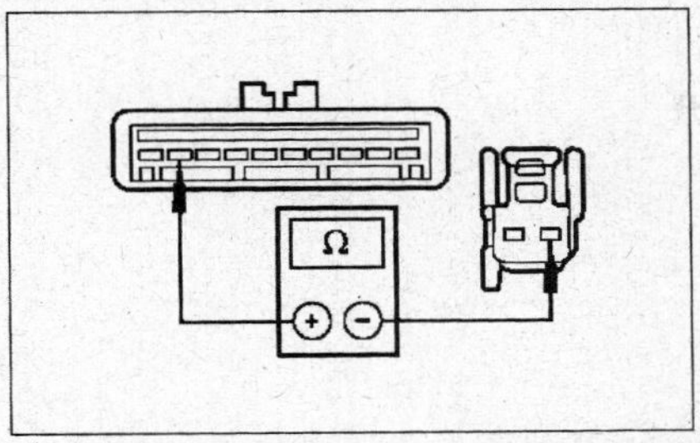

1

Measure the resistance between speed control servo C152 Pin 9, Circuit 636 (OG), harness side and deactivator switch C218, Circuit 636 (OG), harness side.

- **Is the resistance less than 5 ohms?**

➔ **Yes**

INSTALL a new deactivator switch. CLEAR the DTCs. TEST the system for normal operation.

➔ **No**

REPAIR the circuit. CLEAR the DTCs. TEST the system for normal operation.

FM1100100733040X

Fig. 45 Test F: DTC C1127, Deactivator Switch Circuit Failure (Part 4 of 4). 2001–04 Continental

H1 CHECK THE HORN SYSTEM

1 Verify the horn system operates by pressing the horn switch.

- **Does the horn system operate properly?**

➔ **Yes**

Go to «H2».

➔ **No**

Diagnose horn fault condition.

FM1100100735010X

Fig. 47 Test H: Speed Control Inoperative, No DTCs (Part 1 of 9). 2001–04 Continental

G1 CHECK THE SPEED CONTROL ACTUATOR CABLE ADJUSTMENT

1 Carry out the speed control actuator cable adjustment.

2 CLEAR the DTCs. REPEAT the self-test.

3

Retrieve and document DTCs.

- **Is DTC C1179 retrieved?**

➔ **Yes**

INSTALL a new speed control servo. TEST the system for normal operation.

➔ **No**

System is OK.

FM1100100734000X

Fig. 46 Test G: DTC C1179, Speed Control Cable Slack Failure. 2001–04 Continental

H2 CHECK THE SPEED CONTROL ACTUATOR SWITCH ON

1

2

Speed Control Servo C152

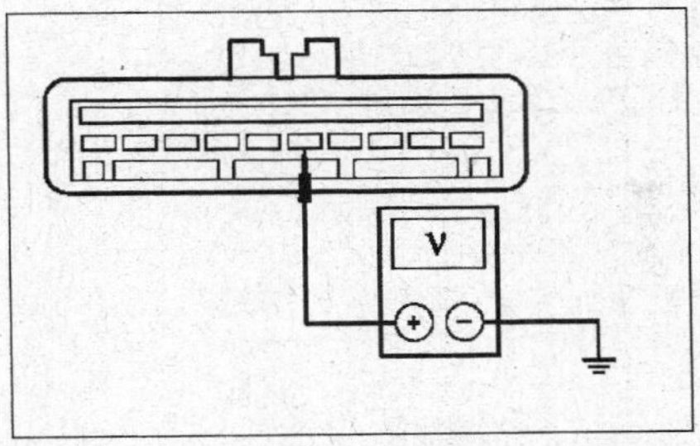

3

Measure the voltage between speed control servo C152 Pin 5, Circuit 151 (LB/BK), harness side and ground while pressing the speed control actuator switch ON.

FM1100100735020X

Fig. 47 Test H: Speed Control Inoperative, No DTCs (Part 2 of 9). 2001–04 Continental

- **Is the voltage greater than 10 volts?**

➔ **Yes**

Go to «H3».

➔ **No**

Go to «H4».

FM1100100735030X

Fig. 47 Test H: Speed Control Inoperative, No DTCs (Part 3 of 9). 2001–04 Continental

H3 CHECK THE SPEED CONTROL ACTUATOR SWITCH SET/ACCEL

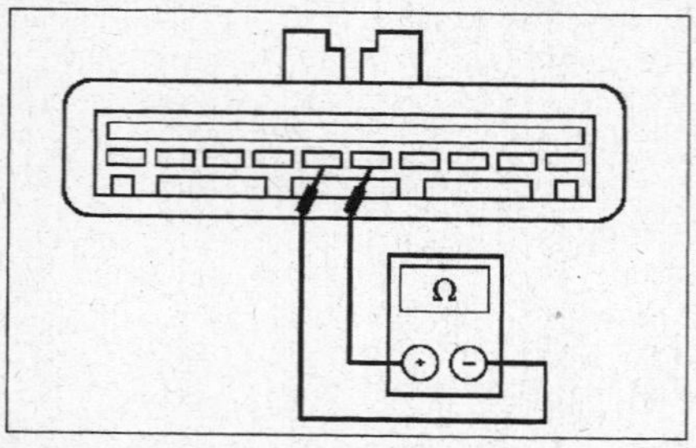

1

Measure the resistance between speed control servo C152 Pin 5, Circuit 151 (LB/BK), harness side and speed control servo C152 Pin 6, Circuit 133 (BK), harness side while pressing the speed control actuator switch SET/ACCEL.

- **Is the resistance between 612 and 748 ohms with the switch pressed, and greater than 10,000 ohms with the switch released?**

→ **Yes**

INSTALL a new speed control servo. TEST the system for normal operation.

→ **No**

INSTALL a new speed control actuator switch. TEST the system for normal operation.

FM1100100735040X

Fig. 47 Test H: Speed Control Inoperative, No DTCs (Part 4 of 9). 2001–04 Continental

- **Is the resistance less than 5 ohms?**

→ **Yes**

Go to «H5».

→ **No**

REPAIR the circuit. TEST the system for normal operation.

FM1100100735060X

Fig. 47 Test H: Speed Control Inoperative, No DTCs (Part 6 of 9). 2001–04 Continental

H5 CHECK THE AIR BAG SLIDING CONTACT

1 Remove the driver side air bag.

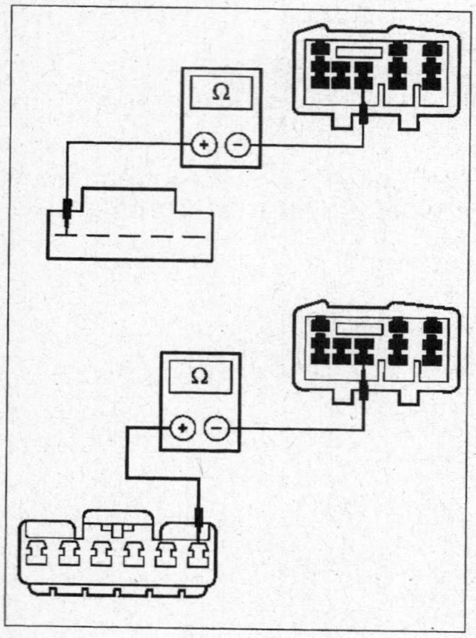

2

FM1100100735070X

Fig. 47 Test H: Speed Control Inoperative, No DTCs (Part 7 of 9). 2001–04 Continental

H4 CHECK CIRCUIT 151 (LB/BK) FOR AN OPEN

1

2 *Air Bag Sliding Contact C2012*

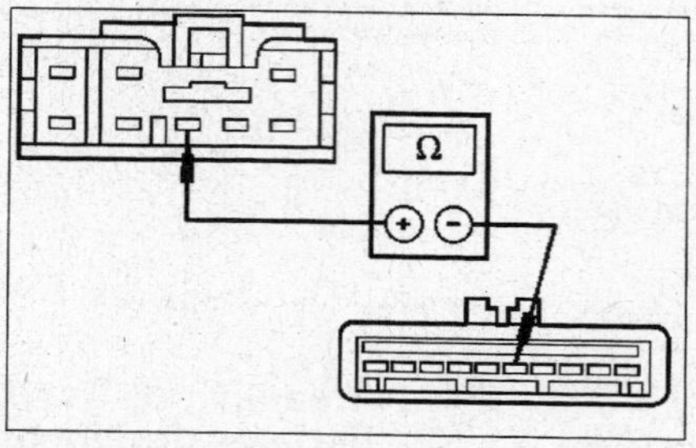

3

Measure the resistance between air bag sliding contact C2012F Pin 6, Circuit 151 (LB/BK), harness side and speed control servo C152 Pin 5, Circuit 151 (LB/BK), harness side.

FM1100100735050X

Fig. 47 Test H: Speed Control Inoperative, No DTCs (Part 5 of 9). 2001–04 Continental

If not equipped with remote audio/climate controls, measure the resistance between top of air bag sliding contact Pin 1 and air bag sliding contact C2012M Pin 6. If equipped with remote audio/climate controls, measure the resistance between top of air bag sliding contact Pin 6 and air bag sliding contact C2012M-6.

- **Is the resistance less than 1 ohm?**

→ **Yes**

If not equipped with remote audio/climate controls, INSTALL a new speed control actuator switch.
TEST the system for normal operation. If equipped with remote audio/climate controls, Go to «H6».

→ **No**

INSTALL a new air bag sliding contact. TEST the system for normal operation.

FM1100100735080X

Fig. 47 Test H: Speed Control Inoperative, No DTCs (Part 8 of 9). 2001–04 Continental

H6	CHECK THE SPEED CONTROL ACTUATOR SWITCH WIRE HARNESS

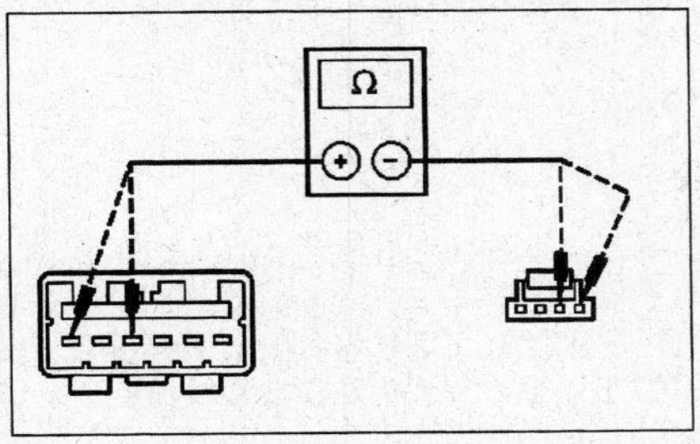

1

Measure the resistance between top of air bag sliding contact connector and speed control actuator switch connector as follows:

Top of Air Bag Sliding Contact Connector	Speed Control Actuator Switch Connector
Pin 6	Pin 1
Pin 4	Pin 2

- **Are the resistances less than 5 ohms?**

➔ **Yes**

INSTALL a new speed control actuator switch. TEST the system for normal operation.

➔ **No**

INSTALL a new speed control actuator switch wire harness. TEST the system for normal operation.

FM1100100735090X

Fig. 47 Test H: Speed Control Inoperative, No DTCs (Part 9 of 9). 2001–04 Continental

J1	CHECK THE SPEED CONTROL ACTUATOR SWITCH COAST PID

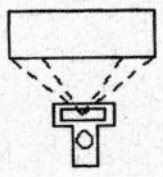

1

Monitor the speed control servo COAST PID. Depress and release the speed control actuator switch COAST button, while slightly turning the steering wheel from side to side.

- **Does the scan tool indicate ACTIVE with the speed control actuator switch depressed and notACT with the speed control actuator switch released?**

➔ **Yes**

System is OK.

➔ **No**

Go to «J2».

FM1100100737010X

Fig. 49 Test J: COAST Switch Inoperative (Part 1 of 3). 2001–04 Continental

actuator switch COAST and slightly turning the steering wheel from side to side.

- **Is the resistance between 108 and 132 ohms with the COAST pressed and greater than 10,000 ohms with the COAST released?**

➔ **Yes**

INSTALL a new speed control servo. TEST the system for normal operation.

➔ **No**

INSTALL a new speed control actuator switch; TEST the system for normal operation.

FM1100100737030X

Fig. 49 Test J: COAST Switch Inoperative (Part 3 of 3). 2001–04 Continental

I1	CHECK THE SPEED CONTROL ACTUATOR CABLE AND THROTTLE LEVER

1 Check the throttle lever and speed control actuator cable for proper operation, while performing the speed control servo slack test on the scan tool.

- **Does the throttle lever operate properly?**

➔ **Yes**

INSTALL a new speed control servo. TEST the system for normal operation.

➔ **No**

REPAIR as necessary. TEST the system for normal operation.

FM1100100736000X

Fig. 48 Test I: Set Speed Fluctuates. 2001–04 Continental

J2	CHECK THE SPEED CONTROL ACTUATOR SWITCH COAST

1

2

Speed Control Servo C152

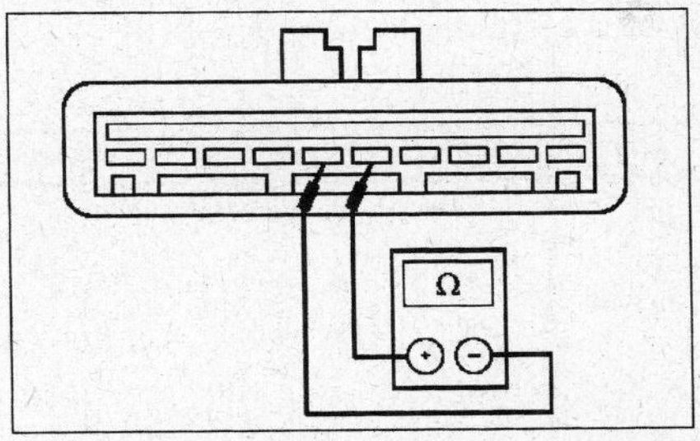

3

Measure the resistance between speed control servo C152 Pin 5, Circuit 151 (LB/BK), harness side and speed control servo C152 Pin 6, Circuit 133 (BK), harness side while pressing the speed control

FM1100100737020X

Fig. 49 Test J: COAST Switch Inoperative (Part 2 of 3). 2001–04 Continental

K1	CHECK THE SPEED CONTROL ACTUATOR SWITCH SET_ACL PID

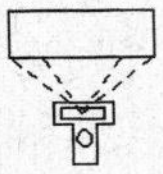

1

Monitor the speed control servo SET_ACL PID. Depress and release the speed control actuator switch SET/ACCEL button, while slightly turning the steering wheel from side to side.

- **Does the scan tool indicate ACTIVE with the speed control actuator switch depressed and notACT with the speed control actuator switch released?**

➔ **Yes**

System is OK.

➔ **No**

Go to «K2».

FM1100100738010X

Fig. 50 Test K: SET/ACCEL Switch Inoperative (Part 1 of 3). 2001–04 Continental

K2 CHECK THE SPEED CONTROL ACTUATOR SWITCH SET_ACL

1

2

Speed Control Servo C152

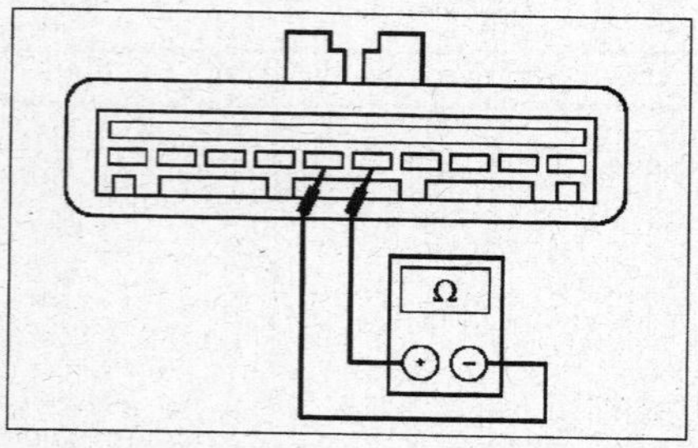

3

Measure the resistance between speed control servo C152 Pin 5, Circuit 151 (LB/BK), harness side and speed control servo C152 Pin 6, Circuit 133 (BK), harness side while pressing the speed control

FM1100100738020X

Fig. 50 Test K: SET/ACCEL Switch Inoperative (Part 2 of 3). 2001–04 Continental

L1 CHECK THE SPEED CONTROL ACTUATOR SWITCH RESUME PID

1

Monitor the speed control servo RESUME PID. Depress and release the speed control actuator switch RESUME button, while slightly turning the steering wheel from side to side.

- **Does the scan tool indicate ACTIVE with the speed control actuator switch depressed and notACT with the speed control actuator switch released?**

→ **Yes**

System is OK.

→ **No**

Go to «L2».

FM1100100739010X

Fig. 51 Test L: RESUME Switch Inoperative (Part 1 of 3). 2001–04 Continental

actuator switch RESUME and slightly turning the steering wheel from side to side.

- **Is the resistance between 1,980 and 2,420 ohms with the RESUME pressed and greater than 10,000 ohms with the RESUME released?**

→ **Yes**

INSTALL a new speed control servo. TEST the system for normal operation.

→ **No**

INSTALL a new speed control actuator switch. TEST the system for normal operation.

FM1100100739030X

Fig. 51 Test L: RESUME Switch Inoperative (Part 3 of 3). 2001–04 Continental

actuator switch SET/ACCEL and slightly turning the steering wheel from side to side.

- **Is the resistance between 612 and 748 ohms with the SET/ACCEL pressed and greater than 10,000 ohms with the SET/ACCEL released?**

→ **Yes**

INSTALL a new speed control servo. TEST the system for normal operation.

→ **No**

INSTALL a new speed control actuator switch. TEST the system for normal operation.

FM1100100738030X

Fig. 50 Test K: SET/ACCEL Switch Inoperative (Part 3 of 3). 2001–04 Continental

L2 CHECK THE SPEED CONTROL ACTUATOR SWITCH RESUME

1

2

Speed Control Servo C152

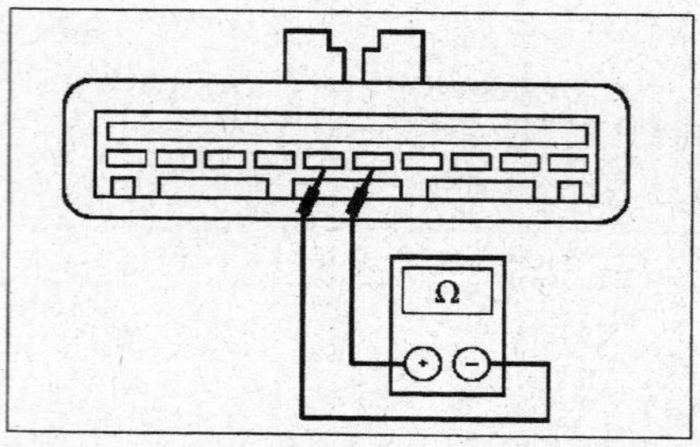

3

Measure the resistance between speed control servo C152 Pin 5, Circuit 151 (LB/BK), harness side and speed control servo C152 Pin 6, Circuit 133 (BK), harness side while pressing the speed control

FM1100100739020X

Fig. 51 Test L: RESUME Switch Inoperative (Part 2 of 3). 2001–04 Continental

M1 CHECK THE SPEED CONTROL ACTUATOR SWITCH SC_OFF PID

1

Monitor the speed control servo SC_OFF PID. Depress and release the speed control actuator switch OFF button, while slightly turning the steering wheel from side to side.

- **Does the scan tool indicate ACTIVE with the speed control actuator switch depressed and notACT with the speed control actuator switch released?**

→ **Yes**

System is OK.

→ **No**

Go to «M2».

FM1100100740010X

Fig. 52 Test M: OFF Switch Inoperative (Part 1 of 3). 2001–04 Continental

M2	CHECK THE SPEED CONTROL ACTUATOR SWITCH OFF

1

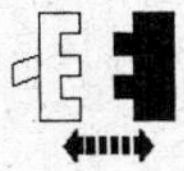

2

Speed Control Servo C152

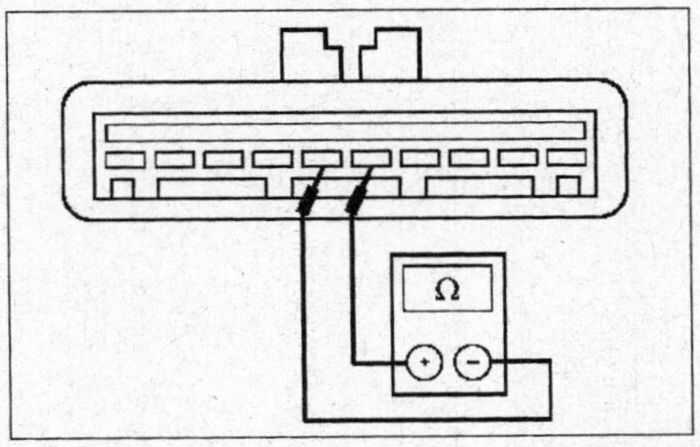

3

Measure the resistance between speed control servo C152 Pin 5, Circuit 151 (LB/BK), harness side and speed control servo C152 Pin 6, Circuit 133 (BK), harness side while pressing the speed control

FM1100100740020X

Fig. 52 Test M: OFF Switch Inoperative (Part 2 of 3). 2001–04 Continental

actuator switch OFF and slightly turning the steering wheel side to side.

- **Is the resistance less than 5 ohms with OFF pressed and greater than 10,000 ohms with the OFF released?**

➔ **Yes**

INSTALL a new speed control servo; TEST the system for normal operation.

➔ **No**

INSTALL a new speed control actuator switch. TEST the system for normal operation.

FM1100100740030X

Fig. 52 Test M: OFF Switch Inoperative (Part 3 of 3). 2001–04 Continental

Symptom Chart

Condition	Possible Sources	Action
• The Speed Control Inoperative	• Circuitry. • BPP switch. • Brake pedal deactivator switch. • Clutch pedal position switch. • Brake pedal deactivator switch. • Speed control/horn switches. • Actuator . • Speed Control Module. • Fuse.	• GO to Pinpoint Test A.
• The Speed Control Does Not Disengage When the Brakes are Appliedr	• Brake pedal deactivator switch. • BPP switch. • Circuitry.	• GO to Pinpoint Test B.
• The OFF Switch is Inoperative	• OFF switch. • Circuitry.	• GO to Pinpoint Test C.
• The Coast Switch is Inoperative	• COAST switch. • Circuit.	• GO to Pinpoint Test D.

FM1109800492010X

Fig. 53 Symptom chart (Part 1 of 2). Contour & Mystique

Condition	Possible Sources	Action
• The SET/ACCL Switch is Inoperative	• SET/ACCL switch. • Circuitry.	• GO to Pinpoint Test E.
• The Resume Switch is Inoperative	• Resume switch. • Circuitry.	• GO to Pinpoint Test F.
• The Set Speed Fluctuates	• VSS • Circuitry.	• GO to Pinpoint Test G.
• The Speed Control Does Not Disengage When the Clutch is Applied	• Clutch pedal position (CPP) switch.	• GO to Pinpoint Test H.
• The Speed Control Does Not Increase or Decrease By One Mile Per Hour When the ACCL or Coast Buttons are Depressed But the ACCL and Coast Normal Functions Operate	• Speed Control Module	• REPLACE the speed control module. TEST the system for normal operation.

FM1109800492020X

Fig. 53 Symptom chart (Part 2 of 2). Contour & Mystique

CONDITIONS	DETAILS/RESULTS/ACTIONS
A1 CHECK FOR VOLTAGE AND GROUND TO SPEED CONTROL MODULE	
1 2 3  Speed Control Module C833	

FM1109800493010X

Fig. 54 Test A: Speed Control Inoperative (Part 1 of 13). Contour & Mystique

CONDITIONS	DETAILS/RESULTS/ACTIONS
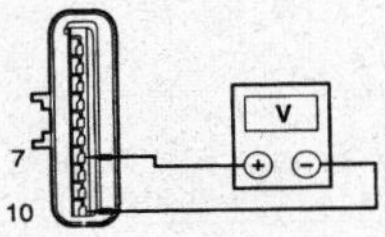	4 Measure the voltage between speed control module C833-7, circuit 14 PG12 (VT/WH) and C833-10, circuit 91 PG12 (BK/WH). • Is the voltage greater than 10 volts? → **Yes** GO to **A2.** → **No** GO to **A13.**
A2 CHECK CIRCUIT 29S-PG17 (OG/BU) FOR SHORT TO POWER	
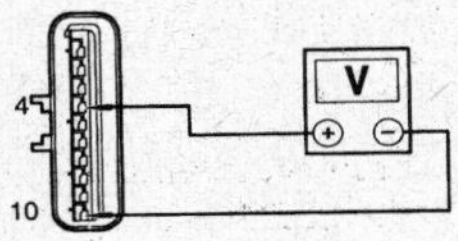	1 Measure the voltage between speed control module C833-4, circuit 29S-PG17 (OG/BU), and C833-10, circuit 91-PG12 (BK/WH). • Is any voltage indicated? → **Yes**] → **No** If the vehicle is equipped with M/T, GO to **A3.** If the vehicle is equipped with A/T, GO to **A4.**
A3 CHECK THE CLUTCH PEDAL POSITION (CPP) SWITCH FOR OPEN	

FM1109800493020X

Fig. 54 Test A: Speed Control Inoperative (Part 2 of 13). Contour & Mystique

CONDITIONS	DETAILS/RESULTS/ACTIONS
1  2  CPP Switch C825	
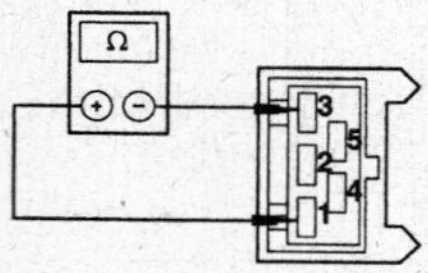	3 Measure the resistance between clutch pedal position (CPP) switch terminals. • Is the resistance less than 5 ohms? → **Yes** GO to **A4.** → **No** REPLACE the CPP. TEST the system for normal operation.
A4 CHECK CIRCUIT 29S PG16 (OG/YE) FOR VOLTAGE	
1 	

FM1109800493030X

Fig. 54 Test A: Speed Control Inoperative (Part 3 of 13). Contour & Mystique

CONDITIONS	DETAILS/RESULTS/ACTIONS
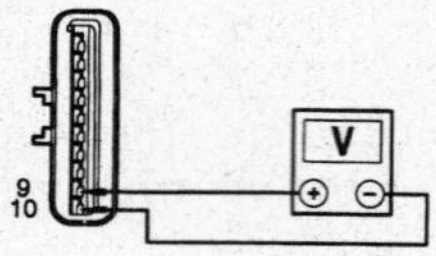	2 Measure the voltage between speed control module C833–9, circuit 29S-PG16 (OG/YE) and C833-10, circuit 91-PG12 (BK/WH). • Is voltage greater than 10 volts? → **Yes** GO to **A5.** → **No** GO to **A15.**
A5 CHECK FOR SHORTED SPEED CONTROL/HORN SWITCHES	
1 	
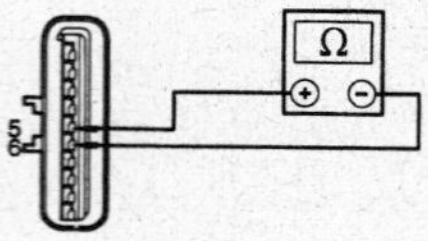	2 Measure the resistance between speed control module C833–5, circuit 8-PG13 (WH), and C833-6, circuit 31-PG13 (BK).

FM1109800493040X

Fig. 54 Test A: Speed Control Inoperative (Part 4 of 13). Contour & Mystique

CONDITIONS	DETAILS/RESULTS/ACTIONS
	• Is resistance greater than 10,000 ohms? → **Yes** GO to **A6.** → **No** REPLACE the speed control/horn switch. TEST the system for normal operation.
A6 CHECK CIRCUIT 31-PG13 (BK) FOR SHORT TO POWER	
1 	
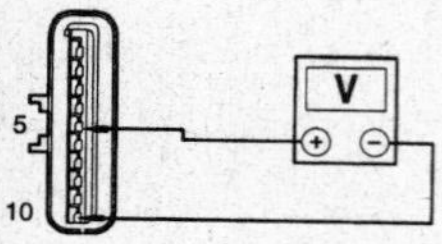 4	2 Measure the voltage between speed control module C833–5, circuit 8-PG13 (WH) and C833-10, circuit 91-PG12 (BK/WH). • Is any voltage indicated? → **Yes** REPAIR circuit 8-PG13 (WH). TEST the system for normal operation. → **No** GO to **A7.**
A7 CHECK CIRCUIT 8-PG13 (WH) FOR SHORT TO GROUND	

FM1109800493050X

Fig. 54 Test A: Speed Control Inoperative (Part 5 of 13). Contour & Mystique

CONDITIONS	DETAILS/RESULTS/ACTIONS
1 	
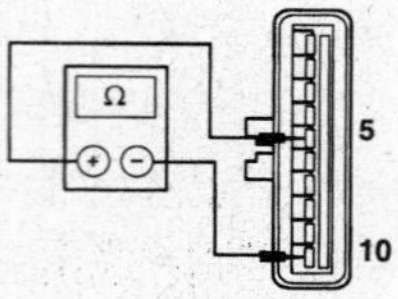	2 Measure the resistance between speed control module C833-5, circuit 8-PG13 (WH) and C833-10, circuit 91-PG12 (BK/WH). • Is resistance greater than 10,000 ohms? → **Yes** GO to **A8.** → **No** REPAIR circuit 8-PG13 (WH). TEST the system for normal operation.
A8 CHECK CIRCUIT 31-PG13 (BK) FOR SHORT TO GROUND	
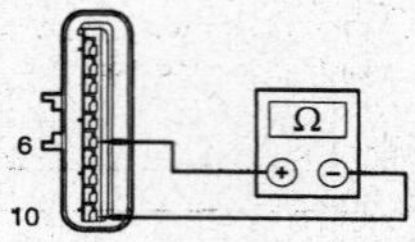	1 Measure the resistance between speed control module C833-5 circuit 31-PG13 (BK), and C833-10,circuit 91-PG12 (BK/WH).

FM1109800493060X

Fig. 54 Test A: Speed Control Inoperative (Part 6 of 13). Contour & Mystique

CONDITIONS	DETAILS/RESULTS/ACTIONS
	• Is the resistance greater than 10,000 ohms? → **Yes** GO to **A9.** → **No** REPAIR circuit 31-PG13 (BK). TEST the system for normal operation.
A9 CHECK CIRCUIT 31-PG13 (BK) FOR SHORT TO POWER	
1 	
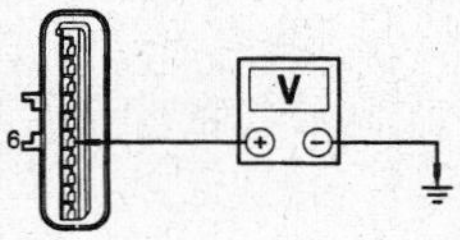	2 Measure the voltage between speed control module C833-6, circuit 31-PG13 (BK) and ground. • Is any voltage indicated.? → **Yes** REPAIR circuit 31-PG13 (BK). TEST the system for normal operation. → **No** GO to **A10.**
A10 CHECK THE ON SWITCH FOR VOLTAGE	

FM1109800493070X

Fig. 54 Test A: Speed Control Inoperative (Part 7 of 13). Contour & Mystique

CONDITIONS	DETAILS/RESULTS/ACTIONS
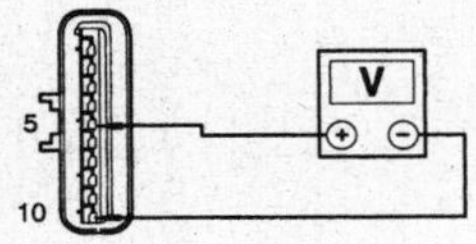	1 Measure the voltage between speed control module C833-5, circuit 8-PG13 (WH), and ground, while depressing the ON switch. • Is the voltage greater than 10 volts? → **Yes** GO to **A11.** → **No** CHECK the horn. IF the horn operates, GO to **A14.** If the horn does not operate.
A11 CHECK THE SET/ACC SWITCH FOR OPEN	
1 	
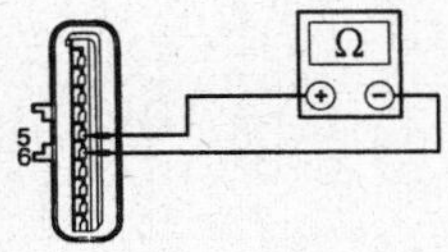	2 Measure the resistance between speed control module C833-5, circuit 8-PG13 (WH), and C833-6, circuit 31-PG13 (BK) while the SET/ACCL switch is depressed.

FM1109800493080X

Fig. 54 Test A: Speed Control Inoperative (Part 8 of 13). Contour & Mystique

CONDITIONS	DETAILS/RESULTS/ACTIONS
	• Is the resistance approximately 680 ohms? → **Yes** GO to **A12.** → **No** If the resistance is less than 640 ohms or greater than 720 ohms, REPLACE speed control/horn switch. TEST the system for normal operation.
A12 CHECK FOR OPEN CIRCUIT BETWEEN THE VSS AND THE SPEED CONTROL MODULE	
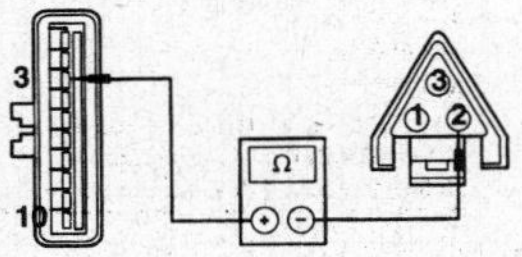 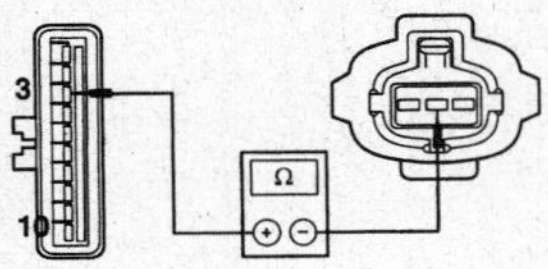	1 Measure the resistance between speed control module C833-3, circuit 8 PG12 (WH/VT) and vehicle speed sensor (VSS) C823–2 [automatic transmission] or C1899-2 [manual transmission], circuit 8-PC60 (WH/BU). • Is the resistance less than 5 ohms? → **Yes** If the speedometer operates correctly, REPLACE the speed control module. TEST the system for normal operation. If the speedometer does not operate correctly. Diagnose Circuit → **No** REPAIR circuits 8-PG12, (WH/VT)/ 8-PC89 (WH/VT)/8-PC89A (WH/VT), 8–PC60 (WH/BU). TEST the system for normal operation.
A13 CHECK CIRCUIT 14-PG12 (VT/WH) FOR VOLTAGE	

FM1109800493090X

Fig. 54 Test A: Speed Control Inoperative (Part 9 of 13). Contour & Mystique

CONDITIONS	DETAILS/RESULTS/ACTIONS
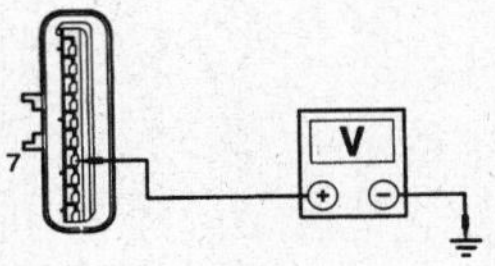	1 Measure the voltage between speed control module C833-7, circuit 14–PG12 (VT/WH) and ground. • Is the voltage greater than 10 volts? → **Yes** REPAIR circuit 91–PG12 (BK/WH). TEST the system for normal operation. → **No** REPAIR CIRCUIT 14 PG12 (VT/WH). TEST the system for normal operation.
A14 CHECK OFF SWITCH	
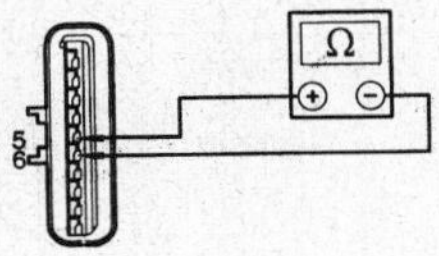	1 Measure the resistance between speed control C833-5, circuit 8-PG13 (WH) and C833-6, circuit 31-PG13 (BK), while depressing the OFF switch. • Is the resistance less than 5 ohms? → **Yes** REPLACE speed control/horn switch. TEST the system for normal operation. → **No** REPAIR circuit 8-PG13 (WH)/clockspring. TEST the system for normal operation.

FM1109800493100X

Fig. 54 Test A: Speed Control Inoperative (Part 10 of 13). Contour & Mystique

CONDITIONS	DETAILS/RESULTS/ACTIONS
A15 CHECK THE BRAKE PEDAL DEACTIVATOR SWITCH FOR OPEN	
1 2 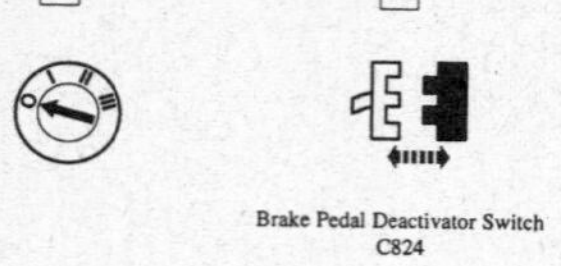	
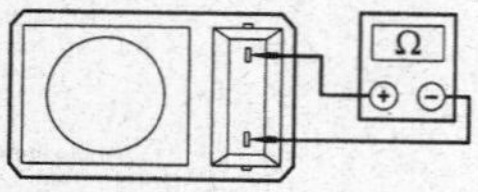	3 Measure the resistance between brake pedal deactivator switch terminals . • Is the resistance less than 5 ohms? → **Yes** GO to **A16.** → **No** REPLACE the brake pedal deactivator switch. TEST the system for normal operation.
A16 CHECK THE VOLTAGE TO THE BRAKE PEDAL DEACTIVATOR-CIRCUIT 29-PG6 (OG/YE)	
1 	

FM1109800493110X

Fig. 54 Test A: Speed Control Inoperative (Part 11 of 13). Contour & Mystique

CONDITIONS	DETAILS/RESULTS/ACTIONS
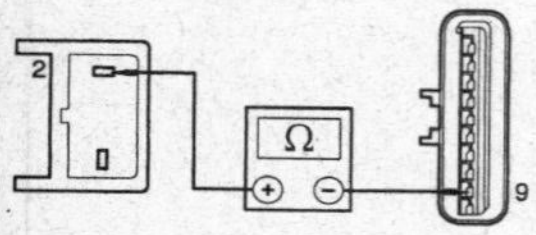	3 Measure the resistance between brake pedal deactivator switch C833-2, circuit 29S-PG16 (OG/YE), and speed control module C833-9, circuit 29S-PG16 (OG/YE). • Is the resistance less than 5 ohms? → **Yes** REPLACE speed control module. TEST the system for normal operation. → **No** REPAIR circuit 29S-PG16 (OG/YE). TEST the system for normal operation.

FM1109800493130X

Fig. 54 Test A: Speed Control Inoperative (Part 13 of 13). Contour & Mystique

CONDITIONS	DETAILS/RESULTS/ACTIONS
B1 CHECK FOR STOP LAMP ILLUMINATION WHEN BRAKE PEDAL IS DEPRESSED	
1 	2 Depress the brake pedal. • Do the stop lamps illuminate? → **Yes** GO to **B2.** → **No** Diagnose Circuit

FM1109800494010X

Fig. 55 Test B: Speed Control Does Not Disengage When Brakes are Applied (Part 1 of 3). Contour & Mystique

CONDITIONS	DETAILS/RESULTS/ACTIONS
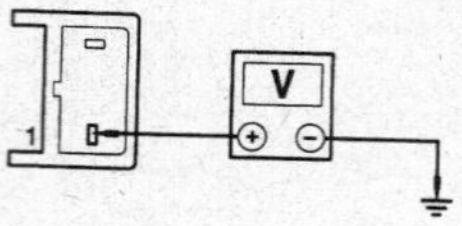	2 Measure the voltage between brake pedal deactivator switch C824-1, circuit 29 PG6 (OG/YE) and ground. • Is the voltage greater than 10 volts? → **Yes** GO to **A17.** → **No** REPAIR circuit 29-PG6 (OG/YE). TEST the system for normal operation.
A17 CHECK CIRCUIT 29S-PG16 (OG/YE) FOR OPEN	
1 2 	

FM1109800493120X

Fig. 54 Test A: Speed Control Inoperative (Part 12 of 13). Contour & Mystique

CONDITIONS	DETAILS/RESULTS/ACTIONS
B2 CHECK THE BRAKE PEDAL DEACTIVATOR SWITCH	
1 2 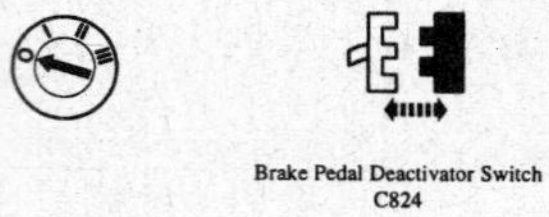	
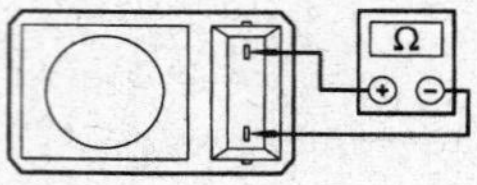	3 Measure the resistance between brake pedal deactivator switch terminals, while depressing the brake pedal completely to the floor. • Is the resistance greater than 10,000 ohms? → **Yes** GO to **B3.** → **No** REPLACE the brake pedal deactivator switch. TEST the system for normal operation.
B3 CHECK CIRCUIT 29S-PG16 (OG/YE) FOR VOLTAGE	
1 2 	

FM1109800494020X

Fig. 55 Test B: Speed Control Does Not Disengage When Brakes are Applied (Part 2 of 3). Contour & Mystique

CONDITIONS	DETAILS/RESULTS/ACTIONS
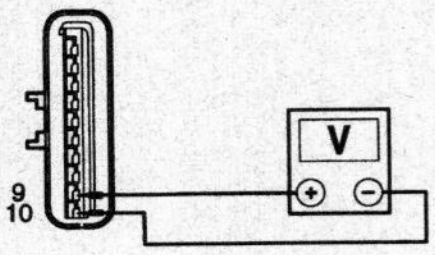	3 Measure the voltage between speed control module C833–9, circuit 29S-PG16 (OG/YE) and C833-10, circuit 91-PG12 (BK/WH). • Is any voltage indicated? → Yes REPAIR circuit 29S–PG16 (OG/YE). TEST the system for normal operation. → No GO to **B4.**
B4 CHECK CIRCUIT 29S-PG17 FOR OPENR	
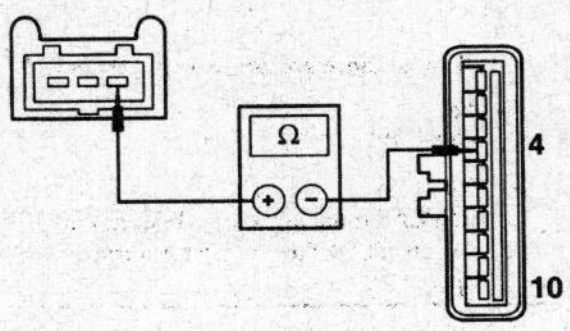	1 Measure the resistance between BPP switch C444–3, circuit 29S-PG7 (OG/BU) and speed control module C833-4, circuit 29S-PG17 (OG/BU). • Is the resistance less than 5 ohms? → Yes REPLACE the speed control module. TEST the system for normal operation. → No REPAIR circuit 29S-PG17 (OG/BU), and circuit 29S-PG7 (OG/BU) on vehicles equipped with a manual transaxle. TEST the system for normal operation.

FM1109800494030X

Fig. 55 Test B: Speed Control Does Not Disengage When Brakes are Applied (Part 3 of 3). Contour & Mystique

CONDITIONS	DETAILS/RESULTS/ACTIONS
D1 CHECK COAST SWITCH	
1  2  Speed Control Module C833 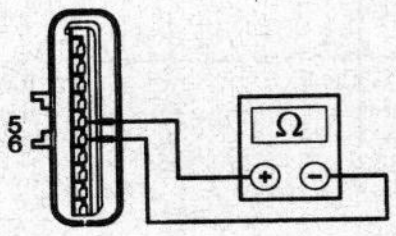	3 Measure the resistance between speed control module C833-5, circuit 8–PG13 (WH) and C833-6, circuit 31 PG13 (BK), while the coast switch is depressed. • Is the resistance measured approximately 120 ohms? → Yes REPLACE the speed control module. TEST the system for normal operation. → No If the resistance is less than 114 ohms or greater than 126 ohms. REPLACE speed control/horn switch. TEST the system for normal operation.

FM1109800496000X

Fig. 57 Test D: Coast Switch Inoperative. Contour & Mystique

CONDITIONS	DETAILS/RESULTS/ACTIONS
C1 CHECK OFF SWITCH	
1  2  Speed Control Module C833 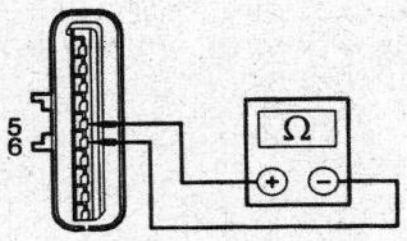	3 Measure the resistance between speed control module C833-5, circuit 8-PG13 (WH) and C833-6, circuit 31–PG13 (BK), while the off switch is depressed. • Is the resistance less than 5 ohms? → Yes REPLACE speed control module. TEST the system for normal operation. → No REPLACE speed control/horn switch. TEST the system for normal operation.

FM1109800495000X

Fig. 56 Test C: OFF Switch Inoperative. Contour & Mystique

CONDITIONS	DETAILS/RESULTS/ACTIONS
E1 CHECK SET/ACCL SWITCH	
1  2  Speed Control Module C833 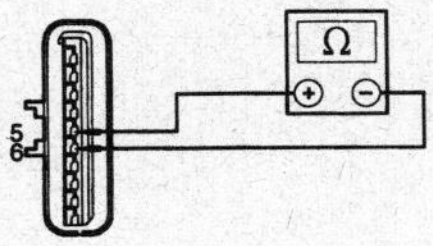	3 Measure the resistance between speed control module C833-5, circuit 8 PG13 (WH) and C833-6, circuit 31 PG13 (BK), while the SET/ACCL is switch depressed. • Is the resistance approximately 680 ohms? → Yes REPLACE the speed control module. TEST the system for normal operation. → No If the resistance is less than 646 ohms or greater than 714 ohms, REPLACE speed control/horn switch. TEST the system for normal operation.

FM1109800497000X

Fig. 58 Test E: SET/ACCEL Switch Inoperative. Contour & Mystique

CONDITIONS	DETAILS/RESULTS/ACTIONS
F1 CHECK RESUME SWITCH	

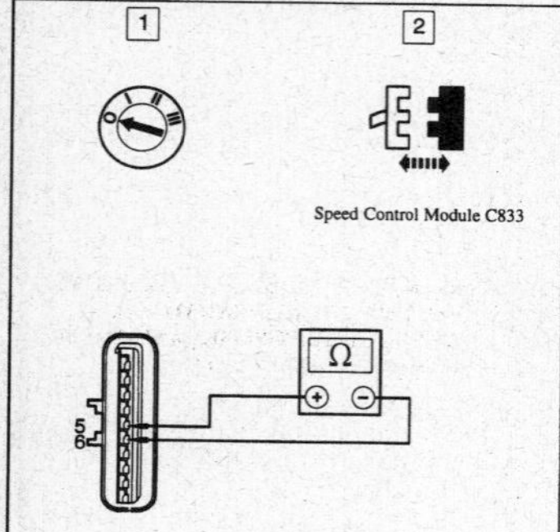

3 Measure the resistance between speed control module C833-5, circuit 8 PG13 (WH) and C833-6, circuit 31 PG13 (BK) while the RES switch is depressed.

- Is the resistance approximately 2200 ohms?
  - → **Yes** REPLACE speed control module. TEST the system for normal operation.
  - → **No** If the resistance is less than 2090 ohms or greater than 2310 ohms, REPLACE the speed control/horn switch. TEST the system for normal operation.

FM1109800498000X

Fig. 59 Test F: Resume Switch Inoperative. Contour & Mystique

CONDITIONS	DETAILS/RESULTS/ACTIONS

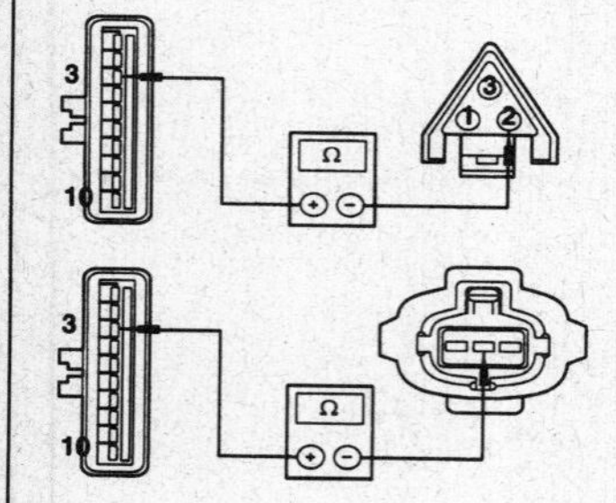

4 Measure the resistance between speed control module C833-3, circuit 8-PG12 (WH/VT), and VSS C823-2 (A/T) or C1899-2 (M/T), circuit 8-PC60 (WH/BU).

- Is the resistance less than 5 ohms?
  - → **Yes** If the speedometer operates correctly, REPLACE the speed control module. TEST the system for normal operation. If the speedometer does not operate correctly. Diagnose Circuit
  - → **No** REPAIR circuits 8-PG12 (WH/VT)/8-PC89 (WH/VT), 8-PC89A (WH/VT)/8-PC60 (WH/BU). TEST the system for normal operation.

FM1109800499020X

Fig. 60 Test G: Set Speed Fluctuates (Part 2 of 2). Contour & Mystique

CONDITIONS	DETAILS/RESULTS/ACTIONS
G1 CHECK FOR OPEN CIRCUIT BETWEEN THE VSS AND THE SPEED CONTROL MODULE	

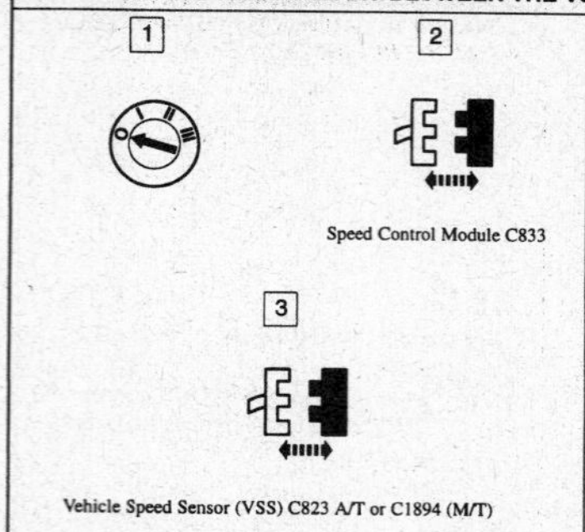

FM1109800499010X

Fig. 60 Test G: Set Speed Fluctuates (Part 1 of 2). Contour & Mystique

CONDITIONS	DETAILS/RESULTS/ACTIONS
H1 CHECK OFF SWITCH	

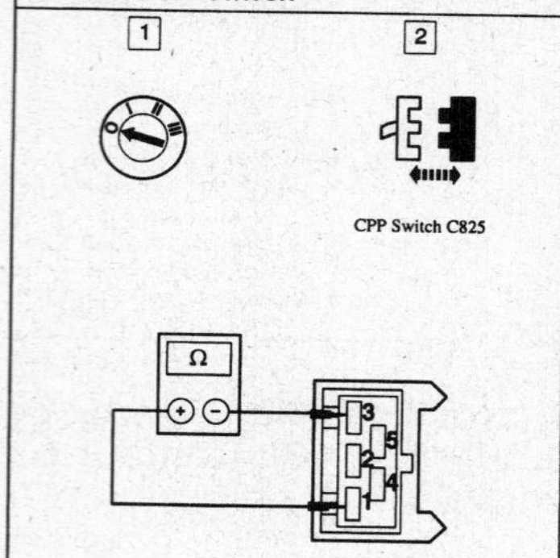

3 Measure the resistance between CPP, switch terminals 1 and 3, while depressing the clutch pedal.

- Is the resistance greater than 10,000 ohms?
  - → **Yes** REPLACE speed control module. TEST the system for normal operation.
  - → **No** REPLACE the CPP switch. TEST the system for normal operation.

FM1109800500000X

Fig. 61 Test H: Speed Control Does Not Disengage When Clutch Is Applied. Contour & Mystique

Condition	Possible Sources	Action
• The vehicle speed control is inoperative	• Circuit(s). • Brake pedal position switch. • Clutch pedal position switch. • Speed control deactivator switch. • Speed control switches. • Speed control actuator. • Fuse(s).	• GO to Pinpoint Test A .
• The vehicle speed control does not disengage when the brakes are applied	• Brake pedal position switch. • Circuit.	• GO to Pinpoint Test B .
• The coast switch is inoperative	• Coast switch. • Circuit.	• Go to Pinpoint Test C .
• The resume switch is inoperative	• Resume switch. • Circuit.	• GO to Pinpoint Test D .
• The vehicle speed control does not disengage when the clutch is applied	• Clutch pedal position switch. • Circuit.	• GO to Pinpoint Test E .
• The set speed fluctuates	• Vehicle speed sensor. • Circuit.	• GO to Pinpoint Test F .
• The OFF switch is inoperative	• Speed control switch.	• INSTALL a new speed control switch.

FM1100200840000X

Fig. 62 Speed control symptom chart. Cougar

CONDITIONS	DETAILS/RESULTS/ACTIONS

A1 CHECK OPERATION OF THE HORN

1 Press the horn switches.

- **Does the horn sound?**

→ **Yes**
GO to A2 .

→ **No**
Diagnose Horn

A2 CHECK ON SWITCH OPERATION

1

Speed Control Actuator C833

2

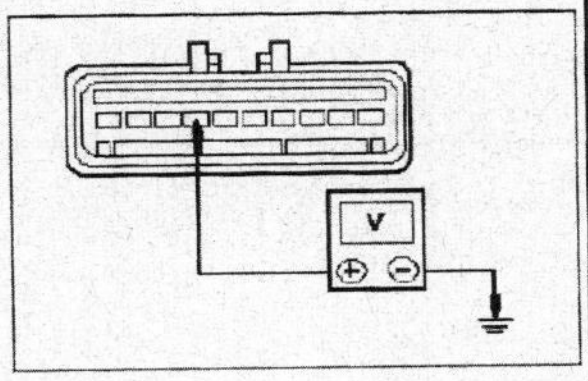

2 Measure the voltage between pin 5 and ground while pressing the ON switch.

- **Is the voltage greater than 10 volts?**

→ **Yes**
GO to A3 .

→ **No**
INSTALL a new speed control switch. TEST the system for normal operation.

FM1100200834010X

Fig. 63 Test A: Speed Control Inoperative (Part 1 of 9). Cougar

A3 CHECK SWITCH INPUT TO SPEED CONTROL ACTUATOR

1

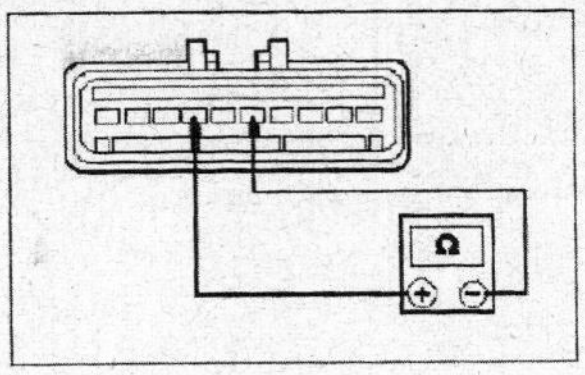

1 Measure the resistance between the speed control actuator C833 pin 5, circuit 8-PG13 (WH), harness side and the speed control actuator C833 pin 6, circuit 31-PG13 (BK), harness side while pressing the OFF switch.

- **Is the resistance less than 5 ohms?**

→ **Yes**
GO to A6 .

→ **No**
GO to A4 .

A4 CHECK CIRCUIT 8-PG13

1

Airbag Sliding Contact C896

2

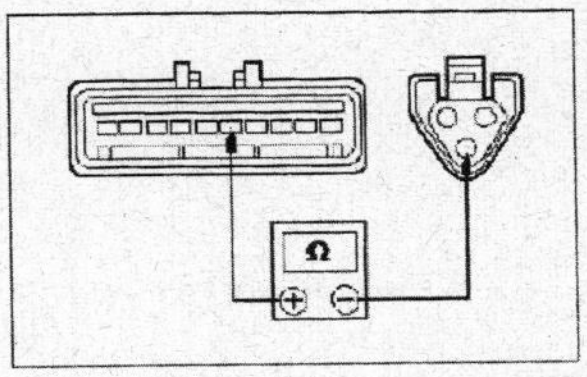

2 Measure the resistance between the speed control actuator C833 pin 5, circuit 8-PG13 (WH), harness side and the air bag sliding contact C896 pin 3, circuit 8-PG13 (WH), harness side.

- **Is the resistance less than 5 ohms?**

→ **Yes**
GO to A5 .

→ **No**
REPAIR circuit 8-PG13 TEST the system for normal operation.

FM1100200834020X

Fig. 63 Test A: Speed Control Inoperative (Part 2 of 9). Cougar

A5 CHECK CONTINUITY OF AIR BAG SLIDING CONTACT

1

Speed Control Switch

2

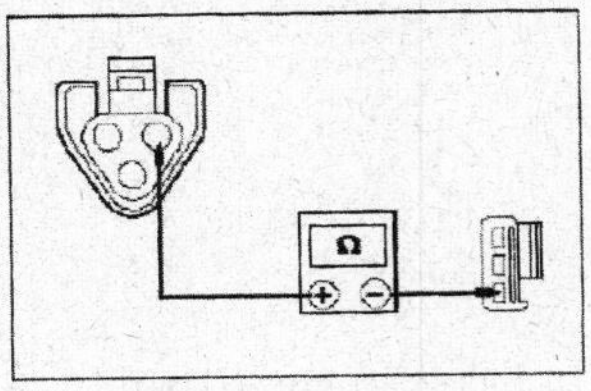

2 Measure the resistance between the air bag sliding contact connector, pin A (BK), component side, and the air bag sliding contact connector, pin 1 (BK), component side, and between the air bag sliding contact connector, pin B (RD/OG), component side, and the air bag sliding contact connector, pin 2 (RD/OG), component side, and between the air bag sliding contact connector, pin C (BK/BU), component side, and the air bag sliding contact connector, pin 3 (BK/BU), component side.

- **Is the resistance less than 5 ohms?**

→ **Yes**
INSTALL a new speed control switch. TEST the system for normal operation.

→ **No**
INSTALL a new air bag sliding contact. TEST the system for normal operation.

FM1100200834030X

Fig. 63 Test A: Speed Control Inoperative (Part 3 of 9). Cougar

A6 CHECK CIRCUIT 91-PG12

1

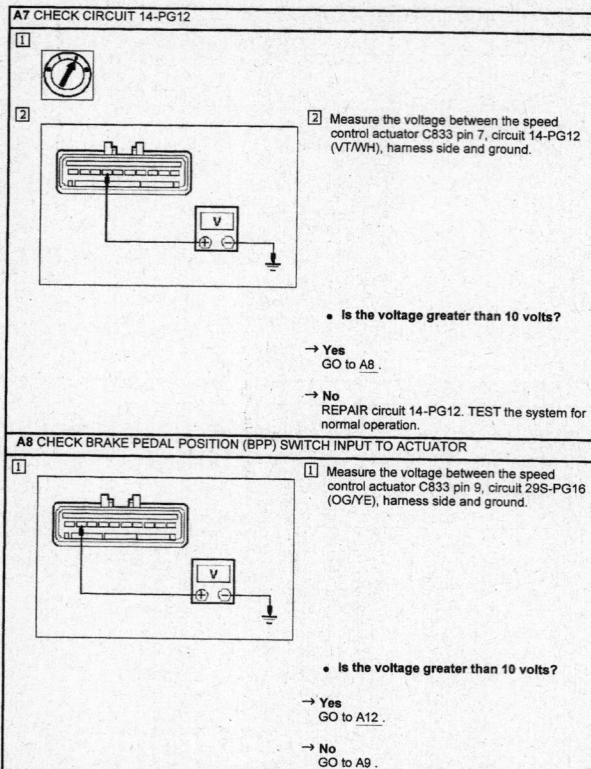

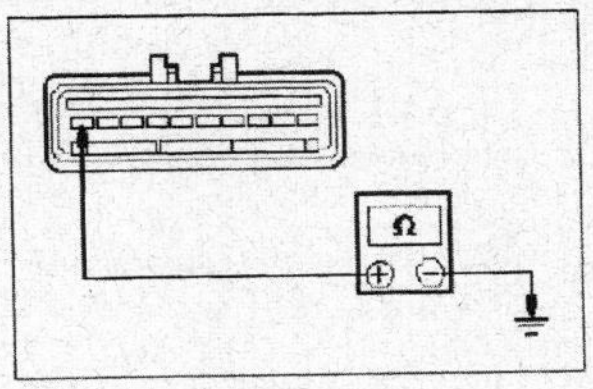

1 Measure the resistance between the speed control actuator C833 pin 10, circuit 91-PG12 (BK/WH), harness side and ground.

- **Is the resistance less than 5 ohms?**

→ **Yes**
GO to A7 .

→ **No**
REPAIR circuit 91-PG12. TEST the system for normal operation.

FM1100200834040X

Fig. 63 Test A: Speed Control Inoperative (Part 4 of 9). Cougar

A7 CHECK CIRCUIT 14-PG12

1

2

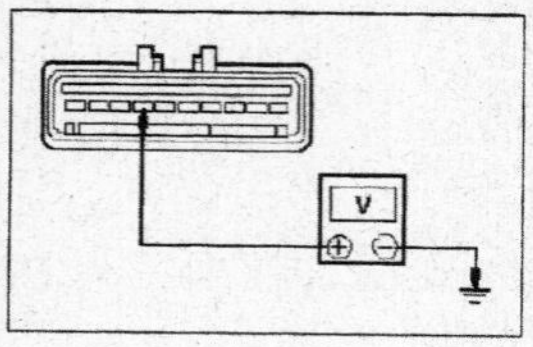

2 Measure the voltage between the speed control actuator C833 pin 7, circuit 14-PG12 (VT/WH), harness side and ground.

- **Is the voltage greater than 10 volts?**

→ **Yes**
GO to A8 .

→ **No**
REPAIR circuit 14-PG12. TEST the system for normal operation.

A8 CHECK BRAKE PEDAL POSITION (BPP) SWITCH INPUT TO ACTUATOR

1

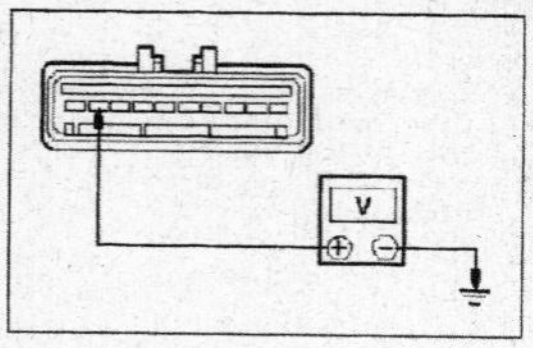

1 Measure the voltage between the speed control actuator C833 pin 9, circuit 29S-PG16 (OG/YE), harness side and ground.

- **Is the voltage greater than 10 volts?**

→ **Yes**
GO to A12 .

→ **No**
GO to A9 .

FM1100200834050X

Fig. 63 Test A: Speed Control Inoperative (Part 5 of 9). Cougar

A9 CHECK BRAKE PEDAL POSITION (BPP) SWITCH

1

BPP Switch C824

2

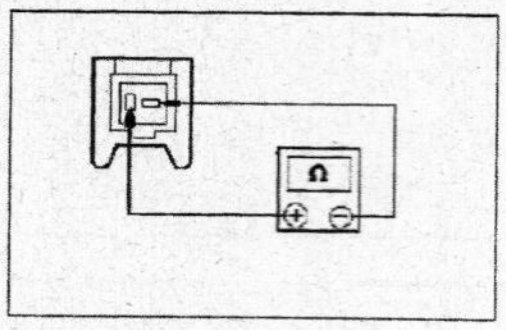

2 Measure the resistance between the BPP switch pin 1 and pin 2, component side, while pressing the switch plunger in and also with the plunger released.

- **Are the resistances greater than 10,000 ohms with the plunger pressed and less than 5 ohms with the plunger released?**

→ **Yes**
GO to A10 .

→ **No**
INSTALL a new BPP switch. TEST the system for normal operation.

A10 CHECK CIRCUIT 29-PG6 (OG/YE)

1

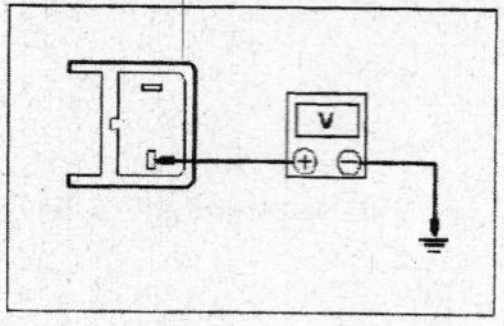

1 Measure the voltage between the BPP switch C824 pin 1, circuit 29-PG6 (OG/YE), harness side and ground.

- **Is the voltage greater than 10 volts?**

→ **Yes**
GO to A11 .

→ **No**
REPAIR circuit 29-PG6 (OG/YE). TEST the system for normal operation.

FM1100200834060X

Fig. 63 Test A: Speed Control Inoperative (Part 6 of 9). Cougar

A11 CHECK CIRCUIT 29S-PG16 (OG/YE)

1

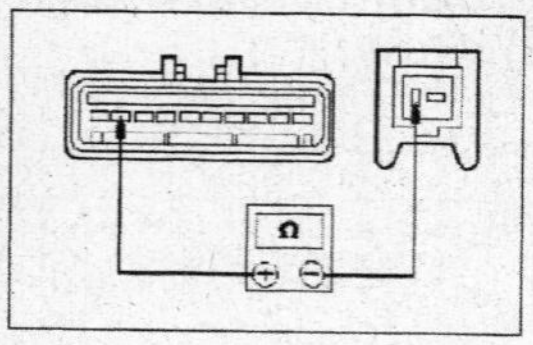

1 Measure the resistance between speed control actuator C833 pin 9, circuit 29-PG16 (OG/YE), harness side and BPP switch C824 pin 2, circuit 29S-PG16 (OG/YE) harness side.

- **Is the resistance less than 5 ohms?**

→ **Yes**
Adjust the BPP switch. TEST the system for normal operation

→ **No**
REPAIR circuit 29S-PG16 (OG/YE). TEST the system for normal operation.

A12 CHECK STOPLAMP SWITCH SIGNAL TO ACTUATOR

1

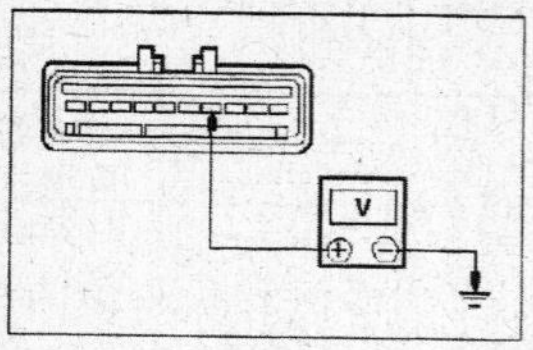

1 Measure the voltage between the speed control actuator C833 pin 4, circuit 29S-PG17 (OG/BU) , harness side and ground while depressing the brake pedal.

- **Is the voltage greater than 10 volts ?**

→ **Yes**
For vehicles with automatic transaxle. GO to A15 .
For vehicles with manual transaxle. GO to A13 .

→ **No**
If the stoplamps operate correctly, REPAIR circuit 29S-PG17. TEST the system for normal operation.

FM1100200834070X

Fig. 63 Test A: Speed Control Inoperative (Part 7 of 9). Cougar

A13 CHECK POWER TO CLUTCH PEDAL POSITION (CPP) SWITCH

1

CPP Switch C825

2

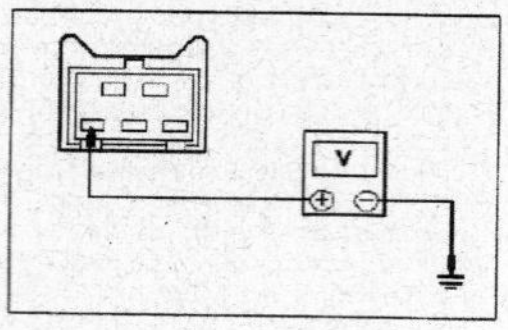

2 Measure the voltage between the CPP switch C825 pin 3, circuit 29S-PG7 (OG/BU), harness side and ground while depressing the brake pedal.

- **Is the voltage greater than 10 volts?**

→ **Yes**
GO to A14 .

→ **No**
REPAIR circuit 29S-PG7. TEST the system for normal operation.

A14 CHECK CPP SWITCH

1

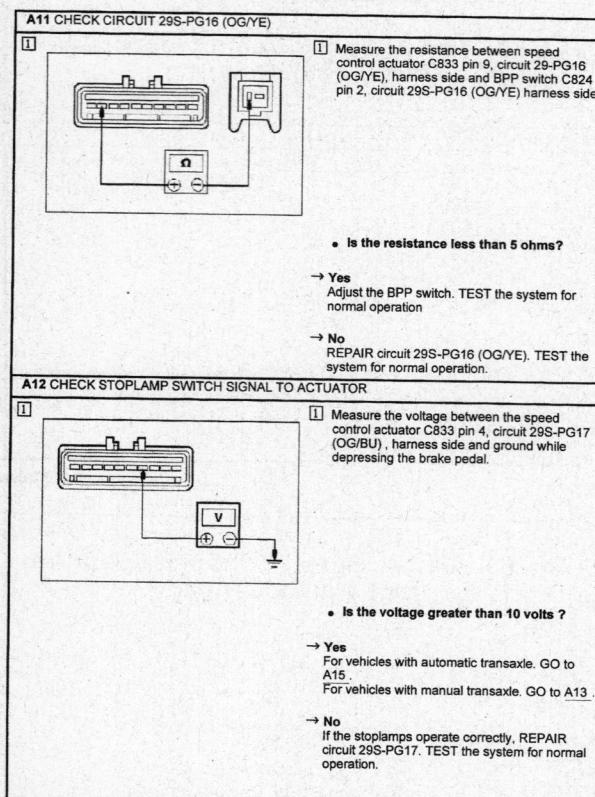

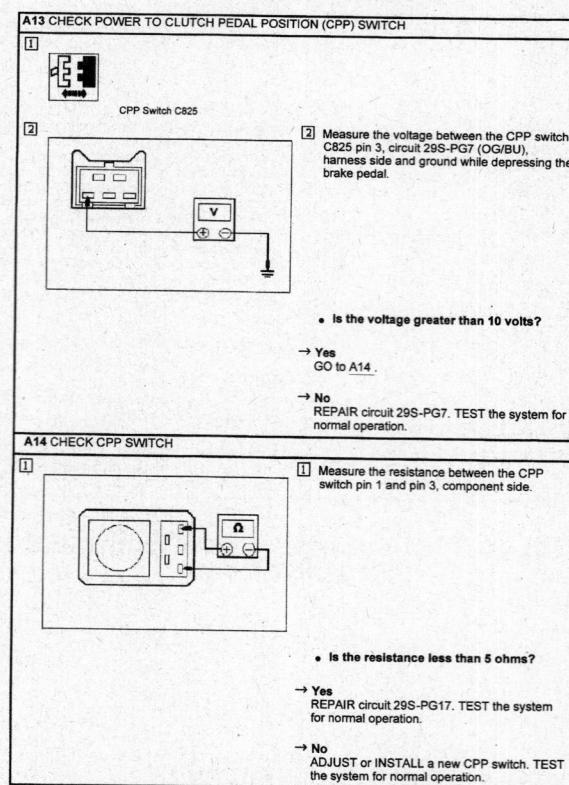

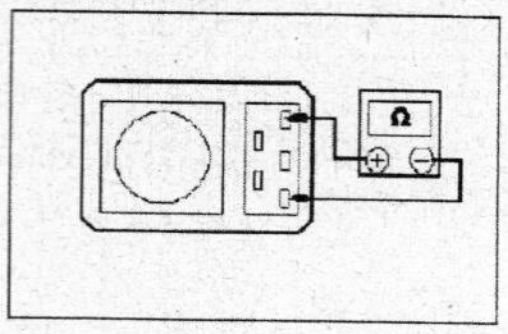

1 Measure the resistance between the CPP switch pin 1 and pin 3, component side.

- **Is the resistance less than 5 ohms?**

→ **Yes**
REPAIR circuit 29S-PG17. TEST the system for normal operation.

→ **No**
ADJUST or INSTALL a new CPP switch. TEST the system for normal operation.

FM1100200834080X

Fig. 63 Test A: Speed Control Inoperative (Part 8 of 9). Cougar

A15 CHECK VEHICLE SPEED SENSOR (VSS) SIGNAL TO ACTUATOR

1

Instrument Cluster C606

2

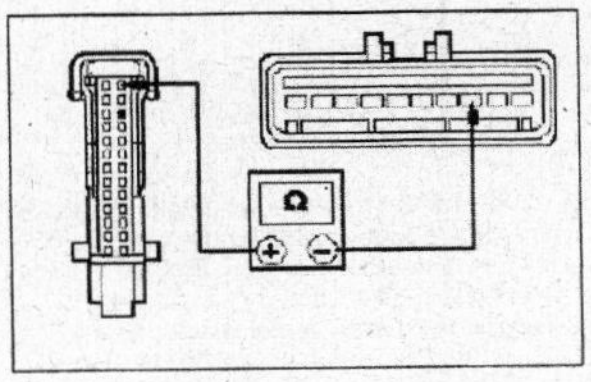

2 Measure the resistance between the instrument cluster C606 pin 26, circuit 8GB8 (WH/BU), harness side and the speed control actuator C833 pin 3, circuit 8PG18.

- **Is the resistance greater than 10,000 ohms?**

→ **Yes**
REPAIR circuit 8PG18/8GB8. Test the system for normal operation.

→ **No**
If there are no DTCs. INSTALL a new speed control actuator. TEST the system for normal operation.

FM1100200834090X

Fig. 63 Test A: Speed Control Inoperative (Part 9 of 9). Cougar

CONDITIONS	DETAILS/RESULTS/ACTIONS

B1 CHECK BRAKE PEDAL POSITION (BPP) SWITCH

1

2

BPP Switch C824

3

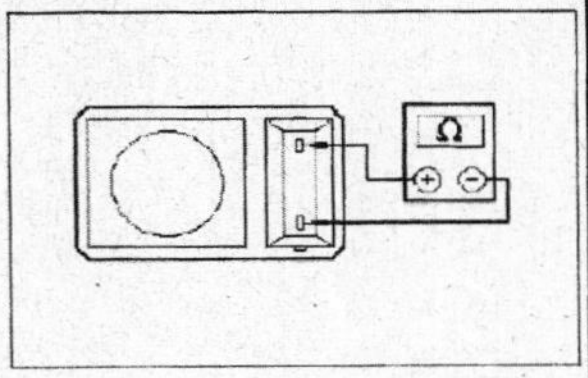

3 Measure the resistance between the BPP switch, pin 1 and pin 2, component side, with no brakes applied.

- **Is the resistance less than 5 ohms?**

→ **Yes**
GO to B2 .

→ **No**
ADJUST or INSTALL a new BPP switch. TEST the system for normal operation.

FM1100200835010X

Fig. 64 Test B: System Does Not Disengage When Brakes Are Applied (Part 1 of 3). Cougar

B2 CHECK BRAKE PEDAL POSITION POWER CIRCUITS 29 -PG6 (OG/YE)

1

2

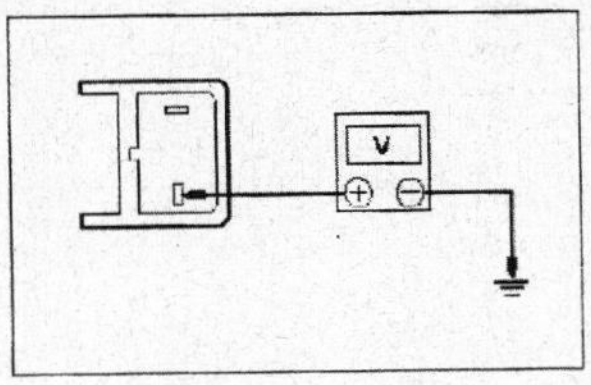

2 Measure the voltage between the BPP switch C824 pin 1, circuit 29PG6 (OG/YE) harness side and ground.

- **Is the voltage greater than 10 volts?**

→ **Yes**
GO to B3 .

→ **No**
If the stoplamps operate, REPAIR circuit 29PG6. TEST the system for normal operation

FM1100200835020X

Fig. 64 Test B: System Does Not Disengage When Brakes Are Applied (Part 2 of 3). Cougar

B3 CHECK CIRCUIT 29S-PG16(OG/YE)

1

2

Speed Control Actuator

3

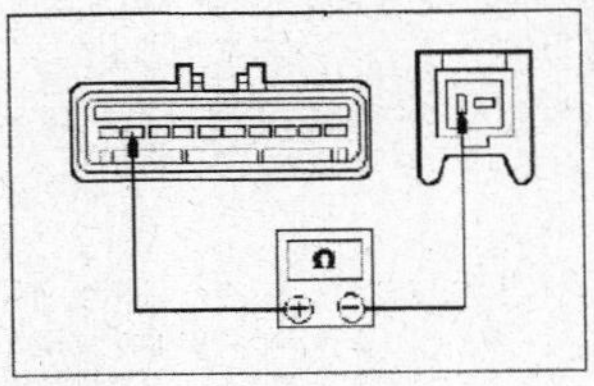

3 Measure the resistance between the BPP switch C824, pin 2, circuit 29S-PG16 (OG/YE) and the speed control C833, pin 9, circuit 29S-PG 16 (OG/YE), harness side.

- **Is the resistance less than 5 ohms?**

→ **Yes**
INSTALL a new speed control actuator. TEST the system for normal operation.

→ **No**
REPAIR circuit 29S-PG16. TEST the system for normal operation.

FM1100200835030X

Fig. 64 Test B: System Does Not Disengage When Brakes Are Applied (Part 3 of 3). Cougar

CONDITIONS	DETAILS/RESULTS/ACTIONS
C1 CHECK RESUME SWITCH	
1 	
2  Speed Control Actuator C833	
3 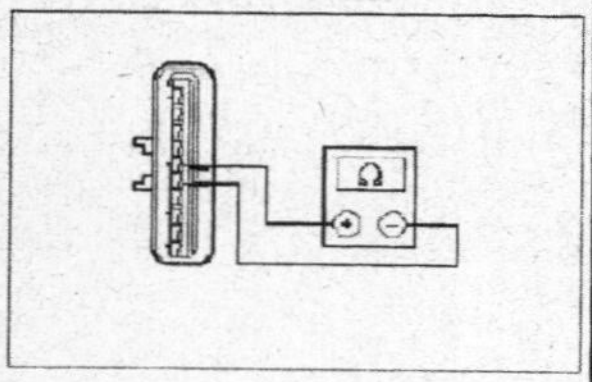	3 Measure the resistance between the speed control actuator C833 pin 5, circuit 8-PG13 (WH) and C833 pin 6, circuit 31-PG13 (BK), harness side while the COAST switch is depressed. • **Is the resistance between 110 and 130 ohms?** → **Yes** INSTALL a new speed control actuator. TEST the system for normal operation. → **No** INSTALL a new the speed control switch. TEST the system for normal operation.

FM1100200836000X

Fig. 65 Test C: Coast Switch Inoperative. Cougar

CONDITIONS	DETAILS/RESULTS/ACTIONS
D1 CHECK RESUME SWITCH	
1 	
2  Speed Control Actuator C833	
3 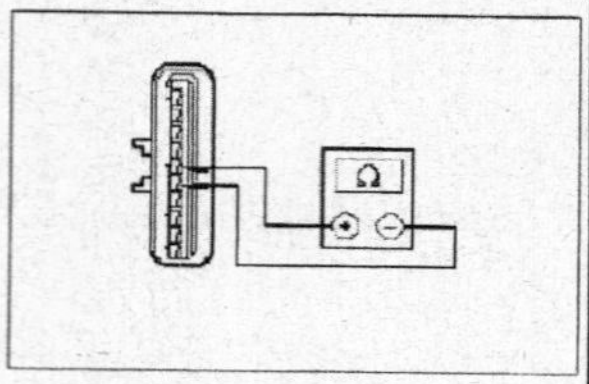	3 Measure the resistance between the speed control actuator C833 pin 5, circuit 8-PG13 (WH), harness side and C833 pin 6, circuit 31-PG13 (BK), harness side while the RESUME switch is depressed. • **Is the resistance approximately 2,200 ohms?** → **Yes** INSTALL a new speed control actuator. TEST the system for normal operation. → **No** INSTALL a new speed control switch. TEST the system for normal operation.

FM1100200837000X

Fig. 66 Test D: Resume Switch Inoperative. Cougar

CONDITIONS	DETAILS/RESULTS/ACTIONS
E1 CHECK THE CLUTCH PEDAL POSITION (CPP) SWITCH	
1  CPP Switch C825	
2 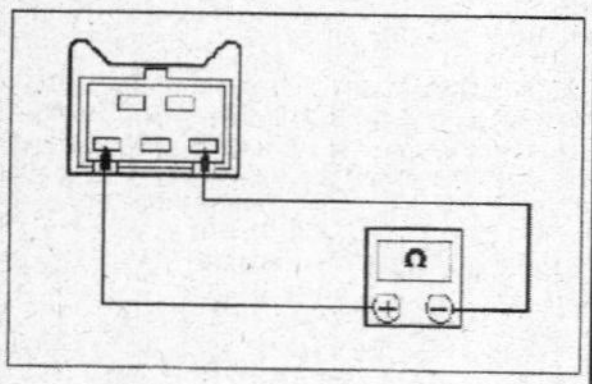	2 Measure the resistance between the CPP switch C825 pin 1, and pin 3, component side. Note the reading while depressing the plunger and with the plunger at rest. • **Is the resistance greater than 10,000 ohms while the plunger is depressed and less than 5 ohms with the plunger at rest?** → **Yes** ADJUST the CPP switch. → **No** INSTALL a new CPP switch.

FM1100200838000X

Fig. 67 Test E: Speed Control Does Not Deactivate When Clutch Is Depressed. Cougar

CONDITIONS	DETAILS/RESULTS/ACTIONS
F1 CHECK FOR SHORT TO GROUND BETWEEN THE VSS AND THE SPEED CONTROL ACTUATOR	
1 	
2  Speed Control Actuator C833	
3  Instrument Cluster C606	
4 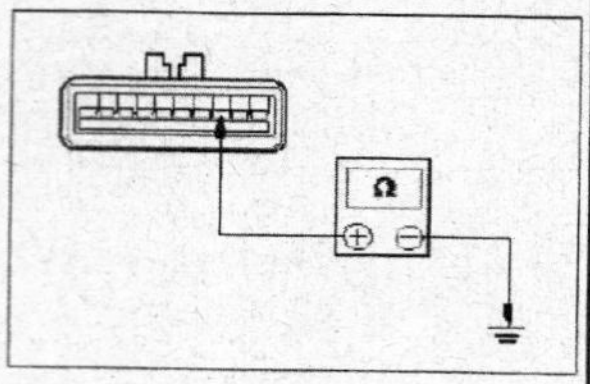	4 Measure the resistance between C833 pin 3, circuit 8-PG18 and ground • **Is the resistance greater than 10,000 ohms?** → **Yes** If there no DTCs, INSTALL a new speed control actuator. TEST the system for normal operation. → **No** REPAIR circuit 8-PG18/8-GB8. TEST for normal operation.

FM1100200839000X

Fig. 68 Test F: Set Speed Fluctuates. Cougar

3. A lamp flash with the last button (SET/ACCEL) indicates that the STATIC test passed. If the lamp does not flash with the last button and there are no additional flashes of the lamp, the switch is defective.

   If the lamp does not flash with the last button, and additional flashes occur, follow the chart below for trouble codes:

   — 2 flashes: BPP defective, circuit is defective, brake applied.

   — 3 flashes: Deactivator switch is open or circuit defective.

4. Immediately after the static test, the speed control servo carries out a dynamic test by automatically actuating the throttle lever from 8 mm (0.32 in) to 10 mm (0.4 in) of travel from the idle position. During the dynamic throttle pull, observe throttle movement to witness any binding or sticking of the actuator cable and proper connection of actuator cable to throttle lever. Make sure the throttle returns back to idle position.

5. Return ignition switch to the OFF position and proceed to the Symptom Chart.

Symptom Chart

Condition(s):

☐ The speed control is inoperative

Possible Source(s):
- Actuator cable not attached to throttle.
- Central junction box (CJB) fuses:
  - 15 (15A).
  - 22 (15A).
- Circuitry.
- Brake pedal position (BPP) switch.
- Speed control actuator switch (9C888).
- Vehicle speed sensor (VSS).
- Speed control servo (9C735).
- Clockspring.

Action(s) to take:
- GO to «Pinpoint Test A».

☐ The set speed fluctuates

Possible Source(s):
- Speed control servo.
- Speed control actuator switch.
- Circuitry.
- Loose fit or binding between speed control actuator cable and throttle body.

Action(s) to take:
- GO to «Pinpoint Test B».

Possible Source(s):
- Engine controls.

Action(s) to take:
- Diagnose engine control fault condition.

FM1100000742010X

Fig. 69 Symptom chart (Part 1 of 4). Crown Victoria, Grand Marquis & Marauder

☐ The speed control does not disengage when the brakes are applied

Possible Source(s):
- BPP switch.
- Speed control servo.
- Circuitry.
- Binding speed control actuator cable.

Action(s) to take:
- GO to «Pinpoint Test C».

☐ The coast switch is inoperative

Possible Source(s):
- Speed control actuator switch.
- Speed control servo.

Action(s) to take:
- GO to «Pinpoint Test D».

☐ The SET/ACCEL switch is inoperative

Possible Source(s):
- Speed control actuator switch.
- Speed control servo.

Action(s) to take:
- GO to «Pinpoint Test E».

☐ The resume switch is inoperative

Possible Source(s):
- Speed control actuator switch.
- Speed control servo.

Action(s) to take:
- GO to «Pinpoint Test F».

☐ The OFF switch is inoperative

Possible Source(s):
- Speed control actuator switch.
- Speed control servo.

Action(s) to take:
- GO to «Pinpoint Test G».

☐ Flash with last switch pressed and dynamic pull occurs at throttle (electronic cluster)

Possible Source(s):
- —

Action(s) to take:
- Test passed.

FM1100000742020X

Fig. 69 Symptom chart (Part 2 of 4). Crown Victoria, Grand Marquis & Marauder

☐ Flash with last switch pressed, but no dynamic pull occurs at throttle and speed control inoperative (electronic cluster)

Possible Source(s):
- Speed control actuator cable.
- Speed control servo.

Action(s) to take:
- GO to «Pinpoint Test H».

☐ Flash with last switch pressed, dynamic pull occurs at throttle and speed control inoperative (electronic cluster)

Possible Source(s):
- Circuitry.
- Speed control servo.

Action(s) to take:
- GO to «Pinpoint Test K».

☐ Flash Code 2 (electronic cluster)

Possible Source(s):
- Circuitry.
- BPP switch.
- Clutch pedal position (CPP) switch or jumper.
- Speed control servo.

Action(s) to take:
- GO to «Pinpoint Test I».

☐ Flash Code 3 (electronic cluster)

Possible Source(s):
- CJB fuse 22 (15A).
- Circuitry.
- Deactivator switch.
- Speed control servo.

Action(s) to take:
- GO to «Pinpoint Test J».

☐ The speed control is inoperative — no flash codes (electronic cluster)

Possible Source(s):
- CJB fuse 15 (15A).
- Circuitry.
- BPP switch.
- Speed control actuator cable.
- Speed control actuator switches (9D743).
- Anti-lock brake control module.
- Speed control servo.
- Clockspring.

Action(s) to take:
- GO to «Pinpoint Test A».

FM1100000742030X

Fig. 69 Symptom chart (Part 3 of 4). Crown Victoria, Grand Marquis & Marauder

☐ The speed control indicator lamp is always on

Possible Source(s):
- Circuitry.
- Speed control servo.
- Instrument cluster.

Action(s) to take:
- Diagnose instrument cluster fault condition.

☐ The speed control indicator is inoperative

Possible Source(s):
- Circuitry.
- Bulb.
- Instrument cluster.
- Speed control servo.

Action(s) to take:
- Diagnose instrument cluster fault condition.

FM1100000742040X

Fig. 69 Symptom chart (Part 4 of 4). Crown Victoria, Grand Marquis & Marauder

A1 CHECK THE SPEED CONTROL ACTUATOR ATTACHMENT TO THROTTLE

1

2 Remove the accelerator control splash shield. Inspect the speed control actuator cable attachment.

- **Is the speed control actuator cable snapped on to the throttle body?**

→ **Yes**

Go to «A2».

→ **No**

REATTACH the speed control actuator cable. TEST the system for normal operation.

FM1100000743010X

Fig. 70 Test A: Speed Control Inoperative (Part 1 of 17). Crown Victoria, Grand Marquis & Marauder

speed control servo C234 pin 10, circuit 676 (PK/OG), harness side.

- **Is the voltage greater than 10 volts?**

→ **Yes**

Go to «A4».

→ **No**

Go to «A3».

FM1100000743030X

Fig. 70 Test A: Speed Control Inoperative (Part 3 of 17). Crown Victoria, Grand Marquis & Marauder

A3 CHECK THE SPEED CONTROL SERVO GROUND CIRCUIT 676 (PK/OG)

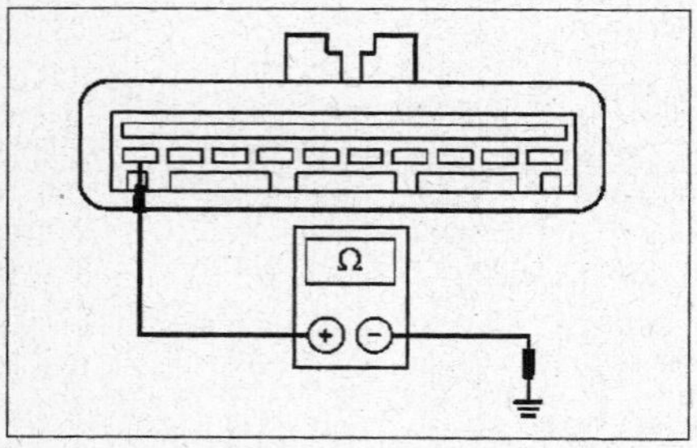

1

Measure the resistance between speed control servo C234 pin 10, circuit 676 (PK/OG), harness side and ground.

- **Is the resistance less than 5 ohms?**

→ **Yes**

REPAIR circuit 296 (WH/PK). TEST the system for normal operation.

→ **No**

REPAIR circuit 676 (PK/OG). TEST for normal operation.

FM1100000743040X

Fig. 70 Test A: Speed Control Inoperative (Part 4 of 17). Crown Victoria, Grand Marquis & Marauder

A2 CHECK THE VOLTAGE TO THE SPEED CONTROL SERVO

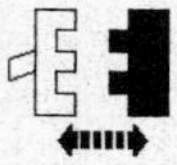

1 *Speed Control Servo C234*

2

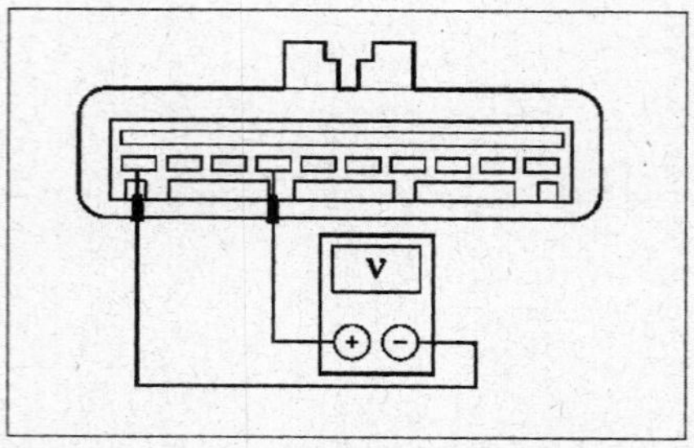

3

Measure the voltage between speed control servo C234 pin 7, circuit 296 (WH/PK), harness side and

FM1100000743020X

Fig. 70 Test A: Speed Control Inoperative (Part 2 of 17). Crown Victoria, Grand Marquis & Marauder

A4 CHECK FOR BRAKE PEDAL POSITION (BPP) SWITCH INPUT WITH NO BRAKES APPLIED

1

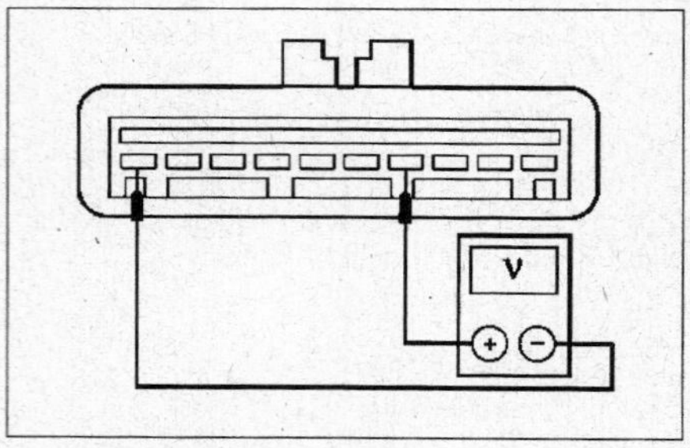

2

Measure the voltage between speed control servo C234 pin 4, circuit 511 (LG), harness side and speed control servo C234 pin 10, circuit 676 (PK/OG), harness side.

- **Is voltage present?**

→ **Yes**

INSTALL a new BPP switch; TEST the system for normal operation.

→ **No**

Go to «A5».

FM1100000743050X

Fig. 70 Test A: Speed Control Inoperative (Part 5 of 17). Crown Victoria, Grand Marquis & Marauder

A5 CHECK THE BRAKE CIRCUIT

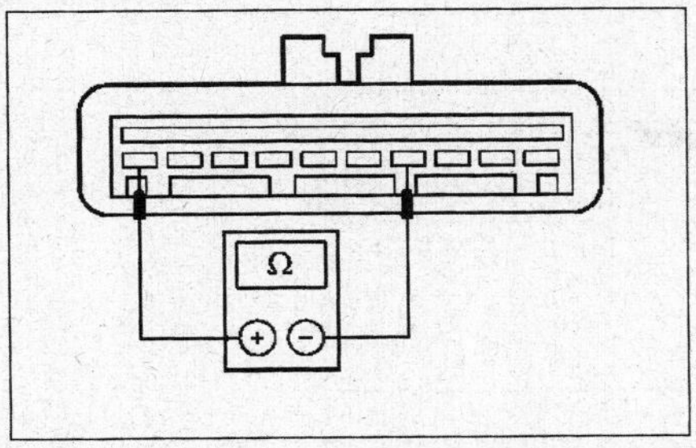

1

Measure the resistance between speed control servo C234 pin 4, circuit 511 (LG), harness side and speed control servo C234 pin 10, circuit 676 (PK/OG), harness side.

- **Is the resistance less than 20 ohms?**

➔ **Yes**

Go to «A6».

➔ **No**

REPAIR the center high mount stoplamp or brake circuit as necessary. TEST the system for normal operation.

FM1100000743060X

Fig. 70 Test A: Speed Control Inoperative (Part 6 of 17). Crown Victoria, Grand Marquis & Marauder

A7 CHECK THE DEACTIVATOR SWITCH

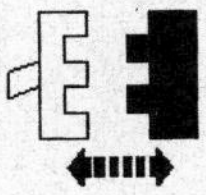

1

Deactivator Switch C233

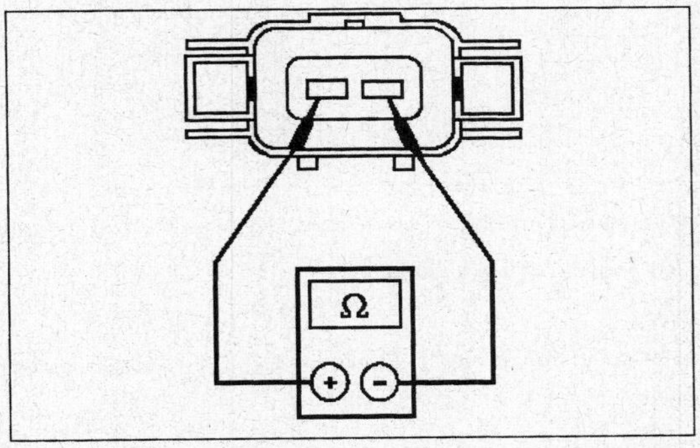

2

Measure the resistance between the deactivator switch pin 1 and pin 2.

- **Is the resistance less than 5 ohms?**

➔ **Yes**

Go to «A8».

➔ **No**

Replace deactivator switch. Test system for normal operation.

FM1100000743080X

Fig. 70 Test A: Speed Control Inoperative (Part 8 of 17). Crown Victoria, Grand Marquis & Marauder

A6 CHECK THE DEACTIVATOR SWITCH INPUT TO SPEED CONTROL SERVO

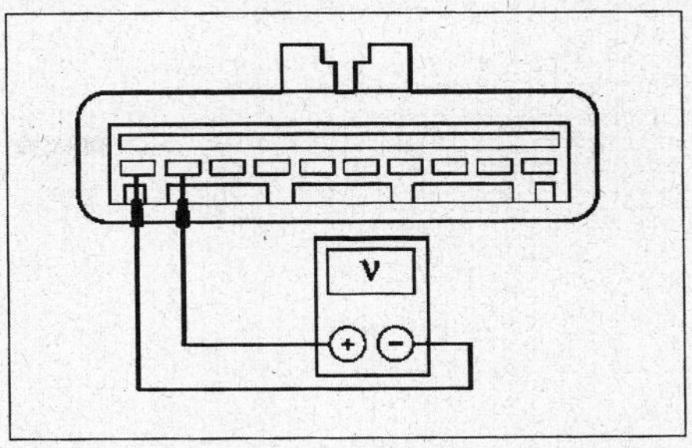

1

Measure the voltage between speed control servo C234 pin 9, circuit 636 (OG), harness side and speed control servo C234 pin 10, circuit 676 (PK/OG), harness side.

- **Is the voltage greater than 10 volts?**

➔ **Yes**

Go to «A9».

➔ **No**

Go to «A7».

FM1100000743070X

Fig. 70 Test A: Speed Control Inoperative (Part 7 of 17). Crown Victoria, Grand Marquis & Marauder

A8 CHECK DEACTIVATOR SWITCH POWER

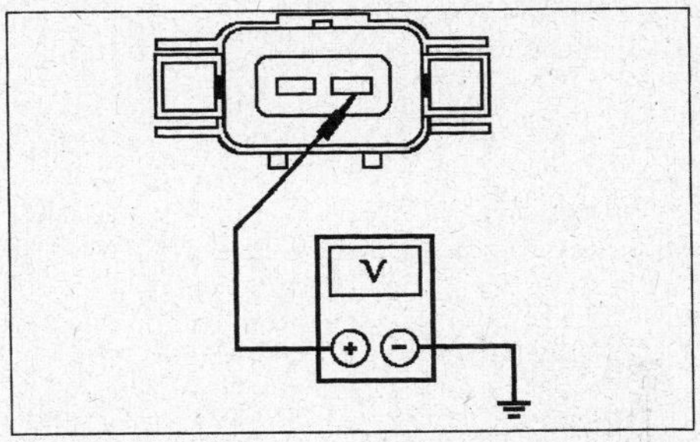

1

Measure the voltage between deactivator switch C233, circuit 10 (LG/RD), harness side and ground.

- **Is the voltage greater than 10 volts?**

➔ **Yes**

REPAIR circuit 636 (OG). TEST the system for normal operation.

➔ **No**

REPAIR circuit 10 (LG/RD). TEST the system for normal operation.

FM1100000743090X

Fig. 70 Test A: Speed Control Inoperative (Part 9 of 17). Crown Victoria, Grand Marquis & Marauder

A9	CHECK FOR STUCK SPEED CONTROL ACTUATOR SWITCH

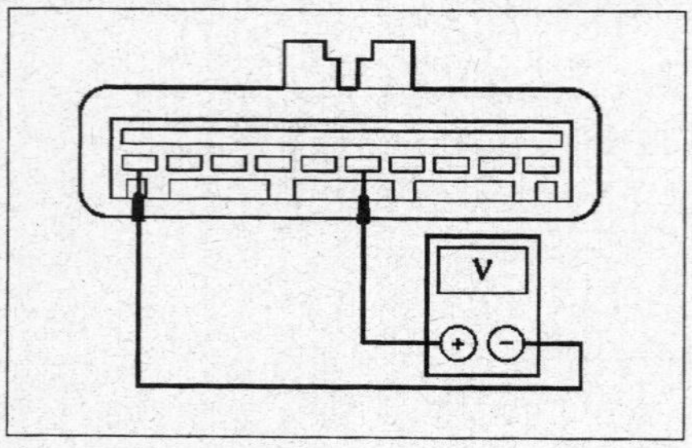

1

Measure the voltage between speed control servo C234 pin 5, circuit 151 (LB/BK), harness side and speed control servo C234 pin 10, circuit 676 (PK/OG), harness side.

- **Is the voltage greater than 10 volts?**

→ **Yes**

INSTALL a new speed control actuator switch. TEST the system for normal operation.

→ **No**

Go to «A10».

FM1100000743100X

Fig. 70 Test A: Speed Control Inoperative (Part 10 of 17). Crown Victoria, Grand Marquis & Marauder

A11	CHECK CIRCUIT 848 (DG/OG) FOR AN OPEN

1 *Clockspring C283*

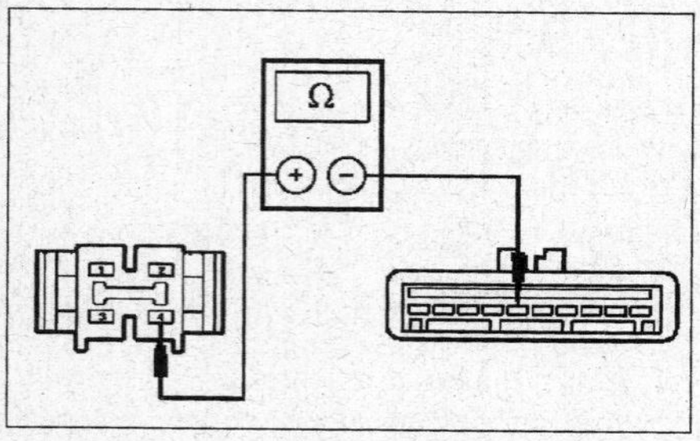

2

Measure the resistance between speed control servo C234 pin 6, circuit 848 (DG/OG) clockspring C283F pin 4, circuit 848 (DG/OG).

- **Is the resistance less than 5 ohms?**

→ **Yes**

Go to «A12».

→ **No**

REPAIR the circuit. TEST the system for normal operation.

FM1100000743120X

Fig. 70 Test A: Speed Control Inoperative (Part 12 of 17). Crown Victoria, Grand Marquis & Marauder

A10	CHECK THE SPEED CONTROL ACTUATOR SWITCH OPERATION

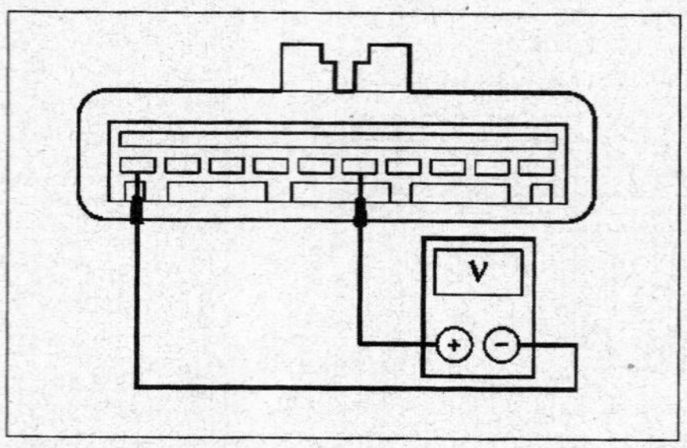

1

With the speed control actuator switch depressed to the ON position, measure the voltage between speed control servo C234 pin 5, circuit 151 (LB/BK), harness side and speed control servo C234 pin 10, circuit 676 (PK/OG), harness side.

- **Is the voltage greater than 10 volts?**

→ **Yes**

Go to «A13».

→ **No**

Go to «A11».

FM1100000743110X

Fig. 70 Test A: Speed Control Inoperative (Part 11 of 17). Crown Victoria, Grand Marquis & Marauder

A12	CHECK THE AIR BAG SLIDING CONTACT FOR AN OPEN

1 Remove the driver side air bag,

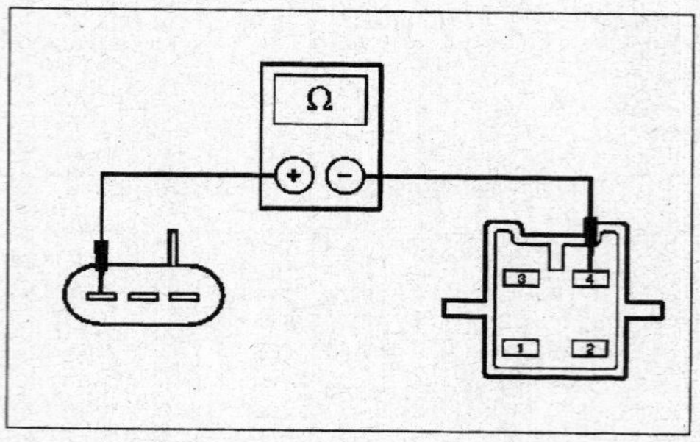

2

Measure the resistance between the clockspring C283M pin 4 and top of clockspring pin 3.

- **Is the resistance less than 1 ohm?**

→ **Yes**

INSTALL a new speed control actuator switch. TEST the system for normal operation.

→ **No**

INSTALL a new clockspring. TEST the system for normal operation.

FM1100000743130X

Fig. 70 Test A: Speed Control Inoperative (Part 13 of 17). Crown Victoria, Grand Marquis & Marauder

A13 CHECK THE SET/ACCEL SWITCH

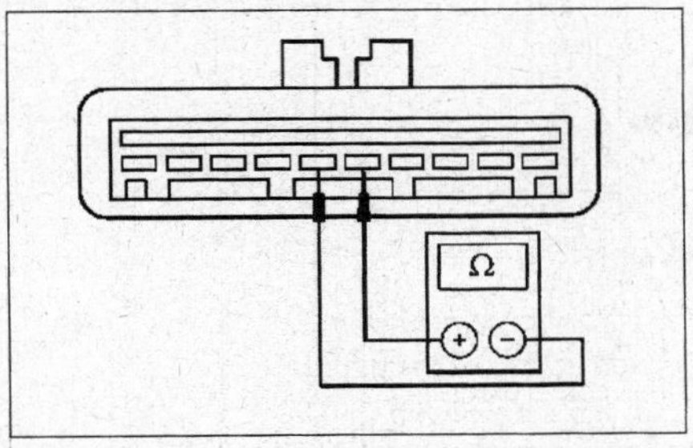

1

With the SET/ACCEL switch depressed, measure the resistance between speed control servo C234 pin 5, circuit 151 (LB/BK), harness side and speed control servo C234 pin 6, circuit 848 (DG/OG), harness side.

- **Is the resistance between 640 and 720 ohms?**

➔ **Yes**

Go to «A14».

➔ **No**

INSTALL a new speed control actuator switch. TEST the system for normal operation.

FM1100000743140X

Fig. 70 Test A: Speed Control Inoperative (Part 14 of 17). Crown Victoria, Grand Marquis & Marauder

A15 CHECK CIRCUIT 679 (GY/BK) FOR AN OPEN

1

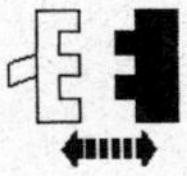

2 *VSS C1020*

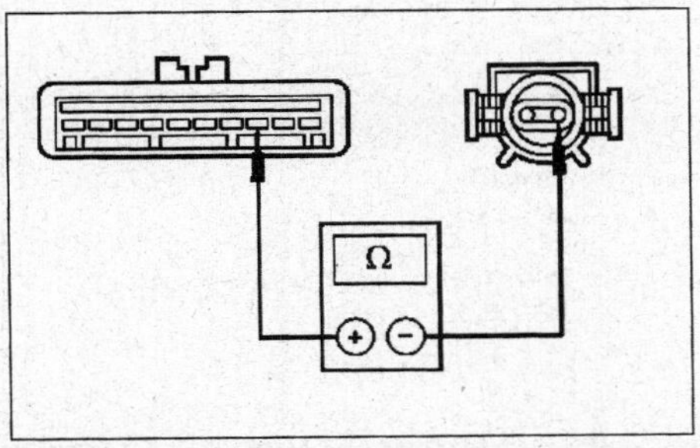

3

Measure the resistance between VSS C1020, circuit 679 (GY/BK), harness side and the speed control servo C234 pin 3, circuit 679 (GY/BK), harness side.

FM1100000743160X

Fig. 70 Test A: Speed Control Inoperative (Part 16 of 17). Crown Victoria, Grand Marquis & Marauder

A14 CHECK THE SPEEDOMETER

1 Check the speedometer for correct operation by driving the vehicle.

- **Does the speedometer operate correctly?**

➔ **Yes**

Go to «A15».

➔ **No**

Diagnose speedometer fault condition.

FM1100000743150X

Fig. 70 Test A: Speed Control Inoperative (Part 15 of 17). Crown Victoria, Grand Marquis & Marauder

- **Is the resistance less than 5 ohms?**

➔ **Yes**

INSTALL a new speed control servo.
REPEAT the self-test.

➔ **No**

REPAIR the circuit. REPEAT the self-test.

FM1100000743170X

Fig. 70 Test A: Speed Control Inoperative (Part 17 of 17). Crown Victoria, Grand Marquis & Marauder

B1 CHECK SPEED CONTROL ACTUATOR CABLE/THROTTLE BODY LINKAGE

1

2 Remove the speed control actuator cable from the speed control servo. Visually inspect the core wire and check the speed control actuator cable by pulling on the cable and noting the throttle movement.

- **Is the speed control actuator cable OK?**

➔ **Yes**

Go to «B2».

➔ **No**

INSTALL a new speed control actuator cable and/or REPAIR the throttle body linkage. TEST the system for normal operation.

FM1100000744010X

Fig. 71 Test B: Set Speed Fluctuates (Part 1 of 2). Crown Victoria, Grand Marquis & Marauder

B2 CHECK THE SPEEDOMETER

1 Check the speedometer for correct operation by driving the vehicle.

- **Does the speedometer fluctuate?**

➔ **Yes**

Diagnose speedometer fault condition.

➔ **No**

INSTALL a new speed control servo. TEST the system for normal operation.

FM1100000744020X

Fig. 71 Test B: Set Speed Fluctuates (Part 2 of 2). Crown Victoria, Grand Marquis & Marauder

C1 CHECK THE STOPLAMP OPERATION

1 Check the stoplamps for correct operation by pressing and releasing the brake pedal and observing the stoplamps.

- **Do the stoplamps operate correctly?**

➔ **Yes**

Go to «C2».

➔ **No**

Diagnose stop lamp fault condition.

FM1100000745010X

Fig. 72 Test C: Speed Control Does Not Disengage When Brakes Are Applied (Part 1 of 6). Crown Victoria, Grand Marquis & Marauder

C3 CHECK THE DEACTIVATOR SWITCH CIRCUITRY

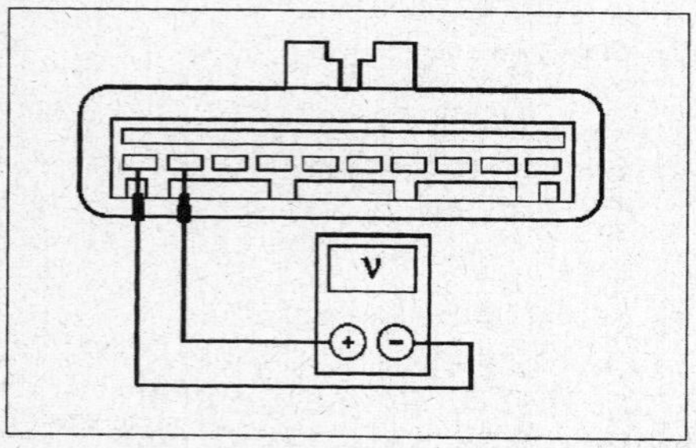

1

Measure the voltage between speed control servo C234 pin 9, circuit 636 (OG), harness side and speed control servo C234 pin 10, circuit 676 (PK/OG), harness side while firmly pressing and releasing the brake pedal.

- **Is the voltage 0 volts with the brake pedal firmly pressed and greater than 10 volts with the brake pedal released?**

➔ **Yes**

INSTALL a new speed control servo.
TEST the system for normal operation.

➔ **No**

Go to «C4».

FM1100000745030X

Fig. 72 Test C: Speed Control Does Not Disengage When Brakes Are Applied (Part 3 of 6). Crown Victoria, Grand Marquis & Marauder

C4 CHECK THE DEACTIVATOR SWITCH

1 *Deactivator Switch C233*

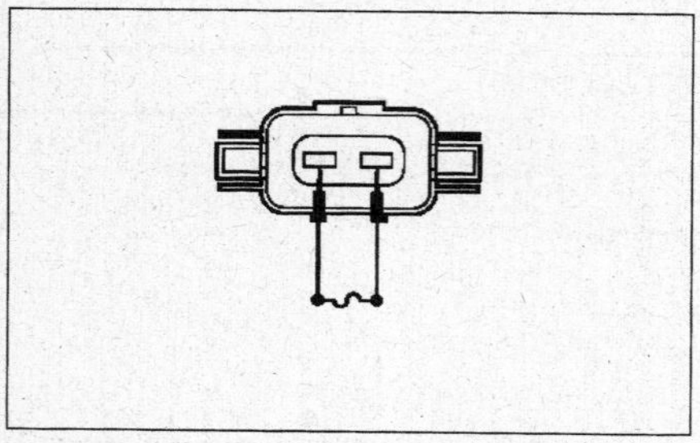

2

Note:
The jumper must be fused with a 15A fuse.

Connect a fused jumper wire between the deactivator switch C233 circuit 10 (LG/RD), harness side and the deactivator switch C233 circuit 636 (OG), harness side.

FM1100000745040X

Fig. 72 Test C: Speed Control Does Not Disengage When Brakes Are Applied (Part 4 of 6). Crown Victoria, Grand Marquis & Marauder

C2 CHECK CIRCUIT 511 (LG) FOR AN OPEN

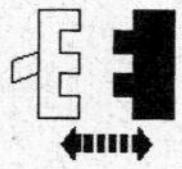

1 *Speed Control Servo C234*

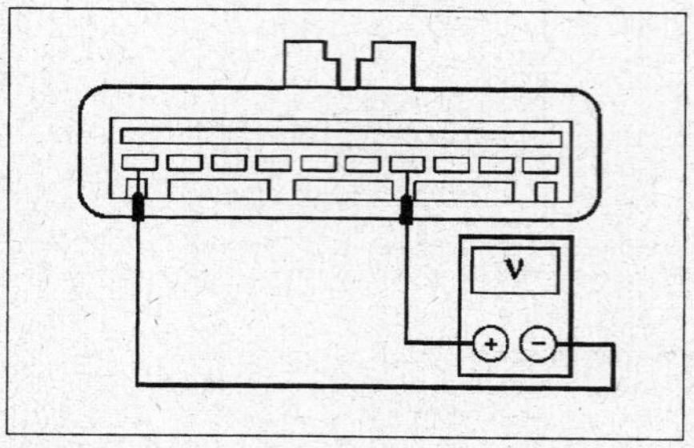

2

Measure the voltage between speed control servo C234 pin 4, circuit 511 (LG), harness side and speed control servo C234 pin 10, circuit 676 (PK/OG), harness side while pressing the brake pedal.

- **Is the voltage greater than 10 volts?**

➔ **Yes**

Go to «C3».

➔ **No**

Repair the circuit. Test system for normal operation.

FM1100000745020X

Fig. 72 Test C: Speed Control Does Not Disengage When Brakes Are Applied (Part 2 of 6). Crown Victoria, Grand Marquis & Marauder

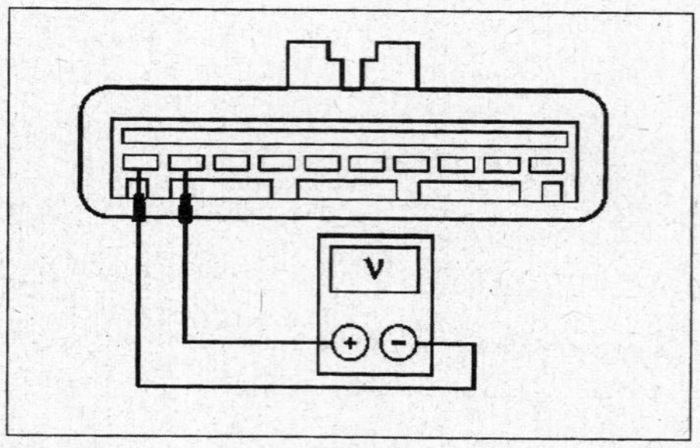

3

Measure the voltage between speed control servo C234 pin 9, circuit 636 (OG), harness side and speed control servo C234 pin 10, circuit 676 (PK/OG), harness side.

- **Is the voltage greater than 10 volts?**

➔ **Yes**

INSTALL a new deactivator switch. TEST the system for normal operation.

➔ **No**

Go to «C5».

FM1100000745050X

Fig. 72 Test C: Speed Control Does Not Disengage When Brakes Are Applied (Part 5 of 6). Crown Victoria, Grand Marquis & Marauder

C5	CHECK CIRCUIT 636 (OG) FOR AN OPEN

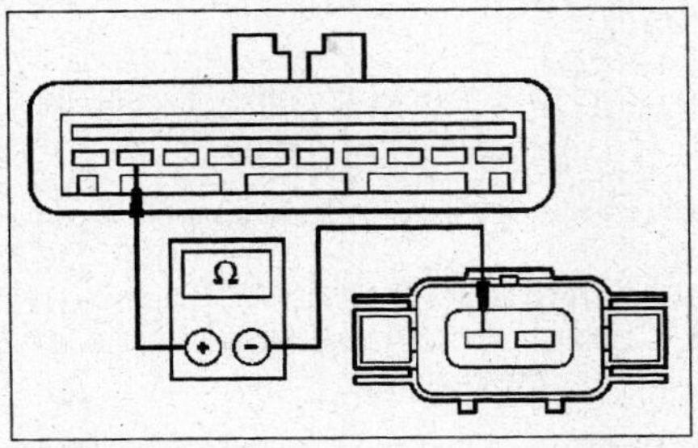

1

Measure the resistance between speed control servo C234 pin 9, circuit 636 (OG), harness side and deactivator switch C233, circuit 636 (OG), harness side.

- **Is the resistance less than 5 ohms?**

→ **Yes**

REPAIR circuit 10 (LG/RD). TEST the system for normal operation.

→ **No**

REPAIR circuit 636 (OG). TEST the system for normal operation.

FM1100000745060X

Fig. 72 Test C: Speed Control Does Not Disengage When Brakes Are Applied (Part 6 of 6). Crown Victoria, Grand Marquis & Marauder

- **Is the resistance between 114 and 126 ohms?**

→ **Yes**

INSTALL a new speed control servo. TEST the system for normal operation.

→ **No**

INSTALL a new speed control actuator switch. TEST the system for normal operation.

FM1100000746020X

Fig. 73 Test D: COAST Switch Inoperative (Part 2 of 2). Crown Victoria, Grand Marquis & Marauder

E1	CHECK THE SET/ACCEL SWITCH OPERATION

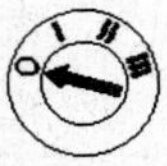

1

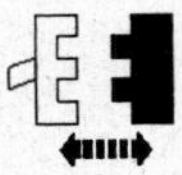

2

Speed Control Servo C234

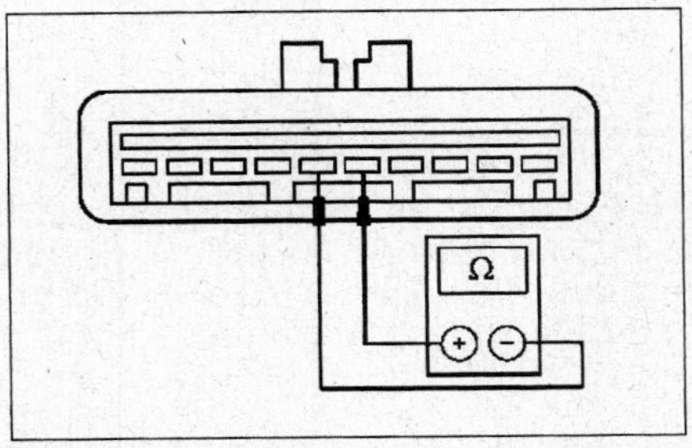

3

With the SET/ACCEL switch depressed and while rotating the steering wheel from stop to stop, measure the resistance between speed control servo C234 pin 5, circuit 151 (LB/BK), harness side

FM1100000747010X

Fig. 74 Test E: SET/ACCEL Switch Inoperative (Part 1 of 2). Crown Victoria, Grand Marquis & Marauder

D1	CHECK THE COAST SWITCH OPERATION

1

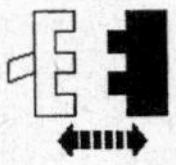

2

Speed Control Servo C234

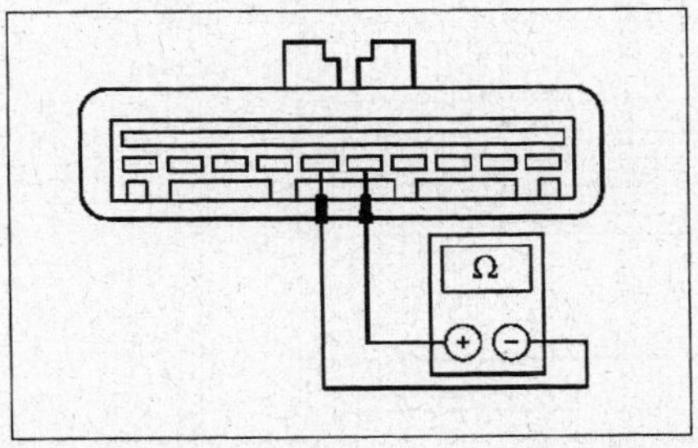

3

With the COAST switch depressed, measure the resistance between speed control servo C234 pin 5, circuit 151 (LB/BK) harness side and speed control servo C234 pin 6, circuit 848 (DG/OG), harness side.

FM1100000746010X

Fig. 73 Test D: COAST Switch Inoperative (Part 1 of 2). Crown Victoria, Grand Marquis & Marauder

and speed control servo C234 pin 6, circuit 848 (DG/OG), harness side.

- **Is the resistance between 646 and 714 ohms at all times?**

→ **Yes**

INSTALL a new speed control servo. TEST the system for normal operation.

→ **No**

INSTALL a new speed control actuator switch. TEST the system for normal operation.

FM1100000747020X

Fig. 74 Test E: SET/ACCEL Switch Inoperative (Part 2 of 2). Crown Victoria, Grand Marquis & Marauder

F1 CHECK THE RESUME SWITCH OPERATION

1

2

Speed Control Servo C234

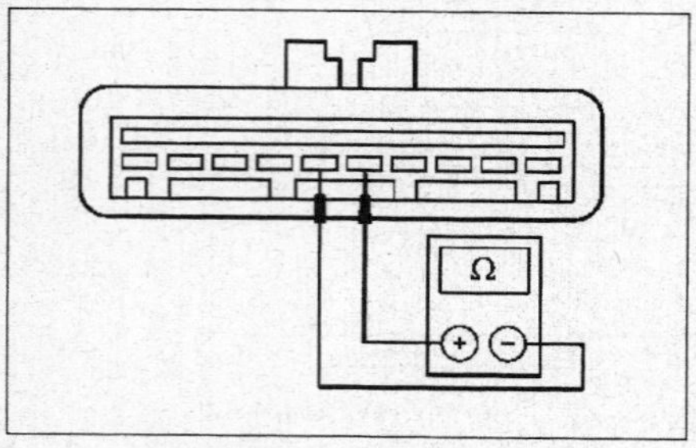

3

With the RESUME switch depressed and while rotating the steering wheel from stop to stop, measure the resistance between speed control servo C234 pin 5, circuit 151 (LB/BK), harness side

FM1100000748010X

Fig. 75 Test F: RESUME Switch Inoperative (Part 1 of 2). Crown Victoria, Grand Marquis & Marauder

G1 CHECK THE OFF SWITCH OPERATION

1

2

Speed Control Servo C234

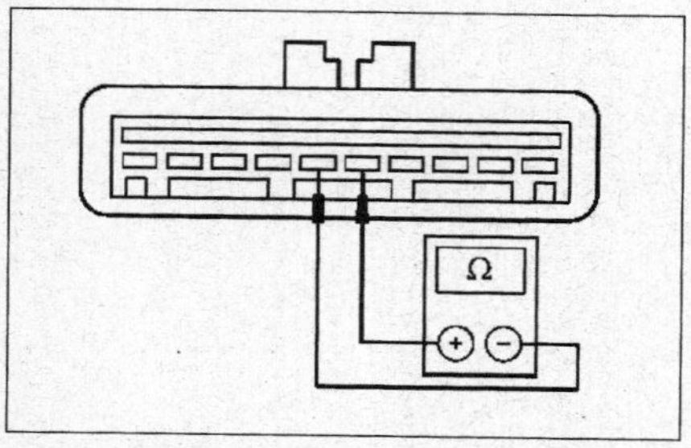

3

With the OFF switch depressed and while rotating the steering wheel from stop to stop, measure the resistance between the speed control servo C234 pin 5, circuit 151 (LB/BK), harness side and speed

FM1100000749010X

Fig. 76 Test G: OFF Switch Inoperative (Part 1 of 2). Crown Victoria, Grand Marquis & Marauder

and speed control servo C234 pin 6, circuit 848 (DG/OG), harness side.

- Is the resistance between 2,090 and 2,310 ohms?

→ Yes

INSTALL a new speed control servo. TEST the system for normal operation.

→ No

INSTALL a new speed control actuator switch. TEST the system for normal operation.

FM1100000748020X

Fig. 75 Test F: RESUME Switch Inoperative (Part 2 of 2). Crown Victoria, Grand Marquis & Marauder

control servo C234 pin 6, circuit 848 (DG/OG), harness side.

- Is the resistance less than 5 ohms with the switch pressed and greater than 10,000 ohms with the switch released?

→ Yes

INSTALL a new speed control servo. TEST the system for normal operation.

→ No

INSTALL a new speed control actuator switch. TEST the system for normal operation.

FM1100000749020X

Fig. 76 Test G: OFF Switch Inoperative (Part 2 of 2). Crown Victoria, Grand Marquis & Marauder

H1 CHECK THE SPEED CONTROL ACTUATOR CABLE

- 1 Check the speed control actuator cable for proper attachment at the speed control servo and throttle body.

- Is the speed control actuator cable attached correctly?

→ Yes

Go to «H2».

→ No

RECONNECT the speed control actuator cable. REPEAT the self-test.

FM1100000750010X

Fig. 77 Test H: Flash w/Last Switch Pressed, But No Dynamic Pull Occurs At Throttle & Speed Control Inoperative (Part 1 of 3). Crown Victoria, Grand Marquis & Marauder

H2 CHECK FOR CORRECT AMOUNT OF SLACK IN THE SPEED CONTROL ACTUATOR CABLE

- 1 Disconnect the speed control actuator cable from the throttle lever.
- 2 Check for 3 mm of slack (extra length) in the speed control actuator cable beyond the throttle attachment.

- Is there approximately 3 mm of slack in the speed control actuator cable?

→ Yes

Go to «H3».

→ No

ADJUST the speed control actuator cable. REPEAT the self-test.

FM1100000750020X

Fig. 77 Test H: Flash w/Last Switch Pressed, But No Dynamic Pull Occurs At Throttle & Speed Control Inoperative (Part 2 of 3). Crown Victoria, Grand Marquis & Marauder

H3	CHECK FOR A STICKING OR BINDING SPEED CONTROL ACTUATOR CABLE

1 Check the speed control actuator cable for sticking or binding.

- **Is the speed control actuator cable OK?**

→ **Yes**

INSTALL a new speed control servo. REPEAT the self-test.

→ **No**

REPAIR or INSTALL a new speed control actuator cable. REPEAT the self-test.

FM1100000750030X

Fig. 77 Test H: Flash w/Last Switch Pressed, But No Dynamic Pull Occurs At Throttle & Speed Control Inoperative (Part 3 of 3). Crown Victoria, Grand Marquis & Marauder

I2	CHECK CIRCUIT 511 (LG)

1

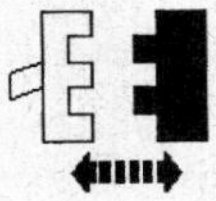

2 *Speed Control Servo C234*

3

FM1100000751020X

Fig. 78 Test I: Flash Code 2, BPP Switch Failure (Part 2 of 3). Crown Victoria, Grand Marquis & Marauder

J1	CHECK STOPLAMP OPERATION

1 Press and release the brake pedal while observing the stoplamps.

- **Do the stoplamps operate correctly?**

→ **Yes**

Go to «J2».

→ **No**

Diagnose stop lamp fault condition.

FM1100000752010X

Fig. 79 Test J: Flash Code 3, Deactivator Switch Circuit Failure (Part 1 of 6). Crown Victoria, Grand Marquis & Marauder

I1	CHECK STOPLAMP OPERATION

1 Press and release the brake pedal while observing the stoplamps.

- **Do the stoplamps operate correctly?**

→ **Yes**

Go to «I2».

→ **No**

Diagnose stop lamp fault condition.

FM1100000751010X

Fig. 78 Test I: Flash Code 2, BPP Switch Failure (Part 1 of 3). Crown Victoria, Grand Marquis & Marauder

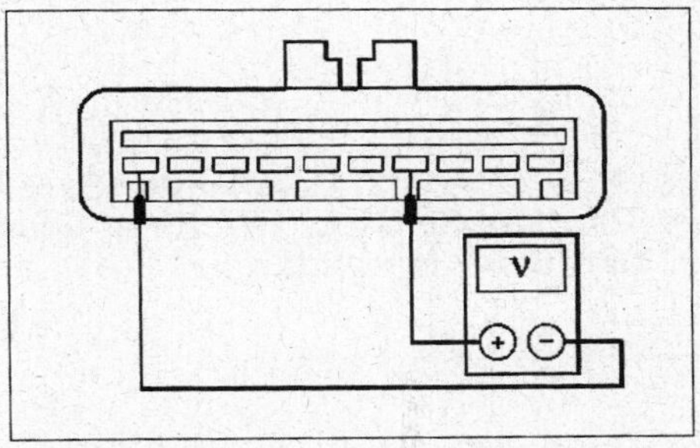

4

While depressing the brake pedal, measure the voltage between speed control servo C234 pin 4, circuit 511 (LG), harness side and speed control servo C234 pin 10, circuit 676 (PK/OG), harness side.

- **Is the voltage greater than 10 volts?**

→ **Yes**

INSTALL a new speed control servo. TEST the system for normal operation.

→ **No**

REPAIR the circuit.

FM1100000751030X

Fig. 78 Test I: Flash Code 2, BPP Switch Failure (Part 3 of 3). Crown Victoria, Grand Marquis & Marauder

J2	CHECK THE DEACTIVATOR SWITCH CIRCUITRY

1

2 *Speed Control Servo C234*

3

FM1100000752020X

Fig. 79 Test J: Flash Code 3, Deactivator Switch Circuit Failure (Part 2 of 6). Crown Victoria, Grand Marquis & Marauder

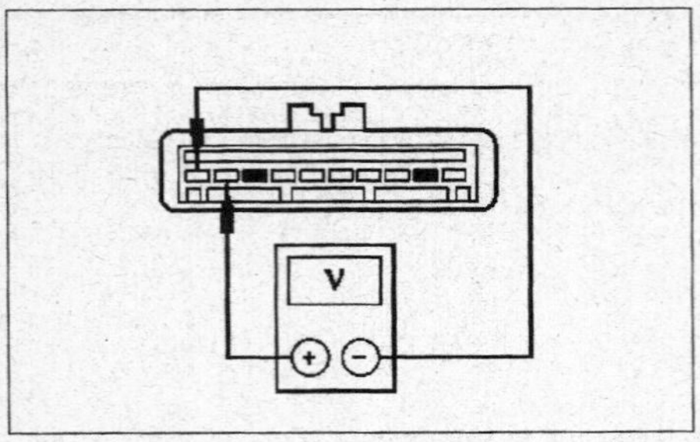

4

Measure the voltage between speed control servo C234 pin 9, circuit 636 (OG), harness side and speed control servo C234 pin 10, circuit 676 (PK/OG), harness side.

- **Is the voltage greater than 10 volts?**

➔ **Yes**

INSTALL a new speed control servo. REPEAT the self-test.

➔ **No**

Go to «J3».

FM1100000752030X

Fig. 79 Test J: Flash Code 3, Deactivator Switch Circuit Failure (Part 3 of 6). Crown Victoria, Grand Marquis & Marauder

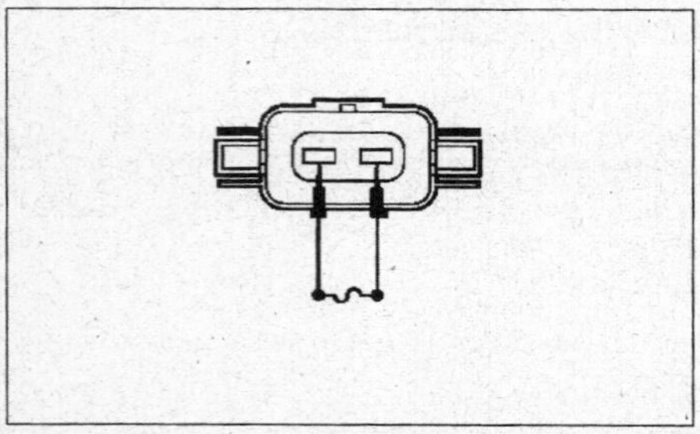

4

Connect a fused jumper wire between deactivator switch C233 circuit 10 (LG/RD), harness side and deactivator switch C236 circuit 636 (OG), harness side.

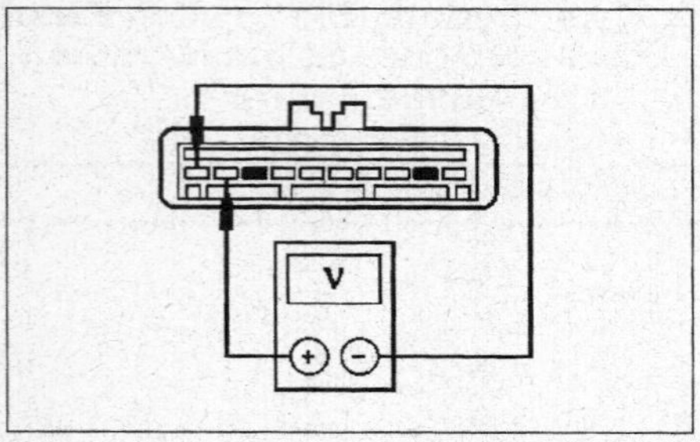

5

Measure the voltage between speed control servo C234 pin 9, circuit 636 (OG), harness side and speed control servo C234 pin 10, circuit 676 (PK/OG), harness side.

- **Is the voltage greater than 10 volts?**

➔ **Yes**

INSTALL a new deactivator switch. REPEAT the self-test.

➔ **No**

Go to «J4».

FM1100000752050X

Fig. 79 Test J: Flash Code 3, Deactivator Switch Circuit Failure (Part 5 of 6). Crown Victoria, Grand Marquis & Marauder

J3 CHECK THE DEACTIVATOR SWITCH

1

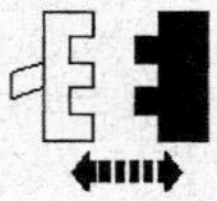

2 *Deactivator Switch C233*

3

FM1100000752040X

Fig. 79 Test J: Flash Code 3, Deactivator Switch Circuit Failure (Part 4 of 6). Crown Victoria, Grand Marquis & Marauder

J4 CHECK CIRCUIT 636 (OG) FOR AN OPEN

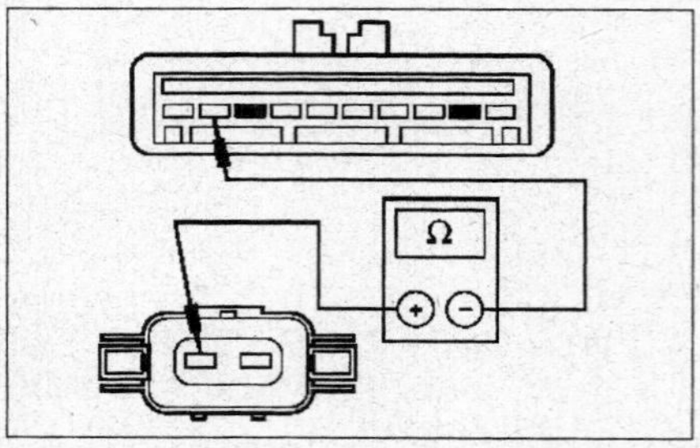

1

Measure the resistance between speed control servo C234 pin 9, circuit 636 (OG), harness side and deactivator switch C233, circuit 636 (OG), harness side.

- **Is the resistance less than 5 ohms?**

➔ **Yes**

REPAIR circuit 10 (LG/RD). REPEAT the self-test.

➔ **No**

REPAIR the circuit.

FM1100000752060X

Fig. 79 Test J: Flash Code 3, Deactivator Switch Circuit Failure (Part 6 of 6). Crown Victoria, Grand Marquis & Marauder

K1 CHECK THE SPEEDOMETER OPERATION

1 Check the speedometer for correct operation by driving the vehicle.

- **Does the speedometer operate correctly?**

→ **Yes**

Go to «K2».

→ **No**

Diagnose speedometer fault condition.

FM1100000753010X

Fig. 80 Test K: Flash w/Last Switch Pressed, Dynamic Pull Occurs At Throttle & Speed Control Inoperative (Part 1 of 3). Crown Victoria, Grand Marquis & Marauder

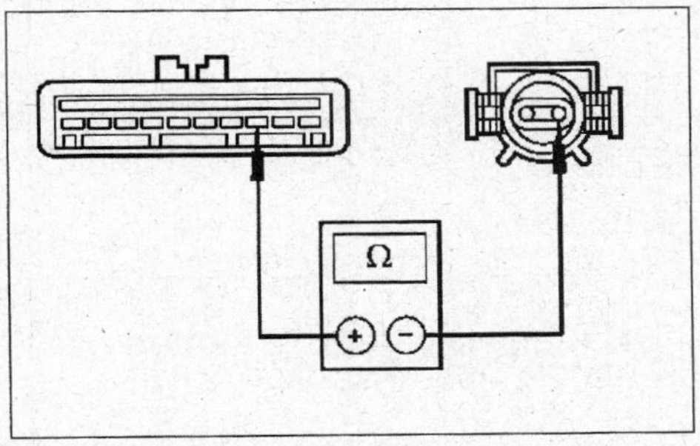

4

Measure the resistance between VSS C1020 circuit 679 (GY/BK), harness side and the speed control servo C234 pin 3, circuit 679 (GY/BK), harness side.

- **Is the resistance less than 5 ohms?**

→ **Yes**

INSTALL a new speed control servo. REPEAT the self-test.

→ **No**

REPAIR the circuit. REPEAT the self-test.

FM1100000753030X

Fig. 80 Test K: Flash w/Last Switch Pressed, Dynamic Pull Occurs At Throttle & Speed Control Inoperative (Part 3 of 3). Crown Victoria, Grand Marquis & Marauder

Condition	Possible Source	Action
• Speed Control Inoperative	• Actuator cable not attached to throttle. • Blown fuse. • Circuitry. • Brake on/off (BOO) switch. • Deactivator switch. • Speed control actuator switch. • Vehicle speed sensor (VSS). • Speed control servo.	• GO to Pinpoint Test A.
• Set Speed Fluctuates	• Speed control servo. • Speed control actuator switch. • Circuitry. • Vehicle speed sensor (VSS). • Loose or binding speed control actuator cable between speed control actuator and throttle body.	• GO to Pinpoint Test B.
• Speed Control Does Not Disengage When Brakes Are Applied	• Deactivator switch. • Binding speed control actuator cable.	• GO to Pinpoint Test C.
• Speed Control Does Not Disengage When Clutch Pedal is Depressed	• Clutch pedal position (CPP) switch.	• REPLACE faulty clutch switch.
• COAST Switch Inoperative	• Speed control actuator switch. • Speed control servo. • Circuitry.	• GO to Pinpoint Test D.
• SET/ACCEL Switch Inoperative	• Speed control actuator switch. • Speed control servo. • Circuitry.	• GO to Pinpoint Test E.
• RESUME Switch Inoperative	• Speed control actuator switch. • Speed control servo. • Circuitry.	• GO to Pinpoint Test F.
• OFF Switch Inoperative	• Speed control actuator switch. • Circuitry.	• GO to Pinpoint Test G.

FM1109700439000X

Fig. 81 Speed control diagnostic symptom chart. 2000 Escort & ZX2

K2 CHECK CIRCUIT 679 (GY/BK) FOR AN OPEN

1

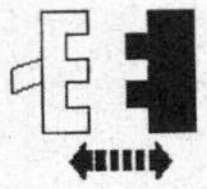

2 *Speed Control C234*

3 *VSS C1020*

FM1100000753020X

Fig. 80 Test K: Flash w/Last Switch Pressed, Dynamic Pull Occurs At Throttle & Speed Control Inoperative (Part 2 of 3). Crown Victoria, Grand Marquis & Marauder

TEST CONDITIONS	TEST DETAILS/RESULTS/ACTIONS
A1 CHECK FUSE	
1 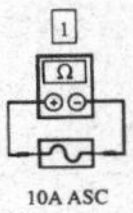	• Is the fuse OK? → **Yes** REINSTALL the 10A ASC fuse. GO to **A4**. → **No** GO to **A2**.
A2 CHECK SYSTEM	
2  3 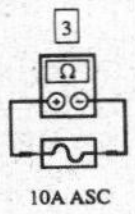	1 Replace the 10A ASC fuse. • Is the fuse OK? → **Yes** REINSTALL the 10A ASC fuse. GO to **A4**. → **No** GO to **A3**.

FM1109700440010X

Fig. 82 Test A: Speed Control Inoperative (Part 1 of 8). 2000 Escort & ZX2

TEST CONDITIONS	TEST DETAILS/RESULTS/ACTIONS
A3 CHECK FOR SHORT TO GROUND	
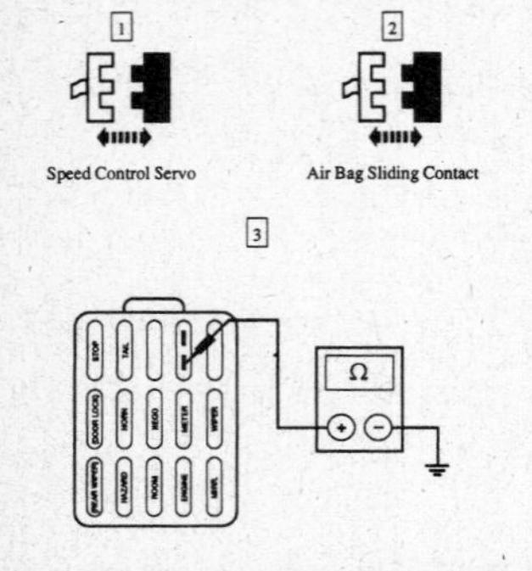	3 Measure the resistance between the bottom terminal of the 10A ASC fuse holder and ground. • Is the resistance greater than 10,000 ohms? → **Yes** REINSTALL the 10A ASC fuse. GO to **A4**. → **No** REPAIR circuit 65 (Y).
A4 CHECK POWER TO THE SPEED CONTROL SERVO	
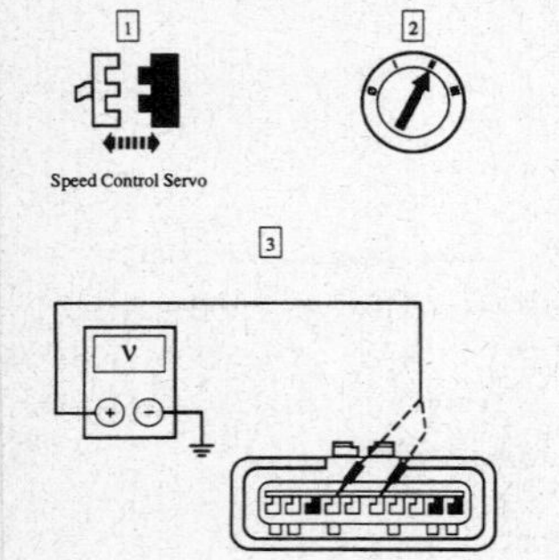	3 With the speed control actuator switch in the ON position, measure the voltage between speed control servo connector pin 7, circuit 65 (Y), and ground; and between pin 5, circuit 356 (R/Y), and ground. • Are the voltages greater than 10 volts? → **Yes** GO to **A5**. → **No** If circuit 356 (R/Y), GO to **A11**. If both, REPAIR circuit 65 (Y).

FM1109700440020X

Fig. 82 Test A: Speed Control Inoperative (Part 2 of 8). 2000 Escort & ZX2

TEST CONDITIONS	TEST DETAILS/RESULTS/ACTIONS
A7 CHECK DEACTIVATOR SWITCH POWER	
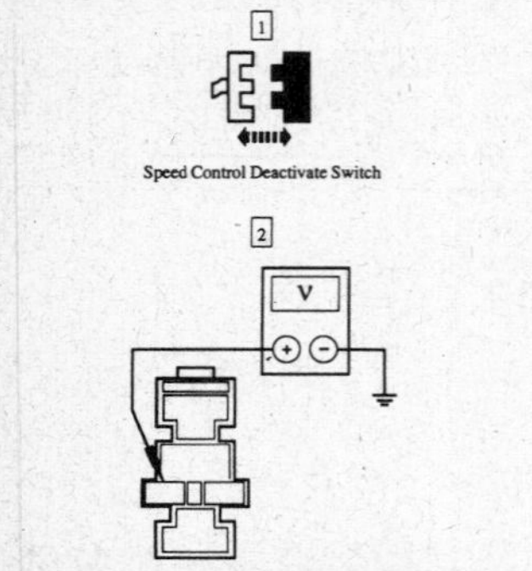	2 Measure the voltage between the deactivator switch connector pin 2, circuit 350C (GN/W), and ground. • Is the voltage greater than 10 volts? → **Yes** GO to **A8**. → **No** REPAIR circuit 350 (GN/W).
A8 CHECK THE DEACTIVATOR SWITCH	
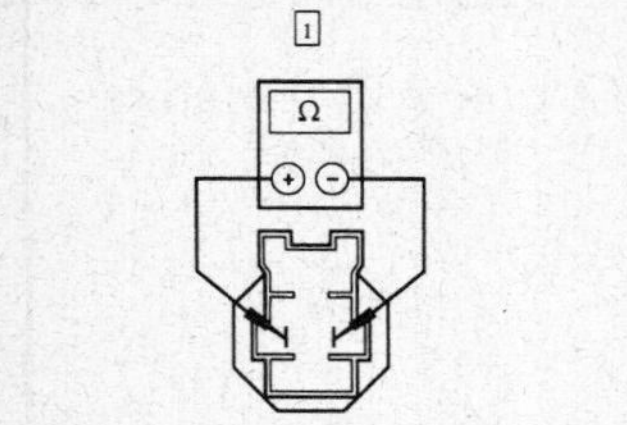	1 **NOTE:** The speed control deactivate switch is located next to the BOO switch. Measure the resistance between the deactivator switch terminal 1 and terminal 2. • Is the resistance less than 5 ohms? → **Yes** REPAIR circuit 65 (Y). → **No** REPLACE the deactivator switch.

FM1109700440040X

Fig. 82 Test A: Speed Control Inoperative (Part 4 of 8). 2000 Escort & ZX2

TEST CONDITIONS	TEST DETAILS/RESULTS/ACTIONS
A5 CHECK FOR BRAKE ON/OFF (BOO) SWITCH INPUT WITHOUT BRAKES APPLIED	
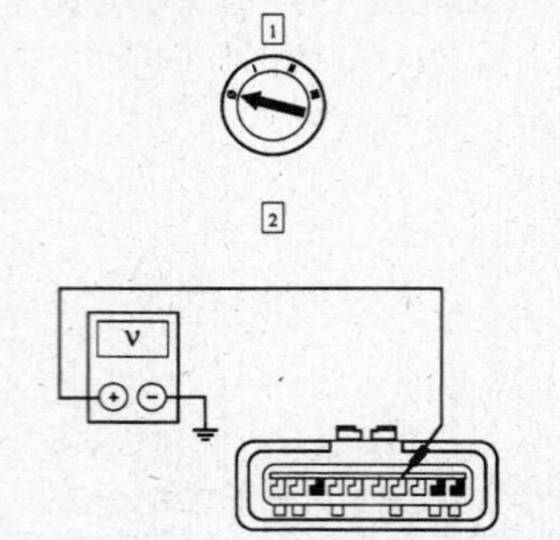	2 Measure the voltage between the speed control servo connector pin 4, circuit 409 (GN), and ground. • Is the voltage greater than 10 volts? → **Yes** REPLACE the BOO switch. → **No** GO to **A6**.
A6 CHECK THE DEACTIVATOR SWITCH INPUT TO SPEED CONTROL SERVO	
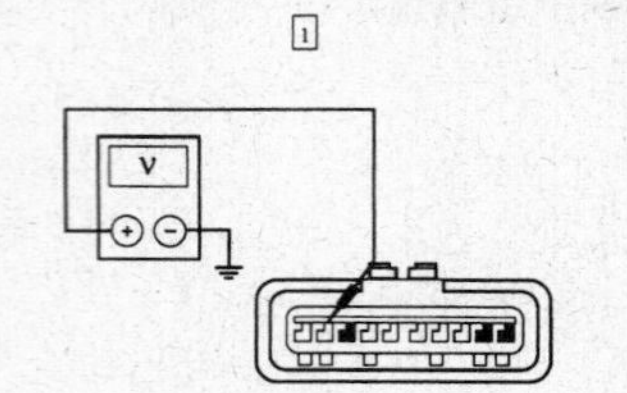	1 Measure the voltage between speed control servo connector pin 9, circuit 355 (GN/Y) and ground. • Is the voltage greater than 10 volts? → **Yes** GO to **A9**. → **No** GO to **A7**.

FM1109700440030X

Fig. 82 Test A: Speed Control Inoperative (Part 3 of 8). 2000 Escort & ZX2

TEST CONDITIONS	TEST DETAILS/RESULTS/ACTIONS
A9 CHECK SPEED CONTROL ACTUATOR SWITCH POWER	
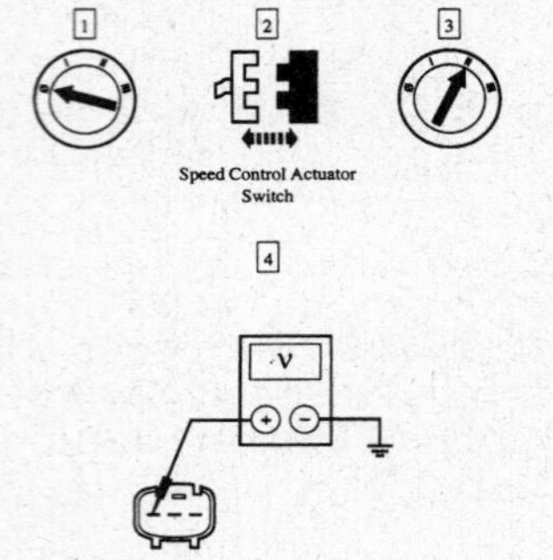	4 Measure the voltage between the speed control actuator switch connector GN wire and ground. • Is the voltage greater than 10 volts? → **Yes** GO to **A11**. → **No** GO to **A10**.

FM1109700440050X

Fig. 82 Test A: Speed Control Inoperative (Part 5 of 8). 2000 Escort & ZX2

TEST CONDITIONS	TEST DETAILS/RESULTS/ACTIONS
A10 CHECK POWER AT AIR BAG SLIDING CONTACT CONNECTOR	
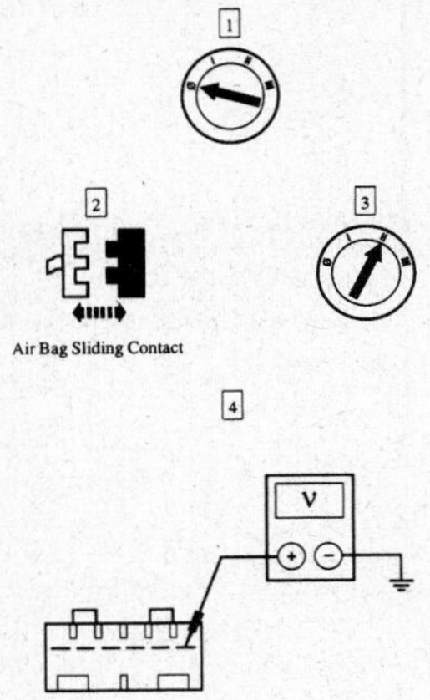	1 **NOTE:** Before attempting to disconnect the air bag sliding contact connector, the air bag system must be disabled. 4 Measure the voltage between the air bag sliding contact connector pin 6, circuit 65A (Y), and ground. • Is the voltage greater than 10 volts? → **Yes** REPLACE the air bag sliding contact. → **No** REPAIR circuit 65A (Y).

FM1109700440060X

Fig. 82 Test A: Speed Control Inoperative (Part 6 of 8). 2000 Escort & ZX2

TEST CONDITIONS	TEST DETAILS/RESULTS/ACTIONS
A13 ISOLATE FAULT	
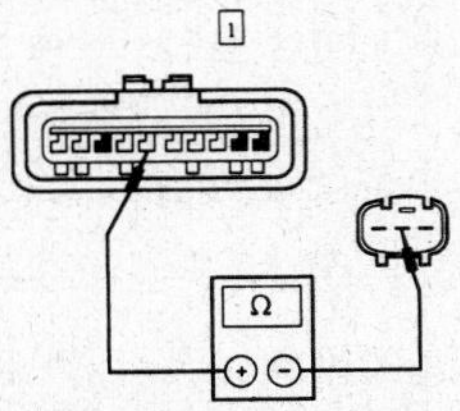	1 Measure the resistance between speed control actuator switch connector BK/W wire and speed control servo connector pin 6, circuit 359 (R/BL). • Is the resistance less than 5 ohms? → **Yes** REPLACE the speed control actuator switch. → **No** GO to **A14**.
A14 CHECK CIRCUIT 359 (R/BL)	
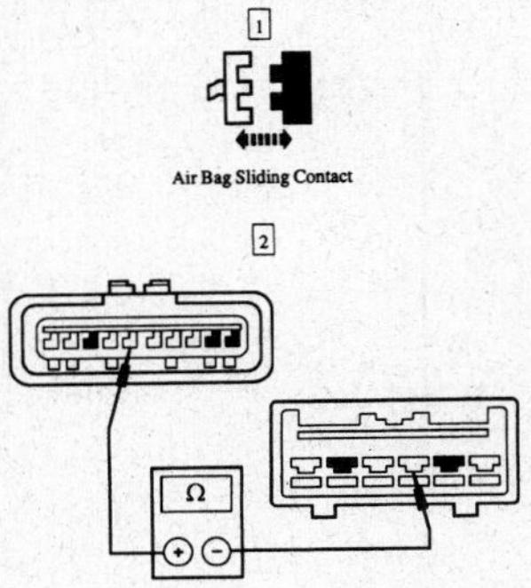	2 Measure the resistance between air bag sliding contact connector pin 4, circuit 359 (R/BL), and speed control servo connector pin 6. • Is the resistance less than 5 ohms? → **Yes** REPLACE the air bag sliding contact. → **No** REPAIR circuit 359 (R/BL).

FM1109700440080X

Fig. 82 Test A: Speed Control Inoperative (Part 8 of 8). 2000 Escort & ZX2

TEST CONDITIONS	TEST DETAILS/RESULTS/ACTIONS
A11 CHECK CIRCUIT 356 (R/Y)	
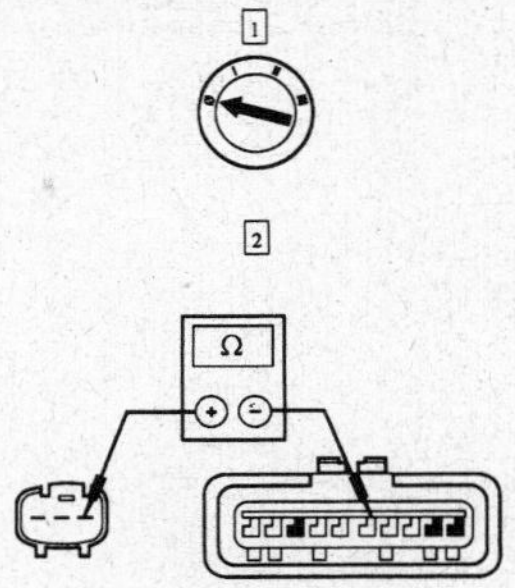	2 Measure the resistance between the speed control actuator switch connector BL wire and speed control servo connector pin 5, circuit 356 (R/Y). • Is the resistance less than 5 ohms? → **Yes** GO to **A13.** → **No** GO to **A12.**
A12 CHECK AIR BAG SLIDING CONTACT	
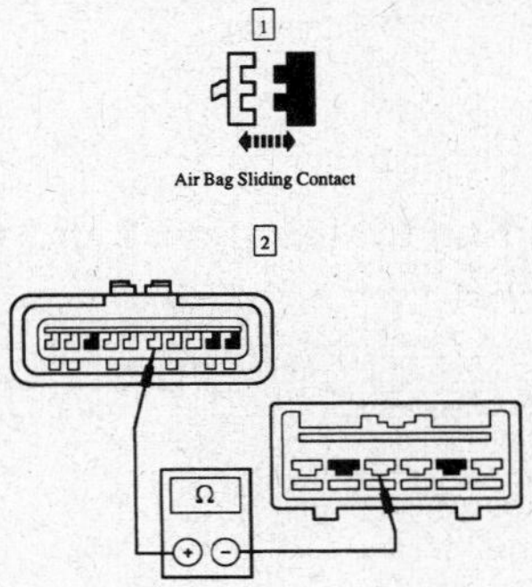	2 Measure the resistance between air bag sliding contact connector pin 3, circuit 356 (R/Y), and speed control servo connector pin 5. • Is the resistance less than 5 ohms? → **Yes** REPLACE the air bag sliding contact. → **No** REPAIR circuit 356 (R/Y).

FM1109700440070X

Fig. 82 Test A: Speed Control Inoperative (Part 7 of 8). 2000 Escort & ZX2

TEST CONDITIONS	TEST DETAILS/RESULTS/ACTIONS
B1 VERIFY CONDITION OCCURS ONLY WHILE USING SPEED CONTROL	
	1 Perform a vehicle test drive. Verify that the condition does not occur without speed control. • Does condition occur without speed control? → **Yes** REPAIR engine as required. → **No** GO to **B2.**
B2 CHECK SPEED CONTROL ACTUATOR CABLE/THROTTLE BODY LINKAGE	
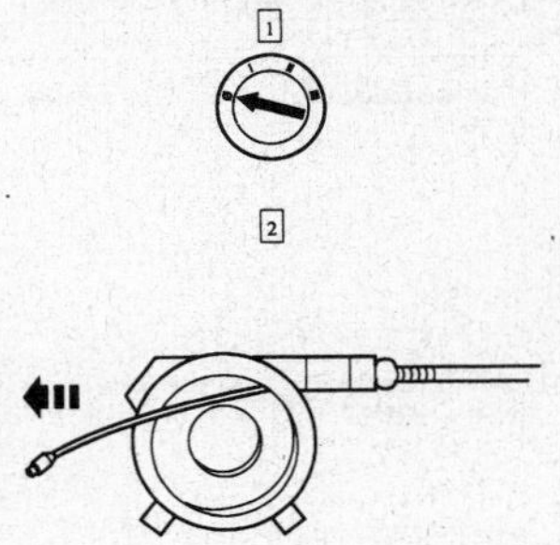	2 Remove the speed control actuator cable from the speed control servo. Visually inspect the core wire; check the speed control actuator cable by pulling on it and noting the throttle movement.

FM1109700441010X

Fig. 83 Test B: Set Speed Fluctuates (Part 1 of 3). 2000 Escort & ZX2

TEST CONDITIONS	TEST DETAILS/RESULTS/ACTIONS
B2 CHECK SPEED CONTROL ACTUATOR CABLE/THROTTLE BODY LINKAGE (Continued)	
3 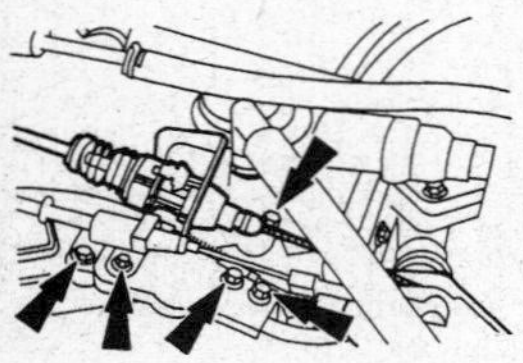	3 Make sure the throttle cable bracket is securely fastened.
4 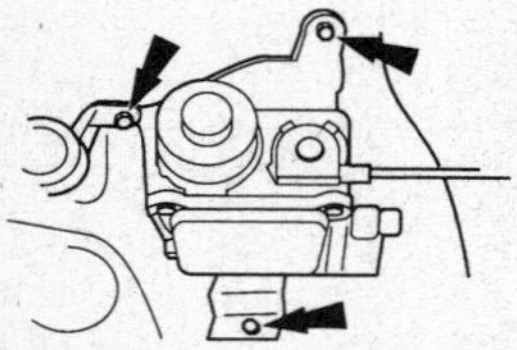	4 Make sure the speed control servo bracket is securely fastened. • Are the components OK? → **Yes** GO to **B3**. → **No** REPAIR as necessary.

FM1109700441020X

Fig. 83 Test B: Set Speed Fluctuates (Part 2 of 3). 2000 Escort & ZX2

TEST CONDITIONS	TEST DETAILS/RESULTS/ACTIONS
C1 CHECK SPEED CONTROL ACTUATOR CABLE/THROTTLE BODY LINKAGE	
1 	
2 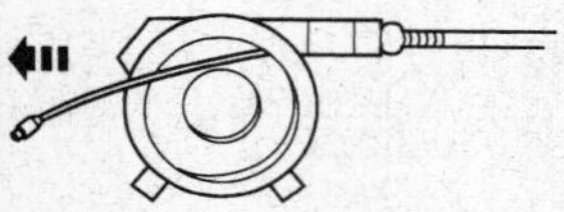	2 Remove the speed control actuator cable from the speed control servo. Visually inspect the core wire; check the speed control actuator cable by pulling on it and noting the throttle movement.

FM1109700442010X

Fig. 84 Test C: Speed Control Does Not Disengage When Brakes Are Applied (Part 1 of 2). 2000 Escort & ZX2

TEST CONDITIONS	TEST DETAILS/RESULTS/ACTIONS
C1 CHECK SPEED CONTROL ACTUATOR CABLE/THROTTLE BODY LINKAGE (Continued)	
3 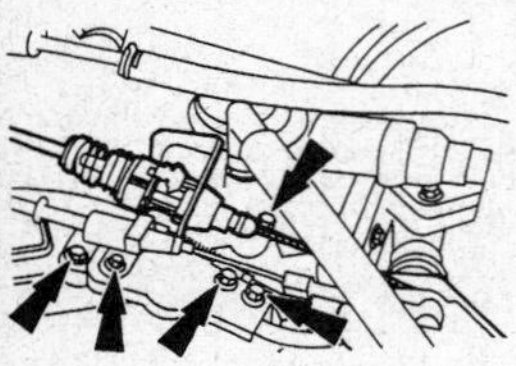	3 Make sure the throttle cable bracket is securely fastened.
4 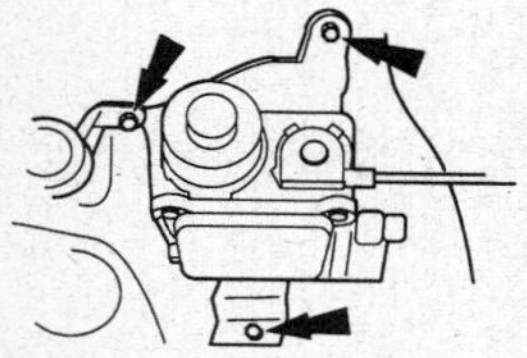	4 Make sure the speed control servo bracket is securely fastened. • Are the components OK? → **Yes** REPLACE the speed control deactivate switch. → **No** REPAIR as necessary.

FM1109700442020X

Fig. 84 Test C: Speed Control Does Not Disengage When Brakes Are Applied (Part 2 of 2). 2000 Escort & ZX2

TEST CONDITIONS	TEST DETAILS/RESULTS/ACTIONS
B3 CHECK THE VEHICLE SPEED SENSOR (VSS) CIRCUIT	
1  2  Speed Control Servo	
3 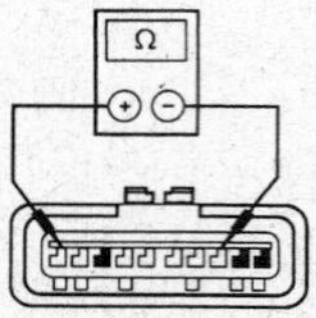	3 Measure the resistance between the speed control servo connector pin 3, circuit 159A (W/BK), and pin 10, circuit 57C (BL). • Is the resistance between 200 and 300 ohms? → **Yes** GO to **B5**. → **No** GO to **B4**.
B4 CHECK THE VEHICLE SPEED SENSOR (VSS)	
1  VSS	
2 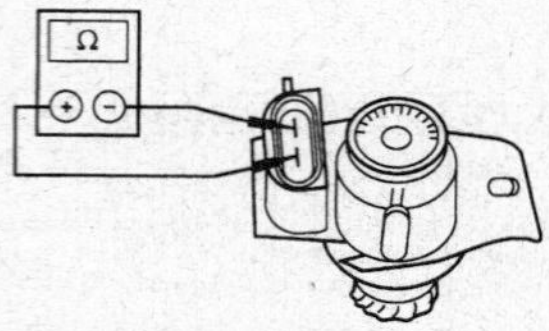	2 Measure the resistance between the terminals of the VSS. • Is the resistance between 200 and 300 ohms? → **Yes** REPAIR circuit 159 (W/BK) and/or circuit 57 (BL). → **No** REPLACE the vehicle speed sensor.
B5 CHECK THE SPEED CONTROL SERVO	
	1 Substitute a known good speed control servo.

FM1109700441030X

Fig. 83 Test B: Set Speed Fluctuates (Part 3 of 3). 2000 Escort & ZX2

TEST CONDITIONS	TEST DETAILS/RESULTS/ACTIONS
D1 CHECK COAST SWITCH OPERATION	
1  2 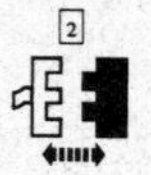 Speed Control Servo	
3 	3 With the COAST switch depressed and while turning steering wheel from stop to stop, measure the resistance between the speed control servo connector pin 5, circuit 356 (R/Y), and pin 6, circuit 359 (R/BL). • Is the resistance between 114 and 126 ohms? → **Yes** GO to **D2**. → **No** REPLACE the speed control actuator switch.
D2 CHECK SPEED CONTROL ACTUATOR CABLE/THROTTLE BODY LINKAGE	
1 	
2 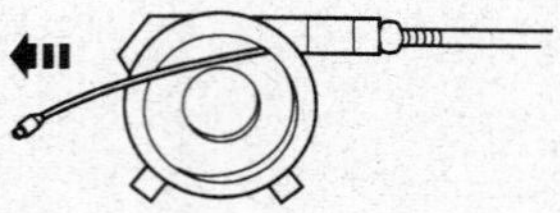	2 Remove the speed control actuator cable from the speed control servo. Visually inspect the core wire; check the speed control actuator cable by pulling on it and noting the throttle movement.

FM1109700443010X

Fig. 85 Test D: Coast Switch Inoperative (Part 1 of 2). 2000 Escort & ZX2

TEST CONDITIONS	TEST DETAILS/RESULTS/ACTIONS
D2 CHECK SPEED CONTROL ACTUATOR CABLE/THROTTLE BODY LINKAGE (Continued)	
3 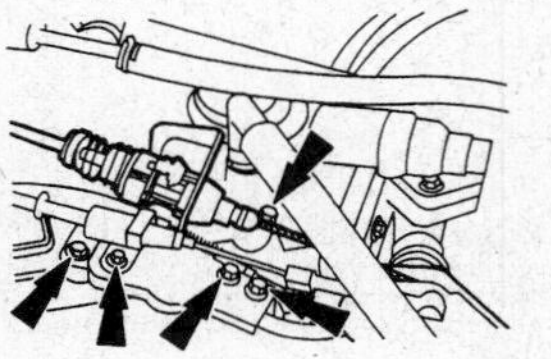	3 Make sure the throttle cable bracket is securely fastened.
4 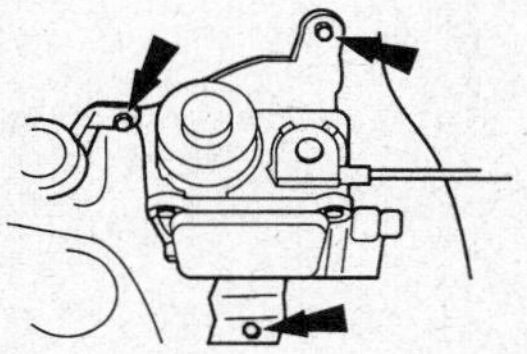	4 Make sure the speed control servo bracket is securely fastened. • Are the components OK? → **Yes** REPLACE the speed control servo. → **No** REPAIR as necessary.

FM1109700443020X

Fig. 85 Test D: Coast Switch Inoperative (Part 2 of 2). 2000 Escort & ZX2

TEST CONDITIONS	TEST DETAILS/RESULTS/ACTIONS
E2 CHECK SPEED CONTROL ACTUATOR CABLE/THROTTLE BODY LINKAGE (Continued)	
3 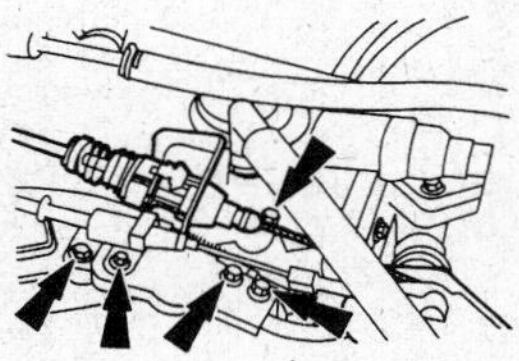	3 Make sure the throttle cable bracket is securely fastened.
4 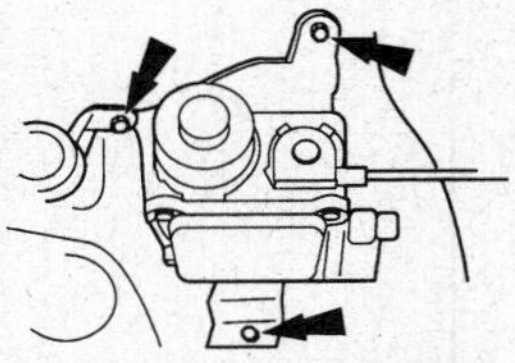	4 Make sure the speed control servo bracket is securely fastened. • Are the components OK? → **Yes** REPLACE the speed control servo. → **No** REPAIR as necessary.

FM1109700444020X

Fig. 86 Test E: SET/ACCEL Switch Inoperative (Part 2 of 2). 2000 Escort & ZX2

TEST CONDITIONS	TEST DETAILS/RESULTS/ACTIONS
E1 CHECK SET/ACCEL SWITCH OPERATION	
1  2  Speed Control Servo	
3 	3 With the SET/ACCEL switch depressed and while turning the steering wheel from stop to stop, measure the resistance between the speed control servo connector pin 5, circuit 356 (R/Y), and pin 6, circuit 359 (R/BL). • Is the resistance between 546 and 614 ohms? → **Yes** GO to **E2**. → **No** REPLACE the speed control actuator switch.
E2 CHECK SPEED CONTROL ACTUATOR CABLE/THROTTLE BODY LINKAGE	
1 	
2 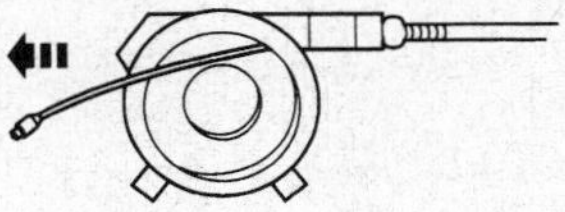	2 Remove the speed control actuator cable from the speed control servo. Visually inspect the core wire; check the speed control actuator cable by pulling on it and noting the throttle movement.

FM1109700444010X

Fig. 86 Test E: SET/ACCEL Switch Inoperative (Part 1 of 2). 2000 Escort & ZX2

TEST CONDITIONS	TEST DETAILS/RESULTS/ACTIONS
F1 CHECK RESUME SWITCH OPERATION	
1  2  Speed Control Servo	
3 	3 With the RESUME switch depressed and while turning the steering wheel from stop to stop, measure the resistance between the speed control servo connector pin 5, circuit 356 (R/Y) and pin 6, circuit 359 (R/BL). • Is the resistance between 2090 and 2310 ohms? → **Yes** GO to **F2**. → **No** REPLACE the speed control actuator switch.
F2 CHECK SPEED CONTROL ACTUATOR CABLE/THROTTLE BODY LINKAGE	
1 	
2 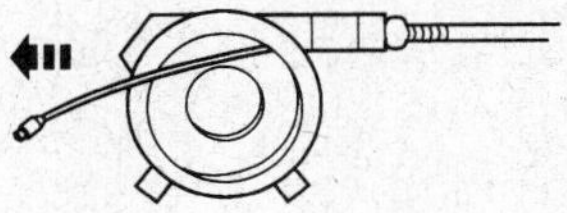	2 Remove the speed control actuator cable from the speed control servo. Visually inspect the core wire; check the speed control actuator cable by pulling on it and noting the throttle movement.

FM1109700445010X

Fig. 87 Test F: Resume Switch Inoperative (Part 1 of 2). 2000 Escort & ZX2

TEST CONDITIONS	TEST DETAILS/RESULTS/ACTIONS
F2 CHECK SPEED CONTROL ACTUATOR CABLE/THROTTLE BODY LINKAGE (Continued)	
3 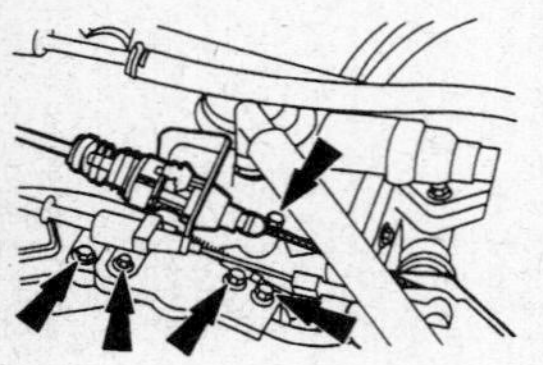	3 Make sure the throttle cable bracket is securely fastened.
4 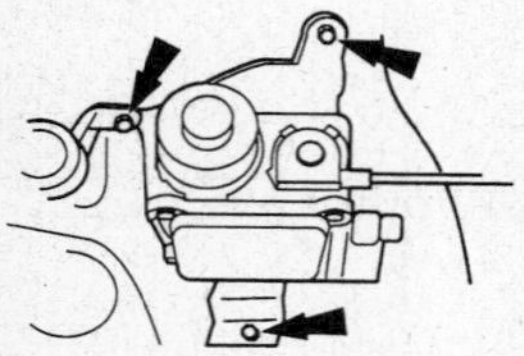	4 Make sure the speed control servo bracket is securely fastened. • Are the components OK? → **Yes** REPLACE the speed control servo. → **No** REPAIR as necessary.

FM1109700445020X

Fig. 87 Test F: Resume Switch Inoperative (Part 2 of 2). 2000 Escort & ZX2

TEST CONDITIONS	TEST DETAILS/RESULTS/ACTIONS
G2 CHECK SPEED CONTROL ACTUATOR CABLE/THROTTLE BODY LINKAGE (Continued)	
3 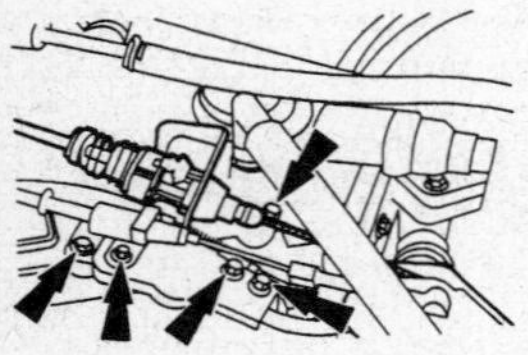	3 Make sure the throttle cable bracket is securely fastened.
4 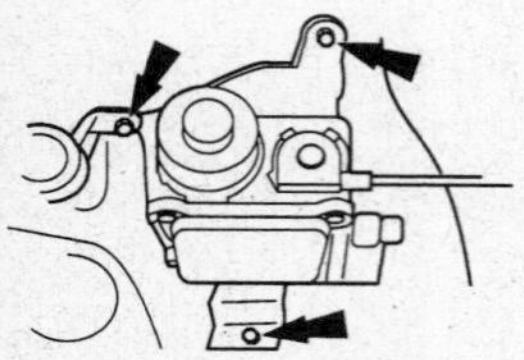	4 Make sure the speed control servo bracket is securely fastened. • Are the components OK? → **Yes** REPLACE the speed control servo. → **No** REPAIR as necessary.

FM1109700446020X

Fig. 88 Test G: Off Switch Inoperative (Part 2 of 2). 2000 Escort & ZX2

TEST CONDITIONS	TEST DETAILS/RESULTS/ACTIONS
G1 CHECK OFF SWITCH OPERATION	
1  2  Speed Control Servo	
3 	3 With the OFF switch depressed and while turning the steering wheel from stop to stop, measure the resistance between the speed control servo connector pin 5, circuit 356 (R/Y) and pin 6, circuit 359 (R/BL). • Is the resistance less than 4 ohms? → **Yes** GO to **G2**. → **No** REPLACE the speed control actuator switch.
G2 CHECK SPEED CONTROL ACTUATOR CABLE/THROTTLE BODY LINKAGE	
1 	
2 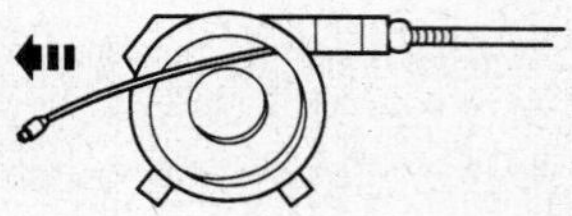	2 Remove the speed control actuator cable from the speed control servo. Visually inspect the core wire; check the speed control actuator cable by pulling on it and noting the throttle movement.

FM1109700446010X

Fig. 88 Test G: Off Switch Inoperative (Part 1 of 2). 2000 Escort & ZX2

Condition(s):

☐ The Speed Control Is Inoperative

Possible Source(s):
- Air bag sliding contact.
- Fuse.
- Circuitry.
- Brake pedal position (BPP) switch.
- Deactivator switch.
- Speed control actuator switch.
- Vehicle speed sensor (VSS).
- Speed control servo.

Action(s) to take:
- GO to «Pinpoint Test A».

☐ The Set Speed Fluctuates

Possible Source(s):
- Speed control servo.
- Circuitry.
- VSS.
- Base engine problem.
- Loose or binding speed control actuator cable between speed control servo and throttle body.

Action(s) to take:
- GO to «Pinpoint Test B».

☐ The Speed Control Does Not Disengage When the Brakes Are Applied

Possible Source(s):
- Deactivator switch.
- BPP switch.
- Circuitry.

Action(s) to take:
- GO to «Pinpoint Test C».

FM1100100702010X

Fig. 89 Speed control diagnostic symptom chart (Part 1 of 2). 2001–04 Escort & ZX2

- ☐ The Speed Control Does Not Disengage When the Clutch Is Applied

  Possible Source(s):
  - Clutch pedal position (CPP) switch.
  - Circuitry.

    Action(s) to take:
    - GO to «Pinpoint Test D».

- ☐ The COAST Switch Is Inoperative

  Possible Source(s):
  - Speed control actuator switch.
  - Speed control servo.

    Action(s) to take:
    - GO to «Pinpoint Test E».

- ☐ The SET/ACCL Switch Is Inoperative

  Possible Source(s):
  - Speed control actuator switch.
  - Speed control servo.

    Action(s) to take:
    - GO to «Pinpoint Test F».

- ☐ The RESUME Switch Is Inoperative

  Possible Source(s):
  - Speed control actuator switch.
  - Speed control servo.

    Action(s) to take:
    - GO to «Pinpoint Test G».

- ☐ The OFF Switch Is Inoperative

  Possible Source(s):
  - Speed control actuator switch.
  - Speed control servo.

    Action(s) to take:
    - GO to «Pinpoint Test H».

FM1100100702020X

Fig. 89 Speed control diagnostic symptom chart (Part 2 of 2). 2001–03 Escort & ZX2

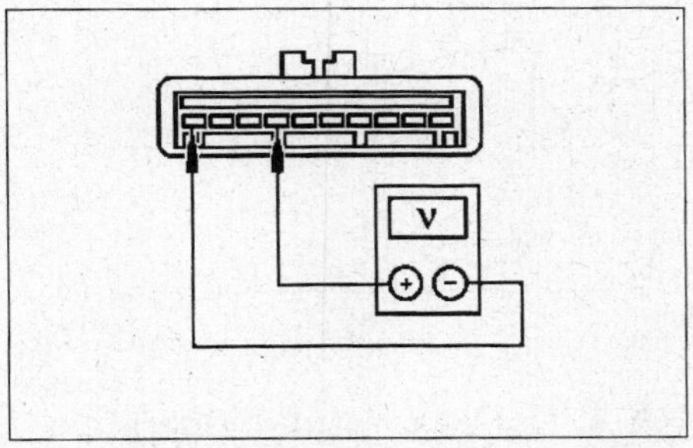

4

Measure the voltage between speed control servo C177-7, circuit 65 (Y), and speed control servo C177-10, circuit 57 (BL).

- **Is the voltage greater than 10 volts?**

→ **Yes**

Go to «A4».

→ **No**

Go to «A2».

FM1100100703020X

Fig. 90 Test A: Speed Control Inoperative (Part 2 of 27). 2001–04 Escort & ZX2

A1	CHECK POWER AND GROUND TO THE SPEED CONTROL SERVO

1

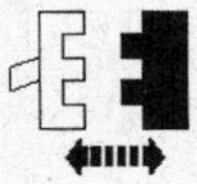

2 *Speed Control Servo C177*

3

FM1100100703010X

Fig. 90 Test A: Speed Control Inoperative (Part 1 of 27). 2001–04 Escort & ZX2

A2	CHECK THE FUSE

1

2 *Fuse Junction Panel ASC Fuse (10A)*

- **Is the fuse OK?**

→ **Yes**

Go to «A3».

→ **No**

REPLACE ASC Fuse (10A). TEST the system for normal operation. If the fuse fails again, CHECK for short to ground. REPAIR as necessary. TEST the system for normal operation.

FM1100100703030X

Fig. 90 Test A: Speed Control Inoperative (Part 3 of 27). 2001–04 Escort & ZX2

A3	CHECK THE SPEED CONTROL SERVO GROUND CIRCUIT

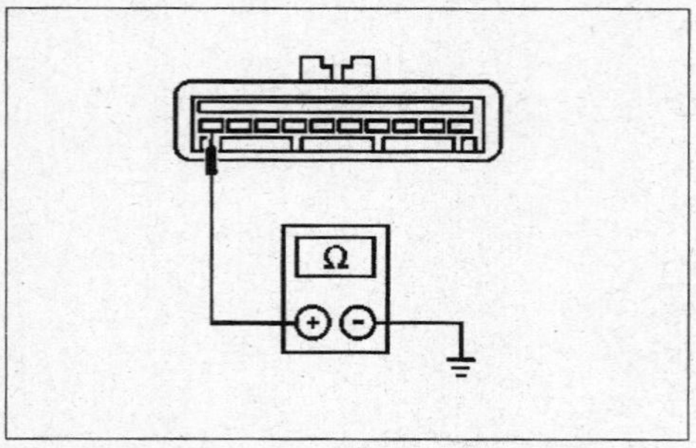

1

Measure the resistance between speed control servo C177-10, circuit 57 (BL), and ground.

- **Is the resistance less than 5 ohms?**

➔ **Yes**

REPAIR circuit 65 (Y). TEST the system for normal operation.

➔ **No**

REPAIR circuit 57 (BL). TEST the system for normal operation.

FM1100100703040X

Fig. 90 Test A: Speed Control Inoperative (Part 4 of 27). 2001–04 Escort & ZX2

A5	CHECK THE BRAKE CIRCUIT

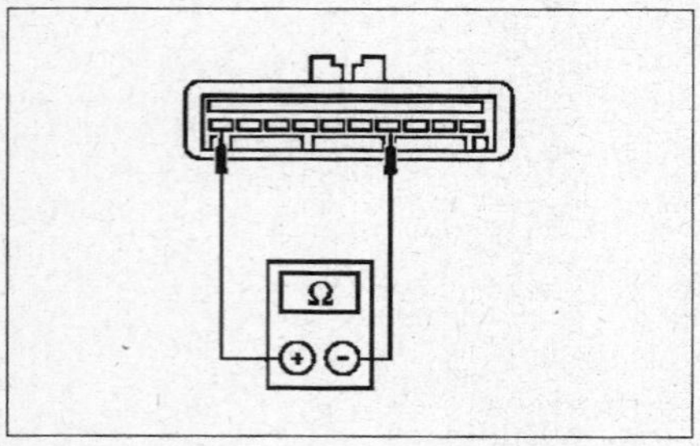

1

Measure the resistance between speed control servo C177-4, circuit 409 (GN), and speed control servo C177-10, circuit 57 (BL).

- **Is the resistance less than 20 ohms?**

➔ **Yes**

Go to «A8».

➔ **No**

If the vehicle is equipped with an automatic transmission, REPAIR circuit 409 (GN). TEST the system for normal operation. If the vehicle is equipped with a manual transmission, Go to «A6».

FM1100100703060X

Fig. 90 Test A: Speed Control Inoperative (Part 6 of 27). 2001–04 Escort & ZX2

A4	CHECK THE STOPLAMPS FOR PROPER OPERATION

1 Check the stoplamps for proper operation by depressing and releasing the brake pedal.

- **Do the stoplamps operate properly?**

➔ **Yes**

Go to «A5».

➔ **No**

Diagnose stop lamp fault.

FM1100100703050X

Fig. 90 Test A: Speed Control Inoperative (Part 5 of 27). 2001–04 Escort & ZX2

A6	CHECK THE CLUTCH PEDAL POSITION (CPP) SWITCH

1

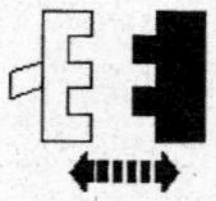

2

CPP Switch C292

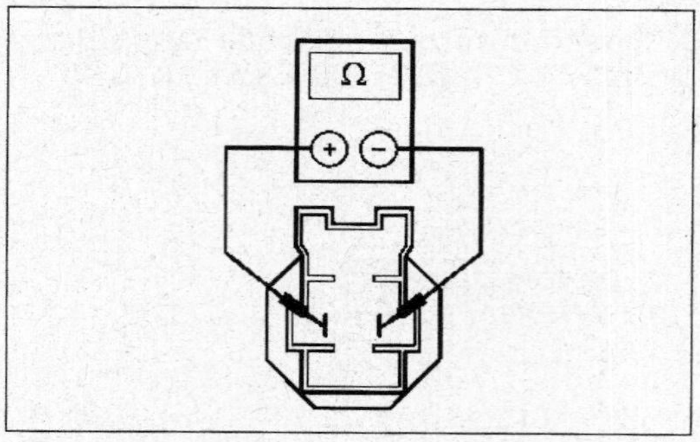

3

Measure the resistance between the CPP switch terminals (component side).

FM1100100703070X

Fig. 90 Test A: Speed Control Inoperative (Part 7 of 27). 2001–04 Escort & ZX2

- **Is the resistance less than 5 ohms?**

➔ **Yes**

Go to «A7».

➔ **No**

REPLACE the CPP switch. TEST the system for normal operation.

FM1100100703080X

Fig. 90 Test A: Speed Control Inoperative (Part 8 of 27). 2001–04 Escort & ZX2

A7 CHECK CIRCUIT 351 (GN) FOR AN OPEN

1

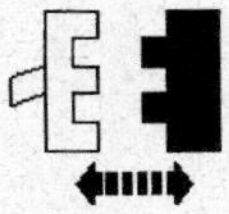

2 *CPP Switch C292*

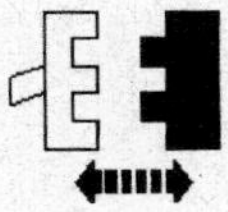

3 *BPP Switch C245*

FM1100100703090X

Fig. 90 Test A: Speed Control Inoperative (Part 9 of 27). 2001–04 Escort & ZX2

A8 CHECK THE DEACTIVATOR SWITCH INPUT TO THE SPEED CONTROL SERVO

1

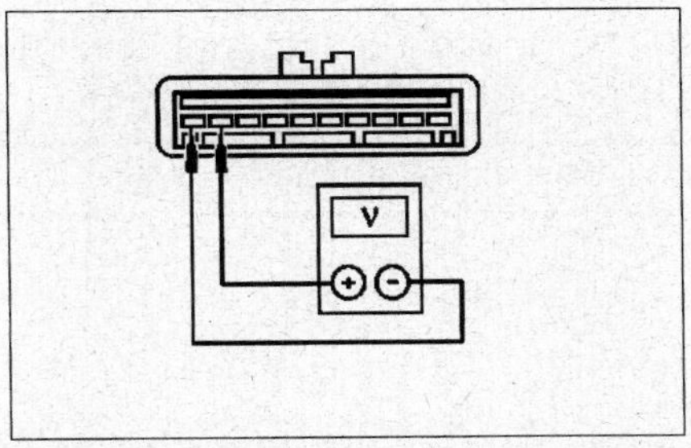

2

Measure voltage between speed control servo C177-9, circuit 355 (GN/Y), and speed control servo C177-10, circuit 57 (BL).

- **Is the voltage greater than 10 volts?**

→ **Yes**

Go to «A11».

→ **No**

Go to «A9 ».

FM1100100703110X

Fig. 90 Test A: Speed Control Inoperative (Part 11 of 27). 2001–04 Escort & ZX2

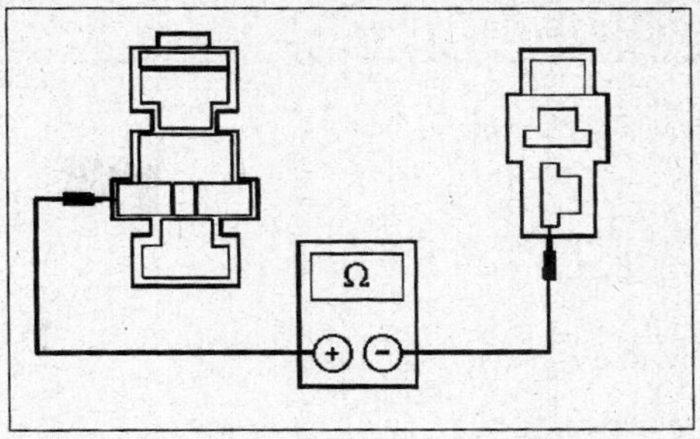

4

Measure the resistance between CPP switch C292-3, circuit 351 (GN), and brake pedal position (BPP) switch C245, circuit 351 (GN).

- **Is the resistance less than 5 ohms?**

→ **Yes**

REPAIR circuit 407 (W), circuit 408 (GN) or circuit 409 (GN). TEST the system for normal operation.

→ **No**

REPAIR circuit 351 (GN). TEST the system for normal operation.

FM1100100703100X

Fig. 90 Test A: Speed Control Inoperative (Part 10 of 27). 2001–04 Escort & ZX2

A9 CHECK THE DEACTIVATOR SWITCH

1

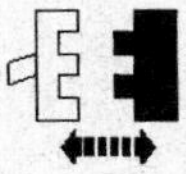

2 *Deactivator Switch C208*

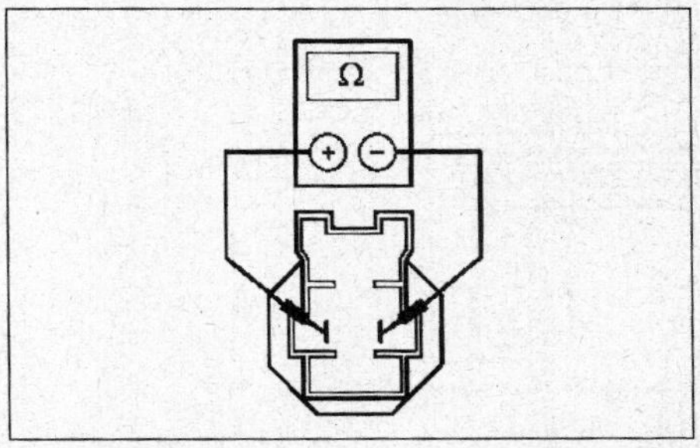

3

Measure the resistance between the deactivator switch terminals (component side).

FM1100100703120X

Fig. 90 Test A: Speed Control Inoperative (Part 12 of 27). 2001–04 Escort & ZX2

- **Is the resistance less than 5 ohms?**

→ **Yes**

Go to «A10».

→ **No**

REPLACE the deactivator switch, TEST the system for normal operation.

FM1100100703130X

Fig. 90 Test A: Speed Control Inoperative (Part 13 of 27). 2001–04 Escort & ZX2

A10 CHECK DEACTIVATOR SWITCH POWER

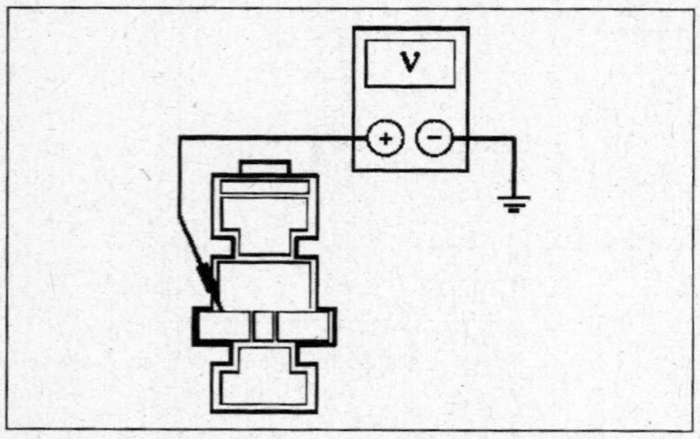

1

Measure the voltage between deactivator switch C208, circuit 350 (GN/W), and ground.

- **Is the voltage greater than 10 volts?**

➔ **Yes**

REPAIR circuit 355 (GN/Y). TEST the system for normal operation.

➔ **No**

REPAIR circuit 350 (GN/W). TEST the system for normal operation.

FM1100100703140X

Fig. 90 Test A: Speed Control Inoperative (Part 14 of 27). 2001–04 Escort & ZX2

A12 CHECK FOR STUCK SPEED CONTROL ACTUATOR SWITCH

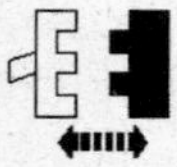

1 *Speed Control Actuator Switch C269*

2

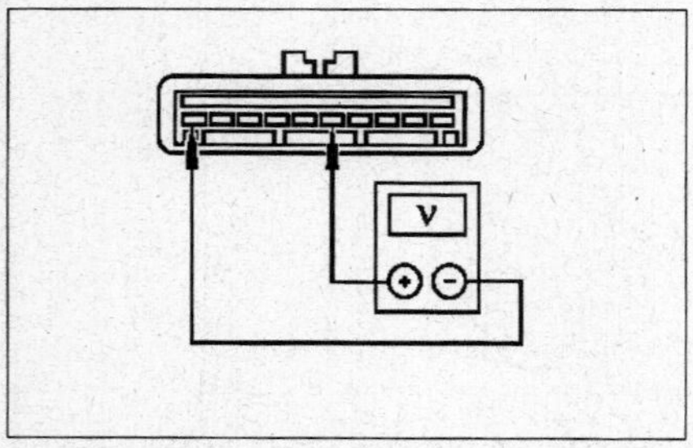

3

Measure the voltage between speed control servo C177-5, circuit 356 (R/Y), and speed control servo C177-10, circuit 57 (BL).

FM1100100703160X

Fig. 90 Test A: Speed Control Inoperative (Part 16 of 27). 2001–04 Escort & ZX2

A11 CHECK FOR SHORT TO POWER ON CIRCUIT 356 (R/Y)

1

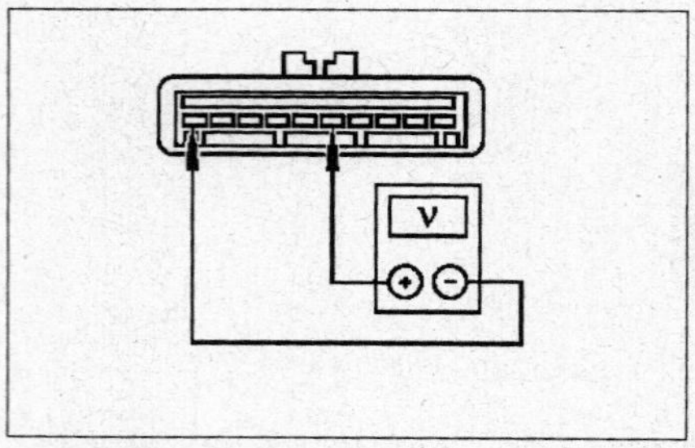

2

Measure the voltage between speed control servo C177-5, circuit 356 (R/Y), and speed control servo C177-10, circuit 57 (BL).

- **Is voltage present?**

➔ **Yes**

Go to «A12».

➔ **No**

Go to «A14».

FM1100100703150X

Fig. 90 Test A: Speed Control Inoperative (Part 15 of 27). 2001–04 Escort & ZX2

- **Is voltage present?**

➔ **Yes**

Go to «A13».

➔ **No**

REPLACE the speed control actuator switch. TEST the system for normal operation.

FM1100100703170X

Fig. 90 Test A: Speed Control Inoperative (Part 17 of 27). 2001–04 Escort & ZX2

A13 CHECK CIRCUIT 356 (R/Y) FOR SHORT TO POWER

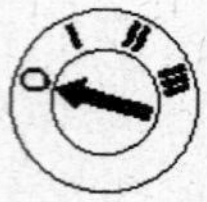

1

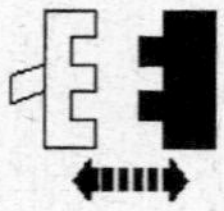

2 *Air Bag Sliding Contact C248*

3

FM1100100703180X

Fig. 90 Test A: Speed Control Inoperative (Part 18 of 27). 2001–04 Escort & ZX2

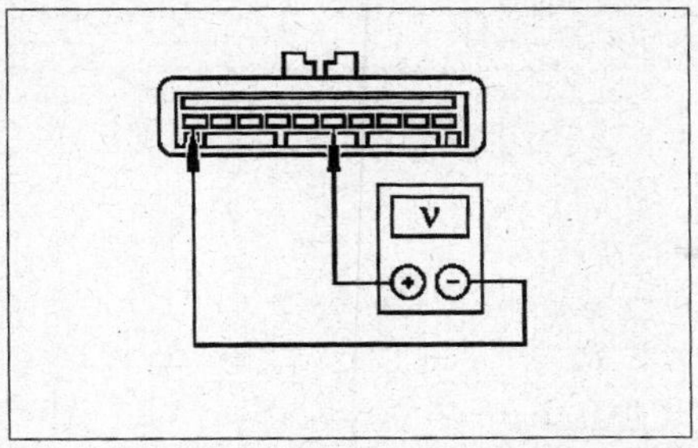

4

Measure the voltage between speed control servo C177-5, circuit 356 (R/Y), and speed control servo C177-10, circuit 57 (BL).

- **Is voltage present?**

➔ **Yes**

REPAIR circuit 356 (R/Y). TEST the system for normal operation.

➔ **No**

REPLACE the air bag sliding contact. TEST the system for normal operation.

FM1100100703190X

Fig. 90 Test A: Speed Control Inoperative (Part 19 of 27). 2001–04 Escort & ZX2

A14 CHECK THE SPEED CONTROL ACTUATOR SWITCH OPERATION

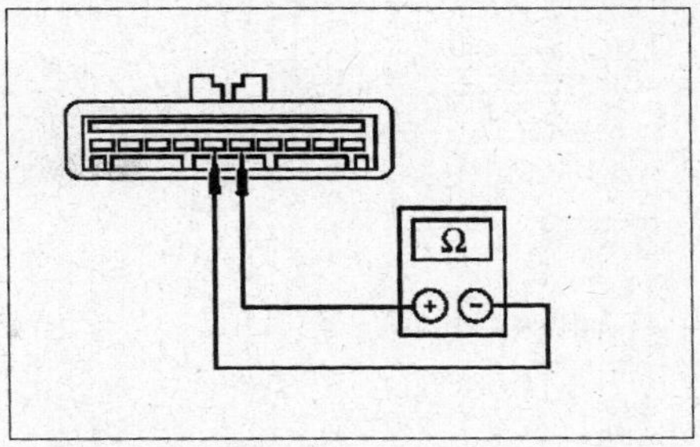

1

Measure the resistance between speed control servo C177-5, circuit 356 (R/Y), and speed control servo C177-6, circuit 359 (R/BL), while depressing speed control actuator switch SET/ACCEL.

- **Is the resistance between 640 and 720 ohms?**

➔ **Yes**

Go to «A15».

➔ **No**

Go to «A16».

FM1100100703200X

Fig. 90 Test A: Speed Control Inoperative (Part 20 of 27). 2001–04 Escort & ZX2

A15 CHECK THE SPEED CONTROL ACTUATOR SWITCH ON OPERATION

1

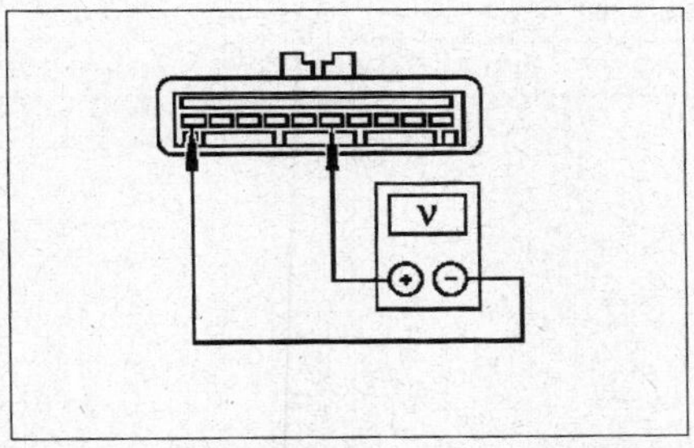

2

Measure the voltage between speed control servo C177-5, circuit 356 (R/Y), and speed control servo C177-10, circuit 57 (BL), while depressing the speed control actuator switch ON.

- **Is the voltage greater than 10 volts?**

➔ **Yes**

Go to «A19».

➔ **No**

Replace speed control actuator switch. Test system for normal operation.

FM1100100703210X

Fig. 90 Test A: Speed Control Inoperative (Part 21 of 27). 2001–04 Escort & ZX2

A16 CHECK CIRCUIT 356 (R/Y) FOR AN OPEN

1

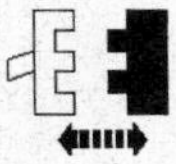

2 *Air Bag Sliding Contact C248*

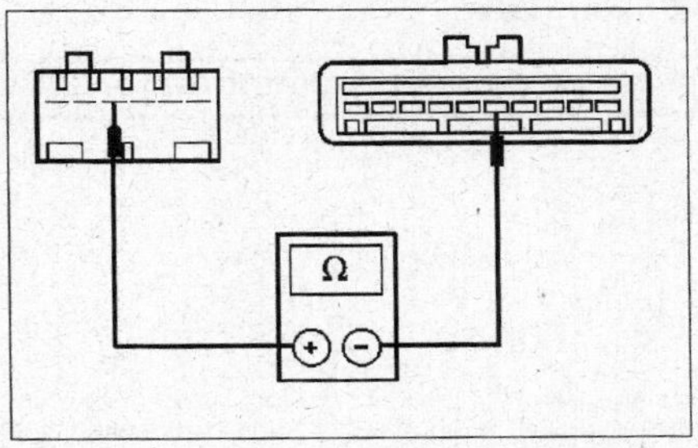

3

Measure the resistance between air bag sliding contact C248M, circuit 356 (R/Y), and speed control servo C177-5, circuit 356 (R/Y).

FM1100100703220X

Fig. 90 Test A: Speed Control Inoperative (Part 22 of 27). 2001–04 Escort & ZX2

- **Is the resistance less than 5 ohms?**

➔ **Yes**

Go to «A17».

➔ **No**

REPAIR circuit 356 (R/Y). TEST the system for normal operation.

FM1100100703230X

Fig. 90 Test A: Speed Control Inoperative (Part 23 of 27). 2001–04 Escort & ZX2

A17 CHECK CIRCUIT 359 (R/BL) FOR AN OPEN

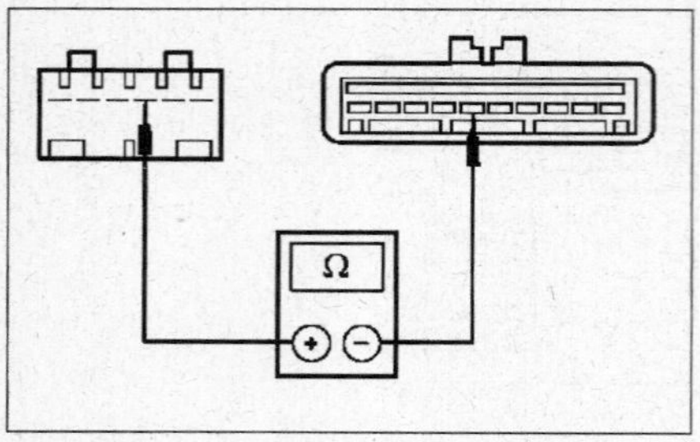

1

Measure the resistance between air bag sliding contact C248M, circuit 359 (R/BL), and speed control servo C177-6, circuit 359 (R/BL).

- **Is the resistance less than 5 ohms?**

➔ **Yes**

Go to «A18».

➔ **No**

REPAIR circuit 359 (R/BL). TEST the system for normal operation.

FM1100100703240X

Fig. 90 Test A: Speed Control Inoperative (Part 24 of 27). 2001–04 Escort & ZX2

A19 CHECK THE SPEEDOMETER OPERATION

1 Drive the vehicle and observe the speedometer operation.

- **Does the speedometer operate properly?**

➔ **Yes**

Go to «A20».

➔ **No**

Diagnose speedometer fault condition.

FM1100100703260X

Fig. 90 Test A: Speed Control Inoperative (Part 26 of 27). 2001–04 Escort & ZX2

B1 CHECK THE SPEED CONTROL ACTUATOR CABLE/THROTTLE BODY LINKAGE

1

2 Remove the speed control actuator cable from the speed control servo. Visually inspect the core wire and check the speed control actuator cable by pulling on it and noting the throttle movement.

- **Is the speed control actuator cable and throttle body linkage OK?**

➔ **Yes**

Go to «B2».

➔ **No**

REPLACE the speed control actuator cable or REPAIR the throttle body linkage. TEST the system for normal operation.

FM1100100704010X

Fig. 91 Test B: Set Speed Fluctuates (Part 1 of 2). 2001–04 Escort & ZX2

A18 CHECK THE AIR BAG SLIDING CONTACT

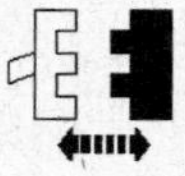

1 *Speed Control Actuator Switch C269*

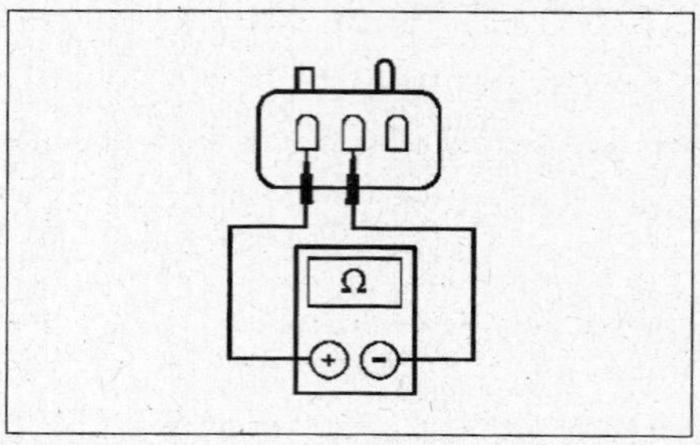

2

Measure the resistance between speed control actuator switch C269-1, and speed control actuator switch C269-2, while depressing speed control actuator switch SET/ACCEL.

- **Is the resistance between 640 and 720 ohms with the speed control actuator switch SET/ACCEL depressed?**

➔ **Yes**

REPLACE the air bag sliding contact, TEST the system for normal operation.

➔ **No**

REPLACE the speed control actuator switch TEST the system for normal operation.

FM1100100703250X

Fig. 90 Test A: Speed Control Inoperative (Part 25 of 27). 2001–04 Escort & ZX2

A20 CHECK THE SPEED CONTROL ACTUATOR CABLE/THROTTLE BODY LINKAGE

1

2 Remove the speed control actuator cable from the speed control servo. Visually inspect the core wire and check the speed control actuator cable by pulling on it and noting the throttle movement.

- **Is the speed control actuator cable and throttle body linkage OK?**

➔ **Yes**

REPLACE the speed control servo. TEST the system for normal operation.

➔ **No**

REPLACE the speed control actuator cable or REPAIR the throttle body linkage. TEST the system for normal operation.

FM1100100703270X

Fig. 90 Test A: Speed Control Inoperative (Part 27 of 27). 2001–04 Escort & ZX2

B2 CHECK THE SPEEDOMETER OPERATION

1 Drive the vehicle and observe the speedometer operation.

- **Does the speedometer needle fluctuate?**

➔ **Yes**

Diagnose speedometer fault condition.

➔ **No**

REPLACE the speed control servo. TEST the system for normal operation.

FM1100100704020X

Fig. 91 Test B: Set Speed Fluctuates (Part 2 of 2). 2001–04 Escort & ZX2

C1	CHECK THE STOPLAMPS FOR PROPER OPERATION

1 Check the stoplamps for proper operation by depressing and releasing the brake pedal.

- **Do the stoplamps operate properly?**

➔ **Yes**

Go to «C2».

➔ **No**

Diagnose stop lamp fault condition.

FM1100100705010X

Fig. 92 Test C: Speed Control Does Not Disengage When Brakes Are Applied (Part 1 of 6). 2001–04 Escort & ZX2

C3	CHECK THE CLUTCH PEDAL POSITION (CPP) SWITCH

1

2 *CPP Switch C292*

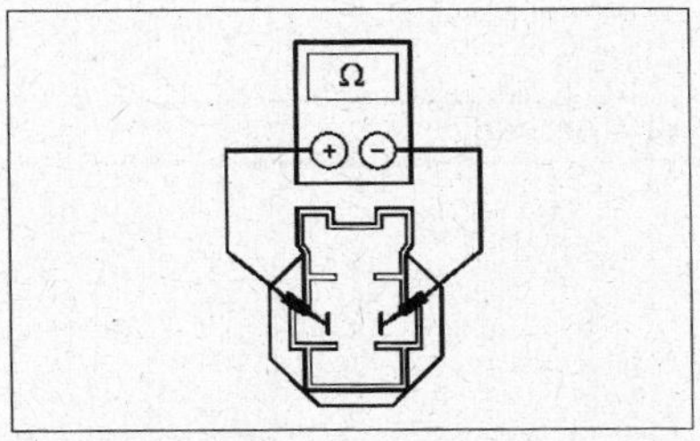

3

Measure the resistance between the CPP switch terminal 3, and terminal 4 (component side).

FM1100100705030X

Fig. 92 Test C: Speed Control Does Not Disengage When Brakes Are Applied (Part 3 of 6). 2001–04 Escort & ZX2

C4	CHECK CIRCUIT 351 (GN) FOR AN OPEN

1

2 *BPP Switch C245*

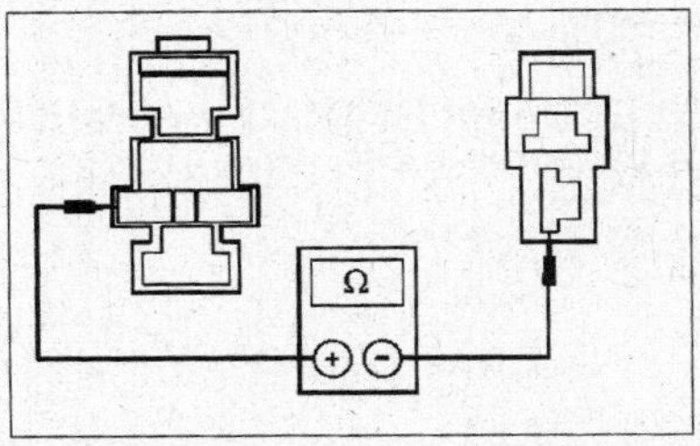

3

Measure the resistance between CPP switch C292-3, circuit 351 (GN), and BPP switch C245, circuit 351 (GN).

FM1100100705050X

Fig. 92 Test C: Speed Control Does Not Disengage When Brakes Are Applied (Part 5 of 6). 2001–04 Escort & ZX2

C2	CHECK THE BRAKE CIRCUIT

1 *Speed Control Servo C177*

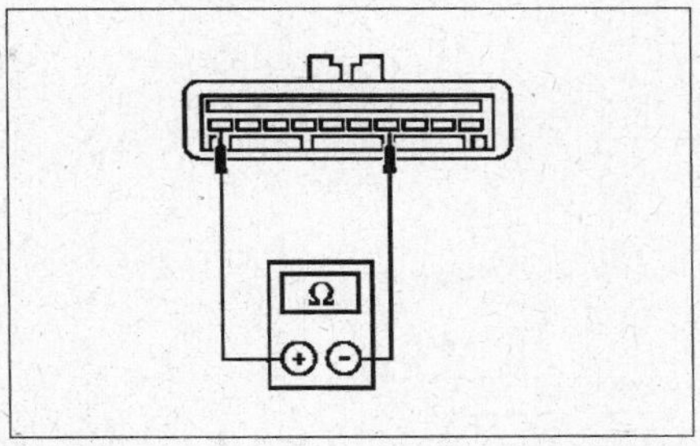

2

Measure the resistance between speed control servo C177-4, circuit 409(GN), and speed control servo C177-10, circuit 57 (BL).

- **Is the resistance less than 20 ohms?**

➔ **Yes**

REPLACE the speed control servo. TEST the system for normal operation.

➔ **No**

If the vehicle is equipped with an automatic transmission, REPAIR circuit 409 (GN). TEST the system for normal operation. If the vehicle is equipped with a manual transmission, Go to «C3».

FM1100100705020X

Fig. 92 Test C: Speed Control Does Not Disengage When Brakes Are Applied (Part 2 of 6). 2001–04 Escort & ZX2

- **Is the resistance less than 5 ohms?**

➔ **Yes**

Go to «C4».

➔ **No**

REPLACE the CPP switch. TEST the system for normal operation.

FM1100100705040X

Fig. 92 Test C: Speed Control Does Not Disengage When Brakes Are Applied (Part 4 of 6). 2001–04 Escort & ZX2

- **Is the resistance less than 5 ohms?**

➔ **Yes**

REPAIR circuit 407 (W), circuit 408 (GN) or circuit 409 (GN). TEST the system for normal operation.

➔ **No**

REPAIR circuit 351 (GN). TEST the system for normal operation.

FM1100100705060X

Fig. 92 Test C: Speed Control Does Not Disengage When Brakes Are Applied (Part 6 of 6). 2001–04 Escort & ZX2

D1 CHECK THE CLUTCH PEDAL POSITION (CPP) SWITCH

1

2 *CPP Switch C292*

3 Depress the clutch pedal and hold.

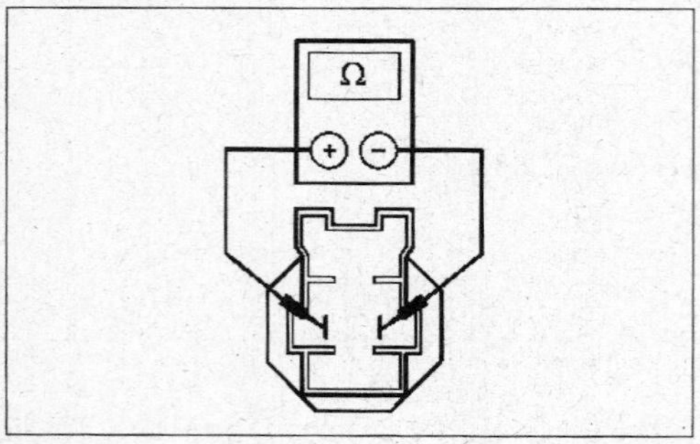

4

FM1100100706010X

Fig. 93 Test D: Speed Control Does Not Disengage When Clutch Is Applied (Part 1 of 4). 2001–04 Escort & ZX2

D2 CHECK CIRCUIT 409 (GN), CIRCUIT 408 (GN), AND CIRCUIT 407 (GN) FOR SHORT TO GROUND

1

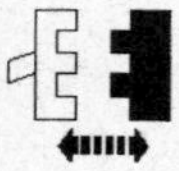

2 *Speed Control Servo C177*

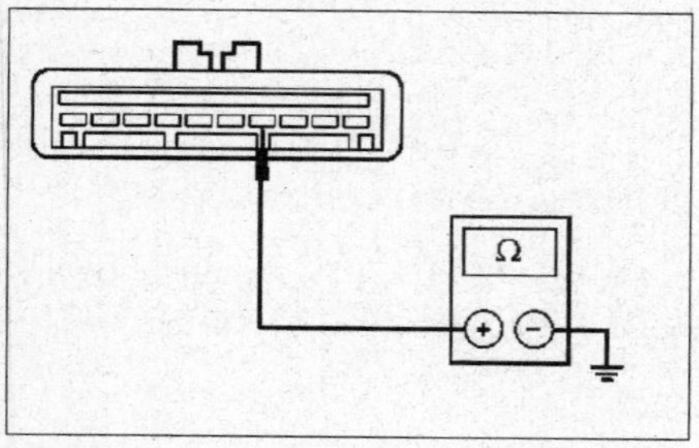

3

FM1100100706030X

Fig. 93 Test D: Speed Control Does Not Disengage When Clutch Is Applied (Part 3 of 4). 2001–04 Escort & ZX2

Measure the resistance between the clutch pedal position (CPP) switch terminal 3, and CPP switch terminal 4 (component side).

- **Is the resistance greater than 10,000 ohms?**

→ **Yes**

Go to «D2».

→ **No**

REPLACE the CPP switch. TEST the system for normal operation.

FM1100100706020X

Fig. 93 Test D: Speed Control Does Not Disengage When Clutch Is Applied (Part 2 of 4). 2001–04 Escort & ZX2

Measure the resistance between speed control servo C177-4, circuit 409 (GN), and ground, while the clutch pedal is depressed.

- **Is the resistance greater than 10,000 ohms?**

→ **Yes**

REPLACE the speed control servo. TEST the system for normal operation.

→ **No**

REPAIR circuit 409 (GN), circuit 408 (GN), or circuit 407 (GN). TEST the system for normal operation.

FM1100100706040X

Fig. 93 Test D: Speed Control Does Not Disengage When Clutch Is Applied (Part 4 of 4). 2001–04 Escort & ZX2

E1 CHECK COAST SWITCH OPERATION

1

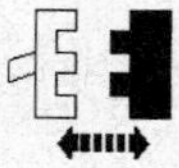

2 *Speed Control Servo C177*

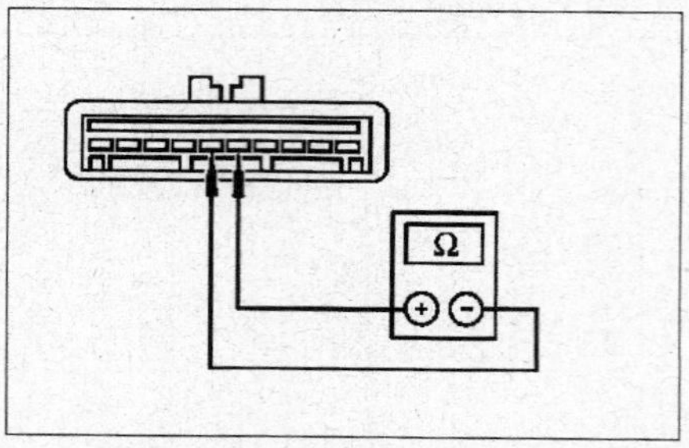

3

With the speed control actuator switch COAST depressed, measure the resistance between speed control servo C177-5, circuit 356 (R/Y), and speed control servo C177-6, circuit 359 (R/BL).

FM1100100707010X

Fig. 94 Test E: Coast Switch Inoperative (Part 1 of 2). 2001–04 Escort & ZX2

- **Is the resistance between 114 and 126 ohms?**

➔ **Yes**

REPLACE the speed control servo.
TEST the system for normal operation.

➔ **No**

REPLACE the speed control actuator switch.
TEST the system for normal operation.

FM1100100707020X

Fig. 94 Test E: Coast Switch Inoperative (Part 2 of 2). 2001–04 Escort & ZX2

- **Is the resistance between 646 and 714 ohms?**

➔ **Yes**

REPLACE the speed control servo.
TEST the system for normal operation.

➔ **No**

REPLACE the speed control actuator switch.
TEST the system for normal operation.

FM1100100708020X

Fig. 95 Test F: SET/ACCEL Switch Inoperative (Part 2 of 2). 2001–04 Escort & ZX2

G1 CHECK RESUME SWITCH OPERATION

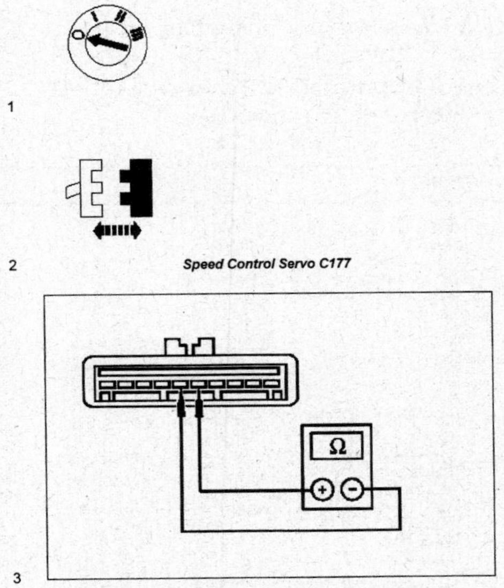

With the speed control actuator switch RESUME depressed, measure the resistance between speed control servo C177-5, circuit 356 (R/Y), and speed control servo C177-6, circuit 359 (R/BL).

FM1100100709010X

Fig. 96 Test G: Resume Switch Inoperative (Part 1 of 2). 2001–04 Escort & ZX2

F1 CHECK SET/ACCEL SWITCH OPERATION

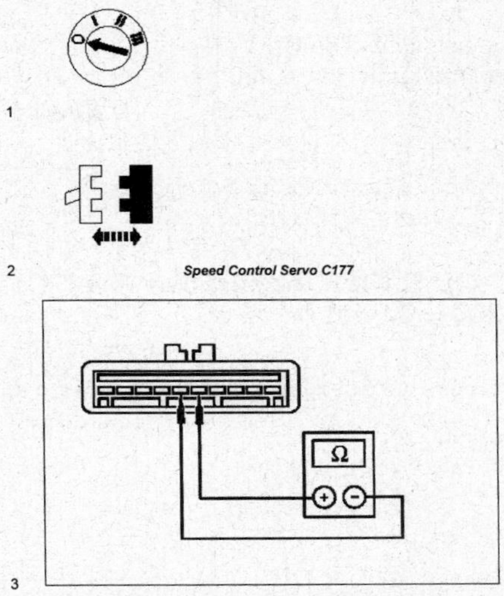

With the speed control actuator switch SET/ACCEL depressed, measure the resistance between speed control servo C177-5, circuit 356 (R/Y), and speed control servo C177-6, circuit 359 (R/BL).

FM1100100708010X

Fig. 95 Test F: SET/ACCEL Switch Inoperative (Part 1 of 2). 2001–04 Escort & ZX2

- **Is the resistance between 2090 and 2310 ohms?**

➔ **Yes**

REPLACE the speed control servo.
TEST the system for normal operation.

➔ **No**

REPLACE the speed control actuator switch.
TEST the system for normal operation.

FM1100100709020X

Fig. 96 Test G: Resume Switch Inoperative (Part 2 of 2). 2001–04 Escort & ZX2

H1 CHECK OFF SWITCH OPERATION

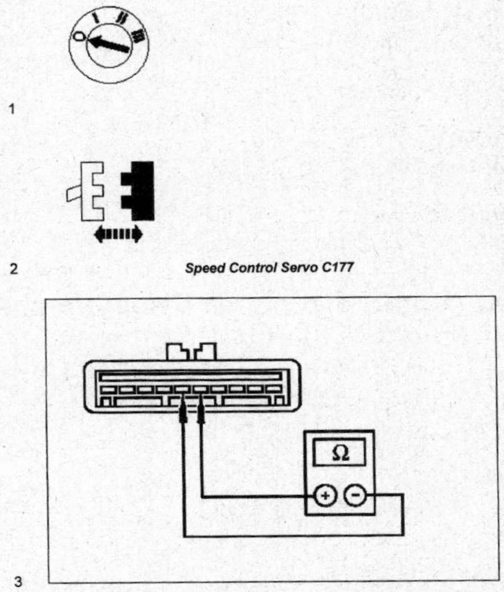

With the speed control actuator switch OFF depressed, measure the resistance between speed control servo C177-5, circuit 356 (R/Y), and speed control servo C177-6, circuit 359 (R/BL).

FM1100100710010X

Fig. 97 Test H: Off Switch Inoperative (Part 1 of 2). 2001–04 Escort & ZX2

- **Is the resistance less than 5 ohms?**

➔ **Yes**

REPLACE the speed control servo.
TEST the system for normal operation.

➔ **No**

REPLACE the speed control actuator switch.
TEST the system for normal operation.

FM1100100710020X

Fig. 97 Test H: Off Switch Inoperative (Part 2 of 2). 2001–04 Escort & ZX2

☐ The speed control does not disengage when the brakes are applied

Possible Source(s):
- Brake Pedal Position (BPP) switch.
- Circuit.

Action(s) to take:
- GO to «Pinpoint Test B».

☐ The - (COAST) switch is inoperative

Possible Source(s):
- - (COAST) switch.
- Circuit.

Action(s) to take:
- Go to «Pinpoint Test C».

☐ The = (RESUME) switch is inoperative

Possible Source(s):
- = (RESUME) switch.
- Circuit.

Action(s) to take:
- GO to «Pinpoint Test D».

☐ The speed control does not disengage when the clutch is applied

Possible Source(s):
- Clutch pedal position (CPP) switch.
- Circuit.

Action(s) to take:
- GO to «Pinpoint Test E».

☐ The OFF switch is inoperative

Possible Source(s):
- Speed control switch.

Action(s) to take:
- INSTALL a new speed control switch.

FM1100100765020X

Fig. 98 Speed control diagnostic symptom chart (Part 2 of 2). Focus

Symptom Chart

Condition(s):

☐ The speed control is inoperative

Possible Source(s):
- Circuit(s).
- Brake pedal position (BPP) switch.
- Clutch pedal position (CPP) switch.
- Stop lamp switch.
- Speed control switches.
- Speed control actuator.
- Fuse(s).

Action(s) to take:
- GO to «Pinpoint Test A».

FM1100100765010X

Fig. 98 Speed control diagnostic symptom chart (Part 1 of 2). Focus

A1	**CHECK OPERATION OF THE HORN**

1 Press the horn switch.

- **Does the horn sound?**

➔ **Yes**

Go to «A2».

➔ **No**

DIAGNOSE the air-bag sliding contact.

FM1100100766010X

Fig. 99 Test A: Speed Control Inoperative (Part 1 of 16). Focus

A2	**CHECK ON SWITCH OPERATION**

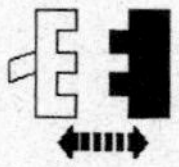

1 *Speed Control Actuator C831*

2 Remove fuse 53 (10A).

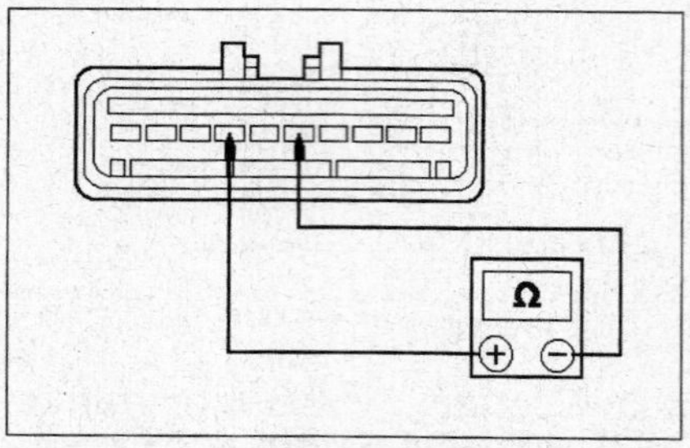

3

Measure the resistance between the speed control actuator C831 pin 5, circuit 8-PG13 (WH), harness side and speed control actuator C831 pin 7, circuit 15-PG12 (GN/WH), harness side, while pressing the ON switch.

- **Is the resistance between 810 and 840 ohms?**

➔ **Yes**

Install fuse 53 (10A). Go to «A3».

➔ **No**

Install fuse 53 (10A). Go to «A5».

FM1100100766020X

Fig. 99 Test A: Speed Control Inoperative (Part 2 of 16). Focus

A3 CHECK SWITCH INPUT TO SPEED CONTROL ACTUATOR

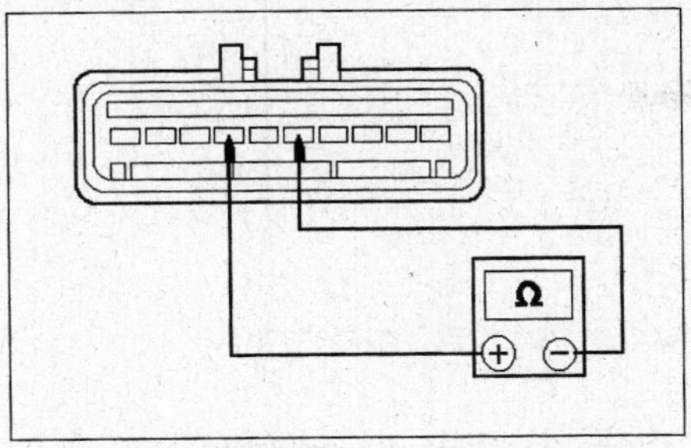

1

Measure the resistance between the speed control actuator C831 pin 5, circuit 8-PG13 (WH), harness side and the speed control actuator C831 pin 6, circuit 9-PG13 (BN), harness side while pressing the OFF switch.

- **Is the resistance less than 5 ohms?**

➔ **Yes**

Go to «A6».

➔ **No**

Go to «A4».

FM1100100766030X

Fig. 99 Test A: Speed Control Inoperative (Part 3 of 16). Focus

A5 CHECK CONTINUITY OF AIR-BAG SLIDING CONTACT

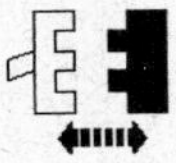

1 *Speed Control Switch C921*

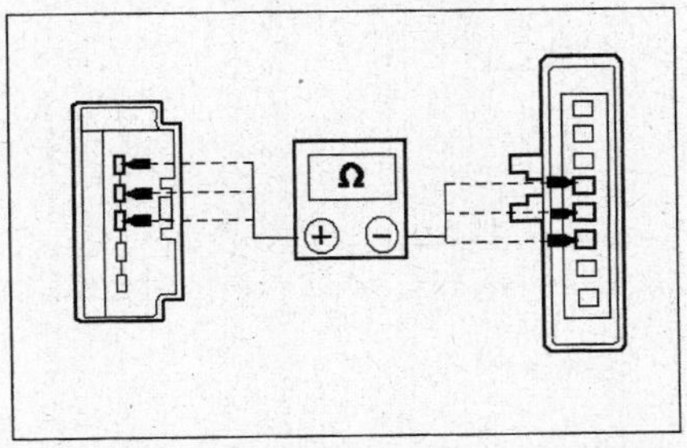

2

Measure the resistance between the air-bag sliding contact C896 pin 4 (WH), component side, and the air-bag sliding contact C921 pin 3 component side, and between the air-bag sliding contact C896 pin 5 (BN), component side, and the air-bag sliding contact C921 pin 2 component side, and between the air-bag sliding contact C896 pin 6 (GN/YE), component side, and the air-bag sliding contact C921 pin 1 component side.

- **Is the resistance less than 5 ohms?**

➔ **Yes**

INSTALL a new speed control switch. TEST the system for normal operation.

➔ **No**

INSTALL a new air-bag sliding contact. TEST the system for normal operation.

FM1100100766050X

Fig. 99 Test A: Speed Control Inoperative (Part 5 of 16). Focus

A4 CHECK CIRCUIT 8-PG13 (WH) FOR OPEN

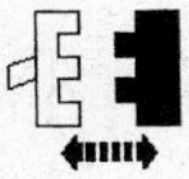

1 *Air-bag Sliding Contact C896*

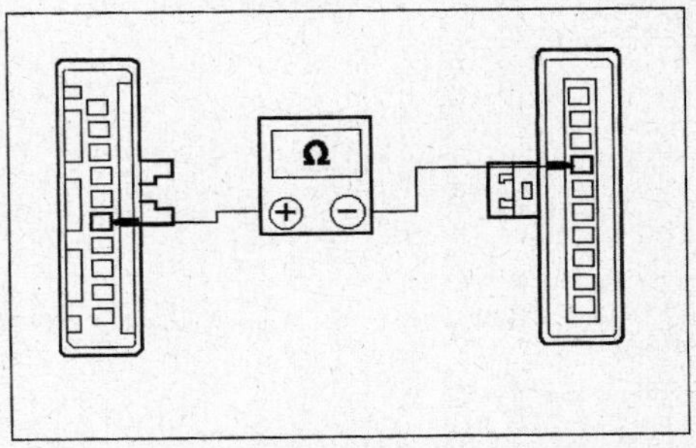

2

Measure the resistance between the speed control actuator C831 pin 5, circuit 8-PG13 (WH), harness side and the air-bag sliding contact C896 pin 4, circuit 8-PG13 (WH), harness side.

- **Is the resistance less than 5 ohms?**

➔ **Yes**

Go to «A5».

➔ **No**

REPAIR circuit 8-PG13 (WH). TEST the system for normal operation.

FM1100100766040X

Fig. 99 Test A: Speed Control Inoperative (Part 4 of 16). Focus

A6 CHECK CIRCUIT 91-PG12 (BK/WH) FOR OPEN

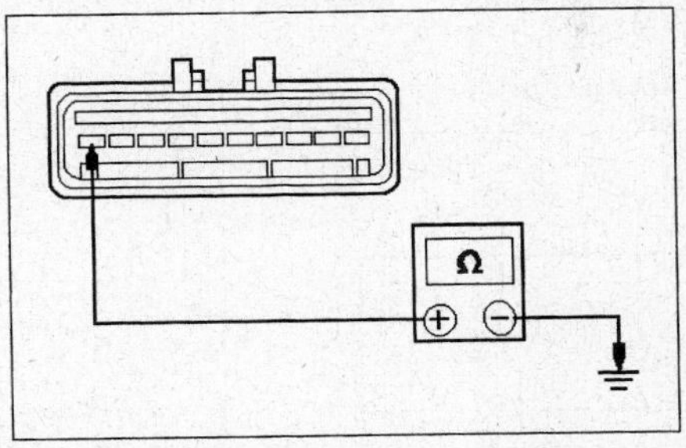

1

Measure the resistance between the speed control actuator C831 pin 10, circuit 91-PG12 (BK/WH), harness side and ground.

- **Is the resistance less than 5 ohms?**

➔ **Yes**

Go to «A7».

➔ **No**

REPAIR circuit 91-PG12 (BK/WH). TEST the system for normal operation.

FM1100100766060X

Fig. 99 Test A: Speed Control Inoperative (Part 6 of 16). Focus

A7 CHECK CIRCUIT 15-PG12 (GN/WH) FOR VOLTAGE

1

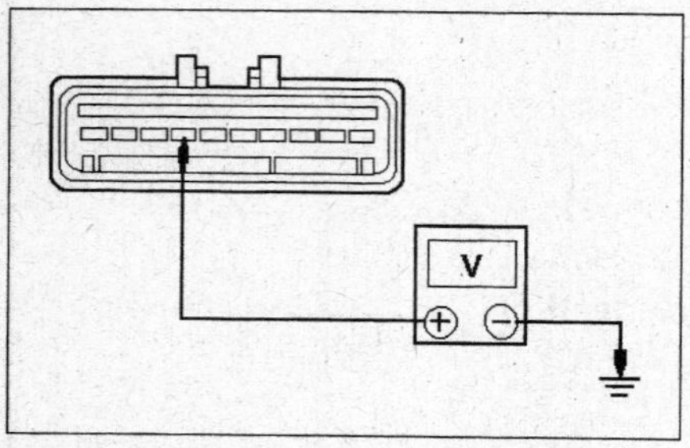

2

Measure the voltage between the speed control actuator C831 pin 7, circuit 15-PG12 (GN/WH), harness side and ground.

- **Is the voltage greater than 10 volts?**

→ **Yes**

Go to «A8».

→ **No**

CHECK fuse 53 (10A). If blown INSTALL a new fuse. TEST the system for normal operation, if the fuse blows again then check for short to ground. If the fuse is OK then REPAIR circuit 15-PG12 (GN/WH). TEST the system for normal operation.

FM1100100766070X

Fig. 99 Test A: Speed Control Inoperative (Part 7 of 16). Focus

A9 CHECK BRAKE PEDAL POSITION (BPP) SWITCH

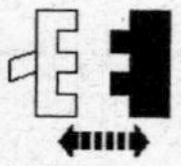

1 *BPP Switch C824*

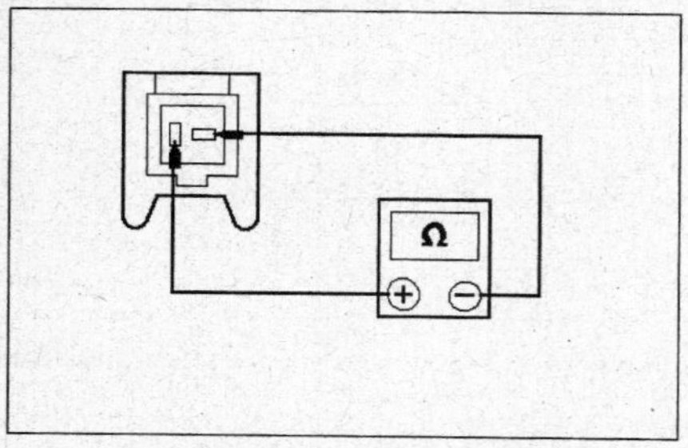

2

Measure the resistance between the BPP switch C824 pin 1 and pin 2, component side, with the switch plunger pressed and also with the plunger released.

- **Are the resistances greater than 10,000 ohms with the plunger pressed in and less than 5 ohms with the plunger released?**

→ **Yes**

Go to «A10».

→ **No**

Install new BPP switch. Test system for normal operation.

FM1100100766090X

Fig. 99 Test A: Speed Control Inoperative (Part 9 of 16). Focus

A8 CHECK BRAKE PEDAL POSITION (BPP) SWITCH INPUT

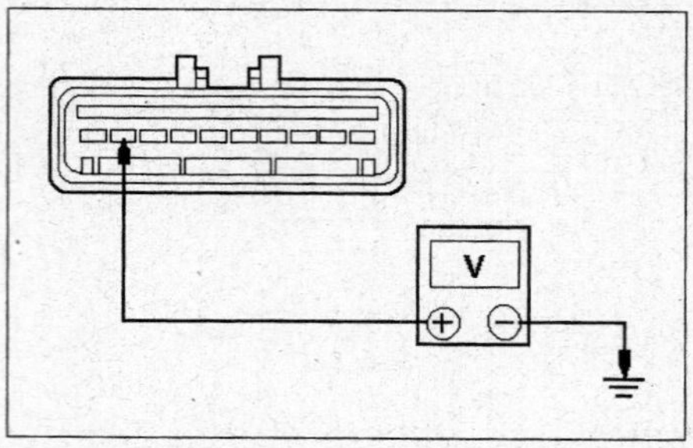

1

Measure the voltage between the speed control actuator C831 pin 9, circuit 15S-PG16 (GN/YE), harness side and ground.

- **Is the voltage greater than 10 volts?**

→ **Yes**

Go to «A12».

→ **No**

Go to «A9».

FM1100100766080X

Fig. 99 Test A: Speed Control Inoperative (Part 8 of 16). Focus

A10 CHECK CIRCUIT 15-PG6 (GN/YE) FOR VOLTAGE

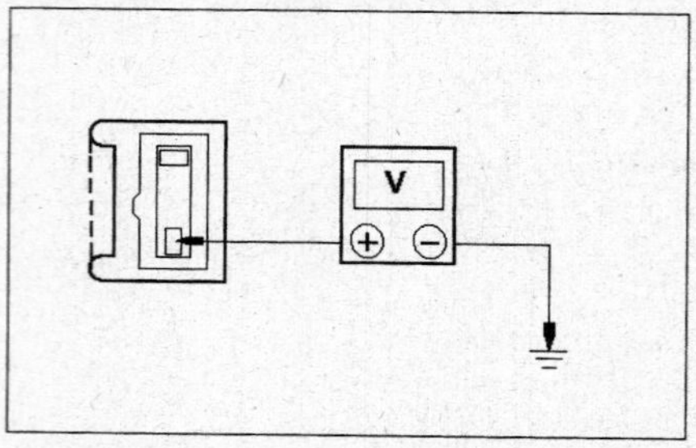

1

Measure the voltage between the BPP switch C824 pin 2, circuit 15-PG6 (GN/YE), harness side and ground.

- **Is the voltage greater than 10 volts?**

→ **Yes**

Go to «A11».

→ **No**

CHECK fuse 54 (15A). If blown INSTALL a new fuse. TEST the system for normal operation, if the fuse blows again then check for short to ground. If the fuse is OK then REPAIR circuit 15-PG6 (GN/YE). TEST the system for normal operation.

FM1100100766100X

Fig. 99 Test A: Speed Control Inoperative (Part 10 of 16). Focus

A11 CHECK CIRCUIT 15S-PG16 (GN/YE) FOR OPEN

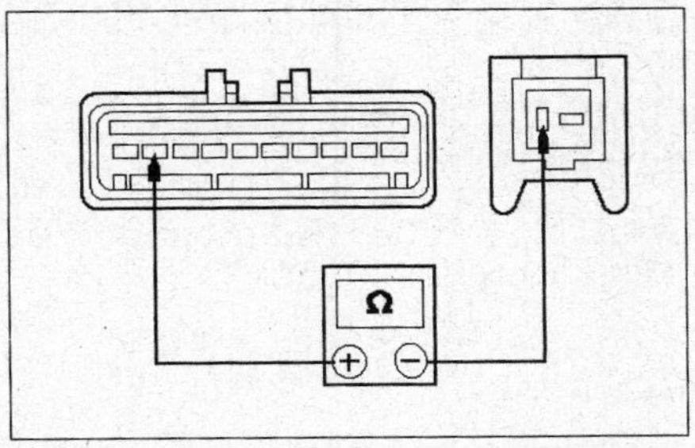

1

Measure the resistance between the speed control actuator C831 pin 9, circuit 15S-PG16 (GN/YE), harness side and the BPP switch C824 pin 1, circuit 15S-PG16 (GN/YE) harness side.

- **Is the resistance less than 5 ohms?**

➔ **Yes**

ADJUST the BPP switch. TEST the system for normal operation.

➔ **No**

REPAIR circuit 15S-PG16 (GN/YE). TEST the system for normal operation.

FM1100100766110X

Fig. 99 Test A: Speed Control Inoperative (Part 11 of 16). Focus

A12 CHECK STOP LAMP SWITCH SIGNAL TO ACTUATOR

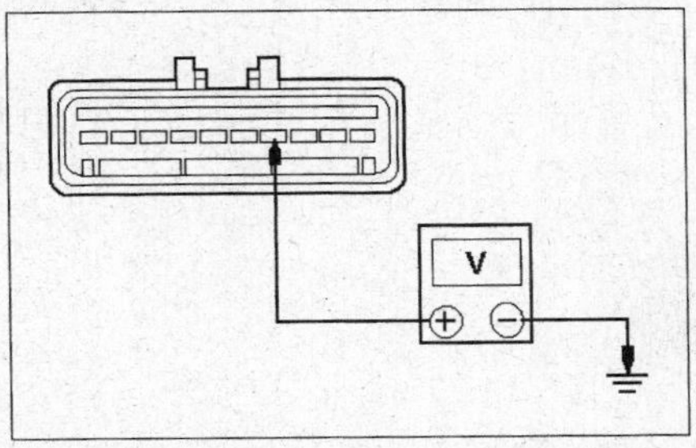

1

Measure the voltage between the speed control actuator C831 pin 4, circuit 15S-PG17 (GN/BU), harness side and ground while the brake pedal is depressed.

- **Is the voltage greater than 10 volts ?**

➔ **Yes**

Go to «A15».

➔ **No**

Vehicles with manual transaxle. Go to «A13».If the stop lamps operate correctly, REPAIR circuit 15S-PG17 (GN/BU). TEST the system for normal operation.

IF the stop lamps do not operate correctly, diagnose and repair as required.

FM1100100766120X

Fig. 99 Test A: Speed Control Inoperative (Part 12 of 16). Focus

A13 CHECK POWER TO CLUTCH PEDAL POSITION (CPP) SWITCH

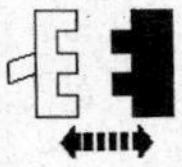

1

CPP Switch C825

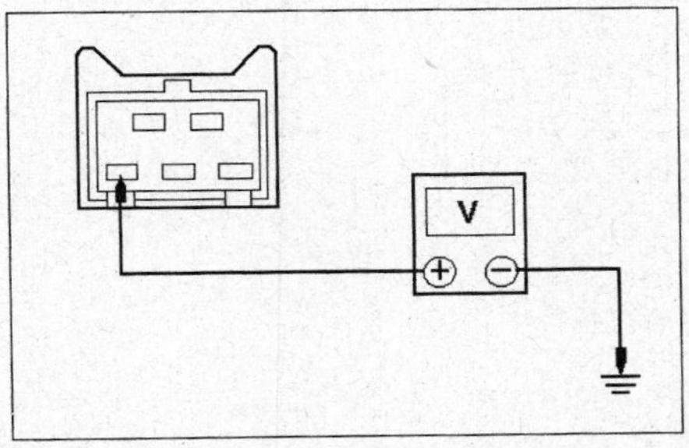

2

Measure the voltage between the CPP switch C825 pin 3, circuit 15S-PG7 (GN/BU), harness side and ground, while depressing the clutch pedal.

- **Is the voltage greater than 10 volts?**

➔ **Yes**

Go to «A14».

➔ **No**

Repair circuit 15S-PG7 (GN/BU). Test system for normal operation.

FM1100100766130X

Fig. 99 Test A: Speed Control Inoperative (Part 13 of 16). Focus

A14 CHECK CLUTCH PEDAL POSITION (CPP) SWITCH

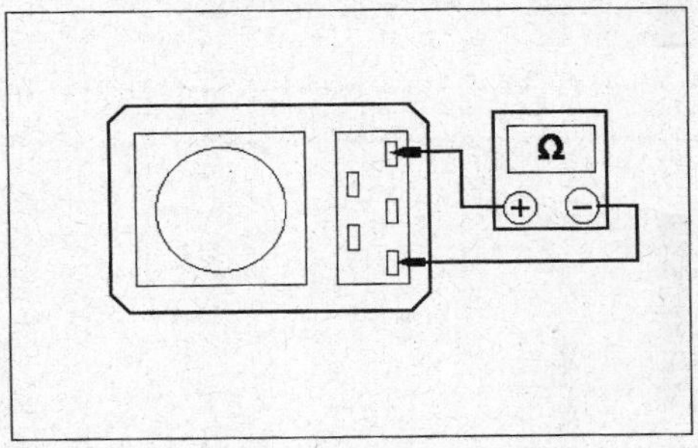

1

Measure the resistance between the CPP switch C825 pin 1 and pin 3, component side.

- **Is the resistance less than 5 ohms?**

➔ **Yes**

REPAIR circuit 15S-PG17 (GN/BU). TEST the system for normal operation.

➔ **No**

ADJUST or INSTALL a new CPP switch. TEST the system for normal operation.

FM1100100766140X

Fig. 99 Test A: Speed Control Inoperative (Part 14 of 16). Focus

A15 CHECK VEHICLE SPEED SENSOR (VSS) SIGNAL FOR ACTUATOR

1 *Instrument Cluster C809*

2 *Powertrain Control Module (PCM) C415*

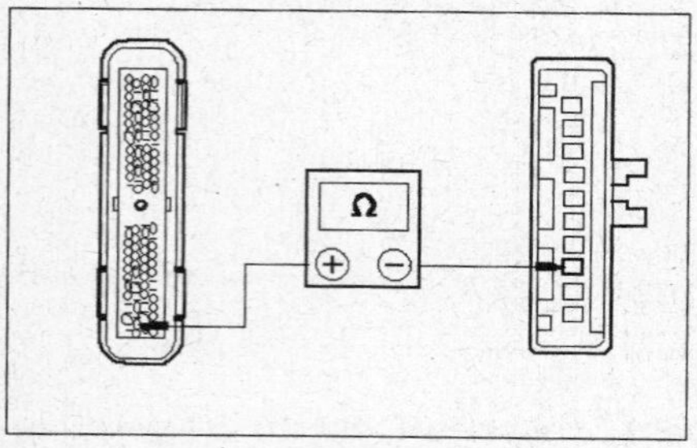

3

Measure the resistance between the PCM C415 pin 28 (pin 4 on 60-pin PCM), circuit 8-RE22 (WH/GN), harness side and the speed control actuator C831 pin 3, circuit 8-PG18 (WH/BU) harness side.

FM1100100766150X

Fig. 99 Test A: Speed Control Inoperative (Part 15 of 16). Focus

B1 CHECK BRAKE PEDAL POSITION (BPP) SWITCH

1

2 *BPP Switch C824*

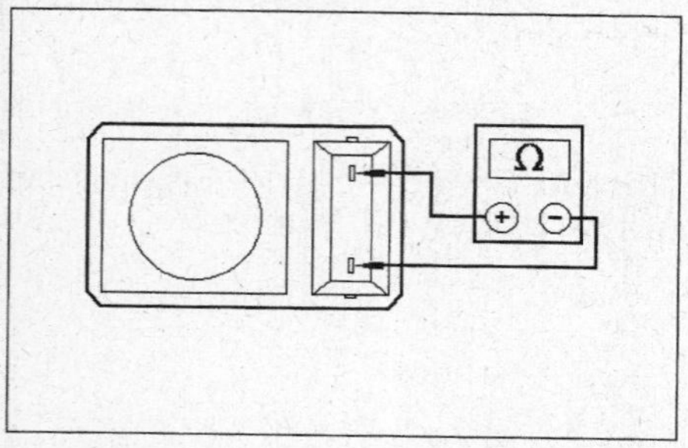

3

Measure the resistance between the BPP switch C824 pin 1 and pin 2, component side, with no brakes applied.

FM1100100767010X

Fig. 100 Test B: System Does Not Disengage When Brakes Are Applied (Part 1 of 5). Focus

- **Is the resistance greater than 10,000 ohms?**

→ **Yes**

REPAIR circuit 8-PG18 (WH/BU) or 8-RE22 (WH/GN). Test the system for normal operation.

→ **No**

Use FDS 2000 to retrieve any stored DTCs. If there are no DTCs. INSTALL a new speed control actuator. TEST the system for normal operation.

FM1100100766160X

Fig. 99 Test A: Speed Control Inoperative (Part 16 of 16). Focus

- **Is the resistance less than 5 ohms?**

→ **Yes**

Go to «B2».

→ **No**

ADJUST or INSTALL a new BPP switch. TEST the system for normal operation.

FM1100100767020X

Fig. 100 Test B: System Does Not Disengage When Brakes Are Applied (Part 2 of 5). Focus

B2 CHECK BRAKE PEDAL POSITION CIRCUIT 15-PG6 (GN/YE) FOR VOLTAGE

1

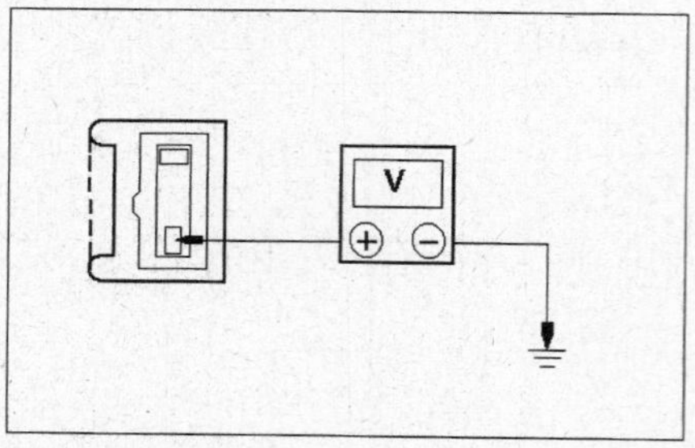

2

Measure the voltage between the BPP switch C824 pin 2, circuit 15-PG6 (GN/YE), harness side and ground.

- **Is the voltage greater than 10 volts?**

→ **Yes**

Go to «B3».

→ **No**

If the stop lamps operate, REPAIR circuit 15-PG6 (GN/YE). TEST the system for normal operation

If the stop lamps do not operate, diagnose and repair as required.

FM1100100767030X

Fig. 100 Test B: System Does Not Disengage When Brakes Are Applied (Part 3 of 5). Focus

B3	CHECK CIRCUIT 15S-PG16 (GN/YE) FOR OPEN

1

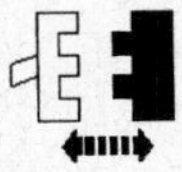

2

Speed Control Actuator C831

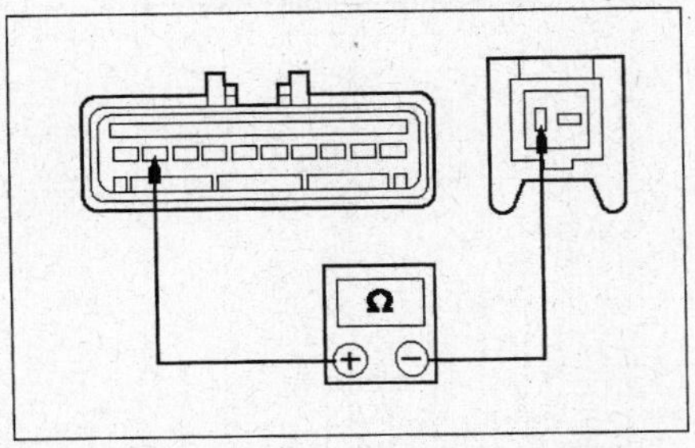

3

Measure the resistance between the BPP switch C824, pin 1, circuit 15S-PG16 (GN/YE), and the speed control C831 pin 9, circuit 15S-PG16 (GN/YE), harness side.

FM1100100767040X

Fig. 100 Test B: System Does Not Disengage When Brakes Are Applied (Part 4 of 5). Focus

C1	CHECK COAST SWITCH

1

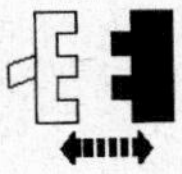

2

Speed Control Actuator C831

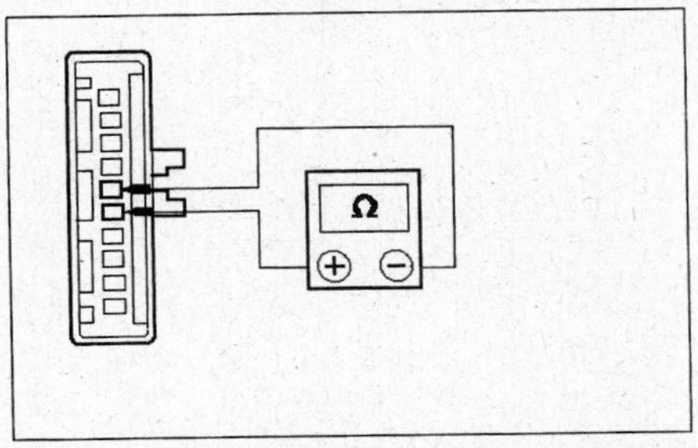

3

Measure the resistance between the speed control actuator C831 pin 5, circuit 8-PG13 (WH), and C831 pin 6, circuit 9-PG13 (BN), harness side, while the (COAST) switch is pressed.

FM1100100768010X

Fig. 101 Test C: COAST Switch Inoperative (Part 1 of 3). Focus

- **Is the resistance less than 5 ohms?**

→ **Yes**

INSTALL a new speed control actuator. TEST the system for normal operation.

→ **No**

REPAIR circuit 15S-PG16 (GN/YE). TEST the system for normal operation.

FM1100100767050X

Fig. 100 Test B: System Does Not Disengage When Brakes Are Applied (Part 5 of 5). Focus

- **Is the resistance between 110 and 130 ohms?**

→ **Yes**

INSTALL a new speed control actuator. TEST the system for normal operation.

→ **No**

Go to «C2».

FM1100100768020X

Fig. 101 Test C: COAST Switch Inoperative (Part 2 of 3). Focus

C2	CHECK RESUME SWITCH

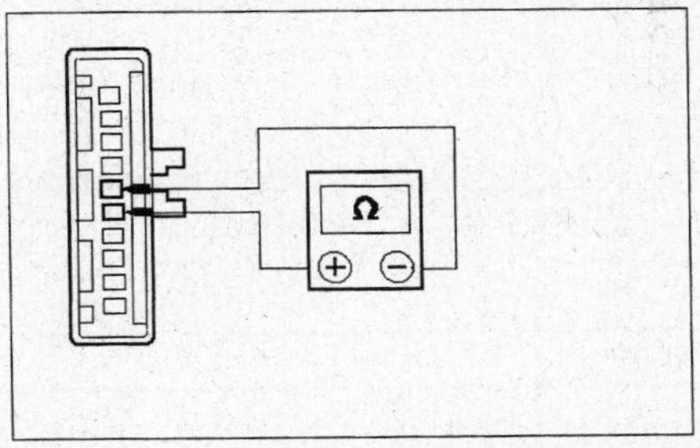

1

Measure the resistance between the speed control actuator C831 pin 5, circuit 8-PG13 (WH), and C831 pin 6, circuit 9-PG13 (BN), harness side, while the (RESUME) switch is pressed.

- **Is the resistance between 110 and 130 ohms?**

→ **Yes**

INSTALL a new COAST switch. TEST the system for normal operation.

→ **No**

Go to «A4».

FM1100100768030X

Fig. 101 Test C: COAST Switch Inoperative (Part 3 of 3). Focus

D1 CHECK RESUME SWITCH

1

2

Speed Control Actuator C831

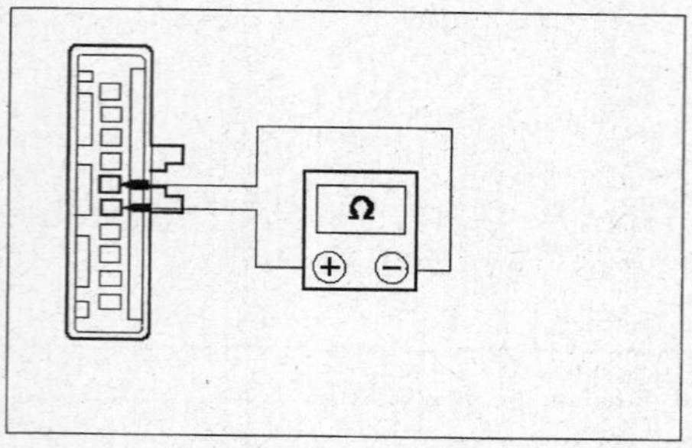

3

Measure the resistance between the speed control actuator C831 pin 5, circuit 8-PG13 (WH), harness side and C831 pin 6, circuit 9-PG13 (BN), harness side, while the (RESUME) switch is pressed.

FM1100100769010X

Fig. 102 Test D: RESUME Switch Inoperative (Part 1 of 3). Focus

D2 CHECK COAST SWITCH

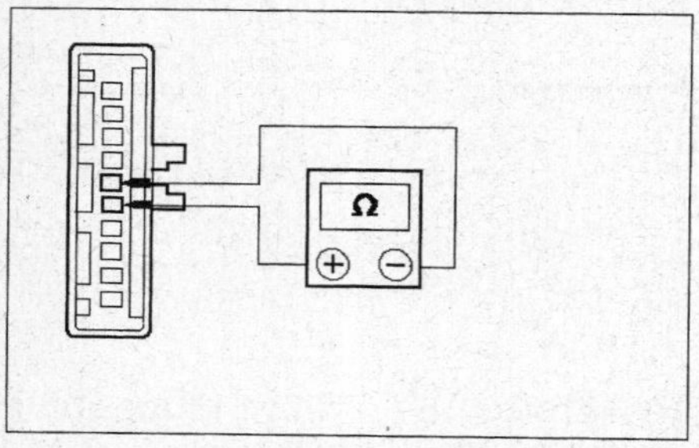

1

Measure the resistance between the speed control actuator C831 pin 5, circuit 8-PG13 (WH) and C831 pin 6, circuit 9-PG13 (BN), harness side, while the (COAST) switch is pressed.

- **Is the resistance between 110 and 130 ohms?**

➔ **Yes**

INSTALL a new RESUME switch. TEST the system for normal operation.

➔ **No**

Go to «A4».

FM1100100769030X

Fig. 102 Test D: RESUME Switch Inoperative (Part 3 of 3). Focus

- **Is the resistance between 110 and 130 ohms?**

➔ **Yes**

INSTALL a new speed control actuator. TEST the system for normal operation.

➔ **No**

Go to «D2»..

FM1100100769020X

Fig. 102 Test D: RESUME Switch Inoperative (Part 2 of 3). Focus

E1 CHECK CLUTCH PEDAL POSITION (CPP) SWITCH

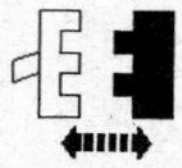

1

CPP Switch C825

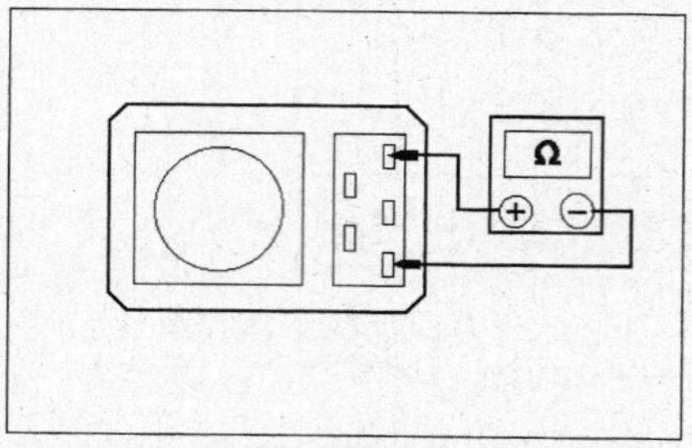

2

Measure the resistance between the CPP switch C825 pin 1 and pin 3, component side, with the switch plunger pressed and also with the plunger released.

- **Are the resistances greater than 10,000 ohms with the plunger pressed in and less than 5 ohms with the plunger released?**

➔ **Yes**

ADJUST the CPP switch.

➔ **No**

INSTALL a new CPP switch.

FM1100100770000X

Fig. 103 Test E: Speed Control Does Not Deactivate When Clutch Is Depressed. Focus

☐ No communication with the powertrain control module

Possible Source(s):
- Underhood auxiliary junction box (AJB) Fuse 118 (40A).
- CJB Fuse F204 (5A).
- CJB Fuse 207 (5A).
- Circuitry.
- PCM.

Action(s) to take:
- GO to «Pinpoint Test A».

☐ Unable to enter self-test

Possible Source(s):
- PCM.

Action(s) to take:
- GO to «Pinpoint Test B».

☐ The speed control switch is inoperative—no DTCs

Possible Source(s):
- Speed control actuator switch.

Action(s) to take:
- INSTALL a new speed control actuator switch.

☐ The speed control indicator is always on

Possible Source(s):
- Instrument cluster.

Action(s) to take:

☐ The speed control is inoperative—no DTC's

Possible Source(s):
- Circuitry.
- Parking brake switch.
- Clutch pedal position (CPP) switch (for M/T only).
- Digital transmission range (DTR) sensor (for A/T only).
- Low battery voltage.

Action(s) to take:
- GO to «Pinpoint Test H».

FM1109900686000X

Fig. 104 Speed control symptom chart. LS & Thunderbird

A2	CHECK THE PCM GROUND CIRCUITS

1

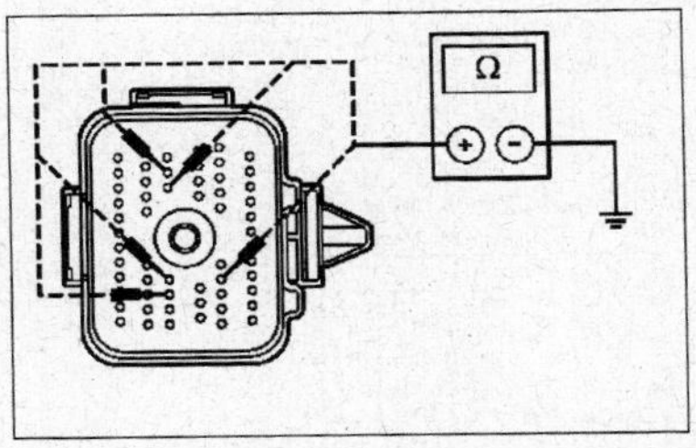

2

Measure the resistance between PCM C175a, and ground, as follows:

Pin	Circuit
24	31-RE8
25	31-RE21
26	31-RE26
27	31-RE25
43	91-RE27

- **Are the resistances less than 5 ohms?**

➔ **Yes**

➔ **No**

REPAIR the circuit. CLEAR the DTCs. REPEAT the self-test.

FM1109900687020X

Fig. 105 Test A: No Communication w/PCM (Part 2 of 2). LS & Thunderbird

A1	CHECK THE PCM POWER CIRCUITS

1

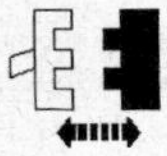

2 PCM C175a

3

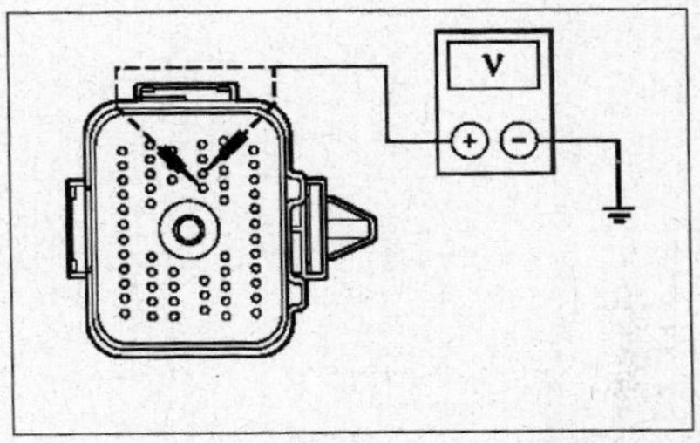

4

Measure the voltage between PCM C175a pin 32, circuit 15S-RE8 (GN/YE), harness side, and ground; and between PCM C175a pin 33, circuit 15S-RE21 (GN/OG), harness side, and ground.

- **Are the voltages greater than 10 volts?**

➔ **Yes**

Go to «A2».

➔ **No**

REPAIR the circuit. CLEAR the DTCs. REPEAT the self-test.

FM1109900687010X

Fig. 105 Test A: No Communication w/PCM (Part 1 of 2). LS & Thunderbird

B1	CHECK THE COMMUNICATION TO THE PCM

1 Check the communication to the PCM.

- **Does the NGS Tester communicate with the PCM?**

➔ **Yes**

Go to «B2».

➔ **No**

GO to «Pinpoint Test A».

FM1109900688010X

Fig. 106 Test B: Unable To Enter Self-Test (Part 1 of 2). LS & Thunderbird

B2	CHECK THE PCM COMMUNICATION PID

1 Monitor the PCM SCINT_F PID.

- **Does the PCM SCINT_F PID indicate NO?**

→ **Yes**

→ **No**

INSTALL a new PCM. REPEAT the self-test.

FM1109900688020X

Fig. 106 Test B: Unable To Enter Self-Test (Part 2 of 2). LS & Thunderbird

C2	CHECK FOR OPEN CIRCUIT

1

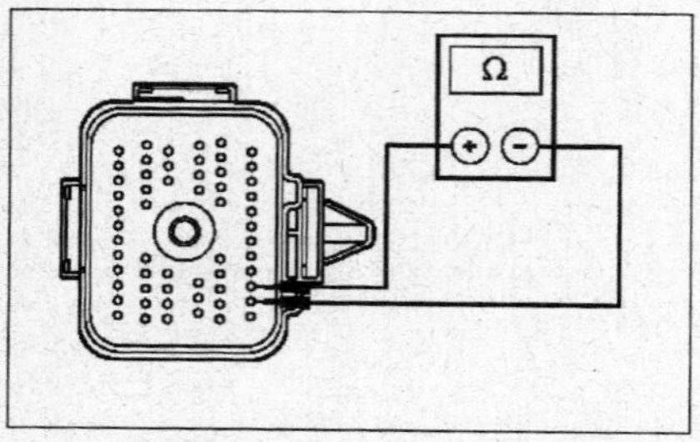

2

Measure the resistance between PCM C175a pin 57, circuit 7PG-24 (YE/BU), harness side, and PCM C175a pin 56, circuit 31S-PG24, (BK/OG), harness side.

- **Is the resistance greater than 10,000 ohms?**

→ **Yes**

Go to «C3».

→ **No**

INSTALL a new PCM. CLEAR the DTCs. REPEAT the self-test.

FM1109900689020X

Fig. 107 Test C: Code P1565, Speed Control Command Switches High/Out Of Range (Part 2 of 6). LS & Thunderbird

C1	CHECK FOR SHORT TO POWER

1

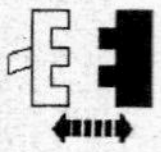

2 *PCM C175a*

3

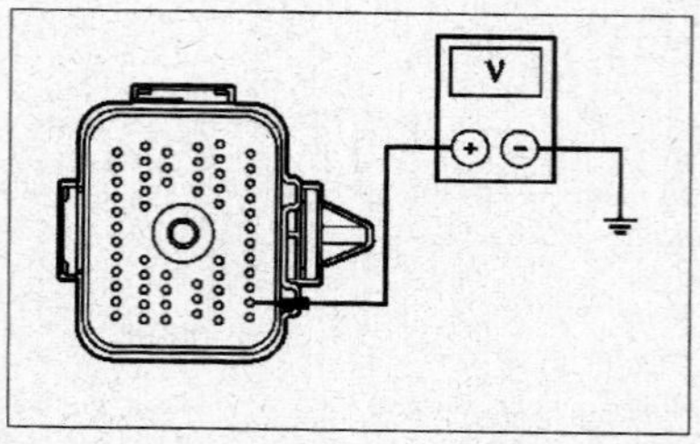

4

Measure the voltage between PCM C175a pin 57, circuit 7PG-24 (YE/BU), harness side and ground.

- **Is any voltage present?**

→ **Yes**

Go to «C6».

→ **No**

Go to «C2».

FM1109900689010X

Fig. 107 Test C: Code P1565, Speed Control Command Switches High/Out Of Range (Part 1 of 6). LS & Thunderbird

C3	CHECK CIRCUIT 31S-PG24 (BK/OG) FOR OPEN

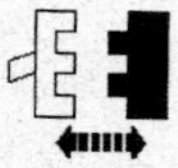

1 *Air Bag Sliding Contact C218a*

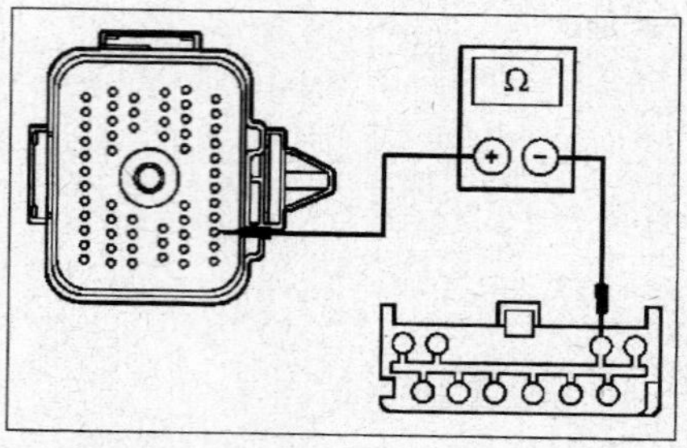

2

Measure the resistance between PCM C175a pin 56, circuit 31S-PG24 (BK/OG), harness side and air bag sliding contact C218a pin 8, circuit 31S-PG24 (BK/OG), harness side.

- **Is the resistance less than 5 ohms?**

→ **Yes**

Go to «C4».

→ **No**

REPAIR the circuit. CLEAR the DTCs. REPEAT the self-test.

FM1109900689030X

Fig. 107 Test C: Code P1565, Speed Control Command Switches High/Out Of Range (Part 3 of 6). LS & Thunderbird

C4	CHECK THE AIR BAG SLIDING CONTACT

1 Remove the driver side air bag.

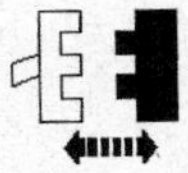

2 *Horn Switch C217*

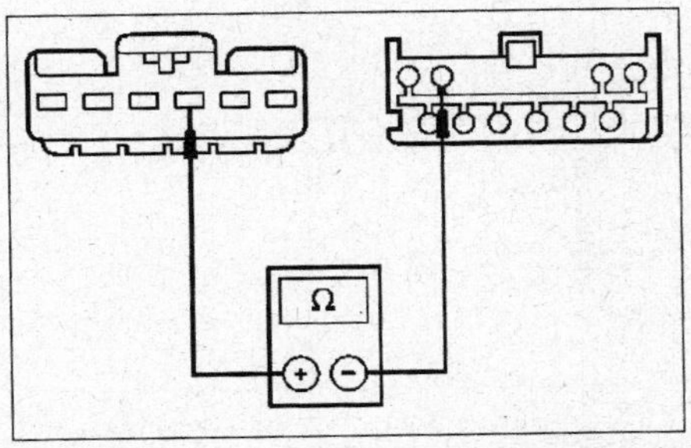

3

Measure the resistance between air bag sliding contact C218a pin 8, circuit 31S-PG24 (BK/OG), (component side), and horn switch C217 pin 3, harness side (top of the air bag sliding contact).

- **Is the resistance less than 5 ohms?**

→ **Yes**

Go to «C5».

→ **No**

INSTALL a new air bag sliding contact. CLEAR the DTCs. REPEAT the self-test.

FM1100100755000X

Fig. 107 Test C: Code P1565, Speed Control Command Switches High/Out Of Range (Part 4 of 6). LS & Thunderbird

C6	CHECK THE AIR BAG SLIDING CONTACT

1 *Air Bag Sliding Contact C218a*

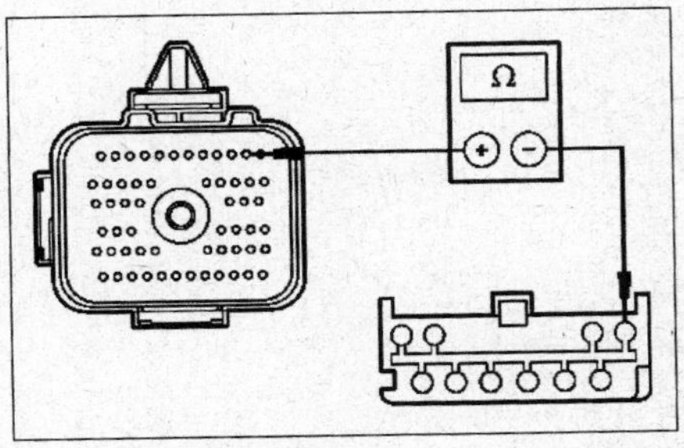

2

Measure the resistance between PCM C175a pin 57, circuit 7PG-24 (YE/BU), harness side, and air bag sliding contact C218a pin 7, circuit 7PG-24 (YE/BU), harness side.

- **Is the resistance less than 5 ohms?**

→ **Yes**

INSTALL a new air bag sliding contact. CLEAR the DTCs. REPEAT the self-test.

→ **No**

REPAIR the circuit. CLEAR the DTCs. REPEAT the self-test.

FM1100100756000X

Fig. 107 Test C: Code P1565, Speed Control Command Switches High/Out Of Range (Part 6 of 6). LS & Thunderbird

C5	CHECK THE SPEED CONTROL ACTUATOR SWITCHES

1 *Speed Control Actuator Switch C203*

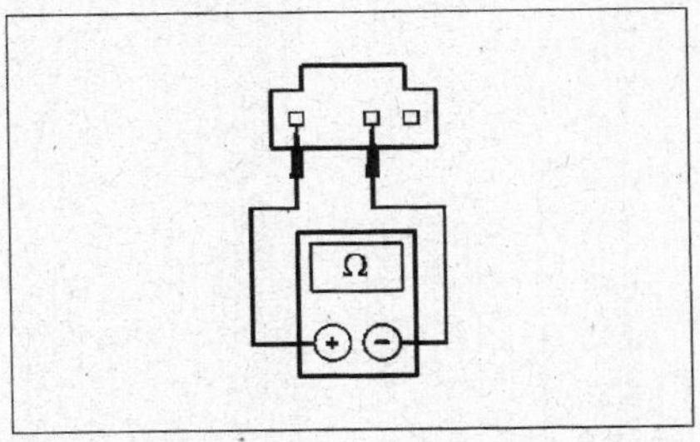

2

Measure the resistance between speed control actuator switch pin 2 (component side), and speed control actuator switch pin 4 (component side).

- **Is the resistance approximately 4.3k ohms?**

→ **Yes**

INSTALL a new horn switch. CLEAR the DTCs. REPEAT the self-test.

→ **No**

INSTALL a new speed control actuator switch. CLEAR the DTCs. REPEAT the self-test.

FM1109900689050X

Fig. 107 Test C: Code P1565, Speed Control Command Switches High/Out Of Range (Part 5 of 6). LS & Thunderbird

D1	CHECK FOR SHORT TO GROUND OR STUCK ACTUATOR SWITCH

1

2 Monitor the PCM PIDs SET/ACL, COAST, RESUME, CANCEL, and SC_ON without depressing any speed control actuator switch.

- **Do any of the PCM PIDs indicate YES?**

→ **Yes**

INSTALL a new speed control actuator switch. CLEAR the DTCs. REPEAT the self-test.

→ **No**

Go to «D2».

FM1109900690010X

Fig. 108 Test D: Code P1566, Speed Control Command Switches Low/Out Of Range (Part 1 of 8). LS & Thunderbird

D2	CHECK CIRCUIT 7-PG24 (YE/BU) AND 31S-PG24 (BK/OG)

1

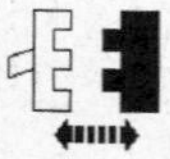

2

PCM C175a

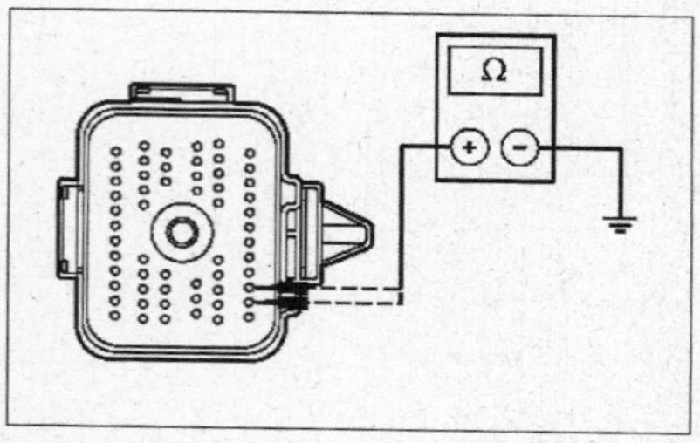

3

Measure the resistance between PCM C175a pin 57, circuit 7PG-24 (YE/BU), harness side, and ground; and between PCM C175a pin 56, circuit 31S-PG24 (BK/OG), harness side, and ground.

- **Are the resistances greater than 10,000 ohms?**

→ **Yes**

Go to «D5».

→ **No**

Go to «D3».

FM1109900690020X

Fig. 108 Test D: Code P1566, Speed Control Command Switches Low/Out Of Range (Part 2 of 8). LS & Thunderbird

D3	CHECK THE HORN SWITCH FOR A SHORT

1 Remove the driver side air bag.

2

Horn Switch C217

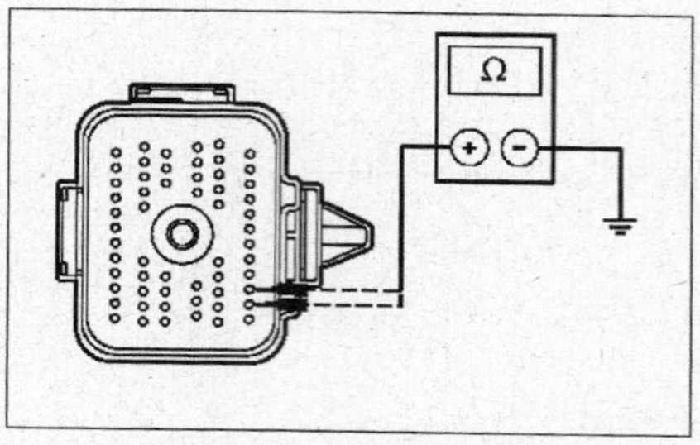

3

Measure the resistance between PCM C175a pin 57, circuit 7PG-24 (YE/BU), harness side, and ground; and between PCM C175a pin 56, circuit 31S-PG24 (BK/OG), harness side, and ground.

- **Are the resistances greater than 10,000 ohms?**

→ **Yes**

INSTALL a new horn switch. CLEAR the DTCs. REPEAT the self-test.

→ **No**

Go to «D4».

FM1109900690030X

Fig. 108 Test D: Code P1566, Speed Control Command Switches Low/Out Of Range (Part 3 of 8). LS & Thunderbird

D4	CHECK THE AIR BAG SLIDING CONTACT

1

Air Bag Sliding Contact C218a

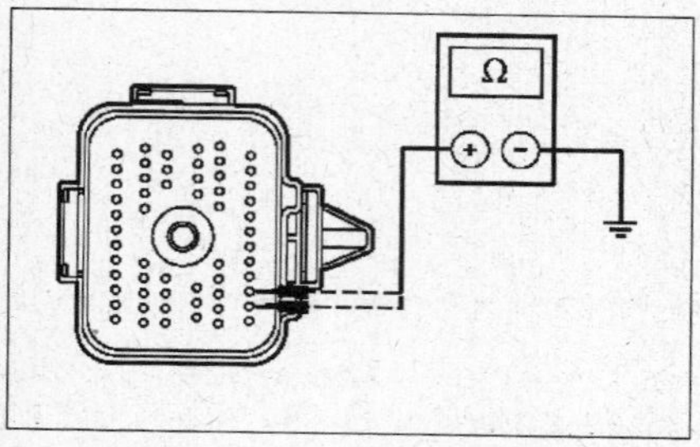

2

Measure the resistance between PCM C175a pin 57, circuit 7PG-24 (YE/BU), harness side, and ground; and between PCM C175a pin 56, circuit 31S-PG24 (BK/OG), harness side, and ground.

- **Are the resistances greater than 10,000 ohms?**

→ **Yes**

INSTALL a new air bag sliding contact. CLEAR the DTCs. REPEAT the self-test.

→ **No**

REPAIR circuit 7-PG24 (YE/BU) and circuit 31S-PG24 (BK/OG) as necessary. CLEAR the DTCs. REPEAT the self-test.

FM1109900690040X

Fig. 108 Test D: Code P1566, Speed Control Command Switches Low/Out Of Range (Part 4 of 8). LS & Thunderbird

D5	CHECK FOR A SHORT CIRCUIT

1

2

PCM C175a

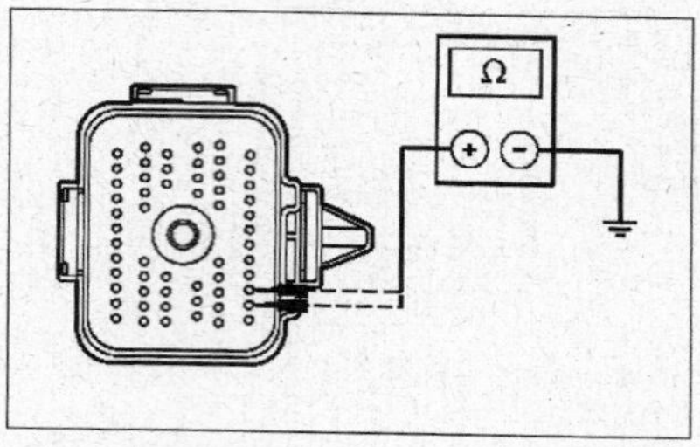

3

Measure the resistance between PCM C175a pin 57, circuit 7-PG24 (YE/BU), harness side, and PCM C175a pin 56, circuit 31S-PG24 (BK/OG), harness side.

- **Is the resistance greater than 10,000 ohms?**

→ **Yes**

INSTALL a new PCM. CLEAR the DTCs. REPEAT the self-test.

→ **No**

Go to «D6».

FM1109900690050X

Fig. 108 Test D: Code P1566, Speed Control Command Switches Low/Out Of Range (Part 5 of 8). LS & Thunderbird

D6 CHECK THE SPEED CONTROL ACTUATOR SWITCH

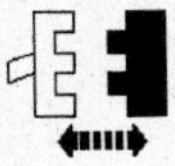

1 *Speed Control Actuator Switch C203*

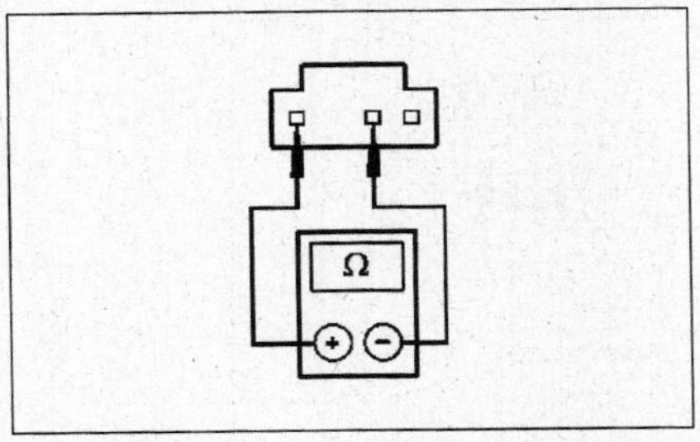

2

Measure the resistance between speed control actuator switch pin 2 (component side), and speed control actuator switch pin 4 (component side).

- **Is the resistance approximately 4.3k ohms?**

→ **Yes**

Go to «D7».

→ **No**

INSTALL a new speed control actuator switch.
CLEAR the DTCs. REPEAT the self-test.

FM1109900690060X

Fig. 108 Test D: Code P1566, Speed Control Command Switches Low/Out Of Range (Part 6 of 8). LS & Thunderbird

D7 CHECK THE HORN SWITCH

1 Remove the driver side air bag.

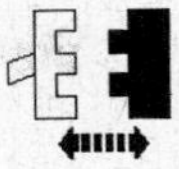

2 *Horn Switch C217*

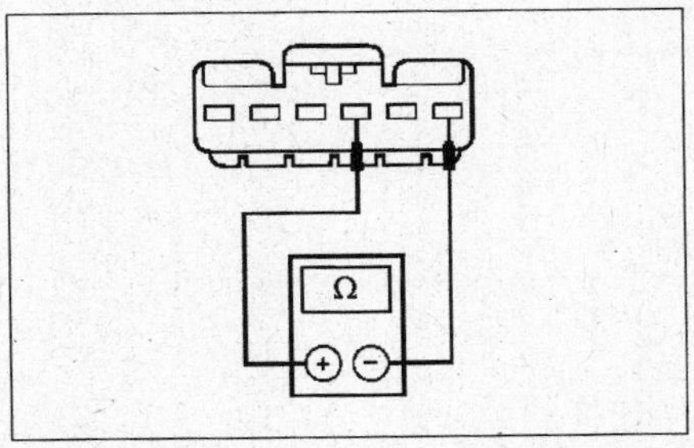

3

Measure the resistance between horn switch C217 pin 1, harness side, and horn switch C217 pin 3, harness side.

- **Is the resistance greater than 10,000 ohms?**

→ **Yes**

Go to «D8».

→ **No**

INSTALL a new horn switch. CLEAR the DTCs. REPEAT the self-test.

FM1100100757000X

Fig. 108 Test D: Code P1566, Speed Control Command Switches Low/Out Of Range (Part 7 of 8). LS & Thunderbird

D8 CHECK THE AIR BAG SLIDING CONTACT FOR A SHORT

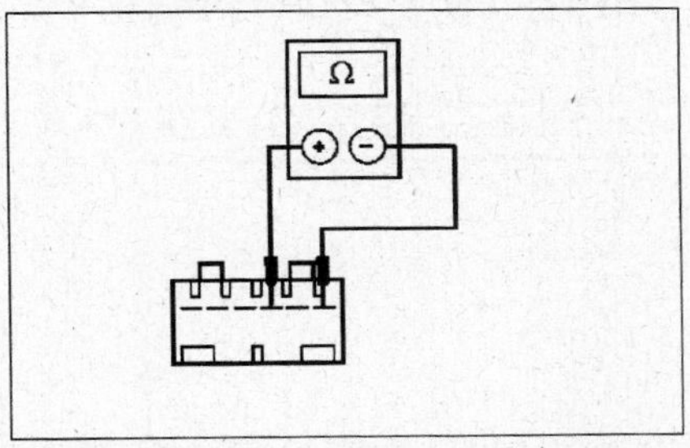

1

Measure the resistance between horn switch C217 pin 1 (component side), and horn switch C217 pin 3 (component side).

- **Is the resistance greater than 10,000 ohms?**

→ **Yes**

REPAIR circuit 7-PG24 (YE/BU) and circuit 31S-PG24 (BK/OG) as necessary. CLEAR the DTCs. REPEAT the self-test.

→ **No**

INSTALL a new air bag sliding contact. CLEAR the DTCs.
REPEAT the self-test.

FM1109900690080X

Fig. 108 Test D: Code P1566, Speed Control Command Switches Low/Out Of Range (Part 8 of 8). LS & Thunderbird

E1 CHECK THE PCM PIDS

1 Test drive the vehicle above 48 km/h (30 mph) with and without the speed control engaged, while monitoring the PCM PID SCINT_F and SC_HW_F.

- **Does either PCM PID SCINT_F or SC_HW_F indicate YES?**

→ **Yes**

If the PCM PID SCINT_F indicates YES, INSTALL a new PCM.
CLEAR the DTCs. REPEAT the self-test.

If the PCM PID SC_HW_F indicates YES, Go to «E2».

→ **No**

Go to «E7».

FM1109900691010X

Fig. 109 Test E: Code P1567, NGSC Driver Fault (Part 1 of 11). LS & Thunderbird

E2 CHECK CIRCUIT 15S-PG12 (GN/WH) FOR AN OPEN

1

2 Speed Control Servo C122

3

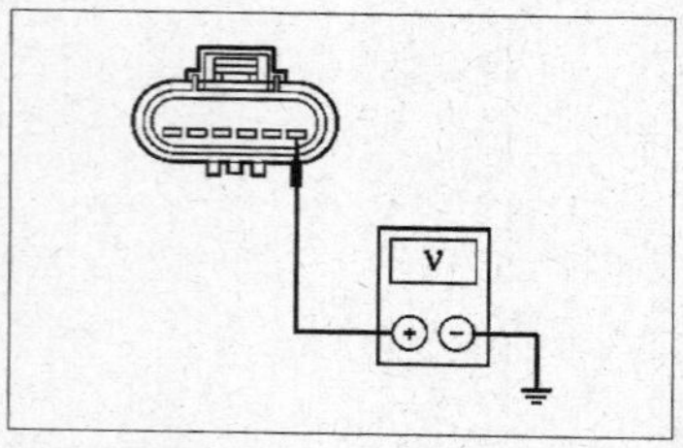

4

Measure the voltage between speed control servo C122 pin 1, circuit 15S-PG12 (GN/WH), harness side, and ground.

- **Is the voltage greater than 10 volts?**

→ **Yes**

Go to «E3».

→ **No**

REPAIR the circuit. CLEAR the DTCs. REPEAT the self-test.

FM1109900691020X

Fig. 109 Test E: Code P1567, NGSC Driver Fault (Part 2 of 11). LS & Thunderbird

E3 CHECK THE SPEED CONTROL SERVO

1

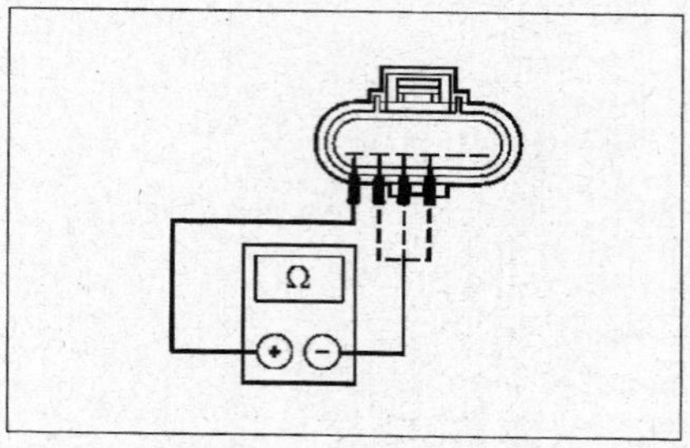

2

Measure the resistance between speed control servo pins (component side), as follows:

Speed Control Servo	Speed Control Servo
Pin 1	Pin 2
Pin 1	Pin 3
Pin 1	Pin 4

- **Are the resistances between 2 and 3 ohms?**

→ **Yes**

Go to «E4».

→ **No**

INSTALL a new speed control servo. CLEAR the DTCs. REPEAT the self-test.

FM1109900691030X

Fig. 109 Test E: Code P1567, NGSC Driver Fault (Part 3 of 11). LS & Thunderbird

E4 CHECK THE SPEED CONTROL SERVO CIRCUITRY FOR SHORT TO POWER

1 PCM C175a

2

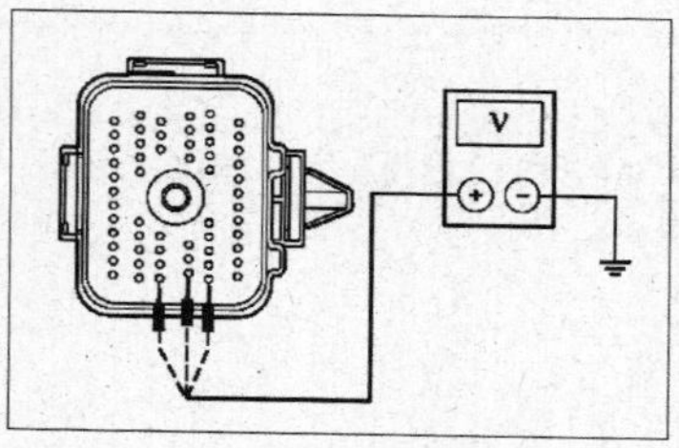

3

Measure the voltage between PCM C175a, harness side and ground, as follows:

PCM C175a	Circuit
Pin 29	10-PG12 (GY/WH)
Pin 36	8-PG21 (WH/GN)
Pin 46	10-PG21 (GY/OG)

- **Is any voltage present?**

→ **Yes**

REPAIR the circuit(s). CLEAR the DTCs. REPEAT the self-test.

→ **No**

Go to «E5».

FM1109900691040X

Fig. 109 Test E: Code P1567, NGSC Driver Fault (Part 4 of 11). LS & Thunderbird

E5 CHECK THE SPEED CONTROL SERVO CIRCUITRY FOR AN OPEN

1

2 Measure the resistance between PCM C175a, harness side, and speed control servo C122, harness side, as follows:

PCM C175a	Speed Control Servo C122	Circuit
Pin 29	Pin 4	10-PG12 (GY/WH)
Pin 36	Pin 3	8-PG21 (WH/GN)
Pin 46	Pin 2	10-PG21 (GY/OG)

- **Are the resistances less than 5 ohms?**

→ **Yes**

Go to «E6».

→ **No**

REPAIR the circuit(s). CLEAR the DTCs. REPEAT the self-test.

FM1109900691050X

Fig. 109 Test E: Code P1567, NGSC Driver Fault (Part 5 of 11). LS & Thunderbird

E6 CHECK THE SPEED CONTROL SERVO CIRCUITRY FOR SHORT TO GROUND

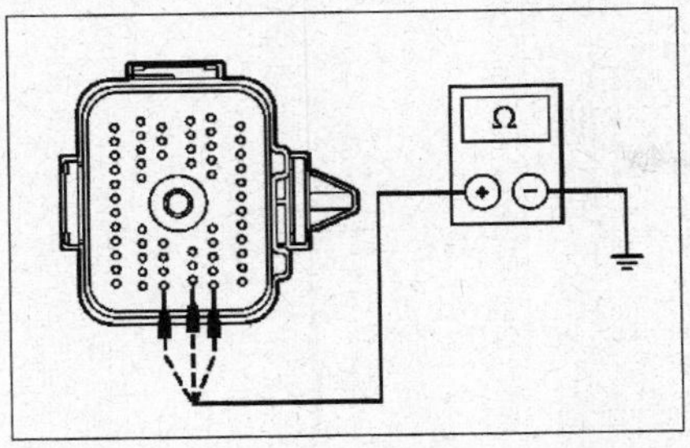

1

Measure the resistance between PCM C175a, harness side, and ground, as follows:

PCM C175a	Circuit
Pin 29	10-PG12 (GY/WH)
Pin 36	8-PG21 (WH/GN)
Pin 46	10-PG21 (GY/OG)

- **Are the resistances greater than 10,000 ohms?**

→ **Yes**

Go to «E7».

→ **No**

REPAIR the circuit(s). CLEAR the DTCs. REPEAT the self-test.

FM1109900691060X

Fig. 109 Test E: Code P1567, NGSC Driver Fault (Part 6 of 11). LS & Thunderbird

E8 CHECK THE SPEED CONTROL SERVO

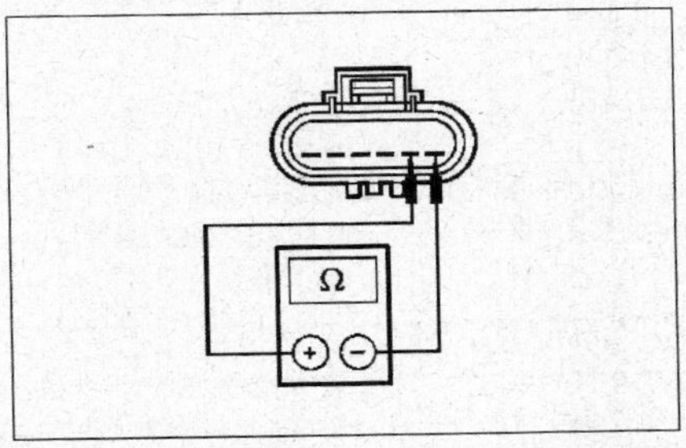

1

Measure the resistance between speed control servo pin 5 (component side), and speed control servo pin 6 (component side).

- **Is the resistance between 20 and 30 ohms?**

→ **Yes**

Go to «E9».

→ **No**

INSTALL a new speed control servo. CLEAR the DTCs. REPEAT the self-test.

FM1109900691080X

Fig. 109 Test E: Code P1567, NGSC Driver Fault (Part 8 of 11). LS & Thunderbird

E7 CHECK THE DEACTIVATOR SWITCH CIRCUITRY FOR AN OPEN

1

2 *Speed Control Servo C122*

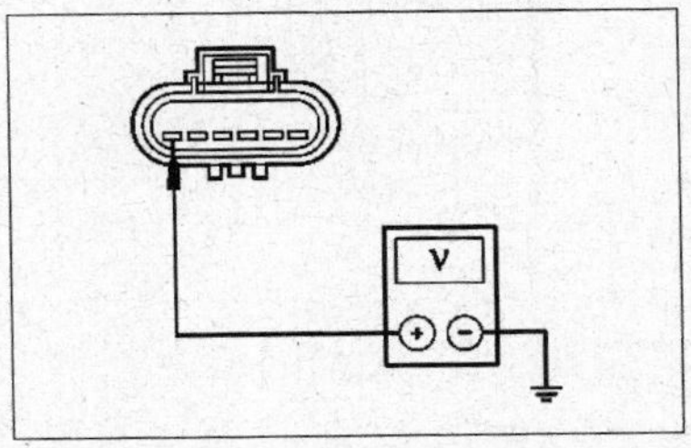

3

Measure the voltage between speed control servo C122 pin 6, circuit 29S-PG16 (OG/YE), harness side, and ground.

- **Is the voltage greater than 10 volts?**

→ **Yes**

Go to «E8».

→ **No**

REPAIR circuit 29S-PG16 (OG/YE) or circuit 29S-PG1 (OG/YE). CLEAR the DTCs. REPEAT the self-test.

FM1109900691070X

Fig. 109 Test E: Code P1567, NGSC Driver Fault (Part 7 of 11). LS & Thunderbird

E9 CHECK CIRCUIT 8-PG12 (WH/VT) FOR SHORT TO POWER

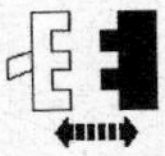

1 *PCM C175a*

2

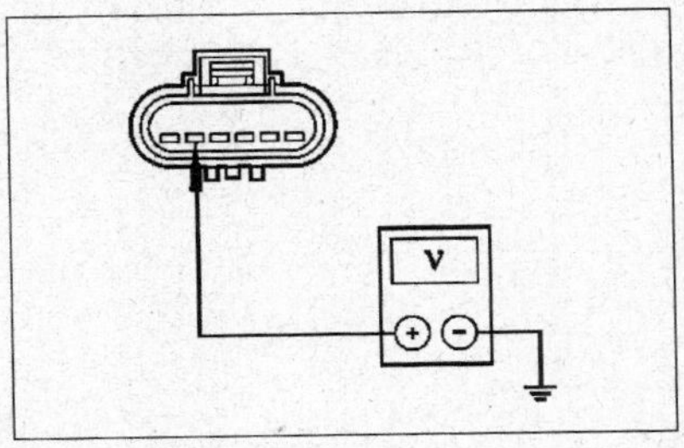

3

Measure the voltage between speed control servo C122 pin 5, circuit 8-PG12 (WH/VT), harness side, and ground.

- **Is any voltage present?**

→ **Yes**

REPAIR the circuit. CLEAR the DTCs. REPEAT the self-test.

→ **No**

Go to «E10».

FM1109900691090X

Fig. 109 Test E: Code P1567, NGSC Driver Fault (Part 9 of 11). LS & Thunderbird

E10 CHECK CIRCUIT 8-PG12 (WH/VT) FOR AN OPEN

1

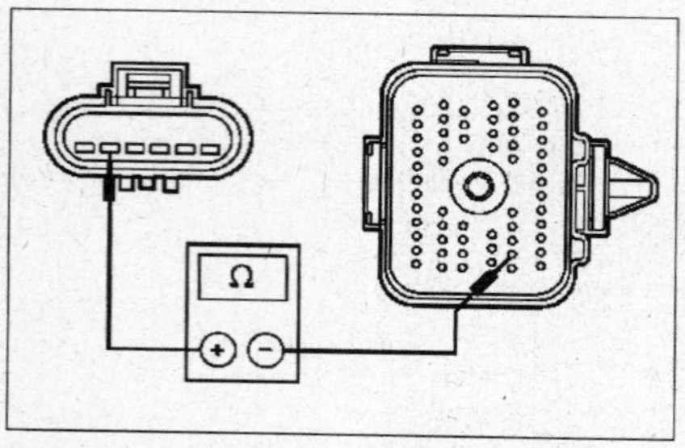

2

Measure the resistance between speed control servo C122 pin 5, circuit 8-PG12 (WH/VT), harness side, and PCM C175a pin 45, circuit 8-PG12 (WH/VT), harness side.

- **Is the resistance less than 5 ohms?**

→ **Yes**

Go to «E11».

→ **No**

REPAIR the circuit. CLEAR the DTCs. REPEAT the self-test.

FM1109900691100X

Fig. 109 Test E: Code P1567, NGSC Driver Fault (Part 10 of 11). LS & Thunderbird

F1 CHECK THE SPEED CONTROL ACTUATOR CABLE

1 Disconnect the speed control actuator cable at the throttle body.

2 Check the speed control actuator cable slack by pulling the speed control cable end taut from within the speed control cable housing.

- **Is the speed control actuator cable slack greater than 0 mm (0 in) and less than 6 mm (0.24 in)?**

→ **Yes**

Go to «F2».

→ **No**

INSTALL a new speed control actuator cable.
CLEAR the DTCs. REPEAT the self-test.

FM1109900692010X

Fig. 110 Test F: Code P1568, NGSC Servo Self-Test Failure (Part 1 of 9). LS & Thunderbird

E11 CHECK CIRCUIT 8-PG12 (WH/VT) FOR SHORT TO GROUND

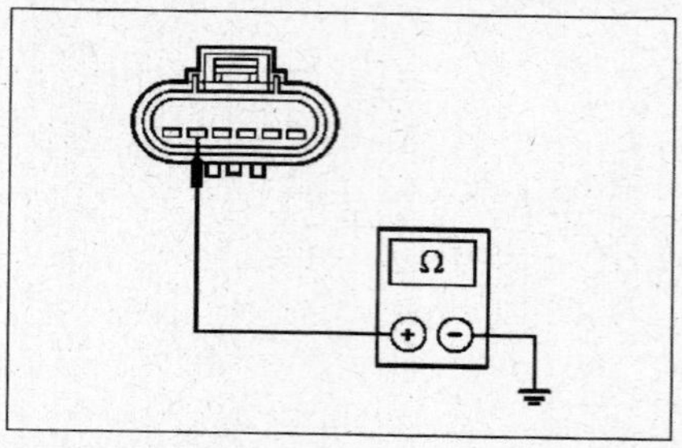

1

Measure the resistance between speed control servo C122 pin 5, circuit 8-PG12 (WH/VT), harness side, and ground.

- **Is the resistance greater than 10,000 ohms?**

→ **Yes**

INSTALL a new PCM. CLEAR the DTCs. REPEAT the self-test.

→ **No**

REPAIR the circuit. CLEAR the DTCs. REPEAT the self-test.

FM1109900691110X

Fig. 109 Test E: Code P1567, NGSC Driver Fault (Part 11 of 11). LS & Thunderbird

F2 CHECK FOR DAMAGE, STICKING OR BINDING SPEED CONTROL ACTUATOR CABLE

1 Disconnect the speed control actuator cable from the speed control servo.

2 Check the speed control actuator cable for damage, sticking or binding.

- **Is the speed control actuator cable OK?**

→ **Yes**

Go to «F3».

→ **No**

INSTALL a new speed control actuator cable.
CLEAR the DTCs. REPEAT the self-test.

FM1109900692020X

Fig. 110 Test F: Code P1568, NGSC Servo Self-Test Failure (Part 2 of 9). LS & Thunderbird

F3 CHECK THE SPEED CONTROL SERVO OUTPUT

1 Check the speed control servo pulley for movement while triggering the on-demand self-test.

- **Does the speed control servo pulley move?**

→ **Yes**

→ **No**

Go to «F4».

FM1109900692030X

Fig. 110 Test F: Code P1568, NGSC Servo Self-Test Failure (Part 3 of 9). LS & Thunderbird

F4	CHECK THE SPEED CONTROL SERVO

1

2 *Speed Control Servo C122*

3 Measure the resistance between speed control servo pins (component side), as follows:

Speed Control Servo	Speed Control Servo	Expected Value
Pin 1	Pin 2	Between 2 and 3 ohms
Pin 1	Pin 3	Between 2 and 3 ohms
Pin 1	Pin 4	Between 2 and 3 ohms
Pin 5	Pin 6	Between 20 and 30 ohms

- **Are the resistances OK?**

→ **Yes**

Go to «F5».

→ **No**

INSTALL a new speed control servo. CLEAR the DTCs. REPEAT the self-test.

FM1109900692040X

Fig. 110 Test F: Code P1568, NGSC Servo Self-Test Failure (Part 4 of 9). LS & Thunderbird

F5	CHECK THE SPEED CONTROL SERVO CIRCUITRY FOR SHORT TO POWER

1

2 *PCM C175a*

3

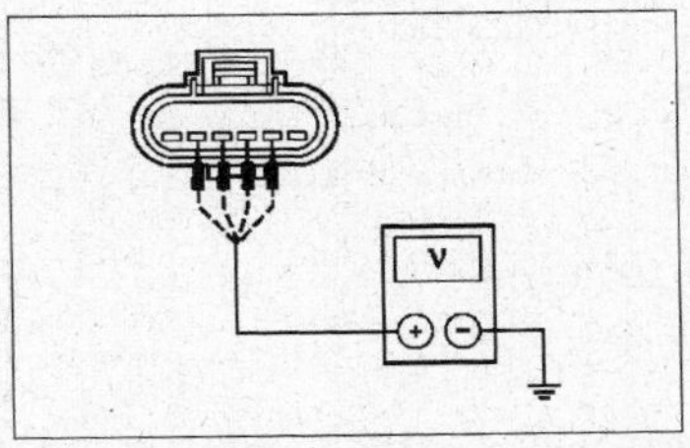

4

Measure the voltage between speed control servo C122, harness side and ground, as follows:

Speed Control Servo C122	Circuit
Pin 5	8-PG12 (WH/VT)
Pin 4	10-PG12 (GY/WH)
Pin 3	8-PG21 (WH/GN)
Pin 2	10-PG21 (GY/OG)

- **Is any voltage present?**

→ **Yes**

REPAIR the circuit(s). CLEAR the DTCs. REPEAT the self-test.

→ **No**

Go to «F6».

FM1109900692050X

Fig. 110 Test F:Code P1568, NGSC Servo Self-Test Failure (Part 5 of 9). LS & Thunderbird

F6	CHECK THE SPEED CONTROL SERVO CIRCUITRY FOR AN OPEN CIRCUIT

1

2 Measure the resistance between PCM C175a, harness side and speed control servo C122, harness side, as follows:

PCM C175a	Speed control servo C122	Circuit
Pin 45	Pin 5	8-PG12 (WH/VT)
Pin 29	Pin 4	10-PG12 (GY/WH)
Pin 36	Pin 3	8-PG21 (WH/GN)
Pin 46	Pin 2	10-PG21 (GY/OG)

- **Are the resistances less than 5 ohms?**

→ **Yes**

Go to «F7».

→ **No**

REPAIR the circuit(s). CLEAR the DTCs. REPEAT the self-test.

FM1109900692060X

Fig. 110 Test F:Code P1568, NGSC Servo Self-Test Failure (Part 6 of 9). LS & Thunderbird

F7	CHECK THE SPEED CONTROL SERVO CIRCUITRY FOR SHORT TO GROUND

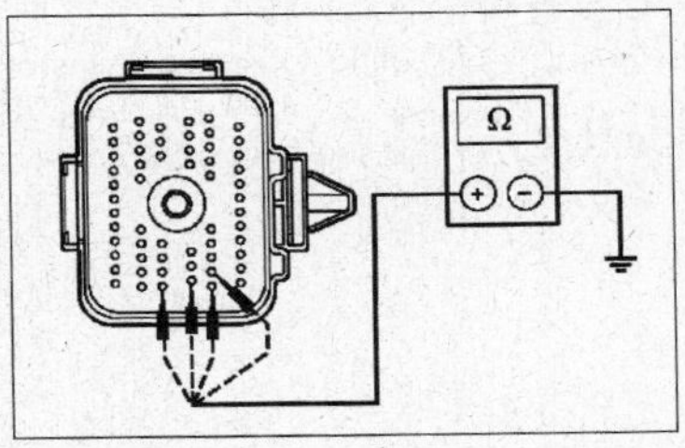

1

Measure the resistances between PCM C175a, harness side, and ground, as follows:

PCM C175a	Circuit
Pin 45	8-PG12 (WH/VT)
Pin 29	10-PG12 (GY/WH)
Pin 36	8-PG21 (WH/GN)
Pin 46	10-PG21 (GY/OG)

- **Are the resistances greater than 10,000 ohms?**

→ **Yes**

Go to «F8».

→ **No**

REPAIR the circuit(s). CLEAR the DTCs. REPEAT the self-test.

FM1109900692070X

Fig. 110 Test F:Code P1568, NGSC Servo Self-Test Failure (Part 7 of 9). LS & Thunderbird

F8	CHECK CIRCUIT 15S-PG12 (GN/WH) FOR AN OPEN

1

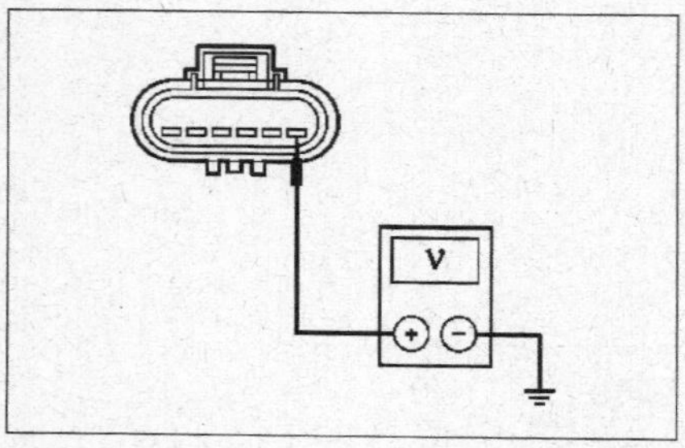

2

Measure the voltage between speed control servo C122 pin 1, circuit 15S-PG12 (GN/WH), harness side and ground.

- **Is the voltage greater than 10 volts?**

→ **Yes**

Go to «F9».

→ **No**

REPAIR the circuit. CLEAR the DTCs. REPEAT the self-test.

FM1109900692080X

Fig. 110 Test F:Code P1568, NGSC Servo Self-Test Failure (Part 8 of 9). LS & Thunderbird

G1	MONITOR THE PCM PID BPA_SW

1

2 Monitor the PCM PID BPA_SW without depressing the brake pedal.

- **Does the PCM BPA_SW PID indicate ON?**

→ **Yes**

Go to «G2».

→ **No**

Go to «G5».

FM1109900693010X

Fig. 111 Test G: Code P1572/P0703, Brake On/Off Failure (Part 1 of 5). LS & Thunderbird

F9	CHECK THE DEACTIVATOR SWITCH CIRCUITRY FOR AN OPEN

1

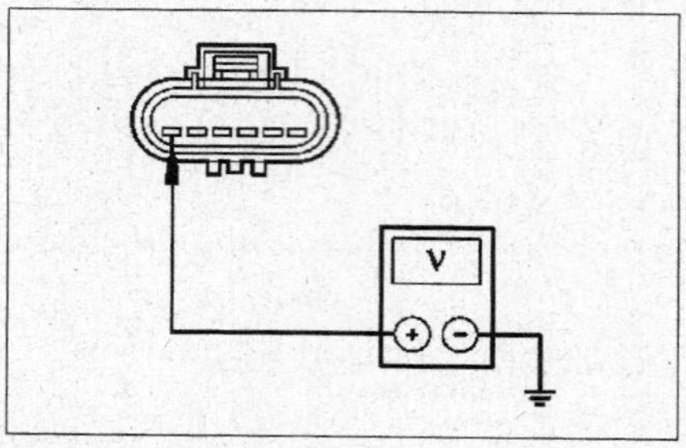

2

Measure the voltage between speed control servo C122 pin 6, circuit 29S-PG16 (OG/YE), harness side and ground.

- **Is the voltage greater than 10 volts?**

→ **Yes**

INSTALL a new speed control servo. CLEAR the DTCs. REPEAT the self-test.

→ **No**

REPAIR circuit 29S-PG16 (OG/YE) or circuit 29S-PG1 (OG/YE) as necessary. CLEAR the DTCs. REPEAT the self-test.

FM1109900692090X

Fig. 110 Test F:Code P1568, NGSC Servo Self-Test Failure (Part 9 of 9). LS & Thunderbird

G2	CHECK FOR AN OPEN CIRCUIT

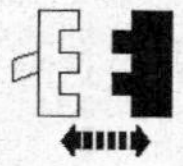

1 *PCM C175a*

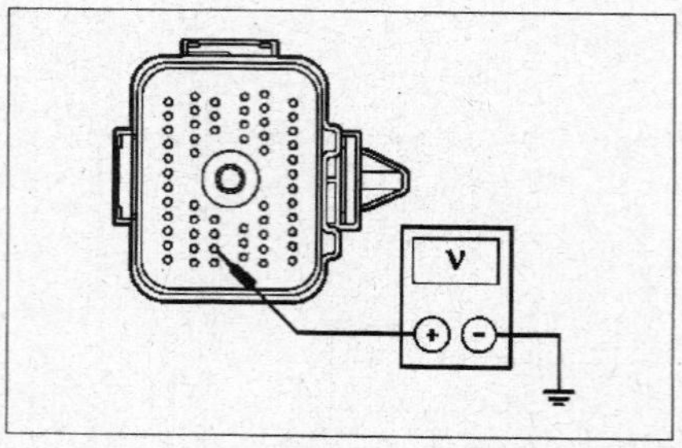

2

Measure the voltage between PCM C175a pin 28, circuit 29S-RE21 (OG/GN), harness side and ground.

- **Is the voltage greater than 10 volts?**

→ **Yes**

INSTALL a new PCM. CLEAR the DTCs. REPEAT the self-test.

→ **No**

Go to «G3».

FM1109900693020X

Fig. 111 Test G: Code P1572/P0703, Brake On/Off Failure (Part 2 of 5). LS & Thunderbird

G3	CHECK CIRCUIT 29S-PG1 (OG/YE)

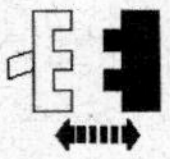

1 *Deactivator Switch C277*

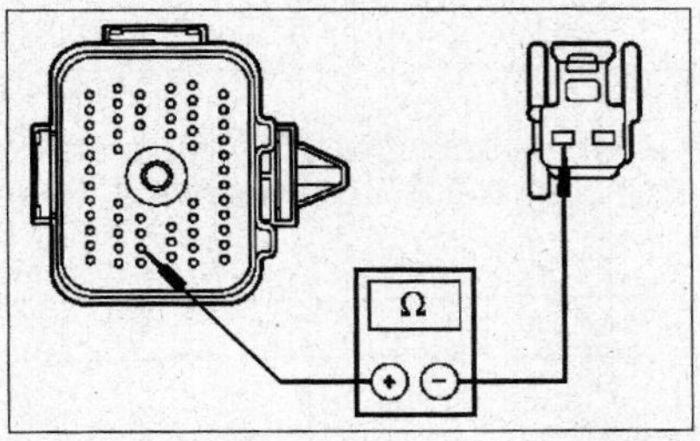

2

Measure the resistance between PCM C175a pin 28, circuit 29S-RE21 (OG/GN), harness side, and deactivator switch C277 pin 2, circuit 29S-PG1 (OG/YE), harness side.

- **Is the resistance less than 5 ohms?**

→ **Yes**

Go to «G4».

→ **No**

REPAIR circuit 29S-RE21 (OG/GN) and circuit 29S-PG1 (OG/YE) as necessary. CLEAR the DTCs. REPEAT the self-test.

FM1109900693030X

Fig. 111 Test G: Code P1572/P0703, Brake On/Off Failure (Part 3 of 5). LS & Thunderbird

G5	CHECK THE BRAKE PEDAL POSITION (BPP) INPUT TO PCM

1

2 *PCM C175a*

3

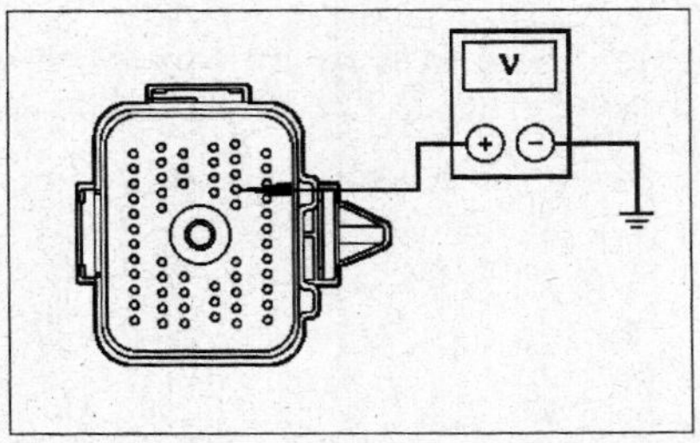

4

Measure the voltage between PCM C175a pin 40, circuit 29S-RE13 (OG), harness side, and ground while depressing the brake pedal.

- **Is the voltage greater than 10 volts?**

→ **Yes**

INSTALL a new PCM. CLEAR the DTCs. REPEAT the self-test.

→ **No**

REPAIR the circuit. CLEAR the DTCs. REPEAT the self-test.

FM1109900693050X

Fig. 111 Test G: Code P1572/P0703, Brake On/Off Failure (Part 5 of 5). LS & Thunderbird

G4	CHECK THE DEACTIVATOR SWITCH

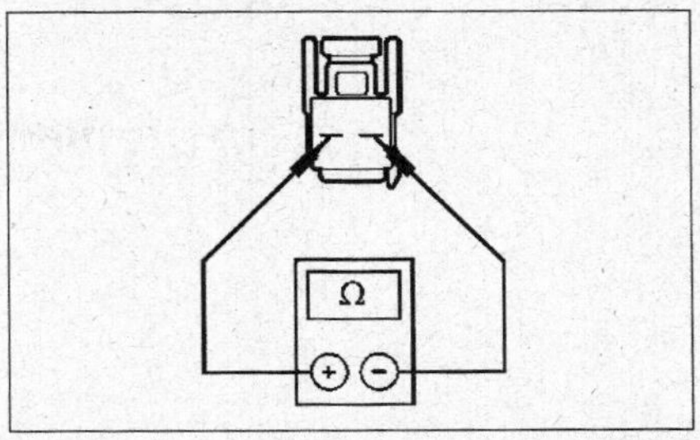

1

Measure the resistance between deactivator switch pins, (component side) while depressing and releasing the brake pedal.

- **Is the resistance less than 5 ohms with the brake pedal released and greater than 10,000 ohms with the brake pedal depressed?**

→ **Yes**

REPAIR circuit 29-PG6 (OG/YE). CLEAR the DTCs. REPEAT the self-test.

→ **No**

INSTALL a new deactivator switch. CLEAR the DTCs. REPEAT the self-test.

FM1109900693040X

Fig. 111 Test G: Code P1572/P0703, Brake On/Off Failure (Part 4 of 5). LS & Thunderbird

H1	CHECK THE PCM PID IDBRKSW

1 Monitor the PCM PID IDBRKSW.

- **Does the PCM PID IDBRKSW indicate OFF?**

→ **Yes**

Go to «H3».

→ **No**

Go to «H2».

FM1109900694010X

Fig. 112 Test H: Speed Control Inoperative (Part 1 of 12). LS & Thunderbird

H2	CHECK THE BPP INPUT TO THE PCM

1

2 *PCM C175a*

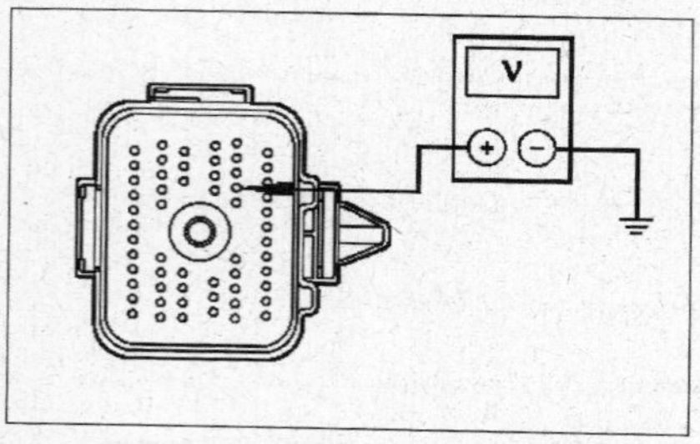

3

Measure the voltage between PCM C175a pin 40, circuit 29S-RE13 (OG), harness side, and ground.

- **Is any voltage present?**

➔ **Yes**

➔ **No**

INSTALL a new PCM. CLEAR the DTCs. REPEAT the self-test.

FM1109900694020X

Fig. 112 Test H: Speed Control Inoperative (Part 2 of 12). LS & Thunderbird

H4	CHECK THE PCM PID CPP

1 Monitor the PCM PID CPP.

- **Does the PCM PID CPP indicate NO?**

➔ **Yes**

Go to «H11».

➔ **No**

Go to «H5».

FM1109900694040X

Fig. 112 Test H: Speed Control Inoperative (Part 4 of 12). LS & Thunderbird

H3	CHECK THE PCM PID PBA_SW

1 Monitor the PCM PID PBA_SW.

- **Does the PCM PID PBA_SW indicate OFF with the parking brake released?**

➔ **Yes**

If equipped with a manual transmission, Go to «H4».

If equipped with an automatic transmission, Go to «H8».

➔ **No**

FM1109900694030X

Fig. 112 Test H: Speed Control Inoperative (Part 3 of 12). LS & Thunderbird

H5	CHECK THE CPP SWITCH

1

2 *CPP Switch C258*

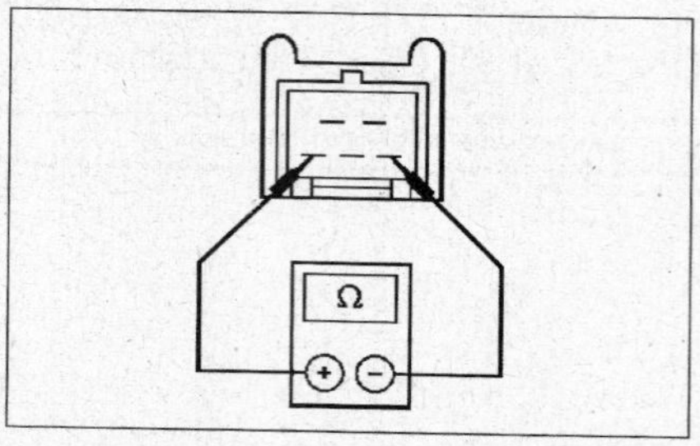

3

Measure the resistance between CPP switch pins 1 (component side), and CPP switch pin 3 (component side), while depressing and releasing the switch.

- **Is the resistance less than 5 ohms in one direction and greater than 10,000 ohms in the other?**

➔ **Yes**

Go to «H6».

➔ **No**

INSTALL a new CPP switch. CLEAR the DTCs. REPEAT the self-test.

FM1109900694050X

Fig. 112 Test H: Speed Control Inoperative (Part 5 of 12). LS & Thunderbird

H6 CHECK CIRCUIT 8-TC18 (WH) FOR AN OPEN

1

PCM C175b

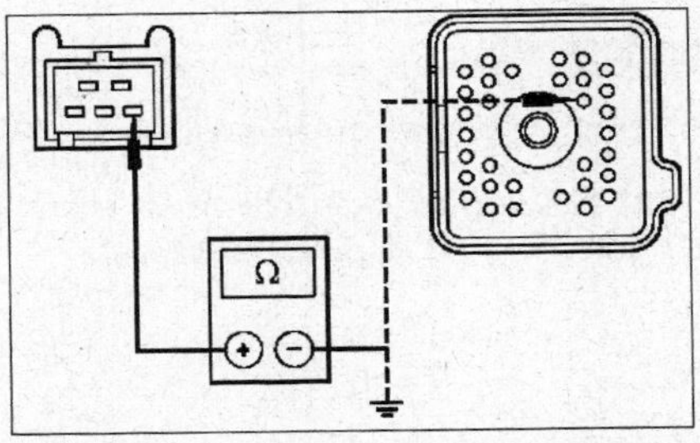

2

Measure the resistance between CPP switch C258 pin 1, circuit 8-TC18 (WH), harness side, and PCM C175b pin 22, circuit 8-TC18 (WH), harness side; and between CPP switch C258 pin 1, circuit 8-TC18 (WH), harness side and ground.

- **Is the resistance less than 5 ohms between the CPP switch and PCM; and greater than 10,000 ohms between the CPP switch and ground?**

→ **Yes**

Go to «H7».

→ **No**

REPAIR the circuit. CLEAR the DTCs. REPEAT the self-test.

FM1109900694060X

Fig. 112 Test H: Speed Control Inoperative (Part 6 of 12). LS & Thunderbird

H8 CHECK THE DTR SENSOR

1

2

DTR Sensor C167

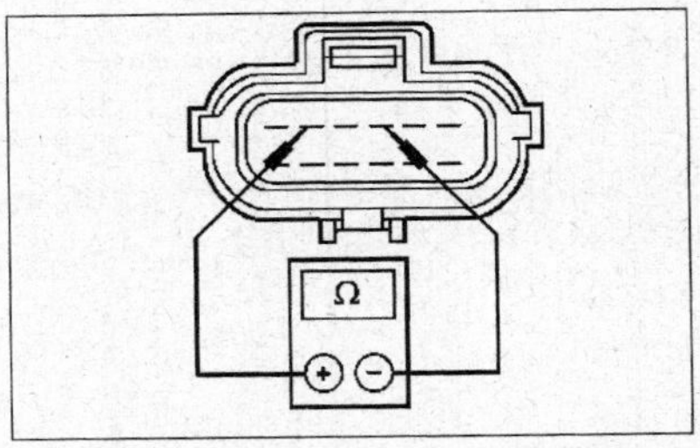

3

Measure the resistance between DTR sensor pin 2 (component side), and DTR sensor pin 4 (component side), while placing the transmission selector in P and D5.

- **Is the resistance less than 5 ohms when the transmission selector is in P and greater than 10,000 ohms when the transmission selector is in D5?**

→ **Yes**

Go to «H9».

→ **No**

INSTALL a new DTR sensor. CLEAR the DTCs. REPEAT the self-test.

FM1109900694080X

Fig. 112 Test H: Speed Control Inoperative (Part 8 of 12). LS & Thunderbird

H7 CHECK CIRCUIT 9-RE8 (BN)

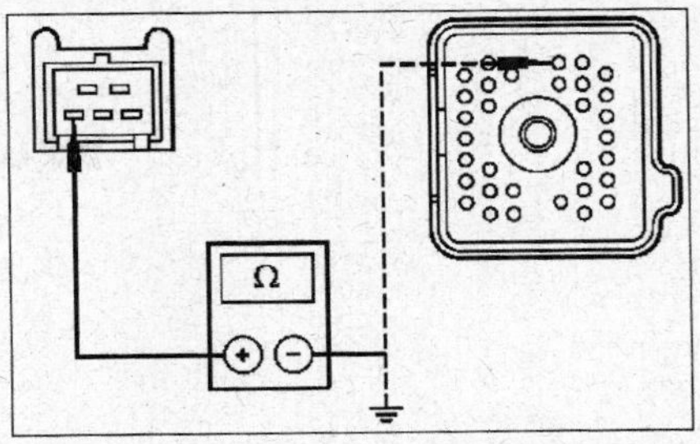

1

Measure the resistance between CPP switch C258 pin 3, circuit 9-RE8 (BN), harness side, and PCM C175a pin 17, circuit 9-RE8 (BN), harness side; and between CPP switch C258 pin 3, circuit 9-RE8 (BN), harness side, and ground.

- **Is the resistance less than 5 ohms between the CPP switch and PCM; and greater than 10,000 ohms between the CPP switch and ground?**

→ **Yes**

INSTALL a new PCM. CLEAR the DTCs. REPEAT the self-test.

→ **No**

REPAIR the circuit. CLEAR the DTCs. REPEAT the self-test.

FM1109900694070X

Fig. 112 Test H: Speed Control Inoperative (Part 7 of 12). LS & Thunderbird

H9 CHECK CIRCUIT 8-TA40 (WH/GN) FOR AN OPEN

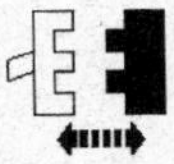

1

PCM C175b

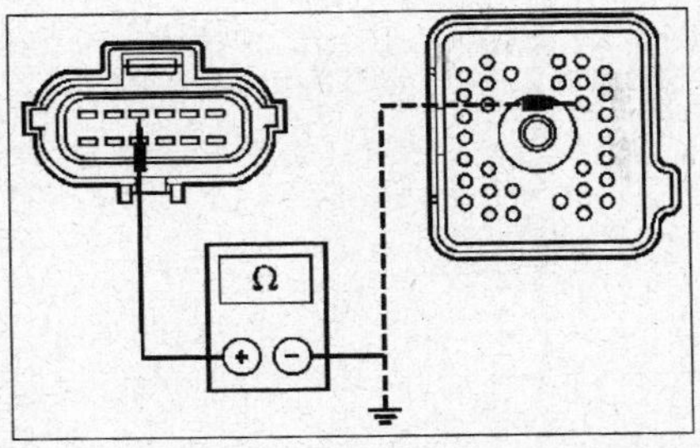

2

Measure the resistance between DTR sensor C167 pin 4, circuit 8-TA40 (WH/GN), harness side, and PCM C175b pin 22, circuit 8-TA40 (WH/GN), harness side; and between DTR sensor C167 pin 4, circuit 8-TA40 (WH/GN), harness side and ground.

- **Is the resistance less than 5 ohms between the DTR sensor and PCM; and greater than 10,000 ohms between the DTR sensor and ground?**

→ **Yes**

Go to «H10».

→ **No**

REPAIR the circuit. CLEAR the DTCs. REPEAT the self-test.

FM1109900694090X

Fig. 112 Test H: Speed Control Inoperative (Part 9 of 12). LS & Thunderbird

H10	CHECK CIRCUIT 9-TA1 (BN) AND CIRCUIT 9-TA18 (BN/YE)

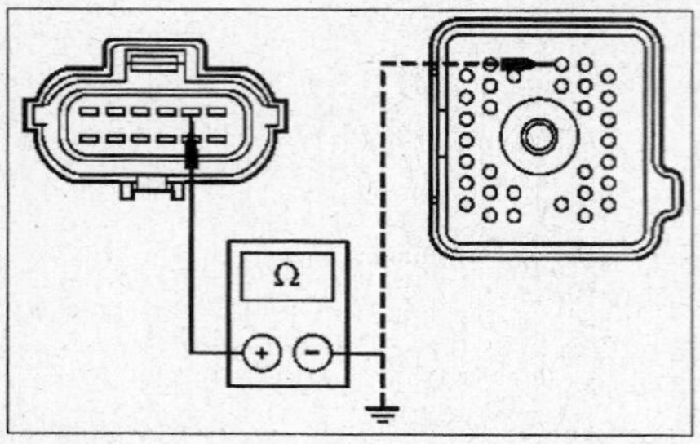

1 Measure the resistance between DTR sensor C167 pin 2, circuit 9-TA18 (BN/YE), harness side, and PCM C175b pin 17, circuit 9-TA1 (BN/YE), harness side; and between DTR sensor C167 pin 2, circuit 9-TA18 (BN/YE), harness side, and ground.

- **Is the resistance less than 5 ohms between the DTR sensor and PCM; and greater than 10,000 ohms between the DTR sensor and ground?**

➔ **Yes**

Go to «H11».

➔ **No**

REPAIR the circuit. CLEAR the DTCs. REPEAT the self-test.

FM1100100758000X

Fig. 112 Test H: Speed Control Inoperative (Part 10 of 12). LS & Thunderbird

H12	CHECK THE PCM PID VBAT

1 Monitor the PCM PID VBAT.

- **Does the PCM PID VBAT indicate greater than 10 volts with the engine running?**

➔ **Yes**

Diagnose Powertrain Control system.

➔ **No**

Diagnose module communications network.

FM1100100759000X

Fig. 112 Test H: Speed Control Inoperative (Part 12 of 12). LS & Thunderbird

Condition	Possible Source	Action
• The speed control is inoperative	• CJB Fuse 17 (15A), 33 (15A). • BJB fuse HORN (20A). • Circuitry. • Deactivator switch. • CPP switch. • Speed control actuator switch. • Speed control servo. • PCM.	• GO to Pinpoint Test A.
• The set speed fluctuates	• Circuitry. • Speed control servo. • PCM. • Engine.	• GO to Pinpoint Test B.
• The speed control does not disengage when the brakes are applied	• CJB Fuse 33 (15A). • Circuitry. • BPP switch. • Speed control servo.	• GO to Pinpoint Test C.
• The speed control does not disengage when the clutch is applied	• CPP switch. • Speed control servo.	• GO to Pinpoint Test D.
• The speed control switch is inoperative— COAST	• Speed control actuator switch. • Speed control servo.	• GO to Pinpoint Test E.
• The speed control switch is inoperative—SET/ACCEL	• Speed control actuator switch. • Speed control servo.	• GO to Pinpoint Test F.
• The speed control switch is inoperative—RESUME	• Speed control actuator switch. • Speed control servo.	• GO to Pinpoint Test G.
• The speed control switch is inoperative—OFF	• Speed control actuator switch. • Speed control servo.	• GO to Pinpoint Test H.

FM1109900675000X

Fig. 113 Speed control diagnostic symptom chart. Mustang

H11	CHECK THE PCM PID SCCS

1 Monitor the PCM PID SCCS, while depressing and releasing the speed control actuator switches. For additional information, refer to the PCM Parameter Identification (PID) Index.

- **Does the PCM PID SCCS operate correctly?**

➔ **Yes**

Go to «H12».

➔ **No**

INSTALL a new speed control actuator switch.
CLEAR the DTCs. REPEAT the self-test.

FM1109900694110X

Fig. 112 Test H: Speed Control Inoperative (Part 11 of 12). LS & Thunderbird

TEST CONDITIONS	TEST DETAILS/RESULTS/ACTIONS
A1 CHECK THE SPEED CONTROL SERVO VOLTAGE AND GROUND	
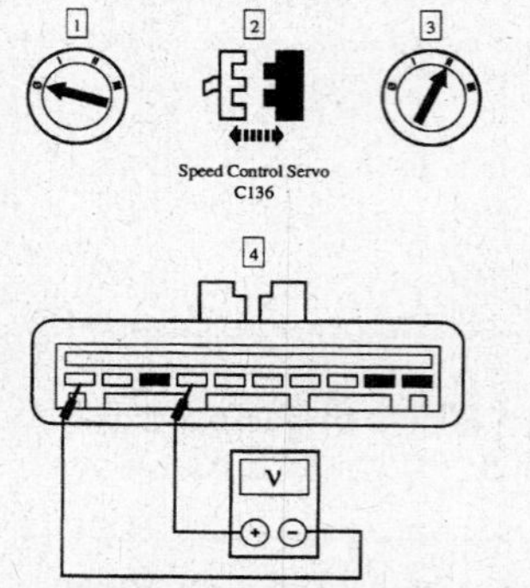	4 Measure the voltage between speed control servo C136 Pin 7, Circuit 294 (WH/LB), harness side and speed control servo C136 Pin 10, Circuit 1205 (BK), harness side. • Is voltage greater than 10 volts? → **Yes** GO to **A3.** → **No** GO to **A2.**
A2 CHECK THE CIRCUIT 1205 (BK) FOR AN OPEN	
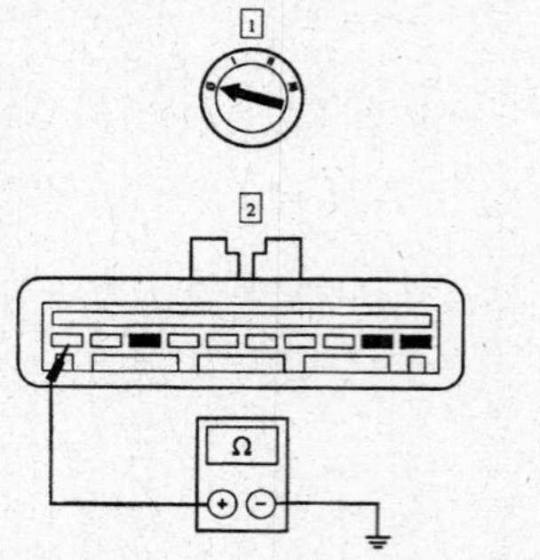	2 Measure the resistance between speed control servo C136 Pin 10, Circuit 1205 (BK), harness side and ground. • Is the resistance less than 5 ohms? → **Yes** REPAIR Circuit 294 (WH/LB). TEST the system for normal operation. → **No** REPAIR Circuit 1205 (BK). TEST the system for normal operation.

FM1109900676010X

Fig. 114 Test A: Speed Control Inoperative (Part 1 of 9). Mustang

TEST CONDITIONS	TEST DETAILS/RESULTS/ACTIONS
A3 CHECK DEACTIVATOR SWITCH CIRCUITRY	
1 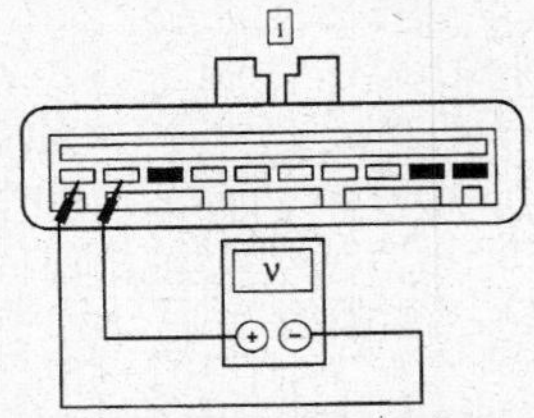	1 Measure the voltage between speed control servo C136 Pin 9, Circuit 636 (OG), harness side and speed control servo C136 Pin 10, Circuit 1205 (BK), harness side. • Is the voltage greater than 10 volts? → **Yes** GO to **A6**. → **No** GO to **A4**.
A4 CHECK CIRCUIT 10 (LG/RD) FOR AN OPEN	
1 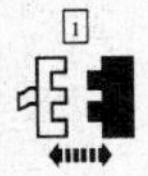 Deactivator Switch C261 2 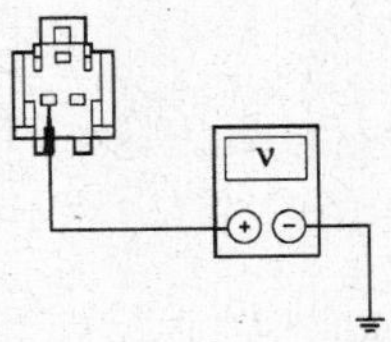	2 Measure the voltage between deactivator switch C216 Pin 1, Circuit 10 (LG/RD), harness side and ground. • Is the voltage greater than 10 volts? → **Yes** GO to **A5**. → **No** REPAIR the circuit. TEST the system for normal operation.

FM1109900676020X

Fig. 114 Test A: Speed Control Inoperative (Part 2 of 9). Mustang

TEST CONDITIONS	TEST DETAILS/RESULTS/ACTIONS
A5 CHECK CIRCUIT 636 (OG) FOR AN OPEN	
1 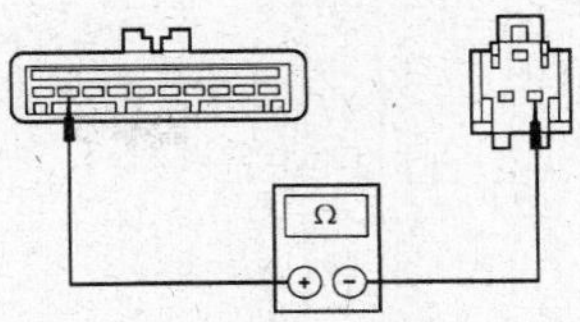	1 Measure the resistance between speed control servo C136 Pin 9, Circuit 636 (OG), harness side and deactivator switch C261 Pin 2, Circuit 636 (OG), harness side. • Is the resistance less than 5 ohms? → **Yes** INSTALL a new deactivator switch; TEST the system for normal operation. → **No** REPAIR the circuit. TEST the system for normal operation.
A6 CHECK THE SPEED CONTROL ACTUATOR SWITCH ON CIRCUITRY	
1 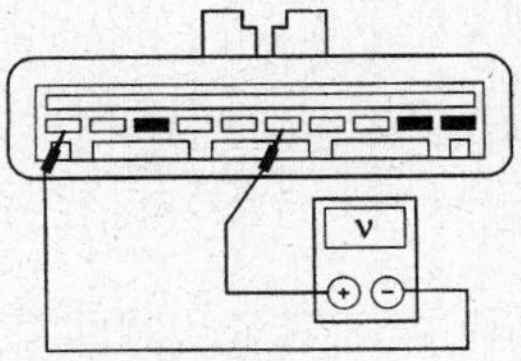	1 Measure the voltage between speed control servo C136 Pin 5, Circuit 151 (LB/BK), harness side and speed control servo C136 Pin 10, Circuit 1205 (BK), harness side, while the speed control actuator switch ON is depressed. • Is the voltage greater than 10 volts? → **Yes** GO to **A9**. → **No** GO to **A7**.

FM1109900676030X

Fig. 114 Test A: Speed Control Inoperative (Part 3 of 9). Mustang

TEST CONDITIONS	TEST DETAILS/RESULTS/ACTIONS
A7 CHECK CIRCUIT 151 (LB/BK) FOR AN OPEN	
1  Air Bag Sliding Contact C233 2 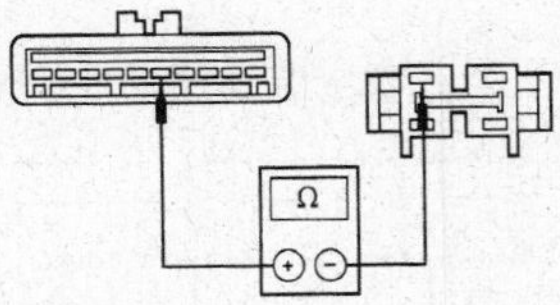	2 Measure the resistance between speed control servo C136 Pin 5, Circuit 151 (LB/BK), harness side and air bag sliding contact C233 Pin 1, Circuit 151 (LB/BK), harness side. • Is the resistance less than 5 ohms? → **Yes** GO to **A8**. → **No** REPAIR the circuit. TEST the system for normal operation.
A8 CHECK THE AIR BAG SLIDING CONTACT	
2  Speed Control Actuator Switch 3 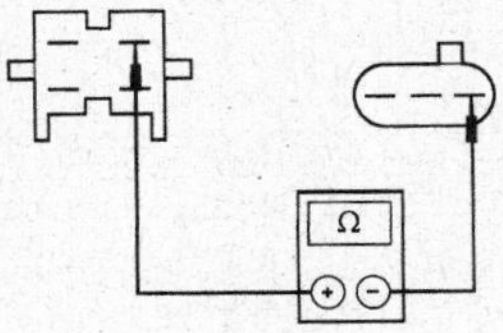	1 Remove the air bag. 3 Measure the resistance between bottom of air bag sliding contact Pin 1 (component side) and top of air bag sliding contact Pin 3 (component side). • Is the resistance less than 5 ohms? → **Yes** INSTALL a new speed control actuator switch. TEST the system for normal operation. → **No** INSTALL a new air bag sliding contact; TEST the system for normal operation.

FM1109900676040X

Fig. 114 Test A: Speed Control Inoperative (Part 4 of 9). Mustang

TEST CONDITIONS	TEST DETAILS/RESULTS/ACTIONS
A9 CHECK THE SPEED CONTROL ACTUATOR SWITCH ON CIRCUITRY FOR SHORT TO POWER	
1  2 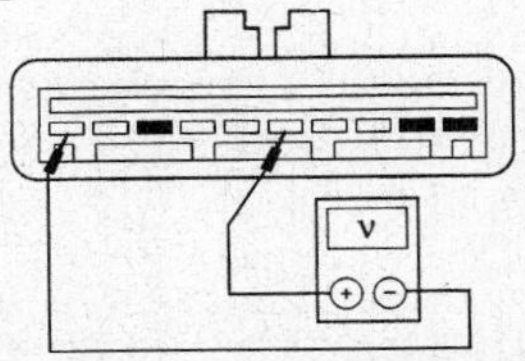	2 Measure the voltage between speed control servo C136 Pin 5, Circuit 151 (LB/BK), harness side and speed control servo C136 Pin 10, Circuit 1205 (BK), harness side. • Is any voltage present? → **Yes** GO to **A10**. → **No** GO to **A12**.
A10 CHECK CIRCUIT 151 (LB/BK) FOR SHORT TO POWER	
1 2 3  Air Bag Sliding Contact C233 4 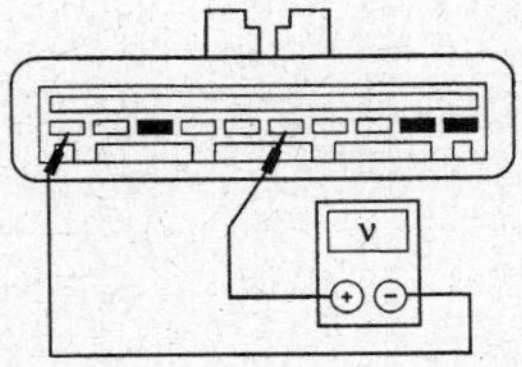	4 Measure the voltage between speed control servo C136 Pin 5, Circuit 151 (LB/BK), harness side and speed control servo C136 Pin 10, Circuit 1205 (BK), harness side. • Is any voltage present? → **Yes** REPAIR the circuit. TEST the system for normal operation. → **No** GO to **A11**

FM1109900676050X

Fig. 114 Test A: Speed Control Inoperative (Part 5 of 9). Mustang

TEST CONDITIONS	TEST DETAILS/RESULTS/ACTIONS
A11 CHECK THE AIR BAG SLIDING CONTACT	
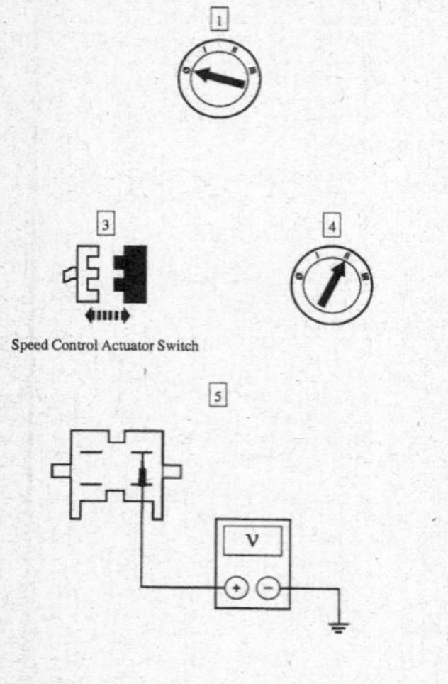	[2] Remove the air bag. [5] Measure the voltage between bottom of air bag sliding contact Pin 1 (component side) and ground. • Is any voltage present? → **Yes** INSTALL a new air bag sliding contact. TEST the system for normal operation. → **No** INSTALL a new speed control actuator switch. TEST the system for normal operation.

FM1109900676060X

Fig. 114 Test A: Speed Control Inoperative (Part 6 of 9). Mustang

TEST CONDITIONS	TEST DETAILS/RESULTS/ACTIONS
A14 CHECK CIRCUIT 511 (LG) AND CIRCUIT 810 (RD/LG) FOR AN OPEN	
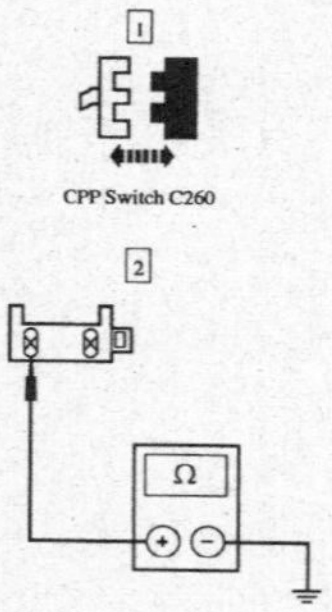	[2] Measure the resistance between CPP Switch C260 Pin 1, Circuit 511 (LG), harness side and ground. • Is the resistance less than 20 ohms? → **Yes** GO to **A15**. → **No** REPAIR Circuit 511 (LG) and Circuit 810 (LG/RD) as necessary. TEST the system for normal operation.
A15 CHECK CIRCUIT 511 (LG) FOR AN OPEN	
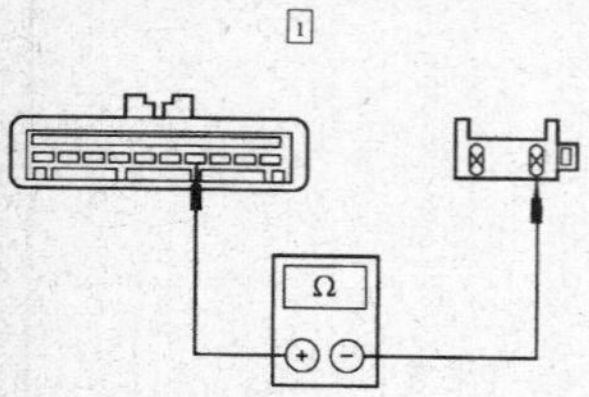	[1] Measure the resistance between speed control servo C136 Pin 4, Circuit 511 (LG), harness side and CPP switch C260 Pin 2, Circuit 511 (LG), harness side. • Is the resistance less than 5 ohms? → **Yes** INSTALL a new CPP switch. TEST the system for normal operation. → **No** REPAIR the circuit. TEST the system for normal operation.
A16 CHECK CIRCUIT 239 (WH/OG) FOR AN OPEN	
	[2] Connect EEC-V 104-Pin Breakout Box.

FM1109900676080X

Fig. 114 Test A: Speed Control Inoperative (Part 8 of 9). Mustang

TEST CONDITIONS	TEST DETAILS/RESULTS/ACTIONS
A12 CHECK THE SPEED CONTROL ACTUATOR SET/ACCEL CIRCUITRY	
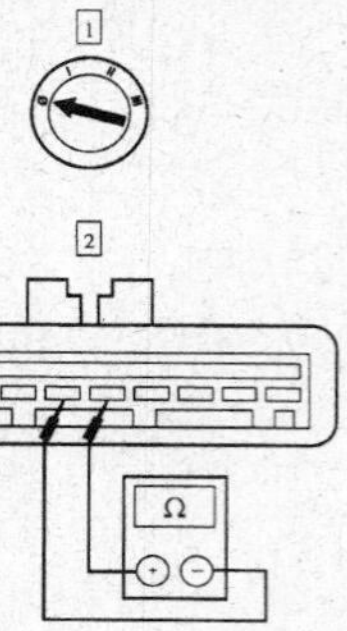	[2] Measure the resistance between speed control servo C136 Pin 5, Circuit 151 (LB/BK), harness side and speed control servo C136 Pin 6, Circuit 848 (DG/OG), harness side, while the speed control actuator switch SET/ACCEL is depressed. • Is the resistance between 612 and 748 ohms? → **Yes** GO to **A13**. → **No** INSTALL a new speed control actuator switch. TEST the system for normal operation.
A13 CHECK THE BPP SWITCH CIRCUITRY	
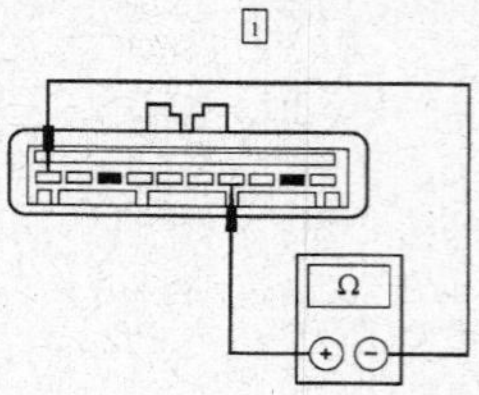	[1] Measure the resistance between speed control servo C136 Pin 4, Circuit 511 (LG), harness side, and speed control servo C136 Pin 10, Circuit 1205 (BK), harness side. • Is the resistance less than 20 ohms? → **Yes** GO to **A16**. → **No** If automatic transmission, REPAIR Circuit 511 (LG) and Circuit 810 (LG/RD) as necessary. TEST the system for normal operation. If manual transmission, GO to **A14**.

FM1109900676070X

Fig. 114 Test A: Speed Control Inoperative (Part 7 of 9). Mustang

TEST CONDITIONS	TEST DETAILS/RESULTS/ACTIONS
A16 CHECK CIRCUIT 239 (WH/OG) FOR AN OPEN (Continued)	
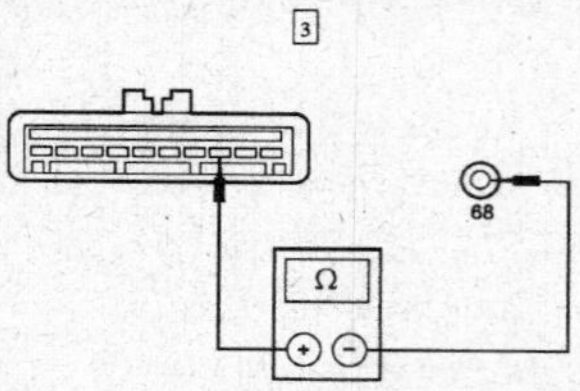	[3] Measure the resistance between speed control servo Pin 3, Circuit 239 (WH/OG), harness side and EEC-V 104-Pin Breakout Box Pin 68, Circuit 239 (WH/OG), harness side. • Is the resistance less than 5 ohms? → **Yes** GO to **A17**. → **No** REPAIR the circuit. TEST the system for normal operation.
A17 CHECK THE SPEED CONTROL SERVO	
	[1] INSTALL a known good speed control servo. [2] Test drive the vehicle for correct operation. • Does the speed control operate correctly? → **Yes** INSTALL a new speed control servo. TEST the system for normal operation. → **No** INSTALL a new PCM. TEST the system for normal operation.

FM1109900676090X

Fig. 114 Test A: Speed Control Inoperative (Part 9 of 9). Mustang

TEST CONDITIONS	TEST DETAILS/RESULTS/ACTIONS
B1 CHECK THAT CONDITION OCCURS ONLY WHILE USING SPEED CONTROL	
	[1] Check that the condition does not occur when driving without speed control. • Does the condition occur without speed control? → **Yes** REPAIR engine as necessary. TEST the system for normal operation. → **No** GO to **B2**

FM1109900677010X

Fig. 115 Test B: Set Speed Fluctuates (Part 1 of 2). Mustang

TEST CONDITIONS | **TEST DETAILS/RESULTS/ACTIONS**

B2 CHECK THE SPEED CONTROL ACTUATOR CABLE

1 **NOTE:** The speed control actuator cable must be disconnected at both ends while carrying out this test.

Check the speed control actuator cable for sticking or binding at the speed control servo and throttle body.

- Is the speed control actuator cable OK?

→ **Yes**
GO to **B3**.

→ **No**
INSTALL a new speed control actuator cable. TEST the system for normal operation.

B3 CHECK THE SPEED CONTROL SERVO

1 INSTALL a known good speed control servo.

2 Test drive the vehicle for correct operation.

- Does the speed control operate correctly?

→ **Yes**
INSTALL a new speed control servo. TEST the system for normal operation.

→ **No**
INSTALL a new PCM. TEST the system for normal operation.

FM1109900677020X

Fig. 115 Test B: Set Speed Fluctuates (Part 2 of 2). Mustang

TEST CONDITIONS | **TEST DETAILS/RESULTS/ACTIONS**

D1 CHECK THE CLUTCH PEDAL POSITION (CPP) SWITCH

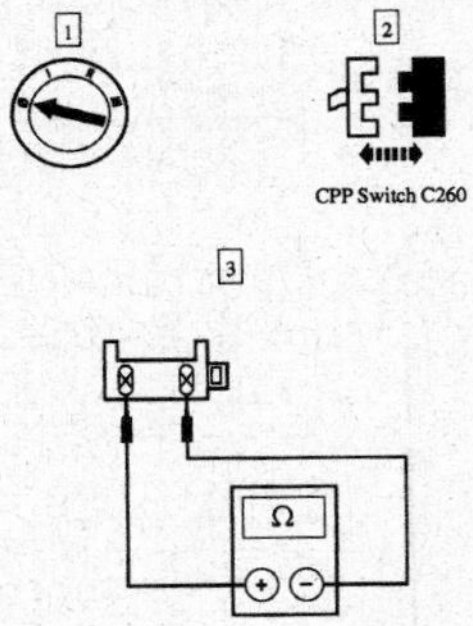

3 Measure the resistance between CPP switch Pin 3 (component side) and CPP switch Pin 4 (component side), while depressing and releasing clutch pedal.

- Is the resistance greater than 10,000 ohms with the clutch pedal depressed and less than 5 ohms with the clutch pedal released?

→ **Yes**
INSTALL a new speed control servo. TEST the system for normal operation.

→ **No**
INSTALL a new CPP switch. TEST the system for normal operation.

FM1109900679000X

Fig. 117 Test D: Speed Control Does Not Disengage When Clutch Is Applied. Mustang

TEST CONDITIONS | **TEST DETAILS/RESULTS/ACTIONS**

F1 CHECK THE SPEED CONTROL ACTUATOR SWITCH

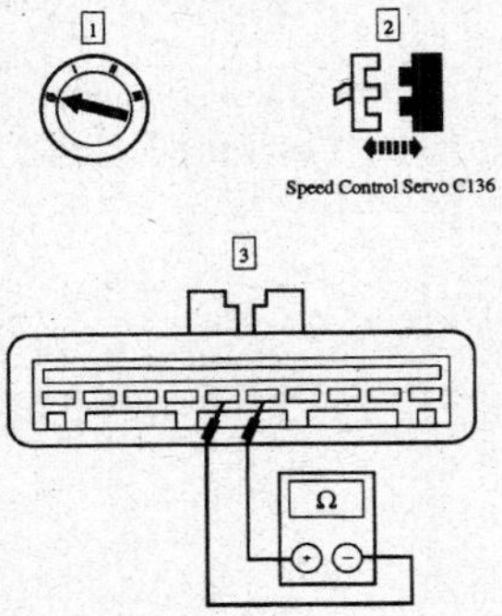

3 Measure the resistance between speed control servo C136 Pin 5, Circuit 151 (LB/BK), harness side and speed control servo C136 Pin 6, Circuit 848 (DG/OG), harness side, while pressing the speed control actuator switch SET/ACCEL.

- Is the resistance between 612 and 748 ohms?

→ **Yes**
INSTALL a new speed control servo. TEST the system for normal operation.

→ **No**
INSTALL a new speed control actuator switch. TEST the system for normal operation.

FM1109900681000X

Fig. 119 Test F: Speed Control Switch Is Inoperative, SET/ACCEL. Mustang

TEST CONDITIONS | **TEST DETAILS/RESULTS/ACTIONS**

C1 CHECK THE BPP SWITCH CIRCUITRY

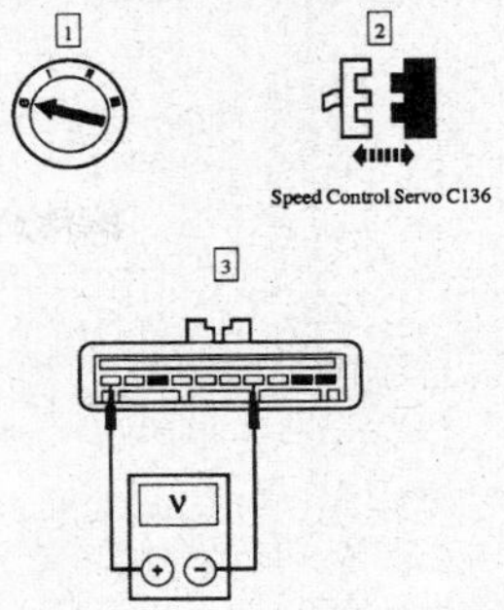

3 Measure the voltage between speed control servo C136 Pin 4, Circuit 511 (LG), harness side and speed control servo C136 Pin 10, Circuit 1205 (BK), harness side, while depressing the brake pedal.

- Is the voltage greater than 10 volts?

→ **Yes**
INSTALL a new speed control servo. TEST the system for normal operation.

→ **No**
REPAIR Circuit 810 (RD/LG) and Circuit 511 (LG) as necessary. TEST the system for normal operation.

FM1109900678000X

Fig. 116 Test C: Speed Control Does Not Disengage When Brakes Are Applied. Mustang

TEST CONDITIONS | **TEST DETAILS/RESULTS/ACTIONS**

E1 CHECK THE SPEED CONTROL ACTUATOR SWITCH

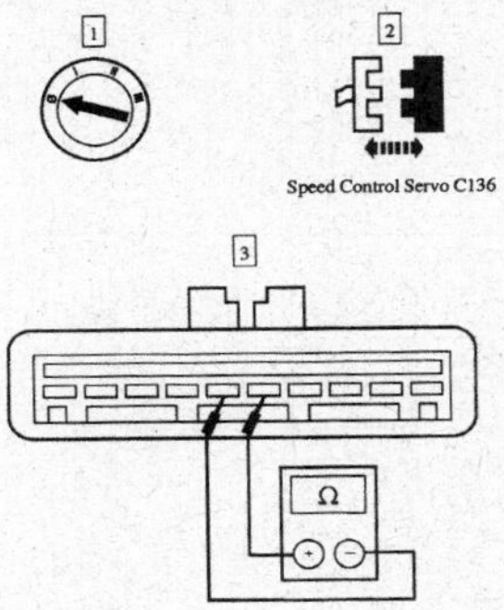

3 Measure the resistance between speed control servo C136 Pin 5, Circuit 151 (LB/BK), harness side and speed control servo C136 Pin 6, Circuit 848 (DG/OG), harness side, while pressing the speed control actuator switch COAST.

- Is the resistance between 108 and 132 ohms?

→ **Yes**
INSTALL a new speed control servo. TEST the system for normal operation.

→ **No**
INSTALL a new speed control actuator switch. TEST the system for normal operation.

FM1109900680000X

Fig. 118 Test E: Speed Control Switch Is Inoperative, Coast. Mustang

TEST CONDITIONS | **TEST DETAILS/RESULTS/ACTIONS**

G1 CHECK THE SPEED CONTROL ACTUATOR SWITCH

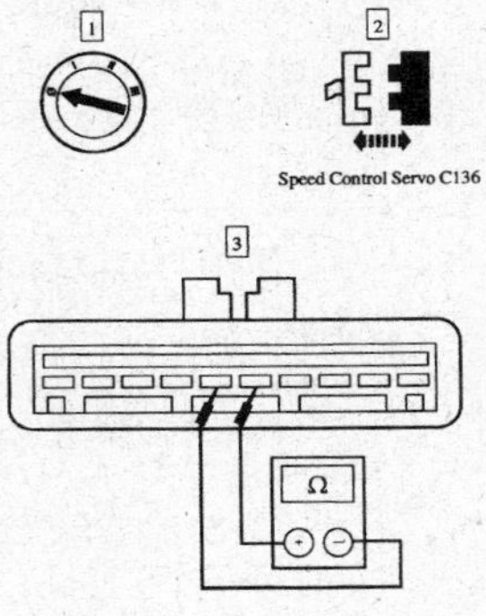

3 Measure the resistance between speed control servo C136 Pin 5, Circuit 151 (LB/BK), harness side and speed control servo C136 Pin 6, Circuit 848 (DG/OG), harness side while pressing the speed control actuator switch RESUME.

- Is the resistance between 1,980 and 2,420 ohms?

→ **Yes**
INSTALL a new speed control servo. TEST the system for normal operation.

→ **No**
INSTALL a new speed control actuator switch. TEST the system for normal operation.

FM1109900682000X

Fig. 120 Test G: Speed Control Switch Is Inoperative, Resume. Mustang

TEST CONDITIONS	TESTDETAILS/RESULTS/ACTIONS
H1 CHECK THE SPEED CONTROL ACTUATOR SWITCH	
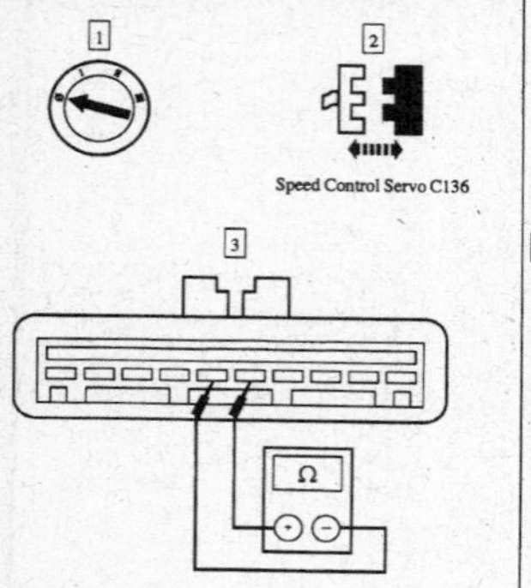	3 Measure the resistance between speed control servo C136 Pin 5, Circuit 151 (LB/BK), harness side and speed control servo C136 Pin 6, Circuit 848 (DG/OG), harness side while pressing the speed control actuator switch OFF. • Is the resistance less than 5 ohms? → **Yes** INSTALL a new speed control servo: TEST the system for normal operation. → **No** INSTALL a new speed control actuator switch. TEST the system for normal operation.

FM1109900683000X

Fig. 121 Test H: Speed Control Switch Is Inoperative, Off. Mustang

Condition	Possible Source	Action
• OFF Switch Inoperative	• Speed control actuator switches. • Speed control servo. • Circuitry.	• GO to Pinpoint Test L.
• Set Speed Fluctuates	• Vehicle speed sensor or anti-lock brake control module (SHO). • Speed control servo. • Speed control actuator switches. • Circuitry. • Loose or binding condition between speed control actuator cable and throttle body. • Engine.	• GO to Pinpoint Test M.

FM1109800534020X

Fig. 122 Symptom Chart (Part 2 of 2). 2000 Sable & Taurus

Test Step		Result	▶ Action to Take
B1	CHECK THE STOPLAMP OPERATION		
	• Check the stoplamps while pressing the brake pedal. • **Do the stoplamps operate properly?**	Yes No	▶ GO to **B2**. ▶ Diagnose Stoplamps
B2	CHECK THE BRAKE PEDAL POSITION (BPP) SWITCH INPUT		
	• Disconnect the speed control servo C102. • Measure the voltage between speed control servo C102-4, circuit 810 (R/LG), and ground, while pressing the brake pedal. • **Is the voltage greater than 10 volts?**	Yes No	▶ GO to **B3**. ▶ REPAIR circuit 810 (R/LG). RESTORE vehicle. PERFORM the Self-Test Diagnostics.
B3	CHECK CIRCUIT 810 (R/LG) FOR SHORT TO POWER		
	• Measure the voltage between speed control servo C102-4, circuit 810 (R/LG), and ground. • **Is voltage present?**	Yes No	▶ GO to **B4**. ▶ REPLACE the speed control servo. RESTORE vehicle. PERFORM the Self-Test Diagnostics.
B4	CHECK THE BPP SWITCH		
	• Disconnect the BPP switch C2016. • Measure the voltage between speed control servo C102-4, circuit 810 (R/LG), and ground. • **Is voltage present?**	Yes No	▶ REPAIR circuit 810 (R/LG). RESTORE vehicle. PERFORM the Self-Test Diagnostics. ▶ REPLACE the BPP switch. RESTORE vehicle. PERFORM the Self-Test Diagnostics.

FM1109800546000X

Fig. 124 Test B: Flash Code 2, Brake Pedal Position Switch Circuity. 2000 Sable & Taurus

C2	CHECK THE DEACTIVATOR SWITCH INPUT		
	• Disconnect the speed control servo C102. • Measure the voltage between speed control servo C102-9, circuit 248 (T/O), and ground. • **Is the voltage greater than 10 volts?**	Yes No	▶ REPLACE the speed control servo. RESTORE vehicle. PERFORM the Self-Test Diagnostics. ▶ GO to **C3**.
C3	CHECK CIRCUIT 10 (LG/R) FOR AN OPEN		
	• Disconnect the deactivator switch C246. • Measure the voltage between deactivator switch C246, circuit 10 (LG/R), and ground. • **Is the voltage greater than 10 volts?**	Yes No	▶ GO to **C4**. ▶ REPAIR circuit 10 (LG/R). RESTORE vehicle. PERFORM the Self-Test Diagnostics.
C4	CHECK CIRCUIT 248 (T/O) FOR AN OPEN		
	• Measure the resistance between speed control servo C102-9, circuit 248 (T/O), and deactivator switch C246, circuit 248 (T/O). • **Is the resistance less than 5 ohms?**	Yes No	▶ REPLACE the deactivator switch. RESTORE vehicle. PERFORM the Self-Test Diagnostics. ▶ REPAIR circuit 248 (T/O). RESTORE vehicle. PERFORM the Self-Test Diagnostics.

FM1109800536020X

Fig. 125 Test C: Flash Code 3, Deactivator Switch Circuitry (Part 2 of 2). 2000 Sable & Taurus

Condition	Possible Source	Action
• Flash Code 1	• —	• Test Passed.
• Flash Code 1 — No Dynamic Pull at Throttle Body	• Speed control actuator cable.	• REPLACE the speed control actuator cable. PERFORM the Self-Test Diagnostics.
• Flash Code 1 — No Dynamic Pull at Speed Control Servo	• Speed control actuator cable. • Speed control servo.	• GO to Pinpoint Test A.
• Flash Code 1 — Speed Control Inoperative	• Circuitry. • Speed control servo.	• GO to Pinpoint Test D.
• Flash Code 2	• Brake pedal position (BPP) switch. • Circuitry.	• GO to Pinpoint Test B.
• Flash Code 3	• Fuse. • Circuitry. • Deactivator switch.	• GO to Pinpoint Test C.
• Flash Code 4	• Circuitry. • Vehicle speed sensor or anti-lock brake control module (SHO).	• GO to Pinpoint Test D.
• Flash Code 5	• Speed control servo.	• REPLACE the speed control servo. PERFORM the Self-Test Diagnostics.
• Speed Control Inoperative — No Flash Codes	• Fuse. • Circuitry. • Deactivator switch. • Brake pedal position (BPP) switch. • Burned out stoplamp bulb. • Speed control actuator switches. • Vehicle speed sensor or anti-lock brake control module (SHO). • Speed control servo.	• GO to Pinpoint Test E.
• Speed Control Indicator Does Not Turn On	• Circuitry. • Instrument cluster. • Speed control servo.	• GO to Pinpoint Test F.
• Speed Control Indicator Does Not Turn Off	• Circuitry. • Speed control servo. • Instrument cluster.	• GO to Pinpoint Test G.
• COAST Switch Inoperative	• Speed control actuator switches. • Speed control servo. • Circuitry.	• GO to Pinpoint Test H.
• SET/ACCEL Switch Inoperative	• Speed control actuator switches. • Speed control servo. • Deactivator switch. • Circuitry.	• GO to Pinpoint Test J.
• RESUME Switch Inoperative	• Speed control actuator switches. • Speed control servo. • Circuitry.	• GO to Pinpoint Test K.

FM1109800534010X

Fig. 122 Symptom Chart (Part 1 of 2). 2000 Sable & Taurus

Test Step		Result	▶ Action to Take
A1	CHECK THE SPEED CONTROL ACTUATOR CABLE		
	• Place the ignition switch in the OFF position. • Disconnect the speed control actuator cable from the speed control servo. • Check the speed control actuator cable for sticking or binding. • **Is the speed control actuator cable OK?**	Yes No	▶ REPLACE speed control servo. PERFORM the Self-Test Diagnostics. ▶ REPAIR or REPLACE the speed control actuator cable. PERFORM the Self-Test Diagnostics.

FM1109800535000X

Fig. 123 Test A: Flash Code 1, No Dynamic Pull At Speed Control Servo. 2000 Sable & Taurus

Test Step		Result	▶ Action to Take
C1	CHECK THE STOPLAMP OPERATION		
	• Check the stoplamps while pressing the brake pedal. • **Do the stoplamps operate properly?**	Yes No	▶ GO to **C2**. ▶ Diagnose Stoplamps

FM1109800536010X

Fig. 125 Test C: Flash Code 3, Deactivator Switch Circuitry (Part 1 of 2). 2000 Sable & Taurus

Test Step		Result	▶ Action to Take
D1	CHECK THE SPEEDOMETER OPERATION		
	• Check the speedometer while driving the vehicle. • **Does the speedometer operate properly?**	Yes No	▶ GO to **D2**. ▶ DIAGNOSE speedometer.
D2	CHECK CIRCUIT 679 (GY/BK) FOR AN OPEN		
	• Disconnect the vehicle speed sensor C1043 or anti-lock brake control module C1057 (SHO). • Measure the resistance between speed control servo C102-3, circuit 679 (GY/BK), and vehicle speed sensor C1043, circuit 679 (GY/BK), or anti-lock brake control module C1057-12, circuit 679 (GY/BK) (SHO). • **Is the resistance less than 5 ohms?**	Yes No	▶ REPLACE the speed control servo. RESTORE vehicle. PERFORM the Self-Test Diagnostics. ▶ REPAIR circuit 679 (GY/BK). RESTORE vehicle. PERFORM the Self-Test Diagnostics.

FM1109800537000X

Fig. 126 Test D: Flash Code 4, Vehicle Speed Signal Input Circuitry. 2000 Sable & Taurus

Test Step		Result	Action to Take
E1	CHECK POWER TO SPEED CONTROL SERVO		
	• Disconnect speed control servo C102. • Turn ignition switch to RUN. • Measure voltage between speed control servo C102-7, Circuit 1087 (O), and speed control servo C102-10, Circuit 57 (BK). • **Is voltage greater than 10 volts?**	Yes No	GO to **E4**. GO to **E2**.
E2	CHECK FUSE JUNCTION PANEL FUSE 6 (15A)		
	• Check the fuse junction panel fuse 6 (15A). • **Is the fuse OK?**	Yes No	GO to **E3**. REPLACE the fuse. PERFORM the Self-Test Diagnostics. If fuse fails again, CHECK for short to ground. REPAIR as necessary. PERFORM the Self-Test Diagnostics.
E3	CHECK SPEED CONTROL SERVO GROUND CIRCUIT		
	• Measure resistance between speed control servo C102-10, Circuit 57 (BK), and ground. • **Is resistance less than 5 ohms?**	Yes No	REPAIR circuit 1087 (O). RESTORE vehicle. PERFORM the Self-Test Diagnostics. REPAIR Circuit 57 (BK). RESTORE vehicle. PERFORM the Self-Test Diagnostics.

FM1109800538010X

Fig. 127 Test E: No Flash Codes, Speed Control Inoperative (Part 1 of 3). 2000 Sable & Taurus

Test Step		Result	Action to Take
E12	CHECK FOR BROKEN OR BINDING CABLE		
	• Remove the speed control actuator cable from speed control servo. • Check for broken or binding cable by pulling on the cable ball slug to make sure throttle moves freely. • **Is the speed control actuator cable OK?**	Yes No	REPLACE the speed control servo. RESTORE vehicle. PERFORM the Self-Test Diagnostics. REPLACE the speed control actuator cable. RESTORE vehicle. PERFORM the Self-Test Diagnostics.
E13	CHECK CIRCUIT SPEED CONTROL ACTUATOR SWITCH		
	• Disconnect the speed control actuator switch. • Measure the voltage between speed control servo C102-5, circuit 916 (LG), and speed control actuator C102-10, circuit 57 (BK). • **Is voltage present?**	Yes No	GO to **E14**. REPLACE the speed control actuator switch. RESTORE vehicle. PERFORM the Self-Test Diagnostics.
E14	CHECK CIRCUIT 916 (LG) FOR SHORT TO POWER		
	• Disconnect the air bag sliding contact. • Measure the voltage between speed control servo C102-5, circuit 916 (LG), and speed control actuator C102-10, circuit 57 (BK). • **Is voltage present?**	Yes No	REPAIR circuit 916 (DG). RESTORE vehicle. PERFORM the Self-Test Diagnostics. REPLACE the air bag sliding contact. RESTORE vehicle. PERFORM the Self-Test Diagnostics.

FM1109800538030X

Fig. 127 Test E: No Flash Codes, Speed Control Inoperative (Part 3 of 3). 2000 Sable & Taurus

Test Step		Result	Action to Take
F1	CHECK VOLTAGE AT SPEED CONTROL SERVO ASSEMBLY CONNECTOR		
	• Disconnect speed control servo connector. • With ignition switch in RUN, measure voltage between speed control servo C102-1, Circuit 203 (O/LB), and speed control servo C102-10, Circuit 57 (BK). • **Is voltage greater than 10 volts?**	Yes No	REPLACE the speed control servo. RESTORE vehicle. PERFORM the Self-Test Diagnostics. GO to **F2**.
F2	CHECK CIRCUIT CONTINUITY		
	• Disconnect instrument cluster C251. • Measure resistance between speed control servo C102-1, circuit 203 (O/LB), and instrument cluster C251-5, circuit 203 (O/LB). • **Is resistance less than 5 ohms?**	Yes No	REPLACE the instrument cluster. REPAIR Circuit 203 (O/LB). RESTORE vehicle. PERFORM the Self-Test Diagnostics.

FM1109800539000X

Fig. 128 Test F: Speed Control Indicator Does Not Turn On. 2000 Sable & Taurus

Test Step		Result	Action to Take
H1	CHECK COAST SWITCH OPERATION		
	• Disconnect speed control servo C102. • With COAST switch pressed, measure resistance between speed control servo C102-5, Circuit 916 (LG), and speed control servo C102-6, Circuit 848 (DG/O), while rotating steering wheel through full range. • **Is the resistance between 114 and 126 ohms?**	Yes No	REPLACE speed control servo. PERFORM the Self-Test Diagnostics. REPLACE speed control actuator switch. RECONNECT speed control servo. PERFORM the Self-Test Diagnostics.

FM1109800541000X

Fig. 130 Test H: Coast Switch Inoperative. 2000 Sable & Taurus

Test Step		Result	Action to Take
K1	CHECK RESUME SWITCH OPERATION		
	• Disconnect speed control servo C102. • With RESUME switch pressed, measure resistance between speed control servo C102-5, Circuit 916 (LG), and speed control servo C102-6, Circuit 848 (DG/O), while rotating steering wheel through full range. • **Is the resistance between 2090 and 2310 ohms?**	Yes No	REPLACE speed control servo. PERFORM the Self-Test Diagnostics. REPLACE speed control actuator switch. RECONNECT speed control servo. PERFORM the Self-Test Diagnostics.

FM1109800543000X

Fig. 132 Test K: Resume Switch Inoperative. 2000 Sable & Taurus

Test Step		Result	Action to Take
E4	CHECK FOR STUCK ON SPEED CONTROL ACTUATOR SWITCH		
	• Turn ignition switch to RUN. • With no speed control switches pressed, measure voltage between speed control servo C102-5, Circuit 916 (LG) and speed control servo C102-10, Circuit 57 (BK). • **Is voltage present?**	Yes No	GO to **E13**. GO to **E5**.
E5	CHECK ON SWITCH OPERATION		
	• With speed control ON switch pressed, measure voltage between speed control servo C102-5, Circuit 916 (LG), and speed control servo C102-10, Circuit 57 (BK). • **Is voltage greater than 10 volts?**	Yes No	GO to **E6**. GO to **E7**.
E6	CHECK HORN OPERATION		
	• Press horn button. • **Does horn system operate properly?**	Yes No	GO to **E9**. REPAIR horn system. RESTORE vehicle. PERFORM the Self-Test Diagnostics.
E7	CHECK AIR BAG SLIDING CONTACT		
	• Disconnect air bag sliding contact at the base of steering column. • Disconnect speed control actuator switch. • Measure resistance across each of the air bag sliding contact windings between the air bag sliding contact connector at the base of steering column and speed control switches connector in the steering wheel. • **Is each resistance reading between 0.25-0.5 ohm?**	Yes No	GO to **E8**. REPLACE air bag sliding contact. RESTORE vehicle. PERFORM the Self-Test Diagnostics.
E8	CHECK CIRCUIT 916 (LG) FOR AN OPEN		
	• Measure the resistance between speed control servo C102-5, circuit 916 (LG), and air bag sliding contact C228M, circuit 916 (LG). • **Is the resistance less than 5 ohms?**	Yes No	REPLACE the speed control actuator switch. RESTORE vehicle. PERFORM the Self-Test Diagnostics. REPAIR circuit 916 (LG). RESTORE vehicle. PERFORM the Self-Test Diagnostics.
E9	CHECK THE SPEED CONTROL SWITCH CIRCUITRY		
	• Measure the resistance between speed control servo C102-5, circuit 916 (LG), and speed control servo C102-6, circuit 848 (DG/O), while pressing the speed control actuator SET/ACCEL switch. • **Is the resistance between 646 and 714 ohms?**	Yes No	GO to **E10**. REPLACE the speed control actuator switch. RESTORE vehicle. PERFORM the Self-Test Diagnostics.
E10	CHECK THE SPEED CONTROL ACTUATOR SWITCH		
	• Measure the resistance between speed control servo C102-5, circuit 916 (LG), and speed control servo C102-6, circuit 848 (DG/O), while pressing the speed control actuator OFF switch.. • **Is the resistance less than 5 ohms?**	Yes No	GO to **E11**. REPLACE the speed control actuator switch. RESTORE vehicle. PERFORM the Self-Test Diagnostics.
E11	CHECK THE SPEED CONTROL INDICATOR CIRCUITRY		
	• Place the ignition switch in the RUN position. • Measure the voltage between the speed control servo C102-1, circuit (O/LB), and ground. • **Is the voltage greater than 10 volts?**	Yes No	GO to **E12**. GO to Pinpoint Test F.

FM1109800538020X

Fig. 127 Test E: No Flash Codes, Speed Control Inoperative (Part 2 of 3). 2000 Sable & Taurus

Test Step		Result	Action to Take
G1	CHECK SPEED CONTROL SERVO		
	• Disconnect speed control servo C102. • Turn ignition switch to RUN. • **Is the speed control indicator illuminated?**	Yes No	GO to **G2**. REPLACE speed control servo. PERFORM the Self-Test Diagnostics.
G2	CHECK CIRCUIT 203 (O/LB) FOR SHORT TO GROUND		
	• Disconnect instrument cluster C251. • Measure resistance between instrument cluster C251-5, Circuit 203 (O/LB) and ground. • **Is the resistance greater than 10,000 ohms?**	Yes No	REPLACE instrument cluster. REPAIR Circuit 203 (O/LB). RESTORE vehicle. PERFORM the Self-Test Diagnostics.

FM1109800540000X

Fig. 129 Test G: Speed Control Indicator Does Not Turn Off. 2000 Sable & Taurus

Test Step		Result	Action to Take
J1	CHECK SET/ACCEL SWITCH OPERATION		
	• Disconnect speed control servo C102. • With SET/ACCEL switch pressed, measure resistance between speed control servo C102-5, Circuit 916 (LG), and speed control servo C102-6, Circuit 848 (DG/O), while rotating steering wheel through full range. • **Is the resistance between 646 and 714 ohms?**	Yes No	REPLACE speed control servo. PERFORM the Self-Test Diagnostics. REPLACE speed control actuator switch. RECONNECT speed control servo. PERFORM the Self-Test Diagnostics.

FM1109800542000X

Fig. 131 Test J: SET/ACCEL Switch Inoperative. 2000 Sable & Taurus

Test Step		Result	Action to Take
L1	CHECK OFF SWITCH OPERATION		
	• Disconnect speed control servo C102. • With OFF switch pressed, measure resistance between speed control servo C102-5, Circuit 916 (LG), and speed control servo C102-6, Circuit 848 (DG/O), while rotating steering wheel through full range. • **Is the resistance less than 5 ohms?**	Yes No	REPLACE speed control servo. PERFORM the Self-Test Diagnostics. REPLACE speed control actuator switch. RECONNECT speed control servo. PERFORM the Self-Test Diagnostics.

FM1109800544000X

Fig. 133 Test L: Off Switch Inoperative. 2000 Sable & Taurus

Test Step		Result	Action to Take
M1	VERIFY CONDITION OCCURS ONLY WHILE USING SPEED CONTROL		
	• Verify that engine is properly tuned. • Verify that condition does not occur when driving without speed control. • **Does condition occur without speed control?**	Yes	REPAIR engine as required.
		No	GO to **M2**.

FM1109800545010X

Fig. 134 Test M: Set Speed Fluctuates (Part 1 of 2). 2000 Sable & Taurus

Test Step		Result	Action to Take
M2	CHECK FOR BINDING IN SPEED CONTROL ACTUATOR CABLE AND THROTTLE BODY LINKAGE		
	• Check for binding or sticking of speed control actuator cable or throttle linkage and throttle plate. • Make sure throttle cable bracket and speed control servo bracket are not loose. • **Are components OK?**	Yes	GO to **M3**.
		No	REPAIR as required. PERFORM the Self-Test Diagnostics.
M3	CHECK THE SPEEDOMETER FOR PROPER OPERATION		
	• Check the speedometer for proper operation while driving the vehicle. • **Does the speedometer operate properly?**	Yes	GO to **M4**.
		No	**Diagnose speedometer.**
M4	CHECK CIRCUIT 679 (GY / BK) FOR AN OPEN		
	• Disconnect the vehicle speed sensor C1043 or anti-lock brake control module C1057 (SHO). • Measure the resistance between speed control servo C102-3, circuit 679 (GY / BK), and vehicle speed sensor C1043, circuit 679 (GY / BK), or anti-lock brake control module C1057-12, circuit 679 (GY / BK) (SHO). • **Is the resistance less than 5 ohms?**	Yes	REPLACE the speed control servo. RESTORE vehicle. PERFORM the Self-Test Diagnostics.
		No	REPAIR circuit 679 (GY / BK). RESTORE vehicle. PERFORM the Self-Test Diagnostics.

FM1109800545020X

Fig. 134 Test M: Set Speed Fluctuates (Part 2 of 2). 2000 Sable & Taurus

☐ Flash code 1 — system pass

Possible Source(s):
- —

Action(s) to take:
- Test Passed.

☐ Flash code 1 — with last switch depressed and no dynamic pull occurs at the throttle

Possible Source(s):
- Speed control actuator cable.
- Speed control servo.

Action(s) to take:
- Pinpoint Test A.

☐ Flash code 1 — dynamic pull occurs at throttle and speed control inoperative

Possible Source(s):
- Circuitry.
- Speed control servo.

Action(s) to take:
- GO to «Pinpoint Test D».

☐ Flash code 2—brake pedal position switch or circuit failure

Possible Source(s):
- Central junction box (CJB) fuse F217 (15A).
- BPP switch or circuitry.
- Speed control servo.

Action(s) to take:
- GO to «Pinpoint Test B».

☐ Flash code 3—deactivator switch or circuit failure

Possible Source(s):
- CJB fuse F217 (15A).
- Deactivator switch or circuitry.
- Speed control servo.

Action(s) to take:
- GO to «Pinpoint Test C».

☐ Flash code 5

Possible Source(s):
- Speed control servo.

Action(s) to take:
- INSTALL a new speed control servo. TEST the system for normal operation.

☐ The speed control is inoperative — no flash codes

Possible Source(s):
- CJB fuse F232 (10A).
- Circuitry.
- Speed control actuator cable.
- Speed control actuator switches.
- Powertrain control module (PCM).
- Speed control servo.

Action(s) to take:
- GO to «Pinpoint Test E».

☐ The speed control switch is inoperative

Possible Source(s):
- Speed control actuator switch.
- Speed control servo.

Action(s) to take:
- GO to «Pinpoint Test F».

☐ The speed control indicator lamp is always on

Possible Source(s):
- Circuitry.
- Speed control servo.
- Instrument cluster.

Action(s) to take:
- GO to «Pinpoint Test G».

☐ The speed control indicator lamp is inoperative

Possible Source(s):
- Circuitry.
- Bulb.
- Instrument cluster.
- Speed control servo.

Action(s) to take:
- Diagnose instrument cluster fault condition.

☐ The set speed fluctuates

Possible Source(s):
- PCM.
- Speed control servo.
- Circuitry.
- Speed control actuator cable.

Action(s) to take:
- GO to «Pinpoint Test H».

Possible Source(s):
- Engine.

Action(s) to take:
- REPAIR engine as required.

FM1100100712010X

Fig. 135 Symptom chart (Part 1 of 2). 2001–04 Sable & Taurus

FM1100100712020X

Fig. 135 Symptom chart (Part 2 of 2). 2001–04 Sable & Taurus

A1 CHECK THE SPEED CONTROL ACTUATOR CABLE

1 Check the speed control actuator cable for correct attachment at the speed control servo and throttle body.

- **Is the speed control actuator cable attached correctly?**

→ **Yes**

Go to «A2».

→ **No**

RECONNECT the speed control actuator cable. TEST the system for normal operation.

FM1100100713010X

Fig. 136 Test A: Flash Code 1, With Last Switch Depressed & No Dynamic Pull Occurs At Throttle (Part 1 of 3). 2001–04 Sable & Taurus

A2 CHECK FOR CORRECT AMOUNT OF SLACK IN THE SPEED CONTROL ACTUATOR CABLE

1 Remove the speed control actuator cable from the throttle lever.

2 Check for 3 mm (0.12 in) of slack (extra length) in the speed control actuator cable, beyond the throttle attachment.

- **Is there less than 10mm (0.39 in) of slack in the cable at the throttle connection?**

→ **Yes**

Go to «A3».

→ **No**

INSTALL a new speed control actuator cable. TEST the system for normal operation.

FM1100100713020X

Fig. 136 Test A: Flash Code 1, With Last Switch Depressed & No Dynamic Pull Occurs At Throttle (Part 2 of 3). 2001–04 Sable & Taurus

A3	CHECK FOR A STICKING OR BINDING SPEED CONTROL ACTUATOR CABLE

1 Disconnect the speed control actuator cable from the speed control servo.

2 Check the speed control actuator cable for sticking or binding.

- **Is the speed control actuator cable OK?**

➔ **Yes**

INSTALL a new speed control servo.
TEST the system for normal operation.

➔ **No**

REPAIR or INSTALL a new speed control actuator cable.
TEST the system for normal operation.

FM1100100713030X

Fig. 136 Test A: Flash Code 1, With Last Switch Depressed & No Dynamic Pull Occurs At Throttle (Part 3 of 3). 2001–04 Sable & Taurus

B2	CHECK CIRCUIT 810 (RD/LG) FOR SHORT TO POWER

1

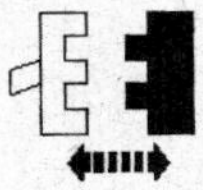

2 *Speed Control Servo C122*

3

FM1100100714020X

Fig. 137 Test B: Flash Code 2, BPP Switch Or Circuit Failure (Part 2 of 5). 2001–04 Sable & Taurus

B3	CHECK CIRCUIT 810 (RD/LG) FOR AN OPEN

1

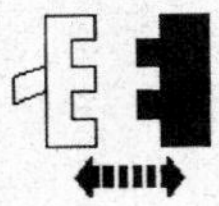

2 *Speed Control Servo C122*

3

FM1100100714040X

Fig. 137 Test B: Flash Code 2, BPP Switch Or Circuit Failure (Part 4 of 5). 2001–04 Sable & Taurus

B1	CHECK THE STOPLAMP OPERATION

1 Depress the brake pedal.

- **Do the brake lights come on?**

➔ **Yes**

Go to «B2».

➔ **No**

Diagnose brake lamp fault condition.

FM1100100714010X

Fig. 137 Test B: Flash Code 2, BPP Switch Or Circuit Failure (Part 1 of 5). 2001–04 Sable & Taurus

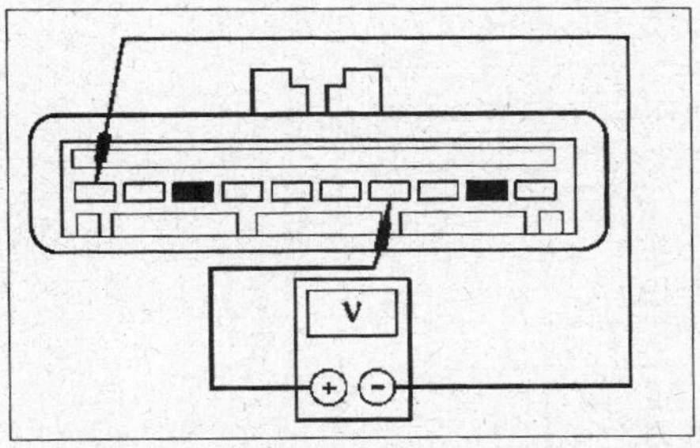

4

Measure the voltage between the speed control servo C122 pin 4, circuit 810 (RD/LG), harness side, and the speed control servo C122 pin 10, circuit 57 (BK), harness side.

- **Is voltage greater than 10 volts?**

➔ **Yes**

REPAIR the circuit. TEST the system for normal operation.

➔ **No**

Go to «B3».

FM1100100714030X

Fig. 137 Test B: Flash Code 2, BPP Switch Or Circuit Failure (Part 3 of 5). 2001–04 Sable & Taurus

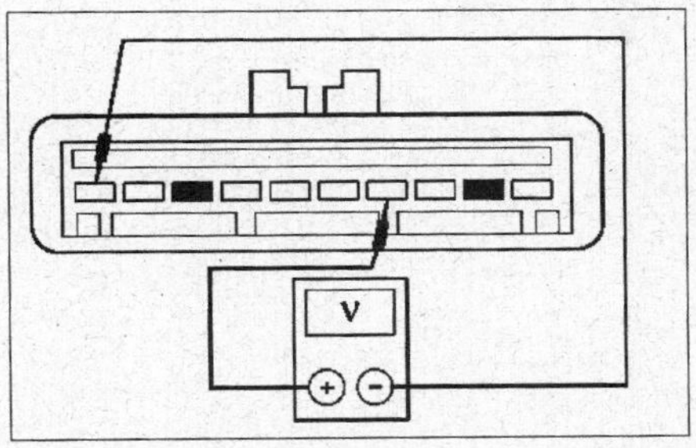

4

Measure the voltage between the speed control servo C122 pin 4, circuit 810 (RD/LG), harness side, and the speed control servo C122 pin 10, circuit 57 (BK), harness side, while depressing the brake pedal.

- **Is voltage greater than 10 volts?**

➔ **Yes**

INSTALL a new speed control servo. TEST the system for normal operation.

➔ **No**

REPAIR the circuit. TEST the system for normal operation.

FM1100100714050X

Fig. 137 Test B: Flash Code 2, BPP Switch Or Circuit Failure (Part 5 of 5). 2001–04 Sable & Taurus

C1 CHECK THE DEACTIVATOR SWITCH CIRCUITRY

1

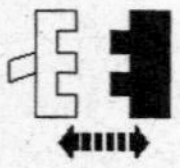

2

Speed Control Servo C122

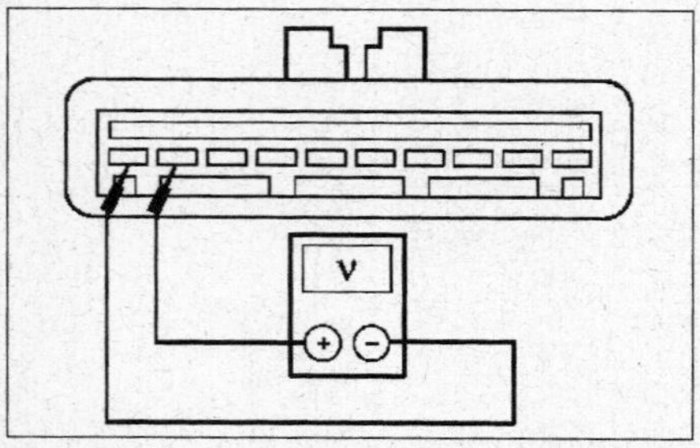

3

Measure the voltage between the speed control servo C122 pin 9, circuit 248 (TN/OG), harness side and the speed control servo C122 pin 10, circuit 57 (BK), harness side.

FM1100100715010X

Fig. 138 Test C: Flash Code 3, Deactivator Switch Or Circuit Failure (Part 1 of 4). 2001–04 Sable & Taurus

C2 CHECK CIRCUIT 10 (LG/RD) FOR AN OPEN

1

Deactivator Switch C277

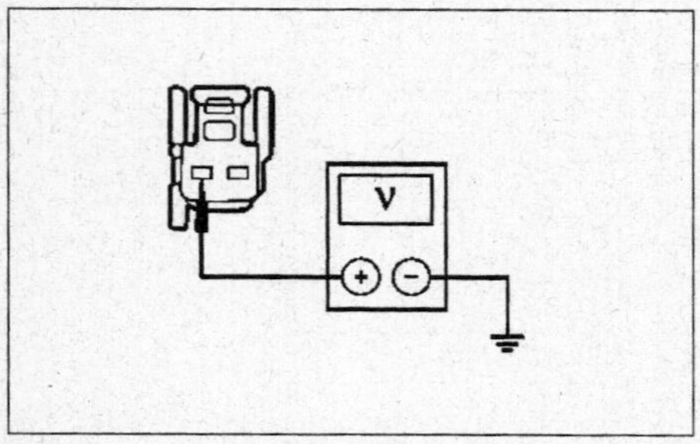

2

Measure the voltage between the deactivator switch C277, circuit 10 (LG/RD), harness side and ground.

- **Is the voltage greater than 10 volts?**

➔ **Yes**

Go to «C3».

➔ **No**

Repair the circuit. Test system for normal operation.

FM1100100715030X

Fig. 138 Test C: Flash Code 3, Deactivator Switch Or Circuit Failure (Part 3 of 4). 2001–04 Sable & Taurus

- **Is the voltage greater than 10 volts?**

➔ **Yes**

INSTALL a new speed control servo. TEST the system for normal operation.

➔ **No**

Go to «C2».

FM1100100715020X

Fig. 138 Test C: Flash Code 3, Deactivator Switch Or Circuit Failure (Part 2 of 4). 2001–04 Sable & Taurus

C3 CHECK CIRCUIT 248 (TN/OG) FOR AN OPEN

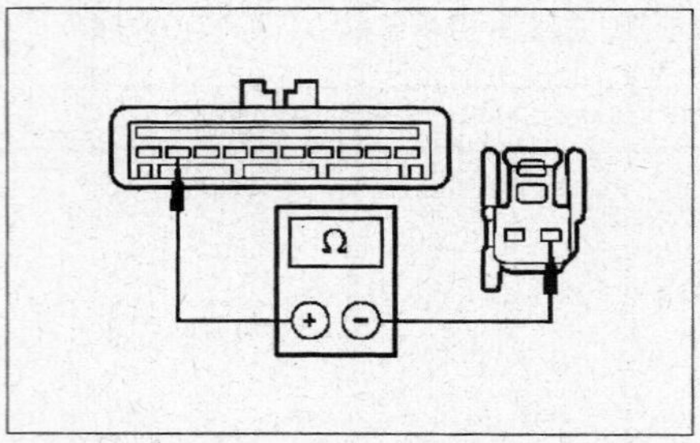

1

Measure the resistance between the speed control servo C122 pin 9, circuit 248 (TN/OG), harness side and the deactivator switch C277, circuit 248 (TN/OG), harness side.

- **Is the resistance less than 5 ohms?**

➔ **Yes**

INSTALL a new deactivator switch. TEST the system for normal operation.

➔ **No**

REPAIR the circuit. TEST the system for normal operation.

FM1100100715040X

Fig. 138 Test C: Flash Code 3, Deactivator Switch Or Circuit Failure (Part 4 of 4). 2001–04 Sable & Taurus

D1 CHECK THE SPEEDOMETER OPERATION

1 Check the speedometer for correct operation by driving the vehicle.

- **Does the speedometer operate correctly?**

➔ **Yes**

Go to «D2».

➔ **No**

Diagnose speedometer fault condition.

FM1100100716010X

Fig. 139 Test D: Flash Code 1, Dynamic Pull Occurs At Throttle & Speed Control Inoperative (Part 1 of 3). 2001–04 Sable & Taurus

D2 CHECK CIRCUIT 679 (GY/BK) FOR AN OPEN

1

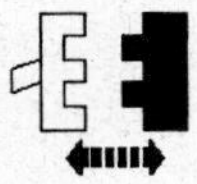

2 *Speed Control Servo C122*

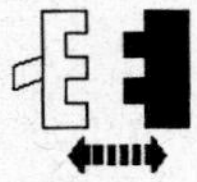

3 *PCM C175*

FM1100100716020X

Fig. 139 Test D: Flash Code 1, Dynamic Pull Occurs At Throttle & Speed Control Inoperative (Part 2 of 3). 2001–04 Sable & Taurus

E1 CHECK CIRCUIT 1087 (OG) FOR AN OPEN

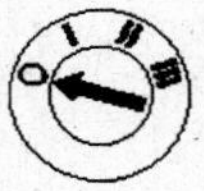

1

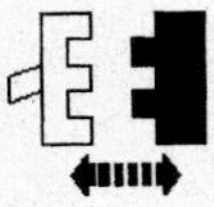

2 *Speed Control Servo C122*

3

FM1100100717010X

Fig. 140 Test E: Speed Control Inoperative, No Flash Codes (Part 1 of 13). 2001–04 Sable & Taurus

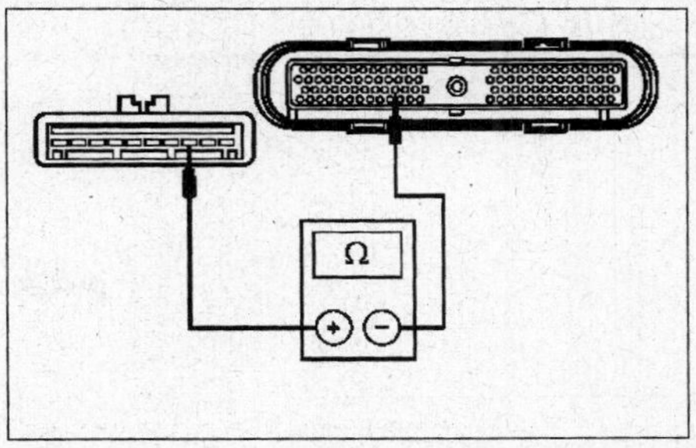

4

Measure the resistance between the speed control servo C122 pin 3, circuit 679 (GY/BK), harness side and the PCM C175 pin 68, circuit 679 (GY/BK), harness side.

- **Is the resistance less than 5 ohms?**

→ **Yes**

INSTALL a new speed control servo. TEST the system for normal operation.

→ **No**

REPAIR the circuit. TEST the system for normal operation.

FM1100100716030X

Fig. 139 Test D: Flash Code 1, Dynamic Pull Occurs At Throttle & Speed Control Inoperative (Part 3 of 3). 2001–04 Sable & Taurus

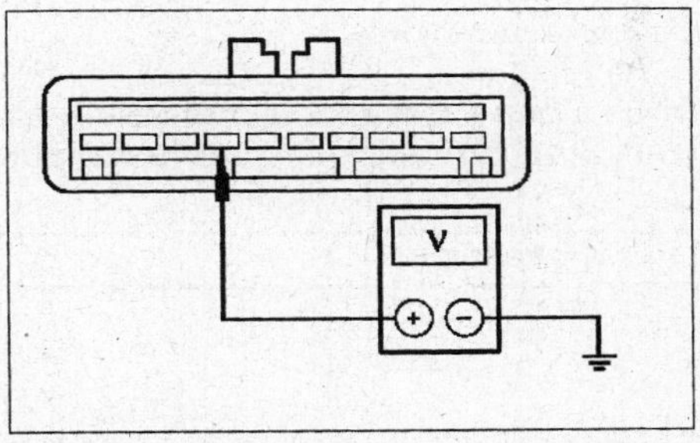

4

Measure the voltage between the speed control servo C122 pin 7, circuit 1087 (OG), harness side and ground.

- **Is the voltage greater than 10 volts?**

→ **Yes**

Go to «E2».

→ **No**

REPAIR the circuit. TEST the system for normal operation.

FM1100100717020X

Fig. 140 Test E: Speed Control Inoperative, No Flash Codes (Part 2 of 13). 2001–04 Sable & Taurus

E2	CHECK CIRCUIT 57 (BK) FOR AN OPEN

1

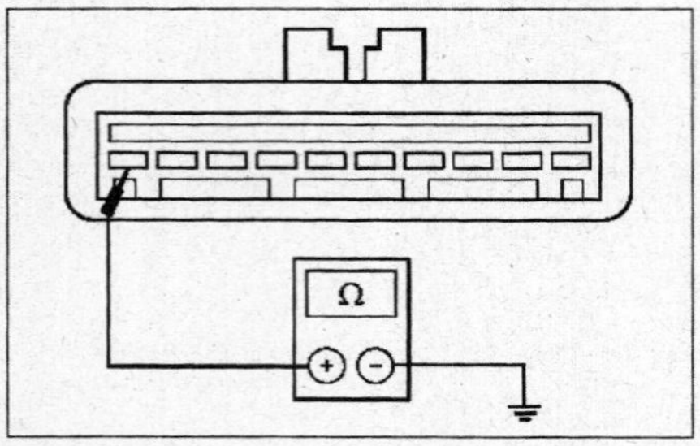

2

Measure the resistance between the speed control servo C122 pin 10, circuit 57 (BK), harness side and ground.

- **Is the resistance less than 5 ohms?**

→ **Yes**

Go to «E3».

→ **No**

Repair the circuit. Test system for normal operation.

FM1100100717030X

Fig. 140 Test E: Speed Control Inoperative, No Flash Codes (Part 3 of 13). 2001–04 Sable & Taurus

E3	CHECK THE SPEED CONTROL ACTUATOR SWITCH CIRCUITRY

1

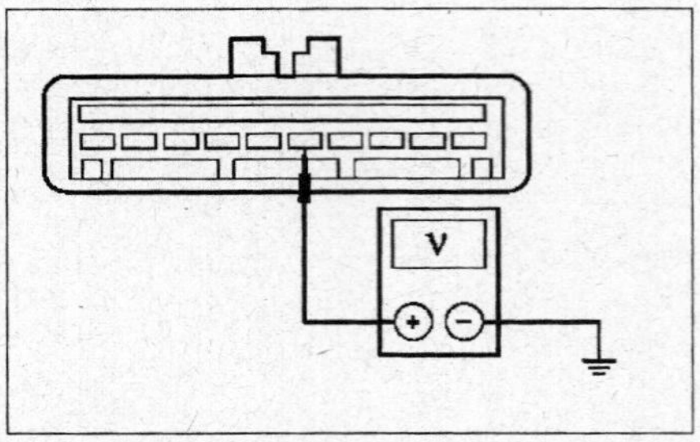

2

Measure the voltage between the speed control servo C122 pin 5, circuit 916 (LG), harness side and ground, while depressing the speed control actuator switch ON.

- **Is the voltage greater than 10 volts?**

→ **Yes**

Go to «E6».

→ **No**

Go to «E4».

FM1100100717040X

Fig. 140 Test E: Speed Control Inoperative, No Flash Codes (Part 4 of 13). 2001–04 Sable & Taurus

E4	CHECK CIRCUIT 916 (LG) FOR AN OPEN

1

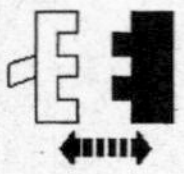

2 *Air Bag Sliding Contact C218b*

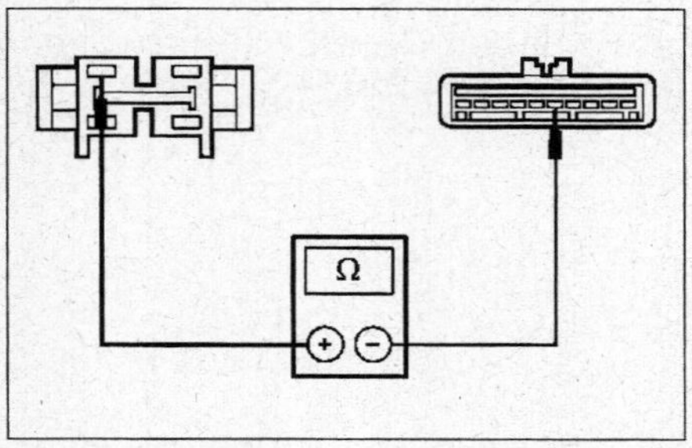

3

Measure the resistance between the air bag sliding contact C218b pin 3, circuit 916 (LG), harness

FM1100100717050X

Fig. 140 Test E: Speed Control Inoperative, No Flash Codes (Part 5 of 13). 2001–04 Sable & Taurus

side and the speed control servo C122 pin 5, circuit 916 (LG), harness side.

- **Is the resistance less than 5 ohms?**

→ **Yes**

Go to «E5».

→ **No**

REPAIR the circuit. TEST the system for normal operation.

FM1100100717060X

Fig. 140 Test E: Speed Control Inoperative, No Flash Codes (Part 6 of 13). 2001–04 Sable & Taurus

E5 CHECK THE AIR BAG SLIDING CONTACT

1 Remove the driver side air bag.

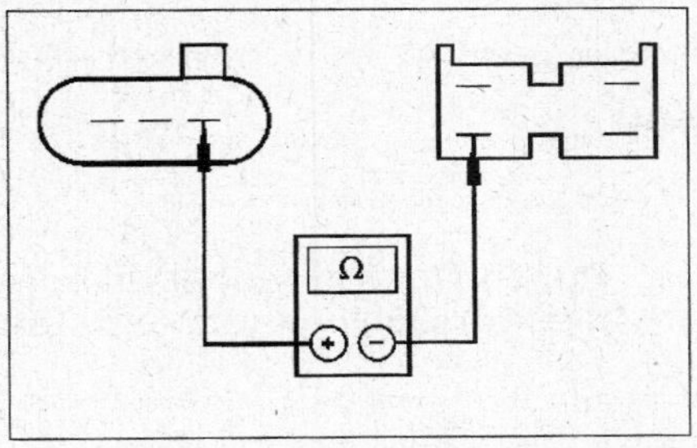

2

Measure the resistance between the top of the air bag sliding contact pin 3 (component side) and the air bag sliding contact C218b pin 3 (component side).

- **Is the resistance less than 5 ohms?**

→ **Yes**

INSTALL a new speed control actuator switch.
TEST the system for normal operation.

→ **No**

INSTALL a new air bag sliding contact.
TEST the system for normal operation.

FM1100100717070X

Fig. 140 Test E: Speed Control Inoperative, No Flash Codes (Part 7 of 13). 2001–04 Sable & Taurus

E7 CHECK CIRCUIT 848 (DG/OG) FOR AN OPEN

1

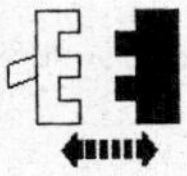

2 *Air Bag Sliding Contact C218b*

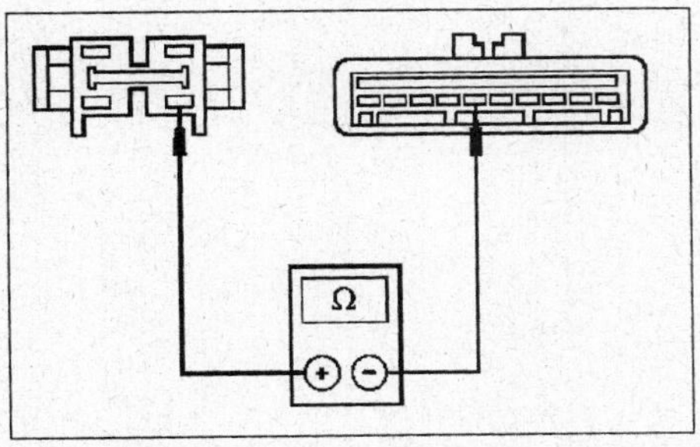

3

Measure the resistance between the air bag sliding contact C218b pin 2, circuit 848 (DG/OG), harness side and the speed control servo C122 pin 6, circuit 848 (DG/OG), harness side.

FM1100100717090X

Fig. 140 Test E: Speed Control Inoperative, No Flash Codes (Part 9 of 13). 2001–04 Sable & Taurus

E6 CHECK THE SPEED CONTROL ACTUATOR SWITCH OPERATION

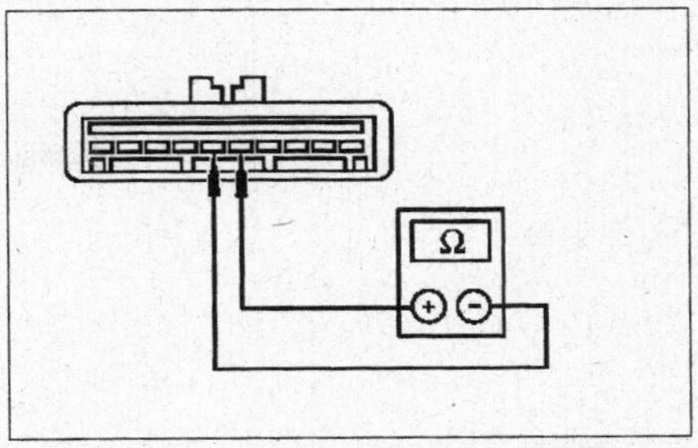

1

Measure the resistance between the speed control servo C122 pin 5, circuit 916 (LG), harness side and the speed control servo C122 pin 6, circuit 848 (DG/OG), harness side while depressing the speed control actuator switch OFF.

- **Is the resistance less than 5 ohms?**

→ **Yes**

Go to «E8».

→ **No**

Go to «E7».

FM1100100717080X

Fig. 140 Test E: Speed Control Inoperative, No Flash Codes (Part 8 of 13). 2001–04 Sable & Taurus

- **Is the resistance less than 5 ohms?**

→ **Yes**

INSTALL a new air bag sliding contact.
TEST the system for normal operation.

→ **No**

REPAIR the circuit. TEST the system for normal operation.

FM1100100717100X

Fig. 140 Test E: Speed Control Inoperative, No Flash Codes (Part 10 of 13). 2001–04 Sable & Taurus

E8 CHECK THE SPEED CONTROL INDICATOR LAMP

1

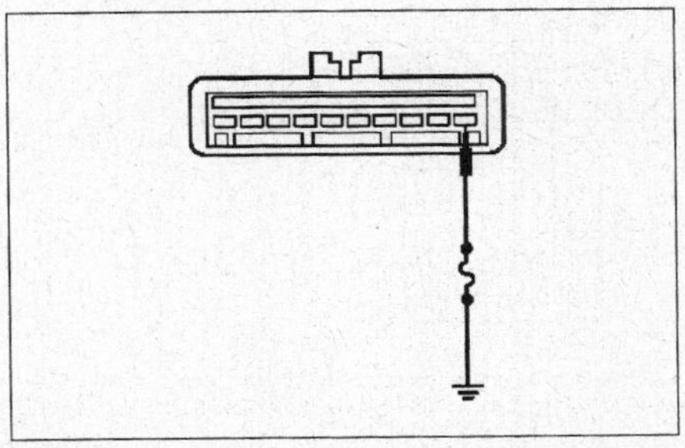

2

Connect a 10A fused jumper wire between the speed control servo C122 pin 1, circuit 203 (OG/LB), harness side and ground.

- **Is the speed control indicator lamp illuminated?**

→ **Yes**

INSTALL a new speed control servo. TEST the system for normal operation.

→ **No**

Go to E9.

FM1100100717110X

Fig. 140 Test E: Speed Control Inoperative, No Flash Codes (Part 11 of 13). 2001–04 Sable & Taurus

E9 CHECK CIRCUIT 203 (OG/LB) FOR AN OPEN

1

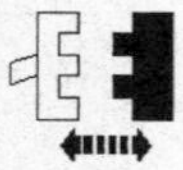

2

Instrument Cluster C220b

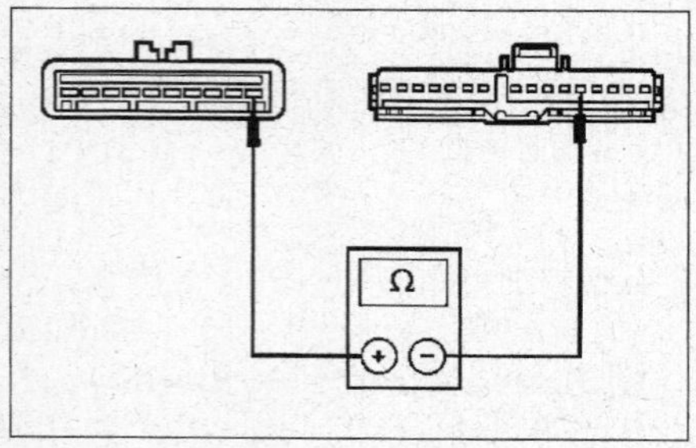

3

Measure the resistance between the speed control servo C122 pin 1, circuit 203 (OG/LB), harness

FM1100100717120X

Fig. 140 Test E: Speed Control Inoperative, No Flash Codes (Part 12 of 13). 2001–04 Sable & Taurus

F1 CHECK THE SPEED CONTROL ACTUATOR SWITCH

1

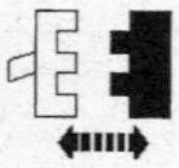

2

Speed Control Servo C122

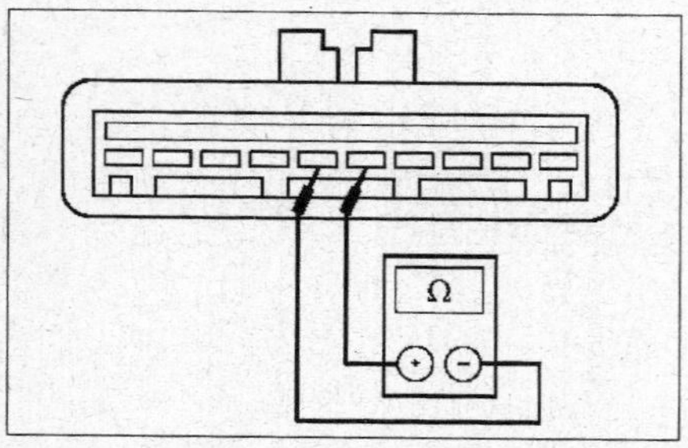

3

Measure the resistance between the speed control servo C122 pin 5, circuit 916 (LG), harness side and the speed control servo C122 pin 6, circuit 848 (DG/OG), harness side while depressing the

FM1100100718010X

Fig. 141 Test F: Speed Control Switch Inoperative (Part 1 of 2). 2001–04 Sable & Taurus

side and the instrument cluster C220b pin 5, circuit 203 (OG/LB), harness side.

- **Is the resistance less than 5 ohms?**

➔ **Yes**

INSTALL a new instrument cluster printed circuit. TEST the system for normal operation.

➔ **No**

REPAIR the circuit. TEST the system for normal operation.

FM1100100717130X

Fig. 140 Test E: Speed Control Inoperative, No Flash Codes (Part 13 of 13). 2001–04 Sable & Taurus

inoperative speed control actuator switch. Use the following table for the speed control actuator switch in question.

•

Speed Control Actuator Switch	Resistance Value
COAST	Between 108 and 132
SET/ACCEL	Between 612 and 748
RESUME	Between 1,980 and 2,420
OFF	Less than 5 ohms

- **Is the speed control actuator switch resistance OK?**

➔ **Yes**

INSTALL a new speed control servo.
TEST the system for normal operation.

➔ **No**

INSTALL a new speed control actuator switch.
TEST the system for normal operation.

FM1100100718020X

Fig. 141 Test F: Speed Control Switch Inoperative (Part 2 of 2). 2001–04 Sable & Taurus

G1 CHECK SPEED CONTROL SERVO FOR SHORT TO GROUND

1

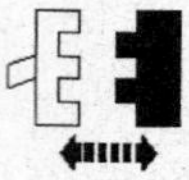

2

Speed Control Servo C122

3

- **Is the indicator lamp illuminated?**

➔ **Yes**

Go to «G2».

➔ **No**

INSTALL a new speed control servo. TEST the system for normal operation.

FM1100100719010X

Fig. 142 Test G: Speed Control Indicator Lamp Always On (Part 1 of 3). 2001–04 Sable & Taurus

G2	CHECK CIRCUIT 203 (OG/LB) FOR SHORT TO GROUND

1

2 *Instrument Cluster C220b*

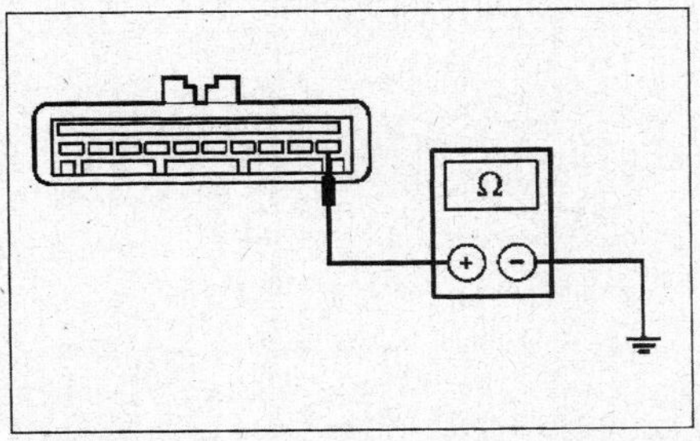

3

Measure the resistance between the speed control servo C122 pin 1, circuit 203 (OG/LB), harness side and ground.

- **Is the resistance greater than 10,000 ohms?**

➔ **Yes**

INSTALL a new instrument cluster printed circuit. TEST the system for normal operation.

➔ **No**

REPAIR the circuit. TEST the system for normal operation.

FM1100100719030X

Fig. 142 Test G: Speed Control Indicator Lamp Always On (Part 2 of 3). 2001–04 Sable & Taurus

Fig. 142 Test G: Speed Control Indicator Lamp Always On (Part 3 of 3). 2001–04 Sable & Taurus

FM1100100719020X

H1	CHECK THE SPEED CONTROL ACTUATOR CABLE/THROTTLE BODY LINKAGE

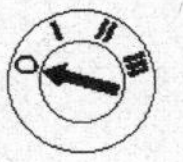

1

2 Remove the speed control actuator cable from the speed control servo. Visually inspect the core wire and check the speed control actuator cable by pulling on it and noting the throttle movement.

- **Is the speed control actuator cable OK?**

➔ **Yes**

Go to «H2».

➔ **No**

INSTALL a new speed control actuator cable or repair the throttle body linkage. TEST the system for normal operation.

FM1100100720010X

Fig. 143 Test H: Set Speed Fluctuates (Part 1 of 2). 2001–04 Sable & Taurus

H2	CHECK THE SPEEDOMETER OPERATION

1 Drive the vehicle and observe the speedometer operation.

- **Does the speedometer needle fluctuate?**

➔ **Yes**

Diagnose speedometer fault condition.

➔ **No**

INSTALL a new speed control servo. TEST the system for normal operation.

FM1100100720020X

Fig. 143 Test H: Set Speed Fluctuates (Part 2 of 2). 2001–04 Sable & Taurus

Condition	Possible Source	Action
• No Communication With The Module — Speed Control Servo	• Fuse(s). • Circuitry. • Speed control servo.	• GO to Pinpoint Test F.
• The Speed Control Is Inoperative — No DTCs	• Circuitry. • Speed control actuator switch. • Speed control servo.	• GO to Pinpoint Test G.
• The Set Speed Fluctuates	• Anti-lock brake control module. • Speed control actuator cable. • Throttle lever. • Speed control servo.	• GO to Pinpoint Test H.
• The Coast Switch Is Inoperative	• Speed control actuator switch. • Speed control servo.	• GO to Pinpoint Test J.
• The SET/ACCL Switch Is Inoperative	• Speed control actuator switch. • Speed control servo.	• GO to Pinpoint Test K.
• The Resume Switch Is Inoperative	• Speed control actuator switch. • Speed control servo.	• GO to Pinpoint Test L.
• The OFF Switch Is Inoperative	• Speed control actuator switch. • Speed control servo.	• GO to Pinpoint Test M.

FM1109800584000X

Fig. 144 Speed control symptom chart. Town Car

DTCS	DTC Caused By	Description	Action
B1318	Speed Control Servo	Battery Voltage Low	GO to Pinpoint Test A.
B1342	Speed Control Servo	ECU Is Defective	REPLACE the speed control servo TEST the system for normal operation.
C1109	Speed Control Servo	Throttle Position Did Not Return to Idle After Self-Test	GO to Pinpoint Test B.
C1126	Speed Control Servo	Speed Control Actuator Switch Stuck for Two Minutes or Longer	GO to Pinpoint Test C.
C1127	Speed Control Servo	Deactivator Switch Circuit Failure	GO to Pinpoint Test D.
C1179	Speed Control Servo	Speed Control Cable Slack Failure	GO to Pinpoint Test E.
U1027	PCM	SCP Invalid or Missing Data for Engine RPM	PERFORM PCM Self-Test.
U1041	ABS	SCP Invalid or Missing Data for Vehicle Speed	PERFORM ABS Self-Test.
U1051	LCM	SCP Invalid or Missing Data for Brakes	PERFORM LCM Self-Test.
U1059	PCM	SCP Invalid or Missing Data for Transmission/Transaxle/ PRNDL	PERFORM PCM Self-Test.

FM1109800585000X

Fig. 145 Diagnostic trouble code chart. Town Car

TEST CONDITIONS	TEST DETAILS/RESULTS/ACTIONS
A1 CHECK CIRCUIT 676 (PK/O) FOR AN OPEN	
1 2  Speed Control Servo C123 3 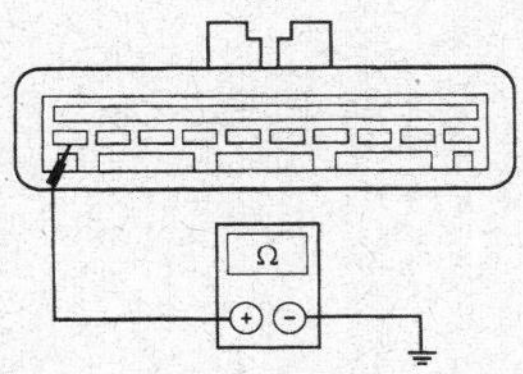	3 Measure the resistance between speed control servo C123-10, circuit 676 (PK/O), and ground. • Is the resistance less than 5 ohms? → **Yes** REPLACE SERVO → **No** REPAIR circuit 676 (PK/O). CLEAR the DTCs. TEST the system for normal operation.

FM1109800586000X

Fig. 146 Test A: DTC 1318, Battery Voltage Low. Town Car

TEST CONDITIONS	TEST DETAILS/RESULTS/ACTIONS
B1 CHECK THE SPEED CONTROL ACTUATOR CABLE	
	1 Check the speed control actuator cable for sticking or binding. • Is the speed control actuator cable OK? → **Yes** GO to **B2**. → **No** REPLACE the speed control actuator cable CLEAR the DTCs. TEST the system for normal operation.
B2 CHECK THE THROTTLE LEVER	
	1 Check the throttle lever for sticking or binding. • Is the throttle lever OK? → **Yes** GO to **B3**. → **No** REPAIR and/or REPLACE as necessary. CLEAR the DTCs. TEST the system for normal operation.
B3 CHECK THE SPEED CONTROL ACTUATOR CABLE ADJUSTMENT	
	1 Perform the speed control actuator cable adjustment; refer to Cable Adjustment. 2 Retrieve and document DTCs. • Is DTC C1109 retrieved? → **Yes** REPLACE the speed control servo TEST the system for normal operation. → **No** System is OK.

FM1109800587000X

Fig. 147 Test B: DTC C1109, Throttle Position Did Not Return to Idle After Self-Test. Town Car

TEST CONDITIONS	TEST DETAILS/RESULTS/ACTIONS
C1 CHECK THE SPEED CONTROL SERVO PIDS	
	1 Monitor the speed control servo COAST, RESUME, SC__OFF, SC__ON, and SET/ACL PIDS. 2 Depress and release the speed control actuator switches. • Does NGS Tester indicate ACTIVE with the speed control actuator switch depressed and notACT with the speed control actuator switch released? → **Yes** System is OK. → **No** GO to **C2**.
C2 CHECK THE SPEED CONTROL ACTUATOR SWITCH	
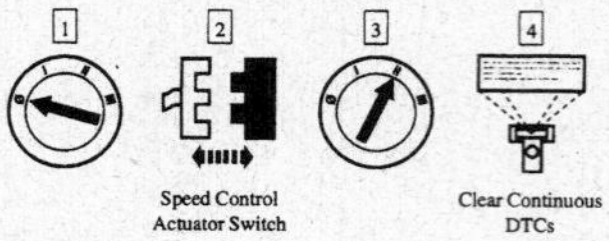 	5 Wait three minutes. 6 Retrieve and document continuous DTCs. • Is DTC C1126 retrieved? → **Yes** GO to **C3**. → **No** REPLACE the speed control actuator switch; TEST the system for normal operation.

FM1109800588010X

Fig. 148 Test C: DTC C1126, Speed Control Actuator Switch Stuck for Two Minutes or Longer (Part 1 of 2). Town Car

TEST CONDITIONS	TEST DETAILS/RESULTS/ACTIONS
C3 CHECK CIRCUIT 151 (LB/BK) FOR SHORT TO GROUND	
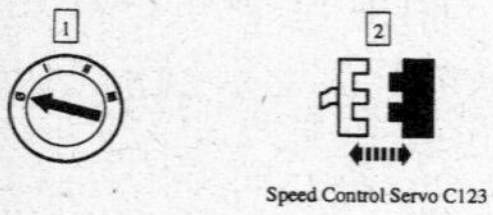 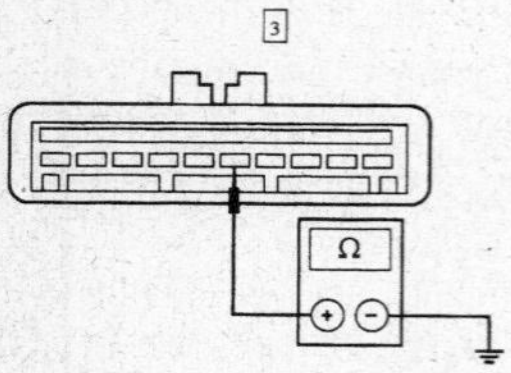	3 Measure the resistance between speed control servo C123-5, circuit 151 (LB/BK), and ground. • Is the resistance greater than 10,000 ohms? → **Yes** REPLACE the speed control servo CLEAR the DTCs. TEST the system for normal operation. → **No** GO to **C4**.
C4 CHECK THE AIR BAG SLIDING CONTACT	
 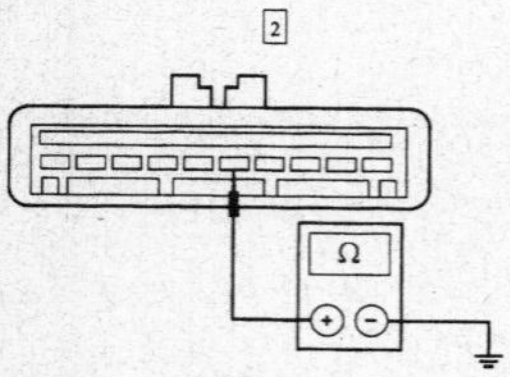	2 Measure the resistance between speed control servo C123-5, circuit 151 (LB/BK), and ground. • Is the resistance greater than 10,000 ohms? → **Yes** REPLACE the air bag sliding contact; CLEAR the DTCs. TEST the system for normal operation. → **No** REPAIR circuit 151 (LB/BK). CLEAR the DTCs. TEST the system for normal operation.

FM1109800588020X

Fig. 148 Test C: DTC C1126, Speed Control Actuator Switch Stuck for Two Minutes or Longer (Part 2 of 2). Town Car

TEST CONDITIONS	TEST DETAILS/RESULTS/ACTIONS
D1 CHECK FUSE JUNCTION PANEL FUSE 10 (20A)	
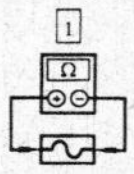	• Is the fuse junction panel fuse 10 (20A) OK? → **Yes** GO to **D2**. → **No** REPLACE the failed fuse. TEST the system for normal operation. If the fuse fails again, CHECK for short to ground. REPAIR as necessary. CLEAR the DTCs. TEST the system for normal operation.
D2 CHECK THE SPEED CONTROL SERVO	
 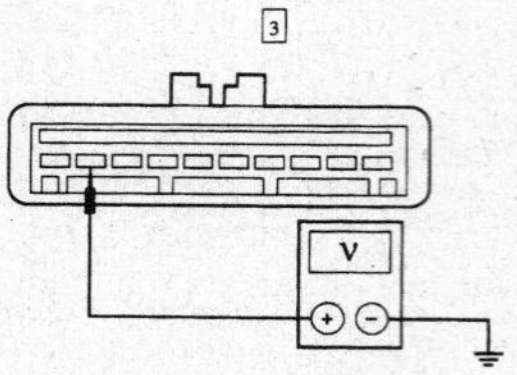	3 Measure the voltage between speed control servo C123-9, circuit 636 (O), and ground, while firmly applying and releasing the brake pedal. • Is the voltage greater than 10 volts with the brake pedal released and zero volts with the brake pedal applied? → **Yes** REPLACE the speed control servo TEST the system for normal operation. → **No** GO to **D3**.

FM1109800589010X

Fig. 149 Test D: DTC C1127, Deactivator Switch Circuit Failure (Part 1 of 2). Town Car

TEST CONDITIONS	TEST DETAILS/RESULTS/ACTIONS
D3 CHECK CIRCUIT 10 (LG/R) FOR AN OPEN	
1 	
2 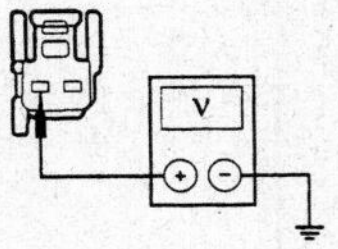	2 Measure the voltage between deactivator switch C219, circuit 10 (LG/R), and ground. • Is the voltage greater than 10 volts? → **Yes** GO to **D4**. → **No** REPAIR circuit 10 (LG/R). CLEAR the DTCs. TEST the system for normal operation.
D4 CHECK CIRCUIT 636 (O) FOR AN OPEN	
1 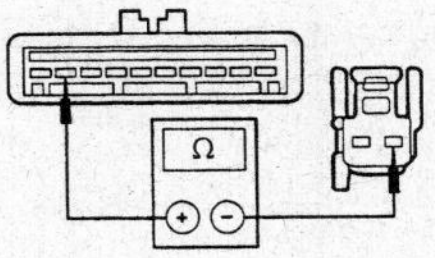	1 Measure the resistance between speed control servo C123-9, circuit 636 (O), and deactivator switch C219, circuit 636 (O). • Is the resistance less than 5 ohms? → **Yes** REPLACE the deactivator switch CLEAR the DTCs. TEST the system for normal operation. → **No** REPAIR circuit 636 (O). CLEAR the DTCs. TEST the system for normal operation.

FM1109800589020X

Fig. 149 Test D: DTC C1127, Deactivator Switch Circuit Failure (Part 2 of 2). Town Car

TEST CONDITIONS	TEST DETAILS/RESULTS/ACTIONS
F1 CHECK THE FUSE JUNCTION PANEL FUSE 8 (10A)	
1 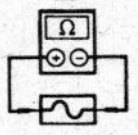	• Is fuse junction panel fuse 8 (10A) OK? → **Yes** GO to **F2**. → **No** REPLACE the failed fuse. TEST the system for normal operation. If the fuse fails again, CHECK for short to ground. REPAIR as necessary. TEST the system for normal operation.

FM1109800591010X

Fig. 151 Test F: No Communication with Module, Speed Control Servo (Part 1 of 2). Town Car

TEST CONDITIONS	TEST DETAILS/RESULTS/ACTIONS
E1 CHECK THE SPEED CONTROL ACTUATOR CABLE ADJUSTMENT	
	1 Perform the speed control actuator cable adjustment.

FM1109800590010X

Fig. 150 Test E: DTC C1179, Speed Control Cable Slack Failure (Part 1 of 2). Town Car

TEST CONDITIONS	TEST DETAILS/RESULTS/ACTIONS
E1 CHECK THE SPEED CONTROL ACTUATOR CABLE ADJUSTMENT (Continued)	
2 	2 Retrieve and document DTCs. • Is DTC C1179 retrieved? → **Yes** REPLACE the speed control servo TEST the system for normal operation. → **No** System is OK.

FM1109800590020X

Fig. 150 Test E: DTC C1179, Speed Control Cable Slack Failure (Part 2 of 2). Town Car

TEST CONDITIONS	TEST DETAILS/RESULTS/ACTIONS
F2 CHECK CIRCUIT 296 (W/P) FOR AN OPEN	
1  2  3 	
4 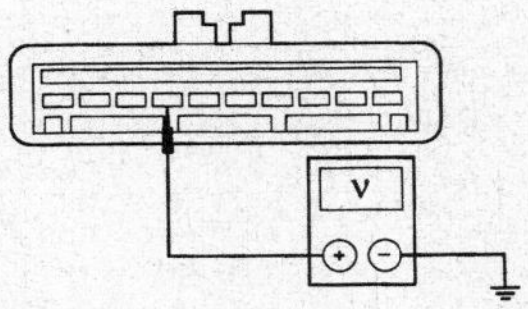	4 Measure the voltage between speed control servo C123-7, circuit 296 (W/P), and ground. • Is the voltage greater than 10 volts? → **Yes** GO to **F3**. → **No** REPAIR circuit 296 (W/P). TEST the system for normal operation.
F3 CHECK CIRCUIT 676 (PK/O) FOR AN OPEN	
1 	
2 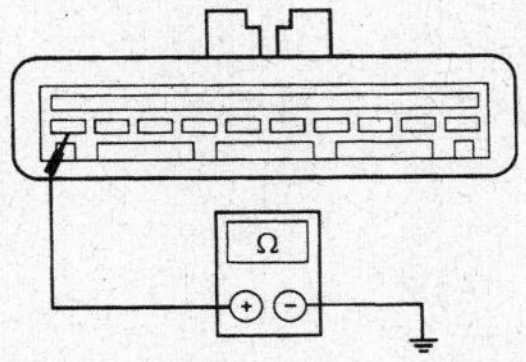	2 Measure the resistance between speed control servo C123-10, circuit 676 (PK/O), and ground. • Is the resistance less than 5 ohms? → **Yes** Diagnose module communications. → **No** REPAIR circuit 676 (PK/O). TEST the system for normal operation.

FM1109800591020X

Fig. 151 Test F: No Communication with Module, Speed Control Servo (Part 2 of 2). Town Car

TEST CONDITIONS	TEST DETAILS/RESULTS/ACTIONS
G1 CHECK THE HORN SYSTEM	
	1 Verify the horn system operates by pressing the horn switch. • Does the horn system operate properly? → **Yes** GO to **G2**. → **No** Diagnose ID cluster.
G2 CHECK THE SPEED CONTROL ACTUATOR SWITCH ON	
1 2 	
3 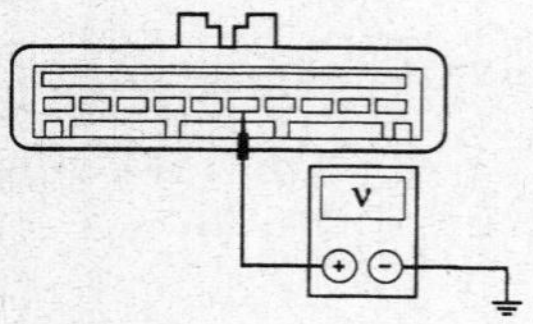	3 Measure the voltage between speed control servo C123-5, circuit 151 (LB/BK), and ground, while pressing the speed control actuator switch ON. • Is the voltage greater than 10 volts? → **Yes** GO to **G3**. → **No** REPLACE the speed control actuator switch; TEST the system for normal operation.

FM1109800592010X

Fig. 152 Test G: Speed Control Inoperative, No DTCs (Part 1 of 2). Town Car

TEST CONDITIONS	TEST DETAILS/RESULTS/ACTIONS
H1 CHECK THE SPEED CONTROL ACTUATOR CABLE	
	1 Check the throttle lever and speed control actuator cable for proper operation while performing the speed control servo slack test on NGS Tester. • Does the throttle lever operate properly? → **Yes** REPLACE the speed control servo TEST the system for normal operation. → **No** REPAIR and/or REPLACE as necessary. TEST the system for normal operation.

FM1109800593000X

Fig. 153 Test H: Set Speed Fluctuates. Town Car

TEST CONDITIONS	TEST DETAILS/RESULTS/ACTIONS
G3 CHECK THE SET/ACCEL SWITCH	
1 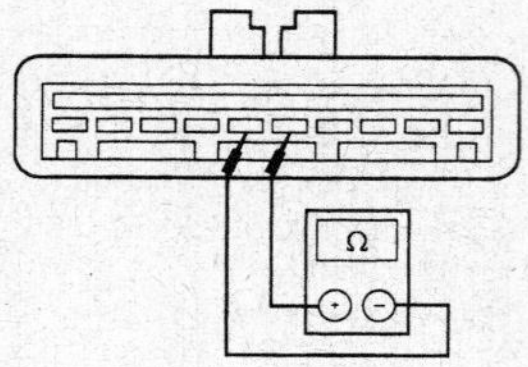	1 Measure the resistance between speed control servo C123-5, circuit 151 (LB/BK), and speed control servo C123-6, circuit 848 (DG/O), while pressing the speed control actuator switch SET/ACCEL. • Is the resistance between 612-748 ohms with the switch pressed and greater than 10,000 ohms with the switch released? → **Yes** REPLACE the speed control servo. TEST the system for normal operation. → **No** REPLACE the speed control actuator switch; TEST the system for normal operation.

FM1109800592020X

Fig. 152 Test G: Speed Control Inoperative, No DTCs (Part 2 of 2). Town Car

TEST CONDITIONS	TEST DETAILS/RESULTS/ACTIONS
J1 CHECK THE SPEED CONTROL ACTUATOR SWITCH COAST PID	
1 	1 Monitor the speed control servo COAST PID. Depress and release the speed control actuator switch COAST button while slightly turning the steering wheel from side to side. • Does NGS Tester indicate ACTIVE with the speed control actuator switch depressed and notACT with the speed control actuator switch released? → **Yes** System is OK. → **No** GO to **J2**.
J2 CHECK THE SPEED CONTROL ACTUATOR SWITCH COAST	
1 2 	
3 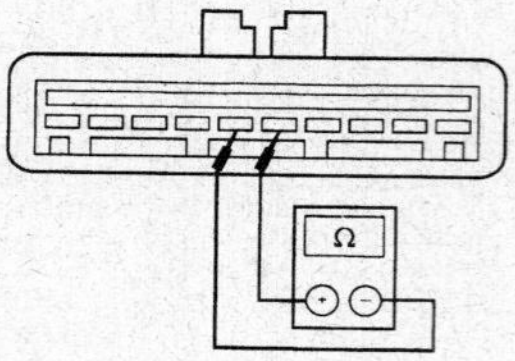	3 Measure the resistance between speed control servo C123-5, circuit 151 (LB/BK), and speed control servo C123-6, circuit 848 (DG/O), while pressing the speed control actuator switch COAST and slightly turning the steering wheel from side to side. • Is the resistance between 105-135 ohms with COAST pressed and greater than 10,000 ohms with COAST released? → **Yes** REPLACE the speed control servo TEST the system for normal operation. → **No** REPLACE the speed control actuator switch; TEST the system for normal operation.

FM1109800594000X

Fig. 154 Test J: Coast Switch Inoperative. Town Car

TEST CONDITIONS	TEST DETAILS/RESULTS/ACTIONS
K1 CHECK THE SPEED CONTROL ACTUATOR SWITCH SET/ACL PID	
1 	1 Monitor the speed control servo SET/ACL PID. Depress and release the speed control actuator switch SET/ACCEL button while slightly turning the steering wheel from side to side. • Does NGS Tester indicate ACTIVE with the speed control actuator switch depressed and notACT with the speed control actuator switch released? → **Yes** System is OK. → **No** GO to **K2**.
K2 CHECK THE SPEED CONTROL ACTUATOR SWITCH SET/ACCEL	
1 2 3 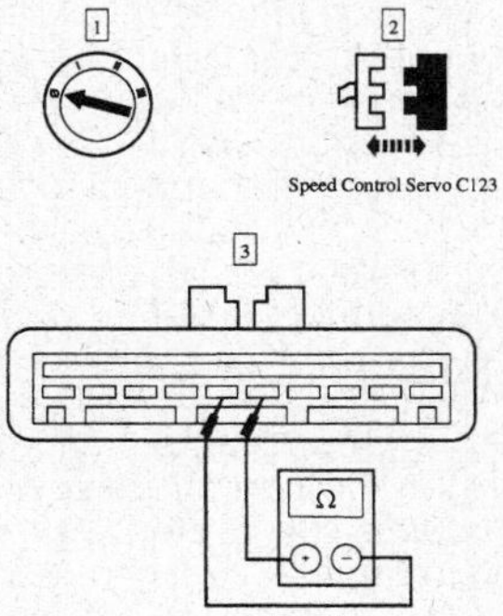	3 Measure the resistance between speed control servo C123-5, circuit 151 (LB/BK), and speed control servo C123-6, circuit 848 (DG/O), while pressing the speed control actuator switch SET/ACCEL and slightly turning the steering wheel from side to side. • Is the resistance between 612-748 ohms with SET/ACCEL pressed and greater than 10,000 ohms with SET/ACCEL released? → **Yes** REPLACE the speed control servo TEST the system for normal operation. → **No** REPLACE the speed control actuator switch; TEST the system for normal operation.

FM1109800595000X

Fig. 155 Test K: SET/ACCEL Switch Inoperative. Town Car

TEST CONDITIONS	TEST DETAILS/RESULTS/ACTIONS
M1 CHECK THE SPEED CONTROL ACTUATOR SWITCH SC__OFF PID	
1 	1 Monitor the speed control servo SC__OFF PID. Depress and release the speed control actuator switch OFF button while slightly turning the steering wheel from side to side. • Does NGS Tester indicate ACTIVE with the speed control actuator switch depressed and notACT with the speed control actuator switch released? → **Yes** System is OK. → **No** GO to **M2**.
M2 CHECK THE SPEED CONTROL ACTUATOR SWITCH OFF	
1 2 3 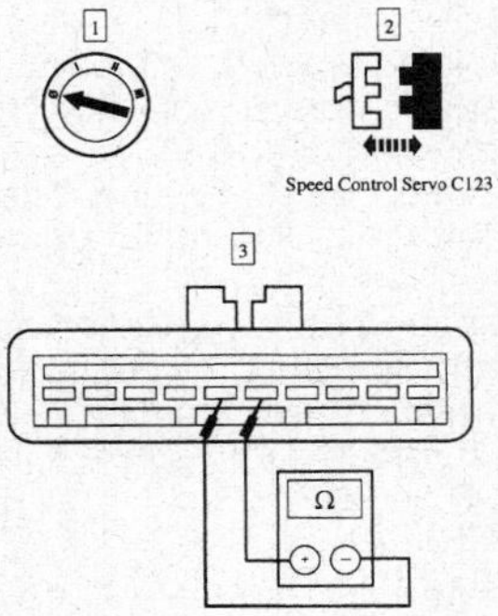	3 Measure the resistance between speed control servo C123-5, circuit 151 (LB/BK), and speed control servo C123-6, circuit 848 (DG/O), while pressing the speed control actuator switch OFF and slightly turning the steering wheel from side to side. • Is the resistance less than 5 ohms with OFF pressed and greater than 10,000 ohms with OFF released? → **Yes** REPLACE the speed control servo TEST the system for normal operation. → **No** REPLACE the speed control actuator switch; TEST the system for normal operation.

FM1109800597000X

Fig. 157 Test M: OFF Switch Inoperative. Town Car

TEST CONDITIONS	TEST DETAILS/RESULTS/ACTIONS
L1 CHECK THE SPEED CONTROL ACTUATOR SWITCH RESUME PID	
1 	1 Monitor the speed control servo RESUME PID. Depress and release the speed control actuator switch RESUME button while slightly turning the steering wheel from side to side. • Does NGS Tester indicate ACTIVE with the speed control actuator switch depressed and notACT with the speed control actuator switch released? → **Yes** System is OK. → **No** GO to **L2**.
L2 CHECK THE SPEED CONTROL ACTUATOR SWITCH RESUME	
1 2 3 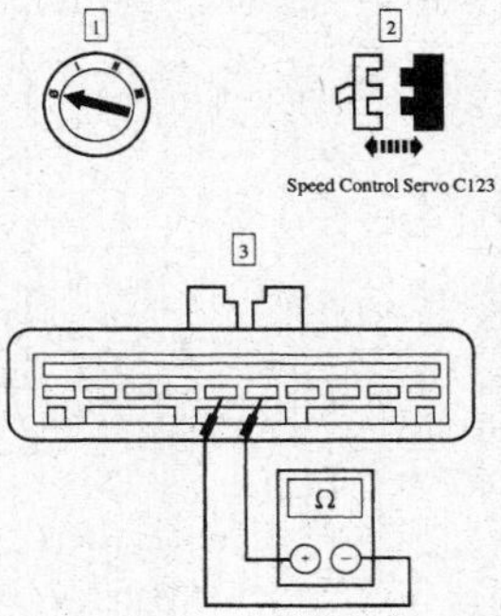	3 Measure the resistance between speed control servo C123-5, circuit 151 (LB/BK), and speed control servo C123-6, circuit 848 (DG/O), while pressing the speed control actuator switch RESUME and slightly turning the steering wheel from side to side. • Is the resistance between 1980-2420 ohms with RESUME pressed and greater than 10,000 ohms with RESUME released? → **Yes** REPLACE the speed control servo TEST the system for normal operation. → **No** REPLACE the speed control actuator switch; TEST the system for normal operation.

FM1109800596000X

Fig. 156 Test L: Resume Switch Inoperative. Town Car

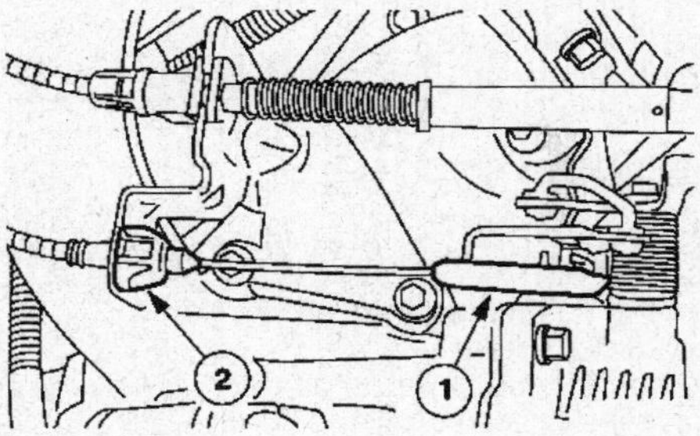

FM1109900698000X

Fig. 158 Actuator cable replacement. LS & Thunderbird

COMPONENT REPLACEMENT

Servo (Throttle Actuator) Assembly Actuator Cable

CONTINENTAL

1. Depress locking tab and rotate speed control actuator cable cap. Rotate counterclockwise to remove.
2. Open throttle to remove speed control actuator cable tension, then gently push actuator cable retaining spring.
3. Disconnect speed control actuator cable from servo pulley.
4. Disconnect speed control cable slug from control servo pulley.
5. Remove air cleaner outlet tube.
6. Disconnect electrical connector from accelerator control splash shield and position aside.
7. Remove accelerator control splash shield mounting fasteners, then the shield.
8. Disconnect actuator cable from throttle body cam by pulling outward, then remove mounting bolt.
9. Remove speed control actuator cable.
10. Reverse procedure to install, noting the following:
    a. Compress cable spring and retain it in a compressed state.
    b. Release tension spring after actuator cable slug is seated in the slot.
    c. Be sure to seat speed control actuator cable cap and seal squarely around servo pulley.

CONTOUR & MYSTIQUE

1. Disconnect speed control cable from throttle body lever.
2. Remove cable retaining clip from accelerator cable bracket.
3. Remove control cable cap from speed control servo by pressing cap locking arm and rotating cap counterclockwise.
4. Remove cable slug from speed control servo pulley, then gently push actuator cable slug past retaining spring using a small screwdriver.
5. Reverse procedure to install.

COUGAR

2.0L ENGINE

1. Disconnect speed control cable from engine cover.
2. Disconnect intake air resonator.
3. Disconnect speed control cable from throttle body cam.
4. Remove speed control cable from throttle bracket.
5. Disconnect speed control actuator electrical connector.
6. Remove speed control actuator bolt.
7. Disconnect speed control actuator.
8. Remove speed control cable cap from speed control actuator.
9. Remove speed control cable from speed control actuator pulley.

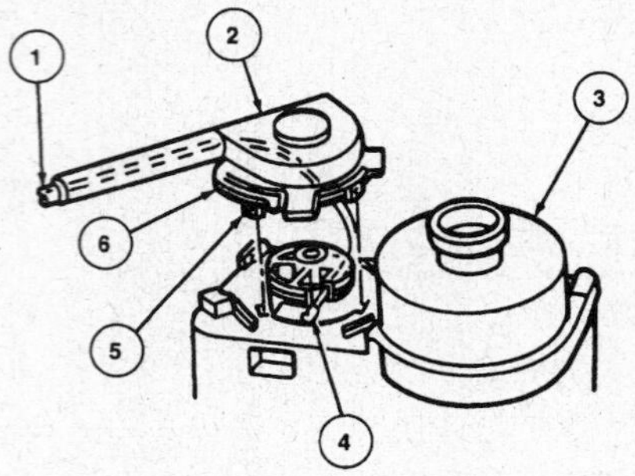

Item	Description
1	Speed Control Actuator
2	Actuator Cable Cap
3	Speed Control Servo
4	Cable Ball Slug
5	Cap Locking Tabs
6	Locking Arm

FM1109500319000X

Fig. 159 Actuator and servo. Contour, Mystique, Sable & Taurus w/electronic system

10. Reverse procedure to install.

2.5L ENGINE

1. Disconnect speed control cable.
2. Disconnect air intake temperature sensor electrical connector.
3. Disconnect speed control cable from securing clip.
4. Disconnect speed control actuator electrical connector.
5. Remove speed control actuator bolt, then the actuator.
6. Remove speed control cable cap from speed control actuator.
7. Remove speed control cable from speed control actuator pulley.
8. Reverse procedure to install.

CROWN VICTORIA, GRAND MARQUIS, MARAUDER & TOWN CAR

1. Remove engine cover retaining nut, then the cover.
2. Remove air cleaner outlet tube as required.
3. Remove speed control actuator cable to throttle lever mounting bolt, then the cable at lever.
4. Remove screw retaining speed control cable to accelerator cable bracket.
5. Disconnect speed control cable from throttle body lever.
6. Remove speed control cable cap from control servo by depressing cap locking arm and rotating cap counterclockwise.
7. Depress spring retainer, then remove speed control actuator cable from servo pulley.
8. Reverse procedure to install, noting the following:
    a. Insert speed control cable slug securely into servo pulley slot.
    b. Ensure rubber seal is fully seated onto speed control actuator cable cap.
    c. **Improper wrapping of actuator cable around servo pulley may result in a high idle condition.**
    d. Adjust actuator cable as outlined in "Adjustments."

ESCORT & ZX2

SOHC ENGINE

1. Disconnect speed control cable from throttle control lever and remove bolt from bracket.
2. Remove cable retaining clip, then compress cable housing retainer and rotate cable housing clockwise.
3. Slide cable end from servo cable actuator groove and disconnect speed control servo electrical connector.
4. Remove three bolts, then the servo.
5. Reverse procedure to install.

DOHC ENGINE

1. Disconnect speed control actuator cable from throttle control lever, then disengage cable sleeve from retainer and remove retainer.
2. Remove speed control actuator cable retaining clips.
3. Depress speed control actuator cable cap retaining tab, then rotate speed control actuator cable cap counterclockwise.
4. Slide speed control actuator cable end from actuator cable groove, then remove actuator cable.
5. Reverse procedure to install.

FOCUS

1. Remove air cleaner outlet tube.
2. Disconnect speed control cable from throttle body.
3. Unhook cable from its two retaining clips.
4. Disconnect actuator cable cover.
5. Remove speed control cable from speed control actuator pulley.
6. Reverse procedure to install.

LS & THUNDERBIRD

1. Remove speed control servo as outlined in "Servo Assembly."
2. Remove engine cover, if equipped.
3. Remove speed control actuator cable from throttle lever, **Fig. 158.**
4. Detach speed control actuator cable end from throttle nail head by pushing forward.
5. Remove speed control actuator cable from throttle bracket by squeezing locking ears and pulling forward.
6. Reverse procedures to install.

MUSTANG

1. Remove lefthand front wheel and tire assembly.
2. Remove lefthand side splash shield retainers, screws and splash shield.
3. Depress locking tabs and rotate speed control actuator cable cap to remove.
4. Remove speed control actuator cable from throttle body.
5. Lift speed control cable from throttle nailhead, then release cable from throttle bracket.

6. Remove cable from retaining clips.
7. Disconnect speed control actuator cable from servo pulley.
8. Reverse procedure to install.

SABLE & TAURUS

1. Remove accelerator control splash shield retainers, then the shield.
2. Rotate throttle valve.
3. Disconnect speed control cable from throttle cam.
4. Squeeze speed control cable tabs and remove cable from cable bracket. **Ensure cable is removed in direction illustrated on cable where it attaches to throttle cam.**
5. Depress speed control cable cap retaining tab.
6. Rotate speed control cable cap counterclockwise, then pull cable cap away from servo housing.
7. Remove speed control cable by depressing spring retainer, sliding core wire end out of servo pulley, then removing the cable.
8. Reverse procedure to install.

Servo Assembly

CONTINENTAL

1. Disconnect speed control cable from throttle body.
2. Remove speed control cable retaining bolt from accelerator control mounting bracket.
3. Disconnect harness connector at speed control servo, then remove two nuts attaching servo mounting bracket to lefthand shock tower.
4. Remove control actuator cable cap from servo. Start by compressing auxiliary throttle return spring on throttle end of actuator, then depressing cap locking arm rotating cap counterclockwise.
5. Remove speed control actuator cable slug from speed control servo pulley.
6. Remove bracket from speed control servo. Retain bracket and screws for installation on new servo.
7. Reverse procedure to install.

CONTOUR & MYSTIQUE

1. Disconnect actuator cable from throttle body lever.
2. Remove actuator cable retaining clip from accelerator cable bracket.
3. Remove actuator cable cap, **Fig. 159,** from servo by pressing cap locking arm and rotating cap counterclockwise.
4. Remove actuator cable slug from servo pulley. Gently push actuator cable slug past retaining spring using a small screwdriver.
5. Remove servo.
6. Reverse procedure to install, noting:
   a. Ensure throttle lever is at idle position after cable installation.

CROWN VICTORIA, GRAND MARQUIS, MARAUDER & TOWN CAR

1. Disconnect speed control actuator

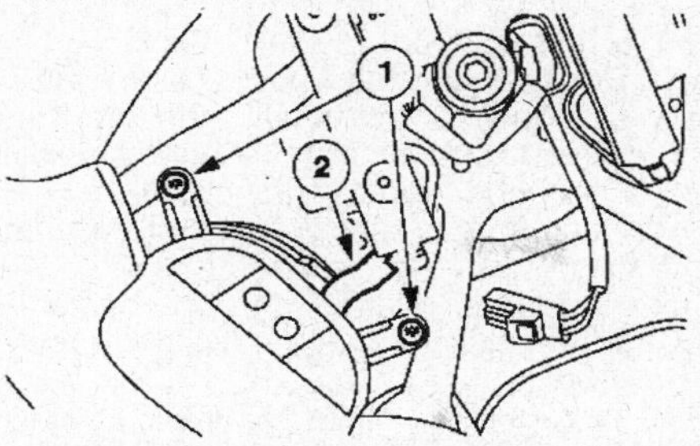

1. Actuator switch retaining screws.
2. Electrical connector.

FM1109900695000X

Fig. 160 Speed control actuator switch replacement. LS & Thunderbird

cable from throttle lever as outlined in "Servo (Throttle Actuator) Assembly Actuator Cable."
2. Depress locking tab, then remove speed control actuator cable cap by rotating in a counterclockwise direction.
3. Disconnect electrical connector from servo.
4. Remove servo assembly and bracket attaching nuts, then the servo and bracket as an assembly.
5. Remove servo to bracket mounting screws, then separate servo from bracket.
6. Reverse procedure to install, noting the following:
   a. **Torque** servo to bracket mounting screws to 71–97 inch lbs.
   b. **Torque** bracket assembly attaching nuts to 45–62 inch lbs.

ESCORT & ZX2

1. Disconnect cable from throttle control lever, then remove cable to bracket mounting bolt as required.
2. Slide cable end from servo cable actuator groove, then disconnect servo electrical connector.
3. Remove servo assembly mounting bolts, then the servo from vehicle.
4. Reverse procedure to install, noting the following:
   a. **On models equipped with SOHC engines, torque** servo mounting bolts to 70–95 inch lbs.
   b. **On models equipped with DOHC engines, torque** servo mounting bolts to 62 inch lbs.

LS & THUNDERBIRD

1. Detach speed control actuator cable end from throttle nailhead by pushing it forward.
2. Remove lefthand front wheel and tire.
3. Remove lefthand front inner splash shield.
4. Disconnect servo electrical connector.
5. Remove servo bracket mounting bolts, then position bracket assembly aside.
6. Remove bolts and separate bracket from servo.
7. Remove speed control actuator cable cap by depressing locking tab.
8. Disconnect speed control actuator cable from servo pulley.
9. Reverse procedure to install, noting the following:
   a. Improperly wrapping actuator cable around servo pulley may lead to high idle conditions.
   b. Ensure rubber seal is fully seated onto actuator cable cap.
   c. **Torque** servo to bracket bolts to 80 inch lbs.
   d. **Torque** bracket mounting bolts to 80 inch lbs.
   e. **Torque** engine cover mounting bolts to 80 inch lbs.

MUSTANG

1. Remove lefthand tire and wheel assembly.
2. Remove lefthand splash shield.
3. Disconnect speed control servo electrical connector.
4. Depress locking tab, then rotate speed control actuator cable cap to remove.
5. Disconnect speed control cable from throttle nailhead.
6. Gently push in retaining spring, then disconnect speed control cable slug from speed control servo pulley.
7. Remove bolts, then the speed control servo.
8. Reverse procedure to install.

SABLE & TAURUS

1. Disconnect speed control servo electrical connector.
2. Remove accelerator control splash shield from accelerator bracket.
3. Remove actuator cable from accelerator cable bracket.
4. Remove actuator cable from throttle body.
5. Remove actuator cable cap, **Fig. 159,** from servo by pressing cap locking arm and rotating cap counterclockwise.
6. Remove actuator cable slug from servo pulley. Gently push actuator cable slug past retaining spring using a small screwdriver.
7. Remove actuator by lifting upward.
8. Reverse procedure to install, noting the following:
   a. Ensure throttle lever is at idle position after cable installation.
   b. **On 2000 models, torque** accelerator bracket screw to 27–44 inch lbs., and splash shield screws to 44–62 inch lbs.
   c. **On 2001–03 models, torque** servo mounting nuts to 15 ft. lbs., and servo to bracket screws to 80 inch lbs.

Actuator Switch(es)

CONTINENTAL

LESS REMOTE AUDIO/CLIMATE CONTROLS

1. Remove driver's air bag module from steering wheel as outlined in "Passive Restraint Systems" chapter.
2. Remove bolt holding steering wheel to steering column.
3. Remove steering wheel using puller tool No. T67L-3600-A, or equivalent,

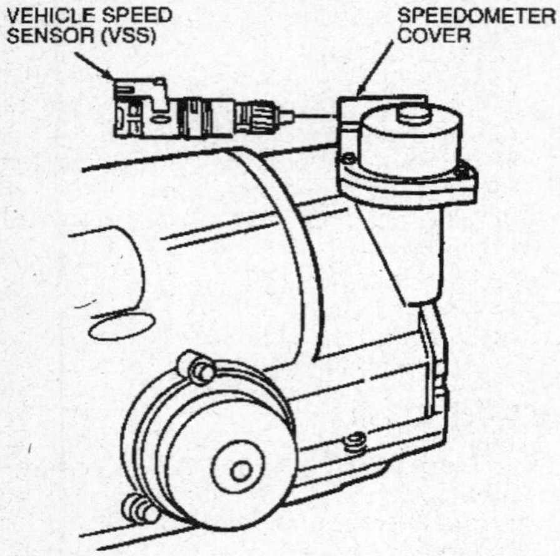

FM1109700721000X

Fig. 161 Speed sensor replacement. Sable & Taurus w/AX4N transaxle

then three screws from back of wheel and plastic cover.
4. Pry lower edge of switch housing from steering wheel until switch housing is clear of wheel using a small screwdriver.
5. Push actuator switches out towards face of steering wheel.
6. Position switches through steering wheel openings and remove.
7. Reverse procedure to install.

WITH REMOTE AUDIO/CLIMATE CONTROLS

1. Carefully pry out speed control switch using a suitable blunt tool.
2. Separate switch from steering wheel, then disconnect switch electrical connector.
3. Reverse procedure to install.

CONTOUR & MYSTIQUE

1. Remove upper and lower steering column shrouds.
2. Rotate steering wheel to gain access to driver side air bag module retaining bolts on rear of steering wheel, then remove driver air bag module from steering wheel.
3. Disconnect actuator switch wiring connectors.
4. Remove actuator switches.
5. Reverse procedure to install.

COUGAR

1. Remove driver's air bag module as outlined in "Passive Restraint Systems" chapter.
2. Disconnect speed control actuator switch assembly electrical connector.
3. Remove speed control actuator switches.
4. Reverse procedure to install.

CROWN VICTORIA, GRAND MARQUIS & MARAUDER

1. Remove driver's air bag module as outlined in "Passive Restraint Systems" chapter.
2. Remove and discard steering wheel retaining bolt.
3. Remove steering wheel using a suitable puller tool.
4. Position steering wheel cover aside.
5. Disconnect electrical connector and wire harness from steering wheel cover, then remove the cover.
6. Push speed control actuator switches out toward face of wheel.
7. Position switches through steering wheel openings and carefully remove them.
8. Reverse procedure to install.

ESCORT & ZX2

1. Ensure front wheels are in straight-ahead position.
2. Remove lefthand and righthand driver's air bag module bolts, then lift air bag module from steering wheel and disconnect air bag, horn and speed control switch electrical connectors.
3. Remove steering wheel bolt, then using puller tool No. T67L-3600-A, or equivalent, remove steering wheel.
4. Tape air bag sliding contact to steering column housing to ensure alignment, then remove four screws and steering wheel trim.
5. Remove four screws and speed control switches.
6. Reverse procedure to install, noting the following:
   a. Ensure all wiring and electrical connectors are properly routed to avoid pinching.
   b. Tighten all fasteners to specifications.
   c. Arm air bag system as outlined in "Air Bag System Arming & Disarming."

FOCUS

1. Remove driver's air bag module as outlined in "Passive Restraint Systems" chapter.
2. Disconnect speed control switch electrical connector.
3. Remove speed control switches.
4. Reverse procedure to install.

LS & THUNDERBIRD

1. Remove driver's air bag module as outlined in "Passive Restraint Systems" chapter.
2. Remove screws and disconnect electrical connector, then remove speed control actuator switch, **Fig. 160.**
3. Reverse procedure to install.

MUSTANG

1. Remove steering wheel using puller tool No. T67L-3600-A, or equivalent.
2. Remove screws from rear steering wheel cover and rear cover.
3. Remove ribbon harness from clips.
4. Remove horn contact electrical connectors.
5. Remove righthand side horn contact.
6. Remove speed control actuator switch mounting screws, then the switch.
7. Reverse procedure to install.

SABLE & TAURUS

EXCEPT SHO

1. Remove driver's air bag module.

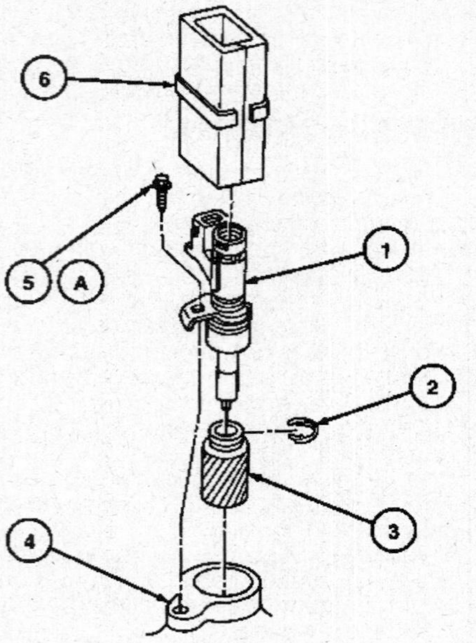

Item	Description
1	Vehicle Speed Sensor (VSS)
2	Speedometer Driven Gear Retainer
3	Speedometer Gear
4	Transaxle Case
5	Vehicle Speed Sensor (VSS) Retaining Bolt
6	Vehicle Speed Sensor Shield
A	Tighten to 4-6 N-m (36-53 Lb-In)

FM1109700722000X

Fig. 162 Speed sensor replacement. Sable & Taurus w/AX4S transaxle

2. Disconnect wiring connectors for actuator switches by depressing locking tang and pulling switch printed circuit and connector out of electrical socket in steering wheel.
3. Remove two Torx head screws retaining each speed control actuator switch to steering wheel, then switches from steering wheel.
4. Reverse procedure to install.

SHO

1. Ensure front wheels are in straight-ahead position.
2. Remove driver's air bag module.
3. Remove and discard bolt retaining steering wheel to steering column.
4. Remove steering wheel using puller tool No. T67L-3600-A, or equivalent. Route air bag sliding contact wiring harness through wheel as it is removed.
5. Remove puller, then turn steering wheel over and remove four screws retaining rear cover to wheel.
6. Remove steering wheel cover, then turn wheel over.
7. The speed control switches are one piece, connected by wiring.

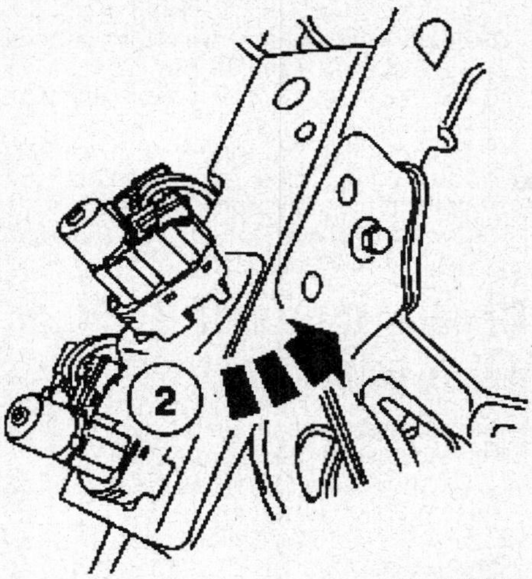

FM1100000760000X

Fig. 163 Deactivator switch removal. LS & Thunderbird

8. Disconnect horn plate wire connector on each side of steering wheel, then disconnect single inline wire connector in purple wire at center of steering wheel.
9. Remove four screws retaining lefthand steering wheel, then switches from steering wheel.
10. Reverse procedure to install.

TOWN CAR

LESS REMOTE AUDIO & CLIMATE CONTROLS

1. Remove driver's air bag module as outlined in "Passive Restraint Systems" chapter.
2. Remove and discard steering wheel retaining bolt.
3. Remove steering wheel using a suitable puller tool.
4. Position steering wheel cover aside.
5. Disconnect electrical connector and wire harness from steering wheel cover, then remove the cover.
6. Push speed control actuator switches out toward face of wheel.
7. Position switches through steering wheel openings and carefully remove them.
8. Reverse procedure to install.

WITH REMOTE AUDIO & CLIMATE CONTROLS

1. Carefully pry speed control actuator switch out of steering wheel.
2. Disconnect actuator switch electrical connector.
3. Remove actuator switch.
4. Reverse procedure to install.

Digital Transmission Range (TR) Sensor

LS & THUNDERBIRD

REMOVAL

1. Raise and safely support vehicle.
2. Remove 3-way catalytic converter.

FM1100000761000X

Fig. 164 Unlocking lock knob. LS & Thunderbird

3. Remove heat shield retainers, then the shield.
4. **Make suitable index-marks with color paint on bolts, washers, nuts, and flex coupling to transmission flange and pinion flange to ensure assembly in original locations. Components improperly assembled could cause driveshaft imbalance.**
5. Loosen flex coupling nut using suitable ratchets and holder tool No. 205-474, or equivalent. **Do not remove flex coupling to driveshaft retaining bolts.**
6. Slide front shaft assembly rearward and support it securely.
7. Tighten nut to prevent front and rear shaft assemblies from separating.
8. Secure transmission to a suitable transmission jack with a safety chain.
9. Remove transmission rear mount.
10. Lower the transmission just enough to access TR sensor.
11. Disconnect transmission shift cable.
12. Disconnect TR sensor electrical connector.
13. Remove TR sensor mounting bolts, then the sensor.

INSTALLATION

1. Ensure sensor fits flush against case boss to prevent damage.
2. Install sensor and loosely install screws. Tightening one screw before the other may cause sensor damage or binding.
3. Ensure manual lever is in Neutral position.
4. Align sensor and **torque** screws in an alternating sequence to 89 inch lbs., using alignment tool No. 307-351, or equivalent.
5. Connect sensor electrical connector.
6. Connect transmission shift cable.
7. Install transmission rear mount. **Torque** mounting bolts to 41 ft. lbs.
8. Adjust transmission shift cable as required.
9. Add one gram of grease to both align-

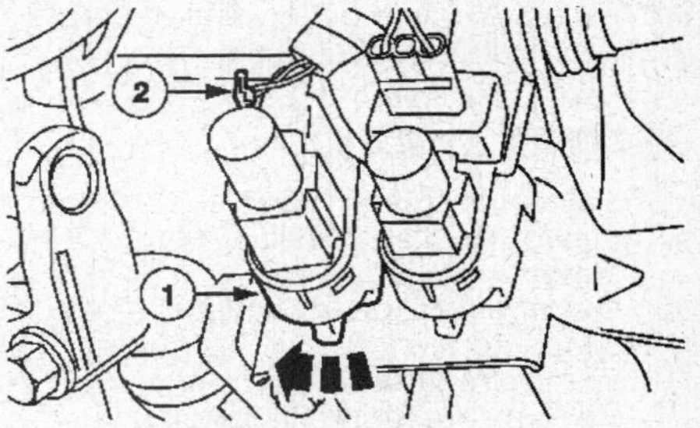

1. Deactivator switch.
2. Electrical connector.

FM1100000762000X

Fig. 165 Deactivator switch installation. LS & Thunderbird

ment bushing cavities.

10. Loosen flex coupling nut and slide front shaft assembly forward.
11. Align index marks and position alignment bushing on transmission flange piloting system.
12. **Install bolts, washers and nuts in their original positions or driveshaft imbalance could occur. Install flex coupling bolts with head of bolt seated against flange and nuts seated against flex coupling. Install short bolts in front and the long bolts in rear. Coat nut and bolt threads with suitable threadlock sealer.**
13. Install heat shield.
14. Install 3-way catalytic converter.

Output Shaft Speed (OSS) Sensor

MUSTANG w/MANUAL TRANSAXLE

1. Raise and safely support vehicle.
2. Disconnect OSS sensor electrical connector.
3. Remove OSS sensor mounting bolts, then the sensor.
4. Reverse procedure to install. **Torque** sensor mounting bolts to 89 inch lbs.

Vehicle Speed Sensor

CONTINENTAL

1. Raise and support vehicle.
2. Remove speed sensor mounting clip to transaxle retaining bolt, then the sensor and driven gear from transaxle.
3. Disconnect electrical connector from speed sensor.
4. Remove driven gear retainer, then the driven gear from sensor.
5. Reverse procedure to install.

CROWN VICTORIA, GRAND MARQUIS, MARAUDER & TOWN CAR

1. Raise and support vehicle.
2. Remove speed sensor mounting clip to transmission retaining bolt.
3. Disconnect electrical connector from sensor.

4. Remove driven gear retainer, then the driven gear from sensor.
5. Reverse procedure to install.

ESCORT & ZX2

1. Raise and support vehicle, then loosen sensor to transmission retaining fastener.
2. Disconnect speed sensor electrical connector.
3. Remove speed sensor.
4. Reverse procedure to install.

SABLE & TAURUS

1. Raise and support vehicle.
2. Remove dual converter Y-pipe and HO2 sensors from exhaust system as required.
3. Remove Vehicle Speed Sensor (VSS) shield.
4. Remove bolt retaining speed sensor mounting clip to transaxle.
5. Remove sensor and driven gear from transaxle, **Figs. 161 and 162.**
6. Disconnect electrical connector and speedometer cable from speed sensor.
7. Remove driven gear retainer, then the driven gear from sensor.
8. Reverse procedure to install, noting the following:
   a. Ensure internal O-ring is properly seated in sensor housing.
   b. Lower vehicle and verify proper speedometer/odometer operation.
   c. Ensure there is no exhaust system leakage.

Deactivator Switch

CONTOUR & MYSTIQUE

Deactivator switch is located above stop lamp switch on pedal bracket in driver footwell.

1. Disconnect battery ground cable.
2. Disconnect deactivator switch wiring connector.
3. Rotate switch 45° counterclockwise and remove from bracket.
4. Reverse procedure to install.

COUGAR

1. Remove driver's side lower instrument panel.
2. Disconnect speed control deactivator switch electrical connector.
3. Remove speed control deactivator switch.
4. Reverse procedure to install.

CROWN VICTORIA, GRAND MARQUIS, MARAUDER & TOWN CAR

REMOVAL

1. Disconnect deactivator switch electrical connector.
2. Remove deactivator switch from brake pedal support by rotating counterclockwise.

INSTALLATION

1. Pull plunger out to its full travel.
2. Completely depress and hold brake pedal.
3. Install deactivator switch into brake pedal support and rotate clockwise.
4. Release brake pedal.
5. Connect switch electrical connector.

ESCORT & ZX2

1. Disconnect deactivator switch electrical connector.
2. Remove deactivator switch by twisting as required.
3. Reverse procedure to install.

LS & THUNDERBIRD

REMOVAL

1. Disconnect footwell lamp electrical connector.
2. Remove instrument panel insulator.
3. Disconnect deactivator switch electrical connector.
4. Rotate and remove deactivator switch, **Fig. 163.**

INSTALLATION

Initial installation of the deactivator switch allows for only one adjustment. If additional adjustments are needed, a new switch will be required.

1. Unlock the lock knob by rotating counterclockwise to its stop, **Fig. 164.**
2. Start engine, then fully depress and hold brake pedal.
3. Position deactivator switch in bracket and rotate clockwise, **Fig. 165,** then connect electrical connector.
4. Release brake pedal.

MUSTANG

1. Disconnect deactivator switch electrical connector.
2. Detach deactivator switch lower hook.
3. Detach deactivator upper pivot.
4. Remove deactivator switch.
5. Reverse procedures to install.

SABLE & TAURUS

2000

1. Disconnect deactivator switch hook from plastic pedal adapter stem.
2. Depress deactivator switch hook and plunger assembly fully. Ensure that hook is against deactivator switch body and locking tab snaps into place in deactivator switch hook.
3. Depress brake pedal fully and attach deactivator switch hook, then release brake pedal and allow brake pedal to return to its normal position.

2001-02

Removal

1. Disconnect deactivator switch electrical connector.
2. Rotate counterclockwise 45°, then remove deactivator switch.

Installation

1. Release plunger lock, if equipped, by turning lock knob counterclockwise until first click is felt and fully depressing brake pedal.
2. Place deactivator switch in bracket and rotate 45° clockwise.
3. Connect deactivator switch electrical connector.
4. **On models equipped with locking tab,** slowly release brake pedal and pull moderately once it reaches rest position. Listen for an extra audible "click" sound.

Brake On/Off Switch

REMOVAL

Locking tab on connector must be lifted before connector can be removed.

1. Disconnect wire harness at connector from brake switch.
2. Since switch side plate nearest brake pedal is slotted, it is not required to remove brake master cylinder push rod and one brake master cylinder push rod spacer from brake pedal pin.
3. Remove hairpin retainer, slide brake switch, push rod and brake master cylinder push rod spacer and brake master cylinder push rod bushing away from brake pedal and remove brake switch by sliding brake switch up and down.

INSTALLATION

1. Position brake switch so that U-shaped side is nearest brake pedal and directly over/under pin.
2. Slide brake switch up and down, trapping master cylinder push rod and blade bushing between brake switch side plates.
3. Push brake switch and push rod assembly firmly toward brake pedal arm. Assemble outside white plastic washer to pin and install hairpin retainer to trap whole assembly.
4. Brake switch wire harness must have sufficient length to travel with brake switch during full stroke of brake pedal. If wire length is insufficient, route harness or service as required.
5. Assemble wire harness connector to brake switch and install wires in retaining clip.
6. Inspect brake switch for proper operation.

Clutch Pedal Position (CPP) Switch

ESCORT & ZX2

1. Disconnect Clutch Pedal Position switch electrical connector, then remove CPP switch locknut.
2. Remove CPP switch.
3. Reverse procedure to install. **Torque** locknut to 12 ft. lbs.

MUSTANG

1. Disconnect electrical connector.
2. Remove bolt and clutch pedal position switch.
3. Reverse procedure to install.

WIPER SYSTEMS

TABLE OF CONTENTS

Front Wiper System

NOTE: On Air Bag Equipped Models, Refer To "Air Bag System Precautions" Located In The Front Of This Manual For System Disarming & Arming Procedures.

NOTE: Refer To "Computer Relearn Procedures" Located In The Front Of This Manual When Battery Power To The Computer Has Been Interrupted.

NOTE: "Electrical Symbol & Wire Color Code Identification" Located In The Front Of This Manual May Be Used As An Aid When Using Wiring Circuits Found In This Section.

INDEX

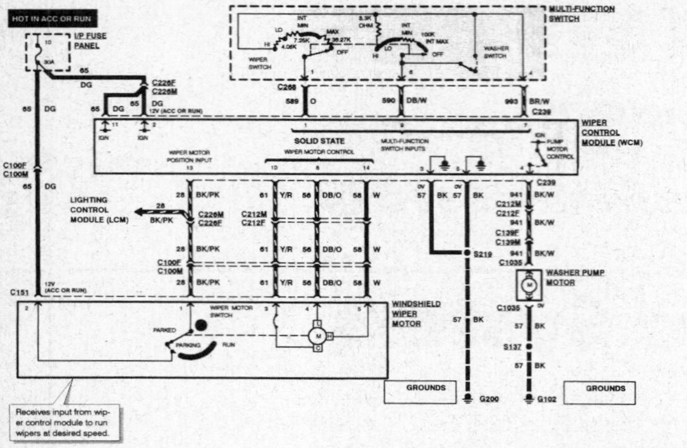

FM9029800572000X

Fig. 1 Wiring diagram. Continental

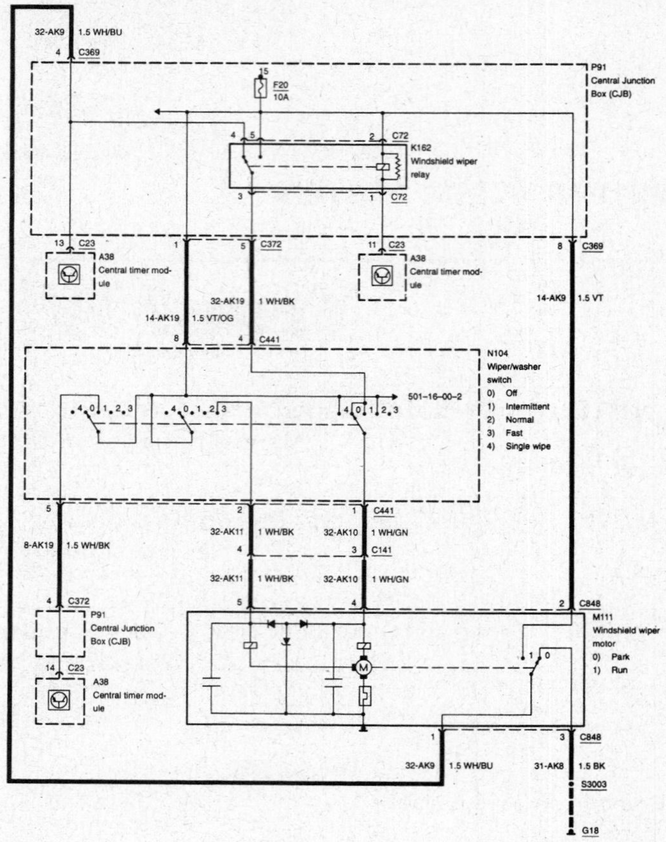

FM9029800559010X

Fig. 2 Wiring diagram (Part 1 of 2). Contour, Mystique & 2000 Cougar w/fixed intermittent wipers

PRECAUTIONS

Air Bag Systems

Refer to "Air Bag System Precautions" in front of this manual for system disarming and arming procedures.

Battery Ground Cable

Prior to service, disconnect battery ground cable and isolate as required.

SYSTEM DIAGNOSIS & TESTING

Wiring Diagrams

Refer to **Figs. 1 through 20,** for wiper and washer system wiring diagrams.

Diagnostic Procedure

Refer to **Figs. 21 through 34,** for diagnosis procedures.

Pinpoint Tests

Pinpoint tests are used to locate specific system faults to be serviced. Refer to the "Diagnostic Chart Index" and system wiring diagrams when performing diagnosis.

CONTINENTAL

Refer to **Figs. 35 through 42,** for pinpoint test procedures.

CONTOUR & MYSTIQUE

Refer to **Figs. 43 through 49,** for pinpoint test procedures.

COUGAR

Refer to **Figs. 50 through 57,** for pinpoint test procedures.

CROWN VICTORIA, GRAND MARQUIS & MARAUDER

Refer to **Figs. 58 through 71,** for pinpoint test procedures.

ESCORT & ZX2

Refer to **Figs. 72 through 81,** for pinpoint procedures.

FOCUS

Refer to **Figs. 82 through 85,** for pinpoint test procedures.

LS

Refer to **Figs. 86 through 93,** for pinpoint test procedures.

MUSTANG

Refer to **Figs. 94 through 96,** for pinpoint test procedures.

SABLE & TAURUS

Refer to **Figs. 97 through 101,** for pinpoint test procedures.

TOWN CAR

Refer to **Figs. 102 through 115,** for pinpoint test procedures.

THUNDERBIRD

Refer to **Figs. 116 through 121,** for pinpoint test procedures.

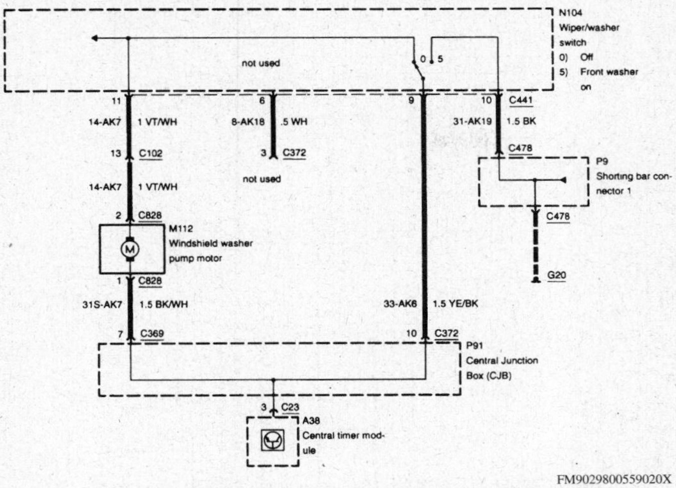

Fig. 2 Wiring diagram (Part 2 of 2). Contour, Mystique & 2000 Cougar w/fixed intermittent wipers

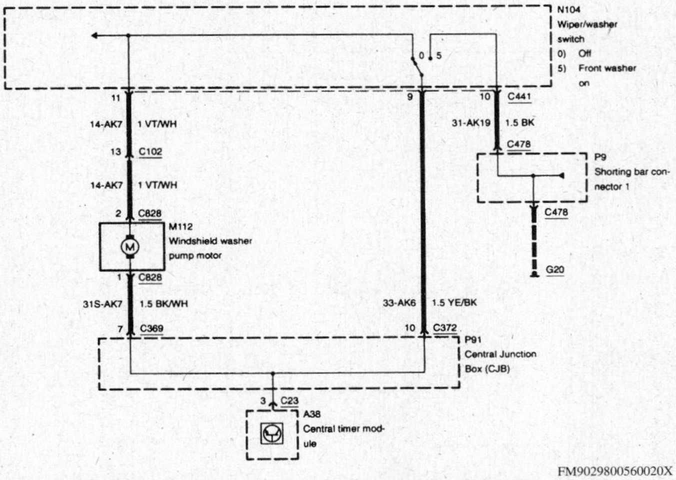

Fig. 3 Wiring diagram (Part 2 of 2). Contour, Mystique & 2000 Cougar w/variable intermittent wipers

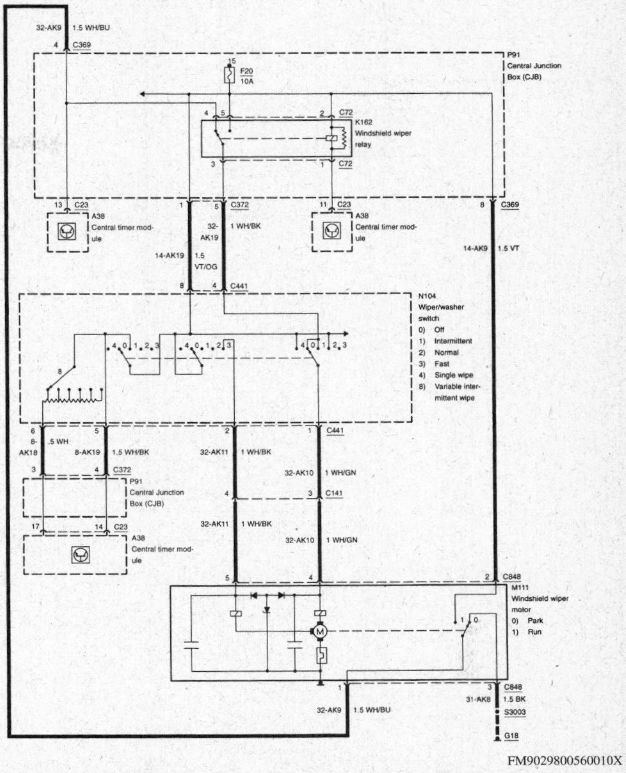

Fig. 3 Wiring diagram (Part 1 of 2). Contour, Mystique & 2000 Cougar w/variable intermittent wipers

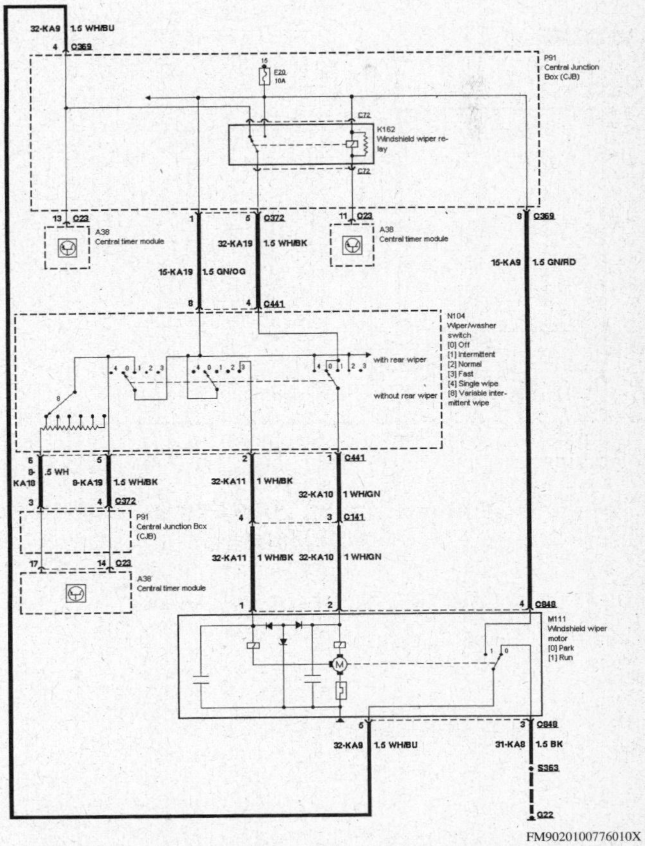

Fig. 4 Wiring diagram (Part 1 of 2). 2001–02 Cougar

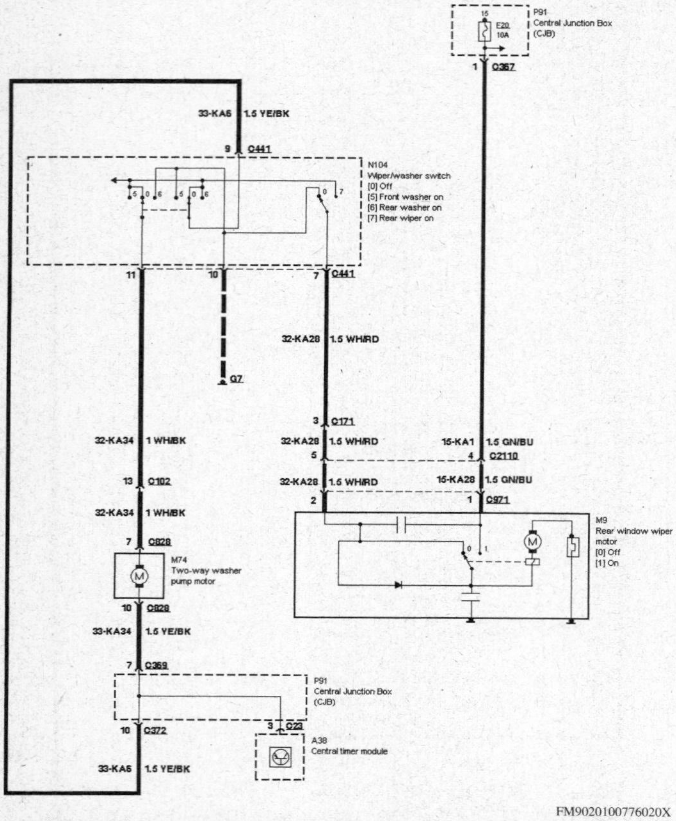

Fig. 4 Wiring diagram (Part 2 of 2). 2001–02 Cougar

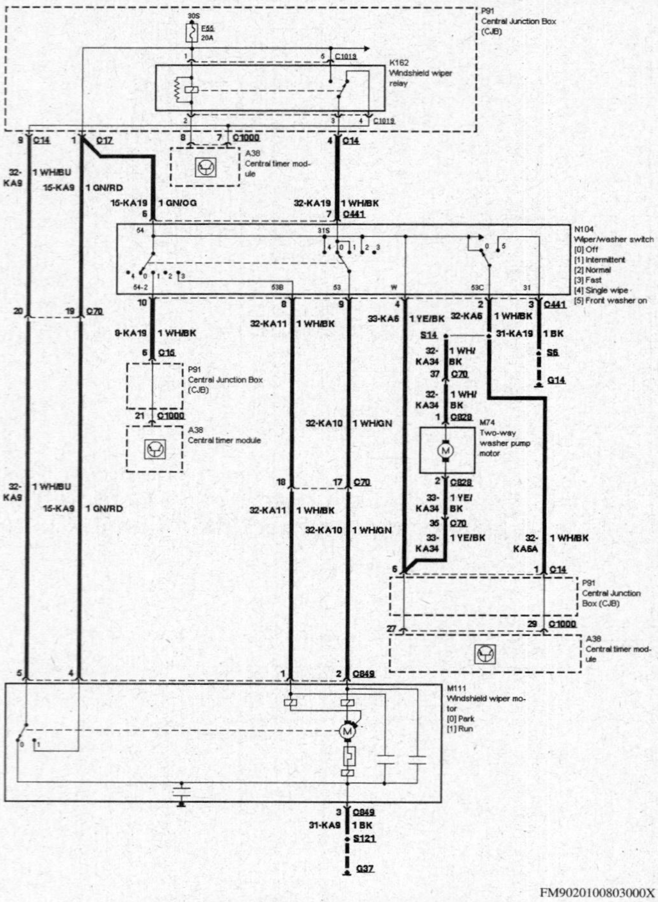

Fig. 5 Wiring diagram. Focus

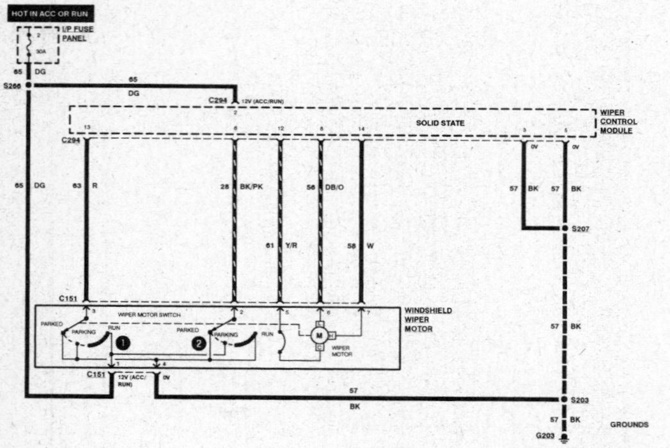

Fig. 6 Wiring diagram. 2000 Crown Victoria & Grand Marquis

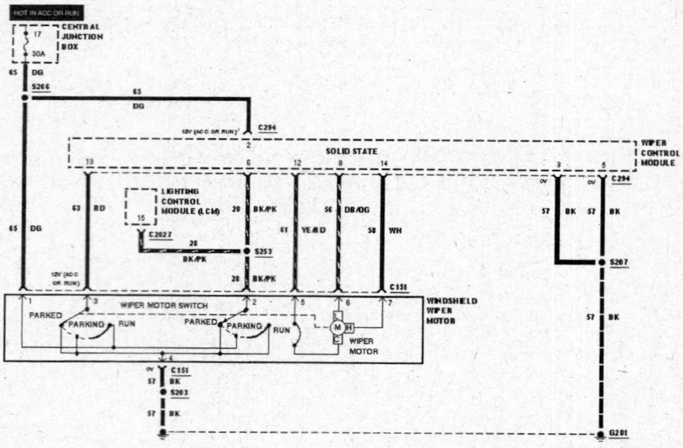

Fig. 7 Wiring diagram (Part 1 of 2). 2001 Crown Victoria & Grand Marquis

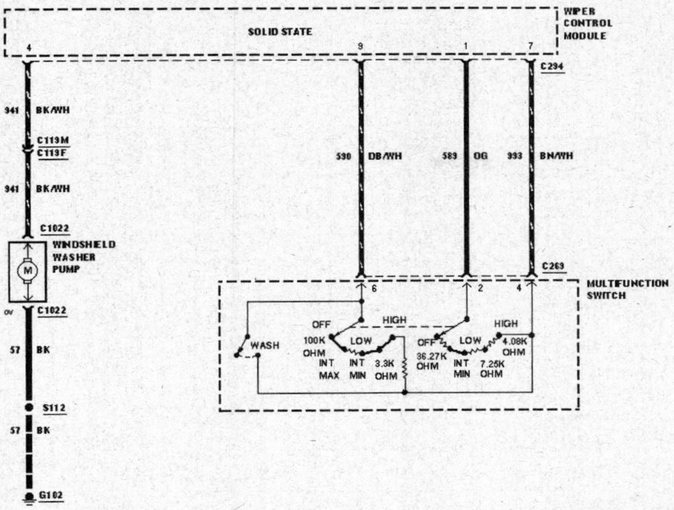

Fig. 7 Wiring diagram (Part 2 of 2). 2001 Crown Victoria & Grand Marquis

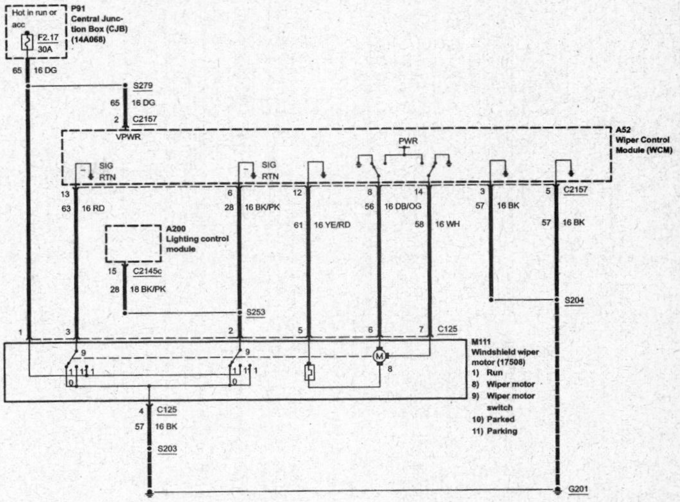

Fig. 8 Wiring diagram. 2002 Crown Victoria & Grand Marquis

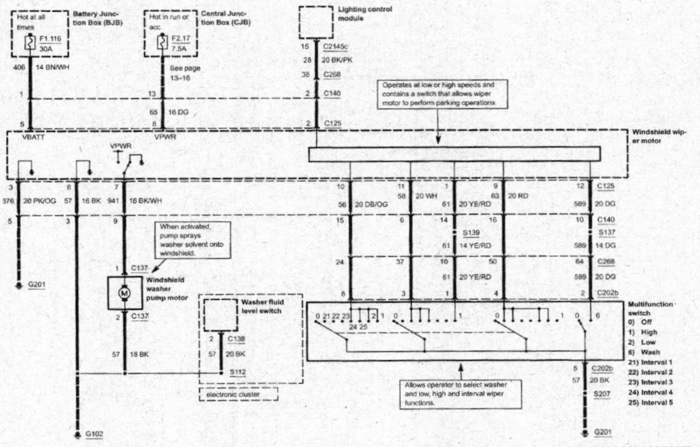

Fig. 9 Wiring diagram. 2003–04 Crown Victoria, Grand Marquis & Marauder

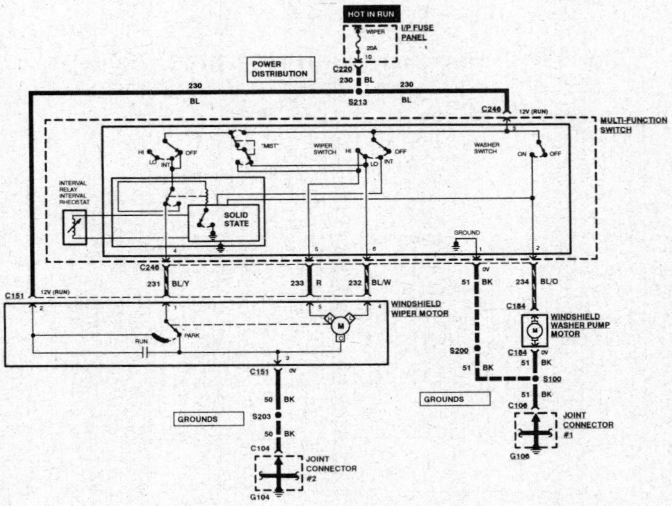

Fig. 10 Wiring diagram. Escort & ZX2

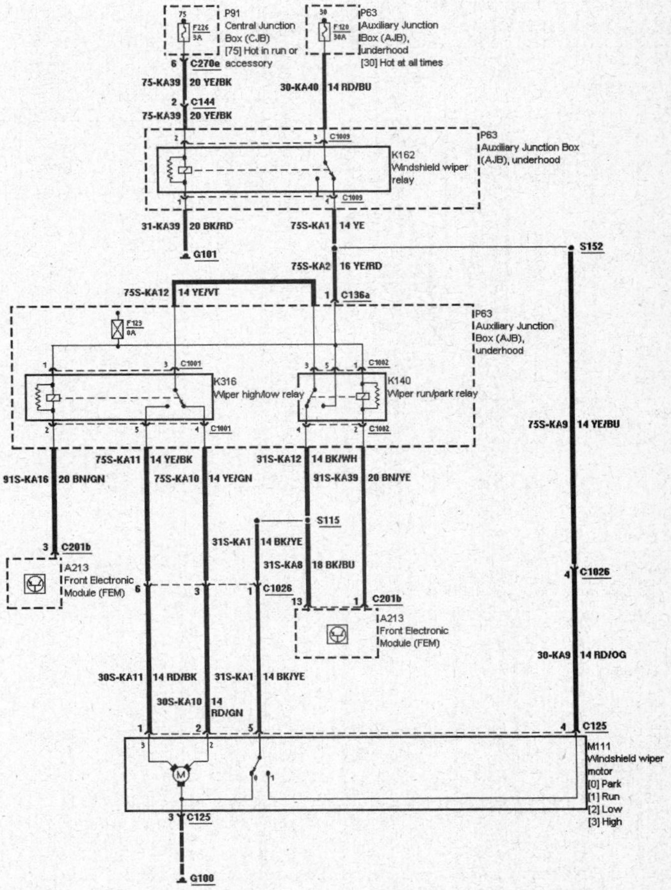

Fig. 11 Wiring diagram (Part 1 of 3). 2000–01 LS

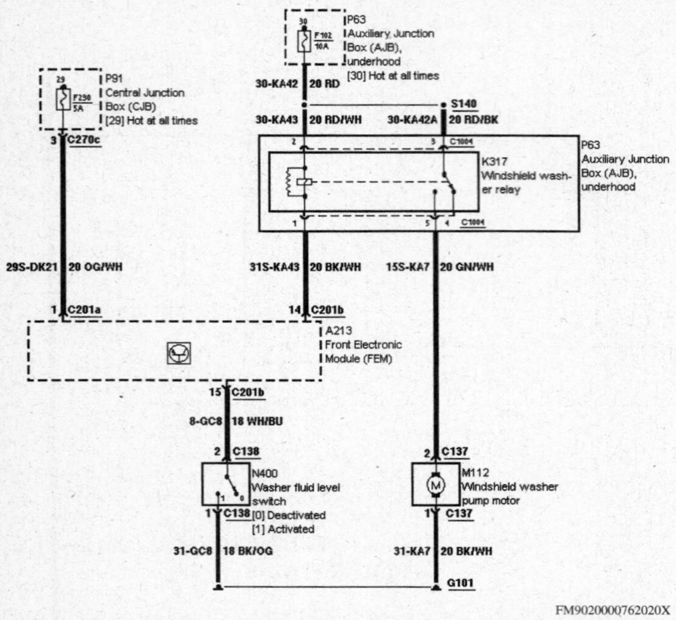

Fig. 11 Wiring diagram (Part 2 of 3). 2000–01 LS

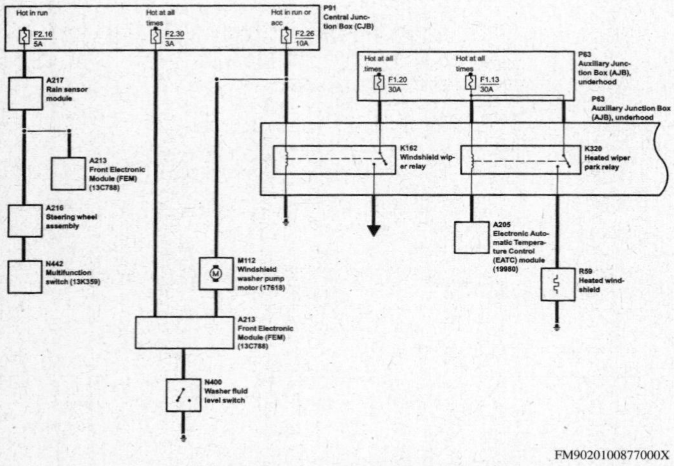

Fig. 12 Wiring diagram. 2002–04 LS

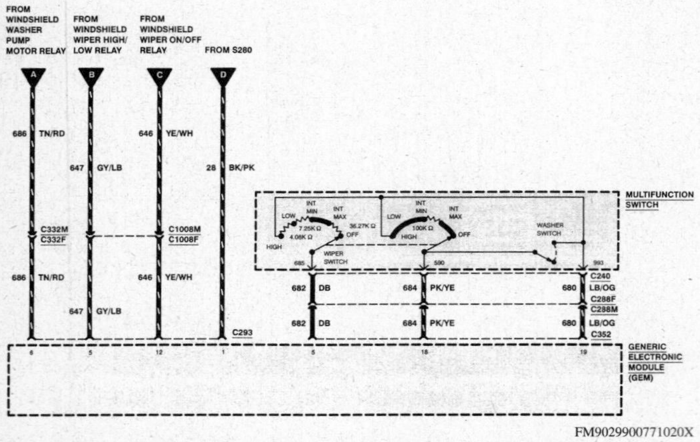

Fig. 13 Wiring diagram (Part 2 of 2). 2000–01 Mustang

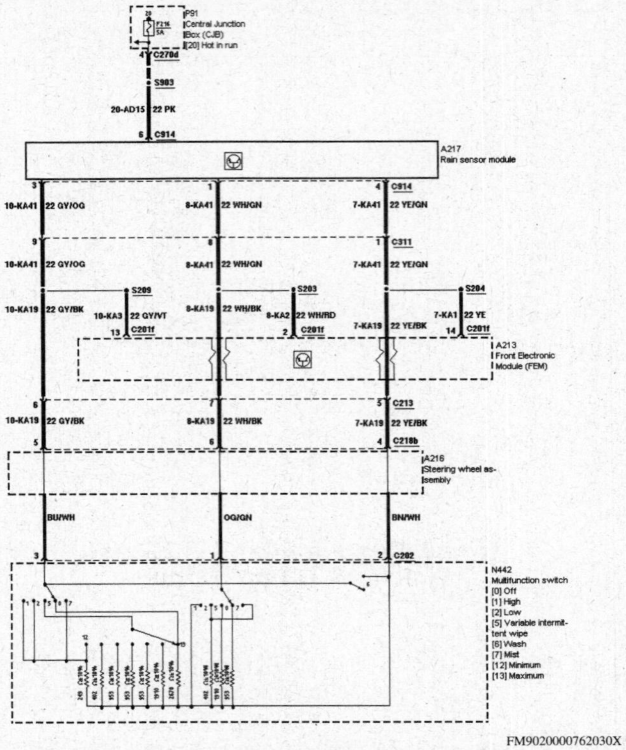

Fig. 11 Wiring diagram (Part 3 of 3). 2000–01 LS

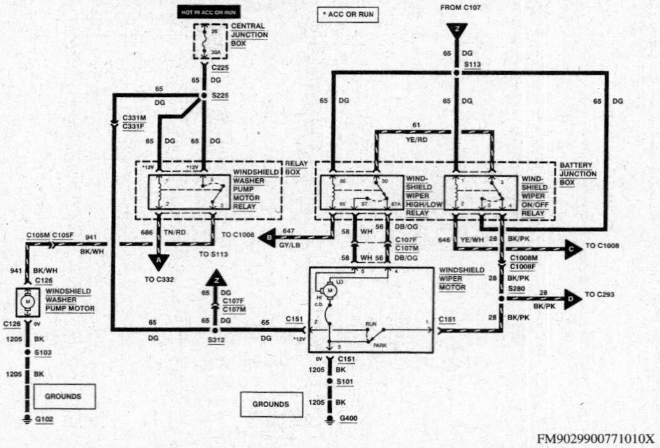

Fig. 13 Wiring diagram (Part 1 of 2). 2000–01 Mustang

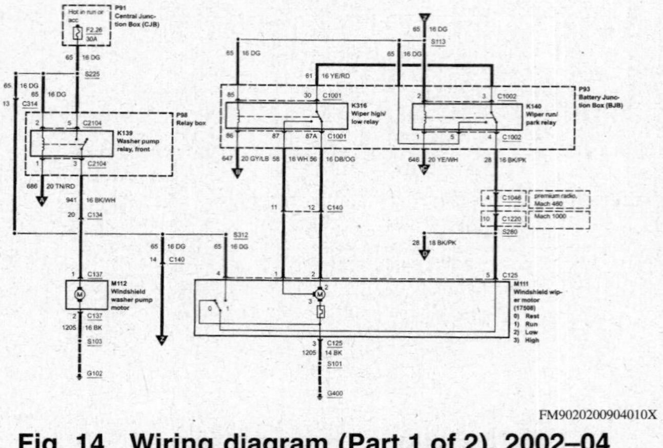

Fig. 14 Wiring diagram (Part 1 of 2). 2002–04 Mustang

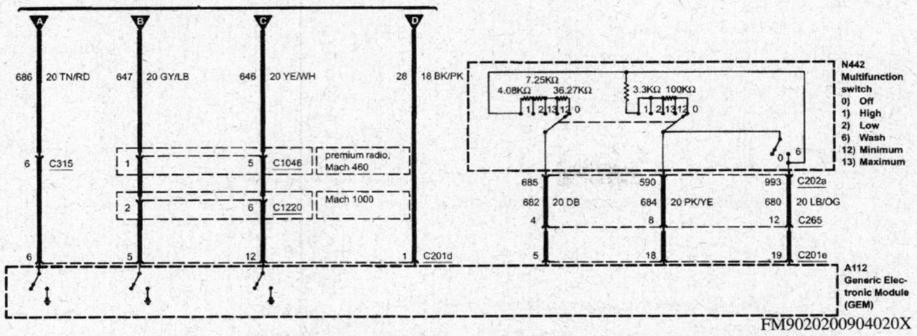

Fig. 14 Wiring diagram (Part 2 of 2). 2002–04 Mustang

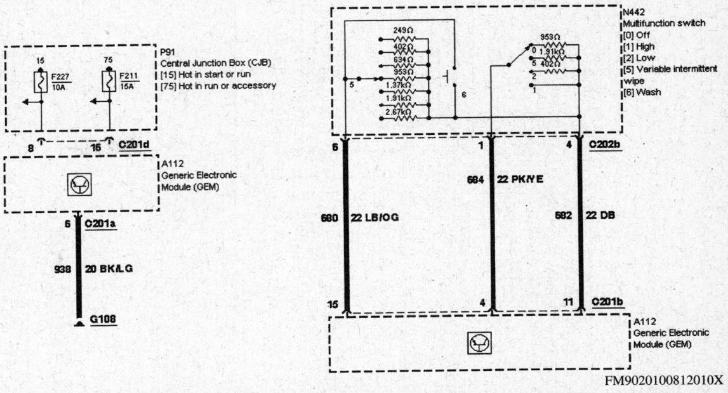

Fig. 15 Wiring diagram (Part 1 of 3). 2000–01 Sable & Taurus

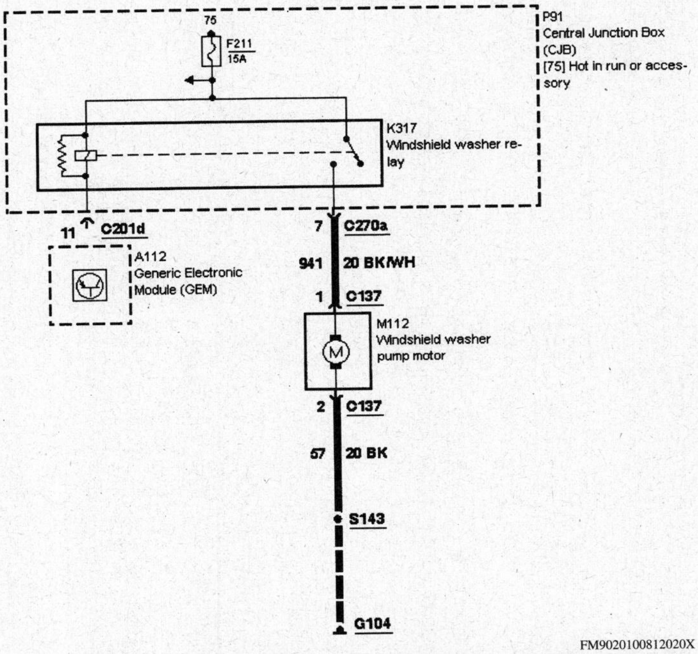

Fig. 15 Wiring diagram (Part 2 of 3). 2000–01 Sable & Taurus

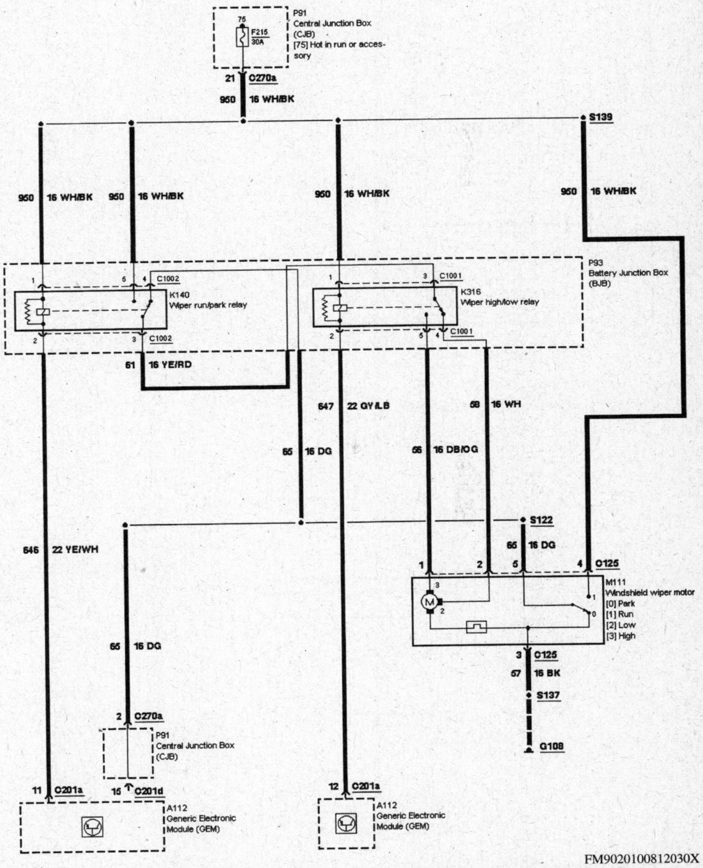

Fig. 15 Wiring diagram (Part 3 of 3). 2000–01 Sable & Taurus

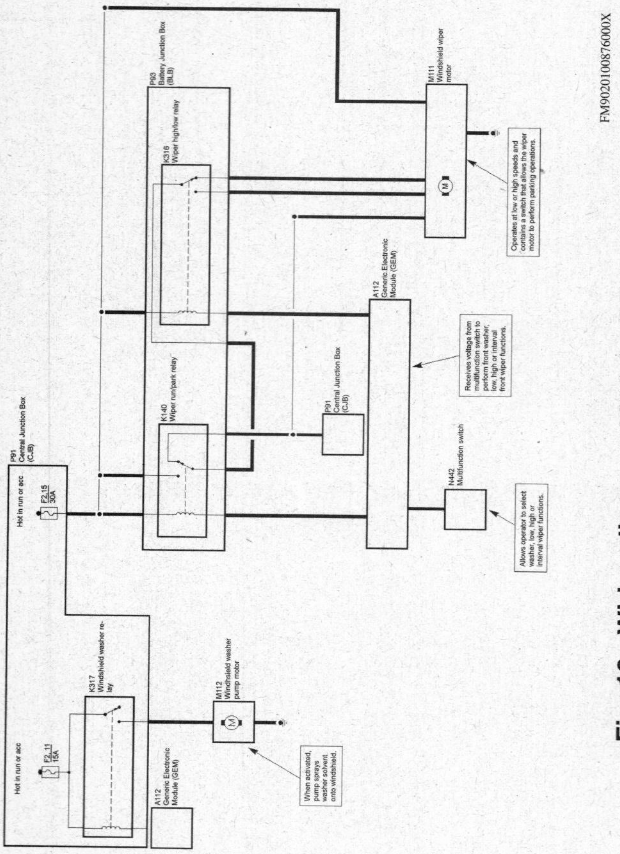

Fig. 16 Wiring diagram. 2002–04 Sable & Taurus

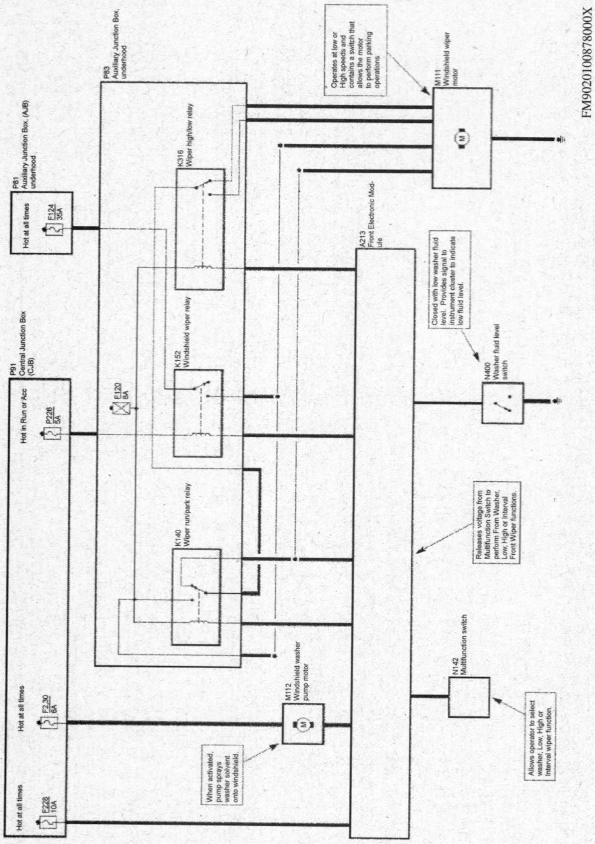

Fig. 17 Wiring diagram. Thunderbird

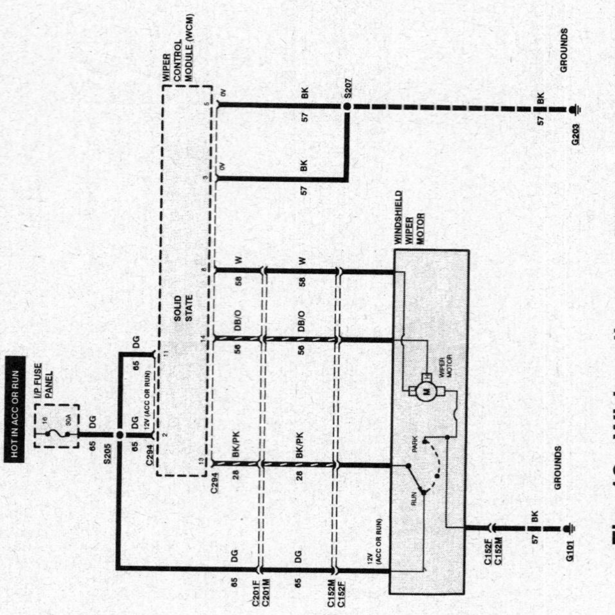

Fig. 18 Wiring diagram (Part 1 of 2). 2000–01 Town Car

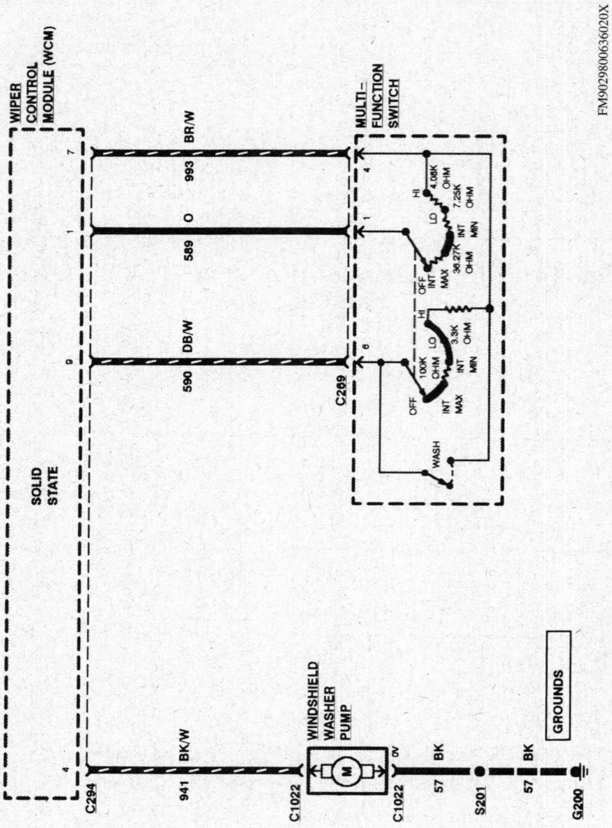

Fig. 18 Wiring diagram (Part 2 of 2). 2000–01 Town Car

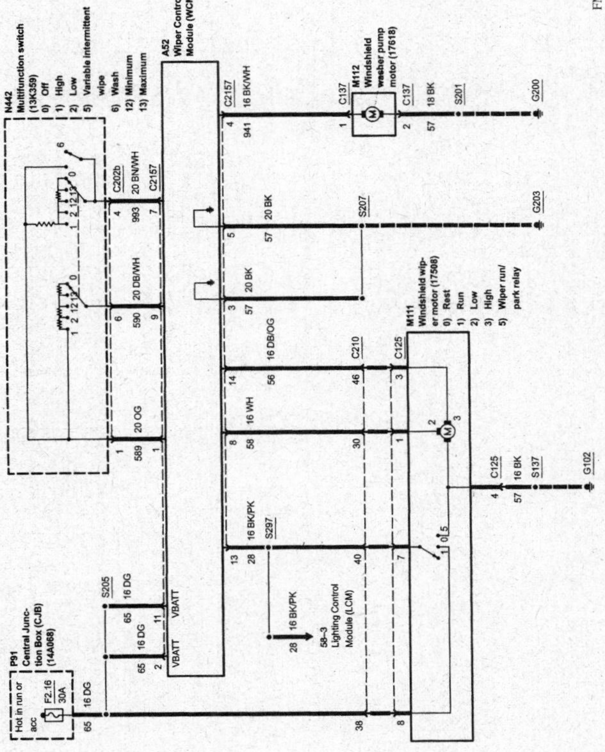

FM9020100874000X

Fig. 19 Wiring diagram. 2002 Town Car

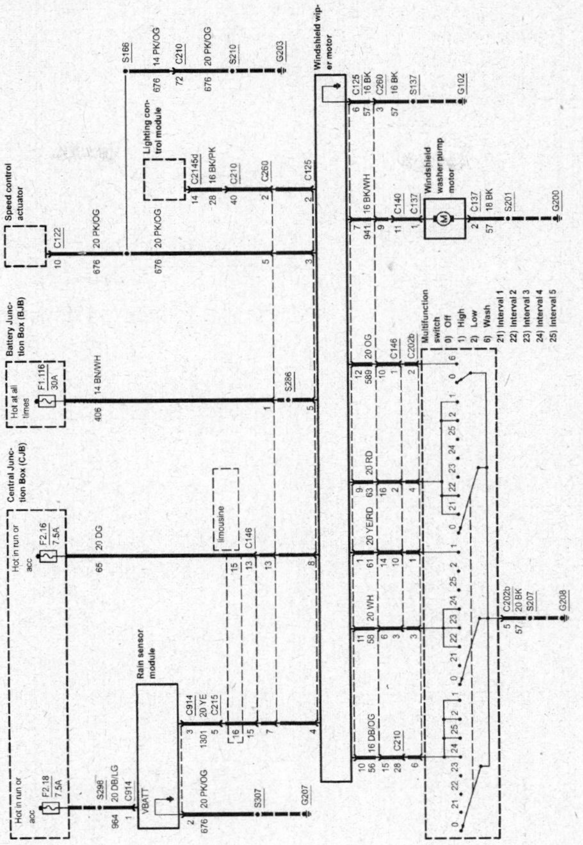

FM9020200905000X

Fig. 20 Wiring diagram. 2003–04 Town Car

Condition	Possible Source	Action
• The Washer Pump Is Inoperative	• Circuitry. • Multi-function switch. • Wiper control module. • Washer pump.	• GO to Pinpoint Test A.
• The Low Washer Fluid Indicator Does Not Operate Properly	• Washer pump. • Sensor. • Virtual image cluster (VIC). • Circuitry.	• INSPECT Message Center
• The Wipers are Inoperative	• Fuse. • Wiper motor. • Multi-function switch. • Circuitry. • Wiper control module.	• GO to Pinpoint Test B.
• The Low Wiper Speed Does Not Operate Properly	• Multi-function switch. • Wiper motor. • Circuitry. • Wiper control module.	• GO to Pinpoint Test C.
• The High Wiper Speed Does Not Operate Properly	• Multi-function switch. • Wiper motor. • Circuitry. • Wiper control module.	• GO to Pinpoint Test D.
• The Intermittent Wiper Speed Does Not Operate Properly	• Multi-function switch. • Circuitry. • Wiper control module. • Wiper motor.	• GO to Pinpoint Test E.
• The Wipers Will Not Park at the Proper Position	• Wiper motor. • Wiper control module. • Circuitry.	• GO to Pinpoint Test F.
• The Wipers Stay On Continuously	• Multi-function switch. • Wiper motor. • Wiper control module. • Circuitry.	• GO to Pinpoint Test G.
• The Headlamps Do Not Illuminate When the Wipers Are On	• Circuitry. • Wiper control module. • Lighting control module (LCM).	• GO to Pinpoint Test H.

FM9029800652000X

Fig. 21 Diagnostic procedure. Continental

Condition	Possible Sources	Action
• The High Speed Does Not Operate Propery (Intermittent Wiper Mode OK)	• Wiper/washer switch. • CTM. • Wiper motor. • Circuitry.	• GO to Pinpoint Test C.
• The Low Speed Does Not Operate Properly (Intermittent Wiper Mode OK)	• Wiper/washer switch. • CTM. • Wiper motor. • Circuitry.	• GO to Pinpoint Test D.
• The Intermittent Wiper Speed Does Not Operate Properly (High/Low Speeds OK)rrr	• CTM. • Circuitry. • Wiper relay. • Wiper/washer switch.	• GO to Pinpoint Test E.
• The Wipers Will Not Park At The Proper Position	• Front wiper motor (park position switch) • Circuitry. • Wiper/washer switch. • CTM.	• GO to Pinpoint Test F.
• The Washer Pump Is Inoperative	• Wiper/washer switch. • Washer pump. • Circuitry. • CTM.	• GO to Pinpoint Test G.
• The High Speed, Intermittent and Single Wipe Do Not Operate	• Circuitry. • Central junction box (CJB).	• Check circuit 14-AK19 (VT/OG) for open. If open, REPAIR circuit 14-AK19 (VT/OG). If OK, REPLACE the CJB.

FM9029800655020X

Fig. 22 Diagnostic procedure (Part 2 of 2). Contour & Mystique

Condition	Possible Sources	Action
• The Wipers Are Inoperative	• Wiper /washer switch. • Circuity. • Wiper motor. • Fuse. • Wiper relay.	• GO to Pinpoint Test A.
• The Wipers Stay On Continuously	• Wiper/washer switch. • Wiper motor. • Wiper relay. • CTM. • Circuitry.	• GO to Pinpoint Test B.

FM9029800655010X

Fig. 22 Diagnostic procedure (Part 1 of 2). Contour & Mystique

Condition	Possible Sources	Action
• The wipers are inoperative – front	• Wiper/washer switch. • Wiper motor. • Fuse. • Circuit.	• GO to Pinpoint Test A.
• The wipers stay on continuously – front	• Wiper/washer switch. • Wiper motor. • Wiper relay. • CTM. • Circuit.	• GO to Pinpoint Test B.
• The high wiper speed does not operate correctly – front (intermittent wiper mode OK)	• Wiper/washer switch. • Wiper motor. • Circuit.	• GO to Pinpoint Test C.
• The low wiper speed does not operate correctly – front (intermittent wiper mode OK)	• Wiper/washer switch. • Wiper motor. • Circuit.	• GO to Pinpoint Test D.
• The intermittent wiper speed does not operate correctly – front (high/low speeds OK)	• Wiper/washer switch. • Central junction box (CJB). • Front wiper relay. • Central timer module (CTM). • Circuit.	• GO to Pinpoint Test E.
• The wash and wipe function does not operate correctly – front	• Wiper/washer switch. • Central junction box (CJB). • Central timer module (CTM).	• GO to Pinpoint Test F.
• The wipers will not park at the correct position – front	• Winshield wiper motor. • Wiper/washer switch. • Central timer module (CTM). • Central junction box (CJB). • Circuit.	• GO to Pinpoint Test G.

FM9020100777010X

Fig. 23 Diagnostic procedure (Part 1 of 2). Cougar

Condition	Possible Sources	Action
• The washer pump is inoperative	• Washer pump. • Wiper/Washer swich. • Central junction box (CJB). • Circuit.	• GO to Pinpoint Test H.
• The low washer fluid indicator does not operate correctly	• Bulb. • Instrument cluster. • Low washer fluid switch. • Circuit.	• Diagnose Instrument Cluster
• The wiper is inoperative – rear	• Wiper/washer switch. • Rear window wiper motor. • Circuit.	• GO to Pinpoint Test I.
• The wiper stay on continouosly – rear	• Wiper/washer switch. • Rear window wiper motor. • Circuit.	• GO to Pinpoint Test J.
• The washer is inoperative – rear	• Wiper/washer switch.	• GO to Pinpoint Test H.
• The wiper will not park at the correct postion – rear	• Rear window wiper motor. • Circuit. • Central junction box (CJB).	• GO to Pinpoint Test K.

FM9020100777020X

Fig. 23 Diagnostic procedure (Part 2 of 2). Cougar

Condition	Possible Sources	Action
• The washer pump is inoperative	• Fluid level. • Washer hose. • Circuitry. • Multifunction switch. • Washer pump motor. • Wiper control module.	• GO to Pinpoint Test A.
• The washer pump is inoperative — runs continuously	• Circuitry. • Multifunction switch. • Washer pump motor. • Wiper control module.	• GO to Pinpoint Test B.
• The wipers are inoperative	• Central junction box (CJB) fuse 17 (30A). • Wiper motor. • Multifunction switch. • Windshield wiper assembly. • Wiper control module. • Circuitry.	• GO to Pinpoint Test C.
• The high wiper speeds do not operate correctly	• Wiper motor. • Wiper control module. • Circuitry. • Multifunction switch.	• GO to Pinpoint Test D.
• The low wiper speeds do not operate correctly	• Wiper motor. • Wiper control module. • Circuitry. • Multifunction switch.	• GO to Pinpoint Test E.

FM9020100879010X

Fig. 24 Diagnostic procedure (Part 1 of 2). 2000–02 Crown Victoria & Grand Marquis

Condition	Possible Sources	Action
• The wipers are inoperative	• Multifunction switch. • Circuitry. • Ignition switch. • Windshield wiper motor.	• Go To Pinpoint Test A .
• The wipers stay on continuously	• Windshield wiper motor. • Multifunction switch. • Circuitry.	• Go To Pinpoint Test B .
• The high/low wiper speeds do not operate correctly (intermittent wiper mode OK)	• Multifunction switch. • Circuitry. • Windshield wiper motor.	• Go To Pinpoint Test C .
• The intermittent windshield wiper speed does not operate correctly (high/low speeds OK)	• Multifunction switch. • Circuitry. • Windshield wiper motor.	• Go To Pinpoint Test D .
• The wipers will not park at correct position	• Wiper motor. • Pivot arm adjustment. • Linkage.	• Windshield Wiper Blade and Pivot Arm Adjustment
• The wipers do not operate correctly in the MIST position	• Multifunction switch. • Circuitry. • Washer pump. • Windshield wiper motor.	• Go To Pinpoint Test E .
• The washer pump is inoperative	• Washer pump. • Multifunction switch. • Wiper motor. • Circuitry.	• Go To Pinpoint Test F .

FM9020200906000X

Fig. 25 Diagnostic procedure. 2003–04 Crown Victoria, Grand Marquis & Marauder

Condition	Possible Sources	Action
• The intermittent wiper speed does not operate correctly	• Wiper motor. • Wiper control module. • Circuitry. • Multifunction switch.	• GO to Pinpoint Test F.
• The wipers will not park at the correct position	• Wiper motor. • Wiper control module. • Circuitry. • Multifunction switch. • Bent/cracked linkages. • Mispositioned arms.	• GO to Pinpoint Test G.
• The wipers stay on continuously	• Wiper motor. • Wiper control module. • Circuitry. • Multifunction switch.	• GO to Pinpoint Test H.

FM9020100879020X

Fig. 24 Diagnostic procedure (Part 2 of 2). 2000–02 Crown Victoria & Grand Marquis

Condition	Possible Source	Action
• The Wipers Are Inoperative — Front, All Positions	• Fuse. • Circuitry. • Multi-function switch. • Windshield wiper motor. • Windshield wiper motor.	• GO to Pinpoint Test A.
• The Wipers Stay On Continuously — Front	• Multi-function switch. • Circuitry.	• GO to Pinpoint Test B.
• The High Wiper Speed Does Not Operate Properly	• Circuitry. • Multi-function switch. • Windshield wiper motor.	• GO to Pinpoint Test C.

FM9029800642010X

Fig. 26 Diagnostic procedure (Part 1 of 2). 2000–01 Escort & ZX2

Condition	Possible Source	Action
• The Low Wiper Speed Does Not Operate Properly	• Multi-function switch.	• REPLACE the multi-function switch TEST the system for normal operation.
• The Intermittent Wiper Speed Does Not Operate Properly	• Multi-function switch.	• REPLACE the multi-function switch TEST the system for normal operation.
• The Wipers Will Not Park at the Proper Position — Front	• Circuitry. • Windshield wiper motor. • Multi-function switch.	• GO to Pinpoint Test D.
• The Washer Pump Is Inoperative — Front	• Circuitry. • Windshield washer pump motor. • Multi-function switch.	• GO to Pinpoint Test E.
• The Wash and Wipe Function Does Not Operate Properly	• Multi-function switch.	• If the washer pump is inoperative, GO to Pinpoint Test E. If the washer pump operates, REPLACE the multi-function switch TEST the system for normal operation.
• The Wipers Are Inoperative — Mist Position Only	• Multi-function switch.	• REPLACE the multi-function switch TEST the system for normal operation.
• The Wipers Are Inoperative — Rear	• Fuse. • Circuit. • Rear window wiper motor. • Rear window wiper/washer switch.	• GO to Pinpoint Test F.
• The Washer Pump Is Inoperative — Rear	• Fuse. • Circuit. • Rear window washer pump. • Rear window wiper/washer switch.	• GO to Pinpoint Test G.
• The Wipers Stay On Continuously — Rear	• Circuit. • Rear window wiper/washer switch. • Rear window wiper motor.	• GO to Pinpoint Test H.
• The Wipers Will Not Park at the Proper Position — Rear	• Rear window wiper motor.	• REPLACE the rear window wiper motor TEST the system for normal operation.

FM9029800642020X

Fig. 26 Diagnostic procedure (Part 2 of 2). 2000–01 Escort & ZX2

Condition	Possible Sources	Action
• The Wipers Are Inoperative — Front, All Positions	• Fuse. • Circuitry. • Multi-function switch (13K359). • Windshield wiper motor. • Windshield wiper motor.	• GO to Pinpoint Test A.
• The Wipers Stay On Continuously — Front	• Multi-function switch. • Circuitry.	• GO to Pinpoint Test B.
• The High Wiper Speed Does Not Operate Properly	• Circuitry. • Multi-function switch. • Windshield wiper motor.	• GO to Pinpoint Test C.
• The Low Wiper Speed Does Not Operate Properly	• Multi-function switch.	• REPLACE the multi-function switch TEST the system for normal operation.
• The Intermittent Wiper Speed Does Not Operate Properly	• Multi-function switch.	• REPLACE the multi-function switch TEST the system for normal operation.
• The Wipers Will Not Park at the Proper Position — Front	• Circuitry. • Windshield wiper motor. • Multi-function switch.	• GO to Pinpoint Test D.
• The Washer Pump Is Inoperative — Front	• Circuitry. • Windshield washer pump motor. • Multi-function switch.	• GO to Pinpoint Test E.
• The Wash and Wipe Function Does Not Operate Properly	• Multi-function switch.	• If the washer pump is inoperative, GO to Pinpoint Test E. If the washer pump operates, REPLACE the multi-function switch TEST the system for normal operation.
• The Wipers Are Inoperative — Mist Position Only	• Multi-function switch.	• REPLACE the multi-function switch TEST the system for normal operation.

FM9020100888000X

Fig. 27 Diagnostic procedure. 2002–04 Escort & ZX2

Condition	Possible Sources	Action
•Intermittent wipe is inoperative (fast/slow wipe OK)	•Multifunction switch. •Front wiper relay. •CTM. •CJB. •Wiring.	•Diagnose With Worldwide Diagnostic Scans Tool or Equivalent
•After switching off, the windshield wipers do not return to the park position	•Front wiper motor. •Front wiper relay. •CJB. •CTM. •Wiring.	•Diagnose With Worldwide Diagnostic Scans Tool or Equivalent
•Windshield wiper one-touch function is inoperative	•Multifunction switch.	•INSTALL a new multifunction switch.
•Rear wiper is inoperative	•Fuse F43 (15 A). •Multifunction switch. •CTM. •Rear wiper motor. •CJB. •Wiring.	•Diagnose With Worldwide Diagnostic Scans Tool or Equivalent
•Rear wiper is on continuously	•Rear wiper motor (limit switch). •Rear wiper relay. •CTM. •CJB. •Wiring.	•GO to system test E.
•After switching off, the rear wiper does not return to the park position	•Rear wiper motor. •CJB. •Wiring.	•GO to system test F.
•Headlamp washer system is inoperative	•Fuse F13 (30 A). •Headlamp washer pump. •Headlamp washer system relay. •Battery junction box (BJB). •Wiring.	•GO to system test G.

FM9020100798020X

Fig. 28 Diagnostic procedure (Part 2 of 2). Focus

Condition	Possible Sources	Action
•No communication with the CTM	•CTM •Wiring, data bus (ISO 9141).	• Diagnose Communications Network Components
•Windshield wipers are inoperative	•Fuse F55 (20 A). •Multifunction switch. •Front wiper motor. •Wiring. •Central junction box (CJB).	•GO to system test A.
•Windshield wipers are on continuously	•Multifunction switch. •Front wiper motor. •Front wiper relay. •CTM. •CJB. •Wiring.	•GO to system test B.
•Fast windshield wipe is inoperative (intermittent OK)	•Multifunction switch. •Front wiper motor. •Wiring.	•GO to system test C.
•Slow windshield wipe is inoperative (intermittent OK)	•Multifunction switch.	•INSTALL a new multifunction switch.
•The wash and wipe function is inoperative or does not operate correctly	•CTM. •Multifunction switch. •Front wiper relay. •CJB. •Wiring.	•GO to system test D.

FM9020100798010X

Fig. 28 Diagnostic procedure (Part 1 of 2). Focus

Condition	Possible Sources	Action
• No communication with the front electronic module (FEM)	• BJB Fuses 425 (40A) and 422 (20A). • Front electronic module (FEM).	• GO to Pinpoint Test A.
• The wipers are inoperative	• Underhood AJB Fuse 120 (30A). • CJB Fuse 226 (3A). • Windshield wiper relay. • Wiper park relay. • Wiper high/low relay. • Multifunction switch. • Circuitry. • Wiper motor. • FEM. • Rain sensor module (If equipped).	• GO to Pinpoint Test B.
• The wipers stay on continuously	• Wiper park relay. • Wiper high/low relay. • Multifunction switch. • Circuitry. • Wiper motor. • FEM. • Rain sensor module (If equipped).	• GO to Pinpoint Test C.
• The high/low wiper speeds do not operate correctly	• Wiper high/low relay. • Multifunction switch. • Circuitry. • FEM. • Rain sensor module (If equipped).	• GO to Pinpoint Test D.
• The wash and wipe function does not operate correctly	• Multifunction switch. • Circuitry. • FEM • Rain sensor module (If equipped).	• GO to Pinpoint Test E.
• The washer pump is inoperative/on continuously	• Underhood AJB Fuse 102 (10A). • Washer pump relay. • Circuitry. • Pump motor. • FEM.	• GO to Pinpoint Test F.
• The speed dependent interval mode does not operate correctly	• Wiper park relay. • Multifunction switch. • Circuitry. • Wiper motor. • FEM. • Rain sensor module (If equipped).	• GO to Pinpoint Test G.
• The low washer fluid indicator does not operate correctly	• Multifunction switch. • Circuitry. • FEM.	• Diagnose multifunction switch & circuit.
• The rain moisture sensitive function does not operate correctly	• CJB Fuse 216 (5A). • Multifunction switch. • Circuitry. • Rain sensor module.	• GO to Pinpoint Test H.

FM9020100894000X

Fig. 29 Diagnostic procedure. LS

Condition	Possible Source	Action
• No communication with the generic electronic module	• CJB Fuse 39 (5A). • Circuitry. • GEM.	• GO to Pinpoint Test A.
• The wipers are inoperative	• CJB Fuse 26 (30A). • Ignition switch. • Circuitry. • GEM. • Multifunction switch (13K359). • Wiper ON/OFF relay. • Wiper HIGH/LOW relay. • Wiper motor.	• GO to Pinpoint Test B.
• The wipers stay on continuously	• Circuitry. • GEM. • Multifunction switch. • Wiper ON/OFF relay. • Wiper HIGH/LOW relay. • Wiper motor.	• GO to Pinpoint Test B.
• The HIGH and LOW wiper speeds do not operate correctly	• Circuitry. • GEM. • Multifunction switch. • Wiper HIGH/LOW relay. • Wiper motor. • DTC B1434.	• GO to Pinpoint Test B.
• The intermittent wiper mode does not operate correctly	• Circuitry. • GEM. • Multifunction switch. • Wiper motor.	• GO to Pinpoint Test B.
• The washer pump is inoperative	• CJB Fuse 26 (30A). • Circuitry. • GEM. • Multifunction switch. • Washer pump relay. • Washer pump. • Ignition switch.	• GO to Pinpoint Test C.

FM9029900772010X

Fig. 30 Diagnostic procedure (Part 1 of 2). Mustang

Condition	Possible Source	Action
• No communication with the generic electronic module (GEM)	• Circuitry. • Generic electronic module (GEM).	• **Diagnose Multifunction Electronic Control Modules**
• The windshield wipers are inoperative	• Central junction box (CJB) Fuse 215 (30A). • Multifunction switch. • Wiper run/park relay. • Windshield wiper motor. • Circuitry. • Generic electronic module (GEM).	• GO to Pinpoint Test A.
• The windshield wipers stay on continuously	• Multifunction switch. • Wiper run/park relay. • Circuitry. • Windshield wiper motor. • Central Junction box (JB). • Generic electronic module (GEM).	• GO to Pinpoint Test B.
• The windshield wipers do not operate correctly	• Wiper high/low relay. • Multifunction switch. • Circuitry. • Windshield wiper motor. • Generic electronic module (GEM).	• GO to Pinpoint Test C.
• The windshield washer pump is inoperative	• Central junction box (CJB) Fuse 211 (15A). • Multifunction switch. • Circuitry. • Windshield washer pump. • Central junction box (CJB). • Generic electronic module (GEM).	• GO to Pinpoint Test D.
• The windshield washer pump stays on continuously	• Circuitry. • Central junction box (CJB). • Generic electronic module (GEM).	• GO to Pinpoint Test E.

FM9020100792000X

Fig. 31 Diagnostic procedure. Sable & Taurus

Condition	Possible Source	Action
• The Washer Pump Is Inoperative	• Circuitry. • Multi-function switch. • Wiper control module. • Washer pump.	• GO to Pinpoint Test A.
• The Wipers are Inoperative	• Fuse. • Wiper motor. • Multi-function switch. • Circuitry. • Wiper control module.	• GO to Pinpoint Test B.
• The Low Wiper Speed Does Not Operate Properly	• Multi-function switch. • Wiper motor. • Circuitry. • Wiper control module.	• GO to Pinpoint Test C.
• The High Wiper Speed Does Not Operate Properly	• Multi-function switch. • Wiper motor. • Circuitry. • Wiper control module.	• GO to Pinpoint Test D.
• The Intermittent Wiper Speed Does Not Operate Properly	• Multi-function switch. • Circuitry. • Wiper control module. • Wiper motor.	• GO to Pinpoint Test E.
• The Wipers Will Not Park at the Proper Position	• Wiper motor. • Wiper control module. • Circuitry.	• GO to Pinpoint Test F.
• The Wipers Stay On Continuously	• Multi-function switch. • Wiper motor. • Wiper control module. • Circuitry.	• GO to Pinpoint Test G.

FM9029800641000X

Fig. 33 Diagnostic procedure. 2000–02 Town Car

Condition	Possible Source	Action
• The low wiper speed does not operate correctly	• Circuitry. • Multifunction switch. • Wiper HIGH/LOW relay. • Wiper motor. • GEM. • DTC B1473. • DTC B1434.	• GO to Pinpoint Test B.

FM9029900772020X

Fig. 30 Diagnostic procedure (Part 2 of 2). Mustang

Condition	Possible Sources	Action
• The wipers are inoperative	• Front power distribution box (FPDB) fuse 124 (30A). • Central junction box (CJB) fuse 226 (3A). • Windshield wiper relay. • Wiper run/park relay. • Wiper high/low relay. • Multifunction switch. • Circuitry. • Wiper motor. • Front electronic module (FEM).	• Go To Pinpoint Test A .
• The wipers stay on continuously	• Wiper run/park relay. • Wiper high/low relay. • Multifunction switch. • Circuitry. • Wiper motor. • FEM.	• Go To Pinpoint Test B .
• The high/low wiper speeds do not operate correctly	• Wiper high/low relay. • Multifunction switch. • Circuitry. • FEM. • Wiper motor. • FPDB.	• Go To Pinpoint Test C .
• The wash and wipe function does not operate correctly	• Multifunction switch. • Circuitry. • FEM.	• Go To Pinpoint Test D .
• The washer pump is inoperative/on continuously	• FPDB fuse 102 (15A). • Washer pump relay. • Circuitry. • Pump motor. • FEM.	• Go To Pinpoint Test E .
• The speed dependent interval mode does not operate correctly	• Wiper run/park relay. • Multifunction switch. • Circuitry. • Wiper motor. • FEM.	• Go To Pinpoint Test F .
• The low washer fluid indicator does not operate correctly	• Instrument cluster. • Circuitry. • FEM. • Low washer fluid switch.	• DIAGNOSE cluster & switch

FM9020100895000X

Fig. 32 Diagnostic procedure. Thunderbird

Condition	Possible Sources	Action
• The wipers are inoperative	• Multifunction switch. • Circuitry. • Ignition switch. • Windshield wiper motor.	• Go To Pinpoint Test A .
• The wipers stay on continuously	• Windshield wiper motor. • Multifunction switch. • Circuitry.	• Go To Pinpoint Test B .
• The high/low wiper speeds do not operate correctly (intermittent wiper mode OK)	• Multifunction switch. • Circuitry. • Windshield wiper motor.	• Go To Pinpoint Test C .
• The intermittent windshield wiper speed does not operate correctly (high/low speeds OK)	• Multifunction switch. • Circuitry. • Windshield wiper motor.	• Go To Pinpoint Test D .
• The wipers will not park at correct position	• Wiper motor. • Pivot arm adjustment. • Linkage.	• Windshield Wiper Blade and Pivot Arm Adjustment
• The wipers do not operate correctly in the MIST position	• Multifunction switch. • Circuitry. • Washer pump. • Windshield wiper motor.	• Go To Pinpoint Test E .
• The washer pump is inoperative	• Washer pump. • Multifunction switch. • Wiper motor. • Circuitry.	• Go To Pinpoint Test F .
• The moisture sensitive wipers do not operate correctly	• Wiper motor. • Circuitry. • Rain sensor module (RSM).	• Go To Pinpoint Test G .

FM9020200913000X

Fig. 34 Diagnostic procedure. 2003–04 Town Car

DIAGNOSTIC CHART INDEX

Continued

DIAGNOSTIC CHART INDEX—Continued

TEST CONDITIONS	TEST DETAILS/RESULTS/ACTIONS
A1 CHECK THE WASHER PUMP OPERATION	
	2 Press the washer button. • Does the washer pump operate properly? → **Yes** GO to **A2**. → **No** GO to **A3**.
A2 CHECK FOR BLOCKAGE OR OBSTRUCTION	
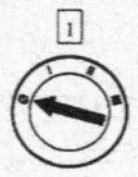	2 Inspect the washer nozzles, washer hoses and washer pump for blockages or obstructions. • Are any blockages or obstructions present? → **Yes** REPAIR or REPLACE as required. TEST the system for normal operation. → **No** REPLACE the washer pump motor TEST the system for normal operation.

FM9029800574010X

Fig. 35 Test A: Washer Pump Inoperative (Part 1 of 3). Continental

TEST CONDITIONS	TEST DETAILS/RESULTS/ACTIONS
A3 CHECK THE WASHER PUMP MOTOR FOR VOLTAGE — CIRCUIT 941 (BK/W)	
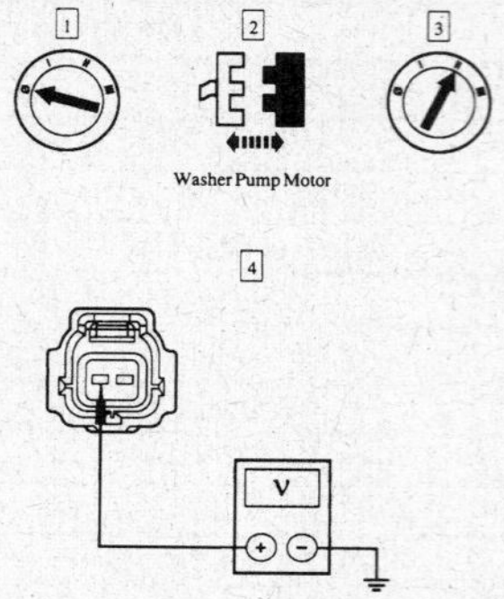	4 Measure the voltage between washer pump motor and ground while pressing the washer button. • Is the voltage greater than 10 volts? → **Yes** GO to **A4**. → **No** GO to **A5**.
A4 CHECK THE WASHER PUMP MOTOR GROUND — CIRCUIT 57 (BK)	
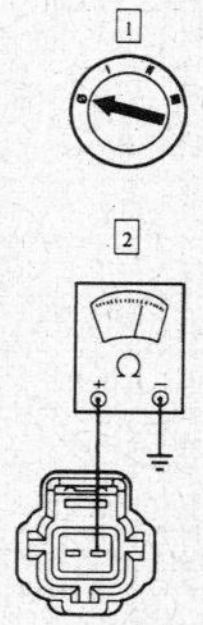	2 Measure the resistance between washer pump motor C1035, circuit 57 (BK), and ground. • Is the resistance less than 5 ohms? → **Yes** REPLACE the washer pump motor. TEST the system for normal operation. → **No** REPAIR circuit. TEST the system for normal operation.

FM9029800574020X

Fig. 35 Test A: Washer Pump Inoperative (Part 2 of 3). Continental

TEST CONDITIONS	TEST DETAILS/RESULTS/ACTIONS
A5 CHECK CIRCUIT 941 (BK/W) FOR SHORT TO GROUND	
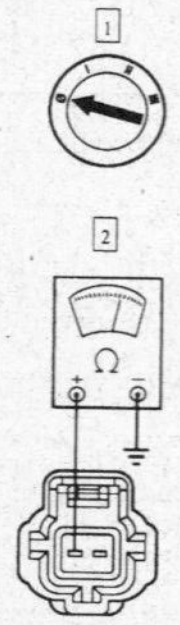	2 Measure the resistance between washer pump motor C1035, circuit 941 (BK/W), and ground. • Is the resistance greater than 10,000 ohms? → **Yes** GO to **A6**. → **No** REPLACE the multi-function switch; TEST the system for normal operation.
A6 CHECK CIRCUIT 941 (BK/W) FOR OPEN	
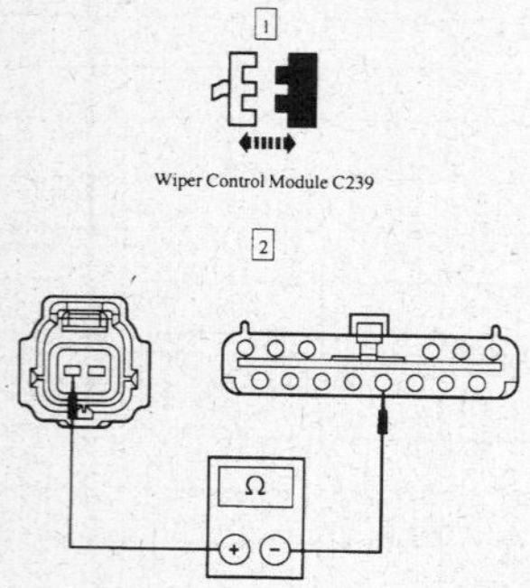	2 Measure the resistance between washer pump motor, and control module • Is the resistance less than 5 ohms? → **Yes** REPLACE the wiper control module; TEST the system for normal operation. → **No** REPAIR circuit 941 (BK/W). TEST the system for normal operation.

FM9029800574030X

Fig. 35 Test A: Washer Pump Inoperative (Part 3 of 3). Continental

TEST CONDITIONS	TEST DETAILS/RESULTS/ACTIONS
B1 CHECK FUSE JUNCTION PANEL FUSE 10 (30A)	
	• Is the fuse OK? → **Yes** GO to **B2**. → **No** REPLACE the fuse. TEST the system for normal operation. If the fuse fails again, CHECK for a short to ground. REPAIR as necessary.
B2 CHECK FOR VOLTAGE TO THE WIPER CONTROL MODULE — CIRCUIT 65 (DG)	
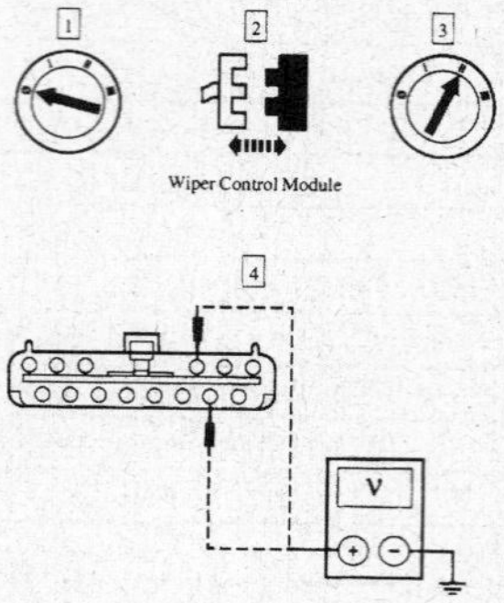	4 Measure the voltage between wiper control module and ground; and between wiper control module and ground. • Is the voltage greater than 10 volts? → **Yes** GO to **B3**. → **No** REPAIR circuit. TEST the system for normal operation.

FM9029800575010X

Fig. 36 Test B: Wipers Are Inoperative (Part 1 of 4). Continental

TEST CONDITIONS	TEST DETAILS/RESULTS/ACTIONS
B3 CHECK CIRCUIT 57 (BK) FOR OPEN	
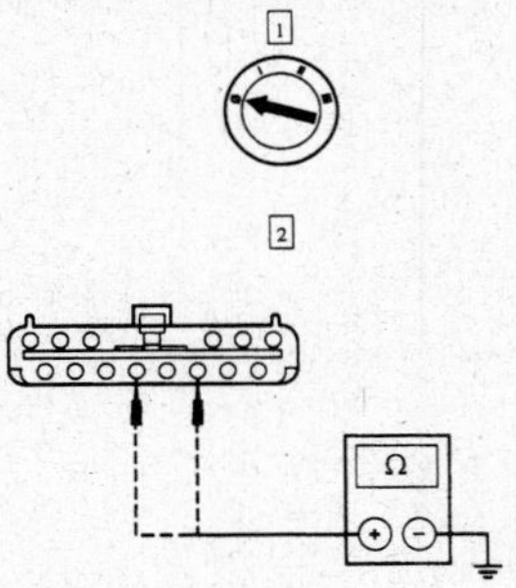	2 Measure the resistance between wiper control module ground; and between wiper control module and ground. • Are the resistances less than 5 ohms? → **Yes** GO to **B4**. → **No** REPAIR circuit. TEST the system for normal operation.
B4 CHECK THE MULTI-FUNCTION SWITCH	
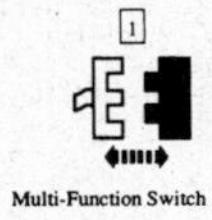	2 Check the multi-function switch. • Is the multi-function switch OK? → **Yes** GO to **B5**. → **No** REPLACE the multi-function switch; TEST the system for normal operation.

FM9029800575020X

Fig. 36 Test B: Wipers Are Inoperative (Part 2 of 4). Continental

TEST CONDITIONS	TEST DETAILS/RESULTS/ACTIONS
B5 CHECK CIRCUIT 993 (BR/W) FOR OPEN	
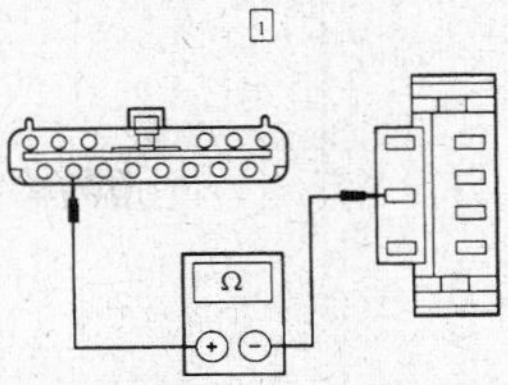	1 Measure the resistance between multi-function switch and wiper control module • Is the resistance less than 5 ohms? → **Yes** GO to **B6**. → **No** REPAIR circuit. TEST the system for normal operation.
B6 CHECK CIRCUIT 589 (O) FOR OPEN	
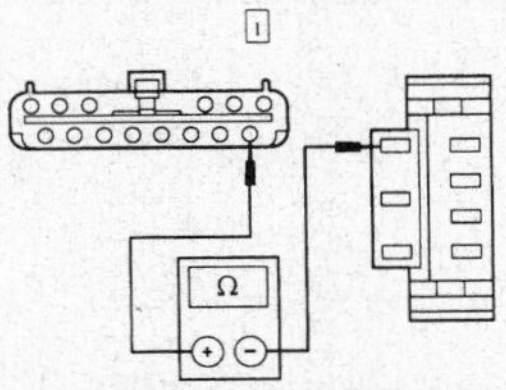	1 Measure the resistance between multi-function switch and wiper control module • Is the resistance less than 5 ohms? → **Yes** GO to **B7**. → **No** REPAIR circuit. TEST the system for normal operation.
B7 CHECK THE WIPER CONTROL MODULE OUTPUT FOR VOLTAGE	
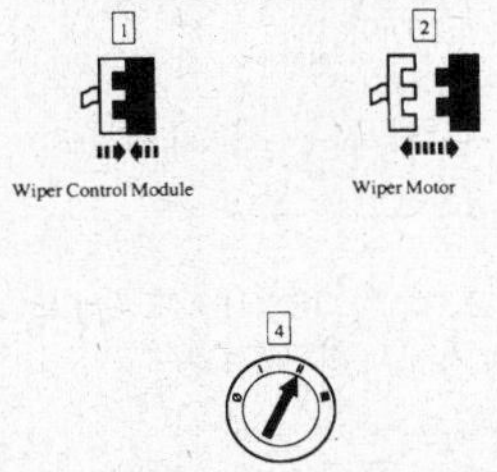	3 Turn the multi-function switch to the HI position.

FM9029800575030X

Fig. 36 Test B: Wipers Are Inoperative (Part 3 of 4). Continental

TEST CONDITIONS	TEST DETAILS/RESULTS/ACTIONS
B7 CHECK THE WIPER CONTROL MODULE OUTPUT FOR VOLTAGE (Continued)	
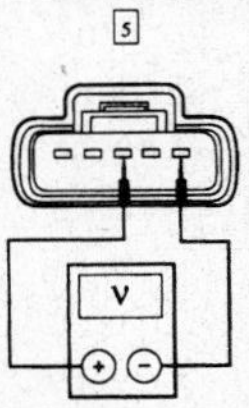	5 Measure the voltage between wiper motor terminals. • Is the voltage greater than 10 volts? → **Yes** REPLACE the wiper motor. TEST the system for normal operation. → **No** GO to **B8**.
B8 CHECK CIRCUIT 61 (Y/R) FOR OPEN	
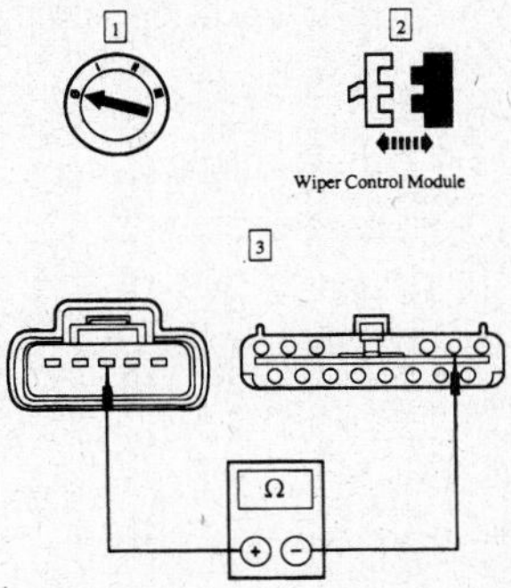	3 Measure the resistance between wiper control module and wiper motor • Is the resistance less than 5 ohms? → **Yes** REPLACE the wiper control module. TEST the system for normal operation. → **No** REPAIR circuit. TEST the system for normal operation.

FM9029800575040X

Fig. 36 Test B: Wipers Are Inoperative (Part 4 of 4). Continental

TEST CONDITIONS	TEST DETAILS/RESULTS/ACTIONS
C1 CHECK THE VOLTAGE TO THE WIPER MOTOR — CIRCUIT 56 (DB/O)	
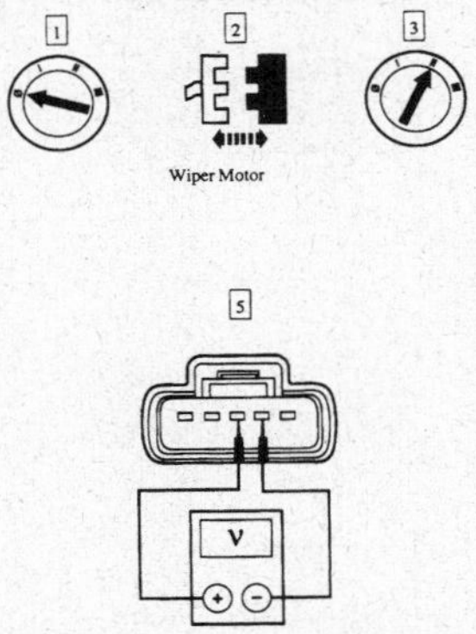	4 Turn the multi-function switch to the LO position. 5 Measure the voltage between wiper motor • Is the voltage greater than 10 volts? → **Yes** REPLACE the wiper motor. TEST the system for normal operation. → **No** GO to **C2**.
C2 CHECK CIRCUIT 56 (DB/O) FOR SHORT TO GROUND	
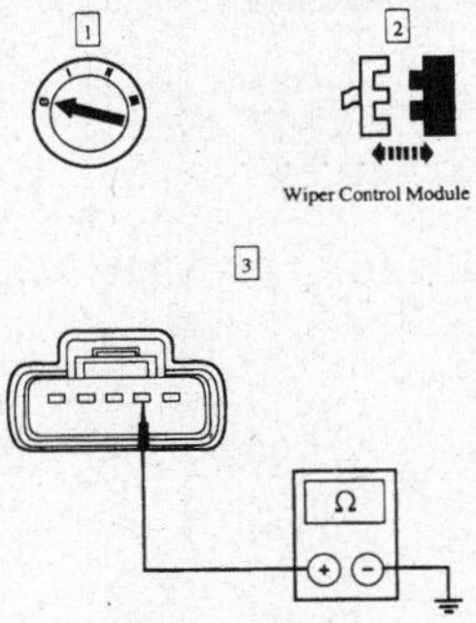	3 Measure the resistance between wiper motor and ground. • Is the resistance greater than 10,000 ohms? → **Yes** GO to **C3**. → **No** REPAIR circuit. TEST the system for normal operation.

FM9029800576010X

Fig. 37 Test C: Low Wiper Speed Does Not Operate Properly (Part 1 of 2). Continental

TEST CONDITIONS	TEST DETAILS/RESULTS/ACTIONS
C3 CHECK CIRCUIT 56 (DB/O) FOR OPEN	
1 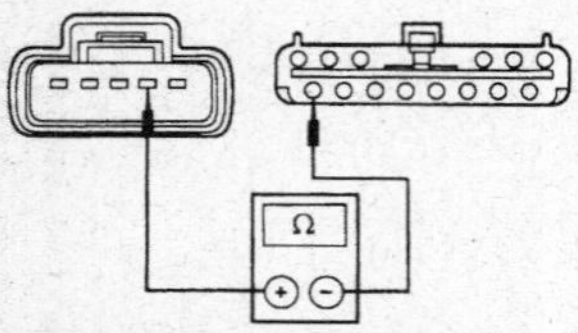	1 Measure the resistance between wiper control module and wiper motor • Is the resistance less than 5 ohms? → **Yes** GO to **C4**. → **No** REPAIR circuit. TEST the system for normal operation.
C4 CHECK THE MULTI-FUNCTION SWITCH	
1  Multi-Function Switch	2 Check the multi-function switch. • Is the multi-function switch OK? → **Yes** REPLACE the wiper control module. TEST the system for normal operation. → **No** REPLACE the multi-function switch. TEST the system for normal operation.

FM9029800576020X

Fig. 37 Test C: Low Wiper Speed Does Not Operate Properly (Part 2 of 2). Continental

TEST CONDITIONS	TEST DETAILS/RESULTS/ACTIONS
D3 CHECK CIRCUIT 58 (W) FOR OPEN	
1 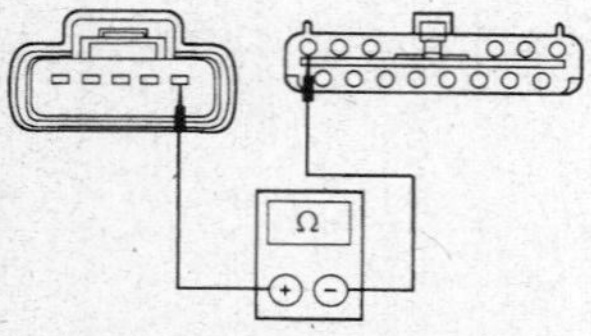	1 Measure the resistance between wiper control module and wiper motor • Is the resistance less than 5 ohms? → **Yes** GO to **D4**. → **No** REPAIR circuit. TEST the system for normal operation.
D4 CHECK THE MULTI-FUNCTION SWITCH	
1  Multi-Function Switch	2 Check the multi-function switch. • Is the multi-function switch OK? → **Yes** REPLACE the wiper control module. TEST the system for normal operation. → **No** REPLACE the multi-function switch. TEST the system for normal operation.

FM9029800581020X

Fig. 38 Test D: High Speed Does Not Operate Properly (Part 2 of 2). Continental

TEST CONDITIONS	TEST DETAILS/RESULTS/ACTIONS
D1 CHECK THE VOLTAGE TO THE WINDSHIELD WIPER MOTOR — CIRCUIT 58 (W)	
1 2  Wiper Motor 4 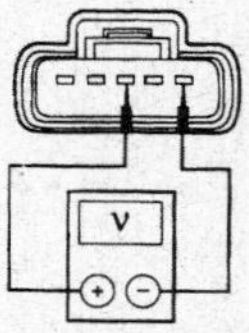	3 Turn the multi-function switch to the HI position. 4 Measure the voltage between wiper motor terminals. • Is the voltage greater than 10 volts? → **Yes** REPLACE the wiper motor. TEST the system for normal operation. → **No** GO to **D2**.
D2 CHECK CIRCUIT 58 (W) FOR SHORT TO GROUND	
1 2  Wiper Control Module 3 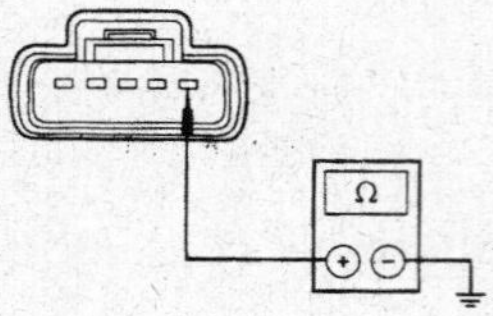	3 Measure the resistance between wiper motor and ground. • Is the resistance greater than 10,000 ohms? → **Yes** GO to **D3**. → **No** REPAIR circuit 58 (W). TEST the system for normal operation.

FM9029800581010X

Fig. 38 Test D: High Speed Does Not Operate Properly (Part 1 of 2). Continental

TEST CONDITIONS	TEST DETAILS/RESULTS/ACTIONS
E1 CHECK THE MULTI-FUNCTION SWITCH	
1 2  Multi-Function Switch	3 Check the multi-function switch. • Is the multi-function switch OK? → **Yes** GO to **E2**. → **No** REPLACE the multi-function switch; TEST the system for normal operation.
E2 CHECK CIRCUIT 590 (DB/W) FOR SHORT TO GROUND	
1  Wiper Control Module 2 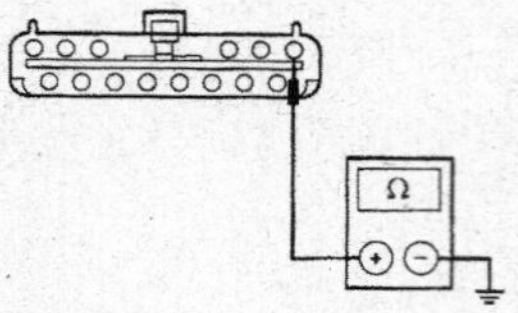	2 Measure the resistance between wiper control module and ground. • Is the resistance greater than 10,000 ohms? → **Yes** GO to **E3**. → **No** REPAIR circuit. TEST the system for normal operation.

FM9029800577010X

Fig. 39 Test E: Intermittent Wiper Speed Does Not Operate Properly (Part 1 of 2). Continental

TEST CONDITIONS	TEST DETAILS/RESULTS/ACTIONS

E3 CHECK CIRCUIT 590 (DB/W) FOR OPEN

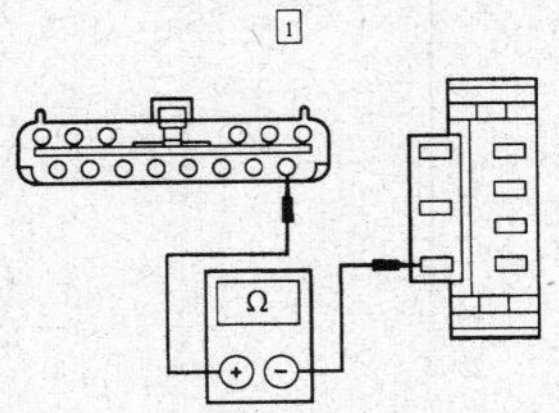

1 Measure the resistance between wiper control module and multi-function switch

- Is the resistance less than 5 ohms?

→ **Yes**
REPLACE the wiper control module. TEST the system for normal operation.

→ **No**
REPAIR circuit. TEST the system for normal operation.

FM9029800577020X

Fig. 39 Test E: Intermittent Wiper Speed Does Not Operate Properly (Part 2 of 2). Continental

TEST CONDITIONS	TEST DETAILS/RESULTS/ACTIONS

F1 CHECK THE WIPER MOTOR FOR VOLTAGE — CIRCUIT 65 (DG)

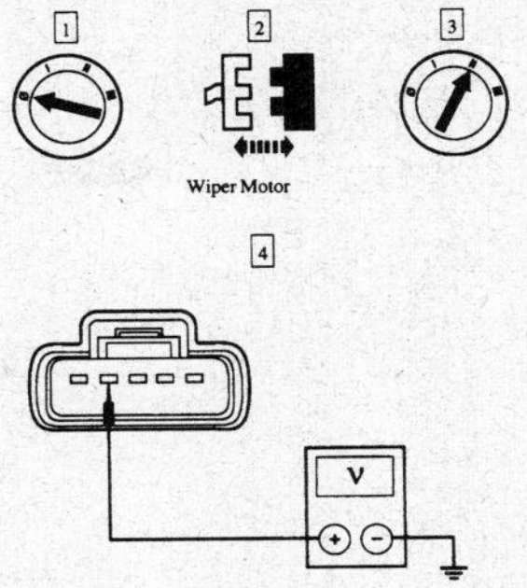

4 Measure the voltage between wiper motor and ground.

- Is the voltage greater than 10 volts?

→ **Yes**
GO to **F2**.

→ **No**
REPAIR circuit. TEST the system for normal operation.

FM9029800578010X

Fig. 40 Test F: Wipers Will Not Park At Proper Position (Part 1 of 3). Continental

TEST CONDITIONS	TEST DETAILS/RESULTS/ACTIONS

F2 CHECK THE WIPER CONTROL MODULE RETURN CIRCUITS FOR OPEN — CIRCUIT 28 (BK/PK) AND CIRCUIT 61 (Y/R)

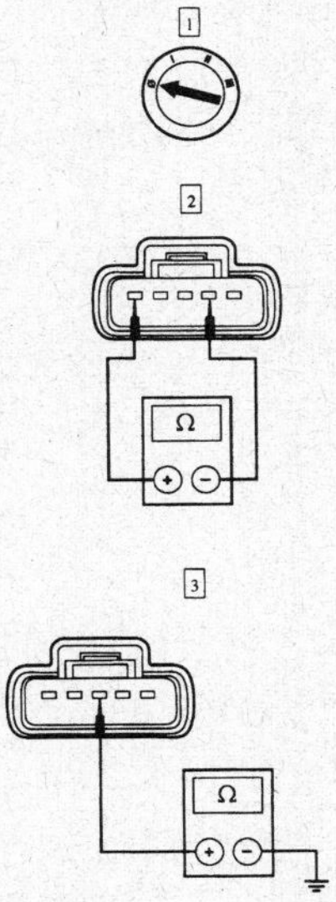

2 Measure the resistance between wiper motor terminals.

3 Measure the resistance between wiper motor and ground.

- Are the resistances less than 5 ohms?

→ **Yes**
GO to **F4**.

→ **No**
GO to **F3**.

FM9029800578020X

Fig. 40 Test F: Wipers Will Not Park At Proper Position (Part 2 of 3). Continental

TEST CONDITIONS	TEST DETAILS/RESULTS/ACTIONS

F3 CHECK THE WIPER CONTROL MODULE/WIPER MOTOR CIRCUITS FOR OPEN

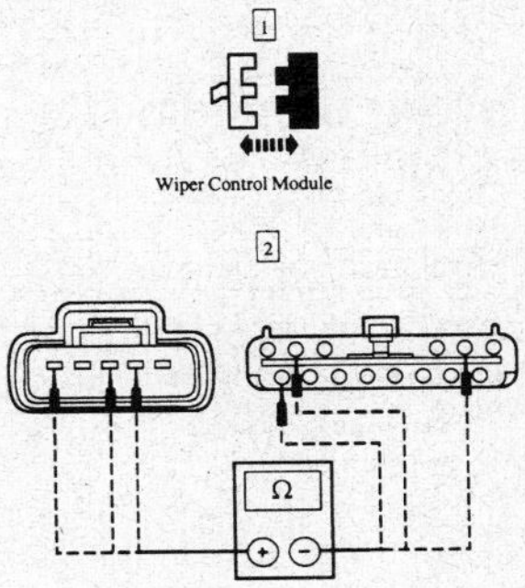

2 Measure the resistance between wiper motor and wiper control module; refer to the following chart:

Wiper Motor Connector	Circuit	Wiper Control Module Connector
C151-1	C151-3	C151-4
28 (BK/PK)	61 (Y/R)	56 (DB/O)
C239-13	C239-10	C239-8

- Are the resistances less than 5 ohms?

→ **Yes**
REPLACE the wiper control module. TEST the system for normal operation.

→ **No**
REPAIR the circuit in question. TEST the system for normal operation.

F4 CHECK THE WIPER LINKAGE

1 Verify the wiper linkage is not bent, cracked or mispositioned from the wiper motor shaft.

- Is the wiper linkage OK?

→ **Yes**
REPLACE the wiper motor, Motor. TEST the system for normal operation.

→ **No**
REPAIR or REPLACE the wiper mounting arm and pivot shaft.
TEST the system for normal operation.

FM9029800578030X

Fig. 40 Test F: Wipers Will Not Park At Proper Position (Part 3 of 3). Continental

TEST CONDITIONS	TEST DETAILS/RESULTS/ACTIONS
G1 CHECK THE MULTI-FUNCTION SWITCH	
	1 Check the multi-function switch. • Is the multi-function switch OK? → **Yes** GO to **G2**. → **No** REPLACE the multi-function switch. TEST the system for normal operation.
G2 CHECK CIRCUIT 589 (O) FOR SHORT TO GROUND	
1 2 3 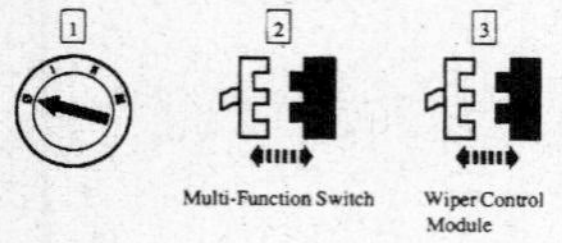 	
4 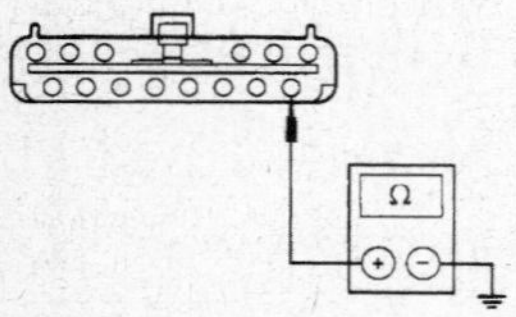 	4 Measure the resistance between wiper control module and ground. • Is the resistance greater than 10,000 ohms? → **Yes** GO to **G3**. → **No** REPAIR circuit. TEST the system for normal operation.

FM9029800579010X

Fig. 41 Test G: Wipers Stay On Continuously (Part 1 of 2). Continental

TEST CONDITIONS	TEST DETAILS/RESULTS/ACTIONS
H1 CHECK THE HEADLAMP OPERATION	
	1 Turn the headlamp switch to the on position. • Do the headlamps illuminate? → **Yes** GO to **H2**. → **No**

FM9029800580010X

Fig. 42 Test H: Headlamps Do Not Illuminate When Wipers Are On (Part 1 of 2). Continental

TEST CONDITIONS	TEST DETAILS/RESULTS/ACTIONS
H2 CHECK THE WIPER MOTOR POSITION INPUT TO THE LCM — CIRCUIT 28 (BK/PK)	
1 2  	3 Turn the multi-function switch to the LO position.
4 	
5 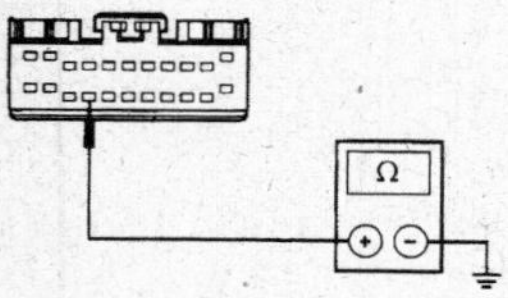 	5 **NOTE:** Wait a minimum of 15 seconds before performing this step. Measure the resistance between LCM and ground. • Does the voltage vary between 0 and 10 volts? → **Yes** REPLACE the LCM. TEST the system for normal operation. → **No** REPAIR circuit. TEST the system for normal operation.

FM9029800580020X

Fig. 42 Test H: Headlamps Do Not Illuminate When Wipers Are On (Part 2 of 2). Continental

TEST CONDITIONS	TEST DETAILS/RESULTS/ACTIONS
G3 CHECK CIRCUIT 993 (BR/W) FOR SHORT TO GROUND	
1 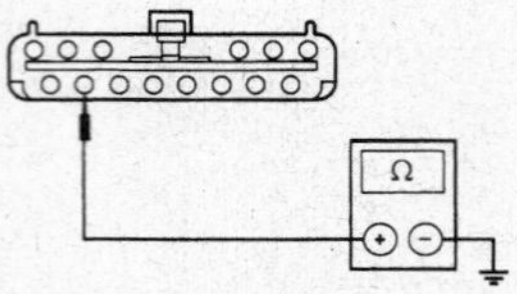 	1 Measure the resistance between wiper control module and ground. • Is the resistance greater than 10,000 ohms? → **Yes** GO to **G4**. → **No** REPAIR circuit. TEST the system for normal operation.
G4 CHECK THE CIRCUIT 590 (DB/W) FOR SHORT TO GROUND	
1 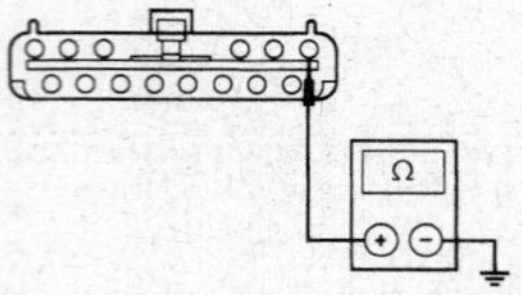 	1 Measure the resistance between wiper control module and ground. • Is the resistance greater than 10,000 ohms? → **Yes** REPLACE the wiper control module. TEST the system for normal operation. → **No** REPAIR circuit. TEST the system for normal operation.

FM9029800579020X

Fig. 41 Test G: Wipers Stay On Continuously (Part 2 of 2). Continental

CONDITIONS	DETAILS/RESULTS/ACTIONS
A1 CHECK FUSE 20 (10A)	
1  	• Is fuse 20 (10 A) OK? → **Yes** GO to **A2**. → **No** REPLACE the fuse. TEST the system for normal operation. If the fuse fails again, CHECK for short to ground. REPAIR as necessary.
A2 CHECK VOLTAGE SUPPLY TO WIPER SWITCH – CIRCUIT 14-AK19 (VT/OG)	
1 2 3  	
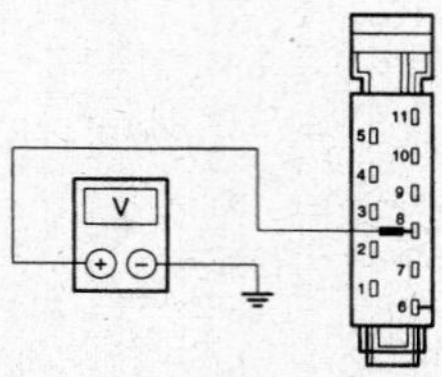 	4 Measure the voltage between wiper/washer switch C441-8, circuit14-AK19 (VT/OG) and ground.

FM9029800562010X

Fig. 43 Test A: Wipers Are Inoperative (Part 1 of 3). Contour & Mystique

CONDITIONS	DETAILS/RESULTS/ACTIONS
	• Is the voltage greater than 10 volts? → **Yes** GO to **A4.** → **No** GO to **A3.**
A3 CHECK CIRCUIT 14-AK19 (VT/OG) FOR OPEN	
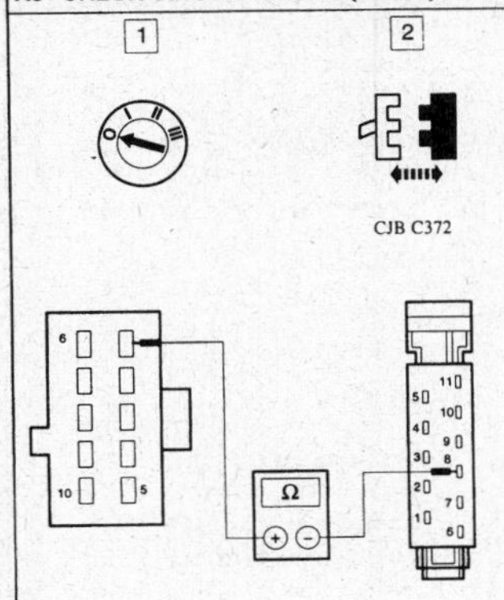	3 Measure the resistance between CJB C372-1, circuit 14-AK19 (VT/OG), and wiper/washer switch C441-8, circuit 14-AK19 (VT/OG). • Is the resistance less than 5 ohm? → **Yes** REPAIR the CJB. TEST the system for normal operation. → **No** REPAIR circuit 14-AK19 (VT/OG). TEST the system for normal operation.
A4 CHECK THE WIPER/WASHER SWITCH FOR PROPER OPERATION	

FM9029800562020X

Fig. 43 Test A: Wipers Are Inoperative (Part 2 of 3). Contour & Mystique

CONDITIONS	DETAILS/RESULTS/ACTIONS
B1 DETERMINE WINDSHIELD WIPER OPERATING SPEED	
	1 Place the wiper switch in the OFF position.

FM9029800563010X

Fig. 44 Test B: Wipers Stay On Continuously (Part 1 of 6). Contour & Mystique

CONDITIONS	DETAILS/RESULTS/ACTIONS
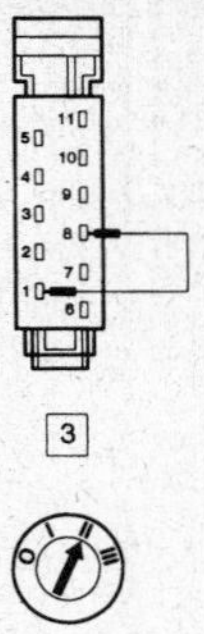	2 Connect a jumper wire between wiper/washer switch C441-8, circuit 14-AK19 (VT/OG) and wiper/washer switch C441-1, circuit 32-AK10 (WH/GN). • Do the wipers operate? → **Yes** REPLACE the wiper/washer switch. TEST the system for normal operation. → **No** REPLACE the wiper motor. TEST the system for normal operation.

FM9029800562030X

Fig. 43 Test A: Wipers Are Inoperative (Part 3 of 3). Contour & Mystique

CONDITIONS	DETAILS/RESULTS/ACTIONS
	• Do the wiper operate at high speed? → **Yes** GO to **B2.** → **No** GO to **B4.**
B2 CHECK THE WIPER SWITCH	
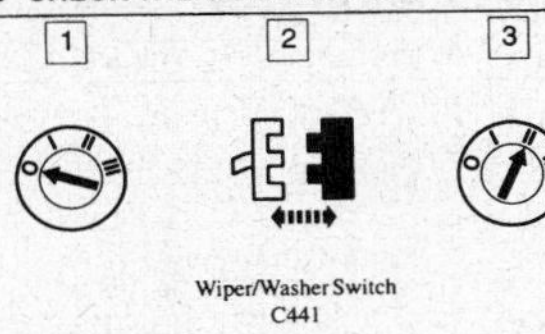	• Do the wiper operate at high speed? → **Yes** GO to **B3.** → **No** REPLACE the wiper/washer switch. TEST the system for normal operation.
B3 CHECK CIRCUIT 32-AK11 (WH/BK) FOR SHORT TO POWER	
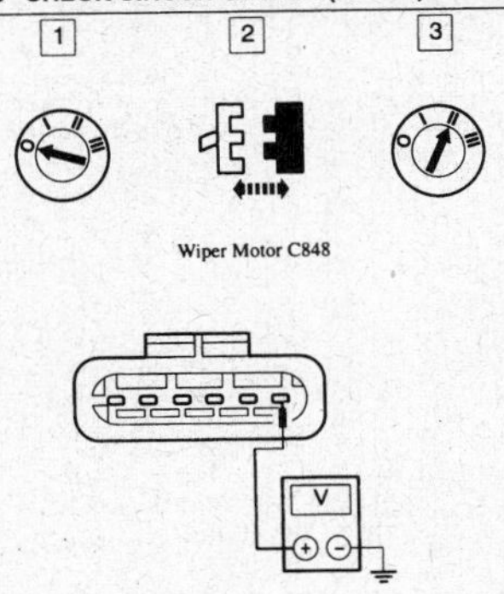	4 Measure the voltage between wiper motor C848-6, circuit 32-AK11 (WH/BK), and ground.

FM9029800563020X

Fig. 44 Test B: Wipers Stay On Continuously (Part 2 of 6). Contour & Mystique

CONDITIONS	DETAILS/RESULTS/ACTIONS
	• Is any voltage present? → **Yes** REPAIR circuit 32-AK11 (WH/BK). TEST the system for normal operation. → **No** REPLACE the wiper motor. TEST the system for normal operation.
B4 DETERMINE VOLTAGE SOURCE OF FRONT WIPER MOTORR	
1 2 3 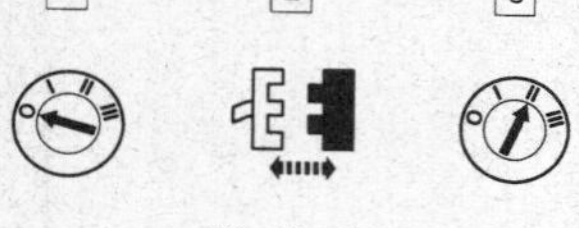 	• Is the wiper motor operating? → **Yes** GO to **B5.** → **No** GO to **B9.**
B5 CHECK THE WIPER SWITCH	
1 2 3 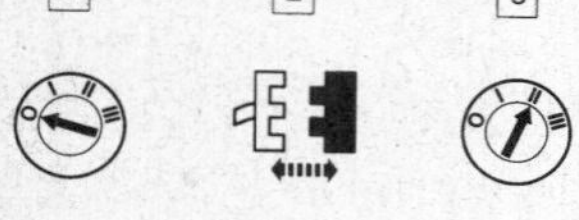 	• Is the wiper motor operating? → **Yes** GO to **B6.** → **No** GO to **B7.**

FM9029800563030X

Fig. 44 Test B: Wipers Stay On Continuously (Part 3 of 6). Contour & Mystique

CONDITIONS	DETAILS/RESULTS/ACTIONS
B6 CHECK CIRCUIT 32-AK10 (WH/GN) FOR SHORT TO POWERRR	
1 2 3 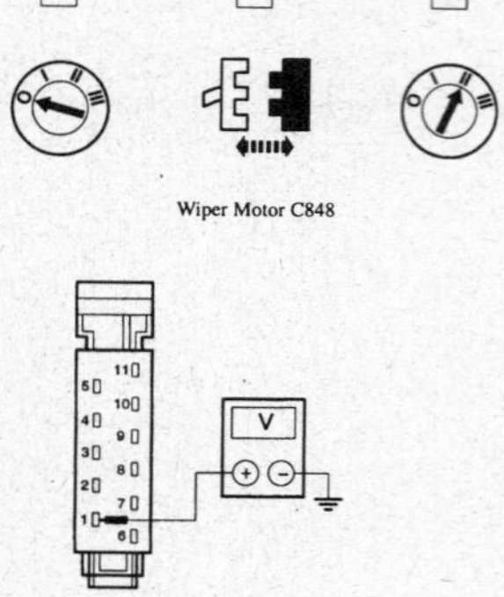 	4 Measure the voltage between wiper/washer switch C441-1, circuit 32-AK10 (WH/GN), and ground. • Is any voltage present? → **Yes** REPAIR circuit 32-AK10 (WH/GN). TEST the system for normal operation. → **No** REPLACE the wiper motor. TEST the system for normal operation.
B7 CHECK CIRCUIT 32-AK19 (WH/BK) FOR SHORT TO POWER – CENTRAL JUNCTION BOX (CJB) CONNECTEDTR	
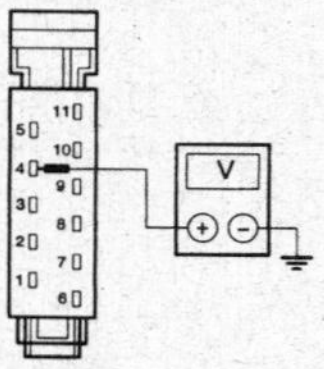	1 Measure the voltage between wiper/washer switch C441-4, circuit 32-AK19 (WH/BK), and ground.

FM9029800563040X

Fig. 44 Test B: Wipers Stay On Continuously (Part 4 of 6). Contour & Mystique

CONDITIONS	DETAILS/RESULTS/ACTIONS
	• Is any voltage present? → **Yes** GO to **B8.** → **No** REPLACE the wiper/washer switch. TEST the system for normal operation.
B8 CHECK CIRCUIT 32-AK19 (WH/BK) FOR SHORT TO POWER – CJB DISCONNECTED	
1 2 3 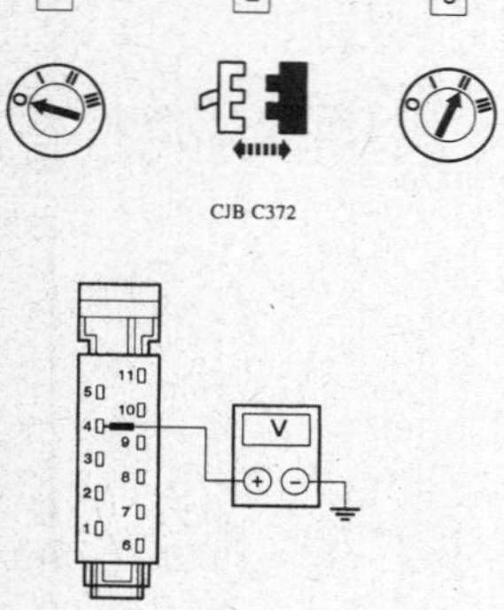 	4 Measure the voltage between wiper/washer switch C441-4, circuit 32-AK19 (WH/BK), and ground. • Is any voltage present? → **Yes** REPAIR circuit 32-AK19 (WH/BK). TEST the system for normal operation. → **No** REPAIR the CJB. TEST the system for normal operation.
B9 CHECK THE WIPER RELAY	
	1 Check the wiper relay; refer to component test Relay-5 Pin in this Section. • Is the wiper relay OK? → **Yes** GO to **B10.** → **No** REPLACE the wiper relay. TEST the system for normal operation.

FM9029800563050X

Fig. 44 Test B: Wipers Stay On Continuously (Part 5 of 6). Contour & Mystique

CONDITIONS	DETAILS/RESULTS/ACTIONS
B10 CHECK THE CENTRAL JUNCTION BOX (CJB) BETWEEN THE CTM AND WIPER RELAY FOR SHORT TO GROUND – CTM DISCONNECTED	
1 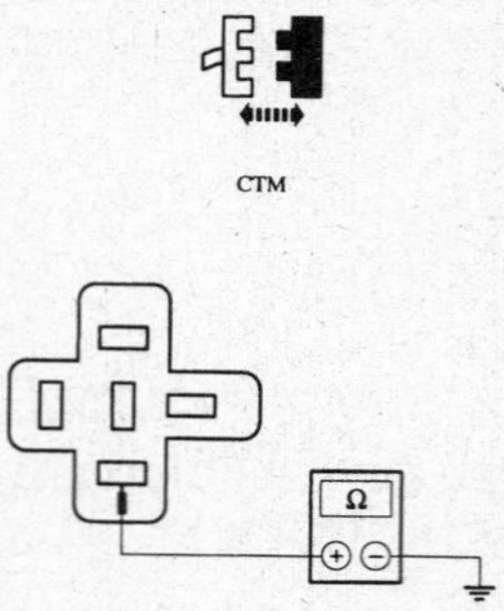 	2 Measure the resistance between wiper relay C72-1, and ground. • Is the resistance greater than 10,000 ohms? → **Yes** REPLACE the CTM. TEST the system for normal operation. → **No** REPLACE the CJB. TEST the system for normal operation.

FM9029800563060X

Fig. 44 Test B: Wipers Stay On Continuously (Part 6 of 6). Contour & Mystique

CONDITIONS	DETAILS/RESULTS/ACTIONS
C1 CHECK WIPER/WASHER SWITCH FOR PROPER OPERATION	
1 2 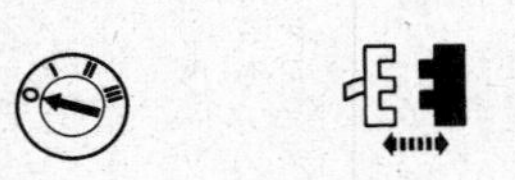	

FM9029800564010X

Fig. 45 Test C: High Speed Does Not Operate Properly w/Intermittent Wiper Mode Satisfactory (Part 1 of 3). Contour & Mystique

CONDITIONS	DETAILS/RESULTS/ACTIONS
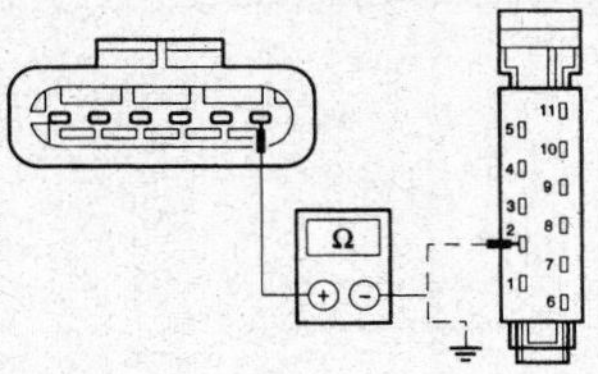	3 Measure the resistance between wiper/washer switch C441-2, circuit 32-AK11 (WH/BK), and wiper motor C848-6, circuit 32-AK11 (WH/BK); and between wiper motor C848-6, circuit 32-AK11 (WH/BK), and ground. • Is the resistance less than 5 ohms between the two connectors and greater than 10,000 ohms between the wiper/washer switch connector and ground? → **Yes** REPLACE the wiper motor. TEST the system for normal operation. → **No** REPAIR circuit 32-AK11 (WH/BK). TEST the system for normal operation.

FM9029800564030X

Fig. 45 Test C: High Speed Does Not Operate Properly w/Intermittent Wiper Mode Satisfactory (Part 3 of 3). Contour & Mystique

CONDITIONS	DETAILS/RESULTS/ACTIONS
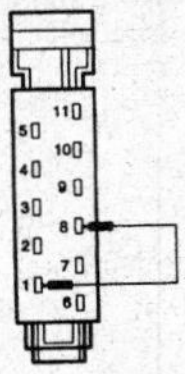 4	3 Connect a jumper wire between wiper/washer switch C441-1, circuit 32-AK10 (WH/GN), and wiper/washer switch C441-8, circuit 14-AK19 (VT/OG). • Do the wipers operate? → **Yes** REPLACE the wiper/washer switch. TEST the system for normal operation. → **No** GO to **D2.**
D2 CHECK CIRCUIT 32-AK10 (WH/GN) FOR OPEN AND SHORT TO GROUND	
1 2 	

FM9029800565020X

Fig. 46 Test D: Low Wiper Speed Does Not Operate Properly w/Intermittent Wiper Mode Satisfactory (Part 2 of 3). Contour & Mystique

CONDITIONS	DETAILS/RESULTS/ACTIONS
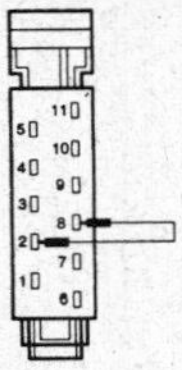 4	3 Connect a jumper wire between wiper/washer switch C441-8, circuit 14-AK19 (VT/OG), and wiper/washer switch C441-2, circuit 32-AK11 (WH/BK). • Do the wipers operate? → **Yes** REPLACE the wiper/washer switch. TEST the system for normal operation. → **No** GO to **C2.**
C2 CHECK CIRCUIT 32-AK11 FOR OPEN AND SHORT TO GROUND	
1 2 	

FM9029800564020X

Fig. 45 Test C: High Speed Does Not Operate Properly w/Intermittent Wiper Mode Satisfactory (Part 2 of 3). Contour & Mystique

CONDITIONS	DETAILS/RESULTS/ACTIONS
D1 CHECK THE WIPER/WASHER SWITCH FOR PROPER OPERATION	
1 2 	

FM9029800565010X

Fig. 46 Test D: Low Wiper Speed Does Not Operate Properly w/Intermittent Wiper Mode Satisfactory (Part 1 of 3). Contour & Mystique

CONDITIONS	DETAILS/RESULTS/ACTIONS
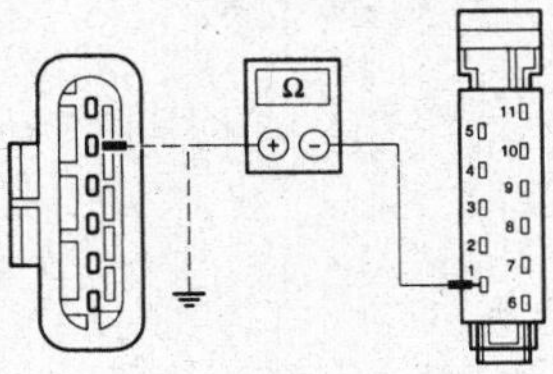	3 Measure the resistance between wiper/washer switch C441-1, circuit 32-AK10 (WH/GN), and wiper motor C848-5, circuit 32-AK10 (WH/GN); and between wiper/washer switch C441-1, circuit 32-AK10 (WH/GN), and ground. • Is the resistance less than 5 ohms between the two connectors and greater than 10,000 ohms between the wiper/washer switch connector and ground? → **Yes** REPLACE the wiper motor. TEST the system for normal operation. → **No** REPAIR circuit 32-AK10 (WH/GN). TEST the system for normal operation.

FM9029800565030X

Fig. 46 Test D: Low Wiper Speed Does Not Operate Properly w/Intermittent Wiper Mode Satisfactory (Part 3 of 3). Contour & Mystique

CONDITIONS	DETAILS/RESULTS/ACTIONS
E1 CHECK FOR VOLTAGE TO THE WIPER RELAY	
1 2 3  Wiper Relay C72	

FM9029800566010X

Fig. 47 Test E: Intermittent Wiper Speed Does Not Operate Properly w/High/Low Speeds Satisfactory (Part 1 of 8). Contour & Mystique

CONDITIONS	DETAILS/RESULTS/ACTIONS
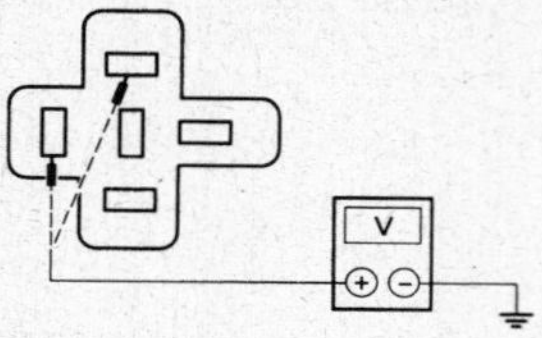	4 Measure the voltage between wiper relay C72-5, and ground and between wiper relay C72-2, and ground. • Are the voltages greater than 10 volts? → **Yes** GO to **E2.** → **No** REPLACE the central junction box. TEST the system for normal operation.
E2 CHECK THE WIPER RELAY	
	1 Check the wiper relay. • Is the wiper relay OK? → **Yes** GO to **E3.** → **No** REPLACE the wiper relay. TEST the system for normal operation.

FM9029800566020X

Fig. 47 Test E: Intermittent Wiper Speed Does Not Operate Properly w/High/Low Speeds Satisfactory (Part 2 of 8). Contour & Mystique

CONDITIONS	DETAILS/RESULTS/ACTIONS
E3 CHECK THE CENTRAL JUNCTION BOX (CJB) FOR OPEN BETWEEN THE CTM AND WIPER RELAYRR	
1 2  CTM C23	
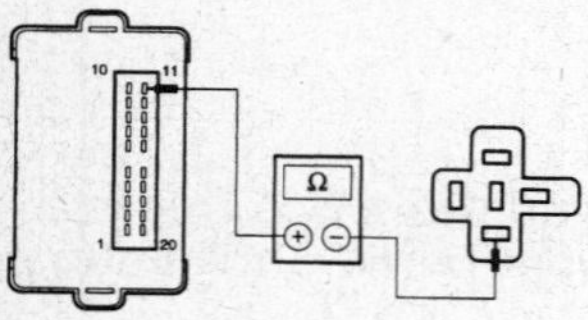	3 Measure the resistance between wiper relay C72-1, and CTM C23-11. • Is the resistance less than 5 ohms? → **Yes** GO to **E4.** → **No** REPLACE the CJB. TEST the system for normal operation.
E4 CHECK THE WIPER/WASHER SWITCH FOR OPEN	
1  Wiper/Washer Switch C441	

FM9029800566030X

Fig. 47 Test E: Intermittent Wiper Speed Does Not Operate Properly w/High/Low Speeds Satisfactory (Part 3 of 8). Contour & Mystique

CONDITIONS	DETAILS/RESULTS/ACTIONS
	2 Set the wiper/washer switch to intermittent.
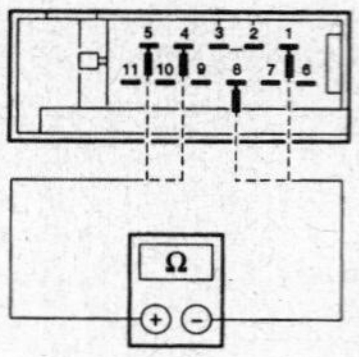	3 Measure the resistance between wiper/washer switch terminal 1 and terminal 4; and between wiper/washer switch terminal 8 and terminal 5. • Are the resistances less than 5 ohms? → **Yes** GO to **E5.** → **No** REPLACE the wiper/washer switch. TEST the system for normal operation.
E5 CHECK CIRCUIT 32-AK19 (WH/BK) FOR OPEN AND SHORT TO GROUND	
1  CJB C372	

FM9029800566040X

Fig. 47 Test E: Intermittent Wiper Speed Does Not Operate Properly w/High/Low Speeds Satisfactory (Part 4 of 8). Contour & Mystique

CONDITIONS	DETAILS/RESULTS/ACTIONS
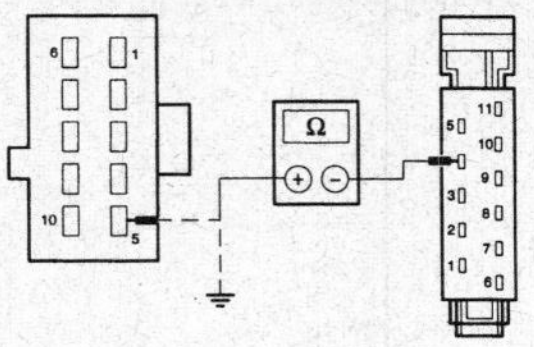	[2] Measure the resistance between wiper/washer switch C441-4, circuit 32-AK19 (WH/BK), and CJB C372-5, circuit 32-AK19 (WH/BK); and between wiper/washer switch C441-4, circuit 32-AK19 (WH/BK), and ground. • Is the resistance less than 5 ohms between the two connectors and greater than 10,000 ohms between the wiper/washer switch connector and ground? → **Yes** GO to **E6.** → **No** REPAIR circuit 32-AK19 (WH/BK). TEST the system for normal operation.
E6 CHECK THE CJB FOR OPEN AND SHORT TO GROUND BETWEEN THE WIPER RELAY AND CIRCUIT 32-AK19 (WH/BK)	
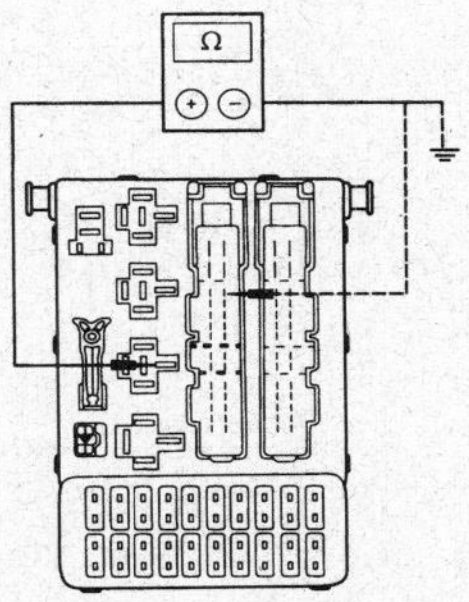	[1] Measure the resistance between CJB terminal 5 and wiper relay C72-3; and between wiper relay C72-3, and ground.

FM9029800566050X

Fig. 47 Test E: Intermittent Wiper Speed Does Not Operate Properly w/High/Low Speeds Satisfactory (Part 5 of 8). Contour & Mystique

CONDITIONS	DETAILS/RESULTS/ACTIONS
	• Is the resistance less than 5 ohms? → **Yes** If equipped with a fixed intermittent wiper/washer switch, REPLACE the CTM. TEST the system for normal operation. If equipped with a variable intermittent wiper/washer switch, GO to **E9.** → **No** REPLACE the CJB. TEST the system for normal operation.
E9 CHECK CIRCUIT 8-AK18 (WH) FOR OPEN	
[1]  CJB C372	
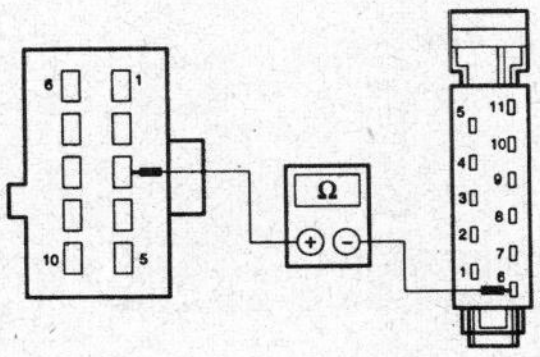	[2] Measure the resistance between CJB C372-3, circuit 8-AK18 (WH), and wiper/washer switch C441-6, circuit 8-AK18 (WH). • Is the resistance less than 5 ohms? → **Yes** RECONNECT CJB. GO to **E10.** → **No** REPAIR circuit 8-AK18 (WH). TEST the system for normal operation.

FM9029800566070X

Fig. 47 Test E: Intermittent Wiper Speed Does Not Operate Properly w/High/Low Speeds Satisfactory (Part 7 of 8). Contour & Mystique

CONDITIONS	DETAILS/RESULTS/ACTIONS
	• Is the resistance less than 5 ohms between the two connectors and greater than 10,000 ohms between the wiper relay connector and ground? → **Yes** GO to **E7.** → **No** REPLACE the CJB. TEST the system for normal operation.
E7 CHECK CIRCUIT 8-AK19 (WH/BK) FOR OPENRTR	
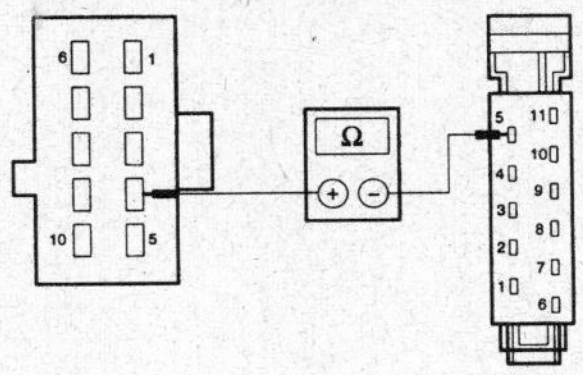	[1] Measure the resistance between wiper/washer switch C441-5, circuit 8-AK19 (WH/BK), and CJB C372-4, circuit 8-AK19 (WH/BK). • Is the resistance less than 5 ohms? → **Yes** RECONNECT wiper/washer switch C441. GO to **E8.** → **No** REPAIR circuit 8-AK19 (WH/BK). TEST the system for normal operation.
E8 CHECK THE CJB FOR OPEN BETWEEN THE CTM AND CIRCUIT 8-AK19 (WH/BK).	
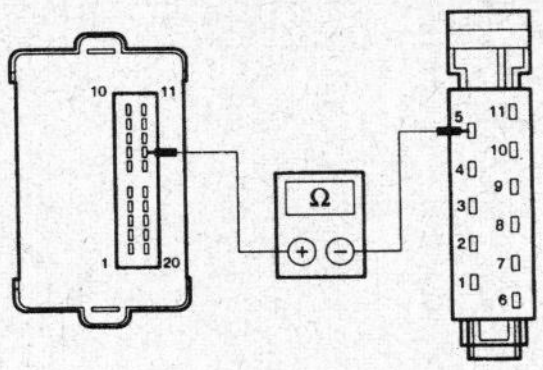	[1] Measure the resistance between wiper/washer switch C441-5, circuit 8-AK19 (WH/BK), and CTM C23-14.

FM9029800566060X

Fig. 47 Test E: Intermittent Wiper Speed Does Not Operate Properly w/High/Low Speeds Satisfactory (Part 6 of 8). Contour & Mystique

CONDITIONS	DETAILS/RESULTS/ACTIONS
E10 CHECK FOR OPEN BETWEEN CJB AND CIRCUIT 8-AK18 (WH)	
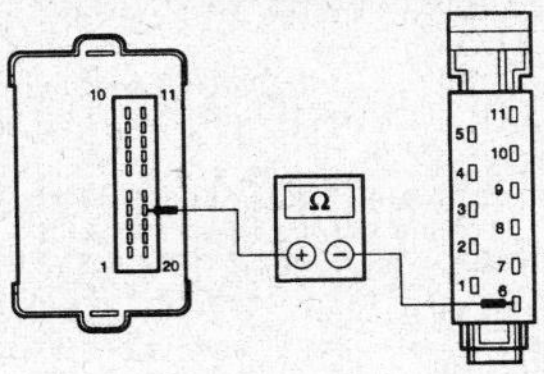	[1] Measure the resistance between wiper/washer switch C441-6, circuit 8-AK18 (WH), and CTM C23-17. • Is the resistance less than 5 ohms? → **Yes** REPLACE the CTM. TEST the system for normal operation. → **No** REPLACE the CJB. TEST the system for normal operation.

FM9029800566080X

Fig. 47 Test E: Intermittent Wiper Speed Does Not Operate Properly w/High/Low Speeds Satisfactory (Part 8 of 8). Contour & Mystique

CONDITIONS	DETAILS/RESULTS/ACTIONS
F1 CHECK CIRCUIT 32-AK9 (WH/BU) FOR VOLTAGE	
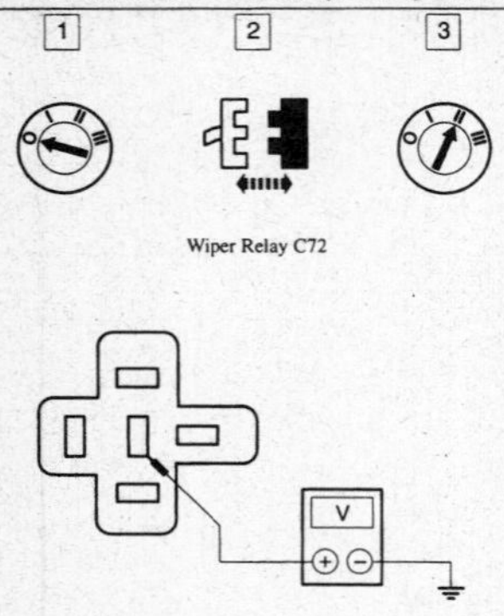	**NOTE:** The wipers must not be in the park position. 4 Measure the voltage between wiper relay C72-4, and ground.

FM9029800567010X

Fig. 48 Test F: Wipers Will Not Park At Proper Position (Part 1 of 6). Contour & Mystique

CONDITIONS	DETAILS/RESULTS/ACTIONS
	• Is the voltage greater than 10 volts? → **Yes** GO to **F2.** → **No** GO to **F3.**
F2 CHECK THE WIPER RELAY	
	1 Check the wiper relay. • Is the wiper relay OK? → **Yes** REPLACE the wiper/washer switch. TEST the system for normal operation. → **No** REPLACE the wiper relay. TEST the system for normal operation.
F3 CHECK CIRCUIT 14-AK9 (VT) FOR VOLTAGE	
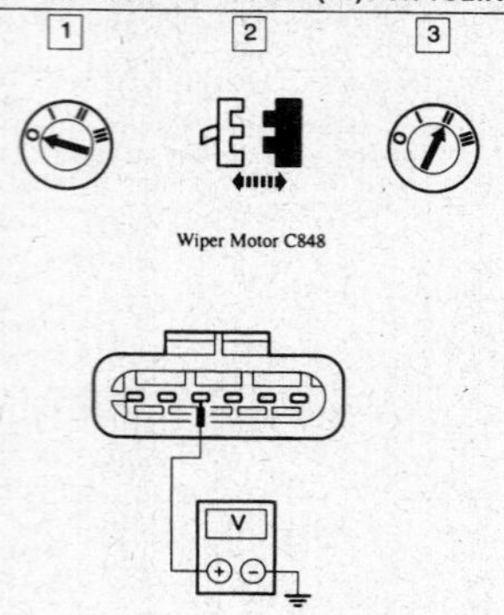	4 Measure the voltage between wiper motor C848-3, circuit 14-AK9 (VT), and ground. • Is the voltage greater than 10 volts? → **Yes** GO to **F5.** → **No** GO to **F4.**

FM9029800567020X

Fig. 48 Test F: Wipers Will Not Park At Proper Position (Part 2 of 6). Contour & Mystique

CONDITIONS	DETAILS/RESULTS/ACTIONS
F4 CHECK CIRCUIT 14-AK9 (VT) FOR OPEN	
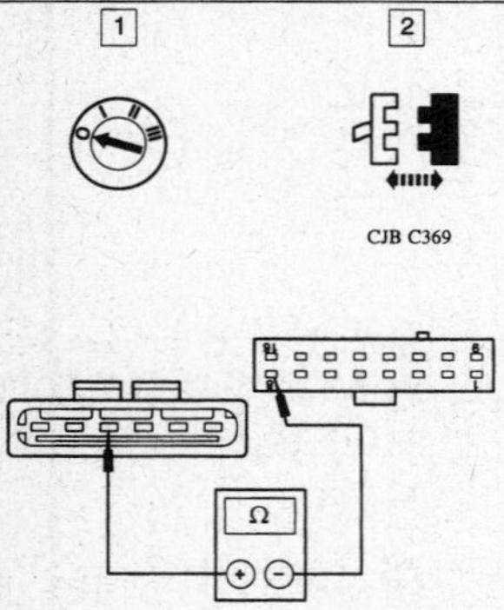	3 Measure the resistance between CJB C369-8, circuit 14-AK9 (VT), and wiper motor C848-3, circuit 14-AK9 (VT). • Is the resistance less than 5 ohms? → **Yes** REPLACE the CJB. TEST the system for normal operation. → **No** REPAIR circuit 14-AK9 (VT). TEST the system for normal operation.
F5 CHECK CIRCUIT 32-AK9 (WH/BU) FOR OPEN AND SHORT TO GROUND	
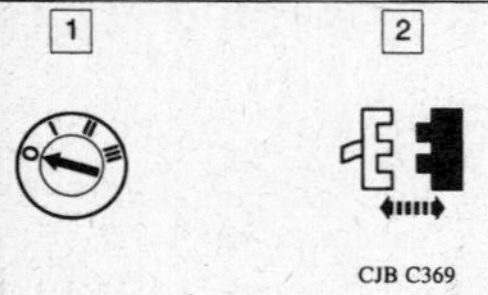	

FM9029800567030X

Fig. 48 Test F: Wipers Will Not Park At Proper Position (Part 3 of 6). Contour & Mystique

CONDITIONS	DETAILS/RESULTS/ACTIONS
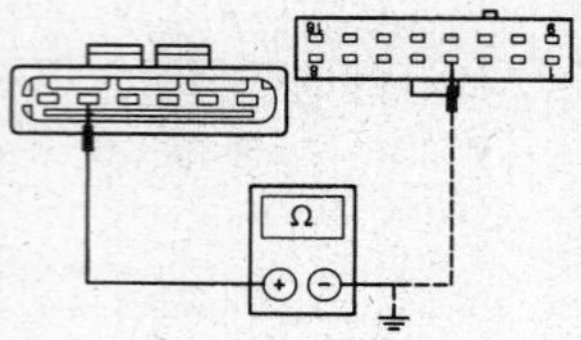	3 Measure the resistance between wiper motor C848-2, circuit 32-AK9 (WH/BU), and CJB C369-4, circuit 32-AK9 (WH/BU); and between wiper motor C848-2, circuit 32-AK9 (WH/BU), and ground. • Is the resistance less than 5 ohms between the two connectors and greater than 10,000 ohms between the wiper motor connector and ground? → **Yes** GO to **F6.** → **No** REPAIR circuit 32-AK9 (WH/BU). TEST the system for normal operation.
F6 CHECK PARK POSITION SWITCH GROUND FOR OPEN – CIRCUIT 31-AK8 (BK)	
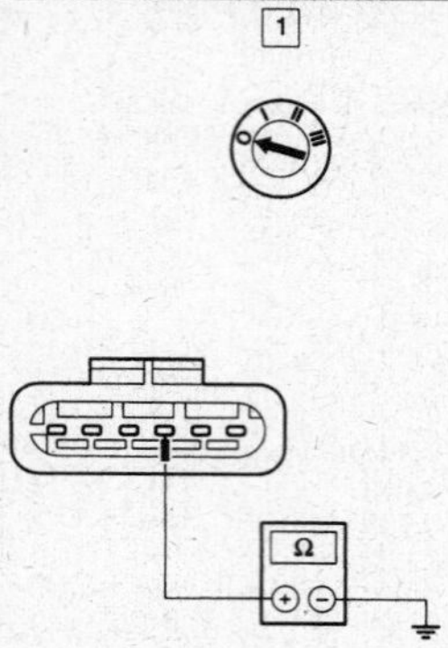	2 Measure the resistance between wiper motor C848-4, circuit 31-AK8 (BK), and ground.

FM9029800567040X

Fig. 48 Test F: Wipers Will Not Park At Proper Position (Part 4 of 6). Contour & Mystique

CONDITIONS	DETAILS/RESULTS/ACTIONS
	• Is the resistance less than 5 ohms? → **Yes** GO to **F7.** → **No** REPAIR circuit 31-AK8 (BK). TEST the system for normal operation.
F7 CHECK THE CJB FOR AN OPEN	
1  CTM C23 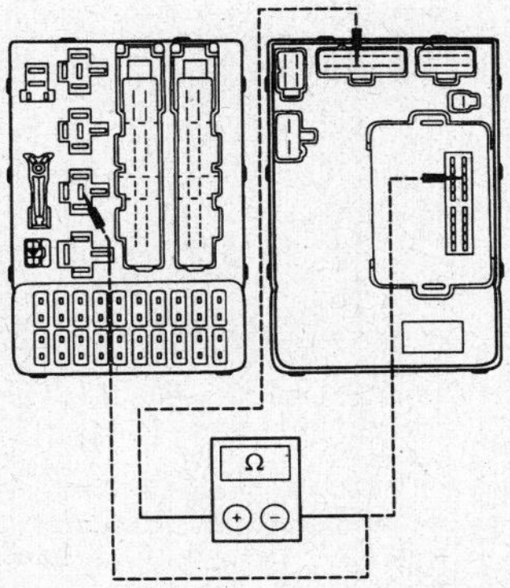	2 Measure the resistance between wiper relay C72-4, and CJB terminal 4; and between CJB terminal 4 and CTM C23-13.

FM9029800567050X

Fig. 48 Test F: Wipers Will Not Park At Proper Position (Part 5 of 6). Contour & Mystique

CONDITIONS	DETAILS/RESULTS/ACTIONS
G1 CHECK WIPE AND WASH FUNCTION FOR PROPER OPERATION	
1  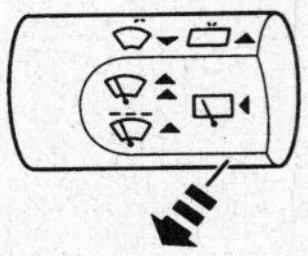	2 Pull the wiper/washer switch toward the steering wheel.

FM9029800568010X

Fig. 49 Test G: Washer Pump Inoperative (Part 1 of 8). Contour & Mystique

CONDITIONS	DETAILS/RESULTS/ACTIONS
	• Is the resistances less than 5 ohms? → **Yes** GO to **F8.** → **No** REPLACE the CJB. TEST the system for normal operation.
F8 CHECK THE WIPER MOTOR	
	1 Check the wiper motor. • Is the wiper motor OK? → **Yes** REPLACE the CTM. TEST the system for normal operation. → **No** REPLACE the wiper motor. TEST the system for normal operation.

FM9029800567060X

Fig. 48 Test F: Wipers Will Not Park At Proper Position (Part 6 of 6). Contour & Mystique

CONDITIONS	DETAILS/RESULTS/ACTIONS
	• Do the wipers cycle three times? → **Yes** GO to **G2.** → **No** GO to **G6.**
G2 CHECK CIRCUIT 31S-AK7 (BK/WH) FOR OPENR	
1  2  Washer Pump C828 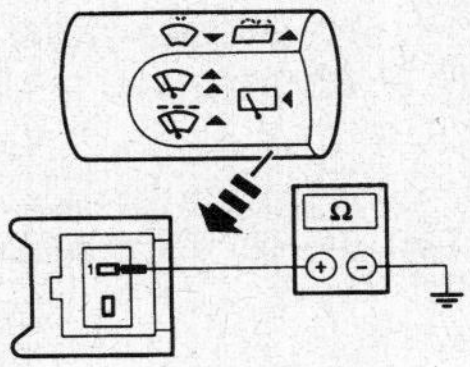	3 Measure the resistance between washer pump C828-1, circuit 31S-AK7 (BK/WH), and ground while holding the wiper/washer switch in the wash position. • Is the resistance less than 5 ohms? → **Yes** GO to **G4.** → **No** GO to **G3.**
G3 CHECK THE CJB FOR OPEN	
1  CJB C369 2  CJB C372	

FM9029800568020X

Fig. 49 Test G: Washer Pump Inoperative (Part 2 of 8). Contour & Mystique

CONDITIONS	DETAILS/RESULTS/ACTIONS
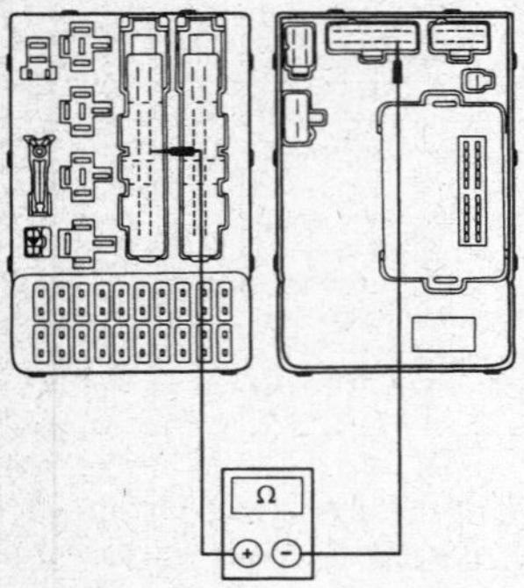	3 Measure the resistance between CJB terminal 7 and CJB terminal 10. • Is the resistance less than 5 ohms? → **Yes** REPAIR circuit 31S-AK7 (BK/WH). TEST the system for normal operation. → **No** REPLACE the CJB. TEST the system for normal operation.
G4 CHECK CIRCUIT 14-AK7 (VT/WH) FOR OPEN	
1  Wiper/Washer Switch C444	

FM9029800568030X

Fig. 49 Test G: Washer Pump Inoperative (Part 3 of 8). Contour & Mystique

CONDITIONS	DETAILS/RESULTS/ACTIONS
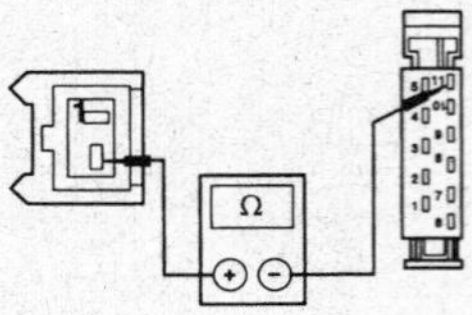	2 Measure the resistance between wiper/washer switch C441-11, circuit 14-AK7 (VT/WH), and washer pump motor C828-2, circuit 14-AK7 (VT/WH). • Is the resistance less than 5 ohms? → **Yes** GO to **G5**. → **No** REPAIR circuit 14-AK7 (VT/WH). TEST the system for normal operation.
G5 CHECK THE WASHER SWITCH FOR PROPER OPERATION	
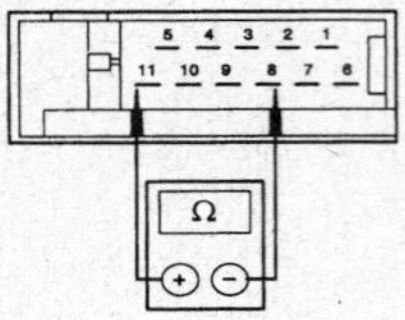	1 Measure the resistance between wiper/washer switch terminal 11 and terminal 8. • Is the resistance less than 5 ohms? → **Yes** REPLACE the washer pump motor. TEST the system for normal operation. → **No** REPLACE the wiper/washer switch. TEST the system for normal operation.

FM9029800568040X

Fig. 49 Test G: Washer Pump Inoperative (Part 4 of 8). Contour & Mystique

CONDITIONS	DETAILS/RESULTS/ACTIONS
G6 CHECK THE WASH AND WIPE FUNCTION – WIPER/WASHER SWITCH DISCONNECTED	
1  2  Wiper/Washer Switch C441 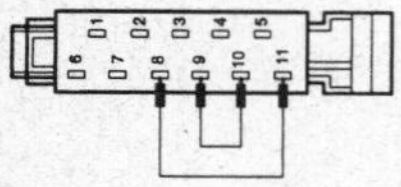 4 	3 Connect a jumper wire between wiper/washer switch C441-9, circuit 33-AK6 (YE/BK), and wiper/washer switch C441-10, circuit 31-AK19 (BK); and between wiper/washer switch C441-11, circuit 14-AK7 (VT/WH), and wiper/washer switch C441-8, circuit 14-AK19 (VT/OG). • Does the wiper and wash function operate? → **Yes** REPLACE the wiper/washer switch. TEST the system for normal operation. → **No** GO to **G7**.

FM9029800568050X

Fig. 49 Test G: Washer Pump Inoperative (Part 5 of 8). Contour & Mystique

CONDITIONS	DETAILS/RESULTS/ACTIONS
G7 CHECK THE 33-AKG (YE/BK) FOR OPEN	
1  2  CJB C372 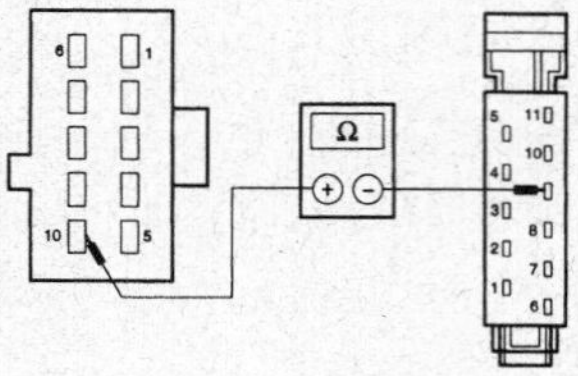	3 Measure the resistance between wiper/washer switch C441-9, circuit 33-AK6 (YE/BK), and CJB C372-10, circuit 33-AK6 (YE/BK). • Is the resistance less than 5 ohms? → **Yes** GO to **G8**. → **No** REPAIR circuit 33-AK6 (YE/BK). TEST the system for normal operation.
G8 CHECK THE CJB FOR OPEN	
1  CJB C369	

FM9029800568060X

Fig. 49 Test G: Washer Pump Inoperative (Part 6 of 8). Contour & Mystique

CONDITIONS	DETAILS/RESULTS/ACTIONS
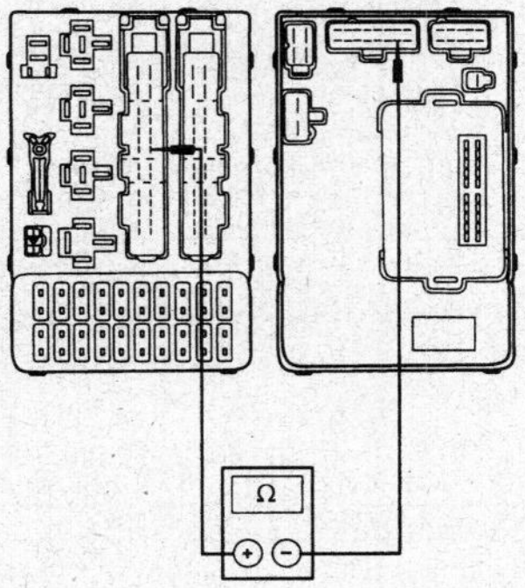	2 Measure the resistance between CJB terminal 7 and CJB terminal 10. • Is the resistance less than 5 ohms? → **Yes** GO to **G9.** → **No** REPLACE the CJB. TEST the system for normal operation.
G9 CHECK CIRCUIT 31-AK19 (BK) FOR OPEN	
1  Shorting Bar #1 C478	

FM9029800568070X

Fig. 49 Test G: Washer Pump Inoperative (Part 7 of 8). Contour & Mystique

CONDITIONS	DETAILS/RESULTS/ACTIONS
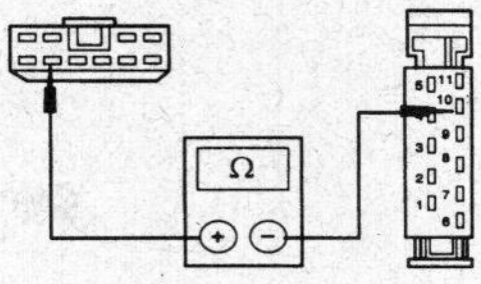	2 Measure the resistance between wiper/washer switch C441-10, circuit 31-AK19 (BK), and shorting bar #1 C478-6, circuit 31-AK19 (BK). • Is the resistance less than 5 ohms? → **Yes** GO to **G10.** → **No** REPAIR circuit 31-AK19 (BK). TEST the system for normal operation.
G10 CHECK SHORTING BAR #1 FOR OPEN	
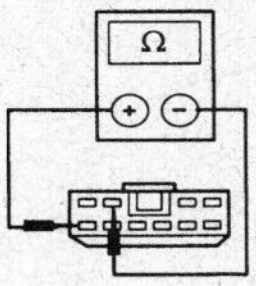	1 Measure the resistance between shorting bar #1 terminal 10 and terminal 3. • Is the resistance less than 5 ohms? → **Yes** REPLACE the CTM. TEST the system for normal operation. → **No** REPLACE the shorting bar #1. TEST the system for normal operation.

FM9029800568080X

Fig. 49 Test G: Washer Pump Inoperative (Part 8 of 8). Contour & Mystique

CONDITIONS	DETAILS/RESULTS/ACTIONS
⚠ **CAUTION: Electronic modules are sensitive to electrical charge. If exposed to these charges, damage may result.**	
A1 DETERMINE FUNCTION OF THE WASHER	
	1 Determine function of the washer. • Does the washer operate? → **Yes** GO to **A5.** → **No** GO to **A2.**

FM9020100778010X

Fig. 50 Test A: Wipers Inoperative (Part 1 of 4). Cougar

CONDITIONS	DETAILS/RESULTS/ACTIONS
A2 CHECK FUSE 20 (10A)	
1  Fuse 20 (10A)	• Is fuse 20 (10A) OK? → **Yes** GO to **A3.** → **No** INSTALL a new fuse. TEST the system for normal operation. If the fuse fails again, CHECK for short to ground. REPAIR circuit as necessary.
A3 CHECK VOLTAGE SUPPLY TO WIPER SWITCH – CIRCUIT 14–AK19 (VT/OG)	
1  2  wiper/washer switch C441 3  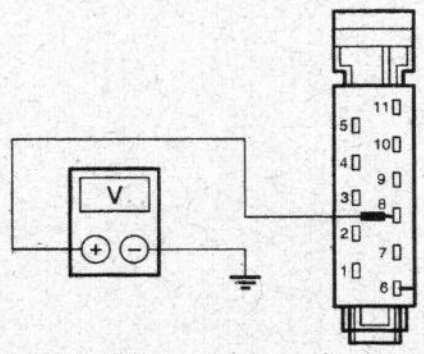	4 Measure the voltage between wiper/washer switch C441 pin 8, circuit14–AK19 (VT/OG), harness side and ground. • Is the voltage greater than 10 volts? → **Yes** GO to **A5.** → **No** GO to **A4.**

FM9020100778020X

Fig. 50 Test A: Wipers Inoperative (Part 2 of 4). Cougar

CONDITIONS	DETAILS/RESULTS/ACTIONS
A4 CHECK CIRCUIT 14–AK19 (VT/OG) FOR OPEN	
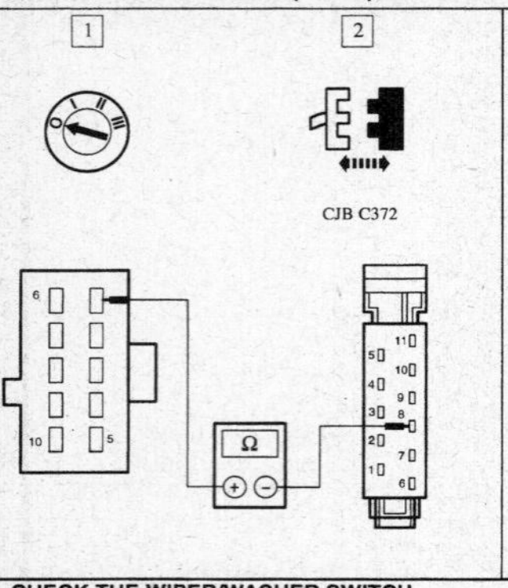	3 Measure the resistance between CJB C372, circuit 14–AK19 (VT/OG), harness side and wiper/washer switch C441 pin 8, circuit 14–AK19 (VT/OG) harness side. • Is the resistance less than 5 ohms? → **Yes** INSTALL a new CJB. TEST the system for normal operation. → **No** REPAIR circuit 14–AK19. TEST the system for normal operation.
A5 CHECK THE WIPER/WASHER SWITCH	
	2 Check the wiper/washer switch. • Is the wiper switch OK? → **Yes** GO to **A6.** → **No** INSTALL a new wiper/washer switch. TEST the system for normal operation.

FM9020100778030X

Fig. 50 Test A: Wipers Inoperative (Part 3 of 4). Cougar

CONDITIONS	DETAILS/RESULTS/ACTIONS
CAUTION: Electronic modules are sensitive to electrical charge. If exposed to these charges, damage may result.	
B1 DETERMINE WINDSHIELD WIPER OPERATION SPEED	
	1 Place the wiper/washer switch in the OFF position. • Do the wipers operate at high speed? → **Yes** GO to **B2.** → **No** GO to **B4.**

FM9020100779010X

Fig. 51 Test B: Wipers Stay On Continuously (Part 1 of 5). Cougar

CONDITIONS	DETAILS/RESULTS/ACTIONS
A6 CHECK THE WINDSHIELD WIPER MOTOR FOR GROUND	
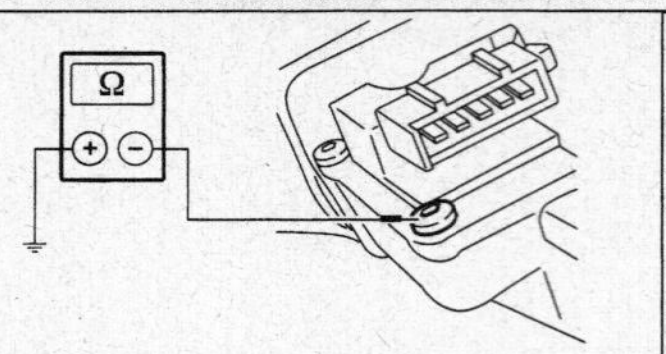	1 Measure the resistance between the housing of the windshield wiper motor and ground. • Is the resistance less than 5 ohms? → **Yes** INSTALL a new windshield wiper motor. TEST the system for normal operation. → **No** REPAIR ground connection of the windshield wiper motor. TEST the system for normal operation.

FM9020100778040X

Fig. 50 Test A: Wipers Inoperative (Part 4 of 4). Cougar

CONDITIONS	DETAILS/RESULTS/ACTIONS
B2 CHECK THE WIPER SWITCH	
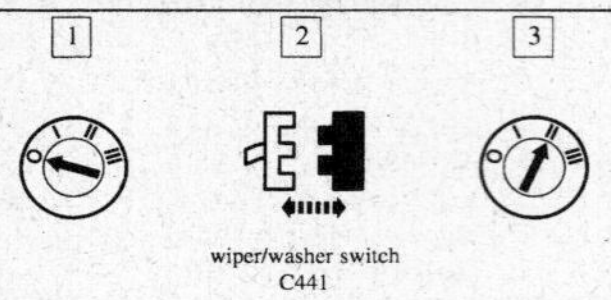	• Do the wipers operate at high speed? → **Yes** GO to **B3.** → **No** INSTALL a new wiper/washer switch. TEST the system for normal operation.
B3 CHECK CIRCUIT 32–AK11 (WH/BK) FOR SHORT TO POWER	
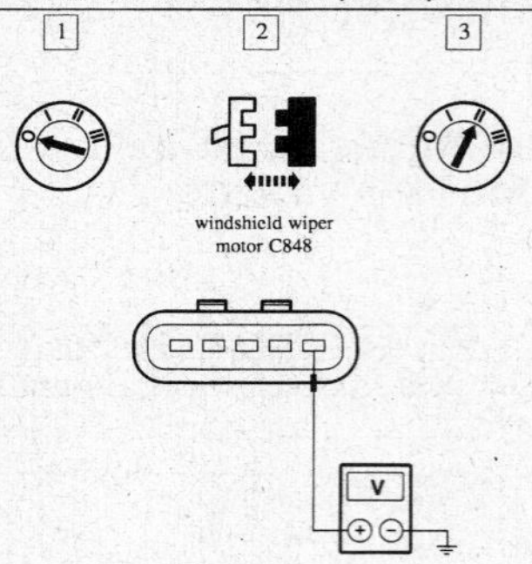	4 Measure the voltage between wiper motor C848, circuit 32–AK11 (WH/BK), harness side and ground. • Is the voltage equal to 0 volts? → **Yes** INSTALL a new windshield wiper motor. TEST the system for normal operation. → **No** REPAIR circuit 32–AK11. TEST the system for normal operation.

FM9020100779020X

Fig. 51 Test B: Wipers Stay On Continuously (Part 2 of 5). Cougar

CONDITIONS	DETAILS/RESULTS/ACTIONS
B4 DETERMINE VOLTAGE SOURCE OF WINDSHIELD WIPER MOTOR	
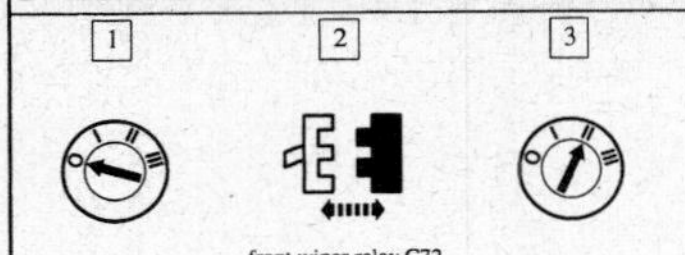 front wiper relay C72	• Is the wiper motor operating? → **Yes** GO to **B5.** → **No** GO to **B9.**
B5 CHECK THE WIPER/WASHER SWITCH	
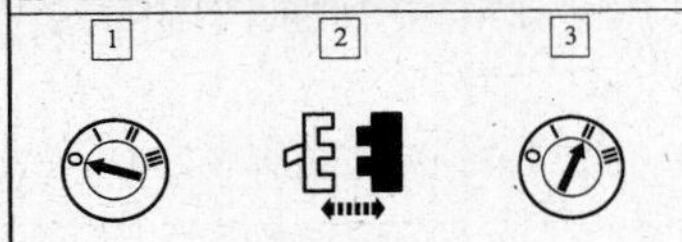 wiper/washer switch C441	• Is the wiper motor operating? → **Yes** GO to **B6.** → **No** GO to **B7.**
B6 CHECK CIRCUIT 32–AK10 (WH/GN) FOR SHORT TO POWER	
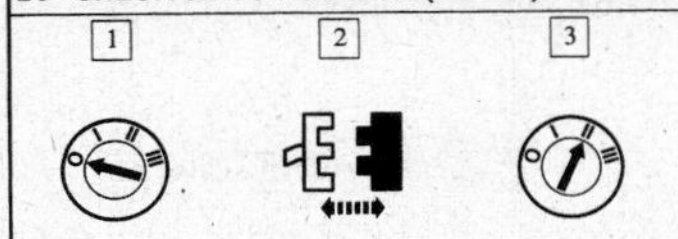 winshield wiper motor C848	

FM9020100779030X

Fig. 51 Test B: Wipers Stay On Continuously (Part 3 of 5). Cougar

CONDITIONS	DETAILS/RESULTS/ACTIONS
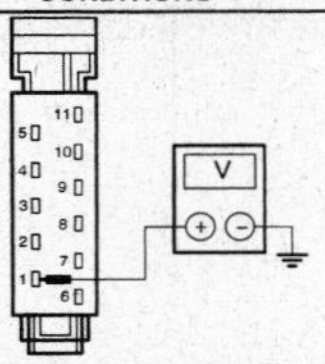	4 Measure the voltage between wiper/washer switch C441 pin 1, circuit 32–AK10 (WH/GN), harness side and ground. • Is the voltage equal to 0 volts? → **Yes** INSTALL a new windshield wiper motor. TEST the system for normal operation. → **No** REPAIR circuit 32–AK10. TEST the system for normal operation.
B7 CHECK CIRCUIT 32–AK19 (WH/BK) FOR SHORT TO POWER – CENTRAL JUNCTION BOX (CJB) CONNECTED	
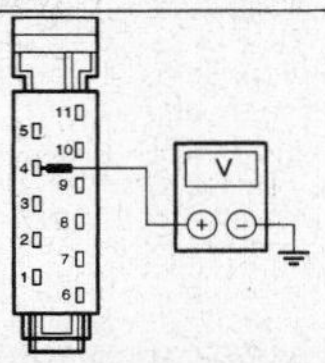	1 Measure the voltage between wiper/washer switch C441 pin 4, circuit 32–AK19 (WH/BK), harness side and ground. • Is the voltage equal to 0 volts? → **Yes** INSTALL a new wiper/washer switch. TEST the system for normal operation. → **No** GO to **B8.**
B8 CHECK CIRCUIT 32–AK19 (WH/BK) FOR SHORT TO POWER – CJB DISCONNECTED	
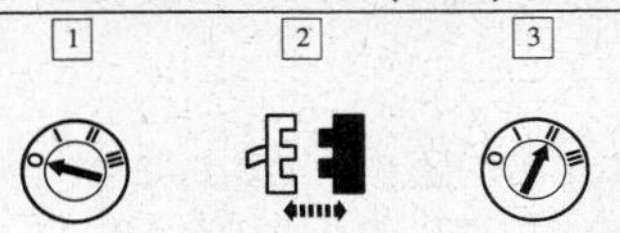 CJB C372	
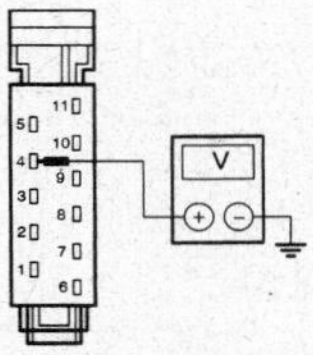	4 Measure the voltage between wiper/washer switch C441 pin 4, circuit 32–AK19 (WH/BK), harness side and ground. • Is the voltage equal to 0 volts? → **Yes** INSTALL a new CJB. TEST the system for normal operation. → **No** REPAIR circuit 32–AK19. TEST the system for normal operation.

FM9020100779040X

Fig. 51 Test B: Wipers Stay On Continuously (Part 4 of 5). Cougar

CONDITIONS	DETAILS/RESULTS/ACTIONS
B9 CHECK THE FRONT WIPER RELAY	
	1 Check the front wiper relay. • Is the front wiper relay OK? → **Yes** GO to **B10.** → **No** INSTALL a new front wiper relay. TEST the system for normal operation.
B10 CHECK THE CENTRAL JUNCTION BOX (CJB) BETWEEN THE CTM AND FRONT WIPER RELAY FOR SHORT TO GROUND	
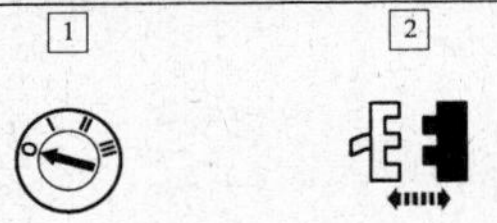 CTM C23	
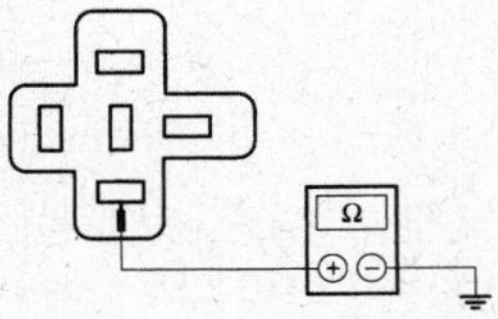	3 Measure the resistance between front wiper relay C72 pin 1, CJB and ground. • Is the resistance greater than 10,000 ohms? → **Yes** INSTALL a new CTM. TEST the system for normal operation. → **No** INSTALL a new CJB. TEST the system for normal operation.

FM9020100779050X

Fig. 51 Test B: Wipers Stay On Continuously (Part 5 of 5). Cougar

CONDITIONS	DETAILS/RESULTS/ACTIONS
⚠ **CAUTION: Electronic modules are sensitive to electrical charge. If exposed to these charges, damage may result.**	

FM9020100780010X

Fig. 52 Test C: High Speed Wiper Does Not Operate Properly, Intermittent Wiper Mode Functioning Properly (Part 1 of 3). Cougar

CONDITIONS	DETAILS/RESULTS/ACTIONS
C1 CHECK WIPER/WASHER SWITCH FOR CORRECT OPERATION	
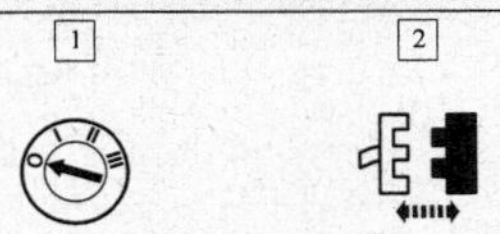 wiper/washer switch C441	3 Check the wiper/washer switch • Is the wiper/washer switch OK? → **Yes** GO to **C2.** → **No** INSTALL a new wiper/washer switch. TEST the system for normal operation.

FM9020100780020X

Fig. 52 Test C: High Speed Wiper Does Not Operate Properly, Intermittent Wiper Mode Functioning Properly (Part 2 of 3). Cougar

CONDITIONS	DETAILS/RESULTS/ACTIONS
C2 CHECK CIRCUIT 32–AK11 (WH/BK) FOR OPEN AND SHORT TO GROUND	
1  windshield wiper motor C848	
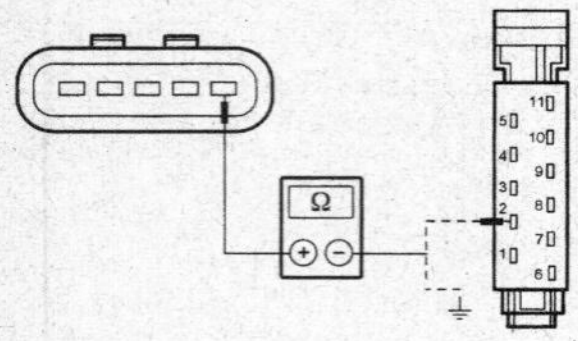	2 Measure the resistance between wiper/washer switch C441 pin 2, circuit 32–AK11 (WH/BK), harness side and wiper motor C848, circuit 32–AK11 (WH/BK), harness side; and between wiper motor C848, circuit 32–AK11 (WH/BK), harness side and ground. • Is the resistance less than 5 ohms between the two connectors and greater than 10,000 ohms between the wiper/washer switch connector and ground? → **Yes** INSTALL a new windshield wiper motor. TEST the system for normal operation. → **No** REPAIR circuit 32–AK11. TEST the system for normal operation.

FM9020100780030X

Fig. 52 Test C: High Speed Wiper Does Not Operate Properly, Intermittent Wiper Mode Functioning Properly (Part 3 of 3). Cougar

CONDITIONS	DETAILS/RESULTS/ACTIONS
	3 Check the wiper/washer switch • Is the wiper/washer switch OK? → **Yes** GO to **D2.** → **No** INSTALL a new wiper/washer switch. TEST the system for normal operation.
D2 CHECK CIRCUIT 32–AK10 (WH/GN) FOR OPEN AND SHORT TO GROUND	
1  windshield wiper motor C848	
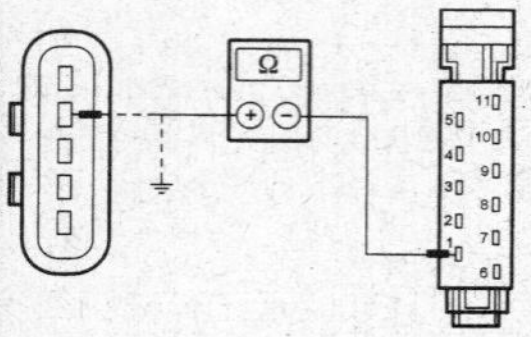	2 Measure the resistance between wiper/washer switch C441 pin 1, circuit 32-AK10 (WH/GN), harness side and wiper motor C848, circuit 32-AK10 (WH/GN), harness side; and between wiper/washer switch C441 pin 1, circuit 32-AK10 (WH/GN), harness side and ground. • Is the resistance less than 5 ohms between the two connectors and greater than 10,000 ohms between the wiper/washer switch connector and ground? → **Yes** INSTALL a new windshield wiper motor. TEST the system for normal operation. → **No** REPAIR circuit. TEST the system for normal operation.

FM9020100781020X

Fig. 53 Test D: Low Wiper Speed Does Not Operate Properly, Intermittent Mode Functioning Properly (Part 2 of 2). Cougar

CONDITIONS	DETAILS/RESULTS/ACTIONS
⚠ **CAUTION: Electronic modules are sensitive to electrical charge. If exposed to these charges, damage may result.**	
D1 CHECK THE WIPER/WASHER SWITCH FOR CORRECT OPERATION	
1 2  wiper/washer switch C441	

FM9020100781010X

Fig. 53 Test D: Low Wiper Speed Does Not Operate Properly, Intermittent Mode Functioning Properly (Part 1 of 2). Cougar

CONDITIONS	DETAILS/RESULTS/ACTIONS
⚠ **CAUTION: Electronic modules are sensitive to electrical charge. If exposed to these charges, damage may result.**	

FM9020100782010X

Fig. 54 Test E: Intermittent Wiper Speed Does Not Operate Properly, High & Low Speeds Functioning Properly (Part 1 of 7). Cougar

CONDITIONS	DETAILS/RESULTS/ACTIONS
E1 CHECK FOR VOLTAGE TO THE RELAY	
1 2 3  front wiper relay	
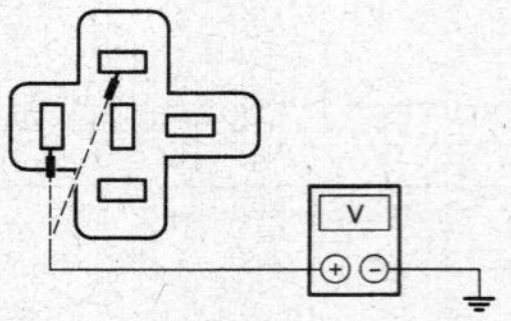	4 Measure the voltage between front wiper relay C72 pin 5, CJB and ground and between front wiper relay C72 pin 2, CJB and ground. • Is the voltage greater than 10 volts? → **Yes** GO to **E2.** → **No** INSTALL a new CJB. TEST the system for normal operation.
E2 CHECK THE FRONT WIPER RELAY	
1 	
	2 Check the front wiper relay • Is the front wiper relay OK? → **Yes** GO to **E3.** → **No** INSTALL an new front wiper relay. TEST the system for normal operation.

FM9020100782020X

Fig. 54 Test E: Intermittent Wiper Speed Does Not Operate Properly, High & Low Speeds Functioning Properly (Part 2 of 7). Cougar

CONDITIONS	DETAILS/RESULTS/ACTIONS
E3 CHECK THE CENTRAL JUNCTION BOX (CJB) FOR OPEN BETWEEN CENTRAL TIMER MODULE (CTM) AND FRONT WIPER RELAY SOCKET	
1  CTM 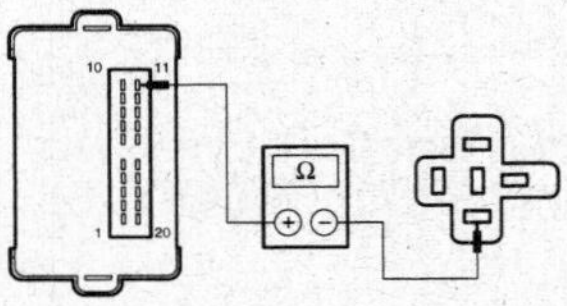	2 Measure the resistance between front wiper relay C72 pin 1, CJB and CTM C23 pin 11, CJB. • Is the resistance less than 5 ohms? → **Yes** GO to **E4.** → **No** INSTALL a new CJB. TEST the system for normal operation.
E4 CHECK THE WIPER/WASHER SWITCH	
1  wiper/washer switch C441	2 Check the wiper/washer switch • Is the wiper/washer switch OK? → **Yes** GO to **E5.** → **No** INSTALL a new wiper/washer switch. TEST the system for normal operation.

FM9020100782030X

Fig. 54 Test E: Intermittent Wiper Speed Does Not Operate Properly, High & Low Speeds Functioning Properly (Part 3 of 7). Cougar

CONDITIONS	DETAILS/RESULTS/ACTIONS
E6 CHECK THE CJB FOR OPEN AND SHORT TO GROUND BETWEEN THE FRONT WIPER RELAY AND CIRCUIT 32–AK19 (WH/BK)	
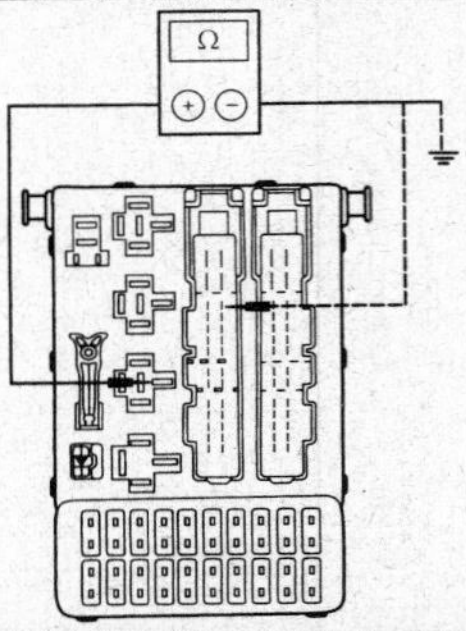	1 Measure the resistance between CJB C372 and front wiper relay C72 pin 3, CJB; and between front wiper relay C72 pin 3, CJB and ground. • Is the resistance less than 5 ohms between the two connectors and greater than 10,000 ohms between the front wiper relay connector and ground? → **Yes** GO to **E7.** → **No** INSTALL a new CJB. TEST the system for normal operation.
E7 CHECK CIRCUIT 8–AK19 (WH/BK) FOR OPEN	
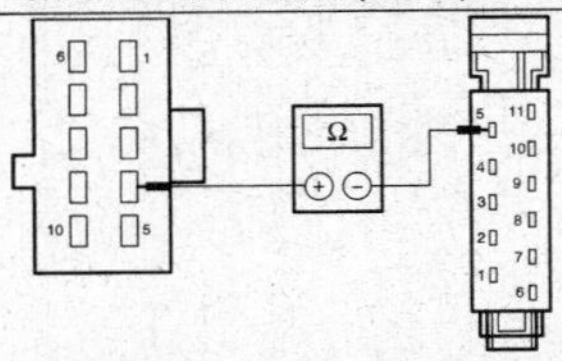	1 Measure the resistance between wiper/washer switch C441 pin 5, circuit 8–AK19 (WH/BK), harness side and CJB C372, circuit 8–AK19 (WH/BK), harness side. • Is the resistance less than 5 ohms? → **Yes** GO to **E8.** → **No** REPAIR circuit 8–AK18. TEST the system for normal operation.
E8 CHECK THE CJB FOR OPEN BETWEEN THE CTM AND CIRCUIT 8–AK19 (WH/BK)	
1  CJB C372	

FM9020100782050X

Fig. 54 Test E: Intermittent Wiper Speed Does Not Operate Properly, High & Low Speeds Functioning Properly (Part 5 of 7). Cougar

CONDITIONS	DETAILS/RESULTS/ACTIONS
E5 CHECK CIRCUIT 32–AK19 (WH/BK) FOR OPEN AND SHORT TO GROUND	
1  CJB C372 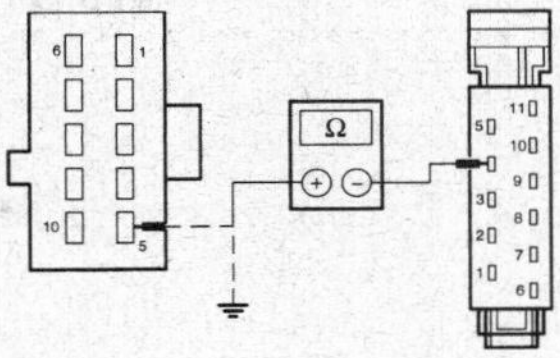	2 Measure the resistance between wiper/washer switch C441 pin 4, circuit 32–AK19 (WH/BK), harness side and CJB C372, circuit 32–AK19 (WH/BK), harness side; and between wiper/washer switch C441 pin 4, circuit 32-AK19 (WH/BK), harness side and ground. • Is the resistance less than 5 ohms between the two connectors and greater than 10,000 ohms between the wiper/washer switch connector and ground? → **Yes** GO to **E6.** → **No** REPAIR circuit 32–AK19. TEST the system for normal operation.

FM9020100782040X

Fig. 54 Test E: Intermittent Wiper Speed Does Not Operate Properly, High & Low Speeds Functioning Properly (Part 4 of 7). Cougar

CONDITIONS	DETAILS/RESULTS/ACTIONS
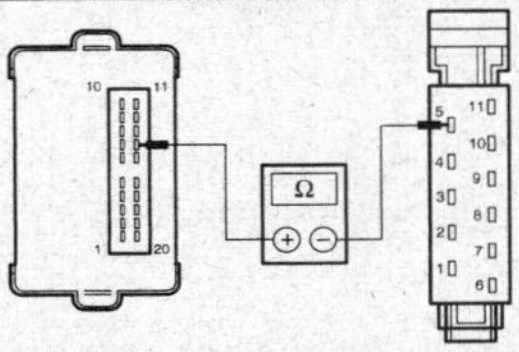	2 Measure the resistance between wiper/washer switch C441 pin 5, circuit 8–AK19 (WH/BK), harness side and CTM C23 pin 14, CJB. • Is the resistance less than 5 ohms? → **Yes** GO to **E9.** → **No** INSTALL a new CJB. TEST the system for normal operation.
E9 CHECK CIRCUIT 8–AK18 (WH) FOR OPEN	
1  CJB C372 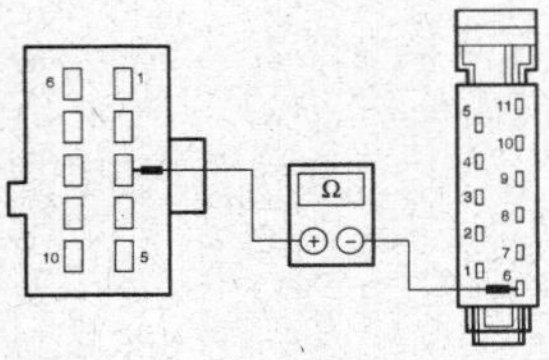	2 Measure the resistance between CJB C372, circuit 8–AK18 (WH), harness side and wiper/washer switch C441 pin 6, circuit 8–AK18 (WH), harness side. • Is the resistance less than 5 ohms? → **Yes** GO to **E10.** → **No** REPAIR circuit 8–AK18. TEST the system for normal operation.

FM9020100782060X

Fig. 54 Test E: Intermittent Wiper Speed Does Not Operate Properly, High & Low Speeds Functioning Properly (Part 6 of 7). Cougar

CONDITIONS	DETAILS/RESULTS/ACTIONS
E10 CHECK THE CJB FOR OPEN BETWEEN THE CTM AND CIRCUIT 8–AK18 (WH)	
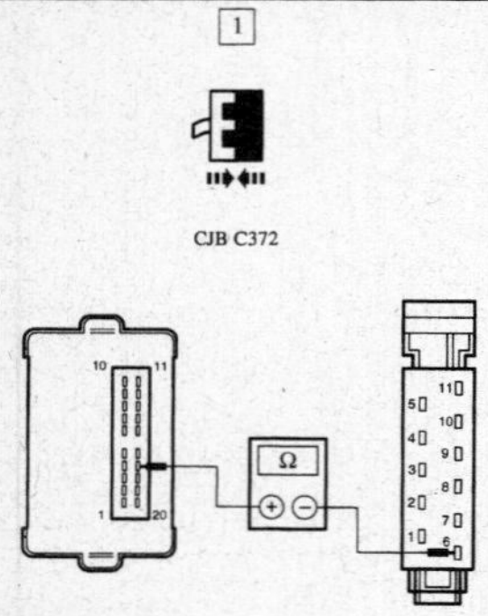	2 Measure the resistance between wiper/washer switch C441 pin 6, circuit 8–AK18 (WH), harness side and CTM C23 pin 17, CJB. • Is the resistance less than 5 ohms? → **Yes** INSTALL a new CTM. TEST the system for normal operation. → **No** INSTALL a new CJB. TEST the system for normal operation.

FM9020100782070X

Fig. 54 Test E: Intermittent Wiper Speed Does Not Operate Properly, High & Low Speeds Functioning Properly (Part 7 of 7). Cougar

CONDITIONS	DETAILS/RESULTS/ACTIONS
	3 Check the wiper/washer switch • Is the wiper/washer switch OK? → **Yes** GO to **F2.** → **No** INSTALL a new wiper/washer switch. TEST the system for normal operation.
F2 CHECK THE CENTRAL JUNCTION BOX (CJB) FOR OPEN BETWEEN CTM AND CIRCUIT 33–AK6 (YE/BK)	
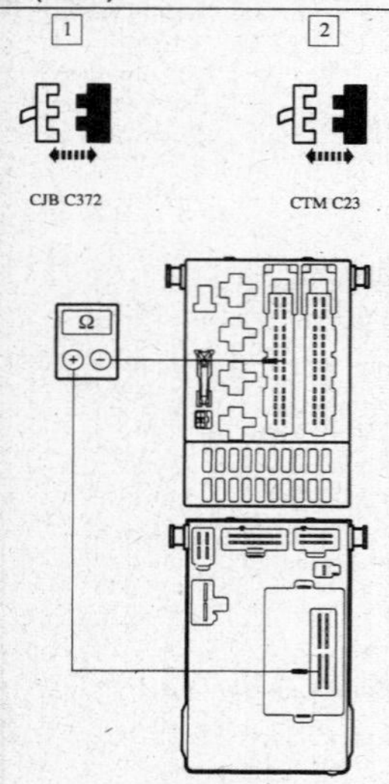	3 Measure the resistance between CJB C372 and CTM C23 pin 3, CJB. • Is the resistance less than 5 ohms? → **Yes** INSTALL a new CTM. TEST the system for normal operation. → **No** INSTALL a new CJB. TEST the system for normal operation.

FM9020100783020X

Fig. 55 Test F: Wash/Wipe Function Does Not Operate Properly (Part 2 of 2). Cougar

CONDITIONS	DETAILS/RESULTS/ACTIONS
⚠ **CAUTION: Electronic modules are sensitive to electrical charge. If exposed to these charges, damage may result.**	
F1 CHECK THE WIPER/WASHER SWITCH	

FM9020100783010X

Fig. 55 Test F: Wash/Wipe Function Does Not Operate Properly (Part 1 of 2). Cougar

CONDITIONS	DETAILS/RESULTS/ACTIONS
⚠ **CAUTION: Electronic modules are sensitive to electrical charge. If exposed to these charges, damage may result.**	
G1 DETECT NEED OF MECHANICAL ADJUSTMENT	
	1 Detect need of mechanical adjustment. • Do the wipers park always at the same postion? → **Yes** **Adjust Wiper Linkage** → **No** GO to **G2.**
G2 DETERMINE FUNCTION OF INTERMITTENT WIPE	
	1 Determine function of the intermittent wipe. • Does the intermittent wipe function operate? → **Yes** GO to **G3.** → **No** GO to Pinpoint Test E.
G3 CHECK CIRCUIT 32–AK9 (WH/BU) FOR VOLTAGE	
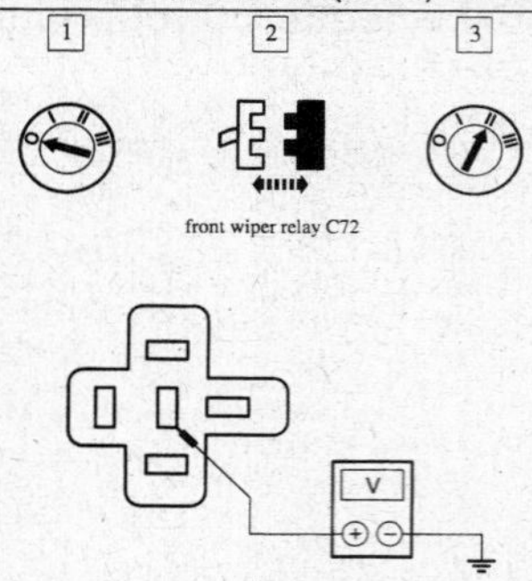	4 Measure the voltage between front wiper relay C72 pin 4, CJB and ground. • Is the voltage greater than 10 volts? → **Yes** INSTALL a new wiper/washer switch. TEST the system for normal operation. → **No** GO to **G4.**

FM9020100784010X

Fig. 56 Test G: Wipers Will Not Park At Correct Position (Part 1 of 4). Cougar

CONDITIONS	DETAILS/RESULTS/ACTIONS
G4 CHECK CIRCUIT 14–AK9 (VT) FOR VOLTAGE	
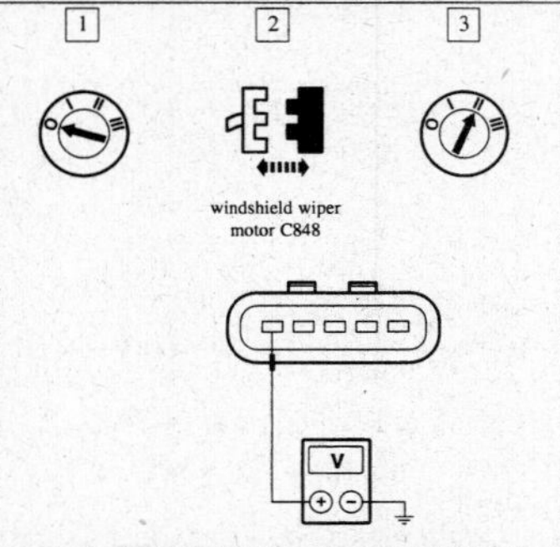	4 Measure the voltage between wiper motor C848, circuit 14–AK9 (VT), harness side and ground. • Is the voltage greater than 10 volts? → **Yes** GO to **G6.** → **No** GO to **G5.**
G5 CHECK CIRCUIT 14–AK9 (VT) FOR OPEN	
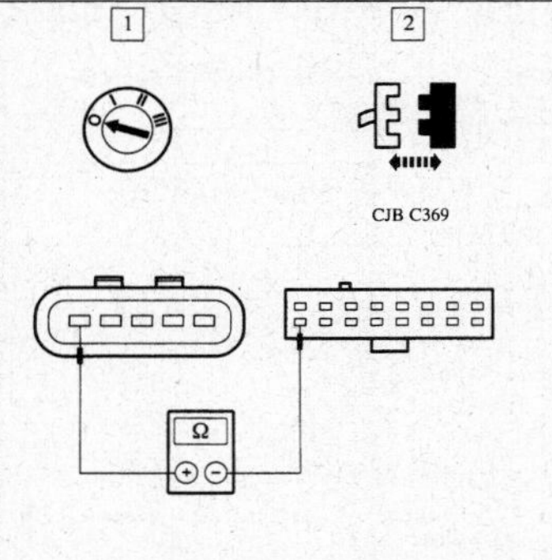	3 Measure the resistance between CJB C369, circuit 14–AK9 (VT), harness side and wiper motor C848, circuit 14–AK9 (VT), harness side. • Is the resistance less than 5 ohms? → **Yes** INSTALL a new CJB. TEST the system for normal operation. → **No** REPAIR circuit 14–AK9. TEST the system for normal operation.

FM9020100784020X

Fig. 56 Test G: Wipers Will Not Park At Correct Position (Part 2 of 4). Cougar

CONDITIONS	DETAILS/RESULTS/ACTIONS
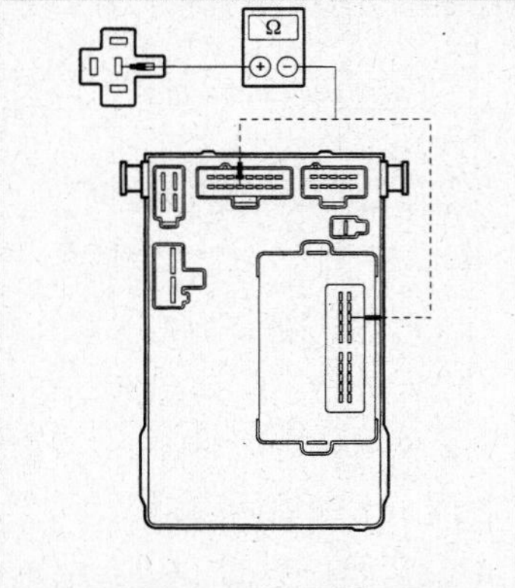	2 Measure the resistance between front wiper relay pin 4, CJB and CJB C369, and between front wiper relay pin 4, CJB and CTM, C23 pin 13, CJB. • Is the resistance less than 5 ohms? → **Yes** GO to **G9.** → **No** INSTALL a new CJB. TEST the system for normal operation.
G9 CHECK THE WINDSHIELD WIPER MOTOR	
	1 Check the wiper motor • Is the wiper motor OK? → **Yes** INSTALL a new CTM. TEST the system for normal operation. → **No** INSTALL a new wiper motor. TEST the system for normal operation.

FM9020100784040X

Fig. 56 Test G: Wipers Will Not Park At Correct Position (Part 4 of 4). Cougar

CONDITIONS	DETAILS/RESULTS/ACTIONS
G6 CHECK CIRCUIT 32–AK9 (WH/BU) FOR OPEN AND SHORT TO GROUND	
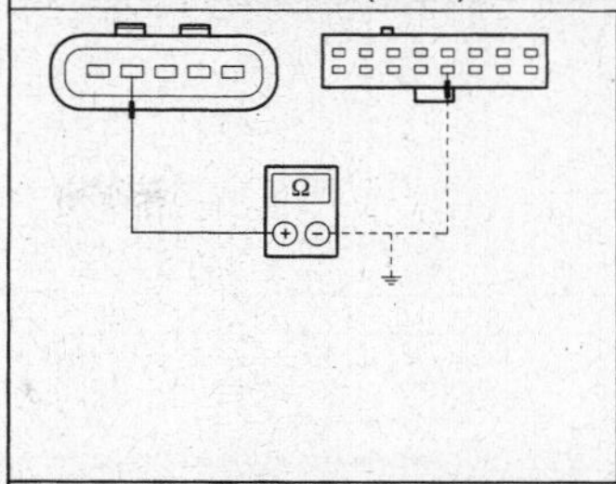	1 Measure the resistance between wiper motor C848, circuit 32–AK9 (WH/BU), harness side and CJB C369, circuit 32–AK9 (WH/BU), harness side; and between wiper motor C848, circuit 32–AK9 (WH/BU), harness side and ground. • Is the resistance less than 5 ohms between the two connectors and greater than 10,000 ohms between the wiper motor connector and ground? → **Yes** GO to **G7.** → **No** REPAIR circuit 32–AK9. TEST the system for normal operation.
G7 CHECK POSITION SWITCH GROUND FOR OPEN – CIRCUIT 31–AK8 (BK)	
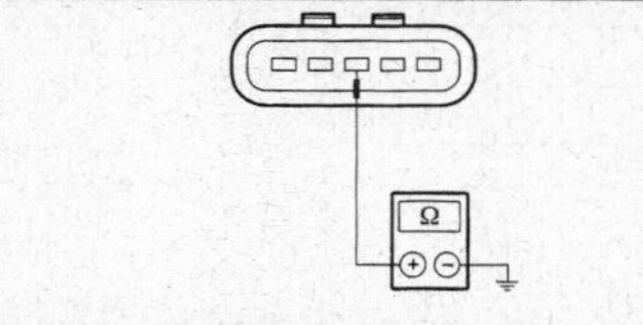	1 Measure the resistance between wiper motor C848, circuit 31–AK8 (BK), harness side and ground. • Is the resistance less than 5 ohms? → **Yes** GO to **G8.** → **No** REPAIR circuit 31–AK8. TEST the system for normal operation.
G8 CHECK THE CJB FOR OPEN	
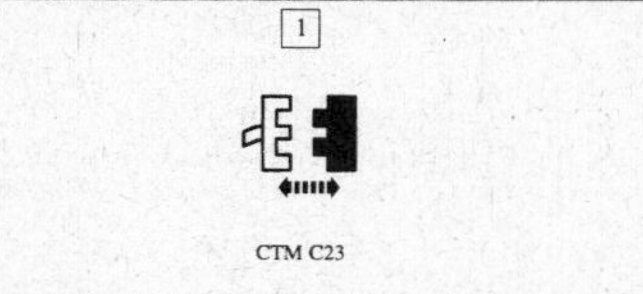	

FM9020100784030X

Fig. 56 Test G: Wipers Will Not Park At Correct Position (Part 3 of 4). Cougar

CONDITIONS	DETAILS/RESULTS/ACTIONS
⚠ **CAUTION: Electronic modules are sensitive to electrical charge. If exposed to these charges, damage may result.**	

FM9020100785010X

Fig. 57 Test H: Washer Pump Is Inoperative (Part 1 of 5). Cougar

CONDITIONS	DETAILS/RESULTS/ACTIONS
H1 DETERMINE FUNCTION OF THE WASHER	
	1 Determine function of the washer. • Are both front and rear washers inoperative? → **Yes** GO to **H2.** → **No** INSTALL a new wiper/washer switch. TEST the system for normal operation.
H2 CHECK WASHER PUMP FOR OPERATION	
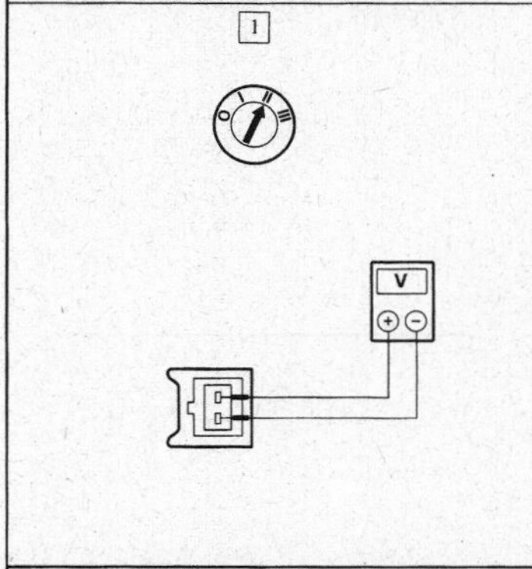	2 Measure the voltage between washer pump C828 pin 2, circuit 32–AK34 (WH/BK), harness side and washer pump C828 pin 1, circuit 33–AK34 (YE/BK), harness side while holding the wiper/washer switch in the rear washer position. • Is the voltage greater than 10 volts? → **Yes** INSTALL a new washer pump. TEST the system for normal operation. → **No** GO to **H3.**
H3 CHECK THE WIPER/WASHER SWITCH	
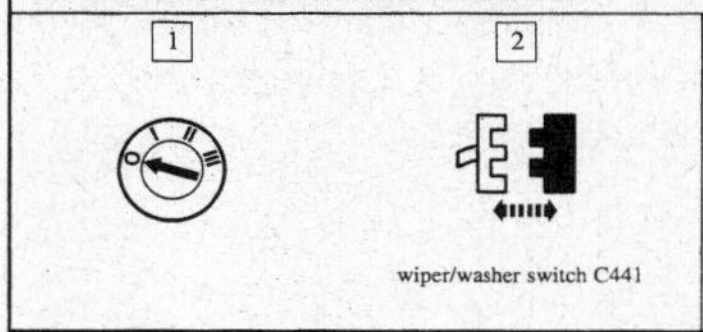	

FM9020100785020X

Fig. 57 Test H: Washer Pump Is Inoperative (Part 2 of 5). Cougar

CONDITIONS	DETAILS/RESULTS/ACTIONS
	3 Check the wiper/washer switch • Is the wiper/washer switch OK? → **Yes** GO to **H4.** → **No** INSTALL a new wiper/washer switch. TEST the system for normal operation.
H4 CHECK CIRCUIT 31–AK18 (BK) FOR OPEN	
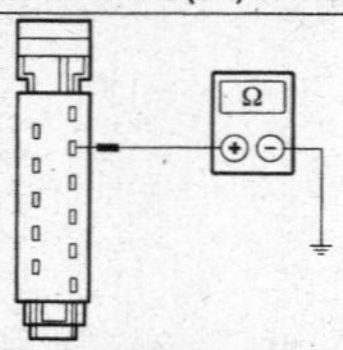	1 Measure the resistance between wiper/washer switch C441 pin 10, circuit 31–AK19 (BK), harness side and ground. • Is the resistance less than 5 ohms? → **Yes** GO to **H5.** → **No** REPAIR circuit 31–AK19. TEST the system for normal operation.
H5 CHECK CIRCUIT 32–AK34 (WH/BK) FOR OPEN	
1  washer pump C828	
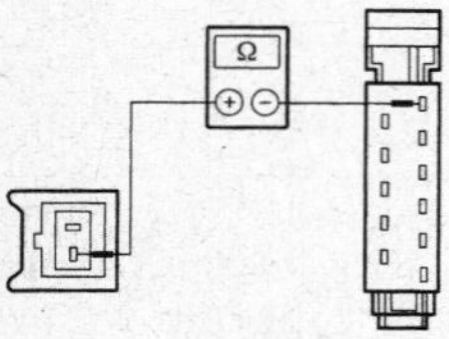	2 Measure the resistance between wiper/washer switch C441 pin 11, circuit 32–AK34 (WH/BK), harness side and washer pump C828 pin 2, circuit 32–AK34 (WH/BK), harness side. • Is the resistance less than 5 ohms? → **Yes** GO to **H6.** → **No** REPAIR circuit 32–AK34. TEST the system for normal operation.

FM9020100785030X

Fig. 57 Test H: Washer Pump Is Inoperative (Part 3 of 5). Cougar

CONDITIONS	DETAILS/RESULTS/ACTIONS
H7 CHECK CJB FOR OPEN	
1  CJB C369	
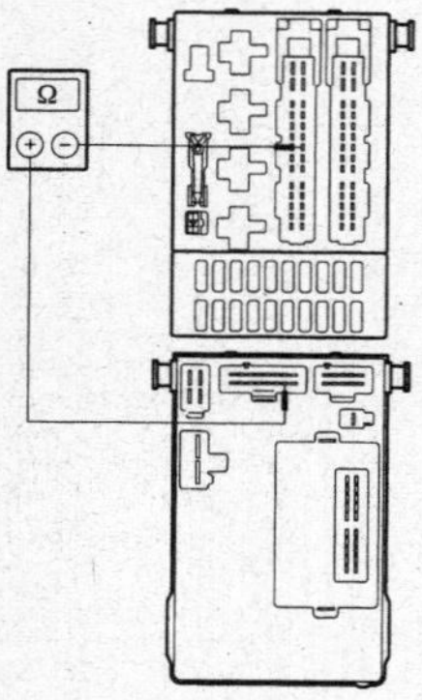	2 Measure the resistance between CJB C372 and CJB C369. • Is the resistance less than 5 ohms? → **Yes** REPAIR circuit 33–AK34. TEST the system for normal operation. → **No** INSTALL a new CJB. TEST the system for normal operation.

FM9020100785050X

Fig. 57 Test H: Washer Pump Is Inoperative (Part 5 of 5). Cougar

CONDITIONS	DETAILS/RESULTS/ACTIONS
H6 CHECK CIRCUIT 33–AK6 (YE/BK) FOR OPEN	
1  CJB C372	
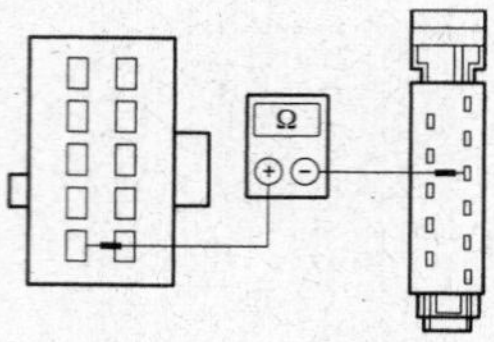	2 Measure the resistance between wiper/washer switch C441 pin 9, circuit 33–AK6 (YE/BK), harness side and CJB C372, circuit 33–AK6 (YE/BK), harness side. • Is the resistance less than 5 ohms? → **Yes** GO to **H7.** → **No** REPAIR circuit 33–AK6. TEST the system for normal operation.

FM9020100785040X

Fig. 57 Test H: Washer Pump Is Inoperative (Part 4 of 5). Cougar

CONDITIONS	DETAILS/RESULTS/ACTIONS
A1 CHECK THE WASHER PUMP OPERATION	
1 	2 Press the wash button on the multifunction switch. • Does the washer pump motor operate correctly? → **Yes** GO to **A2.** → **No** GO to **A3.**

FM9020100880010X

Fig. 58 Test A: Washer Pump Inoperative (Part 1 of 4). 2000–02 Crown Victoria & Grand Marquis

CONDITIONS	DETAILS/RESULTS/ACTIONS
A2 INSPECT FOR BLOCKAGE OR OBSTRUCTION	
	1 Inspect the washer nozzle, washer hoses, and the washer pump for blockages or obstructions. • Are any blockages or obstructions present? → **Yes** INSTALL a new component or REPAIR as necessary. TEST the system for normal operation. → **No** INSTALL a new washer pump motor. TEST the system for normal operation.
A3 CHECK THE WASHER PUMP MOTOR FOR VOLTAGE—CIRCUIT 941 (BK/WH)	
1 2 3  Washer Pump Motor	
4 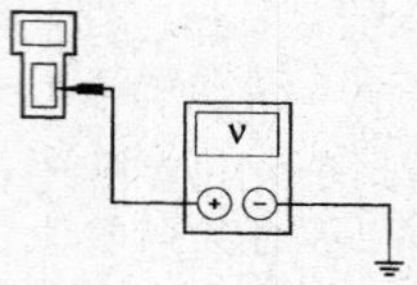	4 Press the wash button on the multifunction switch while measuring the voltage between washer pump motor (BK/WH), harness side and ground. • Is the voltage greater than 10 volts? → **Yes** GO to **A4.** → **No** GO to **A5.**

FM9020100880020X

Fig. 58 Test A: Washer Pump Inoperative (Part 2 of 4). 2000–02 Crown Victoria & Grand Marquis

CONDITIONS	DETAILS/RESULTS/ACTIONS
A4 CHECK THE WASHER PUMP MOTOR GROUND	
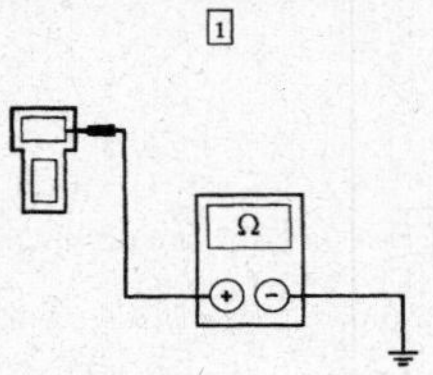	1 Measure the resistance between washer pump motor (BK), harness side and ground. • Is the resistance less than 5 ohms? → **Yes** INSTALL a new washer pump motor. TEST the system for normal operation. → **No** REPAIR circuit 57 (BK). TEST the system for normal operation.
A5 CHECK CIRCUIT 941 (BK/WH) FOR SHORT TO GROUND	
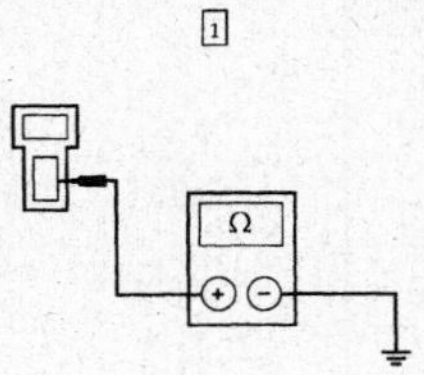	1 Measure the resistance between washer pump motor (BK/WH), harness side and ground. • Is the resistance greater than 10,000 ohms? → **Yes** INSTALL a new multifunction switch. TEST the system for normal operation. → **No** GO to **A6**.
A6 CHECK CIRCUIT 941 (BK/WH) FOR OPEN	
 Wiper Control Module C2157	

FM9020100880030X

Fig. 58 Test A: Washer Pump Inoperative (Part 3 of 4). 2000–02 Crown Victoria & Grand Marquis

CONDITIONS	DETAILS/RESULTS/ACTIONS
A6 CHECK CIRCUIT 941 (BK/WH) FOR OPEN (Continued)	
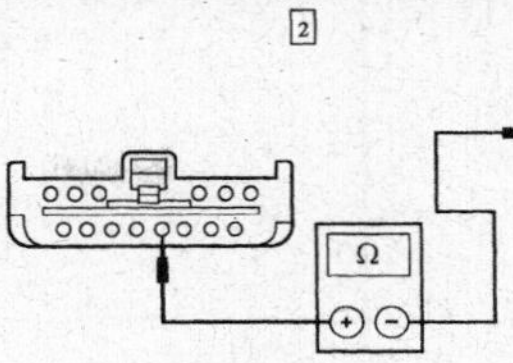	2 Measure the resistance between wiper control module C2157 pin 4, circuit 941 (BK/WH), harness side and washer pump motor C137, circuit 941 (BK/WH), harness side. • Is the resistance less than 5 ohms? → **Yes** INSTALL a new wiper control module. → **No** REPAIR circuit (BK/WH). TEST the system for normal operation.

FM9020100880040X

Fig. 58 Test A: Washer Pump Inoperative (Part 4 of 4). 2000–02 Crown Victoria & Grand Marquis

CONDITIONS	DETAILS/RESULTS/ACTIONS
B1 CHECK THE WIPER CONTROL MODULE FOR SHORT TO POWER	
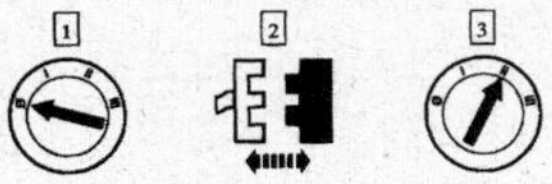 Wiper Control Module	• Does the washer pump motor operate? → **Yes** GO to **B2**. → **No** RECONNECT the wiper control module. GO to **B3**.

FM9020100881010X

Fig. 59 Test B: Washer Pump Inoperative Runs Continuously (Part 1 of 2). 2000–02 Crown Victoria & Grand Marquis

CONDITIONS	DETAILS/RESULTS/ACTIONS
B2 CHECK CIRCUIT 941 (BK/WH) FOR SHORT TO POWER	
 Washer Pump Motor	• Does the washer pump motor operate? → **Yes** INSTALL a new washer pump motor. TEST the system for normal operation. → **No** REPAIR circuit 941 (BK/WH). TEST the system for normal operation.
B3 CHECK MULTIFUNCTION SWITCH	
 Multifunction Switch	• Does the washer pump motor operate? → **Yes** INSTALL a new wiper control module. TEST the system for normal operation. → **No** INSTALL a new multifunction switch. TEST the system for normal operation.

FM9020100881020X

Fig. 59 Test B: Washer Pump Inoperative Runs Continuously (Part 2 of 2). 2000–02 Crown Victoria & Grand Marquis

CONDITIONS	DETAILS/RESULTS/ACTIONS
C1 CHECK FOR VOLTAGE TO THE WIPER CONTROL MODULE — CIRCUIT 65 (DG)	
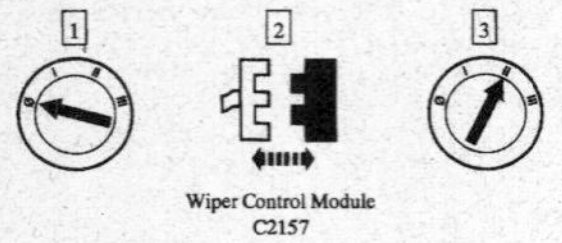	
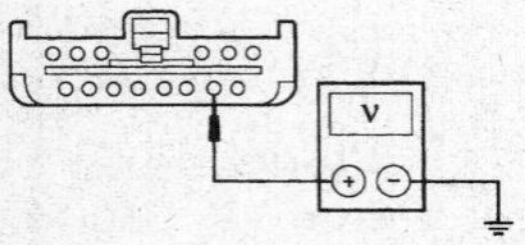	4 Measure the voltage between wiper control module (DG), harness side and ground. • Is the voltage greater than 10 volts? → **Yes** GO to **C2**. → **No** REPAIR (DG). TEST the system for normal operation.
C2 CHECK CIRCUIT 57 (BK) FOR OPEN	

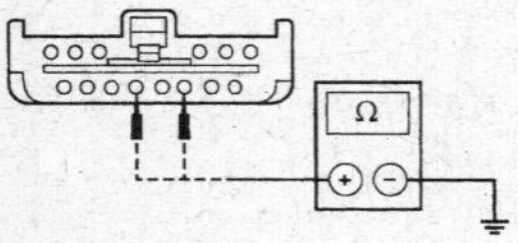	2 Measure the resistance between wiper control module (BK), harness side and ground; and between wiper control module (BK), harness side and ground. • Is the resistance less than 5 ohms? → **Yes** GO to **C3**. → **No** REPAIR (BK). TEST the system for normal operation.

FM9020100882010X

Fig. 60 Test C: Wipers Are Inoperative (Part 1 of 4). 2000–02 Crown Victoria & Grand Marquis

CONDITIONS	DETAILS/RESULTS/ACTIONS
C5 CHECK CIRCUIT 589 (OG) FOR OPEN	
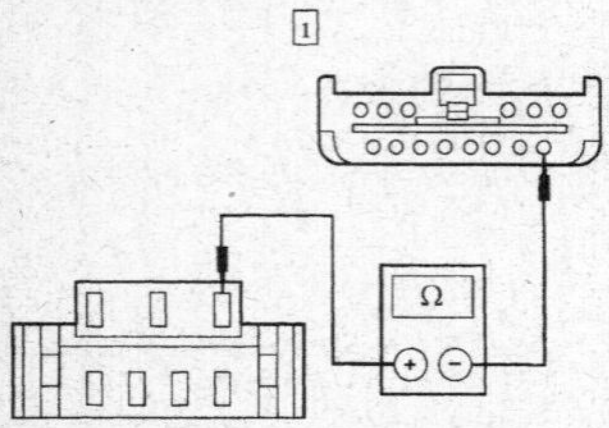	1 Measure the resistance between multifunction switch (OG), harness side and wiper control module (OG), harness side. • Is the resistance less than 5 ohms? → **Yes** INSTALL a new multifunction switch. TEST the system for normal operation. → **No** REPAIR(OG). TEST the system for normal operation.
C6 CHECK THE WIPER CONTROL MODULE OUTPUT FOR VOLTAGE	
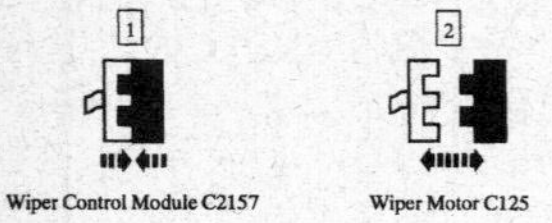	3 Turn the multifunction switch to the HI position.

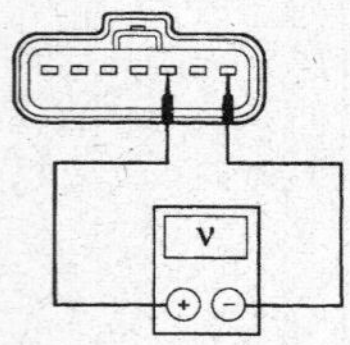	5 Measure the voltage between wiper motor harness side and wiper), motor (WH), harness side. • Is the voltage greater than 10 volts? → **Yes** CARRY OUT the Windshield Wiper Motor Test. TEST the system for normal operation. → **No** GO to **C7**.

FM9020100882030X

Fig. 60 Test C: Wipers Are Inoperative (Part 3 of 4). 2000–02 Crown Victoria & Grand Marquis

CONDITIONS	DETAILS/RESULTS/ACTIONS
C3 CHECK MULTIFUNCTION SWITCH OUTPUT	
	2 Turn the multifunction switch to the HI position.
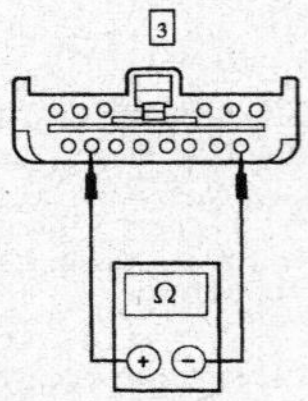	3 Measure the resistance between wiper control module (BN/WH), harness side and wiper control module (OG), harness side. • Is the resistance less than 5 ohms? → **Yes** GO to **C6**. → **No** GO to **C4**.
C4 CHECK CIRCUIT 993 (BN/WH) FOR OPEN	
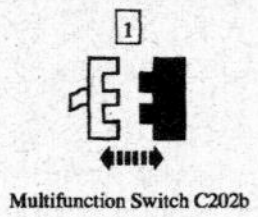	
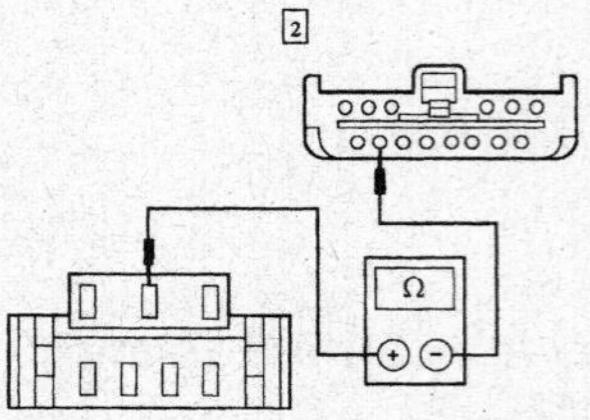	2 Measure the resistance between multifunction switch (BN/WH), harness side and wiper control module (BN/WH), harness side. • Is the resistance less than 5 ohms? → **Yes** GO to **C5**. → **No** REPAIR circuit 993 (BN/WH). TEST the system for normal operation.

FM9020100882020X

Fig. 60 Test C: Wipers Are Inoperative (Part 2 of 4). 2000–02 Crown Victoria & Grand Marquis

CONDITIONS	DETAILS/RESULTS/ACTIONS
C7 CHECK CIRCUIT 61 (YE/RD) FOR OPEN	
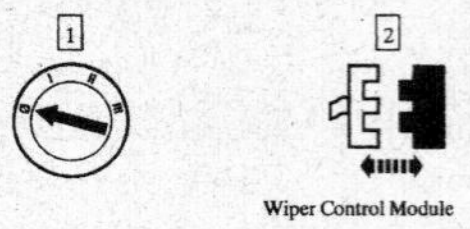	
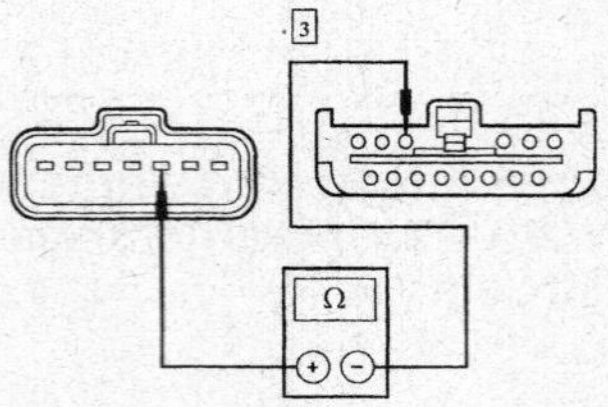	3 Measure the resistance between wiper motor C125 (YE/RD), harness side and wiper control module (Y/RD), harness side. • Is the resistance less than 5 ohms? → **Yes** INSTALL a new wiper control module. TEST the system for normal operation. → **No** REPAIR circuit 61 (YE/RD). TEST the system for normal operation.

FM9020100882040X

Fig. 60 Test C: Wipers Are Inoperative (Part 4 of 4). 2000–02 Crown Victoria & Grand Marquis

CONDITIONS	DETAILS/RESULTS/ACTIONS
D1 CHECK THE VOLTAGE TO THE WIPER MOTOR — CIRCUIT 58 (WH)	
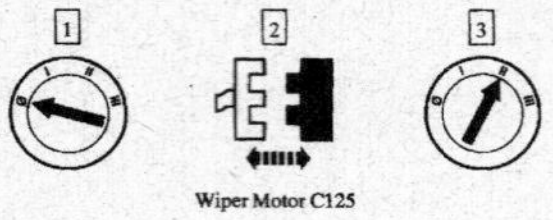	4 Turn the multifunction switch to the HI position.

FM9020100883010X

Fig. 61 Test D: High Wiper Speeds Do Not Operate Correctly (Part 1 of 3). 2000–02 Crown Victoria & Grand Marquis

CONDITIONS	DETAILS/RESULTS/ACTIONS
D1 CHECK THE VOLTAGE TO THE WIPER MOTOR — CIRCUIT 58 (WH) (Continued)	
5 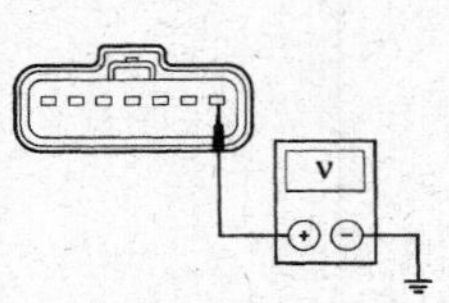	5 Measure the voltage between wiper motor C125 pin 7, circuit 58 (WH), harness side and ground. • Is the voltage greater than 10 volts? → **Yes** CARRY OUT the Windshield Wiper Motor Test. TEST the system for normal operation. → **No** GO to **D2**.
D2 CHECK CIRCUIT 58 (WH) FOR OPEN	
1 2 3 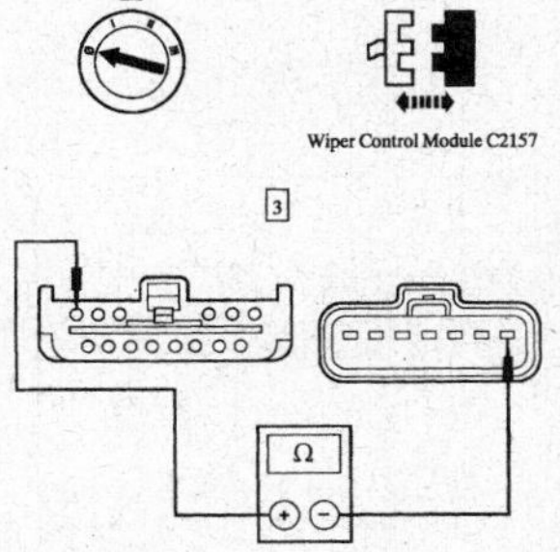	3 Measure the resistance between wiper control module C2157 pin 14, circuit 58 (WH), harness side and wiper motor C125 pin 7, circuit 58 (WH), harness side. • Is the resistance less than 5 ohms? → **Yes** GO to **D3**. → **No** REPAIR circuit 58 (WH). TEST the system for normal operation.

FM9020100883020X

Fig. 61 Test D: High Wiper Speeds Do Not Operate Correctly (Part 2 of 3). 2000–02 Crown Victoria & Grand Marquis

CONDITIONS	DETAILS/RESULTS/ACTIONS
D3 CHECK CIRCUIT 58 (WH) FOR SHORT TO GROUND	
1 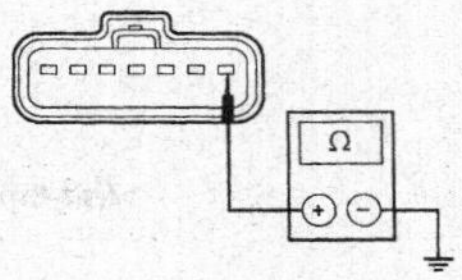	1 Measure the resistance between wiper motor (WH), harness side and ground. • Is the resistance greater than 10,000 ohms? → **Yes** GO to **D4**. → **No** REPAIR (WH). TEST the system for normal operation.
D4 CHECK MULTIFUNCTION SWITCH INPUT	
2 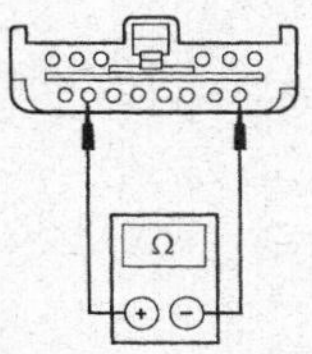	1 Turn the multifunction switch to the HI position. 2 Measure the resistance between wiper control module (OG), harness side and wiper control module (BN/WH), harness side. • Is the resistance less than 5 ohms? → **Yes** INSTALL a new wiper control module. TEST the system for normal operation. → **No** INSTALL a new multifunction switch. TEST the system for normal operation.

FM9020100883030X

Fig. 61 Test D: High Wiper Speeds Do Not Operate Correctly (Part 3 of 3). 2000–02 Crown Victoria & Grand Marquis

CONDITIONS	DETAILS/RESULTS/ACTIONS
E1 CHECK FOR VOLTAGE TO WIPER MOTOR — CIRCUIT 56 (DB/OG)	
1 2 	3 Turn the multifunction switch to the LO position.

FM9020100884010X

Fig. 62 Test E: Low Wiper Speeds Do Not Operate Correctly (Part 1 of 3). 2000–02 Crown Victoria & Grand Marquis

CONDITIONS	DETAILS/RESULTS/ACTIONS
E1 CHECK FOR VOLTAGE TO WIPER MOTOR — CIRCUIT 56 (DB/OG) (Continued)	
4 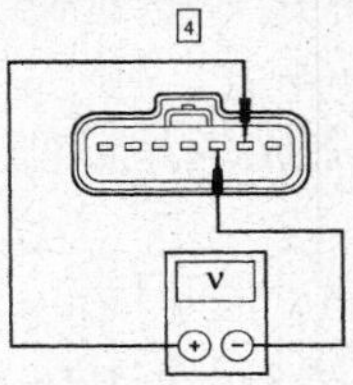	4 Measure the voltage between wiper motor (DB/OG), harness side and wiper motor (YE/RD), harness side. • Is the voltage greater than 10 volts? → **Yes** CARRY OUT the Windshield Wiper Motor Test. TEST the system for normal operation. → **No** GO to **E2**.
E2 CHECK CIRCUIT 56 (DB/OG) FOR SHORT TO GROUND	
1 2 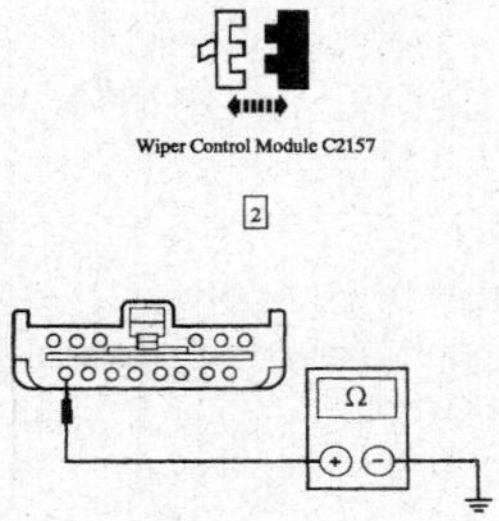	2 Measure the resistance between wiper control module (DB/OG), harness side and ground. • Is the resistance greater than 10,000 ohms? → **Yes** GO to **E3**. → **No** REPAIR (DB/OG). TEST the system for normal operation.

FM9020100884020X

Fig. 62 Test E: Low Wiper Speeds Do Not Operate Correctly (Part 2 of 3). 2000–02 Crown Victoria & Grand Marquis

CONDITIONS	DETAILS/RESULTS/ACTIONS
E3 CHECK CIRCUIT 56 (DB/OG) FOR OPEN	
1 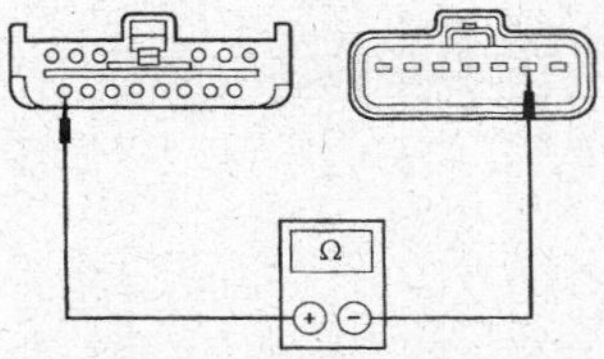	1 Measure the resistance between wiper control module (DB/OG), harness side and wiper motor (DB/OG), harness side. • Is the resistance less than 5 ohms? → **Yes** GO to **E4**. → **No** REPAIR (DB/OG). TEST the system for normal operation.
E4 CHECK THE MULTIFUNCTION SWITCH INPUT	
2 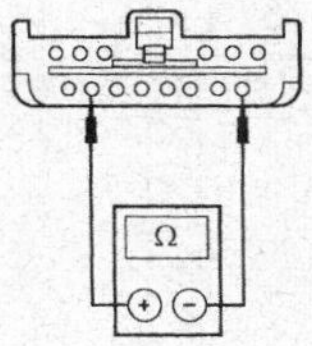	1 Turn the multifunction switch (wiper/washer switch) to the LO position. 2 Measure the resistance between wiper control module (BN/WH), harness side and wiper control module (OG), harness side. • Is the resistance between 3,500 and 4,500 ohms? → **Yes** INSTALL a new wiper control module. TEST the system for normal operation. → **No** INSTALL a new multifunction switch. TEST the system for normal operation.

FM9020100884030X

Fig. 62 Test E: Low Wiper Speeds Do Not Operate Correctly (Part 3 of 3). 2000–02 Crown Victoria & Grand Marquis

CONDITIONS	DETAILS/RESULTS/ACTIONS
F1 CHECK THE MULTIFUNCTION SWITCH INTERVAL INPUT TO THE WASHER CONTROL MODULE	
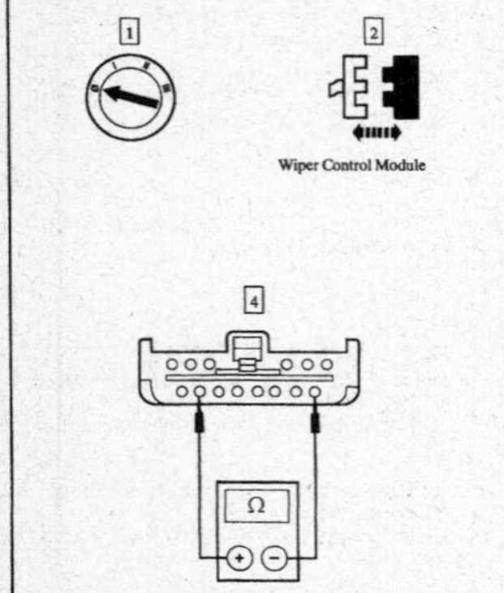	3 Turn the multifunction switch interval to the INT position. 4 Measure the resistance between wiper control module (BN/WH), harness side and wiper control module (OG), harness side. • Is the resistance between 10,500 and 12,000 ohms? → **Yes** GO to **F2**. → **No** INSTALL a new multifunction switch. TEST the system for normal operation.
F2 CHECK THE INTERVAL SETTING INPUT	
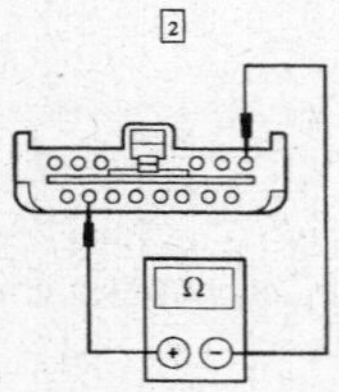	1 Turn the multifunction switch to any interval position. 2 Measure the resistance between wiper control module (BN/WH), harness side and wiper control module (DB/WH), harness side. • Is the resistance between 3,300 and 10,000 ohms? → **Yes** INSTALL a new wiper control module. TEST the system for normal operation. → **No** GO to **F3**.

FM9020100885010X

Fig. 63 Test F: Intermittent Wiper Speed Does Not Operate Correctly (Part 1 of 2). 2000–02 Crown Victoria & Grand Marquis

CONDITIONS	DETAILS/RESULTS/ACTIONS
G1 CHECK CIRCUIT 57 (BK) FOR OPEN	
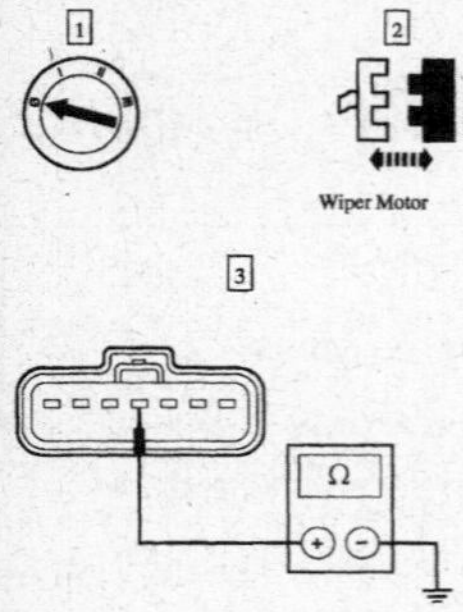	3 Measure the resistance between wiper motor (BK), harness side and ground. • Is the resistance less than 5 ohms? → **Yes** GO to **G2**. → **No** REPAIR (BK). TEST the system for normal operation.
G2 CHECK THE WIPER MOTOR FOR VOLTAGE — CIRCUIT 65 (DG)	
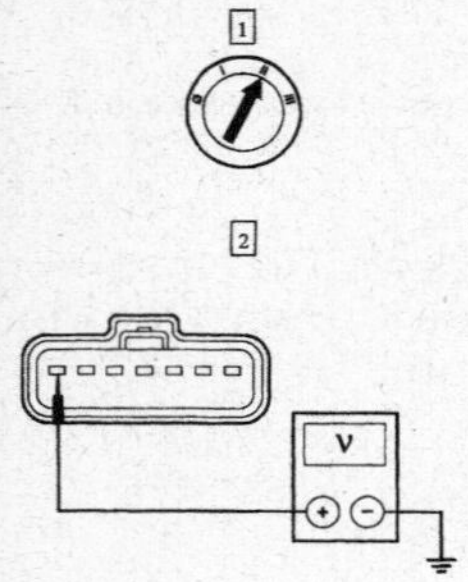	2 Measure the voltage between wiper motor (DG), harness side and ground. • Is the voltage greater than 10 volts? → **Yes** GO to **G3**. → **No** REPAIR (DG). TEST the system for normal operation.

FM9020100886010X

Fig. 64 Test G: Wipers Will Not Park At The Correct Position (Part 1 of 3). 2000–02 Crown Victoria & Grand Marquis

CONDITIONS	DETAILS/RESULTS/ACTIONS
F3 CHECK CIRCUIT 590 (DB/WH) FOR SHORT TO GROUND	
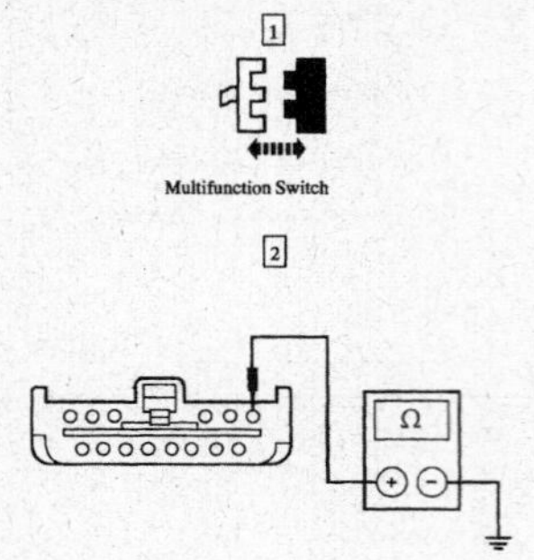	2 Measure the resistance between wiper control module (DB/WH), harness side and ground. • Is the resistance greater than 10,000 ohms? → **Yes** GO to **F4**. → **No** REPAIR (DB/WH). TEST the system for normal operation.
F4 CHECK CIRCUIT 590 (DB/WH) FOR OPEN	
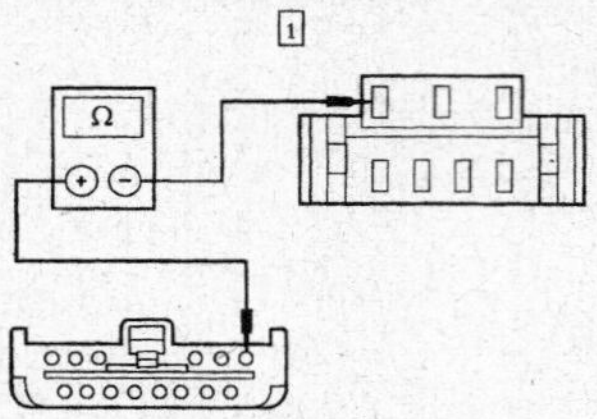	1 Measure the resistance between wiper control module (DB/WH), harness side and multifunction switch C202b pin 6, (DB/WH), harness side. • Is the resistance less than 5 ohms? → **Yes** INSTALL a new multifunction switch. TEST the system for normal operation. → **No** REPAIR (DB/WH). TEST the system for normal operation.

FM9020100885020X

Fig. 63 Test F: Intermittent Wiper Speed Does Not Operate Correctly (Part 2 of 2). 2000–02 Crown Victoria & Grand Marquis

CONDITIONS	DETAILS/RESULTS/ACTIONS
G3 CHECK CIRCUIT 63 (RD) FOR OPEN	
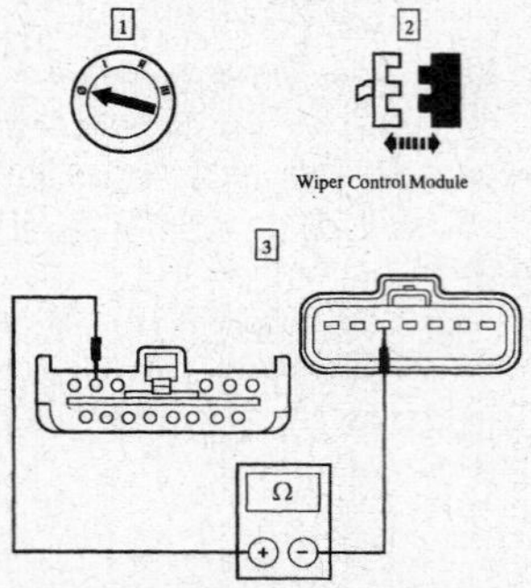	3 Measure the resistance between wiper control module (RD), harness side and wiper motor (RD), harness side. • Is the resistance less than 5 ohms? → **Yes** GO to **G4**. → **No** REPAIR (RD). TEST the system for normal operation.
G4 CHECK CIRCUIT 63 (RD) FOR SHORT TO GROUND	
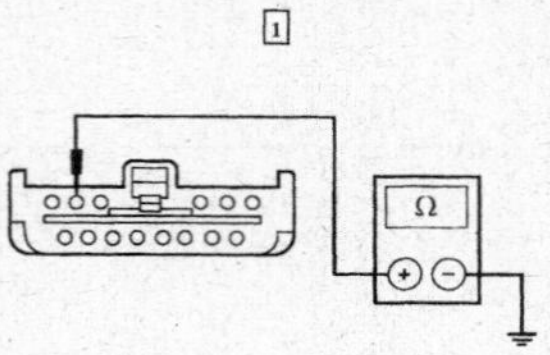	1 Measure the resistance between wiper control module C2157 pin 13, circuit 63 (RD), harness side and ground. • Is the resistance greater than 10,000 ohms? → **Yes** GO to **G5**. → **No** REPAIR circuit 63 (RD). TEST the system for normal operation.

FM9020100886020X

Fig. 64 Test G: Wipers Will Not Park At The Correct Position (Part 2 of 3). 2000–02 Crown Victoria & Grand Marquis

CONDITIONS	DETAILS/RESULTS/ACTIONS
G5 CHECK CIRCUIT 28 (BK/PK) FOR OPEN	
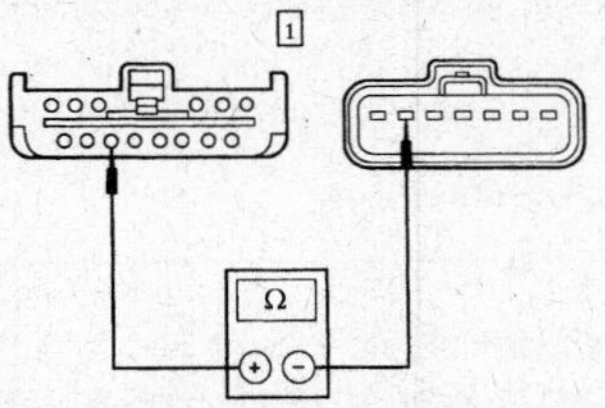	1 Measure the resistance between wiper control module (BK/PK), harness side and wiper motor (BK/PK), harness side. • Is the resistance less than 5 ohms? → **Yes** GO to **G6**. → **No** REPAIR (BK/PK). TEST the system for normal operation.
G6 CHECK CIRCUIT 28 (BK/PK) FOR SHORT TO GROUND	
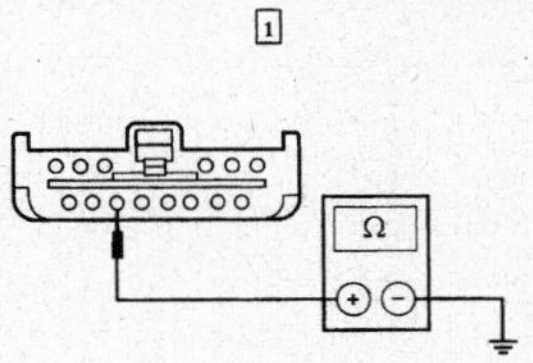	1 Measure the resistance between wiper control module C2157 pin 6, circuit 28 (BK/PK), harness side and ground. • Is the resistance greater than 10,000 ohms? → **Yes** INSTALL a new wiper control module. TEST the system for normal operation. → **No** REPAIR circuit 28 (BK/PK). TEST the system for normal operation.

FM9020100886030X

Fig. 64 Test G: Wipers Will Not Park At The Correct Position (Part 3 of 3). 2000–02 Crown Victoria & Grand Marquis

CONDITIONS	DETAILS/RESULTS/ACTIONS
H1 CHECK CIRCUIT 589 (OG) FOR SHORT TO GROUND (Continued)	
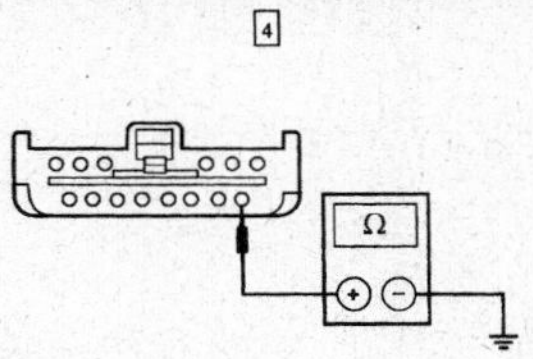	4 Measure the resistance between wiper control module (OG), harness side and ground. • Is the resistance greater than 10,000 ohms? → **Yes** GO to **H2**. → **No** REPAIR (OG). TEST the system for normal operation.
H2 CHECK CIRCUIT 993 (BN/WH) FOR SHORT TO GROUND	
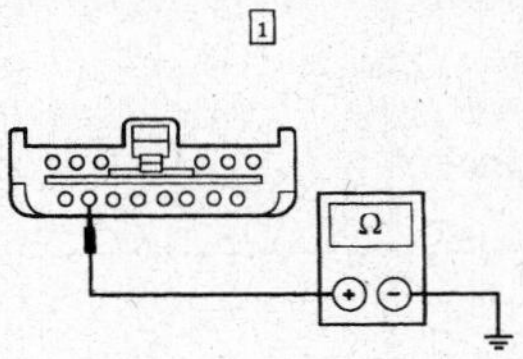	1 Measure the resistance between wiper control module (BN/WH), harness side and ground. • Is the resistance greater than 10,000 ohms? → **Yes** RECONNECT the multifunction switch. GO to **H3**. → **No** REPAIR (BN/WH). TEST the system for normal operation.
H3 CHECK THE MULTIFUNCTION SWITCH FOR SHORT TO GROUND	
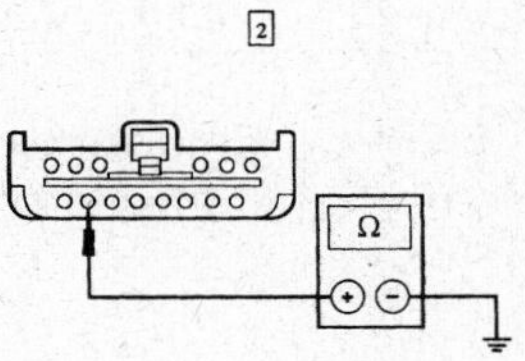	1 Turn the multifunction switch to the HI position. 2 Measure the resistance between wiper control module (BN/WH), harness side and ground. • Is the resistance greater than 10,000 ohms? → **Yes** INSTALL a new wiper control module. TEST the system for normal operation. → **No** INSTALL a new multifunction switch. TEST the system for normal operation.

FM9020100887020X

Fig. 65 Test H: Wipers Stay On Continuously (Part 2 of 2). 2000–02 Crown Victoria & Grand Marquis

CONDITIONS	DETAILS/RESULTS/ACTIONS
H1 CHECK CIRCUIT 589 (OG) FOR SHORT TO GROUND	
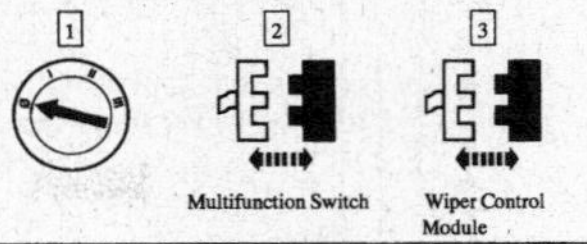	

FM9020100887010X

Fig. 65 Test H: Wipers Stay On Continuously (Part 1 of 2). 2000–02 Crown Victoria & Grand Marquis

Test Step	Result / Action to Take
A1 CHECK CIRCUITS 65 (DG) AND 406 (BN/WH) FOR VOLTAGE	
• Key in OFF position. • Disconnect: Windshield Wiper Motor C125. • Key in ON position. • Measure the voltage between windshield wiper C125 pin 5, circuit 406 (BN/WH), harness side and ground; and between windshield wiper motor C125 pin 8, circuit 65 (DG), harness side and ground. 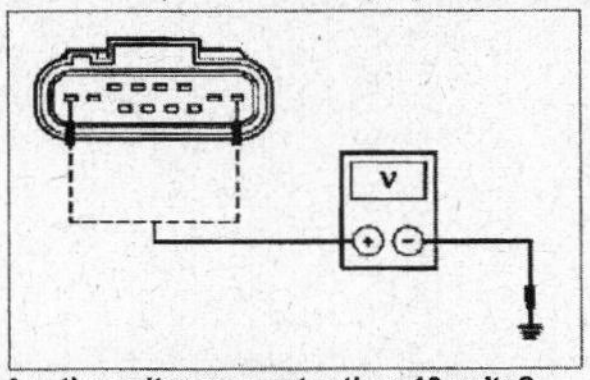 • **Are the voltages greater than 10 volts?**	**Yes** GO to A2 . **No** REPAIR the circuit(s) in question. TEST the system for normal operation.
A2 CHECK CIRCUITS 57 (BK) AND 676 (PK/OG) FOR OPENS	
• Key in OFF position. • Measure the resistance between windshield wiper C125 pin 6, circuit 57 (BK), harness side and ground; and between windshield wiper motor C125 pin 3, circuit 676 (PK/OG), harness side and ground. 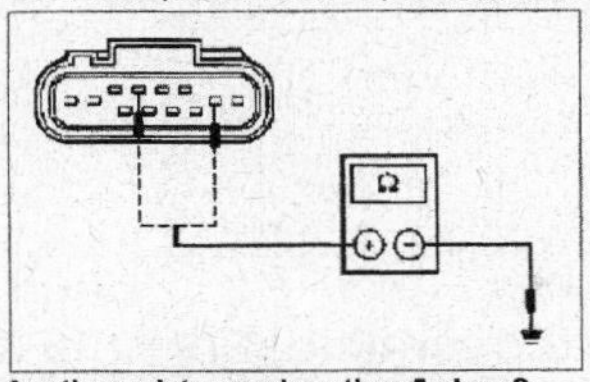 • **Are the resistances less than 5 ohms?**	**Yes** GO to A3 . **No** REPAIR the circuit(s) in question. TEST the system for normal operation.
A3 CHECK THE MULTIFUNCTION SWITCH	
• Disconnect: Multifunction Switch C202b. • Carry out the multifunction switch component test. • **Did the multifunction switch pass the component test?**	**Yes** GO to A4 . **No** INSTALL a new multifunction switch.

FM9020200907010X

Fig. 66 Test A: Wipers Inoperative (Part 1 of 3). 2003–04 Crown Victoria, Grand Marquis & Marauder

A4 CHECK CIRCUIT 57 (BK) FOR AN OPEN	
• Measure the resistance between C202b pin 5, circuit 57 (BK), harness side and ground. 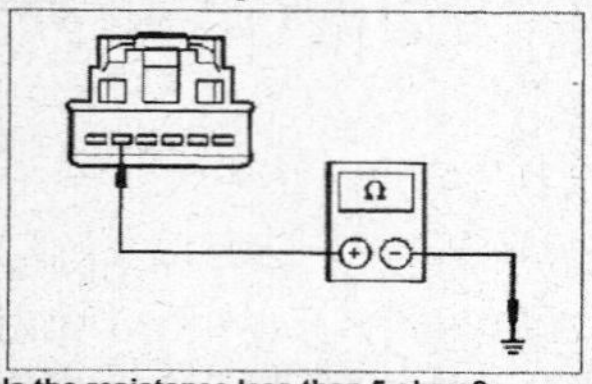 • **Is the resistance less than 5 ohms?**	**Yes** GO to A5 . **No** REPAIR the circuit. TEST the system for normal operation.
A5 CHECK CIRCUITS 56 (DB/OG), 58 (WH), 61 (YE/RD), AND 63 (RD) FOR OPENS	
• Using the following table, measure the resistance between the multifunction switch C202b harness side and the windshield wiper motor C125 harness side: (see table below) 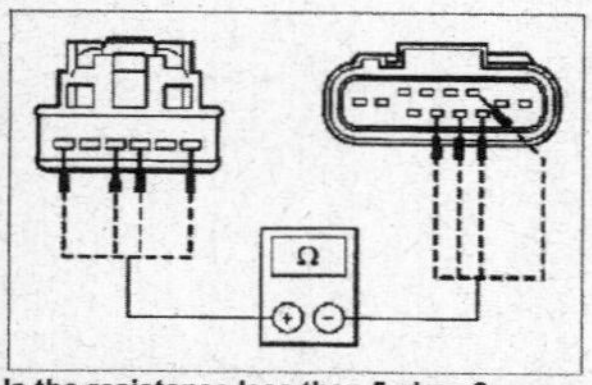 • **Is the resistance less than 5 ohms?**	**Yes** GO to A6 . **No** REPAIR the circuit(s) in question. TEST the system for normal operation.
A6 CHECK FOR CORRECT WIPER MOTOR OPERATION	
• Disconnect all wiper motor connectors. • Check for: ◦ corrosion ◦ pushed-out pins • Connect all wiper motor connectors and make sure they seat correctly. • Operate the system and verify the concern is still present. • **Is the concern still present?**	**Yes** GO to A7 . **No** The system is operating correctly at this time. Concern may have been caused by a loose or corroded connector. TEST the system for normal operation.

Multifunction Switch C202b	Windshield Wiper Motor C125
pin 6, circuit 56 (DB/OG)	pin 10, circuit 56 (DB/OG)
pin 3, circuit 58 (WH)	pin 11, circuit 58 (WH)
pin 1, circuit 61 (YE/RD)	pin 1, circuit 61 (YE/RD)
pin 4, circuit 63 (RD)	pin 9, circuit 63 (RD)

FM9020200907020X

Fig. 66 Test A: Wipers Inoperative (Part 2 of 3). 2003–04 Crown Victoria, Grand Marquis & Marauder

Test Step	Result / Action to Take
B1 CHECK THE MULTIFUNCTION SWITCH	
• Key in OFF position. • Disconnect: Multifunction Switch C202b. • Carry out the multifunction switch component test. Refer to Wiring Diagrams Cell 149 for schematic and connector information. • **Did the multifunction switch pass the component test?**	**Yes** GO to B2 . **No** INSTALL a new multifunction switch.
B2 CHECK CIRCUIT 57 (BK) FOR AN OPEN	
• Measure the resistance between C202b pin 5, circuit 57 (BK), harness side and ground. 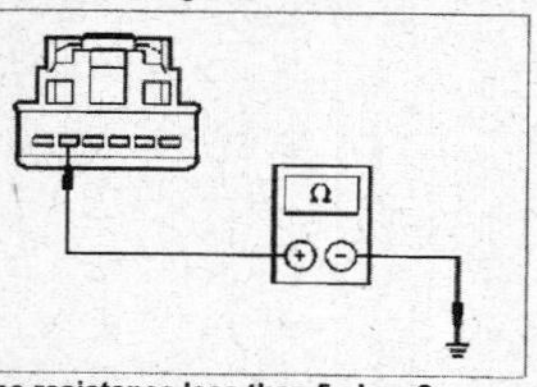 • **Is the resistance less than 5 ohms?**	**Yes** GO to B3 . **No** REPAIR the circuit. TEST the system for normal operation.

FM9020200908010X

Fig. 67 Test B: Wipers Stay On Continuously (Part 1 of 3). 2003–04 Crown Victoria, Grand Marquis & Marauder

A7 CHECK THE WINDSHIELD WIPER MOTOR	
• Key in OFF position. • Disconnect: Windshield Wiper Motor C125. • Carry out the windshield wiper motor component test as outlined in this section. • **Did the windshield wiper motor pass the component test?**	**Yes** The system is operating correctly at this time. Concern may have been caused by binding or incorrect pivot arm adjustment. TEST the system for normal operation. **No** INSTALL a new windshield wiper motor.

FM9020200907030X

Fig. 66 Test A: Wipers Inoperative (Part 3 of 3). 2003–04 Crown Victoria, Grand Marquis & Marauder

B3 CHECK CIRCUITS 56 (DB/OG), 58 (WH), 61 (YE/RD), AND 63 (RD) FOR SHORTS	
• Disconnect: Windshield Wiper Motor C125. • Using the following table, measure the resistance between the windshield wiper motor C125 harness side and ground: (see table below) 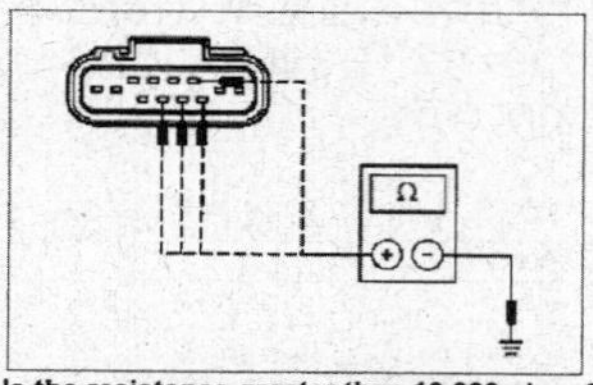 • **Is the resistance greater than 10,000 ohms?**	**Yes** GO to B4 . **No** REPAIR the circuit(s) in question. TEST the system for normal operation.
B4 CHECK FOR CORRECT WIPER MOTOR OPERATION	
• Disconnect all wiper motor connectors. • Check for: ◦ corrosion ◦ pushed-out pins • Connect all wiper motor connectors and make sure they seat correctly. • Operate the system and verify the concern is still present. • **Is the concern still present?**	**Yes** GO to B5 . **No** The system is operating correctly at this time. Concern may have been caused by a loose or corroded connector. TEST the system for normal operation.

Windshield Wiper Motor C125	Ground
pin 10, circuit 56 (DB/OG)	ground
pin 11, circuit 58 (WH)	ground
pin 1, circuit 61 (YE/RD)	ground
pin 9, circuit 63 (RD)	ground

FM9020200908020X

Fig. 67 Test B: Wipers Stay On Continuously (Part 2 of 3). 2003–04 Crown Victoria, Grand Marquis & Marauder

B5 CHECK THE WINDSHIELD WIPER MOTOR	
• Key in OFF position. • Disconnect: Windshield Wiper Motor C125. • Carry out the windshield wiper motor component test as outlined in this section. • **Did the windshield wiper motor pass the component test?**	**Yes** The system is operating correctly at this time. Concern may have been caused by binding or incorrect pivot arm adjustment. TEST the system for normal operation. **No** INSTALL a new windshield wiper motor.

FM9020200908030X

Fig. 67 Test B: Wipers Stay On Continuously (Part 3 of 3). 2003–04 Crown Victoria, Grand Marquis & Marauder

Test Step	Result / Action to Take
C1 CHECK THE MULTIFUNCTION SWITCH	
• Key in OFF position. • Disconnect: Multifunction Switch C202b. • Carry out the multifunction switch component test. • **Did the multifunction switch pass the component test?**	**Yes** GO to C2 . **No** INSTALL a new multifunction switch.
C2 CHECK CIRCUIT 57 (BK) FOR AN OPEN	
• Measure the resistance between C202b pin 5, circuit 57 (BK), harness side and ground. 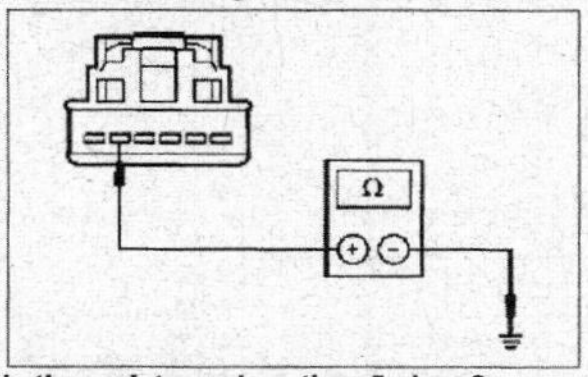 • **Is the resistance less than 5 ohms?**	**Yes** GO to C3 . **No** REPAIR the circuit. TEST the system for normal operation.

FM9020200909010X

Fig. 68 Test C: High/Low Wiper Speeds Do Not Operate Correctly, Intermittent Mode OK (Part 1 of 2). 2003–04 Crown Victoria, Grand Marquis & Marauder

Test Step	Result / Action to Take
D1 CHECK THE MULTIFUNCTION SWITCH	
• Key in OFF position. • Disconnect: Multifunction switch C202b. • Carry out the multifunction switch component test. • **Did the multifunction switch pass the component test?**	**Yes** GO to D2 . **No** INSTALL a new multifunction switch.
D2 CHECK CIRCUIT 57 (BK) FOR AN OPEN	
• Measure the resistance between C202b pin 5, circuit 57 (BK), harness side and ground. 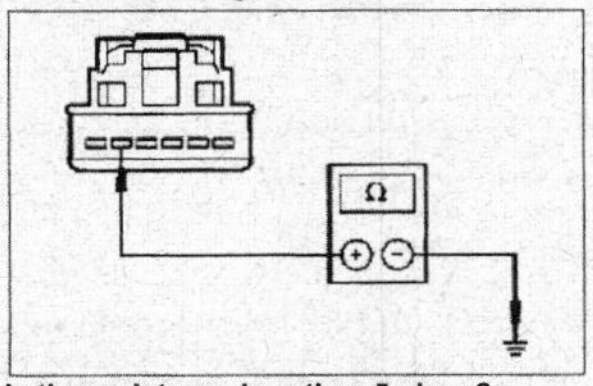 • **Is the resistance less than 5 ohms?**	**Yes** GO to D3 . **No** REPAIR the circuit. TEST the system for normal operation.

FM9020200910010X

Fig. 69 Test D: Intermittent Wiper Speed Does Not Operate Correctly, High/Low Speeds OK (Part 1 of 2). 2003–04 Crown Victoria, Grand Marquis & Marauder

C3 CHECK CIRCUITS 56 (DB/OG), 61 (YE/RD), AND 63 (RD) FOR OPENS	
• Disconnect: Windshield Wiper Motor C125. • Using the following table, measure the resistance between the multifunction switch C202b harness side and the windshield wiper motor C125 harness side:	**Yes** GO to C4 . **No** REPAIR the circuit(s) in question. TEST the system for normal operation.

Multifunction Switch C202b	Windshield Wiper Motor C125
pin 6, circuit 56 (DB/OG)	pin 10, circuit 56 (DB/OG)
pin 1, circuit 61 (YE/RD)	pin 1, circuit 61 (YE/RD)
pin 4, circuit 63 (RD)	pin 9, circuit 63 (RD)

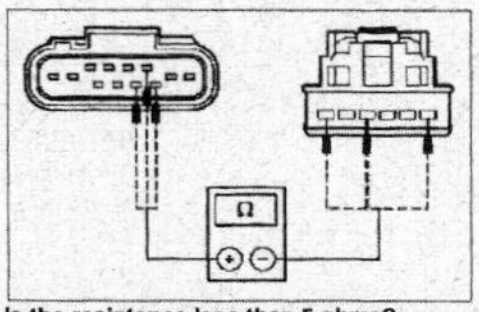

• **Is the resistance less than 5 ohms?**

C4 CHECK FOR CORRECT WIPER MOTOR OPERATION	
• Disconnect all wiper motor connectors. • Check for: • corrosion • pushed-out pins • Connect all wiper motor connectors and make sure they seat correctly. • Operate the system and verify the concern is still present. • **Is the concern still present?**	**Yes** GO to C5 . **No** The system is operating correctly at this time. Concern may have been caused by a loose or corroded connector. TEST the system for normal operation.
C5 CHECK THE WINDSHIELD WIPER MOTOR	
• Key in OFF position. • Disconnect: Windshield Wiper Motor C125. • Carry out the windshield wiper motor component test as outlined in this section. • **Did the windshield wiper motor pass the component test?**	**Yes** The system is operating correctly at this time. Concern may have been caused by binding or incorrect pivot arm adjustment. TEST the system for normal operation. **No** INSTALL a new windshield wiper motor.

FM9020200909020X

Fig. 68 Test C: High/Low Wiper Speeds Do Not Operate Correctly, Intermittent Mode OK (Part 2 of 2). 2003–04 Crown Victoria, Grand Marquis & Marauder

D3 CHECK CIRCUITS 56 (DB/OG), 61 (YE/RD), AND 63 (RD) FOR OPENS	
• Disconnect: Windshield Wiper Motor C125. • Using the following table, measure the resistance between the multifunction switch C202b harness side and the windshield wiper motor C125 harness side:	**Yes** GO to D4 . **No** REPAIR the circuit(s) in question. TEST the system for normal operation.

Multifunction Switch C202b	Windshield Wiper Motor C125
pin 6, circuit 56 (DB/OG)	pin 10, circuit 56 (DB/OG)
pin 1, circuit 61 (YE/RD)	pin 1, circuit 61 (YE/RD)
pin 4, circuit 63 (RD)	pin 9, circuit 63 (RD)

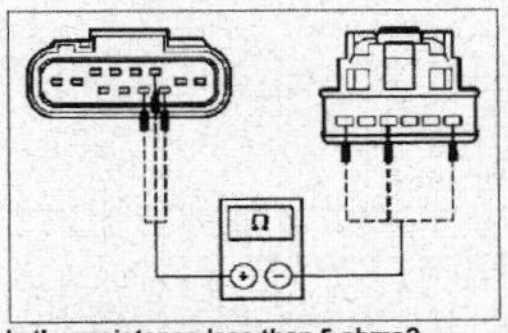

• **Is the resistance less than 5 ohms?**

D4 CHECK FOR CORRECT WIPER MOTOR OPERATION	
• Disconnect all wiper motor connectors. • Check for: • corrosion • pushed-out pins • Connect all wiper motor connectors and make sure they seat correctly. • Operate the system and verify the concern is still present. • **Is the concern still present?**	**Yes** GO to D5 . **No** The system is operating correctly at this time. Concern may have been caused by a loose or corroded connector. TEST the system for normal operation.
D5 CHECK THE WINDSHIELD WIPER MOTOR	
• Key in OFF position. • Disconnect: Windshield Wiper Motor C125. • Carry out the windshield wiper motor component test as outlined in this section. • **Did the windshield wiper motor pass the component test?**	**Yes** The system is operating correctly at this time. Concern may have been caused by binding or incorrect pivot arm adjustment. TEST the system for normal operation. **No** INSTALL a new windshield wiper motor.

FM9020200910020X

Fig. 69 Test D: Intermittent Wiper Speed Does Not Operate Correctly, High/Low Speeds OK (Part 2 of 2). 2003–04 Crown Victoria, Grand Marquis & Marauder

Test Step	Result / Action to Take
E1 CHECK THE MULTIFUNCTION SWITCH	
• Key in OFF position. • Disconnect: Multifunction Switch C202b. • Carry out the multifunction switch component test. • **Did the multifunction switch pass the component test?**	**Yes** GO to E2 . **No** INSTALL a new multifunction switch.
E2 CHECK CIRCUIT 57 (BK) FOR AN OPEN	
• Measure the resistance between C202b pin 5, circuit 57 (BK), harness side and ground. 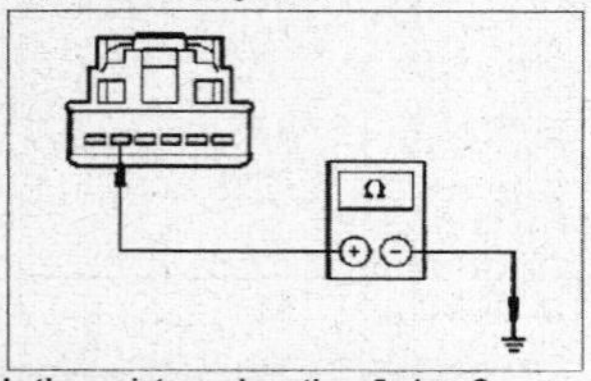 • **Is the resistance less than 5 ohms?**	**Yes** GO to E3 . **No** REPAIR the circuit. TEST the system for normal operation.
E3 CHECK CIRCUIT 589 (OG) FOR AN OPEN	
• Disconnect: Windshield Wiper Motor C125. • Measure the resistance between C202b pin 2, circuit 589 (OG), harness side and C125 pin 12, circuit 589 (OG), harness side. 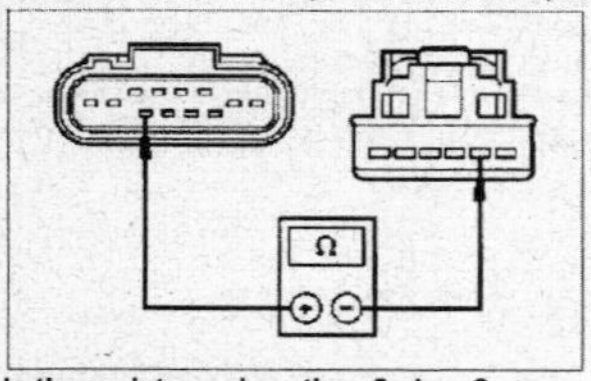 • **Is the resistance less than 5 ohms?**	**Yes** Go To Pinpoint Test F . **No** REPAIR the circuit. TEST the system for normal operation

FM9020200911000X

Fig. 70 Test E: Wipers Do Not Operate Correctly In Mist Mode. 2003–04 Crown Victoria, Grand Marquis & Marauder

Test Step	Result / Action to Take
F3 CHECK CIRCUIT 941 (BK/WH) FOR AN OPEN	
• Key in OFF position. • Disconnect: Windshield Wiper Motor C125. • Measure the resistance between C125 pin 7, circuit 941 (BK/WH), harness side and C137 pin 1, circuit 941 (BK/WH), harness side. 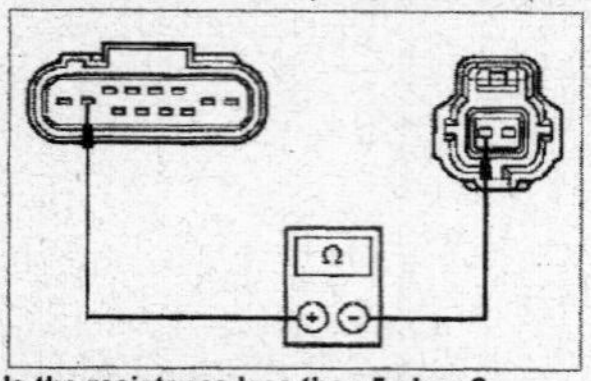 • **Is the resistance less than 5 ohms?**	**Yes** GO to F4 . **No** REPAIR the circuit. TEST the system for normal operation.
F4 CHECK THE MULTIFUNCTION SWITCH	
• Key in OFF position. • Disconnect: Multifunction Switch C202b. • Carry out the multifunction switch component test. • **Did the multifunction switch pass the component test?**	**Yes** GO to F5 . **No** INSTALL a new multifunction switch.
F5 CHECK CIRCUIT 57 (BK) FOR AN OPEN	
• Measure the resistance between C202b pin 5, circuit 57 (BK), harness side and ground. 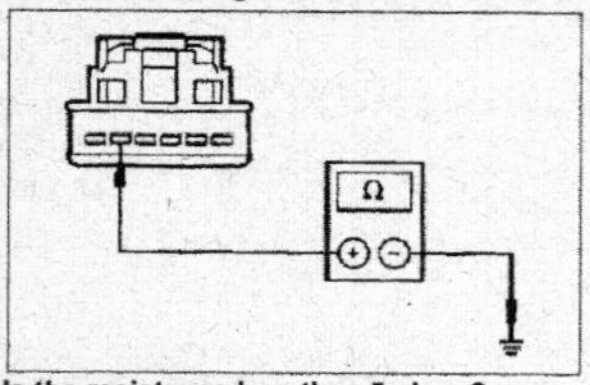 • **Is the resistance less than 5 ohms?**	**Yes** GO to F6 . **No** REPAIR the circuit. TEST the system for normal operation.

FM9020200912020X

Fig. 71 Test F: Washer Pump Inoperative (Part 2 of 3). 2003–04 Crown Victoria, Grand Marquis & Marauder

Test Step	Result / Action to Take
F1 CHECK WASHER PUMP MOTOR FOR VOLTAGE	
• Key in OFF position. • Disconnect: Washer Pump Motor C137. • Key in ON position. • Measure the voltage between C137 pin 1, circuit 941 (BK/WH) harness side and ground while depressing the multifunction switch to the wash position. 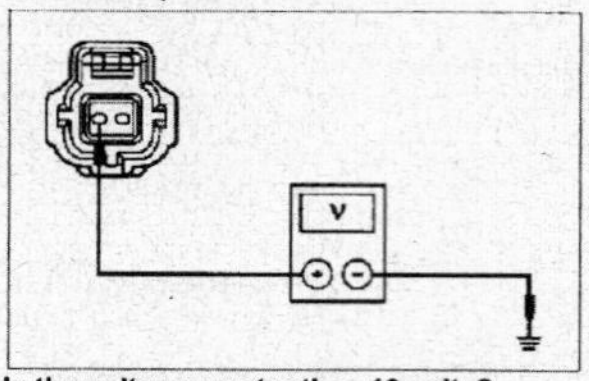 • **Is the voltage greater than 10 volts?**	**Yes** GO to F2 . **No** GO to F3 .
F2 CHECK CIRCUIT 57 (BK) FOR GROUND	
• Measure the resistance between C137 pin 2, circuit 57 (BK) harness side and ground. 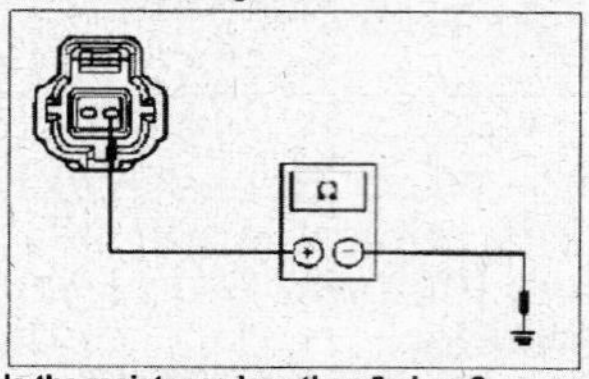 • **Is the resistance less than 5 ohms?**	**Yes** INSTALL a new washer pump. **No** REPAIR the circuit. TEST the system for normal operation.

FM9020200912010X

Fig. 71 Test F: Washer Pump Inoperative (Part 1 of 3). 2003–04 Crown Victoria, Grand Marquis & Marauder

F6 CHECK CIRCUIT 589 (OG) FOR AN OPEN	
• Measure the resistance between C125 pin 12, circuit 589 (OG), harness side and C202b pin 2, circuit 589 (OG), harness side. 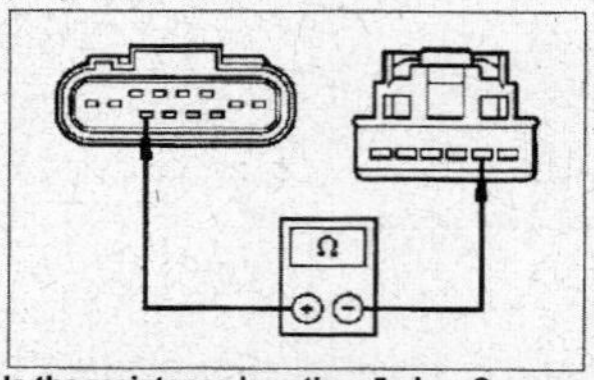 • **Is the resistance less than 5 ohms?**	**Yes** GO to F7 . **No** REPAIR the circuit. TEST the system for normal operation.
F7 CHECK FOR CORRECT WIPER MOTOR OPERATION	

• Disconnect all wiper motor connectors.
• Check for:
  • corrosion
  • pushed-out pins
• Connect all wiper motor connectors and make sure they seat correctly.
• Operate the system and verify the concern is still present.
• **Is the concern still present?**
	Yes
	GO to F8 .
	
	No
	The system is operating correctly at this time. Concern may have been caused by a loose or corroded connector. TEST the system for normal operation.

F8 CHECK THE WINDSHIELD WIPER MOTOR	
• Key in OFF position. • Disconnect: Windshield Wiper Motor C125. • Carry out the windshield wiper motor component test as outlined in this section. • **Did the windshield wiper motor pass the component test?**	**Yes** The system is operating correctly at this time. Concern may have been caused by binding or incorrect pivot arm adjustment. TEST the system for normal operation. **No** INSTALL a new windshield wiper motor.

FM9020200912030X

Fig. 71 Test F: Washer Pump Inoperative (Part 3 of 3). 2003–04 Crown Victoria, Grand Marquis & Marauder

TEST CONDITIONS	TEST DETAILS/RESULTS/ACTIONS
A1 CHECK WIPER FUSE (20A)	
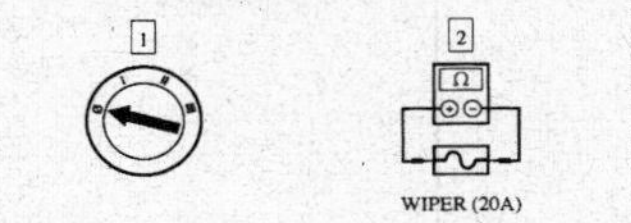	• Is the fuse OK? → **Yes** REINSTALL WIPER fuse (20A). GO to **A2**. → **No** REPLACE the fuse. TEST the system for normal operation. If the fuse fails again, CHECK for a short to ground condition. REPAIR as necessary.
A2 CHECK THE GROUND TO THE WINDSHIELD WIPER MOTOR — CIRCUIT 50 (BK)	
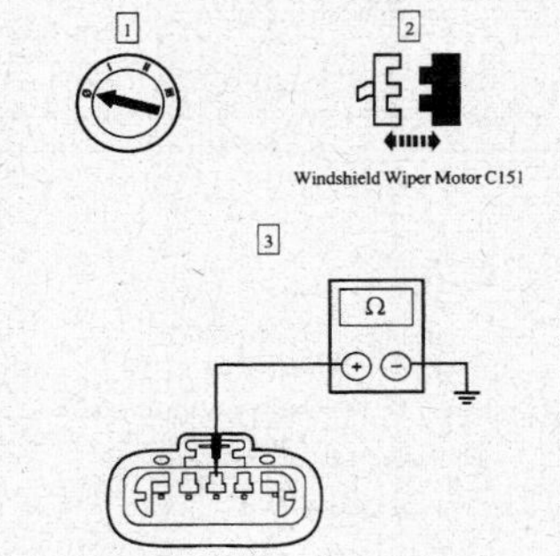	3 Measure the resistance between windshield wiper motor C151-3, circuit 50 (BK), and ground. • Is the resistance less than 5 ohms? → **Yes** GO to **A3**. → **No** REPAIR circuit 50 (BK). TEST the system for normal operation.

FM9020100787010X

Fig. 72 Test A: Wipers Are Inoperative In All Positions (Part 1 of 3). 2000–01 Escort & ZX2

TEST CONDITIONS	TEST DETAILS/RESULTS/ACTIONS
A3 CHECK THE VOLTAGE TO THE MULTI-FUNCTION SWITCH — CIRCUIT 230 (BL)	
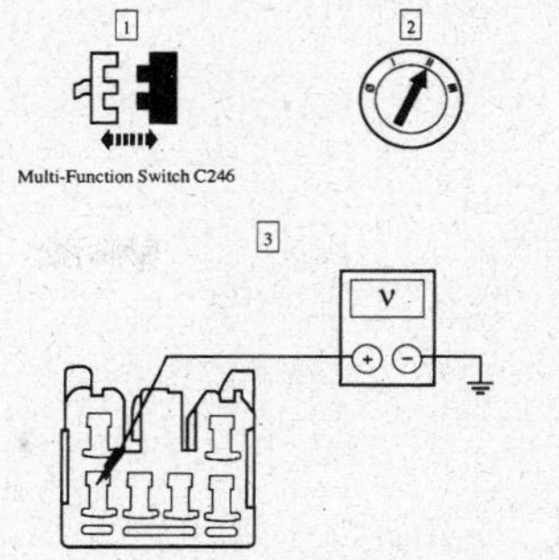	3 Measure the voltage between multi-function switch C246-3, circuit 230 (BL), and ground. • Is the voltage greater than 10 volts? → **Yes** GO to **A4**. → **No** REPAIR circuit 230 (BL). TEST the system for normal operation.
A4 CHECK THE GROUND TO THE MULTI-FUNCTION SWITCH — CIRCUIT 51 (BK)	
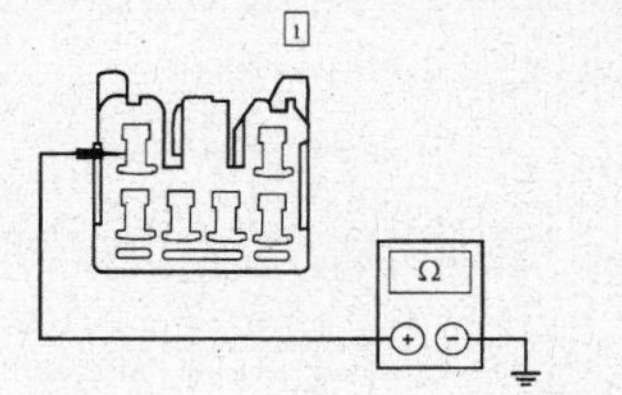	1 Measure the resistance between multi-function switch C246-1, circuit 51 (BK), and ground. • Is the resistance less than 5 ohms? → **Yes** GO to **A5**. → **No** REPAIR circuit 51 (BK). TEST the system for normal operation.

FM9020100787020X

Fig. 72 Test A: Wipers Are Inoperative In All Positions (Part 2 of 3). 2000–01 Escort & ZX2

TEST CONDITIONS	TEST DETAILS/RESULTS/ACTIONS
A5 PERFORM THE MULTI-FUNCTION SWITCH COMPONENT TEST	
	1 Check the multi-function switch. • Is the multi-function switch OK? → **Yes** CHECK the windshield wiper motor. REFER to Component Test. → **No** REPLACE the multi-function switch TEST the system for normal operation.

FM9020100787030X

Fig. 72 Test A: Wipers Are Inoperative In All Positions (Part 3 of 3). 2000–01 Escort & ZX2

TEST CONDITIONS	TEST DETAILS/RESULTS/ACTIONS
B1 CHECK THE MULTI-FUNCTION SWITCH	
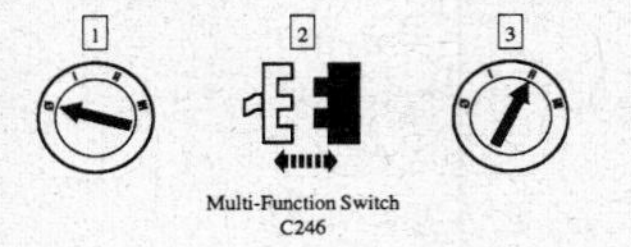	• Do the windshield wipers turn off? → **Yes** REPLACE the multi-function switch TEST the system for normal operation. → **No** GO to **B2**.

FM9020100788010X

Fig. 73 Test B: Wipers Stay On Continuously (Part 1 of 2). 2000–01 Escort & ZX2

TEST CONDITIONS	TEST DETAILS/RESULTS/ACTIONS
B2 CHECK CIRCUIT 233 (R) AND CIRCUIT 232 (BL/W) FOR SHORT TO POWER	
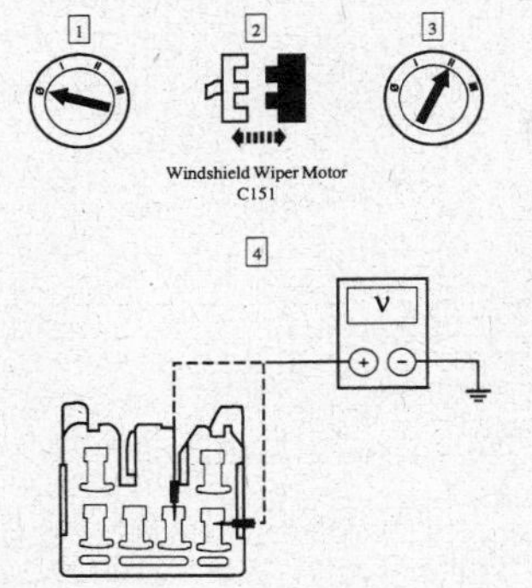	4 Measure the voltage between multi-function switch C246-5, circuit 233 (R), and ground; and between multi-function switch C246-6, circuit 232 (BL/W), and ground. • Is any voltage indicated? → **Yes** REPAIR circuit 233 (R) and/or circuit 232 (BL/W). TEST the system for normal operation. → **No** REPLACE the windshield wiper motor; TEST the system for normal operation.

FM9020100788020X

Fig. 73 Test B: Wipers Stay On Continuously (Part 2 of 2). 2000–01 Escort & ZX2

TEST CONDITIONS	TEST DETAILS/RESULTS/ACTIONS
C1 CHECK HIGH SPEED INPUT TO WINDSHIELD WIPER MOTOR — CIRCUIT 233 (R)	
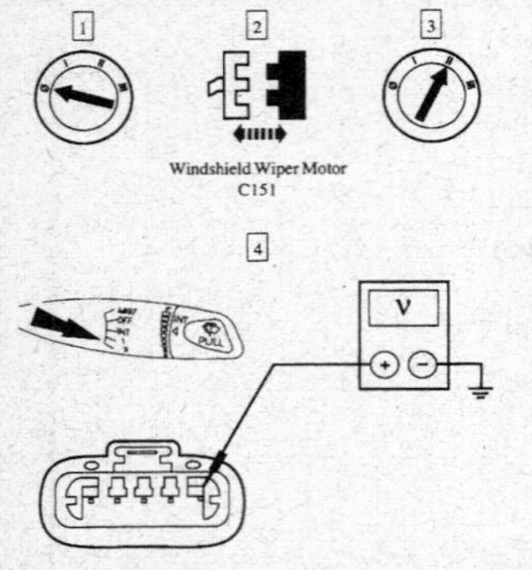	4 With the multi-function switch set to position 2 (high), measure the voltage between windshield wiper motor C151-5, circuit 233 (R), and ground. • Is the voltage greater than 10 volts? → **Yes** CHECK the windshield wiper motor. → **No** GO to **C2**.
C2 CHECK THE MULTI-FUNCTION SWITCH	
	1 Check the multi-function switch. • Is the multi-function switch OK? → **Yes** REPAIR circuit 233 (R). TEST the system for normal operation. → **No** REPLACE the multi-function switch TEST the system for normal operation.

FM9020100789000X

Fig. 74 Test C: High Wiper Speed Does Not Operate Properly. 2000–01 Escort & ZX2

TEST CONDITIONS	TEST DETAILS/RESULTS/ACTIONS
D1 CHECK THE VOLTAGE TO THE WINDSHIELD WIPER MOTOR — CIRCUIT 230 (BL)	
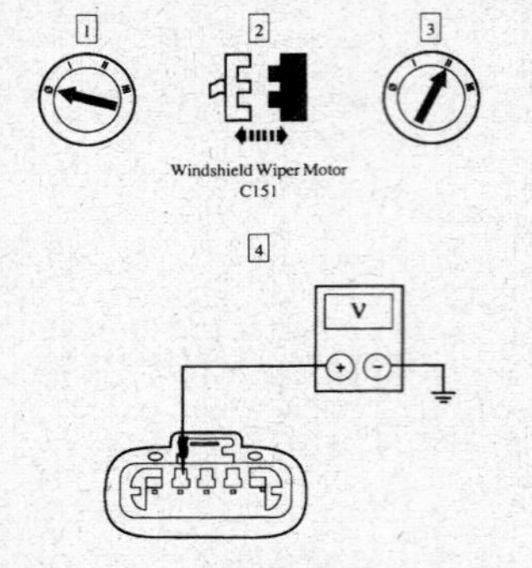	4 Measure the voltage between windshield wiper motor C151-2, circuit 230 (BL), and ground. • Is the voltage greater than 10 volts? → **Yes** GO to **D2**. → **No** REPAIR circuit 230 (BL). TEST the system for normal operation.
D2 CHECK CIRCUIT 231 (BL/Y) FOR OPEN	
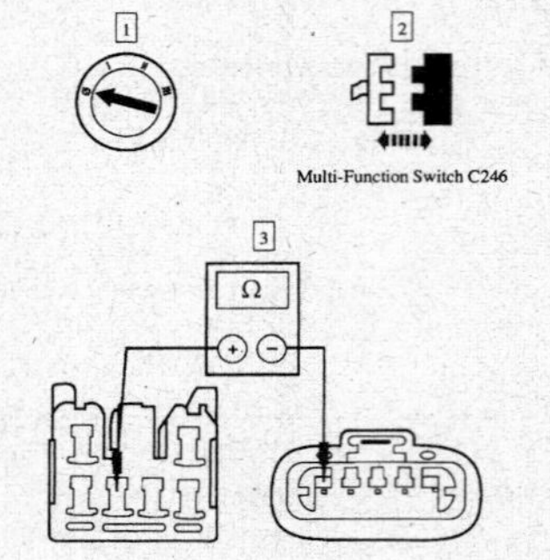	3 Measure the resistance between multi-function switch C246-4, circuit 231 (BL/Y), and windshield wiper motor C151-1, circuit 231 (BL/Y). • Is the resistance less than 5 ohms? → **Yes** GO to **D3**. → **No** REPAIR circuit 231 (BL/Y). TEST the system for normal operation.

FM9020100790010X

Fig. 75 Test D: Wipers Will Not Park At The Proper Position (Part 1 of 2). 2000–01 Escort & ZX2

TEST CONDITIONS	TEST DETAILS/RESULTS/ACTIONS
D3 CHECK CIRCUIT 231 (BL/Y) FOR SHORT TO GROUND	
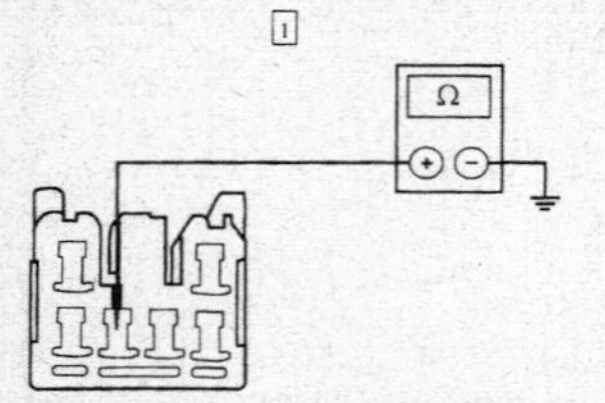	1 Measure the resistance between multi-function switch C246-4, circuit 231 (BL/Y), and ground. • Is the resistance greater than 10,000 ohms? → **Yes** GO to **D4**. → **No** REPAIR circuit 231 (BL/Y). TEST the system for normal operation.
D4 CHECK THE MULTI-FUNCTION SWITCH	
	1 Check the multi-function switch • Is the multi-function switch OK? → **Yes** REPLACE the windshield wiper motor; TEST the system for normal operation. → **No** REPLACE the multi-function switch TEST the system for normal operation.

FM9020100790020X

Fig. 75 Test D: Wipers Will Not Park At The Proper Position (Part 2 of 2). 2000–01 Escort & ZX2

TEST CONDITIONS	TEST DETAILS/RESULTS/ACTIONS
E1 CHECK THE VOLTAGE TO THE WINDSHIELD WASHER PUMP MOTOR — CIRCUIT 234 (BL/O)	
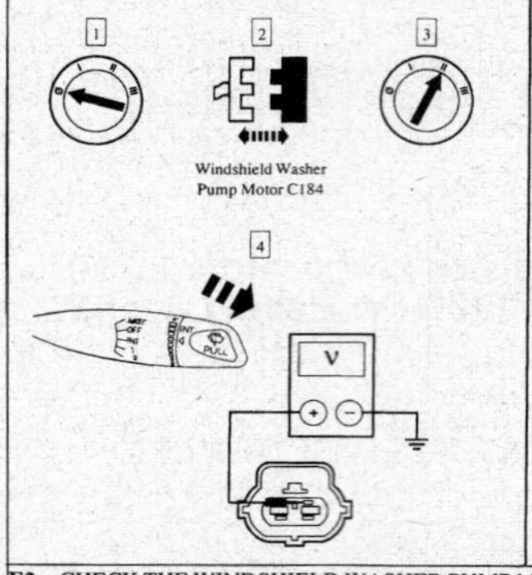	4 Measure the voltage between windshield washer pump motor C184, circuit 234 (BL/O), and ground, while pulling the multi-function switch toward you. • Is the voltage greater than 10 volts? → **Yes** GO to **E2**. → **No** GO to **E3**.
E2 CHECK THE WINDSHIELD WASHER PUMP MOTOR GROUND — CIRCUIT 51 (BK)	
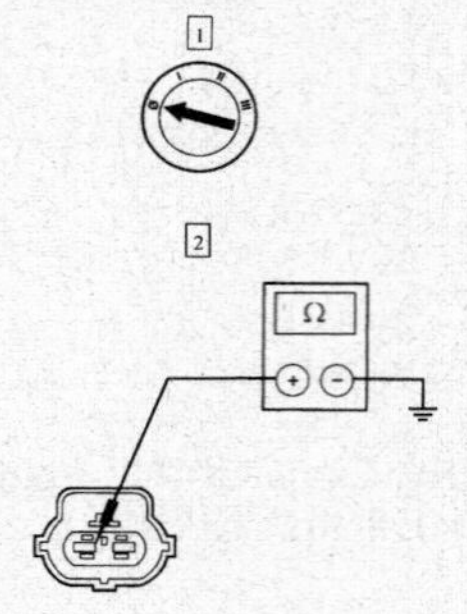	2 Measure the resistance between windshield washer pump motor C184, circuit 51 (BK), and ground. • Is the resistance less than 5 ohms? → **Yes** RECONNECT the windshield washer pump and activate the system. If pump does not operate properly, REPLACE the windshield washer pump motor; TEST the system for normal operation. → **No** REPAIR circuit 51 (BK). TEST the system for normal operation.

FM9020100791010X

Fig. 76 Test E: Washer Pump Is Inoperative (Part 1 of 2). 2000–01 Escort & ZX2

TEST CONDITIONS	TEST DETAILS/RESULTS/ACTIONS
E3 CHECK THE MULTI-FUNCTION SWITCH	
1 2 	3 Check the multi-function switch. • Is the multi-function switch OK? → **Yes** REPAIR circuit 234 (BL/O). TEST the system for normal operation. → **No** REPLACE the multi-function switch TEST the system for normal operation.

FM9020100791020X

Fig. 76 Test E: Washer Pump Is Inoperative (Part 2 of 2). 2000–01 Escort & ZX2

CONDITIONS	DETAILS/RESULTS/ACTIONS
A3 CHECK THE VOLTAGE TO THE MULTI-FUNCTION SWITCH — CIRCUIT 230 (BL)	
1 2  3 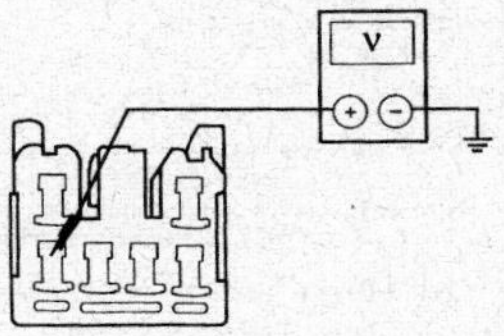	3 Measure the voltage between multi-function switch (BL), and ground. • Is the voltage greater than 10 volts? → **Yes** GO to **A4**. → **No** REPAIR (BL). TEST the system for normal operation.
A4 CHECK THE GROUND TO THE MULTI-FUNCTION SWITCH — CIRCUIT 51 (BK)	
1 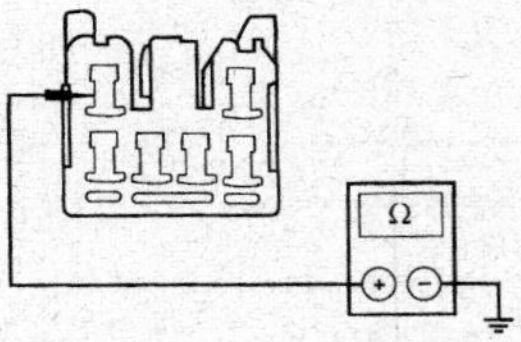	1 Measure the resistance between multi-function switch C246-1, circuit 51 (BK), and ground. • Is the resistance less than 5 ohms? → **Yes** GO to **A5**. → **No** REPAIR (BK). TEST the system for normal operation.

FM9020100889020X

Fig. 77 Test A: Wipers Are Inoperative All Positions (Part 2 of 3). 2002–04 Escort & ZX2

CONDITIONS	DETAILS/RESULTS/ACTIONS
B1 CHECK THE MULTI-FUNCTION SWITCH	
1 2 3 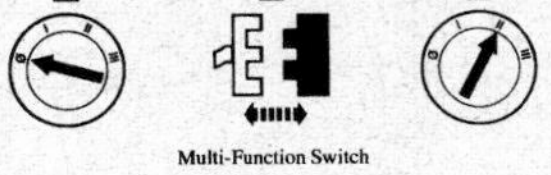	• Do the windshield wipers turn off? → **Yes** REPLACE the multi-function switch. TEST the system for normal operation. → **No** GO to **B2**.
B2 CHECK CIRCUIT 233 (R) AND CIRCUIT 232 (BL/W) FOR SHORT TO POWER	
1 2 3 	

FM9020100890010X

Fig. 78 Test B: Wipers Stay On Continuously (Part 1 of 2). 2002–04 Escort & ZX2

CONDITIONS	DETAILS/RESULTS/ACTIONS
A1 CHECK WIPER FUSE (20A)	
1 2 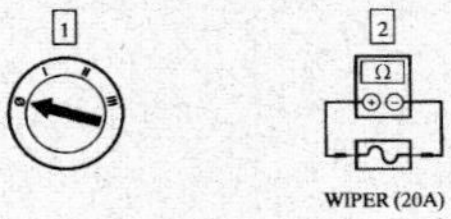	• Is the fuse OK? → **Yes** REINSTALL WIPER fuse (20A). GO to **A2**. → **No** REPLACE the fuse. TEST the system for normal operation. If the fuse fails again, CHECK for a short to ground condition. REPAIR as necessary.
A2 CHECK THE GROUND TO THE WINDSHIELD WIPER MOTOR — CIRCUIT 50 (BK)	
1 2 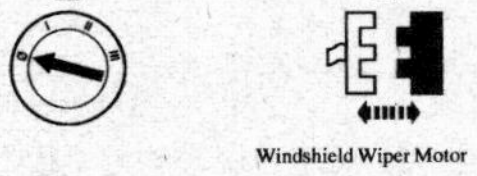 3 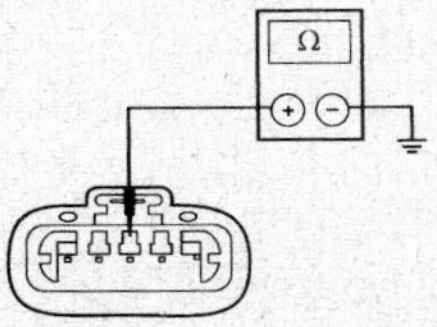	3 Measure the resistance between windshield wiper motor (BK), and ground. • Is the resistance less than 5 ohms? → **Yes** GO to **A3**. → **No** REPAIR (BK). TEST the system for normal operation.

FM9020100889010X

Fig. 77 Test A: Wipers Are Inoperative All Positions (Part 1 of 3). 2002–04 Escort & ZX2

CONDITIONS	DETAILS/RESULTS/ACTIONS
A5 PERFORM THE MULTI-FUNCTION SWITCH COMPONENT TEST	
	1 Check the multi-function switch. • Is the multi-function switch OK? → **Yes** CHECK the windshield wiper motor. → **No** REPLACE the multi-function switch. TEST the system for normal operation.

FM9020100889030X

Fig. 77 Test A: Wipers Are Inoperative All Positions (Part 3 of 3). 2002–04 Escort & ZX2

CONDITIONS	DETAILS/RESULTS/ACTIONS
B2 CHECK CIRCUIT 233 (R) AND CIRCUIT 232 (BL/W) FOR SHORT TO POWER (Continued)	
4 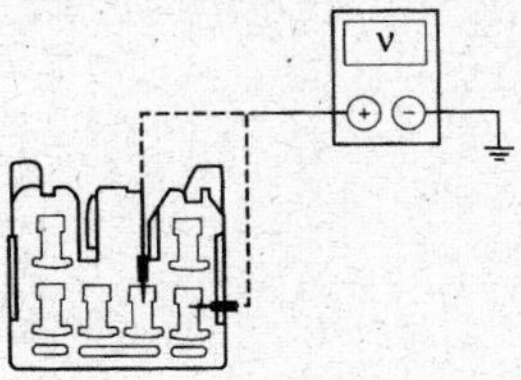	4 Measure the voltage between multi-function switch C246-5, circuit 233 (R), and ground; and between multi-function switch C246-6, circuit 232 (BL/W), and ground. • Is any voltage indicated? → **Yes** REPAIR circuit 233 (R) and/or circuit 232 (BL/W). TEST the system for normal operation. → **No** REPLACE the windshield wiper motor. TEST the system for normal operation.

FM9020100890020X

Fig. 78 Test B: Wipers Stay On Continuously (Part 2 of 2). 2002–04 Escort & ZX2

CONDITIONS	DETAILS/RESULTS/ACTIONS
C1 CHECK HIGH SPEED INPUT TO WINDSHIELD WIPER MOTOR — CIRCUIT 233 (R)	
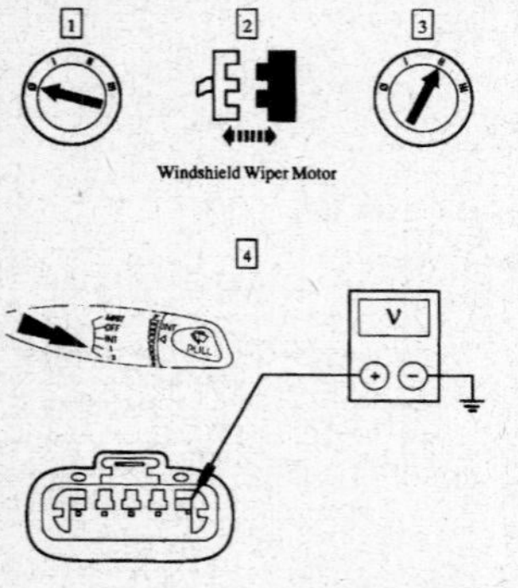	4 With the multi-function switch set to position 2 (high), measure the voltage between windshield wiper motor C151-5, circuit 233 (R), and ground. • Is the voltage greater than 10 volts? → **Yes** CHECK the windshield wiper motor. → **No** GO to **C2**.

FM9020100891010X

Fig. 79 Test C: High Wiper Speed Does Not Operate Properly (Part 1 of 2). 2002–04 Escort & ZX2

CONDITIONS	DETAILS/RESULTS/ACTIONS
C2 CHECK THE MULTI-FUNCTION SWITCH	
	1 Check the multi-function switch. • Is the multi-function switch OK? → **Yes** REPAIR (R). TEST the system for normal operation. → **No** REPLACE the multi-function switch. TEST the system for normal operation.

FM9020100891020X

Fig. 79 Test C: High Wiper Speed Does Not Operate Properly (Part 2 of 2). 2002–04 Escort & ZX2

CONDITIONS	DETAILS/RESULTS/ACTIONS
D1 CHECK THE VOLTAGE TO THE WINDSHIELD WIPER MOTOR — CIRCUIT 230 (BL)	
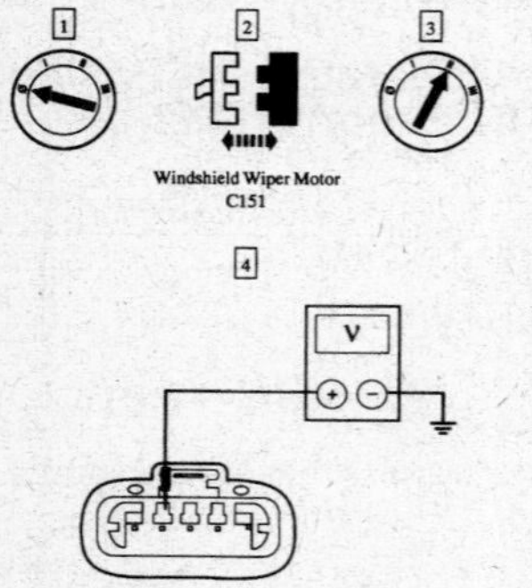	4 Measure the voltage between windshield wiper motor (BL), and ground. • Is the voltage greater than 10 volts? → **Yes** GO to **D2**. → **No** REPAIR (BL). TEST the system for normal operation.
D2 CHECK CIRCUIT 231 (BL/Y) FOR OPEN	
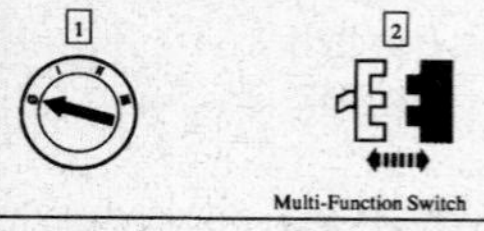	

FM9020100892010X

Fig. 80 Test D: Wipers Will Not Park Proper Position (Part 1 of 2). 2002–04 Escort & ZX2

CONDITIONS	DETAILS/RESULTS/ACTIONS
D2 CHECK CIRCUIT 231 (BL/Y) FOR OPEN (Continued)	
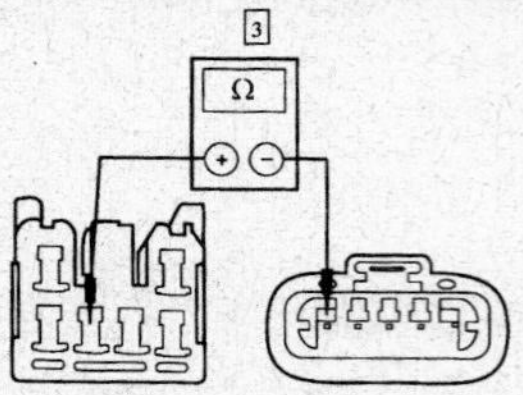	3 Measure the resistance between multi-function switch C246-4, circuit 231 (BL/Y), and windshield wiper motor C151-1, circuit 231 (BL/Y). • Is the resistance less than 5 ohms? → **Yes** GO to **D3**. → **No** REPAIR circuit 231 (BL/Y). TEST the system for normal operation.
D3 CHECK CIRCUIT 231 (BL/Y) FOR SHORT TO GROUND	
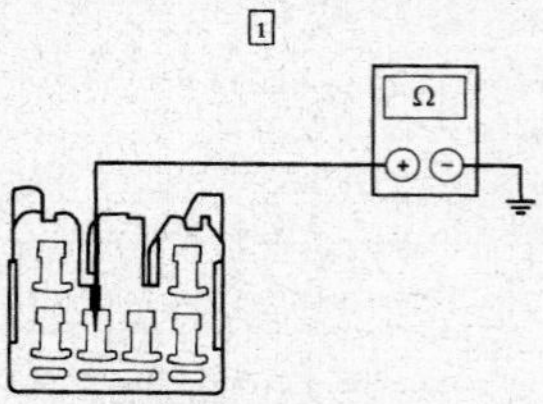	1 Measure the resistance between multi-function switch C246-4, circuit 231 (BL/Y), and ground. • Is the resistance greater than 10,000 ohms? → **Yes** GO to **D4**. → **No** REPAIR circuit 231 (BL/Y). TEST the system for normal operation.
D4 CHECK THE MULTI-FUNCTION SWITCH	
	1 Check the multi-function switch • Is the multi-function switch OK? → **Yes** REPLACE the windshield wiper motor; TEST the system for normal operation. → **No** REPLACE the multi-function switch. TEST the system for normal operation.

FM9020100892020X

Fig. 80 Test D: Wipers Will Not Park Proper Position (Part 2 of 2). 2002–04 Escort & ZX2

CONDITIONS	DETAILS/RESULTS/ACTIONS
E1 CHECK THE VOLTAGE TO THE WINDSHIELD WASHER PUMP MOTOR — CIRCUIT 234 (BL/O)	
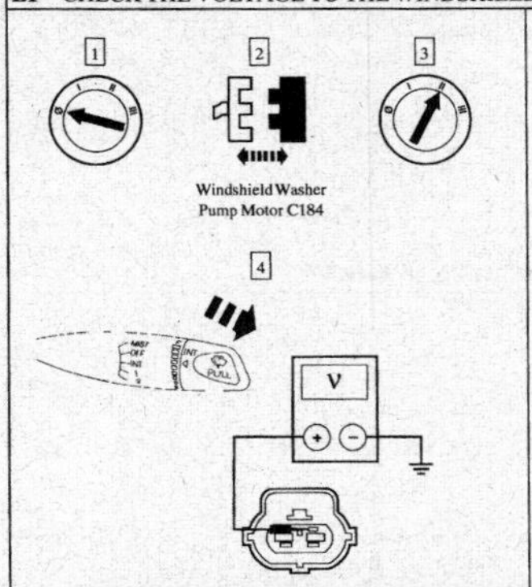	4 Measure the voltage between windshield washer pump motor (BL/O), and ground, while pulling the multi-function switch toward you. • Is the voltage greater than 10 volts? → **Yes** GO to **E2**. → **No** GO to **E3**.
E2 CHECK THE WINDSHIELD WASHER PUMP MOTOR GROUND — CIRCUIT 51 (BK)	
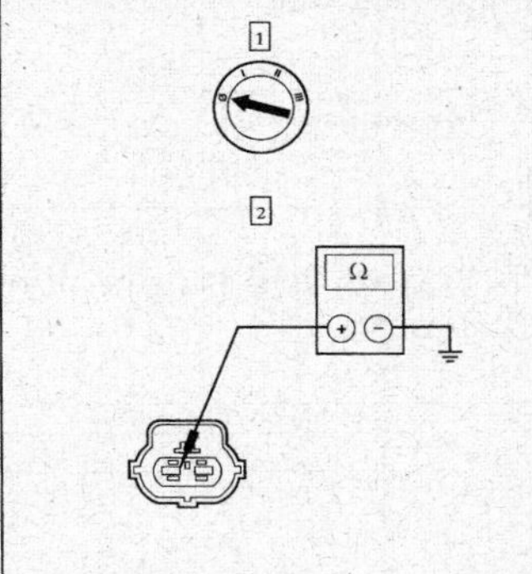	2 Measure the resistance between windshield washer pump motor C184, circuit 51 (BK), and ground. • Is the resistance less than 5 ohms? → **Yes** RECONNECT the windshield washer pump and activate the system. If pump does not operate properly, REPLACE the windshield washer pump motor. TEST the system for normal operation. → **No** REPAIR (BK). TEST the system for normal operation.

FM9020100893010X

Fig. 81 Test E: Washer Pump Is Inoperative (Part 1 of 2). 2002–04 Escort & ZX2

CONDITIONS	DETAILS/RESULTS/ACTIONS
A1: CHECK FUSE F55	
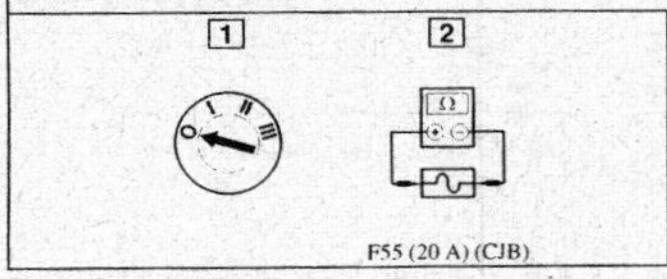	

FM9020100799010X

Fig. 82 Test A: Windshield Wipers Are Inoperative (Part 1 of 5). Focus

CONDITIONS	DETAILS/RESULTS/ACTIONS
E3 CHECK THE MULTI-FUNCTION SWITCH	
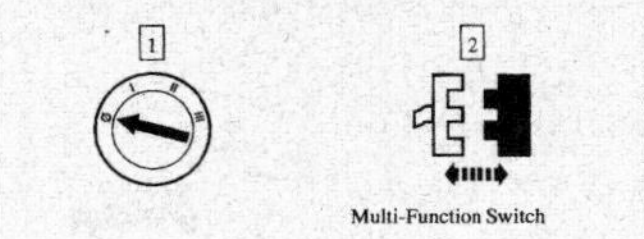	3 Check the multi-function switch. • Is the multi-function switch OK? → **Yes** REPAIR (BL/O). TEST the system for normal operation. → **No** REPLACE the multi-function switch. TEST the system for normal operation.

FM9020100893020X

Fig. 81 Test E: Washer Pump Is Inoperative (Part 2 of 2). 2002–04 Escort & ZX2

CONDITIONS	DETAILS/RESULTS/ACTIONS
	3 Remove fuse F55 (20 A) (CJB) and check it. • Is the fuse OK? → **Yes** GO TO **A2** → **No** INSTALL a new fuse. If the fuse blows again, LOCATE and REPAIR the short circuit using the wiring diagram. TEST the system for normal operation.
A2: CHECK VOLTAGE SUPPLY	
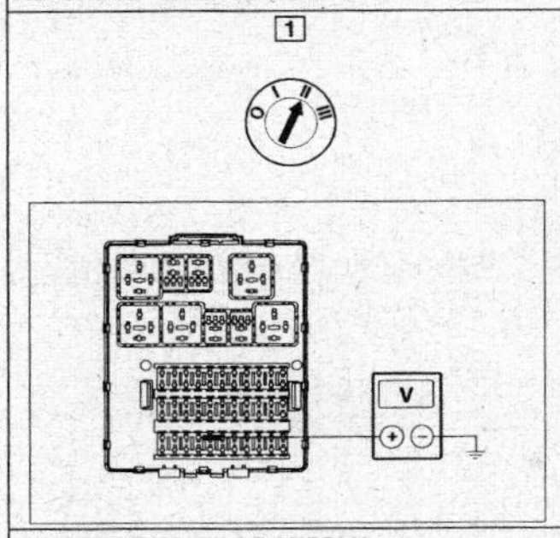	2 Measure the voltage between CJB, connector base F55, supply side and ground. • Is the voltage greater than 10 volts? → **Yes** GO TO **A3** → **No** LOCATE and REPAIR the break in the power supply to F55. TEST the system for normal operation.
A3: CHECK VOLTAGE SUPPLY	
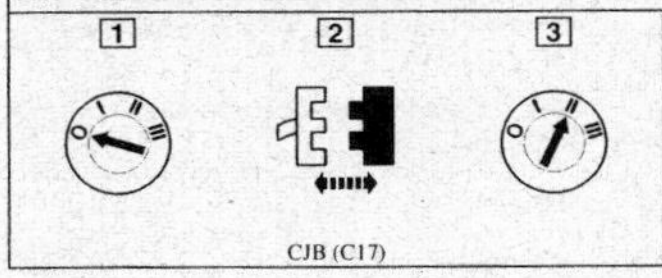	

FM9020100799020X

Fig. 82 Test A: Windshield Wipers Are Inoperative (Part 2 of 5). Focus

CONDITIONS	DETAILS/RESULTS/ACTIONS
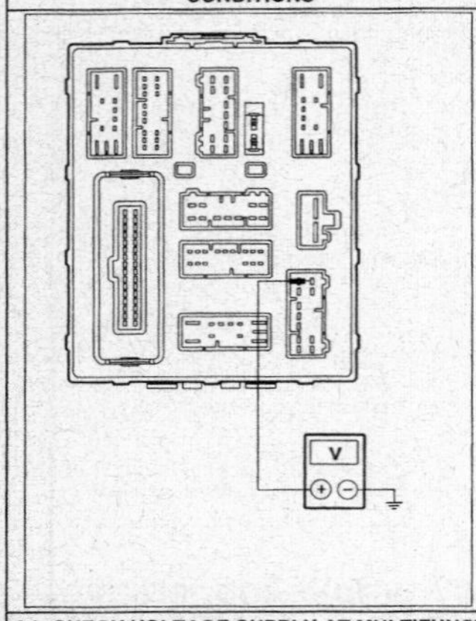	4 Measure the voltage between CJB, connector C17, pin 1, component side and ground. • Is the voltage greater than 10 volts? → **Yes** GO TO **A4** → **No** INSTALL a new CJB. TEST the system for normal operation.
A4: CHECK VOLTAGE SUPPLY AT MULTIFUNCTION SWITCH	
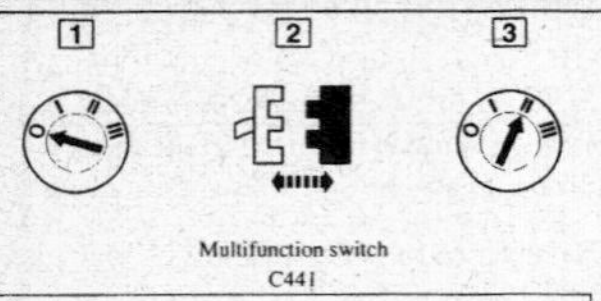 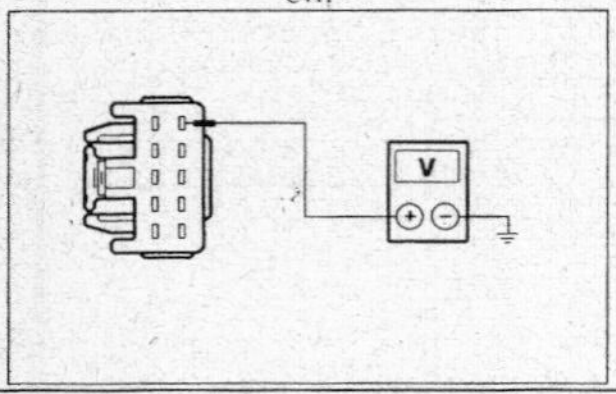	4 Measure the voltage between multifunction switch, connector C441, pin 6, circuit 15-KA19 (GN/OG), harness side and ground. • Is the voltage greater than 10 volts? → **Yes** GO TO **A5** → **No** REPAIR circuit 15-KA19. TEST the system for normal operation.

FM9020100799030X

Fig. 82 Test A: Windshield Wipers Are Inoperative (Part 3 of 5). Focus

CONDITIONS	DETAILS/RESULTS/ACTIONS
A7: CHECK CIRCUITS 32-KA10 AND 32-KA11 FOR CONTINUITY	
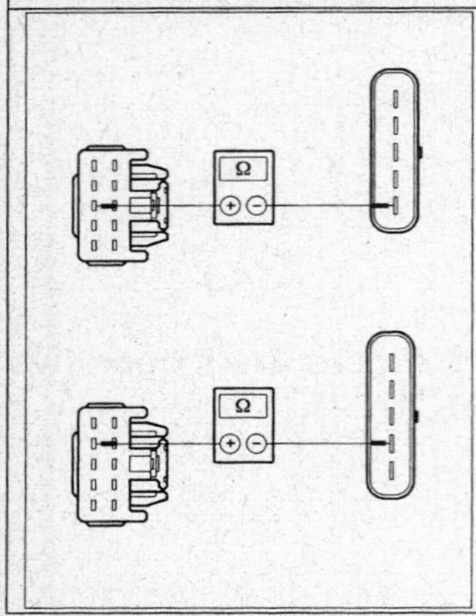	1 Measure the resistance between windshield wiper motor, connector C849, pin 1 and multifunction switch, connector C441, pin 8, circuit 32-KA11 (WH/BK), harness side or between connector C849, pin 2 and connector C441, pin 9, circuit 32-KA10 (WH/GN), harness side. • Is the resistance less than 2 ohms in both cases? → **Yes** INSTALL a new windshield wiper motor TEST the system for normal operation. → **No** REPAIR circuits 32-KA10 or 32-KA11. TEST the system for normal operation.

FM9020100799050X

Fig. 82 Test A: Windshield Wipers Are Inoperative (Part 5 of 5). Focus

CONDITIONS	DETAILS/RESULTS/ACTIONS
A5: CHECK WINDSHIELD WIPER SWITCH	
	1 Check the multifunction switch (windshield wiper switch) according to the components tests in this section. • Is the switch OK? → **Yes** GO TO **A6** → **No** INSTALL a new multifunction switch TEST the system for normal operation.
A6: CHECK GROUND CONNECTION AT WINDSHIELD WIPER MOTOR	
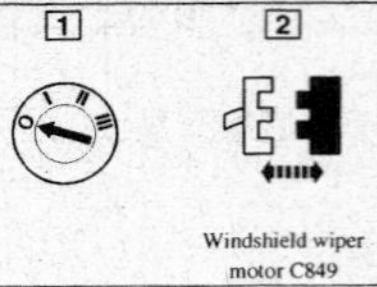 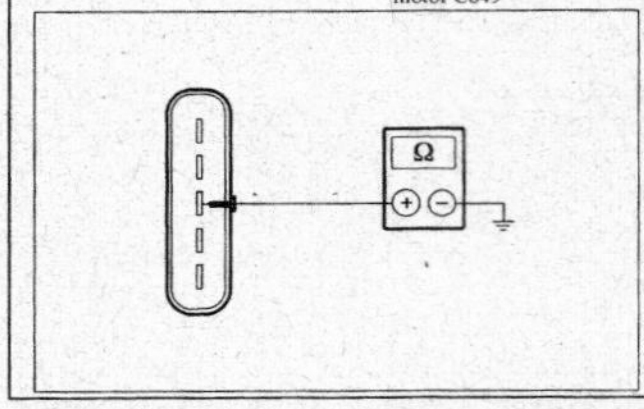	3 Measure the resistance between windshield wiper motor, connector C849, pin 3, circuit 31-KA9 (BK), harness side and ground. • Is the resistance less than 2 ohms? → **Yes** GO TO **A7** → **No** REPAIR circuit 31-KA9. TEST the system for normal operation.

FM9020100799040X

Fig. 82 Test A: Windshield Wipers Are Inoperative (Part 4 of 5). Focus

CONDITIONS	DETAILS/RESULTS/ACTIONS
B1: DETERMINE WIPE SPEED	
	1 Move the wiper lever to "Off". • Do the windshield wipers move at fast rate? → **Yes** GO TO **B2** → **No** GO TO **B4**

FM9020100800010X

Fig. 83 Test B: Windshield Wipers Are On Continuously (Part 1 of 4). Focus

CONDITIONS	DETAILS/RESULTS/ACTIONS
B2: CHECK WIPER SWITCH	
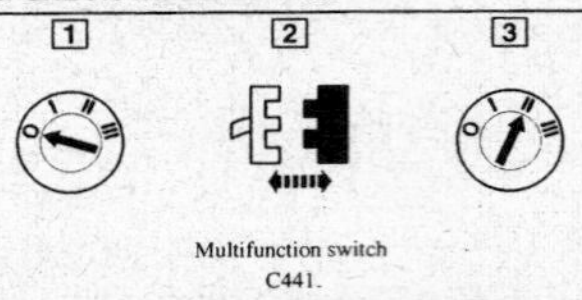	• Do the windshield wipers move at fast rate? → **Yes** GO TO **B3** → **No** CHECK the multifunction switch (windshield wiper switch) according to the component tests in this section. If necessary, INSTALL a new multifunction switch. TEST the system for normal operation.
B3: CHECK CIRCUIT 32-KA11 FOR SHORT TO POWER	
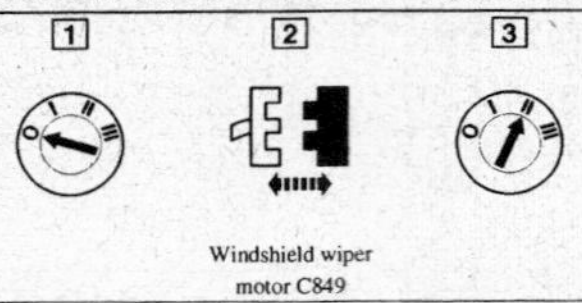 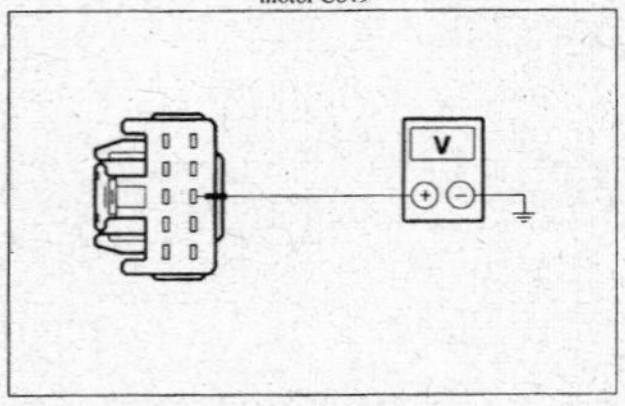	4 Measure the voltage between the multifunction switch, connector C441, pin 8, circuit 32-KA11 (WH/BK), harness side and ground. • Is the voltage greater than 10 volts? → **Yes** REPAIR circuit 32-KA11. TEST the system for normal operation. → **No** CHECK the windshield wiper motor (fast speed winding) according to the component tests in this section. If necessary, INSTALL a new windshield wiper motor. TEST the system for normal operation.
B4: CHECK MULTIFUNCTION SWITCH	
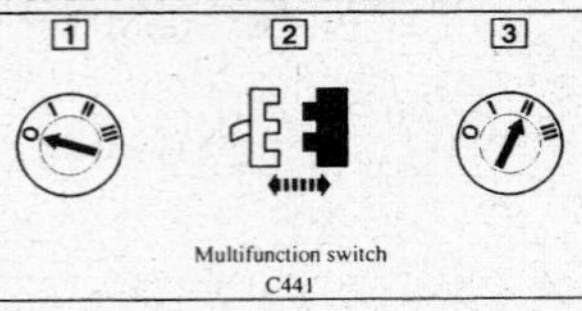	• Do the front wipers move at slow rate? → **Yes** GO TO **B5** → **No** GO TO **B6**

FM9020100800020X

Fig. 83 Test B: Windshield Wipers Are On Continuously (Part 2 of 4). Focus

CONDITIONS	DETAILS/RESULTS/ACTIONS
B5: CHECK CIRCUIT 32-KA10 FOR CONTINUITY	
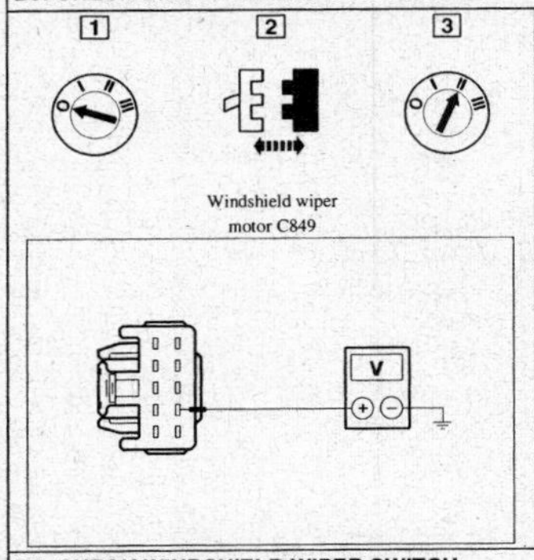	4 Measure the voltage between multifunction switch, connector C441, pin 9, circuit 32-KA10 (WH/GN), harness side and ground. • Is the voltage greater than 10 volts? → **Yes** REPAIR circuit 32-KA10. TEST the system for normal operation. → **No** INSTALL a new windshield wiper motor. TEST the system for normal operation.
B6: CHECK WINDSHIELD WIPER SWITCH	
	1 Check the multifunction switch as described in the component test in this section. • Is the multifunction switch OK? → **Yes** GO TO **B7** → **No** INSTALL a new multifunction switch. TEST the system for normal operation.
B7: CHECK CIRCUIT 32-KA19	
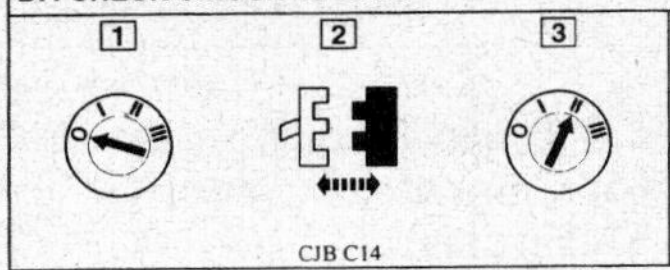	• Do the windshield wipers move at slow rate? → **Yes** REPAIR circuit 32-KA19 (WH/BK). TEST the system for normal operation. → **No** GO TO **B8**

FM9020100800030X

Fig. 83 Test B: Windshield Wipers Are On Continuously (Part 3 of 4). Focus

CONDITIONS	DETAILS/RESULTS/ACTIONS
C1: CHECK FRONT WIPER SWITCH	
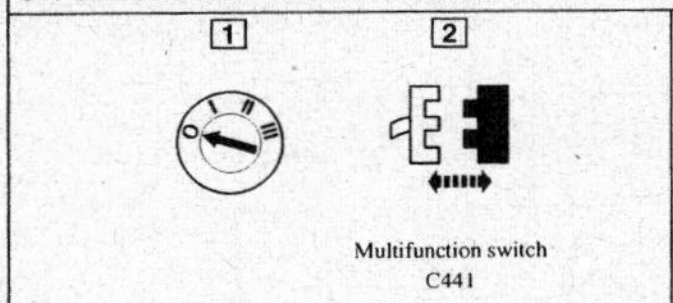	3 CHECK multifunction switch as described in the component test in this section. • Is the switch OK? → **Yes** GO TO **C2** → **No** INSTALL a new multifunction switch TEST the system for normal operation.

FM9020100801010X

Fig. 84 Test C: Fast Windshield Wiper Inoperative, Intermittent Mode Satisfactory (Part 1 of 2). Focus

CONDITIONS	DETAILS/RESULTS/ACTIONS
D1: DETERMINE FAULT	
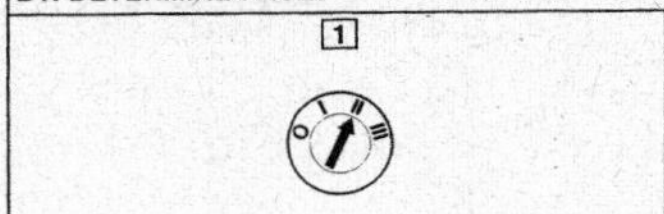	2 Turn the multifunction switch to the wash and wipe function and check for proper function. • Do the wipers work? → **Yes** GO TO **D2** → **No** GO TO **D5**
D2: CHECK VOLTAGE OF WASHER PUMP	
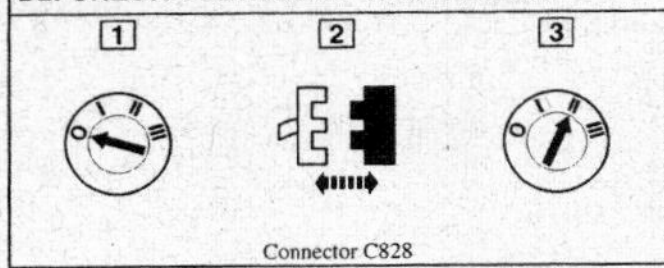	

FM9020100802010X

Fig. 85 Test D: Wash & Wipe Function Is Inoperative Or Does Not Operate Correctly (Part 1 of 5). Focus

CONDITIONS	DETAILS/RESULTS/ACTIONS
B8: CHECK WINDSHIELD WIPER RELAY	
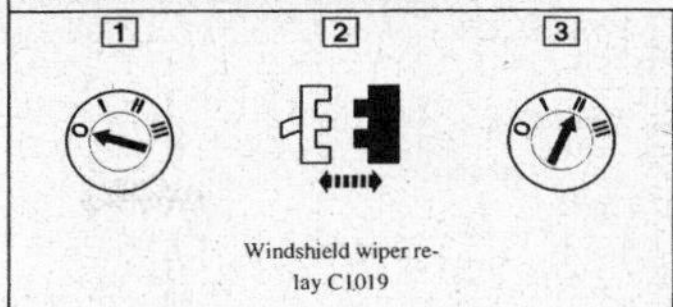	• Do the windshield wipers move at slow rate? → **Yes** INSTALL a new CJB. TEST the system for normal operation. → **No** CHECK the windshield wiper relay according to the component tests in this section. If necessary, INSTALL a new windshield wiper relay. TEST the system for normal operation. Is the windshield wiper relay OK: GO TO **B9**
B9: CHECK CTM OR CJB	
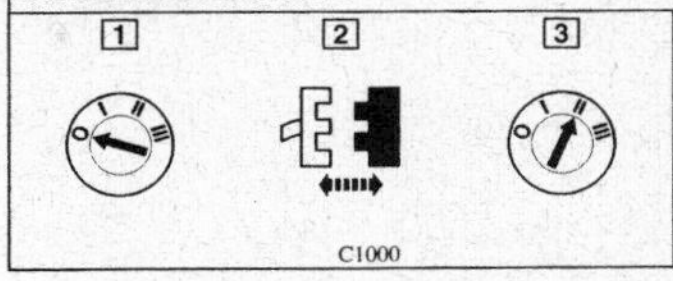	• Do the windshield wipers move at slow rate? → **Yes** INSTALL a new CJB. TEST the system for normal operation. → **No** INSTALL a new CTM. TEST the system for normal operation.

FM9020100800040X

Fig. 83 Test B: Windshield Wipers Are On Continuously (Part 4 of 4). Focus

CONDITIONS	DETAILS/RESULTS/ACTIONS
C2: CHECK CIRCUIT 32-KA11 FOR CONTINUITY	
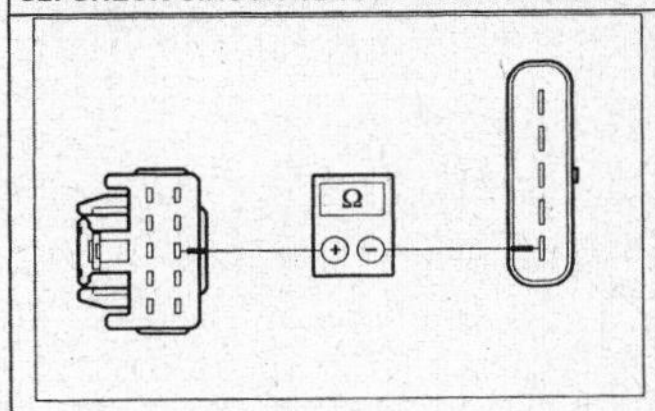	1 Measure the resistance between multifunction switch, connector C441, pin 8 and windshield wiper motor, connector C849, pin 1, circuit 32-KA11 (WH/BK), wiring harness side. • Is the resistance less than 5 ohms? → **Yes** CHECK the windshield wiper motor (fast speed winding) according to the component tests in this section. If necessary, INSTALL a new windshield wiper motor. TEST the system for normal operation. → **No** REPAIR circuit 32-KA11. TEST the system for normal operation.

FM9020100801020X

Fig. 84 Test C: Fast Windshield Wiper Inoperative, Intermittent Mode Satisfactory (Part 2 of 2). Focus

CONDITIONS	DETAILS/RESULTS/ACTIONS
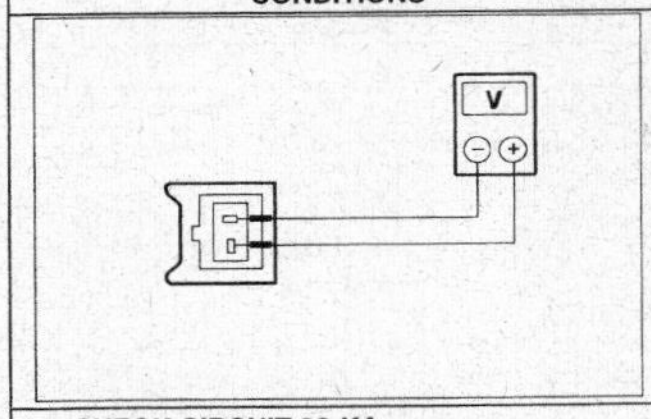	4 Turn the multifunction switch to the wash and wipe function and measure the voltage at connector C828 between pin 1 and 2. • Is the voltage greater than 10 volts? → **Yes** INSTALL a new washer pump. TEST the system for normal operation. → **No** GO TO **D3**
D3: CHECK CIRCUIT 32-KA	
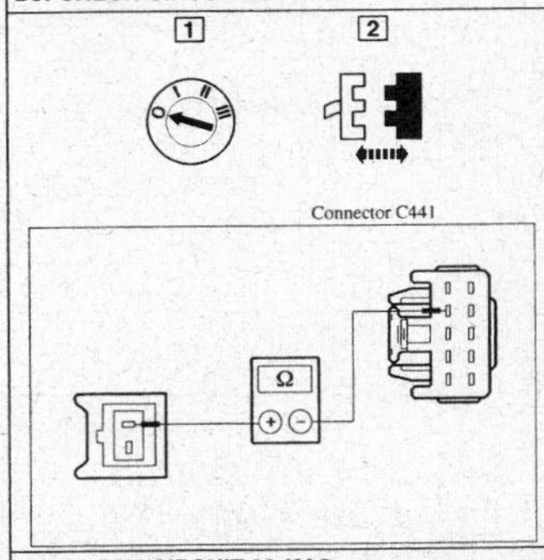	3 Measure the resistance between connector C828, pin 1 and connector C441, pin 2, harness side. • Is the voltage greater than 10 volts? → **Yes** GO TO **D4** → **No** REPAIR circuit 32-KA6/KA34 (WH/BK). TEST the system for normal operation.
D4: CHECK CIRCUIT 33-KA6	
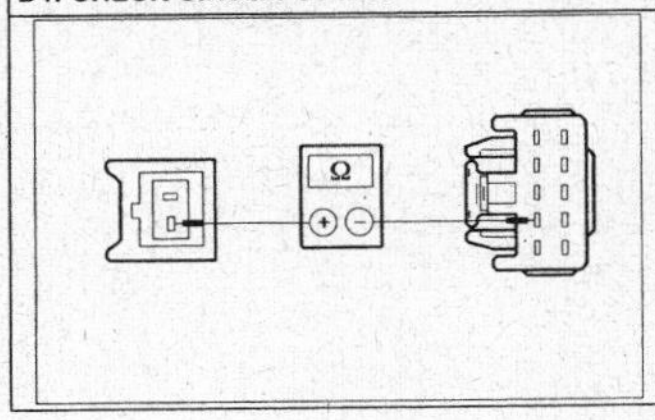	1 Measure the resistance between connector C828, pin 2 and connector C441, pin 4, harness side. • Is the resistance less than 2 ohms? → **Yes** INSTALL a new multifunction switch. TEST the system for normal operation. → **No** REPAIR circuit 33-KA6 (YE/BK). TEST the system for normal operation.

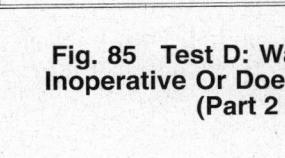

FM9020100802020X

Fig. 85 Test D: Wash & Wipe Function Is Inoperative Or Does Not Operate Correctly (Part 2 of 5). Focus

CONDITIONS	DETAILS/RESULTS/ACTIONS
D5: CHECK INTERMITTENT WIPE	
	1 Turn the multifunction switch to the intermittent wipe function. • Do the wipers work? → **Yes** GO TO **D6** → **No** Check the central timer module with the WDS. Worldwide Diagnostic Scan Tool Or Equivalent
D6: CHECK POWER SUPPLY OF CTM	
1 2 3  Connector C1000 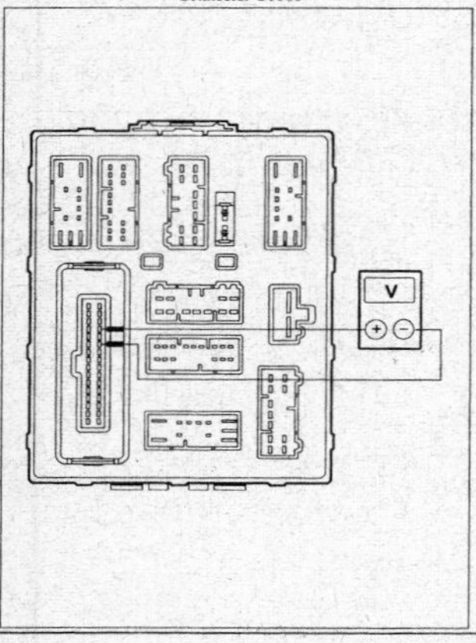	4 Turn the multifunction switch to the wash and wipe function and measure the voltage at connector C1000, between pin 27 and pin 29. • Is the voltage greater than 10 volts? → **Yes** INSTALL a new CTM. TEST the system for normal operation. → **No** GO TO **D7**

FM9020100802030X

Fig. 85 Test D: Wash & Wipe Function Is Inoperative Or Does Not Operate Correctly (Part 3 of 5). Focus

CONDITIONS	DETAILS/RESULTS/ACTIONS
D8: CHECK THE CJB	
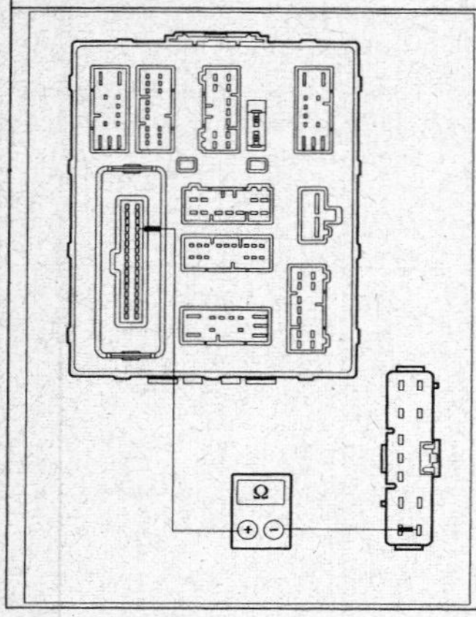	1 Measure the resistance between connector C1000, pin 29 and connector C14, pin 1. • Is the resistance less than 2 ohms? → **Yes** REPAIR circuit 32-KA6A (WH/BK). TEST the system for normal operation. → **No** INSTALL a new CJB. TEST the system for normal operation.

FM9020100802050X

Fig. 85 Test D: Wash & Wipe Function Is Inoperative Or Does Not Operate Correctly (Part 5 of 5). Focus

CONDITIONS	DETAILS/RESULTS/ACTIONS
D7: CHECK CJB	
1 2  Connector C14 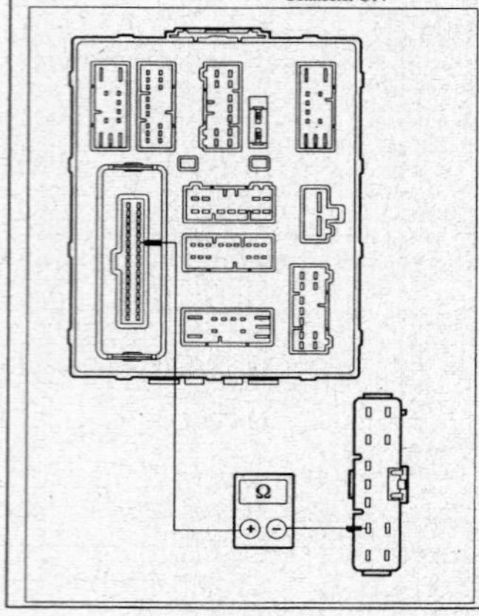	3 Measure the resistance between connector C1000, pin 27 and connector C14, pin 6. • Is the resistance less than 2 ohms? → **Yes** GO TO **D8** → **No** INSTALL a new CJB. TEST the system for normal operation.

FM9020100802040X

Fig. 85 Test D: Wash & Wipe Function Is Inoperative Or Does Not Operate Correctly (Part 4 of 5). Focus

A1 CHECK CIRCUITS 29-DK20 (OG/GN) AND 29S-DK22 (OG/YE) FOR VOLTAGE

Note:
Cycle ignition switch from OFF to RUN to enable the switched system power feature.

1

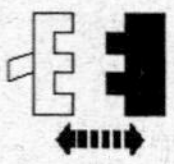

2 *FEM C201c*

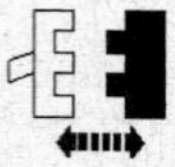

3 *FEM C201f*

4

FM902000076301AX

Fig. 86 Test A: No Communications w/Front Electronic Module (FEM, Part 1 of 4). LS

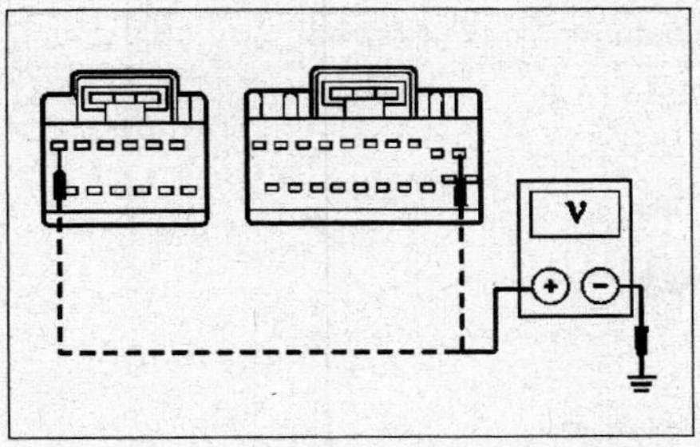

5

Measure the voltage between FEM C201c pin 6, circuit 29-DK20 (OG/GN), harness side and ground; and between FEM C201f pin 1, circuit 29S-DK22 (OG/YE) harness side and ground.

- **Are the voltages greater than 10 volts?**

➔ **Yes**

Go to «A2».

➔ **No**

REPAIR the circuit(s) in question. TEST the system for normal operation.

FM902000076301BX

Fig. 86 Test A: No Communications w/Front Electronic Module (FEM, Part 2 of 4). LS

- **Is the resistance less than 5 ohms?**

➔ **Yes**

Diagnose Module Communication Network.

➔ **No**

REPAIR the circuit(s) in question. TEST the system for normal operation.

FM902000076302BX

Fig. 86 Test A: No Communications w/Front Electronic Module (FEM, Part 4 of 4). LS

B1 CHECK THE FEM PID WPMODE

1

2 Monitor the FEM PID WPMODE, while activating the multifunction switch to the OFF, Low, High, Pulse, Intermittent, and Positions 1 through 7.

- **Do the FEM PID WPMODE values agree with the multifunction switch position?**

➔ **Yes**

Go to «B10».

➔ **No**

If equipped with rain sensor module,Go to «B2». OtherwiseGo to «B3».

FM9020000764010X

Fig. 87 Test B: Wipers Are Inoperative (Part 1 of 38). LS

A2 CHECK CIRCUITS 31-DK20 (BK/RD), 31-DK20A (BK/RD), 31-DK20B (BK/RD), 31-DK20C (BK/RD) AND 31-DK20D (BK/RD) FOR OPENS

1

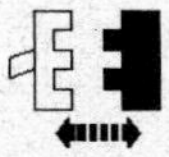

2 *FEM C201a*

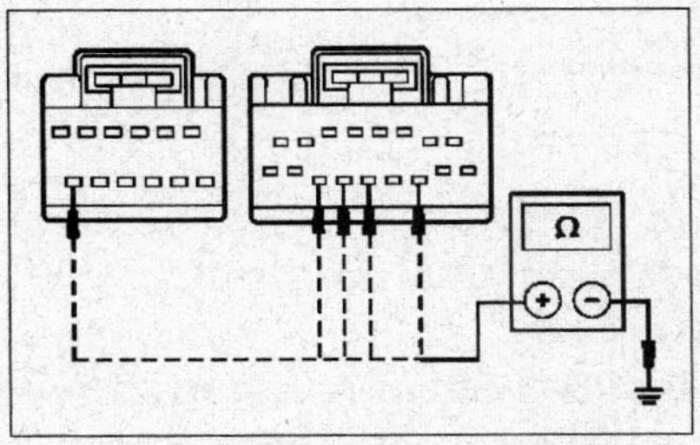

3

Using the following table, measure the resistance between FEM connectors, harness side and ground:

FEM	Pin	Circuit
C201c	12	31-DK20 (BK/RD)
C201a	11	31-DK20A (BK/RD)
C201a	13	31-DK20B (BK/RD)
C201a	14	31-DK20C (BK/RD)
C201a	15	31-DK20D (BK/RD)

FM902000076302AX

Fig. 86 Test A: No Communications w/Front Electronic Module (FEM, Part 3 of 4). LS

B2 CHECK THE RAIN SENSOR MODULE

1

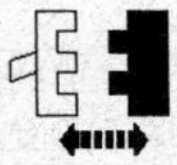

2 *Rain Sensor Module C914 (If equipped)*

3

4 Monitor the FEM PID WPMODE, while activating the multifunction switch to the OFF, Low, Medium, High, Pulse, intermittent, and positions 1 through 7.

- **Do the wiper FEM PID WPMODE values agree with the multifunction switch?**

➔ **Yes**

INSTALL a new rain sensor module. TEST the system for normal operation.

➔ **No**

Go to «B3».

FM9020000764020X

Fig. 87 Test B: Wipers Are Inoperative (Part 2 of 38). LS

B3 CHECK THE MULTIFUNCTION SWITCH OPERATION

1

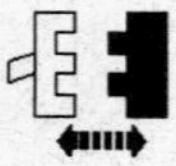

2 *Multifunction Switch C202*

3 Carry out the multifunction switch component test.

- **Is the multifunction switch OK?**

➔ **Yes**

Go to «B4».

➔ **No**

INSTALL a new multifunction switch. TEST the system for normal operation.

FM9020000764030X

Fig. 87 Test B: Wipers Are Inoperative (Part 3 of 38). LS

B5 CHECK THE MULTIFUNCTION SWITCH FOR SHORT TO POWER

1

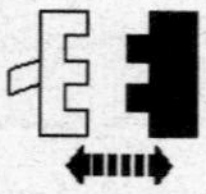

2 *FEM C201f*

3

FM902000076405AX

Fig. 87 Test B: Wipers Are Inoperative (Part 5 of 38). LS

B4 CHECK VOLTAGE TO THE MULTIFUNCTION SWITCH

1

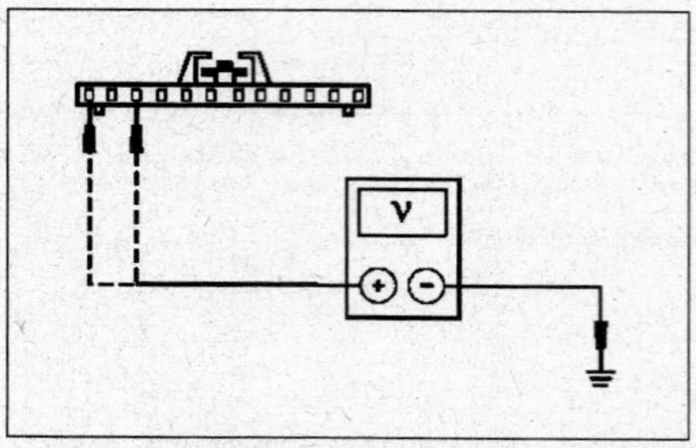

2

Measure the voltage between multifunction switch C202 pin1, circuit (OG/GN) harness side and ground; and between multifunction switch C202 pin 3, circuit (BU/WH), harness side and ground.

- **Are the voltages greater than 10 volts?**

➔ **Yes**

Go to «B5».

➔ **No**

Go to «B8».

FM9020000764040X

Fig. 87 Test B: Wipers Are Inoperative (Part 4 of 38). LS

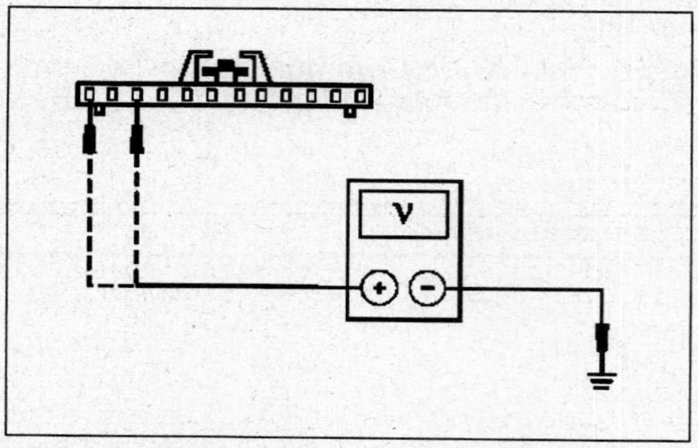

4

Measure the voltage between multifunction switch C202 pin1, circuit (OG/GN) harness side and ground; and between multifunction switch C202 pin 3, circuit (BU/WH), harness side and ground.

- **Are the voltages greater than 10 volts?**

➔ **Yes**

REPAIR the circuit(s) in question. TEST the system for normal operation.

➔ **No**

Go to «B6».

FM902000076405BX

Fig. 87 Test B: Wipers Are Inoperative (Part 6 of 38). LS

B6 CHECK CIRCUIT 7-KA19 (YE/BK) FOR SHORT TO POWER

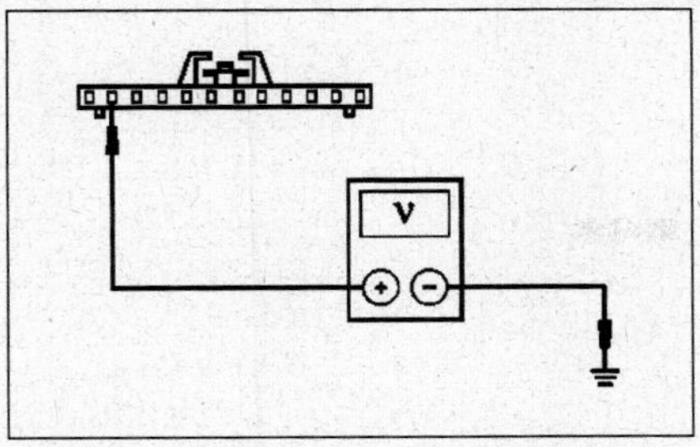

1

Measure the voltage between multifunction switch C202 pin 2, circuit (BN/WH), harness side and ground.

- **Is the voltage greater than 10 volts?**

➔ **Yes**

REPAIR the circuit. TEST the system for normal operation.

➔ **No**

Go to «B7».

FM9020000764060X

Fig. 87 Test B: Wipers Are Inoperative (Part 7 of 38). LS

B7 CHECK CIRCUIT 7-KA19 (YE/BK) AND CIRCUIT 7-KA1 (YE/RD) FOR AN OPEN

1

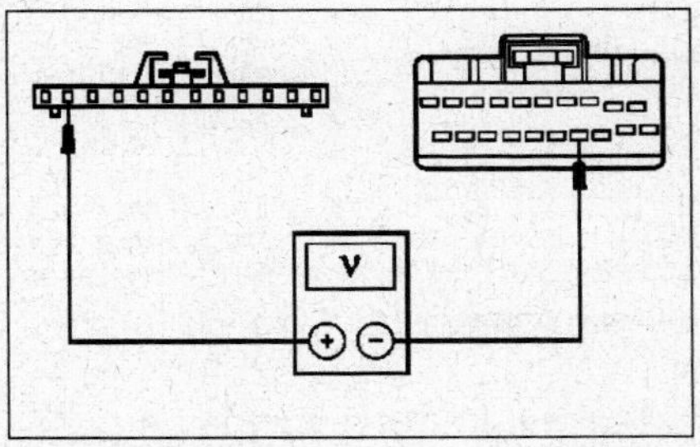

2

Measure the resistance between multifunction switch C202 pin 2, circuit (BN/WH), harness side and FEM C201f pin 14, circuit 7-KA1 (YE/RD), harness side.

- **Is the resistance less than 5 ohms?**

➔ **Yes**

INSTALL a new FEM. TEST the system for normal operation.

➔ **No**

REPAIR the circuit(s) in question. TEST the system for normal operation.

FM9020000764070X

Fig. 87 Test B: Wipers Are Inoperative (Part 8 of 38). LS

B8 CHECK CIRCUITS 7-KA1 (YE/BK), 8-KA2 (WH/RD) AND 10-KA3 (GY/VT) FOR OPENS

1

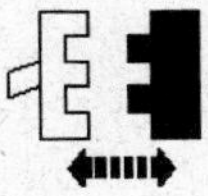

2 *FEM C201f*

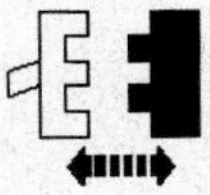

3 *Multifunction Switch C202*

FM902000076408AX

Fig. 87 Test B: Wipers Are Inoperative (Part 9 of 38). LS

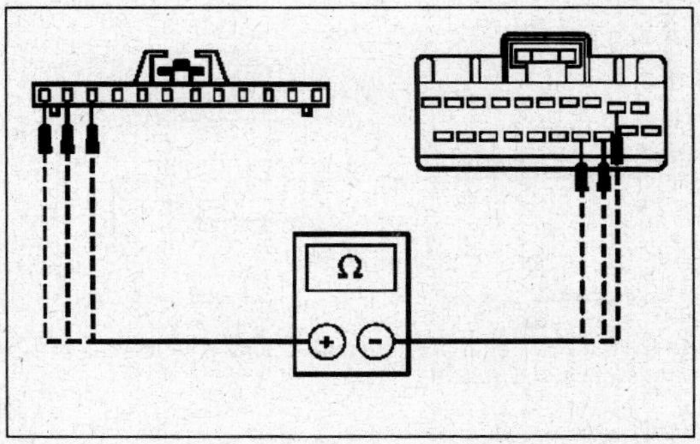

4

Using the following table measure the resistance between multifunction switch C202 harness side and FEM C201f harness side:

Multifunction Switch C202	FEM C201f
pin 1, circuit (OG/GN)	pin 2, circuit 8-KA2 (WH/RD)
pin 2, circuit (BN/WH)	pin 14, circuit 7-KA1 (YE/BK)
pin 3, circuit (BU/WH)	pin 13, circuit 10-KA3 (GY /VT)

- **Is the resistance less than 5 ohms?**

➔ **Yes**

Go to «B9».

➔ **No**

REPAIR the circuit(s) in question. TEST the system for normal operation.

FM902000076408BX

Fig. 87 Test B: Wipers Are Inoperative (Part 10 of 38). LS

B9 CHECK WIPER DELAY AND WIPER MODE CIRCUITS FOR SHORTS TO GROUND

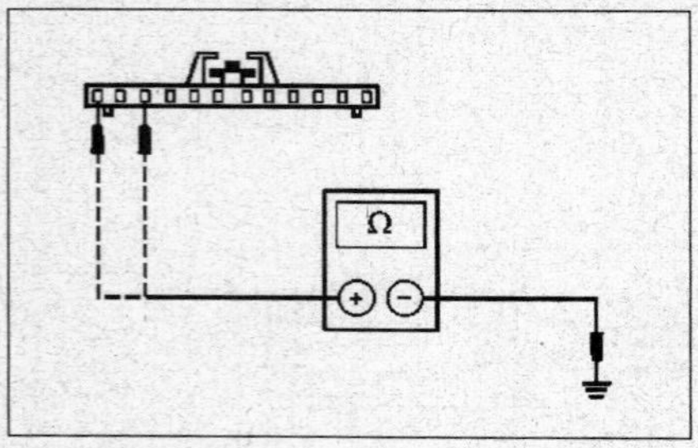

1

Measure the resistance between multifunction switch C202 pin 1, (OG/GN) harness side and ground; and between multifunction switch C202 pin 3, (BU/WH) harness side and ground.

- **Is the resistance greater than 10,000 ohms?**

➔ **Yes**

INSTALL a new FEM. CLEAR the DTCs. REPEAT the self-test.

➔ **No**

REPAIR the circuit(s) in question. CLEAR the DTCs. REPEAT the self-test.

FM9020000764090X

Fig. 87 Test B: Wipers Are Inoperative (Part 11 of 38). LS

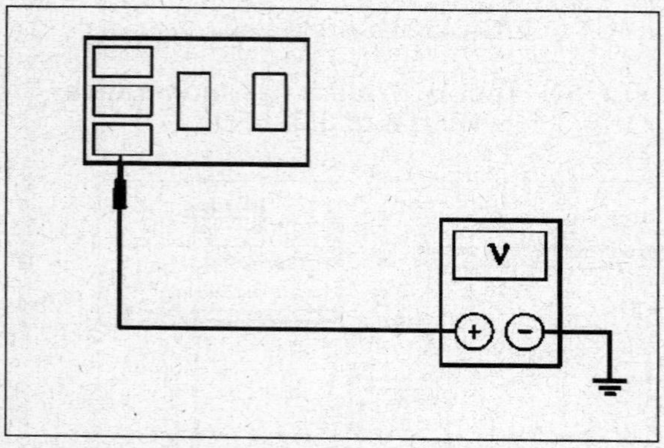

4

Measure the voltage between wiper park relay C1002 pin 2, Circuit 91S-KA39 (BK/RD), harness side and ground.

- **Is the voltage greater than 10 volts?**

➔ **Yes**

Go to «B11».

➔ **No**

Go to «B12».

FM902000076410BX

Fig. 87 Test B: Wipers Are Inoperative (Part 13 of 38). LS

B10 CHECK CIRCUIT 91S-KA39 (BN/YE) FOR VOLTAGE

1

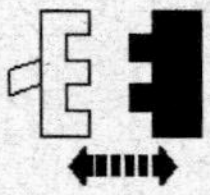

2 *Underhood AJB Wiper Park Relay*

3

FM902000076410AX

Fig. 87 Test B: Wipers Are Inoperative (Part 12 of 38). LS

B11 CHECK CIRCUIT 91S-KA39 (BN/YE) FOR SHORT TO POWER

1

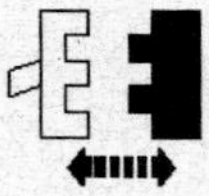

2 *FEM C201b*

3

FM902000076411AX

Fig. 87 Test B: Wipers Are Inoperative (Part 14 of 38). LS

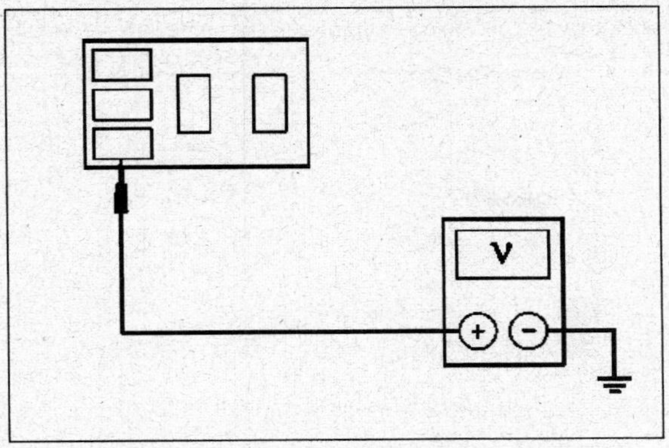

4

Measure the voltage between wiper park relay C1002 Pin 2, Circuit 91S-KA39 (BN/YE), harness side and ground.

- **Is the voltage greater than 10 volts?**

➔ **Yes**

REPAIR the circuit. TEST the system for normal operation.

➔ **No**

INSTALL a new FEM. TEST the system for normal operation.

FM902000076411BX

Fig. 87 Test B: Wipers Are Inoperative (Part 15 of 38). LS

B13 CHECK CIRCUIT 91S-KA39 (BN/YE) FOR AN OPEN

1

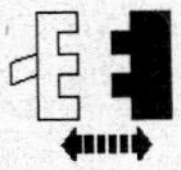

2 *FEM C201b*

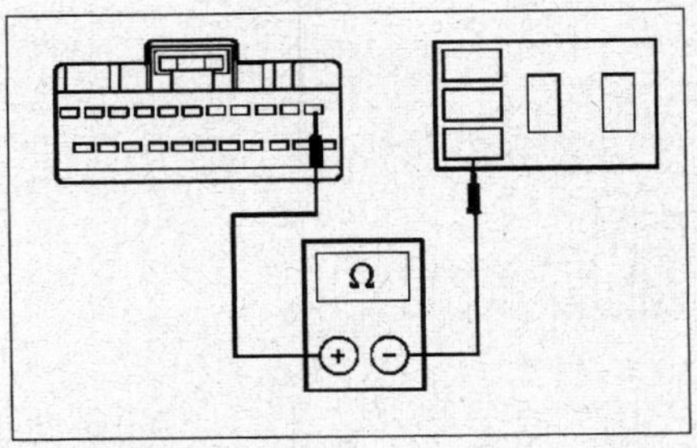

3

Measure the resistance between wiper park relay C1002 Pin 2, Circuit 91S-KA39 (BN/YE), harness side and FEM C201b Pin 1, Circuit 91S-KA39 (BN/YE), harness side.

- **Is the resistance less than 5 ohms?**

➔ **Yes**

INSTALL a new FEM. TEST the system for normal operation.

➔ **No**

REPAIR the circuit. TEST the system for normal operation.

FM9020000764130X

Fig. 87 Test B: Wipers Are Inoperative (Part 17 of 38). LS

B12 ACTIVATE WIPER PARK RELAY COMMAND AND TEST FOR GROUNDING FROM FEM

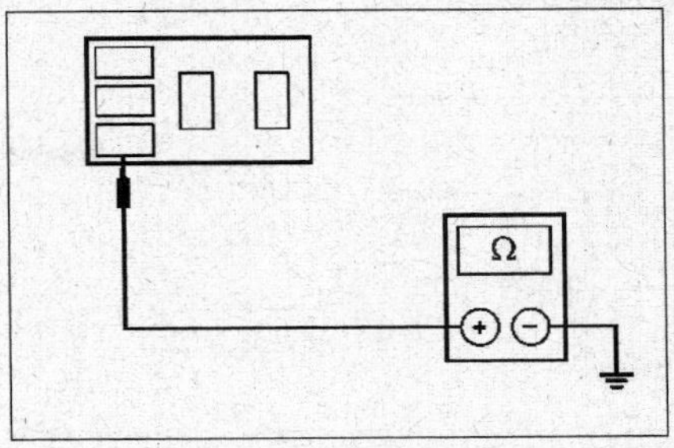

1

Trigger the FEM active command WIPER RLY to ON, while measuring the resistance between wiper park relay C1002 Pin 2, Circuit 91S-KA39 (BN/YE), harness side and ground.

- **Is the resistance less than 5 ohms?**

➔ **Yes**

Go to «B14».

➔ **No**

Go to «B13».

FM9020000764120X

Fig. 87 Test B: Wipers Are Inoperative (Part 16 of 38). LS

B14 CHECK UNDERHOOD AJB FUSE 120 (30A) FOR VOLTAGE

1

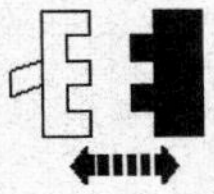

2 *Underhood AJB Fuse 120 (30A)*

3

FM902000076414AX

Fig. 87 Test B: Wipers Are Inoperative (Part 18 of 38). LS

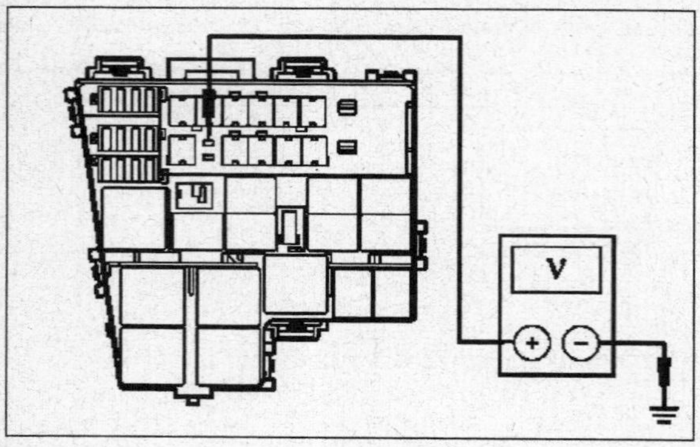

4

Measure the voltage between underhood AJB Fuse 120 (30 A) input side and ground.

- **Is the voltage greater than 10 volts?**

➔ **Yes**

Go to «B15».

➔ **No**

REPAIR the power source. TEST the system for normal operation.

FM902000076414BX

Fig. 87 Test B: Wipers Are Inoperative (Part 19 of 38). LS

B16 CHECK CIRCUIT 75-KA39 (YE/BK) FOR VOLTAGE

1

Windshield Wiper Relay C1009

2

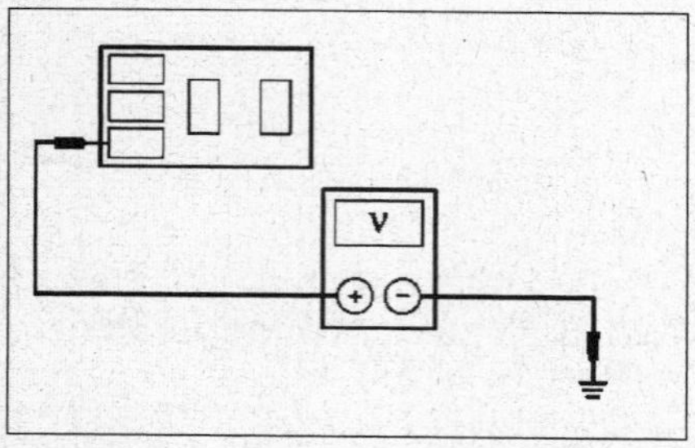

3

Measure the voltage between windshield wiper relay C1009 pin 2, circuit 75-KA39 (YE/BK) and ground.

- **Is the voltage greater than 10 volts?**

➔ **Yes**

Go to «B20».

➔ **No**

Go to «B17».

FM9020000764160X

Fig. 87 Test B: Wipers Are Inoperative (Part 21 of 38). LS

B15 CHECK BETWEEN UNDERHOOD AJB FUSE 120 (30A) AND WIPER PARK RELAY FOR OPENS

1

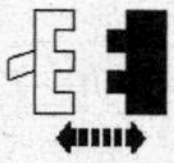

2

Underhood AJB Wiper Park Relay

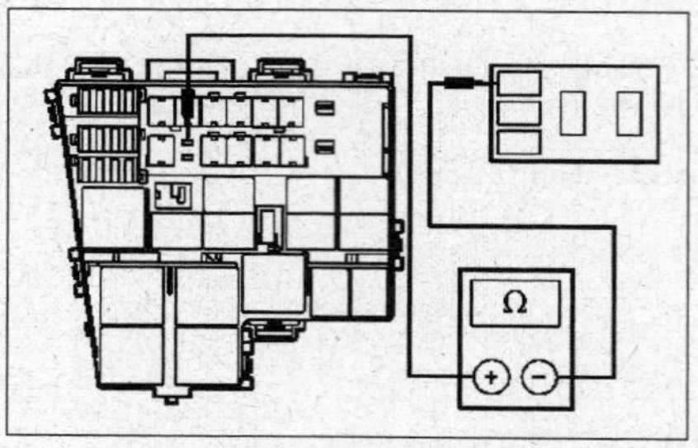

3

Measure the resistance between underhood AJB Fuse 120 (30A), input side, and wiper park relay C1002 Pin 1.

- **Is the resistance less than 5 ohms?**

➔ **Yes**

INSTALL a new underhood AJB Fuse 120 (30A).Go to «B16».

➔ **No**

INSTALL a new underhood AJB. TEST the system for normal operation.

FM9020000764150X

Fig. 87 Test B: Wipers Are Inoperative (Part 20 of 38). LS

B17 CHECK CIRCUIT 75-DD1 (YE) FOR VOLTAGE

1

CJB Fuse 226 (3A)

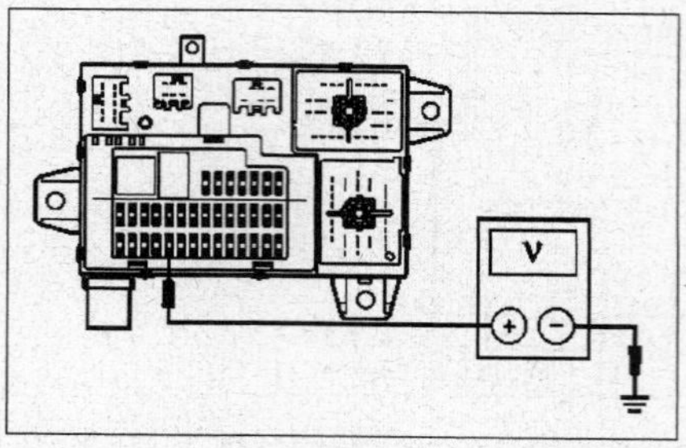

2

Measure the voltage between CJB fuse 226 (3A) input side and ground.

- **Is the voltage greater than 10 volts?**

➔ **Yes**

Go to «B18».

➔ **No**

Go to «B19».

FM9020000764170X

Fig. 87 Test B: Wipers Are Inoperative (Part 22 of 38). LS

B18 CHECK CIRCUIT 75-KA39 (YE/BK) FOR OPENS

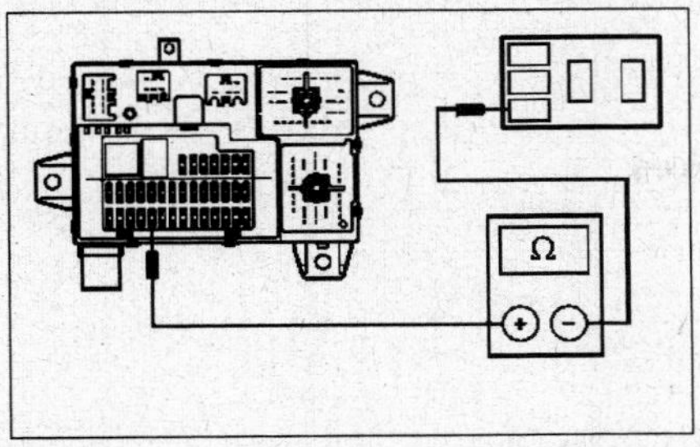

1

Measure the resistance between windshield wiper relay C1009 pin 3, circuit 75-KA39 (YE/BK), and CJB fuse 226 (3A), circuit 75-KA39 (YE/BK) output side.

- **Is the resistance less than 5 ohms?**

→ **Yes**

INSTALL a new AJB. TEST the system for normal operation.

→ **No**

REPAIR the circuit. TEST the system for normal operation.

FM9020000764180X

Fig. 87 Test B: Wipers Are Inoperative (Part 23 of 38). LS

B20 CHECK CIRCUIT 31-KA39 (BK/RD) FOR OPENS

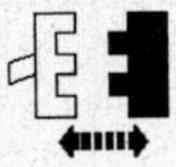

1 *Windshield Wiper Relay C1009*

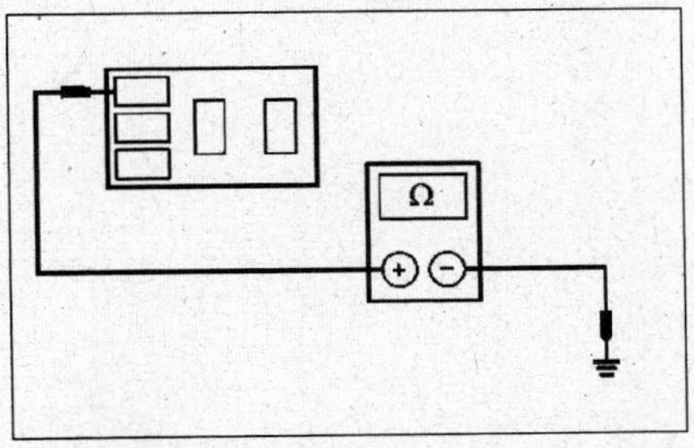

2

Measure the resistance between windshield wiper relay C1009 pin 1, circuit 31-KA39 (BK/RD), harness side and ground.

- **Is the resistance less than 5 ohms?**

→ **Yes**

Go to «B21».

→ **No**

REPAIR the circuit. TEST the system for normal operation.

FM9020000764200X

Fig. 87 Test B: Wipers Are Inoperative (Part 25 of 38). LS

B19 CHECK CIRCUIT 75-DD1 (YE) FOR OPENS

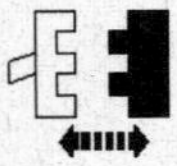

1 *Ignition Switch C250*

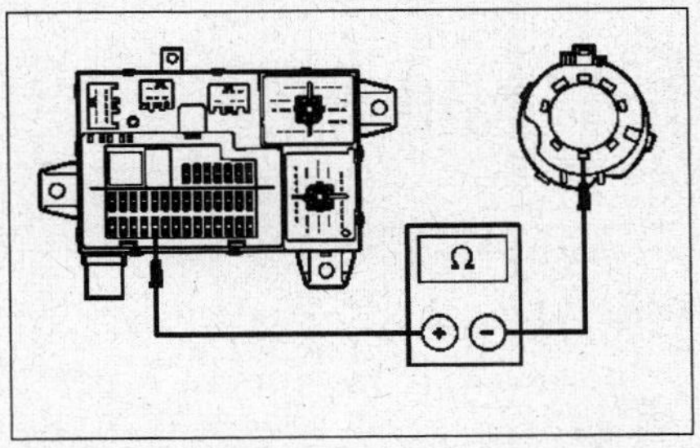

2

Measure the resistance between ignition switch C250 pin 4, circuit 75-DD1 (YE), harness side and CJB fuse 226 (3A), circuit 75-DD1 (YE) input side.

- **Is the resistance less than 5 ohms?**

→ **Yes**

INSTALL a new CJB. TEST the system for normal operation.

→ **No**

REPAIR the circuit. TEST the system for normal operation.

FM9020000764190X

Fig. 87 Test B: Wipers Are Inoperative (Part 24 of 38). LS

B21 CHECK WIPER PARK AND WIPER HIGH/LOW RELAYS

1

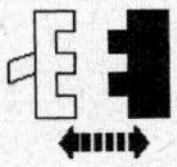

2 *Underhood AJB Wiper High/Low Relay C1001*

3 Carry out the wiper park and wiper high/low relay component tests.

- **Are the wiper park and wiper high/low relays OK?**

→ **Yes**

Go to «B22».

→ **No**

INSTALL a new relay(s) as necessary. TEST the system for normal operation.

FM9020000764210X

Fig. 87 Test B: Wipers Are Inoperative (Part 26 of 38). LS

B22	CHECK CIRCUIT 75S-KA12 (YE/VT) FOR OPENS

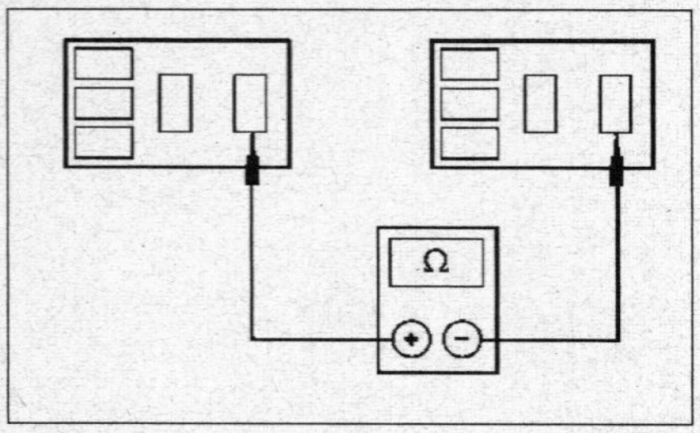

1

Measure the resistance between wiper park relay C1002 pin 3, circuit 75S-KA12 (YE/VT), harness side and wiper high/low relay C1001 pin 3, circuit 75S-KA12 (YE/VT), harness side.

- **Is the resistance less than 5 ohms?**

→ **Yes**

Go to «B23».

→ **No**

REPAIR the circuit. TEST the system for normal operation.

FM9020000764220X

Fig. 87 Test B: Wipers Are Inoperative (Part 27 of 38). LS

B24	CHECK AJB BETWEEN WIPER PARK AND WIPER HIGH/LOW RELAYS FOR OPENS

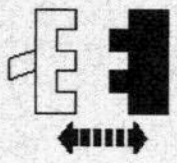

1 *Wiper Run/Park Relay C1002*

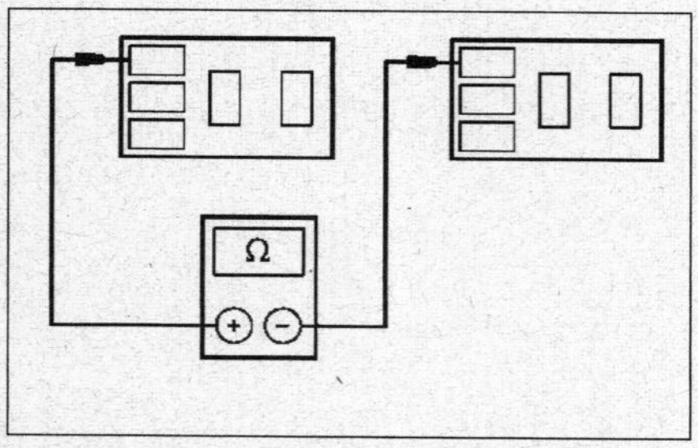

2

Measure the resistance between wiper run/park relay C1002 pin 1, harness side and wiper high/low relay C1001 pin 1, harness side

- **Is the resistance less than 5 ohms?**

→ **Yes**

Go to «B25».

→ **No**

INSTALL a new AJB. TEST the system for normal operation.

FM9020000764240X

Fig. 87 Test B: Wipers Are Inoperative (Part 29 of 38). LS

B23	CHECK AJB FOR OPENS

1 *Wiper Run/Park Relay C1002*

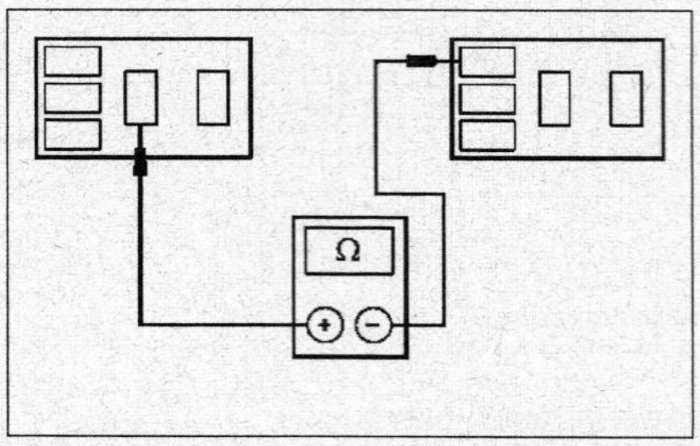

2

Measure the resistance between wiper run/park relay C1002 pin 1, harness side and wiper run/park relay C1002 pin 5, harness side

- **Is the resistance less than 5 ohms?**

→ **Yes**

Go to «B24».

→ **No**

INSTALL a new AJB. TEST the system for normal operation.

FM9020000764230X

Fig. 87 Test B: Wipers Are Inoperative (Part 28 of 38). LS

B25	CHECK CIRCUIT 31S-KA12 (BK/WH) FOR VOLTAGE

1

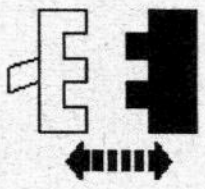

2 *Wiper Motor C125*

3

FM902000076425AX

Fig. 87 Test B: Wipers Are Inoperative (Part 30 of 38). LS

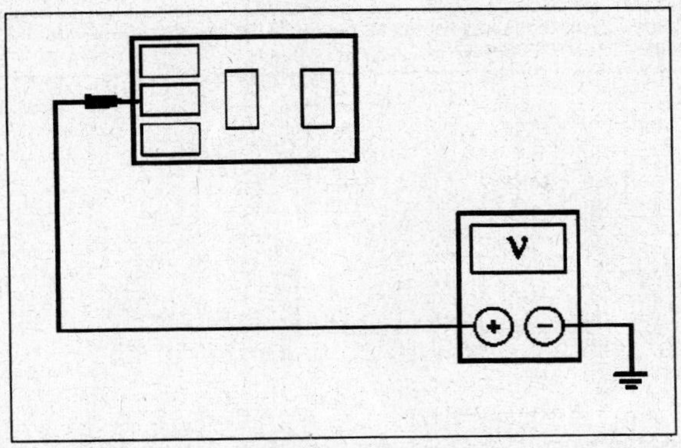

4

Measure the voltage between wiper park relay C1002 Pin 4, Circuit 31S-KA12 (BK/WH), harness side and ground.

- **Is the voltage greater than 10 volts?**

➔ **Yes**

Go to «B26».

➔ **No**

Go to «B27».

FM902000076425BX

Fig. 87 Test B: Wipers Are Inoperative (Part 31 of 38). LS

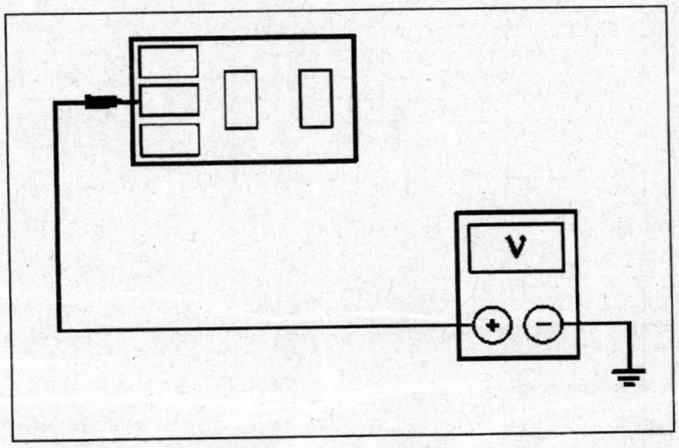

4

Measure the voltage between wiper park relay C1002 Pin 4, Circuit 31S-KA12 (BK/WH), harness side and ground.

- **Is the voltage greater than 10 volts?**

➔ **Yes**

REPAIR the circuit(s) in question. CLEAR the DTCs. REPEAT the self-test.

➔ **No**

INSTALL a new FEM. TEST the system for normal operation.

FM902000076426BX

Fig. 87 Test B: Wipers Are Inoperative (Part 33 of 38). LS

B26	CHECK CIRCUITS 31S-KA12 (BK/WH), 31S-KA1 (BK/YE), AND 31S-KA8 (BK/BU) FOR SHORTS TO POWER

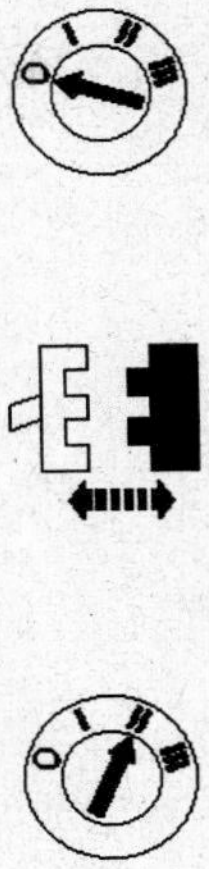

1

2 *FEM C201b*

3

FM902000076426AX

Fig. 87 Test B: Wipers Are Inoperative (Part 32 of 38). LS

B27	CHECK CIRCUIT 31S-KA12 (BK/WH) FOR CONTINUITY

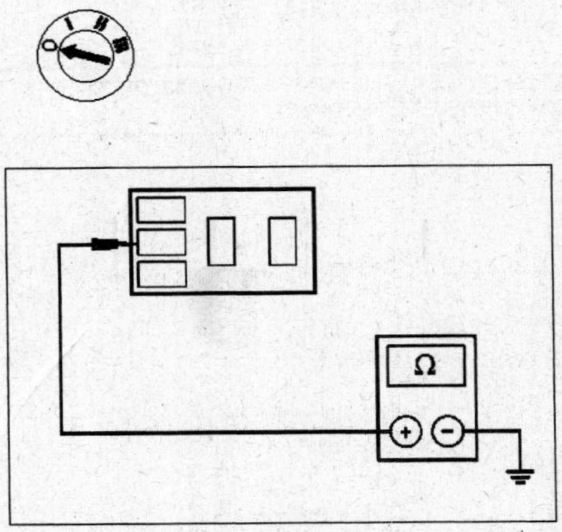

1

2

Measure the resistance between wiper park relay C1002 Pin 4, Circuit 31S-KA12 (BK/WH), harness side and ground.

- **Is the resistance greater than 10,000 ohms?**

➔ **Yes**

Go to «B29».

➔ **No**

Go to «B28».

FM9020000764270X

Fig. 87 Test B: Wipers Are Inoperative (Part 34 of 38). LS

B28 CHECK CIRCUIT 31S-KA12 (BK/WH), 31S-KA1 (BK/YE) AND 31S-KA8 (BK/BU) FOR SHORTS TO GROUND

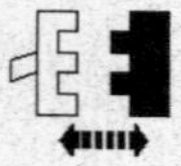

1 *FEM C201b*

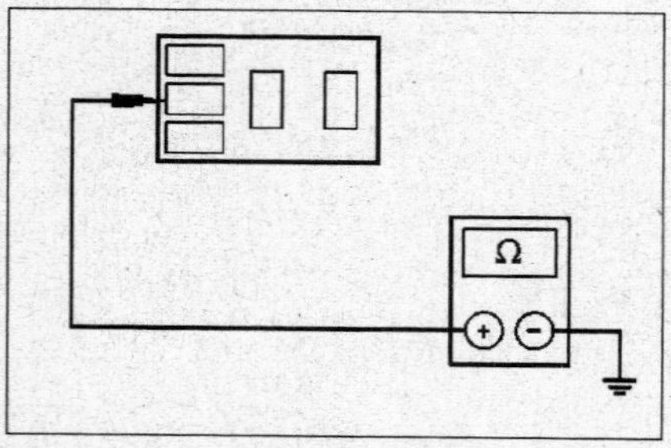

2

Measure the resistance between wiper park relay C1002 Pin 4, Circuit 31S-KA12 (BK/WH), harness side and ground.

- **Is the resistance greater than 10,000 ohms?**

→ **Yes**

INSTALL a new FEM. TEST the system for normal operation.

→ **No**

REPAIR Circuit 31S-KA12 (BK/WH), Circuit 31S-KA1 (BK/YE) or Circuit 31S-KA8 (BK/BU). CLEAR the DTCs. REPEAT the self-test.

FM9020000764280X

Fig. 87 Test B: Wipers Are Inoperative (Part 35 of 38). LS

B29 CHECK CIRCUIT 75S-KA2 (YE/RD) BETWEEN WIPER RUN/PARK AND WINDSHIELD WIPER RELAYS FOR OPENS

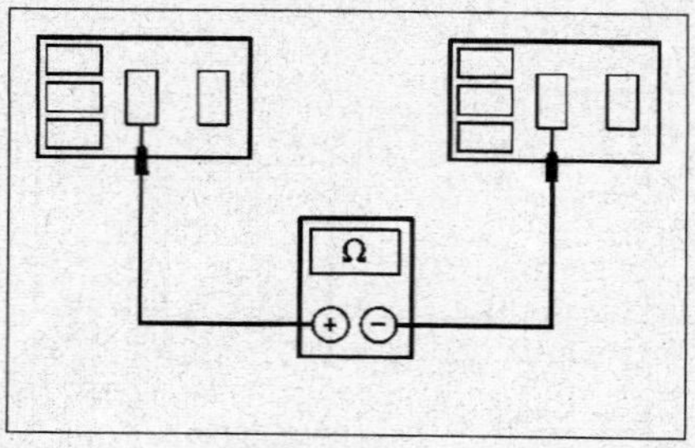

1

Measure the resistance between wiper run/park relay C1002 pin 5, circuit 75S-KA2 (YE/RD) harness side and windshield wiper relay C1009 pin 5, circuit 75S-KA1 (YE/BK) harness side.

- **Is the resistance less than 5 ohms?**

→ **Yes**

Go to «B30».

→ **No**

REPAIR the circuit(s) in question. TEST the system for normal operation.

FM9020000764290X

Fig. 87 Test B: Wipers Are Inoperative (Part 36 of 38). LS

B30 CHECK CIRCUITS 75S-KA2 (YE/RD) AND 30–KA9 (RD/OG)BETWEEN WIPER MOTOR AND WINDSHIELD WIPER RELAYS FOR OPENS

1 *Wiper Motor C125*

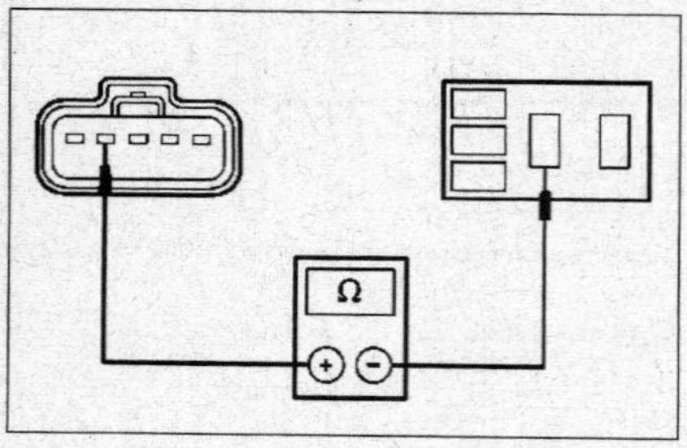

2

Measure the resistance between wiper run/park relay C1002 pin 5, circuit 75S-KA2 (YE/RD), harness side and windshield wiper motor C125 pin 4, circuit 30–KA9 (RD/OG), harness side.

- **Is the resistance less than 5 ohms?**

→ **Yes**

Go to «B31».

→ **No**

REPAIR the circuit(s) in question. TEST the system for normal operation.

FM9020000764300X

Fig. 87 Test B: Wipers Are Inoperative (Part 37 of 38). LS

B31 CHECK CIRCUIT 31-KA9 (BK) FOR OPENS

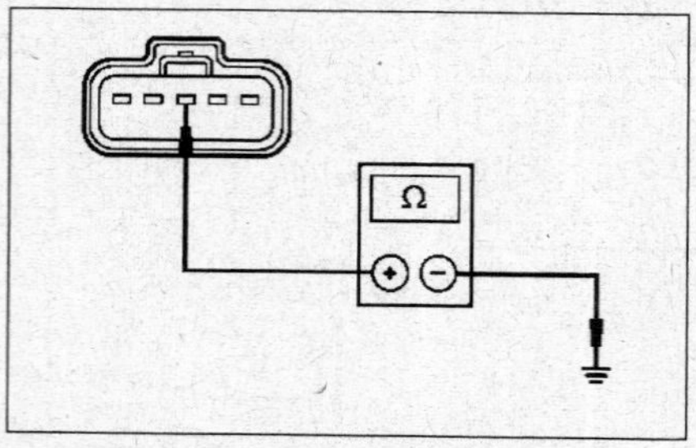

1

Measure the resistance between wiper motor C125 Pin 3, Circuit 31-KA9 (BK), harness side and ground.

- **Is the resistance less than 5 ohms?**

→ **Yes**

CHECK the wiper motor; If the wiper motor does not pass the test, INSTALL a new wiper motor. TEST the system for normal operation.

→ **No**

REPAIR the circuit. TEST the system for normal operation.

FM9020000764310X

Fig. 87 Test B: Wipers Are Inoperative (Part 38 of 38). LS

C1 CHECK THE MULTIFUNCTION SWITCH OPERATION

1

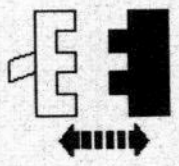

2 *Multifunction Switch C202*

3 Carry out the multifunction switch component test.

- **Is the multifunction switch OK?**

➔ **Yes**

Go to «C2».

➔ **No**

INSTALL a new multifunction switch. TEST the system for normal operation.

FM9020000765010X

Fig. 88 Test C: Wipers Stay On Continuously (Part 1 of 9). LS

C3 CHECK FOR A FAULTY RAIN SENSOR MODULE

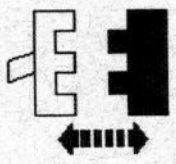

1 *Rain Sensor Module C914*

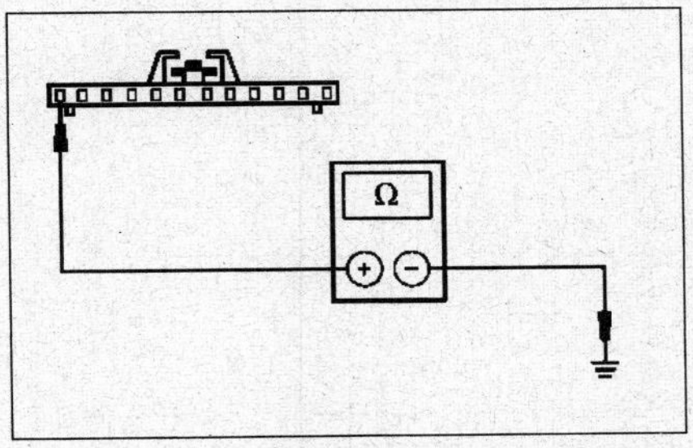

2

Measure the resistance between multifunction switch C202 pin 1, (OG/GN), harness side and ground.

- **Is the resistance greater than 10,000 ohms?**

➔ **Yes**

INSTALL a new rain sensor module.

➔ **No**

Go to «C4».

FM9020000765030X

Fig. 88 Test C: Wipers Stay On Continuously (Part 3 of 9). LS

C2 CHECK CIRCUIT 8–KA41 (WH/GN), 8–KA19 (WH/BK) AND 8–KA2 (WH/RD) FOR SHORTS TO GROUND

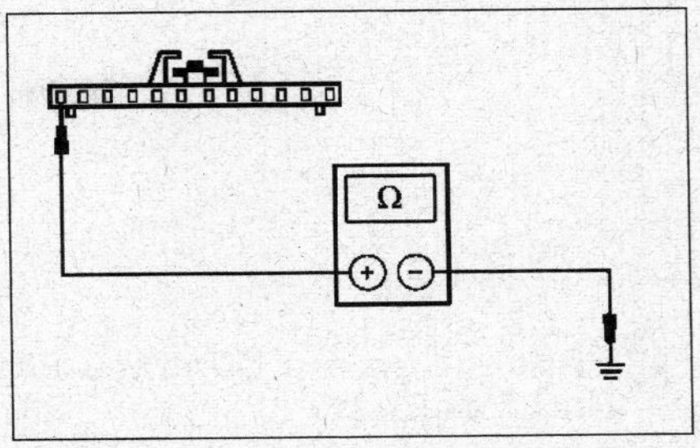

1

Measure the resistance between multifunction switch C202 pin 1, (OG/GN), harness side and ground.

- **Is the resistance greater than 10,000 ohms?**

➔ **Yes**

Go to «C5».

➔ **No**

If equipped with moisture sensitive wipersGo to «C3».

All othersGo to «C4».

FM9020000765020X

Fig. 88 Test C: Wipers Stay On Continuously (Part 2 of 9). LS

C4 CHECK CIRCUITS 8–KA2 (WH/RD), 8–KA19 (WH/BK) AND 8–KA41 (WH/GN) FOR SHORTS TO GROUND

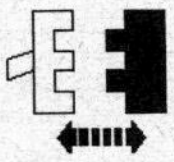

1 *FEM C201f*

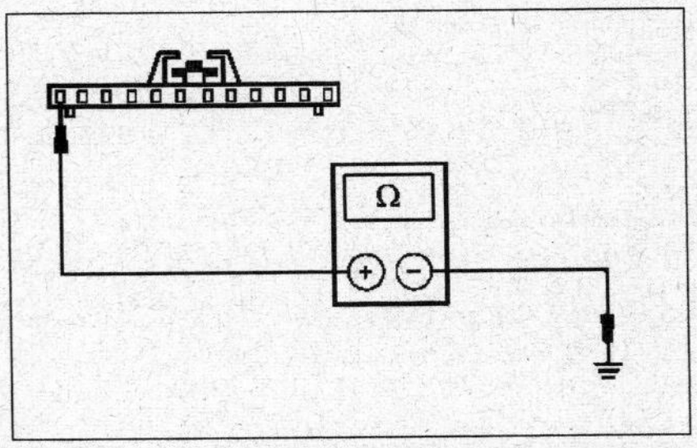

2

Measure the resistance between multifunction switch C202 pin 1, (OG/GN), harness side and ground.

- **Is the resistance greater than 10,000 ohms?**

➔ **Yes**

INSTALL a new FEM. TEST the system for normal operation.

➔ **No**

REPAIR circuit(s) in question. TEST the system for normal operation.

FM9020000765040X

Fig. 88 Test C: Wipers Stay On Continuously (Part 4 of 9). LS

C5 CHECK WIPER PARK AND WIPER HIGH/LOW RELAYS

1 Remove the AJB wiper park and wiper high/low relays.

2 Carry out the relay component test.

- **Are both relays OK?**

→ **Yes**

Go to «C6».

→ **No**

INSTALL a new relay(s). TEST the system for normal operation.

FM9020000765050X

Fig. 88 Test C: Wipers Stay On Continuously (Part 5 of 9). LS

C7 CHECK CIRCUIT 91S-KA39 (BN/YE) FOR SHORTS TO GROUND

1 *FEM C201b*

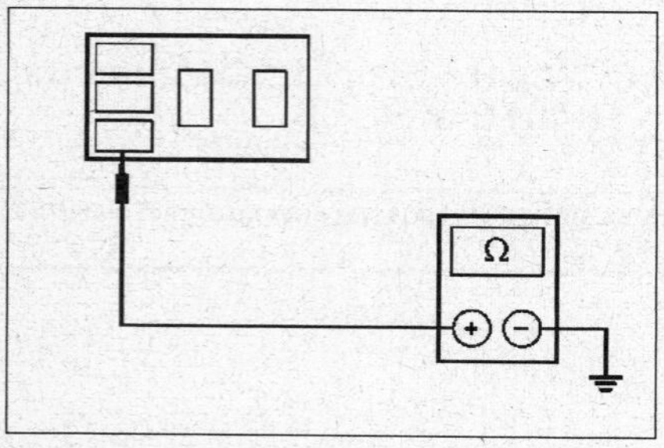

2

Measure the resistance between wiper park relay C1002 Pin 2, Circuit 91S-KA39 (BN/YE), harness side and ground.

- **Is the resistance greater than 10,000 ohms?**

→ **Yes**

INSTALL a new FEM. TEST the system for normal operation.

→ **No**

REPAIR the circuit. TEST the system for normal operation.

FM9020000765070X

Fig. 88 Test C: Wipers Stay On Continuously (Part 7 of 9). LS

C8 CHECK CIRCUIT 75S–KA12 (YE/VT) FOR SHORTS TO BATTERY

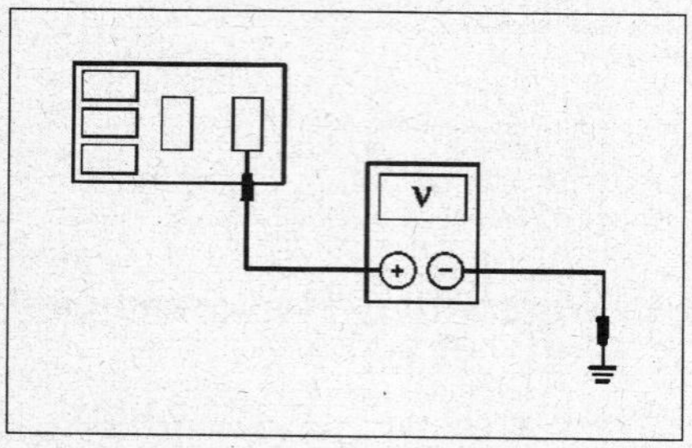

1

Measure the voltage between wiper park relay C1002 pin 3, circuit 75S–KA12 (YE/VT) and ground.

- **Is the voltage greater than 10 volts?**

→ **Yes**

REPAIR the circuit. TEST the system for normal operation.

→ **No**

Go to «C9».

FM9020000765080X

Fig. 88 Test C: Wipers Stay On Continuously (Part 8 of 9). LS

C6 CHECK CIRCUIT 91S-KA39 (BN/YE) FOR CONTINUITY

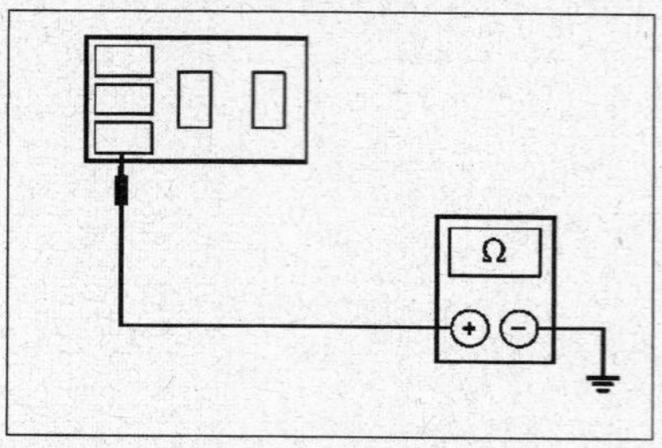

1

Measure the resistance between wiper park relay C1002 Pin 2, Circuit 91S-KA39 (BN/YE), harness side and ground.

- **Is the resistance greater than 10,000 ohms?**

→ **Yes**

Go to «C8».

→ **No**

Go to «C7».

FM9020000765060X

Fig. 88 Test C: Wipers Stay On Continuously (Part 6 of 9). LS

C9 CHECK CIRCUIT 75S–KA11 (YE/BK) AND CIRCUIT 75S–KA10 (YE/GN) FOR SHORT TO BATTERY

1 *Wiper Motor C125*

2

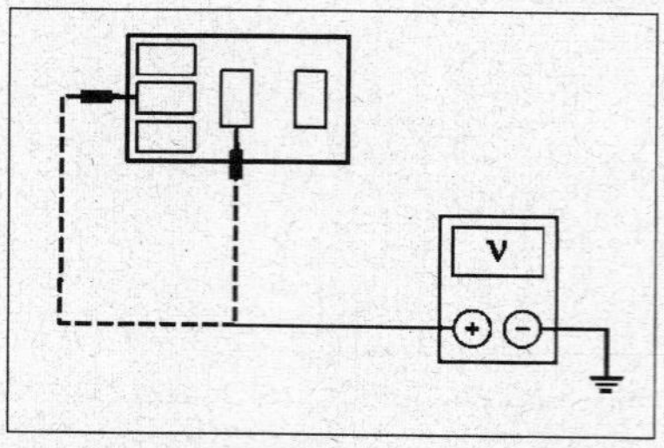

3

Measure the voltage between wiper high/low relay C1001 pin 4, circuit 75S–KA10 (YE/GN), harness side and ground; and between wiper high/low relay C1001 pin 5, circuit 75S–KA11 (YE/BK), harness side and ground.

- **Is the voltage greater than 10 volts?**

→ **Yes**

REPAIR circuit(s) in question. TEST the system for normal operation.

→ **No**

INSTALL a new FEM. TEST the system for normal operation.

FM9020000765090X

Fig. 88 Test C: Wipers Stay On Continuously (Part 9 of 9). LS

D1 CHECK THE FEM PID WPMODE

1 Monitor the FEM PID WPMODE, while activating the multifunction switch to the high and low positions.

- **Do the FEM PID WPMODE values agree with the multifunction switch positions?**

→ **Yes**

Go to «D2».

→ **No**

Go to «D3».

FM9020000766010X

Fig. 89 Test D: High/Low Wiper Speeds Do No Operate Correctly (Part 1 of 17). LS

D2 ACTIVATE THE FRONT WINDSHIELD WIPER/WASHER COMMAND

1

2 Trigger the FEM active command SPEED RLY to the LOW and HIGH speeds.

- **Do the wipers work in LOW and HIGH?**

➔ **Yes**

INSTALL a new FEM. TEST the system for normal operation.

➔ **No**

Go to «D6».

FM9020000766020X

Fig. 89 Test D: High/Low Wiper Speeds Do No Operate Correctly (Part 2 of 17). LS

D4 CHECK RAIN SENSOR MODULE

1 *Multifunction Switch C202*

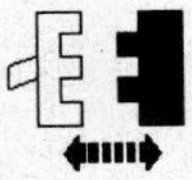

2 *Rain Sensor Module C914*

3

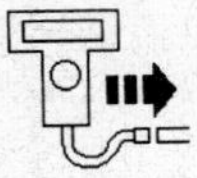

4

Monitor the FEM PID WPMODE while activating the multifunction switch to the high and low positions.

- **Does the FEM PID WPMODES agree with the multifunction switch positions?**

➔ **Yes**

INSTALL a new rain sensor module. TEST the system for normal operation.

➔ **No**

Go to «D5».

FM9020000766040X

Fig. 89 Test D: High/Low Wiper Speeds Do No Operate Correctly (Part 4 of 17). LS

D3 CHECK THE MULTIFUNCTION SWITCH OPERATION

1

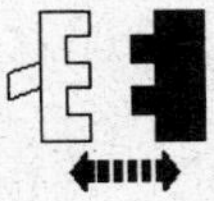

2 *Multifunction Switch C202*

3 Carry out the multifunction switch component test.

- **Is the multifunction switch OK?**

➔ **Yes**

If equipped with moisture sensitive wipers.Go to «D4».

All othersGo to «D5».

➔ **No**

INSTALL a new multifunction switch. TEST the system for normal operation.

FM9020000766030X

Fig. 89 Test D: High/Low Wiper Speeds Do No Operate Correctly (Part 3 of 17). LS

D5 CHECK CIRCUITS 8–KA2 (WH/RD), 8–KA19 (WH/GN) AND 8–KA41 (WH/GN) FOR SHORTS TO GROUND

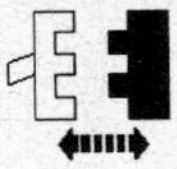

1 *FEM C201f*

2 *Multifunction Switch C202*

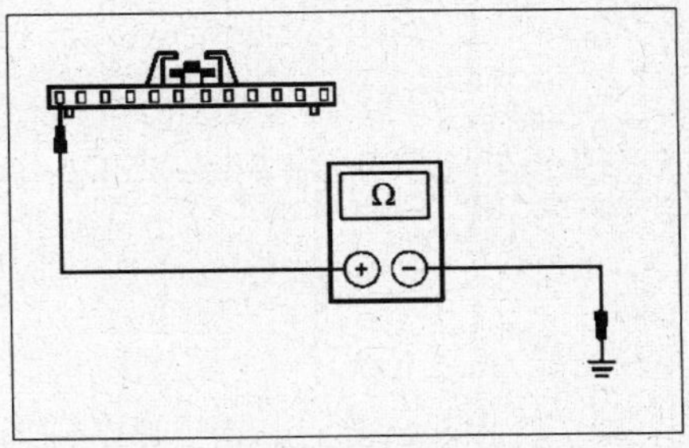

3

Measure the resistance between multifunction switch C202 pin 1, circuit (OG/GN), harness side and ground.

- **Is the resistance greater than 10,000 ohms?**

➔ **Yes**

INSTALL a new FEM. TEST the system for normal operation.

➔ **No**

REPAIR circuit(s) in question. TEST the system for normal operation.

FM9020000766050X

Fig. 89 Test D: High/Low Wiper Speeds Do No Operate Correctly (Part 5 of 17). LS

D6 CHECK WIPER HIGH/LOW RELAY PIN 2 FOR VOLTAGE

1

2 *Underhood AJB Wiper HIGH/LOW Relay*

3

FM902000076606AX

Fig. 89 Test D: High/Low Wiper Speeds Do No Operate Correctly (Part 6 of 17). LS

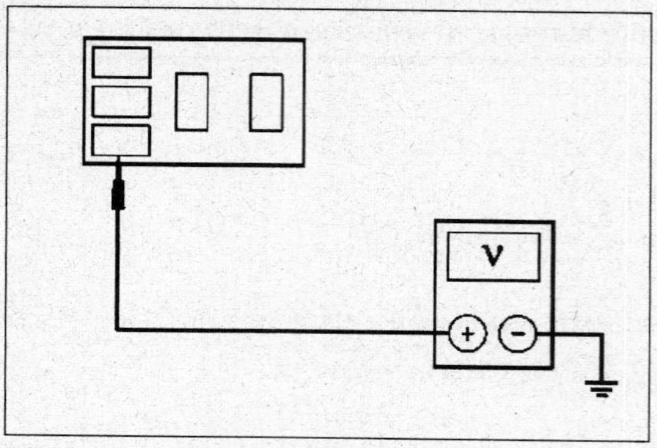

4

Measure the voltage between wiper high/low relay C1001 pin 2, circuit 91S-KA16 (BN/GN), harness side and ground.

- **Is the voltage greater than 10 volts?**

➔ **Yes**

Go to «D7».

➔ **No**

Go to «D8».

FM902000076606BX

Fig. 89 Test D: High/Low Wiper Speeds Do No Operate Correctly (Part 7 of 17). LS

D7 CHECK CIRCUIT 91S-KA16 (BN/GR) FOR SHORTS TO POWER

1

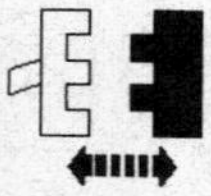

2 *FEM C201b*

3

FM902000076607AX

Fig. 89 Test D: High/Low Wiper Speeds Do No Operate Correctly (Part 8 of 17). LS

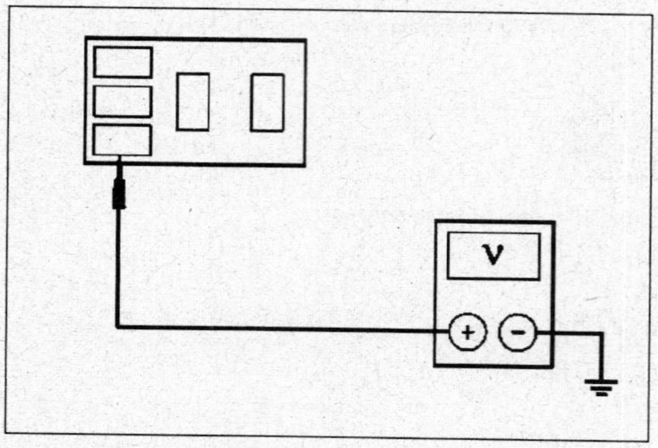

4

Measure the voltage between wiper high/low relay C1001 pin 2, circuit 91S-KA16 (BN/GN), harness side and ground.

- **Is the voltage greater than 10 volts?**

➔ **Yes**

REPAIR the circuit. TEST the system for normal operation.

➔ **No**

INSTALL a new FEM. TEST the system for normal operation.

FM902000076607BX

Fig. 89 Test D: High/Low Wiper Speeds Do No Operate Correctly (Part 9 of 17). LS

D8 CHECK WIPER HIGH/LOW RELAY PIN 2 FOR CONTINUITY TO GROUND

1

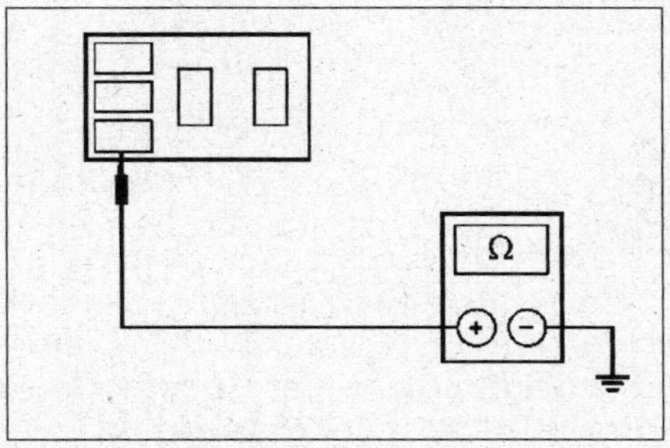

2

Measure the resistance between wiper high/low relay C1001 pin 2, circuit 91S-KA16 (BN/GN), harness side and ground.

- **Is the resistance greater than 10,000 ohms?**

→ **Yes**

Go to «D10».

→ **No**

Go to «D9».

FM9020000766080X

Fig. 89 Test D: High/Low Wiper Speeds Do No Operate Correctly (Part 10 of 17). LS

D9 CHECK CIRCUIT 91S-KA16 (BN/GN) FOR SHORTS TO GROUND

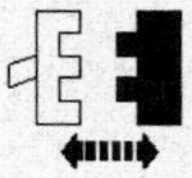

1 *FEM C201b*

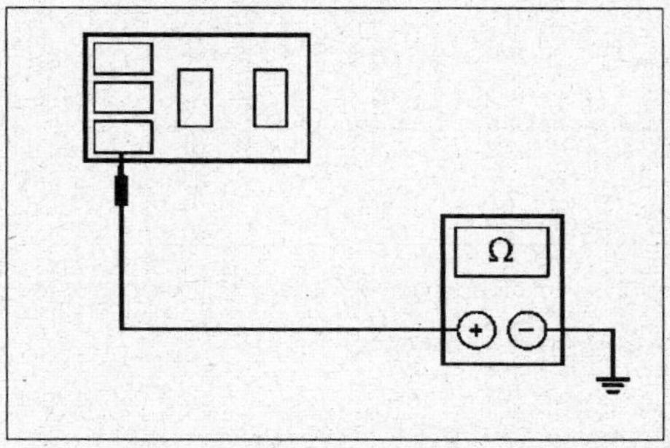

2

Measure the resistance between wiper high/low relay C1001 pin 2, circuit 91S-KA16 (BN/GN), harness side and ground.

- **Is the resistance greater than 10,000 ohms?**

→ **Yes**

INSTALL a new FEM. TEST the system for normal operation.

→ **No**

REPAIR the circuit. TEST the system for normal operation.

FM9020000766090X

Fig. 89 Test D: High/Low Wiper Speeds Do No Operate Correctly (Part 11 of 17). LS

D10 ACTIVATE WIPER HIGH/LOW RELAY

1

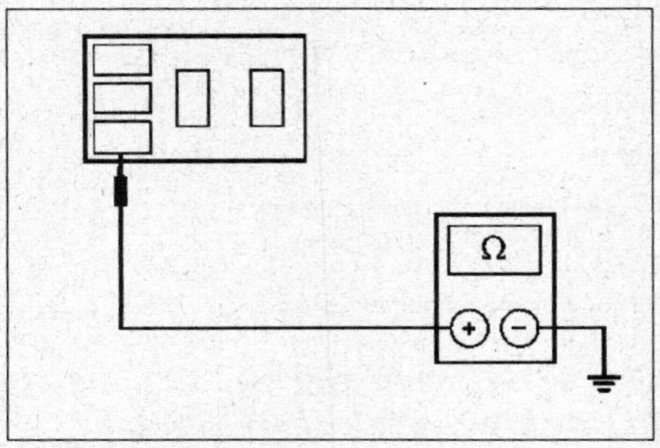

2

Trigger the FEM active command SPEED RLY to ON, while measuring the resistance between wiper high/low relay C1001 Pin 2, Circuit 91S-KA16 (BN/GN) and ground.

- **Is the resistance less than 5 ohms?**

→ **Yes**

Go to «D11».

→ **No**

Go to «D14».

FM9020000766100X

Fig. 89 Test D: High/Low Wiper Speeds Do No Operate Correctly (Part 12 of 17). LS

D11 CHECK UNDERHOOD AJB WIPER HIGH/LOW RELAY

1 Carry out the wiper high/low relay component test.

- **Is the wiper high/low relay OK?**

→ **Yes**

Go to «D12».

→ **No**

INSTALL a new wiper high/low relay. TEST the system for normal operation.

FM9020000766110X

Fig. 89 Test D: High/Low Wiper Speeds Do No Operate Correctly (Part 13 of 17). LS

D12 CHECK WIPER HIGH/LOW RELAY PIN 1 FOR VOLTAGE

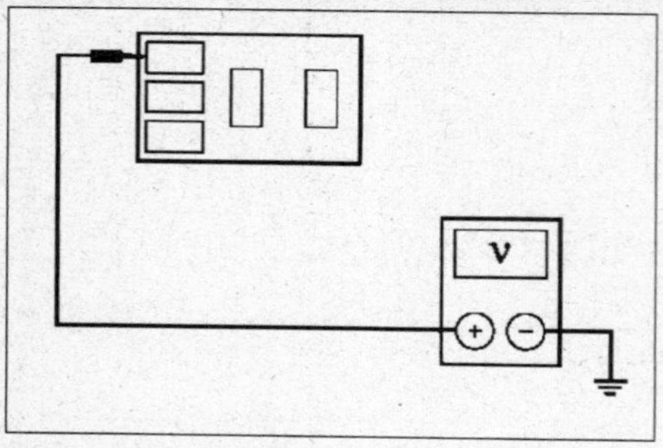

1

Measure the voltage between wiper high/low relay C1001 Pin 1, harness side and ground.

- **Is the voltage greater than 10 volts?**

➔ **Yes**

Go to «D13».

➔ **No**

INSTALL a new underhood AJB. TEST the system for normal operation.

FM9020000766120X

Fig. 89 Test D: High/Low Wiper Speeds Do No Operate Correctly (Part 14 of 17). LS

D13 CHECK CIRCUITS 75S-KA10 (YE/GN) AND 75S-KA11 (YE/BK) FOR OPENS

1

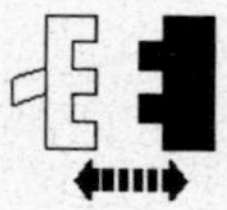

2

Wiper Motor C125

FM902000076613AX

Fig. 89 Test D: High/Low Wiper Speeds Do Not Operate Correctly (Part 15 of 17). LS

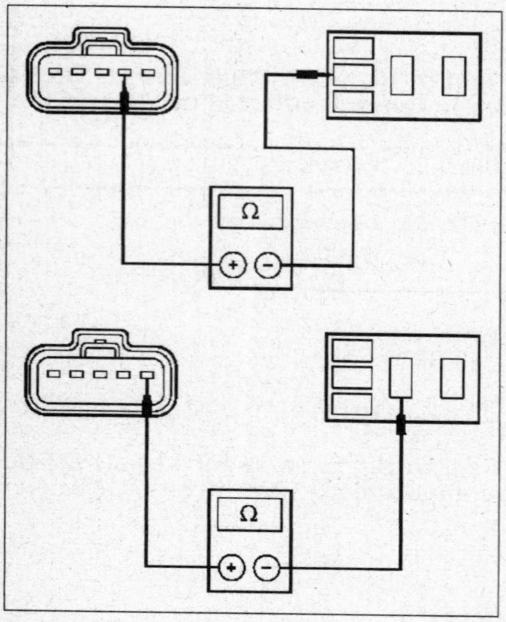

3

Measure the resistance between wiper high/low relay C1001 pin 4, circuit 75S-KA10 (YE/GN), harness side and wiper motor C125 pin 4, circuit 75S-KA10 (YE/GN), harness side; and between wiper high/low relay C1001 pin 5, circuit 75S-KA11 (YE/BK), harness side and wiper motor C125 Pin 5, circuit 75S-KA11 (YE/BK), harness side.

- **Is the resistance greater than 10,000 ohms?**

➔ **Yes**

CHECK the wiper motor; If the wiper motor does not pass the test, INSTALL a new wiper motor, TEST the system for normal operation.

➔ **No**

REPAIR circuits in question. TEST the system for normal operation.

FM902000076613BX

Fig. 89 Test D: High/Low Wiper Speeds Do Not Operate Correctly (Part 16 of 17). LS

D14 CHECK CIRCUIT 91S-KA16 (BN/GN) FOR OPENS

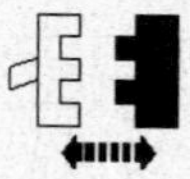

1

FEM C201b

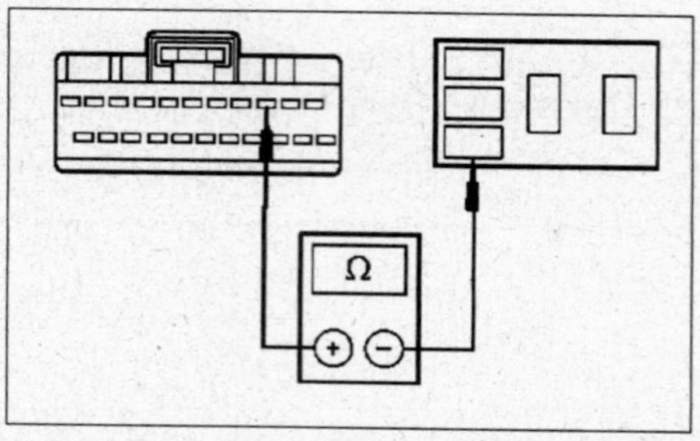

2

Measure the resistance between wiper high/low relay C1001 pin 2, circuit 91S-KA16 (BN/GN), harness side and FEM C201b pin 3, circuit 91S-KA16 (BN/GN), harness side.

- **Is the resistance less than 5 ohms?**

➔ **Yes**

INSTALL a new FEM. TEST the system for normal operation.

➔ **No**

REPAIR the circuit. TEST the system for normal operation.

FM9020000766140X

Fig. 89 Test D: High/Low Wiper Speeds Do Not Operate Correctly (Part 17 of 17). LS

E1 MONITOR THE FEM PID WPMODE

1

2 Monitor the FEM PID WPMODE while activating the wash and wipe functions.

- **Do the FEM PID WPMODE values agree with the multifunction switch positions?**

→ **Yes**

Go to «E6».

→ **No**

If equipped with moisture sensitive wipersGo to «E2».

All othersGo to «E3».

FM9020000767010X

Fig. 90 Test E: Wash & Wipe Function Does Not Operate Correctly (Part 1 of 6). LS

E3 CHECK THE MULTIFUNCTION SWITCH OPERATION

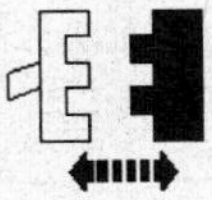

1 *Multifunction Switch C202*

2 Carry out the multifunction switch component test.

- **Is the multifunction switch OK?**

→ **Yes**

Go to «E4».

→ **No**

INSTALL a new multifunction switch. TEST the system for normal operation.

FM9020000767030X

Fig. 90 Test E: Wash & Wipe Function Does Not Operate Correctly (Part 3 of 6). LS

E2 CHECK RAIN SENSOR MODULE

1

2 *Rain Sensor Module C914*

3 Monitor the FEM PID WPMODE while activating the wash and wipe functions.

- **Do the FEM PID WPMODE values agree with the multifunction switch positions?**

→ **Yes**

INSTALL a new rain sensor module. TEST the system for normal operation.

→ **No**

Go to «E3».

FM9020000767020X

Fig. 90 Test E: Wash & Wipe Function Does Not Operate Correctly (Part 2 of 6). LS

E4 CHECK CIRCUITS 10-KA3 (GY/VT), 10–KA19 (GY/BK) AND 10–KA41 (GY/OG) FOR SHORTS TO GROUND

1 *FEM C201f*

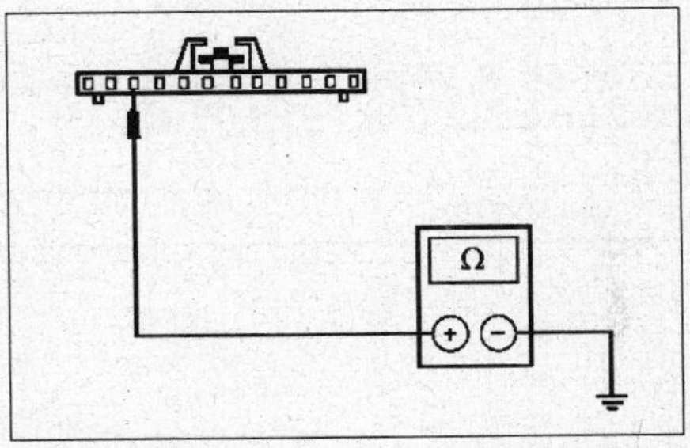

2

Measure the resistance between multifunction switch C202 pin 3, circuit (BU/WH), harness side and ground.

- **Is the resistance greater than 10,000 ohms?**

→ **Yes**

Go to «E5».

→ **No**

REPAIR circuit(s) in question. TEST the system for normal operation.

FM9020000767040X

Fig. 90 Test E: Wash & Wipe Function Does Not Operate Correctly (Part 4 of 6). LS

E5	CHECK CIRCUITS 10-KA3 (GY/VT), 10–KA19 (GY/BK) AND 10–KA41 (GY/OG) FOR OPENS

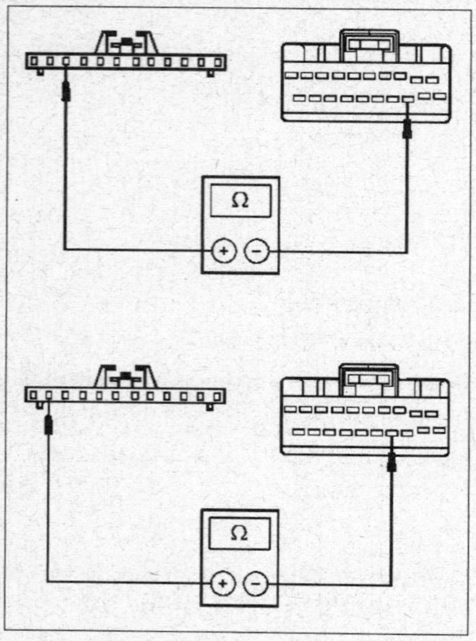

1

Measure the resistance between multifunction switch C202 pin 3, circuit (BU/WH), harness side and FEM C201f pin 13, circuit 10-KA3 (GY/VT); and between multifunction switch C202 pin 2, circuit (BN/WH), harness side and FEM C201f pin 14, circuit 7-KA1 (YE), harness side.

- **Is the resistance less than 5 ohms?**

→ **Yes**

Go to «E6».

→ **No**

REPAIR the circuit(s) in question. TEST the system for normal operation.

FM9020000767050X

Fig. 90 Test E: Wash & Wipe Function Does Not Operate Correctly (Part 5 of 6). LS

F1	VERIFY THE WASHER PUMP SYMPTOM

1

2

3 **Note:**
If the wipers are also inoperative, REFER to the Symptom Chart. If the wash and wipe function does not operate correctly, REFER to «Pinpoint Test E».

Verify if the washer pump is never ON or if the pump is always ON.

- **Is the washer pump always on?**

→ **Yes**

Go to «F12».

→ **No**

Go to «F2».

FM9020000768010X

Fig. 91 Test F: Washer Pump Is Inoperative/On Continuously (Part 1 of 16). LS

E6	CHECK CIRCUITS 31S–KA8 (BK/BU) AND 31S–KA1 (BK/YE) FOR OPENS

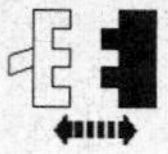

1 *FEM C201b*

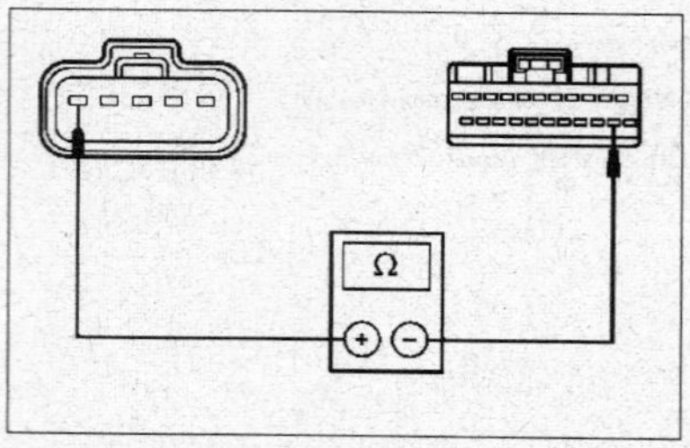

2

Measure the resistance between wiper motor C125 pin 5, circuit 31S-KA1 (BK/YE), and FEM C201b pin 13, circuit 31S-KA8 (BK/BU).

- **Is the resistance less than 5 ohms?**

→ **Yes**

INSTALL a new FEM. CLEAR the DTCs. REPEAT the self-test.

→ **No**

REPAIR the circuit(s) in question. TEST the system for normal operation.

FM9020000767060X

Fig. 90 Test E: Wash & Wipe Function Does Not Operate Correctly (Part 6 of 6). LS

F2	ACTIVATE THE WASHER PUMP

1 Trigger the FEM active command WASH RLY to ON.

- **Did the washer pump work?**

→ **Yes**

INSTALL a new FEM. TEST the system for normal operation.

→ **No**

Go to «F3».

FM9020000768020X

Fig. 91 Test F: Washer Pump Is Inoperative/On Continuously (Part 2 of 16). LS

F3	CHECK FOR VOLTAGE AT UNDERHOOD AJB FUSE 102 (10A)

1 Remove the underhood AJB Fuse 102 (10A).

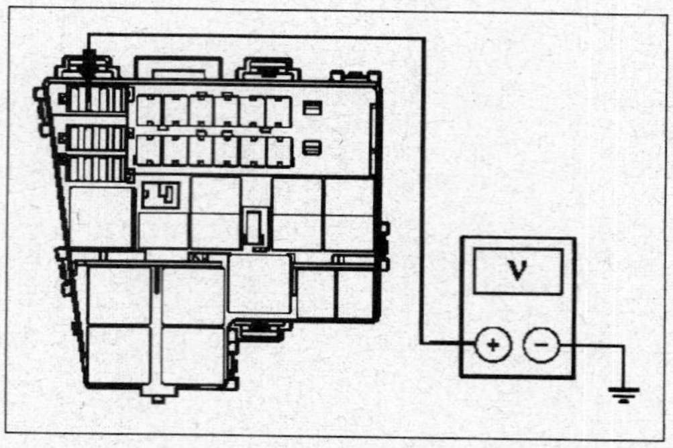

2

Measure the voltage between underhood AJB Fuse 102 (10A) input side and ground.

- **Is the voltage greater than 10 volts?**

→ **Yes**

Go to «F4».

→ **No**

REPAIR the power source. TEST the system for normal operation.

FM9020000768030X

Fig. 91 Test F: Washer Pump Is Inoperative/On Continuously (Part 3 of 16). LS

F4	CHECK WASHER PUMP RELAY

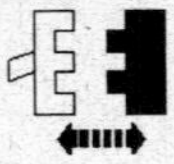

1 *Washer Pump Relay C1004*

2 Carry out the washer pump relay component tests.

- **Did the washer relay pass the component test?**

→ **Yes**

Go to «F5».

→ **No**

INSTALL a new relay. TEST the system for normal operation.

FM9020000768040X

Fig. 91 Test F: Washer Pump Is Inoperative/On Continuously (Part 4 of 16). LS

F5	CHECK CIRCUITS 31-KA42A (RD/BK) AND 30–KA43 (RD/WH) FOR OPENS

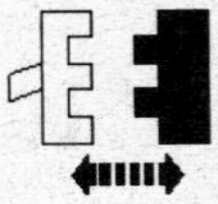

1 *Underhood AJB Fuse 102 (10A)*

2

FM902000076805AX

Fig. 91 Test F: Washer Pump Is Inoperative/On Continuously (Part 5 of 16). LS

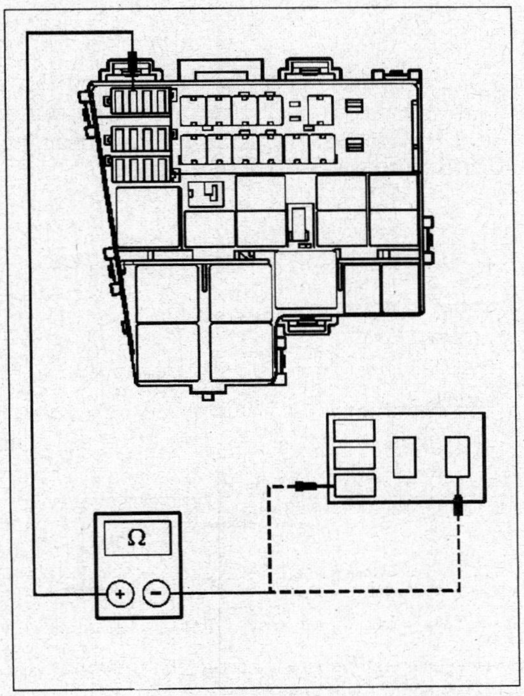

3

Measure the resistance between underhood AJB fuse 102 (10A) output side, circuit 30–KA42 (RD) and washer pump relay C1004 pin 3, circuit 30–KA42A (RD/BK) harness side; and between underhood AJB fuse 102 (10A) output side, circuit 30–KA42 (RD) and washer pump relay C1004 pin 2, circuit 30–KA43 (RD/WH) harness side.

- **Is resistance less than 5 ohms?**

→ **Yes**

Go to «F6».

→ **No**

REPAIR circuit(s) in question. TEST the system for normal operation.

FM902000076805BX

Fig. 91 Test F: Washer Pump Is Inoperative/On Continuously (Part 6 of 16). LS

F6	CHECK CIRCUIT 15S-KA7 (GN/WH) FOR OPENS

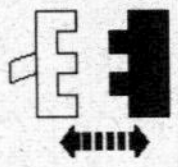

1 *Washer Pump Motor C137*

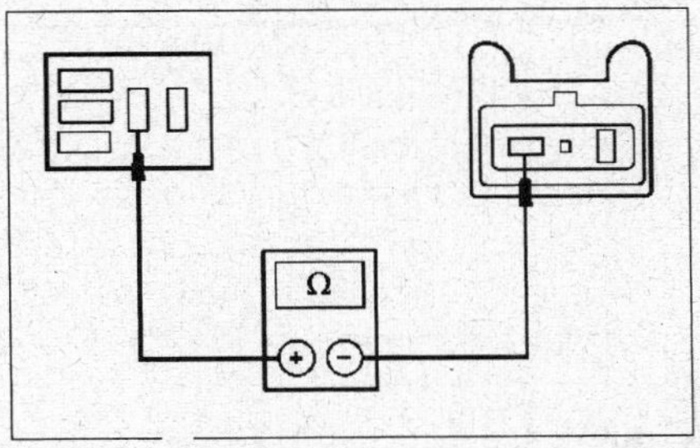

2

Measure the resistance between washer pump motor C137 pin 2, circuit 15S-KA7 (GN/WH), harness side and washer pump relay C1004 pin 5, circuit 15S-KA7 (GN/WH) harness side.

- **Is the resistance less than 5 ohms?**

→ **Yes**

Go to «F7».

→ **No**

REPAIR the circuit. TEST the system for normal operation.

FM9020000768060X

Fig. 91 Test F: Washer Pump Is Inoperative/On Continuously (Part 7 of 16). LS

F7 CHECK CIRCUIT 31-KA7 (BK/WH) FOR OPENS

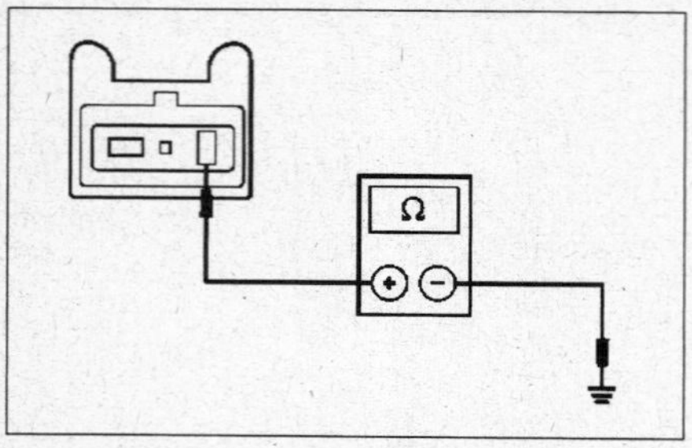

1

Measure the resistance between washer pump motor C137 pin 1, circuit 31S-KA7 (BK/WH), harness side and ground.

- **Is the resistance less than 5 ohms?**

➔ **Yes**

INSTALL underhood AJB fuse 102 (10A). Go to «F8».

➔ **No**

REPAIR the circuit. TEST the system for normal operation.

FM9020000768070X

Fig. 91 Test F: Washer Pump Is Inoperative/On Continuously (Part 8 of 16). LS

F8 CHECK CIRCUIT 31S-KA43 (BK/WH) FOR SHORT TO POWER

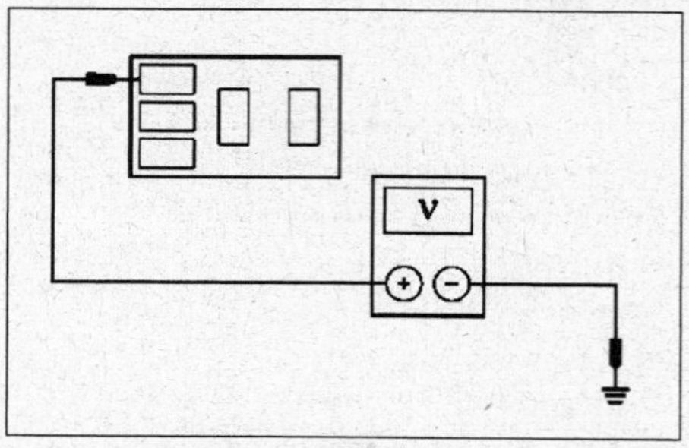

1

Measure the voltage between windshield washer relay C1004 pin 1, circuit 31S-KA43 (BK/WH), harness side and ground.

- **Is the voltage greater than 10 volts?**

➔ **Yes**

Go to «F9».

➔ **No**

Go to «F10».

FM9020000768080X

Fig. 91 Test F: Washer Pump Is Inoperative/On Continuously (Part 9 of 16). LS

F9 CHECK CIRCUIT 31S-KA43 (BK/WH) FOR SHORT TO POWER

1

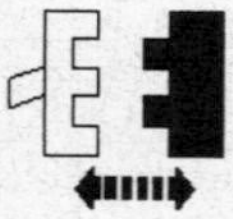

2

FEM C201b

3

FM902000076809AX

Fig. 91 Test F: Washer Pump Is Inoperative/On Continuously (Part 10 of 16). LS

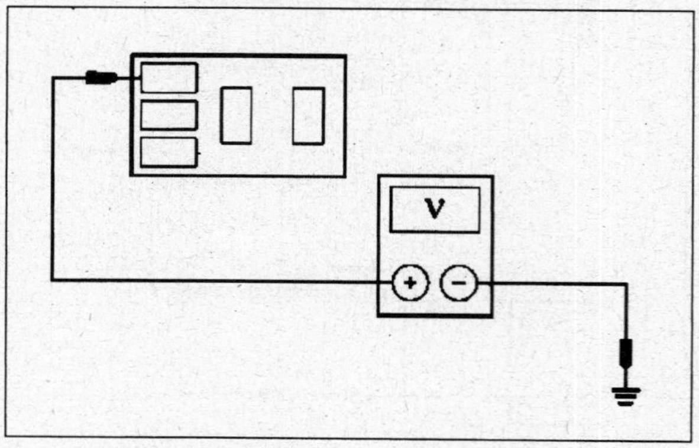

4

Measure the voltage between windshield washer relay C1004 pin 1, circuit 31S-KA43 (BK/WH), harness side and ground.

- **Is the voltage greater than 10 volts?**

➔ **Yes**

REPAIR the circuit. TEST the system for normal operation.

➔ **No**

INSTALL a new FEM. TEST the system for normal operation.

FM902000076809BX

Fig. 91 Test F: Washer Pump Is Inoperative/On Continuously (Part 11 of 16). LS

F10 CHECK CIRCUIT 31S-KA43 (RD/WH) FOR OPEN

1

2 *FEM C201b*

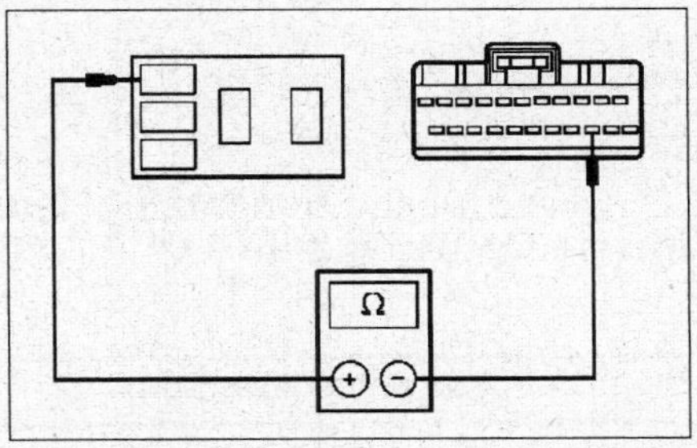

3 Measure the resistance between windshield washer relay C1004 pin 1, circuit 31S-KA43 (BK/WH), harness side and FEM C201b pin 14, circuit 31S-KA43 (BK/WH), harness side.

- **Is the resistance less than 5 ohms?**

→ **Yes**

Go to «F11».

→ **No**

REPAIR the circuit. TEST the system for normal operation.

FM9020000768100X

Fig. 91 Test F: Washer Pump Is Inoperative/On Continuously (Part 12 of 16). LS

F12 CHECK WASHER PUMP RELAY

1 *Washer Pump Relay C1004*

2 Carry out the washer pump relay component tests.

- **Did the washer relay pass the component test?**

→ **Yes**

Go to «F13».

→ **No**

INSTALL a new relay. TEST the system for normal operation.

FM9020000768120X

Fig. 91 Test F: Washer Pump Is Inoperative/On Continuously (Part 14 of 16). LS

F11 CHECK WINDSHIELD WASHER PUMP

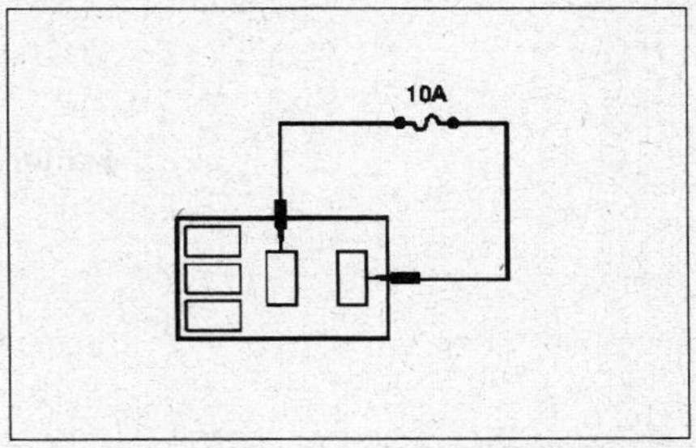

1 Using a fused (10A) jumper wire, jumper windshield washer relay C1004 pin 3, circuit 30–KA42 (RD/BK), harness side and windshield washer relay C1004 pin 5, circuit 15S–KA7 (GN/WH), harness side.

- **Does the washer pump turn ON?**

→ **Yes**

INSTALL a new FEM. TEST the system for normal operation.

→ **No**

INSTALL a new washer pump motor.

FM9020000768110X

Fig. 91 Test F: Washer Pump Is Inoperative/On Continuously (Part 13 of 16). LS

F13 CHECK CIRCUIT 15S-KA7 (GN/WH) FOR SHORT POWER

1 *Washer Pump Motor C137*

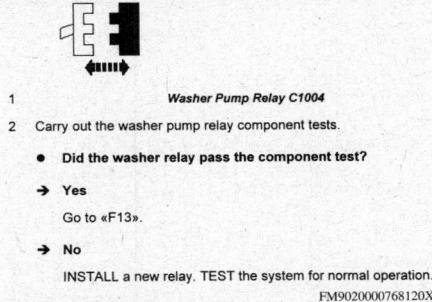

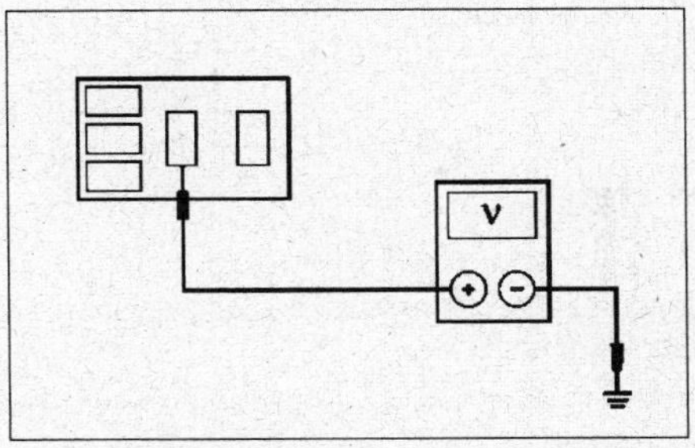

2 Measure the voltage between washer pump relay C1004 pin 5, circuit 15S-KA7 (GN/WH), harness side and ground.

- **Is the voltage greater than 10 volts?**

→ **Yes**

REPAIR the circuit. TEST the system for normal operation.

→ **No**

Go to «F14».

FM9020000768130X

Fig. 91 Test F: Washer Pump Is Inoperative/On Continuously (Part 15 of 16). LS

F14 ISOLATE FEM AND CIRCUIT 31S-KA43 (BK/WH) FOR SHORTS TO GROUND

1 Verify motor is running.

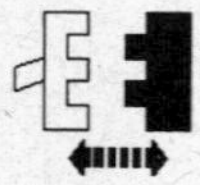

2 *FEM C201b*

- **Did washer pump motor stop running?**

→ **Yes**

INSTALL a new FEM. TEST the system for normal operation.

→ **No**

REPAIR the circuit. TEST the system for normal operation.

FM9020000768140X

Fig. 91 Test F: Washer Pump Is Inoperative/On Continuously (Part 16 of 16). LS

G2 CHECK THE RAIN SENSOR MODULE

1

2 *Rain Sensor Module C914*

3

4 Monitor the FEM PID WPMODE, while activating the intermittent washers through all speeds (positions) at the multifunction switch.

- **Do the FEM PID WPMODE values agree with the multifunction switch position?**

→ **Yes**

INSTALL a new rain sensor module. TEST the system for normal operation.

→ **No**

Go to «G3».

FM9020000769020X

Fig. 92 Test G: Speed Dependent Interval Mode Does Not Operate Correctly (Part 2 of 13). LS

G1 CHECK THE FEM PID WPMODE

1

2 Monitor the FEM PID WPMODE, while activating the intermittent washers through all speeds (positions) at the multifunction switch.

- **Do the FEM PID WPMODE values agree with the multifunction switch position?**

→ **Yes**

Go to «G7».

→ **No**

If equipped with moisture sensitive wipers.Go to «G2».

All othersGo to «G3».

FM9020000769010X

Fig. 92 Test G: Speed Dependent Interval Mode Does Not Operate Correctly (Part 1 of 13). LS

G3 CHECK THE MULTIFUNCTION SWITCH OPERATION

1

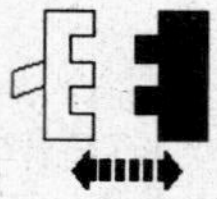

2 *Multifunction Switch C202*

3

4 Carry out the multifunction switch component test.

- **Is the multifunction switch OK?**

→ **Yes**

Go to «G4».

→ **No**

INSTALL a new multifunction switch. TEST the system for normal operation.

FM9020000769030X

Fig. 92 Test G: Speed Dependent Interval Mode Does Not Operate Correctly (Part 3 of 13). LS

G4	CHECK CIRCUITS 10–KA3 (GY/VT), 10–KA19 (GY/BK) AND 10–KA41 (GY/OG) FOR VOLTAGE

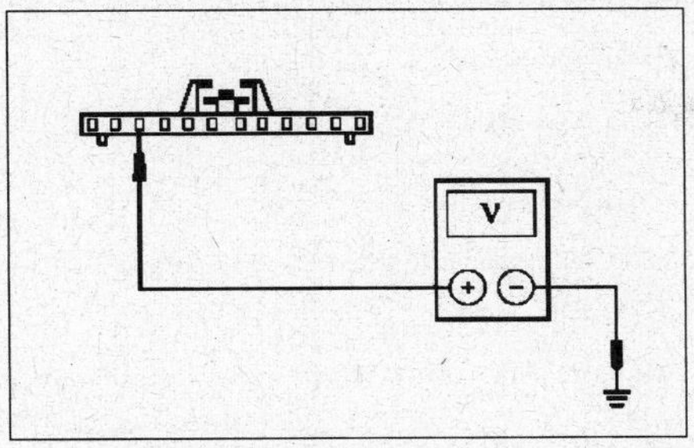

1

Measure the voltage between multifunction switch C202 pin 3, (BU/WH), harness side and ground.

- **Is the voltage greater than 10 volts?**

➔ **Yes**

Go to «G5».

➔ **No**

Go to «G6».

FM9020000769040X

Fig. 92 Test G: Speed Dependent Interval Mode Does Not Operate Correctly (Part 4 of 13). LS

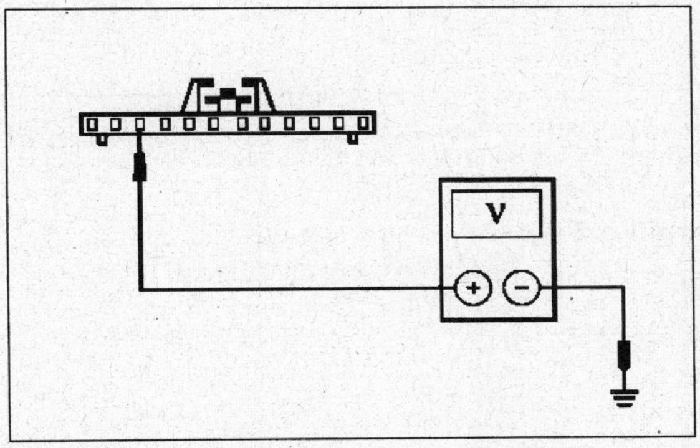

4

Measure the voltage between multifunction switch C202 pin 3, circuit (BU/WH), harness side and ground.

- **Is the voltage greater than 10 volts?**

➔ **Yes**

REPAIR the circuit(s) in question. TEST the system for normal operation.

➔ **No**

INSTALL a new FEM. TEST the system for normal operation.

FM902000076905BX

Fig. 92 Test G: Speed Dependent Interval Mode Does Not Operate Correctly (Part 6 of 13). LS

G5	CHECK CIRCUITS 10–KA3 (GY/VT), 10–KA19 (GY/BK) AND 10–KA41 (GY/OG) FOR SHORTS TO POWER

1

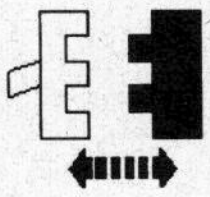

2 *FEM C201f*

3

FM902000076905AX

Fig. 92 Test G: Speed Dependent Interval Mode Does Not Operate Correctly (Part 5 of 13). LS

G6	CHECK CIRCUITS 10–KA3 (GY/VT), 10–KA19 (GY/BK) AND 10–KA41 (GY/OG) FOR OPENS

1

2 *FEM C201f*

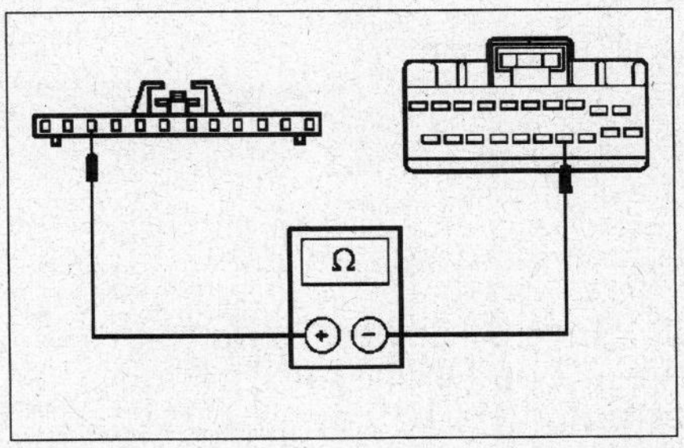

3

Measure the resistance between multifunction switch pin 3, circuit (BU/WH), harness side and FEM C201f pin 13, circuit 10–KA3 (GY/VT), harness side.

- **Is the resistance less than 5 ohms?**

➔ **Yes**

INSTALL a new FEM. TEST the system for normal operation.

➔ **No**

REPAIR the circuit(s) in question. TEST the system for normal operation.

FM9020000769060X

Fig. 92 Test G: Speed Dependent Interval Mode Does Not Operate Correctly (Part 7 of 13). LS

G7 MONITOR THE FEM PID WPPRKSW

1

2 Trigger the FEM active command WIPER RLY ON and OFF while monitoring the FEM PID WPPRKSW.

- **Did the PID change from PARKED to not PRK?**

➔ **Yes**

INSTALL a new FEM. TEST the system for normal operation.

➔ **No**

Go to «G8».

FM9020000769070X

Fig. 92 Test G: Speed Dependent Interval Mode Does Not Operate Correctly (Part 8 of 13). LS

G8 CHECK WIPER PARK RELAY

1 Remove the underhood AJB wiper park relay.

2 Carry out the relay component test.

- **Is the wiper park relay OK?**

➔ **Yes**

Go to «G9».

➔ **No**

INSTALL a new wiper park relay. TEST the system for normal operation.

FM9020000769080X

Fig. 92 Test G: Speed Dependent Interval Mode Does Not Operate Correctly (Part 9 of 13). LS

G9 CHECK THE WIPER MOTOR

1 

2 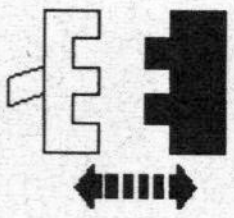

Wiper Motor C125

3 

FM902000076909AX

Fig. 92 Test G: Speed Dependent Interval Mode Does Not Operate Correctly (Part 10 of 13). LS

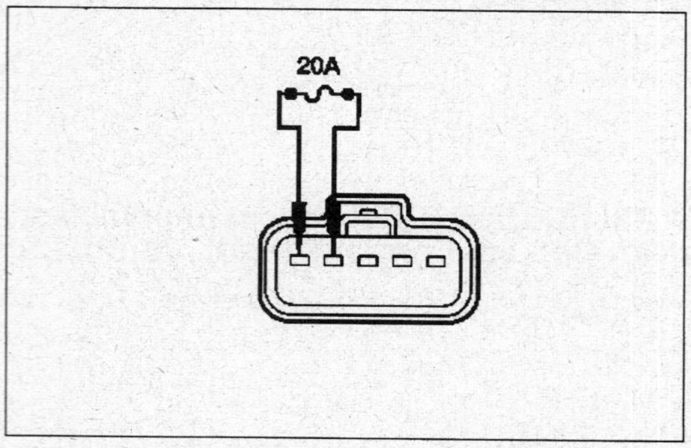

4

Monitor the FEM PID WPPRKSW while connecting a (20 A) fused jumper wire between wiper motor C125 pin 5, circuit 31S-KA1 (BK/YE), harness side and wiper motor C125 pin 4, circuit 75S–KA9 (YE/BU), harness side.

- **Did the PID change from notPRK to PARKED?**

➔ **Yes**

INSTALL a new wiper motor. TEST the system for normal operation.

➔ **No**

Go to «G10».

FM902000076909BX

Fig. 92 Test G: Speed Dependent Interval Mode Does Not Operate Correctly (Part 11 of 13). LS

G10 CHECK CIRCUITS 31S-KA1 (BK/YE) AND 31S-KA12 (BK/WH) FOR OPENS

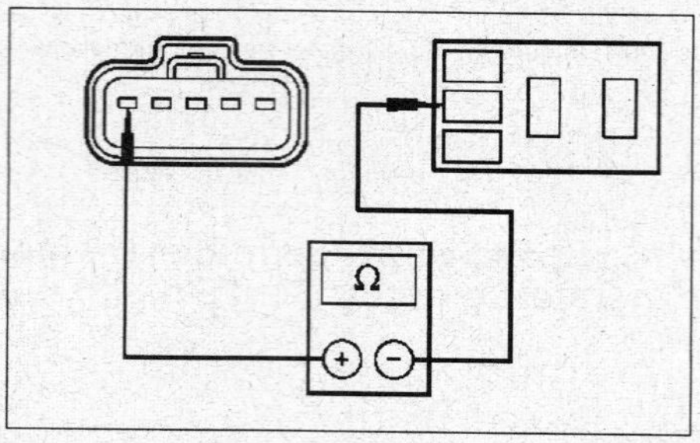

1

Measure the resistance between the wiper park relay C1002 Pin 4, Circuit 31S-KA12 (BK/WH), harness side and wiper motor C125 pin 5, circuit 31S-KA1 (BK/YE), harness side.

- **Is the resistance less than 5 ohms?**

➔ **Yes**

Go to «G11».

➔ **No**

REPAIR the circuit(s) in question. TEST the system for normal operation.

FM9020000769100X

Fig. 92 Test G: Speed Dependent Interval Mode Does Not Operate Correctly (Part 12 of 13). LS

G11 CHECK CIRCUIT 31S-KA8 (BK/BU) FOR OPENS

1

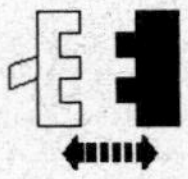

2 *FEM C201b*

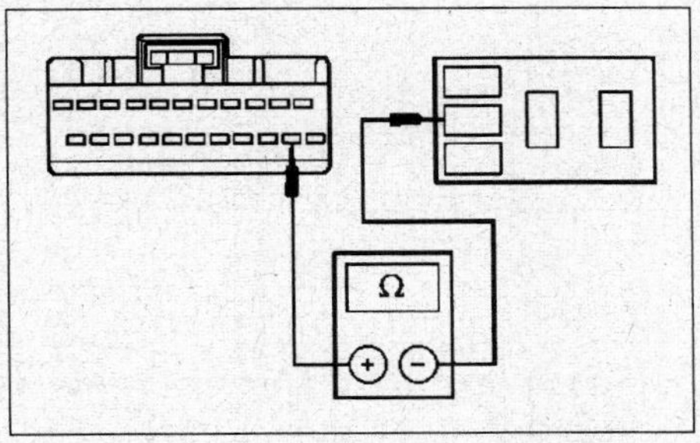

3

Measure the resistance between the wiper park relay C1002 pin 4, circuit 31S-KA12 (BK/WH), harness side and FEM C201b pin 13, circuit 31S-KA8 (BK/BU), harness side.

- **Is the resistance less than 5 ohms?**

➔ **Yes**

INSTALL a new FEM. TEST the system for normal operation.

➔ **No**

REPAIR the circuit(s) in question. TEST the system for normal operation.

FM9020000769110X

Fig. 92 Test G: Speed Dependent Interval Mode Does Not Operate Correctly (Part 13 of 13). LS

H2 QUICK VISUAL CHECKS

1 Check if the rain sensor module is mounted correctly.
— Interior side of the windshield.
— Near and behind the mirror.
— The optical windows must be within the wiper pattern.

2 Check if the rain sensor module connector is in place.

3 Check if the green slides are fully closed.

4 Check presence and proper coupling of silicon pads (About 80% of pad area should form a seal to the glass).

5 Check if brackets are in place (not broken off the windscreen).

6 Check windscreen, over the optical windows, for cracks, scratches, covered, etc.

7 Make sure multifunction switch was set in AUTO, in order for the moisture sensitive wiper function to work.

- **Does everything check out OK?**

➔ **Yes**

Go to «H3».

➔ **No**

REPAIR as necessary. TEST the system for normal operation.

FM9020000770020X

Fig. 93 Test H: Rain Moisture Sensitive Function Does Not Operate Correctly (Part 2 of 9). LS

H1 RETRIEVE THE FEM DIAGNOSTIC TROUBLE CODES

1 Using recorded results from the FEM self-test.

- **Are any DTCs recorded?**

➔ **Yes**

GO to the FEM Diagnostic Trouble Code (DTC) Index.

➔ **No**

Go to «H2».

FM9020000770010X

Fig. 93 Test H: Rain Moisture Sensitive Function Does Not Operate Correctly (Part 1 of 9). LS

H3 VERIFY WIPER AUTO FUNCTION

1 Verify the moisture sensitive wiper system is continuously wiping when the multifunction switch is placed in AUTO.

- **Do wipers wipe continuously when switch is placed in AUTO?**

➔ **Yes**

Go to «H10».

➔ **No**

Go to «H4».

FM9020000770030X

Fig. 93 Test H: Rain Moisture Sensitive Function Does Not Operate Correctly (Part 3 of 9). LS

H4 VERIFY SYMPTOM

1 Verify if the wipers are totally inoperative or working erratically.

- **Are the wipers totally inoperative?**

➔ **Yes**

Go to «H5».

➔ **No**

REMOVE rain sensor module, clean the interior windshield glass and RE-INSTALL. TEST system for normal operation.

FM9020000770040X

Fig. 93 Test H: Rain Moisture Sensitive Function Does Not Operate Correctly (Part 4 of 9). LS

H5 CHECK THE FEM PID WPMODE

1

2 Monitor the FEM PID WPMODE, while activating the multifunction switch to the AUTO position.

- **Do the wiper FEM PID WPMODE values agree with the multifunction switch?**

➔ **Yes**

Go to «H7».

➔ **No**

Go to «H6».

FM9020000770050X

Fig. 93 Test H: Rain Moisture Sensitive Function Does Not Operate Correctly (Part 5 of 9). LS

H6	CHECK THE FEM PID WPMODE WHILE SELECTING OTHER POSITIONS WITH THE MULTIFUNCTION SWITCH

1 Monitor the FEM PID WPMODE, while activating the multifunction switch positions 2 through 7.

- **Do the wiper FEM PID WPMODE values agree with the multifunction switch?**

→ **Yes**

INSTALL a new multifunction switch. TEST the system for normal operation.

→ **No**

GO to the Symptom Chart for further diagnosis.

FM9020000770060X

Fig. 93 Test H: Rain Moisture Sensitive Function Does Not Operate Correctly (Part 6 of 9). LS

H8	CHECK CJB FUSE 216 (5A) VOLTAGE SUPPLY

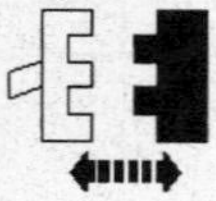

1 *CJB Fuse 216 (5A)*

2

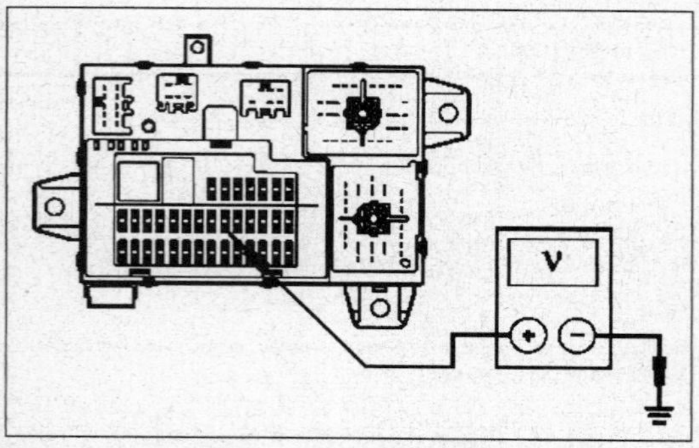

3

Measure the voltage between CJB Fuse 216 (5A) input side and ground.

- **Is the voltage greater than 10 volts?**

→ **Yes**

REPAIR the circuit(s) in question. TEST the system for normal operation.

→ **No**

INSTALL a new CJB power supply. TEST the system for normal operation.

FM9020000770080X

Fig. 93 Test H: Rain Moisture Sensitive Function Does Not Operate Correctly (Part 8 of 9). LS

H7	CHECK RAIN SENSOR MODULE CIRCUIT 20–AD15 (PK) FOR VOLTAGE

1 *Rain Sensor Module C914*

2

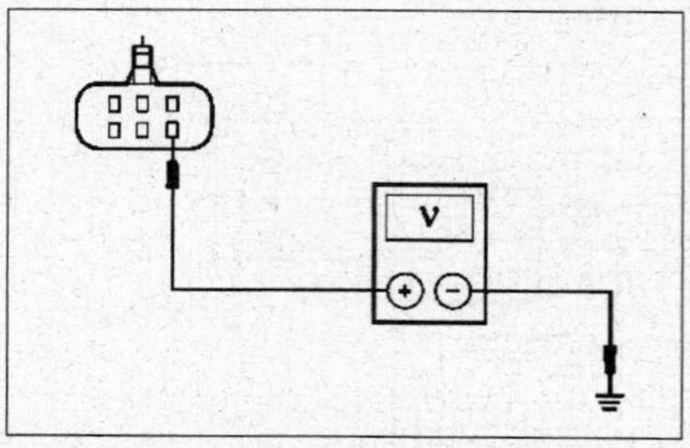

3

Measure the voltage between the rain sensor module C914 pin 6, circuit 20–AD15 (PK), harness side and ground.

- **Is the voltage greater than 10 volts?**

→ **Yes**

Go to «H9».

→ **No**

Go to «H8».

FM9020000770070X

Fig. 93 Test H: Rain Moisture Sensitive Function Does Not Operate Correctly (Part 7 of 9). LS

H9	CHECK CIRCUITS 7–KA41 (YE/GN), 8-KA41 (WH/GN) AND 10–KA41 (GY/OG) FOR AN OPEN

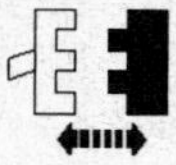

1 *Multifunction Switch C202*

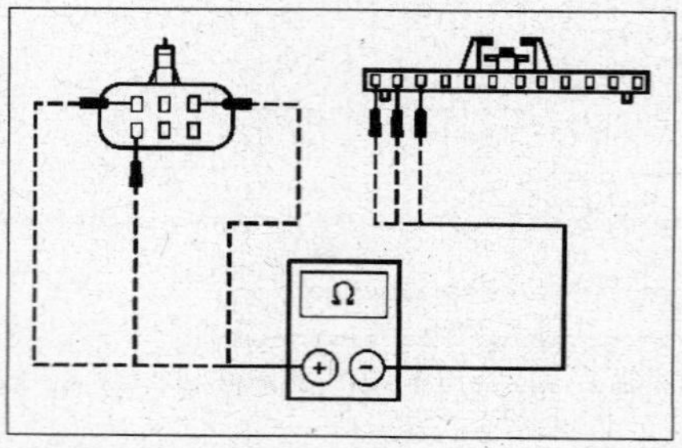

2

Using the following table measure the resistance between multifunction switch C202 harness side and rain sensor module C914 harness side:

Multifunction Switch C202	Rain Sensor Module C914
pin 1, circuit (OG/GN)	pin 1, circuit 8-KA41 (WH/GN)
pin 2, circuit (BN/WH)	pin 4, circuit 7-KA41 (YE/GN)
pin 3, circuit (BU/WH)	pin 3, circuit 10-KA41 (GY /OG)

- **Is the resistance less than 5 ohms?**

→ **Yes**

INSTALL a new rain sensor module.

→ **No**

REPAIR the circuit(s) in question. TEST the system for normal operation.

FM9020000770090X

Fig. 93 Test H: Rain Moisture Sensitive Function Does Not Operate Correctly (Part 9 of 9). LS

TEST CONDITIONS	TEST DETAILS/RESULTS/ACTIONS
A1 CHECK CIRCUIT 1001 (WH/YE) FOR VOLTAGE	
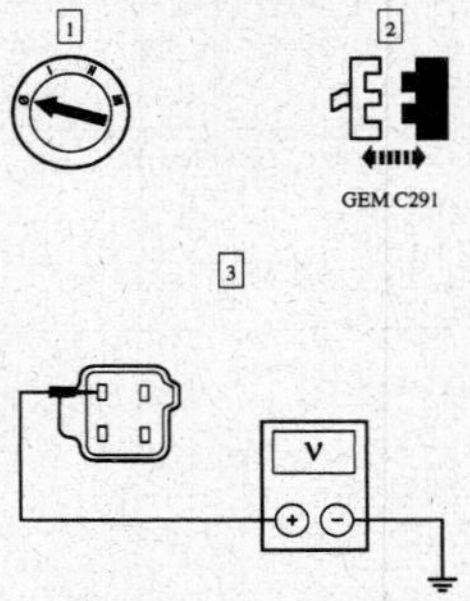	3 Measure the voltage between GEM C291 Pin 2, Circuit 1001 (WH/YE), harness side and ground. • Is the voltage greater than 10 volts? → **Yes** GO to **A2**. → **No** GO to **A3**.

FM9029900773010X

Fig. 94 Test A: No Communications w/Generic Electronic Module (Part 1 of 3). Mustang

TEST CONDITIONS	TEST DETAILS/RESULTS/ACTIONS
A4 CHECK CIRCUIT 397 (BK/WH) FOR SHORT TO VOLTAGE	
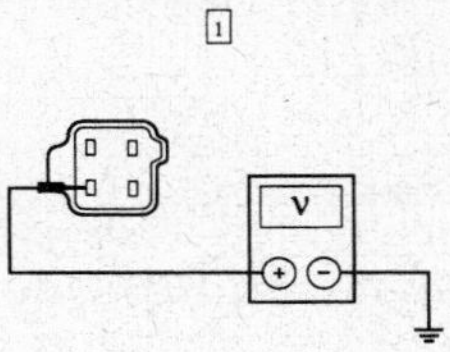	1 Measure the voltage between GEM C291 Pin 4, Circuit 397 (BK/WH), harness side and ground. • Is the voltage greater than 10 volts? → **Yes** REPAIR Circuit 397 (BK/WH). REPEAT the self-test. CLEAR the DTCs. → **No** Diagnose Module Communications Network.

FM9029900773030X

Fig. 94 Test A: No Communications w/Generic Electronic Module (Part 3 of 3). Mustang

TEST CONDITIONS	TEST DETAILS/RESULTS/ACTIONS
B1 DETERMINE IF GEM IS RECEIVING CORRECT IGNITION SWITCH STATUS	
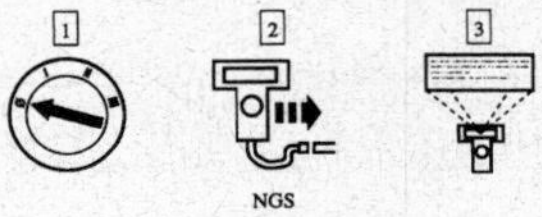	3 **NOTE:** If the vehicle is equipped with a manual transmission, depress the clutch while turning the ignition switch to START. Monitor the GEM PIDs IGN__S, IGN__R IGN__A, and IGN__KEY while turning the ignition switch through the START, RUN, OFF and ACC positions. • Do the GEM PID values agree with the ignition switch positions? → **Yes** GO to **B2**. → **No** Inspect guages.
B2 DETERMINE IF GEM IS RECEIVING CORRECT WIPER SWITCH STATUS FROM MULTIFUNCTION SWITCH	
	2 Monitor PID WPMODE, while moving through all wiper control positions on the multifunction switch. • Do the GEM PID values agree with switch positions? → **Yes** GO to **B3**. → **No** GO to **B6**.

FM9029900774010X

Fig. 95 Test B: Windshield Wipers Do Not Operate/ Operate Correctly (Part 1 of 14). Mustang

TEST CONDITIONS	TEST DETAILS/RESULTS/ACTIONS
A2 CHECK CIRCUIT 397 (BK/WH) FOR OPEN	
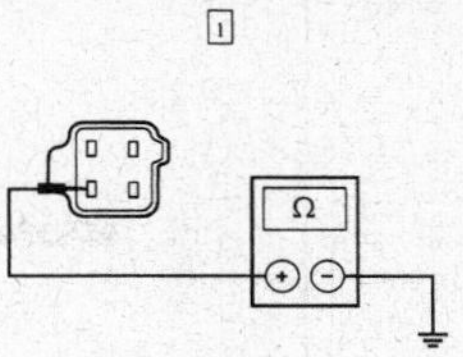	1 Measure the resistance between GEM 291 Pin 4, Circuit 397 (BK/WH), harness side and ground. • Is the resistance less than 5 ohms? → **Yes** GO to **A4**. → **No** REPAIR Circuit 397 (BK/WH). REPEAT the self-test. CLEAR the DTCs.
A3 CHECK CIRCUIT 1002 (BK/PK) FOR VOLTAGE	
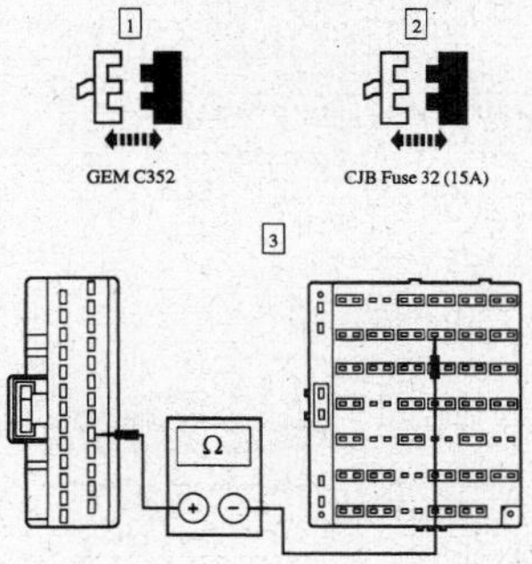	3 Measure the resistance between GEM C352 Pin 22, Circuit 1002 (BK/PK), harness side and CJB Fuse 32 (15A) Pin 1, Circuit 1002 (BK/PK), harness side. • Is the resistance less than 5 ohms? → **Yes** GO to **A4**. → **No** REPAIR Circuit 1002 (BK/PK). REPEAT the self-test. CLEAR the DTCs.

FM9029900773020X

Fig. 94 Test A: No Communications w/Generic Electronic Module (Part 2 of 3). Mustang

TEST CONDITIONS	TEST DETAILS/RESULTS/ACTIONS
B3 TEST GEM CONTROL OF WIPER ON/OFF RELAY	
	1 Trigger the GEM active command WIPER RLY ON and OFF. • Do the wipers turn ON and OFF? → **Yes** GO to **B4**. → **No** GO to **B10**.
B4 TEST THE GEM CONTROL OF WIPER HIGH/LOW RELAY	
	1 Trigger the GEM active command WIPER RLY to ON.
	2 Trigger the GEM active command SPEED RLY ON and OFF. • Does wiper speed change on activation and deactivation of SPEED RLY command? → **Yes** GO to **B5**. → **No** GO to **B16**.
B5 DETERMINE IF GEM IS RECEIVING CORRECT WIPER POSITION STATUS	
	1 Monitor GEM PID WPPRKSW while turning the wipers ON using the multifunction switch. • Do the PID values agree with the wiper position? → **Yes** INSTALL a new GEM. CLEAR the DTCs. REPEAT the self-test. → **No** GO to **B27**.

FM9029900774020X

Fig. 95 Test B: Windshield Wipers Do Not Operate/ Operate Correctly (Part 2 of 14). Mustang

TEST CONDITIONS	TEST DETAILS/RESULTS/ACTIONS
B6 TEST THE MULTIFUNCTION SWITCH FOR NORMAL OPERATION	

1 

Multifunction Switch C240

2 Check the multifunction switch.

- Is the multifunction switch OK?

→ **Yes**
GO to **B7**.

→ **No**
INSTALL a new multifunction switch; REPEAT the self-test. CLEAR the DTCs.

B7 CHECK CIRCUITS 682 (DB), 684 (PK/YE), AND 680 (LB/OG) FOR SHORT TO BATTERY BETWEEN THE GEM AND THE MULTIFUNCTION SWITCH

1 

GEM C352

2 

3 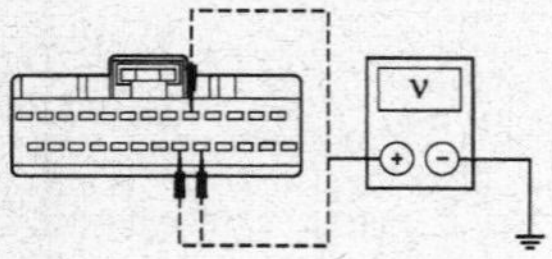

3 Using the following table, measure the voltage between the GEM C352 Pins, harness side and ground.

Pin	Circuit
5	682 (DB)
18	684 (PK/YE)
19	680 (LB/OG)

FM9029900774030X

Fig. 95 Test B: Windshield Wipers Do Not Operate/ Operate Correctly (Part 3 of 14). Mustang

TEST CONDITIONS	TEST DETAILS/RESULTS/ACTIONS
B7 CHECK CIRCUITS 682 (DB), 684 (PK/YE), AND 680 (LB/OG) FOR SHORT TO BATTERY BETWEEN THE GEM AND THE MULTIFUNCTION SWITCH (Continued)	

- Are the voltages greater than 10 volts?

→ **Yes**
REPAIR the circuit(s) in question. REPEAT the self-test. CLEAR the DTCs.

→ **No**
GO to **B8**.

B8 CHECK CIRCUITS 682 (DB), 684 (PK/YE), AND 680 (LB/OG) FOR SHORT TO GROUND BETWEEN THE GEM AND THE MULTIFUNCTION SWITCH

1 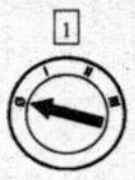

2 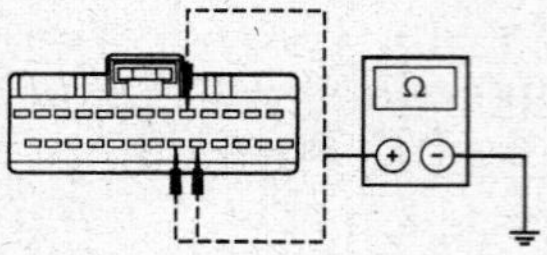

2 Using the following table, measure the resistance between the GEM C352 Pins, harness side and ground.

Pin	Circuit
5	682 (DB)
18	684 (PK/YE)
19	680 (LB/OG)

- Are the resistances greater than 10,000 ohms?

→ **Yes**
REPAIR the circuit(s) in question. REPEAT the self-test. CLEAR the DTCs.

→ **No**
GO to **B9**.

FM9029900774040X

Fig. 95 Test B: Windshield Wipers Do Not Operate/ Operate Correctly (Part 4 of 14). Mustang

TEST CONDITIONS	TEST DETAILS/RESULTS/ACTIONS
B9 CHECK CIRCUITS 682 (DB), 684 (PK/YE), AND 680 (LB/OG) FOR AN OPEN CONDITION BETWEEN GEM AND MULTIFUNCTION SWITCH	

1 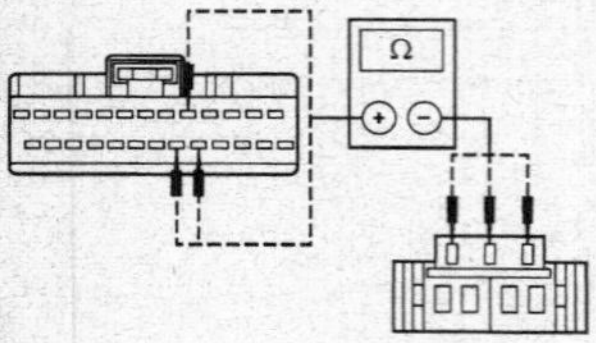

1 Using the following table, measure the resistance between the GEM C352 Pins, harness side and multifunction switch C240 Pins, harness side.

GEM	Multifunction Switch	Circuit
C352 Pin 5	C240 Pin 685	682 (DB)
C352 Pin 18	C240 Pin 590	684 (PK/YE)
C352 Pin 19	C240 Pin 993	680 (LB/OG)

- Are the resistances less than 5 ohms?

→ **Yes**
INSTALL a new GEM. For additional information.
REPEAT the self-test. CLEAR the DTCs.

→ **No**
REPAIR circuit(s) in question. REPEAT the self-test. CLEAR the DTCs.

FM9029900774050X

Fig. 95 Test B: Windshield Wipers Do Not Operate/ Operate Correctly (Part 5 of 14). Mustang

TEST CONDITIONS	TEST DETAILS/RESULTS/ACTIONS
B10 CHECK CIRCUITS 65 (DG) FOR OPEN CIRCUIT CONDITION BETWEEN BJB AND CJB	
NOTE: Verify voltage at CJB F26 (30A) before carrying out this test.	

1 

Wiper On/Off Relay

2 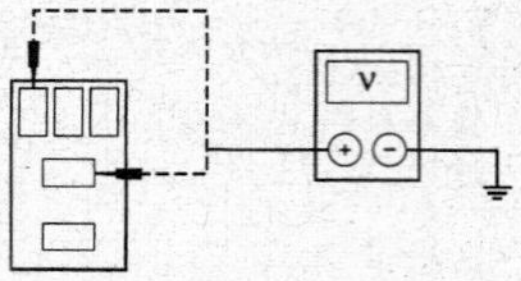

2 Measure the voltage between BJB ON and OFF wiper relay Pin 5, Circuit 65 (DG), harness side and ground; and between BJB wiper ON/OFF relay Pin 2, Circuit 65 (DG), harness side and ground.

- Are the voltages greater than 10 volts?

→ **Yes**
GO to **B11**.

→ **No**
REPAIR circuit(s) in question. REPEAT the self-test. CLEAR the DTCs.

B11 ISOLATE PROBLEM BETWEEN GEM AND BJB

1 

2 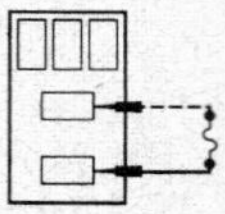

2 Connect a fused jumper wire (30A) between wiper ON/OFF relay Pin 3 and Pin 5, harness side.

FM9029900774060X

Fig. 95 Test B: Windshield Wipers Do Not Operate/ Operate Correctly (Part 6 of 14). Mustang

TEST CONDITIONS	TEST DETAILS/RESULTS/ACTIONS
B11 ISOLATE PROBLEM BETWEEN GEM AND BJB (Continued)	
3 	• Did the wiper motor activate? → **Yes** GO to **B12**. → **No** GO to **B22**.
B12 CARRY OUT THE WIPER ON/OFF RELAY COMPONENT TEST	
	1 Check the wiper ON and OFF relay. • Is the ON/OFF wiper relay OK? → **Yes** GO to **B13**. → **No** INSTALL a new wiper ON/OFF relay. REPEAT the self-test. CLEAR the DTCs.
B13 CHECK CIRCUIT 646 (YE/WH) FOR SHORT TO BATTERY BETWEEN GEM AND BJB	
1  Wiper On/Off Relay 2  GEM C293	
3 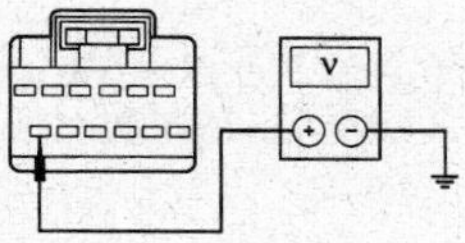	3 Measure the voltage between GEM C293 Pin 12, Circuit 646 (YE/WH), harness side and ground. • Is the voltage greater than 10 volts? → **Yes** REPAIR Circuit 646 (YE/WH). REPEAT the self-test. CLEAR the DTCs. → **No** GO to **B14**.

FM9029900774070X

Fig. 95 Test B: Windshield Wipers Do Not Operate/ Operate Correctly (Part 7 of 14). Mustang

TEST CONDITIONS	TEST DETAILS/RESULTS/ACTIONS
B16 CHECK CIRCUITS 65 (DG) AND 61 (YE/RD) FOR OPEN CONDITION BETWEEN BJB AND CJB (Continued)	
3 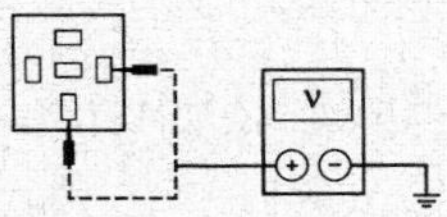	3 Measure the voltages between BJB wiper HIGH/LOW relay Pin 86, Circuit 65 (DG), harness side and ground; and between BJB wiper HIGH/LOW relay Pin 30, Circuit 61 (YE/RD), harness side and ground. • Are the voltages greater than 10 volts? → **Yes** GO to **B17**. → **No** REPAIR circuit in question. REPEAT the self-test. CLEAR the DTCs.
B17 ISOLATE THE PROBLEM BETWEEN THE GEM AND THE BJB	
1 	1 Trigger the GEM active command WIPER RLY to ON.
2 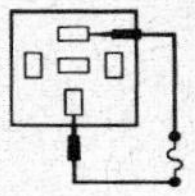	2 Connect a fused jumper wire (30A) between wiper HIGH/LOW relay Pin 30, Circuit 61 (YE/RD), harness side and Pin 87, Circuit 58 (WH), harness side. • Did the wiper motor speed increase with the jumper installed and slow down with the jumper removed? → **Yes** GO to **B18**. → **No** GO to **B26**.
B18 CARRY OUT COMPONENT TEST ON WIPER HIGH/LOW RELAY	
	1 Check the wiper HIGH/LOW relay. • Is the wiper HIGH/LOW relay OK? → **Yes** GO to **B19**. → **No** INSTALL a new wiper HIGH/LOW relay. REPEAT the self-test. CLEAR the DTCs.

FM9029900774090X

Fig. 95 Test B: Windshield Wipers Do Not Operate/ Operate Correctly (Part 9 of 14). Mustang

TEST CONDITIONS	TEST DETAILS/RESULTS/ACTIONS
B14 CHECK CIRCUIT 646 (YE/WH) FOR SHORT TO GROUND BETWEEN GEM AND BJB	
1 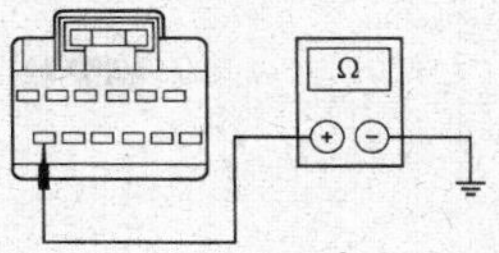	1 Measure the resistance between GEM C293 Pin 12, Circuit 646 (YE/WH), harness side and ground. • Is the resistance greater than 10,000 ohms? → **Yes** GO to **B15**. → **No** REPAIR Circuit 646 (YE/WH). REPEAT the self-test. CLEAR the DTCs.
B15 CHECK CIRCUIT 646 (YE/WH) FOR OPEN BETWEEN GEM AND BJB	
1 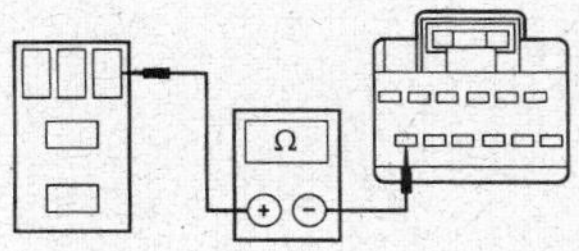	1 Measure the resistance between GEM C293 Pin 12, Circuit 646 (YE/WH), harness side and BJB wiper ON/OFF relay Pin 1, Circuit 646 (YE/WH), harness side. • Is the resistance less than 5 ohms? → **Yes** INSTALL a new GEM. For additional information. REPEAT the self-test. CLEAR the DTCs. → **No** REPAIR Circuit 646 (YE/WH). REPEAT the self-test. CLEAR the DTCs.
B16 CHECK CIRCUITS 65 (DG) AND 61 (YE/RD) FOR OPEN CONDITION BETWEEN BJB AND CJB	
1  Wiper HIGH/LOW Relay 2 	2 Trigger the GEM active command WIPER RLY to ON.

FM9029900774080X

Fig. 95 Test B: Windshield Wipers Do Not Operate/ Operate Correctly (Part 8 of 14). Mustang

TEST CONDITIONS	TEST DETAILS/RESULTS/ACTIONS
B19 CHECK CIRCUIT 647 (GY/LB) FOR SHORT TO BATTERY BETWEEN GEM AND BJB	
1  GEM C293	
2 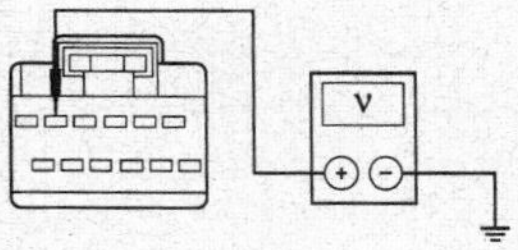	2 Measure voltage between GEM C293 Pin 5, Circuit 647 (GY/LB), harness side and ground. • Is the voltage greater than 10 volts? → **Yes** REPAIR Circuit 647 (GY/LB). REPEAT the self-test. CLEAR the DTCs. → **No** GO to **B20**.
B20 CHECK CIRCUIT 647 (GY/LB) FOR SHORT TO GROUND BETWEEN GEM AND BJB	
1 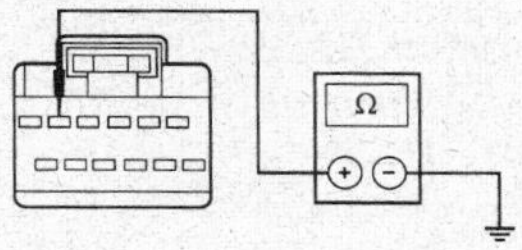	1 Measure the resistance between GEM C293 Pin 5, Circuit 647 (GY/LB), harness side and ground. • Is the resistance greater than 10,000 ohms? → **Yes** GO to **B21**. → **No** REPAIR Circuit 647 (GY/LB). REPEAT the self-test. CLEAR the DTCs.

FM9029900774100X

Fig. 95 Test B: Windshield Wipers Do Not Operate/ Operate Correctly (Part 10 of 14). Mustang

TEST CONDITIONS	TEST DETAILS/RESULTS/ACTIONS
B21 CHECK CIRCUIT 647 (GY/LB) FOR OPEN CONDITION BETWEEN GEM AND BJB	
1 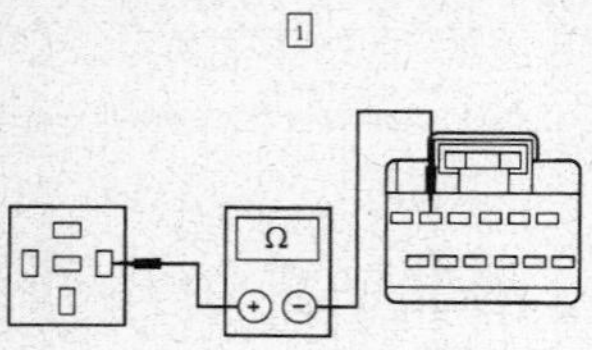	1 Measure the resistance between GEM C293 Pin 5, Circuit 647 (GY/LB), harness side and wiper HIGH/LOW relay Pin 85, Circuit 647 (GY/LB), harness side. • Is the resistance less than 5 ohms? → **Yes** INSTALL a new GEM. REPEAT the self-test. CLEAR the DTCs. → **No** REPAIR Circuit 647 (GY/LB). REPEAT the self-test. CLEAR the DTCs.
B22 CHECK CIRCUIT 61 (YE/RD) FOR OPEN CIRCUIT CONDITION BETWEEN WIPER ON/OFF AND HIGH/LOW RELAYS	
1 2 3 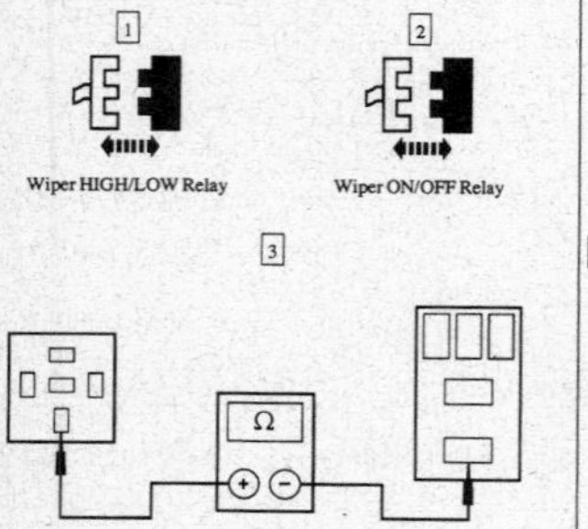	3 Measure the resistance between wiper ON/OFF relay Pin 3, Circuit 61 (YE/RD), harness side and wiper HIGH/LOW relay Pin 30, Circuit 61 (YE/RD), harness side. • Is the resistance less than 5 ohms? → **Yes** GO to **B23**. → **No** REPAIR Circuit 61 (YE/RD). REPEAT the self-test. CLEAR the DTCs.

FM9029900774110X

Fig. 95 Test B: Windshield Wipers Do Not Operate/ Operate Correctly (Part 11 of 14). Mustang

TEST CONDITIONS	TEST DETAILS/RESULTS/ACTIONS
B23 CARRY OUT THE WIPER HIGH/LOW RELAY COMPONENT TEST	
	1 Check the wiper HIGH/LOW relay. • Is the wiper HIGH/LOW relay OK? → **Yes** GO to **B24**. → **No** INSTALL a new wiper HIGH/LOW relay. REPEAT the self-test. CLEAR the DTCs.
B24 CHECK CIRCUIT 56 (DB/OG) FOR AN OPEN CIRCUIT BETWEEN THE WIPER HIGH/LOW RELAY AND THE WIPER MOTOR	
1 2 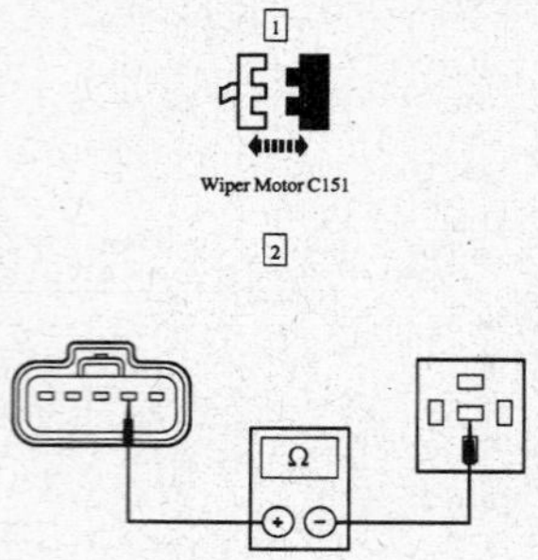	2 Measure the resistance between wiper HIGH/LOW relay Pin 87A, Circuit 56 (DB/OG), harness side and wiper motor C151 Pin 4, Circuit 56 (DB/OG), harness side. • Is the resistance less than 5 ohms? → **Yes** GO to **B25**. → **No** REPAIR Circuit 56 (DB/OG). REPEAT the self-test. CLEAR the DTCs.

FM9029900774120X

Fig. 95 Test B: Windshield Wipers Do Not Operate/ Operate Correctly (Part 12 of 14). Mustang

TEST CONDITIONS	TEST DETAILS/RESULTS/ACTIONS
B25 CHECK CIRCUIT 1205 (BK) FOR OPEN CIRCUIT CONDITION BETWEEN WIPER MOTOR AND GROUND	
1 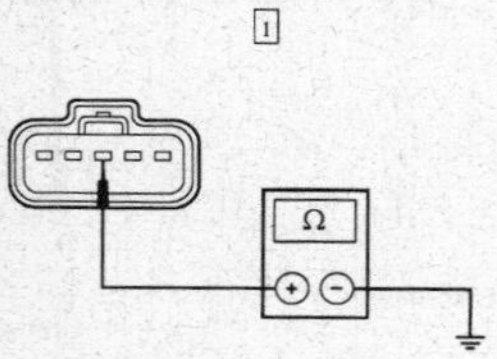	1 Measure the resistance between wiper motor C151 Pin 3, Circuit 1205 (BK), harness side and ground. • Is the resistance less than 5 ohms? → **Yes** CARRY OUT the windshield wiper motor component test. If the component fails, INSTALL a new wiper motor; REPEAT the self-test. CLEAR the DTCs. → **No** REPAIR Circuit 1205 (BK). REPEAT the self-test. CLEAR the DTCs.
B26 CHECK CIRCUIT 58 (WH) FOR AN OPEN CIRCUIT BETWEEN THE WIPER HIGH/LOW RELAY AND THE WIPER MOTOR	
1 2 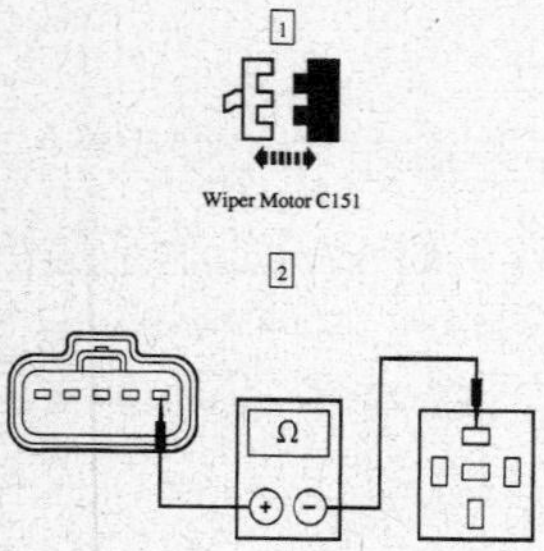	2 Measure the resistance between wiper motor C151 Pin 5, Circuit 58 (WH), harness side and wiper HIGH/LOW relay Pin 87, Circuit 58 (WH), harness side. • Is the resistance less than 5 ohms? → **Yes** CARRY OUT the windshield wiper motor component test. If the component fails, INSTALL a new wiper motor; REPEAT the self-test. CLEAR the DTCs. → **No** REPAIR Circuit 58 (WH). REPEAT the self-test. CLEAR the DTCs.

FM9029900774130X

Fig. 95 Test B: Windshield Wipers Do Not Operate/ Operate Correctly (Part 13 of 14). Mustang

TEST CONDITIONS	TEST DETAILS/RESULTS/ACTIONS
B27 CHECK CIRCUIT 28 (BK/PK) FOR OPEN CIRCUIT CONDITION BETWEEN THE WIPER HIGH/LOW RELAY AND THE WIPER MOTOR	
1 2 3 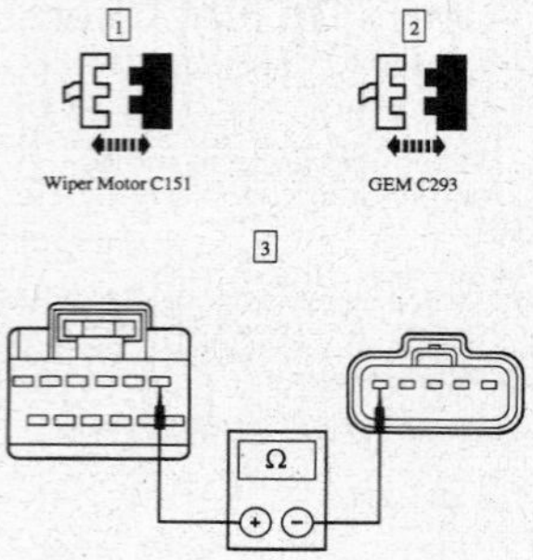	3 Measure the resistance between wiper motor C151 Pin 1, Circuit 28 (BK/PK), harness side and GEM C293 Pin 1, Circuit 58 (WH), harness side. • Is the resistance less than 5 ohms? → **Yes** INSTALL a new wiper motor; REPEAT the self-test. CLEAR the DTCs. → **No** REPAIR Circuit 28 (BK/PK). REPEAT the self-test. CLEAR the DTCs.

FM9029900774140X

Fig. 95 Test B: Windshield Wipers Do Not Operate/ Operate Correctly (Part 14 of 14). Mustang

TEST CONDITIONS	TEST DETAILS/RESULTS/ACTIONS
C1 DETERMINE IF GEM IS RECEIVING CORRECT IGNITION SWITCH STATUS	
1 2 3 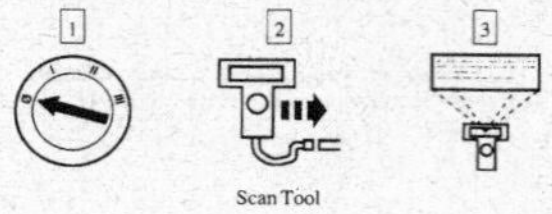	3 **Note:** If the vehicle is equipped with a manual transmission, depress the clutch while turning the ignition switch to START. Monitor the GEM PIDs IGN__S, IGN__R IGN__A, and IGN__KEY while turning the ignition switch through the START, RUN, OFF and ACC positions. • Do the GEM PID values agree with the ignition switch positions? → **Yes** GO to **C2**. → **No** Diagnose & Repair Warning Devices
C2 DETERMINE IF GEM IS RECEIVING CORRECT WIPER SWITCH STATUS FROM MULTIFUNCTION SWITCH	

FM9029900775010X

Fig. 96 Test C: Windshield Washers Do Not Operate/Operate Correctly (Part 1 of 7). Mustang

TEST CONDITIONS	TEST DETAILS/RESULTS/ACTIONS
C2 DETERMINE IF GEM IS RECEIVING CORRECT WIPER SWITCH STATUS FROM MULTIFUNCTION SWITCH	
	2 Monitor GEM PID WPMODE while activating all wiper control positions on the multifunction switch. • Does the GEM PID values agree with switch positions? → **Yes** GO to **C3**. → **No** GO to Pinpoint Test B.
C3 CHECK GEM CONTROL OF THE WASHER ON/OFF RELAY	
	1 Trigger GEM active command WASH RLY ON and OFF. • Do washers turn ON and OFF? → **Yes** INSTALL a new GEM; REPEAT the self-test. CLEAR the DTCs. → **No** GO to **C4**.

FM9029900775020X

Fig. 96 Test C: Windshield Washers Do Not Operate/Operate Correctly (Part 2 of 7). Mustang

TEST CONDITIONS	TEST DETAILS/RESULTS/ACTIONS
C6 CARRY OUT WASHER ON/OFF RELAY COMPONENT TEST	
	1 Check the washer ON/OFF relay. • Is the washer ON/OFF relay OK? → **Yes** GO to C7. → **No** INSTALL a new wiper ON/OFF relay. REPEAT the self-test. CLEAR the DTCs.
C7 CHECK CIRCUIT 686 (TN/RD) FOR SHORT TO BATTERY BETWEEN GEM AND BJB	
 GEM C293 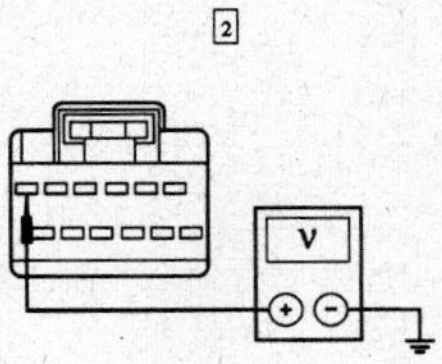	2 Measure the voltage between GEM C293 Pin 6, Circuit 686 (TN/RD), harness side and ground. • Is the voltage greater than 10 volts? → **Yes** REPAIR Circuit 686 (TN/RD). REPEAT the self-test. CLEAR the DTCs. → **No** GO to **C8**.

FM9029900775040X

Fig. 96 Test C: Windshield Washers Do Not Operate/Operate Correctly (Part 4 of 7). Mustang

TEST CONDITIONS	TEST DETAILS/RESULTS/ACTIONS
C4 CHECK CIRCUIT 65 (DG) FOR OPEN CIRCUIT BETWEEN CJB AND WASHER ON/OFF RELAY	
NOTE: Verify voltage at CJB F26 (30A) before carrying out this test.	
 Washer ON/OFF Relay 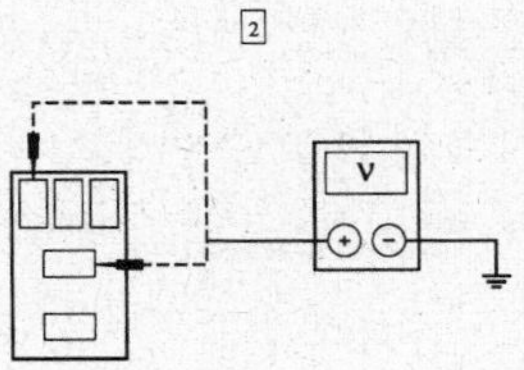	2 Measure the voltage between washer ON/OFF relay Pin 2, Circuit 65 (DG), harness side and ground; and washer ON/OFF relay Pin 3, Circuit 65 (DG), harness side and ground. • Are the voltages greater than 10 volts? → **Yes** GO to **C5**. → **No** REPAIR the circuit in question. REPEAT the self-test. CLEAR the DTCs.
C5 ISOLATE THE PROBLEM BETWEEN GEM AND BJB	
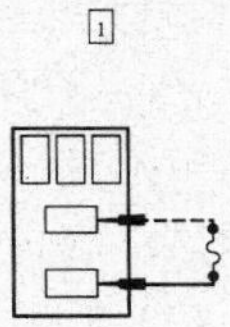	1 Connect a fused jumper wire (30A) between washer ON/OFF relay Pin 3, Circuit 65 (DG), harness side and Pin 5, Circuit 941 (BK/WH), harness side. • Did the washer motor activate? → **Yes** GO to **C6**. → **No** GO to **C10**.

FM9029900775030X

Fig. 96 Test C: Windshield Washers Do Not Operate/Operate Correctly (Part 3 of 7). Mustang

TEST CONDITIONS	TEST DETAILS/RESULTS/ACTIONS
C8 CHECK CIRCUIT 686 (TN/RD) FOR SHORT TO GROUND BETWEEN GEM AND BJB	
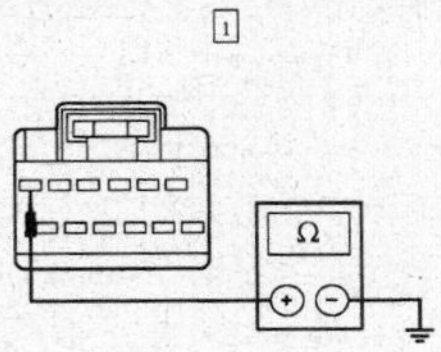	1 Measure the resistance between GEM C293 Pin 6, Circuit 686 (TN/RD), harness side and ground. • Is the resistance greater than 10,000 ohms? → **Yes** GO to **C9**. → **No** REPAIR Circuit 686 (TN/RD). REPEAT the self-test. CLEAR the DTCs.
C9 CHECK CIRCUIT 686 (TN/RD) FOR AN OPEN CIRCUIT BETWEEN GEM AND WASHER ON/OFF RELAY	
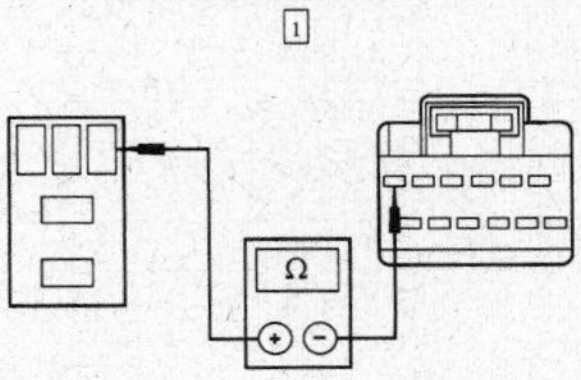	1 Measure the resistance between GEM C293 Pin 6, Circuit 686 (TN/RD), harness side and washer ON/OFF relay Pin 1, Circuit 686 (TN/RD), harness side. • Is the resistance less than 5 ohms? → **Yes** INSTALL a new GEM. REPEAT the self-test. CLEAR the DTCs. → **No** REPAIR Circuit 686 (TN/RD). REPEAT the self-test. CLEAR the DTCs.

FM9029900775050X

Fig. 96 Test C: Windshield Washers Do Not Operate/Operate Correctly (Part 5 of 7). Mustang

TEST CONDITIONS	TEST DETAILS/RESULTS/ACTIONS
C10 CHECK CIRCUIT 941 (BK/WH) FOR SHORT TO BATTERY BETWEEN BJB AND WASHER MOTOR	
1  Washer Pump Motor C126	
2 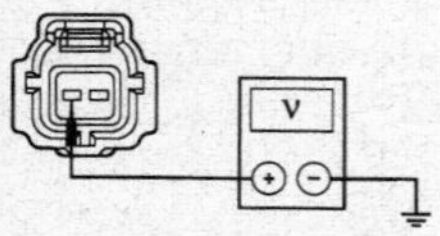	2 Measure the voltage between washer pump C126 Pin 1, Circuit 941 (BK/WH), harness side and ground. • Is the voltage greater than 10 volts? → **Yes** REPAIR Circuit 941 (BK/WH). REPEAT the self-test. CLEAR the DTCs. → **No** GO to **C11**.
C11 CHECK CIRCUIT 941 (BK/WH) FOR OPEN BETWEEN THE BJB AND THE WASHER MOTOR	
1 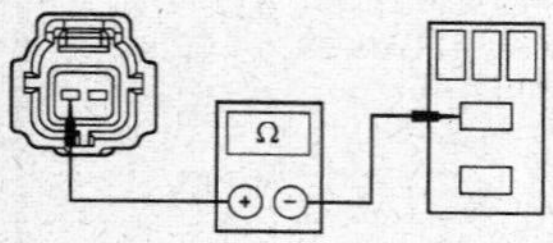	1 Measure the resistance between washer pump C126 Pin 1, Circuit 941 (BK/WH), harness side and washer pump relay Pin 5, Circuit 941 (BK/WH), harness side. • Is the resistance less than 5 ohms? → **Yes** GO to **C12**. → **No** REPAIR Circuit 941 (BK/WH). REPEAT the self-test. CLEAR the DTCs.

FM9029900775060X

Fig. 96 Test C: Windshield Washers Do Not Operate/Operate Correctly (Part 6 of 7). Mustang

TEST CONDITIONS	TEST DETAILS/RESULTS/ACTIONS
A1 RETRIEVE THE RECORDED DTCS FROM BOTH CONTINUOUS AND ON-DEMAND GEM SELF-TEST	
Note: If DTC B1359 is retrieved, repair this DTC before proceeding with this test.	
	1 Use the recorded GEM DTCs. • Are any DTCs recorded? → **Yes** For DTC B1359, For DTC B1465 and B1466, GO to **A13**. For DTC B1432, GO to **A6**. For DTC B1438, GO to **A3**. For DTC B1446, GO to **A6**. For DTC B1450, GO to **A3**. For DTC B1465, GO to **A13**. For DTC B1466, GO to **A3**. → **No** GO to **A2**.
A2 CHECK FOR VOLTAGE AT CENTRAL JUNCTION BOX (CJB) FUSE 215 (30A)	
1 	
	2 Remove CJB Fuse 215 (30A)
3 	

FM9020100793010X

Fig. 97 Test A: Windshield Wipers Are Inoperative (Part 1 of 9). Sable & Taurus

TEST CONDITIONS	TEST DETAILS/RESULTS/ACTIONS
C12 CHECK CIRCUIT 1205 (BK) FOR AN OPEN	
1 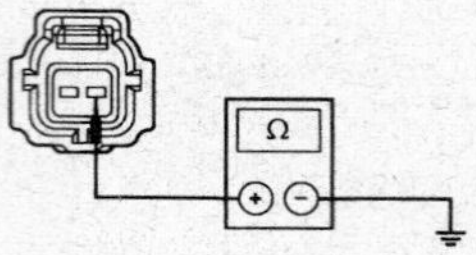	1 Measure the resistance between washer pump C126 Pin 2, Circuit 1205 (BK), harness side and ground. • Is the resistance less than 5 ohms? → **Yes** INSTALL a new washer motor. REPEAT the self-test. CLEAR the DTCs. → **No** REPAIR Circuit 1205 (BK). REPEAT the self-test. CLEAR the DTCs.

FM9029900775070X

Fig. 96 Test C: Windshield Washers Do Not Operate/Operate Correctly (Part 7 of 7). Mustang

TEST CONDITIONS	TEST DETAILS/RESULTS/ACTIONS
A2 CHECK FOR VOLTAGE AT CENTRAL JUNCTION BOX (CJB) FUSE 215 (30A) (Continued)	
4 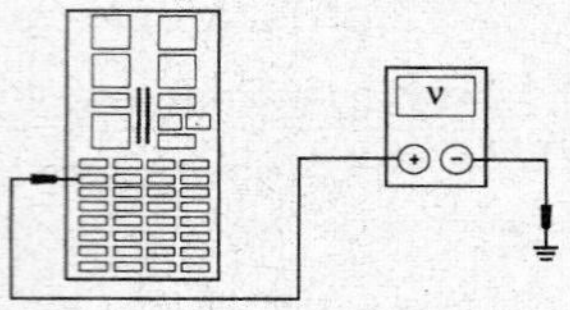	4 Measure the voltage between input terminal of Fuse 215 (30A) and ground. • Is the voltage greater than 10 volts? → **Yes** GO to **A3**. → **No** REPAIR power supply to CJB. TEST system for normal operation.
A3 CHECK THE MULTIFUNCTION SWITCH INPUT TO GEM — MONITOR GEM PID WPMODE	
1  CJB Fuse 215 (30A) 2 	2 Monitor the GEM PID WPMODE while turning the multifunction switch through all positions. • Do the PID values agree with the multifunction switch positions? → **Yes** GO to **A6**. → **No** GO to **A4**.
A4 CHECK THE MULTIFUNCTION SWITCH	
1  2  Multifunction Switch C202a 3  Multifunction Switch C202b	
	4 Carry out the multifunction switch component test. • Is the multifunction switch OK? → **Yes** GO to **A5**. → **No** INSTALL a new multifunction switch. CLEAR the DTCs. REPEAT the self-test.

FM9020100793020X

Fig. 97 Test A: Windshield Wipers Are Inoperative (Part 2 of 9). Sable & Taurus

TEST CONDITIONS	TEST DETAILS/RESULTS/ACTIONS
A5 CHECK CIRCUIT 682 (DB) FOR OPEN	
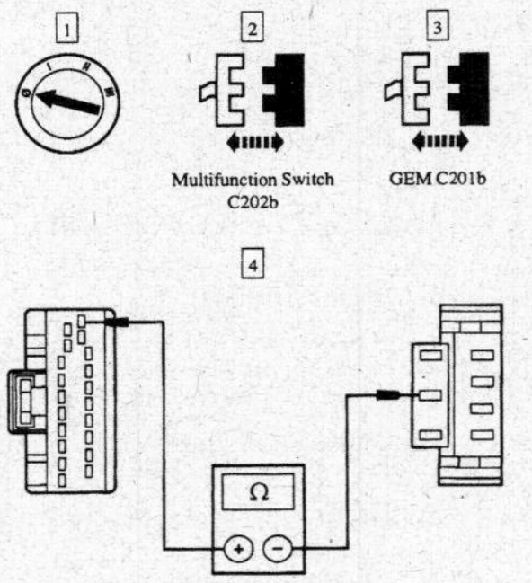	4 Measure the resistance between multifunction switch C202b pin 4, circuit 682 (DB), harness side and GEM C201b pin 11, circuit 682 (DB), harness side. • Is the resistance less than 5 ohms? → **Yes** GO to **A17**. → **No** REPAIR the circuit. CLEAR the DTCs. REPEAT the self-test.
A6 CHECK THE GEM MONITOR THE PID WPMODE	
	2 Monitor the PID WPMODE while turning multifunction switch through all positions. • Does PID indicate SHORTVBAT? → **Yes** GO to **A10**. → **No** GO to **A7**.
A7 CHECK THE GEM OUTPUT	
	2 Select GEM active command WIPER__RLY.

FM9020100793030X

Fig. 97 Test A: Windshield Wipers Are Inoperative (Part 3 of 9). Sable & Taurus

TEST CONDITIONS	TEST DETAILS/RESULTS/ACTIONS
A7 CHECK THE GEM OUTPUT (Continued)	
	3 Trigger WIPER__RLY to ON. • Do the wipers operate? → **Yes** GO to **A17**. → **No** GO to **A8**.
A8 CHECK FOR VOLTAGE AT WIPER RUN/PARK RELAY	
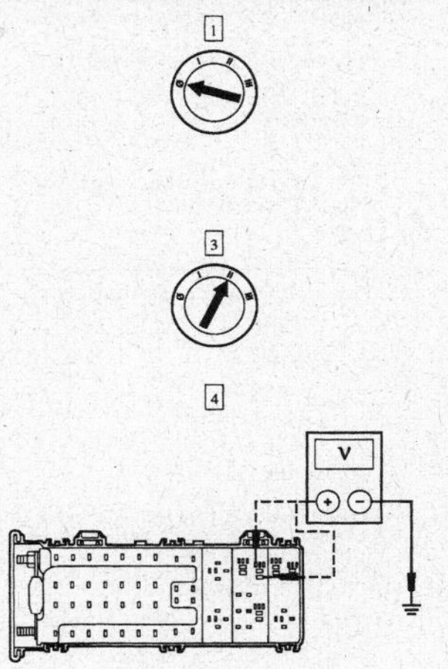	2 Remove wiper run/park relay from BJB 4 Measure the voltage between wiper park/run relay pin 2, circuit 646 (YE/WH), BJB side and ground; and between wiper park/run relay pin 5, circuit 950 (WH/BK), BJB side and ground. • Are the voltages greater than 10 volts? → **Yes** GO to **A9**. → **No** REPAIR power supply to BJB. CLEAR the DTCs. REPEAT the self-test.

FM9020100793040X

Fig. 97 Test A: Windshield Wipers Are Inoperative (Part 4 of 9). Sable & Taurus

TEST CONDITIONS	TEST DETAILS/RESULTS/ACTIONS
A9 CHECK WIPER PARK/RUN RELAY	
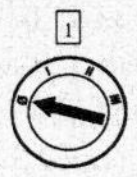	2 Carry out the relay component test on the wiper run/park relay. • Is the wiper run/park relay OK? → **Yes** GO to **A10**. → **No** INSTALL a new wiper run/park relay. CLEAR the DTCs. REPEAT the self-test.
A10 CHECK CIRCUIT 950 (WH/BK) FOR SHORT TO POWER	
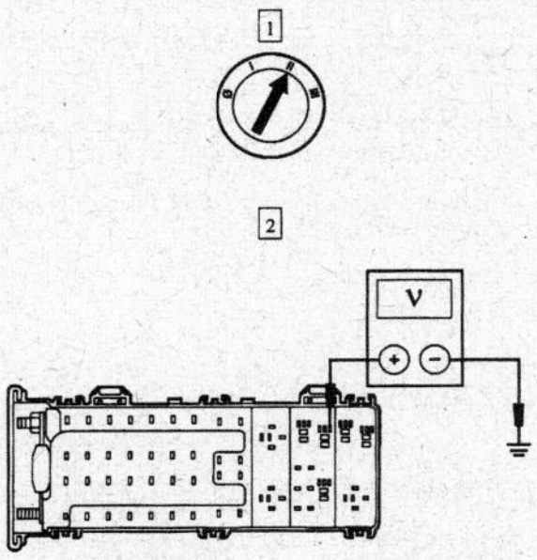	2 Measure the voltage between wiper run/park relay pin 1, circuit 950 (WH/BK), BJB side and ground. • Is any voltage indicated? → **Yes** GO to **A12**. → **No** GO to **A11**.

FM9020100793050X

Fig. 97 Test A: Windshield Wipers Are Inoperative (Part 5 of 9). Sable & Taurus

TEST CONDITIONS	TEST DETAILS/RESULTS/ACTIONS
A11 CHECK CIRCUIT 61 (YE/RD) FOR OPEN	
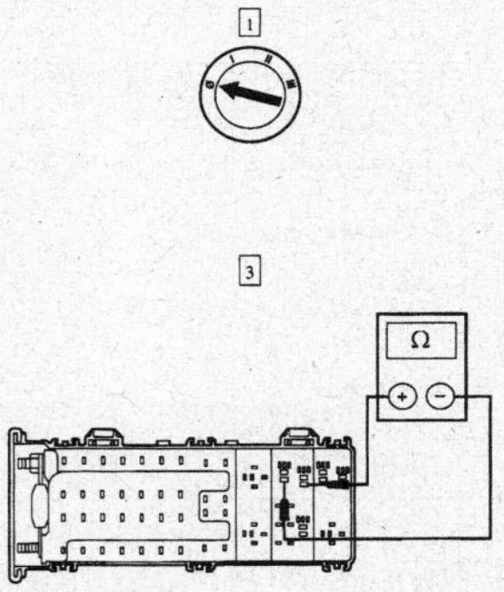	2 Remove wiper hi/lo relay from BJB. 3 Measure the resistance between wiper run/park relay pin 3, circuit 61 (YE/RD), BJB side and wiper hi/lo relay pin 3, circuit 61 (YE/RD), BJB side. • Is the resistance less than 5 ohms? → **Yes** GO to **A13**. → **No** REPAIR the circuit. CLEAR the DTCs. REPEAT the self-test.
A12 CHECK CIRCUIT 646 (BK) FOR SHORT TO POWER	
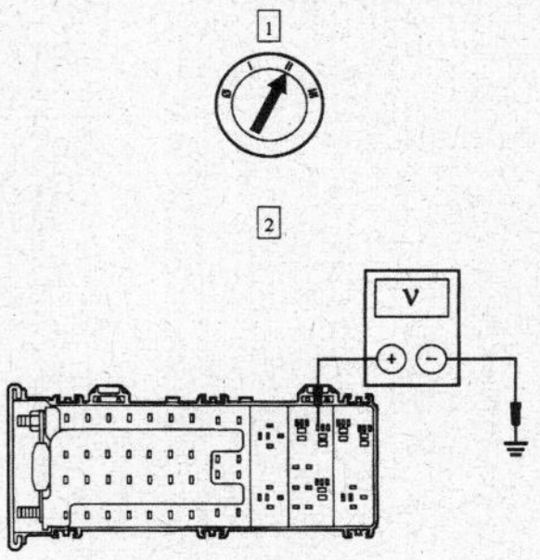	2 Measure the voltage between wiper run/park relay pin 2, circuit 646 (BK), BJB side and ground. • Is any voltage indicated? → **Yes** REPAIR the circuit. CLEAR the DTCs. REPEAT the self-test. → **No** GO to **A17**.

FM9020100793060X

Fig. 97 Test A: Windshield Wipers Are Inoperative (Part 6 of 9). Sable & Taurus

TEST CONDITIONS	TEST DETAILS/RESULTS/ACTIONS
A13 CHECK CIRCUIT 646 (BK) FOR OPEN	
1  GEM C201a 2 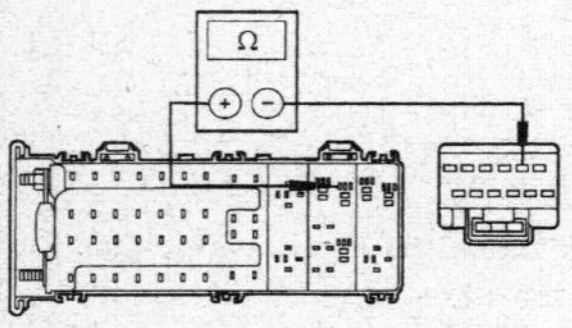	2 Measure the resistance between wiper run/park relay pin 2, circuit 646 (BK), BJB side and GEM C201a pin 11, circuit 646 (BK), harness side. • Is the resistance less than 5 ohms? → **Yes** GO to **A14**. → **No** REPAIR the circuit. CLEAR the DTCs. REPEAT the self-test.
A14 CHECK CIRCUIT 57 (BK) FOR OPEN	
1  2  Wiper Motor C125 3 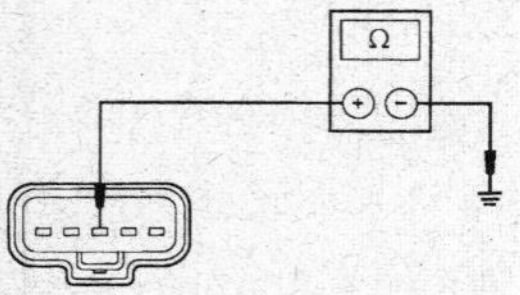	3 Measure the resistance between wiper motor C125 pin 3, circuit 57 (BK), harness side and ground. • Is the resistance less than 5 ohms? → **Yes** GO to **A15**. → **No** REPAIR the circuit. CLEAR the DTCs. REPEAT the self-test.

FM9020100793070X

Fig. 97 Test A: Windshield Wipers Are Inoperative (Part 7 of 9). Sable & Taurus

TEST CONDITIONS	TEST DETAILS/RESULTS/ACTIONS
A15 CHECK GEM OUTPUT	
1  2 	3 Select GEM active command WIPER_RLY. 4 Trigger WIPER_RLY to ON. 5 Measure the voltage between wiper motor C125 pin 2, circuit 58 (WH), harness side and ground. • Is the voltage greater than 10 volts? → **Yes** GO to **A16**. → **No** GO to Pinpoint Test C.
A16 CHECK WIPER MOTOR	
	1 Carry out the wiper motor component test. • Is the wiper motor OK? → **Yes** GO to **A17**. → **No** INSTALL a new wiper motor.
A17 CHECK FOR CORRECT GEM OPERATION	
	1 Disconnect all GEM connectors. 2 Check: • for corrosion • for pushed-out pins 3 Connect all GEM connectors and make sure they seat correctly.

FM9020100793080X

Fig. 97 Test A: Windshield Wipers Are Inoperative (Part 8 of 9). Sable & Taurus

TEST CONDITIONS	TEST DETAILS/RESULTS/ACTIONS
A17 CHECK FOR CORRECT GEM OPERATION (Continued)	
	4 Operate the system and verify the concern is still present. • Is the concern still present? → **Yes** INSTALL a new GEM. → **No** The system is operating correctly at this time. Concern may have been caused by a loose or corroded connector. CLEAR the DTCs. REPEAT the self-test.

FM9020100793090X

Fig. 97 Test A: Windshield Wipers Are Inoperative (Part 9 of 9). Sable & Taurus

TEST CONDITIONS	TEST DETAILS/RESULTS/ACTIONS
B1 RETRIEVE THE RECORDED DTCS FROM BOTH CONTINUOUS AND ON-DEMAND GEM SELF-TEST	
	1 Use the recorded GEM DTCs from the continuous and on-demand self-test: • Are any DTCs recorded? → **Yes** For DTC B1465 and B1466, GO to **B5**. For DTC B1441, GO to **B3**. For DTC B1446, GO to **B5**. For DTC B1448, GO to **B5**. For DTC B1465, GO to **B5**. → **No** GO to **B2**.
B2 CHECK THE MULTIFUNCTION SWITCH INPUT TO GEM — MONITOR GEM PID WPMODE	
1 	1 Monitor the GEM PID WPMODE while turning the multifunction switch through all positions. • Do the PID values agree with the multifunction switch positions? → **Yes** GO to **B5**. → **No** GO to **B3**.

FM9020100794010X

Fig. 98 Test B: Windshield Wipers Stay On Continuously (Part 1 of 8). Sable & Taurus

TEST CONDITIONS	TEST DETAILS/RESULTS/ACTIONS
B3 CHECK THE MULTIFUNCTION SWITCH	
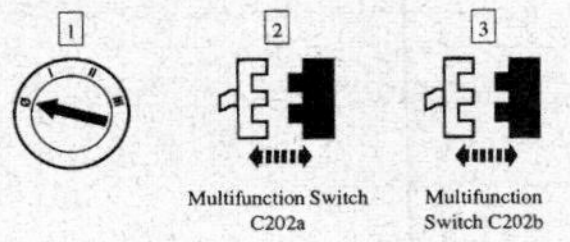	4 Carry out the multifunction switch component test. • Is the multifunction switch OK? → **Yes** GO to **B4**. → **No** INSTALL a new multifunction switch.
B4 CHECK CIRCUIT 684 (PK/YE) FOR A SHORT TO GROUND	
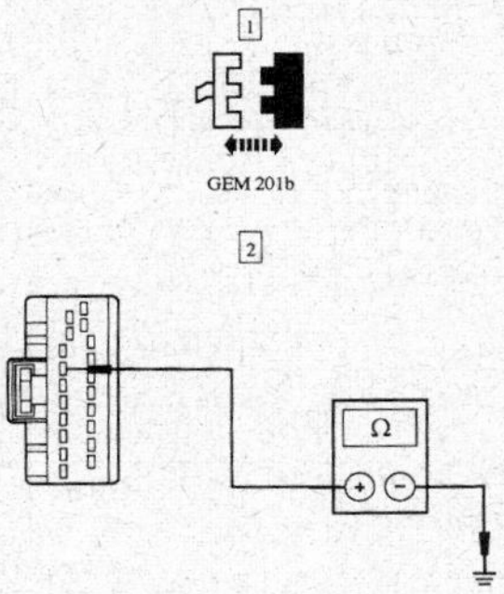	2 Measure the resistance between GEM C201b pin 4, circuit 684 (PK/YE), harness side and ground. • Is the resistance greater than 10,000 ohms? → **Yes** GO to **B15**. → **No** REPAIR the circuit. CLEAR the DTCs. REPEAT the self-test.

FM9020100794020X

Fig. 98 Test B: Windshield Wipers Stay On Continuously (Part 2 of 8). Sable & Taurus

TEST CONDITIONS	TEST DETAILS/RESULTS/ACTIONS
B5 CHECK WIPER PARK/RUN RELAY	
	2 Carry out the relay component test on the wiper run/park relay. • Is the wiper run/park relay OK? → **Yes** GO to **B6**. → **No** INSTALL a new wiper run/park relay. CLEAR the DTCs. REPEAT the self-test.
B6 CHECK CIRCUIT 61 (YE/RD) FOR A SHORT TO POWER	
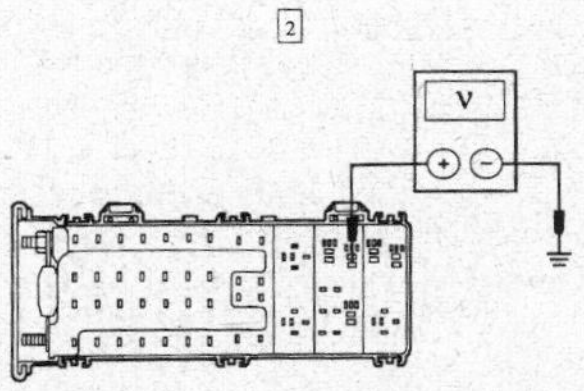	1 Remove the wiper hi/lo relay. 2 Measure the voltage between wiper run/park relay pin 3, circuit 61 (YE/RD), battery junction box (BJB) side and ground. • Is any voltage indicated? → **Yes** REPAIR the circuit. CLEAR the DTCs. REPEAT the self-test. → **No** GO to **B7**.
B7 CHECK CIRCUIT 646 (YE/WH) FOR SHORT TO GROUND	
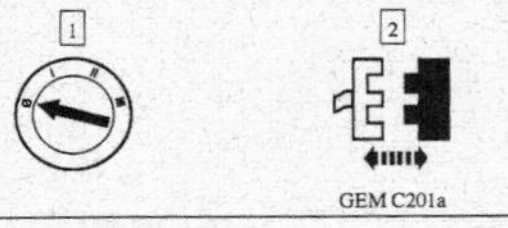	

FM9020100794030X

Fig. 98 Test B: Windshield Wipers Stay On Continuously (Part 3 of 8). Sable & Taurus

TEST CONDITIONS	TEST DETAILS/RESULTS/ACTIONS
B7 CHECK CIRCUIT 646 (YE/WH) FOR SHORT TO GROUND (Continued)	
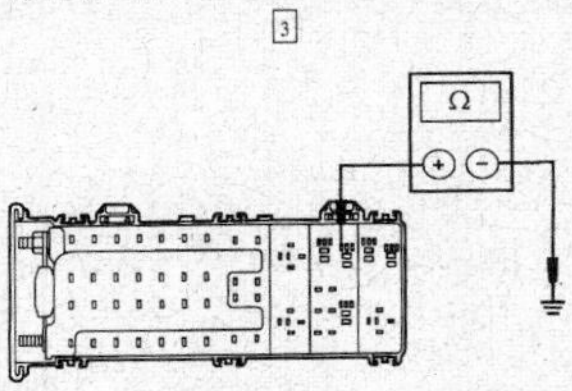	3 Measure the resistance between wiper run/park relay pin 2, circuit 646 (YE/WH) BJB side and ground. • Is the resistance greater than 10,000 ohms? → **Yes** GO to **B8**. → **No** REPAIR the circuit. CLEAR the DTCs. REPEAT the self-test.
B8 CHECK CIRCUITS 56 (DB/OG) AND 58 (WH) FOR SHORT TO VOLTAGE	
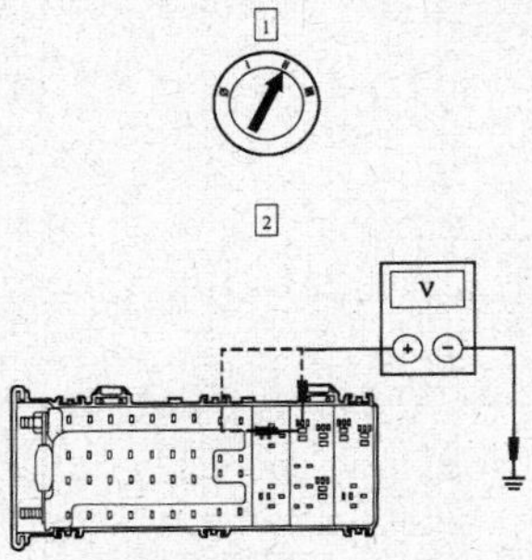	2 Measure the voltage between wiper hi/lo relay pin 5, circuit 56 (DB/OG), BJB side and ground; and between wiper hi/lo relay pin 4, circuit 58 (WH), BJB side and ground. • Is any voltage indicated? → **Yes** GO to **B9**. → **No** GO to **B10**.
B9 ISOLATE CIRCUITS 56 (DB/OG) AND 58 (WH) FOR SHORT TO VOLTAGE	
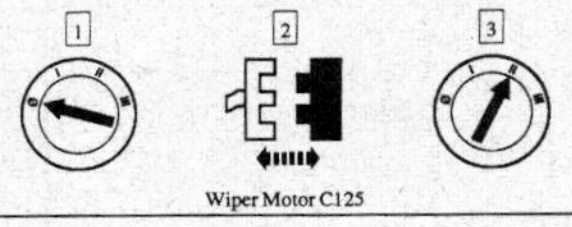	

FM9020100794040X

Fig. 98 Test B: Windshield Wipers Stay On Continuously (Part 4 of 8). Sable & Taurus

TEST CONDITIONS	TEST DETAILS/RESULTS/ACTIONS
B9 ISOLATE CIRCUITS 56 (DB/OG) AND 58 (WH) FOR SHORT TO VOLTAGE (Continued)	
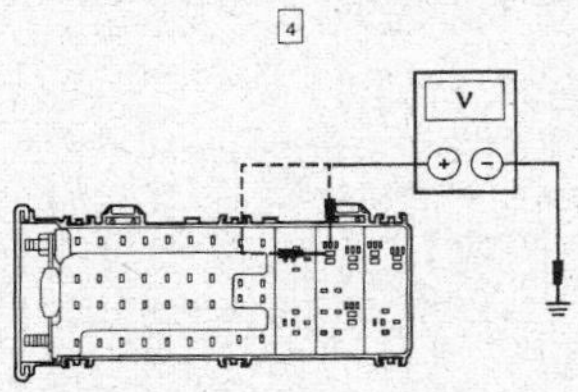	4 Measure the voltage between wiper hi/lo relay pin 5, circuit 56 (DB/OG), BJB side and ground; and between wiper hi/lo relay pin 4, circuit 58 (WH) BJB side and ground. • Is any voltage indicated? → **Yes** REPAIR the circuit(s) in question. CLEAR the DTCs. REPEAT the self-test. → **No** GO to **B10**.
B10 CHECK CIRCUIT 65 (DG) FOR SHORT TO VOLTAGE	
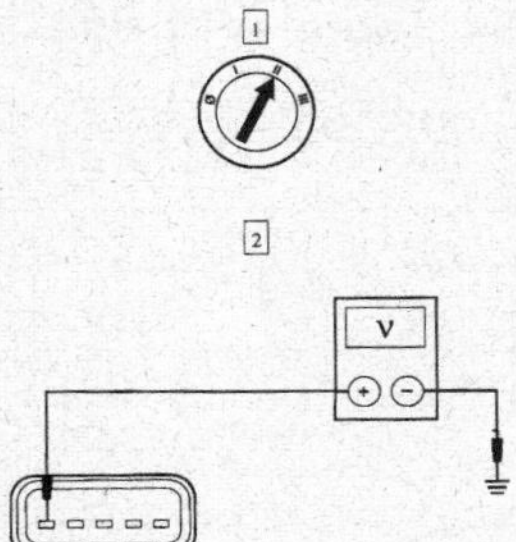	2 Measure the voltage between wiper motor C125 pin 5, circuit 65 (DG), harness side and ground. • Is any voltage indicated? → **Yes** GO to **B11**. → **No** GO to **B13**.
B11 ISOLATE GEM FOR SHORT TO VOLTAGE	

FM9020100794050X

Fig. 98 Test B: Windshield Wipers Stay On Continuously (Part 5 of 8). Sable & Taurus

TEST CONDITIONS	TEST DETAILS/RESULTS/ACTIONS
B11 ISOLATE GEM FOR SHORT TO VOLTAGE (Continued)	
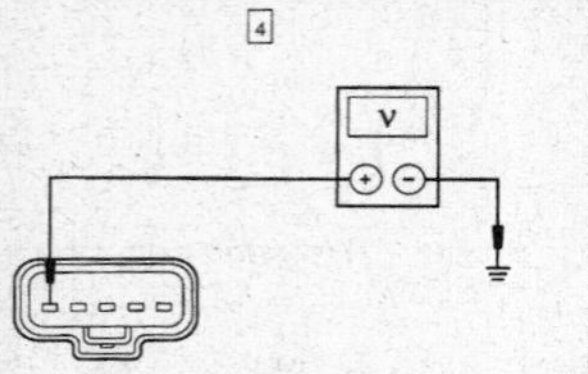	4 Measure voltage between wiper motor C125 pin 5, circuit 65 (DG), harness side and ground. • Is any voltage indicated? → **Yes** GO to **B12**. → **No** GO to **B15**.
B12 ISOLATE CENTRAL JUNCTION BOX (CJB) FOR SHORT TO POWER	
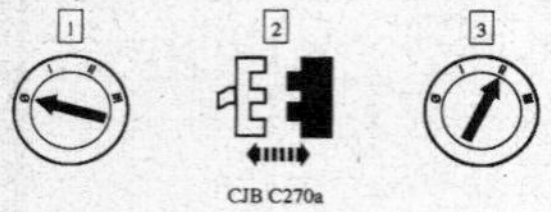	
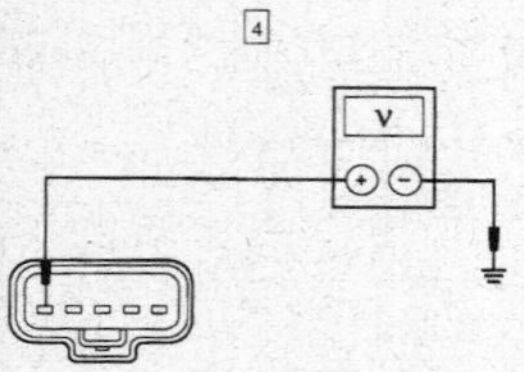	4 Measure the voltage between wiper motor C125 pin 5, circuit 65 (DG), harness side and ground. • Is any voltage indicated? → **Yes** REPAIR the circuit. CLEAR the DTCs. REPEAT the self-test. → **No** REPAIR CJB as necessary. CLEAR the DTCs. REPEAT the self-test.
B13 CHECK WIPER MOTOR FOR SHORT TO POWER	
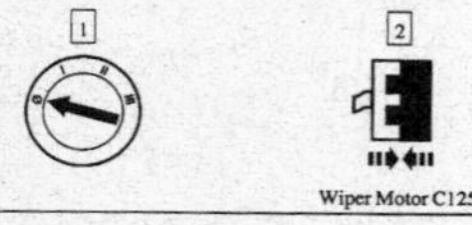	

FM9020100794060X

Fig. 98 Test B: Windshield Wipers Stay On Continuously (Part 6 of 8). Sable & Taurus

TEST CONDITIONS	TEST DETAILS/RESULTS/ACTIONS
B15 CHECK FOR CORRECT GEM OPERATION (Continued)	
	4 Operate the system and verify the concern is still present. • Is the concern still present? → **Yes** INSTALL a new GEM. → **No** The system is operating correctly at this time. Concern may have been caused by a loose or corroded connector. CLEAR the DTCs. REPEAT the self-test.

FM9020100794080X

Fig. 98 Test B: Windshield Wipers Stay On Continuously (Part 8 of 8). Sable & Taurus

TEST CONDITIONS	TEST DETAILS/RESULTS/ACTIONS
C1 RETRIEVE THE RECORDED DTCS FROM BOTH CONTINUOUS AND ON-DEMAND GEM SELF-TEST	
	1 Use the recorded GEM DTCs from the continuous and on-demand self-test: • Are any DTCs recorded? → **Yes** For DTC B1438 and B1450, GO to Pinpoint Test A. For DTC B1434, GO to **C6**. For DTC B1436, GO to **C6**. For DTC B1438, GO to **C3**. For DTC B1446, GO to **C6**. For DTC B1448, GO to **C6**. For DTC B1450, GO to **C3**. For DTC B1466, GO to **C6**. → **No** GO to **C2**.

FM9020100795010X

Fig. 99 Test C: Windshield Wipers Do Not Operate Correctly (Part 1 of 12). Sable & Taurus

TEST CONDITIONS	TEST DETAILS/RESULTS/ACTIONS
B13 CHECK WIPER MOTOR FOR SHORT TO POWER (Continued)	
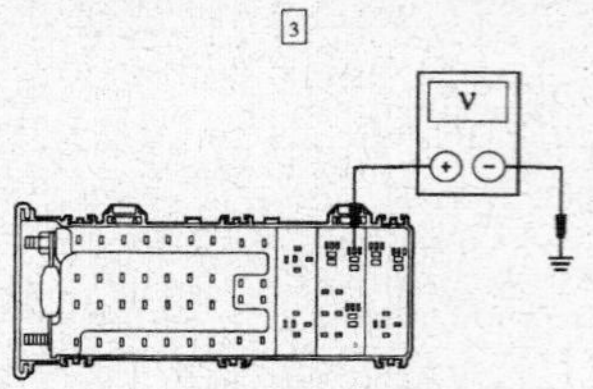	3 Measure the voltage between wiper run/park relay pin 4, circuit 65 (DG), BJB side and ground. • Is any voltage indicated? → **Yes** GO to **B14**. → **No** GO to **B15**.
B14 CHECK WIPER MOTOR	
	1 Carry out the wiper motor component test. • Is the wiper motor OK? → **Yes** GO to **B15**. → **No** INSTALL a new windshield wiper motor. CLEAR the DTCs. REPEAT the self-test.
B15 CHECK FOR CORRECT GEM OPERATION	
	1 Disconnect all GEM connectors. 2 Check: • for corrosion • for pushed-out pins 3 Connect all GEM connectors and make sure they seat correctly.

FM9020100794070X

Fig. 98 Test B: Windshield Wipers Stay On Continuously (Part 7 of 8). Sable & Taurus

TEST CONDITIONS	TEST DETAILS/RESULTS/ACTIONS
C2 CHECK THE MULTIFUNCTION SWITCH INPUT TO GEM	
	3 Monitor GEM PID WP MODE while moving multifunction switch through all switch positions. • Does PID agree with all switch positions? → **Yes** GO to **C6**. → **No** GO to **C3**.
C3 CHECK THE MULTIFUNCTION SWITCH	
	4 Carry out the multifunction switch component test. • Is the multifunction switch OK? → **Yes** GO to **C4**. → **No** INSTALL a new multifunction switch. CLEAR the DTCs. REPEAT the self-test.
C4 CHECK CIRCUITS 684 (PK/YE) AND 680 (LB/OG) FOR SHORT TO VOLTAGE	

FM9020100795020X

Fig. 99 Test C: Windshield Wipers Do Not Operate Correctly (Part 2 of 12). Sable & Taurus

TEST CONDITIONS	TEST DETAILS/RESULTS/ACTIONS
C4 CHECK CIRCUITS 684 (PK/YE) AND 680 (LB/OG) FOR SHORT TO VOLTAGE (Continued)	
4 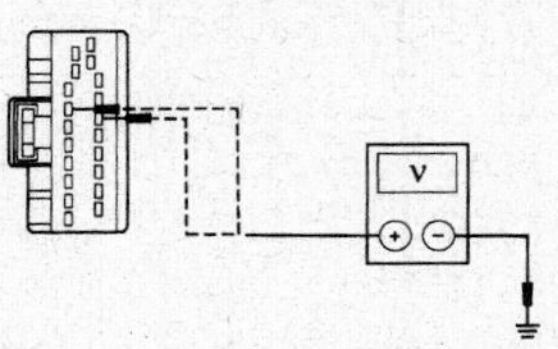	4 Measure the voltage between GEM C201b pin 4, circuit 684 (PK/YE), harness side and ground; and between GEM C201b pin 15, circuit 680 (LB/OG), harness side and ground. • Is any voltage indicated? → **Yes** REPAIR the circuit(s) in question. CLEAR the DTCs. REPEAT the self-test. → **No** GO to **C5**.
C5 CHECK CIRCUIT 684 (PK/YE) FOR AN OPEN	
1  2 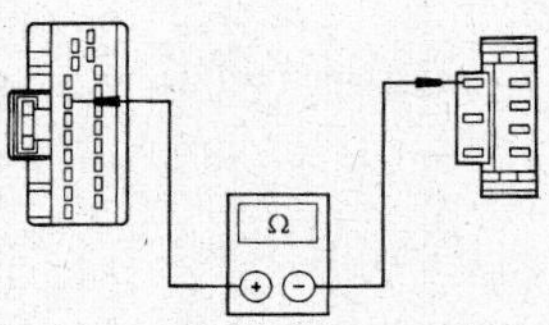	2 Measure the resistance between the GEM C201b pin 4, circuit 684 (PK/YE), harness side and multifunction switch C202b pin 1, circuit 684 (PK/YE), harness side. • Is the resistance less than 5 ohms? → **Yes** GO to **C23**. → **No** REPAIR the circuit. CLEAR the DTCs. REPEAT the self-test.

FM9020100795030X

Fig. 99 Test C: Windshield Wipers Do Not Operate Correctly (Part 3 of 12). Sable & Taurus

TEST CONDITIONS	TEST DETAILS/RESULTS/ACTIONS
C9 CHECK WIPER HI/LO RELAY	
1 	2 Carry out the relay component test on the wiper hi/lo relay. • Is the wiper hi/lo relay OK? → **Yes** GO to **C10**. → **No** INSTALL a new wiper hi/lo relay. CLEAR the DTCs. REPEAT the self-test.
C10 CHECK VOLTAGE TO WIPER HI/LO RELAY	
1  2 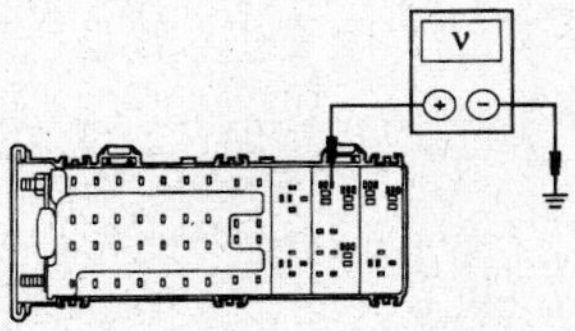	2 Measure the voltage between wiper hi/lo relay pin 1, circuit 647 (GY/LB), BJB side and ground. • Is voltage greater than 10 volts? → **Yes** GO to **C11**. → **No** REPAIR the circuit. CLEAR the DTCs. REPEAT the self-test.

FM9020100795050X

Fig. 99 Test C: Windshield Wipers Do Not Operate Correctly (Part 5 of 12). Sable & Taurus

TEST CONDITIONS	TEST DETAILS/RESULTS/ACTIONS
C6 CHECK THE WIPER HIGH SPEED OPERATION	
1 	2 Actuate the multifunction switch to the wiper high position. • Do the high speed wipers operate? → **Yes** GO to **C16**. → **No** GO to **C7**.
C7 CHECK THE GEM — MONITOR GEM PID WPHISP	
1 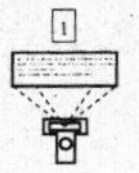	2 Monitor the GEM PID WPHISP while turning multifunction switch to the wiper high position. • Does the GEM PID WPHISP indicate SHORTVBAT? → **Yes** GO to **C11**. → **No** GO to **C8**.
C8 CHECK THE GEM OUTPUT	
	1 Select GEM active command WIPER_RLY. 2 Trigger WIPER_RLY and SPEED_RLY ON. • Do high speed wipers operate? → **Yes** GO to **C23**. → **No** GO to **C9**.

FM9020100795040X

Fig. 99 Test C: Windshield Wipers Do Not Operate Correctly (Part 4 of 12). Sable & Taurus

TEST CONDITIONS	TEST DETAILS/RESULTS/ACTIONS
C11 CHECK CIRCUIT 647 (GY/LB) FOR SHORT TO VOLTAGE	
1 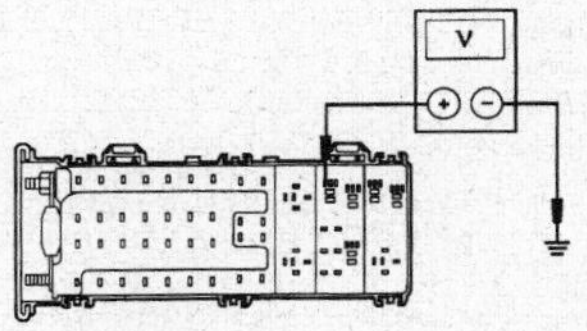	1 Measure the voltage between wiper hi/lo relay pin 2, circuit 647 (GY/LB) battery junction box (BJB) side and ground. • Is any voltage indicated? → **Yes** GO to **C12**. → **No** GO to **C13**.
C12 ISOLATE CIRCUIT 647 (GY/LB) FOR SHORT TO VOLTAGE	
1  2  GEM C201a 3  4 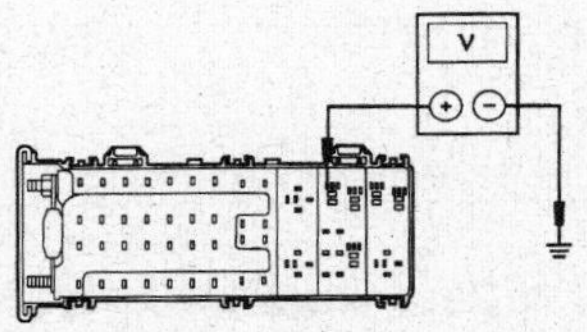	4 Measure the voltage between hi/lo relay pin 2, circuit 647 (GY/LB), BJB side and ground. • Is any voltage indicated? → **Yes** REPAIR the circuit. CLEAR the DTCs. REPEAT the self-test. → **No** GO to **C23**.
C13 CHECK CIRCUIT 647 (GY/LB) FOR AN OPEN	
1 	

FM9020100795060X

Fig. 99 Test C: Windshield Wipers Do Not Operate Correctly (Part 6 of 12). Sable & Taurus

TEST CONDITIONS	TEST DETAILS/RESULTS/ACTIONS
C13 CHECK CIRCUIT 647 (GY/LB) FOR AN OPEN (Continued)	
2 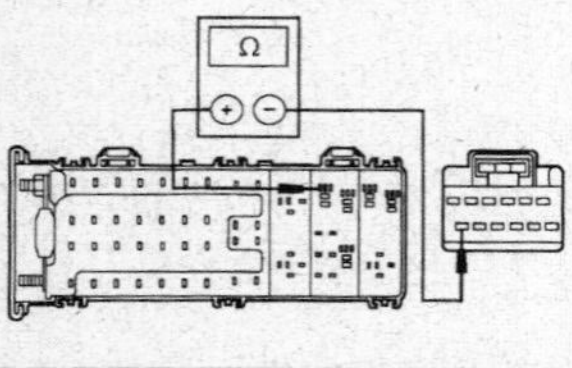	2 Measure the resistance between wiper hi/lo relay pin 2, circuit 647 (GY/LB), BJB side and GEM C201a pin 12, circuit 647 (GY/LB), harness side. • Is the resistance less than 5 ohms? → **Yes** GO to **C14**. → **No** REPAIR the circuit. CLEAR the DTCs. REPEAT the self-test.
C14 CHECK CIRCUIT 647 (GY/LB) FOR SHORT TO GROUND	
1 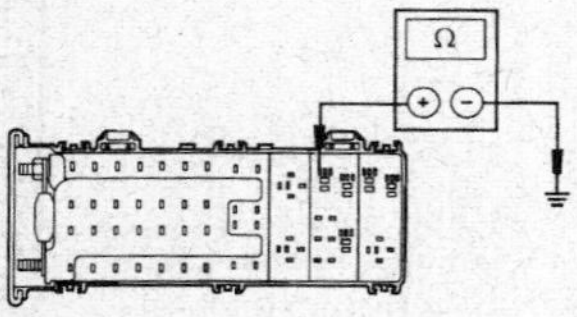	1 Measure the resistance between wiper hi/lo relay pin 2, circuit 647 (GY/LB), BJB side and ground. • Is the resistance greater than 10,000 ohms? → **Yes** GO to **C15**. → **No** REPAIR the circuit. CLEAR the DTCs. REPEAT the self-test.
C15 CHECK CIRCUIT 56 (DB/OG) FOR OPEN	
1  2  Wiper Motor C125	

FM9020100795070X

Fig. 99 Test C: Windshield Wipers Do Not Operate Correctly (Part 7 of 12). Sable & Taurus

TEST CONDITIONS	TEST DETAILS/RESULTS/ACTIONS
C15 CHECK CIRCUIT 56 (DB/OG) FOR OPEN (Continued)	
3 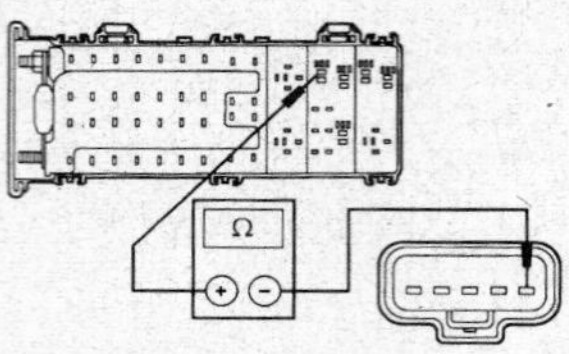	3 Measure the resistance between wiper hi/lo relay pin 5, circuit 56 (DB/OG), BJB side and wiper motor C125 pin 1, circuit 56 (DB/OG), harness side. • Is the resistance less than 5 ohms? → **Yes** GO to **C22**. → **No** REPAIR the circuit. CLEAR the DTCs. REPEAT the self-test.
C16 CHECK WIPER HI/LO RELAY	
1 	2 Carry out the relay component test on the wiper hi/lo relay. • Is the wiper hi/lo relay OK? → **Yes** GO to **C17**. → **No** INSTALL a new wiper hi/lo relay. CLEAR the DTCs. REPEAT the self-test.
C17 CHECK CIRCUIT 58 (WH) FOR OPEN	
1  Wiper Motor C125	

FM9020100795080X

Fig. 99 Test C: Windshield Wipers Do Not Operate Correctly (Part 8 of 12). Sable & Taurus

TEST CONDITIONS	TEST DETAILS/RESULTS/ACTIONS
C17 CHECK CIRCUIT 58 (WH) FOR OPEN (Continued)	
2 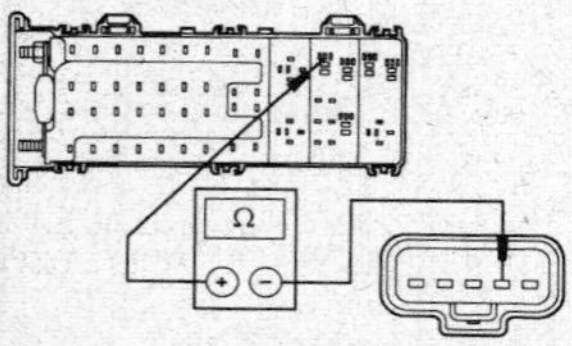	2 Measure the resistance between wiper hi/lo relay pin 4, circuit 58 (WH), BJB side and wiper motor C125 pin 2, circuit 58 (WH), harness side. • Is the resistance less than 5 ohms? → **Yes** GO to **C18**. → **No** REPAIR the circuit. CLEAR the DTCs. REPEAT the self-test.
C18 CHECK CIRCUIT 950 (WH/BK) FOR VOLTAGE	
1 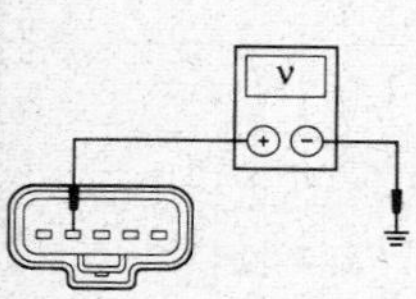	1 Measure the voltage between wiper motor C125 pin 4, circuit 950 (WH/BK), harness side and ground. • Is the voltage greater than 10 volts? → **Yes** GO to **C19**. → **No** REPAIR the circuit. CLEAR the DTCs. REPEAT the self-test.
C19 CHECK CIRCUIT 65 (DG) FOR OPEN	
1 	2 Remove wiper run/park relay.

FM9020100795090X

Fig. 99 Test C: Windshield Wipers Do Not Operate Correctly (Part 9 of 12). Sable & Taurus

TEST CONDITIONS	TEST DETAILS/RESULTS/ACTIONS
C19 CHECK CIRCUIT 65 (DG) FOR OPEN (Continued)	
3 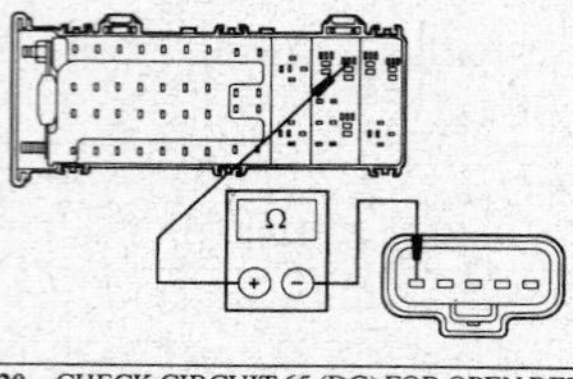	3 Measure the resistance between wiper run/park relay pin 4, circuit 65 (DG), BJB side and wiper motor C125 pin 5, circuit 65 (DG), harness side. • Is the resistance less than 5 ohms? → **Yes** GO to **C20**. → **No** REPAIR the circuit. CLEAR the DTCs. REPEAT the self-test.
C20 CHECK CIRCUIT 65 (DG) FOR OPEN BETWEEN WIPER MOTOR AND CENTRAL JUNCTION BOX (CJB)	
1  CJB C270a 2 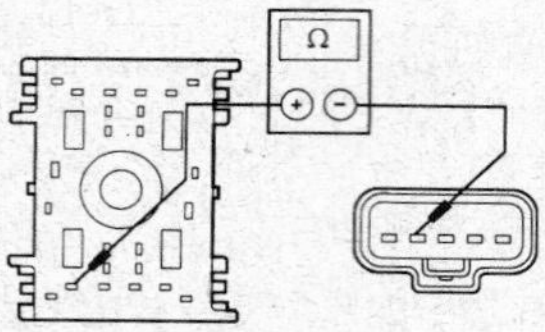	2 Measure the resistance between wiper motor C125 pin 4, circuit 65 (DG), harness side and CJB C270a pin 2, circuit 65 (DG), harness side. • Is the resistance less than 5 ohms? → **Yes** GO to **C21**. → **No** REPAIR the circuit. CLEAR the DTCs. REPEAT the self-test.

FM9020100795100X

Fig. 99 Test C: Windshield Wipers Do Not Operate Correctly (Part 10 of 12). Sable & Taurus

TEST CONDITIONS	TEST DETAILS/RESULTS/ACTIONS
C21 CHECK CIRCUIT 65 (DG) FOR INTERNAL OPEN IN CJB	
1 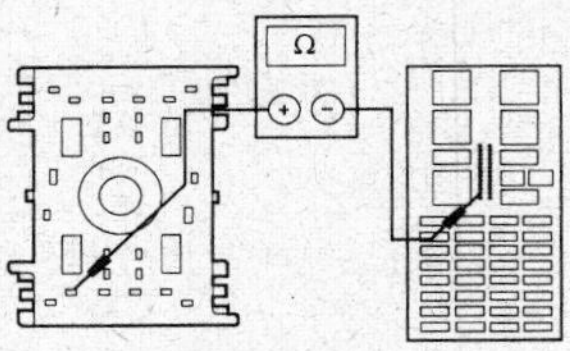	1 Measure the resistance between CJB C270a pin 2, circuit 65 (DG), harness side and GEM/CJB C201d pin 15, circuit 65 (DG), harness side. • Is the resistance less than 5 ohms? → **Yes** GO to **C22**. → **No** REPAIR the circuit. CLEAR the DTCs. REPEAT the self-test.
C22 CHECK WIPER MOTOR	
	1 Carry out the wiper motor component test. • Is the wiper motor OK? → **Yes** GO to **C23** → **No** INSTALL a new wiper motor. CLEAR the DTCs. REPEAT the self-test.
C23 CHECK FOR CORRECT GEM OPERATION	
	1 Disconnect all GEM connectors. 2 Check: • for corrosion • for pushed-out pins 3 Connect all GEM connectors and make sure they seat correctly.

FM9020100795110X

Fig. 99 Test C: Windshield Wipers Do Not Operate Correctly (Part 11 of 12). Sable & Taurus

TEST CONDITIONS	TEST DETAILS/RESULTS/ACTIONS
D1 RETRIEVE THE RECORDED DTCS FROM BOTH CONTINUOUS AND ON-DEMAND GEM SELF-TEST	
	1 Use the recorded GEM DTCs from the continuous and on-demand self-test. • Are any DTCs recorded? → **Yes** For DTC B1359, REFER to DTC. For DTC B1450 and B1438, Go to Pinpoint Test A. For DTC B1458, GO to **D12**. For DTC B1460, GO to **D7**. For DTC B1450, GO to **D3**. For DTC B1453, GO to **D3**. → **No** GO to **D2**.
D2 CHECK CENTRAL JUNCTION BOX (CJB) SUPPLY TO FUSE 211 (15A)	
1 	2 Remove CJB Fuse 211.

FM9020100796010X

Fig. 100 Test D: Windshield Washer Pump Is Inoperative (Part 1 of 8). Sable & Taurus

TEST CONDITIONS	TEST DETAILS/RESULTS/ACTIONS
C23 CHECK FOR CORRECT GEM OPERATION (Continued)	
	4 Operate the system and verify the concern is still present. • Is the concern still present? → **Yes** INSTALL a new GEM. → **No** The system is operating correctly at this time. Concern may have been caused by a loose or corroded connector. CLEAR the DTCs. REPEAT the self-test.

FM9020100795120X

Fig. 99 Test C: Windshield Wipers Do Not Operate Correctly (Part 12 of 12). Sable & Taurus

TEST CONDITIONS	TEST DETAILS/RESULTS/ACTIONS
D2 CHECK CENTRAL JUNCTION BOX (CJB) SUPPLY TO FUSE 211 (15A) (Continued)	
3  4 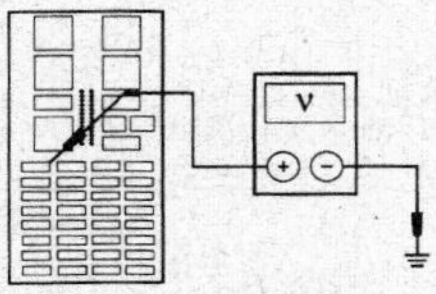	4 Measure the voltage between the input terminal of CJB Fuse 211 (15A) and ground. • Is voltage greater than 10 volts? → **Yes** GO to **D3**. → **No** REPAIR the circuit. TEST the system for normal operation.
D3 CHECK MULTIFUNCTION SWITCH INPUT TO GEM	
1 	2 Monitor the GEM PID WPMODE while actuating the multifunction switch through all switch positions. • Does GEM PID WPMODE agree with all switch positions? → **Yes** GO to **D7**. → **No** GO to **D4**.

FM9020100796020X

Fig. 100 Test D: Windshield Washer Pump Is Inoperative (Part 2 of 8). Sable & Taurus

TEST CONDITIONS	TEST DETAILS/RESULTS/ACTIONS
D4 CHECK THE MULTIFUNCTION SWITCH	
1 2 3 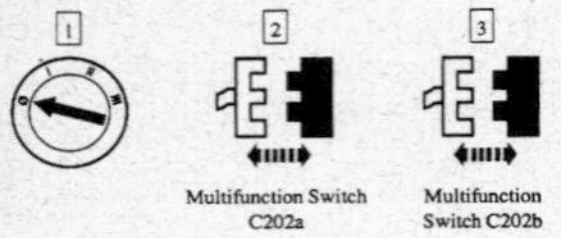	4 Carry out the multifunction switch component test. • Is the multifunction switch OK? → **Yes** GO to **D5**. → **No** INSTALL a new multifunction switch. CLEAR the DTCs. REPEAT the self-test.
D5 CHECK CIRCUIT 680 (LB/OG) FOR OPEN	
1  2 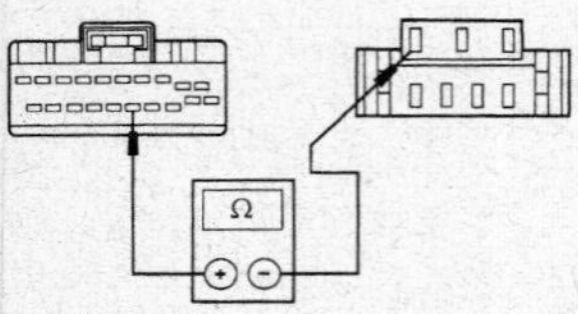	2 Measure the resistance between multifunction switch C202b pin 6, circuit 680 (LB/OG), harness side and GEM C201b pin 15, circuit 680 (LB/OG), harness side. • Is the resistance less than 5 ohms? → **Yes** GO to **D6**. → **No** REPAIR the circuit. CLEAR the DTCs. TEST the system for normal operation.

FM9020100796030X

Fig. 100 Test D: Windshield Washer Pump Is Inoperative (Part 3 of 8). Sable & Taurus

TEST CONDITIONS	TEST DETAILS/RESULTS/ACTIONS
D6 CHECK CIRCUIT 680 (LB/OG) FOR SHORT TO GROUND	
1 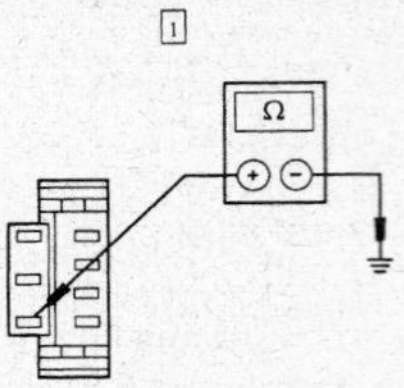	1 Measure the resistance between multifunction switch C202b pin 6, circuit 680 (LB/OG), harness side and ground. • Is the resistance greater than 10,000 ohms? → **Yes** GO to **D14**. → **No** REPAIR the circuit. CLEAR the DTCs. REPEAT the self-test.
D7 CHECK THE GEM RELAY DRIVER FOR SHORT TO VOLTAGE	
1 2 	3 Monitor the GEM PID WASH__RLY while pressing the front washer switch. • Does the PID read SHORTVBAT? → **Yes** GO to **D12**. → **No** GO to **D8**.
D8 CHECK THE GEM OUTPUT	
1 	2 Select GEM active command WASH__RLY.

FM9020100796040X

Fig. 100 Test D: Windshield Washer Pump Is Inoperative (Part 4 of 8). Sable & Taurus

TEST CONDITIONS	TEST DETAILS/RESULTS/ACTIONS
D8 CHECK THE GEM OUTPUT (Continued)	
	3 Trigger WASH__RLY to on. • Does the washer pump operate? → **Yes** GO to **D14**. → **No** GO to **D9**.
D9 CHECK CIRCUIT 941 (BK/WH) FOR VOLTAGE	
1 2 3 4  7 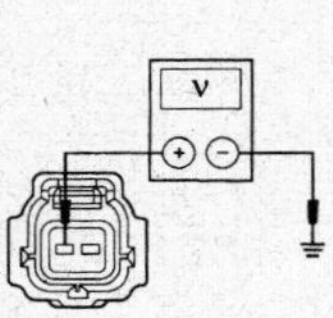	5 Select GEM active command WASH__RLY. 6 Trigger WASH__RLY to on. 7 Measure the voltage between washer pump C137 pin 1, circuit 941 (BK/WH), harness side and ground. • Is the voltage greater than 10 volts? → **Yes** GO to **D10**. → **No** GO to **D11**.
D10 CHECK CIRCUIT 57 (BK) FOR OPEN	
1 	

FM9020100796050X

Fig. 100 Test D: Windshield Washer Pump Is Inoperative (Part 5 of 8). Sable & Taurus

TEST CONDITIONS	TEST DETAILS/RESULTS/ACTIONS
D10 CHECK CIRCUIT 57 (BK) FOR OPEN (Continued)	
2 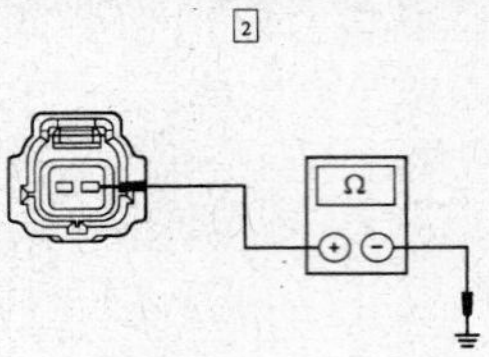	2 Measure the resistance between washer pump C137 pin 2, circuit 57 (BK) harness side and ground. • Is the resistance less than 5 ohms? → **Yes** INSTALL a new washer pump. CLEAR the DTCs. → **No** REPAIR circuit 57 (BK). CLEAR the DTCs. TEST the system for normal operation.
D11 CHECK CIRCUIT 941 (BK/WH) FOR OPEN	
1 2 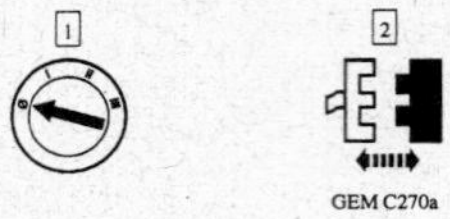 3 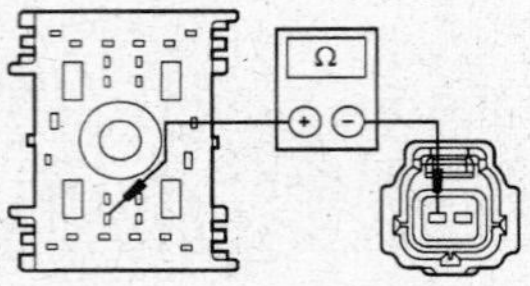	3 Measure the resistance between the washer pump C137 pin 1, circuit 941 (BK/WH), harness side and CJB C270a pin 7, circuit 941 (BK/WH), harness side. • Is the resistance less than 5 ohms? → **Yes** GO to **D12**. → **No** REPAIR the circuit. CLEAR the DTCs. REPEAT the self-test.
D12 CHECK CJB FOR SHORT TO VOLTAGE	
1 2 3 	

FM9020100796060X

Fig. 100 Test D: Windshield Washer Pump Is Inoperative (Part 6 of 8). Sable & Taurus

TEST CONDITIONS	TEST DETAILS/RESULTS/ACTIONS
D12 CHECK CJB FOR SHORT TO VOLTAGE (Continued)	
4 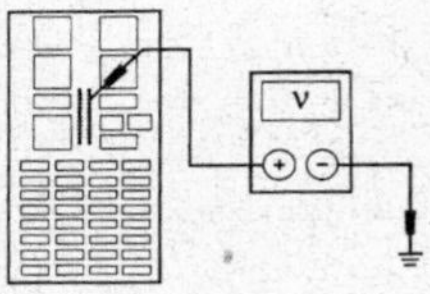	4 Measure the voltage between GEM C201d pin 11, CJB side and ground. • Is any voltage indicated? → **Yes** REPAIR CJB as necessary. CLEAR the DTCs. REPEAT the self-test. → **No** GO to **D13**.
D13 CHECK WASHER RELAY OPERATION	
1  2 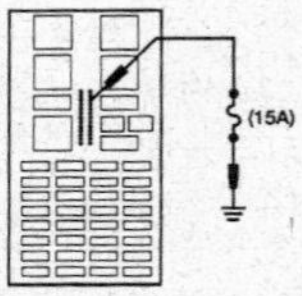	2 Using a jumper wire, jumper GEM/CJB C201d pin 11 CJB side to ground. • Does the washer pump operate? → **Yes** GO to **D14**. → **No** REPAIR CJB as necessary. CLEAR the DTCs. REPEAT the self-test.
D14 CHECK FOR CORRECT GEM OPERATION	
	1 Disconnect all GEM connectors. 2 Check: • for corrosion • for pushed-out pins 3 Connect all GEM connectors and make sure they seat correctly.

FM9020100796070X

Fig. 100 Test D: Windshield Washer Pump Is Inoperative (Part 7 of 8). Sable & Taurus

TEST CONDITIONS	TEST DETAILS/RESULTS/ACTIONS
E1 RETRIEVE THE RECORDED DTCS FROM BOTH CONTINUOUS AND ON-DEMAND GEM SELF-TEST	
	1 Use the recorded GEM DTCs. • Are any DTCs recorded? → **Yes** For DTC B1458, GO to **E4**. → **No** GO to **E2**.
E2 CHECK CENTRAL JUNCTION BOX (CJB) FOR INTERNAL SHORT	
1  3 	2 Remove CJB Fuse 211 (15A).

FM9020100797010X

Fig. 101 Test E: Windshield Washer Pump Stays On Continuously (Part 1 of 3). Sable & Taurus

TEST CONDITIONS	TEST DETAILS/RESULTS/ACTIONS
D14 CHECK FOR CORRECT GEM OPERATION (Continued)	
	4 Operate the system and verify the concern is still present. • Is the concern still present? → **Yes** INSTALL a new GEM. → **No** The system is operating correctly at this time. Concern may have been caused by a loose or corroded connector. CLEAR the DTCs. REPEAT the self-test.

FM9020100796080X

Fig. 100 Test D: Windshield Washer Pump Is Inoperative (Part 8 of 8). Sable & Taurus

TEST CONDITIONS	TEST DETAILS/RESULTS/ACTIONS
E2 CHECK CENTRAL JUNCTION BOX (CJB) FOR INTERNAL SHORT (Continued)	
	• Does the washer pump continue to run? → **Yes** GO to **E3**. → **No** GO to **E4**.
E3 CHECK CIRCUIT 941 (BK/WH) FOR SHORT TO VOLTAGE	
1 2 3 4  5 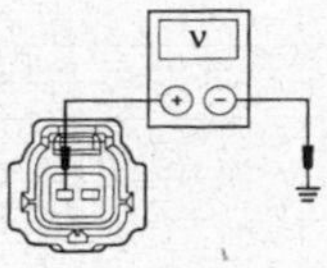	5 Measure the voltage between washer pump C137 pin 1, circuit 941 (BK/WH), harness side and ground. • Is any voltage indicated? → **Yes** REPAIR the circuit. TEST the system for normal operation. → **No** REPAIR CJB as necessary. TEST the system for normal operation.
E4 CHECK CJB FOR INTERNAL SHORT TO GROUND	
1 2 3 	• Does the washer pump run? → **Yes** REPAIR CJB as necessary. CLEAR the DTCs. REPEAT the self-test. → **No** GO to **E5**.

FM9020100797020X

Fig. 101 Test E: Windshield Washer Pump Stays On Continuously (Part 2 of 3). Sable & Taurus

TEST CONDITIONS	TEST DETAILS/RESULTS/ACTIONS
E5 CHECK FOR CORRECT GEM OPERATION	
	1 Disconnect all GEM connectors. 2 Check: • for corrosion • for pushed-out pins 3 Connect all GEM connectors and make sure they seat correctly. 4 Operate the system and verify the concern is still present. • Is the concern still present? → **Yes** INSTALL a new GEM. → **No** The system is operating correctly at this time. Concern may have been caused by a loose or corroded connector. CLEAR the DTCs. REPEAT the self-test.

FM9020100797030X

Fig. 101 Test E: Windshield Washer Pump Stays On Continuously (Part 3 of 3). Sable & Taurus

TEST CONDITIONS	TEST DETAILS/RESULTS/ACTIONS
A1 CHECK THE WASHER PUMP MOTOR OPERATION	
1 	2 Press the washer button. • Does the washer pump motor operate properly? → **Yes** GO to **A2**. → **No** GO to **A3**.
A2 CHECK FOR BLOCKAGE OR OBSTRUCTION	
1 	2 Inspect the washer nozzles, washer hoses, and washer pump for blockages or obstructions. • Are any blockages or obstructions present? → **Yes** REPAIR or REPLACE as required. TEST the system for normal operation. → **No** REPLACE the washer pump motor TEST the system for normal operation.

FM9029800666010X

Fig. 102 Test A: Washer Pump Is Inoperative (Part 1 of 3). 2000–02 Town Car

TEST CONDITIONS	TEST DETAILS/RESULTS/ACTIONS
A3 CHECK THE WASHER PUMP MOTOR FOR VOLTAGE — CIRCUIT 941 (BK/W)	
1 2 3 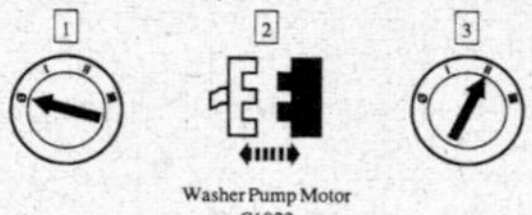	
4 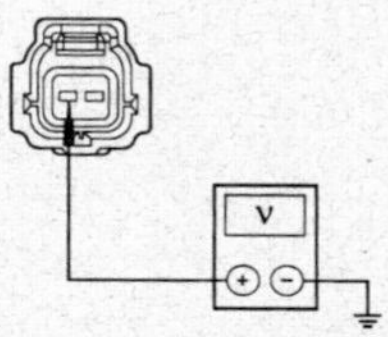	4 Measure the voltage between washer pump motor C1022, circuit 941 (BK/W), and ground while pressing the washer button. • Is the voltage greater than 10 volts? → **Yes** GO to **A4**. → **No** GO to **A5**.
A4 CHECK THE WASHER PUMP MOTOR GROUND — CIRCUIT 57 (BK)	
1  2 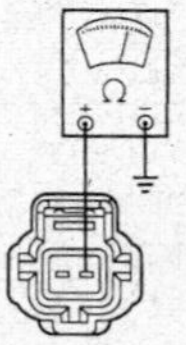	2 Measure the resistance between washer pump motor C1022, circuit 57 (BK), and ground. • Is the resistance less than 5 ohms? → **Yes** REPLACE the washer pump motor TEST the system for normal operation. → **No** REPAIR circuit 57 (BK). TEST the system for normal operation.

FM9029800666020X

Fig. 102 Test A: Washer Pump Is Inoperative (Part 2 of 3). 2000–02 Town Car

TEST CONDITIONS	TEST DETAILS/RESULTS/ACTIONS
A5 CHECK CIRCUIT 941 (BK/W) FOR SHORT TO GROUND	
1  2 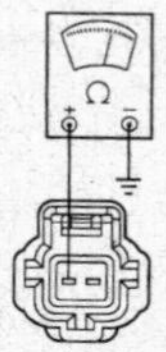	2 Measure the resistance between washer pump motor C1022, circuit 941 (BK/W), and ground. • Is the resistance greater than 10,000 ohms? → **Yes** GO to **A6**. → **No** REPLACE the multi-function switch; TEST the system for normal operation.
A6 CHECK CIRCUIT 941 (BK/W) FOR OPEN	
1  2 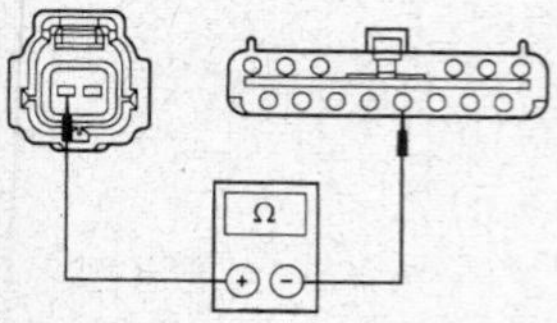	2 Measure the resistance between washer pump motor C1022, circuit 941 (BK/W), and wiper control module C294-4, circuit 941 (BK/W). • Is the resistance less than 5 ohms? → **Yes** REPLACE the wiper control module: TEST the system for normal operation. → **No** REPAIR circuit 941 (BK/W). TEST the system for normal operation.

FM9029800666030X

Fig. 102 Test A: Washer Pump Is Inoperative (Part 3 of 3). 2000–02 Town Car

TEST CONDITIONS	TEST DETAILS/RESULTS/ACTIONS
B1 CHECK FUSE JUNCTION PANEL FUSE 16 (30A)	
1 2 	• Is the fuse OK? → **Yes** GO to **B2**. → **No** REPLACE the fuse. TEST the system for normal operation. If the fuse fails again, CHECK for a short to ground. REPAIR as necessary.
B2 CHECK FOR VOLTAGE TO THE WIPER CONTROL MODULE — CIRCUIT 65 (DG)	
1 2 3  4 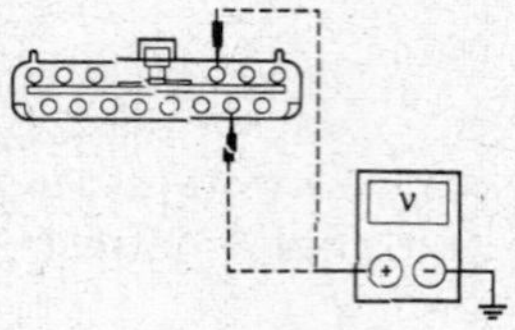	4 Measure the voltage between wiper control module C294-2, circuit 65 (DG), and ground; and between wiper control module C294-11, circuit 65 (DG), and ground. • Is the voltage greater than 10 volts? → **Yes** GO to **B3**. → **No** REPAIR circuit 65 (DG). TEST the system for normal operation.

FM9029800667010X

Fig. 103 Test B: Wipers Are Inoperative (Part 1 of 4). 2000–02 Town Car

TEST CONDITIONS	TEST DETAILS/RESULTS/ACTIONS
B3 CHECK CIRCUIT 57 (BK) FOR OPEN	
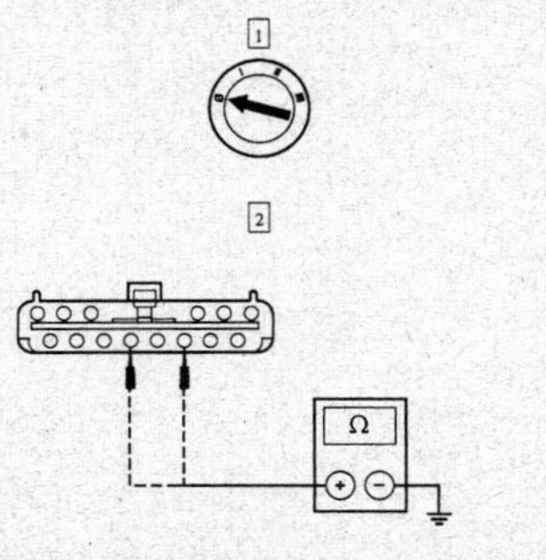	2 Measure the resistance between wiper control module C294-3, circuit 57 (BK), and ground; and between wiper control module C294-5, circuit 57 (BK), and ground. • Are the resistances less than 5 ohms? → **Yes** GO to **B4**. → **No** REPAIR circuit 57 (BK). TEST the system for normal operation.
B4 CHECK THE MULTI-FUNCTION SWITCH	
	2 Check the multi-function switch • Is the multi-function switch OK? → **Yes** GO to **B5**. → **No** REPLACE the multi-function switch; TEST the system for normal operation.

FM9029800667020X

Fig. 103 Test B: Wipers Are Inoperative (Part 2 of 4). 2000–02 Town Car

TEST CONDITIONS	TEST DETAILS/RESULTS/ACTIONS
B7 CHECK THE WIPER CONTROL MODULE OUTPUT FOR VOLTAGE (Continued)	
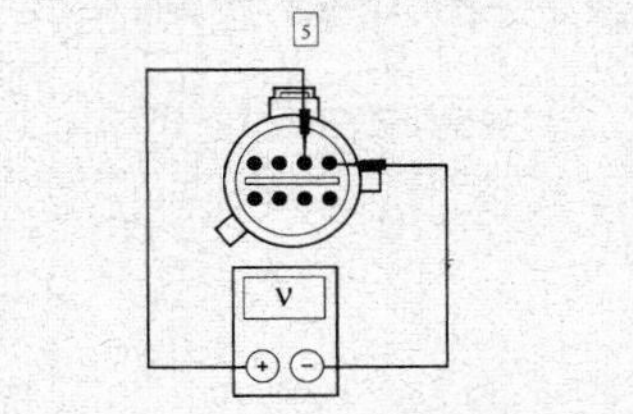	5 Measure the voltage between wiper motor C152-4, circuit 57 (BK), and wiper motor C152-3, circuit 56 (DB/O). • Is the voltage greater than 10 volts? → **Yes** REPLACE the wiper motor TEST the system for normal operation. → **No** GO to **B8**.
B8 CHECK CIRCUIT 57 (BK) FOR OPEN	
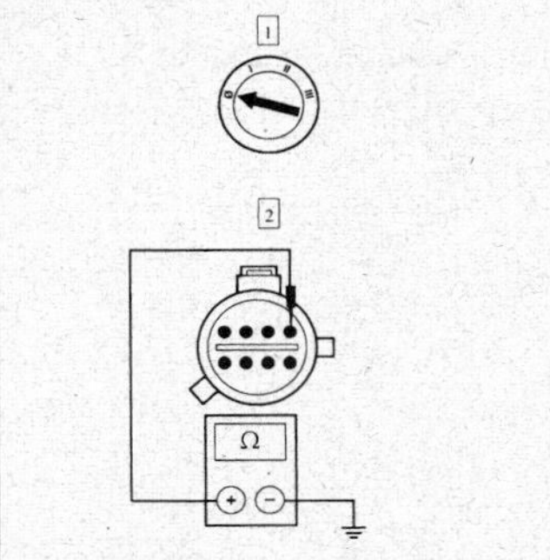	2 Measure the resistance between wiper motor C152-4, circuit 57 (BK), and ground. • Is the resistance less than 5 ohms? → **Yes** REPLACE the wiper control module; TEST the system for normal operation. → **No** REPAIR circuit 57 (BK). TEST the system for normal operation.

FM9029800667040X

Fig. 103 Test B: Wipers Are Inoperative (Part 4 of 4). 2000–02 Town Car

TEST CONDITIONS	TEST DETAILS/RESULTS/ACTIONS
B5 CHECK CIRCUIT 993 (BR/W) FOR OPEN	
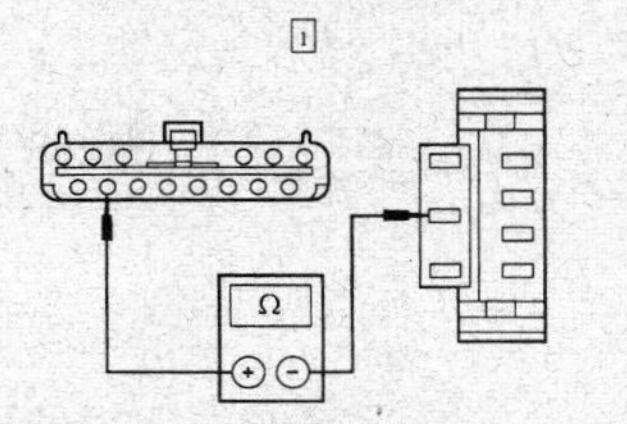	1 Measure the resistance between multi-function switch C269-4, circuit 993 (BR/W), and wiper control module C294-7, circuit 993 (BR/W). • Is the resistance less than 5 ohms? → **Yes** GO to **B6**. → **No** REPAIR circuit 993 (BR/W). TEST the system for normal operation.
B6 CHECK CIRCUIT 589 (O) FOR OPEN	
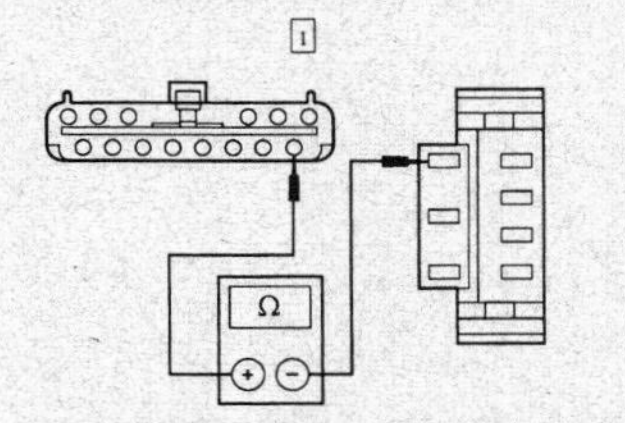	1 Measure the resistance between multi-function switch C269-1, circuit 589 (O), and wiper control module C294-1, circuit 589 (O). • Is the resistance less than 5 ohms? → **Yes** GO to **B7**. → **No** REPAIR circuit 589 (O). TEST the system for normal operation.
B7 CHECK THE WIPER CONTROL MODULE OUTPUT FOR VOLTAGE	
	3 Turn the multi-function switch to the HI position.

FM9029800667030X

Fig. 103 Test B: Wipers Are Inoperative (Part 3 of 4). 2000–02 Town Car

TEST CONDITIONS	TEST DETAILS/RESULTS/ACTIONS
C1 CHECK THE VOLTAGE TO THE WIPER MOTOR — CIRCUIT 58 (W)	
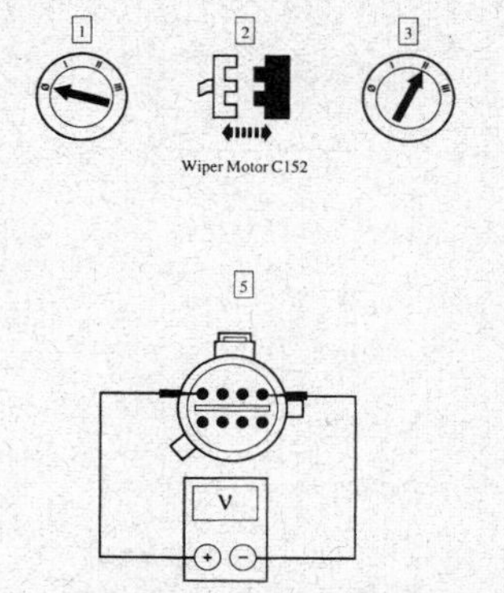	4 Turn the multi-function switch to the LO position. 5 Measure the voltage between wiper motor C152-4, circuit 57 (BK), and wiper motor C152-1, circuit 58 (W). • Is the voltage greater than 10 volts? → **Yes** REPLACE the wiper motor TEST the system for normal operation. → **No** GO to **C2**.
C2 CHECK CIRCUIT 58 (W) FOR SHORT TO GROUND	
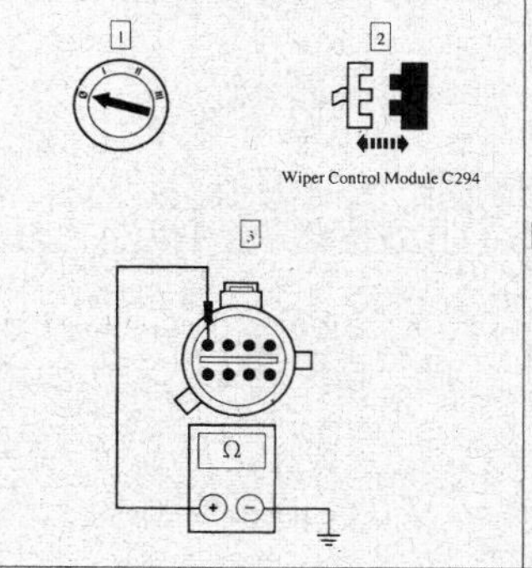	3 Measure the resistance between wiper motor C152-1, circuit 58 (W), and ground. • Is the resistance greater than 10,000 ohms? → **Yes** GO to **C3**. → **No** REPAIR circuit 58 (W). TEST the system for normal operation.

FM9029800668010X

Fig. 104 Test C: Low Wiper Speed Does Not Operative Properly (Part 1 of 2). 2000–02 Town Car

TEST CONDITIONS	TEST DETAILS/RESULTS/ACTIONS
C3 CHECK CIRCUIT 58 (W) FOR OPEN	
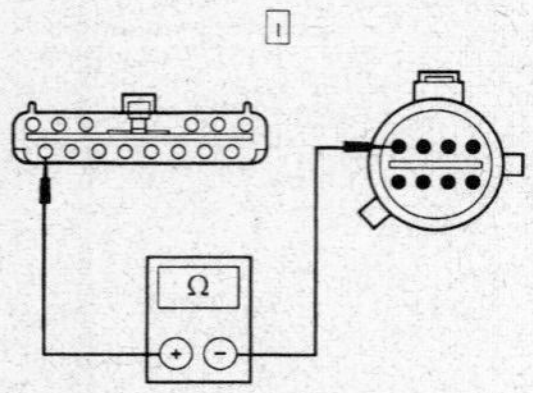	1 Measure the resistance between wiper control module C294-8, circuit 58 (W), and wiper motor C152-1, circuit 58 (W). • Is the resistance less than 5 ohms? → **Yes** GO to **C4**. → **No** REPAIR circuit 58 (W). TEST the system for normal operation.
C4 CHECK THE MULTI-FUNCTION SWITCH	
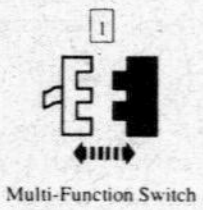	2 Check the multi-function switch • Is the multi-function switch OK? → **Yes** REPLACE the wiper control module; TEST the system for normal operation. → **No** REPLACE the multi-function switch; TEST the system for normal operation.

FM9029800668020X

Fig. 104 Test C: Low Wiper Speed Does Not Operative Properly (Part 2 of 2). 2000–02 Town Car

TEST CONDITIONS	TEST DETAILS/RESULTS/ACTIONS
D3 CHECK CIRCUIT 56 (DB/O) FOR OPEN	
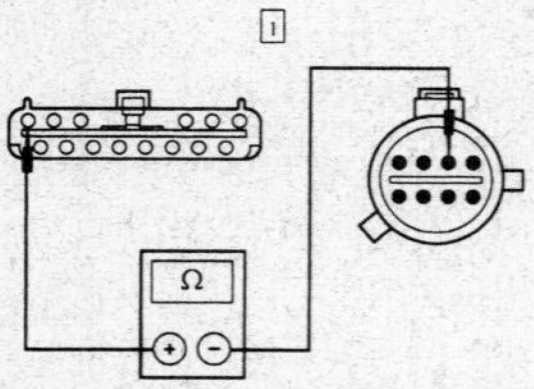	1 Measure the resistance between wiper control module C294-14, circuit 56 (DB/O), and wiper motor C152-3, circuit 56 (DB/O). • Is the resistance less than 5 ohms? → **Yes** GO to **D4**. → **No** REPAIR circuit 56 (DB/O). TEST the system for normal operation.
D4 CHECK THE MULTI-FUNCTION SWITCH	
	2 Check the multi-function switch • Is the multi-function switch OK? → **Yes** REPLACE the wiper control module; TEST the system for normal operation. → **No** REPLACE the multi-function switch TEST the system for normal operation.

FM9029800669020X

Fig. 105 Test D: High Wiper Speed Does Not Operate Properly (Part 2 of 2). 2000–02 Town Car

TEST CONDITIONS	TEST DETAILS/RESULTS/ACTIONS
D1 CHECK THE VOLTAGE TO THE WINDSHIELD WIPER MOTOR — CIRCUIT 56 (DB/O)	
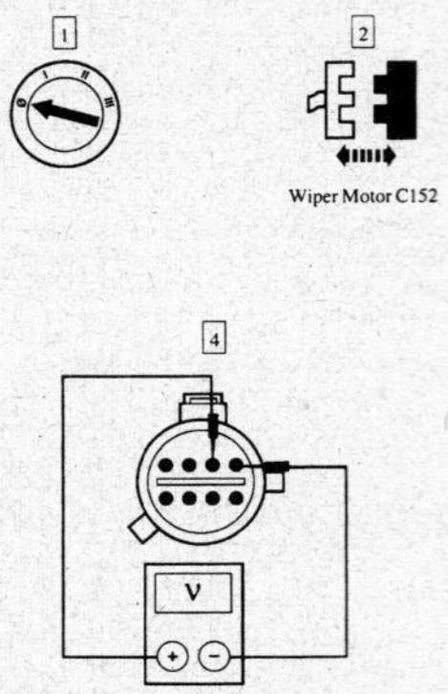	3 Turn the multi-function switch to the HI position. 4 Measure the voltage between wiper motor C152-4, circuit 57 (BK), and wiper motor C152-3, circuit 56 (DB/O). • Is the voltage greater than 10 volts? → **Yes** REPLACE the wiper motor. TEST the system for normal operation. → **No** GO to **D2**.
D2 CHECK CIRCUIT 56 (DB/O) FOR SHORT TO GROUND	
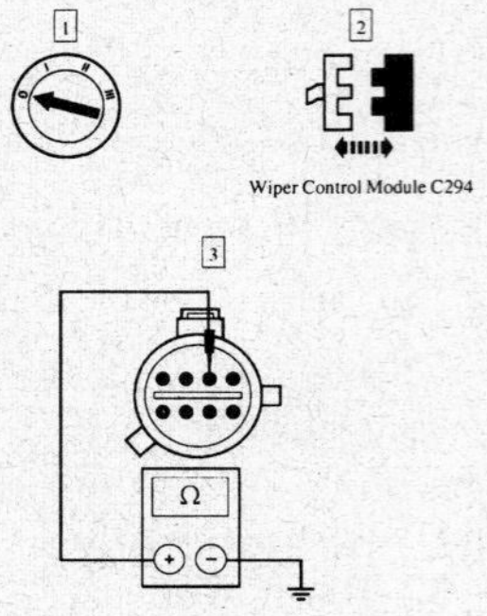	3 Measure the resistance between wiper motor C152-3, circuit 56 (DB/O), and ground. • Is the resistance greater than 10,000 ohms? → **Yes** GO to **D3**. → **No** REPAIR circuit 56 (DB/O). TEST the system for normal operation.

FM9029800669010X

Fig. 105 Test D: High Wiper Speed Does Not Operate Properly (Part 1 of 2). 2000–02 Town Car

TEST CONDITIONS	TEST DETAILS/RESULTS/ACTIONS
E1 CHECK THE MULTI-FUNCTION SWITCH	
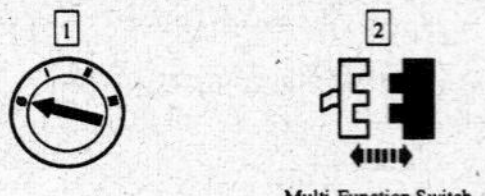	3 Check the multi-function switch • Is the multi-function switch OK? → **Yes** GO to **E2**. → **No** REPLACE the multi-function switch TEST the system for normal operation.
E2 CHECK CIRCUIT 590 (DB/W) FOR SHORT TO GROUND	
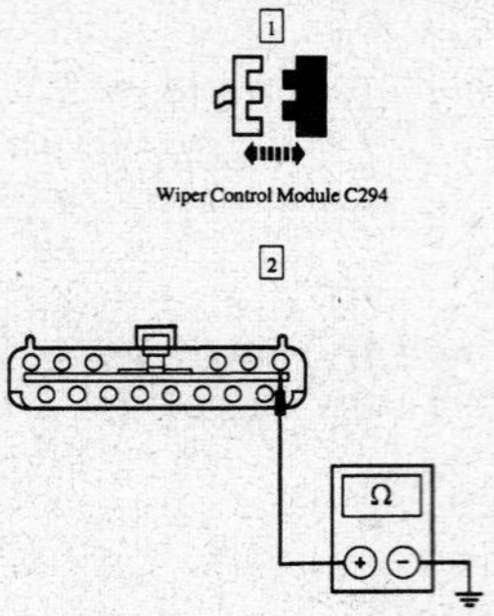	2 Measure the resistance between wiper control module C294-9, circuit 590 (DB/W), and ground. • Is the resistance greater than 10,000 ohms? → **Yes** GO to **E3**. → **No** REPAIR circuit 590 (DB/W). TEST the system for normal operation.

FM9029800670010X

Fig. 106 Test E: Intermittent Wiper Speed Does Not Operate Properly (Part 1 of 2). 2000–02 Town Car

TEST CONDITIONS	TEST DETAILS/RESULTS/ACTIONS
E3 CHECK CIRCUIT 590 (DB/W) FOR OPEN	
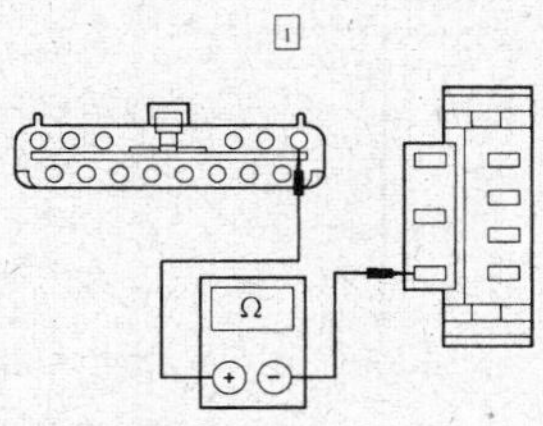	1 Measure the resistance between wiper control module C294-9, circuit 590 (DB/W), and multi-function switch C269-6, circuit 590 (DB/W). • Is the resistance less than 5 ohms? → **Yes** REPLACE the wiper control module; TEST the system for normal operation. → **No** REPAIR circuit 590 (DB/W). TEST the system for normal operation.

FM9029800670020X

Fig. 106 Test E: Intermittent Wiper Speed Does Not Operate Properly (Part 2 of 2). 2000–02 Town Car

TEST CONDITIONS	TEST DETAILS/RESULTS/ACTIONS
F2 CHECK THE WIPER CONTROL MODULE RETURN CIRCUIT FOR OPEN — CIRCUIT 28 (BK/PK)	
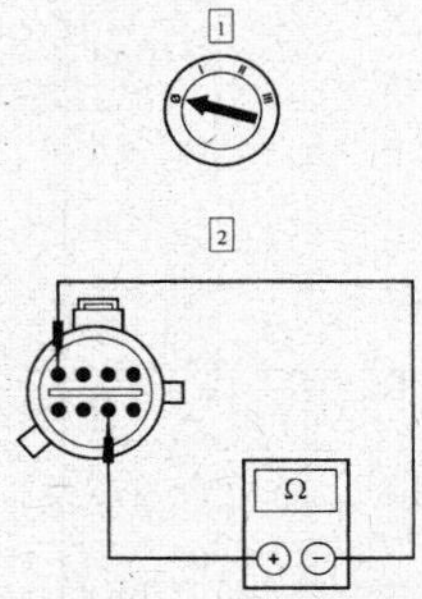	2 Measure the resistance between wiper motor C152-7, circuit 28 (BK/PK), and wiper motor C152-1, circuit 58 (W). • Is the resistance less than 5 ohms? → **Yes** GO to **F4**. → **No** GO to **F3**.
F3 CHECK THE WIPER CONTROL MODULE/WIPER MOTOR CIRCUITS FOR OPEN	
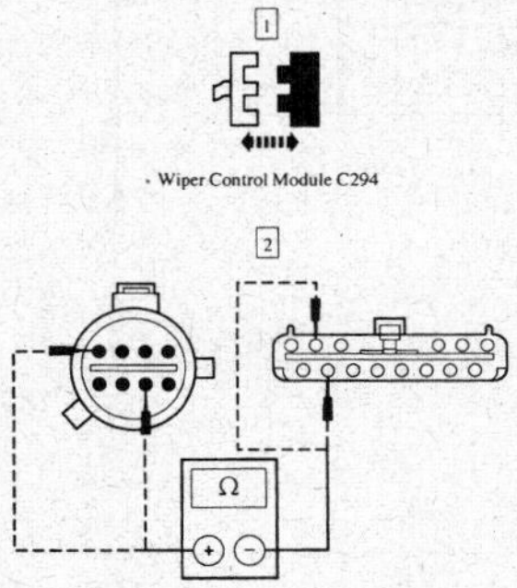	2 Measure the resistance between wiper motor C152 and wiper control module C294 REFER to the following chart

Wiper Motor Connector	Circuit	Wiper Control Module Connector
C152-7	28 (BK/PK)	C294-13
C152-1	58 (W)	C294-8

FM9029800671020X

Fig. 107 Test F: Wipers Will Not Park At Proper Position (Part 2 of 3). 2000–02 Town Car

TEST CONDITIONS	TEST DETAILS/RESULTS/ACTIONS
F1 CHECK THE WIPER MOTOR FOR VOLTAGE — CIRCUIT 65 (DG)	
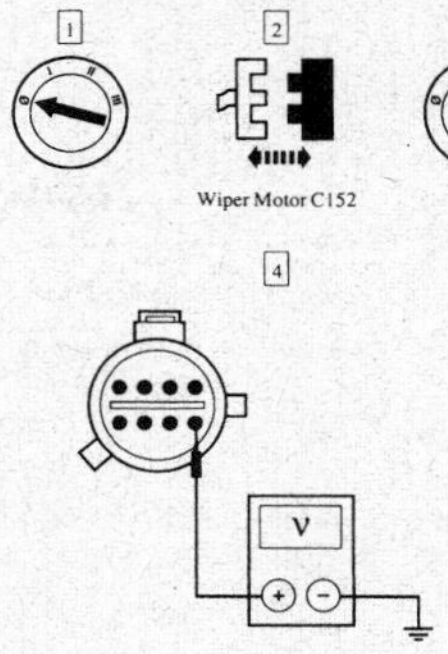	4 Measure the voltage between wiper motor C152-8, circuit 65 (DG), and ground. • Is the voltage greater than 10 volts? → **Yes** GO to **F2**. → **No** REPAIR circuit 65 (DG). TEST the system for normal operation.

FM9029800671010X

Fig. 107 Test F: Wipers Will Not Park At Proper Position (Part 1 of 3). 2000–02 Town Car

TEST CONDITIONS	TEST DETAILS/RESULTS/ACTIONS
F3 CHECK THE WIPER CONTROL MODULE/WIPER MOTOR CIRCUITS FOR OPEN (Continued)	
	• Are the resistances less than 5 ohms? → **Yes** REPLACE the wiper control module TEST the system for normal operation. → **No** REPAIR the circuit in question. TEST the system for normal operation.
F4 CHECK THE WIPER LINKAGE	
	1 Verify the wiper linkage is not bent, cracked, or mispositioned from the wiper motor shaft. • Is the wiper linkage OK? → **Yes** REPLACE the wiper motor TEST the system for normal operation. → **No** REPAIR or REPLACE the wiper mounting arm and pivot shaft TEST the system for normal operation.

FM9029800671030X

Fig. 107 Test F: Wipers Will Not Park At Proper Position (Part 3 of 3). 2000–02 Town Car

TEST CONDITIONS	TEST DETAILS/RESULTS/ACTIONS
G1 CHECK THE MULTI-FUNCTION SWITCH	
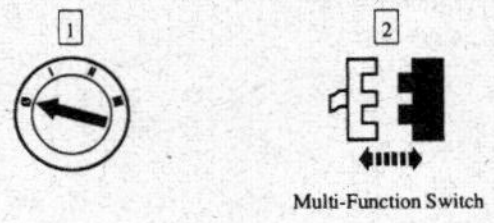	3 Check the multi-function switch • Is the multi-function switch OK? → **Yes** GO to **G2**. → **No** REPLACE the multi-function switch

FM9029800672010X

Fig. 108 Test G: Wipes Stay On Continuously (Part 1 of 3). 2000–02 Town Car

TEST CONDITIONS	TEST DETAILS/RESULTS/ACTIONS
G2 CHECK CIRCUIT 589 (O) FOR SHORT TO GROUND	
1 	
2 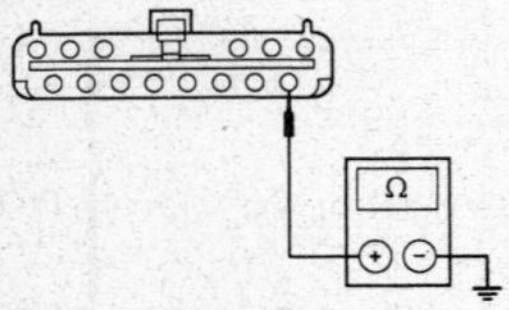	2 Measure the resistance between wiper control module C294-1, circuit 589 (O), and ground. • Is the resistance greater than 10,000 ohms? → **Yes** GO to **G3**. → **No** REPAIR circuit 589 (O). TEST the system for normal operation.
G3 CHECK CIRCUIT 993 (BR/W) FOR SHORT TO GROUND	
1 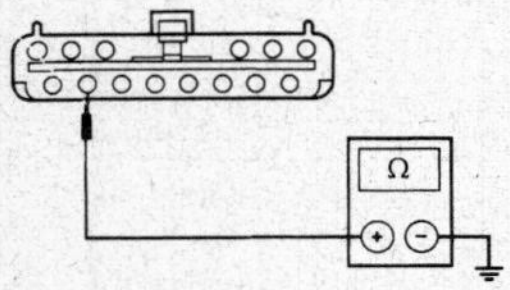	1 Measure the resistance between wiper control module C294-7, circuit 993 (BR/W), and ground. • Is the resistance greater than 10,000 ohms? → **Yes** GO to **G4**. → **No** REPAIR circuit 993 (BR/W). TEST the system for normal operation.

FM9029800672020X

Fig. 108 Test G: Wipes Stay On Continuously (Part 2 of 3). 2000–02 Town Car

Test Step	Result / Action to Take
A1 CHECK CIRCUITS 65 (DG) AND 406 (BN/WH) FOR VOLTAGE	
• Key in OFF position. • Disconnect: Windshield Wiper Motor C125. • Key in ON position. • Measure the voltage between windshield wiper C125 pin 5, circuit 65 (DG), harness side and ground; and between windshield wiper motor C125 pin 8, circuit 406 (BN/WH), harness side and ground. 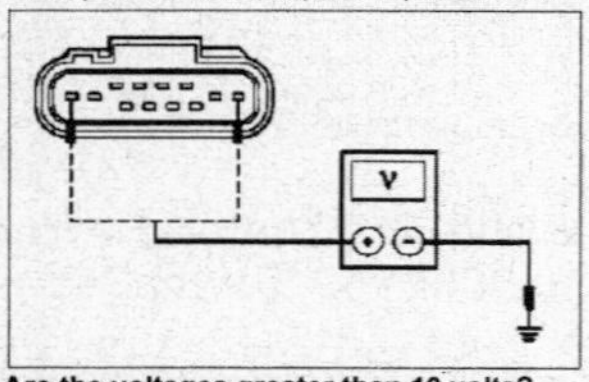 • **Are the voltages greater than 10 volts?**	**Yes** GO to A2 . **No** REPAIR the circuit(s) in question. TEST the system for normal operation.
A2 CHECK CIRCUITS 57 (BK) AND 676 (PK/OG) FOR OPENS	
• Key in OFF position. • Measure the resistance between windshield wiper C125 pin 6, circuit 57 (BK), harness side and ground; and between windshield wiper motor C125 pin 3, circuit 676 (PK/OG), harness side and ground. 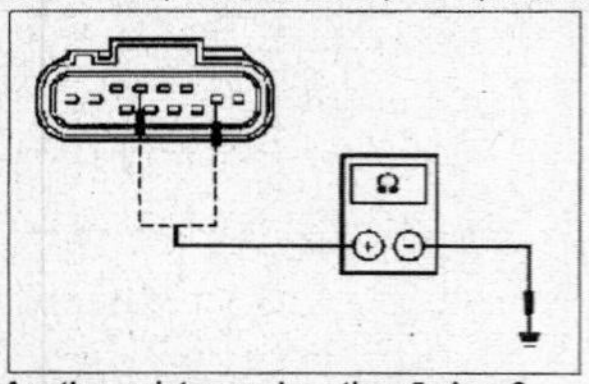 • **Are the resistances less than 5 ohms?**	**Yes** GO to A3 . **No** REPAIR the circuit(s) in question. TEST the system for normal operation.
A3 CHECK THE MULTIFUNCTION SWITCH	
• Disconnect: Multifunction Switch C202b. • Carry out the multifunction switch component test. • **Did the multifunction switch pass the component test?**	**Yes** GO to A4 . **No** INSTALL a new multifunction switch.

FM9020200914010X

Fig. 109 Test A: Wipers Inoperative (Part 1 of 3). 2003–04 Town Car

TEST CONDITIONS	TEST DETAILS/RESULTS/ACTIONS
G4 CHECK CIRCUIT 590 (DB/W) FOR SHORT TO GROUND	
1 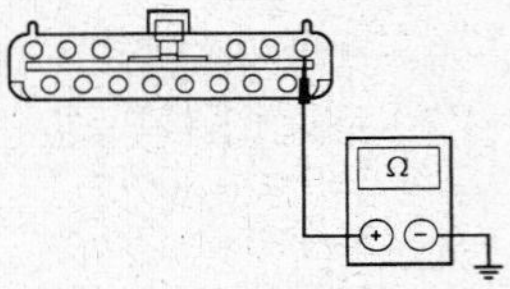	1 Measure the resistance between wiper control module C294-9, circuit 590 (DB/W), and ground. • Is the resistance greater than 10,000 ohms? → **Yes** REPLACE the wiper control module; TEST the system for normal operation. → **No** REPAIR circuit 590 (DB/W). TEST the system for normal operation.

FM9029800672030X

Fig. 108 Test G: Wipes Stay On Continuously (Part 3 of 3). 2000–02 Town Car

A4 CHECK CIRCUIT 57 (BK) FOR AN OPEN	
• Measure the resistance between C202b pin 5, circuit 57 (BK), harness side and ground. 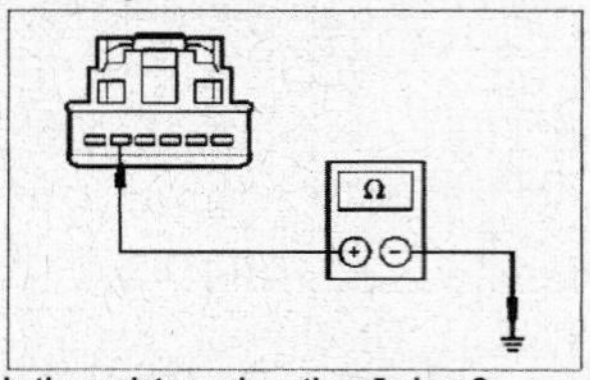 • **Is the resistance less than 5 ohms?**	**Yes** GO to A5 . **No** REPAIR the circuit. TEST the system for normal operation.
A5 CHECK CIRCUITS 56 (DB/OG), 58 (WH), 61 (YE/RD), AND 63 (RD) FOR OPENS	
• Using the following table, measure the resistance between the multifunction switch C202b harness side and the windshield wiper motor C125 harness side: 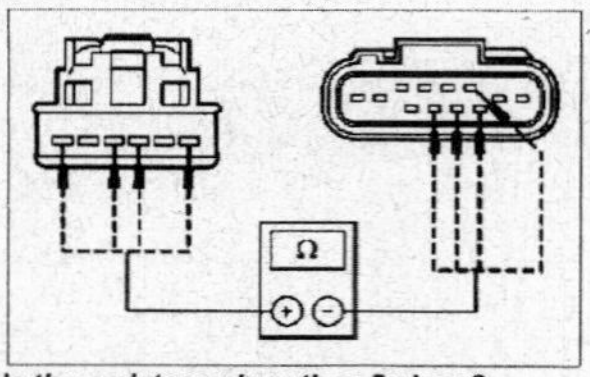 • **Is the resistance less than 5 ohms?**	**Yes** GO to A6 . **No** REPAIR the circuit(s) in question. TEST the system for normal operation

Multifunction Switch C202b	Windshield Wiper Motor C125
pin 6, circuit 56 (DB/OG)	pin 10, circuit 56 (DB/OG)
pin 3, circuit 58 (WH)	pin 11, circuit 58 (WH)
pin 1, circuit 61 (YE/RD)	pin 1, circuit 61 (YE/RD)
pin 4, circuit 63 (RD)	pin 9, circuit 63 (RD)

FM9020200914020X

Fig. 109 Test A: Wipers Inoperative (Part 2 of 3). 2003–04 Town Car

A6 CHECK FOR CORRECT WIPER MOTOR OPERATION	

• Disconnect all wiper motor connectors.
• Check for:
  • corrosion
  • pushed-out pins
• Connect all wiper motor connectors and make sure they seat correctly.
• Operate the system and verify the concern is still present.
• **Is the concern still present?**
	Yes
	GO to A7 .
	No
	The system is operating correctly at this time. Concern may have been caused by a loose or corroded connector. TEST the system for normal operation.

A7 CHECK THE WINDSHIELD WIPER MOTOR	
• Key in OFF position. • Disconnect: Windshield Wiper Motor C125. • Carry out the windshield wiper motor component test as outlined in this section. • **Did the windshield wiper motor pass the component test?**	**Yes** The system is operating correctly at this time. Concern may have been caused by binding or incorrect pivot arm adjustment. TEST the system for normal operation. **No** INSTALL a new windshield wiper motor.

FM9020200914030X

Fig. 109 Test A: Wipers Inoperative (Part 3 of 3). 2003–04 Town Car

Test Step	Result / Action to Take
B1 CHECK THE MULTIFUNCTION SWITCH	
• Key in OFF position. • Disconnect: Multifunction Switch C202b. • Carry out the multifunction switch component test. • **Did the multifunction switch pass the component test?**	**Yes** GO to B2 . **No** INSTALL a new multifunction switch.
B2 CHECK CIRCUIT 57 (BK) FOR AN OPEN	
• Measure the resistance between C202b pin 5, circuit 57 (BK), harness side and ground. 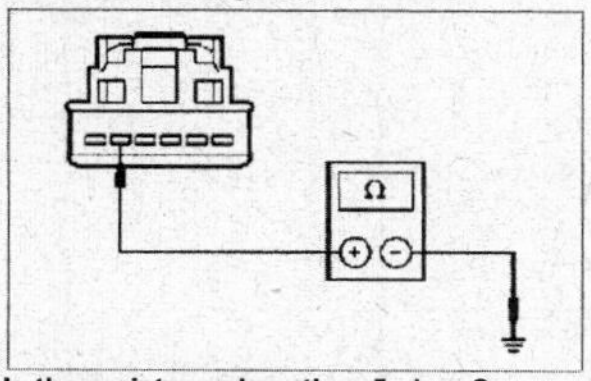 • **Is the resistance less than 5 ohms?**	**Yes** GO to B3 . **No** REPAIR the circuit. TEST the system for normal operation.

FM9020200915010X

Fig. 110 Test B: Wipers Stay On Continuously (Part 1 of 2). 2003–04 Town Car

Test Step	Result / Action to Take
B3 CHECK CIRCUITS 56 (DB/OG), 58 (WH), 61 (YE/RD), AND 63 (RD) FOR SHORTS	
• Disconnect: Windshield Wiper Motor C125. • Using the following table, measure the resistance between the windshield wiper motor C125 harness side and ground:	**Yes** GO to B4 . **No** REPAIR the circuit(s) in question. TEST the system for normal operation.

Windshield Wiper Motor C125	Ground
pin 10, circuit 56 (DB/OG)	ground
pin 11, circuit 58 (WH)	ground
pin 1, circuit 61 (YE/RD)	ground
pin 9, circuit 63 (RD)	ground

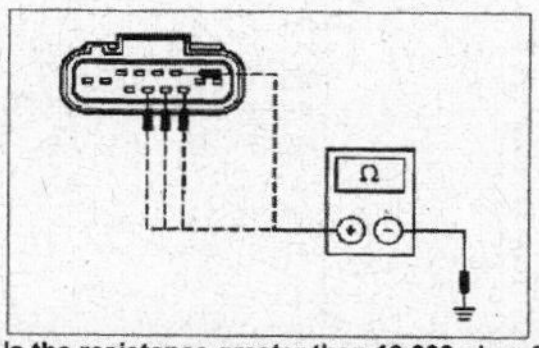

• **Is the resistance greater than 10,000 ohms?**

Test Step	Result / Action to Take
B4 CHECK FOR CORRECT WIPER MOTOR OPERATION	

• Disconnect all wiper motor connectors.
• Check for:
  • corrosion
  • pushed-out pins
• Connect all wiper motor connectors and make sure they seat correctly.
• Operate the system and verify the concern is still present.
• **Is the concern still present?**
	Yes
	GO to B5 .
	
	No
	The system is operating correctly at this time. Concern may have been caused by a loose or corroded connector. TEST the system for normal operation.

B5 CHECK THE WINDSHIELD WIPER MOTOR	
• Key in OFF position. • Disconnect: Windshield Wiper Motor C125. • Carry out the windshield wiper motor component test as outlined in this section. • **Did the windshield wiper motor pass the component test?**	**Yes** The system is operating correctly at this time. Concern may have been caused by binding or incorrect pivot arm adjustment TEST the system for normal operation. **No** INSTALL a new windshield wiper motor. REFER to Windshield Wiper Motor in this section

FM9020200915020X

Fig. 110 Test B: Wipers Stay On Continuously (Part 2 of 2). 2003–04 Town Car

Test Step	Result / Action to Take
C1 CHECK THE MULTIFUNCTION SWITCH	
• Key in OFF position. • Disconnect: Multifunction Switch C202b. • Carry out the multifunction switch component test. • **Did the multifunction switch pass the component test?**	**Yes** GO to C2 . **No** INSTALL a new multifunction switch.
C2 CHECK CIRCUIT 57 (BK) FOR AN OPEN	
• Measure the resistance between C202b pin 5, circuit 57 (BK), harness side and ground. 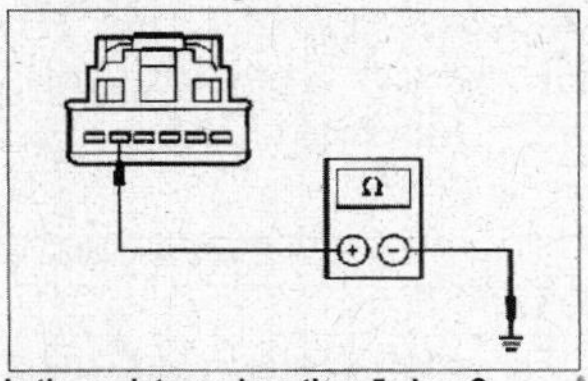 • **Is the resistance less than 5 ohms?**	**Yes** GO to C3 . **No** REPAIR the circuit. TEST the system for normal operation.

FM9020200916010X

Fig. 111 Test C: High/Low Wiper Speeds Do Not Operate Correctly, Intermittent Mode OK (Part 1 of 2). 2003–04 Town Car

Test Step	Result / Action to Take
C3 CHECK CIRCUITS 56 (DB/OG), 61 (YE/RD), AND 63 (RD) FOR OPENS	
• Disconnect: Windshield Wiper Motor C125. • Using the following table, measure the resistance between the multifunction switch C202b harness side and the windshield wiper motor C125 harness side:	**Yes** GO to C4 . **No** REPAIR the circuit(s) in question. TEST the system for normal operation.

Multifunction Switch C202b	Windshield Wiper Motor C125
pin 6, circuit 56 (DB/OG)	pin 10, circuit 56 (DB/OG)
pin 1, circuit 61 (YE/RD)	pin 1, circuit 61 (YE/RD)
pin 4, circuit 63 (RD)	pin 9, circuit 63 (RD)

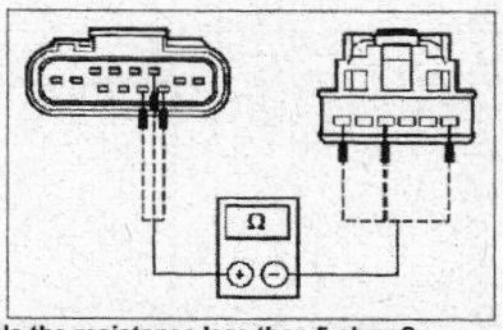

• **Is the resistance less than 5 ohms?**

Test Step	Result / Action to Take
C4 CHECK FOR CORRECT WIPER MOTOR OPERATION	

• Disconnect all wiper motor connectors.
• Check for:
  • corrosion
  • pushed-out pins
• Connect all wiper motor connectors and make sure they seat correctly.
• Operate the system and verify the concern is still present.
• **Is the concern still present?**
	Yes
	GO to C5 .
	
	No
	The system is operating correctly at this time. Concern may have been caused by a loose or corroded connector. TEST the system for normal operation.

C5 CHECK THE WINDSHIELD WIPER MOTOR	
• Key in OFF position. • Disconnect: Windshield Wiper Motor C125. • Carry out the windshield wiper motor component test • **Did the windshield wiper motor pass the component test?**	**Yes** The system is operating correctly at this time. Concern may have been caused by binding or incorrect pivot arm adjustment. TEST the system for normal operation. **No** INSTALL a new windshield wiper motor.

FM9020200916020X

Fig. 111 Test C: High/Low Wiper Speeds Do Not Operate Correctly, Intermittent Mode OK (Part 2 of 2). 2003–04 Town Car

Test Step	Result / Action to Take
D1 CHECK THE MULTIFUNCTION SWITCH	
• Key in OFF position. • Disconnect: Multifunction Switch C202b. • Carry out the multifunction switch component test. • **Did the multifunction switch pass the component test?**	**Yes** GO to D2 . **No** Install a new multifunction switch.
D2 CHECK CIRCUIT 57 (BK) FOR AN OPEN	
• Measure the resistance between C202b pin 5, circuit 57 (BK), harness side and ground. 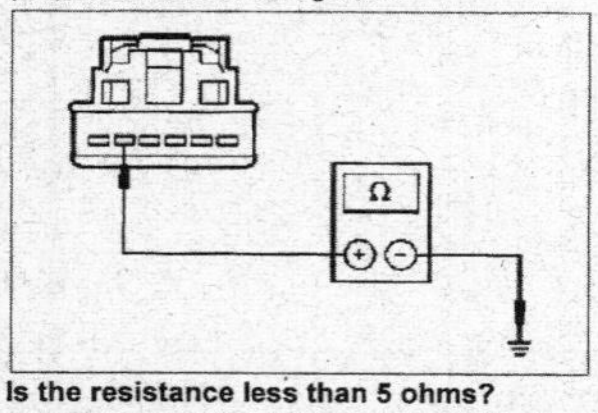 • **Is the resistance less than 5 ohms?**	**Yes** GO to D3 . **No** REPAIR the circuit. TEST the system for normal operation.

FM9020200917010X

Fig. 112 Test D: Intermittent Wiper Does Not Operate Correctly, High/Low Speeds OK (Part 1 of 2). 2003–04 Town Car

<table>
<tr><td>D3 CHECK CIRCUITS 56 (DB/OG), 61 (YE/RD), AND 63 (RD) FOR OPENS</td><td></td></tr>
<tr><td>• Disconnect: Windshield Wiper Motor C125.
• Using the following table, measure the resistance between the multifunction switch C202b harness side and the windshield wiper motor C125 harness side:
<table>
<tr><th>Multifunction Switch C202b</th><th>Windshield Wiper Motor C125</th></tr>
<tr><td>pin 6, circuit 56 (DB/OG)</td><td>pin 10, circuit 56 (DB/OG)</td></tr>
<tr><td>pin 1, circuit 61 (YE/RD)</td><td>pin 1, circuit 61 (YE/RD)</td></tr>
<tr><td>pin 4, circuit 63 (RD)</td><td>pin 9, circuit 63 (RD)</td></tr>
</table>
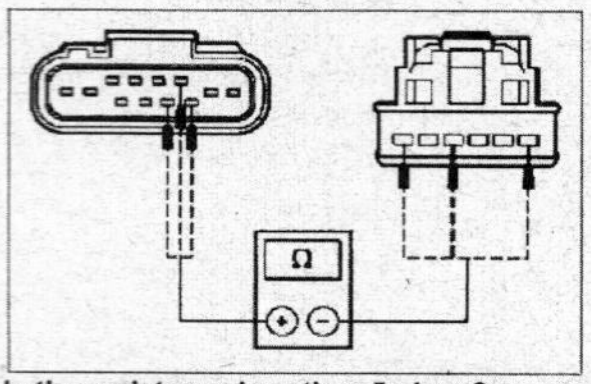
• Is the resistance less than 5 ohms?</td><td>Yes
GO to D4 .
No
REPAIR the circuit(s) in question. TEST the system for normal operation.</td></tr>
<tr><td>D4 CHECK FOR CORRECT WIPER MOTOR OPERATION</td><td></td></tr>
<tr><td>• Disconnect all wiper motor connectors.
• Check for:
  • corrosion
  • pushed-out pins
• Connect all wiper motor connectors and make sure they seat correctly.
• Operate the system and verify the concern is still present.
• Is the concern still present?</td><td>Yes
GO to D5 .
No
The system is operating correctly at this time. Concern may have been caused by a loose or corroded connector. TEST the system for normal operation.</td></tr>
<tr><td>D5 CHECK THE WINDSHIELD WIPER MOTOR</td><td></td></tr>
<tr><td>• Key in OFF position.
• Disconnect: Windshield Wiper Motor C125.
• Carry out the windshield wiper motor component test
• Did the windshield wiper motor pass the component test?</td><td>Yes
The system is operating correctly at this time. Concern may have been caused by binding or incorrect pivot arm adjustment.
TEST the system for normal operation.
No
INSTALL a new windshield wiper motor.</td></tr>
</table>

FM9020200917020X

Fig. 112 Test D: Intermittent Wiper Does Not Operate Correctly, High/Low Speeds OK (Part 2 of 2). 2003–04 Town Car

Test Step	Result / Action to Take
E1 CHECK THE MULTIFUNCTION SWITCH	
• Key in OFF position. • Disconnect: Multifunction Switch C202b. • Carry out the multifunction switch component test. • **Did the multifunction switch pass the component test?**	**Yes** GO to E2 . **No** INSTALL a new multifunction switch.
E2 CHECK CIRCUIT 57 (BK) FOR AN OPEN	
• Measure the resistance between C202b pin 5, circuit 57 (BK), harness side and ground. 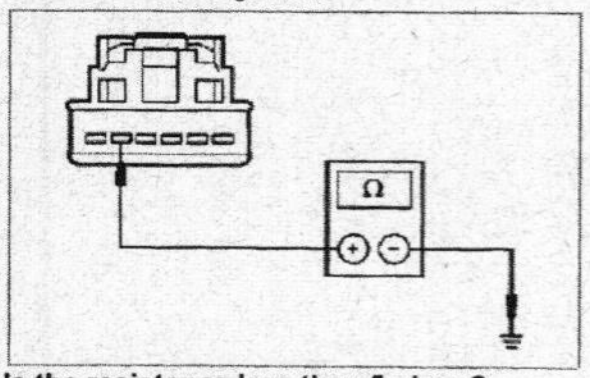 • **Is the resistance less than 5 ohms?**	**Yes** GO to E3 . **No** REPAIR the circuit. TEST the system for normal operation.
E3 CHECK CIRCUIT 589 (OG) FOR AN OPEN	
• Disconnect: Windshield Wiper Motor C125. • Measure the resistance between C202b pin 2, circuit 589 (OG), harness side and C125 pin 12, circuit 589 (OG), harness side. 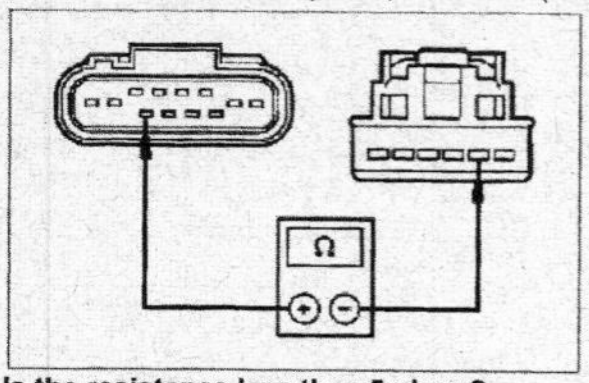 • **Is the resistance less than 5 ohms?**	**Yes** Go To Pinpoint Test F . **No** REPAIR the circuit. TEST the system for normal operation

FM9020200918000X

Fig. 113 Test E: Wipers Do Not Operate Correctly In Mist Mode. 2003–04 Town Car

Test Step	Result / Action to Take
F1 CHECK WASHER PUMP MOTOR FOR VOLTAGE	
• Key in OFF position. • Disconnect: Washer Pump Motor C137. • Key in ON position. • Measure the voltage between C137 pin 1, circuit 941 (BK/WH) harness side and ground while depressing the multifunction switch to the wash position. 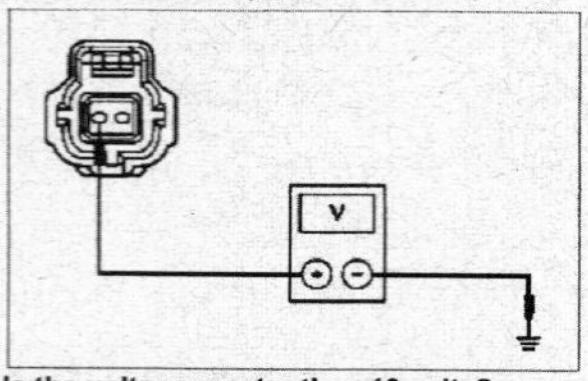 • **Is the voltage greater than 10 volts?**	**Yes** GO to F2 . **No** GO to F3 .
F2 CHECK CIRCUIT 57 (BK) FOR GROUND	
• Measure the resistance between C137 pin 2, circuit 57 (BK) harness side and ground. 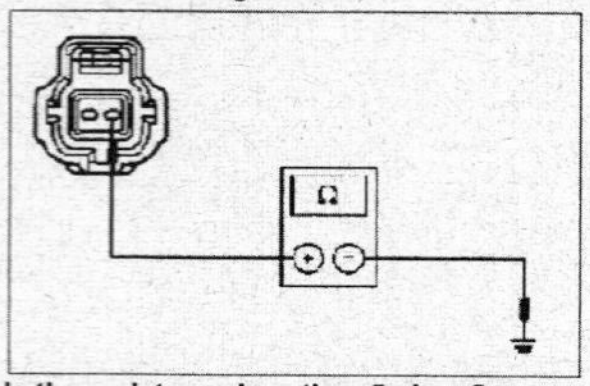 • **Is the resistance less than 5 ohms?**	**Yes** INSTALL a new washer pump. **No** REPAIR the circuit. TEST the system for normal operation.

FM9020200919010X

Fig. 114 Test F: Washer Pump Inoperative (Part 1 of 3). 2003–04 Town Car

F3 CHECK CIRCUIT 941 (BK/WH) FOR AN OPEN	
• Key in OFF position. • Disconnect: Windshield Wiper Motor C125. • Measure the resistance between C125 pin 7, circuit 941 (BK/WH), harness side and C137 pin 1, circuit 941 (BK/WH), harness side. 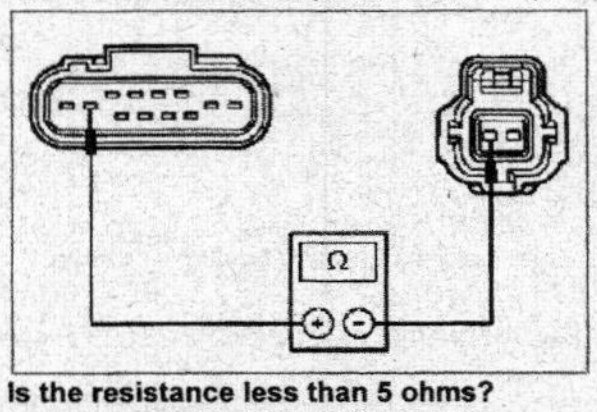 • **Is the resistance less than 5 ohms?**	**Yes** GO to F4 . **No** REPAIR the circuit. TEST the system for normal operation.
F4 CHECK THE MULTIFUNCTION SWITCH	
• Key in OFF position. • Disconnect: Multifunction Switch C202b. • Carry out the multifunction switch component test. • **Did the multifunction switch pass the component test?**	**Yes** GO to F5 . **No** INSTALL a new multifunction switch.
F5 CHECK CIRCUIT 57 (BK) FOR AN OPEN	
• Measure the resistance between C202b pin 5, circuit 57 (BK), harness side and ground. 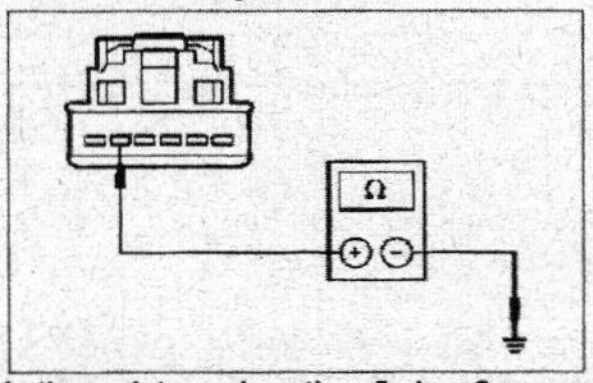 • **Is the resistance less than 5 ohms?**	**Yes** GO to F6 . **No** REPAIR the circuit. TEST the system for normal operation.

FM9020200919020X

Fig. 114 Test F: Washer Pump Inoperative (Part 2 of 3). 2003–04 Town Car

F6 CHECK CIRCUIT 589 (OG) FOR AN OPEN	
• Measure the resistance between C125 pin 12, circuit 589 (OG), harness side and C202b pin 2, circuit 589 (OG), harness side. 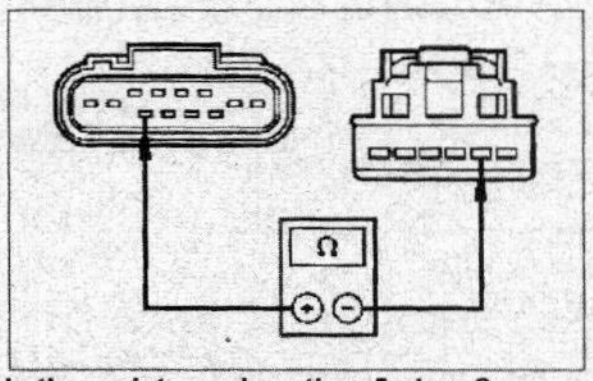 • **Is the resistance less than 5 ohms?**	**Yes** GO to F7 . **No** REPAIR the circuit. TEST the system for normal operation.
F7 CHECK FOR CORRECT WIPER MOTOR OPERATION	

• Disconnect all wiper motor connectors.
• Check for:
  • corrosion
  • pushed-out pins
• Connect all wiper motor connectors and make sure they seat correctly.
• Operate the system and verify the concern is still present.
• **Is the concern still present?**
	Yes
	GO to F8 .
	No
	The system is operating correctly at this time. Concern may have been caused by a loose or corroded connector. TEST the system for normal operation.

F8 CHECK THE WINDSHIELD WIPER MOTOR	
• Key in OFF position. • Disconnect: Windshield Wiper Motor C125. • Carry out the windshield wiper motor component test as outlined in this section. • **Did the windshield wiper motor pass the component test?**	**Yes** The system is operating correctly at this time. Concern may have been caused by binding or incorrect pivot arm adjustment TEST the system for normal operation. **No** INSTALL a new windshield wiper motor.

FM9020200919030X

Fig. 114 Test F: Washer Pump Inoperative (Part 3 of 3). 2003–04 Town Car

Test Step	Result / Action to Take
G1 MONITOR THE RAIN SENSOR MODULE (RSM) INPUT	
• Monitor the RSM PID while pouring water on the windshield over the sensor. • **Does the PID indicate YES?**	**Yes** GO to G6 . **No** GO to G2 .
G2 CHECK CIRCUIT 964 (DB/LG) FOR VOLTAGE	
• Key in OFF position. • Disconnect: RSM C914. • Key in ON position. • Measure the voltage between RSM C914 pin 1, circuit 964 (DB/LG), harness side and ground. 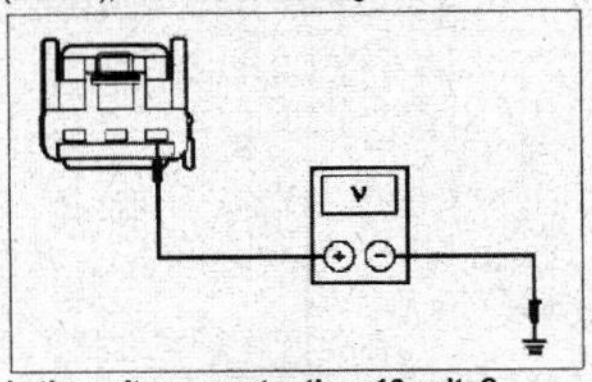 • **Is the voltage greater than 10 volts?**	**Yes** GO to G3 . **No** REPAIR the circuit. TEST the system for normal operation.
G3 CHECK CIRCUIT 57 (BK) FOR AN OPEN	
• Key in OFF position. • Measure the resistance between RSM C914 pin 2, circuit 57 (BK), harness side and ground. 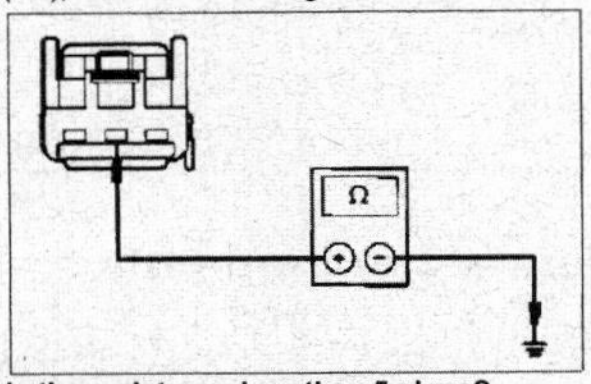 • **Is the resistance less than 5 ohms?**	**Yes** GO to G4 . **No** REPAIR the circuit. TEST the system for normal operation.

FM9020200920010X

Fig. 115 Test G: Moisture Sensitive Wipers Do Not Operate Correctly (Part 1 of 3). 2003–04 Town Car

G4 CHECK CIRCUIT 1301 (YE) FOR AN OPEN	
• Disconnect: Windshield Wiper Motor C125. • Measure the resistance between the RSM C914 pin 3, circuit 1301 (YE), harness side and the windshield wiper motor C125 pin 4, circuit 1301 (YE), harness side. 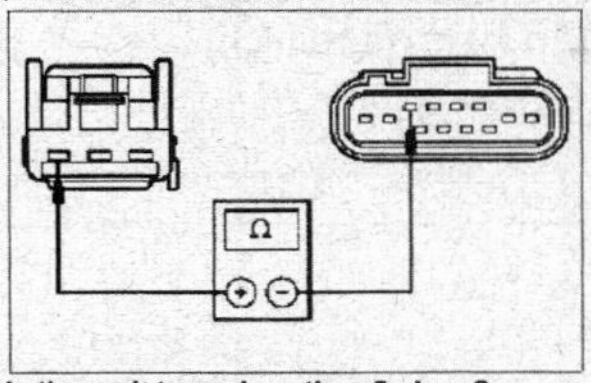 • **Is the resistance less than 5 ohms?**	**Yes** GO to G5 . **No** REPAIR the circuit. TEST the system for normal operation.
G5 CHECK FOR CORRECT RSM OPERATION	

• Disconnect all RSM connectors.
• Check for:
  • corrosion
  • pushed-out pins
• Connect all RSM connectors and make sure they seat correctly.
• Operate the system and verify the concern is still present.
• **Is the concern still present?**
	Yes
	INSTALL a new RSM. REFER to rain sensor module in this section.
	No
	The system is operating correctly at this time. Concern may have been caused by a loose or corroded connector. TEST the system for normal operation.

G6 CHECK FOR CORRECT WIPER MOTOR OPERATION	

• Disconnect all wiper motor connectors.
• Check for:
  • corrosion
  • pushed-out pins
• Connect all wiper motor connectors and make sure they seat correctly.
• Operate the system and verify the concern is still present.
• **Is the concern still present?**
	Yes
	GO to G7 .
	No
	The system is operating correctly at this time. Concern may have been caused by a loose or corroded connector. TEST the system for normal operation.

FM9020200920020X

Fig. 115 Test G: Moisture Sensitive Wipers Do Not Operate Correctly (Part 2 of 3). 2003–04 Town Car

G7 CHECK THE WINDSHIELD WIPER MOTOR	
• Key in OFF position. • Disconnect: Windshield Wiper Motor C125. • Carry out the windshield wiper motor component test as outlined in this section. • **Did the windshield wiper motor pass the component test?**	**Yes** The system is operating correctly at this time. Concern may have been caused by binding or incorrect pivot arm adjustment. TEST the system for normal operation. **No** INSTALL a new windshield wiper motor.

FM9020200920030X

Fig. 115 Test G: Moisture Sensitive Wipers Do Not Operate Correctly (Part 3 of 3). 2003–04 Town Car

CONDITIONS	DETAILS/RESULTS/ACTIONS
A1 CHECK THE FEM PID WPMODE	

1

2 Monitor the FEM PID WPMODE, while activating the multifunction switch to the OFF, low, high, pulse, intermittent, and positions 1 through 7.

• **Do the FEM PID WPMODE values agree with the multifunction switch position?**

→ **Yes**
GO to A6 .

→ **No**
GO to A2 .

FM9020100896010X

Fig. 116 Test A: Wipers Are Inoperative (Part 1 of 19). Thunderbird

A2 CHECK THE MULTIFUNCTION SWITCH OPERATION

1

2

Multifunction Switch

3 Carry out the multifunction switch component test.

• **Is the multifunction switch OK?**

→ **Yes**
GO to A3 .

→ **No**
INSTALL a new multifunction switch.
TEST the system for normal operation.

FM9020100896020X

Fig. 116 Test A: Wipers Are Inoperative (Part 2 of 19). Thunderbird

A3 CHECK VOLTAGE TO THE MULTIFUNCTION SWITCH

1

2

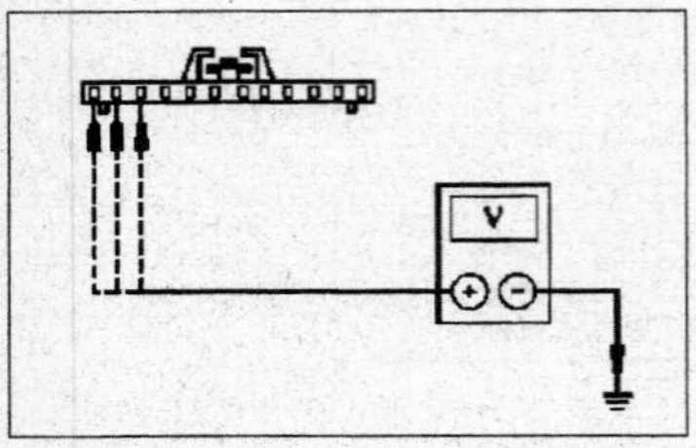

2 Using the following table, measure the voltage between the multifunction switch and ground:

C202	Circuit
Pin 1	8-KA19 (WH/BK)
Pin 2	7-KA19 (YE/BK)
Pin 3	10-KA19 (GY/BK)

• **Are the voltages greater than 10 volts?**

→ **Yes**
GO to A4 .

→ **No**
GO to A5 .

FM9020100896030X

Fig. 116 Test A: Wipers Are Inoperative (Part 3 of 19). Thunderbird

A4 CHECK THE MULTIFUNCTION SWITCH FOR SHORT TO POWER

1

2

FEM

3

4

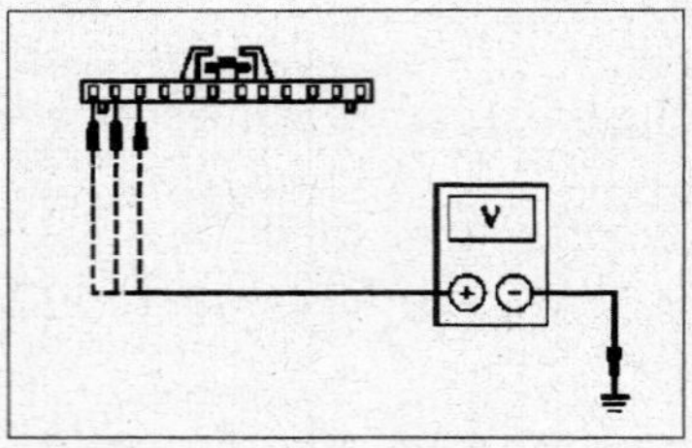

4 Using the following table, measure the voltage between the multifunction switch and ground:

C202	Circuit
Pin 1	8-KA19 (WH/BK)
Pin 2	7-KA19 (YE/BK)
Pin 3	10-KA19 (GY/BK)

• **Are the voltages greater than 10 volts?**

→ **Yes**
REPAIR the circuit(s) in question.
TEST the system for normal operation.

→ **No**
INSTALL a new FEM.
CLEAR the DTCs.
REPEAT the self-test.

FM9020100896040X

Fig. 116 Test A: Wipers Are Inoperative (Part 4 of 19). Thunderbird

A5 CHECK CIRCUITS 7-KA19 (YE/BK), 8-KA19 (WH/BK) AND 10-KA19 (GY/BK) FOR OPENS

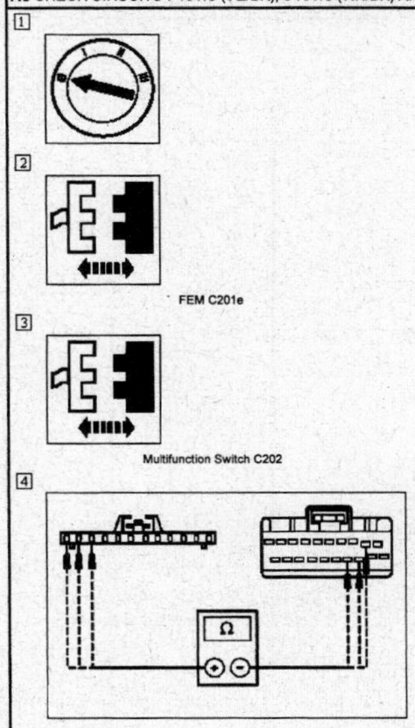

4 Using the following table, measure the resistance between multifunction switch harness side and FEM harness side:

Multifunction Switch C202	FEM C201e
pin 1, circuit 8-KA19 (WH/BK)	pin 2, circuit 8-KA19 (WH/BK)
pin 2, circuit 7-KA19 (YE/BK)	pin 14, circuit 7-KA19 (YE/BK)
pin 3, circuit 10-KA19 (GY/BK)	pin 13, circuit 10-KA19 (GY/BK)

- **Are the resistances less than 5 ohms?**

→ **Yes**
INSTALL a new FEM.
CLEAR the DTCs.
REPEAT the self-test.

→ **No**
REPAIR the circuit(s) in question.
TEST the system for normal operation.

FM9020100896050X

Fig. 116 Test A: Wipers Are Inoperative (Part 5 of 19). Thunderbird

A6 CHECK CIRCUIT 91S-KA39 (BN/YE) FOR VOLTAGE

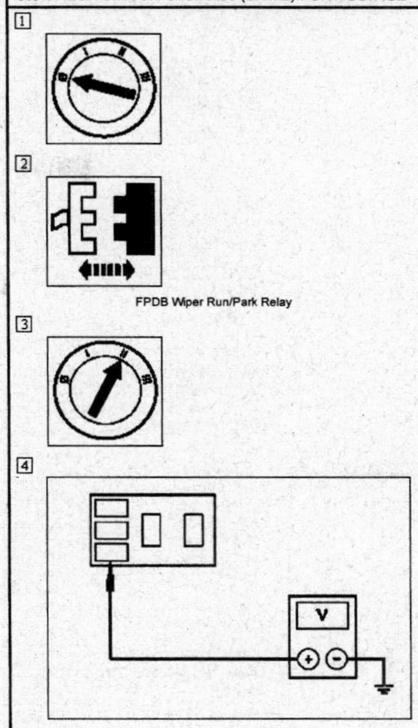

4 Measure the voltage between wiper run/park relay (BN/YE), harness side and ground.

- **Is the voltage greater than 10 volts?**

→ **Yes**
GO to A7.

→ **No**
GO to A8.

FM9020100896060X

Fig. 116 Test A: Wipers Are Inoperative (Part 6 of 19). Thunderbird

A7 CHECK CIRCUIT 91S-KA39 (BN/YE) FOR SHORT TO POWER

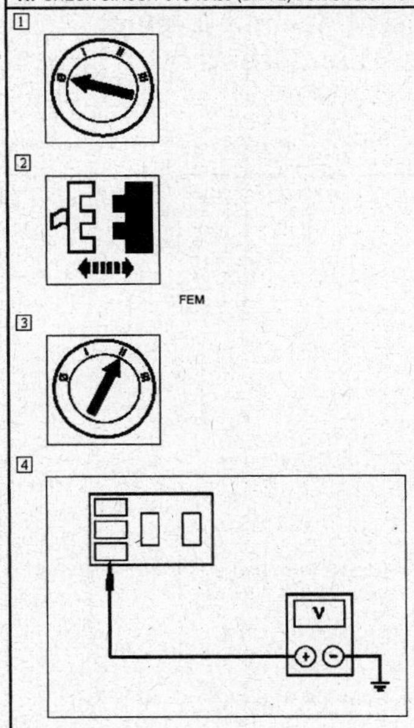

4 Measure the voltage between wiper run/park relay (BN/YE), harness side and ground.

- **Is the voltage greater than 10 volts?**

→ **Yes**
REPAIR the circuit. TEST the system for normal operation.

→ **No**
INSTALL a new FEM.
TEST the system for normal operation.

FM9020100896070X

Fig. 116 Test A: Wipers Are Inoperative (Part 7 of 19). Thunderbird

A8 ACTIVATE WIPER RUN/PARK RELAY COMMAND AND TEST FOR GROUNDING FROM FEM

1

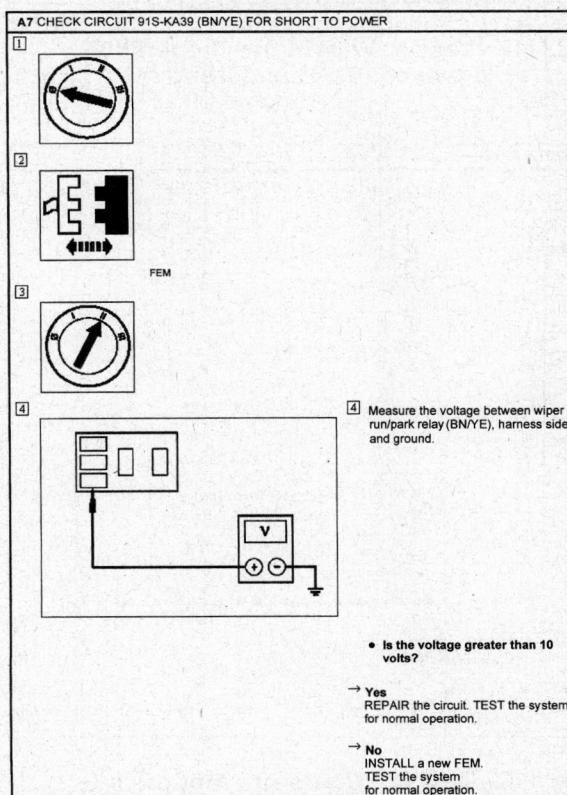

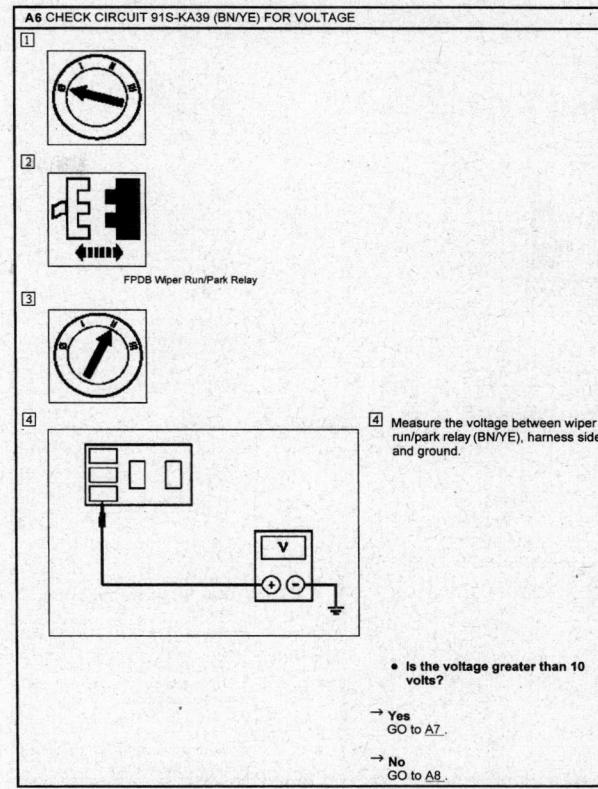

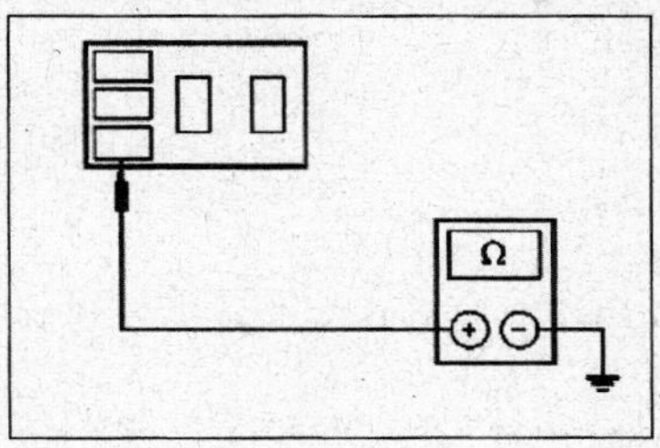

1 Trigger the FEM active command WIPER RLY to ON, while measuring the resistance between wiper run/park relay (BN/YE), harness side and ground.

- **Is the resistance less than 5 ohms?**

→ **Yes**
GO to A10.

→ **No**
GO to A9.

FM9020100896080X

Fig. 116 Test A: Wipers Are Inoperative (Part 8 of 19). Thunderbird

A9 CHECK CIRCUIT 91S-KA39 (BN/YE) FOR AN OPEN

1

2

FEM

3

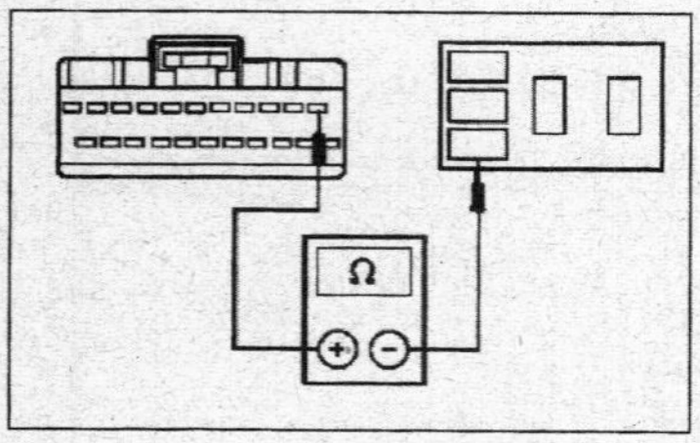

3 Measure the resistance between wiper run/park relay (BN/YE), harness side and FEM circuit (BN/YE), harness side.

- **Is the resistance less than 5 ohms?**

→ **Yes**
INSTALL a new FEM. TEST the system for normal operation.

→ **No**
REPAIR the circuit. TEST the system for normal operation.

FM9020100896090X

Fig. 116 Test A: Wipers Are Inoperative (Part 9 of 19). Thunderbird

A10 CHECK FPDB FUSE 124 (30A) FOR VOLTAGE

1

2

FPDB Fuse 124 (30A)

3

4

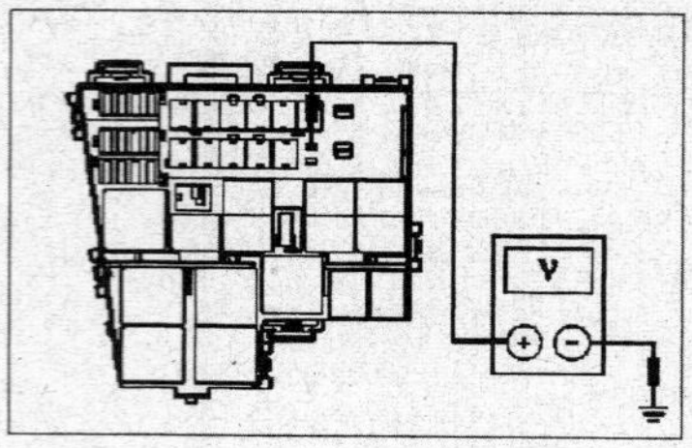

4 Measure the voltage between FPDB fuse 124 (30 A) input side and ground.

- **Is the voltage greater than 10 volts?**

→ **Yes**
GO to A11 .

→ **No**
REPAIR the power source. TEST the system for normal operation.

FM9020100896100X

Fig. 116 Test A: Wipers Are Inoperative (Part 10 of 19). Thunderbird

A11 CHECK BETWEEN FPDB FUSE 124 (30A) AND WIPER RUN/PARK RELAY FOR OPENS

1

2

FPDB Wiper Run/Park Relay

3

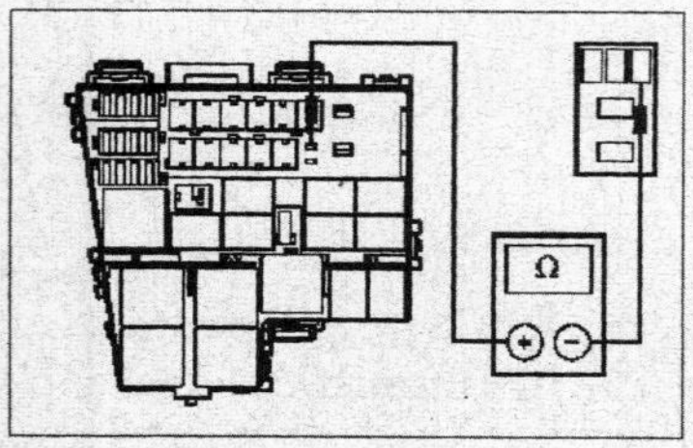

3 Measure the resistance between FPDB fuse 124 (30A), input side, and wiper run/park relay

- **Is the resistance less than 5 ohms?**

→ **Yes**
INSTALL a new FPDB fuse 124 (30A). GO to A12 .

→ **No**
INSTALL a new FPDB. TEST the system for normal operation.

FM9020100896110X

Fig. 116 Test A: Wipers Are Inoperative (Part 11 of 19). Thunderbird

A12 CHECK WIPER RUN/PARK AND WIPER HIGH/LOW RELAYS

1

2

FPDB Wiper High/Low Relay

3 Carry out the wiper run/park and wiper high/low relay component tests.

- **Are the wiper run/park and wiper high/low relays OK?**

→ **Yes**
GO to A13 .

→ **No**
INSTALL a new relay(s) as necessary. TEST the system for normal operation.

FM9020100896120X

Fig. 116 Test A: Wipers Are Inoperative (Part 12 of 19). Thunderbird

A13 CHECK CIRCUIT 30S-KA12 (RD/WH) FOR OPENS

1

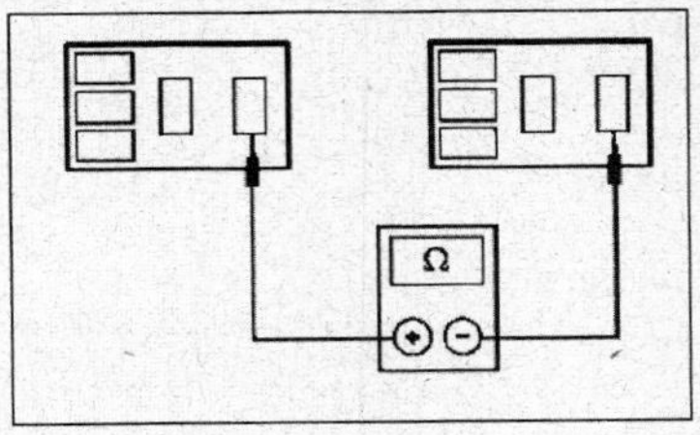

1 Measure the resistance between wiper run/park relay (RD/WH), harness side and wiper high/low relay (RD/WH), harness side.

- **Is the resistance less than 5 ohms?**

→ **Yes**
GO to A14 .

→ **No**
REPAIR the circuit. TEST the system for normal operation.

FM9020100896130X

Fig. 116 Test A: Wipers Are Inoperative (Part 13 of 19). Thunderbird

A14 CHECK CIRCUIT 30S-KA2 (RD/BU) FOR VOLTAGE

1
2
3

FPDB Wiper Run/Park Relay

4

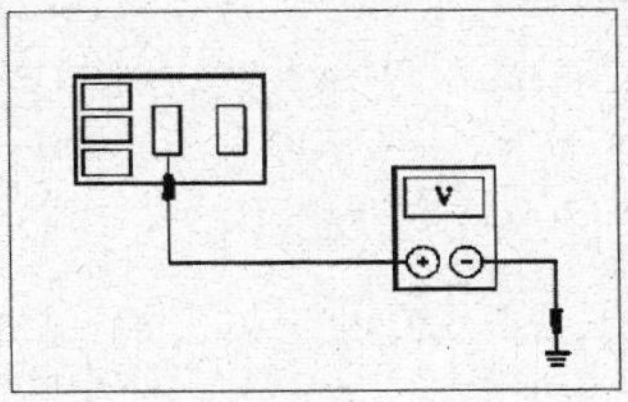

4 Measure the voltage between wiper run/park relay (RD/BU), harness side and ground.

- **Is the voltage greater than 10 volts?**

→ **Yes**
GO to A15 .

→ **No**
INSTALL a new underhood FPDB. TEST the system for normal operation.

FM9020100896140X

Fig. 116 Test A: Wipers Are Inoperative (Part 14 of 19). Thunderbird

A15 CHECK CIRCUIT 31S-KA12 (BK/WH) FOR VOLTAGE

1
2
3

Wiper Motor

4

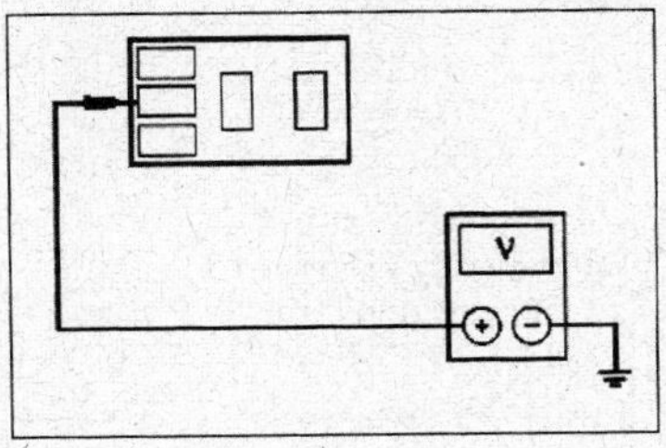

4 Measure the voltage between wiper run/park relay(BK/WH), harness side and ground.

- **Is the voltage greater than 10 volts?**

→ **Yes**
GO to A16 .

→ **No**
GO to A17 .

FM9020100896150X

Fig. 116 Test A: Wipers Are Inoperative (Part 15 of 19). Thunderbird

A16 CHECK CIRCUITS 31S-KA12 (BK/WH), 31S-KA1 (BK/BU), AND 31S-KA8 (BK/BU) FOR SHORTS TO POWER

1
2
3

FEM

4

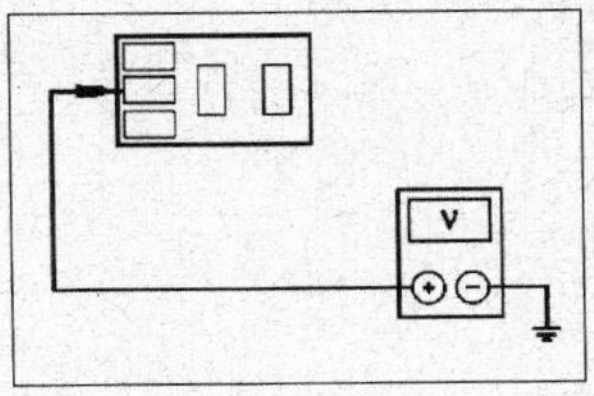

4 Measure the voltage between wiper run/park relay(BK/WH), harness side and ground.

- **Is the voltage greater than 10 volts?**

→ **Yes**
REPAIR the circuit(s) in question. CLEAR the DTCs. REPEAT the self-test.

→ **No**
INSTALL a new FEM. TEST the system for normal operation.

FM9020100896160X

Fig. 116 Test A: Wipers Are Inoperative (Part 16 of 19). Thunderbird

A17 CHECK CIRCUIT 31S-KA12 (BK/WH) FOR CONTINUITY

1

2

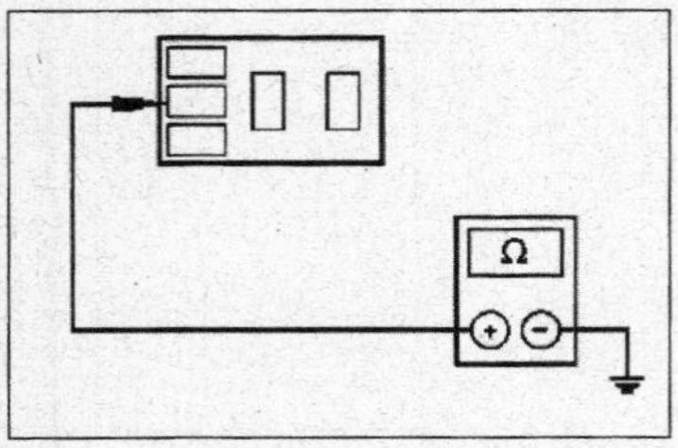

2 Measure the resistance between wiper run/park relay (BK/WH), harness side and ground.

- **Is the resistance greater than 10,000 ohms?**

→ **Yes**
GO to A19.

→ **No**
GO to A18.

FM9020100896170X

Fig. 116 Test A: Wipers Are Inoperative (Part 17 of 19). Thunderbird

A18 CHECK CIRCUITS 31S-KA12 (BK/WH), 31S-KA1 (BK/BU) AND 31S-KA8 (BK/BU) FOR SHORTS TO GROUND

1

FEM

2

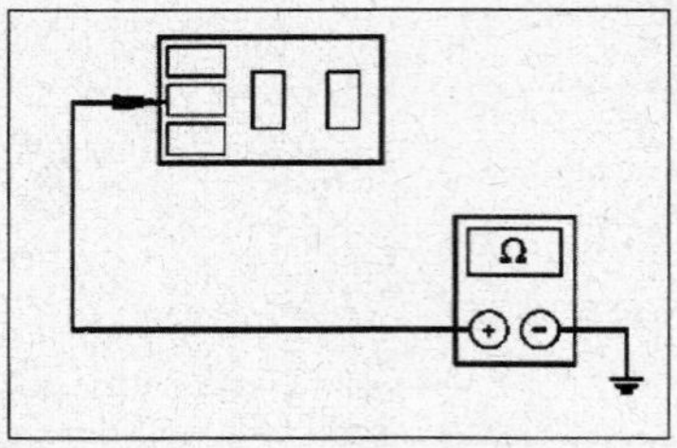

2 Measure the resistance between wiper run/park relay (BK/WH), harness side and ground.

- **Is the resistance greater than 10,000 ohms?**

→ **Yes**
INSTALL a new FEM. TEST the system for normal operation.

→ **No**
REPAIR the circuit(s) in question. CLEAR the DTCs. REPEAT the self-test.

FM9020100896180X

Fig. 116 Test A: Wipers Are Inoperative (Part 18 of 19). Thunderbird

A19 CHECK CIRCUIT 31-KA9 (BK) FOR OPENS

1

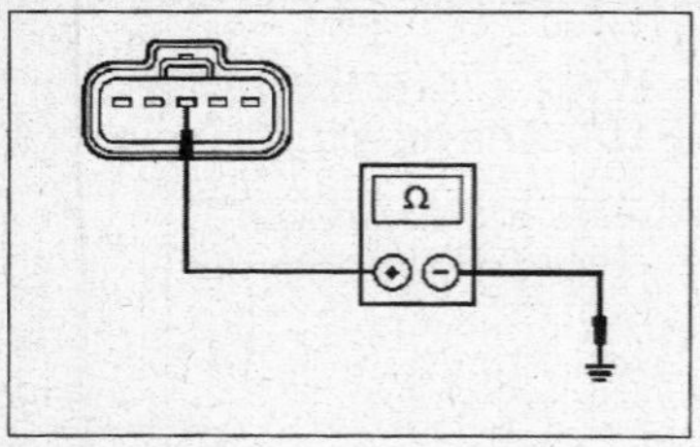

1 Measure the resistance between wiper motor (BK), harness side and ground.

- **Is the resistance less than 5 ohms?**

→ **Yes**
CHECK the wiper motor. If the wiper motor does not pass the test, INSTALL a new wiper motor. TEST the system for normal operation.

→ **No**
REPAIR the circuit. TEST the system for normal operation.

FM9020100896190X

Fig. 116 Test A: Wipers Are Inoperative (Part 19 of 19). Thunderbird

CONDITIONS	DETAILS/RESULTS/ACTIONS
B1 CHECK THE MULTIFUNCTION SWITCH OPERATION	
1  2  Multifunction Switch	3 Carry out the multifunction switch component test. • **Is the multifunction switch OK?** → **Yes** GO to B2. → **No** INSTALL a new multifunction switch. TEST the system for normal operation.

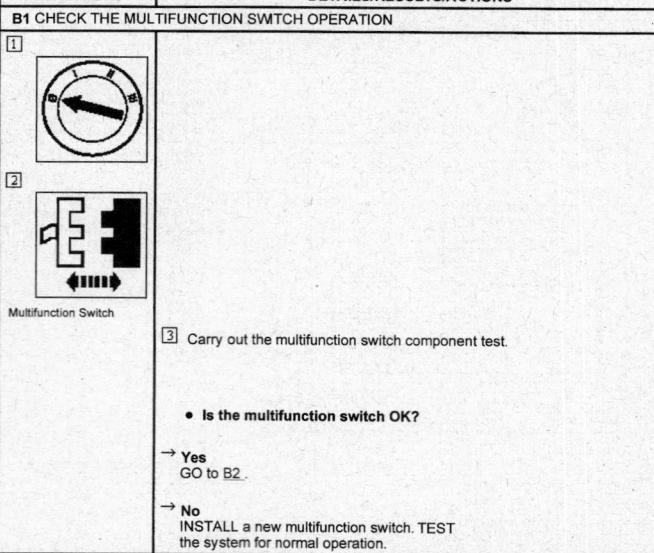

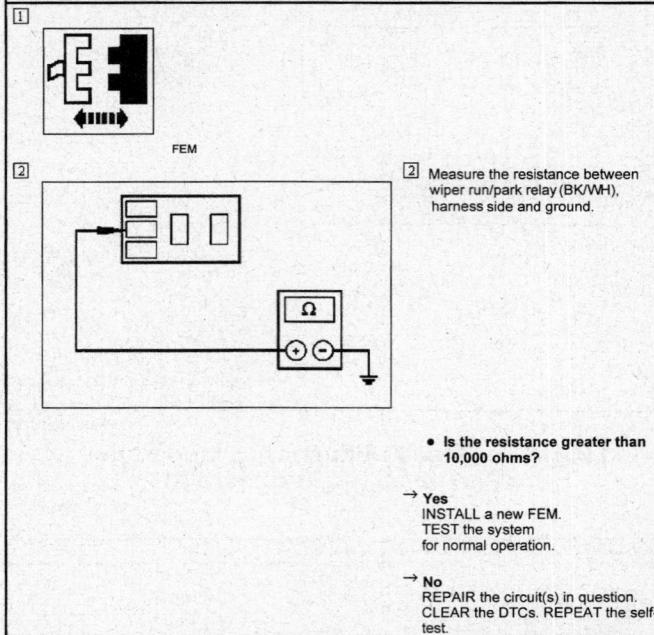

FM9020100897010X

Fig. 117 Test B: Wipers Stay On Continuously (Part 1 of 8). Thunderbird

B2 CHECK CIRCUIT 10–KA19 (GY/BK) FOR RESISTANCE TO GROUND

1

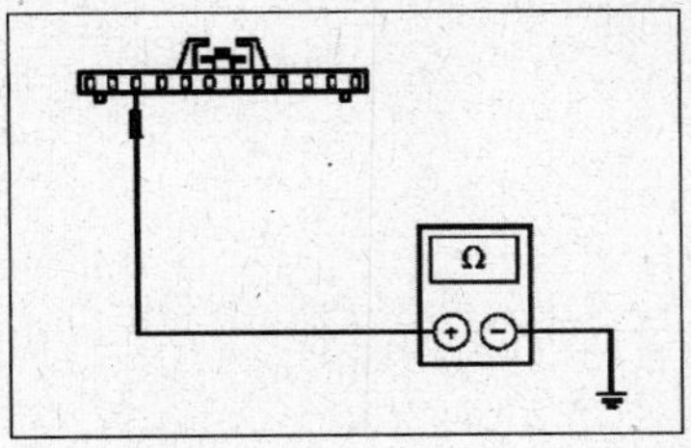

1 Measure the resistance between multifunction switch (GY/BK), harness side and ground.

- **Is the resistance greater than 10,000 ohms?**

→ **Yes**
GO to B4 .

→ **No**
GO to B3 .

FM9020100897020X

Fig. 117 Test B: Wipers Stay On Continuously (Part 2 of 8). Thunderbird

B4 CHECK WIPER RUN/PARK AND WIPER HIGH/LOW RELAYS

1 Remove the FPDB wiper run/park and wiper high/low relays.

2 Carry out the relay component test.

- **Are both relays OK?**

→ **Yes**
GO to B5 .

→ **No**
INSTALL a new relay(s). TEST the system for normal operation.

FM9020100897040X

Fig. 117 Test B: Wipers Stay On Continuously (Part 4 of 8). Thunderbird

B5 CHECK CIRCUIT 91S-KA39 (BN/YE) FOR CONTINUITY

1

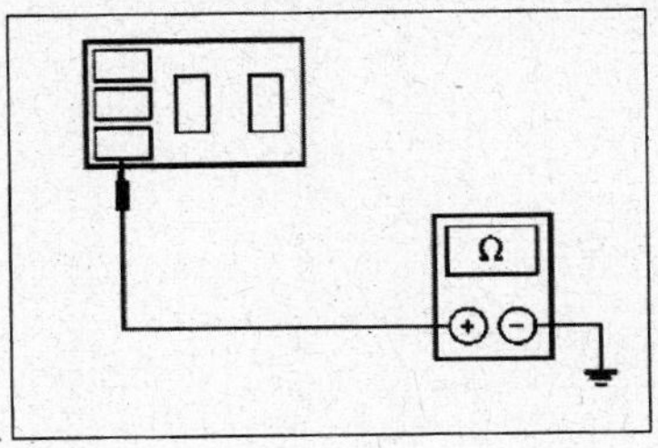

1 Measure the resistance between wiper run/park relay (BN/YE), harness side and ground.

- **Is the resistance greater than 10,000 ohms?**

→ **Yes**
GO to B7 .

→ **No**
GO to B6 .

FM9020100897050X

Fig. 117 Test B: Wipers Stay On Continuously (Part 5 of 8). Thunderbird

B3 CHECK CIRCUIT 10–KA19 (GY/BK) FOR SHORTS TO GROUND

1

FEM

2

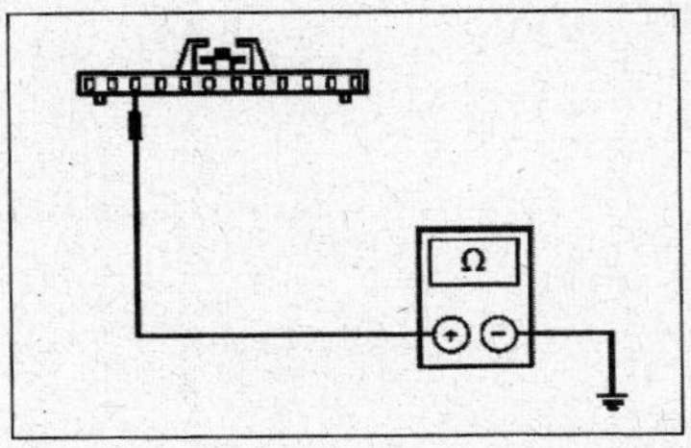

2 Measure the resistance between multifunction switch (GY/BK), 3, harness side and ground.

- **Is the resistance greater than 10,000 ohms?**

→ **Yes**
INSTALL a new FEM.
TEST the system for normal operation.

→ **No**
REPAIR circuit(s) in question. TEST the system for normal operation.

FM9020100897030X

Fig. 117 Test B: Wipers Stay On Continuously (Part 3 of 8). Thunderbird

B6 CHECK CIRCUIT 91S-KA39 (BN/YE) FOR SHORTS TO GROUND

1

FEM

2

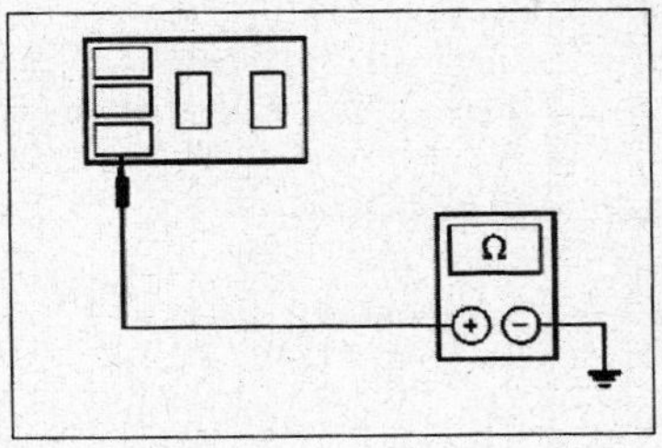

2 Measure the resistance between wiper run/park relay (BN/YE), harness side and ground.

- **Is the resistance greater than 10,000 ohms?**

→ **Yes**
INSTALL a new FEM.
TEST the system for normal operation.

→ **No**
REPAIR the circuit. TEST the system for normal operation.

FM9020100897060X

Fig. 117 Test B: Wipers Stay On Continuously (Part 6 of 8). Thunderbird

B7 CHECK CIRCUIT 30S–KA12 (RD/BK) FOR SHORTS TO BATTERY

1

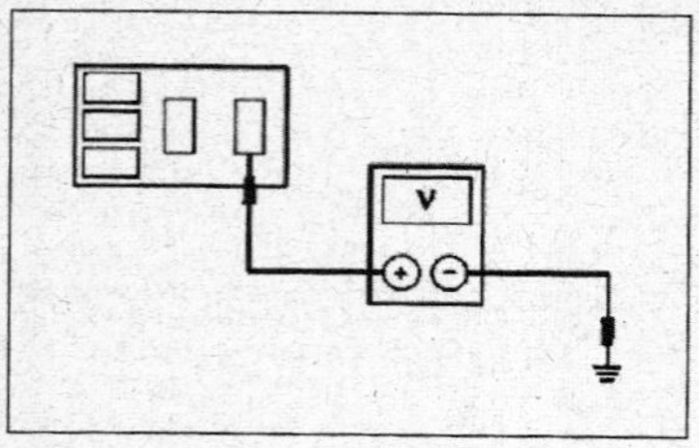

1 Measure the voltage between wiper run/park relay (RD/BK) and ground.

- **Is the voltage greater than 10 volts?**

→ **Yes**
REPAIR the circuit. TEST the system for normal operation.

→ **No**
GO to B8 .

FM9020100897070X

Fig. 117 Test B: Wipers Stay On Continuously (Part 7 of 8). Thunderbird

CONDITIONS	DETAILS/RESULTS/ACTIONS
C1 CHECK THE FEM PID WPMODE	
	1 Monitor the FEM PID WPMODE while activating the multifunction switch to the high and low positions. • **Do the FEM PID WPMODE values agree with the multifunction switch positions?** → **Yes** GO to C2 . → **No** GO to C3 .
C2 ACTIVATE THE FRONT WINDSHIELD WIPER/WASHER COMMAND	
1 	2 Trigger the FEM active command SPEED RLY to the LOW and HIGH speeds. • **Do the wipers work in LOW and HIGH?** → **Yes** INSTALL a new FEM. TEST the system for normal operation. → **No** GO to C5 .

FM9020100898010X

Fig. 118 Test C: High/Low Wiper Speeds Do Not Operate Correctly (Part 1 of 11). Thunderbird

B8 CHECK CIRCUIT 30S–KA11 (RD/BK) AND CIRCUIT 30S–KA10 (RD/GN) FOR SHORT TO BATTERY

1

Wiper Motor

2

3

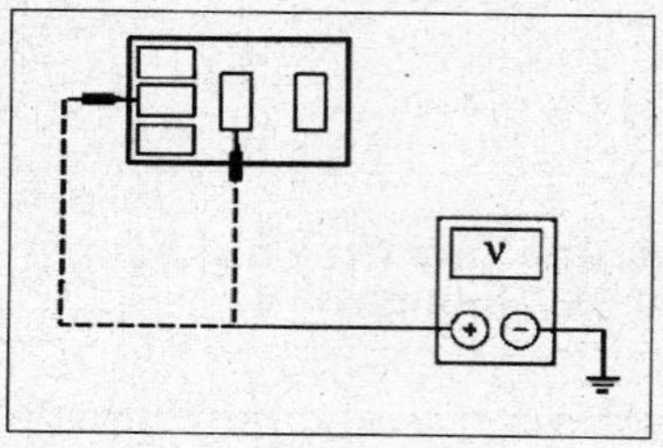

3 Measure the voltage between wiper high/low relay(RD/GN), harness side and ground; and between wiper high/low relay(RD/BK), harness side and ground.

- **Is the voltage greater than 10 volts?**

→ **Yes**
REPAIR circuit(s) in question. TEST the system for normal operation.

→ **No**
INSTALL a new FEM.
TEST the system for normal operation.

FM9020100897080X

Fig. 117 Test B: Wipers Stay On Continuously (Part 8 of 8). Thunderbird

C3 CHECK THE MULTIFUNCTION SWITCH OPERATION

1

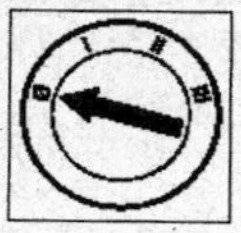

2

Multifunction Switch

3 Carry out the multifunction switch component test.

- **Is the multifunction switch OK?**

→ **Yes**
GO to C4 .

→ **No**
INSTALL a new multifunction switch.
TEST the system for normal operation.

FM9020100898020X

Fig. 118 Test C: High/Low Wiper Speeds Do Not Operate Correctly (Part 2 of 11). Thunderbird

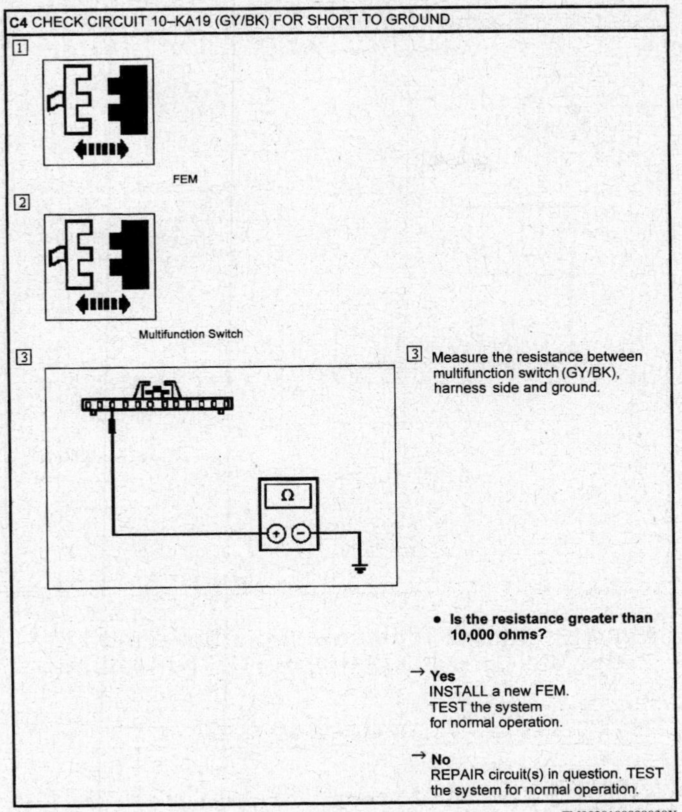

FM9020100898030X

Fig. 118 Test C: High/Low Wiper Speeds Do Not Operate Correctly (Part 3 of 11). Thunderbird

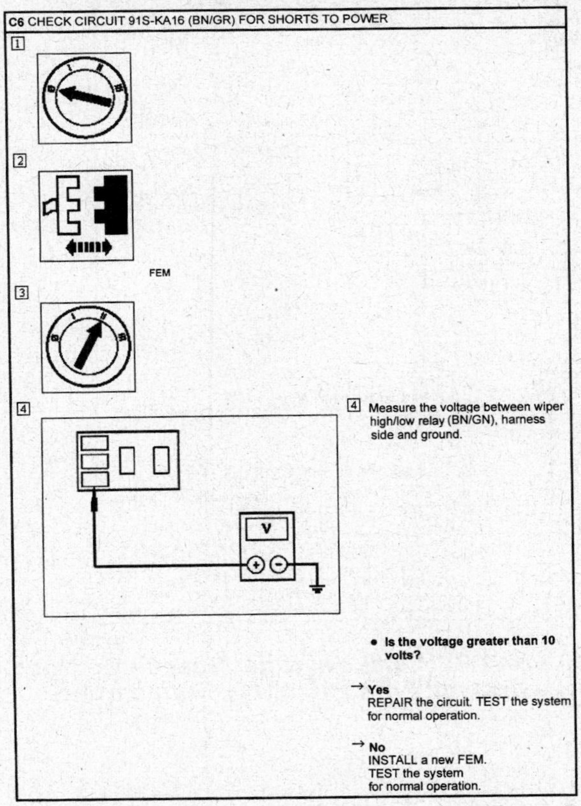

FM9020100898050X

Fig. 118 Test C: High/Low Wiper Speeds Do Not Operate Correctly (Part 5 of 11). Thunderbird

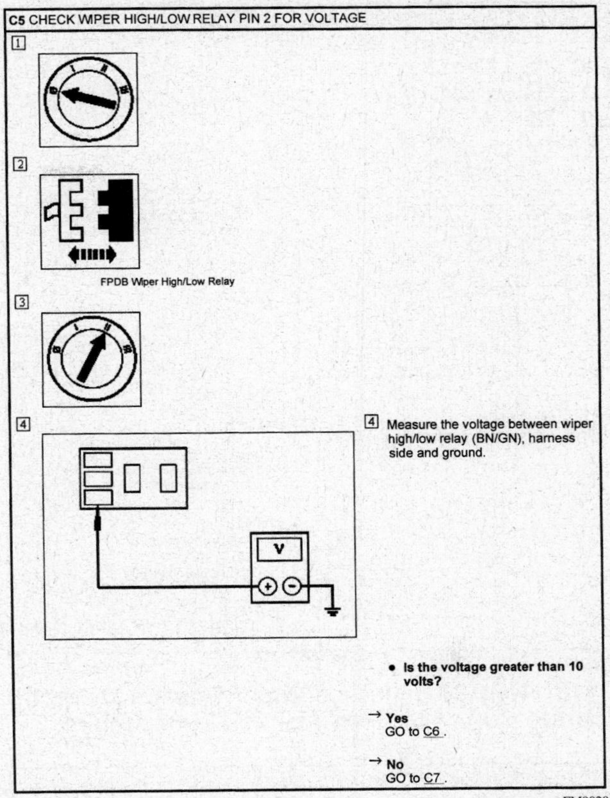

FM9020100898040X

Fig. 118 Test C: High/Low Wiper Speeds Do Not Operate Correctly (Part 4 of 11). Thunderbird

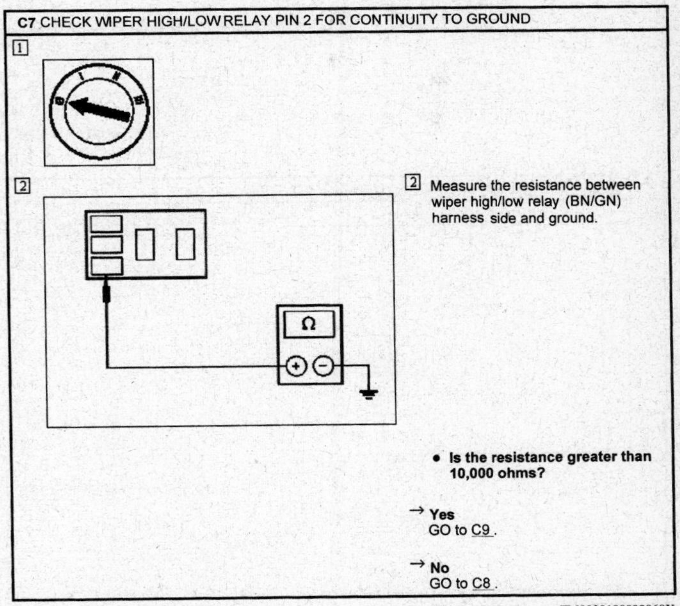

FM9020100898060X

Fig. 118 Test C: High/Low Wiper Speeds Do Not Operate Correctly (Part 6 of 11). Thunderbird

C8 CHECK CIRCUIT 91S-KA16 (BN/GN) FOR SHORTS TO GROUND

1

FEM

2

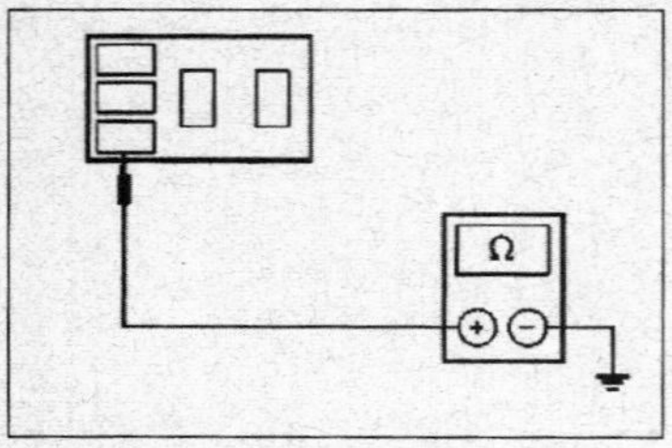

2 Measure the resistance between wiper high/low relay (BN/GN), harness side and ground.

- **Is the resistance greater than 10,000 ohms?**

→ **Yes**
INSTALL a new FEM. TEST the system for normal operation.

→ **No**
REPAIR the circuit. TEST the system for normal operation.

FM9020100898070X

Fig. 118 Test C: High/Low Wiper Speeds Do Not Operate Correctly (Part 7 of 11). Thunderbird

C9 ACTIVATE WIPER HIGH/LOW RELAY

1

2

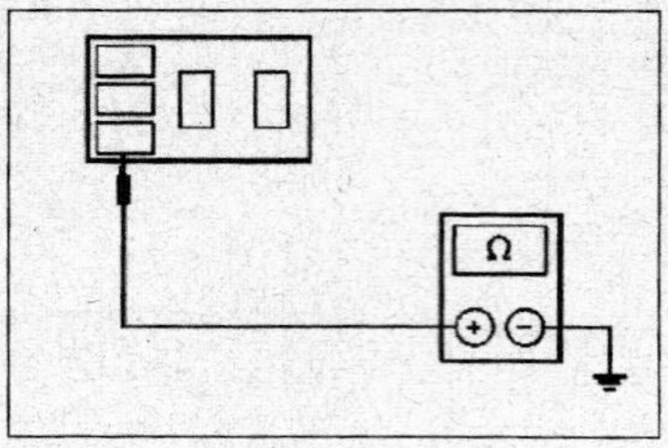

2 Trigger the FEM active command SPEED RLY to ON, while measuring the resistance between wiper high/low relay (BN/GN) and ground.

- **Is the resistance less than 5 ohms?**

→ **Yes**
GO to C10 .

→ **No**
GO to C13 .

FM9020100898080X

Fig. 118 Test C: High/Low Wiper Speeds Do Not Operate Correctly (Part 8 of 11). Thunderbird

C10 CHECK FPDB WIPER HIGH/LOW RELAY

1 Carry out the wiper high/low relay component test.

- **Is the wiper high/low relay OK?**

→ **Yes**
GO to C11 .

→ **No**
INSTALL a new wiper high/low relay. TEST the system for normal operation.

C11 CHECK WIPER HIGH/LOW RELAY PIN 1 FOR VOLTAGE

1

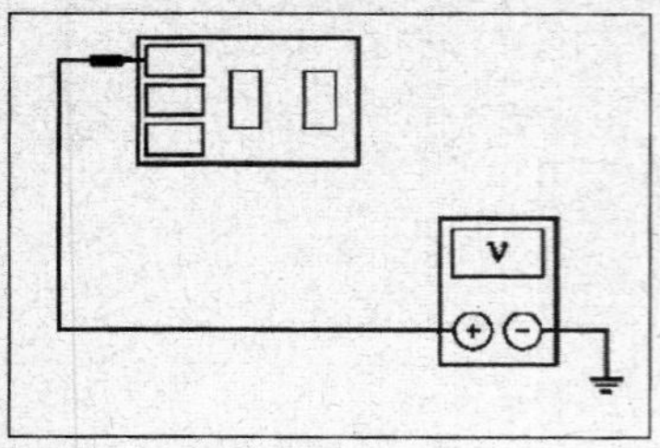

1 Measure the voltage between wiper high/low relay harness side and ground.

- **Is the voltage greater than 10 volts?**

→ **Yes**
GO to C12 .

→ **No**
INSTALL a new underhood AJB. TEST the system for normal operation.

FM9020100898090X

Fig. 118 Test C: High/Low Wiper Speeds Do Not Operate Correctly (Part 9 of 11). Thunderbird

C12 CHECK CIRCUITS 30S-KA10 (RD/GN) AND 30S-KA11 (RD/BK) FOR OPENS

1

2

Wiper Motor

3

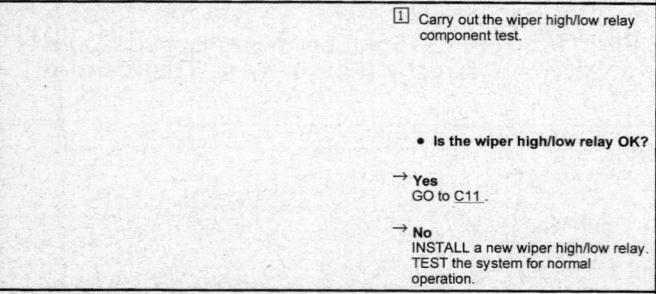

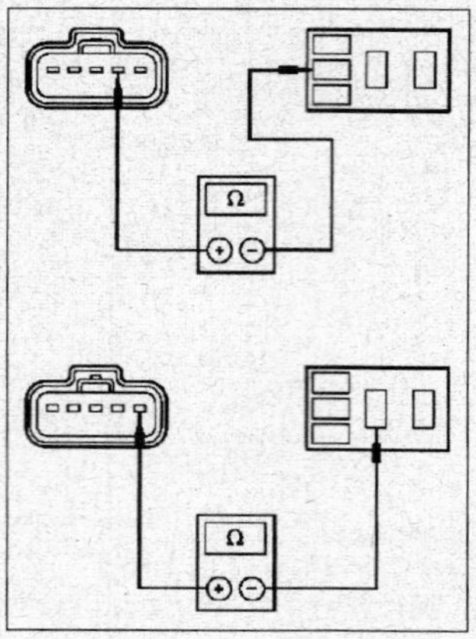

3 Measure the resistance between wiper high/low relay (RD/GN), harness side and wiper motor (RD/GN), harness side; and between wiper high/low relay (RD/BK), harness side and wiper motor (RD/BK), harness side.

- **Is the resistance greater than 10,000 ohms?**

→ **Yes**
CHECK the wiper motor. If the wiper motor does not pass the test, INSTALL a new wiper motor. TEST the system for normal operation.

→ **No**
REPAIR circuit(s) in question. TEST the system for normal operation.

FM9020100898100X

Fig. 118 Test C: High/Low Wiper Speeds Do Not Operate Correctly (Part 10 of 11). Thunderbird

C13 CHECK CIRCUIT 91S-KA16 (BN/GN) FOR OPENS

1

FEM

2

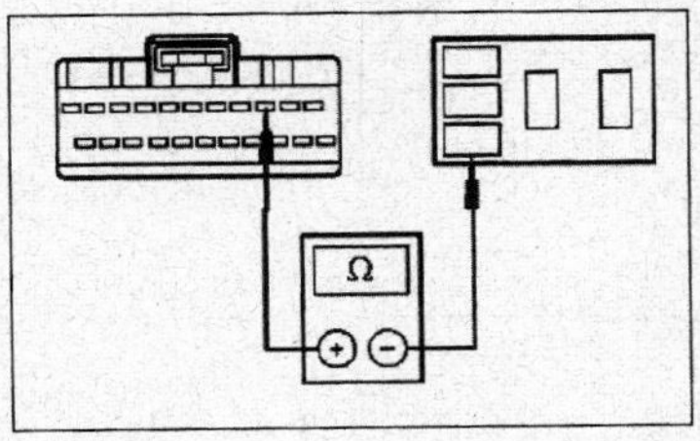

2 Measure the resistance between wiper high/low relay C1001 pin 2, (BN/GN), harness side and FEM circuit (BN/GN), harness side.

- **Is the resistance less than 5 ohms?**

→ **Yes**
INSTALL a new FEM.
TEST the system for normal operation.

→ **No**
REPAIR the circuit. TEST the system for normal operation.

FM9020100898110X

Fig. 118 Test C: High/Low Wiper Speeds Do Not Operate Correctly (Part 11 of 11). Thunderbird

D3 CHECK CIRCUITS 8–KA19 (WH/BK) FOR SHORTS TO GROUND

1

FEM

2

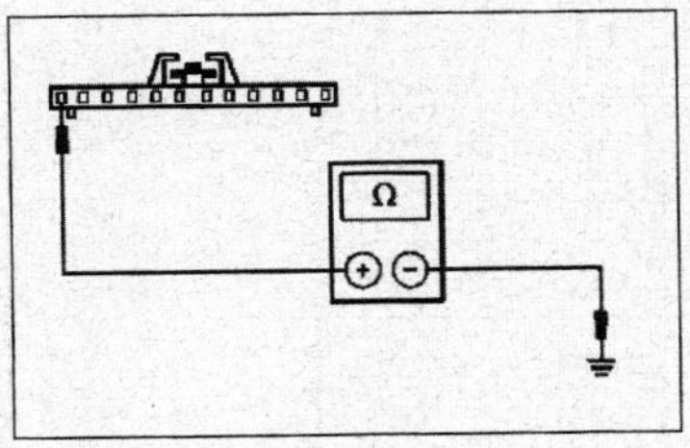

2 Measure the resistance between multifunction switch (WH/BK), harness side and ground.

- **Is the resistance greater than 10,000 ohms?**

→ **Yes**
GO to D4.

→ **No**
REPAIR circuit(s) in question. TEST the system for normal operation.

FM9020100899020X

Fig. 119 Test D: Wash & Wipe Function Does Not Operate Correctly (Part 2 of 4). Thunderbird

CONDITIONS	DETAILS/RESULTS/ACTIONS

D1 MONITOR THE FEM PID WPMODE

1

2 Monitor the FEM PID WPMODE while activating the wash and wipe functions.

- **Do the FEM PID WPMODE values agree with the multifunction switch positions?**

→ **Yes**
GO to D5.

→ **No**
GO to D2.

D2 CHECK THE MULTIFUNCTION SWITCH OPERATION

1

Multifunction Switch C202

2 Carry out the multifunction switch component test.

- **Is the multifunction switch OK?**

→ **Yes**
GO to D3.

→ **No**
INSTALL a new multifunction switch. TEST the system for normal operation.

FM9020100899010X

Fig. 119 Test D: Wash & Wipe Function Does Not Operate Correctly (Part 1 of 4). Thunderbird

D4 CHECK CIRCUITS 7–KA19 (WH/BK) AND 8–KA19 (WH/BK) FOR OPENS

1

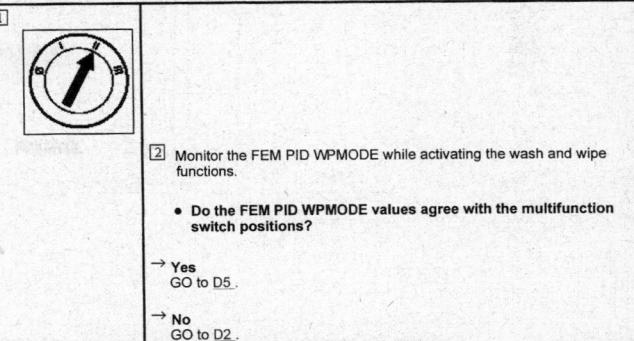

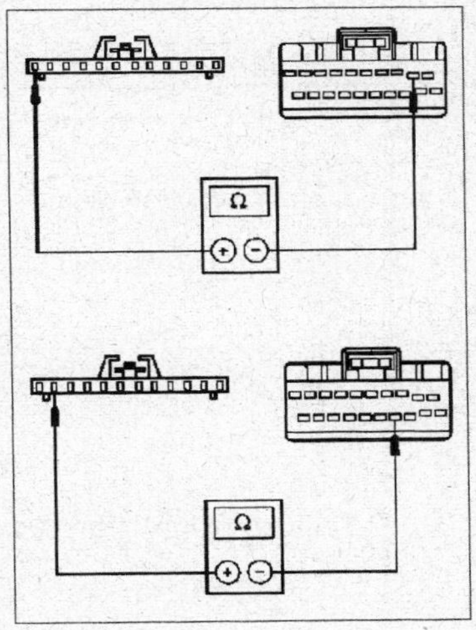

1 Measure the resistance between multifunction switch (WH/BK), harness side and FEM (WH/BK); and between multifunction switch circuit 7-KA19 (YE/BK), harness side and FEM (YE/BK), harness side.

- **Is the resistance less than 5 ohms?**

→ **Yes**
GO to D5.

→ **No**
REPAIR the circuit(s) in question. TEST the system for normal operation.

FM9020100899030X

Fig. 119 Test D: Wash & Wipe Function Does Not Operate Correctly (Part 3 of 4). Thunderbird

D5 CHECK CIRCUITS 31S–KA8 (BK/BU) AND 31S–KA1 (BK/YE) FOR OPENS

1

FEM

2

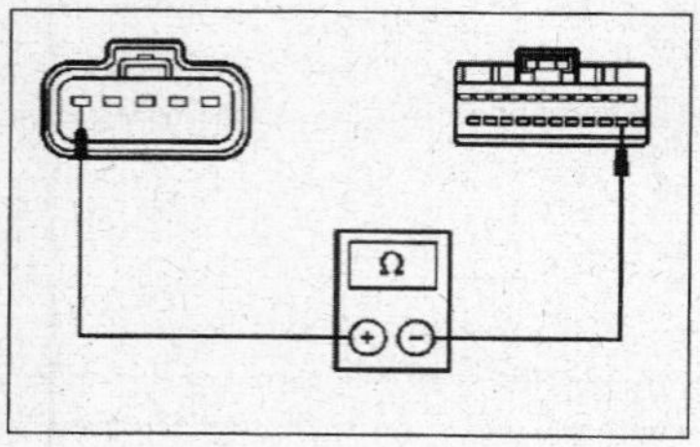

2 Measure the resistance between wiper motor (BK/YE), and FEM (BK/BU).

- **Is the resistance less than 5 ohms?**

→ **Yes**
INSTALL a new FEM.
CLEAR the DTCs.
REPEAT the self-test.

→ **No**
REPAIR the circuit(s) in question.
TEST the system for normal operation.

FM9020100899040X

Fig. 119 Test D: Wash & Wipe Function Does Not Operate Correctly (Part 4 of 4). Thunderbird

E2 ACTIVATE THE WASHER PUMP

1 Trigger the FEM active command WASH RLY to ON.

- **Did the washer pump work?**

→ **Yes**
INSTALL a new FEM.
TEST the system for normal operation.

→ **No**
GO to E3.

E3 CHECK FOR VOLTAGE AT PJB FUSE 225 (10A)

1 Remove the PJB fuse 225 (10A).

2 Measure the voltage between PJB fuse 225 (10A) input side and ground.

2

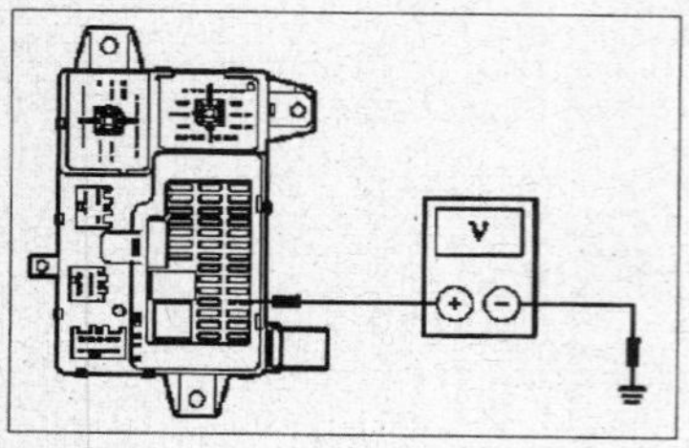

- **Is the voltage greater than 10 volts?**

→ **Yes**
GO to E4.

→ **No**
REPAIR the power source. TEST the system for normal operation.

FM9020100900020X

Fig. 120 Test E: Washer Pump Is Inoperative Or On Continuously (Part 2 of 7). Thunderbird

CONDITIONS	DETAILS/RESULTS/ACTIONS
E1 VERIFY THE WASHER PUMP SYMPTOM	

1

2

3 **NOTE:** If the wipers are also inoperative, refer to the Symptom Chart. If the wash and wipe function does not operate correctly, refer to Pinpoint Test E.

Verify if the washer pump is never ON or if the pump is always ON.

- **Is the washer pump always on?**

→ **Yes**
GO to E2.

→ **No**
GO to E8.

FM9020100900010X

Fig. 120 Test E: Washer Pump Is Inoperative Or On Continuously (Part 1 of 7). Thunderbird

E4 CHECK CIRCUITS 31-KA42A (RD/BK) AND 30–KA43 (RD/WH) FOR OPENS

1

PJB Fuse 225 (10A)

2

3

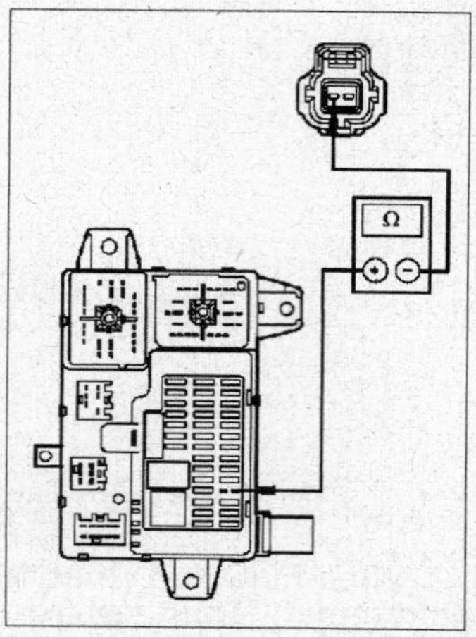

3 Measure the resistance between PJB fuse 102 (15A) output side, (WH) and washer pump motor (WH) harness side.

- **Is resistance less than 5 ohms?**

→ **Yes**
GO to E5.

→ **No**
REPAIR the circuit. TEST the system for normal operation.

FM9020100900030X

Fig. 120 Test E: Washer Pump Is Inoperative Or On Continuously (Part 3 of 7). Thunderbird

E5 CHECK CIRCUIT 31-KA7 (BK/WH) FOR VOLTAGE

1

PJB Fuse 225 (10A)

2

Wiper Motor

3

4

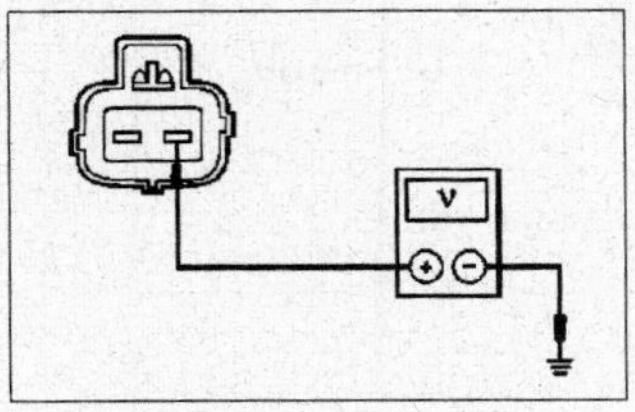

4 Measure the voltage between washer pump motor (BK/WH) harness side and ground.

- **Is voltage greater than 10 volts?**

→ **Yes**
GO to E6.

→ **No**
GO to E7.

FM9020100900040X

Fig. 120 Test E: Washer Pump Is Inoperative Or On Continuously (Part 4 of 7). Thunderbird

E6 CHECK CIRCUIT 31S-KA7 (BK/WH) FOR SHORT TO POWER

1

Washer Pump Motor

2

FEM

3

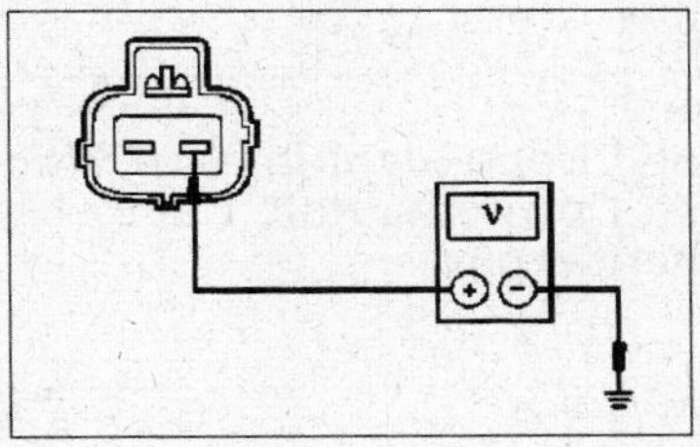

3 Measure the voltage between washer pump motor (BK/WH), harness side and ground.

- **Is the voltage greater than 10 volts?**

→ **Yes**
REPAIR the circuit. TEST the system for normal operation.

→ **No**
INSTALL a new FEM. TEST the system for normal operation.

FM9020100900050X

Fig. 120 Test E: Washer Pump Is Inoperative Or On Continuously (Part 5 of 7). Thunderbird

E7 CHECK CIRCUIT 31-KA7 (BK/WH) FOR OPENS

1

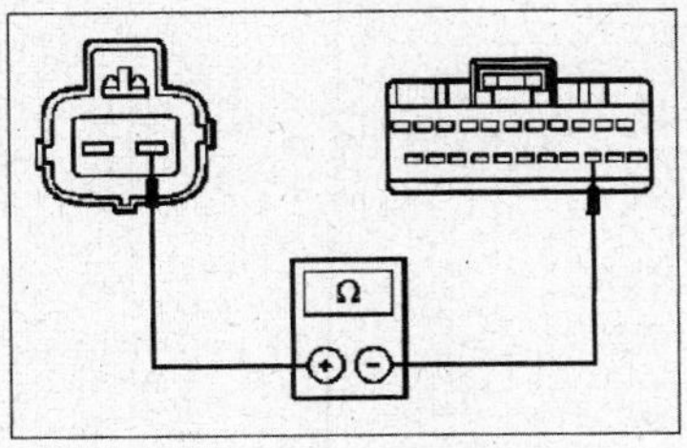

1 Measure the resistance between washer pump motor (BK/WH), harness side and FEM (BK/WH) harness side.

- **Is the resistance less than 5 ohms?**

→ **Yes**
INSTALL a new washer pump motor.

→ **No**
REPAIR the circuit. TEST the system for normal operation.

FM9020100900060X

Fig. 120 Test E: Washer Pump Is Inoperative Or On Continuously (Part 6 of 7). Thunderbird

E8 ISOLATE FEM AND CIRCUIT 31S-KA43 (BK/WH) FOR SHORTS TO GROUND

1 Verify the motor is running.

2

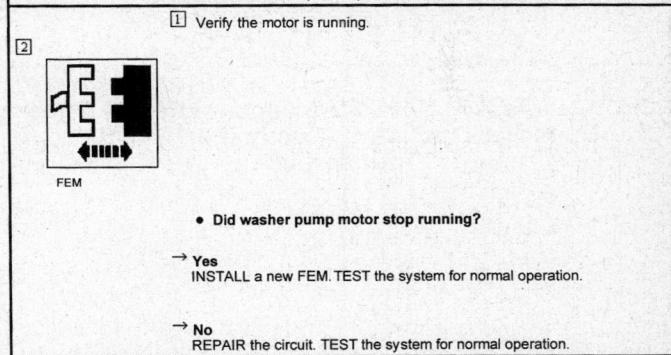

FEM

- **Did washer pump motor stop running?**

→ **Yes**
INSTALL a new FEM. TEST the system for normal operation.

→ **No**
REPAIR the circuit. TEST the system for normal operation.

FM9020100900070X

Fig. 120 Test E: Washer Pump Is Inoperative Or On Continuously (Part 7 of 7). Thunderbird

CONDITIONS	DETAILS/RESULTS/ACTIONS
F1 CHECK THE FEM PID WPMODE	
1 	2 Monitor the FEM PID WPMODE, while activating the intermittent washers through all speeds (positions) at the multifunction switch. • **Do the FEM PID WPMODE values agree with the multifunction switch position?** → **Yes** GO to F6 . → **No** GO to F2 .

FM9020100901010X

Fig. 121 Test F: Speed Dependent Interval Mode Does Not Operate Correctly (Part 1 of 9). Thunderbird

F3 CHECK CIRCUIT 8–KA19 (WH/BK) FOR VOLTAGE

1

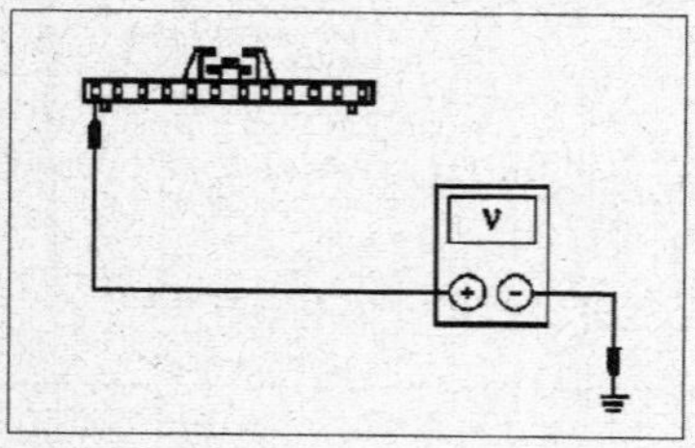

1 Measure the voltage between multifunction switch(WH/BK), harness side and ground.

- **Is the voltage greater than 10 volts?**

→ **Yes**
GO to F4 .

→ **No**
GO to F5 .

FM9020100901030X

Fig. 121 Test F: Speed Dependent Interval Mode Does Not Operate Correctly (Part 3 of 9). Thunderbird

F2 CHECK THE MULTIFUNCTION SWITCH OPERATION

1

2

Multifunction Switch

3

4 Carry out the multifunction switch component test.

- **Is the multifunction switch OK?**

→ **Yes**
GO to F3 .

→ **No**
INSTALL a new multifunction switch.
TEST the system for normal operation.

FM9020100901020X

Fig. 121 Test F: Speed Dependent Interval Mode Does Not Operate Correctly (Part 2 of 9). Thunderbird

F4 CHECK CIRCUITS 8–KA19 (WH/BK) FOR SHORT TO POWER

1

2

FEM

3

4

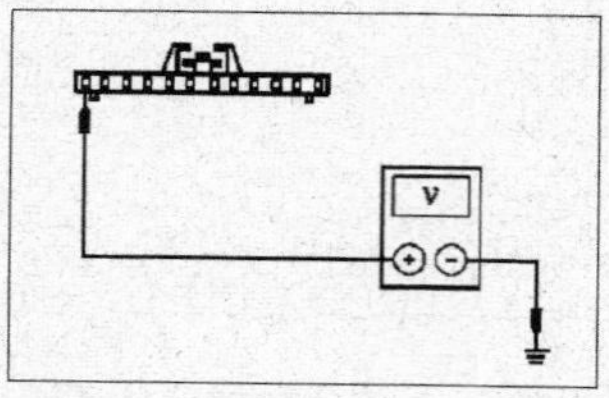

4 Measure the voltage between multifunction switch (WH/BK), harness side and ground.

- **Is the voltage greater than 10 volts?**

→ **Yes**
REPAIR the circuit(s) in question.
TEST the system for normal operation.

→ **No**
INSTALL a new FEM.
TEST the system for normal operation.

FM9020100901040X

Fig. 121 Test F: Speed Dependent Interval Mode Does Not Operate Correctly (Part 4 of 9). Thunderbird

F5 CHECK CIRCUIT 8–KA19 (WH/BK) FOR OPEN

1

2

FEM

3

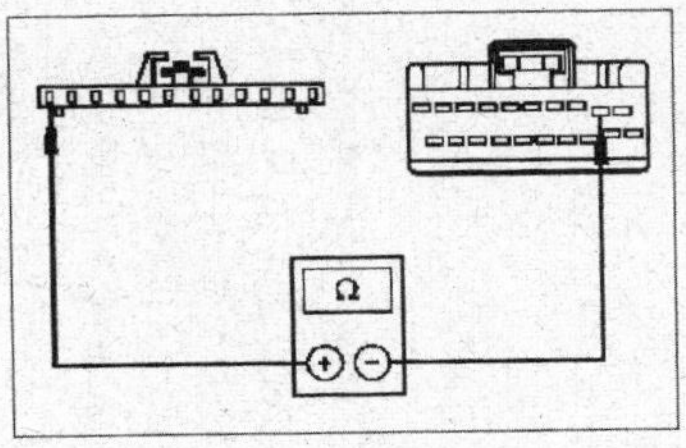

3 Measure the resistance between multifunction switch (WH/BK), harness side and (WH/BK), harness side.

- **Is the resistance less than 5 ohms?**

→ **Yes**
INSTALL a new FEM. TEST the system for normal operation.

→ **No**
REPAIR the circuit(s) in question. TEST the system for normal operation.

FM9020100901050X

Fig. 121 Test F: Speed Dependent Interval Mode Does Not Operate Correctly (Part 5 of 9). Thunderbird

F8 CHECK THE WIPER MOTOR

1

2

Wiper Motor

3

4

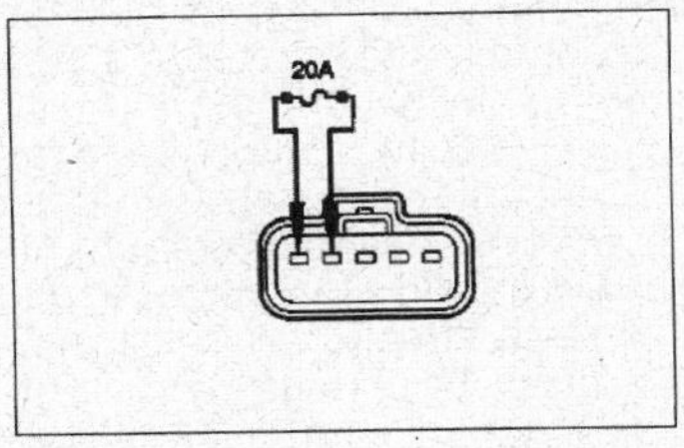

4 Monitor the FEM PID WPPRKSW while connecting a (20 A) fused jumper wire between wiper motor (BK/BU), harness side and wiper motor (RD), harness side.

- **Did the PID change from notPRK to PARKED?**

→ **Yes**
INSTALL a new wiper motor. TEST the system for normal operation.

→ **No**
GO to F9.

FM9020100901070X

Fig. 121 Test F: Speed Dependent Interval Mode Does Not Operate Correctly (Part 7 of 9). Thunderbird

F6 MONITOR THE FEM PID WPPRKSW

1

2 Trigger the FEM active command WIPER RLY ON and OFF while monitoring the FEM PID WPPRKSW.

- **Did the PID change from PARKED to notPRK?**

→ **Yes**
INSTALL a new FEM. TEST the system for normal operation.

→ **No**
GO to F7.

F7 CHECK WIPER RUN/PARK RELAY

1 Remove the FPDB wiper run/park relay.

2 Carry out the relay component test.

Refer to Wiring Diagrams Cell 149 for schematic and connector information.

- **Is the wiper run/park relay OK?**

→ **Yes**
GO to F8.

→ **No**
INSTALL a new wiper run/park relay. TEST the system for normal operation.

FM9020100901060X

Fig. 121 Test F: Speed Dependent Interval Mode Does Not Operate Correctly (Part 6 of 9). Thunderbird

F9 CHECK CIRCUITS 31S-KA1 (BK/BU) AND 31S-KA12 (BK/WH) FOR OPENS

1

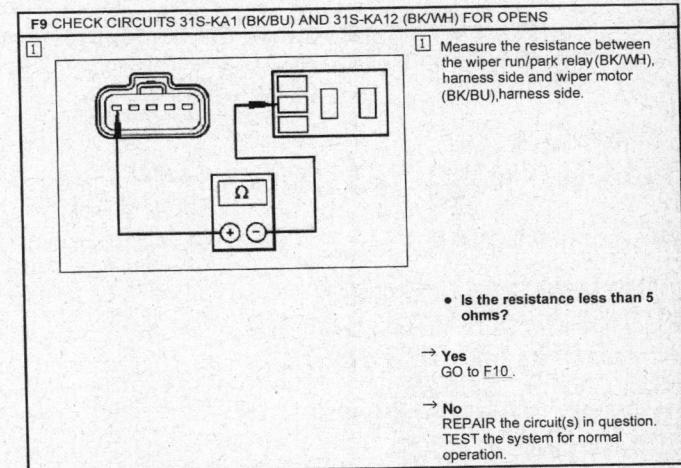

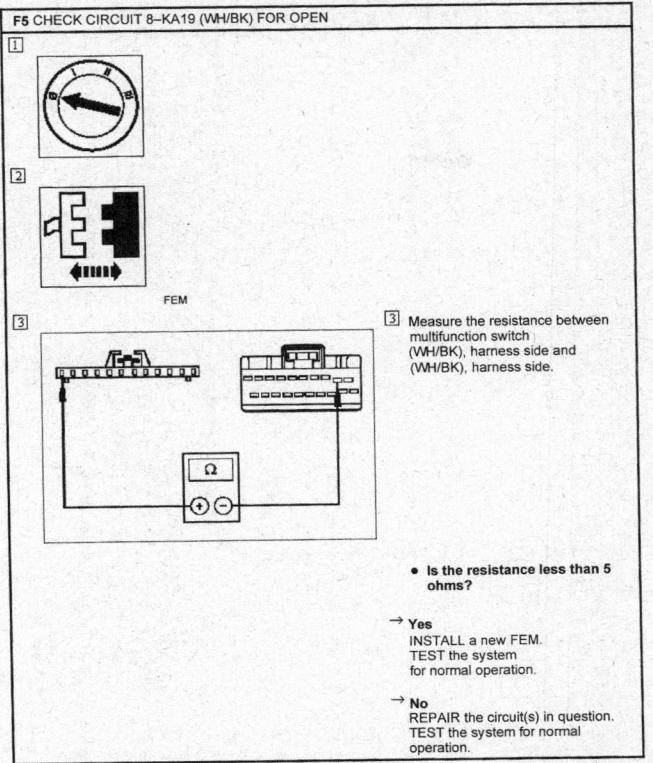

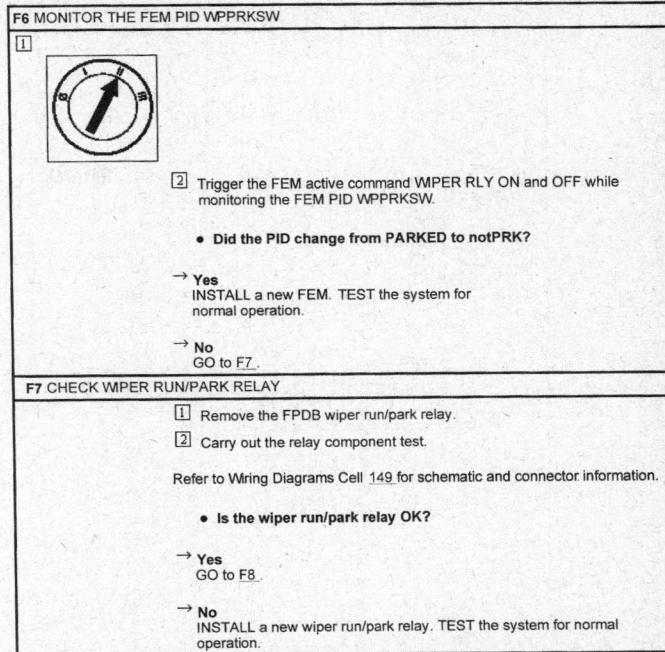

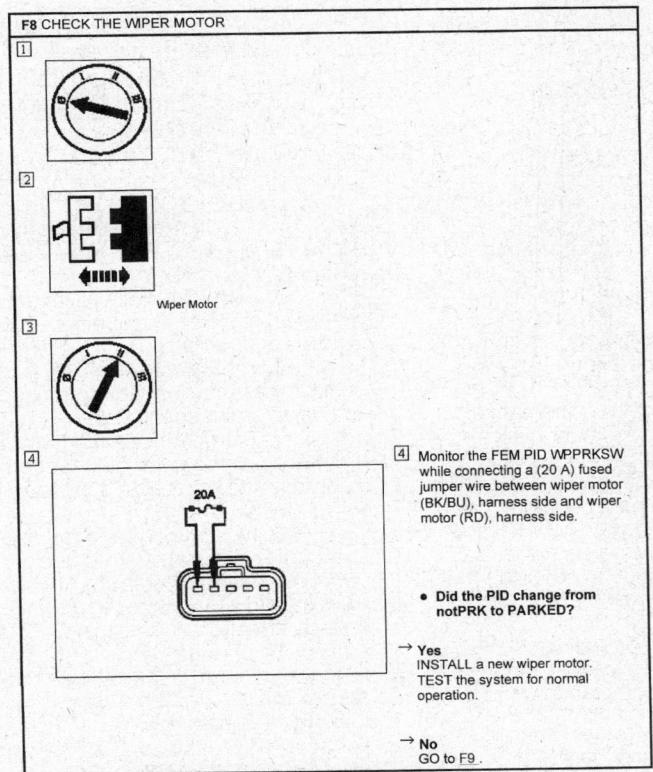

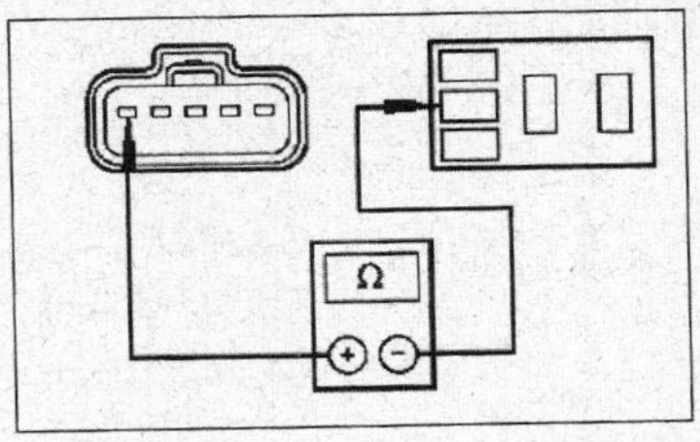

1 Measure the resistance between the wiper run/park relay (BK/WH), harness side and wiper motor (BK/BU), harness side.

- **Is the resistance less than 5 ohms?**

→ **Yes**
GO to F10.

→ **No**
REPAIR the circuit(s) in question. TEST the system for normal operation.

FM9020100901080X

Fig. 121 Test F: Speed Dependent Interval Mode Does Not Operate Correctly (Part 8 of 9). Thunderbird

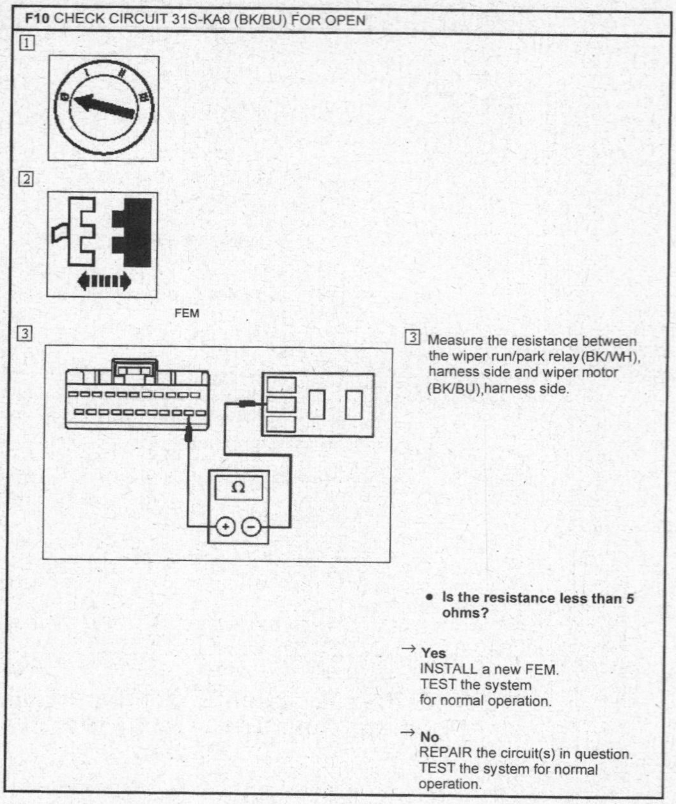

FM9020100901090X

Fig. 121 Test F: Speed Dependent Interval Mode Does Not Operate Correctly (Part 9 of 9). Thunderbird

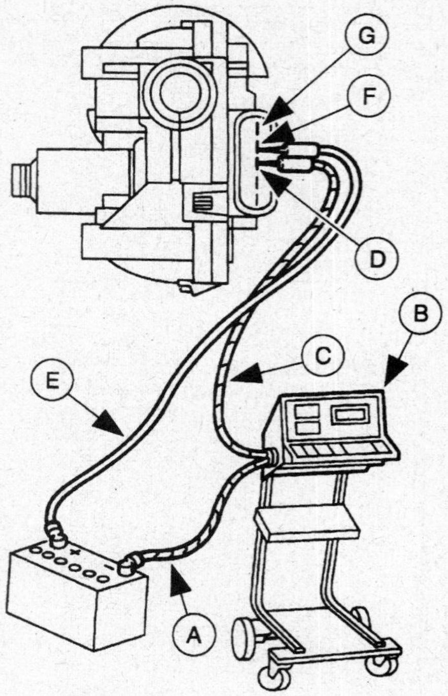

A- Green lead
B- ARBST tester
C- Red lead
D- Wiper motor common brush pin
E- Jumper cable
F- Low speed brush pin
G- High speed brush pin

FM9020100902000X

Fig. 122 Wiper motor test connections. Continental, Crown Victoria, Escort, Grand Marquis, LS, Marauder, Mustang, Sable, Taurus, Thunderbird, Town Car & ZX2

COMPONENT DIAGNOSIS & TESTING

Wiper Motor

CONTINENTAL, CROWN VICTORIA, ESCORT, GRAND MARQUIS, LS, MARAUDER, MUSTANG, SABLE, TAURUS, THUNDERBIRD, TOWN CAR & ZX2

Refer to **Fig. 122,** when performing the following test procedure:

1. Disconnect windshield wiper mounting arm and pivot shaft from wiper motor.
2. Disconnect wiper motor electrical connector.
3. Install green lead from ARBST Tester, or equivalent, to battery ground post.
4. Install red lead from tester to wiper motor common brush pin.
5. Test low speed mode by connecting cable from battery positive post to low speed brush pin, then measure current draw.
6. If current draw is greater than 3.5 amps, replace wiper motor.
7. Test high speed mode by connecting cable from battery ground post to high speed brush pin component side, then measure current draw.
8. If current draw is greater than 5.5 amps, replace wiper motor.

CONTOUR, MYSTIQUE & COUGAR

1. Turn ignition switch to Off position and disconnect motor connector.
2. Connect battery positive terminal to suitable ammeter positive terminal and ground terminal to wiper motor housing.
3. Connect ammeter negative terminal to connector pin No. 6, **Fig. 123.** As motor operates at fast speed, current reading should not be more than 4 amps.
4. Connect ammeter negative terminal to connector pin No. 5. As motor operates at slow speed, current reading should not be more than 2 amps.
5. Ensure motor is not in park position.
6. Measure resistance between connector pin Nos. 2 and 3. If resistance is less than 5 ohms, proceed to next step. If resistance is more than 5 ohms, replace motor.
7. Measure resistance between connector pin Nos. 2 and 4. If resistance is more than 5 ohms, replace wiper motor.

FOCUS

MOTOR

1. Disconnect electrical connector from wiper motor.
2. Remove wiper motor.
3. Connect negative terminal of suitable ammeter to pin No. 1 of windshield wiper motor, **Fig. 124.**
4. Connect 12 volts DC voltage supply negative to pin No. 3 of windshield wiper motor.
5. Connect voltage supply positive lead to positive terminal on ammeter and switch on voltage supply.
6. Read current on meter with windshield wiper motor running at high speed. Current reading should be approximately 3 amps.
7. Switch off voltage supply and disconnect negative terminal of ammeter.
8. Connect negative ammeter to pin No. 2 of windshield wiper motor and switch on voltage supply.
9. Read current on meter as motor runs at slow speed. Current reading should be approximately 2 amps.
10. Switch off voltage supply.

MOTOR LIMIT SWITCH

1. Ensure wiper motor is not at the Rest position.
2. Connect voltage supply positive to pin No. 2 and voltage supply negative to

Apply 12 Volts	Apply Ground	Result
2 and 5	1 and 4	LO wiper operation
2 and 6	1 and 4	HI wiper operation

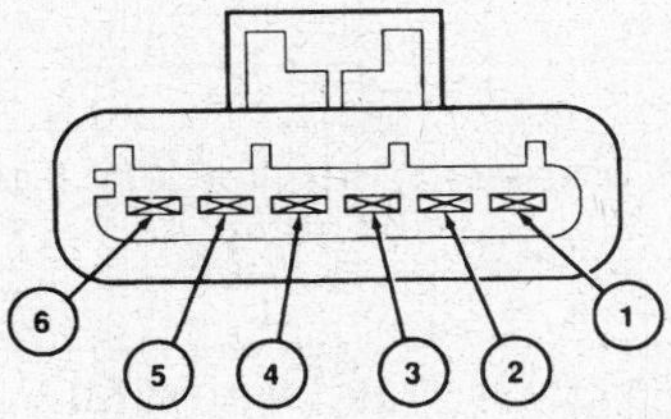

FM9029500595000X

Fig. 123 Wiper motor connector. Contour, Mystique & Cougar

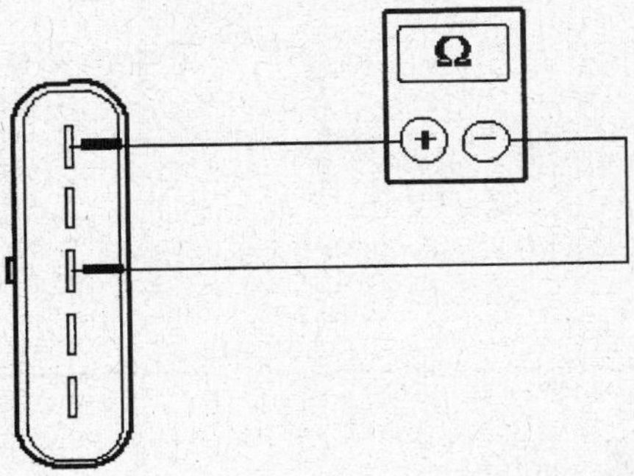

FM9020100806000X

Fig. 126 Wiper motor resistance test. Focus

pin No. 5 of windshield wiper motor.

3. With jumper cable, connect pin No. 3 and No. 4, **Fig. 125.**
4. Motor should run and stop at the Rest position.
5. If motor did not perform as specified, replace wiper motor.
6. Measure resistance between pin No. 5 and pin No. 3 of wiper motor, **Fig. 126.**
7. If resistance is not less than 1 ohm, replace wiper motor.

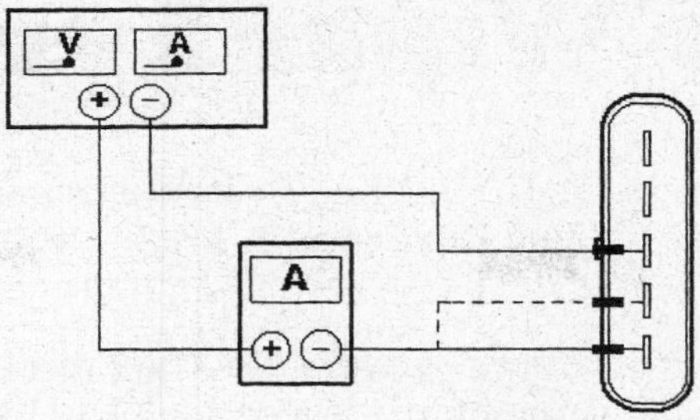

FM9020100804000X

Fig. 124 Wiper motor test. Focus

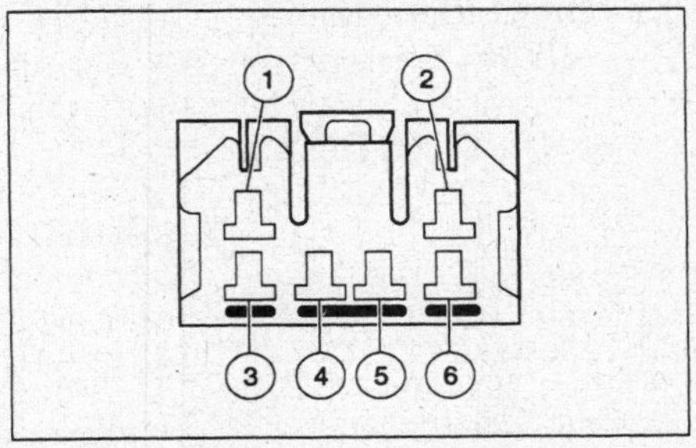

Pin Number	Circuit	Circuit Function
1	51U (BK)	Ground
2	234 (BL/O)	Windshield Washer Pump
3	230 (BL)	Power Supply
4	231 (BL/Y)	Windshield Wiper Motor Intermittent Output
5	233 (R)	Windshield Wiper Motor High Speed Output
6	232 (BL/W)	Windshield Wiper Motor Low Speed Output

FM9029700494010X

Fig. 127 Wiper/washer switch connector test (Part 1 of 2). Escort & ZX2

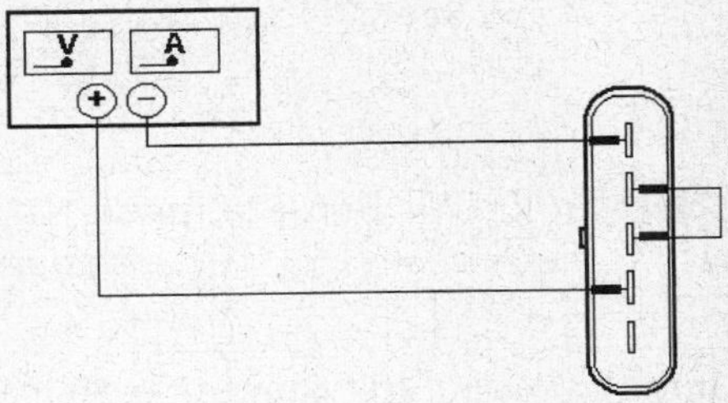

FM9020100805000X

Fig. 125 Wiper motor limiter switch test. Focus

Switch Position	Pin	Resistance
1	6	Less than 5 ohms
2	5	Less than 5 ohms
MIST	5	Less than 5 ohms
Wash (PULL)	2	Less than 5 ohms

FM9029700494020X

Fig. 127 Wiper/washer switch connector test (Part 2 of 2). Escort & ZX2

Wiper Switch

For models not covered here, refer to individual models listed in "Pinpoint Tests."

ESCORT & ZX2

Refer to **Fig. 127,** and test windshield wiper/washer switch using a suitable ohmmeter.

Rear Wiper System

NOTE: On Air Bag Equipped Models, Refer To "Air Bag System Precautions" Located In The Front Of This Manual For System Disarming & Arming Procedures.

NOTE: Refer To "Computer Relearn Procedures" Located In The Front Of This Manual When Battery Power To The Computer Has Been Interrupted.

NOTE: "Electrical Symbol & Wire Color Code Identification" Located In The Front Of This Manual May Be Used As An Aid When Using Wiring Circuits Found In This Section.

INDEX

PRECAUTIONS

Air Bag Systems

Refer to "Air Bag System Precautions" in front of this manual for system disarming and arming procedures.

Battery Ground Cable

Prior to service, disconnect battery ground cable and isolate as required.

SYSTEM DIAGNOSIS & TESTING

Wiring Diagrams

Refer to **Figs. 1 through 3,** for rear wiper/washer system wiring diagrams.

Diagnostic Procedure

Refer to "System Diagnosis & Testing" in "Front Wiper System" for rear wiper diagnostic procedure.

Pinpoint Tests

Pinpoint tests are used to locate specific system faults to be serviced. Refer to the "Diagnostic Chart Index" and system wiring diagrams when performing diagnosis.

ESCORT

Refer to **Figs. 4 through 6,** for pinpoint tests.

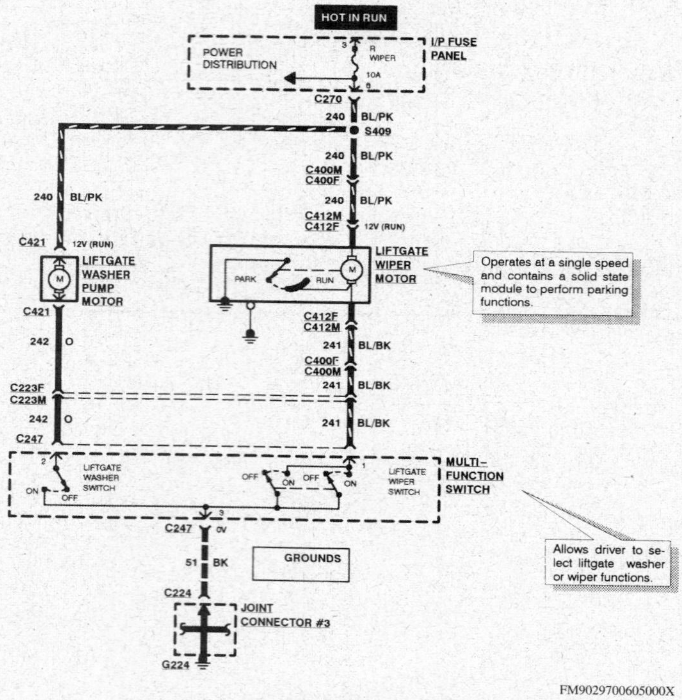

Fig. 1 Wiring diagram. Escort

FOCUS

Refer to **Figs. 7 and 8,** for pinpoint tests.

SABLE & TAURUS

Refer to **Figs. 9 through 12,** for pinpoint tests.

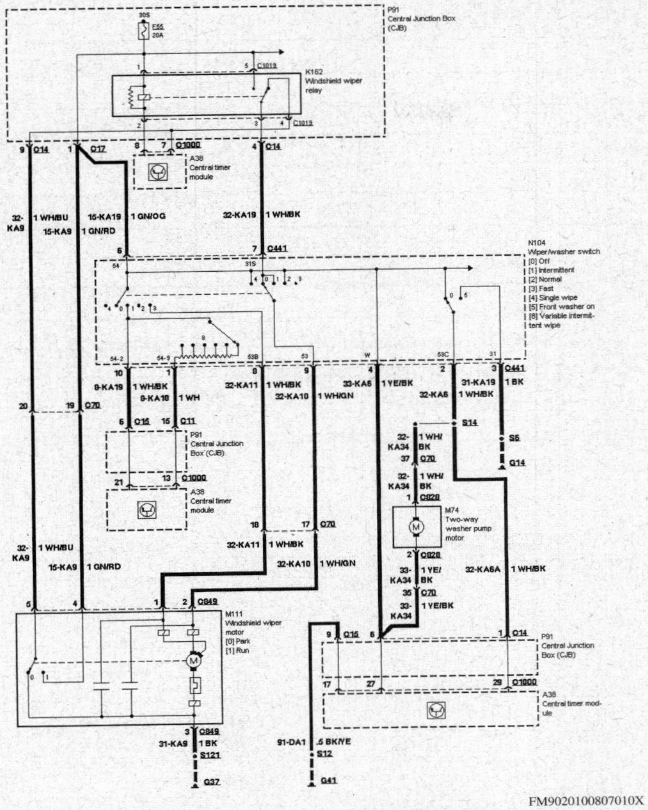

Fig. 2 Wiring diagram (Part 1 of 2). Focus

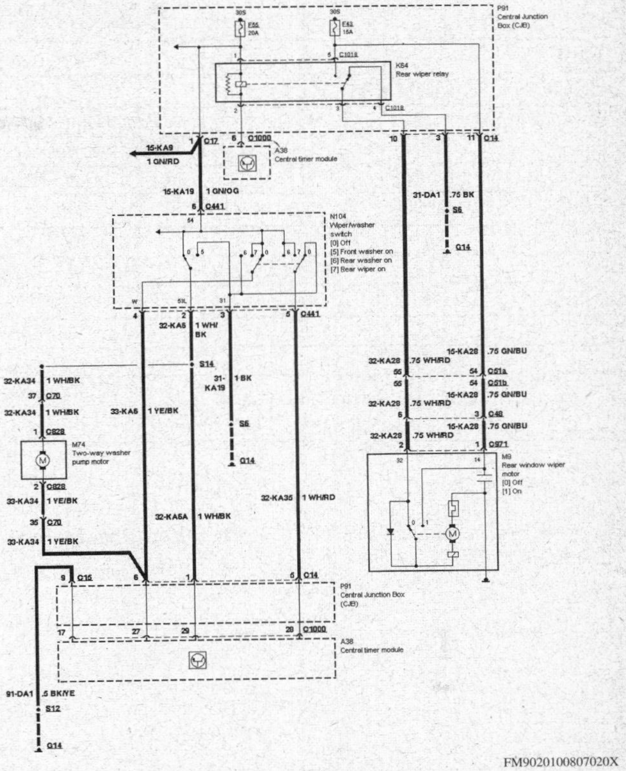

Fig. 2 Wiring diagram (Part 2 of 2). Focus

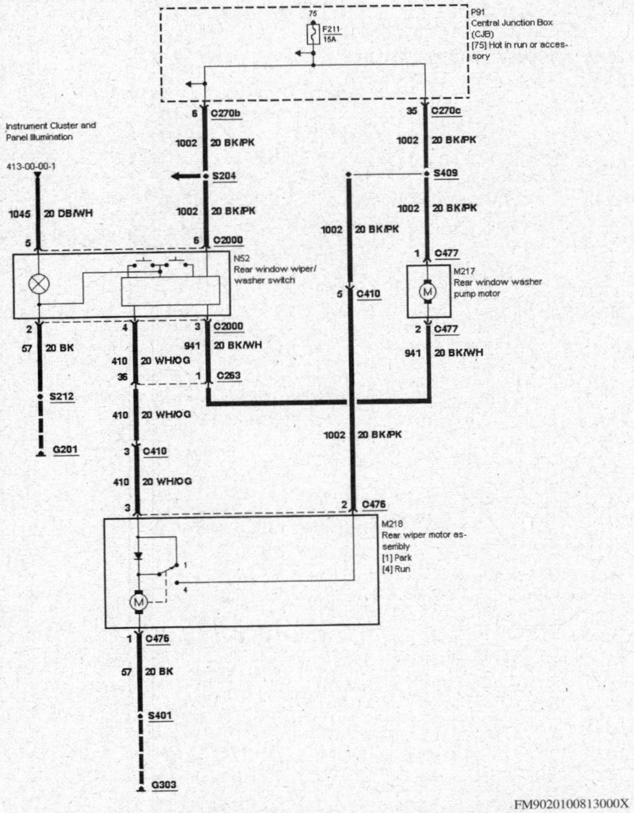

Fig. 3 Wiring diagram. Sable & Taurus

DIAGNOSTIC CHART INDEX

Test	Description	Page No.	Fig. No.
ESCORT & TRACER			
F	Rear Window Wiper Inoperative	3-120	4
G	Rear Window Washer Inoperative	3-121	5
H	Rear Window Wiper Will Not Turn Off	3-121	6
FOCUS			
E	Rear Wiper Is On Continuously	3-122	7
F	After Switching Off, Rear Wiper Doers Not Return To Park Position	3-122	8
SABLE & TAURUS			
F	Rear Wipers Are Inoperative	3-122	9
G	Rear Wipers Stay On Continuously	3-123	10
H	Rear Washer Pump Is Inoperative	3-123	11
I	Rear Washer Pump Stays On Continuously	3-124	12

TEST CONDITIONS	TEST DETAILS/RESULTS/ACTIONS
F1 CHECK FUSE	
1 	• Is the fuse OK? → **Yes** REINSTALL 10A REAR WIPER fuse. GO to **F4**. → **No** GO to **F2**.
F2 REPLACE FUSE AND RETEST SYSTEM	
	1 Replace 10A REAR WIPER fuse.

FM9029700489010X

Fig. 4 Test F: Rear Window Wiper Inoperative (Part 1 of 4). Escort

TEST CONDITIONS	TEST DETAILS/RESULTS/ACTIONS
F2 REPLACE FUSE AND RETEST SYSTEM (Continued)	
2 	• Does the fuse blow? → **Yes** REMOVE the 10A REAR WIPER fuse. GO to **F3**. → **No** GO to **F4**.
F3 CHECK FOR SHORT TO GROUND	
1 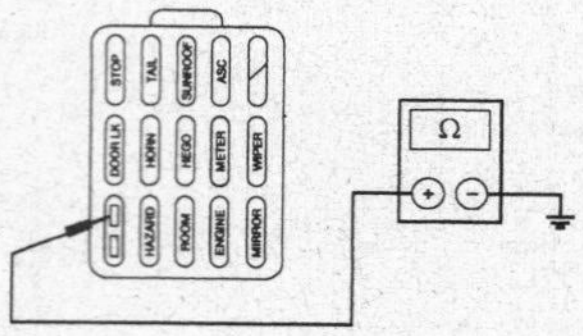	1 Measure the resistance between the 10A REAR WIPER fuse top terminal and ground. • Is the resistance less than 5 ohms? → **Yes** REPAIR circuit 240 (BL/P) and/or 240F (BL/P). → **No** REINSTALL 10A REAR WIPER fuse. GO to **F4**.

FM9029700489020X

Fig. 4 Test F: Rear Window Wiper Inoperative (Part 2 of 4). Escort

TEST CONDITIONS	TEST DETAILS/RESULTS/ACTIONS
F4 CHECK POWER SUPPLY AT THE REAR WINDOW WIPER MOTOR	
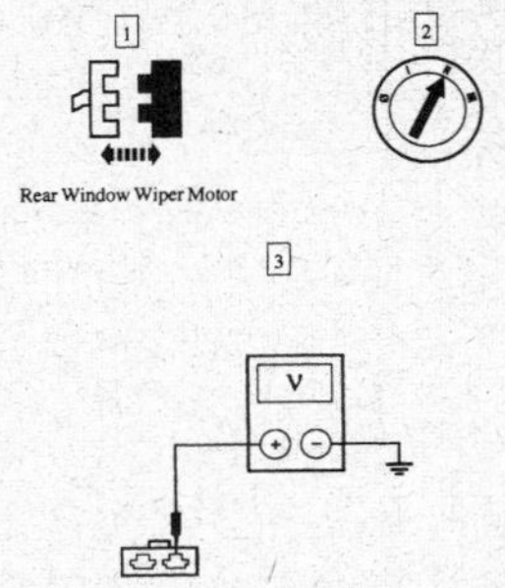	3 Measure the voltage between the rear window wiper motor connector pin 2, circuit 240 (BL/P), and ground. • Is the voltage greater than 10 volts? → **Yes** GO to **F5**. → **No** REPAIR circuit(s) 240 (BL/P).
F5 CHECK REAR WINDOW WIPER MOTOR GROUND	
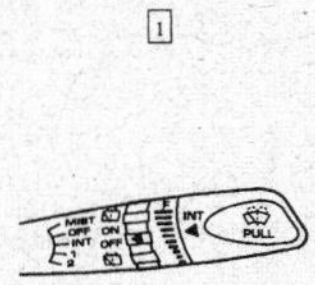	1 Rotate the rear window wiper switch to ON.

FM9029700489030X

Fig. 4 Test F: Rear Window Wiper Inoperative (Part 3 of 4). Escort

TEST CONDITIONS	TEST DETAILS/RESULTS/ACTIONS
F5 CHECK REAR WINDOW WIPER MOTOR GROUND (Continued)	
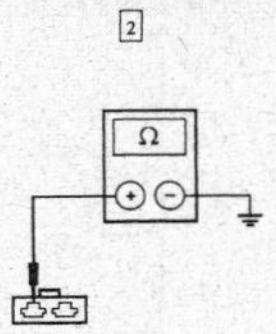	2 Measure the resistance between the rear window wiper motor connector pin 1, circuit 241 (BL/BK), and ground. • Is the resistance less than 5 ohms? → **Yes** REPLACE the rear window wiper motor. → **No** GO to **F6**.
F6 CHECK REAR WINDOW WIPER/WASHER SWITCH	
	1 **NOTE:** The rear window wiper/washer switch is part of the windshield wiper/washer switch. Perform the rear window wiper/washer switch component test in this section. • Is the switch OK? → **Yes** GO to **F7**. → **No** REPLACE the windshield wiper/washer switch.
F7 CHECK REAR WINDOW WIPER/WASHER SWITCH GROUND	
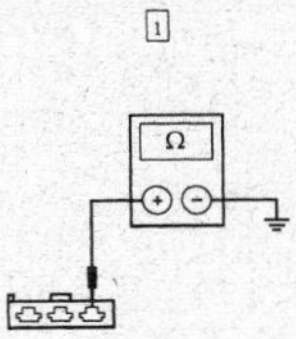	1 Measure the resistance between the rear window wiper/washer switch connector pin 3, circuit 51S (BK), and ground. • Is the resistance less than 5 ohms? → **Yes** REPAIR circuit 241 (BL/BK). → **No** REPAIR the open in circuit 51S (BK).

FM9029700489040X

Fig. 4 Test F: Rear Window Wiper Inoperative (Part 4 of 4). Escort

TEST CONDITIONS	TEST DETAILS/RESULTS/ACTIONS
G1 CHECK POWER SUPPLY TO REAR WINDOW WASHER PUMP	
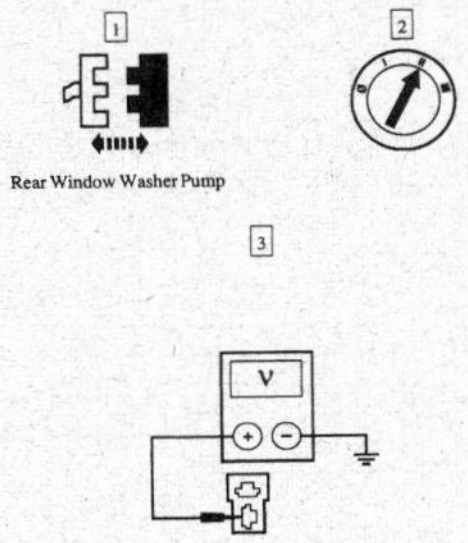	3 Measure the voltage between the rear window washer pump connector pin 1, circuit 240F (BL/P), and ground. • Is the voltage than 10 volts? → **Yes** GO to **G2**. → **No** REPAIR the open in circuit 240F (BL/P).
G2 CHECK REAR WINDOW WASHER PUMP GROUND	
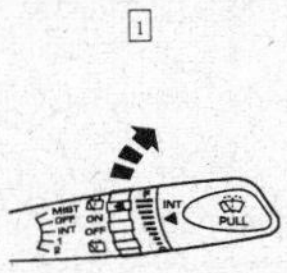	1 Rotate the rear window wiper/washer switch to the wash position.

FM9029700490010X

Fig. 5 Test G: Rear Window Washer Inoperative (Part 1 of 2). Escort

TEST CONDITIONS	TEST DETAILS/RESULTS/ACTIONS
G2 CHECK REAR WINDOW WASHER PUMP GROUND (Continued)	
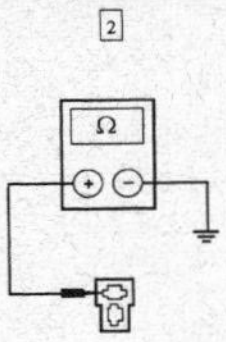	2 Measure the resistance between the rear window washer pump connector pin 2, circuit 242 (O), and ground. • Is the resistance less than 5 ohms? → **Yes** REPLACE the rear window washer pump. → **No** GO to **G3**.
G3 CHECK REAR WINDOW WIPER/WASHER SWITCH	
	1 Perform the rear window wiper/washer switch component test in this section. • Is the switch OK? → **Yes** REPAIR circuit 242 (O). → **No** REPLACE the windshield wiper/washer switch.

FM9029700490020X

Fig. 5 Test G: Rear Window Washer Inoperative (Part 2 of 2). Escort

TEST CONDITIONS	TEST DETAILS/RESULTS/ACTIONS
H1 CHECK REAR WINDOW WIPER MOTOR	
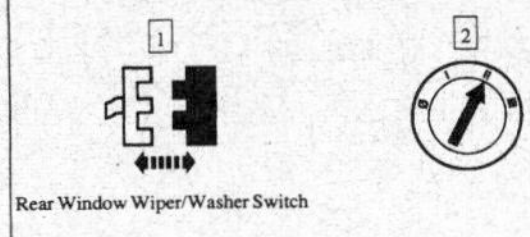	• Does the rear window wiper motor turn off? → **Yes** REPLACE the windshield wiper/washer switch. → **No** GO to **H2**.

FM9029700491010X

Fig. 6 Test H: Rear Window Wiper Will Not Turn Off (Part 1 of 2). Escort

TEST CONDITIONS	TEST DETAILS/RESULTS/ACTIONS
H2 CHECK CIRCUIT	
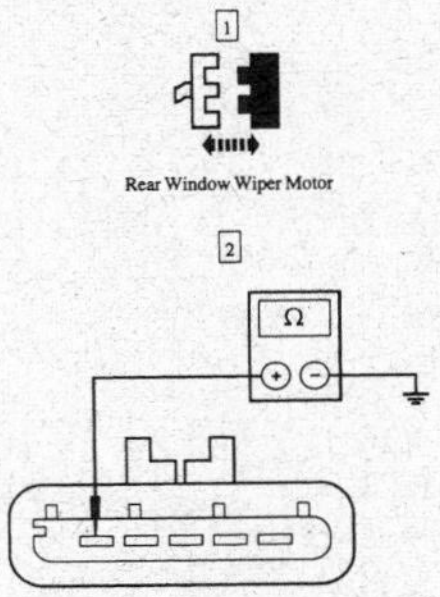	2 Measure the resistance between the rear window wiper motor connector pin 1, circuit 241 (BL/BK) and ground. • Is the resistance greater than 10,000 ohms? → **Yes** REPLACE the rear window wiper motor. → **No** REPAIR circuit 241 (BL/BK).

FM9029700491020X

Fig. 6 Test H: Rear Window Wiper Will Not Turn Off (Part 2 of 2). Escort

CONDITIONS	DETAILS/RESULTS/ACTIONS
E1: CHECK REAR WIPER MOTOR RELAY	
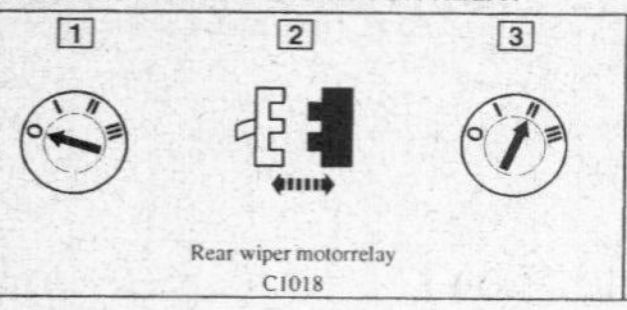	• Does the rear wiper operate? → Yes Check the rear wiper motor according to the component tests in this section. If necessary, INSTALL a new rear wiper motor. TEST the system for normal operation. → No GO TO **E2**

FM9020100808010X

Fig. 7 Test E: Rear Wiper Is On Continuously (Part 1 of 2). Focus

CONDITIONS	DETAILS/RESULTS/ACTIONS
F1: RULE OUT MECHANICAL FAULT	
	1 Check rear wiper adjustment. • Does the rear wiper arm always stop at the same place after the rear wiper is turned off? → Yes Align the wiper arms → No GO TO **F2**

FM9020100809010X

Fig. 8 After Switching Off Rear Wiper Does Not Return To Park (Part 1 of 2). Focus

CONDITIONS	DETAILS/RESULTS/ACTIONS
F2: CHECK VOLTAGE SUPPLY AT REAR WIPER MOTOR	
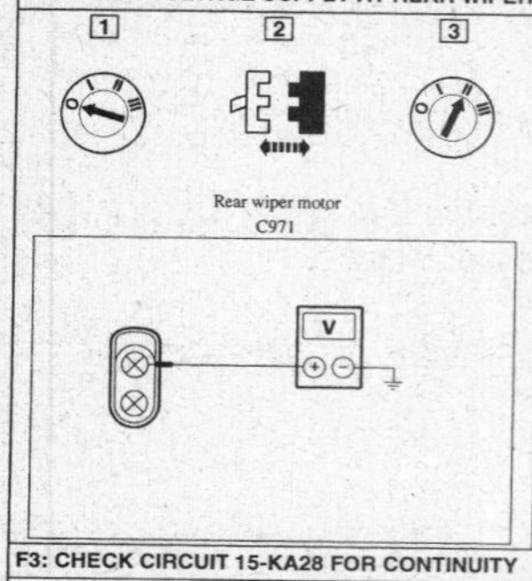	4 Measure the voltage between rear wiper motor, connector C971, pin 1, circuit 15-KA28 (GN/BU), harness side and ground. • Is the voltage greater than 10 volts? → Yes CHECK the rear wiper motor according to the components tests in this section. If necessary, INSTALL a new rear wiper motor. TEST the system for normal operation. → No GO TO **F3**
F3: CHECK CIRCUIT 15-KA28 FOR CONTINUITY	
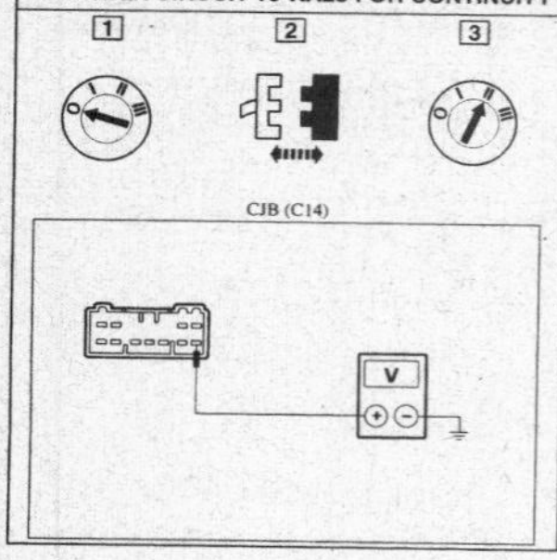	4 Measure the voltage between CJB, connector C14, pin 11, component side and ground. • Is the voltage greater than 10 volts? → Yes REPAIR circuit 15-KA28. TEST the system for normal operation. → No INSTALL a new CJB. TEST the system for normal operation.

FM9020100809020X

Fig. 8 After Switching Off Rear Wiper Does Not Return To Park (Part 2 of 2). Focus

TEST CONDITIONS	TEST DETAILS/RESULTS/ACTIONS
F1 CHECK THE REAR WASHER OPERATION	
	2 Press rear washer switch to verify rear washer operation. • Does the rear washer operate? → **Yes** GO to **F5**. → **No** GO to **F2**.
F2 CHECK CENTRAL JUNCTION BOX (CJB)FUSE 211 (15A)	
	1 Remove CJB Fuse 211 (15A).

FM9020100814010X

Fig. 9 Test F: Rear Wipers Inoperative (Part 1 of 5). Sable & Taurus

CONDITIONS	DETAILS/RESULTS/ACTIONS
E2: CHECK REAR WIPER RELAY	
	1 Check the rear windshield wiper relay according to the components tests in this section. • Is the relay OK? → Yes GO TO **E3** → No INSTALL a new rear wiper relay. TEST the system for normal operation.
E3: CHECK CJB FOR SHORT TO GROUND	
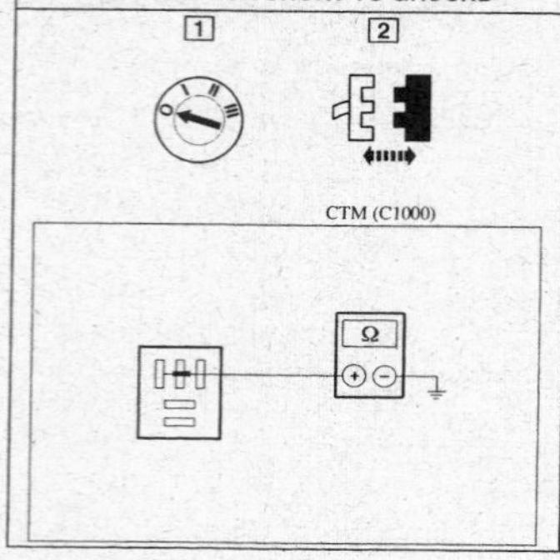	3 Measure the resistance between CJB, rear wiper motor relay, connector C1018, pin 2, component side and ground. • Is the resistance greater than 10,000 ohms? → Yes INSTALL a new CTM. TEST the system for normal operation. → No INSTALL a new CJB. TEST the system for normal operation.

FM9020100808020X

Fig. 7 Test E: Rear Wiper Is On Continuously (Part 2 of 2). Focus

TEST CONDITIONS	TEST DETAILS/RESULTS/ACTIONS
F2 CHECK CENTRAL JUNCTION BOX (CJB)FUSE 211 (15A) (Continued)	
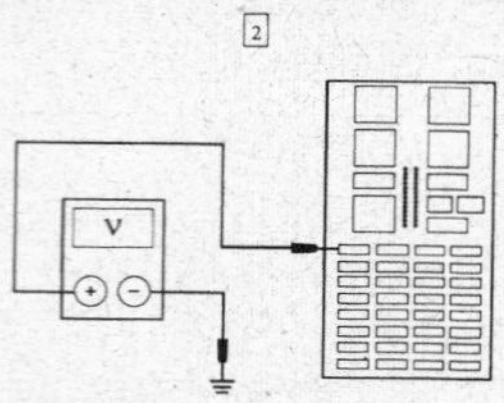	2 Measure the voltage between CJB Fuse 211 (15A) input terminal and ground. • Is the voltage greater than 10 volts? → **Yes** GO to **F3**. → **No** REPAIR the CJB as necessary. TEST the system for normal operation.
F3 CHECK CIRCUIT 1002 (BK/PK) FOR VOLTAGE	
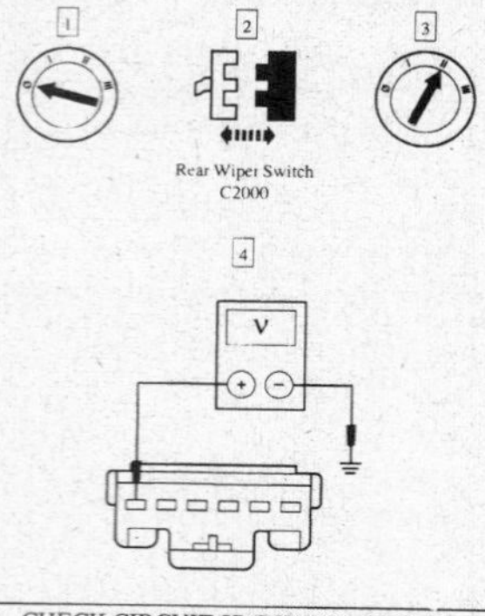	4 Measure the voltage between rear wiper switch C2000 pin 6, circuit 1002 (BK/PK), harness side and ground. • Is the voltage greater than 10 volts? → **Yes** GO to **F4**. → **No** REPAIR the circuit. TEST the system for normal operation.
F4 CHECK CIRCUIT 57 (BK) FOR OPEN	

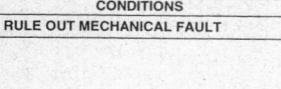

FM9020100814020X

Fig. 9 Test F: Rear Wipers Inoperative (Part 2 of 5). Sable & Taurus

TEST CONDITIONS	TEST DETAILS/RESULTS/ACTIONS
F4 CHECK CIRCUIT 57 (BK) FOR OPEN (Continued)	
2 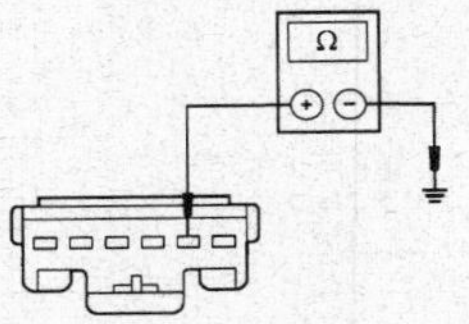	2 Measure the resistance between rear wiper switch C2000 pin 2, circuit 57 (BK), harness side and ground. • Is the resistance less than 5 ohms? → **Yes** INSTALL a new rear wiper switch. TEST the system for normal operation. → **No** REPAIR the circuit. TEST the system for normal operation.
F5 CHECK CIRCUIT 410 (WH/OG) FOR VOLTAGE	
1 2 3  Rear Wiper Motor C476	4 Actuate the rear wiper switch to the ON position.
5 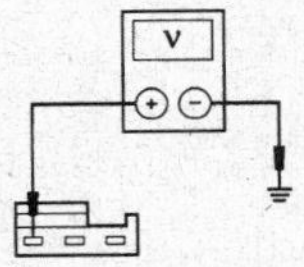	5 Measure the voltage between rear wiper motor C476 pin 3, circuit 410 (WH/OG), harness side and ground. • Is the voltage greater than 10 volts? → **Yes** GO to **F7**. → **No** GO to **F6**.
F6 CHECK CIRCUIT 410 (WH/OG) FOR OPEN	
1 2  Rear Wiper Switch C2000	

FM9020100814030X

Fig. 9 Test F: Rear Wipers Inoperative (Part 3 of 5). Sable & Taurus

TEST CONDITIONS	TEST DETAILS/RESULTS/ACTIONS
F9 CHECK CIRCUIT 1002 (BK/PK) FOR VOLTAGE	
1 	
2 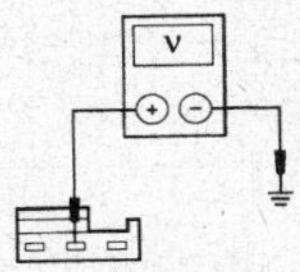	2 Measure the voltage between rear wiper motor C476 pin 2, circuit 1002 (BK/PK), harness side and ground. • Is the voltage greater than 10 volts? → **Yes** INSTALL a new rear window wiper motor. → **No** REPAIR the circuit. TEST the system for normal operation.

FM9020100814050X

Fig. 9 Test F: Rear Wipers Inoperative (Part 5 of 5). Sable & Taurus

TEST CONDITIONS	TEST DETAILS/RESULTS/ACTIONS
G2 CHECK CIRCUIT 410 (WH/OG) FOR SHORT TO VOLTAGE (Continued)	
4 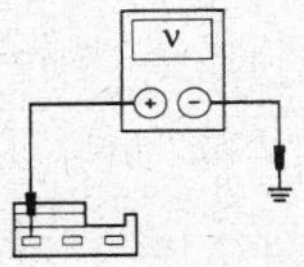	4 Measure the voltage between the rear wiper motor C476 pin 3, circuit 410 (WH/OG), harness side and ground. • Is any voltage indicated? → **Yes** REPAIR the circuit. TEST the system for normal operation. → **No** INSTALL a new rear window wiper motor.

FM9020100815020X

Fig. 10 Test G: Rear Wiper Stays On Continuously (Part 2 of 2). Sable & Taurus

TEST CONDITIONS	TEST DETAILS/RESULTS/ACTIONS
F6 CHECK CIRCUIT 410 (WH/OG) FOR OPEN (Continued)	
3 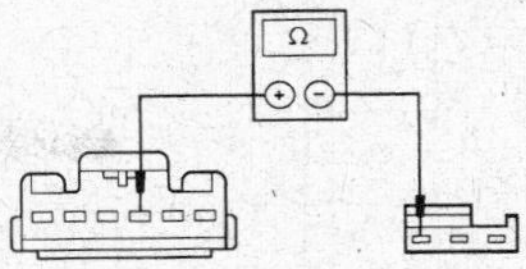	3 Measure the resistance between rear wiper switch C2000 pin 4, circuit 410 (WH/OG), harness side and rear wiper motor C476 pin 3, circuit 410 (WH/OG), harness side. • Is the resistance less than 5 ohms? → **Yes** GO to **F7**. → **No** REPAIR the circuit. TEST the system for normal operation.
F7 CHECK CIRCUIT 410 (WH/OG) FOR SHORT TO GROUND	
1 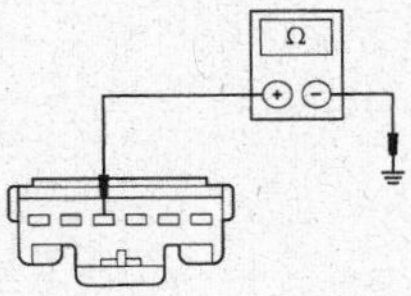	1 Measure the resistance between rear wiper switch C2000 pin 4, circuit 410 (WH/OG), harness side and ground. • Is the resistance greater than 10,000 ohms? → **Yes** GO to **F8**. → **No** REPAIR the circuit. TEST the system for normal operation.
F8 CHECK CIRCUIT 57 (BK) FOR OPEN	
1 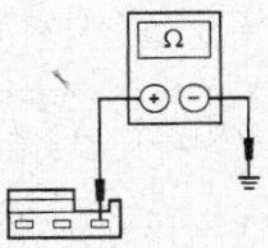	1 Measure the resistance between rear wiper motor C476 pin 1, circuit 57 (BK), harness side and ground. • Is the resistance less than 5 ohms? → **Yes** GO to **F9**. → **No** REPAIR the circuit. TEST the system for normal operation.

FM9020100814040X

Fig. 9 Test F: Rear Wipers Inoperative (Part 4 of 5). Sable & Taurus

TEST CONDITIONS	TEST DETAILS/RESULTS/ACTIONS
G1 CHECK THE REAR WIPER/WASHER SWITCH	
1 2 3  Rear Washer Switch C2000	• Does the rear wiper motor continue to run? → **Yes** GO to **G2**. → **No** INSTALL a new rear wiper/washer switch. TEST the system for normal operation.
G2 CHECK CIRCUIT 410 (WH/OG) FOR SHORT TO VOLTAGE	
1 2 3 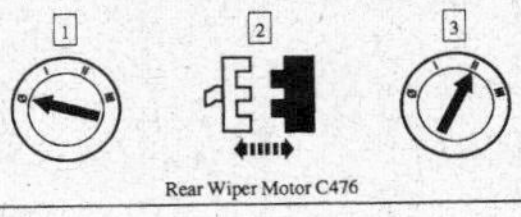 Rear Wiper Motor C476	

FM9020100815010X

Fig. 10 Test G: Rear Wiper Stays On Continuously (Part 1 of 2). Sable & Taurus

TEST CONDITIONS	TEST DETAILS/RESULTS/ACTIONS
H1 CHECK CIRCUIT 1002 (BK/PK) FOR VOLTAGE	
1 2 3  Rear Washer Pump C477	
4 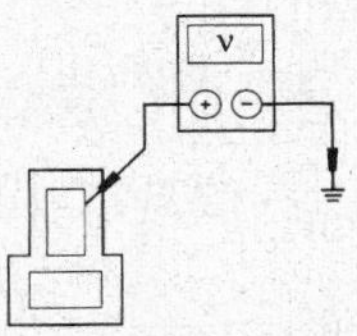	4 Measure the voltage between rear washer pump C477 pin 1, circuit 1002 (BK/PK), harness side and ground. • Is the voltage greater than 10 volts? → **Yes** GO to **H2**. → **No** REPAIR the circuit. TEST the system for normal operation.

FM9020100816010X

Fig. 11 Test H: Rear Washer Pump Is Inoperative (Part 1 of 2). Sable & Taurus

TEST CONDITIONS	TESTDETAILS/RESULTS/ACTIONS
H2 CHECK THE REAR WASHER PUMP OPERATION	
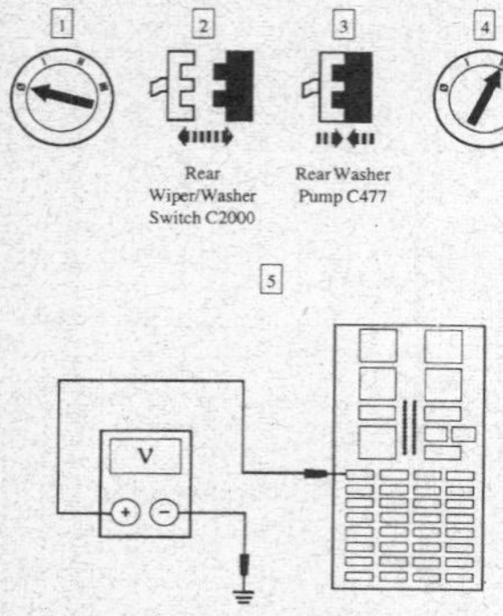	5 With the washer pump connected, connect a jumper wire between the rear washer pump C477 pin 1, circuit 1002 (BK/PK), harness side and ground. • Does the rear washer pump operate? → **Yes** GO to **H3**. → **No** INSTALL a new rear washer pump.
H3 CHECK CIRCUIT 941 BK/WH FOR OPEN	
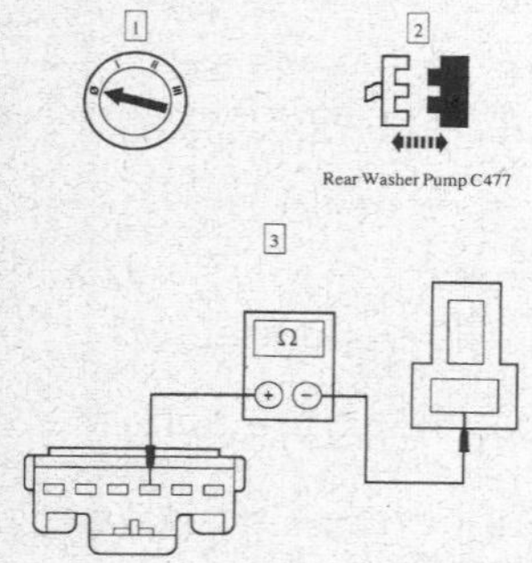	3 Measure the resistance between rear wiper/washer switch C2000 pin 3, circuit 941 (BK/WH), harness side and rear washer pump C477 pin 2, circuit 941 (BK/WH), harness side. • Is the resistance less than 5 ohms? → **Yes** INSTALL a new rear wiper/washer switch. TEST the system for normal operation. → **No** REPAIR the circuit. TEST the system for normal operation

FM9020100816020X

Fig. 11 Test H: Rear Washer Pump Is Inoperative (Part 2 of 2). Sable & Taurus

TEST CONDITIONS	TESTDETAILS/RESULTS/ACTIONS
I1 CHECK THE OPERATION OF THE REAR WIPER/WASHER SWITCH	
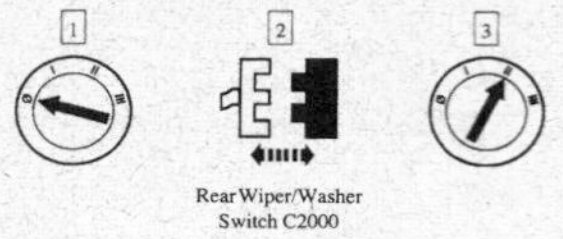	• Does the rear washer pump continue to run? → **Yes** GO to **I2**. → **No** INSTALL a new rear window wiper/washer switch. TEST the system for normal operation.
I2 CHECK CIRCUIT 941 (BK/WH) FOR SHORT TO GROUND	
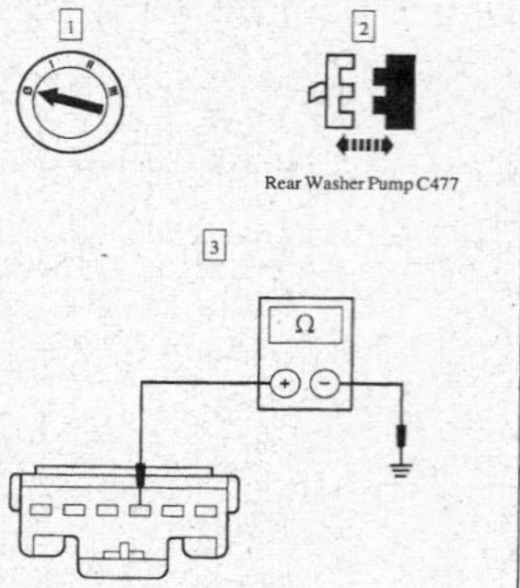	3 Measure the resistance between rear window wiper/washer switch C2000 pin 3, circuit 941 (BK/WH), harness side and ground. • Is the resistance greater than 10,000 ohms? → **Yes** INSTALL a new rear window washer pump. TEST the system for normal operation. → **No** REPAIR the circuit. TEST the system for normal operation.

FM9020100817000X

Fig. 12 Test I: Rear Washer Pump Stays On Continuously. Sable & Taurus

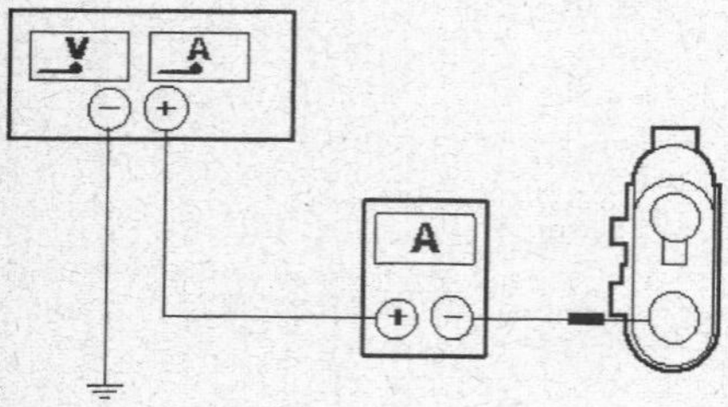

FM9020100810000X

Fig. 13 Rear wiper motor test. Focus

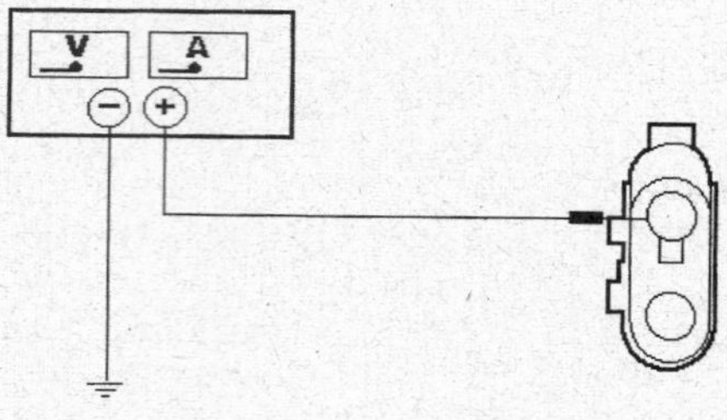

FM9020100811000X

Fig. 14 Limit switch test. Focus

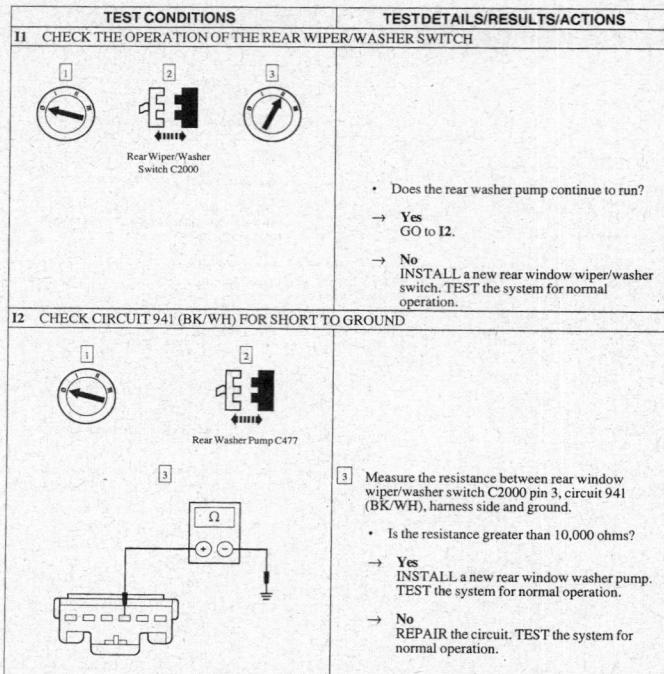

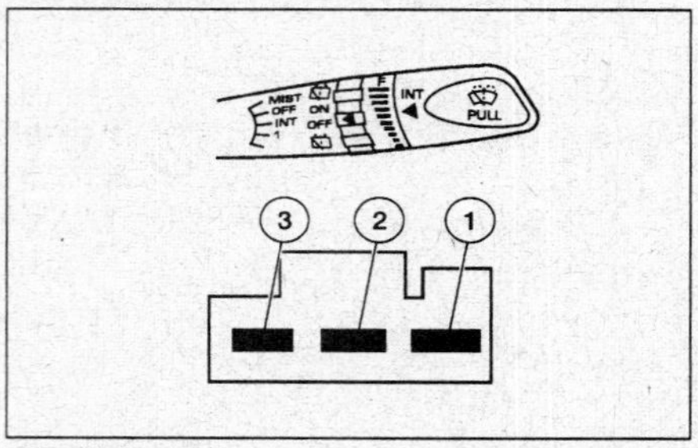

Switch Position	Pin(s)	Resistance
ON	1	Less than 5 ohms
Wash (Top) or Mist Wash (Down)	2 or 1	Less than 5 ohms

FM9029700497000X

Fig. 15 Rear wiper/washer switch inspection. Escort & Tracer

COMPONENT DIAGNOSIS & TESTING

Wiper Motor

FOCUS

1. Disconnect wiper motor electrical connector from motor.
2. Connect negative terminal of ammeter to pin No. 2 of rear wiper motor, **Fig. 13.**
3. Connect voltage supply negative to rear wiper motor housing.
4. Connect voltage supply positive to positive terminal of ammeter and switch on voltage supply.
5. Read current on meter as motor runs. Ammeter reading should be approximately 2 amps.
6. Switch off voltage and remove all connections.
7. Ensure wiper motor is at Rest position.
8. Connect voltage supply negative to rear wiper motor housing.
9. Connect voltage positive to pin No. 1 of rear wiper motor, **Fig. 14.**
10. Switch on voltage supply and ensure motor runs and stops in Rest position.
11. If motor does not perform as specified, replace wiper motor.

Wiper Switch

ESCORT & TRACER

1. Key Off, disconnect switch and measure resistance between "BK" wire and "O" wire switch under following conditions, **Fig.15.**

Washer Pump

ESCORT & TRACER

1. With key Off, disconnect washer pump.
2. Apply 12 volts to "BL/PK" wire terminal at washer pump.
3. Ground "O" wire terminal at washer pump, pump should operate.
4. If rear washer pump tests satisfactory, return to Pinpoint Test, otherwise, replace washer pump.

PASSIVE RESTRAINT SYSTEMS
Air Bag System

NOTE: Refer To "Computer Relearn Procedures" Located In The Front Of This Manual When Battery Power To The Computer Has Been Interrupted.

NOTE: Prior To Performing Any Service Operations Listed In This Section, Consult The "Technical Service Bulletins" Section For Related Information.

INDEX

AIR BAG SYSTEM DISARMING & ARMING

Do not use radio key code savers when servicing the air bag system. Failure to take this precaution may cause air bag deployment and personal injury.

After the battery has been disconnected and connected again, abnormal drive conditions may be present while the powertrain control module relearns its adaptive strategy. The vehicle may need to be driven 10 miles or more to relearn the strategy.

Disarming

Prior to disconnecting battery, record preset radio frequencies.

1. Disconnect and isolate battery ground cable.
2. Allow at least one minute for back-up power supply to deplete.

Arming

1. Connect battery positive cable, then the ground cable.
2. From a safe location at sides of or below air bag modules, turn ignition On.
3. The SRS warning lamp should light for 3–8 seconds, then go off.
4. If SRS indicator does not perform as outlined, refer to **MOTOR's "Air Bag Manual" or "Air Bag Diagnosis CD."**
5. Reset radio stations and clock.

DESCRIPTION & OPERATION

Air Bag System

The Supplemental Air Bag Restraint System (SRS) consists of the driver's, passenger's air bag module, sliding contact, impact sensors, air bag control module and warning lamp.

The Focus, LS, Thunderbird, Continental and Town Car, 2001–04 Sable and Taurus and 2003–04 Crown Victoria, Grand Marquis & Marauder models are also equipped with side air bags modules. These are optional on Cougar models. These modules mount on the outer side edges of the front seatbacks and will deploy if a side collision of sufficient force is detected by the corresponding side impact sensor.

Driver's Air Bag Module

The driver's air bag module is mounted in the center of the steering wheel. The module consists of an igniter assembly, inflator, mounting plate, retainer ring, bag and liner assembly and steering wheel trim cover, **Fig. 1.** This unit may not be disassembled or serviced.

Passenger's Air Bag Module

The passenger's air bag module is mounted in the righthand side of the instrument panel, **Fig. 2.** The module consists of an igniter assembly, inflator, and reaction housing. This unit may not be disassembled or serviced.

Igniter & Inflator Assembly

The igniter/inflator is an integral part of the inflator assembly and is not a serviceable item. When the air bag monitor assembly signals the igniter, the igniter assembly converts the electrical signal to thermal energy, causing the ignition of the inflator gas generant. This ignition reaction will ignite the sodium azide/copper oxide or potassium generant in the inflator, to produce nitrogen gas, causing the air bag to inflate.

Air Bag Assembly

The air bag is constructed of neoprene coated nylon. The air bag fills to full volume in approximately 40 milliseconds. The air bag is not a serviceable item.

Driver's Air Bag Mounting Plate & Retainer Ring

The mounting plate and retainer ring attaches and seals the bag assembly to the inflator. The mounting bracket is also used to attach the trim cover and to mount the entire module to the steering wheel. These items are components of the air bag module and cannot be serviced.

Driver's Air Bag Liner & Steering Wheel Trim Cover

The liner is an injection molded plastic component which encases the air bag assembly and provides support for the steering wheel trim cover assembly. When the air bag is activated, fail seams molded into the liner and steering wheel trim cover separate to allow inflation of the air bag assembly. The liner is a component of the air bag module and is not a serviceable item.

Passenger's Air Bag Reaction Housing

The reaction housing provides support and a reaction surface for the inflator. It is also used to attach the trim cover. the reaction housing also provides a means for mounting the air bag module to the instrument panel.

Passenger's Air Bag Trim Cover

The trim cover is attached to the reaction housing. It is textured to match the instrument panel. The trim cover retains the air bag in the reaction housing. Some trim covers incorporate a mounded tear seam which separates when the air bag inflates. Other trim covers incorporate a corrugated hinge which allows the trim cover up and out of the way when the air bag inflates.

Electrical System

The air bag is powered directly from the battery and back-up power supply. The system can function with the ignition switch in any position, including off and lock. The system can also function when no one is sitting in the driver's seat. The electrical system performs three main functions; it detects an impact, switches electric power to the igniter assembly and monitors the system to determine readiness.

The electrical system components include an electronic monitor assembly, air bag system readiness indicator lamp, wiring harness, sensors and an igniter assembly.

Air Bag Diagnostic Monitor

The air bag diagnostic monitor assembly contains a microcomputer that monitors the electrical system components and connections. The assembly performs a self inspection of the microcomputer internal circuits and energizes the system indicator lamp during prove out and whenever a fault occurs. System defects can be detected and translated into a coded lamp display. If certain faults occur, the system will be disarmed by a firing disarm device built into the diagnostic monitor assembly.

Air Bag Indicator Lamp

The air bag indicator lamp is an instrument cluster mounted lamp that will momentarily light whenever the ignition switch is turned from Off to Run if the air bag system is working properly. If the system is not functioning properly, the lamp will fail to light, stay on continuously or light in a flashing mode, if a system defect exists and the lamp is faulting, an audible tone will be heard. If a fault occurs after the system prove out, the lamp will light either continuously or in a coded flashing mode.

Tone Generator

On some models a series of five sets of five tones will be heard if the readiness lamp is out and a fault occurs in the system. The tone pattern will repeat periodically until the fault and lamp outage are serviced.

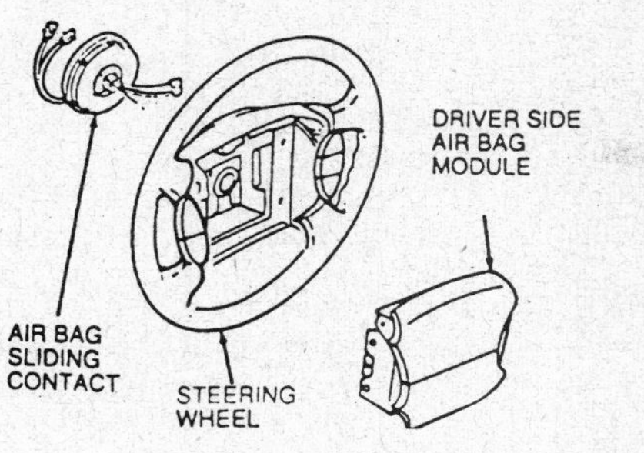

Fig. 1 Driver's air bag module

Crash Sensors

The sensor assembly is an electrical switch which reacts to impacts according to direction and force. It discriminates between impacts that require air bag inflation and impacts that do not require air bag inflation. When an impact occurs that requires air bag inflation, the sensor contacts close, completing the electrical circuit required for system operation. At least two sensors must be activated to inflate the air bag.

Knee Diverter

The knee diverter is located under the steering column behind the steering column opening trim panel, **Fig. 3.** It is designed to divert some of the impact when contacted by the driver's knees, and to protect the knees during impact.

Seat Belt Pretensioner System

As part of supplemental restraint system, the seat belt retractors are equipped with pretensioners. These pretensioners rotate the retractors to remove excess slack from the belt webbing. The pretensioners are activated by the Restraints Control Module (RCM) when the module detects a crash force in excess of a programmed limit.

Seat Belt Switches

The seat belt buckles on models with pretensioners are equipped with switches. The switches indicate to the restraints control module (RCM) whether the belts are connected or disconnected. The RCM uses this information in determining the air bag module deployment rates.

Seat Track Position Sensor

The seat track position sensor informs the restraints control module (RCM) of the driver's seat position. The RCM uses this information in calculating the deployment rate of the air bag modules.

Seat Occupant Sensor

This sensor informs the seat occupant sensor control module of the weight of any occupant or object in the passenger's seat. Based on predetermined limits, the seat occupant sensor control module will inform the Restraints Control Module (RCM) if the passenger air bag module is to be deactivated. The RCM uses this information to determine if the passenger air bag module requires deployment during a deployable crash.

PRECAUTIONS

General Safety Precautions

Do not use radio key code savers when servicing the air bag system. Failure to take this precaution may cause air bag deployment and personal injury.

Always wear safety glasses when servicing a vehicle equipped with air bags and when handling an air bag module.

Avoid working in front of air bag modules. It is safer to approach them from the side or below.

Because of the critical operating requirements of the system, do not attempt to repair sensor assemblies, the slip ring/clockspring assembly, the monitor assembly or the air bag module. Corrections are made by replacement only.

Never probe the connectors on the air bag module. Doing so may result in air bag deployment which could result in personal injury.

All component replacements and wiring repairs must be made with the air bag system disarmed.

The "Disconnect" instruction always refers to a connector. Never detach a part when instructed to "Disconnect."

If a vehicle equipped with an air bag system is involved in a crash where the fenders or grille area have been damaged, the sensors in the area of damage must be replaced whether or not the air bags deployed.

Handling & Storage Of Live Air Bag Module

When carrying a live air bag module, ensure bag and trim cover are pointed away from body. In the unlikely event of an accidental deployment, the bag will then deploy with minimal chance of injury. In addition, when placing a live air bag module on a bench or other surface, always place bag and trim cover face up, away from the surface. This will reduce the motion of the module if it is accidentally deployed.

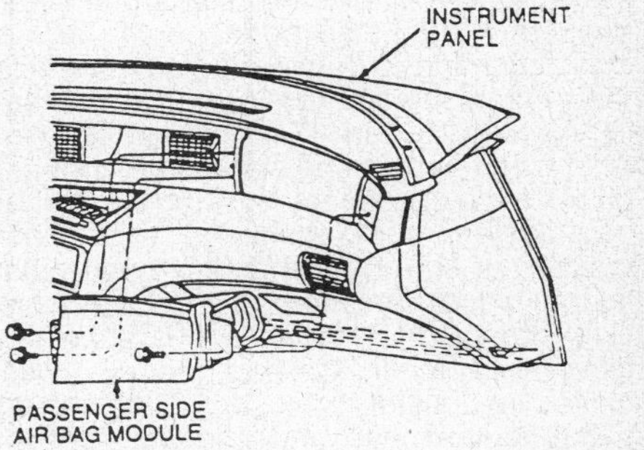

Fig. 2 Passenger's air bag module

Handling Of Deployed Air Bag Module

After deployment, the air bag surface may contain deposits of sodium hydroxide, a product of the gas generant combustion that is irritating to the skin. Always wear gloves and safety glasses when handling a deployed air bag module.

WIRING DIAGRAMS

Refer to **MOTOR's "Air Bag Manual" or "Air Bag Diagnosis CD."** for wiring diagrams.

WIRE HARNESS & CONNECTOR REPAIR

Refer to **MOTOR's "Air Bag Manual" or "Air Bag Diagnosis CD."** for wiring harness and connector repair information.

DIAGNOSIS & TESTING

Refer to **MOTOR's "Air Bag Manual" or "Air Bag Diagnosis CD."** for system diagnosis and testing procedures.

COLLISION INSPECTION

On vehicles that have experienced an air bag system deployment, certain air bag system components must be replaced. To determine which air bag system components require replacement, refer to MOTOR's "Air Bag Manual" or "Air Bag Diagnosis CD."

To ensure proper system operation on any vehicle involved in a collision, perform procedures outlined in "Diagnosis & Testing." All system components should be inspected for dents, cracks, exposure to excessive heat and other damage. The air bag sliding contact, steering wheel and steering column should also be inspected. All air bag system wiring should be inspected for chafing and interference with other vehicle components. If a vehicle has any degree of frontal body damage, the dash sensors should be inspected for dents, cracks, deformation and other damage and replaced with a new unit as required. Dash sensors should also be inspected for secure mounting. When repairing the vehicle, the system should be disarmed as outlined in "Air Bag System Disarming & Arming." Also when performing service procedures, do not expose sensors or wiring or other air bag system components to heat guns, welding or spray guns. If deployment has taking place, the air bag module(s) and clockspring should be replaced. When handling a deployed air bag module, wear gloves and safety glasses. Deployed air bag modules may contain deposits of sodium hydroxide.

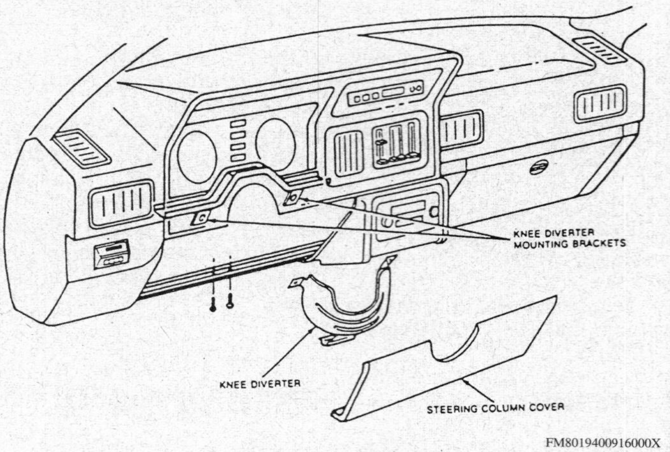

Fig. 3 Knee diverter

COMPONENT SERVICE

Prior to disconnecting any air bag system electrical connectors or servicing any system components or other components located near an air bag system electrical connector, the system must be disarmed, refer to "Air Bag System Disarming & Arming." Failure to disarm air bag system could result in system deployment and personal injury. Also refer to "Precautions" before servicing the component. After completing the service procedure, the air bag system must be armed. Refer to "Air Bag System Disarming & Arming" for procedure.

Fasteners used on air bag components must be replaced after removal. The fasteners are coated with an epoxy adhesive, making them non-reusable.

Driver's Air Bag Module, Replace

CONTINENTAL, CROWN VICTORIA, GRAND MARQUIS, MARAUDER, MUSTANG & TOWN CAR

1. Disarm air bag system as outlined in "Air Bag System Disarming & Arming."
2. Remove two steering wheel spoke bolt covers, if equipped.
3. Remove two air bag module bolts at rear or sides of steering wheel.
4. Carefully lift air bag module away from steering wheel, then tag and disconnect air bag module and horn to clockspring electrical connectors.
5. Remove air bag module.
6. Reverse procedure to install, noting the following:
   a. Ensure electrical connectors are properly connected per tags made during removal.
   b. Tighten air bag module mounting bolts to specifications.
   c. Arm air bag system as outlined in "Air Bag System Disarming & Arming."

CONTOUR, MYSTIQUE & COUGAR

1. Disarm air bag system as outlined in "Air Bag System Disarming & Arming."
2. Rotate steering wheel 90° to access and remove air bag module Torx mounting screw.
3. Rotate steering wheel 180° to access and remove air bag module Torx mounting screw.
4. Disconnect electrical connector.
5. Remove driver air bag module.
6. Reverse procedure to install, noting the following:
   a. Tighten air bag module mounting bolts to specifications.
   b. Arm air bag system as outlined in "Air Bag System Disarming & Arming."

ESCORT & ZX2

1. Disarm air bag system as outlined in "Air Bag System Disarming & Arming."
2. Remove two air bag module bolts, then disconnect air bag sliding contact and horn electrical connectors.
3. Carefully lift module away from steering wheel.
4. Reverse procedure to install, noting the following:
   a. Tighten air bag module mounting bolts to specifications.
   b. Arm air bag system as outlined in "Air Bag System Disarming & Arming."

FOCUS

1. Disarm air bag system as outlined in "Air Bag System Disarming & Arming."
2. Rotate steering wheel as required to undo driver air bag module captive bolts.
3. Detach driver air bag module retaining clips.
4. Carefully remove air bag module from steering wheel.
5. Disconnect electrical connector.
6. Reverse procedure to install, noting the following:
   a. Tighten air bag module mounting bolts to specifications.
   b. Arm air bag system as outlined in "Air Bag System Disarming & Arming."

LS & THUNDERBIRD

1. Disarm air bag system as outlined in "Air Bag System Disarming & Arming."
2. Remove steering wheel plugs and two driver's air bag module mounting bolts.
3. Slide and disengage driver's air bag electrical connector locking clip.
4. Depress locking tabs and disconnect driver's air bag module electrical connector.
5. Remove driver's air bag module.
6. Reverse procedure to install, noting the following:
   a. Tighten air bag module mounting bolts to specifications.
   b. Arm air bag system as outlined in "Air Bag System Disarming & Arming."

SABLE & TAURUS

In the event of an air bag module (soft pack) deployment, the module and the steering wheel must be replaced as an assembly.

1. Disarm air bag system as outlined in "Air Bag System Disarming & Arming."
2. Remove steering column lower opening cover with reinforcement.
3. Disconnect 4-pin air bag sliding contact electrical connector at steering column base.
4. Carefully pry access door open using a suitable thin-bladed screwdriver.
5. Disconnect accessory and air bag module electrical connectors.
6. Rotate pinion shaft 120–130 revolutions to release steering wheel from column shaft using anti-theft socket tool No. 501-052, or equivalent.
7. Release retaining tabs to remove steering wheel rear cover.
8. Note orientation of steering wheel armature.
9. Remove steering wheel armature mounting nuts, then the armature.
10. Disconnect horn electrical connector.
11. Remove horn wiring harness from wire shield retaining clip.
12. Carefully slide horn electrical connector off wire shield, then disconnect connector.
13. Remove air bag module wire harness from wire shield retaining clips.
14. Release retaining tab, then remove air bag module electrical connector from wire shield.

15. Remove component feed electrical connector from wire shield.
16. Position all wire harnesses and electrical connectors aside.
17. Carefully pry up between air bag module backing plate and steering wheel, then remove air bag module.
18. Reverse procedure to install, noting the following:
    a. When positioning air bag module into steering wheel, route horn wire harness through opening in module backing plate to ensure extra harness is not in steering wheel cavity or pinched between module and wheel.
    b. Align steering wheel armature onto wheel with worm gear bolt head facing two electrical connectors.
    c. Ensure steering wheel rear cover is seated completely in wheel mating groove.
    d. Position steering wheel and tighten pinion shaft to specifications.
    e. Arm air bag system as outlined in "Air Bag System Disarming & Arming."

Passenger's Air Bag Module, Replace

CONTINENTAL

1. Disarm air bag system as outlined in "Air Bag System Disarming & Arming."
2. Open glove compartment, push in on door tabs and rotate down completely, past stops.
3. Disconnect passenger's air bag electrical connector.
4. Remove four bolts securing passenger's air bag module.
5. Carefully remove passenger's air bag by pushing on air bag assembly from inside panel. **Do not handle air bag by deployment door edges.**
6. Reverse procedure to install, noting the following:
    a. Ensure all electrical connectors are securely in place.
    b. Tighten mounting bolts to specifications.
    c. Arm air bag system as outlined in "Air Bag System Disarming & Arming."

CONTOUR, MYSTIQUE & COUGAR

1. Disarm air bag system as outlined in "Air Bag System Disarming & Arming."
2. Open glove compartment, push sides inward and lower glove compartment to floor.
3. Disconnect glove compartment lamp and remove glove compartment upper cover.
4. Remove A/C evaporator register duct.
5. Through glove compartment opening, remove two passenger's air bag module mounting bolts.
6. Remove two remaining passenger's air bag module mounting nuts, disconnect electrical connector and remove passenger's air bag module.
7. Reverse procedure to install, noting the following:
    a. Tighten passenger's air bag module mounting fasteners to specifications.
    b. Arm air bag system as outlined in "Air Bag System Disarming & Arming."

CROWN VICTORIA, GRAND MARQUIS & MARAUDER

1. Disarm air bag system as outlined in "Air Bag System Disarming & Arming."
2. Open glove compartment and disconnect glove compartment locator.
3. Push inward on glove compartment door tabs and position door downward.
4. Detach trim panel located below air bag module from instrument panel by pulling straight out to release clips.
5. Disconnect clock and rear window defroster switch electrical connectors and remove trim panel.
6. Disconnect passenger's air bag module electrical connector.
7. Remove two passenger's air bag module mounting bolts and two screws.
8. Place one hand in glove compartment opening and push passenger's air bag module from instrument panel.
9. Reverse procedure to install, noting the following:
    a. Ensure all electrical connectors are securely in place.
    b. Tighten mounting screws to specifications.
    c. Arm air bag system as outlined in "Air Bag System Disarming & Arming."

ESCORT & ZX2

1. Disarm air bag system as outlined in "Air Bag System Disarming & Arming."
2. Push in on glove compartment door tabs and position downward, then remove door.
3. Remove four air bag module bolts and carefully pull module out of instrument panel.
4. Disconnect air bag module electrical connector.
5. Reverse procedure to install, noting the following:
    a. Tighten mounting bolts to specifications.
    b. Arm air bag system as outlined in "Air Bag System Disarming & Arming."

FOCUS

1. Disarm air bag system as outlined in "Air Bag System Disarming & Arming."
2. Carefully release passenger air bag module trim cover retaining clips using a suitable trim tool, starting at front outer edge.
3. Lift trim cover, moving it toward windshield to disengage retaining clips.
4. Remove passenger air bag module and reinforcement bracket mounting bolts.
5. Disconnect passenger air bag module electrical connector.
6. Reverse procedure to install, noting the following:
    a. **If a new passenger air bag module is being installed because of air bag deployment, replace the instrument panel as well or personal injury may result.**
    b. Ensure all air bag trim cover retaining clips are properly engaged and trim cover sits flush with instrument panel.
    c. Tighten mounting bolts to specifications.
    d. Arm air bag system as outlined in "Air Bag System Disarming & Arming."

LS & THUNDERBIRD

1. Place steering wheel in straight ahead position.
2. Disarm air bag system as outlined in "Air Bag System Disarming & Arming."
3. Remove driver's side air bag module as outlined in "Driver's Air Bag Module, Replace."
4. Apply parking brake.
5. **On models equipped with manual transmission,** place selector lever in fourth gear and remove gearshift lever knob.
6. **On models equipped with automatic transmission,** place selector lever in Neutral position.
7. **On all models,** remove ashtray finish panel and disconnect electrical connectors.
8. Disconnect cellular phone electrical connectors.
9. Remove console finish panel assembly by pulling upward from front first.
10. Disconnect traction control switch electrical connector and release cellular phone wiring harness from console finish panel assembly.
11. Remove console rear finish panel assembly by unclipping and pulling rearward.
12. Unclip parking brake boot from console base.
13. Remove console assembly front screws and rear bolts.
14. Remove console air condition duct mounting screw.
15. Remove console assembly by sliding rearward.
16. **On models equipped with automatic transmission,** proceed as follows:
    a. Slide automatic transmission selector lever assembly cover down, remove mounting screws, then the handle and cover.
    b. Remove shift bezel and PRNDL indicator bulb.
    c. Remove rear A/C air duct.
    d. Remove shift interlock cable from bracket and disconnect cable from lever.
    e. Raise and support vehicle then disconnect transmission shift cable from selector lever.
    f. Lower vehicle.
    g. Remove mounting bolts and shifter assembly.
17. **On all models,** remove lefthand and righthand instrument panel insulators, then the scuff plates.
18. Position lefthand and righthand door weatherstrips aside.

19. Remove lefthand and righthand A-pillar lower trim panels, then lefthand and righthand windshield side garnish moldings.
20. Remove instrument panel defroster opening grille assembly and disconnect electrical connector.
21. Remove instrument panel cowl top screws and instrument panel upper reinforcement bolts.
22. Remove lefthand and righthand instrument panel side finish panels.
23. Remove mounting screws and position hood release handle and cable aside.
24. Loosen mounting bolt and disconnect upper righthand bulkhead electrical connector.
25. Disconnect righthand electrical connectors through instrument panel side opening.
26. Disconnect passenger side tunnel electrical connector.
27. Remove pinch bolt and separate intermediate shaft from steering column. **Secure steering wheel to prevent any rotation or damage to air bag sliding contact.**
28. Position carpet aside and disconnect lefthand junction box electrical connector.
29. Disconnect lefthand electrical connectors through instrument panel side opening.
30. Disconnect ignition shift interlock electrical connector.
31. Position carpet aside and remove four instrument panel tunnel brace bolts.
32. Remove driver side outer instrument panel cowl side cover and reinforcement bolt.
33. Remove lefthand instrument panel cowl side bolt and nut.
34. Remove righthand instrument panel cowl side bolt and nut.
35. Remove instrument panel.
36. Position instrument panel face down on suitable bench.
37. Push in mounting clips and remove passenger side air conditioning register.
38. Remove passenger side A/C and demister duct mounting screws.
39. Remove A/C duct mounting screw and position it out of way.
40. Remove mounting screws and position defrost nozzle out of way with demister duct.
41. Remove righthand instrument panel insulator.
42. Remove righthand floor heat duct.
43. Release assist cable from glove compartment arm from under instrument panel.
44. Open glove compartment.
45. Remove instrument panel finish panel.
46. Push down on glove compartment arms and lower glove compartment door.
47. Remove mounting screws and glove compartment instrument panel finish panel, then disconnect electrical connectors.
48. Remove mounting bolts and glove compartment.
49. Disconnect glove compartment electrical connector.
50. Slide and disengage passenger's air bag module electrical connector locking clip.
51. Push in two release tabs and disconnect passenger's air bag module electrical connector.
52. Remove push and pin-type retainers and reposition wire harness.
53. Remove mounting bolts, then the passenger's air bag module through glove box.
54. Reverse procedure to install, noting the following:
    a. Install new air bag module mounting nuts and bolts.
    b. Adjust shifter cable.
    c. Arm air bag system as outlined in "Air Bag System Disarming & Arming."

MUSTANG

2000

1. Disarm air bag system as outlined in "Air Bag System Disarming & Arming."
2. Open glove compartment door and push inward on side of glove compartment. Lower glove compartment assembly to floor.
3. Remove two mounting screws, then the righthand A/C duct.
4. Disconnect passenger's air bag module electrical connector.
5. Remove two passenger's air bag module to instrument panel mounting bolts.
6. Remove passenger's air bag module by pushing on it from inside instrument panel opening.
7. Reverse procedure to install, noting the following:
    a. Tighten passenger's air bag module bolts to specifications.
    b. Arm air bag system as outlined in "Air Bag System Disarming & Arming."

2001-04

1. Disarm air bag system as outlined in "Air Bag System Disarming & Arming."
2. Remove passenger air bag module electrical connector from instrument panel bracket. **Do not handle module by deployment door edges.**
3. Remove passenger air bag module mounting bolts.
4. Reach through glove compartment opening with one hand and carefully push module out of instrument panel.
5. Disconnect module electrical connector.
6. Reverse procedure to install, noting the following:
    a. Ensure all wiring and electrical connectors are properly routed to avoid pinching.
    b. Tighten passenger's air bag module bolts to specifications.
    c. Arm air bag system as outlined in "Air Bag System Disarming & Arming."

SABLE & TAURUS

1. Disarm air bag system as outlined in "Air Bag System Disarming & Arming."
2. Open glove compartment to fullest extent by pushing in on and releasing tabs.
3. Reach through glove compartment opening and remove air bag module mounting bolts.
4. Pull lefthand corner of air bag module trim cover away from instrument panel.
5. Slide across seam from left to right between trim cover and instrument panel, releasing trim cover retaining clips.
6. Pull air bag module and trim cover away from instrument panel, but do not remove it.
7. Disconnect passenger air bag module electrical connector.
8. Remove wire harness pin-type retainer from air bag module.
9. Carefully remove passenger air bag module.
10. Reverse procedure to install, noting the following:
    a. Ensure air bag module alignment channels are properly seated into instrument panel alignment rails.
    b. Tighten fasteners to specifications.
    c. Arm air bag system as outlined in "Air Bag System Disarming & Arming."

TOWN CAR

2000

1. Disarm air bag system as outlined in "Air Bag System Disarming & Arming."
2. Open glove compartment and disconnect compartment isolator.
3. Through glove compartment opening, disconnect passenger's air bag module electrical connector.
4. Remove air bag module mounting bolts, then the module. **Do not handle air bag module by deployment door edges.**
5. Reverse procedure to install, noting the following:
    a. Tighten mounting bolts to specifications.
    b. Ensure electrical connector is securely in place.
    c. Arm air bag system as outlined in "Air Bag System Disarming & Arming."

2001-04

1. Disarm air bag system as outlined in "Air Bag System Disarming & Arming."
2. Remove audio unit, using radio removal tool No. T87P-19061-A, or equivalent. Disconnect electrical connectors and antenna lead-in cable.
3. Remove instrument cluster finish panel from instrument panel.
4. Open glove compartment, then disconnect compartment isolator.
5. Position glove compartment downward while pushing in on two compartment door tabs.
6. Working through glove compartment opening, remove air bag module vehicle wire harness pin-type retainers from instrument panel.
7. Remove passenger air bag module bolts through glove compartment opening.
8. Place one hand in compartment opening and push air bag module out from

instrument panel. Do not handle module by grabbing deployment door edges.
9. Disconnect air bag module electrical connector.
10. Reverse procedure to install, noting the following:
    a. Ensure electrical connector is securely in place.
    b. Arm air bag system as outlined in "Air Bag System Disarming & Arming."

Side Impact Air Bag Module, Replace

CONTINENTAL & TOWN CAR

1. Position front seat fully rearward.
2. Remove front seat track covers and bolts.
3. Position front seat forward.
4. Remove rear seat track covers and bolts.
5. Disarm air bag system as outlined in "Air Bag System Disarming & Arming."
6. Disconnect front seat electrical connector and remove front seat.
7. Push upward on seatback trim panel.
8. Pull outward on bottom corners of trim panel to detach J-hooks.
9. Slide back trim panel down to remove. If seatback trim panel or J-hooks are damaged, replace trim panel.
10. Release four seatback trim cover J-clips.
11. Unzip side air bag module deployment chute.
12. Remove two side air bag module mounting nuts, **Fig. 4.**
13. Position seatback trim cover and pad forward enough to access air bag module.
14. Separate side air bag module from seat frame.
15. Disconnect side air bag module electrical connector and remove air bag module.
16. Reverse procedure to install, noting the following:
    a. Ensure electrical connector is securely in place.
    b. Arm air bag system as outlined in "Air Bag System Disarming & Arming."

COUGAR

1. Position front seat fully rearward.
2. Remove front seat track covers and bolts.
3. Position front seat forward.
4. Remove rear seat track covers and bolts.
5. Disarm air bag system as outlined in "Air Bag System Disarming & Arming."
6. Disconnect front seat electrical connector and remove front seat.
7. Remove mounting screws, then release front and rear mounting clips and remove seat base side trim panel.
8. Disconnect electrical connectors at seat base.
9. Remove seat backrest cover and foam.
10. Remove two seat backrest mounting screws from each side, then the seat backrest.
11. Disconnect side air bag module electrical connector.
12. Remove two side air bag module mounting nuts, then the air bag module, **Fig. 5.**
13. Reverse procedure to install, noting the following:
    a. Ensure side air bag module electrical connector faces seat base.
    b. Ensure electrical connector is securely in place.
    c. Arm air bag system as outlined in "Air Bag System Disarming & Arming."

CROWN VICTORIA, GRAND MARQUIS & MARAUDER

1. Disarm air bag system as outlined in "Air Bag System Disarming & Arming."
2. Remove front seat track covers and bolts.
3. Disconnect front seat electrical connectors and remove seat.
4. Remove screws from bottom of seat back trim panel.
5. Pull out at bottom and slide seat back trim panel up to disengage retaining hooks.
6. Release four seat back trim cover J-clips.
7. Remove side air bag module retaining nuts.
8. Position side air bag module and deployment chute away from mounting bracket and seat back frame.
9. Position seat back trim cover and seat back pad forward enough to access side air bag module.
10. Pull side air bag module mounting studs back through deployment chute openings and remove side air bag module from deployment chute.
11. Disconnect side air bag module electrical connectors and remove side air bag module.
12. Reverse procedure to install noting the following:
    a. Position side air bag module into deployment chute with alignment pin offset to top and electrical connector to bottom.
    b. Arm air bag system as outlined in "Air Bag System Disarming & Arming."

FOCUS

1. Disarm air bag system as outlined in "Air Bag System Disarming & Arming."
2. Remove side air bag module deployment sleeve retainer. **Do not use plastic retaining rivet again. Use new rivet from service kit.**
3. Remove black plastic production rivet and discard.
4. Carefully separate plastic retaining strips securing air bag deployment sleeve.
5. Detach side air bag module wiring harness from seat frame.
6. Remove side air bag module and disconnect electrical connector.
7. Reverse procedure to install, noting the following:
    a. Side air bag modules are designed for specific lefthand or righthand installation. Module wiring harness will face seat base when properly installed.
    b. Install module with new self locking nuts.
    c. Arm air bag system as outlined in "Air Bag System Disarming & Arming."

LS & THUNDERBIRD

REMOVAL

Front seatback trim covers installed on seats equipped with side air bags cannot be repaired. They must be replaced.

If a side air bag has deployed, replace the seatback pad and trim cover. Inspect the seatback frame and replace if required.

1. Move seat forward, then remove seat track rear covers and track to floor nuts.
2. Remove seat belt cover by placing fingers behind cover and pushing outward. **Do not use screwdriver to remove seat belt cover.**
3. Remove mounting nut and front safety belt.
4. Move seat rearward.
5. Remove seat track to floor mounting bolts.
6. Disarm air bag system as outlined in "Air Bag System Disarming & Arming."
7. Disconnect electrical connectors and remove seat.
8. Pull and release pin-type retainers at seatback trim panel bottom.
9. Pushing inward on top of seatback trim panel, slide trim panel down to disengage J-hooks.
10. Pull seatback trim panel top out evenly and remove.
11. Inspect seatback trim panel J-hooks and pin-type retainers for damage. **If seatback trim panel J-hooks are damaged, install new seatback trim panel.**
12. Disconnect electrical connectors.
13. Separate seatback frame pin-type retainers and remove seatback trim cover J-clips.
14. Position seatback trim cover and pad aside, then remove side air bag module mounting nut cover.
15. Push wire harness and grommet through seatback frame.
16. Remove side air bag module mounting nuts.
17. Position seatback trim cover and pad forward enough to access side air bag module.
18. Separate side air bag module and deployment chute from seatback mounting bracket.
19. Pull side air bag module mounting studs back through deployment chute openings and remove side air bag module from deployment chute.
20. Slide side air bag electrical connector locking clip.

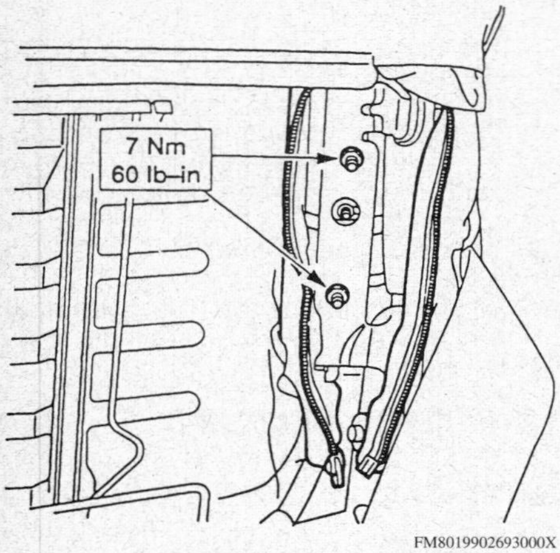

Fig. 4 Side air bag module mounting nut locations. Continental & Town Car

21. Release two connector tabs by pushing in and disconnect side air bag module.
22. Remove side air bag module.

INSTALLATION

1. Connect side air bag module connector.
2. Slide side air bag module electrical connector locking clip to secure connector to side air bag module. Ensure electrical connector is securely fastened to side air bag module.
3. Position side air bag module into deployment chute with alignment pin offset towards top of seatback and electrical connector towards bottom. This will properly position alignment pin when side air bag module and deployment chute are mounted to seatback frame mounting bracket.
4. Side air bag module mounting studs must come through deployment chute stud openings.
5. Install side air bag module onto front seatback frame mounting bracket, noting the following:
   a. Deployment chute should not have any wrinkles or folds where it contacts seatback frame mounting bracket.
   b. If installing new side air bag module, use new mounting nuts.
6. Pull wire harness back through hole in seatback frame and seat grommet.
7. Reposition seatback pad and trim cover to seatback frame.
8. Attach side air bag mounting nuts cover. Ensure all three mounting clips on side air bag nuts cover are properly installed around side air bag mounting bracket.
9. Attach seatback trim cover J-clips.
10. Install pin-type retainers.
11. Connect electrical connectors.
12. **Inspect seatback trim panel J-hooks for damage. If damaged, install new seatback trim panel.**
13. Angle top of seatback trim panel inward and up to engage upper J-hooks to seatback frame.
14. While holding seatback trim panel up, align pin-type retainers at bottom of seatback trim panel and install them into seatback frame.
15. Install seat.
16. Ensure electrical connectors are securely in place.
17. Arm air bag system as outlined in "Air Bag System Disarming & Arming."

SABLE & TAURUS

If a side impact air bag module has deployed the seatback pad, trim cover, and side impact air bag module must be replaced. Replace the seatback frame if required.

1. Disarm air bag system as outlined in "Air Bag System Disarming & Arming."
2. **On models equipped with power seats and adjustable pedals,** disconnect their electrical connectors.
3. **On all models,** remove recliner handle.
4. Remove side shield attaching screw.
5. Pull out on outer side shield to release two hidden clips to inner side shield and two hidden clips to recliner mechanism.
6. Pull forward on side shield, releasing hidden clip at front of seat cushion frame.
7. Slide side shield forward to clear recliner handle while routing wire harness out of seat cushion frame and remove outer side shield.
8. Remove inner side shield.
9. **On models equipped with manual lumbar seat,** proceed as follows:
   a. Pull and remove lumbar adjustment knob.
   b. Reach in seat cushion frame, turn manual lumbar mechanism counterclockwise and separate it from frame.
   c. From inside lumbar adjustment mechanism, push screw stop in toward center.
   d. Rotate lumbar adjustment mechanism counterclockwise while pushing screw stop toward center. Screw stop will pass clear of internal stop, releasing manual lumbar adjustment screw.
   e. Continue to turn manual lumbar mechanism counterclockwise until cable support comes out.
   f. Push screw out enough to remove cable end.
   g. Route manual lumbar cable out from between seat track and cushion frame.
10. **On all models,** separate air bag module wire harness from underside of seat cushion frame and from side of seat track.
11. Remove pivot bolt.
12. Remove seatback from seat cushion.
13. Release seatback trim cover lower J-clips.
14. Remove and discard lower and upper rows of hog rings.
15. Remove pin-type retainers and separate air bag module wire harness from seatback frame.
16. Remove side air bag module retaining nuts. **These nuts may be used if old module will be installed again, but must be discarded if a new module is being installed.**

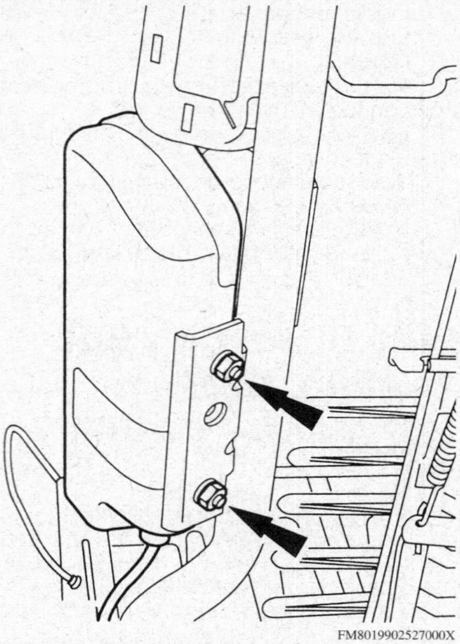

Fig. 5 Side air bag module mounting nut locations. Cougar

17. Carefully remove side air bag module with wire harness through opening in front outboard side of seatback cushion.
18. Reverse procedure to install, noting the following:
   a. Install new pin-type retainers if damaged.
   b. Front seat back trim covers installed on seats equipped with side air bags cannot be repaired.
   c. Arm air bag system as outlined in "Air Bag System Disarming & Arming."

Air Bag Slip Ring/ Sliding Contact, Replace

CONTINENTAL

1. Place front wheels in straight-ahead position and turn ignition to Lock and remove key.
2. Disarm air bag system as outlined in "Air Bag System Disarming & Arming."
3. Remove driver's air bag module as outlined in "Driver's Air Bag Module, Replace."
4. Remove steering wheel mounting bolt or nut.
5. Remove steering wheel from upper shaft using puller tool No. T67L-3600-A, or equivalent.
6. **To prevent rotor from turning, tape clockspring in place prior to removing from steering shaft, Fig. 6.**
7. Remove mounting screws, then the steering column lower finish panel.
8. Remove parking brake and hood release lever to lower instrument panel

mounting screws, then position levers out of way.
9. Remove mounting bolts, then the steering column opening lower finish panel reinforcement.
10. Position steering column fully downward.
11. Unscrew tilt wheel handle and shank.
12. Remove four screws, then the steering column lower shroud.
13. Place ignition in Run position, push upward on release tab using suitable tool and remove lock cylinder.
14. Remove screw and carefully pull straight out on instrument panel center finish panel to access ATC sensor assembly.
15. Remove instrument panel center finish panel.
16. Loosen, but do not remove, four steering column mounting nuts.
17. Remove upper steering column shroud.
18. Remove Passive Anti-Theft System (PATS) transmitter mounting screw and position transmitter aside.
19. **On models equipped with hands-free microphone,** remove microphone from air bag sliding contact.
20. **On all models,** remove sliding contact electrical connectors from bracket and disconnect connectors.
21. Remove sliding contact wiring harness from harness holders.
22. Pry sliding contact mounting clips loose and remove sliding contact.
23. **If installing a new sliding contact,** the new component has a key preventing accidental rotation. Remove this key while keeping sliding contact in its centered position.
24. **If sliding contact requires centering,** proceed as follows:
    a. Hold sliding contact outer housing stationary.
    b. Carefully turn rotor clockwise while feeling for ribbon wire to run out of length until a slight resistance is encountered. **Stop turning at this point.**
    c. Carefully turn rotor counterclockwise approximately 2 ½ turns. Center point has been reached. **Do not permit rotor to turn from this position.**
25. Reverse procedure to install, noting the following:
    a. Ensure all wiring and electrical connectors are properly routed to avoid pinching.
    b. Tighten all fasteners to specifications.
    c. After installation has been completed, arm air bag system as outlined in "Air Bag System Disarming & Arming."

CONTOUR, MYSTIQUE & COUGAR

1. Place front wheels in straight-ahead position, then turn ignition to Lock and remove key.
2. Disarm air bag system as outlined in "Air Bag System Disarming & Arming."
3. Remove driver's air bag module as outlined in "Driver's Air Bag Module, Replace." **Before removing air bag clockspring type slip ring from steering shaft, clockspring must be taped** to prevent rotor from being turned accidentally and damaging clockspring, **Fig. 6.**
4. Remove steering wheel mounting bolt or nut.
5. Remove steering wheel from upper shaft using puller tool No. T67L-3600-A, or equivalent.
6. Remove steering column upper and lower shrouds and instrument panel steering column cover as required.
7. Sliding contact has a service lock preventing accidental rotation when steering wheel is removed.
8. Disconnect air bag slip ring connector from column harness.
9. Disconnect all required electrical connectors, release all three sliding contact retainers using a suitable thin-bladed screwdriver and remove sliding contact while carefully routing electrical connectors through steering column opening.
10. Reverse procedure to install. If sliding contact alignment is required, proceed as follows:
    a. Gently rotate inner rotor against outer rotor fully counterclockwise until it stops.
    b. Rotate inner rotor clockwise approximately 2 ¾ turns until alignment marks (1 and 2), **Figs. 7 and 8,** are aligned and locking tab locates into slot.
    c. Sliding contact is now properly aligned and ready for installation.
11. After installation has been completed, arm air bag system as outlined in "Air Bag System Disarming & Arming."

CROWN VICTORIA, GRAND MARQUIS, MARAUDER & TOWN CAR

1. Place front wheels in straight-ahead position, then turn ignition to Lock and remove key.
2. Disarm air bag system as outlined in "Air Bag System Disarming & Arming."
3. Remove driver's air bag module as outlined in "Driver's Air Bag Module, Replace."
4. Remove steering wheel mounting bolt or nut.
5. Remove steering wheel from upper shaft using puller tool No. T67L-3600-A, or equivalent.
6. **Before removing air bag clockspring type slip ring from steering shaft, clockspring must be taped** to prevent rotor from being turned accidentally and damaging clockspring, **Fig. 6.**
7. Move tilt steering column to lowest position and remove tilt handle and shank.
8. Remove two steering column lower cover bolts.
9. Position parking brake release handle aside and remove steering column lower cover.
10. Remove steering column lower reinforcement cover bolts, then the reinforcement.
11. Remove steering column lower shroud mounting screws, then the shroud.
12. Turn ignition to Run position.
13. Push upward on lock cylinder release tab using a suitable tool, while pulling cylinder outward.
14. Remove instrument panel lower insulator.
15. Loosen two steering column forward mounting nuts.
16. Disconnect PRNDL indicator cable.
17. Loosen two steering column rear mounting nuts, allowing column to drop and provide clearance to remove column upper shroud.
18. Depress cellular telephone microphone mounting tab and remove microphone.
19. Remove Passive Anti-Theft System (PATS) transmitter mounting screw and transmitter.
20. Remove Key-In-Ignition warning switch.
21. **On Town Car models,** cut and remove sliding contact electrical connector wiring harness tie strap as required.
22. **On all models,** remove steering column upper and lower shrouds and instrument panel steering column cover as required.
23. Sliding contact has a service lock preventing accidental rotation when steering wheel is removed.
24. Disconnect air bag slip ring connector from column harness.
25. Disconnect all required electrical connectors, release all three sliding contact retainers using a suitable thin-bladed screwdriver and remove sliding contact while carefully routing electrical connectors through steering column opening.
26. Reverse procedure to install, noting the following:
    a. Ensure all wiring and electrical connectors are connected per tags made during removal.
    b. **If sliding contact requires centering,** hold sliding contact outer housing stationary.
    c. Carefully turn rotor counterclockwise while feeling for ribbon wire to run out of length until a slight resistance is encountered. **Stop turning at this point.**
    d. Carefully turn rotor clockwise approximately three turns. Center point has been reached. **Do not permit rotor to turn from this position.**
    e. After installation has been completed, arm air bag system as outlined in "Air Bag System Disarming & Arming."

ESCORT & ZX2

1. Place front wheels in straight-ahead position, then turn ignition to Lock and remove key.
2. Disarm air bag system as outlined in "Air Bag System Disarming & Arming."
3. Remove driver's air bag module as outlined in "Driver's Air Bag Module, Replace."

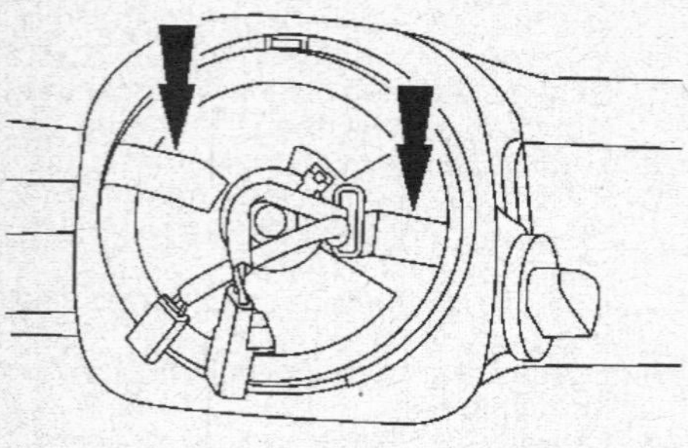

Fig. 6 Slip ring/sliding contact

4. Remove steering wheel mounting bolt or nut.
5. Remove steering wheel from upper shaft using puller tool No. T67L-3600-A, or equivalent.
6. **Before removing air bag clockspring type slip ring from steering shaft, clockspring must be taped** to prevent rotor from being turned accidentally and damaging clockspring, **Fig. 6.**
7. Remove steering column upper and lower shrouds and instrument panel steering column cover as required.
8. Sliding contact has a service lock preventing accidental rotation when steering wheel is removed.
9. Disconnect air bag slip ring connector from column harness.
10. Disconnect sliding contact electrical connectors, then remove four sliding contact mounting screws and sliding contact.
11. New sliding contacts arrive in a centered position and are held in place with a key. Remove key from clockspring, but hold rotor in its centered position.
12. Reverse procedure to install. If sliding contact alignment is required, proceed as follows:
    a. Carefully rotate sliding contact clockwise to its lock position.
    b. **On 2000 models,** if instruction label on sliding contact is yellow, rotate 3½ turns counterclockwise and align arrows as illustrated, **Fig. 9.** If instruction label on sliding contact is orange, rotate 2½ turns counterclockwise and align arrows.
    c. **On 2001–04 models,** rotate approximately 2¾ turns counterclockwise and align arrows, **Fig. 9.**
    d. **On all models,** sliding contact is now properly aligned and ready for installation.
13. After installation has been completed, arm air bag system as outlined in "Air Bag System Disarming & Arming."

FOCUS

1. Ensure wheels are in straight-ahead position.
2. Disarm air bag system as outlined in "Air Bag System Disarming & Arming."
3. Remove driver's air bag module as outlined in "Driver's Air Bag Module, Replace."
4. Disconnect horn and speed control electrical connectors as required.
5. Remove steering wheel mounting bolt.
6. Remove steering wheel using a suitable puller tool.
7. Remove instrument panel lower panel.
8. Remove steering column shrouds.
9. Detach multifunction switches by depressing each retaining tang in turn, then sliding each switch from sliding contact.
10. Disconnect sliding contact electrical connector.
11. Release sliding contact retaining tangs on both sides of steering column.
12. Note position of spacing collar within center of sliding contact, then remove sliding contact.
13. Reverse procedure to install, noting the following:
    a. Ensure spacing collar is properly located. Do not assemble if collar is missing.
    b. To properly center sliding contact, rotate sliding contact counterclockwise approximately 2 ½ turns from central position until a resistance is felt. Then rotate clockwise 2 ½ turns until arrow on center of sliding contact aligns with raised "V" section at 12 o'clock position on sliding contact outer cover.
    c. Tighten all fasteners to specifications.
    d. Arm air bag system as outlined in "Air Bag System Disarming & Arming."

LS & THUNDERBIRD

1. Ensure wheels are in straight-ahead position.
2. Disarm air bag system as outlined in "Air Bag System Disarming & Arming."
3. Remove driver's air bag module outlined in "Driver's Air Bag Module, Replace."
4. Remove steering wheel as outlined in "Electrical" section of "Lincoln LS" chassis chapter.
5. Apply two strips of masking tape across air bag sliding contact to prevent accidental rotation when air bag sliding contact is removed.
6. Remove two mounting screws and pull lower steering column opening finish panel enough to access electrical connector.
7. Disconnect electrical connectors and remove lower steering column opening finish panel.
8. Remove two mounting screws and lower steering column shroud.
9. Pull out and remove ignition switch finish panel.
10. Pull headlight switch finish panel outward and disconnect electrical connectors.
11. Remove mounting screws and separate hood release assembly from steering column opening reinforcement.
12. Remove mounting screw and heater duct.
13. Remove mounting screws and steering column opening reinforcement.
14. Remove two steering column mounting nuts, then loosen two steering column mounting nuts enough to pivot steering column.
15. Remove instrument cluster finish panel and lower steering column.
16. Remove four mounting screws and instrument cluster finish panel enough to access automatic temperature control sensor assembly.
17. Separate automatic temperature control sensor assembly from instrument cluster finish panel by pushing in and releasing tabs.
18. Remove instrument cluster finish panel.
19. **On models equipped with hands-free microphone,** remove upper steering column shroud and disconnect microphone connector.
20. **On all models,** disconnect steering column position sensor.
21. Disconnect three electrical connectors, release four connector mounting clips and remove air bag sliding contact electrical connector.
22. Release three clips and remove air bag sliding contact with multi-function switch.
23. Cut tie strap and disconnect electrical connector.
24. Release tabs and separate air bag sliding contact from multi-function switch.
25. Reverse procedure to install, noting the following:
    a. Tighten mounting bolts, nuts and screws to specifications.
    b. Arm air bag system as outlined in "Air Bag System Disarming & Arming."

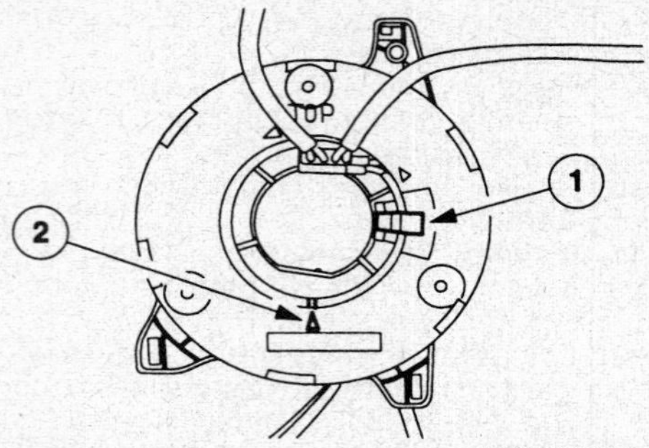

Fig. 7 Sliding contact alignment. Contour & Mystique

MUSTANG

2000

1. Place front wheels in straight-ahead position, then turn ignition to Lock and remove key.
2. Disarm air bag system as outlined in "Air Bag System Disarming & Arming."
3. Remove driver's air bag module as outlined in "Driver's Air Bag Module, Replace."
4. Remove steering wheel mounting bolt or nut.
5. Remove steering wheel from upper shaft using puller tool No. T67L-3600-A, or equivalent.
6. **Before removing air bag clockspring type slip ring from steering shaft, clockspring must be taped** to

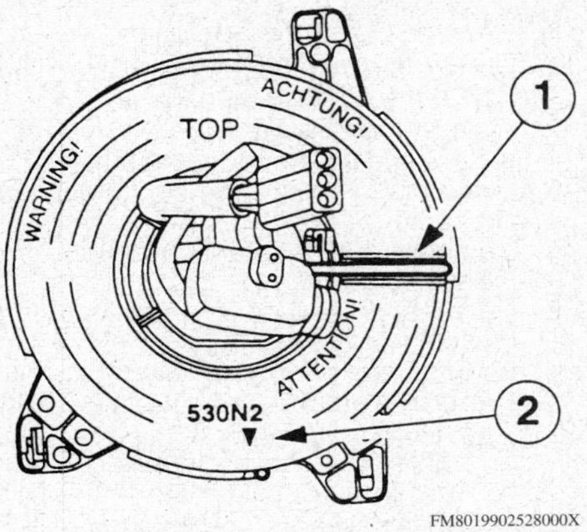

FM8019902528000X

Fig. 8 Sliding contact alignment. Cougar

prevent rotor from being turned accidentally and damaging clockspring, **Fig. 6.**

7. Place tilt steering column in full down position if required.
8. Remove headlamp switch knob.
9. Remove two instrument cluster finish panel mounting screws, then the finish panel.
10. Remove two instrument panel steering column lower cover bolts, then the cover.
11. Remove two instrument panel steering column lower cover reinforcement bolts, then the reinforcement.
12. Remove tilt wheel handle and shank.
13. Remove four mounting screws, then the lower steering column shroud.
14. Turn ignition lock cylinder to Run.
15. Push upward on release tab and remove lock cylinder using suitable tool.
16. Remove upper steering column shroud.
17. Remove anti-theft system transmitter mounting screws and position transmitter out of way.
18. Remove ignition key in warning indicator switch.
19. Disconnect air bag sliding contact electrical connectors.
20. Remove wiring harness from holder.
21. Pry sliding contact mounting clips loose and remove sliding contact.
22. Reverse procedure to install. After installation has been completed, arm air bag system as outlined in "Air Bag System Disarming & Arming."

2001-04

1. Place front wheels in straight-ahead position, then turn ignition to Lock and remove key.
2. Disarm air bag system as outlined in "Air Bag System Disarming & Arming."
3. Remove driver's air bag module as outlined in "Driver's Air Bag Module, Replace."
4. Remove steering wheel mounting bolt or nut.
5. Remove steering wheel from upper shaft using puller tool No. T67L-3600-A, or equivalent.
6. **Before removing air bag clockspring type slip ring from steering shaft, clockspring must be taped** to prevent rotor from being turned accidentally and damaging clockspring, **Fig. 6.**
7. Remove steering column lower shroud.
8. Turn ignition to Run position.
9. Push upward on cylinder release tab while pulling ignition lock cylinder outward using a suitable tool.
10. Raise steering column upper shroud.
11. Position PATS transmitter aside.
12. Remove key-in-ignition warning indicator switch.
13. Remove two clockspring electrical connectors from bracket. Disconnect remaining connector.
14. Remove wire harness from holders.
15. Carefully pry clockspring retaining clips loose, then remove clockspring.
16. New clocksprings arrive in a centered position and are held by a key. Remove this key, but do not allow rotor to turn.
17. Reverse procedure to install, noting the following:
    a. If clockspring requires alignment, hold outer housing stationary, depress clockspring locking tab to release rotor, then while holding locking tab in released position, turn rotor counterclockwise until a slight resistance is felt. Stop turning at this point. Now turn clockwise approximately three turns. This is center point of the clockspring. Release locking tab.
    b. Tighten all fasteners to specifications.
    c. Arm air bag system as outlined in "Air Bag System Disarming & Arming."

SABLE & TAURUS

1. Place front wheels in straight-ahead position, then turn ignition to Lock and remove key.
2. Disarm air bag system as outlined in "Air Bag System Disarming & Arming."
3. Remove driver's air bag module as outlined in "Driver's Air Bag Module, Replace."
4. Apply two strips of masking tape across clockspring to prevent rotation during removal.
5. Move steering column into full down tilt position, then remove tilt wheel handle and shank.
6. Turn ignition to Run position.
7. Push upward on lock cylinder release tab while pulling cylinder outward using a suitable tool.
8. Remove steering column lower and upper shrouds.
9. Remove PATS transmitter mounting screw, then position transmitter aside.
10. Remove key-in-ignition warning indicator switch.
11. **On models equipped with column shift,** disconnect shift indicator tube.
12. **On all models,** route clockspring wire harness out of wire holders along steering column.
13. Carefully pry clockspring retaining clips to release them from steering column.
14. New clocksprings arrive in centered position and are held there with a key. Remove key from clockspring while holding rotor in its centered position. Prevent rotor from turning.
15. Reverse procedure to install, noting the following:
    a. If clockspring requires alignment, hold outer housing stationary, depress clockspring locking tab to release rotor, then while holding locking tab in released position, turn rotor counterclockwise until a slight resistance is felt. Stop turning at this point. Now turn clockwise approximately three turns. This is center point of the clockspring. Release locking tab.
    b. Tighten all fasteners to specifications.
    c. Arm air bag system as outlined in "Air Bag System Disarming & Arming."

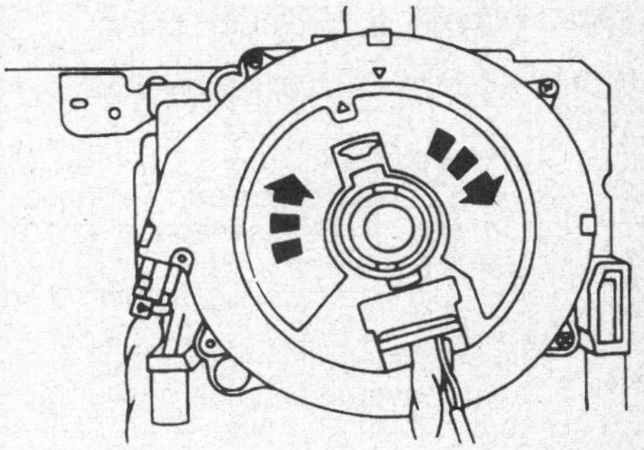

FM8019801986000X

Fig. 9 Sliding contact alignment marks. Escort & ZX2

Front Crash Sensor, Replace

CONTINENTAL

ELECTRONIC CRASH SENSOR (ECS)

1. Disarm air bag system as outlined in "Air Bag System Disarming & Arming."
2. Remove console glove compartment.
3. Disconnect cellular phone electrical connectors.
4. Remove compact disc changer by disconnecting electrical connector and removing screws.
5. Disconnect cigar lighter electrical connector and ash tray receptacle lamp.
6. Remove console top panel.
7. Remove floor console to gear shift bracket screws.
8. Slide floor console rearward, disconnect three electrical connectors and remove floor console.
9. Remove rear seat flow duct.
10. Disconnect ECS module electrical connector locking clip, then the connector.
11. Remove ECS module mounting bolts, then the ECS module.
12. Reverse procedure to install.

CONTOUR & MYSTIQUE

ELECTRONIC CRASH SENSOR (ECS)

1. Disarm air bag system as outlined in "Air Bag System Disarming & Arming."
2. Disconnect crash sensor electrical connector.
3. Remove grille mounting screws, then the grille.
4. Raise and support vehicle.
5. Remove lower radiator shroud.
6. Remove wiring harness from behind lower edge of radiator side panel.
7. Remove wiring harness from mounting clips noting harness routing.
8. Lower vehicle.
9. Remove mounting bolts and remove crash sensor.
10. Reverse procedure to install.

SAFING SENSOR

1. Disarm air bag system as outlined in "Air Bag System Disarming & Arming."
2. Remove powertrain control module.
3. Disconnect safing sensor electrical connector.
4. Remove two mounting bolts, safing sensor and bracket from righthand kick panel.
5. Reverse procedure to install, noting the following:
   a. Tighten mounting bolts to specifications.
   b. Arm air bag system as outlined in "Air Bag System Disarming & Arming."

COUGAR

ELECTRONIC CRASH SENSOR (ECS)

1. Disarm air bag system as outlined in "Air Bag System Disarming & Arming."
2. Disconnect crash sensor electrical connector.
3. Remove grille mounting screws, then the grille.
4. Raise and support vehicle.
5. Remove lower radiator shroud.
6. Remove wiring harness from behind lower edge of radiator side panel.
7. Remove wiring harness from mounting clips noting harness routing.
8. Lower vehicle.
9. Remove mounting bolts and crash sensor.
10. Reverse procedure to install.

SAFING SENSOR

Refer to "Safing Sensor" in "Contour & Mystique."

CROWN VICTORIA, GRAND MARQUIS, MARAUDER & TOWN CAR

1. Disarm air bag system as outlined in "Air Bag System Disarming & Arming."
2. Remove radiator upper sight shield.
3. Disconnect front sensor electrical connector.
4. Remove three screws mounting sensor to radiator front support, then the sensor.
5. Reverse procedure to install, noting the following:
   a. Position sensor with arrow toward front of vehicle.
   b. Tighten mounting screws to specifications.
   c. Arm air bag system as outlined in "Air Bag System Disarming & Arming."

ESCORT & ZX2

ELECTRONIC CRASH SENSOR (ECS)

1. Move both front seats forward and remove two screws from parking brake console panel.
2. Disarm air bag system as outlined in "Air Bag System Disarming & Arming."
3. Engage parking brake.
4. Pull upward and remove parking brake console panel.
5. Remove shift console panel screws, then the pushpins.
6. Place gearshift lever into low gear position.
7. Remove gearshift lever knob.
8. Remove beverage holder from shift console base.
9. Lift upward and remove shift console panel.
10. Place gearshift lever in Park position.
11. Disconnect ECS module electrical connector locking clip and connector.
12. Remove ECS module mounting bolts, then the ECS module.
13. Reverse procedure to install. Arm air bag system as outlined in "Air Bag System Disarming & Arming."

MUSTANG

RIGHTHAND FRONT SENSOR

1. Disarm air bag system as outlined in "Air Bag System Disarming & Arming."
2. Remove air cleaner assembly.
3. Disconnect righthand front sensor electrical connector.
4. Remove screws mounting and sensor.
5. Reverse procedure to install, noting the following:
   a. Position sensor with arrow toward front of vehicle.
   b. Tighten mounting screws to specifications.
   c. Arm air bag system as outlined in "Air Bag System Disarming & Arming."

LEFTHAND FRONT SENSOR

1. Disarm air bag system as outlined in "Air Bag System Disarming & Arming."
2. Remove battery and plastic wiring shield.
3. Disconnect lefthand front sensor electrical connector.
4. Remove lefthand sensor support bracket.
5. Remove mounting screws and sensor.
6. Reverse procedure to install, noting the following:
   a. Tighten mounting screws to specifications.
   b. Arm air bag system as outlined in "Air Bag System Disarming & Arming."

SABLE & TAURUS

1. Disarm air bag system as outlined in "Air Bag System Disarming & Arming."
2. Open hood, then remove pin-type retainers and header opening panel.
3. Disconnect crash sensor electrical connector.
4. Remove sensor retaining bolts, then the sensor.
5. Reverse procedure to install, noting the following:
   a. Ensure all wiring and electrical connectors are properly routed to avoid pinching.
   b. Tighten fasteners to specifications.
   c. Arm air bag system as outlined in "Air Bag System Disarming & Arming."

Side Air Bag Crash Sensor, Replace

CONTINENTAL

1. Move front seat to full forward position.
2. Disarm air bag system as outlined in "Air Bag System Disarming & Arming."
3. Access side air bag crash through carpet opening located under front seat.
4. Remove wiring harness push pin (1) from side air bag crash sensor bracket, **Fig. 10.**
5. Disconnect side air bag crash sensor electrical connector.
6. Remove two side air bag crash sensor bracket mounting screws (2), then the sensor (3) and bracket.
7. Reverse procedure to install, noting the following:
   a. Tighten mounting bolts and screws to specifications.
   b. Ensure electrical connector is securely in place.
   c. Arm air bag system as outlined in "Air Bag System Disarming & Arming."

COUGAR

1. Position front seat fully rearward.
2. Remove front seat track covers and bolts.
3. Position front seat forward.
4. Remove rear seat track covers and bolts.
5. Disarm air bag system as outlined in "Air Bag System Disarming & Arming."
6. Disconnect front seat electrical connector and remove front seat.
7. Remove scuff plate.
8. Lift hood latch release handle and release two mounting clips.
9. Remove cowl side panel.
10. Fold back floor carpeting and sound deadening covering.
11. Remove three side air bag sensor mounting bolts, **Fig. 11.**
12. Disconnect electrical connector and remove side air bag sensor.
13. Reverse procedure to install, noting the following:
    a. Tighten mounting bolts and screws to specifications.
    b. Ensure electrical connector is securely in place.

c. Arm air bag system as outlined in "Air Bag System Disarming & Arming."

CROWN VICTORIA, GRAND MARQUIS & MARAUDER

1. Disarm air bag system as outlined in "Air Bag System Disarming & Arming."
2. Remove front seat track covers and bolts.
3. Disconnect front seat electrical connectors and remove seat.
4. Position carpet back to access side impact sensor.
5. Disconnect electrical connector, then remove side impact sensor with bracket.
6. Reverse procedure to install. Arm air bag system as outlined in "Air Bag System Disarming & Arming."

LS & THUNDERBIRD

1. Remove front seat as outlined in "Side Impact Air Bag Module, Replace."
2. Disarm air bag system as outlined in "Air Bag System Disarming & Arming."
3. **On LS models,** remove front and rear door scuff plates, then the B-pillar lower trim panel.
4. **On Thunderbird models,** remove safety belt anchor, then position carpet back to access sensor.
5. **On all models,** disconnect side crash sensor electrical connector.
6. Remove two mounting bolts and side crash sensor with bracket.
7. Reverse procedure to install, noting the following:
   a. Tighten mounting bolts to specifications.
   b. Ensure electrical connector is securely in place.
   c. Arm air bag system as outlined in "Air Bag System Disarming & Arming."

SABLE & TAURUS

1. Disarm air bag system as outlined in "Air Bag System Disarming & Arming."
2. Pull up to release retaining clips and remove front door scuff plate.
3. From behind seat belt guide, release tabs on each side, then pull out and remove belt guide cover. Replace cover if it is damaged or does not remain closed.
4. Remove belt guide bolt, then the guide.
5. Remove belt anchor bolt, then the anchor.
6. Pull out to release retaining clips and remove B-pillar upper trim panel.
7. Separate B-pillar lower trim panel at retaining button.
8. Pull up and out to release retaining clips and remove B-pillar lower trim panel.
9. Move carpet aside as required to access side crash sensor.
10. Disconnect sensor electrical connector.
11. Remove sensor mounting bolts.
12. Remove side crash sensor with bracket.
13. Reverse procedure to install, noting the following:
    a. Ensure all wiring and electrical connectors are properly routed to avoid pinching.
    b. Tighten mounting bolts to specifications.
    c. Arm air bag system as outlined in "Air Bag System Disarming & Arming."

TOWN CAR

1. Position front seat fully rearward.
2. Remove seat track front covers and bolts.
3. Position front seat fully forward.
4. Remove seat track rear covers and bolts.
5. Disarm air bag system as outlined in "Air Bag System Disarming & Arming."
6. Disconnect front seat electrical connector and remove front seat.
7. Remove carpet to access side air bag sensor.
8. Remove side air bag sensor mounting bolts (1) and position sensor (3) to disconnect electrical connector (2), **Fig. 12.**
9. Remove side air bag sensor and bracket.
10. Reverse procedure to install, noting the following:
    a. Tighten mounting bolts and screws to specifications.
    b. Ensure electrical connector is securely in place.
    c. Arm air bag system as outlined in "Air Bag System Disarming & Arming."

Diagnostic Monitor, Replace

CONTINENTAL

1. Disarm air bag system as outlined in "Air Bag System Disarming & Arming."
2. Remove screws mounting steering column opening cover to instrument panel, then the cover.
3. Remove four mounting bolts and bolster.
4. Disconnect diagnostic monitor electrical wiring connectors.
5. Remove screws mounting diagnostic monitor and bracket assembly to instrument panel brace, then the assembly.
6. Reverse procedure to install, noting the following:
   a. Tighten mounting screws to specifications.
   b. Arm air bag system as outlined in "Air Bag System Disarming & Arming."

CONTOUR & MYSTIQUE

1. Disarm air bag system as outlined in "Air Bag System Disarming & Arming."
2. Remove righthand console front finish panel.
3. Depress tabs on air bag monitor bracket and slide monitor off bracket.
4. Disconnect electrical connectors.
5. Reverse procedure to install, noting the following:
   a. Tighten mounting screws to specifications.
   b. Arm air bag system as outlined in "Air Bag System Disarming & Arming."

CROWN VICTORIA, GRAND MARQUIS & TOWN CAR

1. Disarm air bag system as outlined in "Air Bag System Disarming & Arming."
2. Remove righthand side cowl trim panel.
3. Open glove compartment door, then depress sides to depress mounting tabs and allow door to drop downward.
4. Move righthand cowl trim panel padding out of way.
5. Disconnect diagnostic monitor electrical connectors.
6. Remove diagnostic monitor to righthand cowl panel mounting screws, then the monitor.
7. Reverse procedure to install, noting the following:
   a. Tighten mounting screws to specifications.
   b. Arm air bag system as outlined in "Air Bag System Disarming & Arming."

MUSTANG

1. Disarm air bag system as outlined in "Air Bag System Disarming & Arming."
2. Remove radio and disconnect diagnostic monitor (blue box with two connectors mounted below climate control head).
3. Remove screws mounting diagnostic monitor and bracket on instrument panel brace and remove assembly.
4. Reverse procedure to install, noting the following:
   a. Tighten mounting screws to specifications.
   b. Arm air bag system as outlined in "Air Bag System Disarming & Arming."

SABLE & TAURUS

1. Disarm air bag system as outlined in "Air Bag System Disarming & Arming."
2. Move door lock relays and remote anti-theft module to access diagnostic monitor, if equipped.
3. Disconnect diagnostic monitor electrical connectors.
4. Loosen diagnostic monitor to bracket mounting screws until monitor can be removed. Screw is part of diagnostic monitor and cannot be removed.
5. Reverse procedure to install, noting the following:
   a. Tighten mounting screws to specifications.
   b. Arm air bag system as outlined in "Air Bag System Disarming & Arming."

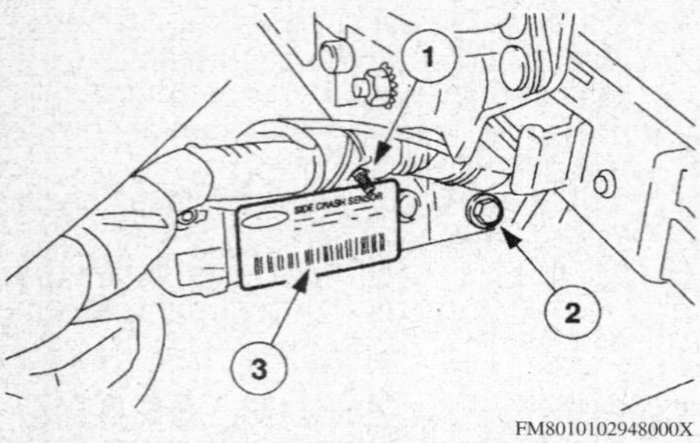

Fig. 10 Side air bag crash sensor replacement. Continental

Air Bag Control Module (ACM), Replace

COUGAR

1. Disarm air bag system as outlined in "Air Bag System Disarming & Arming."
2. Remove instrument panel lower panel fasteners, then the panel.
3. Disconnect ACM electrical connector.
4. Remove ACM mounting bolts, then the ACM.
5. Reverse procedure to install, noting the following:
   a. Tighten fasteners to specifications.
   b. Ensure electrical connector is securely in place.
   c. Arm air bag system as outlined in "Air Bag System Disarming & Arming."

FOCUS

1. Disarm air bag system as outlined in "Air Bag System Disarming & Arming."
2. Remove cupholder insert.
3. Disconnect front of center console from floor panel bracket.
4. **On models equipped with traction control,** disconnect control switch electrical connectors.
5. **On models less center console armrest,** remove rear cup holder insert, then disconnect rear of center console from floor panel bracket.
6. **On models equipped with center console armrest,** remove armrest trim panel and armrest.
7. **On all models,** disconnect boots for shift lever and parking brake handle from center console.
8. Raise parking brake control lever to its full position.
9. **On models equipped with automatic transaxle,** place shift lever in Neutral position.
10. **On all models,** remove center console from vehicle.
11. Disconnect ACM electrical connector.
12. Remove ACM mounting bolts, then the ACM.
13. Reverse procedure to install, noting the following:
   a. Tighten mounting bolts to specifications.
   b. Ensure electrical connector is securely in place.
   c. Arm air bag system as outlined in "Air Bag System Disarming & Arming."

Restraints Control Module (RCM), Replace

CONTINENTAL

1. Disarm air bag system as outlined in "Air Bag System Disarming & Arming."
2. **On models equipped with floor console,** proceed as follows:
   a. Remove floor console assembly.
   b. Remove rear seat air flow duct.
   c. Remove center console mounting bracket.
   d. Position carpet aside to access and remove RCM mounting bolts.
3. **On models equipped with bench seat,** proceed as follows:
   a. Remove driver's side bench seat.
   b. Disconnect RCM electrical connectors.
   c. Remove RCM mounting bolts.
4. **On all models,** remove RCM and its bracket.
5. Reverse procedure to install, noting the following:
   a. Ensure all wiring and electrical connectors are properly routed to avoid pinching.
   b. Tighten all fasteners to specifications.
   c. Arm air bag system as outlined in "Air Bag System Disarming & Arming."

CROWN VICTORIA, GRAND MARQUIS & MARAUDER

1. Disarm air bag system as outlined in "Air Bag System Disarming & Arming."
2. **On models equipped with column shift,** proceed as follows:
   a. Release ashtray locking tabs, then remove ashtray.
   b. Remove two ashtray bracket screws, then slide bracket forward to release retainers and position out of the way.
3. **On models equipped with center console,** proceed as follows:
   a. Set parking brake and shift transmission to neutral position.
   b. Pull out on gauges and finish panel to release retaining clips, then position aside.
   c. Pull up on center console finish panel to release retaining clips, then rotate out of the way.
   d. Remove shifter cable socket from shifter ball, then push in on release tab and separate shifter cable from shifter assembly.
   e. Push in on release tab and separate shift inter-lock cable from shifter assembly, then remove shift inter-lock cable from shifter assembly.
4. **On all models,** disconnect RCM electrical connectors.
5. Remove RCM mounting bolts, then the RCM.

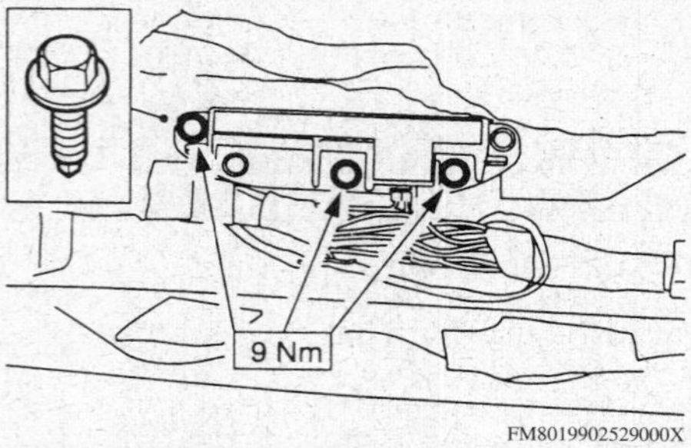

Fig. 11 Side impact air bag crash sensor replacement. Cougar

6. Reverse procedure to install, noting the following:
   a. Ensure all wiring and electrical connectors are properly routed to avoid pinching.
   b. Tighten all fasteners to specifications.
   c. Arm air bag system as outlined in "Air Bag System Disarming & Arming."

LS

1. Apply parking brake.
2. **On models equipped with manual transmission,** place selector lever in fourth gear and remove knob.
3. **On models equipped with automatic transmission,** place selector lever in neutral.
4. **On all models,** disarm air bag system as outlined in "Air Bag System Disarming & Arming."
5. Remove ashtray finish panel.
6. Disconnect cellular phone and traction control switch electrical connectors.
7. Release cellular phone wiring harness from console finish panel.
8. Remove console rear finish panel assembly.
9. Unclip parking brake boot from console base.
10. Remove console assembly front and rear screws.
11. Remove console air conditioning duct mounting screw.
12. Remove console assembly by sliding rearward.
13. Remove rear vent duct.
14. **On models equipped with automatic transmission,** proceed as follows:
   a. Disconnect and separate shifter interlock cable and casing from shifter.
   b. Remove shifter retaining bolts.
   c. Position shifter aside.
15. **On all models,** remove extension duct.
16. Disconnect RCM electrical connectors.
17. Remove RCM mounting bolts, then the RCM.
18. Reverse procedure to install, noting the following:
   a. Ensure RCM arrow faces front of vehicle.
   b. Tighten fasteners to specifications.
   c. Arm air bag system as outlined in "Air Bag System Disarming & Arming."

MUSTANG

1. Disarm air bag system as outlined in "Air Bag System Disarming & Arming."
2. Remove RCM bracket righthand retaining bolt.
3. Position carpet back at righthand side of instrument panel center support bracket.
4. Remove RCM bracket retaining bolt.
5. Position carpet back at lefthand side of instrument panel center support bracket.
6. Disconnect RCM electrical connector.
7. Remove RCM bracket retaining bolts, then the RCM with bracket.
8. Reverse procedure to install, noting the following:
   a. Ensure RCM arrow faces front of vehicle.
   b. Tighten fasteners to specifications.
   c. Arm air bag system as outlined in "Air Bag System Disarming & Arming."

SABLE & TAURUS

1. Disarm air bag system as outlined in "Air Bag System Disarming & Arming."
2. Move carpet aside at righthand side of center tunnel area under instrument panel.
3. Remove RCM righthand mounting bolts.
4. Move carpet aside at lefthand side of center tunnel area under instrument panel.
5. Disconnect RCM electrical connector.
6. Remove RCM lefthand mounting bolt, then the RCM and its bracket.
7. Reverse procedure to install, noting the following:
   a. Ensure RCM arrow faces front of vehicle.
   b. Tighten fasteners to specifications.
   c. Arm air bag system as outlined in "Air Bag System Disarming & Arming."

THUNDERBIRD

1. Disarm air bag system as outlined in "Air Bag System Disarming & Arming."
2. Remove retaining clips, then the center console finish panel.
3. Remove lower center instrument panel, then position aside.
4. **RCM is located on top of transmission tunnel under instrument panel.** Slide and disengage RCM electrical connector, then disconnect.
5. Remove bolts, then the restraint control module.
6. Reverse procedure to install. Arm air bag system as outlined in "Air Bag System Disarming & Arming."

TOWN CAR

1. Disarm air bag system as outlined in "Air Bag System Disarming & Arming."
2. Remove ashtray by releasing retaining tabs, then pulling out of instrument panel.
3. Remove carpet patch covering RCM.
4. Remove RCM cover bolts, then the cover.
5. Disconnect RCM electrical connectors.

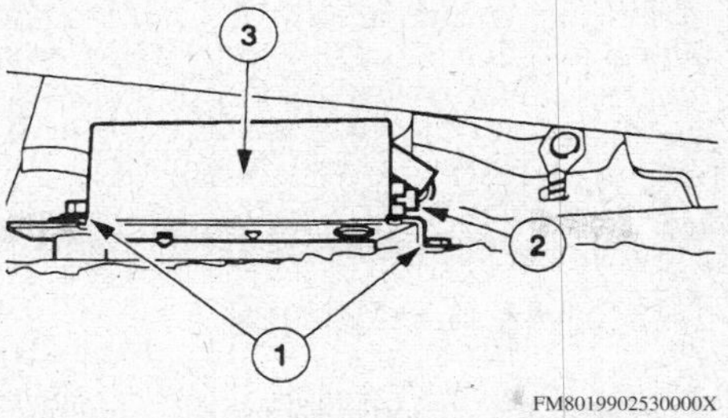

Fig. 12 Side air bag crash sensor replacement. Town Car

6. Remove RCM mounting bolt, then the RCM.
7. Reverse procedure to install, noting the following:
   a. Ensure RCM arrow faces front of vehicle.
   b. Tighten fasteners to specifications.
   c. Arm air bag system as outlined in "Air Bag System Disarming & Arming."

Seat Position Sensor, Replace

CROWN VICTORIA, GRAND MARQUIS & MARAUDER

1. Disarm air bag system as outlined in "Air Bag System Disarming & Arming."
2. Remove front seat track covers and bolts.
3. Disconnect front seat electrical connectors and remove seat.
4. **On models equipped with power seat,** proceed as follows:
   a. Disconnect electrical connector, then remove seat position sensor bolt.
   b. Press seat position sensor tab inward, then remove sensor.
   c. Remove magnet assembly bolt, then slide back and remove magnet assembly.
5. **On models equipped with manual seat,** disconnect electrical connector, then remove bolt and seat position sensor.
6. **On all models,** reverse procedure to install. Arm air bag system as outlined in "Air Bag System Disarming & Arming."

Back-Up Power Supply, Replace

The back-up power supply is combined into the diagnostic monitor. Refer to "Diagnostic Monitor, Replace" for removal procedure.

Air Bag & Seat Belt Pretensioner Disposal

Several situations may arise to require some form of disposal action: scrapping a vehicle containing a deployed air bag, scrapping a vehicle with a live air bag, disposal of a live but electrically inoperative air bag module, scrapping a deployed air bag, etc.

AIR BAG DEPLOYMENT

REMOTE DEPLOYMENT OF AIR BAGS

Remote deployment is to be performed outdoors with all personnel a minimum of 20 feet away to ensure personal safety.

1. Disarm air bag system as outlined in "Air Bag System Disarming & Arming."
2. Remove air bag module from vehicle.
3. **On models equipped with single stage air bags,** cut two module connector wires and strip one inch of insulation from ends.
4. **On models equipped with dual stage air bags,** proceed as follows:
   a. Cut clockspring wire harness, then remove sheathing over wires.
   b. Strip one inch of insulation from all four wires.
   c. Inspect ohms from stripped end of each wire to connector end, **Fig. 13.** If any wire reads more than .5 ohms, use another connector.
   d. Connect two electrical connectors cut from clockspring to air bag module, then twist together one wire from each pair.
5. **On all models,** obtain two wires a minimum of 20 feet long.
6. Connect one end of each wire to each of air bag module wires or connector pin.
7. Place module with trim cover facing upward on a flat surface in a remote area such as a parking lot or field. **Do not place module with trim cover facing down, as forces of deploying air bag may cause module to ricochet and cause personal injury.**
8. Ensure no people, animals or objects are within 20 feet of module.
9. Remaining at least 20 feet away from module, deploy air bag by touching other ends of two wires to terminals of a fully charged 12 volt vehicle battery.
10. If successful, a loud report will be heard and air bag material will be visible coming from top of module. Allow at least ten minutes for cooling before handling air bag components.
11. If air bag module fails to deploy, contact Ford Motor Company.

SEAT BELT PRETENSIONER DISPOSAL

REMOTE DEPLOYMENT OF SEAT BELT PRETENSIONER

1. Disarm air bag system as outlined in "Air Bag System Disarming & Arming."
2. Remove seat belt pretensioner from vehicle.
3. Cut connector wires, then strip one inch of insulation from ends. Obtain two wires a minimum of 20 feet long. Connect one end of each wire to each of the seat belt pretensioner wires.
4. Place seat belt pretensioner on a flat surface in a remote area such as a parking lot or field.
5. Ensure no people, animals or objects

are within 20 feet of seat belt pretensioner.

6. Remaining at least 20 feet away from pretensioner, deploy pretensioner by touching other ends of two wires to terminals of a fully charged 12 volt vehicle battery.
7. Allow at least 10 minutes before handling air bag components to allow for cooling.
8. If seat belt pretensioner fails to deploy, contact Ford Motor Company.

TECHNICAL SERVICE BULLETINS

Discolored Or Marred Air Bag Module Covers

Driver's and passenger's air bag modules must not be painted. This could affect air bag performance during deployment and may increase risk of injury during a collision. Air bag modules which have been damaged or marred must be replaced.

New Design Air Bag Sliding Contact

SABLE & TAURUS

A design change has been made to the mounting of the sliding contact. The previous design had three mounting screws. The new design has three snaps. Previous design and new design sliding contacts are interchangeable. When installing the new design sliding contact, snap the contact into the same three locations where the sliding contact mounting screws would have been installed. After completing installation of the new design sliding contact, remove the yellow pull ring.

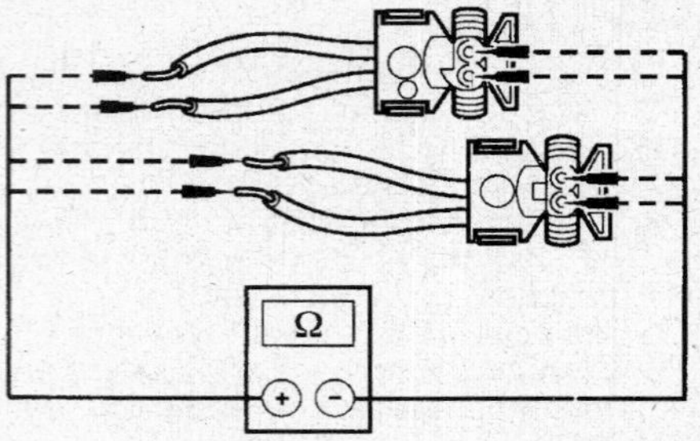

FM8010205211000X

Fig. 13 Connector ohms inspect

TIGHTENING SPECIFICATIONS

Year	Component	Torque/Ft. Lbs.
CONTINENTAL		
2000–04	Air Bag Control Module	17
	Bench Seat Front Track Mounting Bolts	18
	Bench Seat Rear Inner Track Mounting Bolts	59
	Bench Seat Rear Outer Track Mounting Bolts	18
	Driver's Air Bag Module	108①
	Floor Console To Bracket Screws	24–33①
	Passenger's Air Bag Module	80①
	Side Impact Air Bag Module	62①
	Side Impact Air Bag Sensor	108①
	Steering Column Nuts	11
	Steering Wheel	②
CONTOUR & MYSTIQUE		
2000	Crash Sensor Bolts	96①
	Driver's Air Bag Bolts	44①
	Passenger's Air Bag Module	12
	Safing Sensor Bolts	96①
COUGAR		
2000–02	Air Bag Control Module	53①
	Crash Sensor	80①
	Driver's Air Bag Module (2000)	32–44①
	Driver's Air Bag Module (2001–02)	44①
	Passenger's Air Bag Module	12
	Side Impact Air Bag Module	12
	Side Impact Air Bag Sensor	80①
	Steering Wheel	37

Continued

TIGHTENING SPECIFICATIONS—Continued

Year	Component	Torque/Ft. Lbs.
CROWN VICTORIA, GRAND MARQUIS & MARAUDER		
2000	Air Bag Control Module	108①
	Air Bag Front Sensor & Bracket	108①
	Crash Sensor To Radiator Support	108–132①
	Driver's Air Bag Module	24–32①
	Passenger's Air Bag Module, Bolts	66–91①
	Passenger's Air Bag Module, Screws	18–24①
	Steering Wheel	25–34
2001–04	Crash Sensor	108①
	Driver's Air Bag Module Bolts	108①
	Passenger's Air Bag Module Bolts (Through Glove Box)	80①
	Passenger's Air Bag Module Bolts (Under Trim Panel)	27①
	Restraints Control Module	108①
	Side Impact Air Bag Module	62
	Side Impact Air Bar Sensor	108①
	Steering Column Nuts	11
ESCORT & ZX2		
2000–04	Air Bag Control Module Bolts	8–10
	Driver's Air Bag Module Bolts	70–103①
	Passenger's Air Bag Module Bolts	70–103①
	Steering Wheel Bolt	34–46
FOCUS		
2000–04	Air Bag Control Module Bolts	80①
	Driver's Air Bag Module Bolts	44①
	Passenger's Air Bag Module Bolts	12
	Passenger's Air Bag Module Trim Cover Bolts	96①
	Side Impact Air Bag Crash Sensor Bolts	80①
	Side Impact Air Bag Module Nuts	44①
	Steering Column Mounting Bolts	112①
	Steering Wheel Bolt	37
LS & THUNDERBIRD		
2000–04	Air Bag Control Module	108①
	Driver's Air Bag Module	108①
	Front Seat Track To Floor Fasteners	18
	Ground Screw Repair Weld-Nuts	108①
	I/P Reinforcement & Cowl Side Bolts	15
	Passenger's Air Bag Module	80①
	Side Impact Air Bag Module	80①
	Side Crash Sensor	108①
	Steering Column Pinch Bolt	26
MUSTANG		
2000–04	Air Bag Control Module Bracket	108①
	Driver's Air Bag Module	80①
	Passenger's Air Bag Module	80①

Continued

TIGHTENING SPECIFICATIONS—Continued

Year	Component	Torque/Ft. Lbs.
SABLE & TAURUS		
2000–04	Air Bag Control Module Bolts	17
	Crash Sensor	108①
	Grounding Screw	108①
	Passenger's Air Bag Module Bolts	71①
	Seat Belt Anchor Bolts	30
	Seat Belt Guide Bolts	30
	Seatback Pivot Bolt	38
	Side Impact Air Bag Module Nuts	84①
	Steering Column Lower Opening Cover Screws	62①
	Steering Wheel Armature Nuts	12
	Steering Wheel Pinion Shaft	13
TOWN CAR		
2000	Air Bag Control Module	96–120①
	Air Bag Front Sensor & Bracket	86–126①
	Driver's Air Bag Module	96–120①
	Front Crash Sensor	108①
	Instrument Cluster Finish Panel	18–27①
	Instrument Cluster Mounting	8–12①
	Passenger's Air Bag Module	96–120①
	Primary Crash Sensor	18–24①
	PRNDL Indicator	62–97①
	Side Impact Air Bag Crash Sensor	108①
	Side Impact Air Module	62①
	Steering Column Lower Cover	18–27①
	Steering Column Lower Reinforcement	27–44①
	Steering Column Support	10–13
	Steering Wheel	25–34
2001–04	Air Bag Control Module Bolts	108①
	Driver's Air Bag Module Bolts	③
	Front Crash Sensor Bolts	108①
	Ground Screw Repair Weld-Nuts	108①
	Passenger's Air Bag Module Bolts	80①
	Side Impact Air Bag Module Nuts	62①
	Side Impact Sensor Bolts	108①
	Steering Column Lower Reinforcement Bolts	35①
	Steering Column Mounting Nuts	11
	Steering Wheel Bolt	30

① — Inch Lbs.
② — On 2000 models, 25–34 ft. lbs. On 2001–04 models, 23–25 ft. lbs.
③ — On 2001–02 models, 108 inch lbs. On 2003–04 models, 80 inch lbs.

DASH PANEL SERVICE

NOTE: Refer To "Dash Gauges" Section For Information Related To Analog Instrumentation.

NOTE: On Air Bag Equipped Models, Refer To "Air Bag System Precautions" Located In The Front Of This Manual For System Disarming & Arming Procedures.

NOTE: Refer To "Computer Relearn Procedures" Located In The Front Of This Manual When Battery Power To The Computer Has Been Interrupted.

NOTE: Refer To The "Electronic Instrumentation" Section In MOTOR's "Domestic Engine Performance & Driveability Manual" For Information Related To Electronic Instrumentation.

INDEX

PRECAUTIONS

Air Bag Systems

Refer to "Air Bag System Precautions" in the front of this manual for system disarming and arming procedures.

Battery Ground Cable

Prior to service, disconnect battery ground cable and isolate as required.

DASH PANEL

REPLACE

Continental

1. Remove driver's and passenger's air bag modules as outlined in "Passive Restraint Systems" chapter.
2. Remove floor console, mini console and rear seat climate control air duct sleeve.
3. Remove lefthand instrument panel insulator pushpins, then the panel insulator.
4. Remove instrument panel steering column cover retaining screws, then the column cover.
5. Remove hood release handle retaining screws and position hood release handle aside.
6. Remove parking brake release handle and cable, then the instrument panel steering column opening cover reinforcement, **Fig. 1.**
7. Release cable from parking brake actuator.
8. Remove steering column as outlined in "Steering Columns" chapter.
9. Disconnect inboard and outboard bulkhead electrical connectors.
10. **On models equipped with heated seats,** disconnect heated seat switch electrical connectors, **Fig. 2.**
11. **On all models,** remove steering column mounting support to instrument cowl brace bolts, then the instrument panel brace to instrument panel bolt.
12. Remove righthand instrument panel insulator pushpins, then the panel insulator.
13. Disconnect vacuum harness connector, then the in line electrical harness connector, **Fig. 3.**
14. Position righthand scuff plate aside, then remove righthand cowl trim panel.
15. Disconnect antenna inline connector.
16. Remove ignition/shifter interlock cable from bracket and shifter interlock cam.
17. Remove lefthand lower instrument panel trim.
18. Remove nuts and lower steering column, **Fig. 4.**
19. Remove ignition/shifter interlock bracket retaining screws, **Fig. 5.**
20. Disconnect shift interlock electrical connector, then remove ignition/shifter interlock cable from bracket.
21. Remove ignition shifter interlock cable.
22. Pry upward to release instrument panel defroster opening grille assembly from instrument panel.
23. Disconnect two electrical connectors and remove defroster opening grille.
24. Remove instrument panel cowl top screws, then the righthand and lefthand instrument panel support to cowl side nut and bolts.
25. Loosen lefthand instrument panel support to cowl side captive bolt, **Fig. 6.**
26. Position instrument panel away from cowl, then disconnect electronic air temperature control hose from heater plenum.
27. Remove instrument panel.
28. Reverse procedures to install noting following:
    a. **Torque** cowl side captive bolt 13–16 ft. lbs.
    b. **Torque** panel support to cowl side nut 7–11 ft. lbs.
    c. **Torque** steering column mounting support to cowl brace bolts 13–16 ft. lbs.

Contour & Mystique

1. Remove driver side instrument panel lower cover.
2. Center steering wheel and lock in position.
3. Remove steering column upper and lower shroud.
4. Disconnect steering column shaft from flexible coupling.
5. Disconnect electrical connectors on right and left sides of steering column.
6. Unclip wiring harness, remove mounting bolts and slide steering column outward to disengage retaining tab.
7. Remove floor console, then the radio chassis.
8. Remove control opening finishing panel retaining screws, then the finishing panel.
9. Remove climate control assembly, then disconnect electrical connectors and vacuum lines.
10. Pull lever and swing central junction

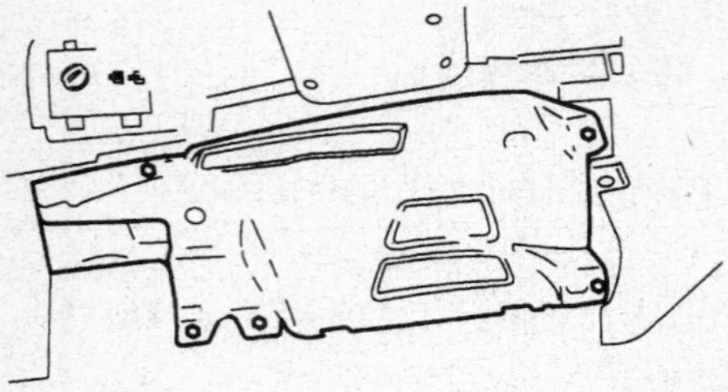

FM9149800123000X

Fig. 1 Steering column opening cover reinforcement removal. Continental

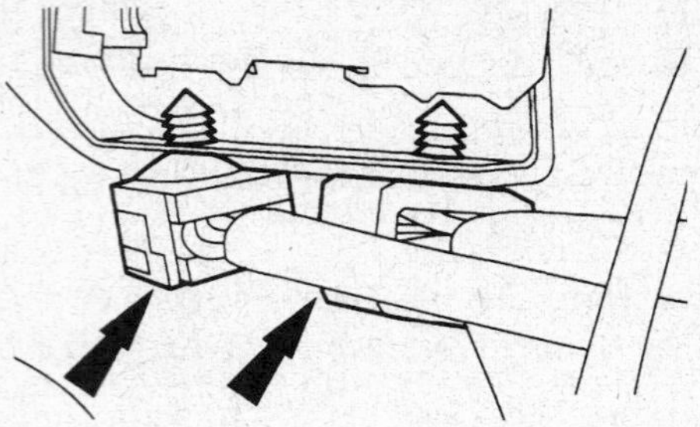

FM9149800124000X

Fig. 2 Heated seat switch connectors. Continental

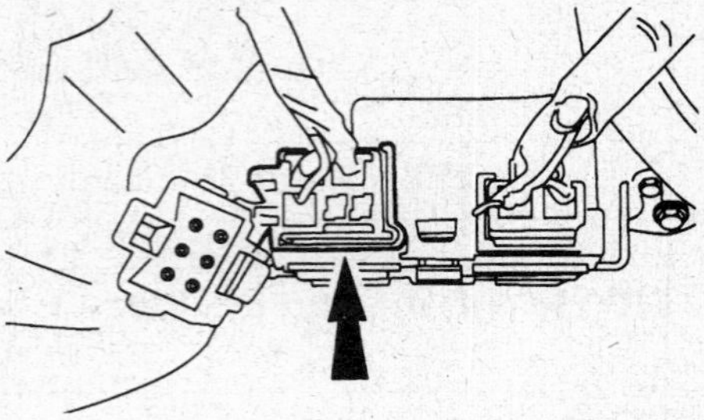

FM9149800125000X

Fig. 3 Inline electrical harness connector location. Continental

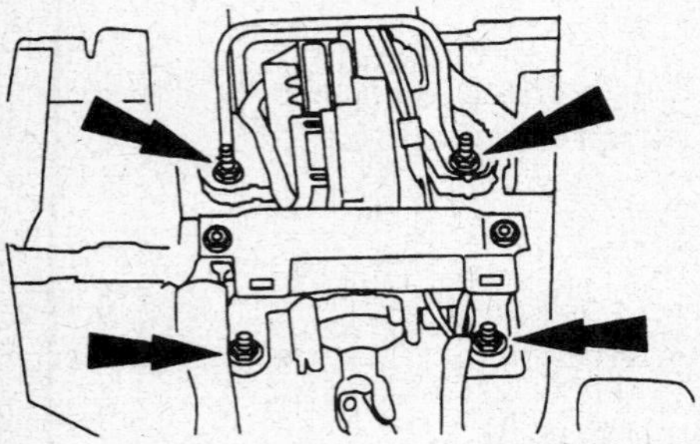

FM9149800121000X

Fig. 4 Steering column retaining nuts. Continental

FM9149800122000X

Fig. 5 Ignition/shifter interlock retaining screws location. Continental

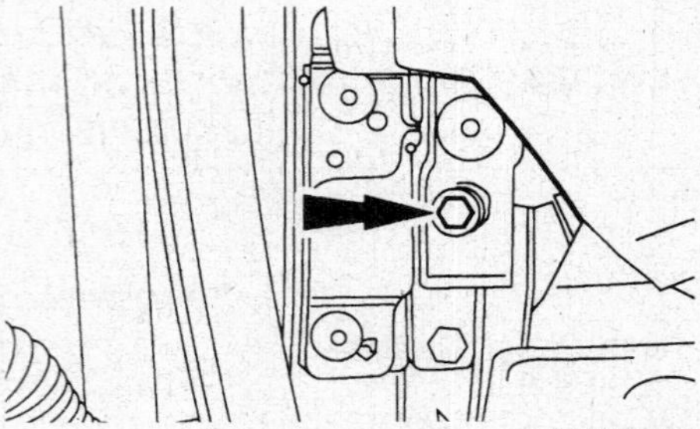

FM9149800126000X

Fig. 6 Captive bolt location. Continental

box down, **Fig. 7,** then disconnect electrical connectors and position kick panel aside.

11. Remove righthand kick panel push pin and screw.
12. Disconnect righthand kickpanel electrical connectors, antenna wire connector, and ground strap bolt.
13. Remove "A" pillar trim panels, then the center lefthand and righthand instrument panel retaining bolts.
14. Remove passenger air bag module as outlined in "Passive Restraint Systems" chapter.
15. Remove lefthand and righthand instrument panel mounting bolts, **Fig. 8.**
16. Partially remove instrument panel to access and disconnect following components:
    a. Instrument interface module electrical connector.
    b. Assembly line diagnostic link connector bracket.
    c. Defroster tubes.
    d. Radio amplifier electrical connector.
    e. A/C electronic door actuator motor.
    f. Anti-theft module electrical connector.
17. Remove instrument panel, then the support, **Fig. 9.**
18. Reverse procedure to install.

Cougar

1. Center and lock steering wheel.
2. Remove upper and lower steering column shrouds.
3. Disconnect steering column shaft from flexible coupling.
4. Disconnect electrical connectors from steering column.
5. Cut cable tie, then disconnect air bag control module connector.
6. Unclip wiring harnesses and remove steering column mounting bolts, then slide column outwards to disengage retaining tab.
7. **On models equipped with automatic transaxle,** remove floor console as follows:
    a. Raise armrest or remove rear cup holder to gain access to floor console rear screws, then remove screws.
    b. Fully apply parking brake lever.
    c. Remove ashtray and cigar lighter bezel.
    d. Remove stowage tray by pulling down on power socket aperture and pulling outward.
    e. Remove bezel screw, carefully lift bezel partially up and disconnect electrical connectors.
    f. Remove terminal spacer from selector lever electrical connector, **Fig. 10.**
    g. Remove overdrive switch terminals from electrical connector and remove selector lever indicator bezel, **Fig. 11.**
    h. Remove floor console front screws, **Fig. 12.**
    i. Disconnect cigar lighter/power socket electrical connector, then remove console.
8. **On models equipped with manual transaxle,** remove floor console as follows:
    a. Remove gearshift knob, then the spring and damping sleeve, **Fig. 13.**
    b. Remove gearshift lever boot.
    c. Raise armrest or remove rear cup holder.
    d. Remove console rear screws, **Fig. 14.**
    e. Remove ashtray and cigar lighter bezel and stowage tray.
    f. Remove floor console front screws, **Fig. 12.**
    g. Fully raise parking brake lever, then remove console.
9. **On all models,** remove radio assembly.
10. Remove switch assembly and heater control/audio unit bezel, **Figs. 15 and 16.**
11. Remove exterior lamp switch and panel.
12. Pull lever and swing central junction box down, then disconnect wiring harnesses and connectors from central junction box, **Fig. 17.**
13. Disconnect instrument interface module electrical connectors, **Fig. 18.**
14. Remove liftgate release switch.
15. Release data link connector retaining clip, then slide data link connector down, **Fig. 19.**
16. Remove right side scuff panel and pull back insulation.
17. Disconnect antenna cable connector, ground strap bolt and electrical connectors, **Fig. 20.**
18. Remove "A" pillar trim panels.
19. Remove center left side instrument panel bolts, **Fig. 21.**
20. Remove passenger air bag module as outlined in "Passive Restraint Systems" chapter.
21. Disconnect air conditioning door actuator motor, anti-theft module, heater blower motor and heater blower resistor electrical connectors, **Fig. 22.**
22. Remove ground strap bolts, then disconnect power seat relay, **Fig. 23.**
23. Remove instrument panel mounting bolts, **Figs. 24 and 25.**

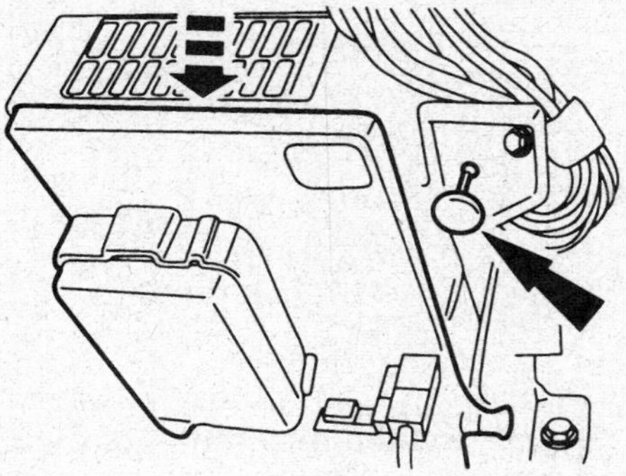

Fig. 7 Central junction box removal. Contour & Mystique

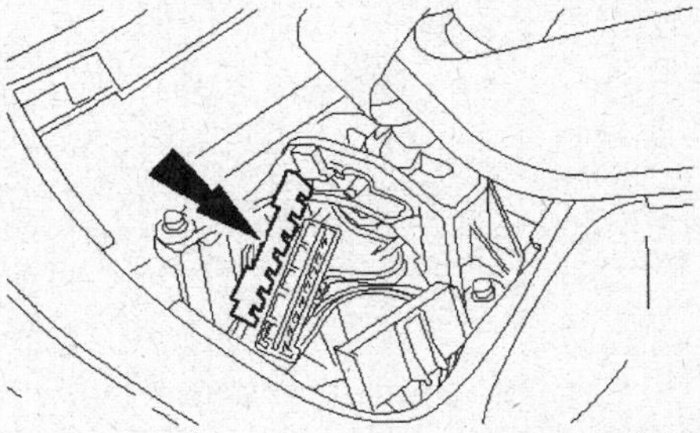

Fig. 10 Selector lever terminal spacer. Cougar w/automatic transaxle

24. Partially remove instrument panel, then remove defroster tubes.
25. Remove instrument panel from vehicle.
26. Reverse procedure to install.

Crown Victoria, Grand Marquis & Marauder

2000-02

1. Remove driver's and passenger's air bag modules as outlined in "Passive Restraint Systems" chapter.
2. Disconnect electrical connector, then remove speed control servo and set aside.
3. Disconnect electrical connectors from lefthand engine compartment, brake fluid sensor and windshield wiper motor.
4. Unseat lefthand wiring harness grommet.
5. Disconnect electrical connectors from blower motor, A/C pressure cutoff switch and righthand engine compartment electrical harness.
6. Disconnect vacuum line at intake manifold and blower motor electrical connector.
7. Remove right front tire and wheel.
8. Remove right upper front fender splash shield bolts and lower splash shield bolt and locator, then position splash shield away from instrument panel.
9. Unlock wiring harness guide and unseat righthand wiring harness grommet.
10. Install right side wheel and tire.
11. Remove right side lower instrument panel lower insulator, right and left scuff plates and right and left cowl side trim panels.
12. Disconnect Electronic Crash Sensor (ECS) module.
13. Disconnect antenna cable lead in connector, righthand ground bolts and righthand bulkhead electrical connectors, **Figs. 26 and 27.**
14. Disconnect Electronic Automatic Temperature Control (EATC) hose from evaporator housing, if equipped.
15. Pull left and right side door weatherstrips loose, position to one side.
16. Feed righthand wiring harness through instrument panel.
17. Remove carpet insert.
18. Disconnect climate control head vacuum harness connector, **Fig. 28.**
19. Remove instrument panel tunnel brace.
20. Remove lefthand instrument panel insulator, lower steering column opening cover and steering column opening cover reinforcement.
21. Disconnect parking brake release vacuum connector and instrument panel vacuum connector, **Figs. 29 and 30.**
22. Position steering column brace to one side.
23. Separate intermediate shaft from steering column.
24. Disconnect transmission shift cable from steering column.
25. Remove lefthand ground bolt and wiring harness connectors.
26. Remove instrument panel defroster grille, three instrument panel top screws, right and left instrument panel cowl nuts and the left side panel cowl side bolt.
27. Remove instrument panel from vehicle.
28. Reverse procedure to install.

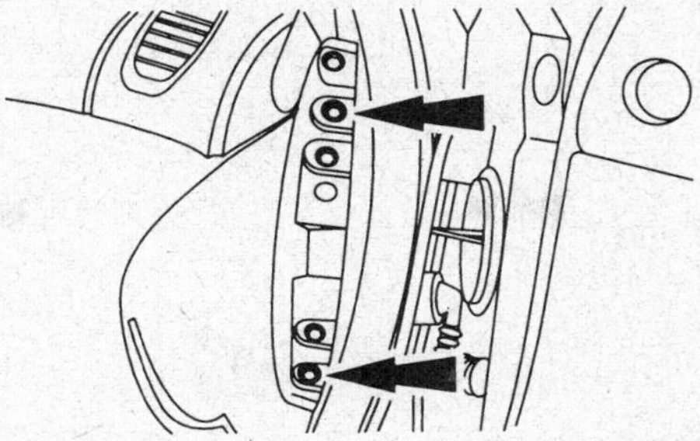

Fig. 8 Mounting bolt locations. Contour & Mystique

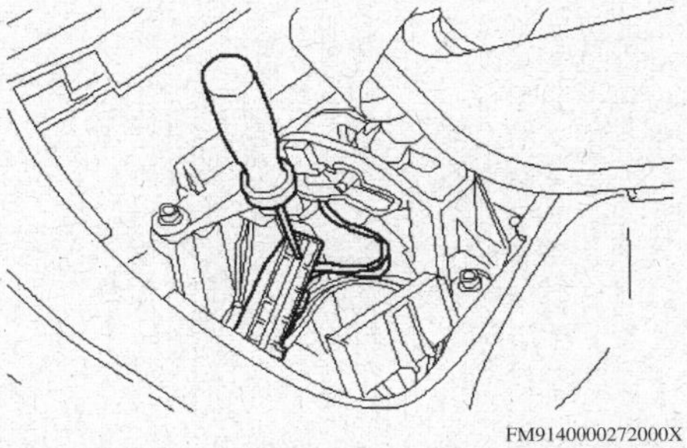

Fig. 11 Overdrive switch terminal location. Cougar w/automatic transaxle

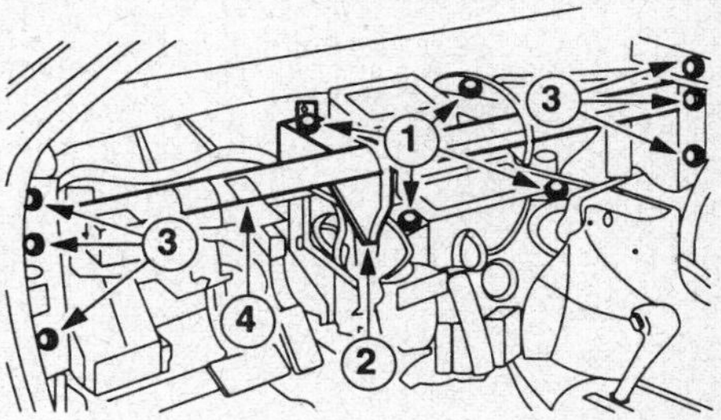

Fig. 9 Instrument panel support removal. Contour & Mystique

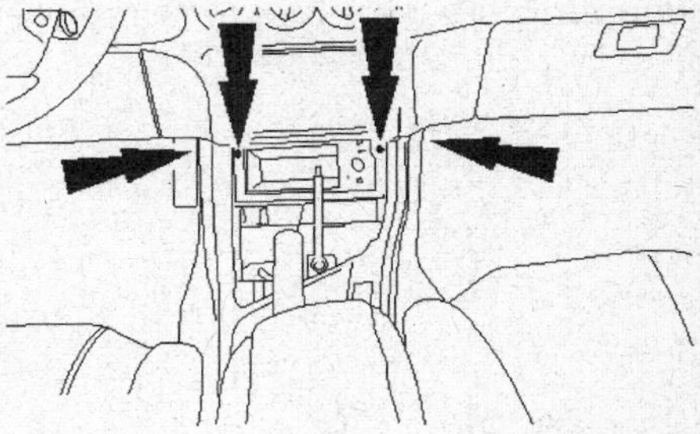

Fig. 12 Floor console front screw location. Cougar

2003-04

1. Remove driver's and passenger's air bag modules as outlined in "Passive Restraint Systems" chapter.
2. **On models equipped with floor console,** remove floor console as follows:
   a. Remove floor console finish panel.
   b. Remove floor console storage bin.
   c. Remove transmission range selector lever assembly bolts, then position range selector aside.
   d. Remove floor console bolts, then remove floor console by sliding rearward.
3. **On all models,** position speed control actuator aside.
4. Loosen bolt and disconnect lefthand bulkhead electrical connector.
5. Release retainers, then position bulkhead electrical connector through instrument panel.
6. Disconnect A/C temperature sensor electrical connector.
7. Disconnect righthand engine compartment inline wiring harness connectors.
8. Remove righthand splash shield.
9. Remove righthand instrument panel lower insulator.
10. Remove scuff plates, then the A-pillar lower trim panels.
11. Disconnect antenna cable inline connector.
12. Remove righthand ground bolts.
13. Loosen bolt, then disconnect righthand bulkhead electrical connectors.
14. Disconnect righthand wiring harness electrical connector.

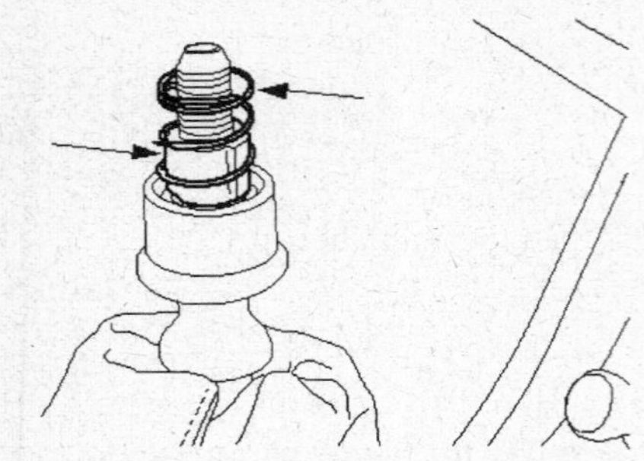

FM9140000274000X

Fig. 13 Gearshift knob, spring & damping sleeve. Cougar w/manual transaxle

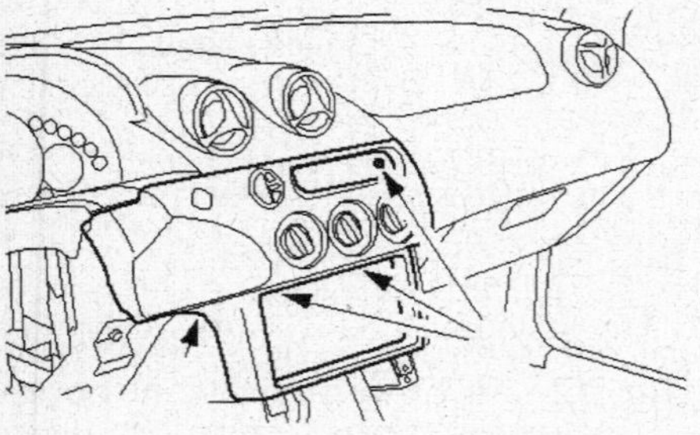

FM9140000277000X

Fig. 16 Heater/audio unit bezel removal. Cougar

15. Disconnect electronic automatic temperature control hose from evaporator housing.
16. Position front door weatherstrip seals aside.
17. Feed righthand wiring harness through instrument panel.
18. Disconnect climate control head vacuum harness connector.
19. **On models equipped with floor console,** remove pin retainer and position carpet aside.
20. **On models equipped with column shift,** remove pin retainer and instrument panel tunnel brace cover.
21. **On all models,** remove nuts, then the instrument panel tunnel brace.
22. Remove lefthand instrument panel insulator.
23. Remove instrument panel steering column opening cover, then the reinforcement.
24. Disconnect parking brake release vacuum connector.
25. Remove nut, then position steering column brace aside.
26. Remove and discard pinch bolt, then separate intermediate shaft from steering column shaft.
27. **On models equipped with column shift,** disconnect transmission shift cable from steering column.
28. **On all models,** remove lefthand ground bolt, then disconnect wiring harness electrical connectors.
29. Remove defroster opening grille.
30. Remove instrument panel cowl top screws.
31. Remove righthand instrument panel cowl side nut.
32. Remove upper lefthand instrument

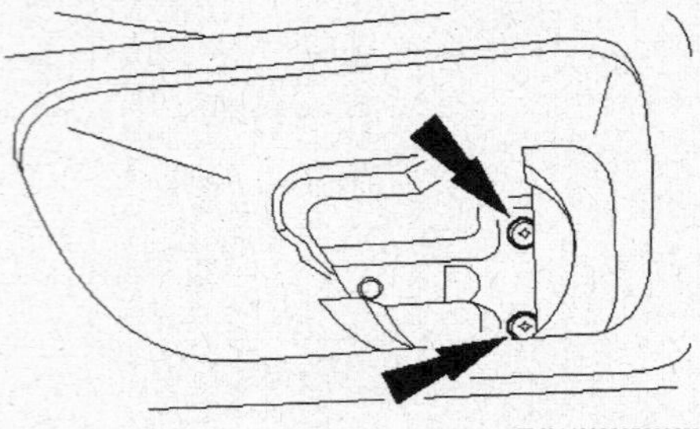

FM9140000275000X

Fig. 14 Floor console rear attaching screws. Cougar w/manual transaxle

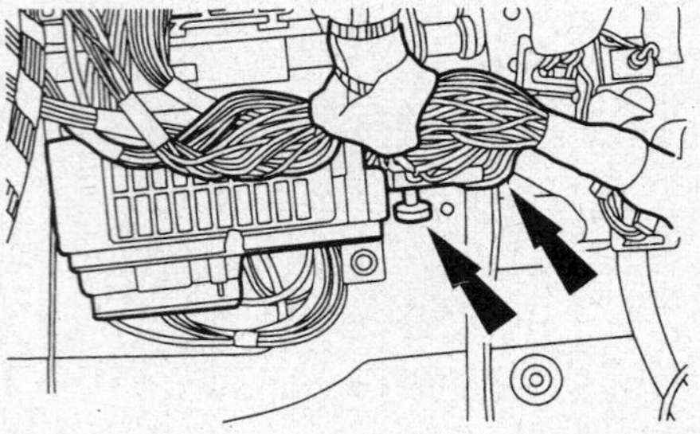

FM9140000278000X

Fig. 17 Central junction box. Cougar

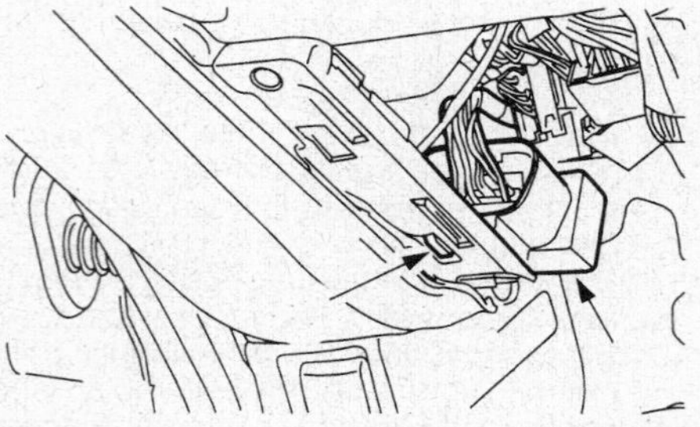

FM9140000280000X

Fig. 19 Data link connector location. Cougar

panel cowl side nut.

33. Remove lower lefthand instrument panel cowl side bolt.
34. Remove instrument panel from vehicle.
35. Reverse procedure to install.

Escort & ZX2

1. Remove parking brake and shift console.
2. Remove instrument panel center finish panel.
3. Remove cigar lighter.
4. Remove pushpins and both control box side covers.
5. Remove antenna lead from instrument panel reinforcement, then disconnect lead.
6. **On models equipped with stereo amplifier,** disconnect its electrical connector.
7. **On models equipped with automatic transaxle,** remove four screws from PRNDL bezel, then position bezel aside.

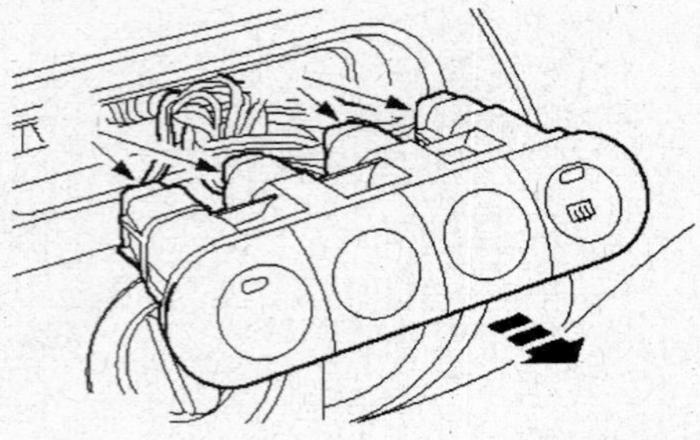

FM9140000276000X

Fig. 15 Switch assembly removal. Cougar

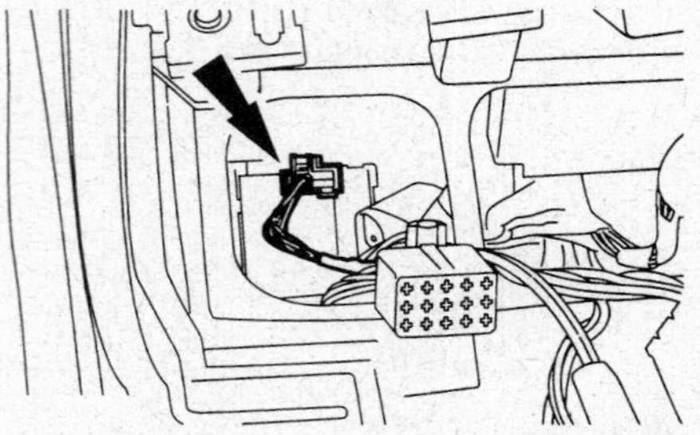

FM9140000279000X

Fig. 18 Instrument interface module electrical connector location. Cougar

8. **On all models,** remove bolt from PCM connector to allow moving it aside.
9. Remove PCM and bracket as an assembly.
10. Rotate temperature control switch to cool position, then disconnect heater temperature cable.
11. Remove steering wheel as outlined in "Steering Columns" chapter.
12. Position hood release control aside.
13. Remove instrument panel steering column cover.
14. Remove two steering column bracket bolts, then move column downward.
15. Remove instrument cluster finish panel and cluster assembly.
16. Remove both front door scuff plates by pulling upward.
17. Remove both cowl side trim panels and door seam welts.
18. Remove fuse panel cover and disconnect main fuse junction panel electrical connectors.
19. Remove glove compartment, then the passenger side air bag module as outlined in "Passive Restraint Systems" chapter.
20. Disconnect vacuum line harness connector.
21. Disconnect in line electrical connector on righthand side of lower instrument panel reinforcement, then the blower motor electrical connection.
22. Remove righthand and lefthand center and lower instrument panel reinforcement bolts.
23. Remove round upper instrument panel reinforcement bolt cover.
24. Ensure all electrical connectors are unplugged and gently pull instrument panel slightly away from normal mounting position.

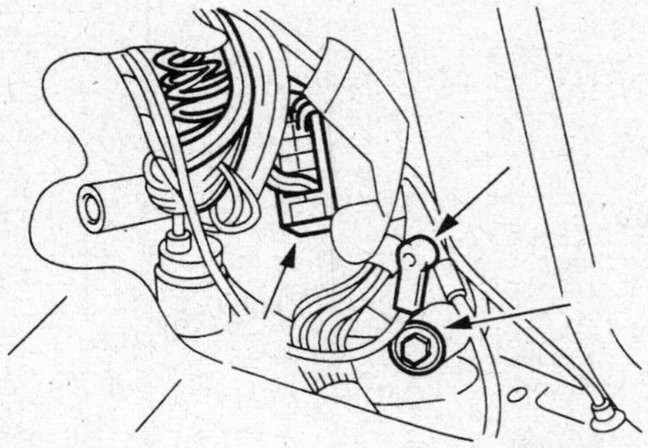

FM9140000281000X

Fig. 20 Electrical connector location (behind right scuff panel). Cougar

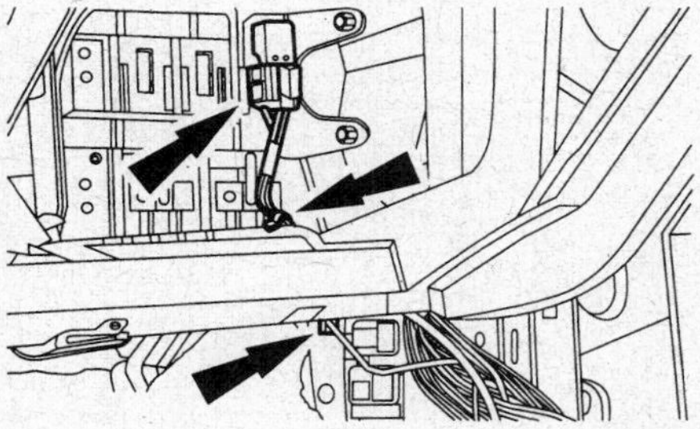

FM9140000284000X

Fig. 23 Ground strap bolts & power seat relay location. Cougar

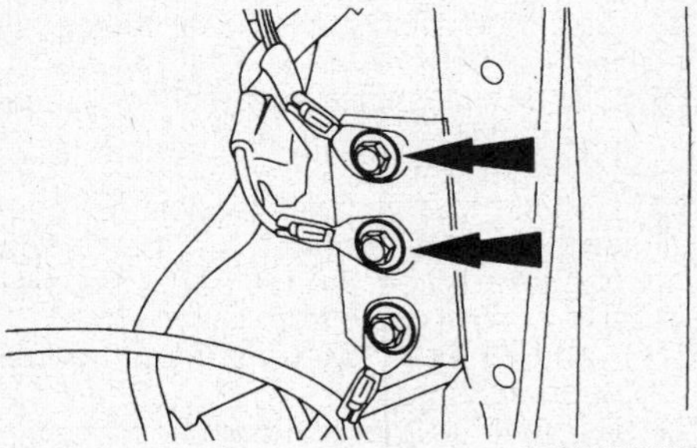

FM9149900127000X

Fig. 26 Righthand ground bolt location. 2000–02 Crown Victoria, Grand Marquis & Town Car

25. Remove instrument panel and its reinforcement from vehicle.
26. Reverse procedure to install.

Focus

1. Center steering wheel, then remove ignition key.
2. Remove instrument panel lower cover.
3. Disconnect hood release cable and data link connector, then remove instrument panel lower cover.
4. Release clip at each side of steering column upper shroud using a suitable thin bladed screwdriver, then remove upper shroud.
5. Release steering column locking lever and lower shroud.
6. Disconnect electrical connectors at right and left side of steering column, then detach harnesses from column.
7. Disconnect steering column shaft from

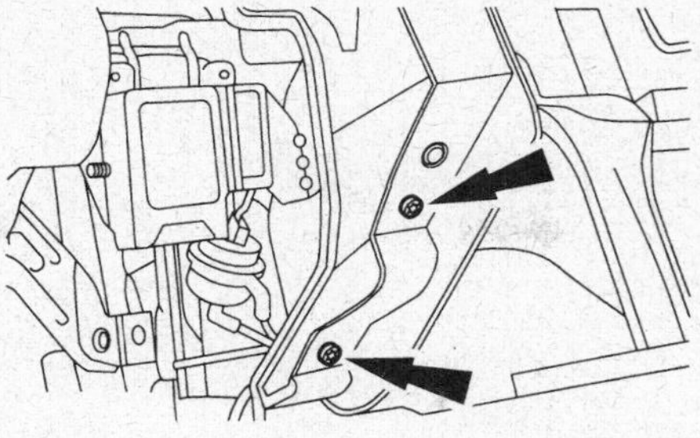

FM9140000282000X

Fig. 21 Left side instrument panel bolts. Cougar

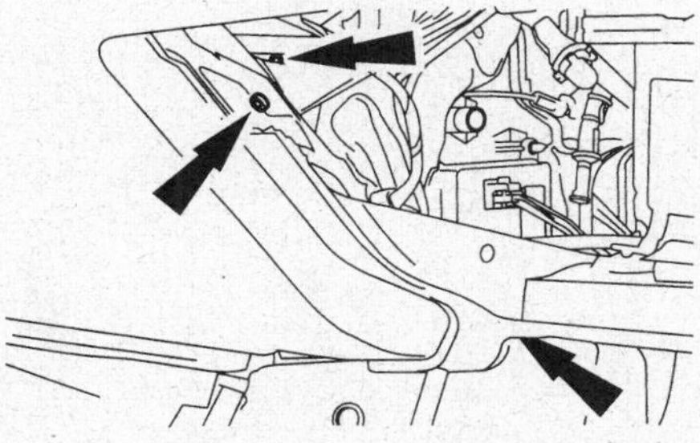

FM9140000285000X

Fig. 24 Right center instrument panel mounting bolts. Cougar

steering gear pinion extension.

8. Remove steering column from vehicle.
9. Partially remove instrument cluster bezel from cluster.
10. Disconnect luggage compartment release switch connector, then remove bezel.
11. Release locking tang, disconnect electrical connector from cluster, then remove cluster from vehicle. **Instrument cluster must be kept upright to prevent silicone liquid from leaking from the gauges.**
12. Remove floor console, radio and glove compartment.
13. Remove passenger air bag module as outlined in "Passive Restraint Systems" chapter.
14. Remove screws and clips from climate control bezel, then the bezel, **Fig. 31.**
15. Remove heater core housing assembly panel.
16. Install bolt into release clip (1) finger tight, then release clip using a suitable pry tool and pad to prevent damage to instrument panel, **Fig. 32.**
17. Remove "A" pillar trim panels, then the bolts at both sides.
18. Remove glove compartment catch.
19. Remove instrument panel mounting bolts, **Fig. 33.**
20. Remove defroster tubes and cable clips, then the instrument panel.
21. Reverse procedure to install.

LS

1. Place steering wheel in straight ahead position.
2. Remove driver's side air bag module as outlined in "Passive Restraint Systems" chapter.

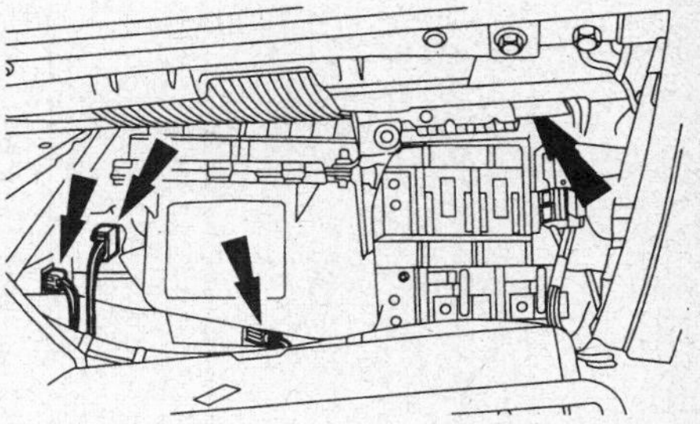

FM9140000283000X

Fig. 22 Electrical connector location. Cougar

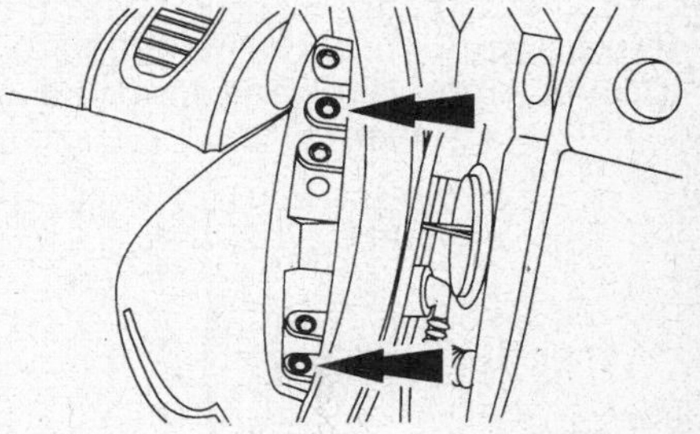

FM9140000286000X

Fig. 25 Right & left instrument panel mounting bolts. Cougar

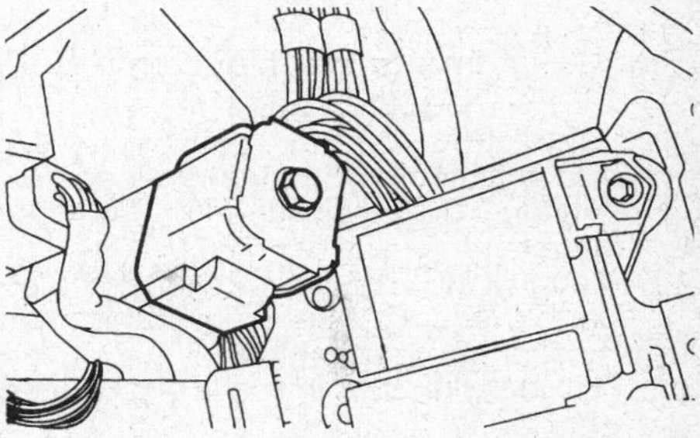

FM9149900128000X

Fig. 27 Righthand bulkhead connector. 2000–02 Crown Victoria, Grand Marquis & Town Car

3. **On models equipped with manual transmission,** place shift lever in fourth gear, then remove gearshift knob.
4. **On models equipped with automatic transmission,** place shift lever in neutral position.
5. **On all models,** disconnect traction control and cellular phone connectors.
6. Remove console rear finish panel assembly.
7. Unclip parking brake boot from console.
8. Remove console front, rear and air conditioning duct mounting screws, then the console.
9. **On all models,** remove console air duct.
10. **On models equipped with automatic transmission,** remove shift selector lever assembly.
11. **On all models,** remove three pin type

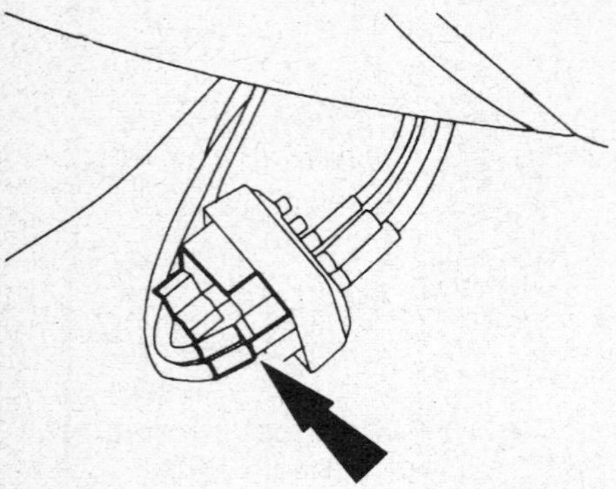

FM9149900129000X

Fig. 28 Climate control vacuum head harness connector. 2000–02 Crown Victoria, Grand Marquis & Town Car

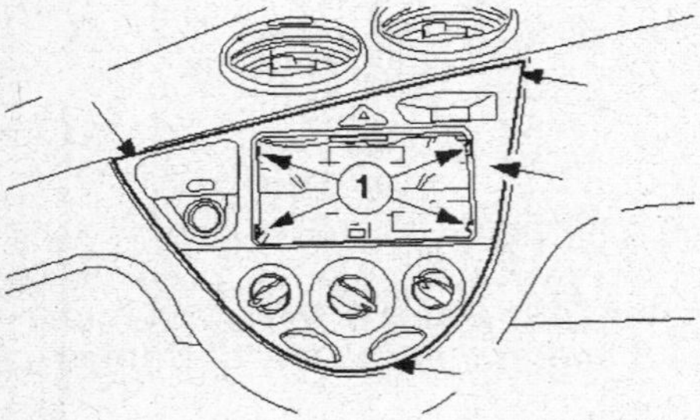

FM9140000147000X

Fig. 31 Climate control/audio unit bezel. Focus

retainers, lefthand instrument panel insulator, then disconnect courtesy lamp.

12. Remove two pin type retainers, righthand instrument panel insulator, then disconnect courtesy lamp.
13. Remove right and left scuff plates, then door weather-strips.
14. Remove "A" pillar lower trim panels.
15. Remove windshield side garnish moldings, then instrument panel defroster opening grille assembly.
16. Remove instrument panel cowl top screws, upper reinforcement bolts, then right and left instrument panel side finish panels.
17. Remove hood release handle and cable, place aside.
18. Disconnect upper righthand bulkhead electrical connector, **Fig. 34.**
19. Separate intermediate shaft from steering column by removing pinch bolt. **Secure steering wheel to prevent any rotation or damage to air bag sliding contact.**
20. Disconnect left side junction box electrical connector, **Fig. 35.**
21. Disconnect ignition shift interlock electrical connector.
22. Remove four instrument panel tunnel brace bolts. Position carpet aside to gain access to bolts.
23. Remove driver side outer instrument panel cowl side cover and reinforcement bolt, **Fig. 36.**
24. Remove righthand and lefthand instrument panel cowl side bolts and nuts, **Fig. 37.**
25. Remove instrument panel.

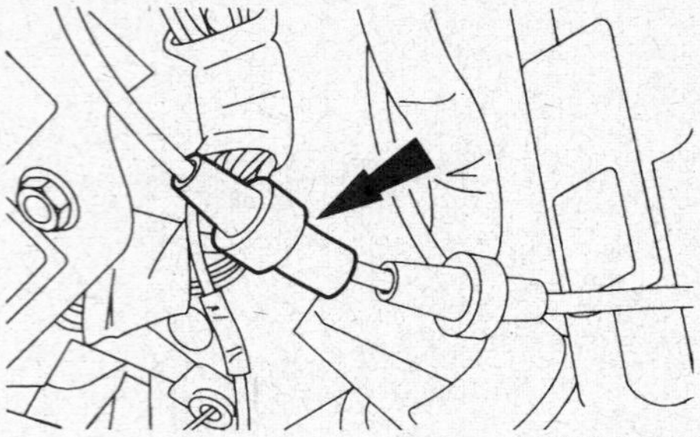

FM9149900130000X

Fig. 29 Parking brake release vacuum connector. 2000–02 Crown Victoria, Grand Marquis & Town Car

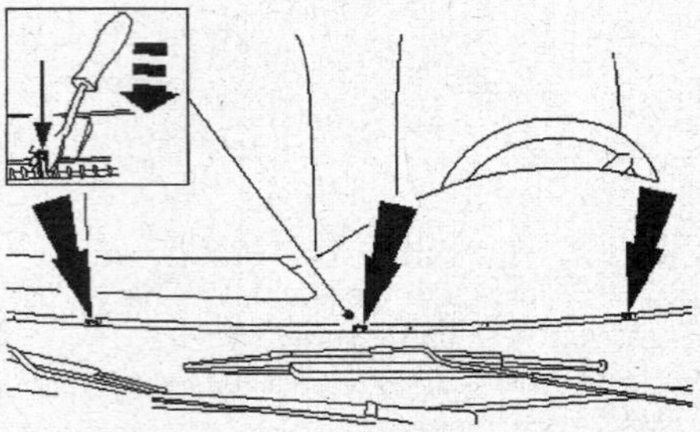

FM9140000148000X

Fig. 32 Instrument panel clip removal. Focus

26. Reverse procedure to install.

Mustang

1. Disconnect battery to starter relay cable and wait one minute for backup power supply to be depleted.
2. Remove left front wheel and tire.
3. Position lefthand splash shield away from instrument panel.
4. Disconnect bulkhead electrical connector from inside of fender opening, then release connector from instrument panel, **Fig. 38.**
5. Remove left front tire and wheel.
6. Remove floor console.
7. Remove driver and passenger air bag modules as outlined in "Passive Restraint Systems" chapter.
8. Disconnect antenna lead and climate control vacuum harness connector, **Fig. 39.**
9. Remove right upper instrument panel support bolt, right and left scuff plates, "A" pillar lower trim panels and windshield garnish moldings.
10. Position right and left door weather-strips aside.
11. Disconnect right side main wiring harnesses connectors, **Fig. 40.**
12. Disconnect climate control wiring harness connector.
13. Remove instrument panel steering column cover and reinforcement.
14. Separate intermediate shaft from steering column.
15. Pull corner of carpeting back slightly to access electrical connectors.
16. Disconnect lefthand main wiring harness, generic electronic module (GEM) and electronic crash sensor

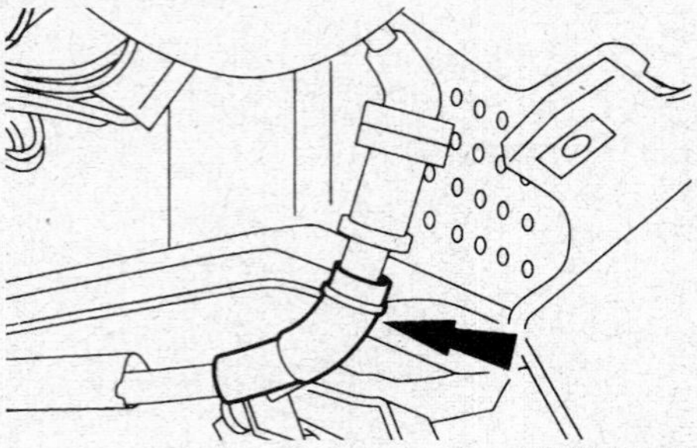

FM9149900131000X

Fig. 30 Instrument panel vacuum connector. 2000–02 Crown Victoria & Grand Marquis

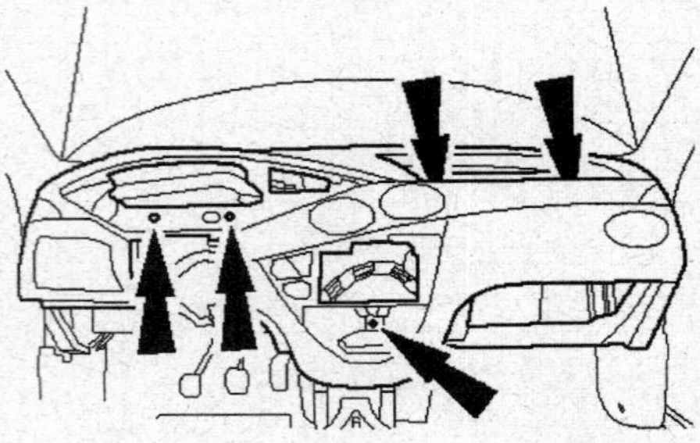

FM9140000149000X

Fig. 33 Instrument panel mounting bolts. Focus

(ECS) connectors, **Figs. 41 and 42.**

17. Disconnect shift interlock assembly from selector lever.
18. Disconnect shifter assembly electrical connector.
19. Remove radio.
20. Reach through radio chassis opening and rotate temperature control switch to cool position, then release temperature control cable from blend door.
21. Remove four center instrument panel support bolts.
22. Remove lefthand instrument panel support bolt and nut and righthand support bolt.
23. Remove instrument panel upper finish panel, then the instrument panel upper support bolts.
24. Remove instrument panel.
25. Reverse procedure to install.

Sable & Taurus

1. Remove passenger and driver air bags as outlined in "Passive Restraint Systems" chapter.
2. Close glove compartment door.
3. **On models equipped with floor console,** remove selector lever as follows:
   a. Remove floor console.
   b. Disconnect ignition/shifter interlock cable from bracket, then disconnect cable from shift cam.
   c. Remove selector lever cable from transaxle range selector.
   d. Depress tab on selector lever cable and remove cable from selector lever housing.
   e. Disconnect electrical connector.
   f. Remove attaching nuts and bolts, then the selector lever.

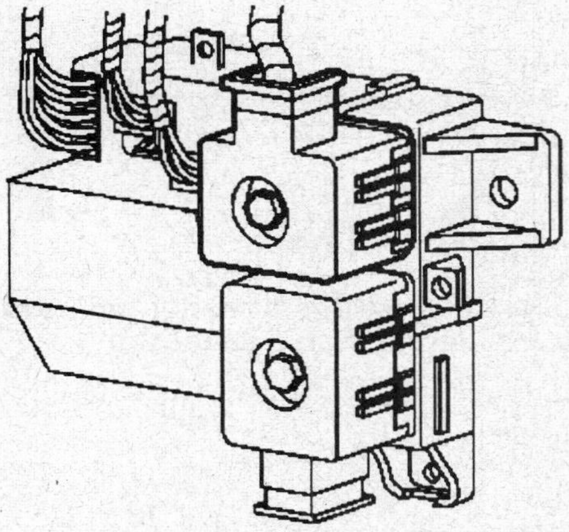

FM9149900138000X

Fig. 34 Upper righthand bulkhead electrical connector. LS

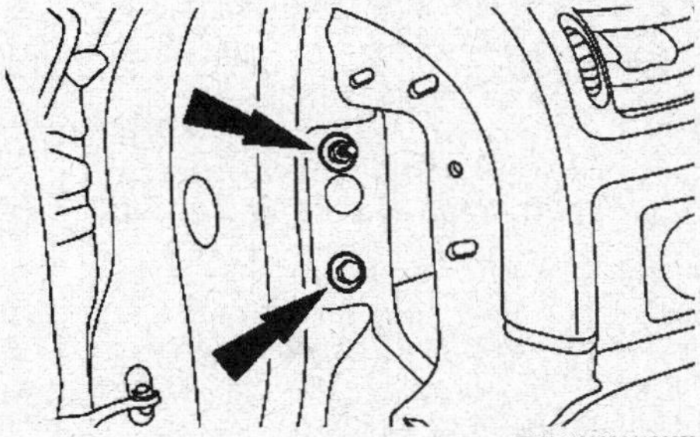

FM9149900141000X

Fig. 37 Instrument panel cowl side bolts & nuts. LS

4. **On all models,** remove front door scuff plates.
5. Position front door weather-strips aside, then remove "A" pillar trim panels.
6. Lift rear edge of defroster grille upwards, then slide rearward to remove.
7. Disconnect sunload/headlamp sensor electrical connector.
8. Remove instrument panel cowl top bolts, **Fig. 43.**
9. Release parking brake cable and conduit from parking brake actuator, **Fig. 44.**
10. Remove retainer clip, then the parking brake release handle.
11. Disconnect Generic Electronic Module (GEM) electrical connector, **Fig. 45.**
12. Disconnect bulkhead and steering column bulkhead electrical connectors.
13. Remove pinch bolt, then disconnect intermediate shaft from steering column, **Fig. 46.**
14. **On models equipped with steering column selector,** disconnect transmission shift cable from steering column shift tube lever and steering column bracket.
15. **On all models,** remove passenger side instrument panel insulator from behind glove compartment.
16. Disconnect blower motor, resistor block and blend door actuator jumper harness.
17. Remove two instrument panel side finish panels.
18. Remove instrument panel side cowl

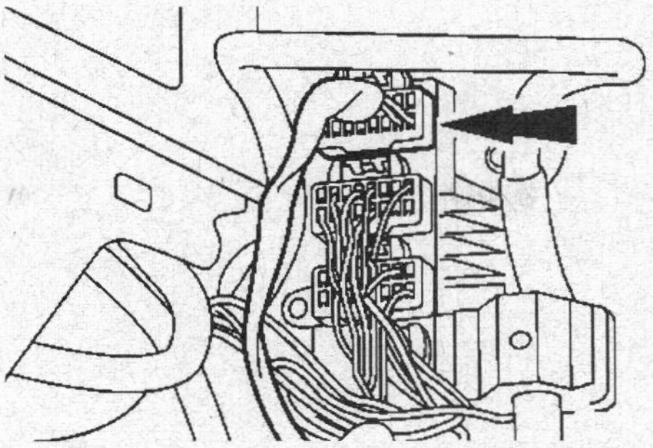

FM9149900139000X

Fig. 35 Lefthand junction box electrical connector. LS

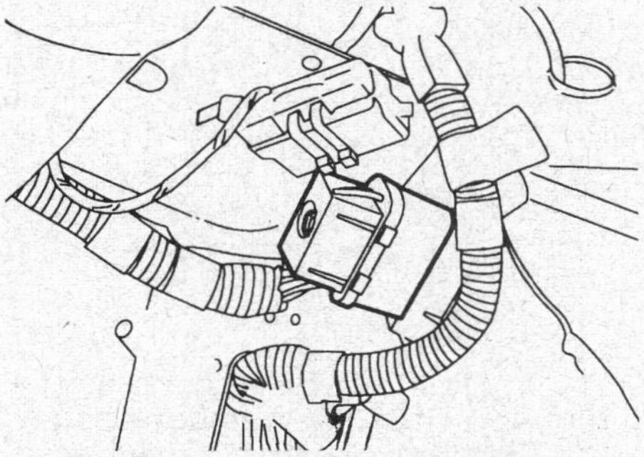

FM9149900132000X

Fig. 38 Bulkhead electrical connector. Mustang

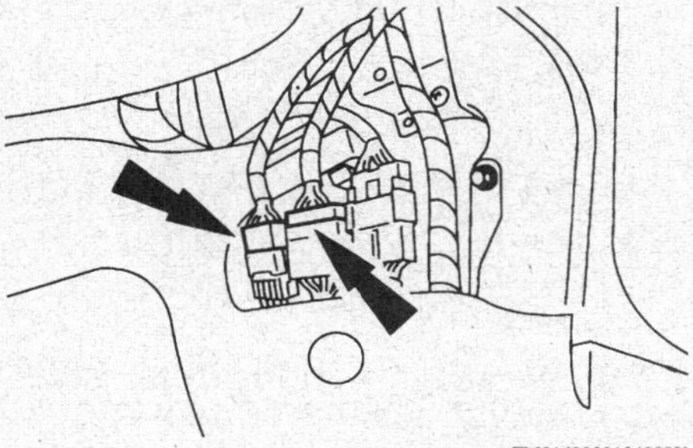

FM9149900134000X

Fig. 40 Main wiring harness electrical connectors (right side). Mustang

bolts, **Fig. 47.**

19. Remove instrument panel from vehicle.
20. Reverse procedure to install.

Thunderbird

1. Remove driver and passenger air bag modules as outlined in "Passive Restraint Systems" chapter.
2. Apply parking brake, then place transmission selector lever in neutral.
3. Remove console finish panel assembly, then release parking brake boot from console base.
4. Remove console retaining screws, then the console.
5. Remove instrument panel insulators, then disconnect courtesy lamp.
6. Remove scuff plates, then position lefthand and righthand door weatherstrips aside.

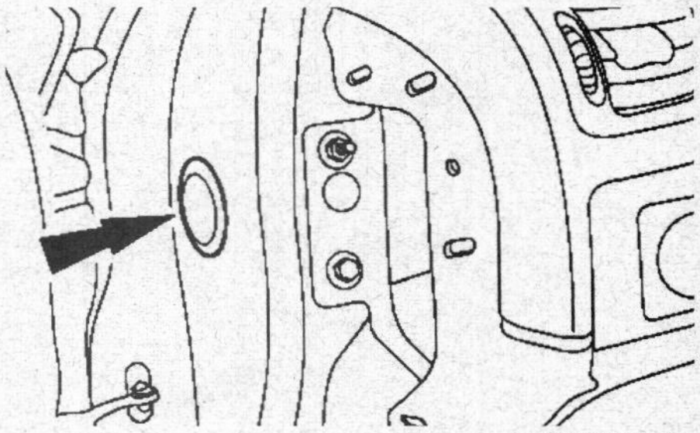

FM9149900140000X

Fig. 36 Driver side outer instrument panel cowl cover & bolt. LS

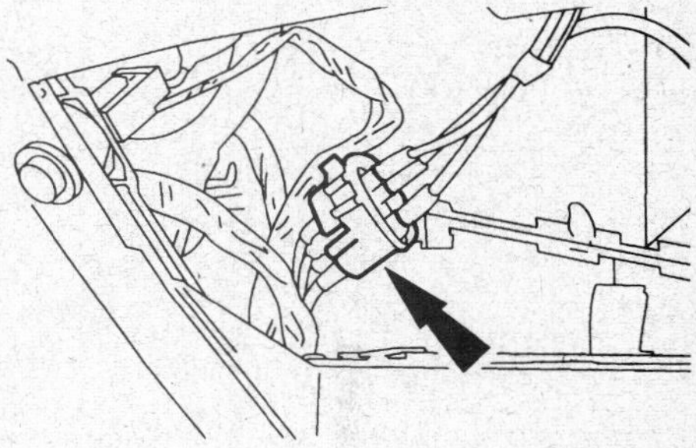

FM9149900133000X

Fig. 39 Climate control vacuum harness connector. Mustang

7. Remove both A-pillar lower trim panels, then the windshield side garnish mouldings.
8. Remove instrument panel defroster opening grille and disconnect electrical connector.
9. Remove instrument panel cowl top screws, then loosen instrument panel upper reinforcement bolts.
10. Remove instrument panel side finish panels.
11. Remove screws, then the floor heat duct.
12. Release assist cable from glove compartment door arm, then open compartment door.
13. Pull up on glove compartment door arms, then lower door.
14. Remove assist cable bracket screws, then the glove compartment screws and bin.
15. Remove bolts, then the glove compartment door. Disconnect electrical connector.
16. Loosen bolt, then disconnect upper righthand bulkhead electrical connector through glove compartment opening.
17. Disconnect passenger side tunnel electrical connector.
18. Remove screws, then position hood release handle and cable aside.
19. Remove retainers, then release instrument panel steering column cover and disconnect electrical connectors.
20. Remove instrument panel steering column cover reinforcement, then the pinch bolt and separate intermediate shaft from steering column.
21. Remove steering column brace, then position carpet aside to gain access

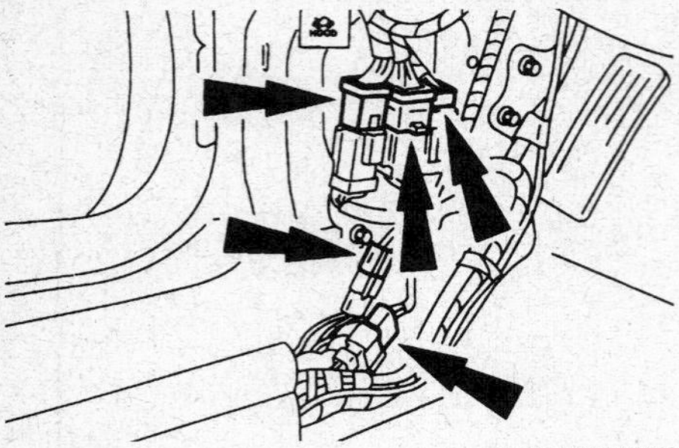

Fig. 41 Main wiring harness electrical connectors (left side). Mustang

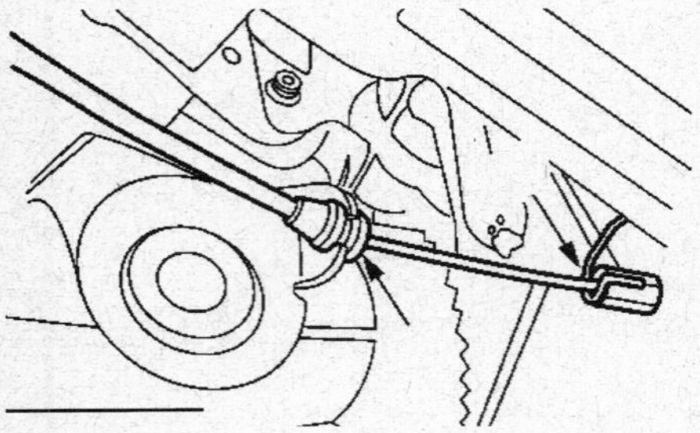

Fig. 44 Parking brake cable removal. Sable & Taurus

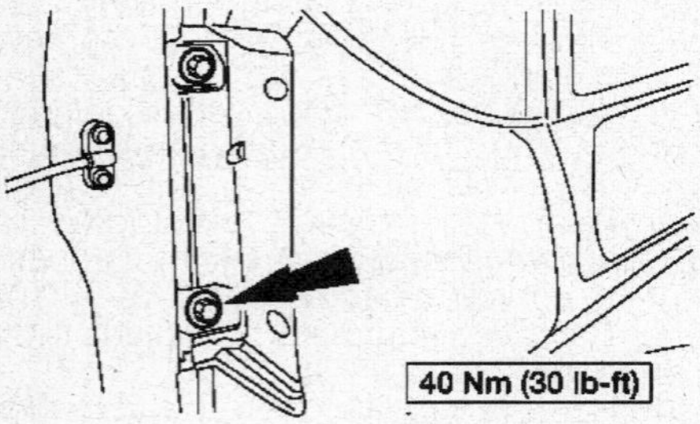

Fig. 47 Instrument panel side cowl bolts. Sable & Taurus

and disconnect lefthand junction box electrical connector.

22. Disconnect lefthand electrical connectors through instrument panel side opening.
23. Position lefthand electrical connector block aside, then remove bolt.
24. Remove instrument panel tunnel bolts, then the lefthand and righthand instrument panel cowl side bolts and nuts
25. Remove instrument panel from vehicle. **Electronic modules are sensitive to static electrical charges. If exposed to these charges, damage may result.**
26. Reverse procedure to install.

Town Car

2000-02

Refer to "Crown Victoria, Grand Marquis & Marauder" for instrument panel replacement procedures.

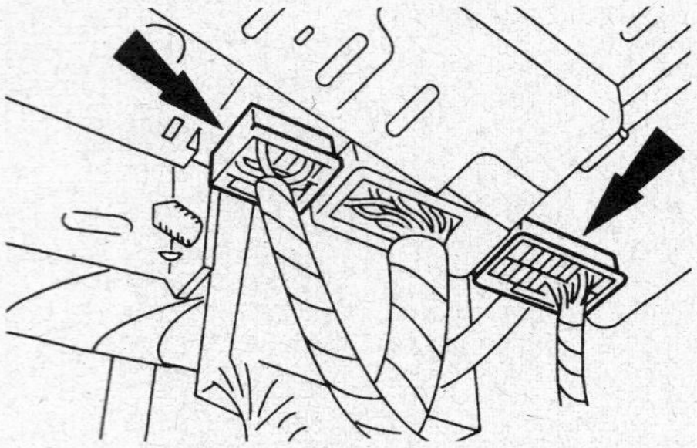

Fig. 42 GEM module connectors. Mustang

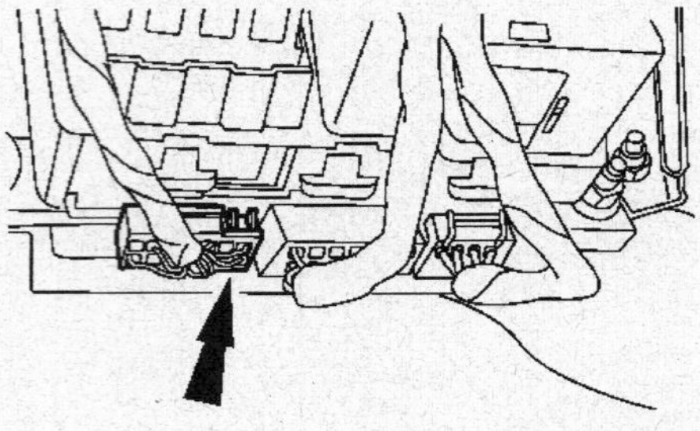

Fig. 45 GEM module connector location. Sable & Taurus

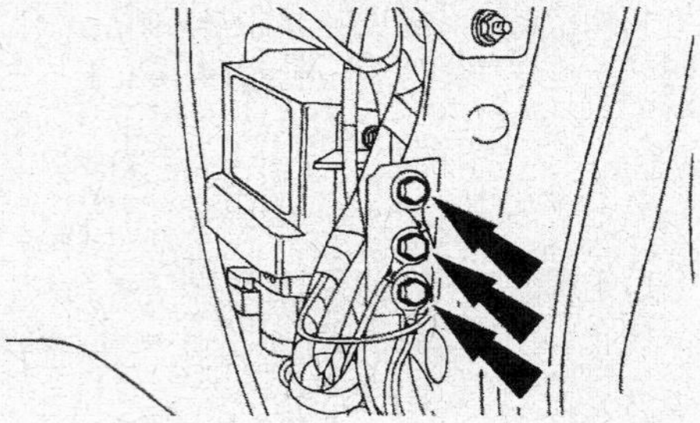

Fig. 48 Righthand ground bolt removal. 2003–04 Town Car

2003-04

1. Remove steering column as outlined in "Steering Columns" chapter.
2. Remove passenger's air bag module as outlined in "Passive Restraint Systems" chapter.
3. Through glove compartment opening, remove instrument panel support brace bolt, then close glove compartment door.
4. Remove righthand side splash shield.
5. Remove speed control servo and position aside.
6. Loosen bolt and disconnect lefthand bulkhead connector, then release connector from instrument panel.
7. Release wiring harness retaining strap from instrument panel.
8. Remove lefthand and righthand instrument panel lower insulators.
9. Unseat wiring grommet and feed wiring harness through instrument panel.
10. Remove A-pillar lower trim panels, then the windshield side garnish moldings.

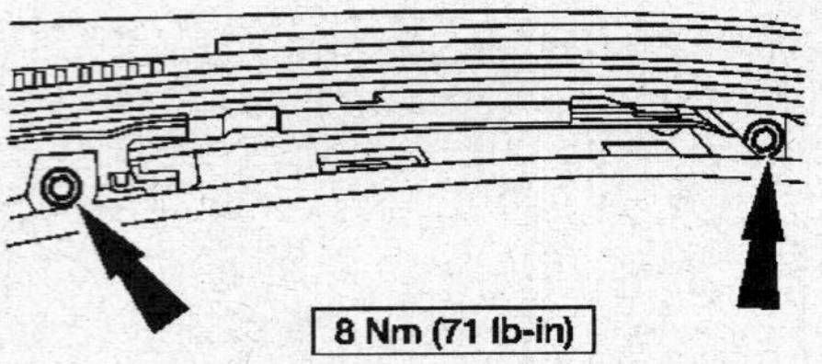

Fig. 43 Instrument panel top cowl bolts. Sable & Taurus

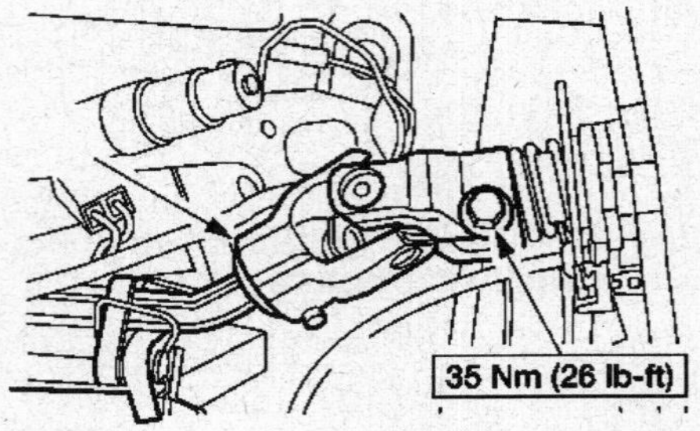

Fig. 46 Intermediate shaft removal. Sable & Taurus

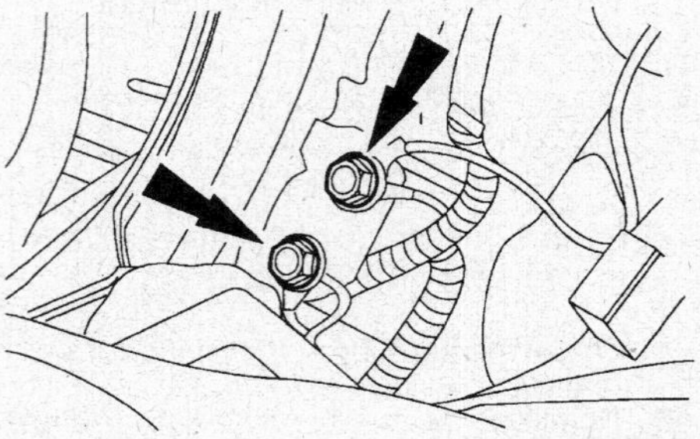

Fig. 49 Lefthand ground bolt removal. 2003–04 Town Car

11. Disconnect antenna cable inline connector.
12. Remove righthand side ground bolts, **Fig. 48.**
13. Loosen bolt and disconnect righthand bulkhead connector.
14. Position door weatherstrip seals aside.
15. Remove two pin retainers, then the tunnel brace trim cover.
16. Disconnect climate control head vacuum harness connector.
17. Remove eight nuts, then the two instrument panel tunnel braces.
18. Remove lefthand ground bolts, **Fig. 49.**
19. Disconnect lefthand wiring harness connectors, then the parking brake switch connector.
20. Remove instrument panel defroster grille, then the three instrument panel cowl top screws.
21. Remove righthand instrument panel cowl nut.
22. Remove upper lefthand instrument panel cowl nut, then the lower cowl bolt.
23. Remove instrument panel from vehicle.
24. Reverse procedure to install.

ANTI-LOCK BRAKES

TABLE OF CONTENTS

Continental, Sable & Taurus

NOTE: On Air Bag Equipped Models, Refer To "Air Bag System Precautions" Located In The Front Of This Manual For System Disarming & Arming Procedures.

NOTE: Refer To "Computer Relearn Procedures" Located In The Front Of This Manual When Battery Power To The Computer Has Been Interrupted.

NOTE: "Electrical Symbol & Wire Color Code Identification" Located In The Front Of This Manual May Be Used As An Aid When Using Wiring Circuits Found In This Section.

NOTE: Prior To Performing Any Service Operations Listed In This Section, Consult The "Technical Service Bulletins" Section For Related Information.

INDEX

PRECAUTIONS

Air Bag Systems

Refer to "Air Bag System Precautions" in the front of this manual for system disarming and arming procedures.

Battery Ground Cable

Prior to service, disconnect battery ground cable and isolate as required.

Hydraulic Brake Fluid Color

Hydraulic brake fluid must conform with the requirements of Federal Motor Vehicle Safety Standard 116. Under this standard, brake fluids are visually different from other automotive fluids such as transmission, power steering and engine.

Fluid color in a normal brake system may vary from its original color for many reasons. A brake master cylinder may show significantly different shades fluid color between the two brake master cylinder reservoirs. Color may also appear to vary between cast steel and die cast aluminum reservoirs. Some reasons for discoloration include the following:

1. Heat and/or aging.
2. Different operation temperatures or different rates of normal oxidation between two reservoir compartments.
3. Different brands and/or shades of fluid are used when topping off during normal service.
4. Dissolution of color dye used on master cylinder internal springs during assembly.
5. Brake fluid contaminated with hydrocarbon/mineral based fluid (power steering or transmission fluid) can be detected by an obvious swelling of the master cylinder cap gasket. If the master cylinder cap gasket is swollen, all brake system rubber components must be replaced. All brake tubes and hoses must be thoroughly flushed with heavy duty brake fluid part No. C6AZ-19542-AA or -BA or DOT-3 equivalent before the vehicle returns to service.

DESCRIPTION

Continental

The anti-lock brake system prevents wheel lock-up by automatically modulating brake pressure during an emergency stop. It allows driver to maintain steering control and stop the vehicle in the shortest possible distance under most conditions. The traction control system controls wheelspin by modulating engine torque and applying or releasing appropriate rear brake to restore traction when driving on slippery or loose surfaces, **Fig. 1.**

Sable & Taurus

The anti-lock system (ABS), **Fig. 2,** controls each brake separately. The brake pedal force required to engage the system may vary with road surface conditions. A dry surface will require a high force, while a slippery surface will require a much less force. During system operation, the driver will sense a slight brake pedal pulsation accompanied by a rise in brake pedal height and a clicking sound. The pedal effort and pedal feel during normal braking are similar to a conventional power brake system.

System Components

VACUUM BOOSTER

The diaphragm type brake booster is self-contained and is mounted on the left side of engine compartment. The vacuum brake booster uses engine intake manifold vacuum and atmospheric pressure for power.

MASTER CYLINDER

This unit is a tandem master cylinder. The primary (rear) circuit feeds right front and left rear brakes. The secondary circuit (front) feeds left front and right rear brakes. The reservoir is a clear translucent plastic container. An integral fluid level switch is part of reservoir cap assembly, with one electrical connector pointing rearward for wire harness connection.

HYDRAULIC CONTROL UNIT

The Hydraulic Control Unit (HCU) is located on the front lefthand side of the engine compartment. It consists of a valve body assembly, pump, motor assembly and brake fluid reservoir with fluid lever indicator assembly. During normal braking, fluid from master cylinder enters the HCU through two inlet ports at the rear of the HCU. The fluid passes through four normally open inlet valves, one to each wheel. When the ABS module (Electronic Control Unit (ECU) senses wheel lock conditions, the ABS module (ECU) produces a pulse to the appropriate inlet valve, which then closes the valve. This prevents any more fluid from entering the affected brake. The ABS module (ECU) senses the wheel again. If the wheel is still decelerating, the ABS module (ECU) then pulses open the normally closed valve, which decreases the pressure trapped inline.

ABS MODULE (ELECTRONIC CONTROL UNIT)

The ABS module (ECU) is located in the engine compartment. This unit is a self-test non-repairable unit consisting of two microprocessors which are programmed identically. The ABS module (ECU) monitors system operation during normal driving as well as during anti-lock braking. Under normal driving conditions, the microprocessors transmit short test pulses to the solenoid valves to inspect the electrical system. Under wheel lock conditions, the ABS module (ECU) produces signals to open and close the appropriate solenoid valves. This results in moderate pulsations in brake pedal. During anti-lock braking, moderate pulsation in the brake pedal is accompanied by a change in pedal height. This rise in pedal height will continue until the pedal travel switch closes and the pump shuts off. During normal braking, the brake pedal feel will be identical to a standard brake system.

WHEEL SENSORS

This system uses four sets of variable resistance sensors and toothed speed indicator rings to determine each wheel's rotational speed. The sensors operate on a magnetic induction principle. For example, as the teeth on the speed indicator ring rotate past a stationary sensor, a signal, proportional to the speed sensor rotation, is generated and transmitted to the ABS module (ECU) through a coaxial cable.

The front wheel sensors are attached to the suspension knuckles and the front speed indicators are pressed onto the outer constant velocity joints. The rear wheel sensors are attached to the rear caliper adapter plates, and the rear speed indicator rings are pressed onto the rear hub assemblies.

PEDAL TRAVEL SWITCH

This system uses a pedal travel switch which monitors brake pedal travel and sends information to the ABS module (ECU) through the wiring harness. Switch adjustment is critical to pedal feel during ABS cycling. The switch is mounted on the right side of the brake pedal support, near the dump valve adapter bracket.

The switch is normally closed. When brake pedal travel exceeds the switch setting during an anti-lock stop, the electronic controller senses the switch is open and grounds the pump motor relay coil. This energizes the relay and turns the pump motor on. When the pump motor is running, the master cylinder fills with high pressure brake fluid, pushing the brake pedal up until the switch closes. When the switch closes, the pump turns off and the pedal drops with each ABS control cycle until the travel switch opens and the pump is turned back on. This minimizes pedal feedback during ABS cycling.

If the pedal travel switch is not adjusted properly or is not electrically connected, it will cause an incorrect pedal feel during ABS stops. Some problems with the switch or its installation will result in the pump running during an entire ABS stop. The pedal will become very firm, pushing the driver's foot up to a very high position.

Operation

ANTI-LOCK BRAKES

When brakes are applied, fluid is forced from the master cylinder outlet ports to the Hydraulic Control Unit (HCU) inlet ports. This pressure is transmitted through four normally open solenoid valves contained inside the HCU, then through outlet ports of the HCU to each wheel. The primary (rear) circuit of the master cylinder feeds the right

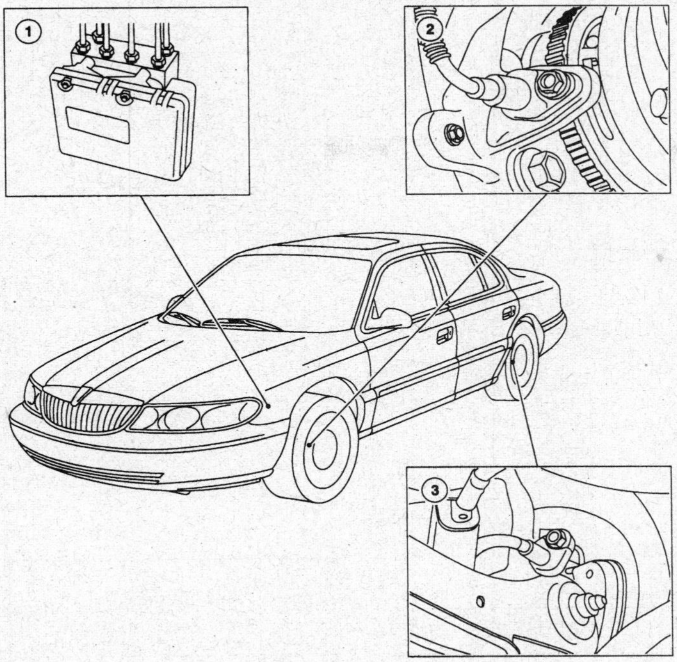

Item	Description
1	Anti-Lock Brake Control Module With Hydraulic Control Unit
2	Front Brake Anti-Lock Sensor
3	Rear Brake Anti-Lock Sensor

FM4029701244000X

Fig. 1 Anti-lock system. Continental

front and left rear brakes. The secondary (front) circuit feeds the left front and right rear brakes.

When the ABS module (ECU) senses wheel lock conditions based on wheel speed sensor data, it pulses against the normally open solenoid valve, closing the circuit. This prevents any more fluid from entering the circuit. The ABS module (ECU) senses the wheel again. If the wheel is still decelerating, the module pulses the normally closed valve open, decreasing the pressure trapped inline.

The ABS module (ECU) monitors the electro-mechanical components of the system. An anti-lock brake system fault will cause the module to shut off or inhibit the anti-lock function, while retaining the normal power assisted braking. Faults are indicated by one or two warning lamps inside the vehicle.

Loss of hydraulic fluid in the HCU reservoir will disable the anti-lock brake system.

The four wheel anti-lock brake system is self-monitoring. When the ignition switch is turned to the RUN position, the ABS module (ECU) will perform a preliminary self-inspection on the anti-lock electrical system, indicated by a three or four second illumination of the amber "Check Anti-Lock Brakes" lamp on the instrument cluster. During vehicle operation, including normal and anti-lock braking, the ABS module (ECU) monitors all electrical anti-lock functions and some hydraulic system operation.

For most faults of the anti-lock brake system, the amber "Check Anti-Lock Brakes" and/or the red "Brake" lamp will be illuminated. The sequence of illumination of these warning lamps, combined with the problem symptoms, can determine the appropriate diagnostic test to perform. Most faults are recorded as a coded number in the controller memory, pinpointing the exact component requiring service.

Traction Assist

Traction Assist (TA) is designed to control wheel spin when accelerating on loose or slippery surfaces. During acceleration, if one or both rear wheels lose traction and begin to spin, the TA system will rapidly apply and release the appropriate rear brake to reduce wheel spin and aid traction. The accompanying isolation valve will also close and the ABS pump will run. The isolation valve permits brake operation only to the rear brake of the circuit by closing off pressure to the front brake.

If brakes are applied during TA operation, the ABS module receives a signal from the stop lamp switch or the pressure switch and automatically stops TA cycling.

TROUBLESHOOTING

Pre-Test Checks

1. Verify parking brake is completely released. If parking brake is applied, "Brake" lamp will be illuminated.
2. Inspect brake fluid. **As fluid level drops, red "Brake" lamp will illuminate. If fluid level continues to fall, amber "Check Anti-Lock Brake" lamp will illuminate and anti-lock function will be inhibited.**
3. Verify all of the following connectors are properly connected and in good operating condition:
   a. Connector of the computer module.
   b. Connector of HCU valve body.
   c. Connectors of pump motor relay.
   d. Connector of master cylinder reservoir.
   e. Connector of HCU reservoir.
   f. Connector of main power relay.
   g. Connector of each wheel sensor.
   h. Connector of pedal travel switch.
   i. Connector of stop lamp switch.
4. Inspect fuses and diode for damage.
5. Ensure all battery connections are clean and tight.
6. Inspect ground connections for anti-lock system located near computer module and pump.

DIAGNOSIS & TESTING

Diagnostic Procedure

Ensure the following diagnosis procedures are used in the sequence and step-by-step order indicated. Following the wrong sequence or bypassing steps will only lead to unrequired replacement of system components and/or incorrect resolution of the problem. The diagnostic procedure consists of five sub-tests: Pre-test Checks, On-Board Self-Tests, Manual Quick Tests, Warning Lamp Symptom Chart and the Diagnostic Tests.

Accessing Diagnostic Trouble Codes

The anti-lock brake/traction assist electronic control module is capable of performing a self-test using New Generation Star (NGS) tester 007-00500, or equivalent, scan tool.

The anti-lock control module monitors system operation and stores all defined diagnostic trouble codes in its memory. It is important to understand the control module cannot recognize some failures. Therefore, if a problem exists and no diagnostic trouble codes are stored by the control module, other diagnostic steps must be followed. The module cannot store a diagnostic trouble code if there is no power to the module. This diagnostic trouble code can be found by using Quick-Check Tests.

1. Connect New Generation Star (NGS) tester to Data Link Connector (DLC) located under instrument panel.
2. Plug NGS into cigarette lighter.
3. Turn ignition switch to Run position.
4. Follow instructions on tester screen and record all diagnostic trouble codes.
5. Refer to "Diagnostic Trouble Code Interpretation" for DTC's. Any DTC preceded by "U" indicates a fault with the

Powertrain Control Module (PCM).
6. If NGS reports "System Passed," proceed to Anti-Lock Quick Tests Checks.

Diagnostic Trouble Code Interpretation

Refer to **Figs. 3 and 4,** for diagnostic trouble code interpretation.

Quick Checks

To properly conduct Quick Checks, an EEC-IV breakout box tool No. T83L-50-EEC-IV, anti-lock harness adapter tool No. T90P-50-ALA and digital volt/ohmmeter tool No. 007-00001, or equivalents, must be used. This group of tests will lead to specific diagnostic Pinpoint Tests that will, in most cases, identify the fault. If fault is not determined by the Quick Check procedure, use the following Diagnostic Lamp Symptom Chart to identify the proper diagnostic procedure to use.

Wiring Diagrams

CONTINENTAL

Refer to **Figs. 5 and 6,** for wiring diagrams.

SABLE & TAURUS

Refer to **Figs. 7 and 8,** for wiring diagram.

Pinpoint Tests

CONTINENTAL

Refer to **Fig. 9,** for symptom chart and **Figs. 10 through 35,** for diagnosis and testing.

SABLE & TAURUS

Refer to **Fig. 36,** for symptom chart and **Figs. 37 through 52,** for diagnosis and testing.

Clearing Diagnostic Trouble Codes

The original error diagnostic trouble codes in the computer from the assembly plant will erase automatically if everything is in working order and vehicle is driven about (25 mph). All error diagnostic trouble codes must be output, all faults corrected (anti-lock lamp off), and vehicle driven (25 mph) before memory will clear. NGS tester can also be used to erase DTCs.

SYSTEM SERVICE

Brake System Bleed

Refer to "Hydraulic Brake Systems" for bleed procedure.

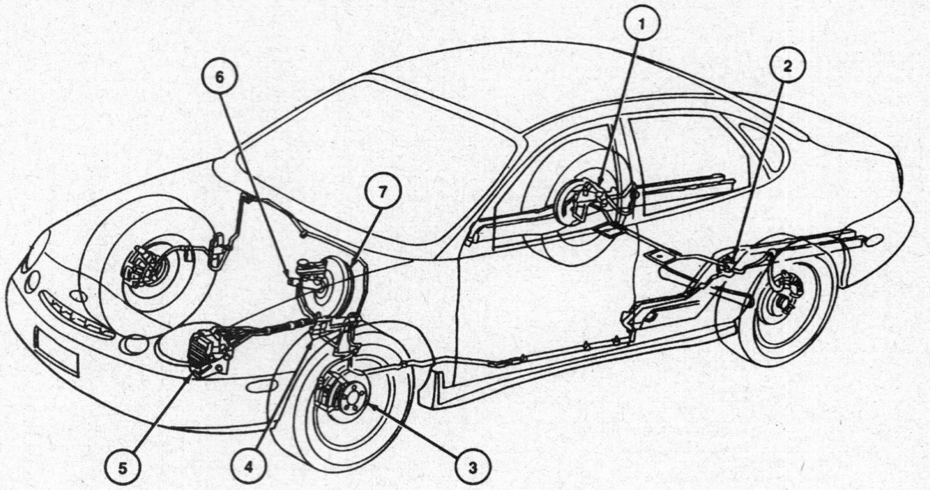

Item	Description
1	Rear Brake Anti-Lock Sensor
2	Brake Load Sensor Proportioning Valve (Sedan Only)
3	Front Brake Anti-Lock Sensor
4	Brake Pressure Control Valve (Station Wagon Only)
5	Anti-Lock Brake Control Module
6	Brake Master Cylinder
7	Power Brake Booster

FM4029601242000X

Fig. 2 Anti-lock brake system. Sable & Taurus

Component Replacement

HYDRAULIC CONTROL UNIT

CONTINENTAL

1. Remove engine air cleaner and air cleaner outlet tube.
2. Disconnect connector attaching anti-lock brake module to wire harness.
3. Remove tubes from inlet ports of pump motor and tubes from outlet ports of brake pressure control valve block. Plug each port to prevent brake fluid from spilling on paint and wiring.
4. Remove HCU to mounting bracket retaining nuts, then tip rear of HCU up and pull rearward to slide forward mounting pins out of the retaining grommets.
5. Remove HCU from vehicle.
6. Reverse procedure to install, noting the following:
   a. **Torque** HCU retaining nuts and tube fittings to 12–18 ft. lbs.
   b. Bleed system as outlined in "Brake System Bleed."

SABLE & TAURUS

1. Remove battery from vehicle.
2. Remove battery tray and mounting bracket from vehicle.
3. Disconnect ABS control module electrical connector, **Fig. 53.**
4. Remove inlet and outlet tubes from ABS Hydraulic Control Unit (HCU). Plug ports to prevent brake fluid from spilling onto paint and wiring.
5. Remove ABS pump motor and ground strap.
6. Remove ABS module assembly to HCU bracket retaining nuts.
7. Remove HCU and ABS control module assembly from vehicle.
8. Reverse procedure to install, noting the following:
   a. **Torque** HCU bracket mounting bolts to 19–25 ft. lbs.
   b. **Torque** ABS module to HCU bracket retaining bolts to 12–18 ft. lbs.
   c. **Torque** inlet and outlet tube fittings to 10–18 ft. lbs.

ABS MODULE (ECU)

CONTINENTAL

1. Disconnect pump motor electrical connector, then release brake control module connector locking tab.
2. Disconnect anti-lock brake control module electrical connector.
3. Remove bolts, then control module.
4. Reverse procedure to install.

SABLE & TAURUS

Refer to "Hydraulic Control Unit" for ABS module replacement procedure.

FRONT WHEEL SENSOR

CONTINENTAL

1. Raise and support vehicle, then remove tire and wheel assembly.
2. Remove inner splash shield.

DTC	Description	DTC Caused By	Action
B1342	ECU Internal Failure	ABS/TC	GO to Pinpoint Test M.
B1485	Brake Pedal Input Open Circuit	ABS/TC	GO to Pinpoint Test N.
B1676	Battery Voltage Out of Range	ABS/TC	GO to Pinpoint Test O.
C1095	ABS Hydraulic Pump Motor Circuit Failure	ABS/TC	GO to Pinpoint Test D.
C1145	RF Anti-Lock Brake Sensor Input Circuit Failure	ABS/TC	GO to Pinpoint Test E.
C1155	LF Anti-Lock Brake Sensor Input Circuit Failure	ABS/TC	GO to Pinpoint Test F.
C1165	RR Anti-Lock Brake Sensor Input Circuit Failure	ABS/TC	GO to Pinpoint Test G.
C1175	LR Anti-Lock Brake Sensor Input Circuit Failure	ABS/TC	GO to Pinpoint Test H.
C1233	LF Anti-Lock Brake Sensor Input Signal Missing	ABS/TC	GO to Pinpoint Test I.
C1234	RF Anti-Lock Brake Sensor Input Signal Missing	ABS/TC	GO to Pinpoint Test J.
C1235	RR Anti-Lock Brake Sensor Input Signal Missing	ABS/TC	GO to Pinpoint Test K.
C1236	LR Anti-Lock Brake Sensor Input Signal Missing	ABS/TC	GO to Pinpoint Test L.
U1009	SCP Invalid or Missing Data for Engine Torque	PCM	CARRY OUT the PCM Self-Test.
U1027	SCP Invalid or Missing Data for Engine RPM	PCM	CARRY OUT the PCM Self-Test.
U1041	SCP Invalid or Missing Data for Vehicle Speed	NGSC, VDM, DDM, LCM	CARRY OUT the NGSC Self-Test. CARRY OUT the VDM Self-Test. CARRY OUT the DDM Self-Test. CARRY OUT the LCM Self-Test.
U1051	SCP Invalid or Missing Data for Brakes	LCM	CARRY OUT the LCM Self-Test.
U1059	SCP Invalid or Missing Data for Transmission/Transaxle/PRNDL	PCM	CARRY OUT the PCM Self-Test.
U1123	SCP Invalid or Missing Data for Odometer	LCM, VIC	CARRY OUT the VIC Self-Test. CARRY OUT the LCM Self-Test.

FM4020001603000X

Fig. 3 Diagnostic trouble code interpretation. Continental

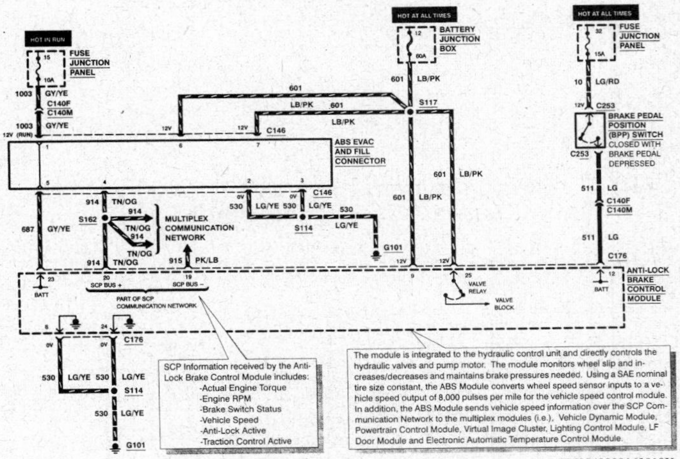

FM9049900163010X

Fig. 5 Wiring diagram (Part 1 of 2). 2000–01 Continental

DTC	Description	Source	Action
B1318	Battery Voltage Low	ABS/TC	GO to Pinpoint Test C.
B1342	ABS Control Module Internal Failure	ABS/TC	CLEAR the DTCs. REPEAT the self-test. If DTC B1342 is retrieved again, INSTALL a new electronic control unit (ECU). REPEAT the self-test.
B1484	Brake Pedal Input Open Circuit	ABS/TC	GO to Pinpoint Test D.
B1596	Repair Continuous Codes	ABS/TC	REPAIR DTCs retrieved.
B1596	Repair Continuous Codes	ABS/TC	REPAIR DTCs retrieved.
C1095	ABS Hydraulic Pump Motor Circuit Failure	ABS/TC	GO to Pinpoint Test E.
C1145	RF Wheel Speed Sensor Input Circuit Failure	ABS/TC	GO to Pinpoint Test F.
C1155	LF Wheel Speed Sensor Input Circuit Failure	ABS/TC	GO to Pinpoint Test F.
C1165	RR Wheel Speed Sensor Input Circuit Failure	ABS/TC	GO to Pinpoint Test F.
C1175	LR Wheel Speed Sensor Input Circuit Failure	ABS/TC	GO to Pinpoint Test F.
C1222	Wheel Speed Signal Mismatch	ABS/TC	GO to Pinpoint Test G.
C1233	LF Wheel Speed Input Signal Missing	ABS/TC	GO to Pinpoint Test H.
C1234	RF Wheel Speed Input Signal Missing	ABS/TC	GO to Pinpoint Test H.
C1235	RR Wheel Speed Input Signal Missing	ABS/TC	GO to Pinpoint Test H.
C1236	LR Wheel Speed Input Signal Missing	ABS/TC	GO to Pinpoint Test H.
C1266	ABS Valve Power Relay Circuit Failure	ABS/TC	INSTALL a new Hydraulic Control Unit (HCU). REPEAT the self-test.
U1009	SCP Invalid or Missing Data for Engine Torque	PCM	CARRY OUT the PCM self-test.
U1262	SCP Communication Bus Fault	SCP Network	DIAGNOSE SCP Network.
C1805	Mismatched Powertrain Control Module (PCM) and/or ABS Control Module	ABS/TC	CARRY OUT the PCM self-test.

FM4020001570000X

Fig. 4 Diagnostic trouble code interpretation. 2000–02 Sable & Taurus

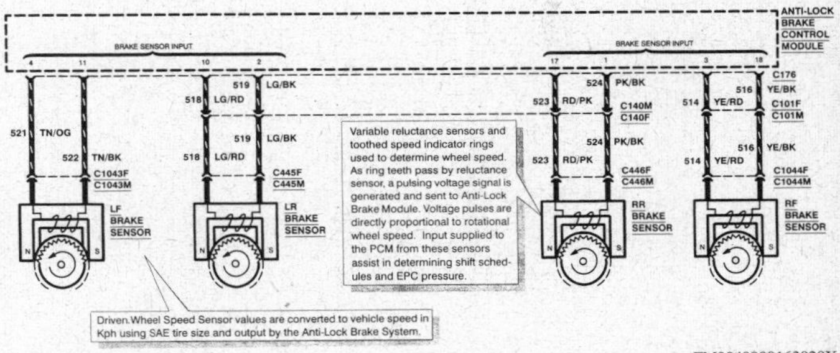

FM9049900163020X

Fig. 5 Wiring diagram (Part 2 of 2). 2000–01 Continental

3. Disconnect front brake sensor electrical connector, then remove harness from clip.
4. Remove sensor bolt, then sensor **Fig. 54.**
5. Reverse procedure to install. **Torque** mounting bolt 44 inch lbs.

SABLE & TAURUS

1. Raise and support vehicle.
2. Remove front wheel sensor bolt, sensor, then wiring from routing brackets, **Fig. 55.**
3. Remove fender splash shield retainer.
4. Pull back on splash shield, then disconnect sensor wiring.
5. Reverse procedure to install. **Torque** attaching bolt to 108 inch lbs.

REAR WHEEL SENSOR

CONTINENTAL

1. Remove rear seat, then disconnect rear ABS brake sensor electrical connector.
2. Remove harness from clips.
3. Remove sensor attaching bolt, then the sensor, **Fig. 56.**
4. Reverse procedure to install. **Torque** attaching bolt to 80 inch lbs.

SABLE & TAURUS

1. Raise and support vehicle.
2. Disconnect wiring connector, then remove from wiring clips.
3. Remove bolt, then rear wheel speed sensor, **Fig. 57.**
4. Reverse procedure to install. **Torque** attaching bolt to 80 inch lbs.

FRONT SPEED INDICATOR RING

Refer to "Front Wheel Drive Axles" for anti-lock indicator ring removal.

REAR SPEED INDICATOR RING

If anti-lock sensor is damaged, replace rear hub.

STOP LAMP SWITCH

REMOVAL

Locking tab must be lifted before stop lamp switch connector can be removed.

1. Disconnect connector from brake pedal position switch.
2. Remove brake master cylinder pushrod black bushing or white speed control deactivate switch bracket nearest pedal arm from brake pedal pin.
3. Remove hairpin retainer and white nylon washer.
4. Slide brake pedal position switch and

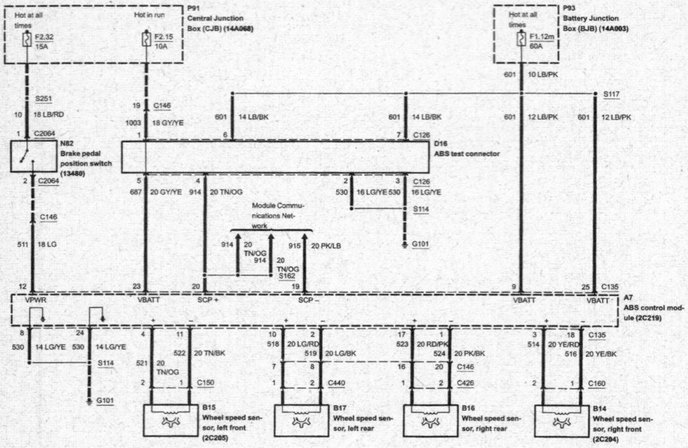

FM4020101794000X

Fig. 6 Wiring diagram. 2002–04 Continental

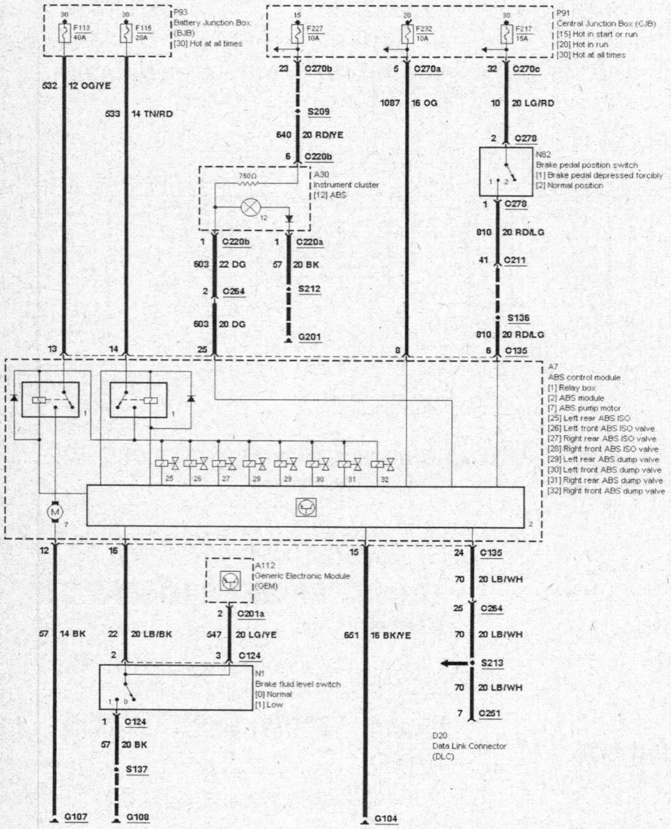

FM4020001588000X

Fig. 7 Wiring diagram (Part 1 of 2). 2001 Sable & Taurus less traction control

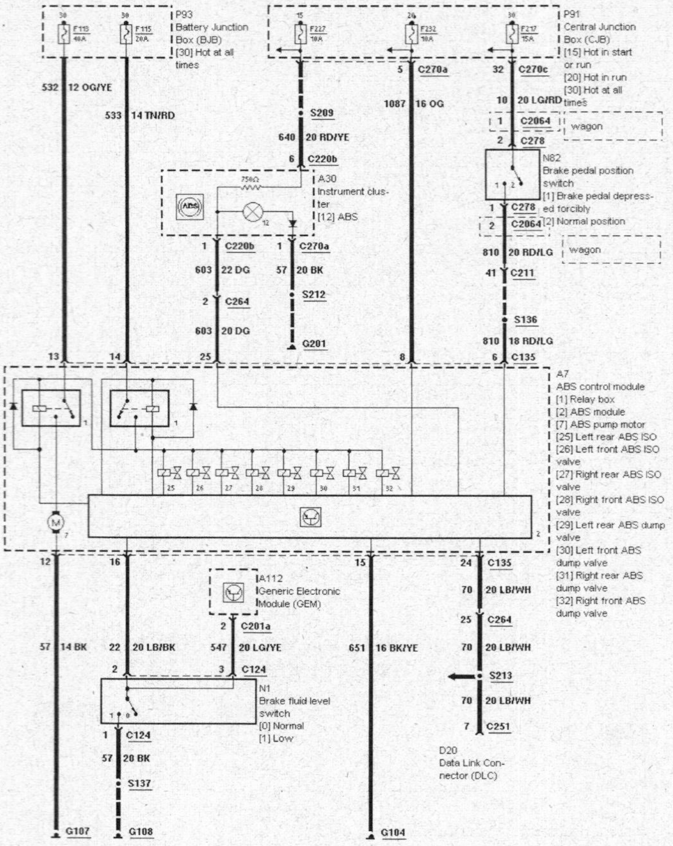

FM4020001571010X

Fig. 7 Wiring diagram (Part 1 of 2). 2000 Sable & Taurus less traction control

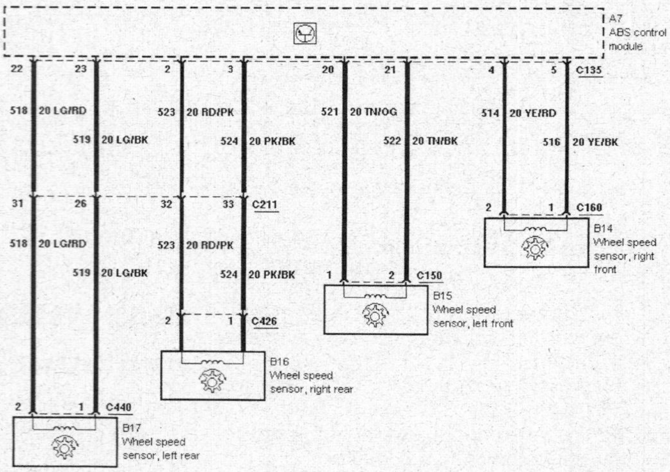

FM4020001571020X

Fig. 7 Wiring diagram (Part 2 of 2). 2000–01 Sable & Taurus less traction control

push rod away from pedal, then brake pedal position switch by sliding it down, **Fig. 58.**

INSTALLATION

1. Position stop lamp switch so U-shaped side is nearest pedal and directly over/under pin. Black bushing must be in position in pushrod eyelet with washer face on side away from brake pedal arm.
2. Slide stop lamp switch up and down, trapping master cylinder pushrod and black bushing between switch side plates. Push stop lamp switch and push rod assembly firmly toward brake pedal arm.
3. Assemble outside white nylon washer to brake pedal pin, then install hairpin retainer to trap whole assembly.
4. Stop lamp switch wire harness must have sufficient length to travel with stop lamp switch during full stroke at pedal. If wire length is insufficient, reroute harness or service as required.
5. Assemble wire harness connector to stop lamp switch.
6. Inspect stop lamp switch for proper operation. Stop lamp should illuminate with less than 6 lbs. applied to brake pedal at pad.

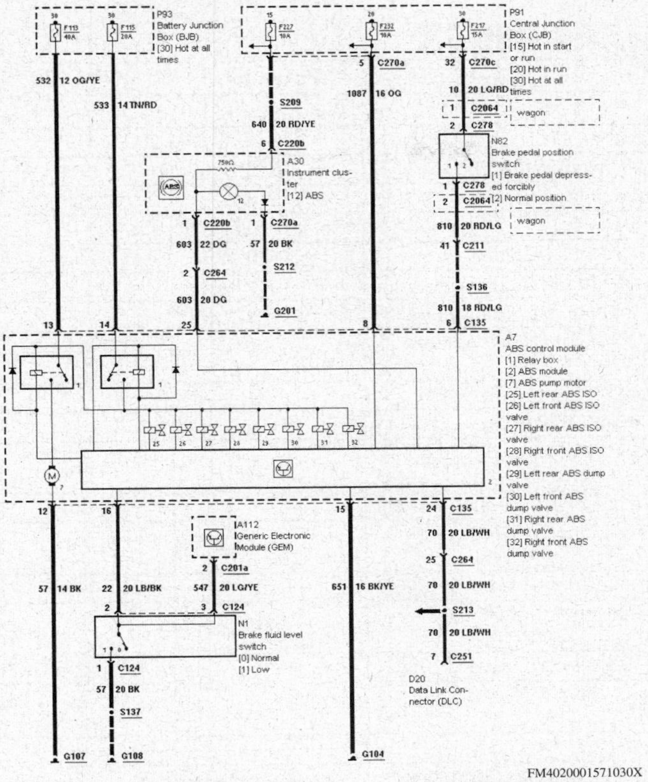

Fig. 8 Wiring diagram (Part 1 of 3). 2000 Sable & Taurus w/traction control

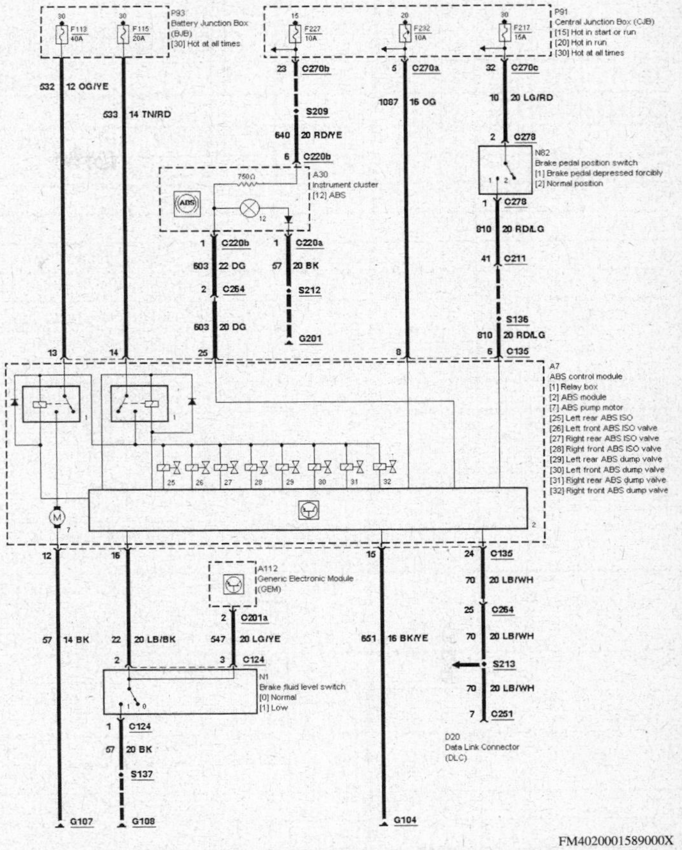

Fig. 8 Wiring diagram (Part 1 of 3). 2001–04 Sable & Taurus w/traction control

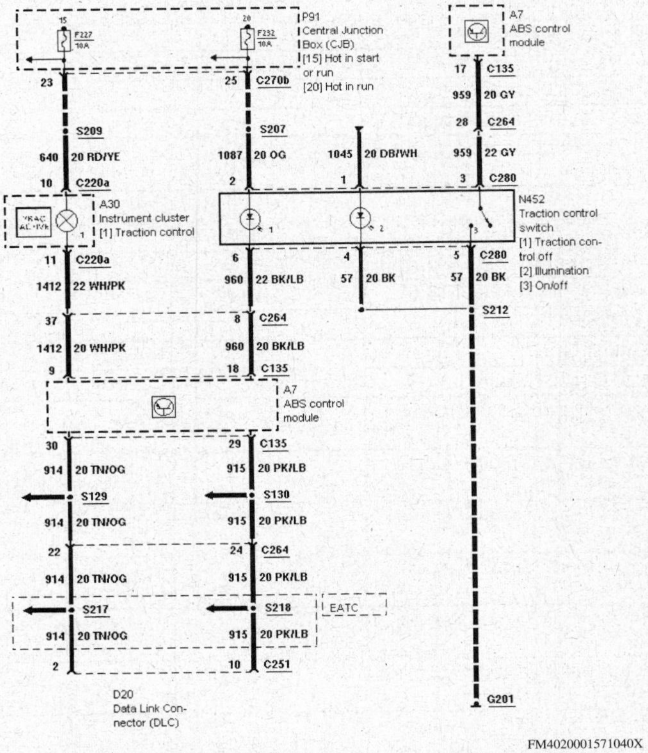

Fig. 8 Wiring diagram (Part 2 of 3). 2000–04 Sable & Taurus w/traction control

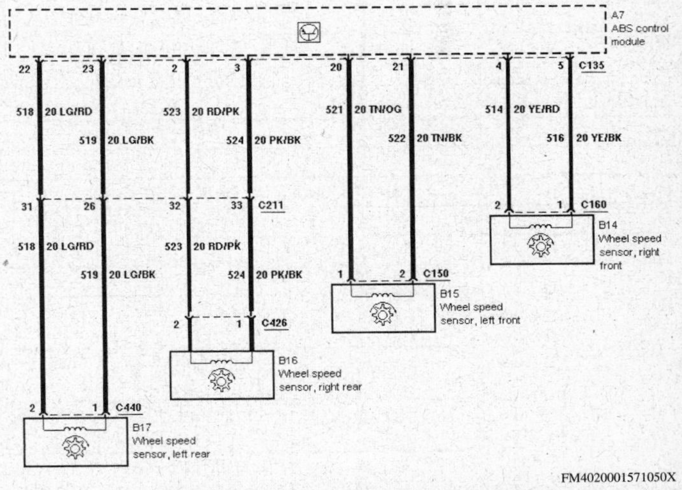

Fig. 8 Wiring diagram (Part 3 of 3). 2000–04 Sable & Taurus w/traction control

DIAGNOSTIC CHART INDEX

Test	Code	Description	Page No.	Fig. No.
CONTINENTAL				
—	—	Symptom Chart	6-9	9
A	—	No Communication w/Anti-Lock Brake Control Module	6-9	10
B	—	No Communication w/Virtual Image Cluster	6-10	11
C	—	Unable To Enter Self Test	6-10	12
D	C1095	ABS Hydraulic Pump Motor Circuit Failure	6-10	13
E	C1145	Right Front Anti-Lock Brake Sensor Input Circuit Failure	6-11	14
F	C1155	Anti-Lock Brake Sensor Left Front Input Circuit Failure (2000)	6-12	15
		Anti-Lock Brake Sensor Left Front Input Circuit Failure (2001–04)	6-13	16
G	C1165	Right Rear Anti-Lock Brake Sensor Input Circuit Failure	6-14	17
H	C1175	Left Rear Anti-Lock Brake Sensor Input Circuit Failure (2000)	6-15	18
		Left Rear Anti-Lock Brake Sensor Input Circuit Failure (2001–04)	6-16	19
I	C1233	Left Front Anti-Lock Brake Sensor Input Signal Missing (2000)	6-17	20
		Left Front Anti-Lock Brake Sensor Input Signal Missing (2001–04)	6-17	21
J	C1234	Right Front Anti-Lock Brake Sensor Input Signal Missing (2000)	6-18	22
		Right Front Anti-Lock Brake Sensor Input Signal Missing (2001–04)	6-18	23
K	C1235	Right Rear Anti-Lock Brake Sensor Input Signal Missing (2000)	6-19	24
		Right Rear Anti-Lock Brake Sensor Input Signal Missing (2001–04)	6-20	25
L	C1236	Left Rear Anti-Lock Brake Input Signal Missing (2000)	6-20	26
		Left Rear Anti-Lock Brake Input Signal Missing (2001–04)	6-21	27
M	B1242	ECU Internal Failure	6-22	28
N	B1485	Brake Pedal Input Open Circuit	6-22	29
O	B1676	Battery Voltage Out Of Range (2000)	6-22	30
		Battery Voltage Out Of Range (2001–04)	6-23	31
P	—	Spongy Brake Pedal w/No Warning Indicator	6-24	32
Q	—	Traction Control Is Inoperative	6-24	33
R	—	Yellow ABS Warning Indicator Does Not Self Test	6-24	34
S	—	Yellow ABS Warning Indicator & Traction Control Active Indicator Always On	6-25	35
SABLE & TAURUS				
—	—	Symptom Chart	6-25	36
A	—	No Communication w/ABS Control Module	6-25	37
B	—	Unable To Enter Self Test, Network Communication OK	6-25	38
C	B1318	Battery Voltage Low	6-26	39
D	B1484	Brake Pedal Input Circuit Open	6-26	40
E	C1095	ABS Hydraulic Pump Motor Circuit Failure	6-26	41
F	C1145	Righthand Front Wheel Speed Sensor Input Circuit Failure (2000)	6-27	42
	C1155	Lefthand Front Wheel Speed Sensor Input Circuit Failure (2000)	6-27	42
	C1165	Righthand Rear Wheel Speed Sensor Input Circuit Failure (2000)	6-27	42
	C1175	Lefthand Rear Wheel Speed Sensor Input Circuit Failure (2000)	6-27	42
	C1145	Righthand Front Wheel Speed Sensor Input Circuit Failure (2001–04)	6-28	43
	C1155	Lefthand Front Wheel Speed Sensor Input Circuit Failure (2001–04)	6-28	43
	C1165	Righthand Rear Wheel Speed Sensor Input Circuit Failure (2001–04)	6-28	43
	C1175	Lefthand Rear Wheel Speed Sensor Input Circuit Failure (2001–04)	6-28	43
G	C1222	Wheel Speed Signal Mismatch	6-29	44

Continued

DIAGNOSTIC CHART INDEX—Continued

Test	Code	Description	Page No.	Fig. No.
SABLE & TAURUS				
H	C1233	Lefthand Front Wheel Speed Input Signal Missing	6-29	45
	C1234	Righthand Front Wheel Speed Input Signal Missing	6-29	45
	C1235	Righthand Rear Wheel Speed Input Signal Missing	6-29	45
	C1236	Lefthand Rear Wheel Speed Input Signal Missing	6-29	45
I	—	Yellow ABS Warning Lamp Does Not Self Check, Always On w/No DTCs (2000–01)	6-30	46
	—	ABS Indicator Is Always On, No DTC's (2002–04)	6-30	47
J	—	Soft Brake Pedal, No Warning Indicator	6-30	48
K	—	Poor Vehicle Tracking During ABS Function	6-31	49
L	—	Traction Control Inoperative	6-31	50
M	—	Traction Control Switch Indicator Inoperative	6-31	51
N	—	Traction Control Cannot Be Disabled	6-32	52

Condition	Possible Source	Action
• No communication with the anti-lock brake control module	• Anti-lock brake control module. • CJB Fuse 15 (10A). • Circuitry. • Shorting cap in evac and fill connector.	• GO to Pinpoint Test A.
• Unable to enter self-test	• Anti-lock brake control module.	• GO to Pinpoint Test C.
• The red brake warning indicator does not self-check	• Parking brake switch. • Circuitry. • Virtual image cluster.	• DIAGNOSE indicator.
• The red brake warning indicator stays on when the ignition switch is in RUN	• Parking brake switch. • Circuitry. • Virtual image cluster. • Brake fluid level.	•
• Spongy brake pedal with no warning indicator	• Air in brake hydraulic system. • Worn pads/shoes.	• GO to Pinpoint Test P.
• The traction control is inoperative	• Anti-lock brake control module. • Circuitry. • HCU. • Base brake system.	• GO to Pinpoint Test Q.
• The yellow ABS warning indicator does not self-check	• Anti-lock brake control module. • Circuitry. • Virtual image cluster.	• GO to Pinpoint Test R.
• The yellow ABS warning indicator self-checks OK, goes off, then is on continuously	• Circuitry. • Anti-lock brake sensor. • Anti-lock brake control module. • HCU.	• REFER to Anti-Lock Brake Diagnostic Trouble Code (DTC) Index.
• The yellow ABS warning indicator and traction control active indicator always on	• Circuitry. • Virtual image cluster. • Anti-lock brake control module.	• GO to Pinpoint Test S.
• No communication with the virtual image cluster	• Circuitry. • Anti-lock brake control module. • Virtual image cluster.	• GO to Pinpoint Test B.
• The CHECK TRACTION control message is temporarily displayed	• Thermal model (will reset after brakes cool down).	• ALLOW brakes to cool down. TEST the system for normal operation.

FM4029901307000X

Fig. 9 Symptom chart. Continental

TEST CONDITIONS	TESTDETAILS/RESULTS/ACTIONS
A1 CHECK CIRCUIT 530 (LG/YE) FOR OPEN	

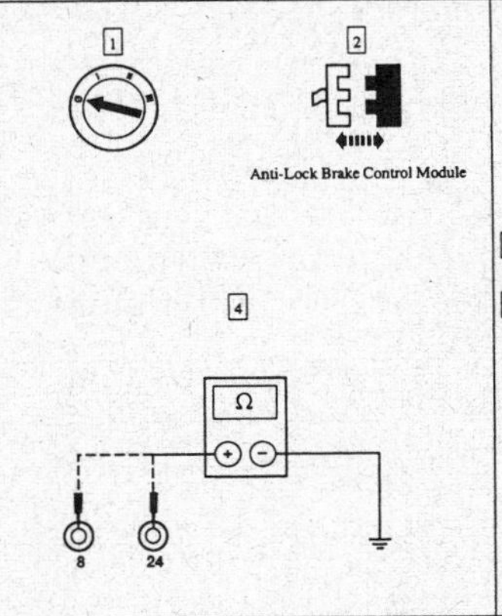

3 Connect EEC-IV 60-Pin Breakout Box.

4 Measure the resistance between EEC-IV 60-Pin Breakout Box Pin 8, Circuit 530 (LG/YE), and ground; and between EEC-IV 60-Pin Breakout Box Pin 24, Circuit 530 (LG/YE), and ground.

• Are the resistances less than 5 ohms?

→ **Yes**
GO to **A2**.

→ **No**
REPAIR the circuit. CLEAR the DTCs. REPEAT the self-test.

FM4029901308010X

Fig. 10 Test A: No Communication w/Anti-Lock Brake Control Module (Part 1 of 2). Continental

TEST CONDITIONS	TESTDETAILS/RESULTS/ACTIONS
A2 CHECK CIRCUITS 601 (LB/BK) FOR AN OPEN	
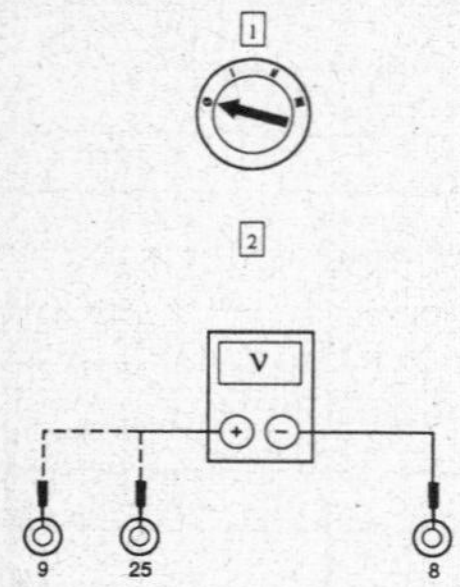	2 Measure the voltage between EEC-IV 60-Pin Breakout Box Pin 25, Circuit 601 (LB/BK), and EEC-IV 60-Pin Breakout Box Pin 8 Circuit 530 (LG/YE); and between EEC-IV 60-Pin Breakout Box Pin 9, Circuit 601 (LB/BK), and EEC-IV 60-Pin Breakout Box pin 8, circuit 530 (LG/YE). • Are the voltages greater than 10 volts? → **Yes** GO to **A3**. → **No** REPAIR the circuit. CLEAR the DTCs. REPEAT the self-test.
A3 CHECK CIRCUIT 687 (GY/YE) FOR AN OPEN	
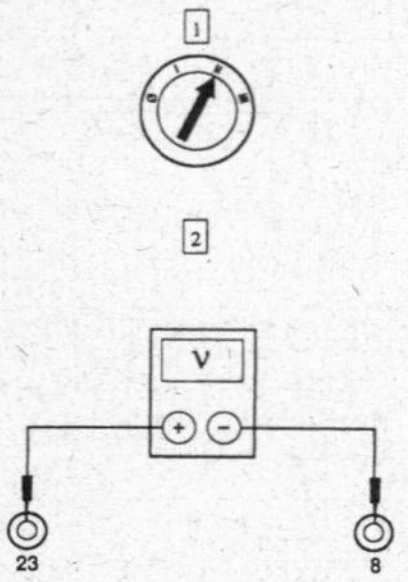	2 Measure the voltage between EEC-IV 60-Pin Breakout Box Pin 23, Circuit 687 (GY/YE), and EEC-IV 60-Pin Breakout Box Pin 8, Circuit 530 (LG/YE). • Are the voltages greater than 10 volts? → **Yes** **Diagnose Communications Network.** → **No** REPAIR the circuit.

FM4029901308020X

Fig. 10 Test A: No Communication w/Anti-Lock Brake Control Module (Part 2 of 2). Continental

TEST CONDITIONS	TESTDETAILS/RESULTS/ACTIONS
C1 CHECK THE COMMUNICATIONS TO THE ANTI-LOCK BRAKE CONTROL MODULE	
	1 Check the communication to the anti-lock brake control module. • Does NGS Tester communicate with the anti-lock brake control module? → **Yes** INSTALL a new anti-lock brake control module. → **No** GO to Pinpoint Test A.

FM4029901310000X

Fig. 12 Test C: Unable To Enter Self Test. Continental

TEST CONDITIONS	TESTDETAILS/RESULTS/ACTIONS
D1 CHECK ABS PUMP	
	• Is the ABS pump motor running all the time? → **Yes** INSTALL a new anti-lock brake control module. CLEAR the DTCs. REPEAT the self-test. → **No** GO to **D2**.

FM4029901311010X

Fig. 13 Test D/Code C1095: ABS Hydraulic Pump Motor Circuit Failure (Part 1 of 4). Continental

TEST CONDITIONS	TESTDETAILS/RESULTS/ACTIONS
B1 VERIFY COMMUNICATION WITH VIRTUAL IMAGE CLUSTER AND ANTI-LOCK BRAKE CONTROL MODULE	
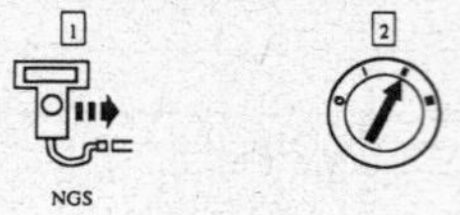	3 Test the diagnostic data link. • Does the virtual image cluster and anti-lock brake module respond to NGS Tester? → **Yes** GO to **B2**. → **No** If the virtual image cluster does not respond to NGS Tester, DIAGNOSE image cluster. If the anti-lock brake control module does not respond to NGS Tester, GO to Pinpoint Test A.
B2 CHECK THE ANTI-LOCK BRAKE CONTROL MODULE	
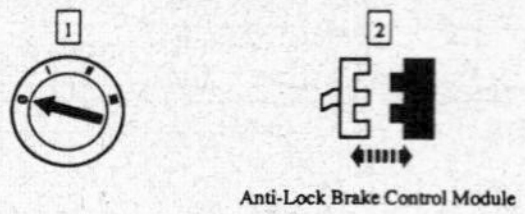	3 Check the virtual image cluster for the yellow ABS warning indicator. • Does the yellow ABS warning indicator illuminate? → **Yes** INSTALL a new anti-lock brake control module. TEST the system for normal operation. → **No** INSTALL a new virtual image cluster. TEST the system for normal operation.

FM4029901309000X

Fig. 11 Test B: No Communication w/Virtual Image Cluster. Continental

TEST CONDITIONS	TESTDETAILS/RESULTS/ACTIONS
D2 CHECK PUMP OPERATION	
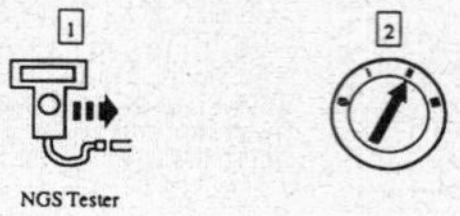	3 Trigger the anti-lock brake control module active command PMP MOTOR ON. • Does the ABS pump motor run for approximately three seconds? → **Yes** CLEAR the DTC. CHECK the yellow ABS warning indicator while driving the vehicle above 32 km/h (20 mph) and no brakes applied until the vehicle exceeds 32 km/h (20 mph). If the yellow ABS warning indicator illuminates, INSTALL a new anti-lock brake control module. CLEAR the DTCs. REPEAT the self-test. If the yellow ABS warning indicator does not illuminate the system is OK. → **No** Trigger the anti-lock brake control module active commands OFF. GO to **D3**.
D3 CHECK SUPPLY TO ANTI-LOCK BRAKE CONTROL MODULE	
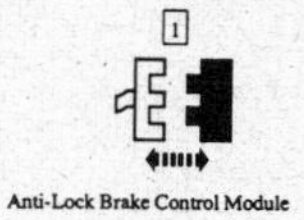	2 Connect EEC-IV 60-Pin Breakout Box.

FM4029901311020X

Fig. 13 Test D/Code C1095: ABS Hydraulic Pump Motor Circuit Failure (Part 2 of 4). Continental

TEST CONDITIONS	TESTDETAILS/RESULTS/ACTIONS
D3 CHECK SUPPLY TO ANTI-LOCK BRAKE CONTROL MODULE	
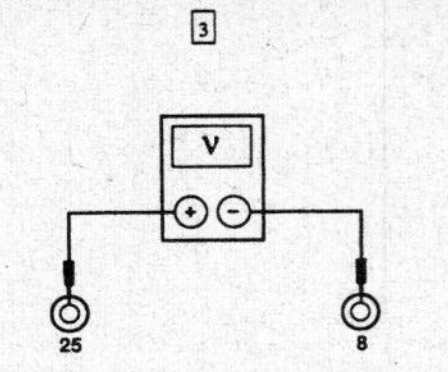	3 Measure the voltage between EEC-IV 60-Pin Breakout Box Pin 25, Circuit 601 (LB/PK), and EEC-IV 60-Pin Breakout Box Pin 8, Circuit 530 (LG/YE). • Is the voltage greater than 10 volts? → **Yes** GO to **D5**. → **No** GO to **D4**.
D4 CHECK CIRCUIT 530 (LG/YE) FOR AN OPEN	
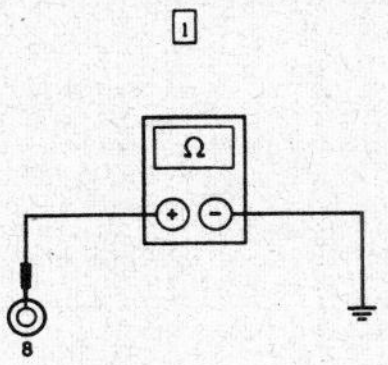	1 Measure the resistance between EEC-IV 60-Pin Breakout Box Pin 8, Circuit 530 (LG/YE), and ground. • Is the resistance less than 5 ohms? → **Yes** REPAIR Circuit 601 (LB/PK). TEST the system for normal operation. → **No** REPAIR Circuit 530 (LG/YE). CLEAR the DTCs. REPEAT the self-test.
D5 CHECK THE CONNECTOR	
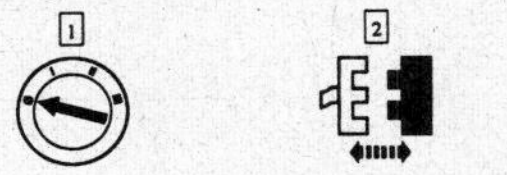 ABS Pump Motor Connector	3 Inspect the ABS pump motor connector and pins. • Are the connector and pins OK? → **Yes** GO to **D6**. → **No** REPAIR as necessary. CLEAR the DTCs. REPEAT the self-test.

FM4029901311030X

Fig. 13 Test D/Code C1095: ABS Hydraulic Pump Motor Circuit Failure (Part 3 of 4). Continental

TEST CONDITIONS	TESTDETAILS/RESULTS/ACTIONS
E1 CHECK THE RF ANTI-LOCK BRAKE SENSOR	
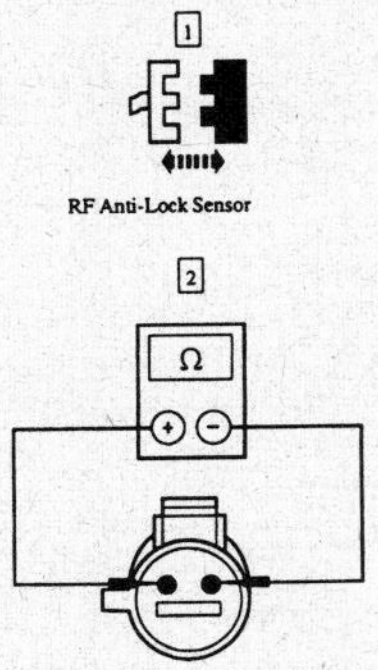	2 Measure the resistance between the RF anti-lock brake sensor pins (component side). • Is the resistance between 1,800 and 3,000 ohms? → **Yes** GO to **E2**. → **No** INSTALL a new RF anti-lock brake sensor. CLEAR the DTCs. REPEAT the self-test.

FM4029901312010X

Fig. 14 Test E/Code C1145: Right Front Anti-Lock Brake Sensor Input Circuit Failure (Part 1 of 4). Continental

TEST CONDITIONS	TESTDETAILS/RESULTS/ACTIONS
D6 CHECK THE ABS PUMP MOTOR	
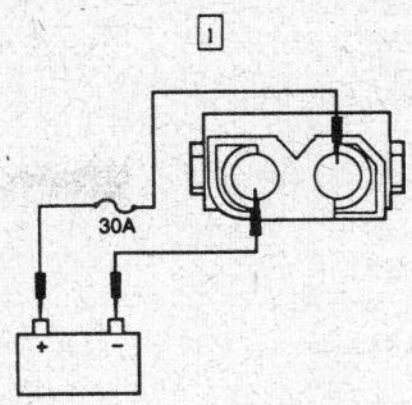	1 **NOTE:** Use heavy jumper wires when carrying out this test. The positive battery post jumper wire must be fused with a 30A fuse. Connect a jumper wire between the positive battery and the red ABS pump motor pin. Connect a jumper wire between the negative battery pin and the brown ABS pump motor pin. • Does the ABS pump motor run? → **Yes** The ABS pump is OK. INSTALL a new anti-lock brake control module. CLEAR the DTCs. REPEAT the self-test. → **No** INSTALL a new hydraulic control unit. CLEAR the DTCs. REPEAT the self-test.

FM4029901311040X

Fig. 13 Test D/Code C1095: ABS Hydraulic Pump Motor Circuit Failure (Part 4 of 4). Continental

TEST CONDITIONS	TESTDETAILS/RESULTS/ACTIONS
E2 CHECK FOR A SHORTED SENSOR	
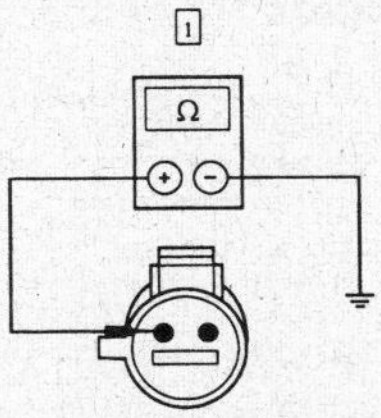	1 Measure the resistance between RF anti-lock brake sensor Pin 1 (component side) and ground. • Is the resistance greater than 10,000 ohms? → **Yes** GO to **E3**. → **No** INSTALL a new RF anti-lock brake sensor. CLEAR the DTCs. REPEAT the self-test.
E3 CHECK THE ANTI-LOCK BRAKE SENSOR CIRCUITRY	
 RF Anti-Lock Brake Sensor / Anti-Lock Brake Control Module	3 Connect EEC-IV 60-Pin Breakout Box.
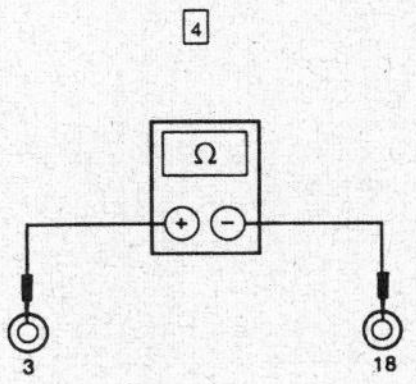	4 Measure the resistance between EEC-IV 60-Pin Breakout Box Pin 3, Circuit 514 (YE/RD), and EEC-IV 60-Pin Breakout Box Pin 18, Circuit 516 (YE/BK). • Is the resistance between 1,800 and 3,000 ohms? → **Yes** GO to **E4**. → **No** REPAIR circuit 514 (YE/RD) and/or circuit 516 (YE/BK). CLEAR the DTCs. REPEAT the self-test.

FM4029901312020X

Fig. 14 Test E/Code C1145: Right Front Anti-Lock Brake Sensor Input Circuit Failure (Part 2 of 4). Continental

TEST CONDITIONS	TEST DETAILS/RESULTS/ACTIONS
E4 CHECK CIRCUIT 514 (YE/RD) AND CIRCUIT 516 (YE/BK) FOR A SHORT TO GROUND	

1

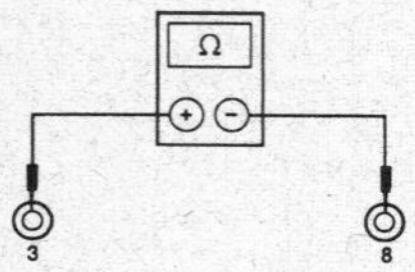

1 Measure the resistance between EEC-IV 60-Pin Breakout Box Pin 3, Circuit 514 (YE/RD), and EEC-IV 60-Pin Breakout Box Pin 8, Circuit 530 (LG/YE).

- Is the resistance greater than 10,000 ohms?

→ **Yes**
GO to **E6**.

→ **No**
GO to **E5**.

E5 CHECK CIRCUIT 514 (YE/RD) FOR A SHORT TO GROUND

1

RF Anti-Lock Brake Sensor

2

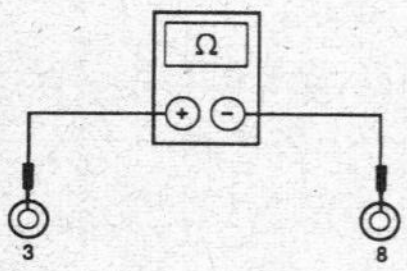

2 Measure the resistance between EEC-IV 60-Pin Breakout Box Pin 3, Circuit 514 (YE/RD), and EEC-IV 60-Pin Breakout Box Pin 8, Circuit 530 (LG/YE).

- Is the resistance greater than 10,000 ohms?

→ **Yes**
REPAIR circuit 516 (YE/BK). CLEAR the DTCs. REPEAT the self-test.

→ **No**
REPAIR circuit 514 (YE/RD). CLEAR the DTCs. REPEAT the self-test.

E6 CHECK FOR DTC

1 Restore the vehicle.

FM4029901312030X

Fig. 14 Test E/Code C1145: Right Front Anti-Lock Brake Sensor Input Circuit Failure (Part 3 of 4). 2000 Continental

CONDITIONS	DETAILS/RESULTS/ACTIONS
E4 CHECK CIRCUIT 514 (YE/RD) AND CIRCUIT 516 (YE/BK) FOR A SHORT TO GROUND	

1

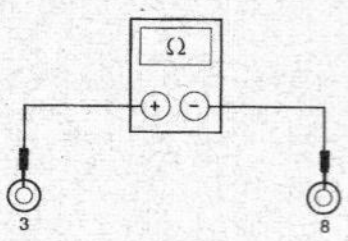

1 Measure the resistance between EEC-IV 60-Pin Breakout Box pin 3, circuit 514 (YE/RD), and EEC-IV 60-Pin Breakout Box pin 8, circuit 530 (LG/YE).

- Is the resistance greater than 10,000 ohms?

→ **Yes**
GO to **E6**.

→ **No**
GO to **E5**.

E5 CHECK CIRCUIT 514 (YE/RD) AND CIRCUIT 516 (YE/BK) FOR A SHORT TO POWER

1 2 3

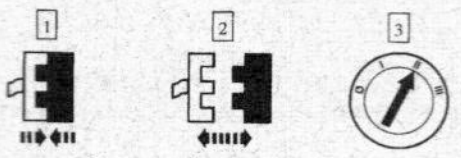

Anti-Lock Brake Control Module C135

RF Anti-Lock Brake Sensor C160

4

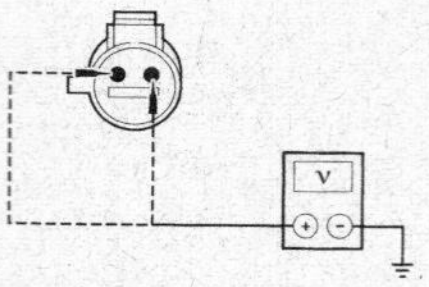

4 Measure the voltage between vehicle harness connector C160, circuit 514 (YE/RD), circuit 516 (YE/BK) and ground.

- Is the voltage greater than 2 volts?

→ **Yes**
REPAIR circuit 516 (YE/BK) and circuit 514 (YE/RD). CLEAR the DTCs. REPEAT the self-test.

→ **No**
GO to **E6**.

E6 CHECK FOR DTC

1

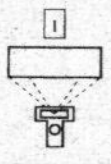

Clear Continuous DTCs

1 Clear the DTCs.

FM4029901312050X

Fig. 14 Test E/Code C1145: Right Front Anti-Lock Brake Sensor Input Circuit Failure (Part 3 of 4). 2001–04 Continental

TEST CONDITIONS	TEST DETAILS/RESULTS/ACTIONS
E6 CHECK FOR DTC	

2 3 4

Clear Continuous DTCs

5 Carry out the anti-lock brake control module On-Demand Self-Test.

- Is DTC C1145 retrieved?

→ **Yes**
INSTALL a new anti-lock brake control module. CLEAR the DTCs. REPEAT the self-test.

→ **No**
INSPECT the connections for an intermittent concern such as corrosion, pushed-out pins or loose connections. REPAIR and/or INSTALL a new component as necessary. CLEAR the DTCs. REPEAT the self-test.

FM4029901312040X

Fig. 14 Test E/Code C1145: Right Front Anti-Lock Brake Sensor Input Circuit Failure (Part 4 of 4). Continental

TEST CONDITIONS	TEST DETAILS/RESULTS/ACTIONS
F1 CHECK THE LF ANTI-LOCK BRAKE SENSOR	

1

LF Anti-Lock Brake Sensor

2

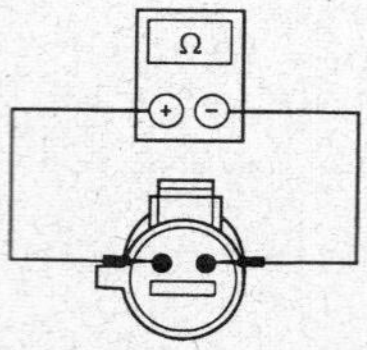

2 Measure the resistance between LF anti-lock brake sensor pins (component side).

- Is the resistance between 1,800 and 3,000 ohms?

→ **Yes**
GO to **F2**.

→ **No**
INSTALL a new LF anti-lock brake sensor. CLEAR the DTCs. REPEAT the self test.

F2 CHECK FOR AN ANTI-LOCK BRAKE SHORTED SENSOR

1

1 Measure the resistance between LF anti-lock brake sensor pin 1 and ground.

- Is the resistance greater than 10,000 ohms?

→ **Yes**
GO to **F3**.

→ **No**
INSTALL a new LF anti-lock brake sensor. CLEAR the DTCs. REPEAT the self test.

F3 CHECK THE ANTI-LOCK BRAKE SENSOR CIRCUITRY

1 2

LF Anti-Lock Brake Sensor

Anti-Lock Brake Control Module

3 Install EEC-IV 60-Pin Breakout Box.

FM4029901313010X

Fig. 15 Test F/Code C1155: Anti-Lock Brake Sensor Left Front Input Circuit Failure (Part 1 of 3). 2000 Continental

TEST CONDITIONS	TEST DETAILS/RESULTS/ACTIONS
F3 CHECK THE ANTI-LOCK BRAKE SENSOR CIRCUITRY	
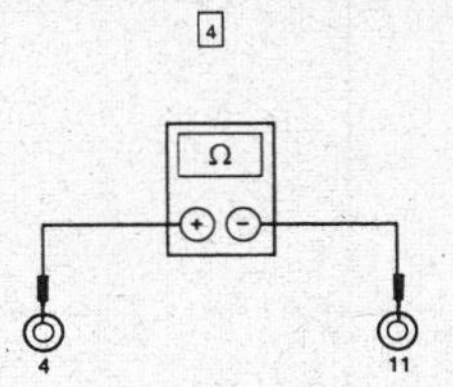	4 Measure the resistance between EEC-IV 60-Pin Breakout Box Pin 4, Circuit 521 (TN/OG), and EEC-IV 60-Pin Breakout Box Pin 11, Circuit 522 (TN/BK). • Is the resistance between 1,800 and 3,000 ohms? → **Yes** GO to **F4**. → **No** REPAIR circuit 521 (TN/OG) and/or circuit 522 (TN/BK) for an open or short to ground and/or short between the anti-lock brake sensor circuit. CLEAR the DTCs. REPEAT the self-test.
F4 CHECK CIRCUIT 521 (TN/OG) AND CIRCUIT 522 (TN/BK) FOR A SHORT TO GROUND	
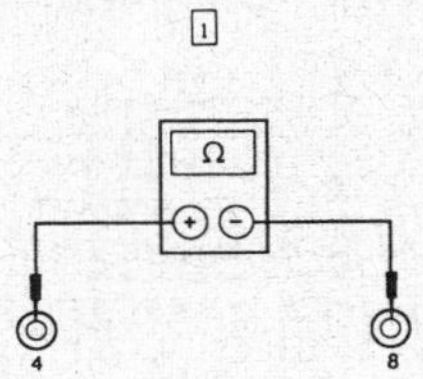	1 Measure the resistance between EEC-IV 60-Pin Breakout Box Pin 4, Circuit 521 (TN/OG), and EEC-IV 60-Pin Breakout Box Pin 8, Circuit 530 (LG/YE). • Is the resistance greater than 10,000 ohms? → **Yes** GO to **F6**. → **No** GO to **F5**.

FM4029901313020X

Fig. 15 Test F/Code C1155: Anti-Lock Brake Sensor Left Front Input Circuit Failure (Part 2 of 3). 2000 Continental

TEST CONDITIONS	TEST DETAILS/RESULTS/ACTIONS
F5 CHECK CIRCUIT 521 (TN/OG) FOR A SHORT TO GROUND	
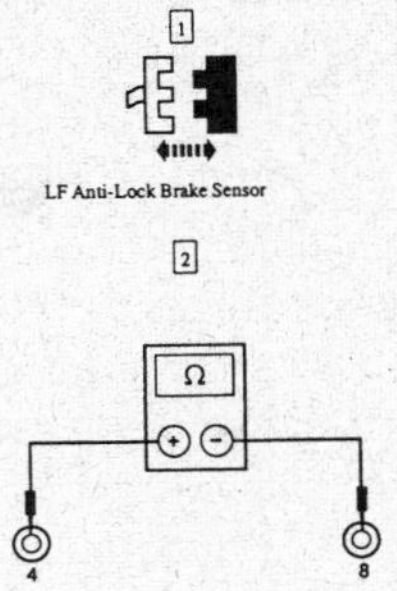	2 Measure the resistance between EEC-IV 60-Pin Breakout Box Pin 4, Circuit 521 (TN/OG), and EEC-IV 60-Pin Breakout Box Pin 8, Circuit 530 (LG/YE). • Is the resistance greater than 10,000 ohms? → **Yes** REPAIR circuit 522 (TN/BK). CLEAR the DTCs. REPEAT the self-test. → **No** REPAIR circuit 521 (TN/OG). CLEAR the DTCs. REPEAT the self-test.
F6 CHECK FOR DTC	
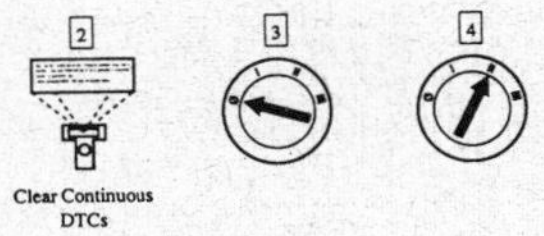	1 Restore the vehicle. 5 Carry out the anti-lock brake control module On-Demand Self-Test. • Is DTC C1155 retrieved? → **Yes** INSTALL a new anti-lock brake control module. CLEAR the DTCs. REPEAT the self-test. → **No** INSPECT the connections for an intermittent concern such as corrosion, pushed-out pin or loose connections. REPAIR as necessary. CLEAR the DTCs. REPEAT the self-test.

FM4029901313030X

Fig. 15 Test F/Code C1155: Anti-Lock Brake Sensor Left Front Input Circuit Failure (Part 3 of 3). 2000 Continental

CONDITIONS	DETAILS/RESULTS/ACTIONS
F1 CHECK THE LF ANTI-LOCK BRAKE SENSOR	
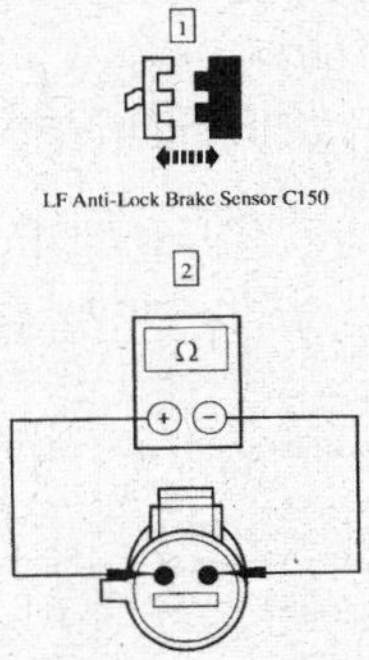	2 Measure the resistance between LF anti-lock brake sensor pins (component side). • Is the resistance between 1,800 and 3,000 ohms? → **Yes** GO to **F2**. → **No** INSTALL a new LF anti-lock brake sensor. CLEAR the DTCs. REPEAT the self test.

FM4020101766010X

Fig. 16 Test F/Code C1155: Anti-Lock Brake Sensor Left Front Input Circuit Failure (Part 1 of 4). 2001–04 Continental

CONDITIONS	DETAILS/RESULTS/ACTIONS
F2 CHECK FOR AN ANTI-LOCK BRAKE SHORTED SENSOR	
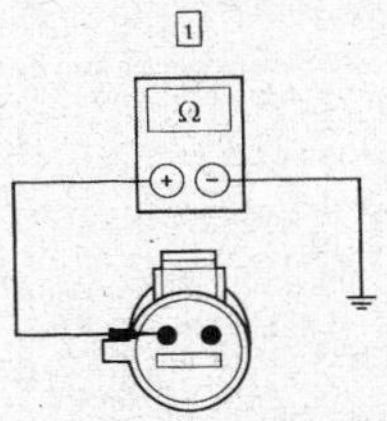	1 Measure the resistance between LF anti-lock brake sensor pin 1 and ground. • Is the resistance greater than 10,000 ohms? → **Yes** GO to **F3**. → **No** INSTALL a new LF anti-lock brake sensor. CLEAR the DTCs. REPEAT the self-test.
F3 CHECK THE ANTI-LOCK BRAKE SENSOR CIRCUITRY	
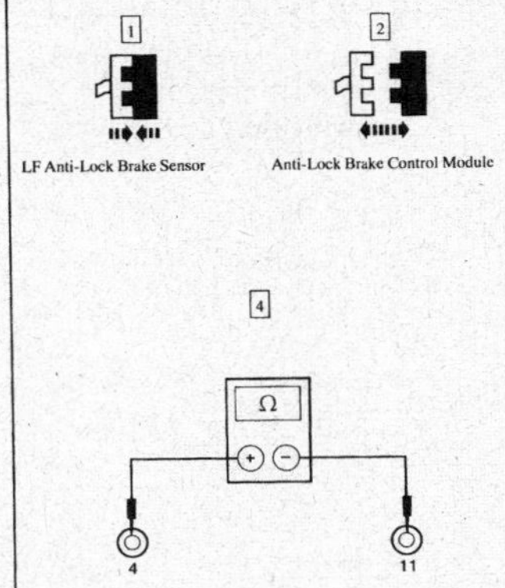	3 Install EEC-IV 60-Pin Breakout Box. 4 Measure the resistance between EEC-IV 60-Pin Breakout Box pin 4, circuit 521 (TN/OG), and EEC-IV 60-Pin Breakout Box pin 11, circuit 522 (TN/BK). • Is the resistance between 1,800 and 3,000 ohms? → **Yes** GO to **F4**. → **No** REPAIR circuit 521 (TN/OG) and/or circuit 522 (TN/BK) for an open or short to ground and/or short between the anti-lock brake sensor circuit. CLEAR the DTCs. REPEAT the self-test.

FM4020101766020X

Fig. 16 Test F/Code C1155: Anti-Lock Brake Sensor Left Front Input Circuit Failure (Part 2 of 4). 2001–04 Continental

CONDITIONS	DETAILS/RESULTS/ACTIONS
F4 CHECK CIRCUIT 521 (TN/OG) AND CIRCUIT 522 (TN/BK) FOR A SHORT TO GROUND	
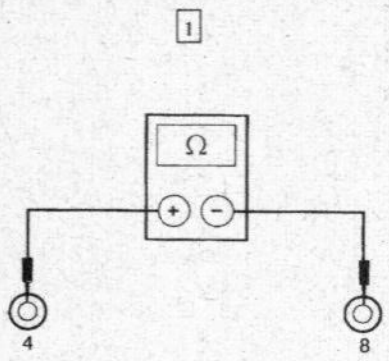	1 Measure the resistance between EEC-IV 60-Pin Breakout Box pin 4, circuit 521 (TN/OG), and EEC-IV 60-Pin Breakout Box pin 8, circuit 530 (LG/YE). • Is the resistance greater than 10,000 ohms? → **Yes** GO to **F6**. → **No** GO to **F5**.
F5 CHECK CIRCUIT 521 (TN/OG) AND CIRCUIT 522 (TN/BK) FOR A SHORT TO POWER	
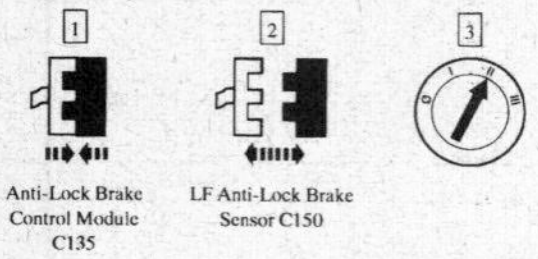	
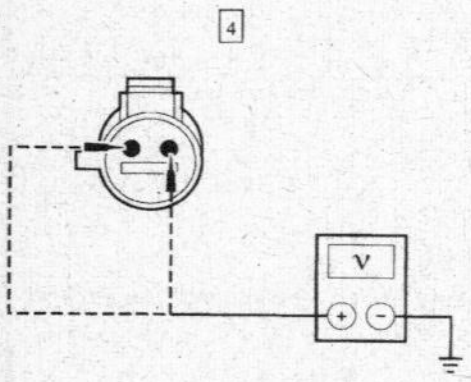	4 Measure the voltage between vehicle harness connector C150 circuit 521 (TN/OG), circuit 522 (TN/BK) and ground. • Is the voltage greater than 2 volts? → **Yes** REPAIR circuit 521 (TN/OG) and circuit 522 (TN/BK). Clear the DTCs. REPEAT the self-test. → **No** GO to **F6**.
F6 CHECK FOR DTC	
	1 Restore the vehicle.

FM4020101766030X

Fig. 16 Test F/Code C1155: Anti-Lock Brake Sensor Left Front Input Circuit Failure (Part 3 of 4). 2001–04 Continental

TEST CONDITIONS	TEST DETAILS/RESULTS/ACTIONS
G1 CHECK RR ANTI-LOCK BRAKE SENSOR	
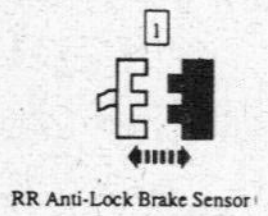	
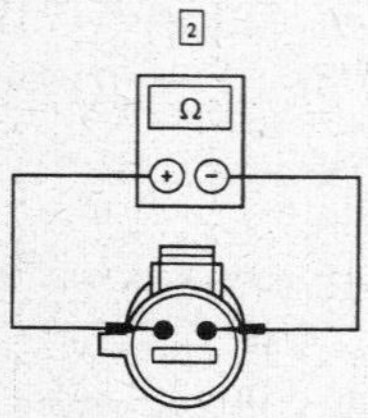	2 Measure the resistance between the RR anti-lock brake sensor pins (component side). • Is the resistance between 800 and 1,400 ohms? → **Yes** GO to **G2**. → **No** INSTALL a new RR anti-lock brake sensor. CLEAR the DTCs. REPEAT the self-test.
G2 CHECK FOR SHORTED ANTI-LOCK BRAKE SENSOR	
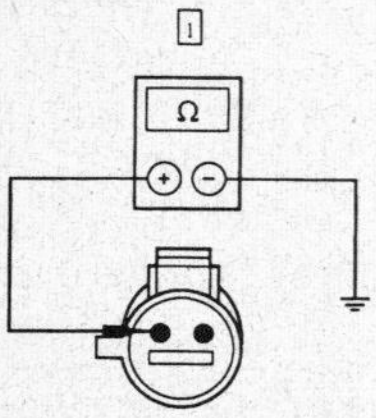	1 Measure the resistance between RR anti-lock brake sensor Pin 1 (component side) and ground. • Is the resistance greater than 10,000 ohms? → **Yes** GO to **G3**. → **No** INSTALL a new RR anti-lock brake sensor. CLEAR the DTCs. REPEAT the self-test.
G3 CHECK THE ANTI-LOCK BRAKE SENSOR CIRCUITRY	
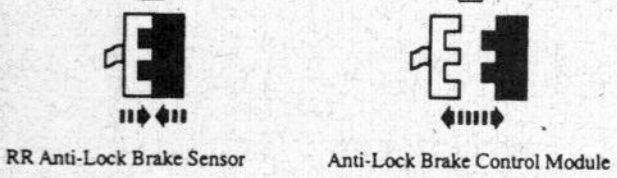	3 Connect EEC-IV 60-Pin Breakout Box.

FM4029901314010X

Fig. 17 Test G/Code C1165: Right Rear Anti-Lock Brake Sensor Input Circuit Failure (Part 1 of 4). Continental

CONDITIONS	DETAILS/RESULTS/ACTIONS
F6 CHECK FOR DTC (Continued)	
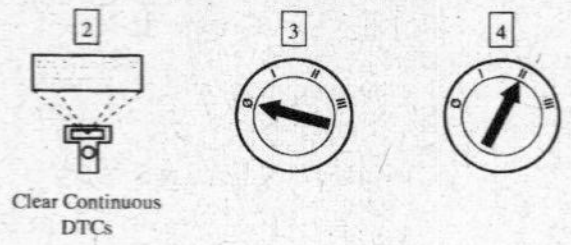	
	5 Carry out the anti-lock brake control module On-Demand Self-Test. • Is DTC C1155 retrieved? → **Yes** INSTALL a new anti-lock brake control module. CLEAR the DTCs. REPEAT the self-test. → **No** INSPECT the connections for an intermittent concern such as corrosion, pushed-out pin or loose connections. REPAIR as necessary. CLEAR the DTCs. REPEAT the self-test.

FM4020101766040X

Fig. 16 Test F/Code C1155: Anti-Lock Brake Sensor Left Front Input Circuit Failure (Part 4 of 4). 2001–04 Continental

TEST CONDITIONS	TEST DETAILS/RESULTS/ACTIONS
G3 CHECK THE ANTI-LOCK BRAKE SENSOR CIRCUITRY (Continued)	
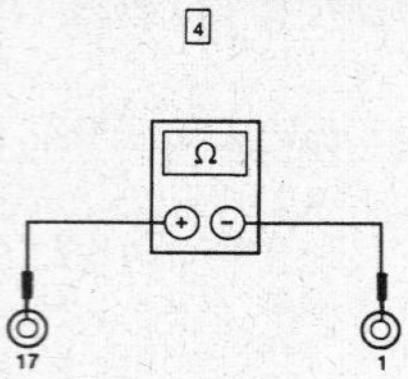	4 Measure the resistance between EEC-IV 60-Pin Breakout Box Pin 17, Circuit 523 (RD/PK), and EEC-IV 60-Pin Breakout Box Pin 1, Circuit 524 (PK/BK). • Is the resistance between 800 and 1,400 ohms? → **Yes** GO to **G4**. → **No** REPAIR circuit 523 (RD/PK) and circuit 524 (PK/BK) as necessary. CLEAR the DTCs. REPEAT the self-test.
G4 CHECK CIRCUIT 523 (RD/PK) AND CIRCUIT 524 (PK/BK) FOR A SHORT TO GROUND	
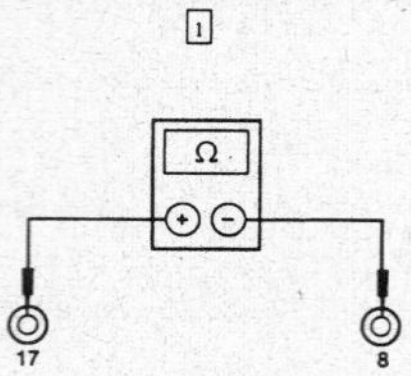	1 Measure the resistance between the EEC-IV 60-Pin Breakout Box Pin 17, Circuit 523 (RD/PK), and EEC-IV 60-Pin Breakout Box Pin 8, Circuit 530 (LG/YE). • Is the resistance greater than 10,000 ohms? → **Yes** GO to **G6**. → **No** GO to **G5**.

FM4029901314020X

Fig. 17 Test G/Code C1165: Right Rear Anti-Lock Brake Sensor Input Circuit Failure (Part 2 of 4). Continental

TEST CONDITIONS	TEST DETAILS/RESULTS/ACTIONS
G5 CHECK CIRCUIT 523 (RD/PK) FOR A SHORT TO GROUND	
1 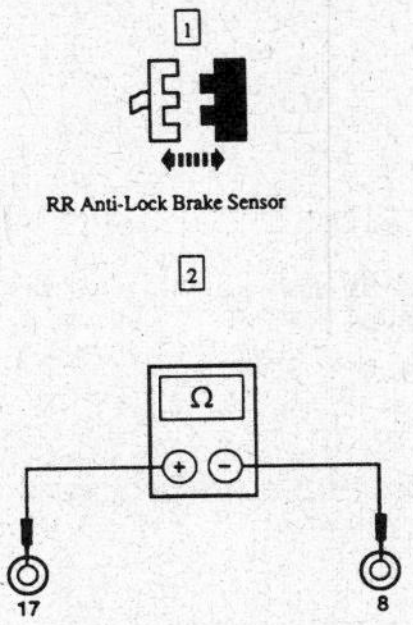 2	2 Measure the resistance between the EEC-IV 60-Pin Breakout Box Pin 17, Circuit 523 (RD/PK), and EEC-IV 60-Pin Breakout Box Pin 8, Circuit 530 (LG/YE). • Is the resistance greater than 10,000 ohms? → Yes REPAIR circuit 524 (PK/BK). CLEAR the DTCs. REPEAT the self-test. → No REPAIR circuit 523 (RD/PK). CLEAR the DTCs. REPEAT the self-test.
G6 CHECK FOR DTC	
2 3 4 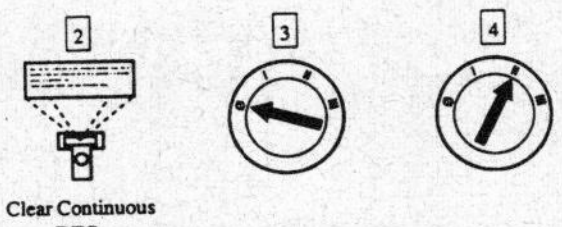	1 Restore the vehicle.

FM4029901314030X

Fig. 17 Test G/Code C1165: Right Rear Anti-Lock Brake Sensor Input Circuit Failure (Part 3 of 4). 2000 Continental

TEST CONDITIONS	TEST DETAILS/RESULTS/ACTIONS
G6 CHECK FOR DTC	
	5 Carry out the anti-lock brake control module On-Demand Self-Test. • Is DTC C1165 retrieved? → Yes INSTALL a new anti-lock brake control module. CLEAR the DTCs. REPEAT the self-test. → No INSPECT the connections for an intermittent concern such as corrosion, pushed-out pin or loose connections. REPAIR or INSTALL a new component as necessary. CLEAR the DTCs. REPEAT the self-test.

FM4029901314040X

Fig. 17 Test G/Code C1165: Right Rear Anti-Lock Brake Sensor Input Circuit Failure (Part 4 of 4). Continental

TEST CONDITIONS	TEST DETAILS/RESULTS/ACTIONS
H1 CHECK THE LR ANTI-LOCK BRAKE SENSOR	
1 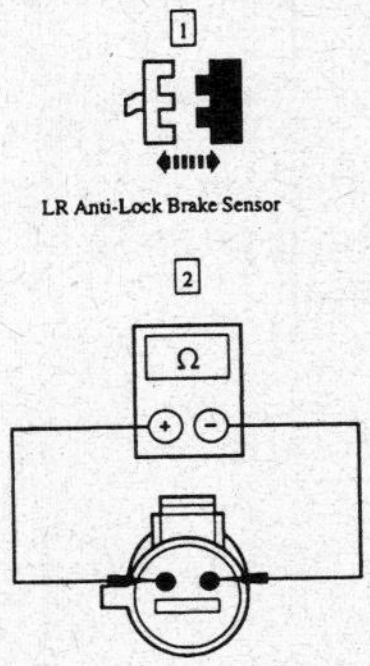 2	2 Measure the resistance between the LR anti-lock brake sensor pins (component side). • Is the resistance between 800 and 1,400 ohms? → Yes GO to **H2**. → No INSTALL a new LR anti-lock brake sensor. CLEAR the DTCs. REPEAT the self-test.

FM4029901315010X

Fig. 18 Test H/Code C1175: Left Rear Anti-Lock Brake Sensor Input Circuit Failure (Part 1 of 4). 2000 Continental

G5 CHECK CIRCUIT 523 (RD/PK) AND CIRCUIT 524 (PK/BK) FOR A SHORT TO POWER	
1 	
2 	
3 	
4 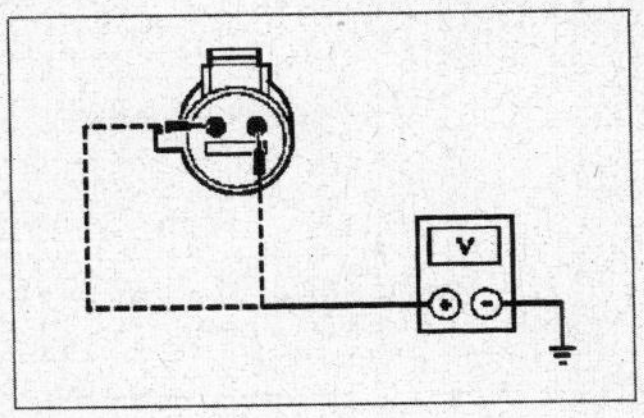	4 Measure the voltage between vehicle harness connector C426 circuit 523 (RD/PK), circuit 524 (PK/BK) and ground. • **Is the voltage greater than 2 volts?** → **Yes** REPAIR circuit 524 (PK/BK) and circuit 523 (RD/PK). CLEAR the DTCs. REPEAT the self-test. → **No** GO to G6 .

FM4029901314050X

Fig. 17 Test G/Code C1165: Right Rear Anti-Lock Brake Sensor Input Circuit Failure (Part 3 of 4). 2001–04 Continental

TEST CONDITIONS	TEST DETAILS/RESULTS/ACTIONS
H2 CHECK FOR A SHORTED ANTI-LOCK BRAKE SENSOR	
1 	1 Measure the resistance between the LR anti-lock brake sensor Pin 1 (component side) and ground. • Is the resistance greater than 10,000 ohms? → Yes GO to **H3**. → No INSTALL a new LR anti-lock brake sensor. CLEAR the DTCs. REPEAT the self-test.
H3 CHECK THE ANTI-LOCK BRAKE SENSOR CIRCUITRY	
1 2  4 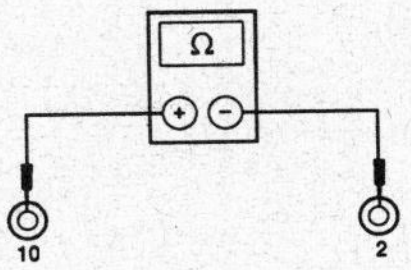	3 Connect EEC-IV 60-Pin Breakout Box. 4 Measure the resistance between EEC-IV 60-Pin Breakout Box Pin 10, Circuit 518 (LG/RD), and EEC-IV 60-Pin Breakout Box Pin 2, Circuit 519 (LG/BK). • Is the resistance between 800 and 1,400 ohms? → Yes GO to **H4**. → No REPAIR circuit 518 (LG/RD) and circuit 519 (LB/BK) as necessary. CLEAR the DTCs. REPEAT the self-test.

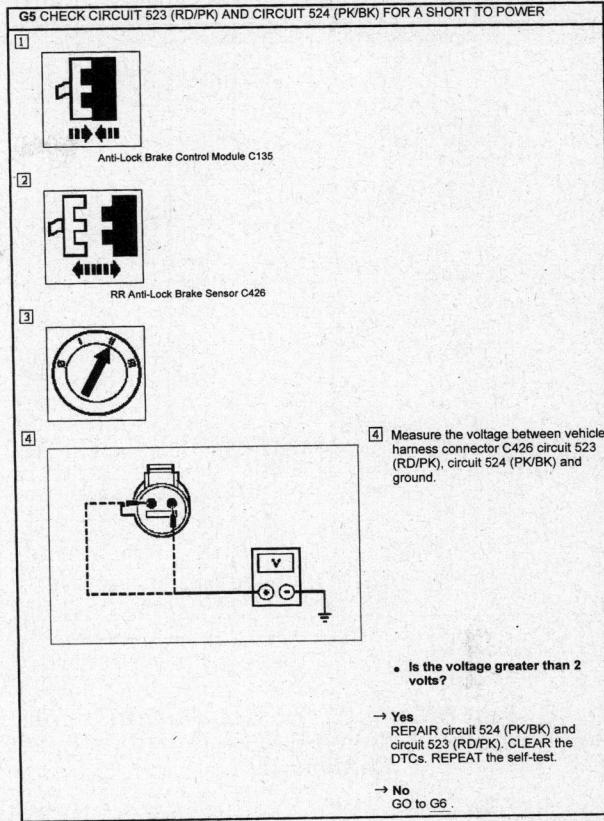

FM4029901315020X

Fig. 18 Test H/Code C1175: Left Rear Anti-Lock Brake Sensor Input Circuit Failure (Part 2 of 4). 2000 Continental

TEST CONDITIONS	TESTDETAILS/RESULTS/ACTIONS
H4 CHECK CIRCUIT 518 (LG/RD) AND CIRCUIT 519 (LG/BK) FOR A SHORT TO GROUND	
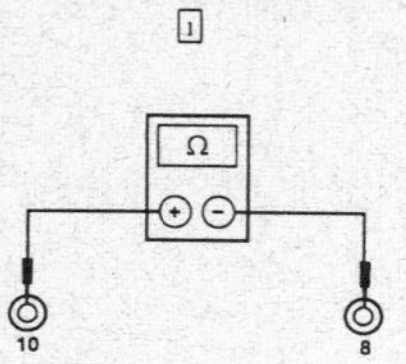	1 Measure the resistance between EEC-IV 60-Pin Breakout Box Pin 10, Circuit 518 (LG/RD), and EEC-IV 60-Pin Breakout Box Pin 8, Circuit 530 (LG/YE). • Is the resistance greater than 10,000 ohms? → **Yes** GO to **H6**. → **No** GO to **H5**.
H5 CHECK CIRCUIT 518 (LG/RD) FOR A SHORT TO GROUND	
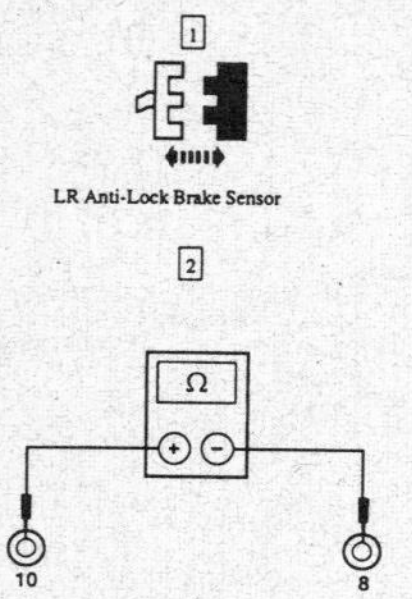	2 Measure the resistance between EEC-IV 60-Pin Breakout Box Pin 10, Circuit 518 (LG/RD), and EEC-IV 60-Pin Breakout Box Pin 8, Circuit 530 (LG/YE). • Is the resistance greater than 10,000 ohms? → **Yes** REPAIR circuit 519 (LG/BK). CLEAR the DTCs. REPEAT the self-test. → **No** REPAIR circuit 518 (LG/RD). CLEAR the DTCs. REPEAT the self-test.
H6 CHECK FOR DTC	
	1 Restore the vehicle.

FM4029901315030X

Fig. 18 Test H/Code C1175: Left Rear Anti-Lock Brake Sensor Input Circuit Failure (Part 3 of 4). 2000 Continental

CONDITIONS	DETAILS/RESULTS/ACTIONS
H1 CHECK THE LR ANTI-LOCK BRAKE SENSOR	
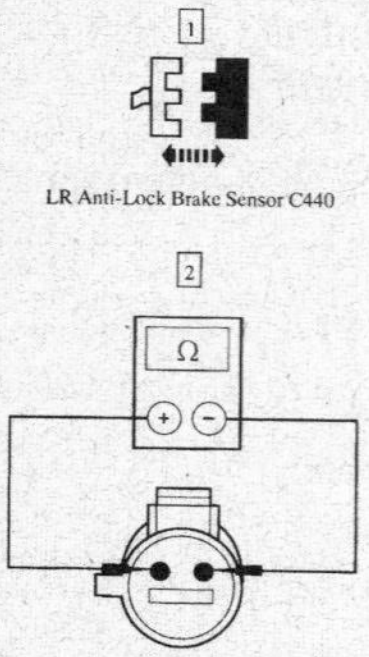	2 Measure the resistance between the LR anti-lock brake sensor pins (component side). • Is the resistance between 800 and 1,400 ohms? → **Yes** GO to **H2**. → **No** INSTALL a new LR anti-lock brake sensor. CLEAR the DTCs. REPEAT the self-test.
H2 CHECK FOR A SHORTED ANTI-LOCK BRAKE SENSOR	
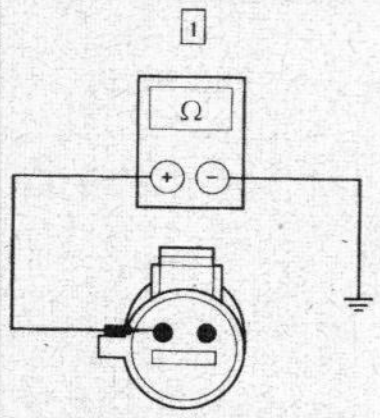	1 Measure the resistance between the LR anti-lock brake sensor pin 1 (component side) and ground. • Is the resistance greater than 10,000 ohms? → **Yes** GO to **H3**. → **No** INSTALL a new LR anti-lock brake sensor. CLEAR the DTCs. REPEAT the self-test.
H3 CHECK THE ANTI-LOCK BRAKE SENSOR CIRCUITRY	
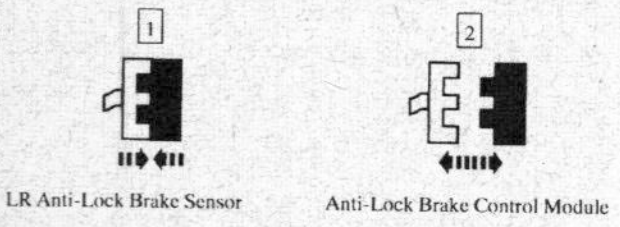	3 Connect EEC-IV 60-Pin Breakout Box.

FM4020101767010X

Fig. 19 Test H/Code C1175: Left Rear Anti-Lock Brake Sensor Input Circuit Failure (Part 1 of 3). 2001–04 Continental

TEST CONDITIONS	TESTDETAILS/RESULTS/ACTIONS
H6 CHECK FOR DTC	
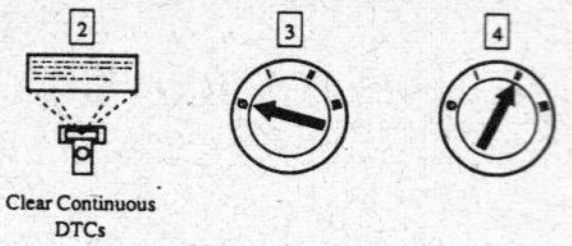	5 Carry out the anti-lock brake control module On-Demand Self-Test. • Is DTC C1175 retrieved? → **Yes** INSTALL a new anti-lock brake control module. CLEAR the DTCs. REPEAT the self-test. → **No** INSPECT the connections for an intermittent concern such as corrosion, pushed-out pin or loose connections. REPAIR and/or INSTALL a new component as necessary. CLEAR the DTCs. REPEAT the self-test.

FM4029901315040X

Fig. 18 Test H/Code C1175: Left Rear Anti-Lock Brake Sensor Input Circuit Failure (Part 4 of 4). 2000 Continental

CONDITIONS	DETAILS/RESULTS/ACTIONS
H3 CHECK THE ANTI-LOCK BRAKE SENSOR CIRCUITRY (Continued)	
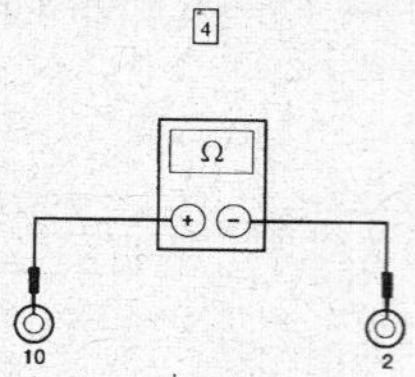	4 Measure the resistance between EEC-IV 60-Pin Breakout Box pin 10, circuit 518 (LG/RD), and EEC-IV 60-Pin Breakout Box pin 2, circuit 519 (LG/BK). • Is the resistance between 800 and 1,400 ohms? → **Yes** GO to **H4**. → **No** REPAIR circuit 518 (LG/RD) and circuit 519 (LG/BK) as necessary. CLEAR the DTCs. REPEAT the self-test.
H4 CHECK CIRCUIT 518 (LG/RD) AND CIRCUIT 519 (LG/BK) FOR A SHORT TO GROUND	
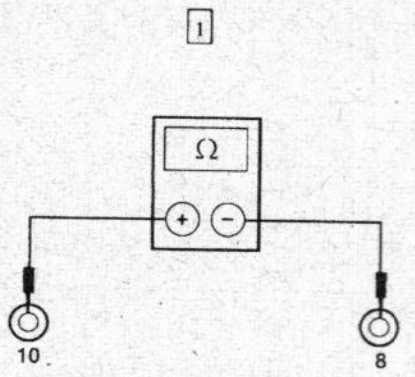	1 Measure the resistance between EEC-IV 60-Pin Breakout Box pin 10, circuit 518 (LG/RD), and EEC-IV 60-Pin Breakout Box pin 8, circuit 530 (LG/YE). • Is the resistance greater than 10,000 ohms? → **Yes** GO to **H6**. → **No** GO to **H5**.
H5 CHECK CIRCUIT 518 (LG/RD) AND CIRCUIT 519 (LG/BK) FOR A SHORT TO POWER	
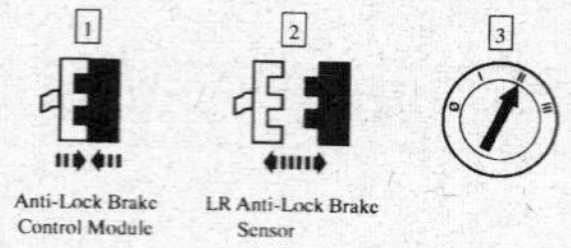	

FM4020101767020X

Fig. 19 Test H/Code C1175: Left Rear Anti-Lock Brake Sensor Input Circuit Failure (Part 2 of 3). 2001–04 Continental

CONDITIONS	DETAILS/RESULTS/ACTIONS
H5 CHECK CIRCUIT 518 (LG/RD) AND CIRCUIT 519 (LG/BK) FOR A SHORT TO POWER (Continued)	
4 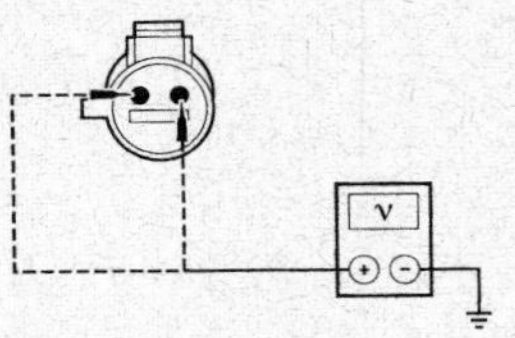	4 Measure the voltage between vehicle harness connector C440 circuit 518 (LG/RD), circuit 519 (LG/BK) and ground. • Is the voltage greater than 2 volts? → **Yes** REPAIR circuit 518 (LG/RD) and circuit 519 (LG/BK). CLEAR the DTCs. REPEAT the self-test. → **No** GO to **H6**.
H6 CHECK FOR DTC	
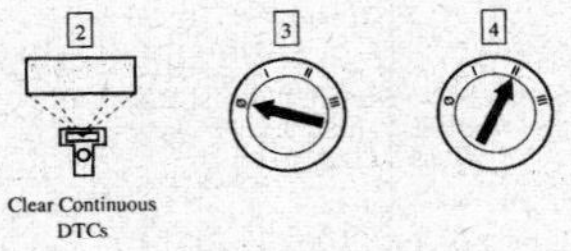	1 Restore the vehicle. 5 Carry out the anti-lock brake control module On-Demand Self-Test. • Is DTC C1175 retrieved? → **Yes** INSTALL a new anti-lock brake control module. CLEAR the DTCs. REPEAT the self-test. → **No** INSPECT the connections for an intermittent concern such as corrosion, pushed-out pin or loose connections. REPAIR and/or INSTALL a new component as necessary. CLEAR the DTCs. REPEAT the self-test.

FM4020101767030X

Fig. 19 Test H/Code C1175: Left Rear Anti-Lock Brake Sensor Input Circuit Failure (Part 3 of 3). 2001–04 Continental

TEST CONDITIONS	TESTDETAILS/RESULTS/ACTIONS
I2 CHECK THE LF ANTI-LOCK BRAKE SENSOR INDICATOR	
	1 Check the LF anti-lock brake sensor indicator for corrosion, nicks, bridged teeth, damaged teeth, proper mounting and alignment with the LF anti-lock brake sensor. Check the air gap. Check the bearing end play. • Is the LF anti-lock brake sensor indicator OK? → **Yes** GO to **I3**. → **No** INSTALL a new LF anti-lock brake sensor indicator. CLEAR the DTCs. REPEAT the self-test.
I3 CHECK THE SIGNAL INPUT	
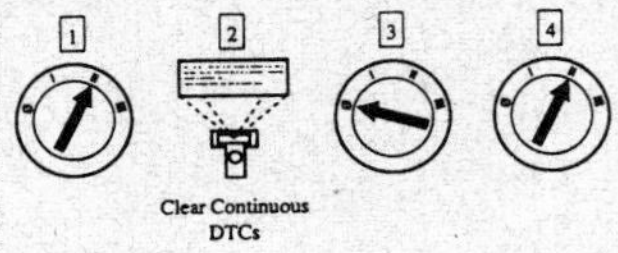	5 Monitor the anti-lock brake control module PID LF__WSPD and RF__WSPD while driving at various speeds. 6 Test drive the vehicle for 16 km (10 miles). • Are the anti-lock brake control module PID readings always approximately the same? → **Yes** INSTALL a new anti-lock brake control module. CLEAR the DTCs. REPEAT the self-test. → **No** INSTALL a new LF anti-lock brake sensor. CLEAR the DTCs. REPEAT the self-test.

FM4029901316020X

Fig. 20 Test I/Code C1233: Left Front Anti-Lock Brake Sensor Input Signal Missing (Part 2 of 2). 2000 Continental

TEST CONDITIONS	TESTDETAILS/RESULTS/ACTIONS
I1 CHECK THE LF ANTI-LOCK BRAKE SENSOR	
	1 Inspect the LF anti-lock brake sensor mounting. Check the sensor for excessive dirt build-up. Check for metal obstructions. Check the sensor for damage. • Is the LF anti-lock brake sensor and mounting OK? → **Yes** GO to **I2**. → **No** REPAIR or INSTALL a new LF anti-lock brake sensor. CLEAR the DTCs. REPEAT the self-test.

FM4029901316010X

Fig. 20 Test I/Code C1233: Left Front Anti-Lock Brake Sensor Input Signal Missing (Part 1 of 2). 2000 Continental

CONDITIONS	DETAILS/RESULTS/ACTIONS
I1 CHECK THE LF ANTI-LOCK BRAKE SENSOR	
	1 Inspect the LF anti-lock brake sensor mounting. Check the sensor for excessive dirt build-up. Check for metal obstructions. Check the sensor for damage. • Is the LF anti-lock brake sensor and mounting OK? → **Yes** GO to **I2**. → **No** REPAIR or INSTALL a new LF anti-lock brake sensor. CLEAR the DTCs. REPEAT the self-test.
I2 CHECK THE LF ANTI-LOCK BRAKE SENSOR INDICATOR	
	1 Check the LF anti-lock brake sensor indicator for corrosion, nicks, bridged teeth, damaged teeth, incorrect mounting and alignment with the LF anti-lock brake sensor. Check the air gap. Check the bearing end play. • Is the LF anti-lock brake sensor indicator OK? → **Yes** GO to **I3**. → **No** INSTALL a new LF anti-lock brake sensor indicator. CLEAR the DTCs. REPEAT the self-test.
I3 CHECK THE SIGNAL INPUT	
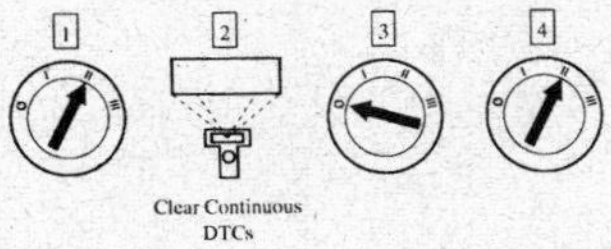	5 Monitor the anti-lock brake control module PID LF__WSPD and RF__WSPD while driving at various speeds.

FM4020101768010X

Fig. 21 Test I/Code C1233: Left Front Anti-Lock Brake Sensor Input Signal Missing (Part 1 of 3). 2001–04 Continental

CONDITIONS	DETAILS/RESULTS/ACTIONS
I3 CHECK THE SIGNAL INPUT (Continued)	
	6 Test drive the vehicle for 16 km (10 miles). • Are the anti-lock brake control module PID readings always approximately the same? → Yes INSTALL a new anti-lock brake control module. CLEAR the DTCs. REPEAT k the self-test. → No GO to **I4**.
I4 CHECK THE SENSOR OUTPUT	
 LF Anti-Lock Brake Sensor C150	2 Raise the vehicle on a hoist.
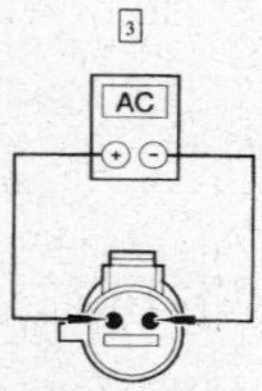	3 SLOWLY rotate the LF wheel while monitoring the signal output in A/C volts. • Is the A/C voltage between 100 and 3500 mV? → Yes GO to **I5**. → No INSTALL a new LF anti-lock brake sensor. LOWER the vehicle. CLEAR the DTCs. REPEAT the self-test.
I5 CHECK THE SENSOR OUTPUT AT THE MODULE CONNECTOR	
 LF Anti-Lock Brake Sensor C150 Anti-Lock Brake Control Module	

FM4020101768020X

Fig. 21 Test I/Code C1233: Left Front Anti-Lock Brake Sensor Input Signal Missing (Part 2 of 3). 2001–04 Continental

TEST CONDITIONS	TESTDETAILS/RESULTS/ACTIONS
J1 CHECK THE RF ANTI-LOCK BRAKE SENSOR	
	1 Inspect the RF anti-lock brake sensor mounting. Check the sensor for excessive dirt build-up. Check for metal obstructions. Check the sensor for damage. • Is the RF anti-lock brake sensor and mounting OK? → Yes GO to **J2**. → No REPAIR or INSTALL a new RF anti-lock brake sensor as necessary. CLEAR the DTCs. REPEAT the self-test.
J2 CHECK THE RF ANTI-LOCK BRAKE SENSOR INDICATOR	
	1 Check the RF anti-lock brake sensor indicator for corrosion, nicks, bridged teeth, damaged teeth, proper mounting and alignment with the RF anti-lock brake sensor. Check the air gap. Check the bearing end play. • Is the RF anti-lock brake sensor indicator OK? → Yes GO to **J3**. → No INSTALL a new RF anti-lock brake sensor indicator. CLEAR the DTCs. REPEAT the self-test.
J3 CHECK THE SIGNAL INPUT	
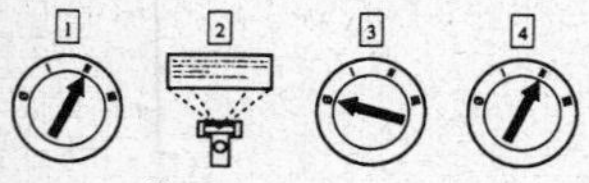 Clear Continuous DTCs	5 Monitor the anti-lock brake control module PIDs LF__WSPD and RF__WSPD while driving at various speeds.

FM4029901317010X

Fig. 22 Test J/Code C1234: Right Front Anti-Lock Brake Sensor Input Signal Missing (Part 1 of 2). 2000 Continental

CONDITIONS	DETAILS/RESULTS/ACTIONS
I5 CHECK THE SENSOR OUTPUT AT THE MODULE CONNECTOR (Continued)	
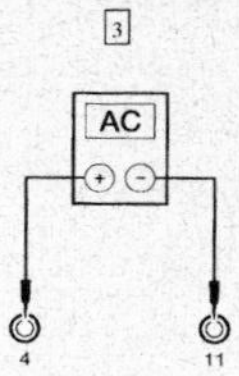	3 Measure the A/C voltage between EEC-IV 60-Pin Breakout Box pin 4, circuit 521 (TN/OG), and pin 11, circuit 522 (TN/BK).
	4 Slowly rotate the LF wheel. • Is the A/C voltage between 100 and 3500 mV? → Yes INSTALL a new module. → No REPAIR circuit 521 (TN/OG) and circuit 522 (TN/BK) as necessary. CLEAR the DTCs. REPEAT the self-test.

FM4020101768030X

Fig. 21 Test I/Code C1233: Left Front Anti-Lock Brake Sensor Input Signal Missing (Part 3 of 3). 2001–04 Continental

TEST CONDITIONS	TESTDETAILS/RESULTS/ACTIONS
J3 CHECK THE SIGNAL INPUT	
	6 Test drive the vehicle for 16 km (10 miles). • Are the anti-lock brake control module PID readings always approximately the same? → Yes INSTALL a new anti-lock brake control module. CLEAR the DTCs. REPEAT the self-test. → No INSTALL a new RF anti-lock brake sensor. CLEAR the DTCs. REPEAT the self-test.

FM4029901317020X

Fig. 22 Test J/Code C1234: Right Front Anti-Lock Brake Sensor Input Signal Missing (Part 2 of 2). 2000 Continental

CONDITIONS	DETAILS/RESULTS/ACTIONS
J1 CHECK THE RF ANTI-LOCK BRAKE SENSOR	
	1 Inspect the RF anti-lock brake sensor mounting. Check the sensor for excessive dirt build-up. Check for metal obstructions. Check the sensor for damage. • Is the RF anti-lock brake sensor and mounting OK? → Yes GO to **J2**. → No REPAIR or INSTALL a new RF anti-lock brake sensor as necessary. CLEAR the DTCs. REPEAT the self-test.

FM4020101769010X

Fig. 23 Test J/Code C1234: Right Front Anti-Lock Brake Sensor Input Signal Missing (Part 1 of 3). 2001–04 Continental

CONDITIONS	DETAILS/RESULTS/ACTIONS
J2 CHECK THE RF ANTI-LOCK BRAKE SENSOR INDICATOR	
	1 Check the RF anti-lock brake sensor indicator for corrosion, nicks, bridged teeth, damaged teeth, incorrect mounting and alignment with the RF anti-lock brake sensor. Check the air gap. Check the bearing end play. • Is the RF anti-lock brake sensor indicator OK? → **Yes** GO to **J3**. → **No** INSTALL a new RF anti-lock brake sensor indicator. CLEAR the DTCs. REPEAT the self-test.
J3 CHECK THE SIGNAL INPUT	
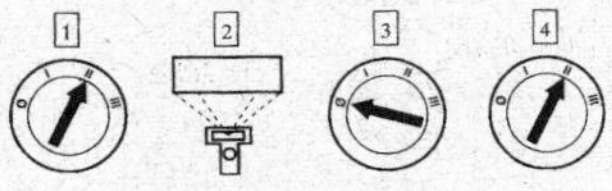 1 2 3 4 Clear Continuous DTCs	5 Monitor the anti-lock brake control module PIDs LF__WSPD and RF__WSPD while driving at various speeds. 6 Test drive the vehicle for 16 km (10 miles). • Are the anti-lock brake control module PID readings always approximately the same? → **Yes** INSTALL a new anti-lock brake control module. CLEAR the DTCs. REPEAT the self-test. → **No** GO to **J4**.

FM4020101769020X

Fig. 23 Test J/Code C1234: Right Front Anti-Lock Brake Sensor Input Signal Missing (Part 2 of 3). 2001–04 Continental

CONDITIONS	DETAILS/RESULTS/ACTIONS
J4 CHECK THE SENSOR OUTPUT	
1  RF Anti-Lock Brake Sensor C160 3 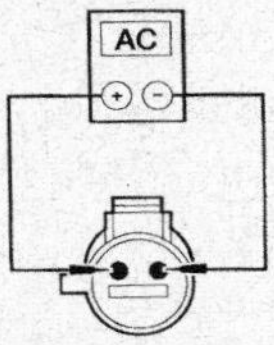	2 Raise the vehicle on a hoist. 3 Slowly rotate the RF wheel while monitoring the signal output in A/C volts. • Is the A/C voltage between 100 and 3500 mV? → **Yes** GO to **J5**. → **No** INSTALL a new RF anti-lock brake sensor. CLEAR the DTCs. REPEAT the self-test.
J5 CHECK THE SENSOR OUTPUT AT THE MODULE CONNECTOR	
 1 RF Anti-Lock Brake Sensor C160 2 Anti-Lock Brake Control Module C135	3 Measure the A/C voltage between EEC-IV 60-Pin Breakout Box pin 3, circuit 514 (YE/RD), and pin 18, circuit 516 (YE/BK).

FM4020101769030X

Fig. 23 Test J/Code C1234: Right Front Anti-Lock Brake Sensor Input Signal Missing (Part 3 of 3). 2001–04 Continental

TEST CONDITIONS	TEST DETAILS/RESULTS/ACTIONS
K1 CHECK THE RR ANTI-LOCK BRAKE SENSOR	
	1 Inspect the RR anti-lock brake sensor mounting. Check the sensor for excessive dirt build-up. Check for metal obstructions. Check the sensor for damage. • Is the RR anti-lock brake sensor and mounting OK? → **Yes** GO to **K2**. → **No** REPAIR or INSTALL a new RR anti-lock brake sensor as necessary. CLEAR the DTCs. REPEAT the self-test.

FM4029901318010X

Fig. 24 Test K/Code C1235: Right Rear Anti-Lock Brake Sensor Input Signal Missing (Part 1 of 2). 2000 Continental

TEST CONDITIONS	TEST DETAILS/RESULTS/ACTIONS
K2 CHECK THE RR ANTI-LOCK BRAKE SENSOR INDICATOR	
	1 Check the RR anti-lock brake sensor indicator for corrosion, nicks, bridged teeth, damaged teeth, proper mounting and alignment with the RR anti-lock brake sensor. Check the air gap. Check the bearing end play. • Is the RR anti-lock brake sensor indicator OK? → **Yes** GO to **K3**. → **No** INSTALL a new anti-lock brake sensor indicator. CLEAR the DTCs. REPEAT the self-test.
K3 CHECK THE SIGNAL INPUT	
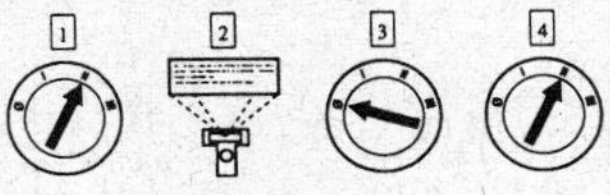 1 2 3 4 Clear Continuous DTCs	5 Monitor the anti-lock brake control module PIDs LR__WSPD and RR__WSPD while driving at various speeds. 6 Test drive the vehicle for 16 km (10 miles). • Are the anti-lock brake control module PID readings always approximately the same? → **Yes** INSTALL a new anti-lock brake control module. CLEAR the DTCs. REPEAT the self-test. → **No** INSTALL a new RR anti-lock brake sensor. CLEAR the DTCs. REPEAT the self-test.

FM4029901318020X

Fig. 24 Test K/Code C1235: Right Rear Anti-Lock Brake Sensor Input Signal Missing (Part 2 of 2). 2000 Continental

CONDITIONS	DETAILS/RESULTS/ACTIONS
K1 CHECK THE RR ANTI-LOCK BRAKE SENSOR	
	1 Inspect the RR anti-lock brake sensor mounting. Check the sensor for excessive dirt build-up. Check for metal obstructions. Check the sensor for damage. • Is the RR anti-lock brake sensor and mounting OK? → **Yes** GO to **K2**. → **No** REPAIR or INSTALL a new RR anti-lock brake sensor as necessary. CLEAR the DTCs. REPEAT the self-test.

FM4020101770010X

Fig. 25 Test K/Code C1235: Right Rear Anti-Lock Brake Sensor Input Signal Missing (Part 1 of 4). 2001–04 Continental

CONDITIONS	DETAILS/RESULTS/ACTIONS
K2 CHECK THE RR ANTI-LOCK BRAKE SENSOR INDICATOR	
	1 Check the RR anti-lock brake sensor indicator for corrosion, nicks, bridged teeth, damaged teeth, incorrect mounting and alignment with the RR anti-lock brake sensor. Check the air gap. Check the bearing end play. • Is the RR anti-lock brake sensor indicator OK? → **Yes** GO to **K3**. → **No** INSTALL a new anti-lock brake sensor indicator. CLEAR the DTCs. REPEAT the self-test.
K3 CHECK THE SIGNAL INPUT	
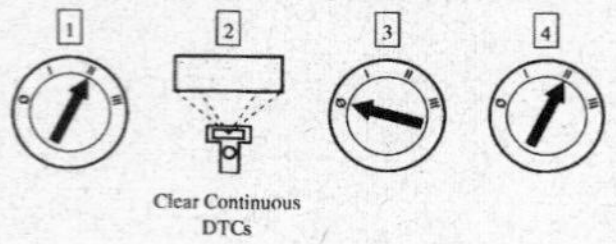	5 Monitor the anti-lock brake control module PIDs LR__WSPD and RR__WSPD while driving at various speeds. 6 Test drive the vehicle for 16 km (10 miles). • Are the anti-lock brake control module PID readings always approximately the same? → **Yes** INSTALL a new anti-lock brake control module. CLEAR the DTCs. REPEAT the self-test. → **No** GO to **K4**.

FM4020101770020X

Fig. 25 Test K/Code C1235: Right Rear Anti-Lock Brake Sensor Input Signal Missing (Part 2 of 4). 2001–04 Continental

CONDITIONS	DETAILS/RESULTS/ACTIONS
K4 CHECK THE SENSOR OUTPUT	
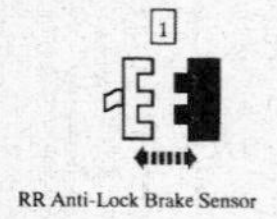	2 Raise the vehicle on a hoist.
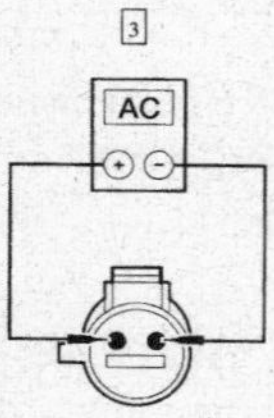	3 Slowly rotate the RR wheel while monitoring the signal output in A/C volts. • Is the A/C voltage between 100 and 3500 mV? → **Yes** GO to **K5**. → **No** INSTALL a new RR anti-lock brake sensor. CLEAR the DTCs. REPEAT the self-test.
K5 CHECK THE SENSOR OUTPUT AT THE MODULE CONNECTOR	
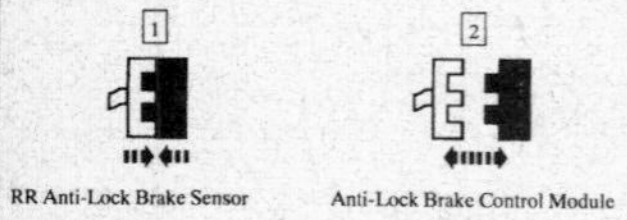	

FM4020101770030X

Fig. 25 Test K/Code C1235: Right Rear Anti-Lock Brake Sensor Input Signal Missing (Part 3 of 4). 2001–04 Continental

CONDITIONS	DETAILS/RESULTS/ACTIONS
K5 CHECK THE SENSOR OUTPUT AT THE MODULE CONNECTOR (Continued)	
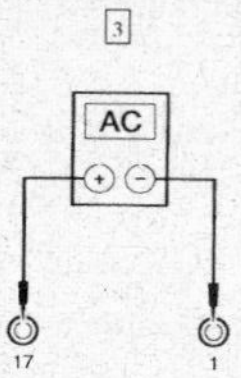	3 Measure the A/C voltage between EEC-IV 60-Pin Breakout Box pin 17, circuit 523 (RD/PK), and pin 1, circuit 524 (PK/BK).
	4 Slowly rotate the RR wheel. • Is the A/C voltage between 100 and 3500 mV? → **Yes** INSTALL a new module. → **No** REPAIR circuit 523 (RD/PK) and circuit 524 (PK/BK) as necessary. CLEAR the DTCs. REPEAT the self-test.

FM4020101770040X

Fig. 25 Test K/Code C1235: Right Rear Anti-Lock Brake Sensor Input Signal Missing (Part 4 of 4). 2001–04 Continental

TEST CONDITIONS	TESTDETAILS/RESULTS/ACTIONS
L1 CHECK THE LR ANTI-LOCK BRAKE SENSOR	
	1 Inspect the LR anti-lock brake sensor mounting. Check the sensor for excessive dirt build-up. Check for metal obstructions. Check the sensor for damage. • Is the LR anti-lock brake sensor and mounting OK? → **Yes** GO to **L2**. → **No** INSTALL a new LR anti-lock brake sensor as necessary. CLEAR the DTCs. REPEAT the self-test.
L2 CHECK THE LR ANTI-LOCK BRAKE SENSOR INDICATOR	
	1 Check the LR anti-lock brake sensor indicator for corrosion, nicks, bridged teeth, damaged teeth, proper mounting and alignment with the LR anti-lock brake sensor. Check the air gap. Check the bearing end play. • Is the LR anti-lock brake sensor indicator OK? → **Yes** GO to **L3**. → **No** INSTALL a new LR anti-lock brake sensor indicator. CLEAR the DTCs. REPEAT the self-test.
L3 CHECK THE SIGNAL INPUT	
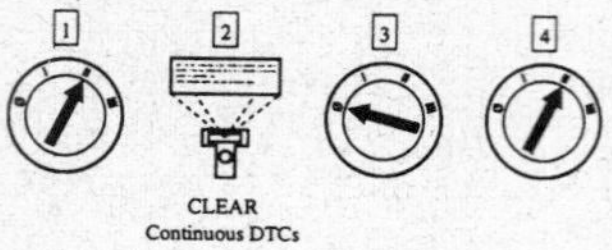	5 Monitor the anti-lock brake control module PIDs RR__WSPD and LR__WSPD while driving at various speeds.

FM4029901319010X

Fig. 26 Test L/Code C1236: Left Rear Anti-Lock Brake Input Signal Missing (Part 1 of 2). 2000 Continental

TEST CONDITIONS	TEST DETAILS/RESULTS/ACTIONS
L3 CHECK THE SIGNAL INPUT	
	6 Test drive the vehicle for 16 km (10 miles). • Are the anti-lock brake control module PID readings approximately the same? → **Yes** INSTALL a new anti-lock brake control module. CLEAR the DTCs. REPEAT the self-test. → **No** INSTALL a new LR anti-lock brake sensor. CLEAR the DTCs. REPEAT the self-test.

FM4029901319020X

Fig. 26 Test L/Code C1236: Left Rear Anti-Lock Brake Input Signal Missing (Part 2 of 2). 2000 Continental

CONDITIONS	DETAILS/RESULTS/ACTIONS
L2 CHECK THE LR ANTI-LOCK BRAKE SENSOR INDICATOR	
	1 Check the LR anti-lock brake sensor indicator for corrosion, nicks, bridged teeth, damaged teeth, incorrect mounting and alignment with the LR anti-lock brake sensor. Check the air gap. Check the bearing end play. • Is the LR anti-lock brake sensor indicator OK? → **Yes** GO to **L3**. → **No** INSTALL a new LR anti-lock brake sensor indicator. CLEAR the DTCs. REPEAT the self-test.
L3 CHECK THE SIGNAL INPUT	
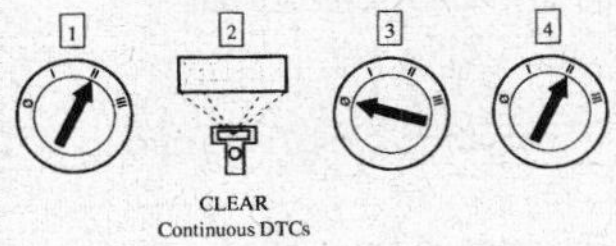	5 Monitor the anti-lock brake control module PIDs RR__WSPD and LR__WSPD while driving at various speeds. 6 Test drive the vehicle for 16 km (10 miles). • Are the anti-lock brake control module PID readings approximately the same? → **Yes** INSTALL a new anti-lock brake control module. CLEAR the DTCs. REPEAT k the self-test. → **No** GO to **L4**.

FM4020101771020X

Fig. 27 Test L/Code C1236: Left Rear Anti-Lock Brake Input Signal Missing (Part 2 of 4). 2001–04 Continental

CONDITIONS	DETAILS/RESULTS/ACTIONS
L1 CHECK THE LR ANTI-LOCK BRAKE SENSOR	
	1 Inspect the LR anti-lock brake sensor mounting. Check the sensor for excessive dirt build-up. Check for metal obstructions. Check the sensor for damage. • Is the LR anti-lock brake sensor and mounting OK? → **Yes** GO to **L2**. → **No** INSTALL a new LR anti-lock brake sensor as necessary. CLEAR the DTCs. REPEAT the self-test.

FM4020101771010X

Fig. 27 Test L/Code C1236: Left Rear Anti-Lock Brake Input Signal Missing (Part 1 of 4). 2001–04 Continental

CONDITIONS	DETAILS/RESULTS/ACTIONS
L4 CHECK THE SENSOR OUTPUT	
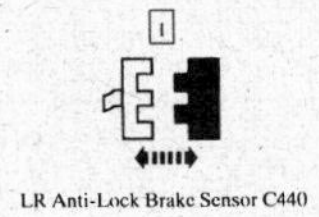	2 Raise the vehicle on a hoist.
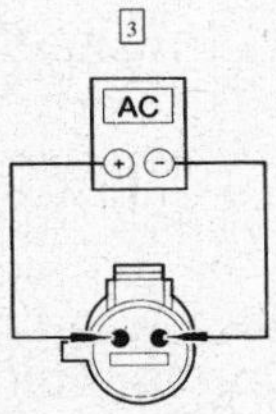	3 Slowly rotate the LR wheel while monitoring the signal output in A/C volts. • Is the A/C voltage between 100 and 3500 mV? → **Yes** GO to **L5**. → **No** INSTALL a new LR anti-lock brake sensor. CLEAR the DTCs. REPEAT the self-test.
L5 CHECK THE SENSOR OUTPUT AT THE MODULE CONNECTOR	
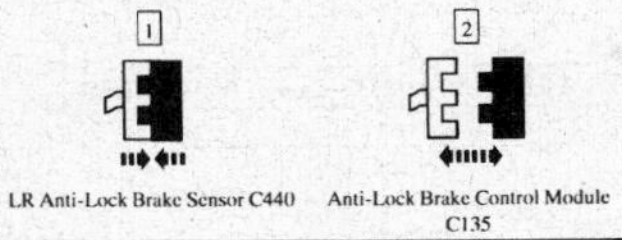	

FM4020101771030X

Fig. 27 Test L/Code C1236: Left Rear Anti-Lock Brake Input Signal Missing (Part 3 of 4). 2001–04 Continental

CONDITIONS	DETAILS/RESULTS/ACTIONS
L5 CHECK THE SENSOR OUTPUT AT THE MODULE CONNECTOR (Continued)	
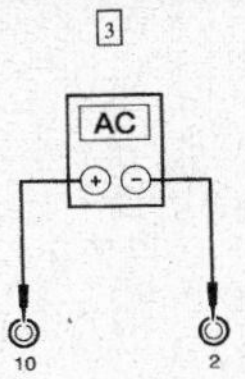	3 Measure the A/C voltage between EEC-IV 60-Pin Breakout Box pin 10, circuit 518 (LG/RD), and pin 2, circuit 519 (LG/BK). 4 Slowly rotate the LR wheel. • Is the A/C voltage between 100 and 3500 mV? → **Yes** INSTALL a new module. → **No** REPAIR circuit 518 (LG/RD) and circuit 519 (LG/BK) as necessary. CLEAR the DTCs. REPEAT the self-test.

FM4020101771040X

Fig. 27 Test L/Code C1236: Left Rear Anti-Lock Brake Input Signal Missing (Part 4 of 4). 2001–04 Continental

TEST CONDITIONS	TEST DETAILS/RESULTS/ACTIONS
M1 CHECK FOR DTC B1342	
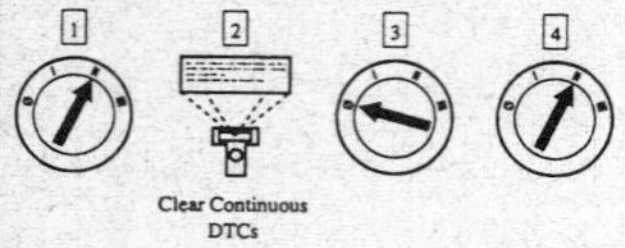	5 Carry out the anti-lock brake control module On-Demand Self-Test. • Is DTC B1342 retrieved? → **Yes** INSTALL a new anti-lock brake control module. CLEAR the DTCs. REPEAT the self-test. → **No** CHECK for loose or corroded connections. CLEAR the DTCs. REPEAT the self-test.

FM4029901320000X

Fig. 28 Test M/Code B1242: ECU Internal Failure. Continental

TEST CONDITIONS	TEST DETAILS/RESULTS/ACTIONS
N3 CHECK THE BRAKE PEDAL POSITION SWITCH OPERATION	
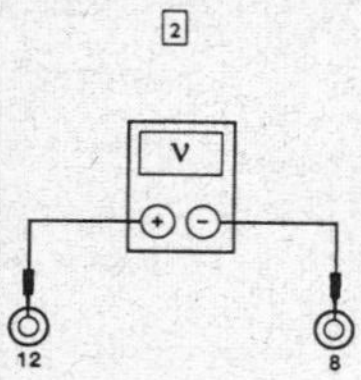	2 Measure the voltage between EEC-IV 60-Pin Breakout Box Pin 12, Circuit 511 (LG), and EEC-IV 60-Pin Breakout Box Pin 8, Circuit 530 (LG/YE). • Is the voltage greater than 10 volts? → **Yes** INSTALL a new anti-lock brake control module. CLEAR the DTCs. REPEAT the self-test. → **No** REPAIR circuit 511 (LG). CLEAR the DTCs. REPEAT the self-test.

FM4029901321020X

Fig. 29 Test N/Code B1485: Brake Pedal Input Open Circuit (Part 2 of 2). Continental

TEST CONDITIONS	TEST DETAILS/RESULTS/ACTIONS
O1 CHECK THE BATTERY VOLTAGE	
	2 Measure the voltage between the positive and negative posts of the battery. • Is the voltage greater than 10 volts? → **Yes** GO to **O2**. → **No** REPAIR the battery or charging system.
O2 CHECK THE CHARGING SYSTEM	
	1 Start the engine. 2 Increase the engine speed to 2,000 rpm.

FM4029901322010X

Fig. 30 Test O/Code B1676: Battery Voltage Out Of Range (Part 1 of 3). 2000 Continental

TEST CONDITIONS	TEST DETAILS/RESULTS/ACTIONS
N1 CHECK THE STOPLAMP OPERATION	
	1 Press the brake pedal. • Do the stoplamps operate correctly? → **Yes** GO to **N2**. → **No** DIAGNOSE stoplamps.
N2 CHECK CIRCUIT 511 (LG) FOR AN OPEN	
NOTE: Make sure the brake pedal is released for this step.	
 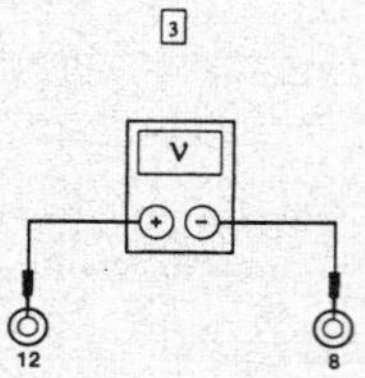	2 Connect EEC-IV 60-Pin Breakout Box. 3 Measure the voltage between EEC-IV 60-Pin Breakout Box Pin 12, Circuit 511 (LG), and EEC-IV 60-Pin Breakout Box Pin 8, Circuit 530 (LG/YE). • Is any voltage indicated? → **Yes** REPAIR circuit 511 (LG). CLEAR the DTCs. REPEAT the self-test. → **No** GO to **N3**.
N3 CHECK THE BRAKE PEDAL POSITION SWITCH OPERATION	
	1 Press the brake pedal and hold.

FM4029901321010X

Fig. 29 Test N/Code B1485: Brake Pedal Input Open Circuit (Part 1 of 2). Continental

TEST CONDITIONS	TEST DETAILS/RESULTS/ACTIONS
O2 CHECK THE CHARGING SYSTEM	
	3 Measure the voltage between the positive and negative posts of the battery. • Is the voltage greater than 16 volts? → **Yes** REPAIR the battery or charging system. → **No** GO to **O3**.
O3 CHECK THE ANTI-LOCK BRAKE CONTROL MODULE GROUND CIRCUIT 530 (LG/YE)	
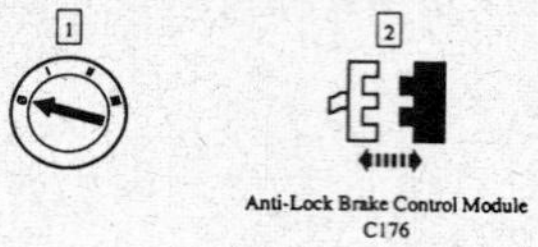 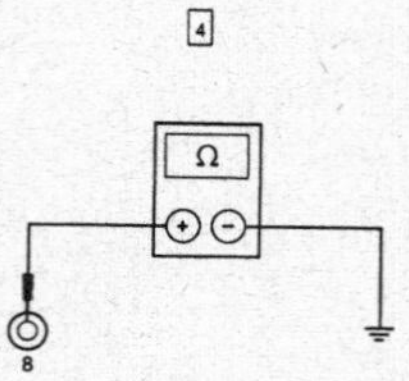	3 Connect EEC-IV 60-Pin Breakout Box. 4 Measure the resistance between EEC-IV 60-Pin Breakout Box Pin 8, Circuit 530 (LG/YE), and ground. • Is the resistance less than 5 ohms? → **Yes** GO to **O4**. → **No** REPAIR the circuit. CLEAR the DTCs. REPEAT the self-test.

FM4029901322020X

Fig. 30 Test O/Code B1676: Battery Voltage Out Of Range (Part 2 of 3). 2000 Continental

TEST CONDITIONS	TEST DETAILS/RESULTS/ACTIONS
O4 CHECK CIRCUIT 530 (LG/YE) FOR AN OPEN	
[1] 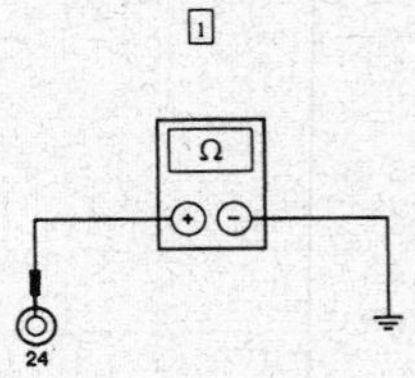	[1] Measure the resistance between EEC-IV 60-Pin Breakout Box Pin 24, Circuit 530 (LG/YE), and ground. • Is the resistance less than 5 ohms? → **Yes** CHECK anti-lock brake control module connector C176 for loose, corroded or pushed-out pins. CLEAR the DTCs. REPEAT the self-test. → **No** REPAIR the circuit. CLEAR the DTCs. REPEAT the self-test.

FM4029901322030X

Fig. 30 Test O/Code B1676: Battery Voltage Out Of Range (Part 3 of 3). 2000 Continental

CONDITIONS	DETAILS/RESULTS/ACTIONS
O3 MEASURE THE VOLTAGE BETWEEN ANTI-LOCK BRAKE CONTROL MODULE C176 CIRCUIT 601 (LB/PK), CIRCUIT 687 (GN/YE) AND GROUND	
[1] 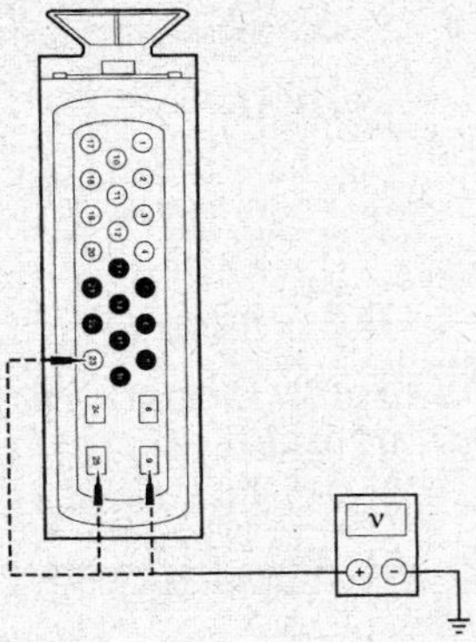	[1] Measure the voltage between the anti-lock brake control module C135 pin 9, circuit 601 (LB/PK), pin 23, circuit 687 (GN/YE) and pin 25, circuit 601 (LB/PK). • Is the voltage less than 16V and greater than 10V? → **Yes** GO to **O4**. → **No** Power feed is open. REPAIR circuit 601 (LB/PK) or circuit 687 (GN/YE) as necessary. CLEAR the DTCs. REPEAT the self-test.
O4 CHECK THE ANTI-LOCK BRAKE CONTROL MODULE GROUND CIRCUIT 530 (LG/YE)	
[1] [2] 	[3] Connect EEC-IV 60-Pin Breakout Box.

FM4020101772020X

Fig. 31 Test O/Code B1676: Battery Voltage Out Of Range (Part 2 of 3). 2001–04 Continental

CONDITIONS	DETAILS/RESULTS/ACTIONS
O1 CHECK THE BATTERY VOLTAGE	
[1] 	[2] Measure the voltage between the positive and negative posts of the battery. • Is the voltage greater than 10 volts? → **Yes** GO to **O2**. → **No** REPAIR the battery or charging system.
O2 CHECK THE CHARGING SYSTEM	
	[1] Start the engine. [2] Increase the engine speed to 2,000 rpm. [3] Measure the voltage between the positive and negative posts of the battery. • Is the voltage greater than 16 volts? → **Yes** REPAIR the battery or charging system. → **No** GO to **O3**.

FM4020101772010X

Fig. 31 Test O/Code B1676: Battery Voltage Out Of Range (Part 1 of 3). 2001–04 Continental

CONDITIONS	DETAILS/RESULTS/ACTIONS
O4 CHECK THE ANTI-LOCK BRAKE CONTROL MODULE GROUND CIRCUIT 530 (LG/YE) (Continued)	
[4] 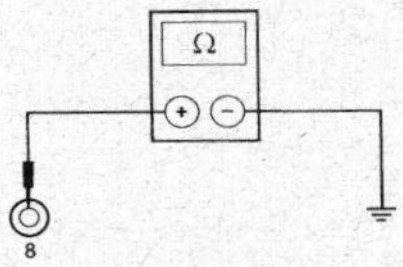	[4] Measure the resistance between EEC-IV 60-Pin Breakout Box pin 8, circuit 530 (LG/YE), and ground. • Is the resistance less than 5 ohms? → **Yes** GO to **O5**. → **No** REPAIR the circuit. CLEAR the DTCs. REPEAT the self-test.
O5 CHECK CIRCUIT 530 (LG/YE) FOR AN OPEN	
[1] 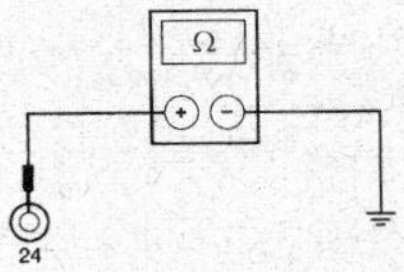	[1] Measure the resistance between EEC-IV 60-Pin Breakout Box pin 24, circuit 530 (LG/YE), and ground. • Is the resistance less than 5 ohms? → **Yes** CHECK anti-lock brake control module connector C135 for loose, corroded or pushed-out pins. CLEAR the DTCs. REPEAT the self-test. → **No** REPAIR the circuit. CLEAR the DTCs. REPEAT the self-test.

FM4020101772030X

Fig. 31 Test O/Code B1676: Battery Voltage Out Of Range (Part 3 of 3). 2001–04 Continental

TEST CONDITIONS	TEST DETAILS/RESULTS/ACTIONS
P1 CHECK THE COMPONENT MOUNTING	
	[1] Inspect the brake pedal and the power brake booster/brake master cylinder for correct attachment. [2] Bleed the brake system. • Is the brake pedal spongy? → **Yes** GO to **P2**. → **No** The brake system is operating correctly at this time. TEST the system for normal operation.
P2 REBLEED THE BRAKE SYSTEM	
	[1] Rebleed the brake system. • Is the brake pedal spongy? → **Yes** REFER to hydraulic brakes. → **No** The brake system is operating correctly at this time. TEST the system for normal operation.

FM4029901323000X

Fig. 32 Test P: Spongy Brake Pedal w/No Warning Indicator. Continental

TEST CONDITIONS	TEST DETAILS/RESULTS/ACTIONS
Q4 CHECK THE BPP SWITCH	
NOTE: Do not depress the brake pedal during this test.	
[1]  Anti-Lock Brake Control Module	
	[2] Connect EEC-IV 60-Pin Breakout Box.
[3] 	
[4] 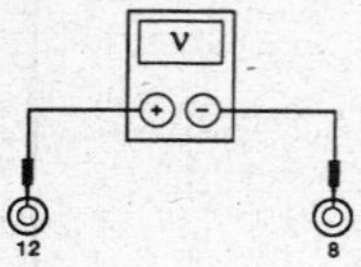	[4] Measure the voltage between EEC-IV 60-Pin Breakout Box Pin 12, circuit 511 (LG), and EEC-IV 60-Pin Breakout Box Pin 8, Circuit 530 (LG/YE). • Is any voltage indicated? → **Yes** DIAGNOSE stoplamps. → **No** INSTALL a new anti-lock brake control module. TEST the system for normal operation.

FM4029901324020X

Fig. 33 Test Q: Traction Control Is Inoperative (Part 2 of 2). Continental

TEST CONDITIONS	TEST DETAILS/RESULTS/ACTIONS
Q1 CHECK FOR DTCS	
	[1] Carry out the anti-lock brake control module On-Demand Self-Test. • Are any DTCs retrieved? → **Yes** GO to the Diagnostic Trouble Code (DTC) Index. → **No** GO to **Q2**.
Q2 CHECK THE ABS OPERATION	
	[1] Test drive the vehicle. Check the ABS operation. • Does the ABS operate correctly? → **Yes** GO to **Q3**. → **No** GO to Symptom Chart.
Q3 CHECK THE DRIVER SETTING	
[1] 	[2] Press the message center vehicle setting switch until the message center displays TRACTION CONTROL. • Does the message read TRACTION CONTROL OFF? → **Yes** ENABLE the traction control. TEST the system for normal operation. → **No** GO to **Q4**.

FM4029901324010X

Fig. 33 Test Q: Traction Control Is Inoperative (Part 1 of 2). Continental

TEST CONDITIONS	TEST DETAILS/RESULTS/ACTIONS
R1 CHECK THE ANTI-LOCK BRAKE WARNING INDICATOR	
[1]  Anti-Lock Brake Control Module [2] 	• Is the yellow ABS warning indicator on? → **Yes** GO to **R2**. → **No** INSTALL a new virtual image cluster. TEST the system for normal operation.
R2 CHECK PROVE OUT	
[1]  Anti-Lock Brake Control Module [2] 	• Does the yellow ABS warning indicator prove out for three seconds and then turn off? → **Yes** The yellow ABS warning indicator is working properly. TEST the system for normal operation. → **No** INSTALL a new anti-lock brake control module. TEST the system for normal operation.

FM4029901325000X

Fig. 34 Test R: Yellow ABS Warning Indicator Does Not Self Test. Continental

TEST CONDITIONS	TESTDETAILS/RESULTS/ACTIONS
S1 CHECK FOR DTCS	
	2 Carry out the anti-lock brake control module On-Demand Self-Test. • Are any DTCs retrieved? → **Yes** GO to Anti-Lock Brake Control Module Diagnostic Trouble Code (DTC) Index. → **No** GO to **S2**.
S2 CHECK THE VIRTUAL IMAGE CLUSTER FOR DTCS	
	2 Carry out the virtual image cluster On-Demand Self-Test. • Is DTC U1123 retrieved? → **Yes** INSTALL a new anti-lock brake control module. TEST the system for normal operation. → **No** INSTALL a new virtual image cluster. TEST the system for normal operation.

FM4029901326000X

Fig. 35 Test S: Yellow ABS Warning Indicator & Traction Control Active Indicator Always On. Continental

TEST CONDITIONS	TESTDETAILS/RESULTS/ACTIONS
A1 CHECK THE FUSE JUNCTION PANEL FUSE 20	
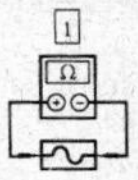	• Is the fuse OK? → **Yes** GO to **A2**. → **No** INSTALL a new fuse. CLEAR the DTCs. REPEAT the self-test. If the fuse fails again, CHECK for short to ground. REPAIR as necessary. CLEAR the DTCs. REPEAT the self-test.
A2 CHECK CIRCUIT 1087 (OG) FOR AN OPEN	

FM4020001573010X

Fig. 37 Test A: No Communication w/ABS Control Module (Part 1 of 2). Sable & Taurus

Condition	Possible Source	Action
• No Communication with the Anti-Lock Brake Control Module	• Fuse. • Circuit. • ABS control module.	• GO to Pinpoint Test A.
• Unable To Enter Self-Test — Communication OK	• ABS control module.	• GO to Pinpoint Test B.
• The Red Brake Warning Indicator Does Not Self-Check	• Low brake fluid warning switch. • Circuit. • Instrument cluster. • Ignition switch. • Parking brake.	• DIAGNOSE Instrument Cluster.
• The Red Brake Warning Indicator Stays On When the Ignition Switch Is In RUN	• Low brake fluid warning switch. • Circuit. • Instrument cluster. • Ignition switch. • Parking brake.	• DIAGNOSE Instrument Cluster.
• The Yellow ABS Warning Indicator Does Not Self-Check — Always On, NO DTCs	• Circuit. • ABS control module. • Instrument cluster.	• GO to Pinpoint Test I.
• Spongy Brake Pedal with No Warning Indicator	• Air in hydraulic brake system. • Base brake svstem.	• GO to Pinpoint Test J. • DIAGNOSE Base Brake System.
• Poor Vehicle Tracking During Anti-Lock Function	• Air in hydraulic brake system. • Hydraulic control unit. • Base brake system.	• GO to Pinpoint Test K. • DIAGNOSE Base Brake System.
• The Traction Control Is Inoperative	• Circuit. • ABS control module. • Hydraulic control unit.	• GO to Pinpoint Test L.
• The Traction Control Switch Indicator Is Inoperative	• Circuit. • Traction control switch. • ABS control module.	• GO to Pinpoint Test M.
• The Traction Control Cannot Be Disabled	• Circuit. • Traction control switch. • ABS control module.	• GO to Pinpoint Test N.
• The Traction Control Indicator Stays On Continuously with No DTCs Retrieved	• Circuit. • Instrument cluster. • ABS control module.	• DIAGNOSE Instrument Cluster.

FM4020001572000X

Fig. 36 Symptom Chart. Sable & Taurus

TEST CONDITIONS	TESTDETAILS/RESULTS/ACTIONS
A2 CHECK CIRCUIT 1087 (OG) FOR AN OPEN (Continued)	
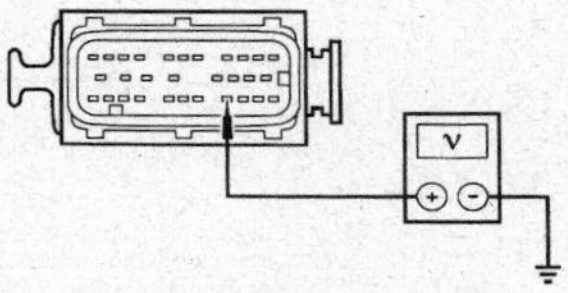	3 Measure the voltage between ABS control module connector C135 pin 8, circuit 1087 (OG), wiring harness side and ground. • Is the voltage greater than 10 volts? → **Yes** GO to **A3**. → **No** REPAIR the circuit. CLEAR the DTCs. REPEAT the self-test.
A3 CHECK CIRCUIT 57 (BK) FOR AN OPEN	
 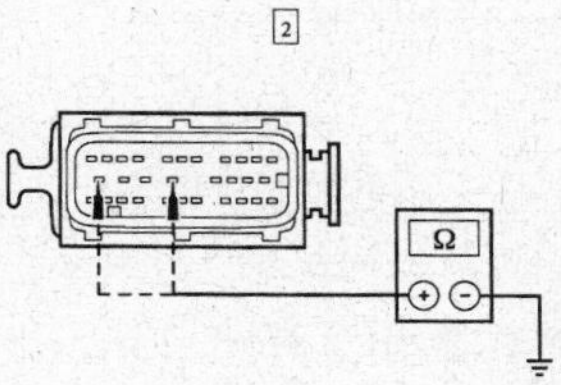	2 Measure the resistance between ABS control module connector C135 pin 12, circuit 57 (BK), harness side and ground. • Is the resistance less than 5 ohms? → **Yes** DIAGNOSE Module Communication System. → **No** REPAIR the circuit. CLEAR the DTCs. REPEAT the self-test.

FM4020001573020X

Fig. 37 Test A: No Communication w/ABS Control Module (Part 2 of 2). Sable & Taurus

TEST CONDITIONS	TESTDETAILS/RESULTS/ACTIONS
B1 CHECK THE COMMUNICATION TO THE ABS CONTROL MODULE	
	1 Check the communication to the ABS control module. • Does scan tool communicate with the ABS control module? → **Yes** INSTALL a new electronic control unit (ECU). REPEAT the self-test. → **No** GO to Pinpoint Test A.

FM4020001574000X

Fig. 38 Test B: Unable To Enter Self Test, Network Communication OK. Sable & Taurus

TEST CONDITIONS	TEST DETAILS/RESULTS/ACTIONS
C1 CHECK THE BATTERY VOLTAGE	
	1 Measure the voltage between the positive and negative battery posts. • Is the voltage greater than 10 volts? → **Yes** GO to **C2**. → **No** REPAIR the charging system.
C2 CHECK CIRCUIT 1087 (OG)	
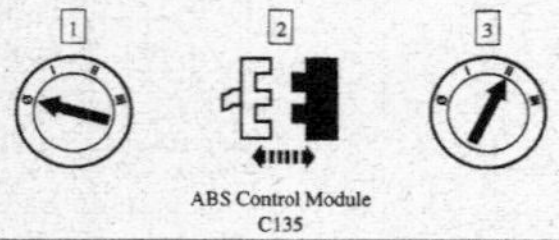	

FM4020001575010X

Fig. 39 Test C/Code B1318: Battery Voltage Low (Part 1 of 2). Sable & Taurus

TEST CONDITIONS	TEST DETAILS/RESULTS/ACTIONS
C2 CHECK CIRCUIT 1087 (OG) (Continued)	
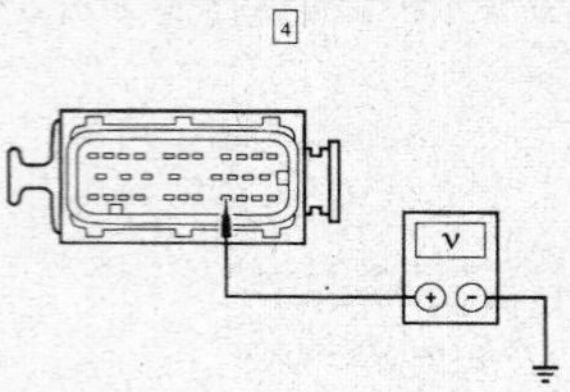	4 Measure the voltage between the ABS control module C135 pin 8, circuit 1087 (OG), harness side and ground. • Is the voltage greater than 10 volts? → **Yes** GO to **C3**. → **No** REPAIR the circuit. CLEAR the DTCs. REPEAT the self-test.
C3 CHECK CIRCUIT 57 (BK) FOR AN OPEN	
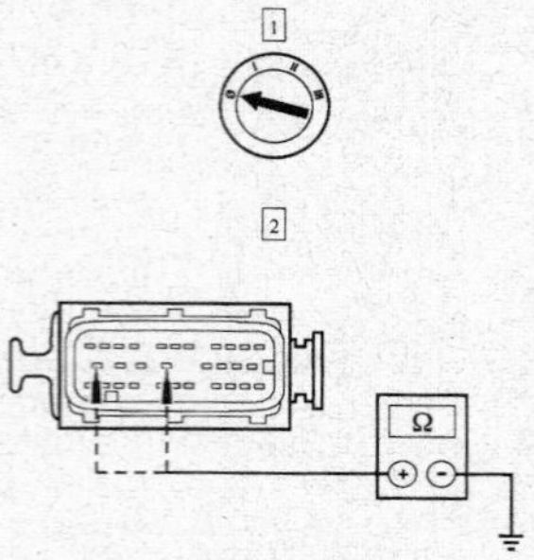	2 Measure the resistance between ABS control module connector C135 pin 12, circuit 57 (BK), harness side and ground, and between ABS control module connector, harness side and ground. • Are the resistances less than 5 ohms? → **Yes** CLEAR the DTCs. REPEAT the self-test. If DTC B1318 is retrieved again, INSTALL a new hydraulic control unit (HCU). REPEAT the self-test. If no DTCs are retrieved the system is operating normally. → **No** REPAIR the circuit. CLEAR the DTCs. REPEAT the self-test.

FM4020001575020X

Fig. 39 Test C/Code B1318: Battery Voltage Low (Part 2 of 2). Sable & Taurus

TEST CONDITIONS	TEST DETAILS/RESULTS/ACTIONS
D1 CHECK THE STOPLAMPS	
	1 Press the brake pedal while checking the stoplamps. • Do the stoplamps illuminate? → **Yes** GO to **D2**. → **No** DIAGNOSE exterior lamps.
D2 CHECK THE ABS CONTROL MODULE BOO__ABS PID	
	2 Monitor the ABS control module PID BOO__ABS, while pressing and releasing the brake pedal. • Does the ABS control module PID BOO__ABS indicate ON with the brake pedal pressed and OFF with the brake pedal released? → **Yes** CLEAR the DTCs. REPEAT the self-test. If the DTC B1484 is retrieved, INSTALL a new electronic control unit (ECU). REPEAT the self-test. → **No** GO to **D3**.
D3 CHECK CIRCUIT 810 (RD/LG) FOR AN OPEN	
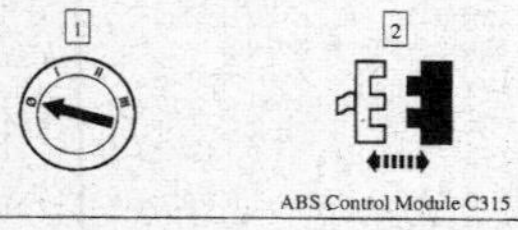	

FM4020001576010X

Fig. 40 Test D/Code B1484: Brake Pedal Input Circuit Open (Part 1 of 2). Sable & Taurus

TEST CONDITIONS	TEST DETAILS/RESULTS/ACTIONS
D3 CHECK CIRCUIT 810 (RD/LG) FOR AN OPEN (Continued)	
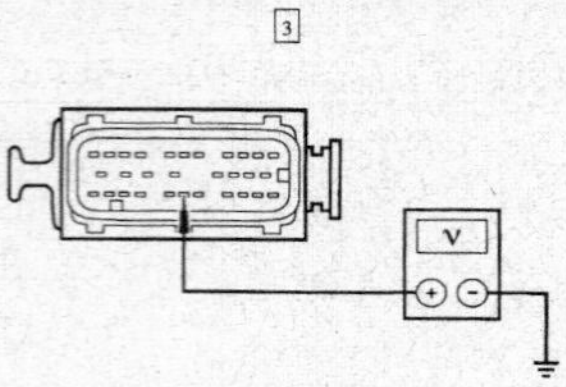	3 Measure the voltage between ABS control module connector C315 pin 6, circuit 810 (RD/LG), harness side and ground while depressing the brake pedal. • Is the voltage greater than 10 volts? → **Yes** INSTALL a new electronic control unit (ECU). REPEAT the self-test. → **No** REPAIR the circuit. CLEAR the DTCs. REPEAT the self-test.

FM4020001576020X

Fig. 40 Test D/Code B1484: Brake Pedal Input Circuit Open (Part 2 of 2). Sable & Taurus

TEST CONDITIONS	TEST DETAILS/RESULTS/ACTIONS
E1 CHECK FOR CONTINUOUS OPERATION OF THE ABS PUMP MOTOR	
	2 Check the ABS pump motor for continuous operation. • Is the ABS pump motor running continuously? → **Yes** INSTALL a new hydraulic control unit (HCU). REPEAT the self-test. → **No** GO to **E2**.

FM4020001577010X

Fig. 41 Test E/Code C1095: ABS Hydraulic Pump Motor Circuit Failure (Part 1 of 3). Sable & Taurus

TEST CONDITIONS	TEST DETAILS/RESULTS/ACTIONS
E2 CHECK THE BATTERY JUNCTION BOX (BJB) FUSE 113	
	1 Check fuse 113 for an open. • Is the fuse OK? → **Yes** GO to **E3**. → **No** INSTALL a new fuse. CLEAR the DTCs. REPEAT the self-test. If the fuse fails again, CHECK for short to ground. REPAIR as necessary. CLEAR the DTCs. REPEAT the self-test.
E3 CHECK CIRCUIT 532 (OG/YE) FOR AN OPEN	

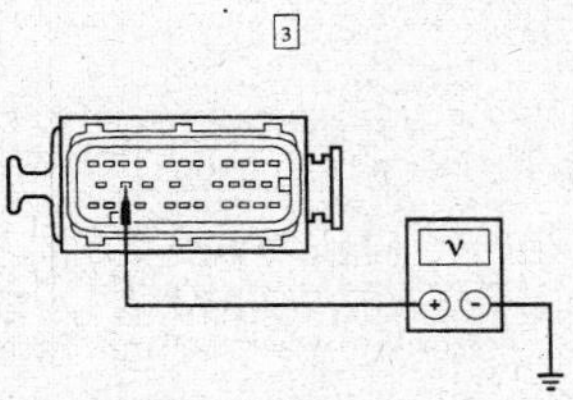	3 Measure the voltage between ABS control module connector C135 pin 13, circuit 532 (OG/YE), harness side and ground. • Is the voltage greater than 10 volts? → **Yes** GO to **E4**. → **No** REPAIR the circuit. CLEAR the DTCs. REPEAT the self-test.

FM4020001577020X

Fig. 41 Test E/Code C1095: ABS Hydraulic Pump Motor Circuit Failure (Part 2 of 3). Sable & Taurus

TEST CONDITIONS	TEST DETAILS/RESULTS/ACTIONS
F1 CHECK THE SUSPECT WHEEL SPEED CIRCUIT FOR SHORT TO POWER	
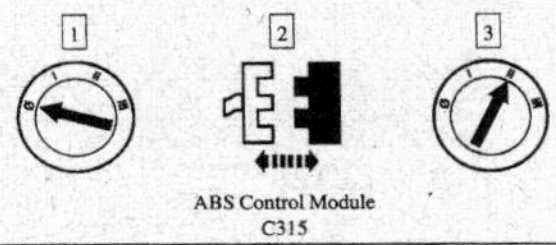	

FM4020001578010X

Fig. 42 Test F/Codes C1145, C1155, C1165 & C1175: Wheel Speed Sensor Input Circuit Failure (Part 1 of 5). 2000 Sable & Taurus

TEST CONDITIONS	TEST DETAILS/RESULTS/ACTIONS
F1 CHECK THE SUSPECT WHEEL SPEED CIRCUIT FOR SHORT TO POWER (Continued)	
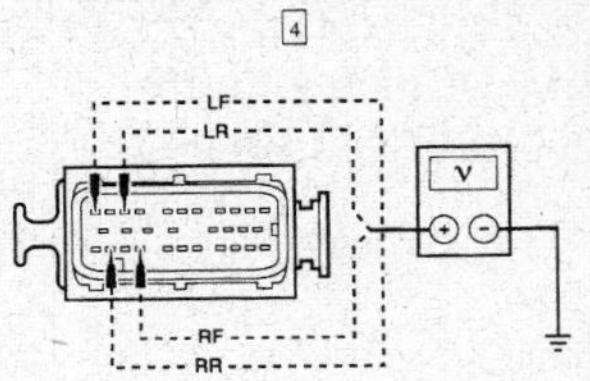	4 Measure the voltage of the suspect wheel speed sensor circuit between: — (RF) ABS control module connector C135 pin 4, circuit 514 (YE/RD), harness side and ground. — (LF) ABS control module connector C135 pin 20, circuit 521 (TN/OG), harness side and ground. — (RR) ABS control module connector C135 pin 2, circuit 523 (RD/PK), harness side and ground. — (LR) ABS control module connector C135 pin 22, circuit 518 (LG/RD), harness side and ground. • Is voltage present? → **Yes** REPAIR the circuit. CLEAR the DTCs. REPEAT the self-test. → **No** GO to **F2**.
F2 CHECK THE SUSPECT WHEEL SPEED SENSOR CIRCUIT FOR SHORT TO GROUND	
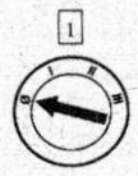	

FM4020001578020X

Fig. 42 Test F/Codes C1145, C1155, C1165 & C1175: Wheel Speed Sensor Input Circuit Failure (Part 2 of 5). 2000 Sable & Taurus

TEST CONDITIONS	TEST DETAILS/RESULTS/ACTIONS
E4 CHECK CIRCUIT 57 (BK) FOR AN OPEN	
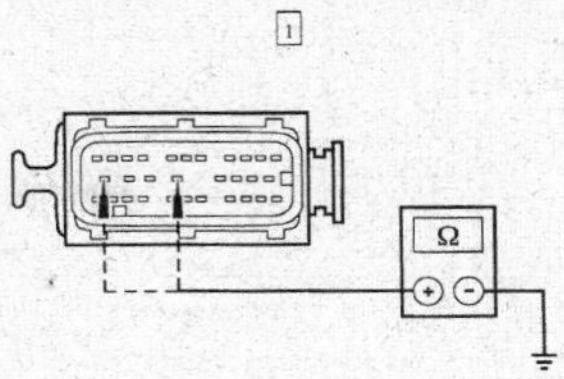	1 Measure the resistance between ABS control module connector C135 pin 12, circuit 57 (BK), harness side and ground. • Is the resistance less than 5 ohms? → **Yes** INSTALL a new electronic control unit (ECU). REPEAT the self-test. → **No** REPAIR the circuit. CLEAR the DTCs. REPEAT the self-test.

FM4020001577030X

Fig. 41 Test E/Code C1095: ABS Hydraulic Pump Motor Circuit Failure (Part 3 of 3). Sable & Taurus

TEST CONDITIONS	TEST DETAILS/RESULTS/ACTIONS
F2 CHECK THE SUSPECT WHEEL SPEED SENSOR CIRCUIT FOR SHORT TO GROUND (Continued)	
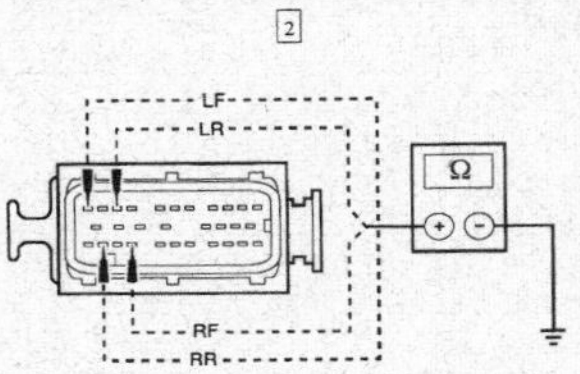	2 Measure the resistance of the suspect wheel speed sensor circuit between: — (RF) ABS control module connector C135 pin 4, circuit 514 (YE/RD), harness side and ground. — (LF) ABS control module connector C135 pin 20, circuit 521 (TN/OG), harness side and ground. — (RR) ABS control module connector C135 pin 2, circuit 523 (RD/PK), harness side and ground. — (LR) ABS control module connector C135 pin 22, circuit 518 (LG/RD), harness side and ground. • Is the resistance infinite? → **Yes** GO to **F4**. → **No** GO to **F3**.
F3 CHECK THE SUSPECT WHEEL SPEED SENSOR FOR SHORT TO GROUND	
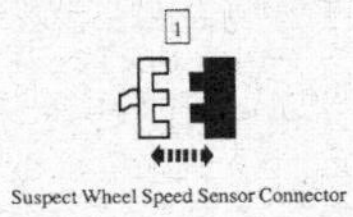	
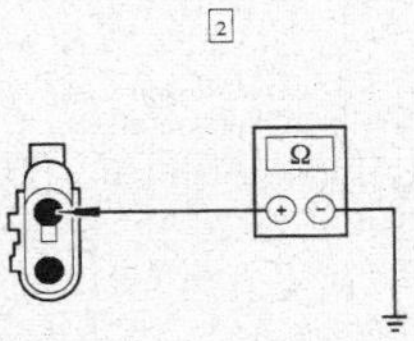	2 Measure the resistance between either suspect wheel speed sensor pin (component side) and ground. • Is the resistance infinite? → **Yes** REPAIR the circuit. CLEAR the DTCs. REPEAT the self-test. → **No** INSTALL a new wheel speed sensor. CLEAR the DTCs. REPEAT the self-test.

FM4020001578030X

Fig. 42 Test F/Codes C1145, C1155, C1165 & C1175: Wheel Speed Sensor Input Circuit Failure (Part 3 of 5). 2000 Sable & Taurus

TEST CONDITIONS	TEST DETAILS/RESULTS/ACTIONS
F4 CHECK THE WHEEL SPEED CIRCUITRY FOR AN OPEN OR SHORT TOGETHER	
1 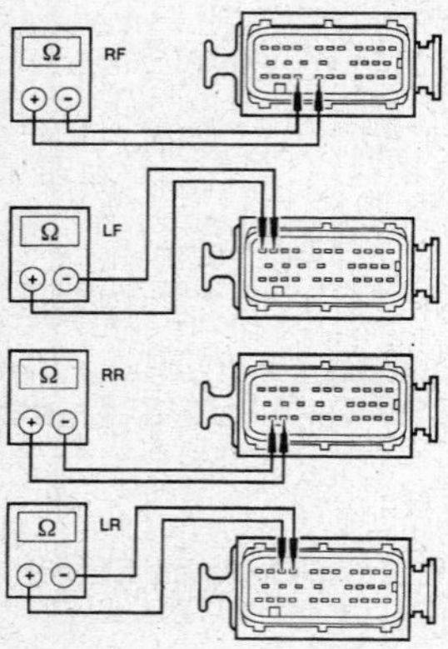	1 Measure the resistance between: — (RF) ABS control module connector C135 pin 4, circuit 514 (YE/RD), harness side and ABS control module connector C135 pin 5, circuit 516 (YE/BK), harness side. — (LF) ABS control module connector C135 pin 20, circuit 521 (TN/OG), harness side and ABS control module connector C135 pin 21, circuit 522 (TN/BK), harness side. — (RR) ABS control module connector C135 pin 2, circuit 523 (RD/PK), harness side and ABS control module connector C135 pin 3, circuit 524 (PK/BK), harness side. — (LR) ABS control module connector C135 pin 22, circuit 518 (LG/RD), harness side and ABS control module connector C135 pin 23, circuit 519 (LG/BK), harness side. • Is the resistance between 1,000 and 1,500 ohms? → **Yes** RECONNECT all connections. CLEAR the DTCs. REPEAT the self-test. If DTC C1145, C1155, C1165 or C1175 is retrieved, INSTALL a new electronic control unit (ECU). REPEAT the self-test. If no DTCs are retrieved the system is operating normally. → **No** GO to **F5**.
F5 CHECK THE SUSPECT WHEEL SPEED SENSOR FOR AN OPEN OR SHORT TOGETHER	
1  Suspect Wheel Speed Sensor Connector	

FM4020001578040X

Fig. 42 Test F/Codes C1145, C1155, C1165 & C1175: Wheel Speed Sensor Input Circuit Failure (Part 4 of 5). 2000 Sable & Taurus

CONDITIONS	DETAILS/RESULTS/ACTIONS
F1 CHECK THE SUSPECT WHEEL SPEED SENSOR FOR AN OPEN OR SHORT TOGETHER	
1  Suspect Wheel Speed Sensor Connector	
2 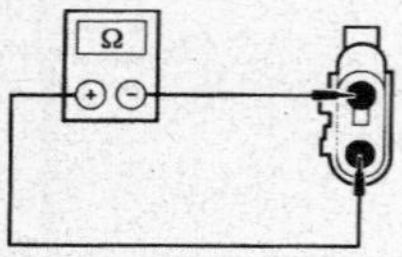	2 Measure the resistance between the suspect wheel speed sensor pins (component side). • Is the resistance between 1,000 and 1,500 ohms? → **Yes** GO to **F2**. → **No** INSTALL a new wheel speed sensor. CLEAR the DTCs. REPEAT the self-test.

FM4020001587010X

Fig. 43 Test F/Codes 1145, C1155, C1165 & C1175: Wheel Speed Sensor Input Circuit Failure (Part 1 of 4). 2001–04 Sable & Taurus

TEST CONDITIONS	TEST DETAILS/RESULTS/ACTIONS
F5 CHECK THE SUSPECT WHEEL SPEED SENSOR FOR AN OPEN OR SHORT TOGETHER (Continued)	
2 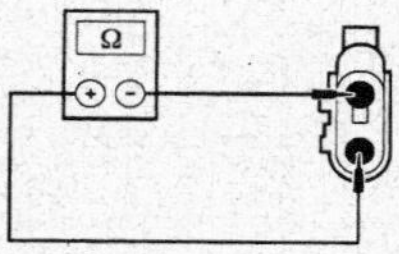	2 Measure the resistance between the suspect wheel speed sensor pins (component side). • Is the resistance between 1,000 and 1,500 ohms? → **Yes** REPAIR the circuit. CLEAR the DTCs. REPEAT the self-test. → **No** INSTALL a new wheel speed sensor. CLEAR the DTCs. REPEAT the self-test.

FM4020001578050X

Fig. 42 Test F/Codes C1145, C1155, C1165 & C1175: Wheel Speed Sensor Input Circuit Failure (Part 5 of 5). 2000 Sable & Taurus

CONDITIONS	DETAILS/RESULTS/ACTIONS
F2 CHECK THE WHEEL SPEED CIRCUITRY FOR AN OPEN OR SHORT TOGETHER	
1 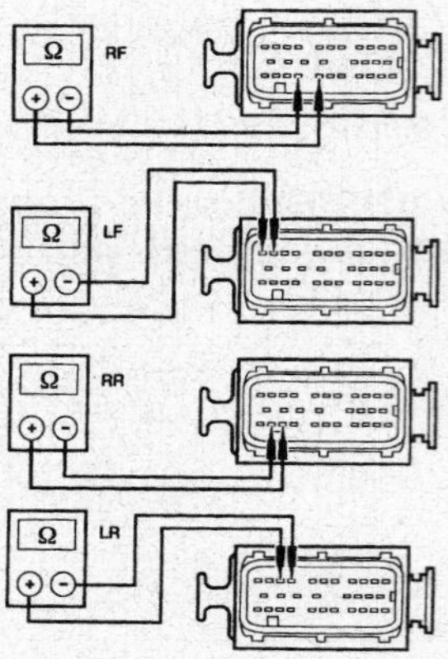	1 Measure the resistance between: — (RF) ABS control module connector C135 pin 4, circuit 514 (YE/RD), harness side and ABS control module connector C135 pin 5, circuit 516 (YE/BK), harness side. — (LF) ABS control module connector C135 pin 20, circuit 521 (TN/OG), harness side and ABS control module connector C135 pin 21, circuit 522 (TN/BK), harness side. — (RR) ABS control module connector C135 pin 2, circuit 523 (RD/PK), harness side and ABS control module connector C135 pin 3, circuit 524 (PK/BK), harness side. — (LR) ABS control module connector C135 pin 22, circuit 518 (LG/RD), harness side and ABS control module connector C135 pin 23, circuit 519 (LG/BK), harness side. • Is the resistance between 1,000 and 1,500 ohms? → **Yes** RECONNECT all connections. CLEAR the DTCs. REPEAT the self-test. If DTC C1145, C1155, C1165 or C1175 is retrieved, INSTALL a new electronic control unit (ECU). REPEAT the self-test. If no DTCs are retrieved the system is operating normally. → **No** GO to **F3**.
F3 CHECK THE SUSPECT WHEEL SPEED SENSOR CIRCUIT FOR SHORT TO GROUND	
1 	

FM4020001587020X

Fig. 43 Test F/Codes 1145, C1155, C1165 & C1175: Wheel Speed Sensor Input Circuit Failure (Part 2 of 4). 2001–04 Sable & Taurus

CONDITIONS	DETAILS/RESULTS/ACTIONS
F3 CHECK THE SUSPECT WHEEL SPEED SENSOR CIRCUIT FOR SHORT TO GROUND (Continued)	
2 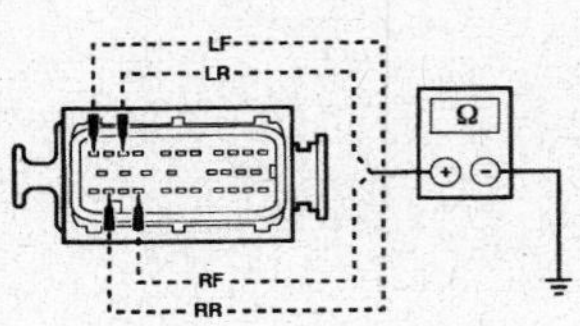	2 Measure the resistance of the suspect wheel speed sensor circuit between: — (RF) ABS control module connector C135 pin 4, circuit 514 (YE/RD), harness side and ground. — (LF) ABS control module connector C135 pin 20, circuit 521 (TN/OG), harness side and ground. — (RR) ABS control module connector C135 pin 2, circuit 523 (RD/PK), harness side and ground. — (LR) ABS control module connector C135 pin 22, circuit 518 (LG/RD), harness side and ground. • Is the resistance infinite? → **Yes** GO to **F5**. → **No** GO to **F4**.
F4 CHECK THE SUSPECT WHEEL SPEED CIRCUIT FOR SHORT TO POWER	
1 2 3 	

FM4020001587030X

Fig. 43 Test F/Codes 1145, C1155, C1165 & C1175: Wheel Speed Sensor Input Circuit Failure (Part 3 of 4). 2001–04 Sable & Taurus

TEST CONDITIONS	TEST DETAILS/RESULTS/ACTIONS
G1 CHECK VEHICLE COMPONENTS	
Note: Any other wheel speed DTC must be diagnosed before proceeding. This DTC C1222 can be set during certain repair procedures with key ON, vehicle towing, on vehicle wheel balance or dynamometer testing with no actual fault.	
	1 Check for correct wheel and tire size, front to rear and side to side. 2 Check for excessive bearing end play. 3 Check the wheel speed sensor indicator for a bent sensor ring or missing teeth. • Are all the conditions OK? → **Yes** GO to **G2**. → **No** REPAIR as necessary. CLEAR the DTCs. REPEAT the self-test.

FM4020001579010X

Fig. 44 Test G/Code C1222: Wheel Speed Signal Mismatch (Part 1 of 2). 2000–01 Sable & Taurus

TEST CONDITIONS	TEST DETAILS/RESULTS/ACTIONS
G2 TEST DRIVE THE VEHICLE	
1 2 3 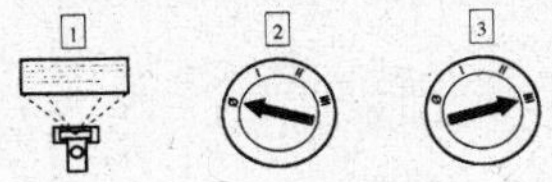	4 Test drive the vehicle over 24 km/h (15 mph).
5 	• Is DTC C1222 retrieved? → **Yes** INSTALL a new electronic control unit (ECU). REPEAT the self-test. → **No** If another DTC is retrieved, GO to the ABS Control Module Diagnostic Trouble Code (DTC) Index. If no DTCs are retrieved, system is operating normally. If not DTCs are retrieved, system is OK.

FM4020001579020X

Fig. 44 Test G/Code C1222: Wheel Speed Signal Mismatch (Part 2 of 2). 2000–01 Sable & Taurus

CONDITIONS	DETAILS/RESULTS/ACTIONS
F4 CHECK THE SUSPECT WHEEL SPEED CIRCUIT FOR SHORT TO POWER (Continued)	
4 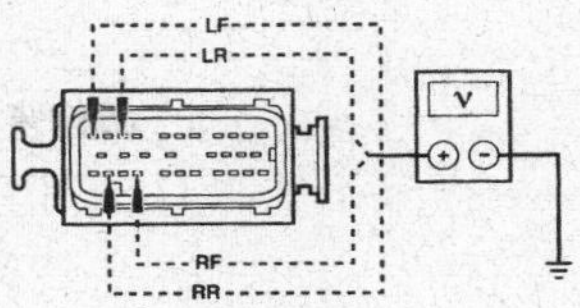	4 Measure the voltage of the suspect wheel speed sensor circuit between: — (RF) ABS control module connector C135 pin 4, circuit 514 (YE/RD), harness side and ground. — (LF) ABS control module connector C135 pin 20, circuit 521 (TN/OG), harness side and ground. — (RR) ABS control module connector C135 pin 2, circuit 523 (RD/PK), harness side and ground. — (LR) ABS control module connector C135 pin 22, circuit 518 (LG/RD), harness side and ground. • Is voltage present? → **Yes** REPAIR the circuit. CLEAR the DTCs. REPEAT the self-test. → **No** GO to **F5**.
F5 CHECK THE SUSPECT WHEEL SPEED SENSOR FOR SHORT TO GROUND	
1 	
2 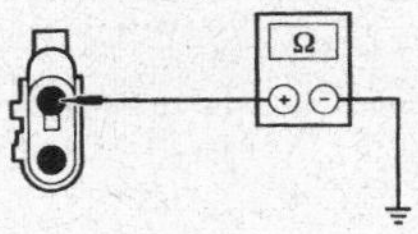	2 Measure the resistance between either suspect wheel speed sensor pin (component side) and ground. • Is the resistance infinite? → **Yes** REPAIR the circuit. CLEAR the DTCs. REPEAT the self-test. → **No** INSTALL a new wheel speed sensor. CLEAR the DTCs. REPEAT the self-test.

FM4020001587040X

Fig. 43 Test F/Codes 1145, C1155, C1165 & C1175: Wheel Speed Sensor Input Circuit Failure (Part 4 of 4). 2001–04 Sable & Taurus

TEST CONDITIONS	TEST DETAILS/RESULTS/ACTIONS
H1 CHECK THE SUSPECT WHEEL SPEED SENSOR	
	1 Inspect the suspect wheel speed sensor mounting. Check the wheel speed sensor for excessive dirt build-up. Check for metal obstructions. Check the wheel speed sensor for damage. • Is the suspect wheel speed sensor and mounting OK? → **Yes** GO to **H2**. → **No** REPAIR or INSTALL a new wheel speed sensor. CLEAR the DTCs. REPEAT the self-test.

FM4020001580010X

Fig. 45 Test H/Code C1233, C1234, C1235 & C1236: Wheel Speed Input Signal Missing (Part 1 of 2). 2000–01 Sable & Taurus

TEST CONDITIONS	TEST DETAILS/RESULTS/ACTIONS
H2 CHECK THE SUSPECT WHEEL SPEED SENSOR INDICATOR	
	1 Check the suspect wheel sensor indicator for corrosion, nicks, bridged teeth, damaged teeth, and correct mounting and alignment with the wheel speed sensor. Check the air gap (less than 1 mm). Check the bearing end play. • Is the suspect ABS sensor indicator OK? → **Yes** GO to **H3**. → **No** INSTALL a new wheel speed sensor indicator. CLEAR the DTCs. REPEAT the self-test.
H3 CHECK THE SUSPECT WHEEL SPEED SENSOR PIDS	
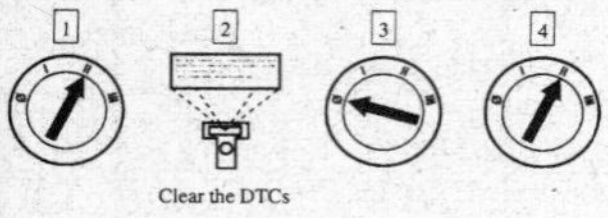	5 Have an assistant monitor the ABS control module PIDs LF__WSPD, RF__WSPD, LR__WSPD and RR__WSPD while driving at various speeds. 6 Test drive the vehicle for 16 km (10 miles). • Are the ABS control module PIDs reading approximately the same at all times? → **Yes** CLEAR the DTCs. REPEAT the self-test. If DTC C1233, C1234, C1235 or C1236 is retrieved, INSTALL a new electronic control unit (ECU). REPEAT the self-test. If no DTCs are retrieved the system is operating normally. → **No** INSTALL a new wheel speed sensor. CLEAR the DTCs. REPEAT the self-test.

FM4020001580020X

Fig. 45 Test H/Code C1233, C1234, C1235 & C1236: Wheel Speed Input Signal Missing (Part 2 of 2). 2000–01 Sable & Taurus

TEST CONDITIONS	TEST DETAILS/RESULTS/ACTIONS
I1 CHECK CIRCUIT 640 (RD/YE) FOR SHORT TO POWER	
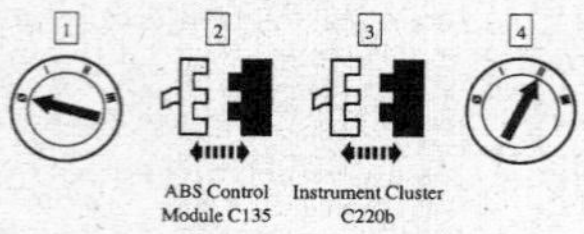 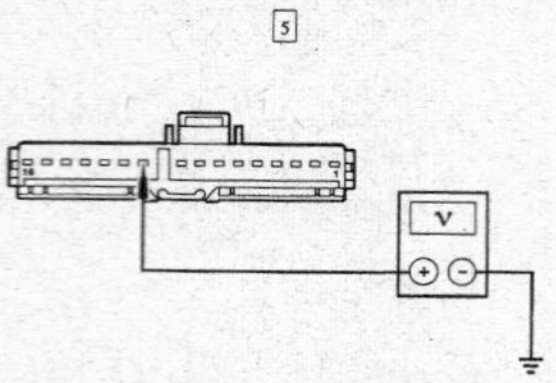	5 Measure the voltage between instrument cluster connector C220b pin 10, circuit 640 (RD/YE), harness side and ground. • Is voltage present? → **Yes** REPAIR the circuit. REPEAT the self-test. → **No** GO to **I2**.
I2 CHECK CIRCUIT 603 (DG) FOR AN OPEN	
 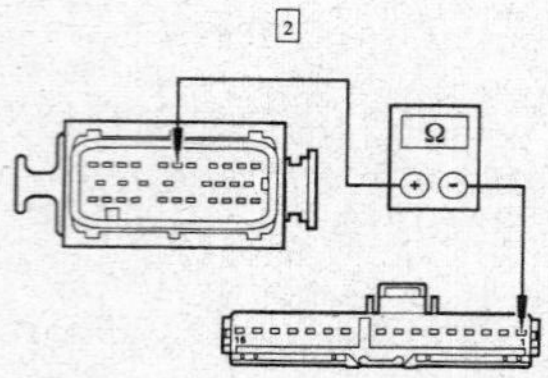	2 Measure the resistance between ABS control module connector C135 pin 28, circuit 603 (DG), harness side and instrument cluster connector C220b pin 1, circuit 603 (DG), harness side. • Is the resistance less than 5 ohms? → **Yes** INSTALL a new electronic control unit (ECU). REPEAT the self-test. → **No** REPAIR the circuit. REPEAT the self-test.

FM4020001581000X

Fig. 46 Test I: Yellow ABS Warning Lamp Does Not Self Check, Always On w/No DTCs. 2000–01 Sable & Taurus

CONDITIONS	DETAILS/RESULTS/ACTIONS
I1 ISOLATE THE ABS CONTROL MODULE	
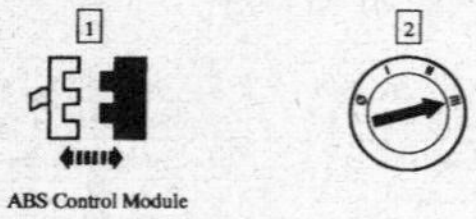	3 Check the ABS indicator light. • Is the indicator light off? → **Yes** INSTALL a new ABS control module. → **No** GO to **I2**.
I2 CHECK CIRCUIT 603 (DG) FOR AN OPEN	
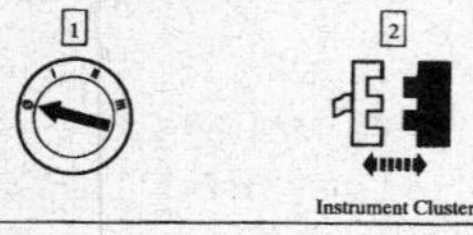	

FM4020101798010X

Fig. 47 Test I: ABS Indicator Light Is Always On, No DTC's (Part 1 of 2). 2002–04 Sable & Taurus

CONDITIONS	DETAILS/RESULTS/ACTIONS
I2 CHECK CIRCUIT 603 (DG) FOR AN OPEN (Continued)	
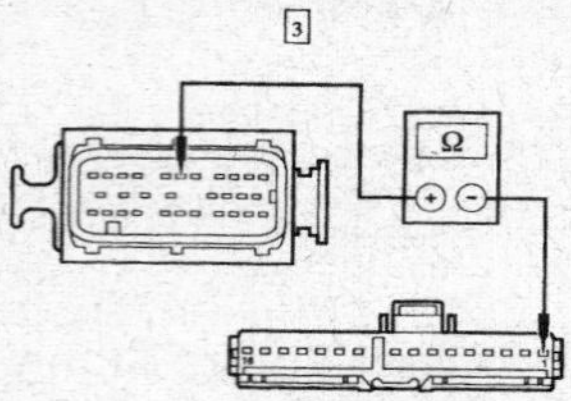	3 Measure the resistance between ABS control module connector C135 pin 25, circuit 603 (DG), harness side and instrument cluster connector C220b pin 1, circuit 603 (DG), harness side. • Is the resistance less than 5 ohms? → **Yes** INSTALL a new instrument cluster. → **No** REPAIR the circuit. REPEAT the self-test.

FM4020101798020X

Fig. 47 Test I: ABS Indicator Light Is Always On, No DTC's (Part 2 of 2). 2002–04 Sable & Taurus

TEST CONDITIONS	TEST DETAILS/RESULTS/ACTIONS
J1 CHECK THE VEHICLE COMPONENT MOUNTING	
	1 Inspect the brake pedal and brake booster/brake master cylinder for correct attachment. 2 Bleed the brake system. • Is the brake pedal spongy? → **Yes** GO to **J2**. → **No** The brake system is operating correctly. REPEAT the self-test.
J2 REBLEED THE BRAKE SYSTEM	
	1 Bleed the brake system using the scan tool. • Is the brake pedal spongy? → **Yes** Diagnose Base Brake System → **No** The brake system is operating correctly. REPEAT self-test.

FM4020001582000X

Fig. 48 Test J: Soft Brake Pedal, No Warning Indicator. Sable & Taurus

TEST CONDITIONS	TESTDETAILS/RESULTS/ACTIONS
K1 BLEED THE BRAKE SYSTEM	
	1 Bleed the brake system. • Does the vehicle track poorly? → **Yes** GO to **K2**. → **No** The brake system is operating correctly. REPEAT the self-test.
K2 CHECK THE ABS INLET VALVE (CLOSED POSITION)	
	1 Raise and support the vehicle. 2 Rotate all the wheels to make sure they rotate freely (the vehicle must be in neutral).

FM4020001583010X

Fig. 49 Test K: Poor Vehicle Tracking During ABS Function (Part 1 of 3). Sable & Taurus

TEST CONDITIONS	TESTDETAILS/RESULTS/ACTIONS
K2 CHECK THE ABS INLET VALVE (CLOSED POSITION) (Continued)	
	3 Apply moderate brake pedal effort. 4 Trigger ABS control module active command LF INLET ON. 5 Have an assistant attempt to rotate the LF wheel. • Does the LF wheel rotate? → **Yes** TRIGGER active command LF INLET OFF. GO to **K3**. → **No** INSTALL a new hydraulic control unit (HCU). REPEAT the self-test.
K3 CHECK THE ABS INLET VALVE (OPEN POSITION)	
	1 Apply moderate brake pedal effort. 2 Have an assistant attempt to rotate the LF wheel. • Does the LF wheel rotate? → **Yes** INSTALL a new hydraulic control unit (HCU). REPEAT the self-test. → **No** GO to **K4**.
K4 CHECK ABS OUTPUT VALVE (OPEN POSITION)	
	1 Apply moderate brake pedal effort. 2 Trigger ABS control module active command LF INLET ON. 3 Trigger ABS control module active command ABS POWER ON (turns on pump motor) for 6 seconds. (Trigger must be depressed 3 times. Each press runs the pump for 2 seconds.) 4 Trigger the ABS control module active command LF OUTLET ON and then OFF, repeat 3 times.

FM4020001583020X

Fig. 49 Test K: Poor Vehicle Tracking During ABS Function (Part 2 of 3). Sable & Taurus

TEST CONDITIONS	TESTDETAILS/RESULTS/ACTIONS
K4 CHECK ABS OUTPUT VALVE (OPEN POSITION) (Continued)	
	5 Have an assistant attempt to rotate the LF wheel. • Does the LF wheel rotate? → **Yes** TRIGGER all active commands OFF. GO to **K5**. → **No** INSTALL a new hydraulic control unit (HCU). REPEAT the self-test.
K5 CHECK ABS INLET AND OUTLET VALVE (CLOSED POSITION)	
	1 Apply moderate brake pedal effort. 2 Have an assistant attempt to rotate the LF wheel. • Does the LF wheel rotate? → **Yes** INSTALL a new hydraulic control unit (HCU). REPEAT the self-test. → **No** REPEAT this procedure (beginning with Step K2) for the RF, LR and RR wheels using the appropriate active commands. IF no failure occurs the system is operating normally.

FM4020001583030X

Fig. 49 Test K: Poor Vehicle Tracking During ABS Function (Part 3 of 3). Sable & Taurus

TEST CONDITIONS	TESTDETAILS/RESULTS/ACTIONS
L1 CHECK FOR DIAGNOSTIC TROUBLE CODES (DTCs)	
	1 Carry out the ABS control module self-test. • Are any DTCs retrieved? → **Yes** GO to the ABS Control Module Diagnostic Trouble Code (DTC) Index. → **No** GO to **L2**.

FM4020001584010X

Fig. 50 Test L: Traction Control Inoperative (Part 1 of 2). Sable & Taurus

TEST CONDITIONS	TESTDETAILS/RESULTS/ACTIONS
L2 CHECK THE ABS OPERATION	
	1 Test drive the vehicle. Check the ABS operation. • Does the ABS operate correctly? → **Yes** GO to **L3**. → **No** GO to the Symptom Chart.
L3 CHECK THE TRACTION CONTROL SWITCH CIRCUIT	
1 2 	
3 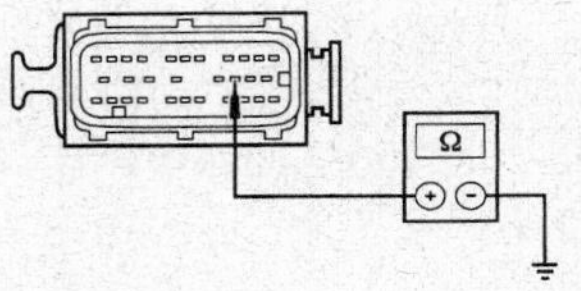	3 Measure the resistance between ABS control module connector C135 pin 17, circuit 959 (GY), harness side and ground while pressing and releasing the traction control switch. • Is the resistance less than 5 ohms with the traction control switch pressed and greater than 10,000 ohms with the traction control switch released? → **Yes** INSTALL a new electronic control unit (ECU). REPEAT the self-test. → **No** GO to Pinpoint Test N.

FM4020001584020X

Fig. 50 Test L: Traction Control Inoperative (Part 2 of 2). Sable & Taurus

TEST CONDITIONS	TESTDETAILS/RESULTS/ACTIONS
M1 CHECK TRACTION CONTROL SWITCH CIRCUIT	
1 2 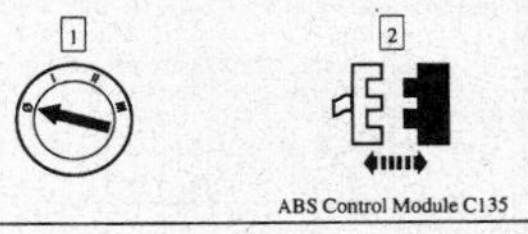	

FM4020001585010X

Fig. 51 Test M: Traction Control Switch Indicator Inoperative (Part 1 of 4). Taurus

TEST CONDITIONS	TESTDETAILS/RESULTS/ACTIONS
M1 CHECK TRACTION CONTROL SWITCH CIRCUIT (Continued)	
3 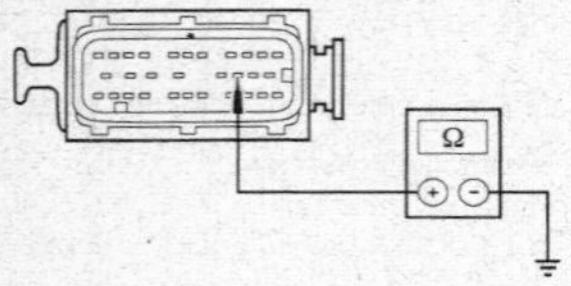	3 Measure the resistance between ABS control module connector C135 pin 17, circuit 959 (GY), harness side and ground while depressing and releasing the traction control switch. • Is the resistance less than 5 ohms with the traction control switch depressed and greater than 10,000 ohms with the traction control switch released? → **Yes** GO to **M4**. → **No** GO to **M2**.
M2 CHECK CIRCUIT 959 (GY) FOR AN OPEN OR SHORT TO GROUND	
1  Traction Control Switch C280	
2 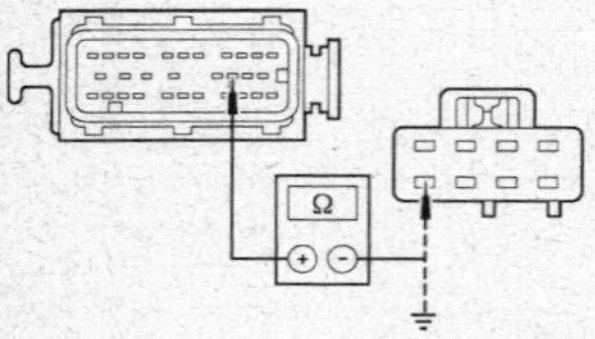	2 Measure the resistance between ABS control module connector C135 pin 17, circuit 959 (GY), harness side and traction control switch connector C280 pin 1, circuit 959 (GY), harness side and between ABS control module connector C135 pin 17, circuit 959 (GY), harness side and ground. • Is the resistance less than 5 ohms between the ABS control module and traction control switch, and greater than 10,000 ohms between the ABS control module and ground? → **Yes** GO to **M3**. → **No** REPAIR the circuit. REPEAT the self-test.

FM4020001585020X

Fig. 51 Test M: Traction Control Switch Indicator Inoperative (Part 2 of 4). Taurus

TEST CONDITIONS	TESTDETAILS/RESULTS/ACTIONS
M3 CHECK CIRCUIT 57 (BK) FOR AN OPEN	
1 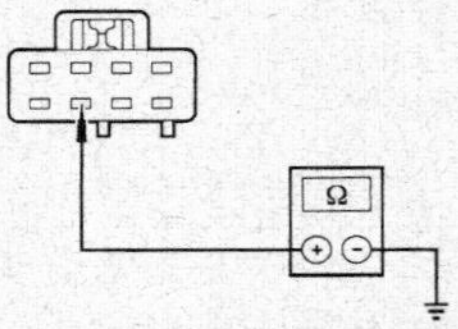	1 Measure the resistance between traction control switch connector C280 pin 2 circuit 57 (BK), harness side and ground. • Is the resistance less than 5 ohms? → **Yes** INSTALL a new traction control switch. REPEAT the self-test. → **No** REPAIR the circuit. REPEAT the self-test.
M4 CHECK THE TRACTION CONTROL SWITCH INDICATOR CIRCUIT	
1 	
2 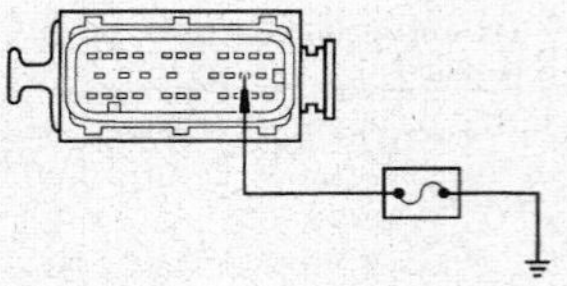	2 **Note:** The jumper wire must be fused with a 10A in-line fuse. Momentarily connect a jumper wire between ABS control module connector C135 pin 18, circuit 960 (BK/LB), harness side and ground while checking the traction control switch indicator. • Does the traction control switch indicator illuminate? → **Yes** INSTALL a new electronic control unit (ECU). REPEAT the self-test. → **No** GO to **M5**.
M5 CHECK CIRCUIT 533 (TN/RO) FOR AN OPEN CIRCUIT	
1 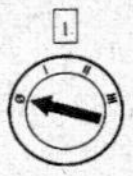 2  Traction Control Switch C280 3 	

FM4020001585030X

Fig. 51 Test M: Traction Control Switch Indicator Inoperative (Part 3 of 4). Taurus

TEST CONDITIONS	TESTDETAILS/RESULTS/ACTIONS
M5 CHECK CIRCUIT 533 (TN/RO) FOR AN OPEN CIRCUIT (Continued)	
4 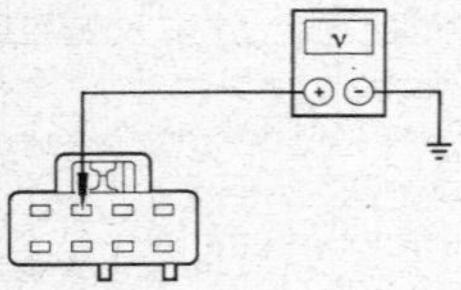	4 Measure the voltage between traction control switch connector C280 pin 6, circuit 533 (TN/RO), harness side and ground. • Is the voltage greater than 10 volts? → **Yes** GO to **M6**. → **No** REPAIR the circuit. REPEAT the self-test.
M6 CHECK CIRCUIT 960 (BK/LB) FOR AN OPEN CIRCUIT	
1 	
2 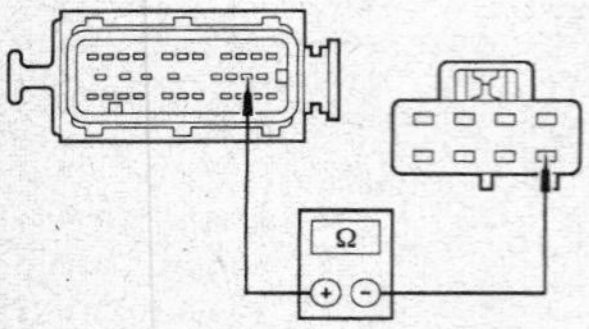	2 Measure the resistance between ABS control module connector C135 pin 18, circuit 960 (BK/LB), harness side and traction control switch connector C280 pin 4, circuit 960 (BK/LB), harness side. • Is the resistance less than 5 ohms? → **Yes** INSTALL a new traction control switch. REPEAT the self-test. → **No** REPAIR the circuit. REPEAT the self-test.

FM4020001585040X

Fig. 51 Test M: Traction Control Switch Indicator Inoperative (Part 4 of 4). Taurus

TEST CONDITIONS	TESTDETAILS/RESULTS/ACTIONS
N1 CHECK TRACTION CONTROL SWITCH CIRCUIT	
1 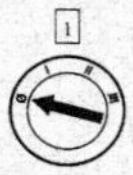 2  ABS Control Module C135	

FM4020001586010X

Fig. 52 Test N: Traction Control Cannot Be Disabled (Part 1 of 4). Sable & Taurus

TEST CONDITIONS	TESTDETAILS/RESULTS/ACTIONS
N1 CHECK TRACTION CONTROL SWITCH CIRCUIT (Continued)	
3 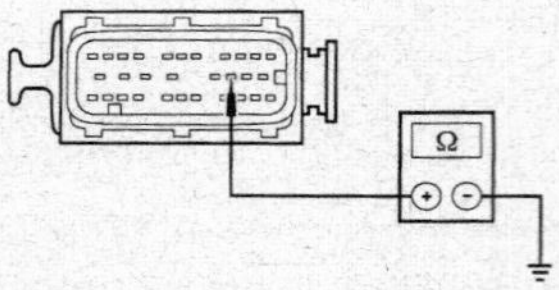	3 Measure the resistance between ABS control module connector C135 pin 17, circuit 959 (GY), harness side and ground while depressing and releasing the traction control switch. • Is the resistance less than 5 ohms with the traction control switch depressed and greater than 10,000 ohms with the traction control switches released? → **Yes** GO to **N4**. → **No** GO to **N2**.
N2 CHECK CIRCUIT 960 (BK/LB) FOR AN OPEN OR SHORT TO GROUND	
1  Traction Control Switch C135	

FM4020001586020X

Fig. 52 Test N: Traction Control Cannot Be Disabled (Part 2 of 4). Sable & Taurus

TEST CONDITIONS	TEST DETAILS/RESULTS/ACTIONS
N2 CHECK CIRCUIT 960 (BK/LB) FOR AN OPEN OR SHORT TO GROUND (Continued)	
2 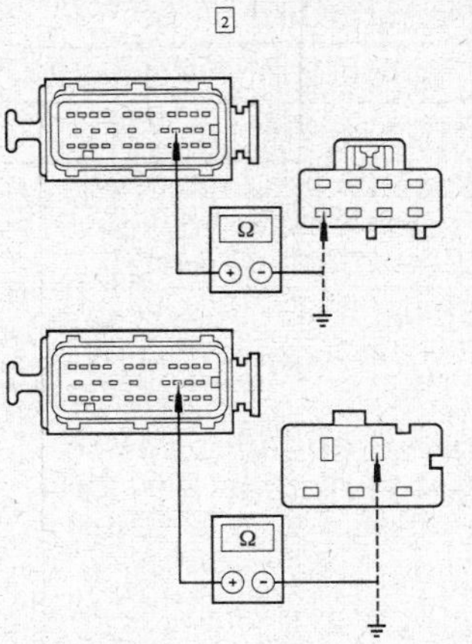	2 Measure the resistance between ABS control module connector C135 pin 17, circuit 959 (GY), harness side and traction control switch connector C280 pin 1, circuit 960 (BK/LB), harness side, and between ABS control module connector C135 pin 17, circuit 959 (GY), harness side and ground. • Is the resistance less than 5 ohms between the ABS control module and traction control switch, and greater than 10,000 ohms between the ABS control module and ground? → **Yes** GO to **N3**. → **No** REPAIR the circuit. REPEAT the self-test.

FM4020001586030X

Fig. 52 Test N: Traction Control Cannot Be Disabled (Part 3 of 4). Sable & Taurus

TEST CONDITIONS	TEST DETAILS/RESULTS/ACTIONS
N3 CHECK CIRCUIT 57 (BK) FOR AN OPEN	
1 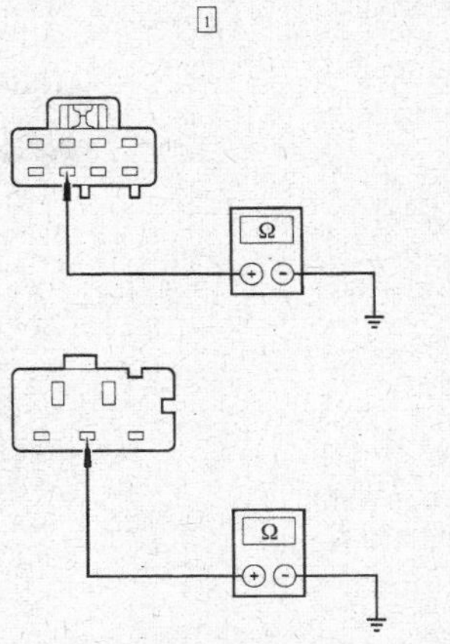	1 Measure the resistance between traction control switch connector C280 pin 4, circuit 57 (BK), harness side and ground. • Is the resistance less than 5 ohms? → **Yes** INSTALL a new traction control switch. REPEAT the self-test. → **No** REPAIR the circuit. REPEAT the self-test.
N4 CHECK CIRCUIT 959 (GY) FOR SHORT TO POWER	
1 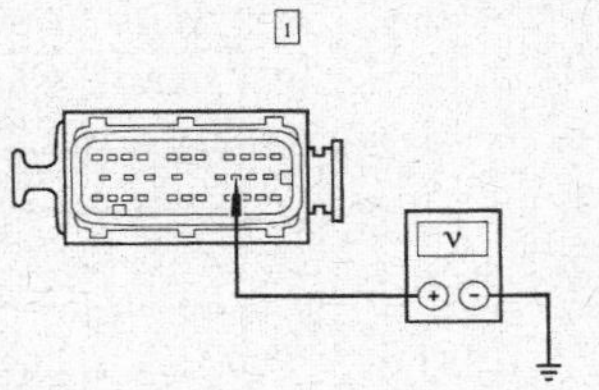	1 Measure the voltage between ABS control module connector C135 pin 17, circuit 959 (GY), harness side and ground. • Is voltage present? → **Yes** REPAIR the circuit. REPEAT the self-test. → **No** INSTALL a new electronic control unit (ECU). REPEAT the self-test.

FM4020001586040X

Fig. 52 Test N: Traction Control Cannot Be Disabled (Part 4 of 4). Sable & Taurus

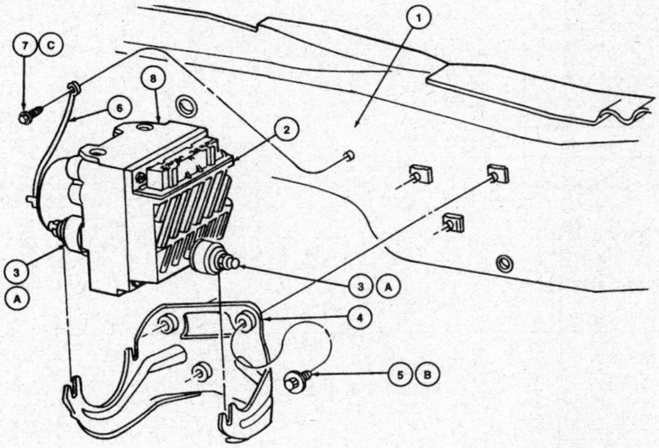

FM4029600712010X

Fig. 53 ABS module & hydraulic control unit assembly (Part 1 of 2). Sable & Taurus

Item	Description
1	Side Member
2	Anti-Lock Brake Control Module (ECU)
3	Insulator Assy (3 Req'd)
4	Anti-Lock Brake Hydraulic Control Bracket
5	Bolt (3 Req'd)
6	Ground Strap
7	Screw
8	Anti-Lock Brake Hydraulic Control Unit
A	Tighten to 12-20 N·m (9-15 Lb-Ft)
B	Tighten to 26-34 N·m (19-25 Lb-Ft)
C	Tighten to 8-10 N·m (67-92 Lb-In)

FM4029600712020X

Fig. 53 ABS module & hydraulic control unit assembly (Part 2 of 2). Sable & Taurus

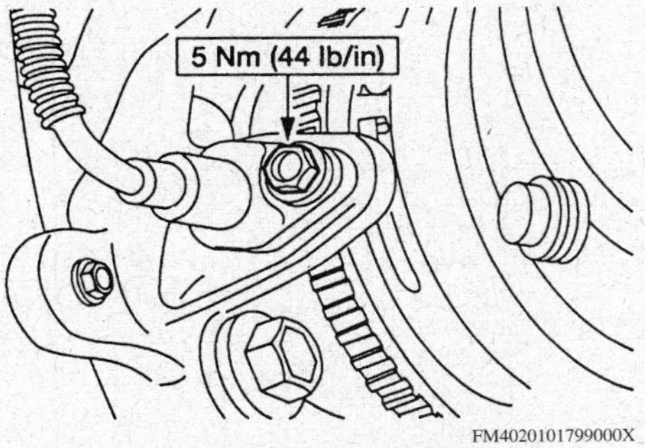

FM4020101799000X

Fig. 54 Front ABS wheel sensor replacement. Continental

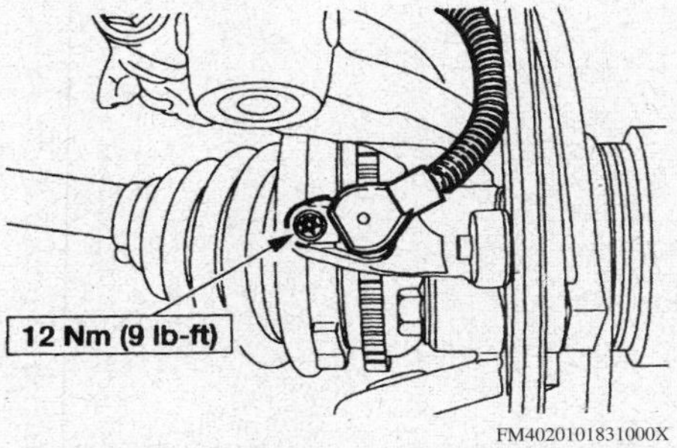

FM4020101831000X

Fig. 55 Front ABS wheel speed sensor replacement. Sable & Taurus

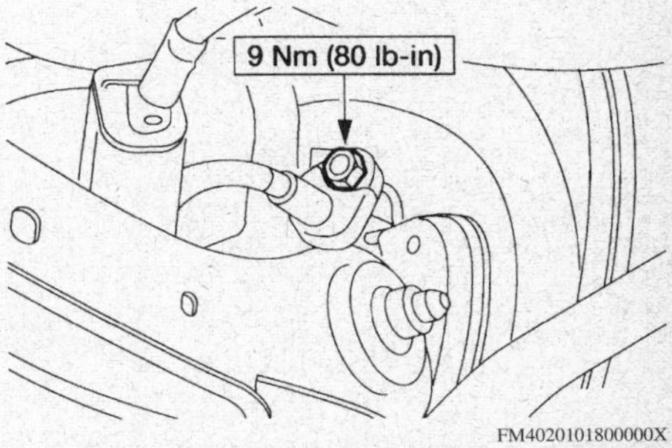

FM4020101800000X

Fig. 56 Rear ABS wheel speed sensor replacement. Continental

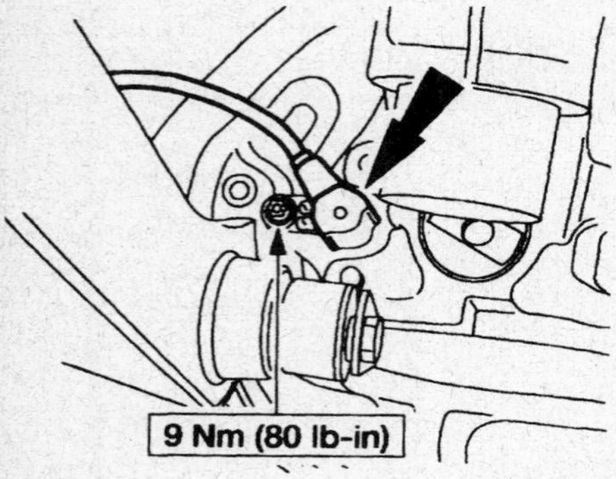

Fig. 57 Rear wheel speed sensor replacement. Sable & Taurus

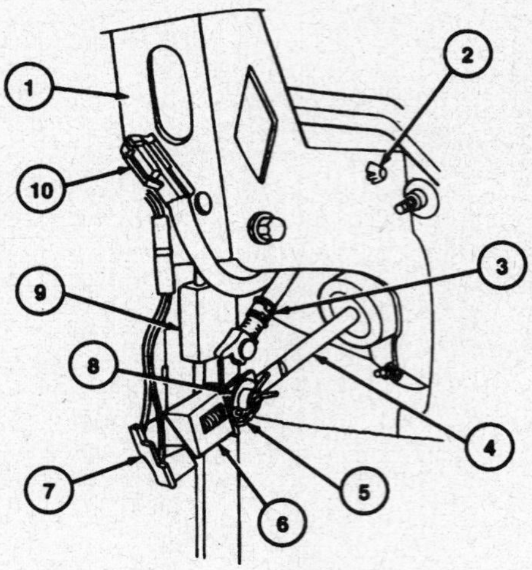

Item	Description
1	Brake Pedal Support Bracket
2	Locking Tabs
3	Speed Control Deactivate Switch
4	Brake Push Rod (Part of Master Cylinder)
5	Hairpin Retainer
6	Stoplight Switch

FM4029701306010X

Fig. 58 Stop lamp switch replacement (Part 1 of 2). Continental, Sable & Taurus

Item	Description
7	Stoplight Switch Connector
8	Nylon Washer
9	Speed Control Deactivate Switch Mounting Bracket (Part of Brake Pedal)
10	Speed Control Deactivate Switch Connector

FM4029701306020X

Fig. 58 Stop lamp switch replacement (Part 2 of 2). Continental, Sable & Taurus

Crown Victoria, Grand Marquis, Marauder & Town Car

NOTE: On Air Bag Equipped Models, Refer To "Air Bag System Precautions" Located In The Front Of This Manual For System Disarming & Arming Procedures.

NOTE: Refer To "Computer Relearn Procedures" Located In The Front Of This Manual When Battery Power To The Computer Has Been Interrupted.

NOTE: "Electrical Symbol & Wire Color Code Identification" Located In The Front Of This Manual May Be Used As An Aid When Using Wiring Circuits Found In This Section.

INDEX

PRECAUTIONS

Air Bag Systems

Refer to "Air Bag System Precautions" in the front of this manual for system disarming and arming procedures.

Battery Ground Cable

Prior to service, disconnect battery ground cable and isolate as required.

Hydraulic Brake Fluid Color

Hydraulic brake fluid must conform with the requirements of Federal Motor Vehicle Safety Standard 116. Under this standard, brake fluids are visually different from other automotive fluids such as transmission, power steering and engine.

Fluid color in a normal brake system may vary from its original color for many reasons. A brake master cylinder may show significantly different shades fluid color between the two brake master cylinder reservoirs. Color may also appear to vary between cast steel and die cast aluminum reservoirs. Some reasons for discoloration include the following:

1. Heat and/or aging.
2. Different operation temperatures or different rates of normal oxidation between two reservoir compartments.
3. Different brands and/or shades of fluid are used when topping off during normal service.
4. Dissolution of color dye used on master cylinder internal springs during assembly.
5. Brake fluid contaminated with hydrocarbon/mineral based fluid (power steering or transmission fluid) can be detected by an obvious swelling of the master cylinder cap gasket. If the master cylinder cap gasket is swollen, all brake system rubber components must be replaced. All brake tubes and hoses must be thoroughly flushed with heavy duty brake fluid part No. C6AZ-19542-AA or -BA or DOT-3 equivalent before the vehicle returns to service.

DESCRIPTION

The anti-lock brake system prevents wheel lock-up by automatically modulating brake pressure during an emergency stop. It allows driver to maintain steering control and stop the vehicle in the shortest possible distance under most conditions. The traction control system controls wheelspin by modulating engine torque and applying or releasing appropriate rear brake to restore traction when driving on slippery or loose surfaces, **Fig. 1**.

System Components

VACUUM BOOSTER

The diaphragm type brake booster is self-contained and is mounted on the left side of engine compartment. The vacuum brake booster uses engine intake manifold vacuum and atmospheric pressure for power.

MASTER CYLINDER

This unit is a tandem master cylinder. The primary (rear) circuit feeds right front and left rear brakes. The secondary circuit (front) feeds left front and right rear brakes. The reservoir is a clear translucent plastic container. An integral fluid level switch is part of reservoir cap assembly, with one

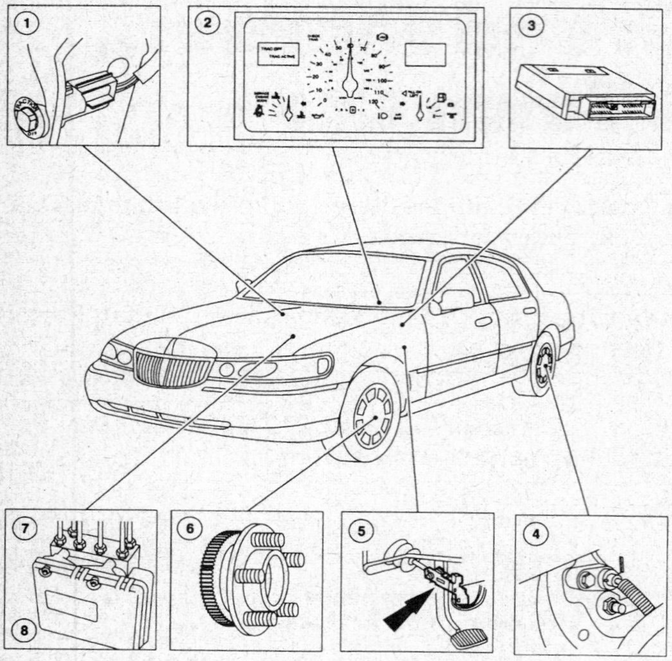

Item	Description
1	Traction Control Switch
2	Hybrid Electronic Cluster (HEC) (includes ABS Warning Indicator; Traction Control Indicator)
3	Powertrain Control Module
4	Anti-Lock Brake Sensor (Rear)

Item	Description
5	Brake Pedal Position (BPP) Switch
6	Anti-Lock Brake Sensor Indicator (Front)
7	Hydraulic Control Unit (HCU)
8	Anti-Lock Brake Control Module

FM4029801243000X

Fig. 1 Anti-lock & traction control system

DTCS	Description	Source	Action
B1342	ECU Is Defective	ABS/TC	INSTALL a new anti-lock brake control module.
B1485	Brake Pedal Input Circuit Short to Battery	ABS/TC	GO to Pinpoint Test F.
B1676	Battery Voltage Out of Range	ABS/TC	GO to Pinpoint Test G.
C1095	ABS Hydraulic Pump Motor Circuit Failure	ABS/TC	GO to Pinpoint Test C.
C1145	RF Anti-Lock Brake Sensor Input Circuit Failure	ABS/TC	GO to Pinpoint Test D.
C1155	LF Anti-Lock Brake Sensor Input Circuit Failure	ABS/TC	GO to Pinpoint Test D.
C1165	RR Anti-Lock Brake Sensor Input Circuit Failure	ABS/TC	GO to Pinpoint Test D.
C1175	LR Anti-Lock Brake Sensor Input Circuit Failure	ABS/TC	GO to Pinpoint Test D.
C1233	LF Anti-Lock Brake Sensor Input Signal Missing	ABS/TC	GO to Pinpoint Test E.
C1234	RF Anti-Lock Brake Sensor Input Signal Missing	ABS/TC	GO to Pinpoint Test E.
C1235	RR Anti-Lock Brake Sensor Input Signal Missing	ABS/TC	GO to Pinpoint Test E.
C1236	LR Anti-Lock Brake Sensor Input Signal Missing	ABS/TC	GO to Pinpoint Test E.
U1009	SCP Invalid or Missing Data for Engine Torque	PCM	CARRY OUT the PCM Self-Test.
U1027	SCP Invalid or Missing Data for Engine RPM	PCM	CARRY OUT the PCM Self-Test.
U1059	SCP Invalid or Missing Data for Transmission/Transaxle/PRNDL	PCM	CARRY OUT the PCM Self-Test.

FM4020005015000X

Fig. 2 Diagnostic trouble code interpretation. 2000 Crown Victoria & Grand Marquis

electrical connector pointing rearward for wire harness connection.

HYDRAULIC CONTROL UNIT

The Hydraulic Control Unit (HCU) is located on the front lefthand side of the engine compartment. It consists of a valve body assembly, pump, motor assembly and brake fluid reservoir with fluid lever indicator assembly. During normal braking, fluid from master cylinder enters the HCU through two inlet ports at the rear of the HCU. The fluid passes through four normally open inlet valves, one to each wheel. When the ABS module (Electronic Control Unit (ECU) senses wheel lock conditions, the ABS module (ECU) produces a pulse to the appropriate inlet valve, which then closes the valve. This prevents any more fluid from entering the affected brake. The ABS module (ECU) senses the wheel again. If the wheel is still decelerating, the ABS module (ECU) then pulses open the normally closed valve, which decreases the pressure trapped inline.

ABS MODULE (ELECTRONIC CONTROL UNIT)

The ABS module (ECU) is located in the engine compartment. This unit is a self-test non-repairable unit consisting of two microprocessors which are programmed identically. The ABS module (ECU) monitors system operation during normal driving as well as during anti-lock braking. Under normal driving conditions, the microprocessors transmit short test pulses to the solenoid valves to inspect the electrical system. Under wheel lock conditions, the ABS module (ECU) produces signals to open and close the appropriate solenoid valves. This results in moderate pulsations in brake pedal. During anti-lock braking, moderate pulsation in the brake pedal is accompanied by a change in pedal height. This rise in pedal height will continue until the pedal travel switch closes and the pump shuts off. During normal braking, the brake pedal feel will be identical to a standard brake system.

WHEEL SENSORS

This system uses four sets of variable resistance sensors and toothed speed indicator rings to determine each wheel's rotational speed. The sensors operate on a magnetic induction principle. For example, as the teeth on the speed indicator ring rotate past a stationary sensor, a signal, proportional to the speed sensor rotation, is generated and transmitted to the ABS module (ECU) through a coaxial cable.

The front wheel sensors are attached to the suspension knuckles and the front speed indicators are pressed onto the outer constant velocity joints. The rear wheel sensors are attached to the rear caliper adapter plates, and the rear speed indicator rings are pressed onto the rear hub assemblies.

PEDAL TRAVEL SWITCH

This system uses a pedal travel switch which monitors brake pedal travel and sends information to the ABS module (ECU) through the wiring harness. Switch adjustment is critical to pedal feel during ABS cycling. The switch is mounted on the right side of the brake pedal support, near the dump valve adapter bracket.

The switch is normally closed. When brake pedal travel exceeds the switch setting during an anti-lock stop, the electronic controller senses the switch is open and grounds the pump motor relay coil. This energizes the relay and turns the pump motor on. When the pump motor is running, the master cylinder fills with high pressure brake fluid, pushing the brake pedal up until the switch closes. When the switch closes, the pump turns off and the pedal drops with each ABS control cycle until the travel switch re-opens and the pump is turned back on. This minimizes pedal feedback during ABS cycling.

If the pedal travel switch is not adjusted properly or is not electrically connected, it will cause an incorrect pedal feel during ABS stops. Some problems with the switch or its installation will result in the pump running during an entire ABS stop. The pedal will become very firm, pushing the driver's foot up to a very high position.

DTCS	DTC Caused By	Description	Action
B1342	ABS/TC	ECU Is Defective	REPLACE the anti-lock brake control module.
B1485	ABS/TC	Brake Pedal Input Circuit Short to Battery	GO to Pinpoint Test D.
B1676	ABS/TC	Battery Voltage Out of Range	GO to Pinpoint Test E.
C1095	ABS/TC	ABS Hydraulic Pump Motor Circuit Failure	GO to Pinpoint Test A.
C1145	ABS/TC	RF Anti-Lock Brake Sensor Input Circuit Failure	GO to Pinpoint Test B.
C1155	ABS/TC	LF Anti-Lock Brake Sensor Input Circuit Failure	GO to Pinpoint Test B.
C1165	ABS/TC	RR Anti-Lock Brake Sensor Input Circuit Failure	GO to Pinpoint Test B.
C1175	ABS/TC	LR Anti-Lock Brake Sensor Input Circuit Failure	GO to Pinpoint Test B.
C1233	ABS/TC	LF Anti-Lock Brake Sensor Input Signal Missing	GO to Pinpoint Test C.
C1234	ABS/TC	RF Anti-Lock Brake Sensor Input Signal Missing	GO to Pinpoint Test C.
C1235	ABS/TC	RR Anti-Lock Brake Sensor Input Signal Missing	GO to Pinpoint Test C.
C1236	ABS/TC	LR Anti-Lock Brake Sensor Input Signal Missing	GO to Pinpoint Test C.
U1009	PCM	SCP Invalid or Missing Data for Engine Torque	PERFORM the PCM Self-Test.
U1027	PCM	SCP Invalid or Missing Data for Engine RPM	PERFORM the PCM Self-Test.
U1041	HEC, DDM, LCM, EATC, Air Suspension Control Module, Speed Control Servo	SCP Invalid or Missing Data for Vehicle Speed	PERFORM the HEC Self-Test. PERFORM the DDM Self-Test. PERFORM the LCM Self-Test. PERFORM the EATC Self-Test. PERFORM the Air Suspension Control Module Self-Test. PERFORM the Speed Control Servo Self-Test.
U1043	HEC	SCP Invalid or Missing Data for Traction Control	PERFORM the HEC Self-Test.
U1059	PCM	SCP Invalid or Missing Data for Transmission/Transaxle/PRNDL	PERFORM the PCM Self-Test.
U1123	HEC, Air Suspension Control Module	SCP Invalid or Missing Data for Odometer	PERFORM the HEC Self-Test. PERFORM the Air Suspension Control Module Self-Test.

FM4029801304000X

Fig. 3 Diagnostic trouble code interpretation. 2000 Town Car

DTCS	DTC Caused By	Description	Action
B1342	ABS/TC	ECU Is Defective	INSTALL a new anti-lock brake control module.
B1484	ABS/TC	Brake Pedal Input Open Circuit	GO to PINPOINT TEST D.
B1676	ABS/TC	Battery Voltage Out of Range	GO to PINPOINT TEST E.
C1300	ABS/TC	ABS Hydraulic Pump Motor Circuit Failure	GO to PINPOINT TEST A.
C1145	ABS/TC	RF Anti-Lock Brake Sensor Input Circuit Failure	GO to PINPOINT TEST B.
C1155	ABS/TC	LF Anti-Lock Brake Sensor Input Circuit Failure	GO to PINPOINT TEST B.
C1165	ABS/TC	RR Anti-Lock Brake Sensor Input Circuit Failure	GO to PINPOINT TEST B.
C1175	ABS/TC	LR Anti-Lock Brake Sensor Input Circuit Failure	GO to PINPOINT TEST B.
C1296	ABS/TC	LF Anti-Lock Brake Sensor Input Signal Missing	GO to PINPOINT TEST C.
C1297	ABS/TC	RF Anti-Lock Brake Sensor Input Signal Missing	GO to PINPOINT TEST C.
C1298	ABS/TC	RR Anti-Lock Brake Sensor Input Signal Missing	GO to PINPOINT TEST C.
C1299	ABS/TC	LR Anti-Lock Brake Sensor Input Signal Missing	GO to PINPOINT TEST C.
C1222	Wheel Tone Ring	Mismatched Wheels or Damaged Tone Ring	Make sure the tires are the same size and correctly inflated. INSPECT the tone rings.
C1805	Data Received by ABS Module Not as Expected	PCM and ABS/TC Modules Do Not Match	CHECK the part numbers. INSTALL the correct module.
C1266	ABS/TC	ABS Valve Power Relay Circuit Failure	INSTALL a new hydraulic control unit (HCU). REPEAT the self-test.
U1009	PCM	SCP Invalid or Missing Data for Engine Torque	CARRY OUT the PCM Self-Test.
U1262	HEC	SCP Invalid or Missing Data for Traction Control	CARRY OUT the HEC Self-Test.

FM4020101775000X

Fig. 4 Diagnostic trouble code interpretation. Marauder & 2001–04 Crown Victoria, Grand Marquis & Town Car

Operation

ANTI-LOCK BRAKES

When brakes are applied, fluid is forced from the master cylinder outlet ports to the Hydraulic Control Unit (HCU) inlet ports. This pressure is transmitted through four normally open solenoid valves contained inside the HCU, then through outlet ports of the HCU to each wheel. The primary (rear) circuit of the master cylinder feeds the right front and left rear brakes. The secondary (front) circuit feeds the left front and right rear brakes.

When the ABS module (ECU) senses wheel lock conditions based on wheel speed sensor data, it pulses against the normally open solenoid valve, closing the circuit. This prevents any more fluid from entering the circuit. The ABS module (ECU) senses the wheel again. If the wheel is still decelerating, the module pulses the normally closed valve open, decreasing the pressure trapped inline.

The ABS module (ECU) monitors the electro-mechanical components of the system. An anti-lock brake system fault will cause the module to shut off or inhibit the anti-lock function, while retaining the normal power assisted braking. Faults are indicated by one or two warning lamps inside the vehicle.

Loss of hydraulic fluid in the HCU reservoir will disable the anti-lock brake system.

The four wheel anti-lock brake system is self-monitoring. When the ignition switch is turned to the RUN position, the ABS module (ECU) will perform a preliminary self-check on the anti-lock electrical system, indicated by a three or four second illumination of the amber "Check Anti-Lock Brakes" lamp on the instrument cluster. During vehicle operation, including normal and anti-lock braking, the ABS module (ECU) monitors all electrical anti-lock functions and some hydraulic system operation.

For most faults of the anti-lock brake system, the amber "Check Anti-Lock Brakes" and/or the red "Brake" lamp will be illuminated. The sequence of illumination of these warning lamps, combined with the problem symptoms, can determine the appropriate diagnostic test to perform. Most faults are recorded as a coded number in the controller memory, pinpointing the exact component requiring service.

Traction Assist

Traction Assist (TA) is designed to control wheel spin when accelerating on loose or slippery surfaces. During acceleration, if one or both rear wheels lose traction and begin to spin, the TA system will rapidly apply and release the appropriate rear brake to reduce wheel spin and aid traction. The accompanying isolation valve will also close and the ABS pump will run. The isolation valve permits brake operation only to the rear brake of the circuit by closing off pressure to the front brake.

If brakes are applied during TA operation, the ABS module receives a signal from the stop lamp switch or the pressure switch and automatically stops TA cycling.

TROUBLESHOOTING

Pre-Test Checks

1. Verify parking brake is completely released. If parking brake is applied, "Brake" lamp will be illuminated.
2. Inspect brake fluid. **As fluid level drops, red "Brake" lamp will illuminate. If fluid level continues to fall, amber "Check Anti-Lock Brake" lamp will illuminate and anti-lock function will be inhibited.**
3. Verify all of the following connectors are properly connected and in good operating condition:
    a. Connector of the computer module.
    b. Connector of HCU valve body.
    c. Connectors of pump motor relay.
    d. Connector of master cylinder reservoir.
    e. Connector of HCU reservoir.
    f. Connector of main power relay.
    g. Connector of each wheel sensor.
    h. Connector of pedal travel switch.
    i. Connector of stop lamp switch.
4. Inspect fuses and diode for damage.
5. Ensure all battery connections are clean and tight.
6. Inspect ground connections for anti-lock system located near computer module and pump.

Item to be Tested	Ignition Switch Position	EEC-IV 60-Pin Breakout Box Pins	Tester Scale/ Range	Specification	Action
Battery Power	OFF or ON	9 and 8 25 and 24	DC Volts DC Volts	10 V min. 10 V min.	GO to Pinpoint Test F. GO to Pinpoint Test F.
Ignition Feed	OFF ON	23 and 8 23 and 8	DC Volts DC Volts	0 V 10 V min.	GO to Pinpoint Test F. GO to Pinpoint Test F.
LF Sensor Resistance	OFF	4 and 11	K Ohms	0.8-1.4 K Ohms	GO to Pinpoint Test B.
RF Sensor Resistance	OFF	3 and 18	K Ohms	0.8-1.4 K Ohms	GO to Pinpoint Test B.

FM4029801305010X

Fig. 5 Quick check (Part 1 of 2). 2000 Crown Victoria, Grand Marquis & Town Car

Item to be Tested	Ignition Switch Position	EEC-IV 60-Pin Breakout Box Pins	Tester Scale/ Range	Specification	Action
LR Sensor Resistance	OFF	10 and 2	K Ohms	0.8-1.4 K Ohms	GO to Pinpoint Test B.
RR Sensor Resistance	OFF	17 and 1	K Ohms	0.8-1.4 K Ohms	GO to Pinpoint Test B.
Sensor Continuity To Ground					
LF	OFF	4 and 8	Continuity	No Continuity	GO to Pinpoint Test B.
RF	OFF	3 and 8	Continuity	No Continuity	GO to Pinpoint Test B.
LR	OFF	10 and 8	Continuity	No Continuity	GO to Pinpoint Test B.
RR	OFF	17 and 8	Continuity	No Continuity	GO to Pinpoint Test B.
Sensor voltage: Rotate wheel @ one revolution per second					
LF	OFF	4 and 11	AC mVolts	100-3500 mV	GO to Pinpoint Test C.
RF	OFF	3 and 18	AC mVolts	100-3500 mV	GO to Pinpoint Test C.
LR	OFF	10 and 2	AC mVolts	100-3500 mV	GO to Pinpoint Test C.
RR	OFF	17 and 1	AC mVolts	100-3500 mV	GO to Pinpoint Test C.

FM4029801305020X

Fig. 5 Quick check (Part 2 of 2). 2000 Crown Victoria, Grand Marquis & Town Car

Item to be Tested	Ignition Switch Position	EEC-IV 60-Pin Breakout Box Pins	Tester Scale/ Range	Specification	Action
Battery Power	OFF or ON	12 and 13 15 and 14	DC Volts DC Volts	10 V min. 10 V min.	GO to PINPOINT TEST F. GO to PINPOINT TEST F.
Ignition Feed	OFF ON	15 and 8 15 and 8	DC Volts DC Volts	0 V 10 V min.	GO to PINPOINT TEST F. GO to PINPOINT TEST F.
LF Sensor Resistance	OFF	20 and 21	K Ohms	0.8-1.4 K Ohms	GO to PINPOINT TEST B.
RF Sensor Resistance	OFF	4 and 5	K Ohms	0.8-1.4 K Ohms	GO to PINPOINT TEST B.
LR Sensor Resistance (Drum/Disc)	OFF	22 and 23	K Ohms	0.8-1.4 K Ohms/1.3-1.9 K Ohms	GO to PINPOINT TEST B.
RR Sensor Resistance (Drum/Disc)	OFF	3 and 1	K Ohms	0.8-1.4 K Ohms/1.3-1.9 K Ohms	GO to PINPOINT TEST B.
Sensor Continuity To Ground					
LF	OFF	20 and 15	Continuity	No Continuity	GO to PINPOINT TEST B.
RF	OFF	4 and 15	Continuity	No Continuity	GO to PINPOINT TEST B.

FM4020001624010X

Fig. 6 Quick check (Part 1 of 2). Marauder & 2001–04 Crown Victoria, Grand Marquis & Town Car

Item to be Tested	Ignition Switch Position	EEC-IV 60-Pin Breakout Box Pins	Tester Scale/ Range	Specification	Action
LR	OFF	22 and 15	Continuity	No Continuity	GO to PINPOINT TEST B.
RR	OFF	1 and 15	Continuity	No Continuity	GO to PINPOINT TEST B.
Sensor voltage: Rotate wheel @ one revolution per second					
LF	OFF	20 and 21	ACmVolts	100-3500 mV	GO to PINPOINT TEST C.
RF	OFF	4 and 5	ACmVolts	100-3500 mV	GO to PINPOINT TEST C.
LR	OFF	22 and 23	ACmVolts	100-3500 mV	GO to PINPOINT TEST C.
RR	OFF	3 and 1	ACmVolts	100-3500 mV	GO to PINPOINT TEST C.

FM4020001624020X

Fig. 6 Quick check (Part 2 of 2). Marauder 2001–04 Crown Victoria, Grand Marquis & Town Car

DIAGNOSIS & TESTING

Diagnostic Procedure

Ensure the following diagnosis procedures are used in the sequence and step-by-step order indicated. Following the wrong sequence or bypassing steps will only lead to unrequired replacement of system components and/or incorrect resolution of the problem. The diagnostic procedure consists of five sub-tests: Pre-test Checks, On-Board Self-Tests, Manual Quick Tests, Warning Lamp Symptom Chart and the Diagnostic Tests.

Accessing Diagnostic Trouble Codes

The anti-lock brake/traction assist electronic control module is capable of performing a self-test using New Generation Star (NGS) tester 007-00500, or equivalent, scan tool.

The anti-lock control module monitors system operation and stores all defined diagnostic trouble codes in its memory. It is important to understand the control module cannot recognize some failures. Therefore, if a problem exists and no diagnostic trouble codes are stored by the control module, other diagnostic steps must be followed. The module cannot store a diagnostic trouble code if there is no power to the module. This diagnostic trouble code can be found by using Quick-Check Tests.

1. Connect New Generation Star (NGS) tester to Data Link Connector (DLC) located under instrument panel.
2. Plug NGS into cigarette lighter.
3. Turn ignition switch to Run position.
4. Follow instructions on tester screen and record all diagnostic trouble codes.
5. Refer to "Diagnostic Trouble Code Interpretation" for DTC's. Any DTC preceded by "U" indicates a fault with the Powertrain Control Module (PCM).
6. If NGS reports "System Passed," proceed to Anti-Lock Quick Tests Checks.

Diagnostic Trouble Code Interpretation

Refer to **Figs. 2 through 4,** for diagnostic trouble code interpretation.

Quick Checks

To properly conduct Quick Checks, an EEC-IV breakout box tool No. T83L-50-EEC-IV, anti-lock harness adapter tool No. T90P-50-ALA and digital volt/ohmmeter tool No. 007-00001, or equivalents, must be used. This group of tests will lead to specific diagnostic Pinpoint Tests that will, in most cases, identify the fault. If fault is not determined by the Quick Check procedure, use the following Diagnostic Lamp Symptom Chart to identify the proper diagnostic procedure to use.

Refer to Quick Check, **Figs. 5 and 6,** for items to be tested, ignition switch mode position, measurement taken between terminal pin numbers, tester scale/range, volt/ohm specifications and the specific pinpoint test to correct the fault.

Wiring Diagrams

CROWN VICTORIA, GRAND MARQUIS & MARAUDER

Refer to **Figs. 7 through 11,** for wiring diagrams.

TOWN CAR

Refer to **Figs. 12 through 15,** for wiring diagrams.

Pinpoint Tests

CROWN VICTORIA, GRAND MARQUIS & MARAUDER

2000

Refer to **Fig. 16,** for symptom chart and **Figs. 17 through 29,** for diagnosis and testing.

2001

Refer to **Fig. 30,** for symptom chart and **Figs. 31 through 43,** for diagnosis and testing.

2002

Refer to **Fig. 44,** for symptom chart and **Figs. 45 through 58,** for diagnosis and testing.

2003-04

Refer to **Fig. 59,** for symptom chart and **Figs. 60 through 70,** for diagnosis and testing.

TOWN CAR

2000

Refer to **Fig. 71,** for symptom chart and **Figs. 72 through 84,** for diagnosis and testing.

2001

Refer to "2001 Crown Victoria, Grand Marquis & Marauder" for pinpoint tests.

2002

Refer to "2002 Crown Victoria, Grand Marquis & Marauder" for pinpoint tests.

2003-04

Refer to "2003–04 Crown Victoria, Grand Marquis & Marauder" for pinpoint tests.

Clearing Diagnostic Trouble Codes

The original error diagnostic trouble codes in the computer from the assembly plant will erase automatically if everything is in working order and vehicle is driven about (25 mph). All error diagnostic trouble codes must be output, all faults corrected (anti-lock lamp off), and vehicle driven (25 mph) before memory will clear. NGS tester can also be used to erase DTCs.

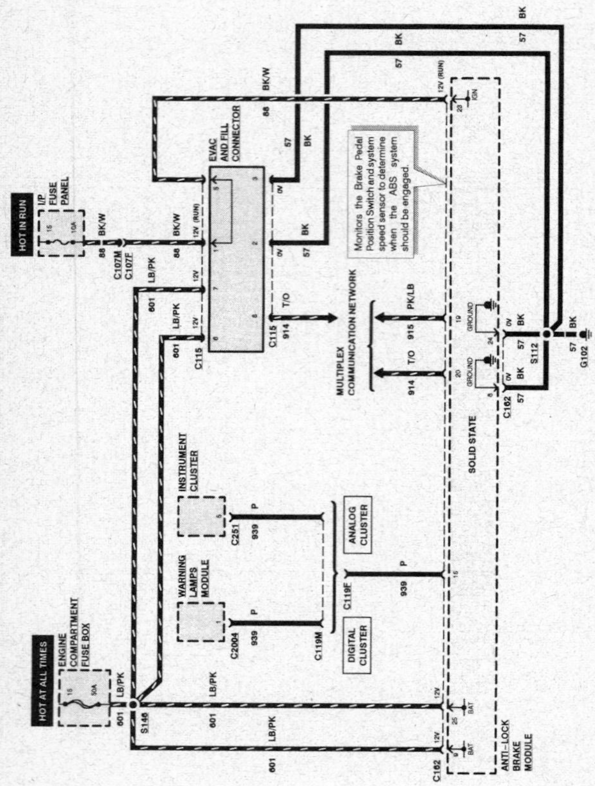

FM4029801247000X

Fig. 7 Wiring diagram. 2000 Crown Victoria & Grand Marquis less traction assist

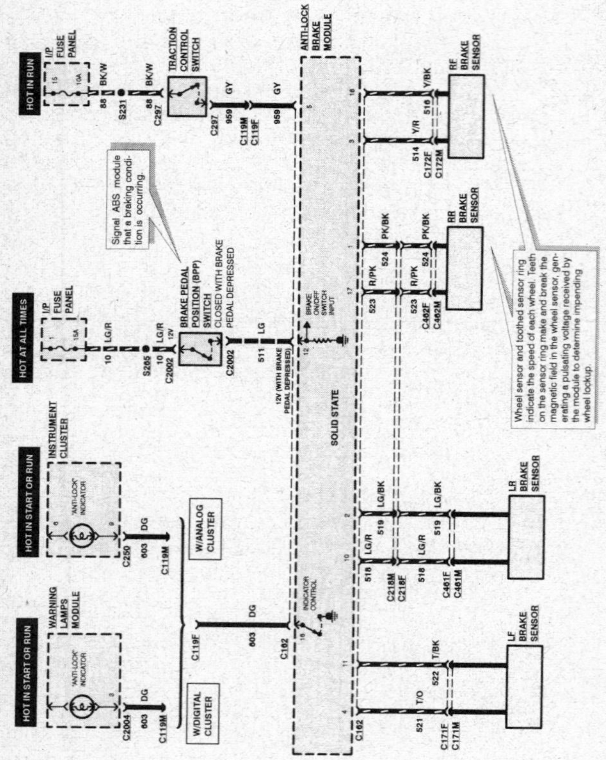

FM4029801248000X

Fig. 8 Wiring diagram. 2000 Crown Victoria & Grand Marquis w/traction assist

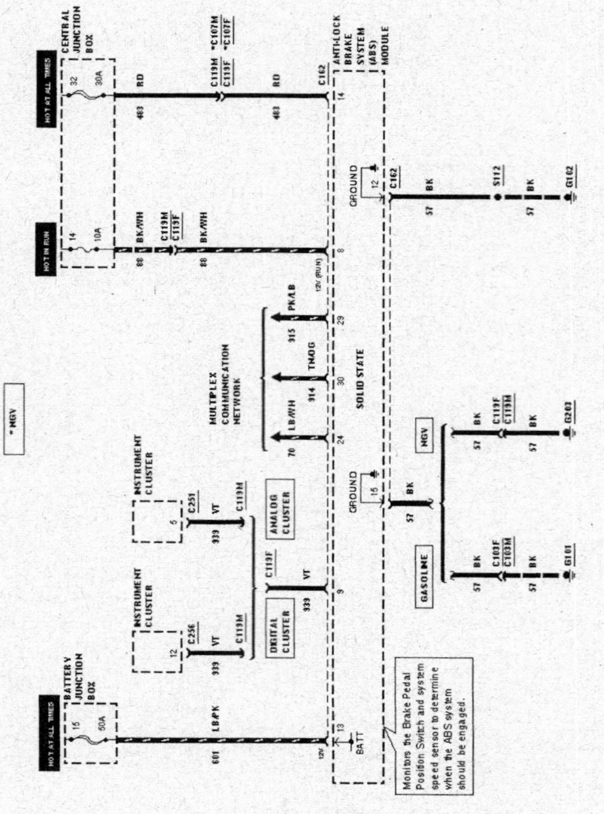

FM4020001625010X

Fig. 9 Wiring diagram (Part 1 of 2). 2001 Crown Victoria & Grand Marquis

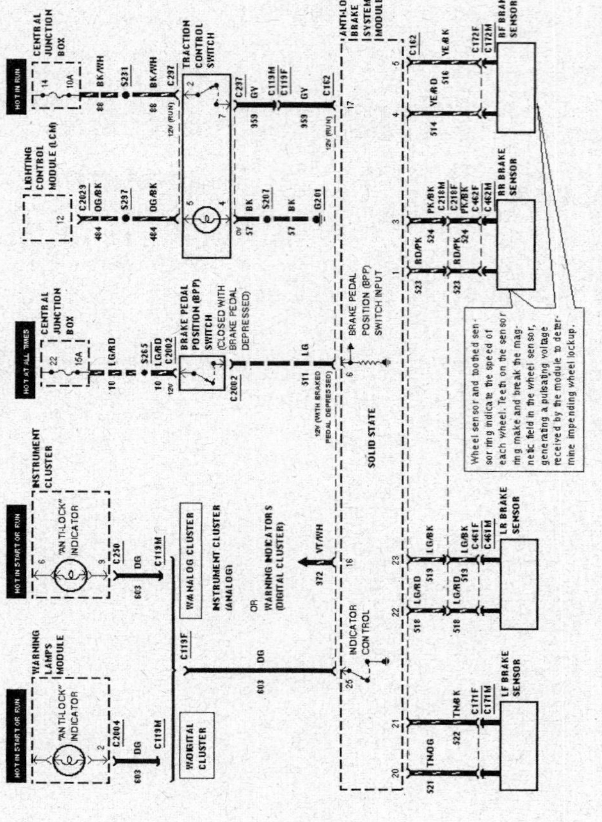

FM4020001625020X

Fig. 9 Wiring diagram (Part 2 of 2). 2001 Crown Victoria & Grand Marquis

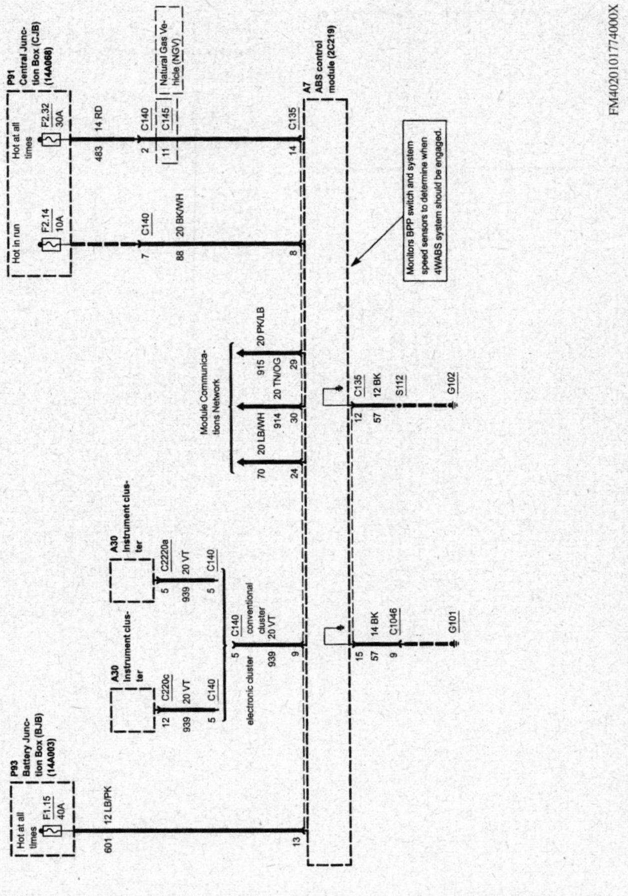

Fig. 10 Wiring diagram (Part 1 of 2). 2002 Crown Victoria & Grand Marquis

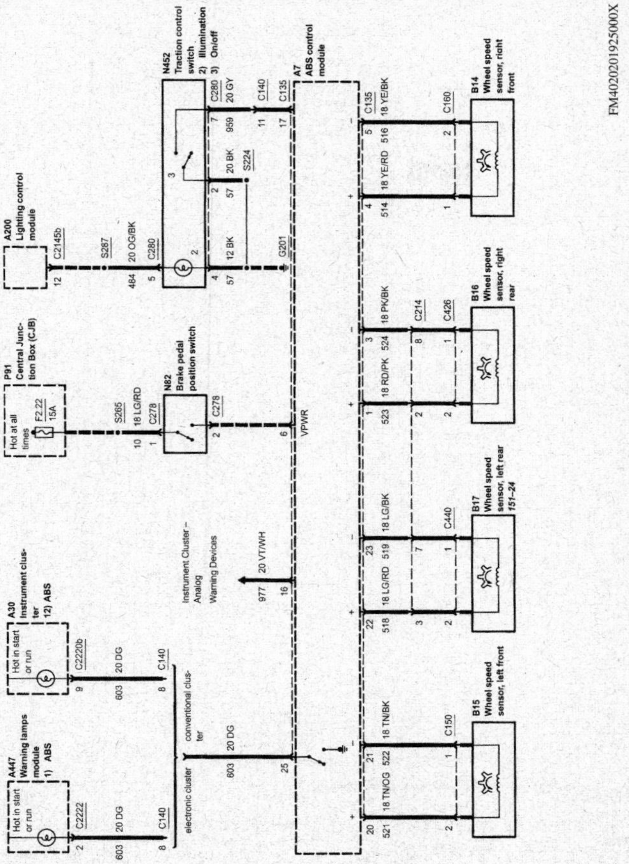

Fig. 10 Wiring diagram (Part 2 of 2). 2002 Crown Victoria & Grand Marquis

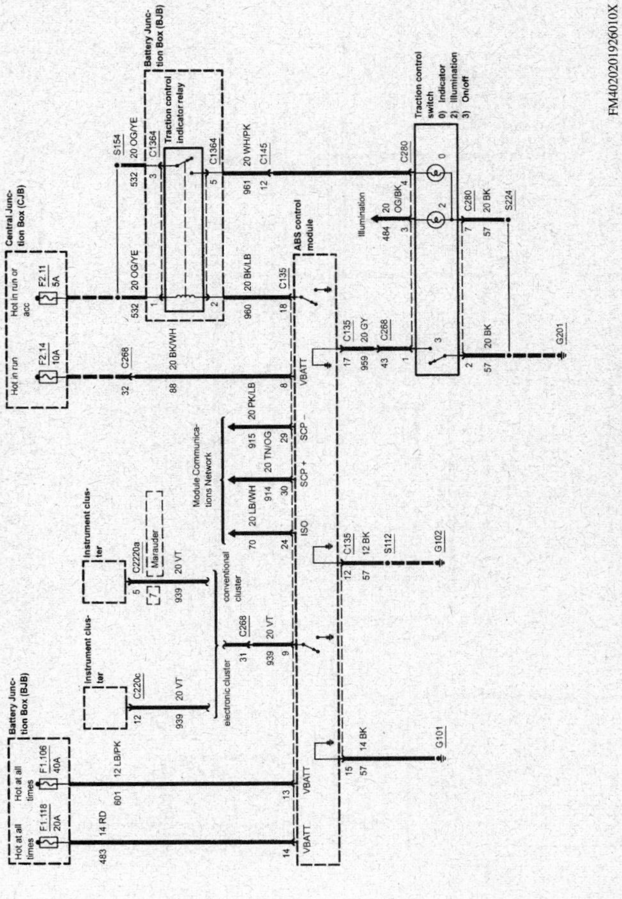

Fig. 11 Wiring diagram (Part 1 of 2). 2003–04 Crown Victoria, Grand Marquis & Marauder

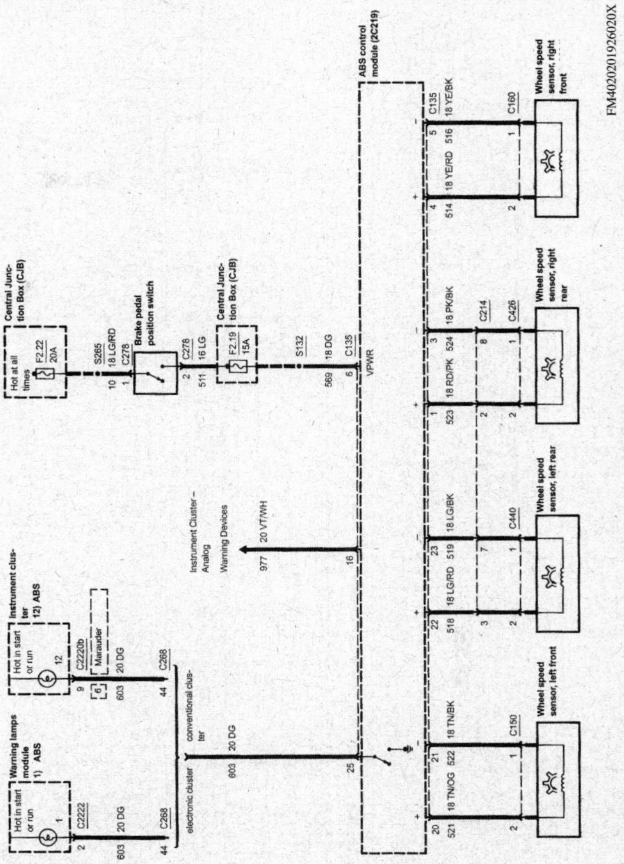

Fig. 11 Wiring diagram (Part 2 of 2). 2003–04 Crown Victoria, Grand Marquis & Marauder

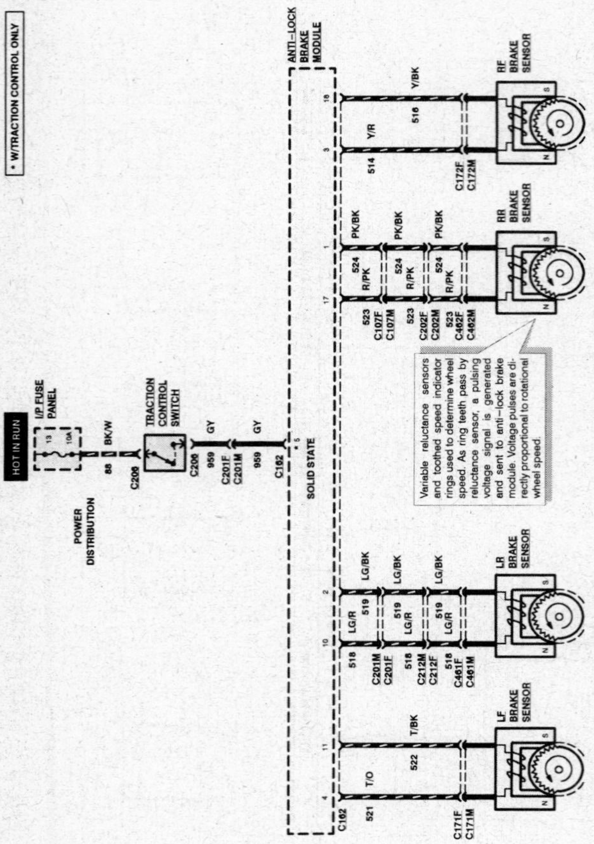

FM4029801252020X

Fig. 12 Wiring diagram (Part 2 of 2). 2000 Town Car

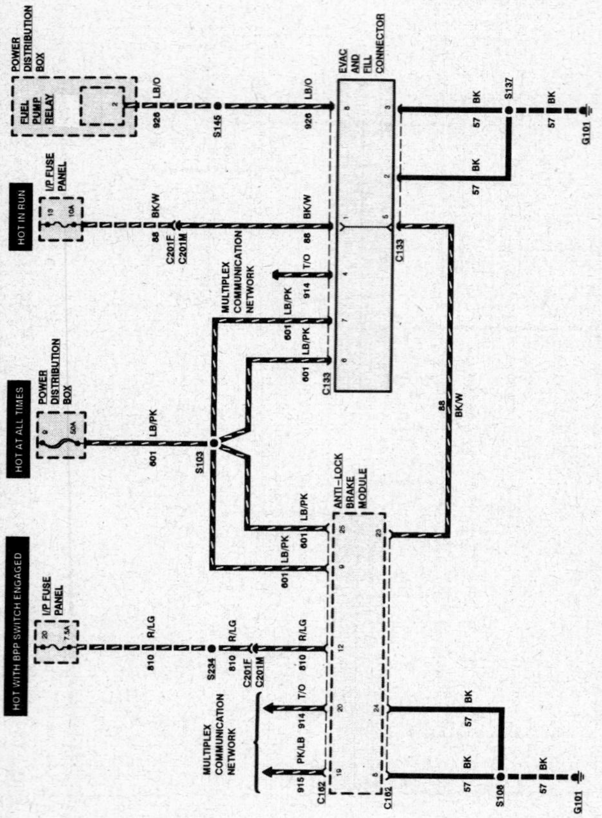

FM4029801252010X

Fig. 12 Wiring diagram (Part 1 of 2). 2000 Town Car

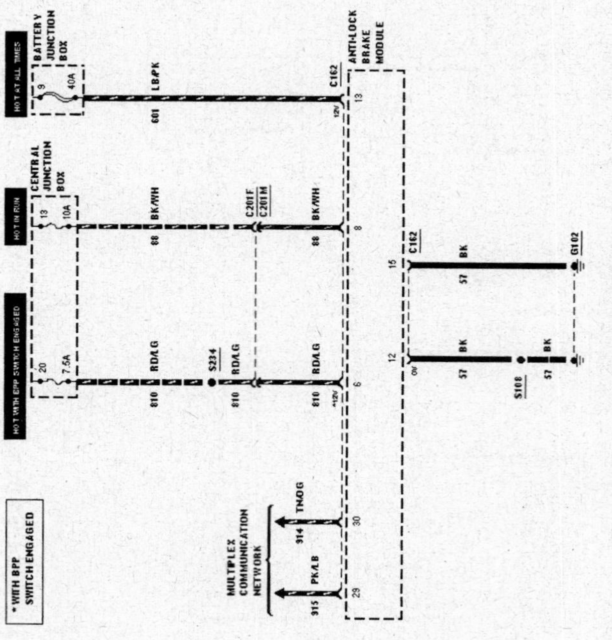

FM4020001639010X

Fig. 13 Wiring diagram (Part 1 of 2). 2001 Town Car

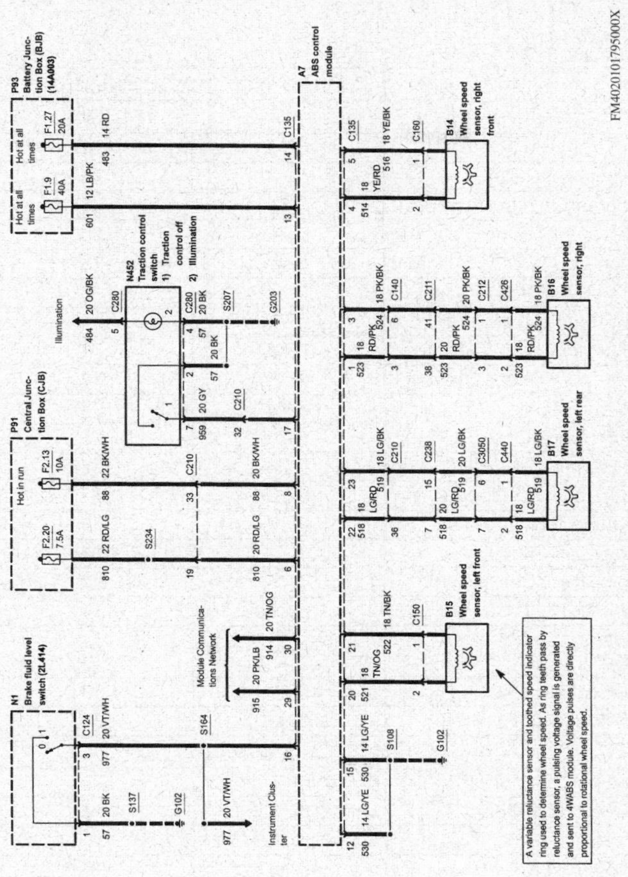

Fig. 14 Wiring diagram. 2002 Town Car

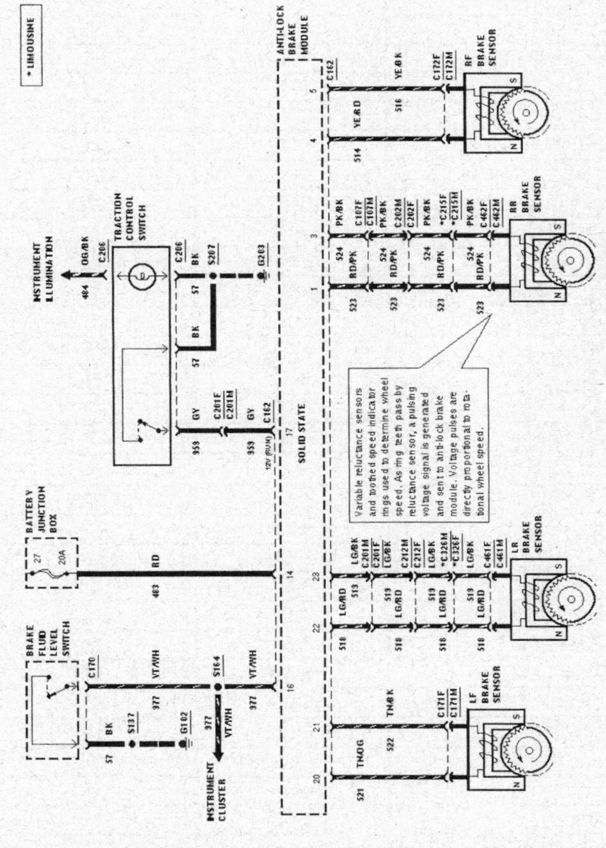

Fig. 13 Wiring diagram (Part 2 of 2). 2001 Town Car

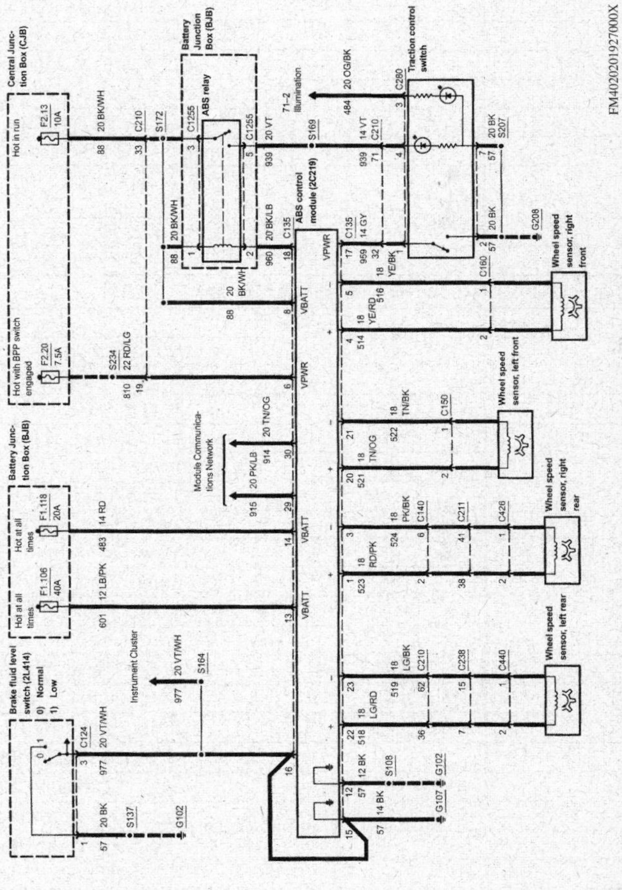

Fig. 15 Wiring diagram. 2003–04 Town Car

DIAGNOSTIC CHART INDEX

Test	Code	Description	Page No.	Fig. No.
2000 TOWN CAR				
—	—	Symptom Chart	6-73	71
A	C1095	ABS Hydraulic Pump Motor Circuit Failure	6-73	72
B	C1145	Righthand Front Anti-Lock Brake Sensor Input Circuit Failure	6-74	73
	C1155	Lefthand Front Anti-Lock Brake Sensor Input Circuit Failure	6-74	73
	C1165	Righthand Rear Anti-Lock Brake Sensor Input Circuit Failure	6-74	73
	C1175	Lefthand Rear Anti-Lock Brake Sensor Input Circuit Failure	6-74	73
C	C1233	Lefthand Front Anti-Lock Brake Sensor Input Signal Missing	6-75	74
	C1234	Righthand Front Anti-Lock Brake Sensor Input Signal Missing	6-75	74
	C1235	Righthand Rear Anti-Lock Brake Sensor Input Signal Missing	6-75	74
	C1236	Lefthand Rear Anti-Lock Brake Sensor Input Signal Missing	6-75	74
D	B1485	Brake Pedal Input Circuit Short To Battery	6-75	75
E	B1676	Battery Voltage Out Of Range	6-76	76
F	—	No Communication w/Anti-Lock Brake Control Module	6-76	77
G	—	Spongy Brake Pedal w/No Warning Indicator	6-77	78
H	—	Poor Vehicle Tracking During Anti-Lock Function	6-77	79
J	—	Traction Control Is Inoperative	6-78	80
K	—	Yellow ABS Warning Indicator Does Not Self Check	6-79	81
L	—	Yellow ABS Warning Indicator & Traction Control Active Indicator Always On	6-79	82
M	—	Traction Control Cannot Be Disabled	6-79	83
N	—	No Communication w/Hybrid Electronic Cluster Module	6-80	84
2000 CROWN VICTORIA & GRAND MARQUIS				
—	—	Symptom Chart	6-46	16
A	—	No Communication w/ABS Control Module	6-46	17
B	—	Unable To Enter Self Test	6-46	18
C	C1095	Hydraulic Pump Motor Circuit Failure	6-46	19
D	C1145	Righthand Front Brake Sensor Input Circuit Failure	6-47	20
	C1155	Lefthand Front Brake Sensor Input Circuit Failure	6-47	20
	C1165	Righthand Rear Brake Sensor Input Circuit Failure	6-47	20
	C1175	Lefthand Rear Brake Sensor Input Circuit Failure	6-47	20
E	C1233	Lefthand Front Brake Sensor Input Signal Missing	6-48	21
	C1234	Righthand Front Brake Sensor Input Signal Missing	6-48	21
	C1235	Righthand Rear Brake Sensor Input Signal Missing	6-48	21
	C1236	Lefthand Rear Brake Sensor Input Signal Missing	6-48	21
F	B1485	Brake Pedal Input Circuit Short To Battery	6-49	22
G	B1676	Battery Voltage Out Of Range	6-49	23
H	—	Spongy Brake Pedal, No Indicator Illuminated	6-50	24
I	—	Poor Vehicle Tracking During Anti-Lock Function	6-50	25
J	—	Traction Control Inoperative	6-51	26
K	—	Yellow ABS Indicator Does Not Self-Check	6-52	27
L	—	Yellow ABS Indicator Always Illuminated	6-52	28
M	—	Traction Control Cannot Be Disabled	6-53	29
2001 CROWN VICTORIA, GRAND MARQUIS & TOWN CAR				
—	—	Symptom Chart	6-53	30
A	C1300	ABS Hydraulic Pump Motor Circuit Failure	6-53	31
B	C1145	Righthand Front ABS Sensor Input Circuit Failure	6-54	32
	C1155	Lefthand Front ABS Sensor Input Circuit Failure	6-54	32
	C1165	Righthand Rear ABS Sensor Input Circuit Failure	6-54	32
	C1175	Lefthand Rear ABS Sensor Input Circuit Failure	6-54	32
C	C1296	Lefthand Front ABS Sensor Input Signal Missing	6-55	33
	C1297	Righthand Front ABS Sensor Input Signal Missing	6-55	33
	C1298	Righthand Rear ABS Sensor Input Signal Missing	6-55	33
	C1299	Lefthand Rear ABS Sensor Input Signal Missing	6-55	33
D	B1484	Brake Pedal Input Circuit Open	6-55	34
E	B1676	Battery Voltage Out Of Range	6-56	35
F	—	No Communications w/ABS Control Module	6-56	36

Continued

DIAGNOSTIC CHART INDEX—Continued

Test	Code	Description	Page No.	Fig. No.
2001 CROWN VICTORIA, GRAND MARQUIS & TOWN CAR				
G	—	Spongy Brake Pedal w/No Warning Indicator	6-57	37
H	—	Improper Vehicle Tracking During ABS Operation	6-57	38
J	—	Traction Control Cannot Be Disabled	6-59	39
K	—	Yellow ABS Indicator Does Not Self-Check	6-59	40
L	—	Yellow ABS Indicator & Traction Control Active Indicator Always On	6-59	41
M	—	Traction Control Inoperative	6-60	42
N	—	No Communication w/Hybrid Electronic Cluster	6-60	43
2002 CROWN VICTORIA, GRAND MARQUIS & TOWN CAR				
—	—	Symptom Chart	6-61	44
A	C1300	ABS Hydraulic Pump Motor Circuit Failure	6-61	45
B	C1145	Righthand Front ABS Sensor Input Circuit Failure	6-62	46
	C1155	Lefthand Front ABS Sensor Input Circuit Failure	6-62	46
	C1165	Righthand Rear ABS Sensor Input Circuit Failure	6-62	46
	C1175	Lefthand Rear ABS Sensor Input Circuit Failure	6-62	46
C	C1296	Lefthand Front ABS Sensor Input Signal Missing	6-63	47
	C1297	Righthand Front ABS Sensor Input Signal Missing	6-63	47
	C1298	Righthand Rear ABS Sensor Input Signal Missing	6-63	47
	C1299	Lefthand Rear ABS Sensor Input Signal Missing	6-63	47
D	B1484	Brake Pedal Input Open Circuit (Crown Victoria & Grand Marquis)	6-63	48
		Brake Pedal Input Open Circuit (Town Car)	6-64	49
E	B1676	Battery Voltage Out Of Range	6-64	50
F	—	No Communication w/Module – ABS Brake Control Module	6-64	51
G	—	Spongy Brake Pedal w/No Warning Indicator	6-65	52
H	—	Poor Vehicle Tracking During ABS Function	6-65	53
I	—	Traction Control Cannot Be Disabled/Is Inoperative	6-66	54
J	—	Yellow ABS Warning Indicator Does Not Self-Check	6-67	55
K	—	Yellow ABS Warning Indicator & Traction Control Active Indicator Always On	6-67	56
L	—	No Communication w/Module-Hybrid Electronic Cluster (HEC, Crown Victoria & Grand Marquis)	6-67	57
	—	No Communication w/Module-Hybrid Electronic Cluster (HEC, Town Car)	6-68	58
2003–04 CROWN VICTORIA, GRAND MARQUIS, MARAUDER & TOWN CAR				
—	—	Symptom Chart	6-69	59
A	C1300	ABS Hydraulic Pump Motor Circuit Failure	6-69	60
B	C1145	Righthand Front ABS Brake Sensor Input Circuit Failure	6-69	61
	C1155	Lefthand Front ABS Brake Sensor Input Circuit Failure	6-69	61
	C1165	Righthand Rear ABS Brake Sensor Input Circuit Failure	6-69	61
	C1175	Lefthand Rear ABS Brake Sensor Input Circuit Failure	6-69	61
C	C1296	Lefthand Front ABS Sensor Input Signal Missing	6-70	62
	C1297	Righthand Front ABS Sensor Input Signal Missing	6-70	62
	C1298	Righthand Rear ABS Sensor Input Signal Missing	6-70	62
	C1299	Lefthand Rear ABS Sensor Input Signal Missing	6-70	62
D	B1484	Brake Pedal Open Circuit	6-70	63
E	B1676	Battery Voltage Out Of Range	6-71	64
F	—	No Communication w/ABS Module	6-71	65
G	—	Poor Vehicle Tracking During ABS Function	6-71	66
H	—	Traction Control Inop/Cannot Be Disabled	6-72	67
I	—	Yellow ABS Warning Indicator Does Not Self Check	6-72	68
J	—	Yellow ABS Warning Indicator & Traction Control Active Indicator Always On	6-72	69
K	—	No Communication w/Hybrid Electronic Cluster	6-73	70

Condition	Possible Source	Action
• No communication with the anti-lock brake control module	• CJB Fuse 10 (15A). • Battery junction box (BJB) Fuse 15 (50A). • Anti-lock brake control module. • Circuit.	• GO to Pinpoint Test A.
• Unable to enter self-test	• Anti-lock brake control module.	• GO to Pinpoint Test B.
• Spongy brake pedal with no warning indicator	• Air in brake hydraulic system.	• GO to Pinpoint Test H.
• Poor vehicle tracking during anti-lock function	• Air in brake hydraulic system. • Hydraulic control unit (HCU). • Base brake system.	• GO to Pinpoint Test I.
• The traction control is inoperative	• Anti-lock brake control module. • Hydraulic control unit (HCU). • Base brake system. • Thermal model (will reset after brakes cool down).	• GO to Pinpoint Test J.
• The yellow ABS warning indicator does not self-check	• Circuit. • Instrument cluster. • Anti-lock brake control module.	• GO to Pinpoint Test K.
• The yellow ABS warning indicator is always on	• Circuit. • Instrument cluster. • Anti-lock brake control module.	• GO to Pinpoint Test L.
• The traction control cannot be disabled	• Circuit. • Traction control switch. • Anti-lock brake control module.	• GO to Pinpoint Test M.

FM4020005001000X

Fig. 16 Symptom Chart. 2000 Crown Victoria & Grand Marquis

TEST CONDITIONS	TEST DETAILS/RESULTS/ACTIONS
B1 CHECK THE COMMUNICATIONS TO THE ANTI-LOCK BRAKE CONTROL MODULE	
	1 Check the communication to the anti-lock brake control module. • Does NGS Tester communicate with the anti-lock brake control module? → **Yes** INSTALL a new anti-lock brake control module. REPEAT the self-test. → **No** GO to Pinpoint Test A.

FM4020005003000X

Fig. 18 Test B: Unable To Enter Self Test. 2000 Crown Victoria & Grand Marquis

TEST CONDITIONS	TEST DETAILS/RESULTS/ACTIONS
A1 CHECK CIRCUITS 601 (LB/PK) AND CIRCUIT 88 (BK/WH) FOR AN OPEN	
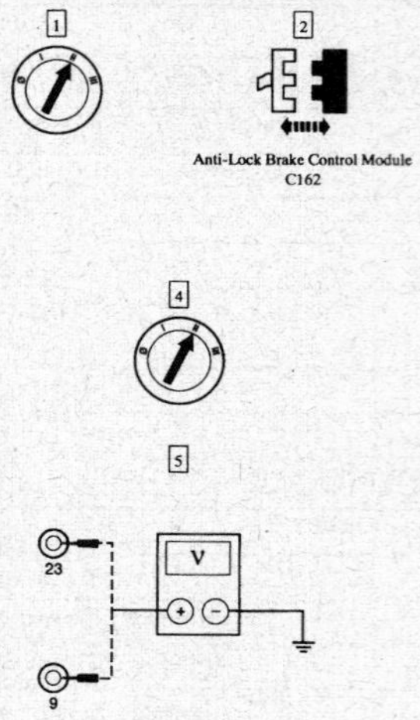	3 Connect EEC-IV 60-Pin Breakout Box. 5 Measure the voltage between EEC-IV 60-Pin Breakout Box Pin 23, Circuit 88 (BK/WH), and ground; and between EEC-IV 60-Pin Breakout Box Pin 9, Circuit 601 (LB/PK), and ground. • Are the voltages greater than 10 volts? → **Yes** GO to **A2**. → **No** REPAIR the circuit in question. REPEAT the self-test.
A2 CHECK CIRCUIT 57 (BK) FOR AN OPEN	
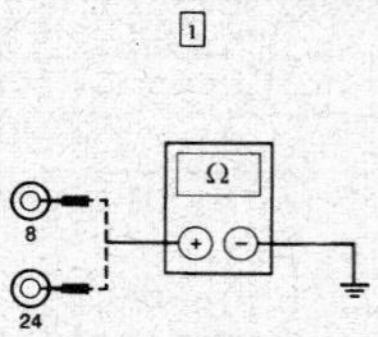	1 Measure the resistance between EEC-IV 60-Pin Breakout Box Pin 24, Circuit 57 (BK), and ground; and between EEC-IV 60-Pin Breakout Box Pin 8, Circuit 57 (BK), and ground. • Are the resistances less than 5 ohms? → **Yes** INSPECT electrical distribution. → **No** REPAIR the circuit. REPEAT the self-test.

FM4020005002000X

Fig. 17 Test A: No Communication w/ABS Control Module. 2000 Crown Victoria & Grand Marquis

TEST CONDITIONS	TEST DETAILS/RESULTS/ACTIONS
C1 CHECK ABS PUMP MOTOR	
	• Is the ABS pump motor running all the time? → **Yes** INSTALL a new anti-lock brake control module. REPEAT the self-test. → **No** GO to C2.

FM4020005004010X

Fig. 19 Test C/Code C1095: Hydraulic Pump Motor Circuit Failure (Part 1 of 4). 2000 Crown Victoria & Grand Marquis

TEST CONDITIONS	TEST DETAILS/RESULTS/ACTIONS
C2 CHECK PUMP OPERATION	
1 	2 Trigger the anti-lock brake control module active command PMP MOTOR ON. • Does the ABS pump motor run for approximately three seconds? → **Yes** CLEAR the DTC. CHECK the yellow ABS warning indicator while driving the vehicle above 32 kph (20 mph) and no brakes applied until the vehicle exceeds 32 kph (20 mph). If the yellow ABS warning indicator illuminates, INSTALL a new anti-lock brake control module. REPEAT the self-test. If the yellow ABS warning indicator does not illuminate, the system is OK. → **No** TRIGGER the anti-lock brake control module active command PMP MOTOR OFF. GO to **C3**.
C3 CHECK CIRCUIT 601 (LB/PK) FOR AN OPEN	
1  Anti-Lock Brake Control Module C162	2 Connect EEC-IV 60-Pin Breakout Box.

FM4020005004020X

Fig. 19 Test C/Code C1095: Hydraulic Pump Motor Circuit Failure (Part 2 of 4). 2000 Crown Victoria & Grand Marquis

TEST CONDITIONS	TEST DETAILS/RESULTS/ACTIONS
C5 CHECK THE PUMP MOTOR FOR PROPER OPERATION	
1  Pump Motor Connector 2 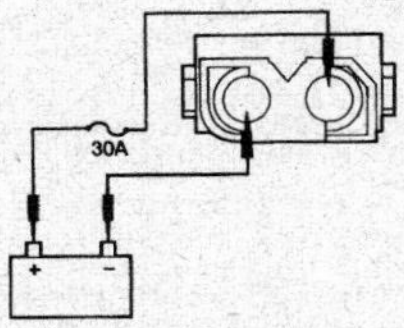	2 Use a heavy gauge jumper to connect a jumper between negative battery post and pump motor connector, brown wire; and momentarily connect a jumper between the positive battery post and pump motor connector, red wire with a 30A in-line fuse. • Does the pump motor run? → **Yes** INSTALL a new anti-lock brake control module. REPEAT the self-test. → **No** INSTALL a new HCU. CLEAR the DTCs. REPEAT the self-test.

FM4020005004040X

Fig. 19 Test C/Code C1095: Hydraulic Pump Motor Circuit Failure (Part 4 of 4). 2000 Crown Victoria & Grand Marquis

TEST CONDITIONS	TEST DETAILS/RESULTS/ACTIONS
C3 CHECK CIRCUIT 601 (LB/PK) FOR AN OPEN	
3 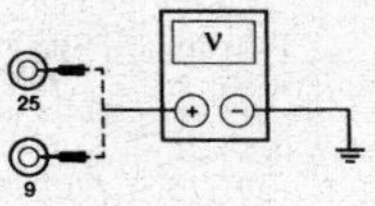	3 Measure the voltage between EEC-IV 60-Pin Breakout Box Pin 9, Circuit 601 (LB/PK), and ground; and between EEC-IV 60-Pin Breakout Box Pin 25, Circuit 601 (LB/PK), and ground. • Are the voltages greater than 10 volts? → **Yes** GO to **C4**. → **No** REPAIR the circuit. CLEAR the DTCs. REPEAT the self-test.
C4 CHECK CIRCUIT 57 (BK) FOR AN OPEN	
1 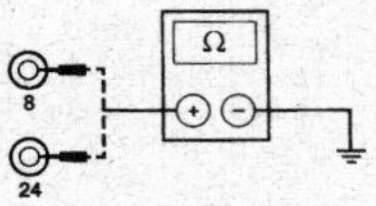	1 Measure the resistance between EEC-IV 60-Pin Breakout Box Pin 8, Circuit 57 (BK), and ground; and between EEC-IV 60-Pin Breakout Box Pin 24, Circuit 57 (BK), and ground. • Are the resistances less than 5 ohms? → **Yes** GO to **C5**. → **No** REPAIR the circuit. CLEAR the DTCs. REPEAT the self-test.

FM4020005004030X

Fig. 19 Test C/Code C1095: Hydraulic Pump Motor Circuit Failure (Part 3 of 4). 2000 Crown Victoria & Grand Marquis

TEST CONDITIONS	TEST DETAILS/RESULTS/ACTIONS
D1 CHECK FOR SHORT TO POWER	
1  2  Anti-Lock Brake Control Module C162 4 	3 Connect EEC-IV 60-Pin Breakout Box.

FM4020005005010X

Fig. 20 Test D/Codes C1145, C1155, C1165, C1175 & C1176: Brake Sensor Input Circuit Failure (Part 1 of 4). 2000 Crown Victoria & Grand Marquis

TEST CONDITIONS	TESTDETAILS/RESULTS/ACTIONS

D1 CHECK FOR SHORT TO POWER

5

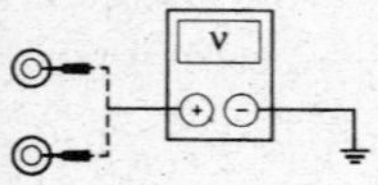

5 Measure the voltage between EEC-IV 60-Pin Breakout Box pins and ground as follows:

DTC	Breakout Box Pin	Breakout Box Pin
C1145 (RF)	3 (Circuit 514 [YE/RD])	18 (Circuit 516 [YE/BK])
C1155 (LF)	4 (Circuit 521 [TN/OG])	11 (Circuit 522 [TN/BK])
C1165 (RR)	17 (Circuit 523 [RD/PK])	1 (Circuit 524 [PK/BK])
C1175 (LR)	10 (Circuit 518 [LG/RD])	2 (Circuit 519 [LG/BK])

- Is voltage present?

→ **Yes**
REPAIR the circuit(s) in question. CLEAR the DTCs. REPEAT the self-test.

→ **No**
GO to **D2**.

D2 CHECK FOR AN OPEN

1

2

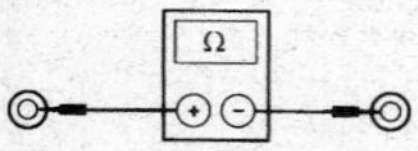

2 Measure the resistance between EEC-IV 60-Pin Breakout Box pins as follows:

DTC	Breakout Box Pin	Breakout Box Pin
C1145 (RF)	3 (Circuit 514 [YE/RD])	18 (Circuit 516 [YE/BK])
C1155 (LF)	4 (Circuit 521 [TN/OG])	11 (Circuit 522 [TN/BK])
C1165 (RR)	17 (Circuit 523 [RD/PK])	1 (Circuit 524 [PK/BK])
C1175 (LR)	10 (Circuit 518 [LG/RD])	2 (Circuit 519 [LG/BK])

FM4020005005020X

Fig. 20 Test D/Codes C1145, C1155, C1165, C1175 & C1176: Brake Sensor Input Circuit Failure (Part 2 of 4). 2000 Crown Victoria & Grand Marquis

TEST CONDITIONS	TESTDETAILS/RESULTS/ACTIONS

D2 CHECK FOR AN OPEN

- Is the resistance between 800 and 1,400 ohms?

→ **Yes**
GO to **D4**.

→ **No**
GO to **D3**.

D3 CHECK THE SUSPECT ANTI-LOCK BRAKE SENSOR FOR AN OPEN

1

Suspect Anti-Lock Brake Sensor

2

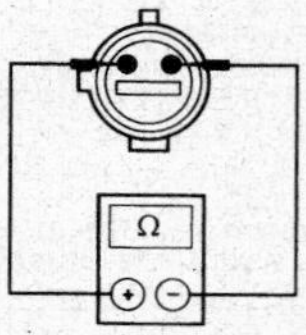

2 Measure the resistance between suspect anti-lock brake sensor pins (component side).

- Is the resistance between 800 and 1,400 ohms?

→ **Yes**
REPAIR the circuit(s) in question. CLEAR the DTCs. REPEAT the self-test.

→ **No**
INSTALL a new anti-lock brake sensor; REFER to Sensor—Anti-Lock Brake, Front or Sensor—Anti-Lock Brake, Rear. CLEAR the DTCs. REPEAT the self-test.

D4 CHECK FOR SHORT TO GROUND

1

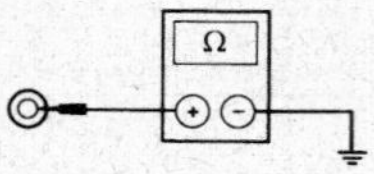

1 Measure the resistance between EEC-IV 60-Pin Breakout Box pins and ground as follows:

DTC	Breakout Box Pin
C1145 (RF)	3 (Circuit 514 [YE/RD])
C1155 (LF)	4 (Circuit 521 [TN/OG])
C1165 (RR)	17 (Circuit 523 [RD/PK])
C1175 (LR)	10 (Circuit 518 [LG/RD])

FM4020005005030X

Fig. 20 Test D/Codes C1145, C1155, C1165, C1175 & C1176: Brake Sensor Input Circuit Failure (Part 3 of 4). 2000 Crown Victoria & Grand Marquis

TEST CONDITIONS	TESTDETAILS/RESULTS/ACTIONS

D4 CHECK FOR SHORT TO GROUND

- Is the resistance greater than 10,000 ohms?

→ **Yes**
INSTALL a new anti-lock brake control module. REPEAT the self-test.

→ **No**
GO to **D5**.

D5 CHECK THE SUSPECT ANTI-LOCK BRAKE SENSOR FOR SHORT TO GROUND

1

Suspect Anti-Lock Brake Sensor

2

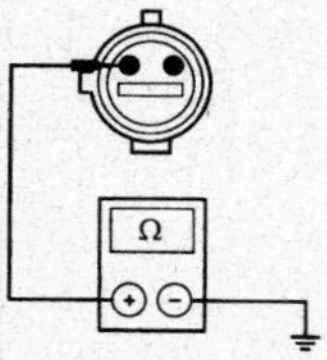

2 Measure the resistance between suspect anti-lock brake sensor pin (component side) and ground.

- Is the resistance greater than 10,000 ohms?

→ **Yes**
REPAIR the circuit(s) in question. CLEAR the DTCs. REPEAT the self-test.

→ **No**
INSTALL a new anti-lock brake sensor. CLEAR the DTCs. REPEAT the self-test.

FM4020005005040X

Fig. 20 Test D/Codes C1145, C1155, C1165, C1175 & C1176: Brake Sensor Input Circuit Failure (Part 4 of 4). 2000 Crown Victoria & Grand Marquis

TEST CONDITIONS	TESTDETAILS/RESULTS/ACTIONS

E1 CHECK THE ANTI-LOCK BRAKE SENSOR

1 Check the suspect anti-lock brake sensor mounting. Check the suspect anti-lock brake sensor for excessive dirt build-up, metal obstructions, improper harness routing, and chafing.

- Is the suspect anti-lock brake sensor OK?

→ **Yes**
GO to **E2**.

→ **No**
REPAIR or INSTALL a new component as necessary. CLEAR the DTCs. REPEAT the self-test.

E2 CHECK THE ANTI-LOCK BRAKE SENSOR INDICATOR

1 Check the suspect anti-lock brake sensor indicator for corrosion, nicks, damaged teeth, proper mounting, alignment, and consistent air gap.

- Is the suspect anti-lock brake sensor indicator OK?

→ **Yes**
GO to **E3**.

→ **No**
REPAIR or INSTALL a new component as necessary. CLEAR the DTCs. REPEAT the self-test.

E3 CHECK THE ANTI-LOCK BRAKE SENSOR OUTPUT

1

2

Anti-Lock Brake Control Module C162

3 Connect EEC-IV 60-Pin Breakout Box.

FM4020005006010X

Fig. 21 Test E/Codes C1233, C1234, C1235 & C1236: Brake Sensor Input Signal Missing (Part 1 of 2). 2000 Crown Victoria & Grand Marquis

TEST CONDITIONS	TESTDETAILS/RESULTS/ACTIONS
E3 CHECK THE ANTI-LOCK BRAKE SENSOR OUTPUT	
4 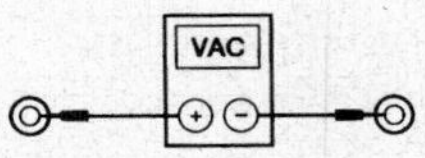	4 While spinning the suspect wheel at one revolution per second, measure the AC voltage between EEC-IV 60-Pin Breakout Box pins as follows: (see table below) • Is the voltage between 100 and 3,500 mVolts AC? → **Yes** INSTALL a new anti-lock brake control module. REPEAT the self-test. → **No** INSTALL a new anti-lock brake sensor; CLEAR the DTCs. REPEAT the self-test.

DTC	Breakout Box Pin	Breakout Box Pin
C1234 (RF)	3 (Circuit 514 [YE/RD])	18 (Circuit 516 [YE/BK])
C1233 (LF)	4 (Circuit 521 [TN/OG])	11 (Circuit 522 [TN/BK])
C1235 (RR)	17 (Circuit 523 [RD/PK])	1 (Circuit 524 [PK/BK])
C1236 (LR)	10 (Circuit 518 [LG/RD])	2 (Circuit 519 [LG/BK])

FM4020005006020X

Fig. 21 Test E/Codes C1233, C1234, C1235 & C1236: Brake Sensor Input Signal Missing (Part 2 of 2). 2000 Crown Victoria & Grand Marquis

TEST CONDITIONS	TESTDETAILS/RESULTS/ACTIONS
F2 CHECK CIRCUIT 511 (LG/RD) FOR SHORT TO POWER	
Note: Make sure the brake pedal is released for this step.	
1 	
	2 Connect EEC-IV 60-Pin Breakout Box.
3 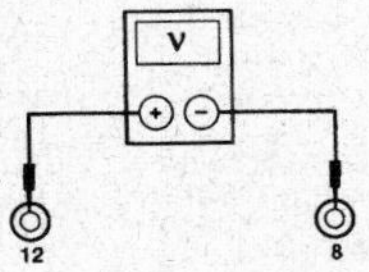	3 Measure the voltage between EEC-IV 60-Pin Breakout Box Pin 12, Circuit 511 (LG/RD), and EEC-IV 60-Pin Breakout Box Pin 8, Circuit 57 (BK). • Is voltage present? → **Yes** REPAIR the circuit. CLEAR the DTCs. REPEAT the self-test. → **No** INSTALL a new anti-lock brake control module. REPEAT the self-test.

FM4020005007020X

Fig. 22 Test F/Code B1485: Brake Pedal Input Circuit Short To Battery (Part 2 of 2). 2000 Crown Victoria & Grand Marquis

TEST CONDITIONS	TESTDETAILS/RESULTS/ACTIONS
F1 CHECK THE STOPLAMP OPERATION	
	1 Press the brake pedal. • Do the stoplamps operate correctly? → **Yes** GO to **F2**. → **No** INSPECT as required.

FM4020005007010X

Fig. 22 Test F/Code B1485: Brake Pedal Input Circuit Short To Battery (Part 1 of 2). 2000 Crown Victoria & Grand Marquis

TEST CONDITIONS	TESTDETAILS/RESULTS/ACTIONS
G1 CHECK THE BATTERY VOLTAGE	
1 	
2 	2 Measure the voltage between positive and negative battery posts with the key ON engine OFF (KOEO) and with the engine running. • Is the voltage between 10 and 13 volts with KOEO, and between 11 and 17 volts with engine running? → **Yes** GO to **G2**. → **No** DIAGNSOE charging system.
G2 CHECK THE ANTI-LOCK BRAKE CONTROL MODULE GROUND	
1  2 	
	3 Connect EEC-IV 60-Pin Breakout Box.
4 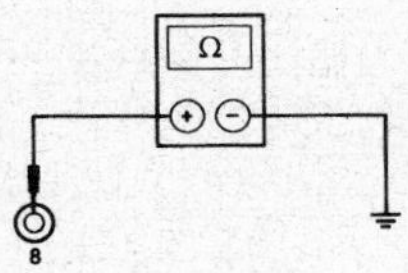	4 Measure the resistance between EEC-IV 60-Pin Breakout Box Pin 8, Circuit 57 (BK), and ground. • Is the resistance less than 5 ohms? → **Yes** GO to **G3**. → **No** REPAIR the circuit. CLEAR the DTCs. REPEAT the self-test.

FM4020005008010X

Fig. 23 Test G/Code B1676: Battery Voltage Out Of Range (Part 1 of 2). 2000 Crown Victoria & Grand Marquis

TEST CONDITIONS	TEST DETAILS/RESULTS/ACTIONS
G3 CHECK CIRCUIT 57 (BK) FOR AN OPEN	
1 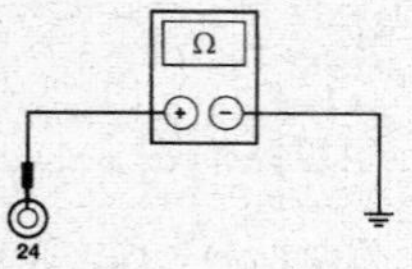	1 Measure the resistance between EEC-IV 60-Pin Breakout Box Pin 24, Circuit 57 (BK), and ground. • Is the resistance less than 5 ohms? → **Yes** INSTALL a new anti-lock brake control module. REPEAT the self-test. → **No** REPAIR the circuit. CLEAR the DTCs. REPEAT the self-test.

FM4020005008020X

Fig. 23 Test G/Code B1676: Battery Voltage Out Of Range (Part 2 of 2). 2000 Crown Victoria & Grand Marquis

TEST CONDITIONS	TEST DETAILS/RESULTS/ACTIONS
I1 BLEED THE BRAKE SYSTEM	
	1 Bleed the brake system. 2 Place the air suspension switch in the ON position after the vehicle is off the hoist. • Does the vehicle track poorly? → **Yes** GO to **I2**. → **No** The brake system is operating correctly. TEST the system for normal operation.
I2 CHECK THE LF HCU VALVE OPERATION	
2 3 	1 Place the air suspension switch in the OFF position. 4 Lift the vehicle and rotate all the wheels to make sure they turn freely (the vehicle must be in Neutral). 5 Trigger the anti-lock brake control module active command PMP MOTOR ON for four seconds. (Trigger must be pushed twice. Each press runs the pump for two seconds.) 6 Apply moderate brake pedal effort. 7 Have an assistant attempt to rotate the LF wheel. • Does the LF wheel rotate? → **Yes** INSTALL a new HCU. TEST the system for normal operation. → **No** GO to **I3**.

FM4020005010010X

Fig. 25 Test I: Poor Vehicle Tracking During Anti-Lock Function (Part 1 of 5). 2000 Crown Victoria & Grand Marquis

TEST CONDITIONS	TEST DETAILS/RESULTS/ACTIONS
H1 CHECK THE COMPONENTS MOUNTING	
	1 Inspect the brake pedal and the power brake booster/brake master cylinder for correct attachment. 2 Bleed the brake system. • Is the brake pedal spongy? → **Yes** GO to **H2**. → **No** The brake system is operating correctly. TEST the system for normal operation.
H2 BLEED THE BRAKE SYSTEM	
	1 Rebleed the brake system. • Is the brake pedal spongy? → **Yes** INSPECT as required → **No** The brake system is operating correctly. TEST the system for normal operation.

FM4020005009000X

Fig. 24 Test H: Spongy Brake Pedal, No Indicator Illuminated. 2000 Crown Victoria & Grand Marquis

TEST CONDITIONS	TEST DETAILS/RESULTS/ACTIONS
I3 CHECK THE LF HCU VALVE RELEASE	
	1 Trigger the anti-lock brake control module active command LF INLET ON and LF OUTLET ON. 2 Have an assistant turn the LF wheel using a two foot lever, such as a breaker bar, immediately after pressing trigger (NGS will energize the valves for only two seconds per trigger press). • Does the LF wheel turn? → **Yes** GO to **I4**. → **No** GO to **I10**.
I4 CHECK THE RF HCU VALVE OPERATION	
1 	2 Trigger the anti-lock brake control module active command PMP MOTOR ON for four seconds. (Trigger must be pushed twice. Each press runs the pump for two seconds.) 3 Apply moderate brake pedal effort. 4 Have an assistant attempt to rotate the RF wheel. • Does the RF wheel rotate? → **Yes** INSTALL a new HCU. TEST the system for normal operation. → **No** GO to **I5**.
I5 CHECK THE RF HCU VALVE RELEASE	
	1 Trigger the anti-lock brake control module active command RF INLET ON and RF OUTLET ON.

FM4020005010020X

Fig. 25 Test I: Poor Vehicle Tracking During Anti-Lock Function (Part 2 of 5). 2000 Crown Victoria & Grand Marquis

TEST CONDITIONS	TEST DETAILS/RESULTS/ACTIONS
I5 CHECK THE RF HCU VALVE RELEASE	
	2 Have an assistant turn the RF wheel using a two foot lever, such as a breaker bar, immediately after pressing trigger (NGS will energize the valves for only two seconds per trigger press). • Does the RF wheel turn? → **Yes** GO to **I6**. → **No** GO to **I10**.
I6 CHECK THE LR HCU VALVE OPERATION	
1  2 	2 Trigger the anti-lock brake control module active command PMP MOTOR ON for four seconds. (Trigger must be pushed twice. Each press runs the pump for two seconds.) 3 Apply moderate brake pedal effort. 4 Have an assistant attempt to rotate the LR wheel. • Does the LR wheel rotate? → **Yes** INSTALL a new HCU. TEST the system for normal operation. → **No** GO to **I7**.
I7 CHECK THE LR HCU VALVE RELEASE	
	1 Trigger the anti-lock brake control module active command LR INLET ON and LR OUTLET ON. 2 Have an assistant turn the LR wheel using a two foot lever, such as a breaker bar, immediately after pressing trigger (NGS will energize the valves for only two seconds per trigger press). • Does the LR wheel turn? → **Yes** GO to **I8**. → **No** GO to **I10**.

FM4020005010030X

Fig. 25 Test I: Poor Vehicle Tracking During Anti-Lock Function (Part 3 of 5). 2000 Crown Victoria & Grand Marquis

TEST CONDITIONS	TEST DETAILS/RESULTS/ACTIONS
I10 CHECK FOR DIAGNOSTIC TROUBLE CODES (DTCS)	
	1 Retrieve and document continuous DTCs. • Are any DTCs retrieved? → **Yes** GO to Anti-Lock Brake Control Module Diagnostic Trouble Code (DTC) Index. → **No** INSTALL a new HCU. TEST the system for normal operation.

FM4020005010050X

Fig. 25 Test I: Poor Vehicle Tracking During Anti-Lock Function (Part 5 of 5). 2000 Crown Victoria & Grand Marquis

TEST CONDITIONS	TEST DETAILS/RESULTS/ACTIONS
I8 CHECK THE RR HCU VALVE OPERATION	
1 	2 Trigger the anti-lock brake control module active command PMP MOTOR ON for four seconds. (Trigger must be pushed twice. Each press runs the pump for two seconds.) 3 Apply moderate brake pedal effort. 4 Have an assistant attempt to rotate the RR wheel. • Does the RR wheel rotate? → **Yes** INSTALL a new HCU. TEST the system for normal operation. → **No** GO to **I9**.
I9 CHECK THE RR HCU VALVE RELEASE	
	1 Trigger the anti-lock brake control module active command RR INLET ON and RR OUTLET ON. 2 Have an assistant turn the RR wheel using a two foot lever, such as a breaker bar, immediately after pressing trigger (NGS will energize the valves for only two seconds per trigger press). • Does the RR wheel turn? → **Yes** The anti-lock brake system is operating properly. TEST the system for normal operation. → **No** GO to **I10**.

FM4020005010040X

Fig. 25 Test I: Poor Vehicle Tracking During Anti-Lock Function (Part 4 of 5). 2000 Crown Victoria & Grand Marquis

TEST CONDITIONS	TEST DETAILS/RESULTS/ACTIONS
J1 CHECK FOR DTCS	
1  NGS	2 Retrieve and document continuous DTCs. • Are any DTCs retrieved? → **Yes** GO to Anti-Lock Brake Control Module Diagnostic Trouble Code (DTC) Index. → **No** GO to **J2**.
J2 CHECK THE ABS OPERATION	
	1 Test drive the vehicle. Check the ABS operation. • Does the ABS operate properly? → **Yes** GO to **J3**. → **No** GO to Symptom Chart.

FM4020005011010X

Fig. 26 Test J: Traction Control Inoperative (Part 1 of 3). 2000 Crown Victoria & Grand Marquis

TEST CONDITIONS	TESTDETAILS/RESULTS/ACTIONS
J3 CHECK CIRCUIT 959 (GY) FOR SHORT TO POWER	
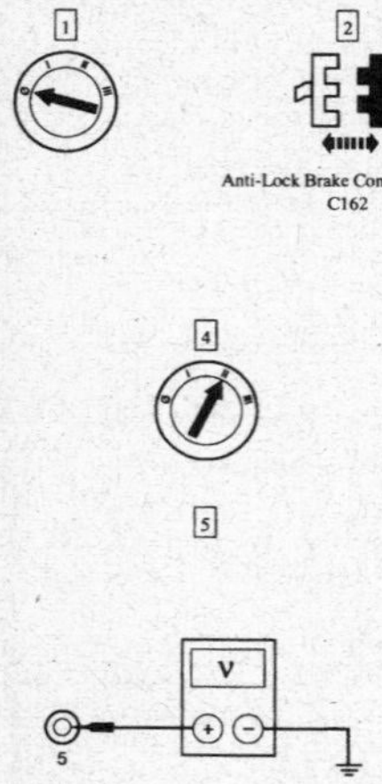	3 Connect EEC-IV 60-Pin Breakout Box. 5 Measure the voltage between EEC-IV 60-Pin Breakout Box Pin 5, Circuit 959 (GY), and ground. • Is voltage present? → **Yes** GO to **J4**. → **No** INSTALL a new HCU. TEST the system for normal operation.

FM4020005011020X

Fig. 26 Test J: Traction Control Inoperative (Part 2 of 3). 2000 Crown Victoria & Grand Marquis

TEST CONDITIONS	TESTDETAILS/RESULTS/ACTIONS
K1 CHECK THE YELLOW ABS WARNING INDICATOR	
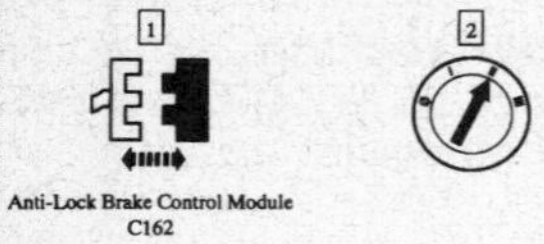	• Is the yellow ABS warning indicator illuminated? → **Yes** GO to **K2**. → **No** INSPECT instrument cluster.
K2 CHECK PROVE OUT	
	• Does the yellow ABS warning indicator prove out for three seconds and then turn off? → **Yes** The yellow ABS warning indicator is working properly. REPEAT the self-test. → **No** INSTALL a new anti-lock brake control module. TEST the system for normal operation.

FM4020005012000X

Fig. 27 Test K: Yellow ABS Indicator Does Not Self-Check. 2000 Crown Victoria & Grand Marquis

TEST CONDITIONS	TESTDETAILS/RESULTS/ACTIONS
J4 CHECK THE TRACTION CONTROL SWITCH	
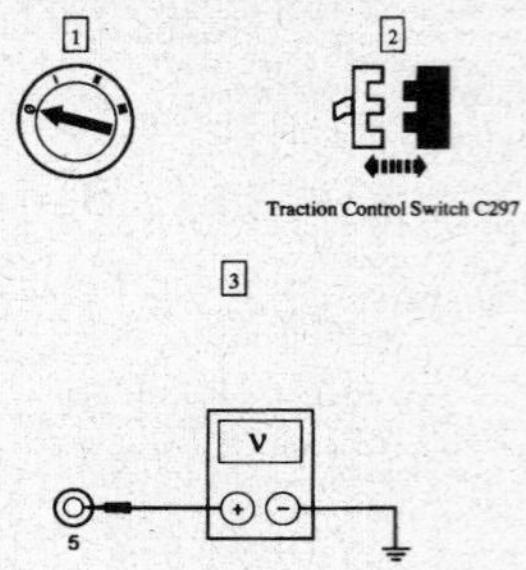	3 Measure the resistance between EEC-IV 60-Pin Breakout Box Pin 5, Circuit 959 (GY), and ground. • Is voltage present? → **Yes** REPAIR the circuit. TEST the system for normal operation. → **No** INSTALL a new traction control switch. TEST the system for normal operation.

FM4020005011030X

Fig. 26 Test J: Traction Control Inoperative (Part 3 of 3). 2000 Crown Victoria & Grand Marquis

TEST CONDITIONS	TESTDETAILS/RESULTS/ACTIONS
L1 CHECK FOR DTCs	
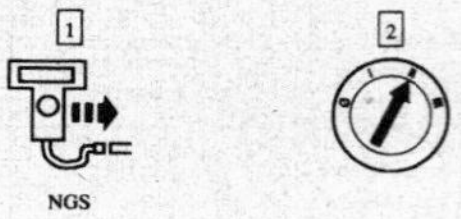	3 Retrieve and document continuous DTCs for the anti-lock brake control module. • Are any DTCs retrieved? → **Yes** GO to Anti-Lock Brake Control Module Diagnostic Trouble Code (DTC) Index. → **No** INSTALL a new instrument cluster (conventional cluster) or indicator lamp module (electronic cluster). TEST the system for normal operation.

FM4020005013000X

Fig. 28 Test L: Yellow ABS Indicator Always Illuminated. 2000 Crown Victoria & Grand Marquis

TEST CONDITIONS	TESTDETAILS/RESULTS/ACTIONS
M1 CHECK CIRCUIT 88 (BK/WH) FOR AN OPEN	
1 2 3 	
4 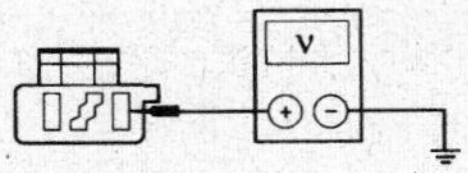	4 Measure the voltage between traction control switch C297, Circuit 88 (BK/WH), harness side and ground. • Is the voltage greater than 10 volts? → **Yes** GO to **M2**. → **No** REPAIR the circuit. TEST the system for normal operation.
M2 CHECK THE TRACTION CONTROL SWITCH	
1 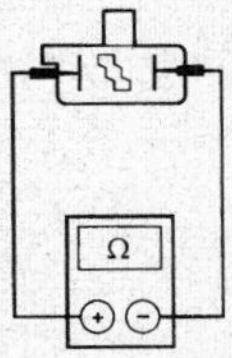	1 Measure the resistance between traction control switch pins (component side) while depressing the traction control switch. • Is the resistance less than 5 ohms? → **Yes** GO to **M3**. → **No** INSTALL a new traction control switch. TEST the system for normal operation.
M3 CHECK CIRCUIT 959 (GY) FOR AN OPEN	
1 	2 Connect EEC-IV 60-Pin Breakout Box.

FM4020005014010X

Fig. 29 Test M: Traction Control Cannot Be Disabled (Part 1 of 2). 2000 Crown Victoria & Grand Marquis

Condition	Possible Sources	Action
• No communication with the module — anti-lock brake control module	• Fuse. • Anti-lock brake control module. • Circuitry.	• GO to PINPOINT TEST F.
• No communication with the module — hybrid electronic cluster (HEC)	• Fuse. • Hybrid electronic cluster. • Circuitry.	• GO to PINPOINT TEST N.
• Spongy brake pedal with no warning indicator	• Air in brake hydraulic system.	• GO to PINPOINT TEST G.
• Poor vehicle tracking during anti-lock function	• Air in brake hydraulic system. • Hydraulic control unit (HCU). • Base brake system.	• GO to PINPOINT TEST H.
• The traction control is inoperative	• Anti-lock brake control module. • Electronic control unit (ECU). • Base brake system.	• GO to PINPOINT TEST M.
• The yellow ABS warning indicator does not self-check	• Circuitry. • Hybrid electronic cluster. • Anti-lock brake control module.	• GO to PINPOINT TEST K.
• The yellow ABS warning indicator and traction control active indicator always on	• Circuitry. • Hybrid electronic cluster. • Anti-lock brake control module.	• GO to PINPOINT TEST L.
• Traction control active indicator always/never on	• Circuitry. • Message center display. • Anti-lock brake control module.	• Diagnose message center.
• The traction control cannot be disabled	• Circuitry. • Traction control switch. • Electronic control unit (ECU).	• GO to PINPOINT TEST J.
• Red brake warning indicator always on with ABS lamp	• ABS subsystem (electronic brake distribution [EBD]). • Circuit. • Parking brake. • Brake fluid level.	• RETRIEVE the DTCs. REFER to DTC Index.

FM4020101773000X

Fig. 30 Symptom Chart. 2001 Crown Victoria, Grand Marquis & Town Car

TEST CONDITIONS	TESTDETAILS/RESULTS/ACTIONS
M3 CHECK CIRCUIT 959 (GY) FOR AN OPEN	
3 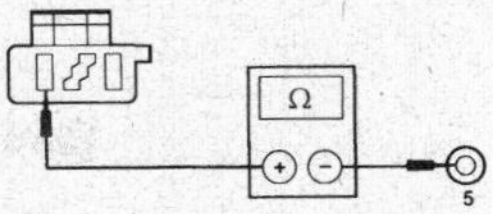	3 Measure the resistance between EEC-IV 60-Pin Breakout Box Pin 5, Circuit 959 (GY), and traction control switch C297, Circuit 959 (GY), harness side. • Is the resistance less than 5 ohms? → **Yes** INSTALL a new HCU. TEST the system for normal operation. → **No** REPAIR the circuit. TEST the system for normal operation.

FM4020005014020X

Fig. 29 Test M: Traction Control Cannot Be Disabled (Part 2 of 2). 2000 Crown Victoria & Grand Marquis

CONDITIONS	DETAILS/RESULTS/ACTIONS
A1 CHECK ABS PUMP MOTOR	
1 	• Is the ABS pump motor running all the time? → **Yes** INSTALL a new anti-lock brake control module. TEST the system for normal operation. → **No** GO to **A2**.
A2 CHECK PUMP OPERATION	
1 2 3 	3 Trigger the anti-lock brake control module active command PMP MOTOR ON. • Does the ABS pump motor run for approximately three seconds? → **Yes** CLEAR the DTC. CHECK the yellow ABS warning indicator while driving the vehicle above 12 kph (7.5 mph) and no brakes applied until the vehicle exceeds 32 kph (20 mph). If the yellow ABS warning indicator illuminates, INSTALL a new anti-lock brake control module. TEST the system for normal operation. If the yellow ABS warning indicator does not illuminate, system is OK. → **No** TRIGGER the anti-lock brake control module active command PMP MOTOR OFF. GO to **A3**.

FM4020001626010X

Fig. 31 Test A/Code C1300: ABS Hydraulic Pump Motor Circuit Failure (Part 1 of 3). 2001 Crown Victoria, Grand Marquis & Town Car

CONDITIONS	DETAILS/RESULTS/ACTIONS

A3 CHECK POWER DISTRIBUTION BOX FUSE 9 (50A)

1

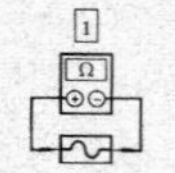

Power Distribution Box Fuse 9 (50A)

- Is the fuse OK?

→ **Yes**
GO to **A4**.

→ **No**
INSTALL a new fuse. TEST the system for normal operation. If the fuse fails again, CHECK for short to ground. REPAIR as necessary. TEST the system for normal operation.

A4 CHECK CIRCUIT 601 (LB/PK) FOR AN OPEN

1

Anti-Lock Brake Control Module

2 Connect the Breakout Box.

3

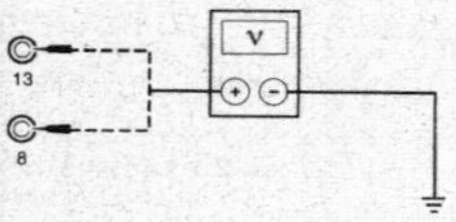

3 Measure the voltage between the Breakout Box pin 8, circuit 601 (LB/PK), and ground; and between the Breakout Box pin 13, circuit 601 (LB/PK), and ground.

- Are the voltages greater than 10 volts?

→ **Yes**
GO to **A5**.

→ **No**
REPAIR circuit 601 (LB/PK). CLEAR the DTCs. TEST the system for normal operation.

FM4020001626020X

Fig. 31 Test A/Code C1300: ABS Hydraulic Pump Motor Circuit Failure (Part 2 of 3). 2001 Crown Victoria, Grand Marquis & Town Car

CONDITIONS	DETAILS/RESULTS/ACTIONS

A5 CHECK CIRCUIT 57 (BK) FOR AN OPEN

1

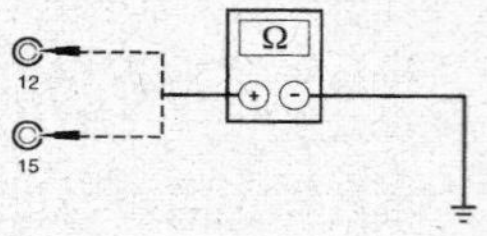

1 Measure the resistance between the Breakout Box pin 12, circuit 57 (BK), and ground; and between the Breakout Box pin 15, circuit 57 (BK), and ground.

- Are the resistances less than 5 ohms?

→ **Yes**
GO to **A6**.

→ **No**
REPAIR circuit 57 (BK). CLEAR the DTCs. TEST the system for normal operation.

A6 CHECK THE PUMP MOTOR FOR PROPER OPERATION

1

Pump Motor Connector

2

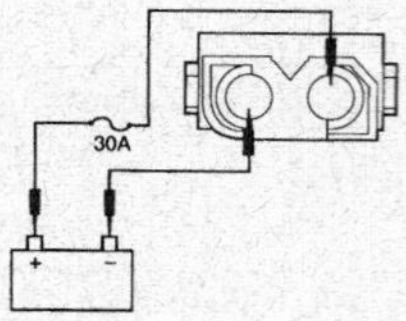

2 Use a heavy gauge jumper to connect a jumper between negative battery post and pump motor connector, brown wire; and momentarily connect a jumper between the positive battery post and pump motor connector, red wire with an in-line 30A in-line fuse.

- Does the pump motor run?

→ **Yes**
INSTALL a new anti-lock brake control module. TEST the system for normal ck operation.

→ **No**
INSTALL a new HCU.
CLEAR the DTCs.
TEST the system for normal operation.

FM4020001626030X

Fig. 31 Test A/Code C1300: ABS Hydraulic Pump Motor Circuit Failure (Part 3 of 3). 2001 Crown Victoria, Grand Marquis & Town Car

CONDITIONS	DETAILS/RESULTS/ACTIONS

B1 CHECK FOR SHORT TO POWER

1

2

Anti-Lock Brake Control Module C162

3 Connect the Breakout Box.

4

5

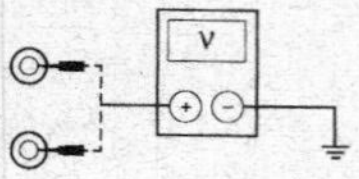

5 Measure the voltage between the Breakout Box Pins, and ground as follows:

DTC	Breakout Box Pin	Breakout Box Pin
C1145 (RF)	4 (circuit 514 [Y/R])	5 (circuit 516 [Y/BK])
C1155 (LF)	20 (circuit 521 [T/O])	21 (circuit 522 [T/BK])
C1165 (RR)	1 (circuit 523 [R/PK])	3 (circuit 524 [PK/BK])
C1175 (LR)	22 (circuit 518 [LG/R])	23 (circuit 519 [LG/BK])

- Is voltage present?

→ **Yes**
REPAIR the suspected anti-lock brake sensor circuit(s) in question. CLEAR the DTCs. TEST the system for normal operation.

→ **No**
GO to **B2**.

B2 CHECK FOR AN OPEN

1

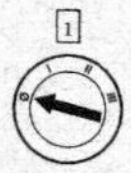

FM4020001627010X

Fig. 32 Test B/Codes C1145, C1155, C1165 & C1175: ABS Sensor Input Circuit Failure (Part 1 of 3). 2001 Crown Victoria, Grand Marquis & Town Car

CONDITIONS	DETAILS/RESULTS/ACTIONS

B2 CHECK FOR AN OPEN (Continued)

2

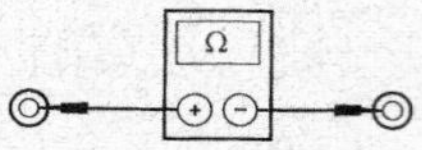

2 Measure the resistance between the Breakout Box Pins as follows:

DTC	Breakout Box Pin	Breakout Box Pin
C1145 (RF)	4 (circuit 514 [Y/R])	5 (circuit 516 [Y/BK])
C1155 (LF)	20 (circuit 521 [T/O])	21 (circuit 522 [T/BK])
C1165 (RR)	1 (circuit 523 [R/PK])	3 (circuit 524 [PK/BK])
C1175 (LR)	22 (circuit 518 [LG/R])	23 (circuit 519 [LG/BK])

- Is the resistance between 800 and 1,400 ohms?

→ **Yes**
GO to **B4**.

→ **No**
GO to **B3**.

B3 CHECK THE SUSPECT ANTI-LOCK BRAKE SENSOR FOR AN OPEN

1

Suspect Anti-Lock Brake Sensor

2

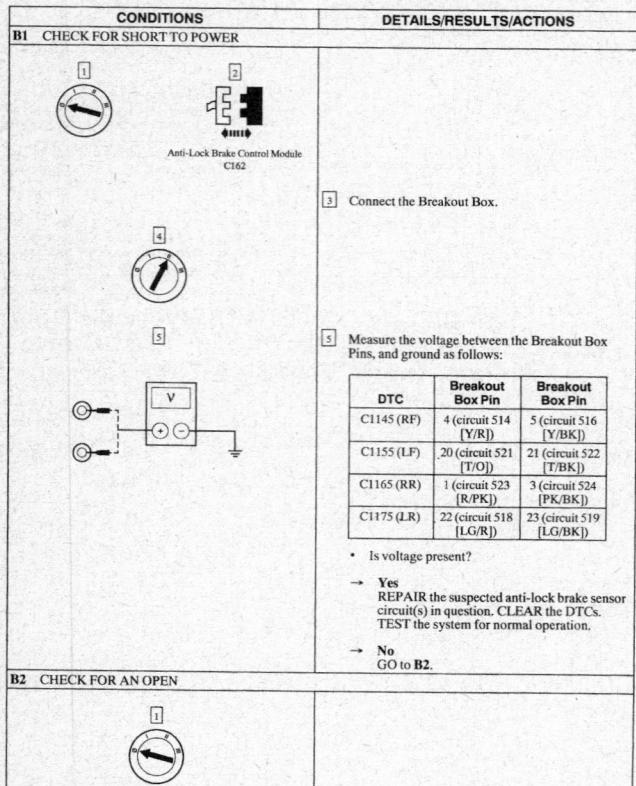

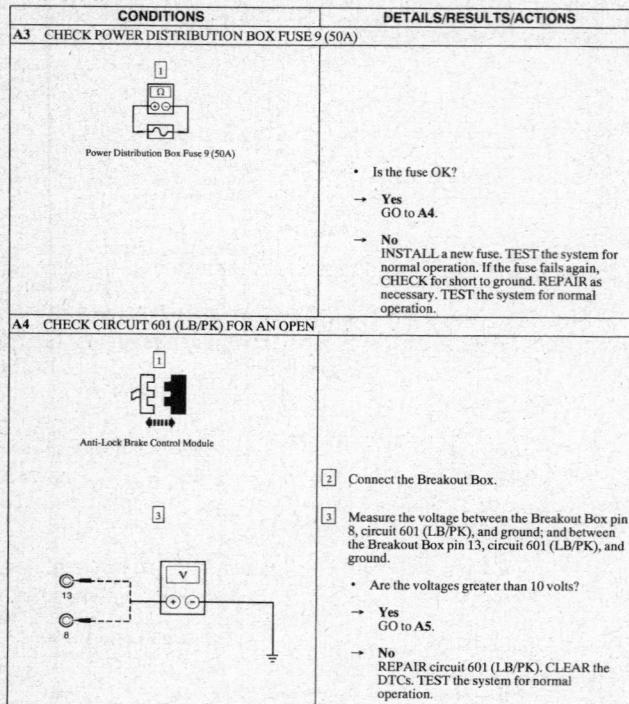

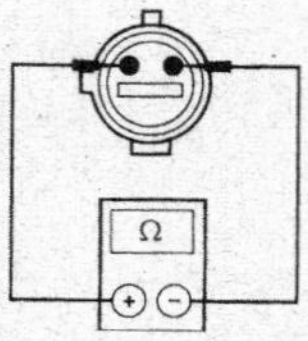

2 Measure the resistance between suspect anti-lock brake sensor terminals.

- Is the resistance between 800 and 1,400 ohms?

→ **Yes**
REPAIR the suspected anti-lock brake sensor circuit(s) in question. CLEAR the DTCs. TEST the system for normal operation.

→ **No**
INSTALL a new anti-lock brake sensor. CLEAR the DTCs. TEST the system for normal operation.

FM4020001627020X

Fig. 32 Test B/Codes C1145, C1155, C1165 & C1175: ABS Sensor Input Circuit Failure (Part 2 of 3). 2001 Crown Victoria, Grand Marquis & Town Car

CONDITIONS	DETAILS/RESULTS/ACTIONS
B4 CHECK FOR SHORT TO GROUND	

[1]

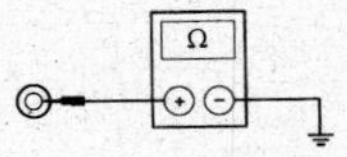

[1] Measure the resistance between the Breakout Box Pins, and ground as follows:

DTC	Breakout Box Pin
C1145 (RF)	4 (circuit 514 [Y/R])
C1155 (LF)	20 (circuit 521 [T/O])
C1165 (RR)	1 (circuit 523 [R/PK])
C1175 (LR)	22 (circuit 518 [LG/R])

- Is the resistance greater than 10,000 ohms?

→ **Yes**
INSTALL a new anti-lock brake control module.
TEST the system for normal operation.

→ **No**
GO to **B5**.

B5 CHECK THE SUSPECT ANTI-LOCK BRAKE SENSOR FOR SHORT TO GROUND

[1]

Suspect Anti-Lock Brake Sensor

[2]

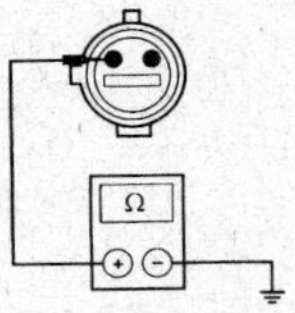

[2] Measure the resistance between suspect anti-lock brake sensor terminal, and ground.

- Is the resistance greater than 10,000 ohms?

→ **Yes**
REPAIR the suspect anti-lock brake sensor circuit(s) in question. CLEAR the DTCs. TEST the system for normal operation.

→ **No**
INSTALL a new anti-lock brake sensor. CLEAR the DTCs. TEST the system for normal operation.

FM4020001627030X

Fig. 32 Test B/Codes C1145, C1155, C1165 & C1175: ABS Sensor Input Circuit Failure (Part 3 of 3). 2001 Crown Victoria, Grand Marquis & Town Car

CONDITIONS	DETAILS/RESULTS/ACTIONS
C3 CHECK THE ANTI-LOCK BRAKE SENSOR OUTPUT (Continued)	

[4]

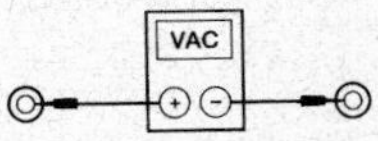

[4] While spinning the suspect wheel at one revolution per second, measure the AC voltage between the Breakout Box Pins as follows:

DTC	Breakout Box Pin	Breakout Box Pin
C1297 (RF)	4 (circuit 514 [Y/R])	5 (circuit 516 [Y/BK])
C1296 (LF)	20 (circuit 521 [T/O])	21 (circuit 522 [T/BK])
C1298 (RR)	1 (circuit 523 [R/PK])	3 (circuit 524 [PK/BK])
C1299 (LR)	22 (circuit 518 [LG/R])	23 (circuit 519 [LG/BK])

- Is the voltage between 100 and 3,500 mVolts AC?

→ **Yes**
INSTALL a new anti-lock brake control module. TEST the system for normal operation.

→ **No**
INSTALL a new anti-lock brake sensor. TEST the system for normal. CLEAR operation.

FM4020001628020X

Fig. 33 Test C/Codes C1296, C1297, C1298 & C1299: ABS Sensor Input Signal Missing (Part 2 of 2). 2001 Crown Victoria, Grand Marquis & Town Car

CONDITIONS	DETAILS/RESULTS/ACTIONS
D1 CHECK CENTRAL JUNCTION BOX (CJB) FUSE 32 (20A)	

[1] Check CJB fuse 32 (20A).

- Is the fuse OK?

→ **Yes**
GO to **D2**.

→ **No**
DIAGNOSE exterior lighting.

FM4020001629010X

Fig. 34 Test D/Code B1484: Brake Pedal Input Circuit Open (Part 1 of 3). 2001 Crown Victoria, Grand Marquis & Town Car

CONDITIONS	DETAILS/RESULTS/ACTIONS
C1 CHECK THE ANTI-LOCK BRAKE SENSOR	

[1] Check the suspect anti-lock brake sensor mounting. Check the suspect anti-lock brake sensor for excessive dirt build-up, metal obstructions, improper harness routing, and chafing.

- Is the suspect anti-lock brake sensor OK?

→ **Yes**
GO to **C2**.

→ **No**
REPAIR or INSTALL a new sensor as necessary. CLEAR the DTCs. TEST the system for normal operation.

C2 CHECK THE ANTI-LOCK BRAKE SENSOR INDICATOR

[1] Check the suspect anti-lock brake sensor indicator for corrosion, nicks, damaged teeth, correct mounting, alignment, and consistent air gap.

- Is the suspect anti-lock brake sensor indicator OK?

→ **Yes**
GO to **C3**.

→ **No**
REPAIR or INSTALL a new indicator as necessary. CLEAR the DTCs. TEST the system for normal operation.

C3 CHECK THE ANTI-LOCK BRAKE SENSOR OUTPUT

[1]

[2]

Anti-Lock Brake Control Module

[3] Connect the Breakout Box.

FM4020001628010X

Fig. 33 Test C/Codes C1296, C1297, C1298 & C1299: ABS Sensor Input Signal Missing (Part 1 of 2). 2001 Crown Victoria, Grand Marquis & Town Car

CONDITIONS	DETAILS/RESULTS/ACTIONS
D2 CHECK THE ABS CONTROL MODULE BOO__ABS PID	

[1]

[2]

[3] Monitor the ABS control module PID BOO__ABS, while pressing and releasing the brake pedal.

- Does the ABS control module PID BOO__ABS indicate ON with the brake pedal pressed and OFF with the brake pedal released?

→ **Yes**
CLEAR the DTCs. REPEAT the self-test. If the DTC B1484 is retrieved, INSTALL a new electronic control unit (ECU). REPEAT the self-test.

→ **No**
GO to **D3**.

D3 CHECK CIRCUIT 511 (LG) FOR OPEN

NOTE: Make sure the brake pedal is released for this step.

[1]

Anti-Lock Brake Control Module C162

[2] Connect the Breakout Box.

FM4020001629020X

Fig. 34 Test D/Code B1484: Brake Pedal Input Circuit Open (Part 2 of 3). 2001 Crown Victoria, Grand Marquis & Town Car

CONDITIONS	DETAILS/RESULTS/ACTIONS
D3 CHECK CIRCUIT 511 (LG) FOR OPEN (Continued)	
3 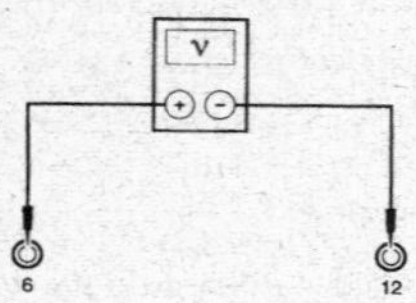	3 Press and hold the brake pedal. 4 Measure the voltage between the Breakout Box pin 6, circuit 511 (LG), and the Breakout Box pin 12, circuit 57 (BK). • Is voltage greater than 10 volts? → **Yes** INSTALL a new anti-lock brake control module. TEST the system for normal operation. → **No** REPAIR circuit 511 (LG) or circuit 57 (BK). CLEAR the DTCs. TEST the system for normal operation.

FM4020001629030X

Fig. 34 Test D/Code B1484: Brake Pedal Input Circuit Open (Part 3 of 3). 2001 Crown Victoria, Grand Marquis & Town Car

CONDITIONS	DETAILS/RESULTS/ACTIONS
E1 CHECK THE BATTERY VOLTAGE (Continued)	
2 	2 Measure the voltage between positive and negative battery post. • Is the voltage between 10 and 16 volts? → **Yes** GO to **E2**. → **No** Diagnose charging system.
E2 CHECK THE ANTI-LOCK BRAKE CONTROL MODULE GROUND	
1 2 	3 Connect the Breakout Box.
4 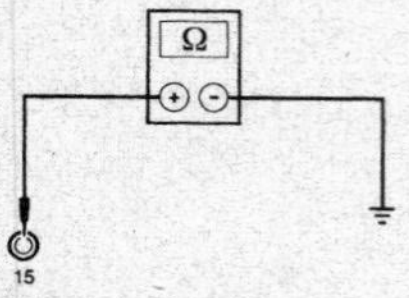	4 Measure the resistance between the Breakout Box pin 15, circuit 57 (BK), and ground. • Is the resistance less than 5 ohms? → **Yes** GO to **E3**. → **No** REPAIR circuit 57 (BK). CLEAR the DTCs. TEST the system for normal operation.

FM4020001630020X

Fig. 35 Test E/Code B1676: Battery Voltage Out Of Range (Part 2 of 3). 2001 Crown Victoria, Grand Marquis & Town Car

E1 CHECK THE BATTERY VOLTAGE

1

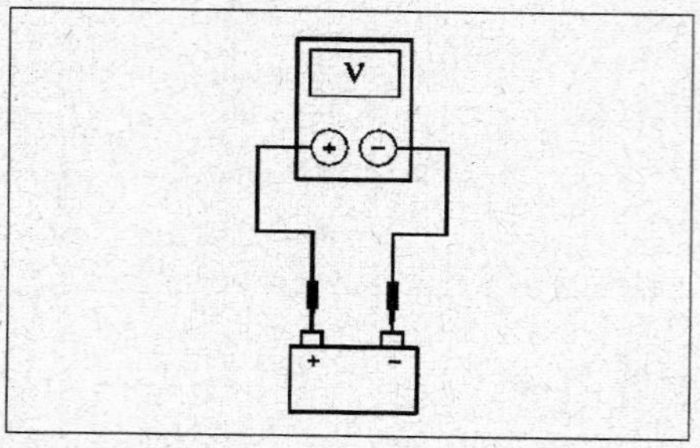

2

Measure the voltage between positive and negative battery post.

- **Is the voltage between 10 and 16 volts?**

→ **Yes**

Go to «E2».

→ **No**

Diagnose Battery & charging system.

FM4020001630010X

Fig. 35 Test E/Code B1676: Battery Voltage Out Of Range (Part 1 of 3). 2001 Crown Victoria, Grand Marquis & Town Car

CONDITIONS	DETAILS/RESULTS/ACTIONS
E3 CHECK CIRCUIT 57 (BK) FOR AN OPEN	
1 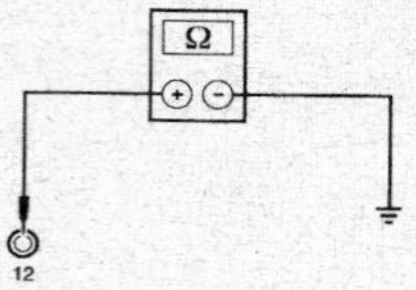	1 Measure the resistance between the Breakout Box pin 12, circuit 57 (BK), and ground. • Is the resistance less than 5 ohms? → **Yes** INSTALL a new anti-lock brake control module. TEST the system for normal operation. → **No** REPAIR circuit 57 (BK). CLEAR the DTCs. TEST the system for normal operation.

FM4020001630030X

Fig. 35 Test E/Code B1676: Battery Voltage Out Of Range (Part 3 of 3). 2001 Crown Victoria, Grand Marquis & Town Car

CONDITIONS	DETAILS/RESULTS/ACTIONS
F1 CHECK THE FUSE JUNCTION PANEL FUSE 13 (10A) AND POWER DISTRIBUTION BOX MAXI FUSE 9 (50A)	
1 2 3 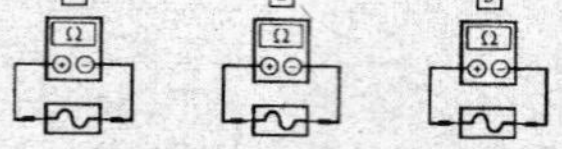	• Are the fuses OK? → **Yes** GO to **F2**. → **No** INSTALL a new fuse(s). TEST the system for normal operation. If the fuse fails again, CHECK for short to ground. REPAIR as necessary. TEST the system for normal operation.

FM4020001631010X

Fig. 36 Test F: No Communications w/ABS Control Module (Part 1 of 3). 2001 Crown Victoria, Grand Marquis & Town Car

CONDITIONS	DETAILS/RESULTS/ACTIONS
F2 CHECK CIRCUITS 601 (LB/BK), AND CIRCUIT 88 (BK/W) FOR AN OPEN	
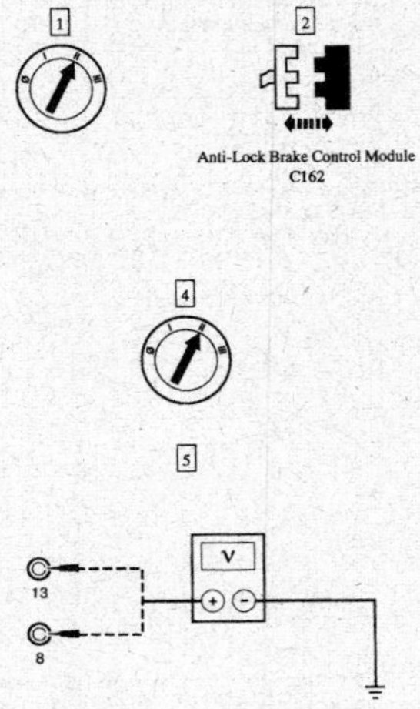	3 Connect the Breakout Box. 5 Measure the voltage between the Breakout Box Pins, and ground as follows: Breakout Box Pin 8 – Circuit 88 (BK/W) Breakout Box Pin 13 – Circuit 601 (LB/PK) • Are the voltages greater than 10 volts? → **Yes** GO to **F3**. → **No** REPAIR the circuit in question. TEST the system for normal operation.

Breakout Box Pin	Circuit
8	Circuit 88 (BK/W)
13	Circuit 601 (LB/PK)

FM4020001631020X

Fig. 36 Test F: No Communications w/ABS Control Module (Part 2 of 3). 2001 Crown Victoria, Grand Marquis & Town Car

CONDITIONS	DETAILS/RESULTS/ACTIONS
G1 CHECK THE COMPONENTS MOUNTING	
	1 Inspect the brake pedal and the power brake booster/brake master cylinder for correct attachment. 2 Bleed the brake system. • Is the brake pedal spongy? → **Yes** GO to **G2**. → **No** The brake system is operating correctly. TEST the system for normal operation.
G2 BLEED THE BRAKE SYSTEM	
	1 Rebleed the brake system. • Is the brake pedal spongy? → **Yes** Diagnose brake system. → **No** The brake system is operating correctly. TEST the system for normal operation.

FM4020001632000X

Fig. 37 Test G: Spongy Brake Pedal w/No Warning Indicator. 2001 Crown Victoria, Grand Marquis & Town Car

CONDITIONS	DETAILS/RESULTS/ACTIONS
F3 CHECK CIRCUIT 57 (BK) FOR AN OPEN	
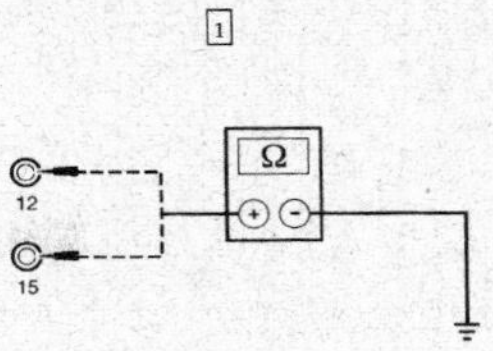	1 Measure the resistance between the Breakout Box pin 15, circuit 57 (BK), and ground; and between the Breakout Box pin 12, circuit 57 (BK), and ground. • Are the resistances less than 5 ohms? → **Yes** **DIAGNOSE module communications.** → **No** REPAIR circuit 57 (BK). TEST the system for normal operation.

FM4020001631030X

Fig. 36 Test F: No Communications w/ABS Control Module (Part 3 of 3). 2001 Crown Victoria, Grand Marquis & Town Car

CONDITIONS	DETAILS/RESULTS/ACTIONS
H1 BLEED THE BRAKE SYSTEM	
	1 Bleed the brake system. 2 Place the air suspension switch in the ON position after the vehicle is off the hoist. • Does the vehicle track poorly? → **Yes** GO to **H2**. → **No** The brake system is operating correctly. TEST the system for normal operation.

FM4020001633010X

Fig. 38 Test H: Improper Vehicle Tracking During ABS Operation (Part 1 of 6). 2001 Crown Victoria, Grand Marquis & Town Car

CONDITIONS	DETAILS/RESULTS/ACTIONS
H2 CHECK THE LF HCU VALVE OPERATION	
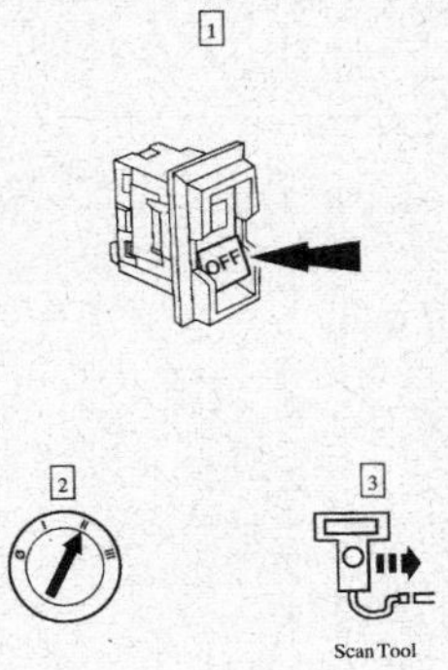	1 Place the air suspension switch in the OFF position. 4 Lift the vehicle and rotate all the wheels to make sure they turn freely (the transmission must be in NEUTRAL). 5 Trigger the anti-lock brake control module active command PMP MOTOR ON for four seconds. (Trigger must be pushed twice. Each press runs the pump for two seconds.) 6 Apply moderate brake pedal effort. 7 Have an assistant attempt to rotate the LF wheel. • Does the LF wheel rotate? → **Yes** INSTALL a new HCU. TEST the system for normal operation. → **No** GO to **H3**.

FM4020001633020X

Fig. 38 Test H: Improper Vehicle Tracking During ABS Operation (Part 2 of 6). 2001 Crown Victoria, Grand Marquis & Town Car

CONDITIONS	DETAILS/RESULTS/ACTIONS
H3 CHECK THE LF HCU VALVE RELEASE	
	1 Trigger the anti-lock brake control module active command LF INLET ON and LF OUTLET ON. 2 Have an assistant turn the LF wheel using a two foot lever, such as a breaker bar, immediately after pressing trigger (the scan tool will energize the valves for only two seconds per trigger press). • Does the LF wheel turn? → **Yes** GO to **H4**. → **No** GO to **H10**.
H4 CHECK THE RF HCU VALVE OPERATION	
	2 Trigger the anti-lock brake control module active command PMP MOTOR ON for four seconds. (Trigger must be pushed twice. Each press runs the pump for two seconds.) 3 Apply moderate brake pedal effort. 4 Have an assistant attempt to rotate the RF wheel. • Does the RF wheel rotate? → **Yes** INSTALL a new HCU. TEST the system for normal operation. → **No** GO to **H5**.

FM4020001633030X

Fig. 38 Test H: Improper Vehicle Tracking During ABS Operation (Part 3 of 6). 2001 Crown Victoria, Grand Marquis & Town Car

CONDITIONS	DETAILS/RESULTS/ACTIONS
H5 CHECK THE RF HCU VALVE RELEASE	
	1 Trigger the anti-lock brake control module active command RF INLET ON and RF OUTLET ON. 2 Have an assistant turn the RF wheel using a two foot lever, such as a breaker bar, immediately after pressing trigger (the scan tool will energize the valves for only two seconds per trigger press). • Does the RF wheel turn? → **Yes** GO to **H6**. → **No** GO to **H10**.
H6 CHECK THE LR HCU VALVE OPERATION	
	2 Trigger the anti-lock brake control module active command PMP MOTOR ON for four seconds. (Trigger must be pushed twice. Each press runs the pump for two seconds.) 3 Apply moderate brake pedal effort. 4 Have an assistant attempt to rotate the LR wheel. • Does the LR wheel rotate? → **Yes** INSTALL a new HCU. TEST the system for). normal operation. → **No** GO to **H7**.

FM4020001633040X

Fig. 38 Test H: Improper Vehicle Tracking During ABS Operation (Part 4 of 6). 2001 Crown Victoria, Grand Marquis & Town Car

CONDITIONS	DETAILS/RESULTS/ACTIONS
H7 CHECK THE LR HCU VALVE RELEASE	
	1 Trigger the anti-lock brake control module active command LR INLET ON and LR OUTLET ON. 2 Have an assistant turn the LR wheel using a two foot lever, such as a breaker bar, immediately after pressing trigger (the scan tool will energize the valves for only two seconds per trigger press). • Does the LR wheel turn? → **Yes** GO to **H8**. → **No** GO to **H10**.
H8 CHECK THE RR HCU VALVE OPERATION	
	2 Trigger the anti-lock brake control module active command PMP MOTOR ON for four seconds. (Trigger must be pushed twice. Each press runs the pump for two seconds.) 3 Apply moderate brake pedal effort. 4 Have an assistant attempt to rotate the RR wheel. • Does the RR wheel rotate? → **Yes** INSTALL a new HCU. TEST the system for normal operation. → **No** GO to **H9**.

FM4020001633050X

Fig. 38 Test H: Improper Vehicle Tracking During ABS Operation (Part 5 of 6). 2001 Crown Victoria, Grand Marquis & Town Car

CONDITIONS	DETAILS/RESULTS/ACTIONS
H9 CHECK THE RR HCU VALVE RELEASE	
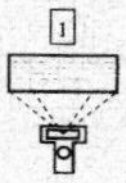	1 Trigger the anti-lock brake control module active command RR INLET ON and RR OUTLET ON. 2 Have an assistant turn the RR wheel using a two foot lever, such as a breaker bar, immediately after pressing trigger (the scan tool will energize the valves for only two seconds per trigger press). • Does the RR wheel turn? → **Yes** The anti-lock brake system is operating correctly. TEST the system for normal operation. → **No** GO to **H10**.
H10 CHECK FOR DIAGNOSTIC TROUBLE CODES (DTCS)	
	1 Retrieve and document continuous DTCs. • Are any DTCs retrieved? → **Yes** GO to Anti-Lock Brake Control Module Diagnostic Trouble Code (DTC) Index. → **No** INSTALL a new HCU. TEST the system for normal operation.

FM4020001633060X

Fig. 38 Test H: Improper Vehicle Tracking During ABS Operation (Part 6 of 6). 2001 Crown Victoria, Grand Marquis & Town Car

CONDITIONS	DETAILS/RESULTS/ACTIONS
J1 CHECK FOR DTCS	
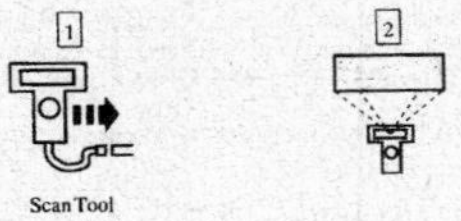	2 Retrieve and document continuous DTCs. • Are any DTCs retrieved? → **Yes** GO to Anti-Lock Brake Control Module Diagnostic Trouble Code (DTC) Index. → **No** GO to **J2**.

FM4020001634010X

Fig. 39 Test J: Traction Control Cannot Be Disabled (Part 1 of 3). 2001 Crown Victoria, Grand Marquis & Town Car

CONDITIONS	DETAILS/RESULTS/ACTIONS
J2 CHECK CIRCUIT 959 (G/W) FOR SHORT TO GROUND	
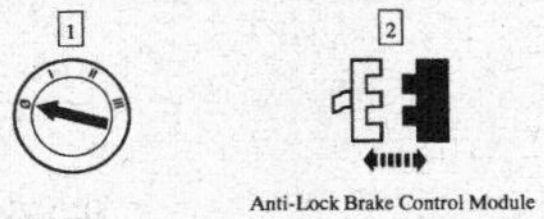	
	3 Connect the Breakout Box.
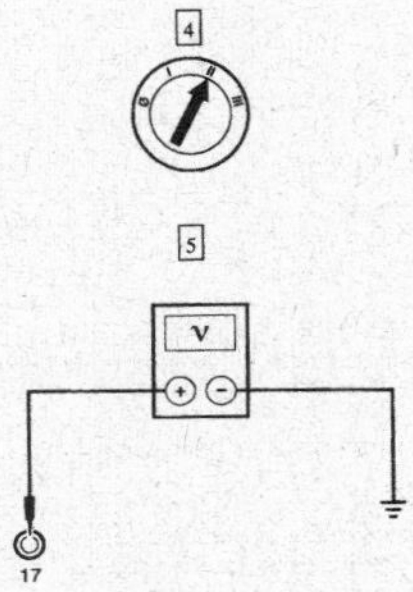	5 Measure the voltage between the Breakout Box pin 17, circuit 959 (G/W), and ground. • Is voltage present? → **Yes** GO to **J3**. → **No** INSTALL a new ECU. TEST the system for normal operation.
J3 CHECK THE TRACTION CONTROL SWITCH	
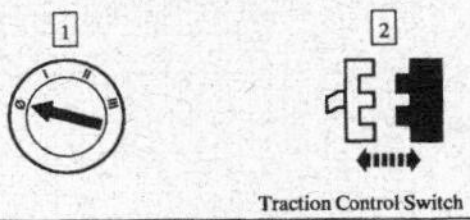	

FM4020001634020X

Fig. 39 Test J: Traction Control Cannot Be Disabled (Part 2 of 3). 2001 Crown Victoria, Grand Marquis & Town Car

CONDITIONS	DETAILS/RESULTS/ACTIONS
J3 CHECK THE TRACTION CONTROL SWITCH (Continued)	
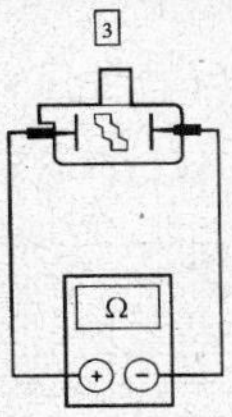	3 Measure the resistance between the traction control switch pin 2, circuit 959 (GY), and pin 1, circuit 57 (BK). • Is the resistance less than 5 ohms? → **Yes** INSTALL a new ECU. TEST the system for normal operation. → **No** INSTALL a new traction control switch. TEST the system for normal operation.

FM4020001634030X

Fig. 39 Test J: Traction Control Cannot Be Disabled (Part 3 of 3). 2001 Crown Victoria, Grand Marquis & Town Car

CONDITIONS	DETAILS/RESULTS/ACTIONS
K1 CHECK THE YELLOW ABS WARNING INDICATOR	
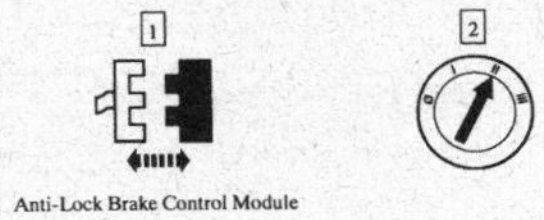	• Is the yellow ABS warning indicator illuminated? → **Yes** GO to **K2**. → **No** DIAGNOSE instrument cluster.

FM4020001635010X

Fig. 40 Test K: Yellow ABS Indicator Does Not Self-Check (Part 1 of 2). 2001 Crown Victoria, Grand Marquis & Town Car

CONDITIONS	DETAILS/RESULTS/ACTIONS
K2 CHECK PROVE OUT	
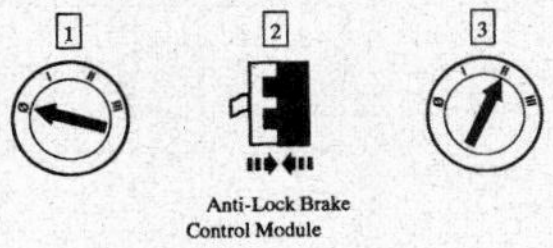	• Does the yellow ABS warning indicator prove out for three seconds and then turn off? → **Yes** The yellow ABS warning indicator is working correctly. TEST the system for normal operation. → **No** INSTALL a new anti-lock brake control module. TEST the system for normal operation.

FM4020001635020X

Fig. 40 Test K: Yellow ABS Indicator Does Not Self-Check (Part 2 of 2). 2001 Crown Victoria, Grand Marquis & Town Car

CONDITIONS	DETAILS/RESULTS/ACTIONS
L1 CHECK FOR DTCs	
	3 Retrieve and document continuous DTCs for the anti-lock brake control module. • Are any DTCs retrieved? → **Yes** GO to Anti-Lock Brake Control Module Diagnostic Trouble Code (DTC) Index. → **No** INSTALL a new HEC. TEST the system for normal operation.

FM4020001636000X

Fig. 41 Test L: Yellow ABS Indicator & Traction Control Active Indicator Always On. 2001 Crown Victoria, Grand Marquis & Town Car

CONDITIONS	DETAILS/RESULTS/ACTIONS
M1 CHECK CIRCUIT 57 (BK) FOR AN OPEN	
1 2 	3 Measure the resistance between traction control switch C206, circuit 57 (BK), and ground. • Is the resistance greater than 10,000 ohms? → **Yes** GO to **M2**. → **No** INSTALL a new traction control switch. TEST the system for normal operation.
M2 CHECK THE TRACTION CONTROL SWITCH	
1 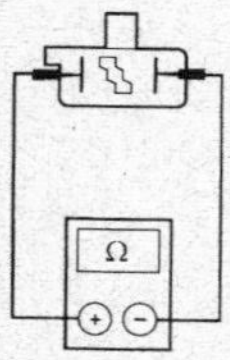	1 Measure the resistance between traction control switch terminals, while depressing the traction control switch. • Is the resistance less than 5 ohms? → **Yes** INSTALL a new ECU. TEST the system for normal operation. → **No** INSTALL a new traction control switch. TEST the system for normal operation.
M3 CHECK CIRCUIT 959 (G/W) FOR AN OPEN	
1 	2 Connect the Breakout Box.

FM4020001637010X

Fig. 42 Test M: Traction Control Inoperative (Part 1 of 2). 2001 Crown Victoria, Grand Marquis & Town Car

CONDITIONS	DETAILS/RESULTS/ACTIONS
N1 CHECK FUSES	
1 2 	• Are the fuses OK? → **Yes** GO to **N2**. → **No** INSTALL new fuse(s). TEST the system for normal operation. If the fuse fails again, CHECK for short to ground. REPAIR as necessary. TEST the system for normal operation.
N2 CHECK HEC POWER SUPPLY	
1 2 3 	

FM4020101638010X

Fig. 43 Test N: No Communication w/Hybrid Electronic Cluster (Part 1 of 3). 2001 Crown Victoria, Grand Marquis & Town Car

CONDITIONS	DETAILS/RESULTS/ACTIONS
M3 CHECK CIRCUIT 959 (G/W) FOR AN OPEN (Continued)	
3 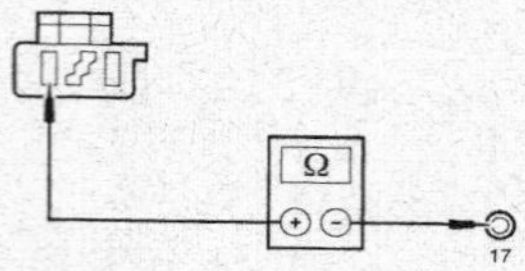	3 Measure the resistance between the Breakout Box pin 17, circuit 959 (G/W), and traction control switch C206, circuit 959 (G/W). • Is the resistance less than 5 ohms? → **Yes** INSTALL a new ECU. TEST the system for normal operation. → **No** REPAIR circuit 959 (G/W). TEST the system for normal operation.

FM4020001637020X

Fig. 42 Test M: Traction Control Inoperative (Part 2 of 2). 2001 Crown Victoria, Grand Marquis & Town Car

CONDITIONS	DETAILS/RESULTS/ACTIONS
N2 CHECK HEC POWER SUPPLY (Continued)	
4 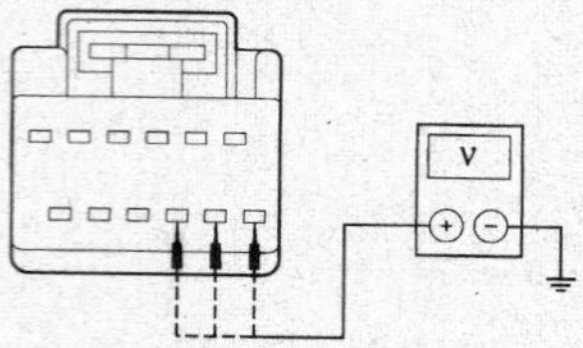	4 Measure the voltage between HEC connector, and ground as follows: HEC Connectors-Pin / Circuit: C255-7 — 729 (R/W) C255-9 — 1003 (GY/Y) C255-8 — 16 (R/LG) • Are the voltages greater than 10 volts? → **Yes** GO to **N3**. → **No** REPAIR the circuit(s) in question. TEST the system for normal operation.
N3 CHECK THE HEC GROUNDS	
1  2 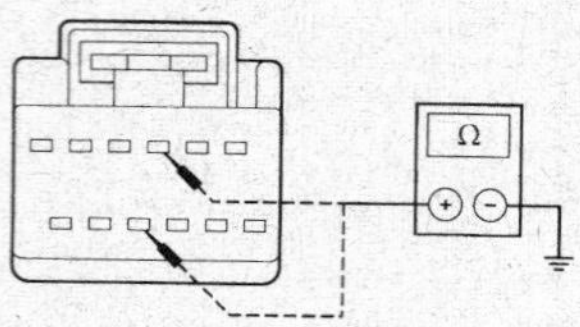	2 Measure the resistance between the HEC connector, and ground as follows: HEC Connectors-Pin / Circuit: C255-3 — 57 (BK) C255-10 — 676 (BK)

HEC Connectors-Pin	Circuit
C255-7	729 (R/W)
C255-9	1003 (GY/Y)
C255-8	16 (R/LG)

HEC Connectors-Pin	Circuit
C255-3	57 (BK)
C255-10	676 (BK)

FM4020101638020X

Fig. 43 Test N: No Communication w/Hybrid Electronic Cluster (Part 2 of 3). 2001 Crown Victoria, Grand Marquis & Town Car

CONDITIONS	DETAILS/RESULTS/ACTIONS
N3 CHECK THE HEC GROUNDS (Continued)	
	• Are the resistances less than 5 ohms? → **Yes** DIAGNOSE module communications. → **No** REPAIR circuit 57 (BK) or circuit 676 (BK). TEST the system for normal operation.

FM4020101638030X

Fig. 43 Test N: No Communication w/Hybrid Electronic Cluster (Part 3 of 3). 2001 Crown Victoria, Grand Marquis & Town Car

Condition	Possible Sources	Action
• No communication with the module — anti-lock brake control module	• Fuse. • Anti-lock brake control module. • Circuitry.	• GO to Pinpoint Test F.
• No communication with the module — hybrid electronic cluster (HEC)	• Fuse. • Hybrid electronic cluster. • Circuitry.	• GO to Pinpoint Test L.
• Spongy brake pedal with no warning indicator	• Air in brake hydraulic system.	• GO to Pinpoint Test G.
• Poor vehicle tracking during anti-lock function	• Air in brake hydraulic system. • Hydraulic control unit (HCU). • Base brake system.	• GO to Pinpoint Test H.
• The traction control is inoperative	• Anti-lock brake control module. • Electronic control unit (ECU). • Base brake system.	• GO to Pinpoint Test I.
• The yellow ABS warning indicator does not self-check	• Circuitry. • Hybrid electronic cluster. • Anti-lock brake control module.	• GO to Pinpoint Test J.
• The yellow ABS warning indicator and traction control active indicator always on	• Circuitry. • Hybrid electronic cluster. • Anti-lock brake control module.	• GO to Pinpoint Test K.
• Traction control active indicator always/never on	• Circuitry. • Message center display. • Anti-lock brake control module.	• DIAGNOSE message center display.
• The traction control cannot be disabled	• Circuitry. • Traction control switch. • Electronic control unit (ECU).	• GO to Pinpoint Test I.
• Red brake warning indicator always on with ABS lamp	• ABS subsystem (electronic brake distribution [EBD]). • Circuit. • Parking brake. • Brake fluid level.	• RETRIEVE the DTCs. REFER to DTC Index.

FM4020101781000X

Fig. 44 Symptom Chart. 2002 Crown Victoria, Grand Marquis & Town Car

CONDITIONS	DETAILS/RESULTS/ACTIONS
A1 CHECK ABS PUMP MOTOR	
	• Is the ABS pump motor running all the time? → **Yes** INSTALL a new anti-lock brake control module. TEST the system for normal operation. → **No** GO to **A2**.
A2 CHECK PUMP OPERATION	
	3 Trigger the anti-lock brake control module active command PMP MOTOR ON. • Does the ABS pump motor run for approximately three seconds? → **Yes** CLEAR the DTC. CHECK the yellow ABS warning indicator while driving the vehicle above 12 kph (7.5 mph) and no brakes applied until the vehicle exceeds 32 kph (20 mph). If the yellow ABS warning indicator illuminates, INSTALL a new anti-lock brake control module. TEST the system for normal operation. If the yellow ABS warning indicator does not illuminate, system is OK. → **No** TRIGGER the anti-lock brake control module active command PMP MOTOR OFF. GO to **A3**.

FM4020101782010X

Fig. 45 Test A/Code C1300: ABS Hydraulic Pump Motor Circuit Failure (Part 1 of 3). 2002 Crown Victoria, Grand Marquis & Town Car

CONDITIONS	DETAILS/RESULTS/ACTIONS
A3 CHECK POWER DISTRIBUTION BOX FUSE 9 (50A)	
	• Is the fuse OK? → **Yes** GO to **A4**. → **No** INSTALL a new fuse. TEST the system for normal operation. If the fuse fails again, CHECK for short to ground. REPAIR as necessary. TEST the system for normal operation.
A4 CHECK CIRCUIT 601 (LB/PK) FOR AN OPEN	
	2 Measure the voltage between the Anti-Lock Brake Control Module Connector (harness side), C135 pin 8, circuit 601 (LB/PK), and ground; and between the Anti-Lock Brake Control Module Connector (harness side), C135 pin 13, circuit 601 (LB/PK), and ground. • Are the voltages greater than 10 volts? → **Yes** GO to **A5**. → **No** REPAIR circuit 601 (LB/PK). CLEAR the DTCs. TEST the system for normal operation.

FM4020101782020X

Fig. 45 Test A/Code C1300: ABS Hydraulic Pump Motor Circuit Failure (Part 2 of 3). 2002 Crown Victoria, Grand Marquis & Town Car

CONDITIONS	DETAILS/RESULTS/ACTIONS
A5 CHECK CIRCUIT 57 (BK) FOR AN OPEN	
	1 Measure the resistance between the Anti-Lock Brake Control Module Connector (harness side), C135 pin 12, circuit 57 (BK), and ground; and between the Anti-Lock Brake Control Module Connector (harness side), C135 pin 15, circuit 57 (BK), and ground. • Are the resistances less than 5 ohms? → **Yes** GO to **A6**. → **No** REPAIR circuit 57 (BK). CLEAR the DTCs. TEST the system for normal operation.
A6 CHECK THE PUMP MOTOR FOR PROPER OPERATION	
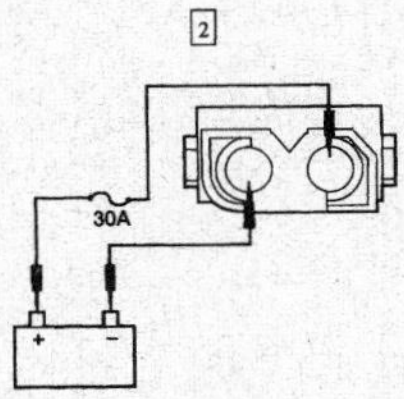	2 Use a heavy gauge jumper to connect a jumper between negative battery post and pump motor connector, brown wire; and momentarily connect a jumper between the positive battery post and pump motor connector, red wire with an in-line 30A fuse. • Does the pump motor run? → **Yes** INSTALL a new anti-lock brake control module. TEST the system for normal operation. → **No** INSTALL a new HCU. CLEAR the DTCs. TEST the system for normal operation.

FM4020101782030X

Fig. 45 Test A/Code C1300: ABS Hydraulic Pump Motor Circuit Failure (Part 3 of 3). 2002 Crown Victoria, Grand Marquis & Town Car

CONDITIONS	DETAILS/RESULTS/ACTIONS

B1 CHECK THE SUSPECT ANTI-LOCK BRAKE SENSOR FOR AN OPEN

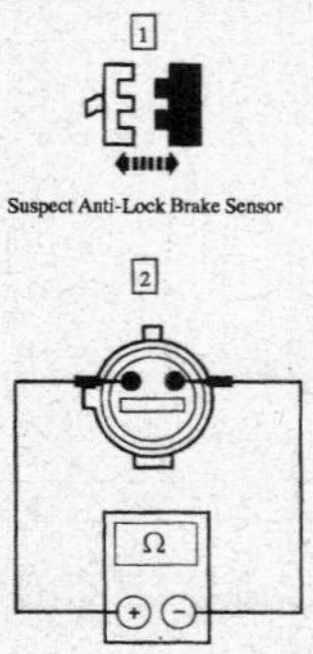

2 Measure the resistance between suspect anti-lock brake sensor terminals.

- Is the resistance between 800 and 1,400 ohms for the front anti-lock brake sensors and the rear anti-lock brake on vehicles equipped with rear drum brakes, and between 1,300 and 1,900 ohms for the rear anti-lock brake sensor on vehicles equipped with rear disc brakes?

→ **Yes**
GO to **B2**.

→ **No**
INSTALL a new anti-lock brake sensor.
CLEAR the DTCs.
TEST the system for normal operation.

B2 CHECK THE SUSPECT ANTI-LOCK BRAKE SENSOR FOR SHORT TO GROUND

1 Measure the resistance between suspect anti-lock brake sensor terminal, and ground.

- Is the resistance greater than 10,000 ohms?

→ **Yes**
GO to **B3**.

→ **No**
INSTALL a new anti-lock brake sensor.
CLEAR the DTCs.
TEST the system for normal operation.

FM4020101783010X

Fig. 46 Test B/Codes C1145, C1155, C1165 & C1175: ABS Sensor Input Circuit Failure (Part 1 of 4). 2002 Crown Victoria, Grand Marquis & Town Car

CONDITIONS	DETAILS/RESULTS/ACTIONS

B3 CHECK FOR SHORT TO POWER

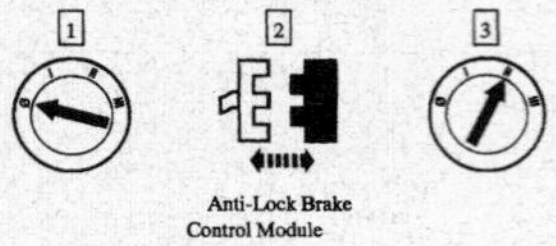

4 Measure the voltage between the Anti-Lock Brake Control Module Connector (harness side), C135 pins, and ground as follows:

DTC	Pin	Pin
C1145 (RF)	4 (circuit 514 [YE/RD])	5 (circuit 516 [YE/BK])
C1155 (LF)	20 (circuit 521 [TN/OG])	21 (circuit 522 [TN/BK])
C1165 (RR)	1 (circuit 523 [RD/PK])	3 (circuit 524 [PK/BK])
C1175 (LR)	22 (circuit 518 [LG/RD])	23 (circuit 519 [LG/BK])

- Is voltage present?

→ **Yes**
REPAIR the suspected anti-lock brake sensor circuit(s) in question. CLEAR the DTCs. TEST the system for normal operation.

→ **No**
GO to **B4**.

FM4020101783020X

Fig. 46 Test B/Codes C1145, C1155, C1165 & C1175: ABS Sensor Input Circuit Failure (Part 2 of 4). 2002 Crown Victoria, Grand Marquis & Town Car

CONDITIONS	DETAILS/RESULTS/ACTIONS

B4 CHECK FOR SHORT TO GROUND

1 Measure the resistance between the Anti-Lock Brake Control Module Connector (harness side), C135 pins, and ground as follows:

DTC	Pins
C1145 (RF)	4 (circuit 514 [YE/RD])/ 5 (circuit 516 [YE/BK])
C1155 (LF)	20 (circuit 521 [TN/OG])/ 21 (circuit 522 [TN/BK])
C1165 (RR)	1 (circuit 523 [RD/PK])/ 3 (circuit 524 [PK/BK])
C1175 (LR)	22 (circuit 518 [LG/RD])/ 23 (circuit 519 [LG/BK])

- Is the resistance greater than 10,000 ohms?

→ **Yes**
INSTALL a new anti-lock brake control module. TEST the system for normal operation.

→ **No**
GO to **B5**.

FM4020101783030X

Fig. 46 Test B/Codes C1145, C1155, C1165 & C1175: ABS Sensor Input Circuit Failure (Part 3 of 4). 2002 Crown Victoria, Grand Marquis & Town Car

CONDITIONS	DETAILS/RESULTS/ACTIONS

B5 CHECK FOR AN OPEN

2 Measure the resistance between the Anti-Lock Brake Control Module Connector (harness side), C135 pins and the corresponding anti-lock brake sensor pin as follows:

DTC	Pin	Pin
C1145 (RF)	4 (circuit 514 [YE/RD])	5 (circuit 516 [YE/BK])
C1155 (LF)	20 (circuit 521 [TN/OG])	21 (circuit 522 [TN/BK])
C1165 (RR)	1 (circuit 523 [RD/PK])	3 (circuit 524 [PK/BK])
C1175 (LR)	22 (circuit 518 [LG/RD])	23 (circuit 519 [LG/BK])

- Is the resistance between 800 and 1,400 ohms for the front anti-lock brake sensors and the rear anti-lock brake on vehicles equipped with rear drum brakes, and between 1,300 and 1,900 ohms for the rear anti-lock brake sensor on vehicles equipped with rear disc brakes?

→ **Yes**
INSTALL a new anti-lock brake control module. TEST the system for normal operation.

→ **No**
INSTALL a new anti-lock brake sensor.
CLEAR the DTCs.
TEST the system for normal operation.

FM4020101783040X

Fig. 46 Test B/Codes C1145, C1155, C1165 & C1175: ABS Sensor Input Circuit Failure (Part 4 of 4). 2002 Crown Victoria, Grand Marquis & Town Car

CONDITIONS	DETAILS/RESULTS/ACTIONS
C1 CHECK THE ANTI-LOCK BRAKE SENSOR	
	1 Check the suspect anti-lock brake sensor mounting. Check the suspect anti-lock brake sensor for excessive dirt build-up, metal obstructions, improper harness routing, and chafing. • Is the suspect anti-lock brake sensor OK? → **Yes** GO to **C2**. → **No** REPAIR or INSTALL a new sensor as necessary. CLEAR the DTCs. TEST the system for normal operation.
C2 CHECK THE ANTI-LOCK BRAKE SENSOR INDICATOR	
	1 Check the suspect anti-lock brake sensor indicator for corrosion, nicks, damaged teeth, correct mounting, alignment, and consistent air gap. • Is the suspect anti-lock brake sensor indicator OK? → **Yes** GO to **C3**. → **No** REPAIR or INSTALL a new indicator as necessary. CLEAR the DTCs. TEST the system for normal operation.

FM4020101784010X

Fig. 47 Test C/Codes C1296, C1297, C1298 & C1299: ABS Sensor Input Signal Missing (Part 1 of 2). 2002 Crown Victoria, Grand Marquis & Town Car

CONDITIONS	DETAILS/RESULTS/ACTIONS
C3 CHECK THE ANTI-LOCK BRAKE SENSOR OUTPUT	
1 2	

Anti-Lock Brake Control Module

3 While spinning the suspect wheel at one revolution per second, measure the AC voltage between the Anti-Lock Brake Control Module Connector (harness side), C135 pins as follows:

DTC	Pin	Pin
C1297 (RF)	4 (circuit 514 [YE/RD])	5 (circuit 516 [YE/BK])
C1296 (LF)	20 (circuit 521 [TN/OG])	21 (circuit 522 [TN/BK])
C1298 (RR)	1 (circuit 523 [RD/PK])	3 (circuit 524 [PK/BK])
C1299 (LR)	22 (circuit 518 [LG/RD])	23 (circuit 519 [LG/BK])

• Is the voltage between 100 and 3,500 mVolts AC?

→ **Yes**
INSTALL a new anti-lock brake control module. TEST the system for normal operation.

→ **No**
INSTALL a new anti-lock brake sensor. CLEAR the DTCs. TEST the system for normal operation.

FM4020101784020X

Fig. 47 Test C/Codes C1296, C1297, C1298 & C1299: ABS Sensor Input Signal Missing (Part 2 of 2). 2002 Crown Victoria, Grand Marquis & Town Car

CONDITIONS	DETAILS/RESULTS/ACTIONS
D1 CHECK CENTRAL JUNCTION BOX (CJB) FUSE 22 (15A)	
	1 Check CJB fuse 22 (15A). • Is the fuse OK? → **Yes** GO to **D2**. → **No** DIAGNOSE exterior lighting.
D2 CHECK THE ABS CONTROL MODULE BOO__ABS PID	
1 2	

3 Monitor the ABS control module PID BOO__ABS, while pressing and releasing the brake pedal.

• Does the ABS control module PID BOO__ABS indicate ON with the brake pedal pressed and OFF with the brake pedal released?

→ **Yes**
CLEAR the DTCs. REPEAT the self-test. If the DTC B1484 is retrieved, INSTALL a new electronic control unit (ECU). REPEAT the self-test.

→ **No**
GO to **D3**.

D3 CHECK CIRCUIT 10 (LG/RD) FOR OPEN

NOTE: Make sure the brake pedal is released for this step.

1

Anti-Lock Brake Control Module C135

2 Press and hold the brake pedal.

FM4020101785010X

Fig. 48 Test D/Code B1484: Brake Pedal Input Open Circuit (Part 1 of 2). 2002 Crown Victoria & Grand Marquis

CONDITIONS	DETAILS/RESULTS/ACTIONS
D3 CHECK CIRCUIT 10 (LG/RD) FOR OPEN (Continued)	
	3 Measure the voltage between the Anti-Lock Brake Control Module Connector (harness side), C135 pin 6, circuit 10 (LG/RD), and the Anti-Lock Brake Control Module Connector (harness side), C135 pin 12, circuit 57 (BK). • Is voltage greater than 10 volts? → **Yes** GO to **D4**. → **No** REPAIR circuit 10 (LG/RD) or circuit 57 (BK). CLEAR the DTCs. TEST the system for normal operation.
D4 CHECK BRAKE PEDAL POSITION (BPP) SWITCH	

1

Brake Pedal Position (BPP) Switch

2 Press and release the brake pedal.

• Is the BPP switch closed when the brake pedal is pressed and open when the brake pedal is released?

→ **Yes**
INSTALL a new anti-lock brake control module. TEST the system for normal operation.

→ **No**
INSTALL a new BPP switch. TEST the system for normal operation.

FM4020101785020X

Fig. 48 Test D/Code B1484: Brake Pedal Input Open Circuit (Part 2 of 2). 2002 Crown Victoria & Grand Marquis

D1 CHECK CENTRAL JUNCTION BOX (CJB) FUSE 32 (20A)

1 Check CJB fuse 32 (20A).

- **Is the fuse OK?**

→ **Yes**
GO to D2.

→ **No**
Diagnose exterior lighting.

D2 CHECK THE ABS CONTROL MODULE BOO_ABS PID

1

2

3 Monitor the ABS control module PID BOO_ABS, while pressing and releasing the brake pedal.

- **Does the ABS control module PID BOO_ABS indicate ON with the brake pedal pressed and OFF with the brake pedal released?**

→ **Yes**
CLEAR the DTCs. REPEAT the self-test. If the DTC B1484 is retrieved, INSTALL a new electronic control unit (ECU). REPEAT the self-test.

→ **No**
GO to D3.

FM4020101796010X

Fig. 49 Test D/Code B1484: Brake Pedal Input Open Circuit (Part 1 of 2). 2002 Town Car

D3 CHECK CIRCUIT 511 (LG) FOR OPEN

NOTE: Make sure the brake pedal is released for this step.

1

Anti-Lock Brake Control Module

2 Press and hold the brake pedal.

3 Measure the voltage between the Anti-Lock Brake Control Module Connector (harness side), C135 pin 6, circuit 511 (LG), and the Anti-Lock Brake Control Module Connector (harness side), C135 pin 12, circuit 57 (BK).

- **Is voltage greater than 10 volts?**

→ **Yes**
INSTALL a new anti-lock brake control module. TEST the system for normal operation.

→ **No**
REPAIR circuit 511 (LG) or circuit 57 (BK). CLEAR the DTCs. TEST the system for normal operation.

FM4020101796020X

Fig. 49 Test D/Code B1484: Brake Pedal Input Open Circuit (Part 2 of 2). 2002 Town Car

CONDITIONS	DETAILS/RESULTS/ACTIONS
E1 CHECK THE BATTERY VOLTAGE	
1 	
2 	2 Measure the voltage between positive and negative battery post. • Is the voltage between 10 and 16 volts? → **Yes** GO to **E2**. → **No** DIAGNOSE charging system.
E2 CHECK THE ANTI-LOCK BRAKE CONTROL MODULE GROUND	
1  2  Anti-Lock Brake Control Module	3 Measure the resistance between the Anti-Lock Brake Control Module Connector (harness side), C135 pin 15, circuit 57 (BK), and ground. • Is the resistance less than 5 ohms? → **Yes** GO to **E3**. → **No** REPAIR circuit 57 (BK). CLEAR the DTCs. TEST the system for normal operation.

FM4020101786010X

Fig. 50 Test E/Code B1676: Battery Voltage Out Of Range (Part 1 of 2). 2002 Crown Victoria, Grand Marquis & Town Car

CONDITIONS	DETAILS/RESULTS/ACTIONS
E3 CHECK CIRCUIT 57 (BK) FOR AN OPEN	
	1 Measure the resistance between the Anti-Lock Brake Control Module Connector (harness side), C135 pin 12, circuit 57 (BK), and ground. • Is the resistance less than 5 ohms? → **Yes** INSTALL a new anti-lock brake control module. TEST the system for normal operation. → **No** REPAIR circuit 57 (BK). CLEAR the DTCs. TEST the system for normal operation.

FM4020101786020X

Fig. 50 Test E/Code B1676: Battery Voltage Out Of Range (Part 2 of 2). 2002 Crown Victoria, Grand Marquis & Town Car

CONDITIONS	DETAILS/RESULTS/ACTIONS
F1 CHECK CIRCUITS 601 (LB/BK), AND CIRCUIT 88 (BK/WH) FOR AN OPEN	
1  2  Anti-Lock Brake Control Module 3 	4 Measure the voltage between the Anti-Lock Brake Control Module Connector (harness side), C135 pins, and ground as follows: Pin 8 – Circuit 88 (BK/WH) Pin 13 – Circuit 601 (LB/PK) Pin 14 – Circuit 483 (RD) • Are the voltages greater than 10 volts? → **Yes** GO to **F2**. → **No** REPAIR the circuit in question. TEST the system for normal operation.

Pin	Circuit
8	Circuit 88 (BK/WH)
13	Circuit 601 (LB/PK)
14	Circuit 483 (RD)

FM4020101787010X

Fig. 51 Test F: No Communication w/Module – ABS Brake Control Module (Part 1 of 2). 2002 Crown Victoria, Grand Marquis & Town Car

CONDITIONS	DETAILS/RESULTS/ACTIONS
F2 CHECK CIRCUIT 57 (BK) FOR AN OPEN	
	1 Measure the resistance between the Anti-Lock Brake Control Module Connector (harness side), C135 pin 15, circuit 57 (BK), and ground; and between the Anti-Lock Brake Control Module Connector (harness side), C135 pin 12, circuit 57 (BK), and ground. • Are the resistances less than 5 ohms? → **Yes** DIAGNOSE module communications. → **No** REPAIR circuit 57 (BK). TEST the system for normal operation.

FM4020101787020X

Fig. 51 Test F: No Communication w/Module – ABS Brake Control Module (Part 2 of 2). 2002 Crown Victoria, Grand Marquis & Town Car

CONDITIONS	DETAILS/RESULTS/ACTIONS
H1 BLEED THE BRAKE SYSTEM	
	1 Bleed the brake system. 2 Place the air suspension switch in the ON position after the vehicle is off the hoist. • Does the vehicle track poorly? → **Yes** GO to **H2**. → **No** The brake system is operating correctly. TEST the system for normal operation.

FM4020101789010X

Fig. 53 Test H: Poor Vehicle Tracking During ABS Function (Part 1 of 6). 2002 Crown Victoria, Grand Marquis & Town Car

CONDITIONS	DETAILS/RESULTS/ACTIONS
H2 CHECK THE LF HCU VALVE OPERATION	
1 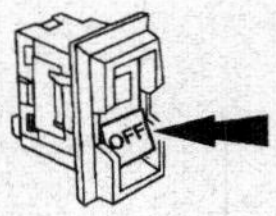 2  3 	1 Place the air suspension switch in the OFF position. 4 Lift the vehicle and rotate all the wheels to make sure they turn freely (the transmission must be in NEUTRAL). 5 Trigger the anti-lock brake control module active command PMP MOTOR ON for four seconds. (Trigger must be pushed twice. Each press runs the pump for two seconds.) 6 Apply moderate brake pedal effort. 7 Have an assistant attempt to rotate the LF wheel. • Does the LF wheel rotate? → **Yes** INSTALL a new HCU. TEST the system for normal operation. → **No** GO to **H3**.

FM4020101789020X

Fig. 53 Test H: Poor Vehicle Tracking During ABS Function (Part 2 of 6). 2002 Crown Victoria, Grand Marquis & Town Car

CONDITIONS	DETAILS/RESULTS/ACTIONS
G1 CHECK THE COMPONENTS MOUNTING	
	1 Inspect the brake pedal and the power brake booster/brake master cylinder for correct attachment. 2 Bleed the brake system. • Is the brake pedal spongy? → **Yes** GO to **G2**. → **No** The brake system is operating correctly. TEST the system for normal operation.
G2 BLEED THE BRAKE SYSTEM	
	1 Rebleed the brake system. • Is the brake pedal spongy? → **Yes** DIAGNOSE brakes. → **No** The brake system is operating correctly. TEST the system for normal operation.

FM4020101788000X

Fig. 52 Test G: Spongy Brake Pedal w/No Warning Indicator. 2002 Crown Victoria, Grand Marquis & Town Car

CONDITIONS	DETAILS/RESULTS/ACTIONS
H3 CHECK THE LF HCU VALVE RELEASE	
1 	1 Trigger the anti-lock brake control module active command LF INLET ON and LF OUTLET ON. 2 Have an assistant turn the LF wheel using a two foot lever, such as a breaker bar, immediately after pressing trigger (the scan tool will energize the valves for only two seconds per trigger press). • Does the LF wheel turn? → **Yes** GO to **H4**. → **No** GO to **H10**.
H4 CHECK THE RF HCU VALVE OPERATION	
1 	2 Trigger the anti-lock brake control module active command PMP MOTOR ON for four seconds. (Trigger must be pushed twice. Each press runs the pump for two seconds.) 3 Apply moderate brake pedal effort. 4 Have an assistant attempt to rotate the RF wheel. • Does the RF wheel rotate? → **Yes** INSTALL a new HCU. TEST the system for normal operation. → **No** GO to **H5**.

FM4020101789030X

Fig. 53 Test H: Poor Vehicle Tracking During ABS Function (Part 3 of 6). 2002 Crown Victoria, Grand Marquis & Town Car

CONDITIONS	DETAILS/RESULTS/ACTIONS
H5 CHECK THE RF HCU VALVE RELEASE	
	1 Trigger the anti-lock brake control module active command RF INLET ON and RF OUTLET ON. 2 Have an assistant turn the RF wheel using a two foot lever, such as a breaker bar, immediately after pressing trigger (the scan tool will energize the valves for only two seconds per trigger press). • Does the RF wheel turn? → **Yes** GO to **H6**. → **No** GO to **H10**.
H6 CHECK THE LR HCU VALVE OPERATION	
	2 Trigger the anti-lock brake control module active command PMP MOTOR ON for four seconds. (Trigger must be pushed twice. Each press runs the pump for two seconds.) 3 Apply moderate brake pedal effort. 4 Have an assistant attempt to rotate the LR wheel. • Does the LR wheel rotate? → **Yes** INSTALL a new HCU. TEST the system for normal operation. → **No** GO to **H7**.

FM4020101789040X

Fig. 53 Test H: Poor Vehicle Tracking During ABS Function (Part 4 of 6). 2002 Crown Victoria, Grand Marquis & Town Car

CONDITIONS	DETAILS/RESULTS/ACTIONS
H9 CHECK THE RR HCU VALVE RELEASE	
	1 Trigger the anti-lock brake control module active command RR INLET ON and RR OUTLET ON. 2 Have an assistant turn the RR wheel using a two foot lever, such as a breaker bar, immediately after pressing trigger (the scan tool will energize the valves for only two seconds per trigger press). • Does the RR wheel turn? → **Yes** The anti-lock brake system is operating correctly. TEST the system for normal operation. → **No** GO to **H10**.
H10 CHECK FOR DIAGNOSTIC TROUBLE CODES (DTCS)	
	1 Retrieve and document continuous DTCs. • Are any DTCs retrieved? → **Yes** GO to Anti-Lock Brake Control Module Diagnostic Trouble Code (DTC) Index. → **No** INSTALL a new HCU. TEST the system for normal operation.

FM4020101789060X

Fig. 53 Test H: Poor Vehicle Tracking During ABS Function (Part 6 of 6). 2002 Crown Victoria, Grand Marquis & Town Car

CONDITIONS	DETAILS/RESULTS/ACTIONS
H7 CHECK THE LR HCU VALVE RELEASE	
	1 Trigger the anti-lock brake control module active command LR INLET ON and LR OUTLET ON. 2 Have an assistant turn the LR wheel using a two foot lever, such as a breaker bar, immediately after pressing trigger (the scan tool will energize the valves for only two seconds per trigger press). • Does the LR wheel turn? → **Yes** GO to **H8**. → **No** GO to **H10**.
H8 CHECK THE RR HCU VALVE OPERATION	
	2 Trigger the anti-lock brake control module active command PMP MOTOR ON for four seconds. (Trigger must be pushed twice. Each press runs the pump for two seconds.) 3 Apply moderate brake pedal effort. 4 Have an assistant attempt to rotate the RR wheel. • Does the RR wheel rotate? → **Yes** INSTALL a new HCU. TEST the system for normal operation. → **No** GO to **H9**.

FM4020101789050X

Fig. 53 Test H: Poor Vehicle Tracking During ABS Function (Part 5 of 6). 2002 Crown Victoria, Grand Marquis & Town Car

CONDITIONS	DETAILS/RESULTS/ACTIONS
I1 CHECK FOR DTCS	
	2 Retrieve and document continuous DTCs. • Are any DTCs retrieved? → **Yes** GO to Anti-Lock Brake Control Module Diagnostic Trouble Code (DTC) Index. → **No** GO to **I2**.
I2 CHECK THE TRACTION CONTROL SWITCH	
 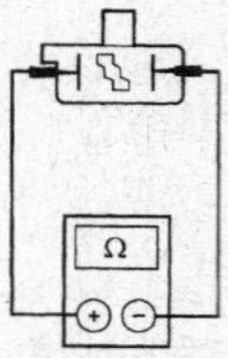	3 Press the traction control switch in the ON position. 4 Measure the resistance between the traction control switch pin 2, circuit 959 (GY), and pin 1, circuit 57 (BK). • Is the resistance greater than 5 ohms? → **Yes** GO to **I3**. → **No** INSTALL a new traction control switch. TEST the system for normal operation.
I3 CHECK CIRCUIT 959 (GY/WH) FOR SHORT	

FM4020101790010X

Fig. 54 Test I: Traction Control Cannot Be Disabled/Is Inoperative (Part 1 of 2). 2002 Crown Victoria, Grand Marquis & Town Car

CONDITIONS	DETAILS/RESULTS/ACTIONS
I3 CHECK CIRCUIT 959 (GY/WH) FOR SHORT (Continued)	
4 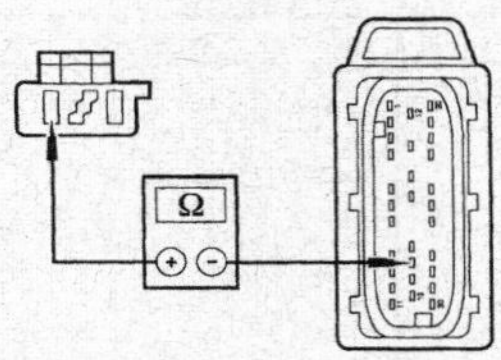	4 Measure the resistance between the Anti-Lock Brake Control Module Connector (harness side), C135 pin 17, circuit 959 (GY/WH) and the traction control switch connector pin 2, circuit 959 (GY/WH). • Is the resistance greater than 5 ohms? → **Yes** REPAIR circuit 959 (GY/WH). TEST the system for normal operation. → **No** GO to **I4**.
I4 CHECK CIRCUIT 57 (BK)	
1 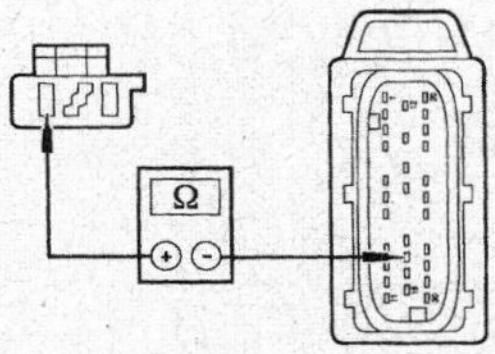	1 Measure the resistance between the traction control switch connector pin 1, circuit 57 (BK) and ground. • Is the resistance greater than 5 ohms? → **Yes** REPAIR circuit 57 (BK). TEST the system for normal operation. → **No** INSTALL a new anti-lock brake control module. REPEAT the self-test. TEST the system for normal operation.

FM4020101790020X

Fig. 54 Test I: Traction Control Cannot Be Disabled/Is Inoperative (Part 2 of 2). 2002 Crown Victoria, Grand Marquis & Town Car

CONDITIONS	DETAILS/RESULTS/ACTIONS
K1 CHECK FOR DTCs	
1 2 3 	3 Retrieve and document continuous DTCs for the anti-lock brake control module. • Are any DTCs retrieved? → **Yes** GO to Anti-Lock Brake Control Module Diagnostic Trouble Code (DTC) Index. → **No** INSTALL a new HEC. TEST the system for normal operation.

FM4020101792000X

Fig. 56 Test K: Yellow ABS Warning Indicator & Traction Control Active Indicator Always On. 2002 Crown Victoria, Grand Marquis & Town Car

CONDITIONS	DETAILS/RESULTS/ACTIONS
L1 CHECK FUSES	
1 2 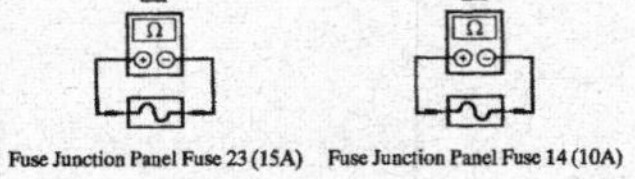	• Are the fuses OK? → **Yes** GO to **L2**. → **No** INSTALL new fuse(s). TEST the system for normal operation. If the fuse fails again, CHECK for short to ground. REPAIR as necessary. TEST the system for normal operation.

FM4020101793010X

Fig. 57 Test L: No Communication w/Module-Hybrid Electronic Cluster (Part 1 of 3). 2002 Crown Victoria & Grand Marquis

CONDITIONS	DETAILS/RESULTS/ACTIONS
J1 CHECK THE YELLOW ABS WARNING INDICATOR	
1 2 	• Is the yellow ABS warning indicator illuminated? → **Yes** GO to **J2**. → **No** DIAGNOSE instrument cluster.
J2 CHECK PROVE OUT	
1 2 3 	• Does the yellow ABS warning indicator prove out for three seconds and then turn off? → **Yes** The yellow ABS warning indicator is working correctly. TEST the system for normal operation. → **No** INSTALL a new anti-lock brake control module. TEST the system for normal operation.

FM4020101791000X

Fig. 55 Test J: Yellow ABS Warning Indicator Does Not Self-Check. 2002 Crown Victoria, Grand Marquis & Town Car

CONDITIONS	DETAILS/RESULTS/ACTIONS
L2 CHECK HEC POWER SUPPLY	
1 2 3  HEC 4 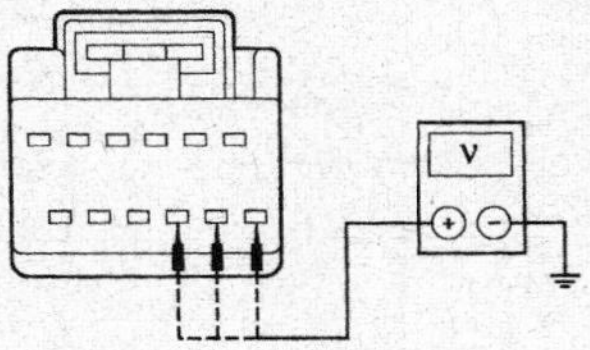	4 Measure the voltage between HEC connector, and ground as follows: (see table below) • Are the voltages greater than 10 volts? → **Yes** GO to **L3**. → **No** REPAIR the circuit(s) in question. TEST the system for normal operation.
L3 CHECK THE HEC GROUNDS	
1 	

HEC Connectors-Pin	Circuit
C220b-7	729 (RD/WH)
C220b-9	1003 (GY/YE)
C220b-8	16 (RD/LG)

FM4020101793020X

Fig. 57 Test L: No Communication w/Module-Hybrid Electronic Cluster (Part 2 of 3). 2002 Crown Victoria & Grand Marquis

CONDITIONS	DETAILS/RESULTS/ACTIONS
L3 CHECK THE HEC GROUNDS (Continued)	
2 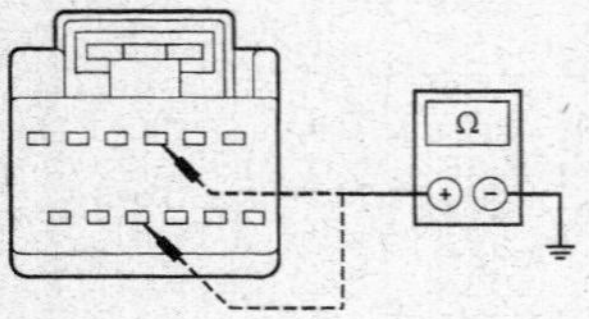	2 Measure the resistance between the HEC connector, and ground as follows: (see table below) • Are the resistances less than 5 ohms? → **Yes** DIAGNOSE network communications. → **No** REPAIR circuit 57 (BK) or circuit 676 (BK). TEST the system for normal operation.

HEC Connec-tors-Pin	Circuit
C220b-3	57 (BK)
C220b-10	676 (BK)

FM4020101793030X

Fig. 57 Test L: No Communication w/Module-Hybrid Electronic Cluster (Part 3 of 3). 2002 Crown Victoria & Grand Marquis

L2 CHECK HEC POWER SUPPLY

1

2

HEC

3

4

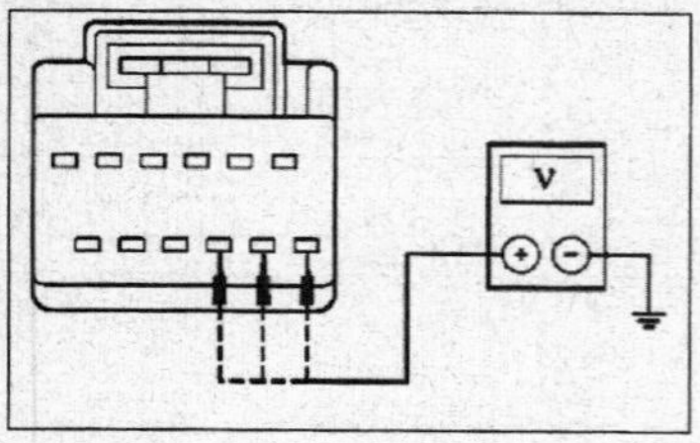

4 Measure the voltage between HEC connector, and ground as follows:

HEC Connectors-Pin	Circuit
C220a-7	729 (RD/WH)
C220a-9	1003 (GY/YE)
C220a-8	16 (RD/LG)

- **Are the voltages greater than 10 volts?**

→ **Yes**
GO to L3 .

→ **No**
REPAIR the circuit(s) in question. TEST the system for normal operation.

FM4020101797020X

Fig. 58 Test L: No Communication w/Module-Hybrid Electronic Cluster (Part 2 of 3). 2002 Town Car

CONDITIONS	DETAILS/RESULTS/ACTIONS

CAUTION: The Flex Probe Kit must be used for all test connections. Use of standard multimeter probes may damage wiring terminals.

L1 CHECK FUSES

1

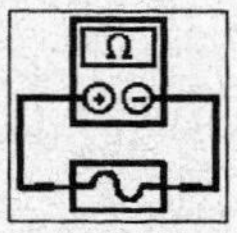

Fuse Junction Panel Fuse 23 (15A)

2

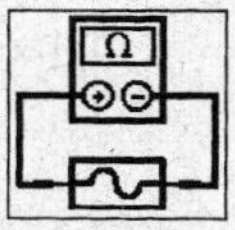

Fuse Junction Panel Fuse 14 (10A)

- **Are the fuses OK?**

→ **Yes**
GO to L2 .

→ **No**
INSTALL new fuse(s). TEST the system for normal operation. If the fuse fails again, CHECK for short to ground. REPAIR as necessary. TEST the system for normal operation.

FM4020101797010X

Fig. 58 Test L: No Communication w/Module-Hybrid Electronic Cluster (Part 1 of 3). 2002 Town Car

L3 CHECK THE HEC GROUNDS

1

2

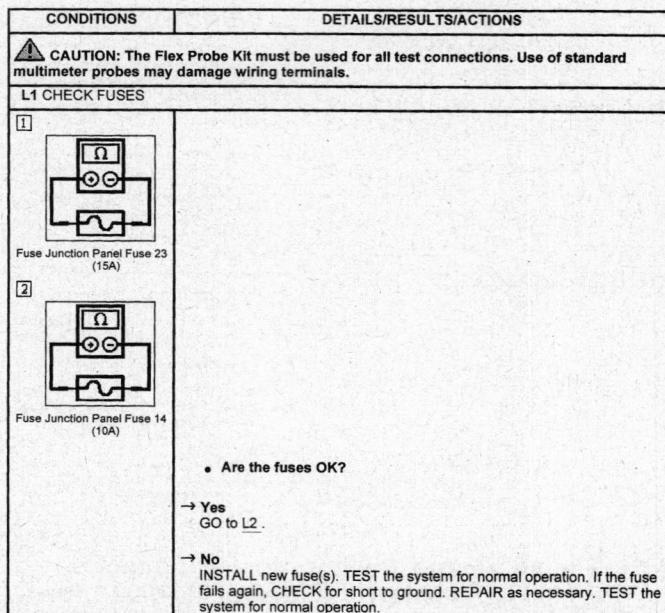

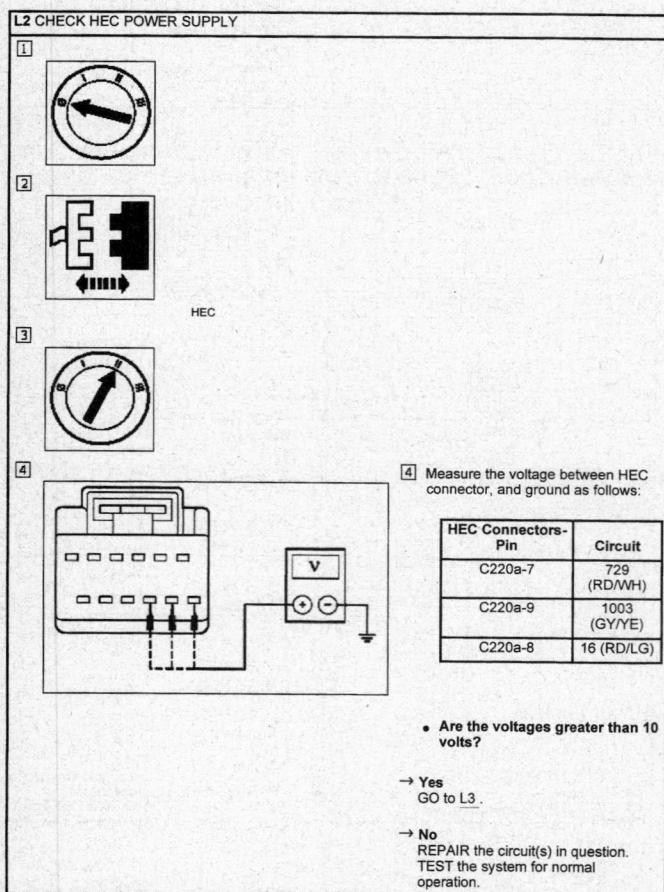

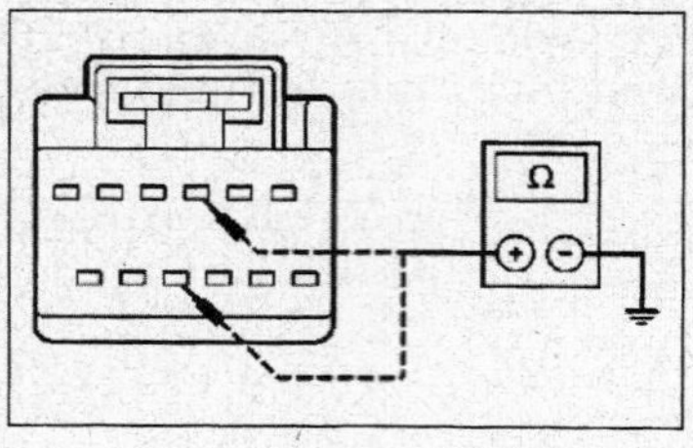

2 Measure the resistance between the HEC connector, and ground as follows:

HEC Connectors-	Circuit
C220a-3	57 (BK)
C220a-10	676

- **Are the resistances less than 5 ohms?**

→ **Yes**
Diagnose module communications.

→ **No**
REPAIR circuit 57 (BK) or circuit 676 (BK). TEST the system for normal operation.

FM4020101797030X

Fig. 58 Test L: No Communication w/Module-Hybrid Electronic Cluster (Part 3 of 3). 2002 Town Car

Condition	Possible Sources	Action
• No communication with the module — anti-lock brake control module	• Fuse. • Anti-lock brake control module. • Circuitry.	• Go To Pinpoint Test F .
• No communication with the module — hybrid electronic cluster (HEC)	• Fuse. • Hybrid electronic cluster. • Circuitry.	• Go To Pinpoint Test K .
• Poor vehicle tracking during anti-lock function	• Air in brake hydraulic system. • Hydraulic control unit (HCU). • Base brake system.	• Go To Pinpoint Test G .
• The traction control is inoperative	• Anti-lock brake control module. • Electronic control unit (ECU). • Base brake system.	• Go To Pinpoint Test H .
• The yellow ABS warning indicator does not self-check	• Circuitry. • Hybrid electronic cluster. • Anti-lock brake control module.	• Go To Pinpoint Test I .
• The yellow ABS warning indicator and traction control active indicator always on	• Circuitry. • Hybrid electronic cluster. • Anti-lock brake control module.	• Go To Pinpoint Test J .
• Traction control active indicator always/never on	• Circuitry. • Message center display. • Anti-lock brake control module.	• DIAGNOSE message center.
• The traction control cannot be disabled	• Circuitry. • Traction control switch. • Electronic control unit (ECU).	• Go To Pinpoint Test H .
• Red brake warning indicator always on with ABS lamp	• ABS subsystem (electronic brake distribution [EBD]). • Circuit. • ABS module connector not connected.	• RETRIEVE the DTCs. REFER to DTC Index. • CONNECT the ABS module connector.
• Red brake warning indicator always on without ABS lamp	• Parking brake. • Brake fluid level.	• DIAGNOSE brake system.

FM4020201939000X

Fig. 59 Symptom Chart. 2003–04 Crown Victoria, Grand Marquis, Marauder & Town Car

A4 CHECK CIRCUITS 601 (LB/PK) AND 483 (RD) FOR AN OPEN	
• Disconnect: Anti-Lock Brake Control Module C135. • Measure the voltage between the Anti-Lock Brake Control Module Connector (harness side), C135 pin 14, circuit 483 (RD), and ground; and between the Anti-Lock Brake Control Module Connector (harness side), C135 pin 13, circuit 601 (LB/PK), and ground. • **Are the voltages greater than 10 volts?**	**Yes** GO to A5 . **No** REPAIR circuit 601 (LB/PK) or 483 (RD). CLEAR the DTCs. TEST the system for normal operation.
A5 CHECK CIRCUIT 57 (BK) FOR AN OPEN	
• Measure the resistance between the Anti-Lock Brake Control Module Connector (harness side), C135 pin 12, circuit 57 (BK), and ground; and between the Anti-Lock Brake Control Module Connector (harness side), C135 pin 15, circuit 57 (BK), and ground. • **Are the resistances less than 5 ohms?**	**Yes** GO to A6 . **No** REPAIR circuit 57 (BK). CLEAR the DTCs. TEST the system for normal operation.
A6 CHECK THE PUMP MOTOR FOR PROPER OPERATION	
• Disconnect: Pump Motor Connector. • Use a heavy gauge jumper to connect a jumper between negative battery post and pump motor connector, brown wire; and momentarily connect a jumper between the positive battery post and pump motor connector, red wire with an in-line 30A fuse. 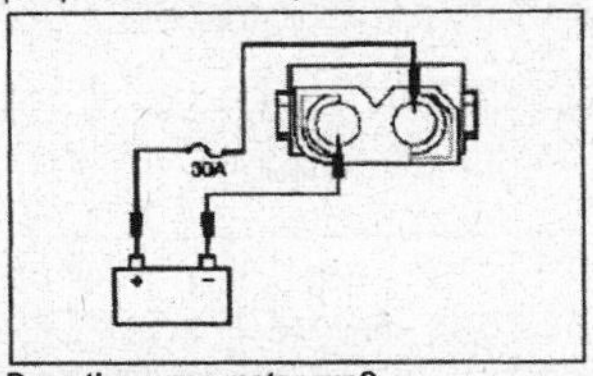 • **Does the pump motor run?**	**Yes** INSTALL a new anti-lock brake control module. TEST the system for normal operation. **No** INSTALL a new HCU. CLEAR the DTCs. TEST the system for normal operation.

FM4020201928020X

Fig. 60 Test A/Code C1300: ABS Hydraulic Pump Motor Circuit Failure (Part 2 of 2). 2003–04 Crown Victoria, Grand Marquis, Marauder & Town Car

Test Step	Result / Action to Take
⚠ **CAUTION: The Flex Probe Kit must be used for all test connections. Use of standard multimeter probes may damage wiring terminals.**	
A1 CHECK ABS PUMP MOTOR	
• Key in ON position. • **Is the ABS pump motor running all the time?**	**Yes** INSTALL a new anti-lock brake control module. TEST the system for normal operation. **No** GO to A2 .
A2 CHECK PUMP OPERATION	
• Connect the diagnostic tool. • Key in ON position. • Trigger the anti-lock brake control module active command PMP MOTOR ON. • **Does the ABS pump motor run for approximately three seconds?**	**Yes** CLEAR the DTC. CHECK the yellow ABS warning indicator while driving the vehicle above 12 kph (7.5 mph) and no brakes applied until the vehicle exceeds 32 kph (20 mph). If the yellow ABS warning indicator illuminates, INSTALL a new anti-lock brake control module. TEST the system for normal operation. If the yellow ABS warning indicator does not illuminate, system is OK. If the yellow ABS warning indicator does illuminate, INSTALL a new HCU. **No** TRIGGER the anti-lock brake control module active command PMP MOTOR OFF. GO to A3 .
A3 CHECK POWER DISTRIBUTION BOX FUSE 106 (40A) and 118 (20A)	
• Check fuse: Power Distribution Box Fuse 118 (20A). • **Is the fuse OK?**	**Yes** GO to A4 . **No** INSTALL a new fuse. TEST the system for normal operation. If the fuse fails again, CHECK for short to ground. REPAIR as necessary. TEST the system for normal operation.

FM4020201928010X

Fig. 60 Test A/Code C1300: ABS Hydraulic Pump Motor Circuit Failure (Part 1 of 2). 2003–04 Crown Victoria, Grand Marquis, Marauder & Town Car

Test Step	Result / Action to Take
⚠ **CAUTION: The Flex Probe Kit must be used for all test connections. Use of standard multimeter probes may damage wiring terminals.**	
B1 CHECK THE SUSPECT ANTI-LOCK BRAKE SENSOR FOR AN OPEN	
• Disconnect: Suspect Anti-Lock Brake Sensor. • Measure the resistance between suspect anti-lock brake sensor terminals. 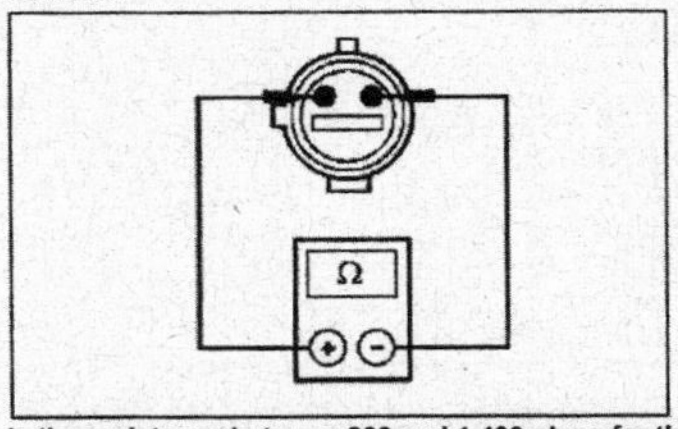 • **Is the resistance between 800 and 1,400 ohms for the front anti-lock brake sensors and the rear anti-lock brake on vehicles equipped with rear drum brakes, and between 1,300 and 1,900 ohms for the rear anti-lock brake sensor on vehicles equipped with rear disc brakes?**	**Yes** GO to B2 . **No** INSTALL a new anti-lock brake sensor. CLEAR the DTCs. TEST the system for normal operation.
B2 CHECK FOR SHORT TO POWER	
• Key in OFF position. • Disconnect: Anti-Lock Brake Control Module C135. • Key in ON position. • Measure the voltage between the Anti-Lock Brake Control Module Connector (harness side), C135 pins, and ground as follows: (see table below) • **Is voltage present?**	**Yes** REPAIR the suspected anti-lock brake sensor circuit(s) in question. CLEAR the DTCs. TEST the system for normal operation. **No** GO to B3 .

DTC	Pin	Pin
C1145 (RF)	4 (circuit 514 [YE/RD])	5 (circuit 516 [YE/BK])
C1155 (LF)	20 (circuit 521 [TN/OG])	21 (circuit 522 [TN/BK])
C1165 (RR)	1 (circuit 523 [RD/PK])	3 (circuit 524 [PK/BK])
C1175 (LR)	22 (circuit 518 [LG/RD])	23 (circuit 519 [LG/BK])

FM4020201929010X

Fig. 61 Test B/Codes C1145, C1155, C1165 & C1175: ABS Brake Sensor Input Circuit Failure (Part 1 of 2). 2003–04 Crown Victoria, Grand Marquis, Marauder & Town Car

B3 CHECK FOR SHORT TO GROUND

- Measure the resistance between the Anti-Lock Brake Control Module Connector (harness side), C135 pins, and ground as follows:

DTC	Pins
C1145 (RF)	4 (circuit 514 [YE/RD])/ 5 (circuit 516 [YE/BK])
C1155 (LF)	20 (circuit 521 [TN/OG])/ 21 (circuit 522 [TN/BK])
C1165 (RR)	1 (circuit 523 [RD/PK])/ 3 (circuit 524 [PK/BK])
C1175 (LR)	22 (circuit 518 [LG/RD])/ 23 (circuit 519 [LG/BK])

- **Is the resistance greater than 10,000 ohms?**

Yes
INSTALL a new anti-lock brake control module.

TEST the system for normal operation.

No
GO to B4 .

B4 CHECK FOR AN OPEN

- Key in OFF position.
- Measure the resistance between the Anti-Lock Brake Control Module Connector (harness side), C135 pins and the corresponding anti-lock brake sensor pin as follows:

DTC	Pin	Pin
C1145 (RF)	4 (circuit 514 [YE/RD])	5 (circuit 516 [YE/BK])
C1155 (LF)	20 (circuit 521 [TN/OG])	21 (circuit 522 [TN/BK])
C1165 (RR)	1 (circuit 523 [RD/PK])	3 (circuit 524 [PK/BK])
C1175 (LR)	22 (circuit 518 [LG/RD])	23 (circuit 519 [LG/BK])

- **Is the resistance between 800 and 1,400 ohms for the front anti-lock brake sensors and the rear anti-lock brake on vehicles equipped with rear drum brakes, and between 1,300 and 1,900 ohms for the rear anti-lock brake sensor on vehicles equipped with rear disc brakes?**

Yes
INSTALL a new anti-lock brake control module.

TEST the system for normal operation.

No
INSTALL a new anti-lock brake sensor.

CLEAR the DTCs. TEST the system for normal operation.

FM4020201929020X

Fig. 61 Test B/Codes C1145, C1155, C1165 & C1175: ABS Brake Sensor Input Circuit Failure (Part 2 of 2). 2003–04 Crown Victoria, Grand Marquis, Marauder & Town Car

C4 CHECK THE SUSPECT ANTI-LOCK BRAKE SENSOR FOR SHORT TO GROUND

- Measure the resistance between suspect anti-lock brake sensor terminal, and ground.

- **Is the resistance greater than 10,000 ohms?**

Yes
INSTALL a new anti-lock brake system (ABS) module.

REPEAT the self-test.

No
INSTALL a new anti-lock brake sensor.

CLEAR the DTCs. TEST the system for normal operation

FM4020201930020X

Fig. 62 Test C/Codes C1296, C1297, C1298 & C1299: ABS Sensor Input Signal Missing (Part 2 of 2). 2003–04 Crown Victoria, Grand Marquis, Marauder & Town Car

Test Step	Result / Action to Take

⚠ **CAUTION: The Flex Probe Kit must be used for all test connections. Use of standard multimeter probes may damage wiring terminals.**

C1 CHECK THE ANTI-LOCK BRAKE SENSOR

- Check the suspect anti-lock brake sensor mounting. Check the suspect anti-lock brake sensor for excessive dirt build-up, metal obstructions, improper harness routing, and chafing.
- **Is the suspect anti-lock brake sensor OK?**

Yes
GO to C2 .

No
REPAIR or INSTALL a new sensor as necessary. CLEAR the DTCs. TEST the system for normal operation.

C2 CHECK THE ANTI-LOCK BRAKE SENSOR INDICATOR

- Check the suspect anti-lock brake sensor indicator for corrosion, nicks, damaged teeth, correct mounting, alignment, and consistent air gap.
- **Is the suspect anti-lock brake sensor indicator OK?**

Yes
GO to C3 .

No
REPAIR or INSTALL a new indicator as necessary. CLEAR the DTCs. TEST the system for normal operation.

C3 CHECK THE ANTI-LOCK BRAKE SENSOR OUTPUT

- Key in OFF position.
- Disconnect: Anti-Lock Brake Control Module C135.
- While spinning the suspect wheel at one revolution per second, measure the AC voltage between the Anti-Lock Brake Control Module Connector (harness side), C135 pins as follows:

DTC	Pin	Pin
C1297 (RF)	4 (circuit 514 [YE/RD])	5 (circuit 516 [YE/BK])
C1296 (LF)	20 (circuit 521 [TN/OG])	21 (circuit 522 [TN/BK])
C1298 (RR)	1 (circuit 523 [RD/PK])	3 (circuit 524 [PK/BK])
C1299 (LR)	22 (circuit 518 [LG/RD])	23 (circuit 519 [LG/BK])

- **Is the voltage between 100 and 3,500 mVolts AC?**

Yes
GO to C4 .

No
INSTALL a new anti-lock brake sensor.

CLEAR the DTCs. TEST the system for normal operation.

FM4020201930010X

Fig. 62 Test C/Codes C1296, C1297, C1298 & C1299: ABS Sensor Input Signal Missing (Part 1 of 2). 2003–04 Crown Victoria, Grand Marquis, Marauder & Town Car

Test Step	Result / Action to Take

⚠ **CAUTION: The Flex Probe Kit must be used for all test connections. Use of standard multimeter probes may damage wiring terminals.**

D1 CHECK CENTRAL JUNCTION BOX (CJB) FUSE 32 (20A)

- Press the brake pedal.
- **Do the brake lamps illuminate?**

Yes
GO to D2 .

No
DIAGNOSE brake lamps.

D2 CHECK THE ABS CONTROL MODULE BOO_ABS PID

- Connect the diagnostic tool.
- Key in ON position.
- Monitor the ABS control module PID BOO_ABS, while pressing and releasing the brake pedal.
- **Does the ABS control module PID BOO_ABS indicate ON with the brake pedal pressed and OFF with the brake pedal released?**

Yes
CLEAR the DTCs. REPEAT the self-test. If the DTC B1484 is retrieved, INSTALL an anti-lock brake system (ABS) module.

REPEAT the self-test.

No
GO to D3 .

D3 CHECK CIRCUIT 810 (RD/LG) FOR OPEN

NOTE: Make sure the brake pedal is released for this step.

- Disconnect: Anti-Lock Brake Control Module C135.
- Press and hold the brake pedal.
- Measure the voltage between the Anti-Lock Brake Control Module Connector (harness side), C135 pin 6, circuit 810 (RD/LG), and the Anti-Lock Brake Control Module Connector (harness side), C135 pin 12, circuit 57 (BK).
- **Is voltage greater than 10 volts?**

Yes
INSTALL a new anti-lock brake control module.

TEST the system for normal operation.

No
REPAIR circuit 810 (RD/LG) or circuit 57 (BK). CLEAR the DTCs. TEST the system for normal operation.

FM4020201931000X

Fig. 63 Test D/Code B1484: Brake Pedal Open Circuit. 2003–04 Crown Victoria, Grand Marquis, Marauder & Town Car

Test Step	Result / Action to Take
⚠ **CAUTION: The Flex Probe Kit must be used for all test connections. Use of standard multimeter probes may damage wiring terminals.**	
E1 CHECK THE BATTERY VOLTAGE	
• Key in OFF position. • Measure the voltage between positive and negative battery post. 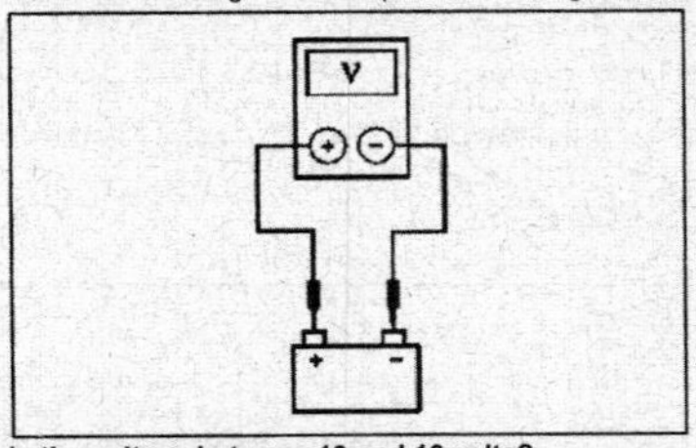 • **Is the voltage between 10 and 16 volts?**	**Yes** GO to E2 . **No** DIAGNOSE battery.
E2 CHECK THE ANTI-LOCK BRAKE CONTROL MODULE GROUND	
• Key in OFF position. • Disconnect: Anti-Lock Brake Control Module C135. • Measure the resistance between the Anti-Lock Brake Control Module Connector (harness side), C135 pin 15, circuit 57 (BK), and ground. • **Is the resistance less than 5 ohms?**	**Yes** GO to E3 . **No** REPAIR circuit 57 (BK). CLEAR the DTCs. TEST the system for normal operation.

FM4020201932010X

Fig. 64 Test E/Code B1676: Battery Voltage Out Of Range (Part 1 of 2). 2003–04 Crown Victoria, Grand Marquis, Marauder & Town Car

Test Step	Result / Action to Take
⚠ **CAUTION: The Flex Probe Kit must be used for all test connections. Use of standard multimeter probes may damage wiring terminals.**	
F1 CHECK CIRCUITS 601 (LB/BK), AND CIRCUIT 88 (BK/WH) FOR AN OPEN	
• Key in ON position. • Disconnect: Anti-Lock Brake Control Module C135. • Key in ON position. • Measure the voltage between the Anti-Lock Brake Control Module Connector (harness side), C135 pins, and ground as follows: Pin 8 – Circuit 88 (BK/WH) Pin 13 – Circuit 601 (LB/PK) Pin 14 – Circuit 483 (RD) • **Are the voltages greater than 10 volts?**	**Yes** GO to F2 . **No** REPAIR the circuit in question. TEST the system for normal operation.
F2 CHECK CIRCUIT 57 (BK) FOR AN OPEN	
• Measure the resistance between the Anti-Lock Brake Control Module Connector (harness side), C135 pin 15, circuit 57 (BK), and ground; and between the Anti-Lock Brake Control Module Connector (harness side), C135 pin 12, circuit 57 (BK), and ground. • **Are the resistances less than 5 ohms?**	**Yes** DIAGNOSE module. **No** REPAIR circuit 57 (BK). TEST the system for normal operation.

FM4020201933000X

Fig. 65 Test F: No Communication w/ABS Module. 2003–04 Crown Victoria, Grand Marquis, Marauder & Town Car

Test Step	Result / Action to Take
E3 CHECK CIRCUIT 57 (BK) FOR AN OPEN	
• Measure the resistance between the Anti-Lock Brake Control Module Connector (harness side), C135 pin 12, circuit 57 (BK), and ground. • **Is the resistance less than 5 ohms?**	**Yes** GO to E4 . **No** REPAIR circuit 57 (BK). CLEAR the DTCs. TEST the system for normal operation.
E4 CHECK CIRCUITS 601 (LB/BK) AND CIRCUIT 88 (BK/WH) FOR AN OPEN	
• Key in ON position. • Disconnect: Anti-Lock Brake Control Module C135. • Key in ON position. • Measure the voltage between the Anti-Lock Brake Control Module Connector (harness side), C135 pins and ground as follows: Pin 8 – Circuit 88 (BK/WH) Pin 13 – Circuit 601 (LB/PK) Pin 14 – Circuit 483 (RD) • **Are the voltages greater than 10 volts?**	**Yes** INSTALL a new anti-lock brake control module. TEST the system for normal operation. **No** REPAIR the circuit in question. TEST the system for normal operation.

FM4020201932020X

Fig. 64 Test E/Code B1676: Battery Voltage Out Of Range (Part 2 of 2). 2003–04 Crown Victoria, Grand Marquis, Marauder & Town Car

Test Step	Result / Action to Take
G1 BLEED THE BRAKE SYSTEM	
• Bleed the brake system. • Place the air suspension switch in the ON position after the vehicle is off the hoist. • **Does the vehicle track poorly?**	**Yes** GO to G2 . **No** The brake system is operating correctly. TEST the system for normal operation.
G2 CHECK THE LF HCU VALVE OPERATION	
• Place the air suspension switch in the OFF position. • Key in ON position. • Connect the diagnostic tool. • Lift the vehicle and rotate all the wheels to make sure they turn freely (the transmission must be in NEUTRAL). • Trigger the anti-lock brake control module active command PMP MOTOR ON for four seconds. (Trigger must be pushed twice. Each press runs the pump for two seconds.) • Apply moderate brake pedal effort. • Have an assistant attempt to rotate the LF wheel. • **Does the LF wheel rotate?**	**Yes** INSTALL a new HCU. TEST the system for normal operation. **No** GO to G3 .
G3 CHECK THE LF HCU VALVE RELEASE	
• Trigger the anti-lock brake control module active command LF INLET ON and LF OUTLET ON. • Have an assistant turn the LF wheel using a two foot lever, such as a breaker bar, immediately after pressing trigger (the scan tool will energize the valves for only two seconds per trigger press). • **Does the LF wheel turn?**	**Yes** GO to G4 . **No** GO to G10 .

FM4020201934010X

Fig. 66 Test G: Poor Vehicle Tracking During ABS Function (Part 1 of 3). 2003–04 Crown Victoria, Grand Marquis, Marauder & Town Car

G4 CHECK THE RF HCU VALVE OPERATION	
• Key in ON position. • Trigger the anti-lock brake control module active command PMP MOTOR ON for four seconds. (Trigger must be pushed twice. Each press runs the pump for two seconds.) • Apply moderate brake pedal effort. • Have an assistant attempt to rotate the RF wheel. • **Does the RF wheel rotate?**	**Yes** INSTALL a new HCU. TEST the system for normal operation. **No** GO to G5 .
G5 CHECK THE RF HCU VALVE RELEASE	
• Trigger the anti-lock brake control module active command RF INLET ON and RF OUTLET ON. • Have an assistant turn the RF wheel using a two foot lever, such as a breaker bar, immediately after pressing trigger (the scan tool will energize the valves for only two seconds per trigger press). • **Does the RF wheel turn?**	**Yes** GO to G6 . **No** GO to G10 .
G6 CHECK THE LR HCU VALVE OPERATION	
• Key in ON position. • Trigger the anti-lock brake control module active command PMP MOTOR ON for four seconds. (Trigger must be pushed twice. Each press runs the pump for two seconds.) • Apply moderate brake pedal effort. • Have an assistant attempt to rotate the LR wheel. • **Does the LR wheel rotate?**	**Yes** INSTALL a new HCU. TEST the system for normal operation. **No** GO to G7 .

FM4020201934020X

Fig. 66 Test G: Poor Vehicle Tracking During ABS Function (Part 2 of 3). 2003–04 Crown Victoria, Grand Marquis, Marauder & Town Car

Test Step	Result / Action to Take
⚠ **CAUTION: The Flex Probe Kit must be used for all test connections. Use of standard multimeter probes may damage wiring terminals.**	
H1 CHECK FOR DTCS	
• Connect the diagnostic tool. • Retrieve and document continuous DTCs. • **Are any DTCs retrieved?**	**Yes** GO to Anti-Lock Brake Control Module Diagnostic Trouble Code (DTC) Index. **No** GO to H2 .
H2 CHECK THE TRACTION CONTROL SWITCH	
• Key in OFF position. • Disconnect: Traction Control Switch C280. • Press the traction control switch in the ON position. • Measure the resistance between the traction control switch C280 pin 1, circuit 959 (GY), and pin 2, circuit 57 (BK). • **Is the resistance less than 5 ohms?**	**Yes** GO to H3 . **No** INSTALL a new traction control switch. TEST the system for normal operation.
H3 CHECK CIRCUIT 959 (GY) FOR OPEN	
• Key in OFF position. • Disconnect: Anti-Lock Brake Control Module C135. • Disconnect: Traction Control Switch C280. • Measure the resistance between the Anti-Lock Brake Control Module Connector (harness side), C135 pin 17, circuit 959 (GY) and the traction control switch connector C280 pin 1, circuit 959 (GY). • **Is the resistance greater than 5 ohms?**	**Yes** REPAIR circuit 959 (GY). TEST the system for normal operation. **No** GO to H4 .

FM4020201935010X

Fig. 67 Test H: Traction Control Inop/Cannot Be Disabled (Part 1 of 2). 2003–04 Crown Victoria, Grand Marquis, Marauder & Town Car

Test Step	Result / Action to Take
I1 CHECK THE YELLOW ABS WARNING INDICATOR	
• Disconnect: Anti-Lock Brake Control Module C135. • Key in ON position. • **Is the yellow ABS warning indicator illuminated?**	**Yes** GO to I2 . **No** DIAGNOSE instrument cluster.
I2 CHECK PROVE OUT	
• Key in OFF position. • Connect: Anti-Lock Brake Control Module C135. • Key in ON position. • **Does the yellow ABS warning indicator prove out for three seconds and then turn off?**	**Yes** The yellow ABS warning indicator is working correctly. TEST the system for normal operation. **No** CONNECT the scan tool and CHECK for DTCs. If no DTCs, INSTALL a new anti-lock brake control module. . TEST the system for normal operation.

FM4020201936000X

Fig. 68 Test I: Yellow ABS Warning Indicator Does Not Self Check. 2003–04 Crown Victoria, Grand Marquis, Marauder & Town Car

G7 CHECK THE LR HCU VALVE RELEASE	
• Trigger the anti-lock brake control module active command LR INLET ON and LR OUTLET ON. • Have an assistant turn the LR wheel using a two foot lever, such as a breaker bar, immediately after pressing trigger (the scan tool will energize the valves for only two seconds per trigger press). • **Does the LR wheel turn?**	**Yes** GO to G8 . **No** GO to G10 .
G8 CHECK THE RR HCU VALVE OPERATION	
• Key in ON position. • Trigger the anti-lock brake control module active command PMP MOTOR ON for four seconds. (Trigger must be pushed twice. Each press runs the pump for two seconds.) • Apply moderate brake pedal effort. • Have an assistant attempt to rotate the RR wheel. • **Does the RR wheel rotate?**	**Yes** INSTALL a new HCU. TEST the system for normal operation. **No** GO to G9 .
G9 CHECK THE RR HCU VALVE RELEASE	
• Trigger the anti-lock brake control module active command RR INLET ON and RR OUTLET ON. • Have an assistant turn the RR wheel using a two foot lever, such as a breaker bar, immediately after pressing trigger (the scan tool will energize the valves for only two seconds per trigger press). • **Does the RR wheel turn?**	**Yes** The anti-lock brake system is operating correctly. TEST the system for normal operation. **No** GO to G10 .
G10 CHECK FOR DIAGNOSTIC TROUBLE CODES (DTCS)	
• Retrieve and document continuous DTCs. • **Are any DTCs retrieved?**	**Yes** GO to Anti-Lock Brake Control Module Diagnostic Trouble Code (DTC) Index. **No** INSTALL a new HCU. TEST the system for normal operation.

FM4020201934030X

Fig. 66 Test G: Poor Vehicle Tracking During ABS Function (Part 3 of 3). 2003–04 Crown Victoria, Grand Marquis, Marauder & Town Car

H4 CHECK CIRCUIT 57 (BK)	
• Measure the resistance between the traction control switch connector pin 2, circuit 57 (BK) and ground. • **Is the resistance greater than 5 ohms?**	**Yes** REPAIR circuit 57 (BK). TEST the system for normal operation. GO to H5 . **No** INSTALL a new anti-lock brake control module. REPEAT the self-test. TEST the system for normal operation.
H5 CHECK CIRCUIT 959 (GY) FOR SHORT TO GROUND	
• Disconnect: Traction Control Switch C280. • Measure the resistance between traction control switch connector C280 (harness side) pin 1, circuit 959 (GY) and ground. • **Is the resistance less than 10,000 ohms?**	**Yes** REPAIR circuit 959 (GY). TEST the system for normal operation. **No** INSTALL a new anti-lock brake control module. TEST the system for normal operation.

FM4020201935020X

Fig. 67 Test H: Traction Control Inop/Cannot Be Disabled (Part 2 of 2). 2003–04 Crown Victoria, Grand Marquis, Marauder & Town Car

Test Step	Result / Action to Take
⚠ **CAUTION: The Flex Probe Kit must be used for all test connections. Use of standard multimeter probes may damage wiring terminals.**	
J1 CHECK FOR DTCs	
• Connect the diagnostic tool. • Key in ON position. • Retrieve and document continuous DTCs for the anti-lock brake control module. • **Are any DTCs retrieved?**	**Yes** GO to Anti-Lock Brake Control Module Diagnostic Trouble Code (DTC) Index. **No** DISCONNECT the anti-lock brake system (ABS) module. If the warning indicator remains on, DIAGNOSE instrument cluster. If the warning indicator is off, INSTALL a new HEC. TEST the system for normal operation.

FM4020201937000X

Fig. 69 Test J: Yellow ABS Warning Indicator & Traction Control Active Indicator Always On. 2003–04 Crown Victoria, Grand Marquis, Marauder & Town Car

Test Step	Result / Action to Take
⚠ **CAUTION: The Flex Probe Kit must be used for all test connections. Use of standard multimeter probes may damage wiring terminals.**	
K1 CHECK FUSES	
• Check fuse: Central Junction Box Fuse 23 (15A). • Check fuse: Central Junction Box Fuse 14 (10A). • **Are the fuses OK?**	**Yes** GO to K2 . **No** INSTALL new fuse(s). TEST the system for normal operation. If the fuse fails again, CHECK for short to ground. REPAIR as necessary. TEST the system for normal operation.
K2 CHECK HEC POWER SUPPLY	
• Key in OFF position. • Disconnect: HEC. • Key in ON position. • Measure the voltage between HEC connector, and ground as follows:	**Yes** GO to K3 . **No** REPAIR the circuit(s) in question. TEST the system for normal operation.

HEC Connectors-Pin	Circuit
C220a-7	729 (RD/WH)
C220a-9	1003 (GY/YE)
C220a-8	16 (RD/LG)

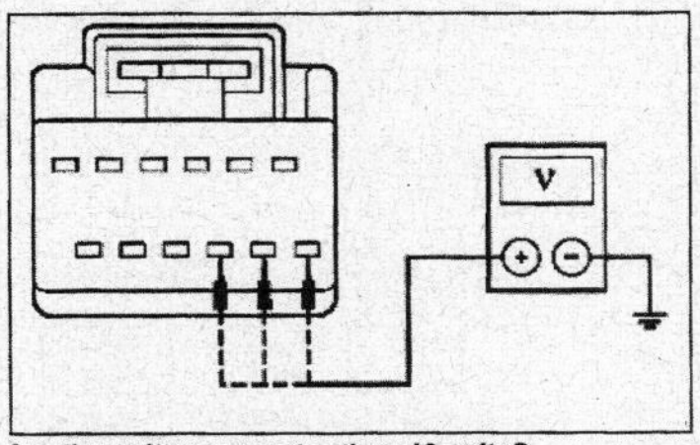

• **Are the voltages greater than 10 volts?**

FM4020201938010X

Fig. 70 Test K: No Communication w/Hybrid Electronic Cluster (Part 1 of 2). 2003–04 Crown Victoria, Grand Marquis, Marauder & Town Car

Condition	Possible Source	Action
• No Communication With the Module — Anti-Lock Brake Control Module	• Fuse. • Anti-lock brake control module. • Circuitry.	• GO to Pinpoint Test F.
• No Communication With the Module — Hybrid Electronic Cluster (HEC)	• Fuse. • Hybrid electronic cluster. • Circuitry.	• GO to Pinpoint Test N.
• Spongy Brake Pedal With No Warning Indicator	• Air in brake hydraulic system.	• GO to Pinpoint Test G.
• Poor Vehicle Tracking During Anti-Lock Function	• Air in brake hydraulic system. • Hydraulic control unit (HCU). • Base brake system.	• GO to Pinpoint Test H.
• The Traction Control Is Inoperative	• Anti-lock brake control module. • Hydraulic control unit (HCU). • Base brake system. • Thermal model (will reset after brakes cool down).	• GO to Pinpoint Test J.
• The Yellow ABS Warning Indicator Does Not Self-Check	• Circuitry. • Hybrid electronic cluster. • Anti-lock brake control module.	• GO to Pinpoint Test K.
• The Yellow ABS Warning Indicator and Traction Control Active Indicator Always On	• Circuitry. • Hybrid electronic cluster. • Anti-lock brake control module.	• GO to Pinpoint Test L.

FM4029801289010X

Fig. 71 Symptom chart (Part 1 of 2). 2000 Town Car

TEST CONDITIONS	TEST DETAILS/RESULTS/ACTIONS
A1 CHECK ABS PUMP MOTOR	
	• Is the ABS pump motor running all the time? → **Yes** REPLACE the anti-lock brake control module. TEST the system for normal operation. → **No** GO to **A2**.

FM4029801290010X

Fig. 72 Test A/Code C1095: ABS Hydraulic Pump Motor Circuit Failure (Part 1 of 4). 2000 Town Car

K3 CHECK THE HEC GROUNDS	
• Key in OFF position. • Measure the resistance between the HEC connector, and ground as follows:	**Yes** DIAGNOSE module. **No** REPAIR circuit 57 (BK) or circuit 676 (BK). TEST the system for normal operation

HEC Connectors-Pin	Circuit
C220a-3	57 (BK)
C220a-10	676 (BK)

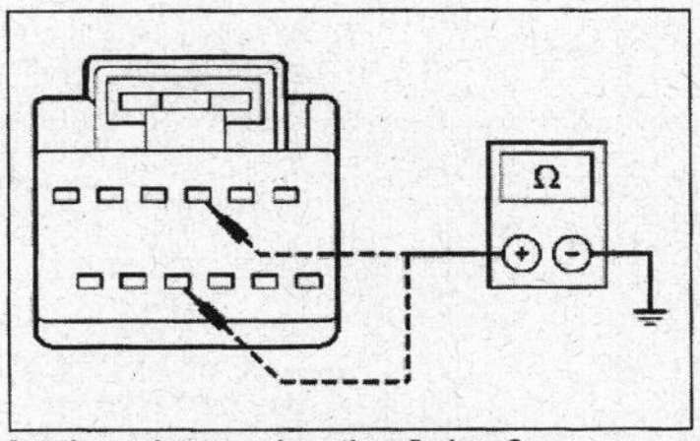

• **Are the resistances less than 5 ohms?**

FM4020201938020X

Fig. 70 Test K: No Communication w/Hybrid Electronic Cluster (Part 2 of 2). 2003–04 Crown Victoria, Grand Marquis, Marauder & Town Car

Condition	Possible Source	Action
• Traction Control Active Indicator Always/Never On	• Circuitry. • Message center display. • Anti-lock brake control module.	• DIAGNOSE instrument cluster.
• The Traction Control Cannot Be Disabled	• Circuitry. • Traction control switch. • Anti-lock brake control module.	• GO to Pinpoint Test M.

FM4029801289020X

Fig. 71 Symptom chart (Part 2 of 2). 2000 Town Car

TEST CONDITIONS	TEST DETAILS/RESULTS/ACTIONS
A2 CHECK PUMP OPERATION	
	3 Trigger the anti-lock brake control module active command PMP MOTOR ON. • Does the ABS pump motor run for approximately three seconds? → **Yes** CLEAR the DTC. CHECK the yellow ABS warning indicator while driving the vehicle above 32 kph (20 mph) and no brakes applied until the vehicle exceeds 32 kph (20 mph). If the yellow ABS warning indicator illuminates, REPLACE the anti-lock brake control module. TEST the system for normal operation. If the yellow ABS warning indicator does not illuminate, system is OK. → **No** TRIGGER the anti-lock brake control module active command PMP MOTOR OFF. GO to **A3**.
A3 CHECK POWER DISTRIBUTION BOX FUSE	
	• Is the fuse OK? → **Yes** GO to **A4**. → **No** REPLACE the fuse. TEST the system for normal operation. If the fuse fails again, CHECK for short to ground. REPAIR as necessary. TEST the system for normal operation.

FM4029801290020X

Fig. 72 Test A/Code C1095: ABS Hydraulic Pump Motor Circuit Failure (Part 2 of 4). 2000 Town Car

TEST CONDITIONS	TEST DETAILS/RESULTS/ACTIONS
A4 CHECK CIRCUIT 601 (LB/PK) FOR AN OPEN	

1

Anti-Lock Brake Control Module C162

2 Connect EEC-IV 60-Pin Breakout Box.

3

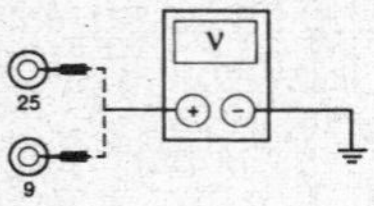

3 Measure the voltage between EEC-IV 60-Pin Breakout Box pin 9, circuit 601 (LB/PK), and ground; and between EEC-IV 60-Pin Breakout Box pin 25, circuit 601 (LB/PK), and ground.

- Are the voltages greater than 10 volts?

→ **Yes**
GO to **A5**.

→ **No**
REPAIR circuit 601 (LB/PK). CLEAR the DTCs. TEST the system for normal operation.

A5 CHECK CIRCUIT 57 (BK) FOR AN OPEN	

1

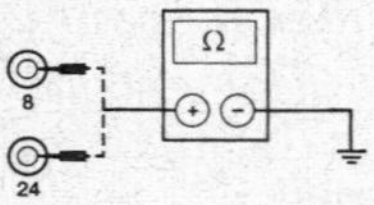

1 Measure the resistance between EEC-IV 60-Pin Breakout Box pin 8, circuit 57 (BK), and ground; and between EEC-IV 60-Pin Breakout Box pin 24, circuit 57 (BK), and ground.

- Are the resistances less than 5 ohms?

→ **Yes**
GO to **A6**.

→ **No**
REPAIR circuit 57 (BK). CLEAR the DTCs. TEST the system for normal operation.

FM4029801290030X

Fig. 72 Test A/Code C1095: ABS Hydraulic Pump Motor Circuit Failure (Part 3 of 4). 2000 Town Car

TEST CONDITIONS	TEST DETAILS/RESULTS/ACTIONS
B1 CHECK FOR SHORT TO POWER	

1 2

Anti-Lock Brake Control Module C162

3 Connect EEC-IV 60-Pin Breakout Box.

4

FM4029801291010X

Fig. 73 Test B/Codes C1145, C1155, C1165 & C1175: Anti-Lock Brake Sensor Input Circuit Failure (Part 1 of 4). 2000 Town Car

TEST CONDITIONS	TEST DETAILS/RESULTS/ACTIONS
A6 CHECK THE PUMP MOTOR FOR PROPER OPERATION	

1

Pump Motor Connector

2

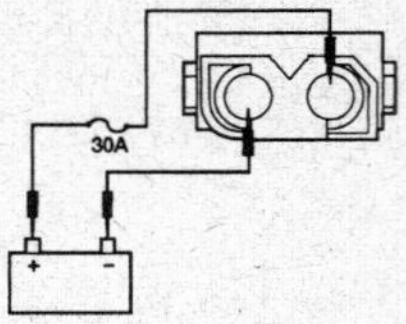

2 Use a heavy gauge jumper to connect a jumper between negative battery post and pump motor connector, brown wire; and momentarily connect a jumper between the positive battery post and pump motor connector, red wire with an in-line 30A in-line fuse.

- Does the pump motor run?

→ **Yes**
REPLACE the anti-lock brake control module. TEST the system for normal operation.

→ **No**
REPLACE the HCU. CLEAR the DTCs. TEST the system for normal operation.

FM4029801290040X

Fig. 72 Test A/Code C1095: ABS Hydraulic Pump Motor Circuit Failure (Part 4 of 4). 2000 Town Car

TEST CONDITIONS	TEST DETAILS/RESULTS/ACTIONS
B1 CHECK FOR SHORT TO POWER	

5

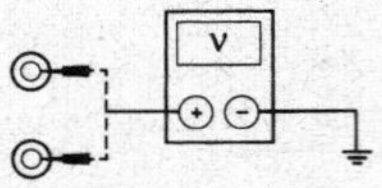

5 Measure the voltage between EEC-IV 60-Pin Breakout Box Pins, and ground as follows:

DTC	Breakout Box Pin	Breakout Box Pin
C1145 (RF)	3 (circuit 514 [Y/R])	18 (circuit 516 [Y/BK])
C1155 (LF)	4 (circuit 521 [T/O])	11 (circuit 522 [T/BK])
C1165 (RR)	17 (circuit 523 [R/PK])	1 (circuit 524 [PK/BK])
C1175 (LR)	10 (circuit 518 [LG/R])	2 (circuit 519 [LG/BK])

- Is voltage present?

→ **Yes**
REPAIR the suspected anti-lock brake sensor circuit(s) in question. CLEAR the DTCs. TEST the system for normal operation.

→ **No**
GO to **B2**.

B2 CHECK FOR AN OPEN	

1

2

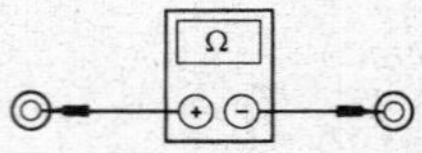

2 Measure the resistance between EEC-IV 60-Pin Breakout Box Pins as follows:

DTC	Breakout Box Pin	Breakout Box Pin
C1145 (RF)	3 (circuit 514 [Y/R])	18 (circuit 516 [Y/BK])
C1155 (LF)	4 (circuit 521 [T/O])	11 (circuit 522 [T/BK])
C1165 (RR)	17 (circuit 523 [R/PK])	1 (circuit 524 [PK/BK])
C1175 (LR)	10 (circuit 518 [LG/R])	2 (circuit 519 [LG/BK])

FM4029801291020X

Fig. 73 Test B/Codes C1145, C1155, C1165 & C1175: Anti-Lock Brake Sensor Input Circuit Failure (Part 2 of 4). 2000 Town Car

TEST CONDITIONS	TEST DETAILS/RESULTS/ACTIONS
B2 CHECK FOR AN OPEN	
	• Is the resistance between 800 and 1400 ohms? → **Yes** GO to **B4**. → **No** GO to **B3**.
B3 CHECK THE SUSPECT ANTI-LOCK BRAKE SENSOR FOR AN OPEN	
1  Suspect Anti-Lock Brake Sensor 2 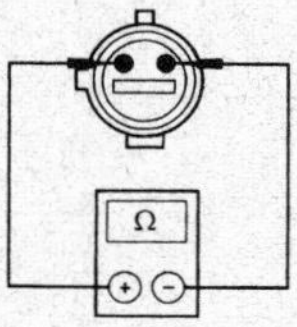	2 Measure the resistance between suspect anti-lock brake sensor terminals. • Is the resistance between 800 and 1400 ohms? → **Yes** REPAIR the suspected anti-lock brake sensor circuit(s) in question. CLEAR the DTCs. TEST the system for normal operation. → **No** REPLACE the anti-lock brake sensor. CLEAR the DTCs. TEST the system for normal operation.
B4 CHECK FOR SHORT TO GROUND	
1 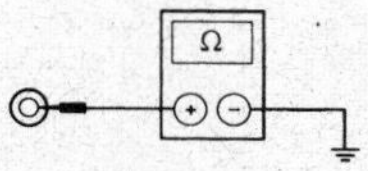	1 Measure the resistance between EEC-IV 60-Pin Breakout Box Pins, and ground as follows:

DTC	Breakout Box Pin
C1145 (RF)	3 (circuit 514 [Y/R])
C1155 (LF)	4 (circuit 521 [T/O])
C1165 (RR)	17 (circuit 523 [R/PK])
C1175 (LR)	10 (circuit 518 [LG/R])

FM4029801291030X

Fig. 73 Test B/Codes C1145, C1155, C1165 & C1175: Anti-Lock Brake Sensor Input Circuit Failure (Part 3 of 4). 2000 Town Car

TEST CONDITIONS	TEST DETAILS/RESULTS/ACTIONS
C1 CHECK THE ANTI-LOCK BRAKE SENSOR	
	1 Check the suspect anti-lock brake sensor mounting. Check the suspect anti-lock brake sensor for excessive dirt build-up, metal obstructions, improper harness routing, and chafing. • Is the suspect anti-lock brake sensor OK? → **Yes** GO to **C2**. → **No** REPAIR or REPLACE as necessary. CLEAR the DTCs. TEST the system for normal operation.
C2 CHECK THE ANTI-LOCK BRAKE SENSOR INDICATOR	
	1 Check the suspect anti-lock brake sensor indicator for corrosion, nicks, damaged teeth, proper mounting, alignment, and consistent air gap. • Is the suspect anti-lock brake sensor indicator OK? → **Yes** GO to **C3**. → **No** REPAIR or REPLACE as necessary. CLEAR the DTCs. TEST the system for normal operation.
C3 CHECK THE ANTI-LOCK BRAKE SENSOR OUTPUT	
1 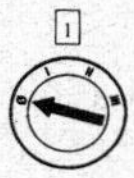 2  Anti-Lock Brake Control Module C162	3 Connect EEC-IV 60-Pin Breakout Box.

FM4029801292010X

Fig. 74 Test C/Codes C1233, C1234, C1235 & C1236: Anti-Lock Brake Sensor Input Signal Missing (Part 1 of 2). 2000 Town Car

TEST CONDITIONS	TEST DETAILS/RESULTS/ACTIONS
B4 CHECK FOR SHORT TO GROUND	
	• Is the resistance greater than 10,000 ohms? → **Yes** REPLACE the anti-lock brake control module. TEST the system for normal operation. → **No** GO to **B5**.
B5 CHECK THE SUSPECT ANTI-LOCK BRAKE SENSOR FOR SHORT TO GROUND	
1  Suspect Anti-Lock Brake Sensor 2 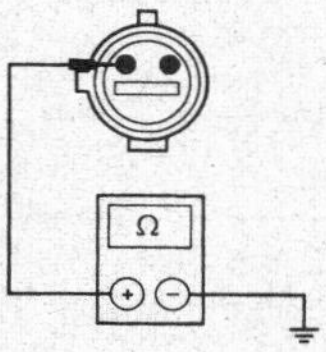	2 Measure the resistance between suspect anti-lock brake sensor terminal, and ground. • Is the resistance greater than 10,000 ohms? → **Yes** REPAIR the suspect anti-lock brake sensor circuit(s) in question. CLEAR the DTCs. TEST the system for normal operation. → **No** REPLACE the anti-lock brake sensor. CLEAR the DTCs. TEST the system for normal operation.

FM4029801291040X

Fig. 73 Test B/Codes C1145, C1155, C1165 & C1175: Anti-Lock Brake Sensor Input Circuit Failure (Part 4 of 4). 2000 Town Car

TEST CONDITIONS	TEST DETAILS/RESULTS/ACTIONS
C3 CHECK THE ANTI-LOCK BRAKE SENSOR OUTPUT	
4 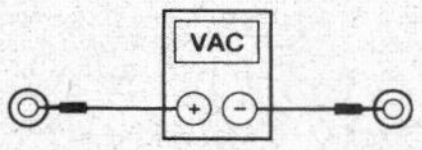	4 While spinning the suspect wheel at one revolution per second, measure the AC voltage between EEC-IV 60-Pin Breakout Box Pins as follows:

DTC	Breakout Box Pin	Breakout Box Pin
C1234 (RF)	3 (circuit 514 [Y/R])	18 (circuit 516 [Y/BK])
C1233 (LF)	4 (circuit 521 [T/O])	11 (circuit 522 [T/BK])
C1235 (RR)	17 (circuit 523 [R/PK])	1 (circuit 524 [PK/BK])
C1236 (LR)	10 (circuit 518 [LG/R])	2 (circuit 519 [LG/BK])

• Is the voltage between 100 and 3500 mVolts AC?

→ **Yes** REPLACE the anti-lock brake control module. TEST the system for normal operation.

→ **No** REPLACE the anti-lock brake sensor. CLEAR the DTCs. TEST the system for normal operation.

FM4029801292020X

Fig. 74 Test C/Codes C1233, C1234, C1235 & C1236: Anti-Lock Brake Sensor Input Signal Missing (Part 2 of 2). 2000 Town Car

TEST CONDITIONS	TEST DETAILS/RESULTS/ACTIONS
D1 CHECK THE STOPLAMP OPERATION	
	1 Press the brake pedal. • Do the stoplamps operate properly? → **Yes** GO to **D2**. → **No** DIAGNOSE stoplamps.

FM4029801293010X

Fig. 75 Test D/Code B1485: Brake Pedal Input Circuit Short To Battery (Part 1 of 2). 2000 Town Car

TEST CONDITIONS	TEST DETAILS/RESULTS/ACTIONS
D2 CHECK CIRCUIT (R/LG) FOR SHORT TO POWER	
NOTE: Make sure the brake pedal is released for this step.	

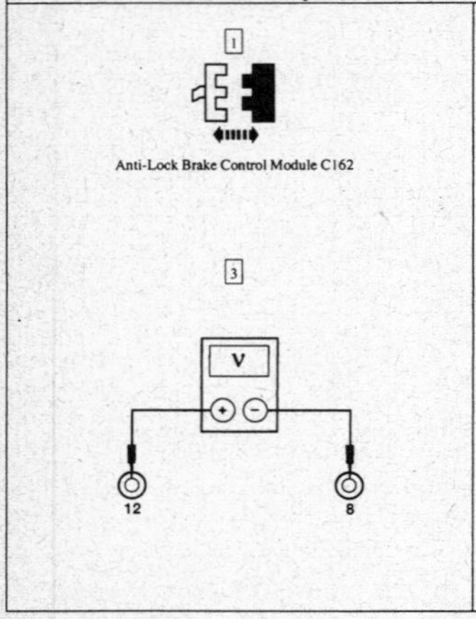

2 Connect EEC-IV 60-Pin Breakout Box.

3 Measure the voltage between EEC-IV 60-Pin Breakout Box pin 12, circuit (LG/R), and EEC-IV 60-Pin Breakout Box pin 8, circuit 57 (BK).

- Is voltage present?

→ **Yes**
REPAIR circuit (LG/R). CLEAR the DTCs. TEST the system for normal operation.

→ **No**
REPLACE the anti-lock brake control module. TEST the system for normal operation.

FM4029801293020X

Fig. 75 Test D/Code B1485: Brake Pedal Input Circuit Short To Battery (Part 2 of 2). 2000 Town Car

TEST CONDITIONS	TEST DETAILS/RESULTS/ACTIONS
E3 CHECK CIRCUIT 57 (BK) FOR AN OPEN	

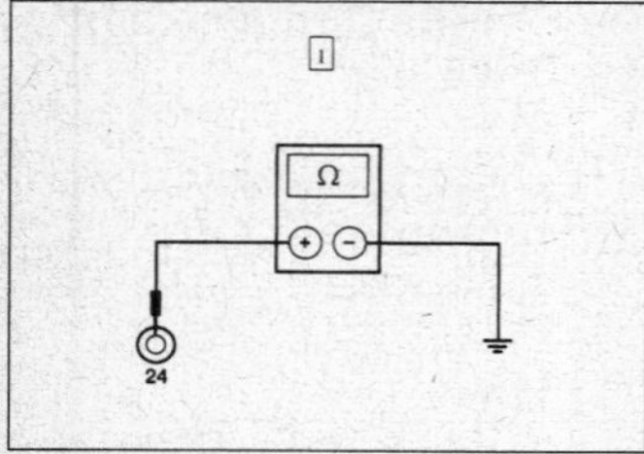

1 Measure the resistance between EEC-IV 60-Pin Breakout Box pin 24, circuit 57 (BK), and ground.

- Is the resistance less than 5 ohms?

→ **Yes**
REPLACE the anti-lock brake control module. TEST the system for normal operation.

→ **No**
REPAIR circuit 57 (BK). CLEAR the DTCs. TEST the system for normal operation.

FM4029801294020X

Fig. 76 Test E/Code B1676: Battery Voltage Out Of Range (Part 2 of 2). 2000 Town Car

TEST CONDITIONS	TEST DETAILS/RESULTS/ACTIONS
F2 CHECK CIRCUITS 601 (LB/BK), AND CIRCUIT 88 (BK/W) FOR AN OPEN	

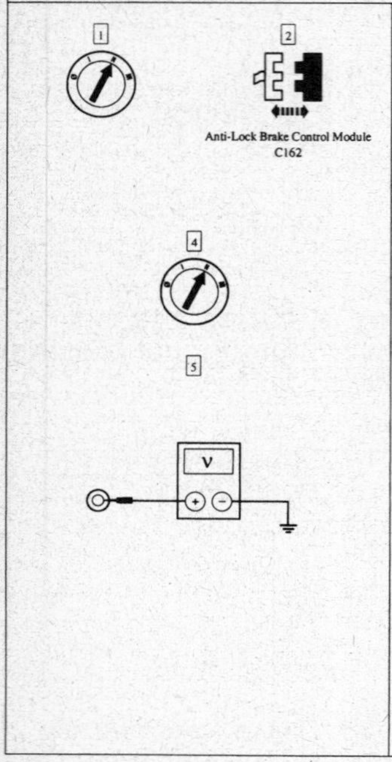

3 Connect EEC-IV 60-Pin Breakout Box.

5 Measure the voltage between EEC-IV 60-Pin Breakout Box Pins, and ground as follows:

Breakout Box Pin	Circuit
23	Circuit 88 (BK/W)
9	Circuit 601 (LB/PK)

- Are the voltages greater than 10 volts?

→ **Yes**
GO to **F3**.

→ **No**
REPAIR the circuit in question. TEST the system for normal operation.

FM4029801295020X

Fig. 77 Test F: No Communication w/Anti-Lock Brake Control Module (Part 2 of 3). 2000 Town Car

TEST CONDITIONS	TEST DETAILS/RESULTS/ACTIONS
E1 CHECK THE BATTERY VOLTAGE	

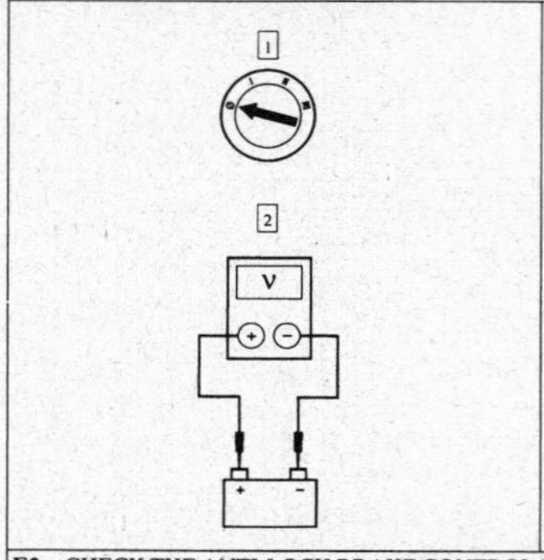

2 Measure the voltage between positive and negative battery post.

- Is the voltage between 10 and 16 volts?

→ **Yes**
GO to **E2**.

→ **No**
DIAGNOSE starter.

TEST CONDITIONS	TEST DETAILS/RESULTS/ACTIONS
E2 CHECK THE ANTI-LOCK BRAKE CONTROL MODULE GROUND	

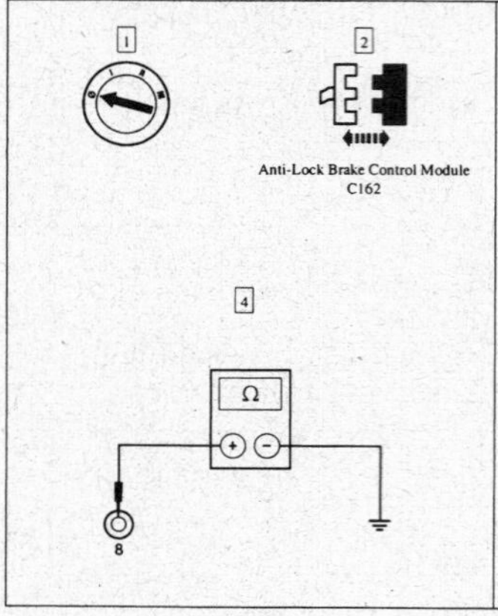

3 Connect EEC-IV 60-Pin Breakout Box.

4 Measure the resistance between EEC-IV 60-Pin Breakout Box pin 8, circuit 57 (BK), and ground.

- Is the resistance less than 5 ohms?

→ **Yes**
GO to E3.

→ **No**
REPAIR circuit 57 (BK). CLEAR the DTCs. TEST the system for normal operation.

FM4029801294010X

Fig. 76 Test E/Code B1676: Battery Voltage Out Of Range (Part 1 of 2). 2000 Town Car

TEST CONDITIONS	TEST DETAILS/RESULTS/ACTIONS
F1 CHECK THE FUSE JUNCTION PANEL FUSE AND POWER DISTRIBUTION BOX MAXI FUSE	

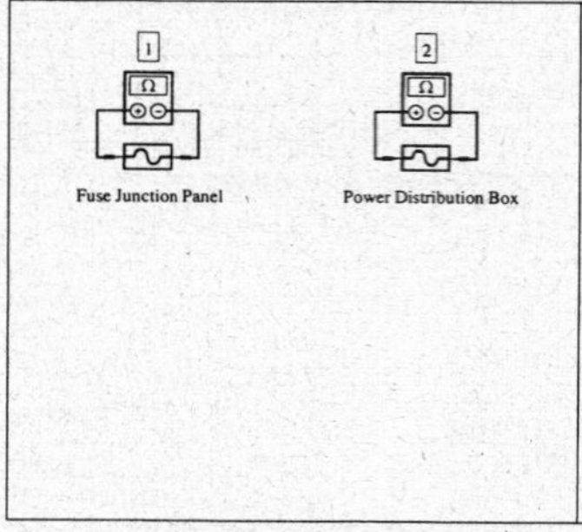

- Are fuse junction panel fuse and power distribution box fuse OK?

→ **Yes**
GO to **F2**.

→ **No**
REPLACE the fuse(s) in question. TEST the system for normal operation. If the fuse fails again, CHECK for short to ground. REPAIR as necessary. TEST the system for normal operation.

FM4029801295010X

Fig. 77 Test F: No Communication w/Anti-Lock Brake Control Module (Part 1 of 3). 2000 Town Car

TEST CONDITIONS	TEST DETAILS/RESULTS/ACTIONS
F3 CHECK CIRCUIT 57 (BK) FOR AN OPEN	

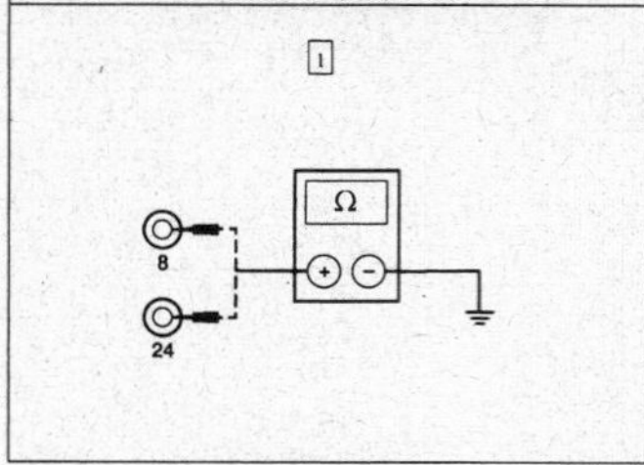

1 Measure the resistance between EEC-IV 60-Pin Breakout Box pin 24, circuit 57 (BK), and ground; and between EEC-IV 60-Pin Breakout Box pin 8, circuit 57 (BK), and ground.

- Are the resistances less than 5 ohms?

→ **Yes**
DIAGNOSE module communications network.

→ **No**
REPAIR circuit 57 (BK). TEST the system for normal operation.

FM4029801295030X

Fig. 77 Test F: No Communication w/Anti-Lock Brake Control Module (Part 3 of 3). 2000 Town Car

TEST CONDITIONS	TEST DETAILS/RESULTS/ACTIONS
G1 CHECK THE COMPONENTS MOUNTING	
	1 Inspect the brake pedal and the power brake booster/brake master cylinder for proper attachment. 2 Bleed the brake system. • Is the brake pedal spongy? → **Yes** GO to **G2**. → **No** The brake system is operating properly. TEST the system for normal operation.
G2 BLEED THE BRAKE SYSTEM	
	1 Rebleed the brake system. • Is the brake pedal spongy? → **Yes** DIAGNOSE hydraulic brake system. → **No** The brake system is operating properly. TEST the system for normal operation.

FM4029801296000X

Fig. 78 Test G: Spongy Brake Pedal w/No Warning Indicator. 2000 Town Car

TEST CONDITIONS	TEST DETAILS/RESULTS/ACTIONS
H2 CHECK THE LF HCU VALVE OPERATION	
	7 Have an assistant attempt to rotate the LF wheel. • Does the LF wheel rotate? → **Yes** REPLACE the HCU. TEST the system for normal operation. → **No** GO to **H3**.
H3 CHECK THE LF HCU VALVE RELEASE	
1 	1 Trigger the anti-lock brake control module active command LF INLET ON and LF OUTLET ON. 2 Have an assistant turn the LF wheel using a two foot lever, such as a breaker bar, immediately after pressing trigger (NGS will energize the valves for only two seconds per trigger press). • Does the LF wheel turn? → **Yes** GO to **H4**. → **No** GO to **H10**.
H4 CHECK THE RF HCU VALVE OPERATION	
1 	2 Trigger the anti-lock brake control module active command PMP MOTOR ON for four seconds. (Trigger must be pushed twice. Each press runs the pump for two seconds.) 3 Apply moderate brake pedal effort.

FM4029801297020X

Fig. 79 Test H: Poor Vehicle Tracking During Anti-Lock Function (Part 2 of 5). 2000 Town Car

TEST CONDITIONS	TEST DETAILS/RESULTS/ACTIONS
H1 BLEED THE BRAKE SYSTEM	
	1 Bleed the brake system. 2 Place the air suspension switch in the ON position after the vehicle is off the hoist. • Does the vehicle track poorly? → **Yes** GO to **H2**. → **No** The brake system is operating properly. TEST the system for normal operation.
H2 CHECK THE LF HCU VALVE OPERATION	
1 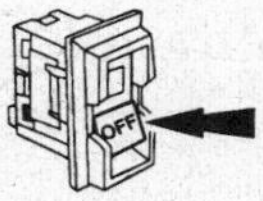 2  3  NGS	1 Place the air suspension switch in the OFF position. 4 Lift the vehicle and rotate all the wheels to make sure they turn freely (the vehicle must be in neutral). 5 Trigger the anti-lock brake control module active command PMP MOTOR ON for four seconds. (Trigger must be pushed twice. Each press runs the pump for two seconds.) 6 Apply moderate brake pedal effort.

FM4029801297010X

Fig. 79 Test H: Poor Vehicle Tracking During Anti-Lock Function (Part 1 of 5). 2000 Town Car

TEST CONDITIONS	TEST DETAILS/RESULTS/ACTIONS
H4 CHECK THE RF HCU VALVE OPERATION	
	4 Have an assistant attempt to rotate the RF wheel. • Does the RF wheel rotate? → **Yes** REPLACE the HCU. TEST the system for normal operation. → **No** GO to **H5**.
H5 CHECK THE RF HCU VALVE RELEASE	
1 	1 Trigger the anti-lock brake control module active command RF INLET ON and RF OUTLET ON. 2 Have an assistant turn the RF wheel using a two foot lever, such as a breaker bar, immediately after pressing trigger (NGS will energize the valves for only two seconds per trigger press). • Does the RF wheel turn? → **Yes** GO to **H6**. → **No** GO to **H10**.
H6 CHECK THE LR HCU VALVE OPERATION	
1 	2 Trigger the anti-lock brake control module active command PMP MOTOR ON for four seconds. (Trigger must be pushed twice. Each press runs the pump for two seconds.) 3 Apply moderate brake pedal effort.

FM4029801297030X

Fig. 79 Test H: Poor Vehicle Tracking During Anti-Lock Function (Part 3 of 5). 2000 Town Car

TEST CONDITIONS	TEST DETAILS/RESULTS/ACTIONS
H6 CHECK THE LR HCU VALVE OPERATION	
	4 Have an assistant attempt to rotate the LR wheel. • Does the LR wheel rotate? → **Yes** REPLACE the HCU. TEST the system for normal operation. → **No** GO to **H7**.
H7 CHECK THE LR HCU VALVE RELEASE	
1 	1 Trigger the anti-lock brake control module active command LR INLET ON and LR OUTLET ON.
	2 Have an assistant turn the LR wheel using a two foot lever, such as a breaker bar, immediately after pressing trigger (NGS will energize the valves for only two seconds per trigger press). • Does the LR wheel turn? → **Yes** GO to **H8**. → **No** GO to **H10**.
H8 CHECK THE RR HCU VALVE OPERATION	
1 	2 Trigger the anti-lock brake control module active command PMP MOTOR ON for four seconds. (Trigger must be pushed twice. Each press runs the pump for two seconds.) 3 Apply moderate brake pedal effort.

FM4029801297040X

Fig. 79 Test H: Poor Vehicle Tracking During Anti-Lock Function (Part 4 of 5). 2000 Town Car

TEST CONDITIONS	TEST DETAILS/RESULTS/ACTIONS
H8 CHECK THE RR HCU VALVE OPERATION	
	4 Have an assistant attempt to rotate the RR wheel. • Does the RR wheel rotate? → **Yes** REPLACE the HCU. TEST the system for normal operation. → **No** GO to **H9**.
H9 CHECK THE RR HCU VALVE RELEASE	
1 	1 Trigger the anti-lock brake control module active command RR INLET ON and RR OUTLET ON.
	2 Have an assistant turn the RR wheel using a two foot lever, such as a breaker bar, immediately after pressing trigger (NGS will energize the valves for only two seconds per trigger press). • Does the RR wheel turn? → **Yes** The anti-lock brake system is operating properly. TEST the system for normal operation. → **No** GO to **H10**.
H10 CHECK FOR DIAGNOSTIC TROUBLE CODES (DTCS)	
1 	1 Retrieve and document continuous DTCs. • Are any DTCs retrieved? → **Yes** GO to Diagnostic Trouble Code (DTC) Index. → **No** REPLACE the HCU. TEST the system for normal operation.

FM4029801297050X

Fig. 79 Test H: Poor Vehicle Tracking During Anti-Lock Function (Part 5 of 5). 2000 Town Car

TEST CONDITIONS	TEST DETAILS/RESULTS/ACTIONS
J1 CHECK FOR DTCS	
1  NGS 2 	2 Retrieve and document continuous DTCs. • Are any DTCs retrieved? → **Yes** GO to Diagnostic Trouble Code (DTC) Index. → **No** GO to **J2**.
J2 CHECK THE ABS OPERATION	
	1 Test drive the vehicle. Check the ABS operation. • Does the ABS operate properly? → **Yes** GO to **J3**. → **No** GO to Symptom Chart.
J3 CHECK CIRCUIT 959 (GY) FOR SHORT TO POWER	
1  2  Anti-Lock Brake Control Module C162	3 Connect EEC-IV 60-Pin Breakout Box.
4 	

FM4029801298010X

Fig. 80 Test J: Traction Control Is Inoperative (Part 1 of 2). 2000 Town Car

TEST CONDITIONS	TEST DETAILS/RESULTS/ACTIONS
J3 CHECK CIRCUIT 959 (GY) FOR SHORT TO POWER	
5 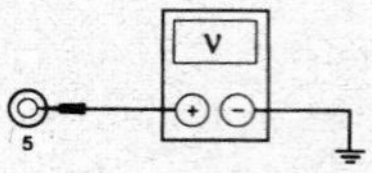	5 Measure the voltage between EEC-IV 60-Pin Breakout Box pin 5, circuit 959 (GY), and ground. • Is voltage present? → **Yes** GO to **J4**. → **No** REPLACE the HCU. TEST the system for normal operation.
J4 CHECK THE TRACTION CONTROL SWITCH	
1  2  Traction Control Switch C206	
3 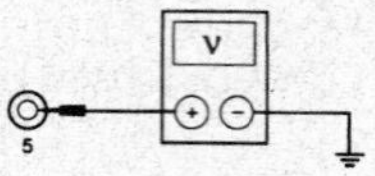	3 Measure the resistance between EEC-IV 60-Pin Breakout Box pin 5, circuit 959 (GY), and ground. • Is voltage present? → **Yes** REPAIR circuit 959 (GY). TEST the system for normal operation. → **No** REPLACE the traction control switch. TEST the system for normal operation.

FM4029801298020X

Fig. 80 Test J: Traction Control Is Inoperative (Part 2 of 2). 2000 Town Car

TEST CONDITIONS	TEST DETAILS/RESULTS/ACTIONS
K1 CHECK THE YELLOW ABS WARNING INDICATOR	
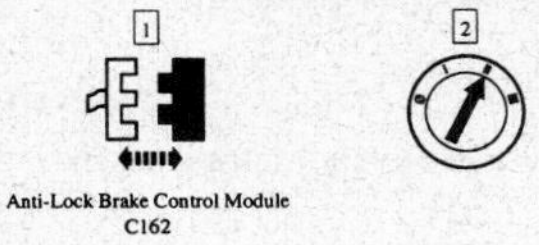	• Is the yellow ABS warning indicator illuminated? → **Yes** GO to **K2**. → **No** DIAGNOSE instrument cluster.
K2 CHECK PROVE OUT	
	• Does the yellow ABS warning indicator prove out for three seconds and then turn off? → **Yes** The yellow ABS warning indicator is working properly. TEST the system for normal operation. → **No** REPLACE the anti-lock brake control module. TEST the system for normal operation.

FM4029801299000X

Fig. 81 Test K: Yellow ABS Warning Indicator Does Not Self Check. 2000 Town Car

TEST CONDITIONS	TEST DETAILS/RESULTS/ACTIONS
M1 CHECK CIRCUIT 88 (BK/W) FOR AN OPEN	
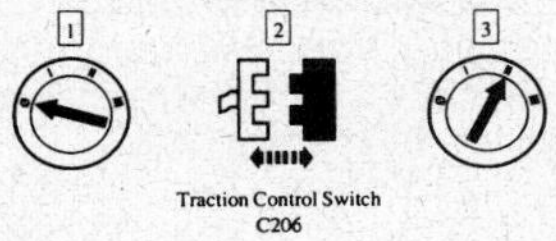	
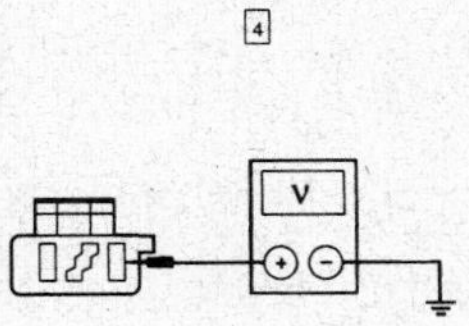	4 Measure the voltage between traction control switch C206, circuit 88 (BK/W), and ground. • Is the voltage greater than 10 volts? → **Yes** GO to **M2**. → **No** REPAIR circuit 88 (BK/W). TEST the system for normal operation.

FM4029801301010X

Fig. 83 Test M: Traction Control Cannot Be Disabled (Part 1 of 2). 2000 Town Car

TEST CONDITIONS	TEST DETAILS/RESULTS/ACTIONS
L1 CHECK FOR DTCs	
	3 Retrieve and document continuous DTCs for the anti-lock brake control module. • Are any DTCs retrieved? → **Yes** GO to Diagnostic Trouble Code (DTC) Index. → **No** REPLACE the HEC. TEST the systemn for normal operation.

FM4029801300000X

Fig. 82 Test L: Yellow ABS Warning Indicator & Traction Control Active Indicator Always On. 2000 Town Car

TEST CONDITIONS	TEST DETAILS/RESULTS/ACTIONS
M2 CHECK THE TRACTION CONTROL SWITCH	
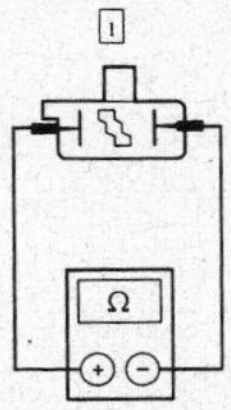	1 Measure the resistance between traction control switch terminals, while depressing the traction control switch. • Is the resistance less than 5 ohms? → **Yes** GO to **M3**. → **No** REPLACE the traction control switch. TEST the system for normal operation.
M3 CHECK CIRCUIT 959 (GY) FOR AN OPEN	
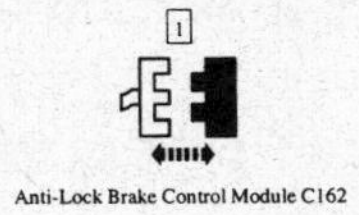	
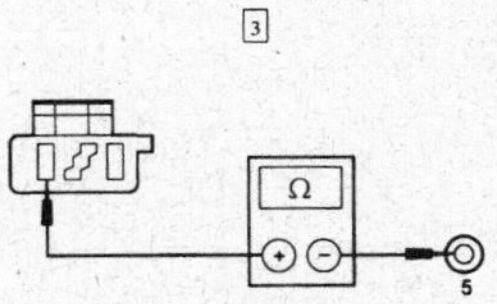	2 Connect EEC-IV 60-**Pin** Breakout Box. 3 Measure the resistance between EEC-IV 60-Pin Breakout Box pin 5, circuit 959 (GY), and traction control switch C206, circuit 959 (GY). • Is the resistance less than 5 ohms? → **Yes** REPLACE the HCU. TEST the system for normal operation. → **No** REPAIR circuit 959 (GY). TEST the system for normal operation.

FM4029801301020X

Fig. 83 Test M: Traction Control Cannot Be Disabled (Part 2 of 2). 2000 Town Car

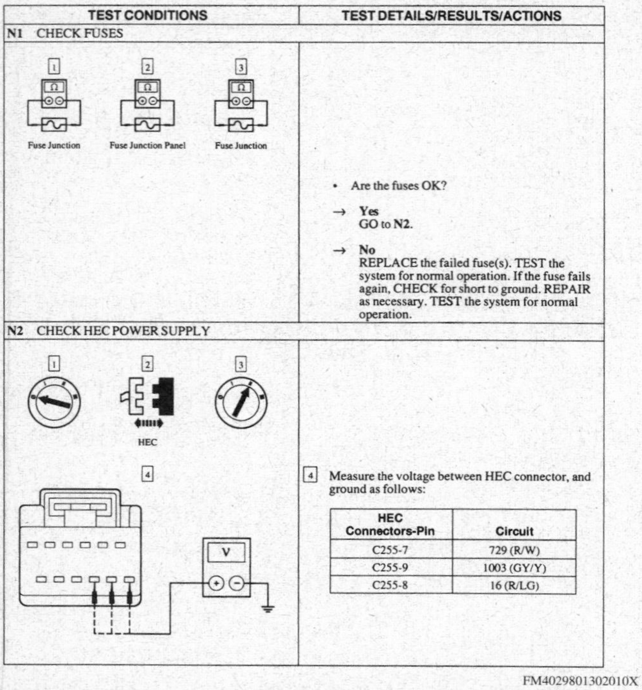

Fig. 84 Test N: No Communication w/Hybrid Electronic Cluster Module (Part 1 of 2). 2000 Town Car

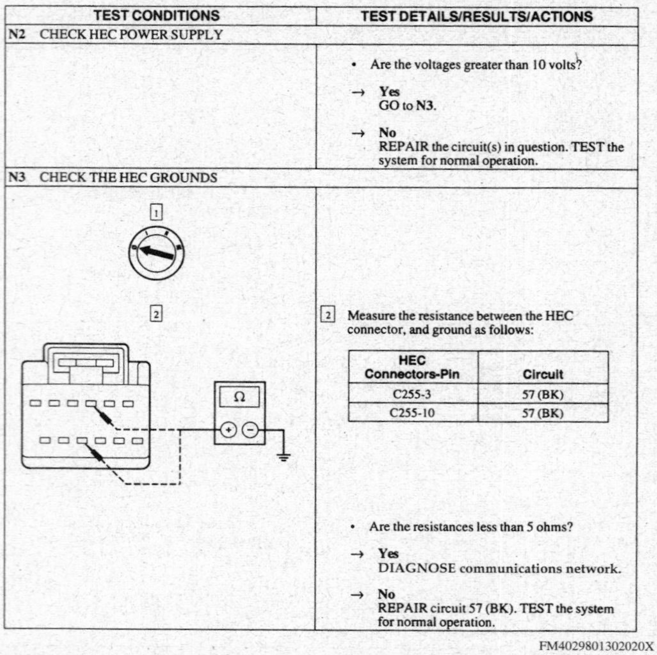

Fig. 84 Test N: No Communication w/Hybrid Electronic Cluster Module (Part 2 of 2). 2000 Town Car

SYSTEM SERVICE

Brake System Bleed

Refer to "Hydraulic Brake Systems" for bleed procedure.

Component Replacement

HYDRAULIC CONTROL UNIT

1. Disconnect brake lines from HCU. Plug each port to prevent fluid from spilling.
2. Disconnect ABS Control Module electrical connectors.
3. Remove mounting bracket to HCU bolts.
4. Remove HCU from vehicle.
5. Remove ABS Control Module.
6. Reverse procedure to install, noting the following:
   a. **Torque** brake lines to 12 ft. lbs.
   b. **Torque** control unit attaching bolts to 81–115 inch lbs.

FRONT WHEEL SENSOR

1. Disconnect front ABS sensor electrical connector.
2. Raise and support vehicle.
3. Remove routing clips.
4. Remove bolt, then ABS wheel speed sensor.
5. Reverse procedure to install. **Torque** wheel speed sensor attaching bolt to 45 inch lbs.

REAR WHEEL SENSOR

1. Remove rear seat bottom.
2. Disconnect rear anti-lock brake sensor connector.
3. Push sensor harness grommet through passenger compartment floor.
4. Raise and support vehicle.
5. Disconnect routing clips, then remove the rear sensor bolt and sensor.
6. Reverse procedure to install, noting the following:
   a. **On 2000 models, torque** rear sensor bolt to 14–91 ft. lbs.
   b. **On 2001–04 models, torque** rear sensor bolt to 64 inch lbs.

FRONT SPEED INDICATOR RING

1. Remove wheel and tire assembly.
2. Remove caliper, rotor and hub assemblies.
3. Remove indicator ring from hub.
4. Reverse procedure to install.

REAR SPEED INDICATOR RING

REMOVAL

1. Remove axle shaft and position on workbench.
2. Strike evenly around flange using a thin blade cold chisel between sensor ring and axle flange, forcing indicator ring off of sensor ring journal. **Do not use a screwdriver or similar tool. Extreme care must be taken not to scratch or nick wheel bearing and seal journal.**

INSTALLATION

1. Prior to installation of new ring, remove any burrs or nicks from journal.
2. Position indicator ring installation tool No. T89P-20202-A, or equivalent, on press with pilot ring facing down.
3. Place new indicator ring over installation tool and insert axle shaft through tool.
4. Place spacer tool No. T85T-4616-AH, or equivalent, over hub end of axle shaft.
5. Press axle shaft until it bottoms out on axle flange.
6. Install axle shaft on vehicle.

STOP LAMP SWITCH

REMOVAL

1. Locking tab on connector must be lifted before connector can be removed.
2. Remove hairpin retainer and slide switch, pushrod, nylon washers and bushings away from brake pedal.

INSTALLATION

1. Position switch so that U-shaped side is nearest brake pedal and directly over or under the pin. Slide switch down or up trapping master cylinder pushrod and black bushing between switch and side plates.
2. Push switch and pushrod assembly firmly toward brake pedal arm. Assemble outside white plastic washer to pin and install hairpin retainer to trap whole assembly.
3. Ensure switch wire harness has sufficient length to travel with switch during full stroke of brake pedal.
4. Inspect switch for proper operation.

Escort & ZX2

NOTE: On Air Bag Equipped Models, Refer To "Air Bag System Precautions" Located In The Front Of This Manual For System Disarming & Arming Procedures.

NOTE: Refer To "Computer Relearn Procedures" Located In The Front Of This Manual When Battery Power To The Computer Has Been Interrupted.

NOTE: "Electrical Symbol & Wire Color Code Identification" Located In The Front Of This Manual May Be Used As An Aid When Using Wiring Circuits Found In This Section.

INDEX

PRECAUTIONS

Air Bag Systems

Refer to "Air Bag System Precautions" in the front of this manual for system disarming and arming procedures.

Battery Ground Cable

Prior to service, disconnect battery ground cable and isolate as required.

Hydraulic Brake Fluid Color

Hydraulic brake fluid must conform with the requirements of Federal Motor Vehicle Safety Standard 116. Under this standard, brake fluids are visually different from other automotive fluids such as transmission, power steering and engine.

Fluid color in a normal brake system may vary from its original color for many reasons. A brake master cylinder may show significantly different shades fluid color between the two brake master cylinder reservoirs. Color may also appear to vary between cast steel and die cast aluminum reservoirs. Some reasons for discoloration include the following:

1. Heat and/or aging.
2. Different operation temperatures or different rates of normal oxidation between two reservoir compartments.
3. Different brands and/or shades of fluid are used when topping off during normal service.
4. Dissolution of color dye used on master cylinder internal springs during assembly.

Brake fluid contaminated with hydrocarbon/mineral based fluid (power steering or transmission fluid) can be detected by an obvious swelling of the master cylinder cap gasket. If the master cylinder cap gasket is swollen, all brake system rubber components must be replaced. All brake tubes and hoses must be thoroughly flushed with Ford Heavy Duty Brake Fluid C6AZ-19542-AA or -BA or DOT-3 equivalent before the vehicle returns to service.

DESCRIPTION

System Components

Refer to **Fig. 1,** for ABS component locations.

HYDRAULIC CONTROL UNIT (HCU)

The hydraulic unit consists of a valve body assembly, pump and a motor assembly. During normal braking, fluid from the brake master cylinder enters the HCU through inlet port located at the bottom of the unit. Then the fluid passes through four normally open isolation valves, one to each of the four wheels.

If anti-lock brake control module senses that a wheel is about to lock, the module pulses the appropriate isolation valve, which in turn closes that valve which prevents any more fluid from entering the affected brake.

ANTI-LOCK BRAKE CONTROL MODULE

The anti-lock brake control module controls the hydraulic control unit during ABS operation and to monitor the system during normal driving and braking. The module is located behind the lefthand side of the instrument panel.

The anti-lock brake control module continuously calculates wheel speed and vehicle speed based on information it receives from the front and rear brake anti-lock sensors. The module has self-diagnostic capabilities and stores diagnostic trouble codes in its memory. If a diagnostic trouble code is present in module memory, the instrument panel ANTI-LOCK indicator will illuminate when the engine is running.

ANTI-LOCK BRAKE SENSORS

The front anti-lock sensor and brackets are mounted on the front wheel knuckles and the rear brake anti-lock sensors are mounted on the rear wheel spindles. The sensors produce electrical pulses by monitoring the rotation of the sensor indicators

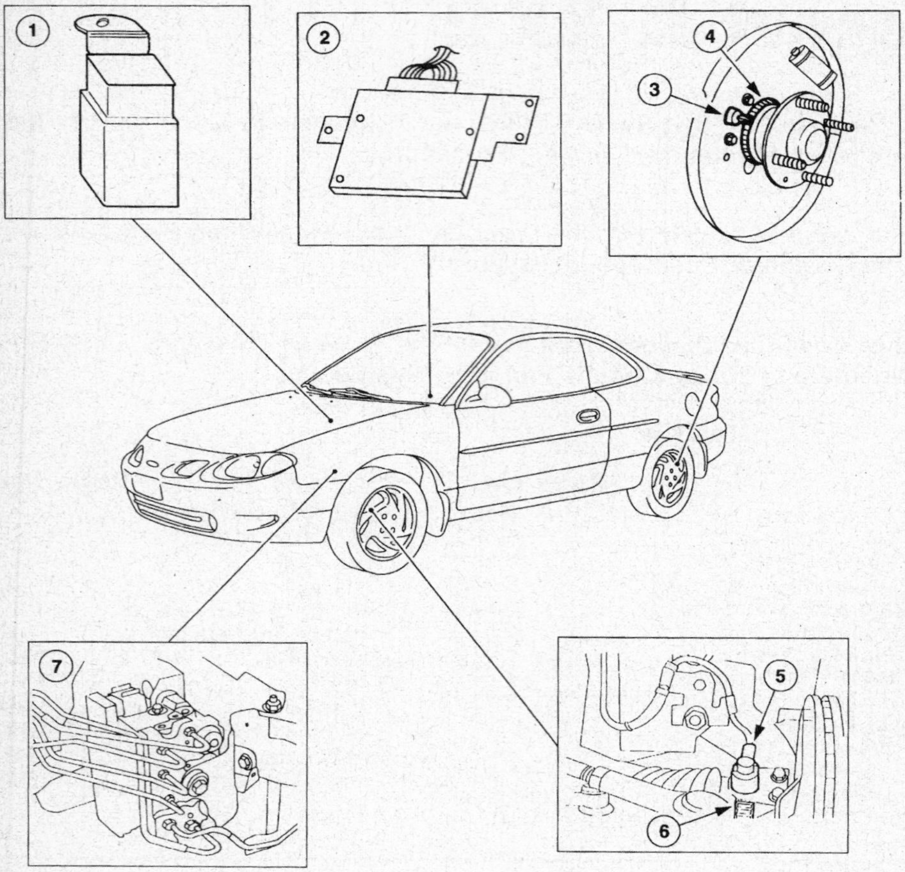

Item	Description
1	Anti-Lock Brake Relay
2	Anti-Lock Brake Control Module
3	Rear Anti-Lock Brake Sensor

Item	Description
4	Rear Anti-Lock Brake Sensor Indicator
5	Front Anti-Lock Brake Sensor
6	Front Anti-Lock Brake Sensor Indicator
7	Hydraulic Control Unit (HCU)

FM4020101841000X

Fig. 1 ABS component locations

which are mounted on the front wheel driveshaft and joints and the rear wheel hubs.

WARNING INDICATOR

The anti-lock brake warning indicator will come on to warn the driver of an ABS failure. Normal brake system operation will still be available. However, the wheels will lock up under hard braking.

Operation

The ABS functions by releasing and applying fluid pressure to the front disc brake calipers and rear wheel cylinders during special braking conditions. The ABS does not function under normal braking conditions, nor does it affect front-to-rear brake proportioning. When one or more wheels approach a slip condition, the ABS automatically senses the slip and activates the pressure control function.

Through its pre-programming, the anti-lock brake control module decides which wheel(s)' brake pressure needs modulation. Once determined, the anti-lock brake control module sends appropriate signals to the solenoid valves located in the hydraulic anti-lock actuator assembly. These solenoid valves allow adjoining flow control valves to modulate fluid pressure, resulting in a pressure reduction at the front disc brake calipers and rear wheel cylinders to prevent further lock-up.

TROUBLESHOOTING

Preliminary Inspection

Verify concern by driving vehicle. Look for problems in other areas which may affect ABS: suspension and steering components, tire integrity and air pressure, wheel bearings and brake components common to all brake systems. **The hydraulic anti-lock actuator assembly is not serviceable and can not be pressure inspected. If any of its components fail, it must be replaced as a complete unit.**

Mechanical	Electrical
• Insufficient brake fluid • Damaged anti-lock brake sensor indicator(s) • Damaged HCU • Damaged hydraulic system lines/hoses • Damaged wheel bearings	• Blown fuse: — 60A ABS — 15A AIR COND — 10A METER — 15A STOP • Damaged wiring harness • Loose or corroded connection(s) • Damaged anti-lock brake control module • Damaged brake pedal position (BPP) switch • Blown anti-lock brake warning indicator miniature bulb • Damaged anti-lock brake sensor(s) • Damaged HCU • Damaged anti-lock relay

FM4020101842000X

Fig. 2 Visual inspection chart

If all systems and components are satisfactory, refer to Visual Inspection Chart, **Fig. 2.** After following Visual Inspection Chart proceed to "Quick Test" in "Diagnosis & Testing."

DIAGNOSIS & TESTING

Accessing Diagnostic Trouble Codes

The anti-lock brake/traction assist electronic control module is capable of performing a self-test using New Generation Star (NGS) tester 007-00500, or equivalent, scan tool.

The ABS control module monitors system operation and stores all defined diagnostic trouble codes in its memory. It is important to understand the control module cannot recognize some failures. Therefore, if a problem exists and no diagnostic trouble codes are stored by the control module, other diagnostic steps must be followed. The module cannot store a diagnostic trouble code if there is no power to the module. This diagnostic trouble code can be found by using System Pre Check, **Fig. 3.**

1. Connect New Generation Star (NGS) tester to data link connector (DLC) located under instrument panel to right of steering column.
2. Plug NGS into cigarette lighter.
3. Turn ignition switch to Run position.
4. Follow instructions on tester screen and record all diagnostic trouble codes.
5. Refer to "Diagnostic Trouble Code Interpretation" for DTC's. Any DTC preceded by "U" indicates a fault with Powertrain Control Module (PCM).

TEST CONDITIONS	TEST DETAILS/RESULTS/ACTIONS
SPC1 CHECK YELLOW ABS WARNING INDICATOR PROVE OUT	
1 	2 Observe the anti-lock brake warning indicator. • Did the yellow ABS warning indicator illuminate and go off after approximately two seconds? → **Yes** The yellow ABS warning indicator prove out normally. GO to **SPC3**. → **No** The yellow ABS warning indicator stays on. GO to **SPC3**. The yellow ABS warning indicator is never illuminated. GO to **SPC2**.
SPC2 CHECK YELLOW ABS WARNING INDICATOR	
1 	2 Connect EEC-IV 60-Pin Breakout Box to the anti-lock brake control module C386.

FM4029700917010A

Fig. 3 System pre-check (Part 1 of 3)

TEST CONDITIONS	TEST DETAILS/RESULTS/ACTIONS
SPC2 CHECK YELLOW ABS WARNING INDICATOR	
3 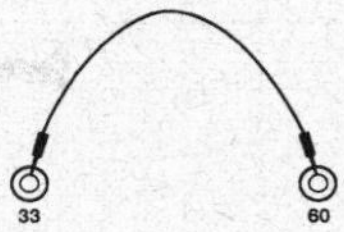	3 Connect a jumper wire between EEC-IV 60-Pin Breakout Box pin 33, circuit 918 (Y/R), and EEC-IV 60-Pin Breakout Box pin 60, circuit 57 (BK).
4 	4 Leave the key ON for ten seconds.
5 	• Did the yellow ABS warning indicator illuminate? → **Yes** REPLACE the anti-lock brake control module → **No** Diagnose Indicator

FM4029700917020A

Fig. 3 System pre-check (Part 2 of 3)

TEST CONDITIONS	TEST DETAILS/RESULTS/ACTIONS
SPC3 RETRIEVE ABS DIAGNOSTIC TROUBLE CODES (DTCs)	
1 2 3 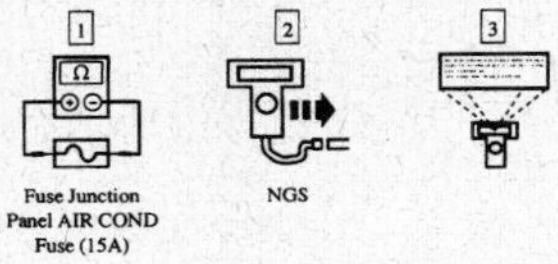	3 **NOTE:** Failure to do so may result in improper diagnosis and unnecessary replacement of good components. Retrieve and document all continuous DTCs. • Are any DTCs present? → **Yes** Starting with the first code recorded, GO to the Anti-Lock Brake Control Module Diagnostic Trouble Code (DTC) Index. → **No** If System Pass is obtained and no DTCs are present, DRIVE the vehicle to CHECK ABS operation. If previous action was taken during Inspection and Verification, the concern is resolved. If System Pass is obtained and the concern is still present, GO to Symptom Chart. If no response is obtained, GO to Pinpoint Test R.

FM4029700917030A

Fig. 3 System pre-check (Part 3 of 3)

DTCs	Description	DTC Caused By	Action
B1318	No/Low Voltage To Anti-Lock Brake Control Module.	ABS	GO to Pinpoint Test Q.
B1342	Anti-Lock Brake Control Module Failure.	ABS	REPLACE the anti-lock brake control module. Control. TEST the system for normal operation.
C1095	Pump Motor Shorted.	ABS	GO to Pinpoint Test B.
C1096	Pump Motor Open.	ABS	GO to Pinpoint Test C.
C1115	Shorted Anti-Lock Relay.	ABS	GO to Pinpoint Test D.
C1140	Excessive Dump Time Fault.	ABS	GO to Pinpoint Test E.
C1145	RF Anti-Lock Brake Sensor (Static).	ABS	GO to Pinpoint Test F.
C1148/C1234	RF Anti-Lock Brake Sensor (Dynamic).	ABS	GO to Pinpoint Test G.
C1155	LF Anti-Lock Brake Sensor (Static).	ABS	GO to Pinpoint Test F.

FM4020001641010X

Fig. 4 Diagnostic trouble code identification (Part 1 of 2)

6. If NGS reports "System Passed," proceed to Anti-Lock Quick Tests Checks.

Diagnostic Trouble Code Interpretation

Refer to **Fig. 4,** for diagnostic trouble code interpretation.

Drive Cycle Test

Refer to **Fig. 5,** for drive cycle test.

Wiring Diagrams

Refer to **Fig. 6,** for wiring diagram.

Pinpoint Tests

Refer to **Fig. 7,** for symptom chart and **Figs. 8 through 23,** for diagnostic tests.

Clearing Diagnostic Trouble Codes

Connect a suitably programmmed scan tool to Data Link Connector (DLC), and follow manufacturer's instructions.

DTCs	Description	DTC Caused By	Action
C1158/C1233	LF Anti-Lock Brake Sensor (Dynamic).	ABS	GO to Pinpoint Test G.
C1165	RR Anti-Lock Brake Sensor (Static).	ABS	GO to Pinpoint Test H.
C1168/C1235	RR Anti-Lock Brake Sensor (Dynamic).	ABS	GO to Pinpoint Test J.
C1175	LR Anti-Lock Brake Sensor (Static).	ABS	GO to Pinpoint Test H.
C1178/C1236	LR Anti-Lock Brake Sensor (Dynamic).	ABS	GO to Pinpoint Test J.
C1184	Excessive ABS Isolation.	ABS	GO to Pinpoint Test K.
C1185	Open Anti-Lock Relay.	ABS	GO to Pinpoint Test L.
C1194/C1196	Open or Shorted LF Dump Valve Solenoid.	ABS	GO to Pinpoint Test N.
C1198/C1200	Open or Shorted LF Isolation (ISO) Valve Solenoid.	ABS	GO to Pinpoint Test M.
C1220	Anti-Lock Brake Warning Indicator Shorted.	ABS	GO to Pinpoint Test P.
C1222	Wheel Speed Error.	ABS	GO to Pinpoint Test K.
C1210/C1212	Open or Shorted RF Dump Valve Solenoid.	ABS	GO to Pinpoint Test N.
C1214/C1216	Open or Shorted RF Isolation (ISO) Valve Solenoid.	ABS	GO to Pinpoint Test M.
C1242/C1244	Open or Shorted LR Dump Valve Solenoid.	ABS	GO to Pinpoint Test N.
C1246/C1248	Open or Shorted RR Dump Valve Solenoid.	ABS	GO to Pinpoint Test N.
C1250/C1252	Open or Shorted LR Isolation (ISO) Valve Solenoid.	ABS	GO to Pinpoint Test M.
C1254/C1256	Open or Shorted RR Isolation (ISO) Valve Solenoid.	ABS	GO to Pinpoint Test M.

FM4020001641020X

Fig. 4 Diagnostic trouble code identification (Part 2 of 2)

TEST CONDITIONS	TEST DETAILS/RESULTS/ACTIONS
DT2 CHECK FOR UNWARRANTED ABS ACTIVITY (Continued)	
	[2] **NOTE:** When conducting the following procedure, the vehicle may pull as soon as the pump motor turns on. The front brake anti-lock sensor opposite the pull should be checked using the ABS Misfire, ABS Too Sensitive, ABS Fires On Normal Stop symptoms on the Symptom Chart. If the pump motor turns on and no pull is felt, the rear brake anti-lock sensors should be checked using the ABS Misfire, ABS Too Sensitive, ABS Fires On Normal Stop conditions on the Symptom Chart. If a vehicle pulls immediately upon braking and the pump motor does not turn on, use the Vehicle Pulls During Braking symptom on the Symptom Chart to diagnose the concern. Perform a light to medium (normal traffic) stop. • Does the pump motor turn on and are brake pedal pulsations felt at any time during the stop? → **Yes** If the yellow ABS warning indicator does not illuminate, GO to ABS Misfire, ABS Too Sensitive, ABS Fires On Normal Stop in the Symptom Chart. If the yellow ABS warning indicator illuminates and stays on, GO to **DT7**. → **No** If other symptoms are detected, GO to **DT6**. If the yellow ABS warning indicator does not illuminate, GO to **DT3**.

FM4029701133020X

Fig. 5 Drive cycle test (Part 2 of 5)

TEST CONDITIONS	TEST DETAILS/RESULTS/ACTIONS
DT1 LOW SPEED ABS STOP	
NOTE: Wetting down the area where the stop is to be performed will aid in performing this test.	
	[1] **NOTE:** An assistant should monitor the wheels during the ABS stop. Momentary lockup is permissible. Drive the vehicle at approximately 6 kph (10 mph). [2] Press the brake pedal hard enough to lock all four wheels. • Does one wheel lock consistently? → **Yes** If the yellow ABS warning indicator does not illuminate, GO to the Symptom Chart condition Wheels Lock Up. If the yellow ABS warning indicator illuminates and stays on, GO to **DT7**. → **No** If the yellow ABS warning indicator does not illuminate and one wheel does not lock up consistently, GO to **DT2**.
DT2 CHECK FOR UNWARRANTED ABS ACTIVITY	
	[1] Drive the vehicle at approximately 12 kph (20 mph).

FM4029701133010X

Fig. 5 Drive cycle test (Part 1 of 5)

TEST CONDITIONS	TEST DETAILS/RESULTS/ACTIONS
DT3 CHECK FOR MARGINALLY HIGH SENSOR GAP AT IDLE	
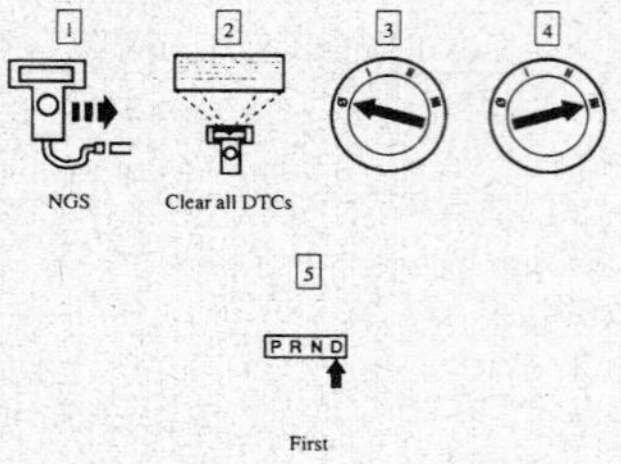	[6] Allow the vehicle to creep forward at idle for at least 45 seconds. • Does the yellow ABS warning indicator illuminate? → **Yes** GO to **DT8**. → **No** GO to **DT4**.
DT4 CHECK FOR MARGINALLY HIGH SENSOR GAP	
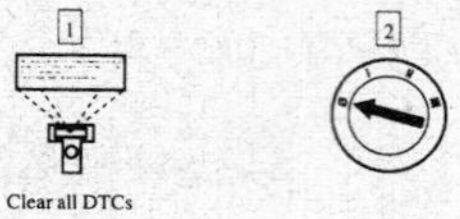	[3] Start the vehicle and accelerate to 15 kph (25 mph). Let at least 45 seconds elapse before reaching 15 kph (25 mph). • Does the yellow ABS warning indicator illuminate? → **Yes** GO to **DT8**. → **No** GO to **DT5**.

FM4029701133030X

Fig. 5 Drive cycle test (Part 3 of 5)

TEST CONDITIONS	TEST DETAILS/RESULTS/ACTIONS
DT5 DETERMINE IF DRIVE TEST IS COMPLETE	
	1 Determine if Drive Cycle Test is complete. • Has the customer concern been addressed and corrected by the previous actions? → **Yes** STOP. Vehicle ABS function has been verified. → **No** REFER to the Symptom Chart.
DT6 DETERMINE NEXT DIAGNOSTIC STEP BASED ON BRAKE SYMPTOM	
	1 Test for the following conditions: — Lack of sufficient vehicle deceleration upon brake application — Vehicle pulls during braking and the pump motor does not come on • Are any of the above symptoms present? → **Yes** GO to the Symptom Chart. → **No** Concern is not in the ABS system.

FM4029701133040X

Fig. 5 Drive cycle test (Part 4 of 5)

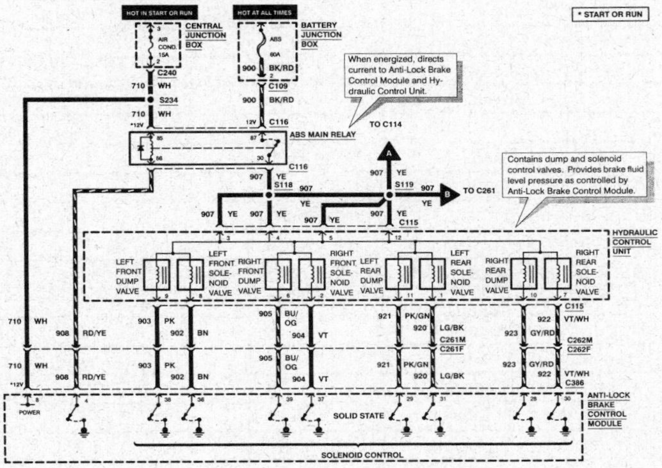

FM9049900368010X

Fig. 6 Wiring diagram (Part 1 of 3)

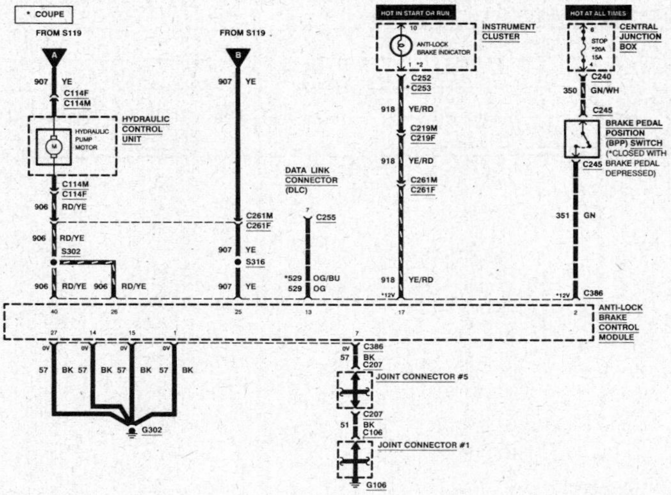

FM9049900368020X

Fig. 6 Wiring diagram (Part 2 of 3)

TEST CONDITIONS	TEST DETAILS/RESULTS/ACTIONS
DT7 RETRIEVE DIAGNOSTIC TROUBLE CODE (DTC)	
1  NGS 2  Retrieve DTCs	• Is the DTC the same as before and is the entire pinpoint test for the DTC completed? → **Yes** DIAGNOSE the intermittent fault. → **No** If the Pinpoint Test is not complete, RETURN to the test step last completed in the pinpoint test. If DTC retrieved is not the same, GO to the pinpoint test for the DTC retrieved. If the module does not respond, GO to the Quick Test.
DT8 DETERMINE WHICH SENSOR SIGNAL IS INCORRECT	
1  Retrieve DTCs	• Is a sensor code obtained? → **Yes** GO to the appropriate pinpoint test. → **No** If system pass is not obtained, GO to the pinpoint test for the DTC retrieved. If no code or system pass is obtained, GO to the Quick Test.

FM4029701133050X

Fig. 5 Drive cycle test (Part 5 of 5)

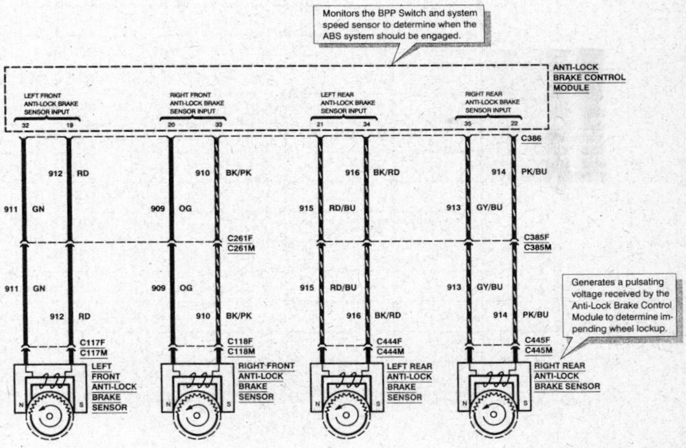

FM9049900368030X

Fig. 6 Wiring diagram (Part 3 of 3)

DIAGNOSTIC CHART INDEX

Test	Code	Description	Page No.	Fig. No.
—	—	Symptom Chart	6-87	7
A	—	ABS Warning Indicator On, System Self-Check Pass	6-87	8
B	C1095	Pump Motor Shorted	6-87	9
C	C1096	Pump Motor Open	6-88	10
D	C1115	Shorted ABS Relay	6-89	11
E	C1140	Excessive Dump Time Fault	6-90	12
F	C1145	Righthand Front ABS Sensor Fault	6-90	13
	C1155	Lefthand Front ABS Sensor Fault	6-90	13
G	C1148	Righthand Front ABS Sensor Fault	6-91	14
	C1158	Lefthand Front ABS Sensor Fault	6-91	14
	C1233	Lefthand Front ABS Sensor Fault	6-91	14
	C1234	Righthand Front ABS Sensor Fault	6-91	14
H	C1165	Righthand Rear ABS Sensor Fault	6-92	15
	C1175	Lefthand Rear ABS Sensor Fault	6-92	15
J	C1168	Righthand Rear ABS Sensor Fault	6-94	16
	C1178	Lefthand Rear ABS Sensor Fault	6-94	16
	C1235	Righthand Rear ABS Sensor Fault	6-94	16
	C1236	Lefthand Rear ABS Sensor Fault	6-94	16
K	C1184	Excessive ABS Isolation Or Wheel Speed Error	6-95	17
	C1222	Excessive ABS Isolation Or Wheel Speed Error	6-95	17
L	C1185	ABS Relay Open	6-96	18
M	C1198	Open Or Shorted Lefthand Front Isolation Valve	6-98	19
	C1200	Open Or Shorted Lefthand Front Isolation Valve	6-98	19
	C1214	Open Or Shorted Righthand Front Isolation Valve	6-98	19
	C1216	Open Or Shorted Righthand Front Isolation Valve	6-98	19
	C1250	Open Or Shorted Lefthand Rear Isolation Valve	6-98	19
	C1252	Open Or Shorted Lefthand Rear Isolation Valve	6-98	19
	C1254	Open Or Shorted Righthand Rear Isolation Valve	6-98	19
	C1256	Open Or Shorted Righthand Rear Isolation Valve	6-98	19
N	C1194	Open Or Shorted Lefthand Front Dump Valve Solenoid	6-99	20
	C1196	Open Or Shorted Lefthand Front Dump Valve Solenoid	6-99	20
	C1210	Open Or Shorted Righthand Front Dump Valve Solenoid	6-99	20
	C1212	Open Or Shorted Righthand Front Dump Valve Solenoid	6-99	20
	C1242	Open Or Shorted Lefthand Rear Dump Valve Solenoid	6-99	20
	C1244	Open Or Shorted Lefthand Rear Dump Valve Solenoid	6-99	20
	C1246	Open Or Shorted Righthand Rear Dump Valve Solenoid	6-99	20
	C1248	Open Or Shorted Righthand Rear Dump Valve Solenoid	6-99	20
P	C1220	Yellow ABS Warning Indicator Shorted	6-101	21
Q	B1318	Low Voltage To ABS Control Module	6-102	22
R	—	No Communication w/ABS Control Module	6-102	23

Condition	Possible Source	Action
• ABS Misfire, ABS Too Sensitive, ABS Activates On Normal Stops	• Rear anti-lock brake sensor indicators. • Front anti-lock brake sensor indicator. • Anti-lock brake sensor circuitry. • Improper harness routing and/or circuitry. • Rear brake adjustment. • Linings are "grabby." • Anti-lock brake sensor output.	• INSPECT the rear anti-lock brake sensor indicators. • INSPECT the front anti-lock brake sensor indicators. • GO to the Intermittent Failures Test. • INSPECT anti-lock brake sensor wiring harnesses. • Diagnose base brake system. • CHECK the front anti-lock brake sensor; GO to Pinpoint Test G. • CHECK the rear anti-lock brake sensor; GO to Pinpoint Test J.
• Wheels Lock Up	• Rear brake shoes and linings, disc brake caliper or rear brakes. • Parking brake. • HCU.	• Diagnose base brake system. • Diagnose base brake system. • REPLACE the HCU.
• Hard or Soft Brake Pedal, Excessive Brake Pedal Travel	• Brake line or hose, master cylinder or disc brake caliper (soft). • Hydraulic system (soft). • Vacuum boost (hard). • Disc brake caliper (hard). • Brake line or hose (hard). • Inlet (isolation) valve (hard) or outlet (dump) valve (soft). • Inlet (isolation) valve during ABS.	• Diagnose base brake system. • BLEED the hydraulic system. • Diagnose base brake system. • REPLACE the HCU. • REPLACE the HCU.
• Lack of Deceleration During Medium/Hard Brake Applications	• Brake line or hose, master cylinder or disc brake caliper. • Hydraulic system. • Vacuum boost (hard). • Wheel cylinder or caliper. • Brake shoes or linings. • Inlet (isolation) valve or outlet (dump) valve (rear axle only).	• Diagnose base brake system. • BLEED the hydraulic system. • Diagnose base brake system. • REPLACE the HCU.
• Vehicle Pulls During Braking	• Front disc brake caliper (one side of vehicle). • Brake shoe and lining wear. • Brake line or hose. • Right front inlet (isolation) valve. • Left front inlet (isolation) valve.	• Diagnose base brake. • system. • Diagnose base brake system. • REPLACE the HCU. • REPLACE the HCU.

FM4020001642010X

Fig. 7 Symptom chart (Part 1 of 2)

TEST CONDITIONS	TEST DETAILS/RESULTS/ACTIONS
A1 CHECK FOR SHORT TO GROUND	
Note: The System Pre-Check must be performed before proceeding.	
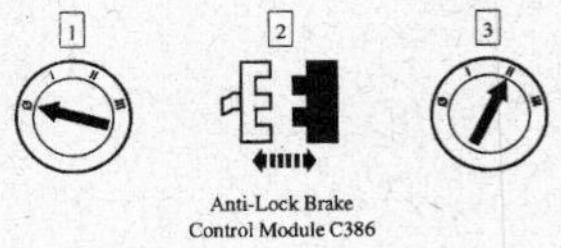	• Does the yellow ABS warning indicator illuminate continuously? → **Yes** REFER to instrument cluster. → **No** REPLACE the anti-lock brake control module; TEST the system for normal operation.

FM4020001643000X

Fig. 8 Test A: ABS Warning Indicator On, System Self-Check Pass

Condition	Possible Source	Action
• Anti-Lock Brake Warning Indicator On With System Pass	• Circuitry. • Anti-lock brake control module.	• GO to Pinpoint Test A.
• No Communication With the Anti-Lock Brake Control Module	• Circuitry. • Anti-lock brake control module.	• GO to Pinpoint Test R.

FM4020001642020X

Fig. 7 Symptom chart (Part 2 of 2)

TEST CONDITIONS	TEST DETAILS/RESULTS/ACTIONS
B1 CHECK FAULT REPEATABILITY	
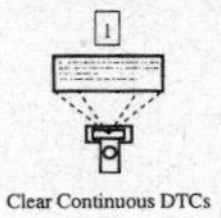	
	2 Perform the drive cycle test. GO to Drive Cycle Test.
	3 Retrieve and document continuous DTCs. • Is DTC C1095 retrieved? → **Yes** GO to **B2**. → **No** If a different DTC is retrieved, GO to Anti-Lock Brake Control Module Diagnostic Trouble Code (DTC) Index. If System Pass is obtained, GO to **B4**.
B2 CHECK PUMP MOTOR	
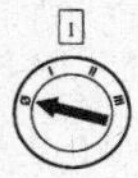	2 Connect EEC-IV 60-Pin Breakout Box to the anti-lock brake control module C386. 3 Replace the power distribution box ABS fuse (60A) with a 20A fuse.

FM4020001644010X

Fig. 9 Test B/Code C1095: Pump Motor Shorted (Part 1 of 4)

TEST CONDITIONS	TEST DETAILS/RESULTS/ACTIONS
B2 CHECK PUMP MOTOR (Continued)	
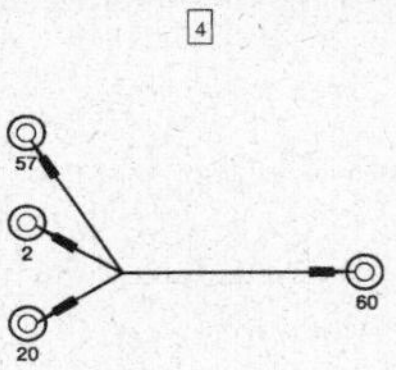	4 Connect a jumper between EEC-IV 60-Pin Breakout Box pin 60, circuit 57 (BK), and EEC-IV 60-Pin Breakout Box pins as follows:
	6 Listen for pump motor operation.
	• Does the pump motor run until the key is turned OFF? → **Yes** REPLACE the anti-lock brake control module. GO to **B4**. → **No** GO to **B3**.
B3 CHECK CIRCUIT 906 (R/Y)	
	1 Replace the failed 20A fuse with another 20A fuse.

EEC-IV 60-Pin Breakout Box Pin	Circuit
57	908 (R/Y)
2	906 (R/Y)
20	906 (R/Y)

FM4020001644020X

Fig. 9 Test B/Code C1095: Pump Motor Shorted (Part 2 of 4)

TEST CONDITIONS	TEST DETAILS/RESULTS/ACTIONS
B3 CHECK CIRCUIT 906 (R/Y) (Continued)	
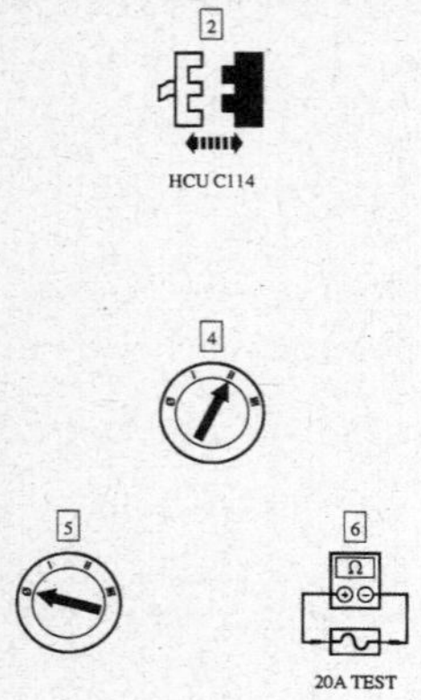	3 Remove all jumpers from EEC-IV 60-Pin Breakout Box. 4 Ignition switch in the RUN position for at least 15 seconds. • Is the fuse OK? → **Yes** REPLACE the HCU. GO to **B4**. → **No** REPLACE the 20A TEST fuse. REPAIR circuit 906 (R/Y). GO to **B4**.
B4 VERIFY REPAIR	
	1 Reconnect all components and restore system. 3 Repeat the Drive Cycle Test.

FM4020001644030X

Fig. 9 Test B/Code C1095: Pump Motor Shorted (Part 3 of 4)

TEST CONDITIONS	TEST DETAILS/RESULTS/ACTIONS
C1 CHECKFAULTREPEATABILITY	
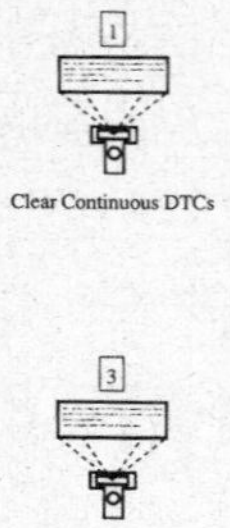	2 Perform the drive cycle test. GO to Drive Cycle Test. 3 Retrieve and document continuous DTCs. • Is C1096 retrieved? → **Yes** GO to **C2**. → **No** If a different DTC is retrieved, GO to Anti-Lock Brake Control Module Diagnostic Trouble Code (DTC) Index. If System Pass is obtained, GO to **C5**.

FM4020001645010X

Fig. 10 Test C/Code C1096: Pump Motor Open (Part 1 of 3)

TEST CONDITIONS	TEST DETAILS/RESULTS/ACTIONS
B4 VERIFY REPAIR (Continued)	
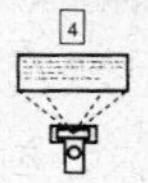	4 Retrieve and document continuous DTCs. • Is System Pass obtained? → **Yes** STOP. Repair is complete. → **No** If original code is retrieved, GO to **B1**. If a different DTC is retrieved, GO to Anti-Lock Brake Control Module Diagnostic Trouble Code (DTC) Index.

FM4020001644040X

Fig. 9 Test B/Code C1095: Pump Motor Shorted (Part 4 of 4)

TEST CONDITIONS	TEST DETAILS/RESULTS/ACTIONS
C2 CHECK PUMP MOTOR OPERATION	
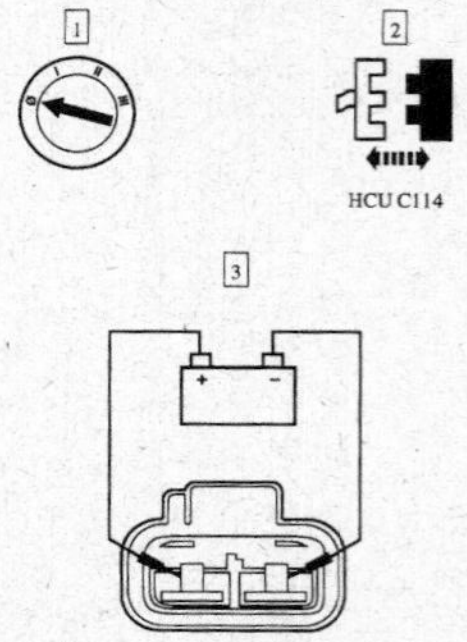	3 Use jumper wires to apply battery voltage and ground to the terminals of the HCU C114. • Does the pump motor operate? → **Yes** GO to **C3**. → **No** REPLACE the HCU. GO to **C5**.
C3 CHECK PUMP MOTOR DRIVE CIRCUIT 906 (R/Y) FOR OPEN	
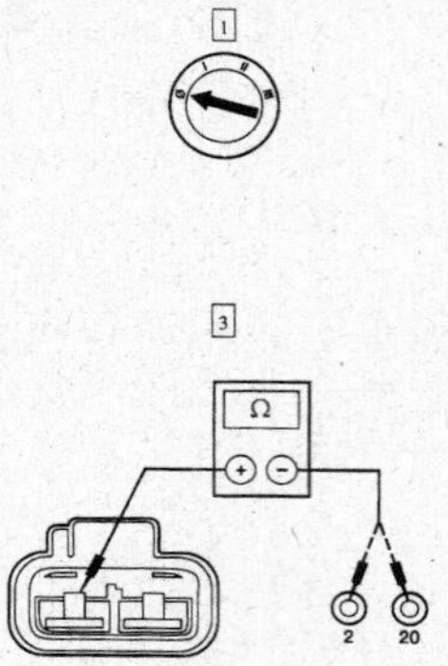	2 Connect EEC-IV 60-Pin Breakout Box to the anti-lock brake control module C386. 3 Measure the resistance between EEC-IV 60-Pin Breakout Box pin 2, circuit 906 (R/Y), and the HCU C114-1, circuit 906 (R/Y), and between EEC-IV 60-Pin Breakout Box pin 20 circuit 906 (R/Y), and HCU C114-1, circuit 906 (R/Y). • Is the resistance less than 5 ohms? → **Yes** GO to **C4**. → **No** REPAIR circuit 906 (R/Y). GO to **C5**.

FM4020001645020X

Fig. 10 Test C/Code C1096: Pump Motor Open (Part 2 of 3)

TEST CONDITIONS	TEST DETAILS/RESULTS/ACTIONS
C4 CHECK PUMP MOTOR POWER SUPPLY CIRCUIT 907 (Y) FOR OPEN	
1 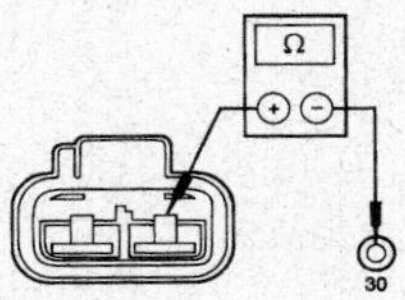	1 Measure the resistance between EEC-IV 60-Pin Breakout Box pin 30, circuit 907 (Y), and HCU C114-2, circuit 907 (Y). • Is the resistance less than 5 ohms? → **Yes** REPLACE the anti-lock brake control module. GO to **C5**. → **No** REPAIR circuit 907 (Y). GO to **C5**.
C5 VERIFY REPAIR	
	1 Reconnect all components and restore system.
2  Clear Continuous DTCs	
	3 Repeat the Drive Cycle Test.
4 	4 Retrieve and document continuous DTCs. • Is System Pass obtained? → **Yes** STOP. Repair is complete. → **No** If the original code is retrieved, GO to **C1**. If a different DTC is retrieved, GO to Anti-Lock Brake Control Module Diagnostic Trouble Code (DTC) Index.

FM4020001645030X

Fig. 10 Test C/Code C1096: Pump Motor Open (Part 3 of 3)

TEST CONDITIONS	TEST DETAILS/RESULTS/ACTIONS
D3 CHECK ANTI-LOCK RELAY	
1 	2 Perform the Anti-Lock Relay Component Test. • Is the anti-lock relay OK? → **Yes** REINSTALL the anti-lock relay. GO to **D4**. → **No** REPLACE the anti-lock relay. GO to **D6**.
D4 CHECK RELAY CONTROL CIRCUIT	
	1 Connect EEC-IV 60-pin Breakout Box to the anti-lock brake control module C386.
2 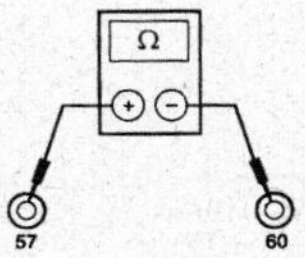	2 Measure the resistance between EEC-IV 60-pin Breakout Box pin 57, circuit 908 (R/Y), and EEC-IV 60-pin Breakout Box pin 60, circuit 57 (BK). • Is the resistance greater than 10,000 ohms? → **Yes** REPLACE the anti-lock brake control module. GO to **D6**. → **No** REPAIR circuit 908 (R/Y). GO to **D6**.

FM4020001646020X

Fig. 11 Test D/Code C1115: Shorted ABS Relay (Part 2 of 3)

TEST CONDITIONS	TEST DETAILS/RESULTS/ACTIONS
D1 CHECK FAULT REPEATABILITY	
1  Clear Continuous DTCs	
	2 Perform the drive cycle test. GO to Drive Cycle Test.
3 	3 Retrieve and document continuous DTCs. • Is DTC C1115 retrieved? → **Yes** DTC C1095 is also retrieved. IGNORE DTC 1095 and GO to **D2**. → **No** If only DTC C1095 is retrieved, GO to Pinpoint Test B. If a different DTC is retrieved, GO to Anti-Lock Brake Control Module Diagnostic Trouble Code (DTC) Index.
D2 CHECK FOR SHORT TO POWER	
1 2 3 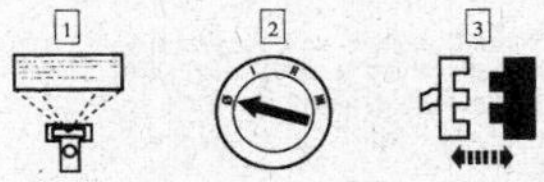 Clear Continuous DTCs; Anti-Lock Relay C116	
	4 Perform the drive cycle test. GO to Drive Cycle Test.
5 	5 Retrieve and document continuous DTCs. • Is DTC C1115 retrieved? → **Yes** GO to **D5**. → **No** If a different DTC is retrieved, IGNORE DTC and GO to **D3**.

FM4020001646010X

Fig. 11 Test D/Code C1115: Shorted ABS Relay (Part 1 of 3)

TEST CONDITIONS	TEST DETAILS/RESULTS/ACTIONS
D5 CHECK CIRCUIT 907 (Y) FOR SHORT TO POWER	
1 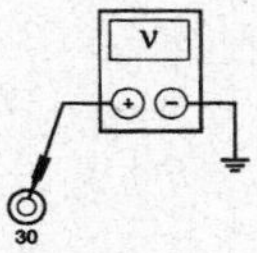	1 Measure the voltage between EEC-IV 60-Pin Breakout Box pin 30, circuit 907 (Y), and ground. • Is the voltage greater than 10 volts? → **Yes** REPAIR short to power in circuit 907 (Y) wire. GO to **D6**. → **No** REPLACE the anti-lock brake control module. GO to **D6**.
D6 VERIFY REPAIR	
	1 Reconnect all the components and restore the system.
2  Clear Continuous DTCs	
	3 Repeat the Drive Cycle Test.
4 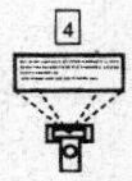	4 Retrieve and document continuous DTCs. • Is System Pass obtained? → **Yes** STOP. Repair is complete. → **No** If the original code is retrieved, REPEAT **D1**. If a different DTC is retrieved, GO to Anti-Lock Brake Control Module Diagnostic Trouble Code (DTC) Index.

FM4020001646030X

Fig. 11 Test D/Code C1115: Shorted ABS Relay (Part 3 of 3)

TEST CONDITIONS	TEST DETAILS/RESULTS/ACTIONS
E1 CHECK FAULT REPEATABILITY	

1

Clear Continuous DTCs

2 Perform the drive cycle test. GO to Drive Cycle Test.

3

3 Retrieve and document continuous DTCs.

- Is DTC C1140 retrieved?

→ **Yes**
GO to **E2**.

→ **No**
REPEAT the System Pre-Check. GO to System Pre-Check.

E2 CHECK LOW SPEED ANTI-LOCK CONTROL OPERATION

Note: Wetting down the test area will aid in performing the test.

1 Drive the vehicle at approximately 16 km/h (10 mph).

2 **Note:** Momentary lock-up is permissible. An assistant should be used to monitor the wheels during the stop.

Apply the brakes hard enough to lock all four wheels.

- Does one wheel lock consistently?

→ **Yes**
GO to the Symptom Chart.

→ **No**
REPEAT the System Pre-Check. GO to System Pre-Check.

FM4020001647000X

Fig. 12 Test E/Code C1140: Excessive Dump Time Fault

TEST CONDITIONS	TEST DETAILS/RESULTS/ACTIONS
F2 CHECK SUSPECT FRONT ANTI-LOCK BRAKE SENSOR CIRCUIT RESISTANCE (Continued)	

- Is the resistance between 2400 and 2800 ohms?

→ **Yes**
GO to **F3**.

→ **No**
GO to **F5**.

F3 CHECK CIRCUITS FOR SHORT TO GROUND

1

Suspected Anti-Lock Brake Sensor Connector

1 RF anti-lock brake sensor C118, or LF anti-lock brake sensor C117.

2

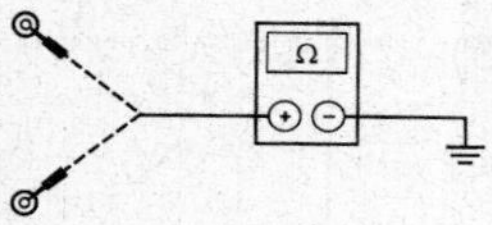

2 Measure the resistance between the suspected anti-lock brake sensor, EEC-IV 60-Pin Breakout Box pins, and ground as follows:

DTC	Breakout Box Pin	Breakout Box Pin
C1145 (RF Anti-Lock Brake Sensor)	53 (circuit 909 [O])	55 (circuit 910 [BK/PK])
C1155 (LF Anti-Lock Brake Sensor)	34 (circuit 912 [R])	26 (circuit 911 [GN])

- Are the resistances greater than 10,000 ohms?

→ **Yes**
GO to **F4**.

→ **No**
REPAIR the circuit(s) in question. GO to **F9**.

FM4020001648020X

Fig. 13 Test F/Codes C1145 & C1155: Front ABS Sensor Fault (Static, Part 2 of 5)

TEST CONDITIONS	TEST DETAILS/RESULTS/ACTIONS
F1 CHECK FAULT REPEATABILITY	

1

Clear Continuous DTCs

2 Perform the drive cycle test. GO to Drive Cycle Test.

3

3 Retrieve and document continuous DTCs

- Is DTC C1145 or DTC C1155 retrieved?

→ **Yes**
GO to **F2**.

→ **No**
If System Pass is obtained, concern is intermittent. GO to **F8**.

If a different DTC is retrieved, REFER to Anti-Lock Brake Control Module Diagnostic Trouble Code (DTC) index.

F2 CHECK SUSPECT FRONT ANTI-LOCK BRAKE SENSOR CIRCUIT RESISTANCE

1

2 Connect EEC-IV 60-Pin Breakout Box.

3

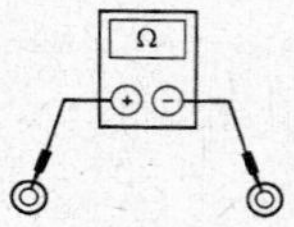

3 Measure the resistance between EEC-IV 60-Pin Breakout Box pins as follows:

DTC	Breakout Box Pin	Breakout Box Pin
C1145 (RF Anti-Lock Brake Sensor)	53 (circuit 909 [O])	55 (circuit 910 [BK/PK])
C1155 (LF Anti-Lock Brake Sensor)	34 (circuit 912 [R])	26 (circuit 911 [GN])

FM4020001648010X

Fig. 13 Test F/Codes C1145 & C1155: Front ABS Sensor Fault (Static, Part 1 of 5)

TEST CONDITIONS	TEST DETAILS/RESULTS/ACTIONS
F4 CHECK THE ANTI-LOCK BRAKE SENSOR FOR A SHORT TO GROUND	

1

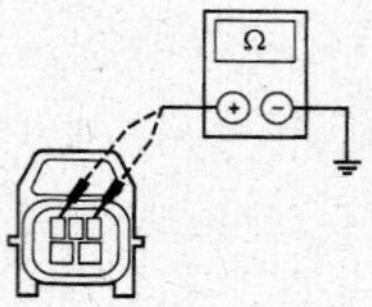

1 Measure the resistance between suspected anti-lock brake sensor terminal, and ground.

- Is the resistance greater than 10,000 ohms?

→ **Yes**
REPLACE the anti-lock brake control module.
GO to **F9**.

→ **No**
REPLACE the anti-lock brake sensor.
GO to **F9**.

F5 CHECK THE SUSPECTED ANTI-LOCK BRAKE CIRCUITS FOR OPEN

1

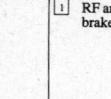

Suspected Anti-Lock Brake Sensor Connector

1 RF anti-lock brake sensor C118, or LF anti-lock brake sensor C117.

2 Measure the resistance in the circuits between EEC-IV 60-Pin Breakout Box pins, and anti-lock brake sensor connector as follows:

Suspected Anti-Lock Brake Sensor	EEC-IV 60-Pin Breakout Box Pin	Anti-Lock Brake Sensor Connector	Circuit
RF Anti-Lock Brake Sensor	53	C118	909 (O)
	55	C118	910 (BK/PK)
LF Anti-Lock Brake Sensor	26	C117	911 (GN)
	34	C117	912 (R)

FM4020001648030X

Fig. 13 Test F/Codes C1145 & C1155: Front ABS Sensor Fault (Static, Part 3 of 5)

TEST CONDITIONS	TEST DETAILS/RESULTS/ACTIONS

F5 CHECK THE SUSPECTED ANTI-LOCK BRAKE CIRCUITS FOR OPEN (Continued)

- Are the resistances less than 5 ohms?

→ **Yes**
GO to **F6**.

→ **No**
REPAIR the circuit(s) in question. GO to **F9**.

F6 CHECK CIRCUITS FOR SHORT TO EACH OTHER

1

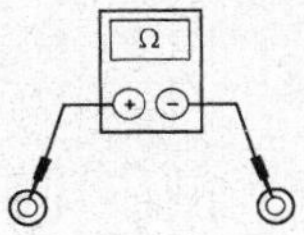

1 Measure the resistance between EEC-IV 60-Pin Breakout Box pins as follows:

DTC	EEC-IV 60-Pin Breakout Box Pins	Circuits
C1145 (RF Anti-Lock Brake Sensor)	53, 55	909 (O), 910 (BK/PK)
C1155 (LF Anti-Lock Brake Sensor)	26, 34	911 (GN), 912 (R)

- Is the resistance greater than 10,000 ohms?

→ **Yes**
GO to **F7**.

→ **No**
REPAIR circuit(s) in question. GO to **F9**.

F7 CHECK THE ANTI-LOCK BRAKE SENSOR

1

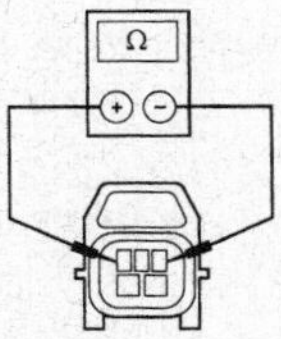

1 Measure the resistance between the suspected anti-lock brake sensor terminals.

- Is the resistance between 2400 and 2800 ohms?

→ **Yes**
REPLACE the anti-lock brake control module.
GO to **F9**.

→ **No**
REPLACE the anti-lock brake sensor.
GO to **F9**.

FM4020001648040X

Fig. 13 Test F/Codes C1145 & C1155: Front ABS Sensor Fault (Static, Part 4 of 5)

TEST CONDITIONS	TEST DETAILS/RESULTS/ACTIONS

F8 INTERMITTENT DIAGNOSIS

1 Conduct the Intermittent Failures Sensor Failure Test for the LF anti-lock brake sensor (DTC C1155) or the RF anti-lock brake sensor (DTC C1145).

- Did the suspect front anti-lock brake sensor pass the Intermittent Failures Test?

→ **Yes**
RECONNECT the suspect front anti-lock brake sensor. GO to **F9**.

→ **No**
GO to **F9**.

F9 VERIFY REPAIR

1 Reconnect all components and restore system.

2

Clear DTCs

3 Repeat the Drive Cycle Test.

4

Retrieve DTCs

- Is System Pass obtained?

→ **Yes**
STOP. Repair is complete.

→ **No**
If the original code is retrieved, GO to **F2**.

If a different DTC is retrieved, GO to Anti-Lock Brake Control Module Diagnostic Trouble Code (DTC) Index.

FM4020001648050X

Fig. 13 Test F/Codes C1145 & C1155: Front ABS Sensor Fault (Static, Part 5 of 5)

TEST CONDITIONS	TEST DETAILS/RESULTS/ACTIONS

G1 RETRIEVE DTCs

1

Retrieve Continuous DTCs

- Is DTC C1145 or C1155 retrieved?

→ **Yes**
GO to Pinpoint Test F. IGNORE all other DTCs retrieved.

→ **No**
If DTC C1148, C1234, C1158 and/or C1233 is/are retrieved, GO to **G2**.

If a different DTC is retrieved, GO to Anti-Lock Brake Control Module Diagnostic Trouble Code (DTC) Index.

G2 REPEATABILITY TEST DRIVE (MISMATCHED OUTPUT)

Note: Recording all speeds for later plotting will eliminate the need of monitoring the NGS while driving.

Note: If a hard turn is made, some variation between all four sensors is expected.

1

1 Monitor anti-lock brake PIDs; LF__WSPI, LR__WSPI, RF__WSPI, and RR__WSPI.

2 Drive the vehicle at various speeds and over rough roads.

- Does the suspect front anti-lock brake sensor signal consistently match the others?

→ **Yes**
Concern is intermittent. GO to **G8**.

→ **No**
Concern is repeatable. GO to **G3**.

G3 CHECK SENSOR FOR INTERNAL SHORT

1

1 Suspect anti-lock brake sensor, RF anti-lock brake sensor C118 or LF anti-lock brake sensor C117.

FM4020001649010X

Fig. 14 Test G/Codes C1148, C1158, C1233 & C1234: Front ABS Sensor Fault (Dynamic, Part 1 of 6)

TEST CONDITIONS	TEST DETAILS/RESULTS/ACTIONS

G3 CHECK SENSOR FOR INTERNAL SHORT (Continued)

2

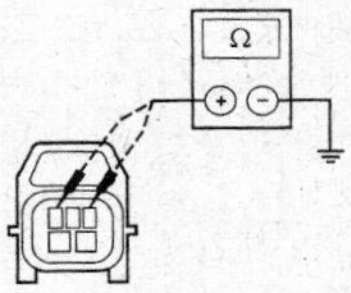

2 Measure the resistance between the suspect front anti-lock brake sensor terminals, and ground.

- Are the resistances greater than 10,000 ohms?

→ **Yes**
GO to **G4**.

→ **No**
REPLACE the suspect front brake anti-lock sensor (2C204).
GO to **G10**.

G4 CHECK SUSPECT FRONT ANTI-LOCK BRAKE SENSOR FOR OPEN

1

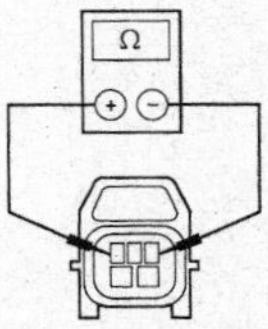

1 Measure the resistance between the suspect front anti-lock brake sensor terminals.

- Is the resistance between 2400 and 2800 ohms?

→ **Yes**
GO to **G5**.

→ **No**
REPLACE the suspect front anti-lock brake sensor.
GO to **G10**.

G5 CHECK ANTI-LOCK BRAKE SENSOR CIRCUITS

1 Connect EEC-IV 60-Pin Breakout Box to the anti-lock brake control module harness.

2

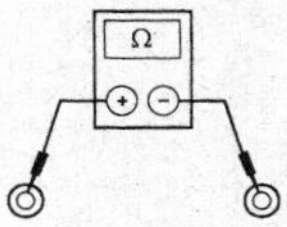

2 Measure the resistance between EEC-IV 60-Pin Breakout Box pins as follows:

DTC	EEC-IV 60-Pin Breakout Box Pin	EEC-IV 60-Pin Breakout Box Pin
C1148/C1234 (RF Anti-Lock Brake Sensor)	53 (circuit 909 [O])	55 (circuit 910 [BK/PK])
C1158/C1233 (LF Anti-Lock Brake Sensor)	34 (circuit 912 [R])	26 (circuit 911 [GN])

FM4020001649020X

Fig. 14 Test G/Codes C1148, C1158, C1233 & C1234: Front ABS Sensor Fault (Dynamic, Part 2 of 6)

TEST CONDITIONS	TEST DETAILS/RESULTS/ACTIONS
G5 CHECK ANTI-LOCK BRAKE SENSOR CIRCUITS (Continued)	
3 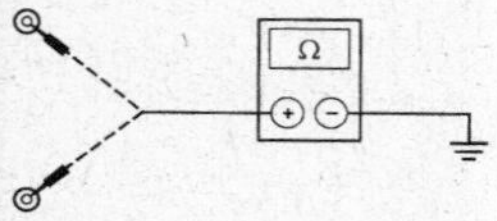	3 Measure the resistance between EEC-IV 60-Pin Breakout Box pins and ground as follows:

DTC	EEC-IV 60-Pin Breakout Box Pin	EEC-IV 60-Pin Breakout Box Pin
C1148/C1234 (RF Anti-Lock Brake Sensor)	53 (circuit 909 [O])	55 (circuit 910 [BK/PK])
C1158/C1233 (LF Anti-Lock Brake Sensor)	34 (circuit 912 [R])	26 (circuit 911 [GN])

TEST CONDITIONS	TEST DETAILS/RESULTS/ACTIONS
	• Are the resistances greater than 10,000 ohms? → **Yes** GO to **G6**. → **No** REPAIR circuits in question. GO to **G10**.
G6 CHECK AIR GAP	
	1 Raise and support the vehicle.
2 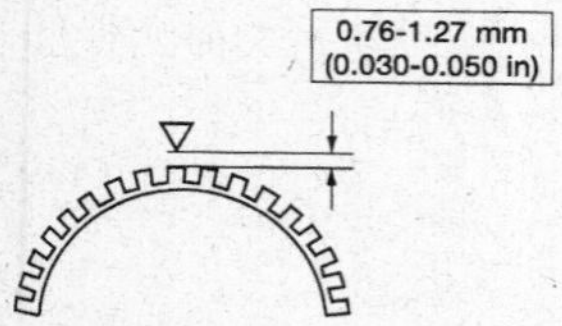	2 **Note:** The air gap is not adjustable. Inspect components for looseness or damage if the air gap is not within specification. Measure the suspect front anti-lock brake sensor air gap. • Is the air gap within specification? → **Yes** GO to **G7**. → **No** REPAIR or REPLACE components as necessary. GO to **G9**.
G7 CHECK COMPONENTS	
Note: Examine all components carefully. Failure to properly diagnose component damage at this time will lead to unnecessary component replacement and wasted diagnostic time.	
	1 Remove the suspect front brake anti-lock sensor.

FM4020001649030X

Fig. 14 Test G/Codes C1148, C1158, C1233 & C1234: Front ABS Sensor Fault (Dynamic, Part 3 of 6)

TEST CONDITIONS	TEST DETAILS/RESULTS/ACTIONS
G9 CHECK COMPONENTS (FOR INTERMITTENT TEST) (Continued)	
	2 Visually inspect the suspect front anti-lock brake sensor indicator, the suspect front anti-lock brake sensor and sensor cable for signs of damage, corrosion or improper fit. • Are the components OK? → **Yes** GO to **G10**. → **No** REPLACE or REPAIR components as necessary. GO to **G9**.
G10 VERIFY REPAIR	
	1 Reconnect all components and restore system.
2  Clear Continuous DTCs	
	3 Repeat the Drive Cycle Test.
4 	4 Retrieve and document continuous DTCs. • Is System Pass obtained? → **Yes** GO to **G11**. → **No** If the original code is retrieved, GO to **G2**. If a different DTC is retrieved, GO to Anti-Lock Brake Control Module Diagnostic Trouble Code (DTC) Index.

FM4020001649050X

Fig. 14 Test G/Codes C1148, C1158, C1233 & C1234: Front ABS Sensor Fault (Dynamic, Part 5 of 6)

TEST CONDITIONS	TEST DETAILS/RESULTS/ACTIONS
G7 CHECK COMPONENTS (Continued)	
	2 Visually inspect the suspect front brake anti-lock sensor indicator, the suspect front brake anti-lock sensor and sensor cable for signs of damage, corrosion or improper fit. • Are the components OK? → **Yes** REPLACE the anti-lock brake control module. GO to **G10**. → **No** REPLACE or REPAIR components as necessary. GO to **G10**.
G8 INTERMITTENT DIAGNOSIS	
	1 Conduct the Intermittent Failures Sensor Failure Test for the LF anti-lock brake sensor (DTCs C1158/C1233) or the RF anti-lock brake sensor (DTCs C1148/C1234). • Did the suspect front anti-lock brake sensor pass the Intermittent Failures test? → **Yes** RECONNECT the suspect front anti-lock brake sensor. GO to **G10**. → **No** GO to **G9**.
G9 CHECK COMPONENTS (FOR INTERMITTENT TEST)	
Note: Examine all components carefully. Failure to properly diagnose component damage at this time will lead to unnecessary component replacement and wasted diagnostic time.	
	1 Remove the suspect front anti-lock brake sensor.

FM4020001649040X

Fig. 14 Test G/Codes C1148, C1158, C1233 & C1234: Front ABS Sensor Fault (Dynamic, Part 4 of 6)

TEST CONDITIONS	TEST DETAILS/RESULTS/ACTIONS
G11 VERIFICATION TEST DRIVE	
Note: Recording all speeds for later plotting will eliminate the need of monitoring the NGS while driving. **Note:** If a hard turn is made, some variation between all four sensors is expected.	
1 	1 Monitor anti-lock brake PIDs; LF__WSPI, LR__WSPI, RF__WSPI, and RR__WSPI.
	2 Gradually and smoothly accelerate the vehicle from a stop to 32.2 km/h (20 mph) several times. • Does the suspect front anti-lock brake sensor signal consistently match the others? → **Yes** STOP. Repair is complete. → **No** Concern is repeatable. GO to **G3**.

FM4020001649060X

Fig. 14 Test G/Codes C1148, C1158, C1233 & C1234: Front ABS Sensor Fault (Dynamic, Part 6 of 6)

TEST CONDITIONS	TEST DETAILS/RESULTS/ACTIONS
H1 CHECK FAULT REPEATABILITY	
1 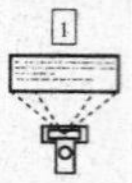 Clear Continuous DTCs	
	2 Perform the drive cycle test. GO to Drive Cycle Test.

FM4020001650010X

Fig. 15 Test H/Code C1165 & C1175: Rear ABS Sensor Fault (Static, Part 1 of 6)

TEST CONDITIONS	TEST DETAILS/RESULTS/ACTIONS

H1 CHECK FAULT REPEATABILITY (Continued)

3 

3 Retrieve and document continuous DTCs.

- Is DTC C1165 or DTC C1175 retrieved?

→ **Yes**
GO to **H2**.

→ **No**
If System Pass is obtained, concern is intermittent. GO to **H8**.

If a different DTC is retrieved, GO to Anti-Lock Brake Control Module Diagnostic Trouble Code (DTC) Index.

H2 CHECK SUSPECT REAR ANTI-LOCK BRAKE SENSOR CIRCUIT RESISTANCE

1 

2 Connect EEC-IV 60-Pin Breakout Box.

3 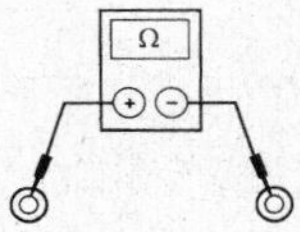

3 Measure the resistance between EEC-IV 60-Pin Breakout Box pins as follows:

DTC	Breakout Box Pin	Breakout Box Pin
C1165 (RR Anti-Lock Brake Sensor)	45 (circuit 914 [PK/BL])	32 (circuit 913 [GY/BL])
C1175 (LR Anti-Lock Brake Sensor)	27 (circuit 915 [R/BK])	38 (circuit 916 [BK/R])

- Is the resistance between 2400 and 2800 ohms?

→ **Yes**
GO to **H3**.

→ **No**
GO to **H5**.

FM4020001650020X

Fig. 15 Test H/Code C1165 & C1175: Rear ABS Sensor Fault (Static, Part 2 of 6)

TEST CONDITIONS	TEST DETAILS/RESULTS/ACTIONS

H5 CHECK THE SUSPECTED ANTI-LOCK BRAKE CIRCUITS FOR OPEN

1 

Suspected Anti-Lock Brake Sensor Connector

1 RR anti-lock brake sensor C445, or LR anti-lock brake sensor C444.

2 Measure the resistance in the circuits between EEC-IV 60-Pin Breakout Box pins, and anti-lock brake sensor connector as follows:

Suspected Anti-Lock Brake Sensor	EEC-IV 60-Pin Breakout Box Pin	Anti-Lock Brake Sensor Connector	Circuit
RR Anti-Lock Brake Sensor	45	C445	914 (PK/BL)
	32	C445	913 (GY/BL)
LR Anti-Lock Brake Sensor	27	C444	915 (R/BK)
	38	C444	916 (BK/R)

- Are the resistances less than 5 ohms?

→ **Yes**
GO to **H6**.

→ **No**
REPAIR the circuit(s) in question. GO to **H9**.

FM4020001650040X

Fig. 15 Test H/Code C1165 & C1175: Rear ABS Sensor Fault (Static, Part 4 of 6)

TEST CONDITIONS	TEST DETAILS/RESULTS/ACTIONS

H3 CHECK CIRCUITS FOR SHORT TO GROUND

1 

Suspected Anti-Lock Brake Sensor Connector

1 RR anti-lock brake sensor C445, or LR anti-lock brake sensor C444.

2 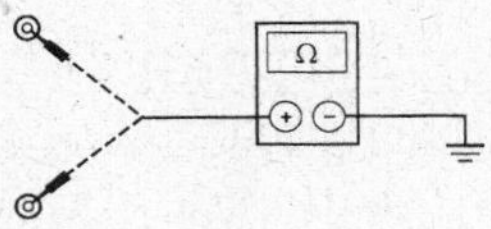

2 Measure the resistance between the suspected anti-lock brake sensor, EEC-IV 60-Pin Breakout Box pins, and ground as follows:

DTC	Breakout Box Pin	Breakout Box Pin
C1165 (RR Anti-Lock Brake Sensor)	45 (circuit 914 [PK/BL])	32 (circuit 913 [GY/BL])
C1175 (LR Anti-Lock Brake Sensor)	27 (circuit 915 [R/BK])	38 (circuit 916 [BK/R])

- Are the resistances greater than 10,000 ohms?

→ **Yes**
GO to **H4**.

→ **No**
REPAIR the circuit(s) in question. GO to **H9**.

H4 CHECK THE ANTI-LOCK BRAKE SENSOR FOR A SHORT TO GROUND

1 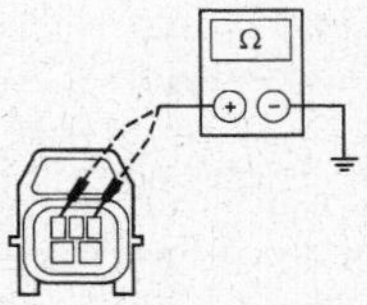

1 Measure the resistance between suspected anti-lock brake sensor terminal, and ground.

- Is the resistance greater than 10,000 ohms?

→ **Yes**
REPLACE the anti-lock brake control module.
GO to **H9**.

→ **No**
REPLACE the anti-lock brake sensor.
GO to **H9**.

FM4020001650030X

Fig. 15 Test H/Code C1165 & C1175: Rear ABS Sensor Fault (Static, Part 3 of 6)

TEST CONDITIONS	TEST DETAILS/RESULTS/ACTIONS

H6 CHECK CIRCUITS A FOR SHORT TO EACH OTHER

1 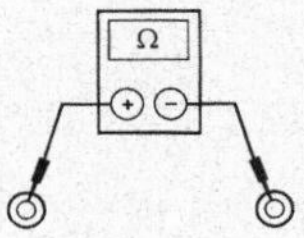

1 Measure the resistance between EEC-IV 60-Pin Breakout Box pins as follows:

DTC	EEC-IV 60-Pin Breakout Box Pins	Circuits
C1165 (RR Anti-Lock Brake Sensor)	45, 32	914 (PK/BL), 913 (GY/BL)
C1175 (LR Anti-Lock Brake Sensor)	27, 38	915 (R/BK), 916 (BK/R)

- Is the resistance greater than 10,000 ohms?

→ **Yes**
GO to **H7**.

→ **No**
REPAIR circuit(s) in question. GO to **H9**.

H7 CHECK THE ANTI-LOCK BRAKE SENSOR

1 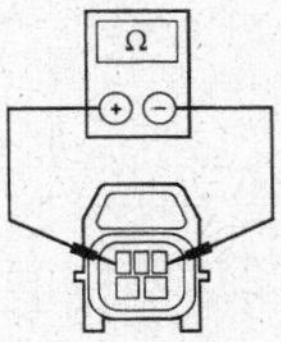

1 Measure the resistance between the suspected anti-lock brake sensor terminals.

- Is the resistance between 2400 and 2800 ohms?

→ **Yes**
REPLACE the anti-lock brake control module.
GO to **H9**.

→ **No**
REPLACE the anti-lock brake sensor.
GO to **H9**.

FM4020001650050X

Fig. 15 Test H/Code C1165 & C1175: Rear ABS Sensor Fault (Static, Part 5 of 6)

TEST CONDITIONS	TEST DETAILS/RESULTS/ACTIONS
H8 INTERMITTENT DIAGNOSIS	
	1 Conduct the Intermittent Failures Sensor Failure Test for the LR brake anti-lock sensor (DTC 1175) or the RR brake anti-lock sensor (DTC C1165). Go to Intermittent Failures test. • Did the suspect rear brake anti-lock sensor pass the Intermittent Failures test? → **Yes** RECONNECT the suspect rear brake anti-lock sensor. GO to **H9**. → **No** GO to **H9**.
H9 VERIFY REPAIR	
	1 Reconnect all components and restore system.
2  Clear DTCs	
	3 Repeat the Drive Cycle Test.
4  Retrieve DTCs	• Is System Pass obtained? → **Yes** STOP. Repair is complete. → **No** If the original code is retrieved, GO to **H2**. If a different DTC is retrieved, GO to Anti-Lock Brake Control Module Diagnostic Trouble Code (DTC) Index.

FM4020001650060X

Fig. 15 Test H/Code C1165 & C1175: Rear ABS Sensor Fault (Static, Part 6 of 6)

TEST CONDITIONS	TEST DETAILS/RESULTS/ACTIONS
J1 RETRIEVE DTCs	
1  Retrieve Continuous DTCs	• Is DTC C1165 or DTC C1175 retrieved? → **Yes** GO to Pinpoint Test H. IGNORE all other DTCs retrieved. → **No** If DTC C1168, C1235, C1178 and/or C1236, is/are retrieved, GO to **J2**. If a different DTC is retrieved, GO to Anti-Lock Brake Control Module Diagnostic Trouble Code (DTC) Index.
J2 REPEATABILITY TEST DRIVE (MISMATCHED OUTPUT)	
Note: Recording all speeds for later plotting will eliminate the need of monitoring NGS while driving. **Note:** If a hard turn is made, some variation between all four sensors is expected.	
1 	1 Monitor anti-lock brake PIDs; LF__WSPI, LR__WSPI, RF__WSPI, and RR__WSPI. 2 Drive the vehicle at various speeds and over rough roads. • Does the suspect rear anti-lock brake sensor signal consistently match the others? → **Yes** GO to **J8**. → **No** GO to **J3**.
J3 CHECK SUSPECT REAR ANTI-LOCK BRAKE SENSOR FOR INTERNAL SHORT	
1 	1 Suspect anti-lock brake sensor RR anti-lock brake sensor C445 or LR anti-lock brake sensor C444.

FM4020001651010X

Fig. 16 Test J/Codes C1168, C1178, C1235 & C1236: Rear ABS Sensor Fault (Dynamic, Part 1 of 6)

TEST CONDITIONS	TEST DETAILS/RESULTS/ACTIONS
J3 CHECK SUSPECT REAR ANTI-LOCK BRAKE SENSOR FOR INTERNAL SHORT (Continued)	
2 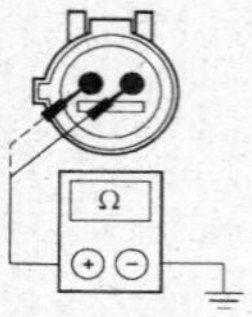	2 Measure the resistance between the suspect rear anti-lock brake sensor terminals, and ground. • Are the resistances greater than 10,000 ohms? → **Yes** GO to **J4**. → **No** REPLACE the suspect rear anti-lock brake sensor. GO to **J10**.
J4 CHECK SUSPECT REAR ANTI-LOCK BRAKE SENSOR FOR OPEN	
1 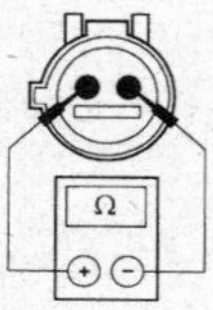	1 Measure the resistance between the suspect rear anti-lock brake sensor terminals. • Is the resistance between 2400 and 2800 ohms? → **Yes** GO to **J5**. → **No** REPLACE the suspect rear anti-lock brake sensor. GO to **J10**.
J5 CHECK CIRCUIT	
	1 Connect EEC-IV 60-Pin Breakout Box to the anti-lock brake control module harness.

FM4020001651020X

Fig. 16 Test J/Codes C1168, C1178, C1235 & C1236: Rear ABS Sensor Fault (Dynamic, Part 2 of 6)

TEST CONDITIONS	TEST DETAILS/RESULTS/ACTIONS
J5 CHECK CIRCUIT (Continued)	
2 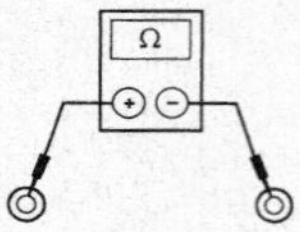	2 Measure the resistance between the following EEC-IV 60-Pin Breakout Box pins.

DTC	EEC-IV 60-Pin Breakout Box Pin	EEC-IV 60-Pin Breakout Box Pin
C1168/C1235 (RR Anti-Lock Brake Sensor)	45 (circuit 914 [PK/BL])	37 (circuit 913 [GY/BL])
C1178/C1236 (LR Anti-Lock Brake Sensor)	27 (circuit 915 [R/BL])	38 (circuit 916 [BK/R])

TEST CONDITIONS	TEST DETAILS/RESULTS/ACTIONS
3 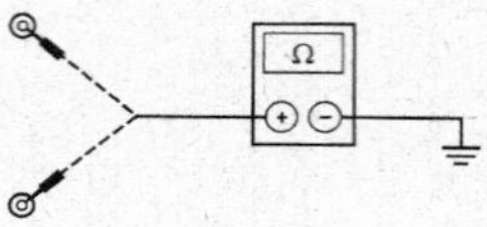	3 Measure the resistance between EEC-IV 60-Pin Breakout Box pins and ground as follows:

DTC	EEC-IV 60-Pin Breakout Box Pin	EEC-IV 60-Pin Breakout Box Pin
C1168/C1235 (RR Anti-Lock Brake Sensor)	45 (circuit 914 [PK/BL])	37 (circuit 913 [GY/BL])
C1178/C1236 (LR Anti-Lock Brake Sensor)	27 (circuit 915 [R/BL])	38 (circuit 916 [BK/R])

TEST CONDITIONS	TEST DETAILS/RESULTS/ACTIONS
	• Are the resistances greater than 10,000 ohms? → **Yes** GO to **J6**. → **No** REPAIR circuit(s) in question. GO to **J9**.
J6 CHECK AIR GAP	
	1 Raise and support the vehicle.

FM4020001651030X

Fig. 16 Test J/Codes C1168, C1178, C1235 & C1236: Rear ABS Sensor Fault (Dynamic, Part 3 of 6)

TEST CONDITIONS	TEST DETAILS/RESULTS/ACTIONS
J6 CHECK AIR GAP (Continued)	
2 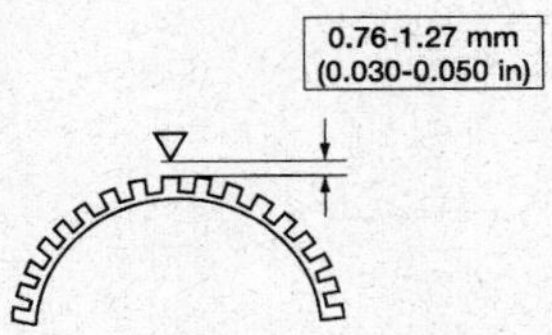	2 **Note:** The air gap is not adjustable. Inspect components for looseness or damage if the air gap is not within specification. Measure the suspect rear anti-lock brake sensor air gap. • Is the air gap within specification? → **Yes** GO to **J7**. → **No** REPAIR or REPLACE components as necessary. GO to **J9**.
J7 CHECK COMPONENTS	
Note: Examine all components carefully. Failure to properly diagnose component damage at this time will lead to unnecessary component replacement and wasted diagnostic time.	
	1 Remove the suspect rear anti-lock brake sensor. 2 Visually inspect the suspect rear anti-lock brake sensor indicator, the suspect rear anti-lock brake sensor and sensor cable for signs of damage, corrosion, or improper fit. • Are the components OK? → **Yes** REPLACE the anti-lock brake control module. GO to **J10**. → **No** REPLACE or REPAIR components as necessary. GO to **J10**.

FM4020001651040X

Fig. 16 Test J/Codes C1168, C1178, C1235 & C1236: Rear ABS Sensor Fault (Dynamic, Part 4 of 6)

TEST CONDITIONS	TEST DETAILS/RESULTS/ACTIONS
J10 VERIFY REPAIR (Continued)	
4 	4 Retrieve and document continuous DTCs. • Is System Pass obtained? → **Yes** GO to **J11**. → **No** If the original DTC is retrieved, GO to **J2**. If a different DTC is retrieved, GO to Anti-Lock Brake Control Module Diagnostic Trouble Code (DTC) Index.
J11 VERIFICATION TEST DRIVE	
Note: Recording all speeds for later plotting will eliminate the need of monitoring NGS while driving. **Note:** If a hard turn is made, some variation between all four sensors is expected.	
1 	1 Monitor anti-lock brake PIDs; LF__WSPI, LR__WSPI, RR__WSPI, and RF__WSPI. 2 Gradually and smoothly accelerate the vehicle from a stop to 32.2 km/h (20 mph) several times. • Does the suspect rear anti-lock brake sensor signal consistently match the others? → **Yes** STOP. Repair is complete. → **No** GO to **J3**.

FM4020001651060X

Fig. 16 Test J/Codes C1168, C1178, C1235 & C1236: Rear ABS Sensor Fault (Dynamic, Part 6 of 6)

TEST CONDITIONS	TEST DETAILS/RESULTS/ACTIONS
J8 INTERMITTENT DIAGNOSIS	
	1 Conduct the Intermittent Failures Sensor Failure test for the LR anti-lock brake sensor (DTCs C1178/C1236) or the RR anti-lock brake sensor (DTCs C1168/C1235). • Did the suspect rear anti-lock brake sensor pass the Intermittent Failures test? → **Yes** RECONNECT the suspect rear anti-lock brake sensor. GO to **J10**. → **No** GO to **J9**.
J9 CHECK COMPONENTS	
Note: Examine all components carefully. Failure to properly diagnose component damage at this time will lead to unnecessary component replacement and wasted diagnostic time.	
	1 Remove the suspect rear anti-lock brake sensor. 2 Visually inspect the suspect rear anti-lock brake sensor indicator, the suspect rear anti-lock brake sensor and sensor cable for signs of damage, corrosion, or improper fit. • Are the components OK? → **Yes** GO to **J10**. → **No** REPLACE or REPAIR components as necessary. GO to **J10**.
J10 VERIFY REPAIR	
2  Clear Continuous DTCs	1 Reconnect all components and restore system. 3 Repeat the Drive Cycle Test.

FM4020001651050X

Fig. 16 Test J/Codes C1168, C1178, C1235 & C1236: Rear ABS Sensor Fault (Dynamic, Part 5 of 6)

TEST CONDITIONS	TEST DETAILS/RESULTS/ACTIONS
K1 VISUAL INSPECTION	
1 	2 Raise and support the vehicle.

FM4020001652010X

Fig. 17 Test K/Codes C1184 & C1222: Excessive ABS Isolation Or Wheel Speed Error (Part 1 of 3)

TEST CONDITIONS	TEST DETAILS/RESULTS/ACTIONS
K1 VISUAL INSPECTION (Continued)	
	3 Inspect the tires for proper size. 4 Inspect the anti-lock brake sensor indicators for damaged or missing teeth. • Are the tires correct and the anti-lock brake sensor indicators OK? → **Yes** GO to **K2**. → **No** CORRECT as necessary. REPEAT the System Pre-Check.
K2 CHECK FAULT REPEATABILITY	
1  Clear Continuous DTCs	2 Perform the drive cycle test. GO to Drive Cycle Test.

FM4020001652020X

Fig. 17 Test K/Codes C1184 & C1222: Excessive ABS Isolation Or Wheel Speed Error (Part 2 of 3)

TEST CONDITIONS	TESTDETAILS/RESULTS/ACTIONS
K2 CHECK FAULT REPEATABILITY (Continued)	
3 	3 Retrieve and document continuous DTCs. • Is DTC C1184 or C1222 retrieved and/or the anti-lock control active on normal stops? → **Yes** If the anti-lock control was active on normal stops, GO to **K3**. If DTC C1222 was retrieved, REPLACE the anti-lock brake control module . REPEAT the System Pre-Check. If DTC 1184 was retrieved and the anti-lock control was not active, REPLACE the anti-lock brake control module. REPEAT the System Pre-Check. If DTC 1184 was retrieved and the anti-lock control was active, GO to **K3**. → **No** A different DTC was retrieved. GO to Anti-Lock Brake Control Module Diagnostic Trouble Code (DTC) Index.
K3 CHECK FOR ERRATIC WHEEL SPEED SIGNAL	
1 2  Clear Continuous DTCs	2 Capture anti-lock brake sensor signals from PIDs; LF__WSPI, LR__WSPI, RF__WSPI, and RR__WSPI. 3 Repeat the Drive Cycle Test. • Does a wheel speed signal drop out while driving or braking? → **Yes** GO to Anti-Lock Brake Control Module Diagnostic Trouble Code (DTC) Index. → **No** REPEAT the capture mode. Intermittent or erratic wheel speed signals may not be recorded the first time. RE-CHECK the anti-lock brake sensor indicators for damage. VERIFY anti-lock brake sensor wiring is routed properly. If OK, REPEAT System Pre-Check.

FM4020001652030X

Fig. 17 Test K/Codes C1184 & C1222: Excessive ABS Isolation Or Wheel Speed Error (Part 3 of 3)

TEST CONDITIONS	TESTDETAILS/RESULTS/ACTIONS
L3 CHECK FOR SHORT IN CIRCUIT 710 (W)	
1 2  Anti-Lock Relay C116 Anti-Lock Brake Control Module C386 3 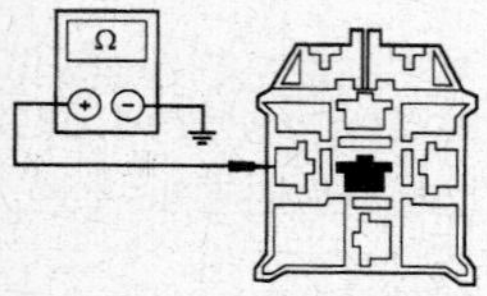	3 Measure the resistance between anti-lock relay C116-85, circuit 710 (W), and ground. • Is the resistance greater than 10,000 ohms? → **Yes** REPLACE the 15A AIR COND fuse. GO to **L4**. → **No** REPAIR circuit 710 (W). GO to **L10**.
L4 CHECK POWER SUPPLY CIRCUIT 900 (BK/R) AND CIRCUIT 710 (W)	
1  2 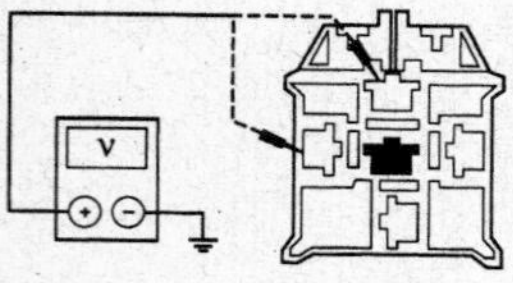	2 Measure the voltage between anti-lock relay C116-87, circuit 900 (BK/R), and ground; and between anti-lock relay C116-85, circuit 710 (W), and ground.

FM4020001653020X

Fig. 18 Test L/Code C1185: ABS Relay Open (Part 2 of 7)

TEST CONDITIONS	TESTDETAILS/RESULTS/ACTIONS
L1 CHECK FUSES 60A ABS AND 15A AIR COND	
1 2  Power Distribution Box ABS Fuse (60A) Fuse Junction Panel AIR COND (15A)	• Are the fuses OK? → **Yes** GO to **L4**. → **No** If the 60A ABS fuse, GO to **L2**. If the 15A AIR COND fuse, GO to **L3**.
L2 CHECK FOR SHORT IN CIRCUIT 900 (BK/R)	
1  Anti-Lock Relay C116 2 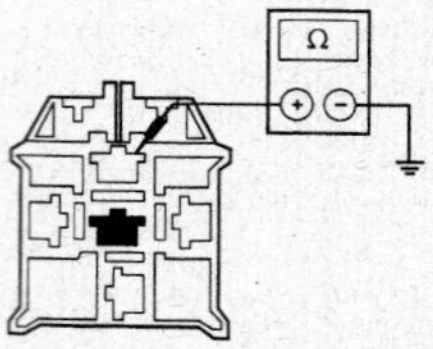	2 Measure the resistance between anti-lock relay C116-87, circuit 900 (BK/R), and ground. • Is the resistance greater than 10,000 ohms? → **Yes** REPLACE the 60A ABS fuse. GO to **L4**. → **No** REPAIR circuit 900 (BK/R). GO to **L10**.

FM4020001653010X

Fig. 18 Test L/Code C1185: ABS Relay Open (Part 1 of 7)

TEST CONDITIONS	TESTDETAILS/RESULTS/ACTIONS
L4 CHECK POWER SUPPLY CIRCUIT 900 (BK/R) AND CIRCUIT 710 (W) (Continued)	
3 	• Are the voltages greater than 10 volts? → **Yes** GO to **L5**. → **No** If voltage is 0 volts, REPAIR circuit 900 (BK/R) and/or circuit 710 (W). GO to **L10**. If voltage is greater than 0 volts but less than 10 volts, there is insufficient voltage to pull in the anti-lock relay. CHECK the charging system and battery for normal operation.
L5 CHECK ANTI-LOCK RELAY	
	1 Perform Anti-Lock Relay Component Test. • Is the anti-lock relay OK? → **Yes** GO to **L6**. → **No** REPLACE the anti-lock relay. GO to **L10**.
L6 CHECK RELAY COIL CIRCUIT 908 (RY)	
2 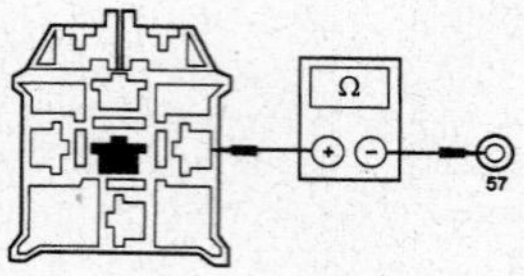	1 Connect EEC-IV 60-Pin Breakout Box to the anti-lock brake control module harness. 2 Measure the resistance between EEC-IV 60-Pin Breakout Box pin 57, circuit 908 (R/Y), and anti-lock relay C116-86, circuit 908 (R/Y).

FM4020001653030X

Fig. 18 Test L/Code C1185: ABS Relay Open (Part 3 of 7)

TEST CONDITIONS	TEST DETAILS/RESULTS/ACTIONS

L6 CHECK RELAY COIL CIRCUIT 908 (RY) (Continued)

3

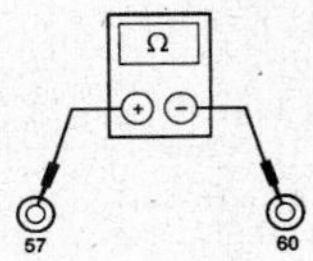

3 Measure the resistance between EEC-IV 60-Pin Breakout Box pin 57, circuit 908 (R/Y), and EEC-IV 60-Pin Breakout Box pin 60, circuit 57 (BK).

- Is the resistance less than 5 ohms between EEC-IV 60-Pin Breakout Box pin 57 and anti-lock relay connector C116-86, and greater than 10,000 ohms between EEC-IV 60-Pin Breakout Box pin 57 and pin 60?

→ **Yes**
GO to **L7**.

→ **No**
REPAIR circuit 908 (R/Y). GO to **L10**.

L7 CHECK RELAY POWER OUTLET CIRCUIT 907 (Y)

1

2

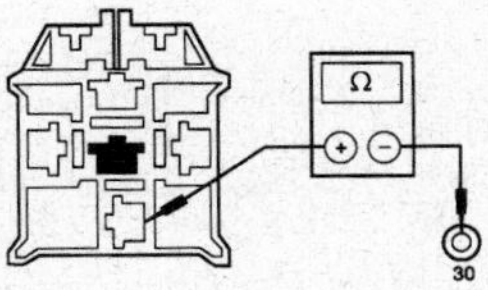

2 Measure the resistance between EEC-IV 60-Pin Breakout Box pin 30, circuit 907 (Y), and anti-lock relay C116-30, 907 (Y).

FM4020001653040X

Fig. 18 Test L/Code C1185: ABS Relay Open (Part 4 of 7)

TEST CONDITIONS	TEST DETAILS/RESULTS/ACTIONS

L7 CHECK RELAY POWER OUTLET CIRCUIT 907 (Y) (Continued)

3

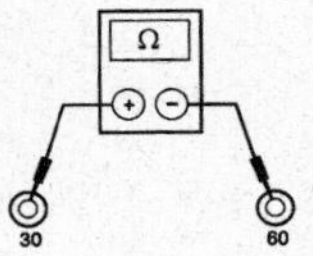

3 Measure the resistance between EEC-IV 60-Pin Breakout Box pin 30, circuit 907 (Y), and EEC-IV 60-Pin Breakout Box pin 60, circuit 57 (BK).

- Is the resistance greater than 10,000 ohms?

→ **Yes**
RECONNECT the anti-lock relay and HCU. GO to **L8**.

→ **No**
REPAIR circuit 907 (Y). GO to **L10**.

L8 CHECK HCU CIRCUITS

1

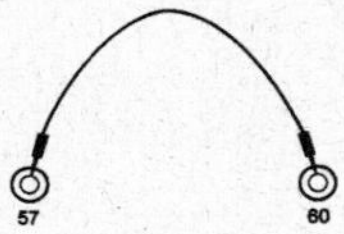

1 Install a jumper wire between EEC-IV 60-Pin Breakout Box pin 57, circuit 908 (R/Y) and EEC-IV 60-Pin Breakout Box pin 60, circuit 57 (BK).

2

FM4020001653050X

Fig. 18 Test L/Code C1185: ABS Relay Open (Part 5 of 7)

TEST CONDITIONS	TEST DETAILS/RESULTS/ACTIONS

L8 CHECK HCU CIRCUITS (Continued)

3

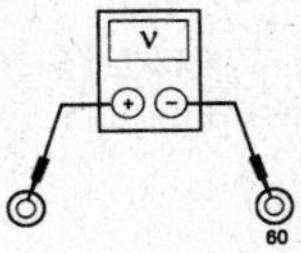

3 Measure the voltage between EEC-IV 60-Pin Breakout Box pin 60, circuit 57 (BK), and EEC-IV 60-Pin Breakout Box pins as follows:

EEC-IV 60-Pin Breakout Box Pin	Circuit
4	923 (GT/W)
8	920 (LG/BK)
9	922 (P/W)
15	921 (PK/GR)
31	903 (PK)
47	902 (BR)
49	904 (P)
50	905 (BL/O)

- Are all the voltages greater than 10 volts?

→ **Yes**
REPLACE the anti-lock brake control module.
GO to **L10**.

→ **No**
Leave jumper in place. GO to **L9**.

L9 CHECK HCU POWER SUPPLY CIRCUIT 907 (Y)

1 2 3

4

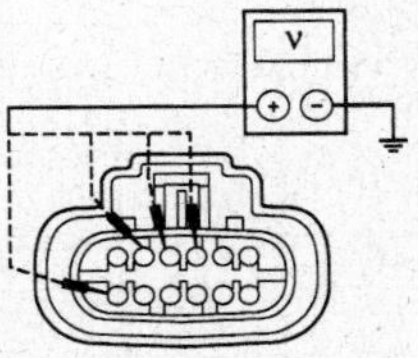

4 Measure the voltage between HCU C115 pins, and ground as follows:

Pin	Circuit
3	907 (Y)
4	907 (Y)
5	907 (Y)
12	907 (Y)

FM4020001653060X

Fig. 18 Test L/Code C1185: ABS Relay Open (Part 6 of 7)

TEST CONDITIONS	TEST DETAILS/RESULTS/ACTIONS

L9 CHECK HCU POWER SUPPLY CIRCUIT 907 (Y) (Continued)

- Are the voltages greater than 10 volts?

→ **Yes**
REPLACE the HCU.
GO to **L10**.

→ **No**
REPAIR circuit 907 (Y). GO to **L10**.

L10 VERIFY REPAIR

1 Reconnect all components and restore system.

2

Clear Continuous DTCs

3 Repeat the Drive Cycle Test.

4

4 Retrieve and document continuous DTCs.

- Is System Pass obtained?

→ **Yes**
STOP. Repair is complete.

→ **No**
If original code is retrieved, GO to **L1**.

If a different DTC is retrieved, GO to Anti-Lock Brake Control Module Diagnostic Trouble Code (DTC) Index.

FM4020001653070X

Fig. 18 Test L/Code C1185: ABS Relay Open (Part 7 of 7)

TEST CONDITIONS	TEST DETAILS/RESULTS/ACTIONS
M1 CHECK FAULT REPEATABILITY	
1  Clear Continuous DTCs	
	2 Perform the drive cycle test. GO to Drive Cycle Test.
3 	3 Retrieve and document continuous DTCs. • Are any DTCs retrieved? → **Yes** If DTC C1198, C1214, C1250, or C1254 is retrieved, GO to **M2**. If DTC C1200, C1216, C1252, or C1256 is retrieved, GO to **M6**. If a different DTC is retrieved, GO to Anti-Lock Brake Control Module Diagnostic Trouble Code (DTC) Index. → **No** System Pass is obtained. GO to **M8**.
M2 CHECK SUSPECT ISO VALVE SOLENOID RESISTANCE	
1 	
	2 Connect EEC-IV 60-Pin Breakout Box to the anti-lock control module harness.

FM4020001654010X

Fig. 19 Test M/Codes C1198, C1200, C1214, C1216, C1250, C1252, C1254 Or C1256: Open Or Shorted Isolation Valve (Part 1 of 6)

TEST CONDITIONS	TEST DETAILS/RESULTS/ACTIONS
M2 CHECK SUSPECT ISO VALVE SOLENOID RESISTANCE (Continued)	
3 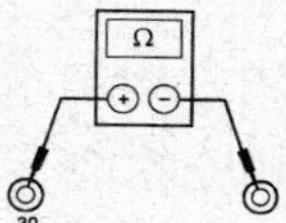 30	3 Measure the resistance between EEC-IV 60-Pin Breakout Box pin 30, circuit 907 (Y), and EEC-IV 60-Pin Breakout Box pins as follows: (see table below) • Is the resistance between 3 and 6 ohms? → **Yes** GO to **M5**. → **No** GO to **M3**.

DTC	Circuit	EEC-IV 60-Pin Breakout Box Pin
C1198	902 (BR)	47
C1214	904 (P)	49
C1250	920 (LG/BK)	8
C1254	922 (P/W)	9

TEST CONDITIONS	TEST DETAILS/RESULTS/ACTIONS
M3 ISOLATE RESISTANCE FAULT	
1  HCU C115	
	2 Measure the resistance between HCU terminals as follows: (see table below) • Are the resistances between 3 and 6 ohms? → **Yes** GO to **M4**. → **No** REPLACE the coil assembly. GO to **M8**.

DTC	Terminals	ISO Coil
C1198	8 and 3	LF
C1214	2 and 4	RF
C1250	1 and 5	LR
C1254	7 and 12	RR

FM4020001654020X

Fig. 19 Test M/Codes C1198, C1200, C1214, C1216, C1250, C1252, C1254 Or C1256: Open Or Shorted Isolation Valve (Part 2 of 6)

TEST CONDITIONS	TEST DETAILS/RESULTS/ACTIONS
M4 CHECK CIRCUIT BETWEEN ANTI-LOCK BRAKE CONTROL MODULE AND HCU	
	1 Measure the resistance between EEC-IV 60-Pin Breakout Box pin and connectors as follows: (see table below) • Is the resistance less than 5 ohms? → **Yes** REPLACE the anti-lock brake control module. GO to **M8**. → **No** If DTC C1198, REPAIR circuit 902 (BR). GO to **M8** If DTC C1214, REPAIR circuit 904 (P). GO to **M8**. If DTC C1250, REPAIR circuit 920 (LG/BK). GO to **M8**. If DTC C1254, REPAIR circuit 922 (P/W). GO to **M8**.

DTC	EEC-IV 60-Pin Break-out Box Pin	C115 Pin	Circuit
C1198	47	8	902 (BR)
C1214	49	2	904 (P)
C1250	8	1	920 (LG/BK)
C1254	9	7	922 (P/W)

FM4020001654030X

Fig. 19 Test M/Codes C1198, C1200, C1214, C1216, C1250, C1252, C1254 Or C1256: Open Or Shorted Isolation Valve (Part 3 of 6)

TEST CONDITIONS	TEST DETAILS/RESULTS/ACTIONS
M5 CHECK FOR SUSPECT ISO VALVE SOLENOID SHORT TO GROUND	
1  HCU C115	
2 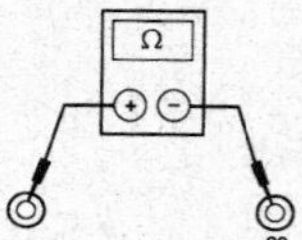 60	2 Measure the resistance between EEC-IV 60-Pin Breakout Box pin 60, circuit 57 (BK), and EEC-IV 60-Pin Breakout Box pins as follows: (see table below) • Is the resistance greater than 10,000 ohms? → **Yes** REPLACE the anti-lock brake control module. GO to **M8**. → **No** If DTC C1198, REPAIR circuit 902 (BR). GO to **M8**. If DTC C1214, REPAIR circuit 904 (P). GO to **M8**. If DTC C1250, REPAIR circuit 920 (LG/BK). GO to **M8**. If DTC C1254, REPAIR circuit 922 (P/W). GO to **M8**.
M6 CHECK SUSPECT ISO VALVE RESISTANCE AT ANTI-LOCK BRAKE CONTROL MODULE CONNECTOR	
	1 Connect EEC-IV 60-Pin Breakout Box to the anti-lock brake control module harness.

DTC	Circuit	EEC-IV 60-Pin Breakout Box Pin
C1198	902 (BR)	47
C1214	904 (P)	49
C1250	920 (LG/BK)	8
C1254	922 (P/W)	9

FM4020001654040X

Fig. 19 Test M/Codes C1198, C1200, C1214, C1216, C1250, C1252, C1254 Or C1256: Open Or Shorted Isolation Valve (Part 4 of 6)

TEST CONDITIONS	TEST DETAILS/RESULTS/ACTIONS
M6 CHECK SUSPECT ISO VALVE RESISTANCE AT ANTI-LOCK BRAKE CONTROL MODULE CONNECTOR (Continued)	
2 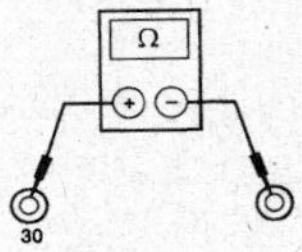	2 Measure the resistance between EEC-IV 60-Pin Breakout Box pin 30, circuit 907 (Y), and EEC-IV 60-Pin Breakout Box pins as follows:

DTC	Circuit	EEC-IV 60-Pin Breakout Box Pin
C1200	902 (BR)	47
C1216	904 (P)	49
C1252	920 (LG/BK)	8
C1256	922 (P/W)	9

- Is the resistance between 3 and 6 ohms?

→ **Yes**
GO to **M7**.

→ **No**
REPLACE the coil assembly.
GO to **M8**.

TEST CONDITIONS	TEST DETAILS/RESULTS/ACTIONS
M7 CHECK CIRCUIT BETWEEN ANTI-LOCK BRAKE CONTROL MODULE AND HCU	
1 	
2 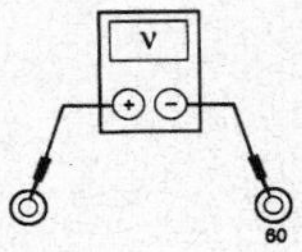	2 Measure the voltage between EEC-IV 60-Pin Breakout Box pin 60, circuit 57 (BK), and EEC-IV 60-Pin Breakout Box pins as follows:

DTC	Circuit	EEC-IV 60-Pin Breakout Box Pin
C1200	902 (BR)	47
C1216	904 (P)	49
C1252	920 (LG/BK)	8
C1256	922 (P/W)	9

FM40200016540 50X

Fig. 19 Test M/Codes C1198, C1200, C1214, C1216, C1250, C1252, C1254 Or C1256: Open Or Shorted Isolation Valve (Part 5 of 6)

TEST CONDITIONS	TEST DETAILS/RESULTS/ACTIONS
M7 CHECK CIRCUIT BETWEEN ANTI-LOCK BRAKE CONTROL MODULE AND HCU (Continued)	

- Is voltage present?

→ **Yes**
If DTC C1200, REPAIR circuit 902 (BR). GO to **M8**.

If DTC C1216, REPAIR circuit 904 (P). GO to **M8**.

If DTC C1252, REPAIR circuit 920 (LG/BK). GO to **M8**.

If DTC C1256, REPAIR circuit 922 (P/W). GO to **M8**.

→ **No**
REPLACE the anti-lock brake control module.
GO to **M8**.

TEST CONDITIONS	TEST DETAILS/RESULTS/ACTIONS
M8 VERIFY REPAIR	
	1 Reconnect all components.
2 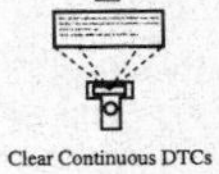	
	3 Repeat the Drive Cycle Test.
4 	4 Retrieve and document continuous DTCs.

- Is System Pass obtained?

→ **Yes**
STOP. Repair is complete.

→ **No**
If original DTC is retrieved, GO to **M1**.

If a different DTC is retrieved, GO to Anti-Lock Brake Control Module Diagnostic Trouble Code (DTC) Index.

FM4020001654060X

Fig. 19 Test M/Codes C1198, C1200, C1214, C1216, C1250, C1252, C1254 Or C1256: Open Or Shorted Isolation Valve (Part 6 of 6)

TEST CONDITIONS	TEST DETAILS/RESULTS/ACTIONS
N1 CHECK FAULT REPEATABILITY	
1 	
	2 Perform the drive cycle test. GO to Drive Cycle Test.
3 	3 Retrieve and document continuous DTCs.

- Are any DTCs retrieved?

→ **Yes**
If DTC C1194, C1210, C1242, or C1246 is retrieved, GO to **N2**.

If DTC C1196, C1212, C1244, or C1248 is retrieved, GO to **N6**.

If a different DTC is retrieved, GO to Anti-Lock Brake Control Module Diagnostic Trouble Code (DTC) Index.

→ **No**
System Pass is obtained. GO to **N8**.

TEST CONDITIONS	TEST DETAILS/RESULTS/ACTIONS
N2 CHECK SUSPECT DUMP VALVE SOLENOID RESISTANCE	
1 	
	2 Connect EEC-IV 60-Pin Breakout Box to the anti-lock brake control module harness.

FM4020001655010X

Fig. 20 Test N/Codes C1194, C1196, C1210, C1212, C1242, C1244, C1246 Or C1248: Open Or Shorted Dump Valve Solenoid (Part 1 of 6)

TEST CONDITIONS	TEST DETAILS/RESULTS/ACTIONS
N2 CHECK SUSPECT DUMP VALVE SOLENOID RESISTANCE (Continued)	
3 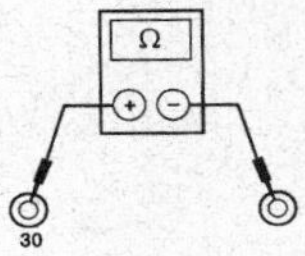	3 Measure the resistance between EEC-IV 60-Pin Breakout Box pin 30, circuit 907 (Y), and EEC-IV 60-Pin Breakout Box pins as follows:

DTC	Circuit	EEC-IV 60-Pin Breakout Box Pin
C1194	903 (PK)	31
C1210	905 (BL/O)	50
C1242	921 (PK/GN)	15
C1246	923 (GN/R)	4

- Is the resistance between 1 and 3 ohms?

→ **Yes**
GO to **N5**.

→ **No**
GO to **N3**.

TEST CONDITIONS	TEST DETAILS/RESULTS/ACTIONS
N3 ISOLATE RESISTANCE FAULT	
1 	
	2 Measure the resistance between HCU terminals as follows:

DTC	Terminals	Dump Coil
C1198	9 and 3	LF
C1214	6 and 4	RF
C1250	11 and 5	LR
C1254	10 and 12	RR

FM4020001655020X

Fig. 20 Test N/Codes C1194, C1196, C1210, C1212, C1242, C1244, C1246 Or C1248: Open Or Shorted Dump Valve Solenoid (Part 2 of 6)

TEST CONDITIONS	TEST DETAILS/RESULTS/ACTIONS
N3 ISOLATE RESISTANCE FAULT (Continued)	
	• Are the resistances between 1 and 3 ohms? → **Yes** GO to **N4**. → **No** REPLACE the coil assembly. GO to **N8**.
N4 CHECK CIRCUIT BETWEEN ANTI-LOCK BRAKE CONTROL MODULE AND HCU	
	1 Measure the resistance between EEC-IV 60-Pin Breakout Box pin and HCU C115 pin as follows:

DTC	Break-out Box Pin	Connector Pin	Circuit
C1194	31	9	903 (PK)
C1210	50	6	905 (BL/O)
C1242	15	11	921 (PK/GN)
C1246	4	10	923 (GY/R)

• Is the resistance less than 5 ohms?

→ **Yes**
REPLACE the anti-lock brake control module.
GO to **N8**.

→ **No**
REPAIR circuit(s) in question. GO to **N8**.

FM4020001655030X

Fig. 20 Test N/Codes C1194, C1196, C1210, C1212, C1242, C1244, C1246 Or C1248: Open Or Shorted Dump Valve Solenoid (Part 3 of 6)

TEST CONDITIONS	TEST DETAILS/RESULTS/ACTIONS
N5 CHECK FOR SUSPECT DUMP VALVE SOLENOID SHORT TO GROUND	

1

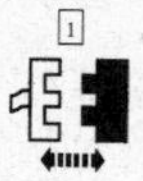

HCU C115

2

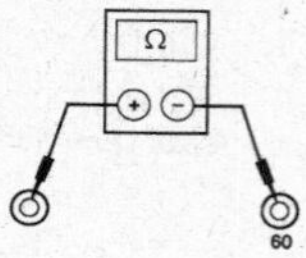

2 Measure the resistance between EEC-IV Breakout Box pin 60, circuit 57 (BK), and EEC-IV Breakout Box pins as follows:

DTC	Circuit	EEC-IV Breakout Box Pin
C1194	903 (PK)	31
C1210	905 (BL/O)	50
C1242	921 (PK/GN)	15
C1246	923 (GY/R)	4

• Is the resistance greater than 10,000 ohms?

→ **Yes**
REPLACE the anti-lock brake control module.
GO to **N8**.

→ **No**
REPAIR circuit(s) is question. GO to **N8**.

N6 CHECK SUSPECT DUMP VALVE RESISTANCE AT ANTI-LOCK BRAKE CONTROL MODULE CONNECTOR

1

2 Connect EEC-IV 60-Pin Breakout Box to the anti-lock brake control module harness.

FM4020001655040X

Fig. 20 Test N/Codes C1194, C1196, C1210, C1212, C1242, C1244, C1246 Or C1248: Open Or Shorted Dump Valve Solenoid (Part 4 of 6)

TEST CONDITIONS	TEST DETAILS/RESULTS/ACTIONS
N6 CHECK SUSPECT DUMP VALVE RESISTANCE AT ANTI-LOCK BRAKE CONTROL MODULE CONNECTOR (Continued)	

3

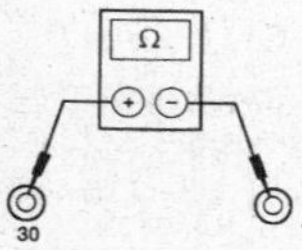

3 Measure the resistance between EEC-IV 60-Pin Breakout Box pin 30, circuit 907 (Y), and EEC-IV 60-Pin Breakout Box pins as follows:

DTC	Circuit	EEC-IV 60-Pin Breakout Box Pin
C1196	903 (PK)	31
C1212	905 (BL/O)	50
C1244	921 (PK/GN)	15
C1248	923 (GY/R)	4

• Is the resistance between 1 and 3 ohms?

→ **Yes**
GO to **N7**.

→ **No**
REPLACE the coil assembly.
GO to **N8**.

N7 CHECK CIRCUIT BETWEEN ANTI-LOCK BRAKE CONTROL MODULE AND HCU

1

2

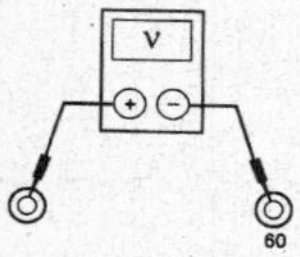

2 Measure the voltage between EEC-IV 60-Pin Breakout Box pin 60, circuit 57 (BK), and EEC-IV 60-Pin Breakout Box pins as follows:

DTC	Circuit	EEC-IV 60-Pin Breakout Box Pin
C1196	903 (PK)	31
C1212	905 (BL/O)	50
C1244	921 (PK/GN)	15
C1248	923 (GY/R)	4

FM4020001655050X

Fig. 20 Test N/Codes C1194, C1196, C1210, C1212, C1242, C1244, C1246 Or C1248: Open Or Shorted Dump Valve Solenoid (Part 5 of 6)

TEST CONDITIONS	TEST DETAILS/RESULTS/ACTIONS
N7 CHECK CIRCUIT BETWEEN ANTI-LOCK BRAKE CONTROL MODULE AND HCU (Continued)	
	• Is voltage present? → **Yes** REPAIR circuit(s) in question. GO to **N8**. → **No** REPLACE the anti-lock brake control module. GO to **N8**.
N8 VERIFY REPAIR	

1 Reconnect all components.

2

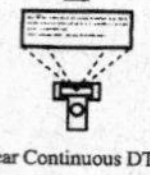

Clear Continuous DTCs

3 Repeat the Drive Cycle Test.

4

4 Retrieve and document continuous DTCs.

• Is System Pass obtained?

→ **Yes**
STOP. Repair is complete.

→ **No**
If original DTC is retrieved, GO to **N1**.

If a different DTC is retrieved, GO to Anti-Lock Brake Control Module Diagnostic Trouble Code (DTC) Index.

FM4020001655060X

Fig. 20 Test N/Codes C1194, C1196, C1210, C1212, C1242, C1244, C1246 Or C1248: Open Or Shorted Dump Valve Solenoid (Part 6 of 6)

TEST CONDITIONS	TEST DETAILS/RESULTS/ACTIONS
P1 CHECK YELLOW ABS WARNING INDICATOR PROVE OUT	
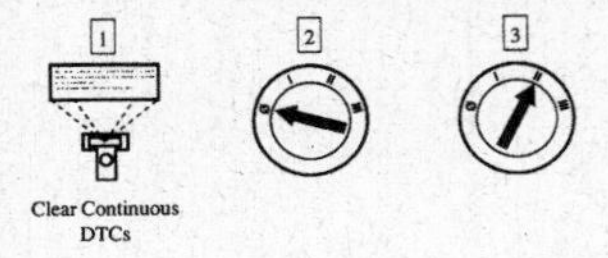	4 Observe the yellow ABS warning indicator. • Does the yellow ABS warning indicator illuminate for approximately 2 seconds and go out? → **Yes** GO to **P2**. → **No** GO to **P3**.
P2 VERIFY ANTI-LOCK BRAKE CONTROL MODULE FUNCTION	
	1 Retrieve and document continuous DTCs. • Is DTC C1220 retrieved? → **Yes** REPLACE the anti-lock brake control module. GO to **P5**. → **No** GO to **P5**.
P3 CHECK FOR SHORT TO POWER	
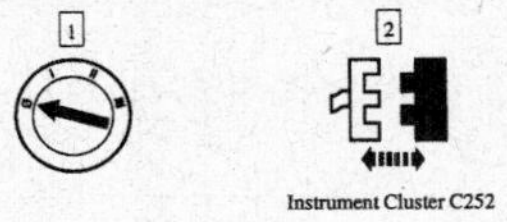	3 Connect EEC-IV 60-Pin Breakout Box to the anti-lock brake control module harness.

FM4020001656010X

Fig. 21 Test P/Code C1220: Yellow ABS Warning Indicator Shorted (Part 1 of 4)

TEST CONDITIONS	TEST DETAILS/RESULTS/ACTIONS
P4 ISOLATE FAULT (Continued)	
	• Did the yellow ABS warning indicator illuminate? → **Yes** If the yellow ABS warning indicator illuminates brightly, REPLACE the anti-lock brake control module. GO to **P6**. If the yellow ABS warning indicator illuminates dimly, REPAIR circuit 918 (Y/R). GO to **P6**. → **No** CHECK the yellow ABS warning indicator.
P5 CHECK INTERMITTENT WIRING CONCERN	
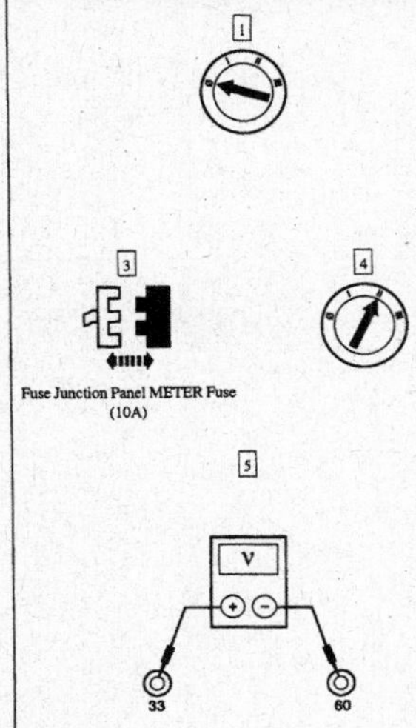	2 Connect EEC-IV 60-Pin Breakout Box to the anti-lock brake control harness. 5 Measure the voltage between EEC-IV 60-Pin Breakout Box pin 33, circuit 918 (Y/R), and EEC-IV 60-Pin Breakout Box pin 60, circuit 57 (BK).

FM4020001656030X

Fig. 21 Test P/Code C1220: Yellow ABS Warning Indicator Shorted (Part 3 of 4)

TEST CONDITIONS	TEST DETAILS/RESULTS/ACTIONS
P3 CHECK FOR SHORT TO POWER (Continued)	
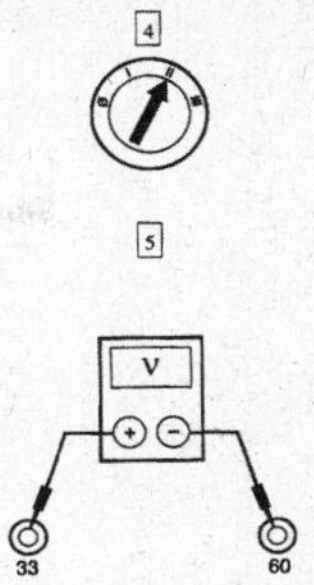	5 Measure the voltage between EEC-IV 60-Pin Breakout Box pin 33, circuit 918 (Y/R), and EEC-IV 60-Pin Breakout Box pin 60, circuit 57 (BK). • Is voltage present? → **Yes** REPAIR circuit 918 (Y/R). GO to **P6**. → **No** RECONNECT instrument cluster C252. GO to **P4**.
P4 ISOLATE FAULT	
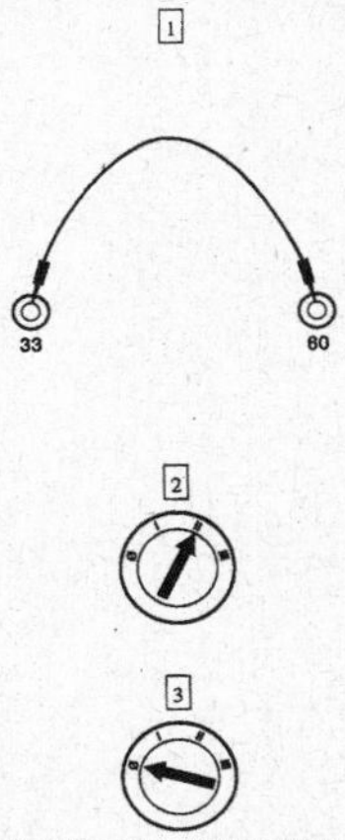	1 Install a jumper wire between EEC-IV 60-Pin Breakout Box pin 33, circuit 918 (Y/R), and EEC-IV 60-Pin Breakout Box pin 60, circuit 57 (BK). 2 Leave the ignition switch in the RUN position for ten seconds.

FM4020001656020X

Fig. 21 Test P/Code C1220: Yellow ABS Warning Indicator Shorted (Part 2 of 4)

TEST CONDITIONS	TEST DETAILS/RESULTS/ACTIONS
P5 CHECK INTERMITTENT WIRING CONCERN (Continued)	
	6 Wiggle the circuit starting at the end points and move toward the middle while monitoring the voltage. • Is voltage detected? → **Yes** REPAIR circuit 918 (Y/R). GO to **P6**. → **No** GO to **P6**.
P6 VERIFY REPAIR	
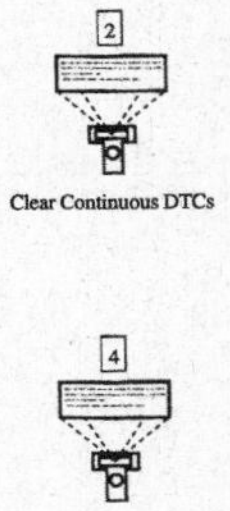	1 Reconnect all components. 3 Repeat the Drive Cycle Test. 4 Retrieve and document continuous DTCs. • Is System Pass obtained? → **Yes** STOP. Repair is complete. → **No** If original DTC is retrieved, GO to **P1**. If a different DTC is retrieved, GO to Anti-Lock Brake Control Module Diagnostic Trouble Code (DTC) Index.

FM4020001656040X

Fig. 21 Test P/Code C1220: Yellow ABS Warning Indicator Shorted (Part 4 of 4)

TEST CONDITIONS	TEST DETAILS/RESULTS/ACTIONS
Q1 CHECK CIRCUIT 710 (W) (Continued)	
2 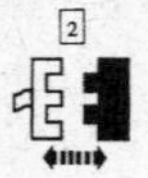 Anti-Lock Relay C116	1 Connect EECIV Breakdown Box to ABS Control Module harness.
	3 Remove fuse junction panel fuse AIR COND (15A).
4 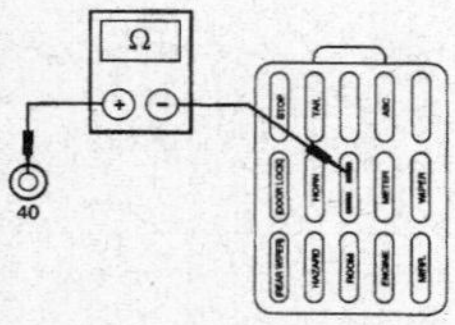	4 Measure the resistance between EEC-IV 60-Pin Breakout Box pin 40, circuit 710 (W), and the top terminal of the 15A AIR COND fuse holder. • Is the resistance less than 5 ohms? → **Yes** REINSTALL the fuse and the anti-lock relay. GO to **Q2**. → **No** REPAIR circuit 710 (W). GO to **Q3**.
Q2 CHECK VEHICLE POWER SUPPLY	
1 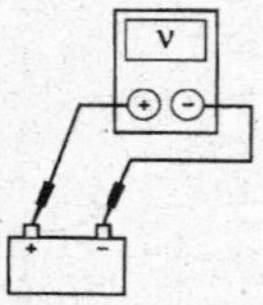	1 Measure the battery voltage. • Is the voltage greater than 9.5 volts? → **Yes** REPLACE the anti-lock brake control module. Brake Control. GO to **Q3**. → **No** CHECK the charging system and battery.
Q3 VERIFY REPAIR	
	1 Reconnect all components.

FM4020001657010X

Fig. 22 Test Q/Code B1318: Low Voltage To ABS Control Module (Part 1 of 2)

TEST CONDITIONS	TEST DETAILS/RESULTS/ACTIONS
R1 VERIFY NGS CONNECTIONS	
1 	
	2 Verify that NGS is properly connected to the data link connector (DLC) and to a known good power source.
3  Retrieve DTCs	

FM4020001658010X

Fig. 23 Test R: No Communication w/ABS Control Module (Part 1 of 5)

TEST CONDITIONS	TEST DETAILS/RESULTS/ACTIONS
Q3 VERIFY REPAIR (Continued)	
2  Clear Continuous DTCs	
	3 Repeat the Drive Cycle Test.
4 	4 Retrieve and document continuous DTCs. • Is System Pass obtained? → **Yes** STOP. Repair is complete. → **No** If the original DTC is retrieved, GO to **Q1**. If a different DTC is retrieved, GO to Anti-Lock Brake Control Module Diagnostic Trouble Code (DTC) Index.

FM4020001657020X

Fig. 22 Test Q/Code B1318: Low Voltage To ABS Control Module (Part 2 of 2)

TEST CONDITIONS	TEST DETAILS/RESULTS/ACTIONS
R1 VERIFY NGS CONNECTIONS (Continued)	
	• Is a valid DTC or System Pass obtained? → **Yes** RETURN to System Pre-Check. → **No** GO to **R2**.
R2 CHECK FUSE JUNCTION PANEL AIR COND FUSE (15A)	
1  Fuse Junction Panel AIR COND Fuse (15A)	• Is the fuse OK? → **Yes** GO to **R3**. → **No** REPLACE the fuse. GO to **R1**.
R3 CHECK ANTI-LOCK BRAKE CONTROL MODULE POWER SUPPLY	
	1 Connect EEC-IV 60-Pin Breakout Box to the anti-lock brake control module harness.
2 	
3 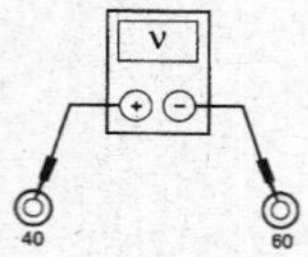	3 Measure the voltage between EEC-IV 60-Pin Breakout Box pin 40, circuit 710 (W), and EEC-IV 60-Pin Breakout Box pin 60, circuit 57 (BK).

FM4020001658020X

Fig. 23 Test R: No Communication w/ABS Control Module (Part 2 of 5)

TEST CONDITIONS	TEST DETAILS/RESULTS/ACTIONS
R3 CHECK ANTI-LOCK BRAKE CONTROL MODULE POWER SUPPLY (Continued)	
4 	• Is the voltage greater than 10 volts? → **Yes** GO to **R5**. → **No** GO to **R4**.
R4 CHECK CIRCUIT	
	1 Disconnect fuse junction panel AIR COND fuse (15A).
2  Anti-Lock Relay C116	
3 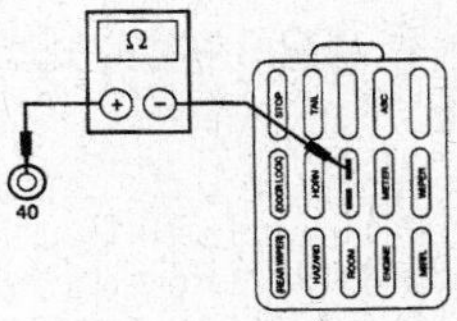	3 Measure the resistance between EEC-IV 60-Pin Breakout Box pin 40, circuit 710 (W), and the top terminal of the fuse junction panel AIR COND fuse holder.

FM4020001658030X

Fig. 23 Test R: No Communication w/ABS Control Module (Part 3 of 5)

TEST CONDITIONS	TEST DETAILS/RESULTS/ACTIONS
R4 CHECK CIRCUIT (Continued)	
4 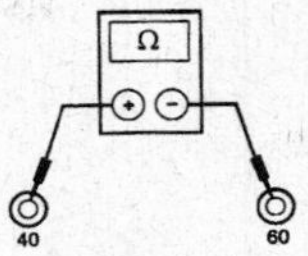	4 Measure the resistance between EEC-IV 60-Pin Breakout Box pin 40, circuit 710 (W), and EEC-IV 60-Pin Breakout Box pin 60, circuit 57 (BK). • Is the resistance less than 5 ohms between EEC-IV 60-Pin Breakout Box pin 40 and the top terminal of the 15A AIR COND fuse holder, and greater than 10,000 ohms between EEC-IV 60-Pin Breakout Box pin 40 and pin 60? → **Yes** REINSTALL the fuse and the anti-lock relay. GO to **R5**. → **No** REPAIR circuit 710 (W). RETURN to the System Pre-Check.
R5 CHECK ECU GROUND	
2 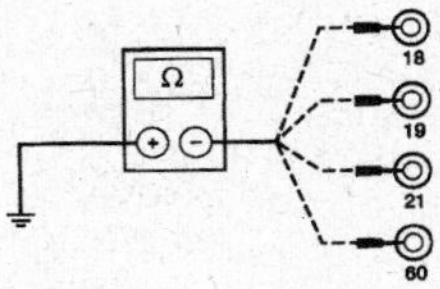	1 Ensure ground bolt is clean and tight. 2 Measure resistance between EEC-IV 60-Pin Breakout Box pins and ground as follows. (see table below) • Is the resistance less than 5 ohms? → **Yes** GO to **R6**. → **No** REPAIR circuit 57 (BK). RETURN to the System Pre-Check.

EEC-IV 60-Pin Breakout Box Pin	Circuit
18	57 (BK)
19	57 (BK)
21	57 (BK)
60	57 (BK)

FM4020001658040X

Fig. 23 Test R: No Communication w/ABS Control Module (Part 4 of 5)

TEST CONDITIONS	TEST DETAILS/RESULTS/ACTIONS
R6 CHECK VEHICLE POWER SUPPLY	
1 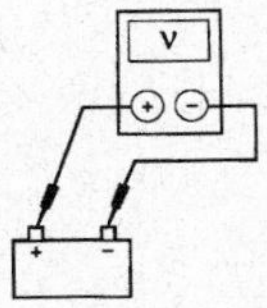	1 Measure the battery voltage. • Is the voltage greater than 10 volts? → **Yes** Diagnose Module Communications Network. → **No** CHECK the charging system and battery.

FM4020001658050X

Fig. 23 Test R: No Communication w/ABS Control Module (Part 5 of 5)

SYSTEM SERVICE

Brake System Bleed

PRESSURE

1. Clean outside of brake master cylinder reservoir.
2. Remove reservoir cap and fill brake master cylinder reservoir with specified brake fluid.
3. Follow manufacturer's instructions when installing master cylinder adapter.
4. Install brake bleeder to brake master cylinder reservoir, and attach brake bleeder tank hose to fitting on adapter.
5. Attach a rubber drain hose to righthand rear bleeder screw and submerge free end of hose in a container partially filled with clean brake fluid.
6. Open valve on brake bleeder tank.
7. Loosen bleeder screw. Leave open until clear, bubble-free brake fluid flows, then close bleeder screw and remove rubber hose.
8. Tighten wheel cylinder bleeder screw.
9. Continue bleeding rest of system, going in order from the lefthand rear wheel to righthand front wheel, ending with lefthand front wheel.
10. Close brake bleeder tank valve and remove tank hose from adapter and remove adapter.
11. Fill brake master cylinder reservoir and install reservoir cap.

GRAVITY

1. Fill brake master cylinder reservoir with specified brake fluid.
2. Inspect brake fluid level in the brake master cylinder reservoir often. Do not let it run dry.
3. Loosen righthand rear wheel cylinder bleeder screw and leave open until clear, bubble-free brake fluid flows. Tighten wheel cylinder bleeder screw.
4. Continue bleeding rest of system, going in order from lefthand rear wheel, to righthand front wheel, ending with lefthand front wheel.
5. Fill brake master cylinder reservoir specified brake fluid and install reservoir cap.

MANUAL

1. Attach a rubber drain hose to righthand rear bleeder screw and submerge free end of hose in a container partially filled with clean brake fluid.
2. Have assistant pump brake pedal ten times and then hold firm pressure on brake pedal.
3. Loosen righthand rear bleeder screw until clear, bubble-free brake fluid flows. Have an assistant maintain pressure on brake pedal while tightening bleeder screw.
4. Tighten wheel cylinder bleeder screw.
5. Continue bleeding rest of system, going in order from lefthand rear wheel, to righthand front wheel, ending with lefthand front wheel.
6. Fill brake master cylinder reservoir and install the reservoir cap.

Component Replacement

HYDRAULIC ABS ACTUATOR ASSEMBLY

1. Remove battery tray.
2. Disconnect two hydraulic control unit (HCU) electrical connectors.
3. Remove brake tubes from hydraulic anti-lock actuator assembly.
4. Remove HCU bolts and HCU.

5. Reverse procedure to install, noting the following:
   a. Ensure electrical connectors are properly routed.
   b. **Torque** HCU bolts to 14–18 ft. lbs.
   c. **Torque** brake tube fittings to 10–16 inch lbs.
   d. Bleed brake system as outlined in "Brake System Bleed."

ABS CONTROL MODULE

The ABS control module is located under the passenger seat, **Fig. 24.**

1. Disconnect control module electrical connectors.
2. Remove two module nuts, then the control module.
3. Reverse procedure to install. **Torque** control module bolts to 60–84 inch lbs.

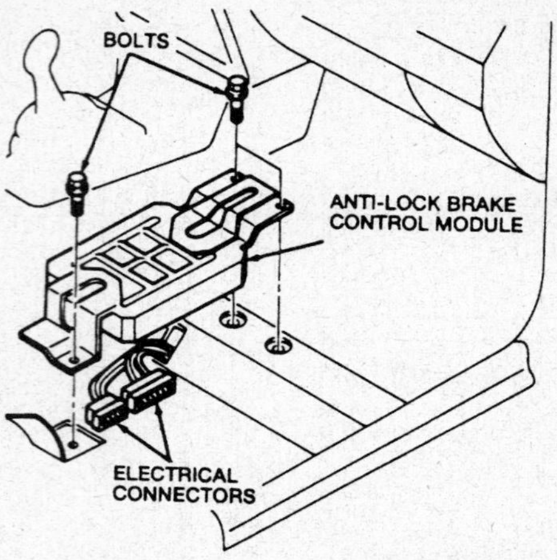

Fig. 24 ABS control module

FRONT BRAKE ABS SENSORS

1. **On righthand sensor,** remove windshield washer pump and reservoir, then peel back foam insulation and disconnect sensor connector.
2. **On lefthand sensor,** disconnect sensor connector.
3. **On all sensors,** raise and support vehicle, then remove wheels.
4. Remove upper sensor cable bracket, then the grommet and pull sensor cable through the opening.
5. Remove sensor bracket attaching bolts, then the sensor and bracket.
6. Reverse procedure to install, noting the following:
   a. **Torque** sensor bolts to 12-16 ft. lbs.
   b. **Torque** wheel lug nuts to 73–99 ft. lbs.
   c. **Torque** upper sensor bracket bolt to 72–84 inch lbs.

REAR BRAKE ABS SENSORS

1. Disconnect sensor electrical connector.
2. Push grommet through hole in chassis.
3. Raise and support vehicle, then remove wheel and tire assembly
4. Remove upper and lower clips.
5. Remove sensor bolt, then the sensor.
6. Reverse procedure to install. **Torque** sensor bolt to 14–18 ft. lbs.

FRONT BRAKE ABS SENSOR INDICATOR

1. Remove front wheel driveshaft and joint as outlined in "Front Wheel Drive Axles" chapter.
2. Use chisel to tap sensor indicator off front wheel driveshaft and joint. Discard sensor.
3. Use dust shield/sensing ring replacer tool T94P-20202-B, or equivalent, to install sensor indicator onto driveshaft and joint.
4. Install front wheel driveshaft and joint as outlined in "Front Wheel Drive Axles" chapter.

REAR BRAKE ABS SENSOR INDICATOR

1. Raise and support vehicle, then remove wheel and tire assembly.
2. Remove brake drum or disc rotor.
3. Unstake, remove and discard rear axle wheel hub retainer, then wheel hub.
4. Remove sensor indicator using suitable chisel. Discard sensor indicator.
5. Press sensor indicator until flush with wheel hub using steel plate wider than outside diameter of sensor indicator.
6. Install wheel hub, then the wheel and tire assembly.

Mustang

NOTE: On Air Bag Equipped Models, Refer To "Air Bag System Precautions" Located In The Front Of This Manual For System Disarming & Arming Procedures.

NOTE: Refer To "Computer Relearn Procedures" Located In The Front Of This Manual When Battery Power To The Computer Has Been Interrupted.

NOTE: "Electrical Symbol & Wire Color Code Identification" Located In The Front Of This Manual May Be Used As An Aid When Using Wiring Circuits Found In This Section.

INDEX

PRECAUTIONS

Air Bag Systems

Refer to "Air Bag System Precautions" in the front of this manual for system disarming and arming procedures.

Battery Ground Cable

Prior to service, disconnect battery ground cable and isolate as required.

Fuel System Pressure Relief

Fuel supply tubes will remain pressurized for long periods of time after engine shutdown. This pressure must be relieved before performing fuel system service. A valve is provided on the fuel injection supply manifold for this purpose.

1. Remove air cleaner assembly.
2. Connect EFI and CFI fuel pressure gauge tool No. T80L-9974-B, or equivalent, to fuel pressure relief valve cap on fuel injection supply manifold.
3. Open manual valve on gauge tool to relieve fuel system pressure.

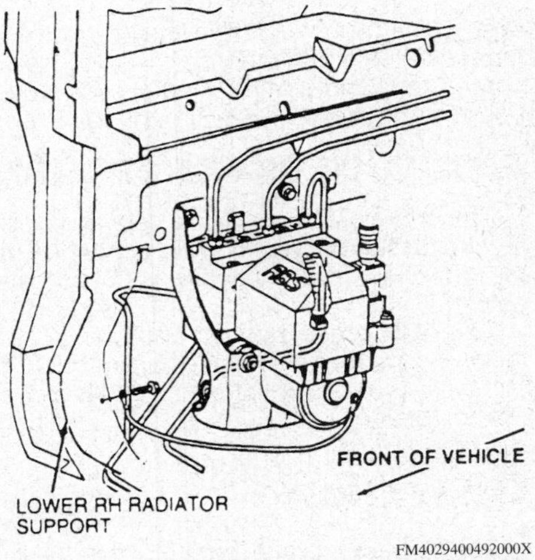

Fig. 1 ABS hydraulic control unit & anti-lock brake control module

Hydraulic Brake Fluid Color

Hydraulic brake fluid must conform with the requirements of Federal Motor Vehicle Safety Standard 116. Under this standard, brake fluids are visually different from other automotive fluids such as transmission, power steering and engine.

Fluid color in a normal brake system may vary from its original color for many reasons. A brake master cylinder may show significantly different shades fluid color between the two brake master cylinder reservoirs. Color may also appear to vary between cast steel and die cast aluminum reservoirs. Some reasons for discoloration include the following:

1. Heat and/or aging.
2. Different operation temperatures or different rates of normal oxidation between two reservoir compartments.
3. Different brands and/or shades of fluid are used when topping off during normal service.
4. Dissolution of color dye used on master cylinder internal springs during assembly.

Brake fluid contaminated with hydrocarbon/mineral based fluid (power steering or transmission fluid) can be detected by an obvious swelling of the master cylinder cap gasket. If the master cylinder cap gasket is swollen, all brake system rubber components must be replaced. All brake tubes and hoses must be thoroughly flushed with Ford Heavy Duty Brake Fluid C6AZ-19542-AA or -BA or DOT-3 equivalent before the vehicle returns to service.

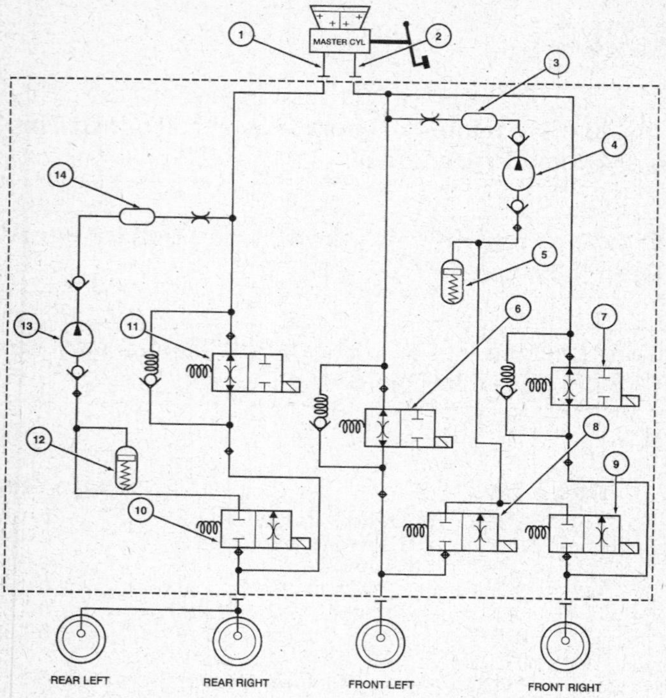

Item	Description
1	Rear Primary Circuit
2	Front Primary Circuit
3	Front Damping Chamber

Item	Description
4	Front Return Pump
5	Front Accumulator Chamber
6	LF Inlet Valve
7	RF Inlet Valve

FM4029801181000X

Fig. 2 ABS hydraulic schematic

Mechanical	Electrical
• Low brake fluid • Anti-lock brake sensor • Anti-lock brake sensor indicator • Base brake system	• Central junction box (CJB)Fuse: — 15 (10A) — 29 (15A) — 33 (15A) — 35 (15A) • Battery junction box (BJB) Fuse: — ABS 1 (50A) — ABS 2 (20A) • Circuitry • Damaged or corroded connectors • Yellow ABS warning indicator • Loose grounds

FM4029901511000X

Fig. 3 ABS inspection chart

Condition	Possible Sources	Action
• No communication with the anti-lock brake control module	• CJB Fuse 29 (15A). • Circuitry. • Anti-lock brake control module.	• GO to Pinpoint Test A.
• Unable to enter self-test.	• Anti-lock brake control module.	• GO to Pinpoint Test B.
• The yellow ABS warning indicator does not self-check	• Circuitry. • Anti-lock brake control module. • Instrument cluster.	• GO to Pinpoint Test I.
• Spongy brake pedal with no warning indicator	• Air in the brake system. • Base brake system.	• GO to Pinpoint Test J.
• Poor vehicle tracking during anti-lock function	• Air in the brake system. • Hydraulic control unit (HCU). • Base brake system.	• GO to Pinpoint Test K.

FM4020101834000X

Fig. 4 ABS symptom chart. 2000–01 less traction control

DESCRIPTION

System Components

POWER BRAKE BOOSTER

The diaphragm-type power brake booster is a self-contained unit, mounted on the firewall. The booster uses engine intake manifold vacuum and atmospheric pressure for its power. Other than the power brake booster check valve, the booster is serviced only as an assembly. The booster must be replaced if it becomes damaged or inoperative.

BRAKE MASTER CYLINDER

The brake master cylinder consists of a fluid reservoir, reservoir control valve and a fluid level indicator. The fluid level indicator is located inside the brake master cylinder reservoir and replaces the previously used pressure differential valve. The fluid level indicator activates the brake warning indicator whenever the brake fluid level is low.

ABS HYDRAULIC CONTROL UNIT & ANTI-LOCK BRAKE CONTROL MODULE

The ABS hydraulic control unit and anti-lock brake control module are a complete assembly. The assembly is located in the righthand lower front corner of the engine compartment, next to the bottom of the white radiator coolant recovery reservoir, **Fig. 1.** The unit is mounted in a bracket, attached to the righthand frame rail. Both the control unit and control module have on-board diagnostics.

ANTI-LOCK BRAKE SENSOR

The front brake anti-lock sensor is attached to the front wheel spindle. It is part of the wheel hub assembly and is not adjustable.

The rear brake anti-lock sensor is attached to the rear disc brake caliper anchor plate. It is pressed onto the axle shaft and is not adjustable.

Operation

The anti-lock brake control module receives wheel speed readings from each brake anti-lock sensor. The module uses this information to compare wheel speeds. The anti-lock brake sensor electrically senses each tooth of the anti-lock brake sensor indicator as it passes through the anti-lock brake sensor's electrical field. This data is sent on to the ABS control module. The control module monitors the frequency created when the anti-lock brake sensor indicator teeth pass the brake sensor to determine wheel rotational speed.

By continuously monitoring and comparing each wheel's rotational speed, the module activates the ABS only when it senses an impending wheel lock-up under severe braking conditions. During ABS cycling, a brake fluid pump motor recirculates the brake fluid, **Fig. 2.**

The module then decides which wheels' brakes need to be controlled and sends the appropriate signals to the hydraulic control unit (hydraulic portion of the assembly). Impending wheel lock conditions trigger signals from the hydraulic control unit which opens and closes the appropriate modulator solenoid valves. This may result in moderate pulsations in the brake pedal when applied. During normal braking, the brake pedal feel will be the same as a vehicle with a standard brake system.

TROUBLESHOOTING

Inspection & Verification

1. Verify customer's original concern by operating anti-lock brakes to duplicate concern.
2. Inspect to determine whether problem is mechanical or electrical, **Fig. 3.**
3. If concern remains after inspection, determine symptom and refer to ABS Symptom Chart, **Figs. 4 through 6.**

DIAGNOSIS & TESTING

Accessing Diagnostic Trouble Codes

USING NEW GENERATION STAR TESTER

1. Connect New Generation Star (NGS)

Condition	Possible Sources	Action
• No communication with the anti-lock brake control module	• CJB Fuse 29 (15A). • Circuitry. • Anti-lock brake control module.	• Go To Pinpoint Test A .
• Unable to enter self-test.	• Anti-lock brake control module.	• Go To Pinpoint Test B .
• The yellow ABS warning indicator does not self-check	• Circuitry. • Anti-lock brake control module. • Instrument cluster.	• Go To Pinpoint Test J .
• Spongy brake pedal with no warning indicator	• Air in the brake system. • Base brake system.	• Go To Pinpoint Test K .
• Poor vehicle tracking during anti-lock function	• Air in the brake system. • Hydraulic control unit (HCU). • Base brake system.	• Go To Pinpoint Test L .

FM4020101835000X

Fig. 5 ABS symptom chart. 2002–04 less traction control

Condition	Possible Source	Action
• The traction control is inoperative—does not operate correctly	• CJB 5 (15A). • Circuitry. • Traction control switch. • Instrument cluster. • Anti-lock brake control module.	• GO to Pinpoint Test L.
• The traction control indicator is inoperative—traction control switch	• Circuitry. • Traction control switch. • Instrument cluster.	• GO to Pinpoint Test M.

FM4020001659000X

Fig. 6 ABS symptom chart (Part 2 of 2). With traction control

DTC	Description	Source	Action
C1233	LF Anti-Lock Brake Sensor Input Signal Missing	ABS	GO to Pinpoint Test H.
C1234	RF Anti-Lock Brake Sensor Input Signal Missing	ABS	GO to Pinpoint Test H.
C1235	RR Anti-Lock Brake Sensor Input Signal Missing	ABS	GO to Pinpoint Test H.
C1236	LR Anti-Lock Brake Sensor Input Signal Missing	ABS	GO to Pinpoint Test H.
C1266	ABS Valve Power Relay Circuit Failure	ABS	INSTALL a new anti-lock brake control module; REPEAT the self-test.

FM4029901513020X

Fig. 7 Diagnostic trouble code Interpretation (Part 2 of 2). 2000–01 less traction control

tester to data link connector (DLC) located under instrument panel.

2. Plug NGS into cigarette lighter.
3. Turn ignition switch to Run position.
4. Follow instructions on screen and record all diagnostic trouble codes.
5. If any DTCs appear during Self-Test, refer to "Diagnostic Trouble Code Interpretation."
6. If NGS reports "System Passed," proceed to symptom chart to continue diagnostics.

Diagnostic Trouble Code Interpretation

Refer to **Figs. 7 through 9,** for diagnostic trouble code interpretation.

Wiring Diagrams

Refer to **Figs. 10 and 11,** for wiring diagrams.

Diagnostic Tests

Refer to **Figs. 12 through 36,** for diagnostic test procedures.

Condition	Possible Source	Action
• No communication with the anti-lock brake control module	• CJB Fuse 29 (15A). • Circuitry. • Anti-lock brake control module.	• GO to Pinpoint Test A.
• Unable to enter self-test.	• Anti-lock brake control module.	• GO to Pinpoint Test B.
• The yellow ABS warning indicator does not self-check	• Circuitry. • Anti-lock brake control module. • Instrument cluster.	• GO to Pinpoint Test I.
• Spongy brake pedal with no warning indicator	• Air in the brake system. • Base brake system.	• GO to Pinpoint Test J.
• Poor vehicle tracking during anti-lock function	• Air in the brake system. • Hydraulic control unit (HCU). • Base brake system.	• GO to Pinpoint Test K.

FM4029901512000X

Fig. 6 ABS symptom chart (Part 1 of 2). With traction control

DTC	Description	Source	Action
B1318	Battery Voltage Low	ABS	GO to Pinpoint Test C.
B1342	ECU Is Defective	ABS	INSTALL a new anti-lock brake control module; REPEAT the self-test.
B1484	Brake Pedal Input Open Circuit	ABS	GO to Pinpoint Test D.
B1596	Repair Continuous Codes	ABS	REPAIR the DTCs retrieved.
C1095	ABS Hydraulic Pump Motor Circuit Failure	ABS	GO to Pinpoint Test E.
C1145	RF Anti-Lock Brake Sensor Input Circuit Failure	ABS	GO to Pinpoint Test F.
C1155	LFAnti-Lock Brake Sensor Input Circuit Failure	ABS	GO to Pinpoint Test F.
C1165	RR Anti-Lock Brake Sensor Input Circuit Failure	ABS	GO to Pinpoint Test F.
C1175	LR Anti-Lock Brake Sensor Input Circuit Failure	ABS	GO to Pinpoint Test F.
C1222	Anti-Lock Brake Sensor Mismatch	ABS	GO to Pinpoint Test G.

FM4029901513010X

Fig. 7 Diagnostic trouble code Interpretation (Part 1 of 2). 2000–01 less traction control

DTC	Description	Source	Action
B1318	Battery Voltage Low	ABS	Go To Pinpoint Test C .
B1342	ECU Is Defective	ABS	INSTALL a new anti-lock brake control module; REPEAT the self-test.
B1484	Brake Pedal Input Open Circuit	ABS	Go To Pinpoint Test D .
B1596	Repair Continuous Codes	ABS	REPAIR the DTCs retrieved.
C1095	ABS Hydraulic Pump Motor Circuit Failure	ABS	Go To Pinpoint Test E .
C1145	RF Anti-Lock Brake Sensor Input Circuit Failure	ABS	Go To Pinpoint Test F .
C1155	LF Anti-Lock Brake Sensor Input Circuit Failure	ABS	Go To Pinpoint Test F .
C1165	RR Anti-Lock Brake Sensor Input Circuit Failure	ABS	Go To Pinpoint Test F .
C1175	LR Anti-Lock Brake Sensor Input Circuit Failure	ABS	Go To Pinpoint Test F .
C1222	Anti-Lock Brake Sensor Mismatch	ABS	Go To Pinpoint Test G .
C1233	LF Anti-Lock Brake Sensor Input Signal Missing	ABS	Go To Pinpoint Test H .
C1234	RF Anti-Lock Brake Sensor Input Signal Missing	ABS	Go To Pinpoint Test H .
C1235	RR Anti-Lock Brake Sensor Input Signal Missing	ABS	Go To Pinpoint Test H .
C1236	LR Anti-Lock Brake Sensor Input Signal Missing	ABS	Go To Pinpoint Test H .
C1266	ABS Valve Power Relay Circuit Failure	ABS	Go To Pinpoint Test I .

FM4020101836000X

Fig. 8 Diagnostic trouble code Interpretation. 2002–04 less traction control

Clearing Diagnostic Trouble Codes

After all DTCs have been retrieved, remove New generation Star Tester. Cycle ignition switch on and off, then start vehicle and drive to more than 15 mph. The stored DTCs will be erased. After erasing the DTCs, perform Quick Test.

DTC	Description	Source	Action
B1318	Battery Voltage Low	ABS/TC	GO to Pinpoint Test C.
B1342	ECU Is Defective	ABS/TC	INSTALL a new anti-lock brake control module. REPEAT the self-test.
B1484	Brake Pedal Input Open Circuit	ABS/TC	GO to Pinpoint Test D.
B1596	Repair Continuous Codes	ABS/TC	REPAIR the DTCs retrieved.
C1095	ABS Hydraulic Pump Motor Circuit Failure	ABS/TC	GO to Pinpoint Test E.
C1145	RF Anti-Lock Brake Sensor Input Circuit Failure	ABS/TC	GO to Pinpoint Test F.
C1155	LF Anti-Lock Brake Sensor Input Circuit Failure	ABS/TC	GO to Pinpoint Test F.
C1165	RR Anti-Lock Brake Sensor Input Circuit Failure	ABS/TC	GO to Pinpoint Test F.
C1175	LR Anti-Lock Brake Sensor Input Circuit Failure	ABS/TC	GO to Pinpoint Test F.
C1222	Anti-Lock Brake Sensor Mismatch	ABS/TC	GO to Pinpoint Test G.
C1233	LF Anti-Lock Brake Sensor Input Signal Missing	ABS/TC	GO to Pinpoint Test H.
C1234	RF Anti-Lock Brake Sensor Input Signal Missing	ABS/TC	GO to Pinpoint Test H.
C1235	RR Anti-Lock Brake Sensor Input Signal Missing	ABS/TC	GO to Pinpoint Test H.
C1236	LR Anti-Lock Brake Sensor Input Signal Missing	ABS/TC	GO to Pinpoint Test H.
C1266	ABS Valve Power Relay Circuit Failure	ABS/TC	INSTALL a new anti-lock brake control module. REPEAT the self-test.

FM40200016660010X

Fig. 9 Diagnostic trouble code interpretation (Part 1 of 2). With traction control

DTC	Description	Source	Action
C1805	Mismatched PCM and/or Anti-Lock Brake Control Module	ABS/TC	CLEAR the DTCs. RETRIEVE the DTCs. If DTC C1805 is retrieved, check the PCM and Anti-Lock Brake Control Module is for the correct vehicle. INSTALL a new PCM or anti-lock brake control module as necessary. CLEAR the DTCs. REPEAT the self-test.
U1009	SCP (J1850) Invalid or Missing Data for Engine Torque	ABS/TC	CARRY OUT the PCM self-test.
U1027	SCP (J1850) Invalid or Missing Data for Engine RPM	ABS/TC	CARRY OUT the PCM self-test.
U1059	SCP (J1850) Invalid or Missing Data for Transmission/Transaxle/PRNDL	ABS/TC	CARRY OUT the PCM self-test.
U1083	SCP (J1850) Invalid or Missing Data for Engine Systems	ABS/TC	CARRY OUT the PCM self-test.
U1262	SCP (J1850) Communication Bus Fault	ABS/TC	DIAGNOSE Vehicle Communications Network

FM40200016660020X

Fig. 9 Diagnostic trouble code interpretation (Part 2 of 2). With traction control

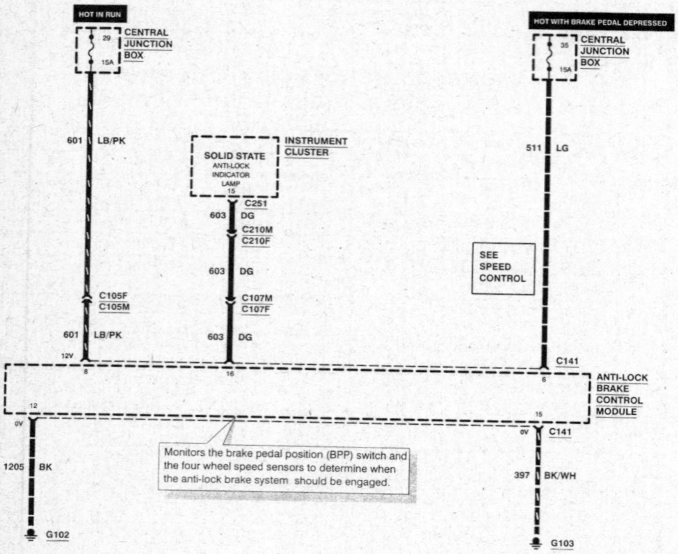

Fig. 10 Wiring diagram (Part 1 of 3). 2000–01

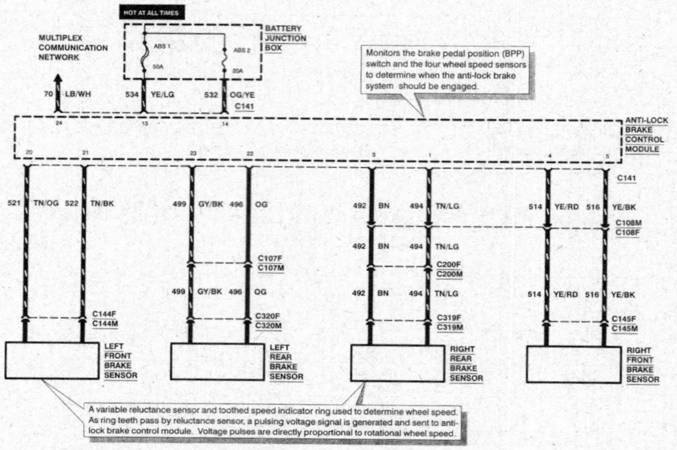

Fig. 10 Wiring diagram (Part 2 of 3). 2000–01

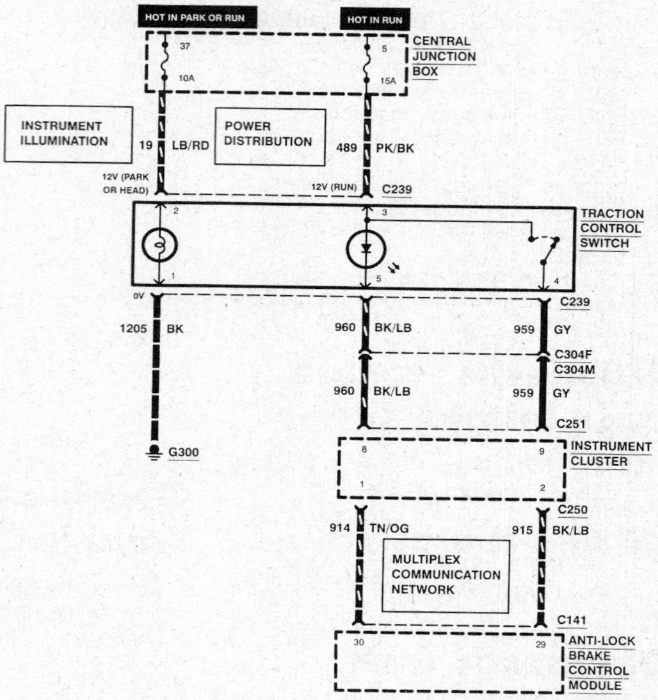

Fig. 10 Wiring diagram (Part 3 of 3). 2000

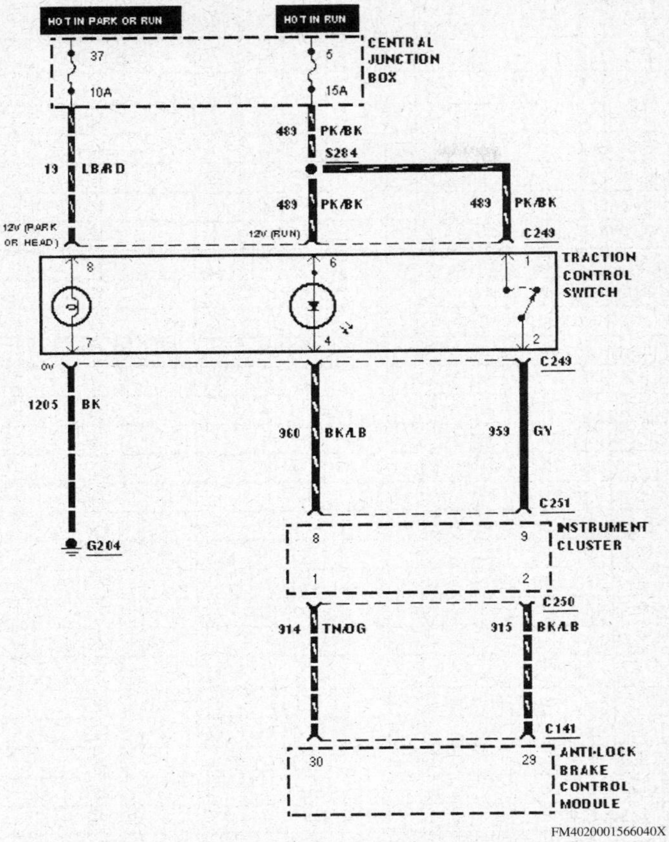

Fig. 10 Wiring diagram (Part 3 of 3). 2001

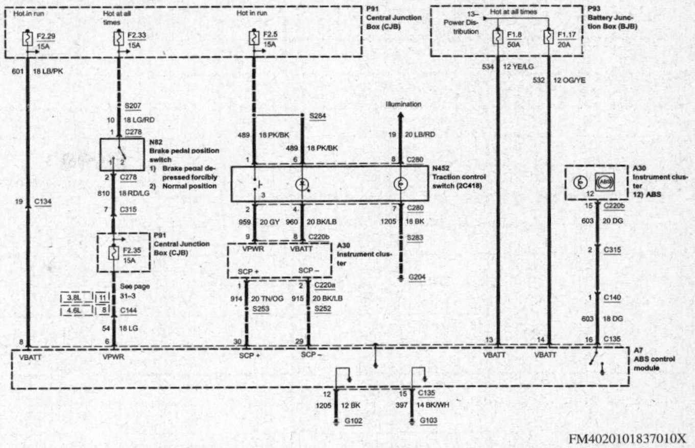

FM4020001566040X

Fig. 11 Wiring diagram (Part 1 of 2). 2002–04

FM4020101837010X

Fig. 11 Wiring diagram (Part 2 of 2). 2002–04

FM4020101837020X

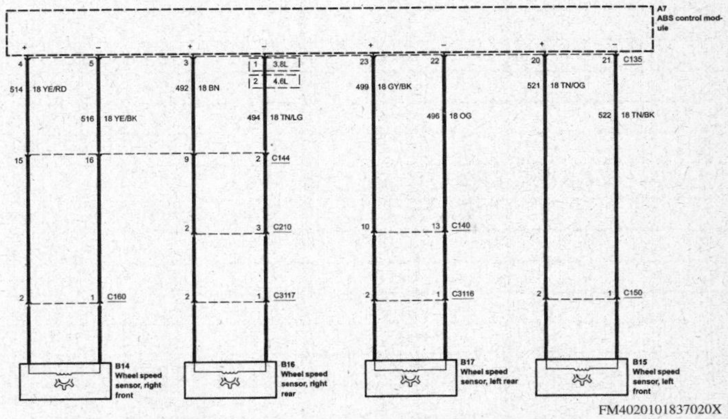

DIAGNOSTIC CHART INDEX

Test	Code	Description	Page No.	Fig. No.
2000–01 LESS TRACTION CONTROL				
A	—	No Communication w/ABS Control Module	6-111	12
B	—	Unable To Enter Self-Test	6-111	13
C	B1318	Battery Voltage Low	6-111	14
D	B1484	Brake Pedal Input Open Circuit	6-112	15
E	C1095	ABS Hydraulic Pump Motor Failure	6-112	16
F	C1145	Righthand Front ABS Sensor Input Circuit Failure	6-112	17
	C1155	Lefthand Front ABS Sensor Input Circuit Failure	6-112	17
	C1165	Righthand Rear ABS Sensor Input Circuit Failure	6-112	17
	C1175	Lefthand Rear ABS Sensor Input Circuit Failure	6-112	17
G	C1222	ABS Sensor Mismatch	6-113	18
H	C1233	Lefthand Front ABS Sensor Input Signal Missing	6-114	19
	C1234	Righthand Front ABS Sensor Input Signal Missing	6-114	19
	C1235	Righthand Rear ABS Sensor Input Signal Missing	6-114	19
	C1236	Lefthand Rear ABS Sensor Input Signal Missing	6-114	19
I	—	Yellow ABS Warning Indicator Does Not Self-Check	6-114	20
J	—	Spongy Brake Pedal w/No Warning Indicator	6-114	21
K	—	Poor Vehicle Tracking During ABS Function	6-115	22
L	—	Traction Control Inoperative	6-116	23
M	—	Traction Control Indicator Inoperative	6-116	24
2002–04 LESS TRACTION CONTROL				
A	—	No Communication w/Anti-Lock Brake Control Module	6-117	25
B	—	Unable To Enter Self-Test	6-117	26
C	C1318	Battery Voltage Low	6-117	27
D	C1484	Brake Pedal Input Open Circuit	6-118	28
E	C1095	ABS Hydraulic Pump Motor Failure	6-119	29
F	C1145	Righthand Front ABS Sensor Input Circuit Failure	6-119	30
	C1155	Lefthand Front ABS Sensor Input Circuit Failure	6-119	30
	C1165	Righthand Rear ABS Sensor Input Circuit Failure	6-119	30
	C1175	Lefthand Rear ABS Sensor Input Circuit Failure	6-119	30
G	C1222	Anti-Lock Brake Sensor Mismatch	6-121	31
H	C1233	Lefthand Front Anti-Lock Brake Sensor Input Signal Missing	6-121	32
	C1234	Righthand Front Anti-Lock Brake Sensor Input Signal Missing	6-121	32
	C1235	Righthand Rear Anti-Lock Brake Sensor Input Signal Missing	6-121	32
	C1236	Lefthand Rear Anti-Lock Brake Sensor Input Signal Missing	6-121	32
I	—	ABS Valve Power Relay Circuit Failure	6-122	33
J	—	Yellow ABS Warning Indicator Does Not Self-Check	6-122	34
K	—	Spongy Pedal w/No Warning Indicator	6-123	35
L	—	Poor Vehicle Tracking During Anti-Lock Function	6-123	36

TEST CONDITIONS	TEST DETAILS/RESULTS/ACTIONS
A1 CHECK CIRCUIT 601 (LB/PK) FOR AN OPEN	
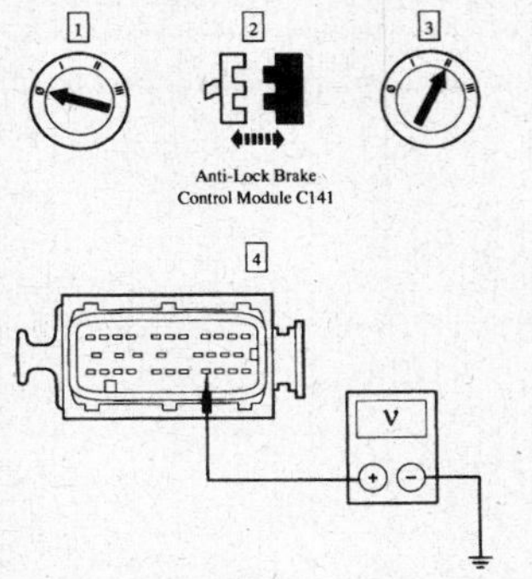	4 Measure the voltage between anti-lock brake control module C141 Pin 8, Circuit 601 (LB/PK), harness side and ground. • Is the voltage greater than 10 volts? → **Yes** GO to **A2**. → **No** REPAIR the circuit. REPEAT the self-test.
A2 CHECK THE ANTI-LOCK BRAKE CONTROL MODULE GROUNDS	
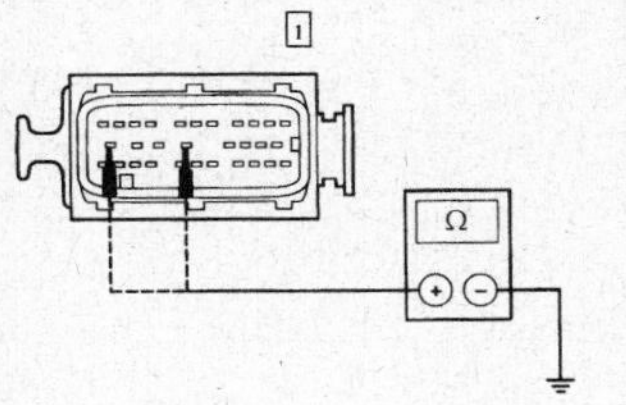	1 Measure the resistance between anti-lock brake control module C141 Pin 12, Circuit 1205 (BK), harness side and ground; and between anti-lock brake control module C141 Pin 15, Circuit 397 (BK/WH), harness side and ground. • Are the resistances less than 5 ohms? → **Yes** INSTALL a new anti-lock brake control module. REPEAT the self-test. → **No** REPAIR the circuit in question. REPEAT the self-test.

FM4029901514000X

Fig. 12 Test A: No Communication w/ABS Control Module. 2000–01 Less Traction Control

TEST CONDITIONS	TEST DETAILS/RESULTS/ACTIONS
C1 CHECK BATTERY VOLTAGE	
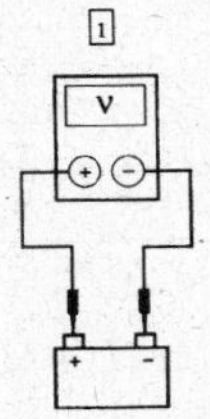	1 Measure the battery voltage between the positive and negative battery posts with the key ON engine OFF (KOEO), and with the engine running. • Is the battery voltage between 10 and 13 volts with KOEO, and between 11 and 17 volts with the engine running? → **Yes** GO to **C2**. → **No** DIAGNOSE charging system.

FM4029901516010X

Fig. 14 Test C/Code B1318: Battery Voltage Low (Part 1 of 2). 2000–01 Less Traction Control

TEST CONDITIONS	TEST DETAILS/RESULTS/ACTIONS
B1 CHECK THE COMMUNICATIONS TO THE ANTI-LOCK BRAKE CONTROL MODULE	
	1 Check the communications to the anti-lock brake control module. • Does the scan tool communicate with the anti-lock brake control module? → **Yes** INSTALL a new anti-lock brake control module. REPEAT the self-test. → **No** GO to Pinpoint Test A.

FM4029901515000X

Fig. 13 Test B: Unable To Enter Self-Test. 2000–01 Less Traction Control

TEST CONDITIONS	TEST DETAILS/RESULTS/ACTIONS
C2 CHECK THE VOLTAGE TO THE ANTI-LOCK BRAKE CONTROL MODULE	
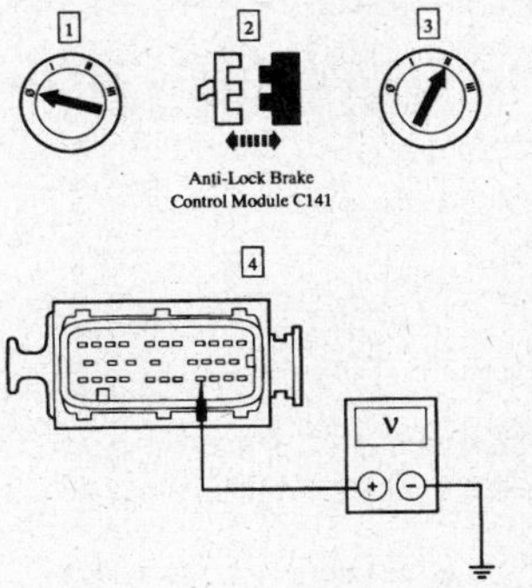	4 Measure the voltage between anti-lock brake control module C141 Pin 8, Circuit 601 (LB/PK), harness side and ground. • Is the voltage greater than 10 volts? → **Yes** GO to **C3**. → **No** REPAIR the circuit. CLEAR the DTCs. REPEAT the self-test.
C3 CHECK THE ANTI-LOCK BRAKE CONTROL MODULE GROUNDS	
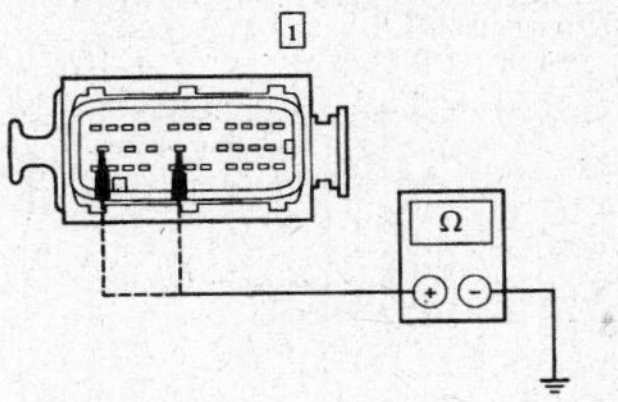	1 Measure the resistance between anti-lock brake control module C141 Pin 12, Circuit 1205 (BK), harness side and ground; and between anti-lock brake control module C141 Pin 15, Circuit 397 (BK/WH), harness side and ground. • Are the resistances less than 5 ohms? → **Yes** INSTALL a new anti-lock brake control module. REPEAT the self-test. → **No** REPAIR the circuit in question. CLEAR the DTCs. REPEAT the self-test.

FM4029901516020X

Fig. 14 Test C/Code B1318: Battery Voltage Low (Part 2 of 2). 2000–01 Less Traction Control

TEST CONDITIONS	TESTDETAILS/RESULTS/ACTIONS
D1 CHECK THE STOPLAMPS FOR CORRECT OPERATION	
	[1] Depress the brake pedal while checking the stoplamps. • Do the stop lamps illuminate? → **Yes** GO to **D2**. → **No** DIAGNOSE stop lamps.
D2 CHECK THE BRAKE PEDAL INPUT TO THE ANTI-LOCK BRAKE CONTROL MODULE	
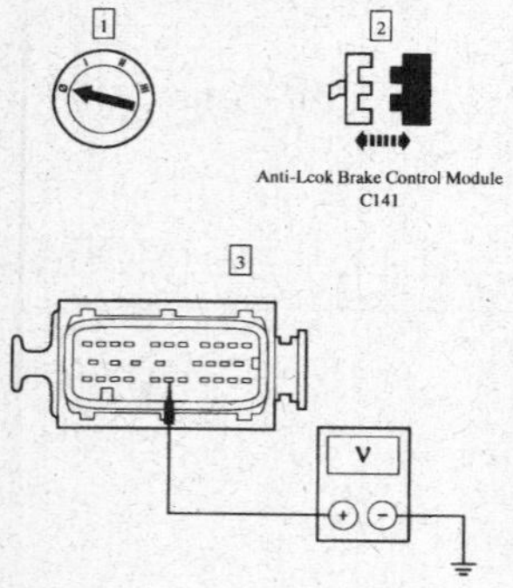	[3] Measure the voltage between anti-lock brake control module C141 Pin 6, Circuit 511 (LG), harness side and ground, while depressing and releasing the brake pedal. • Is the voltage greater than 10 volts with the brake pedal depressed and zero volts with the brake pedal released? → **Yes** INSTALL a new anti-lock brake control module. REPEAT the self-test. → **No** REPAIR Circuit 511 (LG) and Circuit 810 (RD/LG) as necessary. CLEAR the DTCs. REPEAT the self-test.

FM4029901517000X

Fig. 15 Test D/Code B1484: Brake Pedal Input Open Circuit. 2000–01 Less Traction Control

TEST CONDITIONS	TESTDETAILS/RESULTS/ACTIONS
E1 CHECK THE PUMP MOTOR FOR CONTINUOUS OPERATION	
	[1] Check the pump motor for continuous operation. • Is the pump motor running continuously? → **Yes** INSTALL a new anti-lock brake control module. REPEAT the self-test. → **No** GO to **E2**.
E2 CHECK CIRCUIT 534 (YE/LG) FOR AN OPEN	
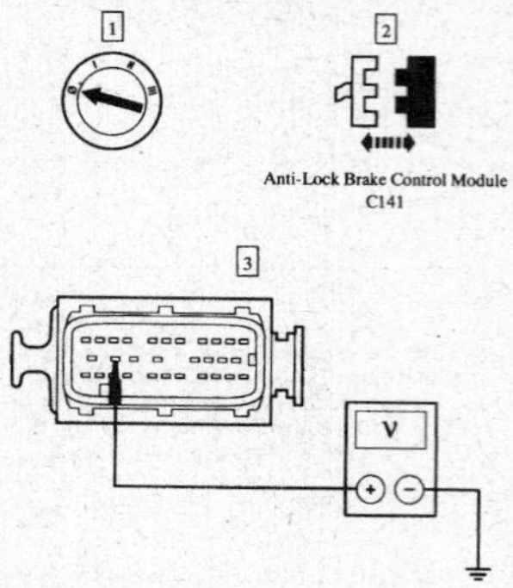	[3] Measure the voltage between anti-lock brake control module C141 Pin 13, Circuit 534 (YE/LG), harness side, and ground. • Is the voltage greater than 10 volts? → **Yes** GO to **E3**. → **No** REPAIR the circuit. CLEAR the DTCs. REPEAT the self-test.

FM4029901518010X

Fig. 16 Test E/Code C1095: ABS Hydraulic Pump Motor Failure (Part 1 of 2). 2000–01 Less Traction Control

TEST CONDITIONS	TESTDETAILS/RESULTS/ACTIONS
E3 CHECK CIRCUIT 1205 (BK) FOR AN OPEN	
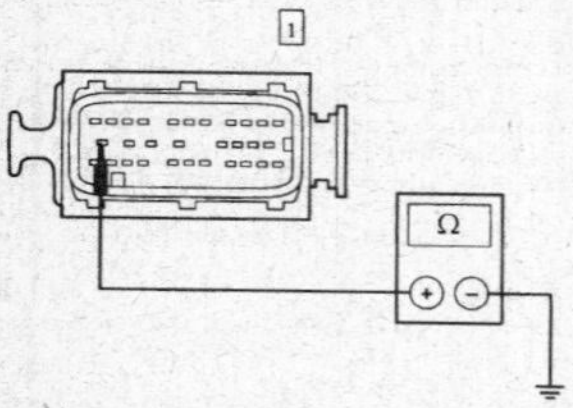	[1] Measure the resistance between anti-lock brake control module C141 Pin 12, Circuit 1205 (BK), harness side and ground. • Is the resistance less than 5 ohms? → **Yes** GO to **E4**. → **No** REPAIR the circuit. CLEAR the DTCs. REPEAT the self-test.
E4 CHECK THE PUMP MOTOR FOR OPERATION	
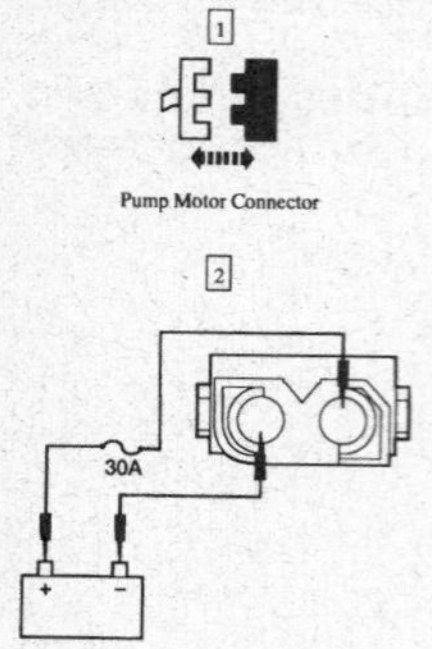	[2] Connect a 30A fused heavy jumper wire between the positive battery post and pump motor connector Pin 1 (component side); and momentarily connect a heavy jumper between negative battery post and pump motor connector Pin 2 (component side). • Does the pump motor operate? → **Yes** INSTALL a new anti-lock brake control module. REPEAT the self-test. → **No** INSTALL a new HCU; REFER to Hydraulic Control Unit. CLEAR the DTCs. REPEAT the self-test.

FM4029901518020X

Fig. 16 Test E/Code C1095: ABS Hydraulic Pump Motor Failure (Part 2 of 2). 2000–01 Less Traction Control

TEST CONDITIONS	TESTDETAILS/RESULTS/ACTIONS
F1 CHECK THE SUSPECT ANTI-LOCK BRAKE SENSOR CIRCUIT FOR SHORT TO POWER	
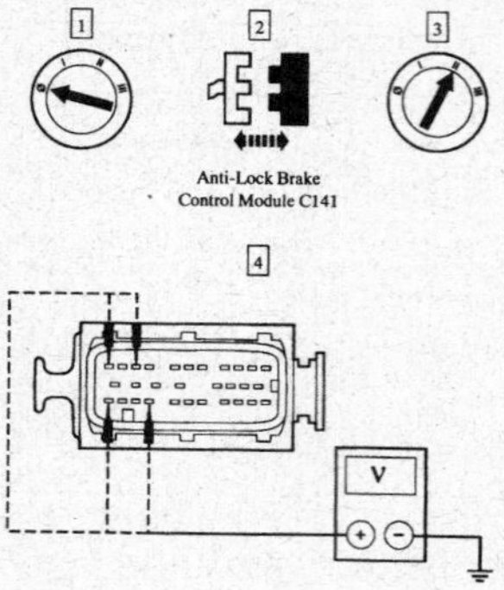	[4] Measure the voltage between anti-lock brake control module C141 Pins, harness side and ground as follows: (see table below) • Is any voltage present? → **Yes** REPAIR the circuit in question. CLEAR the DTCs. REPEAT the self-test. → **No** GO to **F2**.

DTC	Anti-Lock Brake Control Module C141 Pin	Circuit
C1145 (RF)	4	514 (YE/RD)
C1155 (LF)	20	521 (TN/OG)
C1165 (RR)	1	494 (TN/LG)
C1175 (LR)	22	496 (OG)

FM4029901519010X

Fig. 17 Test F/Codes C1145, C1155, C1165 & C1175: ABS Sensor Input Circuit Failure (Part 1 of 5). 2000–01 Less Traction Control

TEST CONDITIONS	TESTDETAILS/RESULTS/ACTIONS
F2 CHECK THE SUSPECT ANTI-LOCK BRAKE SENSOR CIRCUIT FOR SHORT TO GROUND	

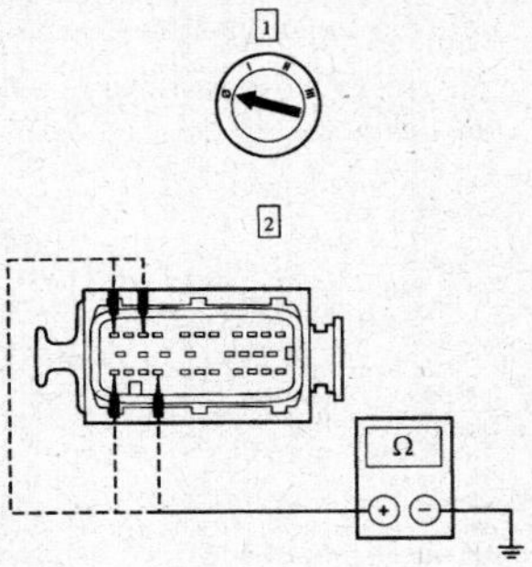

2 Measure the resistance between anti-lock brake control module C141 Pins, harness side and ground as follows:

DTC	Anti-Lock Brake Control Module C141 Pin	Circuit
C1145 (RF)	4	514 (YE/RD)
C1155 (LF)	20	521 (TN/OG)
C1165 (RR)	1	494 (TN/LG)
C1175 (LR)	22	496 (OG)

- Is the resistance greater than 10,000 ohms?

→ **Yes**
GO to **F4**.

→ **No**
GO to **F3**.

FM4029901519020X

Fig. 17 Test F/Codes C1145, C1155, C1165 & C1175: ABS Sensor Input Circuit Failure (Part 2 of 5). 2000–01 Less Traction Control

TEST CONDITIONS	TESTDETAILS/RESULTS/ACTIONS
F4 CHECK THE SUSPECT ANTI-LOCK BRAKE SENSOR CIRCUIT FOR FOR AN OPEN	

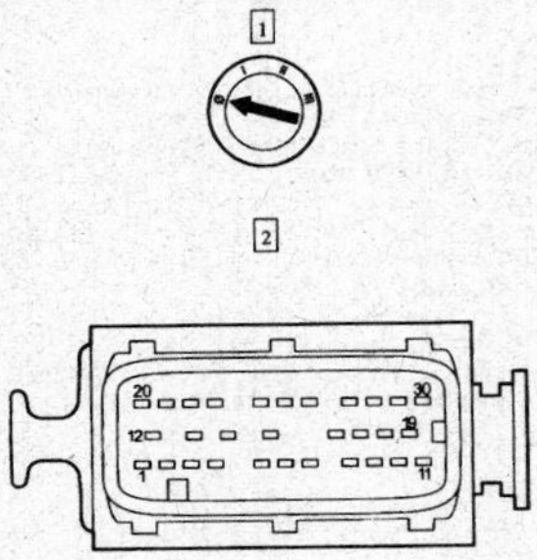

2 Measure the resistance between anti-lock brake control module C141 pins, harness side and suspect anti-lock brake sensor, harness side as follows:

DTC	Anti-Lock Brake Control Module	Anti-Lock Brake Sensor	Circuit
C1145 (RF)	C141 Pin 4	C145 Pin 1	514 (YE/RD)
C1145 (RF)	C141 Pin 5	C145 Pin 2	516 (YE/BK)
C1155 (LF)	C141 Pin 20	C144 Pin 1	521 (TN/OG)
C1155 (LF)	C141 Pin 21	C144 Pin 2	522 (TN/BK)
C1165 (RR)	C141 Pin 1	C319 Pin 2	494 (TN/LG)
C1165 (RR)	C141 Pin 3	C319 Pin 1	492 (BN)
C1175 (LR)	C141 Pin 22	C320 Pin 2	496 (OG)
C1175 (LR)	C141 Pin 23	C320 Pin 1	499 (GY/BK)

- Are the resistances less than 5 ohms?

→ **Yes**
GO to **F5**.

→ **No**
REPAIR the circuit in question. CLEAR the DTCs. REPEAT the self-test.

FM4029901519040X

Fig. 17 Test F/Codes C1145, C1155, C1165 & C1175: ABS Sensor Input Circuit Failure (Part 4 of 5). 2000–01 Less Traction Control

TEST CONDITIONS	TESTDETAILS/RESULTS/ACTIONS
F3 CHECK THE SUSPECT ANTI-LOCK BRAKE SENSOR FOR A SHORT TO GROUND	

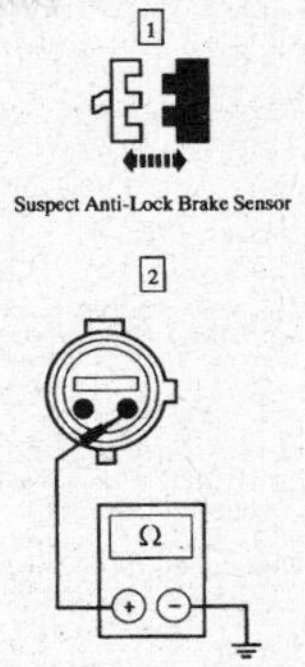

2 Measure the resistance between suspect anti-lock brake sensor Pin 1 (component side) and ground.

- Is the resistance greater than 10,000 ohms?

→ **Yes**
If RF, REPAIR Circuit 514 (YE/RD) and Circuit 516 (YE/BK), as necessary. CLEAR the DTCs. REPEAT the self-test.

If LF, REPAIR Circuit 521 (TN/OG) and Circuit 522 (TN/BK), as necessary. CLEAR the DTCs. REPEAT the self-test.

If RR, REPAIR Circuit 494 (TN/LG) and Circuit 492 (BN), as necessary. CLEAR the DTCs. REPEAT the self-test.

If LR, REPAIR Circuit 496 (OG) and Circuit 499 (GY/BK), as necessary. CLEAR the DTCs. REPEAT the self-test.

→ **No**
INSTALL a new anti-lock brake sensor. CLEAR the DTCs. REPEAT the self-test.

FM4029901519030X

Fig. 17 Test F/Codes C1145, C1155, C1165 & C1175: ABS Sensor Input Circuit Failure (Part 3 of 5). 2000–01 Less Traction Control

TEST CONDITIONS	TESTDETAILS/RESULTS/ACTIONS
F5 CHECK THE ANTI-LOCK BRAKE SENSOR	

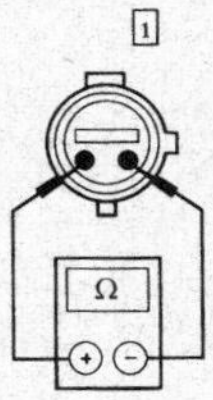

1 Measure the resistance between suspect anti-lock brake sensor Pin 1 (component side) and suspect anti-lock brake sensor Pin 2 (component side).

- Is the resistance between 1280 and 1920 (front) or 1830 and 2760 (rear) ohms?

→ **Yes**
INSTALL a new anti-lock brake control module
REPEAT the self-test.

→ **No**
INSTALL a new anti-lock brake sensor. CLEAR the DTCs. REPEAT the self-test.

FM4029901519050X

Fig. 17 Test F/Codes C1145, C1155, C1165 & C1175: ABS Sensor Input Circuit Failure (Part 5 of 5). 2000–01 Less Traction Control

TEST CONDITIONS	TESTDETAILS/RESULTS/ACTIONS
G1 CHECK THE VEHICLE COMPONENTS	

1 Check for correct wheel and tire size, front-to-rear and side-to-side.

2 Check for excessive bearing end play.

3 Check the anti-lock brake sensor indicator for a deformation or missing teeth.

- Are the conditions OK?

→ **Yes**
GO to **G2**.

→ **No**
REPAIR as necessary. CLEAR the DTCs. REPEAT the self-test.

G2 TEST DRIVE THE VEHICLE

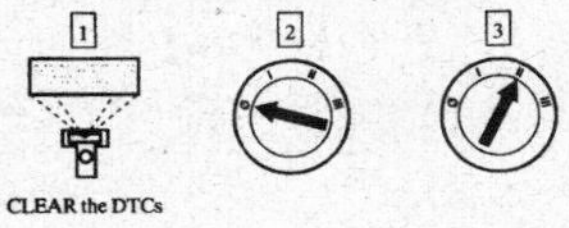

4 Test drive the vehicle over 24 kph (15 mph).

FM4029901520010X

Fig. 18 Test G/Code C1222: ABS Sensor Mismatch (Part 1 of 2). 2000–01 Less Traction Control

TEST CONDITIONS	TEST DETAILS/RESULTS/ACTIONS
G2 TEST DRIVE THE VEHICLE	
5 	• Is DTC C1222 retrieved? → **Yes** INSTALL a new anti-lock brake control module. REPEAT the self-test. → **No** If another DTC is retrieved, GO to the Anti-Lock Brake Control Module Diagnostic Trouble Code (DTC) index. If no DTCs are retrieved, the system is OK.

FM4029901520020X

Fig. 18 Test G/Code C1222: ABS Sensor Mismatch (Part 2 of 2). 2000–01 Less Traction Control

TEST CONDITIONS	TEST DETAILS/RESULTS/ACTIONS
H2 CHECK THE SUSPECT ANTI-LOCK BRAKE SENSOR INDICATOR	
	2 Check the air gap and bearing end play. • Is the suspect anti-lock brake sensor indicator OK? → **Yes** GO to **H3**. → **No** INSTALL a new anti-lock brake sensor indicator. CLEAR the DTCs. REPEAT the self-test.
H3 CHECK THE ANTI-LOCK BRAKE SENSOR OUTPUT	
1 2 3 4 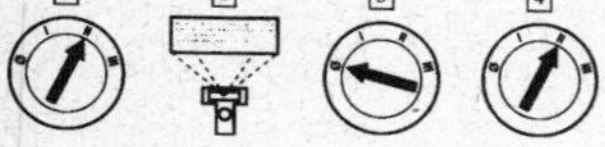	5 Have an assistant monitor the anti-lock brake control module PIDs LF__WSPD, RF__WSPD, LR__WSPD, and RR__WSPD while driving at various speeds. 6 **Note:** The vehicle must be driven 16 km/h (10 miles) during this test step. Test drive the vehicle for 16 kmh (10 miles). • Are the anti-lock brake control module PIDs approximately the same at all times? → **Yes** INSTALL a new anti-lock brake control module. REPEAT the self-test. → **No** INSTALL a new anti-lock brake sensor. CLEAR the DTCs. REPEAT the self-test.

FM4029901521020X

Fig. 19 Test H/Codes C1233, C1234, C1235 & C1236: ABS Sensor Input Signal Missing (Part 2 of 2). 2000–01 Less Traction Control

TEST CONDITIONS	TEST DETAILS/RESULTS/ACTIONS
J1 CHECK THE VEHICLE COMPONENTS	
	1 Check the brake pedal and power booster/brake master cylinder for correct attachment. • Are the components OK? → **Yes** GO to **J2**. → **No** REPAIR as necessary. TEST the system for normal operation.
J2 BLEED THE BRAKE SYSTEM	
	1 Bleed the brake system.

FM4029901523010X

Fig. 21 Test J: Spongy Brake Pedal w/No Warning Indicator (Part 1 of 2). 2000–01 Less Traction Control

TEST CONDITIONS	TEST DETAILS/RESULTS/ACTIONS
H1 CHECK THE SUSPECT ANTI-LOCK BRAKE SENSOR	
	1 Check the suspect anti-lock brake sensor mounting. 2 Check the suspect anti-lock brake sensor for excessive dirt build up, obstructions, and damage. • Is the suspect anti-lock brake sensor and mounting OK? → **Yes** GO to **H2**. → **No** REPAIR as necessary. CLEAR the DTCs. REPEAT the self-test.
H2 CHECK THE SUSPECT ANTI-LOCK BRAKE SENSOR INDICATOR	
	1 Check the suspect anti-lock brake sensor indicator for corrosion, nicks, bridged teeth, damaged teeth, correct mounting, and alignment with the anti-lock brake sensor.

FM4029901521010X

Fig. 19 Test H/Codes C1233, C1234, C1235 & C1236: ABS Sensor Input Signal Missing (Part 1 of 2). 2000–01 Less Traction Control

TEST CONDITIONS	TEST DETAILS/RESULTS/ACTIONS
I1 CHECK THE ABS WARNING INDICATOR CIRCUITRY	
1 2 3 	4 Depress and release the shorting bar connector internal to the anti-lock brake control module C141, harness side, while checking the yellow ABS warning indicator in the instrument cluster. • Does the yellow ABS indicator illuminate with the shorting bar released and turn OFF with the shorting bar depressed? → **Yes** INSTALL a new anti-lock brake control module. TEST the system for normal operation. → **No** DIAGNOSE instrument cluster.

FM4029901522000X

Fig. 20 Test I: Yellow ABS Warning Indicator Does Not Self-Check. 2000–01 Less Traction Control

TEST CONDITIONS	TEST DETAILS/RESULTS/ACTIONS
J2 BLEED THE BRAKE SYSTEM	
	2 Check for spongy brake pedal. • Is the brake pedal spongy? → **Yes** INSTALL a new HCU. TEST the system for normal operation. → **No** The brake system is OK. TEST the system for normal operation.

FM4029901523020X

Fig. 21 Test J: Spongy Brake Pedal w/No Warning Indicator (Part 2 of 2). 2000–01 Less Traction Control

TEST CONDITIONS	TEST DETAILS/RESULTS/ACTIONS
K1 BLEED THE BRAKE SYSTEM	
	[1] Bleed the brake system. [2] Check for vehicle tracking poorly. • Does the vehicle track poorly? → **Yes** GO to **K2**. → **No** The brake system is OK. TEST the system for normal operation.
K2 CHECK THE LF ABS VALVE OPERATION	
	[1] Lift the vehicle and rotate all the wheels to make sure they rotate freely (the vehicle must be in neutral). [2] **NOTE:** Trigger must be depressed twice. Each depress runs the pump motor for two seconds. Trigger the anti-lock brake control module active command PMP MOTOR ON for four seconds. [3] Apply moderate brake pedal effort.

FM4029901524010X

Fig. 22 Test K: Poor Vehicle Tracking During ABS Function (Part 1 of 4). 2000–01 Less Traction Control

TEST CONDITIONS	TEST DETAILS/RESULTS/ACTIONS
K4 CHECK THE RF ABS VALVE OPERATION	
	[3] Have an assistant attempt to rotate the RF wheel while the pump motor is running. • Does the RF wheel rotate? → **Yes** INSTALL a new HCU. TEST the system for normal operation. → **No** GO to **K5**.
K5 CHECK THE RF ABS VALVE RELEASE	
	[1] Apply moderate brake pedal effort. [2] Trigger the anti-lock brake control module active command RF INLET and RF OUTLET. [3] **Note:** The scan tool will energize the valves for only two seconds per trigger press. Have an assistant rotate the RF wheel immediately after depressing trigger. • Does the RF wheel rotate? → **Yes** GO to **K6**. → **No** GO to **K8**.
K6 CHECK THE REAR ABS VALVE OPERATION	
	[1] **Note:** Trigger must be depressed twice.Each press will run the pump motor for two seconds. Trigger the anti-lock brake control module active command PMP MOTOR ON for four seconds. [2] Apply moderate brake pedal effort.

FM4029901524030X

Fig. 22 Test K: Poor Vehicle Tracking During ABS Function (Part 3 of 4). 2000–01 Less Traction Control

TEST CONDITIONS	TEST DETAILS/RESULTS/ACTIONS
K2 CHECK THE LF ABS VALVE OPERATION (Continued)	
	[4] Have an assistant attempt to rotate the LF wheel while the pump motor is running. • Does the LF wheel rotate? → **Yes** INSTALL a new HCU. TEST the system for normal operation. → **No** GO to **K3**.
K3 CHECK THE LF ABS VALVE RELEASE	
	[1] Apply moderate brake pedal effort. [2] Trigger the anti-lock brake control module active command LF INLET and LF OUTLET. [3] **Note:** The scan tool will energize the valves for only two seconds per trigger press. Have an assistant rotate the LF wheel immediately after depressing trigger. • Does the LF wheel rotate? → **Yes** GO to **K4**. → **No** GO to **K8**.
K4 CHECK THE RF ABS VALVE OPERATION	
	[1] **Note:** Trigger must be depressed twice. Each press will run the pump motor for two seconds. Trigger the anti-lock brake control module active command PMP MOTOR ON for four seconds. [2] Apply moderate brake pedal effort.

FM4029901524020X

Fig. 22 Test K: Poor Vehicle Tracking During ABS Function (Part 2 of 4). 2000–01 Less Traction Control

TEST CONDITIONS	TEST DETAILS/RESULTS/ACTIONS
K6 CHECK THE REAR ABS VALVE OPERATION	
	[3] Have an assistant attempt to rotate the LR and RR wheels while the pump motor is running. • Does the LR or RR wheel rotate? → **Yes** INSTALL a new HCU. TEST the system for normal operation. → **No** GO to **K7**.
K7 CHECK THE REAR ABS VALVE RELEASE	
	[1] Apply moderate brake pedal effort. [2] Trigger the anti-lock brake control module active command R INLET and R OUTLET. [3] **Note:** The scan tool will energize the valves for only two seconds per trigger press. Have an assistant rotate the LR and RR wheels immediately after depressing trigger. • Does the LR or RR wheel rotate? → **Yes** The ABS system is operating correctly. → **No** GO to **K8**.
K8 CHECK FOR DTCS	
	[1] Carry out the anti-lock brake control module self-test. • Are any DTCs retrieved? → **Yes** GO to the Anti-Lock Brake Control Module Diagnostic Trouble Code (DTC) Index. → **No** INSTALL a new HCU. TEST the system for normal operation.

FM4029901524040X

Fig. 22 Test K: Poor Vehicle Tracking During ABS Function (Part 4 of 4). 2000–01 Less Traction Control

TEST CONDITIONS	TEST DETAILS/RESULTS/ACTIONS
L1 CHECK THE TRACTION CONTROL SWITCH CIRCUITRY	
1 2 3  	
4 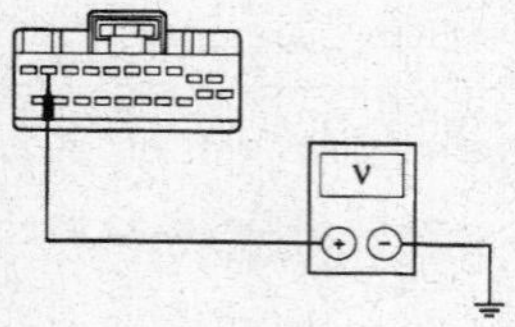 	4 Measure the voltage between instrument cluster C251 Pin 9, Circuit 959 (GY), harness side and ground, while depressing and releasing the traction control switch. • Is the voltage greater than 10 volts with the traction control switch depressed and zero volts with the traction control switch released? → **Yes** INSTALL a new instrument cluster. TEST the system for normal operation. → **No** GO to **L2**.
L2 CHECK CIRCUIT 959 (GY) FOR AN OPEN	
1 2 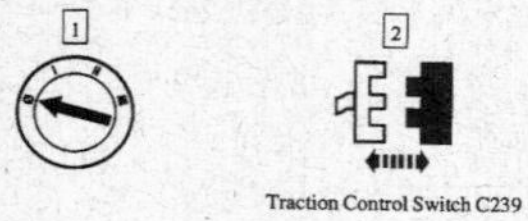 	
3 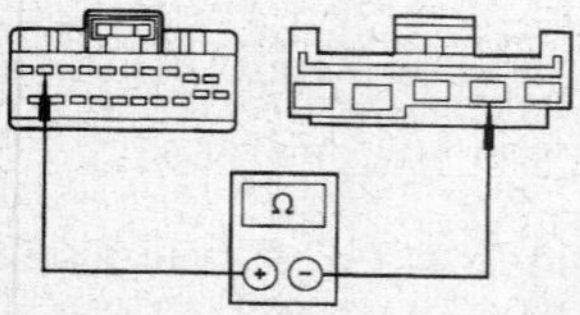 	3 Measure the resistance between instrument cluster C251 Pin 9, Circuit 959 (GY), harness side and traction control switch C239 Pin 4, Circuit 959 (GY), harness side. • Is the resistance less than 5 ohms? → **Yes** GO to **L3**. → **No** REPAIR the circuit. TEST the system for normal operation.

FM4020001661010X

Fig. 23 Test L: Traction Control Inoperative (Part 1 of 2). 2000–01 Less Traction Control

TEST CONDITIONS	TEST DETAILS/RESULTS/ACTIONS
M1 CHECK CIRCUIT 960 (BK/LB)	
1 2 3 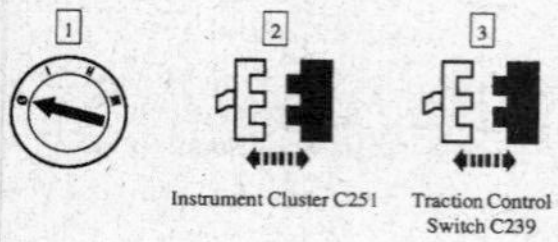 	
4 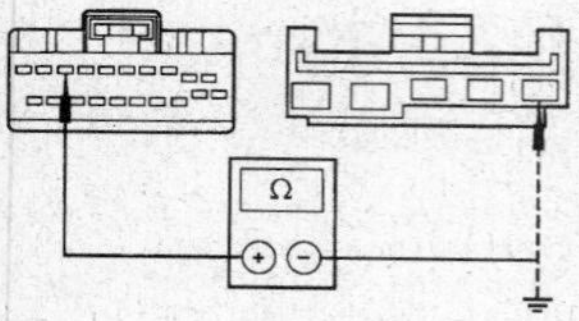 	4 Measure the resistance between instrument cluster C251 Pin 8, Circuit 960 (BK/LB), harness side and traction control switch C239 Pin 5, Circuit 960 (BK/LB), harness side; and between instrument cluster C251 Pin 8, Circuit 960 (BK/LB), harness side and ground. • Is the resistance less than 5 ohms between the instrument cluster and traction control switch and greater than 10,000 ohms between instrument cluster and ground? → **Yes** GO to **M2**. → **No** REPAIR as necessary.
M2 CHECK CIRCUIT 489 (PK/BK) FOR AN OPEN	
1 	
2 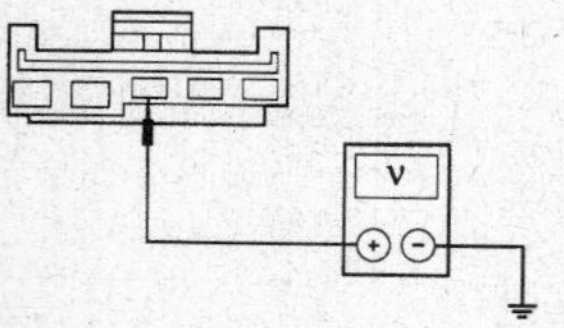 	2 Measure the voltage between traction control switch C239 Pin 3, Circuit 489 (PK/BK), harness side and ground. • Is the voltage greater than 10 volts? → **Yes** GO to **M3**. → **No** REPAIR the circuit. TEST the system for normal operation.

FM4020001662010X

Fig. 24 Test M: Traction Control Indicator Inoperative (Part 1 of 2). 2000–01 Less Traction Control

TEST CONDITIONS	TEST DETAILS/RESULTS/ACTIONS
L3 CHECK CIRCUIT 489 (PK/BK) FOR AN OPEN	
1 	
2 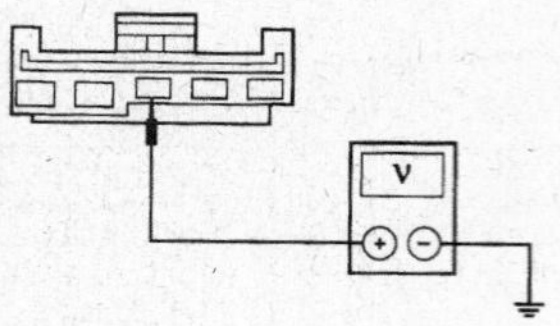 	2 Measure the voltage between traction control switch C239 Pin 3, Circuit 489 (PK/BK), harness side and ground. • Is the voltage greater than 10 volts? → **Yes** INSTALL a new traction control switch. TEST the system for normal operation. → **No** REPAIR the circuit. TEST the system for normal operation.

FM4020001661020X

Fig. 23 Test L: Traction Control Inoperative (Part 2 of 2). 2000–01 Less Traction Control

TEST CONDITIONS	TEST DETAILS/RESULTS/ACTIONS
M3 CHECK THE TRACTION CONTROL SWITCH INDICATOR	
1 2 3 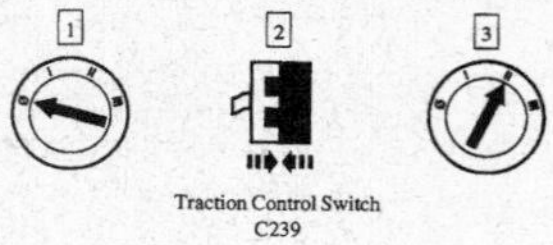 	
4 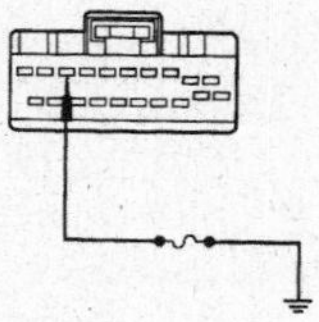	4 Momentarily connect a fused (10A) jumper wire between instrument cluster C251 Pin 8, Circuit 960 (BK/LB), harness side and ground, while observing the traction control switch indicator. • Does the traction control switch indicator illuminate? → **Yes** INSTALL a new instrument cluster. TEST the system for normal operation. → **No** INSTALL a new traction control switch. TEST the system for normal operation.

FM4020001662020X

Fig. 24 Test M: Traction Control Indicator Inoperative (Part 2 of 2). 2000–01 Less Traction Control

CONDITIONS	DETAILS/RESULTS/ACTIONS
A1 CHECK CIRCUIT 601 (LB/PK) FOR AN OPEN	
1 	
2  Anti-Lock Brake Control Module C135	
3 	
4 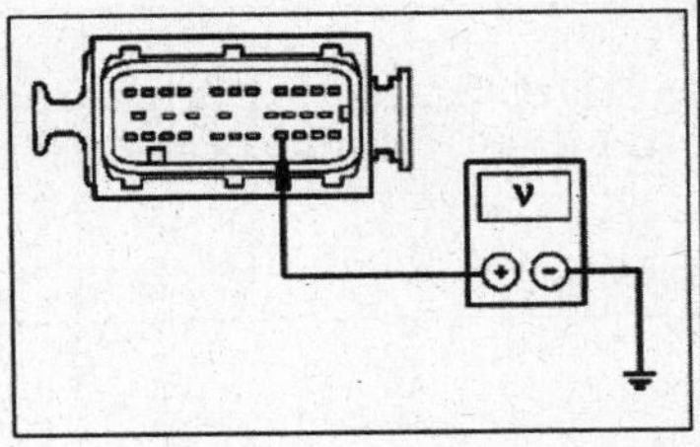	4 Measure the voltage between anti-lock brake control module C135 Pin 8, Circuit 601 (LB/PK), harness side and ground. • **Is the voltage greater than 10 volts?** → **Yes** GO to A2 . → **No** REPAIR the circuit. REPEAT the self-test.

FM4020101838010X

Fig. 25 Test A: No Communication w/Anti-Lock Brake Control Module (Part 1 of 2). 2002–04 Less Traction Control

CONDITIONS	DETAILS/RESULTS/ACTIONS
B1 CHECK THE COMMUNICATIONS TO THE ANTI-LOCK BRAKE CONTROL MODULE	
	1 Check the communications to the anti-lock brake control module. • **Does the scan tool communicate with the anti-lock brake control module?** → **Yes** INSTALL a new anti-lock brake control module. REPEAT the self-test. → **No** Go To Pinpoint Test A .

FM4020101839000X

Fig. 26 Test B: Unable To Enter Self-Test. 2002–04 Less Traction Control

A2 CHECK THE ANTI-LOCK BRAKE CONTROL MODULE GROUNDS	
1 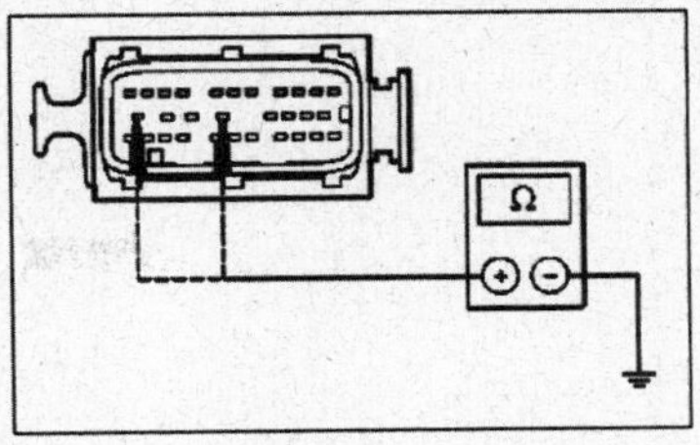	1 Measure the resistance between anti-lock brake control module C135 Pin 12, Circuit 1205 (BK), harness side and ground; and between anti-lock brake control module C135 Pin 15, Circuit 397 (BK/WH), harness side and ground. • **Are the resistances less than 5 ohms?** → **Yes** INSTALL a new anti-lock brake control module. REPEAT the self-test. → **No** REPAIR the circuit in question. REPEAT the self-test.

FM4020101838020X

Fig. 25 Test A: No Communication w/Anti-Lock Brake Control Module (Part 2 of 2). 2002–04 Less Traction Control

CONDITIONS	DETAILS/RESULTS/ACTIONS
C1 CHECK BATTERY VOLTAGE	
1 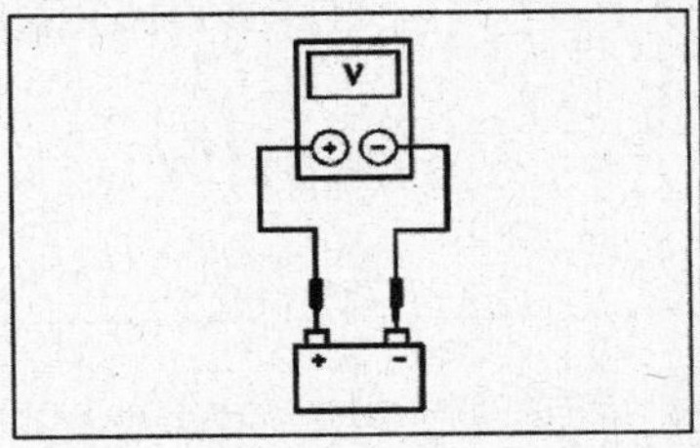	1 Measure the battery voltage between the positive and negative battery posts with the key ON engine OFF (KOEO), and with the engine running. • **Is the battery voltage between 10 and 13 volts with KOEO, and between 11 and 17 volts with the engine running?** → **Yes** GO to C2 . → **No** Diagnose charging system.

FM4020101840010X

Fig. 27 Test C/Code 1318: Battery Voltage Low (Part 1 of 3). 2002–04 Less Traction Control

C2 CHECK THE VOLTAGE TO THE ANTI-LOCK BRAKE CONTROL MODULE

1

2

Anti-Lock Brake Control Module C135

3

4

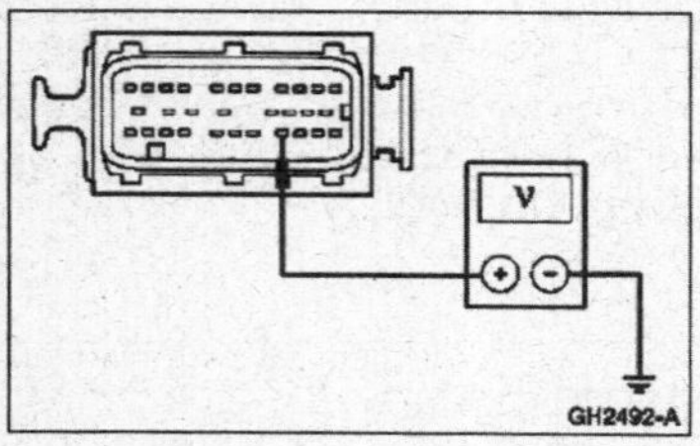

4 Measure the voltage between anti-lock brake control module C135 Pin 8, Circuit 601 (LB/PK), harness side and ground.

- **Is the voltage greater than 10 volts?**

→ **Yes**
GO to C3 .

→ **No**
REPAIR the circuit. CLEAR the DTCs. REPEAT the self-test.

FM4020101840020X

Fig. 27 Test C/Code 1318: Battery Voltage Low (Part 2 of 3). 2002–04 Less Traction Control

CONDITIONS	DETAILS/RESULTS/ACTIONS
D1 CHECK THE STOPLAMPS FOR CORRECT OPERATION	
	1 Depress the brake pedal while checking the stoplamps. • **Do the stop lamps illuminate?** → **Yes** GO to D2 . → **No** Diagnose exterior lighting.

FM4020101852010X

Fig. 28 Test D/Code 1484: Brake Pedal Input Open Circuit (Part 1 of 2). 2002–04 Less Traction Control

C3 CHECK THE ANTI-LOCK BRAKE CONTROL MODULE GROUNDS

1

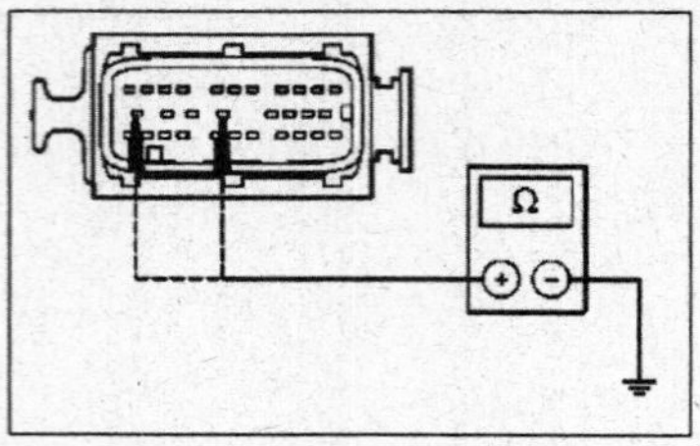

1 Measure the resistance between anti-lock brake control module C135 Pin 12, Circuit 1205 (BK), harness side and ground; and between anti-lock brake control module C135 Pin 15, Circuit 397 (BK/WH), harness side and ground.

- **Are the resistances less than 5 ohms?**

→ **Yes**
INSTALL a new anti-lock brake control module.
REPEAT the self-test.

→ **No**
REPAIR the circuit in question. CLEAR the DTCs. REPEAT the self-test.

FM4020101840030X

Fig. 27 Test C/Code 1318: Battery Voltage Low (Part 3 of 3). 2002–04 Less Traction Control

D2 CHECK THE BRAKE PEDAL INPUT TO THE ANTI -LOCK BRAKE CONTROL MODULE

1

2

Anti-Lock Brake Control Module C135

3

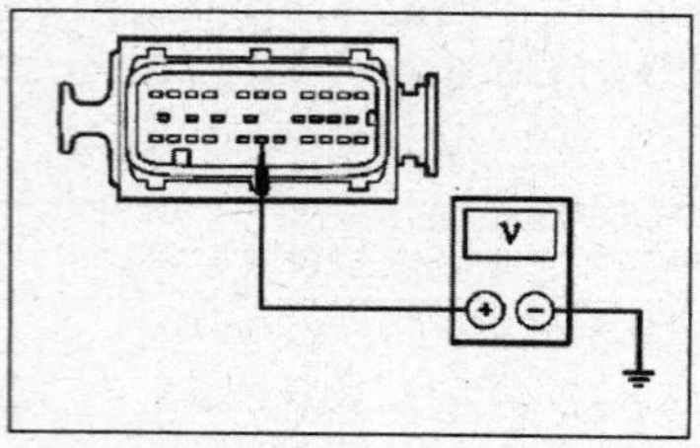

3 Measure the voltage between anti-lock brake control module C135 Pin 6, Circuit 511 (LG), harness side and ground, while depressing and releasing the brake pedal.

- **Is the voltage greater than 10 volts with the brake pedal depressed and zero volts with the brake pedal released?**

→ **Yes**
INSTALL a new anti-lock brake control module.
REPEAT the self-test.

→ **No**
REPAIR Circuit 511 (LG) and Circuit 810 (RD/LG) as necessary. CLEAR the DTCs. REPEAT the self-test.

FM4020101852020X

Fig. 28 Test D/Code 1484: Brake Pedal Input Open Circuit (Part 2 of 2). 2002–04 Less Traction Control

CONDITIONS	DETAILS/RESULTS/ACTIONS
E1 CHECK THE PUMP MOTOR FOR CONTINUOUS OPERATION	
	1 Check the pump motor for continuous operation. • **Is the pump motor running continuously?** → **Yes** INSTALL a new anti-lock brake control module. REPEAT the self-test. → **No** GO to E2 .

FM4020101853010X

Fig. 29 Test E/Code 1095: ABS Hydraulic Pump Motor Failure (Part 1 of 4). 2002–04 Less Traction Control

E2 CHECK CIRCUIT 534 (YE/LG) FOR AN OPEN

1

2

Anti-Lock Brake Control Module C135

3

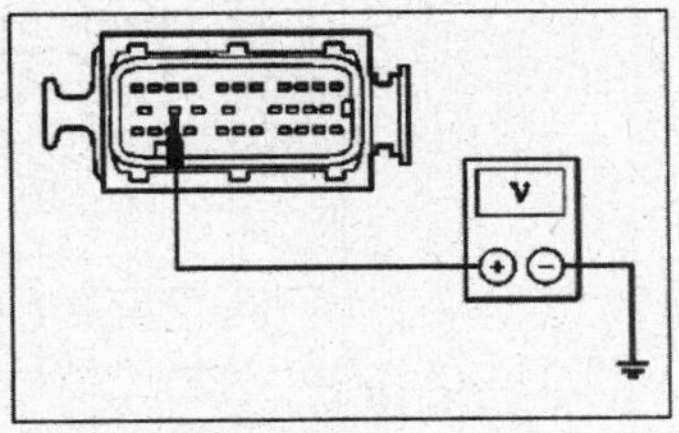

3 Measure the voltage between anti-lock brake control module C135 Pin 13, Circuit 534 (YE/LG), harness side, and ground.

• **Is the voltage greater than 10 volts?**

→ **Yes**
GO to E3 .

→ **No**
REPAIR the circuit. CLEAR the DTCs. REPEAT the self-test.

FM4020101853020X

Fig. 29 Test E/Code 1095: ABS Hydraulic Pump Motor Failure (Part 2 of 4). 2002–04 Less Traction Control

E3 CHECK CIRCUIT 1205 (BK) FOR AN OPEN

1

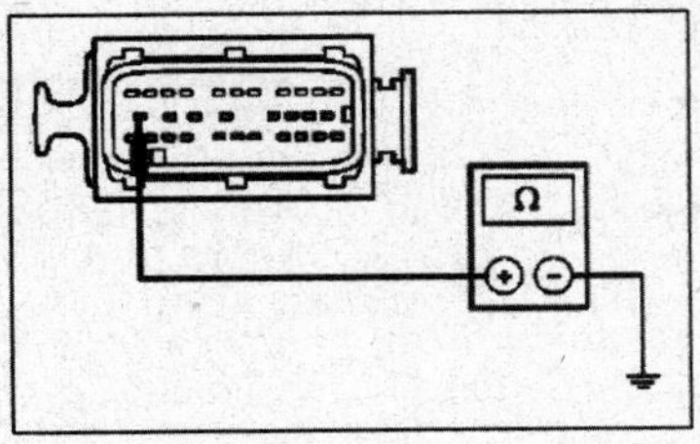

1 Measure the resistance between anti-lock brake control module C135 Pin 12, Circuit 1205 (BK), harness side and ground.

• **Is the resistance less than 5 ohms?**

→ **Yes**
GO to E4 .

→ **No**
REPAIR the circuit. CLEAR the DTCs. REPEAT the self-test.

FM4020101853030X

Fig. 29 Test E/Code 1095: ABS Hydraulic Pump Motor Failure (Part 3 of 4). 2002–04 Less Traction Control

E4 CHECK THE PUMP MOTOR FOR OPERATION

1

Pump Motor Connector

2

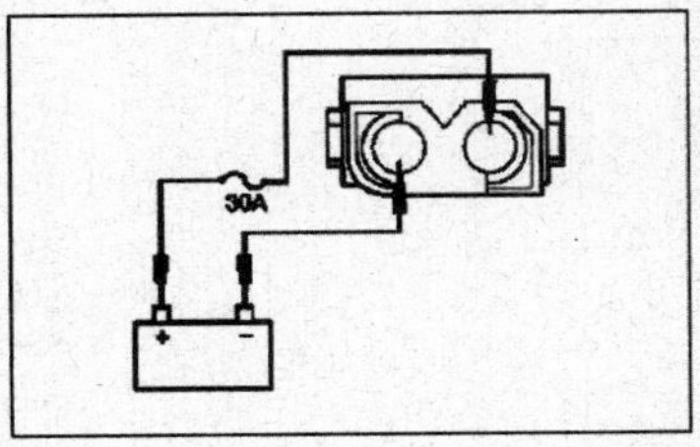

2 Connect a 30A fused heavy jumper wire between the positive battery post and pump motor connector Pin 1 (component side); and momentarily connect a heavy jumper between negative battery post and pump motor connector Pin 2 (component side).

• **Does the pump motor operate?**

→ **Yes**
INSTALL a new anti-lock brake control module.
REPEAT the self-test.

→ **No**
INSTALL a new HCU.
CLEAR the DTCs.
REPEAT the self-test.

FM4020101853040X

Fig. 29 Test E/Code 1095: ABS Hydraulic Pump Motor Failure (Part 4 of 4). 2002–04 Less Traction Control

CONDITIONS	DETAILS/RESULTS/ACTIONS

F1 CHECK THE SUSPECT ANTI-LOCK BRAKE SENSOR CIRCUIT FOR SHORT TO POWER

1

2

Anti-Lock Brake Control Module C135

3

4

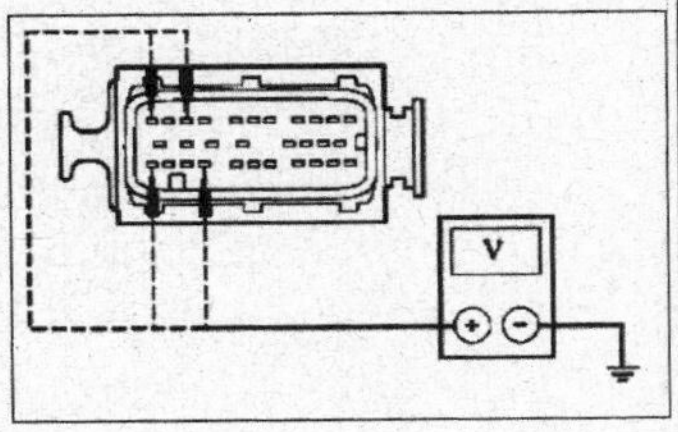

4 Measure the voltage between anti-lock brake control module C135 Pins, harness side and ground as follows:

DTC	Anti-Lock Brake Control Module C135 Pin	Circuit
C1145 (RF)	4	514 (YE/RD)
C1155 (LF)	20	521 (TN/OG)
C1165 (RR)	1	494 (TN/LG)
C1175 (LR)	22	496 (OG)

• **Is any voltage present?**

→ **Yes**
REPAIR the circuit in question. CLEAR the DTCs. REPEAT the self-test.

→ **No**
GO to F2 .

FM4020101854010X

Fig. 30 Test F/Codes C1145, C1155, C1165 & C1175: ABS Sensor Input Circuit Failure (Part 1 of 5). 2002–04 Less Traction Control

F2 CHECK THE SUSPECT ANTI-LOCK BRAKE SENSOR CIRCUIT FOR SHORT TO GROUND

1

2

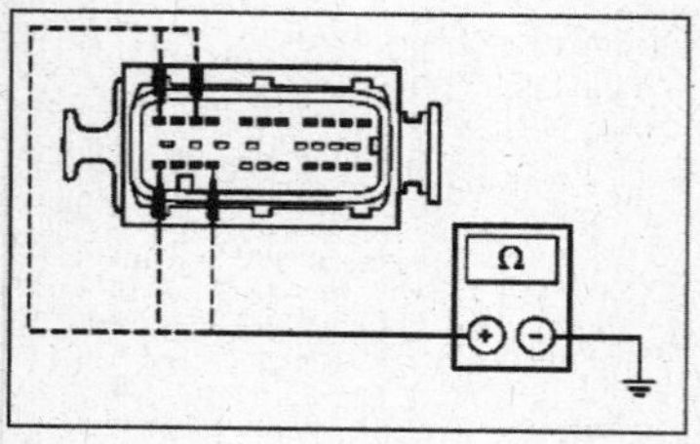

2 Measure the resistance between anti-lock brake control module C135 Pins, harness side and ground as follows:

DTC	Anti-Lock Brake Control Module C135 Pin	Circuit
C1145 (RF)	4	514 (YE/RD)
C1155 (LF)	20	521 (TN/OG)
C1165 (RR)	1	494 (TN/LG)
C1175 (LR)	22	496 (OG)

- **Is the resistance greater than 10,000 ohms?**

→ **Yes**
GO to F4 .

→ **No**
GO to F3 .

FM4020101854020X

Fig. 30 Test F/Codes C1145, C1155, C1165 & C1175: ABS Sensor Input Circuit Failure (Part 2 of 5). 2002–04 Less Traction Control

F4 CHECK THE SUSPECT ANTI-LOCK BRAKE SENSOR CIRCUIT FOR FOR AN OPEN

1

2

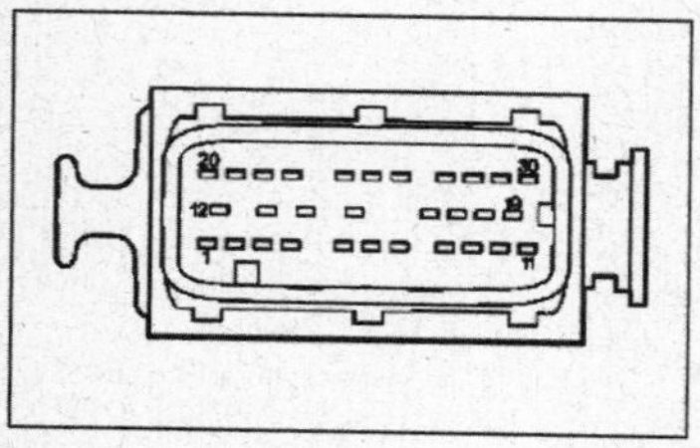

2 Measure the resistance between anti-lock brake control module C135 pins, harness side and suspect anti-lock brake sensor, harness side as follows:

DTC	Anti-Lock Brake Control Module	Anti-Lock Brake Sensor	Circuit
C1145 (RF)	C135 Pin 4	C160 Pin 1	514 (YE/RD)
C1145 (RF)	C135 Pin 5	C160 Pin 2	516 (YE/BK)
C1155 (LF)	C135 Pin 20	C150 Pin 1	521 (TN/OG)
C1155 (LF)	C135 Pin 21	C150 Pin 2	522 (TN/BK)
C1165 (RR)	C135 Pin 1	C3117 Pin 2	494 (TN/LG)
C1165 (RR)	C135 Pin 3	C3117 Pin 1	492 (BN)
C1175 (LR)	C135 Pin 22	C3116 Pin 2	496 (OG)
C1175 (LR)	C135 Pin 23	C3116 Pin 1	499 (GY/BK)

- **Are the resistances less than 5 ohms?**

→ **Yes**
GO to F5 .

→ **No**
REPAIR the circuit in question. CLEAR the DTCs. REPEAT the self-test.

FM4020101854040X

Fig. 30 Test F/Codes C1145, C1155, C1165 & C1175: ABS Sensor Input Circuit Failure ABS Sensor Input Circuit Failure (Part 4 of 5). 2002–04 Less Traction Control

F3 CHECK THE SUSPECT ANTI-LOCK BRAKE SENSOR FOR A SHORT TO GROUND

1

Suspect Anti-Lock Brake Sensor

2

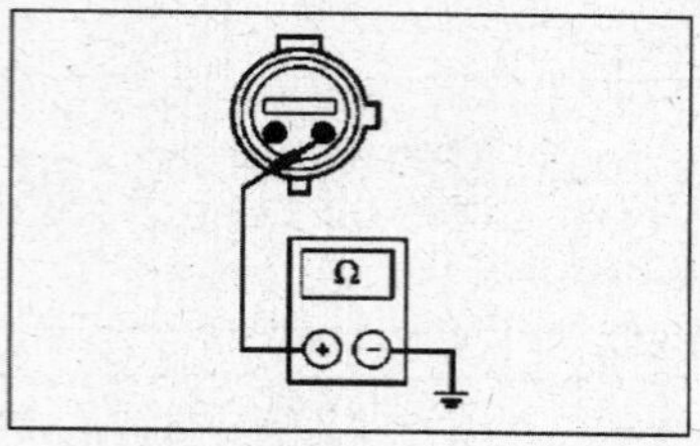

2 Measure the resistance between suspect anti-lock brake sensor Pin 1 (component side) and ground.

- **Is the resistance greater than 10,000 ohms?**

→ **Yes**
If RF, REPAIR Circuit 514 (YE/RD) and Circuit 516 (YE/BK), as necessary. CLEAR the DTCs. REPEAT the self-test.
If LF, REPAIR Circuit 521 (TN/OG) and Circuit 522 (TN/BK), as necessary. CLEAR the DTCs. REPEAT the self-test.
If RR, REPAIR Circuit 494 (TN/LG) and Circuit 492 (BN), as necessary. CLEAR the DTCs. REPEAT the self-test.
If LR, REPAIR Circuit 496 (OG) and Circuit 499 (GY/BK), as necessary. CLEAR the DTCs. REPEAT the self-test.

→ **No**
INSTALL a new anti-lock brake sensor. CLEAR the DTCs. REPEAT the self-test.

FM4020101854030X

Fig. 30 Test F/Codes C1145, C1155, C1165 & C1175: ABS Sensor Input Circuit Failure (Part 3 of 5). 2002–04 Less Traction Control

F5 CHECK THE ANTI-LOCK BRAKE SENSOR

1

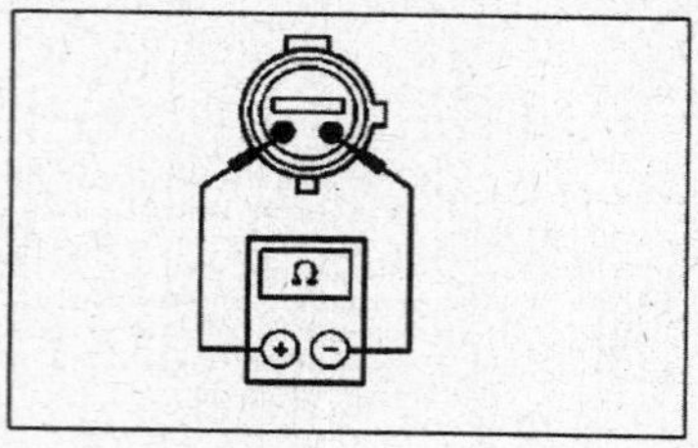

1 Measure the resistance between suspect anti-lock brake sensor Pin 1 (component side) and suspect anti-lock brake sensor Pin 2 (component side).

- **Is the resistance between 1280 and 1920 (front) or 1830 and 2760 (rear) ohms?**

→ **Yes**
INSTALL a new anti-lock brake control module,
REPEAT the self-test.

→ **No**
INSTALL a new anti-lock brake sensor, CLEAR the DTCs.
REPEAT the self-test.

FM4020101854050X

Fig. 30 Test F/Codes C1145, C1155, C1165 & C1175: ABS Sensor Input Circuit Failure (Part 5 of 5). 2002–04 Less Traction Control

CONDITIONS	DETAILS/RESULTS/ACTIONS
G1 CHECK THE VEHICLE COMPONENTS	
	1 Check for correct wheel and tire size, front-to-rear and side-to-side. 2 Check for excessive bearing end play. 3 Check the anti-lock brake sensor indicator for a deformation or missing teeth. • **Are the conditions OK?** → **Yes** GO to G2 . → **No** REPAIR as necessary. CLEAR the DTCs. REPEAT the self-test.

FM4020101855010X

Fig. 31 Test G/Code 1222: Anti-Lock Brake Sensor Mismatch (Part 1 of 2). 2002–04 Less Traction Control

CONDITIONS	DETAILS/RESULTS/ACTIONS
H1 CHECK THE SUSPECT ANTI-LOCK BRAKE SENSOR	
	1 Check the suspect anti-lock brake sensor mounting. 2 Check the suspect anti-lock brake sensor for excessive dirt build up, obstructions, and damage. • **Is the suspect anti-lock brake sensor and mounting OK?** → **Yes** GO to H2 . → **No** REPAIR as necessary. CLEAR the DTCs. REPEAT the self-test.
H2 CHECK THE SUSPECT ANTI-LOCK BRAKE SENSOR INDICATOR	
	1 Check the suspect anti-lock brake sensor indicator for corrosion, nicks, bridged teeth, damaged teeth, correct mounting, and alignment with the anti-lock brake sensor. 2 Check the air gap and bearing end play. • **Is the suspect anti-lock brake sensor indicator OK?** → **Yes** GO to H3 . → **No** INSTALL a new anti-lock brake sensor indicator. CLEAR the DTCs. REPEAT the self-test.

FM4020101856010X

Fig. 32 Test H/Codes C1233, C1234, C1235 & C1236: Anti-Lock Brake Sensor Input Signal Missing (Part 1 of 2). 2002–04 Less Traction Control

G2 TEST DRIVE THE VEHICLE

1

CLEAR the DTCs

2

3

4 Test drive the vehicle over 24 kph (15 mph).

5

Retrieve DTCs

• **Is DTC C1222 retrieved?**

→ **Yes**
INSTALL a new anti-lock brake control module.
REPEAT the self-test.

→ **No**
If another DTC is retrieved, GO to the Anti-Lock Brake Control Module Diagnostic Trouble Code (DTC) index.
If no DTCs are retrieved, the system is OK.

FM4020101855020X

Fig. 31 Test G/Code 1222: Anti-Lock Brake Sensor Mismatch (Part 2 of 2). 2002–04 Less Traction Control

H3 CHECK THE ANTI-LOCK BRAKE SENSOR OUTPUT

1

2

CLEAR the DTCs.

3

4

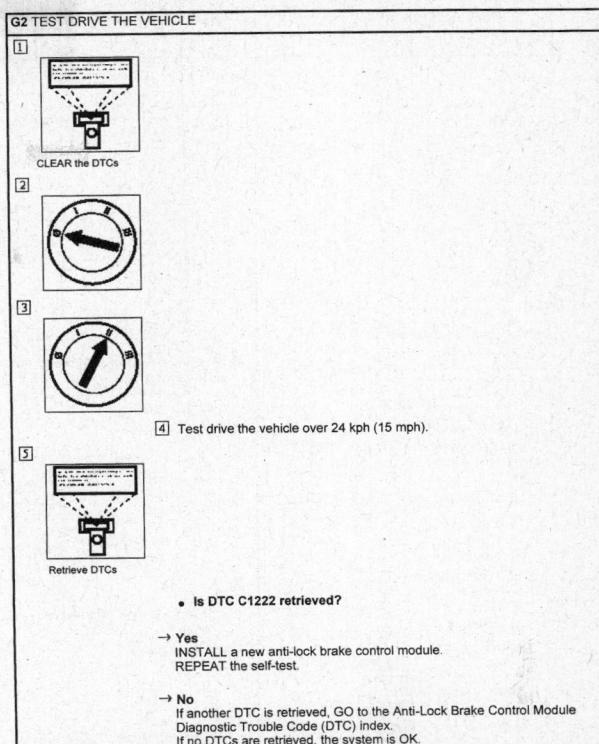

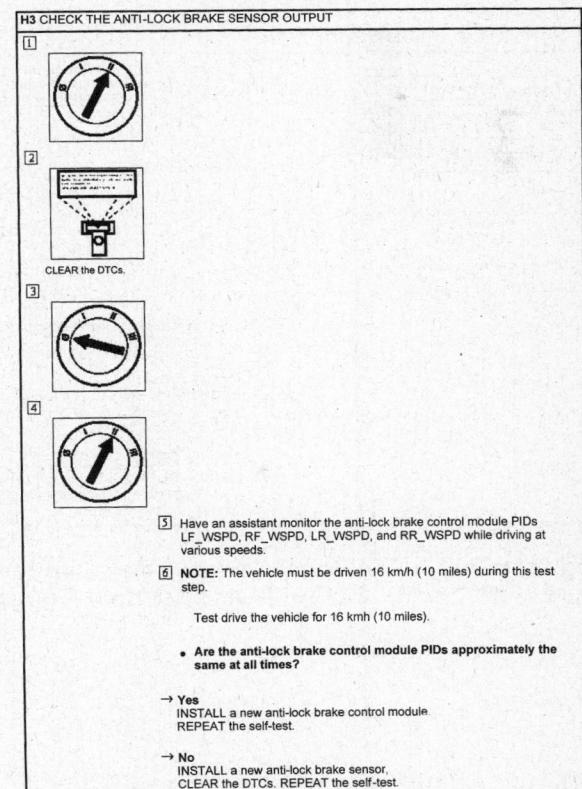

5 Have an assistant monitor the anti-lock brake control module PIDs LF_WSPD, RF_WSPD, LR_WSPD, and RR_WSPD while driving at various speeds.

6 **NOTE:** The vehicle must be driven 16 km/h (10 miles) during this test step.

Test drive the vehicle for 16 kmh (10 miles).

• **Are the anti-lock brake control module PIDs approximately the same at all times?**

→ **Yes**
INSTALL a new anti-lock brake control module.
REPEAT the self-test.

→ **No**
INSTALL a new anti-lock brake sensor,
CLEAR the DTCs. REPEAT the self-test.

FM4020101856020X

Fig. 32 Test H/Codes C1233, C1234, C1235 & C1236: Anti-Lock Brake Sensor Input Signal Missing (Part 2 of 2). 2002–04 Less Traction Control

CONDITIONS	DETAILS/RESULTS/ACTIONS
I1 CHECK CIRCUIT 534 (YE/LG) FOR AN OPEN	
1 	
2  Anti-Lock Brake Control Module C135	
3 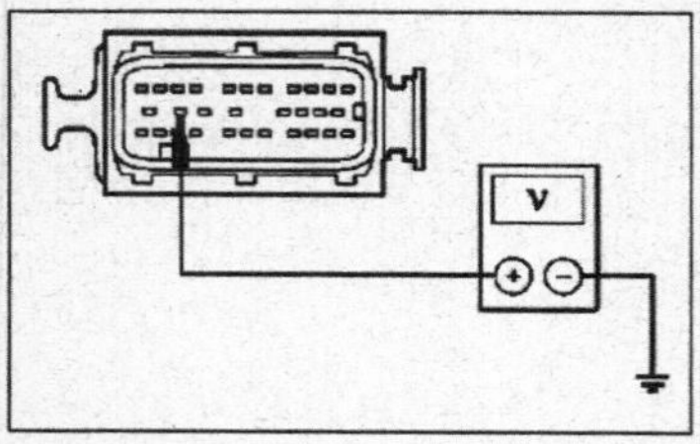	3 Measure the voltage between anti-lock brake control module C135 Pin 13, Circuit 534 (YE/LG), harness side and ground. • **Is the voltage greater than 10 volts?** → **Yes** GO to I2 . → **No** REPAIR the circuit. CLEAR the DTCs. REPEAT the self-test.

FM4020101857010X

Fig. 33 Test I: ABS Valve Power Relay Circuit Failure (Part 1 of 3). 2002–04 Less Traction Control

I2 CHECK CIRCUIT 532 (OG/YE) FOR AN OPEN	
1 	
2 	
3 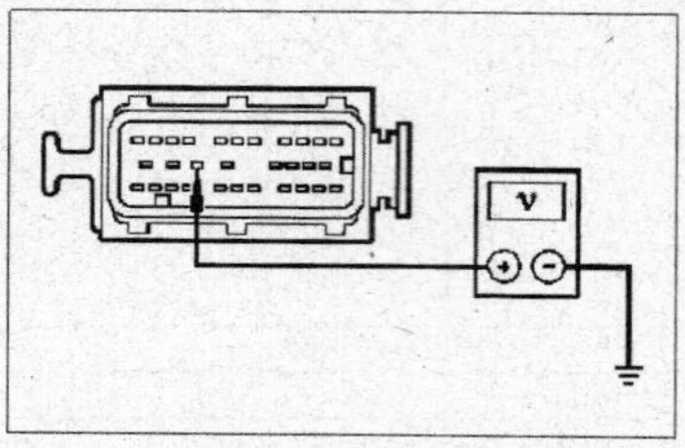	3 Measure the voltage between anti-lock brake control module C135 Pin 14, Circuit 532 (OG/YE), harness side and ground. • **Is the voltage less than 5 volts?** → **Yes** REPAIR the open in Circuit 532 (OG/YE). CLEAR the DTCs. REPEAT the self-test. → **No** GO to I3 .

FM4020101857020X

Fig. 33 Test I: ABS Valve Power Relay Circuit Failure (Part 2 of 3). 2002–04 Less Traction Control

I3 CHECK CIRCUIT 1205 (BK) FOR AN OPEN	
1 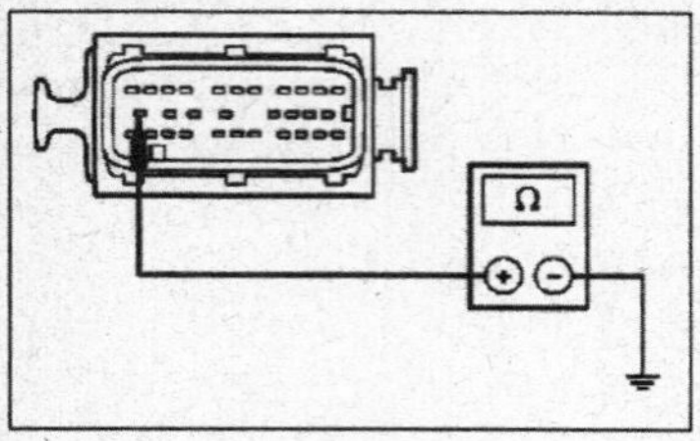	1 Measure the resistance between anti-lock brake control module C135 Pin 12, Circuit 1205 (BK), harness side and ground. • **Is the resistance less than 5 ohms?** → **Yes** INSTALL a new anti-lock brake control module. CLEAR the DTCs. REPEAT the self-test. → **No** REPAIR the circuit. CLEAR the DTCs. REPEAT the self-test.

FM4020101857030X

Fig. 33 Test I: ABS Valve Power Relay Circuit Failure (Part 3 of 3). 2002–04 Less Traction Control

CONDITIONS	DETAILS/RESULTS/ACTIONS
J1 CHECK THE ABS WARNING INDICATOR CIRCUITRY	
1 	
2  Anti-Lock Brake Control Module C135	
3 	
	4 Depress and release the shorting bar connector internal to the anti-lock brake control module C135, harness side, while checking the yellow ABS warning indicator in the instrument cluster. • **Does the yellow ABS indicator illuminate with the shorting bar released and turn OFF with the shorting bar depressed?** → **Yes** INSTALL a new anti-lock brake control module. TEST the system for normal operation. → **No** Diagnose instrument cluster.

FM4020101858000X

Fig. 34 Test J: Yellow ABS Warning Indicator Does Not Self-Check. 2002–04 Less Traction Control

CONDITIONS	DETAILS/RESULTS/ACTIONS
K1 CHECK THE VEHICLE COMPONENTS	
	1 Check the brake pedal and power booster/brake master cylinder for correct attachment. • **Are the components OK?** → **Yes** GO to K2 . → **No** REPAIR as necessary. TEST the system for normal operation.
K2 BLEED THE BRAKE SYSTEM	
	1 Bleed the brake system. 2 Check for spongy brake pedal. • **Is the brake pedal spongy?** → **Yes** INSTALL a new HCU. TEST the system for normal operation. → **No** The brake system is OK. TEST the system for normal operation.

FM4020101859000X

Fig. 35 Test K: Spongy Pedal w/No Warning Indicator. 2002–04 Less Traction Control

CONDITIONS	DETAILS/RESULTS/ACTIONS
L1 BLEED THE BRAKE SYSTEM	
	1 Bleed the brake system. 2 Check for vehicle tracking poorly. • **Does the vehicle track poorly?** → **Yes** GO to L2 . → **No** The brake system is OK. TEST the system for normal operation.
L2 CHECK THE LF ABS VALVE OPERATION	
	1 Lift the vehicle and rotate all the wheels to make sure they rotate freely (the vehicle must be in neutral). 2 **NOTE:** Trigger must be depressed twice. Each press will run the pump motor for two seconds. Trigger the anti-lock brake control module active command PMP MOTOR ON for four seconds. 3 Apply moderate brake pedal effort. 4 Have an assistant attempt to rotate the LF wheel while the pump motor is running. • **Does the LF wheel rotate?** → **Yes** INSTALL a new HCU. TEST the system for normal operation. → **No** GO to L3 .

FM4020101860010X

Fig. 36 Test L: Poor Vehicle Tracking During Anti-Lock Function (Part 1 of 4). 2002–04 Less Traction Control

L3 CHECK THE LF ABS VALVE RELEASE	
1 Apply moderate brake pedal effort. 2 Trigger the anti-lock brake control module active command LF INLET and LF OUTLET. 3 **NOTE:** The scan tool will energize the valves for only two seconds per trigger press. Have an assistant rotate the LF wheel immediately after depressing trigger. • **Does the LF wheel rotate?** → **Yes** GO to L4 . → **No** GO to L8 .	
L4 CHECK THE RF ABS VALVE OPERATION	
1 **NOTE:** Trigger must be depressed twice. Each press will run the pump motor for two seconds. Trigger the anti-lock brake control module active command PMP MOTOR ON for four seconds. 2 Apply moderate brake pedal effort. 3 Have an assistant attempt to rotate the RF wheel while the pump motor is running. • **Does the RF wheel rotate?** → **Yes** INSTALL a new HCU. TEST the system for normal operation. → **No** GO to L5 .	

FM4020101860020X

Fig. 36 Test L: Poor Vehicle Tracking During Anti-Lock Function (Part 2 of 4). 2002–04 Less Traction Control

L5 CHECK THE RF ABS VALVE RELEASE	
1 Apply moderate brake pedal effort. 2 Trigger the anti-lock brake control module active command RF INLET and RF OUTLET. 3 **NOTE:** The scan tool will energize the valves for only two seconds per trigger press. Have an assistant rotate the RF wheel immediately after depressing trigger. • **Does the RF wheel rotate?** → **Yes** GO to L6 . → **No** GO to L8 .	
L6 CHECK THE REAR ABS VALVE OPERATION	
1 **NOTE:** Trigger must be depressed twice.Each press will run the pump motor for two seconds. Trigger the anti-lock brake control module active command PMP MOTOR ON for four seconds. 2 Apply moderate brake pedal effort. 3 Have an assistant attempt to rotate the LR and RR wheels while the pump motor is running. • **Does the LR or RR wheel rotate?** → **Yes** INSTALL a new HCU. TEST the system for normal operation. → **No** GO to L7 .	

FM4020101860030X

Fig. 36 Test L: Poor Vehicle Tracking During Anti-Lock Function (Part 3 of 4). 2002–04 Less Traction Control

L7 CHECK THE REAR ABS VALVE RELEASE

1. Apply moderate brake pedal effort.
2. Trigger the anti-lock brake control module active command R INLET and R OUTLET.
3. **NOTE:** The scan tool will energize the valves for only two seconds per trigger press.

   Have an assistant rotate the LR and RR wheels immediately after depressing trigger.

- **Does the LR or RR wheel rotate?**

→ **Yes**
The ABS system is operating correctly.

→ **No**
GO to L8.

L8 CHECK FOR DTCS

1. Carry out the anti-lock brake control module self-test.

- **Are any DTCs retrieved?**

→ **Yes**
GO to the Anti-Lock Brake Control Module Diagnostic Trouble Code (DTC) Index.

→ **No**
INSTALL a new HCU. TEST the system for normal operation.

FM4020101860040X

Fig. 36 Test L: Poor Vehicle Tracking During Anti-Lock Function (Part 4 of 4). 2002–04 Less Traction Control

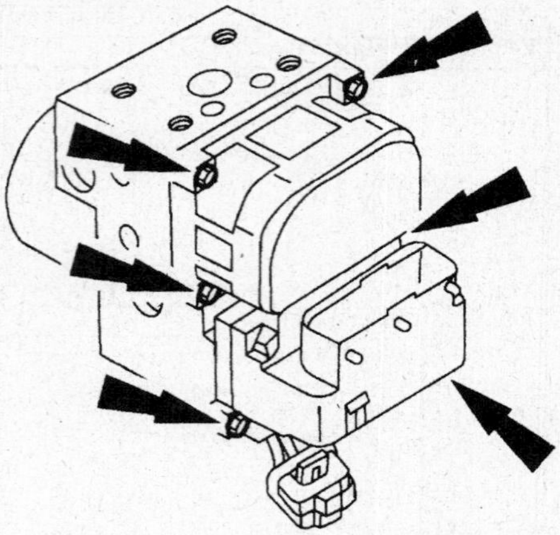

FM4020101861000X

Fig. 37 ABS control module replacement

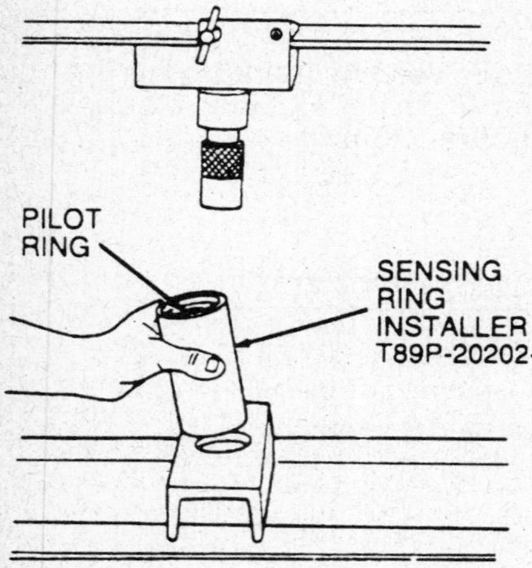

FM4029400508000X

Fig. 38 Sensing ring installer tool positioning

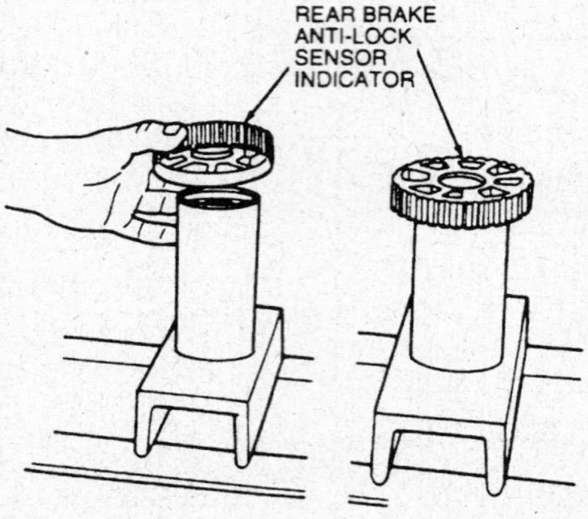

FM4029400509000X

Fig. 39 Anti-lock sensor indicator position

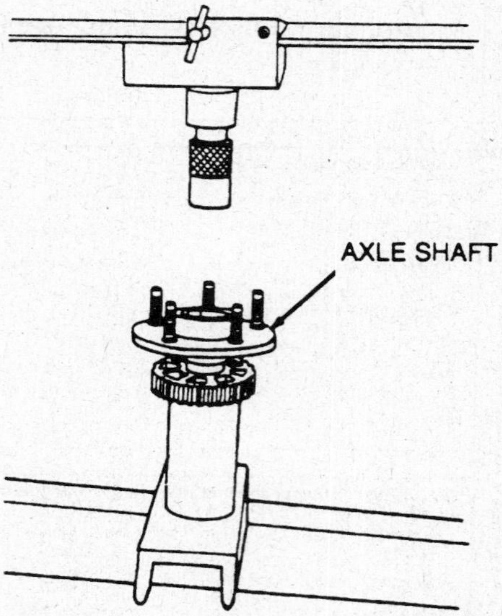

FM4029400510000X

Fig. 40 Axle shaft position

SYSTEM SERVICE

Brake System Bleed

MANUAL

The primary and secondary (front and rear) hydraulic brake systems are individual systems and are bled separately. Bleed longest tube first on individual system being serviced. **During complete bleeding operation, DO NOT allow the master cylinder reservoir to run dry. Never reuse brake fluid that has been drained from hydraulic system or has been allowed to stand in an open container for an extended period of time.**

1. To bleed brake system, position a suitable box wrench on bleeder fitting on brake wheel cylinder. Attach rubber drain hose to bleeder fitting.
2. Submerge free end of tube in a container partially filled with clean brake fluid and loosen bleeder fitting approximately three-quarters of a turn.
3. Have an assistant push brake pedal down slowly through its full travel. Close bleeder fitting and repeat operation until air bubbles cease to appear at submerged end of bleeder hose tube.
4. When fluid is completely free of air bubbles, secure bleeder fitting and remove bleeder tube.
5. Repeat this procedure at brake wheel cylinder on opposite side. Refill master cylinder reservoir after each wheel cylinder is bled and install master cylinder cap and gasket.
6. Make sure diaphragm type gasket is properly positioned in master cylinder cap.
7. When bleeding operation is completed the fluid level should be at the MAX line.
8. If primary (front brake) system is to bled, repeat steps starting at righthand front brake caliper and ending at lefthand front brake caliper. Bleed brake master cylinder at bleed screw after all caliper are bled.
9. After disc brake service, make sure the disc brake pistons are returned to normal positions and shoe and lining assemblies are properly seated. This is accomplished by applying brake pedal several times until normal pedal travel is established.

PRESSURE

For pressure bleeding, use a bladder-type bleeder tank only. Rotunda Brake Bleeder tool No. 104–00064, or equivalent. Bleed longest tubes first on system being bled. The bleeder tank should contain enough new brake fluid to complete bleeding operation. **Never reuse brake fluid that has been drained from hydraulic system.** The pressure bleeder tank should be charged with approximately 10-30 psi of air pressure.

1. Clean all dirt from master cylinder filler cap, then remove cap.
2. Fill master cylinder reservoir with specified brake fluid. Install pressure bleeder adapter tool to master cylinder and adapter.
3. Bleed master cylinder.

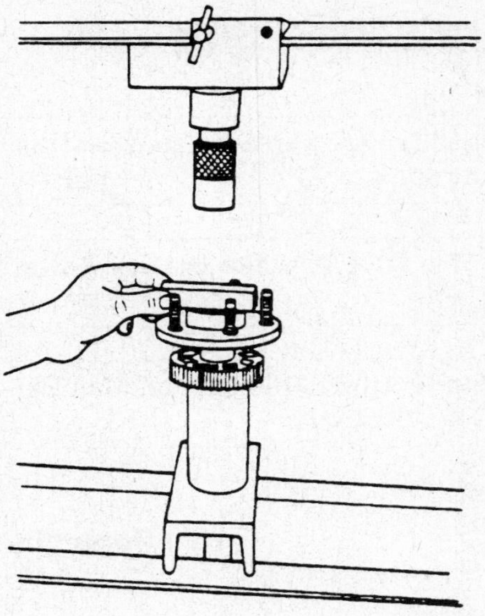

Fig. 41 Steel piece to axle shaft position

4. If rear disc brake calipers are to be bled, start with left rear disc brake caliper and attach bleed tube snugly around wheel cylinder bleeder screw fitting.
5. Open valve on bleeder tank to release pressurized brake fluid into brake master cylinder reservoir.
6. Submerge free end of tube in container partially filled with clean brake fluid and loosen wheel cylinder bleeder screw.
7. When bubbles cease to appear in fluid, close bleeder screw, then remove tube and replace rubber dust cap on bleeder screw.
8. Repeat steps for right rear disc brake caliper.
9. Attach a bleed tube to front brake caliper starting at caliper with longest brake tube and ending with shortest tube.
10. After all calipers have been bled, bleed brake master cylinder using bleed screws on master cylinder.
11. When bleeding operation is completed, close bleeder tank valve and remove tank hose from adapter fitting.
12. After disc brake service, make sure disc brake pistons are returned to their normal position and shoe lining assemblies are properly seated. Press brake pedal several times until normal pedal travel is established.
13. Remove pressure bleeder adapter tool from master cylinder, then fill master cylinder and install cap.

Component Replacement

HYDRAULIC CONTROL UNIT (HCU)

1. Disconnect ABS control module electrical connector.
2. Disconnect brake lines from HCU, then remove bracket nuts to HCU.
3. Remove HCU.
4. Reverse procedure to install noting the following:
   a. **Torque** HCU attaching nuts to 13 ft. lbs.
   b. **Torque** brake lines to 14 ft. lbs.
   c. Bleed brake system.

ABS CONTROL MODULE

1. Remove hydraulic control unit as outlined in "Hydraulic Control Unit."
2. Disconnect pump motor electrical connector.
3. Remove ABS control module screws, **Fig. 37.**
4. Reverse procedure to install. Bleed brake system.

FRONT BRAKE ABS SENSORS

1. Raise and support vehicle, then remove front wheel and tire assembly.
2. Remove inner fender splash shield, then disconnect ABS wheel sensor electrical connector.
3. Remove wheel sensor harness from harness clips.
4. Remove sensor bolt, then the wheel sensor.
5. Reverse procedure to install. **Torque** sensor bolt to 62 inch lbs.

REAR BRAKE ABS SENSORS

1. Remove rear passenger seat, then disconnect ABS brake sensor electrical connector.
2. Raise and support vehicle, then remove rear ABS sensor harness from floor pan.
3. Remove sensor harness bracket bolt.
4. Remove bolt, then the wheel speed sensor.
5. Reverse procedure noting the following:
   a. Apply Nickel Anti-Sieze Lubricant part No. F6AZ-9L494-AA, or equivalent, to wheel sensor bolt.
   b. **Torque** wheel sensor bolt to 62 inch lbs.

FRONT ABS SENSOR INDICATOR

The front brake anti-lock sensor indicator is not serviceable. If the sensor indicator is damaged, the wheel hub must be replaced.

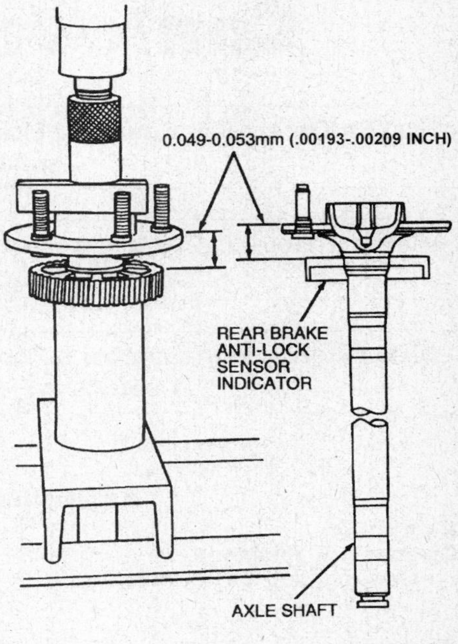

Fig. 42 Rear brake anti-lock sensor indicator installation clearance

REAR ABS SENSOR INDICATOR

Do not allow axle shaft flange to contact press bed during rear brake anti-lock sensor indicator removal.

Once a rear brake anti-lock sensor indicator has been removed, it must be replaced with a new rear brake anti-lock sensor indicator.

1. Remove axle shaft as outlined in "Rear Drive Axles" chapter.
2. Place axle shaft in press, and remove sensor indicator using bearing pulling attachment tool No. D79L-4621-A, or equivalent.
3. Position sensing ring installer tool No. T89P-20202-A, or equivalent, on press with pilot ring up, **Fig. 38.**
4. Place new sensor indicator on sensor ring installer tool, **Fig. 39. Ensure sensor indicator is positioned as outlined.**
5. Position axle shaft, **Fig. 40,** then flat piece of steel on shaft, **Fig. 41.**
6. Press sensor indicator onto shaft to specified dimension, **Fig. 42.**
7. Install axle shaft as outlined in "Rear Drive Axles" chapter.

Contour, Cougar & Mystique

NOTE: On Air Bag Equipped Models, Refer To "Air Bag System Precautions" Located In The Front Of This Manual For System Disarming & Arming Procedures.

NOTE: Refer To "Computer Relearn Procedures" Located In The Front Of This Manual When Battery Power To The Computer Has Been Interrupted.

NOTE: "Electrical Symbol & Wire Color Code Identification" Located In The Front Of This Manual May Be Used As An Aid When Using Wiring Circuits Found In This Section.

INDEX

PRECAUTIONS

Air Bag Systems

Refer to "Air Bag System Precautions" in the front of this manual for system disarming and arming procedures.

Battery Ground Cable

Prior to service, disconnect battery ground cable and isolate as required.

Hydraulic Brake Fluid Color

Hydraulic brake fluid must conform with the requirements of Federal Motor Vehicle Safety Standard 116. Under this standard, brake fluids are visually different from other automotive fluids such as transmission, power steering and engine.

Fluid color in a normal brake system may vary from its original color for many reasons. A brake master cylinder may show significantly different shades fluid color between the two brake master cylinder reservoirs. Color may also appear to vary between cast steel and die cast aluminum reservoirs. Some reasons for discoloration include the following:

1. Heat and/or aging.
2. Different operation temperatures or different rates of normal oxidation between two reservoir compartments.
3. Different brands and/or shades of fluid are used when topping off during normal service.
4. Dissolution of color dye used on master cylinder internal springs during assembly.

Brake fluid contaminated with hydrocarbon/mineral based fluid (power steering or transmission fluid) can be detected by an obvious swelling of the master cylinder cap gasket. If the master cylinder cap gasket is swollen, all brake system rubber components must be replaced. All brake tubes and hoses must be thoroughly flushed with Ford Heavy Duty Brake Fluid C6AZ-19542-AA or -BA or DOT-3 equivalent before the vehicle returns to service.

DESCRIPTION

The anti-lock brake system operates using a control unit and sensors as follows, wheel lock-up is prevented during heavy braking by modulating brake pressure. The system permits the driver to maintain steering control and stop vehicle in the shortest possible distance under most conditions. During the anti-lock brake operation, the driver will sense a pulsation in the brake pedal and hear a clicking sound. The pedal effort and pedal feel during normal braking are similar to that of a conventional power brake system.

The Hydraulic Control Unit (HCU) is an integrated unit and is located below the brake booster. The HCU consists of an electronic control unit equipped with relays, valve body, pump motor, anti-lock control module and an anti-lock brake relay, **Fig. 1.** The HCU is a non-repairable unit, must be replaced as an assembly.

The Anti-lock Braking System (ABS) control module receives wheel speed readings from each wheel speed sensor and processes this information to determine if an ABS event is required. The wheel speed sensor electrically senses each tooth of the ABS sensor indicators as it passes through the wheel speed sensors magnetic field. The ABS control module continuously monitors and compares the rotational speed of each wheel. When the module detects an impending wheel lock, it modulates brake pressure to the appropriate brake caliper. This is accomplished by triggering the HCU to open and close the appropriate solenoid valves.

The ABS control module is self-monitoring. When the ignition switch is turned to the RUN position, the ABS control module will do a preliminary electrical inspection. At 12 mph, the pump motor is turned on for approximately one-half second. Also, during all phases of operation the ABS control module inspects for correct operation of the wheel speed sensors. Any fault of the ABS system will cause the ABS to shut off however, normal power assisted braking is maintained. The ABS control module has the ability to store three DTC's in its memory.

TROUBLESHOOTING

Inspection & Verification

1. Verify customer concern by operating the system.
2. Visually inspect for obvious signs of mechanical or electrical damage, **Fig. 2.**
3. If an obvious cause for an observed or reported concern is found, correct the cause before proceeding on the further steps.

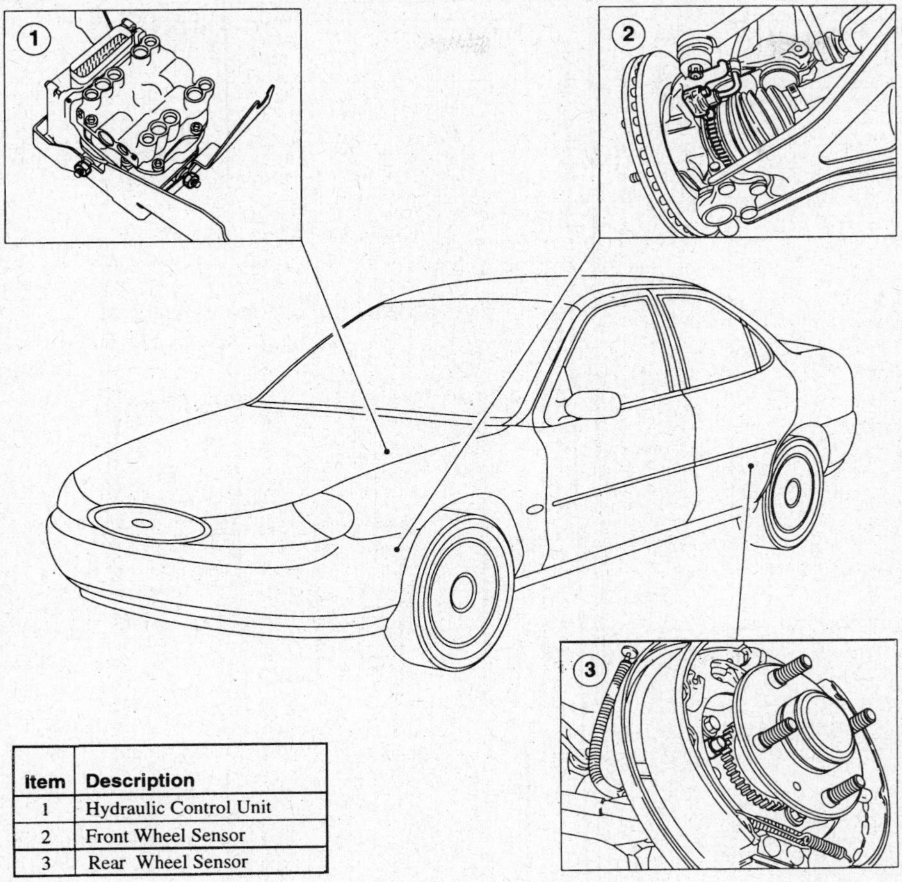

Item	Description
1	Hydraulic Control Unit
2	Front Wheel Sensor
3	Rear Wheel Sensor

Fig. 1 Anti-lock brake system component locations

4. If the concern remains after the inspection, connect scan tool to data link connector (DLC).
5. Perform DATA LINK DIAGNOSTIC TEST. If scan tool responds with:
   a. CKT914, CKT915 or CKT70 – ALL ECUS NO RESP/NOT EQUIP.
   b. NO RESP/NOT EQUIP for anti-lock brake control module, go to Test A.
   c. SYSTEM PASSED, retrieve and record the continuous diagnostic trouble codes, erase the continuous DTC's and perform self-test diagnostics for the anti-lock brake control module.
6. If the DTCs retrieved are related to the concern, go to Anti-Lock Brake Module Diagnostic Trouble Code DTC Index to continue diagnostics.
7. If DTCs are not related to the concern, proceed to Symptom Chart to continue diagnostics.

Symptom Chart Index

Refer to **Fig. 3,** for symptom chart conditions and procedures.

DIAGNOSIS & TESTING

Accessing Diagnostic Trouble Codes

If the ABS warning lamp indicates a fault, diagnostic trouble codes are present and should be retrieved prior to ABS service. Diagnostic trouble codes may be retrieved using a Rotunda New Generation Star (NGS) tester or a suitable OBD II scan tool. The data link connector is located under the instrument panel.

Mechanical	Electrical
• Low brake fluid	• Failed fuse(s): Fuse 3 (60A), Fuse 7 (20A)
• ABS sensor(s)	• Failed ABS indicator lamp
• ABS toothed wheel(s)	• Circuit(s)
• Brake lines	• Loose or corroded connections
• Wheel bearings	

FM4020101802000X

Fig. 2 ABS visual inspection

Diagnostic Trouble Code Interpretation

Refer to **Fig. 4,** for diagnostic trouble code interpretation.

Wiring Diagrams

CONTOUR & MYSTIQUE

Refer to **Figs. 5 and 6,** for wiring diagrams.

COUGAR

Refer to **Figs. 7 through 10,** for wiring diagrams.

Diagnostic Tests

Refer to **Figs. 11 through 24,** for diagnostic test procedures.

Clearing Diagnostic Trouble Codes

Follow instructions on NGS tester or scan tool screen to erase diagnostic trouble codes from memory.

Condition	Possible Sources	Action
• No communication with the anti-lock brake control module	• Fuse. • Circuit. • ABS control module.	• GO to Pinpoint Test A.
• Unable to enter self-test – communication OK	• ABS control module.	• GO to Pinpoint Test B.
• The red brake warning indicator does not self-check	• Low brake fluid warning switch. • Circuit. • Instrument cluster. • Ignition switch. • Parking brake.	
• The red brake warning indicator stays on when the ignition switch is in RUN	• Low brake fluid warning switch. • Circuit. • Instrument cluster. • Ignition switch . • Parking brake.	
• The yellow ABS warning indicator does not self-check – Always on, NO DTCs	• Circuit. • ABS control module. • Instrument cluster.	• GO to Pinpoint Test I.
• Spongy brake pedal with no warning indicator	• Air in hydraulic brake system. • Base brake system.	• GO to Pinpoint Test J.
• Poor vehicle tracking during anti-lock function	• Air in hydraulic brake system. • Hydraulic control unit. • Base brake system.	• GO to Pinpoint Test K.

FM4020101803010X

Fig. 3 Symptom chart index (Part 1 of 2)

DTC	Description	Source	Action
B1318	Battery Voltage Low	ABS/TC	GO to Pinpoint Test C.
B1484	Brake Pedal Input Open Circuit	ABS/TC	GO to Pinpoint Test D.
C1095	ABS Hydraulic Pump Motor Circuit Failure	ABS/TC	GO to Pinpoint Test E.
C1145	RF Wheel Speed Sensor Input Circuit Failure	ABS/TC	GO to Pinpoint Test F.
C1155	LF Wheel Speed Sensor Input Circuit Failure	ABS/TC	GO to Pinpoint Test F.
C1165	RR Wheel Speed Sensor Input Circuit Failure	ABS/TC	GO to Pinpoint Test F.
C1175	LR Wheel Speed Sensor Input Circuit Failure	ABS/TC	GO to Pinpoint Test F.
C1222	Wheel Speed Signal Mismatch	ABS/TC	GO to Pinpoint Test G.
C1233	LF Wheel Speed Input Signal Missing	ABS/TC	GO to Pinpoint Test H.
C1234	RF Wheel Speed Input Signal Missing	ABS/TC	GO to Pinpoint Test H.
C1235	RR Wheel Speed Input Signal Missing	ABS/TC	GO to Pinpoint Test H.
C1236	LR Wheel Speed Input Signal Missing	ABS/TC	GO to Pinpoint Test H.

FM4020101805000X

Fig. 4 Diagnostic trouble code interpretation

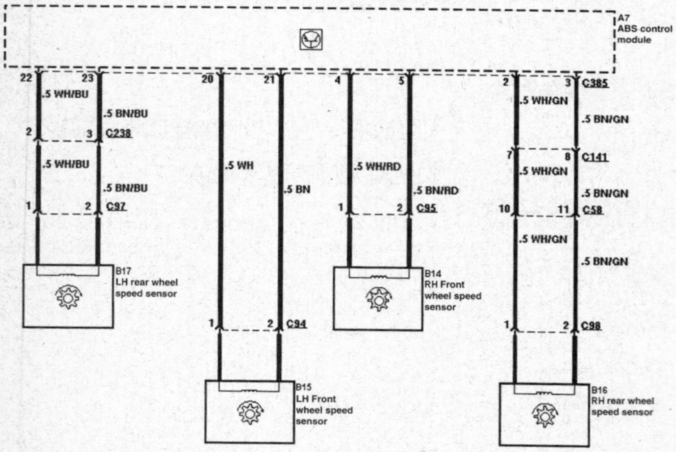

FM4029901332020X

Fig. 5 Wiring diagram (Part 2 of 2). Contour & Mystique less traction control

Condition	Possible Sources	Action
• The traction control is inoperative	• Circuit. • ABS control module. • Hydraulic control unit.	• GO to Pinpoint Test L.
• The traction control switch indicator is inoperative	• Circuit. • Traction control switch. • ABS control module.	• GO to Pinpoint Test M.
• The traction control cannot be disabled	• Circuit. • Traction control switch. • ABS control module.	• GO to Pinpoint Test N.
• The traction control indicator stays on continuously with no DTCs retrieved	• Circuit. • Instrument cluster. • ABS control module.	

FM4020101803020X

Fig. 3 Symptom chart index (Part 2 of 2)

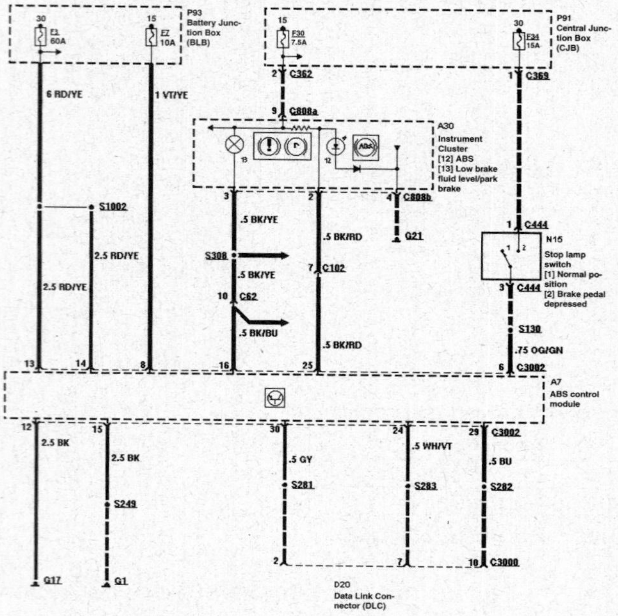

FM4029901332010X

Fig. 5 Wiring diagram (Part 1 of 2). Contour & Mystique less traction control

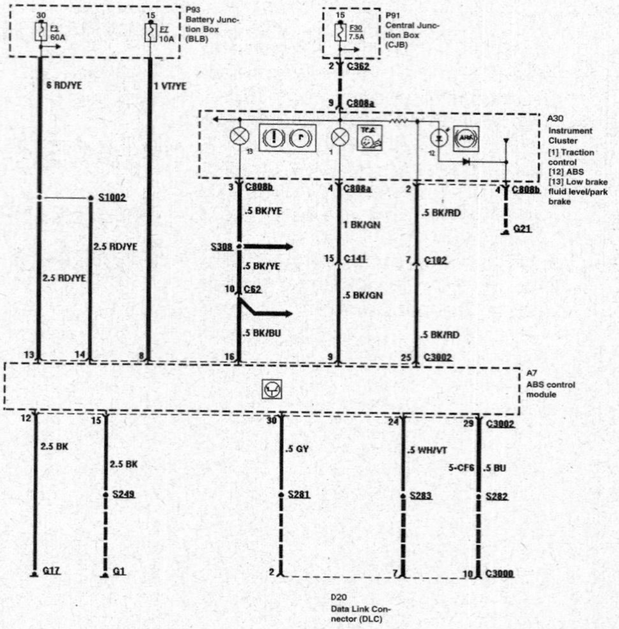

FM4029901333010X

Fig. 6 Wiring diagram (Part 1 of 2). Contour & Mystique w/traction control

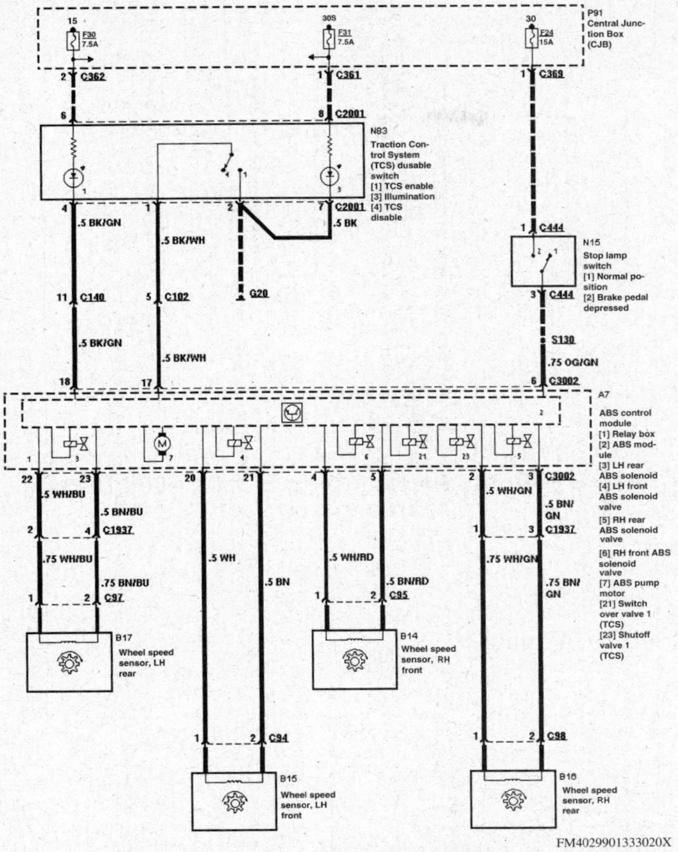

Fig. 6 Wiring diagram (Part 2 of 2). Contour & Mystique w/traction control

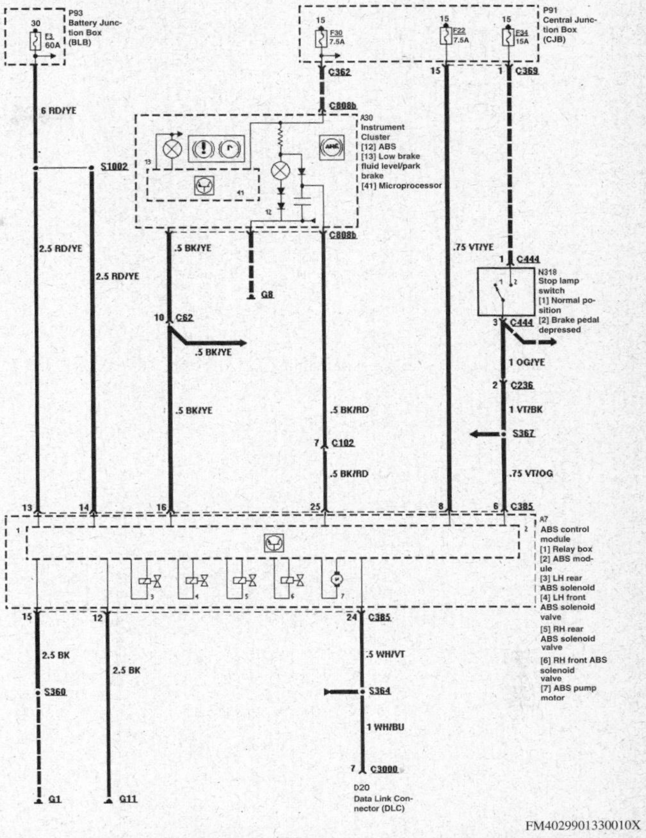

Fig. 7 Wiring diagram (Part 1 of 2). 2000 Cougar less traction control

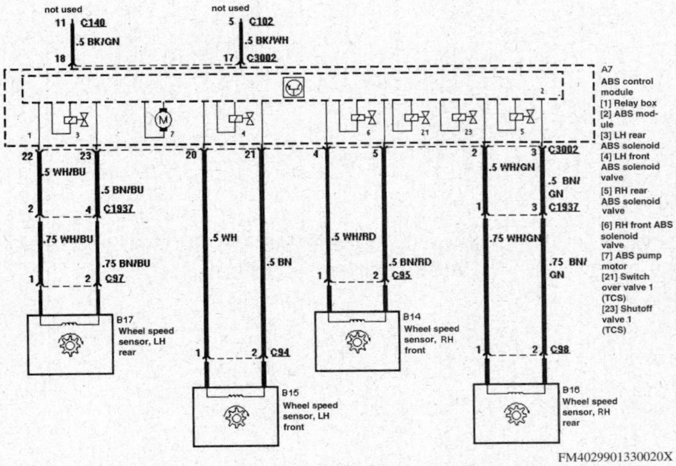

Fig. 7 Wiring diagram (Part 2 of 2). 2000 Cougar less traction control

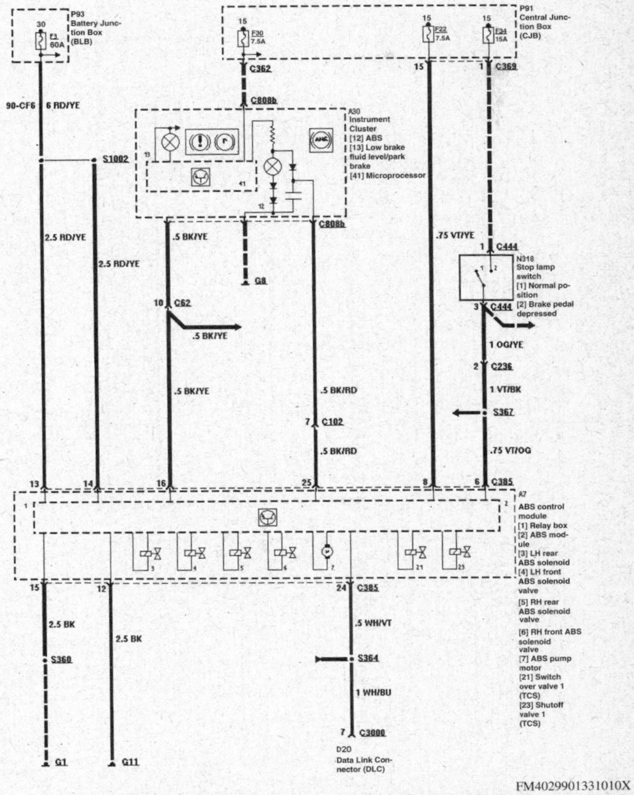

Fig. 8 Wiring diagram (Part 1 of 3). 2000 Cougar w/traction control

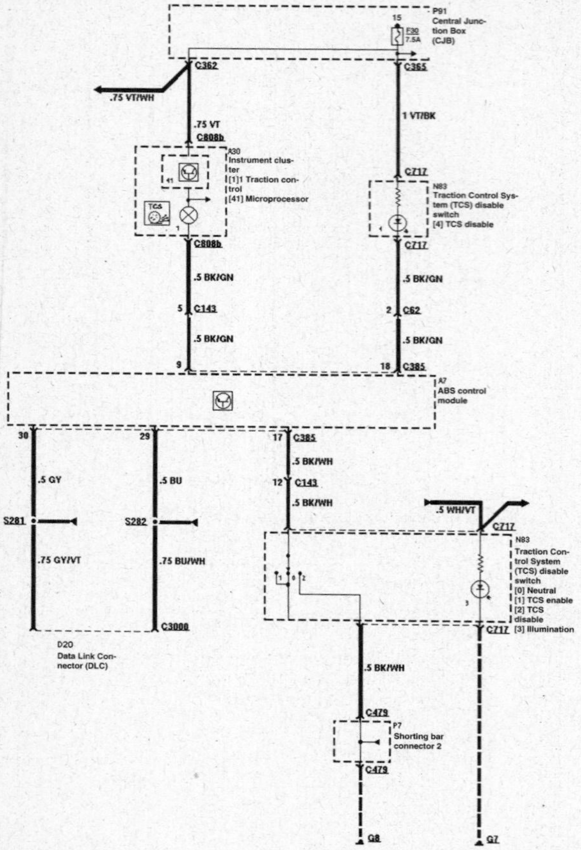

FM4029901331020X

Fig. 8 Wiring diagram (Part 2 of 3). 2000 Cougar w/traction control

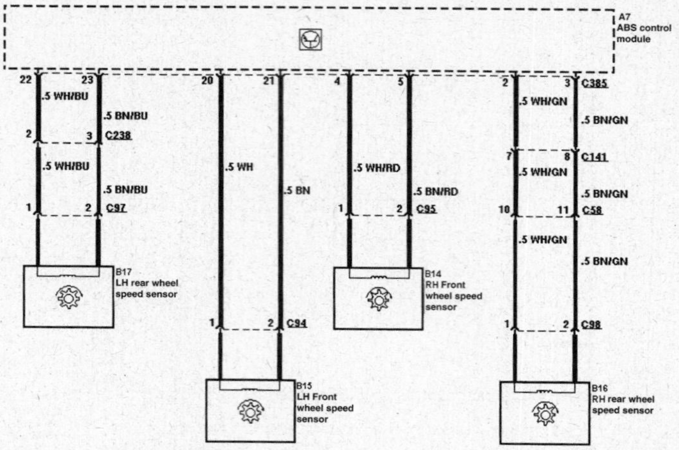

FM4029901331030X

Fig. 8 Wiring diagram (Part 3 of 3). 2000 Cougar w/traction control

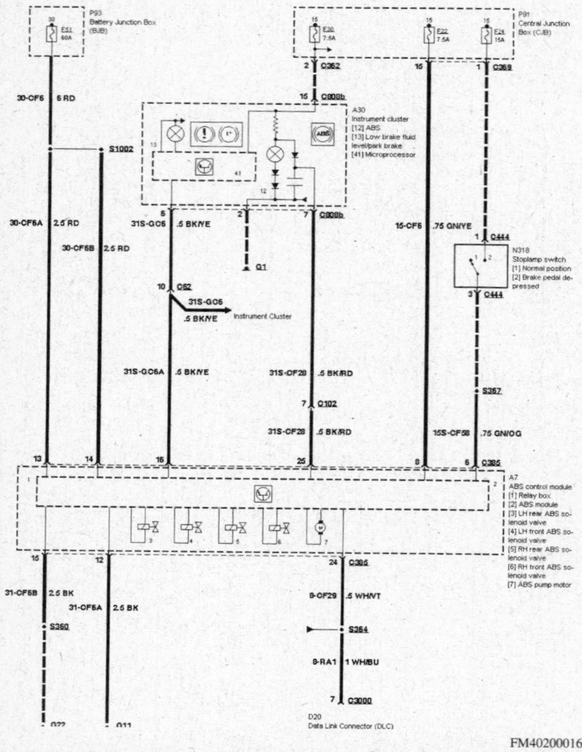

FM4020001663010X

Fig. 9 Wiring diagram (Part 1 of 2). 2001–02 Cougar less traction control

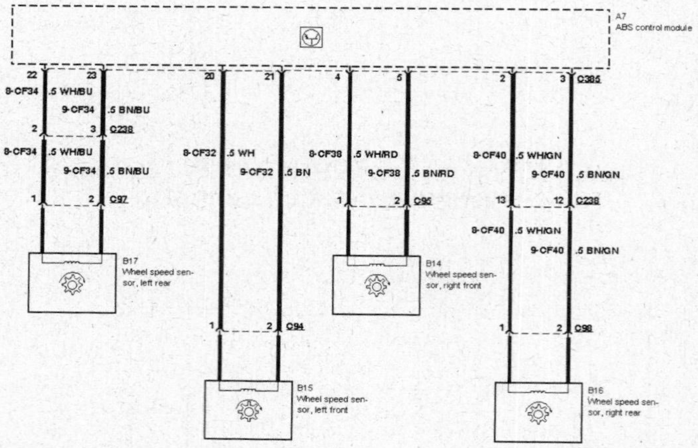

FM4020001663020X

Fig. 9 Wiring diagram (Part 2 of 2). 2001–02 Cougar less traction control

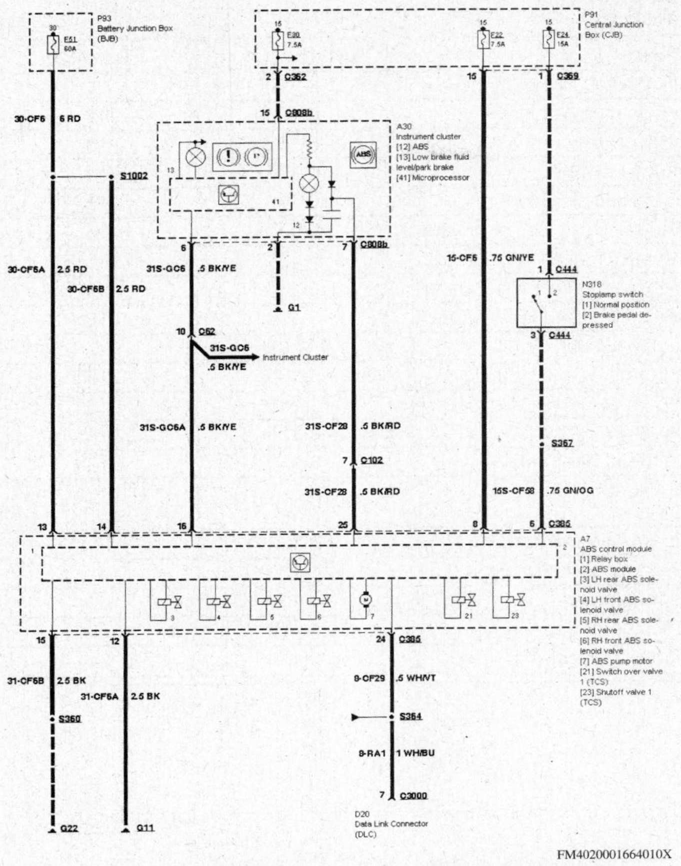

FM4020001664010X

Fig. 10 Wiring diagram (Part 1 of 3). 2001–02 Cougar w/traction control

FM4020001664020X

Fig. 10 Wiring diagram (Part 2 of 3). 2001–02 Cougar w/traction control

FM4020001664030X

Fig. 10 Wiring diagram (Part 3 of 3). 2001–02 Cougar w/traction control

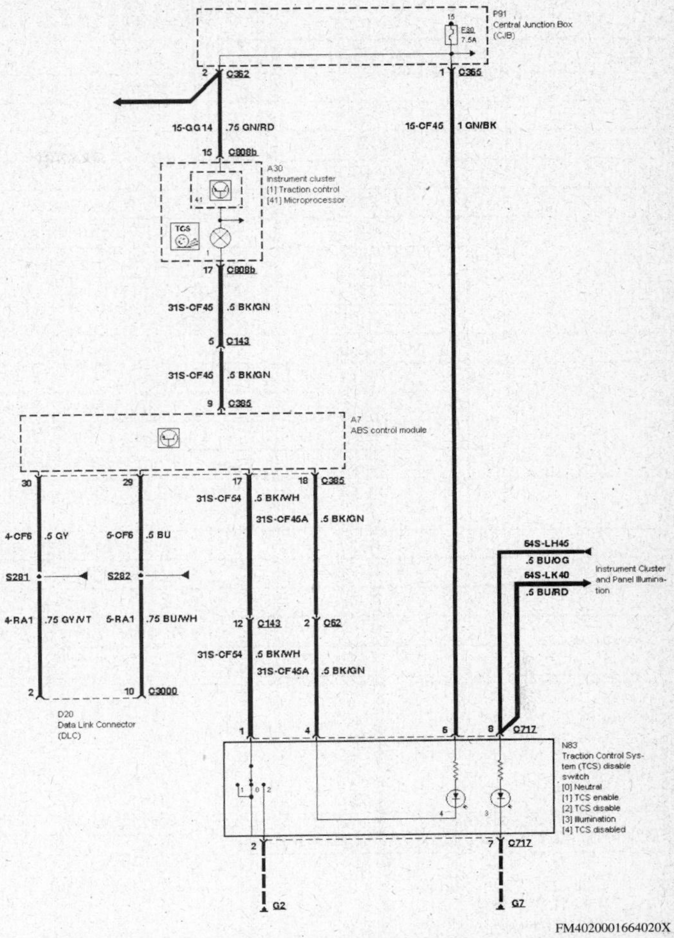

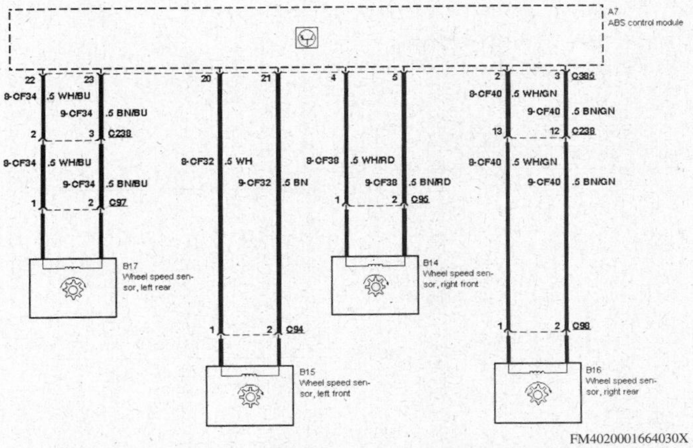

DIAGNOSTIC CHART INDEX

CONDITIONS	DETAILS/RESULTS/ACTIONS
A1 CHECK THE CENTRAL JUNCTION BOX (CJB) FUSE 7 (10A)	
1 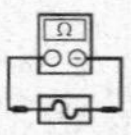 CJB fuse 7 (10A)	

FM4020101815010X

Fig. 11 Test A: No Communication w/Anti-Lock Brake Control Module (Part 1 of 3)

CONDITIONS	DETAILS/RESULTS/ACTIONS
	• Is the fuse OK? → **Yes** GO to **A2.** → **No** INSTALL a new fuse. CLEAR the DTCs. REPEAT the self-test. If the fuse fails again, CHECK for short to ground. REPAIR as necessary. CLEAR the DTCs. REPEAT the self-test.
A2 CHECK CIRCUIT 14-CF6 (VT/YE) FOR AN OPEN	
1  ABS Control Module 2 	3 Measure the Voltage between ABS control module connector pin 8, circuit 14-CF6 (VT/YE), wiring harness side and ground. • Is the voltage greater than 10 volts? → **Yes** GO to **A3.** → **No** REPAIR the circuit. CLEAR the DTCs. REPEAT the self-test.

FM4020101815020X

Fig. 11 Test A: No Communication w/Anti-Lock Brake Control Module (Part 2 of 3)

CONDITIONS	DETAILS/RESULTS/ACTIONS
A3 CHECK CIRCUIT 31-CF6A (BK) AND CIRCUIT 31-CF6B (BK) FOR AN OPEN CIRCUIT	
1 	2 Measure the resistance between ABS control module connector pin 12, circuit 31-CF6A (BK), harness side and ground, and between ABS control module connector pin 15, circuit 31-CF6B (BK), harness side and ground. • Are the resistances less than 5 ohms? → **Yes** → **No** REPAIR the circuit. CLEAR the DTCs. REPEAT the self-test.

FM4020101815030X

Fig. 11 Test A: No Communication w/Anti-Lock Brake Control Module (Part 3 of 3)

CONDITIONS	DETAILS/RESULTS/ACTIONS
B1 CHECK THE COMMUNICATION TO THE ABS CONTROL MODULE	
	1 Check the communication to the ABS control module. • Does NGS Tester communicate with the ABS control module? → **Yes** Diagnose Module Communications → **No** GO to Pinpoint Test A.

FM4020101816000X

Fig. 12 Test B: Unable To Enter Self-Test Communication OK

CONDITIONS	DETAILS/RESULTS/ACTIONS
C1 CHECK THE BATTERY VOLTAGE	
	1 Measure the voltage between the positive and negative battery posts. • Is the voltage greater than 10 volts? → **Yes** GO to **C2.** → **No** REPAIR the charging system.
C2 CHECK CIRCUIT 14-CF6 (VT/YE)	
1 2 3 	4 Measure the voltage between ABs control module C3002 pin 8, circuit 14-CF6 (VT/YE), harness side and ground. • Is the voltage greater than 10 volts? → **Yes** GO to **C3.** → **No** REPAIR the circuit. CLEAR the DTCs. REPEAT the self-test.

FM4020101817010X

Fig. 13 Test C/Code B1318: Battery Voltage Low (Part 1 of 2)

CONDITIONS	DETAILS/RESULTS/ACTIONS
C3 CHECK CIRCUIT 31-CF6A (BK) AND CIRCUIT 31-CF6B (BK) FOR AN OPEN	
1 	2 Measure the resistance between ABS control module connector pin 12, circuit 31-CF6A (BK), harness side and ground, and between ABS control module connector pin 15, circuit 31-CF6B (BK), harness side and ground. • Are the resistances less than 5 ohms? → **Yes** CLEAR the DTCs. REPEAT the self-test. If DTC B1318 is retrieved again, INSTALL a new hydraulic control unit (HCU). REPEAT the self-test. If no DTCs are retrieved the system is operating normally. → **No** REPAIR the circuit. CLEAR the DTCs. REPEAT the self-test.

FM4020101817020X

Fig. 13 Test C/Code B1318: Battery Voltage Low (Part 2 of 2)

CONDITIONS	DETAILS/RESULTS/ACTIONS
D1 CHECK THE STOPLAMPS	
	1 Depress the brake pedal while checking the stoplamps. • Do the stoplamps illuminate? → **Yes** GO to **D2.** → **No** Diagnose Exterior Lighting

FM4020101818010X

Fig. 14 Test D/Code B1484: Brake Pedal Input Open Circuit (Part 1 of 3)

CONDITIONS	DETAILS/RESULTS/ACTIONS
D2 CHECK THE ABS CONTROL MODULE BOO_ABS PID	
1 	2 Monitor the ABS control module PID BOO_ABS, while depressing and releasing the brake pedal. • Does the ABS control module PID BOO_ABS indicate ON with the brake pedal depressed and OFF with the brake pedal released? → **Yes** CLEAR the DTCs. REPEAT the self-test. If the DTC B1484 is retrieved, INSTALL a new hydraulic control unit (HCU). REPEAT the self-test. → **No** GO to **D3.**

FM4020101818020X

Fig. 14 Test D/Code B1484: Brake Pedal Input Open Circuit (Part 2 of 3)

CONDITIONS	DETAILS/RESULTS/ACTIONS
D3 CHECK CIRCUIT 29S-CF58 (OG/GN) FOR AN OPEN CIRCUIT	
1 2 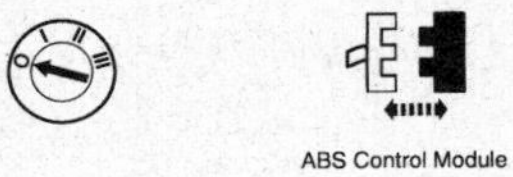	3 Measure the voltage between ABS control module connector pin 6, harness side and ground while depressing the brake pedal. • Is the voltage greater than 10 volts? → **Yes** INSTALL a new hydraulic control unit (HCU). REPEAT the self-test. → **No** REPAIR the circuit. CLEAR the DTCs. REPEAT the self-test.

FM4020101818030X

Fig. 14 Test D/Code B1484: Brake Pedal Input Open Circuit (Part 3 of 3)

CONDITIONS	DETAILS/RESULTS/ACTIONS
E1 CHECK FOR CONTINUOUS OPERATION OF THE ABS PUMP MOTOR	
1 	

FM4020101819010X

Fig. 15 Test E/Code C1095: ABS Hydraulic Pump Motor Circuit Failure (Part 1 of 3)

CONDITIONS	DETAILS/RESULTS/ACTIONS
	2 Check the ABS pump motor for continuous operation. • Is the ABS pump motor running continuously? → **Yes** INSTALL a new hydraulic control unit (HCU). REPEAT the self-test. → **No** GO to **E2.**
E2 CHECK THE BATTERY JUNCTION BOX (BJB) FUSE 3 (60A)	
1 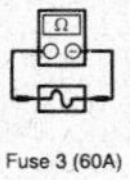	• Is the fuse OK? → **Yes** GO to **E3.** → **No** INSTALL a new fuse. CLEAR the DTCs. REPEAT the self-test. If the fuse fails again, CHECK for short to ground. REPAIR as necessary. CLEAR the DTCs. REPEAT the self-test.
E3 CHECK CIRCUIT 90-CF6A (RD/YE) FOR AN OPEN	
1 2 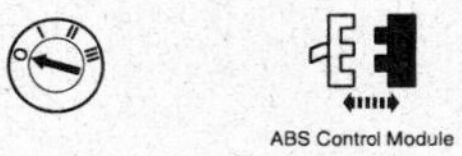	

FM4020101819020X

Fig. 15 Test E/Code C1095: ABS Hydraulic Pump Motor Circuit Failure (Part 2 of 3)

CONDITIONS	DETAILS/RESULTS/ACTIONS
	3 Measure the voltage between ABS control module connector pin 13, circuit 90-CF6A (RD/YE), harness side and ground. • Is the voltage greater than 10 volts? → **Yes** GO to **E4.** → **No** REPAIR the circuit. CLEAR the DTCs. REPEAT the self-test.
E4 CHECK CIRCUIT 31-CF6A (BK) FOR AN OPEN	
	1 Measure the resistance between ABS control module connector pin 12, circuit 31-CF6A (BK), harness side and ground. • Is the resistance less than 5 ohms? → **Yes** INSTALL a new hydraulic control unit (HCU). REPEAT the self-test. → **No** REPAIR the circuit. CLEAR the DTCs. REPEAT the self-test.

FM4020101819030X

Fig. 15 Test E/Code C1095: ABS Hydraulic Pump Motor Circuit Failure (Part 3 of 3)

CONDITIONS	DETAILS/RESULTS/ACTIONS
	4 Measure the voltage of the suspect wheel speed sensor circuit between: – (RF) ABS control module connector pin 4, circuit 8-CF38 (WH/RD), harness side and ground. – (LF) ABS control module connector pin 20, circuit 8-CF32 (WH), harness side and ground. – (RR) ABS control module connector pin 2, circuit 8-CF40 (WH/GN), harness side and ground. – (LR) ABS control module connector pin 22, circuit 8-CF34 (WH/BU), harness side and ground. • Is voltage present? → **Yes** REPAIR the circuit. CLEAR the DTCs. REPEAT the self-test. → **No** GO to **F2.**
F2 CHECK THE SUSPECT WHEEL SPEED SENSOR CIRCUIT FOR SHORT TO GROUND	
1 	

FM4020101820020X

Fig. 16 Test F/Codes C1145, C1155, C1165 & C1175: Wheel Speed Sensor Input Circuit Failure (Part 2 of 5)

CONDITIONS	DETAILS/RESULTS/ACTIONS
F1 CHECK THE SUSPECT WHEEL SPEED CIRCUIT FOR SHORT TO POWER	
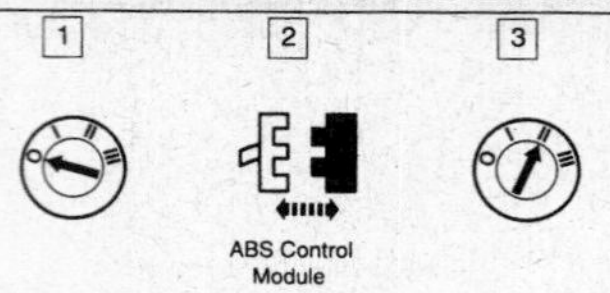	

FM4020101820010X

Fig. 16 Test F/Codes C1145, C1155, C1165 & C1175: Wheel Speed Sensor Input Circuit Failure (Part 1 of 5)

CONDITIONS	DETAILS/RESULTS/ACTIONS
	2 Measure the resistance of the suspect wheel speed sensor circuit between: – (RF) ABS control module connector pin 4, circuit 8-CF38 (WH/RD), harness side and ground. – (LF) ABS control module connector pin 20, circuit 8-CF32 (WH), harness side and ground. – (RR) ABS control module connector pin 2, circuit 8-CF40 (WH/GN), harness side and ground. – (LR) ABS control module connector pin 22, circuit 8-CF34 (WH/BU), harness side and ground. • Is the resistance infinite? → **Yes** GO to **F4.** → **No** GO to **F3.**
F3 CHECK THE SUSPECT WHEEL SPEED SENSOR FOR SHORT TO GROUND	
1 	
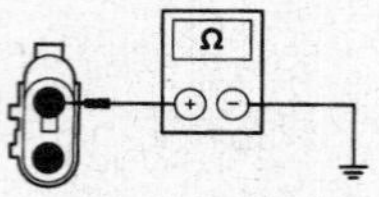	2 Measure the resistance between either suspect wheel speed sensor pin (component side) and ground. • Is the resistance infinite? → **Yes** REPAIR the circuit. CLEAR the DTCs. REPEAT the self-test. → **No** INSTALL a new wheel speed sensor. CLEAR the DTCs. REPEAT the self-test.

FM4020101820030X

Fig. 16 Test F/Codes C1145, C1155, C1165 & C1175: Wheel Speed Sensor Input Circuit Failure (Part 3 of 5)

CONDITIONS	DETAILS/RESULTS/ACTIONS
F4 CHECK THE WHEEL SPEED CIRCUITRY FOR AN OPEN OR SHORT TOGETHER	
	1 Measure the resistance between: – (RF) ABS control module connector pin 4, circuit 8-CF38 (WH/RD), harness side and ABS control module connector pin 5, circuit 9-CF38 (BN/RD), harness side. – (LF) ABS control module connector pin 20, circuit- 8CF32 (WH), harness side and ABS control module connector pin 21, circuit- 9CF32 (BN), harness side. – (RR) ABS control module connector pin 2, circuit- 8CF40 (WH/GN), harness side and ABS control module connector pin 3, circuit- 9CF40 (BN/GN), harness side. – (LR) ABS control module connector pin 22, circuit- 8CF34 (WH/BU), harness side and ABS control module connector pin 23, circuit- 9CF34 (BN/BU), harness side. • Is the resistance between 1,000 and 1,500 ohms? → **Yes** Reconnect all connections. CLEAR the DTCs. REPEAT the self-test. If DTC C1145, C1155 C1165 or C1175 is retrieved INSTALL a new hydraulic control unit (HCU). REPEAT the se-lftest. If no DTCs are retrieved the system is operating normally → **No** GO to **F5.**

FM4020101820040X

Fig. 16 Test F/Codes C1145, C1155, C1165 & C1175: Wheel Speed Sensor Input Circuit Failure (Part 4 of 5)

CONDITIONS	DETAILS/RESULTS/ACTIONS
G1 CHECK VEHICLE COMPONENTS	
NOTE: Any other wheel speed DTC must be diagnosed before proceeding. This DTC C1222 can be set during certain repair procedures with key ON, vehicle towing, on vehicle wheel balance or dynamometer testing with no actual fault.	
	1 Check for correct wheel and tire size, front to rear and side to side. 2 Check for excessive bearing end play. 3 Check the wheel speed sensor indicator for a bent sensor ring or missing teeth. • Are all the conditions OK? → **Yes** GO to **G2.** → **No** REPAIR as necessary. CLEAR the DTCs. REPEAT the self-test.

FM4020101821010X

Fig. 17 Test G/Code C1222: Wheel Speed Signal Mismatch (Part 1 of 2)

CONDITIONS	DETAILS/RESULTS/ACTIONS
F5 CHECK THE SUSPECT WHEEL SPEED SENSOR FOR AN OPEN OR SHORT TOGETHER	
1  Suspect Wheel Speed Sensor Connector	
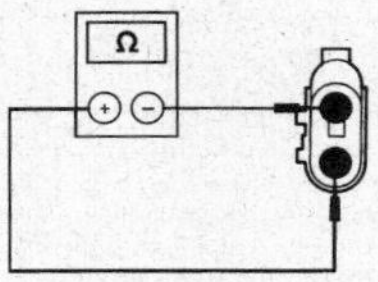	2 Measure the resistance between the suspect wheel speed sensor pins (component side). • Is resistance between 1,000 and 1,500 ohms? → **Yes** REPAIR the circuit. CLEAR the DTCs. REPEAT the self-test. → **No** INSTALL a new wheel speed sensor. CLEAR the DTCs. REPEAT the self-test.

FM4020101820050X

Fig. 16 Test F/Codes C1145, C1155, C1165 & C1175: Wheel Speed Sensor Input Circuit Failure (Part 5 of 5)

CONDITIONS	DETAILS/RESULTS/ACTIONS
G2 TEST DRIVE THE VEHICLE	
1 2 3  Clear the DTCs	
	4 Test drive the vehicle over 24 Km/h (15 mph).
5  Retrieve DTCs	• Is DTC C1222 retrieved? → **Yes** INSTALL a new hydraulic control unit (HCU). REPEAT the self-test. → **No** If another DTC is retrieved, GO to the ABS Control Module Diagnostic Trouble Code (DTC) Index. If no DTCs are retrieved, system is operating normally. If no DTCs are retrieved, system is OK.

FM4020101821020X

Fig. 17 Test G/Code C1222: Wheel Speed Signal Mismatch (Part 2 of 2). Contour, Cougar & Mystique

CONDITIONS	DETAILS/RESULTS/ACTIONS
H1 CHECK THE SUSPECT WHEEL SPEED SENSOR	
	1 Inspect the suspect wheel speed sensor mounting. Check the wheel speed sensor for excessive dirt build-up. Check for metal obstructions. Check the wheel speed sensor for damage. • Is the suspect wheel speed sensor and mounting OK? → **Yes** GO to **H2.** → **No** REPAIR or INSTALL a new wheel speed sensor. CLEAR the DTCs. REPEAT the self-test.
H2 CHECK THE SUSPECT WHEEL SPEED SENSOR INDICATOR	
	1 Check the suspect wheel speed sensor indicator for corrosion, nicks, bridged teeth, damaged teeth, and correct mounting and alignment with the wheel speed sensor. Check the air gap (less than 1 mm). Check the bearing end play. • Is the suspect ABS sensor indicator OK? → **Yes** GO to **H3.** → **No** INSTALL a new wheel speed sensor indicator. CLEAR the DTCs. REPEAT the self-test.
H3 CHECK THE SUSPECT WHEEL SPEED SENSOR PIDS	
1 2  Clear the DTCs	

FM4020101822010X

Fig. 18 Test H/Codes C1233, C1234, C1235 & C1236: Wheel Speed Input Signal Missing (Part 1 of 2)

CONDITIONS	DETAILS/RESULTS/ACTIONS
3 4 	5 Have an assistant monitor the ABS control module PIDs LF_WSPD, RF_WSPD, LR_WSPD, and RR_WSPD while driving at various speeds. 6 Test drive the vehicle for 16 km (10 miles). • Are the ABS control module PIDs reading approximately the same at all times? → **Yes** CLEAR the DTCs. REPEAT the self-test. If DTC C1233, C1234, C1235 or C1236 is retrieved INSTALL a new hydraulic control unit (HCU). REPEAT the self-test. If no DTCs are retrieved the system is operating normally. → **No** INSTALL a new wheel speed sensor. CLEAR the DTCs. REPEAT the self-test.

FM4020101822020X

Fig. 18 Test H/Codes C1233, C1234, C1235 & C1236: Wheel Speed Input Signal Missing (Part 2 of 2)

CONDITIONS	DETAILS/RESULTS/ACTIONS
I1 CHECK CIRCUIT 31S-CF28 (BK/RD) FOR SHORT TO POWER	
1 2 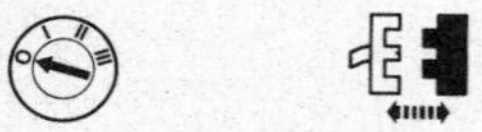 ABS Control Module C3002	

FM4020101823010X

Fig. 19 Test I: Yellow ABS Warning Indicator Does Not Self-Check Always On No DTC's (Part 1 of 3)

CONDITIONS	DETAILS/RESULTS/ACTIONS
3 4  Instrument Cluster C808b	5 Measure the voltage between instrument cluster connector C808b, circuit 31S-CF28 (BK/RD), harness side and ground. • Is voltage present? → **Yes** REPAIR the circuit. REPEAT the self-test. → **No** GO to **I2.**

FM4020101823020X

Fig. 19 Test I: Yellow ABS Warning Indicator Does Not Self-Check Always On No DTC's (Part 2 of 3)

CONDITIONS	DETAILS/RESULTS/ACTIONS
I2 CHECK CIRCUIT 31S-CF28 (BK/RD) FOR OPEN CIRCUIT	
1 	2 Measure the resistance between ABS control module connector, circuit 31S-CF28 (BK/RD), harness side and instrument cluster connector C808b, circuit 31S-CF28 (BK/RD), harness side. • Is the resistance less than 5 ohms? → **Yes** INSTALL a new hydraulic control unit (HCU). REPEAT the self-test. → **No** REPAIR the circuit. REPEAT the self-test.

FM4020101823030X

Fig. 19 Test I: Yellow ABS Warning Indicator Does Not Self-Check Always On No DTC's (Part 3 of 3)

CONDITIONS	DETAILS/RESULTS/ACTIONS
J1 CHECK THE VEHICLE COMPONENT MOUNTING	
	1 Inspect the brake pedal and brake booster/brake master cylinder for proper attachment.

FM4020101824010X

Fig. 20 Test J: Spongy Brake Pedal w/No Warning Indicator (Part 1 of 2)

CONDITIONS	DETAILS/RESULTS/ACTIONS
	2 Bleed the brake system. • Is the brake pedal spongy? → **Yes** GO to **J2.** → **No** The brake system is operating correctly. REPEAT the self-test.
J2 REBLEED THE BRAKE SYSTEM	
	1 Bleed the brake system using the NGS tester. • Is the brake pedal spongy? → **Yes** DIAGNOSE brake system. → **No** The brake system is operating correctly. REPEAT the self-test.

FM4020101824020X

Fig. 20 Test J: Spongy Brake Pedal w/No Warning Indicator (Part 2 of 2)

CONDITIONS	DETAILS/RESULTS/ACTIONS
K1 BLEED THE BRAKE SYSTEM	
	1 Bleed the brake system. • Does the vehicle track poorly? → **Yes** GO to **K2.** → **No** The brake system is operating correctly. REPEAT the self-test.
K2 CHECK THE ABS INLET VALVE (CLOSED POSITION)	
	1 Lift and support the vehicle. 2 Rotate all the wheels to make sure they rotate freely (the vehicle must be in neutral). 3 Apply moderate brake pedal effort.

FM4020101825010X

Fig. 21 Test K: Poor Vehicle Tracking During Anti-Lock Function (Part 1 of 3)

CONDITIONS	DETAILS/RESULTS/ACTIONS
	4 Trigger ABS control module active command LF INLET ON. 5 Have an assistant attempt to rotate the LF wheel. • Does the LF wheel rotate? → **Yes** TRIGGER active command LF INLET OFF. GO to **K3.** → **No** INSTALL a new hydraulic control unit (HCU). REPEAT the self-test.
K3 CHECK THE ABS INLET VALVE (OPEN POSITION)	
	1 Apply moderate brake pedal effort. 2 Have an assistant attempt to rotate the LF wheel. • Does the LF wheel rotate? → **Yes** INSTALL a new hydraulic control unit. REPEAT the self-test. → **No** GO to **K4.**
K4 CHECK ABS OUTLET VALVE (OPEN POSITION)	
	1 Apply moderate brake pedal effort. 2 Trigger ABS control module active command LF INLET ON. 3 Trigger ABS control module active command ABS POWER ON (turns on pump motor) for 6 seconds. (Trigger must be depressed 3 times. Each press runs the pump for 2 seconds.) 4 Trigger the ABS control module active command LF OUTLET ON and then OFF, repeat 3 times. 5 Have an assistant attempt to rotate the LF wheel. • Does the LF wheel rotate? → **Yes** TRIGGER all active commands OFF. GO to K5. → **No** INSTALL a new hydraulic control unit. REPEAT the self-test.

FM4020101825020X

Fig. 21 Test K: Poor Vehicle Tracking During Anti-Lock Function (Part 2 of 3)

CONDITIONS	DETAILS/RESULTS/ACTIONS
K5 CHECK ABS INLET AND OUTLET VALVE (CLOSED POSITION)	
	1 Apply moderate brake pedal effort. 2 Have an assistant attempt to rotate the LF wheel. • Does the LF wheel rotate? → **Yes** INSTALL a new hydraulic control unit. REPEAT the self-test. → **No** REPEAT this procedure (beginning with K2) for the RF, LR and RR wheels using the appropriate active commands. If no failure occurs the system is operating normally.

FM4020101825030X

Fig. 21 Test K: Poor Vehicle Tracking During Anti-Lock Function (Part 3 of 3)

CONDITIONS	DETAILS/RESULTS/ACTIONS
L1 CHECK FOR DIAGNOSTIC TROUBLE CODES (DTCS)	
	1 Carry out the ABS control module self-test. • Are any DTCs retrieved? → **Yes** GO to the ABS Control Module Diagnostic Trouble Code (DTC) Index. → **No** GO to **L2.**
L2 CHECK THE ABS OPERATION	
	1 Test drive the vehicle. Check the ABS operation • Does the ABS operate correctly? → **Yes** GO to **L3.** → **No** GO to Symptom Chart.

FM4020101826010X

Fig. 22 Test L: Traction Control Is Inoperative (Part 1 of 2)

CONDITIONS	DETAILS/RESULTS/ACTIONS
L3 CHECK THE TRACTION CONTROL SWITCH CIRCUIT	
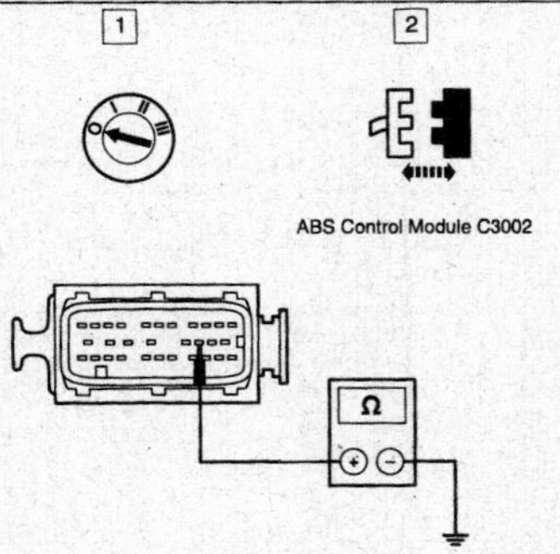	3 Measure the resistance between ABS control module connector C3002 pin 17, circuit 31S-CF54 (BK/WH), harness side and ground while depressing and releasing the traction control switch. • Is the resistance less than 5 ohms with the traction control switch depressed and greater than 10,000 ohms with the traction control switch released? → **Yes** INSTALL a new hydraulic control unit (HCU). REPEAT the self-test. → **No** GO to Pinpoint Test N.

FM4020101826020X

Fig. 22 Test L: Traction Control Is Inoperative (Part 2 of 2)

CONDITIONS	DETAILS/RESULTS/ACTIONS
M1 CHECK TRACTION CONTROL SWITCH CIRCUIT	
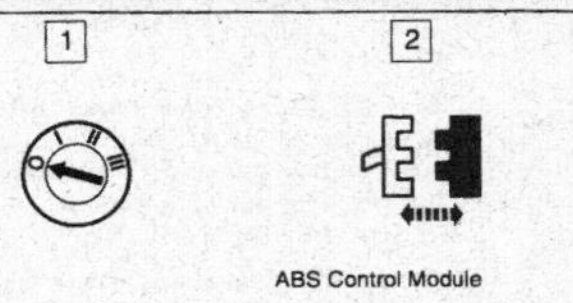	

FM4020101827010X

Fig. 23 Test M: Traction Control Switch Indicator Is Inoperative (Part 1 of 4)

CONDITIONS	DETAILS/RESULTS/ACTIONS
	3 Measure the resistance between ABS control module connector pin 17, circuit 31S-CF54 (BK/WH), harness side and ground while depressing and releasing the traction control switch. • Is the resistance less than 5 ohms with the traction control switch depressed and greater than 10,000 ohms with the traction control switch released? → **Yes** GO to **M4.** → **No** GO to **M2.**
M2 CHECK CIRCUIT 31S-CF54 (BK/WH) FOR AN OPEN OR SHORT TO GROUND	
1  Traction Control Switch	2 Measure the resistance between ABS control module connector pin 17, circuit 31S-CF54 (BK/WH), harness side and traction control switch connector pin 1, circuit 31S-CF54 (BK/WH), harness side and between ABS control module connector pin 17, circuit 31S-CF54 (BK/WH), harness side and ground. • Is the resistance less than 5 ohms between the ABS control module and traction control switch, and greater than 10,000 ohms between the ABS control module and ground.? → **Yes** GO to **M3.** → **No** REPAIR the circuit. REPEAT the self-test.

FM4020101827020X

Fig. 23 Test M: Traction Control Switch Indicator Is Inoperative (Part 2 of 4)

CONDITIONS	DETAILS/RESULTS/ACTIONS
M5 CHECK CIRCUIT 14-CF45 (VT/BK) FOR AN OPEN CIRCUIT	
1  2  Traction Control Switch C2001 3 	4 Measure the voltage between traction control switch connector pin 6, circuit 14-CF45 (VT/BK), harness side and ground. • Is the voltage greater than 10 volts? → **Yes** GO to **M6.** → **No** REPAIR the circuit. REPEAT the self-test.
M6 CHECK CIRCUIT 31S-CF45A (BK/GN) FOR AN OPEN CIRCUIT	
1 	2 Measure the resistance between ABS control module connector pin 18, circuit 31S-CF45A (BK/GN), harness side and traction control switch connector pin 4, circuit 31S-CF45A (BK/GN), harness side. • Is the resistance less than 5 ohms? → **Yes** INSTALL a new traction control switch. REPEAT the self-test. → **No** REPAIR the circuit. REPEAT the self-test.

FM4020101827040X

Fig. 23 Test M: Traction Control Switch Indicator Is Inoperative (Part 4 of 4)

CONDITIONS	DETAILS/RESULTS/ACTIONS
M3 CHECK CIRCUIT 31S-CF54 (BK)FOR AN OPEN CIRCUIT	
	1 Measure the resistance between traction control switch connector pin 2, circuit 31S-CF54 (BK), harness side and ground. • Is the resistance less than 5 ohms? → **Yes** INSTALL a new traction control switch. REPEAT the self-test. → **No** REPAIR the circuit. REPEAT the self-test.
M4 CHECK THE TRACTION CONTROL SWITCH INDICATOR CIRCUIT	
1 	2 NOTE: The jumper wire must be fused with a 10A in-line fuse. Momentarily connect a jumper wire between ABS control module connector pin 18, circuit 31S-CF54A (BK/GN), harness side and ground while checking the traction control switch indicator . • Does the traction control switch indicator illuminate? → **Yes** INSTALL a new hydraulic control unit (HCU). REPEAT the self-test. → **No** GO to **M5.**

FM4020101827030X

Fig. 23 Test M: Traction Control Switch Indicator Is Inoperative (Part 3 of 4)

CONDITIONS	DETAILS/RESULTS/ACTIONS
N1 CHECK TRACTION CONTROL SWITCH CIRCUIT	
1  2  ABS Control Module C3002 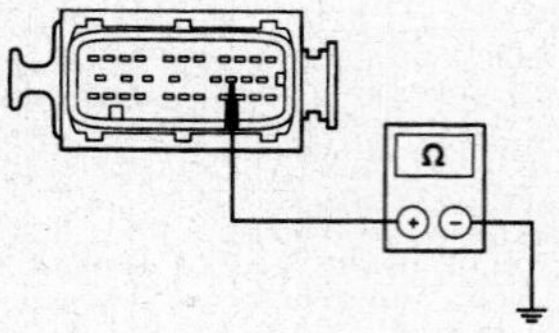	3 Measure the resistance between ABS control module connector pin 17, circuit 31S-CF54 (BK/WH), harness side and ground while depressing and releasing the traction control switch. • Is the resistance less than 5 ohms with the traction control switch depressed and greater than 10,000 ohms with the traction control switch released? → **Yes** GO to **N4.** → **No** GO to **N2.**
N2 CHECK CIRCUIT 31S-CF54 (BK/WH) FOR AN OPEN OR SHORT TO GROUND	
1  Traction Control Switch C2001 (Contour)/C2002 (Mystique)	

FM4020101828010X

Fig. 24 Test N: Traction Control Cannot Be Disabled (Part 1 of 3)

CONDITIONS	DETAILS/RESULTS/ACTIONS
	2 Measure the resistance between ABS control module connector C3002 pin 17, circuit 31S-CF54 (BK/WH), harness side and traction control switch connector C2001 pin 1 (Contour) or connector C2002 pin 2 (Mystique), circuit 31S-CF54 (BK/WH), harness side, and between ABS control module connector C3002 pin 17, circuit 31S-CF54 (BK/WH), harness side and ground. • Is the resistance less than 5 ohms between the ABS control module and traction control switch, and greater than 10,000 ohms between the ABS control module and ground? → **Yes** GO to **N3.** → **No** REPAIR the circuit. REPEAT the self-test.

FM4020101828020X

Fig. 24 Test N: Traction Control Cannot Be Disabled (Part 2 of 3)

CONDITIONS	DETAILS/RESULTS/ACTIONS
N3 CHECK CIRCUIT 91-CF54 (BK/WH) FOR AN OPEN	
	1 Measure the resistance between traction control switch connector pin 2 (Contour) or connector pin 4 (Mystique), circuit 91-CF54 (BK/WH), harness side and ground. • Is the resistance less than 5 ohms? → **Yes** INSTALL a new traction control switch. REPEAT the self-test. → **No** REPAIR the circuit. REPEAT the self-test.
N4 CHECK CIRCUIT 31S-CF54 (BK/WH) FOR SHORT TO POWER	
1	
	2 Measure the voltage between ABS control module connector pin 17, circuit 31S-CF54 (BK/WH), harness side and ground. • Is voltage present? → **Yes** REPAIR the circuit. REPEAT the self-test. → **No** INSTALL a new hydraulic control unit (HCU). REPEAT the self-test.

FM4020101828030X

Fig. 24 Test N: Traction Control Cannot Be Disabled (Part 3 of 3)

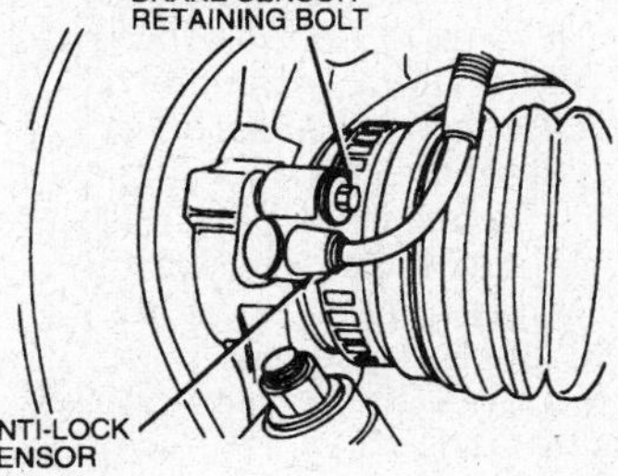

FM4029500761000X

Fig. 25 Front ABS sensor removal

SYSTEM SERVICE

Brake System Bleed

Refer to "Hydraulic Brake Systems" for bleeding procedure.

Component Replacement

HYDRAULIC CONTROL UNIT (HCU)

2.0L ENGINE

1. Remove brake booster, then air cleaner support bracket.
2. Remove instrument panel lower panel.
3. Disconnect brake booster support brackets, then remove brackets.
4. Place air conditioning tube support bracket aside.
5. Disconnect clutch tube (if equipped) and remove bolt, then booster side support bracket.
6. Remove master cylinder fluid feed tubes and hydraulic unit tubes.
7. Disconnect hydraulic control unit connector.
8. Remove control unit nuts and control unit.
9. Reverse procedure to install, noting the following:
   a. **Torque** control unit nuts to 96 inch lbs.
   b. **Torque** brake tube fittings to 11 ft. lbs.
   c. **Torque** air cleaner support bracket bolts to 30 ft. lbs.

2.5L ENGINE

1. Remove brake booster, then brake booster support bracket.
2. Disconnect hydraulic unit brake tubes.
3. Disconnect hydraulic unit connector.
4. Remove hydraulic control unit support bracket rear bolts.
5. Remove hydraulic control unit support bracket side bolts, then hydraulic unit.
6. Reverse procedure to install, noting the following:
   a. **Torque** control unit bolts to 18 ft. lbs.
   b. **Torque** brake tube fittings to 11 ft. lbs.
   c. **Torque** air cleaner support bracket bolts to 30 ft. lbs.

FRONT ABS SENSOR

1. Raise and support vehicle.
2. Remove front brake ABS sensor retaining bolt and front ABS sensor from front wheel knuckle, **Fig. 25.**
3. Remove front fender splash shield.
4. Disconnect sensor electrical connector.
5. Remove sensor.
6. Reverse procedure to install. **Torque** ABS sensor bolt to 84 inch lbs.

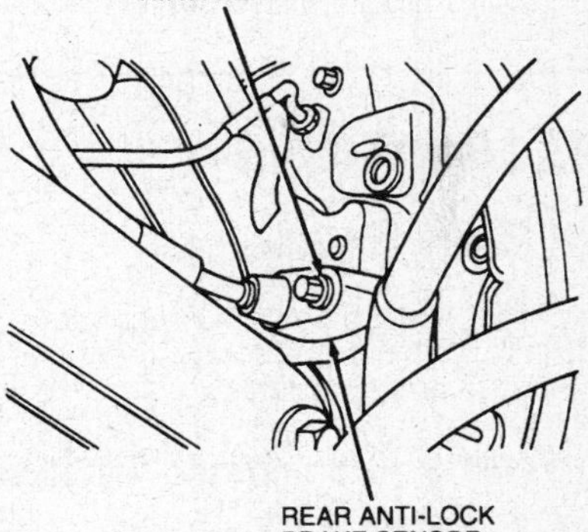

FM4029500762000X

Fig. 26 Rear ABS sensor removal

REAR ABS SENSOR

1. Remove rear seat cushion.
2. Disconnect rear ABS sensor connector. Feed connector through hole in floorpan.
3. Raise and support vehicle.
4. Remove sensor wiring from routing brackets.
5. Remove rear ABS sensor, **Fig. 26.**
6. Reverse procedure to install.

LS & Thunderbird

NOTE: On Air Bag Equipped Models, Refer To "Air Bag System Precautions" Located In The Front Of This Manual For System Disarming & Arming Procedures.

NOTE: Refer To "Computer Relearn Procedure" Located In The Front Of This Manual When Battery Power To The Computer Has Been Interrupted.

NOTE: "Electrical Symbol & Wire Color Code Identification" Located In The Front Of This Manual May Be Used As An Aid When Using Wiring Circuits Found In This Section.

INDEX

PRECAUTIONS

Air Bag Systems

Refer to "Air Bag System Precautions" in the front of this manual for system disarming and arming procedures.

Battery Ground Cable

Prior to service, disconnect battery ground cable and isolate as required.

DESCRIPTION

ABS Control Module

On models less stability control, an ABS control module is used to control ABS and/or traction control. The ABS module is self monitoring. When ignition switch is turned to the run position, the ABS control module performs a preliminary electrical inspection. When vehicle speed reaches 12 mph, the pump motor is actuated for ½ second. A fault in the ABS system will cause ABS operation to deactivate and the yellow ABS warning indicator to illuminate. Normal power assisted braking will still remain available.

When the ABS control module is replaced, it is required to upload current module configuration, and then reconfigure the module. Refer to "Module Configuration" in "System Service" for procedure.

System

LESS TRACTION CONTROL & STABILITY ASSIST

The four wheel anti-lock brake system consists of the following components: anti-lock brake module, front and rear ABS sensors and sensor indicators, hydraulic control unit and the yellow anti-lock brake warning indicator.

The anti-lock brake control module receives wheel speed readings from each wheel speed sensor and uses this data to determine if an ABS event is required. The ABS control module continuously monitors and compares rotational speed of each wheel and modulates pressure to each caliper if the ABS system is activated. Pressure is modulated by the hydraulic control unit which opens and closes the appropriate solenoid valves. When the affected wheel returns to normal speed, solenoid valves are returned to normal position and normal braking resumes.

WITH TRACTION CONTROL, LESS STABILITY ASSIST

The four wheel anti-lock brake system with traction control consists of the following components: anti-lock brake module, front and rear ABS sensors and sensor indicators, hydraulic control unit, traction control event indicator, traction control switch and the yellow anti-lock brake warning indicator.

On vehicles equipped with ABS and traction control, the ABS control module communicates with the PCM to assist in traction control. At speeds under 25 mph, the ABS control module requests the PCM to reduce engine torque while simultaneously applying and releasing appropriate brake to restore traction when one or both drive wheels lose traction and begin to spin. The PCM performs this function by altering ignition timing and injector pulse-width until the ABS control module receives data signifying that wheel speed has returned to normal. At speeds more than 25 mph, the traction control function is accomplished only through PCM control of engine torque.

The traction control function can be disabled by depressing the traction control switch. The traction control system will reset when the ignition switch is cycled or when switch is toggled again.

If the traction control system is cycled excessively, the brake portion of the system will shut down to prevent the rear brakes from overheating. Limited traction control function using only torque reduction will still control wheels from over spinning. After

DTC	Description	Stability Assist Calibration
C1277	Steering Wheel Angle 1 and 2 Circuit Failure	YES
C1278	Steering Wheel Angle 1 and 2 Signal Faulted	YES
C1279	Yaw Rate Sensor Circuit Failure	YES
C1280	Yaw Rate Sensor Signal Fault	YES
C1281	Lateral Accelerometer Circuit Failure	YES
C1282	Lateral Accelerometer Signal Fault	YES
C1283	Switch Test Signal Failure	YES
C1285	Booster Solenoid Circuit Failure	YES
C1286	Booster Mechanical Failure	YES
C1287	Booster Pedal Force Switch Circuit Failure	YES
C1288	Pressure Transducer Main / Primary Input Circuit Failure	YES
C1289	Pressure Transducer Redundant / Secondary Input Circuit Failure	YES
C1730	Reference Voltage Out of Range (+5 V)	YES
C1960	Driver Brake Apply Circuit Fault	NO
C1963	Stability Control Inhibit Warning	NO

FM4029901569000X

Fig. 1 Stability assist calibration list

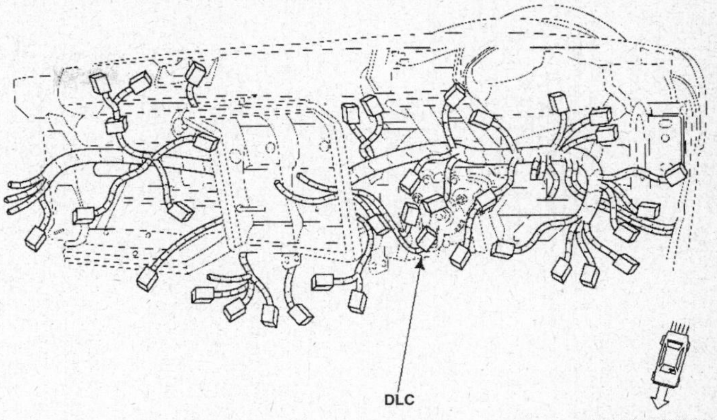

Fig. 2 Data Link Connector (DLC) location

rear brakes are cooled, the system will return to normal function. Anti-lock braking is not affected by this function and will operate normally during rear brake cooling period.

WITH TRACTION CONTROL & STABILITY ASSIST

The four wheel anti-lock brake system with traction control and stability assist consists of the following components: brake booster release switch, front and rear ABS sensors and sensor indicators, hydraulic control unit, stability assist event indicator, stability assist module, lateral accelerometer, steering wheel position sensor, transducers, advance trac control switch, yaw rate sensor and the yellow anti-lock brake warning indicator.

The stability assist system communicates with the PCM. The PCM assists with traction control by altering engine timing and fuel injector pulse. By altering engine timing and fuel injector pulse, the PCM can control torque, which in turn reduces excessive wheel spin. At speeds above 25 mph, traction control is controlled only by PCM command of engine torque output. At speeds up to 25 mph, the stability assist module requests the PCM to reduce engine torque while simultaneously applying and releasing appropriate brake to restore traction when one or both drive wheels lose traction and begin to spin.

The stability assist system continuously monitors vehicle motion relative to the driver's intended course. The driver's intended course is calculated by using sensors to compare steering inputs from driver with actual motion of the vehicle. The driver's steering wheel input is measured from a steering wheel rotation sensor. Vehicle motion is determined using a yaw rate sensor which measures rotation about the vehicle axis, a lateral accelerometer which measures acceleration generated from the vehicle sliding sideways and wheel speed sensors which measure speed of each individual wheel. If there is a discrepancy between driver input and vehicle motion, the stability assist system changes the force at each tire to help control the vehicle.

The stability assist system defaults to on when the engine is started. Stability assist is not active when the vehicle is traveling in reverse, however ABS and traction control are still functional. System status is indicated in the stability assist warning lamp located in the stability assist/traction control switch. Stability assist is an independent function of ABS. The illumination of the stability assist/traction control switch indicates that the stability assist function is off and that ABS will continue to operate normally. Models equipped with a message center will display "ADVANCETRAC OFF."

When the stability assist system is attempting to correct vehicle direction, the following normal conditions may be present: rumble or grinding sound; deceleration or reduction in acceleration of vehicle; stability assist indicator may flash; vibration in brake pedal; brake pedal may move to apply higher brake forces accompanied by whoosh sound from beneath instrument panel. Also, the brake pedal may experience a slight movement when the system self check is performed. The self check is performed after the vehicle reaches a speed of 30 mph after 8 minutes of running time. Self check will only be performed if the vehicle is stable, driver is not braking and accelerator pedal is depressed. If a failure is detected, the stability assist indicator will be illuminated. Anti-lock brake system will continue to function normally unless the yellow ABS warning indicator is illuminated. Normal brake function will continue to occur unless the red brake warning indicator is illuminated.

If the "Active/Fail" lamp is flashing, this indicates the need to calibrate stability assist module. Lamp will flash after the clearing of the following DTCs: C1277, C1278, C1279, C1280, C1281, C1282, C1283, C1285, C1286, C1287, C1288, C1289 and C1730.

Brake Booster

The brake booster operates as any normal brake booster, with the added capability of being electronically actuated by the stability assist module. The electronic actuation of the brake booster is sometimes required in severe stability assist events to ensure that the hydraulic control unit can generate enough brake pressure to improve vehicle stability.

The brake booster houses a solenoid that enables it to be electronically actuated. It also contains a release switch to indicate when the driver is stepping on the brake.

When performing the booster learn cycle using the NGS tester, ensure ignition switch is in the run position with engine running and brakes not applied.

Lateral Accelerometer

The lateral accelerometer measures centrifugal and gravitational acceleration which corresponds to the force required to slide the vehicle sideways. The accelerometer only measures the acceleration along the lateral direction of the vehicle, therefore on level ground, there is no contribution from this acceleration. If the vehicle is parked sideways on a bank or incline, the sensor will measure lateral acceleration due to gravity, even though the vehicle is stationary.

When calibrating the lateral accelerometer using the NGS tester, ensure vehicle is stationary and on a level surface with ignition switch in run position.

Stability Assist Module

On models equipped with stability control, a stability assist module or interactive vehicle dynamic (IVD) module is used in place of the ABS control module. The stability assist module controls ABS, full speed

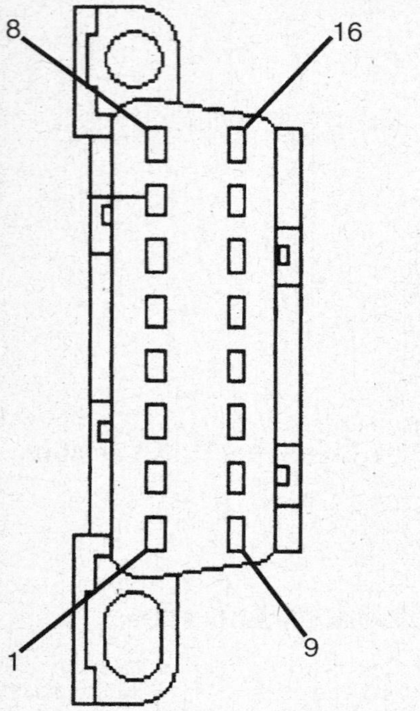

FM4029901568000X

Fig. 3 DLC pin identification

Condition	Possible Source	Action
• No communication with the anti-lock brake control module	• Underhood AJB Maxifuses 114 (30 A) and 122 (30A). • CJB Fuse 203 (5A). • Circuitry. • Anti-Lock brake control module.	• GO to Pinpoint Test A.
• The yellow anti-lock brake warning indicator does not self-check	• Anti-lock brake control module. • Circuitry. • Instrument cluster. • Indicator bulb.	• GO to Pinpoint Test G.
• Spongy brake pedal with no warning indicator	• Air in brake hydraulic system.	• DIAGNOSE brake system.

FM4020101776000X

Fig. 4 Symptom chart. Less traction control

Condition	Possible Source	Action
• No communication with the anti-lock brake control module	• Underhood AJB Maxi Fuses 114 (30 A) and 122 (30A). • CJB Fuses 203 (5A) and 205 (5A). • Circuitry. • Anti-lock brake control module.	• GO to Pinpoint Test A.
• The yellow anti-lock brake warning indicator does not self-check	• Anti-lock brake control module. • Circuitry. • Instrument cluster. • Indicator bulb.	• GO to Pinpoint Test G.
• Spongy brake pedal with no warning indicator	• Air in brake hydraulic system.	• DIAGNOSE brake system.
• The traction control is inoperative	• Circuitry. • Traction control switch. • Anti-lock brake control module. • Hydraulic control unit (HCU). • Base brake system.	• GO to Pinpoint Test H. • DIAGNOSE brake system.
• The traction control cannot be disabled	• Circuitry. • Traction control switch. • Anti-lock brake control module.	• GO to Pinpoint Test I.
• The traction control switch is never/always on	• Circuitry. • Traction control switch. • Anti-lock brake control module.	• GO to Pinpoint Test J.

FM4020101778000X

Fig. 5 Symptom chart. With traction control

traction control and stability assist functions to enhance driver control of the vehicle. Stability assist control determines interactions between anti-lock, traction control and engine control systems to optimize vehicle traction during deceleration and acceleration. Stability assist also controls brake pressure during braking and non-braking conditions as required to counteract excessive vehicle rotation when cornering.

The stability assist module is self-monitoring. When the ignition switch is turned to the run position, stability assist module will perform an electrical inspection. When vehicle speed reaches 12 mph, the pump motor is actuated for ½ second. A fault in the ABS, traction control or stability assist system will cause ABS, traction control and stability assist operation to deactivate and the yellow ABS warning indicator to illuminate. Normal power assisted braking will still remain available.

The stability assist module must be calibrated when a component related to stability assist is disconnected, moved or replaced. Before removing stability assist module, it is required to upload current module configuration, and then reconfigure the module. Refer to **Fig. 1,** for DTCs that require stability assist module re-calibration. If a DTC is present for any component of the stability assist system, the DTC must be cleared before performing calibration procedure. If a DTC is received after calibration, proceed to "Diagnostic Trouble Code & Pinpoint Test Reference Chart" in "Diagnosis & Testing." If module calibration is required, refer to "Module Configuration" in "System Service."

Steering Wheel Rotation Sensor

A sensor ring is mounted to the steering column through which the steering wheel rotation sensor can tell which way the steering wheel is turned, and how far it is turned. This sensor does not tell the stability assist module the position of the steering wheel relative to straight ahead position. The stability assist system learns straight ahead position by comparing steering wheel position with other signals and remembering position learned. Stability assist system confirms this position and modifies it as required during every new driving cycle.

When calibrating the steering wheel rotation sensor using the NGS tester, ensure engine is running and that steering wheel is rotated back-and-forth from lock position to lock position.

Yaw Rate Sensor

The yaw rate sensor measures rotation rate of the vehicle as it turns left and right. The sensor is located under the center console.

When calibrating the yaw rate sensor using the NGS tester, ensure vehicle is stationary and on a level surface with ignition switch in run position.

TROUBLESHOOTING

Inspection & Verification

1. Verify ABS concern by applying brakes under varying conditions.
2. Verify stoplamps are working properly.
3. Verify "PRNDL" indicator on instrument cluster is working properly.
4. Visually inspect the following for mechanical or electrical damage:
   a. Underhood auxiliary junction box fuses.
   b. Central junction box fuses.
   c. Anti-lock brake sensor indicators and sensors.
   d. Base brake concerns.
   e. Tire pressure.
   f. Hydraulic control unit.
   g. Tire size, or mismatched tires.
   h. ABS/stability assist control module.
   i. Brake booster vacuum hose.
   j. Ford specified steering and suspension components.
   k. Steering wheel rotation ring and sensor (if equipped).
   l. Brake booster solenoid and release switch (if equipped).
   m. Brake fluid pressure transducers (if equipped).
   n. Yaw rate and lateral accelerometer switches (if equipped).
   o. Brake pedal position switch.
   p. ABS wiring and connectors.
   q. EVAC and fill connector.
   r. Wiring harness routing.
   s. Traction control/stability assist switch.

DTC	Description	Source	Action
B1342	ECU is Defective	Anti-Lock Brake Control Module	INSTALL a new anti-lock brake control module.
B1485	Brake Pedal Input Circuit Battery Short	Anti-Lock Brake Control Module	GO to Pinpoint Test B.
B1676	Battery Pack Voltage Out of Range	Anti-Lock Brake Control Module	GO to Pinpoint Test C.
B2477	Module Configuration Failure	Anti-Lock Brake Control Module	CONFIGURE the anti-lock brake control module. CLEAR the DTCs. REPEAT the self-test. If DTC B2477 is retrieved again, INSTALL a new anti-lock brake control module Brake System (ABS) Module. REPEAT the self-test.
C1095	Hydraulic Pump Motor Circuit Failure	Anti-Lock Brake Control Module	GO to Pinpoint Test D.
C1145	Speed Wheel Sensor RF Input Circuit Failure	Anti-Lock Brake Control Module	GO to Pinpoint Test E.
C1155	Speed Wheel Sensor LF Input Circuit Failure	Anti-Lock Brake Control Module	GO to Pinpoint Test E.
C1165	Speed Wheel Sensor RR Input Circuit Failure	Anti-Lock Brake Control Module	GO to Pinpoint Test E.
C1175	Speed Wheel Sensor LR Input Circuit Failure	Anti-Lock Brake Control Module	GO to Pinpoint Test E.
C1233	Speed Wheel LF Input Signal Missing	Anti-Lock Brake Control Module	GO to Pinpoint Test F.
C1234	Speed Wheel RF Input Signal Missing	Anti-Lock Brake Control Module	GO to Pinpoint Test F.
C1235	Speed Wheel RR Input Signal Missing	Anti-Lock Brake Control Module	GO to Pinpoint Test F.
C1236	Speed Wheel LR Input Signal Missing	Anti-Lock Brake Control Module	GO to Pinpoint Test F.

FM4020101777000X

Fig. 6 Diagnostic trouble code interpretation

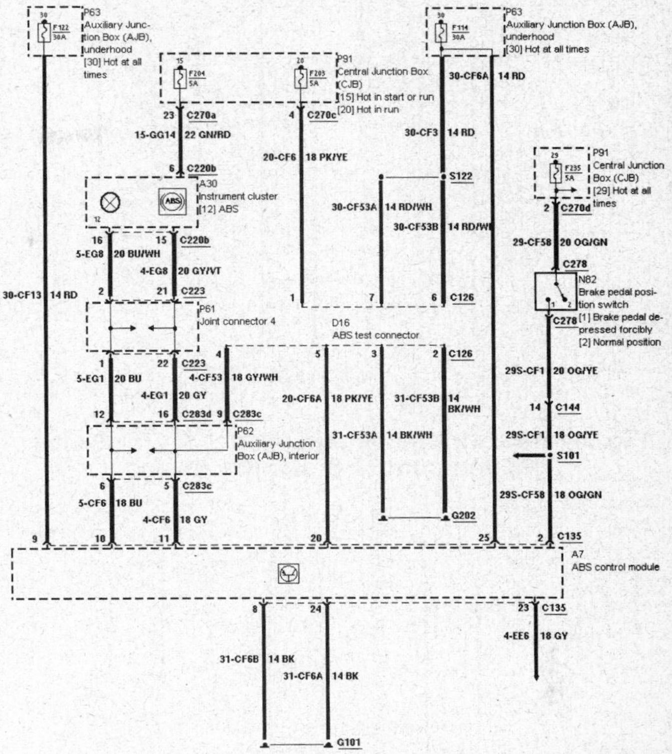

FM4029901551010X

Fig. 7 ABS wiring diagram (Part 1 of 2). LS less traction control & stability assist

5. If a fault is not found during visual inspection, connect the New Generation Star Tester (NGS), or equivalent, to the DLC located beneath the instrument panel, **Figs. 2 and 3,** and follow scan tool instructions to select appropriate vehicle and options. If the NGS does not communicate with the vehicle, proceed as follows:
   a. Ensure NGS program card is properly installed.
   b. Ensure scan tool connections to vehicle are secure.
   c. Ensure ignition switch is in proper position.
6. If NGS still does not communicate with vehicle, refer to scan tool instructions.
7. Perform DATA LINK DIAGNOSTIC TEST and proceed as follows:
   a. If NGS responds with CKT914, CKT915 or CKT70 = ALL ECUS NO RESP/NOT EQUIP, diagnose module communications network.
   b. If NGS responds with NO RESP/NOT EQUIP for anti-lock brake control module, proceed to "Test A" in "Diagnosis & Testing."
   c. If NGS responds with SYSTEM PASSED, retrieve and record continuous diagnostic trouble codes, erase continuous DTCs and perform self test diagnosis for ABS/stability assist control module.
8. If DTCs are related to ABS concern, refer to "Diagnostic Trouble Code & Pinpoint Test Reference Chart" in "Diagnosis & Testing" for DTC index and test step direction. **On models equipped with stability assist,** DTC C1730 must be repaired before DTCs C1279, C1280, C1281, C1282, C1288 and C1289.
9. If no DTCs related to ABS concern are obtained, refer to "Symptom Chart."

Symptom Chart

Refer to **Figs. 4 and 5,** for symptom charts.

DIAGNOSIS & TESTING

Accessing Diagnostic Trouble Codes

Connect the New Generation Star Tester (NGS), or equivalent, to the DLC located beneath the instrument panel, **Figs. 2 and 3,** and follow scan tool instructions to select appropriate vehicle and options.

Diagnostic Trouble Code Interpretation

Refer to **Fig. 6,** for diagnostic trouble code interpretation.

Wiring Diagrams

Refer to **Figs. 7 through 10,** for wiring diagrams.

Pinpoint Tests

Refer to **Figs. 11 through 41,** for pinpoint tests.

Clearing Diagnostic Trouble Codes

Connect a suitably programmed scan tool to Data Link Connector, (DLC), and follow manufacturer's instructions.

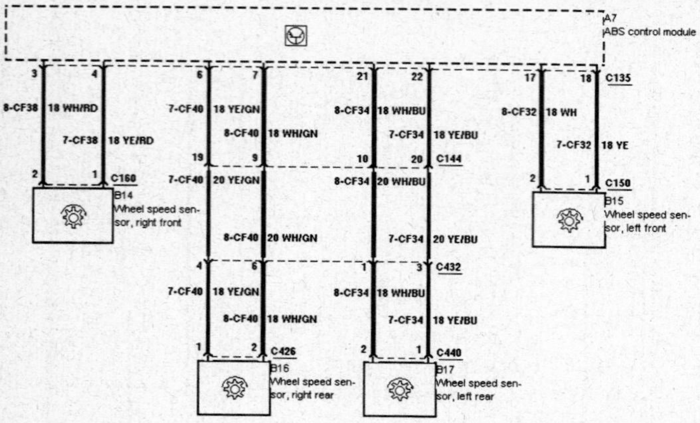

FM4029901551020X

Fig. 7 ABS wiring diagram (Part 2 of 2). LS less traction control & stability assist

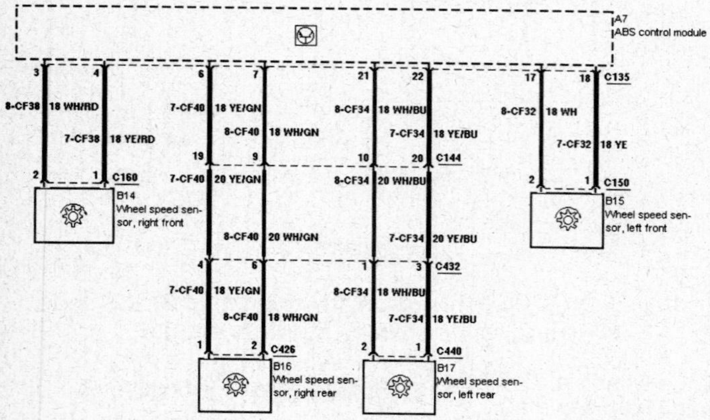

FM4029901552020X

Fig. 8 ABS wiring diagram (Part 2 of 3). LS w/traction control, less stability assist

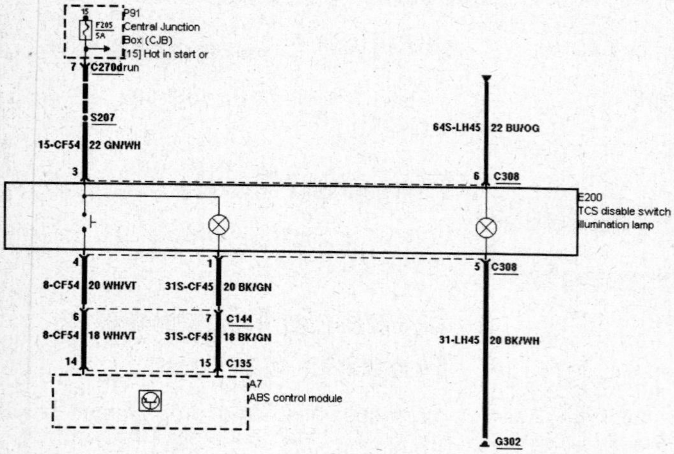

FM4029901552030X

Fig. 8 ABS wiring diagram (Part 3 of 3). LS w/traction control, less stability assist

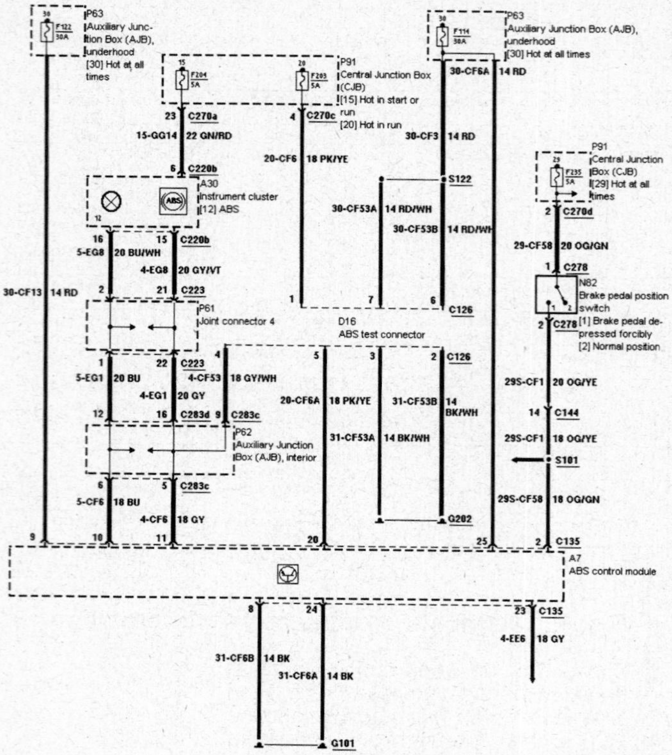

FM4029901552010X

Fig. 8 ABS wiring diagram (Part 1 of 3). LS w/traction control, less stability assist

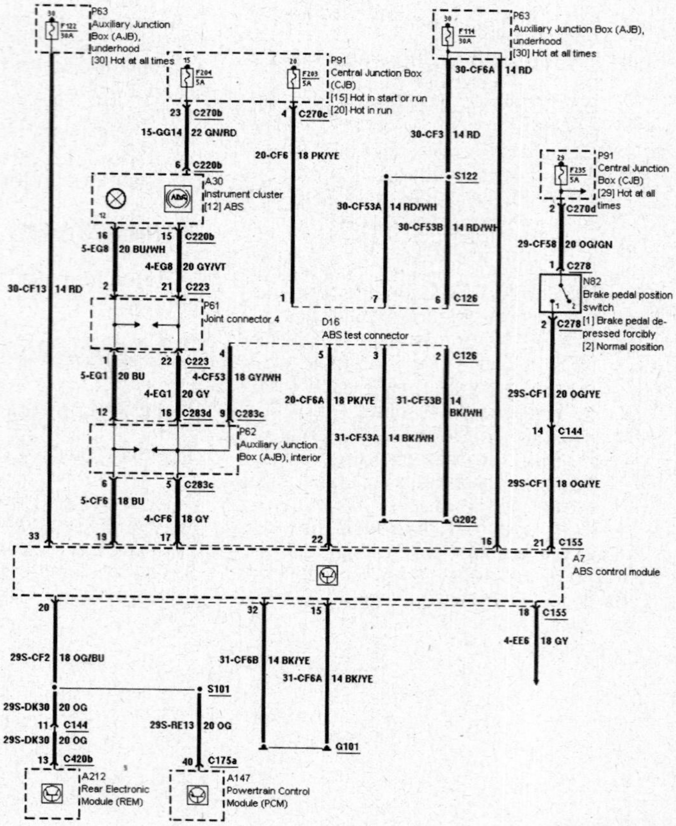

FM4029901553010X

Fig. 9 ABS wiring diagram (Part 1 of 5). LS w/traction control & stability assist

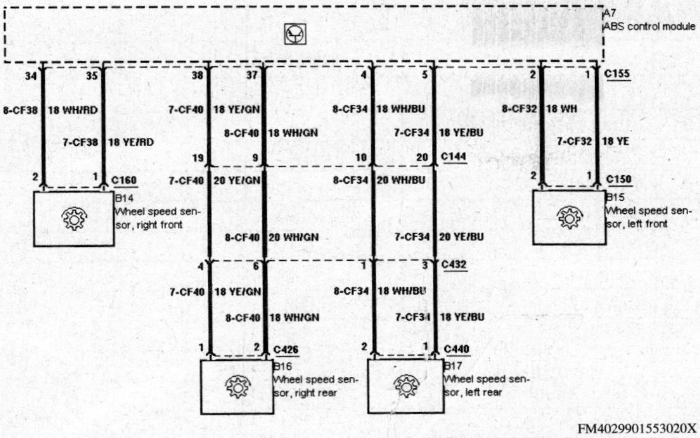

Fig. 9 ABS wiring diagram (Part 2 of 5). LS w/traction control & stability assist

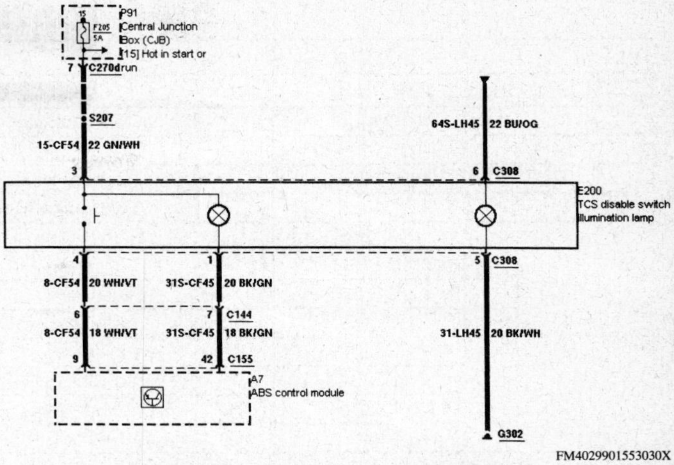

Fig. 9 ABS wiring diagram (Part 3 of 5). LS w/traction control & stability assist

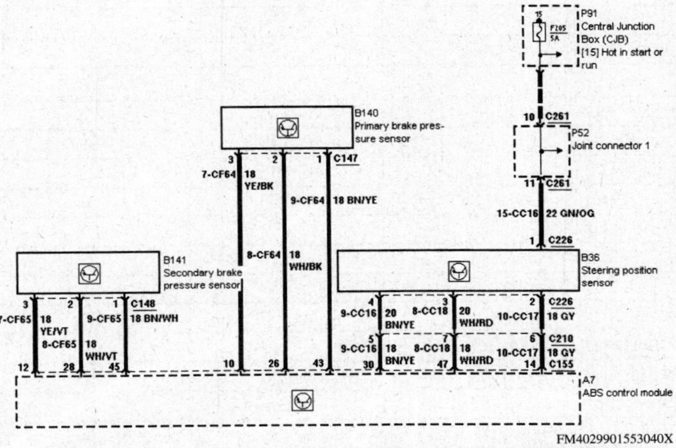

Fig. 9 ABS wiring diagram (Part 4 of 5). LS w/traction control & stability assist

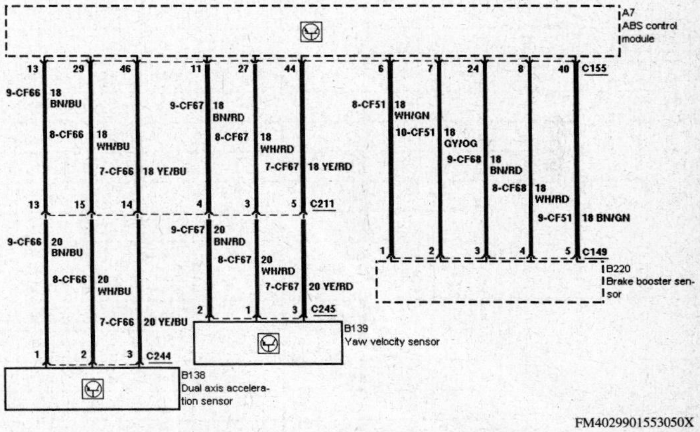

Fig. 9 ABS wiring diagram (Part 5 of 5). LS w/traction control & stability assist

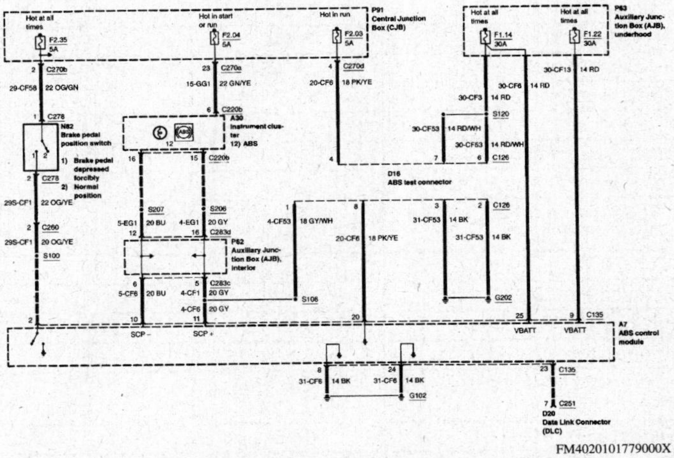

Fig. 10 ABS wiring diagram (Part 1 of 2). Thunderbird

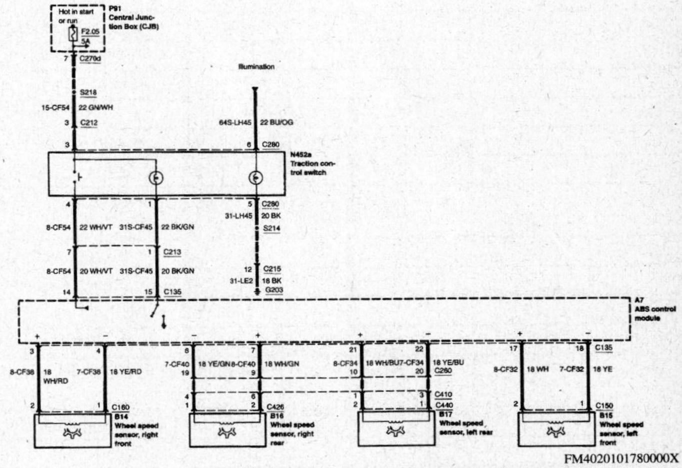

Fig. 10 ABS wiring diagram (Part 2 of 2). Thunderbird

DIAGNOSTIC CHART INDEX

Test	Code	Description	Page No.	Fig. No.
LESS STABILITY ASSIST				
A	—	No Communication w/ABS Control Module	6-147	11
B	B1485	Brake Pedal Input Circuit Battery Short	6-147	12
C	B1676	Battery Pack Voltage Out Of Range	6-148	13
D	C1095	Hydraulic Pump Motor Circuit Failure	6-148	14
E	C1145	Right Front ABS Sensor Circuit Failure	6-149	15
	C1155	Left Front ABS Sensor Circuit Failure	6-149	15
	C1165	Right Rear ABS Sensor Circuit Failure	6-149	15
	C1175	Left Rear ABS Sensor Circuit Failure	6-149	15
F	C1233	Left Front ABS Sensor Input Signal Missing	6-151	16
	C1234	Right Front ABS Sensor Input Signal Missing	6-151	16
	C1235	Right Rear ABS Sensor Input Signal Missing	6-151	16
	C1236	Left Rear ABS Sensor Input Signal Missing	6-151	16
G	—	Yellow ABS Warning Indicator Does Not Self Check	6-151	17
H	—	Traction Control Inoperative	6-152	18
I	—	Traction Control Cannot Be Disabled	6-153	19
J	—	Traction Control Switch Indicator Never/Always On	6-154	20
WITH STABILITY ASSIST				
A	—	No Communication w/Stability Assist Module	6-154	21
B	B1485	Brake Pedal Input Circuit Battery Short	6-155	22
C	B1676	Battery Pack Voltage Out Of Range	6-155	23
D	C1095	ABS Hydraulic Pump Motor Circuit Failure	6-156	24
E	C1145	Right Front ABS Sensor Input Circuit Failure	6-157	25
	C1155	Left Front ABS Sensor Input Circuit Failure	6-157	25
	C1165	Right Rear ABS Sensor Input Circuit Failure	6-157	25
	C1175	Left Rear ABS Sensor Input Circuit Failure	6-157	25
F	C1233	Left Front ABS Sensor Input Signal Missing	6-158	26
	C1234	Right Front ABS Sensor Input Signal Missing	6-158	26
	C1235	Right Rear ABS Sensor Input Signal Missing	6-158	26
	C1236	Left Rear ABS Sensor Input Signal Missing	6-158	26
G	C1277	Steering Wheel Angle 1 & 2 Circuit Failure	6-158	27
	C1278	Steering Wheel Angle 1 & 2 Circuit Fault	6-158	27
H	C1279	Yaw Rate Sensor Circuit Failure	6-160	28
	C1280	Yaw Rate Sensor Signal Fault	6-160	28
I	C1281	Lateral Accelerometer Circuit Failure	6-162	29
	C1282	Lateral Accelerometer Signal Fault	6-162	29
J	C1285	Brake Booster Solenoid Output Failure	6-165	30
K	C1286	Booster Mechanical Failure	6-166	31
L	C1287	Booster Pedal Force Switch Circuit Failure	6-168	32
M	C1288	Pressure Transducer Main/Primary Input Circuit Failure	6-169	33
N	C1289	Pressure Transducer Redundant/Secondary Input Circuit Failure	6-171	34
O	C1730	Reference Voltage Out Of Range	6-172	35
P	C1960	Driver Brake Apply Circuit Fault	6-175	36
Q	—	Yellow ABS Warning Indicator Does Not Self Check	6-175	37
R	—	Traction Control Inoperative	6-175	38
S	—	Stability Assist/Traction Control Switch Indicator Never/Always On	6-176	39
T	—	Stability Assist System Cannot Be Disabled	6-177	40
U	—	Stability Assist Indicator Does Not Self Check	6-178	41

A1 CHECK VOLTAGE TO THE ANTI-LOCK BRAKE CONTROL MODULE

1 

2 

Anti-Lock Brake Control Module C135

3 

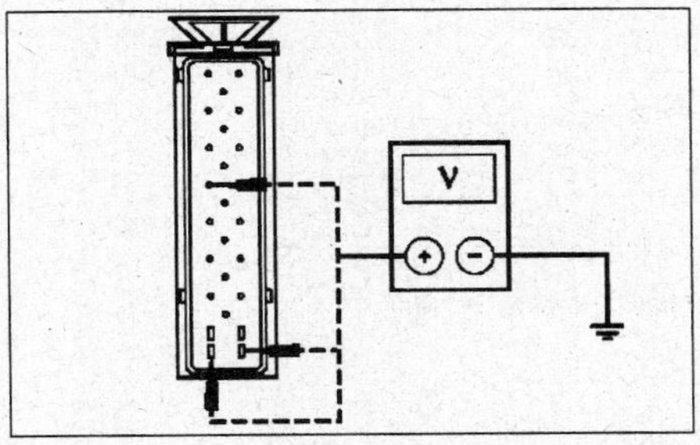

4

Measure the voltage between anti-lock brake control module C135 pins, and ground as follows:

Pin	Circuit
25	30-CF6A (RD)
20	20-CF6A (PK/YE)
9	30-CF13 (RD)

- **Are the voltages greater than 10 volts?**

→ **Yes**

Go to «A2».

→ **No**

REPAIR the circuit in question. TEST the system for normal operation.

FM4029901554010X

Fig. 11 Test A: No Communication w/ABS Control Module (Part 1 of 2). Less Stability Assist

B1 CHECK THE STOPLAMP OPERATION

1 Press the brake pedal.

- **Do the stoplamps operate correctly?**

→ **Yes**

Go to «B2».

→ **No**

DIAGNOSE inoperative stoplamps.

FM4029901555010X

Fig. 12 Test B/Code B1485: Brake Pedal Input Circuit Battery Short (Part 1 of 2). Less Stability Assist

A2 CHECK ANTI-LOCK BRAKE MODULE GROUNDS

1

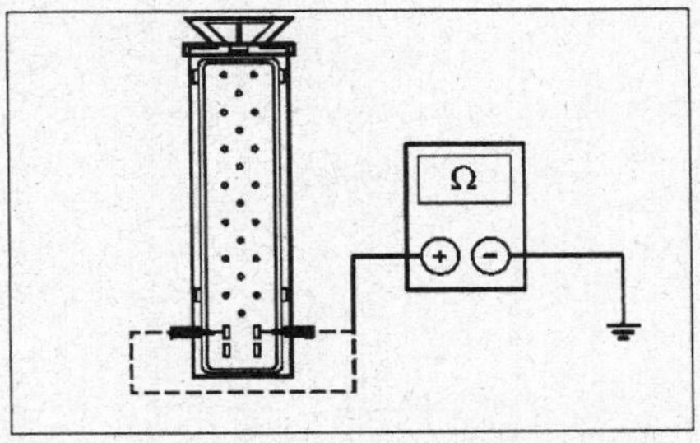

2

Measure the resistance between anti-lock brake control module C135 pin 8, circuit 31-CF6B (BK/YE), harness side and ground; and between anti-lock brake control module C135 pin 24, circuit 31-CF6A (BK/YE), harness side and ground.

- **Are the resistances less than 5 ohms?**

→ **Yes**

DIAGNOSE Module Communications Network.

→ **No**

REPAIR the circuit in question. TEST the system for normal operation.

FM4029901554020X

Fig. 11 Test A: No Communication w/ABS Control Module (Part 2 of 2). Less Stability Assist

B2 CHECK CIRCUIT 29S-CF58 (OG/GN) FOR OPEN

1

2

Anti-Lock Brake Control Module C135

3

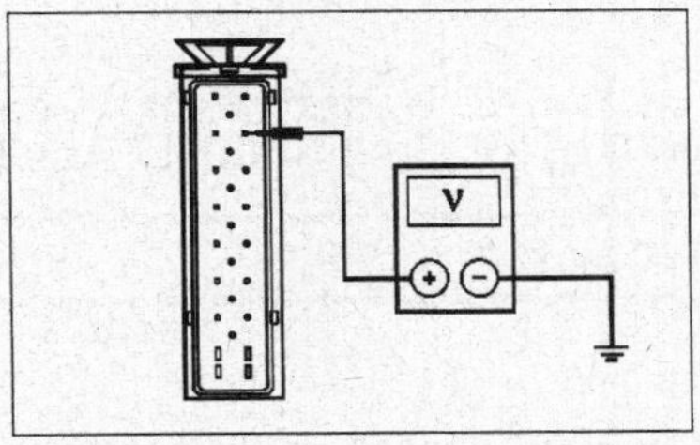

4

Measure the voltage between anti-lock brake control module pin 2 circuit 29S-CF58 (OG/GN), harness side and ground, while depressing the brake pedal.

- **Is the voltage greater than 10 volts?**

→ **Yes**

INSTALL a new anti-lock brake control module.
CLEAR the DTCs. REPEAT the self-test.

No

REPAIR circuit. CLEAR the DTCs. REPEAT the self-test.

FM4029901555020X

Fig. 12 Test B/Code B1485: Brake Pedal Input Circuit Battery Short (Part 2 of 2). Less Stability Assist

C1 CHECK THE BATTERY VOLTAGE

1

2 Measure the voltage between positive and negative battery posts.

- **Is the voltage between 10 and 14 volts?**

→ **Yes**

Go to «C2».

→ **No**

DIAGNOSE charging system concern.

FM4029901556010X

Fig. 13 Test C/Code B1676: Battery Pack Voltage Out Of Range (Part 1 of 3). Less Stability Assist

C2 CHECK VOLTAGE TO THE ANTI-LOCK BRAKE CONTROL MODULE

1

Anti-Lock Brake Control Module C135

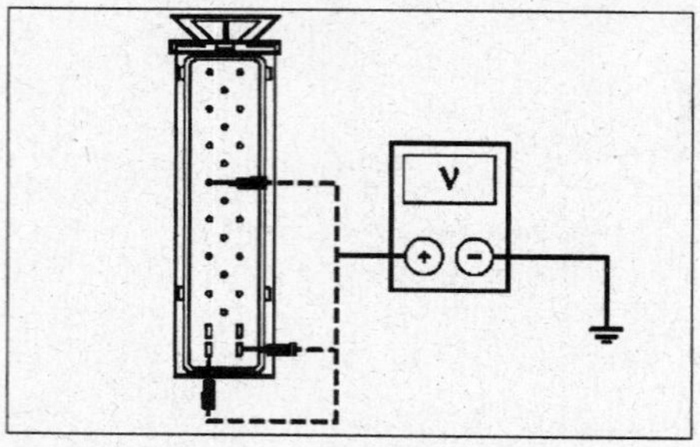

2

Measure the voltage between anti-lock brake control module C135 pins, and ground as follows:

Pin	Circuit
25	30-CF6A (RD)
20	20-CF6A (PK/YE)
9	30-CF13 (RD)

- **Are the voltages greater than 10 volts?**

→ **Yes**

Go to «C3».

→ **No**

REPAIR the circuit in question. CLEAR the DTCs. REPEAT the self-test.

FM4029901556020X

Fig. 13 Test C/Code B1676: Battery Pack Voltage Out Of Range (Part 2 of 3). Less Stability Assist

C3 CHECK THE ANTI-LOCK BRAKE CONTROL MODULE GROUNDS

1

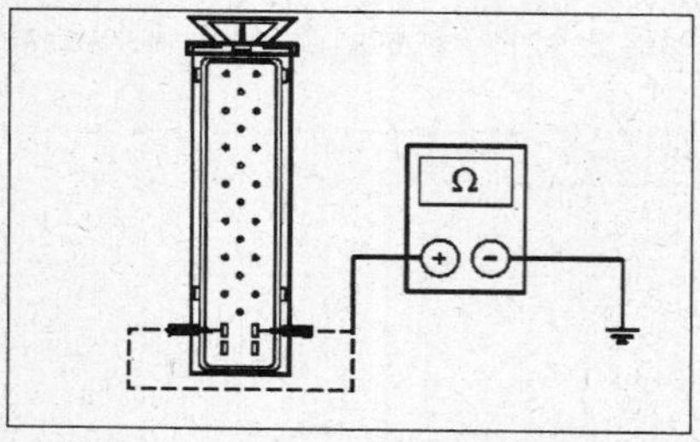

2

Measure the resistance between anti-lock control module pin 24, circuit 31-CF6A (BK/YE), harness side and ground; and between anti-lock control module pin 8, circuit 31-CF6B (BK/YE), harness side and ground.

- **Are the resistances less than 5 ohms?**

→ **Yes**

INSTALL a new anti-lock brake control module.
CLEAR the DTCs. REPEAT the self-test.

→ **No**

REPAIR the circuit in question. CLEAR the DTCs. REPEAT the self-test.

FM4029901556030X

Fig. 13 Test C/Code B1676: Battery Pack Voltage Out Of Range (Part 3 of 3). Less Stability Assist

D1 CHECK ABS PUMP MOTOR

1

- **Is the ABS pump motor running all the time?**

→ **Yes**

INSTALL a new anti-lock brake control module.
REPEAT the self-test.

→ **No**

Go to «D2».

FM4029901557010X

Fig. 14 Test D/Code C1095: Hydraulic Pump Motor Circuit Failure (Part 1 of 5). Less Stability Assist

D2 CHECK PUMP MOTOR OPERATION

1

2 Trigger the anti-lock brake control module active command PMP MOTOR ON.

- **Does the ABS pump motor run for approximately three seconds?**

→ **Yes**

CLEAR the DTCs. CHECK the yellow anti-lock brake warning indicator while driving the vehicle (brakes must not be applied) above 32 km/h (20 mph). If the yellow anti-lock brake warning indicator illuminates, RETRIEVE continuous DTCs. If DTC C1095 is retrieved again, INSTALL a new anti-lock brake control module.
REPEAT the self-test.

If the yellow anti-lock brake warning indicator does not illuminate, the system is OK.

→ **No**

TRIGGER the anti-lock brake control module active command PMP MOTOR OFF. Go to «D3».

FM4029901557020X

Fig. 14 Test D/Code C1095: Hydraulic Pump Motor Circuit Failure (Part 2 of 5). Less Stability Assist

D3	CHECK CIRCUIT 30-CF6A (RD) AND CIRCUIT 30–CF13 (RD) FOR OPEN

1 

2 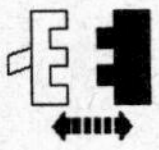

Anti-Lock Brake Control Module

3 

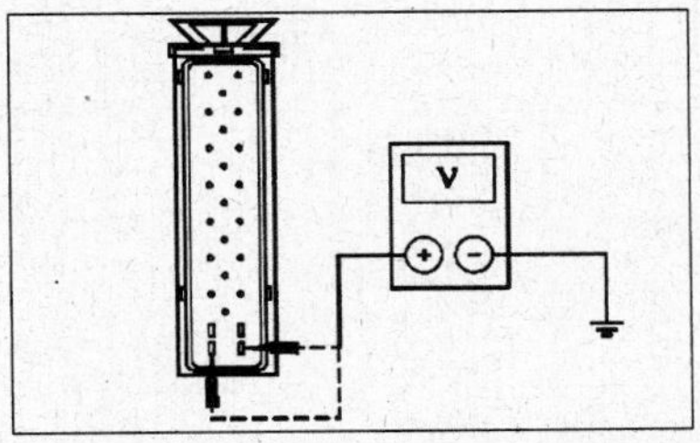

4

Measure the voltage between anti-lock brake control module C135 pin 25 circuit 30-CF6A (RD), harness side and ground; and between anti-lock brake control module C135 pin 9 circuit 30-CF13 (RD), harness side and ground.

- **Are the voltages greater than 10 volts?**

→ **Yes**

Go to «D4».

→ **No**

REPAIR circuit in question. Clear DTC's. REPEAT self-test.

FM4029901557030X

Fig. 14 Test D/Code C1095: Hydraulic Pump Motor Circuit Failure (Part 3 of 5). Less Stability Assist

D5	CHECK THE PUMP MOTOR FOR OPERATION

1 

2 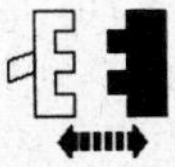 *Pump Motor Connector*

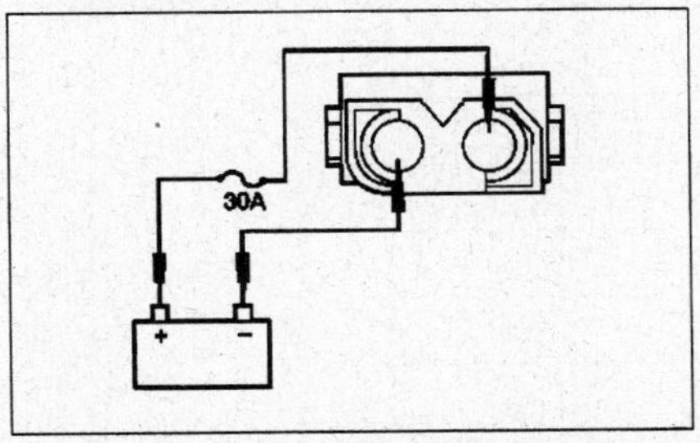

3

Using a heavy gauge wire, make a connection between the negative battery post and the pump motor connector brown wire (HCU side); momentarily connect a fused (30A) jumper wire between the positive battery post and the pump motor connector red wire (HCU side).

- **Does the pump motor run?**

→ **Yes**

INSTALL a new anti-lock brake control module.
CLEAR the DTCs. REPEAT the self-test.

→ **No**

INSTALL a new HCU. CLEAR the DTCs. REPEAT the self-test.

FM4029901557050X

Fig. 14 Test D/Code C1095: Hydraulic Pump Motor Circuit Failure (Part 5 of 5). Less Stability Assist

D4	CHECK CIRCUIT 31-CF6A (BK/YE) AND 31-CF6B (BK/YE) FOR AN OPEN

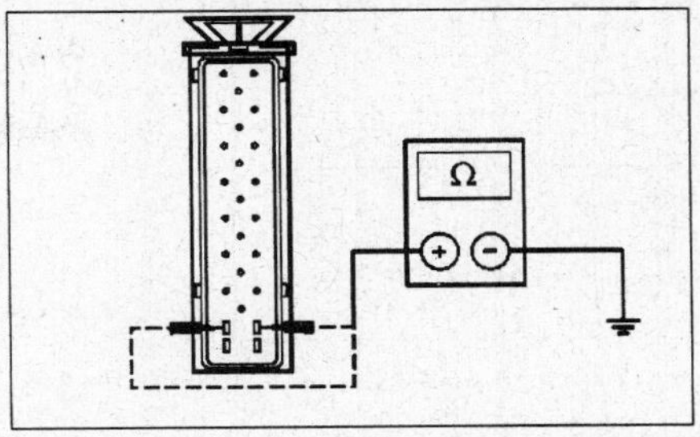

1

Measure the resistance between anti-lock brake control module C135 pin 24, circuit 31-CF6A (BK/YE), harness side and ground; and between anti-lock brake control module C135 pin 8, circuit 31-CF6B (BK/YE), harness side and ground.

- **Are the resistances less than 5 ohms?**

→ **Yes**

Go to «D5».

→ **No**

REPAIR circuit 31-CF6A (BK/YE) or circuit 31-CF6B (BK/YE). CLEAR the DTCs. REPEAT the self-test.

FM4029901557040X

Fig. 14 Test D/Code C1095: Hydraulic Pump Motor Circuit Failure (Part 4 of 5). Less Stability Assist

E1	CHECK FOR SHORT TO POWER

Note:
Both circuits must be checked for each DTC.

1 

2 

Anti-Lock Brake Control Module C135

3 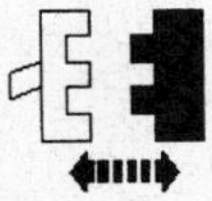

Suspect Anti-Lock Brake Sensor

4 

FM4029901558010X

Fig. 15 Test E/Codes C1145, C1155, C1165 & C1175: ABS Sensor Circuit Failure (Part 1 of 6). Less Stability Assist

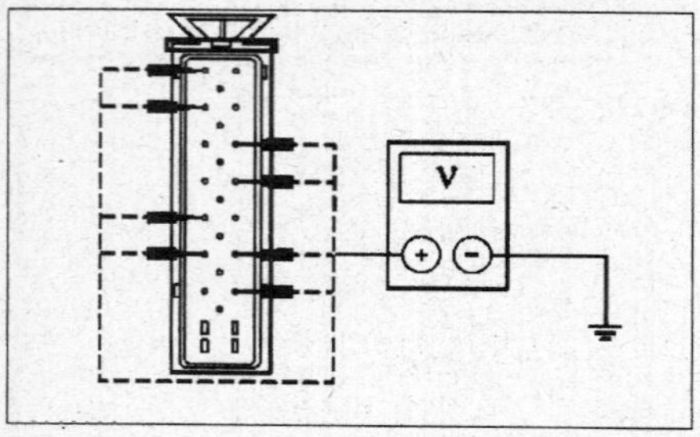

5

Measure the voltage between anti-lock brake control module C135 pin, harness side and ground as follows:

DTC	Anti-Lock Brake Control Module C135	Circuit
C1145 (RF)	Pin 3	8-CF38 (WH/RD)
C1145 (RF)	Pin 4	7-CF38 (YE/RD)
C1155 (LF)	Pin 17	8-CF32 (WH)
C1155 (LF)	Pin 18	7-CF32 (YE)
C1165 (RR)	Pin 7	8-CF40 (WH/GN)
C1165 (RR)	Pin 6	7-CF40 (YE/GN)
C1175 (LR)	Pin 21	8-CF34 (WH/BU)
C1175 (LR)	Pin 22	7-CF34 (YE/BU)

- **Is any voltage present?**

→ **Yes**

If DTC C1145, REPAIR circuit 8-CF38 (WH/RD), or circuit 7-CF38 (YE/RD). CLEAR the DTCs. REPEAT the self-test.

If DTC C1155, REPAIR circuit 8-CF32 (WH), or circuit 7-CF32 (YE). CLEAR the DTCs. REPEAT the self-test.

If DTC C1165, REPAIR circuit 8-CF40 (WH/GN), or circuit 7-CF40 (YE/GN). CLEAR the DTCs. REPEAT the self-test.

If DTC C1175, REPAIR circuit 8-CF34 (WH/BU), or circuit 7-CF34 (YE/BU). CLEAR the DTCs. REPEAT the self-test.

→ **No**

Go to «E2».

FM4029901558020X

Fig. 15 Test E/Codes C1145, C1155, C1165 & C1175: ABS Sensor Circuit Failure (Part 2 of 6). Less Stability Assist

- **Is the resistance greater than 10,000 ohms?**

→ **Yes**

Go to «E3».

→ **No**

If DTC C1145, REPAIR circuit 8-CF38 (WH/RD), or circuit 7-CF38 (YE/RD). CLEAR the DTCs. REPEAT the self-test.

If DTC C1155, REPAIR circuit 8-CF32 (WH), or circuit 7-CF32 (YE). CLEAR the DTCs. REPEAT the self-test.

If DTC C1165, REPAIR circuit 8-CF40 (WH/GN), or circuit 7-CF40 (YE/GN). CLEAR the DTCs. REPEAT the self-test.

If DTC C1175, REPAIR circuit 8-CF34 (WH/BU), or circuit 7-CF34 (YE/BU). CLEAR the DTCs. REPEAT the self-test.

FM4029901558040X

Fig. 15 Test E/Codes C1145, C1155, C1165 & C1175: ABS Sensor Circuit Failure (Part 4 of 6). Less Stability Assist

E2 CHECK FOR SHORT TO GROUND

Note:
Both circuits must be checked for each DTC.

1

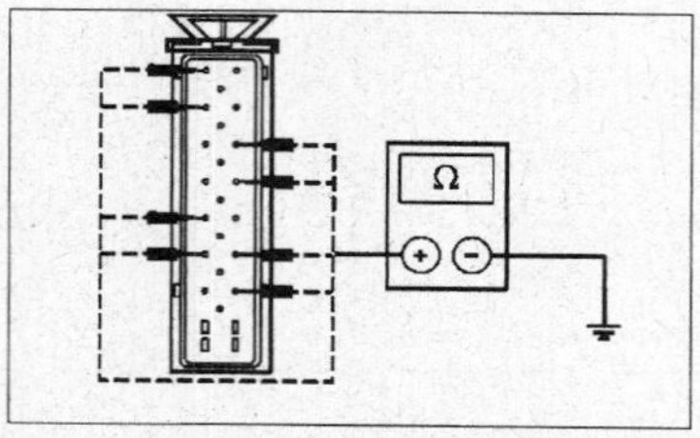

2

Measure the resistance between anti-lock brake control module C135 pin, harness side and ground as follows:

DTC	Anti-Lock Brake Control Module C135	Circuit
C1145 (RF)	Pin 3	8-CF38 (WH/RD)
C1145 (RF)	Pin 4	7-CF38 (YE/RD)
C1155 (LF)	Pin 17	8-CF32 (WH)
C1155 (LF)	Pin 18	7-CF32 (YE)
C1165 (RR)	Pin 7	8-CF40 (WH/GN)
C1165 (RR)	Pin 6	7-CF40 (YE/GN)
C1175 (LR)	Pin 21	8-CF34 (WH/BU)
C1175 (LR)	Pin 22	7-CF34 (YE/BU)

FM4029901558030X

Fig. 15 Test E/Codes C1145, C1155, C1165 & C1175: ABS Sensor Circuit Failure (Part 3 of 6). Less Stability Assist

E3 CHECK FOR AN OPEN

Note:
Both circuits must be checked for each DTC.

1 Measure the resistance between anti-lock brake control module C135 pins, harness side and suspect anti-lock brake sensor connector, harness side as follows:

DTC	Anti-Lock Brake Control Module C135 Pin	Anti-Lock Brake Sensor	Circuit
C1145 (RF)	3	C160 pin 2	8-CF38 (WH /RD)
C1145 (RF)	4	C160 pin 1	7-CF38 (YE /RD)
C1155 (LF)	17	C150 pin 2	8-CF32 (WH)
C1155 (LF)	18	C150 pin 1	7-CF32 (YE)
C1165 (RR)	7	C426 pin 1	8-CF40 (WH /GN)
C1165 (RR)	6	C426 pin 2	7-CF40 (WH /GN)
C1175 (LR)	21	C440 pin 2	8-CF34 (WH /BU)
C1175 (LR)	22	C440 pin 1	7-CF34 (YE /BU)

- **Is the resistance less than 5 ohms?**

→ **Yes**

Go to «E4».

→ **No**

If DTC C1145, REPAIR circuit 8-CF38 (WH/RD), or circuit 7-CF38 (YE/RD). CLEAR the DTCs. REPEAT the self-test.

If DTC C1155, REPAIR circuit 8-CF32 (WH), or circuit 7-CF32 (YE). CLEAR the DTCs. REPEAT the self-test.

If DTC C1165, REPAIR circuit 8-CF40 (WH/GN), or circuit 7-CF40 (YE/GN). CLEAR the DTCs. REPEAT the self-test.

If DTC C1175, REPAIR circuit 8-CF34 (WH/BU), or circuit 7-CF34 (YE/BU). CLEAR the DTCs. REPEAT the self-test.

FM4029901558050X

Fig. 15 Test E/Codes C1145, C1155, C1165 & C1175: ABS Sensor Circuit Failure (Part 5 of 6). Less Stability Assist

E4 CHECK THE ANTI-LOCK BRAKE CONTROL MODULE OUTPUT

1 *Anti-Lock Brake Control Module C135*

2

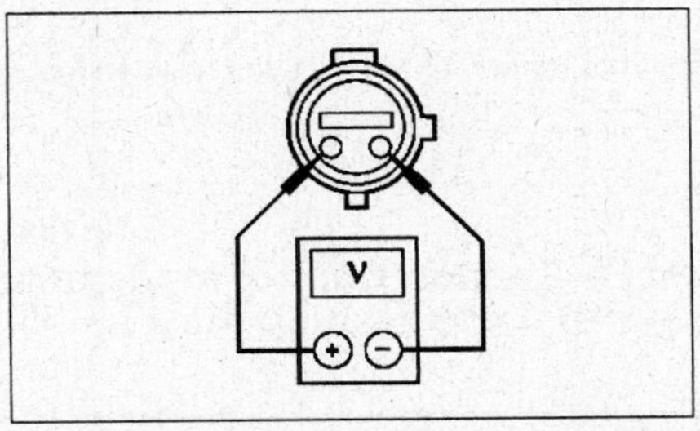

3

Measure the voltage between suspect anti-lock brake sensor connector pins, harness side.

- **Is the voltage greater than 9 volts?**

→ **Yes**

INSTALL a new anti-lock brake sensor.
CLEAR the DTCs. TEST the system for normal operation.

→ **No**

INSTALL a new anti-lock brake control module.
CLEAR the DTCs. TEST the system for normal operation.

FM4029901558060X

Fig. 15 Test E/Codes C1145, C1155, C1165 & C1175: ABS Sensor Circuit Failure (Part 6 of 6). Less Stability Assist

F2 CHECK THE ANTI-LOCK BRAKE SENSOR INDICATOR

1 Check the suspect anti-lock brake sensor indicator for corrosion, nicks, damaged teeth, incorrect mounting, alignment, and consistent air gap.

- **Is the suspect anti-lock brake sensor indicator OK?**

→ **Yes**

INSTALL a new anti-lock brake sensor.
CLEAR the DTCs. TEST the system for normal operation.

→ **No**

REPAIR as necessary. CLEAR the DTCs. TEST the system for normal operation.

FM4029901559020X

Fig. 16 Test F/Codes C1233, C1234, C1235 & C1236: ABS Sensor Input Signal Missing (Part 2 of 2). Less Stability Assist

F1 CHECK THE ANTI-LOCK BRAKE SENSOR

1 Check the suspect anti-lock brake sensor mounting. Check the suspect anti-lock brake sensor for excessive dirt buildup, metal obstructions, incorrect harness routing, and chafing.

- **Is the suspect anti-lock brake sensor OK?**

→ **Yes**

Go to «F2».

→ **No**

REPAIR as necessary. CLEAR the DTCs. TEST the system for normal operation.

FM4029901559010X

Fig. 16 Test F/Codes C1233, C1234, C1235 & C1236: ABS Sensor Input Signal Missing (Part 1 of 2). Less Stability Assist

G1 CHECK THE YELLOW ANTI-LOCK BRAKE WARNING INDICATOR

1

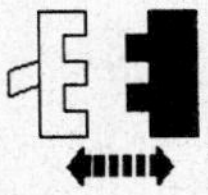

2 *Anti-Lock Brake Control Module C135*

3

- **Is the yellow anti-lock brake warning indicator illuminated?**

→ **Yes**

Go to «G2».

→ **No**

DIAGNOSE instrument cluster.

FM4029901560010X

Fig. 17 Test G: Yellow ABS Warning Indicator Does Not Self Check (Part 1 of 2). Less Stability Assist

G2	CHECK PROVE OUT

1

2 *Anti-Lock Brake Control Module C135*

3

- **Does the yellow anti-lock brake warning indicator prove out for three seconds and then turn off?**

→ **Yes**

The yellow anti-lock brake warning indicator operation is OK.

→ **No**

INSTALL a new anti-lock brake control module.
TEST the system for normal operation.

FM4029901560020X

Fig. 17 Test G: Yellow ABS Warning Indicator Does Not Self Check (Part 2 of 2). Less Stability Assist

H2	CHECK THE ABS OPERATION

1 Test drive the vehicle and carry out several anti-lock stops.

- **Does the ABS operate normally?**

→ **Yes**

Go to «H3».

→ **No**

GO to Symptom Chart.

FM4029901561020X

Fig. 18 Test H: Traction Control Inoperative (Part 2 of 4). Less Stability Assist

H1	CHECK FOR DTCS

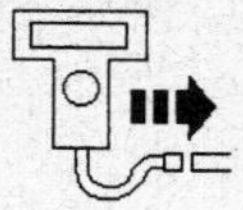

1 ***NGS***

2 Retrieve and document continuous DTCs.

- **Are any DTCs retrieved?**

→ **Yes**

GO to **Diagnostic Trouble Code & Pinpoint Test Reference Chart.**

→ **No**

Go to «H2».

FM4029901561010X

Fig. 18 Test H: Traction Control Inoperative (Part 1 of 4). Less Stability Assist

H3	CHECK THE TRACTION CONTROL OFF INPUT TO THE ANTI-LOCK BRAKE CONTROL MODULE FOR SHORT TO POWER

1

2 *Anti-Lock Brake Control Module C135*

3

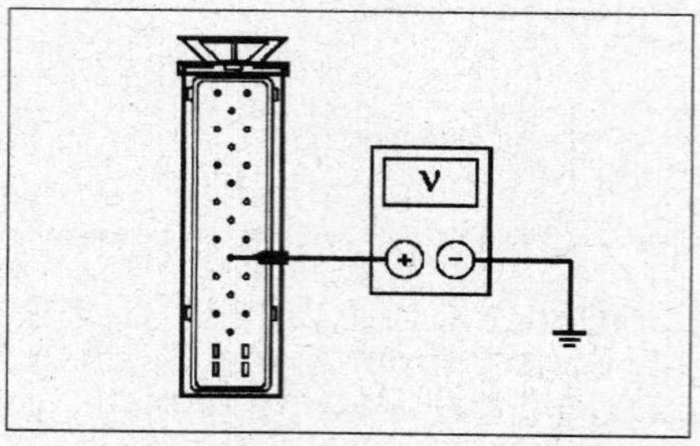

4

Measure the voltage between anti-lock brake control module C135 pin 14, circuit 8-CF54 (WH/VT), harness side and ground.

- **Is any voltage present?**

→ **Yes**

Go to «H4».

→ **No**

Install new ABS Control Module. Test system for normal operation.

FM4029901561030X

Fig. 18 Test H: Traction Control Inoperative (Part 3 of 4). Less Stability Assist

H4	CHECK CIRCUIT 8-CF54 (WH/VT) FOR A SHORT TO POWER

1

2

Traction Control Switch C308

3

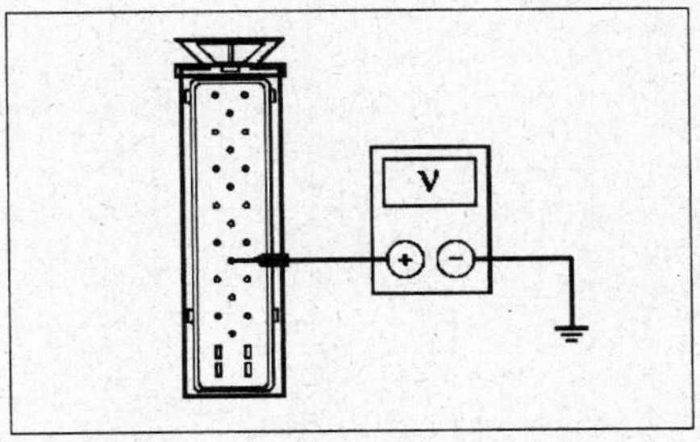

4

Measure the voltage between anti-lock brake control module C135 pin 14, circuit 8-CF54 (WH/VT), harness side and ground.

- **Is any voltage present?**

→ **Yes**

REPAIR the circuit. TEST the system for normal operation.

→ **No**

INSTALL a new traction control switch. TEST the system for normal operation.

FM4029901561040X

Fig. 18 Test H: Traction Control Inoperative (Part 4 of 4). Less Stability Assist

I2	CHECK THE TRACTION CONTROL SWITCH

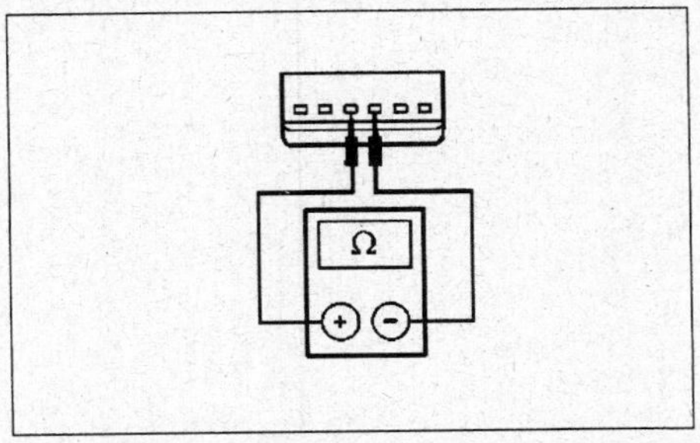

1

Measure the resistance between traction control switch, pin 4 and pin 3 (component side) while depressing the traction control switch.

- **Is the resistance less than 5 ohms?**

→ **Yes**

Go to «I3».

→ **No**

INSTALL a new traction control switch. TEST the system for normal operation.

FM4029901562020X

Fig. 19 Test I: Traction Control Cannot Be Disabled (Part 2 of 3). Less Stability Assist

I1	CHECK CIRCUIT 15-CF54 (GN/WH) FOR AN OPEN

1

2

Traction Control Switch C308

3

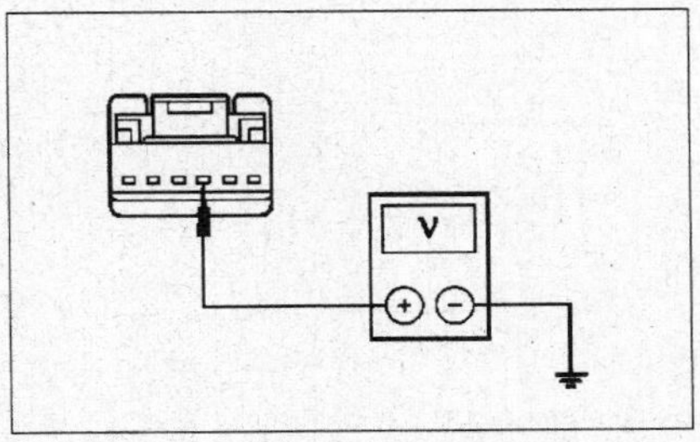

4

Measure the voltage between traction control switch C308, circuit 15-CF54 (GN/WH), harness side and ground.

- **Is any voltage present?**

→ **Yes**

Go to «I2».

→ **No**

REPAIR the circuit 15-CF54 (GN/WH) or circuit 15-DA5 (GN/OG). TEST the system for normal operation.

FM4029901562010X

Fig. 19 Test I: Traction Control Cannot Be Disabled (Part 1 of 3). Less Stability Assist

I3	CHECK CIRCUIT 8-CF54 (WH/VT) FOR AN OPEN

1

2

Anti-Lock Brake Control Module C135

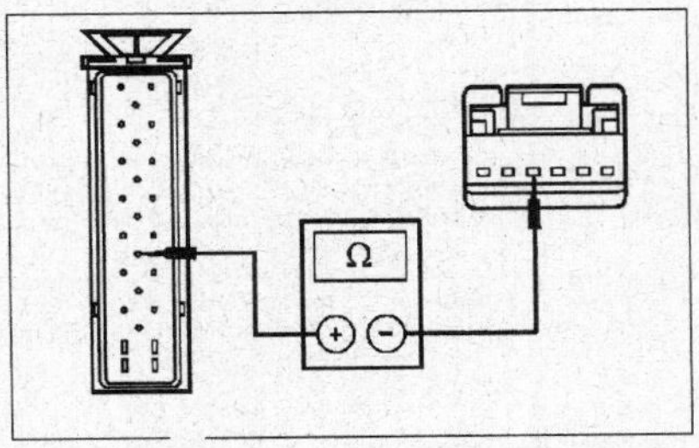

3

Measure the resistance between anti-lock brake control module C135 pin 14, circuit 8-CF54 (WH/VT), harness side and traction control switch C308 pin 4, circuit 8-CF54 (WH/VT), harness side.

- **Is the resistance less than 5 ohms?**

→ **Yes**

INSTALL a new anti-lock brake control module.
TEST the system for normal operation.

→ **No**

REPAIR the circuit. TEST the system for normal operation.

FM4029901562030X

Fig. 19 Test I: Traction Control Cannot Be Disabled (Part 3 of 3). Less Stability Assist

J1 CHECK THE TRACTION CONTROL SWITCH

1 

2 

Traction Control Switch C308

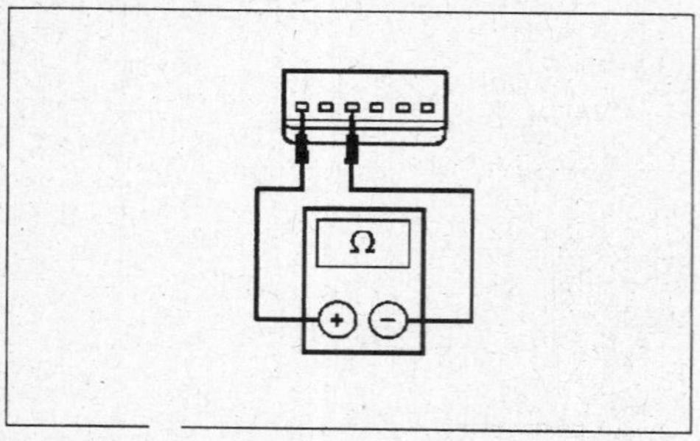

3

Measure the resistance between traction control switch pin 1 and pin 3 (component side).

- **Is the resistance approximately 32 ohms?**

→ **Yes**

Go to «J2».

→ **No**

INSTALL a new traction control switch. Test the system for normal operation.

FM4029901525010X

Fig. 20 Test J: Traction Control Switch Indicator Never/Always On (Part 1 of 3). Less Stability Assist

J3 CHECK CIRCUIT 31S-CF45 (BK/GN)

1 

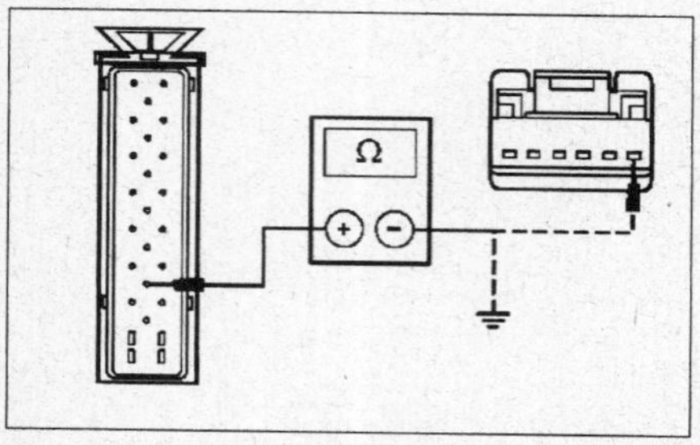

2

Measure the resistance between anti-lock brake control module C135 pin 15, circuit 31S-CF45 (BK/GN), harness side and traction control switch C308 pin 1, circuit 31S-CF45 (BK/GN), harness side; and between anti-lock brake control module C135 pin 15, circuit 31S-CF45 (BK/GN), harness side and ground.

- **Is the resistance less than 5 ohms between the anti-lock brake control module and traction control switch; and greater than 10,000 ohms between anti-lock brake control module and ground?**

→ **Yes**

INSTALL a new anti-lock brake control module.
TEST the system for normal operation.

→ **No**

REPAIR the circuit. TEST the system for normal operation.

FM4029901525030X

Fig. 20 Test J: Traction Control Switch Indicator Never/Always On (Part 3 of 3). Less Stability Assist

J2 CHECK CIRCUIT 31S-CF45 (BK/GN) FOR SHORT TO POWER

1 

Anti-Lock Brake Control Module 135

2 

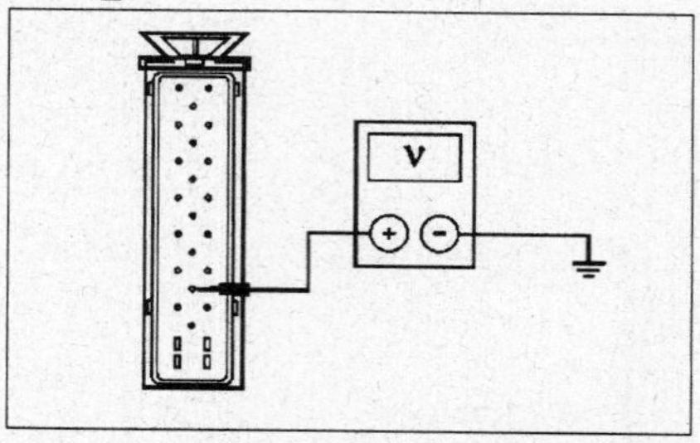

3

Measure the voltage between anti-lock brake control module C135 pin 15, circuit 31S-CF45 (BK/GN), harness side and ground.

- **Is any voltage present?**

→ **Yes**

REPAIR the circuit. TEST the system for normal operation.

→ **No**

Go to «J3».

FM4029901525020X

Fig. 20 Test J: Traction Control Switch Indicator Never/Always On (Part 2 of 3). Less Stability Assist

A1 CHECK THE VOLTAGE TO THE STABILITY ASSIST MODULE

1 

2 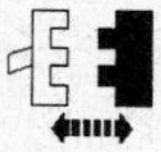

Stability Assist Module C155

3 

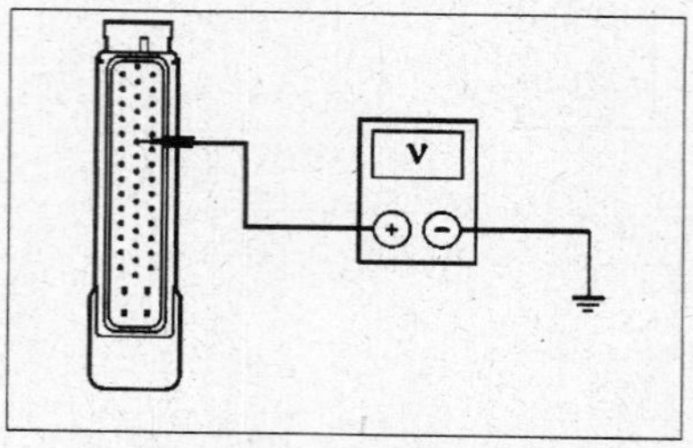

4

Measure the voltage between stability assist module C155 pin 22, circuit 20-CF6A (PK/YE), harness side, and ground.

- **Is the voltage greater than 10 volts?**

→ **Yes**

Go to «A2».

→ **No**

Repair circuit 20-CF6A (PK/YE) or circuit 20-CF6 (PK/YE). Repeat self-test.

FM4029901526010X

Fig. 21 Test A: No Communication w/Stability Assist Module (Part 1 of 2). With Stability Assist

A2	CHECK THE STABILITY ASSIST MODULE GROUNDS

1 

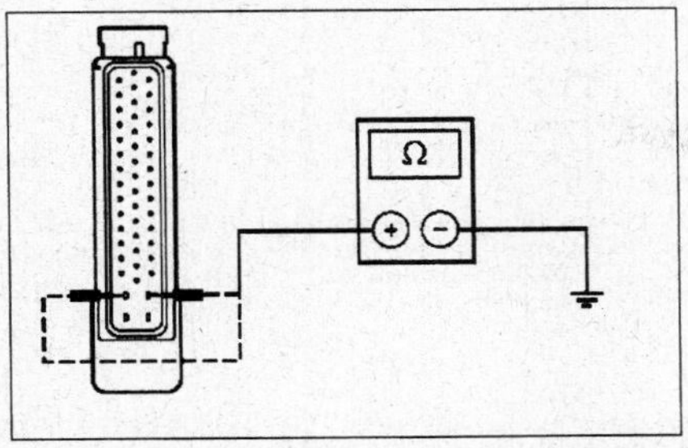

2

Measure the resistance between stability assist module C155 pin 15, circuit 31-CF6A (BK/YE), harness side, and ground; and between stability assist module C155 pin 32, circuit 31-CF6B (BK/YE), harness side, and ground.

- **Are the resistances less than 5 ohms?**

→ **Yes**

DIAGNOSE Network concern.

→ **No**

REPAIR circuit 31-CF6B (BK/YE) or circuit 31-CF6A (BK/YE). REPEAT the self-test.

FM4029901526020X

Fig. 21 Test A: No Communication w/Stability Assist Module (Part 2 of 2). With Stability Assist

C1	CHECK THE BATTERY VOLTAGE

1 Measure the battery voltage between the positive and negative battery posts with the key ON engine OFF (KOEO), and with the engine running.

- **Is the battery voltage between 10 and 13 volts with KOEO, and between 11 and 17 volts with the engine running?**

→ **Yes**

Go to «C2».

→ **No**

DIAGNOSE charging system. TEST the system for normal operation.

FM4029901528010X

Fig. 23 Test C/Code B1676: Battery Pack Voltage Out Of Range (Part 1 of 2). With Stability Assist

B1	CHECK CIRCUIT 29S-CF1 (OG/YE) FOR AN OPEN

1 

2 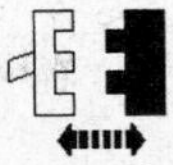

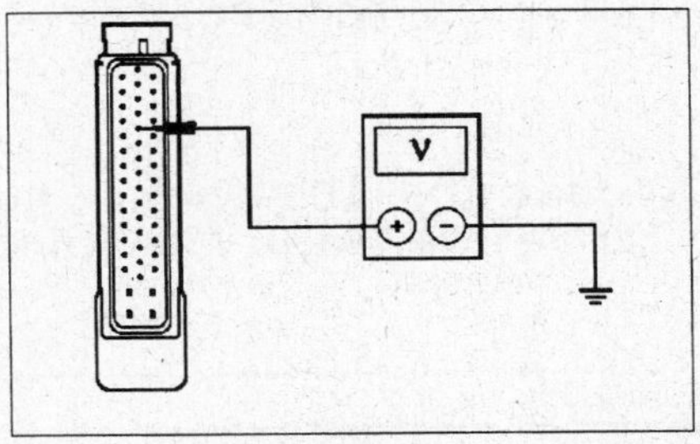

3

Measure the voltage between stability assist module C155 pin 21, circuit 29S-CF1 (OG/YE), harness side, and ground, while depressing and releasing the brake pedal.

- **Is the voltage greater than 10 volts with the brake pedal depressed and zero volts with the brake pedal released?**

→ **Yes**

INSTALL a new stability assist module. REPEAT the self-test.

→ **No**

REPAIR the circuit. CLEAR the DTCs. REPEAT the self-test.

FM4029901527000X

Fig. 22 Test B/Code B1485: Brake Pedal Input Circuit Battery Short. With Stability Assist

C2	CHECK VOLTAGE TO THE STABILITY ASSIST MODULE

1 

2 

3 

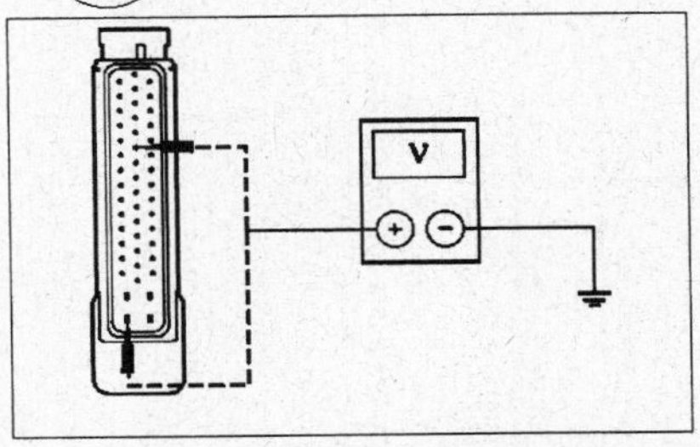

4

Measure the voltage between stability assist module C155 pin 22, circuit 20-CF6A (PK/YE), harness side and ground; and between stability assist module C155 pin 33, circuit 30-CF13 (RD), harness side and ground.

- **Are the voltages greater than 10 volts?**

→ **Yes**

INSTALL a new stability assist module. Repeat self-test.

No

Repair circuit 20-CF6A (PK/YE) or circuit 30-CF13 (RD). Clear DTC's. Repeat self-test.

FM4029901528020X

Fig. 23 Test C/Code B1676: Battery Pack Voltage Out Of Range (Part 2 of 2). With Stability Assist

D1	CHECK ABS PUMP MOTOR

1

- **Is the ABS pump motor running all the time?**

→ **Yes**

INSTALL a new stability assist module. CLEAR the DTCs. REPEAT the self-test.

→ **No**

Go to «D2».

FM4029901529010X

Fig. 24 Test D/Code C1095: ABS Hydraulic Pump Motor Circuit Failure (Part 1 of 4). With Stability Assist

D2	CHECK PUMP MOTOR OPERATION

1

2 Trigger the stability assist module active command PMP MOTOR ON.

- **Does the ABS pump motor run for approximately three seconds?**

→ **Yes**

CLEAR the DTC. CHECK the yellow ABS warning indicator while driving the vehicle (brakes must not be applied) above 32 km/h (20 mph). If the yellow ABS warning indicator illuminates, RETRIEVE the DTCs. If DTC C1095 is retrieved, INSTALL a new HCU.
CLEAR the DTCs. REPEAT the self-test. If the yellow ABS warning indicator does not illuminate, system is OK.

→ **No**

TRIGGER the stability assist module active command PMP MOTOR OFF. Go to «D3».

FM4029901529020X

Fig. 24 Test D/Code C1095: ABS Hydraulic Pump Motor Circuit Failure (Part 2 of 4). With Stability Assist

D3	CHECK CIRCUIT 30-CF13 (RD) FOR AN OPEN

1  *Stability Assist Module C155*

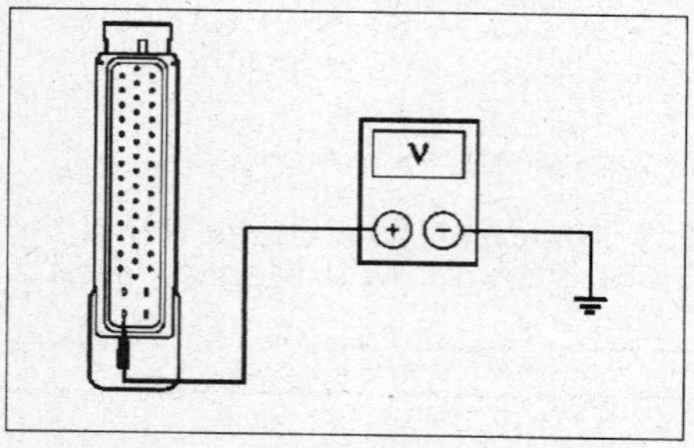

2

Measure the voltage between stability assist module C155 pin 33, circuit 30-CF13 (RD), harness side, and ground.

- **Is the voltage greater than 10 volts?**

→ **Yes**

Go to «D4».

→ **No**

REPAIR the circuit. CLEAR the DTCs. REPEAT the self-test.

FM4029901529030X

Fig. 24 Test D/Code C1095: ABS Hydraulic Pump Motor Circuit Failure (Part 3 of 4). With Stability Assist

D4	CHECK CIRCUIT 31-CF6A (BK/YE) AND 31-CF6B (BK/YE) FOR AN OPEN

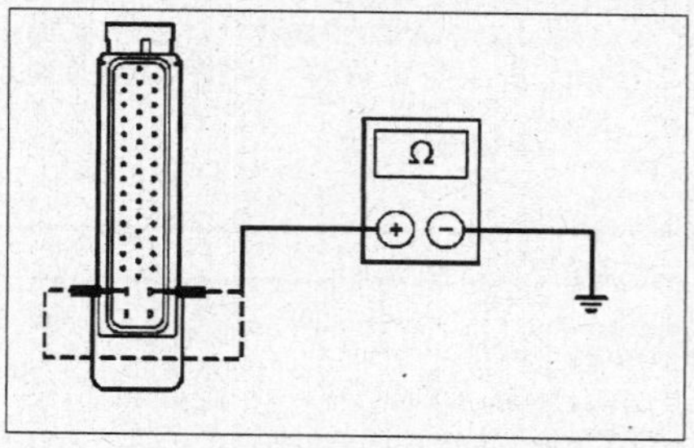

1

Measure the resistance between stability assist module C155 pin 15, circuit 31-CF6A (BK/YE), harness side, and ground; and between stability assist module C155 pin 32, circuit 31-CF6B (BK/YE), harness side, and ground.

- **Are the resistances less than 5 ohms?**

→ **Yes**

INSTALL a new HCU. REPEAT the self-test.

→ **No**

REPAIR circuit 31-CF6B (BK/YE) or circuit 31-CF6A (BK/YE). CLEAR the DTCs. REPEAT the self-test.

FM4029901529040X

Fig. 24 Test D/Code C1095: ABS Hydraulic Pump Motor Circuit Failure (Part 4 of 4). With Stability Assist

E1 CHECK FOR SHORT TO POWER

Note:
Both circuits must be checked for each DTC.

1 

2 

Stability Assist Module C155

3 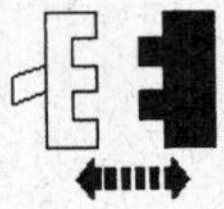

Suspect Anti-lock Brake Sensor

4 

FM4029901530010X

Fig. 25 Test E/Codes C1145, C1155, C1165 & C1175: ABS Sensor Input Circuit Failure (Part 1 of 5). With Stability Assist

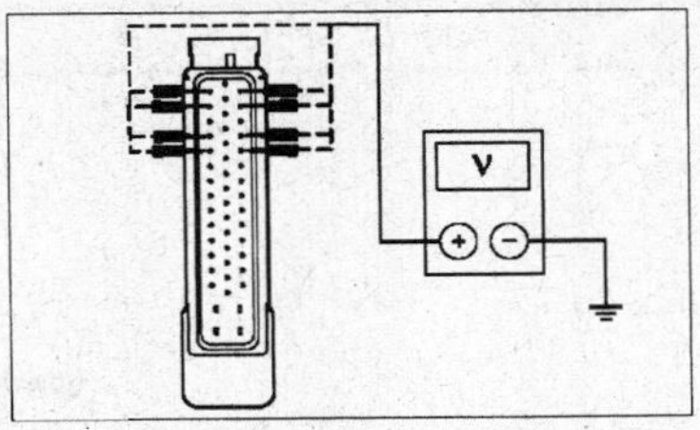

5

Measure the voltage between stability assist module C155 pin, harness side, and ground, as follows:

DTC	Stability Assist Module C155	Circuit
C1145 (RF)	Pin 35	7-CF38 (YE/RD)
C1145 (RF)	Pin 34	8-CF38 (WH/RD)
C1155 (LF)	Pin 1	7-CF32 (YE)
C1155 (LF)	Pin 2	8-CF32 (WH)
C1165 (RR)	Pin 38	7-CF40 (YE/GN)
C1165 (RR)	Pin 37	8-CF40 (WH/GN)
C1175 (LR)	Pin 5	7-CF34 (YE/BU)
C1175 (LR)	Pin 4	8-CF34 (WH/BU)

- **Is voltage present?**

→ **Yes**

If DTC C1145, REPAIR circuit 7-CF38 (YE/RD) or circuit 8-CF38 (YE/BK). CLEAR the DTCs. REPEAT the self-test.

If DTC C1155, REPAIR circuit 7-CF32 (YE) or circuit 8-CF32 (WH). CLEAR the DTCs. REPEAT the self-test.

If DTC C1165, REPAIR circuit 7-CF40 (YE/GN) or circuit 8-CF40 (WH/GN). CLEAR the DTCs. REPEAT the self-test.

If DTC C1175, REPAIR circuit 7-CF34 (YE/BU) or circuit 8-CF34 (WH/BU). CLEAR the DTCs. REPEAT the self-test.

→ **No**

Go to «E2».

FM4029901530020X

Fig. 25 Test E/Codes C1145, C1155, C1165 & C1175: ABS Sensor Input Circuit Failure (Part 2 of 5). With Stability Assist

E2 CHECK FOR SHORT TO GROUND

Note:
Both circuits must be checked for each DTC.

1 

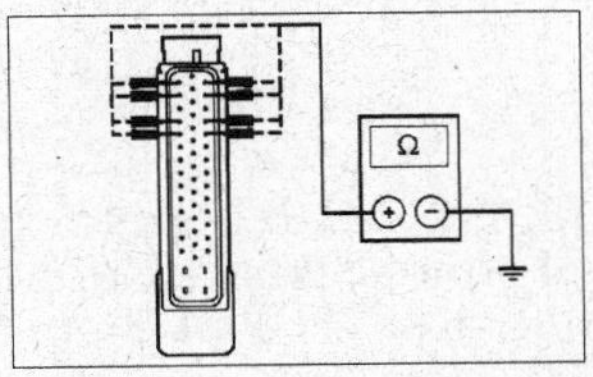

2

Measure the resistance between stability assist module C155 pin, harness side, and ground, as follows:

DTC	Stability Assist Module C155	Circuit
C1145 (RF)	Pin 35	7-CF38 (YE/RD)
C1145 (RF)	Pin 34	8-CF38 (WH/RD)
C1155 (LF)	Pin 1	7-CF32 (YE)
C1155 (LF)	Pin 2	8-CF32 (WH)
C1165 (RR)	Pin 38	7-CF40 (YE/GN)
C1165 (RR)	Pin 37	8-CF40 (WH/GN)
C1175 (LR)	Pin 5	7-CF34 (YE/BU)
C1175 (LR)	Pin 4	8-CF34 (WH/BU)

- **Are the resistances greater than 10,000 ohms?**

→ **Yes**

Go to «E3».

→ **No**

If DTC C1145, REPAIR circuit 7-CF38 (YE/RD) or circuit 8-CF38 (YE/BK). CLEAR the DTCs. REPEAT the self-test.

If DTC C1155, REPAIR circuit 7-CF32 (YE) or circuit 8-CF32 (WH). CLEAR the DTCs. REPEAT the self-test.

If DTC C1165, REPAIR circuit 7-CF40 (YE/GN) or circuit 8-CF40 (WH/GN). CLEAR the DTCs. REPEAT the self-test.

If DTC C1175, REPAIR circuit 7-CF34 (YE/BU) or circuit 8-CF34 (WH/BU). CLEAR the DTCs. REPEAT the self-test.

FM4029901530030X

Fig. 25 Test E/Codes C1145, C1155, C1165 & C1175: ABS Sensor Input Circuit Failure (Part 3 of 5). With Stability Assist

E3 CHECK FOR AN OPEN

Note:
Both circuits must be checked for each DTC.

1 Measure the resistance between stability assist module C155 pins, harness side, and suspect anti-lock brake sensor connector, harness side, as follows:

DTC	Stability Assist Module C155	Anti-lock Brake Sensor	Circuit
C1145 (RF)	Pin 35	C160 Pin 1	7-CF38 (YE /RD)
C1145 (RF)	Pin 34	C160 Pin 1	8-CF38 (YE /BK)
C1155 (LF)	Pin 1	C150 Pin 1	7-CF32 (YE)
C1155 (LF)	Pin 2	C150 Pin 2	8-CF32 (WH)
C1165 (RR)	Pin 38	C426 Pin 1	7-CF40 (YE /GN)
C1165 (RR)	Pin 37	C426 Pin 2	8-CF40 (WH /GN)
C1175 (LR)	Pin 5	C440 Pin 1	7-CF34 (YE /BU)
C1175 (LR)	Pin 4	C440 Pin 2	8-CF34 (WH /BU)

- **Is the resistance less than 5 ohms?**

→ **Yes**

Go to «E4».

→ **No**

If DTC C1145, REPAIR circuit 7-CF38 (YE/RD) or circuit 8-CF38 (YE/BK). CLEAR the DTCs. REPEAT the self-test.

If DTC C1155, REPAIR circuit 7-CF32 (YE) or circuit 8-CF32 (WH). CLEAR the DTCs. REPEAT the self-test.

If DTC C1165, REPAIR circuit 7-CF40 (YE/GN) or circuit 8-CF40 (WH/GN). CLEAR the DTCs. REPEAT the self-test.

If DTC C1175, REPAIR circuit 7-CF34 (YE/BU) or circuit 8-CF34 (WH/BU). CLEAR the DTCs. REPEAT the self-test.

FM4029901530040X

Fig. 25 Test E/Codes C1145, C1155, C1165 & C1175: ABS Sensor Input Circuit Failure (Part 4 of 5). With Stability Assist

E4	CHECK THE STABILITY ASSIST MODULE OUTPUT

1 

Stability Assist Module C155

2 

3 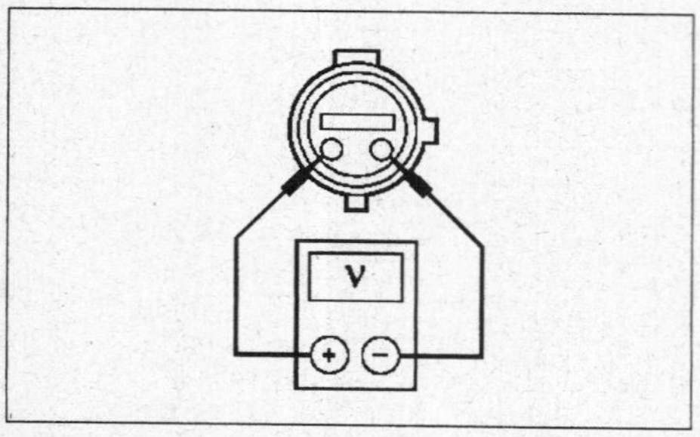

Measure the voltage between suspect anti-lock brake sensor pins, harness side.

- **Is the voltage greater than 9 volts?**

→ **Yes**

INSTALL a new stability assist module. CLEAR the DTCs. REPEAT the self-test.

→ **No**

INSTALL a new anti-lock brake sensor. CLEAR the DTCs. REPEAT the self-test.

FM4029901530050X

Fig. 25 Test E/Codes C1145, C1155, C1165 & C1175: ABS Sensor Input Circuit Failure (Part 5 of 5). With Stability Assist

F2	CHECK THE ANTI-LOCK BRAKE SENSOR INDICATOR

1 Check the suspect anti-lock brake sensor indicator for corrosion, nicks, damaged teeth, correct mounting, alignment, and consistent air gap.

- **Is the suspect anti-lock brake sensor indicator OK?**

→ **Yes**

INSTALL a new anti-lock brake sensor. CLEAR the DTCs. REPEAT the self-test.

→ **No**

REPAIR as necessary. CLEAR the DTCs. REPEAT the self-test.

FM4029901531020X

Fig. 26 Test F/Codes C1233, C1234, C1235 & C1236: ABS Sensor Input Signal Missing (Part 2 of 2). With Stability Assist

F1	CHECK THE ANTI-LOCK BRAKE SENSOR

1 Check the suspect anti-lock brake sensor mounting. Check the suspect anti-lock brake sensor for excessive dirt buildup, metal obstructions, incorrect harness routing, and chafing.

- **Is the suspect anti-lock brake sensor OK?**

→ **Yes**

Go to «F2».

→ **No**

REPAIR as necessary. CLEAR the DTCs. REPEAT the self-test.

FM4029901531010X

Fig. 26 Test F/Codes C1233, C1234, C1235 & C1236: ABS Sensor Input Signal Missing (Part 1 of 2). With Stability Assist

G1	CARRY OUT THE RECALIBRATION PROCEDURE

1 

2 

Clear the DTC

3 Carry out the steering wheel angle recalibration procedure using the NGS Tester.

4 

Retrieve DTCs

- **Are any DTCs retrieved or does the recalibration procedure indicate a fault?**

→ **Yes**

If DTC C1277 or C1278 is retrieved or recalibration procedure indicate a fault, Go to «G2».

If any other DTC, GO to Diagnostic Trouble Code & Pinp[oint Test Reference Chart.

→ **No**

The stability assist system is operating correctly.

FM4029901532010X

Fig. 27 Test G/Codes C1277 & C1278: Steering Wheel Angle 1 & 2 Circuit Failure/Steering Wheel Angle 1 & 2 Circuit Fault (Part 1 of 7). With Stability Assist

G2 CHECK THE VOLTAGE TO THE STEERING WHEEL ROTATION SENSOR

1 

2 

Steering Wheel Rotation Sensor C226

3 

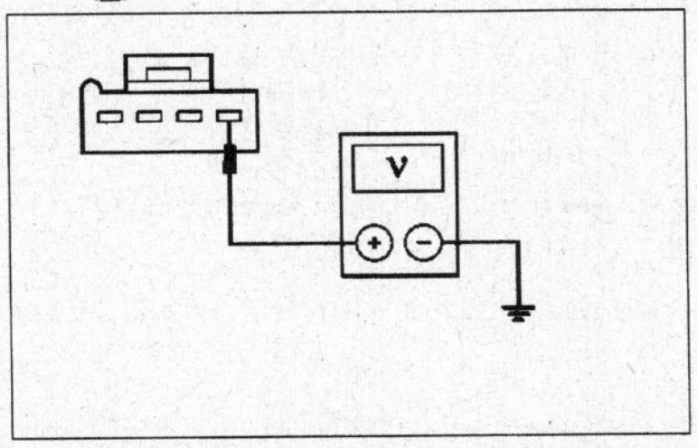

4

Measure the voltage between steering wheel rotation sensor C226 pin 4, circuit 15-CC16 (GN/OG), harness side, and ground.

- **Is the voltage greater than 10 volts?**

➔ **Yes**

Go to «G3».

➔ **No**

Repair the circuit. Clear DTC's. Re-calibrate stability assist module. Repeat self-test

FM4029901532020X

Fig. 27 Test G/Codes C1277 & C1278: Steering Wheel Angle 1 & 2 Circuit Failure/Steering Wheel Angle 1 & 2 Circuit Fault (Part 2 of 7). With Stability Assist

G3 CHECK THE STEERING WHEEL ROTATION SENSOR CIRCUITRY FOR SHORT TO POWER

1 

2 

Stability Assist Module C155

3 

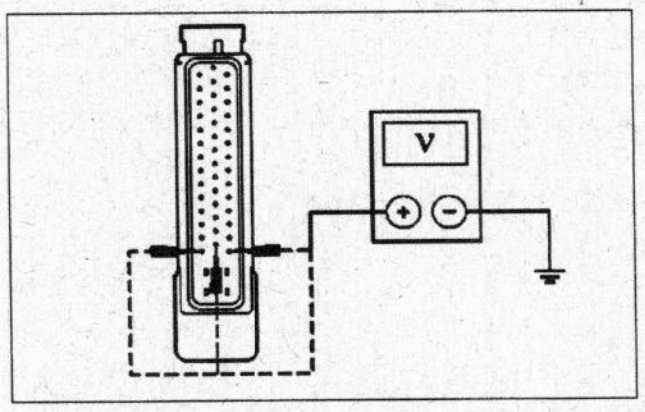

4

Measure the voltage between stability assist module C155 pins, harness side and ground as follows:

Stability Assist Module C155	Circuit
Pin 30	9-CC16 (BN/YE)
Pin 47	8-CC18 (WH/RD)
Pin 14	10-CC17 (GY)

- **Is any voltage present?**

➔ **Yes**

REPAIR the circuit in question. CLEAR the DTCs. RECALIBRATE the stability assist module. REPEAT the self-test.

➔ **No**

Go to «G4».

FM4029901532030X

Fig. 27 Test G/Codes C1277 & C1278: Steering Wheel Angle 1 & 2 Circuit Failure/Steering Wheel Angle 1 & 2 Circuit Fault (Part 3 of 7). With Stability Assist

G4 CHECK THE STEERING WHEEL ROTATION SENSOR CIRCUITRY FOR SHORT TO GROUND

1 

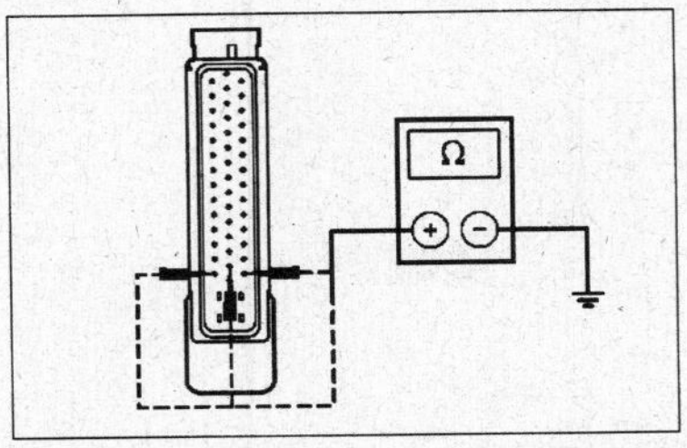

2

Measure the resistance between stability assist module C155 pins, harness side and ground as follows:

Stability Assist Module C155	Circuit
Pin 30	9-CC16 (BN/YE)
Pin 47	8-CC18 (WH/RD)
Pin 14	10-CC17 (GY)

- **Is the resistance greater than 10,000 ohms?**

➔ **Yes**

Go to «G5».

➔ **No**

REPAIR the circuit in question. CLEAR the DTCs. RECALIBRATE the stability assist module. REPEAT the self-test.

FM4029901532040X

Fig. 27 Test G/Codes C1277 & C1278: Steering Wheel Angle 1 & 2 Circuit Failure/Steering Wheel Angle 1 & 2 Circuit Fault (Part 4 of 7). With Stability Assist

G5 CHECK THE STEERING WHEEL ROTATION SENSOR CIRCUITRY FOR AN OPEN

1 

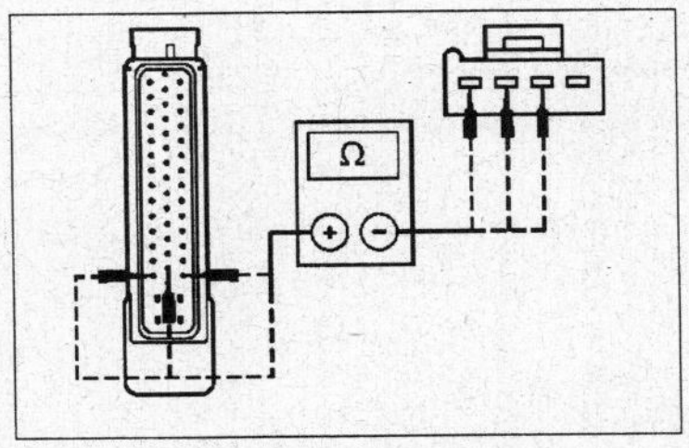

2

Measure the resistance between stability assist module C155 pins, harness side, and steering wheel rotation sensor C226 pins, harness side, as follows:

Stability Assist Module C155	Steering Wheel Rotation Sensor C226	Circuit
Pin 30	Pin 1	9-CC16 (BN/YE)
Pin 47	Pin 2	8-CC18 (WH/RD)
Pin 14	Pin 3	10-CC17 (GY)

- **Is the resistance less than 5 ohms?**

➔ **Yes**

Go to «G6».

➔ **No**

REPAIR the circuit in question. CLEAR the DTCs. RECALIBRATE the stability assist module. REPEAT the self-test.

FM4029901532050X

Fig. 27 Test G/Codes C1277 & C1278: Steering Wheel Angle 1 & 2 Circuit Failure/Steering Wheel Angle 1 & 2 Circuit Fault (Part 5 of 7). With Stability Assist

G6 CHECK THE STEERING WHEEL ROTATION SENSOR OUTPUT

1  *Steering Wheel Rotation Sensor C226*

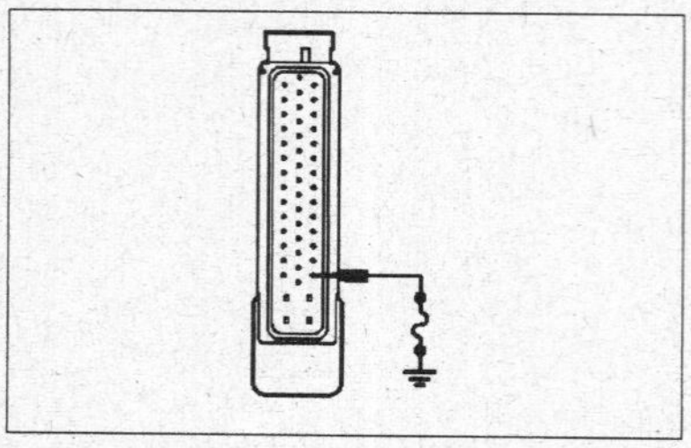

2 Connect a fused (5A) jumper wire between stability assist module C155 pin 14, circuit 10-CC17 (GY), harness side, and ground.

3 Place the 73III Automotive Meter to the diode test position.

4 

FM4029901532060X

Fig. 27 Test G/Codes C1277 & C1278: Steering Wheel Angle 1 & 2 Circuit Failure/Steering Wheel Angle 1 & 2 Circuit Fault (Part 6 of 7). With Stability Assist

H1 CARRY OUT THE RECALIBRATION PROCEDURE

1 

2  *Clear DTC*

3 Carry out the yaw rate sensor recalibration procedure using the NGS Tester.

4  *Retrieve DTCs*

- **Are any DTCs retrieved or does the recalibration procedure indicate a fault?**

→ **Yes**

If DTC C1279 or C1280 is retrieved or recalibration procedure indicate a fault, Go to «H2».

If any other DTC, Go to Diagnostic Trouble Code & Pinpoint Test Reference.

→ **No**

The stability assist system is operating correctly.

FM4029901533010X

Fig. 28 Test H/Codes C1279 & C1280: Yaw Rate Sensor Circuit Failure/Yaw Rate Sensor Signal Fault (Part 1 of 10). With Stability Assist

H2 CHECK THE STABILITY ASSIST MODULE PID YAWRATE

1 Monitor the stability assist module PID YAWRATE.

- **Is the stability assist module PID YAWRATE value between 479 and 545?**

→ **Yes**

INSTALL a new stability assist module. REPEAT the self-test.

→ **No**

Go to «H3».

FM4029901533020X

Fig. 28 Test H/Codes C1279 & C1280: Yaw Rate Sensor Circuit Failure/Yaw Rate Sensor Signal Fault (Part 2 of 10). With Stability Assist

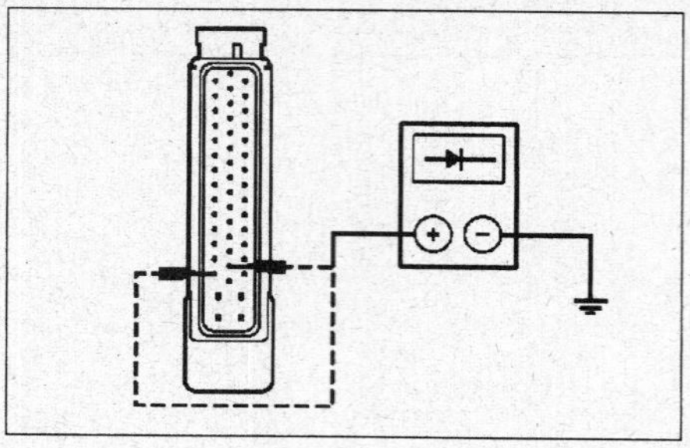

5

Note:
Touch 73III Automotive Meter leads together to be sure the audio (beep) function is operational.

Note:
The 73III Automotive Meter should beep several times while rotating the steering wheel.

Connect 73III Automotive Meter leads between stability assist module C155 pin 30, circuit 9-CC16 (BN/YE), harness side, and ground; and between stability assist module C155 pin 47, circuit 8-CC18 (WH/RD), harness side, and ground. Listen for an audible beep while turning the steering wheel one quarter turn in each direction.

- **Does 73III Automotive Meter beep multiple times in each direction?**

→ **Yes**

INSTALL a new stability assist module. CLEAR the DTCs. REPEAT the self-test.

→ **No**

INSTALL a new steering wheel rotation sensor. CLEAR the DTCs. REPEAT the self-test.

FM4029901532070X

Fig. 27 Test G/Codes C1277 & C1278: Steering Wheel Angle 1 & 2 Circuit Failure/Steering Wheel Angle 1 & 2 Circuit Fault (Part 7 of 7). With Stability Assist

H3 CHECK THE RETURN SIGNAL VOLTAGE

1 

2 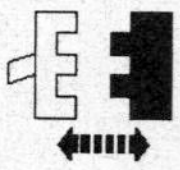 *Stability Assist Module C155*

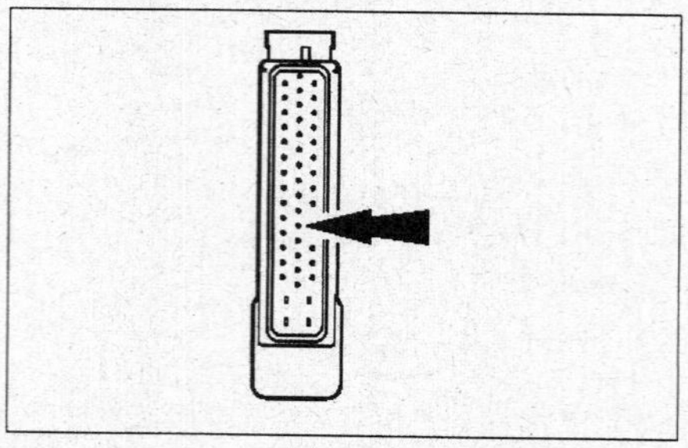

3 Back out the stability assist module C155 pin 27, circuit 8-CF67 (WH/RD), harness side.

4  *Stability Assist Module C155*

5 

FM4029901533030X

Fig. 28 Test H/Codes C1279 & C1280: Yaw Rate Sensor Circuit Failure/Yaw Rate Sensor Signal Fault (Part 3 of 10). With Stability Assist

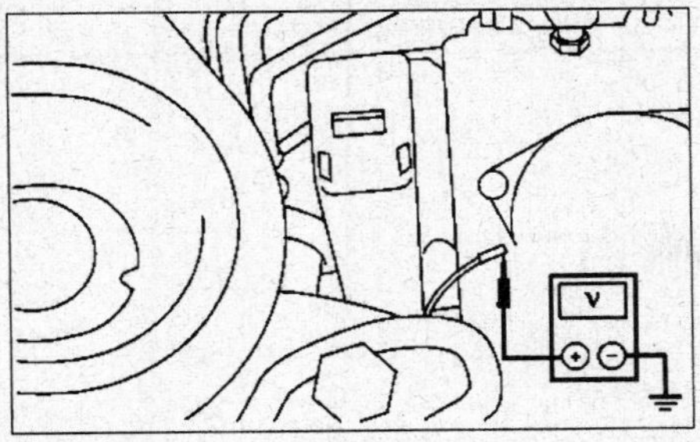

6

Measure the voltage between stability assist module C155 pin 27, circuit 8-CF67 (WH/RD), harness side, and ground.

- **Is the voltage approximately 2.5 volts?**

→ **Yes**

RECONNECT the backed out pin. Go to «H4».

→ **No**

Go to «H5».

FM4029901533040X

Fig. 28 Test H/Codes C1279 & C1280: Yaw Rate Sensor Circuit Failure/Yaw Rate Sensor Signal Fault (Part 4 of 10). With Stability Assist

H5 CHECK YAW RATE SENSOR CIRCUITRY FOR SHORT TO POWER

1

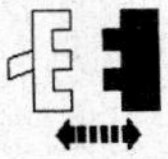

2

Stability Assist Module C155

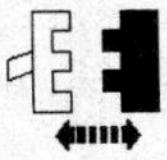

3

Yaw Rate Sensor C245

4

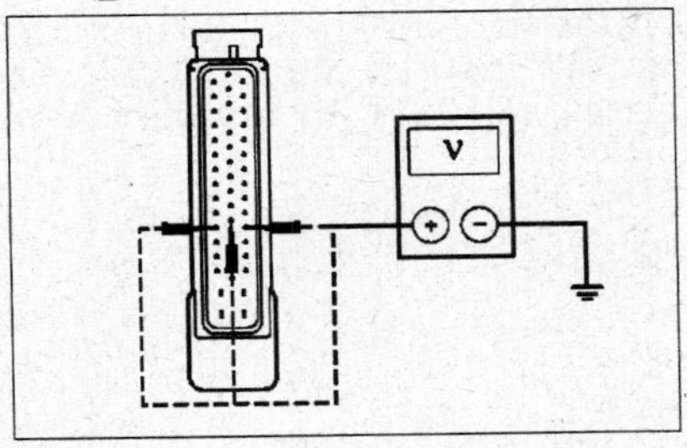

5

FM4029901533060X

Fig. 28 Test H/Codes C1279 & C1280: Yaw Rate Sensor Circuit Failure/Yaw Rate Sensor Signal Fault (Part 6 of 10). With Stability Assist

H4 REVERIFY THE STABILITY ASSIST MODULE PID YAWRATE

1 Monitor the stability assist module PID YAWRATE.

- **Is the stability assist module PID YAWRATE value between 479 and 545?**

→ **Yes**

Check the stability assist module connector for loose or corroded pins. CLEAR the DTCs. REPEAT the self-test.

→ **No**

INSTALL a new stability assist module. REPEAT the self-test.

FM4029901533050X

Fig. 28 Test H/Codes C1279 & C1280: Yaw Rate Sensor Circuit Failure/Yaw Rate Sensor Signal Fault (Part 5 of 10). With Stability Assist

Measure the voltage between stability assist module C155 pins, harness side, and ground as follows:

Stability Assist Module C155	Circuit
Pin 27	8-CF67 (WH/RD)
Pin 11	9-CF67 (BN/RD)
Pin 44	7-CF67 (YE/RD)

- **Is any voltage present?**

→ **Yes**

REPAIR the circuit in question. CLEAR the DTCs. RECALIBRATE the stability assist module. REPEAT the self-test.

→ **No**

Go to «H6».

FM4029901533070X

Fig. 28 Test H/Codes C1279 & C1280: Yaw Rate Sensor Circuit Failure/Yaw Rate Sensor Signal Fault (Part 7 of 10). With Stability Assist

H6 CHECK YAW RATE SENSOR CIRCUITRY FOR SHORT TO GROUND

1

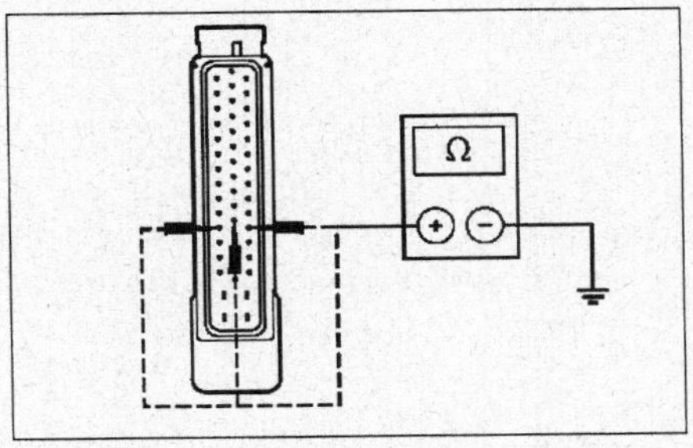

2

Measure the resistance between stability assist module C155 pins, harness side, and ground as follows:

Stability Assist Module C155	Circuit
Pin 27	8-CF67 (WH/RD)
Pin 11	9-CF67 (BN/RD)
Pin 44	7-CF67 (YE/RD)

- **Is the resistance greater than 10,000 ohms?**

→ **Yes**

Go to «H7».

→ **No**

REPAIR the circuit in question. CLEAR the DTCs. RECALIBRATE the stability assist module. REPEAT the self-test.

FM4029901533080X

Fig. 28 Test H/Codes C1279 & C1280: Yaw Rate Sensor Circuit Failure/Yaw Rate Sensor Signal Fault (Part 8 of 10). With Stability Assist

H7 CHECK YAW RATE SENSOR CIRCUITRY FOR AN OPEN

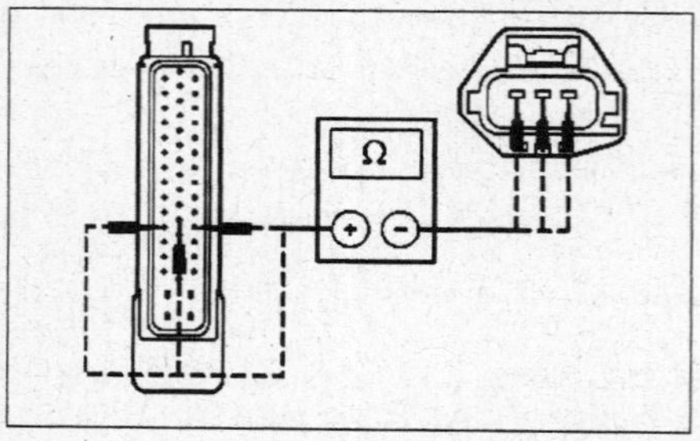

1

Measure the resistance between stability assist module C155 pins, harness side, and yaw rate sensor C245 pins, harness side as follows:

Stability Assist Module C155	Yaw Rate Sensor C245	Circuit
Pin 27	Pin 1	8-CF67 (WH/RD)
Pin 11	Pin 2	9-CF67 (BN/RD)
Pin 44	Pin 3	7-CF67 (YE/RD)

- **Is the resistance less than 5 ohms?**

➔ **Yes**

Go to «H8».

➔ **No**

REPAIR the circuit in question. CLEAR the DTCs. RECALIBRATE the stability assist module. REPEAT the self-test.

FM4029901533090X

Fig. 28 Test H/Codes C1279 & C1280: Yaw Rate Sensor Circuit Failure/Yaw Rate Sensor Signal Fault (Part 9 of 10). With Stability Assist

H8 CHECK THE VOLTAGE FROM THE STABILITY ASSIST MODULE

1

Stability Assist Module C155

2

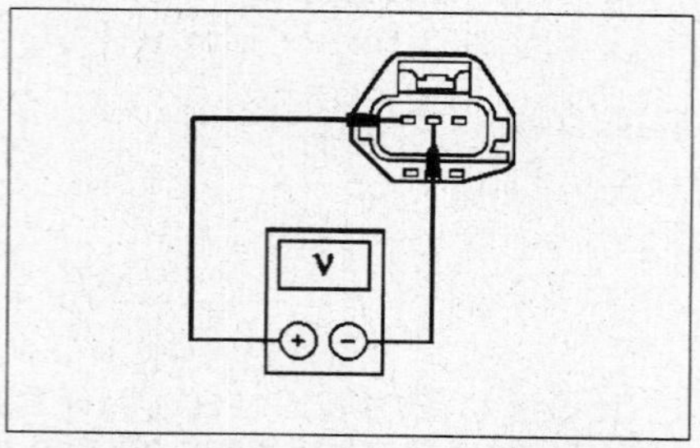

3

Measure the voltage between yaw rate sensor C245 pin 3, circuit 7-CF67 (YE/RD), harness side, and yaw rate sensor C245 pin 2, circuit 9-CF67 (BN/RD), harness side.

- **Is the voltage approximately 5 volts?**

➔ **Yes**

INSTALL a new yaw rate sensor. CLEAR the DTCs. REPEAT the self-test.

➔ **No**

INSTALL a new stability assist module. CLEAR the DTCs. REPEAT the self-test.

FM4029901533100X

Fig. 28 Test H/Codes C1279 & C1280: Yaw Rate Sensor Circuit Failure/Yaw Rate Sensor Signal Fault (Part 10 of 10). With Stability Assist

I1 CARRY OUT THE RECALIBRATION PROCEDURE

1

2 *Clear DTC*

3 Carry out the lateral accelerometer recalibration procedure using the NGS Tester.

4 *Retrieve DTCs*

- **Are any DTCs retrieved or does the recalibration procedure indicate a fault?**

➔ **Yes**

If DTC C1281 or C1282 is retrieved or recalibration procedure indicates a fault, Go to «I2».

If any other DTC, GO to Diagnostic Trouble Code & Pinpoint Test Reference Chart.

➔ **No**

The stability assist system is operating correctly.

FM4029901534010X

Fig. 29 Test I/Codes C1281 & C1282: Lateral Accelerometer Circuit Failure/Lateral Accelerometer Signal Fault (Part 1 of 10). With Stability Assist

I2 CHECK THE STABILITY ASSIST MODULE PID LATACCVL

1 Monitor the stability assist module PID LATACCVL.

- **Is the stability assist module PID LATACCVL value between 547 and 681?**

➔ **Yes**

INSTALL a new stability assist module. REPEAT the self-test.

➔ **No**

Go to «I3».

FM4029901534020X

Fig. 29 Test I/Codes C1281 & C1282: Lateral Accelerometer Circuit Failure/Lateral Accelerometer Signal Fault (Part 2 of 10). With Stability Assist

I3 CHECK THE RETURN SIGNAL VOLTAGE

1 

2 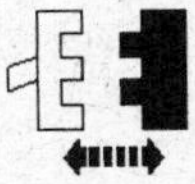

Stability Assist Module C155

3 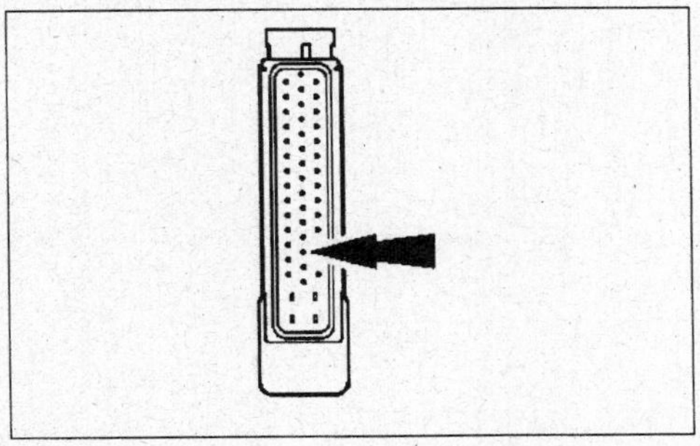

Back out the stability assist module C155 pin 29, circuit 8-CF66 (WH/BU), harness side.

4 

Stability Assist Module C155

5 

6 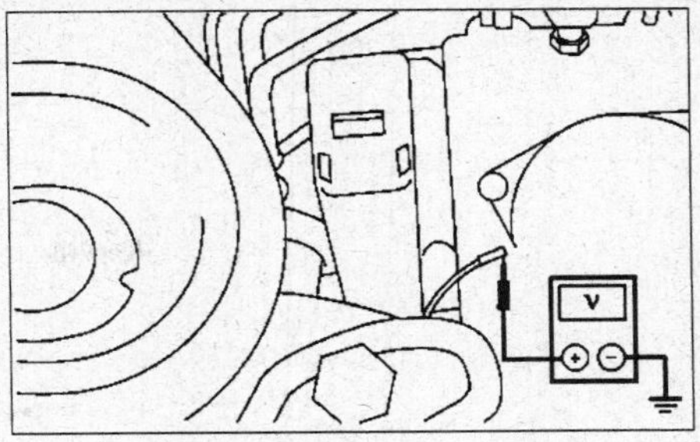

Measure the voltage between stability assist module C155 pin 29, circuit 8-CF66 (WH/BU), harness side, and ground.

- **Is the voltage approximately 3 volts?**

→ **Yes**

RECONNECT the backed out pin. Go to «I4».

→ **No**

Go to «I5».

FM4029901534030X

Fig. 29 Test I/Codes C1281 & C1282: Lateral Accelerometer Circuit Failure/Lateral Accelerometer Signal Fault (Part 3 of 10). With Stability Assist

FM4029901534040X

Fig. 29 Test I/Codes C1281 & C1282: Lateral Accelerometer Circuit Failure/Lateral Accelerometer Signal Fault (Part 4 of 10). With Stability Assist

I4 REVERIFY THE STABILITY ASSIST MODULE PID LATACCVL

1 Monitor the stability assist module PID LATACCVL.

- **Is the stability assist module PID LATACCVL value between 547 and 681?**

→ **Yes**

Check the stability assist module connector for loose or corroded pins. CLEAR the DTCs. REPEAT the self-test.

→ **No**

INSTALL a new stability assist module. REPEAT the self-test.

FM4029901534050X

Fig. 29 Test I/Codes C1281 & C1282: Lateral Accelerometer Circuit Failure/Lateral Accelerometer Signal Fault (Part 5 of 10). With Stability Assist

I5 CHECK LATERAL ACCELEROMETER CIRCUITRY FOR SHORT TO POWER

1 

2 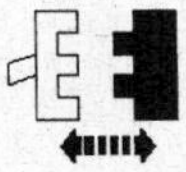

Stability Assist Module C155

3 

Lateral Accelerometer C244

4 

5 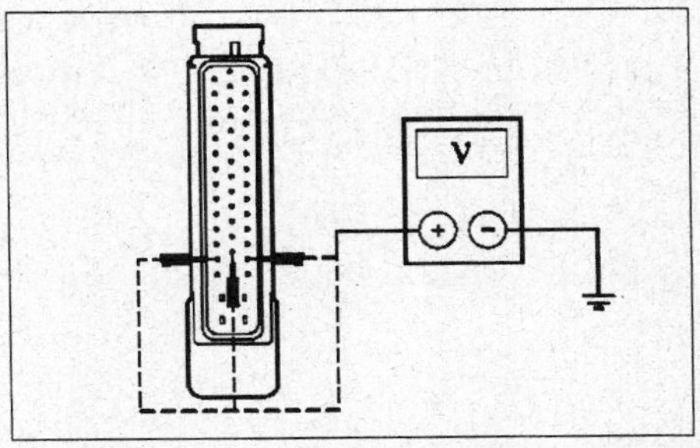

Measure the voltage between stability assist module C155 pins, harness side, and ground, as follows:

FM4029901534060X

Fig. 29 Test I/Codes C1281 & C1282: Lateral Accelerometer Circuit Failure/Lateral Accelerometer Signal Fault (Part 6 of 10). With Stability Assist

Stability Assist Module C155	Circuit
Pin 13	9-CF66 (BN/BU)
Pin 29	8-CF66 (WH/BU)
Pin 46	7-CF66 (YE/BU)

- **Is any voltage present?**

➔ **Yes**

REPAIR the circuit in question. CLEAR the DTCs. RECALIBRATE the stability assist module. REPEAT the self-test.

➔ **No**

Go to «I6».

FM4029901534070X

Fig. 29 Test I/Codes C1281 & C1282: Lateral Accelerometer Circuit Failure/Lateral Accelerometer Signal Fault (Part 7 of 10). With Stability Assist

I7 CHECK LATERAL ACCELEROMETER CIRCUITRY FOR AN OPEN

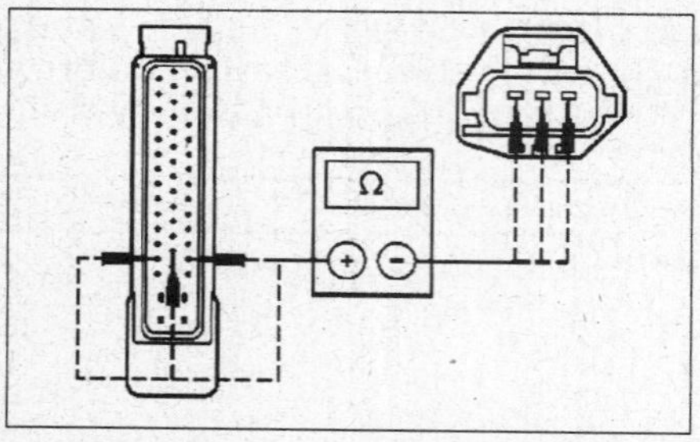

1

Measure the resistance between stability assist module C155 pins, harness side, and lateral accelerometer C244 pin, harness side as follows:

Stability Assist Module C155	Lateral Accelerometer C244	Circuit
Pin 13	Pin 1	9-CF66 (BN/BU)
Pin 29	Pin 2	8-CF66 (WH/BU)
Pin 46	Pin 3	7-CF66 (YE/BU)

- **Is the resistance less than 5 ohms?**

➔ **Yes**

Go to «I8».

➔ **No**

REPAIR the circuit in question. CLEAR the DTCs. RECALIBRATE the stability assist module. REPEAT the self-test.

FM4029901534090X

Fig. 29 Test I/Codes C1281 & C1282: Lateral Accelerometer Circuit Failure/Lateral Accelerometer Signal Fault (Part 9 of 10). With Stability Assist

I6 CHECK LATERAL ACCELEROMETER CIRCUITRY FOR SHORT TO GROUND

1

2

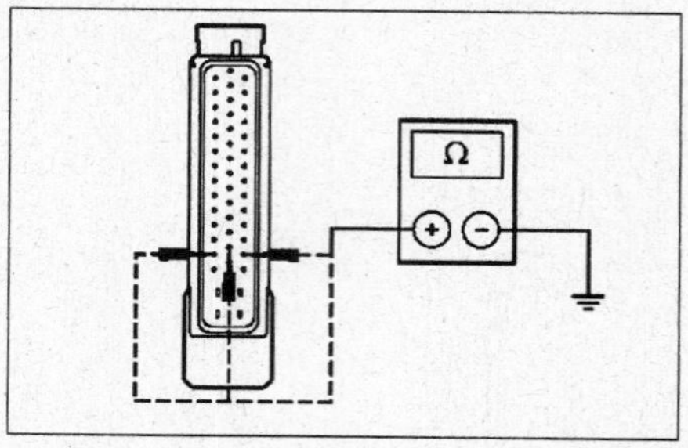

Measure the resistance between stability assist module C155 pins, harness side, and ground as follows:

Stability Assist Module C155	Circuit
Pin 13	9-CF66 (BN/BU)
Pin 29	8-CF66 (WH/BU)
Pin 46	7-CF66 (YE/BU)

- **Is the resistance greater than 10,000 ohms?**

➔ **Yes**

Go to «I7».

➔ **No**

REPAIR the circuit in question. CLEAR the DTCs. RECALIBRATE the stability assist module. REPEAT the self-test.

FM4029901534080X

Fig. 29 Test I/Codes C1281 & C1282: Lateral Accelerometer Circuit Failure/Lateral Accelerometer Signal Fault (Part 8 of 10). With Stability Assist

I8 CHECK THE VOLTAGE FROM THE STABILITY ASSIST MODULE

1

Stability Assist Module C155

2

3

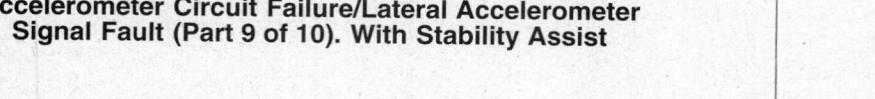

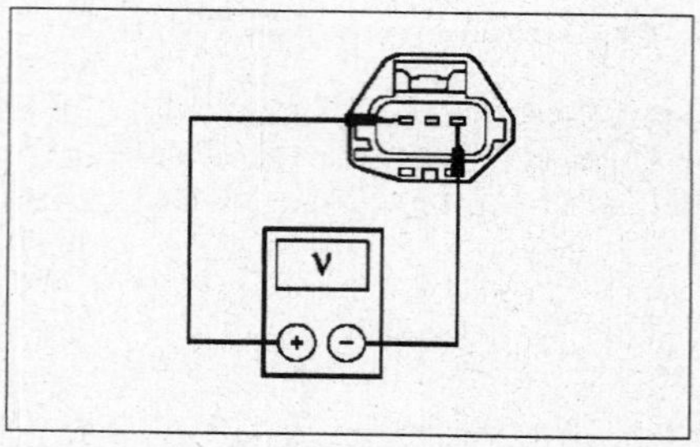

Measure the voltage between lateral accelerometer C244 pin 3, circuit 7-CF66 (YE/BU), harness side, and lateral accelerometer C244 pin 1, circuit 9-CF66 (BN/BU), harness side.

- **Is the voltage approximately 5 volts?**

➔ **Yes**

INSTALL a new lateral accelerometer. CLEAR the DTCs. REPEAT the self-test.

➔ **No**

INSTALL a new stability assist module. CLEAR the DTCs. REPEAT the self-test.

FM4029901534100X

Fig. 29 Test I/Codes C1281 & C1282: Lateral Accelerometer Circuit Failure/Lateral Accelerometer Signal Fault (Part 10 of 10). With Stability Assist

J1 CARRY OUT THE RECALIBRATION PROCEDURE

1 

2  *Clear DTC*

3 Carry out the brake booster recalibration procedure using the NGS Tester.

4 *Retrieve DTCs*

- **Are any DTCs retrieved or does the recalibration procedure indicate a fault?**

→ **Yes**

If DTC C1285 is retrieved or recalibration procedure indicates a fault, Go to «J2».

If any other DTC, GO to Diagnostic Trouble Code & Pinpoint Test Reference Chart.

→ **No**

The stability assist system is operating correctly.

FM4029901535010X

Fig. 30 Test J/Code C1285: Brake Booster Solenoid Output Failure (Part 1 of 6). With Stability Assist

J2 CHECK THE BRAKE BOOSTER SOLENOID

1 

2  *Brake Booster C149*

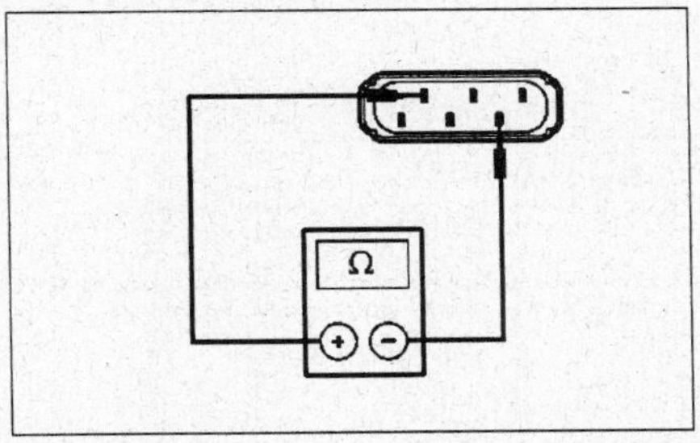

3

Measure the resistance between brake booster pin 3 (component side) and brake booster solenoid pin 4 (component side).

- **Is the resistance between 1 and 2 ohms?**

→ **Yes**

Go to «J3».

→ **No**

INSTALL a new brake booster. CLEAR the DTCs. RECALIBRATE the stability assist module. REPEAT the self-test.

FM4029901535020X

Fig. 30 Test J/Code C1285: Brake Booster Solenoid Output Failure (Part 2 of 6). With Stability Assist

J3 CHECK THE BRAKE BOOSTER SOLENOID CIRCUITRY FOR SHORT TO POWER

1  *Stability Assist Module C155*

2 

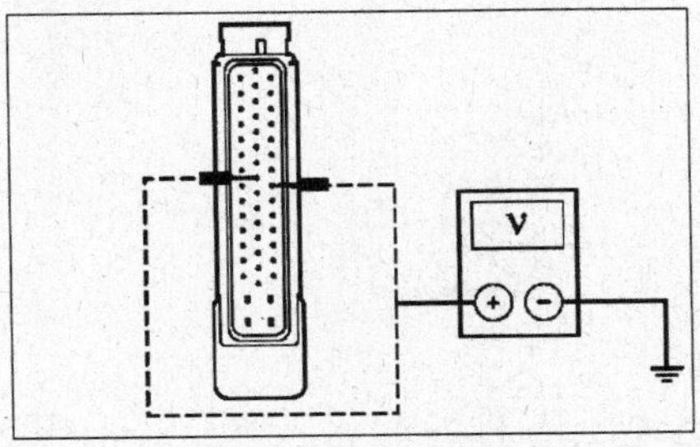

3

Measure the voltage between stability assist module C155 pin 8, circuit 8-CF68 (WH/RD), harness side, and ground; and stability assist module C155 pin 24, circuit 9-CF68 (BN/RD), harness side, and ground.

- **Is the any voltage present?**

→ **Yes**

REPAIR the circuit in question. CLEAR the DTCs. RECALIBRATE the stability assist module. REPEAT the self-test.

→ **No**

Go to «J4».

FM4029901535030X

Fig. 30 Test J/Code C1285: Brake Booster Solenoid Output Failure (Part 3 of 6). With Stability Assist

J4 CHECK CIRCUIT 8-CF68 (WH/RD)

1 

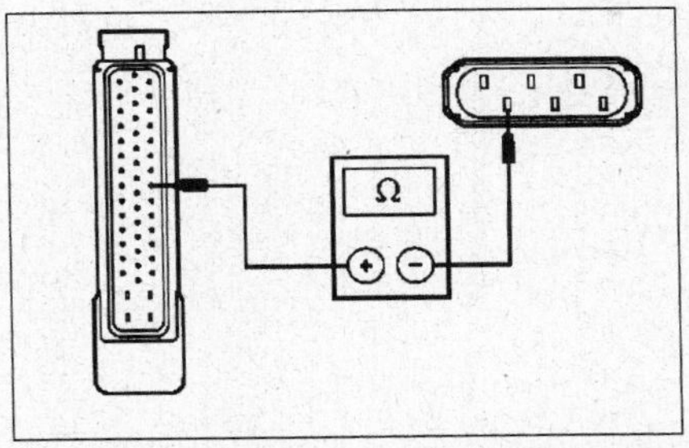

2

Measure the resistance between stability assist module C155 pin 8, circuit 8-CF68 (WH/RD), harness side, and brake booster C149 pin 4, circuit 8-CF68 (WH/RD), harness side; and stability assist module C155 pin 8, circuit 8-CF68 (WH/RD), harness side, and ground.

- **Is the resistance less than 5 ohms between stability assist module and brake booster; and greater than 10,000 ohms between stability assist module and ground?**

→ **Yes**

Go to «J5».

→ **No**

REPAIR the circuit. CLEAR the DTCs. RECALIBRATE the stability assist module. REPEAT the self-test.

FM4029901535040X

Fig. 30 Test J/Code C1285: Brake Booster Solenoid Output Failure (Part 4 of 6). With Stability Assist

J5	CHECK CIRCUIT 9-CF68 (BN/RD)

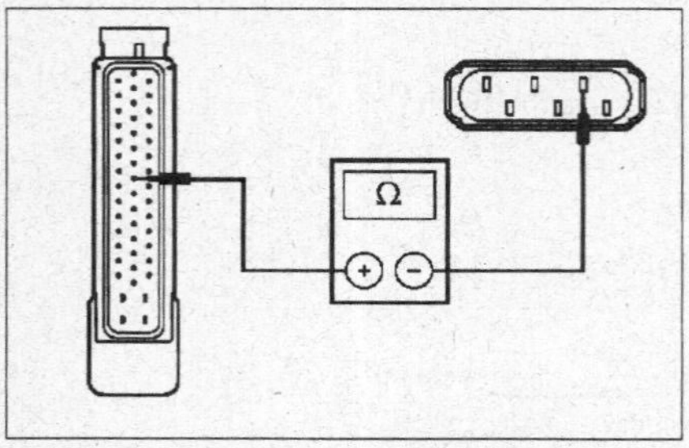

1

Measure the resistance between stability assist module C155 pin 24, circuit 9-CF68 (BN/RD), harness side, and brake booster C149 pin 3, circuit 9-CF68 (BN/RD), harness side; and stability assist module C155 pin 24, circuit 9-CF68 (BN/RD), harness side and ground.

- **Is the resistance less than 5 ohms between stability assist module and brake booster; and greater than 10,000 ohms between stability assist module and ground?**

→ **Yes**

Go to «J6».

→ **No**

REPAIR the circuit. CLEAR the DTCs. RECALIBRATE the stability assist module. REPEAT the self-test.

FM4029901535050X

Fig. 30 Test J/Code C1285: Brake Booster Solenoid Output Failure (Part 5 of 6). With Stability Assist

K1	CARRY OUT THE RECALIBRATION PROCEDURE

1 

2 

Clear DTC

3 Carry out the brake booster recalibration procedure using the NGS Tester.

4 

Clear DTC

5 

Retrieve DTCs

- **Are any DTCs retrieved or does the recalibration procedure indicate a fault?**

→ **Yes**

If DTC C1286 is retrieved or recalibration procedure indicate a fault, Go to «K2».

If any other DTC, GO to Diagnostic Trouble Code & Pinpoint Test Chart.

→ **No**

The stability assist system is operating correctly.

FM4029901536010X

Fig. 31 Test K/Code C1286: Booster Mechanical Failure (Part 1 of 6). With Stability Assist

J6	CHECK THE BRAKE BOOSTER SOLENOID FOR CORRECT OPERATION

1 

Brake Booster C149

2 

3 Wait a few minutes to create engine vacuum in the brake booster and then place the ignition switch in the OFF position.

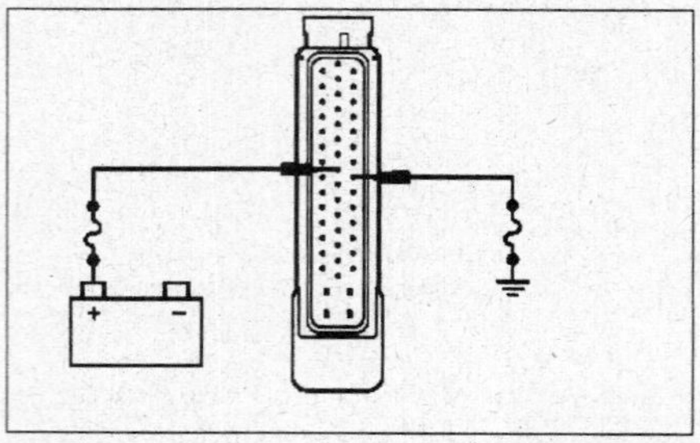

4

Connect a fused (10A) jumper wire between stability assist module pin 8, circuit 8-CF68 (WH/RD), harness side, and ground; and connect a fused (10A) jumper wire for several seconds between stability assist module pin 24, circuit 9-CF68 (WH/RD), harness side, and the positive battery post, while observing the brake pedal for movement.

- **Does the brake pedal move?**

→ **Yes**

INSTALL a new stability assist module. REPEAT the self-test.

→ **No**

INSTALL a new brake booster. CLEAR the DTCs. RECALIBRATE the stability assist module. REPEAT the self-test.

FM4029901535060X

Fig. 30 Test J/Code C1285: Brake Booster Solenoid Output Failure (Part 6 of 6). With Stability Assist

K2	CHECK THE BRAKE BOOSTER SOLENOID

1 

2 

Brake Booster C149

3

Measure the resistance between brake booster pin 3 (component side) and brake booster solenoid pin 4 (component side).

- **Is the resistance between 1 and 2 ohms?**

→ **Yes**

Go to «K3».

→ **No**

INSTALL a new brake booster. CLEAR the DTCs. RECALIBRATE the stability assist module. REPEAT the self-test.

FM4029901536020X

Fig. 31 Test K/Code C1286: Booster Mechanical Failure (Part 2 of 6). With Stability Assist

K3 CHECK THE BRAKE BOOSTER SOLENOID CIRCUITRY FOR SHORT TO POWER

1 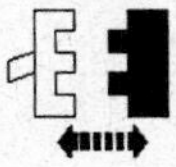

2 

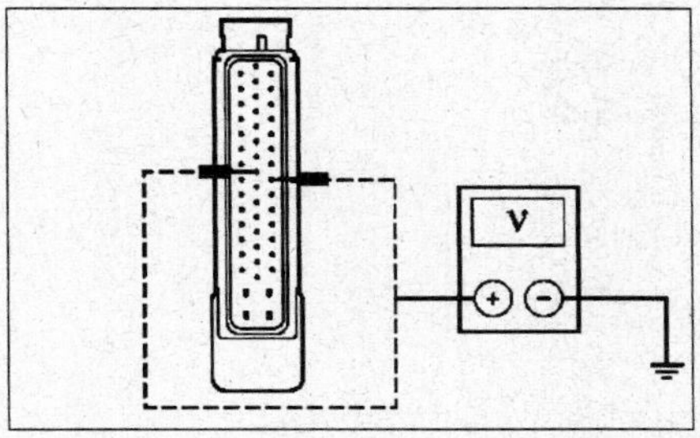

3

Measure the voltage between stability assist module C155 pin 8, circuit 8-CF68 (WH/RD), harness side and ground; and stability assist module C155 pin 24, circuit 9-CF68 (BN/RD), harness side and ground.

- **Is the any voltage present?**

➔ **Yes**

REPAIR the circuit in question. CLEAR the DTCs. RECALIBRATE the stability assist module. REPEAT the self-test.

➔ **No**

Go to «K4».

FM4029901536030X

Fig. 31 Test K/Code C1286: Booster Mechanical Failure (Part 3 of 6). With Stability Assist

K5 CHECK CIRCUIT 9-CF68 (BN/RD)

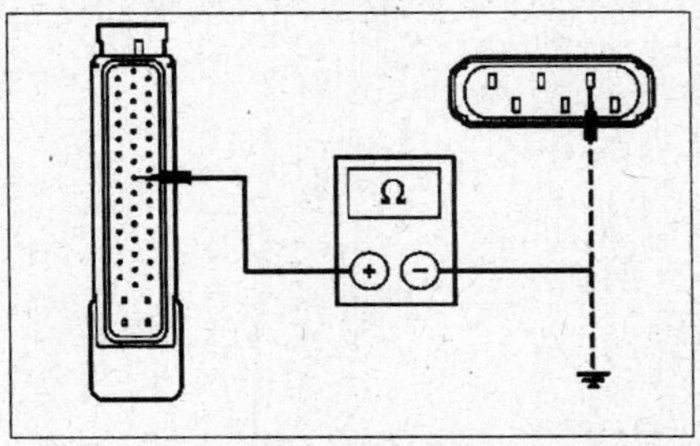

1

Measure the resistance between stability assist module C155 pin 24, circuit 9-CF68 (BN/RD), harness side, and brake booster C149 pin 3, circuit 9-CF68 (BN/RD), harness side; and stability assist module C155 pin 24, circuit 9-CF68 (BN/RD), harness side, and ground.

- **Is the resistance less than 5 ohms between stability assist module and brake booster; and greater than 10,000 ohms between stability assist module and ground?**

➔ **Yes**

Go to «K6».

➔ **No**

REPAIR the circuit. CLEAR the DTCs. RECALIBRATE the stability assist module. REPEAT the self-test.

FM4029901536050X

Fig. 31 Test K/Code C1286: Booster Mechanical Failure (Part 5 of 6). With Stability Assist

K4 CHECK CIRCUIT 8-CF68 (WH/RD)

1 

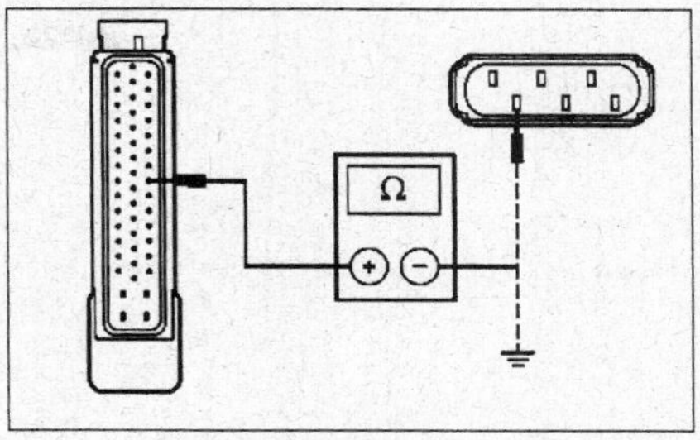

2

Measure the resistance between stability assist module C155 pin 8, circuit 8-CF68 (WH/RD), harness side, and brake booster C149 pin 4, circuit 8-CF68 (WH/RD), harness side; and stability assist module C155 pin 8, circuit 8-CF68 (WH/RD), harness side, and ground.

- **Is the resistance less than 5 ohms between stability assist module and brake booster; and greater than 10,000 ohms between stability assist module and ground?**

➔ **Yes**

Go to «K5».

➔ **No**

REPAIR the circuit. CLEAR the DTCs. RECALIBRATE the stability assist module. REPEAT the self-test.

FM4029901536040X

Fig. 31 Test K/Code C1286: Booster Mechanical Failure (Part 4 of 6). With Stability Assist

K6 CHECK THE BRAKE BOOSTER SOLENOID FOR CORRECT OPERATION

1 

2 

3 Wait a few minutes to create engine vacuum in the brake booster and then place the ignition switch in the OFF position.

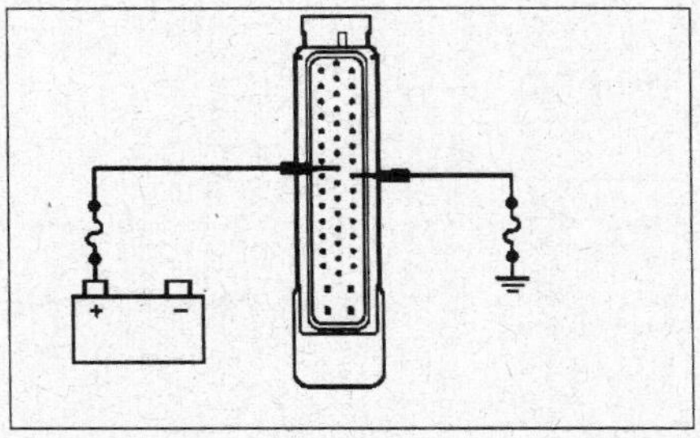

4

Connect a fused (10A) jumper wire between stability assist module pin 8, circuit 8-CF68 (WH/RD), harness side, and ground; and connect a fused (10A) jumper wire for several seconds between stability assist module pin 24, circuit 9-CF68 (BN/RD), harness side, and the positive battery post, while observing the brake pedal for movement.

- **Does the brake pedal move?**

➔ **Yes**

INSTALL a new stability assist module. REPEAT the self-test.

➔ **No**

INSTALL a new brake booster. CLEAR the DTCs. RECALIBRATE the stability assist module. REPEAT the self-test.

FM4029901536060X

Fig. 31 Test K/Code C1286: Booster Mechanical Failure (Part 6 of 6). With Stability Assist

L1	CARRY OUT THE RECALIBRATION PROCEDURE

1 

2 

Clear DTC

3 Carry out the brake booster recalibration procedure using the NGS Tester.

4 *Retrieve DTCs*

- **Are any DTCs retrieved or does the recalibration procedure indicate a fault?**

→ **Yes**

If DTC C1287 is retrieved or recalibration procedure indicates a fault, Go to «L2».

If any other DTC, GO to Diagnostic Trouble Code & Pinpoint Test Chart.

→ **No**

The stability assist system is operating correctly.

FM4029901537010X

Fig. 32 Test L/Code C1287: Booster Pedal Force Switch Circuit Failure (Part 1 of 5). With Stability Assist

L2	CHECK THE NORMALLY CLOSED RELEASE SWITCH

1 

2 

Brake Booster C149

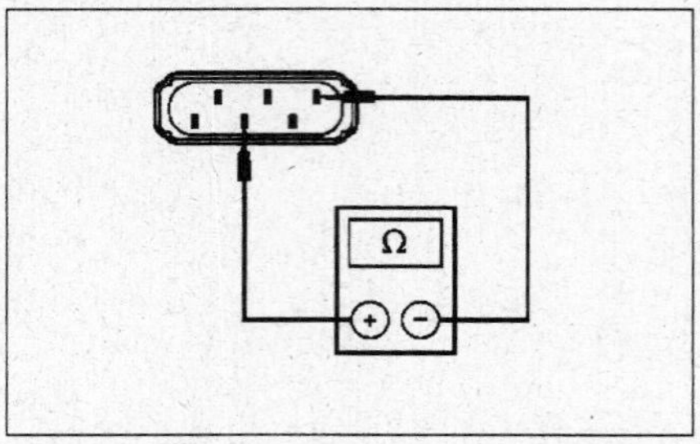

3 Measure the resistance between brake booster pin 1 (component side) and brake booster pin 5 (component side), while depressing and releasing the brake pedal.

- **Is the resistance less than 5 ohms with the brake pedal released and greater than 10,000 ohms with the brake pedal depressed?**

→ **Yes**

Go to «L3».

→ **No**

INSTALL a new brake booster. CLEAR the DTCs. RECALIBRATE the stability assist module. REPEAT the self-test.

FM4029901537020X

Fig. 32 Test L/Code C1287: Booster Pedal Force Switch Circuit Failure (Part 2 of 5). With Stability Assist

L3	CHECK THE NORMALLY OPEN RELEASE SWITCH

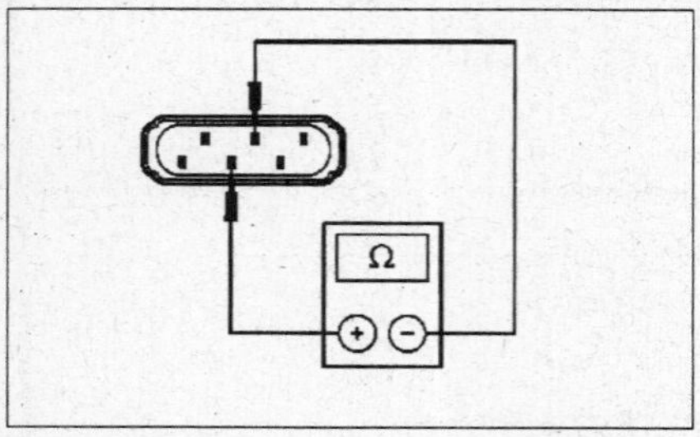

1 Measure the resistance between brake booster pin 2 (component side) and brake booster pin 5 (component side), while depressing and releasing the brake pedal.

- **Is the resistance less than 5 ohms with the brake pedal depressed and greater than 10,000 ohms with the brake pedal released?**

→ **Yes**

Go to «L4».

→ **No**

INSTALL a new brake booster. CLEAR the DTCs. RECALIBRATE the stability assist module. REPEAT the self-test.

FM4029901537030X

Fig. 32 Test L/Code C1287: Booster Pedal Force Switch Circuit Failure (Part 3 of 5). With Stability Assist

L4	CHECK THE BRAKE BOOSTER CIRCUITRY FOR SHORT TO POWER

1 

Stability Assist Module C155

2 

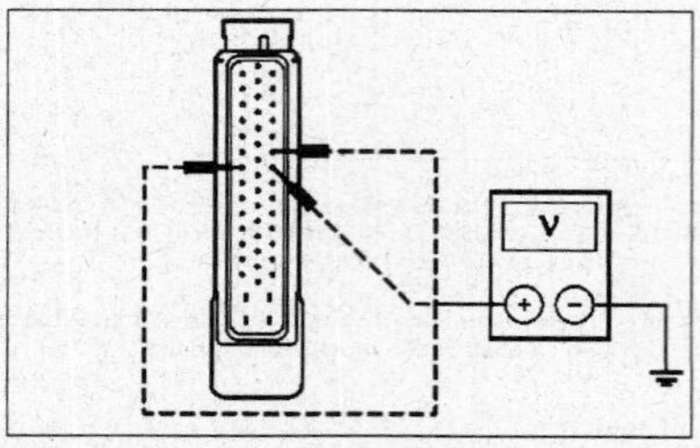

3 Measure the voltage between stability assist module C155 pins, harness side, and ground, as follows:

Stability Assist Module C155	Circuit
Pin 40	9-CF51 (BN/GN)
Pin 7	10-CF51 (GY/OG)
Pin 6	8-CF51 (WH/GN)

- **Is any voltage present?**

→ **Yes**

REPAIR the circuit in question. CLEAR the DTC. RECALIBRATE the stability assist module. REPEAT the self-test.

No

Go to L5.

FM4029901537040X

Fig. 32 Test L/Code C1287: Booster Pedal Force Switch Circuit Failure (Part 4 of 5). With Stability Assist

L5 CHECK THE BRAKE BOOSTER CIRCUITRY

1 

2 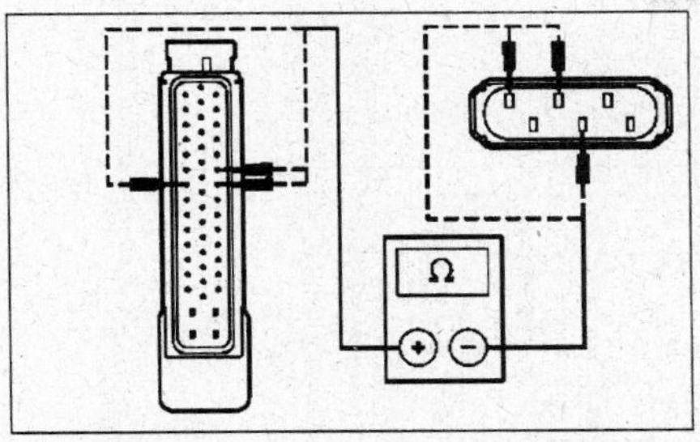

Measure the resistance between stability assist module C155 pins, harness side, and brake booster C149 pins, harness side, as follows:

Stability Assist Module C155	Brake Booster C149	Circuit
Pin 40	Pin 5	9-CF51 (BN/GN)
Pin 7	Pin 2	10-CF51 (GY/OG)
Pin 6	Pin 1	8-CF51 (WH/GN)

- **Are the resistances less than 5 ohms?**

➔ **Yes**

INSTALL a new stability assist module; REPEAT the self-test.

➔ **No**

REPAIR the circuit in question. CLEAR the DTC. RECALIBRATE the stability assist module. REPEAT the self-test.

FM4029901537050X

Fig. 32 Test L/Code C1287: Booster Pedal Force Switch Circuit Failure (Part 5 of 5). With Stability Assist

Measure the voltage between stability assist module C155 pins, harness side, and ground as follows:

Stability Assist Module C155	Circuit
Pin 43	9-CF64 (BN/YE)
Pin 26	8-CF64 (WH/BK)
Pin 10	7-CF64 (YE/BK)

- **Is any voltage present?**

➔ **Yes**

REPAIR the circuit in question. CLEAR the DTCs. REPEAT the self-test.

➔ **No**

Go to «M2».

FM4029901538020X

Fig. 33 Test M/Code C1288: Pressure Transducer Main/Primary Input Circuit Failure (Part 2 of 7). With Stability Assist

M1 CHECK MAIN/PRIMARY PRESSURE TRANSDUCER CIRCUITRY FOR SHORT TO POWER

1 

2 

Stability Assist Module C155

3 

Main/Primary Pressure Transducer C147

4 

5 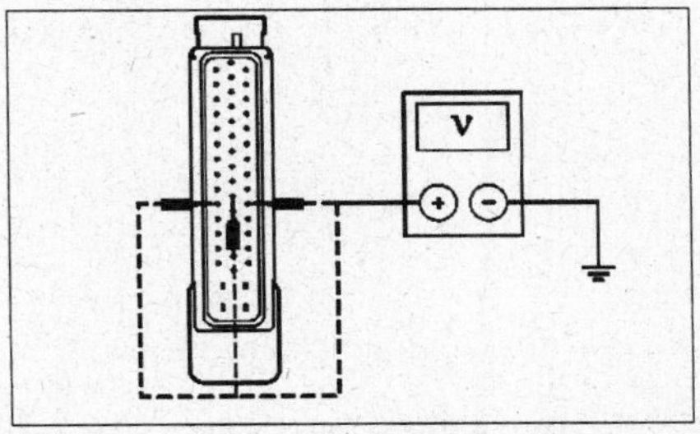

FM4029901538010X

Fig. 33 Test M/Code C1288: Pressure Transducer Main/Primary Input Circuit Failure (Part 1 of 7). With Stability Assist

M2 CHECK MAIN/PRIMARY PRESSURE TRANSDUCER CIRCUITRY FOR SHORT TO GROUND

1 

2 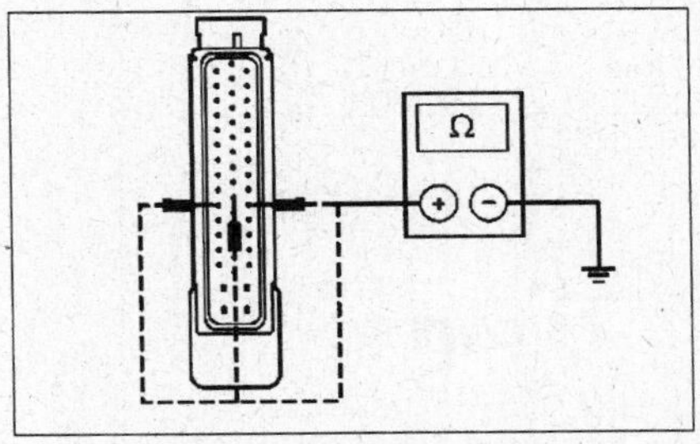

Measure the resistance between stability assist module C155 pins, harness side, and ground, as follows:

Stability Assist Module C155	Circuit
Pin 43	9-CF64 (BN/YE)
Pin 26	8-CF64 (WH/BK)
Pin 10	7-CF64 (YE/BK)

- **Is the resistance greater than 10,000 ohms?**

➔ **Yes**

Go to «M3».

➔ **No**

REPAIR the circuit in question. CLEAR the DTCs. REPEAT the self-test.

FM4029901538030X

Fig. 33 Test M/Code C1288: Pressure Transducer Main/Primary Input Circuit Failure (Part 3 of 7). With Stability Assist

M3 CHECK MAIN/PRIMARY PRESSURE TRANSDUCER CIRCUITRY FOR AN OPEN

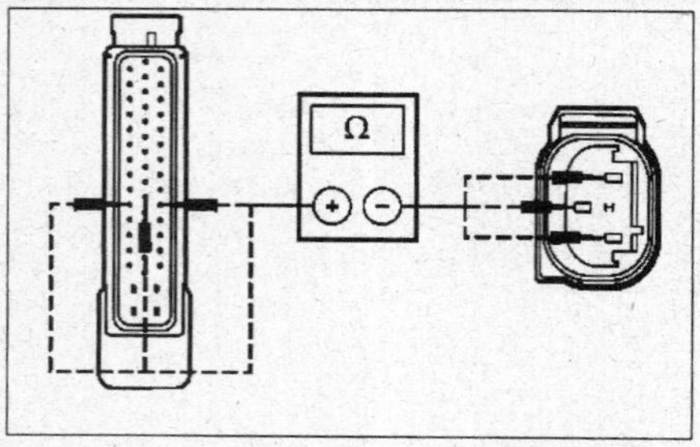

1

Measure the resistance between stability assist module C155 pins, harness side, and main/primary pressure transducer C147 pins, harness side, as follows:

Stability Assist Module C155	Main/Primary Pressure Transducer C147	Circuit
Pin 43	Pin 1	9-CF64 (BN/YE)
Pin 26	Pin 2	8-CF64 (WH/BK)
Pin 10	Pin 3	7-CF64 (YE/BK)

- **Is the resistance less than 5 ohms?**

→ **Yes**

Go to «M4».

→ **No**

REPAIR the circuit in question. CLEAR the DTCs. REPEAT the self-test.

FM4029901538040X

Fig. 33 Test M/Code C1288: Pressure Transducer Main/Primary Input Circuit Failure (Part 4 of 7). With Stability Assist

M4 CHECK THE STABILITY ASSIST MODULE OUTPUT

1  *Stability Assist Module C155*

2 

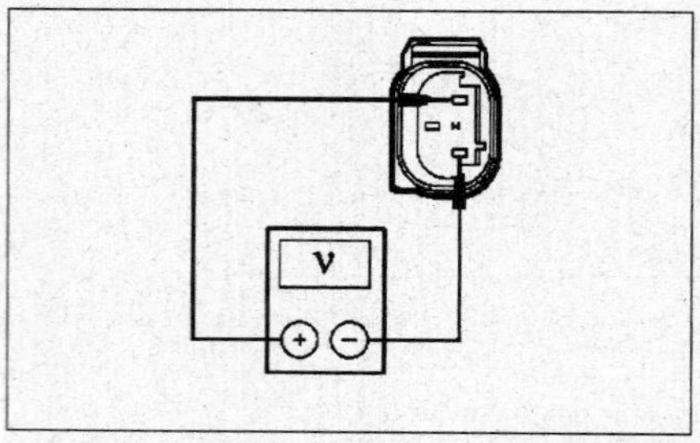

3

Measure the voltage between main/primary pressure transducer C147 pin 3, circuit 7-CF64 (YE/BK), harness side, and main/primary pressure transducer C147 pin 1, circuit 9-CF64 (BN/YE), harness side.

- **Is the voltage approximately 5 volts?**

→ **Yes**

Go to «M5».

→ **No**

INSTALL a new stability assist module. REPEAT the self-test.

FM4029901538050X

Fig. 33 Test M/Code C1288: Pressure Transducer Main/Primary Input Circuit Failure (Part 5 of 7). With Stability Assist

M5 CHECK THE MAIN/PRIMARY PRESSURE TRANSDUCER OUTPUT

1  *Main/Primary Pressure Transducer C147*

2  *Stability Assist Module C155*

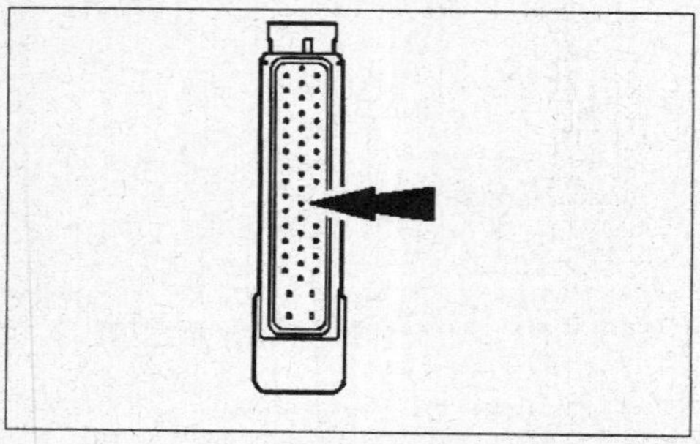

3

Back out the stability assist module C155 pin 26, circuit 8-CF64 (WH/BK), harness side.

4  *Stability Assist Module C155*

5 

FM4029901538060X

Fig. 33 Test M/Code C1288: Pressure Transducer Main/Primary Input Circuit Failure (Part 6 of 7). With Stability Assist

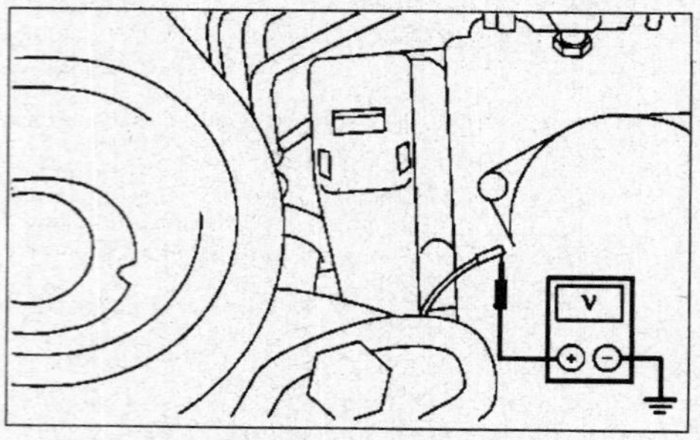

6

Measure the voltage between stability assist module back out pin 26, circuit 8-CF64 (WH/BK), harness side, and ground, while depressing and releasing the brake pedal.

- **Is the voltage between 0.125 and 0.375 volt with the brake pedal released and between 0.125 and 5 volts with the brake pedal depressed?**

→ **Yes**

INSTALL a new stability assist module. REPEAT the self-test.

→ **No**

INSTALL a new main/primary pressure transducer. CLEAR the DTC. RECALIBRATE the stability assist module. REPEAT the self-test.

FM4029901538070X

Fig. 33 Test M/Code C1288: Pressure Transducer Main/Primary Input Circuit Failure (Part 7 of 7). With Stability Assist

N1 CHECK REDUNDANT/SECONDARY PRESSURE TRANSDUCER CIRCUITRY FOR SHORT TO POWER

1 

2 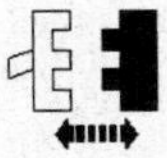 *Stability Assist Module C155*

3 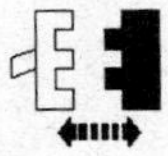 *Redundant/Secondary Pressure Transducer C148*

4 

5 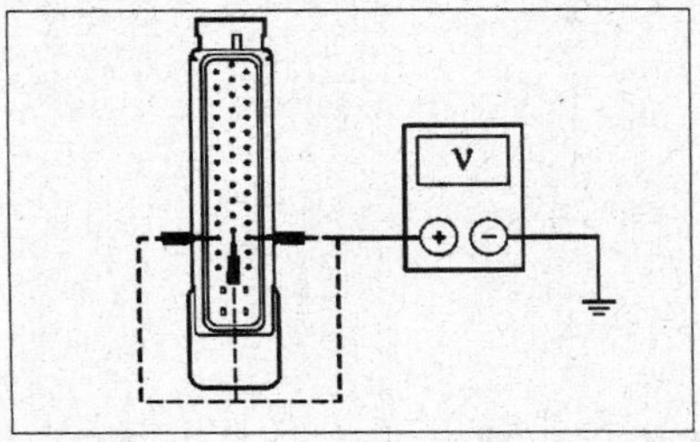

FM4029901539010X

Fig. 34 Test N/Code C1289: Pressure Transducer Redundant/Secondary Input Circuit Failure (Part 1 of 7). With Stability Assist

Measure the voltage between stability assist module C155 pins, harness side, and ground, as follows:

Stability Assist Module C155	Circuit
Pin 45	9-CF65 (BN/WH)
Pin 28	8-CF65 (WH/VT)
Pin 12	7-CF65 (YE/VT)

- **Is any voltage present?**

→ **Yes**

REPAIR the circuit in question. CLEAR the DTCs. REPEAT the self-test.

→ **No**

Go to «N2».

FM4029901539020X

Fig. 34 Test N/Code C1289: Pressure Transducer Redundant/Secondary Input Circuit Failure (Part 2 of 7). With Stability Assist

N2 CHECK REDUNDANT/SECONDARY PRESSURE TRANSDUCER CIRCUITRY FOR SHORT TO GROUND

1 

2 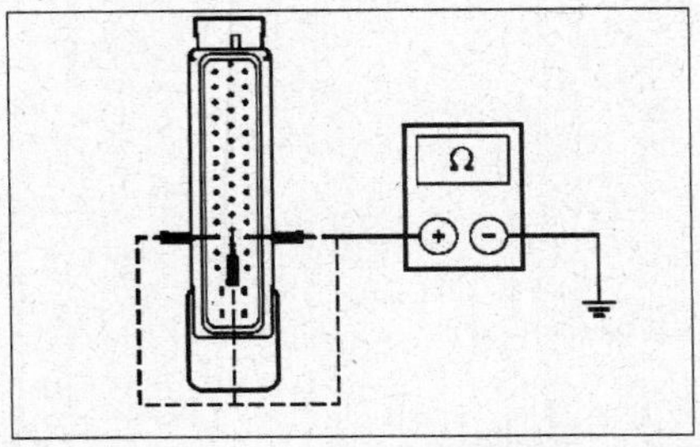

Measure the resistance between stability assist module C155 pins, harness side, and ground, as follows:

Stability Assist Module C155	Circuit
Pin 45	9-CF65 (BN/WH)
Pin 28	8-CF65 (WH/VT)
Pin 12	7-CF65 (YE/VT)

- **Is the resistance greater than 10,000 ohms?**

→ **Yes**

Go to «N3».

→ **No**

REPAIR the circuit in question. CLEAR the DTCs. REPEAT the self-test.

FM4029901539030X

Fig. 34 Test N/Code C1289: Pressure Transducer Redundant/Secondary Input Circuit Failure (Part 3 of 7). With Stability Assist

N3 CHECK REDUNDANT/SECONDARY PRESSURE TRANSDUCER CIRCUITRY FOR AN OPEN

1 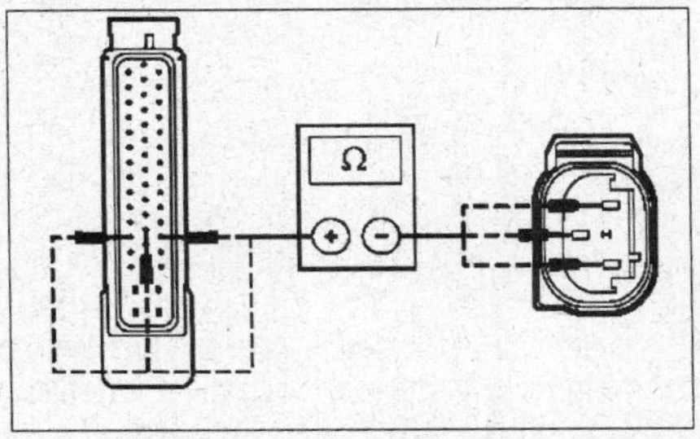

Measure the resistance between stability assist module C155 pins, harness side and redundant/secondary pressure transducer C148 pins, harness side as follows:

Stability Assist Module C155	Redundant/-Secondary-Pressure-Transducer- C148	Circuit
Pin 45	Pin 1	9-CF65 (BN/WH)
Pin 28	Pin 2	8-CF65 (WH/VT)
Pin 12	Pin 3	7-CF65 (YE/VT)

- **Is the resistance less than 5 ohms?**

→ **Yes**

Go to «N4».

→ **No**

REPAIR the circuit in question. CLEAR the DTCs. REPEAT the self-test.

FM4029901539040X

Fig. 34 Test N/Code C1289: Pressure Transducer Redundant/Secondary Input Circuit Failure (Part 4 of 7). With Stability Assist

N4	CHECK THE STABILITY ASSIST MODULE OUTPUT

1

Stability Assist Module C155

2

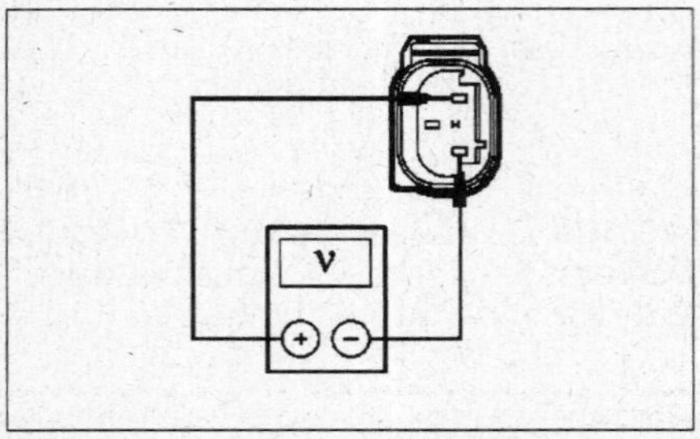

3

Measure the voltage between redundant/secondary pressure transducer C148 pin 3, circuit 7-CF65 (YE/VT), harness side, and redundant/secondary pressure transducer C148 pin 1, circuit 9-CF65 (BN/WH), harness side.

- **Is the voltage approximately 5 volts?**

→ **Yes**

Go to «N5».

→ **No**

INSTALL a new stability assist module. REPEAT the self-test.

FM4029901539050X

Fig. 34 Test N/Code C1289: Pressure Transducer Redundant/Secondary Input Circuit Failure (Part 5 of 7). With Stability Assist

N5	CHECK THE REDUNDANT/SECONDARY PRESSURE TRANSDUCER OUTPUT

1

Redundant/Secondary Pressure Transducer C148

2

Stability Assist Module C155

3
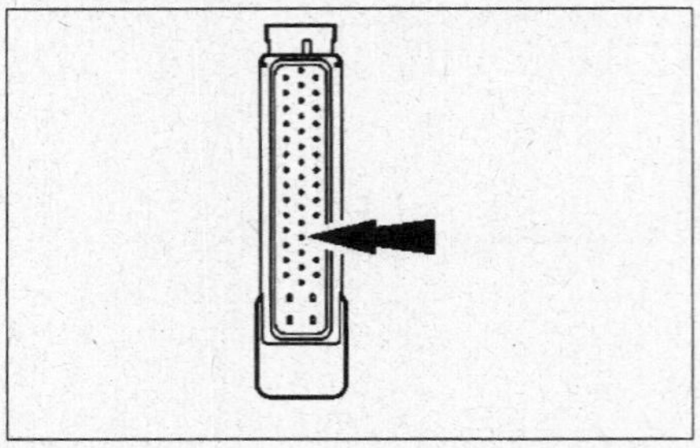

Back out the stability assist module C155 pin 28, circuit 8-CF65 (WH/VT), harness side.

4

Stability Assist Module C155

5

FM4029901539060X

Fig. 34 Test N/Code C1289: Pressure Transducer Redundant/Secondary Input Circuit Failure (Part 6 of 7). With Stability Assist

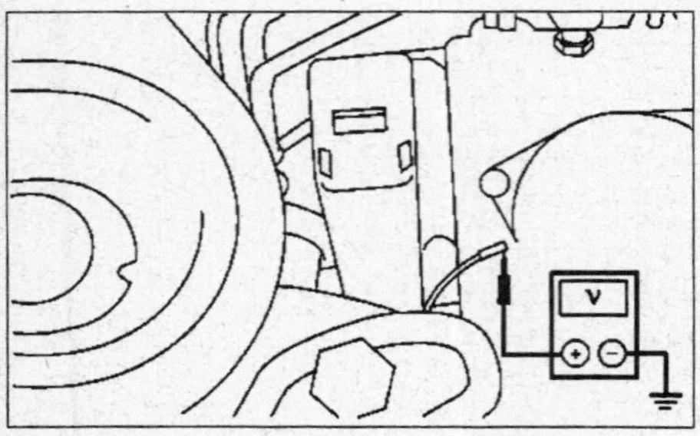

6

Measure the voltage between stability assist module back out pin 28, circuit 8-CF65 (WH/VT), harness side, and ground, while depressing and releasing the brake pedal.

- **Is the voltage between 0.125 and 0.375 volt with the brake pedal released and between 0.125 and 5 volts with the brake pedal depressed?**

→ **Yes**

INSTALL a new stability assist module. REPEAT the self-test.

→ **No**

INSTALL a new secondary pressure transducer. CLEAR the DTCs. RECALIBRATE the stability assist module. REPEAT the self-test.

FM4029901539070X

Fig. 34 Test N/Code C1289: Pressure Transducer Redundant/Secondary Input Circuit Failure (Part 7 of 7). With Stability Assist

O1	CHECK CIRCUIT 7-CF64 (YE/BK) FOR SHORT TO BATTERY

1

2

Stability Assist Module C155

3

Main/Primary Pressure Transducer C147

4

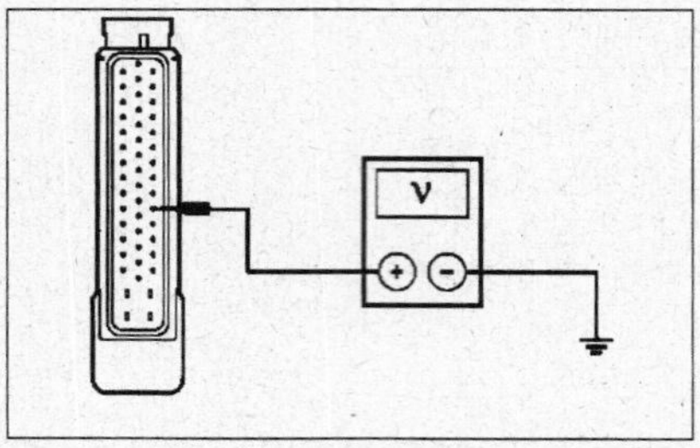

5

Measure the voltage between stability assist module C155 pin 10, circuit 7-CF64 (YE/BK), harness side, and ground.

FM4029901540010X

Fig. 35 Test O/Code C1730: Reference Voltage Out Of Range (Part 1 of 11). With Stability Assist

- **Is any voltage present?**

→ **Yes**

REPAIR the circuit. CLEAR the DTCs. RECALIBRATE the stability assist module. REPEAT the self-test.

→ **No**

Go to «O2».

FM4029901540020X

Fig. 35 Test O/Code C1730: Reference Voltage Out Of Range (Part 2 of 11). With Stability Assist

O3	CHECK CIRCUIT 7-CF65 (YE/VT) FOR SHORT TO BATTERY

1 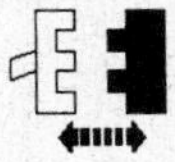

Redundant/Secondary Pressure Transducer C148

2 

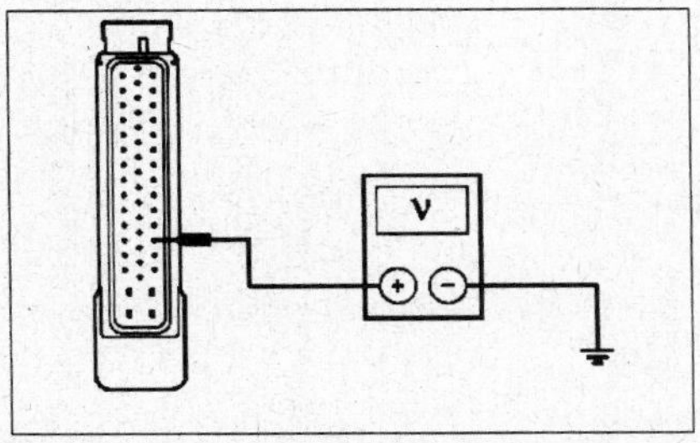

3

Measure the voltage between stability assist module C155 pin 12, circuit 7-CF65 (YE/VT), harness side, and ground.

- **Is any voltage present?**

→ **Yes**

REPAIR the circuit. CLEAR the DTC. RECALIBRATE the stability assist module. REPEAT the self-test.

→ **No**

Go to «O4».

FM4029901540040X

Fig. 35 Test O/Code C1730: Reference Voltage Out Of Range (Part 4 of 11). With Stability Assist

O4	CHECK CIRCUIT 7-CF65 (YE/VT) FOR SHORT TO GROUND

1

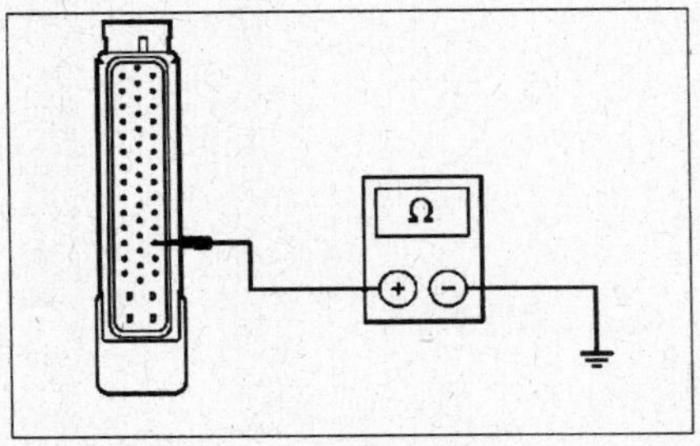

2

Measure the resistance between stability assist module C155 pin 12, circuit 7-CF65 (YE/VT), harness side, and ground.

- **Is the resistance greater than 10,000 ohms?**

→ **Yes**

Go to «O5».

→ **No**

REPAIR the circuit. CLEAR the DTC. RECALIBRATE the stability assist module. REPEAT the self-test.

FM4029901540050X

Fig. 35 Test O/Code C1730: Reference Voltage Out Of Range (Part 5 of 11). With Stability Assist

O2	CHECK CIRCUIT 7-CF64 (YE/BK) FOR SHORT TO GROUND

1

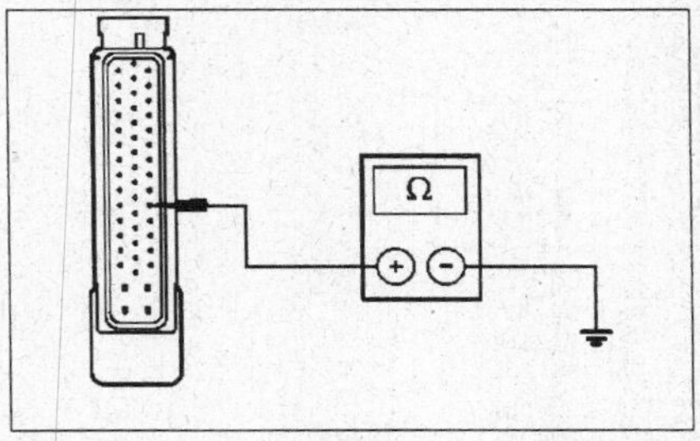

2

Measure the resistance between stability assist module C155 pin 10, circuit 7-CF64 (YE/BK), harness side, and ground.

- **Is the resistance greater than 10,000 ohms?**

→ **Yes**

Go to «O3».

→ **No**

REPAIR the circuit. CLEAR the DTC. RECALIBRATE the stability assist module. REPEAT the self-test.

FM4029901540030X

Fig. 35 Test O/Code C1730: Reference Voltage Out Of Range (Part 3 of 11). With Stability Assist

O5	CHECK CIRCUIT 7-CF66 (YE/BU) FOR SHORT TO BATTERY

1 

Lateral Accelerometer C244

2

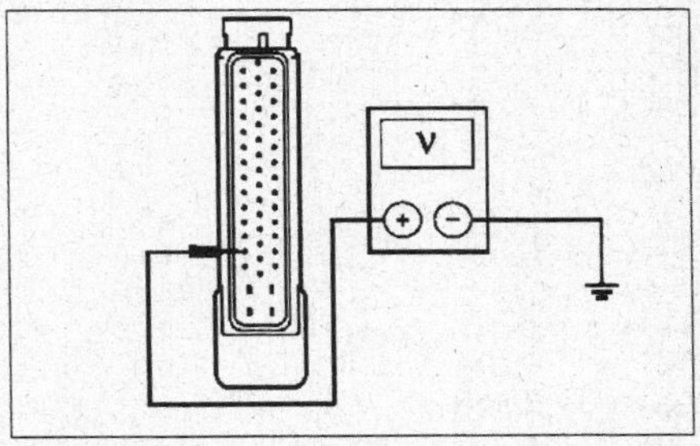

3

Measure the voltage between stability assist module C155 pin 46, circuit 7-CF66 (YE/BU), harness side, and ground.

- **Is any voltage present?**

→ **Yes**

REPAIR the circuit. CLEAR the DTC. RECALIBRATE the stability assist module. REPEAT the self-test.

→ **No**

Go to «O6».

FM4029901540060X

Fig. 35 Test O/Code C1730: Reference Voltage Out Of Range (Part 6 of 11). With Stability Assist

O6 CHECK CIRCUIT 7-CF66 (YE/BU) FOR SHORT TO GROUND

1

2

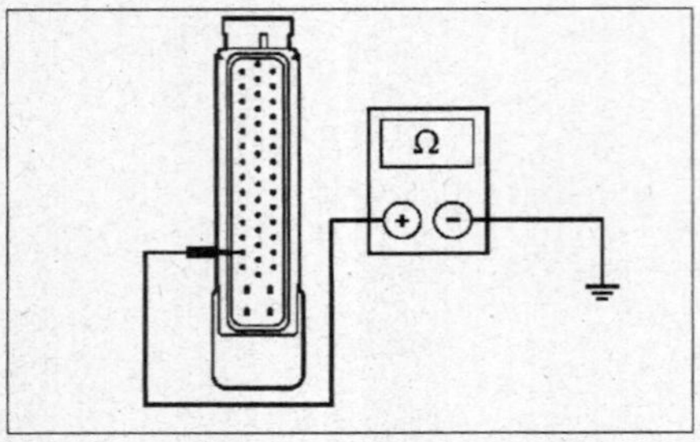

Measure the resistance between stability assist module C155 pin 46, circuit 7-CF66 (YE/BU), harness side, and ground.

- **Is the resistance greater than 10,000 ohms?**

→ **Yes**

Go to «O7».

→ **No**

REPAIR the circuit. CLEAR the DTC. RECALIBRATE the stability assist module. REPEAT the self-test.

FM4029901540070X

Fig. 35 Test O/Code C1730: Reference Voltage Out Of Range (Part 7 of 11). With Stability Assist

O7 CHECK CIRCUIT 7-CF67 (YE/RD) FOR SHORT TO BATTERY

1

Yaw Rate Sensor C245

2

3

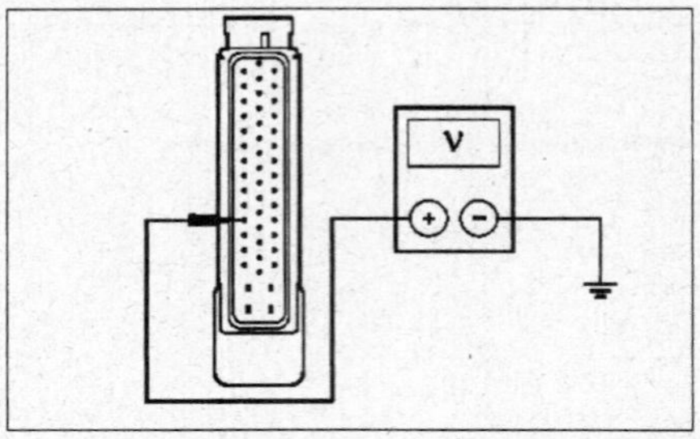

Measure the voltage between stability assist module C155 pin 44, circuit 7-CF67 (YE/RD), harness side, and ground.

- **Is any voltage present?**

→ **Yes**

REPAIR the circuit. CLEAR the DTC. RECALIBRATE the stability assist module. REPEAT the self-test.

→ **No**

Go to «O8».

FM4029901540080X

Fig. 35 Test O/Code C1730: Reference Voltage Out Of Range (Part 8 of 11). With Stability Assist

O8 CHECK CIRCUIT 7-CF66 (YE/BU) FOR SHORT TO GROUND

1

2

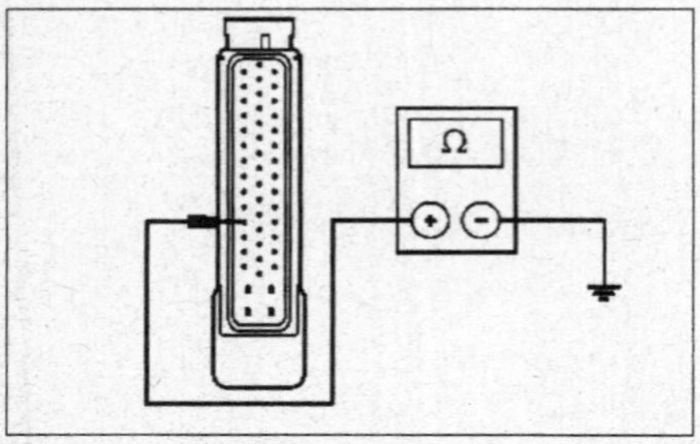

Measure the resistance between stability assist module C155 pin 44, circuit 7-CF67 (YE/RD), harness side, and ground.

- **Is the resistance greater than 10,000 ohms?**

→ **Yes**

Go to «O9».

→ **No**

REPAIR the circuit. CLEAR the DTC. RECALIBRATE the stability assist module. REPEAT the self-test.

FM4029901540090X

Fig. 35 Test O/Code C1730: Reference Voltage Out Of Range (Part 9 of 11). With Stability Assist

O9 CHECK THE STABILITY ASSIST MODULE

1

Stability Assist Module C155

2

3

Clear DTCs

4

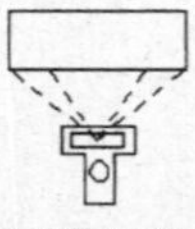

Retrieve DTCs

- **Is DTC C1730 retrieved?**

→ **Yes**

INSTALL a new stability assist module. REPEAT the self-test.

→ **No**

Go to «O10».

FM4029901540100X

Fig. 35 Test O/Code C1730: Reference Voltage Out Of Range (Part 10 of 11). With Stability Assist

O10 CHECK THE STABILITY ASSIST COMPONENTS

1 Reconnect the lateral accelerometer C244, yaw rate sensor C245, main/primary pressure transducer C147, and redundant/secondary pressure transducer C148 one at a time while clearing the DTCs and retrieving the DTCs in between each component being reconnected.

- **Is DTC C1730 retrieved?**

→ **Yes**

INSTALL a new component as necessary. CLEAR the DTCs. RECALIBRATE the stability assist module. REPEAT the self-test.

→ **No**

System is OK.

FM4029901540110X

Fig. 35 Test O/Code C1730: Reference Voltage Out Of Range (Part 11 of 11). With Stability Assist

Q1 CHECK THE YELLOW ANTI-LOCK BRAKE WARNING INDICATOR

1 

2 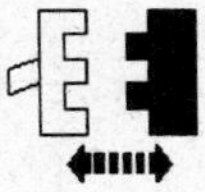

Stability Assist Module C155

3 

- **Is the yellow anti-lock brake warning indicator illuminated?**

→ **Yes**

Go to «Q2».

→ **No**

DIAGNOSE instrument cluster.

FM4029901542010X

Fig. 37 Test Q: Yellow ABS Warning Indicator Does Not Self Check (Part 1 of 2). With Stability Assist

R1 CHECK FOR DTCS

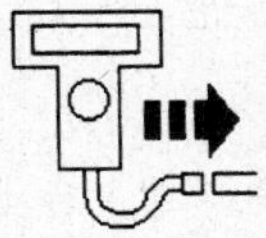

1 *NGS Tester*

2 Retrieve and document continuous DTCs.

- **Are any DTCs retrieved?**

→ **Yes**

GO to Diagnostic Trouble Code & Pinpoint Reference Chart.

→ **No**

Go to «R2».

FM4029901543010X

Fig. 38 Test R: Traction Control Inoperative (Part 1 of 4). With Stability Assist

P1 CHECK FOR OTHER DTCS

1 

2 *Clear DTCs*

3 *Retrieve DTCs*

- **Is DTC C1960 retrieved?**

→ **Yes**

INSTALL a new REM. CLEAR the DTCs. REPEAT the self-test.

→ **No**

If a different DTC is retrieved, GO to Diagnostic Trouble Code & Pinpoint Test Reference Chart.

If no DTCs are retrieved, system is OK.

FM4029901541000X

Fig. 36 Test P/Code C1960: Driver Brake Apply Circuit Fault. With Stability Assist

Q2 CHECK PROVE OUT

1 

2  *Stability Assist Module C162*

3 

- **Does the yellow anti-lock brake warning indicator prove out for three seconds and then turn off?**

→ **Yes**

The yellow anti-lock brake warning indicator is working correctly. TEST the system for normal operation.

→ **No**

INSTALL a new stability assist module. TEST the system for normal operation.

FM4029901542020X

Fig. 37 Test Q: Yellow ABS Warning Indicator Does Not Self Check (Part 2 of 2). With Stability Assist

R2 CHECK THE ABS OPERATION

1 Test drive the vehicle and carry out several anti-lock stops.

- **Does the ABS operate correctly?**

→ **Yes**

Go to «R3».

→ **No**

GO to Symptom Chart.

FM4029901543020X

Fig. 38 Test R: Traction Control Inoperative (Part 2 of 4). With Stability Assist

R3 CHECK THE TRACTION CONTROL OFF INPUT TO THE STABILITY ASSIST MODULE FOR SHORT TO POWER

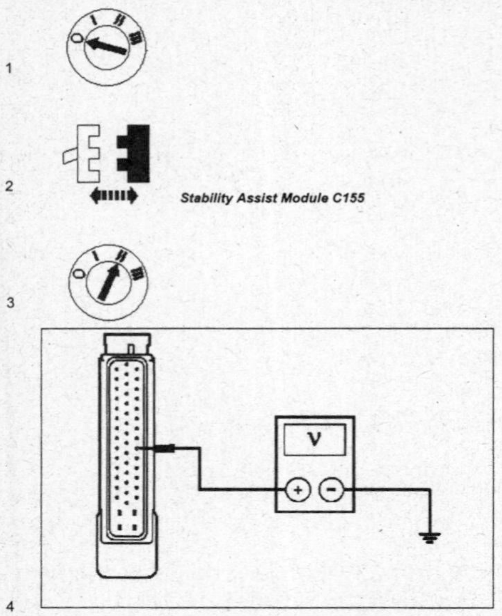

Measure the voltage between stability assist module C155 pin 9, circuit 8-CF54 (BK/GN), harness side, and ground.

- **Is any voltage present?**

→ **Yes**

Go to «R4».

→ **No**

INSTALL new Stability Assist Module. Test system for normal operation.

FM4029901543030X

Fig. 38 Test R: Traction Control Inoperative (Part 3 of 4). With Stability Assist

R4 CHECK CIRCUIT 8-CF54 (BK/GN) FOR SHORT TO POWER

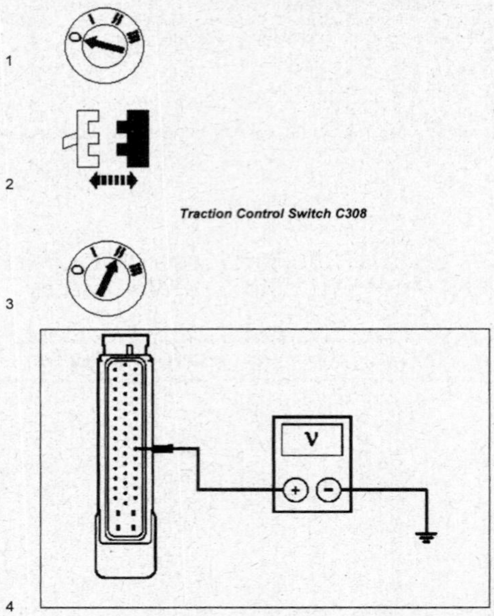

Measure the voltage between stability assist module C155 pin 9, circuit 8-CF54 (BK/GN), harness side, and ground.

- **Is any voltage present?**

→ **Yes**

REPAIR the circuit. TEST the system for normal operation.

→ **No**

INSTALL new traction control switch. TEST system for normal operation.

FM4029901543040X

Fig. 38 Test R: Traction Control Inoperative (Part 4 of 4). With Stability Assist

S1 CHECK THE TRACTION CONTROL SWITCH

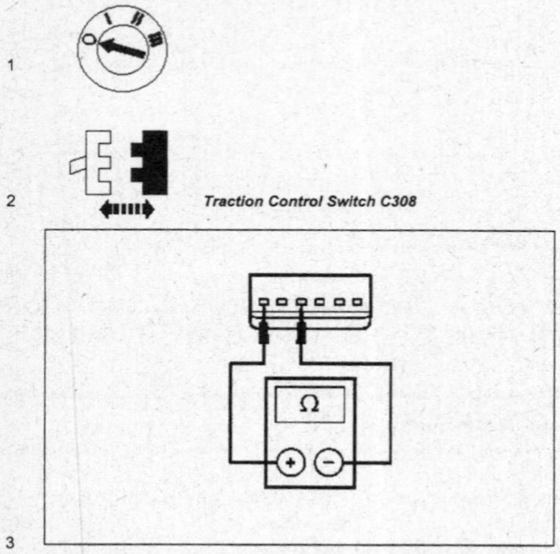

Measure the resistance between traction control switch pin 1 (component side), and traction control switch pin 3 (component side).

- **Is the resistance approximately 32 ohms?**

→ **Yes**

Go to «S2».

→ **No**

INSTALL a new traction control switch. CLEAR the DTC. REPEAT the self-test.

FM4029901544010X

Fig. 39 Test S: Stability Assist/Traction Control Switch Indicator Never/Always On (Part 1 of 3). With Stability Assist

S2 CHECK CIRCUIT 31S-CF45 (BK/GN) FOR SHORT TO POWER

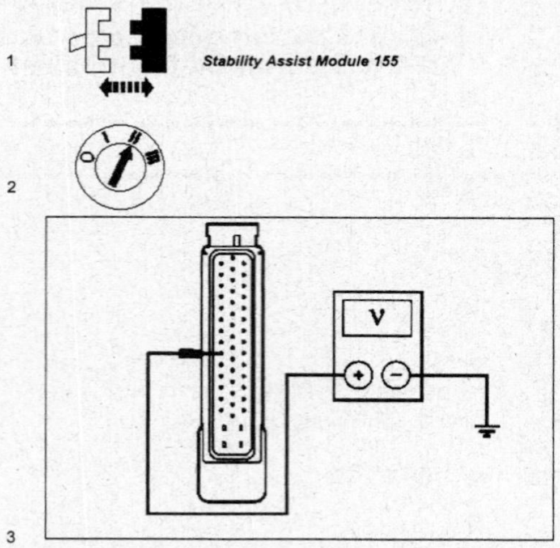

Measure the voltage between stability assist module C155 pin 42, circuit 31S-CF45 (BK/GN), harness side, and ground.

- **Is any voltage present?**

→ **Yes**

REPAIR the circuit. CLEAR the DTC. REPEAT the self-test.

→ **No**

Go to «S3».

FM4029901544020X

Fig. 39 Test S: Stability Assist/Traction Control Switch Indicator Never/Always On (Part 2 of 3). With Stability Assist

S3 CHECK CIRCUIT 31S-CF45 (BK/GN)

1

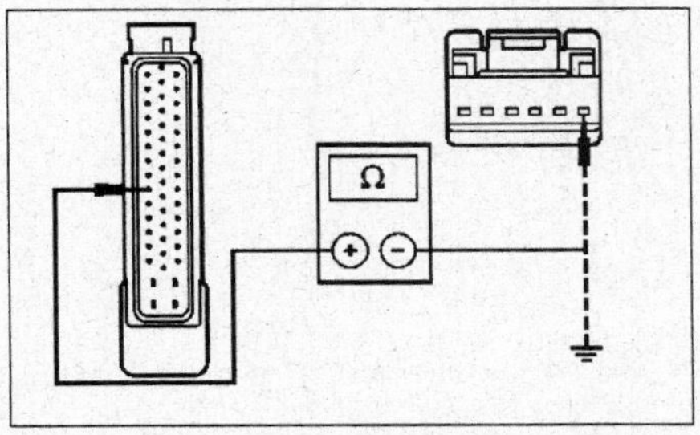

2

Measure the resistance between stability assist module C155 pin 42, circuit 31S-CF45 (BK/GN), harness side and traction control switch C308 pin 1, circuit 31S-CF45 (BK/GN), harness side; and between stability assist module C155 pin 42, circuit 31S-CF45 (BK/GN), harness side and ground.

- **Is the resistance less than 5 ohms between the stability assist module and traction control switch; and greater than 10,000 ohms between stability assist module and ground?**

→ **Yes**

INSTALL a new stability assist module. CLEAR the DTC. REPEAT the self-test.

→ **No**

REPAIR the circuit. CLEAR the DTC. REPEAT the self-test.

FM4029901544030X

Fig. 39 Test S: Stability Assist/Traction Control Switch Indicator Never/Always On (Part 3 of 3). With Stability Assist

T2 CHECK THE TRACTION CONTROL SWITCH

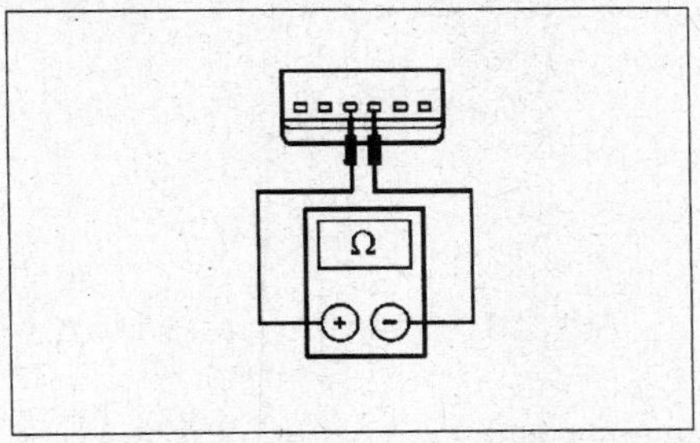

1

Measure the resistance between traction control switch pin 3 (component side), and traction control switch pin 4 (component side), while depressing the traction control switch.

- **Is the resistance less than 5 ohms?**

→ **Yes**

Go to «T3».

→ **No**

INSTALL a new traction control switch. TEST the system for normal operation.

FM4029901545020X

Fig. 40 Test T: Stability Assist System Cannot Be Disabled (Part 2 of 3). With Stability Assist

T1 CHECK CIRCUIT 15-CF54 (GN/WH) FOR AN OPEN

1

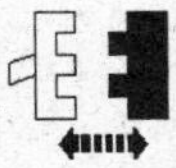

2

Traction Control Switch C308

3

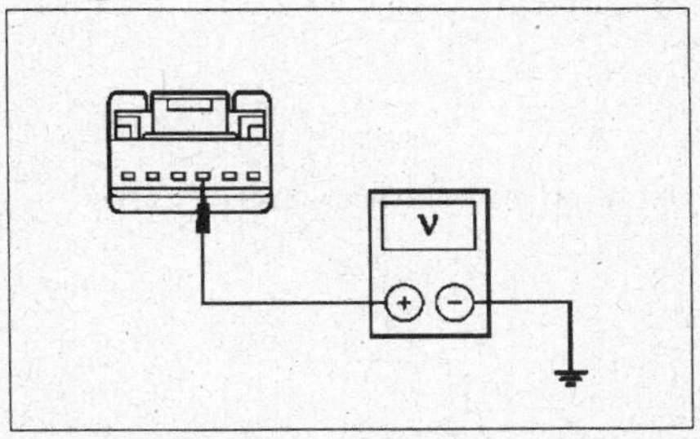

4

Measure the voltage between traction control switch C308 pin 3, circuit 15-CF54 (GN/WH), harness side, and ground.

- **Is the voltage greater than 10 volts?**

→ **Yes**

Go to «T2».

→ **No**

REPAIR circuit 15-CF54 (GN/WH) or circuit 15-DA5 (GN/OG). TEST the system for normal operation.

FM4029901545010X

Fig. 40 Test T: Stability Assist System Cannot Be Disabled (Part 1 of 3). With Stability Assist

T3 CHECK CIRCUIT 8-CF54 (WH/VT) FOR AN OPEN

1

2

Stability Assist Module C155

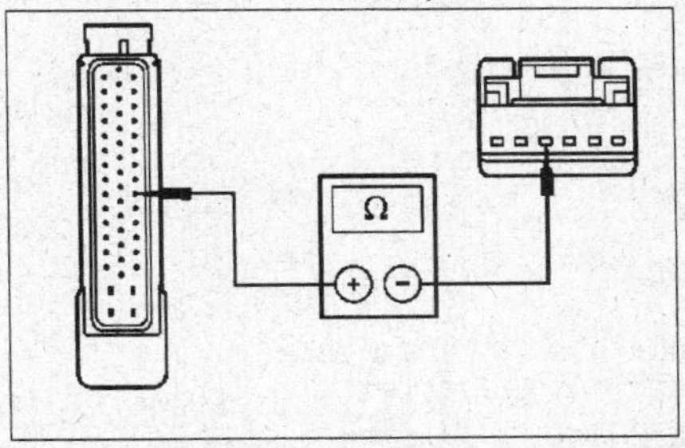

3

Measure the resistance between stability assist module pin 9, circuit 8-CF54 (WH/VT), harness side, and traction control switch C308 pin 4, circuit 8-CF54 (WH/VT), harness side.

- **Is the resistance less than 5 ohms?**

→ **Yes**

INSTALL a new stability assist module. TEST the system for normal operation.

→ **No**

REPAIR the circuit. TEST the system for normal operation.

FM4029901545030X

Fig. 40 Test T: Stability Assist System Cannot Be Disabled (Part 3 of 3). With Stability Assist

U1	CHECK THE STABILITY ASSIST INDICATOR

1 

2 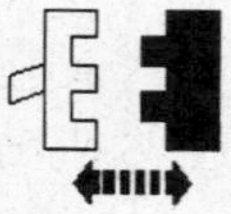 *Stability Assist Module C155*

3 

- **Is the stability assist indicator illuminated?**

➔ **Yes**

Go to «U2».

➔ **No**

DIAGNOSE instrument cluster.

FM4029901546010X

Fig. 41 Test U: Stability Assist Indicator Does Not Self Check (Part 1 of 2). With Stability Assist

U2	CHECK PROVE OUT

1 

2  *Stability Assist Module C162*

3 

- **Does the stability assist indicator prove out for three seconds and then turn off?**

➔ **Yes**

The stability assist indicator is working correctly. TEST the system for normal operation.

➔ **No**

INSTALL a new stability assist module. TEST the system for normal operation.

FM4029901546020X

Fig. 41 Test U: Stability Assist Indicator Does Not Self Check (Part 2 of 2). With Stability Assist

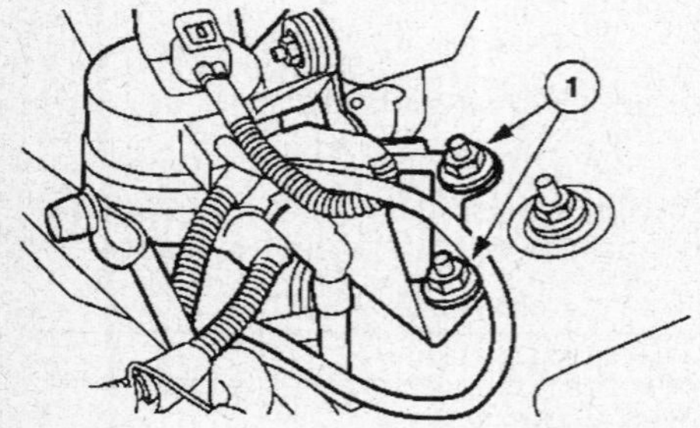

FM4029901547000X

Fig. 42 Vapor management valve

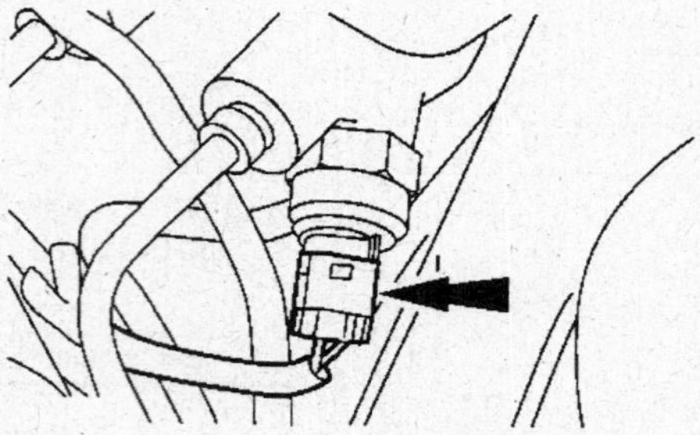

FM4029901548000X

Fig. 43 ABS pressure transducer

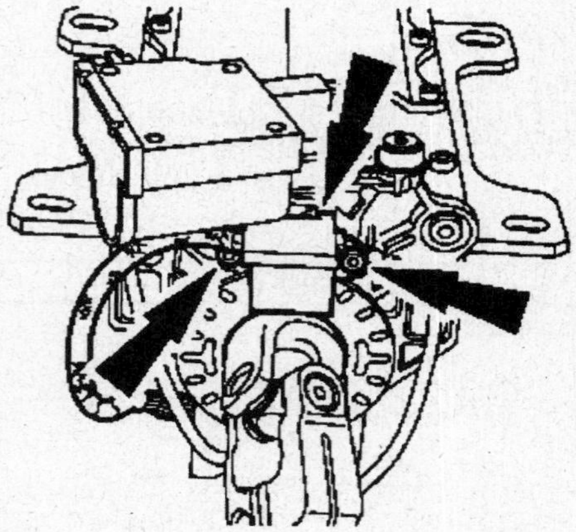

FM4029901565000X

Fig. 44 Steering column rotation sensor

SYSTEM SERVICE

Brake System Bleed

Refer to "Hydraulic Brake Systems" for bleed procedure.

Component Replacement

Refer to "Module Configuration" before performing service procedures.

ABS CONTROL MODULE

1. Disconnect ABS module electrical connector.
2. Release underhood junction block clips and position aside.
3. Remove ABS control module attaching bolts, then the ABS module.
4. Reverse procedure to install noting the following:
   a. **Torque** ABS control module to 18 inch lbs.
   b. Configure ABS control module as outlined in "Module Configuration."

ABS PRESSURE TRANSDUCER (PRIMARY & SECONDARY)

1. Remove vapor management valve bracket bolts (1), and position aside, **Fig. 42.**
2. Disconnect pressure transducer electrical connector, **Fig. 43.**
3. Remove pressure transducer.
4. Reverse procedure to install. Calibrate stability assist module as outlined in "Module Configuration."

BRAKE BOOSTER SOLENOID

If brake booster solenoid requires replacement, the entire booster must be replaced. For brake booster replacement procedures, refer to the "Power Brake Units" chapter.

BRAKE BOOSTER RELEASE SWITCH

If the brake booster release switch requires replacement, the entire booster must be replaced. For brake booster replacement procedures, refer to the "Power Brake Units" chapter.

HYDRAULIC CONTROL UNIT (HCU)

1. Disconnect HCU electrical connector.
2. Disconnect and plug hydraulic lines from HCU.
3. Remove HCU attaching bolts, then the HCU.
4. Reverse procedure to install noting the following:
   a. **Torque** HCU attaching bolts to 96 inch lbs.
   b. **Torque** HCU hydraulic lines to 13 ft. lbs.
   c. Bleed brake system as required.

LATERAL ACCELEROMETER

1. Apply parking brake.
2. **On models equipped with manual transmission,** place gear selector to 4th gear, then remove shift lever knob.
3. **On models equipped with automatic transmission,** place gear selector in neutral.

4. **On all models,** remove ash tray finish panel.
5. Disconnect cellular phone electrical connectors if equipped.
6. Disconnect traction control switch electrical connector, then release cellular phone wiring harness from console finish panel.
7. Remove console rear finish panel.
8. Unclip parking brake boot from console base.
9. Remove console assembly front screws and rear bolts.
10. Remove console air conditioning duct, then slide console rearward and remove.
11. Remove center A/C duct.
12. Remove lateral accelerometer.
13. Reverse procedure to install noting the following:
    a. **Torque** lateral accelerometer sensor to 80 inch lbs.
    b. Calibrate stability assist module as outlined in "Module Configuration."

STABILITY ASSIST MODULE

Refer to "ABS Control Module" for procedure.

STEERING WHEEL ROTATION SENSOR

1. Remove steering column as outlined in "Steering Columns" chapter.
2. Remove steering column rotation sensor attaching screws, then the sensor, **Fig. 44.**
3. Reverse procedure to install.

TRACTION CONTROL SWITCH

1. Apply parking brake.
2. **On models equipped with manual transmission,** place gear selector in 4th gear and remove shifter knob.
3. **On models equipped with automatic transmission,** place gear selector in neutral.
4. **On all models,** remove ash tray finish panel.
5. Disconnect cellular phone electrical connectors if equipped.
6. Remove console finish panel as follows:
    a. Pull upward on front of finish panel.
    b. Disconnect traction control switch.
    c. Release cellular phone wiring harness from console finish panel.
7. Remove traction control switch from finish panel.
8. Reverse procedure to install.

WHEEL SPEED SENSOR

FRONT

This procedure has been revised by a Technical Service Bulletin.

1. Raise and support vehicle.
2. Push up on closed end of ABS sensor retaining clip, then pull sensor from wheel bearing dust cap.
3. Remove retaining ring from dust cap.
4. Inspect end of ABS sensor for water intrusion. If water is found, wheel bearing may be contaminated and should be replaced.

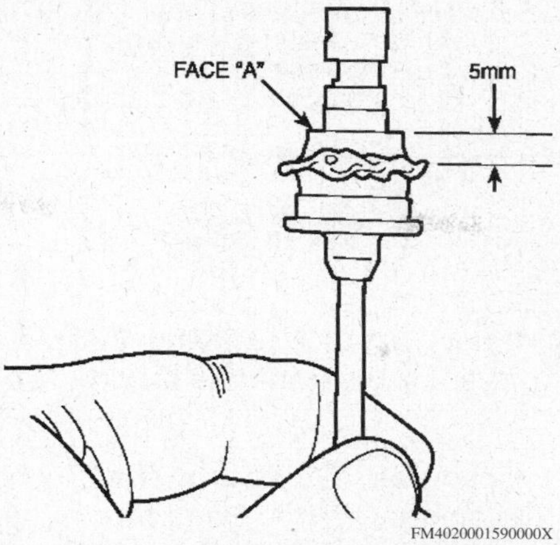

Fig. 45 Front wheel speed sensor installation

5. Remove sensor wire from brake hose attaching clips.
6. Disconnect and remove sensor from vehicle harness.
7. Reverse procedure to install noting the following:
    a. Remove sensor O-ring from steering knuckle.
    b. Clean inside surface of sensor opening using a clean, dry, oil free cloth.
    c. Install new O-ring to sensor opening.
    d. Install new sensor retaining clip.
    e. Apply a .10 inch bead of suitable RTV sealant to new sensor, **Fig. 45.**
    f. Push up on closed end of retainer clip and insert ABS sensor into dust cap. Release clip ensuring open ends of retainer clip are flush with outer surface of dust cap. If ends of clip are not flush, press sensor inward toward bearing to fully seat sensor and clip.

REAR

1. Raise and support vehicle.
2. Disconnect ABS sensor electrical connector.
3. Remove sensor harness from control arm clips.
4. Remove ABS sensor attaching bolt, then the sensor.
5. Reverse procedure to install. **Torque** to 80 inch lbs.

YAW RATE SENSOR

1. Apply parking brake.
2. **On models equipped with manual transmission,** place gear selector to 4th gear, then remove shift lever knob.
3. **On models equipped with automatic transmission,** place gear selector in neutral.
4. **On all models,** remove ash tray finish panel.
5. Disconnect cellular phone electrical connectors if equipped.
6. Disconnect traction control switch electrical connector, then release cellular phone wiring harness from console finish panel.
7. Remove console rear finish panel.
8. Unclip parking brake boot from console base.
9. Remove console assembly front screws and rear bolts.
10. Remove console air conditioning duct, then slide console rearward and remove.
11. Remove center A/C duct.
12. Disconnect yaw rate sensor electrical connector.
13. Remove yaw rate sensor.
14. Reverse procedure to install noting the following:
    a. **Torque** yaw rate sensor to 80 inch lbs.
    b. Calibrate stability assist module as outlined in "Module Configuration."

Module Configuration

Newly released modules will require configuration after being installed on the vehicle. All configurable modules will be packaged in a kit which contains a warning label and multi-language sheet which lists requirements to configure the modules.

There are two types of configuration data. The first type is used by the module so that it can interact with the vehicle correctly. The second type is customer preference driven. These are items that the customer may or may not want to have enabled. To program customer driven preferences, a Ford service function card (FSF) and the New Generation Star Tester (NGS), tool No. 007–00500, or equivalents, must be used to toggle preferences on or off.

The New Generation Star Tester (NGS), tool No. 007–00500, or equivalent, must be used to retrieve configuration data from the old module before it is removed from the vehicle. This information will be transferred into the new module so that the new module will contain the same settings as the old module.

The following modules require configuration when being replaced; ABS control module, ABS control module with traction control, interactive vehicle dynamic (IVD) module, instrument cluster, instrument cluster with message center, rear electronic module (REM), front electronic module (FEM), driver door module (DDM), dual automatic temperature control (DATC) module, remote emergency satellite cellular unit (RESCU) module, and the steering column lock module (SCLM) when PCM is replaced on manual transmission equipped models. If configuring PCM, the NGS tester flash cable tool No. 007–00531, or equivalent, must be used.

To perform the configuration process, proceed as follows:

1. Connect New Generation Star Tester tool No. 007–00500 with Ford service function (FSF) card to vehicle DLC.
2. Follow scan tool instructions to upload configuration data.
3. Install new module. **NGS will not retain configuration data for more than 24 hours.**
4. Download stored configuration information to new module using FSF card and NGS tester.

5. If unable to carry out configuration process, proceed as follows:
   a. Inspect for signs of electrical damage.
   b. If NGS does not communicate with vehicle, ensure program card is correctly installed, vehicle connections are secure and that ignition switch is in run position.
   c. If NGS still does not communicate with vehicle, diagnose module communications network concern.

Focus

NOTE: On Air Bag Equipped Models, Refer To "Air Bag System Precautions" Located In The Front Of This Manual For System Disarming & Arming Procedures.

NOTE: Refer To "Computer Relearn Procedures" Located In The Front Of This Manual When Battery Power To The Computer Has Been Interrupted.

NOTE: "Electrical Symbol & Wire Color Code Identification" Located In The Front Of This Manual May Be Used As An Aid When Using Wiring Circuits Found In This Section.

INDEX

PRECAUTIONS

Air Bag Systems

Refer to "Air Bag System Precautions" in the front of this manual for system disarming and arming procedures.

Battery Ground Cable

Prior to service, disconnect battery ground cable and isolate as required.

DESCRIPTION

Hydraulic & Electronic Control Unit

The ABS control module and hydraulic unit are integrated into one assembly. The unit consists of an aluminum block of solenoid valves, pump motor and ABS control module.

The ABS control module continuously monitors and compares wheel speed information for each wheel. When the module determines that a wheel lockup is going to occur, brake pressure is modulated to the appropriate wheel. Brake pressure modulation is achieved by the hydraulic control unit opening and closing appropriate solenoid valves. When the affected wheel returns to normal speed, solenoid valves are returned to normal position and normal braking resumes.

If a fault exists in the ABS system, the ABS control module can detect it through self-diagnostic capabilities. When the ignition switch is turned on, control module will perform an electrical continuity inspection. When vehicle speed is approximately 12 mph, the hydraulic pump motor is actuated for ½ second, then a wheel speed sensor inspection is carried out. If vehicle is under heavy acceleration during initial vehicle speed to 12 mph, sensor inspection is delayed for 2 minutes.

Any fault in the ABS system will disable ABS function. Normal braking can still resume, if there are no faults in the base brake system.

Wheel Speed Sensors

There are four wheel speed sensors which provide a digital speed signal information to the ABS control module. The signal is generated using an encoder ring with a magnetic profile embedded within the material.

Electronic Brake Distribution (EBD)

The electronic brake force distribution is part of the ABS control module operating strategy. This operating strategy enables greater utilization of the rear brakes up to the point of ABS operation. During EBD, brake force is determined by the amount of wheel slip detected by the ABS control module.

ABS w/Traction Control & Stability Assist

The four wheel anti-lock brake system with traction control and stability assist consists of the following components: brake booster release switch, front and rear ABS sensors and sensor indicators, hydraulic control unit, stability assist event indicator,

DTC	Description	Stability Assist Calibration
C1279	Yaw Rate Sensor Circuit Failure	YES
C1280	Yaw Rate Sensor Signal Fault	YES
C1281	Accelerometer Circuit Failure	YES
C1282	Accelerometer Signal Fault	YES
C1285	Booster Solenoid Circuit Failure	YES
C1286	Booster Mechanical Failure	YES
C1287	Booster Pedal Force Switch Circuit Failure	YES
C1288	Pressure Transducer Main / Primary Input Circuit Failure	YES
C1289	Pressure Transducer Redundant / Secondary Input Circuit Failure	YES
C1730	Reference Voltage Out of Range (+5 V)	YES

FM4020201883000X

Fig. 1 Stability assist calibration list

Condition	Possible Sources	Action
•No communication with the ABS module	•Fuse(s). •Circuit(s). •ABS module.	•GO to Pinpoint Test A.
•Unable to enter self-test	•ABS module.	• GO to Pinpoint Test B.
•The red brake warning indicator does not self-check	•Circuit(s). •Instrument cluster. •ABS module.	•GO to Pinpoint Test H.
•The yellow ABS warning indicator does not self-check	•Circuit(s). •ABS module. •Instrument cluster.	•GO to Pinpoint Test G.

FM4020201913000X

Fig. 2 Symptom chart. Less stability assist

Condition	Possible Sources	Action
•No communication with the stability assist module	•Battery junction box (BJB)Fuse: – F11 (30A). – F21 (20A). •Central junction box (CJB) Fuse: – F20 (10A). – F30 (7.5A). – F36 (7.5A). – F50 (7.5A). – F54 (15A). – F59 (7.5A). •Circuit(s). •stability assist module.	•Go To Pinpoint Test A.
•No brake pedal position input signal	•Circuit(s). •stability assist module.	•Go To Pinpoint Test B.
•The yellow ABS warning indicator does not self-check	•Circuit(s). •stability assist module.	•Go To Pinpoint Test P.
•Spongy brake pedal with no warning indicator	•Air in brake hydraulic system.	•DIAGNOSE brakes.
•The traction control is inoperative	•Circuit(s). •T/C / stability assist switch. •stability assist module.	•Go To Pinpoint Test Q.
	•Base brake system.	•DIAGNOSE traction control.
•The T/C / stability assist indicator is never/always on	•Circuit(s). •ESP/traction control switch. •stability assist module.	•Go To Pinpoint Test R.
•The T/C / stability assist system cannot be disabled	•Circuit(s). •Traction control switch. •stability assist module.	•Go To Pinpoint Test S.
•The T/C / stability assist indicator does not self-check	•Circuit(s). •stability assist module.	•Go To Pinpoint Test T.

FM4020201914000X

Fig. 3 Symptom chart. With stability assist

DTC	Description	Source	Action
B1676	Battery voltage out of range	ABS	GO to Pinpoint Test C.
B1342	ABS module internal failure	ABS	INSTALL a new HCU. CLEAR the DTCs. REPEAT the self-test.
C1095	ABS hydraulic pump motor circuit failure	ABS	GO to Pinpoint Test D.
C1145	RF wheel speed sensor input circuit failure	ABS	GO to Pinpoint Test E.
C1155	LF wheel speed sensor input circuit failure	ABS	GO to Pinpoint Test E.
C1165	RR wheel speed sensor input circuit failure	ABS	GO to Pinpoint Test E.
C1175	LR wheel speed sensor input circuit failure	ABS	GO to Pinpoint Test E.
C1233	LF wheel speed input signal missing	ABS	GO to Pinpoint Test F.
C1234	RF wheel speed input signal missing	ABS	GO to Pinpoint Test F.
C1235	RR wheel speed input signal missing	ABS	GO to Pinpoint Test F.
C1236	LR wheel speed input signal missing	ABS	GO to Pinpoint Test F.
C1267	ABS functions temporarily disabled	ABS	GO to Pinpoint Test C.

FM4020201915000X

Fig. 4 Diagnostic trouble code & pinpoint test reference chart. Less stability assist

stability assist module, lateral accelerometer, steering wheel position sensor, transducers, trac control switch, yaw rate sensor and the yellow anti-lock brake warning indicator.

The stability assist system communicates with the PCM. The PCM assists with traction control by altering engine timing and fuel injector pulse. By altering engine timing and fuel injector pulse, the PCM can control torque, which in turn reduces excessive wheel spin. At speeds above 25 mph, traction control is controlled only by PCM command of engine torque output. At speeds up to 25 mph, the stability assist module requests the PCM to reduce engine torque while simultaneously applying and releasing appropriate brake to restore traction when one or both drive wheels lose traction and begin to spin.

The stability assist system continuously monitors vehicle motion relative to the driver's intended course. The driver's intended course is calculated by using sensors to compare steering inputs from driver with actual motion of the vehicle. The driver's steering wheel input is measured from a steering wheel rotation sensor. Vehicle motion is determined using a yaw rate sensor which measures rotation about the vehicle axis, a lateral accelerometer which measures acceleration generated from the vehicle sliding sideways and wheel speed sensors which measure speed of each individual wheel. If there is a discrepancy between driver input and vehicle motion, the stability assist system changes the force at each tire to help control the vehicle.

The stability assist system defaults to on when the engine is started. Stability assist is not active when the vehicle is traveling in reverse, however ABS and traction control are still functional. System status is indicated in the stability assist warning lamp located in the stability assist/traction control switch. Stability assist is an independent function of ABS. The illumination of the stability assist/traction control switch indicates that the stability assist function is off and that ABS will continue to operate normally.

When the stability assist system is attempting to correct vehicle direction, the following normal conditions may be present: rumble or grinding sound; deceleration or reduction in acceleration of vehicle; ABS indicator may flash; vibration in brake pedal; brake pedal may move to apply higher brake forces accompanied by whoosh sound from beneath instrument panel. Also, the brake pedal may experience a slight movement when the system self check is performed. The self check is performed after the vehicle reaches a speed of 30 mph after 8 minutes of running time. Self check will only be performed if the vehicle is stable, driver is not braking and accelerator pedal is depressed. If a failure is detected, the stability assist indicator will be illuminated. Anti-lock brake system will continue to function normally unless the yellow ABS warning indicator is illuminated. Normal brake function will continue to occur unless the red brake warning indicator is illuminated.

Brake Booster

The brake booster operates as any normal brake booster, with the added capability of being electronically actuated by the stability assist module. The electronic actuation of the brake booster is sometimes required in severe stability assist events to ensure that the hydraulic control unit can generate enough brake pressure to improve vehicle stability.

The brake booster houses a solenoid that enables it to be electronically actuated. It also contains a release switch to indicate when the driver is stepping on the brake.

When performing the booster learn cycle using the NGS tester, ensure ignition switch is in the run position with engine running and brakes not applied.

Lateral Accelerometer

The lateral accelerometer measures centrifugal and gravitational acceleration which corresponds to the force required to slide the vehicle sideways. The accelerometer only measures the acceleration along the lateral direction of the vehicle, therefore on level ground, there is no contribution

DTC	Description	Source	Action
B1342	ECU Is Defective	ESP	CLEAR the DTCs. RETRIEVE the DTCs. If DTC B1342 is retrieved, INSTALL a new stability assist module REPEAT the self-test.
B1676	Battery Voltage Out of Range	ESP	GO to Pinpoint Test C.
B2477	Module Configuration Failure	ESP	CONFIGURE module.
C1095	ABS Hydraulic Pump Motor Circuit Failure	ESP	GO to Pinpoint Test D.
C1145	Speed Wheel Sensor RF Input Circuit Failure	ESP	GO to Pinpoint Test E.
C1155	Speed Wheel Sensor LF Input Circuit Failure	ESP	GO to Pinpoint Test E.
C1165	Speed Wheel Sensor RR Input Circuit Failure	ESP	GO to Pinpoint Test E.

FM4020201916010X

Fig. 5 Diagnostic trouble code & pinpoint reference chart. With stability assist

from this acceleration. If the vehicle is parked sideways on a bank or incline, the sensor will measure lateral acceleration due to gravity, even though the vehicle is stationary.

When calibrating the lateral accelerometer using the NGS tester, ensure vehicle is stationary and on a level surface with ignition switch in run position.

Stability Assist Module

On models equipped with stability control, a stability assist module is used in place of the ABS control module. The stability assist module controls ABS, full speed traction control and stability assist functions to enhance driver control of the vehicle. Stability assist control determines interactions between anti-lock, traction control and engine control systems to optimize vehicle traction during deceleration and acceleration. Stability assist also controls brake pressure during braking and non-braking conditions as required to counteract excessive vehicle rotation when cornering.

The stability assist module is self-monitoring. When the ignition switch is turned to the run position, stability assist module will perform an electrical inspection. When vehicle speed reaches 12 mph, the pump motor is actuated for ½ second. A fault in the ABS, traction control or stability assist system will cause ABS, traction control and stability assist operation to deactivate and the yellow ABS warning indicator to illuminate. Normal power assisted braking will still remain available.

The stability assist module must be calibrated when a component related to stability assist is disconnected, moved or replaced. Before removing stability assist module, it is required to upload current module configuration, and then reconfigure the module. Refer to **Fig. 1,** for DTC's that require stability assist module recalibration. If a DTC is present for any component of the stability assist system, the DTC must be cleared before performing calibration procedure. If a DTC is received after calibration, proceed to "Diagnostic Trouble Code & Pinpoint Test Reference Chart." in "Diagnosis & Testing." If module

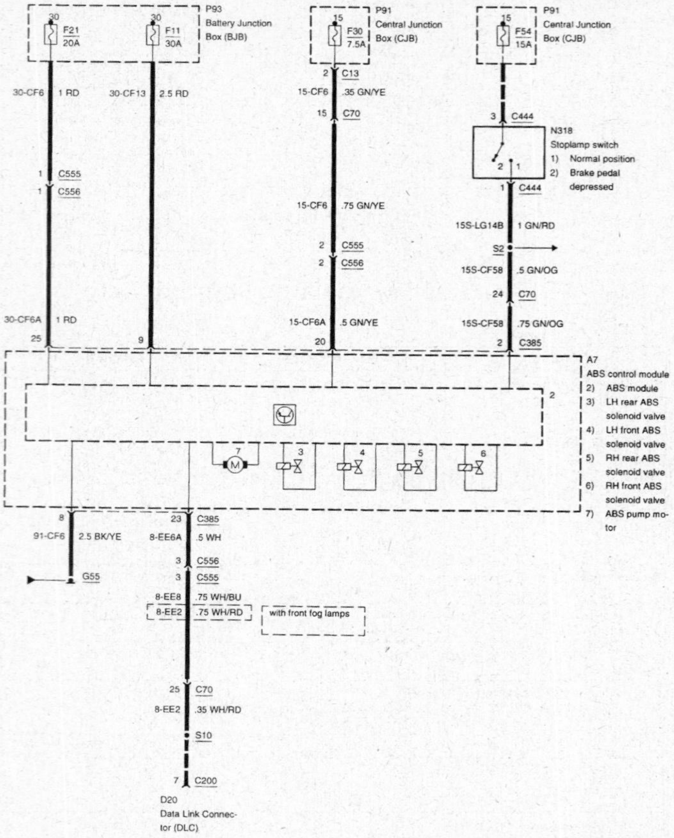

FM4020001600010X

Fig. 6 Wiring diagram (Part 1 of 3). Less stability assist

re-calibration is required, refer to "Module Configuration" in "System Service."

Steering Wheel Rotation Sensor

A sensor ring is mounted to the steering column through which the steering wheel rotation sensor can tell which way the steering wheel is turned, and how far it is turned. This sensor does not tell the stability assist module the position of the steering wheel relative to straight ahead position. The stability assist system learns straight ahead position by comparing steering wheel position with other signals and remembering position learned. Stability assist system confirms this position and modifies it as required during every new driving cycle.

When calibrating the steering wheel rotation sensor using the NGS tester, ensure engine is running and that steering wheel is rotated back-and-forth from lock position to lock position.

Yaw Rate Sensor

The yaw rate sensor measures rotation rate of the vehicle as it turns left and right. The sensor is located under the center console.

When calibrating the yaw rate sensor using the NGS tester, ensure vehicle is stationary and on a level surface with ignition switch in run position.

TROUBLESHOOTING

Inspection & Verification

1. Verify ABS system concern by applying brakes under various driving conditions.
2. Perform a visual inspection of brake system for signs of mechanical or electrical damage.
3. Inspect the following for mechanical faults:
   a. Low brake fluid.
   b. Wheel speed sensors.
   c. Anti-lock brake system sensor indicators.
   d. Base brake system.
   e. Wheel bearings.
4. Inspect the following for mechanical faults:
   a. Fuses and fusible links.
   b. ABS warning indicator lamp.
   c. Red brake warning indicator lamp.
   d. Wiring harness.
   e. Loose, corroded or damaged connectors.
5. If a fault is found during visual inspection, repair as required and verify normal brake system operation.

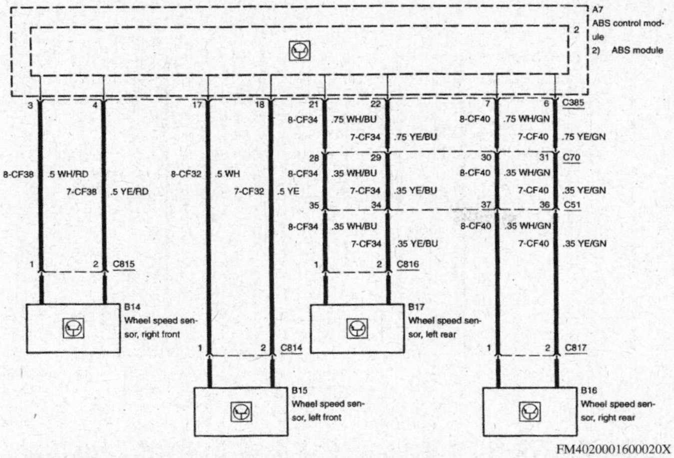

Fig. 6 Wiring diagram (Part 2 of 3). Less stability assist

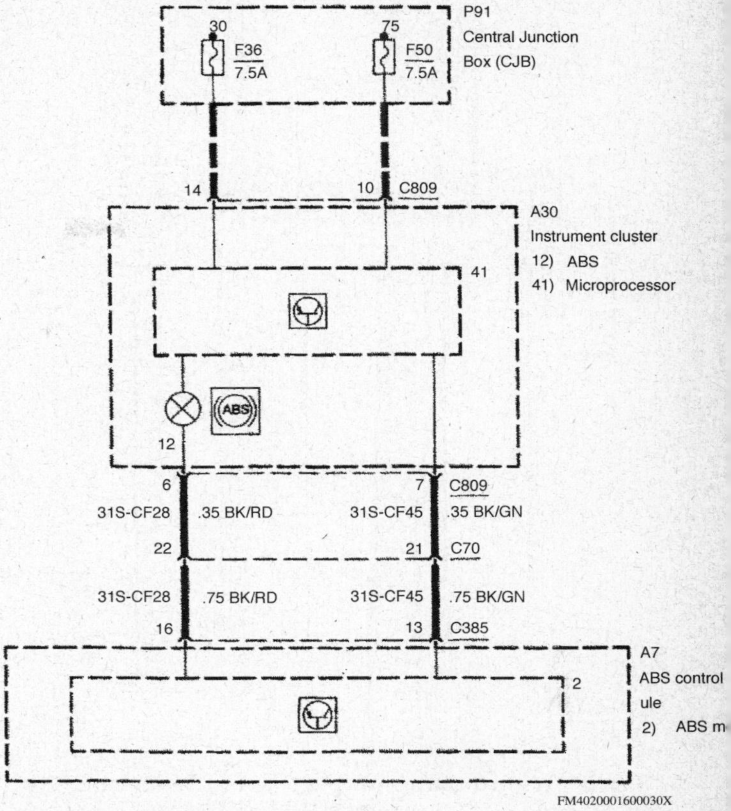

Fig. 6 Wiring diagram (Part 3 of 3). Less stability assist

6. If fault is still present after visual inspection, connect a suitable scan tool to DLC and perform data link diagnostic test. If scan tool will not communicate with vehicle, proceed as follows:
   a. Ensure program card is properly installed to scan tool.
   b. Ensure connections to vehicle are secure.
   c. Ensure ignition switch is in proper position.
   d. If scan tool still does not communicate with vehicle, refer to scan tool instruction manual.
7. If scan tool returns CKT914, CKT915 or CKT70–ALL ECUS NO RESP/NOT EQUIP, diagnose multiplex communication network.
8. If scan tool returns NO RESP/NOT EQUIP for anti-lock brake control module, refer to "Test A" in "Pinpoint Tests."
9. If scan tool returns SYSTEM PASSED, obtain and record continuous DTCs as outlined in "Accessing Diagnostic Trouble Codes." Clear continuous codes as outlined in "Clearing Diagnostic Trouble Codes." Perform self-test diagnostics for ABS control module.
10. If DTCs are related to ABS concern, proceed to "Diagnostic Trouble Code & Pinpoint Test Reference Chart."
11. If no DTCs are present, proceed to "Symptom Chart."

Symptom Chart

Refer to **Figs. 2 and 3,** for symptom chart.

DIAGNOSIS & TESTING

Accessing Diagnostic Trouble Codes

To access diagnostic trouble codes, connect a suitable scan tool to vehicle data link connector and follow scan tool instructions.

Diagnostic Trouble Code & Pinpoint Test Reference Chart

Refer to **Figs. 4 and 5,** for diagnostic trouble code and pinpoint test reference chart.

Wiring Diagrams

Refer to **Figs. 6 and 7,** for wiring diagrams.

Pinpoint Tests

Refer to **Figs. 8 through 44,** for pinpoint tests.

Clearing Diagnostic Trouble Codes

Connect a suitably programmed scan tool to Data Link Connector (DLC), and follow manufacturer's instructions.

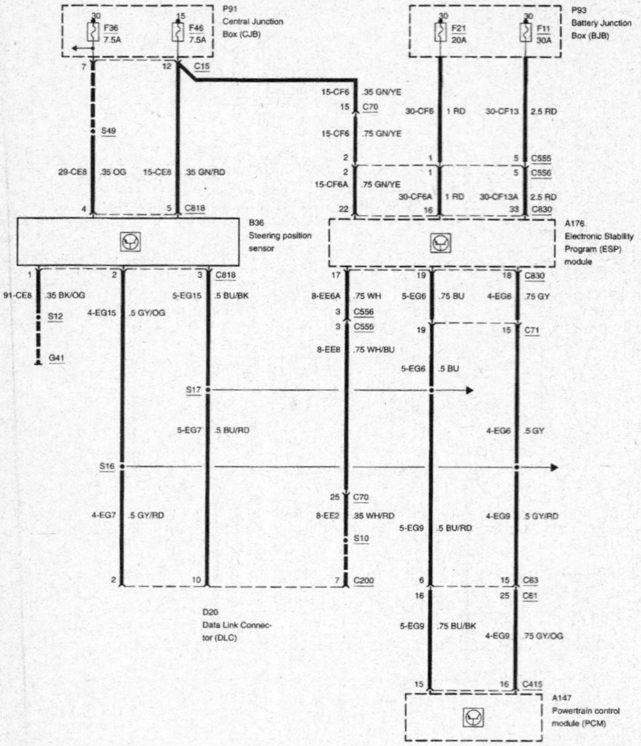

FM4020201917010X

Fig. 7 Wiring diagram (Part 1 of 5). With stability assist

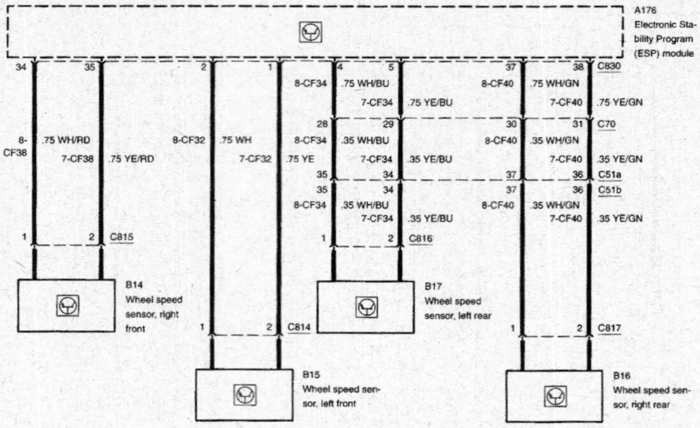

FM4020201917020X

Fig. 7 Wiring diagram (Part 2 of 5). With stability assist

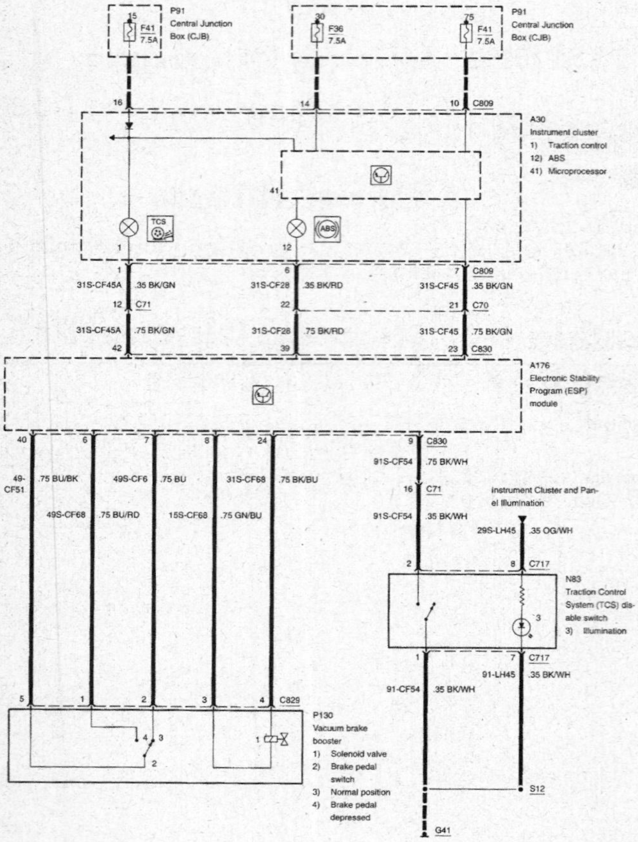

FM4020201917030X

Fig. 7 Wiring diagram (Part 3 of 5). With stability assist

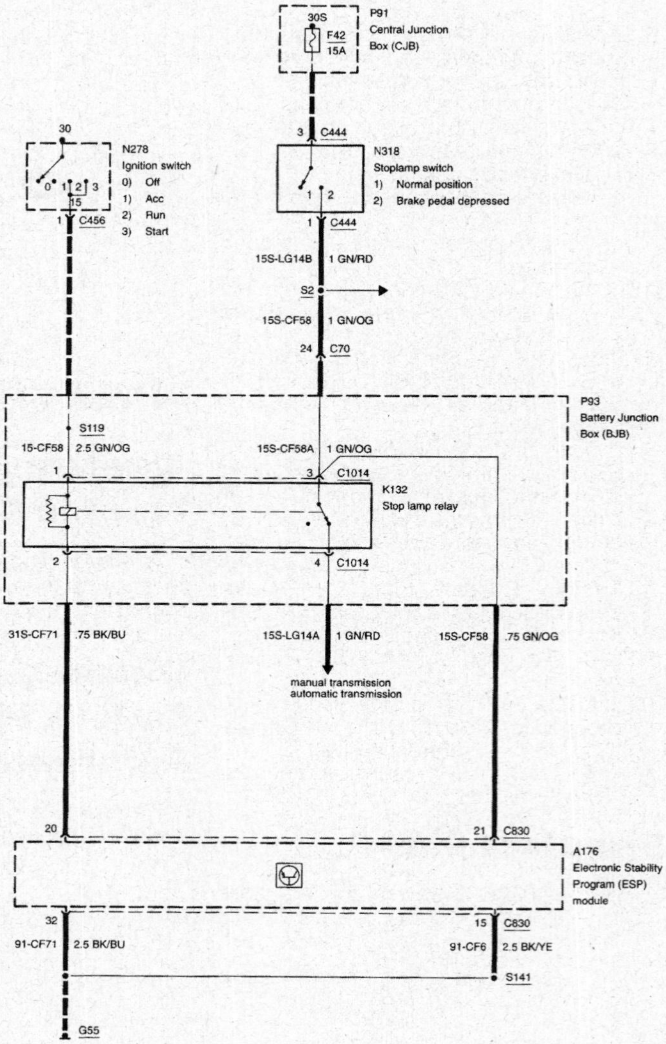

FM4020201917040X

Fig. 7 Wiring diagram (Part 4 of 5). With stability assist

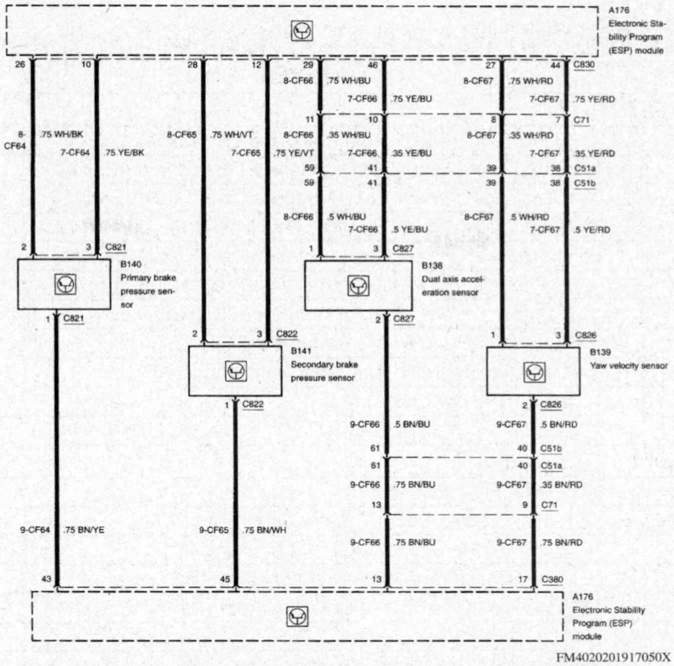

Fig. 7 Wiring diagram (Part 5 of 5). With stability assist

DIAGNOSTIC CHART INDEX

Test	Code	Description	Page No.	Fig. No.
2000–01 LESS STABILITY ASSIST				
A	—	No Communication w/ABS Control Module	6-187	8
B	—	Unable To Enter Self Test	6-187	9
C	B1676	Battery Voltage Out Of Range	6-187	10
D	C1095	ABS Hydraulic Pump Motor Circuit Failure	6-187	11
E	C1145	Righthand Front Wheel Speed Sensor Input Circuit Failure (2000)	6-188	12
		Righthand Front Wheel Speed Sensor Input Circuit Failure (2001)	6-189	13
	C1155	Lefthand Front Wheel Speed Sensor Input Circuit Failure (2000)	6-188	12
		Lefthand Front Wheel Speed Sensor Input Circuit Failure (2001)	6-189	13
	C1165	Righthand Rear Wheel Speed Sensor Input Circuit Failure (2000)	6-188	12
		Righthand Rear Wheel Speed Sensor Input Circuit Failure (2001)	6-189	13
	C1175	Lefthand Rear Wheel Speed Sensor Input Circuit Failure (2000)	6-188	12
		Lefthand Rear Wheel Speed Sensor Input Circuit Failure (2001)	6-189	13
F	C1233	Lefthand Front Wheel Speed Input Signal Missing	6-190	14
	C1234	Righthand Front Wheel Speed Input Signal Missing	6-190	14
	C1235	Righthand Rear Wheel Speed Input Signal Missing	6-190	14
	C1236	Lefthand Rear Wheel Speed Input Signal Missing	6-190	14
G	C1267	Yellow ABS Warning Lamp Does Not Self-Check, Always On & No DTCs	6-190	15
H	C1279	Red Brake Warning Lamp Does Not Self-Check & Always On	6-191	16
2002–04 LESS STABILITY ASSIST				
A	—	No Communication w/ABS Module	6-191	17
B	—	Unable To Enter Self Test	6-192	18
C	B1676	Battery Voltage Out Of Range	6-192	19

Continued

DIAGNOSTIC CHART INDEX—Continued

Test	Code	Description	Page No.	Fig. No.
2002–04 LESS STABILITY ASSIST				
D	C1095	ABS Hydraulic Pump Motor Circuit Failure	6-192	20
E	C1145	Righthand Front Wheel Speed Sensor Input Circuit Failure	6-192	21
	C1155	Lefthand Front Wheel Speed Sensor Input Circuit Failure	6-192	21
	C1165	Righthand Rear Wheel Speed Sensor Input Circuit Failure	6-192	21
	C1175	Lefthand Rear Wheel Speed Sensor Input Circuit Failure	6-192	21
F	C1233	Lefthand Front Wheel Speed Input Signal Missing	6-193	22
	C1234	Righthand Front Wheel Speed Input Signal Missing	6-193	22
	C1235	Righthand Rear Wheel Speed Input Signal Missing	6-193	22
	C1236	Lefthand Rear Wheel Speed Input Signal Missing	6-193	22
G	—	Yellow ABS Warning Indicator Does Not Self Check	6-194	23
H	—	Red Brake Warning Indicator Does Not Self Check	6-194	24
2002–04 W/STABILITY ASSIST				
A	—	No Communication w/Stability Assist Module	6-195	25
B	—	Brake Pedal Position Input Circuit	6-195	26
C	B1676	Battery Voltage Out Of Range	6-195	27
D	C1095	ABS Hydraulic Pump Motor Circuit Failure	6-195	28
E	C1145	Righthand Front ABS Brake Sensor Input Circuit Failure	6-196	29
	C1155	Lefthand Front ABS Brake Sensor Input Circuit Failure	6-196	29
	C1165	Righthand Rear ABS Brake Sensor Input Circuit Failure	6-196	29
	C1175	Lefthand Rear ABS Brake Sensor Input Circuit Failure	6-196	29
F	C1233	Lefthand Front ABS Brake Sensor Input Signal Missing	6-197	30
	C1234	Righthand Front ABS Brake Sensor Input Signal Missing	6-197	30
	C1235	Righthand Rear ABS Brake Sensor Input Signal Missing	6-197	30
	C1236	Lefthand Rear ABS Brake Sensor Input Signal Missing	6-197	30
G	C1276	ABS Function Temporarily Disabled	6-197	31
H	C1279	Yaw Rate Sensor Circuit Failure	6-197	32
	C1280	Yaw Rate Sensor Signal Fault	6-197	32
I	C1281	Accelerometer Circuit Failure	6-199	33
	C1282	Accelerometer Signal Fault	6-199	33
J	C1285	Brake Booster Solenoid Output Failure	6-200	34
K	C1286	Booster Mechanical Failure	6-201	35
L	C1287	Booster Pedal Force Switch Circuit Failure	6-202	36
M	C1288	Primary Brake Pressure Sensor Input Circuit Failure	6-203	37
N	C1289	Secondary Brake Pressure Sensor Input Circuit Failure	6-204	38
O	C1730	Reference Voltage Out Of Range	6-205	39
P	—	Yellow ABS Warning Indicator Does Not Self Check	6-207	40
Q	—	Traction Control Inoperative	6-207	41
R	—	Stability Assist/Traction Control Switch Indicator Is Never/ Always On	6-208	42
S	—	Stability Assist System Cannot Be Disabled	6-209	43
T	—	Stability Assist Indicator Does Not Self Check	6-210	44

CONDITIONS	DETAILS/RESULTS/ACTIONS
A1: CHECK CIRCUIT 15-CF6A (GN/YE) FOR AN OPEN	
1 2 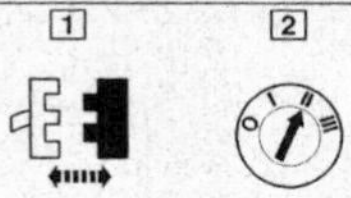 ABS Control Module C385	
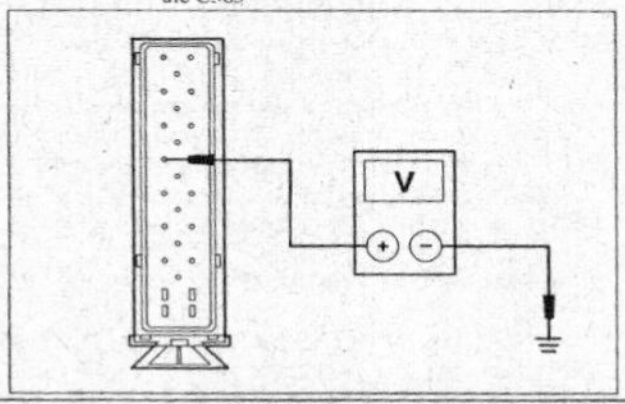	3 Using a digital multimeter, measure the voltage between ABS control module C385 pin 20, circuit 15-CF6A (GN/YE), harness side and ground. • Is the voltage greater than 10 volts? → **Yes** GO TO **A2** → **No** REPAIR circuit 15-CF6A (GN/YE) or 15-CF6 (GN/YE) as necessary. CLEAR the DTCs. REPEAT the self-test.
A2: CHECK CIRCUIT 91CF6 (BK/YE) FOR AN OPEN	
1 	
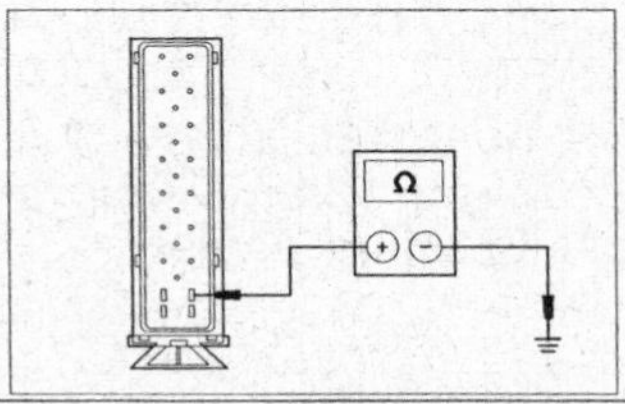	2 Using a digital multimeter, measure the resistance between ABS control module C385 pin 8, circuit 91CF6 (BK/YE), harness side and ground. • Is the resistance less than 5 ohms? → **Yes** DIAGNOSE Module Communication Network. → **No** REPAIR circuit 91CF6 (BK/YE). CLEAR the DTCs. REPEAT the self-test.

FM4020001592000X

Fig. 8 Test A: No Communication w/ABS Control Module. 2000–01 Less Stability Assist

CONDITIONS	DETAILS/RESULTS/ACTIONS
NOTE: Be sure the vehicle has not been recently jump started before proceeding with this pinpoint test.	
C1: CHECK THE BATTERY VOLTAGE	
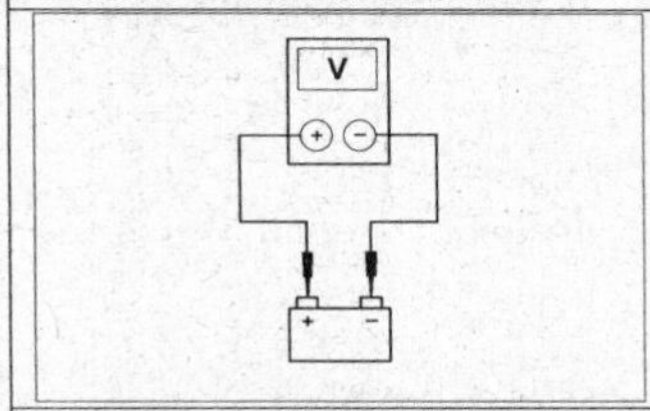	1 Using a digital multimeter, measure the voltage between the positive and negative battery posts. • Is the voltage greater than 10 volts? → **Yes** GO TO **C2** → **No** REPAIR the charging system.
C2: CHECK CIRCUIT 30-CF6A (RD) AND 30-CF13 (RD)	
1 2 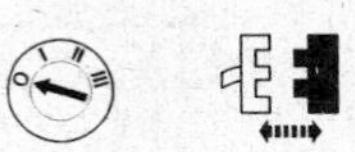 ABS Control Module C385	

FM4020001594010X

Fig. 10 Test C/Code B1676: Battery Voltage Out Of Range (Part 1 of 2). 2000–01 Less Stability Assist

CONDITIONS	DETAILS/RESULTS/ACTIONS
B1: CHECK THE COMMUNICATION TO THE ABS CONTROL MODULE	
	1 Connect the scan tool. 2 Check the communication to the ABS control module. • Does the scan tool communicate with the ABS control module? → **Yes** INSTALL a new hydraulic control unit (HCU). REPEAT the self-test. → **No** GO to Pinpoint Test A.

FM4020001593000X

Fig. 9 Test B: Unable To Enter Self Test. 2000–01 Less Stability Assist

CONDITIONS	DETAILS/RESULTS/ACTIONS
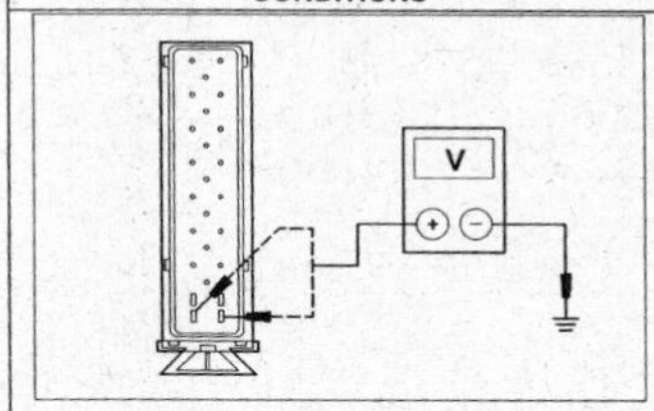	3 Using a digital multimeter, measure the voltage between ABS control module C385 pin 25, circuit 30-CF6A (RD), harness side and ground; and between ABS control module C385 pin 9, circuit 30-CF13 (RD), harness side and ground. • Are the voltages greater than 10 volts? → **Yes** INSTALL a new hydraulic control unit (HCU). CLEAR the DTCs. REPEAT the self-test → **No** REPAIR circuit 30CF6A (RD), 30CF6 (RD), or 30-CF13 (RD) as necessary. CLEAR the DTCs. REPEAT the self-test.

FM4020001594020X

Fig. 10 Test C/Code B1676: Battery Voltage Out Of Range (Part 2 of 2). 2000–01 Less Stability Assist

CONDITIONS	DETAILS/RESULTS/ACTIONS
D1: CHECK FOR CONTINUOUS OPERATION OF THE ABS PUMP MOTOR	
1 	2 Check the ABS pump for continuous operation. • Is the ABS pump motor running continuously? → **Yes** INSTALL a new hydraulic control unit (HCU). CLEAR the DTCs. REPEAT the self-test. → **No** GO TO **D2**
D2: CHECK CIRCUIT 30-CF13 (RD) FOR AN OPEN	
1 2  ABS Control Module C385	

FM4020001595010X

Fig. 11 Test D/Code C1095: ABS Hydraulic Pump Motor Circuit Failure (Part 1 of 2). 2000–01 Less Stability Assist

CONDITIONS	DETAILS/RESULTS/ACTIONS
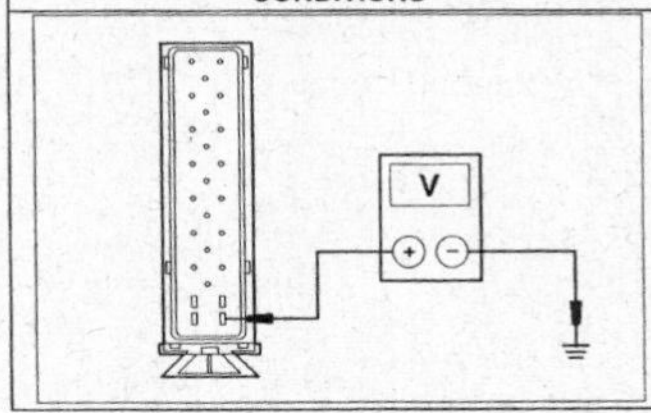	3 Using a digital multimeter, measure the voltage between ABS control module C385 pin 9, circuit 30-CF13 (RD), harness side and ground. • Is the voltage greater than 10 volts? → **Yes** INSTALL a new hydraulic control unit (HCU). CLEAR the DTCs. REPEAT the self-test. → **No** REPAIR circuit 30-CF13 (RD). CLEAR the DTCs. REPEAT the self-test.

FM4020001595020X

Fig. 11 Test D/Code C1095: ABS Hydraulic Pump Motor Circuit Failure (Part 2 of 2). 2000–01 Less Stability Assist

CONDITIONS	DETAILS/RESULTS/ACTIONS
E1: CHECK THE SUSPECT WHEEL SPEED CIRCUIT FOR SHORT TO POWER	
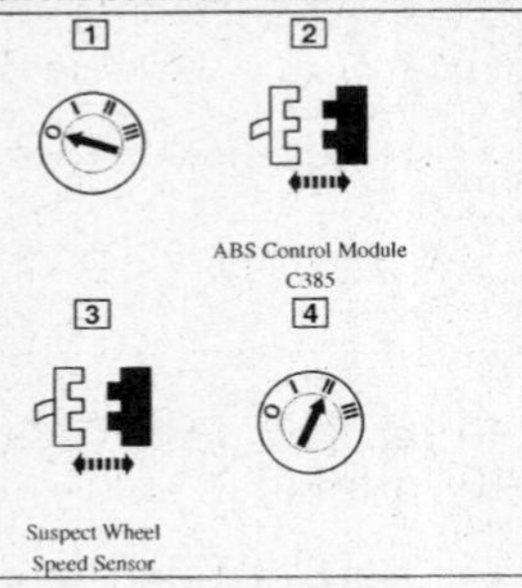	

FM4020001596010X

Fig. 12 Test E/Codes C1145, C1155, C1165 & C1175: Wheel Speed Sensor Input Circuit Failure (Part 1 of 5). 2000 Less Stability Assist

CONDITIONS	DETAILS/RESULTS/ACTIONS
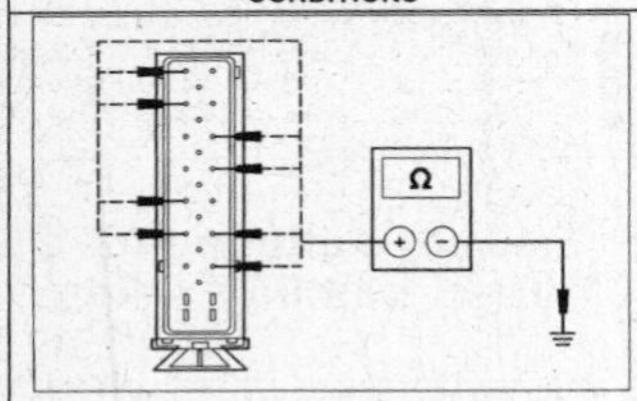	2 Using a digital multimeter, measure the resistance of the suspect wheel speed sensor circuit between: - (RF) ABS control module C385 pin 3, circuit 8-CF38 (WH/RD), harness side and ground; and between ABS control module C385 pin 4, circuit 7-CF38 (YE/RD), harness side and ground. - (LF) ABS control module C385 pin 17, circuit 8-CF32 (WH), harness side and ground; and between ABS control module C385 pin 18, circuit 7-CF32 (YE), harness side and ground. - (RR) ABS control module C385 pin 7, circuit 8-CF40 (WH/GN), harness side and ground; and between ABS module C385 pin 6, circuit 7-CF40 (YE/GN), harness side and ground. - (LR) ABS control module C385 pin 21, circuit 8-CF34 (WH/BU), harness side and ground; and between ABS control module C385 pin 22, circuit 7-CF34 (YE/BU), harness side and ground. • Is the resistance greater than 10,000 ohms? → **Yes** GO TO **E4** → **No** GO TO **E3**
E3: CHECK THE SUSPECT WHEEL SPEED SENSOR CIRCUIT FOR A SHORT TOGETHER	
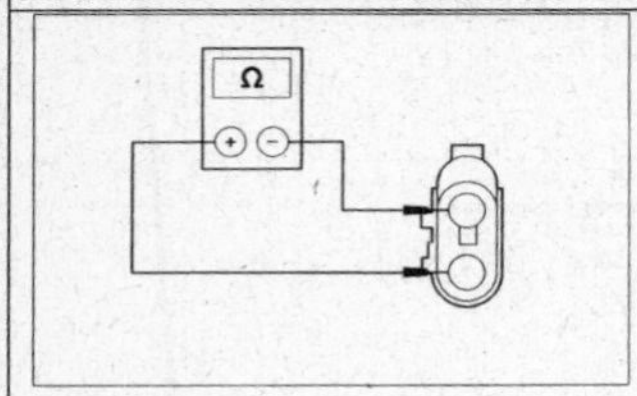	1 Using a digital multimeter, measure the resistance between the suspect wheel speed sensor pins, harness side. • Is the resistance greater than 10,000 ohms? → **Yes** GO TO **E5** → **No** If (RF), REPAIR circuit 7-CF38 (YE/RD) and 8-CF38 (WH/RD). If (LF) REPAIR circuit 7-CF32 (YE) and 8-CF32 (WH). If (RR), REPAIR circuit 7-CF40 (YE/GN) and 8-CF40 (WH/GN). If (LR), REPAIR circuit 7-CF34 (YE/BU) and 8-CF34 (WH//BU). CLEAR the DTC. REPEAT the self-test.

FM4020001596030X

Fig. 12 Test E/Codes C1145, C1155, C1165 & C1175: Wheel Speed Sensor Input Circuit Failure (Part 3 of 5). 2000 Less Stability Assist

CONDITIONS	DETAILS/RESULTS/ACTIONS
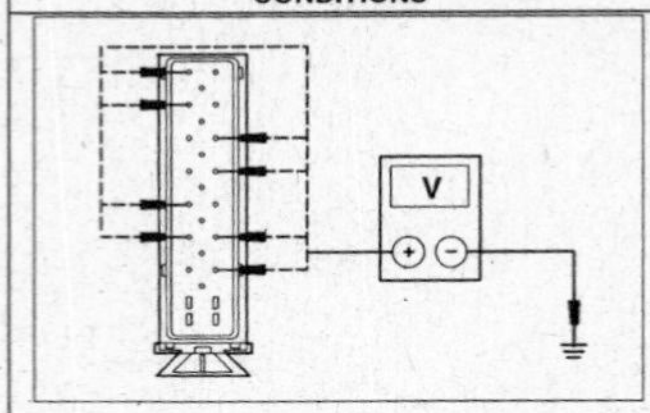	5 Using a digital multimeter, measure the voltage of the suspect wheel speed sensor circuit between: - (RF) ABS control module C385 pin 3, circuit 8-CF38 (WH/RD), harness side and ground; and between ABS control module C385 pin 4, circuit 7-CF38 (YE/RD), harness side and ground. - (LF) ABS control module C385 pin 17, circuit 8-CF32 (WH), harness side and ground; and between ABS control module C385 pin18, circuit 7-CF32 (WH), harness side and ground. - (RR) ABS control module C385 pin 7, circuit 8-CF40 (WH/GN), harness side and ground; and between ABS control module C385 pin 6, circuit 7-CF40 (YE/GN), harness side and ground. - (LR) ABS control module C385 pin 21, circuit 8-CF34 (WH/BU), harness side and ground; and between ABS control module C385 pin 22, circuit 7-CF34 (YE/BU), harness side and ground. • Is voltage present? → **Yes** REPAIR the circuit. CLEAR the DTCs. REPEAT the self-test. → **No** GO TO **E2**
E2: CHECK THE SUSPECT WHEEL SPEED SENSOR CIRCUIT FOR SHORT TO GROUND	

FM4020001596020X

Fig. 12 Test E/Codes C1145, C1155, C1165 & C1175: Wheel Speed Sensor Input Circuit Failure (Part 2 of 5). 2000 Less Stability Assist

CONDITIONS	DETAILS/RESULTS/ACTIONS
E4: CHECK THE SUSPECT WHEEL SPEED SENSOR CIRCUIT FOR OPEN	
	1 Using a digital multimeter, measure the resistance of the suspect wheel speed sensor circuit between: - (RF) ABS control module C385 pin 3, circuit 8-CF38 (WH/RD), harness side and RF wheel speed sensor C815 pin 1, circuit 8-CF38 (WH/RD), harness side: and between ABS control module C385 pin 4, circuit 7-CF38 (YE/RD), harness side and RF wheel speed sensor C815 pin 2, circuit 7-CF38 (YE/RD), harness side. - (LF) ABS control module C385 pin 17, circuit 8-CF32 (WH), harness side and LF wheel speed sensor C814 pin 1, circuit 8-CF32 (WH), harness side: and between ABS control module C385 pin 18, circuit 7-CF32 (YE), harness side and LF wheel speed sensor C814 pin 2 circuit 7-CF32 (YE), harness side. - (RR) ABS control module C385 pin 7, circuit 8-CF40 (WH/GN), harness side and RR wheel speed sensor C817 pin 1, circuit 8-CF40 (WH/GN), harness side: and between ABS control module C385 pin 6, circuit 7-CF40 (YE/GN), harness side and RR wheel speed sensor C817 pin 2, circuit 7-CF40 (YE/GN), harness side. - (LR) ABS control module C385 pin 21, circuit 8-CF32 (WH/BU), harness side and LR wheel speed sensor C816 pin 1, circuit 8-CF32 (WH/BU), harness side: and between ABS control module C385 pin 22, circuit 7-CF32 (YE/BU), harness side and LR wheel speed sensor C816 pin 2, circuit 7-CF32 (YE/BU), harness side. • Is the reistance less than 5 ohms? → **Yes** GO TO **E5** → **No** REPAIR the circuit in question. CLEAR the DTCs. REPEAT the self-test.
E5: CHECK THE ABS CONTROL MODULE OUTPUT	
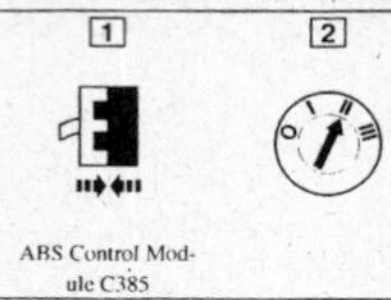	

FM4020001596040X

Fig. 12 Test E/Codes C1145, C1155, C1165 & C1175: Wheel Speed Sensor Input Circuit Failure (Part 4 of 5). 2000 Less Stability Assist

CONDITIONS	DETAILS/RESULTS/ACTIONS
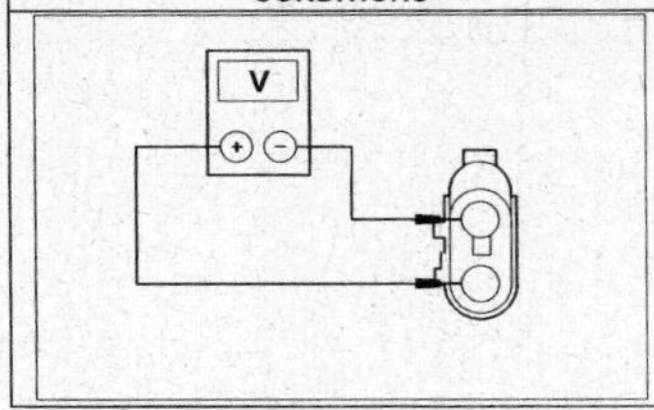	3 Using a digital multimeter, measure the voltage between the suspect wheel speed sensor pins, harness side. • Is the voltage greater than 9 volts? → Yes INSTALL a new hydraulic control unit (HCU). CLEAR the DTCs. REPEAT the self-test. → No INSTALL a new wheel speed sensor. CLEAR the DTCs. REPEAT the self-test.

FM4020001596050X

Fig. 12 Test E/Codes C1145, C1155, C1165 & C1175: Wheel Speed Sensor Input Circuit Failure (Part 5 of 5). 2000 Less Stability Assist

— (RF) ABS control module C385 pin 3, circuit 8-CF38 (WH/RD), harness side and ground; and between ABS control module C385 pin 4, circuit 7-CF38 (YE/RD), harness side and ground.
— (LF) ABS control module C385 pin 17, circuit 8-CF32 (WH), harness side and ground; and between ABS control module C385 pin18, circuit 7-CF32 (WH), harness side and ground.
— (RR) ABS control module C385 pin 7, circuit 8-CF40 (WH/GN), harness side and ground; and between ABS control module C385 pin 6, circuit 7-CF40 (YE/GN), harness side and ground.
— (LR) ABS control module C385 pin 21, circuit 8-CF34 (WH/BU), harness side and ground; and between ABS control module C385 pin 22, circuit 7-CF34 (YE/BU), harness side and ground.

- **Is voltage present?**

→ **Yes**

REPAIR the circuit. CLEAR the DTCs. REPEAT the self-test.

→ **No**

Go to «E2».

FM4020001602020X

Fig. 13 Test E/Codes C1145, C1155, C1165 & C1175: Wheel Speed Sensor Input Circuit Failure (Part 2 of 6). 2001 Less Stability Assist

E2 CHECK THE SUSPECT WHEEL SPEED SENSOR CIRCUIT FOR SHORT TO GROUND

1

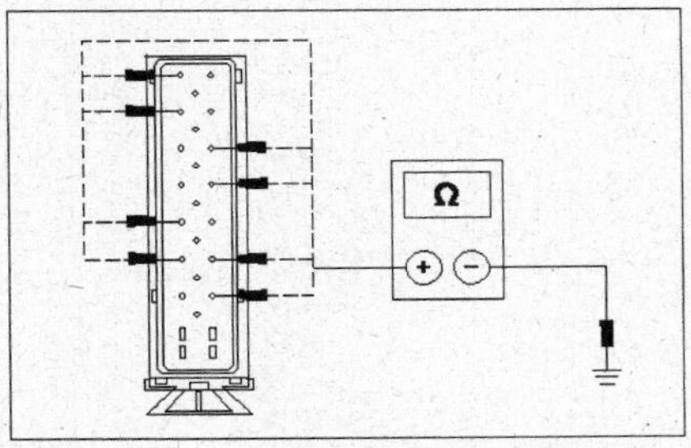

2

Using a digital multimeter, measure the resistance of the suspect wheel speed sensor circuit between:
— (RF) ABS control module C385 pin 3, circuit 8-CF38 (WH/RD), harness side and ground; and between ABS control module C385 pin 4, circuit 7-CF38 (YE/RD), harness side and ground.
— (LF) ABS control module C385 pin 17, circuit 8-CF32 (WH), harness side and ground; and between ABS control module C385 pin 18, circuit 7-CF32 (YE), harness side and ground.
— (RR) ABS control module C385 pin 7, circuit 8-CF40 (WH/GN), harness side and ground; and between ABS module C385 pin 6, circuit 7-CF40 (YE/GN), harness side and ground.
— (LR) ABS control module C385 pin 21, circuit 8-CF34 (WH/BU), harness side and ground; and between ABS control module C385 pin 22, circuit 7-CF34 (YE/BU), harness side and ground.

- **Is the resistance greater than 10,000 ohms?**

→ **Yes**

Go to «E3».

→ **No**

REPAIR the circuit. CLEAR the DTCs. REPEAT the self-test.

FM4020001602030X

Fig. 13 Test E/Codes C1145, C1155, C1165 & C1175: Wheel Speed Sensor Input Circuit Failure (Part 3 of 6). 2001 Less Stability Assist

E1 CHECK THE SUSPECT WHEEL SPEED CIRCUIT FOR SHORT TO POWER

1

2 *ABS Control Module C385*

3 *Suspect Wheel Speed Sensor*

4

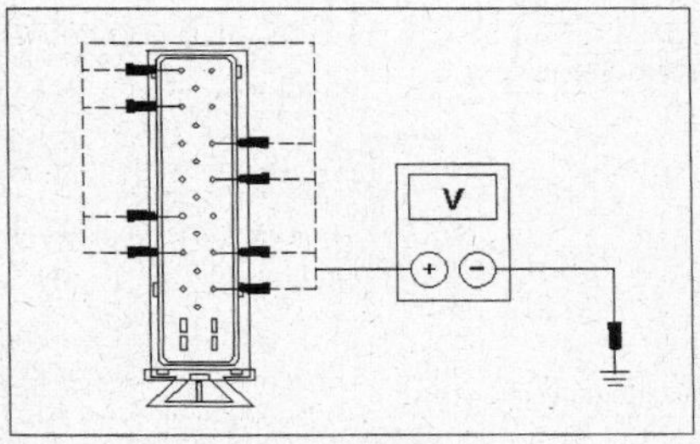

5

Using a digital multimeter, measure the voltage of the suspect wheel speed sensor circuit between:

FM4020001602010X

Fig. 13 Test E/Codes C1145, C1155, C1165 & C1175: Wheel Speed Sensor Input Circuit Failure (Part 1 of 6). 2001 Less Stability Assist

E3 CHECK THE SUSPECT WHEEL SPEED SENSOR CIRCUIT FOR A SHORT TOGETHER

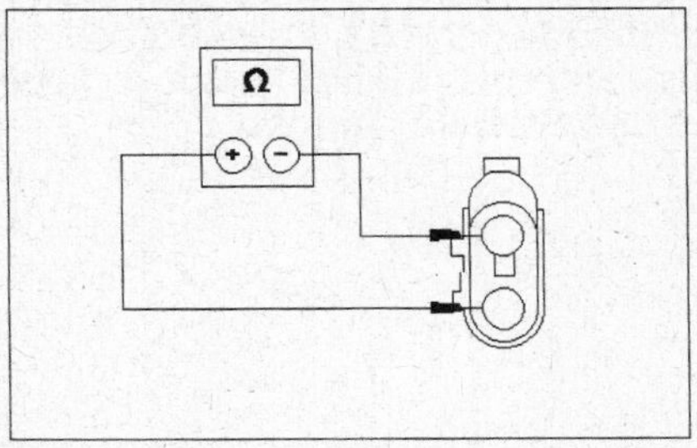

1

Using a digital multimeter, measure the resistance between the suspect wheel speed sensor pins, harness side.

- **Is the resistance greater than 10,000 ohms?**

→ **Yes**

Go to «E4».

→ **No**

If (RF), REPAIR circuit 7-CF38 (YE/RD) and 8-CF38 (WH/RD). If (LF) REPAIR circuit 7-CF32 (YE) and 8-CF32 (WH). If (RR), REPAIR circuit 7-CF40 (YE/GN) and 8-CF40 (WH/GN). If (LR), REPAIR circuit 7-CF34 (YE/BU) and 8-CF34 (WH//BU). CLEAR the DTC. REPEAT the self-test.

FM4020001602040X

Fig. 13 Test E/Codes C1145, C1155, C1165 & C1175: Wheel Speed Sensor Input Circuit Failure (Part 4 of 6). 2001 Less Stability Assist

E4	CHECK THE SUSPECT WHEEL SPEED SENSOR CIRCUIT FOR OPEN

1 Using a digital multimeter, measure the resistance of the suspect wheel speed sensor circuit between:

- (RF) ABS control module C385 pin 3, circuit 8-CF38 (WH/RD), harness side and RF wheel speed sensor C815 pin 1, circuit 8-CF38 (WH/RD), harness side: and between ABS control module C385 pin 4, circuit 7-CF38 (YE/RD), harness side and RF wheel speed sensor C815 pin 2, circuit 7-CF38 (YE/RD), harness side.
- (LF) ABS control module C385 pin 17, circuit 8-CF32 (WH), harness side and LF wheel speed sensor C814 pin 1, circuit 8-CF32 (WH), harness side: and between ABS control module C385 pin 18, circuit 7-CF32 (YE), harness side and LF wheel speed sensor C814 pin 2 circuit 7-CF32 (YE), harness side.
- (RR) ABS control module C385 pin 7, circuit 8-CF40 (WH/GN), harness side and RR wheel speed sensor C817 pin 1, circuit 8-CF40 (WH/GN), harness side: and between ABS control module C385 pin 6, circuit 7-CF40 (YE/GN), harness side and RR wheel speed sensor C817 pin 2, circuit 7-CF40 (YE/GN), harness side.
- (LR) ABS control module C385 pin 21, circuit 8-CF32 (WH/BU), harness side and LR wheel speed sensor C816 pin 1, circuit 8-CF32 (WH/BU), harness side: and between ABS control module C385 pin 22, circuit 7-CF32 (YE/BU), harness side and LR wheel speed sensor C816 pin 2, circuit 7-CF32 (YE/BU), harness side.

- **Is the reistance less than 5 ohms?**

→ **Yes**

Go to «E5».

→ **No**

REPAIR the circuit in question. CLEAR the DTCs. REPEAT the self-test.

FM4020001602050X

Fig. 13 Test E/Codes C1145, C1155, C1165 & C1175: Wheel Speed Sensor Input Circuit Failure (Part 5 of 6). 2001 Less Stability Assist

CONDITIONS	DETAILS/RESULTS/ACTIONS
F1: CHECK THE SUSPECT WHEEL SPEED SENSOR	
	1 Inspect the suspect wheel speed sensor mounting. Check the wheel speed sensor for excessive dirt build-up. Check for metal obstructions. Check the wheel speed sensor for damage. • Is the suspect wheel speed sensor and mounting OK? → Yes GO TO **F2** → No REPAIR or INSTALL a new wheel speed sensor. CLEAR the DTCs. REPEAT the self-test.
F2: CHECK THE SUSPECT ABS SENSOR INDICATOR	
	1 Check the suspect ABS sensor indicator for damage, correct mounting and alignment with the wheel speed sensor. Check the air gap (1.86 mm minimum). • Is the suspect ABS sensor indicator OK? → Yes CLEAR the DTCs. REPEAT the self-test. If DTC C1233, C1234, C1235 or C1236 is retrieved, INSTALL a new hydraulic control unit (HCU). CLEAR the DTCs. REPEAT the self-test. If no DTC is retrieved, system is OK. → No INSTALL a new ABS sensor indicator. CLEAR the DTCs. REPEAT the self-test.

FM4020001597000X

Fig. 14 Test F/Codes C1233, C1234, C1235 & C1236: Wheel Speed Input Signal Missing. 2000–01 Less Stability Assist

E5	CHECK THE ABS CONTROL MODULE OUTPUT

1 *ABS Control Module C385*

2

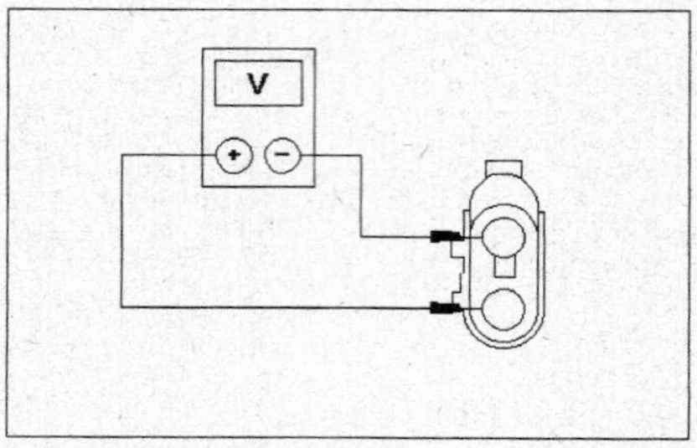

3

Using a digital multimeter, measure the voltage between the suspect wheel speed sensor pins, harness side.

- **Is the voltage greater than 9 volts?**

→ **Yes**

INSTALL a new ABS module. CLEAR the DTCs. REPEAT the self-test.

→ **No**

INSTALL a new wheel speed sensor. CLEAR the DTCs. REPEAT the self-test.

FM4020001602060X

Fig. 13 Test E/Codes C1145, C1155, C1165 & C1175: Wheel Speed Sensor Input Circuit Failure (Part 6 of 6). 2001 Less Stability Assist

CONDITIONS	DETAILS/RESULTS/ACTIONS
G1: CHECK CIRCUIT 31S-CF28 (BK/RD) FOR SHORT TO POWER	
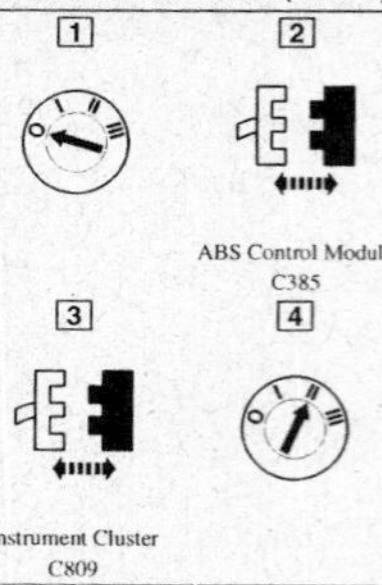	
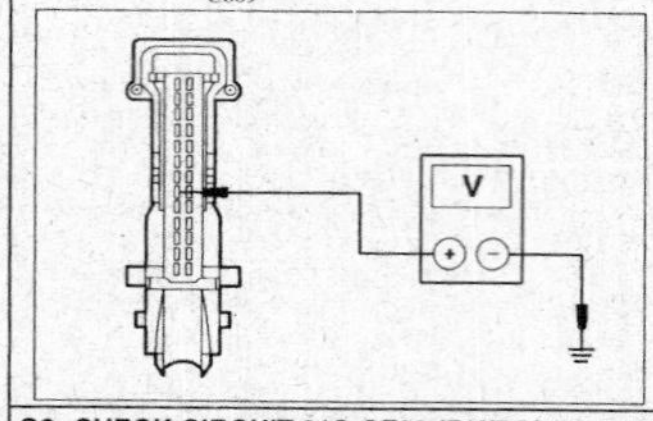	5 Using a digital multimeter, measure the voltage between the instrument cluster C809 pin 6, circuit 31S-CF28 (BK/RD), harness side and ground. • Is voltage present? → Yes REPAIR circuit 31S-CF28 (BK/RD). CLEAR the DTC. REPEAT the self-test. → No GO TO **G2**
G2: CHECK CIRCUIT 31S-CF28 (BK/RD) FOR AN OPEN OR SHORT TO GROUND	

FM4020001598010X

Fig. 15 Test G: Yellow ABS Warning Lamp Does Not Self-Check, Always On & No DTCs (Part 1 of 2). 2000–01 Less Stability Assist

CONDITIONS	DETAILS/RESULTS/ACTIONS
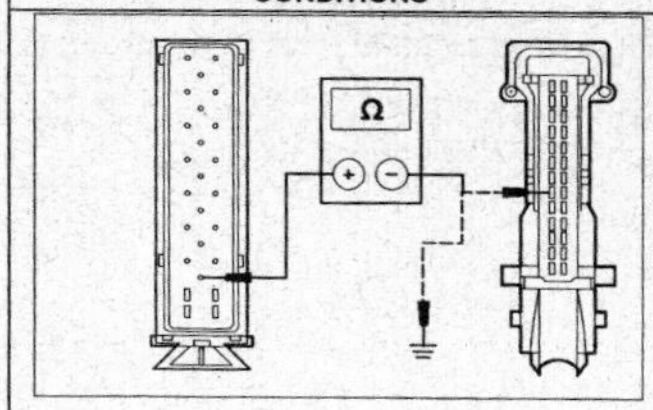	2 Using a digital multimeter, measure the resistance between ABS control module C385 pin 16, circuit 31S-CF28 (BK/RD), harness side and instrument cluster C809 pin 6, circuit 31S-CF28 (BK/RD), harness side; and between ABS control module C385 pin16, circuit 31S-CF28 (BK/RD), harness side and ground. • Is the resistance less than 5 ohms between instrument cluster and ABS control module; and greater than 10,000 ohms between ABS control module and ground? → Yes GO TO **G3** → No REPAIR circuit 31S-CF28 (BK/RD). REPEAT the self-test.
G3: CHECK THE INSTRUMENT CLUSTER	
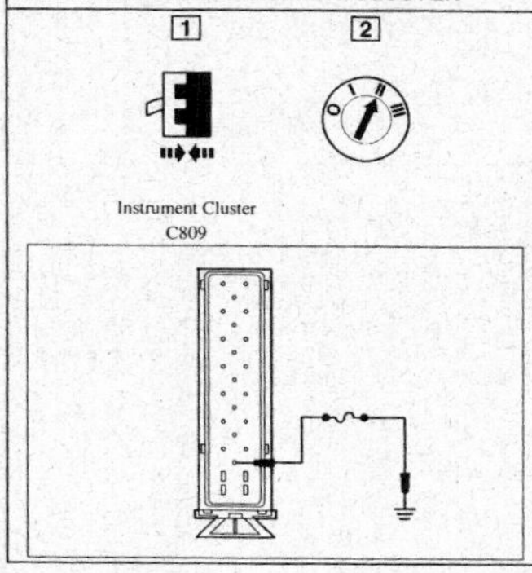	3 Connect a fused (10A) jumper wire between ABS control module C385 pin 16, circuit 31S-CF28 (BK/RD), harness side and ground. • Does the instrument cluster ABS warning indicator turn off? → Yes Install a new ABS module. CLEAR the DTCs. REPEAT the self-test. → No DIAGNOSE Instrument Cluster. CLEAR the DTCs. REPEAT the self-test.

FM4020001598020X

Fig. 15 Test G: Yellow ABS Warning Lamp Does Not Self-Check, Always On & No DTCs (Part 2 of 2). 2000–01 Less Stability Assist

CONDITIONS	DETAILS/RESULTS/ACTIONS
H2: CHECK CIRCUIT 31S-CF45 (BK/GN) FOR AN OPEN OR SHORT TO GROUND	
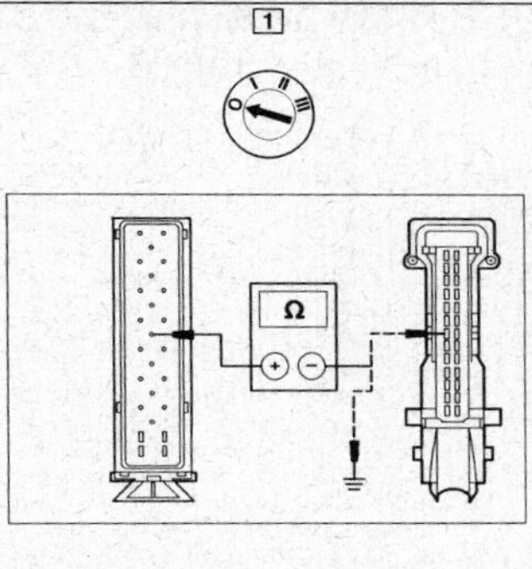	2 Using a digital multimeter, measure the resistance between instrument cluster C809 pin 7, circuit 31S-CF45 (BK/GN), harness side and ABS Control Module C385 pin 13, circuit 31-CF45, harness side and ABS control module C385 pin 13, circuit 31S-CF45 harness side. • Is resistance less than 5 ohms between ABS control module and instrument cluster and greater than 10,000 ohms between ABS control module and ground? → Yes GO TO **H3** → No REPAIR circuit 31S-CF45 (BK/GN). CLEAR the DTCs. REPEAT the self-test.
H3: CHECK THE INSTRUMENT CLUSTER	
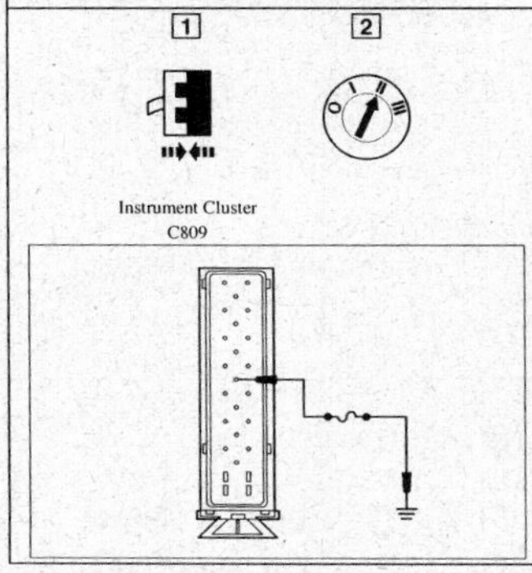	3 Connect a fused (10A) jumper wire between ABS control module C385 pin 13, circuit 31S-CF45 (BK/GN), harness side and ground. • Does the instrument cluster red brake warning indicator turn off? → Yes INSTALL a new ABS control module. CLEAR the DTCs. REPEAT the self-test. → No INSTALL a new instrument cluster.

FM4020001599020X

Fig. 16 Test H: Red Brake Warning Lamp Does Not Self-Check & Always On (Part 2 of 2). 2000–01 Less Stability Assist

CONDITIONS	DETAILS/RESULTS/ACTIONS
H1: CHECK CIRCUIT 31S-CF45 (BK/GN) FOR SHORT TO POWER	
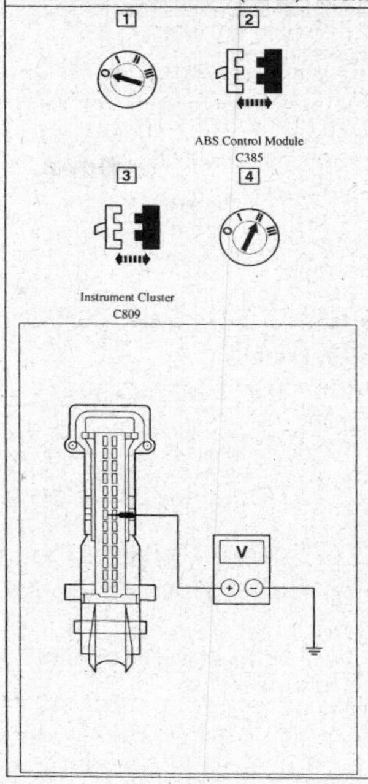	5 Using a digital multimeter, measure the voltage between instrument cluster C809 pin 7, circuit 31S-CF45 (BK/GN), harness side and ground. • Is voltage present? → Yes REPAIR circuit 31S-CF45 (BK/GN). CLEAR the DTCs. REPEAT the self-test. → No GO TO **H2**

FM4020001599010X

Fig. 16 Test H: Red Brake Warning Lamp Does Not Self-Check & Always On (Part 1 of 2). 2000–01 Less Stability Assist

CONDITIONS	DETAILS/RESULTS/ACTIONS
A1: CHECK CIRCUIT 15-CF6A (GN/YE) FOR AN OPEN	
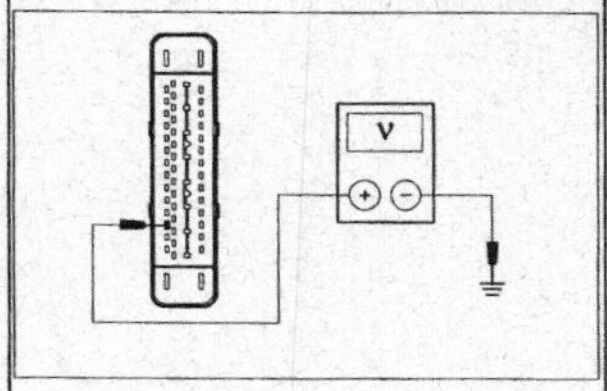	1 Disconnect ABS Module C840. 2 Key in ON position. 3 Measure the voltage between the ABS module C840 pin 4, circuit 15-CF6A (GN/YE), harness side and ground. • Is the voltage greater than 10 volts? → Yes GO to **A2**. → No

FM4020201904010X

Fig. 17 Test A: No Communication w/ABS Module (Part 1 of 2). 2002–04 Less Stability Assist

CONDITIONS	DETAILS/RESULTS/ACTIONS
	REPAIR circuit 15-CF6A (GN/YE) or 15-CF6 (GN/YE) as necessary. CLEAR the DTCs. REPEAT the self-test. TEST the system for normal operation.
A2: CHECK CIRCUIT 91-CF6 (BK/YE) FOR AN OPEN	
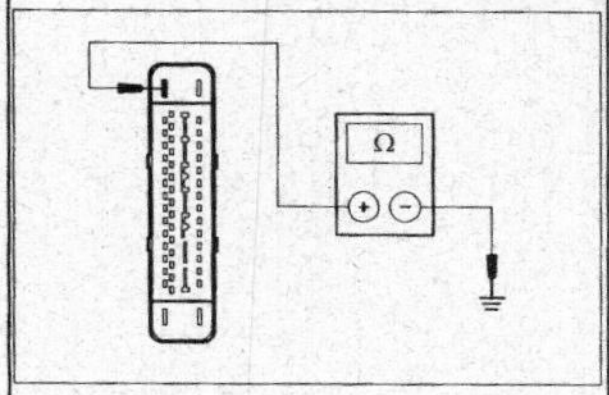	1 Key in OFF position. 2 Measure the resistance between the ABS module C840 pin 16, circuit 91-CF6 (BK/YE), harness side and ground. • Is the resistance less than 5 ohms? → Yes DIAGNOSE module. → No REPAIR circuit 91-CF6 (BK/YE) or 91-CF1 (BK/BU) as necessary. CLEAR the DTCs. REPEAT the self-test. TEST the system for normal operation.

FM4020201904020X

Fig. 17 Test A: No Communication w/ABS Module (Part 2 of 2). 2002–04 Less Stability Assist

CONDITIONS	DETAILS/RESULTS/ACTIONS
B1: CHECK THE COMMUNICATION TO THE ABS MODULE	
	1 Connect the diagnostic tool. 2 Key in ON position. 3 Check the communication to the ABS module. • Does the diagnostic tool communicate with the ABS module? → **Yes** INSTALL a new ABS module. REPEAT the self-test. TEST the system for normal operation. → **No** GO to Pinpoint Test A.

FM4020201905000X

Fig. 18 Test B: Unable To Enter Self Test. 2002–04 Less Stability Assist

CONDITIONS	DETAILS/RESULTS/ACTIONS
	→ **No** REPAIR circuit 30-CF6A (RD), 30-CF6 (RD), or 30-CF13A (RD), 30-CF13 (RD) as necessary. CLEAR the DTCs. REPEAT the self-test. TEST the system for normal operation.

FM4020201906020X

Fig. 19 Test C/Code B1676: Battery Voltage Out Of Range (Part 2 of 2). 2002–04 Less Stability Assist

CONDITIONS	DETAILS/RESULTS/ACTIONS
D1: CHECK FOR CONTINUOUS OPERATION OF THE ABS PUMP MOTOR	
	1 Key in ON position. 2 Check the ABS pump for continuous operation. • Is the ABS pump motor running continuously? → **Yes** INSTALL a new ABS module. CLEAR the DTCs. REPEAT the self-test. Test the system for normal operation. → **No** GO to **D2**.
D2: CHECK CIRCUIT 30-CF13A (RD) FOR AN OPEN	
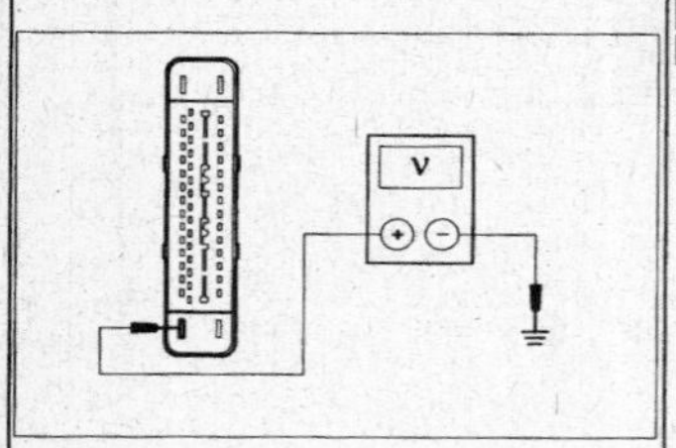	1 Key in OFF position. 2 Disconnect ABS Module C840. 3 Measure the voltage between ABS module C840 pin 1, circuit 30-CF13A (RD), harness side and ground. • Is the voltage greater than 10 volts? → **Yes** INSTALL a new ABS module. CLEAR the DTCs. REPEAT the self-test. TEST the system for normal operation. → **No** REPAIR circuit 30-CF13A (RD), 30-CF13 (RD). CLEAR the DTCs. REPEAT the self-test. TEST the system for normal operation.

FM4020201907000X

Fig. 20 Test D/Code C1095: ABS Hydraulic Pump Motor Circuit Failure. 2002–04 Less Stability Assist

CONDITIONS	DETAILS/RESULTS/ACTIONS
NOTE: Make sure the vehicle has not been recently jump started before proceeding with this pinpoint test.	
C1: CHECK THE BATTERY VOLTAGE	
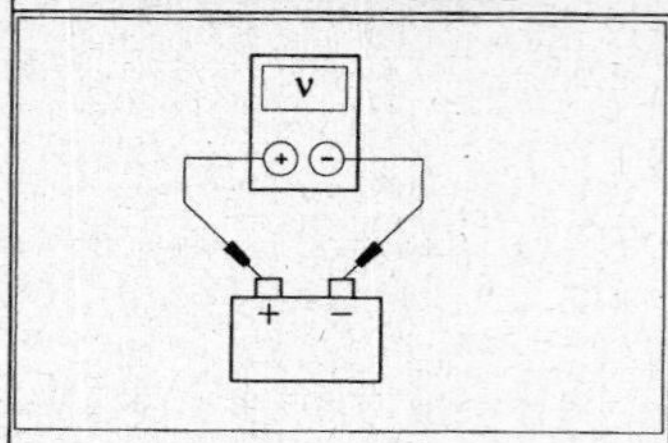	1 Measure the voltage between the battery positive post and the battery negative post. • Is the voltage greater than 10 volts? → **Yes** GO to **C2**. → **No** REPAIR the charging system.
C2: CHECK CIRCUIT 30-CF6A (RD) AND 30-CF13A (RD)	
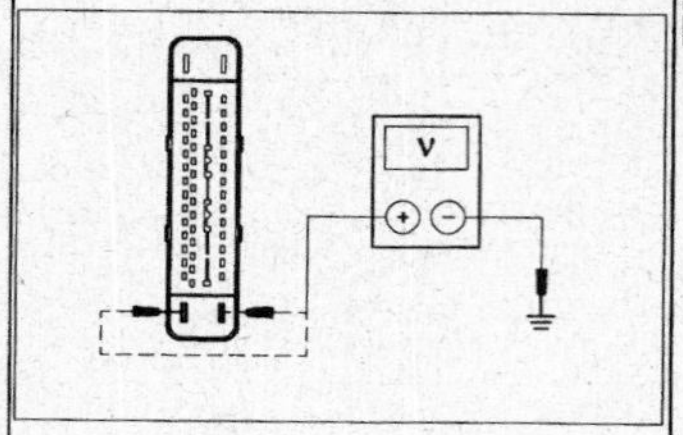	1 Key in OFF position. 2 Disconnect ABS Module C840. 3 Measure the voltage between the ABS module C840 pin 32, circuit 30-CF6A (RD), harness side and ground; and between the ABS module C840 pin 1, circuit 30-CF13A (RD), harness side and ground. • Are the voltages greater than 10 volts? → **Yes** INSTALL a new ABS module. CLEAR the DTCs. REPEAT the self-test. TEST the system for normal operation.

FM4020201906010X

Fig. 19 Test C/Code B1676: Battery Voltage Out Of Range (Part 1 of 2). 2002–04 Less Stability Assist

CONDITIONS	DETAILS/RESULTS/ACTIONS
E1: CHECK THE SUSPECT WHEEL SPEED CIRCUIT FOR SHORT TO POWER	
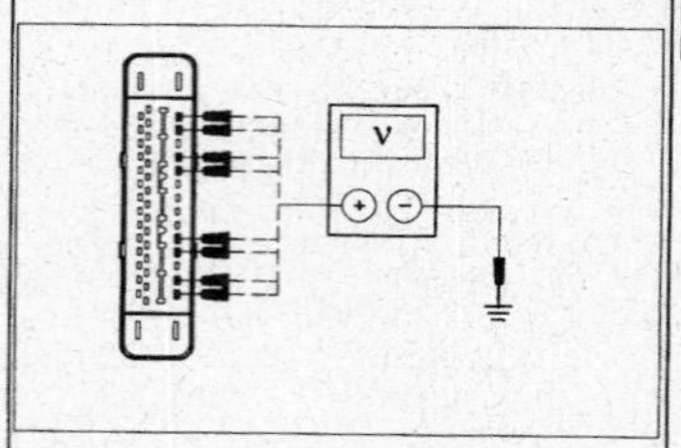	1 Key in OFF position. 2 Disconnect ABS Module C840. 3 Disconnect Suspect Wheel Speed Sensor. 4 Key in ON position. 5 Measure the voltage of the suspect wheel speed sensor circuit between: - (RF) ABS module C840 pin 33, circuit 9-CF38 (BN/RD), harness side and ground; and between the ABS module C840 pin 34, circuit 8-CF38 (WH/RD), harness side and ground. - (LF) ABS module C840 pin 45, circuit 8-CF32 (WH), harness side and ground; and between the ABS module C840 pin 46, circuit 9-CF32 (BN), harness side and ground. - (RR) ABS module C840 pin 43, circuit 8-CF40 (WH/GN), harness side and ground; and between the ABS module C840 pin 42, circuit 9-CF40 (BN/GN), harness side and ground. - (LR) ABS module C840 pin 36, circuit 8-CF34 (WH/BU), harness side and ground; and between the ABS module C840 pin 37, circuit 9-CF34 (BN/BU), harness side and ground. • Is voltage present? → **Yes** REPAIR the circuit. CLEAR the DTCs. REPEAT the self-test. TEST the system for normal operation. → **No** GO to **E2**.
E2: CHECK THE SUSPECT WHEEL SPEED SENSOR CIRCUIT FOR SHORT TO GROUND	
	1 Key in OFF position.

FM4020201908010X

Fig. 21 Test E/Codes C1145, C1155, C1165 & C1175: Wheel Speed Sensor Input Circuit Failure (Part 1 of 4). 2002–04 Less Stability Assist

CONDITIONS	DETAILS/RESULTS/ACTIONS
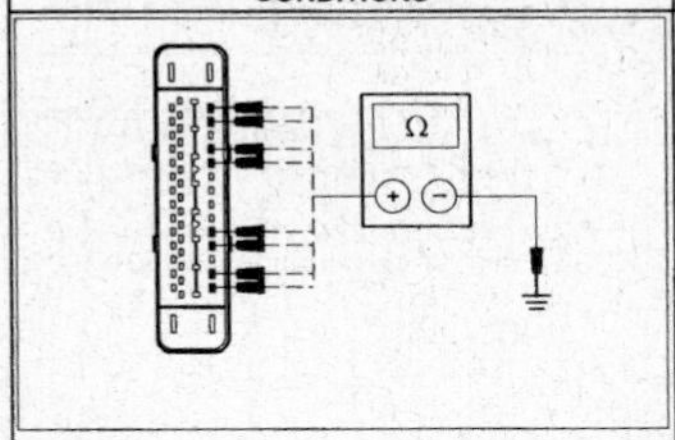	2 Measure the resistance of the suspect wheel speed sensor circuit between: - (RF) ABS module C840 pin 33, circuit 9-CF38 (BN/RD), harness side and ground; and between the ABS module C840 pin 34, circuit 8-CF38 (WH/RD), harness side and ground. - (LF) ABS module C840 pin 45, circuit 8-CF32 (WH), harness side and ground; and between the ABS module C840 pin 46, circuit 9-CF32 (BN), harness side and ground. - (RR) ABS module C840 pin 43, circuit 8-CF40 (WH/GN), harness side and ground; and between the ABS module C840 pin 42, circuit 9-CF40 (BN/GN), harness side and ground. - (LR) ABS module C840 pin 36, circuit 8-CF34 (WH/BU), harness side and ground; and between the ABS module C840 pin 37, circuit 9-CF34 (BN/BU), harness side and ground. • Is the resistance greater than 10,000 ohms? → **Yes** GO to **E3**. → **No** REPAIR the circuit. CLEAR the DTCs. REPEAT the self-test. TEST the system for normal operation.
E3: CHECK THE SUSPECT WHEEL SPEED SENSOR CIRCUIT(S) FOR A SHORT TOGETHER	
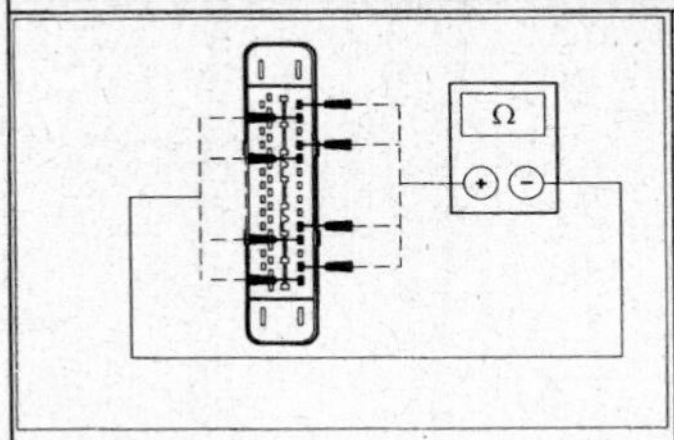	1 Measure the resistance between the suspect wheel speed sensor pins, harness side. • Is the resistance greater than 10,000 ohms? → **Yes** GO to **E4**. → **No**

FM4020201908020X

Fig. 21 Test E/Codes C1145, C1155, C1165 & C1175: Wheel Speed Sensor Input Circuit Failure (Part 2 of 4). 2002–04 Less Stability Assist

CONDITIONS	DETAILS/RESULTS/ACTIONS
	If (RF), REPAIR circuit 9-CF38 (BN/RD) and 8-CF38 (WH/RD). If (LF) REPAIR circuit 9-CF32 (BN) and 8-CF32 (WH). If (RR), REPAIR circuit 9-CF40 (BN/GN) and 8-CF40 (WH/GN). If (LR), REPAIR circuit 9-CF34 (BN/BU) and 8-CF34 (WH//BU). CLEAR the DTCs. REPEAT the self-test. TEST the system for normal operation.
E4: CHECK THE SUSPECT WHEEL SPEED SENSOR CIRCUIT FOR OPEN	
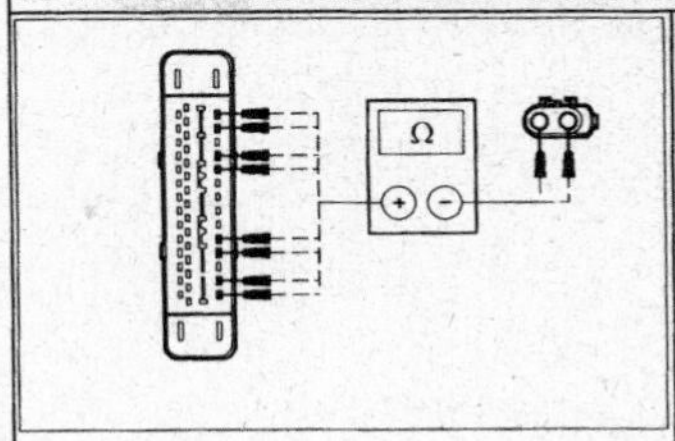	1 Measure the resistance of the suspect wheel speed sensor circuit between: - (RF) ABS module C840 pin 33, circuit 9-CF38 (BN/RD), harness side and the RF wheel speed sensor C815 pin 1, circuit 9-CF38 (BN/RD), harness side: and between the ABS module C840 pin 34, circuit 8-CF38 (WH/RD), harness side and the RF wheel speed sensor C815 pin 2, circuit 8-CF38 (WH/RD), harness side. - (LF) ABS module C840 pin 45, circuit 8-CF32 (WH), harness side and the LF wheel speed sensor C814 pin 2, circuit 8-CF32 (WH), harness side: and between the ABS module C840 pin 46, circuit 9-CF32 (BN), harness side and the LF wheel speed sensor C814 pin 1, circuit 9-CF32 (BN), harness side. - (RR) ABS module C840 pin 43, circuit 8-CF40 (WH/GN), harness side and the RR wheel speed sensor C817 pin 2, circuit 8-CF40 (WH/GN), harness side: and between the ABS module C840 pin 42, circuit 9-CF40 (BN/GN), harness side and the RR wheel speed sensor C817 pin 1, circuit 9-CF40 (BN/GN), harness side. - (LR) ABS module C840 pin 36, circuit 8-CF34 (WH/BU), harness side and the LR wheel speed sensor C816 pin 2, circuit 9-CF34 (WH/BU), harness side: and between the ABS module C840 pin 37, circuit 9-CF34 (BN/BU), harness side and the LR wheel speed sensor C816 pin 1, circuit 9-CF34 (BN/BU), harness side. • Is the resistance less than 5 ohms? → **Yes** GO to **E5**. → **No** REPAIR the circuit in question. CLEAR the DTCs. REPEAT the self-test. TEST the system for normal operation.

FM4020201908030X

Fig. 21 Test E/Codes C1145, C1155, C1165 & C1175: Wheel Speed Sensor Input Circuit Failure (Part 3 of 4). 2002–04 Less Stability Assist

CONDITIONS	DETAILS/RESULTS/ACTIONS
E5: CHECK THE ABS MODULE OUTPUT	
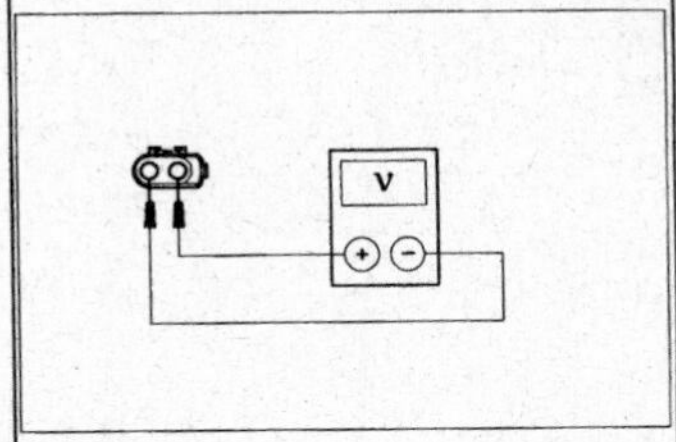	1 Connect ABS Module C840. 2 Key in ON position. 3 Measure the voltage between the suspect wheel speed sensor pins, harness side. • Is the voltage greater than 9 volts? → **Yes** INSTALL a new ABS module. CLEAR the DTCs. REPEAT the self-test. TEST the system for normal operation. → **No** INSTALL a new wheel speed sensor. CLEAR the DTCs. REPEAT the self-test. TEST the system for normal operation.

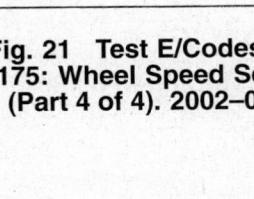

FM4020201908040X

Fig. 21 Test E/Codes C1145, C1155, C1165 & C1175: Wheel Speed Sensor Input Circuit Failure (Part 4 of 4). 2002–04 Less Stability Assist

CONDITIONS	DETAILS/RESULTS/ACTIONS
F1: CHECK THE SUSPECT WHEEL SPEED SENSOR	
	1 Inspect the suspect wheel speed sensor mounting. Check the wheel speed sensor for excessive dirt build-up. Check for metal obstructions. Check the wheel speed sensor for damage. • Is the suspect wheel speed sensor and mounting OK? → **Yes** GO to **F2**. → **No** REPAIR or INSTALL a new wheel speed sensor. CLEAR the DTCs. REPEAT the self-test. TEST the system for normal operation.

FM4020201909010X

Fig. 22 Test F/Codes C1233, C1234, C1235 & C1236: Wheel Speed Input Signal Missing (Part 1 of 2). 2002–04 Less Stability Assist

CONDITIONS	DETAILS/RESULTS/ACTIONS
F2: CHECK THE SUSPECT ABS SENSOR INDICATOR	
	1 Check the suspect ABS sensor indicator for damage, correct mounting and alignment with the wheel speed sensor. Check the air gap (1.86 mm minimum). • Is the suspect ABS sensor indicator OK? → **Yes** CLEAR the DTCs. REPEAT the self-test. If DTC C1233, C1234, C1235 or C1236 is retrieved, INSTALL a new ABS module.CLEAR the DTCs. REPEAT the self-test. TEST the system for normal operation. → **No** INSTALL a new ABS sensor indicator. CLEAR the DTCs. REPEAT the self-test. TEST the system for normal operation.

FM4020201909020X

Fig. 22 Test F/Codes C1233, C1234, C1235 & C1236: Wheel Speed Input Signal Missing (Part 2 of 2). 2002–04 Less Stability Assist

CONDITIONS	DETAILS/RESULTS/ACTIONS
G1: CHECK CIRCUIT 31S-CF28 (BK/RD) FOR SHORT TO POWER	
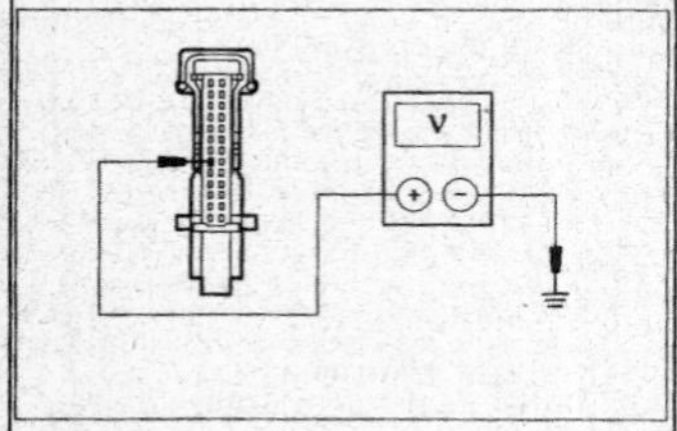	1 Key in OFF position. 2 Disconnect ABS Module C840. 3 Disconnect Instrument Cluster C809. 4 Key in ON position. 5 Measure the voltage between the instrument cluster C809 pin 6, circuit 31S-CF28 (BK/RD), harness side and ground. • Is voltage present? → **Yes** REPAIR the circuit. CLEAR the DTCs. REPEAT the self-test. TEST the system for normal operation. → **No** GO to **G2**.

FM4020201910010X

Fig. 23 Test G: Yellow ABS Warning Indicator Does Not Self Check (Part 1 of 3). 2002–04 Less Stability Assist

CONDITIONS	DETAILS/RESULTS/ACTIONS
	Install a new ABS module. CLEAR the DTCs. REPEAT the self-test. TEST the system for normal operation. → **No** CLEAR the DTCs. REPEAT the self-test.

FM4020201910030X

Fig. 23 Test G: Yellow ABS Warning Indicator Does Not Self Check (Part 3 of 3). 2002–04 Less Stability Assist

CONDITIONS	DETAILS/RESULTS/ACTIONS
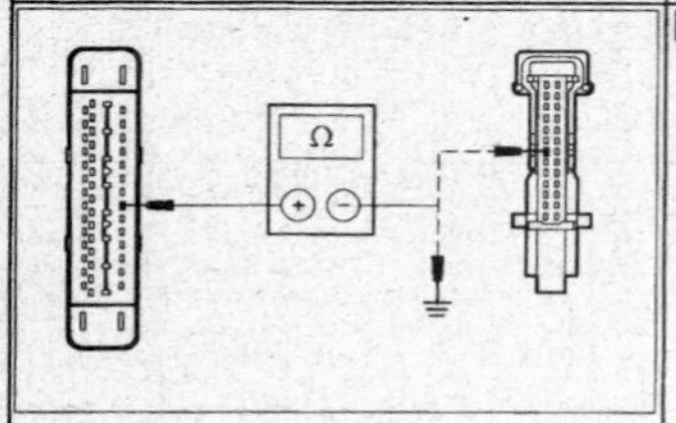	2 Measure the resistance between the instrument cluster C809 pin 7, circuit 31S-CF45 (BK/GN), harness side and the ABS module C840 pin 39, circuit 31S-CF45 (BK/GN), harness side and the ABS module C840 pin 39, circuit 31S-CF45 (BK/GN), harness side, and between the ABS module C840 pin 39, 31S-CF45 (BK/GN), harness side and ground. • Is resistance less than 5 ohms between the ABS module and the instrument cluster and greater than 10,000 ohms between the ABS module and ground? → **Yes** GO to **H3**. → **No** CLEAR the DTCs. REPEAT the self-test. TEST the system for normal operation.
H3: CHECK THE INSTRUMENT CLUSTER	
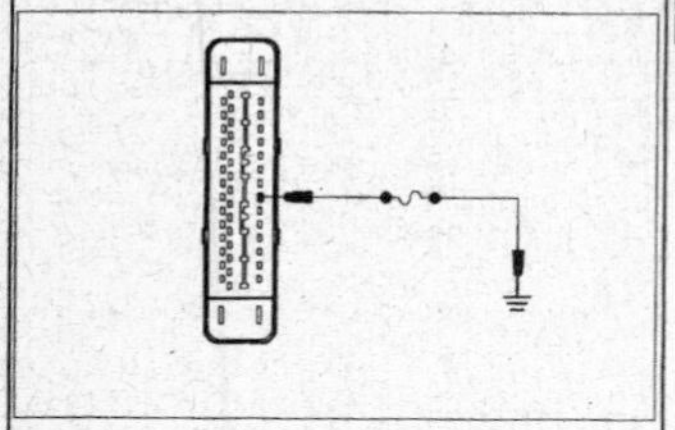	1 Connect Instrument Cluster C809. 2 Key in ON position. 3 Connect a fused (10A) jumper wire between the ABS module C840 pin 39, circuit 31S-CF45 (BK/GN), harness side and ground. • Does the instrument cluster red brake warning indicator turn off? → **Yes** INSTALL a new ABS module. CLEAR the DTCs. REPEAT the self-test. TEST the system for normal operation.

FM4020201911020X

Fig. 24 Test H: Red Brake Warning Indicator Does Not Self Check (Part 2 of 3). 2002–04 Less Stability Assist

CONDITIONS	DETAILS/RESULTS/ACTIONS
G2: CHECK CIRCUIT 31S-CF28 (BK/RD) FOR AN OPEN OR SHORT TO GROUND	
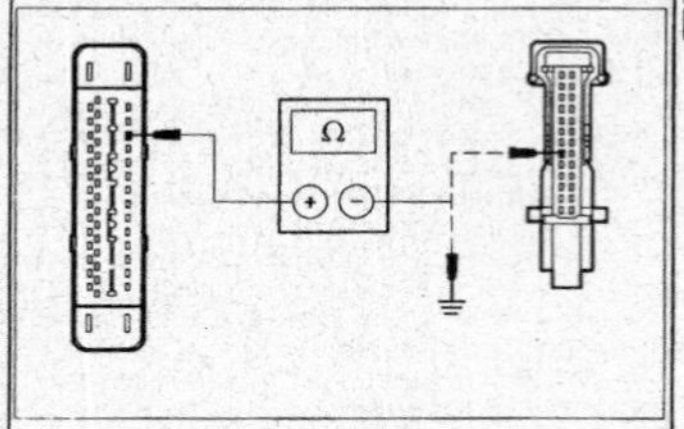	1 Key in OFF position. 2 Measure the resistance between the ABS module C840 pin 44, circuit 31S-CF28 (BK/RD), harness side and the instrument cluster C809 pin 6, circuit 31S-CF28 (BK/RD), harness side; and between the ABS module C840 pin 44, circuit 31S-CF28 (BK/RD), harness side and ground. • Is the resistance less than 5 ohms between the instrument cluster and ABS module; and greater than 10,000 ohms between the ABS module and ground? → **Yes** GO to **G3**. → **No** REPAIR the circuit. REPEAT the self-test. TEST the system for normal operation.
G3: CHECK THE INSTRUMENT CLUSTER	
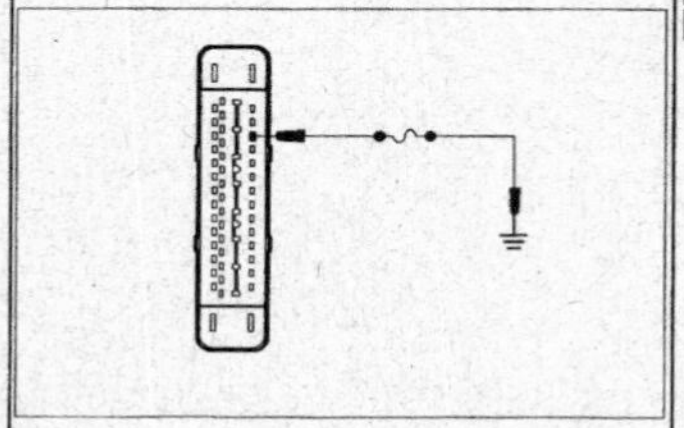	1 Connect Instrument Cluster C809. 2 Key in ON position. 3 Connect a fused (10A) jumper wire between the ABS module C840 pin 44, circuit 31S-CF28 (BK/RD), harness side and ground. • Does the instrument cluster ABS warning indicator turn off? → **Yes**

FM4020201910020X

Fig. 23 Test G: Yellow ABS Warning Indicator Does Not Self Check (Part 2 of 3). 2002–04 Less Stability Assist

CONDITIONS	DETAILS/RESULTS/ACTIONS
H1: CHECK CIRCUIT 31S-CF45 (BK/GN) FOR SHORT TO POWER	
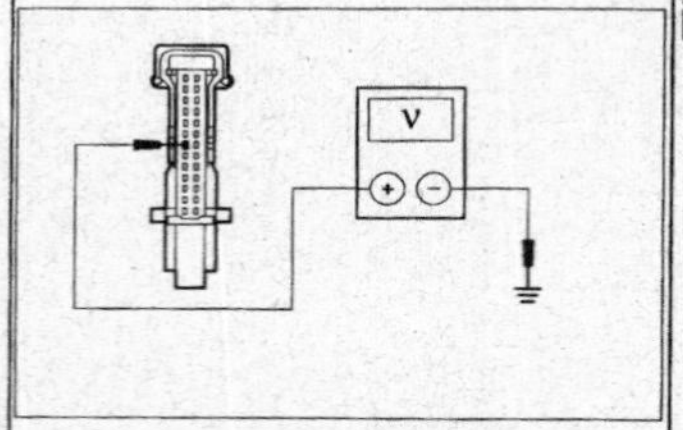	1 Key in OFF position. 2 Disconnect ABS Module C840. 3 Disconnect Instrument Cluster C809. 4 Key in ON position. 5 Measure the voltage between the instrument cluster C809 pin 7, circuit 31S-CF45 (BK/GN), harness side and ground. • Is voltage present? → **Yes** REPAIR the circuit. CLEAR the DTCs. REPEAT the self-test. TEST the system for normal operation. → **No** GO to **H2**.
H2: CHECK CIRCUIT 31S-CF45 (BK/GN) FOR AN OPEN OR SHORT TO GROUND	
	1 Key in OFF position.

FM4020201911010X

Fig. 24 Test H: Red Brake Warning Indicator Does Not Self Check (Part 1 of 3). 2002–04 Less Stability Assist

CONDITIONS	DETAILS/RESULTS/ACTIONS
	→ **No** INSTALL a new instrument cluster.

FM4020201911030X

Fig. 24 Test H: Red Brake Warning Indicator Does Not Self Check (Part 3 of 3). 2002–04 Less Stability Assist

CONDITIONS	DETAILS/RESULTS/ACTIONS
A1: CHECK THE VOLTAGE TO THE STABILITY ASSIST MODULE	
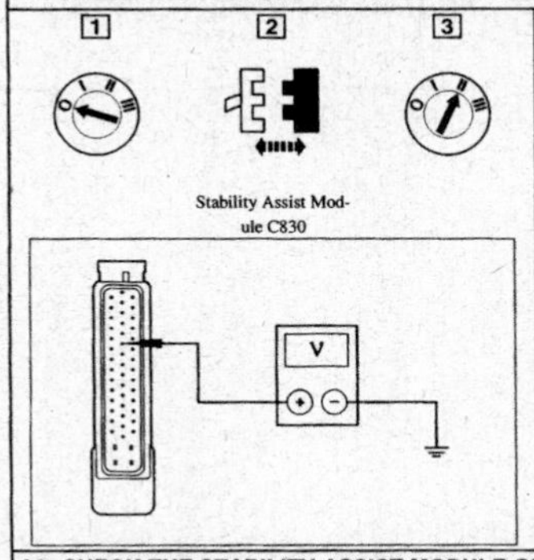	4 Measure the voltage between stability assist module C830 pin 22, circuit 15-CF6A (GN/YE), harness side and ground. • Is the voltage greater than 10 volts? → Yes GO TO **A2** → No REPAIR the circuit. REPEAT the self-test.
A2: CHECK THE STABILITY ASSIST MODULE GROUNDS	
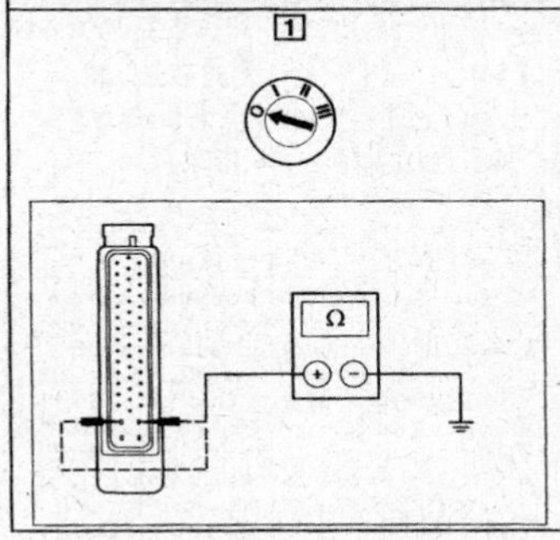	2 Measure the resistance between stability assist module C830 pin 15, circuit 91-CF6 (BK/YE), harness side and ground; and between stability assist module C830 pin 32, circuit 91-CF71 (BK/BU), harness side and ground. • Are the resistances less than 5 ohms? → Yes DIAGNOSE module. → No REPAIR the circuit in question. REPEAT the self-test.

FM4020201884000X

Fig. 25 Test A: No Communication w/Stability Assist Module. 2002–04 w/Stability Assist

CONDITIONS	DETAILS/RESULTS/ACTIONS
C1: CHECK THE BATTERY VOLTAGE	
	1 Measure the battery voltage between the positive and negative battery posts with the key ON engine OFF (KOEO), and with the engine running. • Is the battery voltage between 10 and 13 volts with KOEO, and between 11 and 17 volts with the engine running? → Yes GO TO **C2** → No DIAGNOSE battery. TEST the system for normal operation.

FM4020201886010X

Fig. 27 Test C/Code B1676: Battery Voltage Out Of Range (Part 1 of 2). 2002–04 w/Stability Assist

CONDITIONS	DETAILS/RESULTS/ACTIONS
D1: CHECK ABS PUMP MOTOR	
	• Is the ABS pump motor running all the time? → Yes INSTALL a new stability assist module. CLEAR the DTCs. REPEAT the self-test. → No GO TO **D2**
D2: CHECK PUMP MOTOR OPERATION	

FM4020201887010X

Fig. 28 Test D/Code C0195: ABS Hydraulic Pump Motor Circuit Failure (Part 1 of 3). 2002–04 w/Stability Assist

CONDITIONS	DETAILS/RESULTS/ACTIONS
B1: CHECK CIRCUIT 15S-CF58 (GN/OG) FOR AN OPEN	
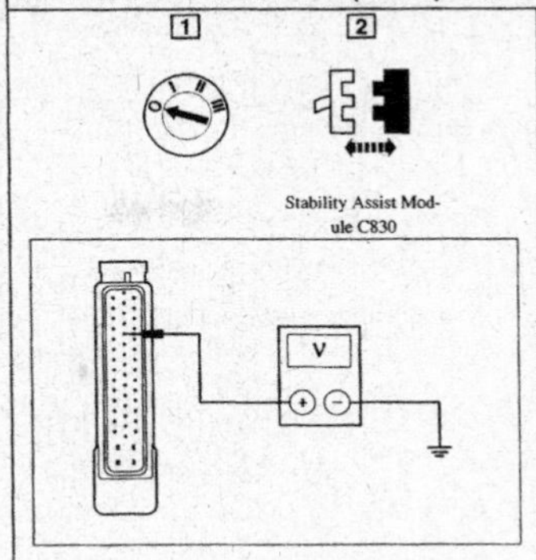	3 Measure the voltage between stability assist module C830 pin 21, circuit 15S-CF58 (GN/OG), harness side and ground while depressing and releasing the brake pedal. • Is the voltage greater than 10 volts with the brake pedal depressed, and zero volts with the brake pedal released? → Yes INSTALL a new stability assist module, REPEAT the self-test. → No REPAIR the circuit. CLEAR the DTCs. REPEAT the self-test.

FM4020201885000X

Fig. 26 Test B: Brake Pedal Position Input Circuit. 2002–04 w/Stability Assist

CONDITIONS	DETAILS/RESULTS/ACTIONS
C2: CHECK VOLTAGE TO THE STABILITY ASSIST MODULE	
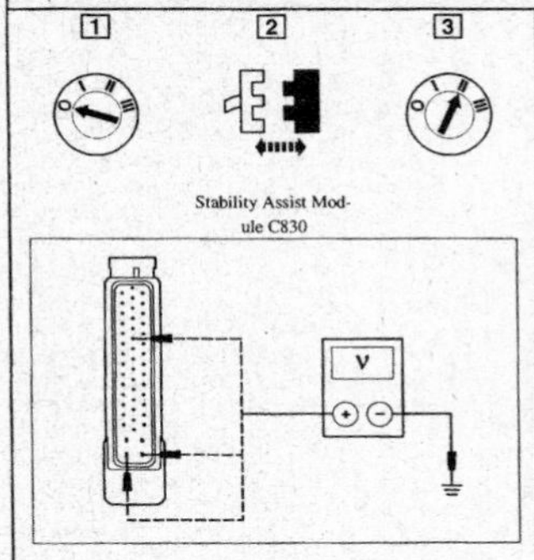	4 Measure the voltage between stability assist module C830 pin 16, circuit 30-CF6 (RD), harness side and ground; and between stability assist module C830 pin 22, circuit 15-CF6A (GN/YE), harness side and ground; and between stability assist module C830 pin 33, circuit 30-CF13 (RD), harness side and ground. • Are the voltages greater than 10 volts? → Yes INSTALL a new stability assist module, REPEAT the self-test. → No REPAIR the circuit in question. CLEAR the DTCs. REPEAT the self-test.

FM4020201886020X

Fig. 27 Test C/Code B1676: Battery Voltage Out Of Range (Part 2 of 2). 2002–04 w/Stability Assist

CONDITIONS	DETAILS/RESULTS/ACTIONS
	2 Trigger the stability assist module active command PMP MOTOR ON. • Does the ABS pump motor run for approximately three seconds? → Yes CLEAR the DTC. CHECK the yellow ABS warning indicator while driving the vehicle (brakes must not be applied) above 32 km/h (20 mph). If the yellow ABS warning indicator illuminates, RETRIEVE the DTCs. If DTC C1095 is retrieved, INSTALL a new HCU. CLEAR the DTCs. REPEAT the self-test. If the yellow ABS warning indicator does not illuminate, system is OK. → No TRIGGER the stability assist module active command PMP MOTOR OFF. GO TO **D3**
D3: CHECK CIRCUIT 30-CF13 (RD) FOR AN OPEN	
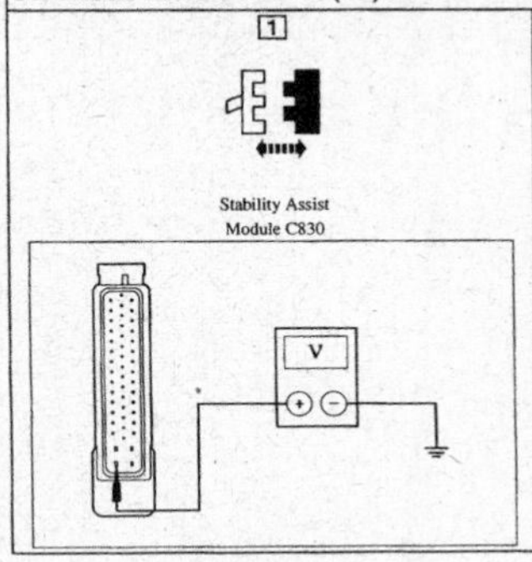	2 Measure the voltage between stability assist module C830 pin 33, circuit 30-CF13 (RD), harness side and ground. • Is the voltage greater than 10 volts? → Yes GO TO **D4** → No REPAIR the circuit. CLEAR the DTCs. REPEAT the self-test.

FM4020201887020X

Fig. 28 Test D/Code C0195: ABS Hydraulic Pump Motor Circuit Failure (Part 2 of 3). 2002–04 w/Stability Assist

CONDITIONS	DETAILS/RESULTS/ACTIONS
D4: CHECK CIRCUIT 91-CF6A (BK/YE) AND 91-CF71 (BK/BU) FOR AN OPEN	
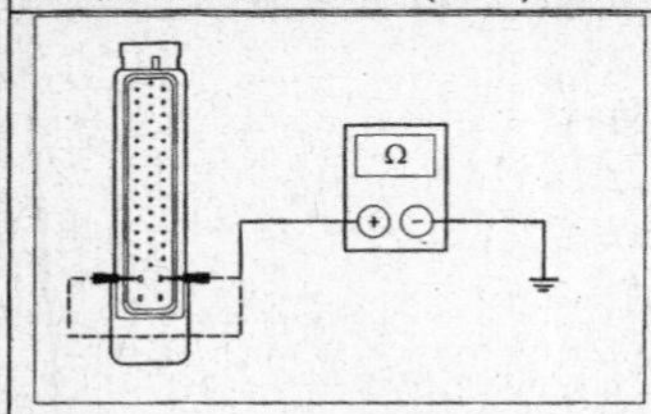	1 Measure the resistance between stability assist module C830 pin 15, circuit 91-CF6 (BK/YE), harness side and ground; and between stability assist module C830 pin 32, circuit 91-CF71 (BK/BU), harness side and ground. • Are the resistances less than 5 ohms? → **Yes** INSTALL a new stability assist module. CLEAR the DTCs. REPEAT the self-test. → **No** REPAIR the circuit in question. CLEAR the DTCs. REPEAT the self-test.

FM4020201887030X

Fig. 28 Test D/Code C0195: ABS Hydraulic Pump Motor Circuit Failure (Part 3 of 3). 2002–04 w/Stability Assist

CONDITIONS	DETAILS/RESULTS/ACTIONS
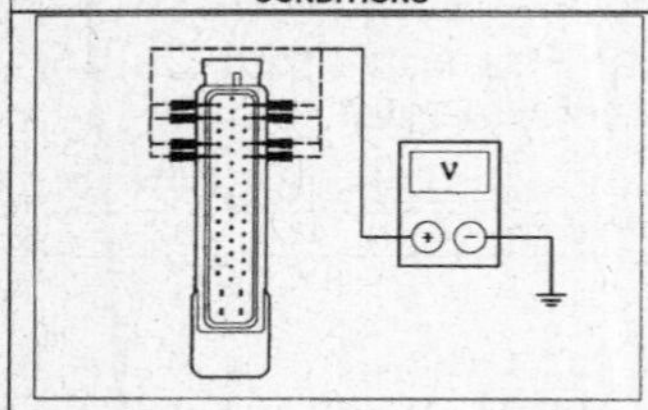	5 DTC C1145 (RF) measure the voltage between stability assist module C830 pin 35, circuit 7-CF38 (YE/RD), harness side and ground; and between stability assist module C830 pin 34, circuit 8-CF38 (WH/RD), harness side and ground; DTC C1155 (LF) measure the voltage between stability assist module C830 pin 1, circuit 7-CF32 (YE), harness side and ground; and between stability assist module pin 2, circuit 8-CF32 (WH), harness side and ground. DTC C1165 (RR) measure the voltage between stability assist module C830 pin 38, circuit 7-CF40 (YE/GN), harness side and ground; and between stability assist module C830 pin 37, circuit 8-CF40 (WH/GN), harness side and ground. DTC C1175 (LR) measure the voltage between stability assist module C830 pin 5, circuit 7-CF34 (YE/BU), harness side and ground; and between stability assist module pin 4, circuit 8-CF34 (WH/BU), harness side and ground. • Is voltage present? → **Yes** If DTC C1145, REPAIR circuit 7-CF38 (YE/RD) or circuit 8-CF38 (WH/RD). CLEAR the DTCs. REPEAT the self-test.If DTC C1155, REPAIR circuit 7-CF32 (YE) or circuit 8-CF32 (WH). CLEAR the DTCs. REPEAT the self-test.If DTC C1165, REPAIR circuit 7-CF40 (YE/GN) or circuit 8-CF40 (WH/GN). CLEAR the DTCs. REPEAT the self-test.If DTC C1175, REPAIR circuit 7-CF34 (YE/BU) or circuit 8-CF34 (WH/BU). CLEAR the DTCs. REPEAT the self-test. → **No** GO TO **E2**
E2: CHECK FOR SHORT TO GROUND	
NOTE: Both circuits must be checked for each DTC.	
1 	

FM4020201888020X

Fig. 29 Test E/Codes C1145, C1155, C1165 & C1175: ABS Brake Sensor Input Circuit Failure (Part 2 of 5). 2002–04 w/Stability Assist

CONDITIONS	DETAILS/RESULTS/ACTIONS
NOTE: Any time an anti-lock brake sensor is removed, thoroughly clean the mounting surfaces and apply High Temperature 4x4 Front Axle and Wheel Bearing Grease E8TZ-19590-A or equivalent meeting Ford specification ESA-M1C198-A.	
E1: CHECK FOR SHORT TO POWER	
NOTE: Both circuits must be checked for each DTC.	
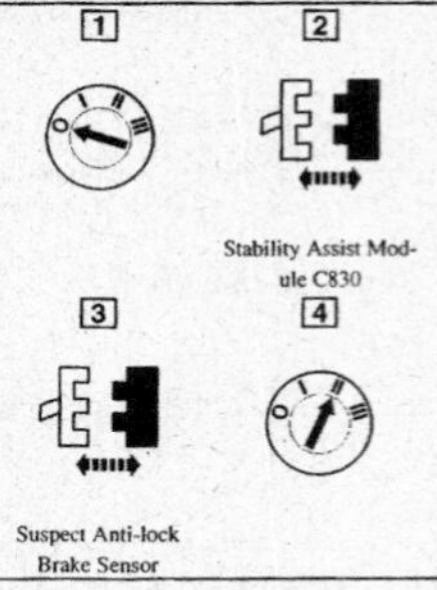	

FM4020201888010X

Fig. 29 Test E/Codes C1145, C1155, C1165 & C1175: ABS Brake Sensor Input Circuit Failure (Part 1 of 5). 2002–04 w/Stability Assist

CONDITIONS	DETAILS/RESULTS/ACTIONS
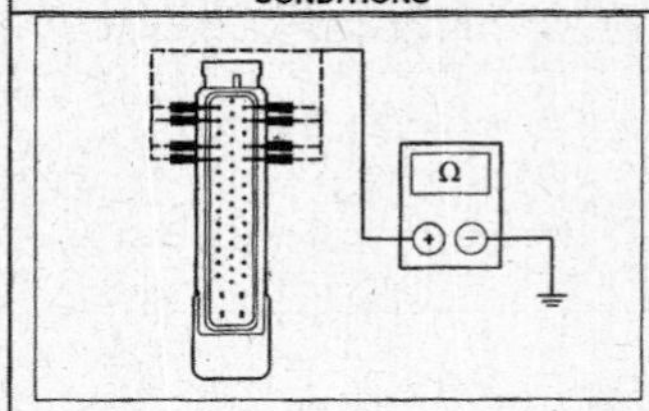	2 DTC C1145 (RF) measure the resistance between stability assist module C830 pin 35, circuit 7-CF38 (YE/RD), harness side and ground; and between stability assist module C830 pin 34, circuit 8-CF38 (WH/RD), harness side and ground. DTC C1155 (LF) measure the resistance between stability assist module C830 pin 1, circuit 7-CF32 (YE), harness side and ground; and between stability assist module C830 pin 2, circuit 8-CF32 (WH), harness side and ground. DTC C1165 (RR) measure the resistance between stability assist module C830 pin 38, circuit 7-CF40 (YE/GN), harness side and ground; and between stability assist module C830 pin 37, circuit 8-CF40 (WH/GN), harness side and ground. DTC C1175 (LR) measure the resistance between stability assist module C830 pin 5, circuit 7-CF34 (YE/BU), harness side and ground; and between stability assist module C830 pin 4, circuit 8-CF34 (WH/BU), harness side and ground. • Are the resistances greater than 10,000 ohms? → **Yes** GO TO **E3** → **No** If DTC C1145, REPAIR circuit 7-CF38 (YE/RD) or circuit 8-CF38 (WH/RD). CLEAR the DTCs. REPEAT the self-test.If DTC C1155, REPAIR circuit 7-CF32 (YE) or circuit 8-CF32 (WH). CLEAR the DTCs. REPEAT the self-test.If DTC C1165, REPAIR circuit 7-CF40 (YE/GN) or circuit 8-CF40 (WH/GN). CLEAR the DTCs. REPEAT the self-test.If DTC C1175, REPAIR circuit 7-CF34 (YE/BU) or circuit 8-CF34 (WH/BU). CLEAR the DTCs. REPEAT the self-test.
E3: CHECK FOR AN OPEN CIRCUIT	
NOTE: Both circuits must be checked for each DTC.	

FM4020201888030X

Fig. 29 Test E/Codes C1145, C1155, C1165 & C1175: ABS Brake Sensor Input Circuit Failure (Part 3 of 5). 2002–04 w/Stability Assist

CONDITIONS	DETAILS/RESULTS/ACTIONS
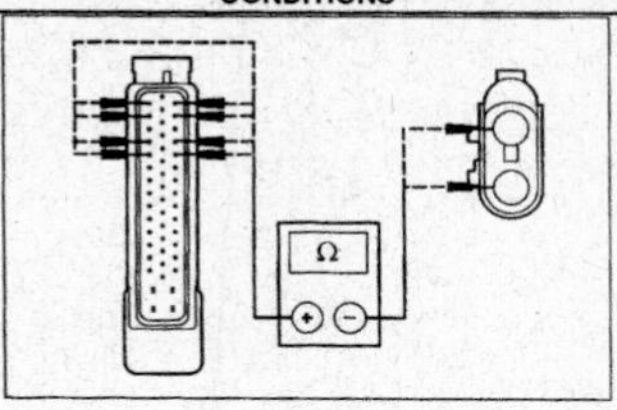	1 DTC C1145 (RF) measure the resistance between stability assist module C830 pin 35 , circuit 7-CF38 (YE/RD), harness side and suspect anti-lock brake sensor connector C815 pin 2, 7-CF38 (YE/RD), harness side; and between stability assist module C830 pin 34, circuit 8-CF38 (WH/RD), harness side and suspect anti-lock brake sensor connector C815 pin 1, circuit 8-CF38 (WH/RD), harness side. DTC C1155 (LF) measure the resistance between stability assist module C830 pin 1, circuit 7-CF32 (YE), harness side and suspect anti-lock brake sensor connector C815 pin 2, circuit 7-CF32 (YE), harness side; and between stability assist module C830 pin 2, circuit 8-CF32 (WH), harness side and suspect anti-lock brake sensor connector C814 pin 1, circuit 8-CF32 (WH), harness side. DTC C1165 (RR) measure the resistance between stability assist module C830 pin 38, circuit 7-CF40 (YE/GN), harness side and suspect anti-lock brake sensor connector C817 pin 2, circuit 7-CF40 (YE/GN), harness side; and between stability assist module C830 pin 37, circuit 8-CF40 (WH/GN), harness side and suspect anti-lock brake sensor connector C817 pin 1, circuit 8-CF40 (WH/GN), harness side. DTC C1175 (LR) measure the resistance between stability assist module C830 pin 5, circuit 7-CF34 (YE/BU), harness side and suspect anti-lock brake sensor connector C816 pin 2, circuit 7-CF34 (YE/BU), harness side; and between stability assist module C830 pin 4, circuit 8-CF34 (WH/BU), harness side and suspect anti-lock brake sensor connector C816 pin 1, circuit 8-CF34 (WH/BU), harness side. • Is the resistance less than 5 ohms? → **Yes** GO TO **E4** → **No** If DTC C1145, REPAIR circuit 7-CF38 (YE/RD) or circuit 8-CF38 (WH/RD). CLEAR the DTCs. REPEAT the self-test.If DTC C1155, REPAIR circuit 7-CF32 (YE) or circuit 8-CF32 (WH). CLEAR the DTCs. REPEAT the self-test.If DTC C1165, REPAIR circuit 7-CF40 (YE/GN) or circuit 8-CF40 (WH/GN). CLEAR the DTCs. REPEAT the self-test.If DTC C1175, REPAIR circuit 7-CF34 (YE/BU) or circuit 8-CF34 (WH/BU). CLEAR the DTCs. REPEAT the self-test.

FM4020201888040X

Fig. 29 Test E/Codes C1145, C1155, C1165 & C1175: ABS Brake Sensor Input Circuit Failure (Part 4 of 5). 2002–04 w/Stability Assist

CONDITIONS	DETAILS/RESULTS/ACTIONS
E4: CHECK THE STABILITY ASSIST MODULE OUTPUT	
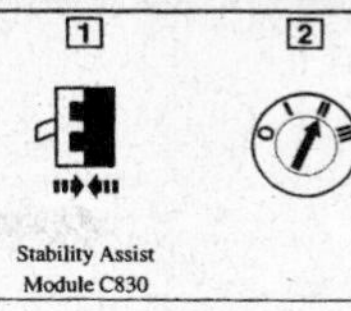 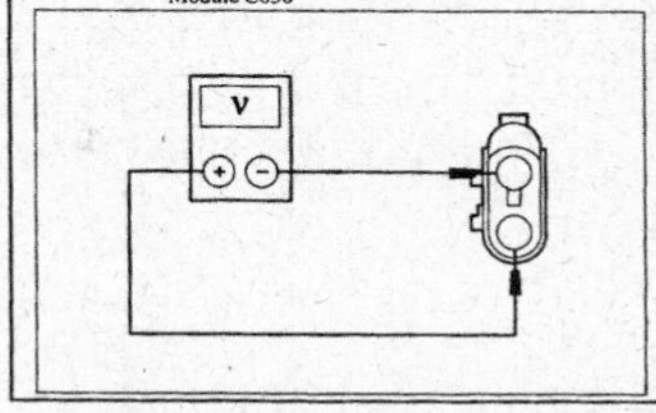	3 Measure the voltage between suspect anti-lock brake sensor pins, harness side. • Is the voltage less than 9 volts? → **Yes** INSTALL a new stability assist module. CLEAR the DTCs. REPEAT the self-test. → **No** INSTALL a new anti-lock brake sensor. CLEAR the DTCs. REPEAT the self-test.

FM4020201888050X

Fig. 29 Test E/Codes C1145, C1155, C1165 & C1175: ABS Brake Sensor Input Circuit Failure (Part 5 of 5). 2002–04 w/Stability Assist

CONDITIONS	DETAILS/RESULTS/ACTIONS
NOTE: Any time an anti-lock brake sensor is removed, thoroughly clean the mounting surfaces and apply High Temperature 4x4 Front Axle and Wheel Bearing Grease E8TZ-19590-A or equivalent meeting Ford specification ESA-M1C198-A.	
F1: CHECK THE ANTI-LOCK BRAKE SENSOR	
	1 Check the suspect anti-lock brake sensor mounting. Check the suspect anti-lock brake sensor for excessive dirt buildup, metal obstructions, incorrect harness routing, and chafing. • Is the suspect anti-lock brake sensor OK? → **Yes** GO TO **F2** → **No** REPAIR as necessary. CLEAR the DTCs. REPEAT the self-test.

FM4020201889010X

Fig. 30 Test F/Code C1233, C1234, C1235 & C1236: ABS Brake Sensor Input Signal Missing (Part 1 of 2). 2002–04 w/Stability Assist

CONDITIONS	DETAILS/RESULTS/ACTIONS
F2: CHECK THE ANTI-LOCK BRAKE SENSOR INDICATOR	
	1 Check the suspect anti-lock brake sensor indicator for corrosion, nicks, damaged teeth, correct mounting, alignment, and consistent air gap. • Is the suspect anti-lock brake sensor indicator OK? → **Yes** INSTALL a new anti-lock brake sensor. CLEAR the DTCs. REPEAT the self-test. → **No** REPAIR as necessary. CLEAR the DTCs. REPEAT the self-test.

FM4020201889020X

Fig. 30 Test F/Code C1233, C1234, C1235 & C1236: ABS Brake Sensor Input Signal Missing (Part 2 of 2). 2002–04 w/Stability Assist

CONDITIONS	DETAILS/RESULTS/ACTIONS
G1: CARRY OUT THE RECALIBRATION PROCEDURE	
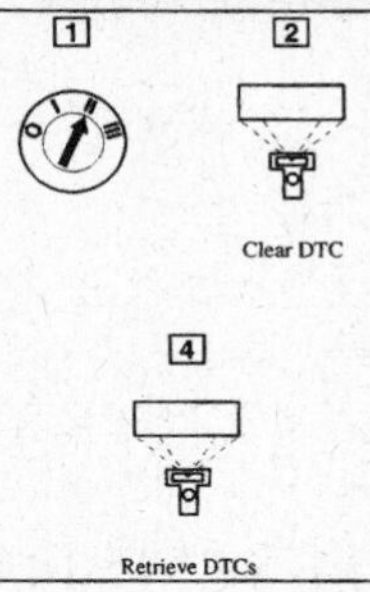	3 Carry out the stability assist module recalibration procedure using the scan tool. • Are any DTCs retrieved? → **Yes** GO to the Stability Assist Module DTC Index. → **No** The stability assist system is operating correctly.

FM4020201890000X

Fig. 31 Test G/Code C1267: ABS Function Temporarily Disabled. 2002–04 w/Stability Assist

CONDITIONS	DETAILS/RESULTS/ACTIONS
H1: CARRY OUT THE RECALIBRATION PROCEDURE	
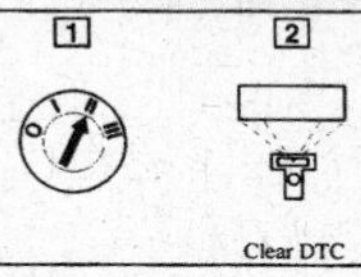	

FM4020201891010X

Fig. 32 Test H/Code C1279 & C1280: Yaw Rate Sensor Circuit Failure (Part 1 of 5). 2002–04 w/Stability Assist

CONDITIONS	DETAILS/RESULTS/ACTIONS
4  Retrieve DTCs	3 Carry out the yaw rate sensor recalibration procedure using the scan tool. • Are any DTCs retrieved or does the recalibration procedure indicate a fault? → **Yes** If DTC C1279 or C1280 is retrieved, or yaw velocity portion of the recalibration procedure indicates failed, GO TO **H2**If any other DTC, GO to the Stability Assist Module DTC Index. → **No** The stability assist system is operating correctly.
H2: CHECK THE STABILITY ASSIST MODULE PID YAWRATE	
	1 Monitor the stability assist module PID YAWRATE. • Is the stability assist module PID YAWRATE value between 479 and 545? → **Yes** INSTALL a new yaw rate sensor. CLEAR DTCs. RECALIBRATE the stability assist module. REPEAT the self-test. → **No** GO TO **H3**
H3: CHECK THE RETURN SIGNAL VOLTAGE	
1 2  Stability Assist Module C830	
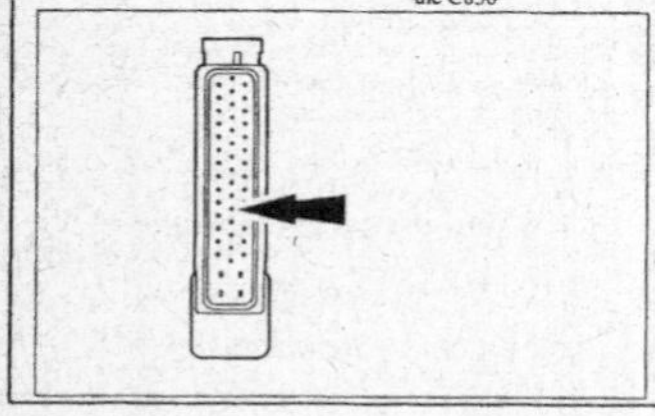	3 Back out the stability assist module C830 pin 27, circuit 8-CF67 (WH/RD), harness side.

FM4020201891020X

Fig. 32 Test H/Code C1279 & C1280: Yaw Rate Sensor Circuit Failure (Part 2 of 5). 2002–04 w/Stability Assist

CONDITIONS	DETAILS/RESULTS/ACTIONS
4 5  Stability Assist Module C830	
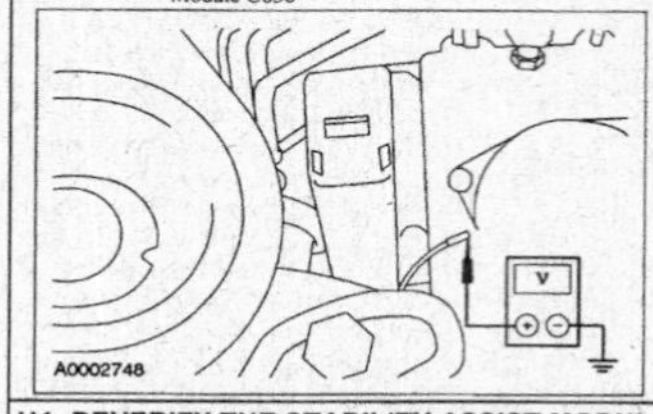	6 Measure the voltage between stability assist module C830 pin 27, circuit 8-CF67 (WH/RD), harness side and ground. • Is the voltage approximately 2.5 volts? → **Yes** RECONNECT the backed out pin. GO TO **H4** → **No** GO TO **H5**
H4: REVERIFY THE STABILITY ASSIST MODULE PID YAWRATE	
	1 Monitor the stability assist module PID YAWRATE. • Is the stability assist module PID YAWRATE value between 479 and 545? → **Yes** CHECK the stability assist module connector for loose or corroded pins. CLEAR the DTCs. REPEAT the self-test. → **No** INSTALL a new stability assist module. REPEAT the self-test.
H5: CHECK YAW RATE SENSOR CIRCUIT FOR SHORT TO POWER	
1 2  Stability Assist Module C830	

FM4020201891030X

Fig. 32 Test H/Code C1279 & C1280: Yaw Rate Sensor Circuit Failure (Part 3 of 5). 2002–04 w/Stability Assist

CONDITIONS	DETAILS/RESULTS/ACTIONS
3 4  Yaw Rate Sensor C826	
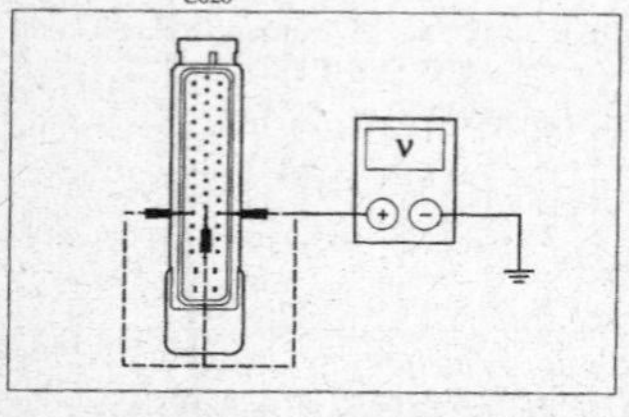	5 Measure the voltage between stability assist module C830 pin 11, circuit 9-CF67 (BN/RD), harness side and ground; and between stability assist module C830 pin 27, circuit 8-CF67 (WH/RD), harness side and ground; and between stability assist module C830 pin 44, circuit 7-CF67 (YE/RD), harness side and ground. • Is any voltage present? → **Yes** REPAIR the circuit in question. CLEAR the DTCs. RECALIBRATE the stability assist module. REPEAT the self-test. → **No** GO TO **H6**
H6: CHECK YAW RATE SENSOR CIRCUIT FOR SHORT TO GROUND	
1 	
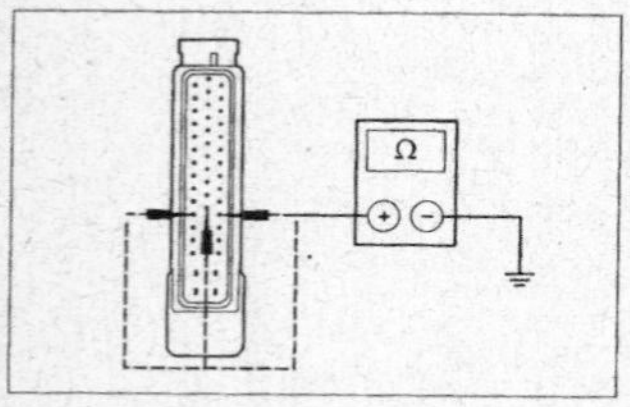	2 Measure the resistance between stability assist module C830 pin 11, circuit 9-CF67 (BN/RD), harness side and ground; and between stability assist module C830 pin 27, circuit 8-CF67 (WH/RD), harness side and ground; and between stability assist module C830 pin 44, circuit 7-CF67 (YE/RD), harness side and ground. • Is the resistance greater than 10,000 ohms? → **Yes** GO TO **H7** → **No** REPAIR the circuit in question. CLEAR the DTCs. RECALIBRATE the stability assist module. REPEAT the self-test.

FM4020201891040X

Fig. 32 Test H/Code C1279 & C1280: Yaw Rate Sensor Circuit Failure (Part 4 of 5). 2002–04 w/Stability Assist

CONDITIONS	DETAILS/RESULTS/ACTIONS
H7: CHECK YAW RATE SENSOR CIRCUIT FOR AN OPEN	
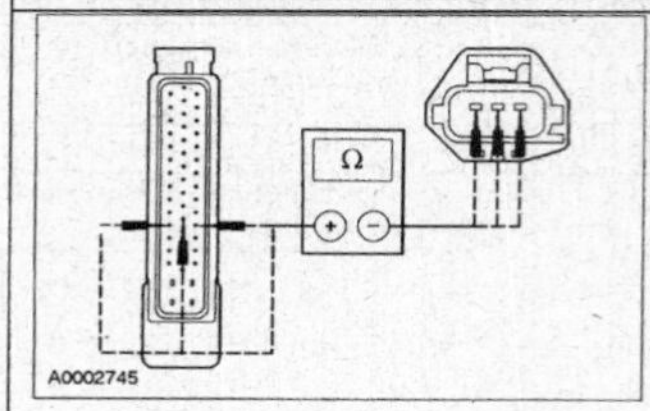	1 Measure the resistance between stability assist module C830 pin 27, circuit 8-CF67 (WH/RD), harness side and the yaw rate sensor C826 pin 1, circuit 8-CF67 (WH/RD), harness side; and between stability assist module C830 pin 11, circuit 8-CF67 (WH/RD), harness side and the yaw rate sensor C826 pin 2, circuit 8-CF67 (WH/RD), harness side; and between stability assist module C830 pin 44, circuit 7-CF67 (YE/RD), harness side and the yaw rate sensor C826 pin 3, circuit 7-CF67 (YE/RD), harness side. • Is the resistance less than 5 ohms? → **Yes** GO TO **H8** → **No** REPAIR the circuit in question. CLEAR the DTCs. RECALIBRATE the stability assist module. REPEAT the self-test.
H8: CHECK THE VOLTAGE FROM THE STABILITY ASSIST MODULE	
1 2  Stability Assist Module C830	
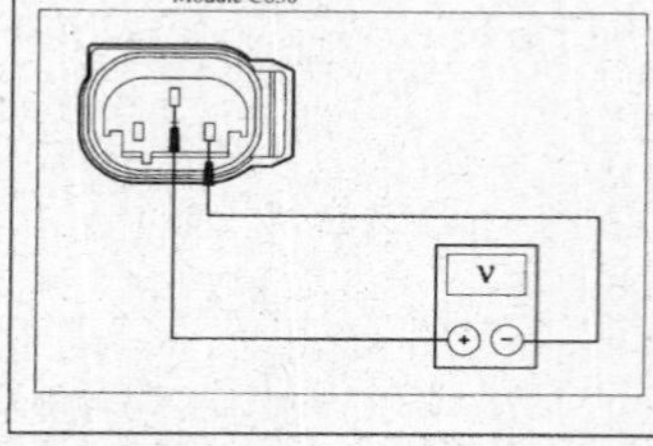	3 Measure the voltage between yaw rate sensor C826 pin 3, circuit 7-CF67 (YE/RD), harness side and yaw rate sensor C826 pin 2, circuit 9-CF67 (BN/RD), harness side. • Is the voltage approximately 5 volts? → **Yes** INSTALL a new yaw rate sensor. CLEAR the DTCs. REPEAT the self-test. → **No** INSTALL a new stability assist module, CLEAR the DTCs. REPEAT the self-test.

FM4020201891050X

Fig. 32 Test H/Code C1279 & C1280: Yaw Rate Sensor Circuit Failure (Part 5 of 5). 2002–04 w/Stability Assist

CONDITIONS	DETAILS/RESULTS/ACTIONS
I1: CARRY OUT THE RECALIBRATION PROCEDURE	
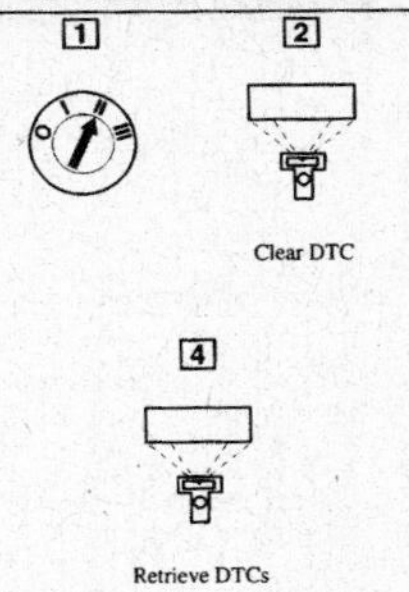	3 Carry out the accelerometer recalibration procedure using the scan tool. • Are any DTCs retrieved or does the recalibration procedure indicate a fault? → **Yes** If DTC C1281 or C1282 is retrieved, or accelerometer portion of the recalibration procedure indicates failed, GO TO **I2**If any other DTC, GO to the Stability Assist Module DTC Index. → **No** The stability assist system is operating correctly.
I2: CHECK THE STABILITY ASSIST MODULE PID LAT_ACC	
	1 Monitor the stability assist module PID LAT_ACC. • Is the stability assist module PID LAT_ACC value between 547 and 681? → **Yes** INSTALL a new accelerometer. . CLEAR DTCs. RECALIBRATE the stability assist module. REPEAT the self-test. → **No** GO TO **I3**
I3: CHECK THE RETURN SIGNAL VOLTAGE	
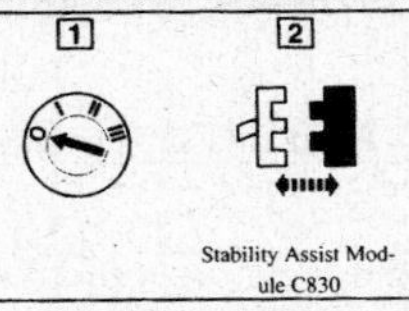	

FM4020201892010X

Fig. 33 Test I/Code C1281 & C1282: Accelerometer Circuit Failure/Signal Fault (Part 1 of 5). 2002–04 w/Stability Assist

CONDITIONS	DETAILS/RESULTS/ACTIONS
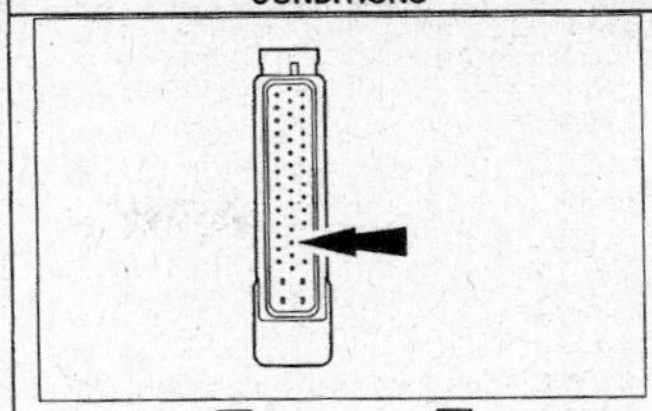	3 Back out the stability assist module C830 pin 29, circuit 8-CF66 (WH/BU), harness side.
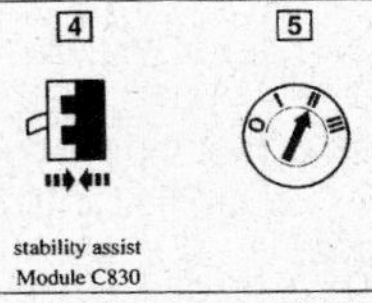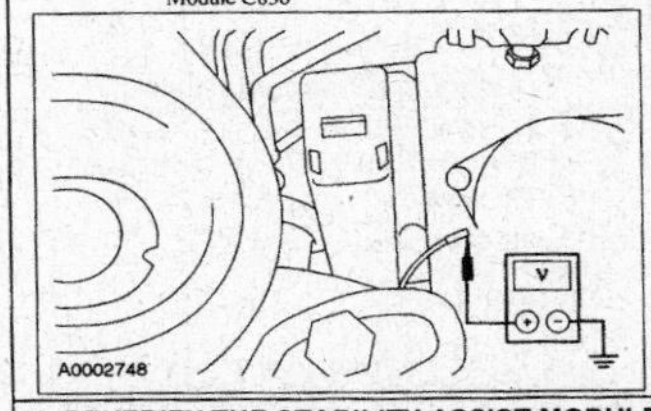	6 Measure the voltage between stability assist module C830 pin 29, circuit 8-CF66 (WH/BU), harness side and ground. • Is the voltage approximately 3 volts? → **Yes** RECONNECT the backed out pin. GO TO **I4** → **No** GO TO **I5**
I4: REVERIFY THE STABILITY ASSIST MODULE PID LAT_ACC	
	1 Monitor the stability assist module PID LAT_ACC. • Is the stability assist module PID LAT_ACC value between 547 and 681? → **Yes** CHECK the stability assist module connector for loose or corroded pins. CLEAR the DTCs. REPEAT the self-test. → **No** INSTALL a new stability assist module. REPEAT the self-test.

FM4020201892020X

Fig. 33 Test I/Code C1281 & C1282: Accelerometer Circuit Failure/Signal Fault (Part 2 of 5). 2002–04 w/Stability Assist

CONDITIONS	DETAILS/RESULTS/ACTIONS
I5: CHECK ACCELEROMETER CIRCUIT FOR SHORT TO POWER	
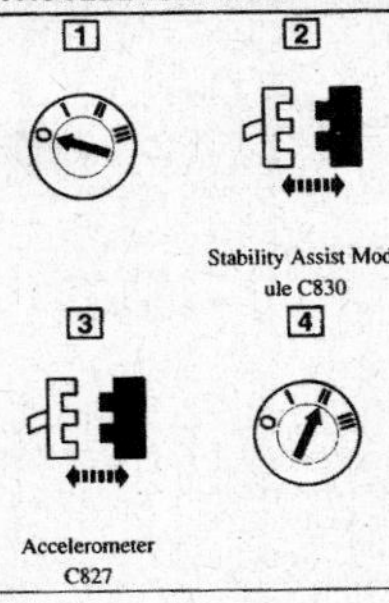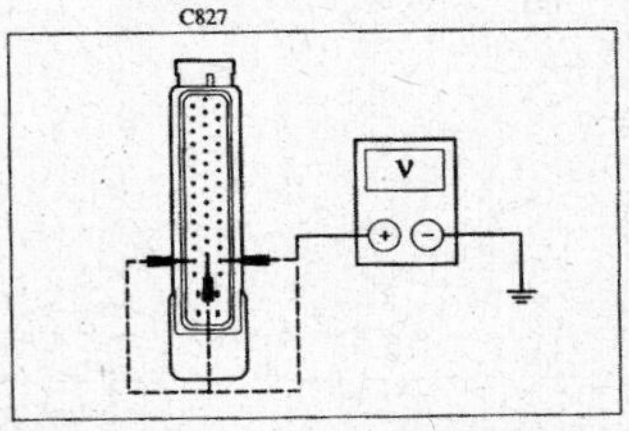	5 Measure the voltage between stability assist module C830 pin 13 circuit 9-CF66 (BN/BU), harness side and ground; and between stability assist module C830 pin 29, circuit 8-CF66 (WH/BU), harness side and ground; and between stability assist module C830 pin 46, circuit 7-CF66 (YE/BU), harness side and ground. • Is any voltage present? → **Yes** REPAIR the circuit in question. CLEAR the DTCs. RECALIBRATE the stability assist module. REPEAT the self-test. → **No** GO TO **I6**
I6: CHECK ACCELEROMETER CIRCUIT FOR SHORT TO GROUND	

FM4020201892030X

Fig. 33 Test I/Code C1281 & C1282: Accelerometer Circuit Failure/Signal Fault (Part 3 of 5). 2002–04 w/Stability Assist

CONDITIONS	DETAILS/RESULTS/ACTIONS
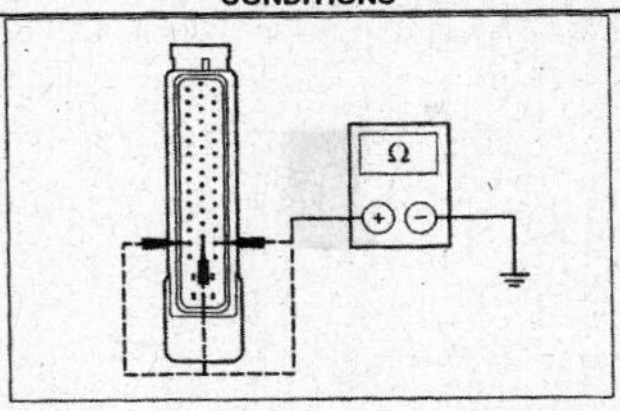	2 Measure the resistance between stability assist module C830 pin 13, circuit 9-CF66 (BN/BU), harness side and ground; and between stability assist module C830 pin 29, circuit 8-CF66 (WH/BU), harness side and ground; and between stability assist module C830 pin 46, circuit 7-CF66 (YE/BU), harness side and ground. • Is the resistance greater than 10,000 ohms? → **Yes** GO TO **I7** → **No** REPAIR the circuit in question. CLEAR the DTCs. RECALIBRATE the stability assist module. REPEAT the self-test.
I7: CHECK ACCELEROMETER CIRCUIT FOR AN OPEN	
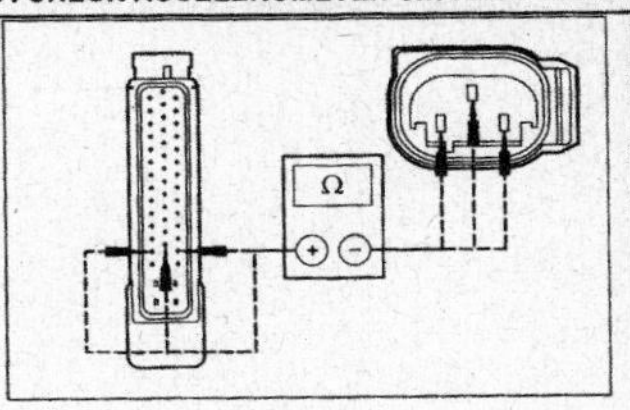	1 Measure the resistance between stability assist module C830 pin 13, circuit 9-CF66 (BN/BU), harness side and accelerometer C827 pin 2, circuit 9-CF66 (BN/BU), harness side; and between stability assist module C830 pin 29, circuit 8-CF66 (WH/BU), harness side and accelerometer C827 pin 1, circuit 8-CF66 (WH/BU), harness side; and between stability assist module C830 pin 46, circuit 7-CF66 (YE/BU), harness side and accelerometer C827 pin 3, circuit 7-CF66 (YE/BU), harness side. • Is the resistance less than 5 ohms? → **Yes** GO TO **I8** → **No** REPAIR the circuit in question. CLEAR the DTCs. RECALIBRATE the stability assist module. REPEAT the self-test.
I8: CHECK THE VOLTAGE FROM THE STABILITY ASSIST MODULE	
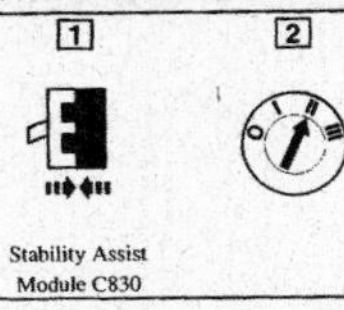	

FM4020201892040X

Fig. 33 Test I/Code C1281 & C1282: Accelerometer Circuit Failure/Signal Fault (Part 4 of 5). 2002–04 w/Stability Assist

CONDITIONS	DETAILS/RESULTS/ACTIONS
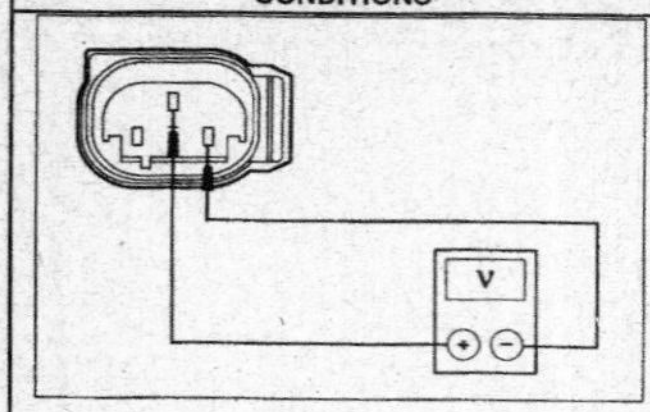	3 Measure the voltage between accelerometer C827 pin 3, circuit 7-CF66 (YE/BU), harness side and accelerometer C827 pin 2, circuit 9-CF66 (BN/BU), harness side. • Is the voltage approximately 5 volts? → Yes INSTALL a new accelerometer. CLEAR DTCs. RECALIBRATE the stability assist module. REPEAT the self-test. → No INSTALL a new stability assist module. CLEAR the DTCs. REPEAT the self-test.

FM4020201892050X

Fig. 33 Test I/Code C1281 & C1282: Accelerometer Circuit Failure/Signal Fault (Part 5 of 5). 2002–04 w/Stability Assist

CONDITIONS	DETAILS/RESULTS/ACTIONS
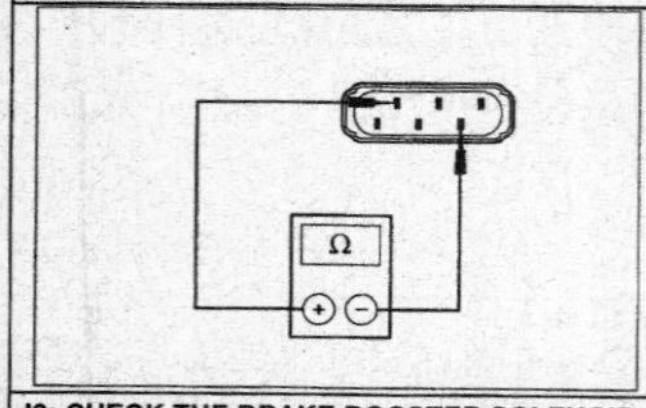	3 Measure the resistance between brake booster pin 3 (component side) and brake booster solenoid pin 4 (component side). • Is the resistance between 1 and 2 ohms? → Yes GO TO **J3** → No INSTALL a new brake booster. CLEAR the DTCs. RECALIBRATE the stability assist module. REPEAT the self-test.
J3: CHECK THE BRAKE BOOSTER SOLENOID CIRCUIT FOR SHORT TO POWER	
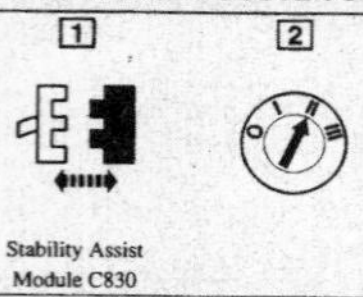 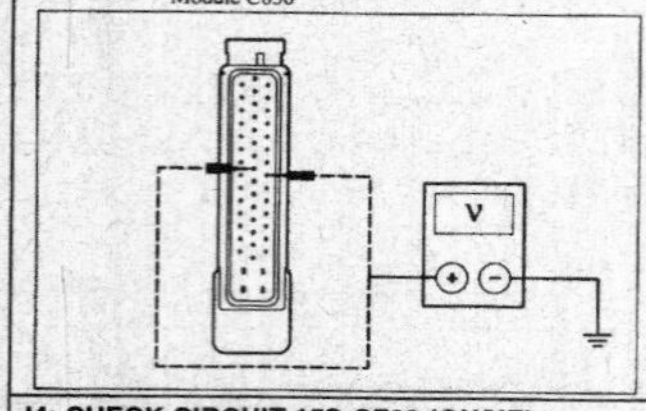	3 Measure the voltage between stability assist module C830 pin 8, circuit 15S-CF68 (GN/YE), harness side and ground; and stability assist module C830 pin 24, circuit 31S-CF68 (BK/YE), harness side and ground. • Is the any voltage present? → Yes REPAIR the circuit in question. CLEAR the DTCs. RECALIBRATE the stability assist module. REPEAT the self-test. → No GO TO **J4**
J4: CHECK CIRCUIT 15S-CF68 (GN/YE)	

FM4020201893020X

Fig. 34 Test J/Code C1285: Brake Booster Solenoid Output Failure (Part 2 of 4). 2002–04 w/Stability Assist

CONDITIONS	DETAILS/RESULTS/ACTIONS
J1: CARRY OUT THE RECALIBRATION PROCEDURE	
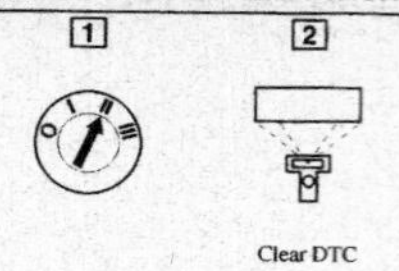 	3 Carry out the brake booster recalibration procedure using the scan tool. • Are any DTCs retrieved or does the recalibration procedure indicate a fault? → Yes If DTC C1285 is retrieved, or brake booster portion of the recalibration procedure indicates failed, GO TO **J2** .If any other DTC, GO to the Stability Assist Module DTC Index. → No The stability assist system is operating correctly.
J2: CHECK THE BRAKE BOOSTER SOLENOID	
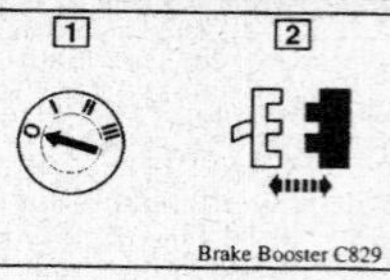	

FM4020201893010X

Fig. 34 Test J/Code C1285: Brake Booster Solenoid Output Failure (Part 1 of 4). 2002–04 w/Stability Assist

CONDITIONS	DETAILS/RESULTS/ACTIONS
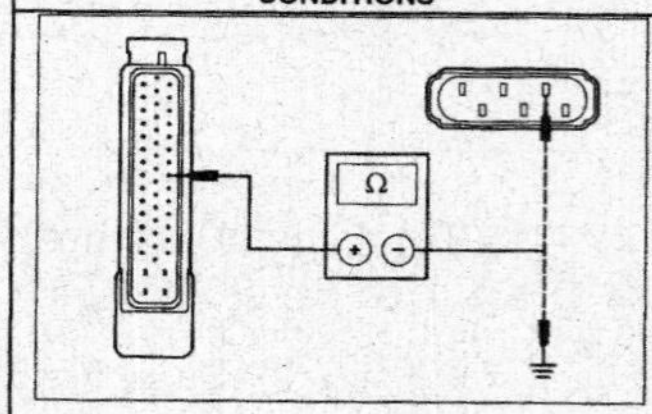	2 Measure the resistance between stability assist module C830 pin 8, circuit 15S-CF68 (GN/YE), harness side and brake booster C829 pin 3, circuit 15S-CF68 (GN/YE), harness side; and between stability assist module C830 pin 8, circuit 15S-CF68 (GN/YE), harness side and ground. • Is the resistance less than 5 ohms between stability assist module and brake booster; and greater than 10,000 ohms between stability assist module and ground? → Yes GO TO **J5** → No REPAIR the circuit. CLEAR the DTCs. RECALIBRATE the stability assist module. REPEAT the self-test.
J5: CHECK CIRCUIT 31S-CF68 (BK/YE)	
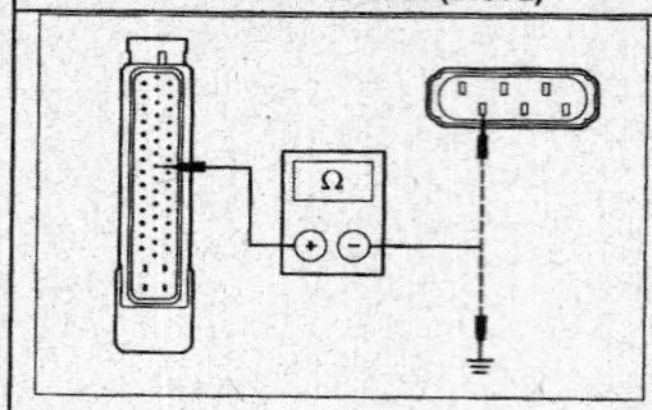	1 Measure the resistance between stability assist module C830 pin 24, circuit 31S-CF68 (BK/YE), harness side and brake booster C829 pin 4, circuit 31S-CF68 (BK/YE), harness side; and stability assist module C830 pin 24, circuit 31S-CF68 (BK/YE), harness side and ground. • Is the resistance less than 5 ohms between stability assist module and brake booster; and greater than 10,000 ohms between stability assist module and ground? → Yes GO TO **J6** → No REPAIR the circuit. CLEAR the DTCs. RECALIBRATE the stability assist module. REPEAT the self-test.
J6: CHECK THE BRAKE BOOSTER SOLENOID FOR CORRECT OPERATION	
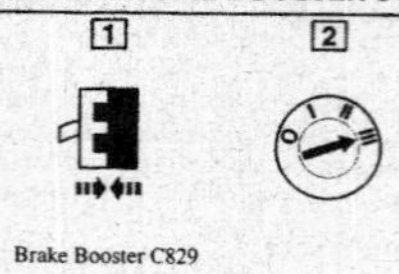	3 Wait a few minutes to create engine vacuum in the brake booster and then place the ignition switch in the OFF position.

FM4020201893030X

Fig. 34 Test J/Code C1285: Brake Booster Solenoid Output Failure (Part 3 of 4). 2002–04 w/Stability Assist

CONDITIONS	DETAILS/RESULTS/ACTIONS
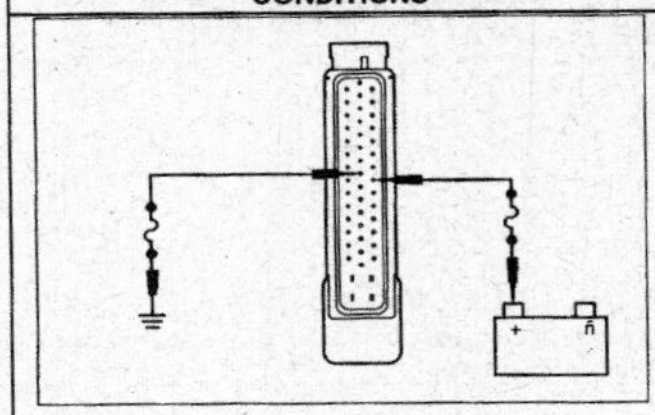	**4** Connect a fused (10A) jumper wire between stability assist module pin 24, circuit 31S-CF68 (BK/YE), harness side and ground; and connect a fused (10A) jumper wire for several seconds between stability assist module pin 8, circuit 15S-CF68 (GN/YE), harness side and the positive battery post while observing the brake pedal for movement. • Does the brake pedal move? → **Yes** INSTALL a new stability assist module. REPEAT the self-test. → **No** INSTALL a new brake booster. CLEAR the DTCs. RECALIBRATE the stability assist module. REPEAT the self-test.

FM4020201893040X

Fig. 34 Test J/Code C1285: Brake Booster Solenoid Output Failure (Part 4 of 4). 2002–04 w/Stability Assist

CONDITIONS	DETAILS/RESULTS/ACTIONS
K1: CARRY OUT THE RECALIBRATION PROCEDURE	
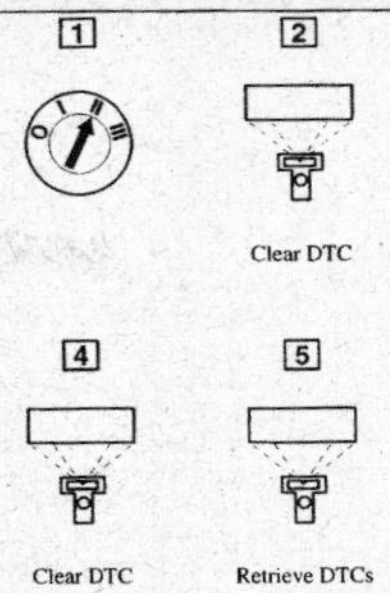	**3** Carry out the brake booster recalibration procedure using the scan tool. • Are any DTCs retrieved or does the recalibration procedure indicate a fault? → **Yes** If DTC C1286 is retrieved or recalibration procedure indicate a fault, GO TO **K2**If any other DTC, GO to the Stability Assist Module DTC Index. → **No** The stability assist system is operating correctly.

FM4020201894010X

Fig. 35 Test K/Code C1286: Booster Mechanical Failure (Part 1 of 4). 2002–04 w/Stability Assist

CONDITIONS	DETAILS/RESULTS/ACTIONS
K2: CHECK THE BRAKE BOOSTER SOLENOID	
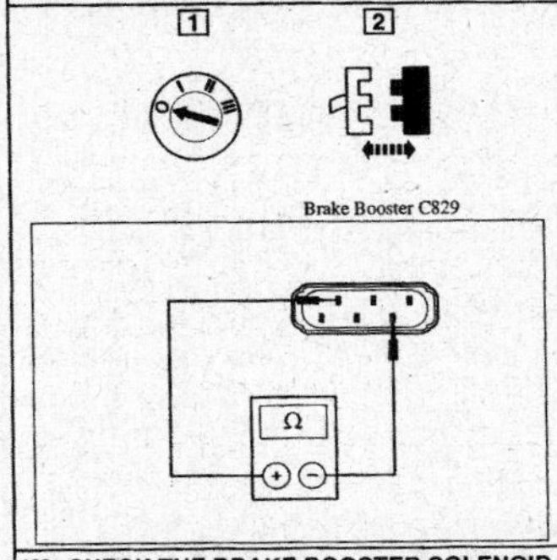	**3** Measure the resistance between brake booster pin 3 (component side) and brake booster solenoid pin 4 (component side). • Is the resistance between 1 and 2 ohms? → **Yes** GO TO **K3** → **No** INSTALL a new brake booster. CLEAR the DTCs. RECALIBRATE the stability assist module. REPEAT the self-test.
K3: CHECK THE BRAKE BOOSTER SOLENOID CIRCUIT FOR SHORT TO POWER	
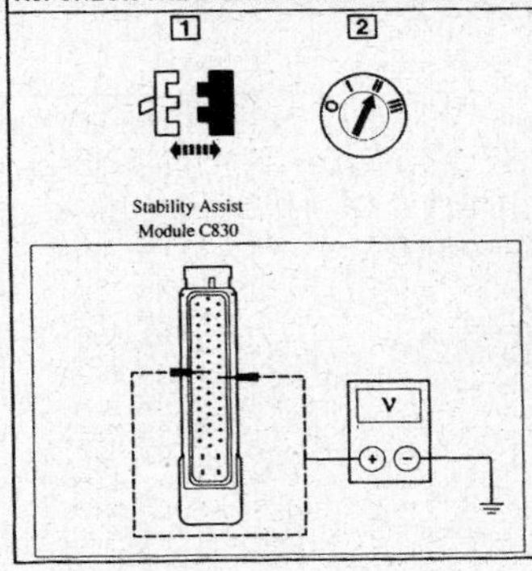	**3** Measure the voltage between stability assist module C830 pin 8, circuit 15S-CF68 (GN/YE), harness side and ground; and stability assist module C830 pin 24, circuit 31S-CF68 (BK/YE), harness side and ground. • Is the any voltage present? → **Yes** REPAIR the circuit in question. CLEAR the DTCs. RECALIBRATE the stability assist module. REPEAT the self-test. → **No** GO TO **K4**

FM4020201894020X

Fig. 35 Test K/Code C1286: Booster Mechanical Failure (Part 2 of 4). 2002–04 w/Stability Assist

CONDITIONS	DETAILS/RESULTS/ACTIONS
K4: CHECK CIRCUIT 15S-CF68 (GN/YE)	
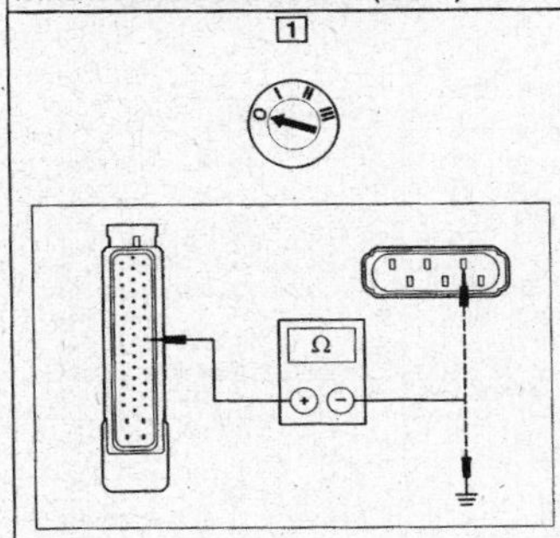	**2** Measure the resistance between stability assist module C830 pin 8, circuit 15S-CF68 (GN/YE), harness side and brake booster C829 pin 3, circuit 15S-CF68 (GN/YE), harness side; and stability assist module C830 pin 8, circuit 15S-CF68 (GN/YE), harness side and ground. • Is the resistance less than 5 ohms between stability assist module and brake booster; and greater than 10,000 ohms between stability assist module and ground? → **Yes** GO TO **K5** → **No** REPAIR the circuit. CLEAR the DTCs. RECALIBRATE the stability assist module. REPEAT the self-test.
K5: CHECK CIRCUIT 31S-CF68 (BK/YE)	
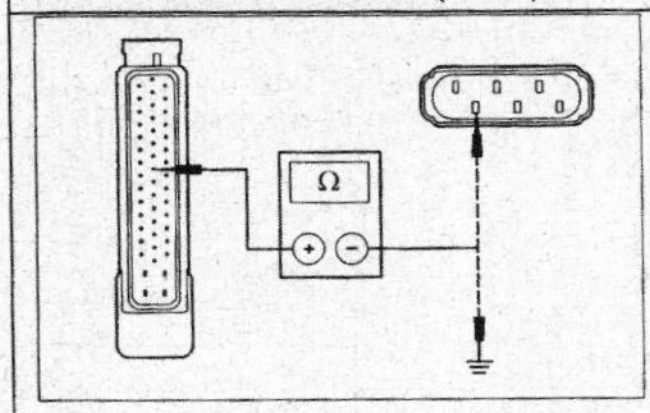	**1** Measure the resistance between stability assist module C830 pin 24, circuit 31S-CF68 (BK/YE), harness side and brake booster C829 pin 4, circuit 31S-CF68 (BK/YE), harness side; and stability assist module C830 pin 24, circuit 31S-CF68 (BK/YE), harness side and ground. • Is the resistance less than 5 ohms between stability assist module and brake booster; and greater than 10,000 ohms between stability assist module and ground? → **Yes** GO TO **K6** → **No** REPAIR the circuit. CLEAR the DTCs. RECALIBRATE the stability assist module. REPEAT the self-test.

FM4020201894030X

Fig. 35 Test K/Code C1286: Booster Mechanical Failure (Part 3 of 4). 2002–04 w/Stability Assist

CONDITIONS	DETAILS/RESULTS/ACTIONS
K6: CHECK THE BRAKE BOOSTER SOLENOID FOR CORRECT OPERATION	
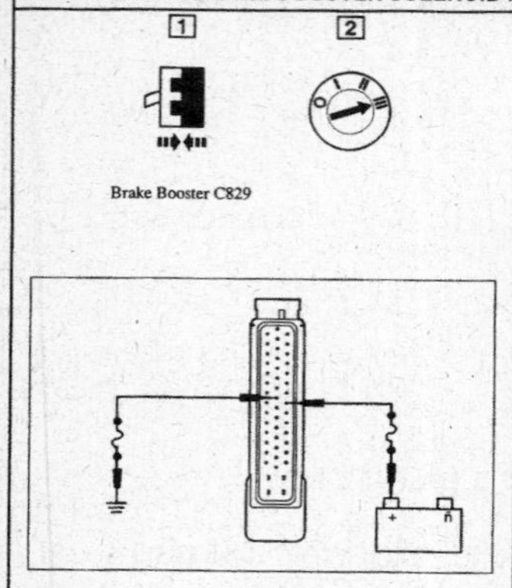	3 Wait a few minutes to create engine vacuum in the brake booster and then place the ignition switch in the OFF position. 4 Connect a fused (10A) jumper wire between stability assist module pin 24, circuit 31S-CF68 (BK/YE), harness side and ground; and connect a fused (10A) jumper wire for several seconds between stability assist module pin 8, circuit 15S-CF68 (GN/YE), harness side and the positive battery post while observing the brake pedal for movement. • Does the brake pedal move? → **Yes** INSTALL a new stability assist module. REPEAT the self-test. → **No** INSTALL a new brake booster. CLEAR the DTCs. RECALIBRATE the stability assist module. REPEAT the self-test.

FM4020201894040X

Fig. 35 Test K/Code C1286: Booster Mechanical Failure (Part 4 of 4). 2002–04 w/Stability Assist

CONDITIONS	DETAILS/RESULTS/ACTIONS
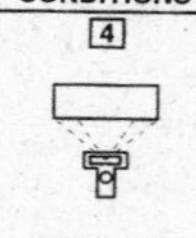	• Are any DTCs retrieved or does the recalibration procedure indicate a fault? → **Yes** If DTC C1287 is retrieved or recalibration procedure indicates a fault, GO TO **L2**If any other DTC, GO to the Stability Assist Module DTC Index. → **No** The stability assist system is operating correctly.
L2: CHECK THE NORMALLY CLOSED RELEASE SWITCH	
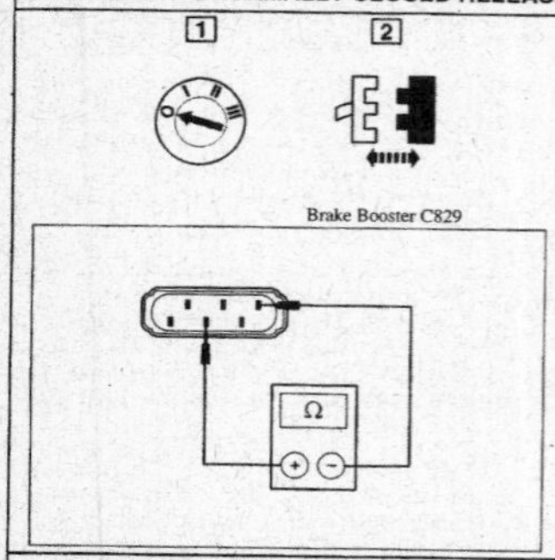	3 Measure the resistance between brake booster pin 1 (component side) and brake booster pin 5 (component side), while depressing and releasing the brake pedal. • Is the resistance less than 5 ohms with the brake pedal depressed and greater than 10,000 ohms with the brake pedal released? → **Yes** GO TO **L3** → **No** INSTALL a new brake booster. CLEAR the DTCs. RECALIBRATE the stability assist module. REPEAT the self-test.
L3: CHECK THE NORMALLY OPEN RELEASE SWITCH	
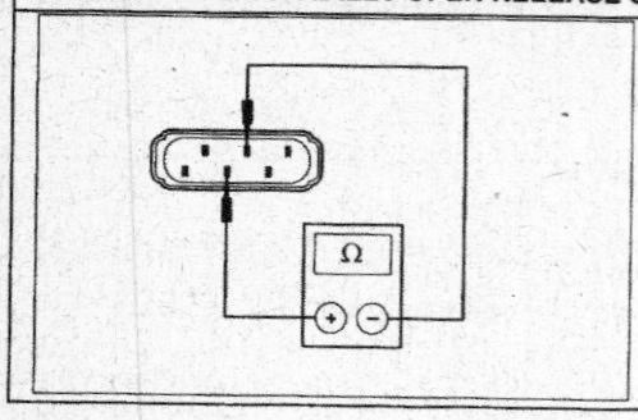	1 Measure the resistance between brake booster pin 2 (component side) and brake booster pin 5 (component side), while depressing and releasing the brake pedal. • Is the resistance less than 5 ohms with the brake pedal released and greater than 10,000 ohms with the brake pedal depressed? → **Yes** GO TO **L4** → **No** INSTALL a new brake booster. CLEAR the DTCs. RECALIBRATE the stability assist module. REPEAT the self-test.

FM4020201895020X

Fig. 36 Test L/Code C1287: Booster Pedal Force Switch Circuit Failure (Part 2 of 4). 2002–04 w/Stability Assist

CONDITIONS	DETAILS/RESULTS/ACTIONS
L1: CARRY OUT THE RECALIBRATION PROCEDURE	
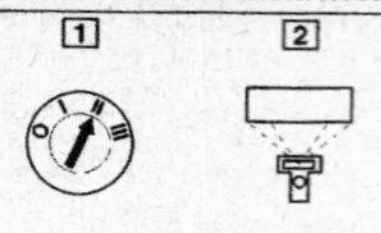	3 Carry out the brake booster recalibration procedure using the scan tool.

FM4020201895010X

Fig. 36 Test L/Code C1287: Booster Pedal Force Switch Circuit Failure (Part 1 of 4). 2002–04 w/Stability Assist

CONDITIONS	DETAILS/RESULTS/ACTIONS
L4: CHECK THE BRAKE BOOSTER CIRCUIT FOR SHORT TO POWER	
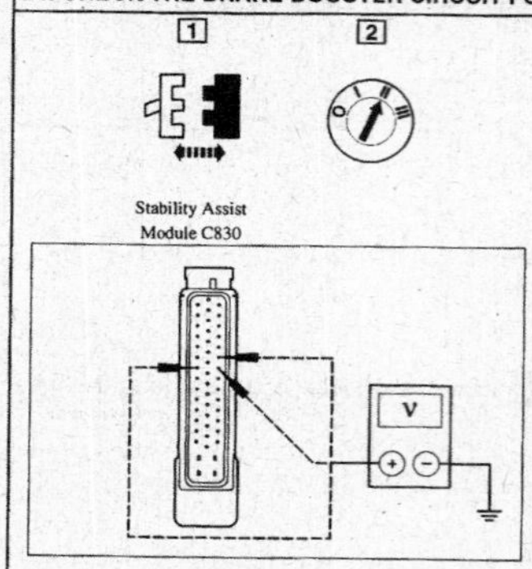	3 Measure the voltage between stability assist module C830 pin 6, circuit 49S-CF68 (BU/RD), harness side and ground; and between stability assist module C830 pin 7, circuit 49S-CF6 (BU/RD), harness side and ground; and between stability assist module C830 pin 40, circuit 49-CF51 (BK), harness side and ground. • Is any voltage present? → **Yes** REPAIR the circuit in question. CLEAR the DTC. RECALIBRATE the stability assist module. REPEAT the self-test. → **No** GO TO **L5**
L5: CHECK THE BRAKE BOOSTER CIRCUIT	

FM4020201895030X

Fig. 36 Test L/Code C1287: Booster Pedal Force Switch Circuit Failure (Part 3 of 4). 2002–04 w/Stability Assist

CONDITIONS	DETAILS/RESULTS/ACTIONS
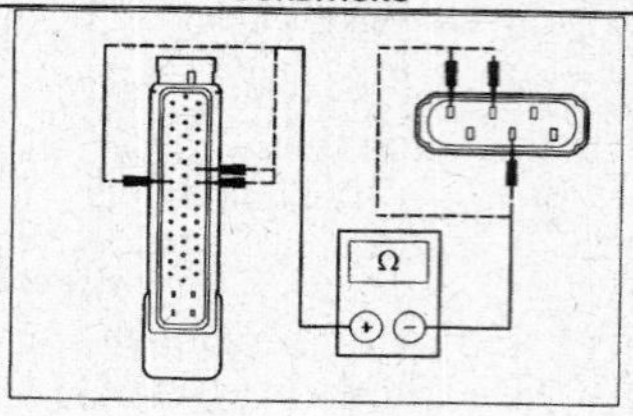	2 Measure the resistance between stability assist module C830 pin 6, circuit 49S-CF68 (BU/RD), harness side and brake booster C829 pin 1, circuit 49S-CF68 (BU/RD), harness side; and between stability assist module C830 pin 7, circuit 49S-CF6 (BU/RD), harness side and brake booster C829 pin 2, circuit 49S-CF6 (BU/RD), harness side; and between stability assist module C830 pin 40, circuit 49-CF51 (BK), harness side and brake booster C829 pin 5, circuit 49-CF51 (BK), harness side. • Are the resistances less than 5 ohms? → **Yes** INSTALL a new stability assist module. REPEAT the self-test. → **No** REPAIR the circuit in question. CLEAR the DTC. RECALIBRATE the stability assist module. REPEAT the self-test.

FM4020201895040X

Fig. 36 Test L/Code C1287: Booster Pedal Force Switch Circuit Failure (Part 4 of 4). 2002–04 w/Stability Assist

CONDITIONS	DETAILS/RESULTS/ACTIONS
NOTE: When diagnosing this DTC, the primary brake pressure sensor is the C821 pin 1, Circuit 9-CF64 (BN/YE). The pressure sensor connectors can be connected to either the primary or the secondary pressure sensor and still operate correctly, therefore the wire color must be looked at before continuing diagnostics.	
M1: CHECK PRIMARY BRAKE PRESSURE SENSOR CIRCUIT FOR SHORT TO POWER	
1 2 3 4 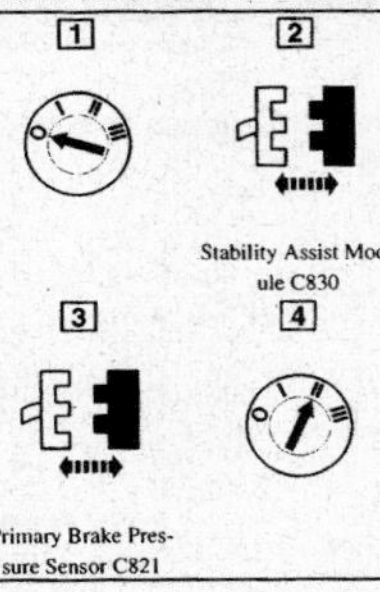	

FM4020201896010X

Fig. 37 Test M/Code C1288: Primary Brake Pressure Sensor Input Circuit Failure (Part 1 of 4). 2002–04 w/Stability Assist

CONDITIONS	DETAILS/RESULTS/ACTIONS
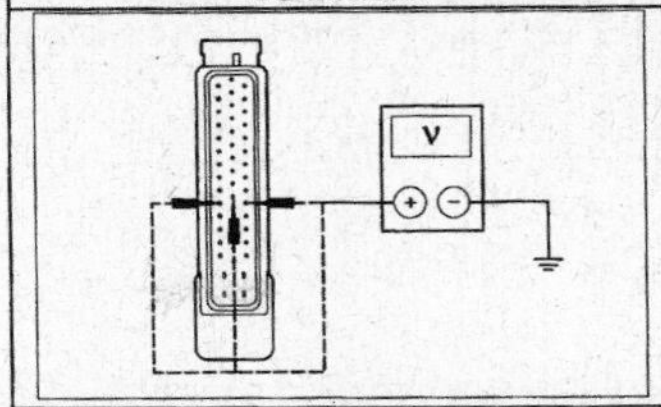	5 Measure the voltage between stability assist module C830 pin 10, circuit 7-CF64 (YE/BK), harness side and ground; and between stability assist module C830 pin 26, circuit 8-CF64 (WH/BK), harness side and ground; and between stability assist module C830 pin 43, circuit 9-CF64 (BN/YE), harness side and ground. • Is any voltage present? → **Yes** REPAIR the circuit in question. CLEAR the DTCs. REPEAT the self-test. → **No** GO TO **M2**
M2: CHECK PRIMARY BRAKE PRESSURE SENSOR CIRCUIT FOR SHORT TO GROUND	
1 	
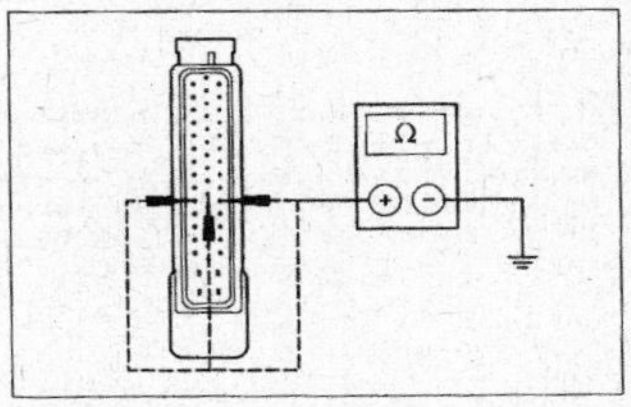	2 Measure the resistance between stability assist module C830 pin 10, circuit 7-CF64 (YE/BK), harness side and ground; and between stability assist module C830 pin 26, circuit 8-CF64 (WH/BK), harness side and ground; and between stability assist module C830 pin 43, circuit 9-CF64 (BN/YE), harness side and ground. • Is the resistance greater than 10,000 ohms? → **Yes** GO TO **M3** → **No** REPAIR the circuit in question. CLEAR the DTCs. REPEAT the self-test.

FM4020201896020X

Fig. 37 Test M/Code C1288: Primary Brake Pressure Sensor Input Circuit Failure (Part 2 of 4). 2002–04 w/Stability Assist

CONDITIONS	DETAILS/RESULTS/ACTIONS
M3: CHECK PRIMARY BRAKE PRESSURE SENSOR CIRCUIT FOR AN OPEN	
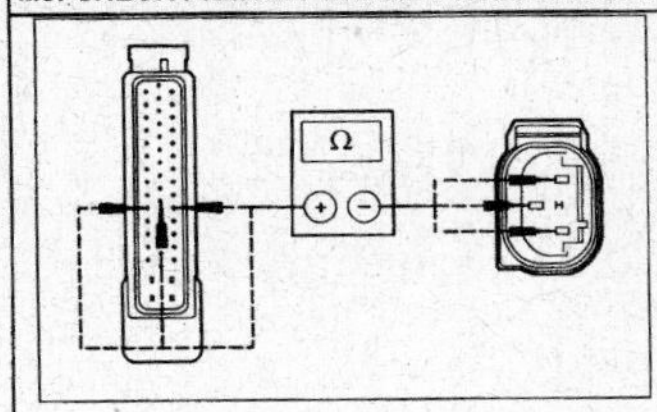	1 Measure the resistance between stability assist module C830 pin 43, circuit 9-CF64 (BN/YE), harness side and primary brake pressure sensor C821 pin 1, circuit 9-CF64 (BN/YE), harness side; and between stability assist module C830 pin 26, circuit 8-CF64 (WH/BK), harness side and primary brake pressure sensor C821 pin 2, circuit 8-CF64 (WH/BK), harness side; and between stability assist module C830 pin 10, circuit 7-CF64 (YE/BK), harness side and primary brake pressure sensor C821 pin 3, circuit 7-CF64 (YE/BK), harness side. • Is the resistance less than 5 ohms? → **Yes** GO TO **M4** → **No** REPAIR the circuit in question. CLEAR the DTCs. REPEAT the self-test.
M4: CHECK THE STABILITY ASSIST MODULE OUTPUT	
1 2 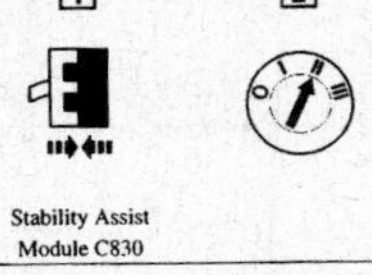	
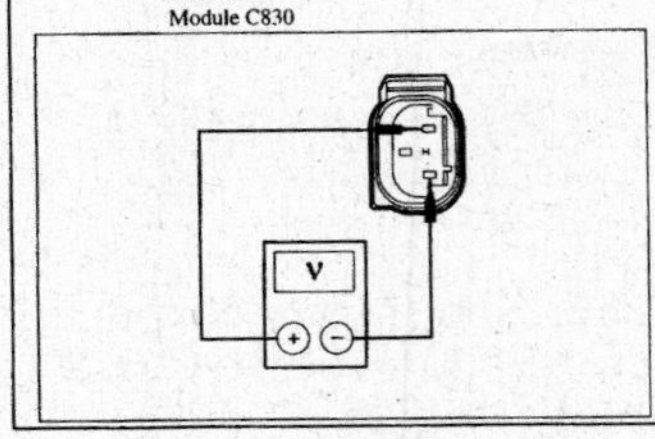	3 Measure the voltage between primary brake pressure sensor C821 pin 3, circuit 7-CF64 (YE/BK), harness side and primary brake pressure sensor C821 pin 1, circuit 9-CF64 (BN/YE), harness side. • Is the voltage approximately 5 volts? → **Yes** GO TO **M5** → **No** INSTALL a new stability assist module. REPEAT the self-test.

FM4020201896030X

Fig. 37 Test M/Code C1288: Primary Brake Pressure Sensor Input Circuit Failure (Part 3 of 4). 2002–04 w/Stability Assist

CONDITIONS	DETAILS/RESULTS/ACTIONS
M5: CHECK THE PRIMARY BRAKE PRESSURE SENSOR OUTPUT	
1 2 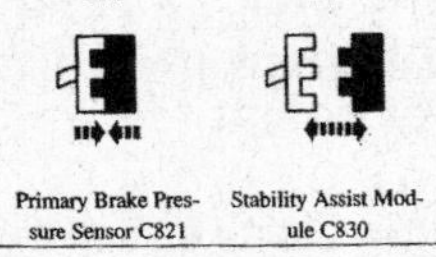	
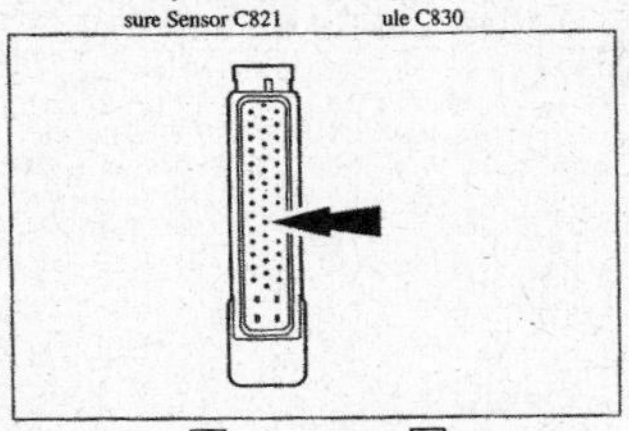	3 Back out the stability assist module C830 pin 26, circuit 8-CF64 (WH/BK), harness side.
4 5 	
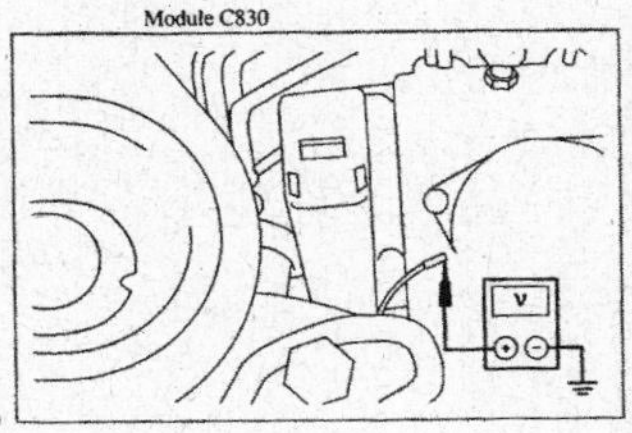	6 Measure the voltage between stability assist module back out pin 26, circuit 8-CF64 (WH/BK), harness side and ground while depressing and releasing the brake pedal. • Is the voltage between 0.125 and 0.375 volt with the brake pedal released and between 0.125 and 5 volts with the brake pedal depressed? → **Yes** INSTALL a new stability assist module. REPEAT the self-test. → **No** INSTALL a new primary brake pressure sensor. CLEAR the DTC. RECALIBRATE the stability assist module. REPEAT the self-test.

FM4020201896040X

Fig. 37 Test M/Code C1288: Primary Brake Pressure Sensor Input Circuit Failure (Part 4 of 4). 2002–04 w/Stability Assist

CONDITIONS	DETAILS/RESULTS/ACTIONS
NOTE: When diagnosing this DTC, the secondary brake pressure sensor is the C822 pin 1, circuit 9-CF65 (BN/WH). The pressure sensor connectors can be connected to either the primary or the secondary pressure sensor and still operate correctly, therefore the wire color must be looked at before continuing diagnostics.	
N1: CHECK SECONDARY BRAKE PRESSURE SENSOR CIRCUIT FOR SHORT TO POWER	
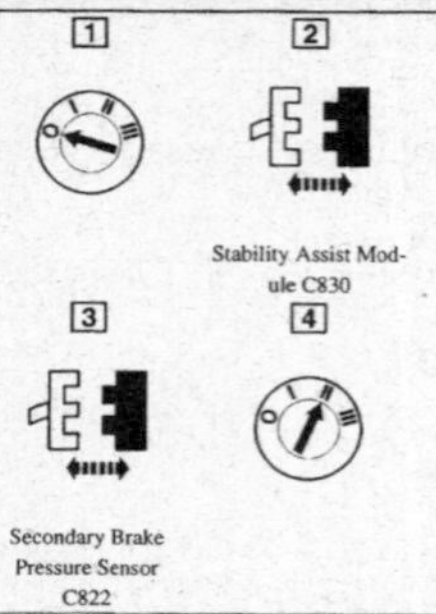	
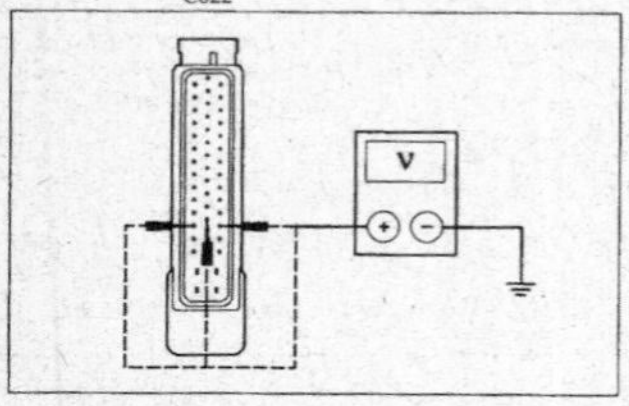	5 Measure the voltage between stability assist module C830 pin 12, circuit 7-CF65 (YE/VT), harness side and ground; and between stability assist module C830 pin 28, circuit 8-CF65 (WH/VT), harness side and ground; and between stability assist module C830 pin 45, circuit 9-CF65 (BN/WH), harness side and ground. • Is any voltage present? → Yes REPAIR the circuit in question. CLEAR the DTCs. REPEAT the self-test. → No GO TO **N2**
N2: CHECK SECONDARY BRAKE PRESSURE SENSOR CIRCUIT FOR SHORT TO GROUND	

FM4020201897010X

Fig. 38 Test N/Code C1289: Secondary Brake Pressure Sensor Input Circuit Failure (Part 1 of 4). 2002–04 w/Stability Assist

CONDITIONS	DETAILS/RESULTS/ACTIONS
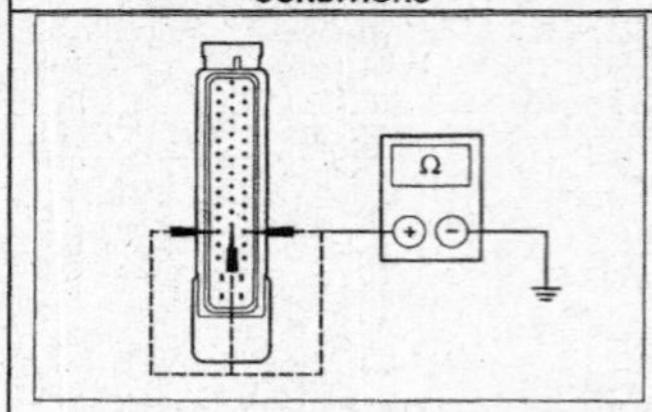	2 Measure the resistance between stability assist module C830 pin 12, circuit 7-CF65 (YE/VT), harness side and ground; and between stability assist module C830 pin 28, circuit 8-CF65 (WH/VT), harness side and ground; and between stability assist module C830 pin 45, circuit 9-CF65 (BN/WH), harness side and ground. • Is the resistance greater than 10,000 ohms? → Yes GO TO **N3** → No REPAIR the circuit in question. CLEAR the DTCs. REPEAT the self-test.
N3: CHECK SECONDARY BRAKE PRESSURE SENSOR CIRCUIT FOR AN OPEN	
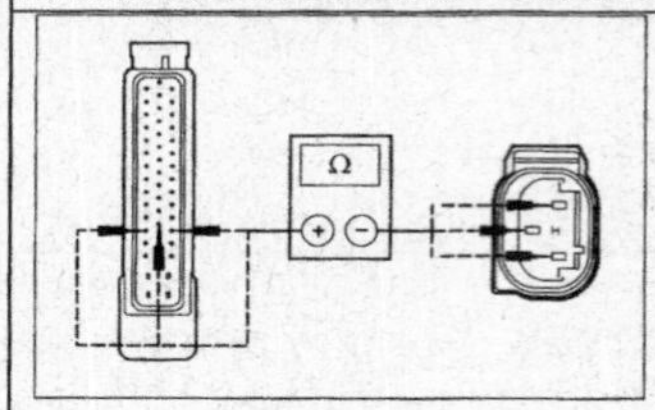	1 Measure the resistance between stability assist module C830 pin 45, circuit 9-CF65 (BN/WH), harness side and secondary brake pressure sensor C822 pin 1, circuit 9-CF65 (BN/WH), harness side; and between stability assist module C830 pin 28, circuit 8-CF65 (WH/VT), harness side and secondary brake pressure sensor C822 pin 2, circuit 8-CF65 (WH/VT), harness side; and between stability assist module C830 pin 12, circuit 7-CF65 (YE/VT), harness side and secondary brake pressure sensor C822 pin 3, circuit 7-CF65 (YE/VT), harness side • Is the resistance less than 5 ohms? → Yes GO TO **N4** → No REPAIR the circuit in question. CLEAR the DTCs. REPEAT the self-test.
N4: CHECK THE STABILITY ASSIST MODULE OUTPUT	
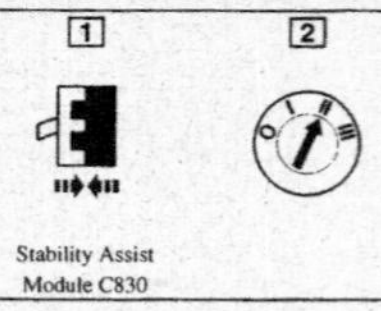	

FM4020201897020X

Fig. 38 Test N/Code C1289: Secondary Brake Pressure Sensor Input Circuit Failure (Part 2 of 4). 2002–04 w/Stability Assist

CONDITIONS	DETAILS/RESULTS/ACTIONS
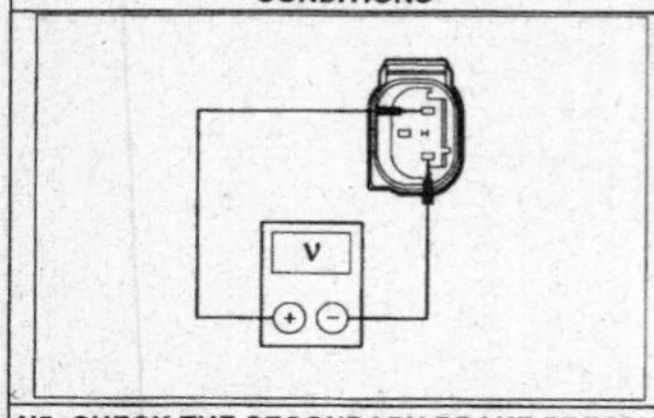	3 Measure the voltage between secondary brake pressure sensor C822 pin 3, circuit 7-CF65 (YE/VT), harness side and secondary brake pressure sensor C822 pin 1, circuit 9-CF65 (BN/WH), harness side. • Is the voltage approximately 5 volts? → Yes GO TO **N5** → No INSTALL a new stability assist module. REPEAT the self-test.
N5: CHECK THE SECONDARY BRAKE PRESSURE SENSOR OUTPUT	
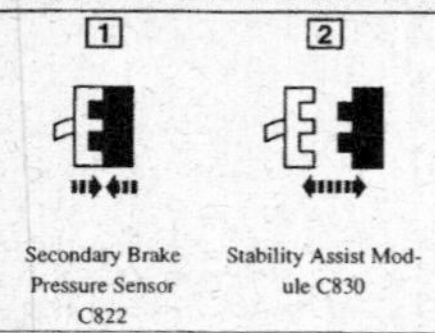	
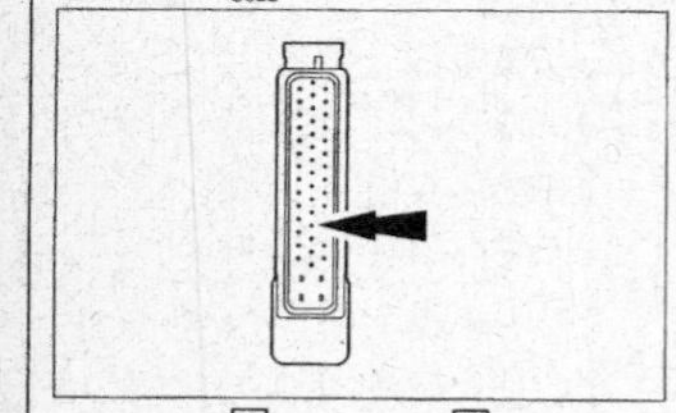	3 Back out the stability assist module C830 pin 28, circuit 8-CF65 (WH/VT), harness side.
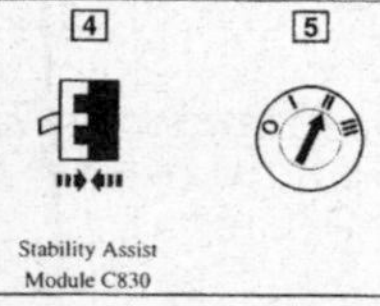	

FM4020201897030X

Fig. 38 Test N/Code C1289: Secondary Brake Pressure Sensor Input Circuit Failure (Part 3 of 4). 2002–04 w/Stability Assist

CONDITIONS	DETAILS/RESULTS/ACTIONS
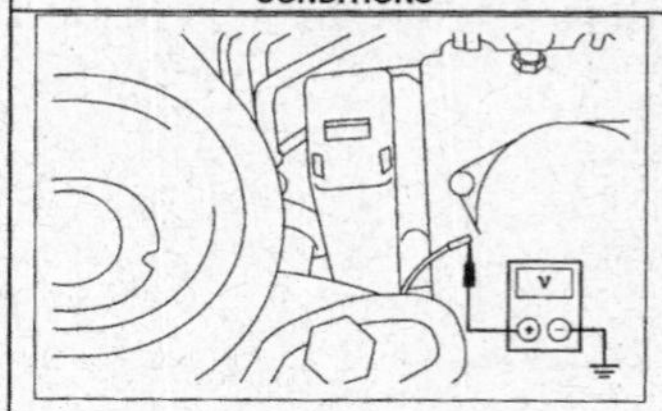	6 Measure the voltage between stability assist module back out pin 28, circuit 8-CF65 (WH/VT), harness side and ground while depressing and releasing the brake pedal. • Is the voltage between 0.125 and 0.375 volt with the brake pedal released and between 0.125 and 5 volts with the brake pedal depressed? → Yes INSTALL a new stability assist module. REPEAT the self-test. → No INSTALL a new secondary brake pressure sensor. CLEAR the DTCs. RECALIBRATE the stability assist module. REPEAT the self-test.

FM4020201897040X

Fig. 38 Test N/Code C1289: Secondary Brake Pressure Sensor Input Circuit Failure (Part 4 of 4). 2002–04 w/Stability Assist

CONDITIONS	DETAILS/RESULTS/ACTIONS
O1: CHECK CIRCUIT 7-CF64 (YE/BK) FOR SHORT TO BATTERY	
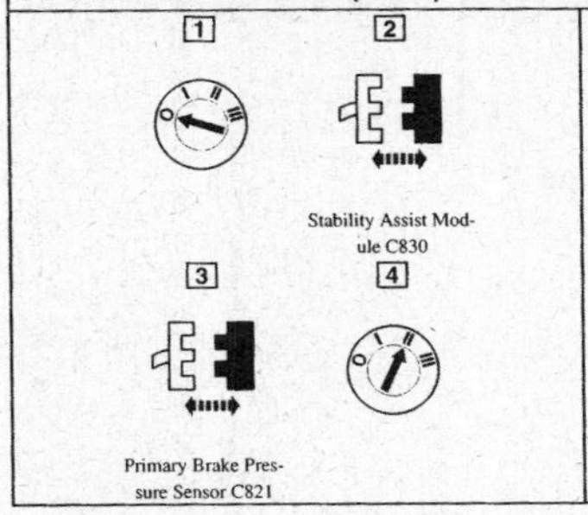	

FM4020201898010X

Fig. 39 Test O/Code C1730: Reference Voltage Out Of Range (Part 1 of 6). 2002–04 w/Stability Assist

CONDITIONS	DETAILS/RESULTS/ACTIONS
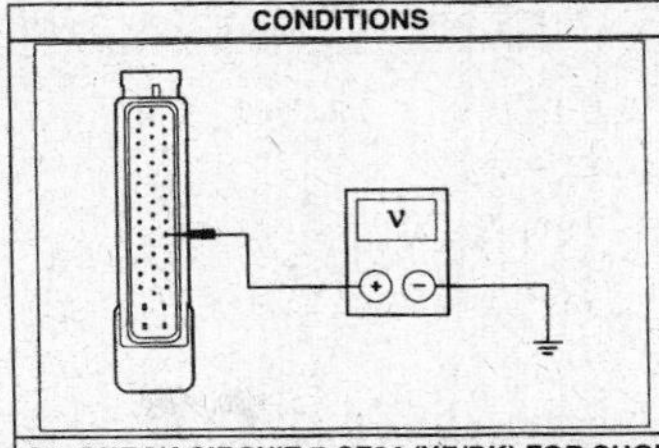	5 Measure the voltage between stability assist module C830 pin 10, circuit 7-CF64 (YE/BK), harness side and ground. • Is any voltage present? → **Yes** REPAIR the circuit. CLEAR the DTCs. RECALIBRATE the stability assist module. REPEAT the self-test. → **No** GO TO **O2**
O2: CHECK CIRCUIT 7-CF64 (YE/BK) FOR SHORT TO GROUND	
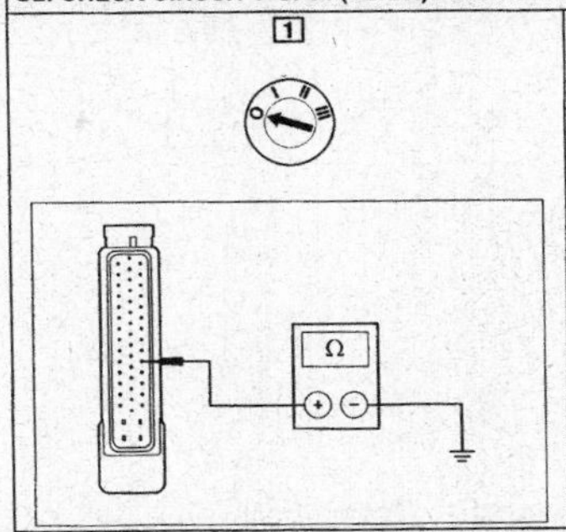	2 Measure the resistance between stability assist module C830 pin 10, circuit 7-CF64 (YE/BK), harness side and ground. • Is the resistance greater than 10,000 ohms? → **Yes** GO TO **O3** → **No** REPAIR the circuit. CLEAR the DTC. RECALIBRATE the stability assist module. REPEAT the self-test.
O3: CHECK CIRCUIT 7-CF65 (YE/VT) FOR SHORT TO BATTERY	
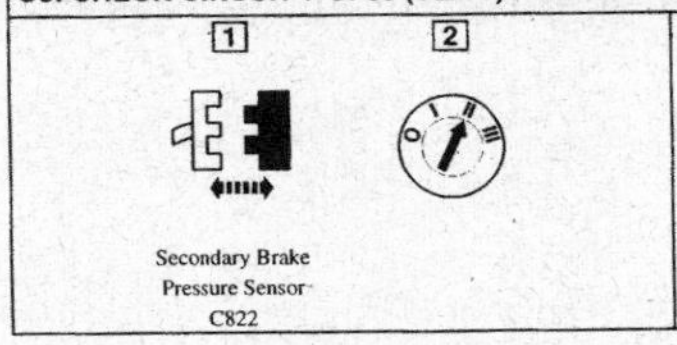	

FM4020201898020X

Fig. 39 Test O/Code C1730: Reference Voltage Out Of Range (Part 2 of 6). 2002–04 w/Stability Assist

CONDITIONS	DETAILS/RESULTS/ACTIONS
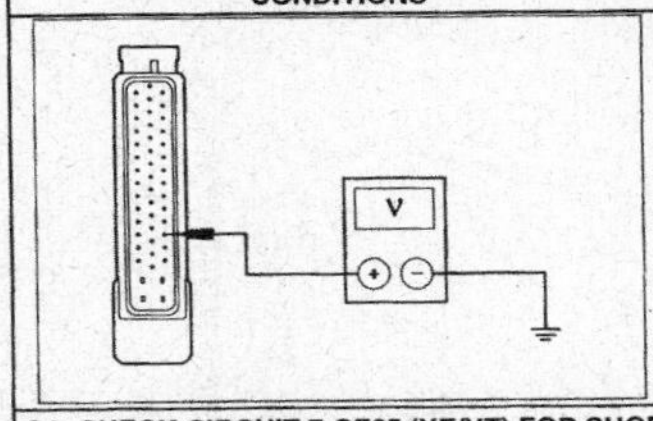	3 Measure the voltage between stability assist module C830 pin 12, circuit 7-CF65 (YE/VT), harness side and ground. • Is any voltage present? → **Yes** REPAIR the circuit. CLEAR the DTC. RECALIBRATE the stability assist module. REPEAT the self-test. → **No** GO TO **O4**
O4: CHECK CIRCUIT 7-CF65 (YE/VT) FOR SHORT TO GROUND	
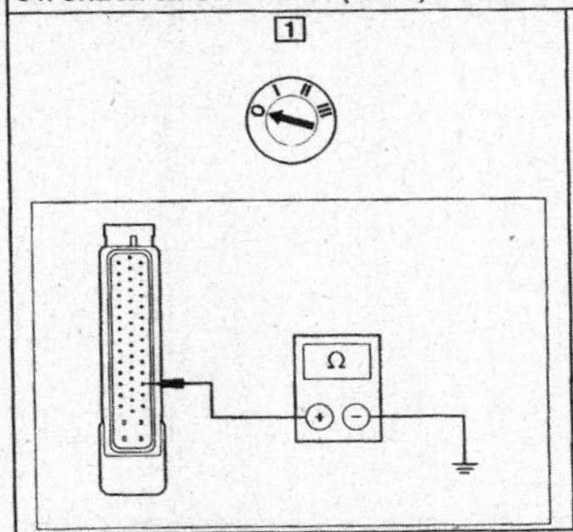	2 Measure the resistance between stability assist module C830 pin 12, circuit 7-CF65 (YE/VT), harness side and ground. • Is the resistance greater than 10,000 ohms? → **Yes** GO TO **O5** → **No** REPAIR the circuit. CLEAR the DTC. RECALIBRATE the stability assist module. REPEAT the self-test.
O5: CHECK CIRCUIT 7-CF66 (YE/BU) FOR SHORT TO BATTERY	
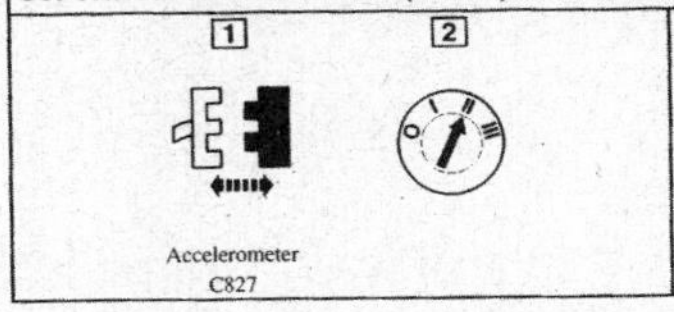	

FM4020201898030X

Fig. 39 Test O/Code C1730: Reference Voltage Out Of Range (Part 3 of 6). 2002–04 w/Stability Assist

CONDITIONS	DETAILS/RESULTS/ACTIONS
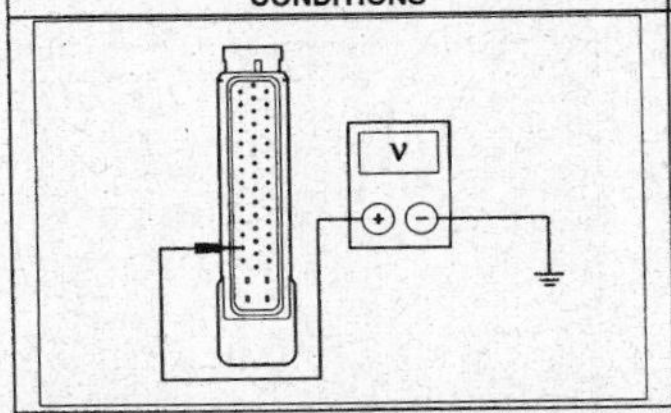	3 Measure the voltage between stability assist module C830 pin 46, circuit 7-CF66 (YE/BU), harness side and ground. • Is any voltage present? → **Yes** REPAIR the circuit. CLEAR the DTC. RECALIBRATE the stability assist module. REPEAT the self-test. → **No** GO TO **O6**
O6: CHECK CIRCUIT 7-CF66 (YE/BU) FOR SHORT TO GROUND	
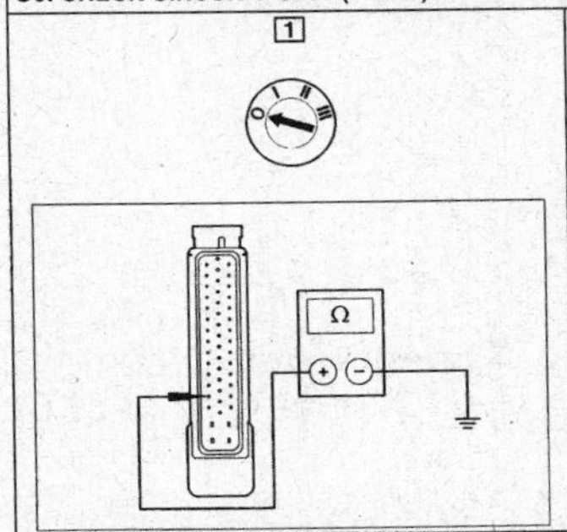	2 Measure the resistance between stability assist module C830 pin 46, circuit 7-CF66 (YE/BU), harness side and ground. • Is the resistance greater than 10,000 ohms? → **Yes** GO TO **O7** → **No** REPAIR the circuit. CLEAR the DTC. RECALIBRATE the stability assist module. REPEAT the self-test.
O7: CHECK CIRCUIT 7-CF67 (YE/RD) FOR SHORT TO BATTERY	
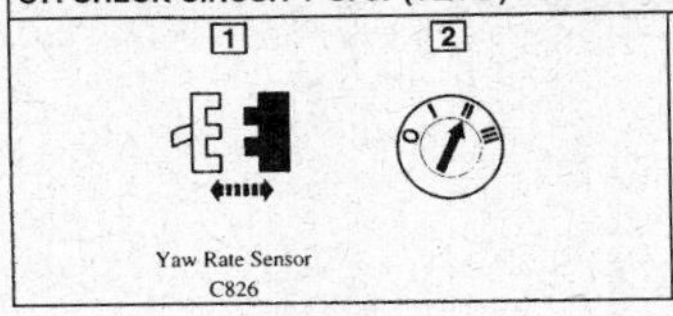	

FM4020201898040X

Fig. 39 Test O/Code C1730: Reference Voltage Out Of Range (Part 4 of 6). 2002–04 w/Stability Assist

CONDITIONS	DETAILS/RESULTS/ACTIONS
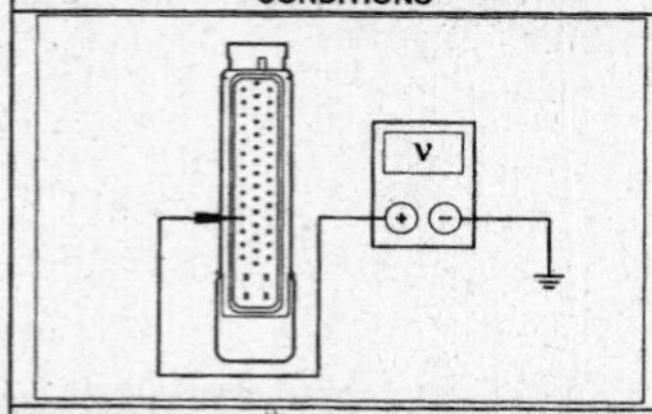	3 Measure the voltage between stability assist module C830 pin 44, circuit 7-CF67 (YE/RD), harness side and ground. • Is any voltage present? → **Yes** REPAIR the circuit. CLEAR the DTC. RECALIBRATE the stability assist module. REPEAT the self-test. → **No** GO TO **O8**
O8: CHECK CIRCUIT 7-CF67 (YE/RD) FOR SHORT TO GROUND	
1 	
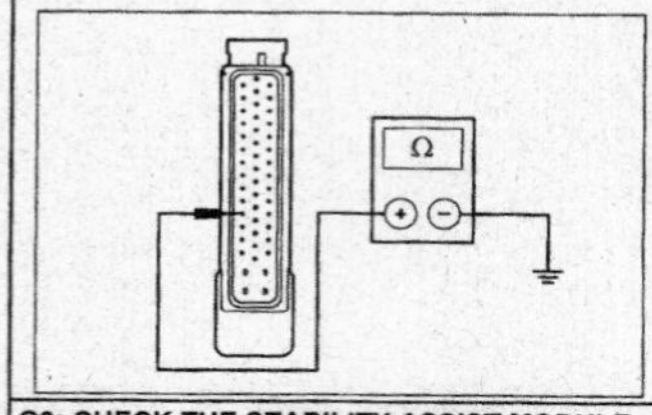	2 Measure the resistance between stability assist module C830 pin 44, circuit 7-CF67 (YE/RD), harness side and ground. • Is the resistance greater than 10,000 ohms? → **Yes** GO TO **O9** → **No** REPAIR the circuit. CLEAR the DTC. RECALIBRATE the stability assist module. REPEAT the self-test.
O9: CHECK THE STABILITY ASSIST MODULE	
1  Stability Assist Module C830 2 	

FM4020201898050X

Fig. 39 Test O/Code C1730: Reference Voltage Out Of Range (Part 5 of 6). 2002–04 w/Stability Assist

CONDITIONS	DETAILS/RESULTS/ACTIONS
3  Clear DTCs 4  Retrieve DTCs	• Is DTC C1730 retrieved? → **Yes** INSTALL a new stability assist module. REPEAT the self-test. → **No** GO TO **O10**
O10: CHECK THE STABILITY ASSIST COMPONENTS	
	1 Reconnect the accelerometer C827, yaw rate sensor C826, primary brake pressure sensor C821, and secondary brake pressure sensor C822 one at a time while clearing the DTCs and retrieving the DTCs in between each component being reconnected. • Is DTC C1730 retrieved? → **Yes** INSTALL a new component as necessary. CLEAR the DTCs. RECALIBRATE the stability assist module. REPEAT the self-test. → **No** System is OK.

FM4020201898060X

Fig. 39 Test O/Code C1730: Reference Voltage Out Of Range (Part 6 of 6). 2002–04 w/Stability Assist

CONDITIONS	DETAILS/RESULTS/ACTIONS
P1: CHECK THE YELLOW ABS WARNING INDICATOR	
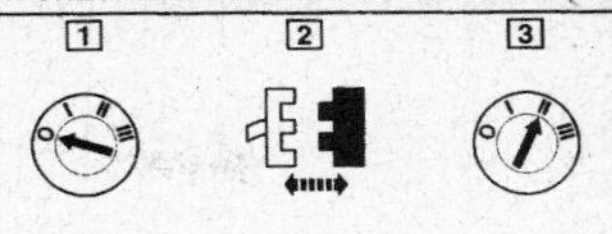 Stability Assist Module C830	• Is the yellow ABS warning indicator illuminated? → **Yes** GO TO **P2** → **No** DIAGNOSE instrument cluster.
P2: CHECK PROVE OUT	
 Stability Assist Module C830	• Does the yellow ABS warning indicator prove out for three seconds and then turn off? → **Yes** The yellow ABS warning indicator is working correctly. TEST the system for normal operation. → **No** INSTALL a new stability assist module. TEST the system for normal operation.

FM4020201899000X

Fig. 40 Test P: Yellow ABS Warning Indicator Does Not Self Check. 2002–04 w/Stability Assist

CONDITIONS	DETAILS/RESULTS/ACTIONS
Q1: CHECK FOR DTCS	
	2 Retrieve and document continuous DTCs. • Are any DTCs retrieved? → **Yes** GO to the Stability Assist Module DTC Index. → **No** GO TO **Q2**
Q2: CHECK THE ABS OPERATION	
	1 Test drive the vehicle and carry out several anti-lock stops. • Does the ABS operate correctly? → **Yes** GO TO **Q3** → **No** GO to the Symptom Chart.
Q3: CHECK THE TRACTION CONTROL OFF INPUT TO THE STABILITY ASSIST MODULE FOR SHORT TO GROUND	
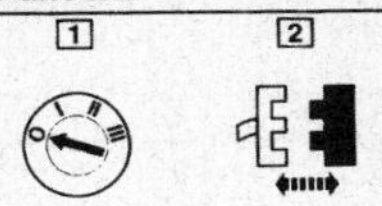 Stability Assist Module C830 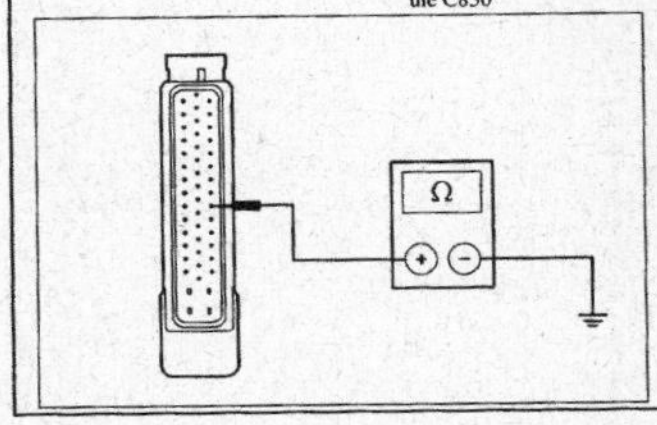	3 Measure the resistance between stability assist module C830 pin 9, circuit 91S-CF54 (BK/WH), harness side and ground. • Is the resistance less than 5 ohms? → **Yes** GO TO **Q4** → **No** INSTALL a new stability assist module. TEST the system for normal operation.

FM4020201900010X

Fig. 41 Test Q: Traction Control Inoperative (Part 1 of 2). 2002–04 w/Stability Assist

CONDITIONS	DETAILS/RESULTS/ACTIONS
Q4: CHECK THE TRACTION CONTROL SWITCH	
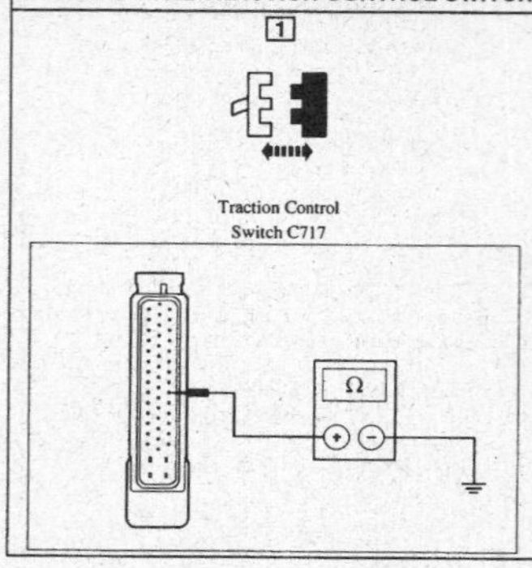	2 Measure the resistance between stability assist module C830 pin 9, circuit 91S-CF54 (BK/WH), harness side and ground. • Is the resistance less than 5 ohms? → **Yes** REPAIR the circuit. TEST the system for normal operation. → **No** INSTALL a new traction control switch. TEST the system for normal operation.

FM4020201900020X

Fig. 41 Test Q: Traction Control Inoperative (Part 2 of 2). 2002–04 w/Stability Assist

CONDITIONS	DETAILS/RESULTS/ACTIONS
R1: CHECK THE INSTRUMENT CLUSTER FOR AN OPEN	
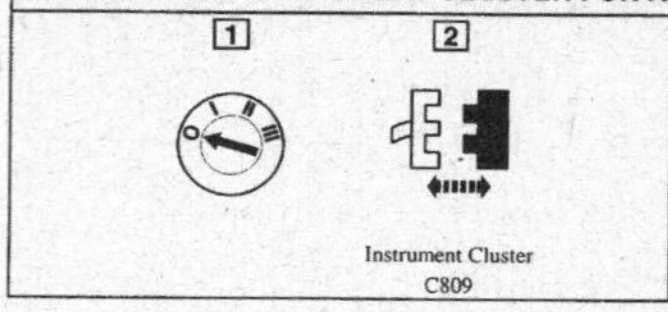	

FM4020201901010X

Fig. 42 Test R: Stability Assist/Traction Control Switch Indicator Is Never/Always On (Part 1 of 3). 2002–04 w/Stability Assist

CONDITIONS	DETAILS/RESULTS/ACTIONS
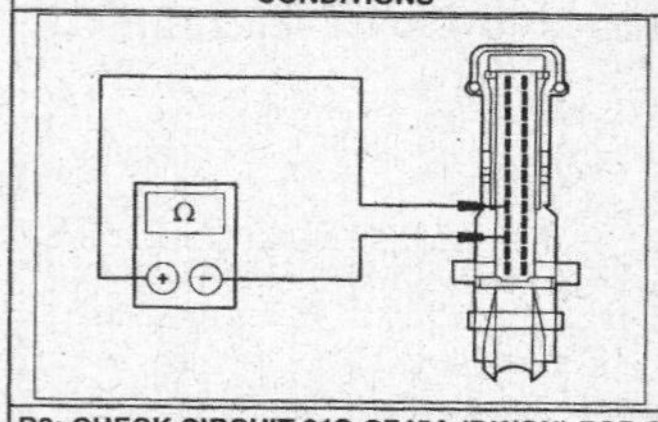	3 Measure the resistance between instrument cluster C809 pin 16 and pin 18 (component side). • Is the resistance less than 5 ohms? → **Yes** GO TO **R2** → **No** CHECK the T/C / stability assist indicator lamp bulb. If OK, INSTALL a new instrument cluster. TEST the system for normal operation.
R2: CHECK CIRCUIT 31S-CF45A (BK/GN) FOR SHORT TO POWER	
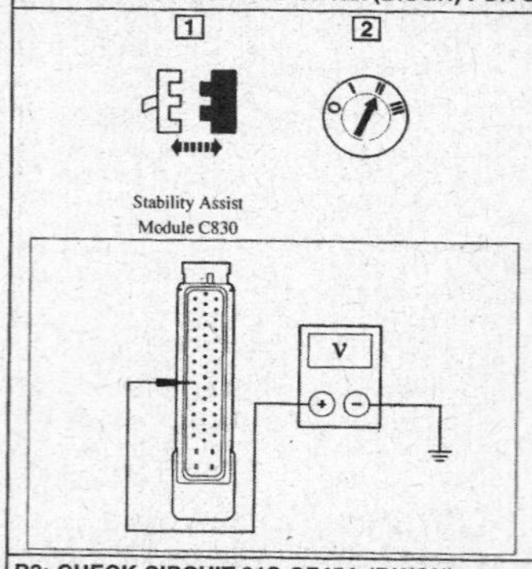	3 Measure the voltage between stability assist module C830 pin 42, circuit 31S-CF45A (BK/GN), harness side and ground. • Is any voltage present? → **Yes** REPAIR the circuit. CLEAR the DTC. REPEAT the self-test. → **No** GO TO **R3**
R3: CHECK CIRCUIT 31S-CF45A (BK/GN)	
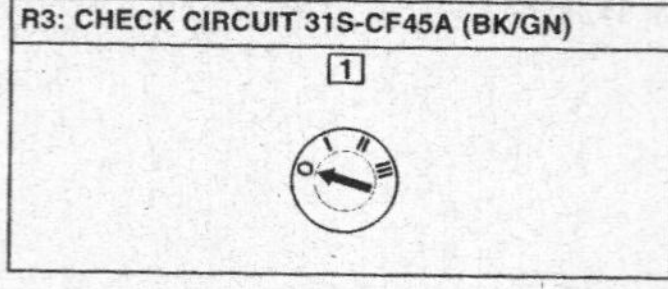	

FM4020201901020X

Fig. 42 Test R: Stability Assist/Traction Control Switch Indicator Is Never/Always On (Part 2 of 3). 2002–04 w/Stability Assist

CONDITIONS	DETAILS/RESULTS/ACTIONS
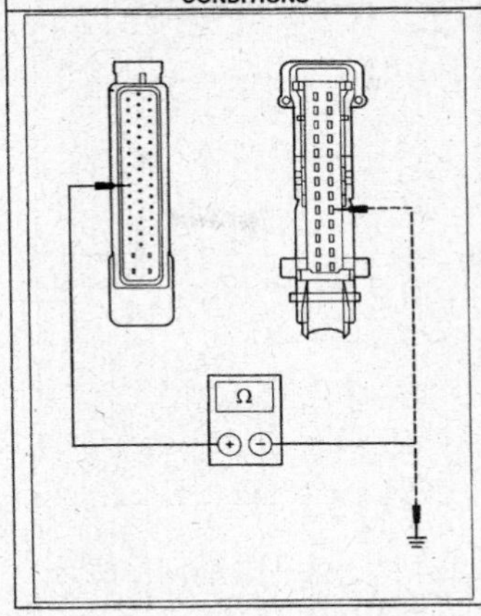	2 Measure the resistance between stability assist module C830 pin 42, circuit 31S-CF45A (BK/GN), harness side and instrument cluster C809 pin 18, circuit 31S-CF45 (BK/GN), harness side; and between stability assist module C830 pin 42, circuit 31S-CF45A (BK/GN), harness side and ground. • Is the resistance less than 5 ohms between the stability assist module and instrument cluster; and greater than 10,000 ohms between stability assist module and ground? → **Yes** INSTALL a new stability assist module. CLEAR the DTC. REPEAT the self-test. → **No** REPAIR the circuit. CLEAR the DTC. REPEAT the self-test.

FM4020201901030X

Fig. 42 Test R: Stability Assist/Traction Control Switch Indicator Is Never/Always On (Part 3 of 3). 2002–04 w/Stability Assist

CONDITIONS	DETAILS/RESULTS/ACTIONS
S1: CHECK CIRCUIT 91S-CF54 (BK/WH) FOR AN OPEN	
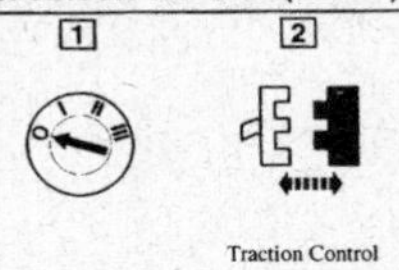	

FM4020201902010X

Fig. 43 Test S: Stability Assist System Cannot Be Disabled (Part 1 of 2). 2002–04 w/Stability Assist

CONDITIONS	DETAILS/RESULTS/ACTIONS
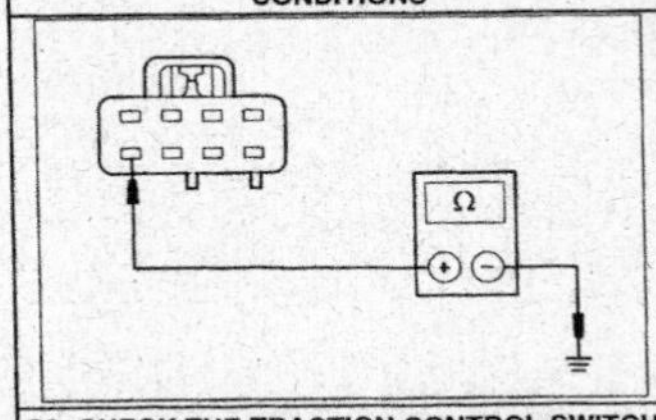	3 Measure the resistance between traction control switch C717 pin 1, circuit 91-CF54 (BK/WH), harness side and ground. • Is the resistance less than 5 ohms? → **Yes** GO TO S2 → **No** REPAIR the circuit. TEST the system for normal operation.
S2: CHECK THE TRACTION CONTROL SWITCH	
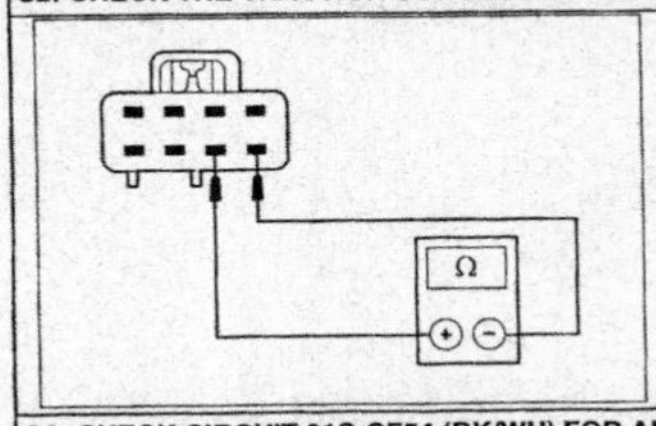	1 Measure the resistance between traction control switch C717, pin 1 and pin 2 (component side) while depressing the traction control switch. • Is the resistance less than 5 ohms? → **Yes** GO TO S3 → **No** INSTALL a new traction control switch. TEST the system for normal operation.
S3: CHECK CIRCUIT 91S-CF54 (BK/WH) FOR AN OPEN	

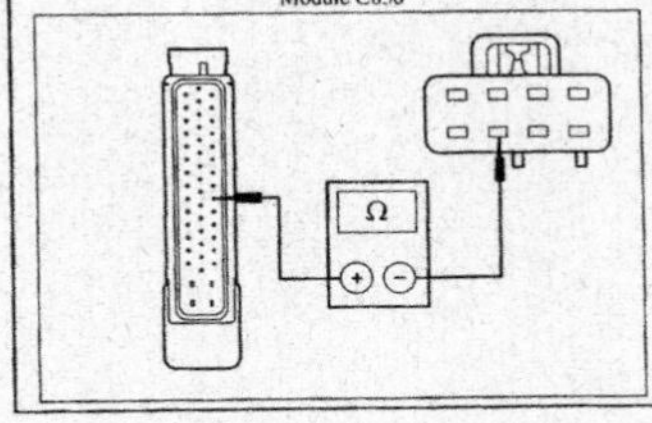	2 Measure the resistance between stability assist module pin 9, circuit 91S-CF54 (BK/WH), harness side and traction control switch C717 pin 2, circuit 91S-CF54 (BK/WH), harness side. • Is the resistance less than 5 ohms? → **Yes** INSTALL a new stability assist module. normal operation. → **No** REPAIR the circuit. TEST the system for normal operation.

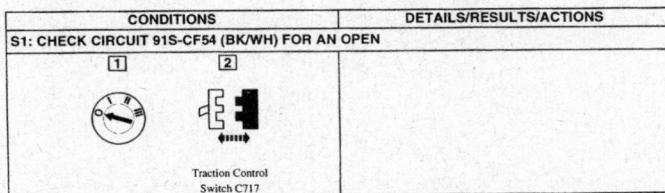

FM4020201902020X

Fig. 43 Test S: Stability Assist System Cannot Be Disabled (Part 2 of 2). 2002–04 w/Stability Assist

CONDITIONS	DETAILS/RESULTS/ACTIONS
T1: CHECK THE T/C / STABILITY ASSIST INDICATOR	
 1 2 3 Stability Assist Module C830	• Is the T/C / stability assist indicator illuminated? → **Yes** GO TO **T2** → **No** DIAGNOSE T/C indicator.
T2: CHECK PROVE OUT	
 1 2 3 Stability Assist Module C830	• Does the T/C / stability assist indicator prove out for three seconds and then turn off? → **Yes** The T/C / stability assist indicator is working correctly. TEST the system for normal operation. → **No** INSTALL a new stability assist module. TEST the system for normal operation.

FM4020201903000X

Fig. 44 Test T: Stability Assist Indicator Does Not Self Check. 2002–04 w/Stability Assist

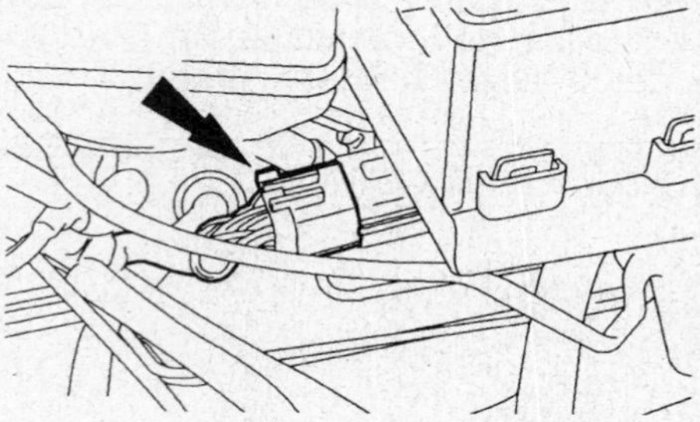

FM4020001601000X

Fig. 45 Hydraulic control unit electrical connector location

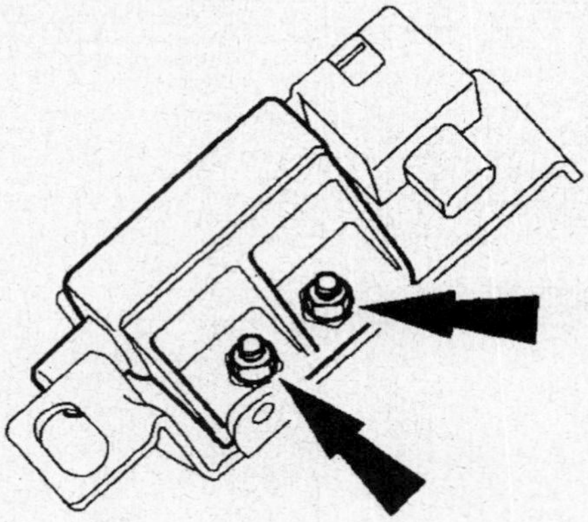

FM4020201918000X

Fig. 46 Yaw rate sensor removal

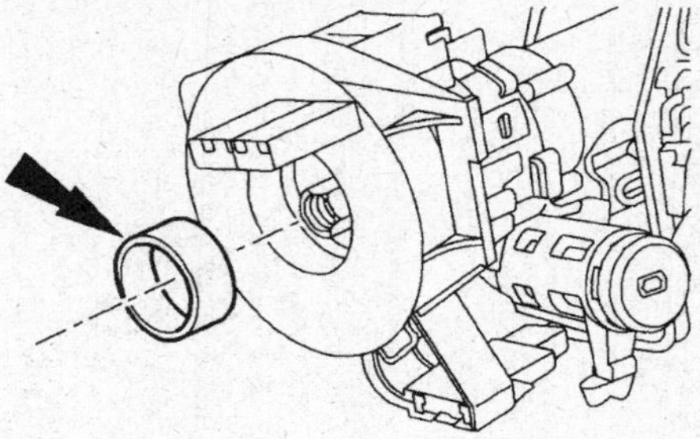
FM4020201920000X

Fig. 47 Tolerance ring removal

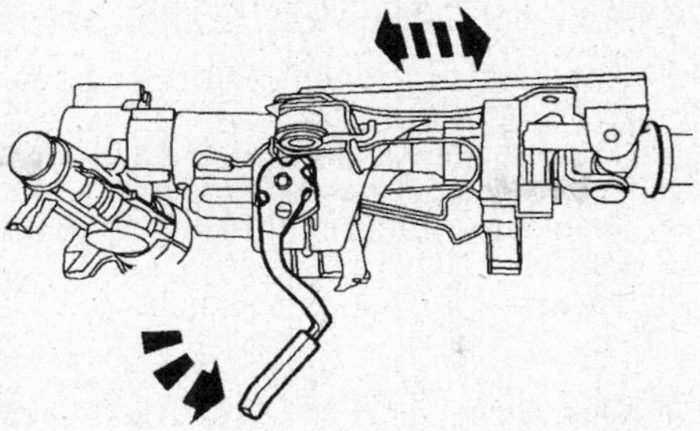
FM4020201921000X

Fig. 48 Steering column extension

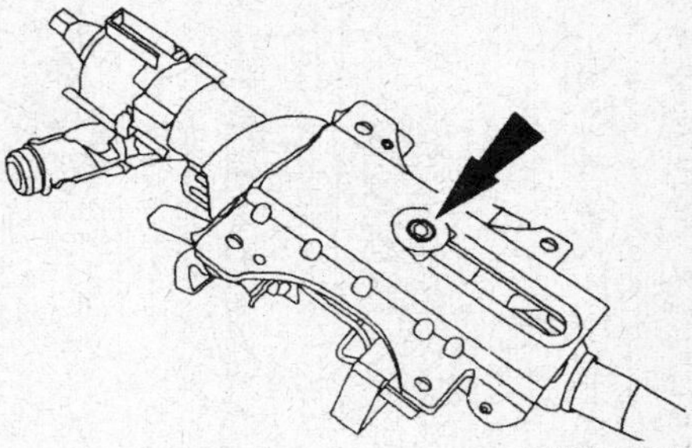
FM4020201922000X

Fig. 49 Allen bolt removal

SYSTEM SERVICE

Brake System Bleed

Refer to "Hydraulic Brake Systems" for bleed procedure.

Component Replacement

HYDRAULIC CONTROL UNIT

1. Remove reservoir cap from master cylinder.
2. Raise and support vehicle, then remove front wheels.
3. Drain fluid from brake system as follows:
   a. Loosen caliper bleeder screw.
   b. Connect a suitable hose and container to bleeder screw.
   c. Open bleeder screw, then depress brake pedal.
   d. Tighten bleeder screw, then release brake pedal.
   e. Repeat procedure for opposite caliper.
4. Lower vehicle, then remove air cleaner assembly.
5. Disconnect electrical connector, **Fig. 45.**
6. Remove underhood fuse panel attaching screws.
7. Disconnect underhood fuse panel from bracket and position aside.
8. **On models equipped with speed control,** disconnect speed control unit electrical connector and remove speed control unit.
9. **On all models,** disconnect hydraulic control unit electrical connector.
10. Remove hydraulic lines from control unit. Seal brake tube connections.
11. Disconnect brake lines from brake line clips.
12. Disconnect hydraulic lines from master cylinder.
13. Remove hydraulic control unit from bracket.
14. Disconnect electrical harness from strut tower.
15. Remove hydraulic control unit.
16. Reverse procedure to install noting the following:
    a. **Torque** control unit to bracket to 80 inch lbs.
    b. **Torque** control unit brake lines to 96 inch lbs.
    c. **Torque** master cylinder hydraulic lines to 13 ft. lbs.
    d. Bleed brake system as outlined in "Brake System Bleed."

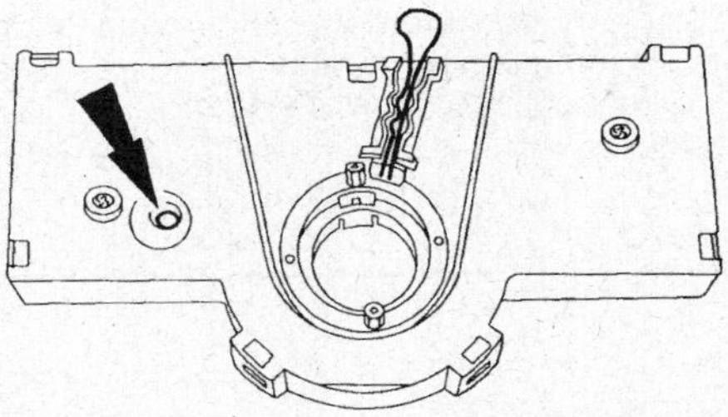
FM4020201923000X

Fig. 50 Steering wheel position sensor alignment indicator

WHEEL SPEED SENSOR

1. Raise and support vehicle.
2. Remove front wheels.
3. Remove wheel speed sensor from wheel hub or drum.
4. Disconnect speed sensor harness from retaining clips, then remove sensor.
5. Reverse procedure to install. **Torque** sensor to 72 inch lbs.

YAW RATE SENSOR

1. Remove door scuff plate trim panel, then detach carpet.
2. Detach sensor bracket, then disconnect electrical connectors.
3. Remove yaw rate sensor, **Fig. 46.**
4. Reverse procedure to install.

STEERING WHEEL ROTATION SENSOR

REMOVAL

1. Remove steering column as outlined in "Steering Columns" chapter.
2. Remove two multifunction switches by depressing retaining clips and lifting upward.
3. Remove driver's air bag module bolts, then detach retaining clips.
4. Remove driver's air bag module, then disconnect electrical connector.
5. Disconnect speed control electrical connector, then remove steering wheel bolt and steering wheel.
6. Remove tolerance ring, **Fig. 47.**
7. Secure air bag sliding contact in central position using suitable tape, then release two retaining clips and remove sliding contact.
8. Release locking lever, then fully extend steering column, **Fig. 48.**
9. Mark two halves of steering column, then remove allen bolt, **Fig. 49.**
10. Separate steering column into two halves.
11. Remove steering wheel rotation sensor clamp.
12. Remove steering wheel rotation sensor retaining screws, then the sensor.

INSTALLATION

1. **Do not install a new steering wheel position sensor if locking pin has been removed.**
2. **Before installing steering wheel position sensor, ensure alignment indicator is in correct position, Fig. 50.**
3. Install steering wheel rotation sensor. **Torque** screws to 11 inch lbs. **Do not over tighten screws.**
4. Install retaining clamp. **Torque** screws to 6 inch lbs. **Do not over tighten screws.**
5. Ensure steering column shafts are aligned correctly, then connect steering column halves.
6. **Ensure breakaway capsules are located in bracket holes. Torque** steering column bolt to 44 inch lbs. **Do not over tighten bolt.**
7. Remove steering wheel rotation locking pin.
8. Centralize air bag sliding contact as follows:
   a. Turn sliding contact counterclockwise approximately 2½ turns from central position, until a resistance is felt.
   b. Turn sliding contact clockwise 2½ turns until arrow marked on center of sliding contact aligns with raised V section at 12 o'clock position on outer cover of sliding contact, **Fig. 51.**
9. Install air bag sliding contact ensuring spacing collar is correctly located.
10. Install steering wheel. **Torque** nut to 37 ft. lbs.
11. Install driver's air bag module, then the multifunction switches.
12. Install steering column as outlined in "Steering Columns" chapter.

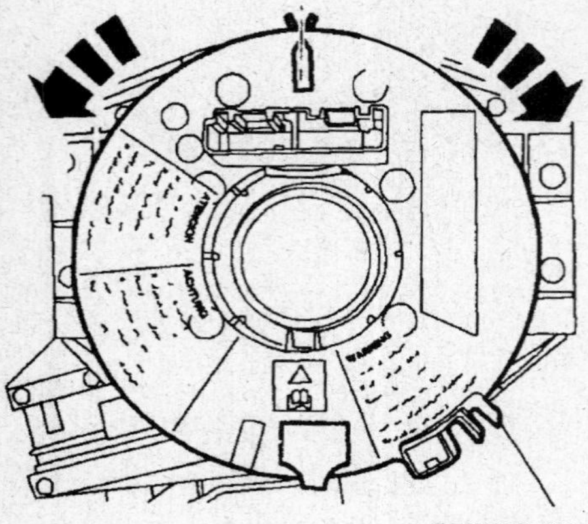

Fig. 51 Air bag sliding contact alignment

ACCELEROMETER SENSOR

1. Remove door scuff plate trim panel, then detach carpet.
2. Detach sensor bracket, then disconnect electrical connectors.
3. Remove accelerometer sensor, **Fig. 52.**
4. Reverse procedure to install.

Module Configuration

1. Connect suitable scan tool to DLC, then follow scan tool manufacturers instructions to upload module configuration.
2. Install new module.
3. Download stored configuration information to new module.
4. Inspect operation of system.

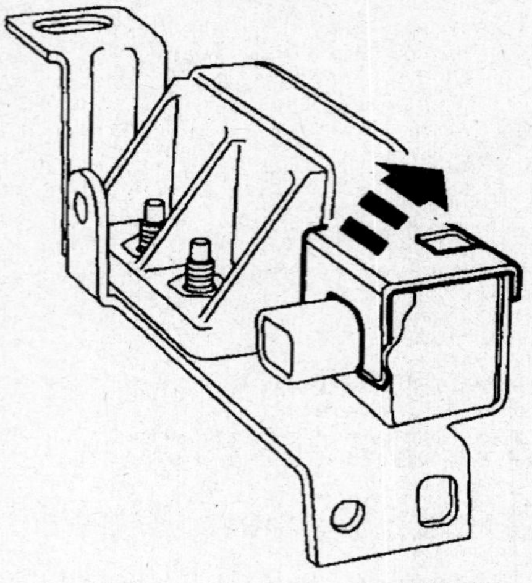

Fig. 52 Accelerometer sensor removal

ACTIVE SUSPENSION SYSTEMS

TABLE OF CONTENTS

Continental

NOTE: On Air Bag Equipped Models, Refer To "Air Bag System Precautions" Located In The Front Of This Manual For System Disarming & Arming Procedures.

NOTE: Refer To "Computer Relearn Procedures" Located In The Front Of This Manual When Battery Power To The Computer Has Been Interrupted.

NOTE: "Electrical Symbol & Wire Color Code Identification" Located In The Front Of This Manual May Be Used As An Aid When Using Wiring Circuits Found In This Section.

INDEX

PRECAUTIONS

Air Bag Systems

Refer to "Air Bag System Precautions" in the front of this manual for system disarming and arming procedures.

Battery Ground Cable

Prior to service, disconnect battery ground cable and isolate as required.

Service

When lifting the vehicle to perform service, position vehicle over hoist and turn ignition switch to OFF position. Turn air suspension switch to OFF position. The switch is located in the luggage compartment on the lefthand side. A body type hoist is the recommended method for lifting the vehicle. When the hoist is used, raise vehicle using standard support procedures. The suspension will be supported in the rebound by the front and rear struts after the vehicle is lifted. As stated previously, ensure to either disconnect battery ground cable or turning the power switch located in the luggage compartment on the lefthand side. Failure to do so may result in unexpected inflation or deflation of the air springs which may result in shifting of the vehicle during these procedures.

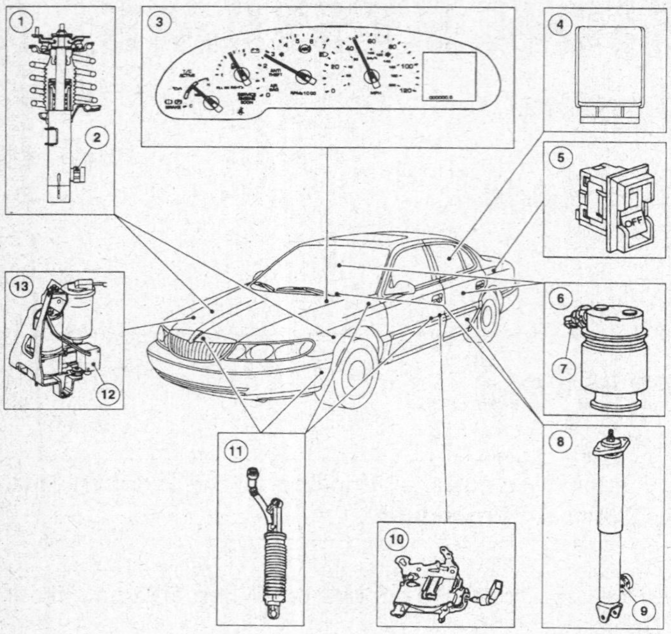

Item	Description
1	Front Spring and Shock Absorber Assembly
2	Shock Actuator (Part of 3C098)
3	Message Center Indicator

Item	Description
4	Vehicle Dynamic Module (VDM)
5	Rear Suspension Leveler Compressor Switch
6	Rear Air Spring

FM2019800374010X

Fig. 1 Rear load leveling & ride control system component locations (Part 1 of 2)

Item	Description
7	Air Spring Solenoid
8	Shock Absorber
9	Shock Actuator
10	Lamp Switch

Item	Description
11	Air Suspension Height Sensor
12	Vent Solenoid
13	Air Compressor

FM2019800374020X

Fig. 1 Rear load leveling & ride control system component locations (Part 2 of 2)

CONDITION	POSSIBLE SOURCE	ACTION
• CHECK RIDE CONTROL is Displayed in Less Than 5 Seconds After Vehicle is Started	• Control module detects an electrical concern before a leveling correction is attempted.	• CHECK vehicle dynamics module.
• CHECK RIDE CONTROL Displayed at Different Times. No Apparent Sequence of Events, Random Order	• Control module detects either an electrical concern or encounters excessive correction time while attempting to level vehicle. Can occur under widely varying conditions.	• CHECK vehicle dynamics module.
• CHECK RIDE CONTROL **Not** Displayed. Vehicle Ride Very Rough or is Very Floaty	• System inactive and cannot turn on CHECK RIDE CONTROL message. • Mechanical failure in shock absorber or strut valve that is not electrically detectable by vehicle dynamics module. • Air suspension height sensor popped off ball stud.	• retrieve DTCs. **WARNING: DO NOT ATTEMPT TO RECALIBRATE RIDE HEIGHT UNTIL THE SYSTEM PASSES ON-DEMAND SELF-TEST.** If On-Demand Self-Test and Pneumatic Test returns SYSTEM PASSED, recalibrate ride height. Refer to Ride Height procedure as outlined.
• CHECK RIDE CONTROL **Not** Displayed. One or More Corners High or Low	• System inactive and cannot turn on CHECK RIDE CONTROL message. • System operating correctly, ride height requires adjustment. • Air suspension height sensor popped off ball stud.	• retrieve DTCs. **WARNING: DO NOT ATTEMPT TO RECALIBRATE RIDE HEIGHT UNTIL THE SYSTEM PASSES ON-DEMAND SELF TEST.** If On-Demand Self Test and Pneumatic Test returns SYSTEM PASSED, recalibrate ride height. Refer to Ride Height procedure as outlined.
• One or More Corners Drop Overnight. Vehicle Achieves Trim When Ignition Switch Turned to RUN	• A large drop in temperature overnight causes the air in the air springs to contract. This will cause lowering of vehicle corners, and is normal. • A minor leak in either air springs or spring solenoid valves.	• CHECK vehicle dynamics module.
• Front Air Springs are Completely High and / or Rear Air Springs are Completely Low. CHECK RIDE CONTROL Displayed 45 to 90 Seconds After Starting Vehicle • One Front Corner is Completely Low. CHECK RIDE CONTROL Displayed 45 to 90 Seconds After Starting Vehicle • Rear Air Springs are Completely Low. CHECK RIDE CONTROL Displayed 45 to 90 Seconds After Starting Vehicle	• Air suspension height sensor is off ball stud. • Air suspension height sensor ground is open on corners that are not trim. Control module does not detect this as an electrical concern. • Wiring harness has intermittent open circuit. • Air suspension height sensor signal is open on corners that are not trim. Control module does not detect this as an electrical concern.	• CHECK vehicle dynamics module.
• One or More Corners Low and CHECK RIDE CONTROL Displayed 90 Seconds to 2 Minutes After Starting Engine	• Control module has detected compressor run time exceeded. This is caused by either: — Compressor will not operate — A large air leak in either the compressor, air springs or the air lines	• CHECK vehicle dynamics module.
• Unable to Enter Auto Test Diagnostics	• Circuits. • Multiplex Communication Network. • Vehicle Dynamics Module.	

FM2019500194010X

Fig. 2 Troubleshooting table (Part 1 of 2)

DESCRIPTION

System

This suspension system incorporates a rear load leveling system that maintains the vehicle at proper ride height under varying conditions of vehicle load. This system also has an optional road calibrated suspension ride control system that varies the damping of the shock absorbers between soft and firm, **Fig. 1.**

The rear load leveling system uses air springs to support vehicle weight. The quantity of air in the rear air spring is controlled by the Vehicle Dynamic Module (VDM). The VDM will maintain a predetermined vehicle ride height. Each air spring has an air spring solenoid to control air flow to each air spring.

The optional ride control system uses four shocks with electronically controlled actuators. The shock actuators are internally mounted on the lower bodies of the shock assemblies. The action of the shock actuators is controlled by the VDM. The VDM sends a signal to the appropriate shock actuator which switches to either soft or firm damping. The shock actuator setting is normally in a soft mode. When driving situations require, the setting is switched to a firm, high performance control mode. The shock actuators are not replaced separately, if testing indicates an actuator failure the entire shock absorber must be replaced.

Vehicle Dynamic Module (VDM)

A microprocessor controls the air suspension and ride control system. The microprocessor and its support hardware are contained in the Vehicle Dynamic Module (VDM). The VDM responds to signals from various sensors in the vehicle to maintain the desired ride height while the vehicle is either moving or stopped. The ride height is controlled by opening and closing solenoid valves and turning on the compressor through the compressor relay. It also controls the shock actuators, if equipped.

Air Compressor

A single cylinder piston type electrically operated air compressor, mounted on the righthand fender apron, supplies the required air pressure for system operation.

A regenerative type dryer is attached to the compressor manifold assembly. All air-flow during the compression or vent cycles, pass through the dryer. A vent solenoid, located on the compressor manifold, controls air exhaustion.

Air required for leveling the vehicle is distributed from the air compressor to each air spring by four nylon air lines which start at the compressor dryer and terminate at the individual air springs. The dryer is a common pressure manifold for all four air lines. The air lines are color coded to identify to which air spring they are attached. **The compressor relay, compressor vent solenoid and all air spring solenoids incorporate internal diodes for electrical noise suppression and are polarity sensitive. Care must be taken when servicing these components not to switch the battery positive and ground cables or system/component damage will result. When charging the battery, the ignition switch must be in the OFF position if the air suspension switch is in the ON position or damage to the air compressor relay or motor may occur.**

CONDITION	POSSIBLE SOURCE	ACTION
• Steering and Ride Hard At All Times	• Vehicle Dynamics Module. • Blown fuses. • Multiplex Communication Network. • Circuitry.	

FM2019500194020X

Fig. 2 Troubleshooting table (Part 2 of 2)

Air Spring & Shock Strut Assembly

The front and rear suspension system incorporate marchers type strut assemblies with integral air springs and two stage (dual) dampening mechanisms. The two stage dampening is achieved by varying the piston orifice area with an externally mounted electronic rotary actuator. The front struts are mounted to the body through a precision ball bearing and rubber mount system. The ball bearing provides a smooth and durable pivot point for the strut/wheel assembly.

The rear struts incorporate a dual path mount which separates the strut and air spring mounting surfaces to provide for maximum isolation.

Electronic Height Sensor

The electronic height sensor is a rotary style design that uses an internal hall effect device to determine ride height. These sensors will indicate conditions above trim, trim and below trim to the control module. The three sensors are located at the lefthand front, righthand front and righthand rear of the vehicle. Each one of the sensors measures the actual difference between known reference points so that the control module can respond to variations in ride height. In the parking mode, additional height positions allow the system to accurately determine if an obstruction was encountered during a parking maneuver. In the driving mode, variations in road surfaces are sensed by inspecting road wheel vertical speed and vertical travel. If the average wheel speed and travel is above a predetermined level, the shock absorbers are switched to the firm position. This reduces the chance of grounding out of the suffrage when traveling over bumpy road surfaces.

Dual Dampening System

The function of the dual dampening system is to automatically switch the shock strut settings from soft to firm when driving conditions require it. The system monitors vehicle accelerations, decelerations, up and down road wheel travel and also steering wheel position and steering wheel turning rates before responding to individual sensor inputs.

TROUBLESHOOTING

Refer to **Fig. 2**, for troubleshooting procedures. As an aid during troubleshooting procedures refer to component locations, **Fig. 1**.

DIAGNOSIS & TESTING

Accessing Diagnostic Trouble Codes

A New Generation Star (NGS) Tester, or equivalent, scan tool must be used to access Diagnostic Trouble Codes (DTCs). Connect tester to Diagnostic Link Connector (DLC) located under the lefthand side of the instrument panel, then follow tool manufacturer's instructions to access Diagnostic Trouble Codes (DTCs).

Diagnostic Procedures, Instructions & Test Modes

Diagnostic test and repair services should be performed in a set sequence to properly access all DTCs and to complete repairs without masking problems or performing redundant procedures.

The correct order of accessing DTCs are as follows:

1. Retrieve/Clear Continuous DTCs.
2. On Demand Self-Test.
3. Pneumatic Test.

If different DTCs are found in each testing sequence, faults found should be corrected in the following order.

1. On Demand Self-Test.
2. Pneumatic Test
3. Retrieve/Clear Continuous DTCs.

Code	Description
B1317	Battery Voltage High
B1318	Battery Voltage Low
B1342	ECU Internal Fault
C1722	Height Sensor Power Circuit Short To Power
C1723	Height Sensor Power Circuit Short To Ground
C1735	Lefthand Rear Corner Up Timeout
C1736	Lefthand Rear Corner Down Timeout
C1737	Righthand Rear Corner Up Timeout
C1738	Righthand Rear Corner Down Timeout
C1770	Vent Solenoid Output Circuit Failure
C1773	Vent Solenoid Output Circuit Short To Ground
C1790	Lefthand Rear Air Spring Solenoid Output Circuit Failure
C1793	Lefthand Rear Air Spring Solenoid Output Circuit Short To Ground
C1795	Righthand Rear Air Spring Solenoid Output Circuit Failure
C1798	Righthand Rear Air Spring Solenoid Output Circuit Short To Ground
C1820	Air Compressor Request Exceeded Maximum Timing
C1840	Disable Switch Circuit Failure
C1842	Disable Switch Circuit Short To Power

Fig. 3 Diagnostic Trouble Code (DTC) table (Part 1 of 2)

DTCs generated in any testing sequence except Continuous DTC mode are not stored in memory. Any DTC stored will be cleared from memory after 80 ignition key cycles from its last occurrence.

When multiple DTCs are generated that relate to the same system always start testing and repairs at the root of the system, then proceed down to the individual component.

There are five individual diagnostic test modes and one monitoring mode available to the technician as follows:

1. Retrieve/Clear Continuous DTCs.
2. On Demand Self-Test.
3. Accurate Trim Test.
4. Pneumatic Test.
5. Wiggle Test.

Select the correct sequence to best diagnose the conditions as outlined by the owner/operator.

RETRIEVE/CLEAR CONTINUOUS DTCS

This menu option is used to retrieve any DTC that may have been stored in control unit memory.

Connect tester per tool manufacturers' instructions to the DLC found under lefthand side of instrument panel, then follow tool manufactures instructions to access this menu option.

ON DEMAND SELF-TEST

This menu option is used to run a preprogrammed series of tests to the suspension electrical system. Any DTCs generated by system faults during this test will NOT be stored in control unit memory. This test series should always be run after any repairs have been performed on the suspension system.

Code	Description
C1881	Righthand Front Height Sensor Circuit Failure
C1884	Righthand Front Height Sensor Circuit Short To Ground
C1885	Righthand Rear Height Sensor Circuit Failure
C1888	Righthand Rear Height Sensor Circuit Short To Ground
C1889	Lefthand Front Height Sensor Circuit Failure
C1892	Lefthand Front Height Sensor Circuit Short To Ground
C1893	Lefthand Rear Height Sensor Circuit Failure
C1896	Lefthand Rear Height Sensor Circuit Short To Ground
C1901	Righthand Rear Shock Actuator Circuit Failure
C1904	Righthand Rear Shock Actuator Short To Ground
C1905	Lefthand Rear Shock Actuator Circuit Failure
C1908	Lefthand Rear Shock Actuator Short To Ground
C1909	Righthand Front Shock Actuator Circuit Failure
C1912	Righthand Front Shock Actuator Short To Ground
C1913	Lefthand Front Shock Actuator Circuit Failure
C1916	Lefthand Front Shock Actuator Short To Ground
C1929	Compressor Relay Circuit Failure
C1931	Compressor Relay Circuit Short To Power

Fig. 3 Diagnostic Trouble Code (DTC) table (Part 2 of 2)

Connect tester per tool manufacturers' instructions to the DLC found under left-hand side of instrument panel, then follow tool manufacturers' instructions to access this menu option.

ACCURATE TRIM TEST

This menu option is used to bring each corner of the vehicle to within plus/minus 2 mm of a predetermined height. Select this menu option when performing ride height measurements or performing wheel alignment.

DTCs will not be displayed in this mode unless it is generated by a system fault during accurate trim test operation.

Connect tester per tool manufacturers' instructions to the DLC found under left-hand side of instrument panel, then follow tool manufacturers' instructions to access this menu option.

PNEUMATIC TEST

This menu option is used to exercise and test the pneumatic components and height sensors of the suspension system. Each suspension unit is pumped then vented for five seconds, in turn, while being monitored by the vehicle control unit. If a suspension unit fails, a DTC is generated recognizing the suspected component or system. The generated DTC is NOT stored in control unit memory.

It should be noted that some compressor relay system short circuit faults and some height sensor open circuit faults may be recognized as a pneumatic system problem, proper component and circuit testing should be performed before component replacement.

Connect tester per tool manufacturers' instructions to the DLC found under left-hand side of instrument panel, then follow tool manufacturers' instructions to access this menu option.

WIGGLE TEST

This menu option is used to allow the technician to test individual components, connectors and circuits for intermittent problems. The tester monitors system signals and will emit an audible tone and increment a incidence counter when it notices a change in those signals.

Connect tester per tool manufacturers' instructions to the DLC found under left-hand side of instrument panel, then follow tool manufacturers' instructions to access this menu option.

PID/DATA MONITOR & RECORD

This menu option is used to used to monitor control unit inputs and outputs on a real-time basis. This can be useful during diagnosis as an aid to understanding why a system is acting in particular manner.

Connect tester per tool manufacturers' instructions to the DLC found under left-hand side of instrument panel, then follow tool manufacturers' instructions to access this menu option.

Active Command Modes

SEMI-ACTIVE RIDE CONTROL

This menu option is used to allow the technician to control the On (soft ride) and Off (firm ride) position of each shock absorber, allowing inspecting of shock unit condition and comparison of shock units.

This mode is also useful while diagnosing an intermittent problem in a shock unit. Turn On a shock solenoid, then by listening for solenoid clicking while moving components, connectors and harness, opens and shorts can be located.

Connect tester per tool manufacturers' instructions to the DLC found under left-hand side of instrument panel, then follow tool manufacturers' instructions to access this menu option.

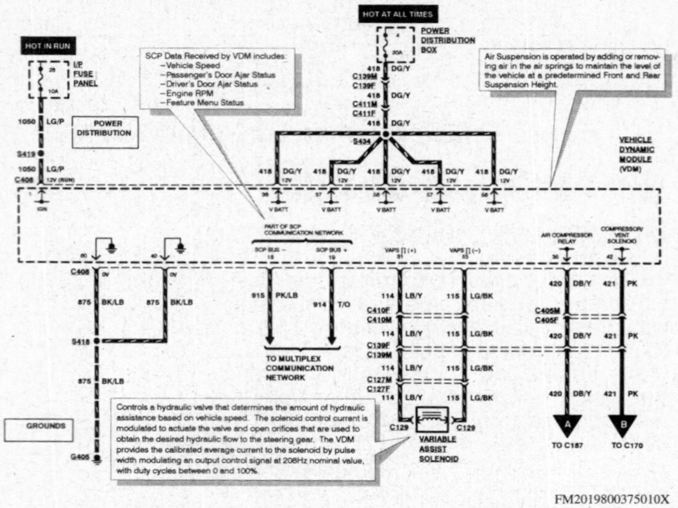

Fig. 4 Wiring diagram (Part 1 of 5). 2000–01

AIR SUSPENSION DIAGNOSTIC CONTROL

The Vent solenoid is turned On and the suspension solenoids are turned Off automatically when the compressor is turned on to reduce compressor load.

This menu option is used to allow the technician to manually control the pumping and venting of individual suspension units. This can be useful when diagnosing sticking or leaking pneumatic components.

This mode also allows technician control of the vent and air spring solenoids, the CHECK RIDE CONTROL message and the height sensor circuit power. This can be useful when diagnosing intermittent problems in these circuits.

This mode is also useful during component replacement, it allows venting of individual units to facilitate service.

Connect tester per tool manufacturers' instructions to the DLC found under left-hand side of instrument panel, then follow tool manufacturers' instructions to access this menu option.

FUNCTION TESTS

This menu option is used to allow the technician to perform Ride Height Calibration. This mode allows the technician to input new ride height calibrations into the control unit to compensate for permanent additions to or subtractions from the vehicle which would affect the ride height. This precludes the necessity of mechanical adjustment of ride height sensors.

Connect tester per tool manufacturers' instructions to the DLC found under left-hand side of instrument panel, then follow

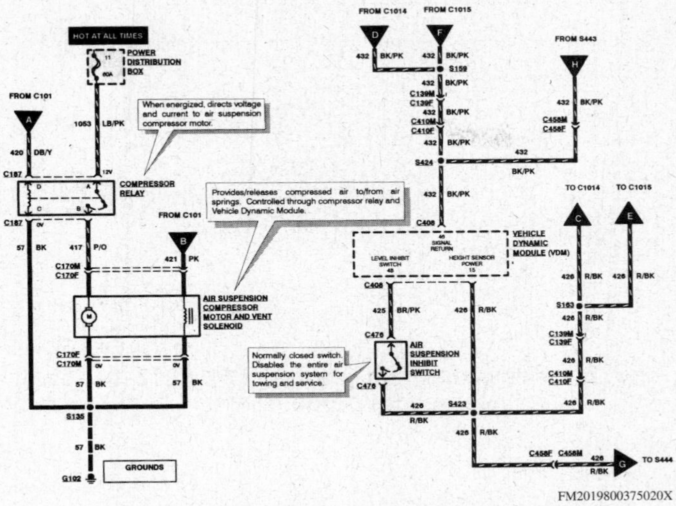

Fig. 4 Wiring diagram (Part 2 of 5). 2000–01

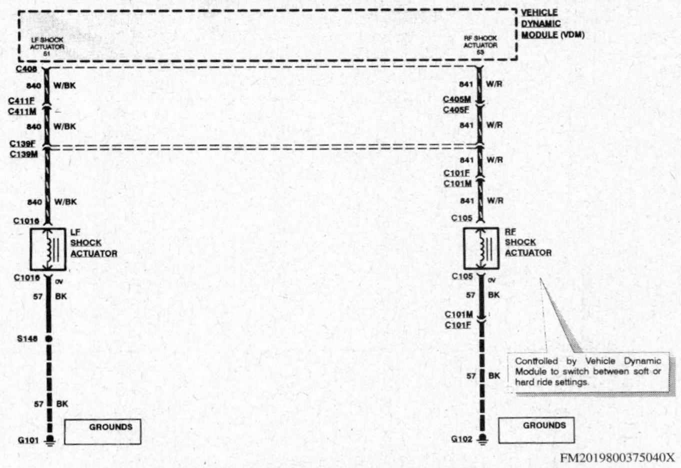

Fig. 4 Wiring diagram (Part 4 of 5). 2000–01

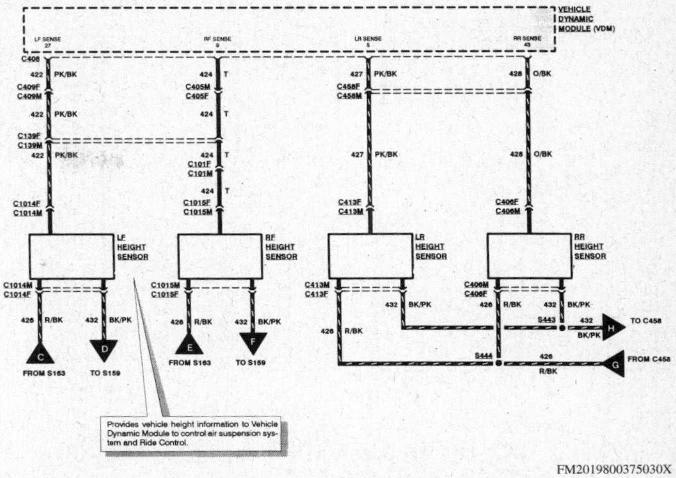

Fig. 4 Wiring diagram (Part 3 of 5). 2000–01

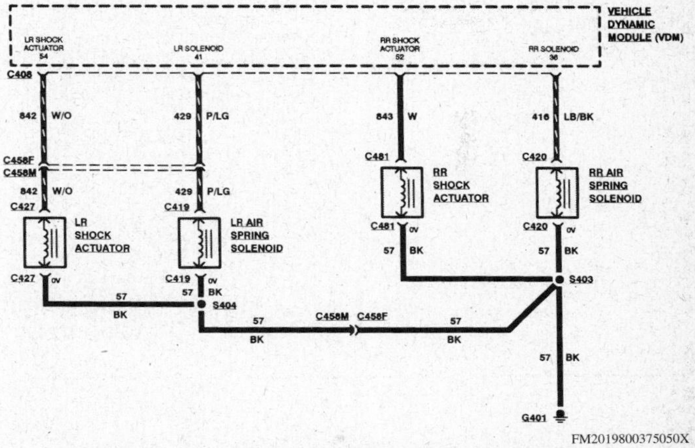

Fig. 4 Wiring diagram (Part 5 of 5). 2000–01

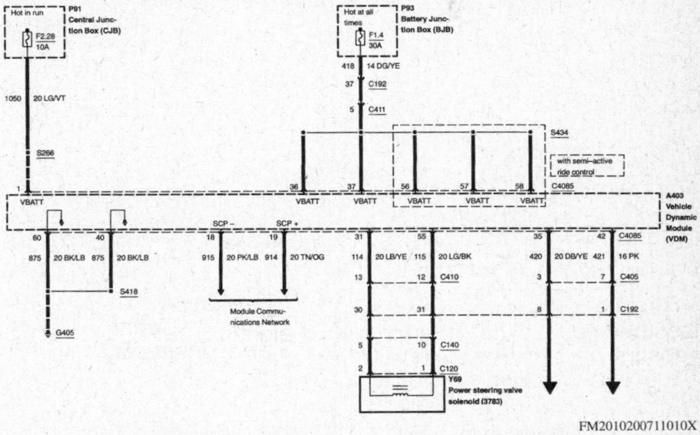

Fig. 5 Wiring diagram (Part 1 of 3). 2002–04

tool manufacturers' instructions to access this menu option.

Diagnostic Trouble Code Interpretation

Refer to **Fig. 3,** for diagnostic trouble code interpretation.

Wiring Diagrams

Refer to **Figs. 4 and 5,** for wiring diagrams.

Pinpoint Tests

2000–01

Refer to **Figs. 6 through 26,** for pinpoint tests.

2002–04

Refer to **Figs. 27 through 48,** for pinpoint tests.

Clearing Diagnostic Trouble Codes

Connect New Generation Star (NGS) tester or equivalent, to Diagnostic Link Connector (DLC) found under lefthand side of instrument panel. Select **Retrieve/Clear Continuous Diagnostic Trouble Codes** from menu. Follow tester instructions to clear codes.

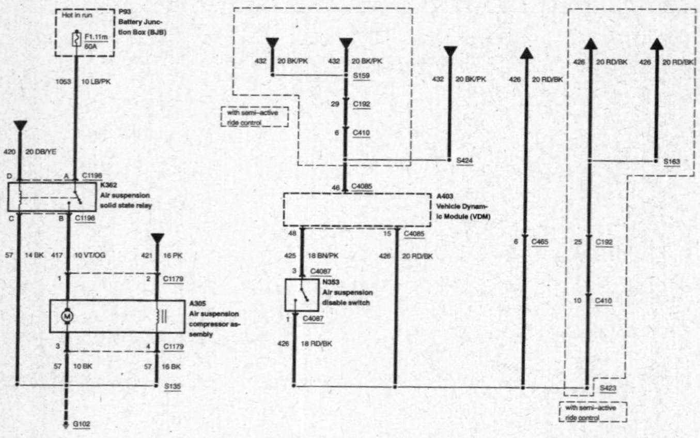

FM2010200711020X

Fig. 5 Wiring diagram (Part 2 of 3). 2002–04

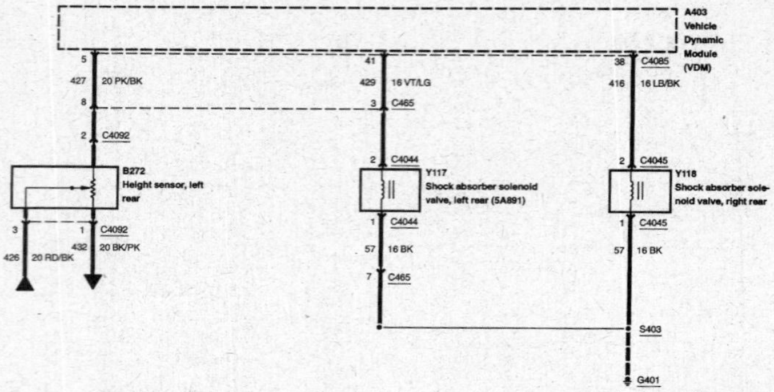

FM2010200711030X

Fig. 5 Wiring diagram (Part 3 of 3). 2002–04 less semi-active ride control

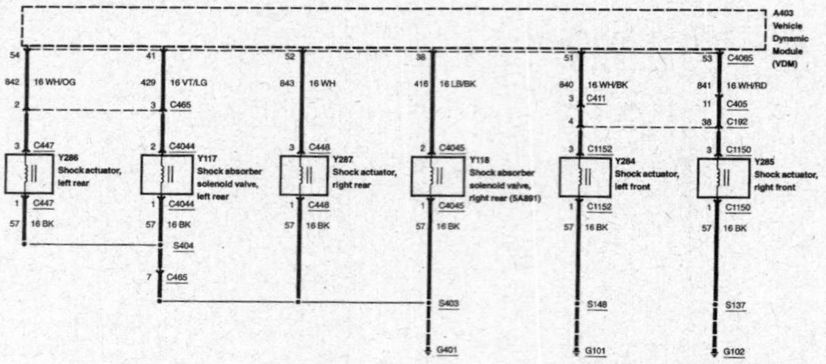

FM2010200711040X

Fig. 5 Wiring diagram (Part 3 of 3). 2002–04 w/semi-active ride control

DIAGNOSTIC CHART INDEX

Pinpoint Test	Code	Description	Page No.	Fig. No.
2000–01				
A	B1317	Battery Voltage High	7-9	6
B	B1318	Battery Voltage Low	7-9	7
C	B1342	ECU Internal Fault	7-9	8
D	C1722	Height Sensor Power Circuit Short To Power	7-10	9
	C1842	Disable Switch Circuit Short To Power	7-10	9
E	C1723	Height Sensor Power Circuit Short To Ground	7-11	10
	C1840	Disable Switch Circuit Failure	7-11	10
F	C1735	Lefthand Rear Corner Up Timeout	7-12	11
	C1737	Righthand Rear Corner Up Timeout	7-12	11
G	C1736	Lefthand Rear Corner Down Timeout	7-13	12
	C1738	Righthand Rear Corner Down Timeout	7-13	12
H	C1770	Vent Solenoid Output Circuit Failure	7-14	13
J	C1773	Vent Solenoid Output Circuit Short To Ground	7-14	14
K	C1790	Lefthand Rear Air Spring Solenoid Output Circuit Failure	7-15	15
	C1795	Righthand Rear Air Spring Solenoid Output Circuit Failure	7-15	15
L	C1793	Lefthand Rear Air Spring Solenoid Output Circuit Short To Ground	7-16	16
	C1798	Righthand Rear Air Spring Solenoid Output Circuit Short To Ground	7-16	16
M	C1820	Air Compressor Request Exceeded Maximum Timing	7-16	17
N	C1881	Righthand Front Height Sensor Circuit Failure	7-17	18
	C1885	Righthand Rear Height Sensor Circuit Failure	7-17	18
	C1889	Lefthand Front Height Sensor Circuit Failure	7-17	18
	C1893	Lefthand Rear Height Sensor Circuit Failure	7-17	18
P	C1884	Righthand Front Height Sensor Circuit Short To Ground	7-19	19
	C1888	Righthand Rear Height Sensor Circuit Short To Ground	7-19	19
	C1892	Lefthand Front Height Sensor Circuit Short To Ground	7-19	19
	C1896	Lefthand Rear Height Sensor Circuit Short To Ground	7-19	19
Q	C1901	Righthand Rear Shock Actuator Circuit Failure	7-20	20
	C1905	Lefthand Rear Shock Actuator Circuit Failure	7-20	20
	C1909	Righthand Front Shock Actuator Circuit Failure	7-20	20
	C1913	Lefthand Front Shock Actuator Circuit Failure	7-20	20
R	C1904	Righthand Rear Shock Actuator Short To Ground	7-21	21
	C1908	Lefthand Rear Shock Actuator Short To Ground	7-21	21
	C1912	Righthand Front Shock Actuator Short To Ground	7-21	21
	C1916	Lefthand Front Shock Actuator Short To Ground	7-21	21
S	C1929	Compressor Relay Circuit Failure	7-21	22
T	C1931	Compressor Relay Circuit Short To Power	7-22	23
U	—	Compressor Is Inoperative	7-22	24
V	—	One Or More Corners Low & Compressor Operates	7-23	25
W	—	No Communication w/Vehicle Dynamic Module	7-24	26
2002–04				
A	—	No Communication w/Module	7-24	27
B	—	Unable To Enter Self-Test Diagnostics	7-25	28
C	B1317	Battery Voltage High	7-25	29
D	B1318	Battery Voltage Low	7-25	30
E	B1342	ECU Internal Fault	7-26	31
F	C1722	Height Sensor Power Circuit Short To Power	7-26	32
	C1842	Disable Switch Circuit Short To Power	7-26	32
G	C1723	Height Sensor Power Circuit Short To Ground	7-27	33
	C1840	Disable Switch Circuit Failure	7-27	33
H	C1735	Lefthand Rear Corner Up Timeout	7-28	34
	C1737	Righthand Rear Corner Up Timeout	7-28	34
I	C1736	Lefthand Rear Corner Down Timeout	7-29	35
	C1738	Righthand Rear Corner Down Timeout	7-29	35
J	C1770	Vent Solenoid Output Circuit Failure	7-30	36

Continued

DIAGNOSTIC CHART INDEX—Continued

Pinpoint Test	Code	Description	Page No.	Fig. No.
2002–04				
K	C1773	Vent Solenoid Output Circuit Short To Ground	7-30	37
L	C1790	Lefthand Rear Air Spring Solenoid Output Circuit Failure	7-31	38
	C1795	Righthand Rear Air Spring Solenoid Output Circuit Failure	7-31	38
M	C1793	Lefthand Rear Air Spring Solenoid Output Circuit Short To Ground	7-32	39
	C1798	Righthand Rear Air Spring Solenoid Output Circuit Short To Ground	7-32	39
N	C1820	Air Compressor Request Exceeded Maximum Timing	7-32	40
O	C1881	Righthand Front Height Sensor Circuit Failure	7-33	41
	C1885	Righthand Rear Height Sensor Circuit Failure	7-33	41
	C1889	Lefthand Front Height Sensor Circuit Failure	7-33	41
	C1893	Lefthand Rear Height Sensor Circuit Failure	7-33	41
P	C1884	Righthand Front Height Sensor Circuit Short To Ground	7-34	42
	C1888	Righthand Rear Height Sensor Circuit Short To Ground	7-34	42
	C1892	Lefthand Front Height Sensor Circuit Short To Ground	7-34	42
	C1896	Lefthand Rear Height Sensor Circuit Short To Ground	7-34	42
Q	C1901	Righthand Rear Shock Actuator Circuit Failure	7-36	43
	C1905	Lefthand Rear Shock Actuator Circuit Failure	7-36	43
	C1909	Righthand Front Shock Actuator Circuit Failure	7-36	43
	C1913	Lefthand Front Shock Actuator Circuit Failure	7-36	43
R	C1904	Righthand Rear Shock Actuator Short To Ground	7-37	44
	C1908	Lefthand Rear Shock Actuator Short To Ground	7-37	44
	C1912	Righthand Front Shock Actuator Short To Ground	7-37	44
	C1916	Lefthand Front Shock Actuator Short To Ground	7-37	44
S	C1929	Compressor Relay Circuit Failure	7-37	45
T	C1931	Compressor Relay Circuit Short To Power	7-38	46
U	—	Compressor Inoperative	7-38	47
V	—	System Inoperative, One Or Corners Low, Compressor Operates	7-39	48

TEST CONDITIONS	TEST DETAILS/RESULTS/ACTIONS
A1 CHECK BATTERY FOR HIGH VOLTAGE	
1 	
	2 Verify that lights, radio and all accessories are off.

FM2019800376010X

Fig. 6 Test A/Code B1317: Battery Voltage High (Part 1 of 2). 2000–01

TEST CONDITIONS	TEST DETAILS/RESULTS/ACTIONS
A1 CHECK BATTERY FOR HIGH VOLTAGE	
3 	3 Measure the voltage between battery terminals. • Is the voltage greater than 14.5 volts? → **Yes** REPAIR the charging system. → **No** If DTC B1317 is a continuous DTC and is not encountered during Self-Test, CLEAR the DTCs and TEST the system for normal operation. If DTC 1317 is a Self-Test DTC, REPLACE the VDM PERFORM Ride Height Adjustments. TEST the system for normal operation.

FM2019800376020X

Fig. 6 Test A/Code B1317: Battery Voltage High (Part 2 of 2). 2000–01

TEST CONDITIONS	TEST DETAILS/RESULTS/ACTIONS
B1 CHECK BATTERY FOR LOW VOLTAGE	
1 	
	2 Verify that lights, radio and all accessories are off.
3 	3 Measure the voltage between battery terminals. • Is the voltage greater than 12.5 volts? → **Yes** GO to **B2**. → **No** REPAIR the charging system.

FM2019800377010X

Fig. 7 Test B/Code B1318: Battery Voltage Low (Part 1 of 3). 2000–01

TEST CONDITIONS	TEST DETAILS/RESULTS/ACTIONS
B2 CHECK VOLTAGE AT VEHICLE DYNAMIC MODULE (VDM)	
1  2 	
	3 Connect the EEC-IV 60-Pin Breakout Box to VDM C408. Do not connect the VDM.
4 	
	5 Verify that lights, radio and all accessories are off.
6 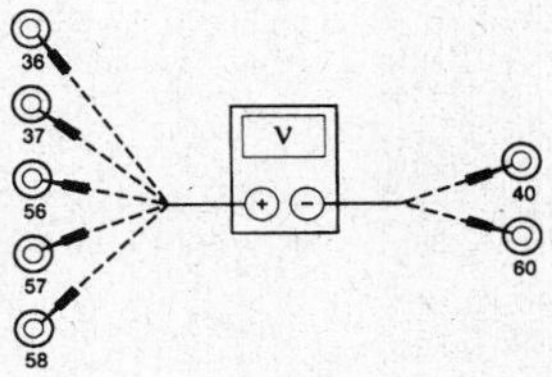	6 Measure the voltage between EEC-IV 60-Pin Breakout Box pins as follows:

EEC-IV 60-Pin Breakout Box Pin, Circuit	EEC-IV 60-Pin Breakout Box Pin, Circuit
36, circuit 418 (DG/Y)	40, circuit 875 (BK/LB)
37, circuit 418 (DG/Y)	40, circuit 875 (BK/LB)
56, circuit 418 (DG/Y)	60, circuit 875 (BK/LB)
57, circuit 418 (DG/Y)	60, circuit 875 (BK/LB)
58, circuit 418 (DG/Y)	60, circuit 875 (BK/LB)

FM2019800377020X

Fig. 7 Test B/Code B1318: Battery Voltage Low (Part 2 of 3). 2000–01

TEST CONDITIONS	TEST DETAILS/RESULTS/ACTIONS
B2 CHECK VOLTAGE AT VEHICLE DYNAMIC MODULE (VDM)	
	• Is voltage greater than 10 volts? → **Yes** If DTC B1318 is a continuous DTC and is not encountered during Self-Test, CLEAR DTCs and TEST the system for normal operation. If DTC 1318 is a Self-Test DTC, REPLACE the VDM. PERFORM Ride Height Adjustments. TEST the system for normal operation. → **No** GO to **B3**.
B3 CHECK VDM GROUND CIRCUITS	
1 	
2 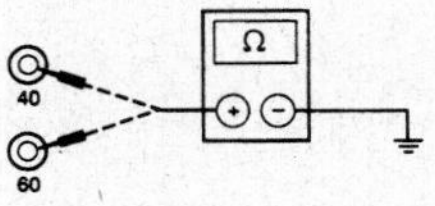	2 Measure the resistance between the following EEC-IV 60-Pin Breakout Box test pins, and ground. — 40, circuit 875 (BK/LB) — 60, circuit 875 (BK/LB) • Are the resistances less than 5 ohms? → **Yes** CHECK circuit 418 (DG/Y) for open. REPAIR as necessary. TEST the system for normal operation. → **No** REPAIR circuit 875 (BK/LB). CLEAR the DTCs. TEST the system for normal operation.

FM2019800377030X

Fig. 7 Test B/Code B1318: Battery Voltage Low (Part 3 of 3). 2000–01

TEST CONDITIONS	TEST DETAILS/RESULTS/ACTIONS
C1 CHECK FOR CONTINUOUS DTCS	
1 	1 Retrieve and document continuous DTCs. • Is DTC B1342 present? → **Yes** REPLACE the VDM. PERFORM Ride Height Adjustments TEST the system for normal operation. → **No** The system is operating normally.

FM2019800378000X

Fig. 8 Test C/Code B1342: ECU Internal Fault. 2000–01

TEST CONDITIONS	TEST DETAILS/RESULTS/ACTIONS
D1 CHECK HEIGHT SENSOR CONNECTORS	
1 	2 DISCONNECT height sensor C413, and if equipped, C406, C1014, and C1015. 3 Check the height sensor connectors for corrosion, bent pins and damaged wires. • Are the height sensor connectors worn or damaged? → **Yes** REPAIR or REPLACE as necessary. CLEAR the DTCs. TEST the system for normal operation. → **No** RECONNECT height sensor(s). GO to **D2**.

FM2019800379010X

Fig. 9 Test D/Codes C1722 & C1842: Height Sensor Power Circuit Short To Power & Disable Switch Circuit Short To Power (Part 1 of 5). 2000–01

TEST CONDITIONS	TEST DETAILS/RESULTS/ACTIONS
D4 CHECK CIRCUIT 425 (BR/PK) FOR SHORT TO POWER	
2  3 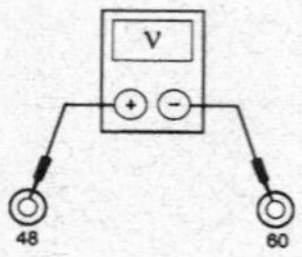	3 Measure the voltage between EEC-IV 60-Pin Breakout Box pin 48, circuit 425 (BR/PK), and EEC-IV 60-Pin Breakout Box pin 60, circuit 875 (BK/LB). • Is voltage present? → **Yes** REPAIR circuit 425 (BR/PK). CLEAR the DTCs. TEST the system for normal operation. → **No** GO to **D5**.
D5 CHECK CIRCUIT 426 (R/BK) FOR SHORT TO POWER	
1 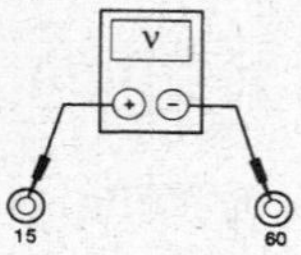	1 Measure the voltage between EEC-IV 60-Pin Breakout Box pin 15, circuit 426 (R/BK), and EEC-IV 60-Pin Breakout Box pin 60, circuit 875 (BK/LB). • Is voltage present? → **Yes** REPAIR circuit 426 (R/BK). CLEAR all DTCs. TEST the system for normal operation. → **No** RECONNECT air suspension switch C476.GO to **D6**.
D6 CHECK VOLTAGE BETWEEN CIRCUIT 426 (R/BK) AND CIRCUIT 432 (BK/PK)	
1 	2 Connect EEC-IV 60-Pin Breakout Box to the VDM.

FM2019800379030X

Fig. 9 Test D/Codes C1722 & C1842: Height Sensor Power Circuit Short To Power & Disable Switch Circuit Short To Power (Part 3 of 5). 2000–01

TEST CONDITIONS	TEST DETAILS/RESULTS/ACTIONS
D2 CHECK AIR SUSPENSION SWITCH CONNECTOR	
1  Air Suspension Switch C476	2 Check air suspension switch C476 for corrosion, bent pins and damaged wires. • Is the air suspension switch C476 worn or damaged? → **Yes** REPAIR or REPLACE as necessary. CLEAR the DTCs. TEST the system for normal operation. → **No** GO to **D3**.
D3 CHECK VEHICLE DYNAMIC MODULE (VDM) CONNECTOR	
1  VDM C408	2 Check VDM C408 for corrosion, bent pins and damaged wires. • Is the VDM C408 worn or damaged? → **Yes** REPAIR or REPLACE as necessary. CLEAR the DTCs. TEST the system for normal operation. → **No** GO to **D4**.
D4 CHECK CIRCUIT 425 (BR/PK) FOR SHORT TO POWER	
	1 Connect EEC-IV 60-Pin Breakout Box to VDM C408.

FM2019800379020X

Fig. 9 Test D/Codes C1722 & C1842: Height Sensor Power Circuit Short To Power & Disable Switch Circuit Short To Power (Part 2 of 5). 2000–01

TEST CONDITIONS	TEST DETAILS/RESULTS/ACTIONS
D6 CHECK VOLTAGE BETWEEN CIRCUIT 426 (R/BK) AND CIRCUIT 432 (BK/PK)	
3 	3 Verify that the air suspension switch is in the ON position.
4  NGS 5 	5 Trigger VDM active command HGT POWER ON.
6 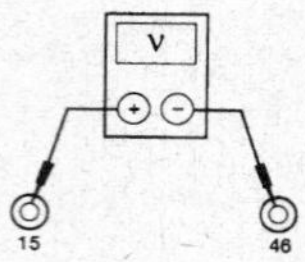	6 Measure the voltage between EEC-IV 60-Pin Breakout Box pin 15, circuit 426 (R/BK), and EEC-IV 60-Pin Breakout Box pin 46, circuit 432 (BK/PK). • Is the voltage between 4.8 volts and 5.2 volts? → **Yes** GO to **D7**. → **No** REPLACE the VDM. PERFORM Ride Height Adjustments. TEST the system for normal operation.

FM2019800379040X

Fig. 9 Test D/Codes C1722 & C1842: Height Sensor Power Circuit Short To Power & Disable Switch Circuit Short To Power (Part 4 of 5). 2000–01

TEST CONDITIONS	TEST DETAILS/RESULTS/ACTIONS
D7 CHECK HEIGHT SENSORS	
1 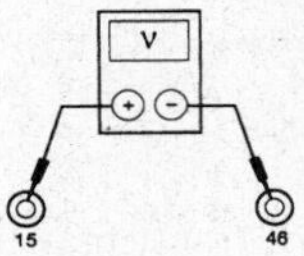	1 Measure the voltage between EEC-IV 60-Pin Breakout Box pin 15, circuit 426 (R/BK), and EEC-IV 60-Pin Breakout Box pin 46, circuit 432 (BK/PK) as each height sensor is reconnected. • Is the voltage between 4.8 volts and 5.2 volts after each height sensor is reconnected? → **Yes** PERFORM the Wiggle Test. REPAIR as necessary. CLEAR the DTCs. TEST the system for normal operation. → **No** REPLACE the suspect height sensor. CLEAR the DTCs. PERFORM Ride Height Adjustments. TEST the system for normal operation.

FM2019800379050X

Fig. 9 Test D/Codes C1722 & C1842: Height Sensor Power Circuit Short To Power & Disable Switch Circuit Short To Power (Part 5 of 5). 2000–01

TEST CONDITIONS	TEST DETAILS/RESULTS/ACTIONS
E1 CHECK HEIGHT SENSOR CONNECTORS	
1 	2 Disconnect height sensor C413, and if equipped, C406, C1014, and C1015. 3 Check the height sensor connectors for corrosion, bent pins and damaged wires. • Are the height sensor connectors worn or damaged? → **Yes** REPAIR or REPLACE as necessary. CLEAR the DTCs. TEST the system for normal operation. → **No** RECONNECT height sensor(s). GO to **E2**.

FM2019800380010X

Fig. 10 Test E/Codes C1723 & C1840: Height Sensor Power Circuit Short To Ground & Disable Switch Circuit Failure (Part 1 of 5). 2000–01

TEST CONDITIONS	TEST DETAILS/RESULTS/ACTIONS
E2 CHECK AIR SUSPENSION SWITCH CONNECTOR	
1 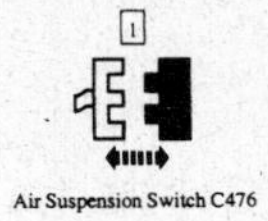	2 Check air suspension switch C476 for corrosion, bent pins and damaged wires. • Is the air suspension switch C476 worn or damaged? → **Yes** REPAIR or REPLACE as necessary. CLEAR the DTCs. TEST the system for normal operation. → **No** GO to **E3**.
E3 CHECK VEHICLE DYNAMIC MODULE (VDM) CONNECTOR	
1 	2 Check VDM C408 for corrosion, bent pins and damaged wires. • Is the VDM C408 worn or damaged? → **Yes** REPAIR or REPLACE as necessary. CLEAR the DTCs. TEST the system for normal operation. → **No** GO to **E4**.

FM2019800380020X

Fig. 10 Test E/Codes C1723 & C1840: Height Sensor Power Circuit Short To Ground & Disable Switch Circuit Failure (Part 2 of 5). 2000–01

TEST CONDITIONS	TEST DETAILS/RESULTS/ACTIONS
E4 CHECK AIR SUSPENSION SWITCH	
1 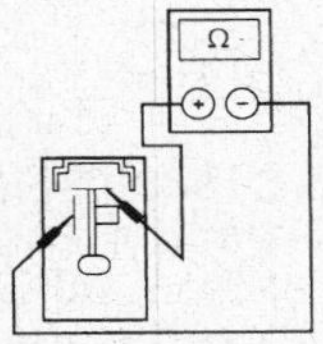	1 Measure the resistance between air suspension switch terminals with the switch ON and then OFF. • Is the resistance with the air suspension switch ON less than 5 ohms and with the air suspension switch OFF greater than 10,000 ohms? → **Yes** GO to **E5**. → **No** REPLACE the air suspension switch. CLEAR the DTCs. TEST the system for normal operation.
E5 CHECK CIRCUIT 425 (BR/PK)	
2 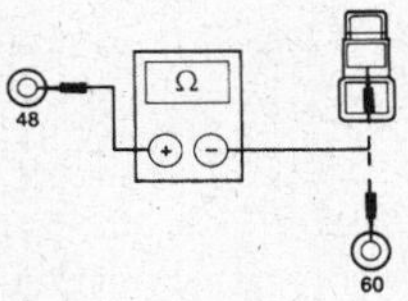	1 Connect EEC-IV 60-Pin Breakout Box to VDM C408. 2 Measure the resistance between EEC-IV 60-Pin Breakout Box pin 48, circuit 425 (BR/PK), and air suspension switch C476, circuit 425 (BR/PK); and between EEC-IV 60-Pin Breakout Box pin 48, circuit 425 (BR/PK), and EEC-IV 60-Pin Breakout Box pin 60, circuit 875 (BK/LB). • Is the resistance less than 5 ohms between EEC-IV 60-Pin Breakout Box and switch, and greater than 10,000 ohms between EEC-IV 60-Pin Breakout Box pins? → **Yes** GO to **E6**. → **No** REPAIR circuit 425 (BR/PK). CLEAR the DTCs. TEST the system for normal operation.

FM2019800380030X

Fig. 10 Test E/Codes C1723 & C1840: Height Sensor Power Circuit Short To Ground & Disable Switch Circuit Failure (Part 3 of 5). 2000–01

TEST CONDITIONS	TEST DETAILS/RESULTS/ACTIONS
E6 CHECK CIRCUIT 426 (R/BK)	
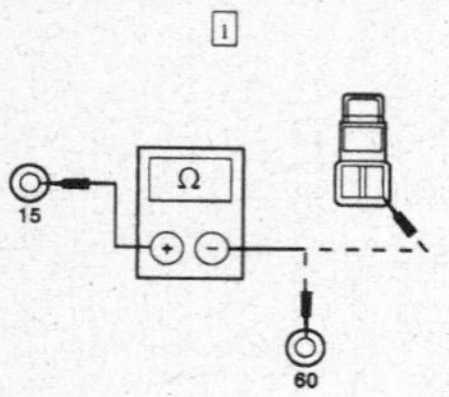	1 Measure the resistance between EEC-IV 60-Pin Breakout Box pin 15, circuit 426 (R/BK), and air suspension switch C476, circuit 426 (R/BK); and between EEC-IV 60-Pin Breakout Box pin 15, circuit 426 (R/BK), and EEC-IV 60-Pin Breakout Box pin 60, circuit 875 (BK/LB). • Is the resistance less than 5 ohms between EEC-IV 60-Pin Breakout Box and air suspension switch; and greater than 10,000 ohms between EEC-IV 60-Pin Breakout Box pins? → **Yes** GO to **E7**. → **No** REPAIR circuit 426 (R/BK). CLEAR the DTCs. TEST the system for normal operation.
E7 CHECK VOLTAGE BETWEEN CIRCUIT 426 (R/BK) AND CIRCUIT 432 (BK/PK)	
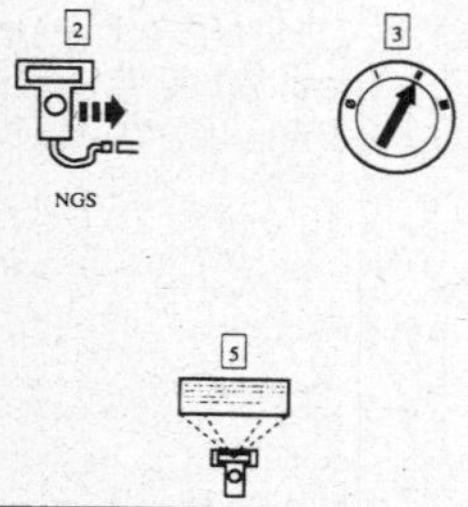	1 Connect EEC-IV 60-Pin Breakout Box to the VDM. 4 Trigger VDM active command HGT POWER ON.

FM2019800380040X

Fig. 10 Test E/Codes C1723 & C1840: Height Sensor Power Circuit Short To Ground & Disable Switch Circuit Failure (Part 4 of 5). 2000–01

TEST CONDITIONS	TEST DETAILS/RESULTS/ACTIONS
E7 CHECK VOLTAGE BETWEEN CIRCUIT 426 (R/BK) AND CIRCUIT 432 (BK/PK)	
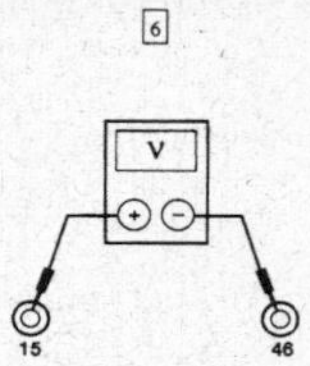	6 Measure the voltage between EEC-IV 60-Pin Breakout Box pin 15, circuit 426 (R/BK), and EEC-IV 60-Pin Breakout Box pin 46, circuit 432 (BK/PK). • Is the voltage between 4.8 volts and 5.2 volts? → **Yes** GO to **E8**. → **No** REPLACE the VDM. CLEAR the DTCs. PERFORM Ride Height Adjustments. TEST the system for normal operation.
E8 CHECK HEIGHT SENSORS	
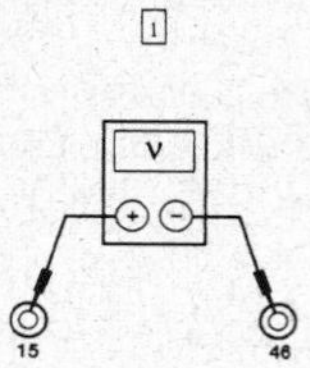	1 Measure the voltage between EEC-IV 60-Pin Breakout Box pin 15, circuit 426 (R/BK), and EEC-IV 60-Pin Breakout Box pin 46, circuit 432 (BK/PK) as each height sensor is reconnected. • Is the voltage between 4.8 volts and 5.2 volts after each height sensor is reconnected? → **Yes** REPLACE the VDM. → **No** REPLACE the suspect height sensor. CLEAR the DTCs. PERFORM Ride Height Adjustments. TEST the system for normal operation.

FM2019800380050X

Fig. 10 Test E/Codes C1723 & C1840: Height Sensor Power Circuit Short To Ground & Disable Switch Circuit Failure (Part 5 of 5). 2000–01

TEST CONDITIONS	TEST DETAILS/RESULTS/ACTIONS
F1 CHECK FOR AIR COMPRESSOR ASSEMBLY OPERATION	
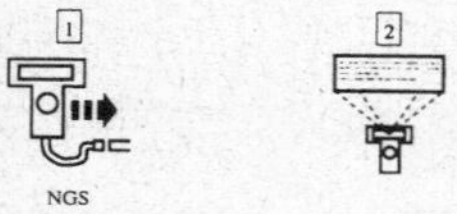	2 Trigger VDM active command COMPRESSR ON then OFF • Does the air compressor turn on and off? → **Yes** GO to **F2**. → **No** GO to Pinpoint Test U.
F2 CHECK FOR AIR SPRING SOLENOID FUNCTION	
	1 Trigger VDM active commands RR SOL or LR SOL, and COMPRESSR ON. • Does a corner raise? → **Yes** TRIGGER VDM active commands RR SOL or LR SOL, and COMPRESSR OFF. GO to **F3**. → **No** TRIGGER VDM active commands RR SOL or LR SOL, and COMPRESSR OFF. GO to Pinpoint Test V.

FM2019800381010X

Fig. 11 Test F/Code C1735 & C1737: Lefthand/Righthand Rear Corner Up Timeout (Part 1 of 3). 2000–01

TEST CONDITIONS	TEST DETAILS/RESULTS/ACTIONS
F3 CHECK HEIGHT SENSOR MOUNTING POINTS	
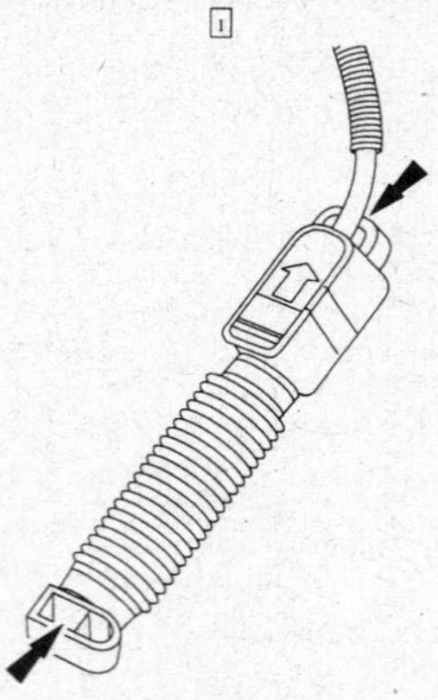	1 Check the height sensor mounting points. • Are the mounting points damaged or are the height sensors disconnected from the ball studs? → **Yes** REPAIR, REPLACE, or REATTACH as necessary. CLEAR the DTCs. PERFORM Ride Height Adjustments. TEST the system for normal operation. → **No** GO to **F4**.
F4 CHECK FOR HEIGHT SENSOR OPERATION	
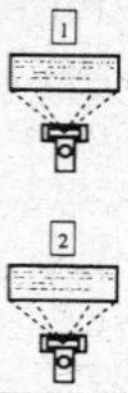	1 Trigger VDM active command HGT POWER ON. 2 Monitor VDM PID LR__HGT or RR__HGT.

FM2019800381020X

Fig. 11 Test F/Codes C1735 & C1737: Lefthand/Righthand Rear Corner Up Timeout (Part 2 of 3). 2000–01

TEST CONDITIONS	TEST DETAILS/RESULTS/ACTIONS
F4 CHECK FOR HEIGHT SENSOR OPERATION	
3 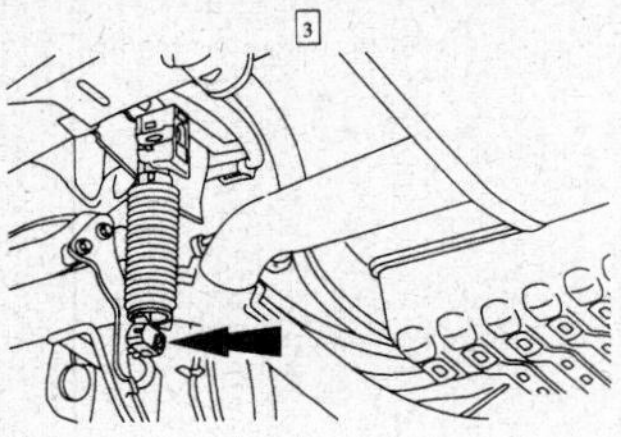	3 Disconnect the selected height sensor from the lower ball stud.
	4 Extend and compress the selected height sensor over its full range of travel. • Does the displayed length for the selected height sensor vary as the length of the height sensor changes? → **Yes** TRIGGER VDM active command HGT POWER OFF. RECONNECT height sensor(s). PERFORM the Accurate Trim Test. CLEAR the DTCs. TEST the system for normal operation. → **No** TRIGGER VDM active command HGT POWER OFF. RECONNECT height sensor(s). GO to Pinpoint Test N.

FM2019800381030X

Fig. 11 Test F/Codes C1735 & C1737: Lefthand/Righthand Rear Corner Up Timeout (Part 3 of 3). 2000–01

TEST CONDITIONS	TEST DETAILS/RESULTS/ACTIONS
G3 CHECK FOR HEIGHT SENSOR OPERATION	
1 	1 Trigger VDM active command HGT POWER ON.
2 	2 Monitor VDM PID LR__HGT or RR__HGT.
3 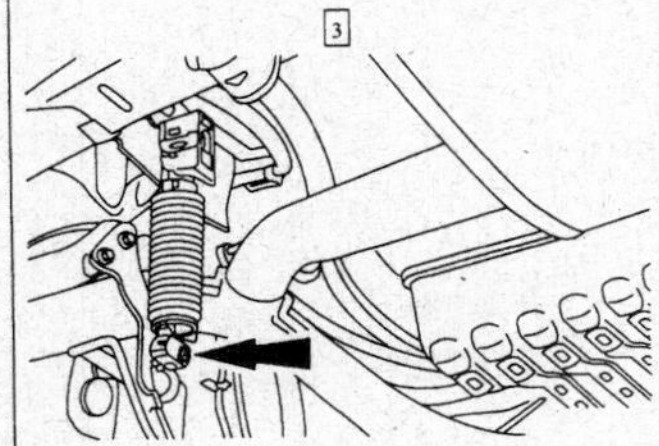	3 Disconnect the selected height sensor from the lower ball stud.
	4 Extend and compress the selected height sensor over its full range of travel. • Does the displayed voltage for the selected height sensor vary as the length of the height sensor changes? → **Yes** REPLACE the VDM. PERFORM Ride Height Adjustment. TEST the system for normal operation. → **No** RECONNECT height sensor(s). GO to Pinpoint Test N.

FM2019800382020X

Fig. 12 Test G/Codes C1736 & C1738: Lefthand/Righthand Rear Corner Down Timeout (Part 2 of 3). 2000–01

TEST CONDITIONS	TEST DETAILS/RESULTS/ACTIONS
G1 CHECK FOR AIR SPRING VENTING	
1 	1 Trigger VDM active commands RR SOL or LR SOL, and VENT ON. • Does a corner lower? → **Yes** TRIGGER VDM active commands RR SOL or LR SOL, and VENT OFF. GO to **G2**. → **No** TRIGGER VDM active commands RR SOL or LR SOL, and VENT OFF. GO to **G4**.
G2 CHECK HEIGHT SENSOR MOUNTING POINTS	
1 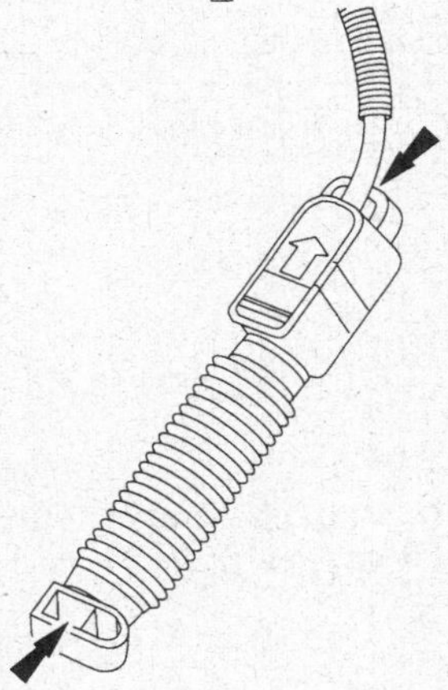	1 Check the height sensor mounting points. • Are the mounting points damaged or are the height sensors disconnected from the ball studs? → **Yes** REPAIR, REPLACE, or REATTACH as necessary. CLEAR the DTCs. PERFORM Ride Height Adjustments. TEST the system for normal operation. → **No** GO to **G3**.

FM2019800382010X

Fig. 12 Test G/Codes C1736 & C1738: Lefthand/Righthand Rear Corner Down Timeout (Part 1 of 3). 2000–01

TEST CONDITIONS	TEST DETAILS/RESULTS/ACTIONS
G4 CHECK FOR RESTRICTED AIR LINE	
	1 Disconnect the air line between the air compressor and the air spring that will not lower. 2 Connect Vacuum Tester to the air line and try to draw a vacuum. • Can a vacuum be drawn and held? → **Yes** REPAIR or REPLACE the air line as necessary. CLEAR the DTCs. TEST the system for normal operation. → **No** GO to **G5**.
G5 CHECK FOR RESTRICTED AIR SPRING SOLENOID VALVE	
1 	1 Trigger VDM active command LR SOL or RR SOL ON. • Does air exhaust from the suspect air spring solenoid? → **Yes** GO to **G6**. → **No** REPLACE the air spring solenoid, CLEAR the DTCs. TEST the system for normal operation.
G6 CHECK AIR COMPRESSOR AIR DRIER	
	1 REMOVE the air compressor air drier from the air compressor. 2 Blow shop air through the air drier from the air line port. • Does air exhaust from the air drier? → **Yes** REPLACE the air compressor. CLEAR the DTCs. TEST the system for normal operation. → **No** REPLACE the air drier. CLEAR the DTCs. TEST the system for normal operation.

FM2019800382030X

Fig. 12 Test G/Codes C1736 & C1738: Lefthand/Righthand Rear Corner Down Timeout (Part 3 of 3). 2000–01

TEST CONDITIONS	TEST DETAILS/RESULTS/ACTIONS
H1 CHECK AIR COMPRESSOR ASSEMBLY CONNECTOR	
1 2 	3 Check air compressor C170 for corrosion, bent pins and damaged wires. • Is the air compressor C170 worn or damaged? → **Yes** REPAIR or REPLACE as necessary. CLEAR the DTCs. TEST the system for normal operation. → **No** GO to **H2**.
H2 CHECK VENT SOLENOID RESISTANCE	
1 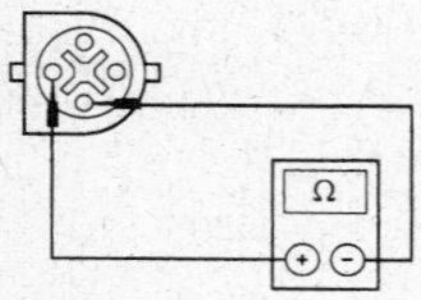	1 Measure the resistance between air compressor terminal 2 and terminal 3. • Is the resistance between 19 and 24 ohms? → **Yes** GO to **H3**. → **No** REPLACE the air compressor. CLEAR the DTCs. TEST the system for normal operation.

FM2019800383010X

Fig. 13 Test H/Code C1770: Vent Solenoid Output Circuit Failure (Part 1 of 3). 2000–01

TEST CONDITIONS	TEST DETAILS/RESULTS/ACTIONS
H3 CHECK CIRCUIT 57 (BK) FOR OPEN	
1 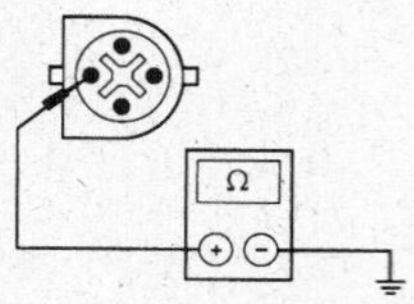	1 Measure the resistance between air compressor C170-3, circuit 57 (BK), and ground. • Is the resistance less than 5 ohms? → **Yes** GO to **H4**. → **No** REPAIR circuit 57 (BK). CLEAR the DTCs. TEST the system for normal operation.
H4 CHECK CIRCUIT 421 (PK) FOR SHORT TO POWER	
1 2 3 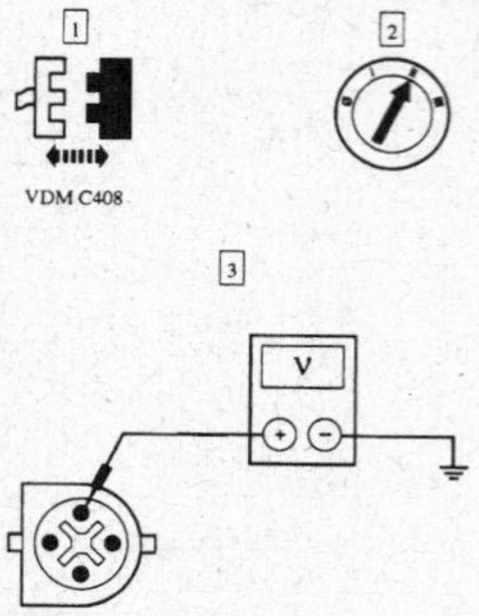	3 Measure the voltage between air compressor C170-2, circuit 421 (PK), and ground. • Is voltage present? → **Yes** REPAIR circuit 421 (PK). CLEAR the DTCs. TEST the system for normal operation. → **No** GO to **H5**.
H5 CHECK CIRCUIT 421 (PK) FOR OPEN	
1 	2 Connect EEC-IV 60-Pin Breakout Box to the VDM C408.

FM2019800383020X

Fig. 13 Test H/Code C1770: Vent Solenoid Output Circuit Failure (Part 2 of 3). 2000–01

TEST CONDITIONS	TEST DETAILS/RESULTS/ACTIONS
H5 CHECK CIRCUIT 421 (PK) FOR OPEN	
3 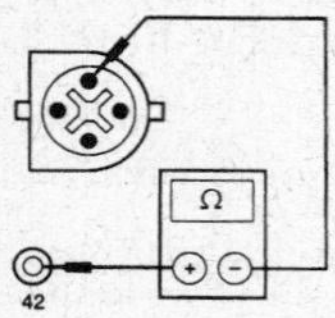	3 Measure the resistance between EEC-IV 60-Pin Breakout Box pin 42, circuit 421 (PK), and air compressor C170-2, circuit 421 (PK). • Is the resistance less than 5 ohms? → **Yes** GO to **H6**. → **No** REPAIR circuit 421 (PK). CLEAR the DTCs. TEST the system for normal operation.
H6 CHECK VDM FUNCTION	
2 3 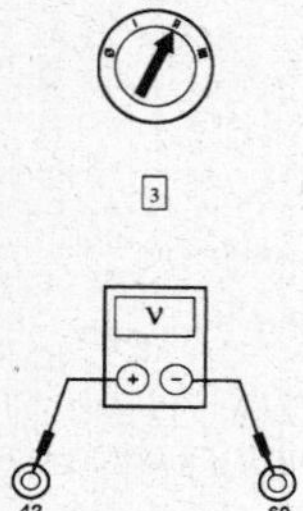	1 CONNECT the EEC-IV 60-Pin Breakout Box to the VDM. 3 Trigger VDM active command VENT ON and then OFF while measuring the voltage between EEC-IV 60-Pin Breakout Box pin 42, circuit 421 (PK), and EEC-IV 60-Pin Breakout Box pin 60, circuit 875 (BK/LB). • Is the voltage greater than 10 volts with VENT ON and equal to zero volts with VENT OFF? → **Yes** TRIGGER VDM active command VENT OFF. PERFORM the Wiggle Test. REPAIR as necessary. CLEAR all DTCs. TEST the system for normal operation. → **No** REPLACE the VDM. CLEAR the DTCs. PERFORM Ride Height Adjustments. TEST the system for normal operation.

FM2019800383030X

Fig. 13 Test H/Code C1770: Vent Solenoid Output Circuit Failure (Part 3 of 3). 2000–01

TEST CONDITIONS	TEST DETAILS/RESULTS/ACTIONS
J1 CHECK AIR COMPRESSOR ASSEMBLY CONNECTOR	
1 2 	3 Check air compressor C170 for corrosion, bent pins and damaged wires. • Is the air compressor C170 worn or damaged? → **Yes** REPAIR or REPLACE as necessary. CLEAR the DTCs. TEST the system for normal operation. → **No** GO to **J2**.
J2 CHECK VENT SOLENOID RESISTANCE	
1 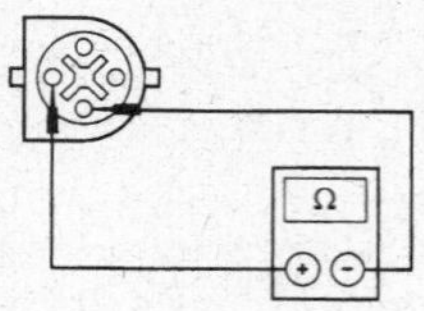	1 Measure the resistance between air compressor terminal 2 and terminal 3. • Is the resistance between 19 and 24 ohms? → **Yes** GO to **J3**. → **No** REPLACE the air compressor. CLEAR the DTCs. TEST the system for normal operation.

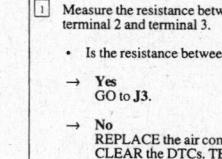

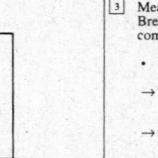

FM2019800384010X

Fig. 14 Test J/Code C1773: Vent Solenoid Output Circuit Short To Ground (Part 1 of 2). 2000–01

TEST CONDITIONS	TEST DETAILS/RESULTS/ACTIONS
J3 CHECK VENT SOLENOID FOR SHORT TO GROUND	
1 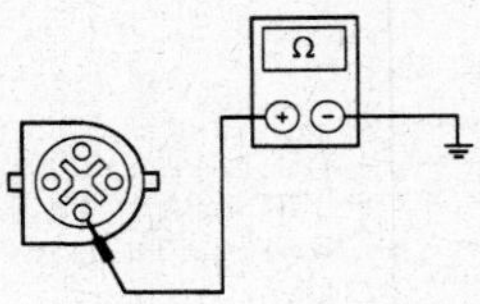	1 Measure the resistance between air compressor terminal 2, and ground. • Is the resistance greater than 10,000 ohms? → **Yes** GO to **J4**. → **No** REPLACE the air compressor.
J4 CHECK CIRCUIT 421 (PK) FOR SHORT TO GROUND	
1  VDM	
2 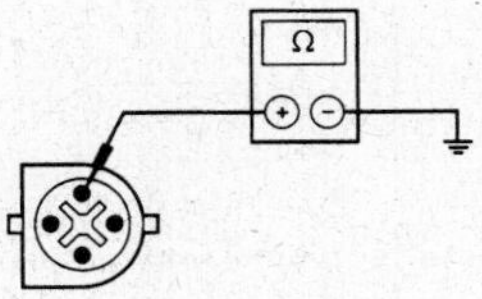	2 Measure the resistance between air compressor C170-2, circuit 421 (PK), and ground. • Is the resistance greater than 10,000 ohms? → **Yes** REPLACE the VDM. PERFORM Ride Height Adjustments. TEST the system for normal operation. → **No** REPAIR circuit 421 (PK). CLEAR the DTCs. TEST the system for normal operation.

FM2019800384020X

Fig. 14 Test J/Code C1773: Vent Solenoid Output Circuit Short To Ground (Part 2 of 2). 2000–01

TEST CONDITIONS	TEST DETAILS/RESULTS/ACTIONS
K1 CHECK AIR SPRING SOLENOID CONNECTOR	
1  2 	2 Disconnect LR air spring solenoid C419 or RR air spring solenoid C420.
	3 Check the suspect air spring solenoid connector for corrosion, bent pins and damaged wires. • Is the suspect air spring solenoid connector worn or damaged? → **Yes** REPAIR or REPLACE as necessary. CLEAR the DTCs. TEST the system for normal operation. → **No** GO to **K2**.
K2 CHECK AIR SPRING SOLENOID RESISTANCE	
1 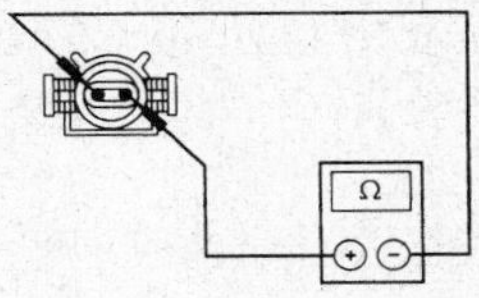	1 Measure the resistance between suspect air spring solenoid terminals. • Is the resistance between 14 and 18 ohms? → **Yes** GO to **K3**. → **No** REPLACE the suspect air spring solenoid. CLEAR the DTCs. TEST the system for normal operation.

FM2019800385010X

Fig. 15 Test K/Codes C1790 & C1795: Lefthand/Righthand Rear Air Spring Solenoid Output Circuit Failure (Part 1 of 4). 2000–01

TEST CONDITIONS	TEST DETAILS/RESULTS/ACTIONS
K3 CHECK CIRCUIT 57 (BK) FOR OPEN	
1 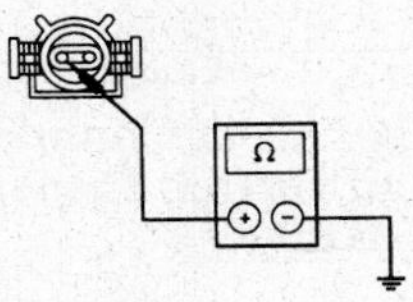	1 Measure the resistance between suspect air spring solenoid (LR C419, RR C420)-1, circuit 57 (BK), and ground. • Is the resistance less than 5 ohms? → **Yes** GO to **K4**. → **No** REPAIR circuit 57 (BK). CLEAR the DTCs. TEST the system for normal operation.
K4 CHECK CIRCUIT 416 (LB/BK) OR CIRCUIT 429 (P/LG) FOR SHORT TO POWER	
1  VDM C408 2 	
3 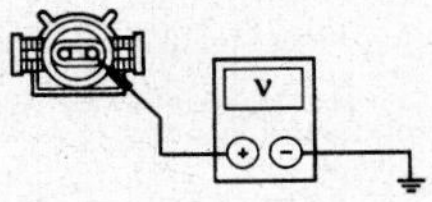	3 Measure the voltage between air spring solenoid (LR C419-2, circuit 429 [P/LG]; RR C420-2, circuit 416 [LB/BK]), and ground. • Is voltage present? → **Yes** REPAIR the circuit in question. CLEAR the DTCs. TEST the system for normal operation. → **No** GO to **K5**.
K5 CHECK CIRCUIT 416 (LB/BK) OR CIRCUIT 429 (P/LG) FOR OPEN	
1 	2 Connect EEC-IV 60-Pin Breakout Box to the VDM C408.

FM2019800385020X

Fig. 15 Test K/Codes C1790 & C1795: Lefthand/Righthand Rear Air Spring Solenoid Output Circuit Failure (Part 2 of 4). 2000–01

TEST CONDITIONS	TEST DETAILS/RESULTS/ACTIONS
K5 CHECK CIRCUIT 416 (LB/BK) OR CIRCUIT 429 (P/LG) FOR OPEN (Continued)	
3 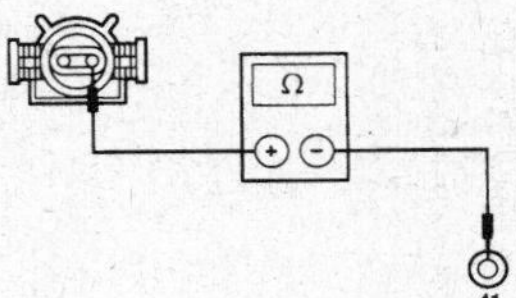 41	3 If suspect air spring solenoid is LR, measure the resistance between EEC-IV 60-Pin Breakout Box pin 41, circuit 429 (P/LG), and air spring solenoid C419-2, circuit 429 (P/LG).
4 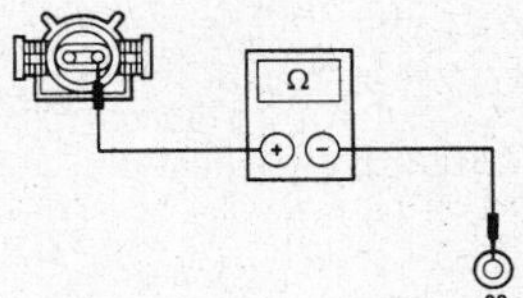 38	4 If suspect air spring solenoid is RR, measure the resistance between EEC-IV 60-Pin Breakout Box pin 38, circuit 416 (LB/BK), and air spring solenoid C420-2, circuit 416 (LB/BK). • Is the resistance less than 5 ohms? → **Yes** RECONNECT air spring solenoid. GO to **K6**. → **No** REPAIR circuit 416 (LB/BK) or circuit 429 (P/LG). CLEAR the DTCs. TEST the system for normal operation.
K6 CHECK VDM FUNCTION	
2  3 	1 Connect the EEC-IV 60-Pin Breakout Box to the VDM. 3 Trigger VDM active command LR SOL or RR SOL ON.

FM2019800385030X

Fig. 15 Test K/Codes C1790 & C1795: Lefthand/Righthand Rear Air Spring Solenoid Output Circuit Failure (Part 3 of 4). 2000–01

TEST CONDITIONS	TEST DETAILS/RESULTS/ACTIONS
K6 CHECK VDM FUNCTION	
4 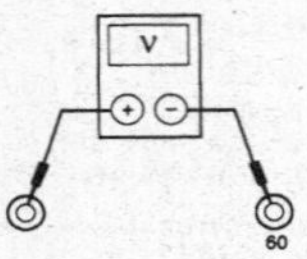	4 Measure the voltage between EEC-IV 60-Pin Breakout Box pin (LR 41, circuit 429 [P/LG] or RR 38, circuit 416 [LB/BK]), and EEC-IV 60-Pin Breakout Box pin 60, circuit 875 (BK/LB). • Is the voltage greater than 10 volts with the solenoid ON and equal to zero volts with the solenoid OFF? → **Yes** TRIGGER VDM active command LR SOL or RR SOL OFF. PERFORM the Wiggle Test. REPAIR as necessary. CLEAR the DTCs. TEST the system for normal operation. → **No** REPLACE the VDM. PERFORM Ride Height Adjustments. TEST the system for normal operation.

FM2019800385040X

Fig. 15 Test K/Codes C1790 & C1795: Lefthand/Righthand Rear Air Spring Solenoid Output Circuit Failure (Part 4 of 4). 2000–01

TEST CONDITIONS	TEST DETAILS/RESULTS/ACTIONS
L2 CHECK AIR SPRING SOLENOID RESISTANCE	
1 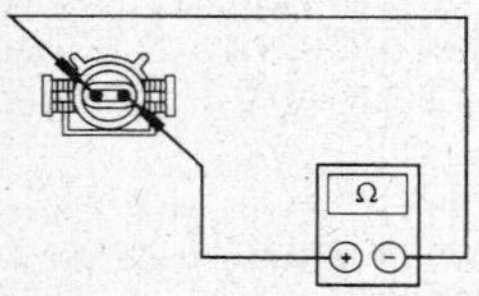	1 Measure the resistance between suspect air spring solenoid terminals. • Is the resistance between 14 and 18 ohms? → **Yes** GO to **L3**. → **No** REPLACE the suspect air spring solenoid. CLEAR the DTCs. TEST the system for normal operation.
L3 CHECK CIRCUIT 416 (LB/BK) OR CIRCUIT 429 (P/LG) FOR SHORT TO GROUND	
2 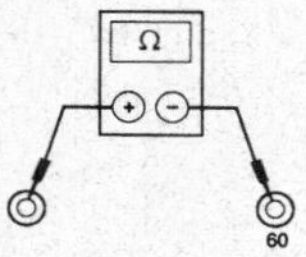	1 Connect the EEC-IV 60-Pin Breakout Box to the VDM C408. 2 Measure the resistance between EEC-IV 60-Pin Breakout Box pin (LR 41, circuit 429 [P/LG] or RR 38, circuit 416 [LB/BK]), and EEC-IV 60-Pin Breakout Box pin 60, circuit 875 (BK/LB). • Is resistance greater than 10,000 ohms? → **Yes** RECONNECT air spring solenoid. GO to **L4**. → **No** REPAIR circuit in question. CLEAR the DTCs. TEST the system for normal operation.
L4 CHECK VDM FUNCTION	
2 3 	1 Connect the EEC-IV 60-Pin Breakout Box to the VDM. 3 Trigger VDM active command LR SOL or RR SOL ON, then OFF.

FM2019800386020X

Fig. 16 Test L/Codes C1793 & C1798: Lefthand/Righthand Rear Air Spring Solenoid Output Circuit Short To Ground (Part 2 of 3). 2000–01

TEST CONDITIONS	TEST DETAILS/RESULTS/ACTIONS
L1 CHECK AIR SPRING SOLENOID CONNECTOR	
1 2 	2 Disconnect LR air spring solenoid C419 or RR air spring solenoid C420. 3 Check the suspect air spring solenoid connector for corrosion, bent pins and damaged wires. • Is the suspect air spring solenoid connector worn or damaged? → **Yes** REPAIR or REPLACE as necessary. CLEAR the DTCs. TEST the system for normal operation. → **No** GO to **L2**.

FM2019800386010X

Fig. 16 Test L/Codes C1793 & C1798: Lefthand/Righthand Rear Air Spring Solenoid Output Circuit Short To Ground (Part 1 of 3). 2000–01

TEST CONDITIONS	TEST DETAILS/RESULTS/ACTIONS
L4 CHECK VDM FUNCTION	
4 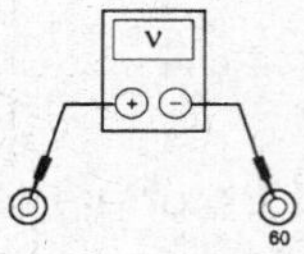	4 Measure the voltage between EEC-IV 60-Pin Breakout Box pin (LR 41, circuit 429 [P/LG] or RR 38, circuit 416 [LB/BK]), and EEC-IV 60-Pin Breakout Box pin 60, circuit 875 (BK/LB). • Is the voltage greater than 10 volts with the solenoid ON and equal to zero volts with the solenoid OFF? → **Yes** RECONNECT air spring solenoid and PERFORM wiggle test. REPAIR as necessary. If no fault is found with wiggle test, REPLACE the air spring solenoid. CLEAR the DTCs. TEST the system for normal operation. → **No** REPLACE the VDM. PERFORM Ride Height Adjustments. TEST the system for normal operation.

FM2019800386030X

Fig. 16 Test L/Codes C1793 & C1798: Lefthand/Righthand Rear Air Spring Solenoid Output Circuit Short To Ground (Part 3 of 3). 2000–01

TEST CONDITIONS	TEST DETAILS/RESULTS/ACTIONS
M1 RETRIEVE CONTINUOUS DTCs	
1 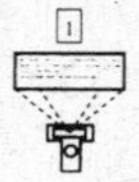	1 Retrieve and document continuous DTCs. • Is DTC C1820 retrieved? → **Yes** GO to **M2**. → **No** System OK. TEST the system for normal operation.
M2 PERFORM PNEUMATIC SELF TEST	
2  Perform Pneumatic Self Test	1 Allow air compressor to cool down for a minimum of 10 minutes before proceeding with this test.

FM2019800387010X

Fig. 17 Test M/Code C1820: Air Compressor Request Exceeded Maximum Timing (Part 1 of 2). 2000–01

TEST CONDITIONS	TEST DETAILS/RESULTS/ACTIONS
M2 PERFORM PNEUMATIC SELF TEST	
	• Did the vehicle pass the Pneumatic Self Test? → **Yes** System OK. Possible prior overloading of vehicle. → **No** GO to Pinpoint Test F.

FM2019800387020X

Fig. 17 Test M/Code C1820: Air Compressor Request Exceeded Maximum Timing (Part 2 of 2). 2000–01

TEST CONDITIONS	TEST DETAILS/RESULTS/ACTIONS
N2 CHECK SENSOR CIRCUIT RESISTANCE	

2

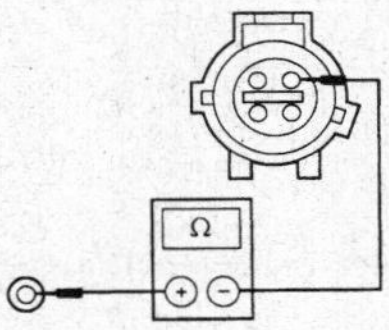

1 Connect EEC-IV 60-Pin Breakout Box to the VDM C408.

2 Measure the resistance between suspect height sensor pin 2, and EEC-IV 60-Pin Breakout Box pin(s) as follows:

DTC	Breakout Box Test Pins	Height Sensor Connector	Circuit
C1881 (RF)	9	C1015	424 (T)
C1885 (RR)	43	C406	428 (O/BK)
C1889 (LF)	27	C1014	422 (PK/BK)
C1893 (LR)	5	C413	427 (PK/BK)

- Is the resistance less than 5 ohms?

→ **Yes**
GO to **N3**.

→ **No**
REPAIR circuit in question. CLEAR the DTCs. TEST the system for normal operation.

N3 CHECK CIRCUIT 426 (R/BK) FOR OPEN

1

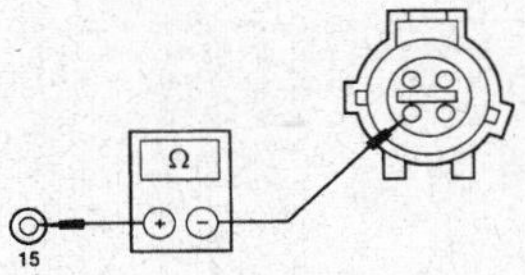

1 Measure the resistance between EEC-IV 60-Pin Breakout Box pin 15, circuit 426 (R/BK) and suspect height sensor pin 3, circuit 426 (R/BK) as follows:

DTC	Height Sensor	Connector
C1881	RF	C1015
C1885	RR	C406
C1889	LF	C1014
C1893	LR	C413

FM2019800388020X

Fig. 18 Test N/Codes C1881, C1885, C1889 & C1893: Height Sensor Circuit Failure (Part 2 of 7). 2000–01

NOTE: Make sure that the vehicle is equipped with the proper air suspension module (with or without ride control) before proceeding with test.

TEST CONDITIONS	TEST DETAILS/RESULTS/ACTIONS
N1 CHECK HEIGHT SENSOR CONNECTOR	

1 2

3 Disconnect the suspect height sensor connector as follows:

DTC	Height Sensor	Connector
C1881	RF	C1015
C1885	RR	C406
C1889	LF	C1014
C1893	LR	C413

4 Check the suspect height sensor connector for corrosion, bent pins and damaged wires.

- Is the suspect height sensor worn or damaged?

→ **Yes**
REPAIR or REPLACE as necessary. CLEAR the DTCs. TEST the system for normal operation.

→ **No**
GO to **N2**.

FM2019800388010X

Fig. 18 Test N/Codes C1881, C1885, C1889 & C1893: Height Sensor Circuit Failure (Part 1 of 7). 2000–01

TEST CONDITIONS	TEST DETAILS/RESULTS/ACTIONS
N3 CHECK CIRCUIT 426 (R/BK) FOR OPEN	
	• Is the resistance less than 5 ohms? → **Yes** GO to **N4**. → **No** REPAIR circuit 426 (R/BK). CLEAR the DTCs. TEST the system for normal operation.

N4 CHECK FOR SHORT BETWEEN CIRCUIT 426 (R/BK) AND CIRCUIT 432 (BK/PK)

1

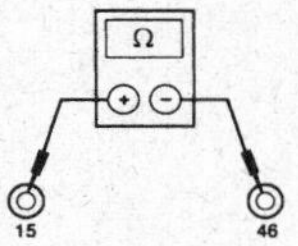

1 Measure the resistance between EEC-IV 60-Pin Breakout Box pin 15, circuit 426 (R/BK), and EEC-IV 60-Pin Breakout Box pin 46, circuit 432 (BK/PK).

- Is the resistance greater than 10,000 ohms?

→ **Yes**
GO to **N5**.

→ **No**
REPAIR circuit 426 (R/BK) and circuit 432 (BK/PK). CLEAR the DTCs. TEST the system for normal operation.

N5 CHECK CIRCUIT 432 (BK/PK) FOR OPEN

1

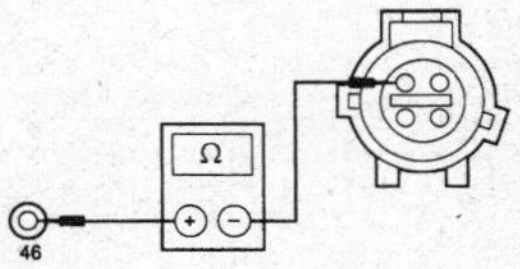

1 Measure the resistance between EEC-IV 60-Pin Breakout Box pin 46, circuit 432 (BK/PK), and suspect height sensor pin 1, circuit 432 (BK/PK) as follows:

DTC	Height Sensor	Connector
C1881	RF	C1015
C1885	RR	C406
C1889	LF	C1014
C1893	LR	C413

- Is the resistance less than 5 ohms?

→ **Yes**
GO to **N6**.

→ **No**
REPAIR circuit 432 (BK/PK). CLEAR the DTCs. TEST the system for normal operation.

FM2019800388030X

Fig. 18 Test N/Codes C1881, C1885, C1889 & C1893: Height Sensor Circuit Failure (Part 3 of 7). 2000–01

TEST CONDITIONS	TEST DETAILS/RESULTS/ACTIONS
N6 CHECK FOR SHORT TO POWER	

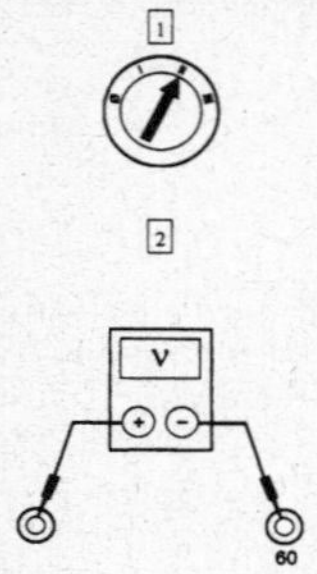

2 Measure the voltage between EEC-IV 60-Pin Breakout Box pin 60, circuit 875 (BK/LB) and EEC-IV 60-Pin Breakout Box pin(s) as follows:

DTC	Breakout Box Test Pins	Circuit
C1881 (RF)	9	424 (T)
C1885 (RR)	43	428 (O/BK)
C1889 (LF)	27	422 (PK/BK)
C1893 (LR)	5	427 (PK/BK)

- Is voltage present?

→ **Yes**
REPAIR the circuit in question. CLEAR the DTCs. TEST the system for normal operation.

→ **No**
GO to **N7**.

FM2019800388040X

Fig. 18 Test N/Codes C1881, C1885, C1889 & C1893: Height Sensor Circuit Failure (Part 4 of 7). 2000–01

TEST CONDITIONS	TEST DETAILS/RESULTS/ACTIONS
N7 CHECK FOR SHORT TO SENSOR VOLTAGE	

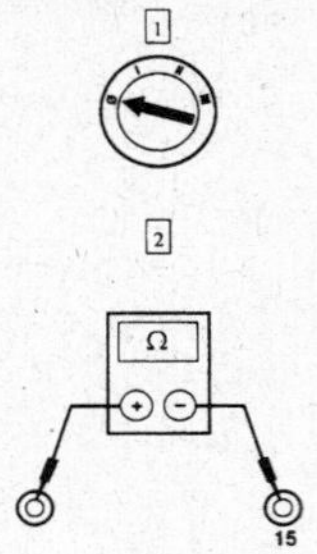

2 Measure the resistance between EEC-IV 60-Pin Breakout Box pin 15, circuit 426 (R/BK), and EEC-IV 60-Pin Breakout Box pin(s) as follows:

DTC	Breakout Box Test Pins	Circuit
C1881 (RF)	9	424 (T)
C1885 (RR)	43	428 (O/BK)
C1889 (LF)	27	422 (PK/BK)
C1893 (LR)	5	427 (PK/BK)

- Is the resistance greater than 10,000 ohms?

→ **Yes**
GO to **N8**.

→ **No**
REPAIR the circuit in question. CLEAR the DTCs. TEST the system for normal operation.

N8 CHECK HEIGHT SENSOR SUPPLY VOLTAGE

1 Connect EEC-IV 60-Pin Breakout Box to the VDM.

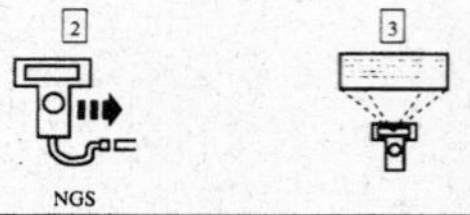

3 Trigger VDM active command HGTPOWER ON.

FM2019800388050X

Fig. 18 Test N/Codes C1881, C1885, C1889 & C1893: Height Sensor Circuit Failure (Part 5 of 7). 2000–01

TEST CONDITIONS	TEST DETAILS/RESULTS/ACTIONS
N8 CHECK HEIGHT SENSOR SUPPLY VOLTAGE (Continued)	

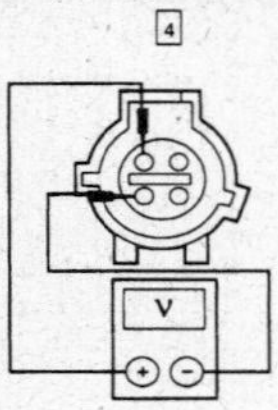

4 Measure the voltage between suspect height sensor pin 3, circuit 426 (R/BK), and suspect height sensor pin 1, circuit 432 (BK/PK) as follows:

DTC	Height Sensor	Connector
C1881	RF	C1015
C1885	RR	C406
C1889	LF	C1014
C1893	LR	C413

- Is the voltage between 4.8 and 5.2 volts?

→ **Yes**
RECONNECT the suspect height sensor connector. GO to **N9**.

→ **No**
REPLACE the VDM.
PERFORM Ride Height Adjustments. TEST the system for normal operation.

N9 CHECK HEIGHT SENSOR SIGNAL RANGE

1 Remove the suspect height sensor from the lower ball stud.

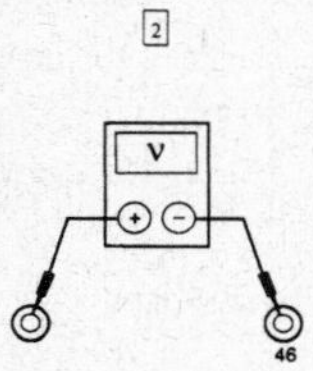

2 While extending and compressing the suspect height sensor, measure the voltage between EEC-IV 60-Pin Breakout Box pin 46, circuit 432 (BK/PK), and EEC-IV 60-Pin Breakout Box pin(s) as follows:

DTC	Breakout Box Test Pins	Circuit
C1881 (RF)	9	424 (T)
C1885 (RR)	43	428 (O/BK)
C1889 (LF)	27	422 (PK/BK)
C1893 (LR)	5	427 (PK/BK)

FM2019800388060X

Fig. 18 Test N/Codes C1881, C1885, C1889 & C1893: Height Sensor Circuit Failure (Part 6 of 7). 2000–01

TEST CONDITIONS	TEST DETAILS/RESULTS/ACTIONS
N9 CHECK HEIGHT SENSOR SIGNAL RANGE	

- Does the voltage range between 0.5 and 4.5 volts as the suspect height sensor length is changed from minimum length to maximum length?

→ **Yes**
GO to **N10**.

→ **No**
REPLACE the suspect height sensor.
CLEAR the DTCs.
PERFORM Ride Height Adjustments.
TEST the system for normal operation.

N10 CHECK FOR CHANGE OF PID VALUES

1 From active command menu, select PID LF_HGT, RF_HGT, LR_HGT, or RR_HGT for the suspect height sensor.

2 Vary the length of the suspect height sensor while monitoring the PID.

- Does the PID value change as the suspect height sensor length is changed from minimum length to maximum length?

→ **Yes**
PERFORM the Wiggle Test. REPAIR as necessary. CLEAR the DTCs. TEST the system for normal operation.

→ **No**
REPLACE the VDM.
PERFORM Ride Height Adjustments. TEST the system for normal operation.

FM2019800388070X

Fig. 18 Test N/Codes C1881, C1885, C1889 & C1893: Height Sensor Circuit Failure (Part 7 of 7). 2000–01

TEST CONDITIONS	TEST DETAILS/RESULTS/ACTIONS

P1 CHECK HEIGHT SENSOR CONNECTOR

2 Disconnect the suspect height sensor connector as follows:

DTC	Height Sensor	Connector
C1884	RF	C1015
C1888	RR	C406
C1892	LF	C1014
C1896	LR	C413

3 Check the suspect height sensor connector for corrosion, bent pins and damaged wires.

- Is the suspect height sensor connector worn or damaged?

→ **Yes**
REPAIR or REPLACE as necessary. CLEAR the DTCs. TEST the system for normal operation.

→ **No**
GO to **P2**.

P2 CHECK FOR SHORT TO GROUND

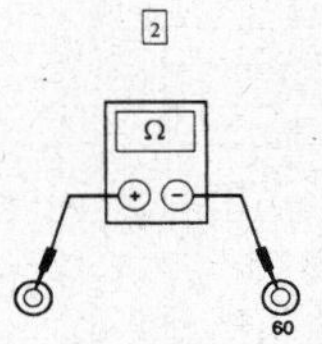

1 Connect EEC-IV 60-Pin Breakout Box to the VDM C408.

2 Measure the resistance between EEC-IV 60-Pin Breakout Box pin 60, circuit 875 (BK/LB), and EEC-IV 60-Pin Breakout Box pin(s) as follows:

DTC	Breakout Box Test Pins	Circuit
C1884 (RF)	9	424 (T)
C1888 (RR)	43	428 (O/BK)
C1892 (LF)	27	422 (PK/BK)
C1896 (LR)	5	427 (PK/BK)

FM2019800389010X

Fig. 19 Test P/Codes C1884, C1888, C1892 & C1896: Height Sensor Circuit Short To Ground (Part 1 of 4). 2000–01

TEST CONDITIONS	TEST DETAILS/RESULTS/ACTIONS

P2 CHECK FOR SHORT TO GROUND

- Is the resistance greater than 10,000 ohms?

→ **Yes**
GO to **P3**.

→ **No**
REPAIR circuit in question. CLEAR the DTCs. TEST the system for normal operation.

P3 CHECK FOR SHORT TO CIRCUIT 432 (BK/PK)

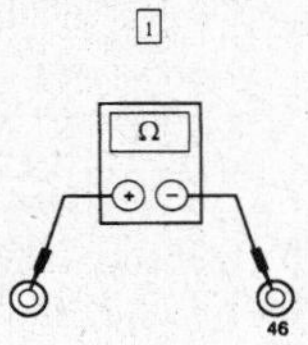

1 Measure the resistance between EEC-IV 60-Pin Breakout Box pin 46, circuit 432 (BL/PK), and EEC-IV 60-Pin Breakout Box pin(s) as follows:

DTC	Breakout Box Test Pins	Circuit
C1884 (RF)	9	424 (T)
C1888 (RR)	43	428 (O/BK)
C1892 (LF)	27	422 (PK/BK)
C1896 (LR)	5	427 (PK/BK)

- Is the resistance greater than 10,000 ohms?

→ **Yes**
GO to **P4**.

→ **No**
REPAIR the circuit in question. CLEAR the DTCs. TEST the system for normal operation.

P4 CHECK HEIGHT SENSOR FOR SHORT TO GROUND

2 Connect EEC-IV 60-Pin Breakout Box to the VDM.

FM2019800389020X

Fig. 19 Test P/Codes C1884, C1888, C1892 & C1896: Height Sensor Circuit Short To Ground (Part 2 of 4). 2000–01

TEST CONDITIONS	TEST DETAILS/RESULTS/ACTIONS

P4 CHECK HEIGHT SENSOR FOR SHORT TO GROUND

3 Trigger VDM active command HGTPOWER ON.

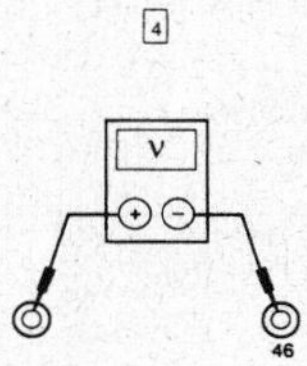

4 Measure the voltage between EEC-IV 60-Pin breakout box pin 46, circuit 432 (BK/PK), and EEC-IV 60-Pin Breakout Box pin(s) as follows:

DTC	Breakout Box Test Pins	Circuit
C1884 (RF)	9	424 (T)
C1888 (RR)	43	428 (O/BK)
C1892 (LF)	27	422 (PK/BK)
C1896 (LR)	5	427 (PK/BK)

- Is the voltage between 2.3 and 2.7 volts?

→ **Yes**
TRIGGER VDM active command HGTPOWER OFF. RECONNECT the height sensor.GO to **P5**.

→ **No**
REPLACE the VDM.
CLEAR the DTCs. PERFORM Ride Height Adjustments.
TEST the system for normal operation.

P5 CHECK FOR SENSOR SIGNAL

1 Trigger VDM active command HGTPOWER ON.

FM2019800389030X

Fig. 19 Test P/Codes C1884, C1888, C1892 & C1896: Height Sensor Circuit Short To Ground (Part 3 of 4). 2000–01

TEST CONDITIONS	TEST DETAILS/RESULTS/ACTIONS

P5 CHECK FOR SENSOR SIGNAL (Continued)

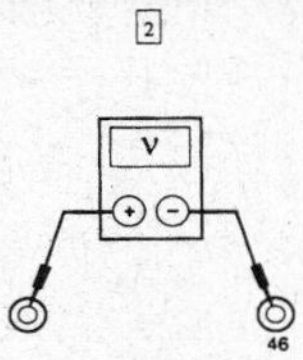

2 Measure the voltage between EEC-IV 60-Pin Breakout Box pin and EEC-IV 60-Pin Breakout Box pin 46, circuit 432 (BK/PK), and EEC-IV 60-Pin Breakout Box pin(s) as follows:

DTC	Breakout Box Test Pins	Circuit
C1884 (RF)	9	424 (T)
C1888 (RR)	43	428 (O/BK)
C1892 (LF)	27	422 (PK/BK)
C1896 (LR)	5	427 (PK/BK)

- Is the voltage between 0.5 volts and 4.5 volts?

→ **Yes**
PERFORM the Wiggle Test. REPAIR as necessary. CLEAR the DTCs. TEST the system for normal operation.

→ **No**
REPLACE the suspect height sensor.
CLEAR the DTCs.
PERFORM Ride Height Adjustments.
TEST the system for normal operation.

FM2019800389040X

Fig. 19 Test P/Codes C1884, C1888, C1892 & C1896: Height Sensor Circuit Short To Ground (Part 4 of 4). 2000–01

NOTE: Make sure that the vehicle is equipped with the proper air suspension module (with or without ride control) before proceeding with test.

TEST CONDITIONS	TEST DETAILS/RESULTS/ACTIONS
Q1 CHECK SHOCK ACTUATOR CONNECTOR	

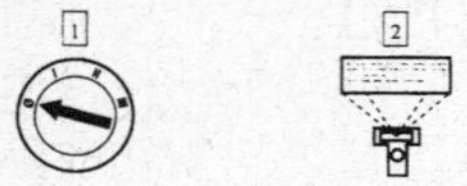

2 Disconnect the suspect shock actuator connector as follows:

DTC	Shock	Connector
C1901	RR	C481
C1905	LR	C427
C1909	RF	C105
C1913	LF	C1016

FM2019800390010X

Fig. 20 Test Q/Codes C1901, C1905, C1909 & C1913: RR/LR/RF/LF Shock Actuator Circuit Failure (Part 1 of 4). 2000–01

TEST CONDITIONS	TEST DETAILS/RESULTS/ACTIONS
Q3 CHECK CIRCUIT 430 (GY) FOR OPEN	

- Is the resistance less than 5 ohms?

→ **Yes**
GO to **Q4**.

→ **No**
REPAIR circuit 430 (GY). CLEAR the DTCs. TEST the system for normal operation.

Q4 CHECK CIRCUIT 843 (W), CIRCUIT 842 (W/O), CIRCUIT 841 (W/R) OR CIRCUIT 840 (W/BK) FOR SHORT TO POWER

3 Measure the voltage between shock actuator connector, and ground as follows:

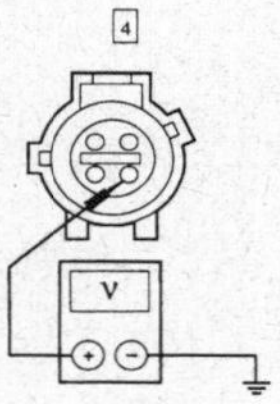

4 Measure the voltage between shock actuator connector, and ground as follows:

DTC	Connector-Pin
C1901	C481-2
C1905	C427-2
C1909	C105-2
C1913	C1016-2

- Is voltage present?

→ **Yes**
REPAIR circuit in question. CLEAR the DTCs. TEST the system for normal operation.

→ **No**
GO to **Q5**.

FM2019800390030X

Fig. 20 Test Q/Codes C1901, C1905, C1909 & C1913: RR/LR/RF/LF Shock Actuator Circuit Failure (Part 3 of 4). 2000–01

TEST CONDITIONS	TEST DETAILS/RESULTS/ACTIONS
Q1 CHECK SHOCK ACTUATOR CONNECTOR	

3 Check the suspect shock actuator connector for corrosion, bent pins and damaged wires.

- Is the suspect shock actuator connector worn or damaged?

→ **Yes**
REPAIR or REPLACE as necessary. CLEAR the DTCs. TEST the system for normal operation.

→ **No**
GO to **Q2**.

Q2 CHECK SHOCK ACTUATOR RESISTANCE

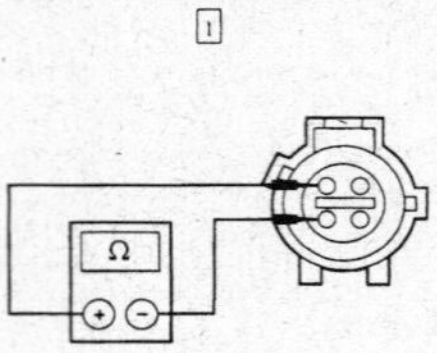

1 Measure the resistance between suspect shock actuator terminals.

- Is the resistance between 15 and 21 ohms?

→ **Yes**
GO to **Q3**.

→ **No**
REPLACE the suspect shock actuator. CLEAR the DTCs. TEST the system for normal operation.

Q3 CHECK CIRCUIT 430 (GY) FOR OPEN

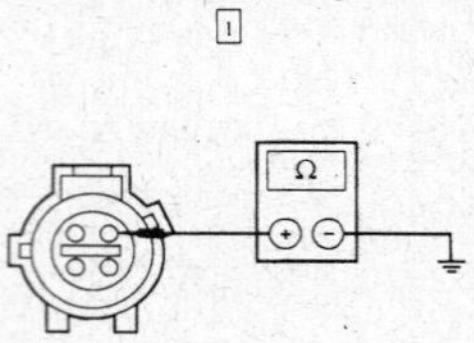

1 Measure the resistance between suspect shock actuator connector, circuit 430 (GY), and ground as follows:

DTC	Connector-Pin
C1901	C481-1
C1905	C427-1
C1909	C105-1
C1913	C1016-1

FM2019800390020X

Fig. 20 Test Q/Codes C1901, C1905, C1909 & C1913: RR/LR/RF/LF Shock Actuator Circuit Failure (Part 2 of 4). 2000–01

TEST CONDITIONS	TEST DETAILS/RESULTS/ACTIONS
Q5 CHECK CIRCUIT 843 (W), CIRCUIT 842 (W/O), CIRCUIT 841 (W/R) OR CIRCUIT 840 (W/BK) FOR OPEN	

2 Connect EEC-IV 60-Pin Breakout Box to the VDM C408.

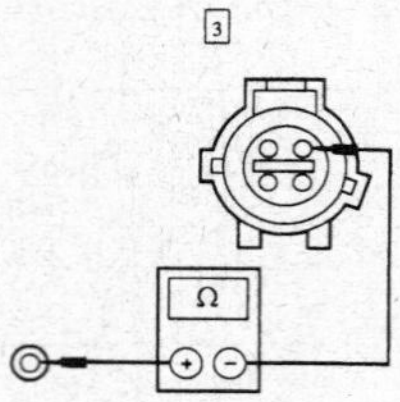

3 Measure the resistance between shock actuator connector, and EEC-IV 60-Pin Breakout Box pin as follows:

DTC	Breakout Box Test Pin	Shock Connector Pin	Circuit
C1901 (RR)	52	C481-2	843 (W)
C1905 (LR)	54	C427-2	842 (W/O)
C1909 (RF)	53	C105-2	841 (W/R)
C1913 (LF)	51	C1016-2	840 (W/BK)

- Is the resistance less than 5 ohms?

→ **Yes**
REPLACE the VDM. PERFORM Ride Height Adjustments. TEST the system for normal operation.

→ **No**
REPAIR circuit in question. CLEAR the DTCs. TEST the system for normal operation.

FM2019800390040X

Fig. 20 Test Q/Codes C1901, C1905, C1909 & C1913: RR/LR/RF/LF Shock Actuator Circuit Failure (Part 4 of 4). 2000–01

TEST CONDITIONS | **TEST DETAILS/RESULTS/ACTIONS**

R1 CHECK SHOCK SOLENOID CONNECTOR

2 Disconnect the suspect shock actuator connector as follows:

DTC	Shock	Connector
C1904	RR	C481
C1908	LR	C427
C1912	RF	C105
C1916	LF	C1016

3 Check the suspect shock actuator connector for corrosion, bent pins and damaged wires.

- Is the suspect shock actuator connector worn or damaged?

→ **Yes**
REPAIR or REPLACE as necessary. CLEAR the DTCs. TEST the system for normal operation.

→ **No**
GO to **R2**.

R2 CHECK SHOCK ACTUATOR RESISTANCE

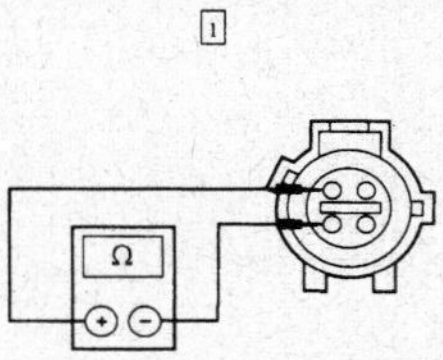

1 Measure the resistance between suspect shock actuator terminals.

- Is the resistance between 15 and 21 ohms?

→ **Yes**
GO to **R3**.

→ **No**
REPLACE the suspect shock actuator. CLEAR the DTCs. TEST the system for normal operation.

R3 CHECK CIRCUIT 843 (W), CIRCUIT 482 (W/O), CIRCUIT 841 (W/R) OR CIRCUIT 840 (W/BK) FOR SHORT TO GROUND

1 Connect EEC-IV 60-Pin Breakout Box to the VDM C408.

FM2019800391010X

Fig. 21 Test R/Codes C1904, C1908, C1912 & C1916: RR/LR/RF/LF Shock Actuator Short To Ground (Part 1 of 2). 2000–01

TEST CONDITIONS | **TEST DETAILS/RESULTS/ACTIONS**

S1 CHECK POWER DISTRIBUTION BOX MAXI FUSE 11 (60A)

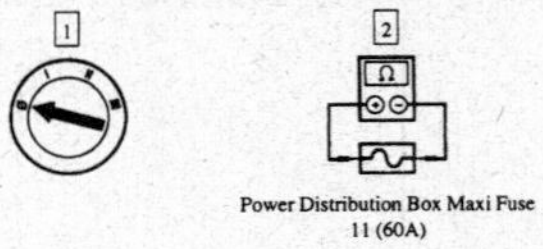

- Is power distribution box maxi fuse 11 (60A) OK?

→ **Yes**
GO to **S2**.

→ **No**
REPLACE the fuse. TEST the system for normal operation. If the fuse fails again, CHECK for short to ground. REPAIR as necessary. TEST the system for normal operation.

S2 CHECK AIR COMPRESSOR RELAY CONNECTOR

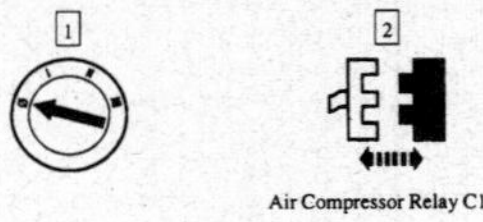

3 Check air compressor relay C187 for corrosion, bent pins and damaged wires.

- Is the air compressor relay C187 worn or damaged?

→ **Yes**
REPAIR or REPLACE as necessary. CLEAR the DTCs. TEST the system for normal operation.

→ **No**
GO to S3.

FM2019800392010X

Fig. 22 Test S/Code C1929: Compressor Relay Circuit Failure (Part 1 of 3). 2000–01

TEST CONDITIONS | **TEST DETAILS/RESULTS/ACTIONS**

R3 CHECK CIRCUIT 843 (W), CIRCUIT 482 (W/O), CIRCUIT 841 (W/R) OR CIRCUIT 840 (W/BK) FOR SHORT TO GROUND

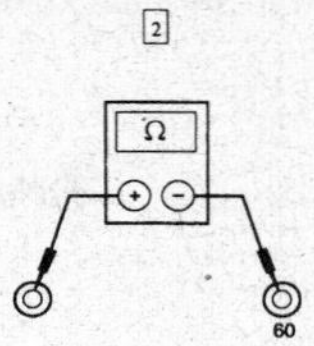

2 Measure the resistance between EEC-IV 60-Pin Breakout Box pin, and ground as follows:

DTC	EEC-IV 60-Pin Breakout Box Pin	Circuit
C1904	52	843 (W)
C1908	54	842 (W/O)
C1912	53	841 (W/R)
C1916	51	840 (W/BK)

- Is resistance greater than 10,000 ohms?

→ **Yes**
REPLACE the VDM.
PERFORM Ride Height Adjustments.
TEST the system for normal operation.

→ **No**
REPAIR the circuit in question. TEST the system for normal operation.

FM2019800391020X

Fig. 21 Test R/Codes C1904, C1908, C1912 & C1916: RR/LR/RF/LF Shock Actuator Short To Ground (Part 2 of 2). 2000–01

TEST CONDITIONS | **TEST DETAILS/RESULTS/ACTIONS**

S3 CHECK CIRCUIT 1053 (LB/PK) FOR OPEN

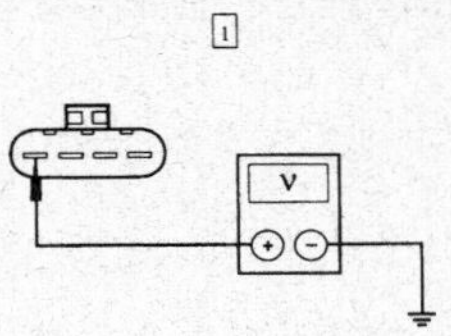

1 Measure the voltage between air compressor relay C187-A, circuit 1053 (LB/PK), and ground.

- Is the voltage greater than 10 volts?

→ **Yes**
GO to **S4**.

→ **No**
REPAIR circuit 1053 (LB/PK). CLEAR the DTCs. TEST the system for normal operation.

S4 CHECK CIRCUIT 57 (BK) FOR OPEN

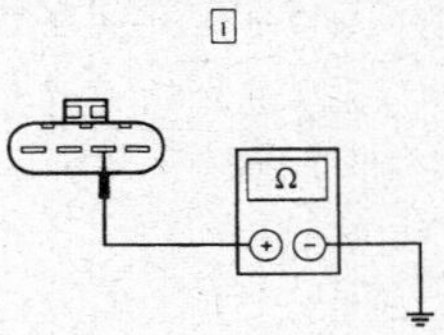

1 Measure the resistance between air compressor relay C187-C, circuit 57 (BK), and ground.

- Is the resistance less than 5 ohms?

→ **Yes**
GO to **S5**.

→ **No**
REPAIR circuit 57 (BK). CLEAR the DTCs. TEST the system for normal operation.

S5 CHECK CIRCUIT 420 (DB/Y)

1 Connect EEC-IV 60-Pin Breakout Box to the VDM C408.

FM2019800392020X

Fig. 22 Test S/Code C1929: Compressor Relay Circuit Failure (Part 2 of 3). 2000–01

TEST CONDITIONS	TEST DETAILS/RESULTS/ACTIONS
S5 CHECK CIRCUIT 420 (DB/Y)	
2 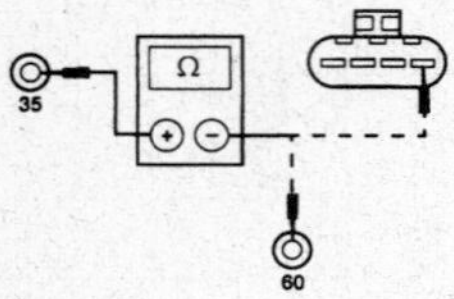	2 Measure the resistance between EEC-IV 60-Pin Breakout Box pin 35, circuit 420 (DB/Y), and air compressor relay C187-D, circuit 420 (DB/Y); and between EEC-IV 60-Pin Breakout Box pin 35, circuit 420 (DB/Y), and EEC-IV 60-Pin Breakout Box pin 60, circuit 875 (BK/LB). • Is the resistance less than 5 ohms between EEC-IV 60-Pin Breakout Box and relay; and greater than 10,000 ohms between EEC-IV 60-Pin Breakout Box pins? → **Yes** RECONNECT air compressor relay C187. GO to **S6**. → **No** REPAIR circuit 420 (DB/Y). CLEAR all DTCs. TEST the system for normal operation.
S6 CHECK VDM	
1 	1 Connect a jumper between EEC-IV 60-Pin Breakout Box pin 35, circuit 420 (DB/Y), and EEC-IV 60-Pin Breakout Box pin 60, circuit 57 (BK). • Does the air compressor operate? → **Yes** REPLACE the VDM. → **No** GO to **S7**.
S7 CHECK COMPRESSOR MOTOR RESISTANCE	
1 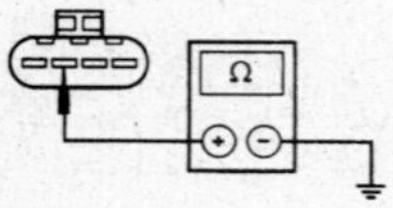	1 Measure the resistance between air compressor relay C187-B, circuit 417 (P/O), and ground. • Is the resistance approximately 39 ohms? → **Yes** REPLACE the air compressor relay. TEST the system for normal operation. → **No** REPLACE the air compressor. TEST the system for normal operation.

FM2019800392030X

Fig. 22 Test S/Code C1929: Compressor Relay Circuit Failure (Part 3 of 3). 2000–01

TEST CONDITIONS	TEST DETAILS/RESULTS/ACTIONS
U1 CHECK POWER DISTRIBUTION BOX MAXI FUSE 11 (60A)	
1  2  Power Distribution Box Maxi-Fuse 11 (60A)	• Is power distribution box maxi-fuse 11 (60A) OK? → **Yes** GO to **U2**. → **No** REPLACE the fuse. TEST the system for normal operation. If the fuse fails again, CHECK for short to ground. REPAIR as necessary. TEST the system for normal operation.
U2 CHECK CONNECTORS	
1  Air Compressor Relay C187 2  Air Compressor C170	3 Inspect the pins and terminals of the air compressor relay C187 and air compressor C170 for corrosion, bent or broken pins, moisture, or other damage. • Are the connectors OK? → **Yes** RECONNECT the air compressor C170. GO to **U3**. → **No** REPAIR or REPLACE as necessary. TEST the system for normal operation.

FM2019800394010X

Fig. 24 Test U: Compressor Is Inoperative (Part 1 of 3). 2000–01

TEST CONDITIONS	TEST DETAILS/RESULTS/ACTIONS
T1 CHECK CIRCUIT 420 (DB/Y) FOR SHORT TO POWER	
1  Air Compressor Relay C187 2  VDM C408	
3 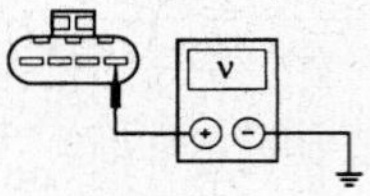	3 Measure the voltage between air compressor relay C187-D, circuit 420 (DB/Y), and ground. • Is voltage present? → **Yes** REPAIR circuit 420 (DB/Y). TEST the system for normal operation. → **No** GO to **T2**.
T2 CHECK AIR COMPRESSOR RELAY	
1  Air Compressor Relay	2 Connect EEC-IV 60-Pin Breakout Box.
3 	3 Connect a jumper between EEC-IV 60-Pin Breakout Box pin 35, circuit 420 (DB/Y), and EEC-IV 60-Pin Breakout Box pin 60, circuit 875 (BK/LB). • Does the air compressor operate? → **Yes** REPLACE the VDM. PERFORM ride height adjustments. TEST the system for normal operation. → **No** REPLACE the air compressor relay. TEST the system for normal operation.

FM2019800393000X

Fig. 23 Test T/Code C1931: Compressor Relay Circuit Short To Power. 2000–01

TEST CONDITIONS	TEST DETAILS/RESULTS/ACTIONS
U3 CHECK COMPRESSOR OPERATION	
1 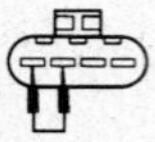	1 Connect a jumper wire between air compressor relay C187-A and air compressor relay C187-B. • Does the air compressor run? → **Yes** GO to **U4**. → **No** GO to **U5**.
U4 CHECK CIRCUIT 430 (GY)	
1 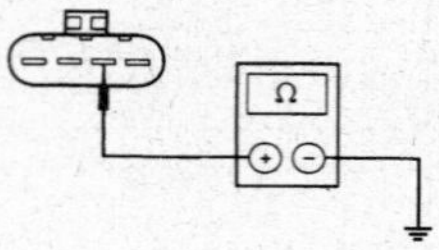	1 Measure the resistance between air compressor relay C187-C, circuit 57 (BK), and ground. • Is the resistance less than 5 ohms? → **Yes** REPLACE the air compressor relay. TEST the system for normal operation. → **No** REPAIR circuit 57 (BK). TEST the system for normal operation.
U5 CHECK CIRCUIT 1053 (LB/PK)	
1 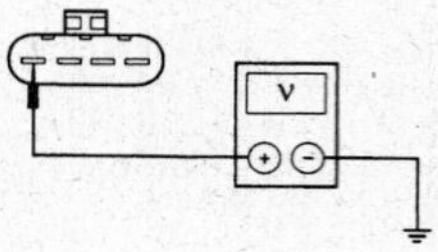	1 Measure the voltage between air compressor relay C187-A, circuit 1053 (LB/PK), and ground. • Is the voltage greater than 10 volts? → **Yes** GO to **U6**. → **No** REPAIR circuit 1053 (LB/PK). TEST the system for normal operation.

FM2019800394020X

Fig. 24 Test U: Compressor Is Inoperative (Part 2 of 3). 2000–01

TEST CONDITIONS	TEST DETAILS/RESULTS/ACTIONS

U6 CHECK CIRCUIT 417 (P/O)

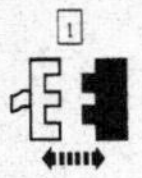
1
Air Compressor C170

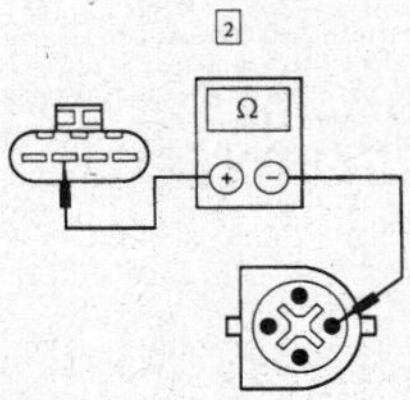

2 Measure the resistance between air compressor relay C187-B, circuit 417 (P/O), and air compressor C170-4, circuit 417 (P/O).

- Is the resistance less than 5 ohms?

→ **Yes**
GO to **U7**.

→ **No**
REPAIR circuit 417 (P/O). TEST the system for normal operation.

U7 CHECK CIRCUIT 57 (BK)

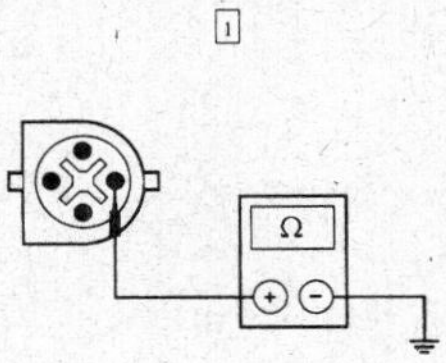

1 Measure the resistance between air compressor C170-3, circuit 57 (BK), and ground.

- Is the resistance less than 5 ohms?

→ **Yes**
REPLACE the air compressor. TEST the system for normal operation.

→ **No**
REPAIR circuit 57 (BK). TEST the system for normal operation.

FM2019800394030X

Fig. 24 Test U: Compressor Is Inoperative (Part 3 of 3). 2000–01

TEST CONDITIONS	TEST DETAILS/RESULTS/ACTIONS

V3 CHECK FOR LEAKS AT AIR SPRING SOLENOID

1
2
3
Air Line at LR Air Spring
Air Line at RR Air Spring
NGS

4 Connect shop air to the air line at the air drier with common fittings.

5 Trigger VDM active command LR SOL and RR SOL ON.

- Do both air springs inflate until full suspension travel is reached?

→ **Yes**
GO to **V4**.

→ **No**
REPLACE the faulty air spring solenoid. TEST the system for normal operation.

V4 PERFORM AIR COMPRESSOR ASSEMBLY LEAK TEST

⚠ **CAUTION: Do not allow the air compressor to run for more than three minutes. The air compressor could overheat and stop operating due to an internal temperature sensitive thermal breaker.**

1 Connect an air pressure gauge with common fittings to the air line.

2
Air Compressor Relay C187

FM2019800395020X

Fig. 25 Test V: One Or More Corners Low & Compressor Operates (Part 2 of 3). 2000–01

TEST CONDITIONS	TEST DETAILS/RESULTS/ACTIONS

V1 CHECK FOR BLOCKED AIR LINE

1
2
Air Line at Air Drier
Air Line at LR Air Spring

3 Use Vacuum Tester to try to draw a vacuum on the air line at the LR air spring.

4
Air Line at RR Air Spring

5 Use Vacuum Tester to try to draw a vacuum on the air line at the RR air spring.

- Does either air line hold a vacuum?

→ **Yes**
REPAIR or REPLACE the air line as necessary. TEST the system for normal operation.

→ **No**
GO to **V2**.

V2 CHECK FOR LEAKS IN AIR LINE

1 ⚠ **CAUTION: Do not use anything as a cap that might be drawn in to the air line.**
Cap both air lines at the air springs.

2 Use Vacuum Tester to try to draw a vacuum on the air line at the air drier.

- Does the air line hold a vacuum?

→ **Yes**
GO to **V3**.

→ **No**
ISOLATE leak in air line. REPLACE the damaged air line. TEST the system for normal operation.

FM2019800395010X

Fig. 25 Test V: One Or More Corners Low & Compressor Operates (Part 1 of 3). 2000–01

TEST CONDITIONS	TEST DETAILS/RESULTS/ACTIONS

V4 PERFORM AIR COMPRESSOR ASSEMBLY LEAK TEST

3 Connect a jumper wire between air compressor relay C187-A, and air compressor relay C187-B.

4 Within 30 seconds, the pressure should reach 1034 kPa (150 psi).

5 Disconnect the jumper wire.

6 The pressure should hold steady.

7 Trigger VDM active command VENT ON.

- Did the air compressor reach and hold a minimum air pressure of 1034 kPa (150 psi)?

→ **Yes**
System OK. TEST the system for normal operation.

→ **No**
REPLACE the air compressor. TEST the system for normal operation.

FM2019800395030X

Fig. 25 Test V: One Or More Corners Low & Compressor Operates (Part 3 of 3). 2000–01

TEST CONDITIONS	TEST DETAILS/RESULTS/ACTIONS
W1 CHECK FUSES	
	1 Check power distribution box mini-fuse 4 (30A), and fuse junction panel fuse 28 (10A). • Are fuses OK? → **Yes** GO to **W2**. → **No** REPLACE the fuse in question. TEST the system for normal operation. If the fuse fails again, CHECK for short to ground. REPAIR as necessary.
W2 CHECK CIRCUIT 875 (BK/LB) FOR OPEN	
2 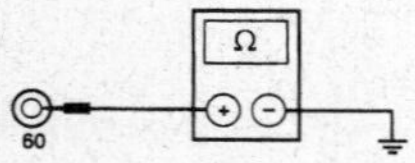	1 Connect the EEC-IV 60-Pin Breakout Box to the VDM C408. 2 Measure the resistance between EEC-IV 60-Pin Breakout Box pin 60, circuit 875 (BK/LB), and ground. • Is the resistance less than 5 ohms? → **Yes** GO to **W3**. → **No** REPAIR circuit 875 (BK/LB). TEST the system for normal operation.

FM2019800396010X

Fig. 26 Test W: No Communication w/Vehicle Dynamic Module (Part 1 of 3). 2000–01

TEST CONDITIONS	TEST DETAILS/RESULTS/ACTIONS
W3 CHECK CIRCUIT 418 (DG/Y) FOR OPEN	
1  Power Distribution Box Mini Fuse 4 (30A) 2 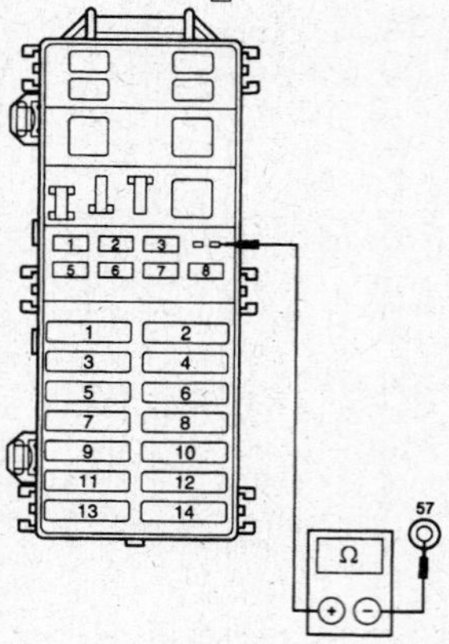	2 Measure the resistance between the load side of power distribution box mini fuse 4 (30A), circuit 418 (DG/Y) and EEC-IV 60-Pin Breakout Box pin 57, circuit 418 (DG/LG). • Is the resistance less than 5 ohms? → **Yes** GO to **W4**. → **No** REPAIR circuit 418 (DG/Y). TEST the system for normal operation.

FM2019800396020X

Fig. 26 Test W: No Communication w/Vehicle Dynamic Module (Part 2 of 3). 2000–01

TEST CONDITIONS	TEST DETAILS/RESULTS/ACTIONS
W4 CHECK CIRCUIT 1050 (LG/P) FOR OPEN	
1  Fuse Junction Panel Fuse 28 (10A) 2 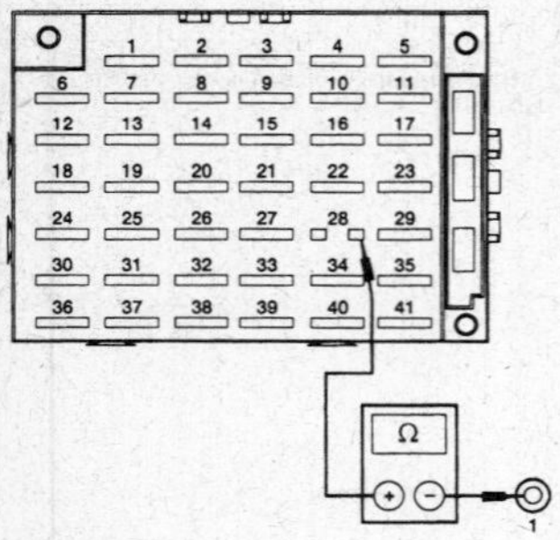	2 Measure the resistance between the load side of fuse junction panel fuse 28 (10A), circuit 1050 (LG/P) and EEC-IV 60-Pin Breakout Box pin 1, circuit 1050 (LG/P). • Is the resistance less than 5 ohms? → **Yes** DIAGNOSE module communictaion netwrok. → **No** REPAIR circuit 1050 (LG/P). TEST the system for normal operation.

FM2019800396030X

Fig. 26 Test W: No Communication w/Vehicle Dynamic Module (Part 3 of 3). 2000–01

CONDITIONS	DETAILS/RESULTS/ACTIONS
A1 CHECK CIRCUIT 875 (BK/LB) FOR OPEN	
	1 Connect the EEC-IV 60-Pin Breakout Box to VDM C4085.

CONDITIONS	DETAILS/RESULTS/ACTIONS
A1 CHECK CIRCUIT 875 (BK/LB) FOR OPEN (Continued)	
2 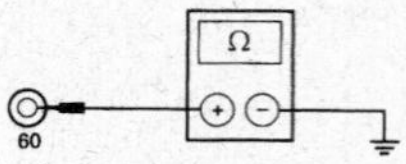	2 Measure the resistance between EEC-IV 60-Pin Breakout Box Pin 60, Circuit 875 (BK/LB), and ground. • Is the resistance less than 5 ohms? → **Yes** GO to **A2**. → **No** REPAIR the circuit. CLEAR the DTCs. REPEAT the self-test.
A2 CHECK CIRCUIT 418 (DG/YE) FOR OPEN	
1  BJB Mini Fuse 4 (30A)	

FM2010200712010X

Fig. 27 Test A: No Communication w/Module (Part 1 of 3). 2002–04

CONDITIONS	DETAILS/RESULTS/ACTIONS
A2 CHECK CIRCUIT 418 (DG/YE) FOR OPEN (Continued)	
2 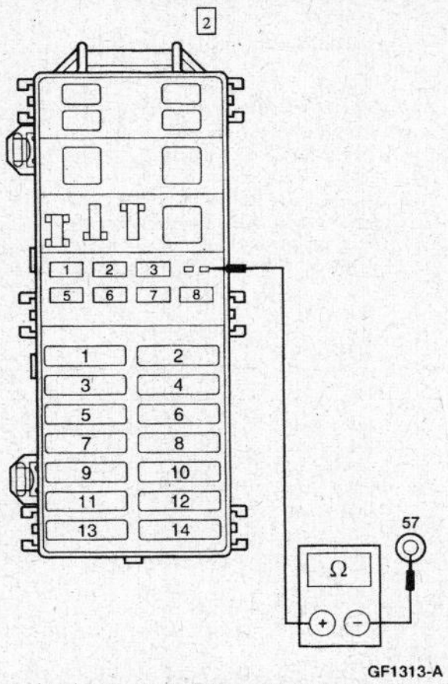	2 Measure the resistance between the load side of BJB mini Fuse 4 (30A), Circuit 418 (DG/YE) and EEC-IV 60-Pin Breakout Box Pin 57, Circuit 418 (DG/LG). • Is the resistance less than 5 ohms? → **Yes** GO to **A3**. → **No** REPAIR the circuit. CLEAR the DTCs. REPEAT the self-test.
A3 CHECK CIRCUIT 1050 (LG/VT) FOR OPEN	
1 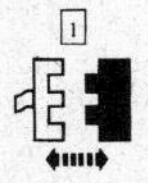 CJB Fuse 28 (10A)	

FM2010200712020X

Fig. 27 Test A: No Communication w/Module (Part 2 of 3). 2002–04

CONDITIONS	DETAILS/RESULTS/ACTIONS
A3 CHECK CIRCUIT 1050 (LG/VT) FOR OPEN (Continued)	
2 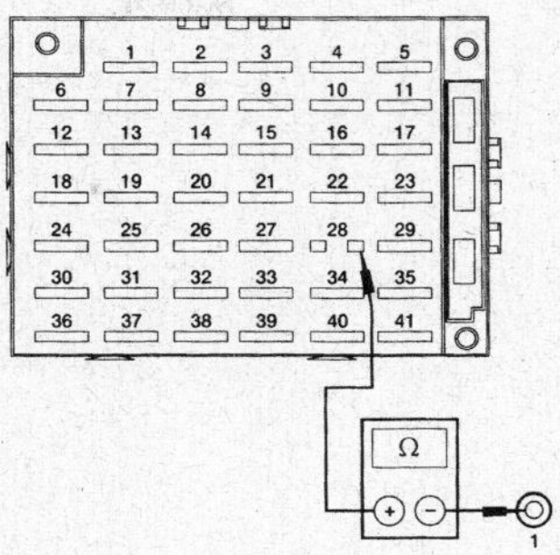	2 Measure the resistance between the load side of CJB Fuse 28 (10A), Circuit 1050 (LG/VT) and EEC-IV 60-Pin Breakout Box Pin 1, Circuit 1050 (LG/VT). • Is the resistance less than 5 ohms? → **Yes** DIAGNOSE module communications. → **No** REPAIR the circuit. CLEAR the DTCs. REPEAT the self-test.

FM2010200712030X

Fig. 27 Test A: No Communication w/Module (Part 3 of 3). 2002–04

CONDITIONS	DETAILS/RESULTS/ACTIONS
B1 CHECK THE COMMUNICATION TO THE VDM	
1 	1 Check the communication to the VDM. • Does scan tool communicate with the VDM? → **Yes** INSTALL a new VDM. CARRY OUT ride height adjustment, REPEAT the self-test. → **No** GO to Pinpoint Test A.

FM2010200713000X

Fig. 28 Test B: Unable To Enter Self-Test Diagnostics. 2002–04

CONDITIONS	DETAILS/RESULTS/ACTIONS
C1 CHECK BATTERY FOR HIGH VOLTAGE	
1 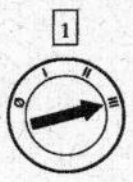	2 Verify that lights, radio and all accessories are off. 3 Measure the voltage between battery terminals. • Is the voltage greater than 14.5 volts? → **Yes** REPAIR the charging system. → **No** If DTC B1317 is a continuous DTC and is not encountered during self-test, CLEAR the DTCs. REPEAT the self-test. If DTC 1317 is a self-test DTC, INSTALL a new VDM. CARRY OUT ride height adjustment, Adjustments. REPEAT the self-test.

FM2010200714000X

Fig. 29 Test C/Code B1317: Battery Voltage High. 2002–04

CONDITIONS	DETAILS/RESULTS/ACTIONS
D1 CHECK BATTERY FOR LOW VOLTAGE	
1 	2 Verify that lights, radio and all accessories are off.

FM2010200716010X

Fig. 30 Test D/Code B1318: Battery Voltage Low (Part 1 of 3). 2002–04

CONDITIONS	DETAILS/RESULTS/ACTIONS
D1 CHECK BATTERY FOR LOW VOLTAGE (Continued)	

[3] Measure the voltage between battery terminals.

- Is the voltage greater than 12.5 volts?

→ **Yes**
GO to **D2**.

→ **No**
REPAIR the charging system.

D2 CHECK VOLTAGE AT VEHICLE DYNAMIC MODULE (VDM)

[3] Connect the EEC-IV 60-Pin Breakout Box to VDM C4085. Do not connect the VDM.

[5] Verify that lights, radio and all accessories are turned off.

[6] Measure the voltage between EEC-IV 60-Pin Breakout Box Pins as follows:

EEC-IV 60-Pin Breakout Box Pin, Circuit	EEC-IV 60-Pin Breakout Box Pin, Circuit
36, Circuit 418 (DG/YE)	40, Circuit 875 (BK/LB)
37, Circuit 418 (DG/YE)	40, Circuit 875 (BK/LB)
56, Circuit 418 (DG/YE)	60, Circuit 875 (BK/LB)
57, Circuit 418 (DG/YE)	60, Circuit 875 (BK/LB)
58, Circuit 418 (DG/YE)	60, Circuit 875 (BK/LB)

FM2010200716020X

Fig. 30 Test D/Code B1318: Battery Voltage Low (Part 2 of 3). 2002–04

CONDITIONS	DETAILS/RESULTS/ACTIONS
E1 CHECK FOR CONTINUOUS DTCS	

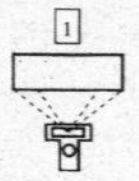

[1] Retrieve and document continuous DTCs.

- Is DTC B1342 present?

→ **Yes**
INSTALL a new VDM
CARRY OUT ride height adjustment;
REPEAT the self-test.

→ **No**
The system is operating normally.

FM2010200717000X

Fig. 31 Test E/Code B1342: ECU Internal Fault. 2002–04

CONDITIONS	DETAILS/RESULTS/ACTIONS
F1 CHECK HEIGHT SENSOR CONNECTORS	

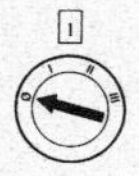

[2] Disconnect height sensor C4092, and if equipped, C4093, C1153, and C1151.

[3] Check the height sensor connectors for corrosion, bent pins and damaged wires.

- Are the height sensor connectors worn or damaged?

→ **Yes**
REPAIR as necessary. CLEAR the DTCs. REPEAT the self-test.

→ **No**
RECONNECT the height sensor(s). GO to F2.

FM2010200718010X

Fig. 32 Test F/Codes C1722 & C1842: Height Sensor Power & Disable Switch Circuits Short To Power (Part 1 of 4). 2002–04

CONDITIONS	DETAILS/RESULTS/ACTIONS
D2 CHECK VOLTAGE AT VEHICLE DYNAMIC MODULE (VDM) (Continued)	

- Is the voltage greater than 10 volts?

→ **Yes**
If DTC B1318 is a continuous DTC and is not encountered during self-test, CLEAR the DTCs. REPEAT the self-test.

If DTC 1318 is a self-test DTC, INSTALL a new VDM. CARRY OUT ride height adjustment, REPEAT the self-test.

→ **No**
GO to **D3**.

D3 CHECK VDM GROUND CIRCUITS

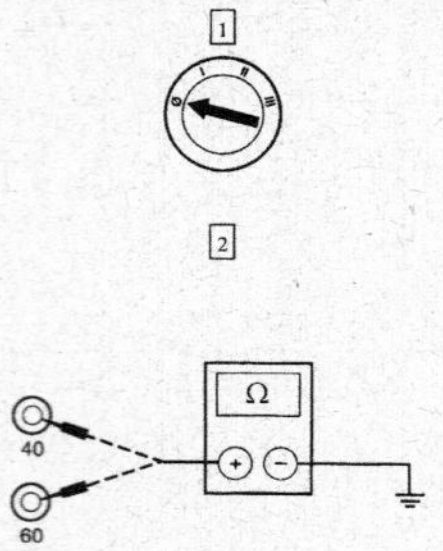

[2] Measure the resistance between the following EEC-IV 60-Pin Breakout Box test pins, and ground.
— 40, Circuit 875 (BK/LB)
— 60, Circuit 875 (BK/LB)

- Are the resistances less than 5 ohms?

→ **Yes**
CHECK Circuit 418 (DG/YE) for open. REPAIR as necessary. REPEAT the self-test.

→ **No**
REPAIR the Circuit. CLEAR the DTCs. REPEAT the self-test.

FM2010200716030X

Fig. 30 Test D/Code B1318: Battery Voltage Low (Part 3 of 3). 2002–04

CONDITIONS	DETAILS/RESULTS/ACTIONS
F2 CHECK AIR SUSPENSION SWITCH CONNECTOR	

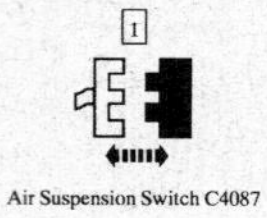

[2] Check air suspension switch C4087 for corrosion, bent pins and damaged wires.

- Is the air suspension switch C4087 worn or damaged?

→ **Yes**
REPAIR as necessary. CLEAR the DTCs. REPEAT the self-test.

→ **No**
GO to **F3**.

F3 CHECK VEHICLE DYNAMIC MODULE (VDM) CONNECTOR

[2] Check VDM C4085 for corrosion, bent pins and damaged wires.

- Is the VDM C4085 worn or damaged?

→ **Yes**
REPAIR as necessary. CLEAR the DTCs. REPEAT the self-test.

→ **No**
GO to **F4**.

F4 CHECK CIRCUIT 425 (BR/PK) FOR SHORT TO POWER

[1] Connect EEC-IV 60-Pin Breakout Box to VDM C4085.

FM2010200718020X

Fig. 32 Test F/Codes C1722 & C1842: Height Sensor Power & Disable Switch Circuits Short To Power (Part 2 of 4). 2002–04

CONDITIONS	DETAILS/RESULTS/ACTIONS
F4 CHECK CIRCUIT 425 (BR/PK) FOR SHORT TO POWER (Continued)	
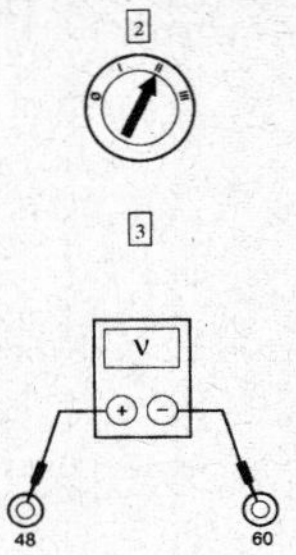	3 Measure the voltage between EEC-IV 60-Pin Breakout Box Pin 48, Circuit 425 (BR/PK), and EEC-IV 60-Pin Breakout Box Pin 60, Circuit 875 (BK/LB). • Is voltage present? → **Yes** REPAIR the circuit. CLEAR the DTCs. REPEAT the self-test. → **No** GO to **F5**.
F5 CHECK CIRCUIT 426 (RD/BK) FOR SHORT TO POWER	
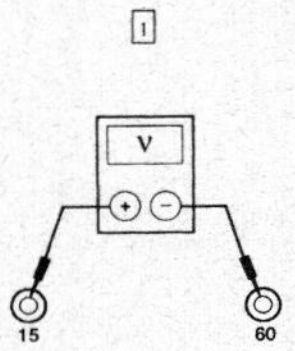	1 Measure the voltage between EEC-IV 60-Pin Breakout Box Pin 15, Circuit 426 (RD/BK), and EEC-IV 60-Pin Breakout Box Pin 60, Circuit 875 (BK/LB). • Is voltage present? → **Yes** REPAIR Circuit 426 (RD/BK). CLEAR the DTCs. REPEAT the self-test. → **No** RECONNECT air suspension switch C4087. GO to **F6**.
F6 CHECK VOLTAGE BETWEEN CIRCUIT 426 (RD/BK) AND CIRCUIT 432 (BK/PK)	
	2 Connect EEC-IV 60-Pin Breakout Box to the VDM.

FM2010200718030X

Fig. 32 Test F/Codes C1722 & C1842: Height Sensor Power & Disable Switch Circuits Short To Power (Part 3 of 4). 2002–04

CONDITIONS	DETAILS/RESULTS/ACTIONS
F6 CHECK VOLTAGE BETWEEN CIRCUIT 426 (RD/BK) AND CIRCUIT 432 (BK/PK) (Continued)	
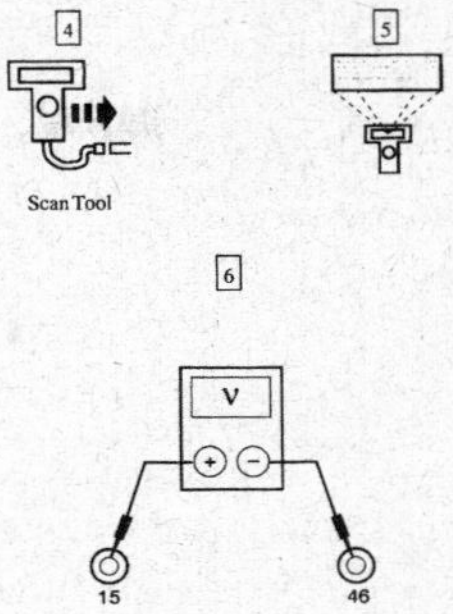	3 Verify that the air suspension switch is in the ON position. 5 Trigger VDM active command HGT POWER ON. 6 Measure the voltage between EEC-IV 60-Pin Breakout Box Pin 15, Circuit 426 (RD/BK), and EEC-IV 60-Pin Breakout Box Pin 46, Circuit 432 (BK/PK). • Is the voltage between 4.8 volts and 5.2 volts? → **Yes** GO to **F7**. → **No** INSTALL a new VDM. CARRY OUT ride height adjustment. REPEAT the self-test.
F7 CHECK HEIGHT SENSORS	
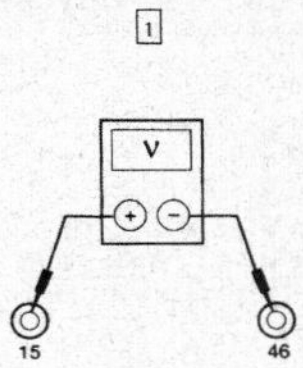	1 Measure the voltage between EEC-IV 60-Pin Breakout Box Pin 15, Circuit 426 (RD/BK), and EEC-IV 60-Pin Breakout Box Pin 46, Circuit 432 (BK/PK) as each height sensor is reconnected. • Is the voltage between 4.8 volts and 5.2 volts after each height sensor is reconnected? → **Yes** CARRY OUT the Wiggle Test. REPAIR as necessary. CLEAR the DTCs. REPEAT the self-test. → **No** INSTALL a new height sensor. CLEAR the DTCs. CARRY OUT ride height adjustment. REPEAT the self-test.

FM2010200718040X

Fig. 32 Test F/Codes C1722 & C1842: Height Sensor Power & Disable Switch Circuits Short To Power (Part 4 of 4). 2002–04

CONDITIONS	DETAILS/RESULTS/ACTIONS
G1 CHECK HEIGHT SENSOR CONNECTORS	
	2 Disconnect height sensor C4092, and if equipped, C4093, C1153, and C1151. 3 Check the height sensor connectors for corrosion, bent pins and damaged wires. • Are the height sensor connectors worn or damaged? → **Yes** REPAIR as necessary. CLEAR the DTCs. REPEAT the self-test. → **No** RECONNECT the height sensor(s). GO to **G2**.
G2 CHECK AIR SUSPENSION SWITCH CONNECTOR	
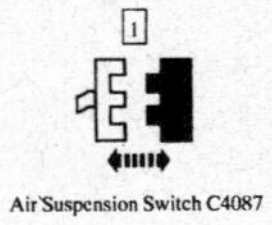	2 Check air suspension switch C4087 for corrosion, bent pins and damaged wires. • Is the air suspension switch C4087 worn or damaged? → **Yes** REPAIR as necessary. CLEAR the DTCs. REPEAT the self-test. → **No** GO to **G3**.

FM2010200719010X

Fig. 33 Test G/Codes C1723 & C1840: Height Sensor Power Circuit Short To Ground & Disable Switch Circuit Failure (Part 1 of 4). 2002–04

CONDITIONS	DETAILS/RESULTS/ACTIONS
G3 CHECK VEHICLE DYNAMIC MODULE (VDM) CONNECTOR	
	2 Check VDM C4085 for corrosion, bent pins and damaged wires. • Is the VDM C4085 worn or damaged? → **Yes** REPAIR as necessary. CLEAR the DTCs. REPEAT the self-test. → **No** GO to **G4**.
G4 CHECK AIR SUSPENSION SWITCH	
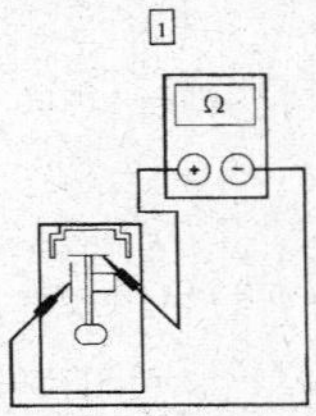	1 Measure the resistance between air suspension switch terminals with the switch ON and then OFF. • Is the resistance with the air suspension switch ON less than 5 ohms and with the air suspension switch OFF greater than 10,000 ohms? → **Yes** GO to **G5**. → **No** INSTALL a new air suspension switch. CLEAR the DTCs. REPEAT the self-test.
G5 CHECK CIRCUIT 425 (BR/PK)	
	1 Connect EEC-IV 60-Pin Breakout Box to VDM C4085.

FM2010200719020X

Fig. 33 Test G/Codes C1723 & C1840: Height Sensor Power Circuit Short To Ground & Disable Switch Circuit Failure (Part 2 of 4). 2002–04

CONDITIONS	DETAILS/RESULTS/ACTIONS
G5 CHECK CIRCUIT 425 (BR/PK) (Continued)	
2 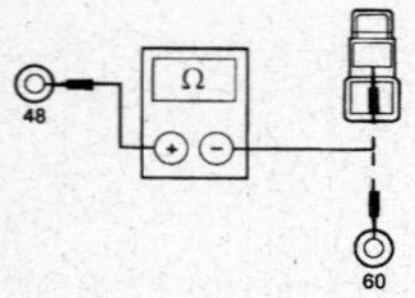	2 Measure the resistance between EEC-IV 60-Pin Breakout Box Pin 48, Circuit 425 (BR/PK), and air suspension switch C4087, Circuit 425 (BR/PK); and between EEC-IV 60-Pin Breakout Box Pin 48, Circuit 425 (BR/PK), and EEC-IV 60-Pin Breakout Box Pin 60, Circuit 875 (BK/LB). • Is the resistance less than 5 ohms between EEC-IV 60-Pin Breakout Box and switch, and greater than 10,000 ohms between EEC-IV 60-Pin Breakout Box pins? → **Yes** GO to **G6**. → **No** REPAIR Circuit 425 (BR/PK). CLEAR the DTCs. REPEAT the self-test.
G6 CHECK CIRCUIT 426 (RD/BK)	
1 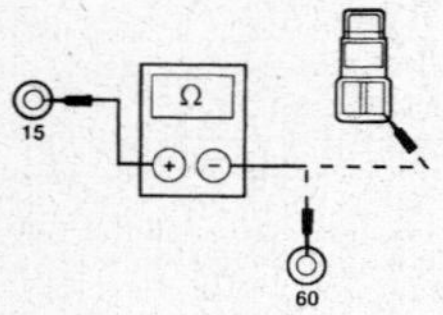	1 Measure the resistance between EEC-IV 60-Pin Breakout Box Pin 15, Circuit 426 (RD/BK), and air suspension switch C4087, Circuit 426 (RD/BK); and between EEC-IV 60-Pin Breakout Box Pin 15, Circuit 426 (RD/BK), and EEC-IV 60-Pin Breakout Box Pin 60, Circuit 875 (BK/LB). • Is the resistance less than 5 ohms between EEC-IV 60-Pin Breakout Box and air suspension switch; and greater than 10,000 ohms between EEC-IV 60-Pin Breakout Box pins? → **Yes** GO to **G7**. → **No** REPAIR Circuit 426 (RD/BK). CLEAR the DTCs. REPEAT the self-test.
G7 CHECK VOLTAGE BETWEEN CIRCUIT 426 (RD/BK) AND CIRCUIT 432 (BK/PK)	
2 3 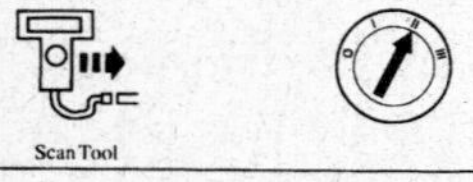	1 Connect EEC-IV 60-Pin Breakout Box to the VDM.

FM2010200719030X

Fig. 33 Test G/Codes C1723 & C1840: Height Sensor Power Circuit Short To Ground & Disable Switch Circuit Failure (Part 3 of 4). 2002–04

CONDITIONS	DETAILS/RESULTS/ACTIONS
H1 CHECK FOR AIR COMPRESSOR ASSEMBLY OPERATION	
1 2 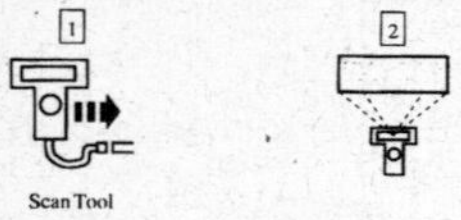	2 Trigger VDM active command COMPRESSR ON then OFF. • Does the air compressor turn on and off? → **Yes** GO to **H2**. → **No** GO to Pinpoint Test U.
H2 CHECK FOR AIR SPRING SOLENOID FUNCTION	
1 	1 Trigger VDM active commands RR SOL or LR SOL, and COMPRESSR ON. • Does a corner raise? → **Yes** TRIGGER VDM active commands RR SOL or LR SOL, and COMPRESSR OFF. GO to **H3**. → **No** TRIGGER VDM active commands RR SOL or LR SOL, and COMPRESSR OFF. GO to Pinpoint Test V.

FM2010200720010X

Fig. 34 Test H/Codes C1735 & C1737: Lefthand/ Righthand Rear Corner Up Timeout (Part 1 of 3). 2002–04

CONDITIONS	DETAILS/RESULTS/ACTIONS
G7 CHECK VOLTAGE BETWEEN CIRCUIT 426 (RD/BK) AND CIRCUIT 432 (BK/PK) (Continued)	
5 	4 Trigger VDM active command HGT POWER ON.
6 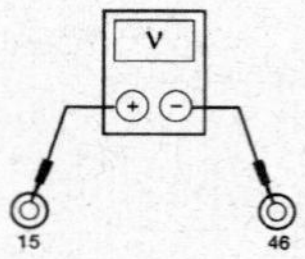	6 Measure the voltage between EEC-IV 60-Pin Breakout Box Pin 15, Circuit 426 (RD/BK), and EEC-IV 60-Pin Breakout Box Pin 46, Circuit 432 (BK/PK). • Is the voltage between 4.8 volts and 5.2 volts? → **Yes** GO to **G8**. → **No** INSTALL a new VDM. CLEAR the DTCs. CARRY OUT ride height adjustment. REPEAT the self-test.
G8 CHECK HEIGHT SENSORS	
1 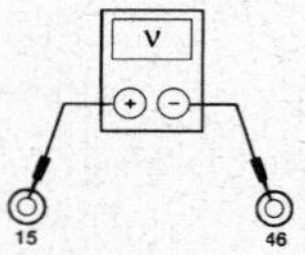	1 Measure the voltage between EEC-IV 60-Pin Breakout Box Pin 15, Circuit 426 (RD/BK), and EEC-IV 60-Pin Breakout Box Pin 46, Circuit 432 (BK/PK) as each height sensor is reconnected. • Is the voltage between 4.8 volts and 5.2 volts after each height sensor is reconnected? → **Yes** INSTALL a new VDM. → **No** INSTALL a new height sensor. CLEAR the DTCs. CARRY OUT ride height adjustment. REPEAT the self-test.

FM2010200719040X

Fig. 33 Test G/Codes C1723 & C1840: Height Sensor Power Circuit Short To Ground & Disable Switch Circuit Failure (Part 4 of 4). 2002–04

CONDITIONS	DETAILS/RESULTS/ACTIONS
H3 CHECK HEIGHT SENSOR MOUNTING POINTS	
1 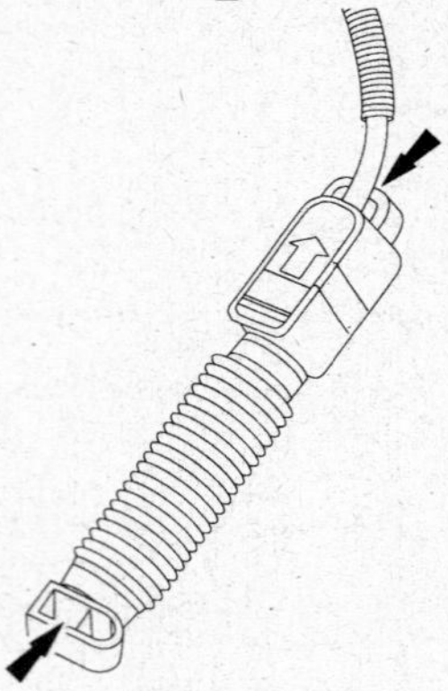	1 Check the height sensor mounting points. • Are the mounting points damaged or are the height sensors disconnected from the ball studs? → **Yes** REPAIR as necessary. CLEAR the DTCs. CARRY OUT ride height adjustment. REPEAT the self-test. → **No** GO to **H4**.
H4 CHECK FOR HEIGHT SENSOR OPERATION	
1 	1 Trigger VDM active command HGT POWER ON.
2 	2 Monitor VDM PID LR__HGT or RR__HGT.

FM2010200720020X

Fig. 34 Test H/Codes C1735 & C1737: Lefthand/ Righthand Rear Corner Up Timeout (Part 2 of 3). 2002–04

CONDITIONS	DETAILS/RESULTS/ACTIONS
H4 CHECK FOR HEIGHT SENSOR OPERATION (Continued)	
3 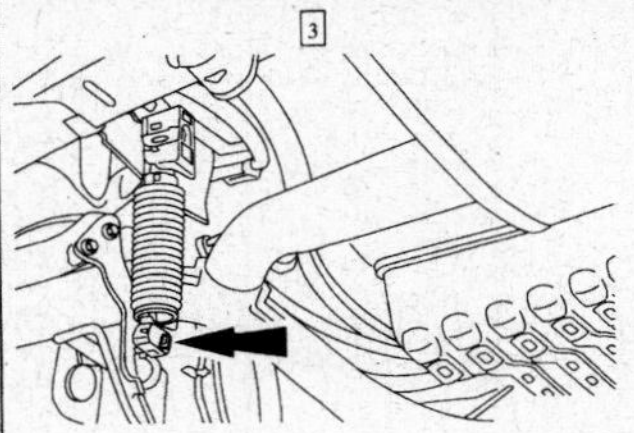	3 Disconnect the selected height sensor from the lower ball stud.
	4 Extend and compress the selected height sensor over its full range of travel. • Does the displayed length for the selected height sensor vary as the length of the height sensor changes? → **Yes** TRIGGER VDM active command HGT POWER OFF. RECONNECT height sensor(s). CARRY OUT the Accurate Trim Test. CLEAR the DTCs. REPEAT the self-test. → **No** TRIGGER VDM active command HGT POWER OFF. RECONNECT height sensor(s). GO to Pinpoint Test O.

FM2010200720030X

Fig. 34 Test H/Codes C1735 & C1737: Lefthand/ Righthand Rear Corner Up Timeout (Part 3 of 3). 2002–04

CONDITIONS	DETAILS/RESULTS/ACTIONS
I1 CHECK FOR AIR SPRING VENTING	
1 	1 Trigger VDM active commands RR SOL or LR SOL, and VENT ON. • Does a corner lower? → **Yes** TRIGGER VDM active commands RR SOL or LR SOL, and VENT OFF. GO to **I2**. → **No** TRIGGER VDM active commands RR SOL or LR SOL, and VENT OFF. GO to **I4**.
I2 CHECK HEIGHT SENSOR MOUNTING POINTS	
1 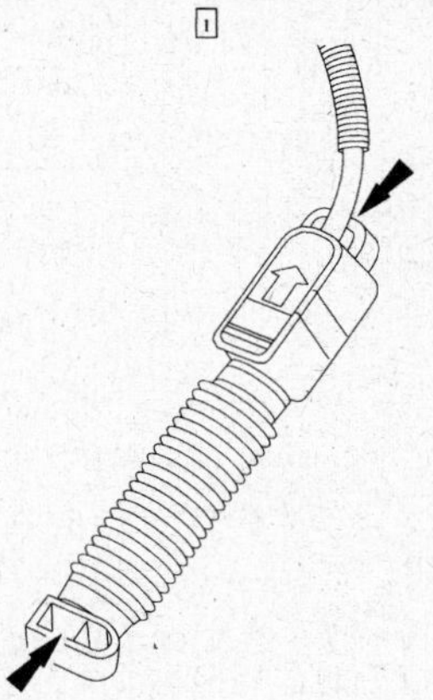	1 Check the height sensor mounting points. • Are the mounting points damaged or are the height sensors disconnected from the ball studs? → **Yes** REPAIR as necessary. CLEAR the DTCs. CARRY OUT ride height adjustment. REPEAT the self-test. → **No** GO to **I3**.

FM2010200721010X

Fig. 35 Test I/Codes C1736 & C1738: Lefthand/ Righthand Rear Corner Down Timeout (Part 1 of 3). 2002–04

CONDITIONS	DETAILS/RESULTS/ACTIONS
I3 CHECK FOR HEIGHT SENSOR OPERATION	
1 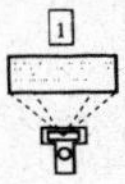	1 Trigger VDM active command HGT POWER ON.
2 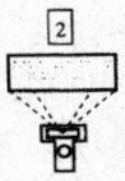	2 Monitor VDM PID LR__HGT or RR__HGT.
3 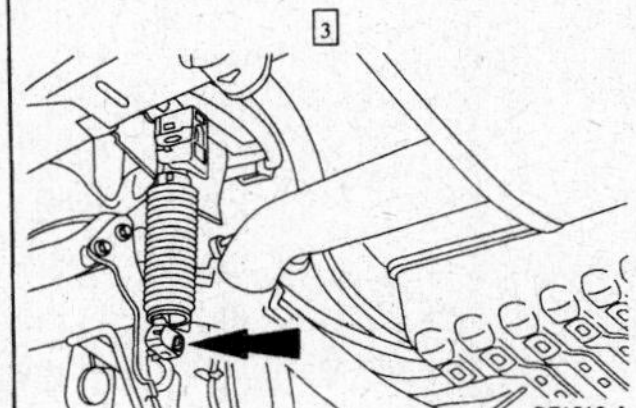 GF1513-A	3 Disconnect the selected height sensor from the lower ball stud.
	4 Extend and compress the selected height sensor over its full range of travel. • Does the displayed voltage for the selected height sensor vary as the length of the height sensor changes? → **Yes** INSTALL a new VDM. CARRY OUT ride height adjustment. REPEAT the self-test. → **No** RECONNECT height sensor(s). GO to Pinpoint Test O.
I4 CHECK FOR RESTRICTED AIR LINE	
	1 Disconnect the air line between the air compressor and the air spring that will not lower.

FM2010200721020X

Fig. 35 Test I/Codes C1736 & C1738: Lefthand/ Righthand Rear Corner Down Timeout (Part 2 of 3). 2002–04

CONDITIONS	DETAILS/RESULTS/ACTIONS
I4 CHECK FOR RESTRICTED AIR LINE (Continued)	
	2 Connect Vacuum Tester to the air line and try to draw a vacuum. • Can a vacuum be drawn and held? → **Yes** REPAIR as necessary. CLEAR the DTCs. REPEAT the self-test. → **No** GO to **I5**.
I5 CHECK FOR RESTRICTED AIR SPRING SOLENOID VALVE	
1 	1 Trigger VDM active command LR SOL or RR SOL ON. • Does air exhaust from the suspect air spring solenoid? → **Yes** GO to **I6**. → **No** INSTALL a new air spring solenoid. CLEAR the DTCs. REPEAT the self-test.
I6 CHECK AIR COMPRESSOR AIR DRIER	
	1 Remove the air compressor air drier from the air compressor. 2 Blow shop air through the air drier from the air line port. • Does air exhaust from the air drier? → **Yes** INSTALL a new air compressor. CLEAR the DTCs. REPEAT the self-test. → **No** INSTALL a new air drier. CLEAR the DTCs. REPEAT the self-test.

FM2010200721030X

Fig. 35 Test I/Codes C1736 & C1738: Lefthand/ Righthand Rear Corner Down Timeout (Part 3 of 3). 2002–04

CONDITIONS	DETAILS/RESULTS/ACTIONS
J1 CHECK AIR COMPRESSOR ASSEMBLY CONNECTOR	
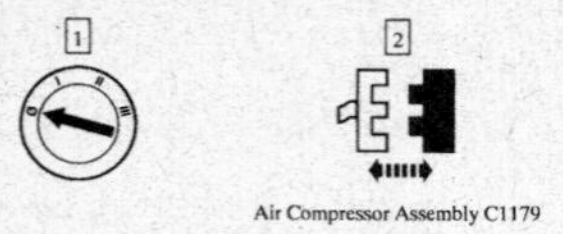	3 Check air compressor C1179 for corrosion, bent pins and damaged wires. • Is the air compressor C1179 worn or damaged? → **Yes** REPAIR as necessary. CLEAR the DTCs. REPEAT the self-test. → **No** GO to **J2**.
J2 CHECK VENT SOLENOID RESISTANCE	
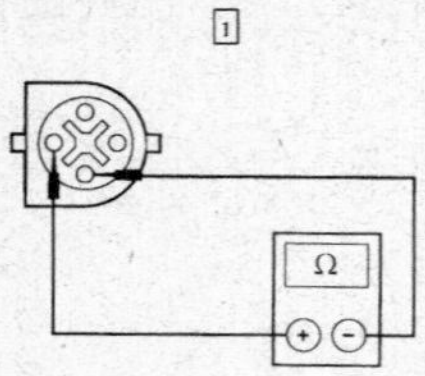	1 Measure the resistance between air compressor assembly C1179F Pin 2 and Pin 3 (component side). • Is the resistance between 19 and 24 ohms? → **Yes** GO to **J3**. → **No** INSTALL a new air compressor. CLEAR the DTCs. REPEAT the self-test.

FM2010200722010X

Fig. 36 Test J/Code C1770: Vent Solenoid Output Circuit Failure (Part 1 of 3). 2002–04

CONDITIONS	DETAILS/RESULTS/ACTIONS
J3 CHECK CIRCUIT 57 (BK) FOR OPEN	
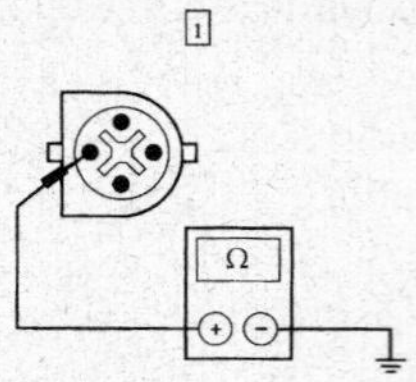	1 Measure the resistance between air compressor C1179 Pin 3, Circuit 57 (BK), harness side and ground. • Is the resistance less than 5 ohms? → **Yes** GO to **J4**. → **No** REPAIR the circuit. CLEAR the DTCs. REPEAT the self-test.
J4 CHECK CIRCUIT 421 (PK) FOR SHORT TO POWER	
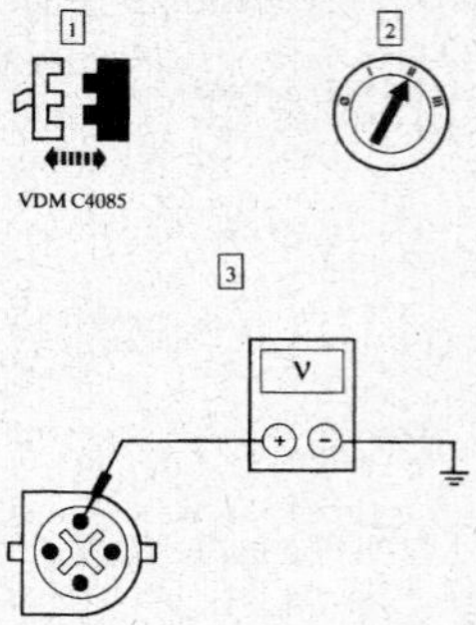	3 Measure the voltage between air compressor C1179 Pin 2, Circuit 421 (PK), harness side and ground. • Is voltage present? → **Yes** REPAIR the circuit. CLEAR the DTCs. REPEAT the self-test. → **No** GO to **J5**.
J5 CHECK CIRCUIT 421 (PK) FOR OPEN	
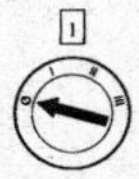	2 Connect EEC-IV 60-Pin Breakout Box to the VDM C4085.

FM2010200722020X

Fig. 36 Test J/Code C1770: Vent Solenoid Output Circuit Failure (Part 2 of 3). 2002–04

CONDITIONS	DETAILS/RESULTS/ACTIONS
J5 CHECK CIRCUIT 421 (PK) FOR OPEN (Continued)	
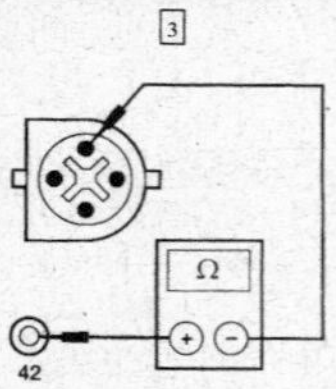	3 Measure the resistance between EEC-IV 60-Pin Breakout Box Pin 42, Circuit 421 (PK), and air compressor C1179 Pin 2, Circuit 421 (PK) harness side. • Is the resistance less than 5 ohms? → **Yes** GO to **J6**. → **No** REPAIR the circuit. CLEAR the DTCs. REPEAT the self-test.
J6 CHECK VDM FUNCTION	
	1 CONNECT the EEC-IV 60-Pin Breakout Box to the VDM.
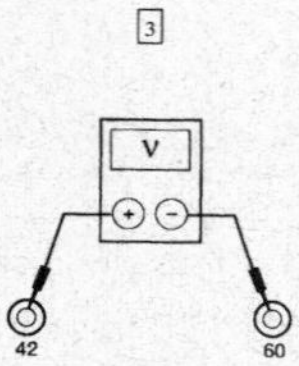	3 Trigger VDM active command VENT ON and then OFF while measuring the voltage between EEC-IV 60-Pin Breakout Box Pin 42, Circuit 421 (PK), and EEC-IV 60-Pin Breakout Box Pin 60, Circuit 875 (BK/LB). • Is the voltage greater than 10 volts with VENT ON and equal to zero volts with VENT OFF? → **Yes** TRIGGER VDM active command VENT OFF. CARRY OUT the Wiggle Test. REPAIR as necessary. CLEAR the DTCs. REPEAT the self-test. → **No** INSTALL a new VDM. CLEAR the DTCs. CARRY OUT ride height adjustment. REPEAT the self-test.

FM2010200722030X

Fig. 36 Test J/Code C1770: Vent Solenoid Output Circuit Failure (Part 3 of 3). 2002–04

CONDITIONS	DETAILS/RESULTS/ACTIONS
K1 CHECK AIR COMPRESSOR ASSEMBLY CONNECTOR	
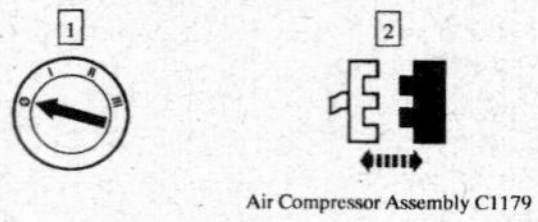	3 Check air compressor C1179 for corrosion, bent pins and damaged wires. • Is the air compressor C1179 worn or damaged? → **Yes** REPAIR as necessary. CLEAR the DTCs. REPEAT the self-test. → **No** GO to **K2**.
K2 CHECK VENT SOLENOID RESISTANCE	
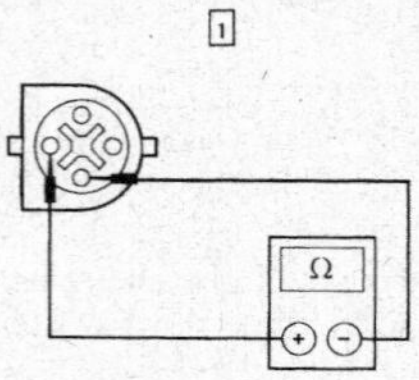	1 Measure the resistance between air compressor C1179F Pin 2 and Pin 3 (component side). • Is the resistance between 19 and 24 ohms? → **Yes** GO to **K3**. → **No** INSTALL a new air compressor. CLEAR the DTCs. REPEAT the self-test.

FM2010200723010X

Fig. 37 Test K/Code C1773: Vent Solenoid Output Circuit Short To Ground (Part 1 of 2). 2002–04

CONDITIONS	DETAILS/RESULTS/ACTIONS
K3 CHECK VENT SOLENOID FOR SHORT TO GROUND	
1 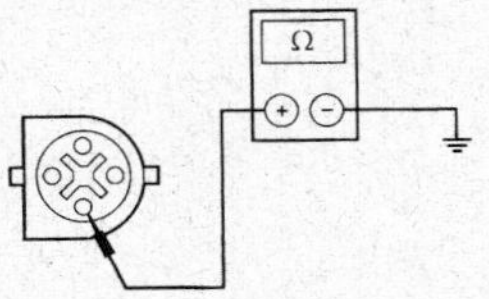	1 Measure the resistance between air compressor C1179F Pin 2, component side and ground. • Is the resistance greater than 10,000 ohms? → **Yes** GO to **K4**. → **No** INSTALL a new air compressor. CLEAR the DTCs. REPEAT the self-test.
K4 CHECK CIRCUIT 421 (PK) FOR SHORT TO GROUND	
1  VDM C4085	
2 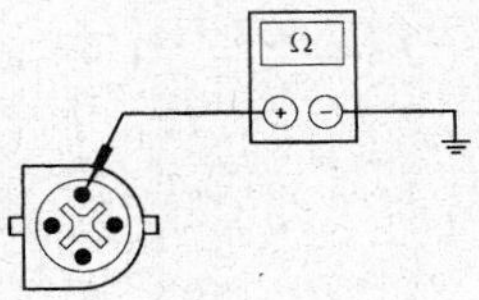	2 Measure the resistance between air compressor C1179 Pin 2, Circuit 421 (PK), harness side and ground. • Is the resistance greater than 10,000 ohms? → **Yes** INSTALL a new VDM. CARRY OUT ride height adjustment. REPEAT the self-test. → **No** REPAIR the circuit. CLEAR the DTCs. REPEAT the self-test.

FM2010200723020X

Fig. 37 Test K/Code C1773: Vent Solenoid Output Circuit Short To Ground (Part 2 of 2). 2002–04

CONDITIONS	DETAILS/RESULTS/ACTIONS
L3 CHECK CIRCUIT 57 (BK) FOR OPEN	
1 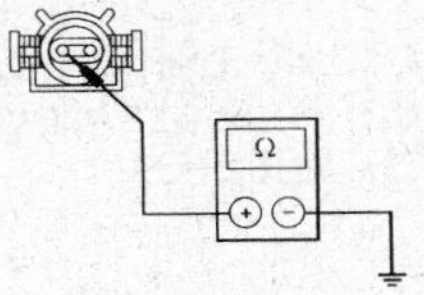	1 Measure the resistance between suspect air spring solenoid (LR C4044, RR C4045) Pin 1, Circuit 57 (BK), harness side and ground. • Is the resistance less than 5 ohms? → **Yes** GO to **L4**. → **No** REPAIR the circuit. CLEAR the DTCs. REPEAT the self-test.
L4 CHECK CIRCUIT 416 (LB/BK) OR CIRCUIT 429 (VT/LG) FOR SHORT TO POWER	
1 2  VDM C4085	
3 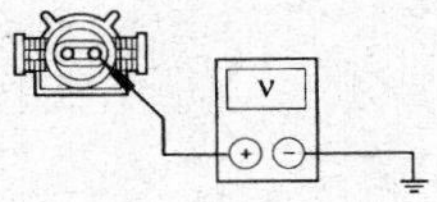	3 Measure the voltage between air spring solenoid (LR C4044 Pin 2, Circuit 429 [VT/LG] harness side; RR C4045 Pin 2, Circuit 416 [LB/BK]), harness side and ground. • Is voltage present? → **Yes** REPAIR the circuit in question. CLEAR the DTCs. REPEAT the self-test. → **No** GO to **L5**.
L5 CHECK CIRCUIT 416 (LB/BK) OR CIRCUIT 429 (VT/LG) FOR OPEN	
1 	2 Connect EEC-IV 60-Pin Breakout Box to the VDM C4085.

FM2010200724020X

Fig. 38 Test L/Codes C1790 & C1795: Lefthand/ Righthand Rear Air Spring Solenoid Output Circuit Failure (Part 2 of 4). 2002–04

CONDITIONS	DETAILS/RESULTS/ACTIONS
L1 CHECK AIR SPRING SOLENOID CONNECTOR	
1 2 	2 Disconnect LR air spring solenoid C4044 or RR air spring solenoid C4045. 3 Check the suspect air spring solenoid connector for corrosion, bent pins and damaged wires. • Is the suspect air spring solenoid connector worn or damaged? → **Yes** REPAIR as necessary. REPEAT the self-test. → **No** GO to **L2**.
L2 CHECK AIR SPRING SOLENOID RESISTANCE	
1 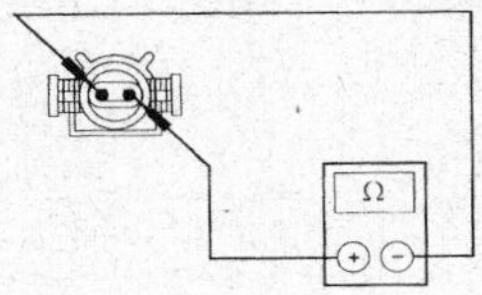	1 Measure the resistance between suspect air spring solenoid pins (component side). • Is the resistance between 14 and 18 ohms? → **Yes** GO to **L3**. → **No** INSTALL a new air spring solenoid. CLEAR the DTCs. REPEAT the self-test.

FM2010200724010X

Fig. 38 Test L/Codes C1790 & C1795: Lefthand/ Righthand Rear Air Spring Solenoid Output Circuit Failure (Part 1 of 4). 2002–04

CONDITIONS	DETAILS/RESULTS/ACTIONS
L5 CHECK CIRCUIT 416 (LB/BK) OR CIRCUIT 429 (VT/LG) FOR OPEN (Continued)	
3 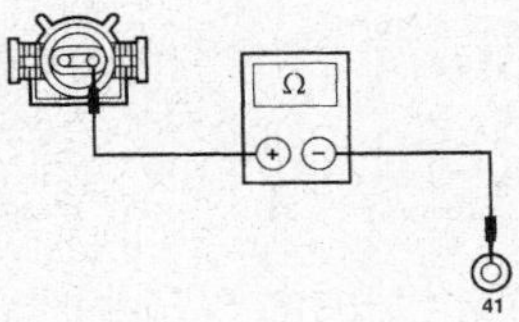	3 If suspect air spring solenoid is LR, measure the resistance between EEC-IV 60-Pin Breakout Box Pin 41, Circuit 429 (VT/LG), and air spring solenoid C4044 Pin 2, Circuit 429 (VT/LG), harness side.
4 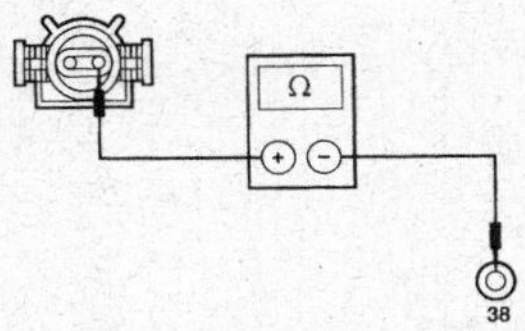	4 If suspect air spring solenoid is RR, measure the resistance between EEC-IV 60-Pin Breakout Box Pin 38, Circuit 416 (LB/BK), and air spring solenoid C4045 Pin 2, Circuit 416 (LB/BK), harness side. • Is the resistance less than 5 ohms? → **Yes** RECONNECT air spring solenoid. GO to **L6**. → **No** REPAIR the circuit in question. CLEAR the DTCs. REPEAT the self-test.
L6 CHECK VDM FUNCTION	
2 3 	1 Connect the EEC-IV 60-Pin Breakout Box to the VDM. 3 Trigger VDM active command LR SOL or RR SOL ON.

FM2010200724030X

Fig. 38 Test L/Codes C1790 & C1795: Lefthand/ Righthand Rear Air Spring Solenoid Output Circuit Failure (Part 3 of 4). 2002–04

CONDITIONS	DETAILS/RESULTS/ACTIONS
L6 CHECK VDM FUNCTION (Continued)	
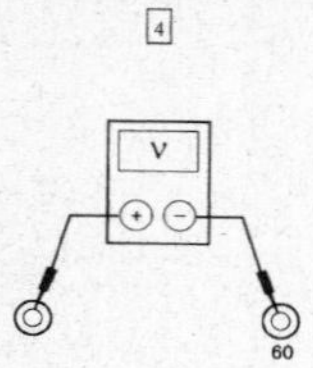	4 Measure the voltage between EEC-IV 60-Pin Breakout Box Pin (LR 41, Circuit 429 [VT/LG] or RR 38, Circuit 416 [LB/BK]), and EEC-IV 60-Pin Breakout Box Pin 60, Circuit 875 (BK/LB). • Is the voltage greater than 10 volts with the solenoid ON and equal to zero volts with the solenoid OFF? → **Yes** TRIGGER VDM active command LR SOL or RR SOL OFF. CARRY OUT the Wiggle Test. REPAIR as necessary. CLEAR the DTCs. REPEAT the self-test. → **No** INSTALL a new VDM. CARRY OUT ride height adjustment. REPEAT the self-test.

FM2010200724040X

Fig. 38 Test L/Codes C1790 & C1795: Lefthand/ Righthand Rear Air Spring Solenoid Output Circuit Failure (Part 4 of 4). 2002–04

CONDITIONS	DETAILS/RESULTS/ACTIONS
M1 CHECK AIR SPRING SOLENOID CONNECTOR	
	2 Disconnect LR air spring solenoid C4044 or RR air spring solenoid C4045. 3 Check the suspect air spring solenoid connector for corrosion, bent pins and damaged wires. • Is the suspect air spring solenoid connector worn or damaged? → **Yes** REPAIR as necessary. CLEAR the DTCs. REPEAT the self-test. → **No** GO to **M2**.

FM2010200725010X

Fig. 39 Test M/Codes C1793 & C1798: Lefthand/ Righthand Rear Air Spring Solenoid Output Circuit Short To Ground (Part 1 of 3). 2002–04

CONDITIONS	DETAILS/RESULTS/ACTIONS
M2 CHECK AIR SPRING SOLENOID RESISTANCE	
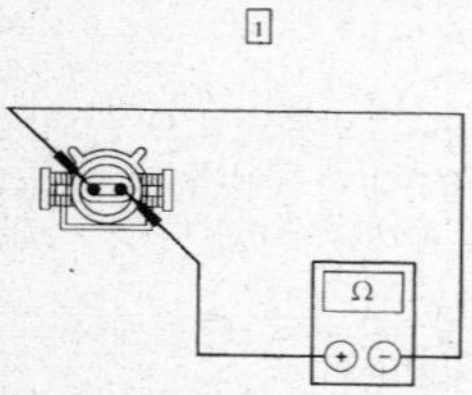	1 Measure the resistance between suspect air spring solenoid pins (component side). • Is the resistance between 14 and 18 ohms? → **Yes** GO to **M3**. → **No** INSTALL a new air spring solenoid. CLEAR the DTCs. REPEAT the self-test.
M3 CHECK CIRCUIT 416 (LB/BK) OR CIRCUIT 429 (VT/LG) FOR SHORT TO GROUND	
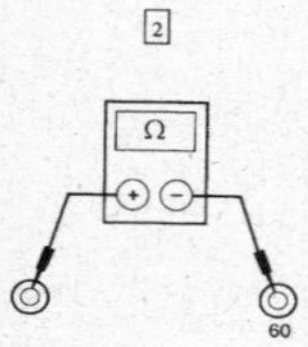	1 Connect the EEC-IV 60-Pin Breakout Box to the VDM C4085. 2 Measure the resistance between EEC-IV 60-Pin Breakout Box Pin (LR 41, Circuit 429 [VT/LG] or RR 38, Circuit 416 [LB/BK]), and EEC-IV 60-Pin Breakout Box Pin 60, Circuit 875 (BK/LB). • Is resistance greater than 10,000 ohms? → **Yes** RECONNECT air spring solenoid. GO to **M4**. → **No** REPAIR Circuit in question. CLEAR the DTCs. REPEAT the self-test.
M4 CHECK VDM FUNCTION	
	1 Connect the EEC-IV 60-Pin Breakout Box to the VDM. 3 Trigger VDM active command LR SOL or RR SOL ON, then OFF.

FM2010200725020X

Fig. 39 Test M/Codes C1793 & C1798: Lefthand/ Righthand Rear Air Spring Solenoid Output Circuit Short To Ground (Part 2 of 3). 2002–04

CONDITIONS	DETAILS/RESULTS/ACTIONS
M4 CHECK VDM FUNCTION (Continued)	
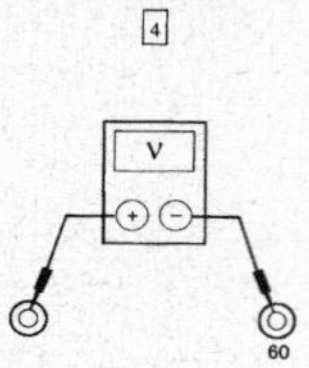	4 Measure the voltage between EEC-IV 60-Pin Breakout Box Pin (LR 41, Circuit 429 [VT/LG] or RR 38, Circuit 416 [LB/BK]), and EEC-IV 60-Pin Breakout Box Pin 60, Circuit 875 (BK/LB). • Is the voltage greater than 10 volts with the solenoid ON and equal to zero volts with the solenoid OFF? → **Yes** RECONNECT air spring solenoid and CARRY OUT wiggle test. REPAIR as necessary. If no fault is found with wiggle test, INSTALL a new air spring solenoid. CLEAR the DTCs. REPEAT the self-test. → **No** INSTALL a new VDM. CARRY OUT ride height adjustment. REPEAT the self-test.

FM2010200725030X

Fig. 39 Test M/Codes C1793 & C1798: Lefthand/ Righthand Rear Air Spring Solenoid Output Circuit Short To Ground (Part 3 of 3). 2002–04

CONDITIONS	DETAILS/RESULTS/ACTIONS
N1 RETRIEVE CONTINUOUS DTCs	
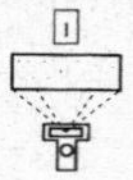	1 Retrieve and document continuous DTCs. • Is DTC C1820 retrieved? → **Yes** GO to **N2**. → **No** System OK. CLEAR the DTCs. TEST the system for normal operation.
N2 CARRY OUT PNEUMATIC SELF-TEST	
 Carry Out Pneumatic Self-Test	1 Allow air compressor to cool down for a minimum of 10 minutes before proceeding with this test.

CONDITIONS	DETAILS/RESULTS/ACTIONS
N2 CARRY OUT PNEUMATIC SELF-TEST (Continued)	
	• Did the vehicle pass the Pneumatic Self-Test? → **Yes** System OK. Possible prior overloading of vehicle. → **No** GO to VDM Diagnostic Trouble Code (DTC) Index.

FM2010200726000X

Fig. 40 Test N/Code C1820: Air Compressor Request Exceeded Maximum Timing. 2002–04

CONDITIONS	DETAILS/RESULTS/ACTIONS
O1 CHECK HEIGHT SENSOR CONNECTOR	

3 Disconnect the suspect height sensor connector as follows:

DTC	Height Sensor	Connector
C1881	RF	C1151
C1885	RR	C4093
C1889	LF	C1153
C1893	LR	C4092

4 Check the suspect height sensor connector for corrosion, bent pins and damaged wires.

- Is the suspect height sensor worn or damaged?

→ **Yes**
REPAIR as necessary. CLEAR the DTCs.

→ **No**
GO to **O2**.

FM2010200727010X

Fig. 41 Test O/Codes C1881, C1885, C1889 & C1893: Height Sensor Circuit Failure (Part 1 of 7). 2002–04

CONDITIONS	DETAILS/RESULTS/ACTIONS
O2 CHECK SENSOR CIRCUIT RESISTANCE	

1 Connect EEC-IV 60-Pin Breakout Box to the VDM C4085.

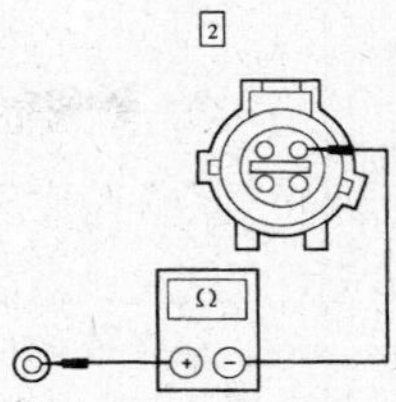

2 Measure the resistance between suspect height sensor Pin 2, harness side and EEC-IV 60-Pin Breakout Box pin(s) as follows:

DTC	Breakout Box Test Pins	Height Sensor Connector	Circuit
C1881 (RF)	9	C1151	424 (TN)
C1885 (RR)	43	C4093	428 (OG/BK)
C1889 (LF)	27	C1153	422 (PK/BK)
C1893 (LR)	5	C4092	427 (PK/BK)

- Is the resistance less than 5 ohms?

→ **Yes**
GO to **O3**.

→ **No**
REPAIR Circuit in question. CLEAR the DTCs. REPEAT the self-test.

CONDITIONS	DETAILS/RESULTS/ACTIONS
O3 CHECK CIRCUIT 426 (RD/BK) FOR OPEN	

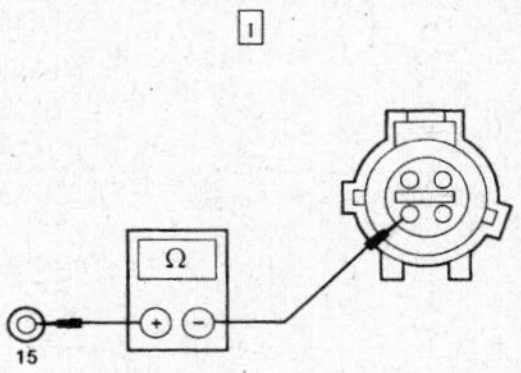

1 Measure the resistance between EEC-IV 60-Pin Breakout Box Pin 15, Circuit 426 (RD/BK) and suspect height sensor Pin 3, Circuit 426 (RD/BK), harness side as follows:

DTC	Height Sensor	Connector
C1881	RF	C1151
C1885	RR	C4093
C1889	LF	C1153
C1893	LR	C4092

FM2010200727020X

Fig. 41 Test O/Codes C1881, C1885, C1889 & C1893: Height Sensor Circuit Failure (Part 2 of 7). 2002–04

CONDITIONS	DETAILS/RESULTS/ACTIONS
O3 CHECK CIRCUIT 426 (RD/BK) FOR OPEN (Continued)	

- Is the resistance less than 5 ohms?

→ **Yes**
GO to **O4**.

→ **No**
REPAIR Circuit 426 (RD/BK). CLEAR the DTCs. REPEAT the self-test.

CONDITIONS	DETAILS/RESULTS/ACTIONS
O4 CHECK FOR SHORT BETWEEN CIRCUIT 426 (RD/BK) AND CIRCUIT 432 (BK/PK)	

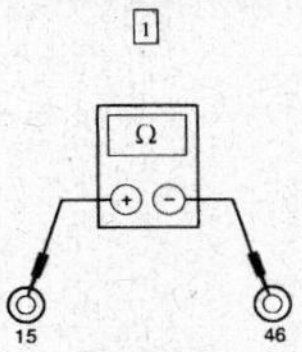

1 Measure the resistance between EEC-IV 60-Pin Breakout Box Pin 15, Circuit 426 (RD/BK), and EEC-IV 60-Pin Breakout Box Pin 46, Circuit 432 (BK/PK).

- Is the resistance greater than 10,000 ohms?

→ **Yes**
GO to **O5**.

→ **No**
REPAIR Circuit 426 (RD/BK) and Circuit 432 (BK/PK). CLEAR the DTCs. REPEAT the self-test.

CONDITIONS	DETAILS/RESULTS/ACTIONS
O5 CHECK CIRCUIT 432 (BK/PK) FOR OPEN	

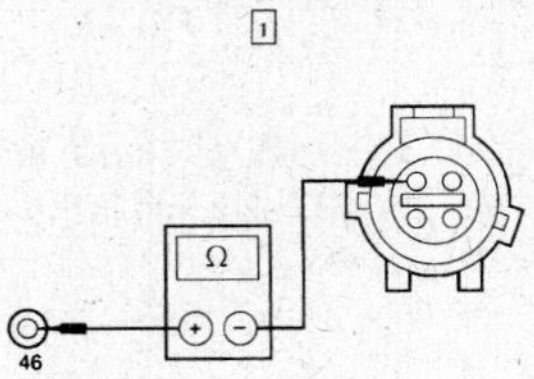

1 Measure the resistance between EEC-IV 60-Pin Breakout Box Pin 46, Circuit 432 (BK/PK), and suspect height sensor Pin 1, Circuit 432 (BK/PK) harness side as follows:

DTC	Height Sensor	Connector
C1881	RF	C1151
C1885	RR	C4093
C1889	LF	C1153
C1893	LR	C4092

- Is the resistance less than 5 ohms?

→ **Yes**
GO to **O6**.

→ **No**
REPAIR the circuit. CLEAR the DTCs. REPEAT the self-test.

FM2010200727030X

Fig. 41 Test O/Codes C1881, C1885, C1889 & C1893: Height Sensor Circuit Failure (Part 3 of 7). 2002–04

CONDITIONS	DETAILS/RESULTS/ACTIONS
O6 CHECK FOR SHORT TO POWER	

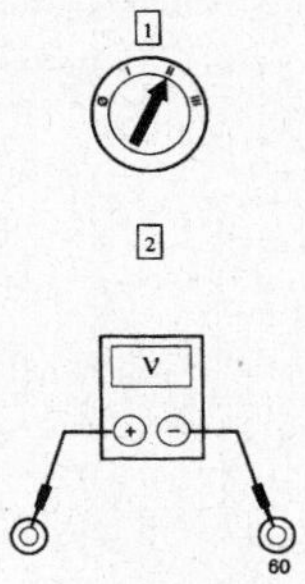

2 Measure the voltage between EEC-IV 60-Pin Breakout Box Pin 60, Circuit 875 (BK/LB) and EEC-IV 60-Pin Breakout Box pin(s) as follows:

DTC	Breakout Box Test Pins	Circuit
C1881 (RF)	9	424 (TN)
C1885 (RR)	43	428 (OG/BK)
C1889 (LF)	27	422 (PK/BK)
C1893 (LR)	5	427 (PK/BK)

- Is voltage present?

→ **Yes**
REPAIR the circuit in question. CLEAR the DTCs. REPEAT the self-test.

→ **No**
GO to **O7**.

CONDITIONS	DETAILS/RESULTS/ACTIONS
O7 CHECK FOR SHORT TO SENSOR VOLTAGE	

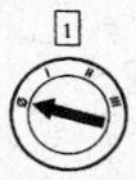

FM2010200727040X

Fig. 41 Test O/Codes C1881, C1885, C1889 & C1893: Height Sensor Circuit Failure (Part 4 of 7). 2002–04

CONDITIONS	DETAILS/RESULTS/ACTIONS
O7 CHECK FOR SHORT TO SENSOR VOLTAGE (Continued)	

2

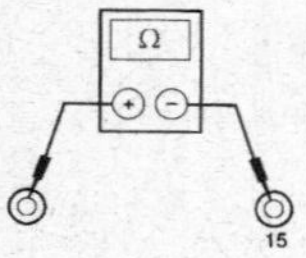

2 Measure the resistance between EEC-IV 60-Pin Breakout Box Pin 15, Circuit 426 (RD/BK), and EEC-IV 60-Pin Breakout Box pin(s) as follows:

DTC	Breakout Box Test Pins	Circuit
C1881 (RF)	9	424 (TN)
C1885 (RR)	43	428 (OG/BK)
C1889 (LF)	27	422 (PK/BK)
C1893 (LR)	5	427 (PK/BK)

- Is the resistance greater than 10,000 ohms?

→ **Yes**
GO to **O8**.

→ **No**
REPAIR the circuit in question. CLEAR the DTCs. REPEAT the self-test.

O8 CHECK HEIGHT SENSOR SUPPLY VOLTAGE

2 3

1 Connect EEC-IV 60-Pin Breakout Box to the VDM.

3 Trigger VDM active command HGTPOWER ON.

4

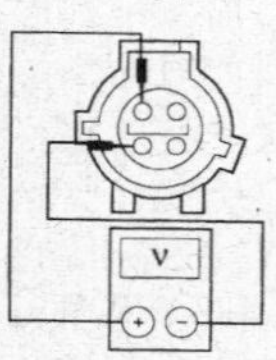

4 Measure the voltage between suspect height sensor Pin 3, Circuit 426 (RD/BK), harness side and suspect height sensor Pin 1, Circuit 432 (BK/PK), harness side as follows:

DTC	Height Sensor	Connector
C1881	RF	C1151
C1885	RR	C4093
C1889	LF	C1153
C1893	LR	C4092

FM2010200727050X

Fig. 41 Test O/Codes C1881, C1885, C1889 & C1893: Height Sensor Circuit Failure (Part 5 of 7). 2002–04

CONDITIONS	DETAILS/RESULTS/ACTIONS
O8 CHECK HEIGHT SENSOR SUPPLY VOLTAGE (Continued)	

- Is the voltage between 4.8 and 5.2 volts?

→ **Yes**
RECONNECT the suspect height sensor connector. GO to **O9**.

→ **No**
INSTALL a new VDM.
CARRY OUT ride height adjustment.
REPEAT the self-test.

O9 CHECK HEIGHT SENSOR SIGNAL RANGE

1 Remove the suspect height sensor from the lower ball stud.

2

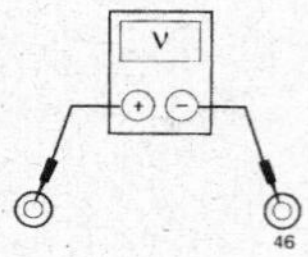

2 While extending and compressing the suspect height sensor, measure the voltage between EEC-IV 60-Pin Breakout Box Pin 46, Circuit 432 (BK/PK), and EEC-IV 60-Pin Breakout Box pin(s) as follows:

DTC	Breakout Box Test Pins	Circuit
C1881 (RF)	9	424 (TN)
C1885 (RR)	43	428 (OG/BK)
C1889 (LF)	27	422 (PK/BK)
C1893 (LR)	5	427 (PK/BK)

- Does the voltage range between 0.5 and 4.5 volts as the suspect height sensor length is changed from minimum length to maximum length?

→ **Yes**
GO to **O10**.

→ **No**
INSTALL a new height sensor.
CLEAR the DTCs. CARRY OUT ride height adjustment.
REPEAT the self-test.

FM2010200727060X

Fig. 41 Test O/Codes C1881, C1885, C1889 & C1893: Height Sensor Circuit Failure (Part 6 of 7). 2002–04

CONDITIONS	DETAILS/RESULTS/ACTIONS
O10 CHECK FOR CHANGE OF PID VALUES	

1

1 From active command menu, select PID LF__HGT, RF__HGT, LR__HGT, or RR__HGT for the suspect height sensor.

2 Vary the length of the suspect height sensor while monitoring the PID.

- Does the PID value change as the suspect height sensor length is changed from minimum length to maximum length?

→ **Yes**
CARRY OUT the Wiggle Test. REPAIR as necessary. CLEAR the DTCs. REPEAT the self-test.

→ **No**
INSTALL a new VDM.
CARRY OUT ride height adjustment.
REPEAT the self-test.

FM2010200727070X

Fig. 41 Test O/Codes C1881, C1885, C1889 & C1893: Height Sensor Circuit Failure (Part 7 of 7). 2002–04

CONDITIONS	DETAILS/RESULTS/ACTIONS
P1 CHECK HEIGHT SENSOR CONNECTOR	

1 2

2 Disconnect the suspect height sensor connector as follows:

DTC	Height Sensor	Connector
C1884	RF	C1151
C1888	RR	C4093
C1892	LF	C1153
C1896	LR	C4092

FM2010200728010X

Fig. 42 Test P/Codes C1884, C1888, C1892 & C1896: Height Sensor Circuit Short To Ground (Part 1 of 5). 2002–04

CONDITIONS	DETAILS/RESULTS/ACTIONS
P1 CHECK HEIGHT SENSOR CONNECTOR (Continued)	
	3 Check the suspect height sensor connector for corrosion, bent pins and damaged wires. • Is the suspect height sensor connector worn or damaged? → **Yes** REPAIR as necessary. CLEAR the DTCs. REPEAT the self-test. → **No** GO to **P2**.
P2 CHECK FOR SHORT TO GROUND	
2 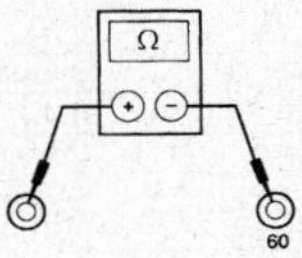	1 Connect EEC-IV 60-Pin Breakout Box to the VDM C4085. 2 Measure the resistance between EEC-IV 60-Pin Breakout Box Pin 60, Circuit 875 (BK/LB), and EEC-IV 60-Pin Breakout Box pin(s) as follows:

DTC	Breakout Box Test Pins	Circuit
C1884 (RF)	9	424 (TN)
C1888 (RR)	43	428 (OG/BK)
C1892 (LF)	27	422 (PK/BK)
C1896 (LR)	5	427 (PK/BK)

- Is the resistance greater than 10,000 ohms?

→ **Yes**
GO to **P3**.

→ **No**
REPAIR the circuit in question. CLEAR the DTCs. REPEAT the self-test.

FM2010200728020X

Fig. 42 Test P/Codes C1884, C1888, C1892 & C1896: Height Sensor Circuit Short To Ground (Part 2 of 5). 2002–04

CONDITIONS	DETAILS/RESULTS/ACTIONS
P3 CHECK FOR SHORT TO CIRCUIT 432 (BK/PK)	
1 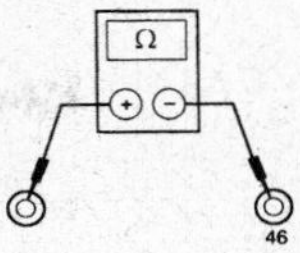	1 Measure the resistance between EEC-IV 60-Pin Breakout Box Pin 46, Circuit 432 (BL/PK), and EEC-IV 60-Pin Breakout Box pin(s) as follows:

DTC	Breakout Box Test Pins	Circuit
C1884 (RF)	9	424 (TN)
C1888 (RR)	43	428 (OG/BK)
C1892 (LF)	27	422 (PK/BK)
C1896 (LR)	5	427 (PK/BK)

- Is the resistance greater than 10,000 ohms?

→ **Yes**
GO to **P4**.

→ **No**
REPAIR the circuit in question. CLEAR the DTCs. REPEAT the self-test.

CONDITIONS	DETAILS/RESULTS/ACTIONS
P4 CHECK HEIGHT SENSOR FOR SHORT TO GROUND	
1 	
	2 Connect EEC-IV 60-Pin Breakout Box to the VDM.
3 	3 Trigger VDM active command HGTPOWER ON.

FM2010200728030X

Fig. 42 Test P/Codes C1884, C1888, C1892 & C1896: Height Sensor Circuit Short To Ground (Part 3 of 5). 2002–04

CONDITIONS	DETAILS/RESULTS/ACTIONS
P4 CHECK HEIGHT SENSOR FOR SHORT TO GROUND (Continued)	
4 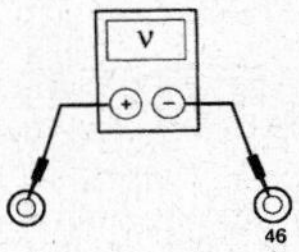	4 Measure the voltage between EEC-IV 60-Pin breakout box Pin 46, Circuit 432 (BK/PK), and EEC-IV 60-Pin Breakout Box pin(s) as follows:

DTC	Breakout Box Test Pins	Circuit
C1884 (RF)	9	424 (TN)
C1888 (RR)	43	428 (OG/BK)
C1892 (LF)	27	422 (PK/BK)
C1896 (LR)	5	427 (PK/BK)

- Is the voltage between 2.3 and 2.7 volts?

→ **Yes**
TRIGGER VDM active command HGTPOWER OFF. RECONNECT the height sensor. GO to **P5**.

→ **No**
INSTALL a new VDM.
CARRY OUT ride height adjustment.
REPEAT the self-test.

CONDITIONS	DETAILS/RESULTS/ACTIONS
P5 CHECK FOR SENSOR SIGNAL	
1 	1 Trigger VDM active command HGTPOWER ON.
2 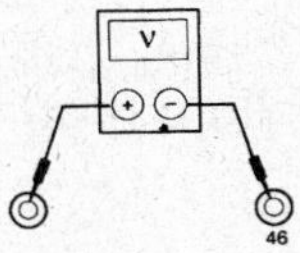	2 Measure the voltage between EEC-IV 60-Pin Breakout Box Pin 46, Circuit 432 (BK/PK), and EEC-IV 60-Pin Breakout Box pin(s) as follows:

DTC	Breakout Box Test Pins	Circuit
C1884 (RF)	9	424 (TN)
C1888 (RR)	43	428 (OG/BK)
C1892 (LF)	27	422 (PK/BK)
C1896 (LR)	5	427 (PK/BK)

FM2010200728040X

Fig. 42 Test P/Codes C1884, C1888, C1892 & C1896: Height Sensor Circuit Short To Ground (Part 4 of 5). 2002–04

CONDITIONS	DETAILS/RESULTS/ACTIONS
P5 CHECK FOR SENSOR SIGNAL (Continued)	
	• Is the voltage between 0.5 volts and 4.5 volts? → **Yes** CARRY OUT the Wiggle Test. REPAIR as necessary. CLEAR the DTCs. REPEAT the self-test. → **No** INSTALL a new height sensor. CARRY OUT ride height adjustment. REPEAT the self-test.

FM2010200728050X

Fig. 42 Test P/Codes C1884, C1888, C1892 & C1896: Height Sensor Circuit Short To Ground (Part 5 of 5). 2002–04

CONDITIONS	DETAILS/RESULTS/ACTIONS

Q1 CHECK SHOCK ACTUATOR CONNECTOR

2 Disconnect the suspect shock actuator connector as follows:

DTC	Shock	Connector
C1901	RR	C448
C1905	LR	C447
C1909	RF	C1150
C1913	LF	C1152

3 Check the suspect shock actuator connector for corrosion, bent pins and damaged wires.

- Is the suspect shock actuator connector worn or damaged?

→ **Yes**
REPAIR as necessary. CLEAR the DTCs. REPEAT the self-test.

→ **No**
GO to **Q2**.

FM2010200729010X

Fig. 43 Test Q/Codes C1901, C1905, C1909 & C1913: Shock Actuator Circuit Failure (Part 1 of 4). 2002–04

CONDITIONS	DETAILS/RESULTS/ACTIONS

Q4 CHECK CIRCUIT 843 (WH), CIRCUIT 842 (WH/OG), CIRCUIT 841 (WH/RD) OR CIRCUIT 840 (WH/BK) FOR SHORT TO POWER (Continued)

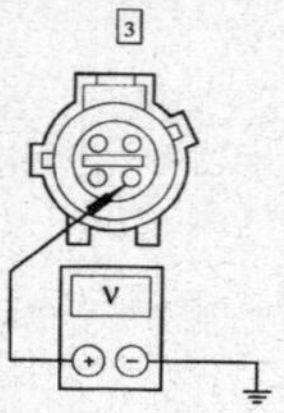

3 Measure the voltage between shock actuator connector, harness side and ground as follows:

DTC	Connector-Pin
C1901	C448 Pin 3
C1905	C447 Pin 3
C1909	C1150 Pin 3
C1913	C1152 Pin 3

- Is voltage present?

→ **Yes**
REPAIR Circuit in question. CLEAR the DTCs. REPEAT the self-test.

→ **No**
GO to **Q5**.

Q5 CHECK CIRCUIT 843 (WH), CIRCUIT 842 (WH/OG), CIRCUIT 841 (WH/RD) OR CIRCUIT 840 (WH/BK) FOR OPEN

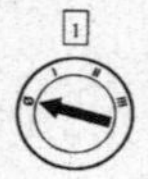

2 Connect EEC-IV 60-Pin Breakout Box to the VDM C4085.

FM2010200729030X

Fig. 43 Test Q/Codes C1901, C1905, C1909 & C1913: Shock Actuator Circuit Failure (Part 3 of 4). 2002–04

CONDITIONS	DETAILS/RESULTS/ACTIONS

Q2 CHECK SHOCK ACTUATOR RESISTANCE

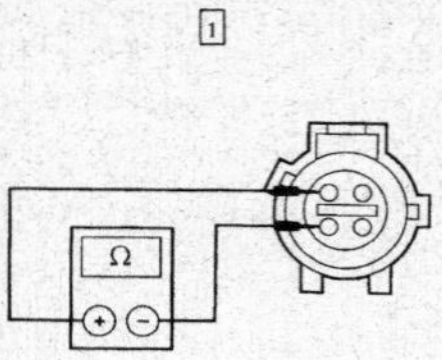

1 Measure the resistance between suspect shock actuator Pin 1 and Pin 3 (component side).

- Is the resistance between 15 and 21 ohms?

→ **Yes**
GO to **Q3**.

→ **No**
INSTALL a new shock actuator. CLEAR the DTCs. REPEAT the self-test.

Q3 CHECK CIRCUIT 57 (BK) FOR OPEN

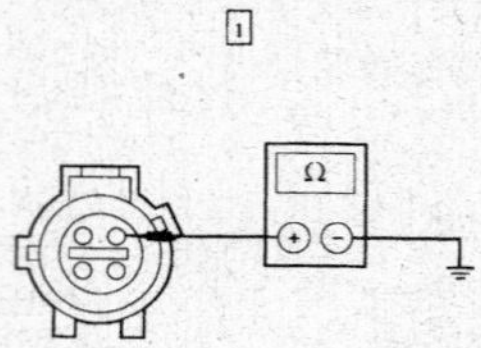

1 Measure the resistance between suspect shock actuator connector, Circuit 57 (BK), harness side and ground as follows:

DTC	Connector-Pin
C1901	C448 Pin 1
C1905	C447 Pin 1
C1909	C1150 Pin 1
C1913	C1152 Pin 1

- Is the resistance less than 5 ohms?

→ **Yes**
GO to **Q4**.

→ **No**
REPAIR the circuit. CLEAR the DTCs. REPEAT the self-test.

Q4 CHECK CIRCUIT 843 (WH), CIRCUIT 842 (WH/OG), CIRCUIT 841 (WH/RD) OR CIRCUIT 840 (WH/BK) FOR SHORT TO POWER

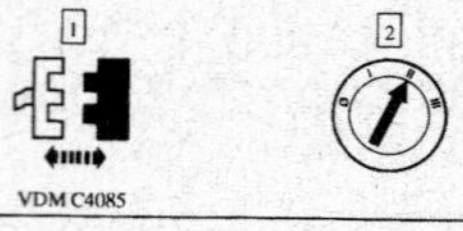

FM2010200729020X

Fig. 43 Test Q/Codes C1901, C1905, C1909 & C1913: Shock Actuator Circuit Failure (Part 2 of 4). 2002–04

CONDITIONS	DETAILS/RESULTS/ACTIONS

Q5 CHECK CIRCUIT 843 (WH), CIRCUIT 842 (WH/OG), CIRCUIT 841 (WH/RD) OR CIRCUIT 840 (WH/BK) FOR OPEN (Continued)

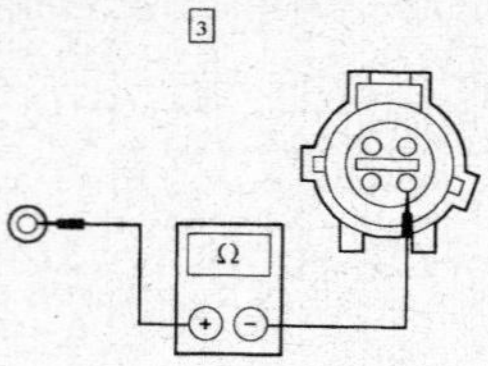

3 Measure the resistance between shock actuator connector, harness side and EEC-IV 60-Pin Breakout Box pin as follows:

DTC	Break-out Box Test Pin	Shock Connector Pin	Circuit
C1901 (RR)	52	C448 Pin 3	843 (WH)
C1905 (LR)	54	C447 Pin 3	842 (WH/OG)
C1909 (RF)	53	C1150 Pin 3	841 (WH/RD)
C1913 (LF)	51	C1152 Pin 3	840 (WH/BK)

- Is the resistance less than 5 ohms?

→ **Yes**
INSTALL a new VDM.
CARRY OUT ride height adjustment.
REPEAT the self-test.

→ **No**
REPAIR Circuit in question. CLEAR the DTCs. REPEAT the self-test.

FM2010200729040X

Fig. 43 Test Q/Codes C1901, C1905, C1909 & C1913: Shock Actuator Circuit Failure (Part 4 of 4). 2002–04

CONDITIONS	DETAILS/RESULTS/ACTIONS
R1 CHECK SHOCK SOLENOID CONNECTOR	

[2] Disconnect the suspect shock actuator connector as follows:

DTC	Shock	Connector
C1904	RR	C448
C1908	LR	C447
C1912	RF	C1150
C1916	LF	C1152

FM2010200730010X

Fig. 44 Test R/Codes C1904, C1908, C1912 & C1916: Shock Actuator Short To Ground (Part 1 of 3). 2002–04

CONDITIONS	DETAILS/RESULTS/ACTIONS
R3 CHECK CIRCUIT 843 (WH), CIRCUIT 482 (WH/OG), CIRCUIT 841 (WH/RD) OR CIRCUIT 840 (WH/BK) FOR SHORT TO GROUND (Continued)	

- Is resistance greater than 10,000 ohms?

→ **Yes**
INSTALL a new VDM.
CARRY OUT ride height adjustment.
REPEAT the self-test.

→ **No**
REPAIR the circuit in question. REPEAT the self-test.

FM2010200730030X

Fig. 44 Test R/Codes C1904, C1908, C1912 & C1916: Shock Actuator Short To Ground (Part 3 of 3). 2002–04

CONDITIONS	DETAILS/RESULTS/ACTIONS
S1 CHECK AIR COMPRESSOR RELAY CONNECTOR	

[3] Check air compressor relay C1198 for corrosion, bent pins and damaged wires.

- Is the air compressor relay C1198 worn or damaged?

→ **Yes**
REPAIR as necessary. CLEAR the DTCs. REPEAT the self-test.

→ **No**
GO to **S2**.

FM2010200731010X

Fig. 45 Test S/Code C1929: Compressor Relay Circuit Failure (Part 1 of 3). 2002–04

CONDITIONS	DETAILS/RESULTS/ACTIONS
R1 CHECK SHOCK SOLENOID CONNECTOR (Continued)	

[3] Check the suspect shock actuator connector for corrosion, bent pins and damaged wires.

- Is the suspect shock actuator connector worn or damaged?

→ **Yes**
REPAIR as necessary. CLEAR the DTCs. REPEAT the self-test.

→ **No**
GO to **R2**.

R2 CHECK SHOCK ACTUATOR RESISTANCE

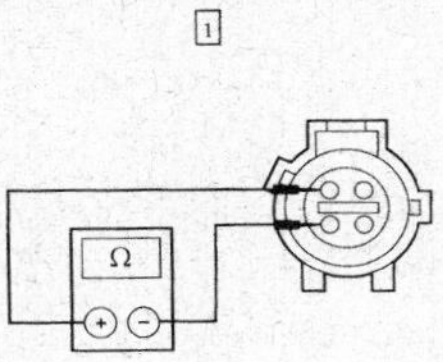

[1] Measure the resistance between suspect shock actuator Pin 1 and Pin 3 (component side).

- Is the resistance between 15 and 21 ohms?

→ **Yes**
GO to **R3**.

→ **No**
INSTALL a new shock actuator. CLEAR the DTCs. REPEAT the self-test.

R3 CHECK CIRCUIT 843 (WH), CIRCUIT 482 (WH/OG), CIRCUIT 841 (WH/RD) OR CIRCUIT 840 (WH/BK) FOR SHORT TO GROUND

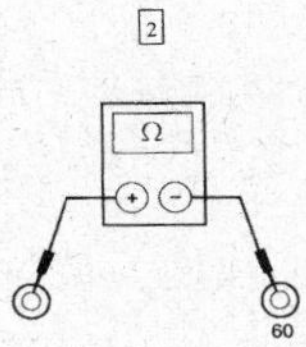

[1] Connect EEC-IV 60-Pin Breakout Box to the VDM C4085.

[2] Measure the resistance between EEC-IV 60-Pin Breakout Box pin, and ground as follows:

DTC	EEC-IV 60-Pin Breakout Box Pin	Circuit
C1904	52	843 (WH)
C1908	54	842 (WH/OG)
C1912	53	841 (WH/RD)
C1916	51	840 (WH/BK)

FM2010200730020X

Fig. 44 Test R/Codes C1904, C1908, C1912 & C1916: Shock Actuator Short To Ground (Part 2 of 3). 2002–04

CONDITIONS	DETAILS/RESULTS/ACTIONS
S2 CHECK CIRCUIT 1053 (LB/PK) FOR OPEN	

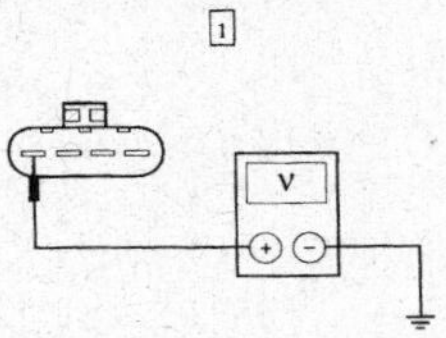

[1] Measure the voltage between air compressor relay C1198 Pin A, Circuit 1053 (LB/PK), harness side and ground.

- Is the voltage greater than 10 volts?

→ **Yes**
GO to **S3**.

→ **No**
REPAIR the circuit. CLEAR the DTCs. REPEAT the self-test.

S3 CHECK CIRCUIT 57 (BK) FOR OPEN

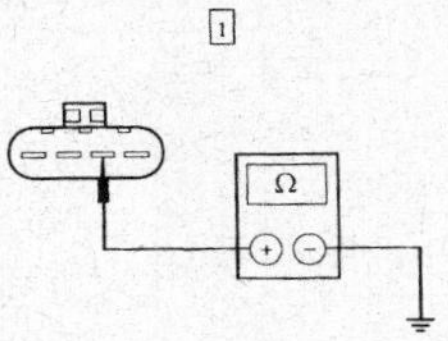

[1] Measure the resistance between air compressor relay C1198 Pin C, Circuit 57 (BK), harness side and ground.

- Is the resistance less than 5 ohms?

→ **Yes**
GO to **S4**.

→ **No**
REPAIR the circuit. CLEAR the DTCs. REPEAT the self-test.

S4 CHECK CIRCUIT 420 (DB/YE)

[1] Connect EEC-IV 60-Pin Breakout Box to the VDM C4085.

FM2010200731020X

Fig. 45 Test S/Code C1929: Compressor Relay Circuit Failure (Part 2 of 3). 2002–04

CONDITIONS	DETAILS/RESULTS/ACTIONS
S4 CHECK CIRCUIT 420 (DB/YE) (Continued)	
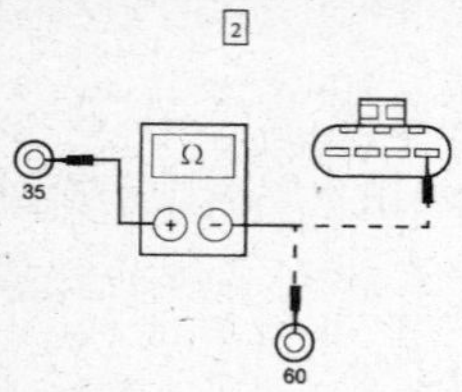	2 Measure the resistance between EEC-IV 60-Pin Breakout Box Pin 35, Circuit 420 (DB/YE), and air compressor relay C1198 Pin D, Circuit 420 (DB/YE), harness side; and between EEC-IV 60-Pin Breakout Box Pin 35, Circuit 420 (DB/YE), and EEC-IV 60-Pin Breakout Box Pin 60, Circuit 875 (BK/LB). • Is the resistance less than 5 ohms between EEC-IV 60-Pin Breakout Box and relay; and greater than 10,000 ohms between EEC-IV 60-Pin Breakout Box pins? → **Yes** RECONNECT air compressor relay C1198. GO to **S5**. → **No** REPAIR Circuit 420 (DB/YE). CLEAR the DTCs. REPEAT the self-test.
S5 CHECK VDM	
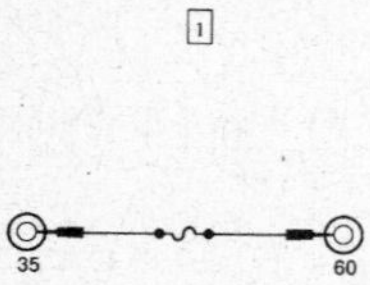	1 Connect a fused jumper (60A) between EEC-IV 60-Pin Breakout Box Pin 35, Circuit 420 (DB/YE), and EEC-IV 60-Pin Breakout Box Pin 60, Circuit 57 (BK). • Does the air compressor operate? → **Yes** INSTALL a new VDM. CARRY OUT ride height adjustment. REPEAT the self-test. → **No** GO to Pinpoint Test U.

FM2010200731030X

Fig. 45 Test S/Code C1929: Compressor Relay Circuit Failure (Part 3 of 3). 2002–04

CONDITIONS	DETAILS/RESULTS/ACTIONS
T1 CHECK CIRCUIT 420 (DB/YE) FOR SHORT TO POWER (Continued)	
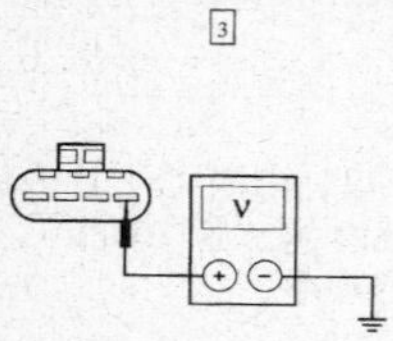	3 Measure the voltage between air compressor relay C1198 Pin D, Circuit 420 (DB/YE), harness side and ground. • Is voltage present? → **Yes** REPAIR the circuit. CLEAR the DTCs. REPEAT the self-test. → **No** GO to **T2**.
T2 CHECK AIR COMPRESSOR RELAY	
 Air Compressor Relay C1198 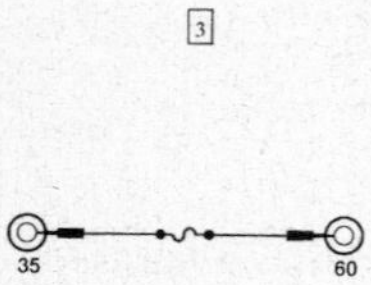	2 Connect EEC-IV 60-Pin Breakout Box. 3 Connect a fused jumper (60A) between EEC-IV 60-Pin Breakout Box Pin 35, Circuit 420 (DB/YE), and EEC-IV 60-Pin Breakout Box Pin 60, Circuit 875 (BK/LB). • Does the air compressor operate? → **Yes** INSTALL a new VDM. CARRY OUT ride height adjustment. REPEAT the self-test. → **No** GO to Pinpoint Test U.

FM2010200732020X

Fig. 46 Test T/Code C1931: Compressor Relay Circuit Short To Power (Part 2 of 2). 2002–04

CONDITIONS	DETAILS/RESULTS/ACTIONS
T1 CHECK CIRCUIT 420 (DB/YE) FOR SHORT TO POWER	
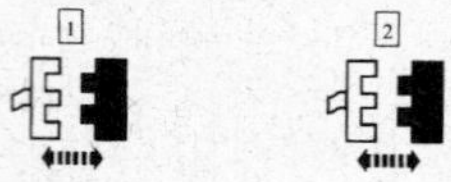 Air Compressor Relay C1198 VDM C4085	

FM2010200732010X

Fig. 46 Test T/Code C1931: Compressor Relay Circuit Short To Power (Part 1 of 2). 2002–04

CONDITIONS	DETAILS/RESULTS/ACTIONS
U1 CHECK CONNECTORS	
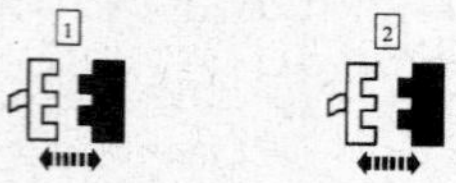 Air Compressor Relay C1198 Air Compressor C1179	3 Inspect the pins and terminals of the air compressor relay C1198 and air compressor C1179 for corrosion, bent or broken pins, moisture, or other damage. • Are the connectors OK? → **Yes** RECONNECT the air compressor C1179. GO to **U2**. → **No** REPAIR as necessary. TEST the system for normal operation.
U2 CHECK COMPRESSOR OPERATION	
	1 Connect a fused jumper (60A) wire between air compressor relay C1198 Pin A and air compressor relay C1198 Pin B, harness side. • Does the air compressor run? → **Yes** GO to **U3**. → **No** GO to **U4**.

FM2010200733010X

Fig. 47 Test U: Compressor Inoperative (Part 1 of 3). 2002–04

CONDITIONS	DETAILS/RESULTS/ACTIONS
U3 CHECK CIRCUIT 57 (BK)	
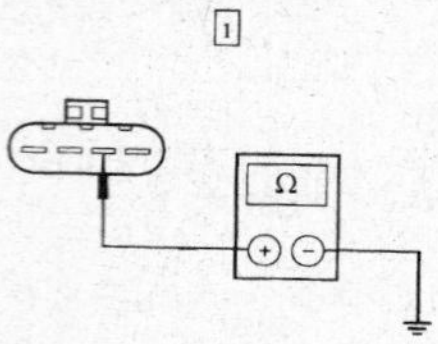	1 Measure the resistance between air compressor relay C1198 Pin C, Circuit 57 (BK), harness side and ground. • Is the resistance less than 5 ohms? → **Yes** INSTALL a new air compressor relay. TEST the system for normal operation. → **No** REPAIR the circuit. TEST the system for normal operation.
U4 CHECK CIRCUIT 1053 (LB/PK)	
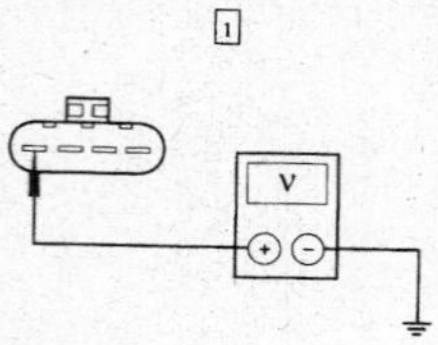	1 Measure the voltage between air compressor relay C1198 Pin A, Circuit 1053 (LB/PK), harness side and ground. • Is the voltage greater than 10 volts? → **Yes** GO to **U5**. → **No** REPAIR the circuit. TEST the system for normal operation.
U5 CHECK CIRCUIT 417 (VT/OG)	
 Air Compressor C1179	

FM2010200733020X

Fig. 47 Test U: Compressor Inoperative (Part 2 of 3). 2002–04

CONDITIONS	DETAILS/RESULTS/ACTIONS
U5 CHECK CIRCUIT 417 (VT/OG) (Continued)	
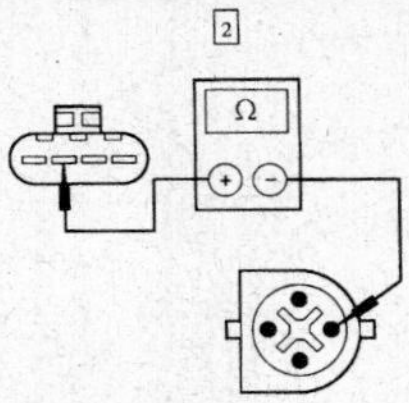	2 Measure the resistance between air compressor relay C1198 Pin B, Circuit 417 (VT/OG), harness side and air compressor C1179 Pin 4, Circuit 417 (VT/OG), harness side. • Is the resistance less than 5 ohms? → **Yes** GO to **U6**. → **No** REPAIR the circuit. TEST the system for normal operation.
U6 CHECK CIRCUIT 57 (BK)	
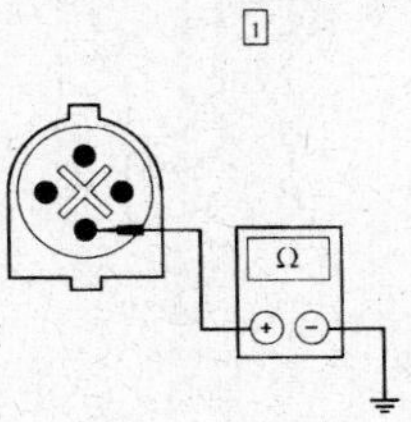	1 Measure the resistance between air compressor C1179 Pin 2, Circuit 57 (BK), harness side and ground. • Is the resistance less than 5 ohms? → **Yes** INSTALL a new air compressor. TEST the system for normal operation. → **No** REPAIR the circuit. TEST the system for normal operation.

FM2010200733030X

Fig. 47 Test U: Compressor Inoperative (Part 3 of 3). 2002–04

CONDITIONS	DETAILS/RESULTS/ACTIONS
V1 CHECK FOR BLOCKED AIR LINE (Continued)	
 Air Line at RR Air Spring	5 Use Vacuum Tester to try to draw a vacuum on the air line at the RR air spring. • Does either air line hold a vacuum? → **Yes** REPAIR air line as necessary. TEST the system for normal operation. → **No** GO to **V2**.
V2 CHECK FOR LEAKS IN AIR LINE	
	1 ⚠ **CAUTION: Do not use anything as a cap that might be drawn in to the air line.** Cap both air lines at the air springs. 2 Use Vacuum Tester to try to draw a vacuum on the air line at the air drier. • Does the air line hold a vacuum? → **Yes** GO to **V3**. → **No** ISOLATE leak in air line. INSTALL a new air line. TEST the system for normal operation.
V3 CHECK FOR LEAKS AT AIR SPRING SOLENOID	
 Air Line at LR Air Spring Air Line at RR Air Spring Scan Tool	4 Connect shop air to the air line at the air drier with common fittings.

FM2010200734020X

Fig. 48 Test V: System Inoperative, One Or Corners Low & Compressor Operates (Part 2 of 4). 2002–04

CONDITIONS	DETAILS/RESULTS/ACTIONS
V1 CHECK FOR BLOCKED AIR LINE	
 Air Line at Air Drier Air Line at LR Air Spring	3 Use Vacuum Tester to try to draw a vacuum on the air line at the LR air spring.

FM2010200734010X

Fig. 48 Test V: System Inoperative, One Or Corners Low & Compressor Operates (Part 1 of 4). 2002–04

CONDITIONS	DETAILS/RESULTS/ACTIONS
V3 CHECK FOR LEAKS AT AIR SPRING SOLENOID (Continued)	
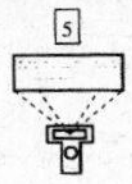	5 Trigger VDM active command LR SOL and RR SOL ON. • Do both air springs inflate until full suspension travel is reached? → **Yes** GO to **V4**. → **No** INSTALL a new air spring solenoid. TEST the system for normal operation.
V4 LEAK TEST THE AIR COMPRESSOR ASSEMBLY	
⚠ **CAUTION: Do not allow the air compressor to run for more than three minutes. The air compressor could overheat and stop operating due to an internal temperature sensitive thermal breaker.**	
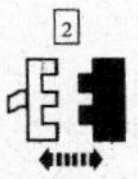 	1 Connect an air pressure gauge with common fittings to the air line.

FM2010200734030X

Fig. 48 Test V: System Inoperative, One Or Corners Low & Compressor Operates (Part 3 of 4). 2002–04

CONDITIONS	DETAILS/RESULTS/ACTIONS
V4 LEAK TEST THE AIR COMPRESSOR ASSEMBLY (Continued)	
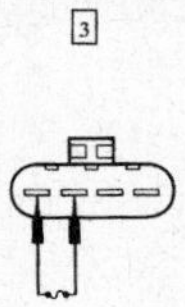	3 Connect a fused jumper (60A) wire between air compressor relay C1198 Pin A, harness side and air compressor relay C1198 Pin B, harness side.
	4 Within 30 seconds, the pressure should reach 1034 kPa (150 psi). 5 Disconnect the jumper wire. 6 The pressure should hold steady.
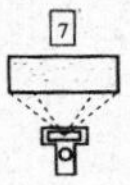	7 Trigger VDM active command VENT ON. • Did the air compressor reach and hold a minimum air pressure of 1034 kPa (150 psi)? → **Yes** System OK. TEST the system for normal operation. → **No** INSTALL a new air compressor. TEST the system for normal operation.

FM2010200734040X

Fig. 48 Test V: System Inoperative, One Or Corners Low & Compressor Operates (Part 4 of 4). 2002–04

COMPRESSOR: ON, LF SOL: ON	Left Front Spring Inflate
COMPRESSOR: ON, LR SOL: ON	Left Rear Spring Inflate
COMPRESSOR: ON, RF SOL: ON	Right Front Spring Inflate
COMPRESSOR: ON, RR SOL: ON	Right Rear Spring Inflate
VENT SOL: ON, LF SOL: ON	Left Front Spring Deflate
VENT SOL: ON, LR SOL: ON	Left Rear Spring Deflate
VENT SOL: ON, RF SOL: ON	Right Front Spring Deflate
VENT SOL: ON, RR SOL: ON	Right Rear Spring Deflate [a]

a Unless otherwise specified, all other outputs should be in the OFF state during this procedure.

FM2019600275000X

Fig. 49 Inflation & deflation of air springs using NGS tool

SYSTEM SERVICE

Deflating & Inflating

Air springs must always be deflated before repairing any component that is a structural part of the suspension. Failure to deflate the air spring prior to suspension repair could lead to component damage. Use the following procedure to deflate and inflate the air springs.

1. Ensure suspension switch is On.
2. Turn ignition switch to Run position.
3. Install battery charger to reduce battery drain.
4. Connect New Generation Star (NGS) Tester, or equivalent, scan tool to DLC connector.
5. Configure NGS Continental, then enter ACTIVE COMMAND MODES on NGS.
6. Enter AIR SUSPENSION DIAGNOSTIC CONTROL. At this time, NGS will present a list of suspension component choices.
7. Select combinations of component choices to inflate or deflate individual air springs, **Fig. 49.**
8. After repairs have been completed follow scan tool instructions to inflate air springs.

Adjustment

RIDE HEIGHT

This procedure should be carried out after a height sensor, VDM module or height sensor attachment bracket is serviced or replaced. This procedure should also be used if their is a ride height lean.

1. Position vehicle on level surface, then connect battery charger to vehicle battery.
2. Turn ignition switch to RUN position, then ensure suspension service switch is ON.
3. Configure NGS for correct model year and VDM module.
4. Select Function Test selection on menu, then the Ride Height Calibration from the menu.
5. Prepare vehicle as specified on NGS screen.
6. NGS will command vehicle to go to its nominal ride height. While this is happening, the NGS will display "RUNNING ACCURATE TRIM TEST."

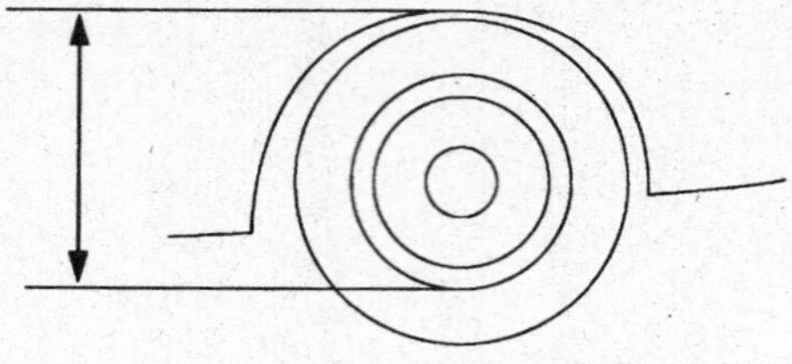

FM2010200735000X

Fig. 50 Ride height measurement

7. When nominal ride height has been reached, then the NGS will prompt the operator to measure wheel lip opening at each corner of vehicle and to enter this measurement into NGS via the thumbwheel. No adjustment will occur if nominal values are entered.
8. Nominal wheel lip opening is 24 1/4 inches for front and rear.
9. Measure and enter each wheel lip opening, **Fig. 50.** Select each corner by pressing trigger button, then press DONE when all four corner wheel lip opening are measured and entered.
10. NGS will first display "DOWNLOADING CALIBRATION," followed by "RUNNING ACCURATE TRIM," which then will be followed by "CALIBRATION COMPLETE." When calibration is complete, measure wheel lip openings to verify that they are close to nominal.
11. If proper wheel lip openings are not attainable by performing this procedure, the height sensor ball studs will require adjustment to attain desired wheel lip opening. Lowering the ball stud will raise the front and lower the rear vehicle ride height and raising the ball stud will lower the front and raise the rear.
12. After making ball stud adjustment, repeat ride height calibration procedure with NGS.
13. Rear air suspension height sensor adjustment is performed by loosening and repositioning the air suspension height sensor ball stud lever adjustment screw.

Component Replacement

ACTUATOR

FRONT

1. Deflate air springs as outlined in "Deflating & Inflating."
2. Place vehicle on a level surface and apply parking brake.
3. Turn ignition switch to OFF or either LOCK position and raise hood.
4. Remove engine compartment covers.
5. Disconnect actuator electrical connector from wiring harness connector.
6. Remove actuator clips from upper mount attaching studs.
7. Remove two attaching screws retaining actuator to mounting bracket.
8. Remove actuator by lifting off.
9. Reverse procedure to install.

REAR

1. Deflate air springs as outlined in "Deflating & Inflating."
2. Disconnect battery ground cable.
3. Remove strut assembly from vehicle as outlined in "Rear Axle & Suspension" section of the "Lincoln" chassis chapter.
4. Remove actuator.
5. Reverse procedure to install.

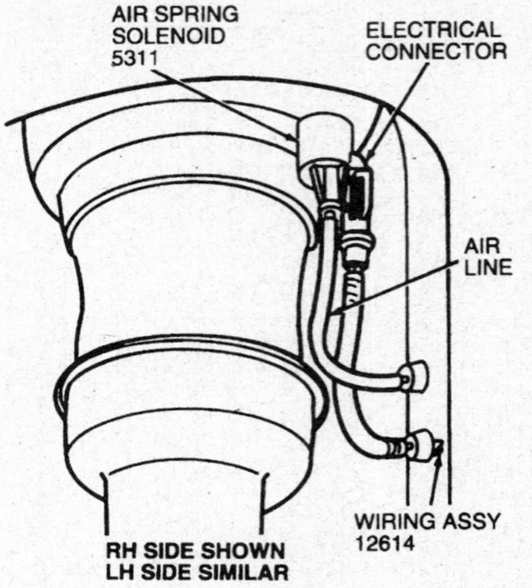

FM2019600276000X

Fig. 51 Air spring solenoid air line & connector

AIR SPRING

1. Deflate air springs as outlined in "Deflating & Inflating."
2. Raise and support vehicle.
3. Disconnect air spring solenoid electrical connector and air line, **Fig. 51.**
4. Depress and hold locking tabs on bottom of air spring seat, then lift bottom of air spring upward.
5. Depress locking air spring locking tabs, then rotate and remove air spring.
6. Reverse procedure to install.

AIR SPRING SOLENOID

1. Deflate air springs as outlined in "Deflating & Inflating."
2. Remove wheel and tire assembly.
3. Disconnect air spring solenoid valve electrical connector and air line, **Fig. 51.**
4. Remove air spring solenoid retainer, then rotate solenoid counterclockwise to first stop.
5. Pull air spring solenoid straight out slowly to second stop to bleed any remaining air from system.
6. After air has fully bled from system, rotate air spring solenoid counterclockwise to third stop and remove solenoid from shock absorber assembly.
7. Reverse procedure to install.

AIR COMPRESSOR & DRYER ASSEMBLY

1. Turn air suspension switch to the OFF position.
2. Remove support bracket, then disconnect electrical connector located on the compressor.

3. Remove air line protector cap from dryer by releasing two latching pins located on bottom of the cap 180° apart.
4. Disconnect air lines from dryer.
5. Remove three air compressor to mounting bolts, then the compressor.
6. Reverse procedure to install.

FRONT HEIGHT SENSOR

1. Deflate air springs as outlined in "Deflating & Inflating."
2. Turn air suspension service switch off.
3. Raise and support vehicle.
4. Disconnect air suspension height sensor electrical connectors. Front air suspension height sensor is located under splash in front of strut tower.
5. Disconnect front height sensor wiring from wire retaining clips.
6. Remove air suspension height sensor from height sensor ball studs.
7. Reverse procedure to install.

REAR HEIGHT SENSOR

1. Deflate air springs as outlined in "Deflating & Inflating."
2. Turn air suspension service switch off.
3. Raise and support vehicle.
4. Disconnect air suspension height sensor electrical connector located on body sheet metal.
5. Remove air suspension height sensor from height sensor ball studs.
6. Reverse procedure to install.

VEHICLE DYNAMIC MODULE (VDM)

1. Turn ignition switch to Off position.
2. Turn air suspension service switch to Off position.
3. Remove upper luggage compartment trim panel and lower the module tray, **Fig. 52.**
4. Disconnect wire harness from control module.
5. Unsnap control module from tray clips and remove control module.
6. Reverse procedure to install.

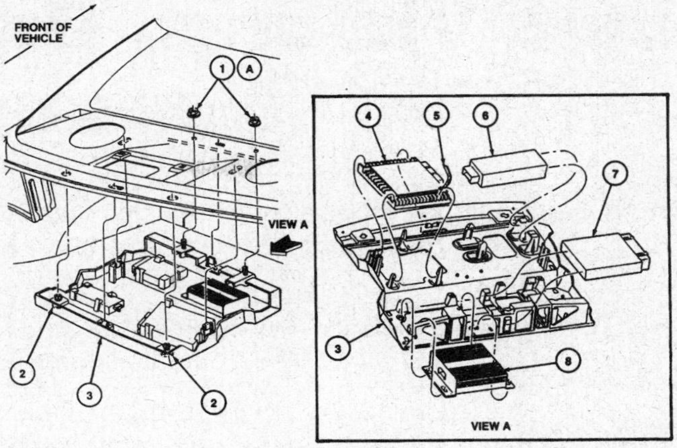

Item	Description
1	Nut (2 Req'd)
2	Push Pin (2 Req'd) (Part of 14A641 Module Tray)
3	Module Tray Assembly (Luggage Compartment)
4	Rear Chassis Unit
5	Bonding Strap (Part of Rear Chassis Unit)

Item	Description
6	Transceiver Assy (Cellular Phone)
7	Control Module
8	Amplifier Assy (Sub-Woofer)
A	Tighten to 10-14 N·m (86-124 Lb-In)

FM2019600277000X

Fig. 52 Vehicle Dynamic Module (VDM) replacement

AIR SUSPENSION SWITCH

1. Disconnect electrical connector.
2. Depress retaining clips attaching switch to brace, and remove switch.
3. Reverse procedure to install.

COMPRESSOR RELAY

1. Disconnect electrical connector.
2. Remove screw retaining relay to relay block, then the relay.
3. Reverse procedure to install.

Crown Victoria, Grand Marquis & Marauder

NOTE: On Air Bag Equipped Models, Refer To "Air Bag System Precautions" Located In The Front Of This Manual For System Disarming & Arming Procedures.

NOTE: Refer To "Computer Relearn Procedures" Located In The Front Of This Manual When Battery Power To The Computer Has Been Interrupted.

NOTE: "Electrical Symbol & Wire Color Code Identification" Located In The Front Of This Manual May Be Used As An Aid When Using Wiring Circuits Found In This Section.

INDEX

PRECAUTIONS

Air Bag Systems

Refer to "Air Bag System Precautions" in the front of this manual for system disarming and arming procedures.

Battery Ground Cable

Prior to service, disconnect battery ground cable and isolate as required.

Service

Before servicing an air suspension component, disconnect power to system by turning air suspension switch to Off position or disconnect battery ground cable. Do not remove air spring when there is pressure in air spring. Do not remove air spring supporting components without exhausting air or supporting air spring. Refer to "Air Spring Refill" to vent air from system.

DESCRIPTION

Air Suspension System

The rear air suspension, **Fig. 1,** is an air operated microprocessor controlled, suspension system which replaces the conventional suspension. This system allows low spring rates for improved ride and automatic rear load leveling.

Two air springs replace the conventional steel springs and support the vehicle load at the rear wheels. The air springs are mounted on the axle spring seats and to the frame upper spring seats.

The system is operational when the ignition is in the Run position and is limited for one hour after the ignition has been turned to the Off position. The air suspension switch, located on the righthand side of the luggage compartment, must in the Off position when the vehicle is on a hoist, being towed or jump started.

The "Check Sir" suspension warning lamp is located in the instrument panel message center, to the righthand of the speedometer. The warning lamp flashes five times and then stays on when the service switch is turned to the Off position or there is a system fault.

The rear leveling system operates by adding or removing air in the springs to maintain the level of the vehicle at a predetermined rear suspension "D" ride height dimension and is controlled by a microcomputer module.

The rear air suspension system module also controls the electronic variable orifice (EVO) steering.

The air required for the leveling is distributed from the air compressor to the air springs by a nylon air line which runs from the compressor dryer through a "Y" fitting to each individual air spring.

Air Compressor

The air compressor assembly consists of a compressor and a vent solenoid, both

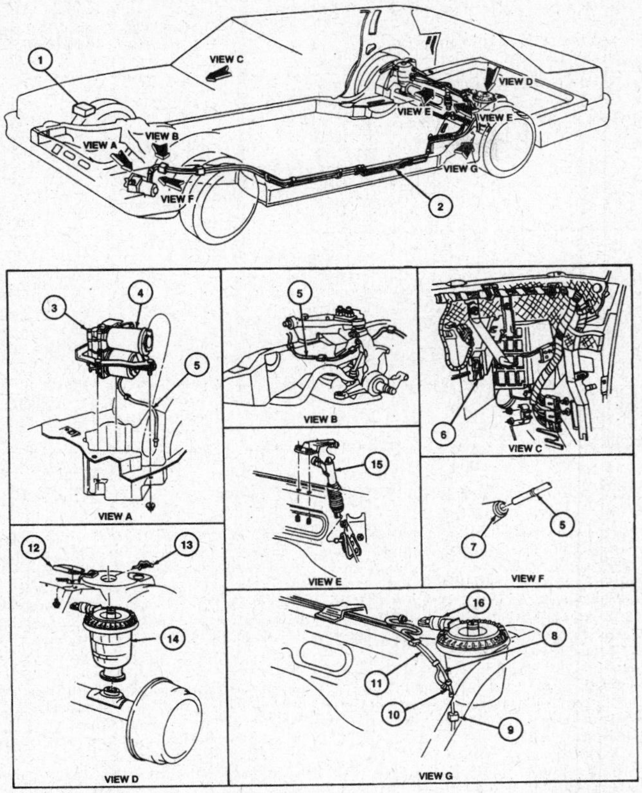

FM2019500209010X

Fig. 1 Component Locations (Part 1 of 2)

Item	Part Number	Description
1	9C392	Compressor Relay Power Junction Block
2	5A897	Air Line (Attached to Brake/Fuel Bundle)
3	5319	Air Compressor
4	5346	Regenerative Air Dryer
5	5A987	Air Line to Compressor
6	5A919	Control Module
7	—	Quick Connect

Item	Part Number	Description
8	—	To LH Air Spring
9	—	From Compressor
10	—	Y-Fitting (Part of 5A911)
11	—	To RH Air Spring
12	5A908	Heat Shield
13	5A966	Spring Retainer Clip
14	5560	Rear Spring
15	5359	Air Suspension Height Sensor
16	14018	Air Spring Solenoid

FM2019500209020X

Fig. 1 Component Locations (Part 2 of 2)

Condition	Possible Source	Action
• No communication with the air suspension control module	• CJB Fuse 5 (15A). • BJB Fuse 8 (30A). • Circuitry. • Air suspension control module.	• GO to Pinpoint Test A.
• Unable to enter auto test	• Air suspension control module. • Circuitry.	• GO to Pinpoint Test B.
• Rear air suspension does not respond to load changes	• Circuitry. • Air compressor. • Air compressor inlet tube. • Air compressor drier. • Air suspension height sensor. • Air suspension control module.	• GO to Pinpoint Test C.
• Rear rides low/high	• Circuitry. • Air spring solenoid. • Air suspension height sensor. • Air suspension control module.	• GO to Pinpoint Test C.
• Poor ride quality	• Circuitry. • Air springs.	• GO to Pinpoint Test C.
• Air suspension warning indicator ON	• Air suspension switch OFF. • Air suspension control module. • Circuitry. • Instrument cluster (conventional cluster) or lamp warning module (electronic cluster).	• Place the air suspension switch in the ON position. • GO to Auto Test.

FM2019900581000X

Fig. 2 Troubleshooting chart. 2000–02

are non-serviceable. The compressor assembly is mounted in the engine compartment on the lefthand fender area below the air cleaner. The air compressor is a single cylinder electric motor which supplies pressurized air as needed. The air compressor is powered by a relay that is controlled by the control module.

The pressurized air from the air compressor passes through the dryer assembly which contains a drying agent (silica gel). The moisture is removed from the air dryer when vented air passes out of the system during vent operation.

Vent Solenoid Valve

The vent solenoid valve allows air to escape the system during venting corrections. The valve is located in the air compressor head and shares an electrical connector with the motor. The valve is enclosed in the cylinder head casting which forms an integral valve housing which allows the valve tip to enter the pressurized side of the system. Leakage is prevented by an O-ring seal.

The vent valve solenoid opens when, the rear of the vehicle is high and the control module determines lowering is required. When the vent solenoid valve is open pressurized air is allowed to escape. However, the vehicle will not lower unless the air spring solenoid valves are also opened to allow air to leave the springs.

The vent solenoid valve has an internal diode for electrical noise suppression and is polarity sensitive. Do not switch battery feed and ground circuits or component damage may result.

Air Spring Solenoid Valve

The air spring solenoid valve allows air to enter and exit the air spring during leveling. The valve is electrically operated and is controlled by the module. The air spring solenoid valve is completely air tight, therefore the air lines are not required to be air tight. The air lines only contain pressurized air during vent and compress operations.

The valve is a two-stage pressure relief system. A clip is removed and rotation of the solenoid out of the seat will release air from the spring before the solenoid can be removed. **Never rotate an air spring solenoid valve to the release slot in the end fitting until all of the pressurized air has escaped the system.**

Compressor Relay

The compressor relay assists the control module in providing the required electrical current required to run the compressor motor.

Height Sensor

The height sensor sends signals to the control module. The three conditions that the control module interprets from the height sensor are that the vehicle is either at, above or below trim height.

The height sensor is attached to the frame crossmember and to the lefthand rear upper control arm. As the rear of the vehicle moves up and down the height sensor lengthens and shortens. Magnets mounted on the lower slide portion of the sensor move relative to the to the sensor housing, generating a signal that is sent to the control module, through two small Hall effect switches that are attached to the sensor housing.

Control Module

The module uses approximately a 45 second averaging interval to determine when compress and vent operations are needed. Door inputs can override the 45 second average interval, so compress and vent operations can begin immediately. This interval is used to keep the module from making unneeded corrections. The module does not allow any vent operations for the first 45 seconds after the ignition has been turned to the ON position.

TROUBLESHOOTING

Refer to troubleshooting table, **Figs. 2 and 3,** when troubleshooting the system.

DIAGNOSIS & TESTING

Accessing Diagnostic Trouble Codes

2000–02

The Super Star II Tester model No. 007-00041B, or equivalent, scan tool is required

Condition	Possible Sources	Action
• **NOTE:** Be sure that air suspension disable switch is in the ON position before determining that a fault condition is present. No communication with the rear air suspension module	• CJB Fuse 16 (15A). • BJB Fuse 114 (30A). • Circuitry. • Data link connector (DLC). • Rear air suspension control module.	• Go To Pinpoint Test A .
• Unable to enter self-test	• Rear air suspension control module.	• Go To Pinpoint Test B .
• Did not detect open and close door signals	• Circuitry. • Door ajar switch. • Lighting control module (LCM). • Rear air suspension control module.	• Go To Pinpoint Test D .
• The compressor is inoperative	• Circuitry. • Air compressor relay. • Air compressor.	• Go To Pinpoint Test L .
• The air compressor continuously cycles with the ignition switch in the OFF position and no DTC is set	• Circuitry. • Air compressor relay. • Air suspension control module.	• Go To Pinpoint Test

FM2010200811010X

Fig. 3 Troubleshooting chart (Part 1 of 2). 2003–04

• Air suspension system works with air suspension switch in the OFF position	• Air suspension switch.	• INSTALL a new air suspension switch. TEST the system for normal operation.
• Uneven vehicle height	• Pneumatic fault. • Air suspension height sensor. • Air spring solenoid. • Air compressor. • Air spring. • Air suspension control module.	• REPAIR as necessary.
• Incorrect vehicle trim height	• Incorrect ride height adjustment. • Incorrect height sensor calibration. • Incorrect air suspension module calibration.	• SET the ride height.
	• Rear suspension component damage.	• INSPECT and REPAIR the rear suspension components as necessary.

FM2010200811020X

Fig. 3 Troubleshooting chart (Part 2 of 2). 2003–04

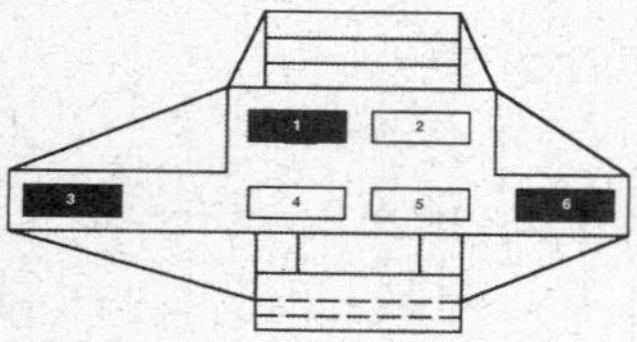

C459F (GRAY)

AIR SUSPENSION TEST CONNECTOR

PIN	CIRCUIT	CIRCUIT FUNCTION
1	—	NOT USED
2	432 (BK/PK)	Ground
3	—	NOT USED
4	419 (DG/LG)	Indicator Output
5	844 (GY/R)	Diagnostic Input
6	—	NOT USED

FM2019900582000X

Fig. 4 Diagnostic Link Connector (DLC)

At the beginning of the automatic portion of the test, the air suspension control module checks for damaged air suspension control module (DTC 70), for unstable battery voltage (DTC 80), then for shorted or open conditions that would create DTC 39 through DTC 46, and DTC 68 through DTC 71. If shorts or opens are detected, the automatic portion of the test is ended and a DTC 13 (auto test failed) will be displayed on the Super Star II Tester. If no shorts or opens are detected, the automatic portion of the test continues. The air suspension control module attempts to raise and lower the vehicle to verify that all three air suspension height sensor states (trim, high, low) can be reached. A properly functioning vehicle will be at trim height at the end of the Auto Test. If all three states are not reached, the Auto Test will end and again a DTC 13 will be displayed. A DTC 12 will be displayed at the end of the Auto Test only if everything checked to this point is functional.

After DTC 12 (or DTC 13) is displayed, the air suspension control module is ready to check for manual inputs. The manual inputs check the steering sensor and door courtesy lamp switch circuits. During the manual test, the air suspension control module continually monitors the door and steering sensor circuits for activity. To pass the manual test, the air suspension control module must detect that four doors have been opened and closed, and the steering wheel has been turned at least one quarter turn in each direction. After the manual test, the Super Star II Tester button must be toggled or the air suspension control module will continue to monitor the manual input tests indefinitely. Either a DTC 11 (air suspension OK) or other DTCs will be displayed at this time.

After the auto and manual input tests, the DTCs will be displayed automatically. Each DTC detected will be displayed for about 15 seconds. The code display will continue until all DTCs have been displayed. The display will repeat the DTC until Super Star II Tester button is released (up). Document all DTCs, then release the depressed Super Star II Tester button. Do not disconnect or turn OFF the Super Star II Tester. The Super Star II Tester is ready to enter the Function Test if a DTC 11 has been displayed.

FM2019900600000X

Fig. 5 Auto test diagnostics

to properly diagnose and test this system. **Do not use Super Star Tester model No. 007-00019.**

Connect scan tool to Diagnostic Link Connector (DLC) **Fig. 4,** which will be found in the trunk compartment near the air suspension On/Off switch. Follow tool manufacturer's instructions for installation and operation of the tool.

Air suspension diagnostics should proceed in a logical sequence. First perform Auto Test Diagnostics, followed by Drive Cycle Diagnostics, then proceed to Functional Tests (if previous testing has not located problem area).

Record any Diagnostic Trouble Codes (DTCs) found during these diagnostic procedures, then refer to "Diagnostic Trouble Code Interpretation" for DTC tables and recommended additional pinpoint tests.

2003-04

A New Generation Star (NGS) Tester, or equivalent, scan tool must be used to access Diagnostic Trouble Codes (DTCs). Connect tester to Diagnostic Link Connector (DLC) located under the lefthand side of the instrument panel, then follow tool manufacturer's instructions to access Diagnostic Trouble Codes (DTCs).

Auto Test/Service Bay Diagnostics

The automatic portion of this test begins with inspecting the control module for shorts or opens that would create STAR codes 39 through 46, and 68 through 71. If shorts or opens are detected, the automatic portion of the test is over and a STAR code 13, auto test failed, will be displayed. If no shorts or opens are detected, the automatic portion of the test continues. The control module attempts to raise and lower the vehicle to verify that all three height positions can be reached. A normally functioning vehicle will be at trim height by the end of the test. If all three height positions are not reached, the auto test will end and STAR code 13 will be displayed. STAR code 12 will be displayed at the end of the auto test if everything is satisfactory.

After STAR code 12 or 13 is displayed the control module will inspect for manual inputs. The manual inputs inspect the steering sensor and the door circuits. To pass the manual test the control module must detect that all four doors have been opened and closed, and the steering wheel has been turned at least ¼ turn in each direction. After the manual test, the tester must be toggled, or the control module will continue to monitor the manual test inputs indefinitely. Either STAR code 11, air suspension normal, or other STAR codes will be displayed.

Refer to **Fig. 5,** to perform auto test diagnostic procedures.

Functional Test

This test is run after the "Auto Test Diagnostic Check." Refer to **Fig. 6,** for test procedures.

Test Step		Result	Action to Take
AB1	CHECK FOR DTCs		
	• Functional Tests are used in some of the DTC Pinpoint Tests to aid in system diagnosis. • The Functional Test mode can only be entered after Auto Test has been performed. A DTC 11 or any other DTCs must be displayed before the Functional Test mode can be entered. • **Are DTCs displayed?**	Yes ▶ No ▶	GO to **AB2.** REPEAT Auto Test. If Auto Test cannot be entered, GO to Pinpoint Test **S.**
AB2	CHECK FOR FUNCTIONAL TEST DTCs		
	• Release Star Tester button to the HOLD (up) position. • Wait at least 20 seconds. • Press Star Tester button to the TEST (down) position. • DTC 23 should be displayed, then DTCs 26, 31, 32 and 33 will be displayed in order. Each DTC will be displayed for about 15 seconds. After all the DTCs are displayed, they will be repeated as long as the Star Test button is in TEST (down) position. • **Are functional test DTCs displayed?**	Yes ▶ No ▶	GO to **AB3.** RELEASE Star Tester button to HOLD (up) position. Wait 20 seconds and press button to TEST (down) position. If Functional Test DTCs are still not displayed, REPEAT Auto Test.
AB3	PERFORM FUNCTIONAL TESTS		
	• The following chart lists the Functional Test DTCs: (see chart below) • Within four seconds after the desired Functional Test DTC is displayed, release the Star Tester button to the HOLD (up) position. NOTE: Waiting longer than four seconds will cause the next Function Test to be entered. • As long as the Star Tester button is in the HOLD (up) position, the Functional Test will continue. NOTE: The Star Tester may or may not display the DTC for the Functional Test selected. • Example: Functional Test DTC 32 is selected. Star Tester may display DTC 31, even though Functional Test 32 is being run. • To exit a Functional Test, depress the Star Tester button to the TEST (down) position. • The Functional Test DTCs will be displayed. The DTCs will be displayed for about 15 seconds each and will cycle. The Functional Tests may be entered and exited as often as desired. • **Are all Functional Tests successful?**	Yes ▶ No ▶	If directed here from Pinpoint Test, RETURN to original test. REFER to Air Suspension Diagnostic Trouble Codes and Pinpoint Test Index.

DTC	Description
23	Vent Rear
26	Compress Rear
31	Toggle Compressor on and off repeatedly
32	Toggle vent solenoid valve on and off repeatedly
33	Toggle air spring solenoid valves on and off repeatedly

FM2019600282000X

Fig. 6 Functional test

Diagnostic Trouble Code Interpretation

Refer to **Figs. 7 and 8,** to locate the problem area description and/or the recommended pinpoint test, then refer to the "Diagnostic Chart Index" to locate the appropriate test.

Wiring Diagrams & Connector Identification

Refer to **Figs. 9 and 10,** for wiring diagrams and **Fig. 11,** for pin and connector locations.

Pinpoint Tests

Refer to the "Diagnostic Chart Index" to locate the appropriate pinpoint test.

Refer to **Figs. 12 through 43,** for Pinpoint Tests.

Clearing Diagnostic Trouble Codes

Connect Star II tester or equivalent, as outlined in "Accessing Diagnostic Trouble Codes" then access menu selection for clearing Diagnostic Trouble Codes (DTC). Follow tool manufacturers instructions to clear DTCs.

DTC	Description	Source	Action
10	Diagnostic auto test in progress	Air suspension control module	—
11	Vehicle system passes	Air suspension control module	—
12	Auto test passed	Air suspension control module	CARRY OUT manual inputs.
13	Auto test failed	Air suspension control module	CARRY OUT manual inputs.
15	No drive cycle errors detected	Air suspension control module	—
16	EVO diagnostic trouble code	Air suspension control module	
17	EVO diagnostic trouble code	Air suspension control module	
18	EVO diagnostic trouble code	Air suspension control module	
23	Vent Rear Function Test	Air suspension control module	GO to Function Tests.
26	Compress Rear Function Test	Air suspension control module	GO to Function Tests.
31	Air Compressor Relay Toggle Function Test	Air suspension control module	GO to Function Tests.

FM2019900602010X

Fig. 7 Diagnostic trouble code table (Part 1 of 2). 2000–02

DTC	Description	Source	Action
32	Vent Solenoid Toggle Function Test	Air suspension control module	GO to Function Tests.
33	Air Spring Solenoid Function Test	Air suspension control module	GO to Function Tests.
35	Drive cycle error codes erased OK	Air suspension control module	—
39	Compressor relay control circuit short to power	Air suspension control module	GO to Pinpoint Test D.
40	Compressor relay control circuit short to ground	Air suspension control module	GO to Pinpoint Test E.
42	Air spring solenoid circuit short to ground	Air suspension control module	GO to Pinpoint Test F.
43	Air spring solenoid circuit short to power	Air suspension control module	GO to Pinpoint Test G.
44	Vent solenoid circuit short to power	Air suspension control module	GO to Pinpoint Test H.
45	Vent solenoid circuit failure	Air suspension control module	GO to Pinpoint Test I.
46	Air suspension height sensor supply circuit failure	Air suspension control module	GO to Pinpoint Test J.
51	Unable to detect lowering of rear	Air suspension control module	GO to Pinpoint Test K.
54	Unable to detect raising of rear	Air suspension control module	GO to Pinpoint Test L.
55	Unable to detect vehicle speed greater than 24 km/h (15 mph)	Air suspension control module	GO to Pinpoint Test M.
60	Air suspension switch short to power	Air suspension control module	GO to Pinpoint Test N.
61	Air suspension switch circuit failure	Air suspension control module	GO to Pinpoint Test O.
68	Air suspension height sensor circuit failure	Air suspension control module	GO to Pinpoint Test P.
70	ECU defective	Air suspension control module	INSTALL a new air suspension control module. REPEAT the Auto Test.
71	Air suspension height sensor circuit open	Air suspension control module	GO to Pinpoint Test Q.
72	Did not detect four open or closed door signals	Air suspension control module	GO to Pinpoint Test R.
74	EVO diagnostic trouble code	Air suspension control module	
80	Battery voltage high or low	Air suspension control module	GO to Pinpoint Test S.

FM2019900602020X

Fig. 7 Diagnostic trouble code table (Part 2 of 2). 2000–02

DTC	Description	Source	Action
B1317	Battery Voltage High	RAS Module	Go To Pinpoint Test C .
B1318	Battery Voltage Low	RAS Module	Go To Pinpoint Test C .
B1342	ECU Is Defective	RAS Module	INSTALL a new rear air suspension control module. REFER to Module—Air Suspension Control in this section. TEST the system for normal operation.
B1566	Door Ajar Circuit Short To Ground	RAS Module	Go To Pinpoint Test D .
B2477	Module Configuration Failure	RAS Module	Diagnose module.
C1445	Vehicle Speed Signal Circuit Failure	Anti-Lock Brake System (ABS) Module	Diagnose brakes.
C1724	Air Suspension Height Sensor Power Circuit Failure	Rear Air Suspension Control Module	Go To Pinpoint Test E .
C1726	Air Suspension Rear Pneumatic Failure	RAS Module	Go To Pinpoint Test F .
C1760	Air Suspension Rear Height Sensor High Signal Circuit Failure	RAS Module	Go To Pinpoint Test G .
C1770	Air Suspension Vent Solenoid Output Circuit Failure	RAS Control Module	Go To Pinpoint Test H .
C1790	Air Suspension LR Air Spring Solenoid Output Circuit Failure	RAS Module	Go To Pinpoint Test I .
C1795	Air Suspension RR Air Spring Solenoid Output Circuit Failure	RAS Module	Go To Pinpoint Test I .
C1830	Air Suspension Compressor Relay Circuit Failure	RAS Module	Go To Pinpoint Test J .
C1840	Air Suspension Disable Switch Circuit Failure	RAS Module	Go To Pinpoint Test K .
C1897	Steering VAPS Circuit Loop Failure	RAS Module	Diagnose steeribg system.
C1964	Air Suspension Air Compressor Request Exceeded Maximum Timing	RAS Module	DTC code C1964 indicates that the air compressor has overheated and is unable to enter the self-test. Allow the air compressor to cool down for approximately five minutes. CLEAR the DTC. REPEAT the self-test.
U1026	SCP Invalid or Missing Data for Engine RPM	PCM	CARRY OUT the PCM Self-Test.

FM2010200812000X

Fig. 8 Diagnostic trouble code table. 2003–04

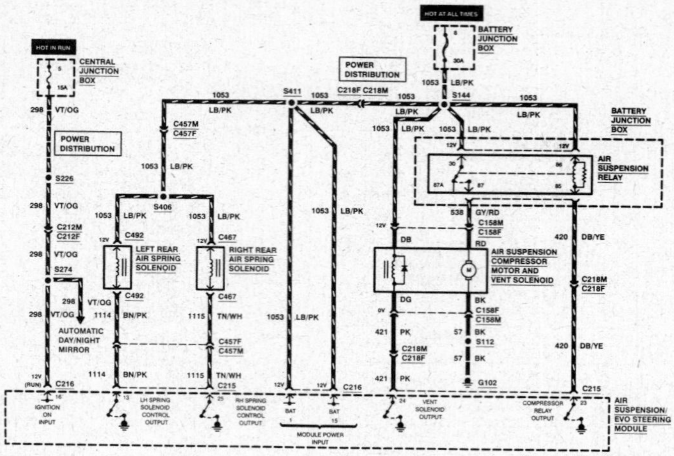

FM2019900579010X

Fig. 9 Wiring diagram (Part 1 of 2). 2000–02

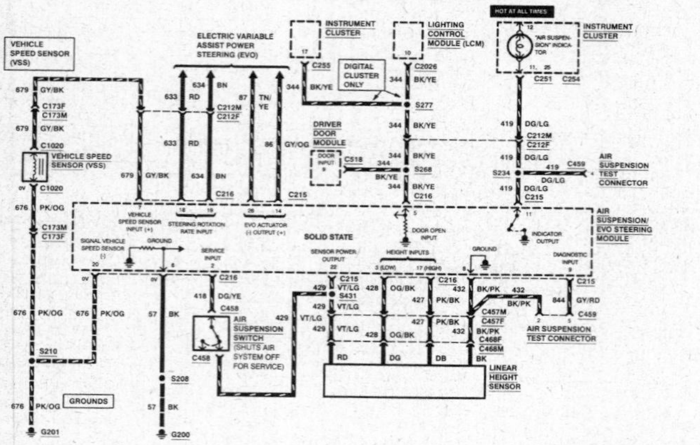

FM2019900579020X

Fig. 9 Wiring diagram (Part 2 of 2). 2000–02

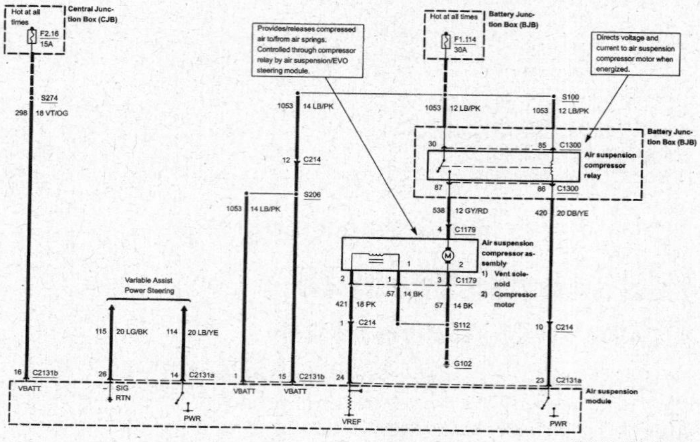

FM2010200813010X

Fig. 10 Wiring diagram (Part 1 of 2). 2003–04

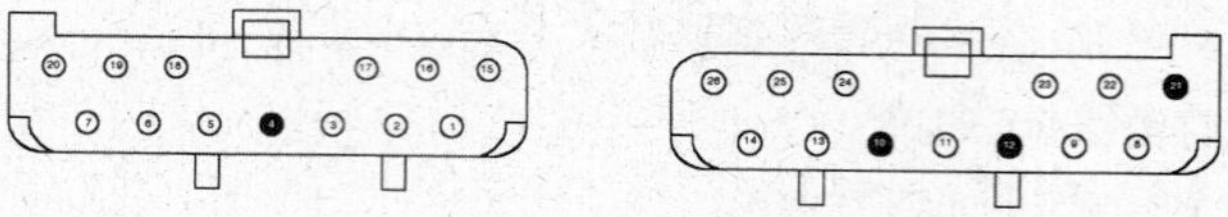

FM2010200813020X

Fig. 10 Wiring diagram (Part 2 of 2). 2003–04

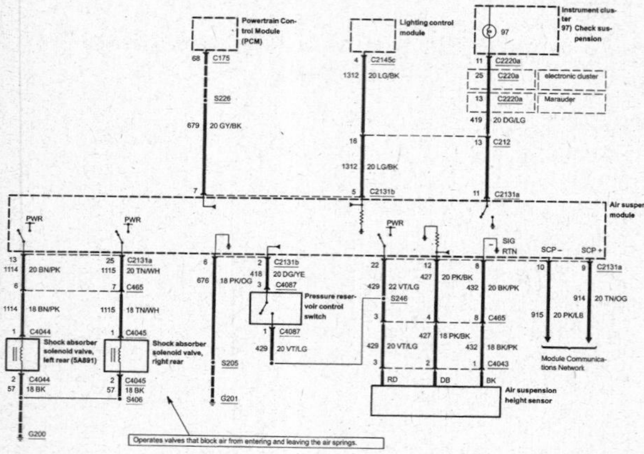

C216F (GRAY)

AIR SUSPENSION/EVO STEERING MODULE

PIN	CIRCUIT	CIRCUIT FUNCTION
1	1053 (LB/PK)	B+
2	418 (DG/Y)	Service Switch Input
3	428 (O/BK)	Linear Height Sensor Input (LOW)
4	—	NOT USED
5	344 (BK/Y)	Door Open Input
6	57 (BK)	Ground
7	679 (GY/BK)	Vehicle Speed Sensor (VSS) Signal Input (+)
15	1053 (LB/PK)	B+
16	298 (P/O)	Ignition On Input
17	427 (PK/BK)	Linear Height Sensor Input (HIGH)
18	633 (R)	Steering Wheel Rotation Rate Input
19	634 (BR)	Steering Wheel Rotation Rate Input
20	676 (PK/O)	Vehicle Speed Sensor (VSS) Signal Input (–)

C215F (BLACK)

AIR SUSPENSION/EVO STEERING MODULE

PIN	CIRCUIT	CIRCUIT FUNCTION
8	432 (BK/PK)	Diagnostic and Height Sensor Ground
9	844 (GY/R)	Diagnostic Input
10	—	NOT USED
11	419 (DG/LG)	Warning Lamp and Diagnostic Output
12	—	NOT USED
13	1114 (BR/PK)	LH Rear Air Spring Solenoid Control
14	86 (GY/O)	Electronic Variable Orifice (EVO) Actuator Control
21	—	NOT USED
22	429 (P/LG)	Linear Height Sensor Power Output
23	420 (DB/Y)	Compressor Relay Control
24	421 (PK)	Vent Solenoid Control
25	1115 (T/W)	RH Rear Air Spring Solenoid Control
26	87 (T/Y)	Electric Variable Orifice (EVO) Actuator Feedback

FM2019900580000X

Fig. 11 Connector & pin diagram

DIAGNOSTIC CHART INDEX

Pinpoint Test	Code	Description	Page No.	Fig. No.
2000–02				
A	—	No Communication w/Air Suspension Control Module	7-48	12
B	—	Unable To Enter Auto Test	7-49	13
C	—	Auto Test	7-50	14
D	39	Compressor Relay Control Circuit Short To Power	7-50	15
E	40	Compressor Relay Control Circuit Failure	7-50	16
F	42	Air Spring Solenoid Circuit Short To Ground	7-51	17
G	43	Air Spring Solenoid Circuit Short To Power	7-51	18
H	44	Vent Solenoid Circuit Short To Power	7-51	19
I	45	Vent Solenoid Circuit Failure	7-52	20
J	46	Air Suspension Height Sensor Supply Circuit Failed	7-52	21
K	51	Unable To Detect Lowering Of Rear	7-53	22
L	54	Unable To Detect Raising Of Rear	7-55	23
M	55	Unable To Detect Vehicle Speed Greater Than 15 mph	7-57	24
N	60	Suspension Switch Short To Power	7-57	25
O	61	Suspension Switch Circuit Failure	7-57	26
P	68	Height Sensor Circuit Failure	7-58	27
Q	71	Height Sensor Circuit Open	7-58	28
R	72	Did Not Detect Four Open Or Closed Door Signals	7-59	29
S	80	Battery Voltage High Or Low	7-60	30
2003–04				
A	—	No Communication w/Rear Air Suspension Control Module	7-60	31
B	—	Unable To Enter Self-Test	7-60	32
C	B1317	Battery Voltage High	7-60	33
	B1318	Battery Voltage Low	7-60	33
D	B1566	Door Ajar Circuit Short To Ground/Did Not Detect Open And Close Signals	7-61	34
E	C1724	Height Sensor Power Circuit Failure	7-61	35
F	C1726	Pneumatic Failure	7-61	36
G	C1760	Rear Height Sensor High Signal Circuit Failure	7-62	37
H	C1770	Vent Solenoid Output Circuit Failure	7-62	38
I	C1790	LR Air Spring Solenoid Output Circuit Failure	7-63	39
	C1795	RR Air Spring Solenoid Output Circuit Failure	7-63	39
J	C1830	Air Compressor Relay Circuit Failure	7-63	40
K	C1840	Air Suspension Switch Circuit Failure	7-63	41
L	—	Compressor Is Inoperative	7-64	42
M	—	Air Compressor Continuously Cycles w/Ignition Switch In Off Position & No DTC Is Set	7-64	43

TEST CONDITIONS	TEST DETAILS/RESULTS/ACTIONS
A1 CHECK CIRCUIT 1053 (LB/PK) AND CIRCUIT 298 (VT/OG) FOR AN OPEN	

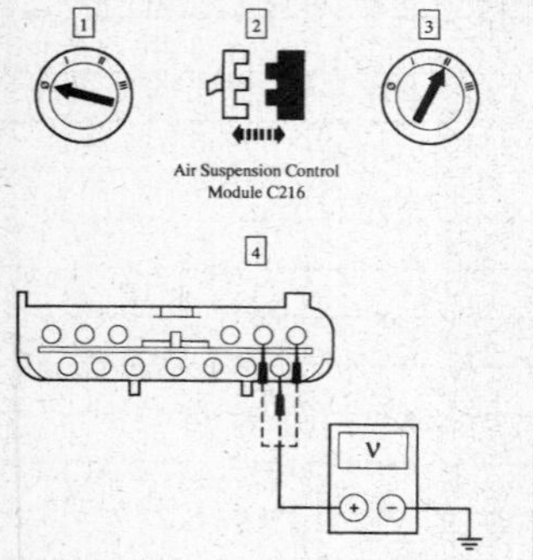

4 Measure the voltage between air suspension control module C216, harness side and ground as follows:

Air Suspension Control Module C216	Circuit
Pin 16	298 (VT/OG)
Pin 1	1053 (LB/PK)
Pin 15	1053 (LB/PK)

- Are the voltages greater than 10 volts?

→ **Yes**
GO to **A2**.

→ **No**
REPAIR the circuit in question. CLEAR the DTCs. REPEAT the Auto Test.

FM2019900603010X

Fig. 12 Test A: No Communication w/Air Suspension Control Module (Part 1 of 7). 2000–02

TEST CONDITIONS	TEST DETAILS/RESULTS/ACTIONS
A4 CHECK CIRCUIT 419 (DG/LG) FOR VOLTAGE AT THE AIR SUSPENSION TEST CONNECTOR	

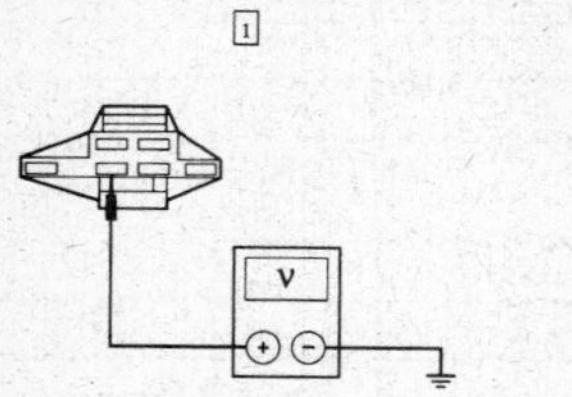

1 Measure the voltage between air suspension test connector C459 Pin 4, Circuit 419 (DG/LG), harness side and ground.

- Is the voltage greater than 10 volts?

→ **Yes**
GO to **A5**.

→ **No**
REPAIR the circuit. CLEAR the DTCs. REPEAT the Auto Test.

A5 CHECK CIRCUIT 844 (GY/RD)

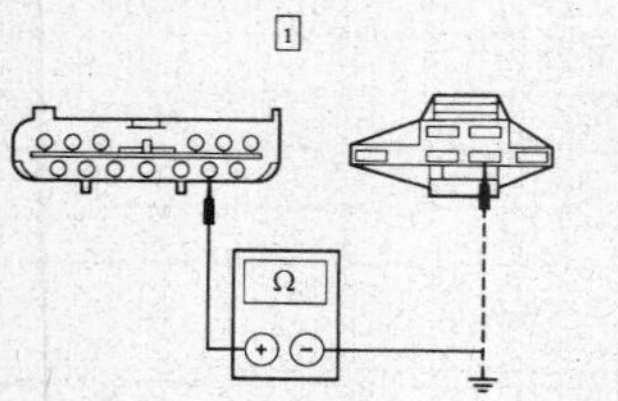

1 Measure the resistance between air suspension control module C215 Pin 9, Circuit 844 (GY/RD), harness side and air suspension test connector C459 Pin 5, Circuit 844 (GY/RD), harness side; and between air suspension control module C215 Pin 9, Circuit 844 (GY/RD), harness side and ground.

- Is the resistance less than 5 ohms between air suspension control module and air suspension test connector; and greater than 10,000 ohms between air suspension control module and ground?

→ **Yes**
GO to **A6**.

→ **No**
REPAIR the circuit. CLEAR the DTCs. REPEAT the Auto Test.

FM2019900603030X

Fig. 12 Test A: No Communication w/Air Suspension Control Module (Part 3 of 7). 2000–02

TEST CONDITIONS	TEST DETAILS/RESULTS/ACTIONS
A2 CHECK CIRCUIT 57 (BK) AND CIRCUIT 676 (PK/OG) FOR AN OPEN	

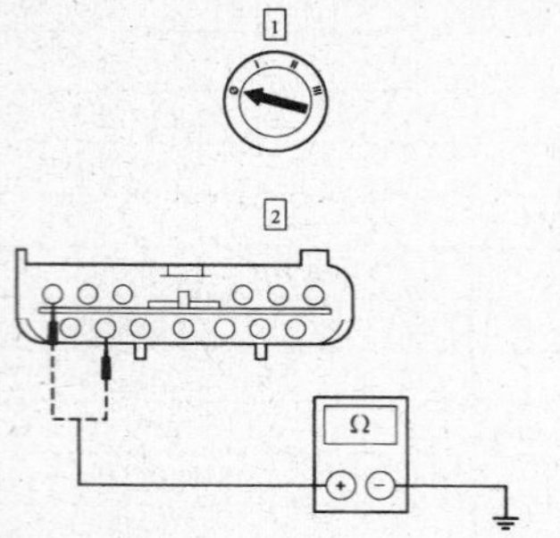

2 Measure the resistance between air suspension control module C216 Pin 6, Circuit 57 (BK), harness side and ground; and between air suspension control module C216 Pin 20, Circuit 676 (PK/OG), harness side and ground.

- Are the resistances less than 5 ohms?

→ **Yes**
GO to **A3**.

→ **No**
REPAIR the circuit in question. CLEAR the DTCs. REPEAT the Auto Test.

A3 CHECK CIRCUIT 419 (DG/LG) FOR VOLTAGE AT THE AIR SUSPENSION CONTROL MODULE

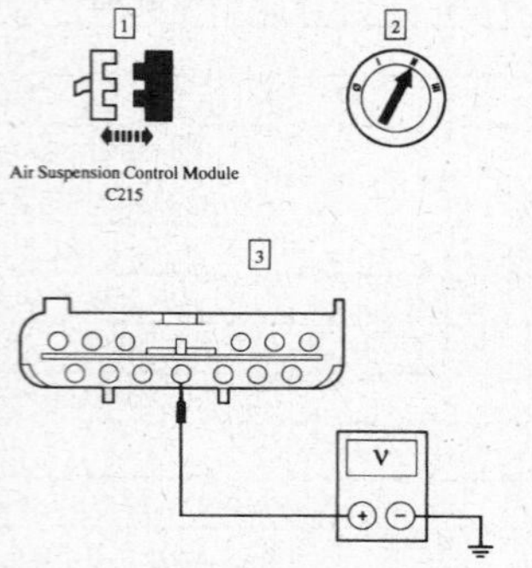

3 Measure the voltage between air suspension control module C215 Pin 11, Circuit 419 (DG/LG), harness side and ground.

- Is the voltage greater than 10 volts?

→ **Yes**
GO to **A4**.

→ **No**
DIAGNOSE instrument cluster.

FM2019900603020X

Fig. 12 Test A: No Communication w/Air Suspension Control Module (Part 2 of 7). 2000–02

TEST CONDITIONS	TEST DETAILS/RESULTS/ACTIONS
A6 CHECK CIRCUIT 432 (BK/PK)	

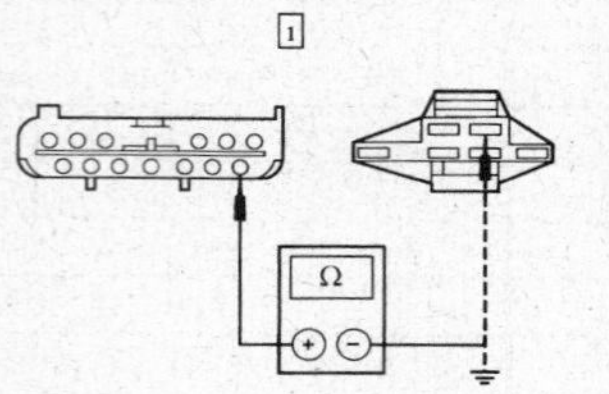

1 Measure the resistance between air suspension control module C215 Pin 8, Circuit 432 (BK/PK), harness side and air suspension test connector C459 Pin 2, Circuit 432 (BK/PK), harness side; and between air suspension control module C215 Pin 9, Circuit 432 (BK/PK), harness side and ground.

- Is the resistance less than 5 ohms between air suspension control module and air suspension test connector; and greater than 10,000 ohms between air suspension control module and ground?

→ **Yes**
GO to **A7**

→ **No**
REPAIR the circuit. CLEAR the DTCs. REPEAT the Auto Test.

A7 CHECK CIRCUIT 419 (DG/LG) FOR SHORT TO POWER

2 Disconnect the instrument cluster C251 (conventional cluster) or C254 (electronic cluster).

FM2019900603040X

Fig. 12 Test A: No Communication w/Air Suspension Control Module (Part 4 of 7). 2000–02

TEST CONDITIONS	TESTDETAILS/RESULTS/ACTIONS
A7 CHECK CIRCUIT 419 (DG/LG) FOR SHORT TO POWER	
[4] 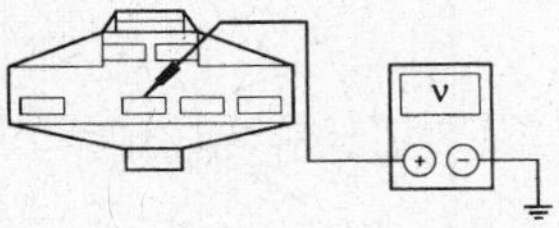	[4] Measure the voltage between air suspension diagnostic connector C459 Pin 4, Circuit 419 (DG/LG), harness side and ground. • Is any voltage indicated? → **Yes** REPAIR the circuit. CLEAR the DTCs. REPEAT the Auto Test. → **No** RECONNECT instrument cluster. GO to **A8**.
A8 CHECK CIRCUIT 432 (BK/PK) FOR SHORT TO POWER	
[1] 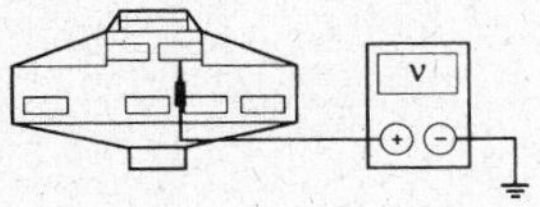	[1] Measure the voltage between air suspension diagnostic connector C459 Pin 2, Circuit 432 (BK/PK), harness side and ground. • Is any voltage indicated? → **Yes** REPAIR the circuit. CLEAR the DTCs. REPEAT the Auto Test. → **No** GO to **A9**.
A9 CHECK CIRCUIT 844 (GY/RD) FOR SHORT TO POWER	
[1] 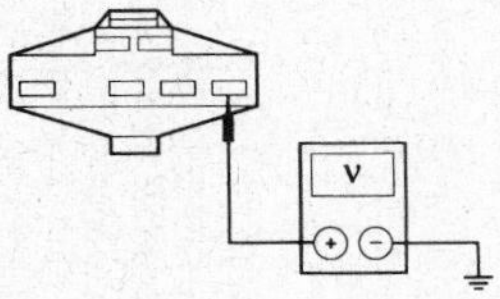	[1] Measure the voltage between air suspension diagnostic connector C459 Pin 2, Circuit 844 (GY/RD), harness side and ground. • Is any voltage indicated? → **Yes** REPAIR the circuit. CLEAR the DTCs. REPEAT the Auto Test. → **No** GO to **A10**.

FM2019900603050X

Fig. 12 Test A: No Communication w/Air Suspension Control Module (Part 5 of 7). 2000–02

TEST CONDITIONS	TESTDETAILS/RESULTS/ACTIONS
A11 CHECK AIR SUSPENSION WARNING INDICATOR	
[4] 	• Does the indicator illuminate? → **Yes** REPEAT the Auto Test. RETEST the system for normal operation. If unable to enter Auto Test, INSTALL a new control module. REPEAT the Auto Test. RETEST the system for normal operation. → **No** INSTALL a new control module. CLEAR the DTCs. REPEAT the Auto Test.

FM2019900603070X

Fig. 12 Test A: No Communication w/Air Suspension Control Module (Part 7 of 7). 2000–02

TEST CONDITIONS	TESTDETAILS/RESULTS/ACTIONS
A10 CHECK AIR SUSPENSION WARNING INDICATOR WIRING	
[1] 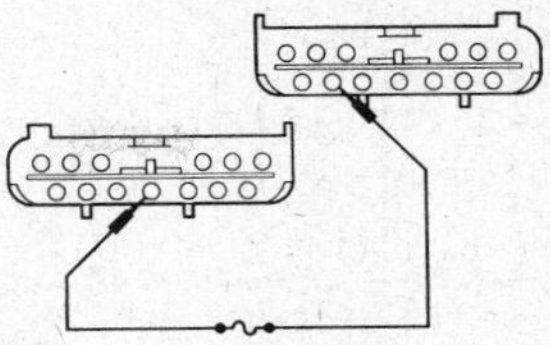	[1] Connect a fused (10A) jumper wire between air suspension control module C216 Pin 6, Circuit 57 (BK), harness side and air suspension control module C215 Pin 11, Circuit 419 (DG/LG), harness side. [2] Check for air suspension warning indicator illumination. • Does the air suspension warning indicator illuminate? → **Yes** DISCONNECT the jumper. RECONNECT the air suspension control module. GO to **A11**. → **No** CHECK the indicator bulb. INSTALL a new bulb as necessary. If OK, REPAIR the instrument cluster. CLEAR the DTCs. REPEAT the Auto Test.
A11 CHECK AIR SUSPENSION WARNING INDICATOR	
[1] 	[2] Place the air suspension switch in the ON position. [3] Place the air suspension switch in the OFF position.

FM2019900603060X

Fig. 12 Test A: No Communication w/Air Suspension Control Module (Part 6 of 7). 2000–02

TEST CONDITIONS	TESTDETAILS/RESULTS/ACTIONS
B1 CHECK COMMUNICATION TO THE AIR SUSPENSION CONTROL MODULE	
	[1] Check communication between the Super Star II Tester and the air suspension control module. • Does the Super Star II Tester communicate? → **Yes** GO to **B2**. → **No** GO to Pinpoint Test A.

FM2019900604010X

Fig. 13 Test B: Unable To Enter Auto Test (Part 1 of 2). 2000–02

TEST CONDITIONS	TESTDETAILS/RESULTS/ACTIONS
B2 CHECK CIRCUIT 298 (VT/OG) AND CIRCUIT 1053 (LB/PK) FOR VOLTAGE	
[1] [2] [3] 	
[4] 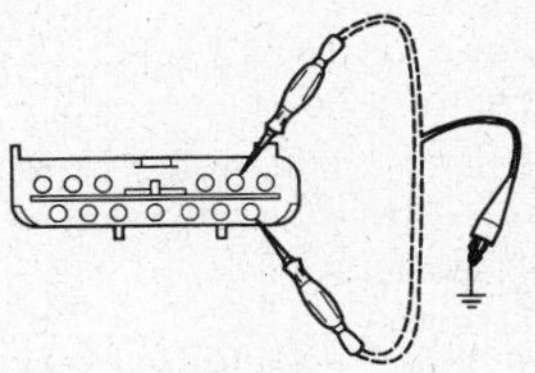	[4] Connect a test light between air suspension control module C216 Pin 16, Circuit 298 (UT/OG), harness side and ground; and between air suspension control module C216 Pin 1, Circuit 1053 (LB/PK), harness side and ground. • Is the test light brightly illuminated on both circuits? → **Yes** INSTALL a new air suspension control module. CLEAR the DTCs. REPEAT the Auto Test. → **No** REPAIR the circuit in question. CLEAR the DTCs. REPEAT the Auto Test.

FM2019900604020X

Fig. 13 Test B: Unable To Enter Auto Test (Part 2 of 2). 2000–02

TEST CONDITIONS	TEST DETAILS/RESULTS/ACTIONS
C1 CHECK FOR DTCS	
	1 Place the Super Star II Tester in the EEC/MCU and FAST settings.
2 	3 Place the air suspension switch in the OFF position and then in the ON position.
	4 **Note:** The Super Star II Tester must be in the HOLD position before connecting the diagnostic connector. Connect the Super Star II Tester to the air suspension control module C459.

FM2019900605010X

Fig. 14 Test C: Auto Test (Part 1 of 3). 2000–02

TEST CONDITIONS	TEST DETAILS/RESULTS/ACTIONS
C1 CHECK FOR DTCS	
5 	6 Wait at least two seconds before depressing the Super Star II Tester to the TEST position. 7 Wait at least 20 seconds for the DTCs to be displayed. • Are any DTCs displayed? → **Yes** GO to **C2**. → **No** GO to Pinpoint Test A.
C2 CHECK FOR DTC 10	
	1 Check the Super Star II Tester for DTC 10. • Is DTC 10 displayed? → **Yes** System is in Auto Test mode. GO to **C4**. → **No** GO to **C3**.
C3 CHECK FOR DTC 15, 55, OR 80	
	1 Check the Super Star II Tester for DTC 15, 55, or 80. • Is DTC 15, 55, or 80 displayed? → **Yes** If DTC 15 or 55 is retrieved, REPAIR Circuit 298 (PK/OG). CLEAR the DTCs. REPEAT the self-test. If DTC 80 is retrieved, GO to Pinpoint Test S. → **No** GO to Pinpoint Test A.
C4 CHECK FOR DTC	
	1 Wait two minutes after DTC 10 is displayed.

FM2019900605020X

Fig. 14 Test C: Auto Test (Part 2 of 3). 2000–02

TEST CONDITIONS	TEST DETAILS/RESULTS/ACTIONS
C4 CHECK FOR DTC	
	2 **Note:** When the Auto Test is complete a DTC 12 (Auto Test passed) or a DTC 13 (Auto Test failed) will be displayed. After the Auto Test is complete, the manual input test can be started. Carry out the manual inputs test by opening and closing all four doors and turning the steering wheel 1/4 turn in both directions. 3 Release the Super Star II Tester TEST button to HOLD position. 4 **Note:** Within 20 seconds of depressing the Super Star II Tester to the TEST position, DTCs will start to be retrieved. Wait two seconds and depress the Super Star II Tester to the TEST position. • Is DTC 11 displayed? → **Yes** If a condition still exists, GO to Symptom Chart. If a condition does not exist, system is OK. → **No** GO to Air Suspension Control Module Diagnostic Trouble Code (DTC) Index.

FM2019900605030X

Fig. 14 Test C: Auto Test (Part 3 of 3). 2000–02

TEST CONDITIONS	TEST DETAILS/RESULTS/ACTIONS
D1 CHECK CIRCUIT 420 (DB/YE) FOR SHORT TO POWER	
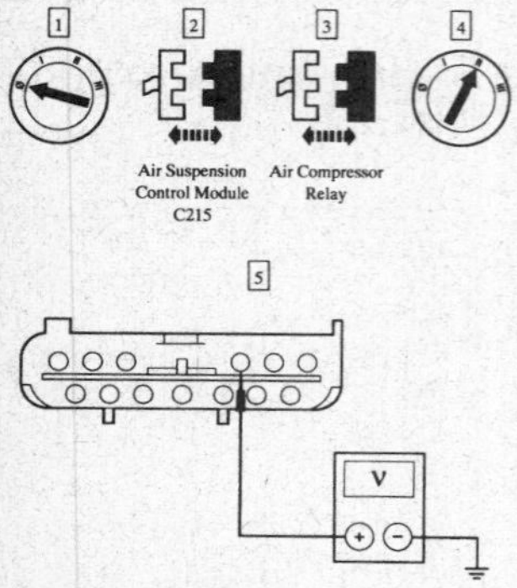	5 Measure the voltage between air suspension control module C215 Pin 23, Circuit 420 (DB/YE), harness side and ground. • Is voltage present? → **Yes** REPAIR the circuit. CLEAR the DTCs. REPEAT the Auto Test. → **No** GO to **D2**.
D2 CHECK THE AIR COMPRESSOR RELAY	
	1 Carry out the air compressor relay component test; • Is the air compressor relay OK? → **Yes** INSTALL a new air suspension control module. REPEAT the Auto Test. → **No** INSTALL a new air compressor relay. CLEAR the DTCs. REPEAT the Auto Test.

FM2019900606000X

Fig. 15 Test D/Code 39: Compressor Relay Control Circuit Short To Power. 2000–02

TEST CONDITIONS	TEST DETAILS/RESULTS/ACTIONS
E1 CHECK CIRCUIT 420 (DB/YE)	
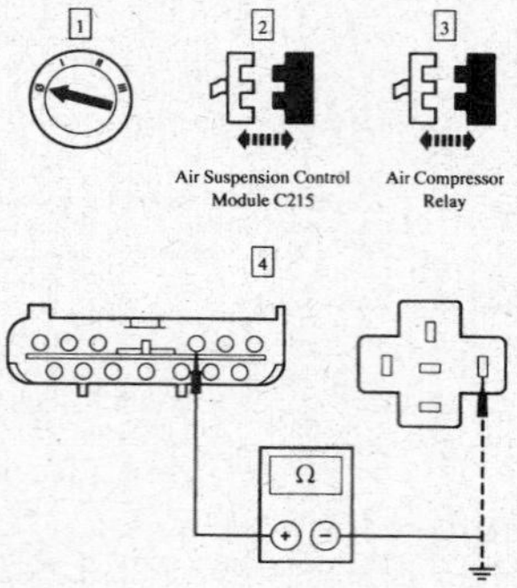	4 Measure the resistance between air suspension control module C215 Pin 23, Circuit 420 (DB/YE), harness side and air compressor relay Pin 85, Circuit 420 (DB/YE), harness side; and between air suspension control module C215 Pin 23, Circuit 420 (DB/YE), harness side and ground. • Is the resistance less than 5 ohms between the air suspension control module and air compressor relay; and greater than 10,000 ohms between the air suspension control module and ground? → **Yes** GO to **E2**. → **No** REPAIR the circuit. CLEAR the DTCs. REPEAT the Auto Test.
E2 CHECK THE AIR COMPRESSOR RELAY	
	1 Carry out the air compressor relay component test; • Is the air compressor relay OK? → **Yes** INSTALL a new air suspension control module. REPEAT the Auto Test. → **No** INSTALL a new air compressor relay. CLEAR the DTCs. REPEAT the Auto Test.

FM2019900607000X

Fig. 16 Test E/Code 40: Compressor Relay Control Circuit Failure. 2000–02

TEST CONDITIONS	TESTDETAILS/RESULTS/ACTIONS
F1 CHECK THE AIR SPRING SOLENOID CIRCUITRY	
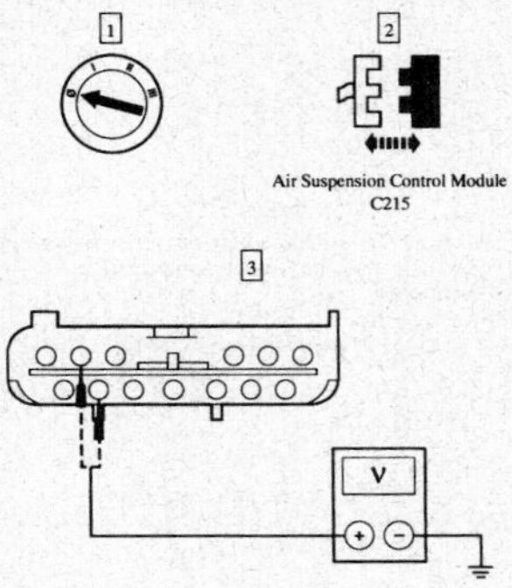	3 Measure the voltage between air suspension control module C215 Pin 13, Circuit 1114 (BN/PK), harness side and ground; and between air suspension control module C215 Pin 25, Circuit 1115 (TN/WH), harness side and ground. • Are the voltages greater than 10 volts? → **Yes** INSTALL a new air suspension control module. REPEAT the Auto Test. → **No** GO to **F2**.
F2 CHECK CIRCUIT 1053 (LB/PK) FOR AN OPEN	
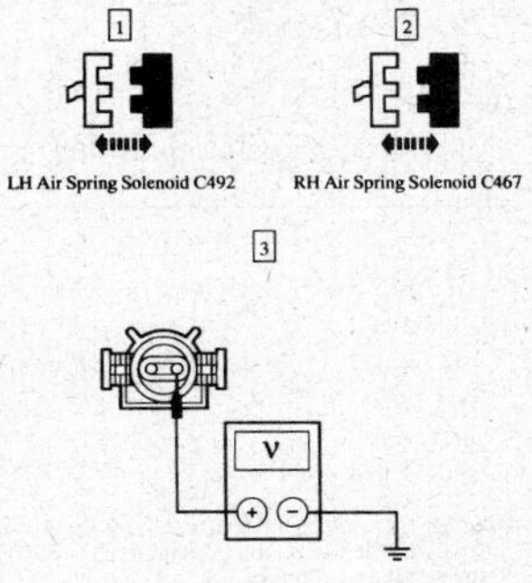	3 Measure the voltage between LH air spring solenoid C492, Circuit 1053 (LB/PK), harness side and ground; and between RH air spring solenoid C467, Circuit 1053 (LB/PK), harness side and ground. • Are the voltages greater than 10 volts? → **Yes** GO to **F3**. → **No** REPAIR the circuit. CLEAR the DTCs. REPEAT the Auto Test.

FM2019900608010X

Fig. 17 Test F/Code 42: Air Spring Solenoid Circuit Short To Ground (Part 1 of 2). 2000–02

TEST CONDITIONS	TESTDETAILS/RESULTS/ACTIONS
G1 CHECK THE RH AIR SPRING SOLENOID	
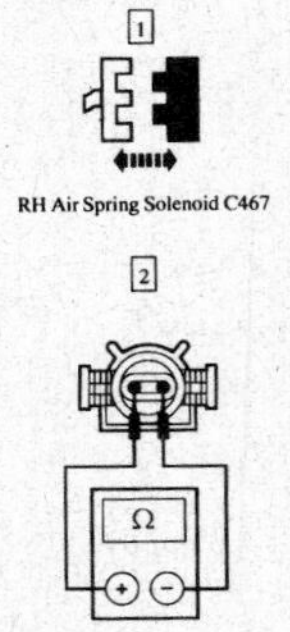	2 Measure the resistance between RH air spring solenoid pins (component side). • Is the resistance between 15 and 18 ohms? → **Yes** GO to **G2**. → **No** INSTALL a new air spring solenoid. CLEAR the DTCs. REPEAT the Auto Test.
G2 CHECK THE LH AIR SPRING SOLENOID	
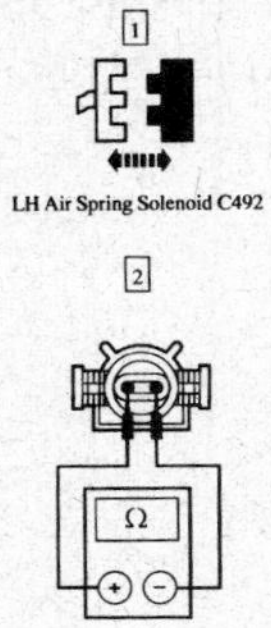	2 Measure the resistance between LH air spring solenoid pins (component side). • Is the resistance between 15 and 18 ohms? → **Yes** GO to **G3**. → **No** INSTALL a new air spring solenoid. CLEAR the DTCs. REPEAT the Auto Test.

FM2019900609010X

Fig. 18 Test G/Code 43 Air Spring Solenoid Circuit Short To Power (Part 1 of 2). 2000–02

TEST CONDITIONS	TESTDETAILS/RESULTS/ACTIONS
F3 CHECK CIRCUIT 1114 (BN/PK)	
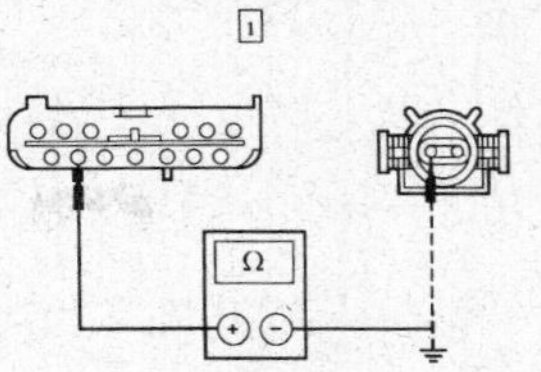	1 Measure the resistance between air suspension control module C215 Pin 13, Circuit 1114 (BN/PK), harness side and air spring solenoid C492, Circuit 1114 (BN/PK), harness side; and between air suspension control module C215 Pin 13, Circuit 1114 (BN/PK), harness side and ground. • Is the resistance less than 5 ohms between the air suspension control module and air spring solenoid; and greater than 10,000 ohms between the air suspension control module and ground? → **Yes** GO to **F4**. → **No** REPAIR the circuit. CLEAR the DTCs. REPEAT the Auto Test.
F4 CHECK CIRCUIT 1115 (TN/WH)	
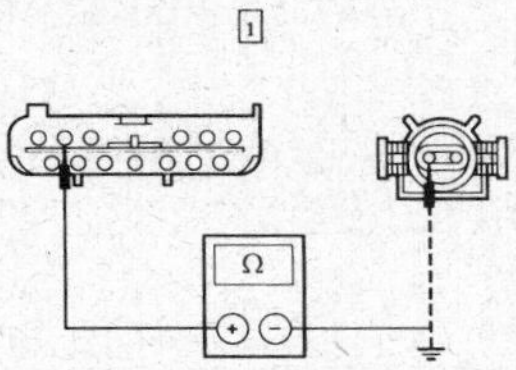	1 Measure the resistance between air suspension control module C215 Pin 25, Circuit 1115 (TN/WH), harness side and air spring solenoid C492, Circuit 1115 (TN/WH), harness side; and between air suspension control module C215 Pin 25, Circuit 1115 (TN/WH), harness side and ground. • Is the resistance less than 5 ohms between the air suspension control module and air spring solenoid; and greater than 10,000 ohms between the air suspension control module and ground? → **Yes** INSTALL a new air spring solenoid in question. CLEAR the DTCs. REPEAT the Auto Test. → **No** REPAIR the circuit. CLEAR the DTCs. REPEAT the Auto Test.

FM2019900608020X

Fig. 17 Test F/Code 42: Air Spring Solenoid Circuit Short To Ground (Part 2 of 2). 2000–02

TEST CONDITIONS	TESTDETAILS/RESULTS/ACTIONS
G3 CHECK CIRCUIT 1115 (TN/WH) AND CIRCUIT 1114 (BN/PK)	
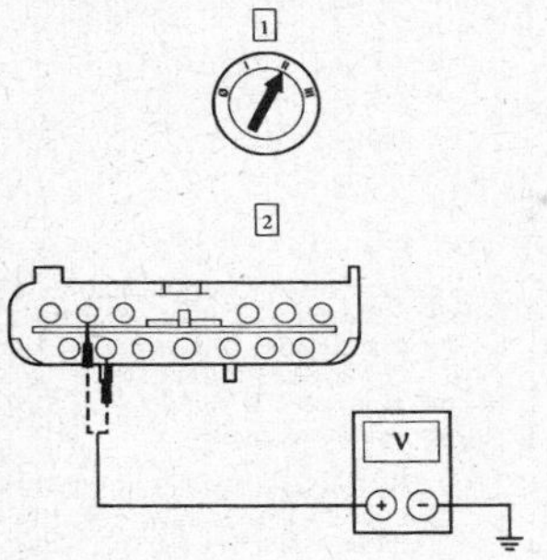	2 Measure the voltage between air suspension control module C215 Pin 25, Circuit 1115 (TN/WH), harness side and ground; and between air suspension control module C215 Pin 13, Circuit 1114 (BN/PK), harness side and ground. • Is voltage present? → **Yes** REPAIR the circuit in question. CLEAR the DTCs. REPEAT the Auto Test. → **No** INSTALL a new air suspension control module. REPEAT the Auto Test.

FM2019900609020X

Fig. 18 Test G/Code 43 Air Spring Solenoid Circuit Short To Power (Part 2 of 2). 2000–02

TEST CONDITIONS	TESTDETAILS/RESULTS/ACTIONS
H1 CHECK THE VENT SOLENOID	
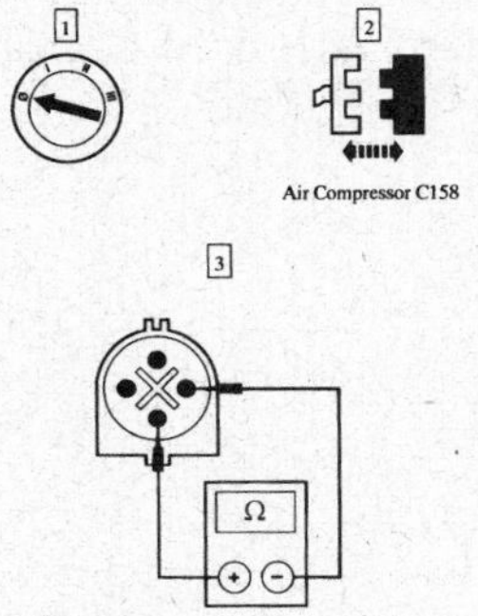	3 Measure the resistance between air compressor pin 1 (component side), and air compressor pin 4 (component side). • Is the resistance between 25 and 35 ohms? → **Yes** GO to **H2**. → **No** INSTALL a new air compressor. CLEAR the DTCs. REPEAT the Auto Test.

FM2019900610010X

Fig. 19 Test H/Code 44: Vent Solenoid Circuit Short To Power (Part 1 of 2). 2000–02

TEST CONDITIONS	TESTDETAILS/RESULTS/ACTIONS
H2 CHECK CIRCUIT 421 (PK) FOR SHORT TO POWER	
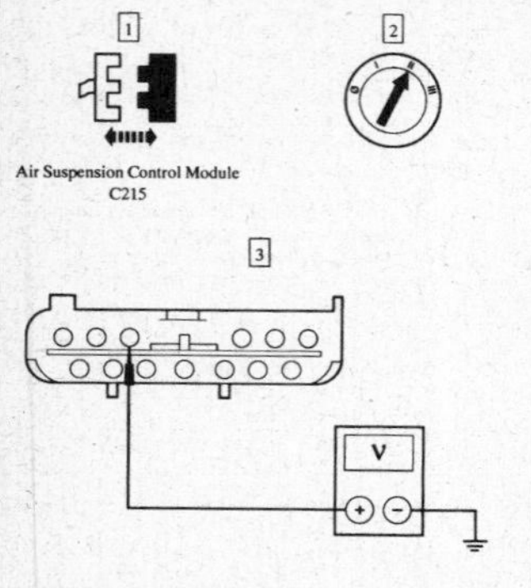	3 Measure the voltage between air suspension control module C215 Pin 24, Circuit 421 (PK), harness side and ground. • Is voltage present? → **Yes** INSTALL a new air suspension control module. REPEAT the Auto Test. → **No** REPAIR the circuit. CLEAR the DTCs. REPEAT the Auto Test.

FM2019900610020X

Fig. 19 Test H/Code 44: Vent Solenoid Circuit Short To Power (Part 2 of 2). 2000–02

TEST CONDITIONS	TESTDETAILS/RESULTS/ACTIONS
I1 CHECK THE VENT SOLENOID	
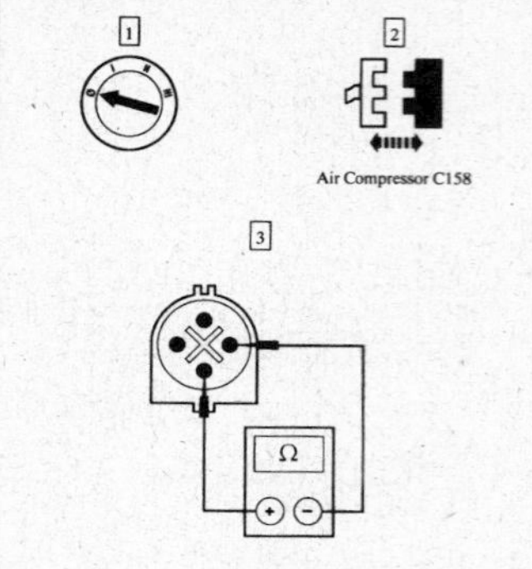	3 Measure the resistance between air compressor pin 1 (component side) and air compressor pin 4 (component side). • Is the resistance between 25 and 35 ohms? → **Yes** GO to **I2**. → **No** INSTALL a new air compressor. CLEAR the DTCs. REPEAT the Auto Test.

FM2019900611010X

Fig. 20 Test I/Code 45: Vent Solenoid Circuit Failure (Part 1 of 2). 2000–02

TEST CONDITIONS	TESTDETAILS/RESULTS/ACTIONS
I2 CHECK CIRCUIT 1053 (LB/PK) FOR AN OPEN	
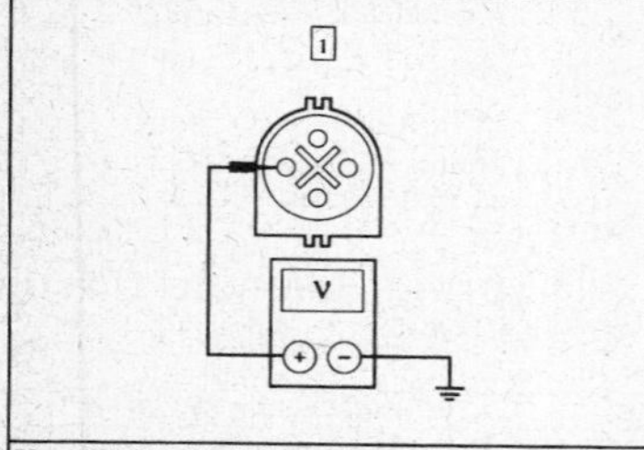	1 Measure the voltage between air compressor C158 Pin 4, Circuit 1053 (LB/PK), harness side and ground. • Is the voltage greater than 10 volts? → **Yes** GO to **I3**. → **No** REPAIR the circuit. CLEAR the DTCs. REPEAT the Auto Test.
I3 CHECK CIRCUIT 421 (PK)	
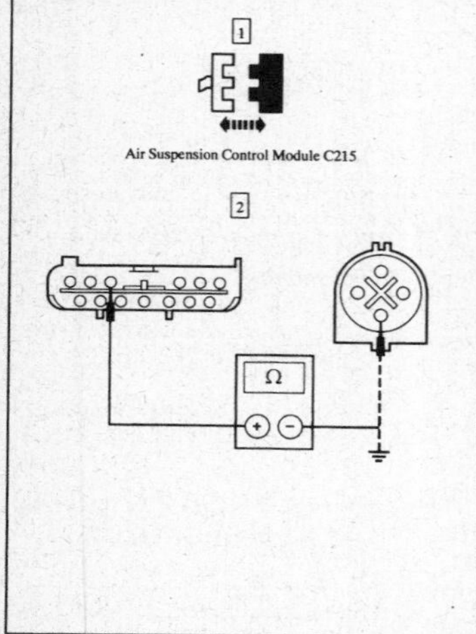	2 Measure the resistance between air suspension control module C215 Pin 24, Circuit 421 (PK), harness side and air compressor C158 Pin 1, Circuit 421 (PK), harness side; and between air suspension control module C215 Pin 24, Circuit 421 (PK), harness side and ground. • Is the resistance less than 5 ohms between the air suspension control module and air compressor; and greater than 10,000 ohms between the air suspension control module and ground? → **Yes** INSTALL a new air suspension control module. REPEAT the Auto Test. → **No** REPAIR the circuit. CLEAR the DTCs. REPEAT the Auto Test.

FM2019900611020X

Fig. 20 Test I/Code 45: Vent Solenoid Circuit Failure (Part 2 of 2). 2000–02

TEST CONDITIONS	TESTDETAILS/RESULTS/ACTIONS
J1 CHECK CIRCUIT 418 (DG/YE) FOR SHORT TO POWER	
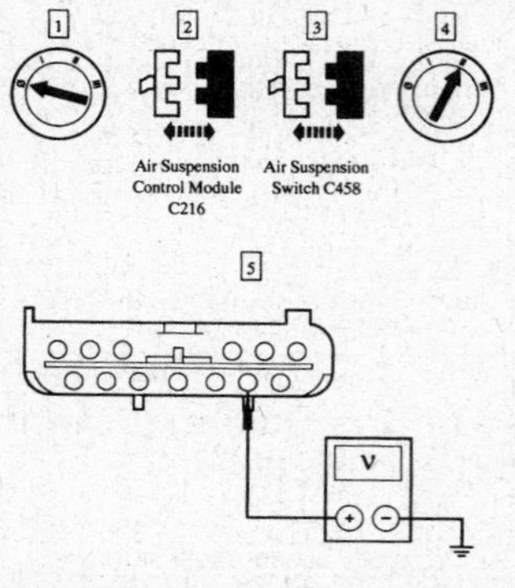	5 Measure the voltage between air suspension control module C216 Pin 2, Circuit 418 (DG/YE), harness side and ground. • Is voltage present? → **Yes** REPAIR the circuit. CLEAR the DTCs. REPEAT the Auto Test. → **No** GO to **J2**.
J2 CHECK CIRCUIT 418 (DG/YE) FOR SHORT TO GROUND	
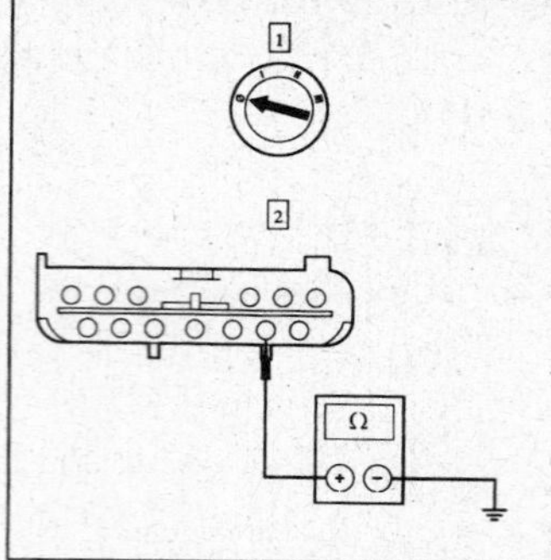	2 Measure the resistance between air suspension control module C216 Pin 2, Circuit 418 (DG/YE), harness side and ground. • Is the resistance greater than 10,000 ohms? → **Yes** GO to **J3**. → **No** REPAIR the circuit. CLEAR the DTCs. REPEAT the Auto Test.

FM2019900612010X

Fig. 21 Test J/Code 46: Height Sensor Supply Circuit Failed (Part 1 of 3). 2000–02

TEST CONDITIONS	TEST DETAILS/RESULTS/ACTIONS
J3 CHECK CIRCUIT 429 (PK/LG)	
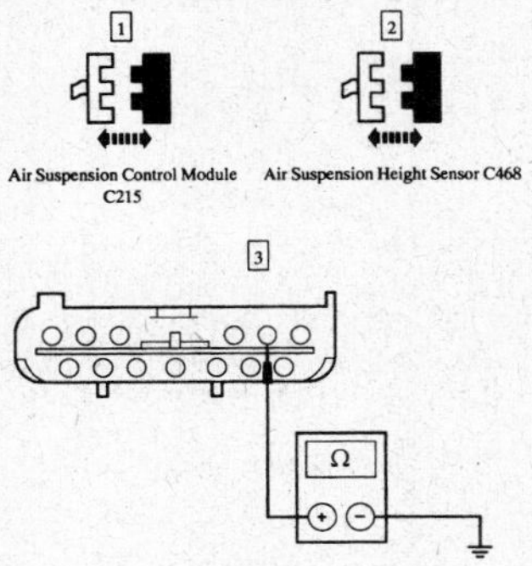	3 Measure the resistance between air suspension control module C215 Pin 22, Circuit 429 (PK/LG), harness side and air suspension height sensor C468 Pin 3, 429 (PK/LG), harness side; and between air suspension control module C215 Pin 22, Circuit 429 (PK/LG), harness side and ground. • Is the resistance less than 5 ohms between the air suspension control module and air suspension height sensor; and greater than 10,000 ohms between the air suspension control module and ground? → **Yes** GO to **J4**. → **No** REPAIR the circuit. CLEAR the DTCs. REPEAT the Auto Test.
J4 CHECK CIRCUIT 427 (PK/BK) FOR SHORT TO GROUND	
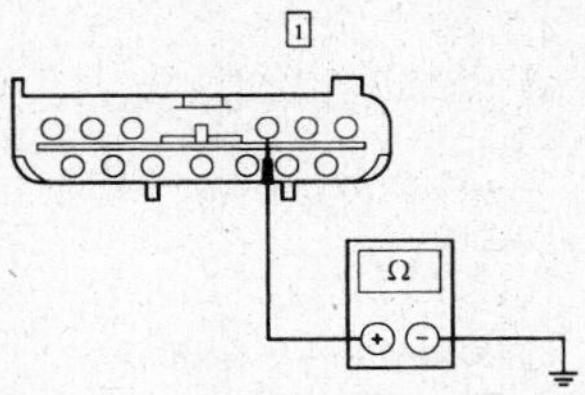	1 Measure the resistance between air suspension control module C216 Pin 17, Circuit 427 (PK/BK), harness side and ground. • Is the resistance greater than 10,000 ohms? → **Yes** GO to **J5**. → **No** REPAIR the circuit. CLEAR the DTCs. REPEAT the Auto Test.
J5 CHECK THE AIR SUSPENSION HEIGHT SENSOR	
	1 Install a known good air suspension height sensor.

FM2019900612020X

Fig. 21 Test J/Code 46: Height Sensor Supply Circuit Failed (Part 2 of 3). 2000–02

TEST CONDITIONS	TEST DETAILS/RESULTS/ACTIONS
K1 CARRY OUT FUNCTION TEST DTC 32	
Note: This test must be done in a quiet environment.	
	1 **Note:** During Function Test DTC 32, the vent solenoid located in the air compressor should cycle ON and OFF repeatedly (one second ON, and one second OFF). As the vent solenoid cycles a clicking noise can be heard at the air compressor. Carry out Function Test DTC 32. • Does the solenoid valve cycle? → **Yes** GO to **K5**. → **No** GO to **K2**.

FM2019900613010X

Fig. 22 Test K/Code 51: Unable To Detect Lowering Of Rear (Part 1 of 7). 2000–02

TEST CONDITIONS	TEST DETAILS/RESULTS/ACTIONS
J5 CHECK THE AIR SUSPENSION HEIGHT SENSOR	
	2 Reconnect the air suspension height sensor C468, air suspension control module, and air suspension switch C458. 3 Retrieve and document DTCs. • Is DTC 46 retrieved? → **Yes** INSTALL a new air suspension control module. REPEAT the Auto Test. → **No** INSTALL a new air suspension height sensor. CLEAR the DTCs. REPEAT the Auto Test.

FM2019900612030X

Fig. 21 Test J/Code 46: Height Sensor Supply Circuit Failed (Part 3 of 3). 2000–02

TEST CONDITIONS	TEST DETAILS/RESULTS/ACTIONS
K2 CHECK CIRCUIT 1053 (LB/PK) FOR AN OPEN	
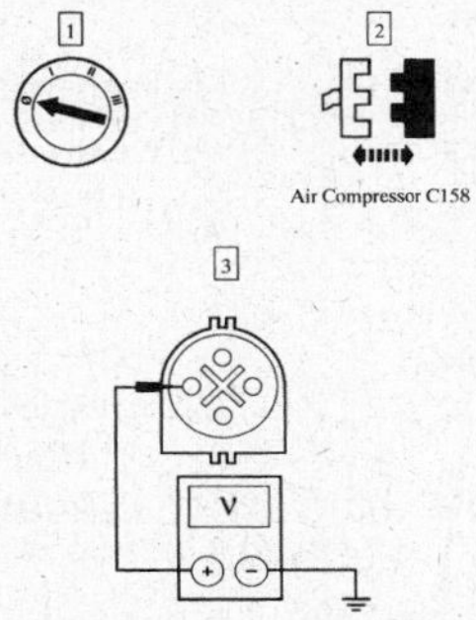	3 Measure the voltage between air compressor C158 Pin 4, Circuit 1053 (LB/PK), harness side and ground. • Is the voltage greater than 10 volts? → **Yes** GO to **K3**. → **No** REPAIR the circuit. CLEAR the DTCs. REPEAT the Auto Test.
K3 CHECK THE AIR SUSPENSION CONTROL MODULE OUTPUT	
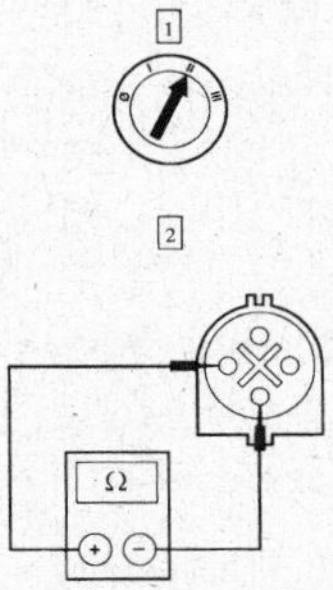	2 Measure the voltage air compressor C158 Pin 4, Circuit 1053 (LB/PK), harness and air compressor C158 Pin 1, Circuit 421 (PK), while running Function Test DTC 32. • Does the voltage cycle between zero and 10 volts? → **Yes** INSTALL a new air compressor. CLEAR the DTCs. REPEAT the Auto Test. → **No** GO to **K4**.

FM2019900613020X

Fig. 22 Test K/Code 51: Unable To Detect Lowering Of Rear (Part 2 of 7). 2000–02

TEST CONDITIONS	TEST DETAILS/RESULTS/ACTIONS
K4 CHECK CIRCUIT 421 (PK) FOR AN OPEN	
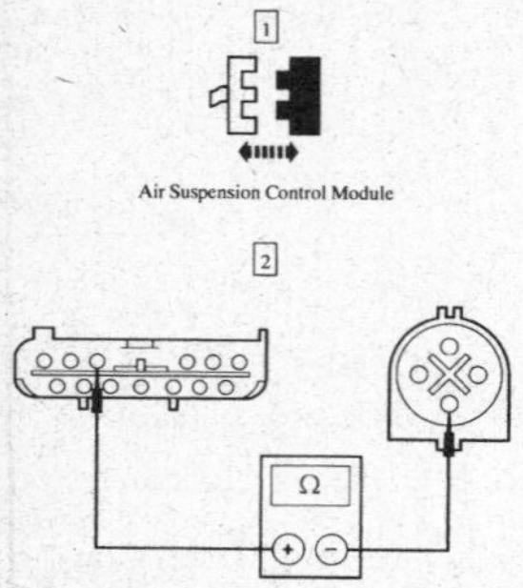	2 Measure the resistance between air suspension control module C215 Pin 24, Circuit 421 (PK), harness side and air compressor C158 Pin 1, Circuit 421 (PK), harness side. • Is the resistance less than 5 ohms? → **Yes** INSTALL a new air suspension control module. REPEAT the Auto Test. → **No** REPAIR the circuit. CLEAR the DTCs. REPEAT the Auto Test.
K5 CHECK THE AIR SPRING SOLENOIDS	
	1 Carry out the Function Test DTC 33. 2 Raise and support the vehicle with the air suspension system ON. 3 **Note:** A clicking vibration should be felt if the air spring solenoid is functioning properly. Check each air spring solenoid for cycling ON and OFF. • Are both air spring solenoids cycling properly? → **Yes** GO to **K9**. → **No** GO to **K6**.

FM2019900613030X

Fig. 22 Test K/Code 51: Unable To Detect Lowering Of Rear (Part 3 of 7). 2000–02

TEST CONDITIONS	TEST DETAILS/RESULTS/ACTIONS
K6 CHECK THE AIR SUSPENSION CONTROL MODULE OUTPUT	
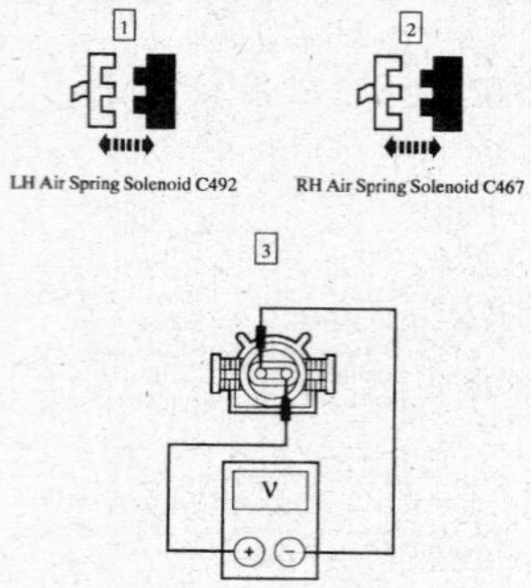	3 Measure the voltage between LH air spring solenoid C492, Circuit 1053 (LB/PK), harness side and LH air spring solenoid C492, Circuit 1114 (BR/PK), harness side; and between RH air spring solenoid C467, Circuit 1053 (LB/PK), harness side and LH air spring solenoid C467, Circuit 1115 (TN/WH), harness side, while running Function Test DTC 33. • Does the voltage cycle between zero and 10 volts? → **Yes** INSTALL a new air spring solenoid. CLEAR the DTCs. REPEAT the Auto Test. → **No** GO to **K7**.
K7 CHECK CIRCUIT 1053 (LB/PK) FOR AN OPEN	
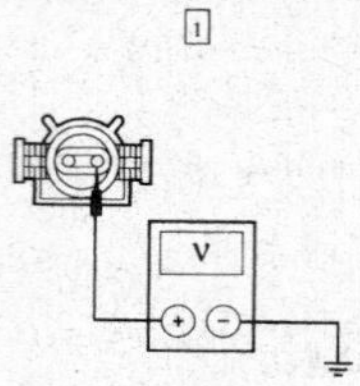	1 Measure the voltage between LH air spring solenoid C492, Circuit 1053 (LB/PK), harness side and ground; and between RH air spring solenoid C467, Circuit 1053 (LB/PK), harness side and ground. • Are the voltages greater than 10 volts? → **Yes** GO to **K8**. → **No** REPAIR the circuit. CLEAR the DTCs. REPEAT the Auto Test.

FM2019900613040X

Fig. 22 Test K/Code 51: Unable To Detect Lowering Of Rear (Part 4 of 7). 2000–02

TEST CONDITIONS	TEST DETAILS/RESULTS/ACTIONS
K8 CHECK CIRCUIT 1114 (BR/PK) AND CIRCUIT 1115 (TN/WH) FOR AN OPEN	
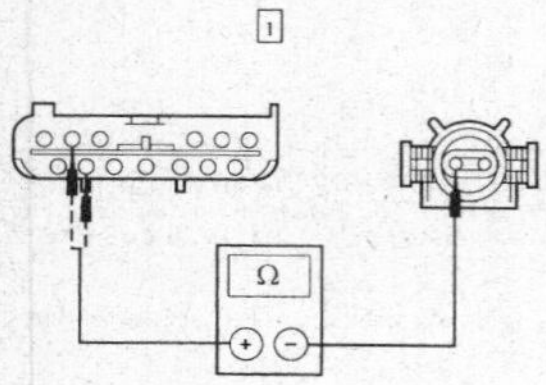	1 Measure the voltage between air suspension control module C215 Pin 13, Circuit 1114 (BR/PK), and LH air spring solenoid C492, Circuit 1053 (LB/PK), harness side; and between air suspension control module C215 Pin 25, Circuit 1115 (TN/WH), harness side and RH air spring solenoid C467, Circuit 1053 (LB/PK), harness side and ground. • Are the resistances less than 5 ohms? → **Yes** INSTALL a new air suspension control module. REPEAT the Auto Test. → **No** REPAIR the circuit in question. CLEAR the DTCs. REPEAT the Auto Test.
K9 CHECK THE AIR SUSPENSION HEIGHT SENSOR FOR PROPER ATTACHMENT	
	1 Check the air suspension height sensor at the upper and lower ball studs for correct attachment. • Is the air suspension height sensor attached correctly? → **Yes** GO to **K10**. → **No** REPAIR or INSTALL a new air suspension height sensor as necessary. CLEAR the DTCs. REPEAT the Auto Test.
K10 CHECK THE AIR FLOW THROUGH THE AIR SPRING SOLENOIDS	
⚠ **CAUTION: Rear of the vehicle must be supported by frame. If rear is supported by the rear axle, rear of vehicle will lower during this test.**	
	1 Disconnect the air lines from the air spring solenoids.

FM2019900613050X

Fig. 22 Test K/Code 51: Unable To Detect Lowering Of Rear (Part 5 of 7). 2000–02

TEST CONDITIONS	TEST DETAILS/RESULTS/ACTIONS
K10 CHECK THE AIR FLOW THROUGH THE AIR SPRING SOLENOIDS (Continued)	
	2 **Note:** The air springs must be filled with some air in order to carry out this test. Carry out Function Test DTC 33 to cycle the air spring solenoids. • Does the air flow from both air springs when the solenoids are cycled open? → **Yes** RECONNECT the air lines to the air springs. GO to **K11**. → **No** INSTALL a new air spring solenoid. CLEAR the DTCs. REPEAT the Auto Test.
K11 CHECK THE AIR LINES	
⚠ **CAUTION: Rear of the vehicle must be supported by frame. If rear is supported by the rear axle, rear of vehicle will lower during this test.**	
	1 Disconnect the air lines from the air compressor drier. 2 **Note:** The air springs must be filled with some air in order to carry out this test. Carry out Function Test DTC 33 to cycle the air spring solenoids. • Does air flow from the air lines? → **Yes** GO to **K12**. → **No** REPAIR the air lines. CLEAR the DTCs. REPEAT the Auto Test.
K12 CHECK THE AIR COMPRESSOR DRIER	
⚠ **CAUTION: Rear of the vehicle must be supported by frame. If rear is supported by the rear axle, rear of vehicle will lower during this test.**	
	1 Disconnect the air compressor drier. 2 Connect the air line to the air compressor drier.

FM2019900613060X

Fig. 22 Test K/Code 51: Unable To Detect Lowering Of Rear (Part 6 of 7). 2000–02

TEST CONDITIONS	TESTDETAILS/RESULTS/ACTIONS
K12 CHECK THE AIR COMPRESSOR DRIER (Continued)	
	3 **Note:** The air springs must be filled with some air in order to carry out this test. Carry out Function Test DTC 33 to cycle the air spring solenoids. • Does little or no air flow from the air compressor drier? → **Yes** INSTALL a new air compressor drier. CLEAR the DTCs. REPEAT the Auto Test. → **No** INSTALL a new air compressor. CLEAR the DTCs. REPEAT the Auto Test.

FM2019900613070X

Fig. 22 Test K/Code 51: Unable To Detect Lowering Of Rear (Part 7 of 7). 2000–02

TEST CONDITIONS	TESTDETAILS/RESULTS/ACTIONS
L3 CHECK VOLTAGE TO THE AIR COMPRESSOR	
1 2 3 	
4 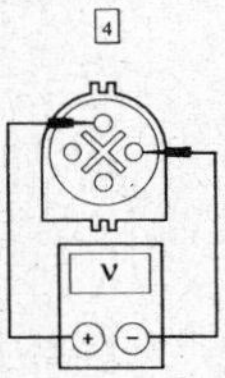	4 Measure the voltage between air compressor C158 Pin 3, Circuit 538 (GY/RD), harness side and air compressor C158 Pin 2, Circuit 57 (BK), harness side, while running Function Test DTC 31. • Does the voltage cycle between zero and 10 volts? → **Yes** RECONNECT the air compressor C158. Wait 15 minutes for the air compressor internal circuit breaker to cool down and close. The circuit breaker may have opened due to excessive run-time during diagnosis. After 15 minutes, run the Function Test DTC 31. If the air compressor does not start to cycle ON and OFF after 15 minutes, INSTALL a new air compressor. CLEAR the DTCs. REPEAT the Auto Test. → **No** GO to **L4**.

FM2019900614020X

Fig. 23 Test L/Code 54: Unable To Detect Raising Of Rear (Part 2 of 7). 2000–02

TEST CONDITIONS	TESTDETAILS/RESULTS/ACTIONS
L1 CARRY OUT THE AIR COMPRESSOR FUNCTION TEST	
	1 **Note:** The air compressor should cycle ON and OFF repeatedly (one second ON and one second OFF) during this test. Carry out Function Test DTC 31. • Does the air compressor cycle ON and OFF? → **Yes** GO to **L6**. → **No** GO to **L2**.
L2 CHECK THE AIR COMPRESSOR RELAY	
	1 Carry out the air compressor relay component test • Is the air compressor relay OK? → **Yes** GO to **L3**. → **No** INSTALL a new air compressor relay. CLEAR the DTCs. REPEAT the Auto Test.

FM2019900614010X

Fig. 23 Test L/Code 54: Unable To Detect Raising Of Rear (Part 1 of 7). 2000–02

TEST CONDITIONS	TESTDETAILS/RESULTS/ACTIONS
L4 CHECK CIRCUIT 1053 (LB/BK) FOR AN OPEN	
1 	
2 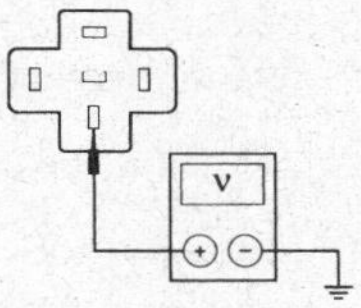	2 Measure the voltage between air compressor relay Pin 30, Circuit 1053 (LB/PK), harness side and ground. • Is the voltage greater than 10 volts? → **Yes** GO to **L5**. → **No** REPAIR the circuit. CLEAR the DTCs. REPEAT the Auto Test.
L5 CHECK CIRCUIT 57 (BK) FOR AN OPEN	
1 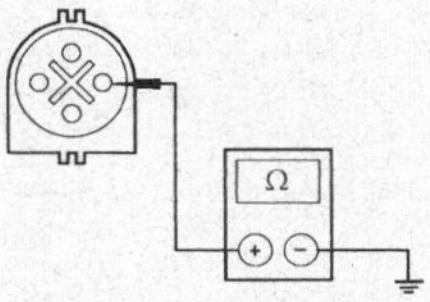	1 Measure the resistance between air compressor C158 Pin 2, Circuit 57 (BK), harness side and ground. • Is the resistance less than 5 ohms? → **Yes** REPAIR Circuit 538 (GY/RD). CLEAR the DTCs. REPEAT the Auto Test. → **No** REPAIR Circuit 57 (BK). CLEAR the DTCs. REPEAT the Auto Test.
L6 CHECK THE AIR SPRING SOLENOIDS	
	1 Raise and support the vehicle with the air suspension switch in the ON position.

FM2019900614030X

Fig. 23 Test L/Code 54: Unable To Detect Raising Of Rear (Part 3 of 7). 2000–02

TEST CONDITIONS	TEST DETAILS/RESULTS/ACTIONS
L6 CHECK THE AIR SPRING SOLENOIDS (Continued)	
	[2] Check both air springs while performing Function Test DTC 33. • Are both air spring solenoids cycling? → **Yes** GO to **L10**. → **No** GO to **L7**.
L7 CHECK THE AIR SUSPENSION CONTROL MODULE OUTPUT	
[1] [2] 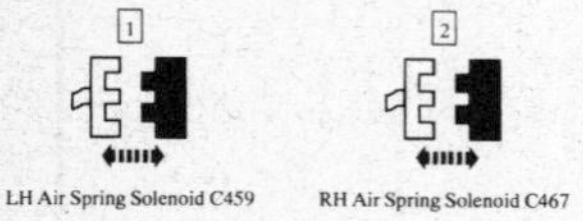 [3] 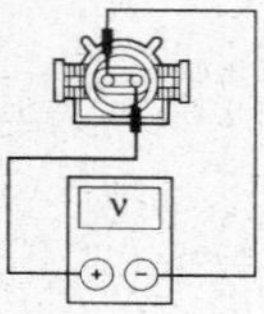	[3] Measure the voltage between LH air spring solenoid C492, Circuit 1053 (LB/PK), harness side and LH air spring solenoid C492, Circuit 1114 (BR/PK), harness side; and between RH air spring solenoid C467, Circuit 1053 (LB/PK), harness side and LH air spring solenoid C467, Circuit 1115 (TN/WH), harness side, while running Function Test DTC 33. • Does the voltage cycle between zero and 10 volts? → **Yes** INSTALL a new air spring solenoid. CLEAR the DTCs. REPEAT the Auto Test. → **No** GO to **L8**.

FM2019900614040X

Fig. 23 Test L/Code 54: Unable To Detect Raising Of Rear (Part 4 of 7). 2000–02

TEST CONDITIONS	TEST DETAILS/RESULTS/ACTIONS
L8 CHECK CIRCUIT 1053 (LB/PK)	
[1] 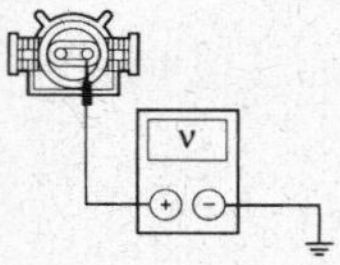	[1] Measure the voltage between LH air spring solenoid C492, Circuit 1053 (LB/PK), harness side and ground; and between RH air spring solenoid C467, Circuit 1053 (LB/PK), harness side and ground. • Are the voltages greater than 10 volts? → **Yes** GO to **L9**. → **No** REPAIR the circuit. CLEAR the DTCs. REPEAT the Auto Test.
L9 CHECK CIRCUIT 1114 (BR/PK) AND CIRCUIT 1115 (TN/WH) FOR AN OPEN	
[1] 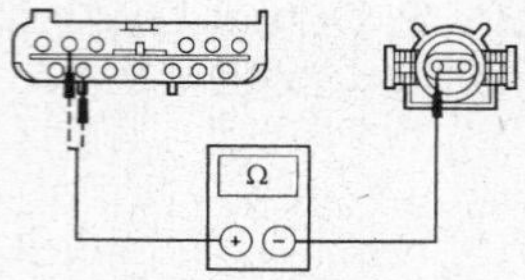	[1] Measure the voltage between air suspension control module C215 Pin 13, Circuit 1114 (BR/PK), and LH air spring solenoid C492, Circuit 1114 (BN/PK), harness side; and between air suspension control module C215 Pin 25, Circuit 1115 (TN/WH), harness side and RH air spring solenoid C467, Circuit 1115 (TN/WH), harness side and ground. • Are the resistances less than 5 ohms? → **Yes** INSTALL a new air suspension control module. REPEAT the Auto Test. → **No** REPAIR the circuit in question. CLEAR the DTCs. REPEAT the Auto Test.
L10 CHECK THE AIR SUSPENSION HEIGHT SENSOR FOR PROPER ATTACHMENT	
	[1] Check the air suspension height sensor at the upper and lower ball studs for correct attachment. • Is the air suspension height sensor attached correctly? → **Yes** GO to **L11**. → **No** REPAIR or INSTALL a new air suspension height sensor as necessary. CLEAR the DTCs. REPEAT the Auto Test.

FM2019900614050X

Fig. 23 Test L/Code 54: Unable To Detect Raising Of Rear (Part 5 of 7). 2000–02

TEST CONDITIONS	TEST DETAILS/RESULTS/ACTIONS
L11 CHECK THE AIR FLOW THROUGH THE AIR SPRING SOLENOIDS	
⚠ CAUTION: **Rear of the vehicle must be supported by frame. If rear is supported by the rear axle, rear of vehicle will lower during this test.**	
	[1] Check the air lines and air spring solenoid for leaks while carry out Function Test DTC 26. • Are any leaks detected? → **Yes** REPAIR the air lines or INSTALL a new air spring solenoid. CLEAR the DTCs. REPEAT the Auto Test. → **No** GO to **L12**.
L12 CHECK THE AIR COMPRESSOR DRIER AIR FLOW	
⚠ CAUTION: **Rear of the vehicle must be supported by frame. If rear is supported by the rear axle, rear of vehicle will lower during this test.**	
	[1] Disconnect the air lines from the air compressor drier. [2] Check the air flow from the air compressor drier while carrying out Function Test DTC 26. • Does air flow from the air compressor drier? → **Yes** RECONNECT the air lines. GO to **L15**. → **No** GO to **L13**.
L13 CHECK FOR A BLOCKED AIR COMPRESSOR INLET TUBE	
	[1] Disconnect the air compressor inlet tube. [2] Check the air flow from the air compressor drier while carrying out Function Test DTC 26. • Does air flow from the air compressor drier? → **Yes** REPAIR the air compressor inlet tube. CLEAR the DTCs. REPEAT the Auto Test. → **No** GO to **L14**.

FM2019900614060X

Fig. 23 Test L/Code 54: Unable To Detect Raising Of Rear (Part 6 of 7). 2000–02

TEST CONDITIONS	TEST DETAILS/RESULTS/ACTIONS
L14 CHECK THE AIR COMPRESSOR	
	[1] Disconnect the air compressor drier. [2] Check the air flow from the air compressor while carrying out Function Test DTC 26. • Does air flow from the air compressor? → **Yes** INSTALL a new air compressor drier. CLEAR the DTCs. REPEAT the Auto Test. → **No** INSTALL a new air compressor. CLEAR the DTCs. REPEAT the Auto Test.
L15 CHECK FOR BLOCKED AIR LINES	
	[1] Disconnect the air lines from both air spring solenoids. [2] Check air flow from both air lines while running Function Test DTC 26. • Does air flow from both air lines? → **Yes** INSTALL a new air suspension control module. REPEAT the Auto Test. → **No** REPAIR the blocked air line. CLEAR the DTCs. REPEAT the Auto Test.

FM2019900614070X

Fig. 23 Test L/Code 54: Unable To Detect Raising Of Rear (Part 7 of 7). 2000–02

TEST CONDITIONS	TEST DETAILS/RESULTS/ACTIONS
M1 CHECK THE SPEEDOMETER	
	1 Check the speedometer for correct operation. • Does the speedometer operate correctly? → **Yes** GO to **M2**. → **No**
M2 CHECK CIRCUIT 679 (GY/BK) FOR AN OPEN	
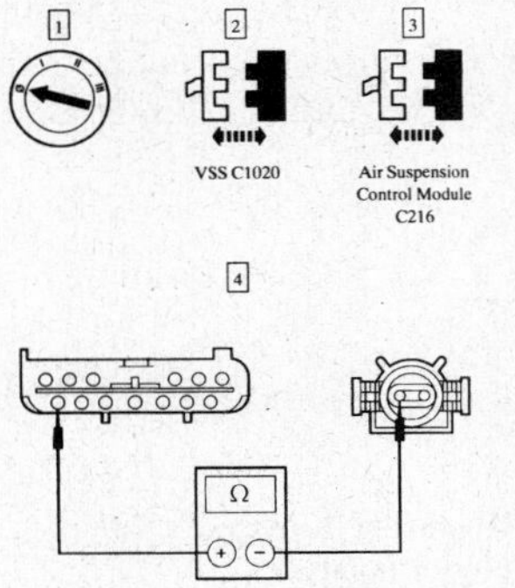	4 Measure the resistance between air suspension control module C216 Pin 7, Circuit 679 (GY/BK), harness side and VSS C1020, Circuit 679 (GY/BK), harness side. • Is the resistance less than 5 ohms? → **Yes** INSTALL a new air suspension control module. REPEAT the Auto Test. → **No** REPAIR the circuit. CLEAR the DTCs. REPEAT the Auto Test.

FM2019900615000X

Fig. 24 Test M/Code 55: Unable To Detect Vehicle Speed Greater Than 15 mph. 2000–02

TEST CONDITIONS	TEST DETAILS/RESULTS/ACTIONS
N2 CHECK CIRCUIT 418 (DG/YE) FOR SHORT TO POWER	
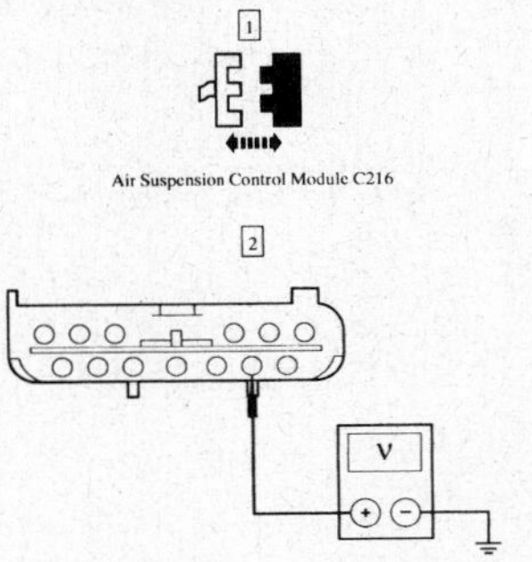	2 Measure the voltage between air suspension control module C216 Pin 2, Circuit 418 (DG/YE), harness side and ground. • Is voltage present? → **Yes** REPAIR the circuit. CLEAR the DTCs. REPEAT the Auto Test. → **No** INSTALL a new air suspension control module. REPEAT the Auto Test.

FM2019900616020X

Fig. 25 Test N/Code 60: Air Suspension Switch Short To Power (Part 2 of 2). 2000–02

TEST CONDITIONS	TEST DETAILS/RESULTS/ACTIONS
O1 CHECK THE AIR SUSPENSION SWITCH POSITION	
	1 Check the air suspension switch. • Is the air suspension switch in the ON position? → **Yes** GO to **O2**. → **No** PLACE the air suspension switch in the ON position. CLEAR the DTCs. REPEAT the Auto Test.

FM2019900617010X

Fig. 26 Test O/Code 61: Air Suspension Switch Circuit Failure (Part 1 of 3). 2000–02

TEST CONDITIONS	TEST DETAILS/RESULTS/ACTIONS
N1 CHECK CIRCUIT 429 (VT/LG) FOR SHORT TO POWER	
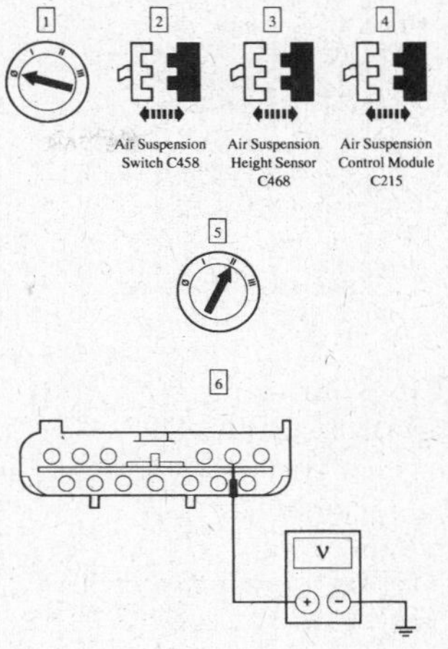	6 Measure the voltage between air suspension control module C215 Pin 22, Circuit 429 (VT/LG), harness side and ground. • Is voltage present? → **Yes** REPAIR the circuit. CLEAR the DTCs. REPEAT the Auto Test. → **No** GO to **N2**.

FM2019900616010X

Fig. 25 Test N/Code 60: Air Suspension Switch Short To Power (Part 1 of 2). 2000–02

TEST CONDITIONS	TEST DETAILS/RESULTS/ACTIONS
O2 CHECK CIRCUIT 429 (VT/LG)	
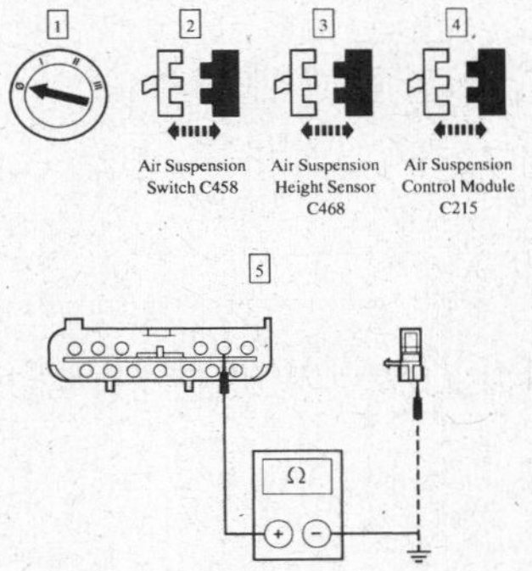	5 Measure the resistance between air suspension control module C215 Pin 22, Circuit 429 (VT/LG), harness side and air suspension switch C458, Circuit 429 (VT/LG), harness side; and between air suspension control module C215 Pin 22, Circuit 429 (VT/LG), harness side and ground. • Is the resistance less than 5 ohms between air suspension control module and air suspension switch; and greater than 10,000 ohms between air suspension control module and ground? → **Yes** GO to **O3**. → **No** REPAIR the circuit. CLEAR the DTCs. REPEAT the Auto Test.
O3 CHECK CIRCUIT 418 (DG/YE)	
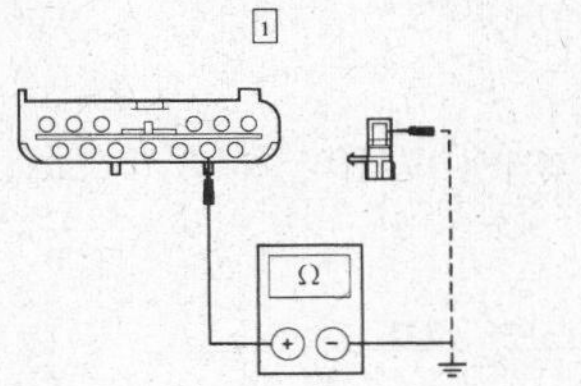	1 Measure the resistance between air suspension control module C216 Pin 2, Circuit 418 (DG/YE), harness side and air suspension switch C458, Circuit 418 (DG/YE), harness side; and between air suspension control module C216 Pin 2, Circuit 418 (DG/YE), harness side and ground. • Is the resistance less than 5 ohms between air suspension control module and air suspension switch; and greater than 10,000 ohms between air suspension control module and ground? → **Yes** GO to **O4**. → **No** REPAIR the circuit. CLEAR the DTCs. REPEAT the Auto Test.

FM2019900617020X

Fig. 26 Test O/Code 61: Air Suspension Switch Circuit Failure (Part 2 of 3). 2000–02

TEST CONDITIONS	TESTDETAILS/RESULTS/ACTIONS
O4 CHECK THE AIR SUSPENSION SWITCH	
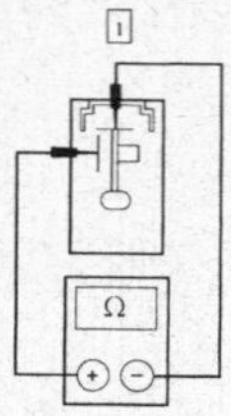	1 Measure the resistance between air suspension switch pins (component side), while in the ON position. • Is the resistance less than 5 ohms? → **Yes** INSTALL a new air suspension control module. REPEAT the Auto Test. → **No** INSTALL a new air suspension switch; CLEAR the DTCs. REPEAT the Auto Test.

FM2019900617030X

Fig. 26 Test O/Code 61: Air Suspension Switch Circuit Failure (Part 3 of 3). 2000–02

TEST CONDITIONS	TESTDETAILS/RESULTS/ACTIONS
P1 CHECK CIRCUIT 429 (VT/LG) FOR SHORT TO POWER	
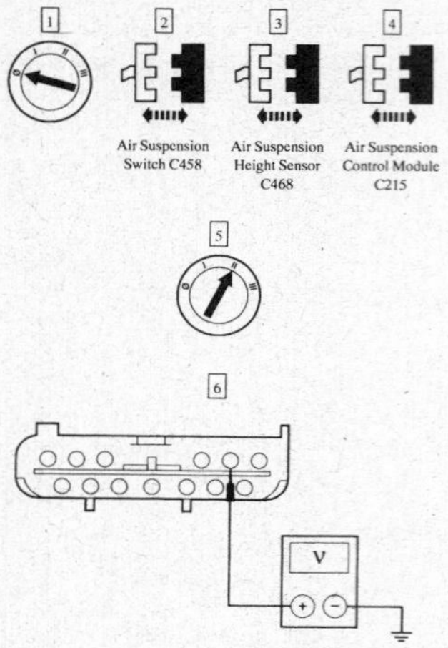	6 Measure the voltage between air suspension control module C215 Pin 22, Circuit 429 (VT/LG), harness side and ground. • Is voltage present? → **Yes** REPAIR the circuit. CLEAR the DTCs. REPEAT the Auto Test. → **No** GO to **P2**.

FM2019900618010X

Fig. 27 Test P/Code 68: Height Sensor Circuit Failure (Part 1 of 2). 2000–02

TEST CONDITIONS	TESTDETAILS/RESULTS/ACTIONS
P2 CHECK CIRCUIT 428 (OG/BK) FOR SHORT TO GROUND	
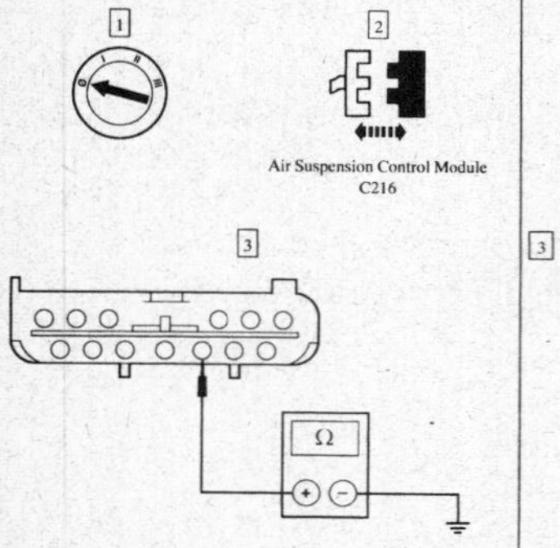	3 Measure the resistance between air suspension control module C216 Pin 3, Circuit 428 (OG/BK), harness side and ground. • Is the resistance greater than 10,000 ohms? → **Yes** GO to **P3**. → **No** REPAIR the circuit. CLEAR the DTCs. REPEAT the Auto Test.
P3 CHECK THE AIR SUSPENSION HEIGHT SENSOR	
	1 Install a known good air suspension height sensor. 2 Reconnect the air suspension height sensor C468, air suspension control module, and air suspension switch C458. 3 Retrieve and document DTCs. • Is DTC 68 retrieved? → **Yes** INSTALL a new air suspension control module. REPEAT the Auto Test. → **No** INSTALL a new air suspension height sensor. CLEAR the DTCs. REPEAT the Auto Test.

FM2019900618020X

Fig. 27 Test P/Code 68: Height Sensor Circuit Failure (Part 2 of 2). 2000–02

TEST CONDITIONS	TESTDETAILS/RESULTS/ACTIONS
Q1 CHECK CIRCUIT 428 (OG/BK) FOR SHORT TO POWER	
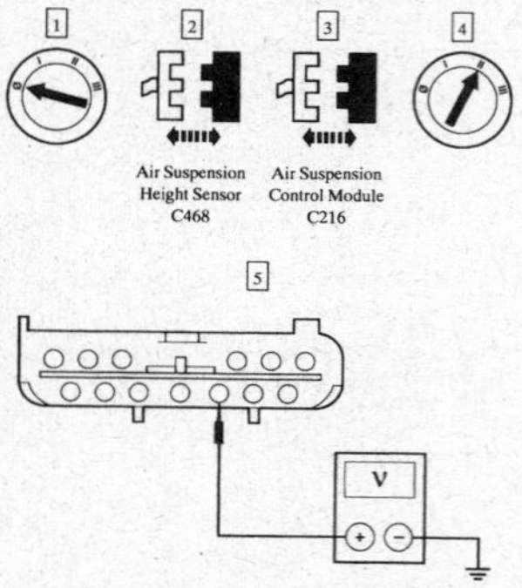	5 Measure the voltage between air suspension control module C216 Pin 3, Circuit 428 (OG/BK), and ground. • Is voltage present? → **Yes** REPAIR the circuit. CLEAR the DTCs. REPEAT the Auto Test. → **No** GO to **Q2**.
Q2 CHECK CIRCUIT 428 (OG/BK) FOR AN OPEN	
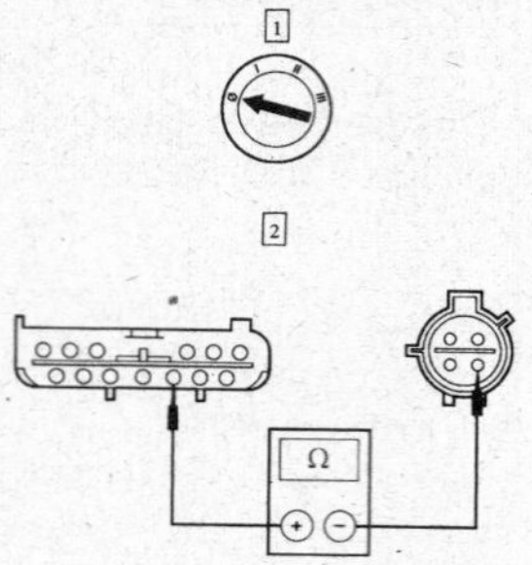	2 Measure the resistance between air suspension control module C216 Pin 3, Circuit 428 (OG/BK), and air suspension height sensor C468 Pin 4, Circuit 428 (OG/BK), harness side. • Is the resistance less than 5 ohms? → **Yes** GO to **Q3**. → **No** REPAIR the circuit. CLEAR the DTCs. REPEAT the Auto Test.

FM2019900619010X

Fig. 28 Test Q/Code 71: Height Sensor Circuit Open (Part 1 of 3). 2000–02

TEST CONDITIONS	TEST DETAILS/RESULTS/ACTIONS
Q3 CHECK CIRCUIT 427 (PK/BK) FOR SHORT TO POWER	
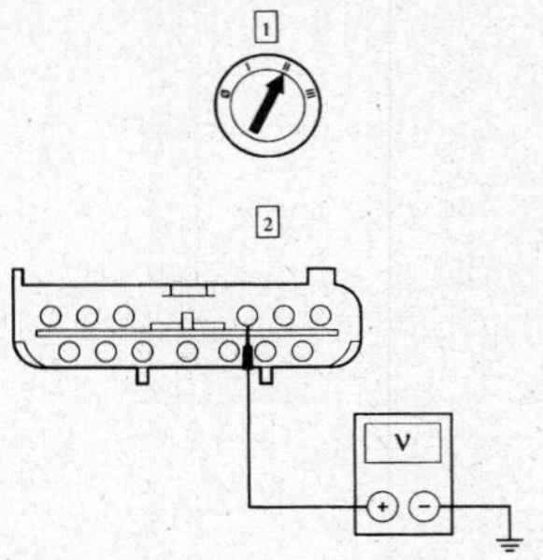	2 Measure the voltage between air suspension control module C216 Pin 17, Circuit 427 (PK/BK), and ground. • Is any voltage present? → **Yes** REPAIR the circuit. CLEAR the DTCs. REPEAT the auto test. → **No** GO to **Q4**.
Q4 CHECK CIRCUIT 427 (PK/BK)	
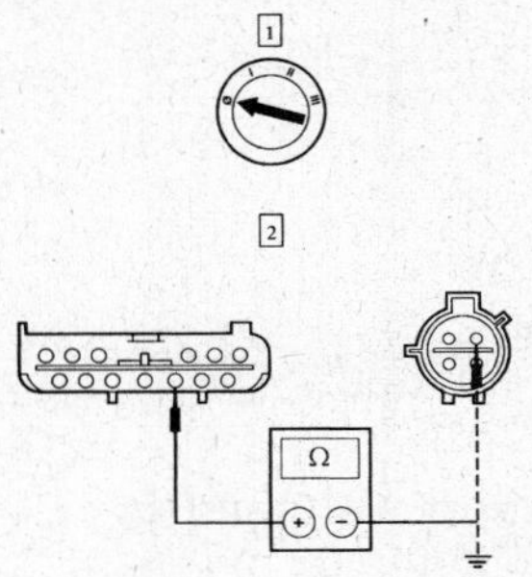	2 Measure the resistance between air suspension control module C216 Pin 3, Circuit 427 (PK/BK), and air suspension height sensor C468 Pin 2, Circuit 427 (PK/BK), harness side; and between air suspension control module C216 Pin 3, Circuit 427 (PK/BK), and ground. • Is the resistance less than 5 ohms between air suspension control module and air suspension height sensor; and greater than 10,000 ohms between air suspension control module and ground? → **Yes** GO to **Q5**. → **No** REPAIR the circuit. CLEAR the DTCs. REPEAT the Auto Test.

FM2019900619020X

Fig. 28 Test Q/Code 71: Height Sensor Circuit Open (Part 2 of 3). 2000–02

TEST CONDITIONS	TEST DETAILS/RESULTS/ACTIONS
R1 CHECK CIRCUIT 344 (BK/YE) FOR SHORT TO POWER	
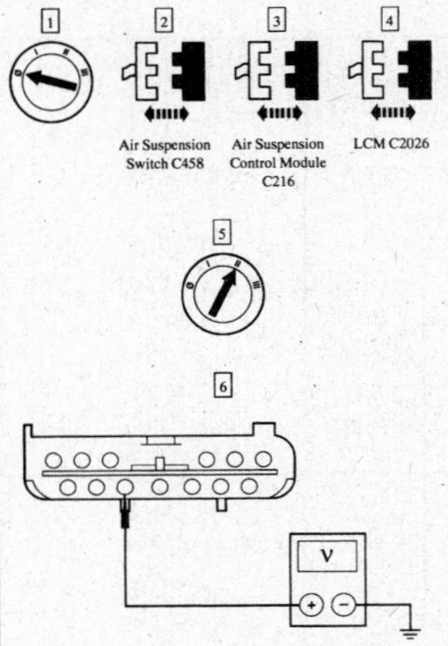	6 Measure the voltage between air suspension control module C216 Pin 5, Circuit 344 (BK/YE), harness side and ground. • Is any voltage present? → **Yes** REPAIR the circuit. CLEAR the DTCs. REPEAT the Auto Test. → **No** GO to **R2**.

FM2019900620010X

Fig. 29 Test R/Code 72: Did Not Detect Four Open Or Closed Door Signals (Part 1 of 3). 2000–02

TEST CONDITIONS	TEST DETAILS/RESULTS/ACTIONS
Q5 CHECK THE AIR SUSPENSION HEIGHT SENSOR	
	1 Install a known good air suspension height sensor. 2 Reconnect the air suspension height sensor C468, and air suspension control module. 3 Retrieve and document DTCs. • Is DTC 71 retrieved? → **Yes** INSTALL a new air suspension control module. REPEAT the Auto Test. → **No** INSTALL a new air suspension height sensor. CLEAR the DTCs. REPEAT the Auto Test.

FM2019900619030X

Fig. 28 Test Q/Code 71: Height Sensor Circuit Open (Part 3 of 3). 2000–02

TEST CONDITIONS	TEST DETAILS/RESULTS/ACTIONS
R2 CHECK CIRCUIT 344 (BK/YE) FOR AN OPEN OR SHORT TO GROUND	
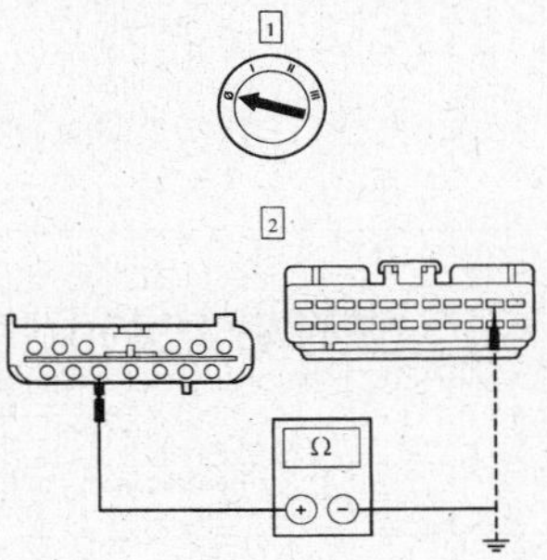	2 Measure the resistance between air suspension control module C216 Pin 5, Circuit 344 (BK/YE), harness side and LCM C2026 Pin 10, Circuit 344 (BK/YE), harness side; and between air suspension control module C216 Pin 5, Circuit 344 (BK/YE), harness side and ground. • Is the resistance less than 5 ohms between air suspension control module and LCM; and greater than 10,000 ohms between air suspension control module and ground? → **Yes** GO to **R3**. → **No** REPAIR the circuit. CLEAR the DTCs. REPEAT the Auto Test.

FM2019900620020X

Fig. 29 Test R/Code 72: Did Not Detect Four Open Or Closed Door Signals (Part 2 of 3). 2000–02

TEST CONDITIONS	TEST DETAILS/RESULTS/ACTIONS
R3 CHECK THE AIR SUSPENSION CONTROL MODULE	
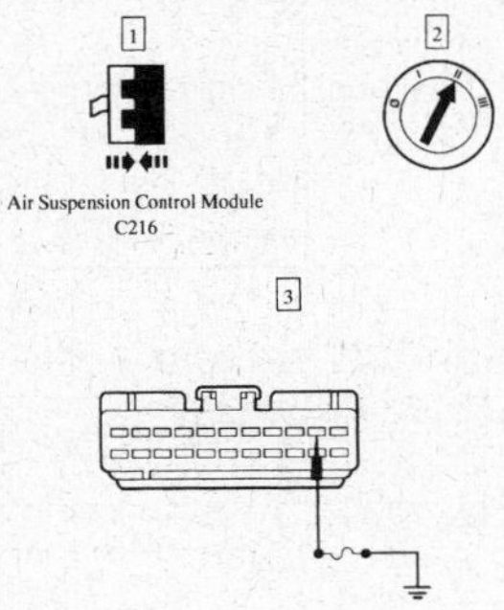	3 **Note:** The Super Star II Tester must be in manual input mode. The jumper wire must be connected and disconnected four times in 5 second intervals. Connect a jumper wire with a 10A in-line fuse to LCM C2026 Pin 10, Circuit 344 (BK/YE), harness side and ground. 4 Retrieve and document DTCs. • Is DTC 72 retrieved? → **Yes** INSTALL a new air suspension control module. REPEAT the Auto Test. → **No** INSTALL a new LCM. REPEAT the Auto Test.

FM2019900620030X

Fig. 29 Test R/Code 72: Did Not Detect Four Open Or Closed Door Signals (Part 3 of 3). 2000–02

TEST CONDITIONS	TESTDETAILS/RESULTS/ACTIONS
S1 CHECKBATTERYVOLTAGE	
1 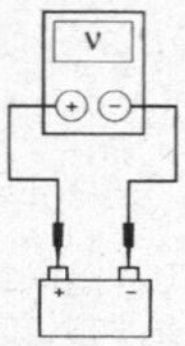	1 Measure the battery voltage between the positive and negative battery posts with the key ON engine OFF (KOEO), and with the engine running. • Is the battery voltage between 10 and 13 volts with KOEO, and between 11 and 17 volts with the engine running? → **Yes** GO to **S2**. → **No**
S2 CHECK CIRCUIT 1053 (LB/PK) FOR AN OPEN	
1  Air Suspension Control Module C216 2 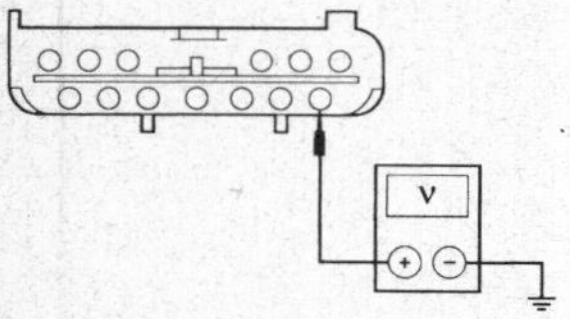	2 Measure the voltage between air suspension control module C216 Pin 1, Circuit 1053 (LB/PK), harness side and ground. • Is the voltage greater than 10 volts? → **Yes** GO to **S3**. → **No** REPAIR the circuit. CLEAR the DTCs. REPEAT the Auto Test.

FM2019900621010X

Fig. 30 Test S/Code 80: Battery Voltage High Or Low (Part 1 of 2). 2000–02

TEST CONDITIONS	TESTDETAILS/RESULTS/ACTIONS
S3 CHECK CIRCUIT 57 (BK) FOR AN OPEN	
1 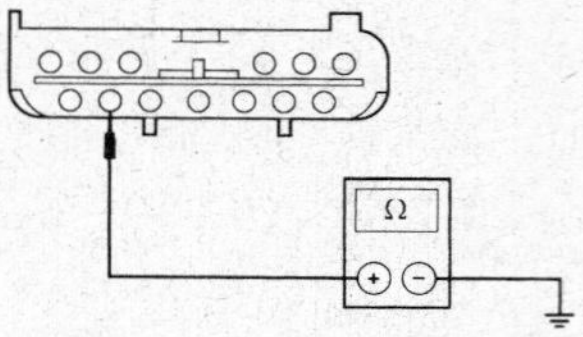	1 Measure the resistance between air suspension control module C216 Pin 6, Circuit 57 (BK), harness side and ground. • Is the resistance less than 5 ohms? → **Yes** GO to **S4**. → **No** REPAIR the circuit. CLEAR the DTCs. REPEAT the Auto Test.
S4 CHECK CIRCUIT 298 (VT/OG) FOR AN OPEN	
1  2 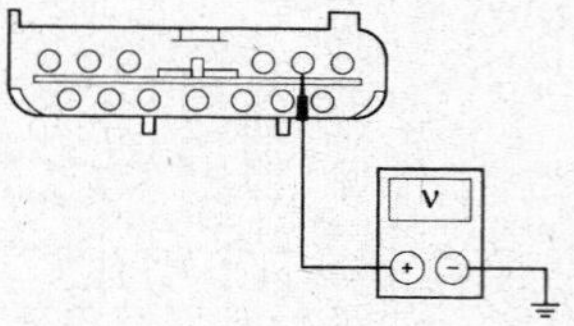	2 Measure the voltage between air suspension control module C216 Pin 16, Circuit 298 (VT/OG), harness side and ground. • Is the voltage greater than 10 volts? → **Yes** INSTALL a new air suspension control module. REPEAT the Auto Test. → **No** REPAIR the circuit. CLEAR the DTCs. REPEAT the Auto Test.

FM2019900621020X

Fig. 30 Test S/Code 80: Battery Voltage High Or Low (Part 2 of 2). 2000–02

Test Step	Result / Action to Take
A1 CHECK CIRCUIT 298 (PK/OG) FOR AN OPEN	
• Key in OFF position. • Disconnect: Rear Air Suspension Control Module C2131a. • Key in ON position. • Measure the voltage between rear air suspension control module C2131a pin 16, circuit 298 (PK/OG), harness side and ground. • **Is the voltage greater than 10 volts?**	**Yes** GO to A2 . **No** REPAIR the circuit. REPEAT the self-test.
A2 CHECK CIRCUIT 1053 (LB/PK) FOR AN OPEN	
• Measure the voltage between rear air suspension control module C2131a pin 1 and pin 15, circuit 1053 (LB/PK), harness side and ground. • **Is the voltage greater than 10 volts?**	**Yes** GO to A3 . **No** REPAIR the circuit. REPEAT the self-test.
A3 CHECK CIRCUIT 676 (PK/OG) FOR AN OPEN	
• Key in OFF position. • Measure the resistance between rear air suspension control module C2131a pin 6, circuit 676 (PK/OG), harness side and ground. • **Is the resistance less than 5 ohms?**	**Yes** Diagnose module. **No** REPAIR the circuit. REPEAT the self-test.

FM2010200814000X

Fig. 31 Test A: No Communication w/Rear Air Suspension Control Module. 2003–04

Test Step	Result / Action to Take
B1 CHECK THE COMMUNICATIONS TO THE REAR AIR SUSPENSION CONTROL MODULE	
• Key in ON position. • Turn the air suspension disable switch ON. • Check the communication to the rear air suspension control module. • **Does the scan tool communicate with the air suspension control module?**	**Yes** INSTALL a new air suspension control module. CLEAR the DTC(s). REPEAT the self-test. **No** GO to Pinpoint Test A .

FM2010200815000X

Fig. 32 Test B: Unable To Enter Self-Test. 2003–04

Test Step	Result / Action to Take
C1 CHECK BATTERY VOLTAGE	
NOTE: A recent jump start can cause these DTCs to set. • Measure the battery voltage between the positive and negative battery posts with the key ON engine OFF (KOEO) and with the engine running. • **Is the battery voltage between 10 and 13 volts with KOEO, and between 11 and 17 volts with the engine running?**	**Yes** GO to C2 . **No** Diagnose battery.
C2 CHECK CIRCUIT 298 (PK/OG) FOR AN OPEN	
• Key in OFF position. • Disconnect: Rear Air Suspension Control Module C2131a. • Key in ON position. • Measure the voltage between rear air suspension control module C2131a pin 16, circuit 298 (PK/OG), harness side and ground. • **Is the voltage greater than 10 volts and less than 17 volts?**	**Yes** GO to C3 . **No** REPAIR the circuit. REPEAT the self-test.
C3 CHECK CIRCUIT 1053 (LB/PK) FOR AN OPEN	
• Measure the voltage between rear air suspension control module C2131a pin 1 and pin 15, circuit 1053 (LB/PK), harness side and ground. • **Is the voltage greater than 10 volts and less than 17 volts?**	**Yes** GO to C4 . **No** REPAIR the circuit. REPEAT the self-test.
C4 CHECK CIRCUIT 676 (PK/OG) FOR AN OPEN	
• Key in OFF position. • Disconnect: Rear Air Suspension Control Module C2131a . • Measure the resistance between rear air suspension control module C2131a pin 6, circuit 676 (PK/OG), harness side and ground. • **Is the resistance less than 5 ohms?**	**Yes** INSTALL a new rear air suspension control module. REPEAT the self-test. **No** REPAIR the circuit. CLEAR the DTC. REPEAT the self-test.

FM2010200816000X

Fig. 33 Test C/Codes B1317 & B1318: Battery Voltage High/Low. 2003–04

Test Step	Result / Action to Take
D1 CHECK THE COURTESY LIGHTS	
• Key in OFF position. • Open a door. • **Did the courtesy lights illuminate?**	**Yes** GO to D2 . **No** GO to D3 .
D2 CHECK THE DOOR SIGNAL	
• Key in ON position. • Monitor the door signal PID. • Open and close a door. • **Does the door signal PID indicate correctly when the door is open and when closed?**	**Yes** The system is OK. **No** GO to D3 .
D3 CHECK CIRCUITS 1312 (LG/BK) FOR AN OPEN	
• Disconnect the battery ground cable. • Disconnect: Air Suspension Control Module C2131a. • Disconnect: Lighting Control Module C2145c. • Measure the resistance between the air suspension control module C2131a pin 5, circuit 1312 (LG/BK) harness side and lighting control module (LCM) C2145c pin 4, harness side. • **Is the resistance less than 5 ohms?**	**Yes** GO to D4 . **No** REPAIR the circuit. REPEAT the self-test.
D4 CHECK CIRCUITS 1312 (LG/BK) FOR A SHORT TO POWER	
• Key in ON position. • Measure the voltage between the rear air suspension control module C2131a pin 5, circuit 1312 (LG/BK) and ground. • **Is voltage present?**	**Yes** REPAIR the circuit. REPEAT the self-test. **No** GO to D5 .
D5 CHECK CIRCUIT 1312 (LG/BK) FOR A SHORT TO GROUND	
• Key in OFF position. • Measure the resistance between the rear air suspension control module C2131a pin 5, circuit 1312 (LG/BK) and ground. • **Is the resistance greater than 10,000 ohms?**	**Yes** Diagnose lighting. **No** REPAIR the circuit. REPEAT the self-test. .

FM2010200817000X

Fig. 34 Test D/Code B1566: Door Ajar Circuit Short To Ground/Did Not Detect Open & Close Signals. 2003–04

Test Step	Result / Action to Take
E1 CHECK CIRCUIT 429 (PK/LG) FOR A SHORT TO POWER	
• Disconnect: Air Suspension Control Module C2131a. • Disconnect: Air Suspension Height Sensor C4043. • Turn the air suspension switch to the OFF position. • Key in ON position. • Measure the voltage between rear air suspension control module C2131a pin 22, circuit 429 (PK/LG), harness side and ground. • **Is the voltage greater than 0 volt?**	**Yes** REPAIR circuit 429 (PK/LG). CLEAR the DTC. REPEAT the self-test. **No** GO to E2 .
E2 CHECK CIRCUIT 429 (PK/LG) FOR A SHORT TO GROUND	
• Key in OFF position. • Measure the resistance between rear air suspension control module C2131a pin 22, circuit 429 (PK/LG), harness side and ground. • **Is the resistance greater than 10,000 ohms?**	**Yes** GO to E3 . **No** REPAIR circuit 429 (PK/LG). CLEAR the DTC. REPEAT the self-test.
E3 CHECK CIRCUIT 429 (PK/LG) FOR AN OPEN	
• Measure the resistance between rear air suspension control module C2131a pin 22, circuit 429 (PK/LG), harness side and air suspension height sensor C4043 pin 3, circuit 429 (PK/LG), harness side. • **Is the resistance greater than 5 ohms?**	**Yes** REPAIR the circuit. CLEAR the DTC. REPEAT the self-test. **No** GO to E4 .
E4 CHECK THE REAR AIR SUSPENSION CONTROL MODULE OUTPUT	
• Connect: Air Suspension Control Module C2131a. • Key in ON position. • Measure the voltage between air suspension height sensor C4043 pin 3, circuit 429 (PK/LG), harness side and ground. • **Is the voltage 5 volts?**	**Yes** INSTALL a new air suspension height sensor. CLEAR the DTC. REPEAT the self-test. **No** INSTALL a new air suspension control module. CLEAR the DTC(s). REPEAT the self-test.

FM2010200818000X

Fig. 35 Test E/Code C1724: Height Sensor Power Circuit Failure. 2003–04

Test Step	Result / Action to Take
NOTE: Repair all other DTCs before repairing DTC C1726.	
NOTE: It can be necessary to partially vent air from the rear air springs during this Pinpoint Test.	
F1 CHECK THE AIR SUSPENSION HEIGHT SENSOR MOUNTING	
• Check the air suspension height sensor for correct installation at the upper and lower ball stud brackets. • Check the air suspension height sensor mounting brackets for damage. • **Are the air suspension height sensor and mounting brackets OK?**	**Yes** GO to F2 . **No** REPAIR as necessary. CLEAR the DTC. REPEAT the self-test.
F2 CHECK THE AIR SUSPENSION HEIGHT SENSOR OPERATION	
• Disconnect the lower end of the air suspension height sensor. • Key in ON position. • Monitor the height sensor PID. • While monitoring the height sensor PID display, slowly move the air suspension height sensor through its full range of motion. • **Does the height sensor PID indicate HIGH, TRIM and LOW?**	**Yes** GO to F3 . **No** INSTALL a new air suspension height sensor. CLEAR the DTC. REPEAT the self-test.
F3 VERIFY THAT THE REAR OF THE VEHICLE CAN BE RAISED	
• Record the voltage level for the rear air suspension height sensor. • Trigger air suspension control module active commands: LR SOLENOID, RR SOLENOID and COMPRESSR ON. • Allow the rear of the vehicle to raise for only 30 seconds. • **Does the rear of the vehicle raise and hold the new height?**	**Yes** TRIGGER air suspension control module active commands. GO to F4 . **No** TRIGGER air suspension control module active command OFF. GO to F5 .
F4 VERIFY THAT THE REAR OF THE VEHICLE CAN BE LOWERED	
• Trigger air suspension control module active commands: LR SOLENOID, RR SOLENOID and COMPRESSR VENT. • Allow the rear to lower until the rear air suspension height sensor voltage reading matches the one recorded in Step F3 or until 30 seconds have passed. • **Does the rear of the vehicle lower?**	**Yes** RESET electronic ride height. CLEAR the DTCs. REPEAT the self-test. **No** GO to F7 .

FM2010200819010X

Fig. 36 Test F/Code C1726: Pneumatic Failure (Part 1 of 3). 2003–04

Test Step	Result / Action to Take
F5 CHECK OPERATION OF THE AIR COMPRESSOR	
⚠ **CAUTION: Do not allow the air compressor to run for more than three minutes. The air compressor could overheat and stop operation due to an internal temperature sensitive thermal breaker.** • Trigger air suspension control module active command: COMPRESSR ON. • **Does the air compressor run (slight buzzing noise from RF fender)?**	**Yes** TRIGGER air suspension control module active command COMPRESSR OFF. GO to F6 . **No** Go To Pinpoint Test I .
F6 CHECK THE AIR COMPRESSOR PRESSURE OUTPUT	
⚠ **CAUTION: Do not allow the air compressor to run for more than three minutes. The air compressor could overheat and stop operation due to an internal temperature sensitive thermal breaker. NOTE:** If fluid is present when disconnecting the air line, clear the air lines. Check the compressor air drier for water or the air compressor for oil contamination. • Disconnect the air line at the air drier. • Connect air pressure gauge (1,723 kPa maximum reading) with common fittings to the air drier. • Trigger air suspension control module active command: COMPRESSR ON. • Run the air compressor for only 30 seconds. • Wait five minutes. • Trigger air suspension control module active command: VENT ON. • **Does the compressor produce 896 kPa (130 psi) within 30 seconds and hold the developed pressure?**	**Yes** TRIGGER air suspension control module active command VENT OFF. GO to F9 . **No** INSTALL a new air suspension compressor.
F7 CHECK THE PNEUMATIC SYSTEM — VENT LR AIR SPRING	
NOTE: If fluid is present when disconnecting the air line, clear the air lines. Check the air compressor drier for water or the air compressor for oil contamination. **NOTE:** The rear springs must be partially inflated in order to carry out this test. Add air as necessary. • Disconnect the air compressor drier air line. • Trigger the LR air spring solenoid ON active command. • **Does the air vent from the air compressor drier air line?**	**Yes** Trigger the LR air spring solenoid OFF active command. GO to F8 . **No** Trigger the LR air spring solenoid OFF active command. GO to F9 .
F8 CHECK THE PNEUMATIC SYSTEM — VENT RR AIR SPRING	
NOTE: The rear springs must be partially inflated in order to carry out this test. Add air as necessary. • Trigger the RR air solenoid ON active command. • **Does the air vent from the air drier?**	**Yes** Trigger the RR air solenoid OFF active command. GO to F10 . **No** Trigger the RR air solenoid OFF active command. GO to F9 .

FM2010200819020X

Fig. 36 Test F/Code C1726: Pneumatic Failure (Part 2 of 3). 2003–04

F9 CHECK THE PNEUMATIC SYSTEM — AIR LINE	
NOTE: If fluid is present when disconnecting the air line, clear the air lines. Refer to Air Line Fluid Purge . Check the air compressor drier for water or the air compressor for oil. • Disconnect the suspected rear air spring solenoid air line. • Connect the vacuum tester to the air line and try to pull a vacuum. • **Can a vacuum be developed?**	**Yes** REPAIR or INSTALL a new air line. CLEAR the DTC. REPEAT the self-test. **No** INSTALL a new air spring solenoid valve. CLEAR the DTC. REPEAT the self-test.
F10 CHECK THE VENT SOLENOID OPERATION	
• Disconnect the air line at the snorkel. • Connect the vacuum tester to the snorkel air line and try to pull a vacuum. • Trigger the vent solenoid ON active command. • Try to pull a vacuum again. • **Can a vacuum be developed with the vent solenoid OFF active command and no vacuum developed with the vent solenoid ON active command?**	**Yes** INSTALL a new air suspension control module. REPEAT the self-test. **No** If no vacuum can be developed with the vent solenoid OFF, GO to F11 . If a vacuum can be developed with the vent solenoid OFF, GO to F12 .
F11 CHECK THE AIR LINE AND CONNECTIONS	
• Check the air line and connections between the vacuum tester and the air compressor. • **Are the air line and connections OK?**	**Yes** INSTALL a new air compressor. CLEAR the DTC. REPEAT the self-test. **No** REPAIR the air line. CLEAR the DTC. REPEAT the self-test.
F12 CHECK THE AIR COMPRESSOR DRIER	
• Disconnect the air compressor drier. • Connect the vacuum tester to the air compressor drier and try to pull a vacuum. • **Can a vacuum be developed?**	**Yes** INSTALL a new air compressor. CLEAR the DTC. REPEAT the self-test. **No** INSTALL a new air compressor drier. CLEAR the DTC. REPEAT the self-test.

FM2010200819030X

Fig. 36 Test F/Code C1726: Pneumatic Failure (Part 3 of 3). 2003–04

G4 CHECK CIRCUIT 427 (PK/BK) FOR AN OPEN AND A SHORT TO GROUND	
• Key in OFF position. • Turn the air suspension switch OFF. • Disconnect: Rear Air Suspension Control module C2131b. • Measure the resistance between the air suspension height sensor C4043 pin 2, circuit 427 (PK/BK), harness side and rear air suspension control module C2131b pin 12, circuit 427 (PK/BK), harness side; and between air suspension height sensor C4043 pin 2, circuit 427 (PK/BK), harness side and ground. • **Is the resistance less than 5 ohms between the air suspension height sensor and the rear air suspension control module, and greater than 10,000 ohms between the air suspension height sensor and ground?**	**Yes** RECONNECT the system. GO to G5 . **No** REPAIR circuit 427 (PK/BK). CLEAR the DTC. REPEAT the self-test.
G5 CHECK FOR AN INTERMITTENT FAULT	
• Connect: Rear Air Suspension Control Module C2131b. • Turn the air suspension switch ON. • Key in ON position. • Monitor the rear air suspension control module PID. • Monitor the PID display while wiggling the wire harness between the air suspension rear height sensor and the air suspension control module. • **Does the air suspension rear height sensor voltage ever indicate less than 0.2 volt or greater than 5 volts?**	**Yes** REPAIR circuits 427 (PK/BK), 432 (BK/PK) and 429 (PK/LG) as necessary. CLEAR the DTC. REPEAT the self-test. **No** INSTALL a new air suspension height sensor. this section. CLEAR the DTC. REPEAT the self-test.

FM2010200820020X

Fig. 37 Test G/Code C1760: Rear Height Sensor High Signal Circuit Failure (Part 2 of 2). 2003–04

Test Step	Result / Action to Take
G1 VERIFY THE DTC	
• Carry out the rear air suspension control module On-Demand self-test. • **Is DTC C1760 present?**	**Yes** GO to G2 . **No** If a different DTC is retrieved, REFER to rear air suspension control Module DTC index.
G2 CHECK THE HEIGHT SENSOR POWER	
• Key in OFF position. • Turn the air suspension switch OFF. • Disconnect: Air Suspension Height Sensor C4043. • Turn the air suspension switch ON. • Key in ON position. • Monitor the air suspension height sensor PID. • Measure the voltage between air suspension height sensor C4043 pin 1, circuit 432 (BK/PK) and pin 3, circuit 429 (PK/LG), harness side. • **Is the voltage approximately 5 volts?**	**Yes** GO to G4 . **No** If the voltage is less than 5 volts, GO to G3 . If the voltage is greater than 5 volts, REPAIR circuit 429 (PK/LG). CLEAR the DTC. REPEAT the self-test.
G3 CHECK THE AIR SUSPENSION HEIGHT SENSOR GROUND	
NOTE: Use the battery negative terminal as ground for this test. • Measure the resistance between the air suspension height sensor C4043 pin 1, circuit 432 (BK/PK), harness side and ground. • **Is the resistance less than 5 ohms?**	**Yes** REPAIR circuit 429 (PK/LG). CLEAR the DTC. REPEAT the self-test. **No** REPAIR circuit 432 (BK/PK) and circuit 676 (PK/OG). CLEAR the DTC. REPEAT the self-test.

FM2010200820010X

Fig. 37 Test G/Code C1760: Rear Height Sensor High Signal Circuit Failure (Part 1 of 2). 2003–04

Test Step	Result / Action to Take
H1 CHECK CIRCUIT 421 (PK) FOR A SHORT TO POWER	
• Key in OFF position. • Disconnect: Rear Air Suspension Control Module C2131a. • Disconnect: Air Compressor C1179. • Key in ON position. • Measure the voltage between the rear air suspension control module C2131b pin 24, circuit 421 (PK), harness side and ground. • **Is the voltage greater than 0 volt?**	**Yes** REPAIR the circuit. CLEAR the DTC. REPEAT the self-test. **No** GO to H2 .
H2 CHECK CIRCUIT 421 (PK) FOR A SHORT TO GROUND	
• Key in OFF position. • Measure the resistance between rear air suspension control module C2131a pin 24, circuit 421 (PK), harness side and ground. • **Is the resistance greater than 10,000 ohms?**	**Yes** GO to H3 . **No** REPAIR circuit 421 (PK). CLEAR the DTC. REPEAT the self-test.
H3 CHECK CIRCUIT 421 (PK) FOR AN OPEN	
• Measure the resistance between the rear air suspension control module C2131b pin 24, circuit 421 (PK) and air compressor C1179 pin 1, circuit 421 (PK), harness side. • **Is the resistance less than 5 ohms?**	**Yes** GO to H4 . **No** REPAIR the circuit. CLEAR the DTC. REPEAT the self-test.

FM2010200821010X

Fig. 38 Test H/Code C1770: Vent Solenoid Output Circuit Failure (Part 1 of 2). 2003–04

H4 CHECK CIRCUIT 57 (BK) FOR AN OPEN	
• Measure the resistance between the air compressor C1179 pin 2, circuit 57 (BK), harness side and ground. • **Is the resistance greater than 5 ohms?**	**Yes** REPAIR the circuit. CLEAR the DTC. REPEAT the self-test. **No** GO to H5 .
H5 CHECK THE AIR COMPRESSOR VENT SOLENOID	
• Measure the resistance between the air compressor C1179 pin 2 and pin 3, component side. • **Is the resistance between 15 and 25 ohms?**	**Yes** INSTALL a new air suspension control module. CLEAR the DTC(s). REPEAT the self-test. **No** INSTALL a new air compressor. CLEAR the DTC. REPEAT the self-test.

FM2010200821020X

Fig. 38 Test H/Code C1770: Vent Solenoid Output Circuit Failure (Part 2 of 2). 2003–04

Test Step	Result / Action to Take
I1 CHECK CIRCUITS 1114 (BN/PK) AND 1115 (TN/WH) FOR AN OPEN	
• Key in OFF position. • Disconnect: Air Suspension Control Module C2131a. • Disconnect: Air Suspension LR Air Spring Solenoid C4044. • Disconnect: Air Suspension RR Air Spring Solenoid C4045. • Measure the resistance between the air suspension control module C2131a pin 13, circuit 1114 (BN/PK) harness side and LR air spring solenoid C4044 pin 1, harness side; and between air suspension control module C2131a pin 25, circuit 1115 (TN/WH) harness side and RR air spring solenoid C4045 pins 1, harness side. • **Are the resistances less than 5 ohms?**	**Yes** GO to I2 . **No** REPAIR the circuit in question. CLEAR the DTC(s). REPEAT the self-test.
I2 CHECK CIRCUITS 1114 (BN/PK) AND 1115 (TN/WH) FOR A SHORT TO POWER	
• Key in ON position. • Measure the voltage between the rear air suspension control module pin 13, circuit 1114 (BN/PK) and ground; and between the rear air suspension control module pin 25, circuit 1115 (TN/WH) and ground. • **Is voltage present?**	**Yes** REPAIR the affected circuit(s). CLEAR the DTC(s). REPEAT the self-test. **No** GO to I3 .
I3 CHECK CIRCUITS 1114 (BN/PK) AND 1115 (TN/WH) FOR A SHORT TO GROUND	
• Key in OFF position. • Measure the resistance between the rear air suspension control module pin 13, circuit 1114 (BN/PK) and ground; and between the rear air suspension control module pin 25, circuit 1115 (TN/WH) and ground. • **Is the resistance greater than 10,000 ohms?**	**Yes** GO to I4 . **No** REPAIR the affected circuit(s). CLEAR the DTC(s). REPEAT the self-test.

FM2010200822010X

Fig. 39 Test I/Codes C1790 & C1795: LR/RR Air Spring Solenoid Output Circuit Failure (Part 1 of 2). 2003–04

I4 CHECK CIRCUIT 57 (BK) FOR AN OPEN	
• Key in OFF position. • Measure the resistance between the LR air suspension solenoid C4044 pin 2, circuit 57 (BK) and ground; and between the RR air suspension solenoid C4045 pin 2, circuit 57 (BK) and ground. • **Is the resistance less than 5 ohms?**	**Yes** GO to I5 . **No** REPAIR the affected circuit(s). CLEAR the DTC(s). REPEAT the self-test.
I5 CHECK THE LR AND RR AIR SPRING SOLENOIDS	
• Key in OFF position. • Measure the resistance between the LR air suspension solenoid C4044 pins 1 and 2; and between the RR air suspension solenoid C4045 pins 1 and 2. • **Are the resistances between 10 and 17 ohms?**	**Yes** INSTALL a new air suspension control module. CLEAR the DTC(s). REPEAT the self-test. **No** INSTALL a new LR or RR air spring solenoid. CLEAR the DTC(s). REPEAT the self-test.

FM2010200822020X

Fig. 39 Test I/Codes C1790 & C1795: LR/RR Air Spring Solenoid Output Circuit Failure (Part 2 of 2). 2003–04

Test Step	Result / Action to Take
J1 CHECK THE AIR COMPRESSOR RELAY CONNECTOR	
• Key in OFF position. • Disconnect: Air Compressor Relay. • Check the air compressor relay connector pins and terminals for corrosion, bent or broken pins, moisture or other damage. • **Is the air compressor relay connector OK?**	**Yes** GO to J2 . **No** REPAIR as necessary. CLEAR the DTC. REPEAT the self-test.
J2 CHECK THE POWER TO THE AIR SUSPENSION RELAY	
• Measure the voltage between air compressor relay pin 1 and pin 3, circuit 1053 (LB/PK), harness side and ground. • **Are the voltages greater than 10 volts?**	**Yes** GO to J3 . **No** REPAIR the circuit. CLEAR the DTC. REPEAT the self-test.
J3 CHECK CIRCUIT 420 (DB/YE) FOR AN OPEN	
• Key in OFF position. • Disconnect: Air Suspension Control Module C2131b. • Measure the resistance between rear air suspension control module C2131b pin 23, circuit 420 (DB/YE), harness side and air compressor relay pin 2, circuit 420 (DB/YE) harness side. • **Is the resistance less than 5 ohms?**	**Yes** GO to J4 . **No** REPAIR the circuit. CLEAR the DTC. REPEAT the self-test.

FM2010200826010X

Fig. 40 Test J/Code C1830: Air Compressor Relay Circuit Failure (Part 1 of 2). 2003–04

J4 CHECK CIRCUIT 420 (DB/YE) FOR A SHORT TO GROUND	
• Measure the resistance between rear air suspension control module C2131b pin 23, circuit 420 (DB/YE), harness side and ground. • **Is the resistance greater than 10,000 ohms?**	**Yes** GO to J5 . **No** REPAIR the circuit. CLEAR the DTC. REPEAT the self-test.
J5 CHECK THE AIR COMPRESSOR RELAY COIL FOR AN OPEN	
• Measure the resistance between air compressor relay pin 1 and pin 2 (component side). • **Is the resistance greater than 10,000 ohms?**	**Yes** INSTALL a new air compressor relay. CLEAR the DTC. REPEAT the self-test. **No** INSTALL a new rear air suspension control module. REPEAT the self-test

FM2010200826020X

Fig. 40 Test J/Code C1830: Air Compressor Relay Circuit Failure (Part 2 of 2). 2003–04

Test Step	Result / Action to Take
K1 CHECK CIRCUIT 418 (DG/YE) FOR AN OPEN	
• Key in OFF position. • Disconnect: Rear Air Suspension Control Module C2131a. • Disconnect: Air Suspension Switch C2130. • Measure the resistance between rear air suspension control module C2131a pin 2, circuit 418 (DG/YE), harness side and air suspension switch C2130 pin 1, circuit 418 (DG/YE), harness side. • **Is the resistance less than 5 ohms?**	**Yes** GO to K2 . **No** REPAIR the circuit. CLEAR the DTC(s). REPEAT the self-test.
K2 CHECK CIRCUIT 418 (DG/YE) FOR A SHORT TO GROUND	
• Measure the resistance between rear air suspension control module C2131a pin 2, circuit 418 (DG/YE), harness side and ground. • **Is the resistance greater than 10,000 ohms?**	**Yes** GO to K3 . **No** REPAIR the circuit. CLEAR the DTC(s). REPEAT the self-test.
K3 CHECK THE AIR SUSPENSION SWITCH POWER	
• Connect: Rear Air Suspension Control Module C2131a. • Key in ON position. • Measure the voltage between air suspension switch C2130 pin 2, circuit 429 (PK/LG), harness side and ground. • **Is the voltage 5 volts?**	**Yes** GO to K4 . **No** REPAIR the circuit. CLEAR the DTC(s). REPEAT the self-test.
K4 CHECK THE AIR SUSPENSION SWITCH	
• Push the air suspension switch to the ON position. • Measure the resistance between air suspension switch pin 1 and pin 2. • **Is the resistance less than 5 ohms?**	**Yes** INSTALL a new air suspension control module. CLEAR the DTC(s). REPEAT the self-test. **No** INSTALL a new air suspension switch. CLEAR the DTC(s). REPEAT the self-test.

FM2010200823000X

Fig. 41 Test K/Code C1840: Suspension Switch Circuit Failure. 2003–04

Test Step	Result / Action to Take
L1 CHECK CIRCUIT 1053 (LB/PK) FOR AN OPEN	
• Key in OFF position. • Disconnect: Air Compressor Relay . • Measure the voltage between air compressor relay pin 3, circuit 1053 (LB/PK), harness side and ground. 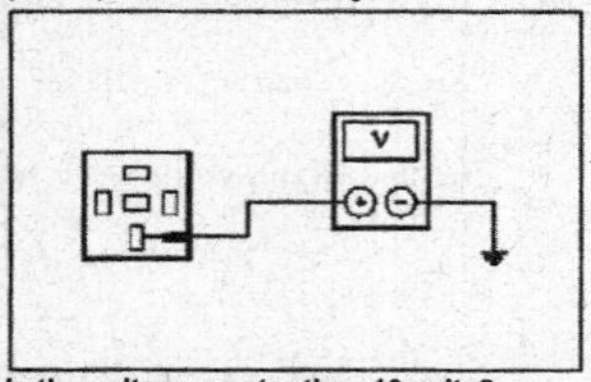 • **Is the voltage greater than 10 volts?**	**Yes** GO to L2 . **No** REPAIR the circuit. REPEAT the self-test.
L2 CHECK CIRCUIT 538 (GY/RD) FOR AN OPEN	
• Disconnect: Air Compressor C1179. • Measure the resistance between air compressor relay pin 5, circuit 538 (GY/RD), harness side and air compressor C1179 pin 3, circuit 538 (GY/RD), harness side. 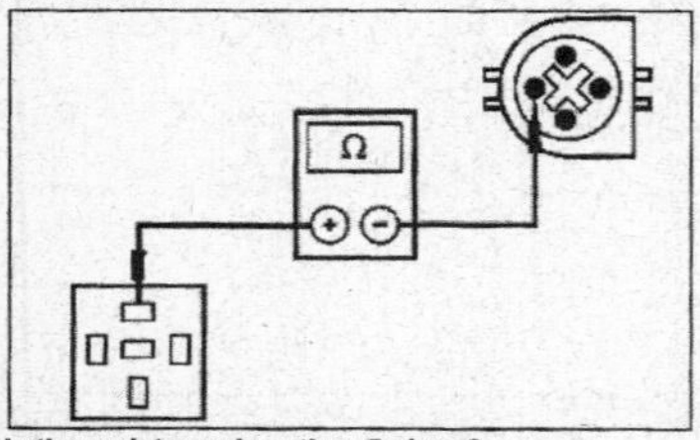 • **Is the resistance less than 5 ohms?**	**Yes** GO to L3 . **No** REPAIR the circuit. REPEAT the self-test.

FM2010200824010X

Fig. 42 Test L: Compressor Is Inoperative (Part 1 of 2). 2003–04

L3 CHECK CIRCUIT 57 (BK) FOR AN OPEN	
• Measure the resistance between air compressor C1179 pin 4, circuit 57 (BK), harness side and ground. 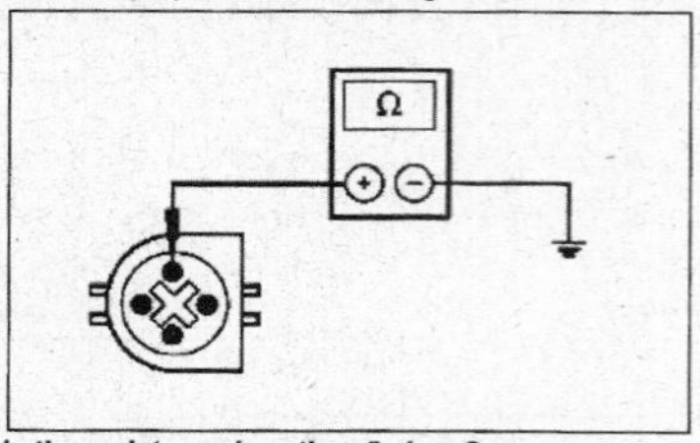 • **Is the resistance less than 5 ohms?**	**Yes** GO to L4 . **No** REPAIR the circuit. REPEAT the self-test.
L4 CHECK CIRCUIT 538 (GY/RD) FOR VOLTAGE	
• Key in ON position. • Trigger the air compressor ON active command. • Measure the voltage between air compressor C1179 pin 3, circuit 538 (GY/RD), harness side and ground. • **Is the voltage greater than 10 volts?**	**Yes** INSTALL a new air compressor. REPEAT the self-test. **No** REPAIR circuit 538 (GY/RD). REPEAT the self-test.

FM2010200824020X

Fig. 42 Test L: Compressor Is Inoperative (Part 2 of 2). 2003–04

Test Step	Result / Action to Take
M1 CHECK FOR MODULE ACTIVITY	
NOTE: The rear air suspension control module is powered for approximately 60 minutes after the ignition switch is placed in the OFF position. During this time, the air suspension will correct for vehicle weight by raising the vehicle. • Key in OFF position. • Turn the air suspension switch to the OFF position. • Verify the air compressor still cycles 60 minutes after the ignition switch is placed in the OFF position. • **Does the air compressor still cycle continuously after the air suspension module is disabled?**	**Yes** GO to M2 . **No** The system is OK.
M2 CHECK THE REAR AIR SUSPENSION CONTROL MODULE	
• Disconnect: Rear Air Suspension Control Module C2131a. • **Does the air compressor still cycle?**	**Yes** GO to M3 . **No** INSTALL a new rear air suspension control module. REPEAT the self-test.
M3 CHECK CIRCUIT 538 (GY/RD) FOR A SHORT TO POWER	
• Disconnect: Air Compressor Relay. • **Does the air compressor still cycle?**	**Yes** REPAIR Circuit 538 (GY/RD). REPEAT the self-test. **No** INSTALL a new air compressor relay. REPEAT the self-test.

FM2010200825000X

Fig. 43 Test M: Air Compressor Continuously Cycles w/Ignition Switch In Off Position & No DTC Is Set. 2003–04

SYSTEM SERVICE

Adjustment

RIDE HEIGHT

2000–02

1. Position vehicle on level surface.
2. Ensure air suspension switch is in ON position, then turn ignition switch to Run position, waiting about 2 minutes.
3. Rock vehicle sideways to remove effect of suspension friction, then allow to settle.
4. Turn air suspension switch to Off position.
5. To determine ride height "D" dimension, position a suitable height gauge between rear axle tube and frame inboard reinforcement rail , **Fig. 44.**
6. Compare measurement with vertical dimension specified in **Fig. 45.**
7. If "D" ride height dimension is not within specifications, adjust by moving rear height sensor attaching bracket up or down. Moving bracket one index mark up or down will change vertical "D" dimension about .35 inch.
8. After adjustment is made, repeat steps 4 through 6.

2003–04

1. Position vehicle on a level surface.
2. Ensure air suspension switch is turned On, then turn ignition switch to Run position and wait at least two minutes.
3. Position measurement tool on rear axle, **Fig. 44.**
4. Release measurement tool set screw, then pull sliding post and scale up until it touches bottom of inboard frame rail to get ride height "D" dimension.
5. Vent or fill air suspension to vertical "D" dimension using suitable scan tool.
6. Monitor suspension height sensor measurement and voltage PIDs.
7. Loosen height sensor ball stud bracket retaining nuts, **Fig. 46.**
8. Slide ball stud bracket until height sensor measurement PID is equal to 0 inches and voltage PID is equal to 2.8 volts.
9. Tighten height sensor ball stud bracket.
10. If ride height dimension "D" is not within specification, **Fig. 47,** use scan tool to vent or fill air suspension to specification and monitor height sensor arm from ball stud.
11. Rotate height sensor link until measurement PID is equal to 0 inches and voltage is 2.8 volts.
12. Disconnect height sensor ball stud, then save the height settings using scan tool.
13. Connect height sensor arm to ball stud.

Air Spring Vent & Refill

1. Turn ignition switch to Run position, then connect suitable scan tool to DLC.
2. Select air suspension control module active command LR_SOL or RR_SOL from off to on.
3. Select air suspension control module active command AS_VENT to deflate air springs or AS_COMP to inflate air

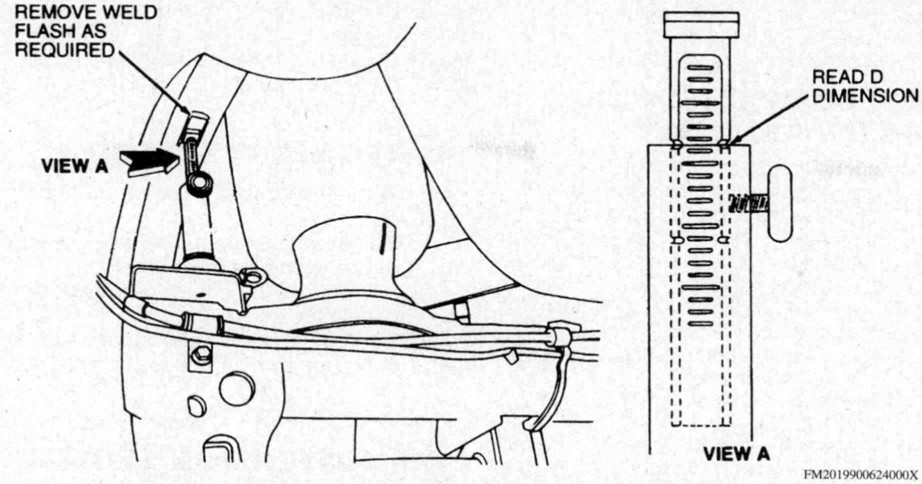

Fig. 44 Ride height "D" dimension measurement

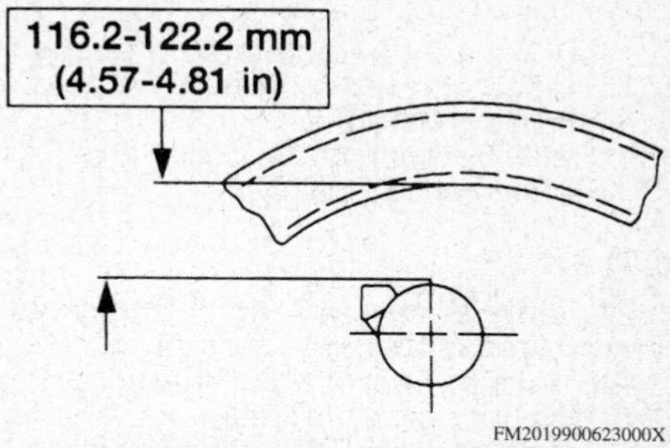

Fig. 45 Vertical "D" dimension. 2000–02

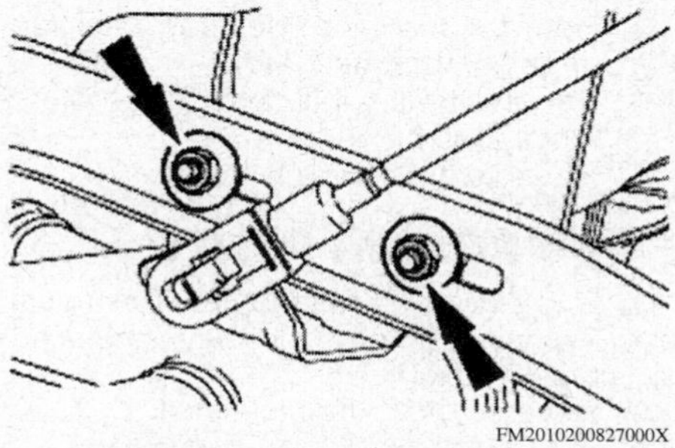

Fig. 46 Height sensor ball retaining bolts. 2003–04

springs. **When using AS_COMP command, do not run air compressor for more than three minutes to prevent overheating.**

Air Spring Refold

1. Place air spring on a flat surface.
2. Remove air spring solenoid to expand collapsed air bag.
3. Push membrane down over piston to correct height, **Fig. 48.**
4. Install solenoid to help maintain correct height.

Component Replacement

AIR SPRING SOLENOID

2000–02

1. Turn air suspension switch to Off position, then vent air from system as outlined in "Air Spring Vent & Refill."
2. Raise and support vehicle, ensure suspension is at full rebound.
3. Remove heat shield.
4. Disconnect air spring solenoid electrical connector.
5. Push down and hold air line plastic release ring, then disconnect attaching air line.
6. Remove air spring solenoid attaching clip.

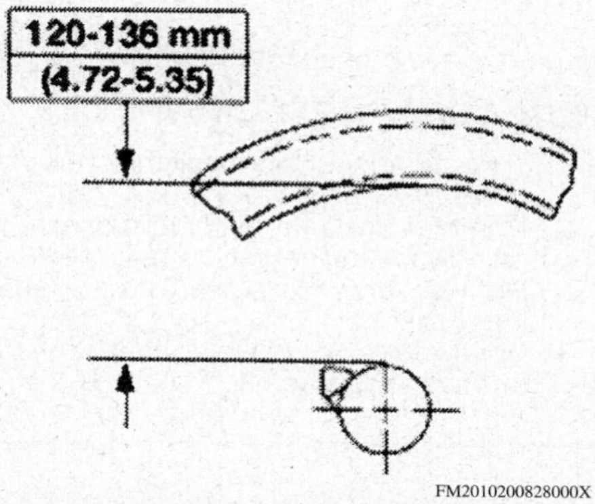

Fig. 47 Ride height dimension "D." 2003–04

7. Rotate solenoid counterclockwise to first stop.
8. Pull solenoid out to second stop, then bleed air from system. **Do not fully release solenoid until air is completely bled from air spring.**
9. Rotate air spring solenoid counterclockwise to third stop, then remove solenoid from housing.
10. Remove O-ring from solenoid housing.
11. Reverse procedure to install.

2003

1. If air spring solenoid valve is functional, vent appropriate air springs as outlined in "Air Spring Vent & Refill."
2. Raise and support vehicle.
3. Disconnect electrical connector, then compress quick connect lock ring and pull out air line.
4. Rotate and remove air spring solenoid valve. **Air spring solenoid valve has a two stage release. When removing a nonfunctional solenoid and air spring is inflated, carefully rotate solenoid counterclockwise until it reaches the first stage to release air from spring. Turn solenoid to second stage to remove.**
5. Reverse procedure to install noting the following:
   a. Replace O-ring if damaged.
   b. Lubricate solenoid seal area with silicone grease.

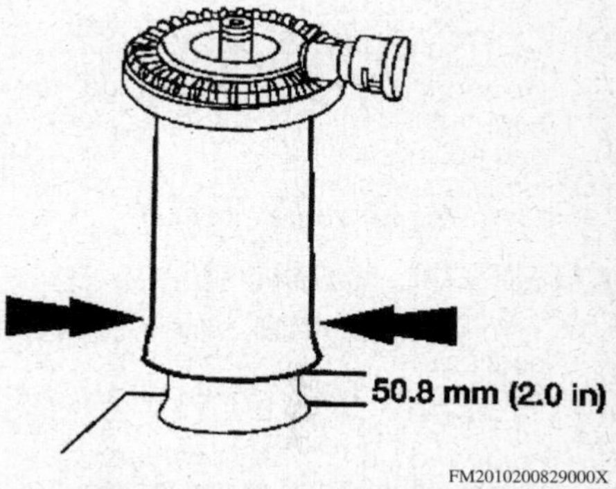

Fig. 48 Air spring height

AIR SPRING

2000–02

Removal

Do not remove an air spring when there is pressure in the air spring.

Do not attempt to install any air spring that has become unfolded.

1. Turn air suspension switch to Off position, then vent air from system as outlined in "Air Spring Vent & Refill."
2. Raise and support vehicle.
3. Remove heat shield attaching screws, then remove heat shield.
4. Remove air spring solenoid as outlined in "Air Spring Solenoid."
5. Remove spring piston to axle spring seat as follows:
   a. Insert air spring removal tool No. T90P-5310-A, or equivalent, between axle and spring seat on forward side of axle.
   b. Position tool so flat end is on piston knob.
   c. Push downward, forcing piston and attaching clip from axle spring seat.
6. Remove air spring.

Installation

1. Install air spring solenoid.
2. Install spring attaching clip to knob of spring cap at top side of frame spring seat.
3. Connect air solenoid air line and electrical connector.
4. Install heat shield.
5. Align air spring piston to axle seats. Squeeze to increase pressure and push downward on piston, then snap

piston to axle seat at rebound. **Air spring may be damaged if suspension is allowed to compress before spring is inflated.**

6. Refill air springs as outlined in "Air Spring Vent & Refill."

2003

Do not remove an air spring when there is pressure in the air spring.

Do not attempt to install any air spring that has become unfolded.

1. Raise and support vehicle until tires are slightly above ground.
2. Vent air springs as outlined in "Air Spring Vent & Refill."
3. Remove air spring retainer, then detach air spring from rear axle.
4. Disconnect air spring electrical connector, then quick connect locking ring and pull out air line.
5. Remove air spring.
6. Reverse procedure to install.

CONTROL MODULE

1. Turn air suspension switch to the Off position.
2. Remove pushpins, then pull lower instrument panel insulator from under righthand side of instrument panel.
3. Disconnect power point and courtesy lamp electrical connectors, then remove insulator panel from vehicle.
4. Disconnect control module electrical connectors.
5. Remove control module retaining screws, then the module.
6. Reverse procedure to install.

AIR COMPRESSOR & DRYER ASSEMBLY

1. Turn air suspension switch to Off position, then vent air from system.
2. Remove air cleaner outlet tube, then disconnect mass air flow (MAF) and intake air temperature (IAT) sensor electrical connectors.
3. Remove air cleaner retaining bolts, then the air cleaner.
4. Remove pushpins and the air compressor dryer cover.
5. Remove snorkel pushpin, then the snorkel.
6. Disconnect air line and electrical connector from compressor.
7. Raise and support vehicle.
8. Remove compressor retaining nuts.
9. Lower vehicle and remove air compressor.
10. Reverse procedure to install.

AIR COMPRESSOR DRYER

1. Turn air suspension switch to the Off position.
2. Remove air compressor and dryer assembly as outlined previously.
3. Remove dryer to compressor attaching screw.
4. Rotate dryer clockwise, then remove from compressor.
5. Remove O-ring seal, then discard O-ring.
6. Reverse procedure to install. **Torque** dryer to compressor attaching screw to 15–25 inch lbs.

REAR HEIGHT SENSOR

1. Turn air suspension switch to Off position.
2. Raise and support vehicle, ensure suspension is at full rebound.
3. Disconnect height sensor electrical connector.
4. Depress spring clip at bottom and top of sensor from ball studs, then pull sensor.
5. Reverse procedure to install.

AIR SUSPENSION SWITCH

1. Turn air suspension switch to the OFF position.
2. Remove pushpins, then peel back luggage compartment trim.
3. Depress switch retaining clips, then remove switch.
4. Reverse procedure to install.

COMPRESSOR RELAY

1. Remove power distribution box cover.
2. Remove compressor relay from distribution box.
3. Reverse procedure to install.

Town Car

NOTE: On Air Bag Equipped Models, Refer To "Air Bag System Precautions" Located In The Front Of This Manual For System Disarming & Arming Procedures.

NOTE: Refer To "Computer Relearn Procedures" Located In The Front Of This Manual When Battery Power To The Computer Has Been Interrupted.

NOTE: "Electrical Symbol & Wire Color Code Identification" Located In The Front Of This Manual May Be Used As An Aid When Using Wiring Circuits Found In This Section.

INDEX

PRECAUTIONS

Air Bag Systems

Refer to "Air Bag System Precautions" in the front of this manual for system disarming and arming procedures.

Battery Ground Cable

Prior to service, disconnect battery ground cable and isolate as required.

Service

Before servicing an air suspension component, disconnect the power to the system by turning the air suspension switch to the Off position or disconnecting the battery ground cable. Do not remove the air spring when there is pressure in the air spring. Do not remove any air spring supporting components without exhausting air or supporting air spring.

DESCRIPTION

Air Suspension System

The rear air suspension is an air operated microprocessor controlled, suspension system which replaces the conventional suspension. This system allows low spring rates for improved ride and automatic rear load leveling.

Two air springs replace the conventional steel springs and support the vehicle load at the rear wheels. The air springs are mounted on the axle spring seats and to the frame upper spring seats.

Air Compressor

The air compressor assembly consists of a compressor pump, electric motor and a vent solenoid, both are non-serviceable. The compressor assembly is mounted in the engine compartment on the lefthand fender area below the air cleaner.

The pressurized air from the air compressor passes through the dryer assembly which contains a drying agent (silica gel). The moisture is removed from the air dryer when vented air passes out of the system during vent operation.

Air Spring Solenoid Valve

The air spring solenoid valve allows air to enter and exit the air spring during leveling. The valve is electrically operated and is controlled by the module.

The valve is a two-stage pressure relief system. A clip is removed and rotation of the solenoid out of the seat will release air from the spring before the solenoid can be removed. **Never rotate an air spring solenoid valve to the release slot in the end fitting until all of the pressurized air has escaped the system.**

Height Sensor

The height sensor sends signals to the control module. The three conditions that the control module interprets from the height sensor are that the vehicle is either at, above or below trim height.

The height sensor is attached to the frame crossmember and to the lefthand rear upper control arm. As the rear of the vehicle moves up and down the height sensor lengthens and shortens. Magnets mounted on the lower slide portion of the sensor move relative to the to the sensor housing, generating a signal that is sent to the control module, through two small Hall effect switches that are attached to the sensor housing.

Control Module

The air suspension control module responds to signals from various sensors in the vehicle to maintain the programmed ride height. The module accomplishes this by opening or closing the solenoid valves to control the amount of air in the air springs. The rear air suspension control module turns on the compressor by applying voltage through the compressor relay to inflate the air spring and raise the vehicle. The

Condition	Possible Sources	Action
• No communication with the module — rear air suspension control module	• CJB Fuse 8 (10A), 17 (10A). • Circuitry. • Data link connector (DLC). • Rear air suspension control module.	• GO to Pinpoint Test A.
• Unable to enter self-test	• Rear air suspension control module.	• GO to Pinpoint Test B.
• Did not detect open and close door signals	• Circuitry. • Door ajar switch. • Lighting control module (LCM). • Rear air suspension control module.	• GO to Pinpoint Test T.
• The compressor is inoperative	• Circuitry. • Air compressor relay. • Air compressor.	• GO to Pinpoint Test U.
• The air compressor continuously cycles with the ignition switch in the OFF position and no DTC is set	• Circuitry. • Air compressor relay. • Rear air suspension control module.	• GO to Pinpoint Test V.
• Air suspension system works with air suspension switch in the OFF position	• Air suspension switch.	• INSTALL a new air suspension switch. TEST the system for normal operation.
• Uneven vehicle height	• Pneumatic fault. • Air suspension height sensor. • Air spring solenoid. • Air compressor. • Air spring. • Rear air suspension control module.	• GO to Pinpoint Test P.

FM2010200865000X

Fig. 1 Troubleshooting chart. 2000–02

Condition	Possible Sources	Action
• The compressor is inoperative	• Circuitry. • Air compressor relay. • Air compressor.	• GO to Pinpoint Test K.
• The air compressor continuously cycles with the ignition switch in the OFF position and no DTC is set	• Circuitry. • Air compressor relay. • Air suspension control module.	• GO to Pinpoint Test L.
• Air suspension system works with air suspension switch in the OFF position	• Air suspension switch.	• INSTALL a new air suspension switch. TEST the system for normal operation.
• Uneven vehicle height	• Pneumatic fault. • Air suspension height sensor. • Air spring solenoid. • Air compressor. • Air spring. • Air suspension control module.	• REPAIR as necessary.
• Incorrect vehicle trim height	• Incorrect ride height adjustment. • Incorrect height sensor calibration. • Incorrect air suspension module calibration. • Rear suspension component damage.	• SET the ride height. • INSPECT and REPAIR the rear suspension components as necessary.

FM2010200866020X

Fig. 2 Troubleshooting chart (Part 2 of 2). 2003–04

• NOTE: Be sure that air suspension disable switch is in the ON position before determining that a fault condition is present. No communication with the rear air suspension module	• BJB Fuses 10 (10A), 101 (50A), or 114 (30A). • Circuitry. • Data link connector (DLC). • Rear air suspension control module.	• GO to Pinpoint Test A.
• Unable to enter self-test	• Rear air suspension control module.	• GO to Pinpoint Test B.
• Did not detect open and close door signals	• Circuitry. • Door ajar switch. • Lighting control module (LCM). • Rear air suspension control module.	• GO to Pinpoint Test M.

FM2010200866010X

Fig. 2 Troubleshooting chart (Part 1 of 2). 2003–04

DTC	Description	Source	Action
B1317	Battery Voltage High	Rear Air Suspension Control Module	GO to Pinpoint Test C.
B1318	Battery Voltage Low	Rear Air Suspension Control Module	GO to Pinpoint Test C.
B1342	ECU Is Defective	Rear Air Suspension Control Module	INSTALL a new rear air suspension control module. TEST the system for normal operation.
C1441	Steering Sensor Channel A Circuit Failure	Rear Air Suspension Control Module	DIAGNOSE steering.
C1442	Steering Sensor Channel B Circuit Failure	Rear Air Suspension Control Module	DIAGNOSE steering.
C1722	Air Suspension Height Sensor Power Circuit Short to Power	Rear Air Suspension Control Module	GO to Pinpoint Test D.
C1723	Air Suspension Height Sensor Power Circuit Short to Ground	Rear Air Suspension Control Module	GO to Pinpoint Test E.
C1760	Air Suspension Rear Height Sensor High Signal Circuit Failure	Rear Air Suspension Control Module	GO to Pinpoint Test F.

FM2010200867010X

Fig. 3 Diagnostic trouble code interpretation (Part 1 of 2). 2000–02

module opens the vent solenoid to lower the vehicle by releasing air from the air spring.

TROUBLESHOOTING

Refer to **Figs. 1 and 2,** for troubleshooting charts.

DIAGNOSIS & TESTING

Accessing Diagnostic Trouble Codes

1. Connect a New Generation STAR (NGS) Tester, or equivalent, to Data Link Connector (DLC) located under the lefthand side of the instrument panel.
2. Follow scan tool instructions to retrieve Diagnostic Trouble Codes (DTC)s.
3. If DTCs are retrieved, refer to "Diagnostic Trouble Code Interpretation" for DTC identification and description.
4. If there are no DTCs present, but symptoms exist, refer to "Troubleshooting."

Diagnostic Trouble Code Interpretation

Refer to **Figs. 3 and 4,** for DTC identification, description and to identify the recommended pinpoint test. Refer to the "Diagnostic Chart Index" for pinpoint test location.

Wiring Diagrams & Connector Identification

Refer to **Figs. 5 and 6,** for wiring diagrams and **Fig. 7,** for connector pin identification.

Pinpoint Tests

2000–02

Refer to **Figs. 8 through 29,** for pinpoint tests.

2003–04

Refer to **Figs. 30 through 42,** for pinpoint tests.

Clearing Diagnostic Trouble Codes

Connect a New Generation STAR (NGS) Tester, or equivalent, to Data Link Connector (DLC) located under the lefthand side of the instrument panel. Follow tool manufacturers' instructions to clear DTCs.

DTC	Description	Source	Action
C1763	Air Suspension Rear Height Sensor High Signal Circuit Short to Ground	Rear Air Suspension Control Module	GO to Pinpoint Test G.
C1765	Air Suspension Rear Height Sensor Low Signal Circuit Failure	Rear Air Suspension Control Module	GO to Pinpoint Test F.
C1768	Air Suspension Rear Height Sensor Low Signal Circuit Short to Ground	Rear Air Suspension Control Module	GO to Pinpoint Test H.
C1770	Air Suspension Vent Solenoid Output Circuit Failure	Rear Air Suspension Control Module	GO to Pinpoint Test I.
C1773	Air Suspension Vent Solenoid Output Circuit Short to Ground	Rear Air Suspension Control Module	GO to Pinpoint Test J.
C1790	Air Suspension LR Air Spring Solenoid Output Circuit Failure	Rear Air Suspension Control Module	GO to Pinpoint Test K.
C1793	Air Suspension LR Air Spring Solenoid Output Circuit Short to Ground	Rear Air Suspension Control Module	GO to Pinpoint Test L.
C1795	Air Suspension RR Air Spring Solenoid Output Circuit Failure	Rear Air Suspension Control Module	GO to Pinpoint Test M.
C1798	Air Suspension RR Air Spring Solenoid Output Circuit Short to Ground	Rear Air Suspension Control Module	GO to Pinpoint Test N.
C1813	Air Suspension Vent Request Exceeded Max Timing	Rear Air Suspension Control Module	GO to Pinpoint Test O.
C1818	Air Suspension Air Compressor Request Exceeded Max Timing	Rear Air Suspension Control Module	GO to Pinpoint Test P.
C1830	Air Compressor Relay Circuit Failure	Rear Air Suspension Control Module	GO to Pinpoint Test Q.
C1832	Air Compressor Relay Circuit Short to Power	Rear Air Suspension Control Module	GO to Pinpoint Test R.
C1840	Air Suspension Switch Circuit Failure	Rear Air Suspension Control Module	GO to Pinpoint Test S.
C1842	Air Suspension Switch Circuit Short to Power	Rear Air Suspension Control Module	GO to Pinpoint Test D.
C1897	Steering VAPS Circuit Loop Failure	Rear Air Suspension Control Module	DIAGNOSE steering.
U1041	SPC Invalid or Missing Data for Vehicle Speed	ABS	CARRY OUT the ABS Self-Test.

FM2010200867020X

Fig. 3 Diagnostic trouble code interpretation (Part 2 of 2). 2000–02

DTC	Description	Source	Action
C1770	Air Suspension Vent Solenoid Output Circuit Failure	RAS Control Module	GO to Pinpoint Test G.
C1790	Air Suspension LR Air Spring Solenoid Output Circuit Failure	RAS Module	GO to Pinpoint Test H.
C1795	Air Suspension RR Air Spring Solenoid Output Circuit Failure	RAS Module	GO to Pinpoint Test H.
C1830	Air Suspension Compressor Relay Circuit Failure	RAS Module	GO to Pinpoint Test I.
C1840	Air Suspension Disable Switch Circuit Failure	RAS Module	GO to Pinpoint Test J.
C1897	Steering VAPS Circuit Loop Failure	RAS Module	DIAGNOSE steering.
C1964	Air Suspension Air Compressor Request Exceeded Maximum Timing	RAS Module	DTC code C1964 indicates that the air compressor has overheated and is unable to enter the self-test. Allow the air compressor to cool down for approximately five minutes. CLEAR the DTC. REPEAT the self-test.
U1026	SCP Invalid or Missing Data for Engine RPM	PCM	CARRY OUT the PCM Self-Test.
U1123	SCP Invalid or Missing Data for Odometer	ABS	CARRY OUT the ABS Self-Test.
U1041	SCP Invalid or Missing Data for Vehicle Speed	ABS	CARRY OUT the ABS Self-Test.
U1099	SCP Invalid or Missing Data for External Access (Vehicle Doors)	DDM	CARRY OUT the Driver Door Module (DDM) Self-Test.

FM2010200868020X

Fig. 4 Diagnostic trouble code interpretation (Part 2 of 2). 2003

DTC	Description	Source	Action
B1317	Battery Voltage High	RAS Module	GO to Pinpoint Test C.
B1318	Battery Voltage Low	RAS Module	GO to Pinpoint Test C.
B1342	ECU Is Defective	RAS Module	INSTALL a new rear air suspension control module. TEST the system for normal operation.
B2477	Module Configuration Failure	RAS Module	DIAGNOSE module.
C1724	Air Suspension Height Sensor Power Circuit Failure	Rear Air Suspension Control Module	GO to Pinpoint Test D.
C1726	Air Suspension Rear Pneumatic Failure	RAS Module	GO to Pinpoint Test E.
C1760	Air Suspension Rear Height Sensor High Signal Circuit Failure	RAS Module	GO to Pinpoint Test F.

FM2010200868010X

Fig. 4 Diagnostic trouble code interpretation (Part 1 of 2). 2003

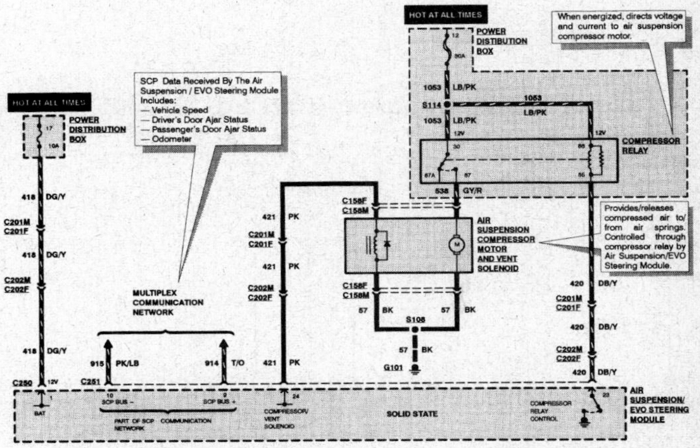

FM2019800508010X

Fig. 5 Wiring diagram (Part 1 of 2). 2000–01

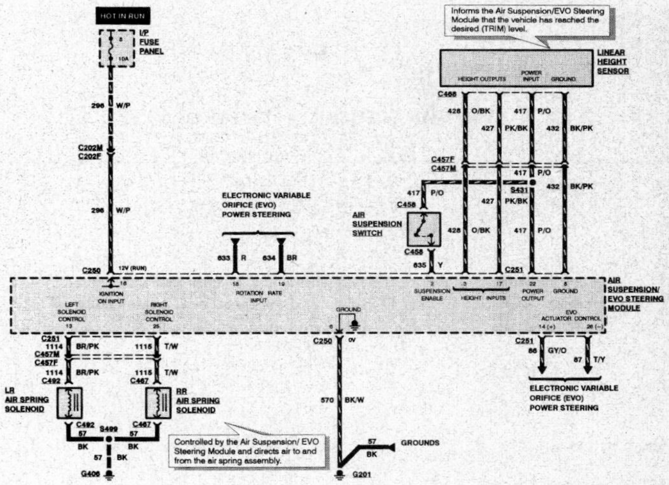

FM2019800508020X

Fig. 5 Wiring diagram (Part 2 of 2). 2000–01

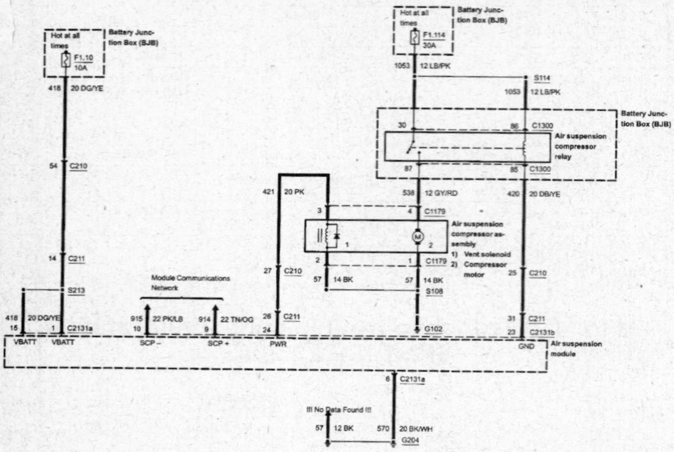

FM2010200869010X

Fig. 6 Wiring diagram (Part 1 of 2). 2002-03

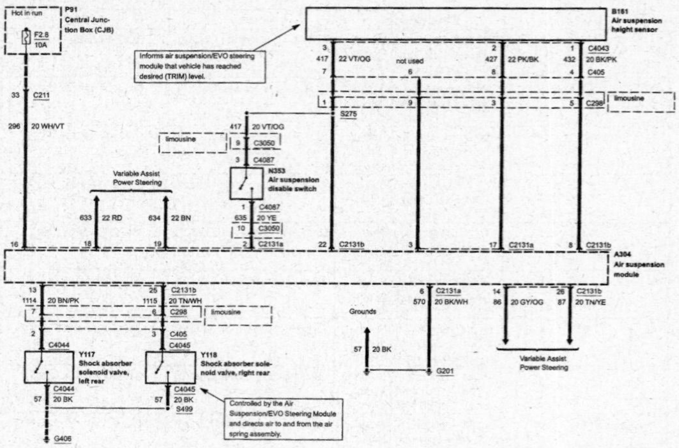

FM2010200869020X

Fig. 6 Wiring diagram (Part 2 of 2). 2002

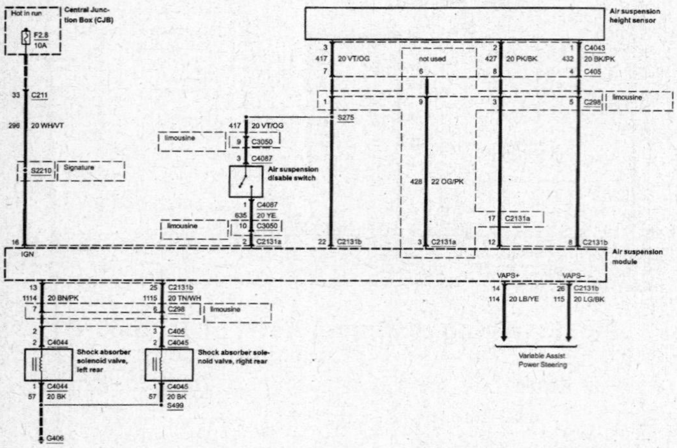

FM2010200869030X

Fig. 6 Wiring diagram (Part 2 of 2). 2003

C250 (GRAY)
AIR SUSPENSION/EVO STEERING MODULE

PIN	CIRCUIT	CIRCUIT FUNCTION
1	418 (DG/Y)	Power (Hot at All Times)
2	635 (Y)	Suspension Enable
3	428 (O/BK)	Linear Height Sensor Input (Low Indicator)
4	—	NOT USED
5	—	NOT USED
6	570 (BK/W)	Ground
7	—	NOT USED
15	—	NOT USED
16	296 (W/P)	Power (Hot in Run)
17	427 (PK/BK)	Linear Height Sensor Input (High Indicator)
18	633 (R)	Steering Wheel Rotation Rate Input
19	634 (BR)	Steering Wheel Rotation Rate Input
20	—	NOT USED

C251 (BLACK)
AIR SUSPENSION/EVO STEERING MODULE

PIN	CIRCUIT	CIRCUIT FUNCTION
8	432 (BK/PK)	Height Sensor Ground
9	914 (T/O)	Data + (SCP Communication Network)
10	915 (PK/LB)	Data– (SCP Communication Network)
11	—	NOT USED
12	—	NOT USED
13	1114 (BR/PK)	LH Rear Air Spring Solenoid Control
14	86 (GY/O)	EVO Actuator Control
21	—	NOT USED
22	417 (P/O)	Linear Height Sensor Power Output
23	420 (DB/Y)	Compressor Relay Control
24	421 (PK)	Vent Solenoid Control
25	1115 (T/W)	RH Rear Air Spring Solenoid Control
26	87 (T/Y)	EVO Actuator Feedback

FM2019800509000X

Fig. 7 Connector pin identification

DIAGNOSTIC CHART INDEX

Pinpoint Test	Code	Description	Page No.	Fig. No.
2000–02				
A	—	No Communication w/Rear Air Suspension Control Module	7-72	8
B	—	Unable To Enter Self-Test	7-72	9
C	B1317	Battery Voltage High	7-72	10
	B1318	Battery Voltage Low	7-72	10
D	C1722	Height Sensor Circuit Short To Power	7-73	11
	C1842	Height Switch Circuit Short To Power	7-73	11
E	C1723	Height Sensor Power Circuit Short To Ground	7-73	12
F	C1760	Rear Height Sensor High Signal Circuit Failure	7-74	13
	C1765	Rear Height Sensor Low Signal Circuit Failure	7-74	13
G	C1763	Height Rear Sensor High Signal Circuit Short To Ground	7-74	14
H	C1768	Rear Height Sensor Low Signal Circuit Short To Ground	7-75	15
I	C1770	Vent Solenoid Output Circuit Failure	7-75	16
J	C1773	Vent Solenoid Output Circuit Short To Ground	7-76	17
K	C1790	LR Air Spring Solenoid Output Circuit Failure	7-76	18
L	C1793	LR Air Spring Solenoid Output Circuit Short To Ground	7-77	19
M	C1795	RR Air Spring Solenoid Output Circuit Failure	7-77	20
N	C1798	RR Air Spring Solenoid Output Circuit Short To Ground	7-78	21
O	C1813	AVent Request Exceeded Maximum Timing	7-78	22
P	C1818	Air Compressor Request Exceeded Maximum Timing	7-79	23
Q	C1830	Air Compressor Relay Circuit Failure	7-82	24
R	C1832	Air Compressor Relay Circuit Short To Power	7-82	25
S	C1840	Air Suspension Switch Circuit Failure	7-83	26
T	—	Did Not Detect Open & Close Door Signals	7-83	27
U	—	Compressor Is Inoperative	7-83	28
V	—	Air Compressor Continuously Cycles w/Ignition Switch In Off Position And No DTC Is Set	7-84	29
2003–04				
A	—	No Communication w/Rear Air Suspension Control Module	7-84	30
B	—	Unable To Enter Self-Test	7-84	31
C	B1317	Battery Voltage High	7-84	32
	B1318	Battery Voltage Low	7-84	32
D	C1724	Height Sensor Power Circuit Failure	7-84	33
E	C1726	Pneumatic Failure	7-85	34
F	C1760	Rear Height Sensor High Signal Circuit Failure	7-85	35
G	C1770	Vent Solenoid Output Circuit Failure	7-85	36
H	C1790	LR Air Spring Solenoid Output Circuit Failure	7-86	37
	C1795	RR Air Spring Solenoid Output Circuit Failure	7-86	37
I	C1830	Air Compressor Relay Circuit Failure	7-86	38
J	C1840	Air Suspension Switch Circuit Failure	7-86	39
K	—	Compressor Is Inoperative	7-86	40
L	—	Air Compressor Continuously Cycles w/Ignition Switch In Off Position And No DTC Is Set	7-87	41
M	—	Did Not Detect Open & Close Door Signals	7-87	42

CONDITIONS	DETAILS/RESULTS/ACTIONS
A1 CHECK CIRCUIT 296 (WH/VT) FOR AN OPEN	
1 2 3  Rear Air Suspension Control Module C250	
4 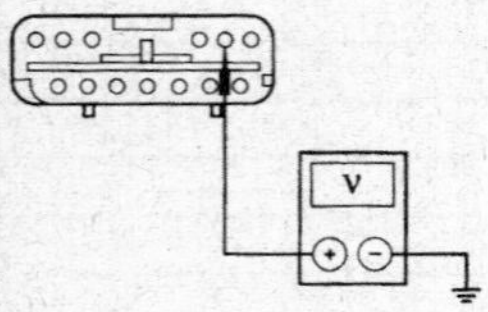	4 Measure the voltage between rear air suspension control module C250 Pin 16, Circuit 296 (WH/VT), harness side and ground. • Is the voltage greater than 10 volts? → **Yes** GO to **A2**. → **No** REPAIR the circuit. REPEAT the Self-Test.
A2 CHECK CIRCUIT 418 (DG/YE) FOR AN OPEN	
1 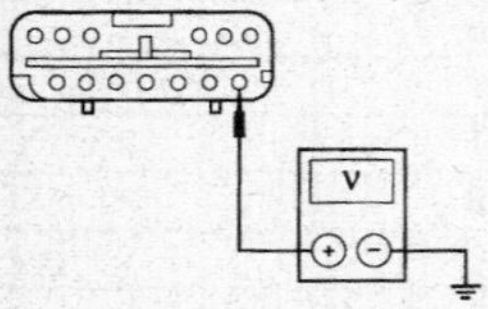	1 Measure the voltage between rear air suspension control module C250 Pin 1, Circuit 418 (DG/YE), harness side and ground. • Is the voltage greater than 10 volts? → **Yes** GO to **A3**. → **No** REPAIR the circuit. REPEAT the Self-Test.
A3 CHECK CIRCUIT 570 (BK/WH) FOR AN OPEN	
1 	

FM2010200830010X

Fig. 8 Test A: No Communication w/Rear Air Suspension Control Module (Part 1 of 2). 2000–02

CONDITIONS	DETAILS/RESULTS/ACTIONS
B1 CHECK THE COMMUNICATIONS TO THE REAR AIR SUSPENSION CONTROL MODULE	
	1 Check the communication to the rear air suspension control module. • Does scan tool communicate to the rear air suspension control module? → **Yes** INSTALL a new rear air suspension control module. REPEAT the Self-Test. → **No** GO to Pinpoint Test A.

FM2010200831000X

Fig. 9 Test B: Unable To Enter Self-Test. 2000–02

CONDITIONS	DETAILS/RESULTS/ACTIONS
A3 CHECK CIRCUIT 570 (BK/WH) FOR AN OPEN (Continued)	
2 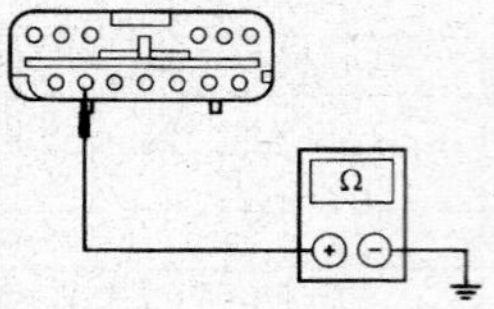	2 Measure the resistance between rear air suspension control module C250 Pin 6, Circuit 570 (BK/WH), harness side and ground. • Is the resistance less than 5 ohms? → **Yes** DIAGNOSE module. → **No** REPAIR the circuit. REPEAT the Self-Test.

FM2010200830020X

Fig. 8 Test A: No Communication w/Rear Air Suspension Control Module (Part 2 of 2). 2000–02

CONDITIONS	DETAILS/RESULTS/ACTIONS
C1 CHECKBATTERYVOLTAGE	
NOTE: A recent jump start may cause these DTCs to set.	
1 	1 Measure the battery voltage between the positive and negative battery posts with the key ON engine OFF (KOEO) and with the engine running. • Is the battery voltage between 10 and 13 volts with KOEO, and between 11 and 17 volts with the engine running? → **Yes** GO to **C2**. → **No** DIAGNOSE battery.
C2 CHECK CIRCUIT 570 (BK/WH) FOR AN OPEN	
1 2  Rear Air Suspension Control Module C250	
3 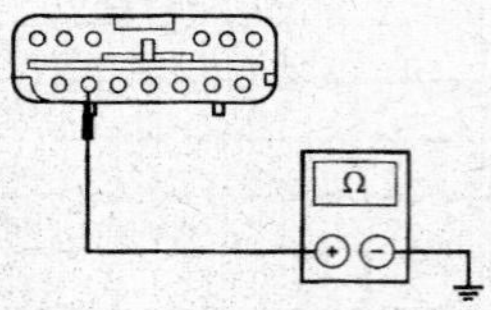	3 Measure the resistance between rear air suspension control module C250 Pin 6, Circuit 570 (BK/WH), harness side and ground. • Is the resistance less than 5 ohms? → **Yes** INSTALL a new rear air suspension control module. REPEAT the Self-Test. → **No** REPAIR the circuit. CLEAR the DTCs. REPEAT the Self-Test.

FM2010200832000X

Fig. 10 Test C/Codes B1317 & B1318: Battery Voltage High/Low. 2000–02

CONDITIONS | **DETAILS/RESULTS/ACTIONS**

D1 CHECK CIRCUIT 635 (YE) FOR SHORT TO POWER

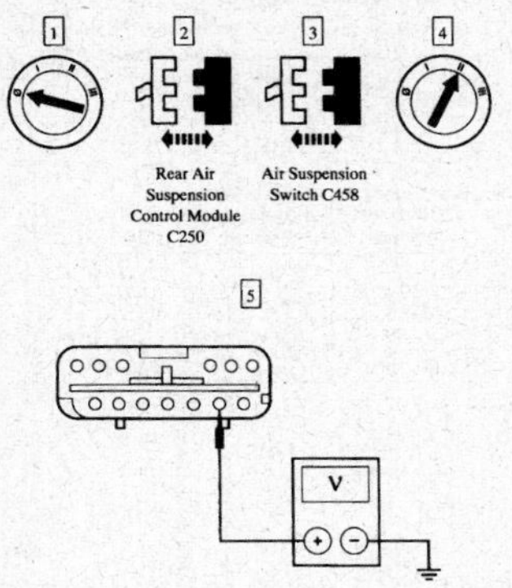

5 Measure the voltage between rear air suspension control module C250 Pin 2, Circuit 635 (YE), harness side and ground.

- Is voltage present?

→ **Yes**
REPAIR the circuit. CLEAR the DTCs. REPEAT the Self-Test.

→ **No**
GO to **D2**.

D2 CHECK CIRCUIT 417 (VT/OG) FOR SHORT TO POWER

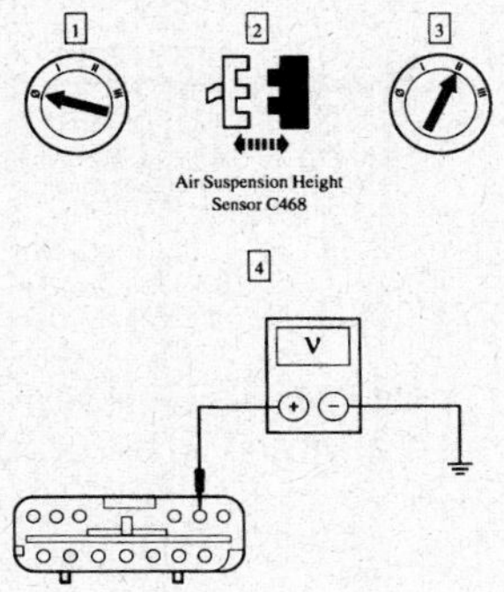

4 Measure the voltage between rear air suspension control module C251 Pin 22, Circuit 417 (VT/OG), harness side and ground.

- Is voltage present?

→ **Yes**
REPAIR the circuit. CLEAR the DTCs. REPEAT the Self-Test.

→ **No**
INSTALL a new rear air suspension control module. REPEAT the Self-Test.

FM2010200833000X

Fig. 11 Test D/Codes C1722 & C1842: Height Sensor/Switch Circuit Short To Power. 2000–02

CONDITIONS | **DETAILS/RESULTS/ACTIONS**

E3 CHECK AIR SUSPENSION SWITCH FOR SHORT TO GROUND

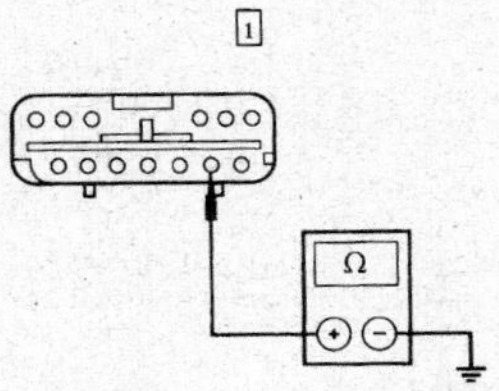

1 Measure the resistance between rear air suspension control module C250 Pin 2, Circuit 635 (YE), harness side and ground.

- Is the resistance greater than 10,000 ohms?

→ **Yes**
RECONNECT air suspension height sensor C468. GO to **E4**.

→ **No**
INSTALL a new air suspension switch. CLEAR the DTCs. REPEAT the Self-Test.

FM2010200834020X

Fig. 12 Test E/Code C1723: Height Sensor Power Circuit Short To Ground (Part 2 of 3). 2000–02

CONDITIONS | **DETAILS/RESULTS/ACTIONS**

E1 CHECK CIRCUIT 635 (YE) FOR SHORT TO GROUND

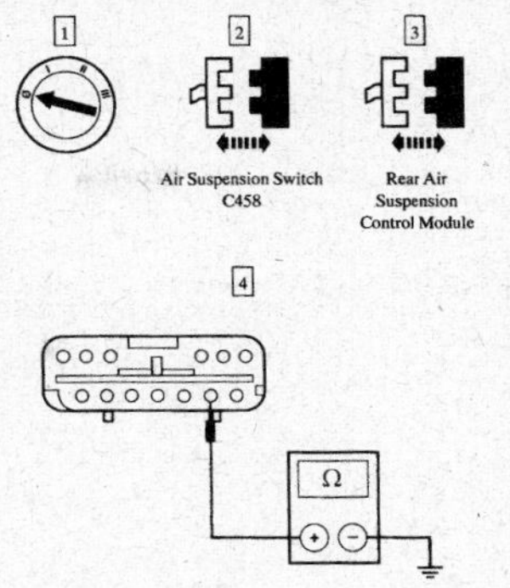

4 Measure the resistance between rear air suspension control module C250 Pin 2, Circuit 635 (YE), harness side and ground.

- Is the resistance greater than 10,000 ohms?

→ **Yes**
GO to **E2**.

→ **No**
REPAIR the circuit. CLEAR the DTCs. REPEAT the Self-Test.

E2 CHECK CIRCUIT 417 (VT/OG) FOR SHORT TO GROUND

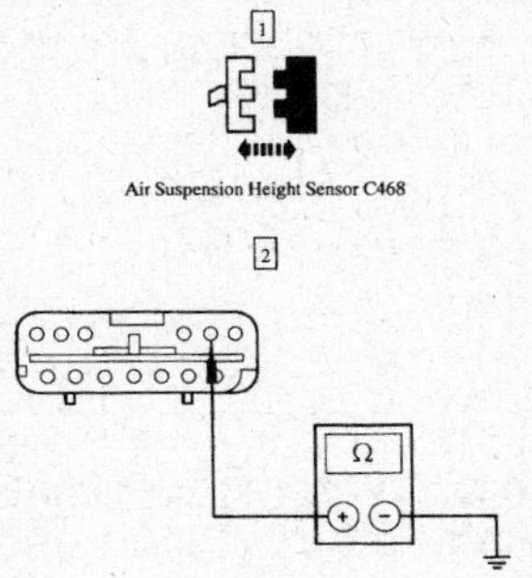

2 Measure the resistance between rear air suspension control module C251 Pin 22, Circuit 417 (VT/OG), harness side and ground.

- Is the resistance greater than 10,000 ohms?

→ **Yes**
RECONNECT air suspension switch C458. GO to **E3**.

→ **No**
REPAIR the circuit. CLEAR the DTCs. REPEAT the Self-Test.

FM2010200834010X

Fig. 12 Test E/Code C1723: Height Sensor Power Circuit Short To Ground (Part 1 of 3). 2000–02

CONDITIONS | **DETAILS/RESULTS/ACTIONS**

E4 CHECK THE AIR SUSPENSION HEIGHT SENSOR

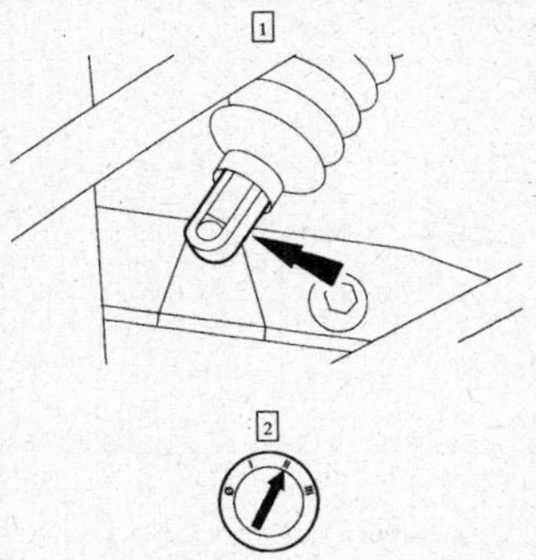

1 Disconnect the lower end of the air suspension height sensor (5359).

3 Monitor the rear air suspension control module PID ASR__HGT.

4 While monitoring the rear air suspension control module PID ASR__HGT display, slowly extend and compress the air suspension height sensor through the full range of motion.

- Does the rear air suspension control module PID ASR__HGT indicate HIGH, TRIM and LOW?

→ **Yes**
INSTALL a new rear air suspension control module. REPEAT the Self-Test.

→ **No**
INSTALL a new air suspension height sensor. CLEAR the DTCs. REPEAT the Self-Test.

FM2010200834030X

Fig. 12 Test E/Code C1723: Height Sensor Power Circuit Short To Ground (Part 3 of 3). 2000–02

CONDITIONS	DETAILS/RESULTS/ACTIONS

F1 CHECK CIRCUIT 428 (OG/BK) FOR SHORT TO POWER

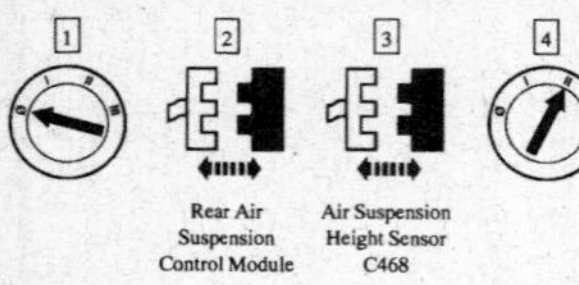

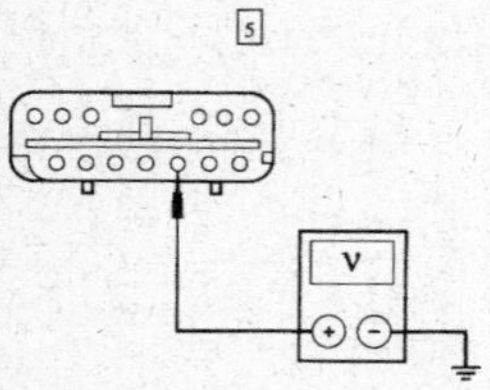

5 Measure the voltage between rear air suspension control module C250 Pin 3, Circuit 428 (OG/BK), harness side and ground.

- Is voltage present?

→ **Yes**
REPAIR the circuit. CLEAR the DTCs. REPEAT the Self-Test.

→ **No**
GO to **F2**.

F2 CHECK CIRCUIT 427 (PK/BK) FOR SHORT TO POWER

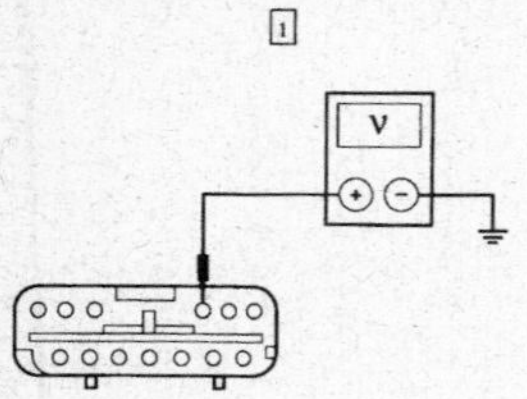

1 Measure the voltage between rear air suspension control module C250 Pin 17, Circuit 427 (PK/BK), harness side and ground.

- Is voltage present?

→ **Yes**
REPAIR the circuit. CLEAR the DTCs. REPEAT the Self-Test.

→ **No**
GO to **F3**.

FM2010200835010X

Fig. 13 Test F/Codes C1760 & C1765: Rear Height Sensor High/Low Signal Circuit Failure (Part 1 of 3). 2000–02

CONDITIONS	DETAILS/RESULTS/ACTIONS

F3 CHECK THE HEIGHT SENSOR CIRCUITRY FOR AN OPEN

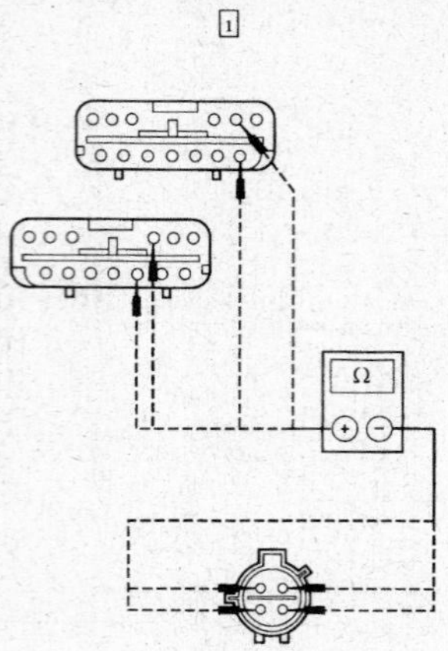

1 Measure the resistance between rear air suspension control module electrical connectors and height sensor electrical connectors; refer to the following table:

Rear Air Suspension Control Module	Air Suspen-sion Height Sensor	Circuit No.
C250 Pin 3	C468 Pin 4	428 (OG/BK)
C250 Pin 17	C468 Pin 2	427 (PK/BK)
C251 Pin 8	C468 Pin 1	432 (BK/PK)
C251 Pin 22	C468 Pin 3	417 (VT/OG)

- Are the resistances less than 5 ohms?

→ **Yes**
RECONNECT the rear air suspension control module C250, C251 and air suspension height sensor C468. GO to **F4**.

→ **No**
REPAIR the circuit in question. CLEAR the DTCs. REPEAT the Self-Test.

FM2010200835020X

Fig. 13 Test F/Codes C1760 & C1765: Rear Height Sensor High/Low Signal Circuit Failure (Part 2 of 3). 2000–02

CONDITIONS	DETAILS/RESULTS/ACTIONS

F4 CHECK THE AIR SUSPENSION HEIGHT SENSOR

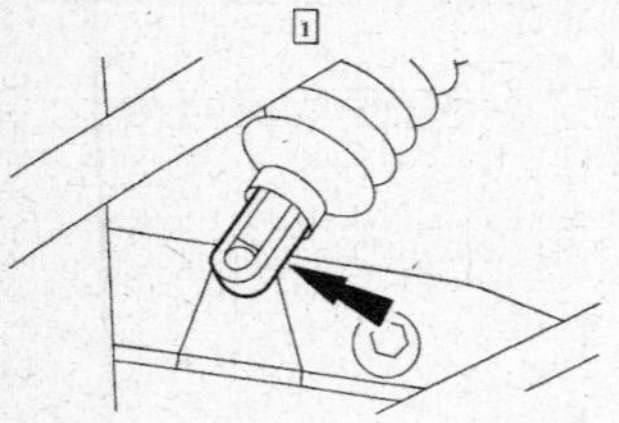

1 Disconnect the lower end of the air suspension height sensor.

3 Monitor the rear air suspension control module PID ASR_HGT.

4 While monitoring the rear air suspension control module PID ASR_HGT display, slowly extend and compress the air suspension height sensor through the full range of motion.

- Does the rear air suspension control module PID ASR_HGT indicate HIGH, TRIM and LOW?

→ **Yes**
INSTALL a new rear air suspension control module.
REPEAT the Self-Test.

→ **No**
INSTALL a new air suspension height sensor.
. REPEAT the Self-Test.

FM2010200835030X

Fig. 13 Test F/Codes C1760 & C1765: Rear Height Sensor High/Low Signal Circuit Failure (Part 3 of 3). 2000–02

CONDITIONS	DETAILS/RESULTS/ACTIONS

G1 CHECK CIRCUIT 427 (PK/BK) FOR SHORT TO GROUND

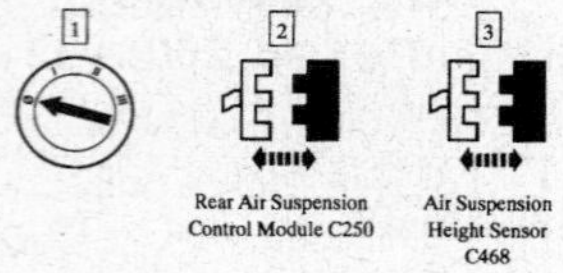

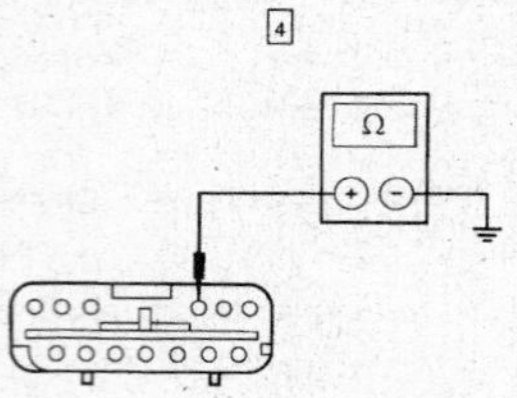

4 Measure the resistance between rear air suspension control module C250 Pin 17, Circuit 427 (PK/BK), harness side and ground.

- Is the resistance greater than 10,000 ohms?

→ **Yes**
RECONNECT the rear air suspension control module C250 and air suspension height sensor C468. GO to **G2**.

→ **No**
REPAIR the circuit. CLEAR the DTCs. REPEAT the Self-Test.

FM2010200836010X

Fig. 14 Test G/Code C1763: Height Rear Sensor High Signal Circuit Short To Ground (Part 1 of 2). 2000–02

CONDITIONS	DETAILS/RESULTS/ACTIONS
G2 CHECK THE AIR SUSPENSION HEIGHT SENSOR	
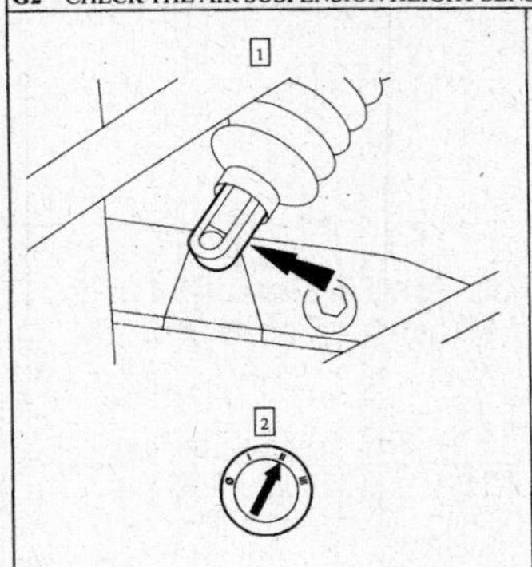	1 Disconnect the lower end of the air suspension height sensor. 3 Monitor the rear air suspension control module PID ASR_HGT. 4 While monitoring the rear air suspension control module PID ASR_HGT display, slowly extend and compress the air suspension height sensor through the full range of motion. • Does the rear air suspension control module PID ASR_HGT indicate HIGH, TRIM and LOW? → **Yes** INSTALL a new rear air suspension control module. REPEAT the Self-Test. → **No** INSTALL a new air suspension height sensor. REPEAT the Self-Test.

FM2010200836020X

Fig. 14 Test G/Code C1763: Height Rear Sensor High Signal Circuit Short To Ground (Part 2 of 2). 2000–02

CONDITIONS	DETAILS/RESULTS/ACTIONS
H2 CHECK THE AIR SUSPENSION HEIGHT SENSOR	
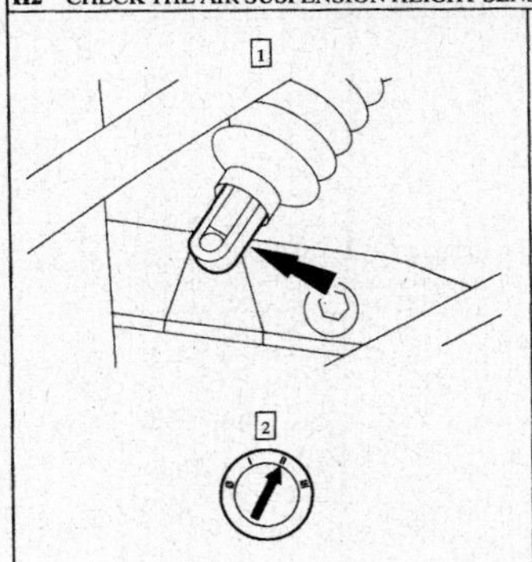	1 Disconnect the lower end of the air suspension height sensor. 3 Monitor the rear air suspension control module PID ASR_HGT. 4 While monitoring the rear air suspension control module PID ASR_HGT display, slowly extend and compress the air suspension height sensor through the full range of motion. • Does the rear air suspension control module PID ASR_HGT indicate HIGH, TRIM and LOW? → **Yes** INSTALL a new rear air suspension control module. REPEAT the Self-Test. → **No** INSTALL a new air suspension height sensor. REPEAT the Self-Test.

FM2010200837020X

Fig. 15 Test H/Code C1768: Rear Height Sensor Low Signal Circuit Short To Ground (Part 2 of 2). 2000–02

CONDITIONS	DETAILS/RESULTS/ACTIONS
H1 CHECK CIRCUIT 428 (OG/BK) FOR SHORT TO GROUND	
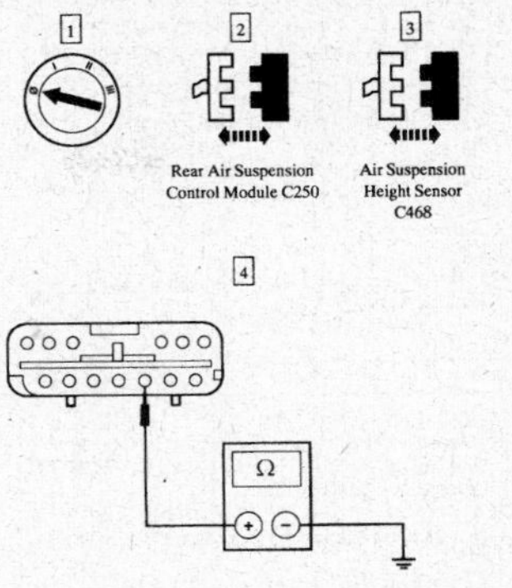	4 Measure the resistance between rear air suspension control module C250 Pin 3, Circuit 428 (OG/BK), harness side and ground. • Is the resistance greater than 10,000 ohms? → **Yes** RECONNECT the rear air suspension control module C250 and air suspension height sensor C468. GO to **H2**. → **No** REPAIR the circuit. CLEAR the DTCs. REPEAT the Self-Test.

FM2010200837010X

Fig. 15 Test H/Code C1768: Rear Height Sensor Low Signal Circuit Short To Ground (Part 1 of 2). 2000–02

CONDITIONS	DETAILS/RESULTS/ACTIONS
I1 CHECK CIRCUIT 421 (PK) FOR SHORT TO POWER	
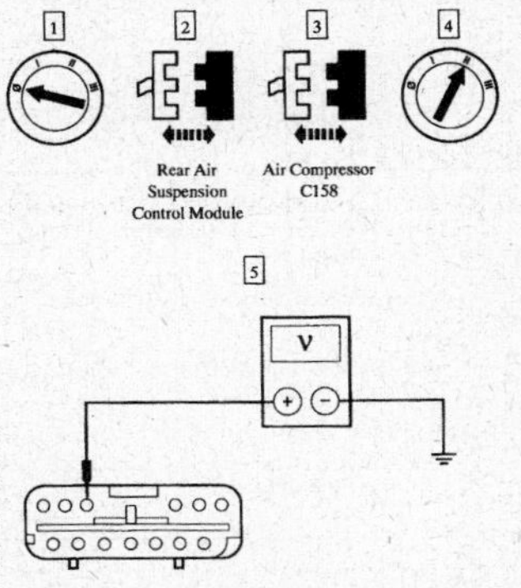	5 Measure the voltage between rear air suspension control module C251 Pin 24, Circuit 421 (PK), harness side and ground. • Is voltage present? → **Yes** REPAIR the circuit. CLEAR the DTCs. REPEAT the Self-Test. → **No** GO to **I2**.
I2 CHECK CIRCUIT 421 (PK) FOR AN OPEN	
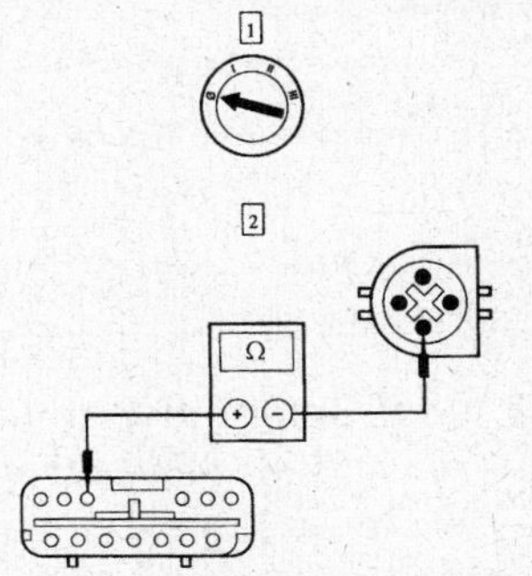	2 Measure the resistance between rear air suspension control module C251 Pin 24, Circuit 421 (PK), harness side and air compressor C158 Pin 2, Circuit 421 (PK), harness side. • Is the resistance less than 5 ohms? → **Yes** GO to **I3**. → **No** REPAIR the circuit. CLEAR the DTCs. REPEAT the Self-Test.

FM2010200838010X

Fig. 16 Test I/Code C1770: Vent Solenoid Output Circuit Failure (Part 1 of 2). 2000–02

CONDITIONS	DETAILS/RESULTS/ACTIONS
I3 CHECK CIRCUIT 57 (BK) FOR AN OPEN	
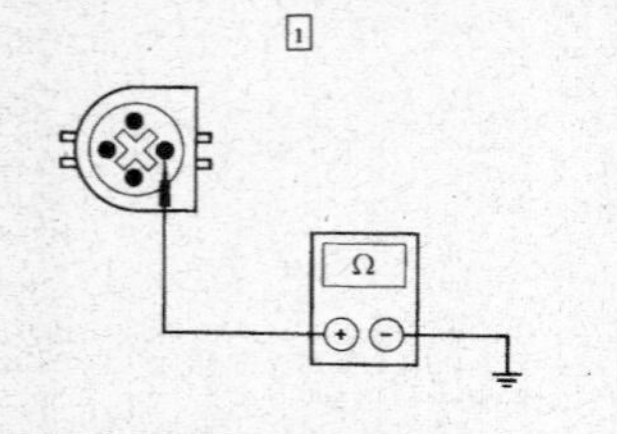	1 Measure the resistance between air compressor C158 Pin 4, Circuit 57 (BK), harness side and ground. • Is the resistance less than 5 ohms? → **Yes** RECONNECT air compressor C158. GO to **I4**. → **No** REPAIR the circuit. CLEAR the DTCs. REPEAT the Self-Test.
I4 CHECK THE AIR COMPRESSOR	
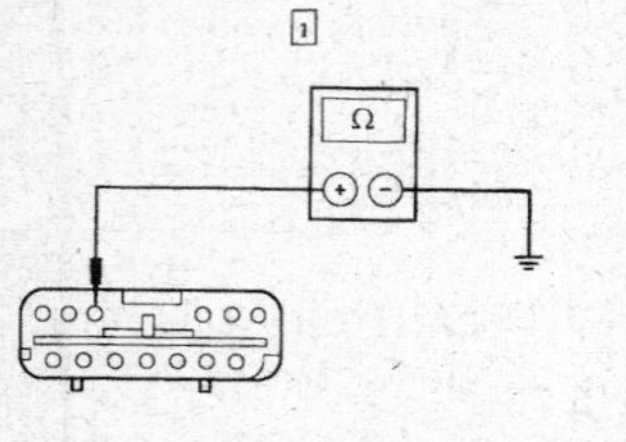	1 Measure the resistance between rear air suspension control module C251 Pin 24, Circuit 421 (PK), harness side and ground. • Is the resistance approximately 31 ohms? → **Yes** INSTALL a new rear air suspension control module. REPEAT the Self-Test. → **No** INSTALL a new air compressor (5319). CLEAR the DTCs. REPEAT the Self-Test.

FM2010200838020X

Fig. 16 Test I/Code C1770: Vent Solenoid Output Circuit Failure (Part 2 of 2). 2000–02

CONDITIONS	DETAILS/RESULTS/ACTIONS
J1 CHECK CIRCUIT 421 (PK) FOR SHORT TO GROUND (Continued)	
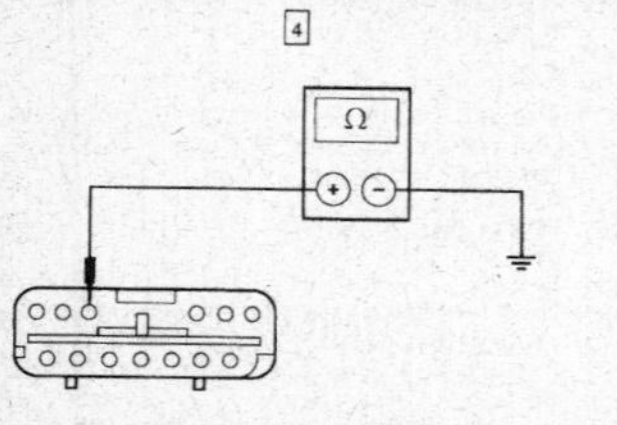	4 Measure the resistance between rear air suspension control module C251 Pin 24, Circuit 421 (PK), harness side and ground. • Is the resistance greater than 10,000 ohms? → **Yes** RECONNECT air compressor C158. GO to **J2**. → **No** REPAIR the circuit. CLEAR the DTCs. REPEAT the Self-Test.
J2 CHECK THE AIR COMPRESSOR	
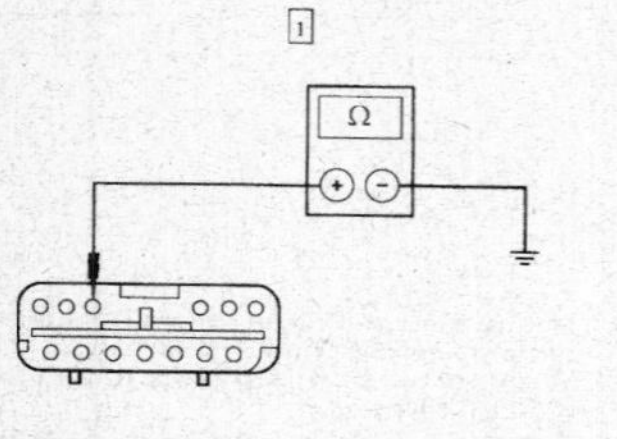	1 Measure the resistance between rear air suspension control module C251 Pin 24, Circuit 421 (PK), harness side and ground. • Is the resistance approximately 31 ohms? → **Yes** INSTALL a new rear air suspension control module. REPEAT the Self-Test. → **No** INSTALL a new air compressor. CLEAR the DTCs. REPEAT the Self-Test.

FM2010200839020X

Fig. 17 Test J/Code C1773: Vent Solenoid Output Circuit Short To Ground (Part 2 of 2). 2000–02

CONDITIONS	DETAILS/RESULTS/ACTIONS
J1 CHECK CIRCUIT 421 (PK) FOR SHORT TO GROUND	
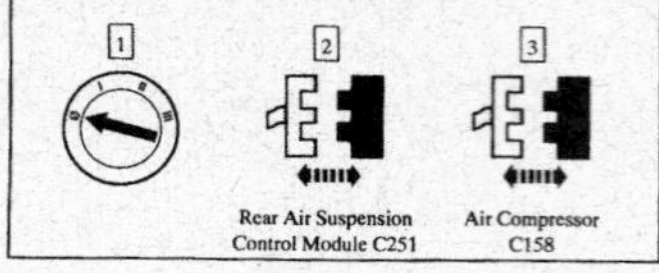	

FM2010200839010X

Fig. 17 Test J/Code C1773: Vent Solenoid Output Circuit Short To Ground (Part 1 of 2). 2000–02

CONDITIONS	DETAILS/RESULTS/ACTIONS
K1 CHECK CIRCUIT 1114 (BN/PK) FOR SHORT TO POWER	
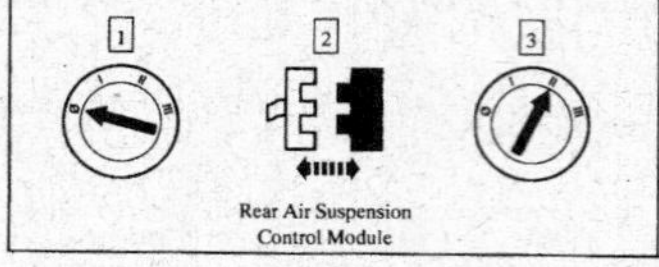	

FM2010200840010X

Fig. 18 Test K/Code C1790: LR Air Spring Solenoid Output Circuit Failure (Part 1 of 3). 2000–02

CONDITIONS	DETAILS/RESULTS/ACTIONS
K1 CHECK CIRCUIT 1114 (BN/PK) FOR SHORT TO POWER (Continued)	
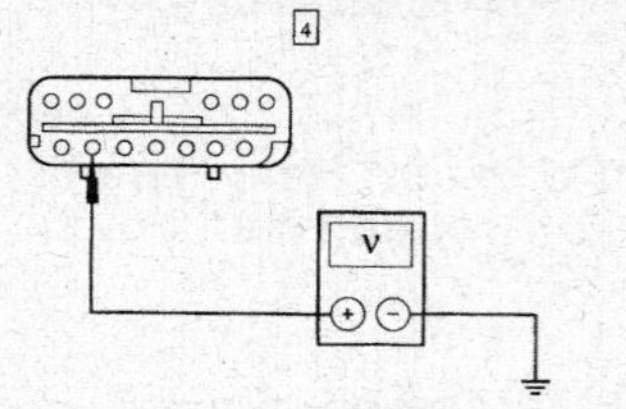	4 Measure the voltage between rear air suspension control module C251 Pin 13, Circuit 1114 (BN/PK), harness side and ground. • Is voltage present? → **Yes** REPAIR the circuit. CLEAR the DTCs. REPEAT the Self-Test. → **No** GO to **K2**.
K2 CHECK THE REAR AIR SUSPENSION CONTROL MODULE	

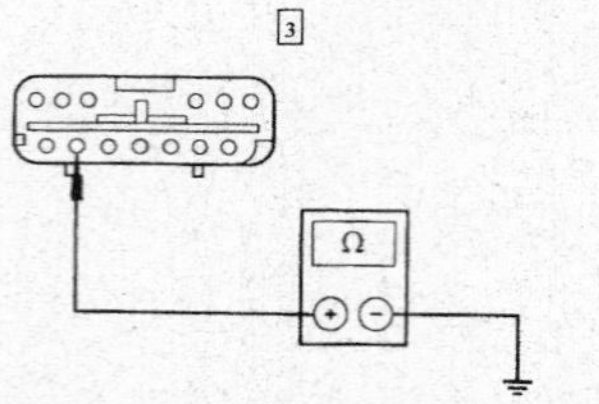	3 Measure the resistance between rear air suspension control module C251 Pin 13, Circuit 1114 (BN/PK), harness side and ground. • Is the resistance approximately 16 ohms? → **Yes** INSTALL a new rear air suspension control module. REPEAT the Self-Test. → **No** GO to **K3**.
K3 CHECK CIRCUIT 1114 (BN/PK) FOR AN OPEN	

FM2010200840020X

Fig. 18 Test K/Code C1790: LR Air Spring Solenoid Output Circuit Failure (Part 2 of 3). 2000–02

CONDITIONS	DETAILS/RESULTS/ACTIONS
K3 CHECK CIRCUIT 1114 (BN/PK) FOR AN OPEN (Continued)	
2 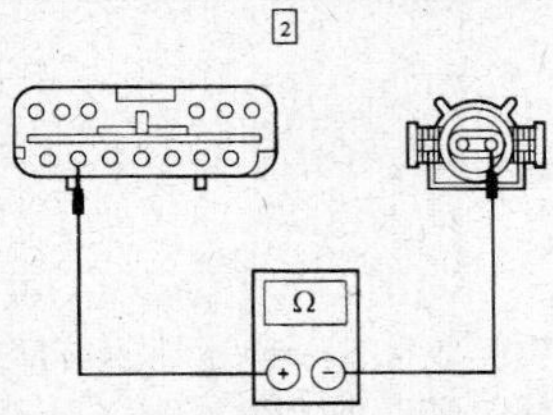	2 Measure the resistance between rear air suspension control module C251 Pin 13, Circuit 1114 (BN/PK), harness side and LR air spring solenoid C492, Circuit 1114 (BN/PK), harness side. • Is the resistance less than 5 ohms? → **Yes** GO to **K4**. → **No** REPAIR the circuit. CLEAR the DTCs. REPEAT the Self-Test.
K4 CHECK CIRCUIT 57 (BK) FOR AN OPEN	
1 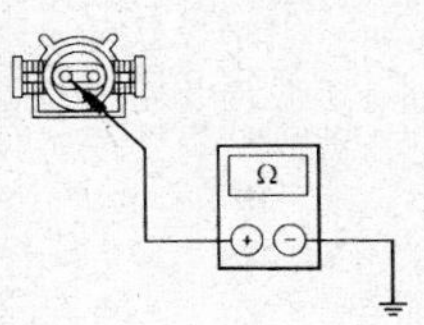	1 Measure the resistance between LR air spring solenoid C492, Circuit 57 (BK), harness side and ground. • Is the resistance less than 5 ohms? → **Yes** INSTALL a new LR air spring solenoid. CLEAR the DTCs. REPEAT the Self-Test. → **No** REPAIR the circuit. CLEAR the DTCs. REPEAT the Self-Test.

FM2010200840030X

Fig. 18 Test K/Code C1790: LR Air Spring Solenoid Output Circuit Failure (Part 3 of 3). 2000–02

CONDITIONS	DETAILS/RESULTS/ACTIONS
L1 CHECK THE REAR AIR SUSPENSION CONTROL MODULE (Continued)	
3 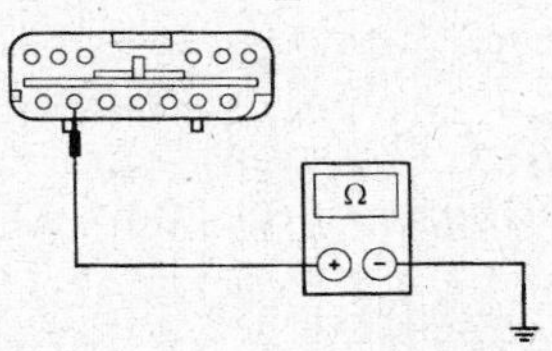	3 Measure the resistance between rear air suspension control module C251 Pin 13, Circuit 1114 (BN/PK), harness side and ground. • Is the resistance approximately 16 ohms? → **Yes** INSTALL a new rear air suspension control module. REPEAT the Self-Test. → **No** GO to **L2**.
L2 CHECK CIRCUIT 1114 (BN/PK) FOR SHORT TO GROUND	
1  LR Air Spring Solenoid C492	
2 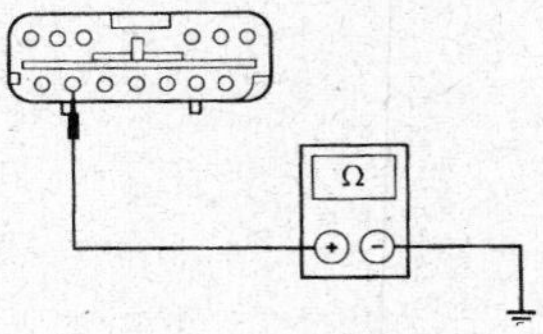	2 Measure the resistance between rear air suspension control module C251 Pin 13, Circuit 1114 (BN/PK), harness side and ground. • Is the resistance greater than 10,000 ohms? → **Yes** INSTALL a new LR air spring solenoid. CLEAR the DTCs. REPEAT the Self-Test. → **No** REPAIR the circuit. CLEAR the DTCs. REPEAT the Self-Test.

FM2010200841020X

Fig. 19 Test L/Code C1793: LR Air Spring Solenoid Output Circuit Short To Ground (Part 2 of 2). 2000–02

CONDITIONS	DETAILS/RESULTS/ACTIONS
L1 CHECK THE REAR AIR SUSPENSION CONTROL MODULE	
1 2  Rear Air Suspension Control Module C251	

FM2010200841010X

Fig. 19 Test L/Code C1793: LR Air Spring Solenoid Output Circuit Short To Ground (Part 1 of 2). 2000–02

CONDITIONS	DETAILS/RESULTS/ACTIONS
M1 CHECK CIRCUIT 1115 (TN/WH) FOR SHORT TO POWER	
1 2 3  Rear Air Suspension Control Module	
4 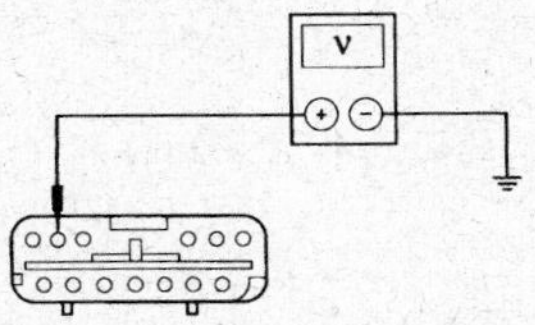	4 Measure the voltage between rear air suspension control module C251 Pin 25, Circuit 1115 (TN/WH), harness side and ground. • Is voltage present? → **Yes** REPAIR the circuit. CLEAR the DTCs. REPEAT the Self-Test. → **No** GO to **M2**.
M2 CHECK THE REAR AIR SUSPENSION CONTROL MODULE	
1 2  RR Air Spring Solenoid C467	
3 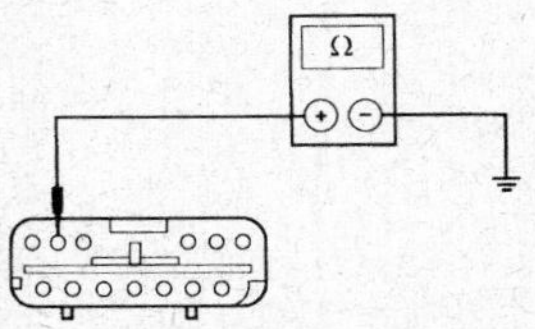	3 Measure the resistance between rear air suspension control module C251 Pin 25, Circuit 1115 (TN/WH), harness side and ground. • Is the resistance approximately 16 ohms? → **Yes** INSTALL a new rear air suspension control module. REPEAT the Self-Test. → **No** GO to **M3**.

FM2010200842010X

Fig. 20 Test M/Code C1795: RR Air Spring Solenoid Output Circuit Failure (Part 1 of 2). 2000–02

CONDITIONS	DETAILS/RESULTS/ACTIONS
M3 CHECK CIRCUIT 1115 (TN/WH) FOR AN OPEN	
[1] 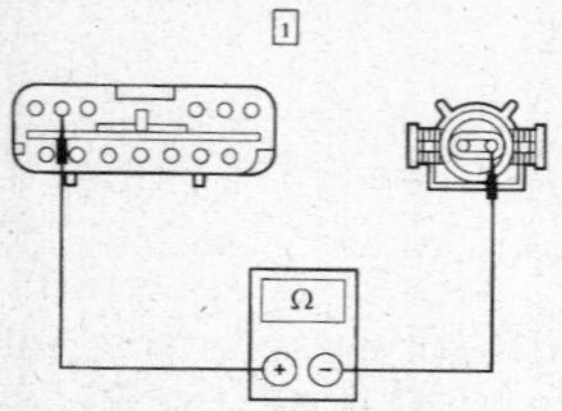	[1] Measure the resistance between rear air suspension control module C251 Pin 25, Circuit 1115 (TN/WH), harness side and RR air spring solenoid C467, Circuit 1114 (BN/PK), harness side. • Is the resistance less than 5 ohms? → **Yes** GO to **M4**. → **No** REPAIR the circuit. CLEAR the DTCs. REPEAT the Self-Test.
M4 CHECK CIRCUIT 57 (BK) FOR AN OPEN	
[1] 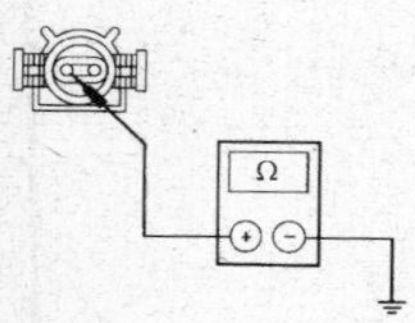	[1] Measure the resistance between RR air spring solenoid C467, Circuit 57 (BK), harness side and ground. • Is the resistance less than 5 ohms? → **Yes** INSTALL a new RR air spring solenoid. CLEAR the DTCs. REPEAT the Self-Test. → **No** REPAIR the circuit. CLEAR the DTCs. REPEAT the Self-Test.

FM2010200842020X

Fig. 20 Test M/Code C1795: RR Air Spring Solenoid Output Circuit Failure (Part 2 of 2). 2000–02

CONDITIONS	DETAILS/RESULTS/ACTIONS
N1 CHECK THE REAR AIR SUSPENSION CONTROL MODULE (Continued)	
[3] 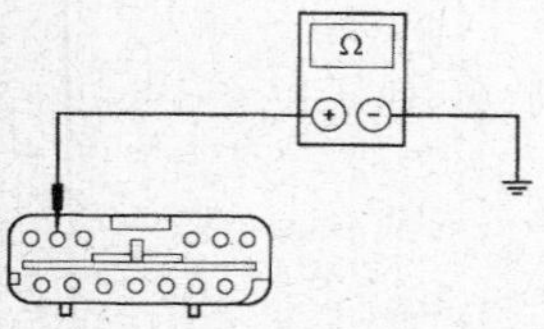	[3] Measure the resistance between rear air suspension control module C251 Pin 25, Circuit 1115 (TN/WH), harness side and ground. • Is the resistance approximately 16 ohms? → **Yes** INSTALL a new rear air suspension control module. REPEAT the Self-Test. → **No** GO to **N2**.
N2 CHECK CIRCUIT 1115 (TN/WH) FOR SHORT TO GROUND	
[1]  RR Air Spring Solenoid C467	
[2] 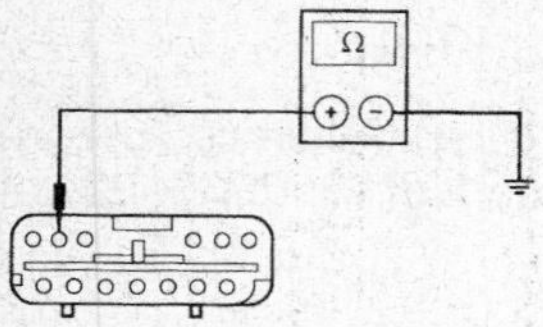	[2] Measure the resistance between rear air suspension control module C251 Pin 25, Circuit 1115 (TN/WH), harness side and ground. • Is the resistance greater than 10,000 ohms? → **Yes** INSTALL a new RR air spring solenoid. CLEAR the DTCs. REPEAT the Self-Test. → **No** REPAIR the circuit. CLEAR the DTCs. REPEAT the Self-Test.

FM2010200843020X

Fig. 21 Test N/Code C1798: RR Air Spring Solenoid Output Circuit Short To Ground (Part 2 of 2). 2000–02

CONDITIONS	DETAILS/RESULTS/ACTIONS
N1 CHECK THE REAR AIR SUSPENSION CONTROL MODULE	
[1] 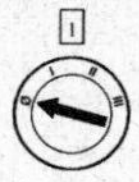 [2]  Rear Air Suspension Control Module C251	

FM2010200843010X

Fig. 21 Test N/Code C1798: RR Air Spring Solenoid Output Circuit Short To Ground (Part 1 of 2). 2000–02

CONDITIONS	DETAILS/RESULTS/ACTIONS
O1 CHECK THE AIR SUSPENSION HEIGHT SENSOR	
[1] 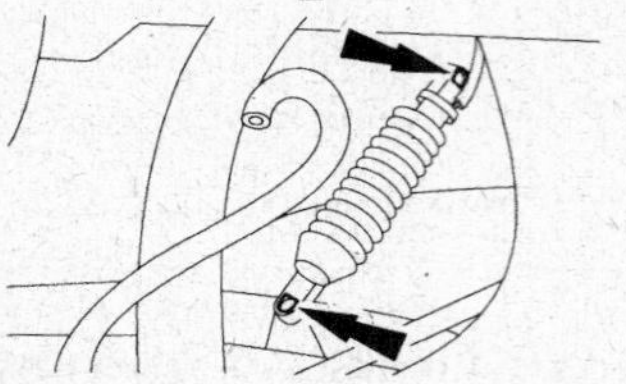	[1] Check the air suspension height sensor for correct installation at the upper and lower ball stud brackets.
	[2] Check the air suspension height sensor mounting brackets for damage. • Are the air suspension height sensor and mounting brackets OK? → **Yes** GO to **O2**. → **No** REPAIR as necessary. CLEAR the DTCs. REPEAT the Self-Test.

FM2010200844010X

Fig. 22 Test O/Code C1813: Vent Request Exceeded Maximum Timing (Part 1 of 5). 2000–02

CONDITIONS	DETAILS/RESULTS/ACTIONS
O2 CHECK AIR SUSPENSION HEIGHT SENSOR OPERATION	
[1] 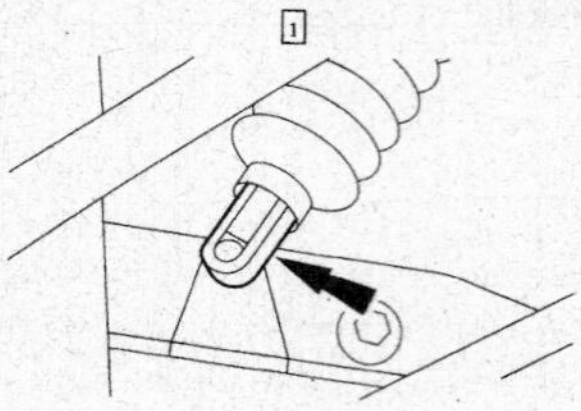	[1] Disconnect the lower end of the air suspension height sensor.
[2] 	
	[3] Monitor the rear air suspension control module PID ASR_HGT.
	[4] While monitoring the rear air suspension control module PID ASR_HGT display, slowly extend and compress the air suspension height sensor through the full range of motion. • Does the rear air suspension control module PID ASR_HGT indicate HIGH, TRIM and LOW? → **Yes** GO to **O3**. → **No** INSTALL a new air suspension height sensor. CLEAR the DTCs. REPEAT the Self-Test.
O3 CHECK PNEUMATIC SYSTEM — VENT LR AIR SPRING	
NOTE: If fluid is present when disconnecting the air line, clear the air lines; refer to Air Line Fluid Purge. Check the air compressor drier for water or the air compressor for oil contamination. **NOTE:** The rear springs must be partially inflated in order to perform this test. Add air as necessary.	
	[1] Disconnect the air compressor drier air line.

FM2010200844020X

Fig. 22 Test O/Code C1813: Vent Request Exceeded Maximum Timing (Part 2 of 5). 2000–02

CONDITIONS	DETAILS/RESULTS/ACTIONS
O3 CHECK PNEUMATIC SYSTEM — VENT LR AIR SPRING (Continued)	
	2 Trigger the rear air suspension control module active command LR SOL ON. • Does the air vent from the air compressor drier air line? → **Yes** Trigger the rear air suspension control module active command LR SOL OFF. GO to **O4**. → **No** Trigger the rear air suspension control module active command LR SOL OFF. GO to **O5**.
O4 CHECK PNEUMATIC SYSTEM — VENT RR AIR SPRING	
NOTE: The rear springs must be partially inflated in order to perform this test. Add air as necessary.	
	1 Trigger the rear air suspension control module active command RR SOL ON. • Does the air vent from the air compressor drier air line? → **Yes** Trigger the rear air suspension control module active command RR SOL OFF. GO to **O6**. → **No** Trigger the rear air suspension control module active command RR SOL OFF. GO to **O5**.
O5 CHECK PNEUMATIC SYSTEM — AIR LINE	
NOTE: If fluid is present when disconnecting the air line, clear the air lines; refer to Air Line Fluid Purge. Check the air compressor drier for water or the air compressor for oil.	
	1 Disconnect the suspected rear air spring solenoid air line.

FM2010200844030X

Fig. 22 Test O/Code C1813: Vent Request Exceeded Maximum Timing (Part 3 of 5). 2000–02

CONDITIONS	DETAILS/RESULTS/ACTIONS
O5 CHECK PNEUMATIC SYSTEM — AIR LINE (Continued)	
	2 Connect Vacuum Tester to the air line and try to pull a vacuum. • Can a vacuum be developed? → **Yes** REPAIR or INSTALL a new air line. CLEAR the DTCs. REPEAT the Self-Test. → **No** INSTALL a new air spring solenoid. CLEAR the DTCs. REPEAT the Self-Test.
O6 CHECK VENT SOLENOID OPERATION	
	1 Disconnect the air line at the snorkel. 2 Connect Vacuum Tester to the snorkel air line and try to pull a vacuum. 3 Trigger the rear air suspension control module active command VENT ON. 4 Try to pull a vacuum again. • Can a vacuum be developed with the rear air suspension control module active command VENT OFF and no vacuum developed with the rear air suspension control module active command VENT ON? → **Yes** INSTALL a new rear air suspension control module REPEAT the Self-Test. → **No** If no vacuum can be developed with the rear air suspension control module active command VENT OFF, GO to **O7**. If a vacuum can be developed with the rear air suspension control module active command VENT ON, GO to **O8**.

FM2010200844040X

Fig. 22 Test O/Code C1813: Vent Request Exceeded Maximum Timing (Part 4 of 5). 2000–02

CONDITIONS	DETAILS/RESULTS/ACTIONS
O7 CHECK THE AIR LINE AND CONNECTIONS	
	1 Check the air line and connections between Vacuum Tester and the air compressor. • Are the air line and connections OK? → **Yes** INSTALL a new air compressor. CLEAR the DTCs. REPEAT the Self-Test. → **No** REPAIR as necessary. CLEAR the DTCs. REPEAT the Self-Test.
O8 CHECK AIR COMPRESSOR DRIER	
	1 Disconnect the air compressor drier. 2 Try to pull a vacuum. • Can a vacuum be developed? → **Yes** INSTALL a new air compressor. CLEAR the DTCs. REPEAT the Self-Test. → **No** INSTALL a new air compressor drier. CLEAR the DTCs. REPEAT the Self-Test.

FM2010200844050X

Fig. 22 Test O/Code C1813: Vent Request Exceeded Maximum Timing (Part 5 of 5). 2000–02

CONDITIONS	DETAILS/RESULTS/ACTIONS
P1 CHECK AIR SUSPENSION HEIGHT SENSOR	
1 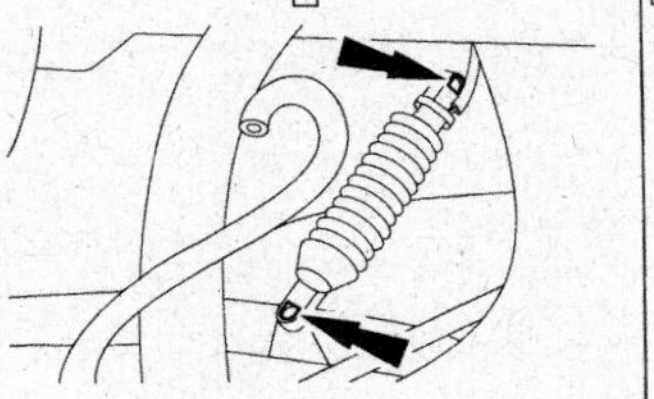	1 Check the air suspension height sensor for correct installation at the upper and lower ball stud brackets. 2 Check the air suspension height sensor mounting brackets for damage. • Are the air suspension height sensor and mounting brackets OK? → **Yes** GO to **P2**. → **No** REPAIR as necessary. CLEAR the DTCs. REPEAT the Self-Test.

FM2010200845010X

Fig. 23 Test P/Code C1818: Air Compressor Request Exceeded Maximum Timing (Part 1 of 10). 2000–02

CONDITIONS	DETAILS/RESULTS/ACTIONS
P2 CHECK AIR SUSPENSION HEIGHT SENSOR OPERATION	
1 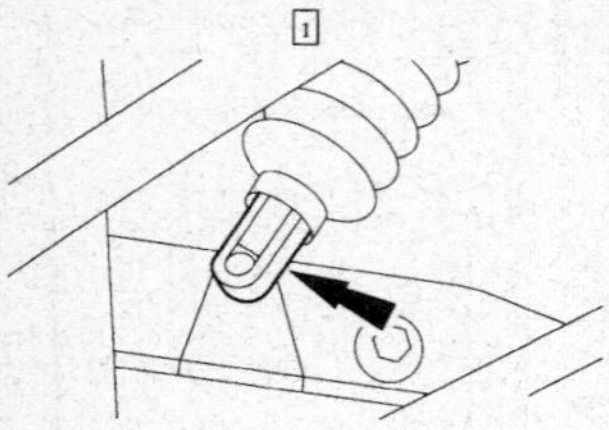 2 	1 Disconnect the lower end of the air suspension height sensor. 3 Monitor the rear air suspension control module PID ASR_HGT. 4 While monitoring the rear air suspension control module PID ASR_HGT display, slowly extend and compress the air suspension height sensor through the full range of motion. • Does the rear air suspension control module PID ASR_HGT indicate HIGH, TRIM and LOW? → **Yes** GO to **P3**. → **No** INSTALL a new air suspension height sensor. CLEAR the DTCs. REPEAT the Self-Test.

FM2010200845020X

Fig. 23 Test P/Code C1818: Air Compressor Request Exceeded Maximum Timing (Part 2 of 10). 2000–02

CONDITIONS	DETAILS/RESULTS/ACTIONS
P3 CHECK OPERATION OF AIR COMPRESSOR	
⚠ **CAUTION: If the air compressor runs in this test, do not allow the air compressor to run for more than three minutes. The air compressor could overheat and stop operation due to an internal temperature sensitive thermal breaker.**	
	1 Trigger the rear air suspension control module active command COMPRESSR ON. • Does the air compressor run? → **Yes** Trigger the rear air suspension control module active command COMPRESSR OFF. GO to **P11**. → **No** Trigger the rear air suspension control module active command COMPRESSR OFF. GO to **P4**.
P4 CHECK AIR COMPRESSOR AFTER COOL DOWN PERIOD	
⚠ **CAUTION: If the air compressor runs in this test, do not allow the air compressor to run for more than three minutes. The air compressor could overheat and stop operation due to an internal temperature sensitive thermal breaker.**	
	1 Allow the vehicle to sit for 60 minutes to give the air compressor time to cool off. 2 Trigger the rear air suspension control module active commands VENT ON and COMPRESSR ON. • Does the air compressor run? → **Yes** Trigger the rear air suspension control module active commands OFF. GO to **P5**. → **No** Trigger the rear air suspension control module active commands OFF. GO to **P6**.

FM2010200845030X

Fig. 23 Test P/Code C1818: Air Compressor Request Exceeded Maximum Timing (Part 3 of 10). 2000–02

CONDITIONS	DETAILS/RESULTS/ACTIONS
P5 CHECK AIR COMPRESSOR THERMAL BREAKER	
⚠ **CAUTION: If the air compressor runs in this test, do not allow the air compressor to run for more than three minutes. The air compressor could overheat and stop operation due to an internal temperature sensitive thermal breaker.**	
	1 Trigger the rear air suspension control module active commands VENT ON and COMPRESSR ON for 60 seconds. • Did the air compressor run for 60 seconds? → **Yes** The thermal breaker was overheated. CLEAR the DTCs. REPEAT the Self-Test. → **No** INSTALL a new air compressor. CLEAR the DTCs. REPEAT the Self-Test.
P6 CHECK AIR COMPRESSOR RELAY	
1  2  Air Compressor Relay	3 Check the air compressor relay connector pins and terminals for corrosion, bent or broken pins, moisture or other damage. • Is the air compressor relay OK? → **Yes** GO to **P7**. → **No** REPAIR as necessary. CLEAR the DTCs. REPEAT the Self-Test.

FM2010200845040X

Fig. 23 Test P/Code C1818: Air Compressor Request Exceeded Maximum Timing (Part 4 of 10). 2000–02

CONDITIONS	DETAILS/RESULTS/ACTIONS
P7 CHECK CIRCUIT 1053 (LB/PK) FOR VOLTAGE	
1 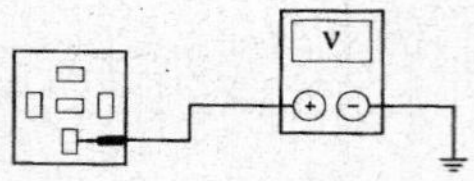	1 Measure the voltage between air compressor relay Pin 30, Circuit 1053 (LB/PK), harness side and ground. • Is the voltage greater than 10 volts? → **Yes** GO to **P8**. → **No** REPAIR the circuit. CLEAR the DTCs. REPEAT the Self-Test.
P8 CHECK CIRCUITRY FROM AIR COMPRESSOR RELAY	
1 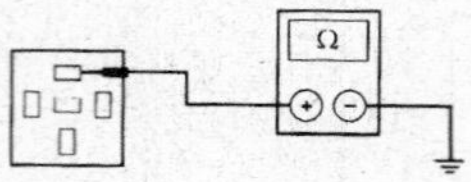	1 Measure the resistance between air compressor relay Pin 87, Circuit 538 (GY/RD), harness side and ground. • Is the resistance less than 5 ohms? → **Yes** INSTALL a new air compressor relay. CLEAR the DTCs. REPEAT the Self-Test. → **No** GO to **P9**.
P9 CHECK CIRCUIT 538 (GY/RD) FOR AN OPEN	
1  Air Compressor C158	

FM2010200845050X

Fig. 23 Test P/Code C1818: Air Compressor Request Exceeded Maximum Timing (Part 5 of 10). 2000–02

CONDITIONS	DETAILS/RESULTS/ACTIONS
P9 CHECK CIRCUIT 538 (GY/RD) FOR AN OPEN (Continued)	
2 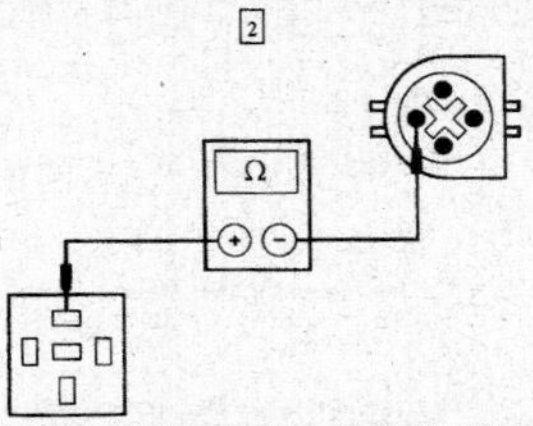	2 Measure the resistance between air compressor relay Pin 87, Circuit 538 (GY/RD), harness side and air compressor C158 Pin 1, Circuit 538 (GY/RD), harness side. • Is the resistance less than 5 ohms? → **Yes** GO to **P10**. → **No** REPAIR the circuit. CLEAR the DTCs. REPEAT the Self-Test.
P10 CHECK CIRCUIT 57 (BK) FOR AN OPEN	
1 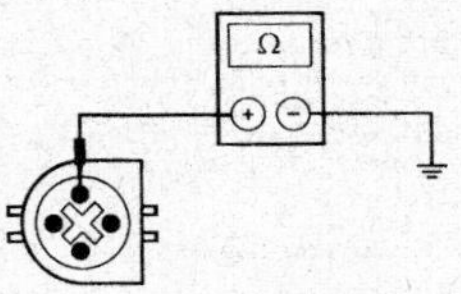	1 Measure the resistance between air compressor C158 Pin 3, Circuit 57 (BK), harness side and ground. • Is the resistance less than 5 ohms? → **Yes** INSTALL a new air compressor. CLEAR the DTCs. REPEAT the Self-Test. → **No** REPAIR the circuit. CLEAR the DTCs. REPEAT the Self-Test.
P11 CHECK AIR COMPRESSOR PRESSURE OUTPUT	
⚠ **CAUTION: If the air compressor runs in this test, do not allow the air compressor to run for more than three minutes. The air compressor could overheat and stop operation due to an internal temperature sensitive thermal breaker.** **NOTE:** If fluid is present when disconnecting the air line, clear the air lines; refer to Air Line Fluid Purge. Check the air compressor drier for water or the air compressor for oil.	
	1 Disconnect the air compressor air line. 2 Connect an air gauge (1,723 kPa [250 psi] maximum reading) with common fittings to the air compressor drier. 3 Trigger the rear air suspension control module active command COMPRESSR ON.

FM2010200845060X

Fig. 23 Test P/Code C1818: Air Compressor Request Exceeded Maximum Timing (Part 6 of 10). 2000–02

CONDITIONS	DETAILS/RESULTS/ACTIONS
P13 CHECK AIR LINES (Continued)	
	2 Try to pull a vacuum. • Can a vacuum be developed? → **Yes** GO to **P16**. → **No** GO to **P14**.
P14 CHECK THE LR AIR SPRING SOLENOID FOR LEAK	
NOTE: If fluid is present when disconnecting the air line, clear the air lines; refer to Air Line Fluid Purge. Check the air compressor drier for water or the air compressor for oil.	
	1 Disconnect the LR air spring solenoid air line. 2 Plug the air line at the LR air spring solenoid. 3 Try to pull a vacuum. • Can a vacuum be developed? → **Yes** INSTALL a new LR air spring solenoid. CLEAR the DTCs. REPEAT the Self-Test. → **No** GO to **P15**.
P15 CHECK RR AIR SPRING SOLENOID FOR LEAK	
NOTE: If fluid is present when disconnecting the air line, clear the air lines; refer to Air Line Fluid Purge. Check the air compressor drier for water or the air compressor for oil.	
	1 Disconnect the RR air spring solenoid air line. 2 Plug the RR air spring solenoid air line.

FM2010200845080X

Fig. 23 Test P/Code C1818: Air Compressor Request Exceeded Maximum Timing (Part 8 of 10). 2000–02

CONDITIONS	DETAILS/RESULTS/ACTIONS
P11 CHECK AIR COMPRESSOR PRESSURE OUTPUT (Continued)	
	4 Trigger the rear air suspension control module active command COMPRESSR OFF after 30 seconds. 5 Wait five minutes. 6 Trigger the rear air suspension control module active command VENT ON long enough to relieve all pressure from the air compressor. • Does the air compressor produce 896 kPa (130 psi) within 30 seconds and hold the developed pressure? → **Yes** GO to **P13**. → **No** CHECK the test fittings for a possible air leak. GO to **P12**.
P12 CHECK AIR COMPRESSOR DRIER	
	1 Disconnect the air compressor drier. 2 Connect the shop air to the air compressor drier port (air compressor side). • Does the air compressor drier leak air? → **Yes** INSTALL a new air compressor drier. CLEAR the DTCs. REPEAT the Self-Test. → **No** INSTALL a new air compressor. CLEAR the DTCs. REPEAT the Self-Test.
P13 CHECK AIR LINES	
	1 Connect Vacuum Tester to the air compressor drier air line.

FM2010200845070X

Fig. 23 Test P/Code C1818: Air Compressor Request Exceeded Maximum Timing (Part 7 of 10). 2000–02

CONDITIONS	DETAILS/RESULTS/ACTIONS
P15 CHECK RR AIR SPRING SOLENOID FOR LEAK (Continued)	
	3 Try to pull a vacuum. • Can a vacuum be developed? → **Yes** INSTALL a new RR air spring solenoid. REFER to Solenoid Valve—Functional. CLEAR the DTCs. REPEAT the Self-Test. → **No** REPAIR or INSTALL a new air line as necessary. CLEAR the DTCs. REPEAT the Self-Test.
P16 CHECK LR AIR SPRING SOLENOID FOR OPERATION	
⚠ **WARNING: Do not over pressurize the rear springs. Over pressurized rear springs may rupture causing personal injury and damage to the vehicle.** **NOTE:** If the rear air spring is fully inflated, partially vent the air before conducting this test. If air cannot be vented, install a new LR air spring solenoid and clear the DTCs. Repeat the Self-Test.	
	1 Connect shop air to the air compressor drier air line. 2 Trigger the rear air suspension control module active command LR SOL ON. 3 Trigger the rear air suspension control module active command LR SOL OFF after 30 seconds or after the left rear is noticeably higher. • Does the left rear raise up? → **Yes** GO to **P17**. → **No** CHECK the LR air spring for air leaks. INSTALL a new LR air spring, if necessary. If no air leak is found, INSTALL a new LR air spring solenoid. CLEAR the DTCs. REPEAT the Self-Test.

FM2010200845090X

Fig. 23 Test P/Code C1818: Air Compressor Request Exceeded Maximum Timing (Part 9 of 10). 2000–02

CONDITIONS	DETAILS/RESULTS/ACTIONS
P17 CHECK RR AIR SPRING SOLENOID FOR OPERATION	
⚠ **WARNING: Do not over pressurize the rear springs. Over pressurized rear springs may rupture causing personal injury and damage to the vehicle.** **NOTE:** If the rear air spring is fully inflated, partially vent the air before conducting this test. If air cannot be vented, install a new RR air spring solenoid. Refer to Solenoid Valve—Functional. and clear the DTCs. Repeat the Self-Test.	
	[1] Connect the shop air to the air compressor drier air line. [2] Trigger the air suspension active command RR SOL ON. [3] Trigger the air suspension active command RR SOL OFF after 30 seconds or after the right rear is noticeably higher. • Does the right rear raise up? → **Yes** INSTALL a new rear air suspension control module. REPEAT the Self-Test. → **No** CHECK the RR air spring for an air leak. INSTALL a new RR air spring, if necessary. If no leak is found, INSTALL a new RR air spring solenoid. CLEAR the DTCs. REPEAT the Self-Test.

FM2010200845100X

Fig. 23 Test P/Code C1818: Air Compressor Request Exceeded Maximum Timing (Part 10 of 10). 2000–02

CONDITIONS	DETAILS/RESULTS/ACTIONS
Q3 CHECK CIRCUIT 420 (DB/YE) FOR AN OPEN/SHORT TO GROUND (Continued)	
[3] 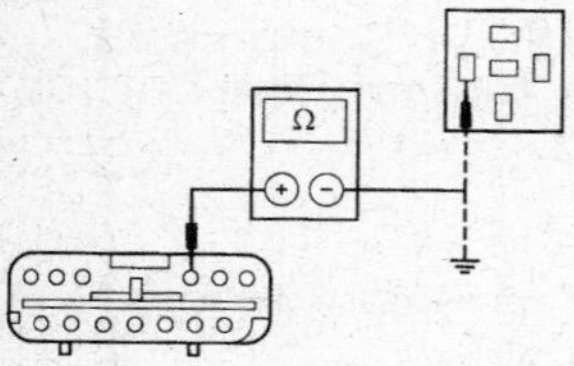	[3] Measure the resistance between rear air suspension control module C251 Pin 23, Circuit 420 (DB/YE), harness side and air compressor relay Pin 85, Circuit 420 (DB/YE) harness side; and between rear air suspension control module C251 Pin 23, Circuit 420 (DB/YE), harness side and ground. • Is the resistance less than 5 ohms between the rear air suspension control module and air compressor relay, and greater than 10,000 ohms between the rear air suspension control module and ground? → **Yes** GO to **Q4**. → **No** REPAIR the circuit. CLEAR the DTCs. REPEAT the Self-Test.
Q4 CHECK AIR COMPRESSOR RELAY COIL FOR AN OPEN	
[1] 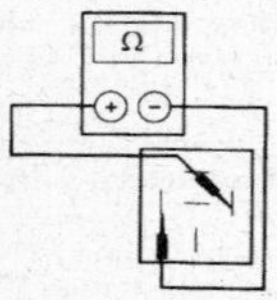	[1] Measure the resistance between air compressor relay Pin 86 and Pin 85 (component side). • Is the resistance greater than 10,000 ohms? → **Yes** INSTALL a new air compressor relay. CLEAR the DTCs. REPEAT the Self-Test. → **No** INSTALL a new rear air suspension control module. REPEAT the Self-Test.

FM2010200846020X

Fig. 24 Test Q/Code C1830: Air Compressor Relay Circuit Failure (Part 2 of 2). 2000–02

CONDITIONS	DETAILS/RESULTS/ACTIONS
R1 CHECK AIR COMPRESSOR RELAY COIL FOR SHORT	
[1] [2]  Air Compressor Relay	

FM2010200847010X

Fig. 25 Test R/Code C1832: Air Compressor Relay Circuit Short To Power (Part 1 of 2). 2000–02

CONDITIONS	DETAILS/RESULTS/ACTIONS
Q1 CHECK AIR COMPRESSOR RELAY CONNECTOR	
[1] [2]  Air Compressor Relay	[3] Check the air compressor relay connector pins and terminals for corrosion, bent or broken pins, moisture or other damage. • Is the air compressor relay connector OK? → **Yes** GO to **Q2**. → **No** REPAIR as necessary. CLEAR the DTCs. REPEAT the Self-Test.
Q2 CHECK POWER TO AIR SUSPENSION RELAY	
[1] 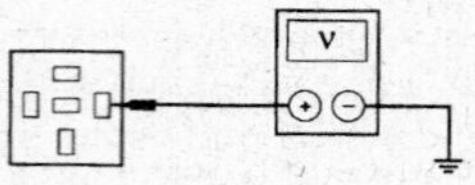	[1] Measure the voltage between air compressor relay Pin 86, Circuit 1053 (LB/PK), harness side and ground. • Is the voltage greater than 10 volts? → **Yes** GO to **Q3**. → **No** REPAIR the circuit. CLEAR the DTCs. REPEAT the Self-Test.
Q3 CHECK CIRCUIT 420 (DB/YE) FOR AN OPEN/SHORT TO GROUND	
[1] [2]  Rear Air Suspension Control Module C251	

FM2010200846010X

Fig. 24 Test Q/Code C1830: Air Compressor Relay Circuit Failure (Part 1 of 2). 2000–02

CONDITIONS	DETAILS/RESULTS/ACTIONS
R1 CHECK AIR COMPRESSOR RELAY COIL FOR SHORT (Continued)	
[3] 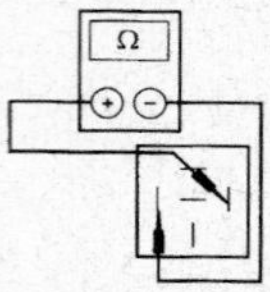	[3] Measure the resistance between air compressor relay Pin 86 and Pin 85 (component side). • Is the resistance less than 5 ohms? → **Yes** INSTALL a new air compressor relay. CLEAR the DTCs. REPEAT the Self-Test. → **No** GO to **R2**.
R2 CHECK CIRCUIT 420 (DB/YE) FOR SHORT TO POWER	
[1] [2]  Rear Air Suspension Control Module C251 [3] 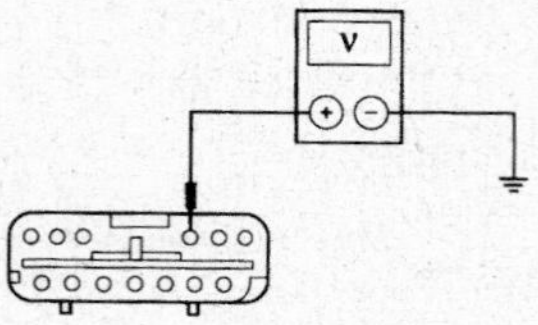	[3] Measure the voltage between rear air suspension control module C251 Pin 23, Circuit 420 (DB/YE), harness side and ground. • Is voltage present? → **Yes** INSTALL a new rear air suspension control module. REPEAT the Self-Test. → **No** REPAIR the circuit. CLEAR the DTCs. REPEAT the Self-Test.

FM2010200847020X

Fig. 25 Test R/Code C1832: Air Compressor Relay Circuit Short To Power (Part 2 of 2). 2000–02

CONDITIONS	DETAILS/RESULTS/ACTIONS
S1 CHECK CIRCUIT 635 (YE) FOR AN OPEN	
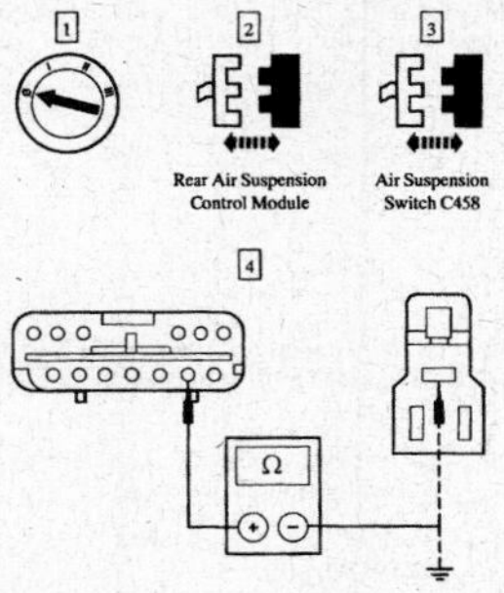	4 Measure the resistance between rear air suspension control module C250 Pin 2, Circuit 635 (YE), harness side and air suspension switch C458, Circuit 635 (YE), harness side. • Is the resistance less than 5 ohms? → **Yes** GO to **S2**. → **No** REPAIR the circuit. CLEAR the DTCs. REPEAT the Self-Test.
S2 CHECK CIRCUIT 417 (VT/OG) FOR AN OPEN	
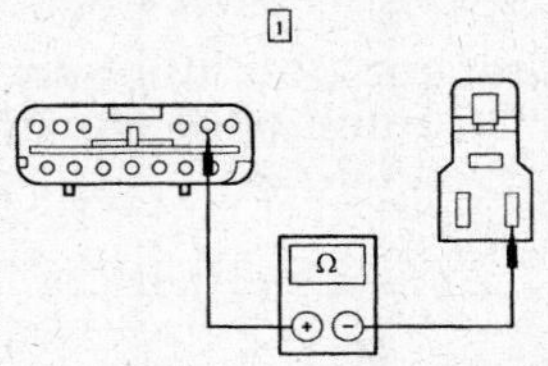	1 Measure the resistance between rear air suspension control module C251 Pin 22, Circuit 417 (VT/OG), harness side and air suspension switch C458, Circuit 417 (VT/OG), harness side. • Is the resistance less than 5 ohms? → **Yes** GO to **S3**. → **No** REPAIR the circuit. CLEAR the DTCs. REPEAT the Self-Test.
S3 CHECK AIR SUSPENSION SWITCH FOR AN OPEN	
	1 Place the air suspension switch in the ON position.

FM2010200848010X

Fig. 26 Test S/Code C1840: Air Suspension Switch Circuit Failure (Part 1 of 2). 2000–02

CONDITIONS	DETAILS/RESULTS/ACTIONS
T1 CHECK THE COURTESY LIGHTS	
	2 Open a door. • Did the courtesy lights illuminate? → **Yes** GO to **T2**. → **No** DIAGNOSE lights.
T2 CHECK REAR AIR SUSPENSION CONTROL MODULE	
	2 Monitor the rear air suspension control module PID D__DRRAS.

FM2010200849010X

Fig. 27 Test T: Did Not Detect Open & Close Door Signals (Part 1 of 2). 2000–02

CONDITIONS	DETAILS/RESULTS/ACTIONS
U1 CHECK CIRCUIT 1053 (LB/PK) FOR AN OPEN	
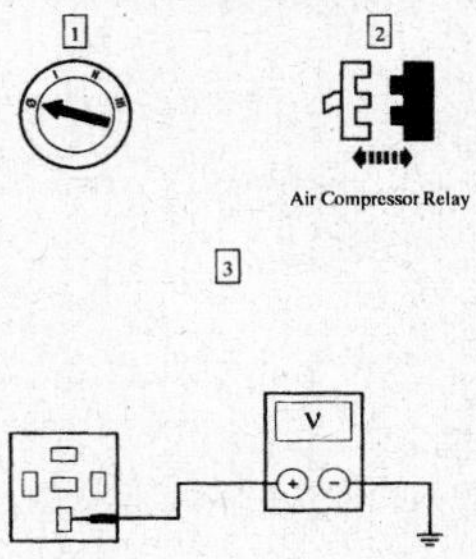	3 Measure the voltage between air compressor relay Pin 30, Circuit 1053 (LB/PK), harness side and ground. • Is the voltage greater than 10 volts? → **Yes** GO to **U2**. → **No** REPAIR the circuit. REPEAT the Self-Test.

FM2010200850010X

Fig. 28 Test U: Compressor Is Inoperative (Part 1 of 3). 2000–02

CONDITIONS	DETAILS/RESULTS/ACTIONS
S3 CHECK AIR SUSPENSION SWITCH FOR AN OPEN (Continued)	
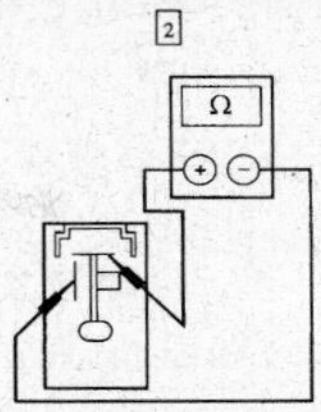	2 Measure the resistance between air suspension switch pins (component side). • Is the resistance less than 5 ohms? → **Yes** INSTALL a new rear air suspension control module. REPEAT the Self-Test. → **No** INSTALL a new air suspension switch. CLEAR the DTCs. REPEAT the Self-Test.

FM2010200848020X

Fig. 26 Test S/Code C1840: Air Suspension Switch Circuit Failure (Part 2 of 2). 2000–02

CONDITIONS	DETAILS/RESULTS/ACTIONS
T2 CHECK REAR AIR SUSPENSION CONTROL MODULE (Continued)	
	3 Open and close a door. • Does the rear air suspension control module PID D__DRRAS indicate AJAR when open and CLOSED when closed? → **Yes** The system is OK. → **No** INSTALL a new rear air suspension control module. REPEAT the Self-Test.

FM2010200849020X

Fig. 27 Test T: Did Not Detect Open & Close Door Signals (Part 2 of 2). 2000–02

CONDITIONS	DETAILS/RESULTS/ACTIONS
U2 CHECK CIRCUITRY FROM AIR COMPRESSOR RELAY	
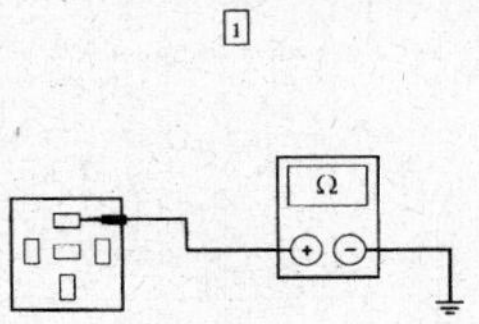	1 Measure the resistance between air compressor relay Pin 87, Circuit 538 (GY/RD) and ground. • Is the resistance less than 5 ohms? → **Yes** INSTALL a new air compressor relay. REPEAT the Self-Test. → **No** GO to **U3**.
U3 CHECK CIRCUIT 538 (GY/RD) FOR AN OPEN	
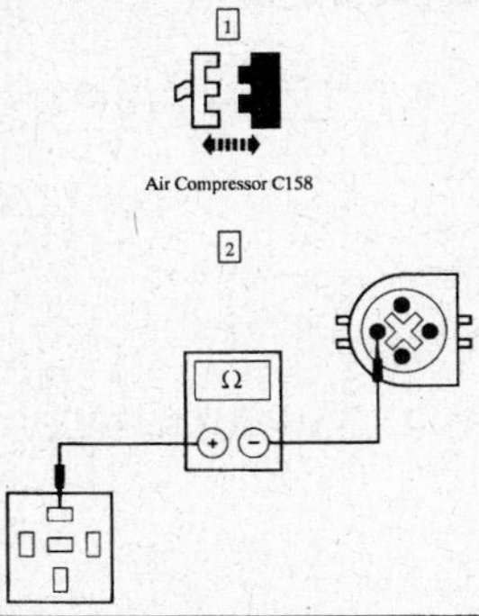	2 Measure the resistance between air compressor relay Pin 87, Circuit 538 (GY/RD), harness side and air compressor C158 Pin 1, Circuit 538 (GY/RD), harness side. • Is the resistance less than 5 ohms? → **Yes** GO to **U4**. → **No** REPAIR the circuit. REPEAT the Self-Test.

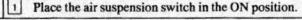

FM2010200850020X

Fig. 28 Test U: Compressor Is Inoperative (Part 2 of 3). 2000–02

CONDITIONS	DETAILS/RESULTS/ACTIONS
U4 CHECK CIRCUIT 57 (BK) FOR AN OPEN	
1 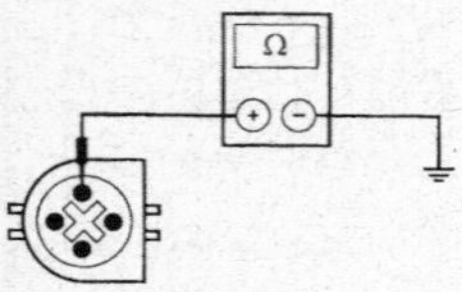	1 Measure the resistance between air compressor C158 Pin 3, Circuit 57 (BK), harness side and ground. • Is the resistance less than 5 ohms? → **Yes** INSTALL a new air compressor. REPEAT the Self-Test. → **No** REPAIR the circuit. REPEAT the Self-Test.

FM2010200850030X

Fig. 28 Test U: Compressor Is Inoperative (Part 3 of 3). 2000–02

CONDITIONS	DETAILS/RESULTS/ACTIONS
V1 CHECK FOR MODULE ACTIVITY	
NOTE: The rear air suspension control module is powered for approximately 60 minutes after the ignition switch is placed in the OFF position. During this time, the air suspension will correct for vehicle weight by raising the vehicle.	
1 	2 Verify the air compressor still cycles 70 minutes after the ignition switch is placed in the OFF position. • Does the air compressor still cycle after the air suspension module powers down? → **Yes** GO to **V2**. → **No** The system is OK.

FM2010200851010X

Fig. 29 Test V: Air Compressor Continuously Cycles w/Ignition Switch In Off Position & No DTC Is Set (Part 1 of 2). 2000–02

CONDITIONS	DETAILS/RESULTS/ACTIONS
V2 CHECK THE REAR AIR SUSPENSION CONTROL MODULE	
1  Rear Air Suspension Control Module C250	• Does the air compressor still cycle? → **Yes** GO to **V3**. → **No** INSTALL a new rear air suspension control module. REPEAT the Self-Test.
V3 CHECK THE AIR COMPRESSOR RELAY	
1  Air Compressor Relay	• Does the air compressor still cycle? → **Yes** REPAIR Circuit 538 (GY/RD). REPEAT the Self-Test. → **No** INSTALL a new air compressor relay. REPEAT the Self-Test.

FM2010200851020X

Fig. 29 Test V: Air Compressor Continuously Cycles w/Ignition Switch In Off Position & No DTC Is Set (Part 2 of 2). 2000–02

	Test Step	Result / Action to Take
A1	**CHECK CIRCUIT 296 (WH/PK) FOR AN OPEN**	
	• Key in OFF position. • Disconnect: Rear Air Suspension Control Module C2131a. • Key in ON position. • Measure the voltage between rear air suspension control module C2131a pin 16, circuit 296 (WH/PK), harness side and ground. • **Is the voltage greater than 10 volts?**	**Yes** GO to **A2**. **No** REPAIR the circuit. REPEAT the self-test.
A2	**CHECK CIRCUIT 418 (DG/YE) FOR AN OPEN**	
	• Measure the voltage between rear air suspension control module C2131a pin 1 and pin 15, circuit 418 (DG/YE), harness side and ground. • **Is the voltage greater than 10 volts?**	**Yes** GO to **A3**. **No** REPAIR the circuit. REPEAT the self-test.
A3	**CHECK CIRCUIT 570 (BK/WH) FOR AN OPEN**	
	• Key in OFF position. • Measure the resistance between rear air suspension control module C2131a pin 6, circuit 570 (BK/WH), harness side and ground. • **Is the resistance less than 5 ohms?**	**Yes** DIAGNOSE module. **No** REPAIR the circuit. REPEAT the self-test.

FM2010200852000X

Fig. 30 Test A: No Communication w/Rear Air Suspension Control Module. 2003–04

	Test Step	Result / Action to Take
B1	**CHECK THE COMMUNICATIONS TO THE REAR AIR SUSPENSION CONTROL MODULE**	
	• Key in ON position. • Turn the air suspension disable switch ON. • Check the communication to the rear air suspension control module. • **Does the scan tool communicate with the air suspension control module?**	**Yes** INSTALL a new air suspension control module. CLEAR the DTC(s). REPEAT the self-test. **No** GO to Pinpoint Test A.

FM2010200853000X

Fig. 31 Test B: Unable To Enter Self-Test. 2003–04

	Test Step	Result / Action to Take
C1	**CHECK THE BATTERY VOLTAGE**	
	NOTE: A recent jump start can cause these DTCs to set. • Measure the battery voltage between the positive and negative battery posts with the key ON engine OFF (KOEO) and with the engine running. • **Is the battery voltage between 10 and 13 volts with KOEO, and between 11 and 17 volts with the engine running?**	**Yes** GO to **C2**. **No** DIAGNOSE battery.
C2	**CHECK CIRCUIT 296 (WH/PK) FOR AN OPEN**	
	• Key in OFF position. • Disconnect: Rear Air Suspension Control Module C2131a. • Key in ON position. • Measure the voltage between rear air suspension control module C2131a pin 16, circuit 296 (WH/PK), harness side and ground. • **Is the voltage greater than 10 volts and less than 17 volts?**	**Yes** GO to **C3**. **No** REPAIR the circuit. CLEAR the DTC(s). REPEAT the self-test.
C3	**CHECK CIRCUIT 418 (DG/YE) FOR AN OPEN**	
	• Measure the voltage between rear air suspension control module C2131a pin 1 and pin 15, circuit 418 (DG/YE), harness side and ground. • **Is the voltage greater than 10 volts and less than 17 volts?**	**Yes** GO to **C4**. **No** REPAIR the circuit. CLEAR the DTC(s). REPEAT the self-test.
C4	**CHECK CIRCUIT 570 (BK/WH) FOR AN OPEN**	
	• Key in OFF position. • Disconnect: Rear Air Suspension Control Module C2131a. • Measure the resistance between rear air suspension control module C2131a pin 6, circuit 570 (BK/WH), harness side and ground. • **Is the resistance less than 5 ohms?**	**Yes** INSTALL a new rear air suspension control module. REPEAT the self-test. **No** REPAIR the circuit. CLEAR the DTC(s). REPEAT the self-test.

FM2010200854000X

Fig. 32 Test C/Codes B1317 & B1318: Battery Voltage High/Low. 2003–04

	Test Step	Result / Action to Take
D1	**CHECK CIRCUIT 417 (PK/OG) FOR A SHORT TO POWER**	
	• Disconnect: Air Suspension Control Module C2131a. • Disconnect: Air Suspension Height Sensor C4043. • Turn the air suspension switch to the OFF position. • Key in ON position. • Measure the voltage between rear air suspension control module C2131a pin 22, circuit 417 (PK/OG), harness side and ground. • **Is the voltage greater than 0 volt?**	**Yes** REPAIR circuit 417 (PK/OG). CLEAR the DTC. REPEAT the self-test. **No** GO to **D2**.
D2	**CHECK CIRCUIT 417 (PK/OG) FOR A SHORT TO GROUND**	
	• Key in OFF position. • Measure the resistance between rear air suspension control module C2131a pin 22, circuit 417 (PK/OG), harness side and ground. • **Is the resistance greater than 10,000 ohms?**	**Yes** GO to **D3**. **No** REPAIR circuit 417 (PK/OG). CLEAR the DTC. REPEAT the self-test.

FM2010200855010X

Fig. 33 Test D/Code C1724: Height Sensor Power Circuit Failure (Part 1 of 2). 2003–04

	Test Step	Result / Action to Take
D3	**CHECK CIRCUIT 417 (PK/OG) FOR AN OPEN**	
	• Measure the resistance between rear air suspension control module C2131a pin 22, circuit 417 (PK/OG), harness side and air suspension height sensor C4043 pin 3, circuit 417 (PK/OG), harness side. • **Is the resistance greater than 5 ohms?**	**Yes** REPAIR the circuit. CLEAR the DTC. REPEAT the self-test. **No** GO to **D4**.
D4	**CHECK THE REAR AIR SUSPENSION CONTROL MODULE OUTPUT**	
	• Connect: Air Suspension Control Module C2131a. • Key in ON position. • Measure the voltage between air suspension height sensor C4043 pin 3, circuit 417 (PK/OG), harness side and ground. • **Is the voltage 5 volts?**	**Yes** INSTALL a new air suspension height sensor. CLEAR the DTC. REPEAT the self-test. **No** INSTALL a new air suspension control module. CLEAR the DTC. REPEAT the self-test.

FM2010200855020X

Fig. 33 Test D/Code C1724: Height Sensor Power Circuit Failure (Part 2 of 2). 2003–04

Test Step	Result / Action to Take
E1 CHECK THE AIR SUSPENSION HEIGHT SENSOR MOUNTING	
• Check the air suspension height sensor for correct installation at the upper and lower ball stud brackets. • Check the air suspension height sensor mounting brackets for damage. • **Are the air suspension height sensor and mounting brackets OK?**	**Yes** GO to **E2**. **No** REPAIR as necessary. CLEAR the DTC. REPEAT the self-test.
E2 CHECK THE AIR SUSPENSION HEIGHT SENSOR OPERATION	
• Disconnect the lower end of the air suspension height sensor. • Key in ON position. • Monitor the height sensor height and voltage PIDs. • While monitoring the height sensor PID display, slowly move the air suspension height sensor through its full range of motion. • **Do the height sensor PIDs correspond to the height sensor movement?**	**Yes** GO to **E3**. **No** INSTALL a new air suspension height sensor. CLEAR the DTC. REPEAT the self-test.
E3 VERIFY THAT THE REAR OF THE VEHICLE CAN BE RAISED	
• Record the voltage level for the rear air suspension height sensor. • Trigger air suspension control module active commands: LR SOLENOID, RR SOLENOID and COMPRESSR ON. • Allow the rear of the vehicle to raise for only 30 seconds. • **Does the rear of the vehicle raise and hold the new height?**	**Yes** TRIGGER air suspension control module active commands. GO to **E4**. **No** TRIGGER air suspension control module active command OFF. GO to **E5**.
E4 VERIFY THAT THE REAR OF THE VEHICLE CAN BE LOWERED	
• Trigger air suspension control module active commands: LR SOLENOID, RR SOLENOID and COMPRESSR VENT. • Allow the rear to lower until the rear air suspension height sensor voltage reading matches the one recorded in Step E3 or until 30 seconds have passed. • **Does the rear of the vehicle lower?**	**Yes** RESET electronic ride height. CLEAR the DTCs. REPEAT the self-test. **No** GO to **E7**.

FM2010200856010X

Fig. 34 Test E/Code C1726: Pneumatic Failure (Part 1 of 3). 2003–04

Test Step	Result / Action to Take
E10 CHECK THE VENT SOLENOID OPERATION	
• Disconnect the air line at the snorkel. • Connect the vacuum tester to the snorkel air line and try to pull a vacuum. • Trigger the vent solenoid ON active command. • Try to pull a vacuum again. • **Can a vacuum be developed with the vent solenoid OFF active command and no vacuum developed with the vent solenoid ON active command?**	**Yes** INSTALL a new air suspension control module. REPEAT the self-test. **No** If no vacuum can be developed with the vent solenoid OFF, GO to **E11**. If a vacuum can be developed with the vent solenoid OFF, GO to **E12**.
E11 CHECK THE AIR LINE AND CONNECTIONS	
• Check the air line and connections between the vacuum tester and the air compressor. • **Are the air line and connections OK?**	**Yes** INSTALL a new air compressor. CLEAR the DTC. REPEAT the self-test. **No** REPAIR the air line. CLEAR the DTC. REPEAT the self-test.
E12 CHECK THE AIR COMPRESSOR DRIER	
• Disconnect the air compressor drier. • Connect the vacuum tester to the air compressor drier and try to pull a vacuum. • **Can a vacuum be developed?**	**Yes** INSTALL a new air compressor. CLEAR the DTC. REPEAT the self-test. **No** INSTALL a new air compressor drier. CLEAR the DTC. REPEAT the self-test.

FM2010200856030X

Fig. 34 Test E/Code C1726: Pneumatic Failure (Part 3 of 3). 2003–04

Test Step	Result / Action to Take
F4 CHECK CIRCUIT 427 (PK/BK) FOR AN OPEN AND SHORT TO GROUND	
• Key in OFF position. • Turn the air suspension switch OFF. • Disconnect: Rear Air Suspension Control module C2131b. • Measure the resistance between the air suspension height sensor C4043 pin 2, circuit 427 (PK/BK), harness side and rear air suspension control module C2131b pin 12, circuit 427 (PK/BK), harness side; and between air suspension height sensor C4043 pin 2, circuit 427 (PK/BK), harness side and ground. • **Is the resistance less than 5 ohms between the air suspension height sensor and the rear air suspension control module, and greater than 10,000 ohms between the air suspension height sensor and ground?**	**Yes** RECONNECT the system. GO to **F5**. **No** REPAIR circuit 427 (PK/BK). CLEAR the DTC. REPEAT the self-test.
F5 CHECK FOR AN INTERMITTENT FAULT	
• Connect: Rear Air Suspension Control Module C2131b. • Turn the air suspension switch ON. • Key in ON position. • Monitor the rear air suspension control module PID. • Monitor the PID display while wiggling the wire harness between the air suspension rear height sensor and the air suspension control module. • **Does the air suspension rear height sensor voltage ever indicate less than 0.2 volt or greater than 5 volts?**	**Yes** REPAIR circuits 427 (PK/BK), 432 (BK/PK) and 417 (PK/OG) as necessary. CLEAR the DTC. REPEAT the self-test. **No** INSTALL a new air suspension height sensor. CLEAR the DTC. REPEAT the self-test.

FM2010200857020X

Fig. 35 Test F/Code C1760: Rear Height Sensor High Signal Circuit Failure (Part 2 of 2). 2003–04

Test Step	Result / Action to Take
E5 CHECK OPERATION OF THE AIR COMPRESSOR	
⚠ **CAUTION: Do not allow the air compressor to run for more than three minutes. The air compressor could overheat and stop operation due to an internal temperature sensitive thermal breaker.** • Trigger air suspension control module active command COMPRESSR ON. • **Does the air compressor run (slight buzzing noise from RF fender)?**	**Yes** TRIGGER air suspension control module active command COMPRESSR OFF. GO to **E6**. **No** GO to Pinpoint Test I.
E6 CHECK THE AIR COMPRESSOR PRESSURE OUTPUT	
⚠ **CAUTION: Do not allow the air compressor to run for more than three minutes. The air compressor could overheat and stop operation due to an internal temperature sensitive thermal breaker.** **NOTE:** If fluid is present when disconnecting the air line, clear the air lines. Check the compressor air drier for water or the air compressor for oil contamination. • Disconnect the air line at the air drier. • Connect air pressure gauge (1,723 kPa maximum reading) with common fittings to the air drier. • Trigger air suspension control module active command COMPRESSR ON. • Run the air compressor for only 30 seconds. • Wait five minutes. • Trigger air suspension control module active command VENT ON. • **Does the compressor produce 896 kPa (130 psi) within 30 seconds and hold the developed pressure?**	**Yes** TRIGGER air suspension control module active command VENT OFF. GO to **E9**. **No** INSTALL a new air suspension compressor.
E7 CHECK THE PNEUMATIC SYSTEM — VENT LR AIR SPRING	
NOTE: If fluid is present when disconnecting the air line, clear the air lines. Check the air compressor drier for water or the air compressor for oil contamination. **NOTE:** The rear springs must be partially inflated in order to carry out this test. Add air as necessary. • Disconnect the air compressor drier air line. • Trigger the LR air spring solenoid ON active command. • **Does the air vent from the air compressor drier air line?**	**Yes** Trigger the LR air spring solenoid OFF active command. GO to **E8**. **No** Trigger the LR air spring solenoid OFF active command. GO to **E9**.
E8 CHECK THE PNEUMATIC SYSTEM — VENT RR AIR SPRING	
NOTE: The rear springs must be partially inflated in order to carry out this test. Add air as necessary. • Trigger the RR air solenoid ON active command. • **Does the air vent from the air drier?**	**Yes** Trigger the RR air solenoid OFF active command. GO to **E10**. **No** Trigger the RR air solenoid OFF active command. GO to **E9**.
E9 CHECK THE PNEUMATIC SYSTEM — AIR LINE	
NOTE: If fluid is present when disconnecting the air line, clear the air lines. Check the air compressor drier for water or the air compressor for oil. • Disconnect the suspected rear air spring solenoid air line. • Connect the vacuum tester to the air line and try to pull a vacuum. • **Can a vacuum be developed?**	**Yes** REPAIR or INSTALL a new air line. CLEAR the DTC. REPEAT the self-test. **No** INSTALL a new air spring solenoid valve. CLEAR the DTC. REPEAT the self-test.

FM2010200856020X

Fig. 34 Test E/Code C1726: Pneumatic Failure (Part 2 of 3). 2003–04

Test Step	Result / Action to Take
F1 VERIFY DTC	
• Carry out the rear air suspension control module On-Demand self-test. • **Is DTC C1760 present?**	**Yes** GO to **F2**. **No** If a different DTC is retrieved, REFER rear air suspension control Module DTC index.
F2 CHECK THE HEIGHT SENSOR POWER	
• Key in OFF position. • Turn the air suspension switch OFF. • Disconnect: Air Suspension Height Sensor C4043. • Turn the air suspension switch ON. • Key in ON position. • Monitor the air suspension height sensor PID. • Measure the voltage between air suspension height sensor C4043 pin 1, circuit 432 (BK/PK) and pin 3, circuit 417 (PK/OG), harness side. • **Is the voltage approximately 5 volts?**	**Yes** GO to **F4**. **No** If the voltage is less than 5 volts, GO to **F3**. If the voltage is greater than 5 volts, REPAIR circuit 417 (PK/OG). CLEAR the DTC. REPEAT the self-test.
F3 CHECK THE AIR SUSPENSION HEIGHT SENSOR GROUND	
NOTE: Use the battery negative terminal as ground for this test. • Measure the resistance between the air suspension height sensor C4043 pin 1, circuit 432 (BK/PK), harness side and ground. • **Is the resistance less than 5 ohms?**	**Yes** REPAIR circuit 417 (PK/OG). CLEAR the DTC. REPEAT the self-test. **No** REPAIR circuit 432 (BK/PK) and circuit 570 (BK/WH). CLEAR the DTC. REPEAT the self-test.

FM2010200857010X

Fig. 35 Test F/Code C1760: Rear Height Sensor High Signal Circuit Failure (Part 1 of 2). 2003–04

PINPOINT TEST G: DTC C1770 — AIR SUSPENSION VENT SOLENOID OUTPUT CIRCUIT FAILURE

Test Step	Result / Action to Take
G1 CHECK CIRCUIT 421 (PK) FOR A SHORT TO POWER	
• Key in OFF position. • Disconnect: Rear Air Suspension Control Module C2131a. • Disconnect: Air Compressor C1179. • Key in ON position. • Measure the voltage between the rear air suspension control module C2131b pin 24, circuit 421 (PK), harness side and ground. • **Is the voltage greater than 0 volts?**	**Yes** REPAIR the circuit. CLEAR the DTC. REPEAT the self-test. **No** GO to **G2**.
G2 CHECK CIRCUIT 421 (PK) FOR A SHORT TO GROUND	
• Key in OFF position. • Measure the resistance between rear air suspension control module C2131a pin 24, circuit 421 (PK), harness side and ground. • **Is the resistance greater than 10,000 ohms?**	**Yes** GO to **G3**. **No** REPAIR circuit 421 (PK). CLEAR the DTC. REPEAT the self-test.
G3 CHECK CIRCUIT 421 (PK) FOR AN OPEN	
• Measure the resistance between the rear air suspension control module C2131b pin 24, circuit 421 (PK) and air compressor C1179 pin 1, circuit 421 (PK), harness side. • **Is the resistance less than 5 ohms?**	**Yes** GO to **G4**. **No** REPAIR the circuit. CLEAR the DTC. REPEAT the self-test.
G4 CHECK CIRCUIT 57 FOR AN OPEN	
• Measure the resistance between the air compressor C1179 pin 2, circuit 57 (BK), harness side and ground. • **Is the resistance greater than 5 ohms?**	**Yes** REPAIR the circuit. CLEAR the DTC. REPEAT the self-test. **No** GO to **G5**.

FM2010200858010X

Fig. 36 Test G/Code C1770: Vent Solenoid Output Circuit Failure (Part 1 of 2). 2003–04

	Test Step	Result / Action to Take
G5	CHECK THE AIR COMPRESSOR VENT SOLENOID	
	• Measure the resistance between the air compressor C1179 pin 2 and pin 3, component side. • **Is the resistance between 15 and 25 ohms?**	**Yes** INSTALL a new air suspension control module. CLEAR the DTC(s). REPEAT the self-test. **No** INSTALL a new air compressor. CLEAR the DTC. REPEAT the self-test.

FM2010200858020X

Fig. 36 Test G/Code C1770: Vent Solenoid Output Circuit Failure (Part 2 of 2). 2003–04

	Test Step	Result / Action to Take
I1	CHECK THE AIR COMPRESSOR RELAY CONNECTOR	
	• Key in OFF position. • Disconnect: Air Compressor Relay. • Check the air compressor relay connector pins and terminals for corrosion, bent or broken pins, moisture or other damage. • **Is the air compressor relay connector OK?**	**Yes** GO to **I2**. **No** REPAIR as necessary. CLEAR the DTC. REPEAT the self-test.
I2	CHECK THE POWER TO THE AIR SUSPENSION RELAY	
	• Measure the voltage between air compressor relay pin 1 and pin 3, circuit 1053 (LB/PK), harness side and ground. • **Are the voltages greater than 10 volts?**	**Yes** GO to **I3**. **No** REPAIR the circuit. CLEAR the DTC. REPEAT the self-test.
I3	CHECK CIRCUIT 420 (DB/YE) FOR AN OPEN	
	• Key in OFF position. • Disconnect: Air Suspension Control Module C2131b. • Measure the resistance between rear air suspension control module C2131b pin 23, circuit 420 (DB/YE), harness side and air compressor relay pin 2, circuit 420 (DB/YE) harness side. • **Is the resistance less than 5 ohms?**	**Yes** GO to **I4**. **No** REPAIR the circuit. CLEAR the DTC. REPEAT the self-test.
I4	CHECK CIRCUIT 420 (DB/YE) FOR A SHORT TO GROUND	
	• Measure the resistance between rear air suspension control module C2131b pin 23, circuit 420 (DB/YE), harness side and ground. • **Is the resistance greater than 10,000 ohms?**	**Yes** GO to **I5**. **No** REPAIR the circuit. CLEAR the DTC. REPEAT the self-test.
I5	CHECK THE AIR COMPRESSOR RELAY COIL FOR AN OPEN	
	• Measure the resistance between air compressor relay pin 1 and pin 2 (component side). • **Is the resistance greater than 10,000 ohms?**	**Yes** INSTALL a new air compressor relay. CLEAR the DTC. REPEAT the self-test. **No** INSTALL a new rear air suspension control module. REPEAT the self-test.

FM2010200860000X

Fig. 38 Test I/Code C1830: Air Compressor Relay Circuit Failure. 2003–04

	Test Step	Result / Action to Take
J4	CHECK THE AIR SUSPENSION SWITCH	
	• Push the air suspension switch to the ON position. • Measure the resistance between air suspension switch pin 1 and pin 2. • **Is the resistance less than 5 ohms?**	**Yes** INSTALL a new air suspension control module. CLEAR the DTC(s). REPEAT the self-test. **No** INSTALL a new air suspension switch. CLEAR the DTC(s). REPEAT the self-test.

FM2010200861020X

Fig. 39 Test J/Code C1840: Air Suspension Switch Circuit Failure (Part 2 of 2). 2003–04

	Test Step	Result / Action to Take
K1	CHECK CIRCUIT 1053 (LB/PK) FOR AN OPEN	
	• Key in OFF position. • Disconnect: Air Compressor Relay. • Measure the voltage between air compressor relay pin 3, circuit 1053 (LB/PK), harness side and ground. 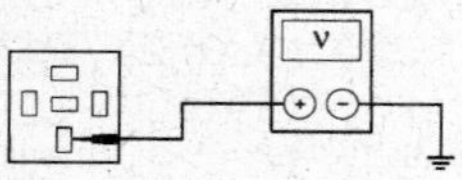 • **Is the voltage greater than 10 volts?**	**Yes** GO to **K2**. **No** REPAIR the circuit. REPEAT the self-test.
K2	CHECK CIRCUIT 538 (GY/RD) FOR AN OPEN	
	• Disconnect: Air Compressor C1179. • Measure the resistance between air compressor relay pin 5, circuit 538 (GY/RD), harness side and air compressor C1179 pin 1, circuit 538 (GY/RD), harness side. 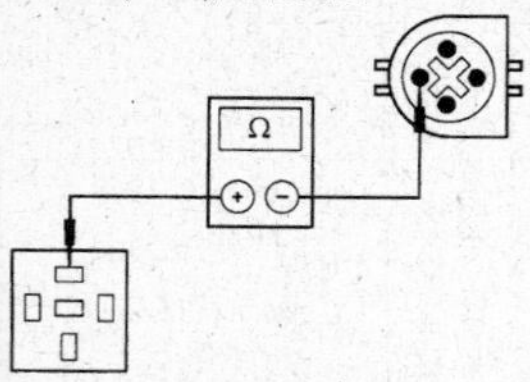 • **Is the resistance less than 5 ohms?**	**Yes** GO to **K3**. **No** REPAIR the circuit. REPEAT the self-test.

FM2010200862010X

Fig. 40 Test K: Compressor Is Inoperative (Part 1 of 2). 2003–04

	Test Step	Result / Action to Take
H1	CHECK CIRCUITS 1114 (BN/PK) AND 1115 (TN/WH) FOR AN OPEN	
	• Key in OFF position. • Disconnect: Air Suspension Control Module C2131a. • Disconnect: Air Suspension LR Air Spring Solenoid C4044. • Disconnect: Air Suspension RR Air Spring Solenoid C4045. • Measure the resistance between the air suspension control module C2131a pin 13, circuit 1114 (BN/PK) harness side and LR air spring solenoid C4044 pin 1, harness side; and between air suspension control module C2131a pin 25, circuit 1115 (TN/WH) harness side and RR air spring solenoid C4045 pin 1, harness side. • **Are the resistances less than 5 ohms?**	**Yes** GO to **H2**. **No** REPAIR the circuit in question. CLEAR the DTC(s). REPEAT the self-test.
H2	CHECK CIRCUITS 1114 (BN/PK) AND 1115 (TN/WH) FOR A SHORT TO POWER	
	• Key in ON position. • Measure the voltage between the rear air suspension control module pin 13, circuit 1114 (BN/PK) and ground; and between the rear air suspension control module pin 25, circuit 1115 (TN/WH) and ground. • **Is voltage present?**	**Yes** REPAIR the affected circuit(s). CLEAR the DTC(s). REPEAT the self-test. **No** GO to **H3**.
H3	CHECK CIRCUITS 1114 (BN/PK) AND 1115 (TN/WH) FOR A SHORT TO GROUND	
	• Key in OFF position. • Measure the resistance between the rear air suspension control module pin 13, circuit 1114 (BN/PK) and ground; and between the rear air suspension control module pin 25, circuit 1115 (TN/WH) and ground. • **Is the resistance greater than 10,000 ohms?**	**Yes** GO to **H4**. **No** REPAIR the affected circuit(s). CLEAR the DTC(s). REPEAT the self-test.
H4	CHECK CIRCUIT 57 (BK) FOR AN OPEN	
	• Key in OFF position. • Measure the resistance between the LR air suspension solenoid C4044 pin 2, circuit 57 (BK) and ground; and between the RR air suspension solenoid C4045 pin 2, circuit 57 (BK) and ground. • **Is the resistance less than 5 ohms?**	**Yes** GO to **H5**. **No** REPAIR the affected circuit(s). CLEAR the DTC(s). REPEAT the self-test.
H5	CHECK THE LR AND RR AIR SPRING SOLENOIDS	
	• Key in OFF position. • Measure the resistance between the LR air suspension solenoid C4044 pins 1 and 2; and between the RR air suspension solenoid C4045 pins 1 and 2. • **Are the resistances between 10 and 17 ohms?**	**Yes** INSTALL a new air suspension control module. CLEAR the DTC(s). REPEAT the self-test. **No** INSTALL a new LR or RR air spring solenoid. CLEAR the DTC(s). REPEAT the self-test.

FM2010200859000X

Fig. 37 Test H/Codes C1790 & C1795: LR/RR Air Spring Solenoid Output Circuit Failure. 2003–04

	Test Step	Result / Action to Take
J1	CHECK CIRCUIT 635 (YE) FOR AN OPEN	
	• Key in OFF position. • Disconnect: Rear Air Suspension Control Module C2131a. • Disconnect: Air Suspension Switch C2130. • Measure the resistance between rear air suspension control module C2131a pin 2, circuit 635 (YE), harness side and air suspension switch C2130 pin 1, circuit 635 (YE), harness side. • **Is the resistance less than 5 ohms?**	**Yes** GO to **J2**. **No** REPAIR the circuit. CLEAR the DTC(s). REPEAT the self-test.
J2	CHECK CIRCUIT 635 (YE) FOR A SHORT TO GROUND	
	• Measure the resistance between rear air suspension control module C2131a pin 2, circuit 635 (YE), harness side and ground. • **Is the resistance greater than 10,000 ohms?**	**Yes** GO to **J3**. **No** REPAIR the circuit. CLEAR the DTC(s). REPEAT the self-test.
J3	CHECK THE AIR SUSPENSION SWITCH POWER	
	• Connect: Rear Air Suspension Control Module C2131a. • Key in ON position. • Measure the voltage between air suspension switch C2130 pin 2, circuit 417 (PK/OG), harness side and ground. • **Is the voltage 5 volts?**	**Yes** GO to **J4**. **No** REPAIR the circuit. CLEAR the DTC(s). REPEAT the self-test.

FM2010200861010X

Fig. 39 Test J/Code C1840: Air Suspension Switch Circuit Failure (Part 1 of 2). 2003–04

	Test Step	Result / Action to Take
K3	CHECK CIRCUIT 57 (BK) FOR AN OPEN	
	• Measure the resistance between air compressor C1179 pin 4, circuit 57 (BK), harness side and ground. 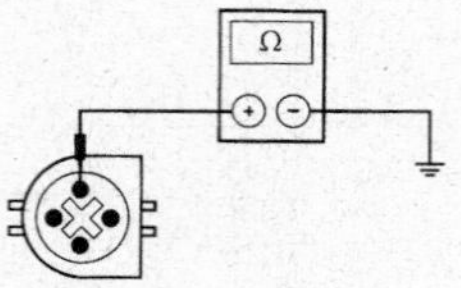 • **Is the resistance less than 5 ohms?**	**Yes** GO to **K4** **No** REPAIR the circuit. REPEAT the self-test.
K4	CHECK CIRCUIT 538 (GY/RD) FOR VOLTAGE	
	• Key in ON position. • Trigger the air compressor ON active command. • Measure the voltage between air compressor C1179 pin 3, circuit 538 (GY/RD), harness side and ground. • **Is the voltage greater than 10 volts?**	**Yes** INSTALL a new air compressor. REPEAT the self-test. **No** REPAIR circuit 538 (GY/RD). REPEAT the self-test.

FM2010200862020X

Fig. 40 Test K: Compressor Is Inoperative (Part 2 of 2). 2003–04

Test Step		Result / Action to Take
L1	**CHECK FOR MODULE ACTIVITY**	
	NOTE: The rear air suspension control module is powered for approximately 60 minutes after the ignition switch is placed in the OFF position. During this time, the air suspension will correct for vehicle weight by raising the vehicle. • Key in OFF position. • Turn the air suspension switch to the OFF position. • Verify the air compressor still cycles 60 minutes after the ignition switch is placed in the OFF position. • **Does the air compressor still cycle continuously after the air suspension module is disabled?**	**Yes** GO to **L2**. **No** The system is OK.
L2	**CHECK THE REAR AIR SUSPENSION CONTROL MODULE**	
	• Disconnect: Rear Air Suspension Control Module C2131a. • **Does the air compressor still cycle?**	**Yes** GO to **L3**. **No** INSTALL a new rear air suspension control module. REPEAT the self-test.
L3	**CHECK CIRCUIT 538 (GY/RD) FOR A SHORT TO POWER**	
	• Disconnect: Air Compressor Relay. • **Does the air compressor still cycle?**	**Yes** REPAIR Circuit 538 (GY/RD). REPEAT the self-test. **No** INSTALL a new air compressor relay. REPEAT the self-test.

FM2010200863000X

Fig. 41 Test L: Air Compressor Continuously Cycles w/Ignition Switch In Off Position And No DTC Is Set. 2003–04

Test Step		Result / Action to Take
M1	**CHECK THE COURTESY LIGHTS**	
	• Key in OFF position. • Open a door. • **Did the courtesy lights illuminate?**	**Yes** GO to **M2**. **No** DIAGNOSE lights.
M2	**CHECK THE DOOR SIGNAL**	
	• Key in ON position. • Monitor the door signal PID. • Open and close a door. • **Does the door signal PID indicate correctly when the door is open and when closed?**	**Yes** The system is OK. **No** DIAGNOSE lights.

FM2010200864000X

Fig. 42 Test M: Did Not Detect Open & Close Door Signals. 2003–04

SYSTEM SERVICE

Air Spring Vent & Refill

1. Ensure air spring is in proper shape with no folds or creases.
2. Turn ignition switch to the RUN position and connect NGS tester, or equivalent, scan tool to Data Link Connector (DLC).
3. Select air suspension control module active command LR_SOL or RR_SOL from off to on.
4. **To vent air from air spring,** select active command AS_VENT.
5. **To refill air spring,** select active command AS_COMP. **To prevent overheating and shutdown when refilling air spring, do not run air compressor for more than three minutes.**

Adjustment

RIDE HEIGHT

2000–02

1. Position vehicle on level surface.
2. Ensure air suspension switch is in ON position, then turn ignition switch to Run position, waiting about 2 minutes.
3. Open driver door and add weight to rear bumper so vehicle rises to trim position.
4. When compressor stops, vehicle is at ride height position, close door and remove weight from bumper.
5. Rock vehicle sideways to remove effect of suspension friction, then allow to settle.
6. Turn air suspension switch to Off position.
7. Position suitable dimension gauge onto rear axle, **Fig. 43.**
8. Measure vertical "D" dimension between rear axle tube to frame inboard reinforcement rail, **Fig. 44**
9. If "D" ride height dimension is not within specifications, adjust by moving rear height sensor attaching bracket inboard (vehicle high) or outboard (vehicle low). Moving bracket one index mark will change vertical "D" dimension about .20 inch.
10. After adjustment is made, repeat steps 4 through 6.

2003–04

1. Position vehicle on a level surface.
2. Ensure air suspension switch is turned on, then turn ignition switch to Run position and wait at least two minutes.
3. Position measurement tool on rear axle, **Fig. 43.**
4. Release measurement tool set screw, then pull sliding post and scale up until it touches bottom of inboard frame rail to get ride height "D" dimension.
5. Vent or fill air suspension to vertical "D" dimension using suitable scan tool.
6. Monitor suspension height sensor measurement and voltage PIDs.
7. Loosen height sensor ball stud bracket retaining nuts.
8. Slide ball stud bracket until height sensor measurement PID is equal to 0 inches and voltage PID is equal to 2.8 volts.
9. Tighten height sensor ball stud bracket.
10. If ride height dimension "D" is not within specification, **Fig. 45** use scan tool to vent or fill air suspension to specification and monitor height sensor arm from ball stud.
11. Rotate height sensor link until measurement PID is equal to 0 inches and voltage is 2.8 volts.
12. Disconnect height sensor ball stud, then save the height settings using scan tool.
13. Connect height sensor arm to ball stud.

Component Replacement

AIR SPRING SOLENOID

2000–02

Functional

1. Vent air from air spring as outlined in "Air Spring Vent & Refill."
2. Remove air spring as outlined in "Air Spring."
3. Rotate solenoid valve counterclockwise to first stop, then pull valve out to stop and release any air remaining in air spring.
4. Rotate solenoid valve counterclockwise to second stop, then remove valve from solenoid valve housing.
5. Reverse procedure to install. Refill air spring as outlined in "Air Spring Vent & Refill."

Non-Functional

1. Vent air from air spring as outlined in "Air Spring Vent & Refill."
2. Turn air suspension switch off.
3. Raise and support vehicle.
4. Disconnect solenoid electrical connector.
5. Compress quick connect locking ring and pull out air line.
6. Remove solenoid retaining clip.
7. Rotate solenoid out of air spring to first detent to release any air remaining in air spring.
8. Twist and remove solenoid valve from air spring.
9. Reverse procedure to install. Refill air spring as outlined in "Air Spring Vent & Refill."

2003–04

1. If air spring solenoid valve is functional, vent appropriate air springs as outlined in "Air Spring Vent & Refill."
2. Raise and support vehicle.
3. Disconnect electrical connector, then compress quick connect lock ring and pull out air line.
4. Remove air spring solenoid valve clip, then rotate and remove air spring solenoid valve. **Air spring solenoid valve has a two stage release. When removing a nonfunctional solenoid and air spring is inflated, carefully rotate solenoid counterclockwise until it reaches the first stage to release air from spring. Turn solenoid to second stage to remove.**
5. Reverse procedure to install noting the following:
   a. Replace O-ring if damaged.
   b. Lubricate solenoid seal area with silicone grease.

AIR SPRING

1. Vent air from air spring as outlined in "Air Spring Vent & Refill."
2. Turn air suspension switch to Off position.
3. Raise and support vehicle.
4. Remove air spring retainer from top of air spring.
5. Lift bottom of air spring off of rear axle.

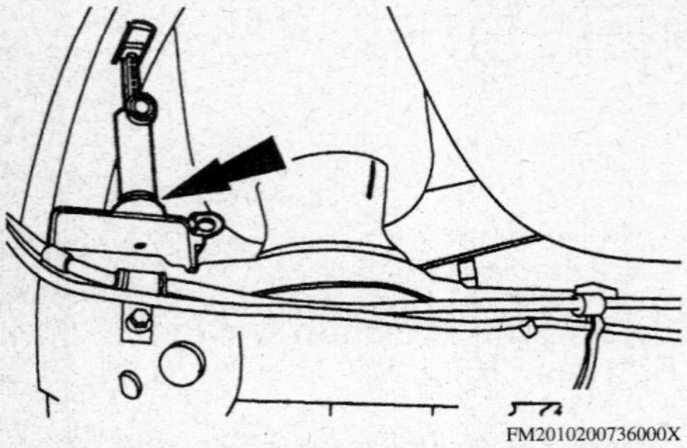

Fig. 43 Ride height measurement

6. Disconnect air spring electrical connector.
7. Compress quick locking ring and pull out air line, then remove air spring.
8. Reverse procedure to install. Refill air spring as outlined in "Air Spring Vent & Refill."

CONTROL MODULE

1. Turn air suspension switch to the Off position.
2. Remove righthand lower instrument panel insulator pushpins.
3. Pull lower instrument panel insulator away from instrument panel and disconnect power point and courtesy lamp electrical connectors.
4. Remove lower instrument panel insulator from in righthand side of instrument panel.
5. Remove control module attaching screws, then disconnect electrical connectors.
6. Remove module from vehicle.
7. Reverse procedure to install.

AIR COMPRESSOR & DRYER ASSEMBLY

1. Turn air suspension switch to Off position.
2. Remove engine appearance cover.
3. Disconnect air cleaner outlet tube and resonator assembly.
4. Remove IAV valve inlet tube and crankcase ventilation hose.
5. Remove air cleaner housing assembly.
6. Remove pushpins, then the air compressor cover.
7. Remove snorkel pushpin and the snorkel.
8. Push dryer air line retainer inward, then pull air line outward to remove.
9. Disconnect compressor electrical connectors.
10. Remove compressor to fender apron attaching bolts, then the compressor and dryer assembly.
11. Reverse to procedure install.

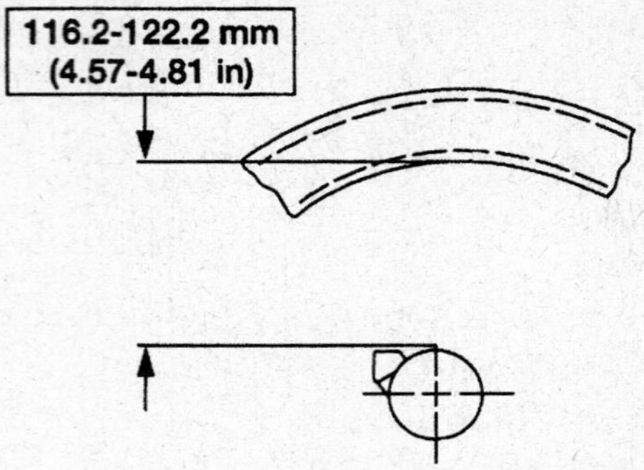

Fig. 44 Vertical "D" Dimension. 2000–02

AIR COMPRESSOR DRYER

1. Turn air suspension switch to the Off position.
2. Remove air compressor and dryer assembly as outlined in "Air Compressor & Dryer Assembly."
3. Remove dryer to compressor attaching screw.
4. Rotate dryer 90° and remove from compressor.
5. Reverse procedure to install. **Torque** dryer to compressor attaching screw to 18–27 inch lbs.

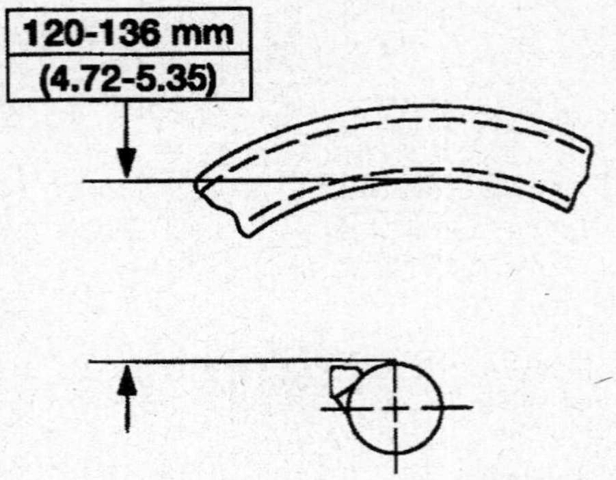

Fig. 45 Ride height measurement "D" Dimension. 2003–04

HEIGHT SENSOR

1. Turn air suspension switch to Off position.
2. Disconnect battery ground cable.
3. Raise and support vehicle, ensure suspension is at full rebound.
4. Disconnect height sensor electrical connector.
5. Depress retaining tabs at bottom and top of sensor, then remove sensor from ball studs.
6. Reverse procedure to install.

AIR SUSPENSION SWITCH

1. Remove pushpins, then peel back luggage compartment trim panel.
2. Depress air suspension switch attaching clips.
3. Pull switch from trim panel and disconnect switch electrical connector.
4. Remove switch from luggage compartment.
5. Reverse procedure to install.

COMPRESSOR RELAY

1. Remove power distribution box cover.
2. Remove compressor relay from distribution box.
3. Reverse procedure to install.

DASH GAUGES & WARNING INDICATORS

NOTE: On Air Bag Equipped Models, Refer To "Air Bag System Precautions" Located In The Front Of This Manual For System Disarming & Arming Procedures.

NOTE: Refer To "Computer Relearn Procedures" Located In The Front Of This Manual When Battery Power To The Computer Has Been Interrupted.

NOTE: "Electrical Symbol & Wire Color Code Identification" Located In The Front Of This Manual May Be Used As An Aid When Using Wiring Circuits Found In This Section.

NOTE: Refer To The "Dash Panel Service" Section For Dash Panel Removal Procedures.

NOTE: Refer To The "Electronic Instrumentation" Section In MOTOR's "Domestic Engine Performance & Driveability Manual" For Information Related To Electronic Instrumentation.

INDEX

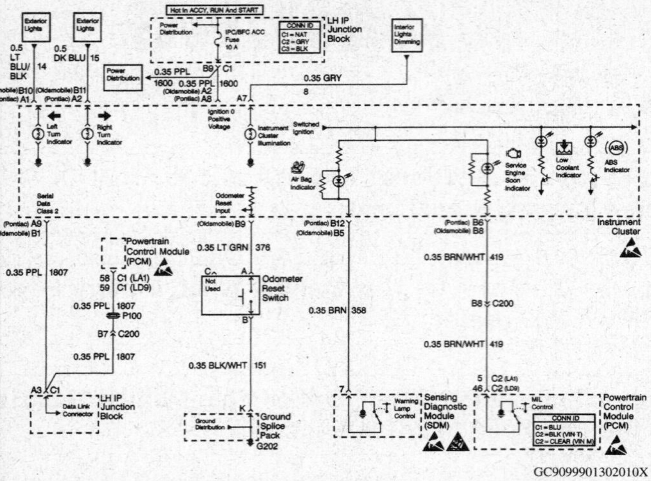

Fig. 1 Instrument cluster (Part 1 of 3). 2000 Alero & Grand Am

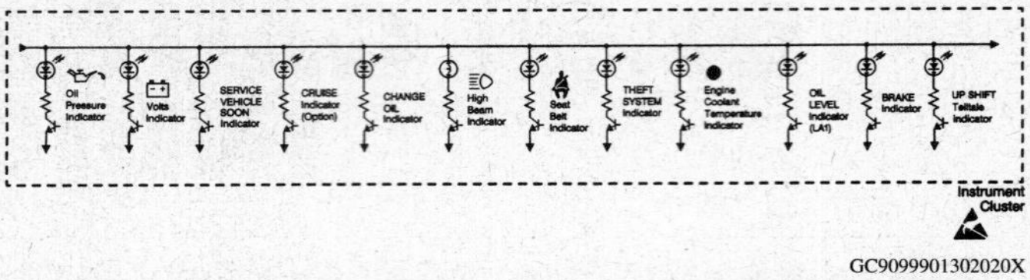

Fig. 1 Instrument cluster (Part 2 of 3). 2000 Alero & Grand Am

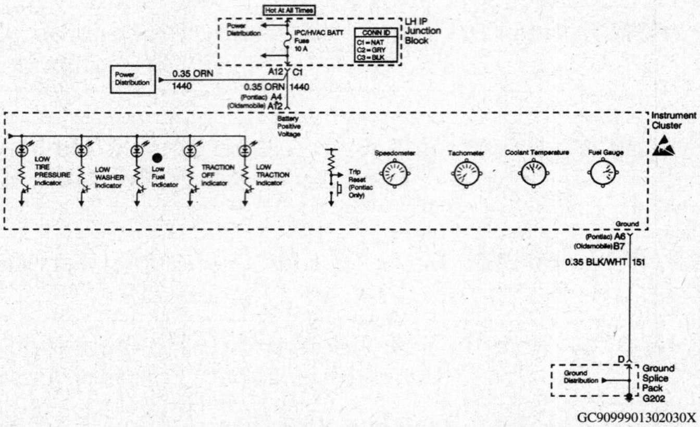

Fig. 1 Instrument cluster (Part 3 of 3). 2000 Alero & Grand Am

PRECAUTION

Air Bag Systems

Refer to "Air Bag System Precautions" in the front of this manual for system disarming and arming procedures.

Battery Ground Cable

Prior to service, disconnect battery ground cable and isolate as required.

TROUBLESHOOTING

Air Bag Warning Lamp

Air bag warning lamp illuminates when there is an air bag system concern.

Refer to **MOTOR's "Air Bag Manual" or "Air Bag Diagnostics CD."**

Anti-Lock Brake Warning Lamp

The anti-lock brake warning lamp will illuminate if the system controller detects any fault in the anti-lock brake system. Normal brake system operation will remain operational, but wheels could lock during panic stop.

Brake Warning Lamp

1. Brake fluid level switch.
2. Low brake fluid level.
3. Park brake system.
4. Instrument cluster.
5. Daytime Running Lights control module.
6. Wiring circuits and bulb.

Charging System Warning Lamp

1. Wiring circuits and bulb.
2. Instrument cluster and battery.
3. Inspect drive belt.
4. Inspect PCM.
5. Inspect for corroded terminals.
6. Alternator.

Check Engine Warning Lamp

Check engine or malfunction indicator lamp (MIL) indicator is illuminated by Powertrain Control Module (PCM). Refer to **MOTOR's "Domestic Engine Performance & Driveability Manual"** for lamp diagnosis.

Low Coolant Warning Lamp

1. Instrument cluster.
2. Wiring circuits and bulb.
3. Low coolant level switch.
4. Inspect BCM.

Low Fuel Level Warning Lamp

1. Fuel gauge and indicator bulb.
2. Instrument cluster circuit.
3. Electrical connections.
4. Low fuel level switch.

Low Oil Pressure Warning Lamp

1. Oil pressure switch.
2. Low engine oil level.
3. Wiring circuits, bulb and fuse.
4. Low engine oil pressure and Instrument cluster.

Low Oil Level Warning Lamp

1. Wiring circuits, bulb and fuse.
2. Low engine oil level.
3. Oil pressure switch.
4. Instrument cluster.

Low Tire Pressure Warning Lamp

1. Low tire pressure.
2. Low tire pressure sensor and bulb.
3. Low tire pressure module.
4. Wiring circuits and fuse.

Low Washer Fluid Warning Lamp

1. Wiring circuits and bulb.
2. Windshield washer low fluid switch.
3. Instrument cluster.
4. Low washer fluid level and washer fluid container.
5. Indicator lamp module and sensor.

Safety Belt Warning Lamp

1. Lefthand belt switch and fuse.
2. Wiring circuits and bulb.
3. Instrument cluster.

WIRING DIAGRAMS

Alero & Grand Am

Refer to **Figs. 1 through 3,** for wiring diagrams.

Aurora

Refer to **Fig. 4,** for wiring diagrams.

Bonneville

Refer to **Fig. 5,** for wiring diagrams.

Camaro & Firebird

Refer to **Figs. 6 and 7,** for wiring diagrams.

Catera

Refer to **Figs. 8 and 9,** for wiring diagrams.

Cavalier & Sunfire

Refer to **Figs. 10 through 12,** for wiring diagrams.

Century & Regal

Refer to **Figs. 13 through 15,** for wiring diagrams.

Corvette

Refer to **Figs. 16 and 17,** for wiring diagrams.

Cutlass & Malibu

Refer to **Figs. 18 through 20,** for wiring diagrams.

CTS

Refer to **Fig. 21,** for wiring diagram.

DeVille & Eldorado

Refer to **Figs. 22 through 25,** for wiring diagrams.

Grand Prix

Refer to **Figs. 26 through 28,** for wiring diagrams.

Impala, Lumina & Monte Carlo

Refer to **Figs. 29 through 31,** for wiring diagrams.

Intrigue

Refer to **Fig. 32,** for wiring diagrams.

LeSabre

Refer to **Figs. 33 and 34,** for wiring diagrams.

Metro

Refer to **Fig. 35,** for wiring diagrams.

Park Avenue

Refer to **Figs. 36 and 37,** for wiring diagrams.

Prizm

Refer to **Fig. 38,** for wiring diagrams.

Saturn

Refer to **Figs. 39 through 42,** for instrument wiring diagrams.

Seville

Refer to **Figs. 43 and 44,** for wiring diagrams.

Vibe

Refer to **Fig. 45,** for wiring diagrams.

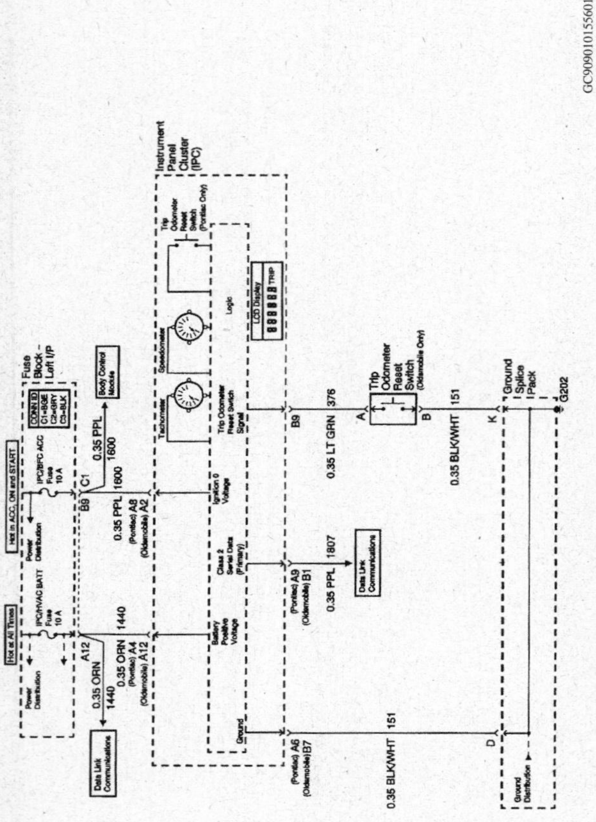

Fig. 2 Instrument cluster (Part 1 of 3). 2001 Alero & Grand Am

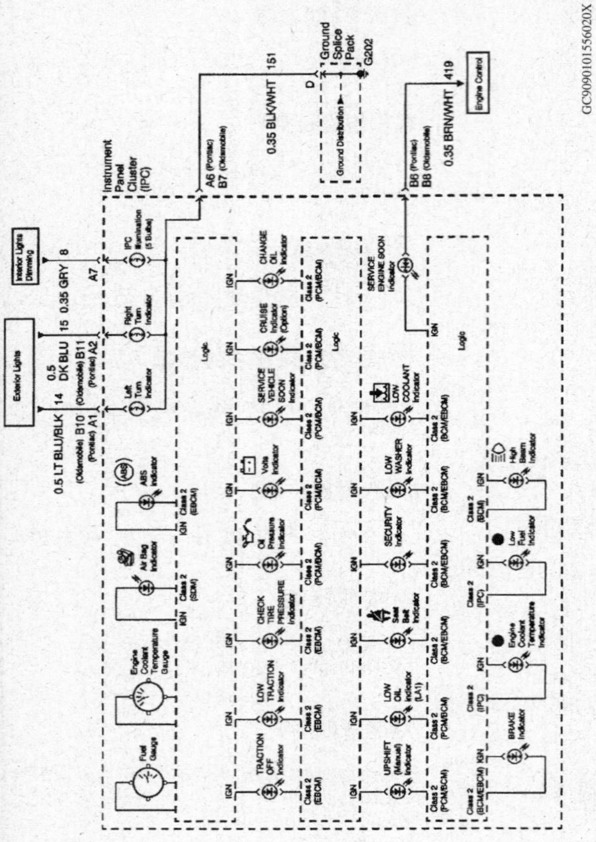

Fig. 2 Instrument cluster (Part 2 of 3). 2001 Alero & Grand Am

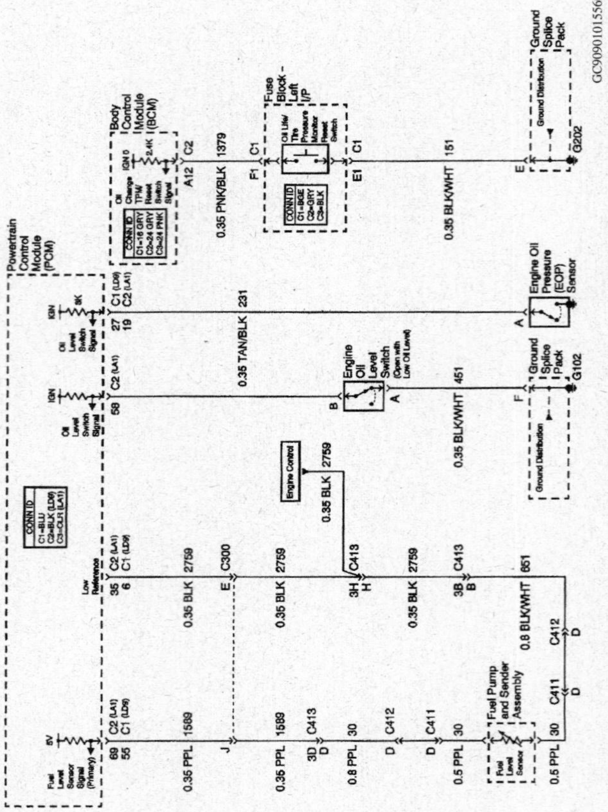

Fig. 2 Instrument cluster (Part 3 of 3). 2001 Alero & Grand Am

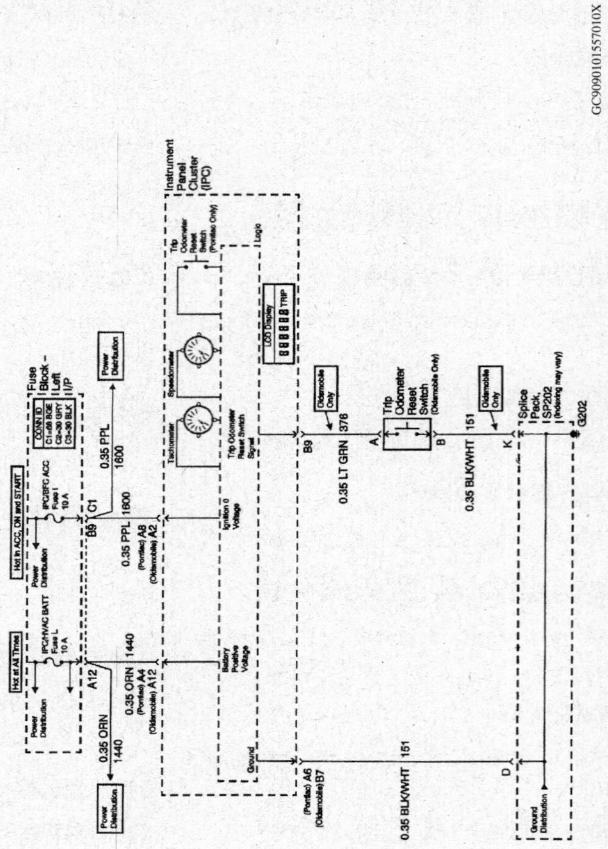

Fig. 3 Instrument cluster (Part 1 of 3). 2002–04 Alero & Grand Am

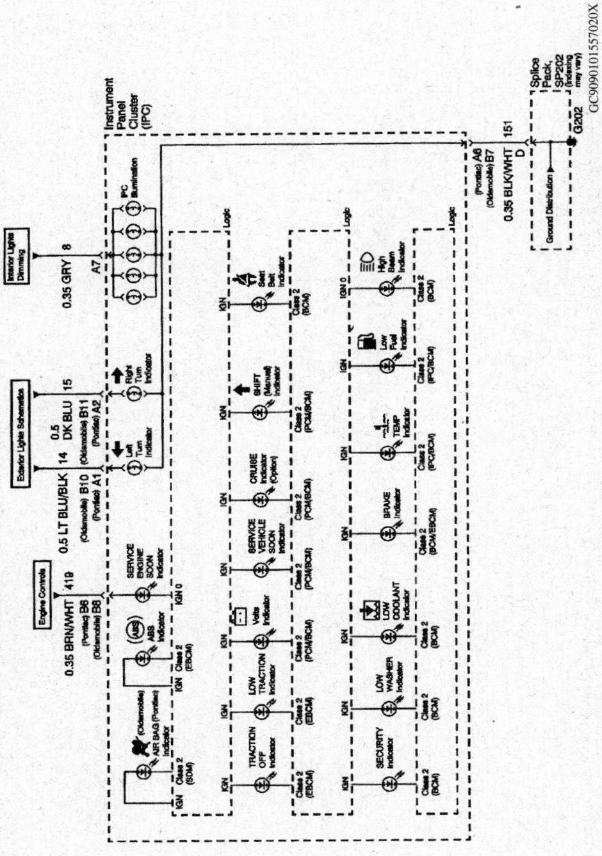

Fig. 3 Instrument cluster (Part 2 of 3). 2002–04 Alero & Grand Am

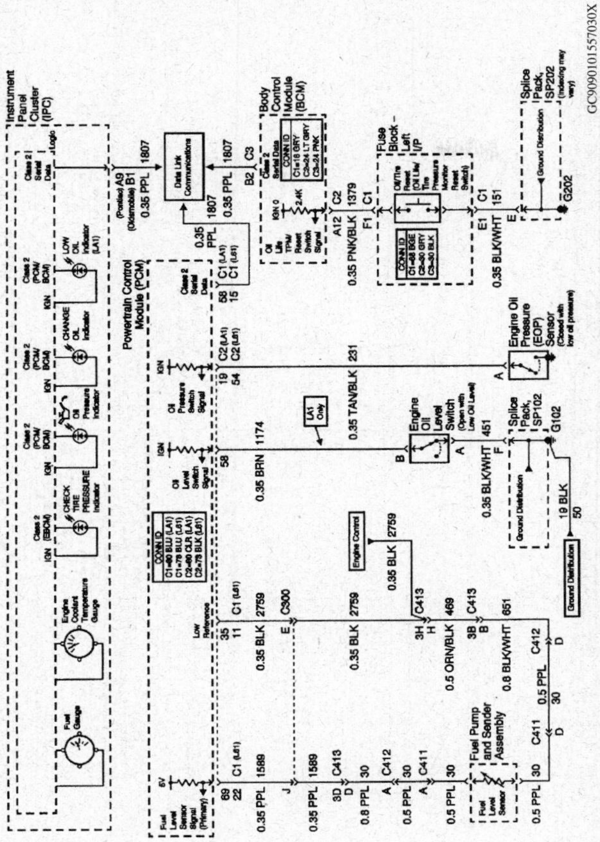

Fig. 3 Instrument cluster (Part 3 of 3). 2002–04 Alero & Grand Am

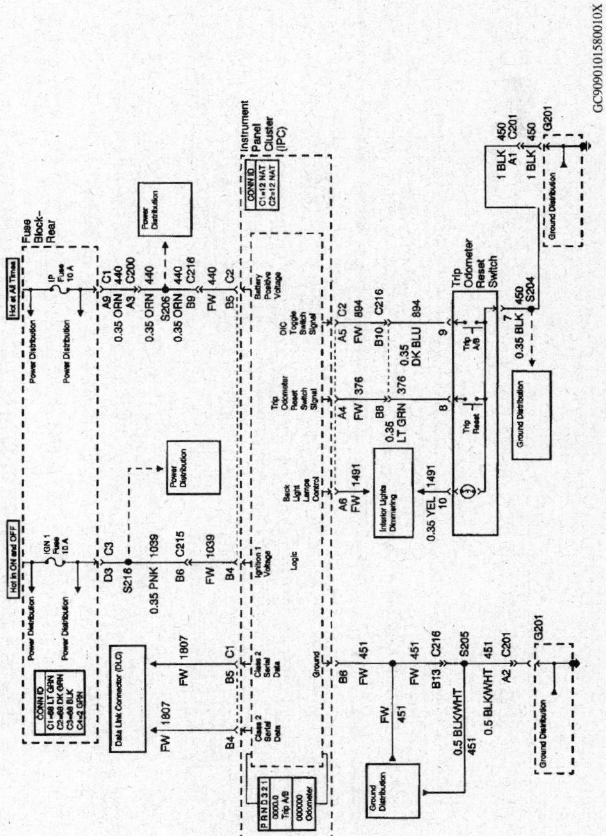

Fig. 4 Instrument cluster (Part 1 of 3). Aurora

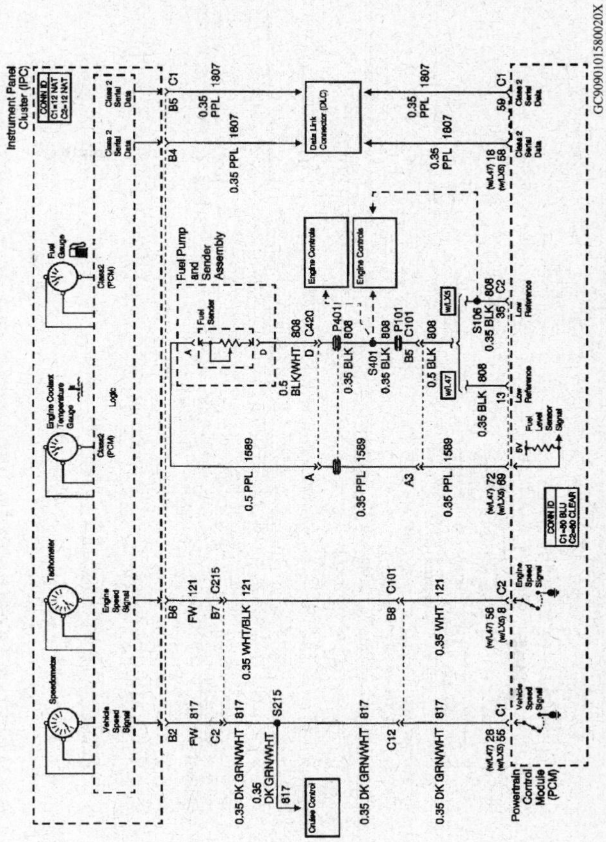

Fig. 4 Instrument cluster (Part 2 of 3). Aurora

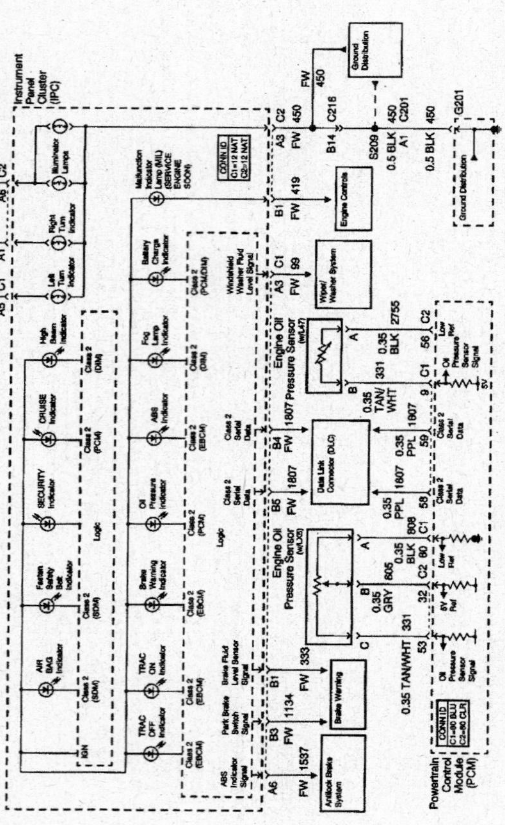

GC9090101580030X

Fig. 4 Instrument cluster (Part 3 of 3). Aurora

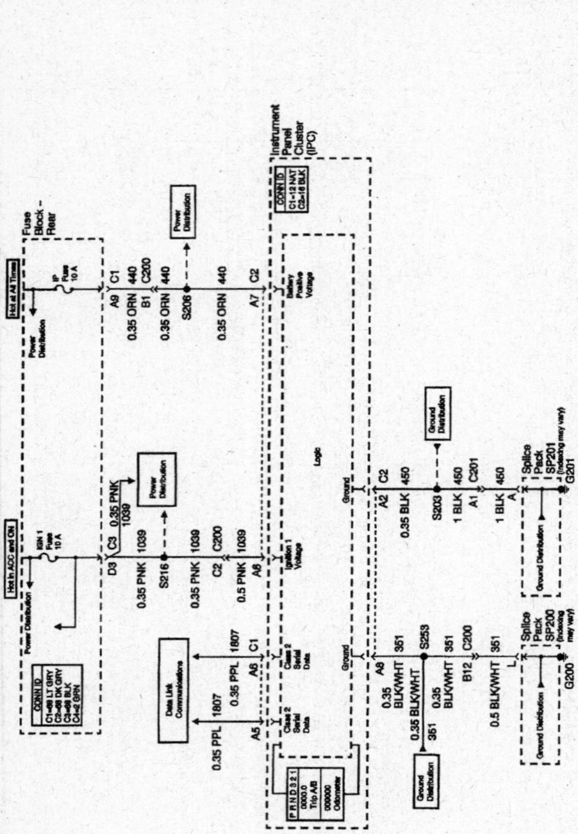

GC9090101561010X

Fig. 5 Instrument cluster (Part 1 of 9). Bonneville

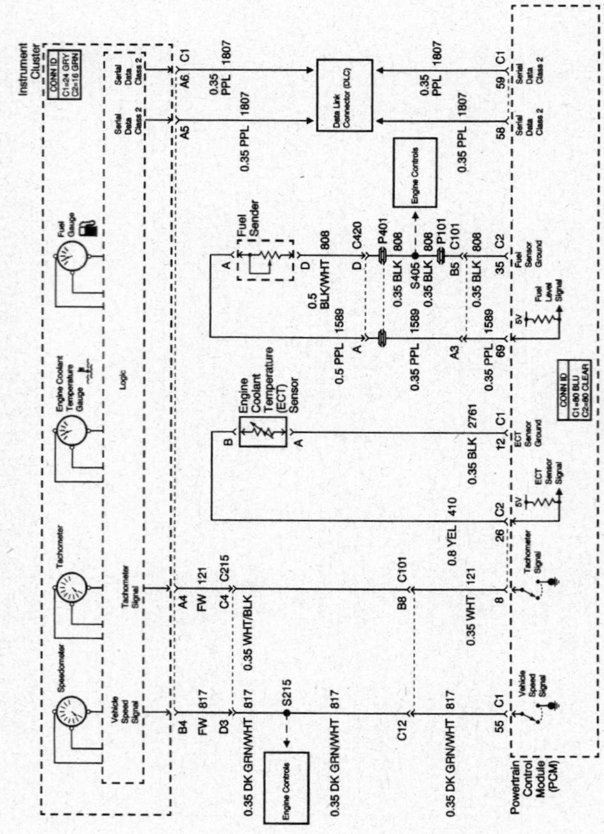

GC9099901322020X

Fig. 5 Instrument cluster (Part 2 of 9). 2000 Bonneville

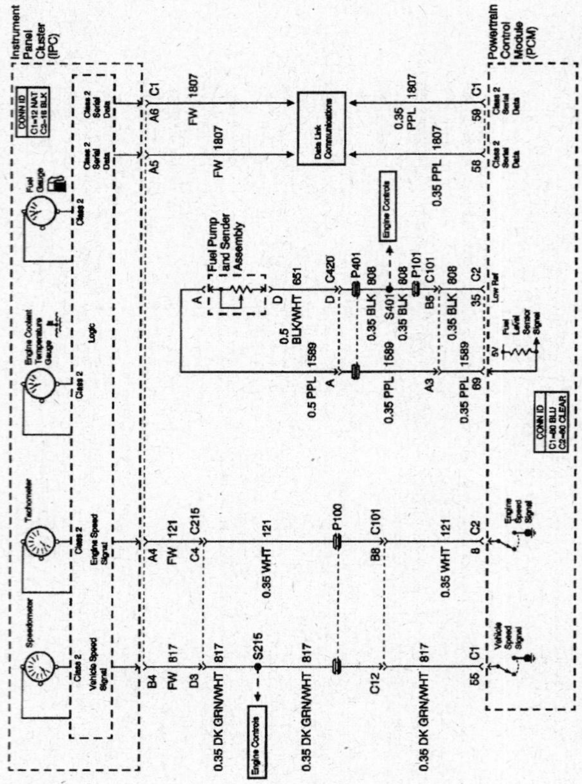

GC9090101561020X

Fig. 5 Instrument cluster (Part 2 of 9). 2001 Bonneville

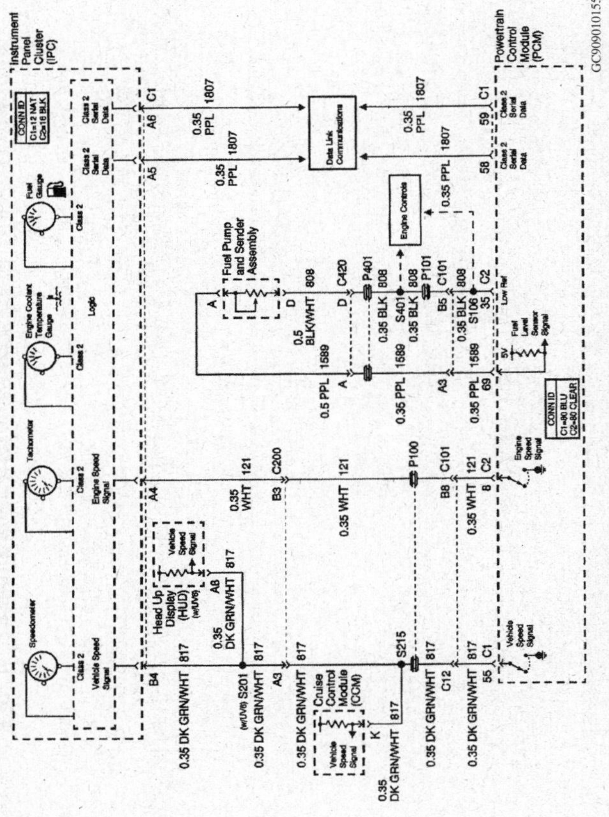

Fig. 5 Instrument cluster (Part 2 of 9). 2002–04 Bonneville

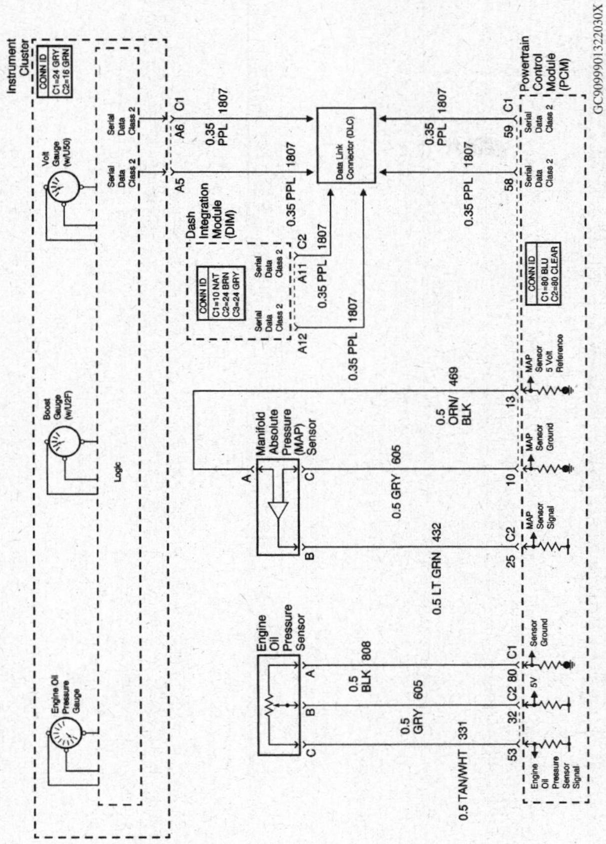

Fig. 5 Instrument cluster (Part 3 of 9). 2000–04 Bonneville

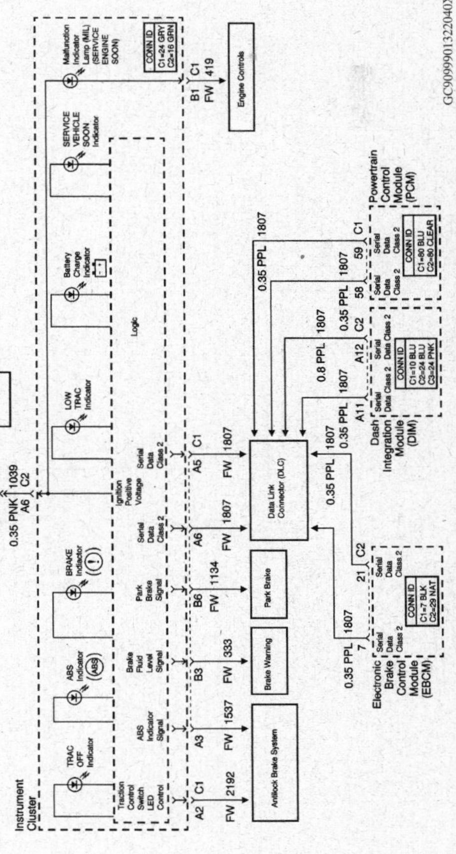

Fig. 5 Instrument cluster (Part 4 of 9). 2000 Bonneville

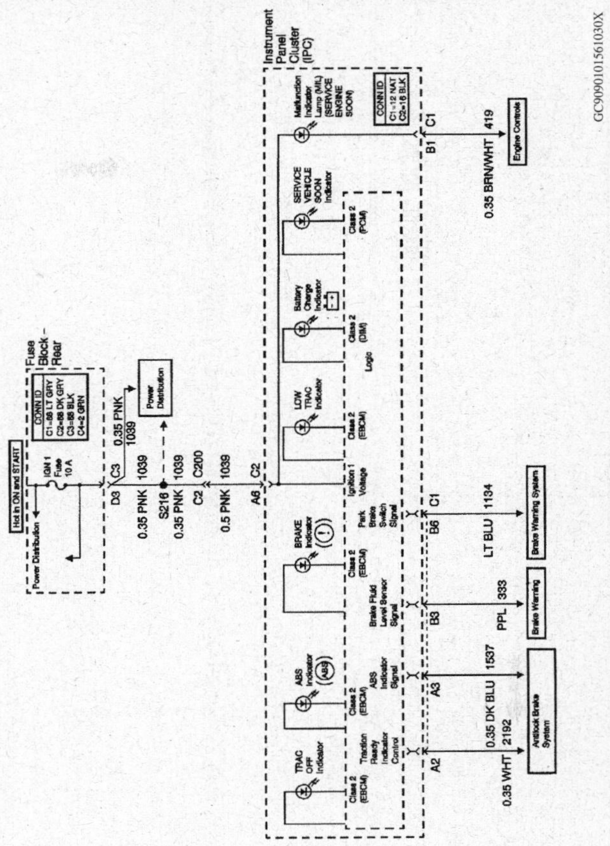

Fig. 5 Instrument cluster (Part 4 of 9). 2001–04 Bonneville

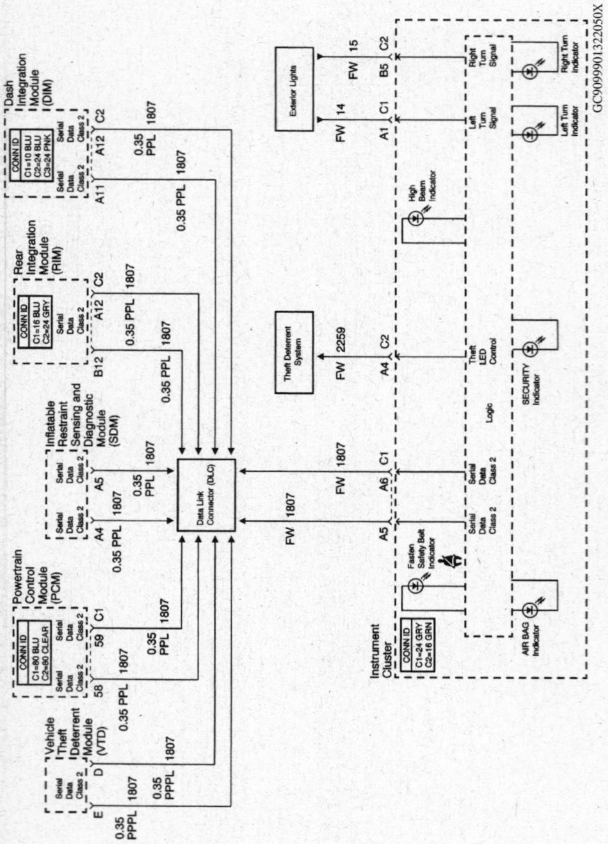

Fig. 5 Instrument cluster (Part 5 of 9). 2000 Bonneville

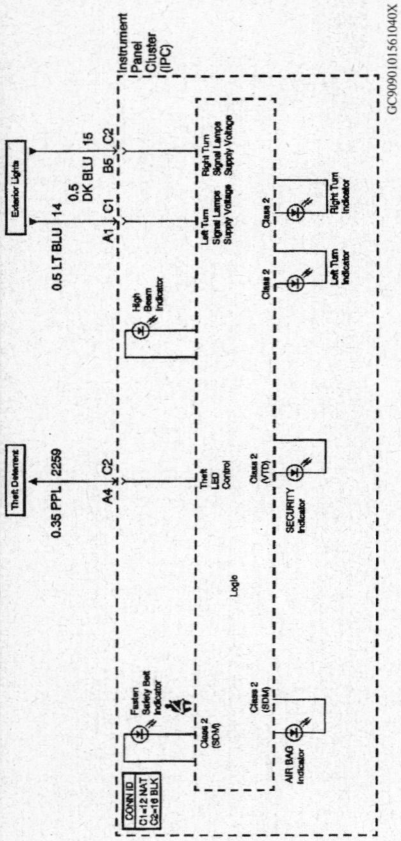

Fig. 5 Instrument cluster (Part 5 of 9). 2001–04 Bonneville

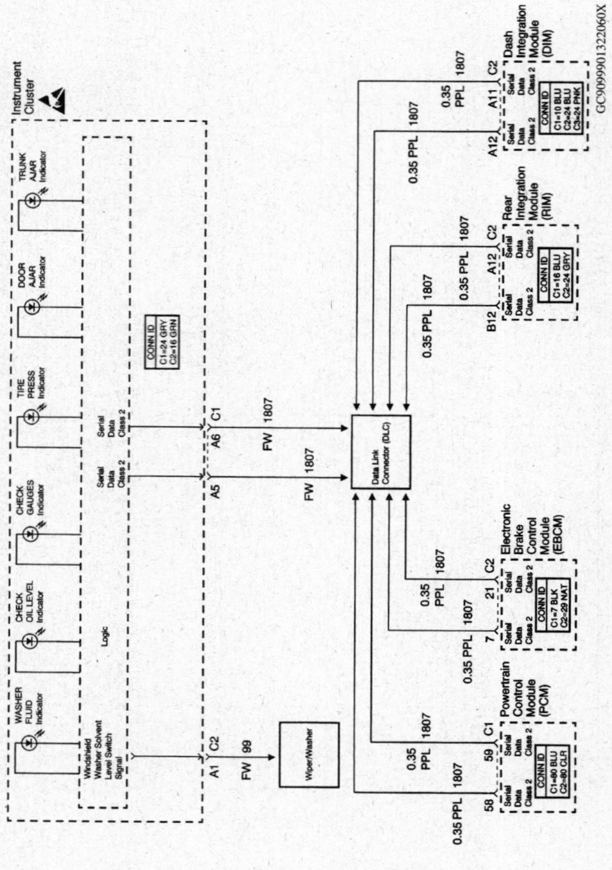

Fig. 5 Instrument cluster (Part 6 of 9). 2000 Bonneville

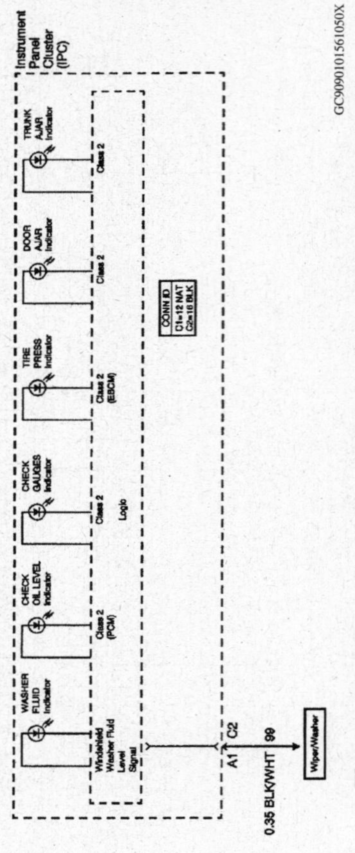

Fig. 5 Instrument cluster (Part 6 of 9). 2001–04 Bonneville

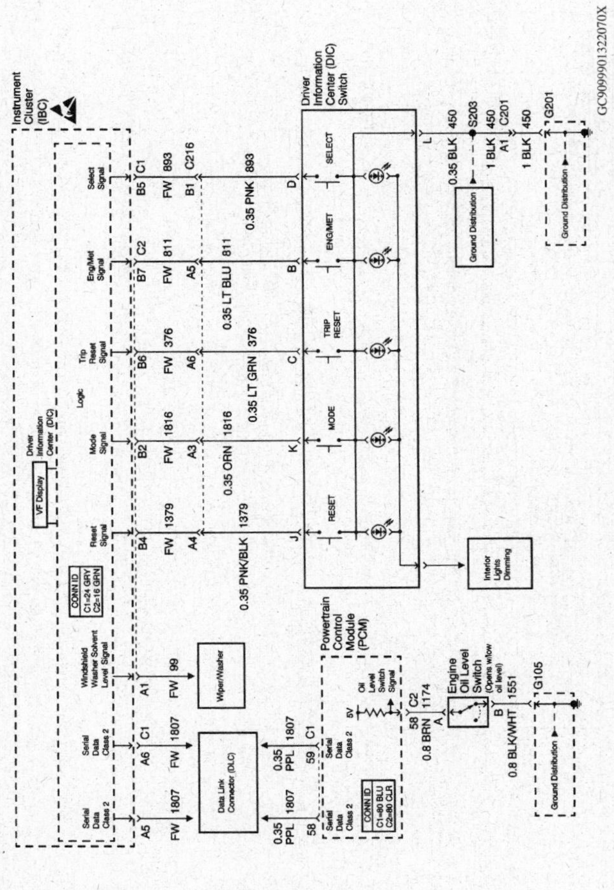

Fig. 5 Instrument cluster (Part 7 of 9). 2000–04 Bonneville

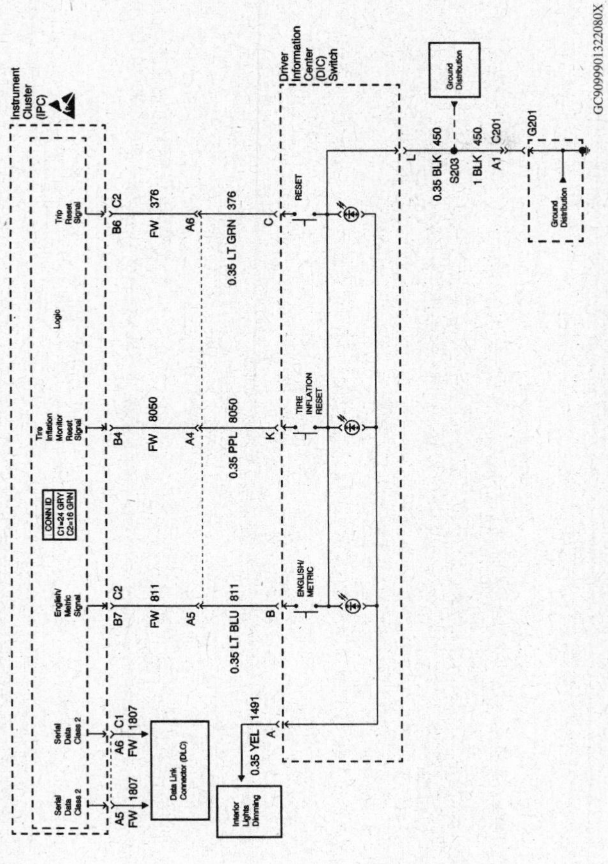

Fig. 5 Instrument cluster (Part 8 of 9). 2000–04 Bonneville

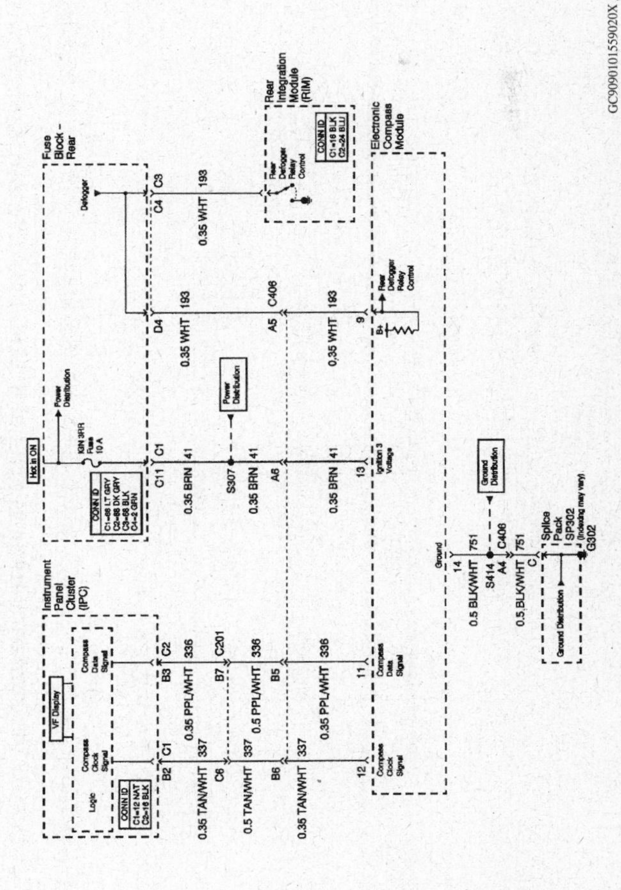

Fig. 5 Instrument cluster (Part 9 of 9). 2000–04 Bonneville

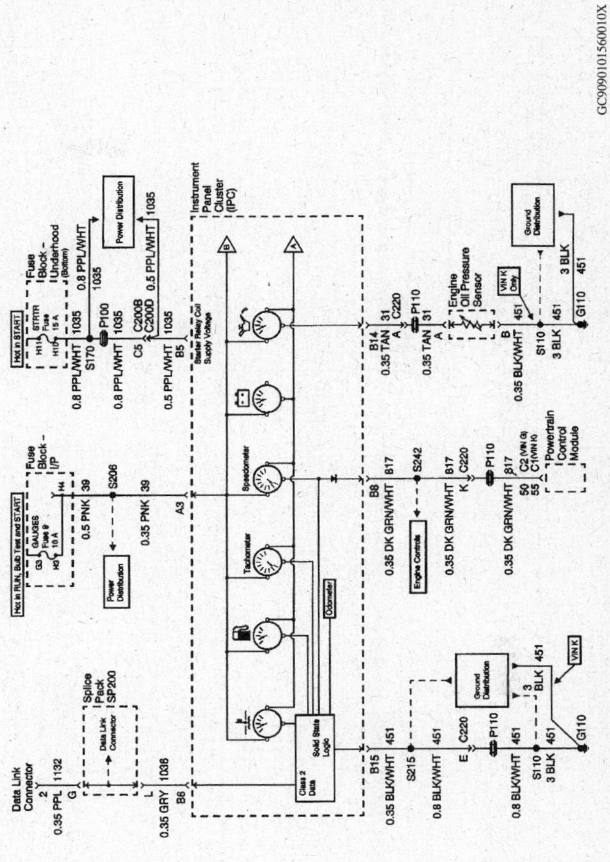

Fig. 6 Instrument cluster (Part 1 of 4). 2000–01 Camaro & Firebird

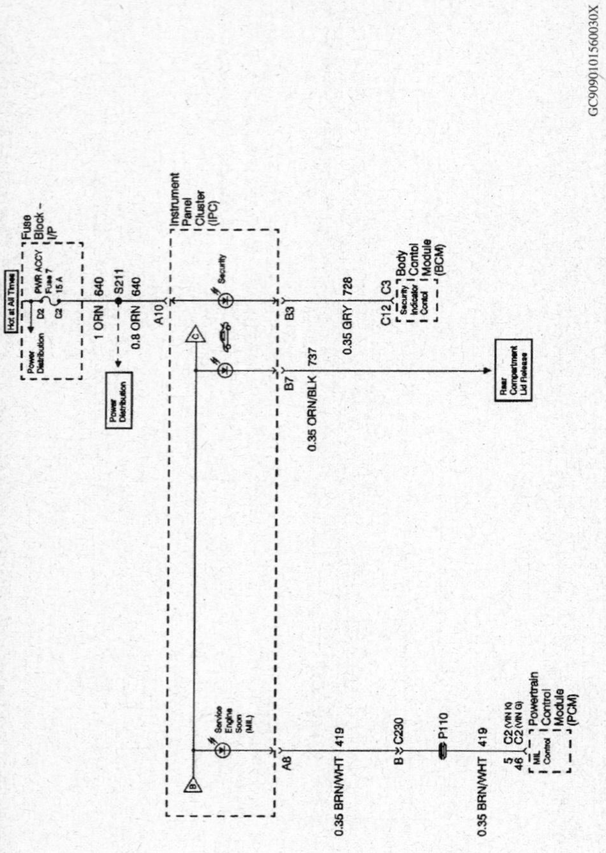

Fig. 6 Instrument cluster (Part 3 of 4). 2000–01 Camaro & Firebird

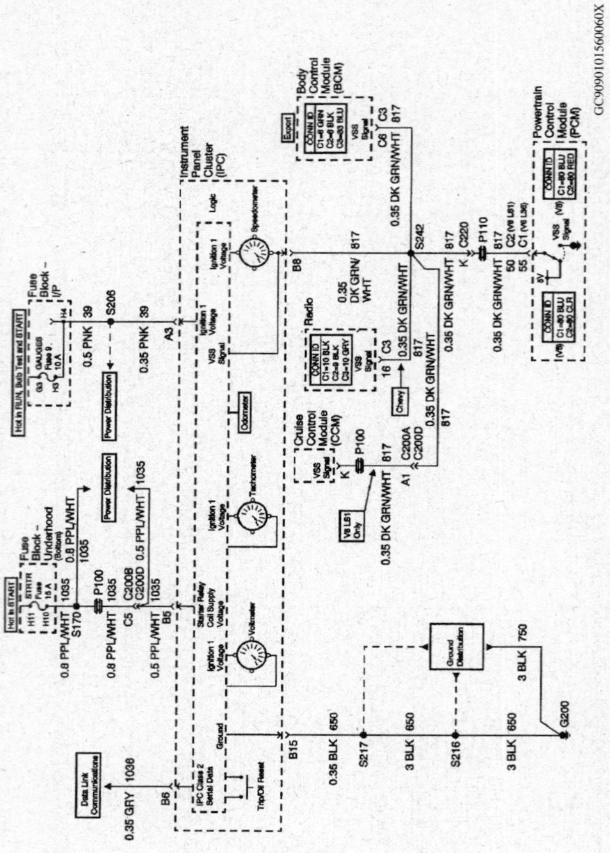

Fig. 7 Instrument cluster (Part 1 of 4). 2002 Camaro & Firebird

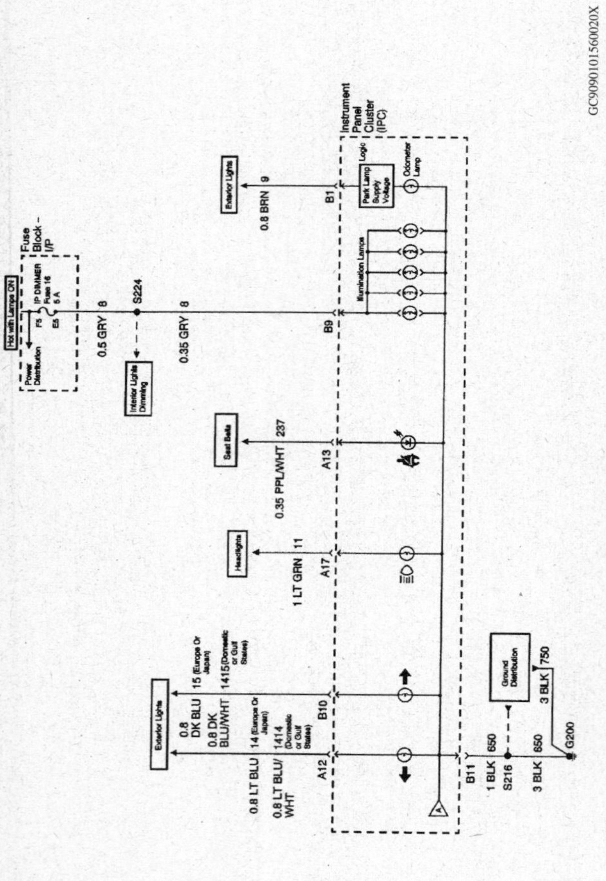

Fig. 6 Instrument cluster (Part 2 of 4). 2000–01 Camaro & Firebird

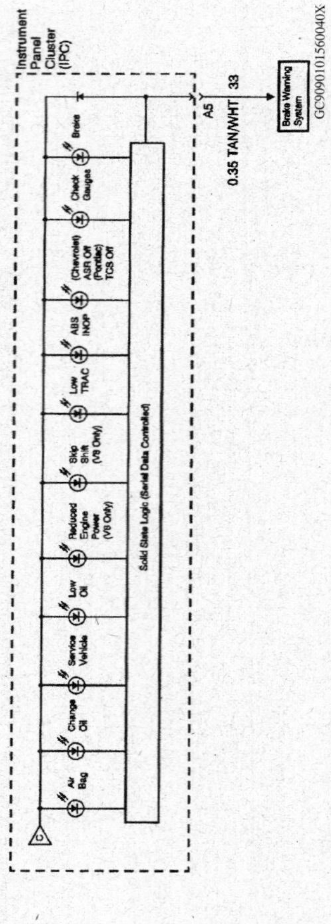

Fig. 6 Instrument cluster (Part 4 of 4). 2000–01 Camaro & Firebird

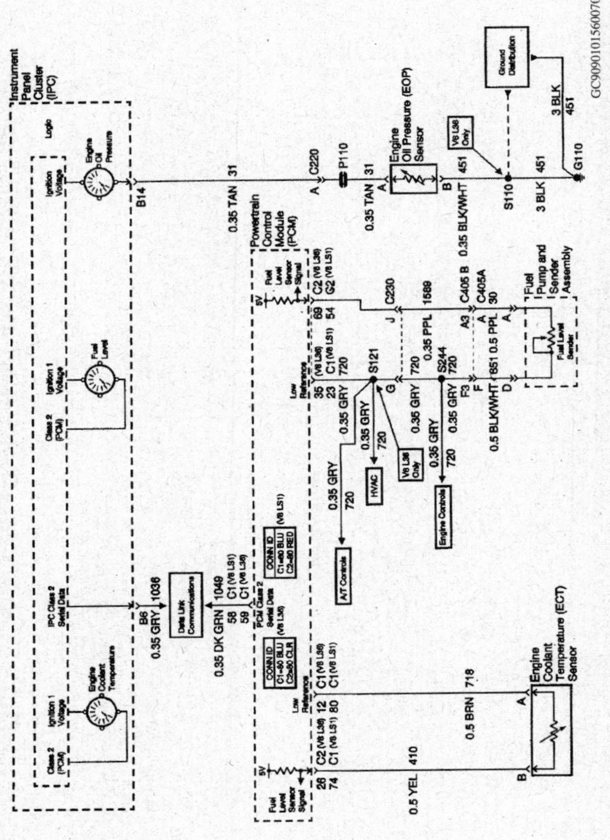

Fig. 7 Instrument cluster (Part 2 of 4). 2002 Camaro & Firebird

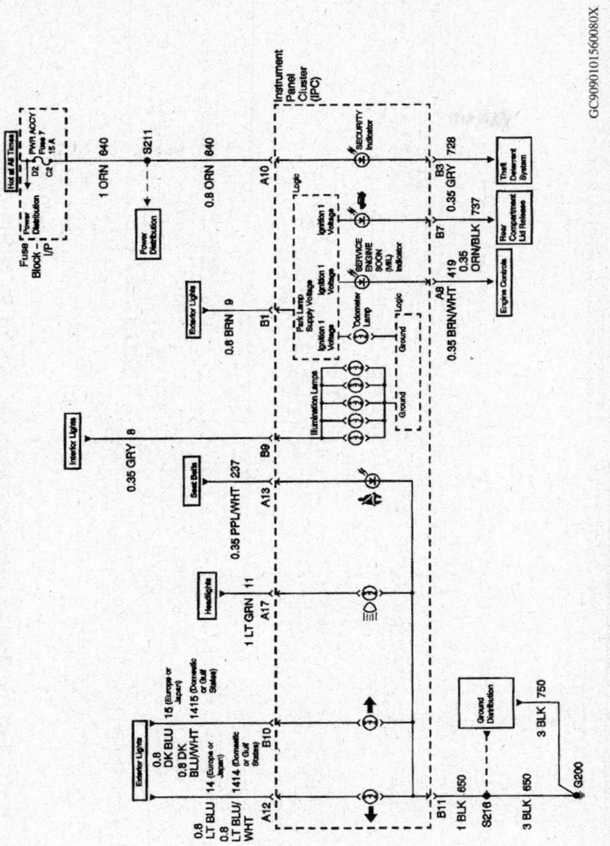

Fig. 7 Instrument cluster (Part 3 of 4). 2002 Camaro & Firebird

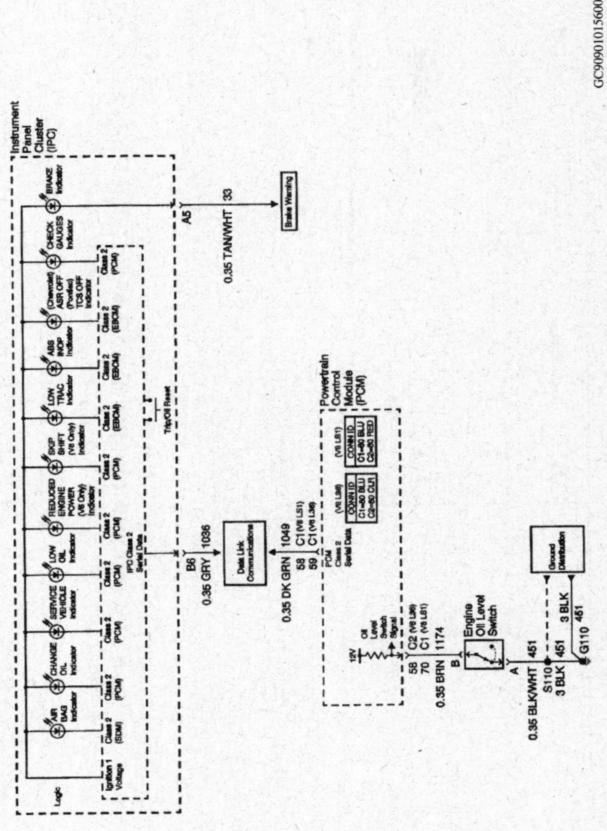

Fig. 7 Instrument cluster (Part 4 of 4). 2002 Camaro & Firebird

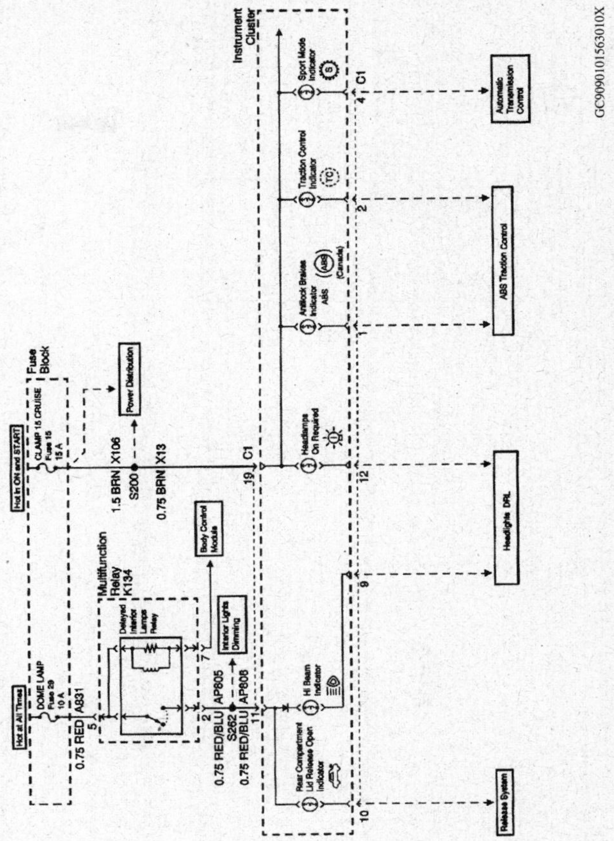

Fig. 8 Instrument cluster (Part 1 of 6). 2000 Catera

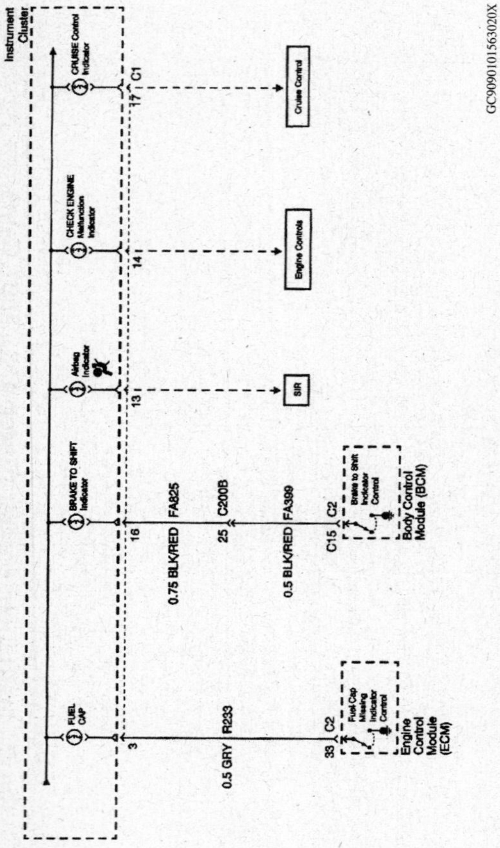

Fig. 8 Instrument cluster (Part 2 of 6). 2000 Catera

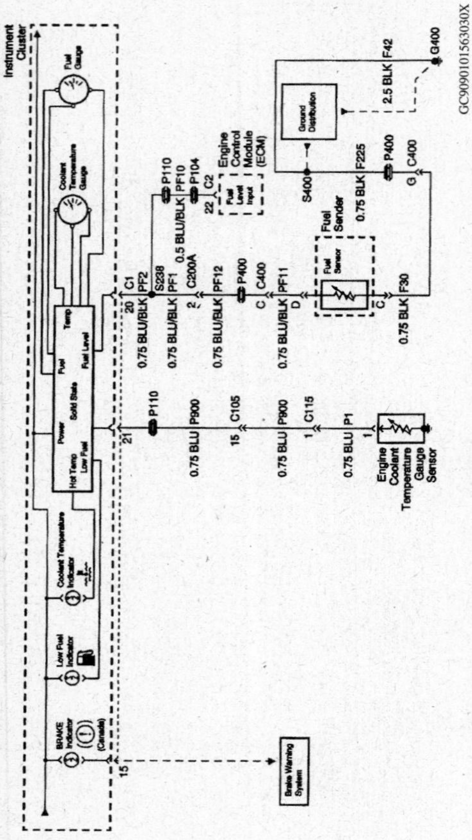

Fig. 8 Instrument cluster (Part 3 of 6). 2000 Catera

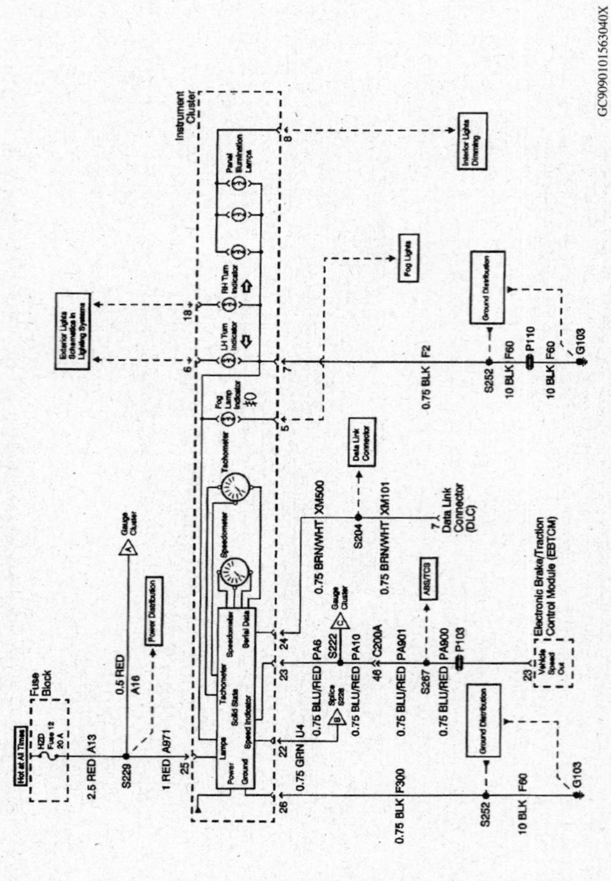

Fig. 8 Instrument cluster (Part 4 of 6). 2000 Catera

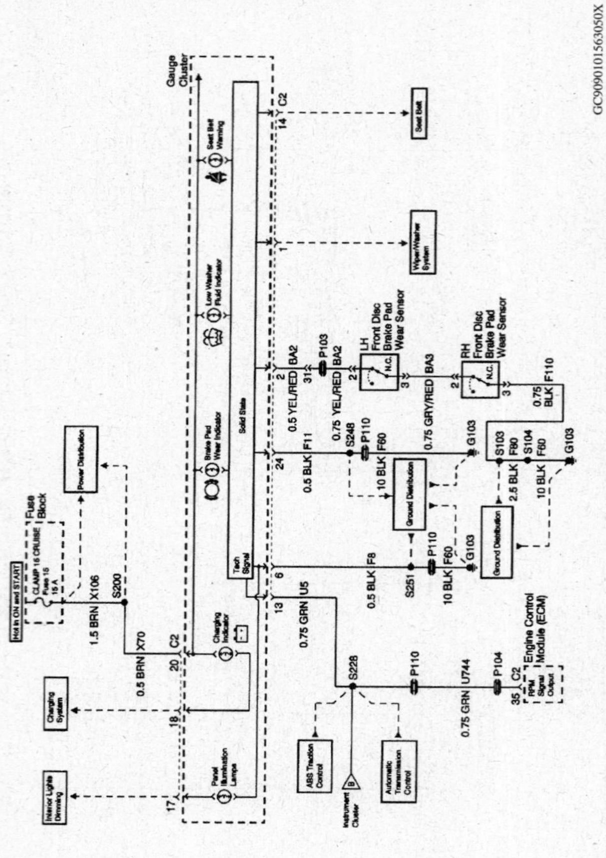

Fig. 8 Instrument cluster (Part 5 of 6). 2000 Catera

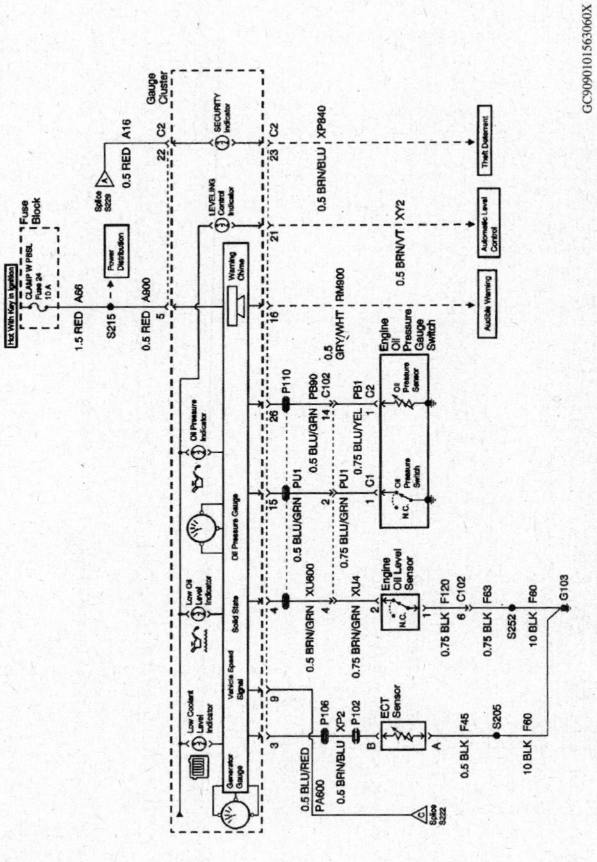

Fig. 8 Instrument cluster (Part 6 of 6). 2000 Catera

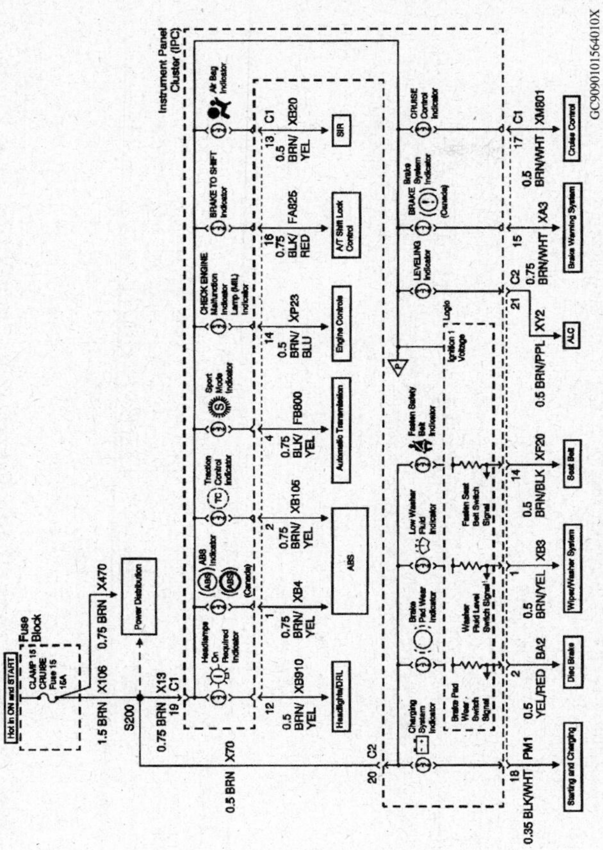

Fig. 9 Instrument cluster (Part 1 of 4). 2001 Catera

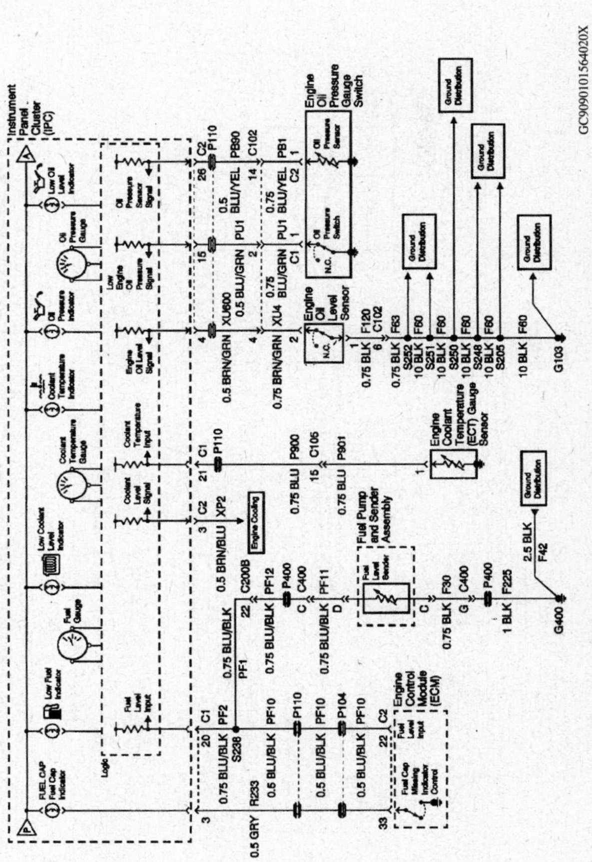

Fig. 9 Instrument cluster (Part 2 of 4). 2001 Catera

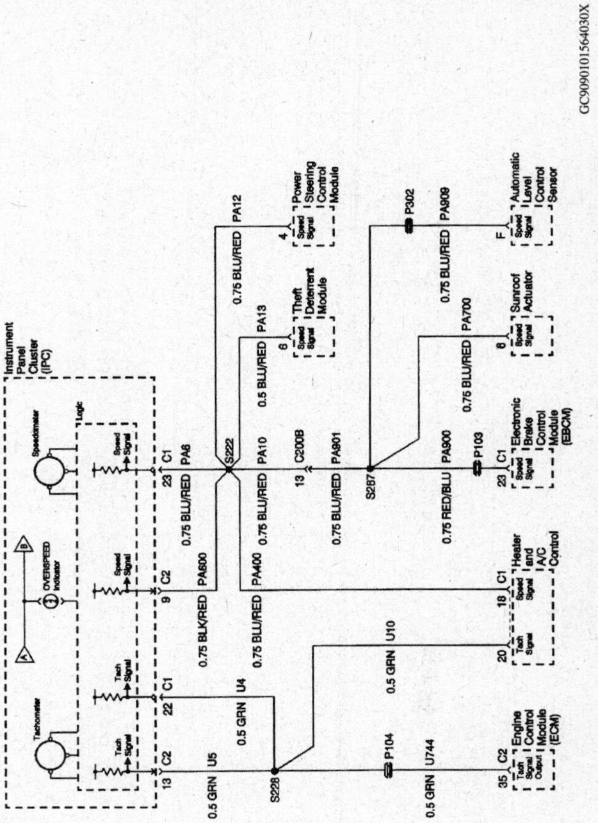

Fig. 9 Instrument cluster (Part 3 of 4). 2001 Catera

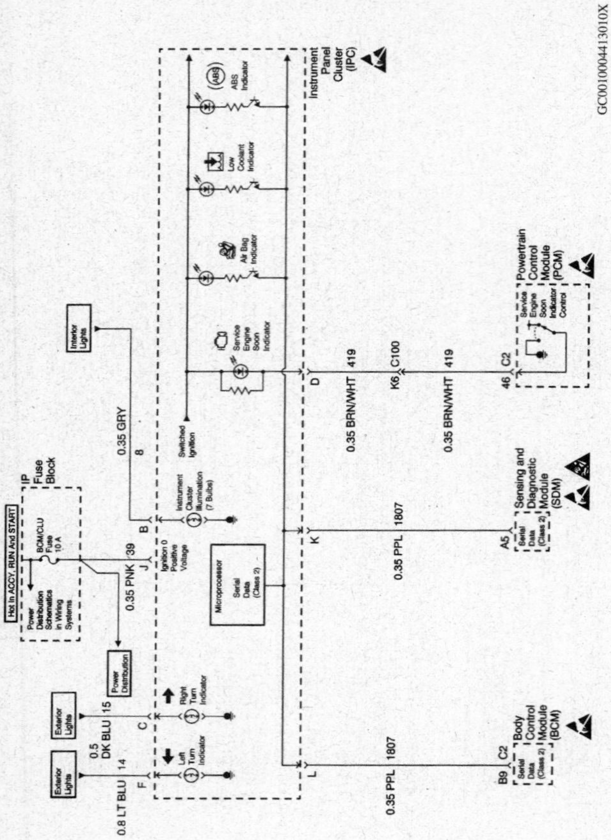

Fig. 10 Instrument cluster (Part 1 of 3). 2000 Cavalier & Sunfire

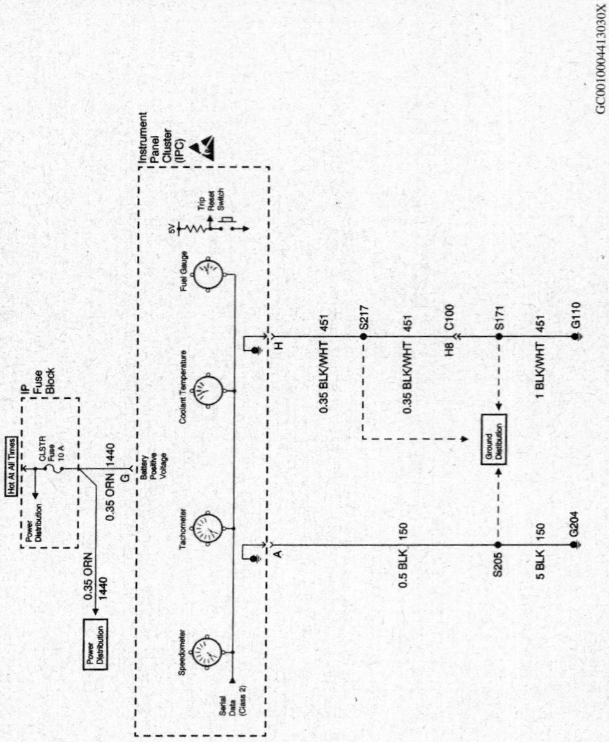

Fig. 10 Instrument cluster (Part 3 of 3). 2000 Cavalier & Sunfire

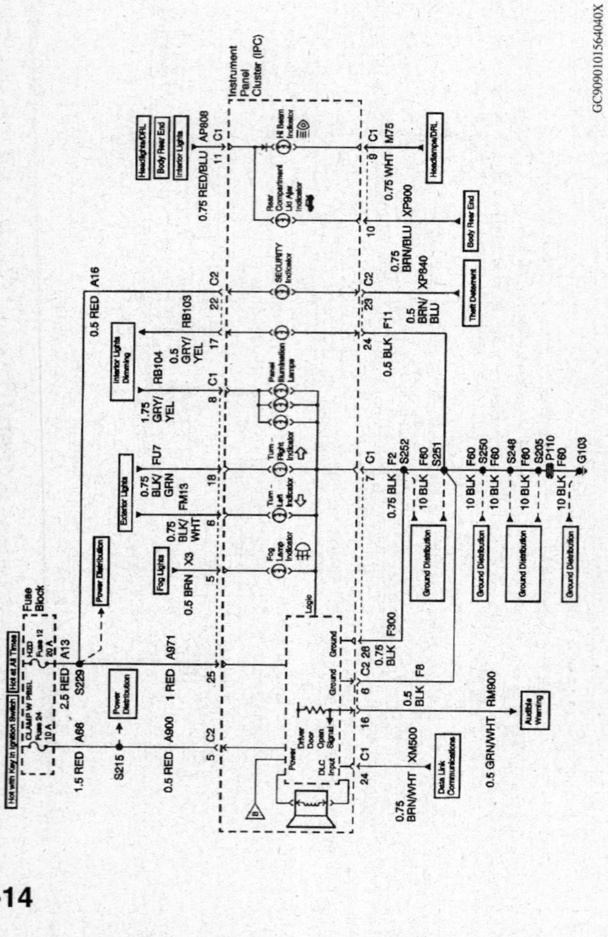

Fig. 9 Instrument cluster (Part 4 of 4). 2001 Catera

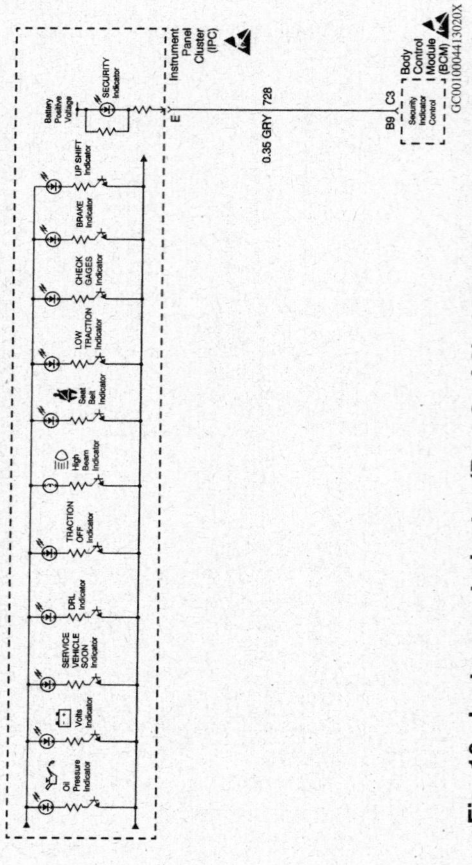

Fig. 10 Instrument cluster (Part 2 of 3). 2000 Cavalier & Sunfire

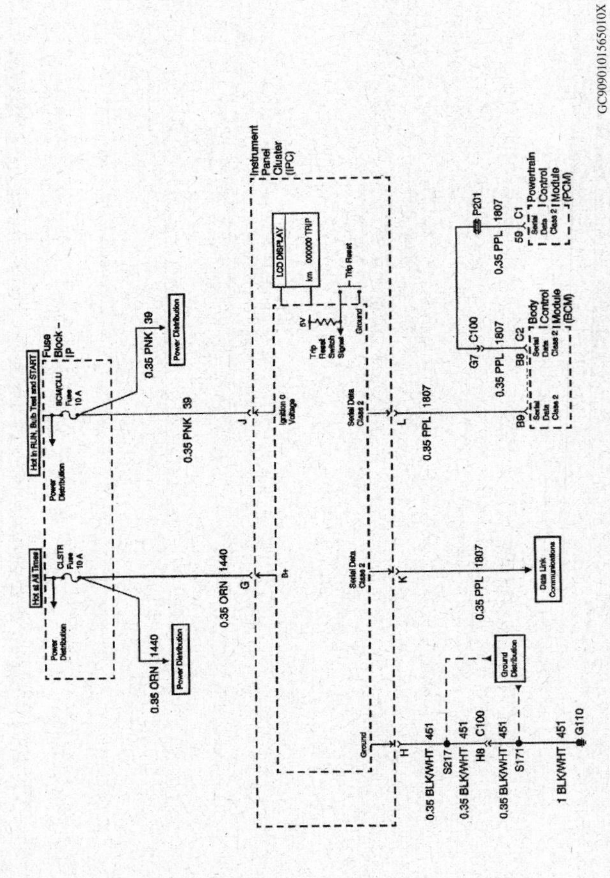

GC90901015565010X

Fig. 11 Instrument cluster (Part 1 of 3). 2001 Cavalier & Sunfire

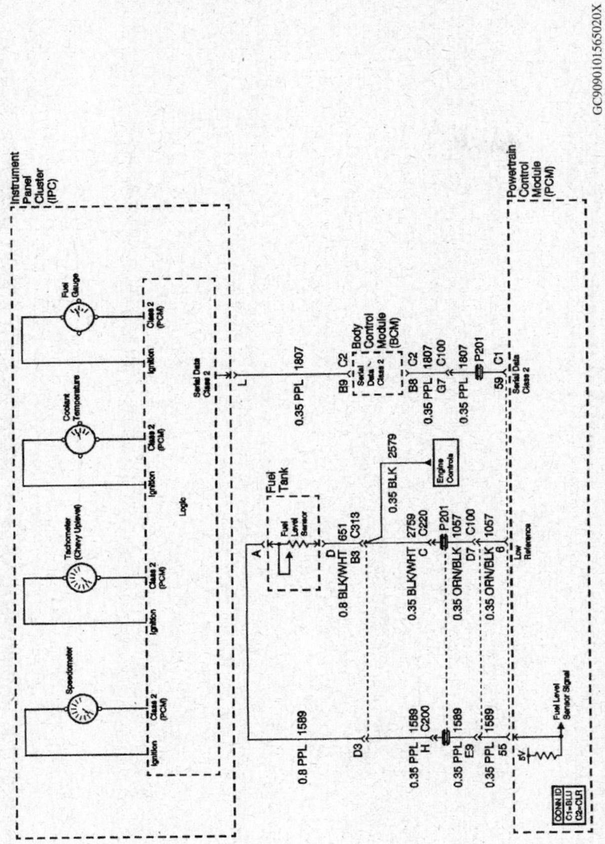

GC90901015565020X

Fig. 11 Instrument cluster (Part 2 of 3). 2001 Cavalier & Sunfire

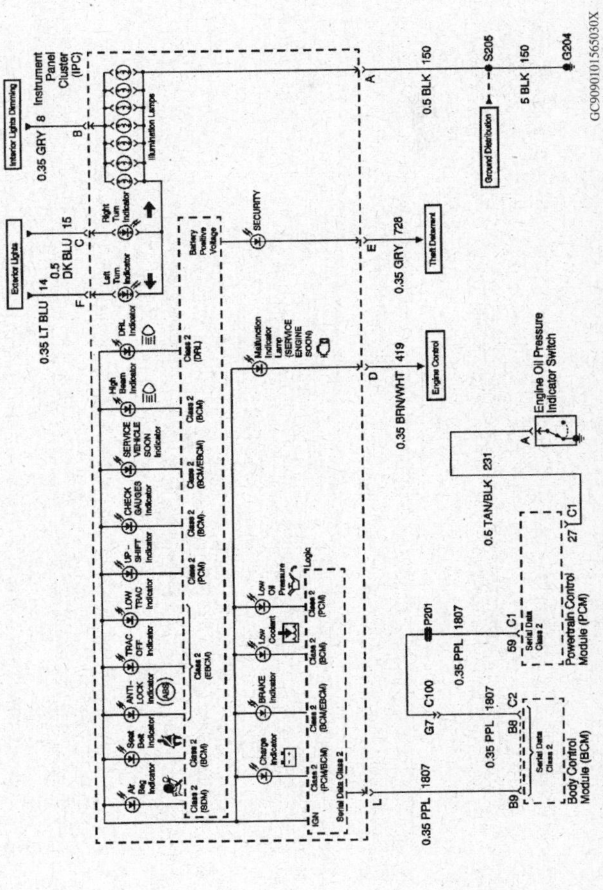

GC90901015565030X

Fig. 11 Instrument cluster (Part 3 of 3). 2001 Cavalier & Sunfire

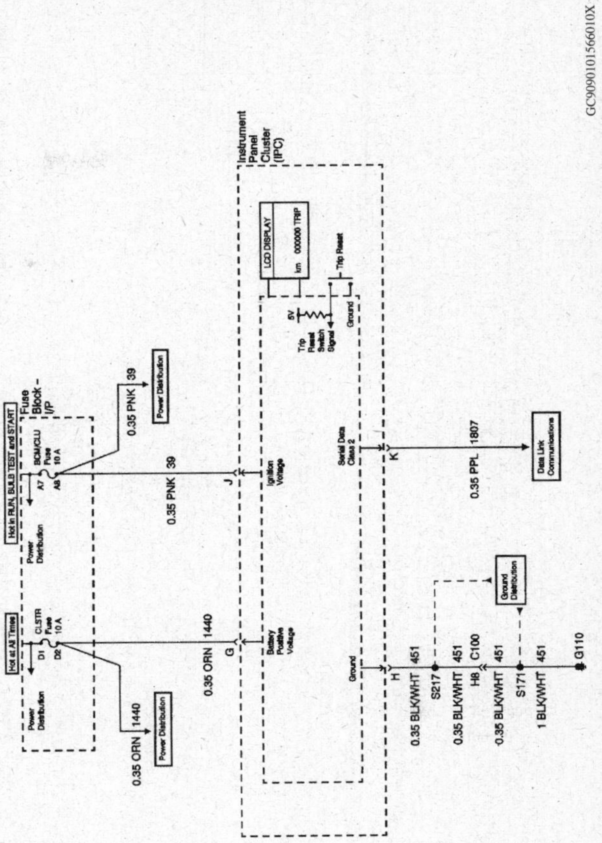

GC90901015566010X

Fig. 12 Instrument cluster (Part 1 of 3). 2002–04 Cavalier & Sunfire

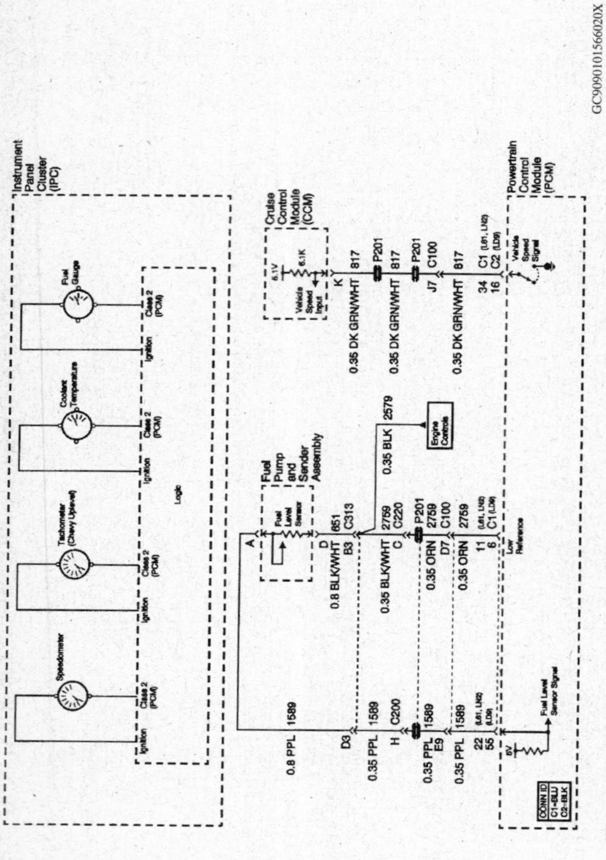

Fig. 12 Instrument cluster (Part 2 of 3). 2002–04 Cavalier & Sunfire

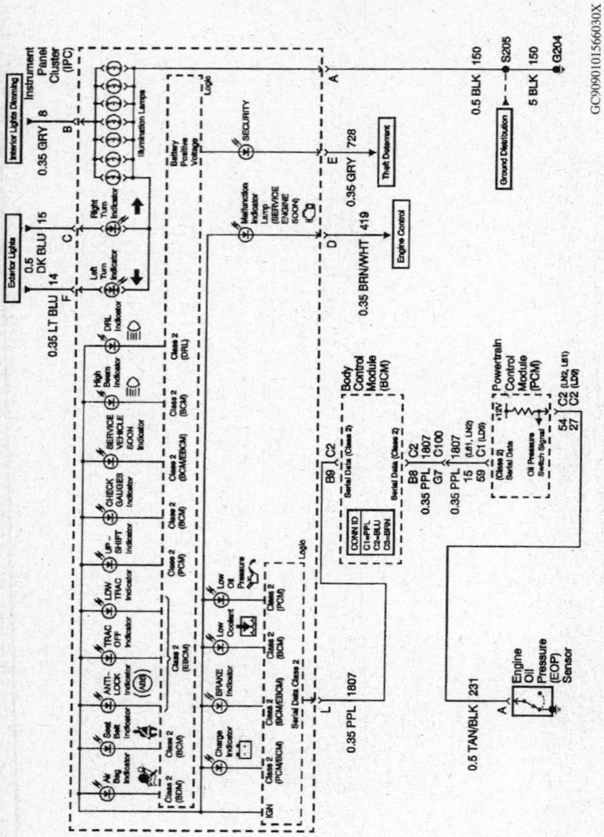

Fig. 12 Instrument cluster (Part 3 of 3). 2002–04 Cavalier & Sunfire

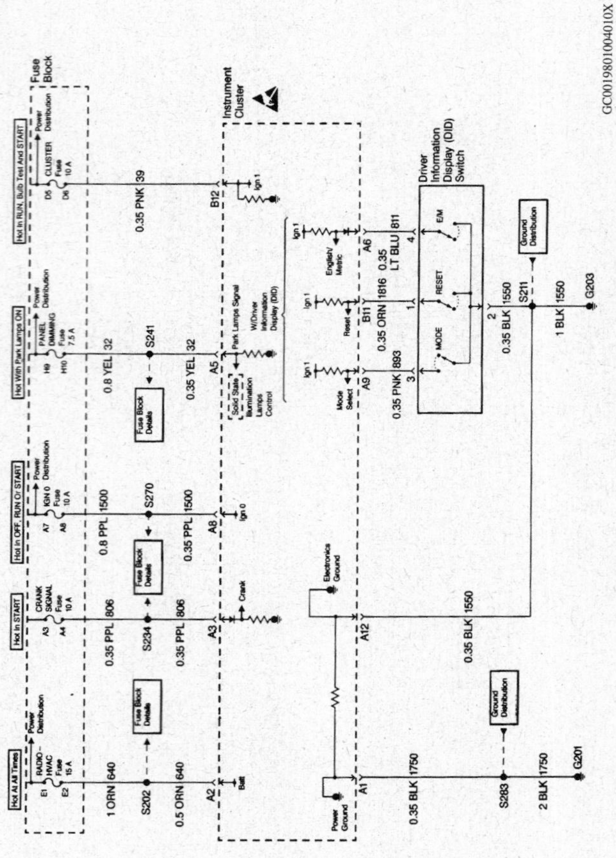

Fig. 13 Instrument cluster (Part 1 of 5). 2000 Century & Regal

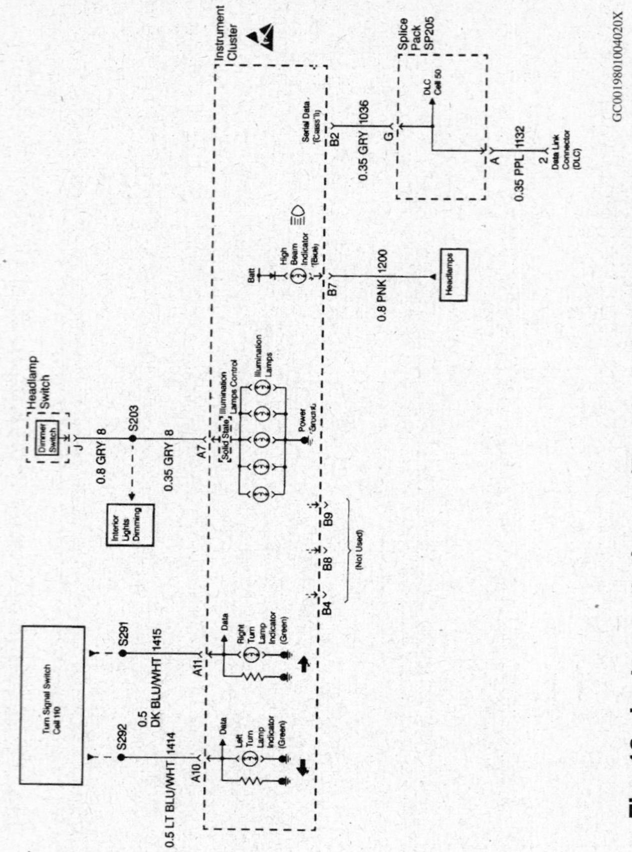

Fig. 13 Instrument cluster (Part 2 of 5). 2000 Century & Regal

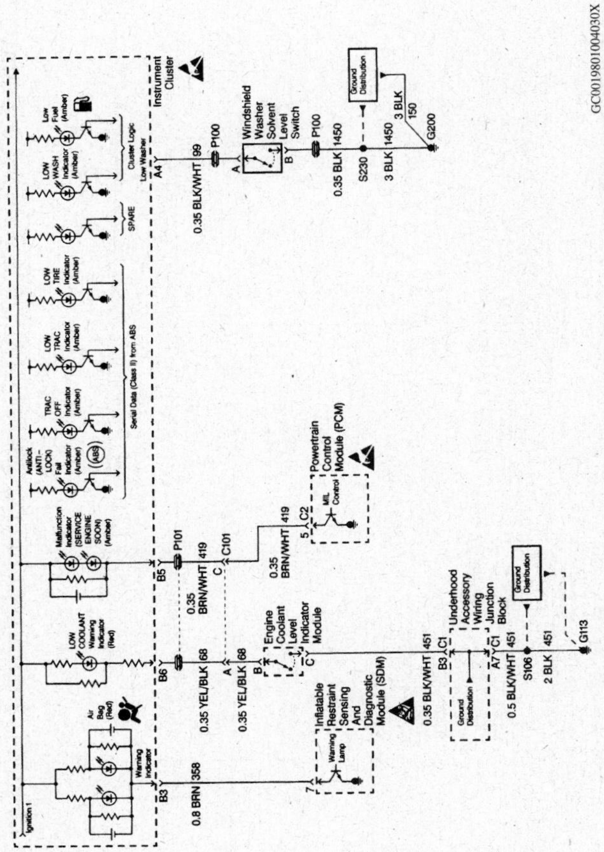

Fig. 13 Instrument cluster (Part 3 of 5). 2000 Century & Regal

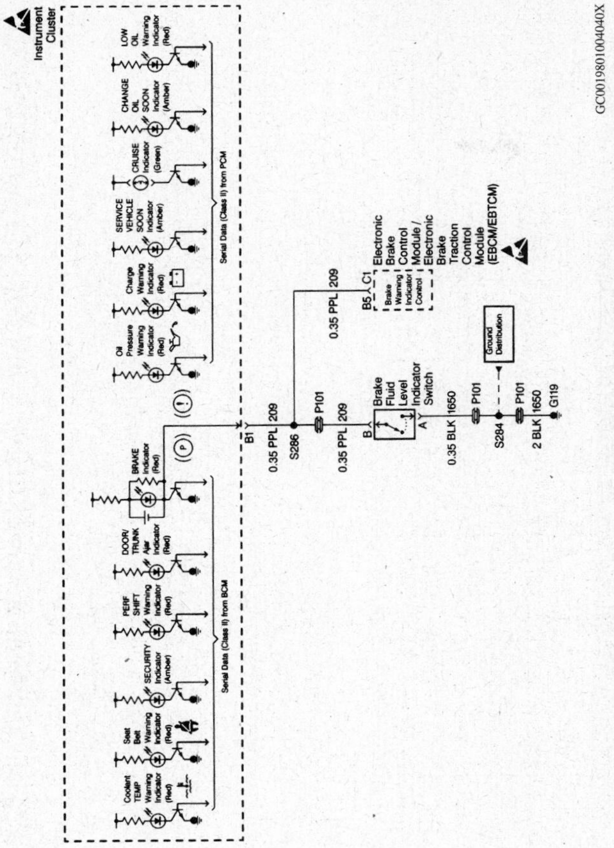

Fig. 13 Instrument cluster (Part 4 of 5). 2000 Century & Regal

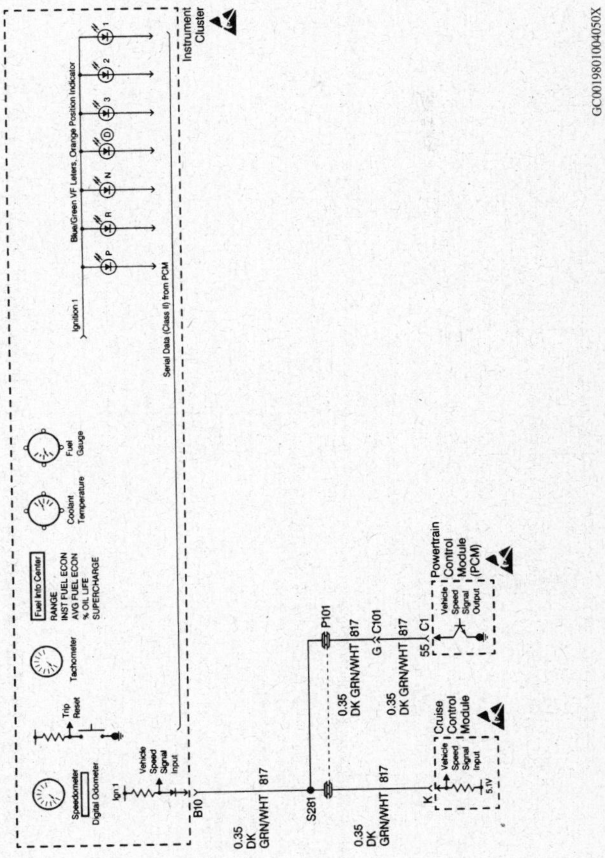

Fig. 13 Instrument cluster (Part 5 of 5). 2000 Century & Regal

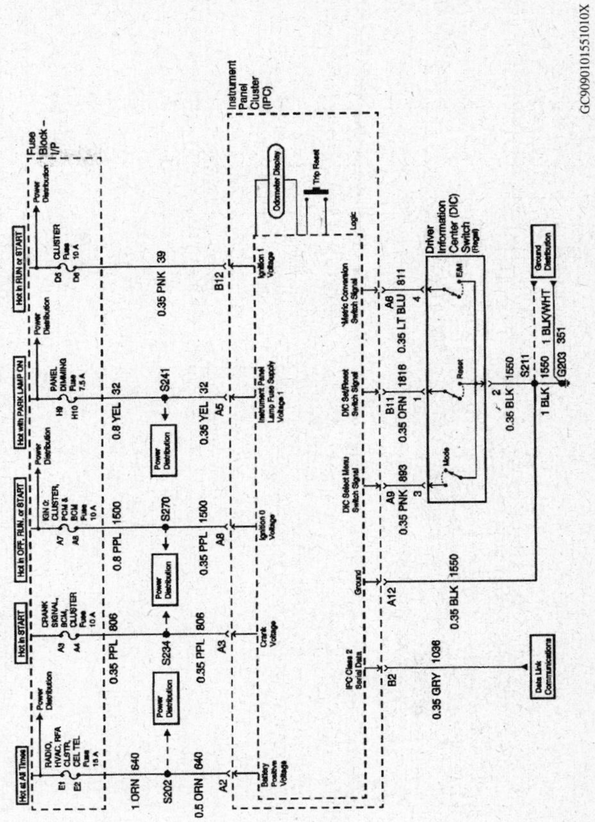

Fig. 14 Instrument cluster (Part 1 of 4). 2001 Century & Regal

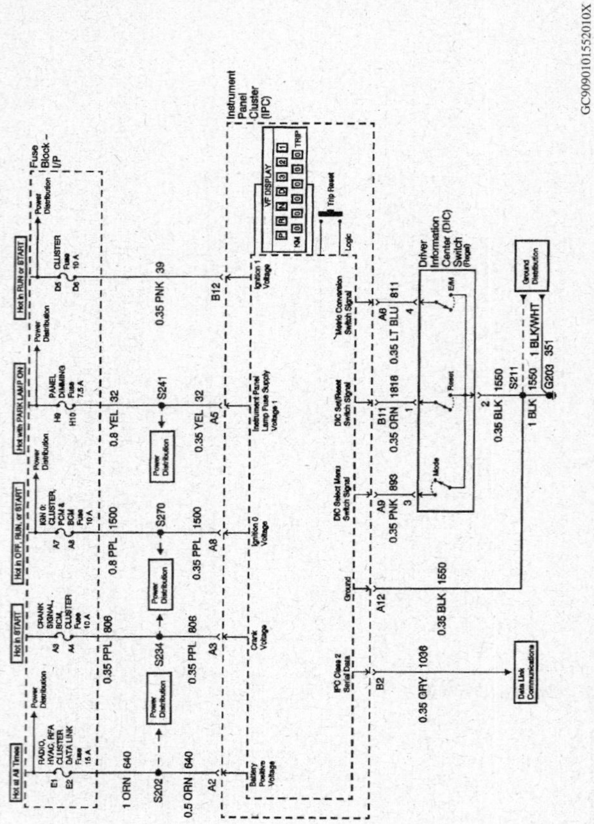

GC9090101552010X

Fig. 15 Instrument cluster (Part 1 of 4). 2002–04 Century & Regal

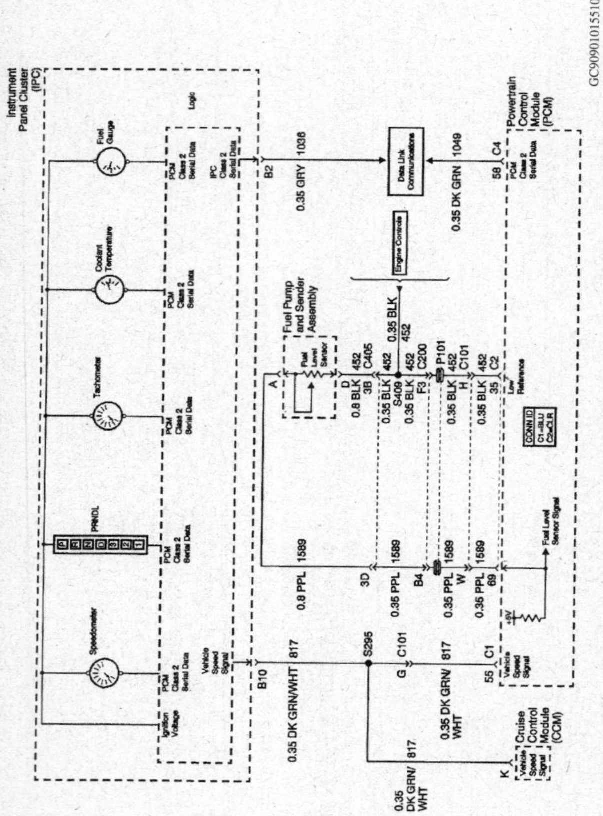

GC9090101551020X

Fig. 14 Instrument cluster (Part 2 of 4). 2001 Century & Regal

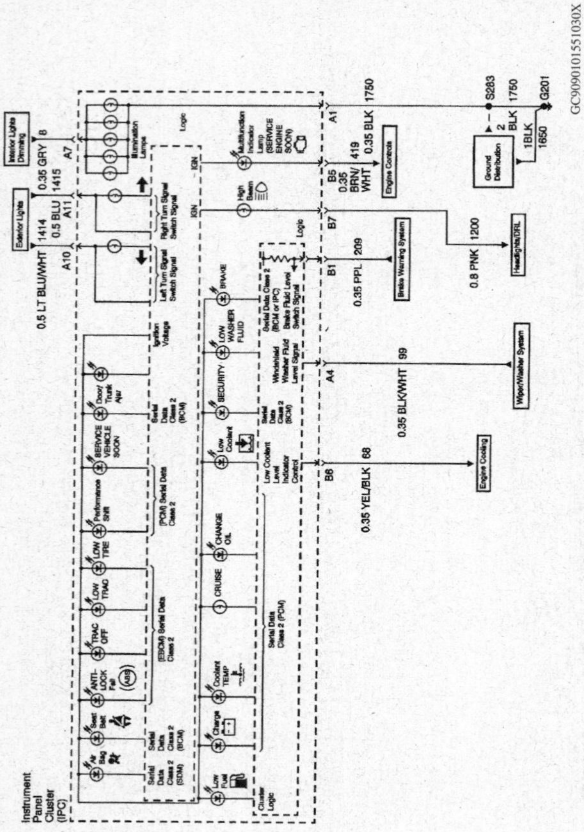

GC9090101551030X

Fig. 14 Instrument cluster (Part 3 of 4). 2001 Century & Regal

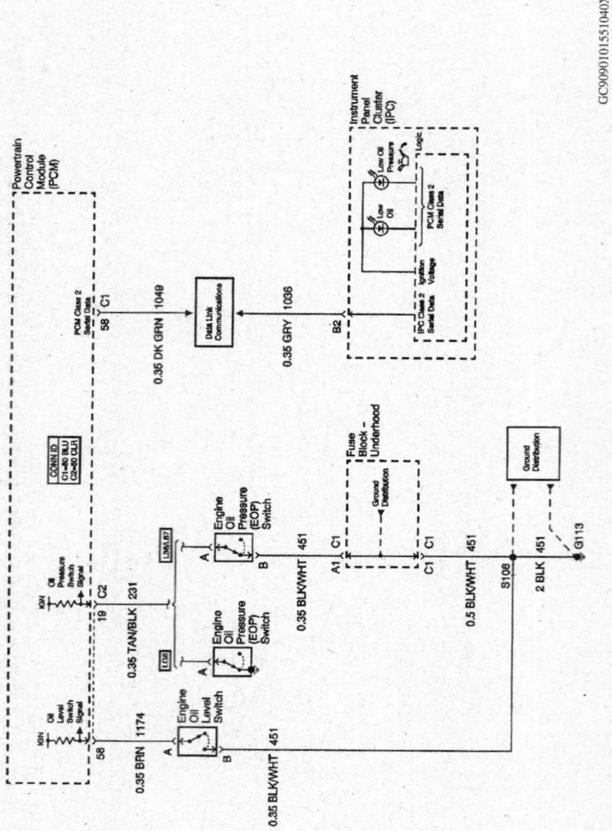

GC9090101551040X

Fig. 14 Instrument cluster (Part 4 of 4). 2001 Century & Regal

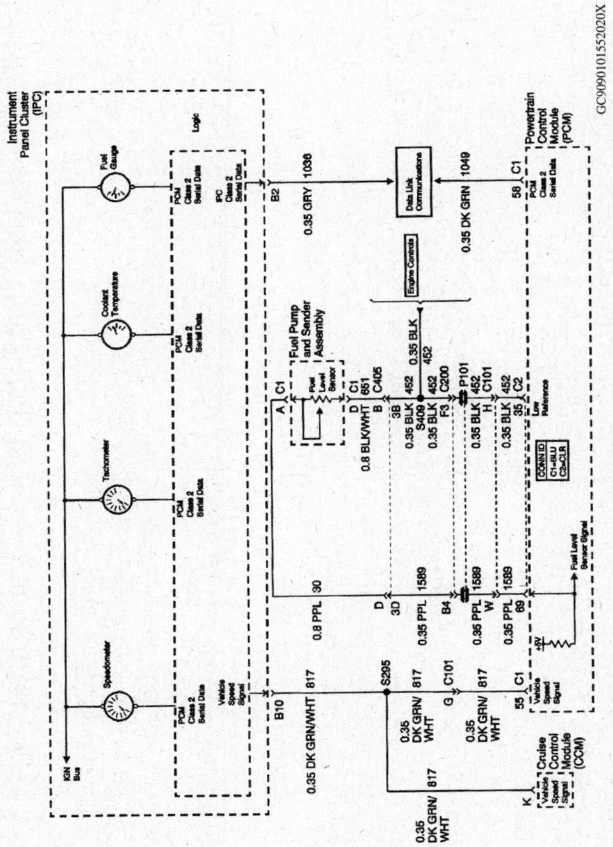

Fig. 15 Instrument cluster (Part 2 of 4). 2002–04 Century & Regal

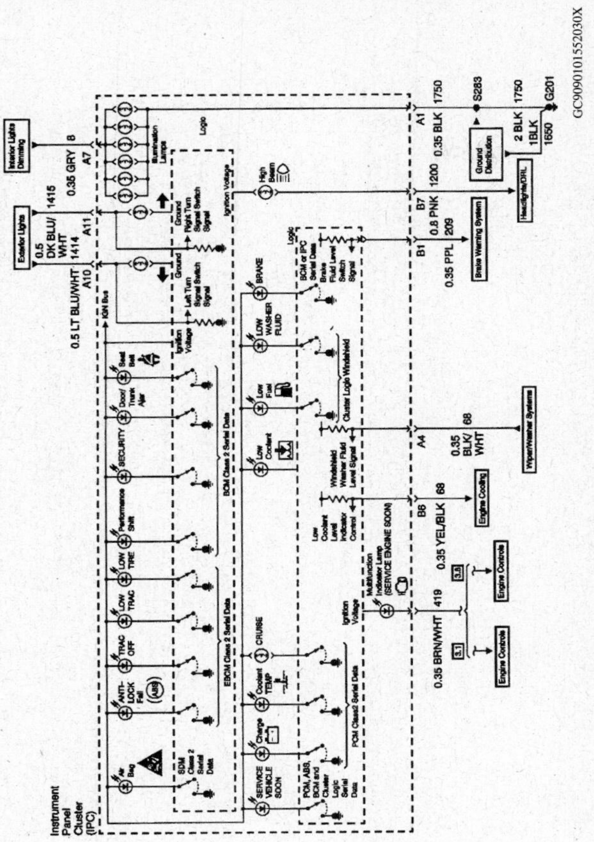

Fig. 15 Instrument cluster (Part 3 of 4). 2002–04 Century & Regal

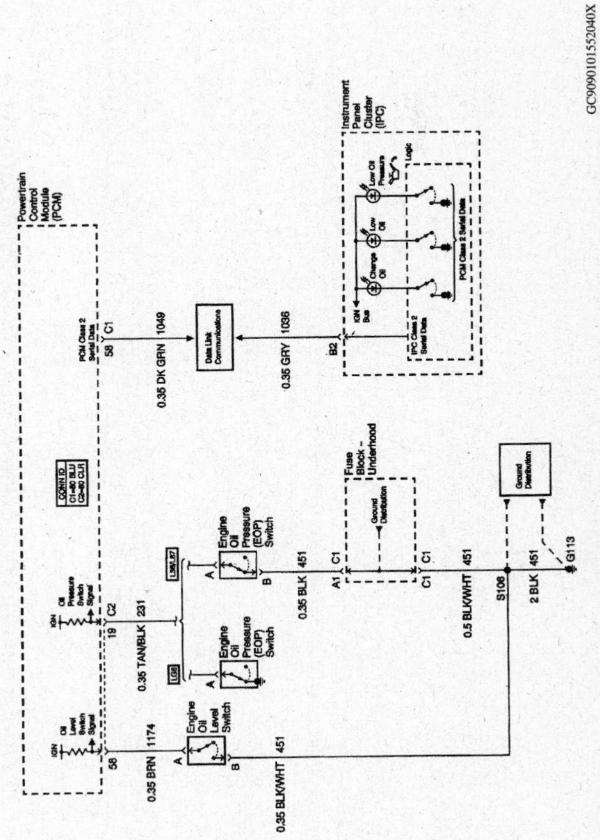

Fig. 15 Instrument cluster (Part 4 of 4). 2002–04 Century & Regal

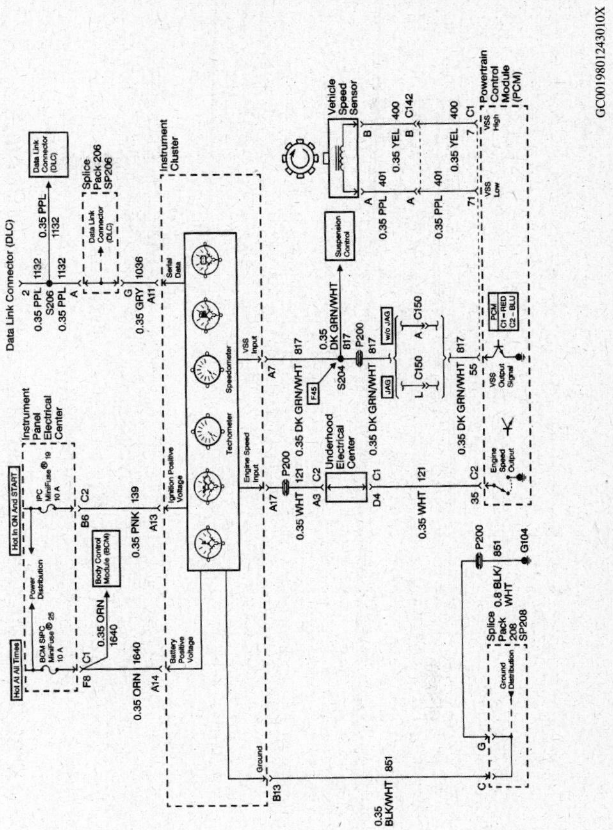

Fig. 16 Instrument cluster (Part 1 of 4). 2000 Corvette

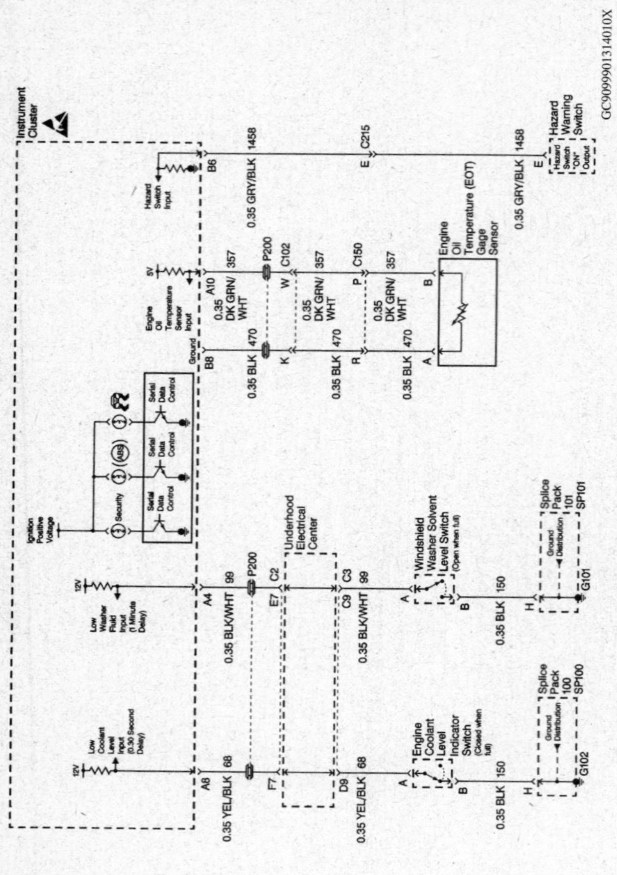

Fig. 16 Instrument cluster (Part 3 of 4). 2000 Corvette

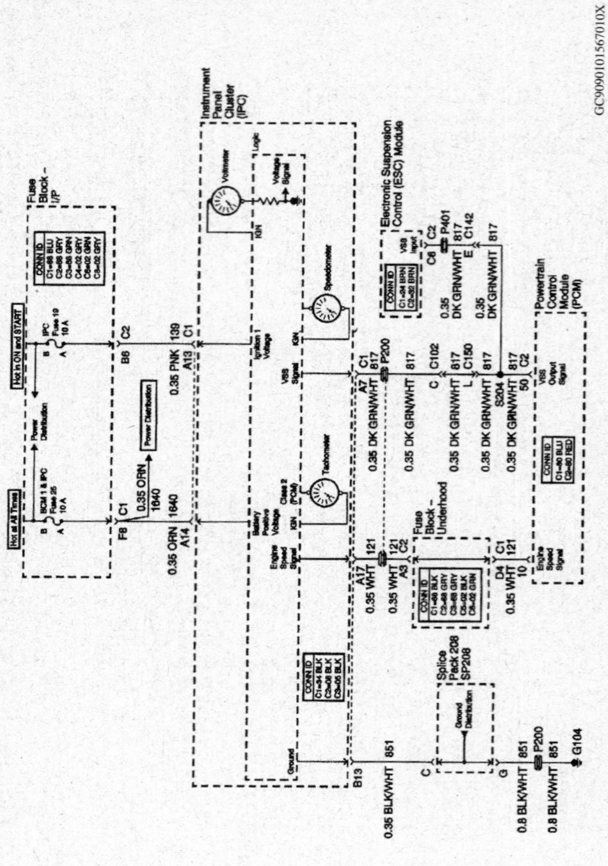

Fig. 17 Instrument cluster (Part 1 of 4). 2001–04 Corvette

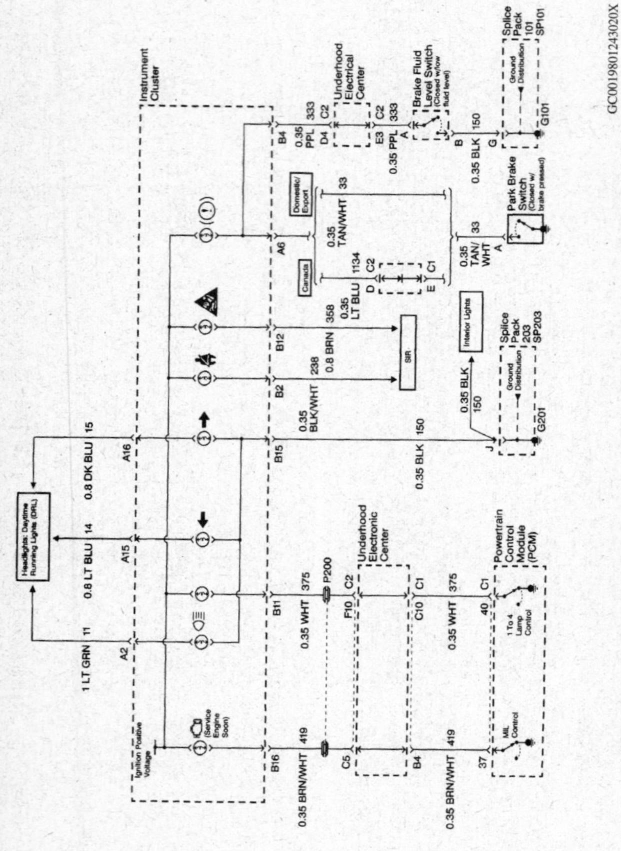

Fig. 16 Instrument cluster (Part 2 of 4). 2000 Corvette

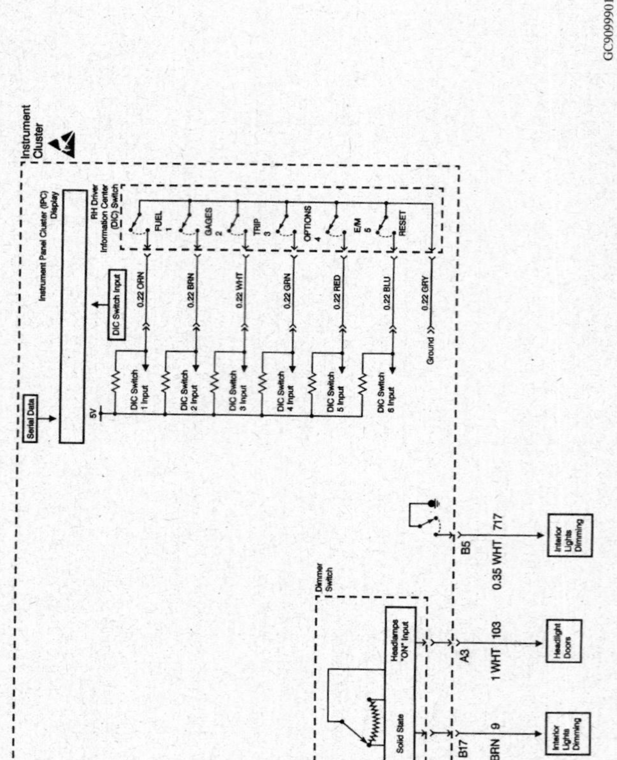

Fig. 16 Instrument cluster (Part 4 of 4). 2000 Corvette

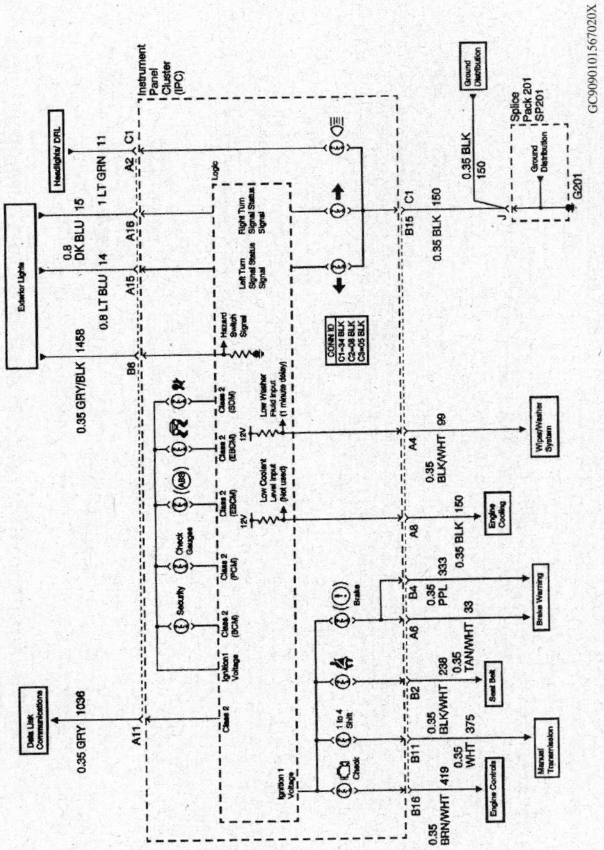

Fig. 17 Instrument cluster (Part 2 of 4). 2001–04 Corvette

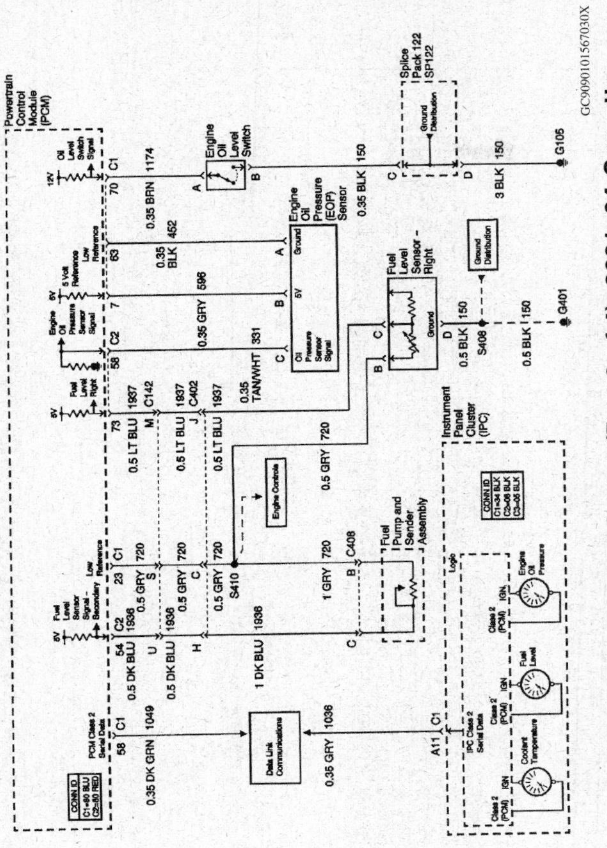

Fig. 17 Instrument cluster (Part 3 of 4). 2001–04 Corvette

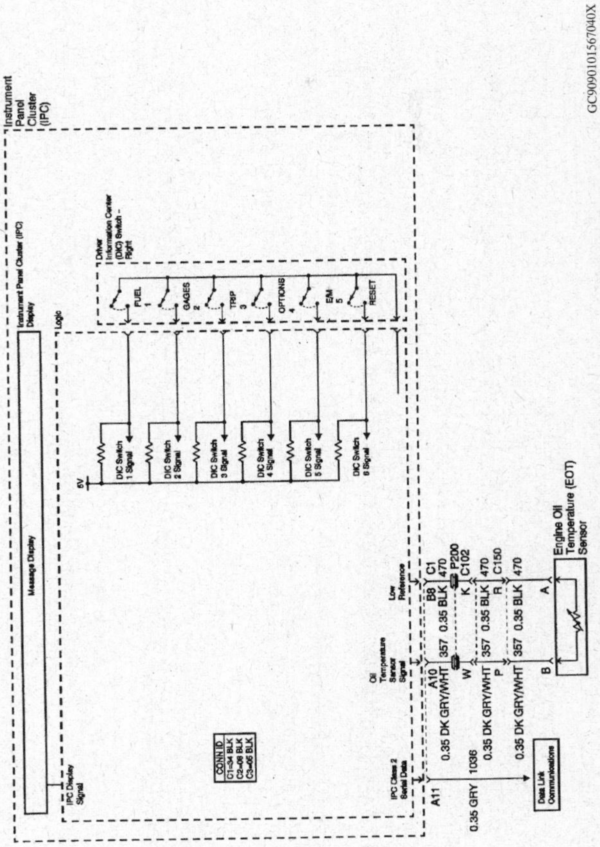

Fig. 17 Instrument cluster (Part 4 of 4). 2001–04 Corvette

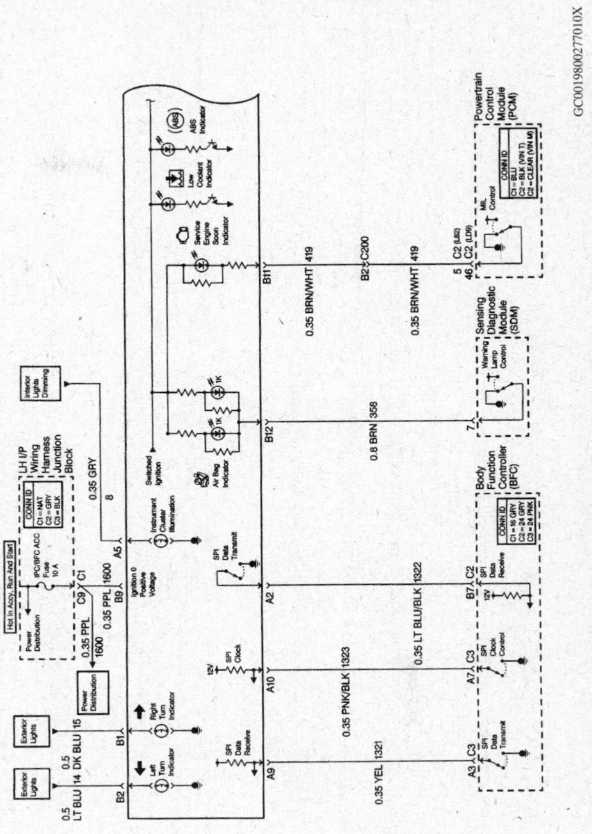

Fig. 18 Instrument cluster (Part 1 of 3). Cutlass & 2000 Malibu

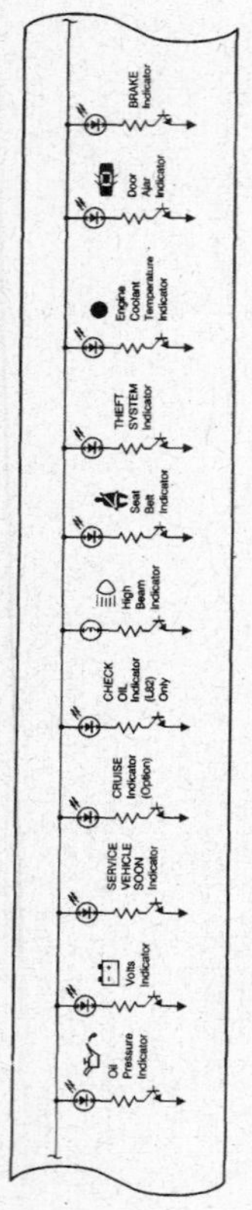

GC0019800277020X

Fig. 18 Instrument cluster (Part 2 of 3). Cutlass & 2000 Malibu

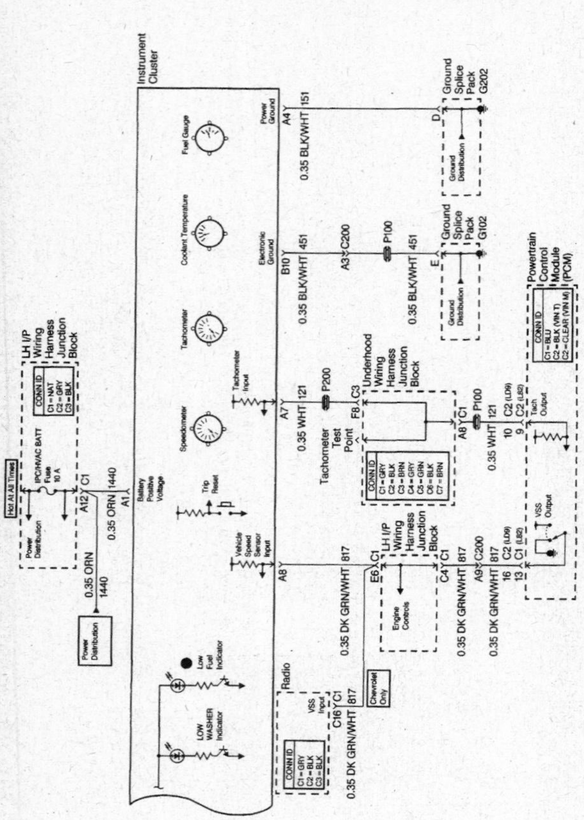

GC0019800277030X

Fig. 18 Instrument cluster (Part 3 of 3). Cutlass & 2000 Malibu

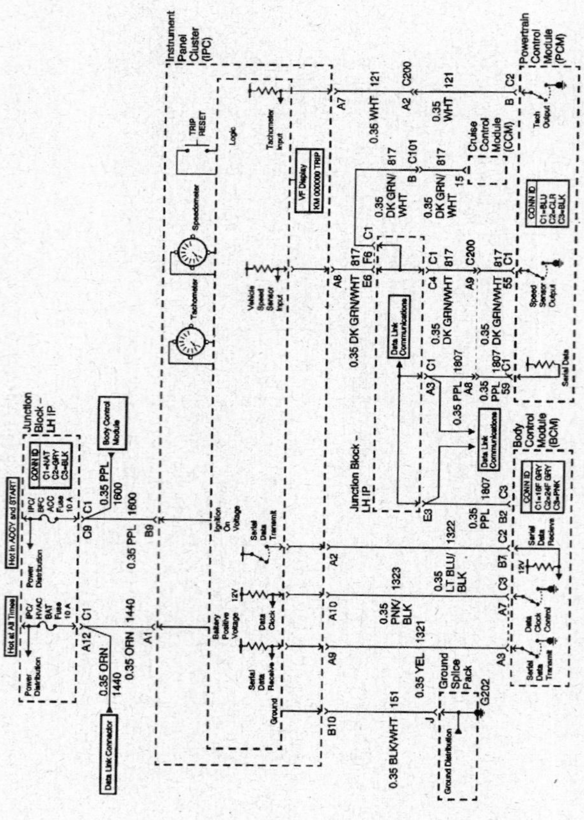

GC9990101568010X

Fig. 19 Instrument cluster (Part 1 of 2). 2001 Malibu

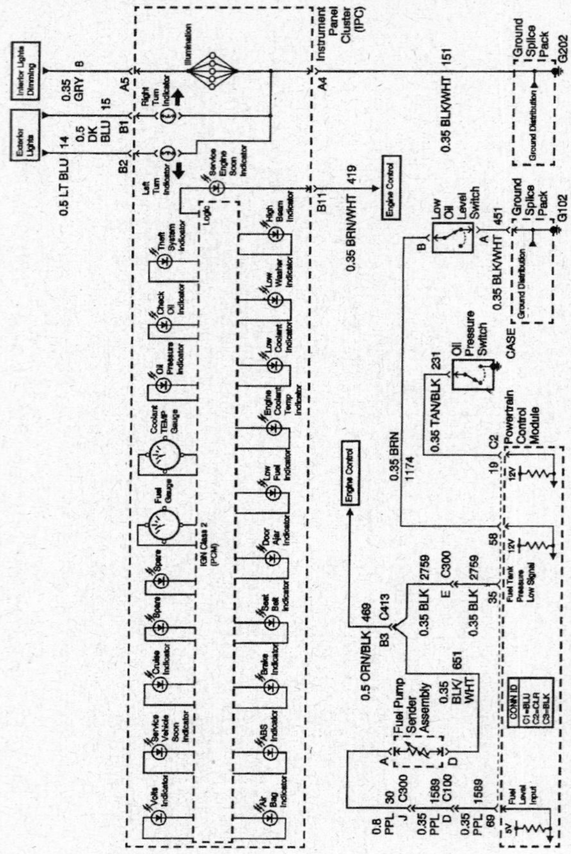

GC9990101568020X

Fig. 19 Instrument cluster (Part 2 of 2). 2001 Malibu

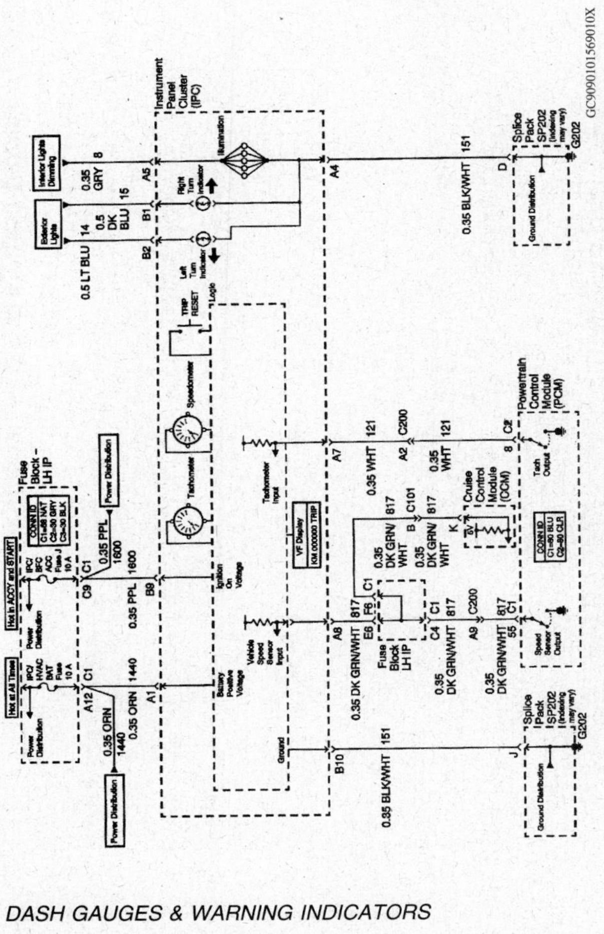

Fig. 20 Instrument cluster (Part 1 of 2). 2002–04 Malibu

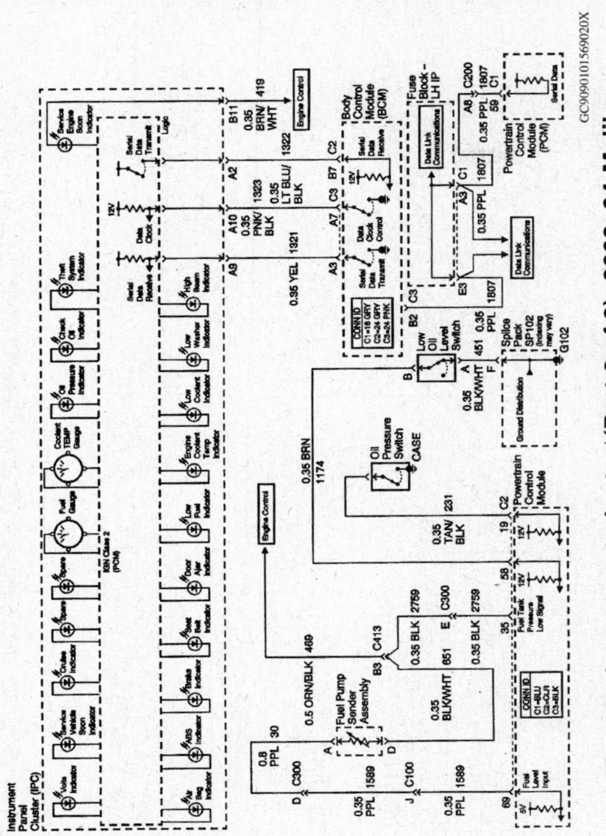

Fig. 20 Instrument cluster (Part 2 of 2). 2002–04 Malibu

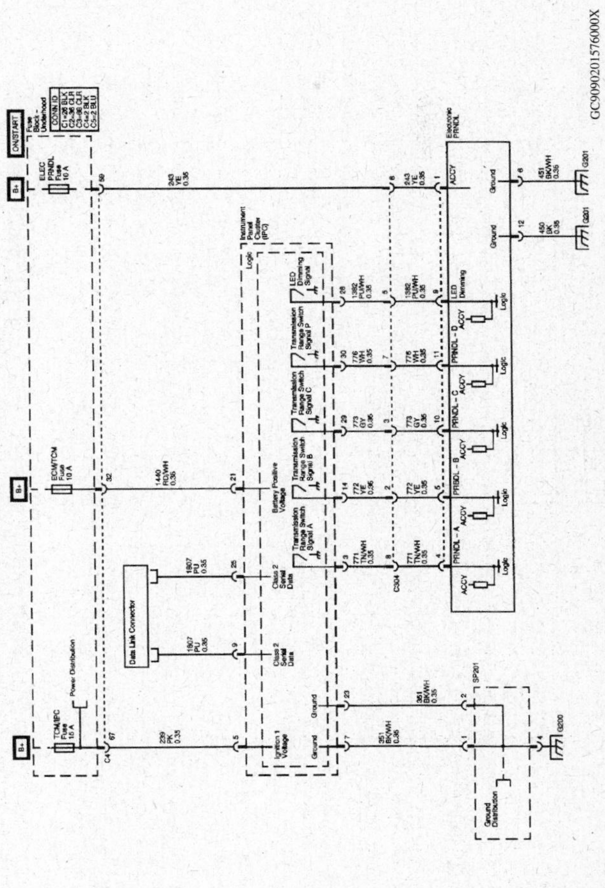

Fig. 21 Instrument cluster. CTS

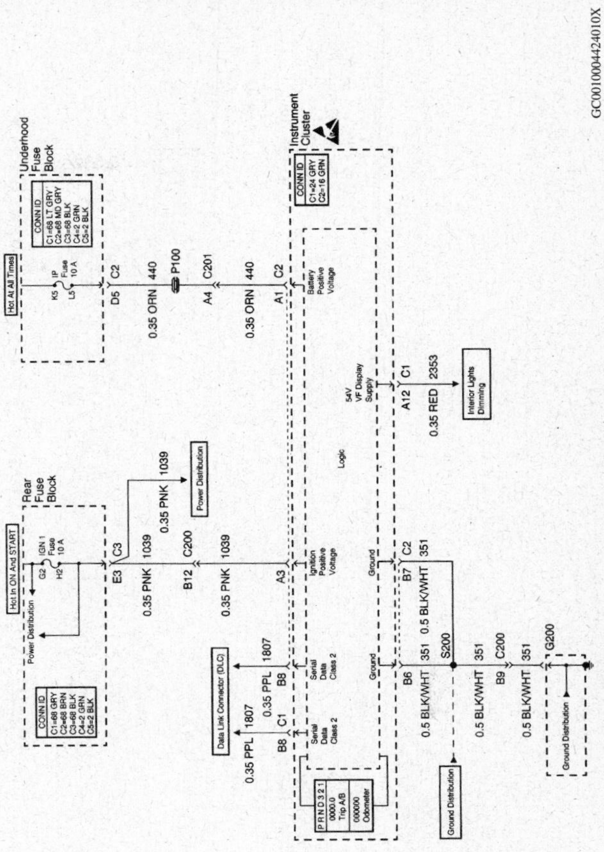

Fig. 22 Instrument cluster (Part 1 of 5). 2000 DeVille

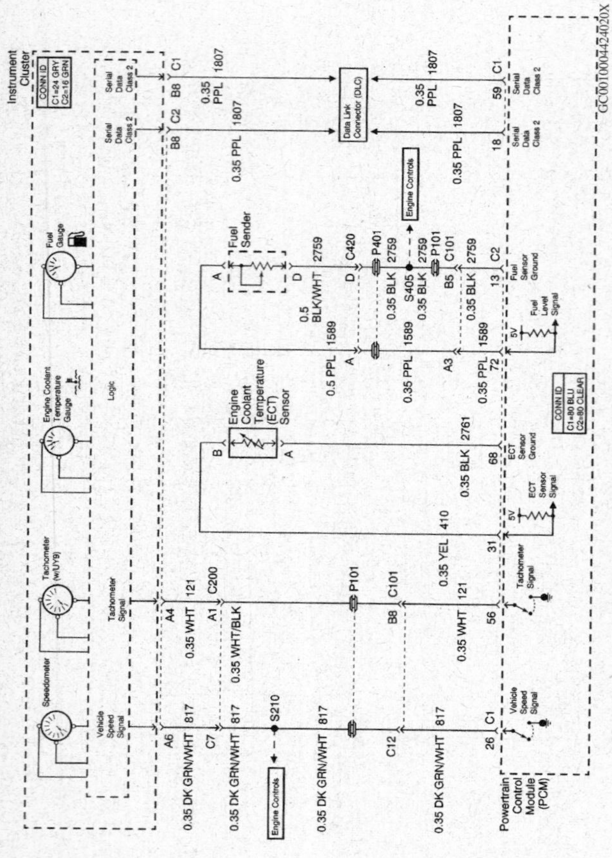

Fig. 22 Instrument cluster (Part 2 of 5). 2000 DeVille

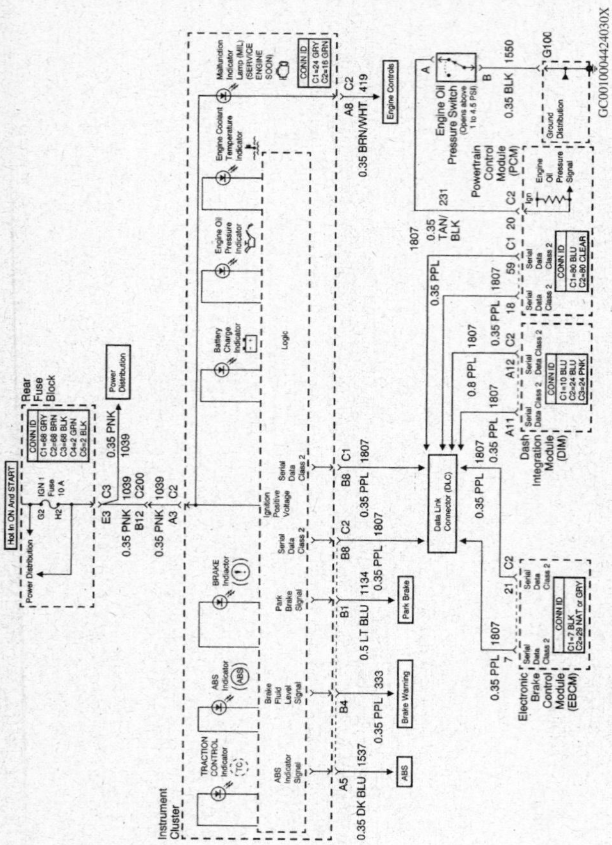

Fig. 22 Instrument cluster (Part 3 of 5). 2000 DeVille

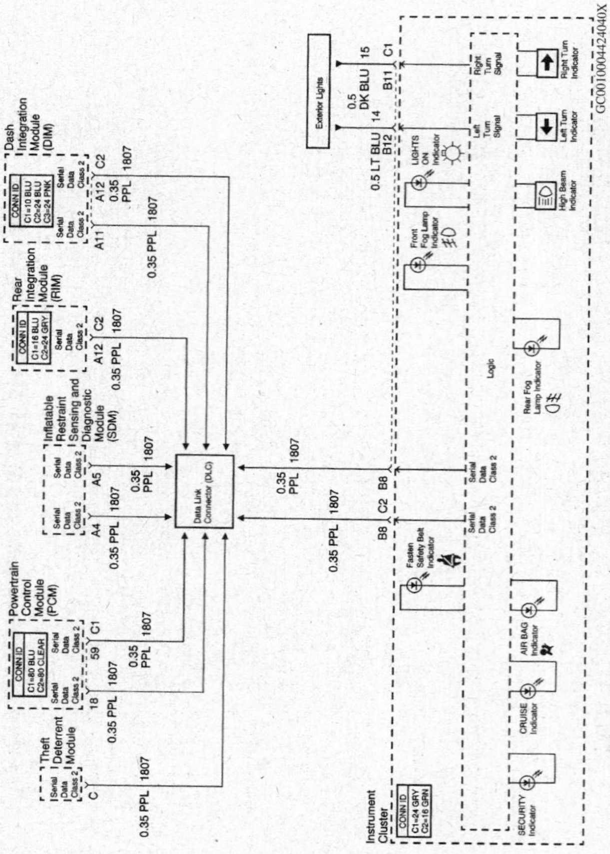

Fig. 22 Instrument cluster (Part 4 of 5). 2000 DeVille

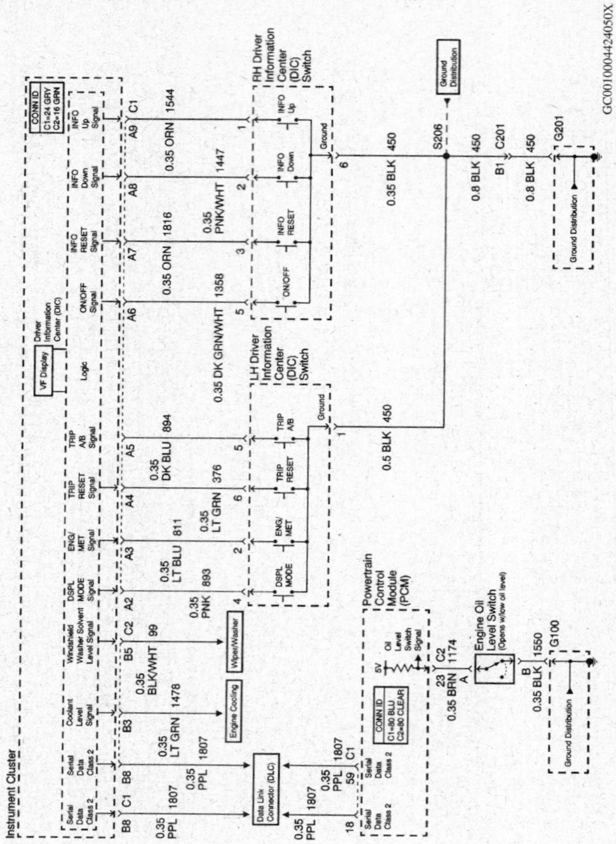

Fig. 22 Instrument cluster (Part 5 of 5). 2000 DeVille

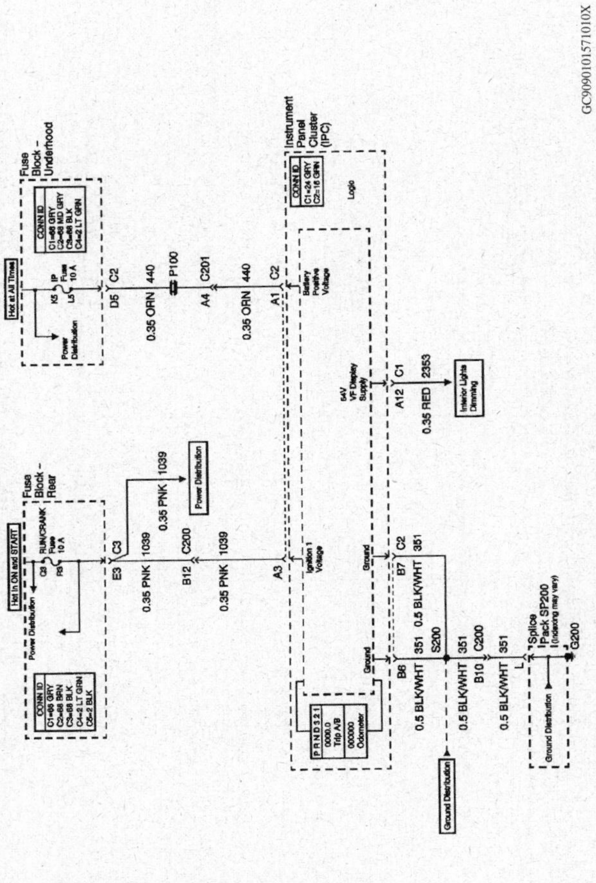

Fig. 23 Instrument cluster (Part 1 of 5). 2001–04 DeVille

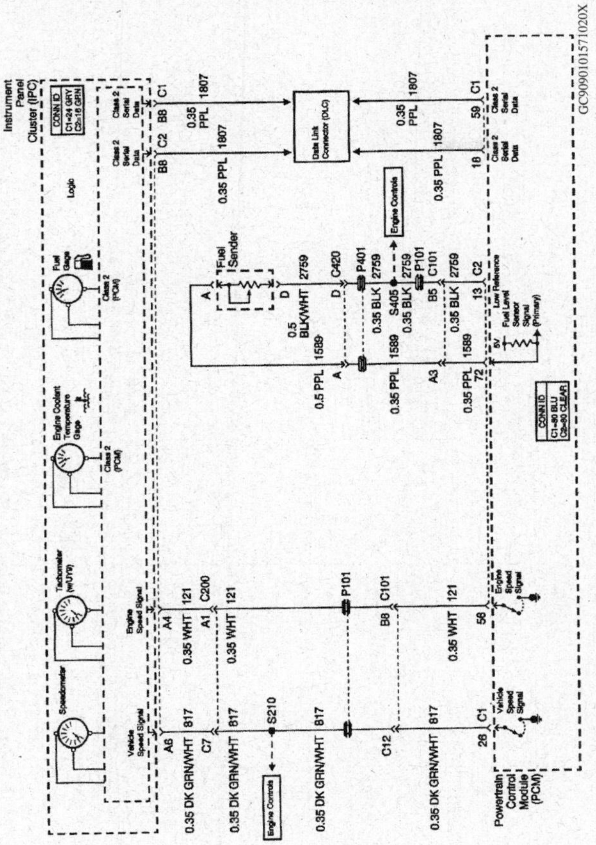

Fig. 23 Instrument cluster (Part 2 of 5). 2001–04 DeVille

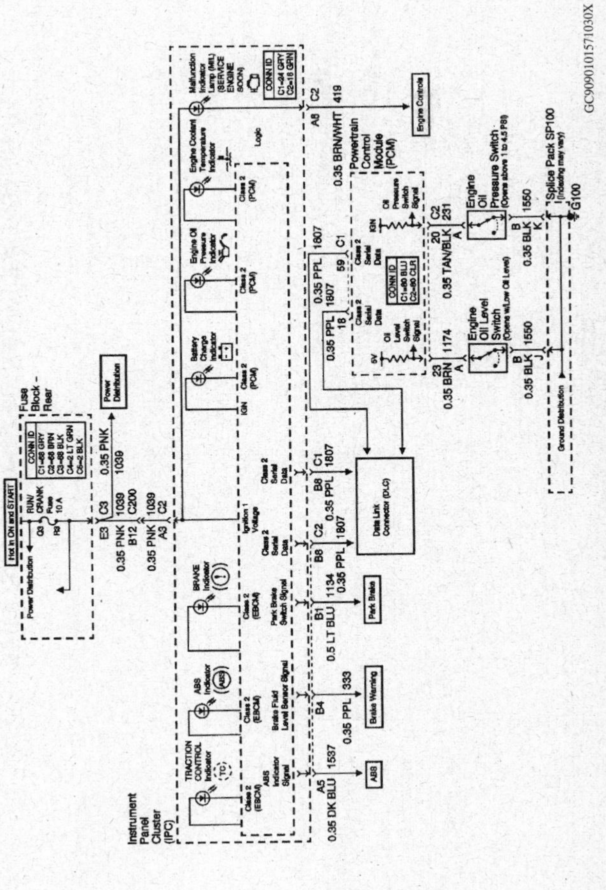

Fig. 23 Instrument cluster (Part 3 of 5). 2001–04 DeVille

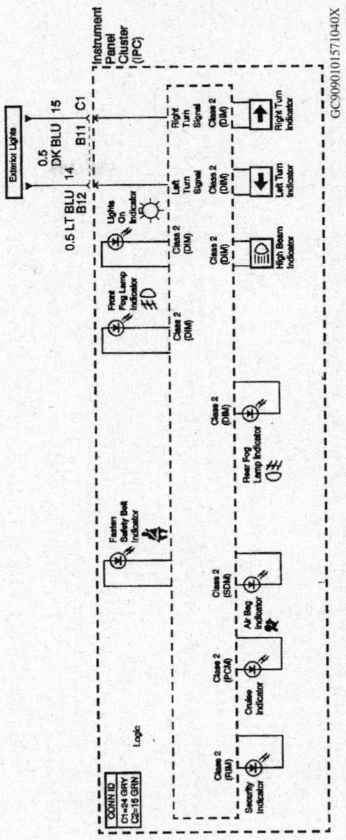

Fig. 23 Instrument cluster (Part 4 of 5). 2001–04 DeVille

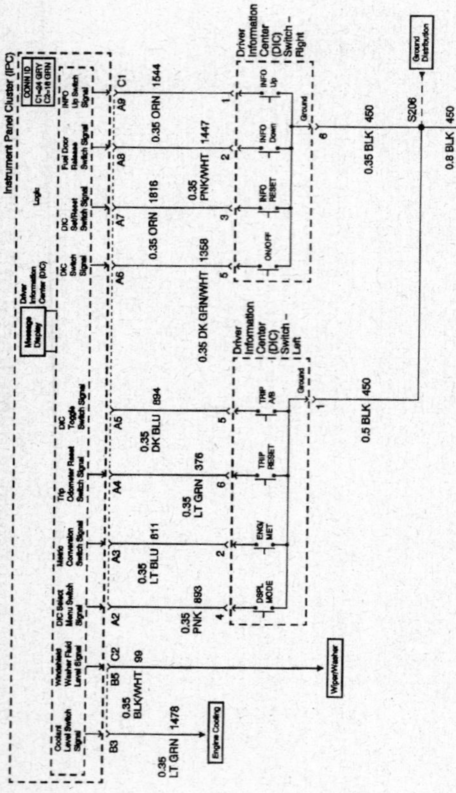

GC9090101571050X

Fig. 23 Instrument cluster (Part 5 of 5). 2001–04 DeVille

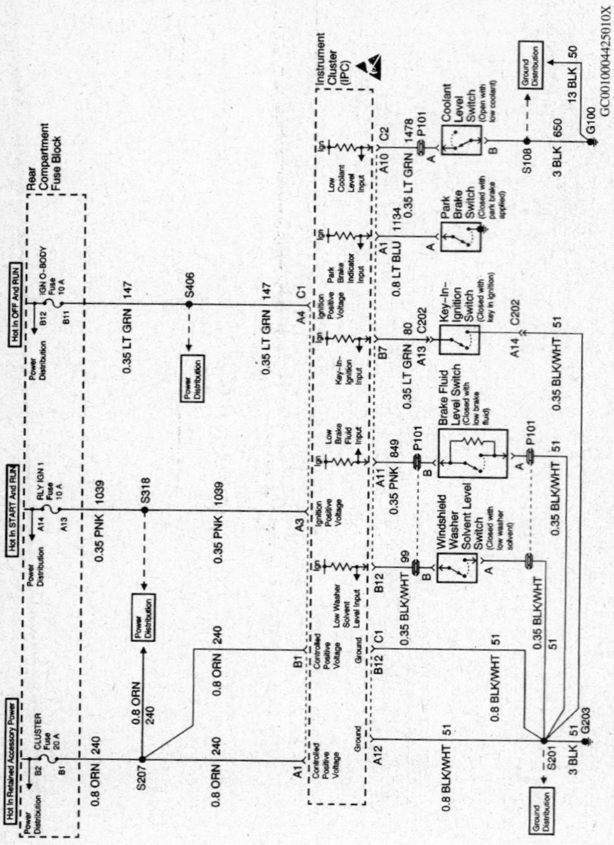

GC0010000442501OX

Fig. 24 Instrument cluster (Part 1 of 9). 2000 Eldorado

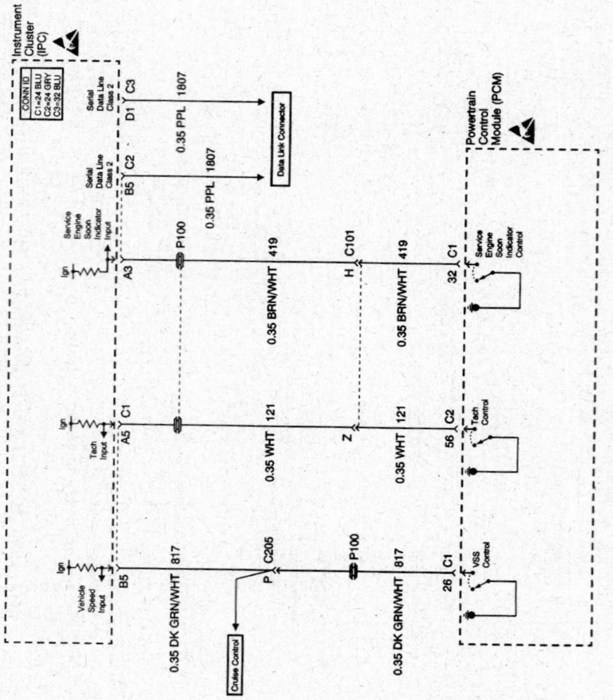

GC0010000442502OX

Fig. 24 Instrument cluster (Part 2 of 9). 2000 Eldorado

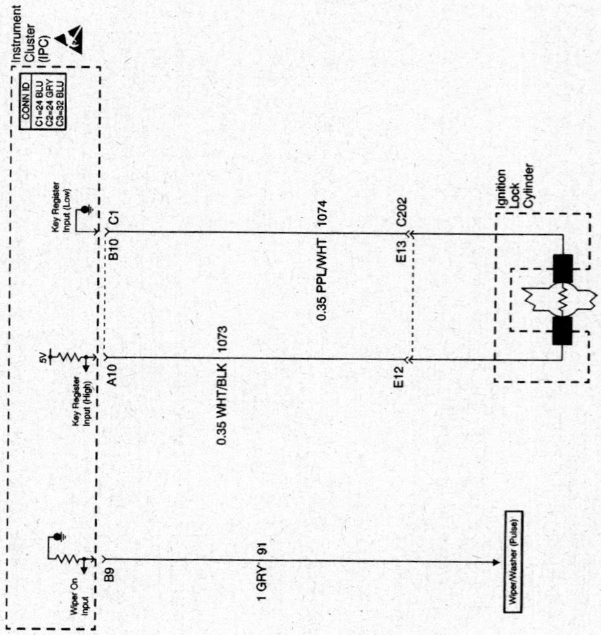

GC0010000442503OX

Fig. 24 Instrument cluster (Part 3 of 9). 2000 Eldorado

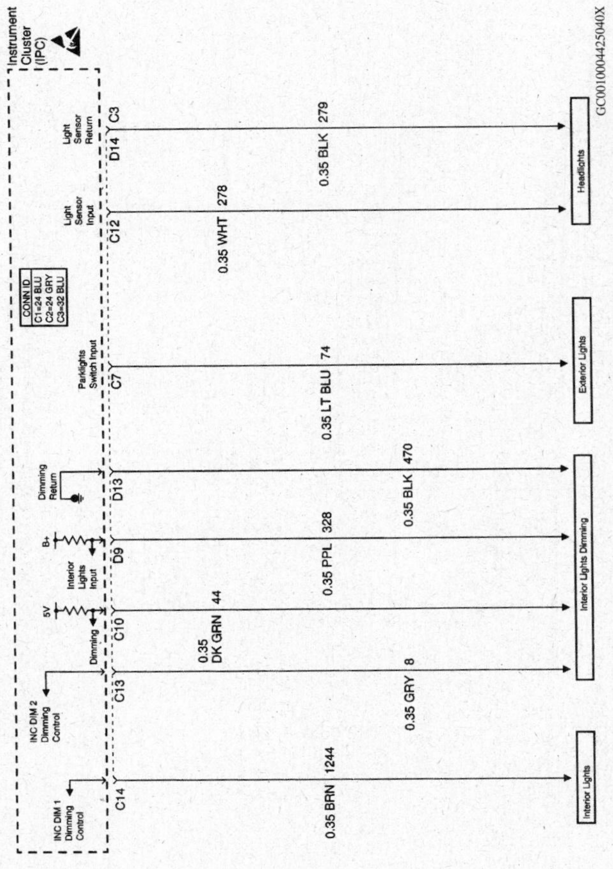

Fig. 24 Instrument cluster (Part 4 of 9). 2000 Eldorado

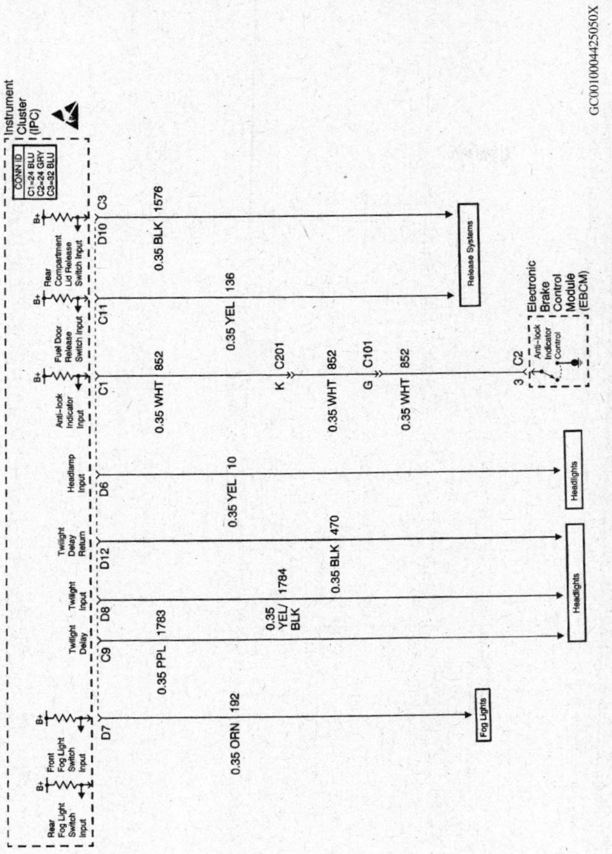

Fig. 24 Instrument cluster (Part 5 of 9). 2000 Eldorado

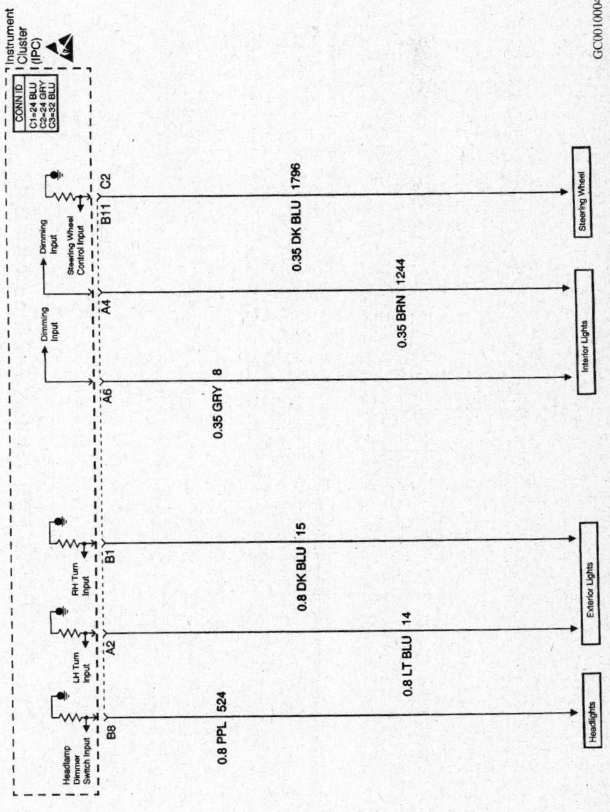

Fig. 24 Instrument cluster (Part 6 of 9). 2000 Eldorado

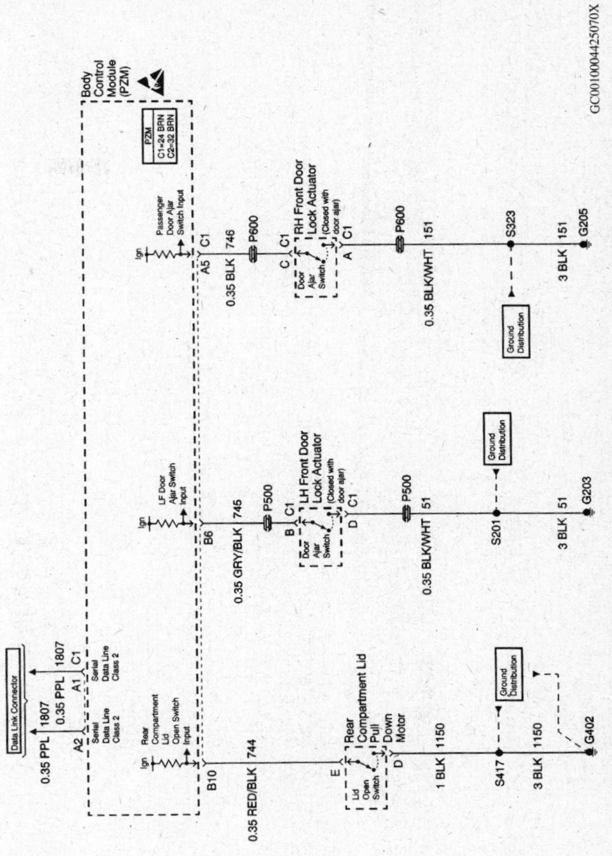

Fig. 24 Instrument cluster (Part 7 of 9). 2000 Eldorado

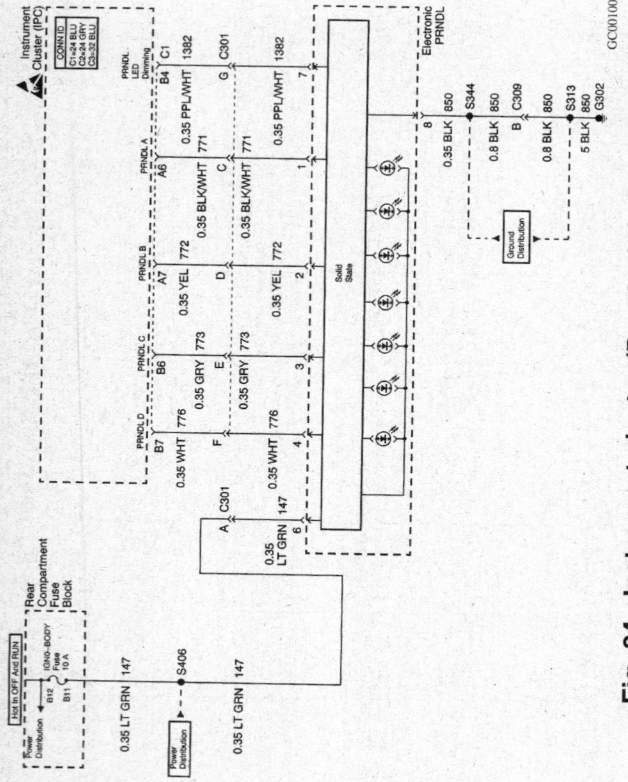

Fig. 24 Instrument cluster (Part 8 of 9). 2000 Eldorado

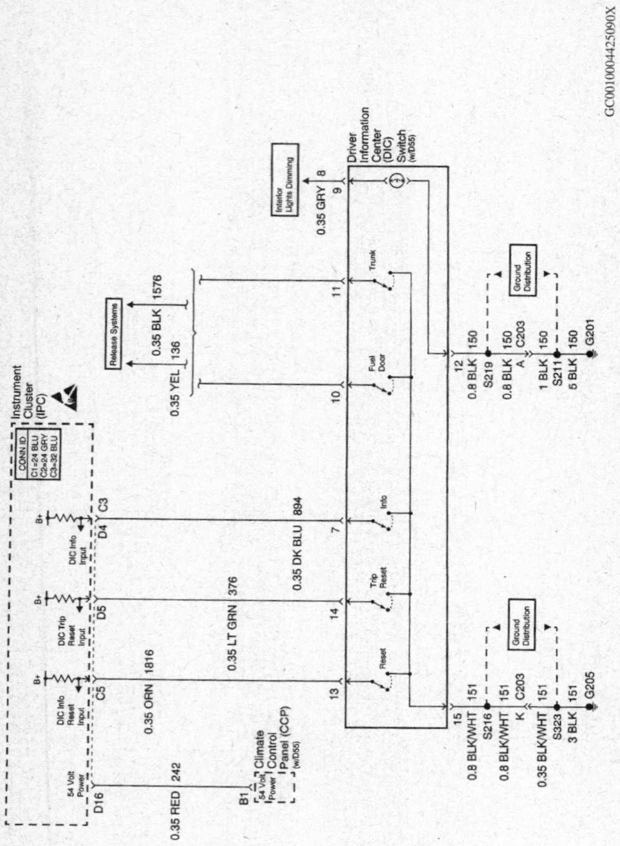

Fig. 24 Instrument cluster (Part 9 of 9). 2000 Eldorado

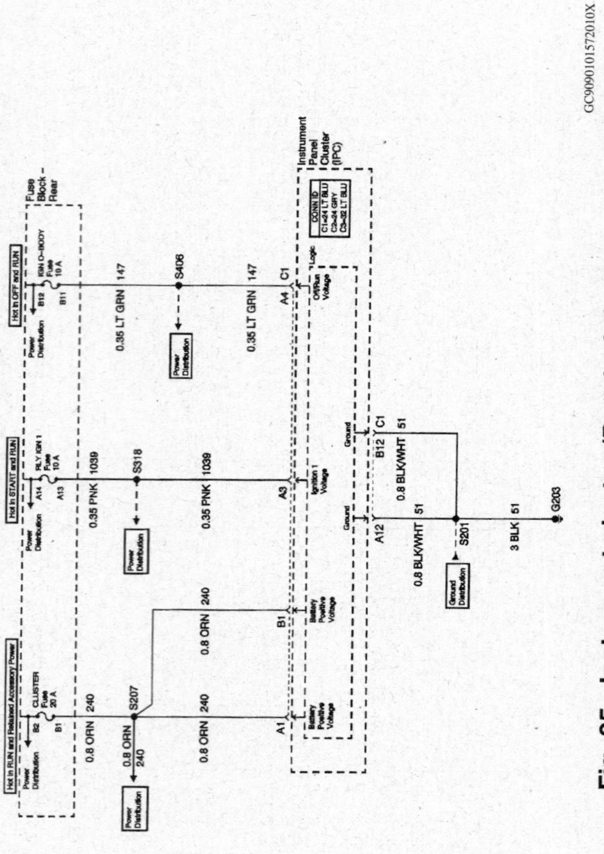

Fig. 25 Instrument cluster (Part 1 of 6). 2001–02 Eldorado

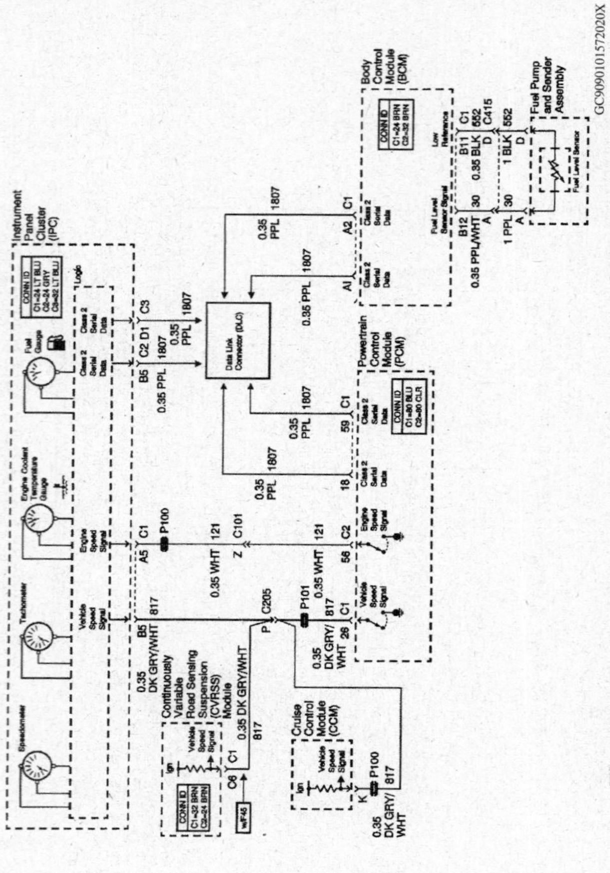

Fig. 25 Instrument cluster (Part 2 of 6). 2001–02 Eldorado

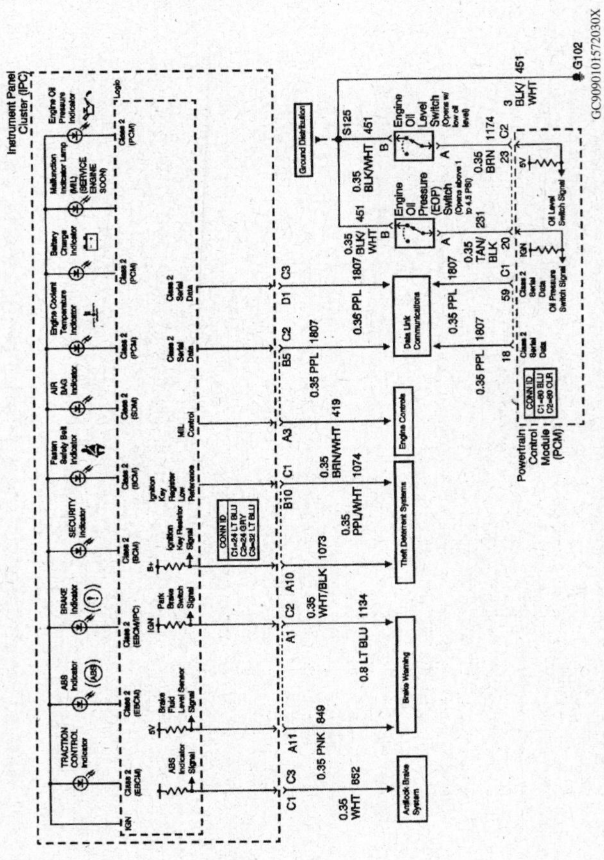

Fig. 25 Instrument cluster (Part 3 of 6). 2001–02 Eldorado

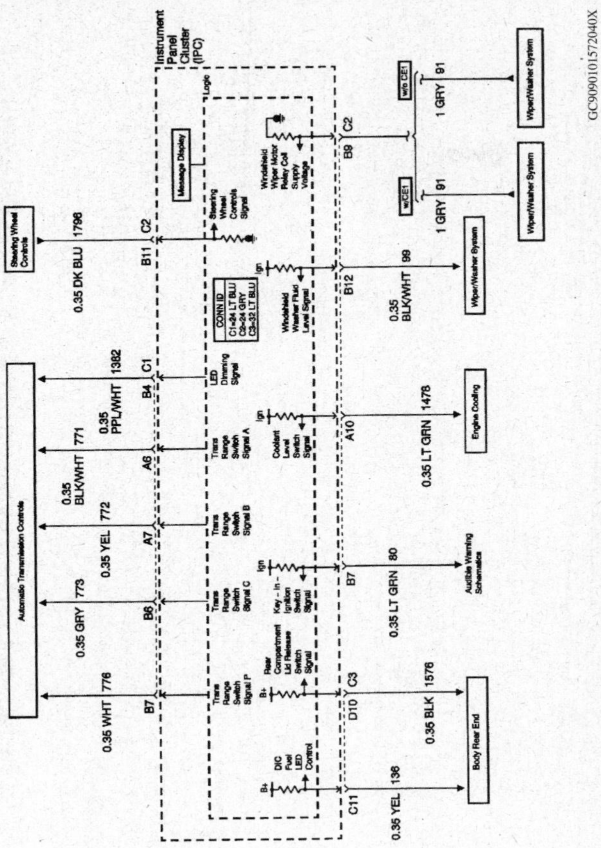

Fig. 25 Instrument cluster (Part 4 of 6). 2001–02 Eldorado

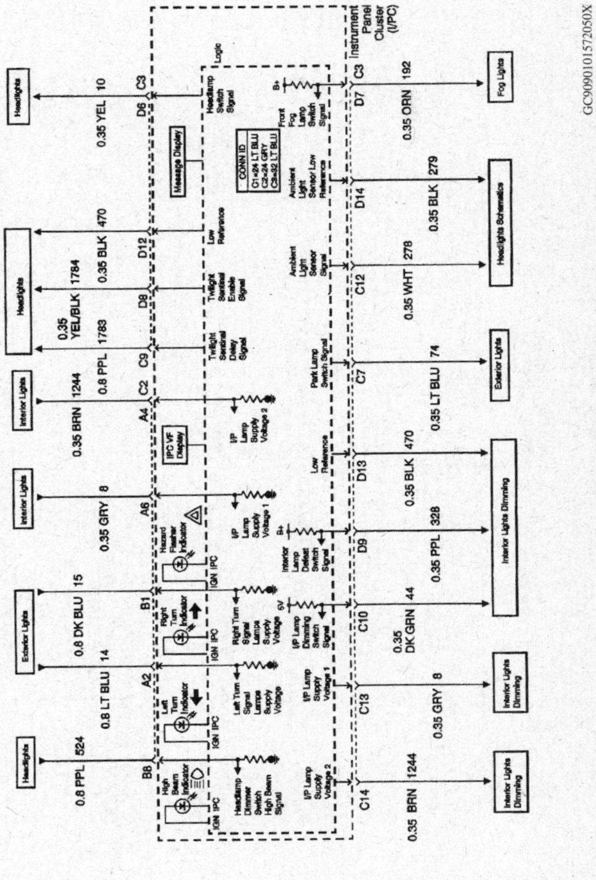

Fig. 25 Instrument cluster (Part 5 of 6). 2001–02 Eldorado

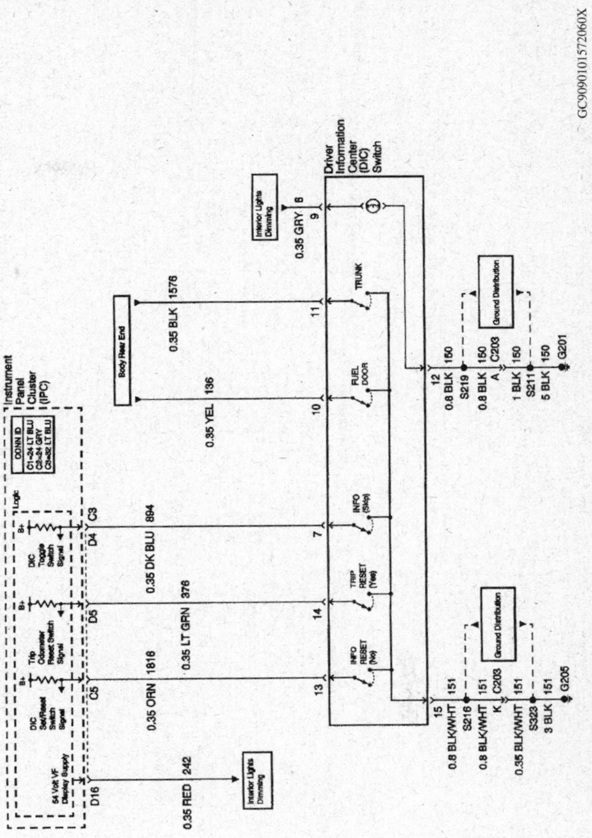

Fig. 25 Instrument cluster (Part 6 of 6). 2001–02 Eldorado

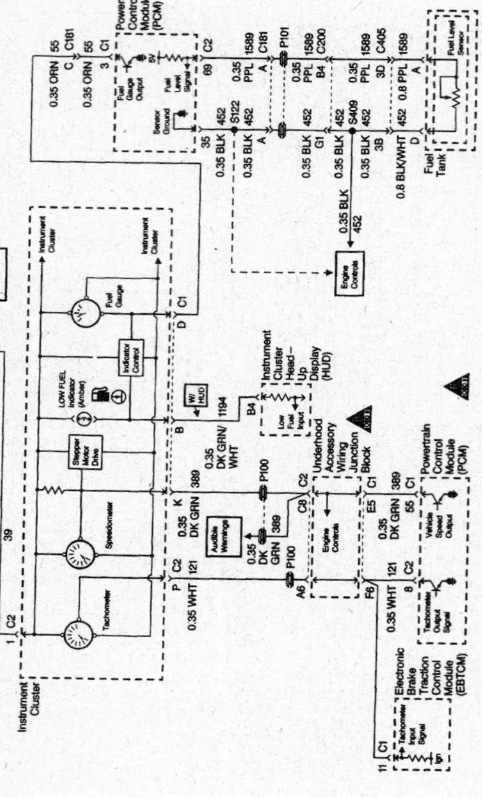

GC0019801118010X

Fig. 26 Instrument cluster (Part 1 of 5). 2000 Grand Prix

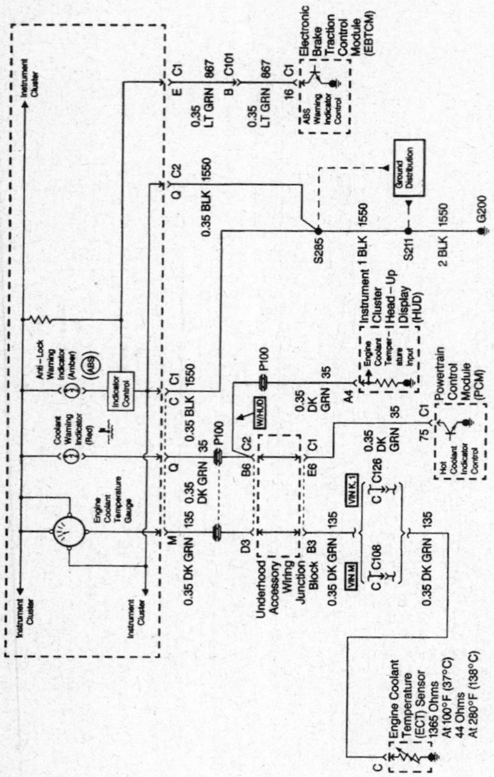

GC0019801118020X

Fig. 26 Instrument cluster (Part 2 of 5). 2000 Grand Prix

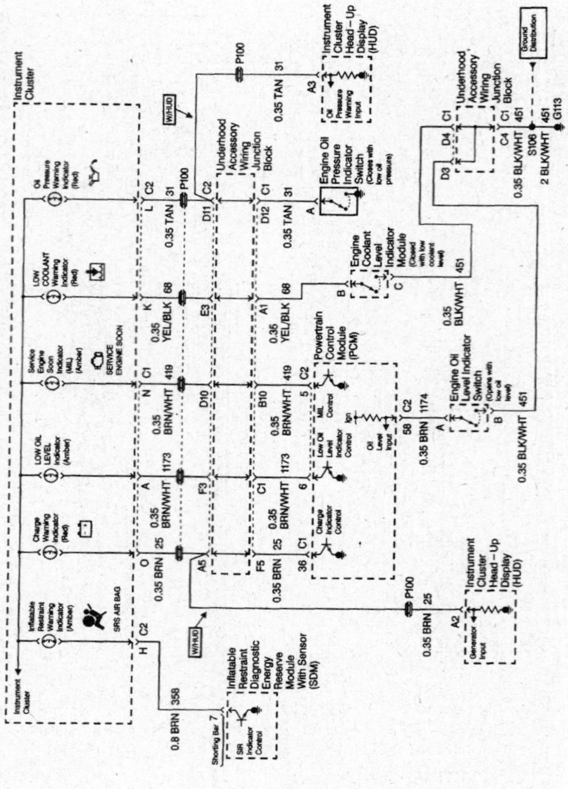

GC0019801118030X

Fig. 26 Instrument cluster (Part 3 of 5). 2000 Grand Prix

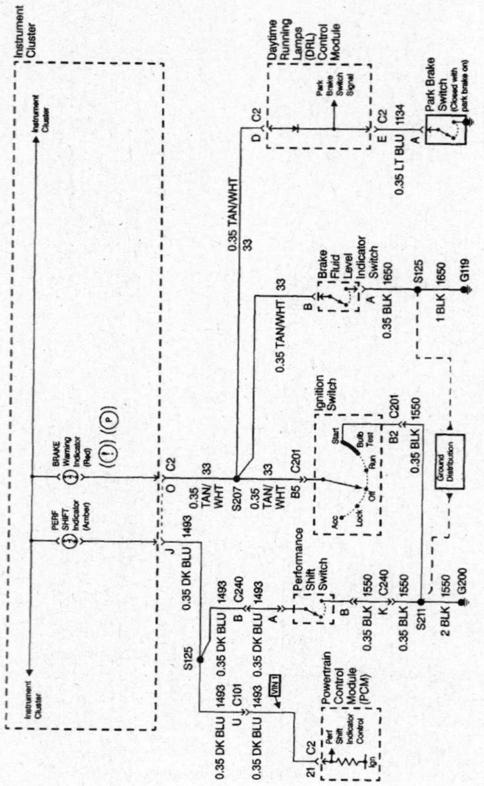

GC0019801118040X

Fig. 26 Instrument cluster (Part 4 of 5). 2000 Grand Prix

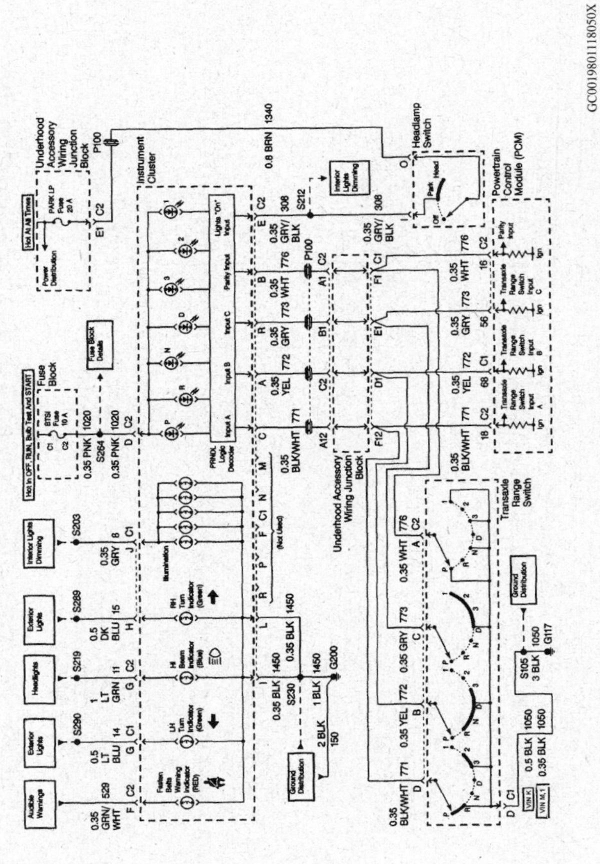

Fig. 26 Instrument cluster (Part 5 of 5). 2000 Grand Prix

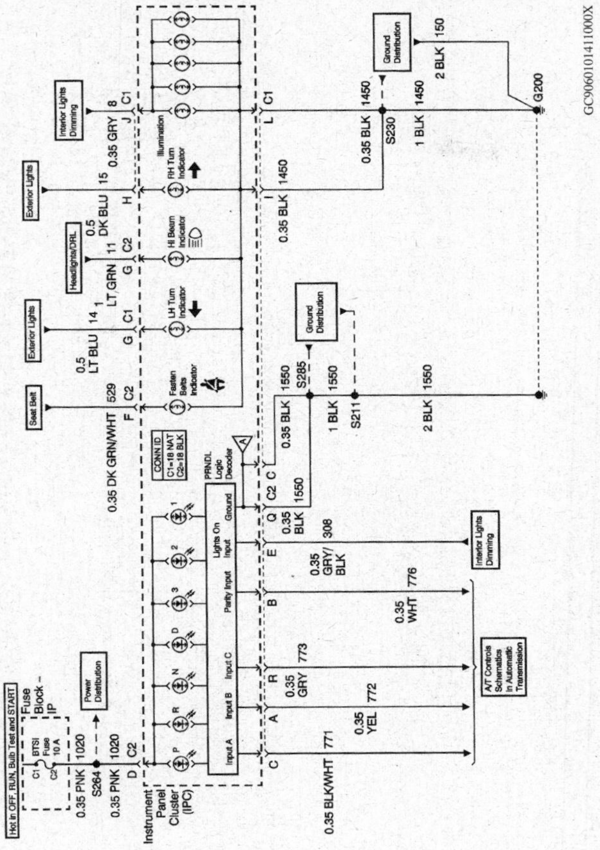

Fig. 27 Instrument cluster (Part 1 of 3) 2001 Grand Prix

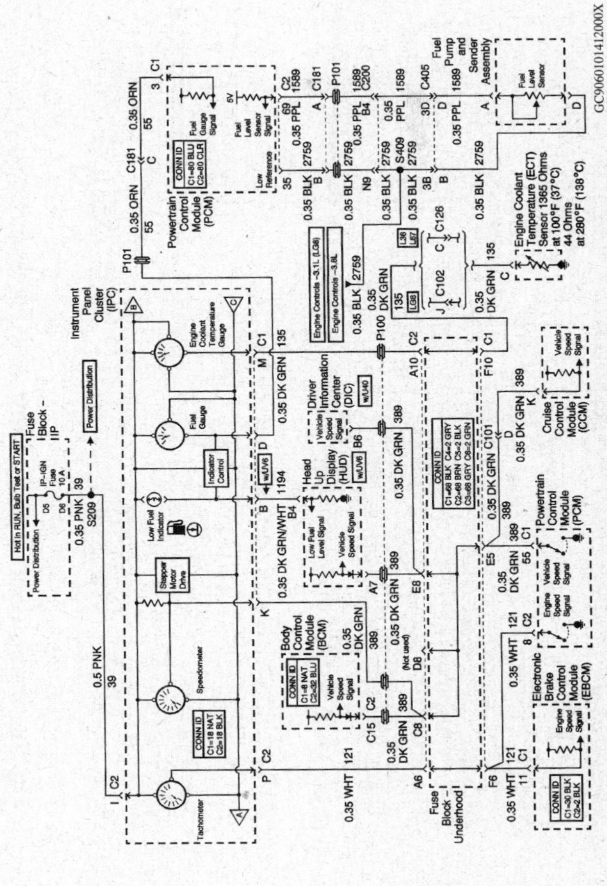

Fig. 27 Instrument cluster (Part 2 of 3) 2001 Grand Prix

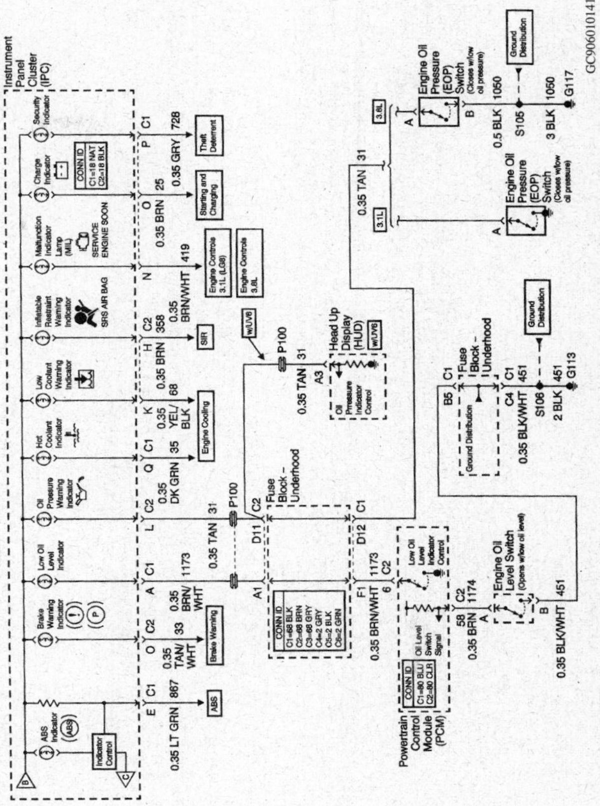

Fig. 27 Instrument cluster (Part 3 of 3) 2001 Grand Prix

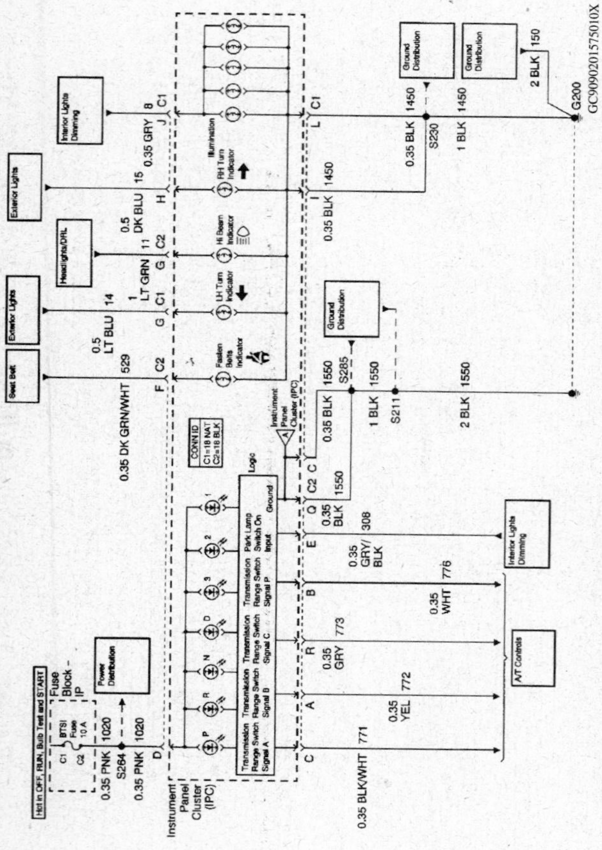

Fig. 28 Instrument cluster (Part 1 of 4). 2002–04 Grand Prix

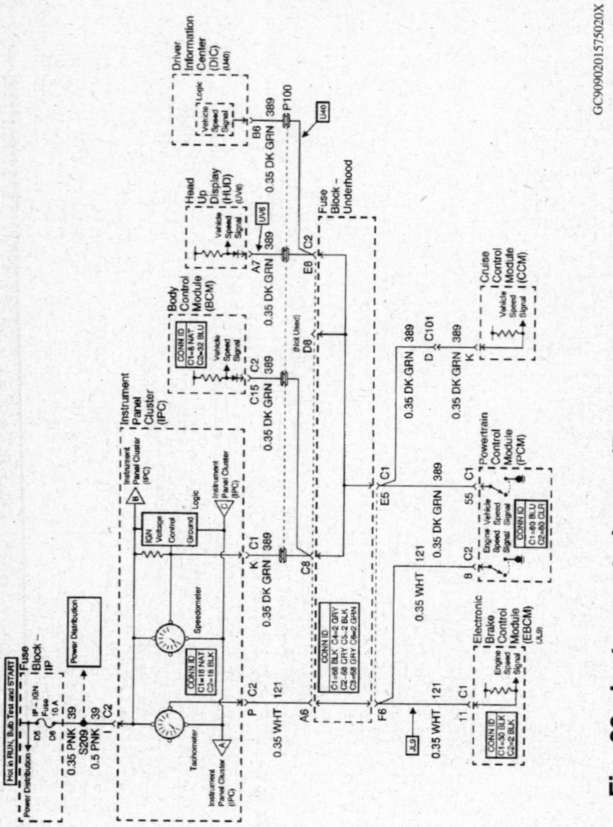

Fig. 28 Instrument cluster (Part 2 of 4). 2002–04 Grand Prix

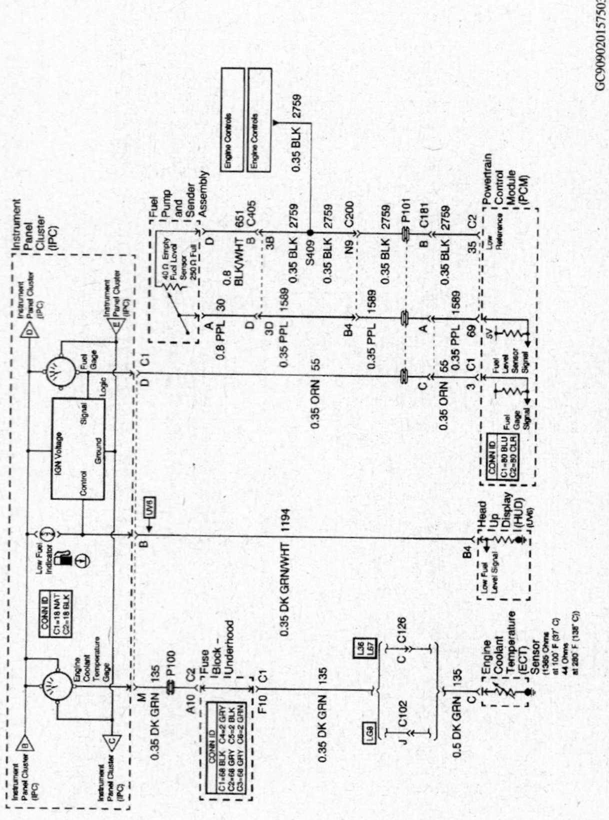

Fig. 28 Instrument cluster (Part 3 of 4). 2002–04 Grand Prix

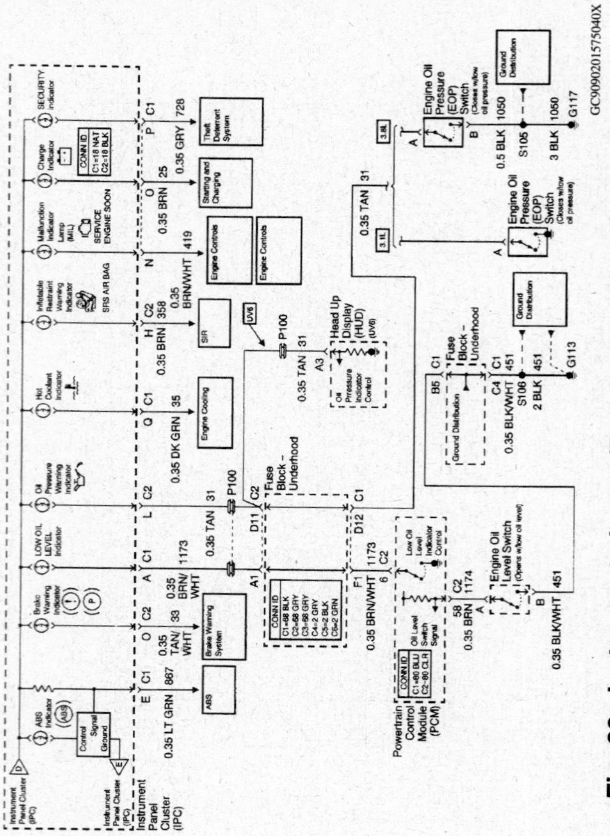

Fig. 28 Instrument cluster (Part 4 of 4). 2002–04 Grand Prix

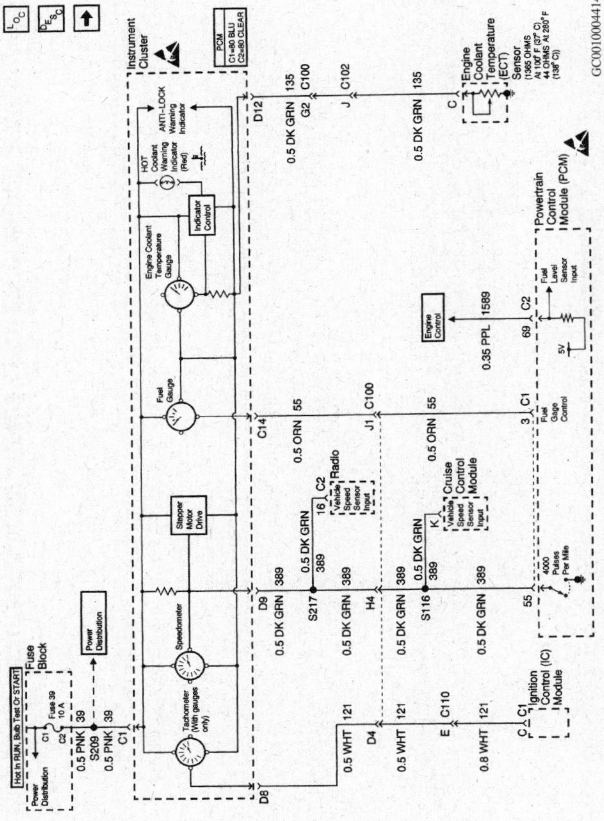

Fig. 29 Instrument cluster (Part 1 of 4). 2000–01 Lumina

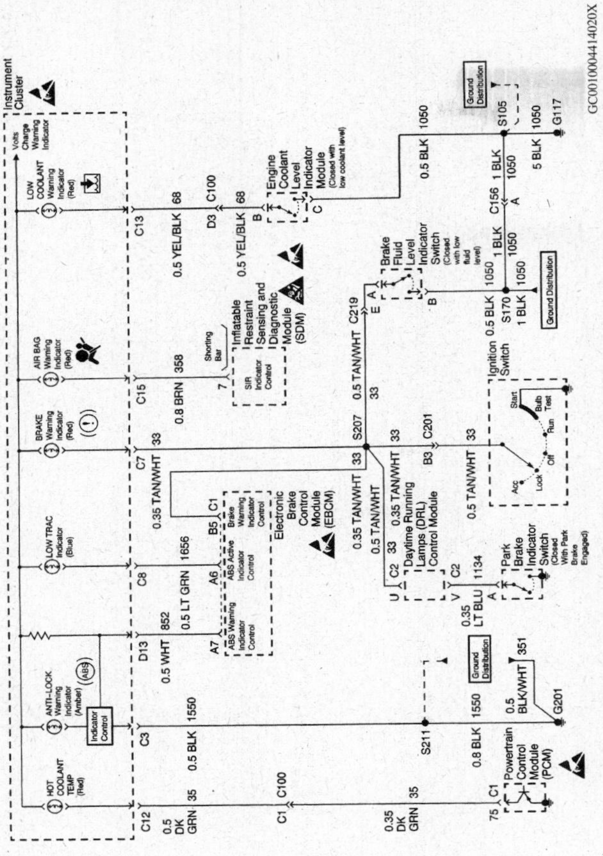

Fig. 29 Instrument cluster (Part 2 of 4). 2000–01 Lumina

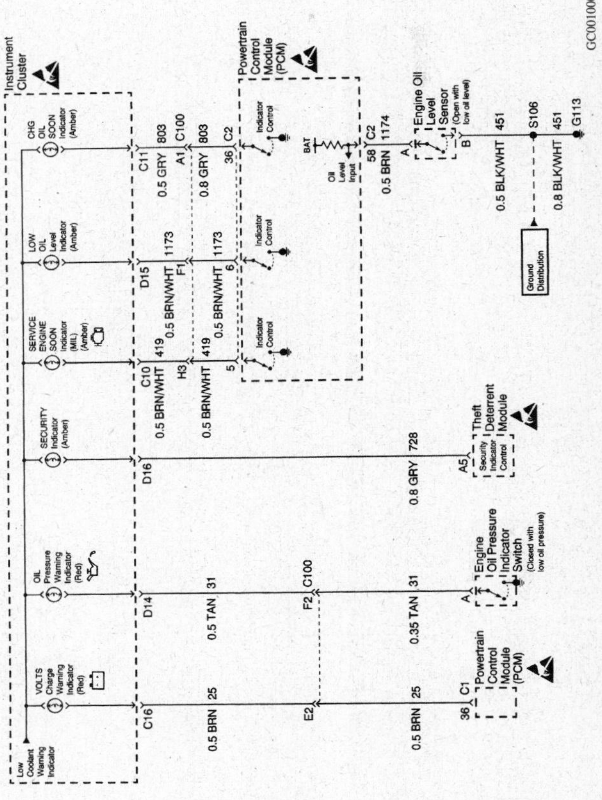

Fig. 29 Instrument cluster (Part 3 of 4). 2000–01 Lumina

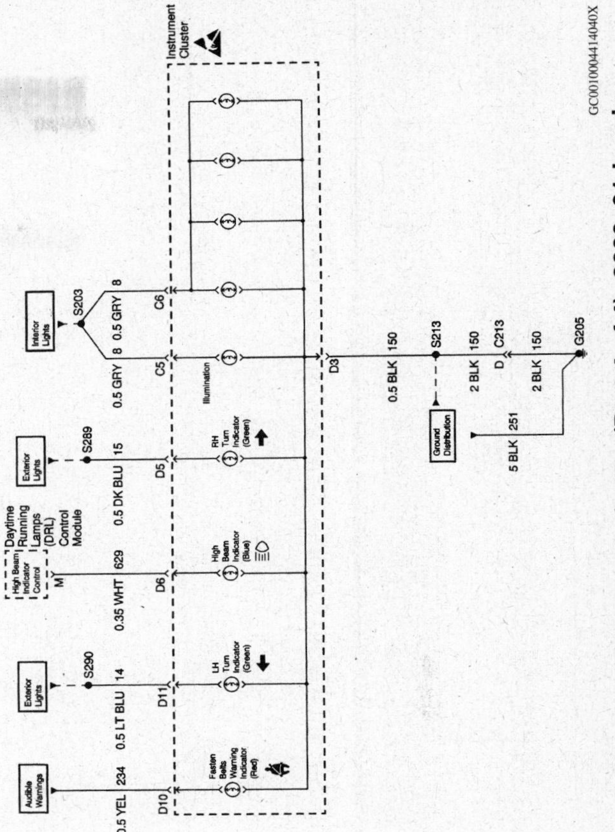

Fig. 29 Instrument cluster (Part 4 of 4). 2000–01 Lumina

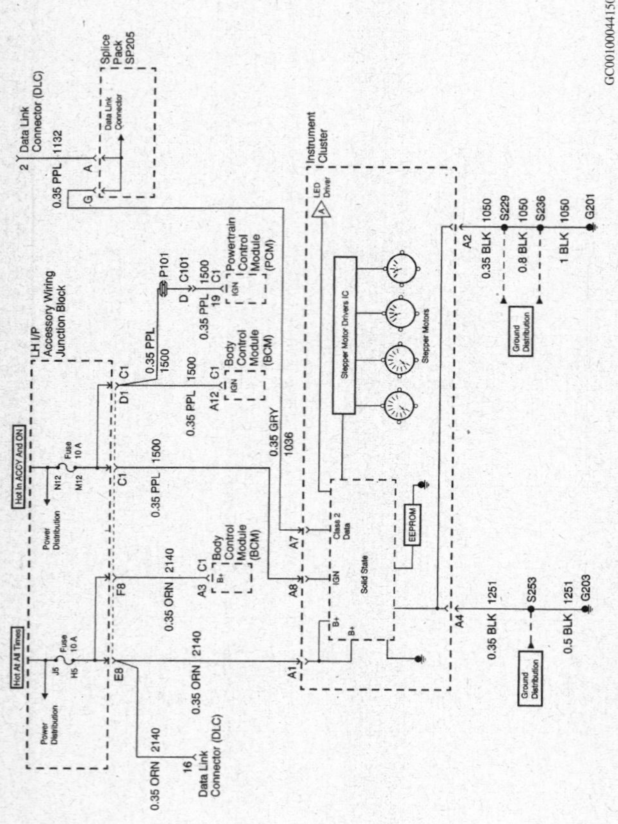

Fig. 30 Instrument cluster (Part 1 of 4). 2000 Impala & Monte Carlo

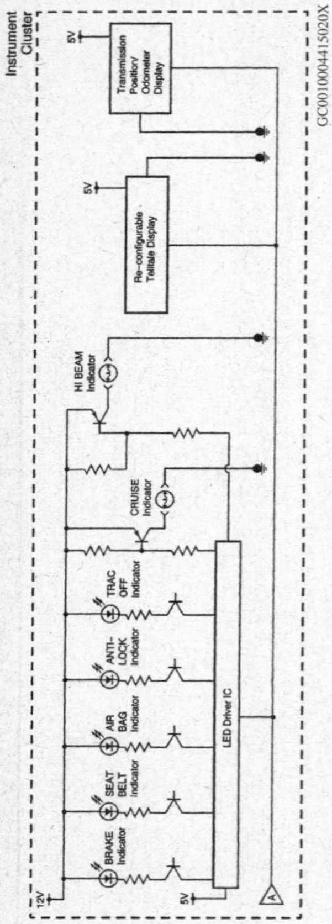

Fig. 30 Instrument cluster (Part 2 of 4). 2000 Impala & Monte Carlo

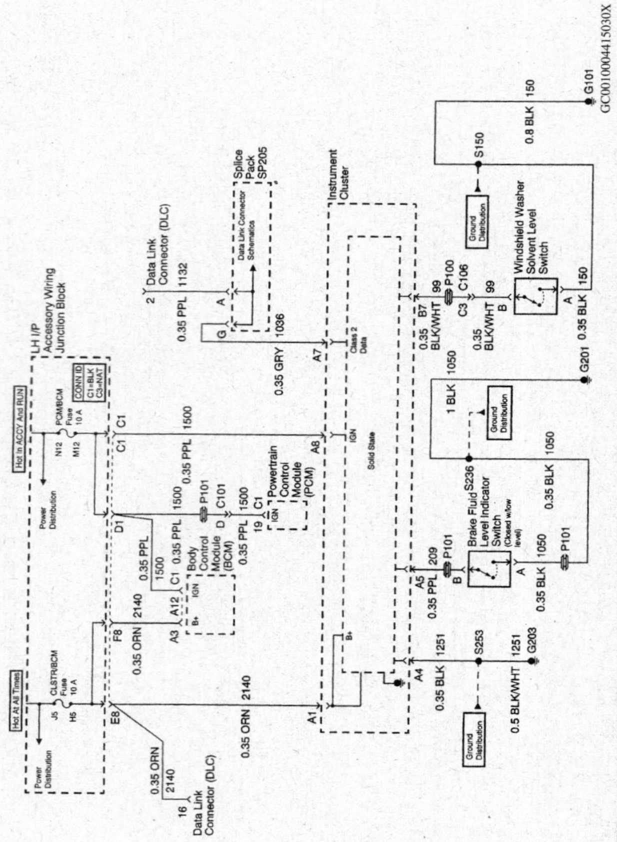

Fig. 30 Instrument cluster (Part 3 of 4). 2000 Impala & Monte Carlo

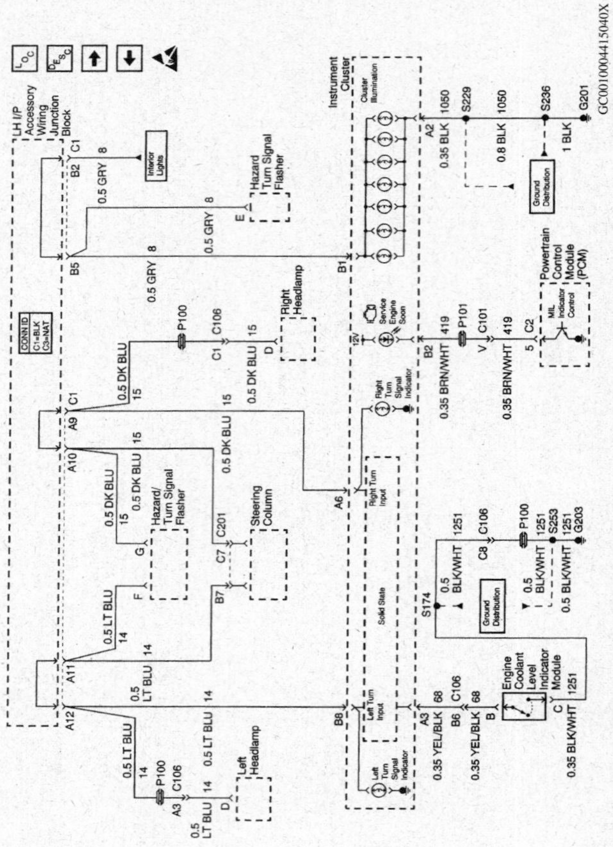

Fig. 30 Instrument cluster (Part 4 of 4). 2000 Impala & Monte Carlo

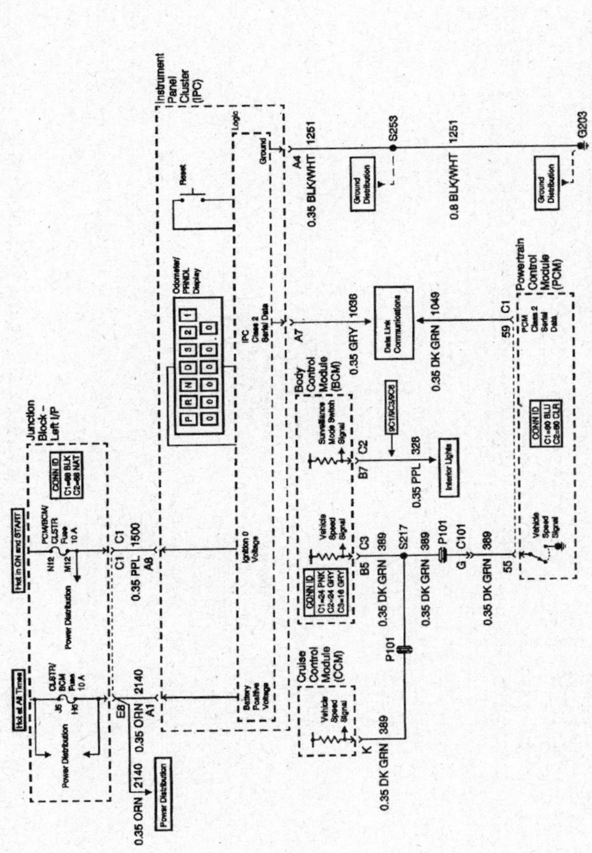

GC9090101570010X

Fig. 31 Instrument cluster (Part 1 of 3). 2001–04 Impala & Monte Carlo

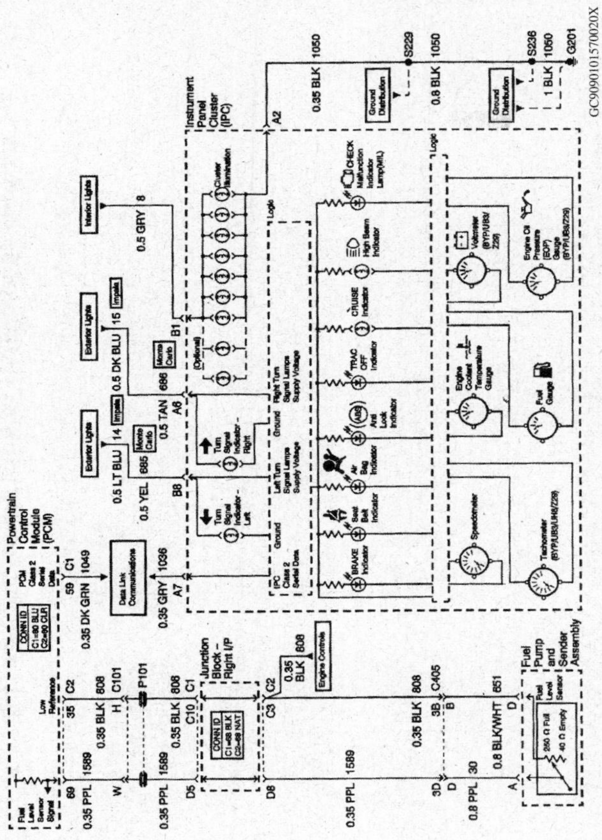

GC9090101570020X

Fig. 31 Instrument cluster (Part 2 of 3). 2001–04 Impala & Monte Carlo

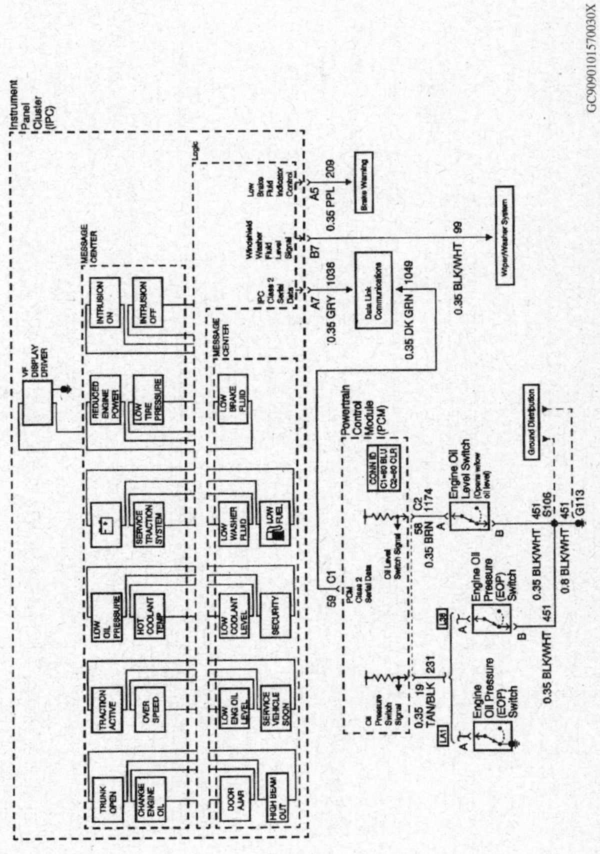

GC9090101570030X

Fig. 31 Instrument cluster (Part 3 of 3). 2001–04 Impala & Monte Carlo

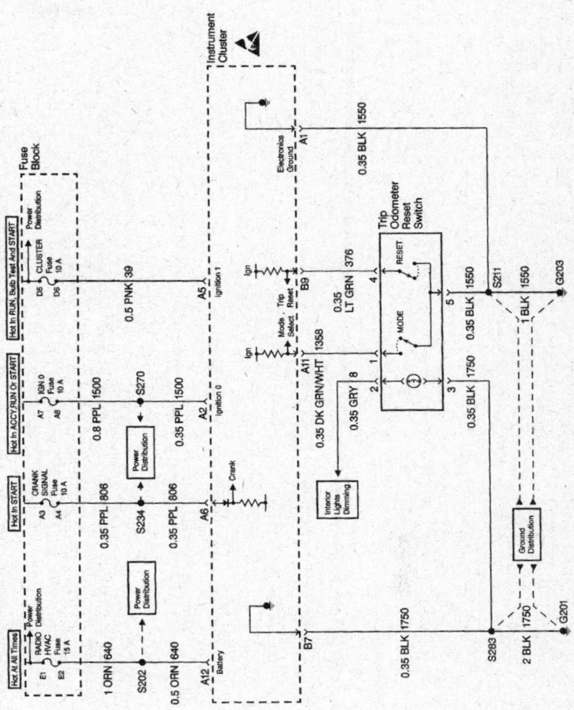

GC0019801545010X

Fig. 32 Instrument cluster (Part 1 of 5). Intrigue

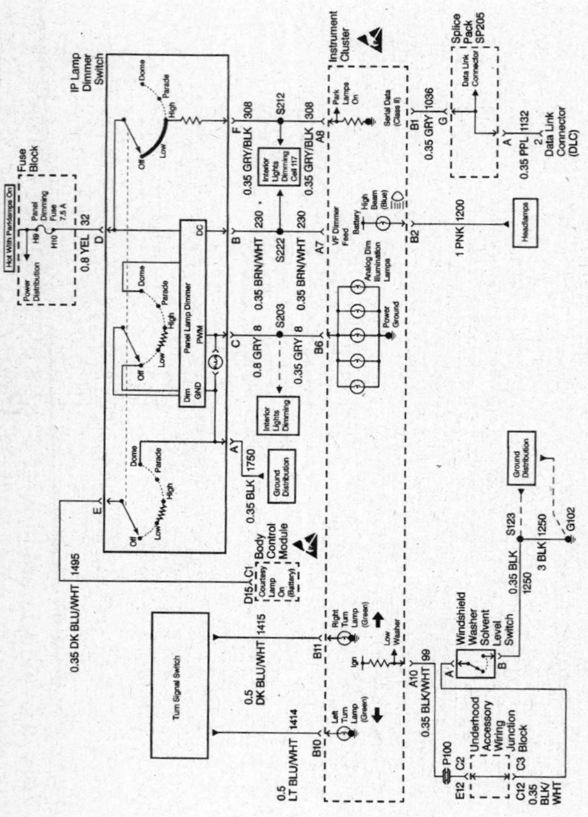

GC0019801545020X

Fig. 32 Instrument cluster (Part 2 of 5). Intrigue

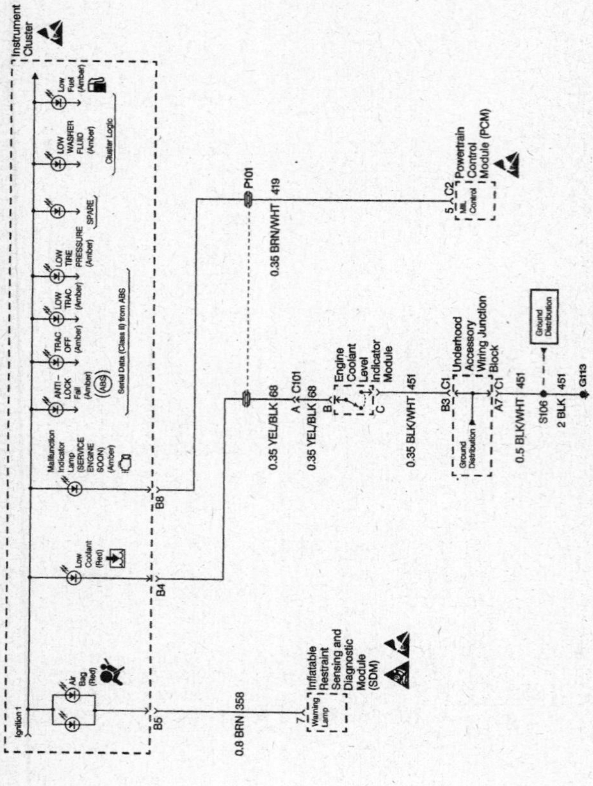

GC0019801545030X

Fig. 32 Instrument cluster (Part 3 of 5). Intrigue

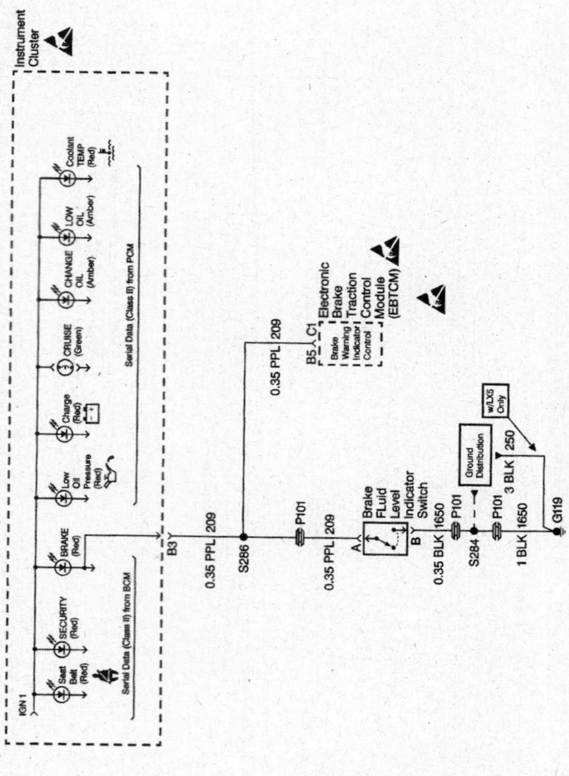

GC0019801545040X

Fig. 32 Instrument cluster (Part 4 of 5). Intrigue

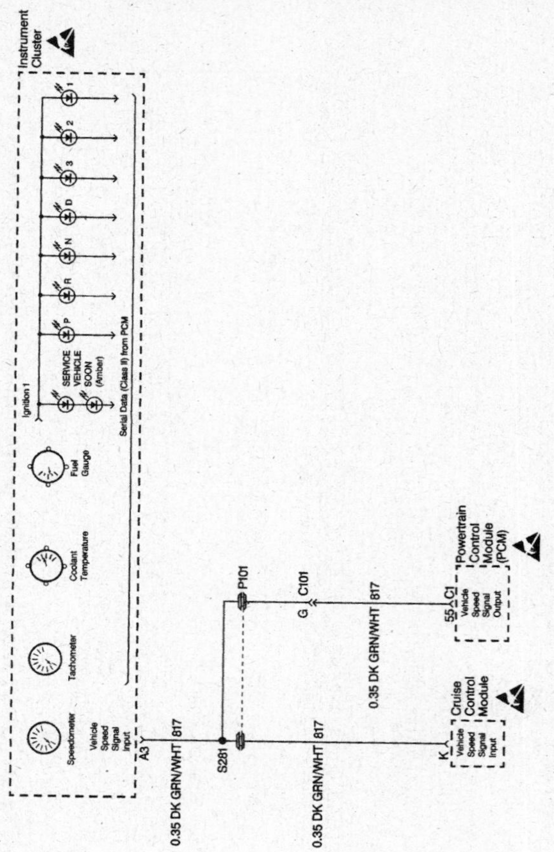

GC0019801545050X

Fig. 32 Instrument cluster (Part 5 of 5). Intrigue

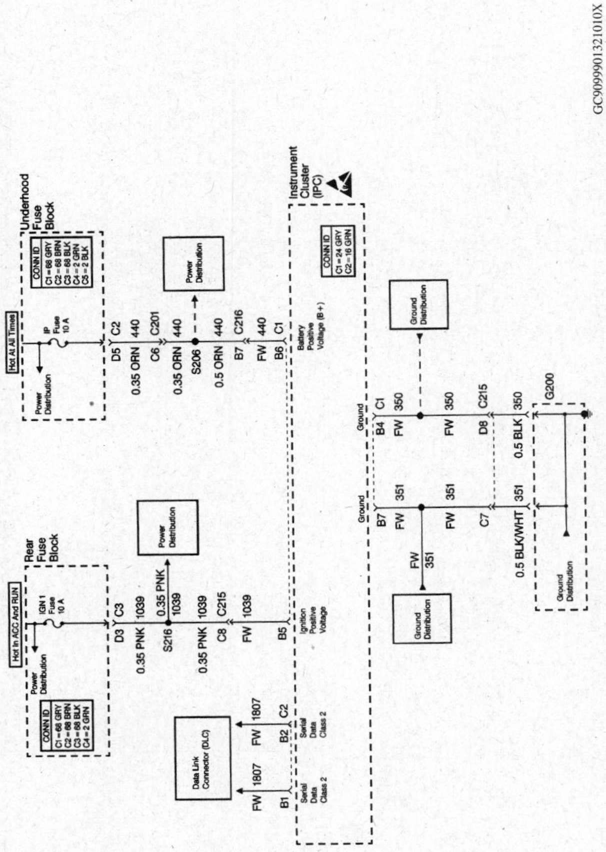

Fig. 33 Instrument cluster (Part 1 of 8). 2000–01 LeSabre

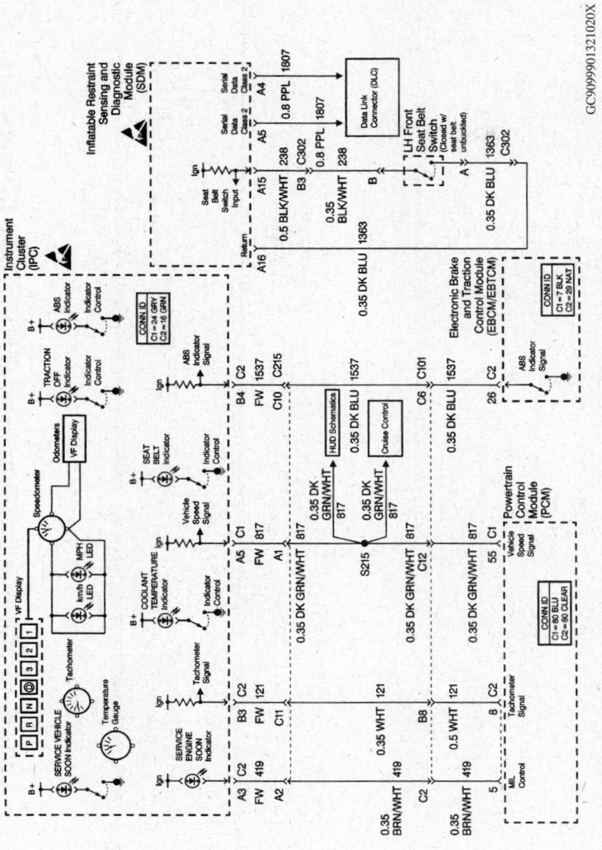

Fig. 33 Instrument cluster (Part 2 of 8). 2000–01 LeSabre

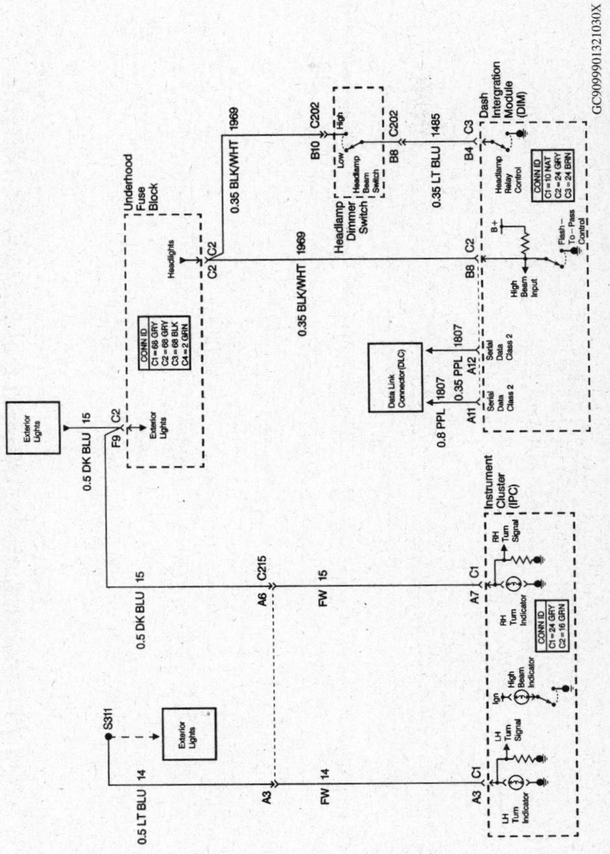

Fig. 33 Instrument cluster (Part 3 of 8). 2000–01 LeSabre

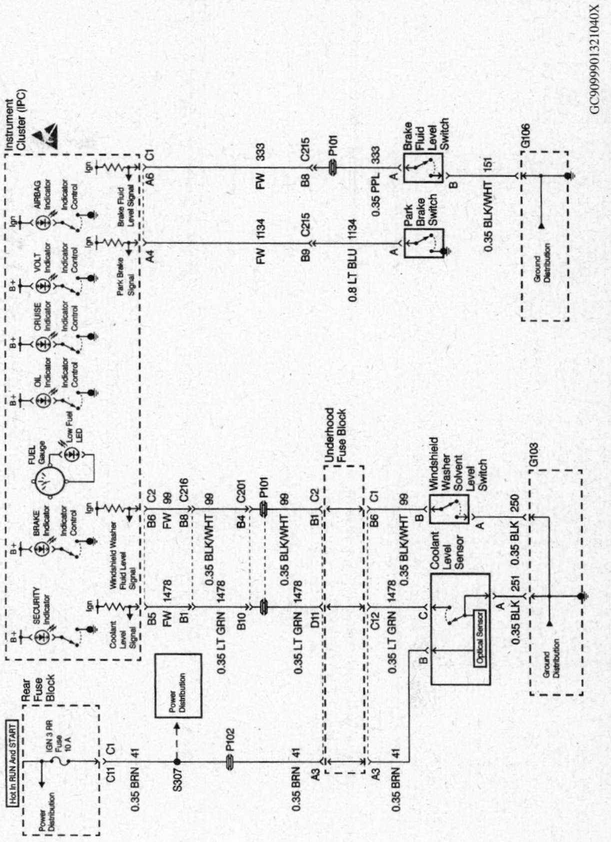

Fig. 33 Instrument cluster (Part 4 of 8). 2000–01 LeSabre

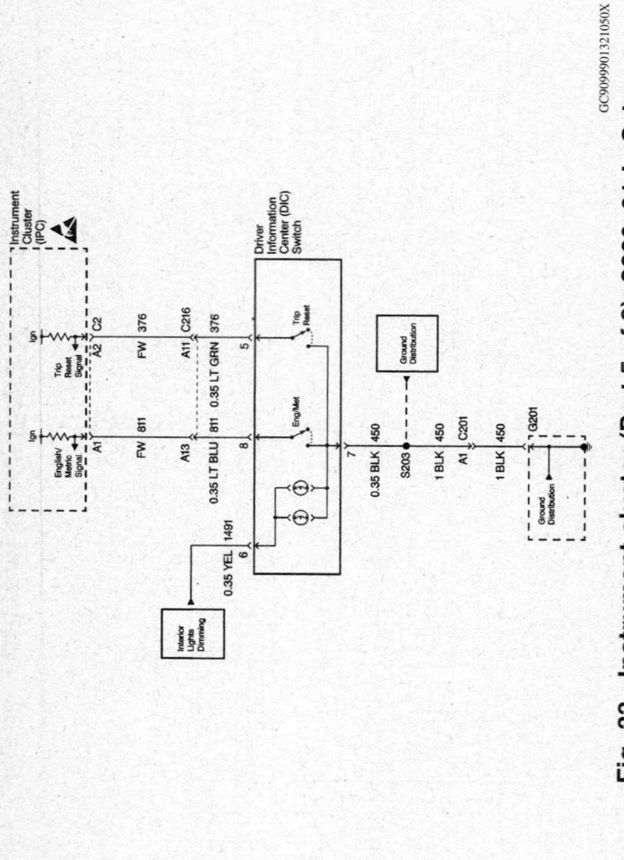

Fig. 33 Instrument cluster (Part 5 of 8). 2000–01 LeSabre

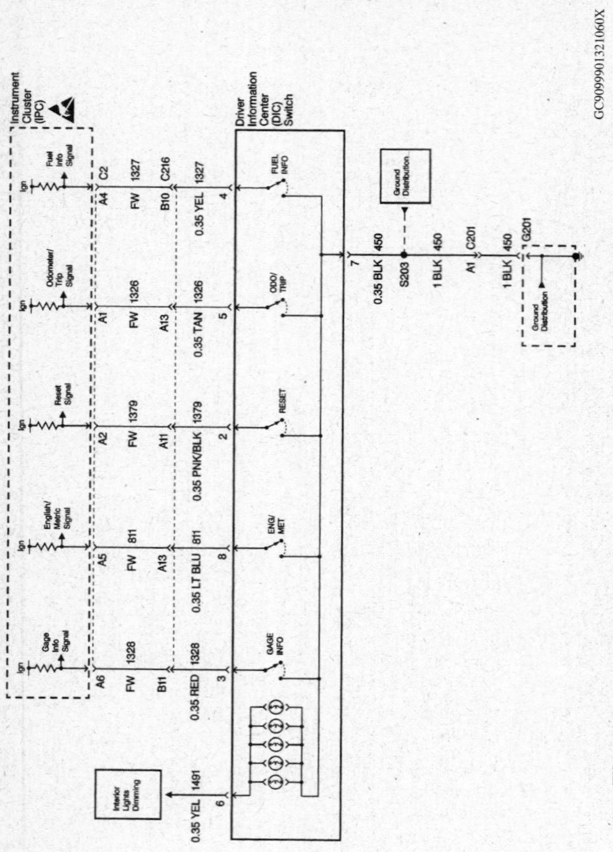

Fig. 33 Instrument cluster (Part 6 of 8). 2000–01 LeSabre

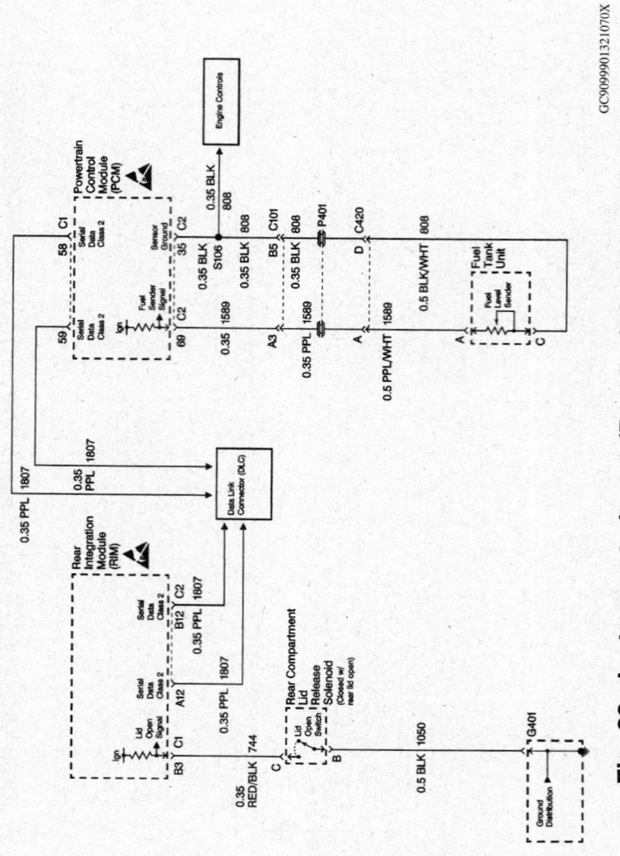

Fig. 33 Instrument cluster (Part 7 of 8). 2000–01 LeSabre

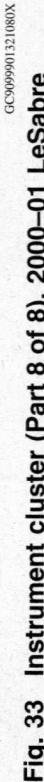

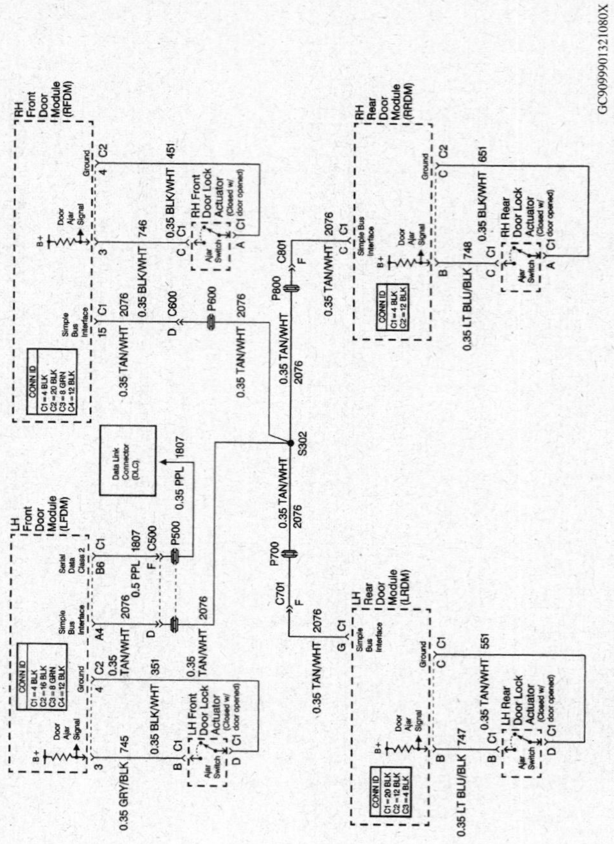

Fig. 33 Instrument cluster (Part 8 of 8). 2000–01 LeSabre

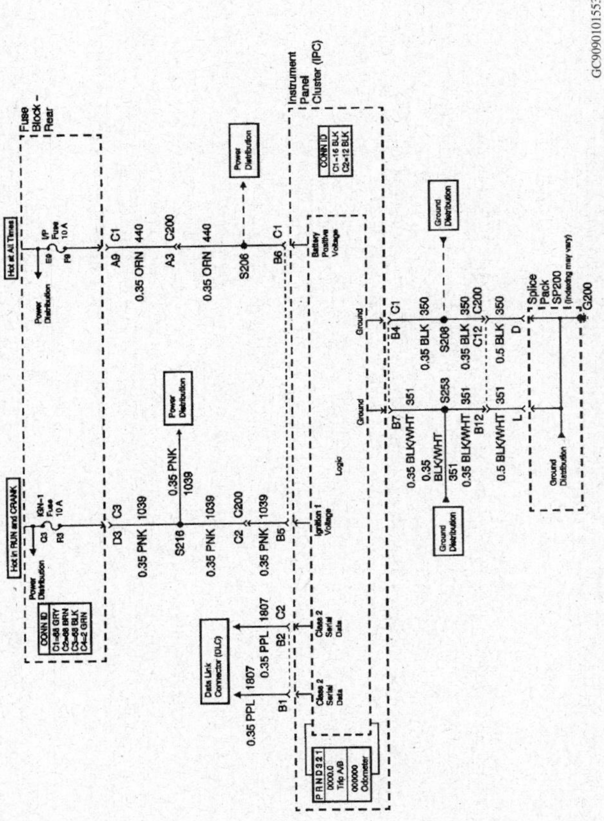

Fig. 34 Instrument cluster (Part 1 of 5). 2002–04 LeSabre

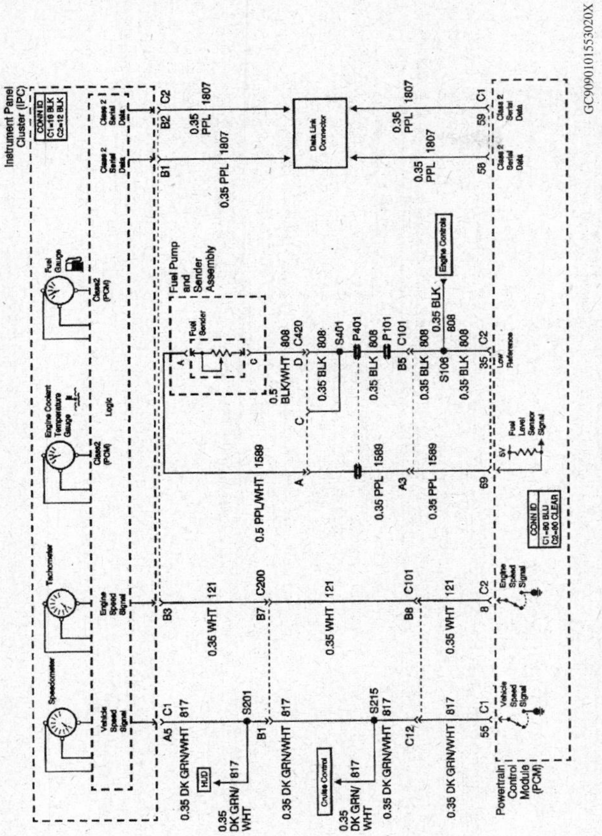

Fig. 34 Instrument cluster (Part 2 of 5). 2002–04 LeSabre

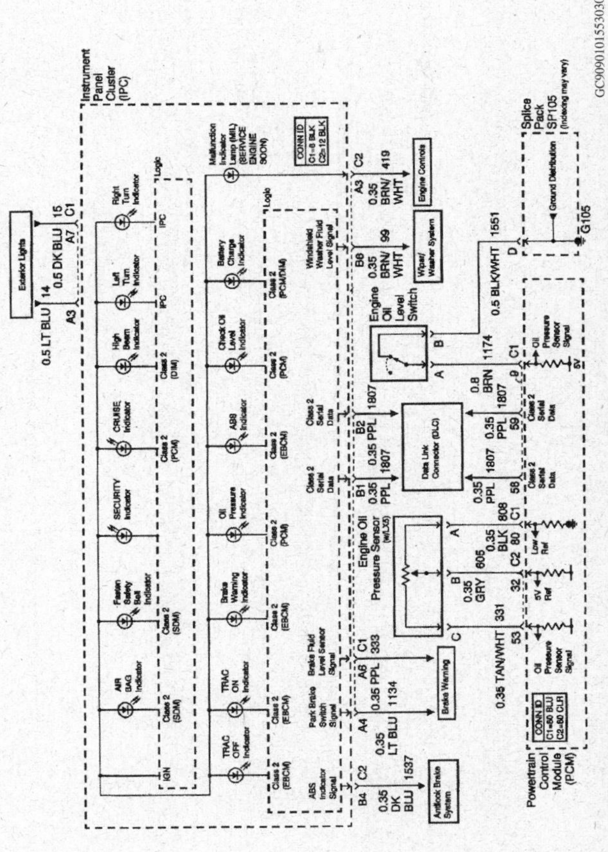

Fig. 34 Instrument cluster (Part 3 of 5). 2002–04 LeSabre

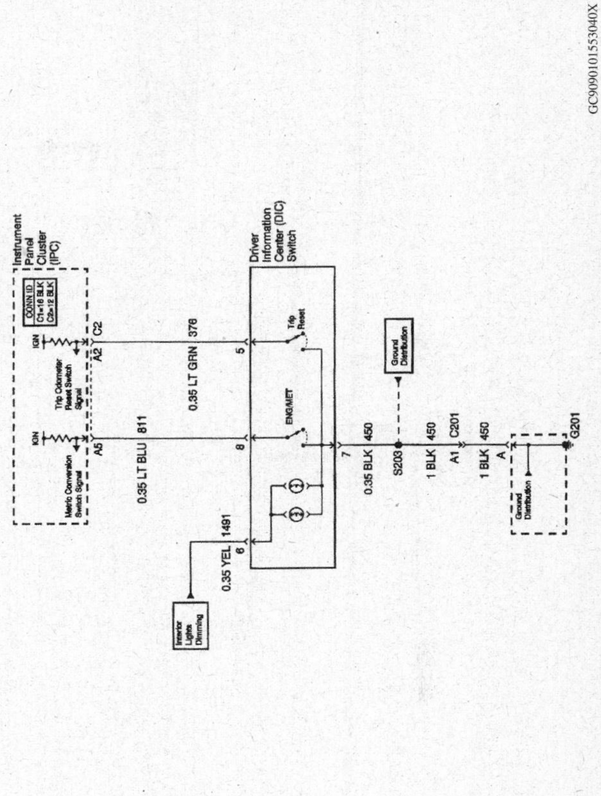

Fig. 34 Instrument cluster (Part 4 of 5). 2002–04 LeSabre

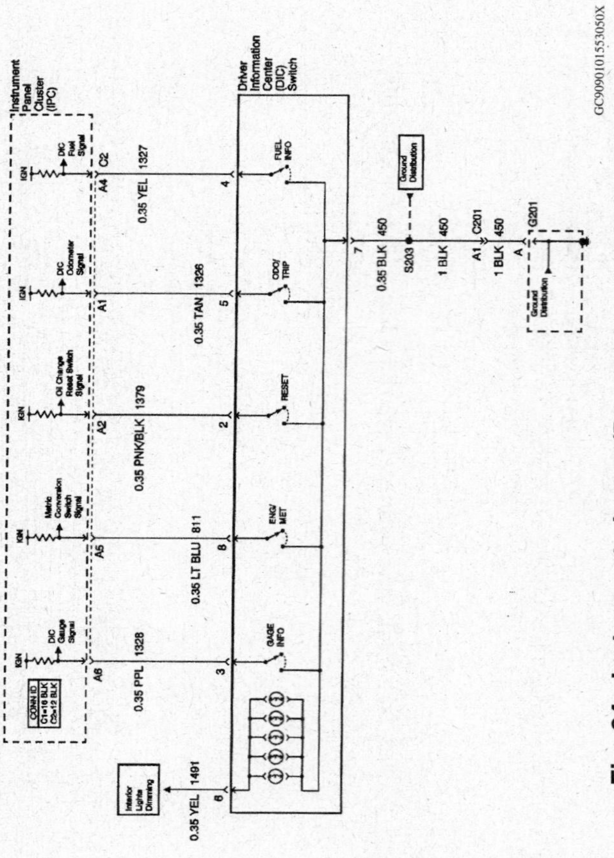

Fig. 34 Instrument cluster (Part 5 of 5). 2002–04 LeSabre

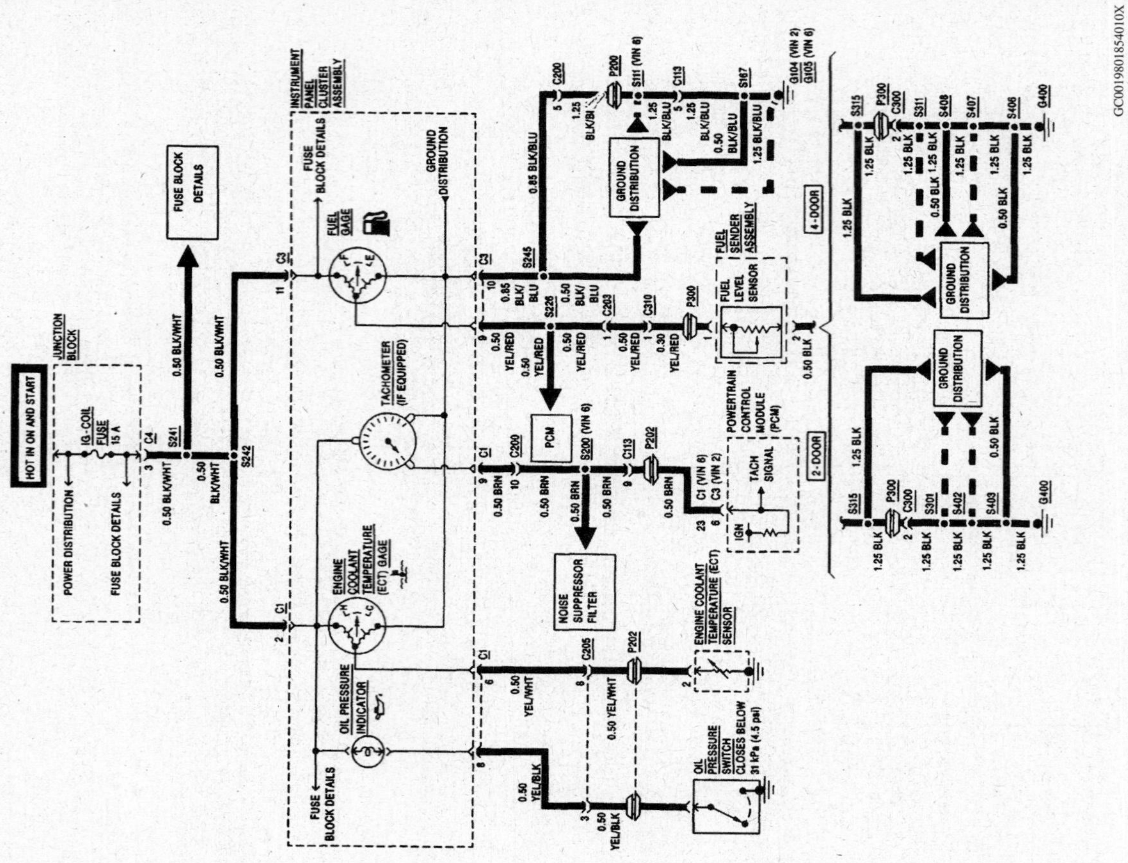

Fig. 35 Instrument cluster (Part 1 of 2). Metro

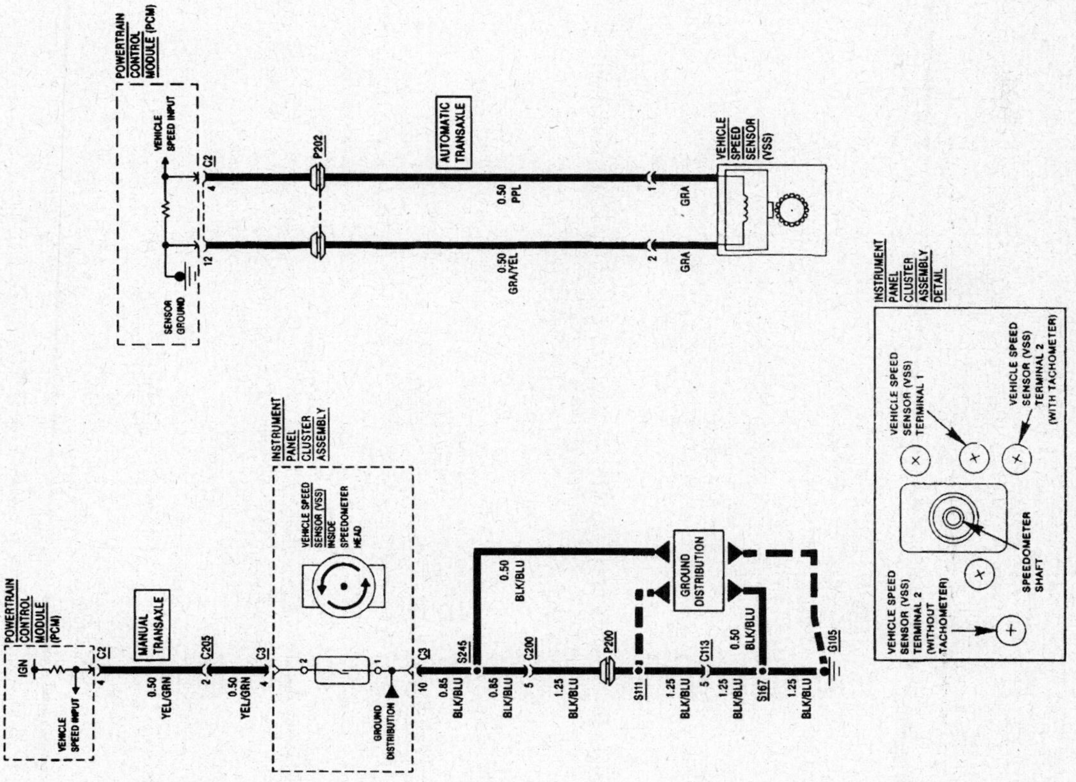

Fig. 35 Instrument cluster (Part 2 of 2). Metro

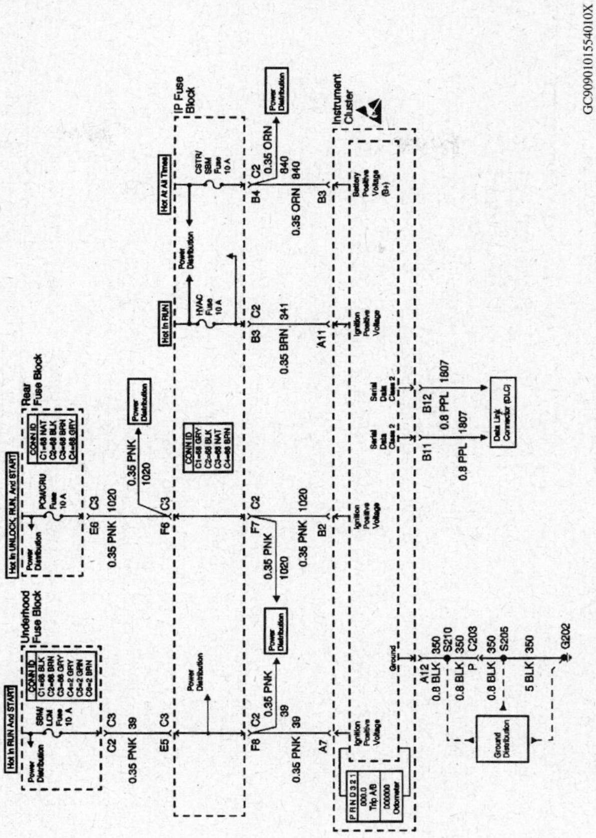

Fig. 36 Instrument cluster (Part 1 of 5). 2000 Park Avenue

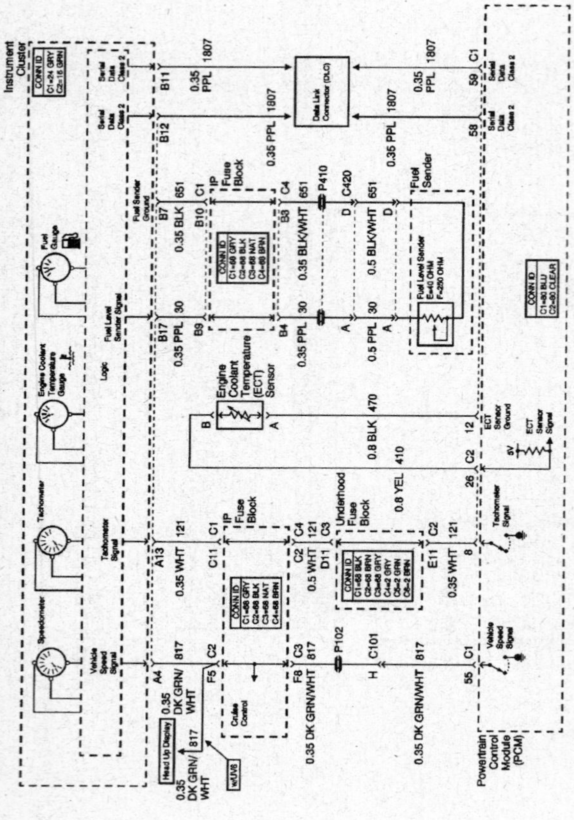
GC909010155402OX

Fig. 36 Instrument cluster (Part 2 of 5). 2000 Park Avenue

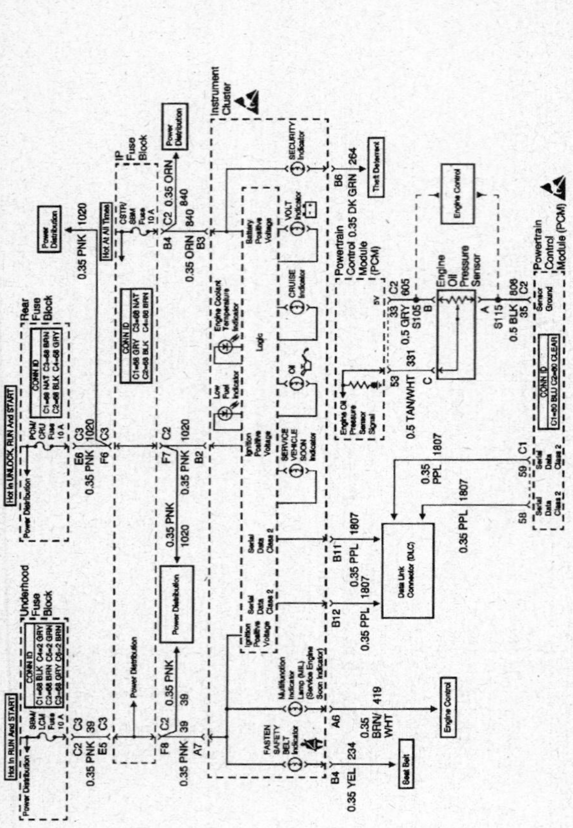
GC909010155403OX

Fig. 36 Instrument cluster (Part 3 of 5). 2000 Park Avenue

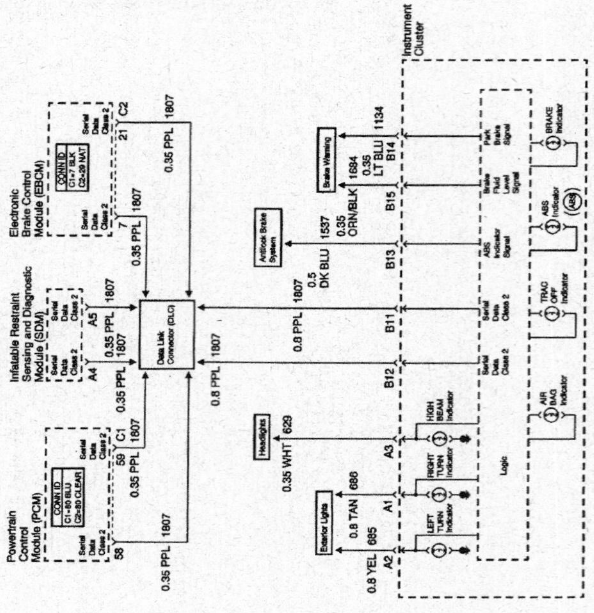
GC909010155404OX

Fig. 36 Instrument cluster (Part 4 of 5). 2000 Park Avenue

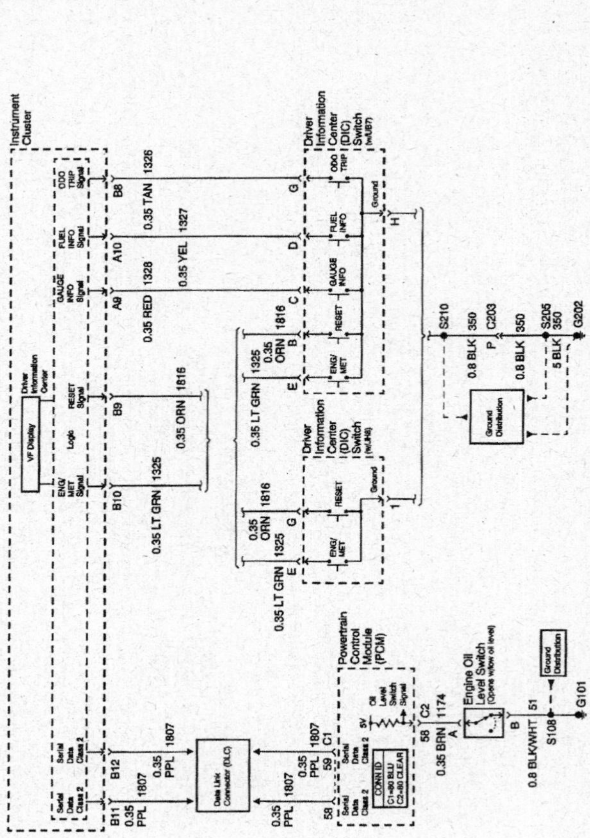
GC909010155405OX

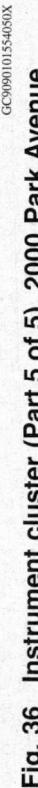

Fig. 36 Instrument cluster (Part 5 of 5). 2000 Park Avenue

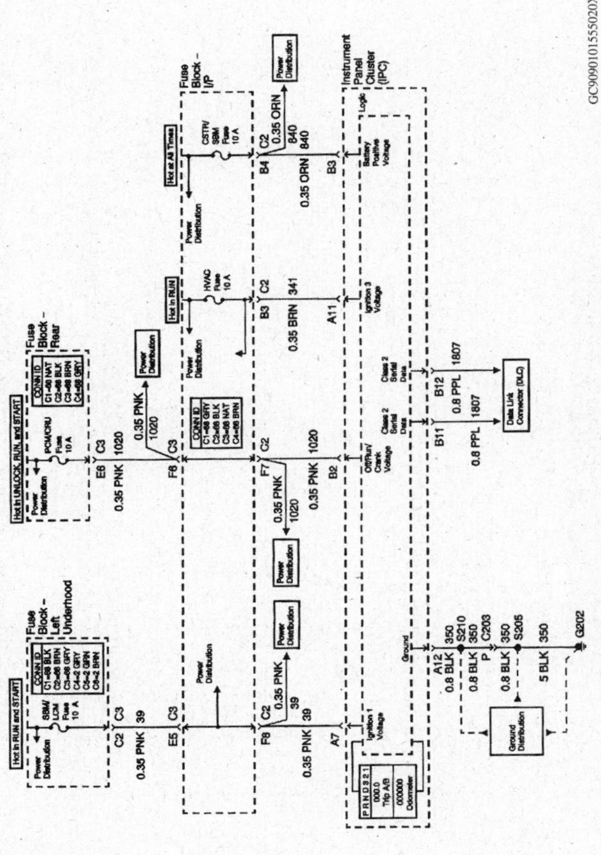

Fig. 37 Instrument cluster (Part 1 of 4). 2001–04 Park Avenue

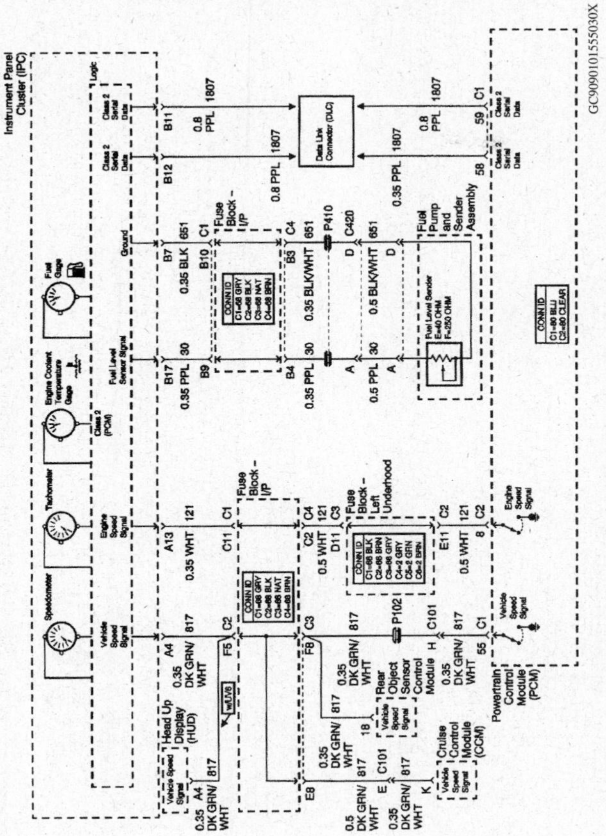

Fig. 37 Instrument cluster (Part 2 of 4). 2001–04 Park Avenue

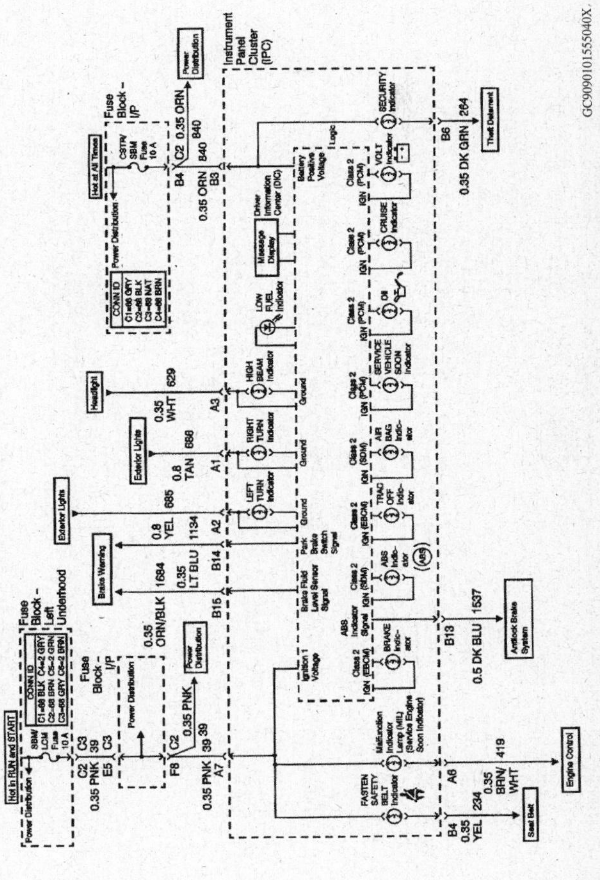

Fig. 37 Instrument cluster (Part 3 of 4). 2001–04 Park Avenue

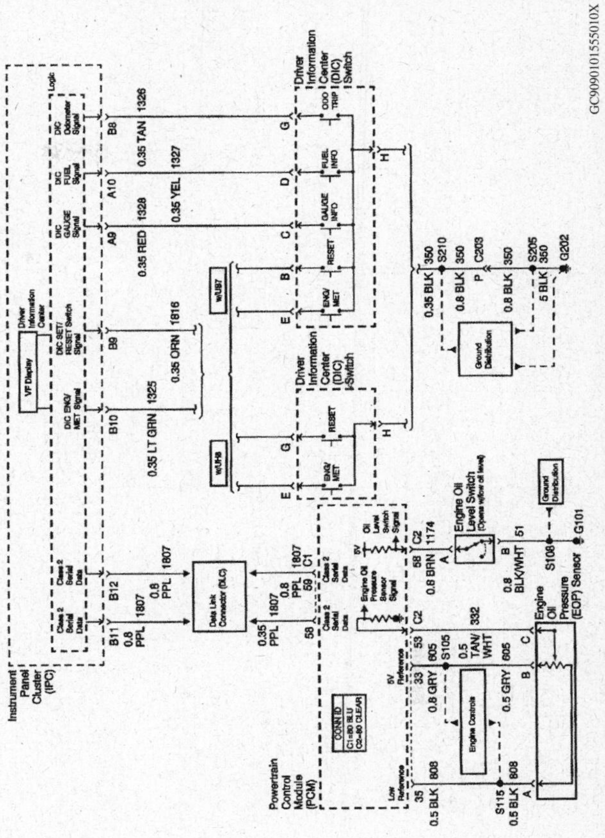

Fig. 37 Instrument cluster (Part 4 of 4). 2001–04 Park Avenue

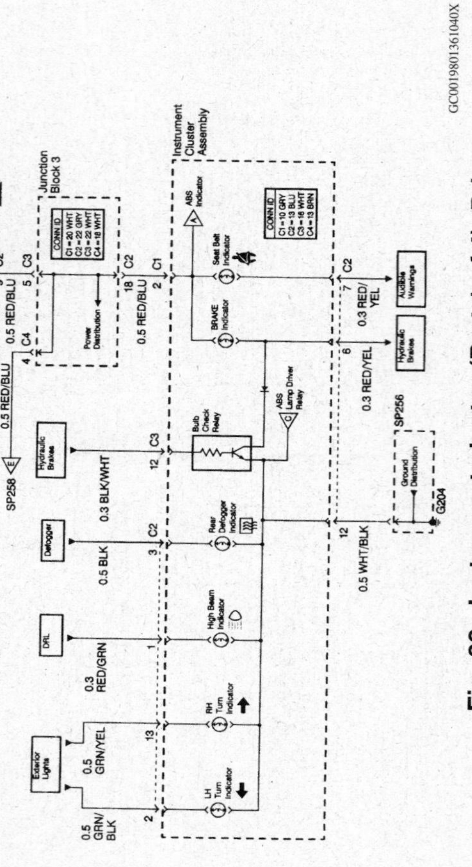

Fig. 38 Instrument cluster (Part 1 of 4). Prizm

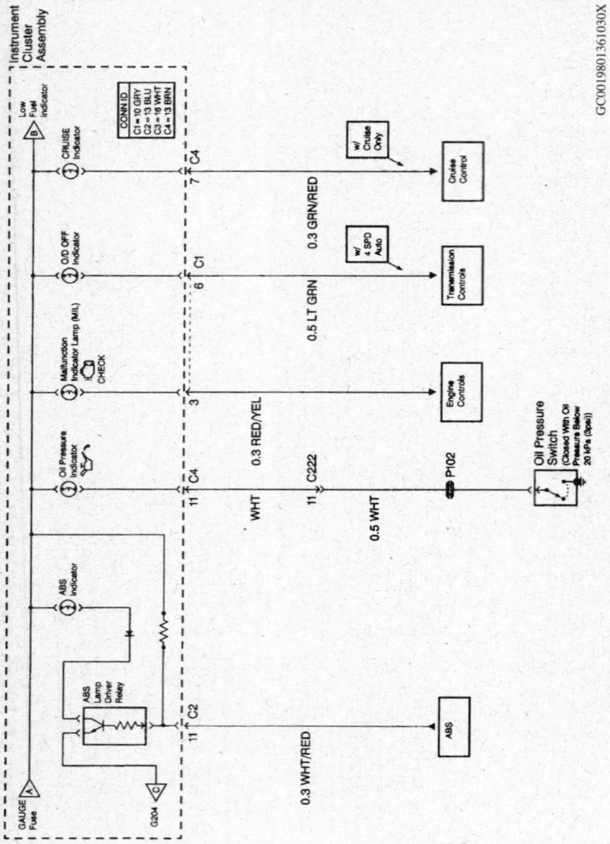

Fig. 38 Instrument cluster (Part 2 of 4). Prizm

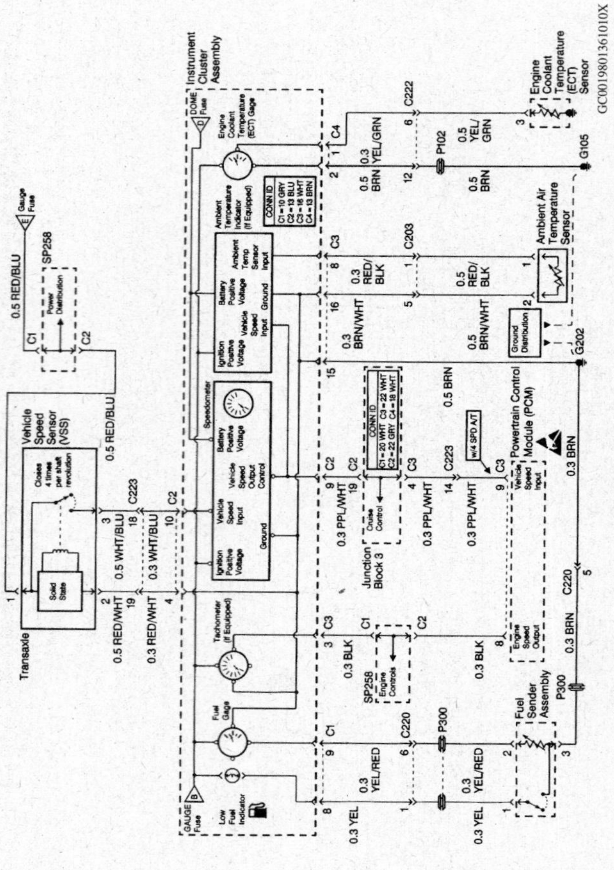

Fig. 38 Instrument cluster (Part 3 of 4). Prizm

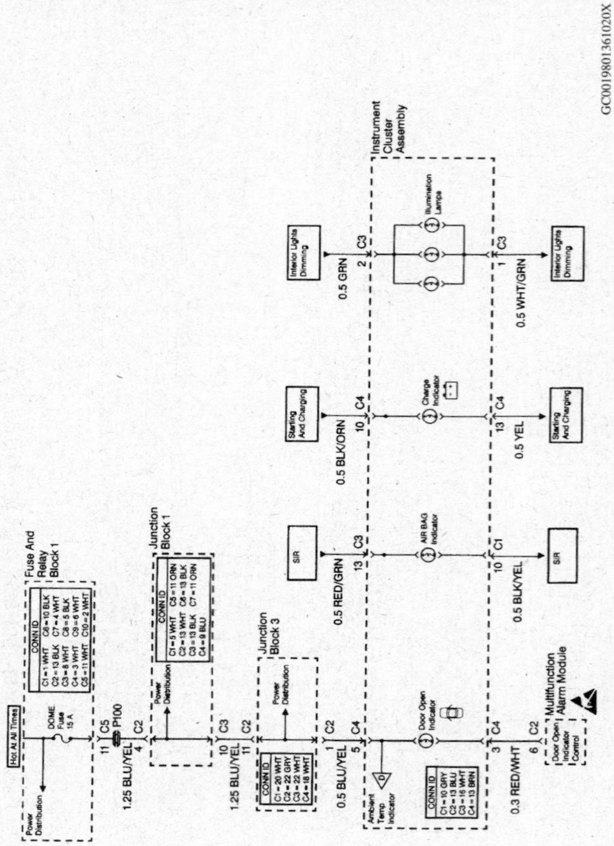

Fig. 38 Instrument cluster (Part 4 of 4). Prizm

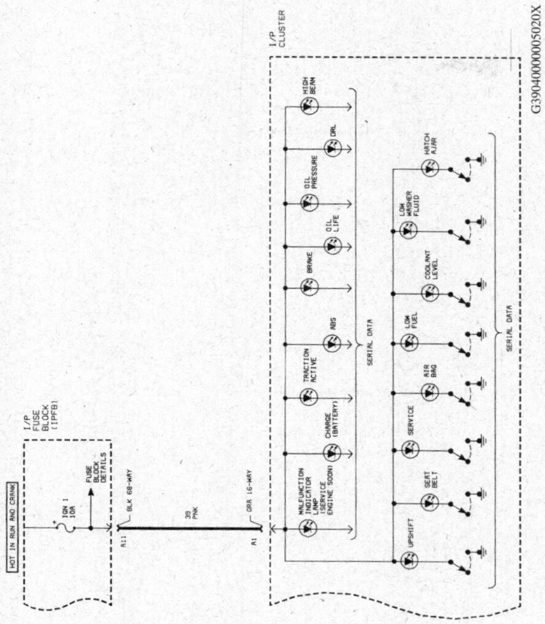

Fig. 39 Instrument cluster (Part 2 of 2). Saturn S-Series

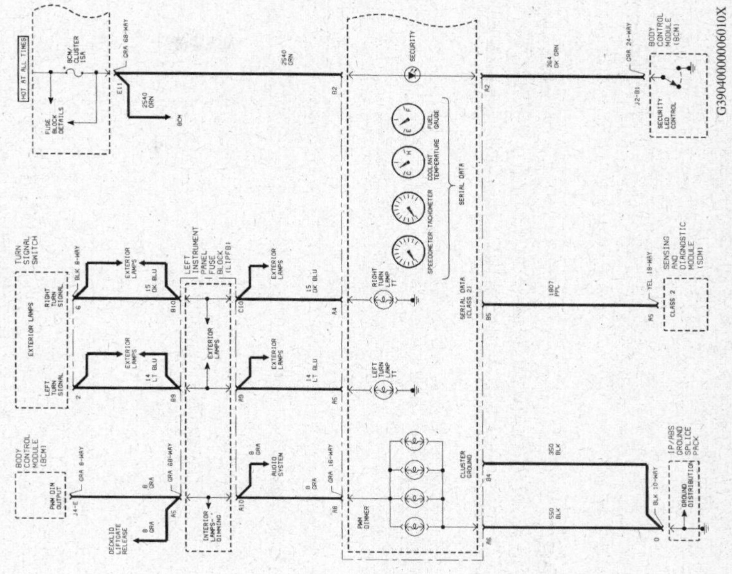

Fig. 40 Instrument cluster (Part 1 of 3). 2000–01 Saturn L-Series

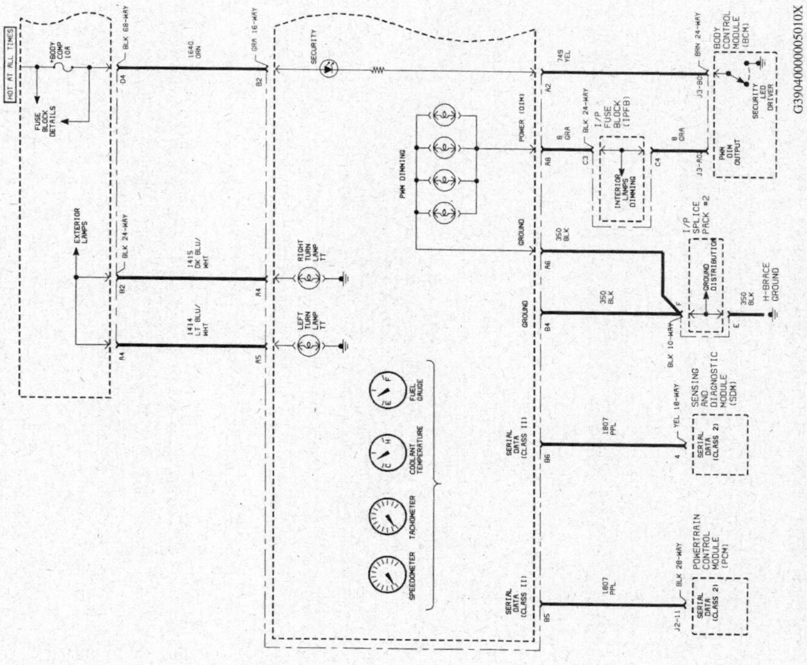

Fig. 39 Instrument cluster (Part 1 of 2). Saturn S-Series

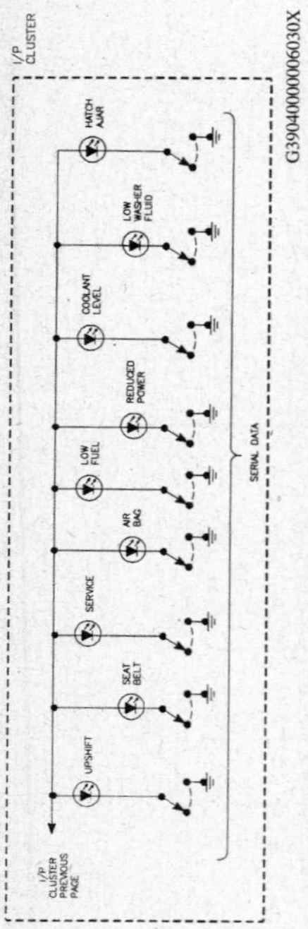

Fig. 40 Instrument cluster (Part 3 of 3). 2000–01 Saturn L-Series

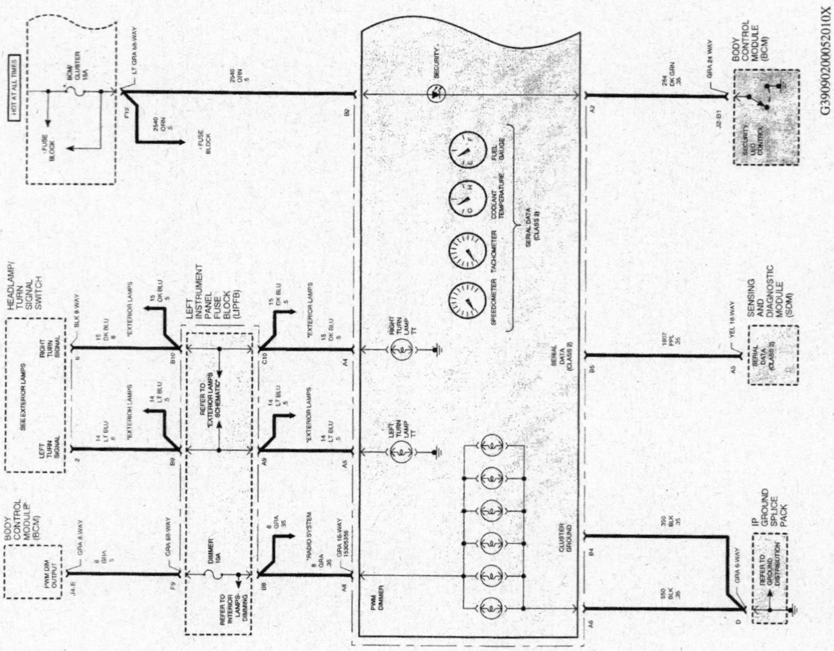

Fig. 41 Instrument cluster (Part 1 of 2). 2002–04 Saturn L-Series

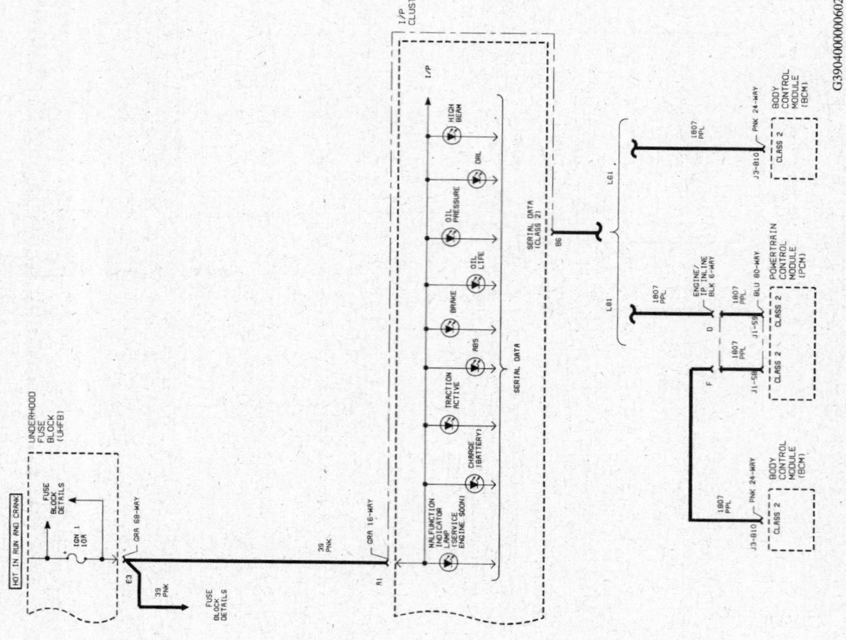

Fig. 40 Instrument cluster (Part 2 of 3). 2000–01 Saturn L-Series

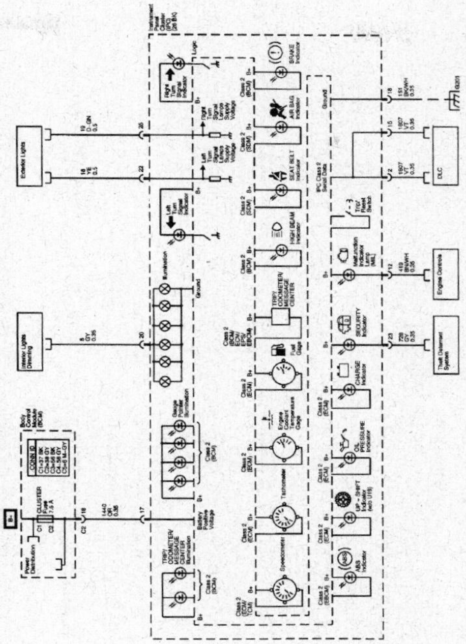

G39090200053010X

Fig. 42 Instrument cluster (Part 1 of 2). Saturn ION

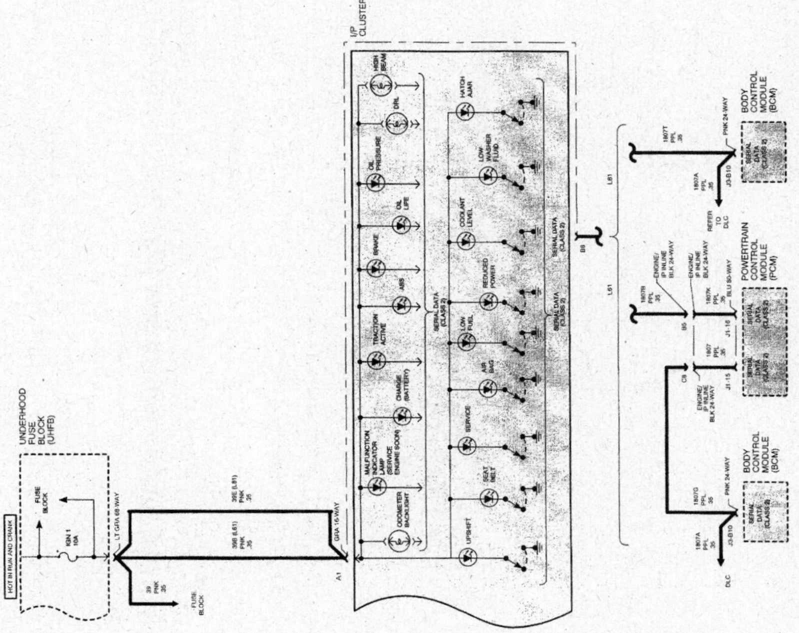

G39090200052020X

Fig. 41 Instrument cluster (Part 2 of 2) 2002–04 Saturn L-Series

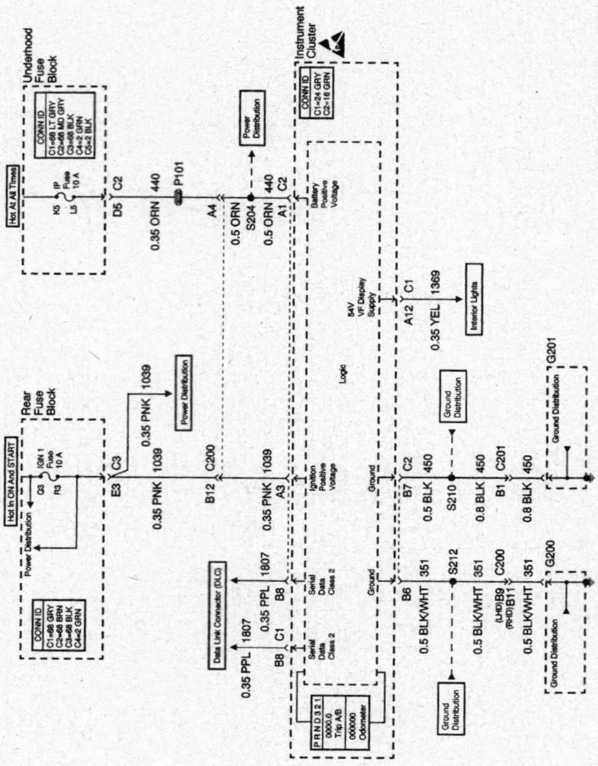

GC0100044260l0X

Fig. 43 Instrument cluster (Part 1 of 5). 2000 Seville

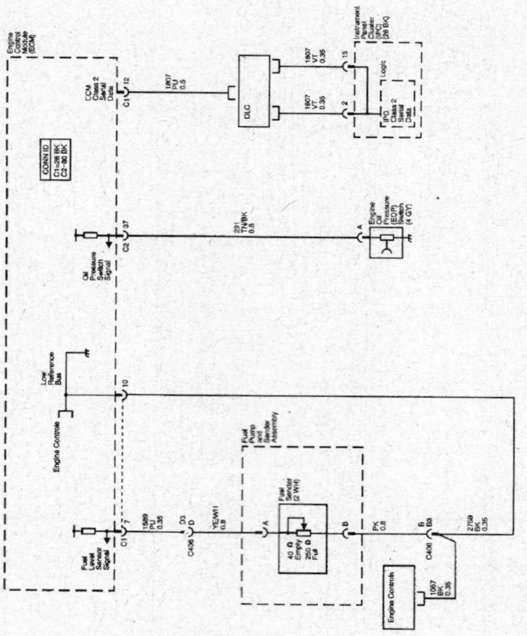

G3909020005302OX

Fig. 42 Instrument cluster (Part 2 of 2). Saturn ION

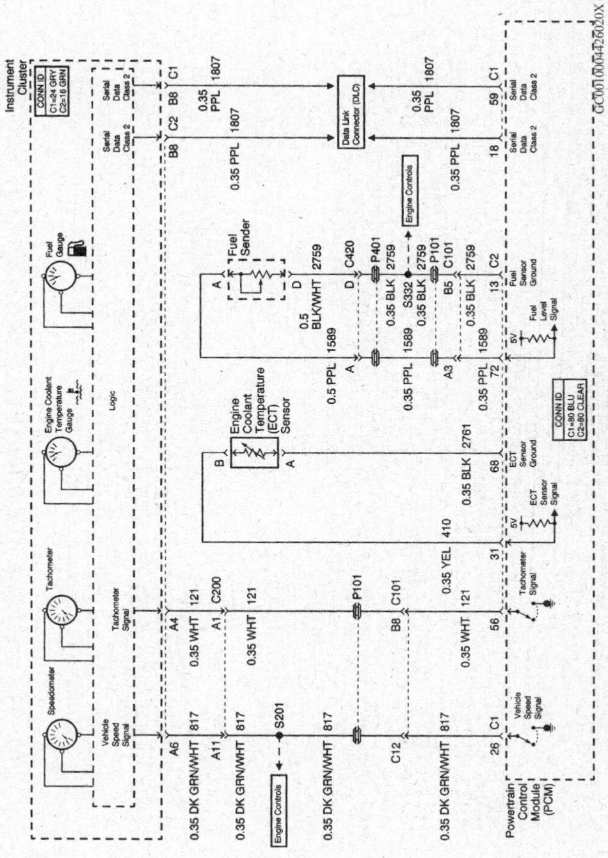

Fig. 43 Instrument cluster (Part 2 of 5). 2000 Seville

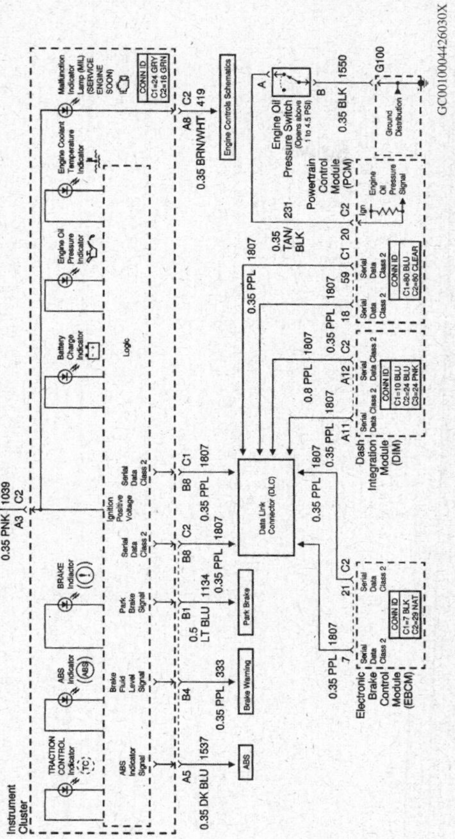

Fig. 43 Instrument cluster (Part 3 of 5). 2000 Seville

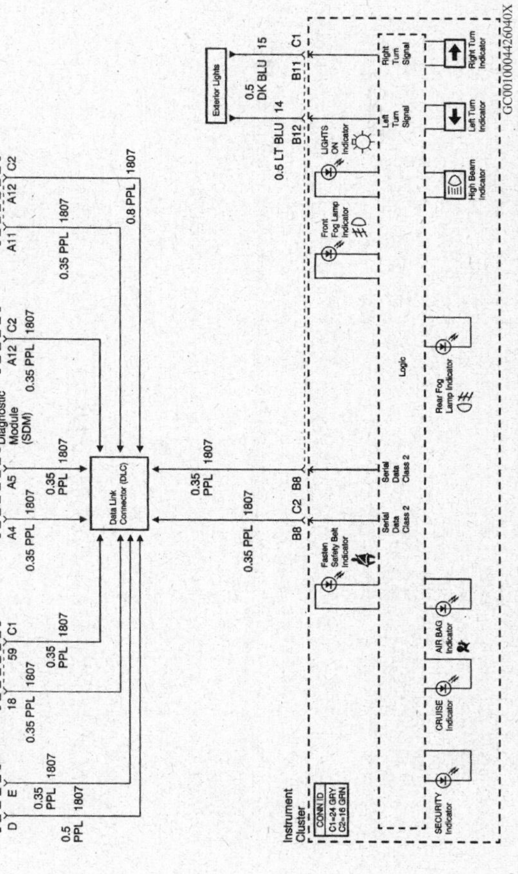

Fig. 43 Instrument cluster (Part 4 of 5). 2000 Seville

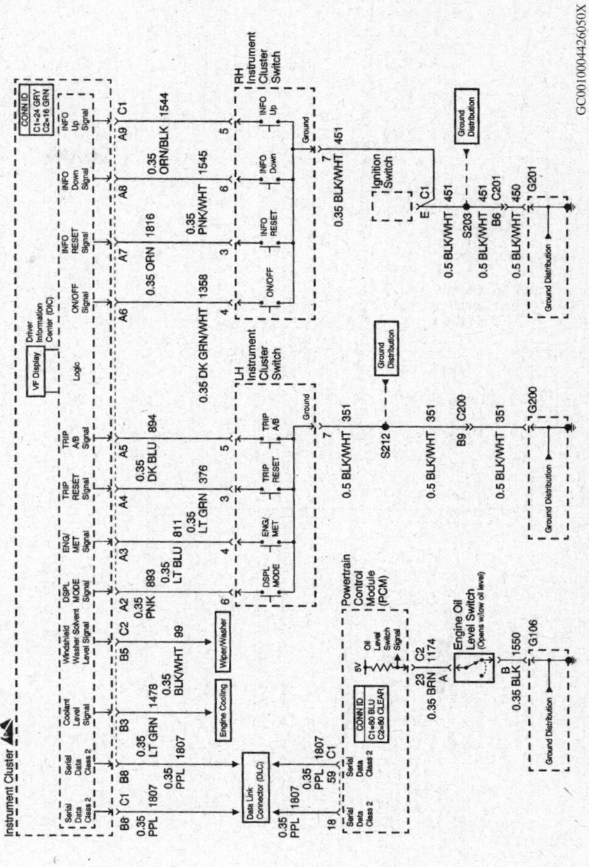

Fig. 43 Instrument cluster (Part 5 of 5). 2000 Seville

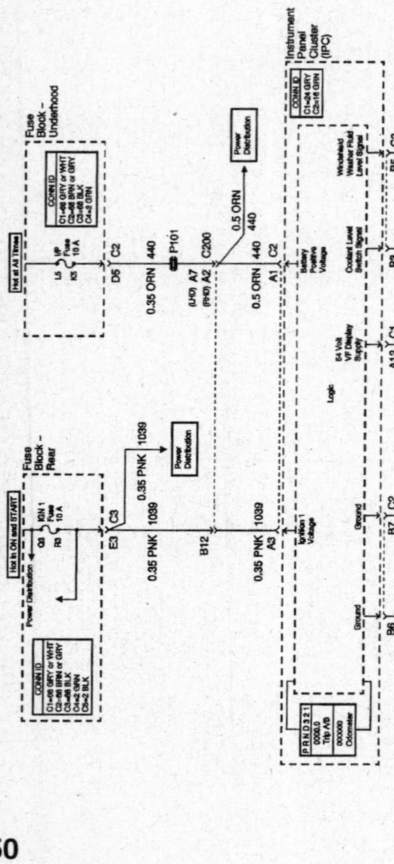

GC909010157301OX

Fig. 44 Instrument cluster (Part 1 of 5). 2001–04 Seville

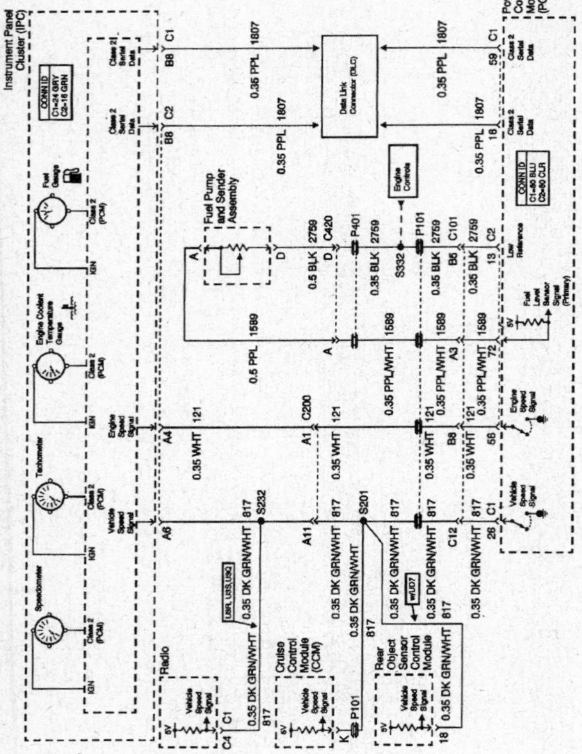

GC909010157302OX

Fig. 44 Instrument cluster (Part 2 of 5). 2001–04 Seville

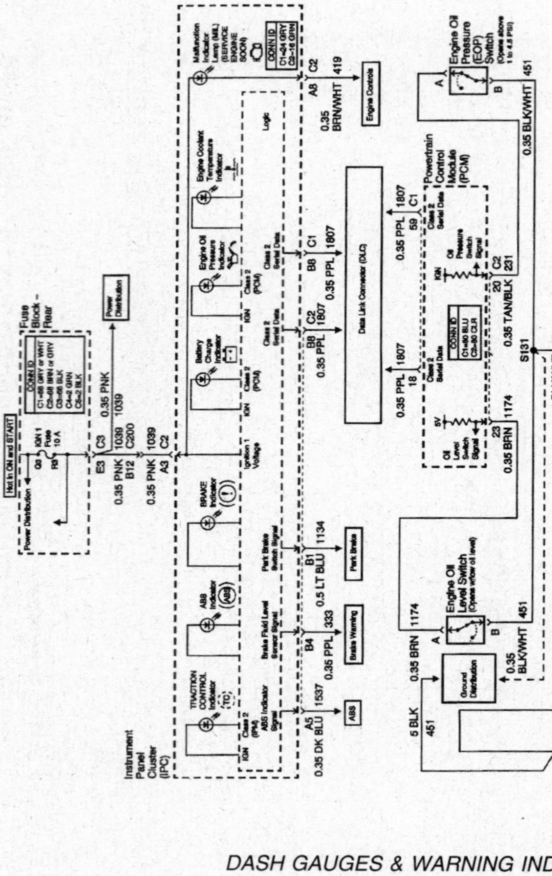

GC909010157303OX

Fig. 44 Instrument cluster (Part 3 of 5). 2001–04 Seville

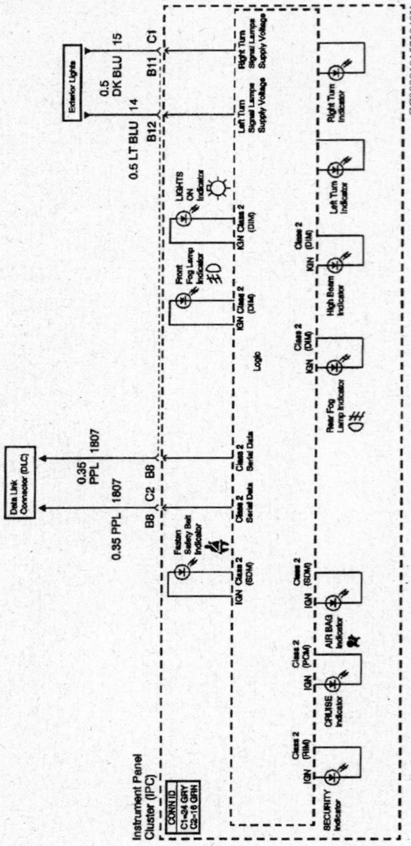

GC909010157304OX

Fig. 44 Instrument cluster (Part 4 of 5). 2001–04 Seville

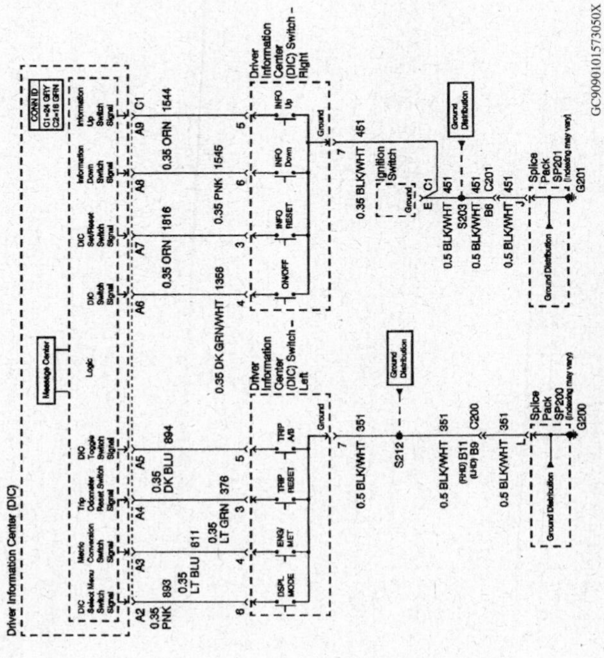

GC0990101573050X

Fig. 44 Instrument cluster (Part 5 of 5). 2001–04 Seville

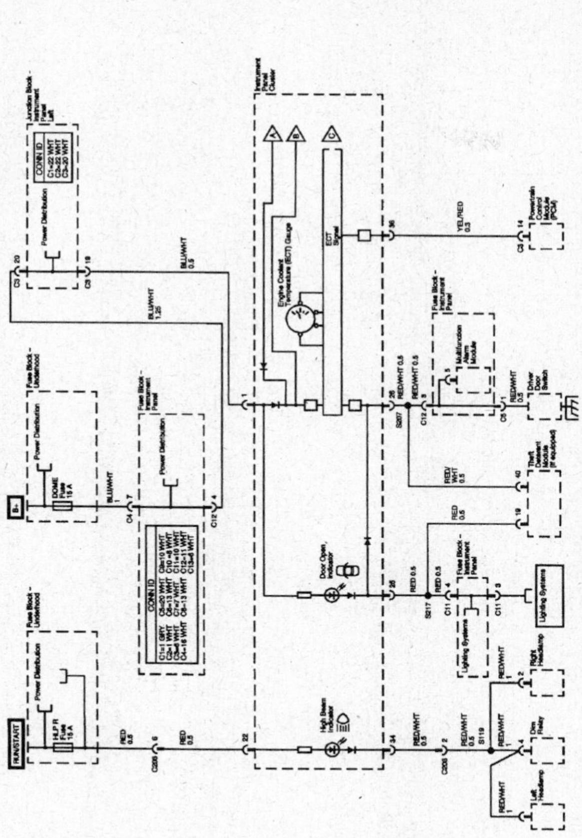

GC0990201606010X

Fig. 45 Instrument cluster (Part 1 of 6). Vibe

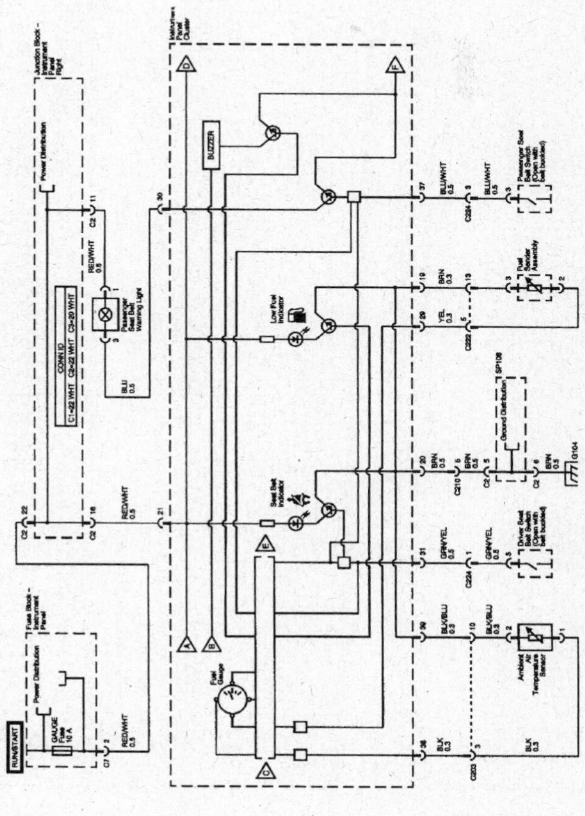

GC0990201606020X

Fig. 45 Instrument cluster (Part 2 of 6). Vibe

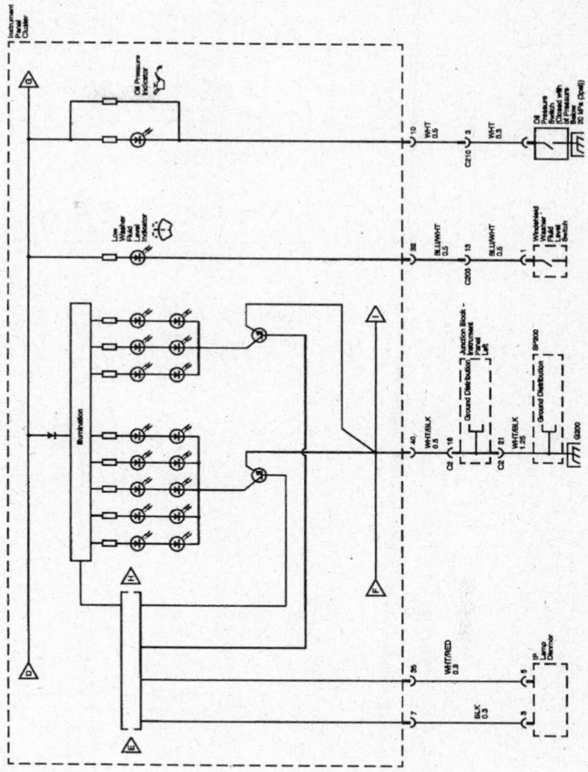

GC0990201606030X

Fig. 45 Instrument cluster (Part 3 of 6). Vibe

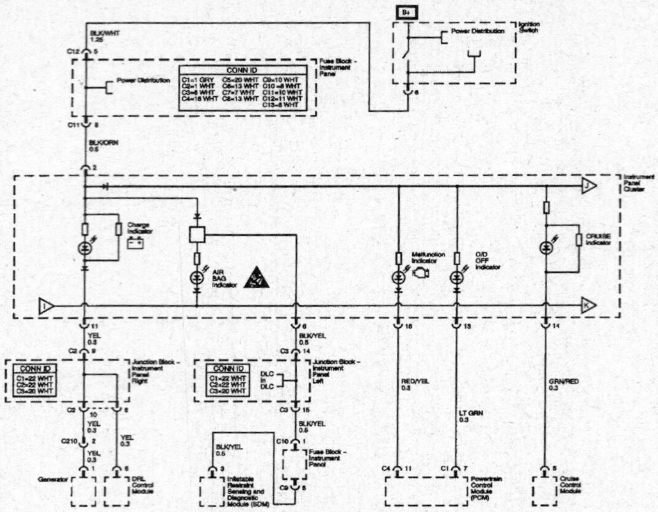

GC9090201606040X

Fig. 45 Instrument cluster (Part 4 of 6). Vibe

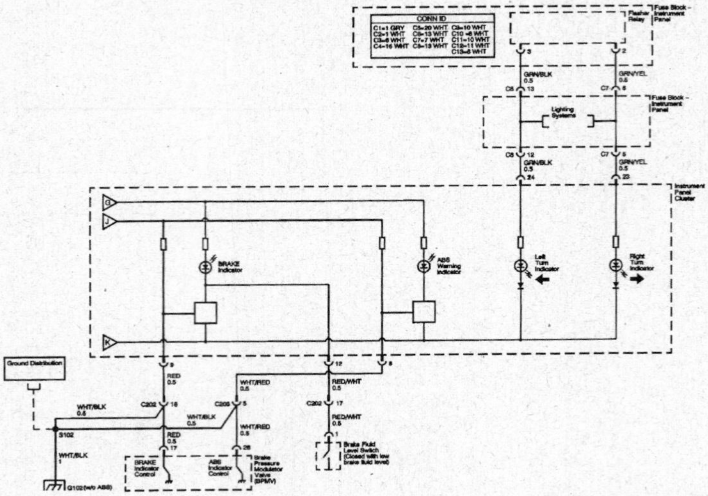

GC9090201606050X

Fig. 45 Instrument cluster (Part 5 of 6). Vibe

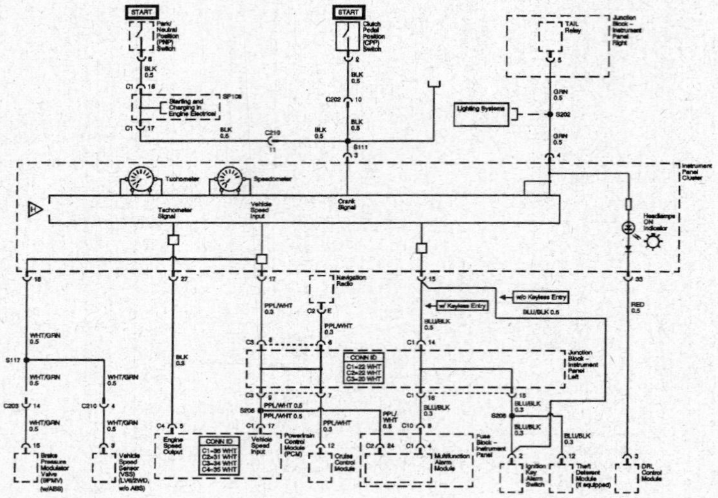

GC9090201606060X

Fig. 45 Instrument cluster (Part 6 of 6). Vibe

SPEED CONTROL SYSTEMS

TABLE OF CONTENTS

Application Chart

Model	Year	Type
BUICK		
Century	2000–04	1
LeSabre	2000–04	1
Park Avenue	2000–04	1
Regal	2000–04	1
CADILLAC		
Catera	2000–01	1
CTS	2003–04	1
DeVille	2000–04	1
Eldorado	2000–02	1
Seville	2000–04	1
CHEVROLET		
Camaro	2000–02	3 or 4①
Cavalier	2000–04	1
Corvette	2000–04	4
Impala	2000–04	1
Lumina	2000–01	1
Malibu	2000–04	1
Monte Carlo	2000–04	1
Prizm	2000–02	2
OLDSMOBILE		
Alero	2000–04	1
Aurora	2001–04	1
Intrigue	2000–02	1
PONTIAC		
Bonneville	2000–04	1
Firebird	2000–02	3 or 4①
Grand Am	2000–04	1
Grand Prix	2000–04	1
Sunfire	2000–04	1
Vibe	2003–04	2
SATURN		
All	2000–04	5

① — Type 3, less Electronic Traction Control (ETC); Type 4, w/ETC.

Type 1

NOTE: On Air Bag Equipped Models, Refer To "Air Bag System Precautions" Located In The Front Of This Manual For System Disarming & Arming Procedures.

NOTE: Refer To "Computer Relearn Procedures" Located In The Front Of This Manual When Battery Power To The Computer Has Been Interrupted.

NOTE: "Electrical Symbol & Wire Color Code Identification" Located In The Front Of This Manual May Be Used As An Aid When Using Wiring Circuits Found In This Section.

INDEX

DESCRIPTION

System

This system consists of a mode control assembly, Electronic Controller Module (ECM), Vehicle Speed Sensor (VSS) buffer amplifier, servo unit, and release switches and valves. The servo unit maintains vehicle speed (throttle position) by trapping vacuum in its diaphragm chamber at servo positions determined by the control module. The module monitors mode control switch position, signals from the VSS buffer amplifier, servo position and release switch operation, then operates vacuum valves within the servo unit to control servo operation and vehicle speed. The module also contains a speed limiting function which prevents system operation at speeds less than 25 mph.

The mode control assembly consists of a three-position slide-type switch and a Set/Coast switch button. To operate the system, the slide switch must be in the On position and vehicle speed must be more than 25 mph. The system is engaged at the desired speed by fully depressing, then releasing the Set/Coast button. Cruise speed can be increased from the set position by accelerating vehicle to desired speed, then pressing and releasing button. In order to decrease speed, the Set/Coast button is held in the fully-depressed position (disengaging system), then released when the desired speed is reached. The system can be disengaged at any time by depressing the brake or clutch pedal, or by moving the slide switch to off position.

If the system is disengaged by depressing the brake or clutch pedal, the last set speed will be retained in the module memory until the slide switch or ignition switch is moved to off position. Momentarily moving the slide switch to the resume/accel position will cause the vehicle to accelerate to the last set speed and maintain that speed. If the slide switch is held in the resume/accel position, the vehicle will continue to accelerate until the switch is released. When the switch is released, the speed that the vehicle accelerated to becomes the new set speed.

The slide switch also allows a tap up function to increase the cruise set speed in one mph increments. With the speed control engaged and operating, tapping-up is done by pressing the slide switch to the resume position, then quickly releasing it. This procedure can be repeated 10 times before the system must be reset to a new speed in the conventional manner.

System Components

SPEED SENSOR

On models with conventional instrument panels, a speedometer frame mounted optic head is used to pick up light reflected by a speedometer cable mounted blade. The reflected light is produced by a light emitting diode (LED). As the speedometer cable mounted blade enters the LED light beam, the light is reflected into the optic head. From there, the light enters a photocell in the optic head and produces a low power speed signal. This signal is sent to a buffer for amplification and conditioning, then to the controller.

On models with electronic speedometers or electronic instrumentation, a transmission mounted speed sensor is used. This sensor utilizes a permanent magnet (PM) to generate vehicle speed information to the controller. Some models use a buffer amplifier to modify the sensor output.

CRUISE CONTROL MODULE

The module will interpret the position of

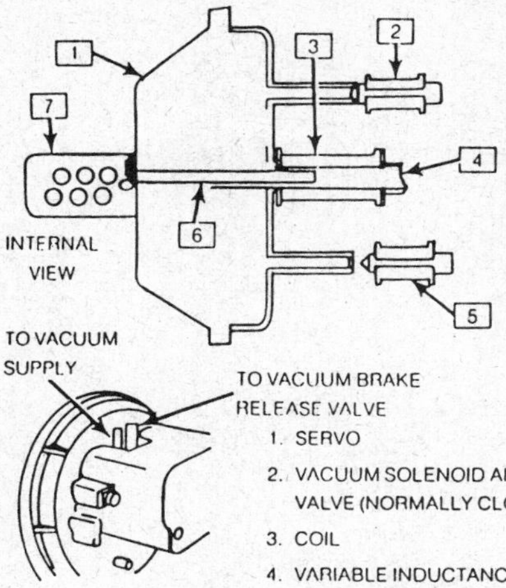

1. SERVO
2. VACUUM SOLENOID AND VALVE (NORMALLY CLOSED)
3. COIL
4. VARIABLE INDUCTANCE POSITION SENSOR
5. VENT SOLENOID AIR VALVE (NORMALLY OPEN)
6. STEEL CORE
7. SERVO BLADE

GC1109100151000X

Fig. 1 Servo unit

the servo, the position of the control switches and the output of the speed sensor. In response to these inputs, the module electrically signals the opening or closing of the vent and vacuum solenoid valves in the servo.

The module is mounted on the dash support bracket at the righthand side of the steering column, but is integral with the ECM on some models with certain engines.

VACUUM RELEASE VALVE

The vacuum release valve provides an additional vent to atmosphere for the servo unit when the brake pedal is held in the depressed position. The venting is spring actuated and occurs within the free travel of the brake pedal arm.

COMBINATION VACUUM RELEASE VALVE/ CONVERTER CLUTCH SWITCH

This combination valve and switch is used on vehicles equipped with a lock-up torque converter. The vacuum release valve portion operates identically to the release valve. At the same time, the converter clutch switch contacts open and the locking clutch mechanism in the transmission is disengaged.

COMBINATION CRUISE/ STOP LIGHT SWITCH

A separately mounted vacuum release valve is used with this combination switch. When the brake pedal is depressed, the switch resets the cruise function to a noncruise condition and illuminates the brake lights. The switch uses two sets of electrical contacts to operate the stop lights and the cruise release function.

CLUTCH SWITCH

When the clutch switch is depressed, the

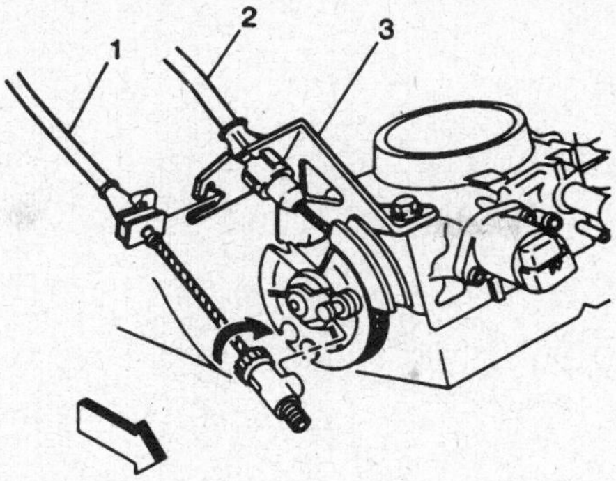

(1) Throttle Body Bracket
(2) Accelerator Cable
(3) Cruise Control Cable

GC1109800537000X

Fig. 2 Cruise control cable adjustment. 2.4L engine

cruise function is disconnected and will remain so after the pedal is released.

SERVO UNIT

The servo unit operates the throttle in response to signals from the electronic controller, **Fig. 1.**

During a steady speed cruise condition, both vacuum and vent valves are closed or sealed. The servo holds a constant vacuum on the diaphragm and places no flow requirements on the vacuum source.

During vehicle deceleration, the vacuum solenoid is energized by the controller to open the vacuum valve to the vacuum source. Throttle angle is then increased by the increased vacuum level in the servo and the vent remains closed.

During vehicle acceleration, the vent solenoid is de-energized by the controller to open the vent valve to atmosphere. This reduces vacuum in the servo and allows throttle return spring to decrease throttle angle while the vacuum valve remains closed.

PRECAUTIONS

Air Bag Systems

Refer to "Air Bag System Precautions" in the front of this manual for system disarming and arming procedures.

Anti-Lock Brake Systems

The hydraulic accumulator, when fully charged contains brake fluid at high pressure. Before disconnecting any lines, hoses or fittings, ensure accumulator is full depressurized. Failure to do so may result in personal injury.

To depressurize the hydraulic accumulator, turn the ignition to the Off position or disconnect battery ground, pump brake pedal a minimum of 40 times at approximately 50 lbs., of force. A noticeable change in pedal feel will occur when accumulator is fully discharged.

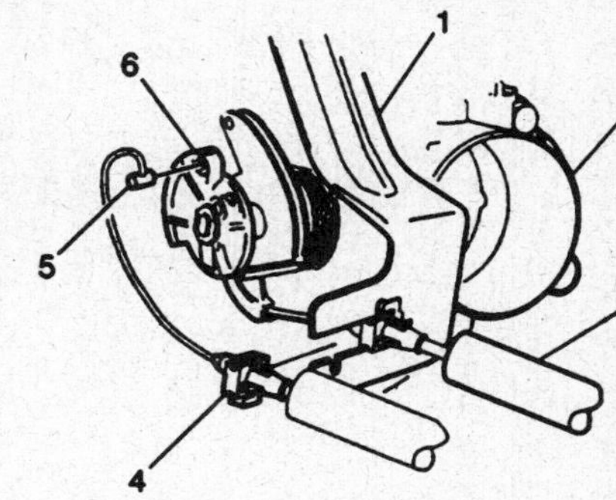

(1) Throttle Body Bracket
(2) Throttle Body
(3) Accelerator Cable
(4) Cruise Control Cable
(5) Cruise Control Cable Cross Slug
(6) Throttle Body Cam

GC1109800538000X

Fig. 3 Cruise control cable adjustment. 3.1L engine

Battery Ground Cable

Prior to service, disconnect battery ground cable and isolate as required.

ADJUSTMENTS

Cable

2.4L ENGINE

1. Ensure throttle plate is closed.
2. Adjust thumb screw to remove any slack in cruise control cable, **Fig. 2.**

3.0L ENGINE

1. Disconnect cruise control cable from clip on heater hose and open adjusting lever on cable.
2. Adjust cable halves until cable has .079–.157 inch of vertical endplay as measured near throttle linkage bracket.
3. Close adjusting lever on cable and connect cruise control cable to clip on heater hose.

3.1L ENGINE

1. Disconnect cruise control cable adjuster lock.
2. With throttle plate closed, remove any slack from cable by sliding adjuster forward, away from module, **Fig. 3.**
3. Connect cruise control cable adjuster lock.

3.5L ENGINE

1. Spread adjuster lock tabs and pull adjuster lock out to disengage adjuster lock.
2. Slide cable adjuster forward, away from module. Remove as much slack as possible without moving throttle lever.
3. Push adjuster lock inward to engage cable adjuster lock.

3800 & 4.0L ENGINES

1. Remove fuel injector sight shield, as

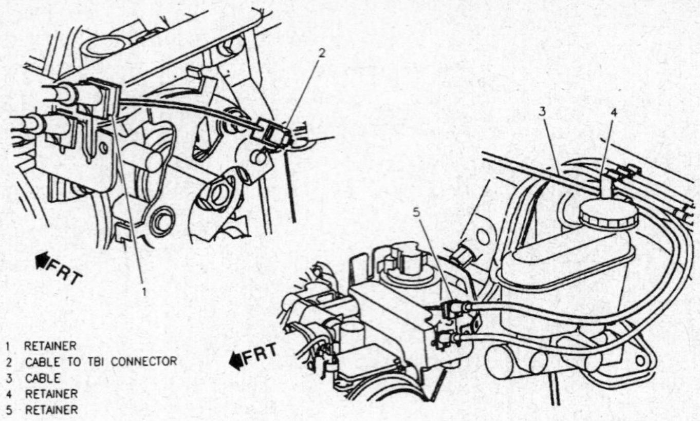

Fig. 4 Cruise control cable adjustment. 3800 & 4.0L engines except Grand Prix, Intrigue & Regal

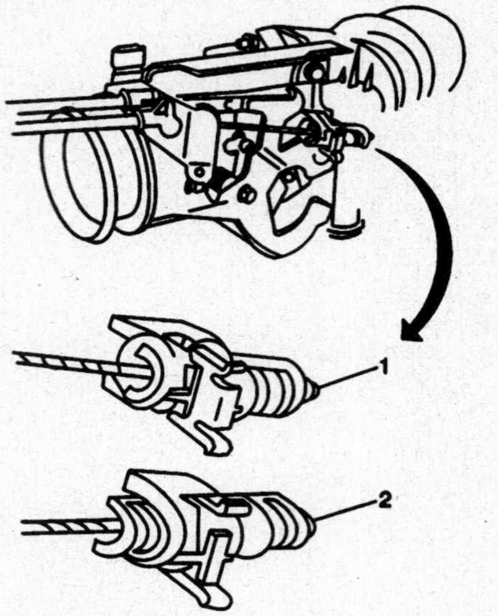

Fig. 5 Cruise control cable adjustment. Grand Prix, Intrigue & Regal w/3800 engine

required, to access cruise control cable lock.

2. Disconnect cruise control cable adjuster lock.
3. **On all models except Grand Prix, Intrigue and Regal,** ensure throttle plate is closed and take up slack by pulling cable, **Fig. 4.**
4. **On Grand Prix, Intrigue and Regal models,** adjuster spring will take up slack in cable, **Fig. 5.** Remove as much cable slack as possible without moving throttle lever.
5. **On all models,** connect cruise control cable adjuster lock.

SYSTEM DIAGNOSIS & TESTING

Accessing Diagnostic Trouble Codes

Connect suitably programmed scan tool to the Data Link Connector (DLC), and follow manufacturer's instructions.

Diagnostic Trouble Code Interpretation

Refer to **Fig. 6,** for Diagnostic Trouble Code (DTC) interpretation.

Wiring Diagrams

Refer to **Figs. 7 through 36,** for system wiring diagrams.

Symptoms

Refer to **Figs. 37 through 56,** for symptoms.

Diagnostic Tests

EXCEPT CTS

Refer to **Figs. 57 through 76,** for diagnostic tests.

CTS

Refer to **Figs. 77 through 90,** for diagnostic tests.

DIAGNOSTIC SYSTEM CHECK

Refer to **Figs. 91 through 98,** for diagnostic tests.

Clearing Diagnostic Trouble Codes

Connect a suitably programmed scan tool to Data Link Connector (DLC), and follow manufacturer's instructions.

COMPONENT DIAGNOSIS & TESTING

Electric Brake Release Switch

1. Turn ignition switch to On position.
2. Connect test light to ground.
3. Probe brown wire at brake switch connector. Lamp should illuminate.
4. Inspect switch adjustment, with probe still at brown wire, depressing brake pedal ⅛–½ inch. Light should go out.
5. If lamp did not illuminate, probe wire in adjacent connector cavity. If lamp illuminates, adjust or replace switch, as required. If light does not illuminate, inspect wiring to switch.

Code	Interpretation
EXCEPT CTS	
55	Cruise Control Module Fault
P0571	Cruise Control Brake Switch Circuit
P0574	PCM Detects Speed More Than 110 mph
P1554	Cruise Control Feedback Circuit
	PCM Detects Cruise Engaged While Inhibiting Cruise Control Operation
P1560	Transaxle Range Switch Indicates Neutral Position w/Cruise Control Engaged
P1564	PCM Detects Extremely Rapid Acceleration
P1566	Engine Speed More Than 6300 RPM w/Cruise Control Engaged
P1567	Active Brake Control System Applied Brakes w/Cruise Control Engaged
P1570	Traction Control Is Active
P1574	Sudden Decrease In Non-Drive Wheel Speed
P1575	PCM Detects Voltage On Extended Travel Brake Switch Circuit
P1585	PCM Detects Improper Voltage Level
P1662	Cruise Lamp Control Circuit
CTS	
P0560	PCM Detects Voltage Out Of Range
P0562	PCM Detects Low Voltage
P0563	PCM Detects High Voltage
P0615	Improper Voltage Level On Output Circuit
P0616	Improper Voltage Level On Output Circuit
P0617	Improper Voltage Level On Output Circuit
P0625	PCM Detects Low PWM Signal
P0704	Insufficient Time Between Gear Changes
P2500	PCM Detects Low Voltage Signal
P2501	PCM Detects High Voltage Signal
B1327	Voltage Falls Below 9 Volts
B1228	Voltage Rises Above 16.5 Volts
B1513	Voltage Falls Below 10.5 Volts For 30 Seconds
B1514	Voltage Falls Below 16.2 Volts For 30 Seconds

Fig. 6 DTC interpretation

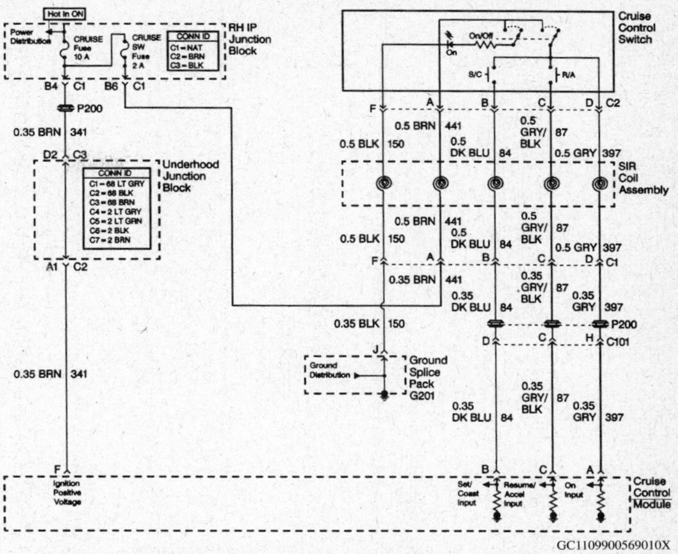

Fig. 7 Wiring diagram (Part 1 of 2). 2000 Alero & Grand Am

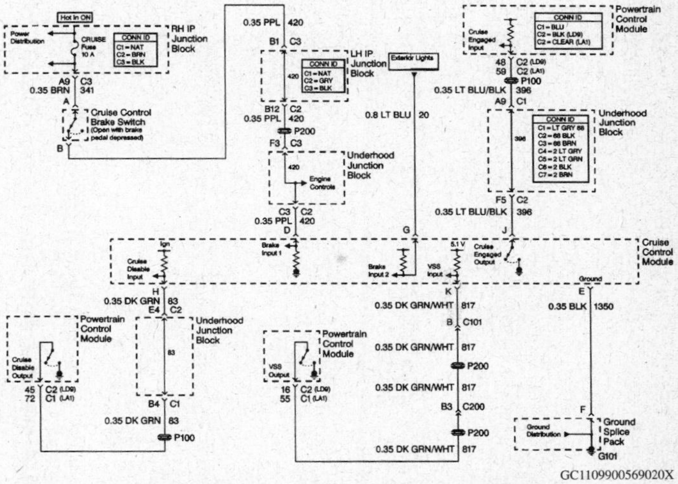

Fig. 7 Wiring diagram (Part 2 of 2). 2000 Alero & Grand Am

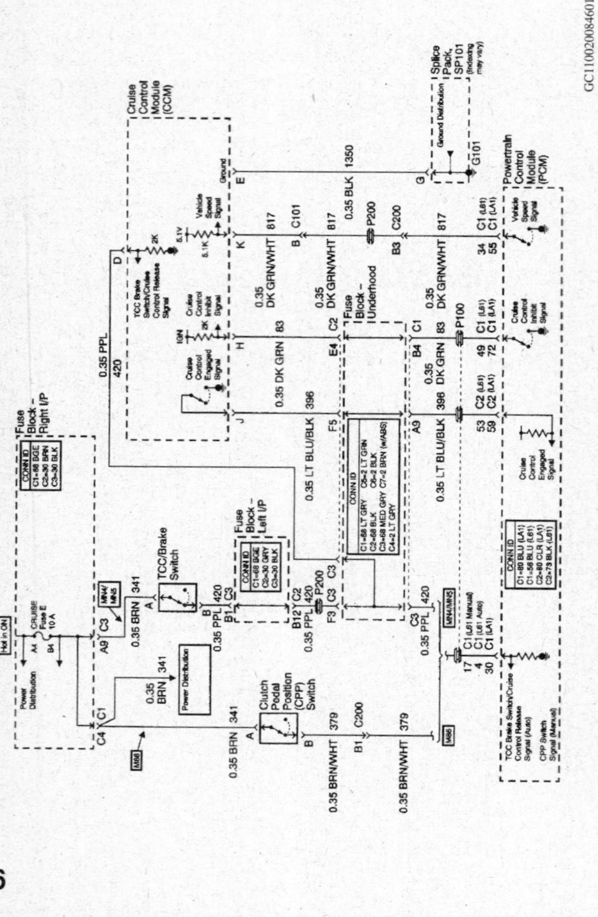

GC1100200846010X

Fig. 8 Wiring diagram (Part 1 of 3). 2001–04 Alero & Grand Am

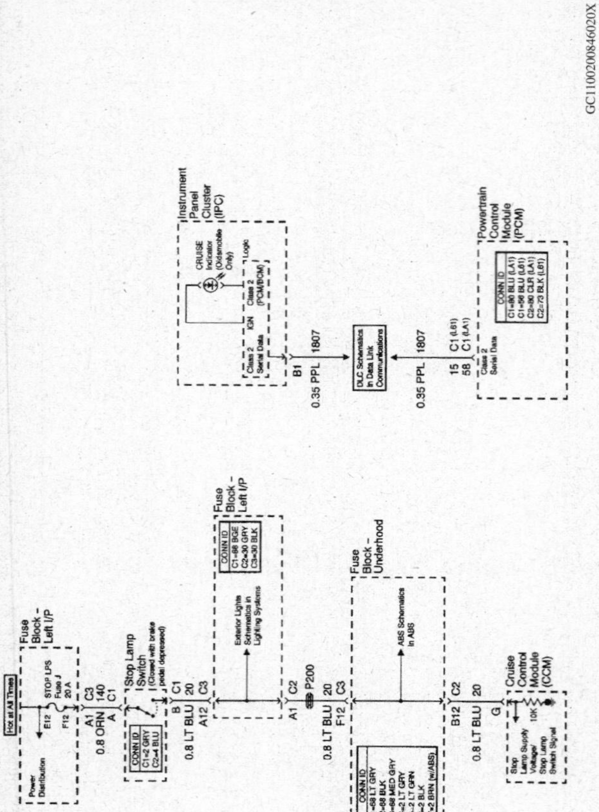

GC1100200846020X

Fig. 8 Wiring diagram (Part 2 of 3). 2001–04 Alero & Grand Am

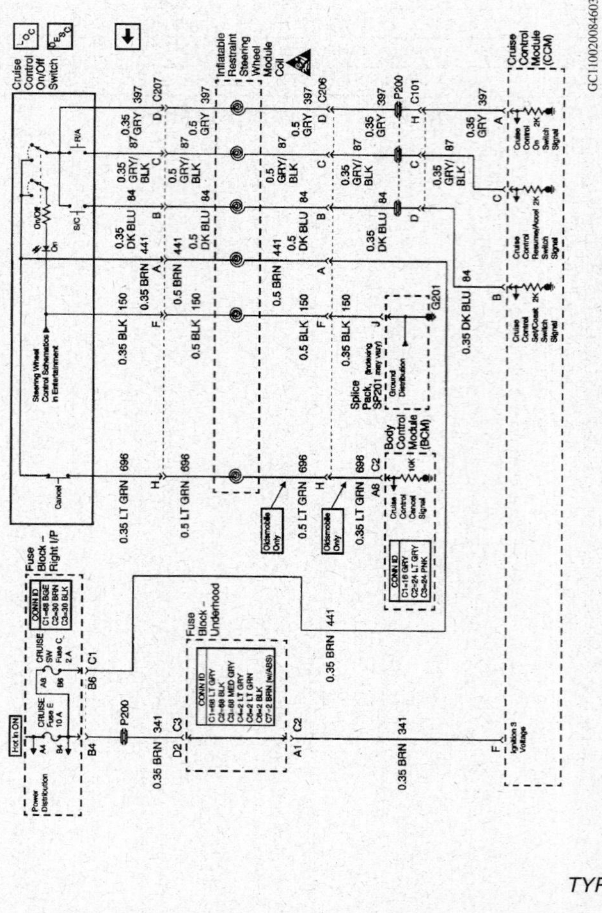

GC1100200846030X

Fig. 8 Wiring diagram (Part 3 of 3). 2001–04 Alero & Grand Am

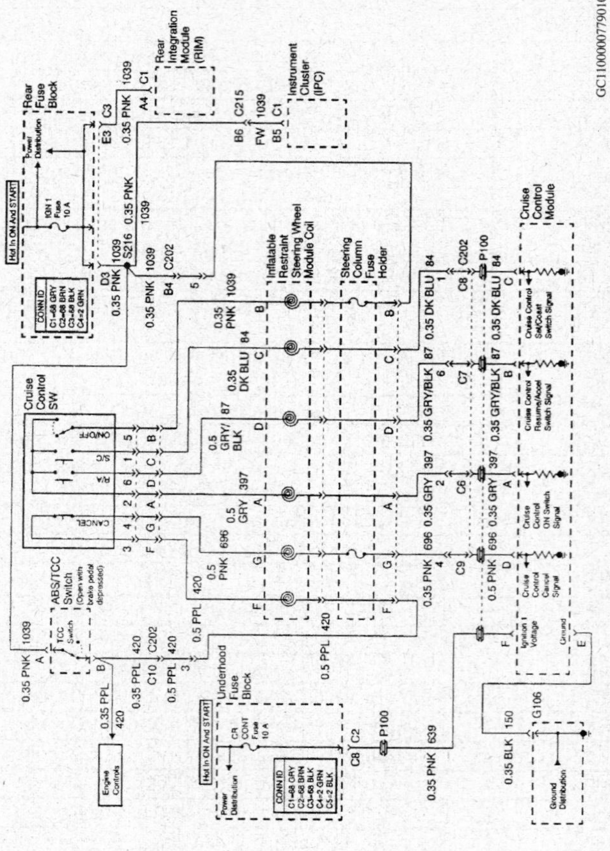

GC1100000779010X

Fig. 9 Wiring diagram (Part 1 of 2). 2001 Aurora

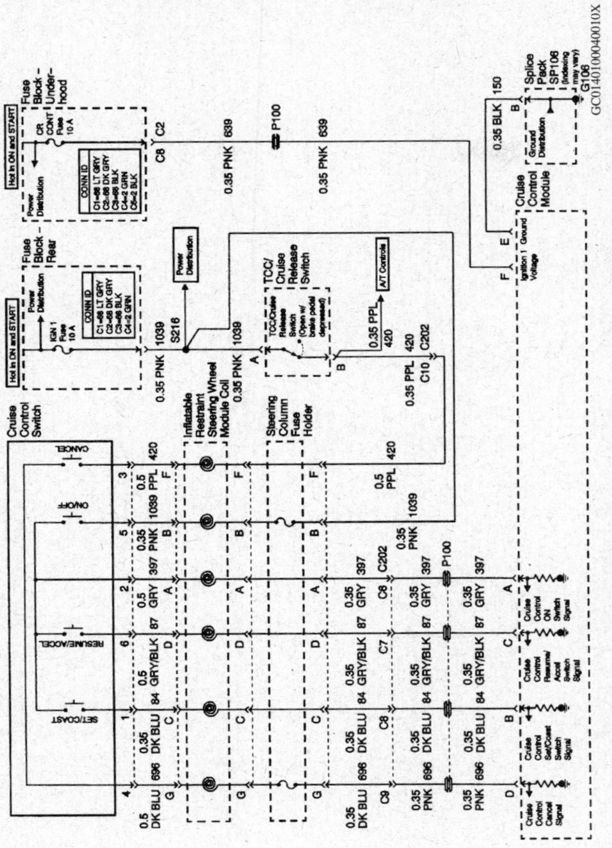

Fig. 10 Wiring diagram (Part 1 of 2). 2002–04 Aurora

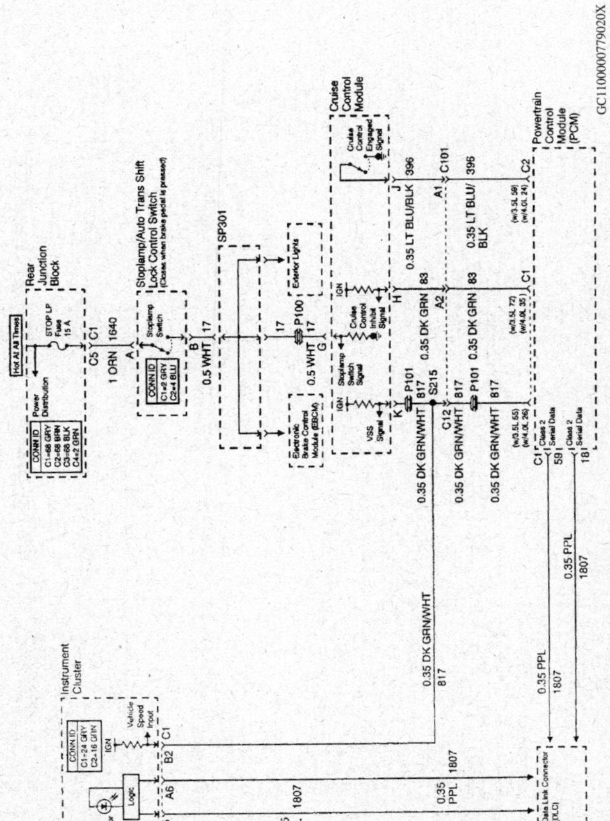

Fig. 9 Wiring diagram (Part 2 of 2). 2001 Aurora

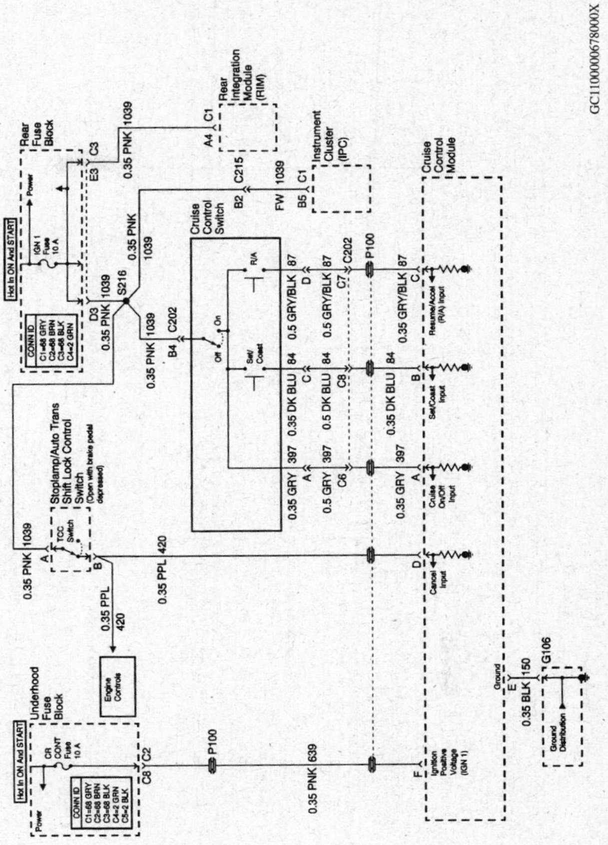

Fig. 11 Wiring diagram (Part 1 of 2). Bonneville

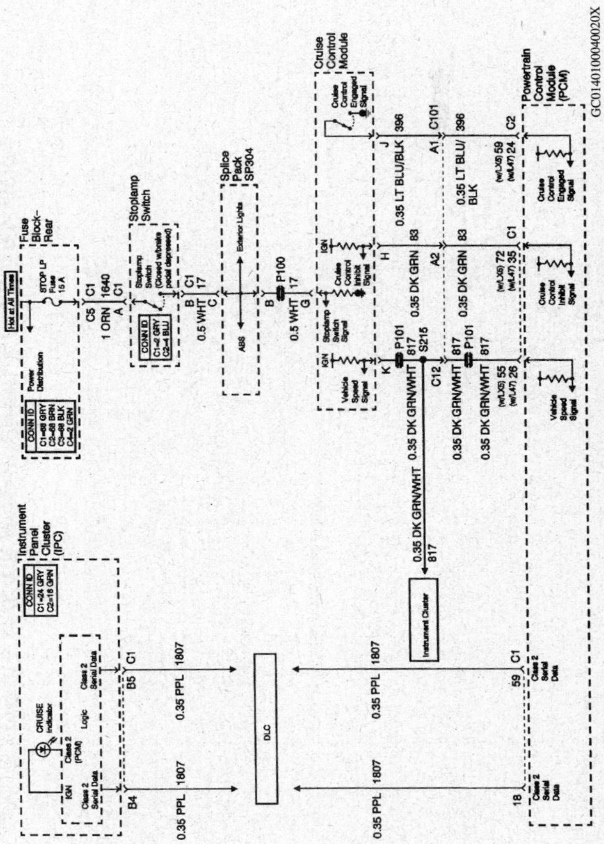

Fig. 10 Wiring diagram (Part 2 of 2). 2002–04 Aurora

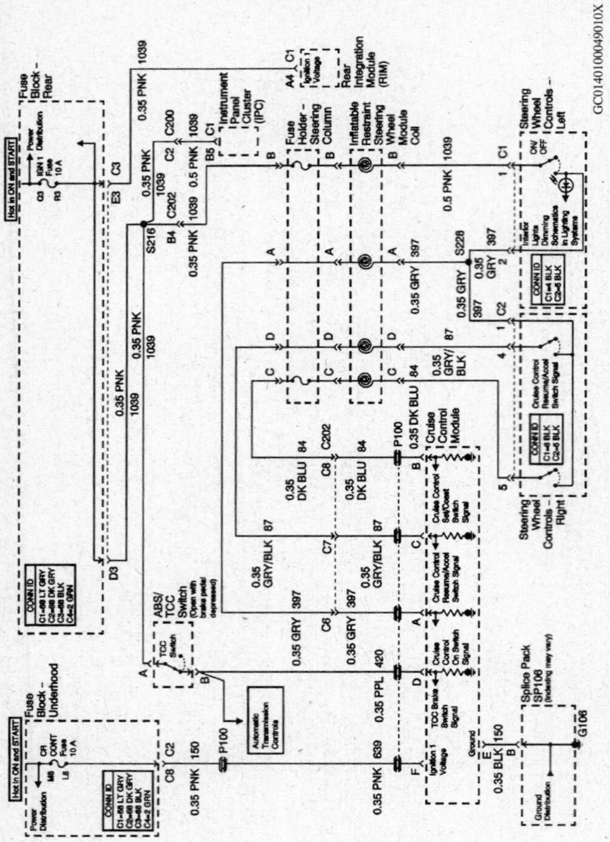

Fig. 12 Wiring diagram (Part 1 of 2). LeSabre

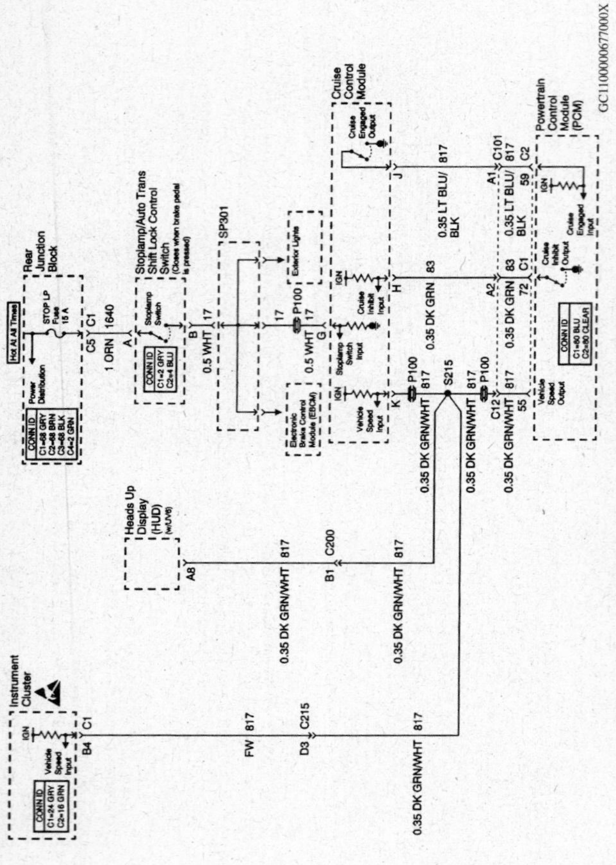

Fig. 11 Wiring diagram (Part 2 of 2). Bonneville

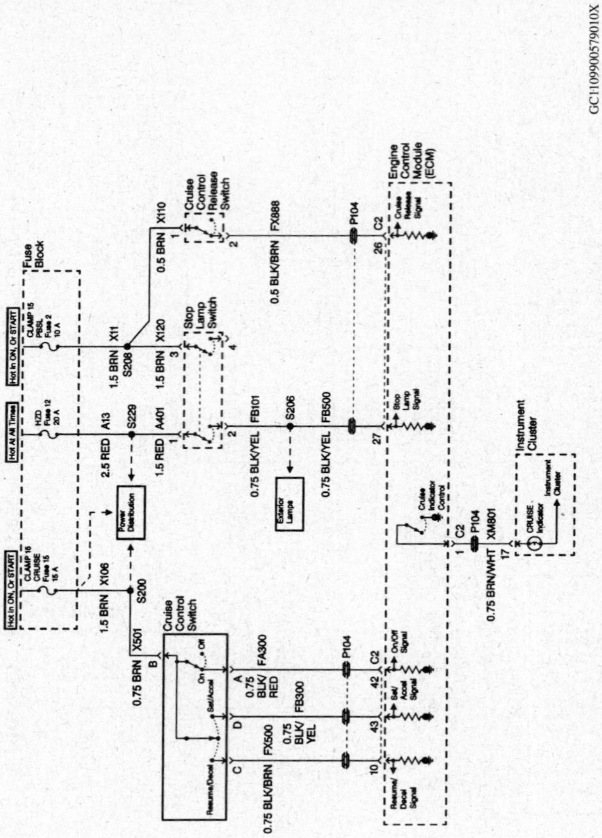

Fig. 13 Wiring diagram (Part 1 of 2). 2000 Catera

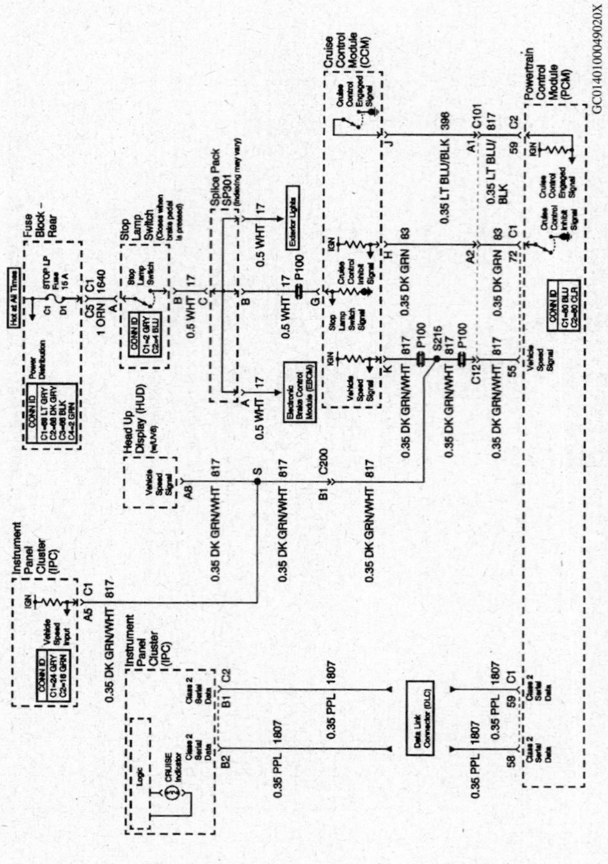

Fig. 12 Wiring diagram (Part 2 of 2). LeSabre

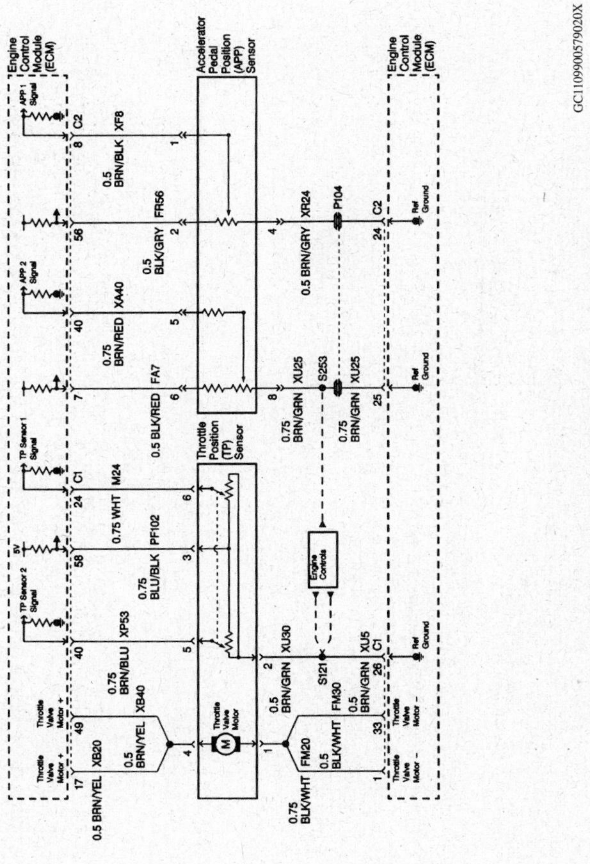

GC1109900579020X

Fig. 13 Wiring diagram (Part 2 of 2). 2000 Catera

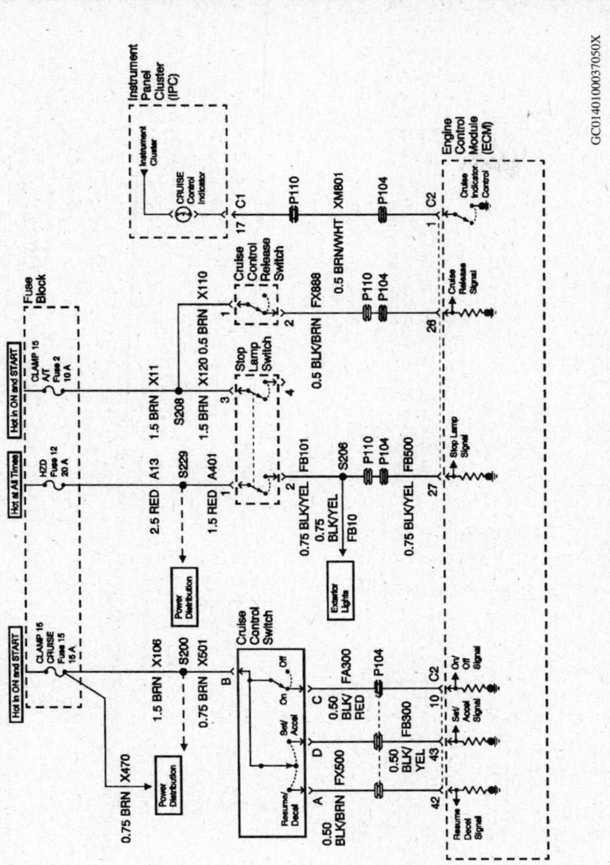

GC0140100037050X

Fig. 14 Wiring diagram. 2001 Catera

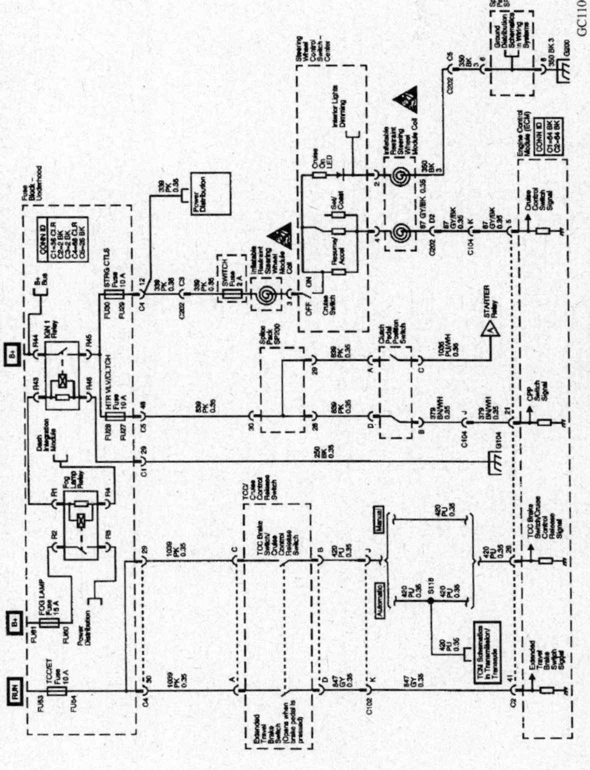

GC1100200848000X

Fig. 15 Wiring diagram. CTS

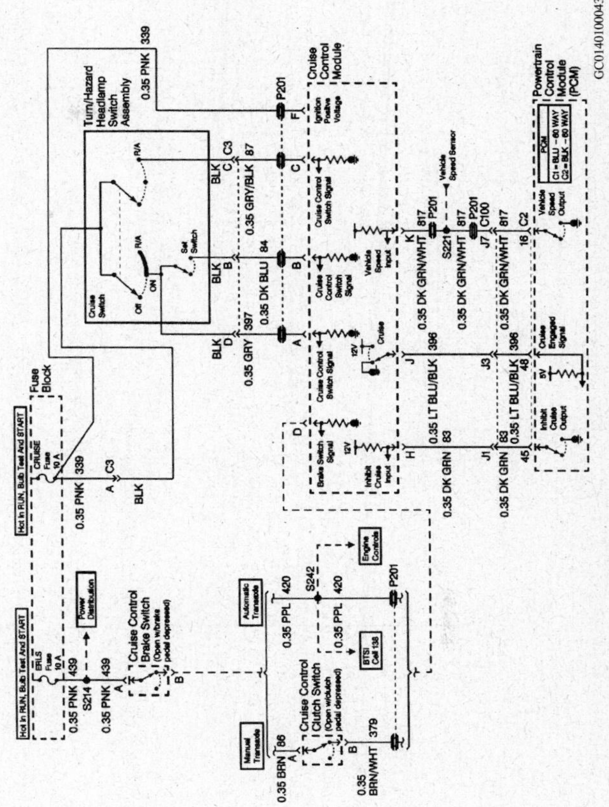

GC0140100043010X

Fig. 16 Wiring diagram (Part 1 of 2). 2000 Cavalier & Sunfire

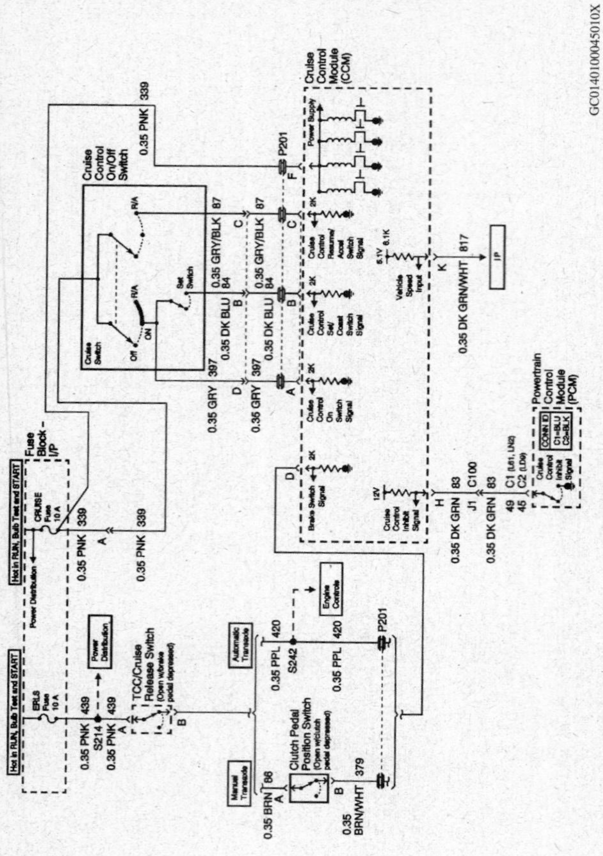

GC01401000045010X

Fig. 17 Wiring diagram (Part 1 of 2). 2001–04 Cavalier & Sunfire

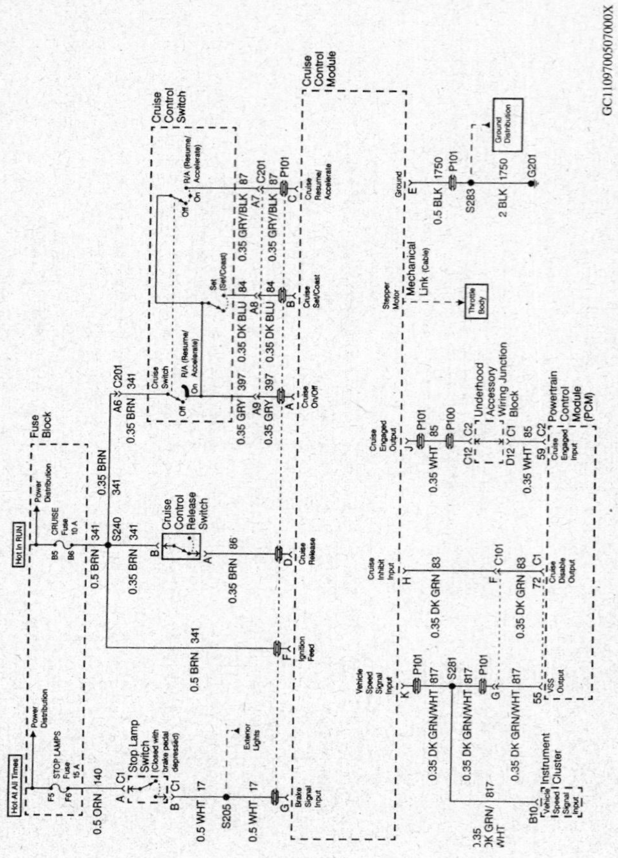

GC11097005007000X

Fig. 18 Wiring diagram. Century & Regal

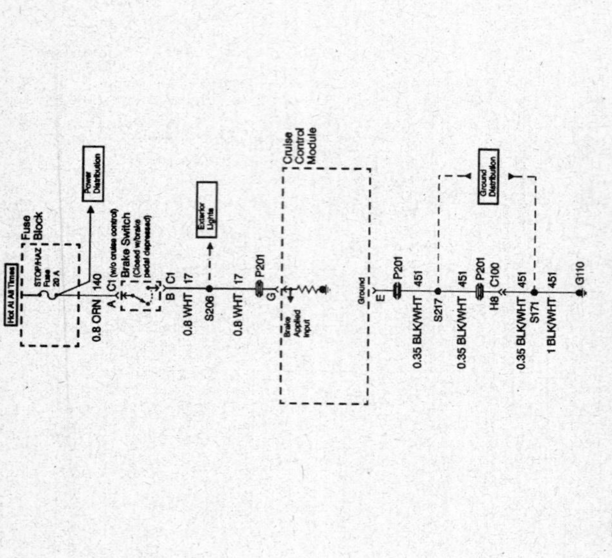

GC01401000043020X

Fig. 16 Wiring diagram (Part 2 of 2). 2000 Cavalier & Sunfire

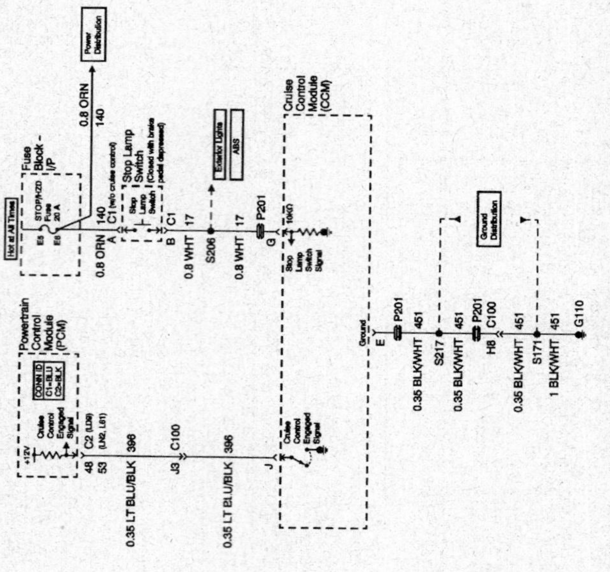

GC01401000045020X

Fig. 17 Wiring diagram (Part 2 of 2). 2001–04 Cavalier & Sunfire

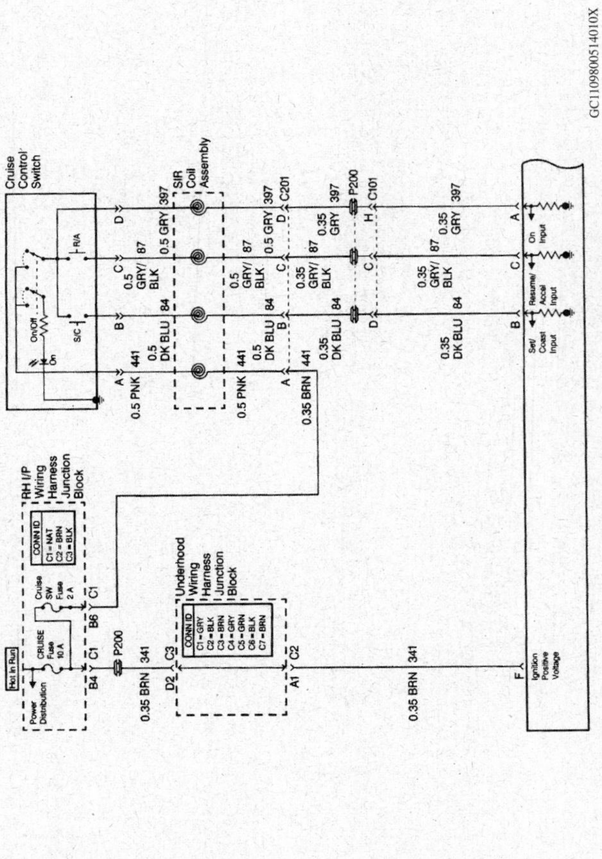

Fig. 19 Wiring diagram (Part 1 of 2). 2000 Malibu

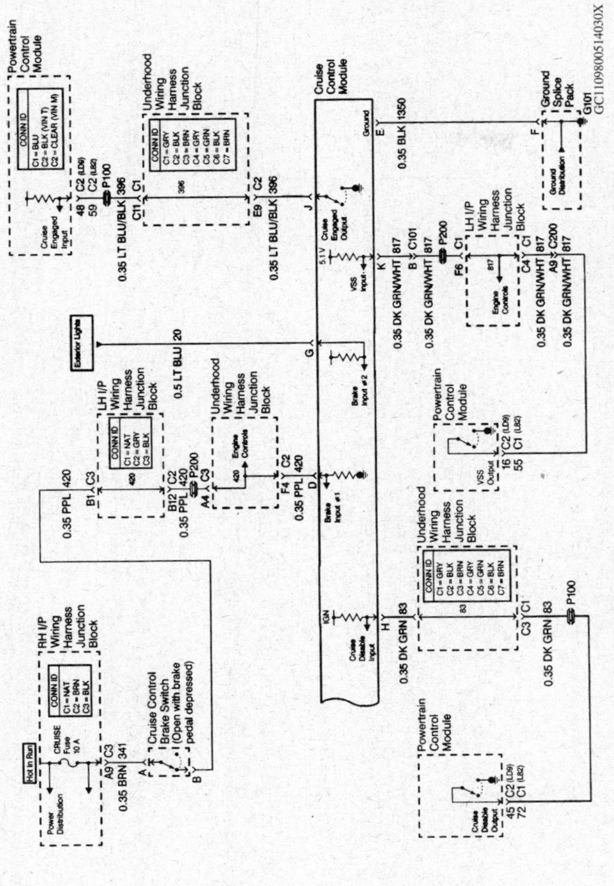

Fig. 19 Wiring diagram (Part 2 of 2). 2000 Malibu

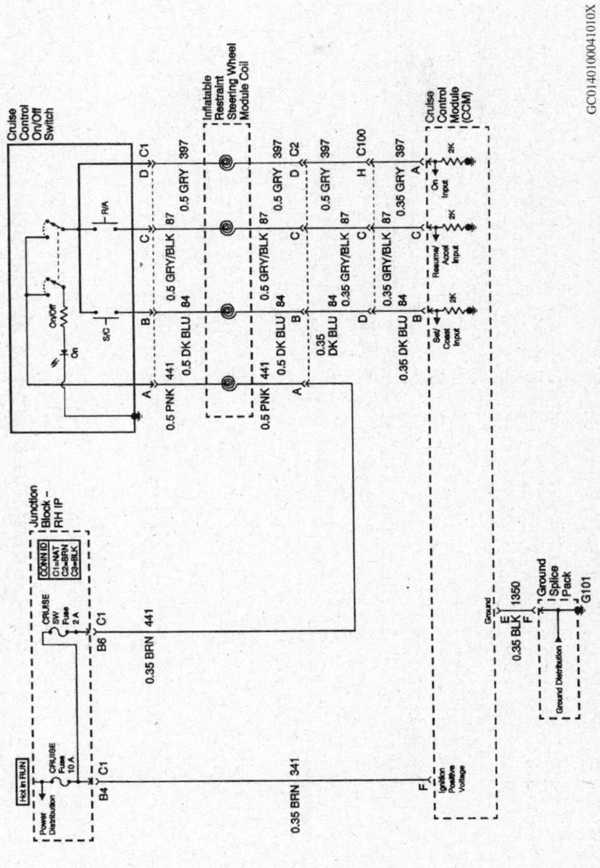

Fig. 20 Wiring diagram (Part 1 of 2). 2001 Malibu

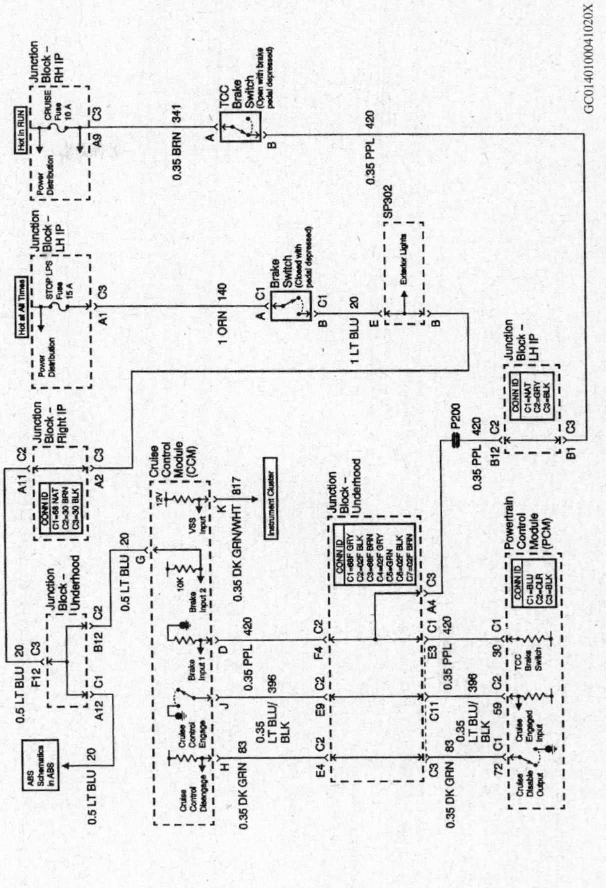

Fig. 20 Wiring diagram (Part 2 of 2). 2001 Malibu

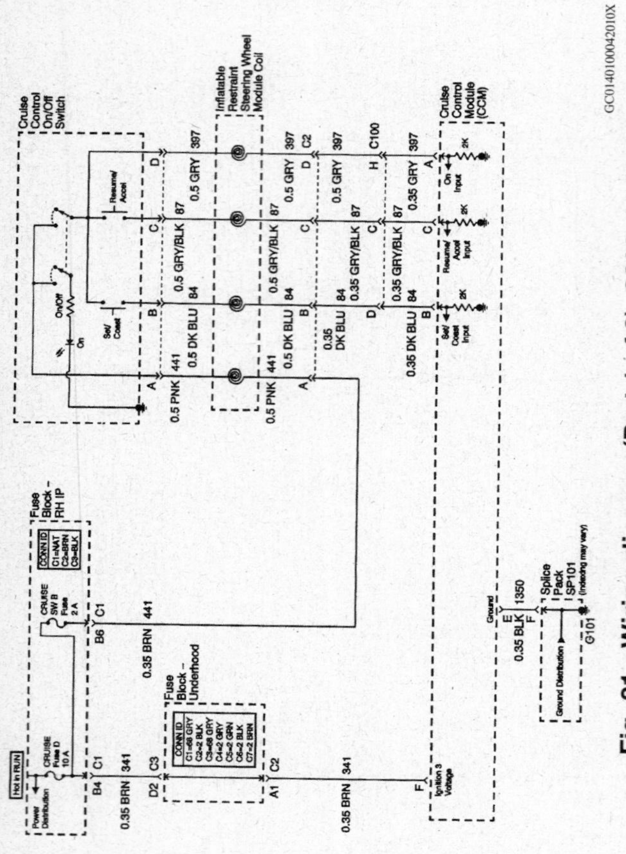

Fig. 21 Wiring diagram (Part 1 of 3). 2002–04 Malibu

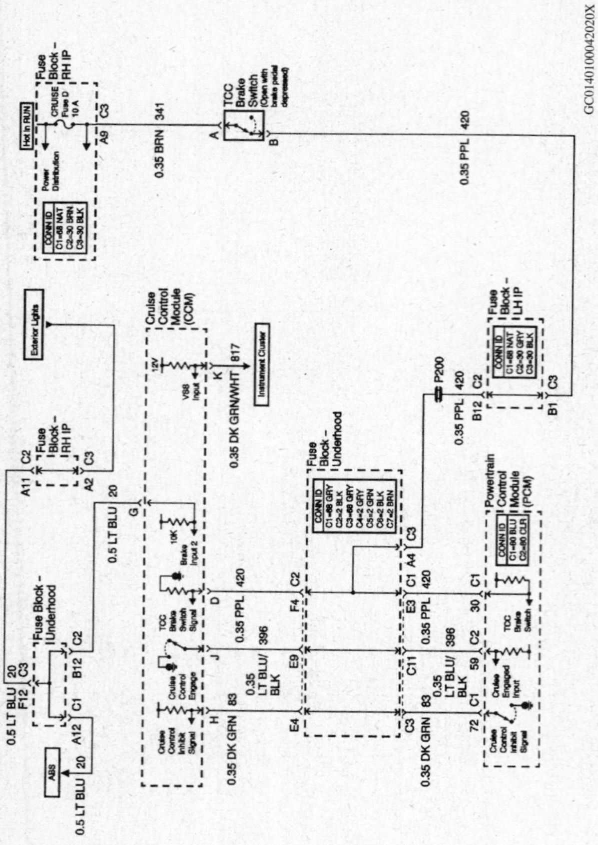

Fig. 21 Wiring diagram (Part 2 of 3). 2002–04 Malibu

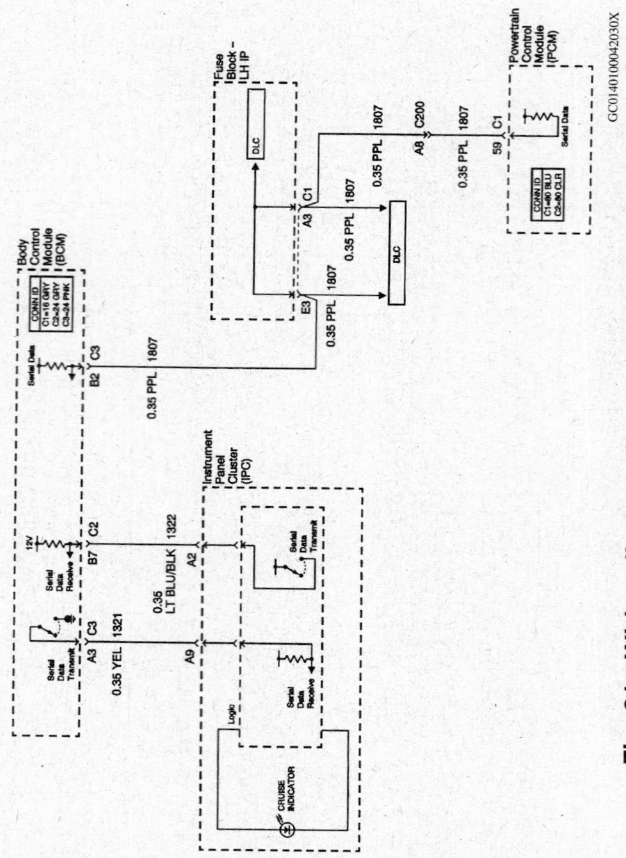

Fig. 21 Wiring diagram (Part 3 of 3). 2002–04 Malibu

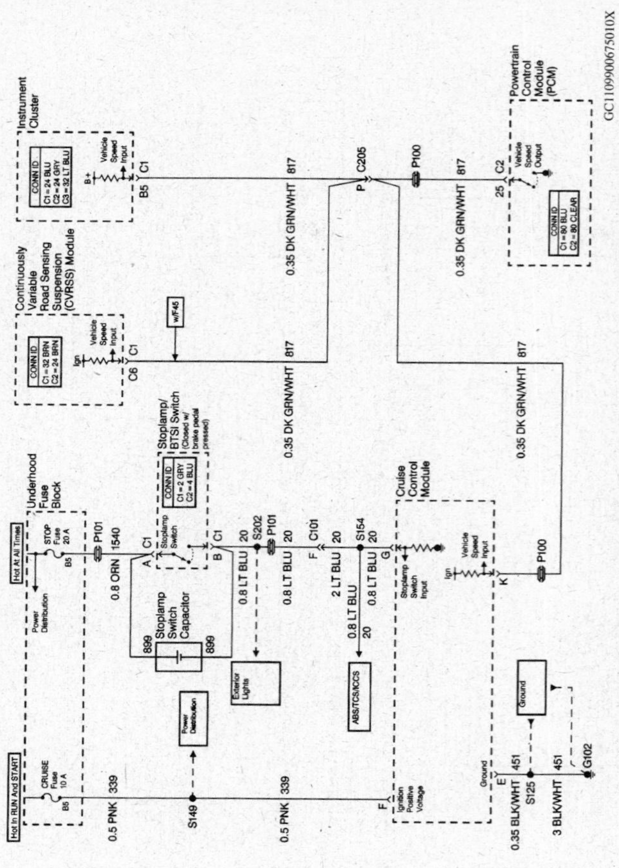

Fig. 22 Wiring diagram (Part 1 of 2). 2000 Eldorado

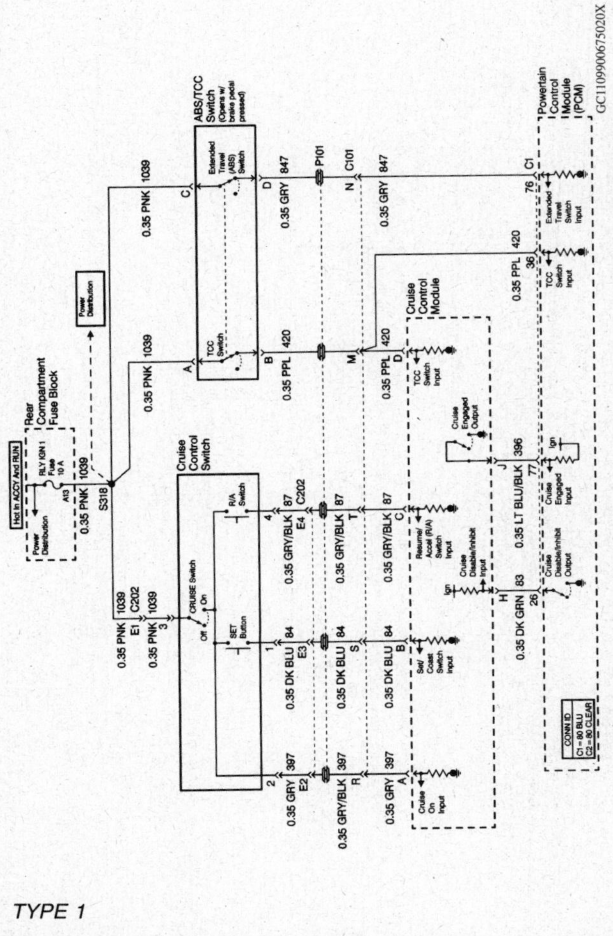

Fig. 22 Wiring diagram (Part 2 of 2). 2000 Eldorado

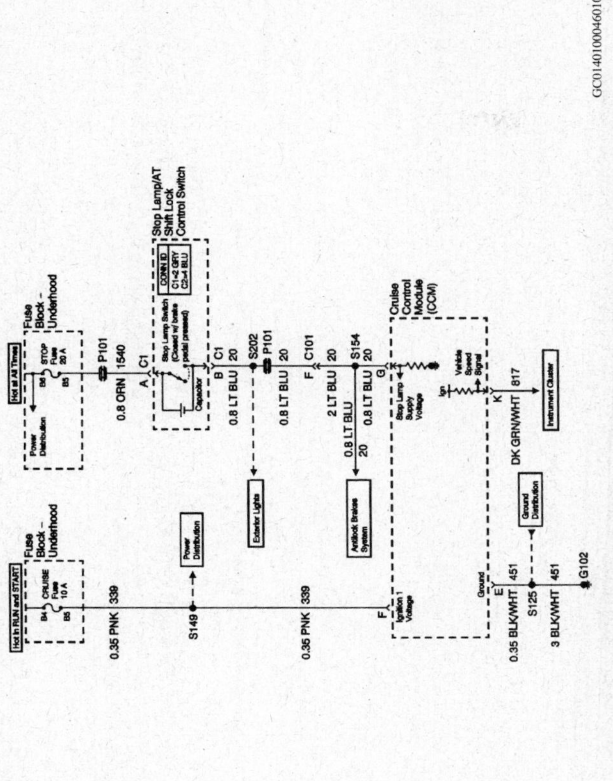

Fig. 23 Wiring diagram (Part 1 of 2). 2001–02 Eldorado

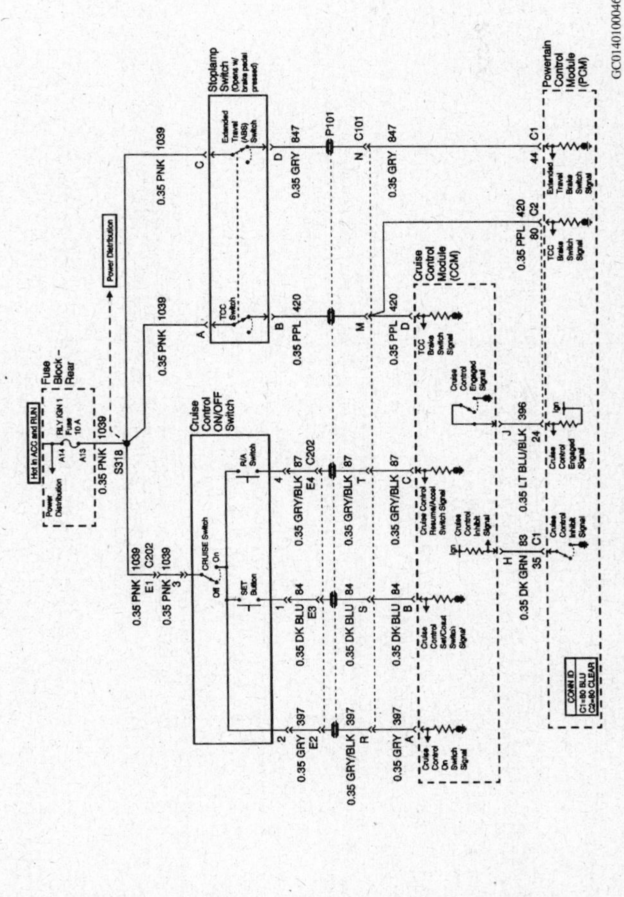

Fig. 23 Wiring diagram (Part 2 of 2). 2001–02 Eldorado

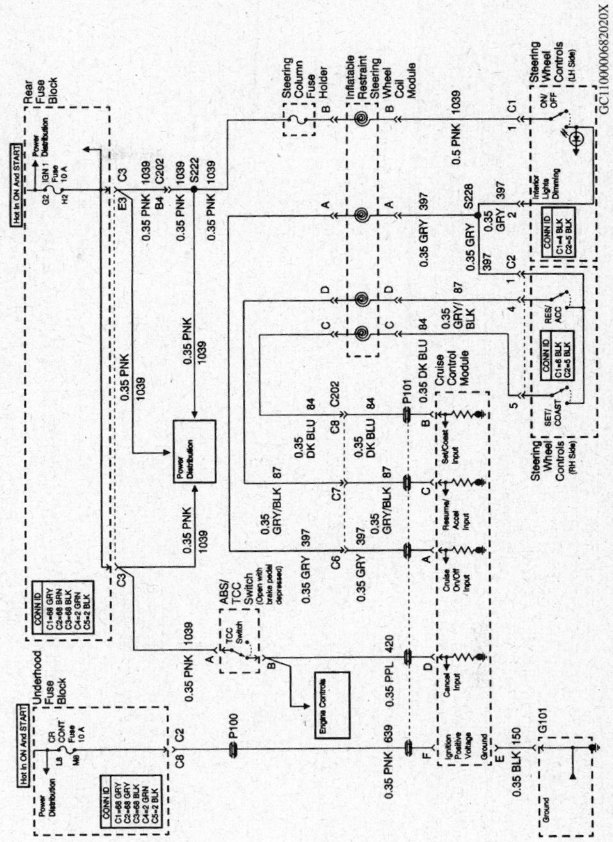

Fig. 24 Wiring diagram (Part 1 of 2). DeVille

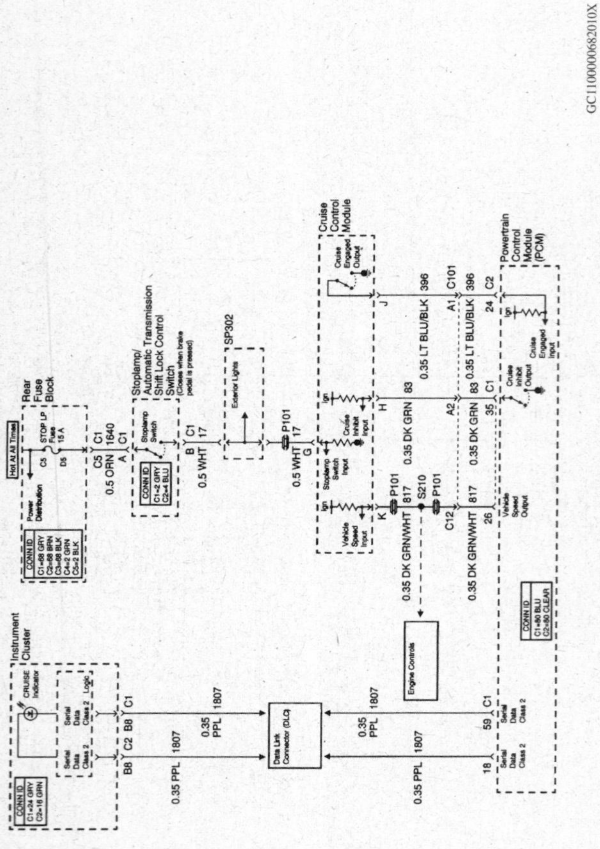

Fig. 24 Wiring diagram (Part 2 of 2). DeVille

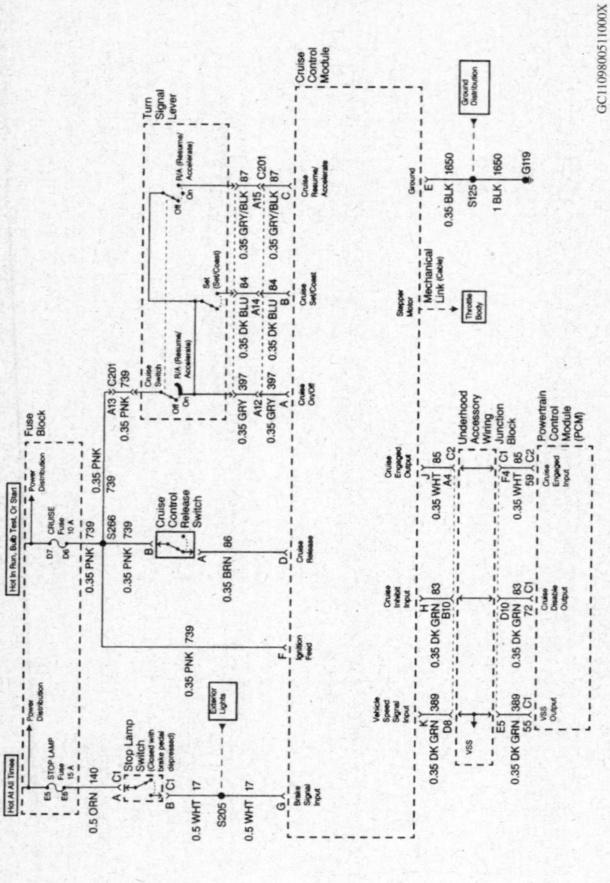

Fig. 25 Wiring diagram. 2000 Grand Prix

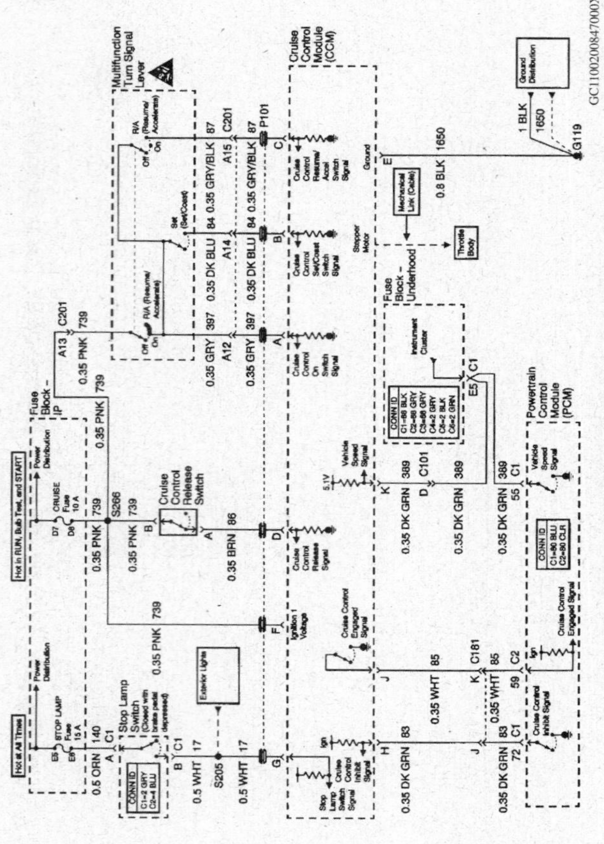

Fig. 26 Wiring diagram. 2001–04 Grand Prix

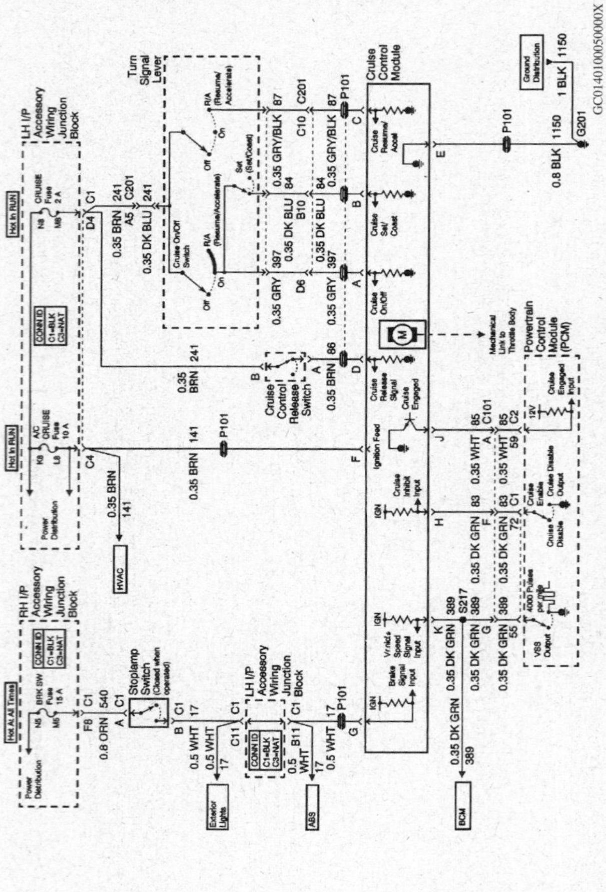

Fig. 27 Wiring diagram. 2000 Impala

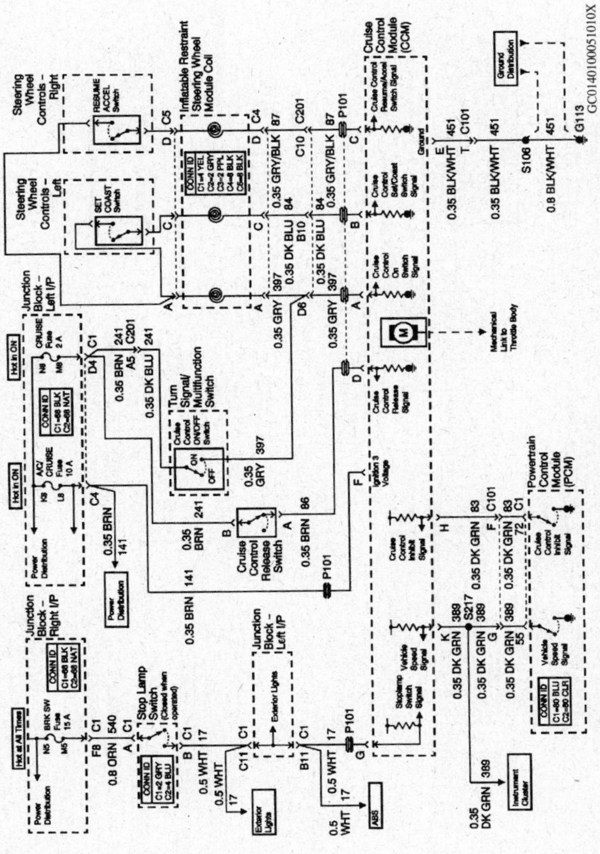

Fig. 28 Wiring diagram (Part 1 of 2). 2001–04 Impala

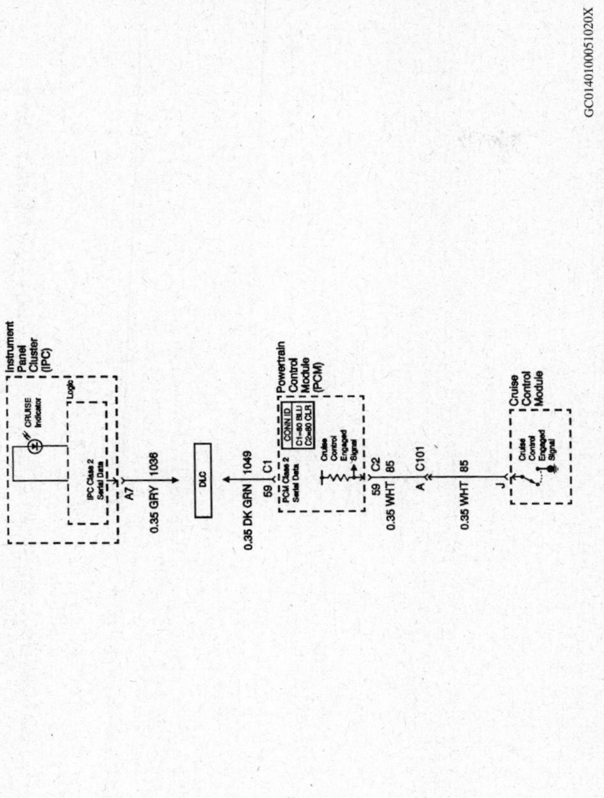

Fig. 28 Wiring diagram (Part 2 of 2). 2001–04 Impala

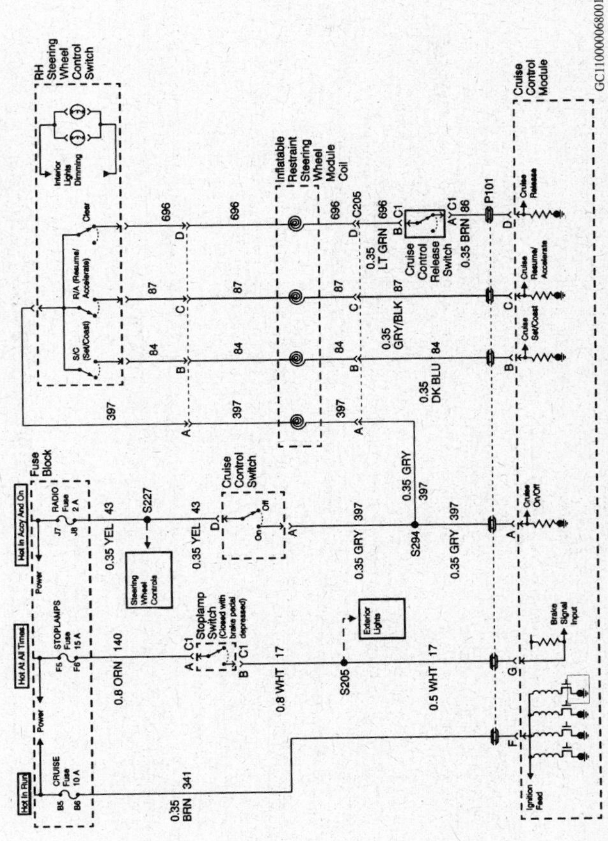

Fig. 29 Wiring diagram (Part 1 of 2). Intrigue

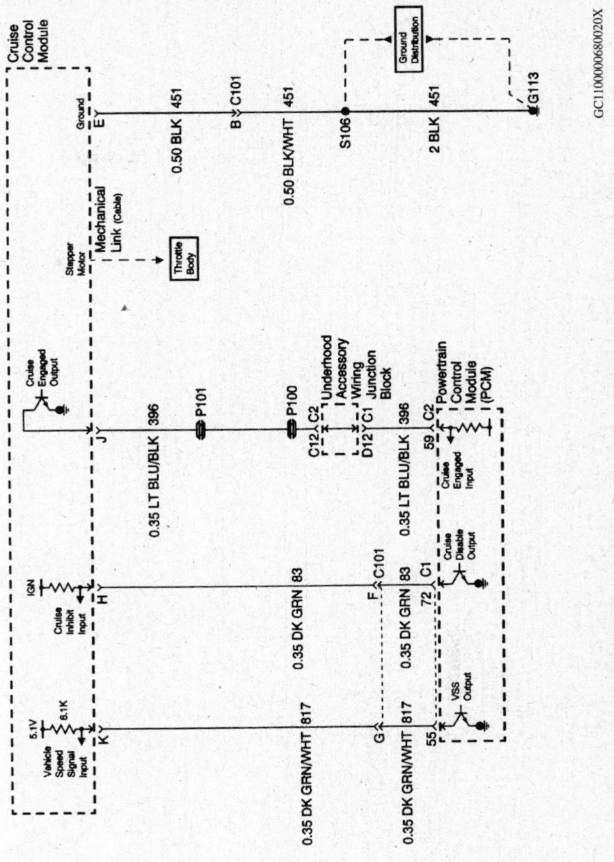

Fig. 29 Wiring diagram (Part 2 of 2). Intrigue

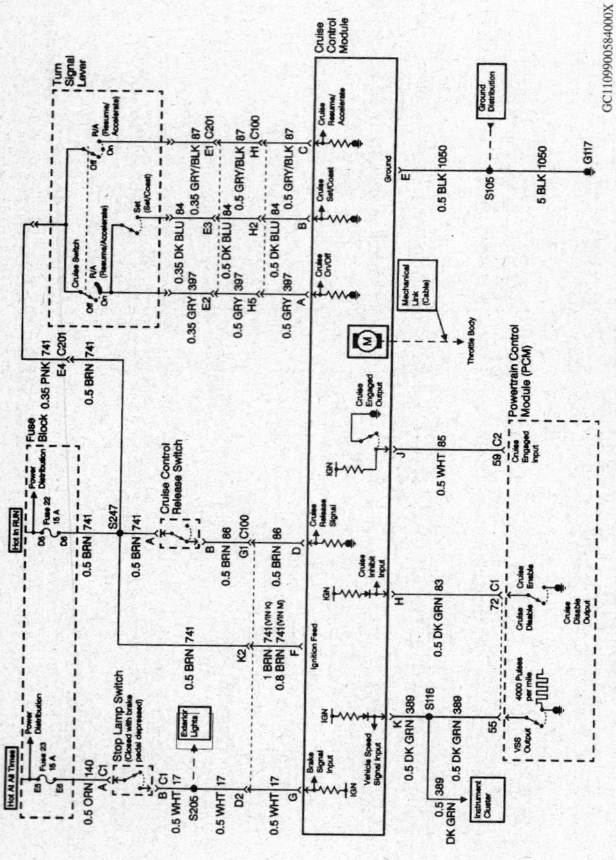

Fig. 30 Wiring diagram. 2000–01 Lumina

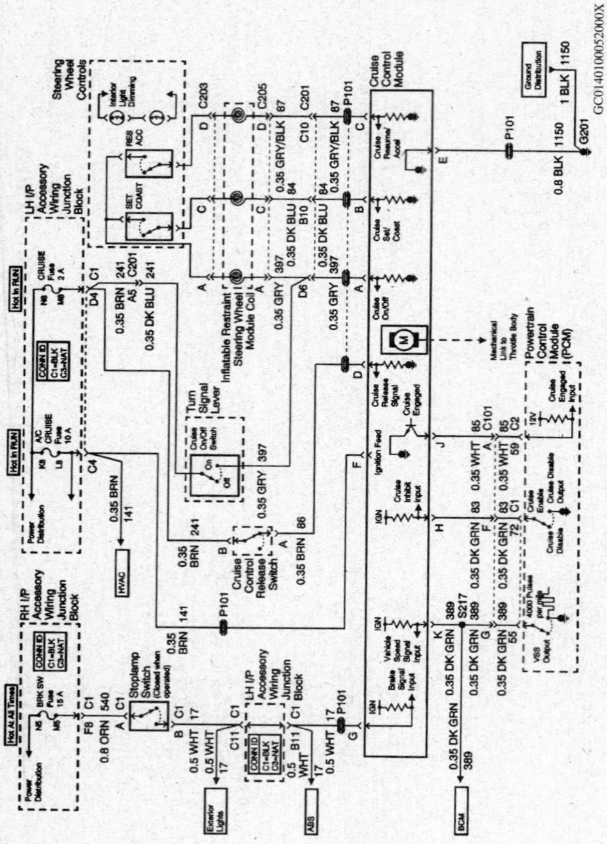

Fig. 31 Wiring diagram. 2000 Monte Carlo

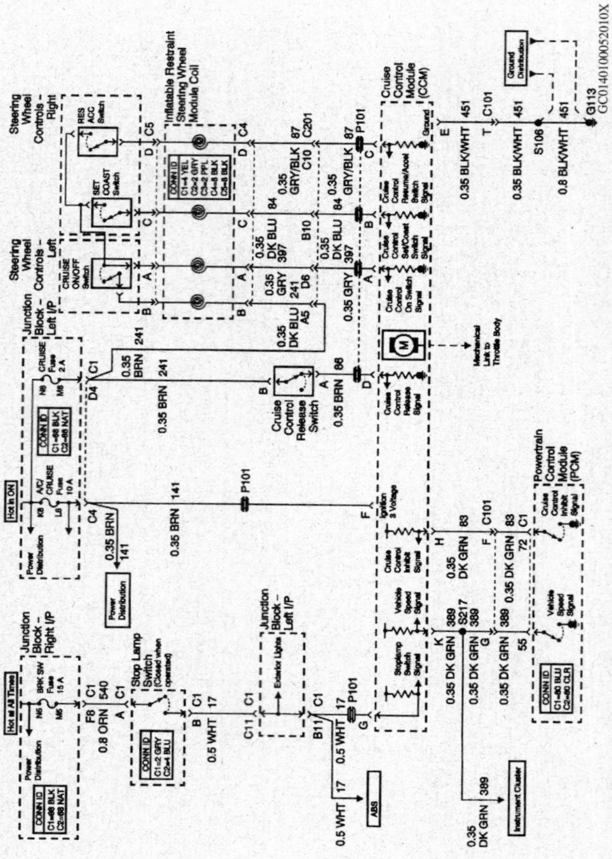

Fig. 32 Wiring diagram (Part 1 of 2). 2001–04 Monte Carlo

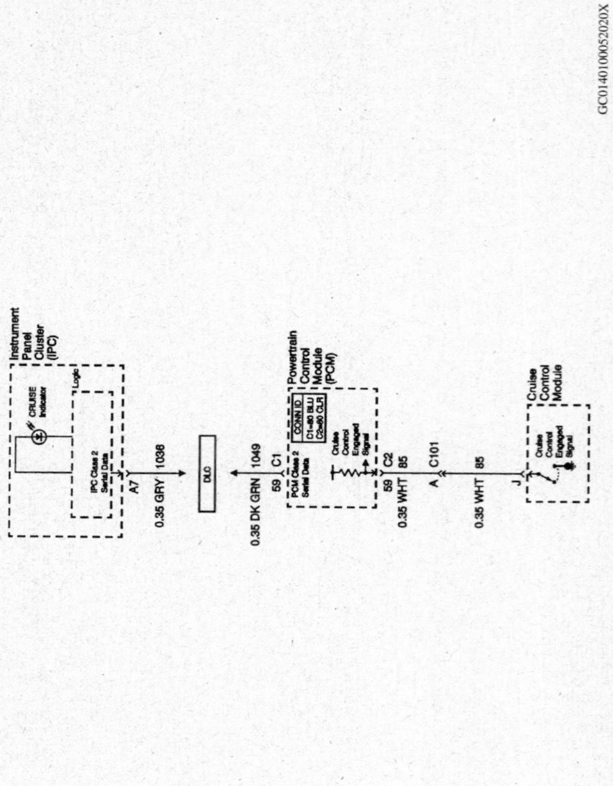

Fig. 32 Wiring diagram (Part 2 of 2). 2001–04 Monte Carlo

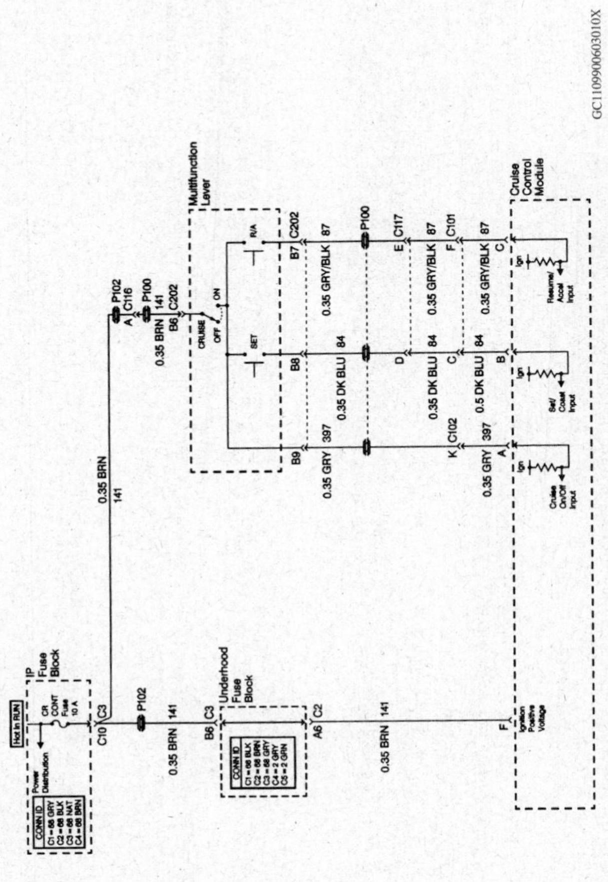

Fig. 33 Wiring diagram (Part 1 of 3). 2000–01 Park Avenue

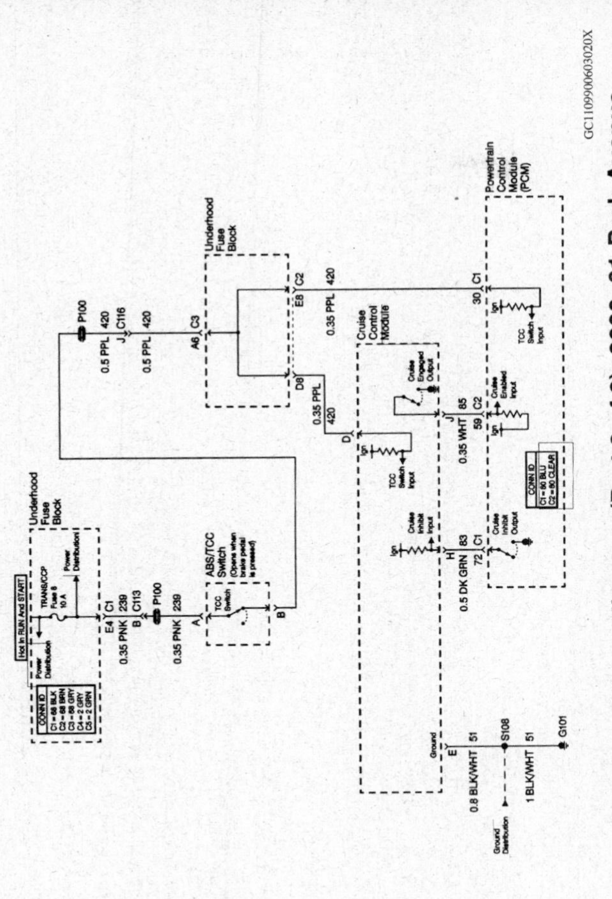

Fig. 33 Wiring diagram (Part 2 of 3). 2000–01 Park Avenue

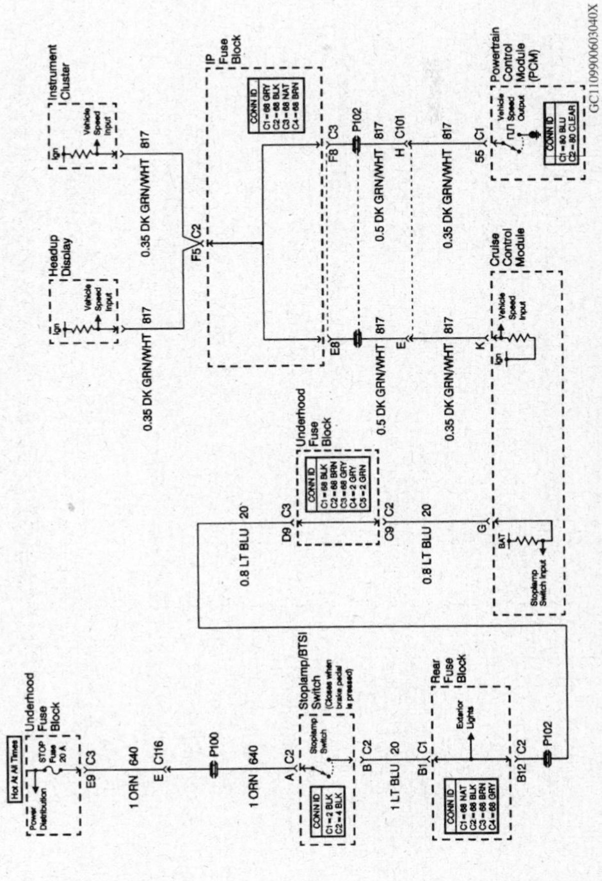

Fig. 33 Wiring diagram (Part 3 of 3). 2000–01 Park Avenue

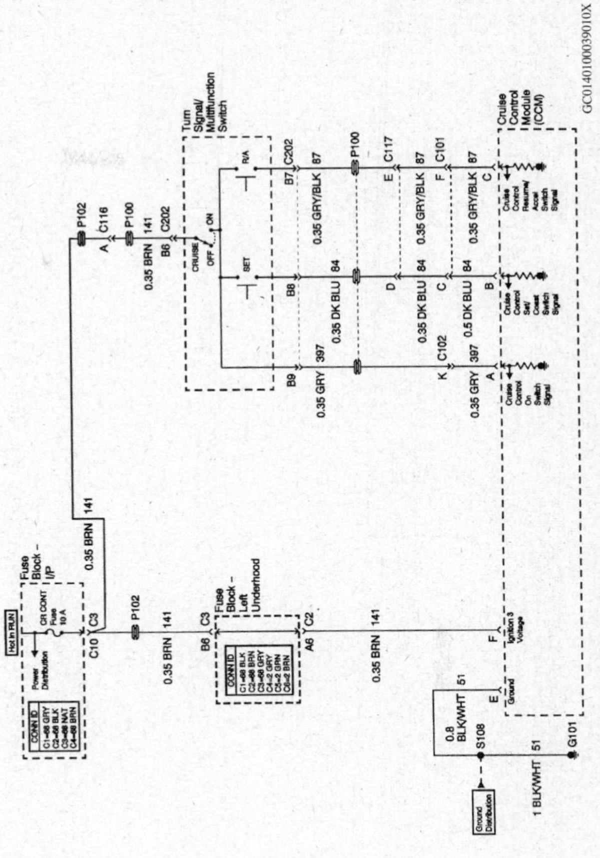

Fig. 34 Wiring diagram (Part 1 of 2). 2002–04 Park Avenue

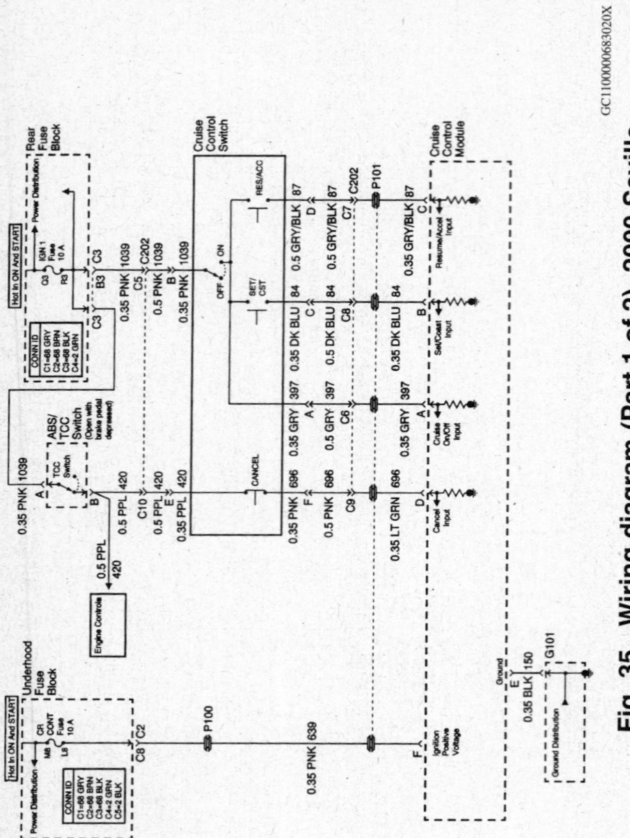

Fig. 35 Wiring diagram (Part 1 of 2). 2000 Seville

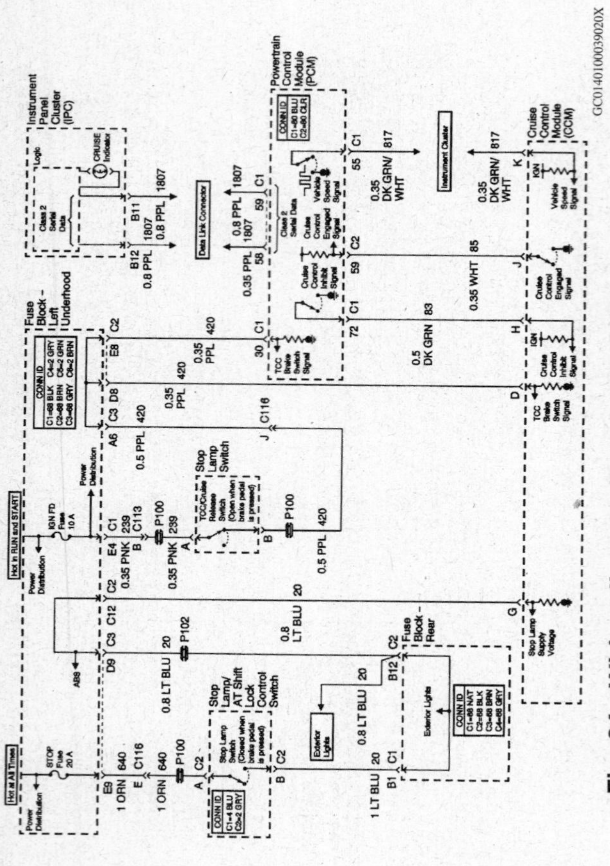

Fig. 34 Wiring diagram (Part 2 of 2). 2002–04 Park Avenue

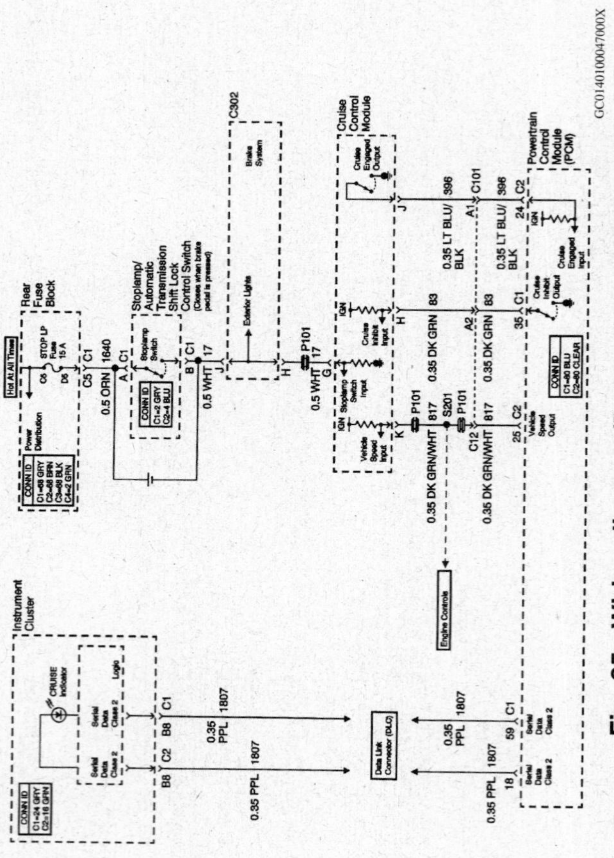

Fig. 35 Wiring diagram (Part 2 of 2). 2000 Seville

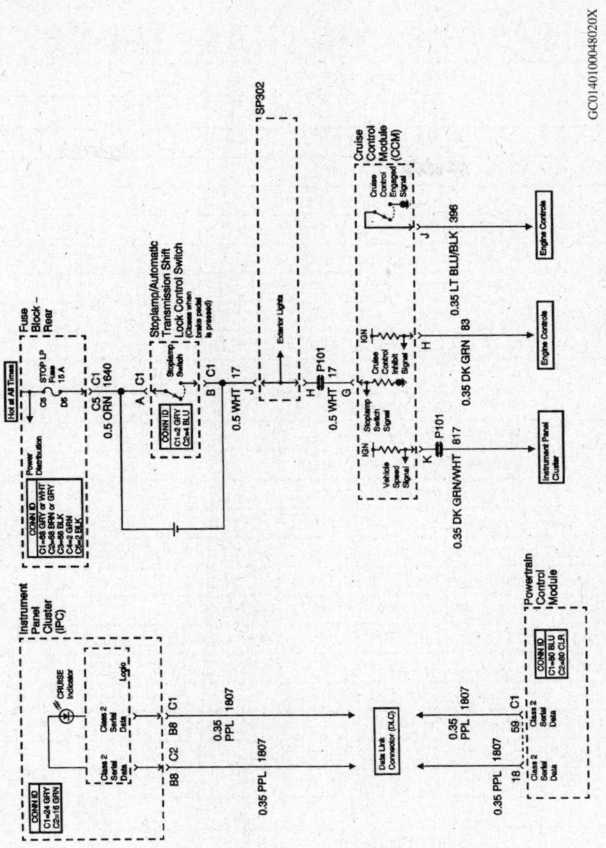

Fig. 36 Wiring diagram (Part 2 of 2). 2001–04 Seville

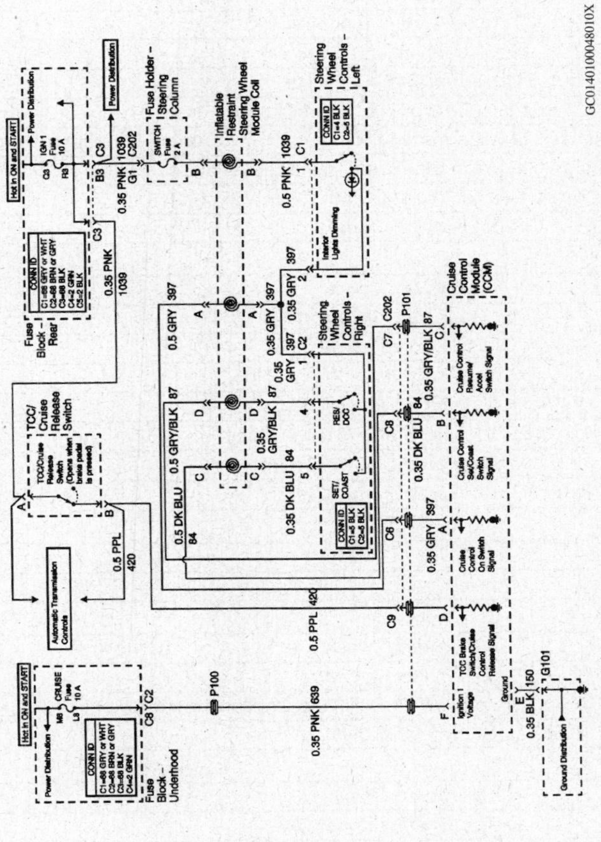

Fig. 36 Wiring diagram (Part 1 of 2). 2001–04 Seville

DIAGNOSTIC CHART INDEX

Code	Description	Page No.	Fig. No.
ALERO & GRAND AM			
—	System Check	2-57	91
—	Cruise Indicator Always On	2-34	45
—	Cruise Control Inoperative	2-23	37
—	Cruise Indicator Inoperative	2-35	50
—	Cruise Indicator Inoperative	2-35	51
P1554	Cruise Control Feedback Circuit	2-40	60
P1585	Cruise Control Inhibit Output Circuit (2000)	2-46	73
P1585	Cruise Control Inhibit Output Circuit (2001–04)	2-47	74
AURORA			
—	System Check	2-57	92
—	Cruise Indicator Always On	2-34	45
—	Cruise Control Inoperative	2-24	38
—	Cruise Indicator Inoperative	2-35	51
P0574	PCM Detects Speed More Than 110 mph	2-39	59
P1554	PCM Detects Cruise Engaged While Inhibiting Cruise Control Operation	2-41	61
P1560	Transaxle Range Switch Indicates Neutral Position w/Cruise Control Engaged	2-41	62
P1564	PCM Detects Extremely Rapid Acceleration	2-42	64
P1566	Engine Speed More Than 6300 RPM w/Cruise Control Engaged	2-42	65
P1567	Active Brake Control System Applied Brakes w/Cruise Control Engaged	2-43	67
P1570	Traction Control Is Active	2-44	69
P1574	Sudden Decrease In Non-Drive Wheel Speed	2-45	71
P1575	PCM Detects Voltage On Extended Travel Brake Switch Circuit	2-45	72
P1585	Cruise Control Inhibit Output Circuit	2-47	74
BONNEVILLE & LESABRE			
—	System Check	2-57	93
—	System Check	2-57	94
—	Cruise Control Inoperative	2-24	38
—	Cruise Indicator Always On	2-34	45
—	Cruise Indicator Inoperative	2-36	52
P1554	Cruise Control Feedback Circuit	2-40	60
P1554	PCM Detects Cruise Engaged While Inhibiting Cruise Control Operation	2-41	61
P1575	PCM Detects Voltage On Extended Travel Brake Switch Circuit	2-45	72
P1585	Cruise Control Inhibit Output Circuit (2000)	2-46	73
P1585	Cruise Control Inhibit Output Circuit (2001–04)	2-47	74
CATERA			
—	System Check	2-58	95
—	Cruise Indicator Always On	2-34	46
—	Cruise Control Inoperative	2-25	39
—	Cruise Indicator Inoperative	2-36	53
P0571	Cruise Control Brake Switch Circuit	2-38	57
P0571	Cruise Control Brake Switch Circuit	2-39	58
P1662	Cruise Lamp Control Circuit	2-48	75
P1662	Cruise Lamp Control Circuit	2-49	76
2000 CAVALIER & SUNFIRE			
—	System Check	2-57	91
—	Cruise Control Inoperative	2-24	38
2001–04 CAVALIER & SUNFIRE			
—	System Check	2-57	93
—	Cruise Control Inoperative	2-28	41
P1554	PCM Detects Cruise Engaged While Inhibiting Cruise Control Operation	2-41	61
P1585	Cruise Control Inhibit Output Circuit	2-47	74
CENTURY & REGAL			
—	System Check	2-57	93
—	Cruise Control Inoperative	2-24	38
—	Cruise Indictor Always On	2-34	47

Continued

DIAGNOSTIC CHART INDEX—Continued

Code	Description	Page No.	Fig. No.
CENTURY & REGAL			
—	Cruise Indictor Always On (2001–04)	2-34	47
—	Cruise Indicator Inoperative (2000–01)	2-36	54
—	Cruise Indicator Inoperative (2002–04)	2-35	50
P1554	PCM Detects Cruise Engaged While Inhibiting Cruise Control Operation	2-41	61
P1575	PCM Detects Voltage On Extended Travel Brake Switch Circuit	2-45	72
P1585	Cruise Control Inhibit Output Circuit (2000)	2-46	73
P1585	Cruise Control Inhibit Output Circuit (2001–04)	2-47	74
MALIBU			
—	System Check	2-57	91
—	Cruise Control Inoperative	2-24	38
—	Cruise Indicator Always On	2-34	45
—	Cruise Indicator Inoperative	2-35	51
P1554	Cruise Control Feedback Circuit	2-40	60
P1585	Cruise Control Inhibit Output Circuit (2000)	2-46	73
P1585	Cruise Control Inhibit Output Circuit (2001–04)	2-47	74
CTS			
—	System Check	2-58	96
—	Cruise Control Inoperative	2-26	40
P0560	PCM Detect Voltage Out Of Range	2-49	77
P0562	PCM Detects Low Voltage	2-50	78
P0563	PCM Detects High Voltage	2-50	79
P0615	Improper Voltage Level On Output Circuit	2-51	80
P0616	Improper Voltage Level On Output Circuit	2-52	81
P0617	Improper Voltage Level On Output Circuit	2-52	82
P0625	PCM Detects Low PWM Signal	2-53	83
P0704	Insufficient Time Between Gear Changes	2-53	84
P2500	PCM Detects Low Voltage Signal	2-54	85
2501	PCM Detects High Voltage Signal	2-55	86
B1327	Voltage Falls Below 9 Volts	2-55	87
B1328	Voltage Rises Above 16 Volts	2-56	88
B1513	Voltage Fall Below 10 Volts For 30 Seconds.	2-56	89
B1514	Voltage Falls Below 16 Volts For 30 Seconds	2-57	90
DEVILLE & ELDORADO			
—	System Check (DeVille)	2-58	97
—	System Check (Eldorado)	2-58	98
—	Cruise Control Inoperative	2-24	38
—	Cruise Indicator Always On	2-35	48
—	Cruise Indicator Inoperative	2-37	55
P0574	PCM Detects Speed More Than 110 mph	2-39	59
P1554	PCM Detects Cruise Engaged While Inhibiting Cruise Control Operation	2-41	61
P1560	Transaxle Range Switch Indicates Neutral Position w/Cruise Control Engaged	2-42	63
P1564	PCM Detects Extremely Rapid Acceleration	2-42	64
P1566	Engine Speed More Than 6300 RPM w/Cruise Control Engaged	2-43	66
P1567	Active Brake Control System Applied Brakes w/Cruise Control Engaged	2-44	68
P1570	Traction Control Is Active	2-44	70
P1574	Sudden Decrease In Non-Drive Wheel Speed	2-45	71
P1575	PCM Detects Voltage On Extended Travel Brake Switch Circuit	2-45	72
P1585	Cruise Control Inhibit Output Circuit	2-47	74
GRAND PRIX			
—	System Check	2-57	93
—	Cruise Control Inoperative	2-24	38
—	Cruise Indictor Always On	2-34	47
P1554	PCM Detects Cruise Engaged While Inhibiting Cruise Control Operation	2-41	61
P1585	Cruise Control Inhibit Output Circuit	2-47	74

Continued

DIAGNOSTIC CHART INDEX—Continued

Code	Description	Page No.	Fig. No.
IMPALA			
—	System Check	2-57	93
—	Cruise Control Inoperative (2000)	2-24	38
—	Cruise Control Inoperative (2001–04)	2-29	42
—	Cruise Indictor Always On	2-34	47
—	Cruise Indicator Inoperative	2-35	50
P1554	PCM Detects Cruise Engaged While Inhibiting Cruise Control Operation	2-41	61
P1585	Cruise Control Inhibit Output Circuit (2000)	2-46	73
P1585	Cruise Control Inhibit Output Circuit (2001–04)	2-47	74
INTRIGUE			
—	System Check	2-57	93
—	Cruise Control Inoperative (2000)	2-24	38
—	Cruise Control Inoperative (2001–02)	2-31	43
—	Cruise Indictor Always On	2-34	47
—	Cruise Indicator Inoperative	2-36	54
P1554	PCM Detects Cruise Engaged While Inhibiting Cruise Control Operation	2-41	61
P1575	PCM Detects Voltage On Extended Travel Brake Switch Circuit	2-45	72
LUMINA			
—	System Check	2-57	93
—	Cruise Control Inoperative	2-24	38
P1554	PCM Detects Cruise Engaged While Inhibiting Cruise Control Operation	2-41	61
P1585	Cruise Control Inhibit Output Circuit (2000)	2-46	73
MONTE CARLO			
—	System Check	2-57	93
—	Cruise Control Inoperative (2000)	2-24	38
—	Cruise Control Inoperative (2001–04)	2-29	42
—	Cruise Indictor Always On	2-34	47
—	Cruise Indicator Inoperative	2-35	50
P1554	PCM Detects Cruise Engaged While Inhibiting Cruise Control Operation	2-41	61
P1585	Cruise Control Inhibit Output Circuit (2000)	2-46	73
P1585	Cruise Control Inhibit Output Circuit (2001–04)	2-47	74
PARK AVENUE			
—	System Check	2-57	93
—	Cruise Indicator Always On	2-34	45
—	Cruise Indicator Inoperative	2-36	52
P1554	Cruise Control Feedback Circuit	2-40	60
P1585	Cruise Control Inhibit Output Circuit (2000)	2-46	73
P1585	Cruise Control Inhibit Output Circuit (2001–04)	2-47	74
SEVILLE			
—	System Check	2-58	97
—	Cruise Control Inoperative	2-32	44
—	Cruise Indicator Always On	2-34	45
—	Cruise Indicator Always On	2-35	49
—	Cruise Indicator Inoperative	2-37	56
P0574	PCM Detects Speed More Than 110 mph	2-39	59
P1554	PCM Detects Cruise Engaged While Inhibiting Cruise Control Operation	2-41	61
P1560	Transaxle Range Switch Indicates Neutral Position w/Cruise Control Engaged	2-42	63
P1564	PCM Detects Extremely Rapid Acceleration	2-42	64
P1566	Engine Speed More Than 6300 RPM w/Cruise Control Engaged	2-43	66
P1567	Active Brake Control System Applied Brakes w/Cruise Control Engaged	2-44	68
P1570	Traction Control Is Active	2-44	70
P1574	Sudden Decrease In Non-Drive Wheel Speed	2-45	71
P1575	PCM Detects Voltage On Extended Travel Brake Switch Circuit	2-45	72
P1585	Cruise Control Inhibit Output Circuit	2-47	74

Important

Perform the following in order to avoid misdiagnosis.

- Inspect for proper operation of brake lamps.
- Inspect throttle linkage for mechanical binding which could cause the system to malfunction.
- Inspect cruise control cable adjustment, should have minimum slack.
- Inspect for stored Diagnostic Trouble Codes (DTCs) in the PCM.
- When testing vehicles with steering wheel controls, the steering wheel must be rotated to each stop position while testing the cruise control signal circuits. This will assure the integrity of the SIR coil.
- EMI on the speed sensor signal circuit may cause erratic cruise control operation.

Conditions for Enabling Cruise Control

- When vehicle speed is more than 40 km/h (25 mph)
- When PARK, REVERSE, NEUTRAL, or 1st gear is not indicated.
- When an over/undercharged battery condition does not exist.
- With normal engine RPM.
- Without high engine RPM (fuel cut-off).

Step	Action	Value (s)	Yes	No
1	Did you perform A Cruise Control System Check ?	--	Go to Step 2	Go to Cruise Control System Check
2	1. Turn OFF the ignition. 2. Disconnect the cruise control module. 3. Turn ON the ignition, with the engine OFF. 4. Probe the ignition positive voltage circuit of the cruise control module with a test lamp that is connected to a good ground. Does the test lamp illuminate?	--	Go to Step 3	Go to Step 40
3	Probe the ignition positive voltage circuit of the cruise control module with a test lamp that is connected to the ground circuit of the cruise control module. Does the test lamp illuminate?	--	Go to Step 4	Go to Step 41

GC0140100056010X

Fig. 37 Cruise Control Inoperative (Part 1 of 6). Alero & Grand Am

Step	Action	Value (s)	Yes	No
4	1. Turn ON the ignition, with the engine OFF. 2. Turn OFF the cruise control. 3. Probe the cruise control on switch signal, the set/coast switch, and the resume/accelerate switch signal circuits with a test lamp that is connected to a good ground. Does the test lamp illuminate on any of the signal circuits?	--	Go to Step 18	Go to Step 5
5	1. Turn ON the ignition, with the engine OFF. 2. Turn ON the cruise control switch. 3. Probe the cruise control on switch signal circuit with a test lamp that is connected to a good ground. Does the test lamp illuminate?	--	Go to Step 6	Go to Step 19
6	1. Probe the cruise control set/coast switch signal circuit with a test lamp that is connected to a good ground. 2. Press and hold the SET/COAST button. Does the test lamp illuminate?	--	Go to Step 7	Go to Step 21
7	1. Probe the cruise control resume/accelerate switch signal circuit with a test lamp that is connected to a good ground. 2. Press and hold the RESUME/ACCEL switch. Does the test lamp illuminate?	--	Go to Step 8	Go to Step 22
8	Probe the cruise control release signal circuit with a test lamp that is connected to a good ground. Does the test lamp illuminate?	--	Go to Step 9	Go to Step 23
9	Press the brake pedal while monitoring the test lamp. Does the test lamp illuminate?	--	Go to Step 24	Go to Step 10
10	Probe the stop lamp signal circuit with a test lamp that is connected to a good ground. Does the test lamp illuminate?	--	Go to Step 25	Go to Step 11
11	Press the brake pedal while monitoring the test lamp. Does the test lamp illuminate?	--	Go to Step 12	Go to Step 26
12	Probe the cruise control inhibit signal circuit with a test lamp that is connected to B+. Does the test lamp illuminate?	--	Go to Step 29	Go to Step 13
13	Use a scan tool in order to command the cruise inhibit/enable OFF. Does the test lamp illuminate?	--	Go to Step 14	Go to Step 30

GC0140100056020X

Fig. 37 Cruise Control Inoperative (Part 2 of 6). Alero & Grand Am

Step	Action	Value (s)	Yes	No
14	Probe the cruise control engaged signal circuit with a DMM that is connected to a good ground. Does the voltage measure near the specified value?	B+	Go to Step 15	Go to Step 31
15	1. Turn OFF the ignition. 2. Disconnect the appropriate BCM harness connector. 3. Turn ON the ignition, with the engine OFF. 4. Probe the cruise control cancel signal circuit with a test lamp connected to a good ground. Does the test lamp illuminate?	--	Go to Step 16	Go to Step 27
16	Press the cruise control cancel switch while monitoring the test lamp. Does the test lamp illuminate?	--	Go to Step 28	Go to Step 17
17	Check the speedometer for proper operation. Does the speedometer operate properly?	--	Go to Step 32	Check Speedometer and/or Odometer
18	Test the signal circuit that illuminated the test lamp for a short to voltage. Did you find and correct the condition?	--	Go to Step 47	Go to Step 34
19	Test the cruise control on switch signal circuit for an open or a high resistance and the set/coast and resume/accel signal circuits for a short to ground. Did you find and correct the condition?	--	Go to Step 47	Go to Step 20
20	Test the ignition positive voltage circuit for an open or high resistance between the IP junction block and the cruise control switch. Did you find and correct the condition?	--	Go to Step 47	Go to Step 38
21	Test the cruise control set/coast signal circuit for an open or a high resistance. Did you find and correct the condition?	--	Go to Step 47	Go to Step 38
22	Test the cruise control resume/accelerate signal circuit for an open or a high resistance. Did you find and correct the condition?	--	Go to Step 47	Go to Step 38

GC0140100056030X

Fig. 37 Cruise Control Inoperative (Part 3 of 6). Alero & Grand Am

Step	Action	Value (s)	Yes	No
23	Test the cruise control release switch signal circuit for an open or a high resistance. Did you find and correct the condition?	--	Go to Step 47	Go to Step 33
24	Test the cruise control release switch signal circuit for a short to voltage. Did you find and correct the condition?	--	Go to Step 47	Go to Step 33
25	Test the stoplamp switch signal circuit for a short to voltage. Did you find and correct the condition?	--	Go to Step 47	Go to Step 34
26	Test the stoplamp switch signal circuit for an open or a high resistance. Did you find and correct the condition?	--	Go to Step 47	Go to Step 34
27	Test the cruise control cancel circuit for an open or high resistance. Did you find and correct the condition?	--	Go to Step 47	Go to Step 38
28	Test the cruise control cancel circuit for a short to voltage. Did you find and correct the condition?	--	Go to Step 47	Go to Step 38
29	Test the cruise inhibit signal circuit for a short to ground. Did you find and correct the condition?	--	Go to Step 47	Go to Step 37
30	Test the cruise inhibit signal circuit for an open, a high resistance, or a short to voltage. Did you find and correct the condition?	--	Go to Step 47	Go to Step 37
31	Test the cruise engaged signal circuit for an open, a high resistance, or a short to voltage. Did you find and correct the condition?	--	Go to Step 47	Go to Step 37
32	Test the speed sensor circuit for an open or a high resistance between the PCM and cruise control module. Did you find and correct the condition?	--	Go to Step 47	Go to Step 39

GC0140100056040X

Fig. 37 Cruise Control Inoperative (Part 4 of 6). Alero & Grand Am

Step	Action	Value (s)	Yes	No
33	Inspect the cruise control release switch for proper adjustment. Did you find and correct the condition?	--	Go to Step 47	Go to Step 35
34	Inspect the stoplamp switch for proper adjustment. Did you find and correct the condition?	--	Go to Step 47	Go to Step 36
35	Inspect for poor connections at the harness connector of the cruise control release switch. Refer to Intermittents Did you find and correct the condition?	--	Go to Step 47	Go to Step 42
36	Inspect for poor connections at the harness connector of the stoplamp switch. Refer to Intermittents Did you find and correct the condition?	--	Go to Step 47	Go to Step 43
37	Inspect for poor connections at the harness connector of the PCM. Refer to Intermittents Did you find and correct the condition?	--	Go to Step 47	Go to Step 44
38	Inspect for poor connections at the harness connector of the cruise control switch. Refer to Intermittents Did you find and correct the condition?	--	Go to Step 47	Go to Step 45
39	Inspect for poor connections at the harness connector of the cruise control module. Refer to Intermittents Did you find and correct the condition?	--	Go to Step 47	Go to Step 46
40	Repair the ignition positive voltage circuit of the cruise control module. Did you complete the repair?	--	Go to Step 47	--
41	Repair the ground circuit of the cruise control module. Did you complete the repair?	--	Go to Step 47	--
42	Replace the cruise control release switch. Did you complete the replacement?	--	Go to Step 47	--

GC0140100056050X

Fig. 37 Cruise Control Inoperative (Part 5 of 6). Alero & Grand Am

Important

Perform the following in order to avoid misdiagnosis.

- Inspect for proper operation of brake lamps.
- Inspect throttle linkage for mechanical binding which could cause the system to malfunction.
- Inspect cruise control cable adjustment, should have minimum slack.
- Inspect for stored Diagnostic Trouble Codes (DTCs) in the PCM.
- EMI on the speed sensor signal circuit may cause erratic cruise control operation.

Conditions for Enabling Cruise Control

- When vehicle speed is more than 40 km/h (25 mph)
- When PARK, REVERSE, NEUTRAL, or 1st gear is not indicated.
- When an over/undercharged battery condition does not exist.
- With normal engine RPM.
- Without high engine RPM (fuel cut-off).

Step	Action	Value (s)	Yes	No
1	Did you perform A Cruise Control System Check ?	--	Go to Step 2	Go to Cruise Control System Check
2	1. Turn OFF the ignition. 2. Disconnect the cruise control module. 3. Turn the ignition to the RUN position. 4. Probe the ignition positive voltage circuit of the cruise control module harness connector with a test lamp that is connected to a good ground. Does the test lamp illuminate?	--	Go to Step 3	Go to Step 36
3	Probe the ignition positive voltage circuit of the cruise control module harness connector with a test lamp that is connected to the ground circuit of the cruise control module harness connector. Does the test lamp illuminate?	--	Go to Step 4	Go to Step 37

GC0140100065010X

Fig. 38 Cruise Control Inoperative (Part 1 of 5). Aurora, Bonneville, LeSabre, Park Avenue, Century, DeVille, Eldorado, Grand Prix, Malibu, Park Avenue, Regal & 2000 Cavalier, Impala, Intrigue, Monte Carlo & Sunfire & 2000–01 Lumina

Step	Action	Value (s)	Yes	No
43	Replace the stop lamp switch. Did you complete the replacement?	--	Go to Step 47	--
44	Replace the PCM. Did you complete the replacement?	--	Go to Step 47	--
45	Replace the cruise control switch. Did you complete the replacement?	--	Go to Step 47	--
46	Replace the cruise control module. Did you complete the replacement?	--	Go to Step 47	--
47	Operate the vehicle within the conditions for cruise control operation. Does the cruise control system operate correctly?	--	System OK	Go to Step 2

GC0140100056060X

Fig. 37 Cruise Control Inoperative (Part 6 of 6). Alero & Grand Am

Step	Action	Value (s)	Yes	No
4	1. Turn OFF the cruise control. 2. Probe the cruise control module harness connector, on/off switch, set/coast switch, and the resume/accelerate switch signal circuits with a test lamp that is connected to a good ground. Does the test lamp illuminate on any of the signal circuits?	--	Go to Step 16	Go to Step 5
5	1. Turn ON the cruise control switch. 2. Probe the cruise control module harness connector on/off switch signal circuit with a test lamp that is connected to a good ground. Does the test lamp illuminate?	--	Go to Step 6	Go to Step 17
6	1. Probe the cruise control module harness connector set/coast switch signal circuit with a test lamp that is connected to a good ground. 2. Press and hold the SET/COAST button. Does the test lamp illuminate?	--	Go to Step 7	Go to Step 19
7	1. Probe the cruise control module harness connector resume/accelerate switch signal circuit with a test lamp that is connected to a good ground. 2. Press and hold the RESUME/ACCEL switch. Does the test lamp illuminate?	--	Go to Step 8	Go to Step 20
8	Probe the cruise control module harness connector Abs/TCC, release signal circuit with a test lamp that is connected to a good ground. Does the test lamp illuminate?	--	Go to Step 9	Go to Step 21
9	Press the brake pedal while monitoring the test lamp. Does the test lamp illuminate?	--	Go to Step 22	Go to Step 10
10	Probe the stop lamp signal circuit with a test lamp that is connected to a good ground. Does the test lamp illuminate?	--	Go to Step 23	Go to Step 11
11	Press the brake pedal while monitoring the test lamp. Does the test lamp illuminate?	--	Go to Step 12	Go to Step 24
12	Probe the cruise control inhibit signal circuit with a test lamp that is connected to B+. Does the test lamp illuminate?	--	Go to Step 25	Go to Step 13
13	Use a scan tool in order to command the cruise inhibit/enable OFF. Does the test lamp illuminate?	--	Go to Step 14	Go to Step 26.

GC0140100065020X

Fig. 38 Cruise Control Inoperative (Part 2 of 5). Aurora, Bonneville, LeSabre, Park Avenue, Century, DeVille, Eldorado, Grand Prix, Malibu, Park Avenue, Regal & 2000 Cavalier, Impala, Intrigue, Monte Carlo & Sunfire & 2000–01 Lumina

Step	Action	Value (s)	Yes	No
14	Probe the cruise control engaged signal circuit with a DMM that is connected to a good ground. Does the voltage measure near the specified value?	B+	Go to Step 15	Go to Step 27
15	Check the speedometer for proper operation. Does the speedometer operate properly?	--	Go to Step 28	Check Speedometer and/or Odometer
16	Test the signal circuit that illuminated the test lamp for a short to voltage. Did you find and correct the condition?	--	Go to Step 43	Go to Step 34
17	Test the cruise control on switch signal circuit for an open or a high resistance and the set/coast and resume/accel signal circuits for a short to ground. Did you find and correct the condition?	--	Go to Step 43	Go to Step 18
18	Test the ignition positive voltage circuit for an open or high resistance between the IP junction block and the cruise control switch. Did you find and correct the condition?	--	Go to Step 43	Go to Step 34
19	Test the cruise control set/coast signal circuit for an open or a high resistance. Did you find and correct the condition?	--	Go to Step 43	Go to Step 34
20	Test the cruise control resume/accelerate signal circuit for an open or a high resistance. Did you find and correct the condition?	--	Go to Step 43	Go to Step 34
21	Test the cruise control release switch signal circuit for an open or a high resistance. Did you find and correct the condition?	--	Go to Step 43	Go to Step 29
22	Test the cruise control release switch signal circuit for a short to voltage. Did you find and correct the condition?	--	Go to Step 43	Go to Step 29
23	Test the stoplamp switch signal circuit for a short to voltage. Did you find and correct the condition?	--	Go to Step 43	Go to Step 30
24	Test the stoplamp switch signal circuit for an open or a high resistance. Did you find and correct the condition?	--	Go to Step 43	Go to Step 30
25	Test the cruise inhibit signal circuit for a short to ground. Did you find and correct the condition?	--	Go to Step 43	Go to Step 33

GC0140100065030X

Fig. 38 Cruise Control Inoperative (Part 3 of 5). Aurora, Bonneville, LeSabre, Park Avenue, Century, DeVille, Eldorado, Grand Prix, Malibu, Park Avenue, Regal & 2000 Cavalier, Impala, Intrigue, Monte Carlo & Sunfire & 2000–01 Lumina

Step	Action	Value (s)	Yes	No
26	Test the cruise inhibit signal circuit for an open, a high resistance, or a short to voltage. Did you find and correct the condition?	--	Go to Step 43	Go to Step 33
27	Test the cruise engaged signal circuit for an open, a high resistance, or a short to voltage. Did you find and correct the condition?	--	Go to Step 43	Go to Step 33
28	Test the speed sensor circuit for an open or a high resistance between the PCM and cruise control module. Did you find and correct the condition?	--	Go to Step 43	Go to Step 35
29	Inspect the cruise control release switch for proper adjustment. Did you find and correct the condition?	--	Go to Step 43	Go to Step 31
30	Inspect the stoplamp switch for proper adjustment. Did you find and correct the condition?	--	Go to Step 43	Go to Step 32
31	Inspect for poor connections at the harness connector of the cruise control release switch. Did you find and correct the condition?	--	Go to Step 43	Go to Step 38
32	Inspect for poor connections at the harness connector of the stoplamp switch. Did you find and correct the condition?	--	Go to Step 43	Go to Step 39
33	Inspect for poor connections at the harness connector of the PCM. Did you find and correct the condition?	--	Go to Step 43	Go to Step 40
34	Inspect for poor connections at the harness connector of the cruise control switch. Did you find and correct the condition?	--	Go to Step 43	Go to Step 39
35	Inspect for poor connections at the harness connector of the cruise control module. Did you find and correct the condition?	--	Go to Step 43	Go to Step 42
36	Repair the ignition positive voltage circuit of the cruise control module. Did you complete the repair?	--	Go to Step 43	--
37	Repair the ground circuit of the cruise control module. Did you complete the repair?	--	Go to Step 43	--

GC0140100065040X

Fig. 38 Cruise Control Inoperative (Part 4 of 5). Aurora, Bonneville, LeSabre, Park Avenue, Century, DeVille, Eldorado, Grand Prix, Malibu, Park Avenue, Regal & 2000 Cavalier, Impala, Intrigue, Monte Carlo & Sunfire & 2000–01 Lumina

Step	Action	Value (s)	Yes	No
38	Replace the cruise control release switch. — Did you complete the replacement?	--	Go to Step 43	--
39	Replace the stop lamp switch. Did you complete the replacement?	--	Go to Step 43	--
40	Replace the PCM. Did you complete the replacement?	--	Go to Step 43	--
41	Replace the cruise control switch. Did you complete the replacement?	--	Go to Step 43	--
42	Replace the cruise control module. Did you complete the replacement?	--	Go to Step 43	--
43	Operate the vehicle within the conditions for cruise control operation. Does the cruise control system operate correctly?	--	System OK	Go to Step 2

GC0140100065050X

Fig. 38 Cruise Control Inoperative (Part 5 of 5). Aurora, Bonneville, LeSabre, Park Avenue, Century, DeVille, Eldorado, Grand Prix, Malibu, Park Avenue, Regal & 2000 Cavalier, Impala, Intrigue, Monte Carlo & Sunfire & 2000–01 Lumina

Diagnostic Aids

To avoid misdiagnosis:

- Inspect for proper operation of the brake lamps.
- Inspect for stored Diagnostic Trouble Codes (DTCs in the ECM).

Conditions for Enabling Cruise Control

- When vehicle speed is more than 40 km/h (25 mph).
- When PARK, REVERSE, NEUTRAL, or 1st gear IS NOT indicated by the Park/Neutral Position Switch.
- When an over/undercharged battery condition DOES NOT exist.

Step	Action	Yes	No
1	Did you perform A Diagnostic System Check - Cruise Control?	Go to Step 2	Go to Check - Cruise Control
2	1. Turn OFF the ignition. 2. Disconnect the appropriate ECM connector. 3. Turn ON the ignition, with the engine OFF. 4. Probe the Resume/Decel and Set/Accel signal circuits of the ECM harness connector with a test lamp that is connected to a good ground. Does the test lamp illuminate?	Go to Step 11	Go to Step 3
3	Probe the ON signal circuit of the ECM harness connector with a test lamp that is connected to a good ground. Does the test lamp illuminate?	Go to Step 5	Go to Step 4
4	1. Turn OFF the ignition. 2. Disconnect the cruise control switch at the multifunction turn signal lever pigtail connector. 3. Turn ON the ignition, with the engine OFF. 4. Probe the ignition positive circuit of the cruise control switch at the multifunction turn signal harness connector with a test lamp connected to a good ground. Does the test lamp illuminate?	Go to Step 12	Go to Step 13

GC0140100087010X

Fig. 39 Cruise Control Inoperative (Part 1 of 4). Catera

Step	Action	Yes	No
5	1. Probe the SET/ACCEL signal circuit of the ECM harness connector with a test lamp that is connected to a good ground. 2. Press and hold the SET/ACCEL switch. Does the test lamp illuminate?	Go to Step 6	Go to Step 14
6	1. Probe the RESUME/DECEL signal circuit of the ECM harness connector with a test lamp that is connected to a good ground. 2. Press and hold the RESUME/DECEL switch. Does the test lamp illuminate?	Go to Step 7	Go to Step 15
7	Probe the stop lamp signal circuit of the ECM harness connector with a test lamp that is connected to a good ground. Does the test lamp illuminate?	Go to Step 21	Go to Step 8
8	Press the brake pedal while monitoring the test lamp. Does the test lamp illuminate?	Go to Step 9	Go to Step 16
9	Probe the cruise release signal circuit of the ECM harness connector with a test lamp that is connected to a good ground. Does the test lamp illuminate?	Go to Step 10	Go to Step 17
10	Press the brake pedal while monitoring the test lamp. Does the test lamp illuminate?	Go to Step 19	Go to Step 23
11	Test the circuit that illuminated the test lamp for a short to voltage. Did you find and correct the condition?	Go to Step 30	Go to Step 23
12	Test the ON signal circuit for a open or high resistance. Did you find and correct the condition?	Go to Step 30	Go to Step 22
13	Test the ignition positive voltage circuit of the cruise control switch for an open or high resistance or a short to ground and the cruise control signal circuits for a short to ground. Did you find and correct the condition?	Go to Step 30	Go to Step 24
14	Test the SET/ACCEL circuit for a open or high resistance or short to ground. Did you find and correct the condition?	Go to Step 30	Go to Step 24

GC0140100087020X

Fig. 39 Cruise Control Inoperative (Part 2 of 4). Catera

Step	Action	Yes	No
25	Inspect for poor connections at the harness connector of the ECM. Refer to Intermittents Did you find and correct the condition?	Go to Step 30	Go to Step 29
26	Replace the cruise control release switch. Did you complete the replacement and adjustment?	Go to Step 30	--
27	Replace the stop lamp switch. Did you complete the replacement?	Go to Step 30	--
28	Replace the multifunction turn signal lever. Did you complete the replacement?	Go to Step 30	--
29	Replace the ECM. Did you complete the replacement?	Go to Step 30	--
30	Operate the vehicle within the conditions for cruise control operation. Does the cruise control system operate correctly?	System OK	Go to Diagnostic Aids

GC0140100087040X

Fig. 39 Cruise Control Inoperative (Part 4 of 4). Catera

Step	Action	Yes	No
15	Test the RESUME/DECEL signal circuit for a open, high resistance or a short to ground. Did you find and correct the condition?	Go to Step 30	Go to Step 24
16	Test the ignition positive voltage circuit of the stop lamp switch for a open, high resistance or a short to ground. Did you find and correct the condition?	Go to Step 30	Go to Step 20
17	Test the cruise release signal circuit for a open, high resistance or a short to ground. Did you find and correct the condition?	Go to Step 30	Go to Step 18
18	Test the ignition positive voltage circuit of the cruise release switch for a open, high resistance or a short to ground. Did you find and correct the condition?	Go to Step 30	Go to Step 22
19	Test the cruise release signal circuit for a short to voltage. Did you find and correct the condition?	Go to Step 30	Go to Step 22
20	Test the stop lamp signal circuit for a open, high resistance or a short to ground. Did you find and correct the condition?	Go to Step 30	Go to Step 23
21	Test the stop lamp signal circuit for a short to voltage. Did you find and correct the condition?	Go to Step 30	Go to Step 23
22	Inspect for poor connections at the harness connector of the cruise control release switch. Refer to Intermittents Did you find and correct the condition?	Go to Step 30	Go to Step 26
23	Inspect for poor connections at the harness connector of the stop lamp switch. Refer to Intermittents Did you find and correct the condition?	Go to Step 30	Go to Step 27
24	Inspect for poor connections at the multifunction turn signal lever harness connector for the cruise control switch. Refer to Intermittents Did you find and correct the condition?	Go to Step 30	Go to Step 28

GC0140100087030X

Fig. 39 Cruise Control Inoperative (Part 3 of 4). Catera

Diagnostic Aids

Disable the inflatable restraint steering wheel module when performing this diagnostic table.

Perform the following in order to avoid misdiagnosis:

- Inspect for proper operation of the brake lamps.
- Inspect for proper adjustment of the TCC/cruise control release switch, if equipped with automatic Transmission.
- Inspect for proper operation of the clutch system, if equipped with manual transmission.
- Rotate the steering wheel to both steering stops while testing the steering wheel control switches. This will eliminate the possibility of a internally open or shorted inflatable restraint steering wheel module coil.

EMI on the speed sensor signal circuit may cause erratic cruise control operation.

Step	Action	Yes	No
1	Did you perform the Cruise Control Diagnostic System Check?	Go to Step 2	Go to Diagnostic System Check

GC1100200850010X

Fig. 40 Cruise Control Inoperative (Part 1 of 6). CTS

2	1. Install a scan tool. 2. Turn the ignition ON, with the engine OFF. 3. Turn the cruise control On/Off switch Off. 4. With the scan tool, observe the following cruise control parameters in the TAC Data list: o Cruise On/Off Switch o Cruise Resume/Accel Switch o Cruise Set/Coast Switch Do all of the parameters listed above display Off?	Go to Step 3	Go to Step 10
3	1. With the scan tool, observe the Cruise On/Off Switch parameter. 2. Turn the cruise On/Off switch On. Does the Cruise On/Off Switch parameter display On?	Go to Step 4	Go to Step 11
4	1. With the scan tool, observe the Cruise Set/Coast Switch parameter. 2. press the "-" switch. Does the Cruise Set/Coast Switch parameter display On?	Go to Step 5	Go to Step 31
5	1. With the scan tool, observe the Cruise Resume/Accel Switch parameter. 2. press the "+" switch. Does the Cruise Resume/Accel Switch parameter display On?	Go to Step 6	Go to Step 31
6	With the scan tool, observe the Extended Travel Brake Switch parameter in the TAC Data list. Does the Extended Travel Brake Switch parameter display Applied?	Go to Step 15	Go to Step 7
7	1. With the scan tool, observe the Extended Travel Brake Switch parameter. 2. Depress the brake pedal. Does the Extended Travel Brake Switch parameter display Applied?	Go to Step 8	Go to Step 14

GC1100200850020X

Fig. 40 Cruise Control Inoperative (Part 2 of 6). CTS

8	With the scan tool, observe the Cruise Release Brake Pedal Switch parameter in the TAC Data list. Does the Cruise Release Brake Pedal Switch parameter display Applied?	Go to Step 18	Go to Step 9
9	1. With the scan tool, observe the Cruise Release Brake Pedal Switch parameter. 2. Press the brake pedal. Does the Cruise Release Brake Pedal Switch parameter display Applied?	Go to Diagnostic Aids	Go to Step 17
10	1. Turn the ignition OFF. 2. Disconnect the cruise switch. 3. Turn the ignition ON, with the engine OFF. 4. Observe the Cruise On/Off Switch parameter in the TAC Data list. Does the Cruise On/Off Switch parameter display Off?	Go to Step 26	Go to Step 20
11	1. Turn the ignition OFF. 2. Disconnect cruise switch. 3. Turn the ignition ON, with the engine OFF. 4. Connect a test lamp between the ignition positive voltage circuit and a good ground. Does the test lamp illuminate?	Go to Step 12	Go to Step 30
12	Connect a test lamp between the ignition positive voltage circuit and the ground circuit of the cruise switch. Does the test lamp illuminate?	Go to Step 13	Go to Step 29
13	1. Connect a 3 ampere fused jumper between the ignition positive voltage circuit and the cruise control switch signal circuit. 2. With the scan tool, observe the Cruise On/Off Switch parameter. Does the Cruise On/Off Switch parameter display On?	Go to Step 26	Go to Step 21
14	1. Turn the ignition OFF. 2. Disconnect the TCC/cruise control release switch. 3. Turn the ignition ON, with the engine OFF. 4. With the scan tool, observe the Extended Travel Brake Switch parameter. Does the Extended Travel Brake Switch parameter display Applied?	Go to Step 27	Go to Step 22

GC1100200850030X

Fig. 40 Cruise Control Inoperative (Part 3 of 6). CTS

15	1. Turn the ignition OFF. 2. Disconnect the TCC/cruise control release switch. 3. Connect a 3 ampere fused jumper between the ignition positive voltage circuit and the extended travel brake switch signal circuit. 4. Turn the ignition ON, with the engine OFF. 5. With the scan tool, observe the Extended Travel Brake Switch parameter. Does the Extended Travel Brake Switch parameter display Applied?	Go to Step 16	Go to Step 27
16	1. Connect a 3 ampere fused jumper between the extended travel brake switch signal circuit and battery voltage. 2. With the scan tool, observe the Extended Travel Brake Switch parameter. Does the Extended Travel Brake Switch parameter display Applied?	Go to Step 23	Go to Step 30
17	1. Turn the ignition OFF. 2. Disconnect the TCC/cruise control release switch. 3. Turn the ignition ON, with the engine OFF. 4. With the scan tool, observe the Cruise Release Brake Pedal Switch parameter. Does the Cruise Release Brake Pedal Switch parameter display Applied?	Go to Step 27	Go to Step 24
18	1. Turn the ignition OFF. 2. Disconnect the TCC/cruise control release switch. 3. Turn the ignition ON, with the engine OFF. 4. Connect a 3 ampere fused jumper between the ignition positive voltage circuit and the TCC brake switch/cruise control release switch signal circuit. 5. With the scan tool, observe the Cruise Release Brake Pedal Switch parameter. Does the Cruise Release Brake Pedal Switch parameter display Applied?	Go to Step 19	Go to Step 27
19	1. Connect a 3 ampere fused jumper between the TCC brake switch/cruise control release switch signal circuit and battery voltage. 2. With the scan tool, observe the Cruise Release Brake Pedal Switch parameter. Does the Cruise Release Brake Pedal Switch parameter display Applied?	Go to Step 25	Go to Step 30

GC1100200850040X

Fig. 40 Cruise Control Inoperative (Part 4 of 6). CTS

20	Test the cruise control switch signal circuit for a short to voltage. Did you find and correct the condition?	Go to Step 34	Go to Step 28
21	Test the cruise control switch signal circuit for an open, for a short to ground, or for a high resistance. Did you find and correct the condition?	Go to Step 34	Go to Step 28
22	Test the extended travel brake switch signal circuit for a short to voltage. Did you find and correct the condition?	Go to Step 34	Go to Step 28
23	Test the extended travel brake switch signal circuit for an open, for a short to ground, or for a high resistance. Did you find and correct the condition?	Go to Step 34	Go to Step 28
24	Test the cruise release brake pedal switch signal circuit for a short to voltage. Did you find and correct the condition?	Go to Step 34	Go to Step 28
25	Test the cruise release brake pedal switch signal circuit for an open, for a short to ground, or high resistance. Did you find and correct the condition?	Go to Step 34	Go to Step 27
26	Inspect for poor connections at the harness connector of the cruise control switch. Did you find and correct the condition?	Go to Step 34	Go to Step 31
27	Inspect for poor connections at the harness connector of the stoplamp switch. Did you find and correct the condition?	Go to Step 34	Go to Step 32

GC1100200850050X

Fig. 40 Cruise Control Inoperative (Part 5 of 6). CTS

28	Inspect for poor connections at the harness connector of the ECM. Did you find and correct the condition?	Go to Step 34	Go to Step 33
29	Repair the open or the high resistance in the ground circuit of the cruise switch. Did you complete the repair?	Go to Step 34	--
30	Repair the open, the short to ground, or the high resistance in the ignition 1 voltage circuit. Did you complete the repair?	Go to Step 34	--
31	Replace the cruise control switch. Did you complete the replacement?	Go to Step 34	--
32	Replace the TCC/cruise control release switch. Did you complete the replacement?	Go to Step 34	--
33	**Important** Program the replacement ECM. Replace the ECM. Did you complete the replacement?	Go to Step 34	--
34	1. Enable the inflatable restraint steering wheel module. 2. Operate the vehicle with in the conditions for cruise control operation. Does the cruise control system operate properly?	System OK	Go to Step 2

GC1100200850060X

Fig. 40 Cruise Control Inoperative (Part 6 of 6). CTS

Step	Action	Value (s)	Yes	No
5	1. Turn ON the ignition, with the engine OFF. 2. Turn ON the cruise control switch. 3. Probe the cruise control on signal circuit with a test lamp that is connected to a good ground. Does the test lamp illuminate?	--	Go to Step 6	Go to Step 19
6	1. Probe the cruise control set/coast signal circuit with a test lamp that is connected to a good ground. 2. Press and hold the SET/COAST switch. Does the test lamp illuminate?	--	Go to Step 7	Go to Step 21
7	1. Probe the cruise control resume/accelerate signal circuit with a test lamp that is connected to a good ground. 2. Press and hold the RESUME/ACCEL switch. Does the test lamp illuminate?	--	Go to Step 8	Go to Step 22
8	Probe the cruise control release signal circuit with a test lamp that is connected to a good ground. Does the test lamp illuminate?	--	Go to Step 13	Go to Step 9
9	Is the vehicle equipped with a manual transmission?	--	Go to Step 10	Go to Step 11
10	1. Turn OFF the ignition. 2. Disconnect the clutch pedal position (CPP) switch. 3. Turn ON the ignition, with the engine OFF. 4. Probe the CPP harness connector ignition positive voltage circuit with a test lamp connected to a good ground. Does the test lamp illuminate?	--	Go to Step 25	Go to Step 11
11	1. Turn OFF the ignition. 2. Disconnect the TCC/Brake switch. 3. Turn ON the ignition, with the engine OFF. 4. Probe the TCC/Brake switch harness connector ignition positive voltage circuit with a test lamp connected to a good ground. Does the test lamp illuminate?	--	Go to Step 23	Go to Step 31
12	Press the brake pedal while monitoring the test lamp. Does the test lamp illuminate?	--	Go to Step 26	Go to Step 13
13	Probe the stop lamp switch signal circuit with a test lamp that is connected to a good ground. Does the test lamp illuminate?	--	Go to Step 27	Go to Step 14
14	Press the brake pedal while monitoring the test lamp. Does the test lamp illuminate?	--	Go to Step 15	Go to Step 25

GC0140100097020X

Fig. 41 Cruise Control Inoperative (Part 2 of 6). Cavalier & Sunfire

Diagnostic Aids

Important

Perform the following in order to avoid misdiagnosis.

- Inspect for proper operation of brake lamps and clutch switch, if equipped.
- Inspect throttle linkage for mechanical binding which could cause the system to malfunction.
- Inspect cruise control cable adjustment, should have minimum slack.
- EMI on the speed sensor signal circuit may cause erratic cruise control operation.

Conditions for Enabling Cruise Control

The vehicle speed is greater than 40 km/h (25 mph).

Step	Action	Value (s)	Yes	No
1	Did you perform the Cruise Control Diagnostic System Check?	--	Go to Step 2	Go to Diagnostic System Check - Cruise Control
2	1. Turn OFF the ignition. 2. Disconnect the cruise control module. 3. Turn ON the ignition, with the engine OFF. 4. Probe the ignition positive voltage circuit of the cruise control module with a test lamp that is connected to a good ground. Does the test lamp illuminate?	--	Go to Step 3	Go to Step 38
3	Probe the ignition positive voltage circuit of the cruise control module with a test lamp that is connected to the ground circuit of the cruise control module. Does the test lamp illuminate?	--	Go to Step 4	Go to Step 39
4	1. Turn ON the ignition, with the engine OFF. 2. Turn OFF the cruise control switch. 3. Probe the cruise control on, set/coast, and the resume/accelerate signal circuits with a test lamp that is connected to a good ground. Does the test lamp illuminate on any of the circuits?	--	Go to Step 18	Go to Step 5

GC0140100097010X

Fig. 41 Cruise Control Inoperative (Part 1 of 6). Cavalier & Sunfire

Step	Action	Value (s)	Yes	No
15	Probe the cruise control engaged signal circuit with a test lamp that is connected to a good ground. Does the test lamp illuminate?	--	Go to Step 16	Go to Step 29
16	1. Connect a scan tool. 2. Probe the cruise inhibit signal circuit with a test lamp that is connected to B+. 3. Using a scan tool, command the cruise control inhibit OFF. Does the test lamp illuminate?	--	Go to Step 17	Go to Step 30
17	Check the speedometer for proper operation. Does the speedometer operate properly?	--	Go to Step 32	Check Instrument Panel, Gauges and Consoles
18	Test the circuit that illuminated the test lamp for a short to voltage. Did you find and correct the condition?	--	Go to Step 46	Go to Step 36
19	Test the cruise control on signal circuit for an open or a high resistance and the cruise control set/coast, resume accel signal circuits for a short to ground. Did you find and correct the condition?	--	Go to Step 46	Go to Step 20
20	Test the ignition positive voltage circuit of the cruise control switch for an open or high resistance. Did you find and correct the condition?	--	Go to Step 46	Go to Step 36
21	Test the cruise control set/coast signal circuit for an open or a high resistance. Did you find and correct the condition?	--	Go to Step 46	Go to Step 36
22	Test the cruise control resume/accelerate signal circuit for an open or a high resistance. Did you find and correct the condition?	--	Go to Step 46	Go to Step 36
23	Check the TCC/Brake switch for proper adjustment. Did you find and correct the condition?	--	Go to Step 46	Go to Step 25

GC0140100097030X

Fig. 41 Cruise Control Inoperative (Part 3 of 6). Cavalier & Sunfire

Step	Action	Value (s)	Yes	No
24	Check the stop lamp switch for proper adjustment. Did you find and correct the condition?	--	Go to Step 46	Go to Step 28
25	Test the TCC Brake switch signal circuit for an open or a high resistance. Did you find and correct the condition?	--	Go to Step 46	Go to Step 33
26	Test the TCC Brake switch signal circuit for a short to voltage. Did you find and correct the condition?	--	Go to Step 46	Go to Step 33
27	Test the stop lamp switch signal circuit for a short to voltage. Did you find and correct the condition?	--	Go to Step 46	Go to Step 34
28	Test the stop lamp switch signal circuit for an open or a high resistance. Did you find and correct the condition?	--	Go to Step 46	Go to Step 34
29	Test the cruise control engaged signal circuit for an open, a high resistance, or a short to voltage. Did you find and correct the condition?	--	Go to Step 46	Go to Step 35
30	Test the cruise inhibit signal circuit for an open, a high resistance, or a short to voltage. Did you find and correct the condition?	--	Go to Step 46	Go to Step 35
31	Test the ignition positive voltage circuit of the TCC/Brake switch for a open, a high resistance. Did you find and correct the condition?	--	Go to Step 46	Go to Step 33
32	Test the speed sensor circuit for an open or a high resistance between the PCM and cruise control module. Did you find and correct the condition?	--	Go to Step 46	Go to Step 37

GC0140100097040X

Fig. 41 Cruise Control Inoperative (Part 4 of 6). Cavalier & Sunfire

Step	Action	Value (s)	Yes	No
33	Inspect for poor connections at the harness connector of the appropriate switch. Refer to Intermittents. Did you find and correct the condition?	--	Go to Step 46	Go to Step 41
34	Inspect for poor connections at the harness connector of the stop lamp switch. Refer to Intermittents. Did you find and correct the condition?	--	Go to Step 46	Go to Step 42
35	Inspect for poor connections at the harness connector of the PCM. Refer to Intermittents. Did you find and correct the condition?	--	Go to Step 46	Go to Step 43
36	Inspect for poor connections at the harness connector of the cruise control switch. Refer to Intermittents. Did you find and correct the condition?	--	Go to Step 46	Go to Step 44
37	Inspect for poor connections at the harness connector of the cruise control module. Refer to Intermittents. Did you find and correct the condition?	--	Go to Step 46	Go to Step 45
38	Repair the ignition positive voltage circuit of the cruise control module. Did you complete the repair?	--	Go to Step 46	--
39	Repair the ground circuit of the cruise control module. Did you complete the repair?	--	Go to Step 46	--
40	Repair the ignition positive voltage circuit of the TCC/Brake switch harness connector. Did you complete the repair?	--	Go to Step 46	--
41	Replace the appropriate switch. Did you complete the replacement?	--	Go to Step 46	--

GC0140100097050X

Fig. 41 Cruise Control Inoperative (Part 5 of 6). Cavalier & Sunfire

Step	Action	Value (s)	Yes	No
42	Replace the stop lamp switch. Did you complete the replacement?	--	Go to Step 46	--
43	**Important** The PCM must be reprogrammed after replacement. Replace the PCM. Did you complete the replacement?	--	Go to Step 46	--
44	Replace the cruise control switch. Did you complete the replacement?	--	Go to Step 46	--
45	Replace the cruise control module. Did you complete the replacement?	--	Go to Step 46	--
46	Operate the vehicle within the conditions for cruise control operation. Does the cruise control system operate correctly?	--	System OK	Go to Step 2

GC0140100097060X

Fig. 41 Cruise Control Inoperative (Part 6 of 6). Cavalier & Sunfire

Diagnostic Aids

To avoid misdiagnosis, inspect for the following:

- Proper operation of the brake lamps.
- The throttle linkage is not binding.
- The cruise control cable is adjusted properly.
- The cruise control release switch is adjusted properly.

EMI on the vehicle speed sensor signal circuit may cause erratic cruise control operation.

Conditions for Enabling Cruise Control

- The vehicle speed is greater than 40 km/h (25 mph)
- The vehicle is not in PARK, REVERSE, NEUTRAL, or 1st gear.
- The system voltage is within 9 volts and 16 volts.

Step	Action	Value (s)	Yes	No
1	Did you perform the Cruise Control Diagnostic System Check?	--	Go to Step 2	Go to Check - Cruise Control
2	1. Raise the vehicles drive wheels. 2. Start the engine. 3. Place the transmission into drive. 4. Observe the speedometer in the IPC. Does the speedometer operate properly?	--	Go to Step 3	Check Instrument Panel Gauges and Console
3	1. Turn the ignition OFF. 2. Disconnect the cruise control module. 3. Turn the ignition ON, with the engine OFF. 4. Connect a test lamp between the ground circuit of the cruise control module and to battery voltage. Does the test lamp illuminate?	--	Go to Step 4	Go to Step 27

GC0140100106010X

Fig. 42 Cruise Control Inoperative (Part 1 of 5). Impala & Monte Carlo

Step	Action	Value (s)	Yes	No
4	1. Turn the cruise control on/off switch OFF. 2. Connect a test lamp between a good ground and each of the following circuits: o The cruise control on switch signal circuit. o The cruise control set/coast switch signal circuit. o The cruise control resume/accel switch signal circuit. Does the test lamp illuminate for any of the signal circuits listed above?	--	Go to Step 12	Go to Step 5
5	1. Turn the cruise control on/off switch ON. 2. Connect a test lamp between the cruise control on switch signal circuit and a good ground. Does the test lamp illuminate?	--	Go to Step 6	Go to Step 13
6	1. Connect a test lamp between the cruise control set/coast switch signal circuit and a good ground. 2. Press the SET/COAST switch. Does the test lamp illuminate?	--	Go to Step 7	Go to Step 15
7	1. Connect a test lamp between the cruise control resume/accel switch signal circuit and a good ground. 2. Press the RESUME/ACCEL switch. Does the test lamp illuminate?	--	Go to Step 8	Go to Step 16
8	Connect a test lamp between the cruise control release signal circuit and a good ground. Does the test lamp illuminate?	--	Go to Step 9	Go to Step 17
9	Apply the brake pedal. Does the test lamp remain illuminated?	--	Go to Step 19	Go to Step 10
10	Connect a test lamp between the cruise control engaged signal circuit at the cruise control module and a good ground. Does the test lamp illuminate?	--	Go to Step 11	Go to Step 21
11	Do the stop lamps operate properly?	--	Go to Step 20	Check Lighting Systems
12	Test the suspected signal circuit for a short to voltage. Did you find and correct the condition?	--	Go to Step 32	Go to Step 25

GC0140100106020X

Fig. 42 Cruise Control Inoperative (Part 2 of 5). Impala & Monte Carlo

Step	Action	Value (s)	Yes	No
13	Test the cruise control on switch signal circuit for an open or for a high resistance. Did you find and correct the condition?	--	Go to Step 32	Go to Step 14
14	Test the ignition 3 voltage circuit of the cruise control on/off switch for an open, for a short to ground, or for a high resistance. Did you find and correct the condition?	--	Go to Step 32	Go to Step 25
15	Test the cruise control set/coast switch signal circuit for an open or for a high resistance. Did you find and correct the condition?	--	Go to Step 32	Go to Step 25
16	Test the cruise control resume/accel switch signal circuit for an open or for a high resistance. Did you find and correct the condition?	--	Go to Step 32	Go to Step 25
17	Test the cruise control release switch signal circuit for an open, for a short to ground, or for a high resistance. Did you find and correct the condition?	--	Go to Step 32	Go to Step 18
18	Test the ignition 3 voltage circuit of the cruise control release switch for an open, for a short to ground, or for high resistance. Did you find and correct the condition?	--	Go to Step 32	Go to Step 23
19	Test the cruise control release switch signal circuit for a short to voltage. Did you find and correct the condition?	--	Go to Step 32	Go to Step 23
20	Test the stop lamp switch signal circuit for an open, for a high resistance, or for a short to voltage between the left IP junction block and the cruise control module. Did you find and correct the condition?	--	Go to Step 32	Go to Step 22
21	Test the cruise control engaged signal circuit for an open, for a high resistance, or for a short to ground. Did you find and correct the condition?	--	Go to Step 32	Go to Step 24

GC0140100106030X

Fig. 42 Cruise Control Inoperative (Part 3 of 5). Impala & Monte Carlo

Step	Action	Value (s)	Yes	No
22	Test the vehicle speed signal circuit for an open or for a high resistance between the cruise control module and S217. Did you find and correct the condition?	--	Go to Step 32	Go to Step 26
23	Inspect for poor connections at the harness connector of the cruise control release switch. Refer to Intermittents Did you find and correct the condition?	--	Go to Step 32	Go to Step 28
24	Inspect for poor connections at the harness connector of the PCM. Refer to Intermittents Did you find and correct the condition?	--	Go to Step 32	Go to Step 29
25	Inspect for poor connections at the harness connector of the turn signal/multifunction lever (Monte Carlo) or of the steering wheel controls (Impala). Refer to Intermittents Did you find and correct the condition?	--	Go to Step 32	Go to Step 30
26	Inspect for poor connections at the harness connector of the cruise control module. Refer to Intermittents Did you find and correct the condition?	--	Go to Step 32	Go to Step 31
27	Repair the open in the ground circuit of the cruise control module. Did you complete the repair?	--	Go to Step 32	--
28	Replace the cruise control release switch. Did you complete the replacement and the adjustment?	--	Go to Step 32	--
29	**Important** Program the replacement PCM. Replace the PCM. Did you complete the replacement?	--	Go to Step 32	--

GC0140100106040X

Fig. 42 Cruise Control Inoperative (Part 4 of 5). Impala & Monte Carlo

Step	Action	Value (s)	Yes	No
30	Replace the turn signal/multifunction switch lever or the steering wheel controls. Did you complete the replacement?	--	Go to Step 32	--
31	Replace the cruise control module. Did you complete the replacement?	--	Go to Step 32	--
32	Operate the vehicle within the conditions for cruise control operation. Does the cruise control system operate correctly?	--	System OK	Go to Step 2

GC0140100106050X

Fig. 42 Cruise Control Inoperative (Part 5 of 5). Impala & Monte Carlo

Important

To avoid misdiagnosis:

- Inspect for proper operation of the brake lamps.
- Inspect throttle linkage for mechanical binding which could cause the system to malfunction.
- Inspect cruise control adjustment, should have minimum slack.
- Inspect for stored Diagnostic Trouble Codes DTCs in the PCM.
- EMI on the speed sensor signal circuit may cause erratic cruise control operation.

Conditions for Enabling Cruise Control

- When vehicle speed is more than 40 km/h (25 mph).
- When PARK, REVERSE, NEUTRAL, or 1st gear IS NOT indicated.
- When an over/undercharged battery condition DOES NOT exist.
- With normal engine RPM.
- Without high engine RPM (fuel cut-off).

Step	Action	Value (s)	Yes	No
1	Did you perform the Cruise Control Diagnostic System Check?	--	Go to Step 2	Go to System Check
2	1. Turn OFF the ignition. 2. Disconnect the cruise control module. 3. Turn ON the ignition, with the engine OFF. 4. Probe the ignition positive voltage circuit of the cruise control module with a test lamp that is connected to a good ground. Does the test lamp illuminate?	--	Go to Step 3	Go to Step 39
3	Probe the ignition positive voltage circuit of the cruise control module with a test lamp that is connected to the ground circuit of the cruise control module. Does the test lamp illuminate?	--	Go to Step 4	Go to Step 40
4	1. Turn ON the ignition, with the engine OFF. 2. Turn OFF the cruise control. 3. Probe the cruise control on/off, set/coast, resume/accel and the release signal circuits with a test lamp that is connected to a good ground. Does the test lamp illuminate on any of the circuits?	--	Go to Step 17	Go to Step 5

GC0140100107010X

Fig. 43 Cruise Control Inoperative (Part 1 of 6). Intrigue

Step	Action	Value (s)	Yes	No
5	1. Turn ON the ignition, with the engine OFF. 2. Turn ON the cruise control switch. 3. Probe the cruise control module harness connector cruise control ON signal circuit with a test lamp that is connected to a good ground. Does the test lamp illuminate?	--	Go to Step 6	Go to Step 18
6	1. Probe the cruise control set/coast signal circuit with a test lamp that is connected to a good ground. 2. Press and hold the SET/COAST switch. Does the test lamp illuminate?	--	Go to Step 7	Go to Step 20
7	1. Probe the cruise control resume/accel signal circuit with a test lamp that is connected to a good ground. 2. Press and hold the RESUME/ACCEL switch. Does the test lamp illuminate?	--	Go to Step 8	Go to Step 21
8	Probe the cruise control release signal circuit with a test lamp that is connected to a good ground. Does the test lamp illuminate?	--	Go to Step 10	Go to Step 9
9	1. Turn OFF the ignition. 2. Disconnect the TCC/Brake, cruise control release switch. 3. Turn ON the ignition, with the engine OFF. 4. Probe the TCC/Brake, cruise control release ignition positive voltage circuit with a test lamp connected to a good ground. Does the test lamp illuminate?	--	Go to Step 31	Go to Step 24
10	Press the brake pedal while monitoring the test lamp. Does the test lamp illuminate?	--	Go to Step 23	Go to Step 11
11	Probe the stoplamp switch signal circuit with a test lamp that is connected to a good ground. Does the test lamp illuminate?	--	Go to Step 25	Go to Step 12
12	Press the brake pedal while monitoring the test lamp. Does the test lamp illuminate?	--	Go to Step 13	Go to Step 26
13	Probe the cruise inhibit signal circuit with a test lamp that is connected to battery positive. Does the test lamp illuminate?	--	Go to Step 27	Go to Step 14
14	Use a scan tool in order to command the cruise disable ON. Does the test lamp illuminate?	--	Go to Step 15	Go to Step 28

GC0140100107020X

Fig. 43 Cruise Control Inoperative (Part 2 of 6). Intrigue

Step	Action	Value (s)	Yes	No
15	Probe the cruise engaged output signal circuit with a DMM that is connected to a good ground. Does the voltage measure near the specified value?	B+	Go to Step 16	Go to Step 29
16	Check the speedometer for proper operation. Does the speedometer operate properly?	--	Go to Step 30	Check Instrument Panel, Gauges and Console
17	Test the signal circuit that illuminated the test lamp for a short to voltage. Did you find and correct the condition?	--	Go to Step 46	Go to Step 36
18	Test the on/off signal circuit for a open, high resistance or short to ground and the cruise control set/coast, resume/accel and cruise release signal circuits for a short to ground. Did you find and correct the condition?	--	Go to Step 46	Go to Step 19
19	Test the ignition positive voltage circuit of the cruise control switch for an open, high resistance or short to ground. Did you find and correct the condition?	--	Go to Step 46	Go to Step 36
20	Test the set/coast signal circuit for a open, high resistance or short to ground. Did you find and correct the condition?	--	Go to Step 46	Go to Step 36
21	Test the resume/accel circuit for a open, high resistance or short to ground. Did you find and correct the condition?	--	Go to Step 46	Go to Step 36
22	Test the cruise control release signal circuit for a open, high resistance or short to ground. Did you find and correct the condition?	--	Go to Step 46	Go to Step 31
23	Test the cruise control release signal circuit for a short to voltage. Did you find and correct the condition?	--	Go to Step 46	Go to Step 31

GC0140100107030X

Fig. 43 Cruise Control Inoperative (Part 3 of 6). Intrigue

Step	Action	Value (s)	Yes	No
24	Test the cruise control release signal circuit between the cruise release switch and the steering wheel switch for a open, high resistance or short to ground. Did you find and correct the condition?	--	Go to Step 46	Go to Step 36
25	Test the stoplamp switch signal circuit for a short to voltage. Did you find and correct the condition?	--	Go to Step 46	Go to Step 32
26	Test the stoplamp switch signal circuit for a open, high resistance or short to ground. Did you find and correct the condition?	--	Go to Step 46	Go to Step 32
27	Test the cruise inhibit signal circuit for a short to ground. Did you find and correct the condition?	--	Go to Step 46	Go to Step 35
28	Test the cruise inhibit signal circuit for a open, high resistance, or a short to voltage. Did you find and correct the condition?	--	Go to Step 46	Go to Step 35
29	Test the cruise engaged output signal circuit for a open, high resistance, or a short to ground. Did you find and correct the condition?	--	Go to Step 46	Go to Step 35
30	Test the VSS signal circuit for an open or a high resistance between the cruise control module and the PCM. Did you find and correct the condition?	--	Go to Step 46	Go to Step 35
31	Inspect the TCC/Brake switch for proper adjustment. Did you find and correct the condition?	--	Go to Step 46	Go to Step 33
32	Inspect the stoplamp/automatic transmission shift lock control switch for proper adjustment. Did you find and correct the condition?	--	Go to Step 46	Go to Step 34

GC0140100107040X

Fig. 43 Cruise Control Inoperative (Part 4 of 6). Intrigue

Step	Action	Value (s)	Yes	No
33	Inspect for poor connections at the harness connector of the TCC/Brake switch. Refer to Intermittents Did you find and correct the condition?	--	Go to Step 46	Go to Step 41
34	Inspect for poor connections at the harness connector of the stoplamp/automatic transmission shift lock control switch. Refer to Intermittents Did you find and correct the condition?	--	Go to Step 46	Go to Step 42
35	Inspect for poor connections at the harness connector of the PCM. Refer to Intermittents Did you find and correct the condition?	--	Go to Step 46	Go to Step 43
36	Inspect for poor connections at the harness connector of the cruise control switch . Refer to Intermittents Did you find and correct the condition?	--	Go to Step 46	Go to Step 44
37	Inspect for poor connections at the harness connector of the cruise control module. Refer to Intermittents Did you find and correct the condition?	--	Go to Step 46	Go to Step 45
38	Repair the ignition positive voltage circuit if the TCC/Brake switch. Did you complete the repair?	--	Go to Step 46	--
39	Repair the ignition positive voltage circuit of the cruise control module. Did you complete the repair?	--	Go to Step 46	--
40	Repair the ground circuit of the cruise control module. Did you complete the repair?	--	Go to Step 46	--
41	Replace the TCC/Brake (cruise release) switch. Did you complete the replacement?	--	Go to Step 46	--

GC0140100107050X

Fig. 43 Cruise Control Inoperative (Part 5 of 6). Intrigue

Important

To avoid misdiagnosis:

- Inspect for proper operation of the brake lamps.
- Inspect throttle linkage for mechanical binding which could cause the system to malfunction.
- Inspect cruise control adjustment, should have minimum slack.
- Inspect for stored Diagnostic Trouble Codes DTCs in the PCM. Refer to Powertrain OBD System check in engine controls.
- EMI on the speed sensor signal circuit may cause erratic cruise control operation.

Conditions for Enabling Cruise Control

- When vehicle speed is more than 40 km/h (25 mph)
- When PARK, REVERSE, NEUTRAL, or 1st gear IS NOT indicated by the Park / Neutral Position Switch.
- When an over / undercharged battery condition DOES NOT exist.
- With normal engine RPM.
- Without high engine RPM (fuel cut-off). Refer to Powertrain Control Module Description in Engine Controls for additional information.

Step	Action	Value (s)	Yes	No
1	Did you perform the Cruise Control Diagnostic System Check?	--	Go to Step 2	Go to System Check
2	1. Turn OFF the ignition. 2. Disconnect the cruise control module. 3. Turn ON the ignition, with the engine OFF. 4. Probe the ignition 1 voltage circuit of the cruise control module with a test lamp that is connected to a good ground. Does the test lamp illuminate?	--	Go to Step 3	Go to Step 40
3	Probe the ignition 1 voltage circuit of the cruise control module with a test lamp that is connected to the ground circuit of the cruise control module. Does the test lamp illuminate?	--	Go to Step 4	Go to Step 41

GC0140100123010X

Fig. 44 Cruise Control Inoperative (Part 1 of 6). Seville

Step	Action	Value (s)	Yes	No
42	Replace the stoplamp/automatic transmission shift lock control switch. Did you complete the replacement?	--	Go to Step 46	--
43	**Important** The powertrain control module must be reprogrammed before replacement. Replace the PCM. Did you complete the replacement?	--	Go to Step 46	--
44	Replace the cruise control switch . Did you complete the replacement?	--	Go to Step 46	--
45	Replace the cruise control module. Did you complete the replacement?	--	Go to Step 46	--
46	Operate the vehicle within the conditions for cruise control operation. Does the cruise control system operate correctly?	--	System OK	Go to Step 2

GC0140100107060X

Fig. 43 Cruise Control Inoperative (Part 6 of 6). Intrigue

Step	Action	Value (s)	Yes	No
4	1. Turn ON the ignition, with the engine OFF. 2. Turn OFF the cruise control. 3. Probe the on/off, the set/coast, and the resume/accel signal circuits with a test lamp that is connected to a good ground. Does the test lamp illuminate on any of the circuits?	--	Go to Step 18	Go to Step 5
5	1. Turn ON the ignition, with the engine OFF. 2. Turn ON the cruise control. 3. Probe the on/off signal circuit with a test lamp that is connected to a good ground. Does the test lamp illuminate?	--	Go to Step 6	Go to Step 19
6	1. Probe the set/coast signal circuit with a test lamp that is connected to a good ground. 2. Press and hold the SET/COAST switch. Does the test lamp illuminate?	--	Go to Step 7	Go to Step 21
7	1. Probe the resume/accel signal circuit with a test lamp that is connected to a good ground. 2. Press and hold the RESUME/ACCEL switch. Does the test lamp illuminate?	--	Go to Step 8	Go to Step 22
8	Probe the ABS/TCC (cruise release) switch signal circuit with a test lamp that is connected to a good ground. Does the test lamp illuminate?	--	Go to Step 9	Go to Step 23
9	1. Turn OFF the ignition. 2. Disconnect the cruise control switch harness connector. 3. Turn ON the ignition, with the engine OFF. 4. Probe the ABS/TCC switch signal circuit with a test lamp connected to a good ground. Does the test lamp illuminate?	--	Go to Step 37	Go to Step 10
10	1. Turn OFF the ignition. 2. Disconnect the ABS/TCC switch. 3. Turn ON the ignition, with the engine OFF. 4. Probe the ABS/TCC ignition positive voltage circuit with a test lamp connected to a good ground. Does the test lamp illuminate?	--	Go to Step 32	Go to Step 39
11	Press the brake pedal while monitoring the test lamp. Does the test lamp illuminate?	--	Go to Step 24	Go to Step 12
12	Probe the stoplamp switch signal circuit with a test lamp that is connected to a good ground. Does the test lamp illuminate?	--	Go to Step 25	Go to Step 13

GC0140100123020X

Fig. 44 Cruise Control Inoperative (Part 2 of 6). Seville

Step	Action	Value (s)	Yes	No
13	Press the brake pedal while monitoring the test lamp. Does the test lamp illuminate?	--	Go to Step 14	Go to Step 26
14	Probe the cruise inhibit signal circuit with a test lamp that is connected to B+. Does the test lamp illuminate?	--	Go to Step 28	Go to Step 15
15	Use a scan tool in order to command the cruise disable ON. Does the test lamp illuminate?	--	Go to Step 16	Go to Step 29
16	Probe the cruise engaged output signal circuit with a DMM that is connected to a good ground. Does the voltage measure near the specified value?	B+	Go to Step 17	Go to Step 30
17	Check the speedometer for proper operation. Does the speedometer operate properly?	--	Go to Step 31	Check Instrument Cluster
18	Test the signal circuit that illuminated the test lamp for a short to voltage. Did you find and correct the condition?	--	Go to Step 47	Go to Step 37
19	Test the on/off signal circuit for a open, high resistance or short to ground and the ABS/TCC switch ignition positive voltage circuits for a short to ground. Did you find and correct the condition?	--	Go to Step 47	Go to Step 20
20	Test the ignition 1 voltage circuit of the cruise control switch for an open, high resistance or short to ground. Did you find and correct the condition?	--	Go to Step 47	Go to Step 37
21	Test the set/coast signal circuit for a open, high resistance or short to ground. Did you find and correct the condition?	--	Go to Step 47	Go to Step 37
22	Test the resume/accel circuit for a open, high resistance or short to ground. Did you find and correct the condition?	--	Go to Step 47	Go to Step 37
23	Test the ABS/TCC (cruise release) switch signal circuit for a open, high resistance or short to ground. Did you find and correct the condition?	--	Go to Step 47	Go to Step 32

GC0140100123030X

Fig. 44 Cruise Control Inoperative (Part 3 of 6). Seville

Step	Action	Value (s)	Yes	No
24	Test the ABS/TCC (cruise release) signal circuit for a short to voltage. Did you find and correct the condition?	--	Go to Step 47	Go to Step 32
25	Test the stoplamp switch signal circuit for a short to voltage. Did you find and correct the condition?	--	Go to Step 47	Go to Step 33
26	Test the stoplamp switch signal circuit for a open, high resistance or short to ground. Did you find and correct the condition?	--	Go to Step 47	Go to Step 33
27	Test the stop lamp/ auto trans shift lock control switch positive battery voltage circuit for a open, high resistance or short to ground. Did you find and correct the condition?	--	Go to Step 47	Go to Step 33
28	Test the cruise inhibit signal circuit for a short to ground. Did you find and correct the condition?	--	Go to Step 47	Go to Step 36
29	Test the cruise inhibit signal circuit for a open, high resistance, or a short to voltage. Did you find and correct the condition?	--	Go to Step 47	Go to Step 36
30	Test the cruise engaged output signal circuit for a open, high resistance, or a short to voltage. Did you find and correct the condition?	--	Go to Step 47	Go to Step 36
31	Test the VSS signal circuit for an open or a high resistance between the cruise control module and the PCM. Did you find and correct the condition?	--	Go to Step 47	Go to Step 36
32	Inspect the ABS/TCC switch for proper adjustment. Did you find and correct the condition?	--	Go to Step 47	Go to Step 34
33	Inspect the stoplamp/automatic transmission shift lock control switch for proper adjustment. Did you find and correct the condition?	--	Go to Step 47	Go to Step 35

GC0140100123040X

Fig. 44 Cruise Control Inoperative (Part 4 of 6). Seville

Step	Action	Value (s)	Yes	No
34	Inspect for poor connections at the harness connector of the TCC brake switch. Refer to Intermittents Did you find and correct the condition?	--	Go to Step 47	Go to Step 42
35	Inspect for poor connections at the harness connector of the stoplamp/automatic transmission shift lock control switch. Refer to Intermittents Did you find and correct the condition?	--	Go to Step 47	Go to Step 43
36	Inspect for poor connections at the harness connector of the PCM. Refer to Intermittents Did you find and correct the condition?	--	Go to Step 47	Go to Step 44
37	Inspect for poor connections at the harness connector of the cruise control switch assembly. Refer to Intermittents Did you find and correct the condition?	--	Go to Step 47	Go to Step 45
38	Inspect for poor connections at the harness connector of the cruise control module. Refer to Intermittents Did you find and correct the condition?	--	Go to Step 47	Go to Step 46
39	Repair the ignition positive voltage circuit if the ABS/TCC switch. Did you complete the repair?	--	Go to Step 47	--
40	Repair the ignition 1 voltage circuit of the cruise control module. Did you complete the repair?	--	Go to Step 47	--
41	Repair the ground circuit of the cruise control module. Did you complete the repair?	--	Go to Step 47	--
42	Replace the ABS/TCC (cruise release) switch. Did you complete the replacement?	--	Go to Step 47	--
43	Replace the stoplamp/automatic transmission shift lock control switch. Did you complete the replacement?	--	Go to Step 47	--

GC0140100123050X

Fig. 44 Cruise Control Inoperative (Part 5 of 6). Seville

Step	Action	Value (s)	Yes	No
44	Replace the PCM. Did you complete the replacement?	--	Go to Step 47	--
45	Replace the cruise control switch assembly. Did you complete the replacement?	--	Go to Step 47	--
46	Replace the cruise control module. Did you complete the replacement?	--	Go to Step 47	--
47	Operate the vehicle within the conditions for cruise control operation. Does the cruise control system operate correctly?	--	System OK	Go to Step 2

GC0140100123060X

Fig. 44 Cruise Control Inoperative (Part 6 of 6). Seville

Step	Action	Value (s)	Yes	No
1	Did you perform A Diagnostic System Check- Instrument Cluster ?	--	Go to Step 2	Go to System Check
2	1. Install a scan tool. 2. Turn ON the ignition, with the engine OFF. 3. With a scan tool, observe the Cruise Lamp parameter in the IPC data list. Does the scan tool indicate that the cruise lamp is commanded On?	--	Go to Step 3	Go to Step 4
3	With a scan tool, observe the Cruise parameter in the PCM data list. Does the scan tool indicate that the cruise control is Engaged?	--	Refer to MOTOR's "Domestic Engine Performance & Driveability Manual"	Go to Step 4
4	Inspect for poor connections at the harness connector of the instrument cluster. Refer to Intermittents Did you find and correct the condition?	--	Go to Step 6	Go to Step 5
5	Replace the instrument panel cluster. Did you complete the replacement?	--	Go to Step 6	--
6	Operate the system in order to verify the repair. Did you correct the condition?	--	System OK	Go to Step 2

GC0140100057000X

Fig. 45 Cruise Indicator Always On. Alero, Bonneville, Grand Am, LeSabre & Park Avenue, Aurora & Malibu

Step	Action	Yes	No
8	**Important** The IPC must be reprogrammed when replaced. Replace the IPC. Did you complete the replacement?	Go to Step 10	--
9	**Important** The PCM must be reprogrammed after replacement. Replace the PCM. Did you complete the replacement?	Go to Step 10	--
10	Operate the vehicle within the conditions for cruise control operation. Did you correct the condition?	System OK	Go to Step 2

GC0140100088020X

Fig. 46 Cruise Indicator Always On (Part 2 of 2). Catera

Step	Action	Yes	No
1	Did you perform A Diagnostic System Check - Cruise Control?	Go to Step 2	Go to Check - Cruise Control
2	Operate the vehicle within the conditions for cruise control operation. Does the cruise control system operate correctly?	Go to Step 3	Go to Cruise Control Inoperative
3	Use a scan tool in order to command the cruise lamp OFF. Does the CRUISE indicator lamp in the IPC turn OFF ?	Refer to MOTOR's "Domestic Engine Performance & Driveability Manual"	Go to Step 4
4	1. Turn OFF the ignition. 2. Disconnect the appropriate PCM harness connector. 3. Turn ON the ignition, with the engine OFF. Is the CRUISE indicator lamp in the IPC OFF?	Go to Step 7	Go to Step 5
5	Test the cruise indicator lamp signal circuit for a short to ground. Did you find and correct the condition?	Go to Step 10	Go to Step 6
6	Inspect for poor connections at the harness connector of the IPC. Refer to Intermittents Did you find and correct the condition?	Go to Step 10	Go to Step 8
7	Inspect for poor connections at the harness connector of the PCM. Refer to Intermittents Did you find and correct the condition?	Go to Step 10	Go to Step 9

GC0140100088010X

Fig. 46 Cruise Indicator Always On (Part 1 of 2). Catera

Step	Action	Yes	No
1	Did you perform A Diagnostic System Check- Cruise Control?	Go to Step 2	Go to System Check
2	1. Install a scan tool. 2. Turn ON the ignition, with the engine OFF. 3. With a scan tool, observe the Cruise Lamp parameter in the IPC data list. Does the scan tool indicate that the cruise lamp is commanded On?	Go to Step 3	Go to Step 4
3	With a scan tool, observe the Cruise parameter in the PCM data list. Does the scan tool indicate that the cruise control is Engaged?	Go to Step 4	Go to Step 5
4	Test th cruise control engaged signal circuit for a short to ground Did you find and correct the condition?	Go to Step 9	Go to Step 6
5	Inspect for poor connections at the harness connector of the instrument cluster. Refer to Intermittents Did you find and correct the condition?	Go to Step 9	Go to Step 7
6	Inspect for poor connections at the harness connector of the PCM. Refer to Intermittents Did you find and correct the condition?	Go to Step 9	Go to Step 8
7	Replace the instrument panel cluster. Did you complete the replacement?	Go to Step 9	--

GC0140100108010X

Fig. 47 Cruise Indictor Always On (Part 1 of 2). Century, Grand Prix, Impala, Intrigue, Monte Carlo & Regal

Step	Action	Yes	No
8	**Important** The PCM must be reprogrammed befroe replacement. Replace the PCM. Did you complete the replacement?	Go to Step 9	--
9	Operate the system in order to verify the repair. Did you correct the condition?	System OK	Go to Step 2

GC0140100108020X

Fig. 47 Cruise Indictor Always On (Part 2 of 2). Century, Grand Prix, Impala, Intrigue, Monte Carlo & Regal

Step	Action	Value (s)	Yes	No
1	Did you perform the Cruise Control Diagnostic System Check?	--	Go to Step 2	Go to System Check
2	1. Turn OFF the ignition. 2. Turn ON the ignition, with the engine OFF. 3. Observe the CRUISE indicator on the instrument cluster (IPC) during the bulb check. Does the suspect indicator illuminate during the bulb check and then turn OFF?	--	Go to Intermittents	Go to Step 3
3	Replace the instrument cluster (IPC). Did you complete the repair?	--	Go to Step 4	--
4	Operate the system in order to verify the repair. Did you correct the condition?	--	System OK	Go to Step 2

GC0140100125000X

Fig. 49 Cruise Indicator Always On. Seville

Step	Action	Value (s)	Yes	No
1	Did you perform the Cruise Control Diagnostic System Check?	--	Go to Step 2	Go to System Check
2	Operate the vehicle within the conditions for cruise control operation. Does the cruise control system operate correctly?	--	Go to Step 3	Go to Cruise Control Inoperative
3	Use a scan tool in order to command the cruise lamp ON/OFF. Does the cruise lamp respond correctly to each command?	--	Refer to MOTOR's "Domestic Engine Performance & Driveability Manual"	Go to Step 4
4	Replace the Instrument Panel Cluster. Did you complete the replacement?	--	System OK	Go to Step 5
5	Operate the system in order to verify the repair. Did you correct the condition?	--	System OK	Go to System Check

GC0140100058000X

Fig. 50 Cruise Indicator Inoperative. 2000 Alero & Grand Am, Impala & Monte Carlo & 2002–04 Century & Regal

Step	Action	Value (s)	Yes	No
1	Did you perform the Cruise Control Diagnostic System Check?	--	Go to Step 2	Go to System Check
2	1. Turn OFF the ignition. 2. Turn ON the ignition, with the engine OFF. 3. Observe the CRUISE indicator on the instrument cluster (IPC) during the bulb check. Does the suspect indicator illuminate during the bulb check and then turn OFF?	--	Go to Intermittent	Go to Step 3
3	Replace the instrument cluster (IPC). Did you complete the repair?	--	Go to Step 4	--
4	Operate the system in order to verify the repair. Did you correct the condition?	--	System OK	Go to Step 2

GC0140100115000X

Fig. 48 Cruise Indicator Always On. DeVille & Eldorado

Step	Action	Yes	No
1	Did you perform A Diagnostic System Check-Cruise Control?	Go to Step 2	Go to System Check
2	Turn ON the ignition, with the engine OFF. Does the cruise indicator illuminate during bulb check?	Go to Step 3	Go to Step 6
3	1. Install a scan tool. 2. Operate the vehicle within the parameters for enabling the cruise control, and set the cruise control. 3. Observe the Cruise Lamp parameter in the IPC data list. Does the scan tool indicate that the cruise lamp is commanded On?	Go to Step 5	Go to Step 4
4	Inspect for poor connections at the harness connector of the PCM. Refer to Intermittents Did you find and correct the condition?	Go to Step 7	Refer to MOTOR's "Domestic Engine Performance & Driveability Manual"
5	Inspect for poor connections at the harness connector of the IPC. Refer to Intermittents Did you find and correct the condition?	Go to Step 7	Go to Step 6
6	Replace the instrument panel cluster. Did you complete the repair?	Go to Step 7	--
7	Operate the system in order to verify the repair. Did you correct the condition?	System OK	Go to Step 2

GC0140100062000X

Fig. 51 Cruise Indicator Inoperative. Aurora, Malibu 2001–04 Alero & Grand Am

Step	Action	Yes	No
1	Did you perform A Diagnostic System Check - Cruise Control?	Go to Step 2	Go to Diagnostic System Check - Cruise Control
2	Turn ON the ignition, with the engine OFF. Does the cruise indicator illuminate during bulb check?	Go to Step 3	Go to Step 6
3	1. Install a scan tool. 2. Operate the vehicle and set the cruise control. 3. Observe the cruise lamp parameter in the IPC data list. Does the scan tool indicate that the cruise lamp is commanded On?	Go to Step 5	Go to Step 4
4	Inspect for poor connections at the harness connector of the PCM. Refer to Testing for Intermittents Did you find and correct the condition?	Go to Step 8	Refer to MOTOR's "Domestic Engine Performance & Driveability Manual"
5	Inspect for poor connections at the harness connector of the IPC. Refer to Testing for Intermittents Did you find and correct the condition?	Go to Step 8	Go to Step 7
6	Inspect for a faulty cruise indicator bulb. Did you find and correct the condition?	Go to Step 8	Go to Step 7
7	Replace the Instrument Panel Cluster. Did you complete the repair?	Go to Step 8	--
8	Operate the system in order to verify the repair. Did you correct the condition?	System OK	Go to Step 2

GC0140100068000X

Fig. 52 Cruise Indicator Inoperative. Bonneville, LeSabre & Park Avenue

Step	Action	Yes	No
1	Did you perform A Diagnostic System Check - Cruise Control?	Go to Step 2	Go to Check - Cruise Control
2	Operate the vehicle within the conditions for cruise control operation. Does the cruise control system operate correctly?	Go to Step 3	Go to Cruise Control Inoperative/Malfunctioning
3	Use a scan tool in order to command the cruise lamp ON. Does the cruise lamp in the IPC illuminate?	Refer to MOTOR's "Domestic Engine Performance & Driveability Manual"	Go to Step 4
4	1. Turn OFF the ignition. 2. Disconnect the appropriate PCM harness connector. 3. Turn ON the ignition, with the engine OFF. 4. Connect a 3 amp fused jumper wire between the cruise indicator lamp signal circuit and a good ground. Does the CRUISE indicator in the IPC illuminate?	Go to Step 10	Go to Step 5
5	Did the 3 amp fuse in the jumper wire open?	Go to Step 8	Go to Step 6
6	Test the cruise indicator lamp signal circuit for a open or a high resistance. Did you find and correct the condition?	Go to Step 13	Go to Step 7
7	Test the CRUISE lamp bulb in the IPC for a open or poor connection. Did you find and correct the condition?	Go to Step 13	Go to Step 9

GC0140100089010X

Fig. 53 Cruise Indicator Inoperative (Part 1 of 2). Catera

Step	Action	Yes	No
8	Test the cruise indicator lamp signal circuit for a short to voltage. Did you find and correct the condition?	Go to Step 13	Go to Step 9
9	Inspect for poor connections at the harness connector of the IPC. Refer to Testing for Intermittents Did you find and correct the condition?	Go to Step 13	Go to Step 11
10	Inspect for poor connections at the harness connector of the PCM. Refer to Testing for Intermittents Did you find and correct the condition?	Go to Step 13	Go to Step 12
11	**Important** The IPC must be reprogrammed when replaced. Replace the IPC. Did you complete the replacement?	Go to Step 13	--
12	**Important** The PCM must be reprogrammed after replacement. Replace the PCM. Did you complete the replacement?	Go to Step 13	--
13	Operate the vehicle within the conditions for cruise control operation. Did you correct the condition?	System OK	Go to Step 2

GC0140100089020X

Fig. 53 Cruise Indicator Inoperative (Part 2 of 2). Catera

Step	Action	Value (s)	Yes	No
1	Did you perform the Cruise Control Diagnostic System Check?	--	Go to Step 2	Go to Check Cruise Control
2	Operate the vehicle within the conditions for cruise control operation. Does the cruise control system operate correctly?	--	Go to Step 3	Go to Cruise Control Inoperative
3	Use a scan tool in order to command the cruise lamp ON/OFF. Does the cruise lamp respond correctly to each command?	--	Refer to MOTOR's "Domestic Engine Performance & Driveability Manual"	Go to Step 4
4	Replace the Instrument Panel Cluster. Did you complete the replacement?	--	Go to Step 2	--

GC0140100105000X

Fig. 54 Cruise Indicator Inoperative. 2000–01 Century, Intrigue & Regal

Step	Action	Value (s)	Yes	No
DEFINITION: The cruise control system operates properly, but the CRUISE Indicator does not illuminate during cruise control operation.				
1	Did you perform the Cruise Control Diagnostic System Check?	--	Go to Step 2	Go to System Check
2	1. Install a scan tool. 2. Start the engine. 3. Carefully drive the vehicle at a speed greater than 40 km/h (25 mph). 4. Engage the cruise control. 5. With a scan tool, observe the Cruise Requested parameter in the powertrain control module (PCM) data list. Does the scan tool display Yes?	--	Go to Step 3	Go to Step 4
3	1. Turn OFF the ignition. 2. Turn ON the ignition, with the engine OFF. 3. Observe the CRUISE indicator on the instrument cluster (IPC) during the bulb check. Does the CRUISE indicator illuminate during the bulb check?	--	Go to Intermittents	Go to Step 9
4	1. Turn OFF the ignition. 2. Disconnect the cruise control module. 3. Connect a 3 amp fused jumper between the cruise engaged signal circuit and a good ground. 4. Carefully drive the vehicle at a speed greater than 40 km/h (25 mph). 5. With a scan tool, observe the Cruise Requested parameter in the powertrain control module (PCM) data list. Does the scan tool display Yes?	--	Go to Step 7	Go to Step 5

GC0140100116010X

Fig. 55 Cruise Indicator Inoperative (Part 1 of 2). DeVille & Eldorado

Step	Action	Value (s)	Yes	No
5	Test the cruise engaged signal circuit for a open, high resistance or short to voltage. Did you find and correct the condition?	--	Go to Step 11	Go to Step 6
6	Inspect for poor connections at the harness connector of the powertrain control module (PCM). Did you find and correct the condition?	--	Go to Step 11	Go to Step 8
7	Inspect for poor connections at the harness connector of the cruise control module. Refer to Intermittents Did you find and correct the condition?	--	Go to Step 11	Go to Step 10
8	Replace the PCM. Did you complete the replacement?	--	Go to Step 11	--
9	Replace the instrument cluster (IPC). Did you complete the replacement?	--	Go to Step 11	--
10	Replace the cruise control module. Did you complete the replacement?	--	Go to Step 11	--
11	Operate the system in order to verify the repair. Did you correct the condition?	--	System OK	Go to Step 2

GC0140100116020X

Fig. 55 Cruise Indicator Inoperative (Part 2 of 2). DeVille & Eldorado

Step	Action	Value (s)	Yes	No
DEFINITION: The cruise control system operates properly, but the CRUISE Indicator does not illuminate during cruise control operation.				
1	Did you perform the Cruise Control Diagnostic System Check?	--	Go to Step 2	Go to System Check
2	1. Install a scan tool. 2. Start the engine. 3. Carefully drive the vehicle at a speed greater than 40 km/h (25 MPH). 4. Engage the cruise control. 5. With a scan tool, observe the Cruise Requested parameter in the powertrain control module (PCM) data list. Does the scan tool display Yes?	--	Go to Step 3	Go to Step 4
3	1. Turn OFF the ignition. 2. Turn ON the ignition, with the engine OFF. 3. Observe the CRUISE indicator on the instrument cluster (IPC) during the bulb check. Does the CRUISE indicator illuminate during the bulb check?	--	Go to Intermittents	Go to Step 9
4	1. Turn OFF the ignition. 2. Disconnect the cruise control module. 3. Connect a 3 amp fused jumper between the cruise engaged signal circuit and a good ground. 4. Carefully drive the vehicle at a speed greater than 40 km/h (25 MPH). 5. With a scan tool, observe the Cruise Requested parameter in the powertrain control module (PCM) data list. Does the scan tool display Yes?	--	Go to Step 7	Go to Step 5

GC0140100124010X

Fig. 56 Cruise Indicator Inoperative (Part 1 of 2). Seville

Step	Action	Value (s)	Yes	No
5	Test the cruise engaged signal circuit for a open, high resistance or short to voltage. Did you find and correct the condition?	--	Go to Step 11	Go to Step 6
6	Inspect for poor connections at the harness connector of the powertrain control module (PCM). Refer to Intermittents Did you find and correct the condition?	--	Go to Step 11	Go to Step 8
7	Inspect for poor connections at the harness connector of the cruise control module. Refer to Intermittents Did you find and correct the condition?	--	Go to Step 11	Go to Step 10
8	Replace the PCM. Did you complete the replacement?	--	Go to Step 11	--
9	Replace the instrument cluster (IPC). Did you complete the replacement?	--	Go to Step 11	--
10	Replace the cruise control module. Did you complete the replacement?	--	Go to Step 11	--
11	Operate the system in order to verify the repair. Did you correct the condition?	--	System OK	Go to Step 2

GC0140100124020X

Fig. 56 Cruise Indicator Inoperative (Part 2 of 2). Seville

Circuit Description

The cruise control switch release is used to disable the cruise control whenever the brake is applied. The switch gets its power from the ignition circuit at the stoplamp switch. The engine control module (ECM) monitors the B+ voltage for the cruise control and stoplamp switch circuits.

Conditions for Setting the DTC

The cruise release signal does not match the stoplamp signal at least 20 times.

Conditions for Running

Ignition is ON.

Action Taken When the DTC Sets

The ECM will not illuminate the malfunction indicator lamp (MIL).

Conditions for Clearing the DTC

- The diagnostic trouble code (DTC) clears after forty consecutive warm-up cycles in which there are no failures reported by this diagnostic or any other non-emission related diagnostic.
- The scan tool clears the DTC.

Diagnostic Aids

Use the J 35616-A connector test adapter kit for any test that requires probing the ECM harness connector or a component harness connector.

Check for the following conditions:

- Poor connections at the ECM or at the component--Inspect the harness connectors for a poor terminal to wire connection. Refer to Intermittents.
- Damaged harness--Inspect the wiring harness for damage. If the harness appears to be OK, observe the scan tool while moving the related connectors and the wiring harnesses. A change in the display may help locate the fault.

Refer to Intermittents.

Step	Action	Values	Yes	No
1	Did you perform the Powertrain On-Board Diagnostic (OBD) System Check?	--	Go to Step 2	Refer to MOTOR's "Domestic Engine Performance & Driveability Manual"

GC0140100090010X

Fig. 57 Code P0571: Cruise Control Brake Switch Circuit (Part 1 of 4). 2000 Catera

Step	Action	Values	Yes	No
2	1. Turn ON the ignition. 2. Monitor the Cruise Release Brake Switch and the Stoplamp Brake Switch Input displays on the scan tool. 3. Depress and release the brake pedal several times while observing the scan tool displays. Do both displays indicate the state of the brake pedal correctly?	--	Go to Diagnostic Aids	Go to Step 3
3	Is the Cruise Release Brake Switch display incorrect?	--	Go to Step 4	Go to Step 8
4	Does the Cruise Release Brake Switch display always indicate Applied?	--	Go to Step 5	Go to Step 7
5	1. Disconnect the cruise control release switch. 2. With an unpowered test lamp connected to ground, probe the cruise control release switch power feed circuit pin 1. Does the test lamp illuminate?	--	Go to Step 6	Go to Step 13
6	1. Jumper the cruise control release switch terminals together using a fused jumper. 2. Monitor the Cruise Release Brake Switch display on the scan tool. Does the display indicate the state of the brake pedal as Released?	--	Go to Step 15	Go to Step 12
7	1. Disconnect the cruise control release switch. 2. Monitor the Cruise Release Brake Switch display on the scan tool. Does the display indicate the state of the brake pedal as Applied?	--	Go to Step 15	Go to Step 14
8	Observe the exterior brake lights while depressing and releasing the brake pedal. Do the exterior brake lights operate normally?	--	Go to Step 12	Go to Step 9
9	1. Disconnect the stoplamp switch. 2. Observe the exterior brake lights with the stoplamp switch disconnected. Are the exterior brake lights illuminated?	--	Go to Step 14	Go to Step 10
10	With an unpowered test lamp connected to ground, probe the stoplamp switch power feed circuit pin 1. Does the test lamp illuminate?	--	Go to Step 11	Go to Step 13
11	1. Jumper the stoplamp switch terminals 1 and 2 together using a fused jumper. 2. Monitor the stoplamp brake switch display on the scan tool. Does the display indicate the state of the brake pedal as Applied?	--	Go to Step 16	Go to Step 12

GC0140100090020X

Fig. 57 Code P0571: Cruise Control Brake Switch Circuit (Part 2 of 4). 2000 Catera

Step	Action	Values	Yes	No
12	1. Turn OFF the ignition. 2. Disconnect the ECM. 3. Using the DMM, check the signal circuit for continuity between the switch and the ECM. The DMM should indicate very low resistance. 4. Inspect for proper terminal contact at the ECM connector. 5. Repair the wiring or connection as necessary. Was a problem found and repaired?	--	Go to Step 18	Go to Step 17
13	1. Inspect for an open fuse. If an open fuse is indicated, repair the cause of the short. 2. Inspect for proper voltage to the fuse. 3. If a problem was not found in the previous inspections, use the DMM and check the switch power feed circuit for continuity between the switch and the fuse. The DMM should indicate very low resistance. 4. Repair the wiring as necessary. Is the action complete?	--	Go to Step 18	--
14	Repair the signal circuit shorted to B+. Is the action complete?	--	Go to Step 18	--
15	Replace the cruise control release switch. Is the action complete?	--	Go to Step 18	--
16	Replace the stoplamp switch. Is the action complete?	--	Go to Step 18	--
17	**Important** • Perform the Idle Learn Procedure when replacing the ECM or throttle body. • This vehicle is equipped with a theft deterrent module that interfaces with the engine control module (ECM). Program the new ECM with the frequency code of the theft deterrent module that is currently on the vehicle. Replace the ECM. Is the action complete?	--	Go to Step 18	--

GC0140100090030X

Fig. 57 Code P0571: Cruise Control Brake Switch Circuit (Part 3 of 4). 2000 Catera

Step	Action	Values	Yes	No
18	1. Use a scan tool in order to clear the DTCs. 2. Start the engine. 3. Allow the engine to idle until the engine reaches the normal operating temperature. 4. Select DTC and the Specific DTC function. 5. Enter the DTC number that was set. 6. Operate the engine within the Conditions for Setting this DTC until the scan tool indicates the diagnostic Ran. Does the scan tool indicate that the diagnostic Passed?	--	Go to Step 2	Go to Step 19
19	Does the scan tool display any additional undiagnosed DTCs?	--	Go to the applicable DTC table	System OK

GC0140100090040X

Fig. 57 Code P0571: Cruise Control Brake Switch Circuit (Part 4 of 4). 2000 Catera

Circuit Description

The cruise control release switch is a normally closed switch. When the cruise control release switch is closed, (brake pedal released) the PCM senses ignition voltage on the cruise control release switch signal circuit.

If the PCM senses a voltage on the cruise control release switch signal circuit when the cruise release switch should be open, this DTC sets.

Conditions for Running the DTC

- The engine speed is greater than 700 RPM.
- The engine operates for greater than 2 seconds.
- The wheel speed is greater than 48 km/h (30 mph) in order to enable the diagnostic. The diagnostic disables when the wheel speed is below 16 km/h (10 mph).

Conditions for Setting the DTC

- The PCM detects voltage on the cruise control release switch circuit when the cruise release switch should be open.
- All above conditions are present for 1.5 seconds.

Action Taken When the DTC Sets

- The PCM stores the DTC information into memory when the diagnostic runs and fails.
- The malfunction indicator lamp (MIL) will not illuminate.
- The PCM records the operating conditions at the time the diagnostic fails. The PCM stores this information in the Failure Records.

Conditions for Clearing the DTC

- A last test failed, or current DTC, clears when the diagnostic runs and does not fail.
- A history DTC will clear after 40 consecutive warm-up cycles, if no failures are reported by this or any other non-emission related diagnostic.
- Use a scan tool in order to clear the DTC.

Diagnostic Aids

Important

- Remove any debris from the PCM connector surfaces before servicing the PCM. Inspect the PCM connector gaskets when diagnosing/replacing the modules. Ensure that the gaskets are installed correctly. The gaskets prevent contaminate intrusion into the PCM.
- For any test that requires probing the PCM or a component harness connector, use the Connector Test Adapter Kit J 35616-A . Using this kit prevents damage to the harness/component terminals.

GC0140100091010X

Fig. 58 Code P0571: Cruise Control Brake Switch Circuit (Part 1 of 3). 2001 Catera

Step	Action	Yes	No
8	Replace the cruise control release switch. Did you complete the repair?	Go to Step 10	--
9	**Important** Program the replacement PCM. Replace the PCM. Is the action complete?	Go to Step 10	--
10	1. Use a scan tool in order to clear the DTCs. 2. Operate the vehicle within the Conditions for Running the DTC as specified in the supporting text. Does the DTC reset?	Go to Step 2	System OK

GC0140100091030X

Fig. 58 Code P0571: Cruise Control Brake Switch Circuit (Part 3 of 3). 2001 Catera

- Test drive the vehicle if a switch or circuit condition cannot be located. An intermittent condition may be duplicated during a test drive.
- For an intermittent, refer to Intermittents.

Test Description

The numbers below refer to the step numbers on the diagnostic table.

2. This step determines if the fault is present.

Step	Action	Yes	No
1	Did you perform A Diagnostic System Check - Cruise Control?	Go to Step 2	Refer to MOTOR's "Domestic Engine Performance & DriveabilityManual"
2	1. Connect a scan tool. 2. Turn ON the ignition, with the engine OFF. 3. Monitor the cruise control release switch parameter in the PCM data list. Does the brake switch parameter indicate Applied?	Go to Step 3	Go to Diagnostic Aids
3	1. Turn OFF the ignition. 2. Disconnect the cruise control release switch. 3. Turn ON the ignition, with the engine OFF. 4. Observe the cruise control release switch parameter in the PCM data list. Does the cruise control release switch parameter indicate Released?	Go to Step 5	Go to Step 4
4	Test the cruise control release switch signal circuit for a short to voltage. Did you find and correct the condition?	Go to Step 10	Go to Step 7
5	Inspect the cruise control release switch for proper adjustment. Did you find and correct the condition?	Go to Step 10	Go to Step 6
6	Inspect for poor connections at the harness connector of the cruise control release switch. Did you find and correct the condition?	Go to Step 10	Go to Step 8
7	Inspect for poor connections at the harness connector of the PCM. Refer to Intermittents. Did you find and correct the condition?	Go to Step 10	Go to Step 9

GC0140100091020X

Fig. 58 Code P0571: Cruise Control Brake Switch Circuit (Part 2 of 3). 2001 Catera

Circuit Description

The cruise control module uses the cruise engaged circuit to request cruise control. If any condition exists that would make cruise control operation undesirable, the PCM will disable cruise control through the cruise inhibit circuit.

Conditions for Running the DTC

- The cruise control is enabled.
- The cruise control is engaged.

Conditions for Setting the DTC

The PCM detects a vehicle speed greater than 176 km/h (110 mph) with the cruise control still engaged.

Action Taken When the DTC Sets

- The PCM disables the cruise control.
- The PCM will not illuminate the malfunction indicator lamp (MIL).
- The PCM will store the conditions which were present when the DTC set, as Fail Records data only.

Conditions for Clearing the DTC

- The History DTC will clear after 40 consecutive warm-up cycles have occurred without a malfunction.
- The DTC can be cleared by using the scan tool's Clear DTC Information function.

Diagnostic Aids

This diagnostic trouble code (DTC) is an information DTC only. The DTC indicates the reason that the PCM disabled the cruise control system. Be sure to verify the conditions that set the DTC with the customer.

Reviewing the Fail Records vehicle mileage since the diagnostic test last failed may assist in diagnosing the condition. The information may help determine how often the condition that set the DTC occurs.

Step	Action	Yes	No
1	Did you perform the Cruise Control Diagnostic System Check?	Go to Step 2	Go to Diagnostic System Check - Cruise Control

GC0140100069010X

Fig. 59 Code P0574: PCM Detects Speed More Than 110 mph (Part 1 of 2). Aurora, DeVille, Eldorado & Seville

Step	Action	Yes	No
2	Since most occurrences of DTC P0574 are caused by wheel spin due to icy, wet or slippery conditions, verify the conditions under which the DTC set with the customer. Did the road conditions cause this DTC to set?	Go to Step 3	Go to Diagnostic Aids
3	Explain system operation to the customer and clear the DTC. Is the action complete?	System OK	--

GC0140100069020X

Fig. 59 Code P0574: PCM Detects Speed More Than 110 mph (Part 2 of 2). Aurora, DeVille, Eldorado & Seville

Remove any debris from the connector surfaces before servicing a component. Inspect the connector gaskets when diagnosing or replacing a component. Ensure that the gaskets are installed correctly. The gaskets prevent contaminate intrusion.

- Loose terminal connection
  - Use a corresponding mating terminal to test for proper tension. Refer to Intermittents
  - Inspect the harness connectors for backed out terminals, improper mating, broken locks, improperly formed or damaged terminals, and faulty terminal to wire connection. Refer to Intermittents
- Damaged harness--Inspect the wiring harness for damage. If the harness inspection does not reveal a problem, observe the display on the scan tool while moving connectors and wiring harnesses related to the sensor. A change in the scan tool display may indicate the location of the fault.
- Inspect the powertrain control module (PCM) and the engine grounds for clean and secure connections.

If the condition is determined to be intermittent, reviewing the Snapshot or Freeze Frame/Failure Records may be useful in determining when the DTC or condition was identified.

Test Description

The numbers below refer to the step numbers on the diagnostic table:

7. This step ensures that the replacement PCM, which utilizes an electrically erasable programmable read only memory (EEPROM), is programmed when installed.

Step	Action	Values	Yes	No
1	Did you perform the Powertrain On Board (OBD) System Check?	--	Go to Step 2	Refer to MOTOR's "Domestic Performance & Driveability Manual"
2	Is DTC P1585 also set?	--	Go to DTC P1585 Cruise Control Inhibit Output Circuit	Go to Step 3
3	1. Turn OFF the ignition. 2. Disconnect the cruise control module. 3. Turn ON the ignition. 4. Using a DMM, measure voltage between the Cruise Engaged Input circuit at the cruise control module harness connector and ground. Is voltage more than the specified value?	7.0 V	Go to Step 4	Go to Step 5

GC0140100059020X

Fig. 60 Code P1554: Cruise Control Feedback Circuit (Part 2 of 3). Alero, Grand Am, Park Avenue, Malibu & 2000 Bonneville & LeSabre

Circuit Description

The stepper motor cruise control module sends the cruise status input to the powertrain control module (PCM) is to indicate when cruise control is engaged. The PCM monitors the cruise status signal while commanding cruise to be disengaged by grounding the cruise inhibit circuit. Any of the following conditions may cause the PCM to inhibit cruise control operation:

- Engine is not running long enough for cruise control operation
- Transaxle range inputs indicate park, neutral, low, or reverse gear selected
- Engine speed is too high or too low
- Vehicle speed is too high or too low
- TCS is active for longer than 2 seconds
- Vehicle acceleration or deceleration rate is too high

Conditions for Running the DTC

The PCM is commanding the cruise module to not allow cruise control operation, Cruise Inhibit circuit grounded.

Conditions for Setting the DTC

- The Cruise Status input to the PCM indicates that cruise control is still active.
- The conditions is present for longer than 1 second.

Action Taken When the DTC Sets

- The PCM will not illuminate the malfunction indicator lamp (MIL).
- The PCM will store conditions which were present when the DTC set as Failure Records only. This information will not be stored as Freeze Frame Records.

Conditions for Clearing the MIL/DTC

- A History DTC will clear after 40 consecutive warm-up cycles have occurred without a malfunction.
- The DTC can be cleared by using a scan tool.

Diagnostic Aids

Inspect for the following conditions:

Many situations may lead to an intermittent condition. Perform each inspection or test as directed.

Important:

GC0140100059010X

Fig. 60 Code P1554: Cruise Control Feedback Circuit (Part 1 of 3). Alero, Grand Am, Park Avenue, Malibu & 2000 Bonneville & LeSabre

Step	Action	Value	Yes	No
4	1. Turn OFF the ignition. 2. Reconnect the cruise control module. 3. Disconnect the PCM. 4. Turn ON the ignition. 5. Probe the Cruise Engaged Input circuit at the PCM harness connector with a test lamp to battery positive voltage. Does the test lamp illuminate?	--	Go to Step 6	Go to Step 7
5	1. Turn OFF the ignition. 2. Disconnect the PCM. 3. Probe the Cruise Engaged Input circuit at the PCM harness connector with a test lamp to battery positive voltage. Does the test illuminate?	--	Go to Step 8	Go to Step 7
6	Replace the cruise control module. Did you complete the replacement?	--	Go to Step 9	--
7	**Important** The replacement PCM must be programmed. Replace the PCM. Did you complete the replacement?	--	Go to Step 9	--
8	Locate and repair short to ground in the Cruise Engaged Input circuit. Did you complete the replacement?	--	Go to Step 9	--
9	1. Clear DTC P1554. 2. Start the engine and observe DTCs. Did DTC P1554 set?	--	Go to Step 2	System OK

GC0140100059030X

Fig. 60 Code P1554: Cruise Control Feedback Circuit (Part 3 of 3). Alero, Grand Am, Park Avenue, Malibu & 2000 Bonneville & LeSabre

Circuit Description

The PCM has the ability to inhibit cruise control operation if conditions exist that would make cruise operation undesirable. The following conditions may inhibit cruise control operation:

- The engine speed is too high or too low.
- The vehicle speed is too high or too low.
- The traction control has been active for longer than 1 second.
- The vehicle acceleration or deceleration rate is too high.

If any of these conditions are present, the PCM will remove the ground from the cruise inhibit circuit.

Conditions for Running the DTC

The PCM is commanding the cruise control module to inhibit cruise control operation.

Conditions for Setting the DTC

The PCM detects a cruise engaged signal from the cruise control module, while inhibiting cruise control operation.

Action Taken When the DTC Sets

- The PCM will not illuminate the malfunction indicator lamp (MIL).
- The PCM will store the conditions present when the DTC sets as Fail Records data only.

Conditions for Clearing the DTC

- The history DTC will clear after 40 consecutive warm-up cycles have occurred without a malfunction.
- The DTC can be cleared by using the scan tool's Clear DTC Information function.

Diagnostic Aids

If the conditions is intermittent, refer to Intermittents.

Test Description

The numbers below refer to the step numbers on the Diagnostic Table.

3. Tests the PCM's ability to correctly read the signal voltage.
5. Tests for a short on the cruise engaged signal circuit.
8. This vehicle is equipped with a PCM which utilizes an electrically erasable programmable read

GC0140100070010X

Fig. 61 Code P1554: PCM Detects Cruise Engaged While Inhibiting Cruise Control Operation (Part 1 of 2). Aurora, Bonneville, Cavalier, Century, DeVille, Eldorado, Grand Prix, Impala, Intrigue, LeSabre, Lumina, Monte Carlo, Regal, Seville & Sunfire

Circuit Description

The cruise control module uses the cruise engaged circuit to request cruise control. If any condition exists that would make cruise control operation undesirable, the PCM will disable cruise control through the cruise inhibit circuit.

Conditions for Running the DTC

- The cruise control is enabled.
- The cruise control is engaged.

Conditions for Setting the DTC

The shift lever is placed in neutral or the transaxle range switch indicates a neutral position with the cruise control engaged.

Action Taken When the DTC Sets

- The PCM disables the cruise control.
- The PCM will not illuminate the malfunction indicator lamp (MIL).
- The PCM will store conditions which were present when the DTC set as Fail Records data only.

Conditions for Clearing the DTC

- The History DTC will clear after 40 consecutive warm-up cycles without a malfunction.
- The DTC can be cleared by using the scan tool's Clear DTC Information function.

Diagnostic Aids

Shifting into neutral while cruise control is engaged will set this DTC.

This diagnostic trouble code (DTC) is an information DTC only. The DTC indicates the reason that the PCM disabled the cruise control system. Be sure to verify the conditions that set the DTC with the customer.

Reviewing the Fail Records vehicle mileage since the diagnostic test last failed may assist in diagnosing the condition. This information may help determine how often the condition that set the DTC occurred.

GC0140100071010X

Fig. 62 Code P1560: Transaxle Range Switch Indicates Neutral Position w/Cruise Control Engaged (Part 1 of 2). Aurora

only memory (EEPROM). When the PCM is replaced, the new PCM must be programmed.

Step	Action	Yes	No
1	Did you perform the Cruise Control Diagnostic System Check?	Go to Step 2	Go to System Check -
2	1. Install a scan tool. 2. Turn ON the ignition, with the engine OFF. 3. With a scan tool, monitor the DTC information for DTC P1585 in the powertrain control module (PCM). Is DTC P1585 also set?	Go to DTC P1585	Go to Step 3
3	With a scan tool, observe the Cruise Control Active display. Does the Cruise Control Active display indicate YES?	Go to Step 5	Go to Step 4
4	1. Review and record the scan tool Fail Records Information. 2. Operate the vehicle within the Fail Records conditions. 3. Using the scan tool, monitor the Specific DTC Information for DTC P1554 until the test runs. Does the scan tool indicate that DTC P1554 failed this ignition?	Go to Step 5	Go to Diagnostic Aids
5	1. Turn OFF the ignition. 2. Disconnect the cruise control module connector. 3. Turn ON the ignition switch, with the engine OFF. 4. Using the scan tool, observe the Cruise Control Active display. Does the Cruise Control Active display indicate YES?	Go to Step 6	Go to Step 7
6	1. Turn OFF the ignition. 2. Disconnect the appropriate PCM connector. 3. Test the cruise control engaged circuit for a short to ground. Did you find and correct the condition?	Go to Step 9	Go to Step 8
7	Replace the cruise control module. Did you complete the replacement?	Go to Step 9	--
8	**Important** The replacement PCM must be programmed. Replace the PCM. Did you complete the replacement?	Go to Step 9	--
9	1. Use the scan tool in order to clear the DTC(s). 2. Operate the vehicle within the conditions for Running the DTC as specified in the supporting text. Does the DTC reset?	Go to Step 2	System OK

GC0140100070020X

Fig. 61 Code P1554: PCM Detects Cruise Engaged While Inhibiting Cruise Control Operation (Part 2 of 2). Aurora, Bonneville, Cavalier, Century, DeVille, Eldorado, Grand Prix, Impala, Intrigue, LeSabre, Lumina, Monte Carlo, Regal, Seville & Sunfire

Step	Action	Yes	No
1	Did you perform the Cruise Control Diagnostic System Check ?	Go to Step 2	Go to System Check
2	Since this DTC will set when the vehicle is shifted into NEUTRAL or PARK while the cruise is engaged, verify the conditions under which the DTC set with the customer. Did the drivers actions cause this DTC to set?	Go to Step 3	Go to Diagnostic Aids
3	Explain system operation to the customer and clear this DTC. Is the action complete?	System OK	--

GC0140100071020X

Fig. 62 Code P1560: Transaxle Range Switch Indicates Neutral Position w/Cruise Control Engaged (Part 2 of 2). Aurora

Circuit Description

The cruise control module uses the cruise engaged circuit to request cruise control. If improper conditions are present, the PCM will disable cruise control via the cruise inhibit control circuit. During cruise control, if the shift lever is place in neutral, or the transaxle range indicates a neutral position, the PCM will inhibit the cruise control system, and set DTC P1560.

Conditions for Running the DTC

- The cruise control is enabled.
- The cruise control is engaged.

Conditions for Setting the DTC

The shift lever is placed in neutral or the transaxle range indicates a neutral position.

Action Taken When the DTC Sets

- The PCM disables cruise control.
- The PCM will not illuminate the Malfunction Indicator Lamp (MIL).
- The PCM will store conditions which were present when the DTC set as Fail Records data only.

Conditions for Clearing the DTC

- The History DTC will clear after 40 consecutive warm-up cycles without a malfunction.
- The DTC can be cleared by using the scan tool Clear DTC Information function.

Diagnostic Aids

Shifting into neutral while cruise control is engaged will set this DTC.

This diagnostic trouble code (DTC) is an information DTC only. The DTC indicates the reason that the PCM disabled the cruise control system. Be sure to check with the customer for the conditions that set the DTC.

Reviewing the Fail Records vehicle mileage since the diagnostic test last failed may assist in diagnosing the condition. The information may help determine how often the condition that set the DTC occurs.

GC0140100117010X

Fig. 63 Code P1560: Transaxle Range Switch Indicates Neutral Position w/Cruise Control Engaged (Part 1 of 2). DeVille, Eldorado & Seville

Circuit Description

The cruise control module uses the cruise engaged circuit to request cruise control. If improper conditions are present, the PCM will disable cruise control via the cruise inhibit control circuit. During cruise control, if a sudden rate of increase in vehicle speed occurs (i.e., vehicle speed sensing problem or traveling on icy roads), the PCM will inhibit the cruise control system, and set DTC P1564.

Conditions for Running the DTC

- The cruise control is enabled.
- The cruise control is engaged.

Conditions for Setting the DTC

The PCM detects an extremely rapid rate of vehicle acceleration.

Action Taken When the DTC Sets

- The PCM disables the cruise control.
- The PCM will not illuminate the malfunction indicator lamp (MIL).
- The PCM will store conditions which were present when the DTC set as Fail Records data only.

Conditions for Clearing the DTC

- The History DTC will clear after 40 consecutive warm-up cycles have occurred without a malfunction.
- The DTC can be cleared by using the scan tool Clear DTC Information function.

Diagnostic Aids

This diagnostic trouble code (DTC) is an information DTC only. The DTC indicates the reason that the PCM disabled the cruise control system. Be sure to check with the customer for the conditions that set the DTC.

Reviewing the Fail Records vehicle mileage since the diagnostic test last failed may assist in diagnosing the condition. The information may help determine how often the condition that set the DTC occurs.

GC0140100072010X

Fig. 64 Code P1564: PCM Detects Extremely Rapid Acceleration (Part 1 of 2). Aurora, DeVille, Eldorado & Seville

Step	Action	Yes	No
1	Did you perform A Diagnostic System Check - Cruise Control?	Go to Step 2	Go to System Check
2	Are any other DTCs also set?	Go to the other DTCs first	Go to Step 3
3	Since this DTC will set when the vehicle is shifted into NEUTRAL or PARK while the cruise is engaged, check with the customer to verify the conditions under which the DTC set. Did the drivers actions cause this DTC to set?	Go to Step 4	Go to Diagnostic Aids
4	Explain system operation to the customer and clear this DTC. Is the action complete?	System OK	--

GC0140100117020X

Fig. 63 Code P1560: Transaxle Range Switch Indicates Neutral Position w/Cruise Control Engaged (Part 2 of 2). DeVille, Eldorado & Seville

Step	Action	Yes	No
1	Did you perform A Diagnostic System Check - Cruise Control?	Go to Step 2	Go to System Check
2	Are any other DTCs also set?	Go to the other DTCs first	Go to Step 3
3	Since this DTC will set when a sudden rate of increase in vehicle speed occurs (i.e., vehicle speed sensing problem or traveling on icy roads) while the cruise is engaged, check with the customer to verify the conditions under which the DTC set. Did the drivers actions or road conditions cause this DTC to set?	Go to Step 4	Go to Diagnostic Aids
4	Explain system operation to the customer and clear this DTC. Is the action complete?	System OK	--

GC0140100072020X

Fig. 64 Code P1564: PCM Detects Extremely Rapid Acceleration (Part 2 of 2). Aurora, DeVille, Eldorado & Seville

Circuit Description

The cruise control module uses the cruise engaged circuit to request cruise control. If any condition exists that would make cruise control operation undesirable, the PCM will disable cruise control through the cruise inhibit control circuit.

Conditions for Running the DTC

- The cruise control is enabled.
- The cruise control is engaged.

Conditions for Setting the DTC

The PCM detects an engine speed greater than 6300 RPM with the cruise control still engaged.

Action Taken When the DTC Sets

- The PCM disables the cruise control.
- The PCM will not illuminate the malfunction indicator lamp (MIL).
- The PCM will store conditions which were present when the DTC set as Fail Records data only.

Conditions for Clearing the DTC

- The History DTC will clear after 40 consecutive warm-up cycles have occurred without a malfunction.
- The DTC can be cleared by using the scan tool's Clear DTC Information function.

Diagnostic Aids

This diagnostic trouble code (DTC) is an information DTC only. The DTC indicates the reason that the PCM disabled the cruise control system. Be sure to verify the conditions that set the DTC with the customer.

Reviewing the Fail Records vehicle mileage since the diagnostic test last failed may assist in diagnosing the condition. This information may help determine how often the condition that set the DTC occurred.

Step	Action	Yes	No
1	Did you perform the Cruise Control Diagnostic System Check ?	Go to Step 2	Go to System Check

GC0140100073010X

Fig. 65 Code P1566: Engine Speed More Than 6300 RPM w/Cruise Control Engaged (Part 1 of 2). Aurora

Step	Action	Yes	No
2	Since most occurrences of DTC P1566 are caused when the engine speed exceeds the maximum allowed RPM, verify the conditions under which the DTC set with the customer. Did an engine RPM condition cause this DTC to set?	Go to Step 3	Go to Diagnostic Aids
3	Explain system operation to the customer and clear this DTC. Is the action complete?	System OK	--

GC0140100073020X

Fig. 65 Code P1566: Engine Speed More Than 6300 RPM w/Cruise Control Engaged (Part 2 of 2). Aurora

Step	Action	Yes	No
2	Are any ABS/TCS DTCs set?	Check ABS/TCS DTCs first	Go to Step 3
3	Are any Transaxle DTCs set?	Check Transaxle DTCs first	Go to Step 4
4	Since most occurrences of DTC P1566 are caused when the engine speed exceeds the maximum allowed RPM. Check with the customer to verify the conditions under which the DTC set. Did an engine RPM condition cause this DTC to set?	Go to Step 5	Go to Diagnostic Aids
5	Explain system operation to the customer and clear this DTC. Is the action complete?	System OK	--

GC0140100118020X

Fig. 66 Code P1566: Engine Speed More Than 6300 RPM w/Cruise Control Engaged (Part 2 of 2). DeVille, Eldorado & Seville

Circuit Description

The cruise control module uses the cruise engaged circuit to request cruise control. If any condition exists that would make cruise control operation undesirable, the PCM will disable cruise control through the cruise inhibit circuit.

Conditions for Running the DTC

- The cruise control is enabled.
- The cruise control is engaged.

Conditions for Setting the DTC

The Active Braking Control system is applying the brakes with the cruise control still engaged.

Action Taken When the DTC Sets

- The PCM disables the cruise control.
- The PCM will not illuminate the malfunction indicator lamp (MIL).
- The PCM will store the conditions which were present when the DTC set as Fail Records data only.

Conditions for Clearing the DTC

- The History DTC will clear after 40 consecutive warm-up cycles have occurred without a malfunction.
- The DTC can be cleared by using the scan tool's Clear DTC Information function.

Diagnostic Aids

This diagnostic trouble code (DTC) is an information DTC only. The DTC indicates the reason that the PCM disabled the cruise control system. Be sure to verify the conditions that set the DTC with the customer.

Reviewing the Fail Records vehicle mileage since the diagnostic test last failed may assist in diagnosing the condition. This information may help determine how often the condition that set the DTC occurred.

Step	Action	Yes	No
1	Did you perform the Cruise Control Diagnostic System Check ?	Go to Step 2	Go to System Check -

GC0140100074010X

Fig. 67 Code P1567: Active Brake Control System Applied Brakes w/Cruise Control Engaged (Part 1 of 2). Aurora

Circuit Description

The cruise control module uses the cruise engaged circuit to request cruise control. If improper conditions are present, the PCM will disable cruise control via the cruise inhibit control circuit. During cruise control, if the engine speed exceeds the calibrated RPM, the PCM will inhibit the cruise control system, and set DTC P1566.

Conditions for Running the DTC

- The cruise control is enabled.
- The cruise control is engaged.

Conditions for Setting the DTC

The PCM detects an engine speed more than the 6300 RPM.

Action Taken When the DTC Sets

- The PCM disables cruise control.
- The PCM will not illuminate the malfunction indicator lamp (MIL).
- The PCM will store conditions which were present when the DTC set as Fail Records data only.

Conditions for Clearing the DTC

- The History DTC will clear after 40 consecutive warm-up cycles have occurred without a malfunction.
- The DTC can be cleared by using the scan tool Clear DTC Information function.

Diagnostic Aids

This diagnostic trouble code (DTC) is an information DTC only. The DTC indicates the reason that the PCM disabled the cruise control system. Be sure to check with the customer for the conditions that set the DTC.

Reviewing the Fail Records vehicle mileage since the diagnostic test last failed may assist in diagnosing the condition. The information may help determine how often the condition that set the DTC occurs.

Step	Action	Yes	No
1	Did you perform A Diagnostic System Check - Cruise Control?	Go to Step 2	Go to System Check -

GC0140100118010X

Fig. 66 Code P1566: Engine Speed More Than 6300 RPM w/Cruise Control Engaged (Part 1 of 2). DeVille, Eldorado & Seville

Step	Action	Yes	No
2	Since most occurrences of DTC P1567 are caused when the Active Braking Control engages while cruise control is active, verify the conditions under which the DTC set with the customer. Did the road conditions cause this DTC to set?	Go to Step 3	Go to Diagnostic Aids
3	Explain system operation to the customer and clear this DTC. Is the action complete?	System OK	--

GC0140100074020X

Fig. 67 Code P1567: Active Brake Control System Applied Brakes w/Cruise Control Engaged (Part 2 of 2). Aurora

Circuit Description

The cruise control module uses the cruise engaged circuit to request cruise control. If improper conditions are present, the PCM will disable cruise control via the cruise inhibit control circuit. During cruise control, if the Active Braking Control system applies the brakes, the PCM will inhibit the cruise control system, and set DTC P1567.

Conditions for Running the DTC

- The cruise control is enabled.
- The cruise control is engaged.

Conditions for Setting the DTC

The Active Braking Control system is applying the brakes.

Action Taken When the DTC Sets

- The PCM disables cruise control.
- The PCM will not illuminate the malfunction indicator lamp (MIL).
- The PCM will store conditions which were present when the DTC set as Fail Records data only.

Conditions for Clearing the DTC

- The History DTC will clear after 40 consecutive warm-up cycles have occurred without a malfunction.
- The DTC can be cleared by using the scan tool Clear DTC Information function.

Diagnostic Aids

This diagnostic trouble code (DTC) is an information DTC only. The DTC indicates the reason that the PCM disabled the cruise control system. Be sure to check with the customer for the conditions that set the DTC.

Reviewing the Fail Records vehicle mileage since the diagnostic test last failed may assist in diagnosing the condition. The information may help determine how often the condition that set the DTC occurs.

Step	Action	Yes	No
1	Did you perform A Diagnostic System Check - Cruise Control?	Go to Step 2	Go to System Check -
2	Are any ABS/TCS DTCs set?	Check ABS/TCS DTCs first	Go to Step 3

GC0140100119010X

Fig. 68 Code P1567: Active Brake Control System Applied Brakes w/Cruise Control Engaged (Part 1 of 2). DeVille, Eldorado & Seville

Step	Action	Yes	No
3	Since most occurrences of DTC P1567 are caused when the active braking control engages while cruise control is active. Check with the customer to verify the conditions under which the DTC set. Did the road conditions cause this DTC to set?	Go to Step 4	Go to Diagnostic Aids
4	Explain system operation to the customer and clear this DTC. Is the action complete?	System OK	--

GC0140100119020X

Fig. 68 Code P1567: Active Brake Control System Applied Brakes w/Cruise Control Engaged (Part 2 of 2). DeVille, Eldorado & Seville

Circuit Description

The cruise control module uses the cruise engaged circuit to request cruise control. If any condition exists that would make cruise control operation undesirable, the PCM will disable cruise control through the cruise inhibit circuit. During cruise control, if traction control is activated, the PCM will inhibit the cruise control system, and set DTC P1570.

Conditions for Running the DTC

- The cruise control is enabled.
- The cruise control is engaged.

Conditions for Setting the DTC

The traction control is active.

Action Taken When the DTC Sets

- The PCM disables the cruise control.
- The PCM will not illuminate the malfunction indicator lamp (MIL).
- The PCM will store the conditions which were present when the DTC set as Fail Records data only.

Conditions for Clearing the DTC

- The History DTC will clear after 40 consecutive warm-up cycles have occurred without a malfunction.
- The DTC can be cleared by using the scan tool's Clear DTC Information function.

Diagnostic Aids

This diagnostic trouble code (DTC) is an information DTC only. The DTC indicates the reason that the PCM disabled the cruise control system. Be sure to verify the conditions that set the DTC with the customer.

Reviewing the Fail Records vehicle mileage since the diagnostic test last failed may assist in diagnosing the condition. This information may help determine how often the condition that set the DTC occurred.

Step	Action	Yes	No
1	Did you perform the Cruise Control Diagnostic System Check ?	Go to Step 2	Go to System Check -

GC0140100075010X

Fig. 69 Code P1570: Traction Control Is Active (Part 1 of 2). Aurora

Step	Action	Yes	No
2	Since most occurrences of DTC P1570 are caused by conditions that causes traction control to activate during cruise control, verify the conditions under which the DTC set with the customer. Did the road conditions cause this DTC to set?	Go to Step 3	Go to Diagnostic Aids
3	Explain system operation to the customer and clear this DTC. Is the action complete?	System OK	--

GC0140100075020X

Fig. 69 Code P1570: Traction Control Is Active (Part 2 of 2). Aurora

The cruise control module uses the cruise engaged circuit to request cruise control. If improper conditions are present, the PCM will disable cruise control via the cruise inhibit control circuit. During cruise control, if the vehicle enters active traction control, the PCM will inhibit the cruise control system, and set DTC P1570.

Conditions for Running the DTC

- The cruise control is enabled.
- The cruise control is engaged.

Conditions for Setting the DTC

Traction control is active.

Action Taken When the DTC Sets

- The PCM disables cruise control.
- The PCM will not illuminate the malfunction indicator lamp (MIL).
- The PCM will store conditions which were present when the DTC set as Fail Records data only.

Conditions for Clearing the DTC

- The History DTC will clear after 40 consecutive warm-up cycles have occurred without a malfunction.
- The DTC can be cleared by using the scan tool Clear DTC Information function.

Diagnostic Aids

This diagnostic trouble code (DTC) is an information DTC only. The DTC indicates the reason that the PCM disabled the cruise control system. Be sure to check with the customer for the conditions that set the DTC.

Reviewing the Fail Records vehicle mileage since the diagnostic test last failed may assist in diagnosing the condition. The information may help determine how often the condition that set the DTC occurs.

Step	Action	Yes	No
1	Did you perform A Diagnostic System Check - Cruise Control?	Go to Step 2	Go to System Check
2	Are any ABS/TCS DTCs set?	Go to the ABS/TCS DTCs first	Go to Step 3

GC0140100120010X

Fig. 70 Code P1570: Traction Control Is Active (Part 1 of 2). DeVille, Eldorado & Seville

Step	Action	Yes	No
3	Since most occurrences of DTC P1570 are caused by conditions that causes traction control to activate during cruise control. Check with the customer to verify the conditions under which the DTC set. Did the road conditions cause this DTC to set?	Go to Step 4	Go to Diagnostic Aids
4	Explain system operation to the customer and clear this DTC. Is the action complete?	System OK	--

GC0140100120020X

Fig. 70 Code P1570: Traction Control Is Active (Part 2 of 2). DeVille, Eldorado & Seville

Step	Action	Yes	No
1	Did you perform the Cruise Control Diagnostic System Check?	Go to Step 2	Go to System Check
2	1. Connect the scan tool. 2. Turn ON the ignition, with the engine OFF. 3. Retrieve the DTCs from the EBCM. Are there any DTCs that begin with a "C" also set?	Go to Diagnostic Trouble Code (DTC) List	Go to Step 3
3	Repair the short to voltage on the stop lamp switch signal circuit. Did you find and correct the condition?	Go to Step 4	--
4	1. Use the scan tool to clear the DTC (s). 2. Operate the vehicle within the conditions for Running the DTC as specified in the supporting text. Does the DTC reset?	Go to Step 2	System OK

GC0140100076020X

Fig. 71 Code P1574: Sudden Decrease In Non-Drive Wheel Speed (Part 2 of 2). Aurora, DeVille, Eldorado & Seville

Circuit Description

This diagnostic test functions on the assumption that a brake application causes a sudden decrease in non-drive wheel speed.

The extended travel brake switch is a normally closed switch. When the extended travel brake switch is closed, the PCM senses ignition voltage on the extended travel brake switch signal circuit.

If the PCM senses voltage on the extended travel brake switch signal circuit when the extended travel brake switch should be open, DTC P1575 will set.

Conditions for Running the DTC

- The engine speed is more than 700 RPM.
- The engine has been operating more than 2 seconds.
- The wheel speed must be more than 30 mph in order to enable the diagnostic. The diagnostic will disable when the wheel speed is below 10 mph.
- The vehicle speed is decreasing at a rate more than 10.4 mph over a 1 second period.

Conditions for Setting the DTC

- The PCM detects voltage on the extended travel brake switch circuit when the extended travel brake switch should be open.
- The above conditions are present for 1.5 seconds.

Action Taken When the DTC Sets

- The PCM stores the DTC information into memory when the diagnostic runs and fails.
- The malfunction indicator lamp (MIL) will not illuminate.
- The PCM records the operating conditions at the time the diagnostic fails. The PCM stores this information in the Failure Records.

Conditions for Clearing the DTC

- A last test failed current DTC clears when the diagnostic runs and does not fail.
- A history DTC clears after 40 consecutive warm-up cycles, if this or any other emission related diagnostic does not report any failures.
- Use a scan tool in order to clear the DTC or disconnect the PCM battery feed.

Diagnostic Aids

Important

Remove any debris from the PCM connector surfaces before servicing the PCM. Inspect the PCM connector gaskets when diagnosing or replacing the modules. Ensure that the gaskets are installed correctly. The gaskets prevent contaminate intrusion into the PCM.

GC0140100077010X

Fig. 72 Code P1575: PCM Detects Voltage On Extended Travel Brake Switch Circuit (Part 1 of 3). Aurora, Bonneville, Century, DeVille, Eldorado, Intrigue, LeSabre, Regal & Seville

Circuit Description

This diagnostic test functions on the assumption that sudden decrease in a non-drive, wheel speed must be caused by a brake application. Non-drive wheel speed and stoplamp switch status are supplied to the PCM through serial data from the electronic brake control Module (EBCM). If there is a 4 km/h (2.5 mph) or greater decrease of non-drive wheel speed in 0.4 seconds and a transition of the TCC or extended travel contacts of the TCC brake switch without a transition of the stop lamp brake switch, DTC P1574 is set.

Conditions for Running the DTC

- DTCs P0502, P0503, P0719, P0724, P1575 and P1602 not set.
- Traction control and antilock brake systems have not failed.
- Traction control and antilock brake systems are not active.
- Non-drive wheel speed goes above 32 km/h (20 mph) and then does not go below 7 km/h (4 mph).

Conditions for Setting the DTC

A 4 km/h (2.5 mph) or greater decrease in non-drive wheel speed in 0.4 seconds and extended travel brake switch or TCC brake switch indicating brakes applied and no transition noticed in the stoplamp contacts of the stop lamp switch.

Action Taken When the DTC Sets

PCM will set the stop lamp switch status to not applied.

- The malfunction indicator lamp (MIL) will not illuminate.
- No message will be displayed.

Conditions for Clearing the DTC

- A History DTC will clear after forty consecutive warm-up cycles with no failures of any non-emission related diagnostic test.
- A Last Test Failed (current) DTC will clear when the diagnostic runs and does not fail.
- Use a scan tool to clear DTCs.
- Interrupting PCM battery voltage may or may not clear DTCs. This practice is not recommended.

Diagnostic Aids

DTC P1574 indicates the stoplamp switch signal to the EBCM or the EBCM's ability to send the stop lamp switch signal to the PCM has failed. Refer to ABS/TCS DTCs for diagnosis of the stop lamp switch signal and the EBCM.

GC0140100076010X

Fig. 71 Code P1574: Sudden Decrease In Non-Drive Wheel Speed (Part 1 of 2). Aurora, DeVille, Eldorado & Seville

In order to adjust the extended travel brake switch perform the following:

1. With the brake pedal pressed, insert the appropriate brake lamp switch into the retainer until the switch body seats in the retainer. You can hear clicks as you push the threaded portion of the switch through the retainer.
2. Slowly pull the brake pedal fully rearward against the stop until you can no longer hear the clicks.

Test Description

The numbers below refer to the step numbers on the diagnostic table.

2. This step determines if the fault is present.

4. This step checks for a Extended Travel Brake Switch circuit for being shorted to B+.

9. This DTC will not report a pass. The scan tool status for this DTC will never report a pass. The scan tool will only display when the diagnostic fails. The repair is not complete if the scan tool indicates that the diagnostic ran and failed.

Step	Action	Values	Yes	No
1	Did you perform A Diagnostic System Check-Cruise Control?	--	Go to Step 2	Go to System Check
2	1. Install a scan tool. 2. Start the engine. 3. Monitor the extended travel brake switch parameter in the PCM data list. 4. Press the brake pedal approximately half-way. Does the extended travel brake switch parameter indicate applied?	--	Go to Diagnostic Aids	Go to Step 3
3	Check for proper adjustment of the appropriate brake switch. Refer to Diagnostic Aids . Did you find and correct the condition?	--	Go to Step 9	Go to Step 4
4	1. Turn OFF the ignition. 2. Disconnect the appropriate brake switch. 3. Turn ON the ignition. 4. Monitor the extended travel brake switch parameter in the PCM data list. Does the extended travel brake switch parameter indicate applied?	--	Go to Step 7	Go to Step 5

GC0140100077020X

Fig. 72 Code P1575: PCM Detects Voltage On Extended Travel Brake Switch Circuit (Part 2 of 3). Aurora, Bonneville, Century, DeVille, Eldorado, Intrigue, LeSabre, Regal & Seville

5	1. Turn OFF the ignition. 2. Disconnect the PCM. 3. Turn ON the ignition, with the engine OFF. 4. Measure the voltage on the extended travel brake switch signal circuit using a DMM connected to a good ground. Does the voltage measure greater than the specified value?	0.5 V	Go to Step 6	Go to Step 8
6	Repair the short to voltage on the extended travel brake switch signal circuit. Did you complete the repair?	--	Go to Step 9	--
7	Replace the appropriate brake switch. Did you complete the replacement?	--	Go to Step 9	--
8	**Important** The replacement PCM must be programmed. Replace the PCM. Did you complete the repair?	--	Go to Step 9	--
9	1. Use the scan tool in order to clear the DTCs. 2. Turn OFF the ignition for 30 seconds. 3. Start the engine. 4. Operate the vehicle within the Conditions for Running the DTC as specified in the supporting text. Does the DTC run and pass?		System OK	Go to Step 2

GC0140100077030X

Fig. 72 Code P1575: PCM Detects Voltage On Extended Travel Brake Switch Circuit (Part 3 of 3). Aurora, Bonneville, Century, DeVille, Eldorado, Intrigue, LeSabre, Regal & Seville

- Loose terminal connection
  - Use a corresponding mating terminal to test for proper tension. Refer to Intermittents
  - Inspect the harness connectors for backed out terminals, improper mating, broken locks, improperly formed or damaged terminals, and faulty terminal to wire connection. Refer to Intermittents
- Damaged harness--Inspect the wiring harness for damage. If the harness inspection does not reveal a problem, observe the display on the scan tool while moving connectors and wiring harnesses related to the sensor. A change in the scan tool display may indicate the location of the fault.
- Inspect the powertrain control module (PCM) and the engine grounds for clean and secure connections.

If the condition is determined to be intermittent, reviewing the Snapshot or Freeze Frame/Failure Records may be useful in determining when the DTC or condition was identified.

Test Description

The numbers below refer to the step numbers on the diagnostic table:

2. This step tests the ignition feed voltage.
3. This step tests for a shorted component or a short to battery positive voltage on the control circuit. Either condition would result in a measured current of over 500 milliamps. Also tests for a component that is going open while being operated, resulting in a measured current of 0 milliamps.
4. This step tests for a short to voltage on the control circuit.
15. This step ensures that the replacement PCM, which utilizes an electrically erasable programmable read only memory (EEPROM), is programmed when installed.

Step	Action	Values	Yes	No
1	Did you perform the Powertrain On Board Diagnostic (OBD) System Check?	--	Go to Step 2	Refer to MOTOR's "Domestic Performance & Driveability Manual"
2	1. Turn OFF the ignition. 2. Disconnect the PCM. 3. Turn ON the ignition. **Important** Normally, ignition feed voltage should be present on the control circuit with the PCM disconnected and the ignition turned ON. 4. Using a DMM, measure voltage between the cruise control module control circuit at the PCM harness connector and ground. Is the voltage near the specified value?	B+	Go to Step 3	Go to Step 6

GC0140100060020X

Fig. 73 Code P1585: Cruise Control Inhibit Output Circuit (Part 2 of 5). 2000–01 Lumina & 2000 Alero, Bonneville, Century, Grand Am, Impala, Malibu, Monte Carlo, LeSabre, Park Avenue & Regal

Circuit Description

Output driver modules (ODMs) are used by the powertrain control module (PCM) to turn ON many of the current-driven devices that are needed to control various engine and transaxle functions. Each ODM is capable of controlling up to 7 separate outputs by applying ground to the device which the PCM is commanding ON. DTC P1585 set indicates an improper voltage level has been detected on the output circuit which controls the stepper motor cruise control inhibit circuit.

Conditions for Running the DTC

The ignition is ON.

Conditions for Setting the DTC

- An improper voltage level has been detected on the output circuit which controls the cruise control inhibit.
- The above condition is present for at least 30 seconds.

Action Taken When the DTC Sets

- The PCM will not illuminate the malfunction indicator lamp (MIL).
- The PCM will store conditions which were present when the DTC set as Failure Records only. This information will not be stored as Freeze Frame Records.

Conditions for Clearing the MIL/DTC

- A History DTC will clear after 40 consecutive warm-up cycles have occurred without a malfunction.
- The DTC can be cleared by using a scan tool.

Diagnostic Aids

Inspect for the following conditions:

Many situations may lead to an intermittent condition. Perform each inspection or test as directed.

Important:

Remove any debris from the connector surfaces before servicing a component. Inspect the connector gaskets when diagnosing or replacing a component. Ensure that the gaskets are installed correctly. The gaskets prevent contaminate intrusion.

GC0140100060010X

Fig. 73 Code P1585: Cruise Control Inhibit Output Circuit (Part 1 of 5). 2000–01 Lumina & 2000 Alero, Bonneville, Century, Grand Am, Impala, Malibu, Monte Carlo, LeSabre, Park Avenue & Regal

Step	Action	Value (s)	Yes	No
3	1. Connect the DMM to measure current between the cruise inhibit control circuit at the PCM harness connector and ground. 2. Monitor the current reading on the DMM for at least 2 minutes. Does the current reading remain between the specified values?	0.001-0.5 amp (1-500 mA)	Go to Step 11	Go to Step 4
4	1. Turn OFF the ignition. 2. Disconnect the cruise control module, leave the PCM disconnected. 3. Turn ON the ignition. 4. Using the DMM, measure voltage between the cruise inhibit control circuit and ground. Is the voltage at the specified value?	0.0 V	Go to Step 10	Go to Step 5
5	Locate and repair short to voltage in the cruise inhibit control circuit. Did you complete the repair?	--	Go to Step 16	--
6	1. Turn OFF the ignition. 2. Inspect the ignition feed fuse for the cruise control module. Is the fuse open?	--	Go to Step 7	Go to Step 8
7	1. Locate and repair short to ground in ignition feed circuit for the cruise control module. 2. Replace the fuse. Did you complete the repair?	--	Go to Step 16	--
8	1. Disconnect the cruise control module. 2. Turn ON the ignition. 3. Measure voltage between the ignition feed circuit for the cruise control module and ground. Is the voltage near the specified value?	B+	Go to Step 9	Go to Step 13
9	Test the cruise inhibit control circuit for an open or a short to ground. Did you find and correct the condition?	--	Go to Step 16	Go to Step 10

GC0140100060030X

Fig. 73 Code P1585: Cruise Control Inhibit Output Circuit (Part 3 of 5). 2000–01 Lumina & 2000 Alero, Bonneville, Century, Grand Am, Impala, Malibu, Monte Carlo, LeSabre, Park Avenue & Regal

Step	Action	Value (s)	Yes	No
10	Inspect for the following conditions: 1. The cruise inhibit control circuit for a faulty connection at the PCM. 2. The cruise inhibit control circuit for a faulty connection at cruise control module. 3. The cruise control module ignition feed circuit for a faulty connection at the cruise control module. Did you find and correct the condition?	--	Go to Step 16	Go to Step 14
11	1. Turn OFF the ignition. 2. Reconnect the PCM. 3. Disconnect the cruise control module. 4. Turn ON the ignition. 5. Connect a test lamp between the cruise inhibit control circuit and the ignition feed circuit at the cruise control module harness connector. 6. Using the scan tool outputs test function, cycle the cruise inhibit output ON and OFF. Does the test lamp flash ON and OFF?	--	Go to Diagnostic Aids	Go to Step 12
12	Test the cruise inhibit control circuit for a faulty connection at the PCM. Did you find and correct the condition?	--	Go to Step 16	Go to Step 15
13	Locate and repair open in ignition feed circuit to the stepper motor cruise control module. Did you complete the repair?	--	Go to Step 16	--
14	Replace the cruise control module. Did you complete the replacement?	--	Go to Step 16	--
15	**Important** The replacement PCM must be programmed. Replace the PCM. Did you complete the replacement?	--	Go to Step 16	--

GC0140100060040X

Fig. 73 Code P1585: Cruise Control Inhibit Output Circuit (Part 4 of 5). 2000–01 Lumina & 2000 Alero, Bonneville, Century, Grand Am, Impala, Malibu, Monte Carlo, LeSabre, Park Avenue & Regal

Circuit Description

Output driver modules (ODMs) are used by the powertrain control module (PCM) in order to turn on many of the current driven devices that are needed to control various engine and transaxle functions. DTC P1558 set indicates that an improper voltage level has been detected on the signal circuit which controls the cruise control inhibit circuit.

Conditions for Running the DTC

- The engine speed is 450 RPM or more.
- System voltage is between 8 and 16 volts.

Conditions for Setting the DTC

- The ignition is on.
- The PCM detects an improper voltage level on the cruise inhibit signal circuit.
- The condition exists for at least 30 seconds.

Action Taken When the DTC Sets

- The PCM will not illuminate the malfunction indicator lamp (MIL).
- The PCM will store the conditions present when the DTC set as Failure Records data only.

Conditions for Clearing the DTC

- The history DTC will clear after 40 consecutive warm-up cycles have occurred without a malfunction.
- The DTC can be cleared by using the scan tool's Clear DTC Information function.

Diagnostic Aids

In order to determine whether an improper voltage level exists on the output circuit, the PCM compares the voltage level to the commanded state.

If the condition is intermittent, refer to Intermittent

Test Description

The number(s) below refer to the step number(s) on the diagnostic table.

2. Normally, ignition positive voltage should be present on the control circuit with the PCM disconnected and the ignition turned ON.

3. Tests for short to voltage on the control circuit.

GC0140100063010X

Fig. 74 Code P1585: Cruise Control Inhibit Output Circuit (Part 1 of 3). 2001–04 Alero, Aurora, Bonneville, Cavalier, Century, DeVille, Eldorado, Grand Prix, Grand Am, Impala, Intrigue, LeSabre, Malibu, Monte Carlo, Park Avenue, Regal, Seville & Sunfire

Step	Action	Value (s)	Yes	No
16	1. Review and record scan tool Fail Records data. 2. Clear the DTCs. 3. Operate the vehicle within Fail Records conditions. 4. Using a scan tool, monitor Specific DTC info for DTC P1585 until the DTC P1585 test runs. Does the scan tool indicate DTC P1585 failed this ignition?	--	Go to Step 2	System OK

GC0140100060050X

Fig. 73 Code P1585: Cruise Control Inhibit Output Circuit (Part 5 of 5). 2000–01 Lumina & 2000 Alero, Bonneville, Century, Grand Am, Impala, Malibu, Monte Carlo, LeSabre, Park Avenue & Regal

8. This vehicle is equipped with a PCM which utilizes an Electrically Erasable Programmable Read Only Memory (EEPROM). When the PCM is being replaced, the new PCM must be programmed.

Step	Action	Value (s)	Yes	No
1	Did you perform the Cruise Control Diagnostic System Check ?	--	Go to Step 2	Go to System Check
2	1. Turn OFF the ignition. 2. Disconnect the PCM harness connector. 3. Turn ON the ignition, with the engine OFF. 4. Using a DMM connected to a good ground, measure the voltage of the cruise control inhibit signal circuit. Does the voltage measure near the specified value?	B+	Go to Step 3	Go to Step 4
3	1. Turn OFF the ignition. 2. Disconnect the cruise control module. 3. Turn ON the ignition, with the engine OFF. 4. Probe the cruise control inhibit signal circuit with a test lamp that is connected to a good ground. Does the test lamp illuminate?	--	Go to Step 7	Go to Step 5
4	Test the cruise control inhibit signal circuit for a open, high resistance or short to ground. Did you find and correct the condition?	--	Go to Step 10	Go to Step 6
5	Inspect for poor connections at the harness connector of the PCM. Did you find and correct the condition?	--	Go to Step 10	Go to Step 8
6	Inspect for poor connections at the harness connector of the cruise control module. Did you find and correct the condition?	--	Go to Step 10	Go to Step 9
7	Repair the short to voltage in the cruise control inhibit signal circuit. Did you complete the repair?	--	Go to Step 10	--

GC0140100063020X

Fig. 74 Code P1585: Cruise Control Inhibit Output Circuit (Part 2 of 3). 2001–04 Alero, Aurora, Bonneville, Cavalier, Century, DeVille, Eldorado, Grand Prix, Grand Am, Impala, Intrigue, LeSabre, Malibu, Monte Carlo, Park Avenue, Regal, Seville & Sunfire

Step	Action	Value (s)	Yes	No
8	**Important** The replacement PCM must be programmed. Replace the PCM. Did you complete the replacement?	--	Go to Step 10	--
9	Replace the cruise control module. Did you complete the replacement?	--	Go to Step 10	--
10	1. Use the scan tool in order to clear the DTCs. 2. Operate the vehicle within normal cruise control operating conditions. Does the DTC reset?	--	Go to Step 2	System OK

GC0140100063030X

Fig. 74 Code P1585: Cruise Control Inhibit Output Circuit (Part 3 of 3). 2001–04 Alero, Aurora, Bonneville, Cavalier, Century, DeVille, Eldorado, Grand Prix, Grand Am, Impala, Intrigue, LeSabre, Malibu, Monte Carlo, Park Avenue, Regal, Seville & Sunfire

Step	Action	Value (s)	Yes	No
3	Check the fuse for the instrument cluster ignition feed circuit. Is the fuse OK?	--	Go to Step 4	Go to Step 9
4	1. Turn OFF the ignition. 2. Disconnect the ECM. 3. Turn ON the ignition. 4. Use a fused jumper in order to jumper the CRUISE indicator control circuit in the ECM harness connector to ground. Is the CRUISE indicator ON?	--	Go to Step 10	Go to Step 5
5	Check for the following conditions: • A damaged bulb- • An open ignition feed to the bulb- • A control circuit open or shorted to B+- Is the action complete?	--	Go to Step 12	--
6	Command the CRUISE indicator OFF using the scan tool. Does the CRUISE indicator turn OFF?	--	Go to Step 11	Go to Step 7
7	1. Turn OFF the ignition. 2. Disconnect the ECM. 3. Turn ON the ignition with the engine OFF. Is the CRUISE indicator ON?	--	Go to Step 8	Go to Step 10
8	Repair the short to ground in the CRUISE control circuit. Is the action complete?	--	Go to Step 12	--
9	Repair the short to ground in the feed circuit to the instrument panel indicator lamps. Is the action complete?	--	Go to Step 12	--
10	Check for a poor connections or poor terminal tension at the ECM harness connector. Did you find and correct a problem?	--	Go to Step 12	Go to Step 11

GC0140100092020X

Fig. 75 Code P1662: Cruise Lamp Control Circuit (Part 2 of 3). 2000 Catera

Circuit Description

The engine control module (ECM) turns the CRUISE lamp ON whenever actual cruise operation is present. The ECM controls the lamp by grounding the control circuit with an internal solid state device called a driver.

Conditions for Running the DTC

- The battery voltage is between 7.5-15 volts.
- The engine speed is more than 40 RPM.
- The cruise control is engaged.

Conditions for Setting the DTC

An open, a short to voltage, or a short to ground is monitored by the ECM.

Action Taken When the DTC Sets

The ECM will not illuminate the malfunction indicator lamp (MIL).

Conditions for Clearing the MIL/DTC

- The diagnostic trouble code (DTC) clears after 40 consecutive warm up cycles in which no failures are reported by this diagnostic or any other non-emission related diagnostic.
- The scan tool clears the MIL/DTC.

Test Description

The numbers below refer to the step numbers on the diagnostic table.

2. The CRUISE lamp should remain OFF when the ignition is turned ON and the engine is OFF.
3. If the other indicator lamps in the instrument cluster are functioning, the feed circuit is OK.
8. If the CRUISE lamp is ON with the ECM connected and OFF with the ECM disconnected there is a problem in the ECM.

   If the CRUISE lamp is OFF with the ECM disconnected and a short to ground is NOT present on the control circuit the fault is within the instrument panel.
12. After cruise is engaged, the CRUISE indicator lamp should illuminate.

Step	Action	Values	Yes	No
1	Did you perform the Powertrain On-Board Diagnostic (OBD) System Check?	--	Go to Step 2	Refer to MOTOR's "Domestic Performance & Driveability Manual "
2	Turn ON the ignition, leaving the engine OFF. Is the CRUISE indicator OFF?	--	Go to Step 3	Go to Step 6

GC0140100092010X

Fig. 75 Code P1662: Cruise Lamp Control Circuit (Part 1 of 3). 2000 Catera

Step	Action	Value (s)	Yes	No
11	**Important** • Perform the Idle Learn Procedure when replacing the ECM or the throttle body. • This vehicle is equipped with a theft deterrent system that interfaces with the ECM. Program the new ECM with the frequency code of the theft deterrent module that is currently on the vehicle. Replace the ECM. Is the action complete?	--	Go to Step 12	--
12	1. Using the scan tool, clear the DTCs. 2. Operate the vehicle within the Conditions for Running this DTC. 3. Operate the vehicle with cruise engaged. Does the scan tool indicate that the diagnostic Passed?	--	System OK	Go to Step 2

GC0140100092030X

Fig. 75 Code P1662: Cruise Lamp Control Circuit (Part 3 of 3). 2000 Catera

Circuit Description

The engine control module (ECM) turns the CRUISE lamp ON whenever actual cruise operation is present. The ECM controls the lamp by grounding the control circuit with an internal solid state device called a driver.

Conditions for Running the DTC

- The battery voltage is between 7.5-15 volts.
- The engine speed is more than 40 RPM.
- The cruise control is engaged.

Conditions for Setting the DTC

An open, a short to voltage, or a short to ground is monitored by the ECM.

Action Taken When the DTC Sets

The ECM will not illuminate the malfunction indicator lamp (MIL).

Conditions for Clearing the MIL/DTC

- The diagnostic trouble code (DTC) clears after 40 consecutive warm up cycles in which no failures are reported by this diagnostic or any other non-emission related diagnostic.
- The scan tool clears the MIL/DTC.

Test Description

The numbers below refer to the step numbers on the diagnostic table.

13. After cruise is engaged, the CRUISE indicator lamp should illuminate.

Step	Action	Yes	No
1	Did you perform the Cruise Control Diagnostic System Check?	Go to Step 2	Go to System Check
2	Does the cruise control operate properly?	Go to Step 3	Go to Cruise Control Inoperative
3	Observe the CRUISE Indicator in the instrument panel cluster (IPC). Is the CRUISE indicator lamp illuminated?	Go to Step 5	Go to Step 4

GC0140100093010X

Fig. 76 Code P1662: Cruise Lamp Control Circuit (Part 1 of 3). 2001 Catera

Step	Action	Yes	No
4	1. Connect a scan tool. 2. Command the CRUISE Indicator lamp ON from the Dash Lamps data list. Did the CRUISE Indicator lamp in the IPC illuminate?	Go to Intermittents	Go to Step 6
5	Test the CRUISE indicator signal circuit for a short to ground. Did you find and correct the condition?	Go to Step 13	Go to Step 9
6	Test the CRUISE indicator signal circuit for a open, high resistance or short to voltage. Did you find and correct the condition?	Go to Step 13	Go to Step 7
7	Inspect the CRUISE Indicator lamp in the IPC. Is the CRUISE Indicator lamp open?	Go to Step 10	Go to Step 8
8	Inspect for poor connections at the harness connector of the IPC. Did you find and correct the condition?	Go to Step 13	Go to Step 11
9	Inspect for poor connections at the harness connector of the PCM. Did you find and correct the condition?	Go to Step 13	Go to Step 12
10	Replace the CRUISE Indicator lamp in the IPC.	Go to Step 13	--
11	Replace the IPC. Did you complete the replacement?	Go to Step 13	--

GC0140100093020X

Fig. 76 Code P1662: Cruise Lamp Control Circuit (Part 2 of 3). 2001 Catera

Step	Action	Yes	No
12	**Important** • The PCM must be reprogrammed after replacement. • This vehicle is equipped with a theft deterrent system that interfaces with the ECM. Program the new ECM with the frequency code of the theft deterrent module that is currently on the vehicle. Replace the ECM. Did you complete the replacement?	Go to Step 13	--
13	1. Using the scan tool, clear the DTCs. 2. Operate the vehicle within the Conditions for Running this DTC. 3. Operate the vehicle with cruise engaged. Does the scan tool indicate that the diagnostic Passed?	System OK	Go to Step 2

GC0140100093030X

Fig. 76 Code P1662: Cruise Lamp Control Circuit (Part 3 of 3). 2001 Catera

Circuit Description

The powertrain control module (PCM) monitors the system voltage to make sure that the voltage stays within the proper range. Damage to components, and incorrect data input can occur when the voltage is out of range. The PCM monitors the system voltage over an extended length of time. If the PCM detects a system voltage outside an expected range for the calibrated length of time, DTC P0560 will set.

Conditions for Running the DTC

- System voltage below 2.5 volts
- Engine speed above 650 RPM

Conditions for Setting the DTC

The PCM detects a system voltage out of range for 30 seconds.

Action Taken When the DTC Sets

- The PCM will not illuminate the malfunction indicator lamp (MIL).
- The PCM will command a message to be displayed.
- The PCM will store conditions which were present when the DTC set as Fail Records data only.

Conditions for Clearing the DTC

- The PCM will command the message OFF after one trip in which the diagnostic test has been run and passed.
- The history DTC will clear after 40 consecutive warm-up cycles have occurred without a malfunction.
- The DTC can be cleared by using the scan tool Clear DTC Information function.

Step	Action	Value	Yes	No
1	Did you perform the Engine Electrical Diagnostic System Check?	--	Go to Step 2	Go to System Check -
2	1. Install a scan tool. 2. Operate the vehicle within the conditions for running the DTC. 3. Using the scan tool, observe the Specific DTC Information for DTC P0560 until the test runs. Does the scan tool indicate that DTC P0560 has passed this ignition cycle?	--	Test for Intermittent and Poor Connections	Go to Step 3

GC1100200851010X

Fig. 77 Code P0560: PCM Detect Voltage Out Of Range (Part 1 of 2). CTS

3	1. Install a scan tool. 2. Turn ON the ignition, with the engine OFF. 3. With a scan tool, observe the Battery Voltage parameter in the PCM data list . Does the scan tool indicate that the Battery Voltage parameter is greater than the specified range?	2.5 V	Go to Step 7	Go to Step 4
4	Using a scan tool compare the battery voltage with the Battery Voltage parameter in the PCM data list Is the battery voltage and PCM Battery Voltage readings different by more than the value specified?	0.5 V	Go to Step 5	Go to Charging System Test
5	Test the battery positive voltage circuit of the PCM for a high resistance or open. Did you find and correct the condition?	--	Go to Step 8	Go to Step 6
6	Inspect for poor connections at the harness connector of the PCM. Did you find and correct the condition?	--	Go to Step 8	Go to Step 7
7	**Important** The replacement PCM must be programmed. Replace the PCM. Did you complete the replacement?	--	Go to Step 8	--
8	1. Review and record the scan tool Fail Records data. 2. Use the scan tool in order to clear the DTC. 3. Operate the vehicle within the conditions for running the DTC. 4. Using the scan tool, observe the specific DTC information for DTC P0560 until the test runs. Does the scan tool indicate that DTC P0560 failed this ignition?	--	Go to Step 3	System OK

GC1100200851020X

Fig. 77 Code P0560: PCM Detect Voltage Out Of Range (Part 2 of 2). CTS

3	1. Maintain engine RPM. 2. Measure the battery voltage at the battery terminals and compare it with the Ignition 1 Signal parameter in the PCM data list. Are the battery voltage and PCM Ignition 1 readings different by more than the value specified?	0.8 V	Go to Step 4	Go to Charging System Test
4	Test the battery positive voltage circuit of the PCM for a high resistance. Did you find and correct the condition?	--	Go to Step 7	Go to Step 5
5	Inspect for poor connections at the harness connector of the PCM. Did you find and correct the condition?	--	Go to Step 7	Go to Step 6
6	**Important** The replacement PCM must be programmed. Replace the PCM. Did you complete the replacement?	--	Go to Step 7	--
7	1. Review and record the scan tool Fail Records data. 2. Use the scan tool in order to clear the DTC. 3. Operate the vehicle within the conditions for running the DTC. 4. Using the scan tool, observe the Specific DTC information for DTC P0562 until the test runs. Does the scan tool indicate that DTC P0562 failed this ignition?	--	Go to Step 2	System OK

GC1100200852020X

Fig. 78 Code P0562: PCM Detects Low Voltage (Part 2 of 2). CTS

Circuit Description

The Powertrain Control Module (PCM) checks the system voltage to make sure that the voltage stays within the proper range. Damage to components, and incorrect input can occur when the voltage is out of range. The PCM monitors the system voltage over an extended length of time. If the PCM detects an excessively low system voltage, DTC P0562 will set.

Conditions for Running the DTC

- Engine speed above 1500 RPM
- System voltage between 9.5-18 volts

Conditions for Setting the DTC

The PCM detects a system voltage below 10 volts for 5 seconds.

Action Taken When the DTC Sets

- The PCM will command a message to be displayed.
- The PCM will not illuminate the malfunction indicator lamp (MIL).
- The PCM will store conditions which were present when the DTC set as Fail Records data only.

Conditions for Clearing the DTC

- The PCM will command the message OFF after one trip in which the diagnostic test has been run and passed.
- The history DTC will clear after 40 consecutive warm-up cycles have occurred without a malfunction.
- The DTC can be cleared by using the scan tool Clear DTC Information function.

Step	Action	Value (s)	Yes	No
1	Did you perform the Engine Electrical Diagnostic System Check?	--	Go to Step 2	Go to System Check -
2	1. Install a scan tool. 2. Start the engine. 3. Raise the engine speed above 1500 RPM. 4. With a scan tool, observe the Ignition 1 Signal parameter in the PCM data list . Does the scan tool indicate that the Ignition 1 Signal parameter is greater than the specified range?	10.0 V	Go to Step 6	Go to Step 3

GC1100200852010X

Fig. 78 Code P0562: PCM Detects Low Voltage (Part 1 of 2). CTS

Circuit Description

The Powertrain Control Module (PCM) checks the system voltage to make sure that the voltage stays within the proper range. Damage to components, and incorrect input can occur when the voltage is out of range. The PCM monitors the system voltage over an extended length of time. If the PCM detects an excessively high system voltage, DTC P0563 will set.

Conditions for Running the DTC

- Engine speed above 1500 RPM
- System voltage between 9.5-18 volts

Conditions for Setting the DTC

The PCM detects a system voltage above 16 volts for less than 1 second.

Action Taken When the DTC Sets

- The PCM will command a message to be displayed.
- The PCM will not illuminate the malfunction indicator lamp (MIL).
- The PCM will store conditions which were present when the DTC set as Fail Records data only.

Conditions for Clearing the DTC

- The PCM will command the message OFF after one trip in which the diagnostic test has been run and passed.
- The history DTC will clear after 40 consecutive warm-up cycles have occurred without a malfunction.
- The DTC can be cleared by using the scan tool Clear DTC Information function.

Step	Action	Value (s)	Yes	No
1	Did you perform the Engine Electrical Diagnostic System Check?	--	Go to Step 2	Go to System Check -
2	1. Install a scan tool. 2. Start the engine. 3. Raise the engine speed above 1500 RPM. 4. With a scan tool, observe the Ignition 1 Signal parameter in the PCM data list . Does the scan tool indicate that the Ignition 1 Signal parameter is less than the specified range?	16.0 V	Go to Step 4	Go to Step 3

GC1100200853010X

Fig. 79 Code P0563: PCM Detects High Voltage (Part 1 of 2). CTS

3	1. Maintain engine RPM. 2. Measure the battery voltage at the battery terminals and compare it with the Ignition 1 Signal parameter in the PCM data list. Are the battery voltage and PCM Ignition 1 readings different by more than the value specified?	0.8 V	Go to Step 4	Diagnose Charging System
4	**Important** The replacement PCM must be programmed. Replace the PCM. Did you complete the replacement?	--	Go to Step 5	--
5	1. Review and record the scan tool Fail Records data. 2. Use the scan tool in order to clear the DTC. 3. Operate the vehicle within the conditions for running the DTC. 4. Using the scan tool, observe the specific DTC information for DTC P0563 until the test runs. Does the scan tool indicate that DTC P0563 failed this ignition?	--	Go to Step 2	System OK

GC1100200853020X

Fig. 79 Code P0563: PCM Detects High Voltage (Part 2 of 2). CTS

2	Turn the ignition back and forth from the OFF to START positions. Does the Starter relay turn ON and OFF with each command?	Test for Intermittent and Poor Connections	Go to Step 3
3	1. Turn OFF the ignition. 2. Disconnect the starter relay. 3. Turn ON the ignition, with the engine OFF. 4. Probe the battery positive voltage of the starter relay coil circuit with a test lamp that is connected to a good ground. 5. Turn ON the ignition. Does the test lamp illuminate?	Go to Step 4	Go to Step 5
4	1. Connect a test lamp between the control circuit of the starter relay and the battery positive voltage of the starter relay coil circuit. 2. Turn the ignition back and forth from the ON to START positions. Does the test lamp turn ON and OFF with each command?	Go to Step 11	Go to Step 9
5	Turn the ignition back and forth from the OFF to ON positions. Does the Run/Crank relay turn ON and OFF with each command?	Go to Step 8	Go to Step 6
6	1. Turn OFF the ignition. 2. Disconnect the Run/Crank relay. 3. Turn ON the ignition, with the engine OFF. 4. Probe the battery positive voltage of the Run/Crank relay coil circuit with a test lamp that is connected to a good ground. Does the test lamp illuminate?	Go to Step 7	Go to Step 13
7	1. Connect a test lamp between the battery positive voltage of the Run/Crank relay coil circuit and the ground of the Run/Crank relay coil circuit. 2. Turn ON the ignition. Does the test lamp illuminate?	Go to Step 10	Go to Step 14

GC1100200854020X

Fig. 80 Code P0615: Improper Voltage Level On Output Circuit (Part 2 of 4). CTS

Circuit Description

The Powertrain Control Module (PCM) supplies a ground path for the starter relay when start enable has been requested. The PCM monitors this circuit for conditions that are incorrect for the commanded state. If the PCM detects an improper circuit condition, starter relay DTC P0615 will set.

Conditions for Running the DTC

- System voltage is between 8-16 volts.
- The engine is running.

Conditions for Setting the DTC

- The PCM detects an improper voltage level on the output circuit that controls the starter relay.
- The condition exists for at least 2 seconds.

Action Taken When the DTC Sets

- The PCM will not illuminate the malfunction indicator lamp (MIL).
- The PCM will store the conditions present when the DTC set as Fail Records data only.

Conditions for Clearing the MIL/DTC

- The history DTC will clear after 40 consecutive warm-up cycles have occurred without a malfunction.
- The DTC can be cleared by using the scan tool Clear DTC Information function.

Test Description

The numbers below refer to the step numbers on the diagnostic table.

2. Listen for an audible click when the Starter relay operates. Turn the ignition switch back and forth from the OFF to START positions. Repeat this as necessary.

5. Listen for an audible click when the Run/Crank relay operates. Turn the ignition switch back and forth from the OFF to ON positions. Repeat this as necessary.

Step	Action	Yes	No
1	Did you perform the Engine Electrical Diagnostic System Check?	Go to Step 2	Go to System Check -

GC1100200854010X

Fig. 80 Code P0615: Improper Voltage Level On Output Circuit (Part 1 of 4). CTS

8	1. Install the starter relay. 2. Connect a 10 A fused jumper wire between the battery positive voltage of the Run/Crank relay switch circuit and the Ignition 1 voltage of the Run/Crank relay switch circuit. 3. Turn the ignition back and forth from the OFF to START positions. Does the starter relay turn ON and OFF with each command?	Go to Step 10	Go to Step 15
9	Test the control circuit of the Starter relay for a high resistance or open. Did you find and correct the condition?	Go to Step 19	Go to Step 12
10	Inspect for poor connections at the Run/Crank relay. Did you find and correct the condition?	Go to Step 19	Go to Step 16
11	Inspect for poor connections at the starter relay. Did you find and correct the condition?	Go to Step 19	Go to Step 17
12	Inspect for poor connections at the PCM. Did you find and correct the condition?	Go to Step 19	Go to Step 18
13	Repair the high resistance or open in the Ignition 1 voltage of the Run/Crank relay coil circuit. Did you complete the repair?	Go to Step 19	--
14	Repair the high resistance or open in the ground of the Run/Crank relay coil circuit. Did you find and correct the condition?	Go to Step 19	--
15	Repair the high resistance or open in the Ignition 1 voltage circuit of the starter relay. Did you complete the repair?	Go to Step 19	--

GC1100200854030X

Fig. 80 Code P0615: Improper Voltage Level On Output Circuit (Part 3 of 4). CTS

16	Replace the Run/Crank relay. Did you complete the replacement?	Go to Step 19	--
17	Replace the starter relay. Did you complete the replacement?	Go to Step 19	--
18	**Important** The replacement PCM must be programmed. Replace the PCM. Did you complete the replacement?	Go to Step 19	--
19	1. Review and record the scan tool Fail Records data. 2. Use the scan tool in order to clear the DTC. 3. Operate the vehicle within the conditions for running the DTC. 4. Using the scan tool, observe the specific DTC information for DTC P0615 until the test runs. Does the scan tool indicate that DTC P0615 failed this ignition?	Go to Step 2	System OK

GC1100200854040X

Fig. 80 Code P0615: Improper Voltage Level On Output Circuit (Part 4 of 4). CTS

	1. Install a scan tool. 2. Operate the vehicle within the conditions for running the DTC. 3. Using the scan tool, observe the specific DTC information for DTC P0616 until the test runs. Does the scan tool indicate that DTC P0616 has passed this ignition cycle?	Test for Intermittent and Poor Connections	Go to Step 3
3	Test the control circuit of the Starter relay for a short to ground. Did you find and correct the condition?	Go to Step 6	Go to Step 4
4	Inspect for poor connections at the PCM. Did you find and correct the condition?	Go to Step 6	Go to Step 5
5	**Important** The replacement PCM must be programmed. Replace the PCM. Did you complete the replacement?	Go to Step 6	--
6	1. Review and record the scan tool Fail Records data. 2. Use the scan tool in order to clear the DTC. 3. Operate the vehicle within the Conditions for Running the DTC as specified in the supporting text. 4. Using the scan tool, observe the Specific DTC Information for DTC P0616 until the test runs. Does the scan tool indicate that DTC P0616 failed this ignition?	Go to Step 2	System OK

GC1100200855020X

Fig. 81 Code P0616: Improper Voltage Level On Output Circuit (Part 2 of 2). CTS

Circuit Description

The Powertrain Control Module (PCM) supplies a ground path for the starter relay when start enable has been requested. The PCM monitors this circuit for conditions that are incorrect for the commanded state. If the PCM detects an improper circuit condition, starter relay DTC P0616 will set.

Conditions for Running the DTC

- System voltage is between 8-16 volts.
- The engine is running.

Conditions for Setting the DTC

- The PCM detects an improper voltage level on the output circuit that controls the starter relay.
- The condition exists for at least 2 seconds.

Action Taken When the DTC Sets

- The PCM will not illuminate the malfunction indicator lamp (MIL).
- The PCM will store the conditions present when the DTC set as Fail Records data only.

Conditions for Clearing the MIL/DTC

- The history DTC will clear after 40 consecutive warm-up cycles have occurred without a malfunction.
- The DTC can be cleared by using the scan tool Clear DTC Information function.

Step	Action	Yes	No
1	Did you perform the Engine Electrical Diagnostic System Check?	Go to Step 2	Go to System Check -

GC1100200856010X

Fig. 82 Code P0617: Improper Voltage Level On Output Circuit (Part 1 of 2). CTS

Circuit Description

The Powertrain Control Module (PCM) supplies a ground path for the starter relay when start enable has been requested. The PCM monitors this circuit for conditions that are incorrect for the commanded state. If the PCM detects an improper circuit condition, starter relay DTC P0616 will set.

Conditions for Running the DTC

- System voltage is between 8-16 volts.
- The engine is running.

Conditions for Setting the DTC

- The PCM detects an improper voltage level on the output circuit that controls the starter relay.
- The condition exists for at least 2 seconds.

Action Taken When the DTC Sets

- The PCM will not illuminate the malfunction indicator lamp (MIL).
- The PCM will store the conditions present when the DTC set as Fail Records data only.

Conditions for Clearing the MIL/DTC

- The history DTC will clear after 40 consecutive warm-up cycles have occurred without a malfunction.
- The DTC can be cleared by using the scan tool Clear DTC Information function.

Step	Action	Yes	No
1	Did you perform the Engine Electrical Diagnostic System Check?	Go to Step 2	Go to System Check -

GC1100200855010X

Fig. 81 Code P0616: Improper Voltage Level On Output Circuit (Part 1 of 2). CTS

2	1. Install a scan tool. 2. Operate the vehicle within the conditions for running the DTC. 3. Using the scan tool, observe the specific DTC information for DTC P0617 until the test runs. Does the scan tool indicate that DTC P0617 has passed this ignition cycle?	Test for Intermittent and Poor Connections	Go to Step 3
3	Test the control circuit of the Starter relay for a short to battery. Did you find and correct the condition?	Go to Step 6	Go to Step 4
4	Inspect for poor connections at the PCM. Did you find and correct the condition?	Go to Step 6	Go to Step 5
5	**Important** The replacement PCM must be programmed. Replace the PCM. Did you complete the replacement?	Go to Step 6	--
6	1. Review and record the scan tool Fail Records data. 2. Use the scan tool in order to clear the DTC. 3. Operate the vehicle within the conditions for running the DTC. 4. Using the scan tool, observe the specific DTC information for DTC P0617 until the test runs. Does the scan tool indicate that DTC P0617 failed this ignition?	Go to Step 2	System OK

GC1100200856020X

Fig. 82 Code P0617: Improper Voltage Level On Output Circuit (Part 2 of 2). CTS

Circuit Description

The engine control module (ECM) uses the generator field duty cycle signal circuit to monitor the duty cycle of the generator and fault indication. The generator field duty cycle signal circuit connects to the high side of the field winding in the generator. A pulse width modulated (PWM) high side driver in the voltage regulator turns the field winding ON and OFF. The ECM uses the PWM signal input to determine the generator load on the engine. This allows the ECM to adjust the idle speed to compensate for high electrical loads.

The Powertrain Control Module (PCM) monitors the state of the generator field duty cycle signal circuit. When the engine is running, the ECM should detect a duty cycle that varies up to 100 percent. The ECM monitors the PWM signal using a key ON test and a RUN test. During the tests, if the ECM detects an out of range PWM signal, a DTC will set. When the DTC sets, the PCM will send a class 2 serial data message to the IPC and DIC to illuminate the charge indicator or display a charging message.

Conditions for Running the DTC

- No generator, CKP sensors, or CMP sensor DTCs are set.
- The engine is less than 3000 RPM.
- The generator has not been commanded OFF by the ECM or scan tool.

Conditions for Setting the DTC

The ECM detects a PWM signal less than 5 percent for at least 15 seconds.

Action Taken When the DTC Sets

- The PCM will not illuminate the malfunction indicator lamp (MIL).
- The PCM will store the conditions present when the DTC set as Fail Records data only.
- The PCM will send a class 2 serial data message to the IPC and DIC to illuminate the charge indicator or display a charging message.

Conditions for Clearing the MIL/DTC

- The conditions for setting DTC P0625 are not present.
- The DTC can be cleared by using the scan tool Clear DTC Information function.

Step	Action	Values	Yes	No
1	Did you perform the Engine Electrical Diagnostic System Check?	--	Go to Step 2	Go to System Check

GC1100200857010X

Fig. 83 Code P0625: PCM Detects Low PWM Signal (Part 1 of 3). CTS

2	1. Install a scan tool. 2. Start the engine. 3. With a scan tool, observe the GEN - F Terminal Signal parameter in the PCM data list . Does the scan tool indicate that the GEN - F Terminal parameter is within the specified range?	5-100%	Test for Intermittent and Poor Connections	Go to Step 3
3	1. Turn OFF the ignition 2. Disconnect the generator harness connector. 3. Turn ON the ignition, with the engine OFF. 4. Connect a test lamp to battery positive voltage and repeatedly probe the generator field duty cycle signal circuit in the harness connector while monitoring the GEN - F Terminal Signal parameter on the scan tool. Is the GEN - F Terminal Signal parameter affected?	--	Go to Step 5	Go to Step 4
4	Test the generator field duty cycle signal circuit for a short to ground or open. Did you find and correct the condition?	--	Go to Step 9	Go to Step 7
5	Test the battery positive voltage cable for an open or high resistance. Did you find and correct the condition?	--	Go to Step 9	Go to Step 6

GC1100200857020X

Fig. 83 Code P0625: PCM Detects Low PWM Signal (Part 2 of 3). CTS

	Inspect for poor connections at the harness connector of the generator. Did you find and correct the condition?	-	Go to Step 9	Diagnose Charging System
7	Inspect for poor connections at the harness connector of the ECM. Did you find and correct the condition?	-	Go to Step 9	Go to Step 8
8	**Important** The replacement ECM must be programmed. Replace the ECM. Did you complete the repair?	-	Go to Step 9	--
9	1. Review and record the scan tool Fail Records data. 2. Use the scan tool in order to clear the DTC. 3. Operate the vehicle within the conditions for running DTC P0625. 4. Using the scan tool, observe the specific DTC information for DTC P0625 until the test runs. Does the scan tool indicate that DTC P0625 failed?	-	Go to Step 2	System OK

GC1100200857030X

Fig. 83 Code P0625: PCM Detects Low PWM Signal (Part 3 of 3). CTS

Circuit Description

The clutch switch is a normally closed switch, clutch pedal released. The ECM detects an ignition voltage on the clutch switch circuit when the clutch switch is closed. The ECM detects 0 volts on the clutch switch circuit when the clutch switch is open, clutch pedal depressed.

This DTC determines if the transmission clutch switch has failed by looking for a clutch switch transition during a predetermined drive cycle.

Conditions for Running the DTC

- No VSS DTCs.
- The vehicle speed is greater than 15 km/h (9 mph).
- The brake switch remains released.

Conditions for Setting the DTC

- The ECM must detect 20 or more gear changes with less than 6 clutch pedal transitions.
- Time between gear changes must be 4 seconds or greater.

Action Taken When the DTC Sets

- The ECM stores the DTC information into memory when the diagnostic runs and fails.
- The malfunction indicator lamp (MIL) will not illuminate.
- The ECM records the operating conditions at the time the diagnostic fails. The ECM stores this information in the Failure Records.

Conditions for Clearing the MIL/DTC

- A last test failed, current DTC, clears when the diagnostic runs and does not fail.
- A History DTC clears after 40 consecutive warm-up cycles, if this or any other emission related diagnostic does not report any failures.
- Use a scan tool in order to clear the MIL/DTC.

Test Description

The number below refers to the step number on the diagnostic table.

2. This step determines if the fault is present.

Step	Action	Values	Yes	No
1	Did you perform the Diagnostic System Check - Manual Transmission ?	--	Go to Step 2	Go to System Check -

GC1100200858010X

Fig. 84 Code P0704: Insufficient Time Between Gear Changes (Part 1 of 4). CTS

2	1. Install a scan tool. 2. Turn ON the ignition leaving the engine OFF. 3. Monitor the Clutch Switch parameter using the scan tool. 4. Depress and release the clutch pedal several times. Does the scan tool display change states when the clutch is depressed and released?	-	Diagnose Intermittent Conditions in Engine Controls	Go to Step 3
3	Inspect the adjustment of the clutch switch. Was an adjustment necessary?	-	Go to Step 15	Go to Step 4
4	1. Turn OFF the ignition. 2. Disconnect the clutch switch connector. 3. Jumper the clutch switch ignition feed to the clutch switch signal circuit using a fused jumper wire. 4. Turn ON the ignition leaving the engine OFF. Does the scan tool display the Clutch Switch Released?	-	Go to Step 5	Go to Step 6
5	Remove the jumper. Does the scan tool display the Clutch Switch Depressed?	-	Go to Step 8	Go to Step 7
6	Probe the clutch switch ignition feed circuit with a test lamp connected to a ground. Is the test lamp illuminated?	-	Go to Step 9	Go to Step 10
7	Test for a short to B+ on the clutch switch signal circuit. Did you find the condition?	-	Go to Step 13	Go to Step 14

GC1100200858020X

Fig. 84 Code P0704: Insufficient Time Between Gear Changes (Part 2 of 4). CTS

14	Replace the ECM. Is the action complete?	-	Go to Step 15	--
15	In order to verify your repair, perform the following procedure: 1. Select DTC. 2. Select Clear Info. 3. Operate the vehicle under the following conditions: o Ensure the vehicle speed is greater than 15 km/h (9 mph). o ECM must detect 6 or more clutch pedal transitions. o The time between gear changes is greater than 2 seconds. 4. Select specific DTC. 5. Enter DTC P0704. Has the test run and passed?	-	Go to Step 16	Go to Step 2
16	With a scan tool observe the stored information, capture info and DTC Info. Does the scan tool display any DTCs that you have not diagnosed?	-	Go to Diagnostic Trouble Code	System OK

GC1100200858040X

Fig. 84 Code P0704: Insufficient Time Between Gear Changes (Part 4 of 4). CTS

8	Inspect for poor terminal contact for the clutch switch signal circuit at the clutch switch connector. Did you find the condition?	-	Go to Step 13	Go to Step 11
9	Test for an open in the clutch switch signal circuit. Did you find the condition?	-	Go to Step 13	Go to Step 12
10	Repair the open in the clutch switch ignition feed circuit. Is the action complete?	-	Go to Step 15	--
11	Replace the clutch switch. Is the action complete?	-	Go to Step 15	--
12	Inspect the terminal tension at the ECM connector for the clutch switch signal circuit. Did you find the condition?	-	Go to Step 13	Go to Step 14
13	Repair as necessary. Is the action complete?	-	Go to Step 15	

GC1100200858030X

Fig. 84 Code P0704: Insufficient Time Between Gear Changes (Part 3 of 4). CTS

Circuit Description

The engine control module (ECM) uses the generator turn on signal circuit to control the load of the generator on the engine. A high side driver in the ECM applies a voltage to the voltage regulator. This signals the voltage regulator to turn the field circuit ON and OFF. When the ECM turns ON the high side driver, the voltage regulator turns ON the field circuit. When the ECM turns OFF the high side driver, the voltage regulator turns OFF the field circuit.

The ECM monitors the state of the generator turn on signal circuit. With the engine running, the ECM should detect a high generator turn on signal circuit.

Conditions for Running the DTC

- No generator, CKP sensors, or CMP sensor DTCs are set.
- The engine is running.
- The generator has not been commanded OFF by the ECM or scan tool.

Conditions for Setting the DTC

The ECM detects a low signal voltage on the generator turn on signal circuit for at least 15 seconds.

Action Taken When the DTC Sets

- The PCM will not illuminate the malfunction indicator lamp (MIL).
- The PCM will store the conditions present when the DTC set as Fail Records data only.
- The PCM will send a class 2 serial data message to the IPC and DIC to illuminate the charge indicator or display a charging message.

Conditions for Clearing the MIL/DTC

- The conditions for setting DTC P2500 are not present.
- The DTC can be cleared by using the scan tool Clear DTC Information function.

Step	Action	Values	Yes	No
1	Did you perform the Engine Electrical Diagnostic System Check?	--	Go to Step 2	Go to System Check -

GC1100200859010X

Fig. 85 Code P2500: PCM Detects Low Voltage Signal (Part 1 of 3). CTS

2	1. Install a scan tool. 2. Start the engine. 3. With a scan tool, observe the GEN - F Terminal Signal parameter in the PCM data list . Does the scan tool indicate that the GEN - F Terminal parameter is within the specified range?	5-100%	Test for Intermittent and Poor Connections	Go to Step 3
3	1. Turn OFF the ignition 2. Disconnect the generator harness connector. 3. Turn ON the ignition, with the engine OFF. 4. Measure the voltage between the generator turn on signal circuit of the generator harness connector and a good ground. Is the voltage within the specified range.	4.5 - 5.5 V	Go to Step 5	Go to Step 4
4	Test the generator turn on signal circuit for a short to ground or open. Did you find and correct the condition?	--	Go to Step 8	Go to Step 6

GC1100200859020X

Fig. 85 Code P2500: PCM Detects Low Voltage Signal (Part 2 of 3). CTS

5	Inspect for poor connections at the harness connector of the generator. Refer to Connector Repairs in Wiring Systems. Did you find and correct the condition?	-	Go to Step 8	Go to Charging System Test
6	Inspect for poor connections at the harness connector of the ECM. Refer to Connector Repairs in Wiring Systems. Did you find and correct the condition?	-	Go to Step 8	Go to Step 7
7	**Important** The replacement ECM must be programmed. Replace the ECM. Refer to Engine Control Module (ECM) Replacement in Engine Controls - 2.6L and 3.2L. Did you complete the repair?	-	Go to Step 8	--
8	1. Review and record the scan tool Fail Records data. 2. Use the scan tool in order to clear the DTC. 3. Operate the vehicle within the conditions for running DTC P2500. 4. Using the scan tool, observe the specific DTC information for DTC P2500 until the test runs. Does the scan tool indicate that DTC P2500 failed?	-	Go to Step 2	System OK

GC1100200859030X

Fig. 85 Code P2500: PCM Detects Low Voltage Signal (Part 3 of 3). CTS

Circuit Description

The engine control module (ECM) uses the generator turn on signal circuit to control the load of the generator on the engine. A high side driver in the ECM applies a voltage to the voltage regulator. This signals the voltage regulator to turn the field circuit ON and OFF. When the ECM turns ON the high side driver, the voltage regulator turns ON the field circuit. When the ECM turns OFF the high side driver, the voltage regulator turns OFF the field circuit.

The ECM monitors the state of the generator turn on signal circuit. The ECM should detect a low generator turn on signal circuit voltage when the key is ON and the engine is OFF, or when the charging system malfunctions. If the ECM detects a high generator turn on signal circuit voltage, DTC P2501 will set.

Conditions for Running the DTC

- No generator, CKP sensors, or CMP sensor DTCs are set.
- The ignition is in the ON position
- The engine is not running.

Conditions for Setting the DTC

The PCM detects a high signal voltage on the generator turn on signal circuit for at least 5 seconds.

Action Taken When the DTC Sets

- The PCM will not illuminate the malfunction indicator lamp (MIL).
- The PCM will store the conditions present when the DTC set as Fail Records data only.
- The PCM will send a class 2 serial data message to the IPC and DIC to illuminate the charge indicator or display a charging message.

Conditions for Clearing the MIL/DTC

- The conditions for setting DTC P2501 are not present.
- The DTC can be cleared by using the scan tool Clear DTC Information function.

Step	Action	Values	Yes	No
1	Did you perform the Engine Electrical Diagnostic System Check?	--	Go to Step 2	Go to Diagnostic System Check - Engine Electrical

GC1100200860010X

Fig. 86 Code P2501: PCM Detects High Voltage Signal (Part 1 of 3). CTS

2	1. Install a scan tool. 2. Start the engine. 3. With a scan tool, observe the GEN - F Terminal Signal parameter in the PCM data list . Does the scan tool indicate that the GEN - F Terminal parameter is within the specified range?	80 - 100%	Go to Step 3	Test for Intermittent and Poor Connections
3	1. Turn OFF the ignition 2. Disconnect the generator harness connector. 3. Turn ON the ignition, with the engine OFF. 4. Measure the voltage between the generator turn on signal circuit of the generator harness connector and a good ground. Is the voltage within the specified range.	Battery Voltage	Go to Step 4	Go to Step 5
4	Test the generator turn on signal circuit for a short to battery voltage. Did you find and correct the condition?	--	Go to Step 8	Go to Step 6

GC1100200860020X

Fig. 86 Code P2501: PCM Detects High Voltage Signal (Part 2 of 3). CTS

5	Inspect for poor connections at the harness connector of the generator. Did you find and correct the condition?	-	Go to Step 8	Go to Charging System Test
6	Inspect for poor connections at the harness connector of the ECM. Did you find and correct the condition?	-	Go to Step 8	Go to Step 7
7	**Important** The replacement ECM must be programmed. Replace the ECM. Did you complete the repair?	-	Go to Step 8	--
8	1. Review and record the scan tool Fail Records data. 2. Use the scan tool in order to clear the DTC. 3. Operate the vehicle within the conditions for running DTC. 4. Using the scan tool, observe the specific DTC information for DTC P2501 until the test runs. Does the scan tool indicate that DTC P2501 failed?	-	Go to Step 2	System OK

GC1100200860030X

Fig. 86 Code P2501: PCM Detects High Voltage Signal (Part 3 of 3). CTS

Circuit Description

The dash integration module (DIM) has an internal voltage sensor with a dedicated circuit that checks the battery positive voltage and battery negative circuit voltage to determine if it is above 9.0 volts.

Conditions for Running the DTC

This DTC shall run only if the DIM has power, ground and the ignition is not in START mode. This DTC shall execute regardless of the battery voltage, except when the DTC B1390 is set current.

Conditions for Setting the DTC

- This DTC shall be set as current when the voltage falls below 9.0 volts for 1200 milliseconds.
- When the vehicle exits START the DIM shall delay checking the voltage for 2 seconds.

Action Taken When the DTC Sets

A message shall be sent out on the class 2 lines to notify all other modules of low battery voltage.

Conditions for Clearing the MIL/DTC

In order to clear the DTC from a current status the voltage shall be greater than 9.54 volts for 1200 milliseconds.

Test Description

The number below refers to the step number on the diagnostic table.

3. Compares battery voltage with the voltage that the DIM calculates.

Step	Action	Value (s)	Yes	No
1	Did you perform the Engine Electrical Diagnostic System Check?	--	Go to Step 2	Go to System Check
2	1. Install a scan tool. 2. Turn ON the ignition, with the engine OFF. 3. With a scan tool, observe the Battery Voltage parameter in the DIM data list. Does the scan tool indicate the battery voltage is greater than the specified value?	9.5 V	Go to Step 4	Go to Step 3

GC1100200861010X

Fig. 87 Code B1327: Voltage Falls Below 9 Volts (Part 1 of 2). CTS

3	1. Measure the voltage across the battery terminals. 2. Compare the battery voltage with the Battery Voltage parameter in the DIM data list. Are the voltages within the specified value?	1.0 Volts	Go to Battery Inspection/Test	Go to Step 4
4	Inspect for poor connections at the harness connector of the DIM. Did you find and correct the condition?	--	Go to Step 6	Go to Step 5
5	**Important** Perform the setup procedure for the DIM. Replace the DIM. Did you complete the replacement?	--	Go to Step 6	--
6	1. Use the scan tool in order to clear the DTC. 2. Operate the vehicle within the conditions for running the DTC. Does the DTC reset?	--	Go to Step 2	System OK

GC1100200861020X

Fig. 87 Code B1327: Voltage Falls Below 9 Volts (Part 2 of 2). CTS

3	1. Measure the voltage across the battery terminals. 2. Compare the battery voltage with the Battery Voltage parameter in the DIM data list. Are the voltages within the specified value?	1.0 Volts	Diagnose Charging System	Go to Step 4
4	Inspect for poor connections at the harness connector of the DIM. Did you find and correct the condition?	--	Go to Step 6	Go to Step 5
5	**Important** Perform the setup procedure for the DIM. Replace the DIM. Did you complete the replacement?	--	Go to Step 6	--
6	1. Use the scan tool in order to clear the DTC. 2. Operate the vehicle within the conditions for running the DTC. Does the DTC reset?	--	Go to Step 2	System OK

GC1100200862020X

Fig. 88 Code B1328: Voltage Rises Above 16.5 Volts (Part 2 of 2). CTS

Circuit Description

The voltage level is monitored by the engine control module (ECM) and is sent as a Class 2 data message to the instrument panel cluster (IPC).

Conditions for Running the DTC

- The key is in the ON position.
- The engine is running.
- Engine speed must be greater than 1,500 RPM
- DTC 1327 is not current.

Conditions for Setting the DTC

This DTC will be set as current when the voltage falls below 10.5 volts for 30 seconds and the engine is running.

Action Taken When the DTC Sets

The charging system indicator message will be set in the drivers information center (DIC).

Conditions for Clearing the MIL/DTC

The DTC clears as a current status when the voltage is greater than 10.5 volts for 30 seconds with the engine running.

Step	Action	Value (s)	Yes	No
1	Did you perform the Engine Electrical Diagnostic System Check?	--	Go to Step 2	Go to System Check -

GC1100200863010X

Fig. 89 Code B1513: Voltage Fall Below 10.5 Volts For 30 Seconds (Part 1 of 2). CTS

Circuit Description

The dash integration module (DIM) has an internal voltage sensor with a dedicated circuit that checks the battery positive voltage and battery negative circuit voltage to determine if it is below 15.5 volts.

Conditions for Running the DTC

This DTC shall run only if the DIM has power, ground and the ignition is not in START mode. This DTC shall execute regardless of the battery voltage, except when the DTC B1390 is set current.

Conditions for Setting the DTC

This DTC shall be set as current when the voltage raises above 16.5 volts for 1200 milliseconds.

Action Taken When the DTC Sets

A message shall be sent out on the class 2 lines to notify the SIR of high battery voltage.

Conditions for Clearing the MIL/DTC

In order to clear the DTC from a current status the voltage shall be less than 15.5 volts for 1200 milliseconds.

Test Description

The number below refers to the step number on the diagnostic table.

3. Compares battery voltage with the voltage that the DIM calculates.

Step	Action	Value (s)	Yes	No
1	Did you perform the Engine Electrical Diagnostic System Check?	--	Go to Step 2	Go to System Check -
2	1. Install a scan tool. 2. Start the engine 3. Increase engine speed to above 1,500 RPM. 4. With a scan tool, observe the Battery Voltage parameter in the DIM data list. Does the scan tool indicate the battery voltage is less than the specified value?	15.5 V	Go to Step 4	Go to Step 3

GC1100200862010X

Fig. 88 Code B1328: Voltage Rises Above 16.5 Volts (Part 1 of 2). CTS

2	1. Install a scan tool. 2. Start the engine. 3. Allow voltage to stabilize. 4. With a scan tool observe the Volts parameter in the IPC data list using the scan tool. Does the scan tool indicate that the volts parameter is within the specified range?	10.5-16.2 V	Go to Step 3	Diagnose Charging System
3	Replace the IPC. Did you complete the replacement?	--	Go to Step 4	--
4	1. Use the scan tool in order to clear the DTC. 2. Operate the vehicle within the conditions for running the DTC. Does the DTC reset?	--	Go to Step 2	System OK

GC1100200863020X

Fig. 89 Code B1513: Voltage Fall Below 10.5 Volts For 30 Seconds (Part 2 of 2). CTS

Circuit Description

The voltage level is monitored by the engine control module (ECM) and is sent as a Class 2 data message to the instrument panel cluster (IPC).

Conditions for Running the DTC

- The key is in the ON position.
- The engine is running.
- Engine speed is greater than 1,500 RPM

Conditions for Setting the DTC

This DTC will be set as current when the voltage is greater than 16.0 volts for 30 seconds with the engine running.

Action Taken When the DTC Sets

The charge indicator and driver warning message will be set in the driver information center (DIC).

Conditions for Clearing the MIL/DTC

The DTC clears as a current status when the voltage falls below 16.2 volts for 30 seconds with the engine running.

Step	Action	Value (s)	Yes	No
1	Did you perform the Engine Electrical Diagnostic System Check?	--	Go to Step 2	Go to Diagnostic System Check - Engine Electrical
2	1. Install a scan tool. 2. Start the engine. 3. Allow voltage to stabilize. 4. With a scan tool observe the Volts parameter in the IPC data list using the scan tool. Does the scan tool indicate that the Volts parameter is within the specified range?	10.5-16.2 V	Go to Step 3	Diagnose Charging System
3	Replace the IPC. Did you complete the replacement?	--	Go to Step 4	--
4	1. Use the scan tool in order to clear the DTC. 2. Operate the vehicle within the conditions for running the DTC. Does the DTC reset?	--	Go to Step 2	System OK

GC1100200864000X

Fig. 90 Code B1514: Voltage Falls Below 16.2 Volts For 30 Seconds. CTS

Step	Action	Yes	No
1	Install a scan tool. Does the scan tool power up?	Go to Step 2	Check Data Link Communications
2	1. Turn ON the ignition, with the engine OFF. 2. Attempt to establish communication with the BCM and the PCM. Does the scan tool communicate with the control modules?	Go to Step 3	Check Data Link Communications
3	Select the BCM and PCM display DTCs function on the scan tool. Does the scan tool display any DTCs?	Go to Step 4	Go to Symptoms
4	Does the scan tool display any DTCs which begin with a "U"?	Check Data Link Communications	Go to Step 5
5	Does the scan tool display DTC B1000, B1004, B1007, B1009?	Check Body Control System	Go to Step 6

GC0140100066010X

Fig. 92 System Check (Part 1 of 2). Aurora

Step	Action	Yes	No
1	Install a scan tool. Does the scan tool power up?	Go to Step 2	Check Data Link Communications
2	1. Turn ON the ignition, with the engine OFF. 2. Attempt to establish communication with the powertrain control module (PCM). Does the scan tool communicate with the PCM?	Go to Step 3	Check Data Link Communications
3	Select the PCM display DTC function on the scan tool. Does the scan tool display any DTCs?	**Refer to MOTOR's "Domestic Engine Performance & Driveability Manual"**	Go to Symptoms

GC0140100080000X

Fig. 93 System Check. Century, Grand Prix, Impala, Intrigue, Monte Carlo, Park Avenue, Regal, Lumina & 2000 Bonneville, LeSabre, Seville & 2001–04 Cavalier & Sunfire

Step	Action	Yes	No
1	Install a scan tool. Does the scan tool power up?	Go to Step 2	Check Data Link Communications
2	1. Turn ON the ignition, with the engine OFF. 2. Attempt to establish communication with the powertrain control module. Does the scan tool communicate with the powertrain control module?	Go to Step 3	Check Data Link Communications
3	Select the powertrain control module display DTCs function on the scan tool. Does the scan tool display any DTCs?	Go to Step 4	**Refer to MOTOR's "Domestic Engine Performance & Driveability Manual"**
4	Does the scan tool display any DTCs which begin with a "U"?	Check Data Link Communications	**Refer to MOTOR's "Domestic Engine Performance & Driveability Manual"**

GC0140100061000X

Fig. 91 System Check. Alero, Grand Am & Malibu & 2000 Cavalier & Sunfire

Step	Action	Yes	No
6	Does the scan tool display DTC B1327 ?	**Refer to MOTOR's "Domestic Engine Performance & Driveability Manual"**	Go to Step 7
7	Does the scan tool display any DTCs that begin with a "C"?	Check Antilock Brake System	Go to Step 8
8	Does the scan tool display the PCM DTCs P0574, P1554, P1560, P1564, P1566, P1567, P1570 or P1585?	Go to Diagnostic Trouble Code (DTC) List	Go to Step 9
9	Does the scan tool display any DTCs which begin with a "P"?	**Refer to MOTOR's "Domestic Engine Performance & Driveability Manual"**	Go to Symptoms - Cruise Control

GC0140100066020X

Fig. 92 System Check (Part 2 of 2). Aurora

Step	Action	Yes	No
1	Install a scan tool. Does the scan tool power up?	Go to Step 2	Check Data Link Communications
2	1. Turn ON the ignition, with the engine OFF. 2. Attempt to establish communication with the Powertrain Control Module and the Electronic Brake Control Module. Does the scan tool communicate with the Powertrain Control Module and the Electronic Brake Control Module?	Go to Step 3	Check Data Link Communications
3	Does the scan tool display any DTCs which begin with a "U"?	Check Data Link Communications	Go to Step 4
4	Select the ABS Control Module display DTCs function on the scan tool. Does the scan tool display any DTCs?	Check ABS	Go to Step 5

GC0140100079010X

Fig. 94 System Check (Part 1 of 2). 2001–04 Bonneville & LeSabre

Step	Action	Yes	No
5	Select the Powertrain Control Module display DTCs function on the scan tool. Does the scan tool display any transaxle DTCs?	**Refer to MOTOR's "Domestic Engine Performance & Driveability Manual"**	Go to Step 6
6	Select the Powertrain Control Module display DTCs function on the scan tool. Does the scan tool display any DTCs?	Go to Diagnostic Trouble Code (DTC)	Go to Symptoms

GC0140100079020X

Fig. 94 System Check (Part 2 of 2). 2001–04 Bonneville & LeSabre

Step	Action	Yes	No
1	Install a scan tool. Does the scan tool power up?	Go to Step 2	Check Data Link Communications
2	1. Turn ON the ignition, with the engine OFF. 2. Attempt to establish communication with the Engine Control Module (ECM). Does the scan tool communicate with the ECM?	Go to Step 3	Check Data Link Communications
3	Select the ECM DTCs function on the scan tool. Does the scan tool display any of the following DTCs? • P0571 • P0603 • P1662	**Refer to MOTOR's "Domestic Engine Performance & Driveability Manual"**	Go to Step 4
4	Does the scan tool display any DTCs which begin with a "U"?	Check Data Link Communications	Go to Symptoms

GC0140100086000X

Fig. 95 System Check. Catera

Test Description

The numbers below refer to the step numbers on the diagnostic table.

2. Lack of communication may be due to a malfunction in the Keyword or the Class 2 serial data circuit. The specified procedure will determine the particular condition.

5. The presence of DTCs which begin with U indicates that some other module is not communicating. The specified procedure will compile all the available information before tests are performed.

Step	Action	Yes	No
1	Install a scan tool. Does the scan tool power up?	Go to Step 2	Diagnose Data Link Communications
2	1. Turn the ignition ON, with the engine OFF. 2. Attempt to establish communication with the following modules: o Engine Control Module (ECM) o Electronic Brake Control Module (EBCM) Does the scan tool communicate with the modules listed above?	Go to Step 3	Diagnose Data Link Communications

GC1100200849010X

Fig. 96 System Check (Part 1 of 2). CTS

Step	Action	Yes	No
3	**Important:** The engine may start during the following step. Turn the engine OFF as soon as you have observed the Crank power mode. 1. With a scan tool, access the Class 2 Power Mode in the Diagnostic Circuit Check. 2. Rotate the ignition switch through all positions while observing the System Power Mode parameter. Does the System Power Mode parameter reading match the ignition switch position for all switch positions?	Go to Step 4	Diagnose Data Link Communications
4	Select the DTCs function on the scan tool for the following modules: • ECM • EBCM Does the scan tool display any DTCs for the modules listed above?	Go to Step 4	Go to Symptoms -
5	Does the scan tool display any DTCs which begin with a "U"?	Diagnose Data Link Communications	Go to Step 6
6	Does the scan tool display DTC P0560, P0562, P0563, P0615, P0616, P0617, P0625, P0626, P2500 or P2501?	Go to Diagnostic Trouble Code	Go to Diagnostic Trouble Code

GC1100200849020X

Fig. 96 System Check (Part 2 of 2). CTS

Step	Action	Yes	No
1	Install a scan tool. Does the scan tool power up?	Go to Step 2	Check Data Link Communications
2	1. Turn ON the ignition, with the engine OFF. 2. Attempt to establish communication with the following Control Modules. o Powertrain Control Module (PCM) o Instrument Cluster (IPC) o Electronic Brake Control Module (EBCM) Does the scan tool communicate with these modules?	Go to Step 3	Check Data Link Communications
3	Select the IPC display DTC function on the scan tool. Does the scan tool display any DTCs?	Check Instrument Panel, Gauges and Console	Go to Step 4
4	Select the ABS/TCS display DTC function on the scan tool. Does the scan tool display any DTCs?	Check Antilock Brake System	Go to Step 5
5	Select the PCM display DTC function on the scan tool. Does the scan tool display any DTCs?	**Refer to MOTOR's "Domestic Engine Performance & Driveability Manual"**	Go to Symptoms

GC0140100114000X

Fig. 97 System Check. DeVille & 2001–04 Seville

Step	Action	Yes	No
1	Install a scan tool. Does the scan tool power up?	Go to Step 2	Check Data Link Communications
2	1. Turn ON the ignition, with the engine OFF. 2. Attempt to establish communication with the Powertrain Control Module. Does the scan tool communicate with the Powertrain Control Module?	Go to Step 3	Check Data Link Communications
3	Select the ABS/TCS display DTC function on the scan tool. Does the scan tool display any DTCs?	Check Antilock Brake System	Go to Step 4
4	Select the PCM display DTC function on the scan tool. Does the scan tool display any DTCs?	**Refer to MOTOR's "Domestic Engine Performance & Driveability Manual"**	Go to Symptoms - Cruise Control

GC0140100121000X

Fig. 98 System Check. Eldorado

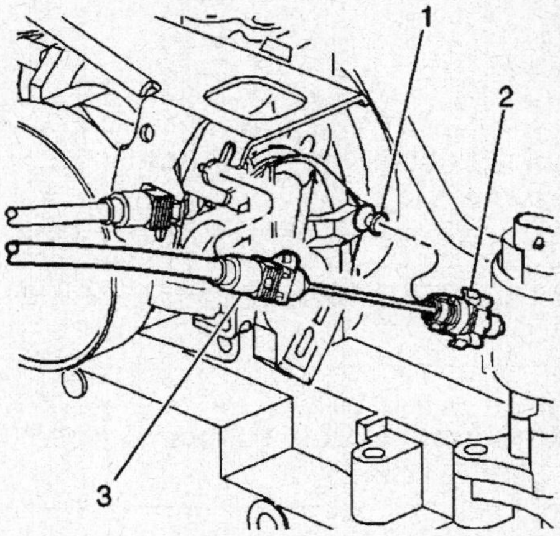

Fig. 99 Cruise cable replacement. Aurora w/3.5L engine

COMPONENT REPLACEMENT

Cruise Control Module

1. Disconnect control cable and electrical connector from speed control module.
2. Remove mounting nuts from shock tower and speed control module.
3. Reverse procedure to install.

Combination Cruise/ Stop Light Switch

1. Remove lefthand instrument panel insulator and disconnect electrical connector from speed control release switch/stop lamp switch.
2. Remove speed control release switch/ stop lamp switch from retainer in brake pedal bracket by pulling out.
3. Reverse procedure to install.

Vehicle Speed Sensor

1. Remove VSS mounting bolt and disconnect electrical connector.
2. Remove VSS from case extension and O-ring from VSS.
3. Reverse procedure to install. Replace O-ring, as required.

Cruise Control Cable

EXCEPT AURORA

1. Disconnect speed control adjuster lock and cruise control cable by rotating cruise control cable counterclockwise.
2. Disconnect cruise control cable from module strap and retainers.
3. Disconnect cruise control cable from throttle lever and accelerator control cable bracket.
4. Remove cruise control cable from engine.
5. Reverse procedure to install.

AURORA

1. Disconnect cruise control cable from cam and throttle body bracket, **Figs. 99 and 100.**
2. Disconnect cruise control cable from cruise control module.
3. Disconnect cable from retainers.
4. Remove cruise control cable.
5. Reverse procedure to install.

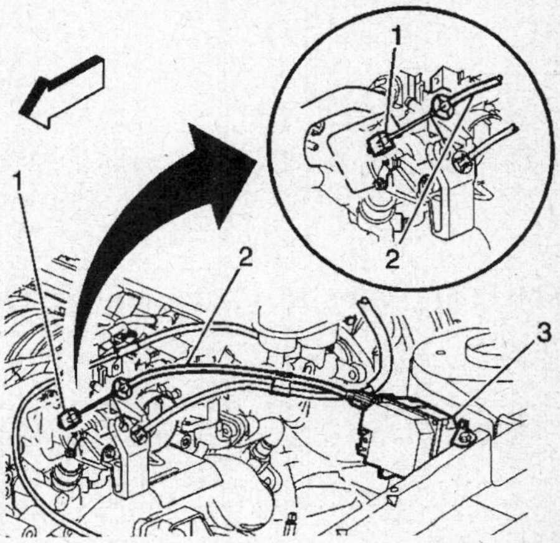

Fig. 100 Cruise cable replacement. Aurora w/4.0L engine

Cruise Control Switch

AURORA

1. Remove steering wheel as outlined in "Electrical" section of chassis chapter.
2. Remove access plate from back of steering wheel.
3. Remove switch mounting screws.
4. Disconnect electrical connector.
5. Reverse procedure to install.

Type 2

NOTE: On Air Bag Equipped Models, Refer To "Air Bag System Precautions" Located In The Front Of This Manual For System Disarming & Arming Procedures.

NOTE: Refer To "Computer Relearn Procedures" Located In The Front Of This Manual When Battery Power To The Computer Has Been Interrupted.

NOTE: "Electrical Symbol & Wire Color Code Identification" Located In The Front Of This Manual May Be Used As An Aid When Using Wiring Circuits Found In This Section.

INDEX

DESCRIPTION

The speed control system maintains a selected speed under normal driving conditions. Steep grades up or down may cause variations in the selected speeds. The speed control system has the ability to cruise, coast, resume speed, accelerate and tap up or tap down.

The main system components of the speed control system are the Cruise Control Module (CCM), the actuator, speed control switch and Vehicle Speed Sensor (VSS).

The speed control module (CCM) monitors vehicle speed and provides speed control actuator with the required command to maintain and change vehicle speed in response to inputs from the speed control switch. Speed control operation is disengaged when the CCM receives a cancel signal from the parking brake switch, stop lamp switch, brake fluid level switch, speed control switch, Park/Neutral Position (PNP) switch (automatic transaxles) or Clutch Pedal Position (CPP) interrupt switch (manual transaxles).

System Components

CRUISE CONTROL MODULE (CCM)

The speed control module is located to the righthand of the instrument panel compartment. On all models, the main function of the CCM is to monitor and act upon input signals from the speed control switch and VSS. There are four different kinds of input signals received by the CCM: ON/OFF, speed control, throttle position and cancel. The ON/OFF signal is provided by the speed control switch and activates and deactivates the speed control system. The speed control input signal to the CCM is provided by the speed control switch and VSS. Speed control input signals from the speed control switch are the RES/ACC (resume/accelerate) signal and the Set/Coast signal; these signals are also used to initiate the tap up and tap down functions. The CCM uses these signals in addition to the signal from the VSS to determine and maintain or alter vehicle speed in accordance with the driver's commands. The throttle position signals to the CCM are provided by the actuator and the idle switch inside the Throttle Position (TP) Sensor. These signals allow the CCM to constantly monitor throttle position during speed control operation. The cancel signals are provided by the speed control switch Cancel signal, the parking brake switch, stop lamp switch, brake fluid level switch, Park/Neutral Position (PNP) switch (automatic transaxles) or Clutch Pedal Position (CPP) interrupt switch (manual transaxles).

CRUISE CONTROL ACTUATOR

The actuator is mounted to the righthand inner fender. The actuator consists of a DC servo motor, a worm gear, a throttle angle sensor (potentiometer) and a magnetic clutch.

VEHICLE SPEED SENSOR (VSS)

The Vehicle Speed Sensor (VSS) is an electronic relay that is mounted on the transaxle. As the transaxle's output shaft turns,

Flash Code	Diagnostic Area	Failure	DTC
11	Servo Motor Circuit	Short	*DTC 11 Servo Motor Circuit Shorted*
12	Servo Magnetic Clutch	Open or short	*DTC 12 Magnetic Clutch CKT Open or Short to Ground*
14	Servo	Mechanical malfunction	*DTC 14 Motor CKT Open or S/Gnd*
15	Servo Motor Circuit	Open	*DTC 11 Servo Motor Circuit Shorted*
21	Vehicle Speed Sensor (VSS)	Open or short	*DTC 21 VSS CKT Open or S/Gnd*
23	Vehicle Speed Sensor (VSS)	Vehicle speed input 16 km/h (10 mph) lower than set speed	*DTC 23 Speed Drops More Than 10 mph*
32	Cruise Control Switch	Short	*DTC 32 Cruise Control Switch Shorted*
34	Cruise Control Switch	Incorrect voltage	*DTC 34 Abnormal Sgnl From Cruise Control Switch*
41	Cruise Control Module	Continuous output to actuator	*DTC 41 Continuous CCM Output to Actuator*
42	Power Supply	Power supply voltage less than 10V	*DTC 42 Low System Voltage*
43	Cruise Control Module	Power supply line is abnormal	*DTC 43 Abnormal Ignition Power Supply*

GC1109900667000X

Fig. 1 DTC interpretation. Prizm

Code/DTC	Interpretation
11/011 Or 015	Servo Motor Circuit
12/012	Magnetic Clutch Circuit Open Or Short To Ground
14/014	Motor Circuit Open Or Short To Ground
21/021	VSS Circuit Open Or Short To Ground
23/023	Speed Drops More Than 10 mph
41/041	Continuous CCM Output To Actuator
42/042	Low System Voltage

Fig. 2 DTC interpretation. Vibe

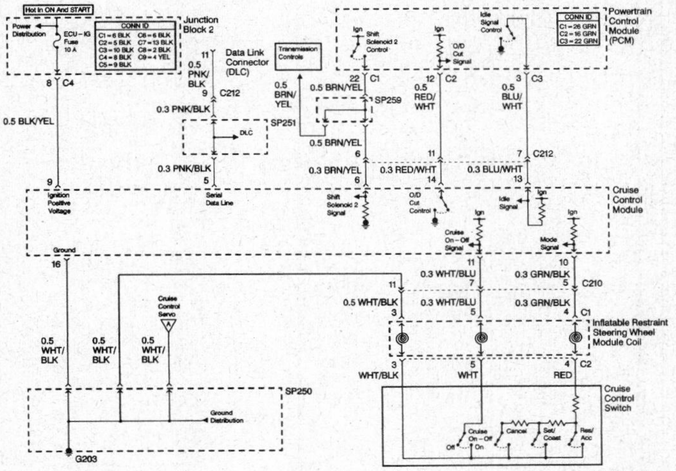

GC1109900554010X

Fig. 3 Wiring diagram (Part 1 of 3). Prizm

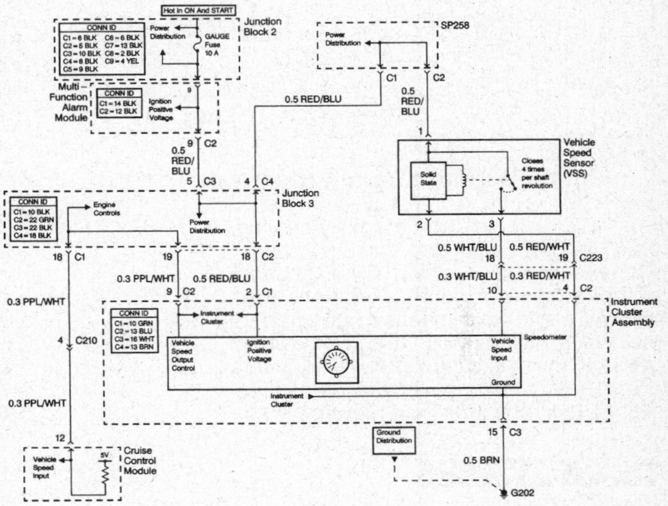

GC1109900554020X

Fig. 3 Wiring diagram (Part 2 of 3). Prizm

the VSS provides the speedometer with vehicle speed input (voltage pulses).

CLUTCH PEDAL POSITION (CPP) INTERRUPT SWITCH (MANUAL TRANSAXLES)

The Clutch Pedal Position (CPP) interrupt switch is mounted directly above the clutch pedal. Whenever the clutch pedal is depressed, the CPP interrupt switch closes and provides a ground to the CCM. The CCM disengages speed control operation when this ground signal is sensed.

PARK/NEUTRAL POSITION (PNP) SWITCH (AUTOMATIC TRANSAXLES)

The Park/Neutral Position (PNP) switch is mounted to the transaxle. Whenever the manual selector lever is placed in Park or Neutral, the PNP closes and provides a ground to the CCM. The CCM disengages speed control operation when this ground signal is sensed.

PARKING BRAKE SWITCH

The parking brake switch is located in the center console directly under the parking brake. Whenever the parking brake is engaged, the switch closes and provides a ground to the CCM. The CCM disengages speed control operation when this ground signal is sensed.

STOP LAMP SWITCH

The stop lamp switch is located under the instrument panel directly above the brake pedal. Whenever the brake pedal is depressed, one set of stop lamp switches close and provide a ground to the CCM. The CCM disengages speed control operation when this ground signal is sensed. When the brake pedal is depressed, another set of stop lamp switch contacts open and the voltage circuit from the CCM to the magnetic clutch inside the actuator is interrupted. With voltage removed from the magnetic clutch, the actuator's DC servo motor is disengaged from the worm gear and the throttle is permitted to return to the idle position. This feature is provided to ensure cancellation of the speed control system operation during vehicle braking.

THROTTLE POSITION (TP) SENSOR

The Throttle Position (TP) sensor is located on the throttle body. Whenever the throttle is in the idle position, the idle switch contacts within the TP sensor close and provide a ground to the CCM.

CRUISE INDICATOR

The CRUISE indicator, located in the gauge cluster. The indicator turns ON to inform the driver that the speed control system is operating.

POWERTRAIN CONTROL MODULE (PCM)

On vehicles equipped with four-speed automatic transaxles, the CCM receives a shift solenoid No. 2 signal. This signal informs the CCM that the transaxle is in second or third gear and is out of the Overdrive mode.

CRUISE ON/OFF SWITCH

The On/Off switch is a temporary contact type button located on the end of the speed control switch. The purpose of the switch is turn the speed control system on and off.

RES/ACC SWITCH

The Res/Acc (resume/accelerate) switch returns speed control operation to the last speed setting after a cancel signal is received by the CCM. If acceleration during cruise speed is desired, move speed control switch upward into Res/Acc position and hold it there until desired speed is attained.

The Res/Acc switch can also be used to tap up vehicle speed. Tapping-up is accomplished by quickly moving speed control switch up into Res/Acc position and releasing it. Tapping-up will increase vehicle speed in one mph increments.

SET/COAST SWITCH

The Set/Coast witch is activated when the speed control switch is moved downward. The vehicle will cruise at the speed

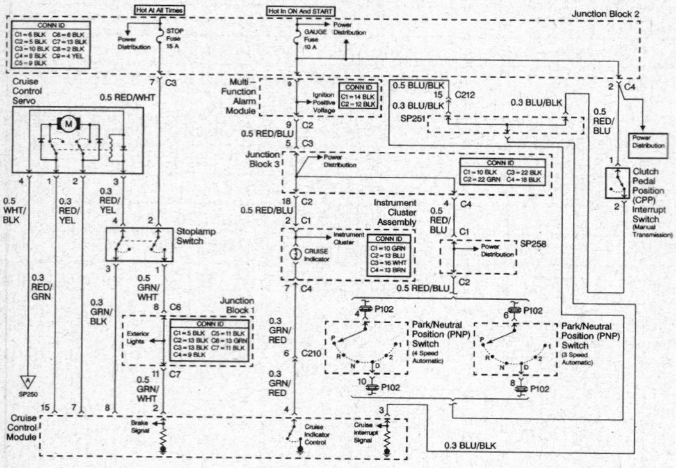

GC1109900554030X

Fig. 3 Wiring diagram (Part 3 of 3). Prizm

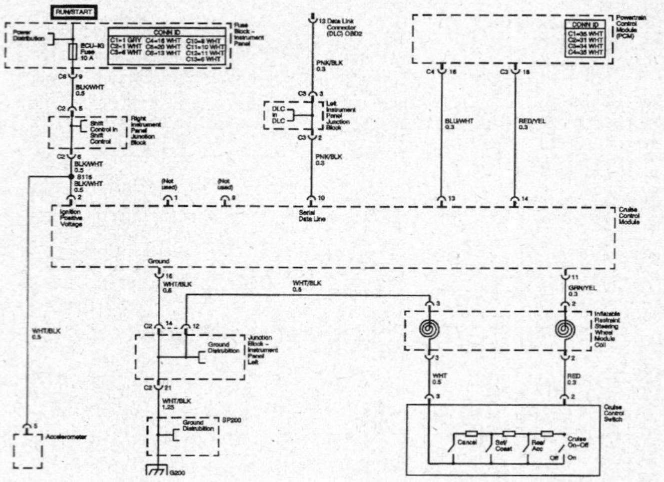

GC1100200947010X

Fig. 4 Wiring diagram (Part 1 of 3). Vibe

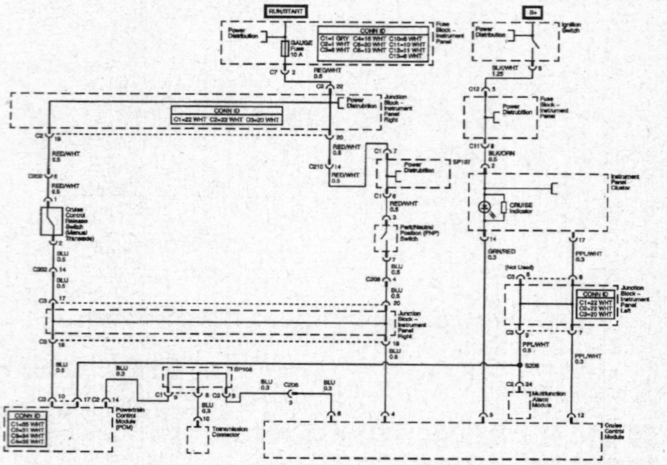

GC1100200947020X

Fig. 4 Wiring diagram (Part 2 of 3). Vibe

when the switch was activated. By moving the switch downward and holding it there, the speed control system will disengage and the throttle will return to idle position. The Set/Coast switch can also be used to tap down vehicle speed. Tapping-down is performed by quickly moving and releasing the Set/Coast switch. This will decrease vehicle speed in one mph increments.

PRECAUTIONS

Air Bag Systems

Refer to "Air Bag System Precautions" in the front of this manual for system disarming and arming procedures.

Battery Ground Cable

Prior to service, disconnect battery ground cable and isolate as required.

SYSTEM DIAGNOSIS & TESTING

Accessing Diagnostic Trouble Codes

LESS SCAN TOOL

1. Turn ignition switch to On position. **Do not start engine.**
2. **On Prizm models,** connect jumper between Data Link Connector (DLC) terminals Tc and E1. DLC is located in lefthand rear of engine compartment, mounted to strut tower.
3. **On Vibe models,**connect a jumper between cavity 4 and cavity 13 . This action pulls cruise control module terminal 10 to ground and signals CCM to enter FLASH DTC diagnostic display mode.
4. Cruise Indicator lamp with flash Diagnostic Trouble Codes (DTCs), as follows:
   a. A series of flashes which represent first DTC digit.
   b. A 2.5 second pause.
   c. A series of flashes which represent second DTC digit.
   d. For example, DTC 32 would be displayed as: three flashes, 2.5 second pause and two more flashes.
5. Each DTC is flashed once before moving on to next DTC.
6. After all DTCs are displayed, entire DTC sequence is continually repeated until jumper is removed from DLC.
7. If there are no DTCs present, CRUISE indicator lamp will flash continuously.

WITH SCAN TOOL

Connect a suitably programmed scan tool to Data Link Connector (DLC), and follow manufacturer's instructions.

Diagnostic Trouble Code Interpretation

Refer to **Figs. 1 and 2,** for Diagnostic Trouble Code (DTC) interpretation.

Wiring Diagrams

Refer to **Figs. 3 and 4,** for wiring diagrams.

Symptoms

Refer to **Figs. 5 through 10,** for symptoms.

Diagnostic Tests

PRIZM

Refer to **Figs. 11 through 21,** for diagnostic test procedures.

VIBE

Refer to **Figs. 22 through 29,** for diagnostic test procedures.

Clearing Diagnostic Trouble Codes

PRIZM

1. Turn ignition switch to Lock position.
2. Remove STOP fuse.
3. Remove ECU-B fuse.
4. Wait 30 seconds.
5. Install STOP and ECU-B fuses.
6. Turn ignition switch to ON position.
7. Connect DLC terminals 11 (Tc) and 3 (E1) using suitable jumper.
8. Ensure CRUISE indicator lamp flashes rapidly.
9. If CRUISE indicator lamp flashes any codes, perform System Check to determine cause of fault within cruise control system.

VIBE

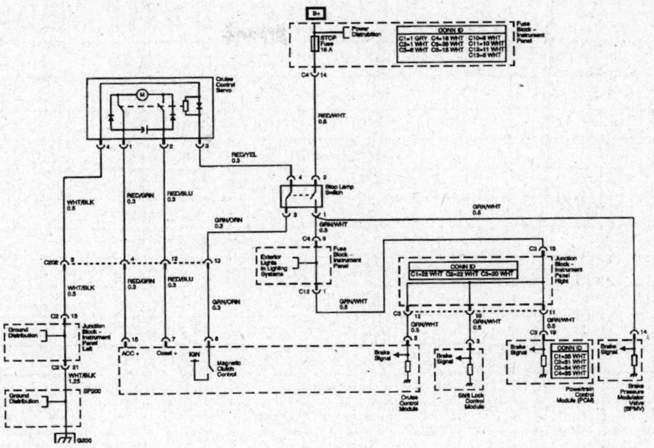

GC1100200947030X

Fig. 4 Wiring diagram (Part 3 of 3). Vibe

1. Place cruise control module in diagnostic mode, then pull cruise control switch to CANCEL position and hold.
2. While holding cruise control switch to CANCEL position, push cruise control ON switch 5 times within 3 seconds.
3. Release cruise control switch, then ensure that CRUISE indicator lamp flashes rapidly. This confirms that any flash codes have been cleared.
4. If CRUISE indicator lamp flashes any flash codes, perform cruise control diagnostic system check to determine cause of fault within cruise control system.

DIAGNOSTIC CHART INDEX

Step	Action	Value(s)	Yes	No
1	Was the Cruise Control System Check performed?	—	*Go to Step 2*	Go to *Cruise Control System Check*
2	1. Turn ignition OFF. 2. Disconnect the inflatable restraint steering wheel module coil connector C2. 3. Connect a *J 39200* between terminal 3 and terminal 4 of connector C2. 4. Move the cruise control switch upward toward the RES/ACC position and hold. Is the resistance within the specified range?	60–80 Ω	*Go to Step 3*	*Go to Step 4*
3	With the ignition still turned OFF and the inflatable restraint steering wheel module coil connector C2 still disconnected. 1. Connect a *J 39200* between terminal 3 and terminal 4 of connector C2. 2. Pull the cruise control switch and hold. Is the resistance within the specified range?	410–420 Ω	*Go to Step 5*	*Go to Step 4*
4	1. Check the cruise control switch connector for poor connection. 2. If OK, replace the cruise control switch. Is the replacement complete?	—	Go to *Cruise Control System Check*	—

GC1109900663010X

Fig. 5 Cruise Control Does Not Resume Or Cancel (Part 1 of 2). Prizm

Step	Action	Value(s)	Yes	No
5	With the ignition still turned OFF and the inflatable restraint steering wheel module coil connector C2 still disconnected. Test for continuity between terminal 3 of the inflatable restraint steering wheel module coil and ground. Is the resistance within the specified range?	0–2 Ω	*Go to Step 7*	*Go to Step 6*
6	Repair the poor ground connection at G203 which is located behind the right hand kick panel. Is the repair complete?	—	Go to *Cruise Control System Check*	—
7	1. Locate the cruise control module which is on the RH side of instrument panel, next to the instrument panel compartment. 2. Check the cruise control module connector for poor terminal contact. 3. If OK, replace the cruise control module. Is the replacement complete?	—	Go to *Cruise Control System Check*	—

GC1109900663020X

Fig. 5 Cruise Control Does Not Resume Or Cancel (Part 2 of 2). Prizm

Step	Action	Value(s)	Yes	No
1	Was the Cruise Control System Check performed?	—	Go to *Step 2*	Go to *Cruise Control System Check*
2	1. Turn ignition ON. 2. Depress and release the CRUISE ON OFF button. Does the cruise indicator lamp light?	—	Go to *Step 10*	Go to *Step 3*
3	Test for an open ECU-IG fuse in junction block 2 located behind the storage box cover on the left hand side of the instrument panel. Is the fuse open?	—	Go to *Step 4*	Go to *Step 7*
4	1. Turn ignition OFF. 2. Disconnect the cruise control module connector. 3. Connect a *J 39200* set to measure resistance between terminal 9 of the cruise control module connector and ground. Is the resistance equal to the specified value?	Infinite	Go to *Step 6*	Go to *Step 5*
5	Repair the short to ground in the BLK/YEL wire between terminal 9 of the cruise control module connector and terminal 8 on connector C4 of junction block 2. Is the repair complete?	—	Go to *Step 44*	—
6	1. Replace the ECU-IG fuse in junction block 2. 2. Reconnect the cruise control module connector. 3. Turn ignition switch to ON. 4. Depress and release the CRUISE ON OFF switch. Does the new fuse open?	—	Go to *Step 43*	Go to *Step 7*
7	1. Turn ignition OFF. 2. Disconnect the cruise control module connector. 3. Connect a *J 39200* set to measure resistance between terminal 16 of the cruise control module connector and ground. Is the resistance within the specified range?	0–2 Ω	Go to *Step 8*	Go to *Step 29*

GC1109900664010X

Fig. 6 Cruise Control Inoperative, Speedometer Inoperative (Part 1 of 5). Prizm

Step	Action	Value(s)	Yes	No
18	Replace the inflatable restraint steering wheel module coil. Is the replacement complete?	—	Go to *Step 44*	—
19	With the cruise control module connector still disconnected. 1. Connect a *J 39200* set to measure resistance between terminal 10 of the cruise control module connector and ground. 2. Pull the cruise control switch toward the CANCEL position and hold. Is the resistance reading within the specified range?	400–440 Ω	Go to*Step 23*	Go to *Step 20*
20	1. Disconnect the cruise control switch connector. 2. Connect a *J 39200* set to measure resistance between terminal 3 and terminal 4 of the cruise control switch. 3. Pull the cruise control switch toward the CANCEL position and hold. Is the resistance reading within the specified range?	400–440 Ω	Go to *Step 21*	Go to *Step 14*
21	With the cruise control switch still disconnected. 1. Disconnect the cruise control module connector. 2. Connect a *J 39200* set to measure resistance between terminal 10 of the cruise control module connector and terminal 4 of the inflatable restraint steering wheel module coil. Is the resistance reading within the specified range?	0–2 Ω	Go to *Step 19*	Go to *Step 22*
22	Repair the open between the inflatable restraint steering wheel module coil and the GRN/BLK wire of terminal 10 of the cruise control module connector. Is the repair complete?	—	Go to *Step 44*	—
23	1. Disconnect the cruise control module connector. 2. Turn ignition to ON. 3. Connect a *J 39200* set to measure voltage between terminal 3 of the cruise control module connector and ground. 4. If the vehicle has an automatic transmission, move the shift lever to the D position. Is the voltage within the specified range?	10–15 V	Go to *Step 25*	Go to *Step 24*
24	Repair the open between terminal 3 (BLU/BLK) wire of the cruise control module connector and B+. Is the repair complete?	—	Go to *Step 44*	—
25	With the ignition turned to OFF. 1. Disconnect the cruise control module connector. 2. Connect a *J 39200* set to measure voltage between terminal 2 of the cruise control module connector and ground. Is the voltage equal to the specified value?	0 V	Go to *Step 30*	Go to *Step 26*
26	Connect a *J 39200* set to measure voltage between terminal 1 of the stoplamp switch connector and ground. Is the voltage equal to the specified value?	0 V	Go to *Step 28*	Go to *Step 27*
27	Adjust or replace the stoplamp switch. Is the adjustment or replacement complete?	—	Go to *Step 44*	—

GC1109900664030X

Fig. 6 Cruise Control Inoperative, Speedometer Inoperative (Part 3 of 5). Prizm

Step	Action	Value(s)	Yes	No
8	1. Turn ignition ON. 2. Connect a *J 39200* set to measure voltage between the cruise control module connector terminal 9 and ground. Is the voltage within the specified range?	10–15 V	Go to *Step 10*	Go to *Step 9*
9	Repair the open between the cruise control module connector terminal 9 (BLK/YEL) and connector C4 terminal 8 of the junction block 2. Is the repair complete?	—	Go to *Step 44*	—
10	1. Turn ignition switch to OFF. 2. Disconnect the cruise control module connector. 3. Connect a *J 39200* set to measure resistance between cruise control module connector terminal 11 and ground. 4. Depress and hold the cruise control ON OFF button. Is the resistance reading within the specified range?	0–2 Ω	Go to *Step 19*	Go to *Step 11*
11	1. Disconnect connector C1 of the inflatable restraint steering wheel module coil. 2. Connect a *J 39200* set to measure resistance between terminal 5 of the inflatable restraint steering wheel module coil connector and terminal 11 of the cruise control module connector. Is the resistance reading within the specified range?	0–2 Ω	Go to *Step 13*	Go to *Step 12*
12	Repair open between terminal 5 of the inflatable restraint steering wheel module coil and the WHT/BLU wire of terminal 11 of the cruise control module. Is the repair complete?	—	Go to *Step 44*	—
13	With the cruise control connector C2 disconnected. 1. Connect the *J 39200* set to measure resistance between the WHT/BLK wire of terminal 3 and the WHT wire of terminal 5 of connector C2. 2. Depress and hold the cruise control button. Is the resistance reading within the specified range?	0–2 Ω	Go to *Step 15*	Go to *Step 14*
14	1. Inspect the cruise control switch for poor connection. 2. Replace the cruise control switch. Is the replacement complete?	—	Go to *Step 44*	—
15	With the cruise control switch connector C2 disconnected. Connect a *J 39200* set to measure resistance between terminal 3 of the inflatable restraint steering wheel module coil and ground. Is the resistance reading within the specified range?	0–2 Ω	Go to *Step 16*	Go to *Step 17*
16	1. Disconnect connector C1 of the inflatable restraint steering wheel module. 2. Connect a *J 39200* set to measure resistance between terminal 3 of connector C2 and terminal 3 of connector C1. Is the resistance reading within the specified range?	0–2 Ω	Go to *Step 10*	Go to *Step 18*
17	Repair open between terminal 3 of the inflatable restraint steering wheel module coil and ground. Is the repair complete?	—	Go to *Step 44*	—

GC1109900664020X

Fig. 6 Cruise Control Inoperative, Speedometer Inoperative (Part 2 of 5). Prizm

Step	Action	Value(s)	Yes	No
28	Repair the short to B+ between the GRN/WHT wire of terminal 2 of the cruise control module connector and terminal 1 of the stoplamp switch connector. Is the repair complete?	—	Go to *Step 44*	—
29	Repair the open between WHT/BLK wire of terminal 16 and ground. Is the repair complete?	—	Go to *Step 44*	—
30	With the ignition turned OFF. 1. Disconnect the cruise control module connector. 2. Connect a *J 39200* set to measure resistance between terminal 8 of the cruise control module connector and ground. Is the resistance reading within the specified range?	30–80 Ω	Go to *Step 39*	Go to *Step 31*
31	1. Disconnect the stoplamp switch connector. 2. Connect the *J 39200* between terminal 3 of the stoplamp switch connector and terminal 8 of the cruise control module connector. Is the resistance reading within the specified range?	0–2 Ω	Go to *Step 33*	Go to *Step 32*
32	Repair the open in the GRN/BLK wire between terminal 3 of the stoplamp switch and terminal 8 of the cruise control module. Is the repair complete?	—	Go to *Step 44*	—
33	With the stoplamp switch still disconnected. Connect a *J 39200* set to measure resistance between Terminal 3 and terminal 4 of the stoplamp switch. Is the resistance within the specified range?	0–2 Ω	Go to *Step 34*	Go to *Step 27*
34	With the stoplamp switch still disconnected. 1. Disconnect the cruise control servo connector. 2. Connect a *J 39200* set to measure resistance between the terminal 3 of the cruise control servo connector and terminal 4 of the stoplamp switch. Is the resistance within the specified range?	0–2 Ω	Go to *Step 36*	Go to *Step 35*
35	Repair the open in the RED/YEL wire between terminal 3 of the cruise control servo connector and terminal 4 of the stoplamp switch connector. Is the repair complete?	—	Go to *Step 44*	—
36	1. With the cruise control servo connector still disconnected. 2. Connect a *J 39200* set to measure resistance between terminlal 3 and terminal 4 of the cruise control servo. Is the resistance within the specified range?	30–50 Ω	Go to *Step 37*	Go to *Step 42*
37	With the cruise control servo connector still disconnected. connect a *J 39200* set to measure resistance between terminal 4 of the cruise control servo connector and ground. Is the resistance within the specified range?	0–2 Ω	Go to *Step 30*	Go to *Step 38*
38	Repair the open between the WHT/BLK wire of terminal 4 of the cruise control servo connector and ground. Is the repair complete?	—	Go to *Step 44*	—

GC1109900664040X

Fig. 6 Cruise Control Inoperative, Speedometer Inoperative (Part 4 of 5). Prizm

Step	Action	Value(s)	Yes	No
39	With the cruise control servo connector still disconnected. 1. Connect the POSITIVE lead of a *J 39200* to terminal 1 of the cruise control servo. 2. Connect the NEGATIVE lead of a *J 39200* to terminal 2 of the cruise control servo. 3. Set the *J 39200* to meaure resistance. Is the resistance within the specified range?	0–2 Ω	*Go to Step 40*	*Go to Step 42*
40	1. Disconnect Connector C2 of the instrument cluster assembly. 2. Connect a *J 39200* set to measure resistance between terminal 9 of C2 of the instrument cluster assembly and terminal 12 of the cruise control module connector. Is the resistance within the specified range?	0–2 Ω	*Go to Step 43*	*Go to Step 41*
41	Repair the open between the PPL/WHT wire of connector C2 terminal 9 of the instrument cluster assembly and terminal 12 of the cruise control module connector. Is the repair complete?	—	*Go to Step 44*	—
42	1. Inspect the cruise control servo connector for poor terminal contact. 2. If OK, replace the cruise control servo. Is the replacement complete?	—	*Go to Step 44*	—
43	1. Inspect the cruise control module connector for poor terminal contact. 2. If OK, replace the cruise control module. Is the replacement complete?	—	*Go to Step 44*	—
44	Install and connect any components removed during diagnosis. Is the repair complete?	—	*Cruise Control System Check*	—

GC1109900664050X

Fig. 6 Cruise Control Inoperative, Speedometer Inoperative (Part 5 of 5). Prizm

Step	Action	Yes	No
1	Did you review the Cruise Control Description and Operation and perform the necessary inspections?	Go to Step 2	Go to Symptoms -
2	1. Turn ON the ignition, with the engine OFF. 2. Observe the cruise indicator located in the instrument cluster. Is the cruise indicator on?	Go to Step 3	Test for Intermittent and Poor Connections
3	1. Turn OFF the ignition . 2. Disconnect the cruise control module. 3. Turn ON the ignition with, the engine OFF. Is the cruise indicator on?	Go to Step 8	Go to Step 4
4	1. Turn OFF the ignition . 2. Reconnect the cruise control module. 3. Disconnect the cruise control switch. 4. Turn ON the ignition with the engine OFF. Is the cruise indicator on?	Go to Step 5	Go to Step 7
5	1. Turn OFF the ignition. 2. Disconnect the cruise control module. 3. Test for a short to ground condition in the cruise on-off circuit between the cruise control module and the cruise control switch. Did you find and correct the condition?	Go to Step 11	Go to Step 6

GC1100200956010X

Fig. 8 Cruise Control Always On (Part 1 of 2). Vibe

6	Inspect for poor connections at the harness connector of the cruise control module. Did you find and correct the condition?	Go to Step 11	Go to Step 9
7	Inspect for poor connections at the harness connector of the cruise control switch. Did you find and correct the condition?	Go to Step 11	Go to Step 10
8	Repair the short to ground condition in the cruise indicator control circuit between the cruise indicator and the cruise control module. Did you complete the repair?	Go to Step 11	--
9	Replace the cruise control module. Did you complete the replacement?	Go to Step 11	--
10	Replace the cruise control switch. Did you complete the replacement?	Go to Step 11	--
11	Operate the system in order to verify the repair. Did you correct the condition?	System OK	Go to Step 3

GC1100200956020X

Fig. 8 Cruise Control Always On (Part 2 of 2). Vibe

Step	Action	Value(s)	Yes	No
1	Was the Cruise Control System Check performed?	—	*Go to Step 2*	Go to *Cruise Control System Check*
2	1. Turn ignition OFF. 2. Locate the cruise control module which is on the RH side of the instrument panel next to the instrument panel compartment. 3. Disconnect the cruise control module connector. 4. Connect a *J 39200* between the cruise control module connector terminal 11 and ground. Is the resistance equal to the specified value?	Infinite	*Go to Step 7*	*Go to Step 3*
3	With the cruise control module still disconnected. 1. Disconnect the inflatable restraint steering wheel module coil connector C2 2. Connect a *J 39200* between terminal 3 and terminal 5 of connector C2. Is the resistance equal to the specified value?	Infinite	*Go to Step 5*	*Go to Step 4*
4	1. Check the cruise control switch connector for poor connection. 2. If OK, replace the cruise control switch. Is the replacement complete?	—	*Go to Step 10*	—
5	With the cruise control module still disconnected. 1. Disconnect the inflatable restraint steering wheel module coil connector C2 2. Connect a *J 39200* between terminal 11 of the cruise control module coil connector and ground. Is the resistance equal to the specified value?	Infinite	*Go to Step 2*	*Go to Step 6*
6	Repair the short to ground between the WHT/BLU wire of terminal 11 of the cruise control module connector and the inflatable restraint steering wheel module coil. Is the repair complete?	—	*Go to Step 10*	—
7	With the cruise control module still disconnected. 1. Disconnect the instrument cluster assembly connector C4. 2. Connect a *J 39200* between terminal 4 of the cruise control module coil and ground. Is the resistance equal to the specified value?	Infinite	*Go to Step 9*	*Go to Step 8*
8	Repair the short to ground between the GRN/RED wire of the cruise control module terminal 4 and terminal 7 of the instrument cluster assembly connector C4. Is the repair complete?	—	*Go to Step 10*	—
9	1. Check the cruise control module connector for poor terminal contact. 2. If OK, replace the cruise control module. Is the replacement complete?	—	*Go to Step 10*	—
10	Install and connect any components removed during diagnosis. Is the repair complete?	—	*Cruise Control System Check*	—

GC1109900665000X

Fig. 7 Cruise Indicator Always On. Prizm

Step	Action	Yes	No
1	Did you review the Cruise Control Description and Operation and perform the necessary inspections?	Go to Step 2	Go to Symptoms
2	1. Turn ON the ignition with the engine OFF. 2. Operate the cruise control switch to the ON position. Does the cruise control indicator illuminate?	Test for Intermittent and Poor Connections	Go to Step 3
3	1. Turn OFF the ignition. 2. Disconnect the cruise control module. 3. Turn ON the ignition with the engine OFF. 4. Connect a fused jumper wire between cavity 4 of the cruise control module connector and ground. Does the cruise control indicator illuminate?	Go to Step 4	Go to Step 8
4	1. Turn OFF the ignition. 2. Operate the cruise control switch to the ON position and hold. 3. Test for a high resistance or an open condition between cavity 11 of the cruise control module and ground. Did you measure a high resistance or an open condition?	Go to Step 5	Go to Step 6
5	Test the cruise control on-off switch for a high resistance or an open condition. Did you measure a high resistance or an open condition?	Go to Step 7	Go to Step 9

GC1100200957010X

Fig. 9 Cruise Control Indicator Inoperative (Part 1 of 2). Vibe

6	Inspect for poor connections at the harness connector of the cruise control module. Did you find and correct the condition?	Go to Step 12	Go to Step 10
7	Inspect for poor connections at the harness connector of the cruise control switch. Did you find and correct the condition?	Go to Step 12	Go to Step 11
8	Repair the open in the cruise indicator circuit between the cruise control module connector and the GAUGE fuse. Did you complete the repair?	Go to Step 12	--
9	Repair the open in the cruise control on-off circuit between the cruise control module connector and ground. Did you complete the repair?	Go to Step 12	--
10	Replace the cruise control module. Did you complete the replacement?	Go to Step 12	--
11	Replace the cruise control switch. Did you complete the replacement?	Go to Step 12	--
12	Operate the system in order to verify the repair. Did you correct the condition?	System OK	Go to Step 3

GC1100200957020X

Fig. 9 Cruise Control Indicator Inoperative (Part 2 of 2). Vibe

4	1. Turn the ignition switch to LOCK. 2. Wait 5 seconds. 3. Turn ON the ignition, with the engine OFF. 4. If the vehicle has an automatic transaxle, Move the gear shift lever to the drive (D) position. 5. Move the cruise control switch downward to the SET/COAST position and hold. 6. Press the CRUISE ON-OFF switch and release. Does the CRUISE indicator lamp flash twice, pause, and then repeat this sequence?	--	Go to Step 5	Go to Step 18
5	Release the Cruise Control switch from the SET/COAST position. Does the CRUISE indicator lamp light continuously?	--	Go to Step 8	Go to Step 6
6	Operation or malfunction of any of the following controls will extinguish the Cruise indicator lamp when in diagnostic mode: • Gear shift lever not in the drive (D) position • Brake pedal depressed • Clutch pedal depressed • Cruise control switch is held in the CANCEL position. Are the controls in their normal position?	--	Go to Step 7	--
7	Test the following control circuits for a short condition: • The brake switch • The Cruise control switch Test the following control circuits for an open condition: • The PNP switch • The cruise release switch Did you find and correct the condition?	--	Go to Step 30	Go to Step 24
8	Move the cruise control switch upward to the RES/ACC position and hold . Does the CRUISE indicator lamp flash 3 times, pause, and then repeat this sequence?	--	Go to Step 9	Go to Step 18

GC1100200958020X

Fig. 10 Cruise Control Inoperative/Fault (Part 2 of 6). Vibe

Test Description

The numbers below refer to the step numbers on the diagnostic table.

3. This step makes sure that none of the DTC's listed are present which would affect cruise control operation.

4. This step places the cruise control module in a functional test mode to allow testing of the; Cruise control switch circuit, brake switch circuit, the vehicle speed sensor (VSS) circuit, PNP switch circuit (if equipped), and the cruise release switch circuit (if equipped)

14. This step checks the vehicle speed circuit (VSS).

Step	Action	Value (s)	Yes	No
DEFINITION: This table diagnoses the cruise control function is totally inoperative. It does not diagnose the lamp(s) only are inoperative.				
1	Did you review the Cruise Control Description and Operation and perform the necessary inspections?	--	Go to Step 2	Go to Symptoms
2	1. Drive the vehicle above 40 km/h (25 mph). 2. Depress and release the CRUISE ON OFF button. 3. Accelerate to the desired speed. 4. Move the cruise control switch downward to the SET/COAST position and release. 5. Take your foot off the accelerator pedal. Does the cruise control system operate normally?	--	Test for Intermittent and Poor Connections	Go to Step 3
3	Verify that the following OBD2 DTCs are not present: • P0505 • P0758 • P0120 • P0500 • P1780 Are any of the DTC's listed stored in Memory?	--		

GC1100200958010X

Fig. 10 Cruise Control Inoperative/Fault (Part 1 of 6). Vibe

9	Pull and release the cruise control switch to the CANCEL position while observing the CRUISE control indicator. Is the CRUISE indicator lamp OFF when the cruise control switch is pulled to the CANCEL position, and ON when the cruise control switch is released?	--	Go to Step 10	Go to Step 18
10	Press and release the brake pedal while observing the CRUISE indicator lamp. Is the CRUISE indicator lamp OFF with the brake pedal is pressed, and ON with the brake pedal released?	--	Go to Step 11	Go to Step 19
11	Does the vehicle have an automatic transaxle?	--	Go to Step 12	Go to Step 13
12	Move the Automatic Transaxle Control Lever to neutral (N), then to drive (D) while observing the CRUISE indicator lamp. Is the CRUISE indicator lamp ON with the manual selector in drive (D), and OFF in neutral (N)?	--	Go to Step 14	Go to Step 20
13	Press the clutch pedal while observing the CRUISE indicator lamp. Is the CRUISE indicator lamp OFF when the clutch pedal is pressed and ON when the clutch pedal is released?	--	Go to Step 14	Go to Step 21
14	1. Turn ignition switch to LOCK. 2. Wait 5 seconds. 3. Start the vehicle. 4. If the vehicle has an automatic transaxle, Move the gear shift lever to the drive (D) position. 5. Move the cruise control switch downward to the SET/COAST position and hold. 6. Press the CRUISE ON-OFF switch and release. 7. The CRUISE indicator lamp will flash twice, pause, and then repeat this sequence 8. Release the cruise control switch from the SET/COAST position 9. Accelerate driving wheels to 40 km/h (25 mph) while observing the CRUISE indicator lamp. Does the CRUISE indicator lamp flash rapidly?	--	Go to Step 15	Go to Step 22

GC1100200958030X

Fig. 10 Cruise Control Inoperative/Fault (Part 3 of 6). Vibe

15	Is vehicle equipped with a 4-speed automatic transaxle?	--	Go to Step 16	Go to Step 17
16	1. Start engine. 2. Set the overdrive (OD) switch to the ON position 3. Accelerate vehicle to 80 km/h (50 mph). 4. press the cruise control switch to the CRUISE ON-OFF position and set speed to engage cruise control. 5. Make sure transaxle is in 4th gear (OD). 6. Press and hold the parking brake release button while pulling up the parking brake gradually (to induce load drag) up to the moment that the transaxle downshifts into 3rd gear. 7. Immediately release the parking brake and notice a 2 second delay before the transaxle upshifts from 3rd gear into OD. Did the transaxle delay OD upshift?	--	Go to Step 17	Go to Step 23
17	1. Turn OFF the ignition. 2. Disconnect the cruise control module (CCM) connector and connector C2 of the PCM. 3. Test the idle signal circuit between cavity 13 of the CCM connector and cavity 16 of C2 of the PCM connector for a short to voltage or an open. Did you find and correct the condition?	--	Go to Step 30	Go to Step 22
18	**Important:** The cruise control switch is part of the inflatable restraint steering wheel module. Refer to Inflatable Restraint Steering Wheel Module Replacement in SIR. disable the SIR system and 1. Disconnect the cruise control switch. 2. Measure the resistance between terminal 2 and terminal 3 of the cruise control switch with the switch in all 3 positions. Did the measurements equal the specified values?	• Cruise ON-OFF 0.0 - 1.0 ohms • RES/ACC 210 - 270 ohms • SET/COAST 560 - 700 ohms • CANCEL 1389 - 1700 ohms	Go to Step 24	Go to Step 25

GC1100200958040X

Fig. 10 Cruise Control Inoperative/Fault (Part 4 of 6). Vibe

24	Inspect for poor connections at the harness connector of the cruise control module. Did you find and correct the condition?	-	Go to Step 30	Go to Step 28
25	Inspect for poor connections at the harness connector of the cruise control switch. Did you find and correct the condition?	-	Go to Step 30	Go to Step 29
26	Repair the open in the stoplamp switch circuit. Did you complete the repair?	-	Go to Step 30	--
27	Repair the open in the cruise release signal circuit. Did you complete the repair?	-	Go to Step 30	--
28	Replace the cruise control module. Did you complete the replacement?	-	Go to Step 30	--
29	Replace the cruise control switch. Did you complete the replacement?	-	Go to Step 30	--
30	Operate the system in order to verify the repair. Did you correct the condition?	-	System OK	Go to Step 3

GC1100200958060X

Fig. 10 Cruise Control Inoperative /Fault (Part 6 of 6). Vibe

19	1. Disconnect the cruise control module connector. 2. Connect a test lamp between cavity 3 of the cruise control module and ground. 3. Depress and release the brake pedal while observing the test lamp. Did the test lamp illuminate when the brake pedal was depressed?	-	Go to Step 24	Go to Step 26
20	1. Disconnect the cruise control module connector. 2. Connect a test lamp between cavity 4 of the cruise control module and ground. 3. Place the PNP switch in the D position. Did the test lamp illuminate when the PNP switch is in the D position?	-	Go to Step 24	Go to Step 27
21	1. Disconnect the cruise control module connector. 2. Connect a test lamp between cavity 3 of the cruise control module and ground. Does the test lamp extinguish when the clutch pedal is depressed and illuminate when the pedal is released?	-	Go to Step 24	Go to Step 27
22	1. Disconnect the cruise control module connector. 2. Test the vehicle speed input circuit between the left instrument panel junction block C3 cavity 7 and cavity 12 of the cruise control module connector for a high resistance or an open. Did you find and correct the condition?	-	Go to Step 30	Go to Step 24
23	1. Disconnect the cruise control module connector. 2. Disconnect Connector C1 of the PCM. 3. Test the O/D cut control circuit between C1 cavity 18 of the PCM connector and cavity 6 of the cruise control module connector for a short to voltage or an open. Did you find and correct the condition?	-	Go to Step 30	Go to Step 24

GC1100200958050X

Fig. 10 Cruise Control Inoperative/Fault (Part 5 of 6). Vibe

Step	Action	Value(s)	Yes	No
1	1. Turn ignition to LOCK. 2. Wait 10 seconds. 3. Turn ignition switch to ON. Is the CRUISE indicator lamp OFF?	—	Go to *Step 2*	Go to *Step 12*
2	Depress the CRUISE ON-OFF switch and release. Is the CRUISE indicator lamp ON steady?	—	Go to *Step 3*	Go to *Step 13*
3	1. Turn ignition switch to LOCK. 2. Wait 5 seconds. 3. Turn ignition switch to ON. 4. If the vehicle has an automatic transaxle, Move the gear shift lever to the drive (D) position. 5. Move the cruise control switch downward to the SET/COAST position and hold. 6. Press the CRUISE ON-OFF switch and release. Does the CRUISE indicator lamp flash twice, pause, and then repeat this sequence?	—	Go to *Step 4*	DIAGNOSE *DTC 32 Cruise Control Switch Shorted*
4	Move the cruise control switch upward to the RES/ACC position. Does the CRUISE indicator lamp flash 3 times, pause, and then repeat this sequence?	—	Go to *Step 5*	DIAGNOSE *DTC 32 Cruise Control Switch Shorted*
5	Pull and release the cruise control switch to the CANCEL position while observing the CRUISE control indicator. Is the CRUISE indicator lamp OFF when the cruise control switch is pulled to the CANCEL position, and ON when the cruise control switch is released?	—	Go to *Step 6*	DIAGNOSE *DTC 32 Cruise Control Switch Shorted*
6	Press and release the brake pedal while observing the CRUISE indicator lamp. Is the CRUISE indicator lamp OFF with the brake pedal is pressed, and ON with the brake pedal released?	—	Go to *Step 7*	Go to *Step 35*
7	Is the vehicle equipped with an automatic transaxle?	—	Go to *Step 8*	Go to *Step 9*
8	Move the Automatic Transaxle Control Lever to neutral (N), then to drive (D) while observing the CRUISE indicator lamp. Is the CRUISE indicator lamp ON with the manual selector in drive (D), and OFF in neutral (N)?	—	Go to *Step 10*	Go to *Step 26*
9	Press the clutch pedal while observing the CRUISE indicator lamp. Is the CRUISE indicator lamp OFF when the clutch pedal is pressed and ON when the clutch pedal is released?	—	Go to *Step 10*	Go to *Step 28*

GC1109900662010X

Fig. 11 System Check (Part 1 of 5). Prizm

Step	Action	Value(s)	Yes	No
10	1. Turn ignition switch to LOCK. 2. Wait 5 seconds. 3. Start the vehicle. 4. If the vehicle has an automatic transaxle, Move the gear shift lever to the drive (D) position. 5. Move the cruise control switch downward to the SET/COAST position and hold. 6. Press the CRUISE ON-OFF switch and release. 7. Accelerate driving wheels to 40 km/h (25 mph) while observing the CRUISE indicator lamp. Does the CRUISE indicator lamp flash?	—	Go to *Step 43*	DIAGNOSE *DTC 21 VSS CKT Open or S/Gnd*
11	1. Turn ignition switch to LOCK. 2. Connect a *J 36169-A* between terminal 3 (E1) and terminal 11 (Tc) of the data link connector which is located in the LH rear of the engine compartment on the strut tower. 3. Turn the ignition switch to ON. Does the cruise control indicator flash at a steady, rapid rate?	—	Go to *Step 34*	Go to *Step 14*
12	1. Turn ignition switch to LOCK. 2. Disconnect the cruise control module connector located next to the instrument panel compartment on the RH side of the instrument panel. 3. Turn the ignition switch to ON. Is the CRUISE indicator lamp ON?	—	Go to *Step 18*	Go to *Step 17*
13	Does the CRUISE indicator lamp flash ON and OFF?	—	Go to *Step 11*	Go to *Cruise Control Inoperative, Speedometer Operative*
14	Does the CRUISE indicator lamp flash any DTCs?	—	Go to the Flash Code DTC Table	Go to *Step 15*
15	1. Turn ignition to the LOCK position. 2. Disconnect the cruise control module connector. 3. Test for continuity between terminal 5 of the cruise control module connector and terminal 11 (Tc) of the DLC. Does continuity exist?	—	Go to *Step 17*	Go to *Step 19*

GC1109900662020X

Fig. 11 System Check (Part 2 of 5). Prizm

Step	Action	Value(s)	Yes	No
16	1. Start engine. 2. Set the overdrive (OD) switch to the ON position 3. Accelerate vehicle to 80 km/h (50 mph). 4. press the cruise control switch to the CRUISE ON-OFF position and set speed to engage cruise control. 5. Make sure transaxle is in 4th gear (OD). 6. Press and hold the parking brake release button while pulling up the parking brake gradually (to induce load drag) up to the moment that the transaxle downshifts into 3rd gear. 7. Immediately release the parking brake and notice a 2 second delay before the transaxle upshifts from 3rd gear into OD. Did the transaxle delay OD upshift?	—	Go to *Step 11*	DIAGNOSE *DTC P0758 Shift Solenoid #2 Electrical*
17	1. Inspect the cruise control module terminal for poor contact. 2. Inspect other wires and connectors for proper connections. 3. If no circuitry problem is found, replace the cruise control module. Is the replacement complete?	—	Go to *Step 34*	—
18	Repair the short to ground in the GRN/RED wire between the cruise control module connector terminal 4 and terminal 7 of connector C4 of the instrument cluster assembly. Is the repair complete?	—	Go to *Step 1*	—
19	Repair the open in the PNK/BLK wire between the cruise control module connector terminal 5 and terminal 11 of the DLC connector. Is the repair complete?	—	Go to *Step 1*	—
20	1. Turn ignition to LOCK. 2. Disconnect the cruise control module (CCM) connector located next to the instrument panel compartment on the RH side of the instrument panel. 3. Test for continuity between terminal 13 of the cruise control module connector and terminal 3 of connector C3 of the Powertrain Control Module (PCM). Does continuity exist?	—	Go to *Step 22*	Go to *Step 21*
21	Repair the open between the BLU/WHT wire of terminal 13 of the cruise control module connector and terminal 3 of connector C3 of the PCM. Is the repair complete?	—	Go to *Step 34*	—
22	With the CCM and PCM connectors still disconnected. Test for continuity between terminal 14 of the CCM and terminal 12 of connector C2 of the PCM. Does continuity exist?	—	Go to *Step 24*	Go to *Step 23*

GC1109900662030X

Fig. 11 System Check (Part 3 of 5). Prizm

Step	Action	Value(s)	Yes	No
23	Repair the open between the RED/WHT wire of terminal 14 of the CCM and terminal 12 of connector C2 of the PCM. Is the repair complete?	—	Go to *Step 34*	—
24	With the CCM and PCM connectors still disconnected. Test for continuity between terminal 6 of the CCM and terminal 22 of connector C1 of the PCM. Does continuity exist?	—	Go to *Step 16*	Go to *Step 25*
25	Repair the open between the BRN/YEL wire of terminal 6 of the CCM and terminal 22 of connector C1 of the PCM. Is the repair complete?	—	Go to *Step 34*	—
26	1. Turn the ignition switch to LOCK. 2. Disconnect the cruise control module connector which is located next to the instrument panel compartment on the RH side of the instrument panel. 3. Test for voltage between terminal 3 of the cruise control module connector and ground. 4. Press firmly on the brake pedal. 5. Shift the manual selector to the drive (D) position. 6. Turn the ignition switch to ON. Is the voltage within the specified range?	10–12 V	Go to *Step 17*	Go to *Step 27*
27	Repair the open in the BLU/BLK wire between terminal 3 of the cruise control module and SP251. Is the repair complete?	—	Go to *Step 34*	—
28	1. Turn the ignition switch to LOCK. 2. Disconnect the cruise control module connector which is located next to the instrument panel compartment on the RH side of the instrument panel. 3. Connect a *J 34142-B* between terminal 3 of the cruise control module connector and ground. 4. Turn the ignition switch to ON. Is the test lamp OFF when the clutch pedal is pressed and ON when the clutch pedal is released?	—	Go to *Step 17*	Go to *Step 29*
29	1. Turn the ignition switch to LOCK. 2. Connect a test lamp between terminal 2 of the clutch pedal position (CPP) interrupt switch and ground. Is the test lamp OFF when the clutch pedal is pressed and ON when the clutch pedal is released?	—	Go to *Step 30*	Go to *Step 31*
30	Repair the open between terminal 3 of the cruise control module connector and terminal 2 of the clutch pedal position (CPP) switch connector. Is the repair complete?	—	Go to *Step 34*	—
31	1. Turn the ignition switch to LOCK. 2. Connect a test lamp between terminal 1 of the clutch pedal position (CPP) interrupt switch connector and ground. Does the test lamp light?	—	Go to *Step 32*	Go to *Step 33*

GC1109900662040X

Fig. 11 System Check (Part 4 of 5). Prizm

Step	Action	Value(s)	Yes	No
32	Adjust or replace the clutch pedal position (CPP) switch. Is the adjustment or replacement complete?	—	Go to *Step 34*	—
33	Repair the open between terminal 1 of the clutch pedal position (CPP) switch connector and terminal 2 of connector C4 of junction block 2. Is the repair complete?	—	Go to *Step 34*	—
34	1. Turn the ignition switch to LOCK. 2. Reconnect all connector(s). 3. Turn the ignition switch to ON. 4. Observe the CRUISE indicator lamp. 5. Press the cruise control switch to the CRUISE ON-OFF position and release. 6. Observe the CRUISE indicator lamp. Was the CRUISE indicator lamp OFF when the ignition switch was turned to ON, then the CRUISE indicator lamp turned ON when the cruise control switch was pressed to the CRUISE ON-OFF position and released?	—	System OK	Go to *Step 1*
35	1. Disconnect the cruise control module connector. 2. Depress the brake pedal and hold. 3. Test for continuity between terminal 2 of the cruise control module connector and terminal 7 of connector C3 of the junction block 2 Is there continuity?	—	Go to *Step 36*	Go to *Step 37*
36	Release the brake pedal while still testing for continuity. Is there continuity after releasing the brake pedal?	—	Go to *Step 38*	Go to *Step 17*
37	Test for continuity between terminal 1 and terminal 2 of the stoplamp switch. Is there continuity when the brake pedal is pressed?	—	Go to *Step 39*	Go to *Step 38*
38	Adjust or replace the stoplamp switch. Is the adjustment or replacement complete?	—	System OK	—
39	Test for continuity between terminal 2 of the cruise control module connector and terminal 1 of the stoplamp switch. Is there continuity?	—	Go to *Step 40*	Go to *Step 42*
40	Test for continuity between terminal 7 of connector C3 of junction block 2 and terminal 2 of the stoplamp switch. Is there continuity?	—	Go to *Step 35*	Go to *Step 41*
41	Repair the RED/WHT wire between terminal 7 of connector C3 of junction block 2 and terminal 2 of the stoplamp switch. Is the repair complete?	—	System OK	—
42	Repair the GRN/WHT wire between terminal 2 of the cruise control module connector and terminal 1 of the stoplamp switch. Is the repair complete?	—	System OK	—
43	Determine if vehicle is equipped with a 3 speed or 4 speed automatic transaxle (4 speed transaxles have an overdrive switch on the automatic transaxle control lever). Does vehicle have a 4 speed automatic transaxle?	—	Go to *Step 16*	Go to *Step 11*

GC1109900662050X

Fig. 11 System Check (Part 5 of 5). Prizm

Step	Action	Value(s)	Yes	No
1	Was the Cruise Control System Check performed?	—	Go to *Step 2*	Go to *Cruise Control System Check*
2	1. Turn the ignition switch to LOCK. 2. Disconnect the cruise control module connector which is located next to the instrument panel compartment on the RH side of the instrument panel. 3. Turn the ignition switch to ON. 4. Connect a DMM set to read voltage between terminal 7 of the cruise control module connector and ground. Is the voltage less than the specified value?	1 V	Go to *Step 3*	Go to *Step 6*
3	Connect a DMM set to read voltage between terminal 15 of the cruise control module connector and ground. Is the voltage less than the specified value?	1 V	Go to *Step 4*	Go to *Step 7*
4	1. Disconnect the cruise control servo connector. 2. Connect a DMM set to measure resistance as follows: • Connect the positive lead of the DMM to terminal 1 of the cruise control servo. • Connect the negative lead of the DMM to terminal 2 of the cruise control servo. Is the resistance within the specified range?	2–4 Ω	Go to *Step 5*	Go to *Step 13*
5	With the cruise control servo still disconnected. Connect a DMM set to measure resistance as follows: 1. Connect the positive lead of the DMM to terminal 2 of the cruise control servo. 2. Connect the negative lead of the DMM to terminal 1 of the cruise control servo. Is the resistance equal to the specified value?	Infinite	Go to *Step 8*	Go to *Step 13*
6	Repair the RED/BLK wire between terminal 7 of the cruise control module and terminal 2 of the cruise control servo. Is the repair complete?	—	Go to *Step 14*	—
7	Repair the RED/GRN wire between terminal 15 of the cruise control module and terminal 1 of the cruise control servo. Is the repair complete?	—	Go to *Step 14*	—
8	1. Disconnect the cruise control cable from the cruise control servo. 2. Move the actuator arm back and forth. Does the actuator arm move freely in both directions?	—	Go to *Step 9*	Go to *Step 13*
9	With the cruise control servo still disconnected. 1. Connect a fused jumper from ground to terminal 4 of the cruise control servo. 2. Connect a fused jumper from B+ to terminal 3 of the cruise control servo. 3. Attempt to move the actuator arm. Does the actuator arm move?	—	Go to *Step 10*	Go to *Step 13*

GC1109900668010X

Fig. 12 Code 11: Servo Motor Circuit (Part 1 of 2). Prizm

Step	Action	Value(s)	Yes	No
10	1. Leave the ground and power connected to the servo. 2. Connect a fused jumper between ground and terminal 2 of the cruise control servo. 3. Connect a fused jumper between B+ and terminal 1. 4. Observe the actuator arm. Does the actuator arm move smoothly to the full open position?	—	Go to *Step 11*	Go to *Step 13*
11	1. Reverse the power and ground connections on terminals 1 and 2. 2. Observe the actuator arm. Does the actuator arm move smoothly to the close position?	—	Go to *Step 12*	Go to *Step 13*
12	1. Test the cruise control module connector for poor terminal contact. 2. If OK, replace the cruise control module. Is the replacement complete?	—	Go to *Step 14*	—
13	1. Test the cruise control servo connector for poor terminal contact. 2. If OK, replace the cruise control servo. Is the replacement complete?	—	Go to *Step 14*	—
14	Install and connect any components removed during diagnosis. Is the repair complete?	—	Go to *Cruise Control System Check*	—

GC1109900668020X

Fig. 12 Code 11: Servo Motor Circuit (Part 2 of 2). Prizm

Step	Action	Value(s)	Yes	No
1	Was the Cruise Control System Check performed?		Go to Step 2	Go to Cruise Control System Check
2	1 Turn the ignition switch to LOCK. 2 Disconnect the cruise control module connector which is located next to the instrument panel compartment on the RH side of the instrument panel. 3 Connect a DMM set to read resistance between terminal 8 of the cruise control module connector and ground. Is the resistance within the specified range?	35–45Ω	Go to Step 3	Go to Step 5
3	With the DMM still connected from the previous step (step 2). Press the brake pedal. Is the resistance reading within the specified range while the pedal is pressed?	Infinite	Go to Step 13	Go to Step 4
4	1 Disconnect the cruise control servo connector. 2 Connect a DMM set to measure resistance between terminal 8 of the cruise control module and ground. Is the resistance within the specified range?	Infinite	Go to Step 5	Go to Step 16
5	1 Disconnect the stoplamp switch connector. 2 Connect a DMM set to measure resistance between terminal 3 and 4 of the stoplamp switch. 3 Observe the resistance reading while pressing and releasing the brake pedal. Does the resistance read infinite Ω while the pedal is pressed, and 0 Ω when the pedal is released?		Go to Step 7	Go to Step 6
6	Adjust or replace the stoplamp switch. Is the adjustment or replacement complete?		Go to Step 20	
7	With the stoplamp switch and cruise control module connectors still disconnected. Connect a DMM set to read resistance between terminal 8 of the cruise control module connector and terminal 3 of the stoplamp switch connector. Is the resistance within the specified range?	0–2Ω	Go to Step 9	Go to Step 8
8	Repair the open in the GRN/BLK wire between terminal 8 of the cruise control module connector and terminal 3 of the stoplamp switch connector. Is the repair complete?		Go to Step 20	
9	With the stoplamp switch still disconnected. 1 Disconnect the cruise control servo connector. 2 Connect a DMM set to measure resistance between terminal 4 of the stoplamp switch connector and terminal 3 of the cruise control servo connector. Is the resistance within the specified range?	0–2Ω	Go to Step 11	Go to Step 10

GC1109900555010X

Fig. 13 Code 12: Magnetic Clutch Circuit Open Or Short To Ground (Part 1 of 2). Prizm

10	Repair the open in the RED/YEL wire between terminal 4 of the stoplamp switch and terminal 3 of the cruise control servo connector. Is the repair complete?		Go to Step 20	
11	1 Disconnect the cruise control servo connector 2 Connect a DMM set to measure resistance between terminal 3 and terminal 4 of the cruise control servo connector. Is the resistance within the specified range?	35–45Ω	Go to Step 12	Go to Step 19
12	With the cruise control servo still disconnected. Connect a DMM set to measure resistance between terminal 4 of the cruise control servo connector and ground. Is the resistance within the specified range?	0–2Ω	Go to Step 13	Go to Step 17
13	1 Disconnect the cruise control cable from the actuator. 2 Move the actuator arm back and forth. Does the actuator arm move freely in both directions?		Go to Step 14	Go to Step 19
14	1 Disconnect the cruise control servo connector. 2 Connect a fused jumper from ground to terminal 4 of the cruise control servo. 3 Connect a fused jumper from B+ to terminal 3 of the cruise control servo. 4 Attempt to move the actuator arm. Does the actuator arm move?		Go to Step 19	Go to Step 18
15	Repair the WHT/GRN wire between terminal 4 of the cruise control servo connector and ground. Is the repair complete?		Go to Step 20	
16	Repair the short to ground between the GRN/BLK wire of terminal 8 of the cruise control module connector and terminal 3 of the cruise control servo connector. Is the repair complete?		Go to Step 20	
17	Repair the WHT/BLK wire between terminal 4 of the cruise control servo and ground. Is the repair complete?		Go to Step 20	
18	Inspect the cruise control module terminals for poor contact. Inspect other wires and connectors for proper connections. If no circuitry problem is found, replace the cruise control module. Is the replacement complete?		Go to Step 20	
19	Inspect the cruise control servo terminals for poor contact. Inspect other wires and connectors for proper connections. If no circuitry problem is found, replace the cruise control servo. Is the replacement complete?		Go to Step 20	
20	Install and connect any components removed during diagnosis. Is the repair complete?		Go to Cruise Control System Check	

GC1109900555020X

Fig. 13 Code 12: Magnetic Clutch Circuit Open Or Short To Ground (Part 2 of 2). Prizm

Step	Action	Value(s)	Yes	No
1	Was the Cruise Control System Check performed?		Go to Step 2	Go to Cruise Control System Check
2	1 Disconnect the cruise control cable from the actuator. 2 Move the actuator arm back and forth. Does the actuator arm move freely in both directions?		Go to Step 3	Go to Step 5
3	1 Disconnect the cruise control servo connector. 2 Connect a fused jumper from ground to terminal 4 of the cruise control servo. 3 Connect a fused jumper from B+ to terminal 3 of the cruise control servo. 4 Attempt to move actuator arm. Does actuator arm move?		Go to Step 5	Go to Step 4

GC1109900556010X

Fig. 14 Code 14: Motor Circuit Open Or Short To Ground (Part 1 of 2). Prizm

Step	Action	Value(s)	Yes	No
1	Was the Cruise Control System Check performed?		Go to Step 2	Go to Cruise Control System Check
2	1 Turn the ignition to LOCK. 2 Disconnect the cruise control module connector located next to the instrument compartment on the RH side of the instrument panel. 3 Disconnect connector C1 on junction block 3 which is located behind the center of the instrument panel. 4 Connect a DMM set to measure resistance between terminal 12 of the cruise control module connector and ground. Is the resistance equal to the specified value?	Infinite	Go to Step 3	Go to Step 6
3	With the cruise control connector and connector C1 of Junction block 3 still disconnected. Connect a DMM set to measure resistance between terminal 12 of the cruise control module connector and terminal 18 of connector C1 of junction block 3. Is the resistance within the specified range?	0–2Ω	Go to Step 4	Go to Step 7
4	1 Disconnect connector C2 of junction block 3 2 Disconnect connector C2 of the instrument cluster assembly. 3 Connect a DMM set to measure resistance between terminal 19 of connector C2 of junction block 3 and ground. Is the resistance equal to the specified value?	Infinite	Go to Step 5	Go to Step 8

GC1109900557010X

Fig. 15 Code 21: VSS Circuit Open Or Short To Ground (Part 1 of 2). Prizm

Step	Action	Value(s)	Yes	No
4	1 Inspect the cruise control module connector for poor terminal contact. 2 If OK, replace the cruise control module. Is the replacement complete?		Go to Step 6	
5	Inspect the cruise control servo terminals for poor contact. Inspect other wires and connectors for proper connections. If no circuitry problem is found, replace the cruise control servo. Is the replacement complete?		Go to Step 6	
6	Install and connect any components removed during diagnosis. Is the repair complete?		Go to Cruise Control System Check	

GC1109900556020X

Fig. 14 Code 14: Motor Circuit Open Or Short To Ground (Part 2 of 2). Prizm

Step	Action	Value(s)	Yes	No
5	With connector C2 of junction block 3 and connector C2 of the instrument cluster assembly still disconnected. Connect a DMM set to measure resistance between terminal 19 of connector C2 of junction block 3 and terminal 9 of connector C2 of the instrument cluster assembly. Is the resistance within the specified range?	0–2Ω	Go to Step 10	Go to Step 9
6	Repair the short to ground in the PPL/WHT wire of terminal 12 of the cruise control module connector and terminal 18 of connector C1 of junction block 3. Is the repair complete?		Go to Step 11	
7	Repair the open in the PPL/WHT wire of terminal 12 of the cruise control module connector and terminal 18 of connector C1 of junction block 3. Is the repair complete?		Go to Step 11	
8	Repair the short to ground in the PPL/WHT wire of terminal 9 of connector C2 of the instrument cluster assembly and terminal 19 of connector C2 of junction block 3. Is the repair complete?		Go to Step 11	
9	Repair the open in the PPL/WHT wire of terminal 9 of connector C2 of the instrument cluster assembly and terminal 19 of connector C2 of junction block 3. Is the repair complete?		Go to Step 11	
10	1 Test the cruise control module connector for poor terminal contact. 2 If OK, replace the cruise control module. Is the replacement complete?		Go to Step 11	
11	Install and connect any components removed during diagnosis. Is the repair complete?		Go to Cruise Control System Check	

GC1109900557020X

Fig. 15 Code 21: VSS Circuit Open Or Short To Ground (Part 2 of 2). Prizm

Step	Action	Value(s)	Yes	No
1	Was the Cruise Control Diagnostic System Check performed?		Go to Step 2	Go to Cruise Control System Check
2	1 Raise and suitably support the vehicle. 2 Disconnect the cruise control module connector. 3 Turn the ignition switch to the on position. 4 Measure the voltage from cavity 12 while slowly rotating the front drive wheel with the transaxle in gear. Does the reading vary within the specified range?	0–5 V	Go to Step 3	Go to Step 4
3	Replace the cruise control module. Is the repair complete?		Go to Cruise Control System Check	
4	Repair the open or high resistance in the PPL/WHT wire between the module and junction block 3. Is the repair complete?		Go to Cruise Control System Check	

GC1109900558000X

Fig. 16 Code 23: Speed Drops More Than 10 mph. Prizm

12	1 Disconnect connector C1 of the inflatable restraint steering wheel module coil. 2 Connect a DMM between terminal 5 of the inflatable restraint steering wheel module and ground. Is the resistance equal to the specified value?	infinite	Go to Step 13	Go to Step 14
13	Connect a DMM between terminal 5 of connector C1 of the inflatable restraint steering wheel module connector and terminal 11 of the cruise control module connector. Is the resistance equal to the specified value?	Infinite	Go to Step 2	Go to Step 15
14	Replace the inflatable restraint steering wheel module coil. Is the replacement complete?		Go to Step 22	
15	Repair the short to ground between the WHT/BLU wire of connector C1 and terminal 11 of the cruise control module connector. Is the repair complete?		Go to Step 22	
16	With the cruise control module connector still disconnected. 1 Disconnect connector C2 of the inflatable restraint steering wheel module coil. 2 Connect a DMM set to measure resistance between terminal 3 and terminal 4 of the cruise control switch connector C2. Is the resistance equal to the specified value?	Infinite	Go to Step 17	Go to Step 21
17	Connect a DMM set to measure resistance between terminal 4 of the inflatable restraint steering wheel module coil and ground. Is the resistance equal to the specified value?	Infinite	Go to Step 4	Go to Step 18
18	1 Disconnect connector C1 of the inflatable restraint steering wheel module coil. 2 Connect a DMM between terminal 4 of the inflatable restraint steering wheel module and ground. Is the resistance equal to the specified value?	Infinite	Go to Step 19	Go to Step 14
19	Connect a DMM between terminal 4 of connector C1 of the inflatable restraint steering wheel module connector and terminal 10 of the cruise control module connector. Is the resistance equal to the specified value?	Infinite	Go to Step 4	Go to Step 20
20	Repair the short to ground between the GRN/BLK wire of terminal 4 of connector C1 and terminal 10 of the cruise control module. Is the repair complete?		Go to Step 22	
21	Test the cruise control switch connector for poor connection. If OK, replace the cruise control switch Is the replacement complete?		Go to Step 22	
22	Install and connect any components removed during diagnosis. Is the repair complete?		Go to Cruise Control System Check	

GC1109900559020X

Fig. 17 Code 32: Cruise Control Switch Shorted (Part 2 of 2). Prizm

Step	Action	Value(s)	Yes	No
1	Was the Cruise Control System Check performed?		Go to Step 2	Go to Cruise Control System Check
2	1 Turn ignition switch to LOCK. 2 Disconnect the cruise control module connector which is located next to the instrument panel compartment on the RH side of the instrument panel. 3 Connect a DMM set to measure resistance between terminal 11 of the cruise control module connector and ground. Is the resistance within the specified range?	Infinite	Go to Step 3	Go to Step 9
3	With the DMM still connected from the previous step (step 2). Press the cruise control switch to the CRUISE ON-OFF position and hold. Is the resistance within the specified range?	0–2Ω	Go to Step 4	Go to Step 9
4	With the cruise control module connector still disconnected. Connect a DMM set to measure resistance between terminal 10 of the cruise control module connector and ground. Is the resistance equal to the specified value?	Infinite	Go to Step 5	Go to Step 16
5	With the DMM still connected from the previous step (step 4). Pull the cruise control switch toward the CANCEL position and hold. Is the resistance within the specified range?	415–425Ω	Go to Step 6	Go to Step 21
6	With the DMM still connected from the previous step (step 5). Move the cruise control switch downward toward the SET/COAST position and hold. Is the resistance within the specified range?	195–205Ω	Go to Step 7	Go to Step 21
7	With the DMM still connected from the previous step (step 6). Move the cruise control switch upward toward the RES/ACC position and hold. Is the resistance within the specified range?	65–75Ω	Go to Step 8	Go to Step 21
8	Test the cruise control module connector for poor terminal contact. If OK, replace the cruise control module. Is the replacement complete?		Go to Step 22	
9	With the cruise control module connector still disconnected. 1 Disconnect connector C2 of the inflatable restraint steering wheel module coil. 2 Connect a DMM set to measure resistance between terminal 3 and terminal 5 of the cruise control switch connector C2. Is the resistance equal to the specified value?	Infinite	Go to Step 10	Go to Step 21
10	With the DMM still connected from the previous step (step 9). Press and hold the cruise control switch to the CRUISE ON/OFF position. Is the resistance within the specified range?	0–2Ω	Go to Step 11	Go to Step 21
11	With the cruise control module connector still disconnected. Connect a DMM set to measure resistance between terminal 5 of the inflatable restraint steering wheel module coil and ground. Is the resistance equal to the specified value?	Infinite	Go to Step 2	Go to Step 12

GC1109900559010X

Fig. 17 Code 32: Cruise Control Switch Shorted (Part 1 of 2). Prizm

Step	Action	Value(s)	Yes	No
1	Was the Cruise Control System Check performed?		Go to Step 2	Go to Cruise Control System Check
2	1 Turn ignition switch to LOCK. 2 Disconnect the cruise control module connector which is located next to the instrument panel compartment on the RH side of the instrument panel. 3 Turn ignition switch to ON. 4 Connect a DMM set to measure resistance between terminal 11 of the cruise control module connector and ground. Is the resistance equal to the specified value?	Infinite	Go to Step 3	Go to Step 9
3	With the DMM still connected from the previous step (step 2). Press the cruise control switch to the CRUISE ON-OFF position and hold. Is the resistance within the specified range?	0–2Ω	Go to Step 4	Go to Step 9
4	With the cruise control module connector still disconnected. Connect a DMM set to measure resistance between terminal 10 of the cruise control module connector and ground. Is the resistance equal to the specified value?	Infinite	Go to Step 5	Go to Step 17
5	With the DMM still connected from the previous step (step 4). Pull the cruise control switch toward the CANCEL position and hold. Is the resistance within the specified range?	415–425Ω	Go to Step 6	Go to Step 23
6	With the DMM still connected from the previous step (step 5). Move the cruise control switch downward toward the SET/COAST position and hold. Is the resistance within the specified range?	195–205Ω	Go to Step 7	Go to Step 23
7	With the DMM still connected from the previous step (step 6). Move the cruise control switch upward toward the RES/ACC position and hold. Is the resistance within the specified range?	65–75Ω	Go to Step 8	Go to Step 23
8	Test the cruise control module connector for poor terminal contact. If OK, replace the cruise control module. Is the replacement complete?		Go to Step 24	

GC1109900560010X

Fig. 18 Code 34: Abnormal Signal From Cruise Control Switch (Part 1 of 3). Prizm

Step	Action	Value(s)	Yes	No
9	With the cruise control module connector still disconnected. 1 Disconnect connector C2 of the inflatable restraint steering wheel module coil. 2 Connect a DMM set to measure resistance between terminal 3 and terminal 5 of the cruise control switch connector C2. Is the resistance equal to the specified value?	Infinite	Go to Step 10	Go to Step 23
10	With the DMM still connected from the previous step (step 9). Press and hold the cruise control switch to the CRUISE ON/OFF position. Is the resistance within the specified range?	0–2Ω	Go to Step 11	Go to Step 23
11	With connector C2 of the inflatable restraint steering wheel module coil still disconnected. Connect a DMM set to measure resistance between terminal 3 of connector C2 of the inflatable restraint steering wheel module and ground. Is the resistance within the specified range?	0–2Ω	Go to Step 12	Go to Step 22
12	With the cruise control module connector still disconnected. Connect a DMM set to measure resistance between terminal 5 of the inflatable restraint steering wheel module coil and ground. Is the resistance equal to the specified value?	Infinite	Go to Step 2	Go to Step 13
13	1 Disconnect connector C1 of the inflatable restraint steering wheel module coil. 2 Connect a DMM set to measure resistance between terminal 5 of the inflatable restraint steering wheel module and ground. Is the resistance equal to the specified value?	infinite	Go to Step 14	Go to Step 15
14	Connect a DMM set to measure resistance between terminal 5 of connector C1 of the inflatable restraint steering wheel module connector and terminal 11 of the cruise control module connector. Is the resistance equal to the specified value?	Infinite	Go to Step 2	Go to Step 16
15	Replace the inflatable restraint steering wheel module coil. Is the replacement complete?		Go to Step 24	

GC1109900560020X

Fig. 18 Code 34: Abnormal Signal From Cruise Control Switch (Part 2 of 3). Prizm

Step	Action	Value(s)	Yes	No
1	Was the Cruise Control Diagnostic System Check performed?		Go to Step 2	Go to Cruise Control System Check
2	1 Turn the ignition switch to the LOCK position. 2 Clear any DTCs present. 3 Test drive the vehicle at approximately 80 km/h (50 mph). 4 Engage the cruise control and observe the performance for one minute. 5 Stop the vehicle and test for DTCs. Does this DTC reset?		Go to Step 3	Go to Step 4
3	Replace the cruise control module. Is the repair complete?		Go to Cruise Control System Check	
4	Malfunction is not present at this time. Is the action complete?		Go to Cruise Control System Check	

GC1109900561000X

Fig. 19 Code 41: Continuous CCM Output To Actuator. Prizm

Step	Action	Value(s)	Yes	No
16	Repair the short to ground between the WHT/BLU wire of connector C1 and terminal 11 of the cruise control module connector. Is the repair complete?		Go to Step 24	
17	With the cruise control module connector still disconnected. 1 Disconnect connector C2 of the inflatable restraint steering wheel module coil. 2 Connect a DMM set to measure resistance between terminal 3 and terminal 4 of the cruise control switch connector C2. Is the resistance equal to the specified value?	Infinite	Go to Step 18	Go to Step 23
18	Connect a DMM set to measure resistance between terminal 4 of the inflatable restraint steering wheel module coil and ground. Is the resistance equal to the specified value?	Infinite	Go to Step 4	Go to Step 19
19	1 Disconnect connector C1 of the inflatable restraint steering wheel module coil. 2 Connect a DMM set to measure resistance between terminal 4 of the inflatable restraint steering wheel module and ground. Is the resistance equal to the specified value?	Infinite	Go to Step 20	Go to Step 15
20	Connect a DMM set to measure resistance between terminal 4 of connector C1 of the inflatable restraint steering wheel module connector and terminal 10 of the cruise control module connector. Is the resistance equal to the specified value?	Infinite	Go to Step 4	Go to Step 21
21	Repair the short to ground between the GRN/BLK wire of terminal 4 of connector C1 and terminal 10 of the cruise control module. Is the repair complete?		Go to Step 24	
22	Repair the open WHT/BLK wire between terminal 3 of the inflatable restraint steering wheel module and ground. Is the repair complete?		Go to Step 24	
23	Test the cruise control switch connector for poor connection. If OK, replace the cruise control switch. Is the replacement complete?		Go to Step 24	
24	Install and connect any components removed during diagnosis. Is the repair complete?		Go to Cruise Control System Check	

GC1109900560030X

Fig. 18 Code 34: Abnormal Signal From Cruise Control Switch (Part 3 of 3). Prizm

Step	Action	Value(s)	Yes	No
1	Was the Cruise Control Diagnostic System Check performed?		Go to Step 2	Go to Cruise Control System Check
2	1 Start the engine. 2 Turn the headlamps on to high beams. 3 Set the blower fan speed to high. 4 Measure the voltage between the positive and negative battery terminals. Is the voltage within the specified range?	10–14 V	Go to Step 3	Go to Step 6
3	1 Turn the ignition switch to the lock position. 2 Disconnect the cruise control module connector Re-start the engine. 3 Measure the voltage between cavity 9 and chassis ground Is the voltage within the specified range?	10–14 V	Go to Step 4	Go to Step 7
4	1 Turn the headlamps off. 2 Turn the blower off. 3 Turn the ignition switch to the lock position. 4 Reconnect the cruise control module. 5 Test drive the vehicle and engage the cruise control to verify the operation. 6 Stop the vehicle. 7 Test for DTCs Did this DTC set?		Go to Step 5	Go to Step 8
5	Inspect wires and connectors for proper connections. If no circuitry problem is found, replace the module. Is the repair complete?		Go to Cruise Control System Check	
6	Inspect Battery charging condition. Is the action complete?		Go to Cruise Control System Check	
7	Repair the high resistance in the BLK/YEL wire between the module and junction block 2. Is the repair complete?		Go to Cruise Control System Check	
8	Malfunction is not present at this time. Is the action complete?		Go to Cruise Control System Check	

GC1109900562000X

Fig. 20 Code 42: Low System Voltage. Prizm

Step	Action	Value(s)	Yes	No
1	Was the Cruise Control Diagnostic System Check performed?		Go to Step 2	Go to Cruise Control System Check
2	1 Turn the ignition switch to the LOCK position. 2 Disconnect the cruise control module. 3 Measure the voltage between cavity 9 and chassis ground. Is the voltage within the specified value?	0–10 V	Go to Step 3	Go to Step 5
3	1 Reconnect the cruise module connector. 2 Test drive the vehicle at approximately 80 km/h (50 mph). 3 Engage the cruise control and observe the performance for one minute. 4 Stop the vehicle and test for DTCs. Does this DTC reset?		Go to Step 6	Go to Step 4
4	Repair the high resistance in the BLK/YEL wire to the module in cavity 9. Is the repair complete?		Go to Cruise Control System Check	
5	Repair the short to voltage in the BLK/YEL wire to the module in cavity 9. Is the repair complete?		Go to Cruise Control System Check	
6	Replace the cruise control module. Is the repair complete?		Go to Cruise Control System Check	

GC1109900563000X

Fig. 21 Code 43: Abnormal Ignition Power Supply. Prizm

5	Repair the open in the serial data circuit between cavity 13 of the DLC and cavity 10 of the cruise control module. Did you complete the repair?	Go to Step 7	--
6	Replace the cruise control module. Did you complete the replacement.	Go to Step 7	--
7	1. Install a scan tool. 2. Turn ON the ignition, with the engine OFF. 3. Note the flash code pattern. Does the CRUISE indicator lamp in the instrument cluster flash rapidly ?	Go to Symptoms -	Go to Diagnostic Trouble Code (DTC) List
8	Note the flash code pattern. Does the CRUISE indicator lamp flash rapidly ?	Go to Symptoms -	Go to Diagnostic Trouble Code (DTC) List

GC1100200948020X

Fig. 22 System Check (Part 2 of 2). Vibe

Test Description

The number(s) below refer to the step number(s) on the diagnostic table.

2. This step ensures that the CRUISE indicator circuit is operational.
3. Lack of communication may be due to a malfunction of the serial data circuit. The specified procedure will determine if the wire between the DLC and the cruise control module is intact.

Step	Action	Yes	No
1	1. Install a scan tool. 2. Turn ON the ignition, with the engine OFF. 3. Select body from the scan tool menu. 4. Start the flash code diagnostics. Does the CRUISE indicator in the instrument cluster flash?	Go to Step 8	Go to Step 2
2	1. Turn ON the ignition, with the engine OFF. 2. Depress the cruise control On - Off switch to the On position. Does the CRUISE indicator Illuminate?	Go to Step 3	Go to Cruise Control Indicator Inoperative
3	1. Disconnect the cruise control module connector. 2. Measure for a high resistance or an open between cavity 13 of the DLC and cavity 10 of the cruise control module. Did you test a high resistance or an open in the serial data line?	Go to Step 5	Go to Step 4
4	Inspect for poor connections at the harness connector of the cruise control module. Did you find and correct the condition?	Go to Step 7	Go to Step 6

GC1100200948010X

Fig. 22 System Check (Part 1 of 2). Vibe

Circuit Description

The cruise control module applies voltage and ground to both the open and close sides of the cruise control servo motor as driving conditions demand changing throttle settings.

Diagnostic Aids

Check for the following:

- Cruise control cable for binding or broken cable
- Short to ground in the RED/GRN or RED/BLU wires between the cruise control module and the servo

An intermittent malfunction may be caused by a fault in the servo motor electrical circuit. Inspect the wiring harness and components for any of the following conditions:

- Backed out terminals
- Improper mating of terminals
- Broken electrical connectors locks
- Improperly formed or damaged terminals
- Faulty terminal to wire connections
- Physical damage to the wiring harness
- A broken wire inside the insulation
- Corrosion of electrical connections, splices, or terminals

Repair any electrical circuit faults that were found.

Test Description

The numbers below refer to the step numbers on the diagnostic table.

4. This step tests to see if the servo motor has the proper resistance.
5. This step tests to see if the servo motor has the proper resistance.
8. This step tests for proper movement of the actuator arm with the magnetic clutch energized.
9. This step tests for proper movement of the actuator arm with the magnetic clutch energized.

GC1100200949010X

Fig. 23 Code 11/011 Or 015: Servo Motor Circuit (Part 1 of 4). Vibe

Step	Action	Value (s)	Yes	No
1	Did you perform the Diagnostic System Check - Cruise Control ?	--	Go to Step 2	Go to Diagnostic System Check -
2	1. Turn the ignition switch to LOCK. 2. Disconnect the cruise control servo connector. 3. Turn ON the ignition, with the engine OFF. 4. Test for a short to voltage or open in the Coast+ control circuit. Did you find and correct the condition?	--	Go to Step 14	Go to Step 3
3	Test for a short to voltage or open in the ACC+ control circuit. Did you find and correct the condition?	--	Go to Step 14	Go to Step 4
4	1. Disconnect the cruise control servo connector. 2. Measure resistance as follows: o Connect the positive lead of the DMM to terminal 1 of the cruise control servo. o Connect the negative lead of the DMM to terminal 2 of the cruise control servo. Is the resistance within the specified range?	2-4 ohms	Go to Step 5	Go to Step 11
5	Measure resistance as follows: • Connect the positive lead of the DMM to terminal 2 of the cruise control servo. • Connect the negative lead of the DMM to terminal 1 of the cruise control servo. Is the resistance equal to the specified value?	infinity	Go to Step 6	Go to Step 11

GC1100200949020X

Fig. 23 Code 11/011 Or 015: Servo Motor Circuit (Part 2 of 4). Vibe

11	Inspect for poor connections at the harness connector of the cruise control servo. Did you find and correct the condition?	-	Go to Step 14	Go to Step 13
12	Replace the cruise control module. Did you Complete the replacement?	-	Go to Step 14	--
13	Replace the cruise control servo. Did you Complete the replacement?	-	Go to Step 14	--
14	1. Install a scan tool. 2. Turn ON the ignition, with the engine OFF. 3. Pull the cruise control switch to the CANCEL position and hold. 4. While holding the cruise control switch to the CANCEL position, push the cruise control ON switch 5 times within 3 seconds. 5. Check that the CRUISE indicator lamp flashes rapidly. This confirms that any flash codes have been cleared. Does the CRUISE indicator lamp flash the same trouble code?	-	Go to Step 2	System Ok

GC1100200949040X

Fig. 23 Code 11/011 Or 015: Servo Motor Circuit (Part 4 of 4). Vibe

6	1. Disconnect the cruise control cable from the cruise control servo. 2. Move the actuator arm back and forth. Does the actuator arm move freely in both directions?	-	Go to Step 7	Go to Step 11
7	With the cruise control servo still disconnected. 1. Connect a fused jumper from ground to terminal 4 of the cruise control servo. 2. Connect a fused jumper from B+ to terminal 3 of the cruise control servo. 3. Attempt to move the actuator arm. Does the actuator arm move?	-	Go to Step 8	Go to Step 11
8	1. Leave the ground and power connected to the servo. 2. Connect a fused jumper between ground and terminal 2 of the cruise control servo. 3. Connect a fused jumper between B+ and terminal 1. 4. Observe the actuator arm. Does the actuator arm move smoothly to the full open position?	-	Go to Step 9	Go to Step 11
9	1. Reverse the power and ground connections on terminals 1 and 2. 2. Observe the actuator arm. Does the actuator arm move smoothly to the close position?	-	Go to Step 10	Go to Step 11
10	Inspect for poor connections at the harness connector of the cruise control module. Did you find and correct the condition?	-	Go to Step 14	Go to Step 12

GC1100200949030X

Fig. 23 Code 11/011 Or 015: Servo Motor Circuit (Part 3 of 4). Vibe

Circuit Description

The cruise control module applies voltage to the magnetic clutch when the cruise control system is engaged. The circuit between the cruise control module and the magnetic clutch in the actuator is interrupted by the stop lamp switch whenever the brake pedal is pressed.

Diagnostic Aids

Check for the following:

- Stop lamp switch out of adjustment, or faulty.
- Open in the cruise control magnetic clutch.
- An open, short, or ground in the WHT/BLK, RED/GRN, RED/BLU, GRN/ORN, or RED/YEL wires.

An intermittent malfunction may be caused by a fault in the magnetic clutch electrical circuit. Inspect the wiring harness and components for any of the following conditions:

- Backed out terminals
- Improper mating of terminals
- Broken electrical connectors locks
- Improperly formed or damaged terminals
- Faulty terminal to wire connections
- Physical damage to the wiring harness
- A broken wire inside the insulation
- Corrosion of electrical connections, splices, or terminals

Repair any electrical circuit faults that were found.

Test Description

The numbers below refer to the step numbers on the diagnostic table.

2. This step tests the resistance of the cruise control servo magnetic clutch circuit.
4. This step tests the stop lamp switch.
7. This step tests the cruise control actuator arm for free movement with the magnetic clutch de-energized.

GC1100200950010X

Fig. 24 Code 12/012: Magnetic Clutch Circuit Open Or Short To Ground (Part 1 of 3). Vibe

Step	Action	Value(s)	Yes	No
1	Did you perform the Diagnostic System Check - Cruise Control ?	--	Go to Step 2	Go to Diagnostic System Check
2	1. Turn OFF the ignition. 2. Disconnect the cruise control module connector which is located behind the instrument panel. 3. Measure the resistance between cavity 8 of the cruise control module connector and ground. Is the resistance within the specified range?	35-45 ohms	Go to Step 3	Go to Step 4
3	1. Disconnect the cruise control servo connector. 2. Test the servo ground circuit for a high resistance or an open condition. Did you find and correct the condition?	--	Go to Step 14	Go to Step 7
4	1. Disconnect the stop lamp switch connector. 2. Measure the resistance between cavity 3 and 4 of the stop lamp switch. 3. Observe the resistance reading while pressing and releasing the brake pedal. Does the resistance read infinite ohms while the pedal is pressed, and 0 ohms when the pedal is released?	--	Go to Step 5	Go to Step 9
5	Test the magnetic clutch control circuit between the cruise control module and the cruise control servo for an open or ground condition. Did you find and correct the condition?	--	Go to Step 14	Go to Step 6
6	1. Disconnect the cruise control servo connector. 2. Measure the resistance between cavity 3 and cavity 4 of the cruise control servo connector. Is the resistance within the specified range?	35-45 ohms	Go to Step 7	Go to Step 11
7	1. Disconnect the cruise control cable from the actuator. 2. Move the actuator arm back and forth. Does the actuaor arm move freely in both directions ?	--	Go to	

GC1100200950020X

Fig. 24 Code 12/012: Magnetic Clutch Circuit Open Or Short To Ground (Part 2 of 3). Vibe

8	1. Disconnect the cruise control servo connector. 2. Connect a fused jumper wire from ground to terminal 4 of the cruise control servo. 3. Connect a fused jumper wire from B+ to terminal 3 of the cruise control servo. 4. Attempt to move the actuator arm. Does the actuator arm move?	-	Go to Step 11	Go to Step 10
9	Adjust or replace the stop lamp switch. Is the adjustment or replacement complete?	-	Go to Step 14	--
10	Inspect for poor connections at the harness connector of the cruise control module. Did you find and correct the condition?	-	Go to Step 14	Go to Step 12
11	Inspect for poor connections at the harness connector of the cruise control servo. Did you find and correct the condition?	-	Go to Step 14	Go to Step 13
12	Replace the cruise control module. Did you complete the replacement?	-	Go to Step 14	--
13	Replace the cruise control servo. Did you complete the replacement?	-	Go to Step 14	--
14	1. Install a scan tool. 2. Turn ON the ignition, with the engine OFF. 3. Pull the cruise control switch to the CANCEL position and hold. 4. While holding the cruise control switch to the CANCEL position, push the cruise control ON switch 5 times within 3 seconds. 5. Check that the CRUISE indicator lamp flashes rapidly. This confirms that any flash codes have been cleared. Does the CRUISE indicator lamp flash the same trouble code?	-	Go to Step 2	System OK

GC1100200950030X

Fig. 24 Code 12/012: Magnetic Clutch Circuit Open Or Short To Ground (Part 3 of 3). Vibe

Diagnostic Aids

An intermittent malfunction may be caused by a fault in the magnetic clutch electrical circuit. Inspect the wiring harness and components for any of the following conditions:

- Backed out terminals
- Improper mating of terminals
- Broken electrical connectors locks
- Improperly formed or damaged terminals
- Faulty terminal to wire connections
- Physical damage to the wiring harness
- A broken wire inside the insulation
- Corrosion of electrical connections, splices, or terminals

Repair any electrical circuit faults that were found. Refer to Wiring Repairs in Wiring Systems.

Test Description

The numbers below refer to the step numbers on the diagnostic table.

2. This step tests for proper arm movement with the magnetic clutch de-energized.

3. This step tests for proper arm movement with the magnetic clutch energized.

Step	Action	Yes	No
1	Did you perform the Diagnostic System Check - Cruise Control ?	Go to Step 2	Go to Diagnostic System Check -
2	1. Disconnect the cruise control cable from the actuator. 2. Move the actuator arm back and forth. Does the actuator arm move freely in both directions?	Go to Step 3	Go to Step 5
3	1. Disconnect the cruise control servo connector. 2. Connect a fused jumper wire from ground to terminal 4 of the cruise control servo. 3. Connect a fused jumper wire from B+ to terminal 3 of the cruise control servo. 4. Attempt to move the actuator arm. Does the actuator arm move?		

GC1100200951010X

Fig. 25 Code 14/014: Motor Circuit Open Or Short To Ground (Part 1 of 2). Vibe

4	Inspect for poor connections at the harness connector of the cruise control module. Did you find and correct the condition?	Go to Step 8	--
5	Inspect for poor connections at the harness connector of the cruise control servo. Did you find and correct the condition?	Go to Step 8	--
6	Replace the cruise control module. Did you complete the replacement?	Go to Step 8	--
7	Replace the cruise control servo. Did you complete the replacement?	Go to Step 8	--
8	1. Install a scan tool. 2. Turn ON the ignition, with the engine OFF. 3. Pull the cruise control switch to the CANCEL position and hold. 4. While holding the cruise control switch to the CANCEL position, push the cruise control ON switch 5 times within 3 seconds. 5. Check that the CRUISE indicator lamp flashes rapidly. This confirms that any flash codes have been cleared. Does the CRUISE indicator lamp flash the same trouble code?	Go to Step 2	System OK

GC1100200951020X

Fig. 25 Code 14/014: Motor Circuit Open Or Short To Ground (Part 2 of 2). Vibe

Circuit Description

The Vehicle speed sensor (VSS) provides vehicle speed input voltage to the instrument cluster and in turn to the cruise control module.

Diagnostic Aids

Check for the following:

Short to ground or an open condition in the PPL/WHT wires between the instrument cluster assembly, the left instrument panel junction block, and the cruise control module.

Inspect the wiring harness and components for any of the following conditions:

- Backed out terminals
- Improper mating of terminals
- Broken electrical connectors locks
- Improperly formed or damaged terminals
- Faulty terminal to wire connections
- Physical damage to the wiring harness
- A broken wire inside the insulation
- Corrosion of electrical connections, splices, or terminals

Repair any electrical circuit faults that were found.

Test Description

The numbers below refer to the step numbers on the diagnostic table.

2. This step tests for a short to ground or an open condition in the PPL/WHT wire which supplies VSS signal voltage to the cruise control module.
3. This step tests for a short to ground in the PPL/WHT wire which supplies VSS signal voltage from the instrument cluster assembly to junction block 3

Step	Action	Yes	No
1	Did you perform the Diagnostic System Check - Cruise Control ?	Go to Step 2	Go to Diagnostic System Check -

GC1100200952010X

Fig. 26 Code 21/021: VSS Circuit Open Or Short To Ground (Part 1 of 4). Vibe

5	Test the magnetic clutch control circuit between the cruise control module and the cruise control servo for an open or ground condition. Did you find and correct the condition?	--	Go to Step 14	Go to Step 6
6	1. Disconnect the cruise control servo connector. 2. Measure the resistance between cavity 3 and cavity 4 of the cruise control servo connector. Is the resistance within the specified range?	35-45 ohms	Go to Step 7	Go to Step 11
7	1. Disconnect the cruise control cable from the actuator. 2. Move the actuator arm back and forth. Does the actuator arm move freely in both directions?	--	Go to Step 8	Go to Step 13
8	1. Disconnect the cruise control servo connector. 2. Connect a fused jumper wire from ground to terminal 4 of the cruise control servo. 3. Connect a fused jumper wire from B+ to terminal 3 of the cruise control servo. 4. Attempt to move the actuator arm. Does the actuator arm move?	--	Go to Step 11	Go to Step 10
9	Adjust or replace the stop lamp switch. Is the adjustment or replacement complete?	--	Go to Step 14	--

GC1100200952030X

Fig. 26 Code 21/021: VSS Circuit Open Or Short To Ground (Part 3 of 4). Vibe

2	1. Turn OFF the ignition. 2. Disconnect the cruise control module connector which is located behind the instrument panel. 3. Measure the resistance between cavity 8 of the cruise control module connector and ground. Is the resistance within the specified range?	35-45 ohms	Go to Step 3	Go to Step 4
3	1. Disconnect the cruise control servo connector. 2. Test the servo ground circuit for a high resistance or an open condition. Did you find and correct the condition?	--	Go to Step 14	Go to Step 7
4	1. Disconnect the stop lamp switch connector. 2. Measure the resistance between cavity 3 and 4 of the stop lamp switch. 3. Observe the resistance reading while pressing and releasing the brake pedal. Does the resistance read infinite ohms while the pedal is pressed, and 0 ohms when the pedal is released?	--	Go to Step 5	Go to Step 9

GC1100200952020X

Fig. 26 Code 21/021: VSS Circuit Open Or Short To Ground (Part 2 of 4). Vibe

10	Inspect for poor connections at the harness connector of the cruise control module. Did you find and correct the condition?	-	Go to Step 14	Go to Step 12
11	Inspect for poor connections at the harness connector of the cruise control servo. Did you find and correct the condition?	-	Go to Step 14	Go to Step 13
12	Replace the cruise control module. Did you complete the replacement?	-	Go to Step 14	--
13	Replace the cruise control servo. Did you complete the replacement?	-	Go to Step 14	--
14	1. Install a scan tool. 2. Turn ON the ignition, with the engine OFF. 3. Pull the cruise control switch to the CANCEL position and hold. 4. While holding the cruise control switch to the CANCEL position, push the cruise control ON switch 5 times within 3 seconds. 5. Check that the CRUISE indicator lamp flashes rapidly. This confirms that any flash codes have been cleared. Does the CRUISE indicator lamp flash the same trouble code?	-	Go to Step 2	System OK

GC1100200952040X

Fig. 26 Code 21/021: VSS Circuit Open Or Short To Ground (Part 4 of 4). Vibe

Circuit Description

This DTC checks for an abnormal VSS input to the cruise control module or a malfunction within the cruise control module.

Diagnostic Aids

Check for the following:

- DTCs in the powertrain control module
- If the speedometer operates normally, the VSS is OK
- Open or high resistance in the PPL/WHT wire between the left instrument panel junction block C 3 and the cruise control module
- Faulty cruise control module

An intermittent may be caused by a poor connection, rubbed through wire insulation or a wire broken inside the insulation. Inspect the following harness connectors for backed out terminals, improper mating, broken lock, improperly formed or damaged terminals or for poor terminal-to-wire connection before replacing the suspect component:

- Cruise control module connector
- Left instrument panel junction block C 3

Test Description

The number below refers to the step number on the diagnostic table.

2. This step tests the resistance of the cruise control servo magnetic clutch circuit.

Step	Action	Value (s)	Yes	No
1	Did you perform the Diagnostic System Check - Cruise Control ?	--	Go to Step 2	Go to Diagnostic System Check -
2	1. Raise and suitably support the vehicle. 2. Disconnect the cruise control module connector. 3. Turn the ignition switch to the on position. 4. Measure the voltage from cavity 12 while Slowly rotating the front drive wheel with the Tranaxle in gear. Does the reading vary within a specific range?	0-8 V		

GC1100200953010X

Fig. 27 Code 23/023: Speed Drops More Than 10 mph (Part 1 of 2). Vibe

3	Inspect for poor connections at the harness connector of the cruise control module. Did you find and correct the condition?	- Go to Step 6	-
4	Repair the open or high resistance in the PPL/WHT wire between the cruise control module and the left instrument panel junction block C 3. Is the repair complete?	- Go to Step 6	-
5	Replace the cruise control module. Is the repair complete?	- Go to Step 6	-
6	1. Install a scan tool. 2. Turn ON the ignition, with the engine OFF. 3. Pull the cruise control switch to the CANCEL position and hold. 4. While holding the cruise control switch to the CANCEL position, push the cruise control ON switch 5 times within 3 seconds. 5. Check that the CRUISE indicator lamp flashes rapidly. This confirms that any flash codes have been cleared. Does the CRUISE indicator lamp flash the same trouble code?	- Go to Step 2	-

GC1100200953020X

Fig. 27 Code 23/023: Speed Drops More Than 10 mph (Part 2 of 2). Vibe

4	Replace the cruise control module. Is the replacement complete?	Go to Step 6	--
5	Malfunction is not present at this time. Is the action complete?	System OK	--
6	1. Install a scan tool. 2. Turn ON the ignition, with the engine OFF. 3. Pull the cruise control switch to the CANCEL position and hold. 4. While holding the cruise control switch to the CANCEL position, push the cruise control ON switch 5 times within 3 seconds. 5. Check that the CRUISE indicator lamp flashes rapidly. This confirms that any flash codes have been cleared. Does the CRUISE indicator lamp flash the same trouble code?	Go to Step 2	System OK

GC1100200954020X

Fig. 28 Code 41/041: Continuous CCM Output To Actuator (Part 2 of 2). Vibe

Circuit Description

This DTC is used to monitor the voltage level available to the cruise control module. If the voltage level drops below 10 Volts at terminal 2 (BLK/WHT wire), DTC 42 will set.

Diagnostic Aids

Check for the following:

- Open or high resistance in the BLK/WHT wire.
- Open, high resistance or low voltage in the power distribution to the ECU-IG fuse in instrument panel fuse block.
- Open or high resistance in the ground distribution to splice pack 200/G200
- Vehicle charging system for poor performance.
- Faulty cruise control module.

An intermittent may be caused by a poor connection, rubbed through wire insulation or a wire broken inside the insulation. Inspect the following harness connectors for backed out terminals, improper mating, broken lock, improperly formed or damaged terminals or for poor terminal-to-wire connection before replacing the suspect component:

- Cruise control module connector
- Instrument panel fuse block C 6
- Splice pack 200
- Ignition switch

Test Description

The numbers below refer to the step numbers on the diagnostic table.

2. This step tests the condition of the vehicles charging system.
3. This step tests the condition of the power feed circuit to the module.
4. This step tests for a faulty cruise control module.

GC1100200955010X

Fig. 29 Code 42/042: Low System Voltage (Part 1 of 3). Vibe

Circuit Description

This DTC allows the cruise control module to check for unwanted application of the servo due to a malfunction within the cruise control module.

Diagnostic Aids

Check for a faulty cruise control module.

Step	Action	Yes	No
1	Did you perform the Diagnostic System Check - Cruise Control ?	Go to Step 2	Go to Diagnostic System Check -
2	1. Install a scan tool. 2. Turn ON the ignition, with the engine OFF. 3. Pull the cruise control switch to the CANCEL position and hold. 4. While holding the cruise control switch to the CANCEL position, push the cruise control ON switch 5 times within 3 seconds. 5. Check that the CRUISE indicator lamp flashes rapidly. This confirms that any flash codes have been cleared. 6. Test drive the vehicle at approximately 80 km/h (50 mph). 7. Engage the cruise control and observe the performance for one minute. 8. Stop the vehicle. 9. Install a scan tool. 10. Turn ON the ignition, with the engine OFF. 11. Pull the cruise control switch to the CANCEL position and hold. 12. While holding the cruise control switch to the CANCEL position, push the cruise control ON switch 5 times within 3 seconds. Does the CRUISE indicator lamp flash the same trouble code?	Go to Step 3	Go to Step 5
3	Inspect for poor connections at the harness connector of the cruise control module. Did you find and correct the condition ?	Go to	

GC1100200954010X

Fig. 28 Code 41/041: Continuous CCM Output To Actuator (Part 1 of 2). Vibe

Step	Action	Value (s)	Yes	No
1	Did you perform the Diagnostic System Check - Cruise Control ?	--	Go to Step 2	Go to Diagnostic System Check -
2	1. Start the engine. 2. Turn the headlamps on to high beams. 3. Set the blower fan speed to high. 4. Measure the voltage between the positive and negative battery terminals. Is the voltage within the specified range?	10-14 V	Go to Step 3	Go to Step 6
3	1. Turn the ignition switch to the lock position. 2. Disconnect the cruise control module connector. 3. Re-start the engine. 4. Measure the voltage between cavity 9 and chassis ground Is the voltage within the specified range?	10-14 V	Go to Step 4	Go to Step 5
4	1. Turn the headlamps off. 2. Turn the blower off. 3. Turn OFF the ignition. 4. Reconnect the cruise control module. 5. Test drive the vehicle and engage the cruise control to verify the operation. 6. Stop the vehicle. 7. Install a scan tool. 8. Turn ON the ignition, with the engine OFF. 9. Pull the cruise control switch to the CANCEL position and hold. 10. While holding the cruise control switch to the CANCEL position, push the cruise control ON switch 5 times within 3 seconds. 11. Check that the CRUISE indicator lamp flashes rapidly. This confirms that any flash codes have been cleared. Does the CRUISE indicator lamp flash the same trouble code?	--	Go to Step 5	Go to Step 9
	Repair the high resistance in the BLK/WHT wire between the module and junction block 2. Is the repair complete?		Go to Step10	

GC1100200955020X

Fig. 29 Code 42/042: Low System Voltage (Part 2 of 3). Vibe

Step	Action	Value(s)	Yes	No
6	In order to diagnose a low charging condition, Diagnose Charging System Is the action complete?	-	Go to Step 10	--
7	Inspect for poor connections at the harness connector of the cruise control module. Did you find and correct the condition?	-	Go to Step 10	Go to Step 8
8	Replace the cruise control module. Is the repair complete?	-	Go to Step 10	--
9	Malfunction is not present at this time. Is the action complete?	-	System OK	--
10	1. Install a scan tool. 2. Turn ON the ignition, with the engine OFF. 3. Pull the cruise control switch to the CANCEL position and hold. 4. While holding the cruise control switch to the CANCEL position, push the cruise control ON switch 5 times within 3 seconds. 5. Check that the CRUISE indicator lamp flashes rapidly. This confirms that any flash codes have been cleared. Does the CRUISE indicator lamp flash the same trouble code?	-	Go to Step 2	System OK

GC1100200955030X

Fig. 29 Code 42/042: Low System Voltage (Part 3 of 3). Vibe

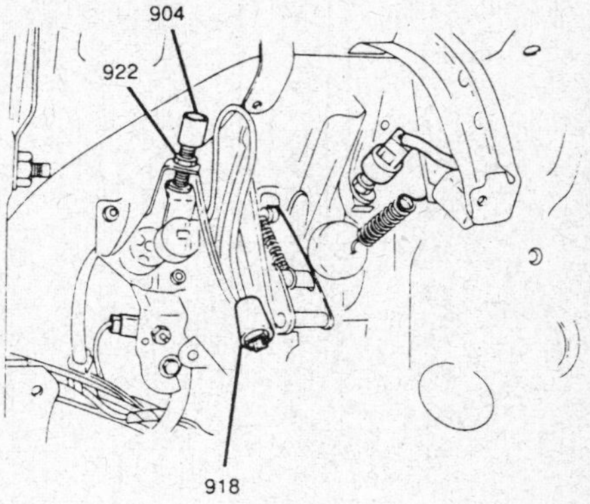

904 CLUTCH PEDAL POSITION (CPP) INTERRUPT SWITCH
918 ELECTRICAL CONNECTOR
922 CPP INTERRUPT SWITCH LOCKNUT

GC1109300264000X

Fig. 30 Clutch pedal position (CPP) interrupt switch replacement

COMPONENT REPLACEMENT

Clutch Pedal Position (CPP) Interrupt Switch

1. Remove two knee bolster cover plates.
2. Disconnect hood release cable from hood release lever and bracket.
3. Remove four bolts and knee bolster.
4. Disconnect ABS Data Link Connector (DLC) electrical connector, as required.
5. Remove screw and side ventilation from lefthand side duct outlet.
6. Disconnect CPP interrupt switch electrical connector and loosen locknut, **Fig. 30.**
7. Remove CPP interrupt switch locknut and switch by turning counterclockwise.
8. Reverse procedure to install. **Torque** CPP interrupt switch locknut and knee bolster bolts to 90 inch lbs.

Cruise Control Servo

PRIZM

1. Remove servo cover and loosen cable locknuts.
2. Loosen accelerator locknut.
3. Remove cruise control servo bracket screw, servo cable and accelerator cable.
4. Disconnect servo electrical connector and remove servo with bracket attached.
5. Remove servo from bracket.
6. Reverse procedure to install, noting the following:
   a. **Torque** servo mounting bolts to 89 inch lbs.
   b. **Torque** accelerator cable locknut to 71 inch lbs.

VIBE

1. Disengage tabs on cruise control cover, then remove cruise control servo cover.
2. Loosen accelerator control cable locknuts, then remove cruise control servo cable bracket screw, cruise control servo cable and accelerator control cable.
3. Disconnect cruise control servo electrical connector, then remove cruise control servo mounting bolts and cruise control servo with bracket attached.
4. Reverse procedure to install, noting the following:
   a. **Torque** servo mounting bolts to 52 inch lbs.
   b. **Torque** accelerator cable locknut to 71 inch lbs.

Cruise Control Cable

1. Loosen cable adjusting locknuts.
2. Remove cruise control servo cable from bracket.
3. Remove cruise control cable from throttle lever. Opening throttle lever by hand will ease removal of cruise control cable.
4. Remove cruise control servo cover by applying slight outward pressure to both sides at base of cover.
5. Remove cruise control cable bracket screw from bracket, **Fig. 31.**
6. Remove cruise control cable from servo lever.
7. Remove cruise control servo cable by removing cable from cable guide clips.
8. Reverse procedure to install, noting the following:
   a. Adjust cable locknuts to allow slight freedom of movement between cruise control cable and throttle lever.
   b. **Torque** cable adjusting locknuts to 71 inch lbs.

Cruise Control Module (CCM)

PRIZM

1. Remove glove compartment.
2. Disconnect cruise control module electrical connector.
3. Remove mounting bolts and CCM.
4. Reverse procedure to install.

VIBE

1. Remove instrument panel cluster trim plate, then the instrument panel cluster assembly.
2. Disconnect cruise control module electrical connector.
3. Remove mounting bolts and CCM.
4. Reverse procedure to install.

Cruise Control Switch

1. Remove driver's air bag as outlined in "Passive Restraint Systems" chapter.
2. Disconnect air bag coil speed control switch electrical connector, **Fig. 32.**
3. Open Terminal Position Assurance (TPA) on top of speed control switch electrical connector.
4. Remove red/blue wire from cruise control switch electrical connector.
5. Remove righthand horn contact and cruise control switch.
6. Reverse procedure to instal.

Park/Neutral Position (PNP) Switch

REMOVAL

1. Place shifter in Neutral position, then raise and support vehicle.

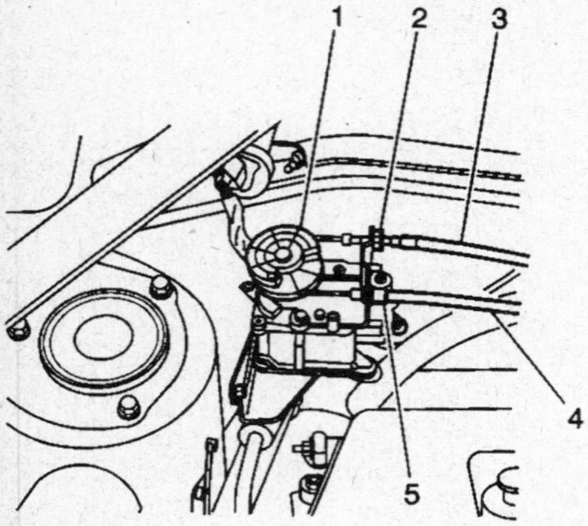

1 Servo Lever
2 Clip
3 Cable
4 Cable

GC1109900666000X

Fig. 31 Cruise control cable bracket

2. Remove six bolts and splash shield.
3. Remove nut, lock washer and shift select cable from manual lever.
4. Disconnect PNP electrical connector.
5. Remove nut, lock washer and manual lever from manual shaft. Unstake lock plate behind manual shaft nut.
6. Remove manual shaft nut and lock plate from PNP switch, then PNP switch bolts and switch.

INSTALLATION

1. **Torque** manual shaft nut to 60 inch lbs.
2. Adjust PNP switch by aligning neutral basic line scribed in PNP switch with groove in PNP switch sleeve, **Fig. 33.**
3. **Torque** PNP switch to 48 inch lbs.
4. **Torque** manual lever nut to 96–108 inch lbs.
5. Rotate manual lever counterclockwise until it reaches Park position.
6. Rotate manual lever clockwise two detent positions until manual lever is in Neutral position.
7. Install shift select cable into manual lever and secure with cable nut.
8. Pull cable taut ensuring no deflection exists.
9. **Torque** shift select cable to 114 inch lbs.
10. **Torque** lefthand splash shield bolts to 44 inch lbs.

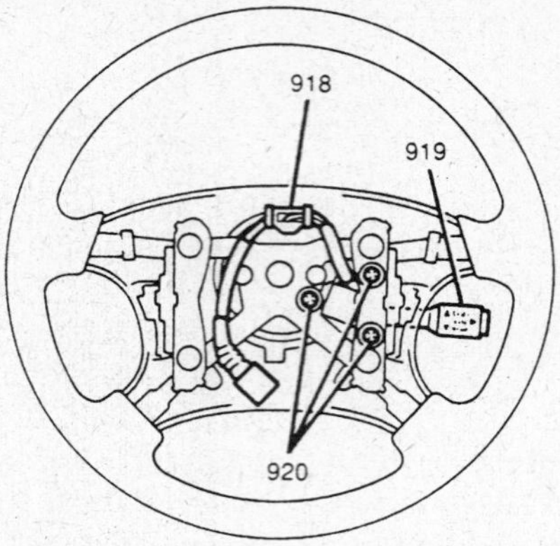

918 ELECTRICAL CONNECTOR
919 CRUISE CONTROL SWITCH
920 CRUISE CONTROL SWITCH SCREWS

GC1109300267000X

Fig. 32 Speed control switch replacement

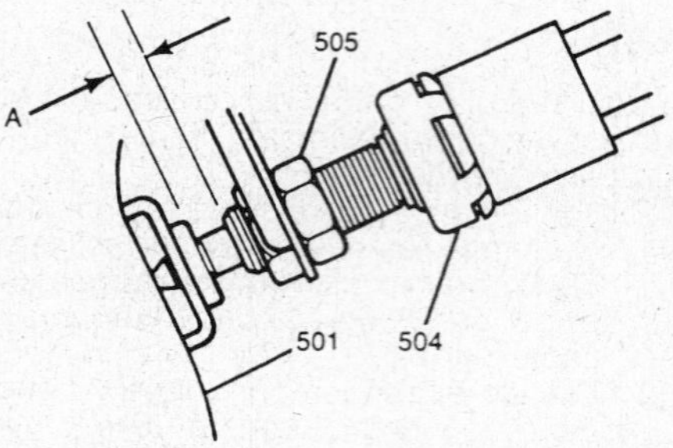

A STOPLAMP SWITCH CLEARANCE 0.5 – 2.4 mm (0.02 – 0.09")
501 BRAKE PEDAL
504 STOPLAMP SWITCH
505 STOPLAMP SWITCH LOCKNUT

GC1109300269000X

Fig. 34 Stop lamp switch clearance inspection

11. **Torque** battery ground cable to 11 ft. lbs.
12. Ensure proper operation of PNP switch, as follows:
    a. Apply parking brake and block wheels.
    b. With shifter in Park and ensure starter operation.
    c. Stop engine and turn engine Off with key in On position.

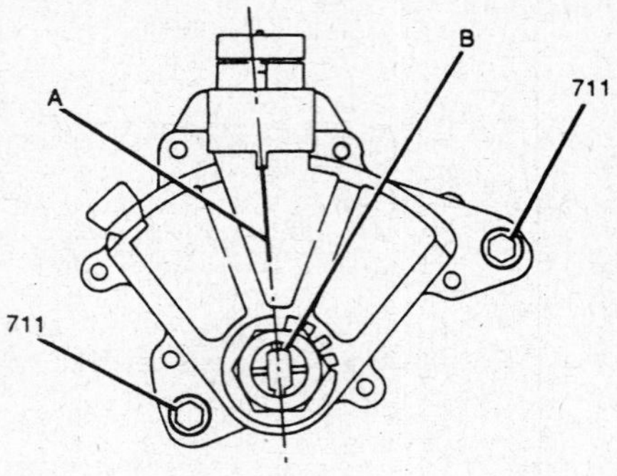

A NEUTRAL BASIC LINE
B PNP SWITCH SLEEVE GROOVE
711 PNP SWITCH BOLTS

GC1109300268000X

Fig. 33 Park/Neutral Position (PNP) switch adjustment

    d. Move shifter to Neutral and ensure starter operation.
    e. Ensure starter does not operate in Drive, 2nd, Low or Reverse.

Stop Lamp Switch

1. Slide hood latch release cable sideways to release from holder.
2. Disconnect hood release cable from hood latch release lever.
3. Remove two screws and hood latch release lever from knee bolster.
4. Remove two cover plates, two screws, four bolts and knee bolster.
5. Remove side ventilation duct from left-hand side duct outlet.
6. Disconnect stop lamp electrical connector and loosen stop lamp switch locknut, **Fig. 34.**
7. Remove locknut and stop lamp switch.
8. Reverse procedure to install, noting the following:
    a. Turn switch until distance between end of switch plunger and end of threaded portion of switch is within .02–.09 inch.
    b. **Torque** stop lamp switch locknut to 84–96 inch lbs.
    c. **Torque** knee bolster bolts to 10 ft. lbs.
    d. **Torque** battery ground cable to 11 ft. lbs.

Type 3

NOTE: On Air Bag Equipped Models, Refer To "Air Bag System Precautions" Located In The Front Of This Manual For System Disarming & Arming Procedures.

NOTE: Refer To "Computer Relearn Procedures" Located In The Front Of This Manual When Battery Power To The Computer Has Been Interrupted.

NOTE: "Electrical Symbol & Wire Color Code Identification" Located In The Front Of This Manual May Be Used As An Aid When Using Wiring Circuits Found In This Section.

INDEX

DESCRIPTION

The main components of the cruise control system are the cruise control module, the function control switches, the vehicle speed sensor (VSS), the cruise control release (brake) switch, the cruise control (clutch) switch and the stoplamp switch.

The cruise control system uses a cruise control module to obtain the desired vehicle cruise speed and operation. The cruise control module has an electronic controller and an electric stepper motor to vary the throttle in each different cruise control mode. Two important components in the module help to do this. The first is the electronic controller and the second is an electric stepper motor. The stepper motor operates in response to the electronic controller to maintain the desired cruise speed. The electronic controller monitors vehicle speed and operates the electric stepper motor. The stepper motor operates in response to the electronic controller, to maintain the desired cruise speed. The electric stepper motor moves a strap that is attached to the cruise control cable which moves the throttle linkage. The cruise control module contains a low speed limit which will prevent system engagement at less than 25 mph. **The module is not serviceable.**

The operation of the electronic controller is controlled by function control switches located on the multi-function turn signal lever.

The cruise control function switch includes the ON/OFF, SET/COAST and R/A (resume/accelerate) switches. The switch provides driver control of the cruise control system.

The cruise control release (brake) switch, the cruise control (clutch) switch and the stoplamp switch are used to disengage the cruise control. The cruise control release (brake) switch and the stoplamp switch mounted on the brake pedal bracket, disengage the system electrically when the driver presses the brake pedal. The cruise control (clutch) switch, mounted on the clutch pedal bracket, will also disengage the system when the driver presses the clutch pedal. When either pedal is pressed, the speed of the vehicle is stored in the cruise module memory.

The VSS is mounted to the automatic or manual transaxle and produces an AC signal. The frequency of this signal is proportional to the speed at which the automatic or manual transaxle output shaft rotates, which in turn is proportional to the speed of the vehicle. The AC signal is supplied to the Powertrain Control Module (PCM) where it is converted to the number of pulses per mile per second to determine vehicle speed. The signal is then sent to the cruise control module and the speedometer rate of 4000 pulses per mile.

With cruise control, you can maintain a speed of approximately 25 mph or more without keeping your foot on the accelerator. When driver turns OFF the ON/OFF switch, or the ignition switch, the cruise control turns off. The vehicle speed stored in the memory of the cruise control module, will be lost.

System Components

SPEED SENSOR

The vehicle speed sensor is mounted to the automatic transmission and produces and Alternating Current (AC) signal. The frequency of this signal is proportional to the speed in which the transmission output shaft rotates, which is proportional to the speed of the vehicle.

The AC signal produced by the sensor is supplied to the Engine Control Module (ECM), speed control module and instrument cluster. The signal is transmitted at a rate of 4000 pulses per mile. The ECM, speed control module and speedometer internally convert the number of pulses per miles per second to determine vehicle speed.

CRUISE CONTROL MODULE

The module is mounted on lefthand engine compartment inner side rail. The module has an electronic controller and an electric stepper motor to vary the throttle with each different cruise mode. The module is not serviceable and must be replaced as an assembly.

PRECAUTIONS

Air Bag Systems

Refer to "Air Bag System Precautions" in the front of this manual for system disarming and arming procedures.

Battery Ground Cable

Prior to service, disconnect battery ground cable and isolate as required.

ADJUSTMENTS

Cruise Control Cable

Cable must not have more than .078 inch slack. Cable should never be adjusted so tightly that cable tension will not allow throttle to close properly.

1. Ensure cable fitting is snapped on to the throttle lever pin.
2. Ensure cable is locked into position on bracket.
3. Pull cable adjustment slider on cable

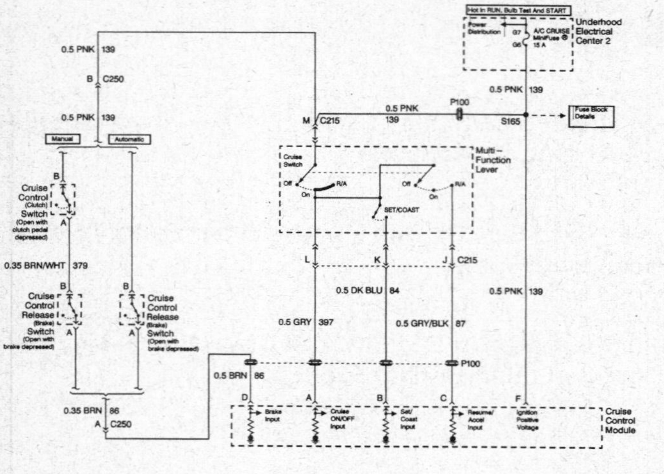

GC1109900564020X

Fig. 1 Wiring diagram (Part 1 of 2)

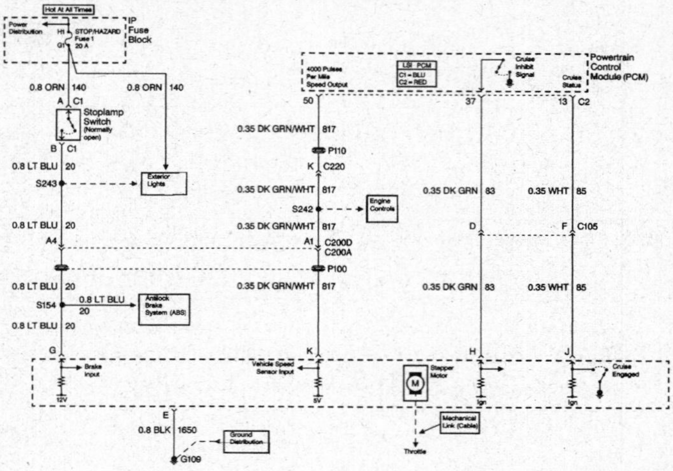

GC1109900564010X

Fig. 1 Wiring diagram (Part 2 of 2)

ACTION	NORMAL RESULTS
[1] • Drive vehicle above 25 mph. • Cruise Switch to "ON." • Depress Set Switch once and release. • Remove foot from accelerator pedal.	Vehicle maintains set speed (at time of button release).
[2] • Depress and hold Set Switch until vehicle speed decreases by 4 to 5 mph. • Release Set Switch.	Vehicle decelerates and maintains a new lower set speed, if speed is above 25 mph.
[3] • Depress and hold R/A Switch until vehicle speed increases by 4 to 5 mph. • Release R/A Switch.	Vehicle accelerates and maintains a new higher set speed.
[4] • Depress brake pedal slightly.	Cruise Control disengages. Memory unchanged.
[5] • Depress R/A Switch once (less than 3/4 second) and release.	Vehicle accelerates to and maintains previous set speed.
[6] • Depress R/A Switch once and release (less than 1/2 of a second).	Vehicle speed increases by 1 mph and maintains new set speed.

GC1109100274010X

Fig. 2 Cruise Control System Inspection (Part 1 of 2)

ACTION	NORMAL RESULTS
[7] • Depress Set Switch once and release (less than 1/2 of a second).	Vehicle speed decreases by 1 mph and maintains new set speed.
[8] • Depress Set and R/A Switches simultaneously.	Vehicle put in Non-Cruise mode with memory unchanged.
[9] • Depress R/A Switch once (less than 3/4 second) and release.	Vehicle accelerates to and maintains previous set speed.
[10] • Cruise Switch to "OFF."	Cruise Control disengages. Memory is lost.

GC1109100274020X

Fig. 2 Cruise Control System Inspection (Part 2 of 2)

end rearward until all slack is removed from cable but without opening throttle.

4. Push down cable adjustment lock button until it snaps and locks in place.
5. Ensure locking tab is secure on both sides.

Clutch Release Switch

1. Ensure cruise control release switch is fully seated in bracket.
2. Slowly pull brake pedal rearward until audible clicking is no longer heard. Switch will be moved in retainer providing adjustment.
3. Release brake pedal.
4. Ensure the following contacts open at 1 inch or less pedal travel:
   a. Release switch.
   b. Stoplamp and torque converter clutch (TCC) switch.
5. Ensure switches open simultaneously or before onset of braking.
6. Brake pedal may travel up to 1 inch before cruise control system disengages.

SYSTEM DIAGNOSIS & TESTING

Wiring Diagrams

Refer to **Fig. 1,** for system wiring diagrams.

Symptoms

Prior to diagnosing system, ensure the Center High Mounted Stop Lamp (CHMSL) is functioning properly.

Refer to **Figs. 2 through 4,** for diagnostic procedures.

Ensure the operation of the cruise control system by performing the following procedure:

1. Set parking brake and start engine.
2. Move cruise switch to Off, move cruise switch to On and wait at least three seconds before proceeding.
3. Fully depress and hold brake pedal, then push cruise switch in and hold.
4. Hold cruise slider switch in R/A position.
5. After 10 seconds, release brake pedal while holding R/A and Set switches.
6. Engine RPM should increase momentarily and return to normal.

DIAGNOSTIC CHART INDEX

Test	Description	Page No.	Fig. No.
—	System Check	2-83	3
—	Cruise Control Inoperative/Faulting	2-83	4

Test Description

The number below refers to the step number on the diagnostic table.

2. Lack of communication may be due to a partial malfunction of the class 2 serial data circuit or due to a total malfunction of the class 2 serial data circuit. The specified procedure will determine the particular condition.

Step	Action	Yes	No
1	Install a scan tool. Does the scan tool power up?	Go to Step 2	Check Data Link Communications
2	1. Turn ON the ignition, with the engine OFF. 2. Attempt to establish communication with the powertrain control module. Does the scan tool communicate with the powertrain control module?	Go to Step 3	Check Data Link Communications
3	Select the powertrain control module display DTCs function on the scan tool. Does the scan tool display any DTCs which begin with a "P"?	Go to Diagnostic Trouble Code (DTC)	Refer to Symptoms

GC0140100013000X

Fig. 3 System Check

Step	Action	Value (s)	Yes	No
10	Probe the brake input circuit with a test lamp that is connected to a good ground. Does the test lamp illuminate?	--	Go to Step 23	Go to Step 11
11	Depress the brake pedal while monitoring the test lamp. Does the test lamp illuminate?	--	Go to Step 12	Go to Step 24
12	Probe the cruise disable/enable circuit with a test lamp that is connected to battery voltage. Does the test lamp illuminate?	--	Go to Step 25	Go to Step 13
13	Use a scan tool in order to command the cruise inhibit/enable OFF. Does the test lamp illuminate?	--	Go to Step 14	Go to Step 26
14	Probe the cruise engaged output circuit with a DMM that is connected to a good ground. Does the voltage measure near the specified value?	B+	Go to Step 15	Go to Step 27
15	1. Raise and suitably support the vehicle. 2. Block one of the drive wheels. 3. Place the Transaxle/Transmission Selector in drive. 4. Set the DMM to the AC scale. 5. Probe the VSS signal circuit with a DMM that is connected to a good ground. 6. Rotate one of the drive wheels. 7. Observe the DMM. Does the voltage displayed on the scan tool vary?	--	Go to Step 35	Go to Step 28
16	Test the circuit that illuminated the test lamp for a short to voltage. Systems. Did you find and correct the condition?	--	Go to Step 43	Go to Step 34
17	Test the on/off circuit for an open or a high resistance. Did you find and correct the condition?	--	Go to Step 43	Go to Step 18
18	Test the ignition positive voltage circuit for an open or high resistance between the cruise control module and the cruise control switch. Did you find and correct the condition?	--	Go to Step 43	Go to Step 34
19	Test the set/coast circuit for an open or a high resistance. Did you find and correct the condition?	--	Go to Step 43	Go to Step 34
20	Test the resume/accelerate circuit for an open or a high resistance. Did you find and correct the condition?	--	Go to Step 43	Go to Step 34
21	Test the cruise cancel circuit for an open or a high resistance. Systems. Did you find and correct the condition?	--	Go to Step 43	Go to Step 29
22	Test the cruise cancel circuit for a short to voltage. Did you find and correct the condition?	--	Go to Step 43	Go to Step 29
23	Test the brake input circuit for a short to voltage. Did you find and correct the condition?	--	Go to Step 43	Go to Step 30

GC1100000689020X

Fig. 4 Cruise Control Inoperative/Faulting (Part 2 of 4)

Step	Action	Value (s)	Yes	No
1	Did you review the system operation and perform the necessary inspections?	--	Go to Step 2	Go to Symptoms
2	1. Turn OFF the ignition. 2. Disconnect the cruise control module. 3. Turn ON the ignition with the engine OFF. 4. Probe the ignition positive voltage circuit of the cruise control module with a test lamp that is connected to a good ground. Does the test lamp illuminate?	--	Go to Step 3	Go to Step 36
3	Probe the ignition positive voltage circuit of the cruise control module with a test lamp that is connected to the ground circuit of the cruise control module. Does the test lamp illuminate?	--	Go to Step 4	Go to Step 37
4	1. Turn ON the ignition with the engine OFF. 2. Turn OFF the cruise control. 3. Probe the on/off, the set/coast, and the resume/accelerate circuits with a test lamp that is connected to a good ground. Does the test lamp illuminate on any of the circuits?	--	Go to Step 16	Go to Step 5
5	1. Turn ON the ignition with the engine OFF. 2. Turn ON the cruise control. 3. Probe the on/off circuit with a test lamp that is connected to a good ground. Does the test lamp illuminate?	--	Go to Step 6	Go to Step 17
6	1. Probe the set/coast circuit with a test lamp that is connected to a good ground. 2. Press and hold the SET/COAST switch. Does the test lamp illuminate?	--	Go to Step 7	Go to Step 19
7	1. Probe the resume/accelerate circuit with a test lamp that is connected to a good ground. 2. Press and hold the RESUME/ACCEL switch. Does the test lamp illuminate?	--	Go to Step 8	Go to Step 20
8	Probe the cruise cancel circuit with a test lamp that is connected to a good ground. Does the test lamp illuminate?	--	Go to Step 9	Go to Step 21
9	Depress the brake pedal while monitoring the test lamp. Does the test lamp illuminate?	--	Go to Step 22	Go to Step 10

GC1100000689010X

Fig. 4 Cruise Control Inoperative/Faulting (Part 1 of 4)

Step	Action	Value (s)	Yes	No
24	Test the brake input circuit for an open or a high resistance. Systems. Did you find and correct the condition?	--	Go to Step 43	Go to Step 30
25	Test the cruise disable/enable circuit for a short to ground. Systems. Did you find and correct the condition?	--	Go to Step 43	Go to Step 33
26	Test the cruise disable/enable circuit for an open, a high resistance, or a short to voltage. Did you find and correct the condition?	--	Go to Step 43	Go to Step 33
27	Test the cruise engaged output circuit for an open, a high resistance, or a short to voltage. Did you find and correct the condition?	--	Go to Step 43	Go to Step 33
28	Test the speed sensor circuit for an open or a high resistance. Did you find and correct the condition?	--	Go to Step 43	Go to Step 33
29	Inspect the cruise control release (brake) switch and cruise control clutch switch for proper adjustment. Did you find and correct the condition?	--	Go to Step 43	Go to Step 31
30	Inspect the stoplamp switch for proper adjustment. Did you find and correct the condition?	--	Go to Step 43	Go to Step 32
31	Inspect for poor connections at the harness connector of the cruise control release (brake) switch and the cruise control (clutch) switch. Did you find and correct the condition?	--	Go to Step 43	Go to Step 38
32	Inspect for poor connections at the harness connector of the stoplamp switch. Did you find and correct the condition?	--	Go to Step 43	Go to Step 39
33	Inspect for poor connections at the harness connector of the PCM. Did you find and correct the condition?	--	Go to Step 43	Go to Step 40
34	Inspect for poor connections at the harness connector of the cruise control switch. Did you find and correct the condition?	--	Go to Step 43	Go to Step 41
35	Inspect for poor connections at the harness connector of the cruise control module. Did you find and correct the condition?	--	Go to Step 43	Go to Step 42
36	Repair the ignition positive voltage circuit of the cruise control module. Did you complete the repair?	--	Go to Step 43	--
37	Repair the ground circuit of the cruise control module. Did you complete the repair?	--	Go to Step 43	--

GC1100000689030X

Fig. 4 Cruise Control Inoperative/Faulting (Part 3 of 4)

Step	Action	Value (s)	Yes	No
38	Replace the cruise control release (brake) switch or the cruise control (clutch) switch. Did you complete the replacement?	--	Go to Step 43	--
39	Replace the stoplamp switch. Did you complete the replacement?	--	Go to Step 43	--
40	Replace the PCM. Did you complete the replacement?	--	Go to Step 43	--
41	Replace the cruise control switch. Did you complete the replacement?	--	Go to Step 43	--
42	Replace the cruise control module. Did you complete the replacement?	--	Go to Step 43	--
43	Operate the vehicle within the conditions for cruise control operation. Does the cruise control system operate correctly?	--	System OK	Go to Step 2

GC1100000689040X

Fig. 4 Cruise Control Inoperative/Faulting (Part 4 of 4)

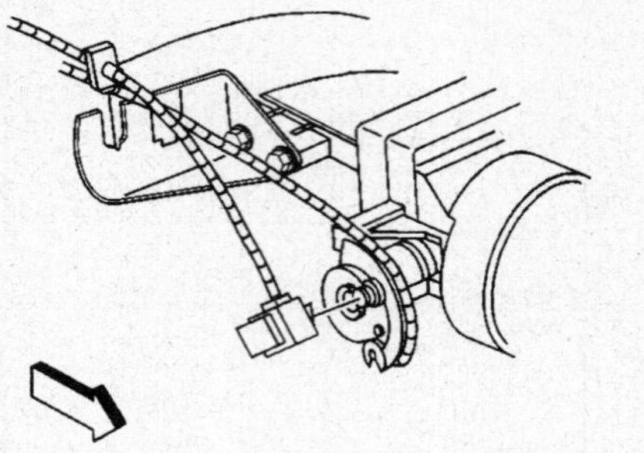

GC1109900653000X

Fig. 5 Cruise control cable end replacement

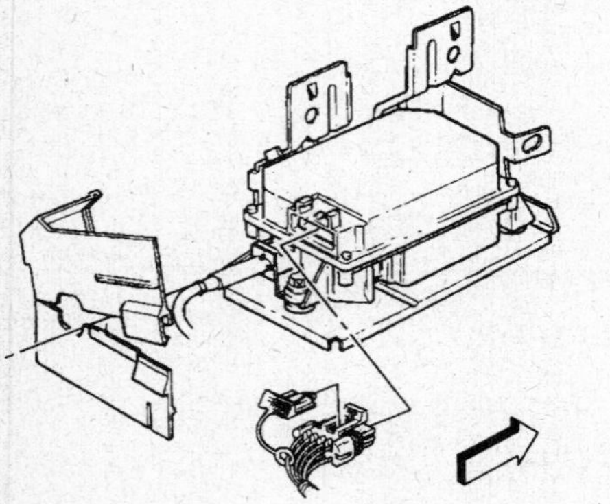

GC1109900654000X

Fig. 6 Cruise control servo cover replacement

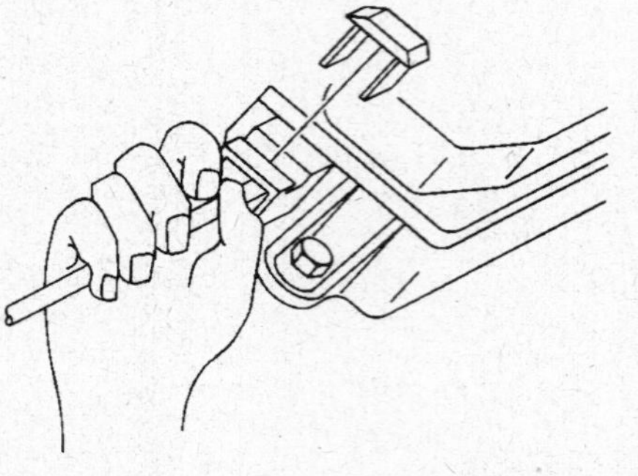

GC1109900655000X

Fig. 7 Cruise control cable replacement

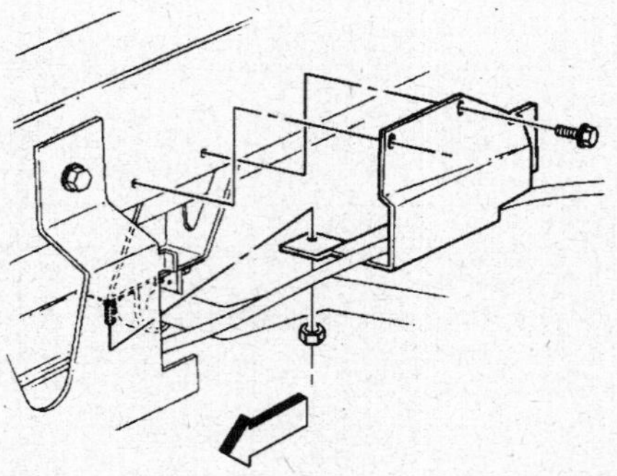

GC1109900657000X

Fig. 8 Cruise control shield replacement

COMPONENT REPLACEMENT

Cruise Control Cable

When removing the cable end fitting from the throttle body, push down in order to disengage the cable. Slide the cable off of the throttle lever.

1. Disconnect cruise control cable from engine bracket.
2. Disconnect cable end fitting from throttle body lever stud, **Fig. 5.**
3. Raise and support vehicle.
4. Remove cruise control servo cover, **Fig. 6.**
5. Remove cruise control servo retainer from cruise control module.
6. Compress conduit tangs and pull cable from cruise control module, **Fig. 7.**
7. Remove cable bead from cruise motor band end fitting on cruise control module.
8. Remove cruise cable from brake pipe clip.
9. Remove bolts, nuts, cruise control shield, **Fig. 8.**
10. Mark cable position on brake booster.
11. Observe routing of cruise control cable for installation reference.
12. Unclip and remove cruise control cable.
13. Reverse procedure to install, noting the following:

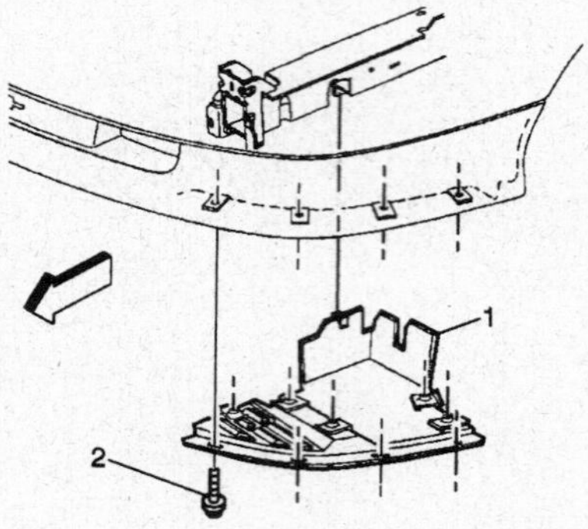

GC1109900660000X

Fig. 9 Front bumper fascia lower deflector replacement

   a. Ribbon cable must not be twisted.
   b. Turn cable ribbon until ribbon is flat and slide cable conduit fitting over ribbon.
   c. Install slug of cruise cable to cam of throttle body before installing cruise cable to engine bracket. Do not bend core wire of cable when installing slug to cam.
   d. Adjust cable as outlined in "Adjustments."

Cruise Control Module

1. Raise and support vehicle.
2. Remove two front end fascia outer mounting bolts and lower deflector, **Fig. 9.**
3. Remove cruise control module cover.
4. Disconnect cruise control cable connector from brake pipe clip.
5. Disconnect cruise control cable from cruise control module.
6. Remove mounting bolts and cruise control module bracket from lefthand side engine compartment inner rail.
7. Remove cruise control module from bracket.
8. Reverse procedure to install, noting the following:
   a. Connect cruise control cable to module as outlined in "Cruise Control Cable" in "Component Replacement."
   b. Adjust cable as outlined in "Adjustments."

CRUISE CONTROL SWITCH

1. Remove lefthand instrument panel sound insulator and disconnect electrical connectors.
2. Remove release switch, stop lamp and TCC switch and clutch switch or clutch anticipate switch, if equipped from pedal with bracket.
3. Reverse procedure to install.

Type 4

NOTE: On Air Bag Equipped Models, Refer To "Air Bag System Precautions" Located In The Front Of This Manual For System Disarming & Arming Procedures.

NOTE: Refer To "Computer Relearn Procedures" Located In The Front Of This Manual When Battery Power To The Computer Has Been Interrupted.

NOTE: "Electrical Symbol & Wire Color Code Identification" Located In The Front Of This Manual May Be Used As An Aid When Using Wiring Circuits Found In This Section.

INDEX

DESCRIPTION

The main components of the cruise control system are the Throttle Actuator Control (TAC) module, the function control switches, the stop lamp switch, the TCC Brake (cruise release) switch, and, if equipped, the clutch pedal position (CPP) sensor.

The cruise control system uses the TAC module to maintain the desired vehicle cruise speed and operation. The TAC and the Powertrain Control Module (PCM) communicate together to vary the throttle opening in each different cruise control mode. The PCM monitors vehicle speed and operates the throttle actuator. The throttle actuator operates in response to the TAC module, to maintain the desired cruise speed. The throttle actuator motor moves the throttle blade. The PCM assembly contains a low speed limit which will prevent system engagement below a minimum speed 25 mph. **The TAC or PCM module assemblies are not serviceable.**

The operation of the TAC module is through the function control switches located on the multifunction turn signal lever.

The cruise control function control switches includes the ON/OFF, SET/COAST, R/A (resume/accelerate). The switch assembly provides driver control of the cruise control system.

The stop lamp switch, TCC Brake switch (cruise release) or CPP switch, is used to disengage the cruise control. A cruise control release switch circuit and a stoplamp switch circuit are used. The stop lamp, TCC Brake and CPP switches are mounted to the brake pedal bracket. To disengage the system the driver presses the brake pedal or clutch pedal. The speed of the vehicle at brake actuation will be stored in the memory of the TAC module.

When the driver turns off the cruise control ON/OFF switch or ignition switch, the cruise control turns off. The vehicle speed stored in the memory of the TAC module will be lost.

Ignition positive voltage is supplied from the Electronic Throttle Control (ETC) fuse, to the TAC module. The TAC module is grounded to chassis. When the cruise control ON/OFF switch is on, ignition positive voltage is applied to the cruise on switch signal terminal of the TAC module. If the driver has not pressed the brake pedal or clutch pedal, ignition positive voltage is supplied through the switches, to the cruise control release switch signal and clutch signal terminals of the PCM.

Cruise control is canceled when the driver presses either the brake pedal or clutch pedal. The stop lamp switch closes, applying battery positive voltage to the stop lamp signal circuit of the TAC module. Voltage is also removed from the cruise release signal circuit and the clutch switch signal circuit at the PCM.

When pressing the SET/COAST button on the multifunction turn signal lever, ignition positive voltage is applied to the set/coast switch signal terminal of the TAC module. When pressing the R/A (resume/accelerate) on the control switch, ignition positive voltage is applied to the resume/accelerate switch signal terminal of the TAC module.

When the cruise switch is in the ON position, and the driver presses the SET/COAST button, the TAC module notifies the PCM that the cruise control is requested. The PCM then inspects to see that the cruise control enable criteria is met. If the cruise control criteria has been met the PCM sends a class 2 message to the Instrument Panel Cluster to illuminate the cruise light.

The PCM will inhibit cruise control: when vehicle speed is less than 25 mph; when in PARK, REVERSE, NEUTRAL, or 1st gear; with low engine RPM; with high engine RPM (fuel cut-off); when vehicle speed is too high; when an over or under charged battery voltage condition exists; when anti-lock brake system/traction control system is active for more than two seconds.

If the PCM determines that any of the cruise control inhibit conditions are present, the PCM will disengage the cruise control. The PCM accomplishes this through data communication with the TAC module. If the PCM disables the cruise control for an inhibiting event it will record the reason for disengagement in the disengage definition data file.

PRECAUTIONS

Air Bag Systems

Refer to "Air Bag System Precautions" in the front of this manual for system disarming and arming procedures.

Battery Ground Cable

Prior to service, disconnect battery ground cable and isolate as required.

Anti-Lock Brake Systems

The hydraulic accumulator, when fully

charged contains brake fluid at high pressure. Before disconnecting any lines, hoses or fittings, ensure accumulator is full depressurized. Failure to do so may result in personal injury.

To depressurize the hydraulic accumulator, turn the ignition to the Off position or disconnect battery ground, pump brake pedal a minimum of 40 times at approximately 50 lbs., of force. A noticeable change in pedal feel will occur when accumulator is fully discharged.

Code	Interpretation
P0567	Resume/Accelerate Switch
P0568	Set/Coast Switch
P0571	TCC Brake Switch
P0574	Cruise Control Module
P0704	Clutch Switch
P1554	Cruise Control Status Circuit
P1574	Stoplamp Switch
P1585	Output Driver Modules
P1586	Cruise Control Brake Switch No. 2. (w/Manual Transmission)

Fig. 1 DTC interpretation

ADJUSTMENTS

Cruise Control Cable

1. Lift adjustment lock button up.
2. Pull cable adjustment slider rearward until all slack is removed from cable, but without opening throttle.
3. Push down cable adjustment lock button until it snaps and locks in place.
4. Ensure locking tabs are secure on both sides.

Clutch Release Switch

1. Ensure cruise control release switch is fully seated in bracket.
2. Slowly pull brake pedal rearward until audible clicking is no longer heard. Switch will be moved in retainer providing adjustment.
3. Release brake pedal.
4. Ensure the following contacts open at 1 inch or less pedal travel:
   a. Release switch.
   b. Stoplamp and torque converter clutch (TCC) switch.
5. Ensure switches open simultaneously or before onset of braking.
6. Brake pedal may travel up to 1 inch before cruise control system disengages.

SYSTEM DIAGNOSIS & TESTING

Accessing Diagnostic Trouble Codes

Connect suitably programmed scan tool to the Data Link Connector (DLC), and follow manufacturer's instructions.

Diagnostic Trouble Code Interpretation

Refer to **Fig. 1,** for Diagnostic Trouble Code (DTC) interpretation.

Intermittents

Intermittent faults may occur which may or may not cause the MIL to come on, or set DTCs in the PCM memory. These intermittent conditions usually result in driveability complaints and cause codes to be set in the PCM memory without turning on the indicator lamp, or are read as intermittent DTCs when testing the system with the scan type tester. However, DTC diagnosis charts cannot be used to diagnose this type of fault as a fault must be present in order to be located using the charts, and use of the charts to diagnose an intermittent condition may result in unrequired replacement of components.

Most intermittent fault conditions are caused by poor electrical or vacuum hose connections, faulty or improperly routed wiring or hoses. The cause for most intermittent faults can usually be located by performing a thorough visual inspection of the system vacuum and wiring harnesses and/or by road testing the vehicle while monitoring the suspected circuit with suitable test equipment. After performing the OBD System Check (Diagnostic Circuit Check) and ensuring the indicator lamp is operating and no hard DTCs are set in the PCM memory, use the following procedure to locate intermittent faults:

1. Inspect vacuum hoses for splits, kinks and proper connection, ensure hoses are routed properly.
2. Inspect fuel system components for proper mounting, fuel, air or vacuum leaks, correct as required.
3. Inspect secondary ignition wiring and replace any wires that are burned, cracked or broken.
4. Inspect engine compartment and emission control system wiring and repair or replace wiring that is broken chafed or damaged.
5. Inspect electrical connectors, noting the following:
   a. Ensure terminal is making proper contact with wire by removing terminal from connector and inspecting for proper crimping and broken wire strands.
   b. Ensure all terminals are fully seated in connector.
   c. Ensure connector terminals are not damaged or deformed, and carefully reform terminals in connectors of suspected circuits to increase spring tension.
   d. Ensure connector halves are properly mated and fully seated.
6. Inspect MIL and DLC wiring for shorts to ground, repair as required.
7. Inspect continuity between PCM connector terminals and engine ground. Repair wiring if no continuity exists.
8. Inspect for electrical interference caused by faulty relays, PCM driven solenoids or switches, and secondary ignition system components, as they may cause voltage surges.
9. Ensure IC (EST) wiring is properly routed and insulated from distributor wiring, distributor, ignition coil and alternator.
10. Inspect added accessories such as lights, two-way radios etc. for proper installation, ensuring no accessories are patched into engine control system wiring.
11. Ensure diodes and resistors installed across accessories such as A/C compressor clutch are not open.
12. Connect suitable programmed scan tool following manufacturer's instructions, or connect suitable voltmeter to suspected circuit and road test vehicle, noting any abnormal readings and conditions under which they occur. Abnormal readings indicate that tested circuit may be cause for fault.

Wiring Diagrams

Refer to **Figs. 2 through 6,** for system wiring diagrams.

Symptoms

Refer to **Figs. 7 through 13,** for symptoms.

Diagnostic Tests

Refer to **Figs. 14 through 22,** for diagnostic tests.

Clearing Diagnostic Trouble Codes

Connect suitable programmed scan tool to Data Link Connector (DLC), and follow manufacturer's instructions.

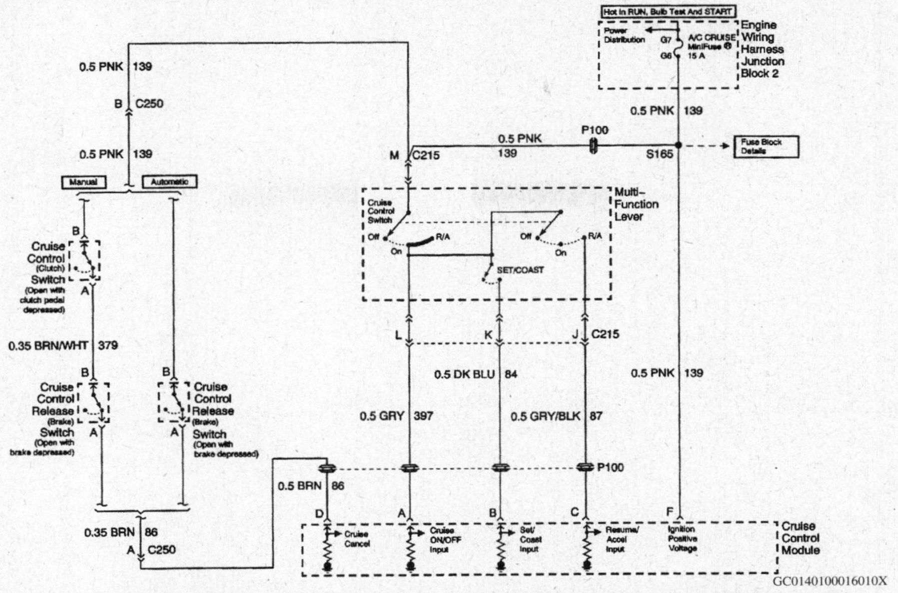

Fig. 2 Wiring diagram (Part 1 of 2). 2000 Camaro & Firebird w/3.8L engine & 2000–02 w/5.7L engine

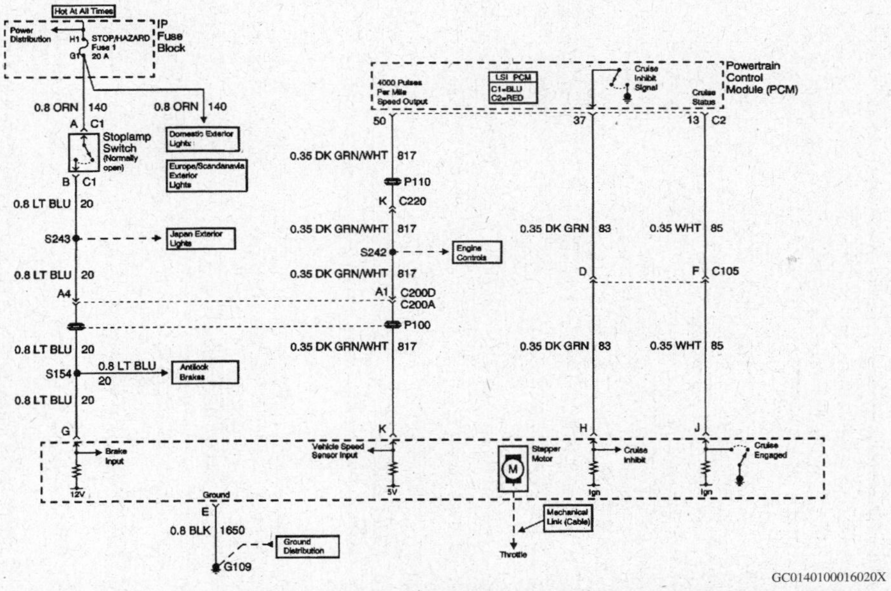

Fig. 2 Wiring diagram (Part 2 of 2). 2000 Camaro & Firebird w/3.8L engine & 2000–02 w/5.7L engine

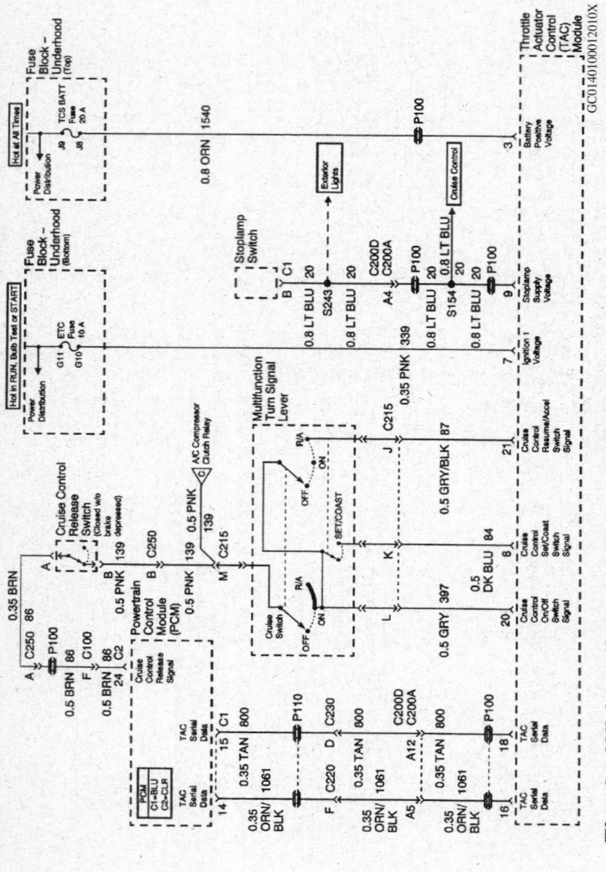

Fig. 3 Wiring diagram (Part 1 of 2). 2001 Camaro & Firebird w/3.8L engine

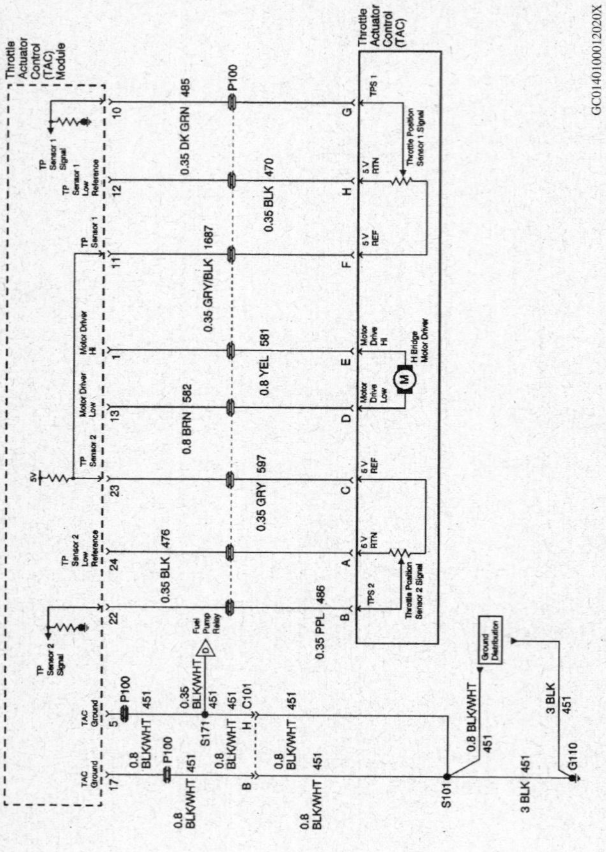

Fig. 3 Wiring diagram (Part 2 of 2). 2001 Camaro & Firebird w/3.8L engine

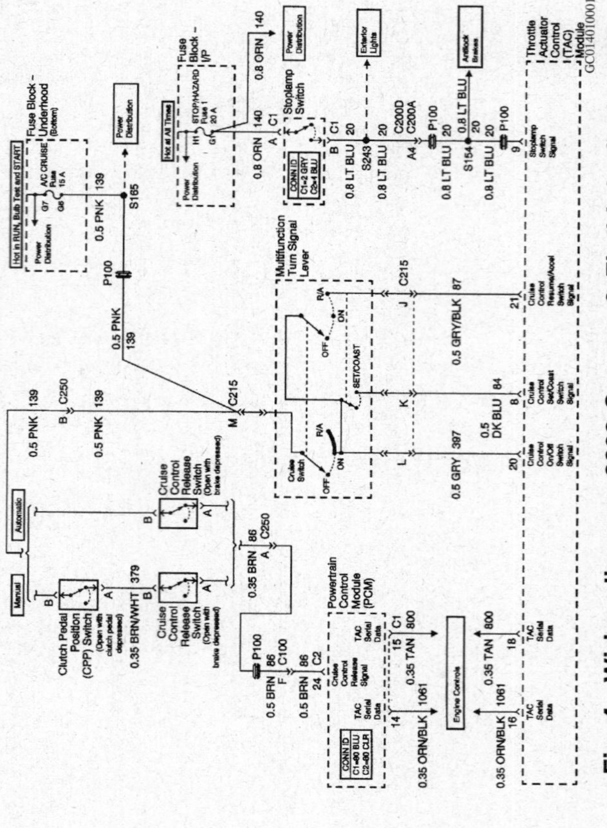

Fig. 4 Wiring diagram. 2002 Camaro & Firebird w/3.8L engine

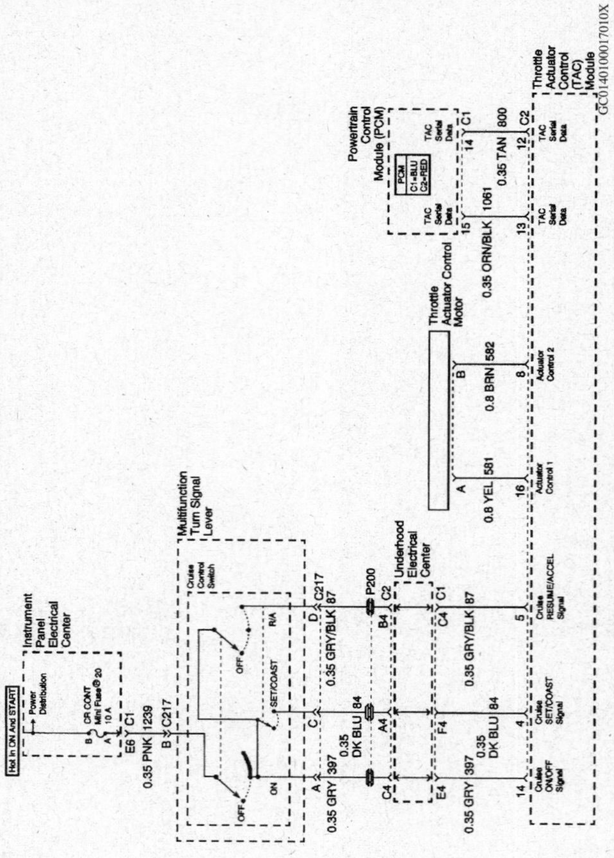

Fig. 5 Wiring diagram (Part 1 of 2). 2000 Corvette

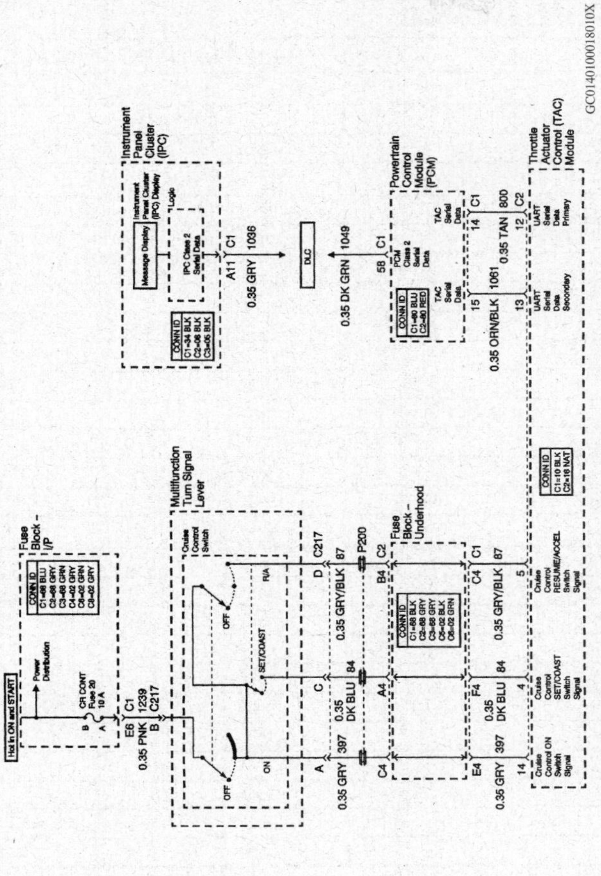

Fig. 6 Wiring diagram (Part 1 of 2). 2001–04 Corvette

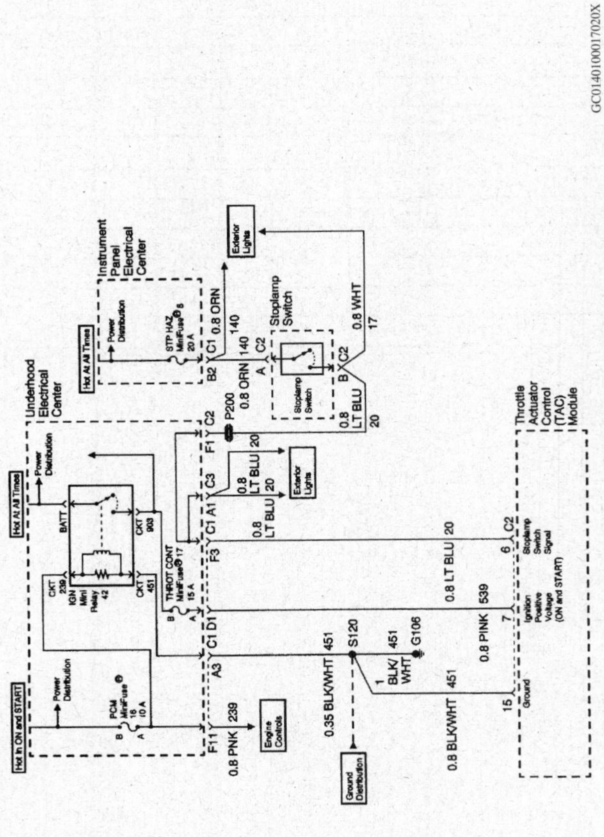

Fig. 5 Wiring diagram (Part 2 of 2). 2000 Corvette

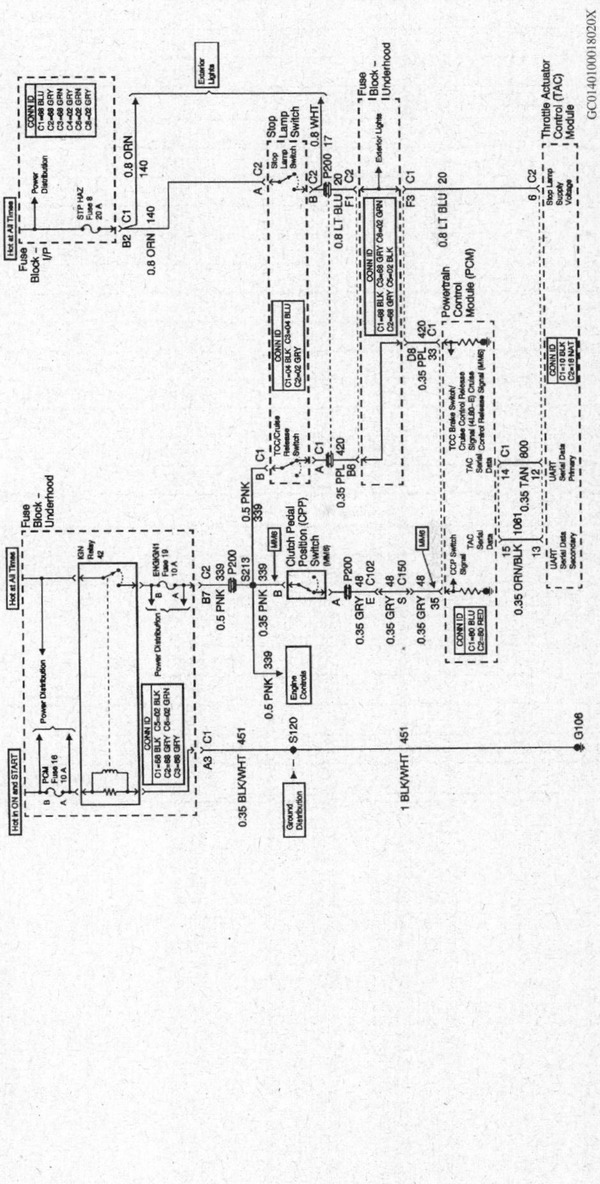

Fig. 6 Wiring diagram (Part 2 of 2). 2001–04 Corvette

DIAGNOSTIC CHART INDEX

The number below refers to the step number on the diagnostic table.

2. Lack of communication may be due to a partial malfunction of the class 2 serial data circuit or due to a total malfunction of the class 2 serial data circuit. The specified procedure will determine the particular condition.

Step	Action	Yes	No
1	Install a scan tool. Does the scan tool power up?	Go to Step 2	Check Data Link Communications
2	1. Turn ON the ignition, with the engine OFF. 2. Attempt to establish communication with the powertrain control module. Does the scan tool communicate with the powertrain control module?	Go to Step 3	Check Data Link Communications
3	Select the powertrain control module display DTCs function on the scan tool. Does the scan tool display any DTCs which begin with a "P"?	Go to Diagnostic Trouble Code (DTC) List/Type 3.8L or Diagnostic Trouble Code (DTC) List/Type 5.7L	Refer to Symptoms

GC0140100023000X

Fig. 7 System Check. Camaro & Firebird

6	1. Observe the Cruise Release switch parameter in the cruise control data list. 2. Press the brake pedal. Did the cruise release switch parameter change state?	Go to Step 7	Go to Step 11
7	Is the vehicle equipped with a manual transmission?	Go to Step 8	Go to Step 29
8	1. Observe the clutch pedal position (CPP) switch parameter in the PCM data list. 2. Press the clutch pedal. Did the CPP switch parameter change state?	Go to Step 29	Go to Step 12
9	1. Turn OFF the ignition. 2. Disconnect the multifunction turn signal lever. 3. Turn ON the ignition, with the engine OFF. 4. Probe the multifunction turn signal lever ignition positive voltage feed circuit with a test lamp connected to a good ground. Did the test lamp illuminate?	Go to Step 13	Go to Step 21
10	1. Turn OFF the ignition. 2. Disconnect the stoplamp switch harness connector. 3. Turn ON the ignition, with the engine OFF. 4. Probe the stop lamp battery positive voltage feed circuit with a test lamp connected to a good ground. Did the test lamp illuminate?	Go to Step 16	Go to Step 22
11	1. Turn OFF the ignition. 2. Disconnect the cruise release switch harness connector. 3. Turn ON the ignition, with the engine OFF. 4. Probe the cruise release switch ignition positive voltage circuit with a test lamp connected to a good ground. Did the test lamp illuminate?	Go to Step 18	Go to Step 23
12	1. Turn OFF the ignition. 2. Disconnect the clutch pedal position (CPP) switch. 3. Turn ON the ignition, with the engine OFF. 4. Probe the CPP switch ignition positive voltage circuit with a test lamp connected to a good ground. Did the test lamp illuminate?	Go to Step 20	Go to Step 24
13	Test the cruise control ON switch signal circuit for a open, high resistance, short to ground or short to voltage. Did you find and correct the condition?	Go to Step 35	Go to Step 28
14	Test the cruise control Set/Coast signal circuit for a open, high resistance, short to ground or short to voltage. Did you find and correct the condition?	Go to Step 35	Go to Step 28

GC0140100021020X

Fig. 8 Cruise Control Inoperative (Part 2 of 5). Camaro & Firebird

Diagnostic Aids

Important

Perform the following in order to avoid misdiagnosis.

- Inspect for proper operation of brake lamps and clutch switch, if equipped.
- EMI on the speed sensor signal circuit may cause erratic cruise control operation.

Conditions for Enabling Cruise Control

The vehicle speed is greater than 40 km/h (25 mph).

Step	Action	Yes	No
1	Did you perform the Cruise Control System Check?	Go to Step 2	Go to Cruise Control System Check
2	1. Connect a scan tool. 2. Monitor the Cruise On switch parameter in the cruise control data list. 3. Turn ON the cruise control switch. Did the scan tool parameter change state?	Go to Step 3	Go to Step 9
3	1. Observe the cruise control Set/Coast parameter in the cruise control data list. 2. Press the cruise control Set button. Did the cruise control Set/Coast parameter change state?	Go to Step 4	Go to Step 14
4	1. Observe the cruise control Resume/Accelerate parameter in the cruise control data list. 2. Press the Resume/Accelerate switch. Did the cruise control Resume Accelerate parameter change state?	Go to Step 5	Go to Step 15
5	1. Observe the stoplamp switch parameter in the cruise control data list. 2. Press the brake pedal. Did the stop lamp switch parameter change state?	Go to Step 6	Go to Step 10

GC0140100021010X

Fig. 8 Cruise Control Inoperative (Part 1 of 5). Camaro & Firebird

15	Test the cruise control Resume/Accelerate signal circuit for a open, high resistance, short to ground or short to voltage. Did you find and correct the condition?	Go to Step 35	Go to Step 28
16	Test the stop lamp switch signal circuit for a open, high resistance, short to ground or short to voltage. Did you find and correct the condition?	Go to Step 35	Go to Step 17
17	Check the stop lamp switch for proper adjustment. Did you find and correct the condition?	Go to Step 35	Go to Step 25
18	Test the cruise release switch signal circuit for a open, high resistance, short to ground or short to voltage. Did you find and correct the condition?	Go to Step 35	Go to Step 19
19	Check the cruise release switch for proper adjustment. Did you find and correct the condition?	Go to Step 35	Go to Step 26
20	Test the CPP switch signal circuit for a open, high resistance, short to ground or short to voltage. Did you find and correct the condition?	Go to Step 35	Go to Step 27
21	Repair the open, high resistance or short to ground in the multifunction turn signal lever ignition positive voltage feed circuit. Did you complete the repair?	Go to Step 35	--
22	Repair the open, high resistance or short to ground in the stop lamp switch battery positive voltage feed circuit. Did you complete the repair?	Go to Step 35	--
23	Repair the open, high resistance or short to ground in the cruise release switch battery positive voltage feed circuit. Did you complete the repair?	Go to Step 35	--
24	Repair the open, high resistance or short to ground in the CPP switch battery positive voltage feed circuit. Did you complete the repair?	Go to Step 35	--

GC0140100021030X

Fig. 8 Cruise Control Inoperative (Part 3 of 5). Camaro & Firebird

25	Inspect for poor connections at the harness connector of the stop lamp switch. Did you find and correct the condition?	Go to Step 35	Go to Step 30
26	Inspect for poor connections at the harness connector of the cruise release switch. Did you find and correct the condition?	Go to Step 35	Go to Step 31
27	Inspect for poor connections at the harness connector of the CPP switch. Did you find and correct the condition?	Go to Step 35	Go to Step 32
28	Inspect for poor connections at the harness connector of the multifunction turn signal lever. Did you find and correct the condition?	Go to Step 35	Go to Step 33
29	Inspect for poor connections at the harness connector of the PCM. Did you find and correct the condition?	Go to Step 35	Go to Step 34
30	Replace the stop lamp switch. Did you complete the repair.	Go to Step 35	--
31	Replace the cruise release switch. Did you complete the repair.	Go to Step 35	--
32	Replace the CPP switch. Did you complete the repair.	Go to Step 35	--
33	Replace the multifunction turn signal lever. Did you complete the repair?	Go to Step 35	--
34	**Important** The PCM must be reprogrammed before replacement. Replace the PCM.	Go to Step 35	--

GC0140100021040X

Fig. 8 Cruise Control Inoperative (Part 4 of 5). Camaro & Firebird

Step	Action	Yes	No
DEFINITION: The cruise control system operates properly, but the CRUISE Indicator does not illuminate during cruise control operation.			
1	Did you perform the Cruise Control Diagnostic System Check?	Go to Step 2	Go to Diagnostic System Check -
2	1. Install a scan tool. 2. Start the engine. 3. Carefully drive the vehicle at a speed greater than 40 km/h (25 mph). 4. Engage the cruise control. 5. With a scan tool, observe the Cruise Requested parameter in the powertrain control module (PCM) data list. Does the scan tool display Yes?	Go to Step 3	Go to Step 4
3	1. Turn OFF the ignition. 2. Turn ON the ignition, with the engine OFF. 3. Observe the CRUISE indicator on the instrument cluster (IPC) during the bulb check. Does the CRUISE indicator illuminate during the bulb check?	Go to Intermittent	Go to Step 9
4	1. Turn OFF the ignition. 2. Disconnect the cruise control module. 3. Connect a 3 amp fused jumper between the cruise engaged signal circuit and a good ground. 4. Carefully drive the vehicle at a speed greater than 40 km/h (25 mph). 5. With a scan tool, observe the Cruise Requested parameter in the powertrain control module (PCM) data list. Does the scan tool display Yes?	Go to Step 7	Go to Step 5
5	Test the cruise engaged signal circuit for a open, high resistance or short to voltage. Did you find and correct the condition?	Go to Step 11	Go to Step 6

GC0140100024010X

Fig. 9 Cruise Indicator Always On (Part 1 of 2). 2002 Camaro & Firebird

35	Operate the vehicle with in the conditions for cruise control operation. Does the cruise control system operate properly?	System OK	Go to Step 2

GC0140100021050X

Fig. 8 Cruise Control Inoperative (Part 5 of 5). Camaro & Firebird

6	Inspect for poor connections at the harness connector of the powertrain control module (PCM). Refer to Intermittent Did you find and correct the condition?	Go to Step 11	Go to Step 8
7	Inspect for poor connections at the harness connector of the cruise control module. Refer to Intermittent Did you find and correct the condition?	Go to Step 11	Go to Step 10
8	**Important** The powertrain control module (PCM) must be reprogrammed after replacement. Replace the PCM. Did you complete the replacement?	Go to Step 11	--
9	Replace the instrument cluster (IPC). Did you complete the replacement?	Go to Step 11	--
10	Replace the cruise control module. Did you complete the replacement?	Go to Step 11	--
11	Operate the system in order to verify the repair. Did you correct the condition?	System OK	Go to Step 2

GC0140100024020X

Fig. 9 Cruise Indicator Always On (Part 2 of 2). 2002 Camaro & Firebird

Step	Action	Yes	No
1	Did you perform the Cruise Control Diagnostic System Check?	Go to Step 2	Go to Diagnostic System Check -
2	1. Turn OFF the ignition. 2. Turn ON the ignition, with the engine OFF. 3. Observe the CRUISE indicator on the instrument cluster (IPC) during the bulb check. Does the suspect indicator illuminate during the bulb check and then turn OFF?	Test for Intermittent and Poor Connections	Go to Step 3
3	Replace the instrument cluster (IPC). Did you complete the repair?	Go to Step 4	--
4	Operate the system in order to verify the repair. Did you correct the condition?	System OK	Go to Step 2

GC0140100025000X

Fig. 10 Cruise Indicator Inoperative. 2002 Camaro & Firebird

Test Description

The number(s) below refer to the step number(s) on the diagnostic table.

2. Lack of communication may be due to a partial malfunction of the class 2 serial data circuit or due to a total malfunction of the class 2 serial data circuit. The specified procedure will determine the particular condition.
3.
4. The presence of DTCs which begin with "U" indicate some other module is not communicating. The specified procedure will compile all the available information before tests are performed.

Step	Action	Yes	No
1	Install a scan tool. Does the scan tool power up?	Go to Step 2	Check in Data Link Communications
2	1. Turn ON the ignition, with the engine OFF. 2. Attempt to establish communication with the following systems: o The powertrain control module o The body control module Does the scan tool communicate with these systems?	Go to Step 3	Data Link Communications
3	1. Select the powertrain control module display DTCs function on the scan tool. 2. Select the body control module display DTCs function on the scan tool. Does the scan tool display any DTCs?	Go to Step 4	Go to Symptoms
4	Does the scan tool display any DTCs which begin with a "U"?	Check in Data Link Communications	Go to Step 5
5	Does the scan tool display DTC B0605?	Check Body Control System	Go to Step 6
6	Does the scan tool display DTC P0562 or P0563?	Powertrain On Board Diagnostic (OBD) System Check	Go to Diagnostic Trouble Code (DTC) List/Type

GC0140100036010X

Fig. 11 System Check (Part 1 of 2). Corvette

GC0140100036020X

Fig. 11 System Check (Part 2 of 2). Corvette

Step	Action	Value (s)	Yes	No
1	Were you sent here from the Cruise Control Diagnostic System Check?	--	Go to Step 2	Go to Diagnostic System Check -
2	1. Install a scan tool and turn the ignition switch on. 2. Display the Powertrain Control Module Cruise Control data list. 3. Turn the Cruise switch ON. Does the scan tool indicate the Cruise Switch is ON?	--	Go to Step 3	Go to Step 8
3	Press the Cruise switch to the R/A position and release to the ON position. Does the scan tool indicate the Resume/Accel switch is ON and OFF?	--	Go to Step 4	Go to Step 16
4	With the Cruise switch in the ON position press and release the SET switch. Does the scan tool indicate the Set switch is ON and OFF?	--	Go to Step 5	Go to Step 17
5	Press and release the brake pedal. Does the scan tool indicate the TCC/CC Brake Switch is Applied and Released?	--	Go to Step 6	Go to Step 23
6	Display the Cruise Control Disengage History 1-8 on the scan tool. Do the last 8 disengage commands listed indicate a malfunction which may be causing the condition?	--	Go to Scan Tool Data Definitions	Go to Step 7
7	Test and repair the cruise control switch signal circuits for an intermittent open or high resistance. Refer to Intermittents . Did you find and correct the condition?	--	Go to Step 29	System OK
8	Test the CR CONT fuse #20 In the Instrument Panel Electrical Center for an open. Is the fuse open?	--	Go to Step 9	Go to Step 14
9	1. Remove the CR CONT fuse #20. 2. Disconnect the multifunction switch connector C217. 3. Test and repair the cruise control switch feed circuit 1239 for a short to ground. Did you find and correct the condition?	--	Go to Step 29	Go to Step 10
10	1. With the multifunction switch connector C217 disconnected. 2. Connect a test light to B+. 3. Probe the cruise control switch feed circuit (terminal B, of the switch side connector C217). A. Turn the cruise switch ON. B. Press and release the SET switch. C. Press and release the R/A switch. Does the test light illuminate while any of the switch functions are ON or OFF?	--	Go to Step 22	Go to Step 11
11	With the test light connected to B+, probe the following circuits from the harness side connector C217. • Cruise ON/OFF signal. • Cruise SET/COAST signal. • Cruise RESUME/ACCEL signal. Do any of the circuits listed illuminate the test light?	--	Go to Step 12	Go to Intermittent
12	1. Disconnect the TAC module connector C2. 2. With the test light connected to B+, probe the following circuits from the harness side connector C217. 3. Cruise ON/OFF signal. 4. Cruise SET/COAST signal. 5. Cruise RESUME/ACCEL signal. Do any of the circuits listed illuminate the test light?	--	Go to Step 13	Go to Step 28
13	Repair the short to ground in the cruise control switch circuits tested in the previous step. Did you complete the repair?	--	Go to Step 29	--
14	1. Disconnect the multifunction switch connector C217. 2. Turn the ignition switch on. 3. Connect a test light from the harness connector C217 terminal B to ground. Does the test light illuminate?	--	Go to Step 15	Go to Step 18

GC0140100035010X

Fig. 12 Cruise Control Inoperative (Part 1 of 4). 2000 Corvette

GC0140100035020X

Fig. 12 Cruise Control Inoperative (Part 2 of 4). 2000 Corvette

15	1. Connect a DMM from the switch side connector C217 terminals B to A. 2. Turn the cruise switch to the on position. 3. Measure the resistance of circuit 397 through the switch. Is the resistance within specified values?	0-2 ohms	Go to Step 19	Go to Step 22
16	1. Disconnect the multifunction switch connector C217. 2. Connect a DMM from the switch side connector C217 terminals B to D. 3. Press the cruise switch to the R/A position. 4. Measure the resistance of circuit 87 through the switch. Is the resistance within specified values?	0-2 ohms	Go to Step 20	Go to Step 22
17	1. Disconnect the multifunction switch connector C217. 2. Connect a DMM from the switch side connector C217 terminals B to C. 3. Turn the cruise switch to the on position. 4. Press the set switch. 5. Measure the resistance of circuit 84 through the switch. Is the resistance within specified values?	0-2 ohms	Go to Step 21	Go to Step 22
18	Repair the open or high resistance in circuit 1239. Is the repair complete?	--	Go to Step 29	--
19	Repair the open or high resistance in circuit 397. If OK replace the TAC Module. Is the repair complete?	--	Go to Step 29	--
20	Repair the open or high resistance in circuit 87. If OK replace the TAC Module. Is the repair complete?	--	Go to Step 29	--
21	Repair the open or high resistance in circuit 84. If OK replace the TAC Module. Is the repair complete?	--	Go to Step 29	--
22	Replace the Multifunction Switch. Is the repair complete?	--	Go to Step 29	--

GC0140100035030X

Fig. 12 Cruise Control Inoperative (Part 3 of 4). 2000 Corvette

Diagnostic Aids

Important

Perform the following in order to avoid misdiagnosis.

- Inspect for proper operation of brake lamps and clutch switch, if equipped.
- Inspect for proper operation of the transmission range switch.
- EMI on the speed sensor signal circuit may cause erratic cruise control operation.

Conditions for Enabling Cruise Control

The vehicle speed is greater than 40 km/h (25 mph).

Step	Action	Yes	No
Schematic Reference: Cruise Control Schematics			
1	Did you perform A Diagnostic System Check - Cruise Control?	Go to Step 2	Go to Diagnostic System Check -
2	1. Connect a scan tool. 2. Monitor the Cruise On switch parameter in the powertrain control module (PCM) data list. 3. Turn ON the cruise control switch. Did the scan tool parameter change state?	Go to Step 3	Go to Step 9
3	1. Observe the cruise control Set/Coast parameter in the PCM data list. 2. Press the cruise control Set button. Did the cruise control Set/Coast parameter change state?	Go to Step 4	Go to Step 14
4	1. Observe the cruise control Resume/Accelerate parameter in the PCM data list. 2. Press the Resume/Accelerate switch. Did the cruise control Resume Accelerate parameter change state?	Go to Step 5	Go to Step 15
5	1. Observe the stop lamp switch parameter in the PCM data list. 2. Press the brake pedal. Did the stop lamp switch parameter change state?	Go to Step 6	Go to Step 10

GC0140100037010X

Fig. 13 Cruise Control Inoperative/Faulting (Part 1 of 4). 2001–04 Corvette

23	1. Inspect the Stoplamp Switch Assembly for proper adjustment. If OK disconnect the Stoplamp Switch Assembly connector C1. 2. Turn the ignition switch on. 3. Connect a test light from the harness connector C1 terminal B to ground. Does the test light illuminate?	--	Go to Step 24	Go to Step 26
24	Test continuity through the TCC/CC Brake Switch, while applying and releasing the brakes. Does the switch open with brakes applied and close with brakes released?	--	Go to Step 25	Go to Step 27
25	Inspect and repair circuit 420 for an open or high resistance. If OK replace the Powertrain Control Module. Is the repair complete?	--	Go to Step 29	--
26	Repair the open or high resistance in circuit 339. Is the repair complete?	--	Go to Step 29	--
27	Replace the Stoplamp Switch Assembly. Is the repair complete?	--	Go to Step 29	--
28	Replace the TAC Module. Did you complete the repair?	--	Go to Step 29	--
29	1. Clear any DTCs which may have set. 2. Operate the system in order to verify the repair. Did you correct the condition?	--	System OK	Go to Diagnostic System Check -

GC0140100035040X

Fig. 12 Cruise Control Inoperative (Part 4 of 4). 2000 Corvette

6	1. Observe the TCC/Brake switch parameter in the PCM data list. 2. Press the brake pedal. Did the cruise release switch parameter change state?	Go to Step 7	Go to Step
7	Is the vehicle equipped with a manual transmission?	Go to Step 8	Go to Step 29
8	1. Observe the clutch pedal position (CPP) switch parameter in the PCM data list. 2. Press the clutch pedal. Did the CPP switch parameter change state?	Go to Step 29	Go to Step 12
9	1. Turn OFF the ignition. 2. Disconnect the multifunction turn signal lever. 3. Turn ON the ignition, with the engine OFF. 4. Probe the multifunction turn signal lever ignition positive voltage circuit with a test lamp connected to a good ground. Did the test lamp illuminate?	Go to Step 13	Go to Step 21
10	1. Turn OFF the ignition. 2. Disconnect the stop lamp switch harness connector. 3. Turn ON the ignition, with the engine OFF. 4. Probe the stop lamp battery positive voltage circuit with a test lamp connected to a good ground. Did the test lamp illuminate?	Go to Step 16	Go to Step 22
11	1. Turn OFF the ignition. 2. Disconnect the TCC/Brake switch harness connector. 3. Turn ON the ignition, with the engine OFF. 4. Probe the TCC/Brake switch ignition positive voltage circuit with a test lamp connected to a good ground. Did the test lamp illuminate?	Go to Step 18	Go to Step 23
12	1. Turn OFF the ignition. 2. Disconnect the clutch pedal position (CPP) switch. 3. Turn ON the ignition, with the engine OFF. 4. Probe the CPP switch ignition positive voltage circuit with a test lamp connected to a good ground. Did the test lamp illuminate?	Go to Step 20	Go to Step 24
13	Test the cruise control ON switch signal circuit for a open, high resistance, short to ground or short to voltage. Did you find and correct the condition?	Go to Step 35	Go to Step 28
14	Test the cruise control Set/Coast signal circuit for a open, high resistance, short to ground or short to voltage. Did you find and correct the condition?	Go to Step 35	Go to Step 28

GC0140100037020X

Fig. 13 Cruise Control Inoperative/Faulting (Part 2 of 4). 2001–04 Corvette

15	Test the cruise control Resume/Accelerate signal circuit for a open, high resistance, short to ground or short to voltage. Did you find and correct the condition?	Go to Step 35	Go to Step 28
16	Test the stop lamp switch signal circuit for a open, high resistance, short to ground or short to voltage. Did you find and correct the condition?	Go to Step 35	Go to Step 17
17	Check the stop lamp switch for proper adjustment. Is the stop lamp switch adjusted properly?	Go to Step 25	Go to Step 25
18	Test the TCC/Brake switch signal circuit for a open, high resistance, short to ground or short to voltage. Did you find and correct the condition?	Go to Step 35	Go to Step 19
19	Check the TCC/Brake switch for proper adjustment. Is the TCC/Brake switch adjusted properly?	Go to Step 26	Go to Step 26
20	Test the CPP switch signal circuit for a open, high resistance, short to ground or short to voltage. Did you find and correct the condition?	Go to Step 35	Go to Step 27
21	Repair the open, high resistance or short to ground in the multifunction turn signal lever ignition positive voltage circuit. Did you complete the repair?	Go to Step 35	--
22	Repair the open, high resistance or short to ground in the stop lamp switch battery positive voltage circuit. Did you complete the repair?	Go to Step 35	--
23	Repair the open, high resistance or short to ground in the TCC/Brake switch battery positive voltage circuit. Did you complete the repair?	Go to Step 35	--
24	Repair the open, high resistance or short to ground in the CPP switch battery positive voltage circuit. Did you complete the repair?	Go to Step 35	--

GC0140100037030X

Fig. 13 Cruise Control Inoperative/Faulting (Part 3 of 4). 2001–04 Corvette

25	Inspect for poor connections at the harness connector of the stop lamp switch. Refer to Intermittents. Did you find and correct the condition?	Go to Step 35	Go to Step 30
26	Inspect for poor connections at the harness connector of the TCC/Brake switch. Refer to Intermittents. Did you find and correct the condition?	Go to Step 35	Go to Step 31
27	Inspect for poor connections at the harness connector of the CPP switch. Refer to Intermittents. Did you find and correct the condition?	Go to Step 35	Go to Step 32
28	Inspect for poor connections at the harness connector of the multifunction turn signal lever. Refer to Intermittents. Did you find and correct the condition?	Go to Step 35	Go to Step 33
29	Inspect for poor connections at the harness connector of the PCM. Refer to Intermittents. Did you find and correct the condition?	Go to Step 35	Go to Step 34
30	Replace the stop lamp switch. Did you complete the replacement?	Go to Step 35	--
31	Replace the TCC/Brake switch. Replacement in Hydraulic Brakes. Did you complete the replacement?	Go to Step 35	--
32	Replace the CPP switch. Did you complete the replacement?	Go to Step 35	--
33	Replace the multifunction turn signal lever. Did you complete the replacement?	Go to Step 35	--
34	**Important** The PCM must be reprogrammed before replacement. Replace the PCM. Did you complete the replacement?	Go to Step 35	--
35	Operate the vehicle within the conditions for cruise control operation. Does the cruise control system operate properly?	System OK	Go to Step 2

GC0140100037040X

Fig. 13 Cruise Control Inoperative/Faulting (Part 4 of 4). 2001–04 Corvette

Circuit Description

The Cruise Resume/Accel switch is an input to the throttle actuator control (TAC) Module. This cruise control information is supplied to the PCM via serial data . This allows the PCM and TAC module to control and hold a requested speed. The Cruise Resume/Accel switch sends an ignition positive voltage signal to the TAC module when the switch is applied. This DTC sets if the TAC module senses a voltage on the Resume/ Accelerate switch signal circuit when voltage is not expected

Conditions for Running the DTC

The cruise control switch is ON.

Conditions for Setting the DTC

The TAC module detects the Resume/Accel switch is ON for longer than 90 seconds.

Action Taken When the DTC Sets

- The PCM stores the DTC information into memory when the diagnostic runs and fails.
- The malfunction indicator lamp (MIL) will not illuminate.
- The PCM records the operating conditions at the time the diagnostic fails. The PCM stores this information in the Failure Records.
- The cruise is disabled.

Conditions for Clearing the MIL/DTC

- A last test failed, or the current DTC, clears when the diagnostic runs and does not fail.
- A history DTC clears after 40 consecutive warm-up cycles, if failures are not reported by this or any other emission related diagnostic.
- Use a scan tool in order to clear the MIL/DTC.

Diagnostic Aids

- Remove any debris from the TAC module connector surfaces before servicing the TAC module. Inspect the TAC module connector gaskets when diagnosing/replacing the module. Ensure that the gaskets are installed correctly.
- For any test that requires probing the PCM or a component harness connector, use the Connector Test Adapter Kit J 35616-A . Using this kit prevents damage to the harness/component terminals.
- Inspect for a resume/accel switch stuck in the engage position or the signal circuit is shorted to voltage.
- For an intermittent, refer to Intermittent

Test Description

The numbers below refer to the step numbers on the diagnostic table.

GC0140100014010X

Fig. 14 Code P0567: Resume/Accelerate Switch (Part 1 of 3). Camaro, Firebird & 2001–04 Corvette

2. This step determines if condition is present.
3. This step determines if the switch is at fault.
4. This steps determines if the circuit is shorted to a voltage.

Step	Action	Yes	No
1	Did you perform A Diagnostic System Check - Cruise Control?	Go to Step 2	Go to Diagnostic System Check
2	**Important** If DTC P1518 is also set, diagnose P1518 first. 1. Install the scan tool. 2. Turn ON the ignition leaving the engine OFF. 3. Turn OFF the cruise control switch. Does the scan tool parameter indicate that the Cruise Resume/Accel switch is ON?	Go to Step 3	Go to Diagnostic Aids
3	1. Turn OFF the ignition. 2. Disconnect the appropriate TAC module harness connector. 3. Turn ON the ignition, with the engine OFF. 4. Monitor the cruise control Resume/Accelerate switch parameter in the PCM data list. Does the scan tool indicate that the cruise control Resume/ Accelerate switch is ON?	Go to Step 6	Go to Step 4
4	Test the cruise control Resume/Accelerate switch signal circuit for a short to voltage. Did you find and correct the condition?	Go to Step 9	Go to Step 5
5	Inspect for poor connections at the harness connector of the cruise control switch. Did you find and correct the condition?	Go to Step 8	Go to Step 7
6	Inspect for poor connections at the harness connector of the TAC module. Did you find and correct the condition?	Go to Step 9	Go to Step 8
7	Replace the cruise control switch. Did you complete the replacement?	Go to Step 9	--

GC0140100014020X

Fig. 14 Code P0567: Resume/Accelerate Switch (Part 2 of 3). Camaro, Firebird & 2001–04 Corvette

8	Replace the TAC module. Did you complete the replacement?	Go to Step 9	--
9	1. Use the scan tool in order to clear the DTCs. 2. Operate the vehicle within the Conditions for Running the DTC as specified in the supporting text. Does the DTC reset?	Go to Step 2	System OK

GC0140100014030X

Fig. 14 Code P0567: Resume/Accelerate Switch (Part 3 of 3). Camaro, Firebird & 2001–04 Corvette

2. This step determines if condition is present.

Step	Action	Yes	No
1	Did you perform A Diagnostic System Check - Cruise Control?	Go to Step 2	Go to Diagnostic System Check -
2	**Important** If DTC P1518 is also set, diagnose P1518 first. 1. Install a scan tool. 2. Turn ON the ignition with the engine OFF. 3. Turn OFF the cruise control switch. 4. Observe the cruise control Set/Coast switch parameter in the PCM data list. Does the scan tool parameter indicate that the cruise control Set/Coast switch is ON?	Go to Step 3	Go to Diagnostic Aids
3	1. Turn OFF the ignition. 2. Disconnect the appropriate TAC module harness connector. 3. Turn On the ignition with the engine OFF. 4. Monitor the cruise control Set/Coast switch parameter with a scan tool. Does the scan tool indicate that the Cruise Set/Coast switch is ON?	Go to Step 6	Go to Step 4
4	Test the cruise control ON switch signal circuit for a short to voltage. Did you find and correct the condition?	Go to Step 9	Go to Step 5
5	Inspect for poor connections at the harness connector of the cruise control switch. Refer to Intermittent Did you find and correct the condition?	Go to Step 9	Go to Step 7
6	Inspect for poor connections at the harness connector of the TAC module. Refer to Intermittent Did you find and correct the condition?	Go to Step 9	Go to Step 8
7	Replace the cruise control switch. Did you complete the replacement?	Go to Step 9	--

GC0140100026020X

Fig. 15 Code P0568: Set/Coast Switch (Part 2 of 3). Camaro, Firebird & 2001–04 Corvette

8	Replace the TAC module. Did you complete the replacement?	Go to Step 9	--
9	1. Use the scan tool in order to clear the DTCs. 2. Operate the vehicle within the Conditions for Running the DTC as specified in the supporting text. Does the DTC reset?	Go to Step 2	System OK

GC0140100026030X

Fig. 15 Code P0568: Set/Coast Switch (Part 3 of 3). Camaro, Firebird & 2001–04 Corvette

Circuit Description

The cruise control Set/Coast switch is an input to the throttle actuator control (TAC) module. The cruise control information is supplied to the PCM via serial data. This input allows the PCM and TAC module to control and hold a requested speed. The cruise control Set/Coast switch sends a ignition positive voltage signal to the TAC module when the momentary switch is applied. This DTC sets if the TAC module senses a voltage on the Set/Coast switch signal circuit when the voltage is not expected.

Conditions for Running the DTC

The Cruise switch is ON.

Conditions for Setting the DTC

The TAC module detects the Set/Coast switch is ON for longer than 90 seconds.

Action Taken When the DTC Sets

- The PCM stores the DTC information into memory when the diagnostic runs and fails.
- The malfunction indicator lamp (MIL) will not illuminate.
- The PCM records the operating conditions at the time the diagnostic fails. The PCM stores this information in the Failure Records.
- The cruise is disabled.

Conditions for Clearing the MIL/DTC

- A last test failed, or the current DTC, clears when the diagnostic runs and does not fail.
- A history DTC clears after 40 consecutive warm-up cycles, if failures are not reported by this or any other emission related diagnostic.
- Use a scan tool in order to clear the MIL/DTC.

Diagnostic Aids

- Remove any debris from the TAC module connector surfaces before servicing the TAC module. Inspect the TAC module connector gaskets when diagnosing/replacing the module. Ensure that the gaskets are installed correctly.
- For any test that requires probing the PCM or a component harness connector, use the Connector Test Adapter Kit J 35616-A . Using this kit prevents damage to the harness/component terminals.
- Inspect for a set/coast switch stuck in the engaged position or the signal circuit is shorted to voltage.
- For an intermittent, refer to Intermittent

Test Description

The number below refers to the step number on the diagnostic table.

GC0140100026010X

Fig. 15 Code P0568: Set/Coast Switch (Part 1 of 3). Camaro, Firebird & 2001–04 Corvette

Circuit Description

The TCC Brake (cruise release) switch is a normally closed switch. When the TCC Brake switch is closed, (brake pedal released) the PCM senses ignition voltage on the TCC Brake switch signal circuit.

If the PCM senses a voltage on the TCC Brake switch signal circuit when the TCC Brake switch should be open, this DTC sets.

Conditions for Running the DTC

- The engine speed is greater than 700 RPM.
- The engine operates for greater than 2 seconds.
- The wheel speed is greater than 48 km/h (30 mph) in order to enable the diagnostic. The diagnostic disables when the wheel speed is below 16 km/h (10 mph).

Conditions for Setting the DTC

- The PCM detects voltage on the TCC Brake switch circuit when the TCC Brake switch should be open.
- All above conditions are present for 1.5 seconds.

Action Taken When the DTC Sets

- The PCM stores the DTC information into memory when the diagnostic runs and fails.
- The malfunction indicator lamp (MIL) will not illuminate.
- The PCM records the operating conditions at the time the diagnostic fails. The PCM stores this information in the Failure Records.

Conditions for Clearing the DTC

- A last test failed, or current DTC, clears when the diagnostic runs and does not fail.
- A history DTC will clear after 40 consecutive warm-up cycles, if no failures are reported by this or any other non-emission related diagnostic.
- Use a scan tool in order to clear the DTC.

Diagnostic Aids

- Remove any debris from the PCM connector surfaces before servicing the PCM. Inspect the PCM connector gaskets when diagnosing/replacing the modules. Ensure that the gaskets are installed correctly. The gaskets prevent contaminate intrusion into the PCM.
- For any test that requires probing the PCM or a component harness connector, use the Connector Test Adapter Kit J 35616-A . Using this kit prevents damage to the harness/component terminals.
- Test drive the vehicle if a switch or circuit condition cannot be located. An intermittent condition may be duplicated during a test drive.

GC0140100027010X

Fig. 16 Code P0571: TCC Brake Switch (Part 1 of 3). Camaro, Firebird & 2001–04 Corvette

- For an intermittent, refer to Intermittents.

Test Description

The number below refers to the step number on the diagnostic table.

2. This step determines if the fault is present.

Step	Action	Yes	No
1	Did you perform A Diagnostic System Check - Cruise Control?	Go to Step 2	Go to Diagnostic System Check -
2	1. Connect a scan tool. 2. Turn ON the ignition, with the engine OFF. 3. Monitor the TCC Brake switch parameter in the PCM data list. Does the brake switch parameter indicate Applied?	Go to Step 3	Go to Diagnostic Aids
3	1. Turn OFF the ignition. 2. Disconnect the TCC Brake switch. 3. Turn ON the ignition, with the engine OFF. 4. Observe the TCC Brake switch parameter in the PCM data list. Does the TCC Brake switch parameter indicate Released?	Go to Step 5	Go to Step 4
4	Test the TCC Brake switch signal circuit for a short to voltage. Did you find and correct the condition?	Go to Step 10	Go to Step 7
5	Inspect the TCC Brake switch for proper adjustment. Did you find and correct the condition?	Go to Step 10	Go to Step 6
6	Inspect for poor connections at the harness connector of the TCC Brake switch. Refer to Intermittent Did you find and correct the condition?	Go to Step 10	Go to Step 8
7	Inspect for poor connections at the harness connector of the PCM. Refer to Intermittent Did you find and correct the condition?	Go to Step 10	Go to Step 9
8	Replace the TCC Brake switch. Did you complete the replacement?	Go to Step 10	--

GC0140100027020X

Fig. 16 Code P0571: TCC Brake Switch (Part 2 of 3). Camaro, Firebird & 2001–04 Corvette

Circuit Description

The cruise control module uses the cruise engaged circuit to request cruise control. If improper conditions are present, the PCM will disable cruise control via the cruise inhibit control circuit. During cruise control, if the PCM detects a vehicle speed above the calibrated value, the PCM will inhibit the cruise control system, and set DTC P0574.

Conditions for Running the DTC

- The cruise control is enabled.
- The cruise control is engaged.

Conditions for Setting the DTC

The PCM detects a vehicle speed above 176 km/h (110 mph).

Action Taken When the DTC Sets

- The PCM disables the cruise control.
- The PCM will not illuminate the malfunction indicator lamp (MIL).
- The PCM will store the conditions present when the DTC set as Fail Records data only.

Conditions for Clearing the DTC

- The History DTC will clear after 40 consecutive warm-up cycles have occurred without a malfunction.
- The DTC can be cleared by using the scan tool Clear DTC Information function.

Diagnostic Aids

This diagnostic trouble code (DTC) is an information DTC only. The DTC indicates the reason that the PCM disabled the cruise control system. Be sure to check with the customer for the conditions that set the DTC.

Reviewing the Fail Records vehicle mileage since the diagnostic test last failed may assist in diagnosing the condition. The Fail Records information may help in determining how often the condition occurs that set the DTC.

Step	Action	Yes	No
1	Did you perform A Diagnostic System Check - Cruise Control?	Go to Step 2	Go to Diagnostic System Check -

GC0140100038010X

Fig. 17 Code P0574: Cruise Control Module (Part 1 of 2). Camaro & Firebird

9	**Important** Program the replacement PCM. Replace the PCM. Is the action complete?	Go to Step 10	--
10	1. Use a scan tool in order to clear the DTCs. 2. Operate the vehicle within the Conditions for Running the DTC as specified in the supporting text. Does the DTC reset?	Go to Step 2	System OK

GC0140100027030X

Fig. 16 Code P0571: TCC Brake Switch (Part 3 of 3). Camaro, Firebird & 2001–04 Corvette

2	Since most occurrences of DTC P0574 are caused by wheel spin due to icy, wet or slippery conditions, verify the conditions under which the DTC set with the customer. Did the road conditions cause this DTC to set?	Go to Step 3	Go to Diagnostic Aids
3	Explain system operation to the customer and clear this DTC. Is the action complete?	System OK	--

GC0140100038020X

Fig. 17 Code P0574: Cruise Control Module (Part 2 of 2). Camaro & Firebird

Circuit Description

The clutch switch is a normally closed switch. The powertrain control module (PCM) receives an ignition voltage on the clutch switch circuit when the clutch switch is closed. The PCM receives 0 voltage on the clutch switch circuit when the clutch switch is open.

This DTC determines if the transmission clutch switch has failed by monitoring for a clutch switch transition within a range from 0-38 km/h (0-24 mph).

Conditions for Running the DTC

No active vehicle speed sensor (VSS) DTCs

Conditions for Setting the DTC

- Vehicle speed goes from 0 to more than 38 km/h (24 mph) and back to 0 km/h (0 mph) for 2 seconds without the PCM detecting a clutch transition.
- This occurs 7 times before the diagnostic reports a fault.

Action Taken When the DTC Sets

- The PCM stores the DTC information into memory when the diagnostic runs and fails.
- The malfunction indicator lamp (MIL) will not illuminate.
- The PCM records the operating conditions at the time the diagnostic fails. The PCM stores this information in the Failure Records.

Conditions for Clearing the DTC

- A last test failed, or current DTC, clears when the diagnostic runs and does not fail.
- A history DTC will clear after 40 consecutive warm-up cycles, if no failures are reported by this or any other non-emission related diagnostic.
- Use a scan tool in order to clear the DTC.

Diagnostic Aids

Important

Remove any debris from the PCM connector surfaces before servicing the PCM. Inspect the PCM connector gaskets when diagnosing or replacing the PCM. Ensure that the gaskets are installed correctly. The gaskets prevent water intrusion into the PCM.

The following may cause an intermittent:

- Poor connections--Refer to Intermittents.
- Corrosion
- Misrouted harness

GC0140100028010X

Fig. 18 Code P0704: Clutch Switch (Part 1 of 3). Camaro, Firebird & 2001–04 Corvette

- Rubbed through wire insulation
- Broken wire inside the insulation

The vehicle may need to be driven to locate an intermittent condition. Monitor the clutch switch parameter on the scan tool. If the parameter changes state while driving, inspect for proper connections.

Using Freeze Frame and Failure Records data may aid in locating an intermittent condition. If you cannot duplicate the DTC, the information included in the Freeze Frame and Failure Records data can aid in determining how many miles since the DTC set. The Fail Counter and Pass Counter can also aid determining how many ignition cycles the diagnostic reported a pass or a fail. Operate the vehicle within the same Freeze Frame conditions, such as RPM, load, vehicle speed, temperature etc., that you observed. This will isolate when the DTC failed. For an intermittent, refer to Intermittent

Test Description

The number below refers to the step number on the diagnostic table.

3. This step determines if the fault is present.

Step	Action	Yes	No
1	Did you perform A Diagnostic System Check - Cruise Control?	Go to Step 2	Go to Diagnostic System Check -
2	1. Turn OFF the ignition. 2. Disconnect the appropriate PCM harness connector. 3. Turn ON the ignition, with the engine OFF. 4. Probe the CPP switch signal circuit with a test lamp connected to a good ground. Does the test lamp illuminate?	Go to Step 3	Go to Step 4
3	1. Press the clutch pedal. 2. Observe the test lamp. Does the test lamp illuminate?	Go to Step 6	Go to Step 9
4	1. Turn OFF the ignition. 2. Disconnect the CPP switch harness connector. 3. Turn On the ignition, with the engine OFF. 4. Probe the ignition positive voltage circuit of the clutch pedal position switch harness connector with a test lamp connected to a good ground. Does the test lamp illuminate?	Go to Step 5	Go to Step 7
5	Test the CPP switch signal circuit for a open or high resistance or short to ground. Did you find and correct the condition?	Go to Step 12	Go to Step 8

GC0140100028020X

Fig. 18 Code P0704: Clutch Switch (Part 2 of 3). Camaro, Firebird & 2001–04 Corvette

Step	Action	Yes	No
6	Test the CPP signal circuit for a short to voltage. Did you find and correct the condition?	Go to Step 12	Go to Step 8
7	Repair the open, high resistance or short to ground in the CPP switch ignition positive voltage circuit . Did you find and correct the condition?	Go to Step 12	--
8	Inspect for poor connection at the harness connector of the CPP switch. Refer to Intermittent Did you find and correct the condition?	Go to Step 12	Go to Step 10
9	Inspect for poor connection at the harness connector of the PCM. Refer to Intermittent Did you find and correct the condition?	Go to Step 12	Go to Step 11
10	Replace the CPP switch. Did you complete the replacement?	Go to Step 12	--
11	**Important** The PCM must be reprogrammed before replacement. Replace the PCM. Did you complete the replacement?	Go to Step 12	--
12	Operate the vehicle with in the condition for cruise control operation. Does the DTC reset?	Go to Step 2	System OK

GC0140100028030X

Fig. 18 Code P0704: Clutch Switch (Part 3 of 3). Camaro, Firebird & 2001–04 Corvette

Circuit Description

The PCM has the ability to disable cruise control if conditions are detected which would make cruise control operation undesirable. The following conditions may cause cruise control to be inhibited by the PCM:

- Engine not running long enough for cruise control operation.
- Transaxle range switch indicates park, neutral, low, or reverse gear selected.
- Engine speed is too high or too low.
- Vehicle speed is too high or too low.
- ABS system is active for longer than 2 seconds.
- Vehicle acceleration or deceleration rate is too high.

If any of these conditions are present, the PCM will interrupt the ground on the cruise inhibit circuit to request that cruise control be disengaged. If the cruise status signal indicates that cruise control is still engaged while the PCM is inhibiting cruise control operation, DTC P1554 will be set.

Conditions for Running the DTC

The PCM is commanding the cruise control module to inhibit cruise control operation.

Conditions for Setting the DTC

- The PCM detects a cruise control engaged signal from the cruise control module, while inhibiting cruise control operation.
- The above conditions are present for more than 1 second.

Action Taken When the DTC Sets

- The PCM will not illuminate the malfunction indicator lamp (MIL).
- The PCM will store conditions which were present when the DTC set as Failure Records only. This information will not be stored as Freeze Frame Records.

Conditions for Clearing the MIL/DTC

- A History DTC will clear after 40 consecutive warm-up cycles have occurred without a malfunction.
- The DTC can be cleared by using a scan tool.

Diagnostic Aids

Check for the following conditions:

- A faulty connection at the PCM. Inspect the harness connectors for backed out terminals, improper mating, broken locks, improperly formed or damaged terminals, and faulty terminal to wire connections. Use a corresponding mating terminal to test for proper terminal tension.

GC0140100029010X

Fig. 19 Code P1554: Cruise Control Status Circuit (Part 1 of 3). Camaro & Firebird

- Inspect the wiring harness for damage. If the harness appears to be OK, observe the Cruise Status display on the scan tool while moving the connectors and wiring harnesses related to the cruise control module. A change in the display will indicate the location of the malfunction.

If DTC P1554 cannot be duplicated, the information included in the Failure Records data can be useful in determining how many ignition cycles have passed since the DTC was last set.

Test Description

The number below refers to the step number on the diagnostic table.

8. This vehicle is equipped with a PCM which utilizes an electrically erasable programmable read-only memory (EEPROM). When the PCM is replaced, the new PCM must be programmed.

Step	Action	Yes	No
1	Did you perform A Diagnostic System Check - Cruise Control?	Go to Step 2	Go to Diagnostic System Check -
2	1. Install a scan tool. 2. Turn ON the ignition, with the engine OFF. 3. With a scan tool, monitor the DTC information for DTC P1585 in the powertrain control module (PCM). Is DTC P1585 also set?	Go to DTC P1585	Go to Step 3
3	With a scan tool, observe the Cruise Requested display. Does the Cruise Requested display indicate YES?	Go to Step 5	Go to Step 4
4	1. Review and record the Failure Records Information. 2. Operate the vehicle within the Failure Records condition. 3. Using a scan tool, monitor the Specific DTC Information for DTC P1554 until the test runs. Does the scan tool indicate that DTC P1554 failed this ignition?	Go to Step 5	Go to Diagnostic Aids
5	1. Turn OFF the ignition. 2. Disconnect the cruise control module harness connector. 3. Turn ON the ignition, with the engine OFF. 4. Using the scan tool, observe the Cruise Requested display. Does the Cruise Requested display indicate YES?	Go to Step 6	Go to Step 7

GC0140100029020X

Fig. 19 Code P1554: Cruise Control Status Circuit (Part 2 of 3). Camaro & Firebird

6	1. Turn OFF the ignition. 2. Disconnect the appropriate PCM connector. 3. Test the Cruise Engaged signal circuit for a short to ground. Did you find and correct the condition?	Go to Step 9	Go to Step 8
7	Replace the cruise control module. Did you complete the replacement?	Go to Step 9	--
8	**Important:** The replacement PCM must be programmed. Replace the PCM. Did you complete the repair?	Go to Step 9	--
9	1. Use a scan tool in order to clear the DTC. 2. Operate the vehicle within the conditions for Running the DTC as specified in the supporting text. Does the DTC reset?	Go to Step 2	System OK

GC0140100029030X

Fig. 19 Code P1554: Cruise Control Status Circuit (Part 3 of 3). Camaro & Firebird

Step	Action	Yes	No
1	Did you perform the Cruise Control Diagnostic System Check?	Go to Step 2	Go to Diagnostic System Check
2	1. Connect the scan tool. 2. Turn ON the ignition, with the engine OFF. 3. Retrieve the DTCs from the EBCM. Are there any DTC's that begin with a "C" also set?	Go to Diagnostic Trouble Code (DTC) List	Go to Step 3
3	Repair the short to voltage on the stop lamp switch signal circuit. Did you find and correct the condition?	Go to Step 4	--
4	1. Use the scan tool to clear the DTC (s). 2. Operate the vehicle within the conditions for Running the DTC as specified in the supporting text. Does the DTC reset?	Go to Step 2	System OK

GC0140100030020X

Fig. 20 Code P1574: Stoplamp Switch (Part 2 of 2). Camaro, Firebird & 2001–04 Corvette

Circuit Description

This diagnostic test functions on the assumption that sudden decrease in a non-drive, wheel speed must be caused by a brake application. Non-drive wheel speed and stoplamp switch status are supplied to the PCM through serial data from the Electronic Brake Control Module (EBCM). If there is a 4 km/h (2.5 mph) or greater decrease of non-drive wheel speed in 0.4 seconds and a transition of the TCC or extended travel contacts of the TCC brake switch without a transition of the stop lamp brake switch, DTC P1574 is set.

Conditions for Running the DTC

- DTCs P0502, P0503, P0719, P0724, P1575 and P1602 not set.
- Traction control and antilock brake systems have not failed.
- Traction control and antilock brake systems are not active.
- Non-drive wheel speed goes above 32.2 km/h (20 mph) and then doesn't go below 6.4 km/h (4 mph).

Conditions for Setting the DTC

A 4.0 km/h (2.5 mph) or greater decrease in non-drive wheel speed in 0.4 second and extended travel brake switch or TCC brake switch indicating brakes applied and no transition noticed in the stoplamp contacts of the stop lamp switch.

Action Taken When the DTC Sets

PCM will set the stoplamp switch status to not applied.

- The Malfunction Indicator Lamp (MIL) will not illuminate.
- No message will be displayed.

Conditions for Clearing the DTC

- A History DTC will clear after forty consecutive warm-up cycles with no failures of any non-emission related diagnostic test.
- A Last Test Failed (current) DTC will clear when the diagnostic runs and does not fail.
- Use a scan tool to clear DTCs.
- Interrupting PCM battery voltage may or may not clear DTCs. This practice is not recommended.

Diagnostic Aids

DTC P1574 indicates the stoplamp switch signal to the EBCM or the EBCM's ability to send the stop lamp switch signal to the PCM has failed. Refer to ABS/TCS DTCs for diagnosis of the stoplamp switch signal and the EBCM.

GC0140100030010X

Fig. 20 Code P1574: Stoplamp Switch (Part 1 of 2). Camaro, Firebird & 2001–04 Corvette

Circuit Description

Output driver modules (ODMs) are used by the powertrain control module (PCM) in order to turn on many of the current driven devices that are needed to control various engine and transaxle functions. DTC P1558 set indicates that an improper voltage level has been detected on the signal circuit which controls the cruise control inhibit circuit.

Conditions for Running the DTC

- The engine speed is 450 RPM or more.
- System voltage is between 8 and 16 volts.

Conditions for Setting the DTC

- The ignition is on.
- The PCM detects an improper voltage level on the cruise inhibit signal circuit.
- The condition exists for at least 30 seconds.

Action Taken When the DTC Sets

- The PCM will not illuminate the malfunction indicator lamp (MIL).
- The PCM will store the conditions present when the DTC set as Failure Records data only.

Conditions for Clearing the DTC

- The history DTC will clear after 40 consecutive warm-up cycles have occurred without a malfunction.
- The DTC can be cleared by using the scan tool's Clear DTC Information function.

Diagnostic Aids

In order to determine whether an improper voltage level exists on the output circuit, the PCM compares the voltage level to the commanded state.

If the condition is intermittent, refer to Intermittents. Systems.

Test Description

The number(s) below refer to the step number(s) on the diagnostic table.

2. Normally, ignition positive voltage should be present on the control circuit with the PCM disconnected and the ignition turned ON.
3. Tests for short to voltage on the control circuit.

GC0140100031010X

Fig. 21 Code P1585: Output Driver Modules (Part 1 of 3). Camaro & Firebird

8. This vehicle is equipped with a PCM which utilizes an Electrically Erasable Programmable Read Only Memory (EEPROM). When the PCM is being replaced, the new PCM must be programmed.

Step	Action	Value (s)	Yes	No
1	Did you perform the Cruise Control Diagnostic System Check ?	--	Go to Step 2	Go to Diagnostic System Check -
2	1. Turn OFF the ignition. 2. Disconnect the PCM harness connector. 3. Turn ON the ignition, with the engine OFF. 4. Using a DMM connected to a good ground, measure the voltage of the cruise control inhibit signal circuit. Does the voltage measure near the specified value?	B+	Go to Step 3	Go to Step 4
3	1. Turn OFF the ignition. 2. Disconnect the cruise control module. 3. Turn ON the ignition, with the engine OFF. 4. Probe the cruise control inhibit signal circuit with a test lamp that is connected to a good ground. Does the test lamp illuminate?	--	Go to Step 7	Go to Step 5
4	Test the cruise control inhibit signal circuit for a open, high resistance or short to ground. Did you find and correct the condition?	--	Go to Step 10	Go to Step 6
5	Inspect for poor connections at the harness connector of the PCM. Testing for Intermittent Did you find and correct the condition?	--	Go to Step 10	Go to Step 8
6	Inspect for poor connections at the harness connector of the cruise control module. Did you find and correct the condition?	--	Go to Step 10	Go to Step 9
7	Repair the short to voltage in the cruise control inhibit signal circuit. Did you complete the repair?	--	Go to Step 10	--

GC0140100031020X

Fig. 21 Code P1585: Output Driver Modules (Part 2 of 3). Camaro & Firebird

8	**Important** The replacement PCM must be programmed. Replace the PCM. Did you complete the replacement?	--	Go to Step 10	--
9	Replace the cruise control module. Did you complete the replacement?	--	Go to Step 10	--
10	1. Use the scan tool in order to clear the DTCs. 2. Operate the vehicle within normal cruise control operating conditions. Does the DTC reset?	--	Go to Step 2	System OK

GC0140100031030X

Fig. 21 Code P1585: Output Driver Modules (Part 3 of 3). Camaro & Firebird

Circuit Description

The TCC/brake switch indicates brake pedal status to the powertrain control module (PCM). The TCC/brake switch is a normally-closed switch that supplies battery voltage to the PCM. Applying the brake pedal opens the switch, interrupting voltage to the PCM. This DTC is for manual transmission vehicles only, this switch is used for TCC operation on automatic transmission vehicles.

Conditions for Running the DTC

- The engine speed is more than 1000 RPM for 1 second.
- The wheel speed is more than 32.2 km/h (20 mph) in order to enable the diagnostic. The diagnostic disables when the wheel speed is less than 8.0 km/h (5 mph).

Conditions for Setting the DTC

- The vehicle speed decreases 1.6 km/h (1 mph) in 0.5 seconds without the PCM sensing a switch transition.
- The condition is present for 10 accel/decel cycles.

Action Taken When the DTC Sets

- The PCM will not illuminate the malfunction indicator lamp (MIL).
- The PCM will store conditions which were present when the DTC set as Failure Records only. This information will not be stored as Freeze Frame Records.

Conditions for Clearing the MIL/DTC

- A History DTC will clear after 40 consecutive warm-up cycles have occurred without a malfunction.
- The DTC can be cleared by using a scan tool.

Diagnostic Aids

Inspect for the following:

- Ask about the customers driving habits. Ask about unusual driving conditions (e.g. stop and go, expressway, etc.).
- Inspect the TCC/brake switch for proper mounting, adjustment and operation.
- Inspect for ABS DTCs. A faulty ABS condition may contribute to setting this DTC.
- An intermittent connection or poor wire terminal tension may contribute to setting the DTC. Refer to Intermittent

GC0140100032010X

Fig. 22 Code P1586: Cruise Control Brake Switch No. 2 (Part 1 of 3). Camaro & Firebird w/Manual Transmission

Step	Action	Yes	No
1	Did you perform the Cruise Control Diagnostic System Check?	Go to Step 2	Go to Diagnostic System Check -
2	1. Connect a scan tool. 2. Turn ON the ignition, with the engine OFF. 3. Observe the TCC/Brake switch parameter in the PCM data list. Does the scan tool indicate the TCC/Brake switch parameter as RELEASED?	Go to Step 3	Go to Step 4
3	Press the brake pedal. Does the scan tool indicate the TCC/Brake switch as APPLIED?	Go to Diagnostic Aids	Go to Step 6
4	Test the TCC/Brake switch signal circuit for a open, high resistance or short to ground. Did you find and correct the condition?	Go to Step 12	Go to Step 5
5	Test the TCC/Brake switch ignition poisitive voltage circuit for a open, high resistance or short to ground. Did you find and corect the condition?	Go to Step 12	Go to Step 7
6	Test the TCC/Brake switch signal circuit for a short to voltage. Did you find and correct the condition?	Go to Step 12	Go to Step 9
7	Test the TCC/Brake switch for proper adjustment. Did you find and correct the condition?	Go to Step 12	Go to Step 8
8	Inspect for poor connection at the harness connector of the TCC/Brake switch. Refer to Intermittents. Did you find and correct the condition?	Go to Step 12	Go to Step 10
9	Inspect for poor connection at the harness connector of the PCM. Refer to Intermittents. Did you find and correct the condition?	Go to Step 12	Go to Step 11

GC0140100032020X

Fig. 22 Code P1586: Cruise Control Brake Switch No. 2 (Part 2 of 3). Camaro & Firebird w/Manual Transmission

10	Replace the TCC/Brake switch. Did you complete the replacement?	Go to Step 12	--
11	**Important** The replacement must be reprogrammed before replacement. Replace the PCM. Did you complete the replacement?	Go to Step 12	--
12	1. Use a scan tool in order to clear the DTCs. 2. Operate the vehicle within the Conditions for Running the DTC as specified in the supporting text. Does the DTC reset?	Go to Step 2	System OK.

GC0140100032030X

Fig. 22 Code P1586: Cruise Control Brake Switch No. 2 (Part 3 of 3). Camaro & Firebird w/Manual Transmission

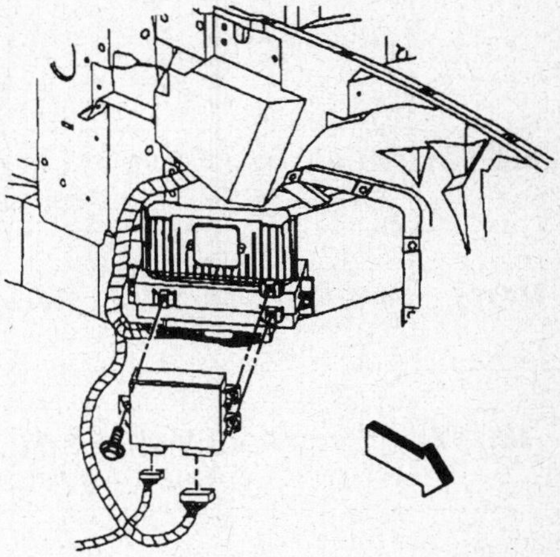

GC1109700536000X

Fig. 23 Electronic throttle control module replacement

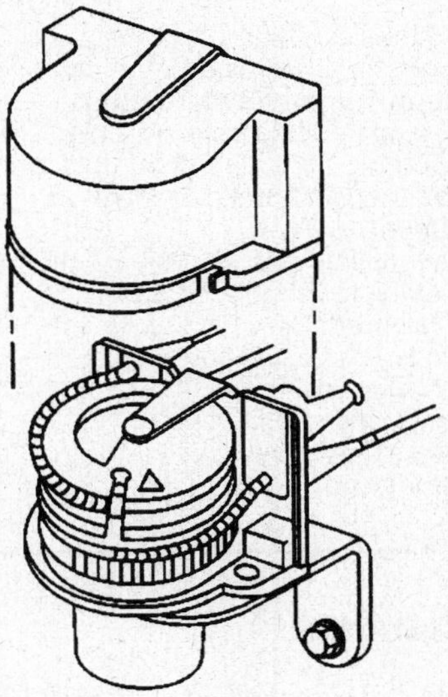

GC1109900658000X

Fig. 24 Cruise control servo cable adjuster cover replacement. Camaro & Firebird

COMPONENT REPLACEMENT

Cruise Release Switch

1. Remove lefthand lower instrument panel insulator panel.
2. Disconnect cruise release switch electrical connector.
3. Remove switch from bracket.
4. Reverse procedure to install. Adjust switch by pulling clutch pedal fully rearward against pedal stop until switch is fully seated.

Electronic Throttle Control Module

1. Raise and support vehicle, then remove righthand front wheel and tire assembly.
2. Remove wheelhouse filler panel and electronic throttle control module mounting screws from PCM bracket, **Fig. 23.**
3. Remove electrical connectors and electronic throttle control module.
4. Reverse procedure to install. **Torque** electronic throttle control module to 17 inch lbs

Cruise Control Cable

1. Remove cruise control servo cable adjuster cover, **Fig. 24.**
2. Remove cruise control cable from servo cable adjuster, **Fig. 25.**
3. Remove cruise control cable from accelerator control cable clip and servo bracket.
4. Remove cruise control cable clip from brake booster.
5. Raise and support vehicle.
6. Disconnect cruise control cable rosebud connector from brake pipe clip.
7. Remove mounting bolts and cruise control module shield.
8. Remove cruise control servo cover.
9. Remove retainer from cruise control module and compress conduit tangs.

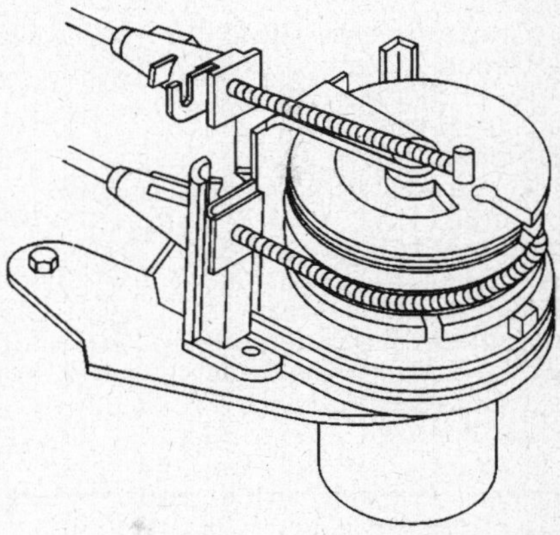

GC1109900659000X

Fig. 25 Cruise control cable at servo cable adjuster replacement. Camaro & Firebird

10. Pull cruise control cable out from module.
11. Disconnect cable bead from ribbon and remove cruise control cable.
12. Reverse procedure to install, noting the following:
    a. Cruise control module ribbon must not be twisted.
    b. Inspect cable and ensure O-ring is in place.
    c. Pull engine end of cruise control cable until cable is taut, install conduit fitting over ribbon and snap cable end into module.
    d. Ensure both tangs are engaged.
    e. Adjust cruise control cable as outlined in "Adjustments."

Type 5

NOTE: On Air Bag Equipped Models, Refer To "Air Bag System Precautions" Located In The Front Of This Manual For System Disarming & Arming Procedures.

NOTE: Refer To "Computer Relearn Procedures" Located In The Front Of This Manual When Battery Power To The Computer Has Been Interrupted.

NOTE: "Electrical Symbol & Wire Color Code Identification" Located In The Front Of This Manual May Be Used As An Aid When Using Wiring Circuits Found In This Section.

INDEX

DESCRIPTION

L-Series

2.2L ENGINE

The electronic cruise control is a system which maintains a desired vehicle speed under normal driving conditions. This cruise control system has the capability to cruise/maintain speed, to coast, to resume speed, to accelerate, to tap up and tap down.

The cruise control system consists of these main components. The PCM, cruise control module, the cruise brake, cruise clutch and stop lamp switches. It also has a cruise throttle cable. The cruise control module contains a low speed limit that will prevent system engagement at speeds of less than 25 mph.

The functional control switches located on the steering wheel control the operation of the controller. A cruise brake switch and a stoplamp switch disengage the system by means of the brake pedal. The switch is mounted on the brake pedal bracket. The cruise clutch switch, located on the clutch pedal bracket will also disengage the system. When the brake/clutch pedal is depressed, the cruise control system electronically disengages and throttle returns to idle position.

3.0L ENGINE

This system consists of cruise On/Off and cruise Set/Resume switches, accelerator pedal position (APP) sensor, cruise/brake and stop lamp switches. Included in the tasks of the ECM is to control the cruise control system. ECM processes switch inputs indicating that the driver has requested cruise control, at which point the ECM regulates throttle angle and other factors to maintain a constant vehicle speed. The ECM also receives inputs directly from the cruise/brake switch and the brake switch to deactivate cruise control and return vehicle control to driver.

This cruise control system is different from conventional systems in that there is no cable to hold the throttle open, nor is there a cruise control module. The electronic throttle control system makes these components unrequired and simplifies cruise control diagnosis. This is because a cruise control failure means that one or more of the sensors or switches associated with the system has failed and correcting this problem will restore the system to a normal working condition.

ION

Refer to "2.2L Engine" in "L-Series" for description.

S-Series

The system consists of a cruise control module, located in the passenger compartment on the driver's side above the accelerator pedal between the steering column and heater and air conditioning control head, control switches, cruise brake switch and, on models equipped with a manual transaxle, a cruise clutch switch.

This system is completely electronic and does not require vacuum or a vacuum servo motor to control throttle movement. A cable from the cruise control module pulls the accelerator linkage at the accelerator pedal.

The on/off switch enables and disables the speed control system. In the on position the cruise control will activate and in the off position the cruise control will immediately be disabled.

When the cruise in enabled, depressing the set/coast switch will engage the cruise. When cruise is engaged the cruise control module will maintain the desired speed within one mph. When the set/coast switch is held down the vehicle speed will coast down until the switch is released.

If the vehicle has been in the cruise control engage mode and cruise has been disabled by pressing the brake or clutch switch, then vehicle can return to the previous cruise set by momentarily depressing the resume/accel switch one time.

The vehicle speed in miles per hour is used for tap up and tap down cruise speed adjustments. Once tap up or tap down button is depressed, vehicle speed will increase or decrease by one mph for each time the switch is depressed.

The cruise control system has five circuits linking it to various input signals and a ground circuit. The IGN3 circuit sends ignition on signal to the module when the switch is in the on position. The cruise control switch supplies battery power to the power-up module, through the enable circuit. The vehicle speed information comes from the powertrain control module (PCM) at 4987 pulses per minute, on all models except Coupe or 4995 pulses per minute on Coupe models. The cruise control module receives input from the set/coast/resume/accel switch, located on the steering wheel. The cruise control module determines the command by the amount of voltage received. Brake and clutch switch inputs are received when the pedal is depressed to disengage the system.

TROUBLESHOOTING

Refer to **Fig. 1**, when troubleshooting speed control system.

COMPLAINT/CONDITION	POSSIBLE CAUSES	CORRECTIONS
NOISE	Cruise module mounting	Missing grommets or loose cruise module fasteners.
	Cruise module rod adjustments	Adjust rod according to procedure.
SURGE Definition: Slight engine power variation under steady throttle or cruise.	Verify surge is not present when cruise control is off.	
	Vehicle speed input	Verify VSS signal is operating properly. No diagnostic trouble codes are present.
SPEED WANDER/ FLUCTUATION	Manual transaxle verify gear selection on steep grades is correct.	Shift to lower gear.
	Speed fluctuation of ± 3 km/h (2 mph) is normal on medium hills	If speed fluctuation seems excessive on hills, check rod adjustment of cruise module.
WILL NOT ENGAGE/ DISENGAGE	Manual transaxle clutch slip	Verify engagement
	Brake switch adjustment	Adjust switch.
	Cruise switch PCM Slip ring/wiring Cruise module	Refer to cruise chart "Cruise Control Function Inoperative"
INTERMITTENT ENGAGE/DISENGAGE	Driver induced disengage.	See DTC P1584 chart.
	Brake switch	Adjust switch

G31109300006000X

Fig. 1 Speed control system troubleshooting chart. S-Series

ADJUSTMENTS

L-Series

2.2L ENGINE

THROTTLE CABLE

1. Partially disengage adjustment lock by depressing tabs, do not remove entirely. This will release spring inside adjuster to take out slack.
2. Ensure throttle cam is closed and cable end is tight against cable snap.
3. Engage adjustment lock.

BRAKE & CLUTCH SWITCH

Adjust switch by depressing the pedal pull out plunger on the switch and release pedal.

3.0L ENGINE

Adjust switch by depressing the pedal pull out plunger on the switch and release pedal.

ION

CRUISE RELEASE SWITCH

1. Ensure cruise control release switch is fully seated in bracket.
2. Slowly pull brake pedal rearward until audible clicking is no longer heard. Switch will be moved in retainer providing adjustment.
3. Release brake pedal, then ensure that release switch, stop lamp and torque converter clutch switch contacts open at 1 inch or less of pedal travel.
4. Ensure switches open simultaneously or before onset of braking.
5. Brake pedal may travel up to 1 inch before cruise control system disengages.

S-Series

CONTROL ROD

The rod and adjuster are not repairable and must be replaced as an assembly. Do not remove rod and adjuster from cruise control module.

1. Disconnect air intake tube at throttle body; then, while observing throttle plate position, depress adjuster release tab and slide adjuster away from bracket, **Fig. 2.**
2. With throttle plate closed, cruise control rod should have .040–.079 inch freeplay. If not as specified, adjust cable rod.

BRAKE & CLUTCH SWITCH

1. Loosen brake switch mounting nut.
2. Install brake switch adjustment gauge, tool No. SA9303BR, or equivalent, between switch actuator pad and switch. Ensure plunger is through slots in gauge.
3. While pulling up on brake pedal, push switch against gauge.
4. **Torque** switch mounting nut to 96 inch lbs.
5. Release brake pedal and tap gauge from side to side. If gauge swings freely, repeat previous steps. If gauge sticks or does not swing freely, proceed as follows:
   a. If .03–.05 inch of plunger is visible between switch and actuator pad on pedal arm, switch is adjusted correctly. Height of rounded crown of plunger is equivalent to .04 inch.
   b. If .05–.30 inch of plunger is visible, repeat previous steps.

SYSTEM DIAGNOSIS & TESTING

Accessing Diagnostic Trouble Codes

Connect a suitably programmed scan tool to Diagnostic Link Connector (DLC), and follow manufacturer's instructions.

Diagnostic Trouble Code Interpretation

S-SERIES & ION

Refer to **Fig. 3**, for Diagnostic Trouble Code (DTC) interpretation.

Wiring Diagrams

Refer to **Figs. 4 through 9**, for system wiring diagrams.

Symptoms

Refer to **Figs. 10 through 24**, for symptoms.

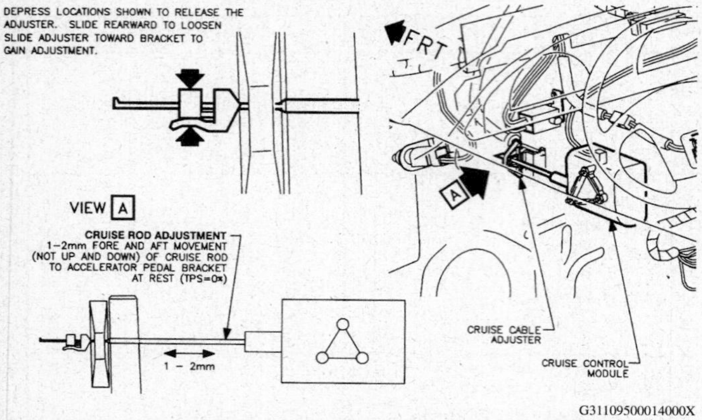

Fig. 2 Speed control rod adjustment. S-Series

Diagnostic Tests

Refer to **Figs. 25 through 43,** for diagnostic test procedures.

Performance Test

Perform the following procedure to confirm speed control system is operating correctly.

1. Test drive vehicle at 25 mph or more, ensure speed controls operate with switch in On position.
2. Depress set/coast switch for at least one second to engage speed controls.
3. Release accelerator pedal, ensure vehicle maintains speed.
4. Depress brake or clutch to disengage system, ensure vehicle decelerates.
5. Depress resume/accelerate switch for at least one second; vehicle should resume original speed.
6. Depress resume/accelerate switch for 1.5–4.5 seconds; vehicle speed should increase by one mph. Repeat this step.
7. Turn speed control on/off switch to Off position, vehicle should decelerate.

Clearing Diagnostic Trouble Codes

Connect a suitably programmed scan tool to Data Link Connector (DLC), and follow manufacturer's instructions.

COMPONENT DIAGNOSIS & TESTING

Brake & Clutch Switch

1. With pedal released, switch contacts should be closed and continuity should exist.
2. With pedal depressed, switch contacts should be open and no continuity should exist.
3. If not as specified, adjust switch as outlined in "Adjustments" or replace as outlined in "Component Replacement."

Code	Interpretation
S-SERIES	
P0565	Cruise Control Switch Circuit
P1580	Cruise Control Move Output Circuit Low Voltage
P1581	Cruise Control Move Output Circuit High Voltage
P1582	Cruise Control Direction Output Circuit Low Voltage
P1583	Cruise Control Direction Output Circuit High Voltage
P1584	Cruise Control Disabled
P1587	Cruise Control Clutch Output Circuit Low Voltage
P1588	Cruise Control Clutch Output Circuit High Voltage
ION	
P0565	Cruise Control Switch Circuit
P0572	Cruise Control Voltage Out Of Range
P0573	No Cruise Control Voltage Detected
P1574	Stop Lamp Switch Out Of Range
P1580	Cruise Control Move Output Circuit Low Voltage
P1581	Cruise Control Direction Output Circuit Low Voltage
P1582	Cruise Control Move Output Circuit High Voltage
P1583	Cruise Control Direction Output Circuit High Voltage
P1584	Cruise Control Disabled
P1587	Cruise Control Clutch Output Circuit Low Voltage
P1588	Cruise Control Clutch Output Circuit High Voltage

Fig. 3 DTC interpretation. S-Series & ION

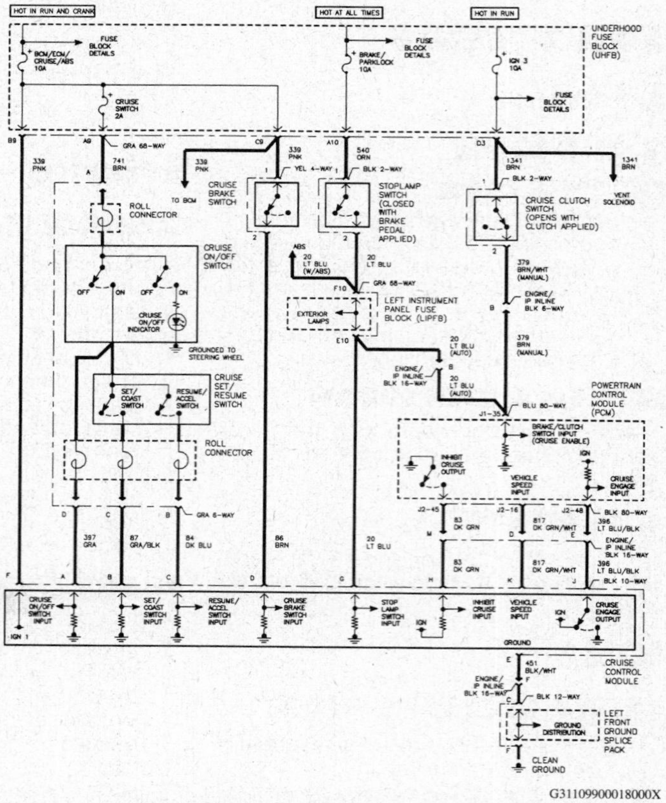

Fig. 4 Wiring diagram. 2000–01 L-Series w/2.2L engine

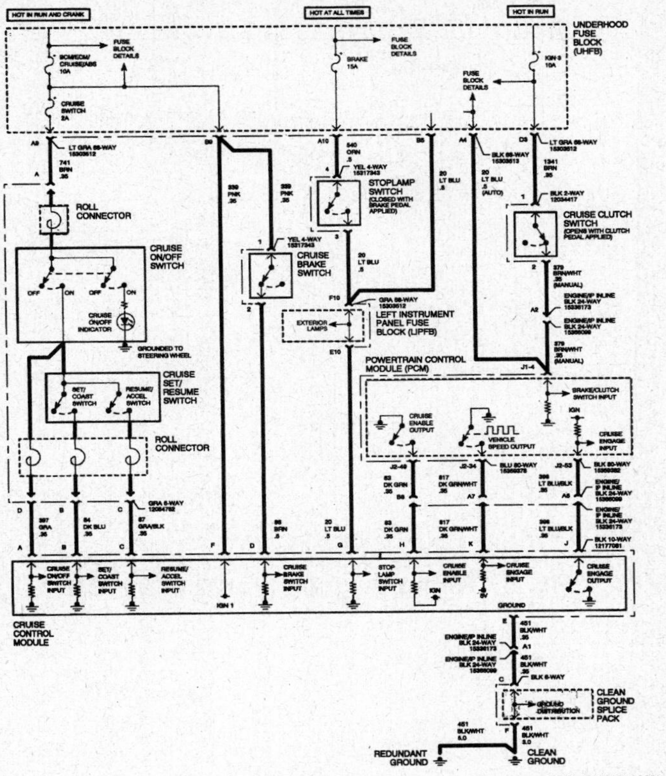

GC0140100001000X

Fig. 5 Wiring diagram. 2002–04 L-Series w/2.2L engine

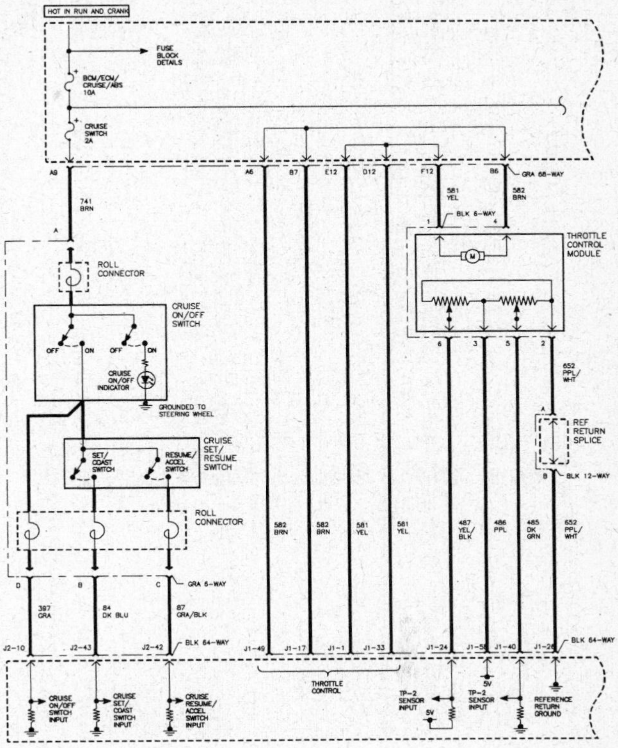

G31109900019010X

Fig. 6 Wiring diagram (Part 1 of 2). 2000–01 L-Series w/3.0L engine

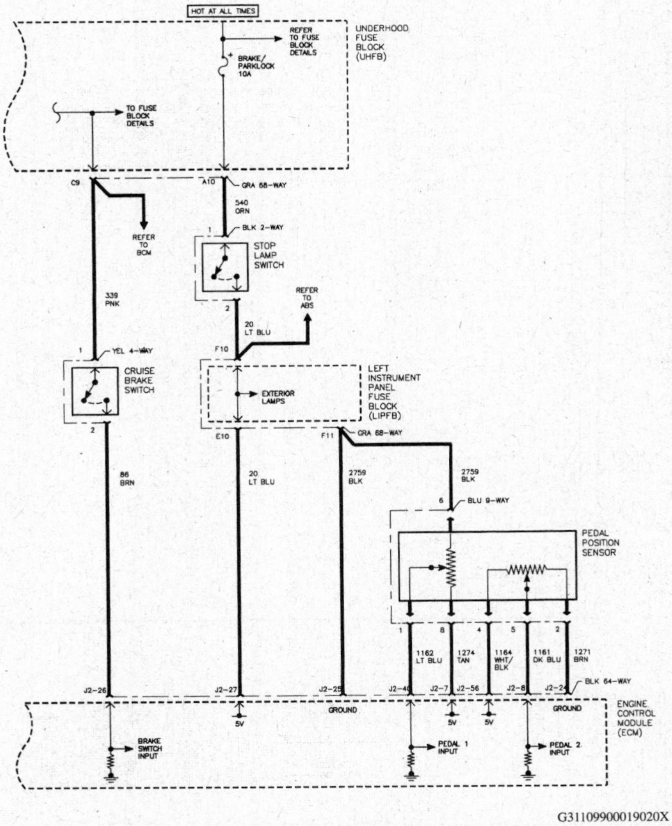

G31109900019020X

Fig. 6 Wiring diagram (Part 2 of 2). 2000–01 L-Series w/3.0L engine

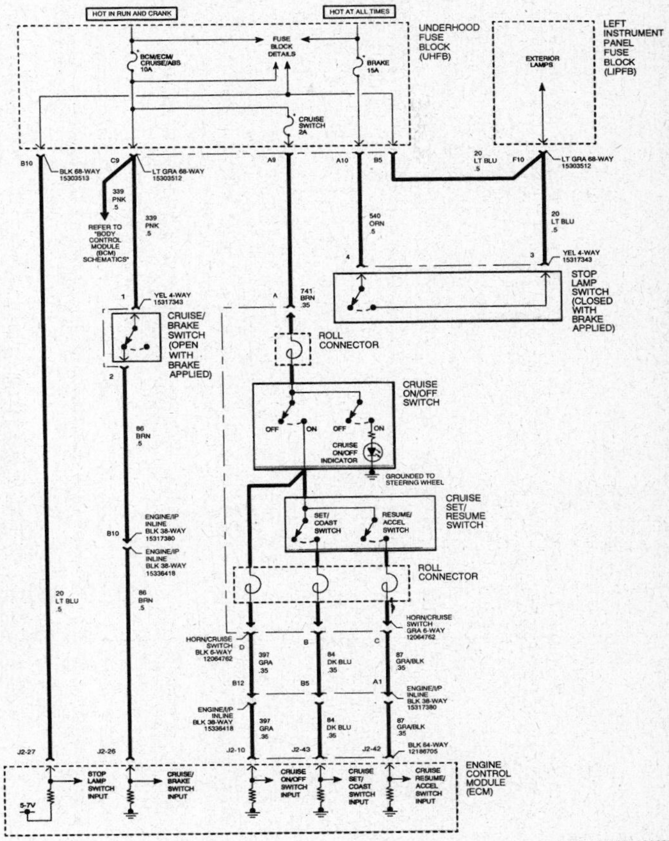

GC0140100002000X

Fig. 7 Wiring diagram. 2002–04 L-Series w/3.0L engine

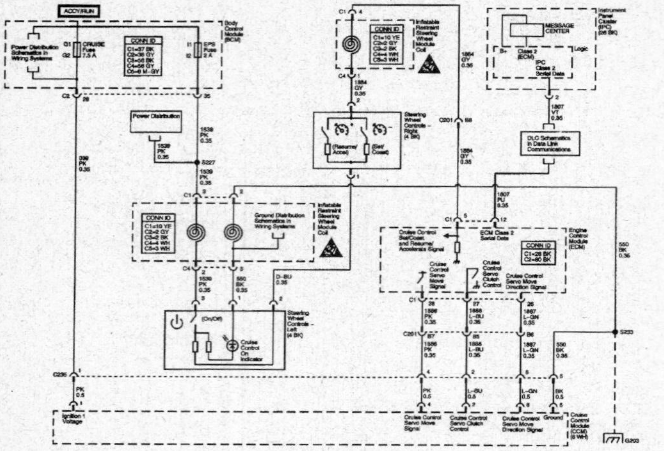

GC1100200865010X

Fig. 8 Wiring diagram (Part 1 of 2). ION

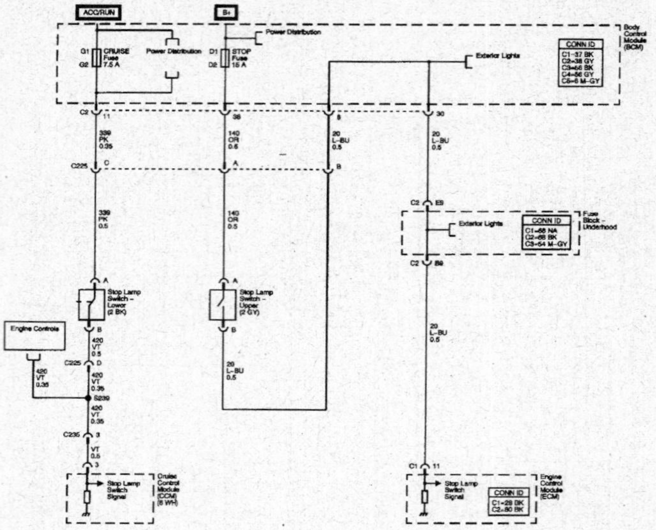

GC1100200865020X

Fig. 8 Wiring diagram (Part 2 of 2). ION

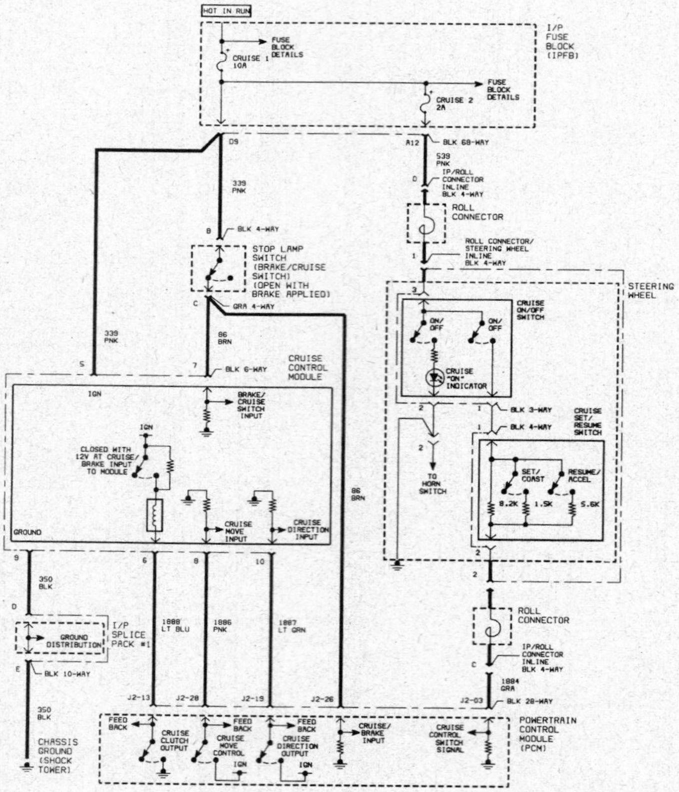

G31109900017000X

Fig. 9 Wiring diagram. S-Series

DIAGNOSTIC CHART INDEX

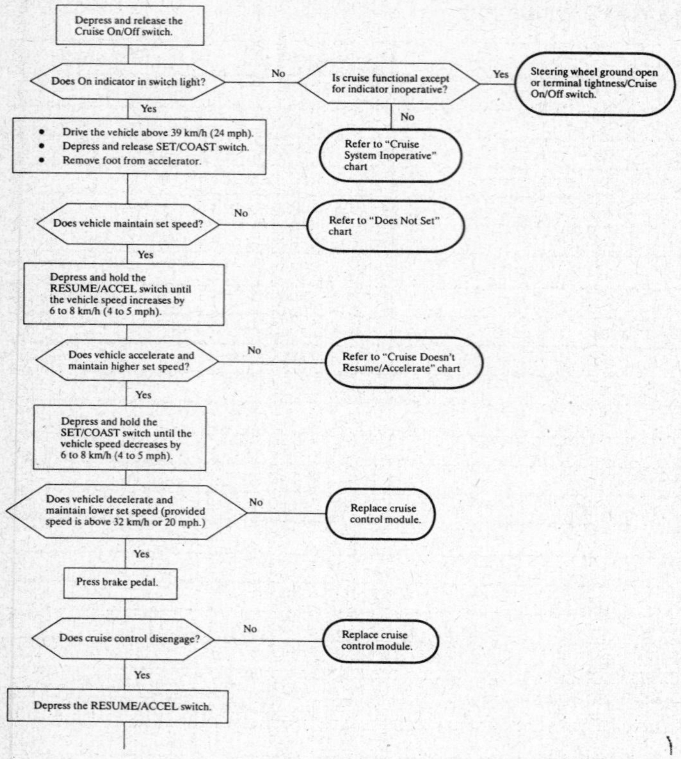

G31109900029010X

Fig. 10 Cruise System Check (Part 1 of 2). 2000–01 L-Series w/2.2L Engine

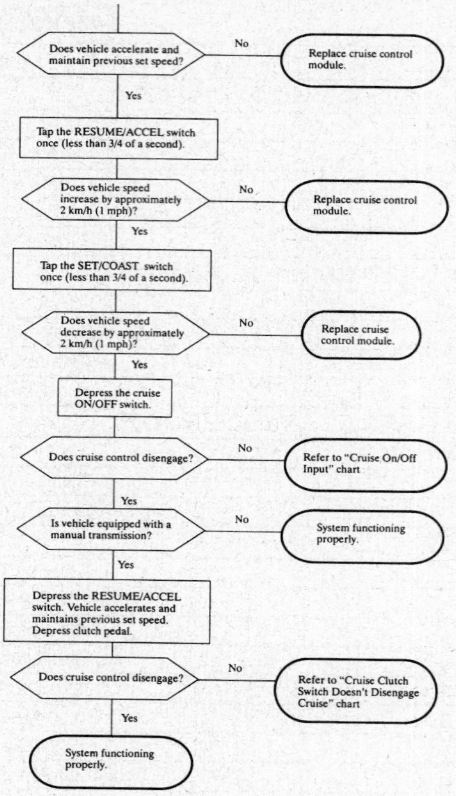

G31109900029020X

Fig. 10 Cruise System Check (Part 2 of 2). 2000–01 L-Series w/2.2L Engine

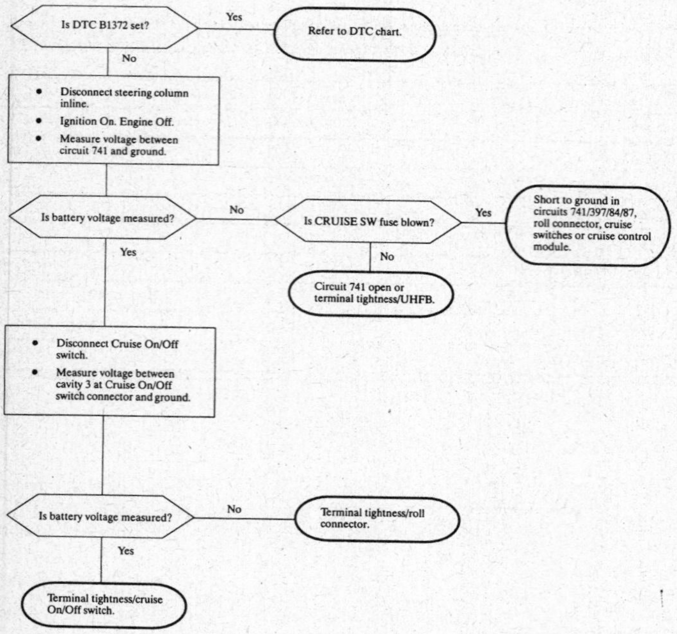

G31109900030000X

Fig. 11 Cruise System Inoperative. 2000–01 L-Series w/2.2L Engine

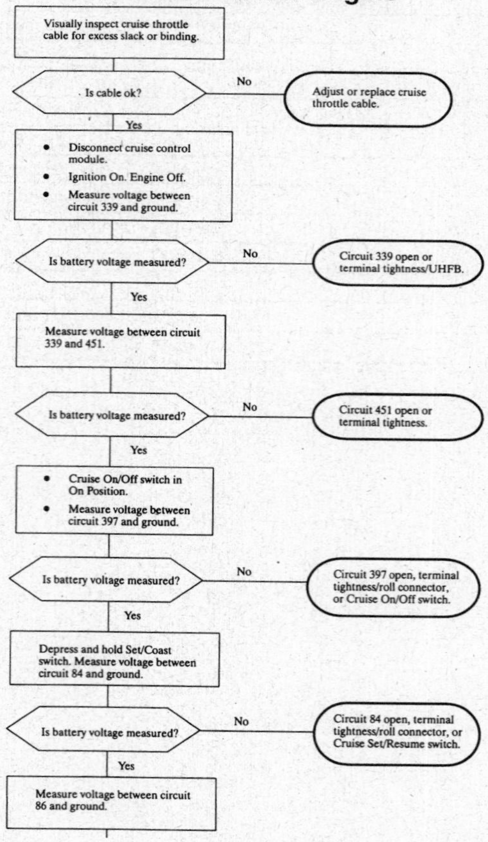

G31109900031010X

Fig. 12 Cruise System Does Not Set (Part 1 of 3). 2000–01 L-Series w/2.2L Engine

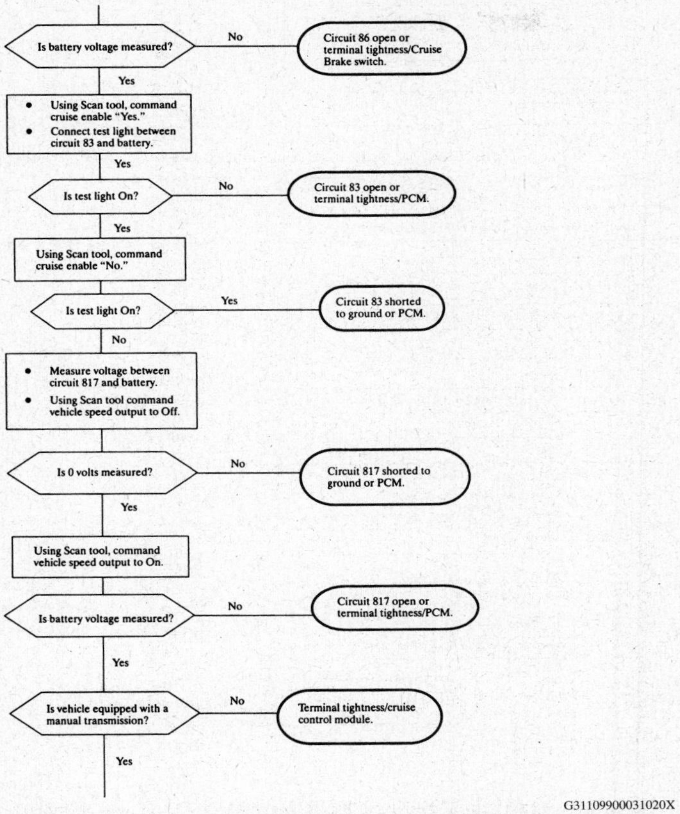

Fig. 12 Cruise System Does Not Set (Part 2 of 3). 2000–01 L-Series w/2.2L Engine

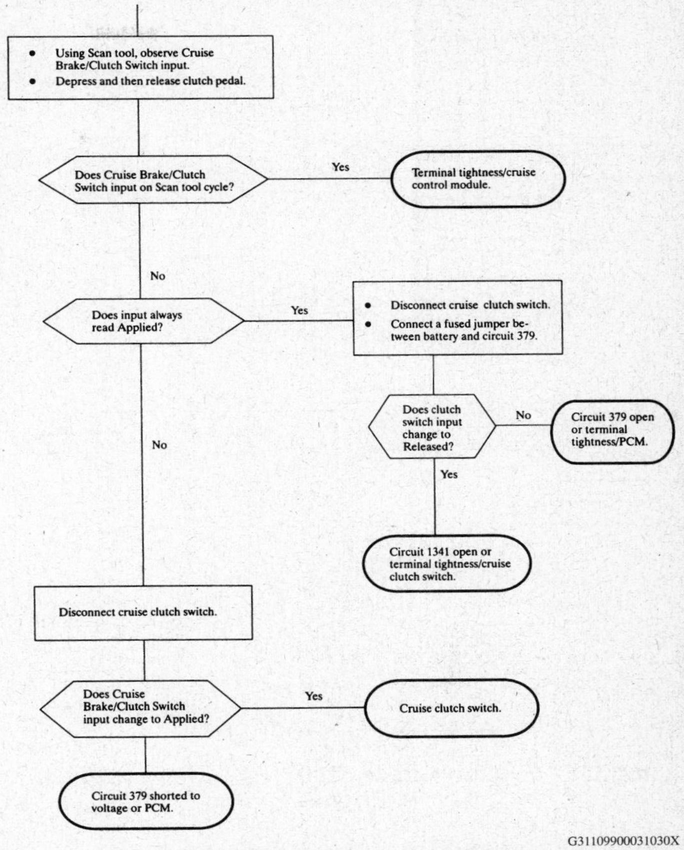

Fig. 12 Cruise System Does Not Set (Part 3 of 3). 2000–01 L-Series w/2.2L Engine

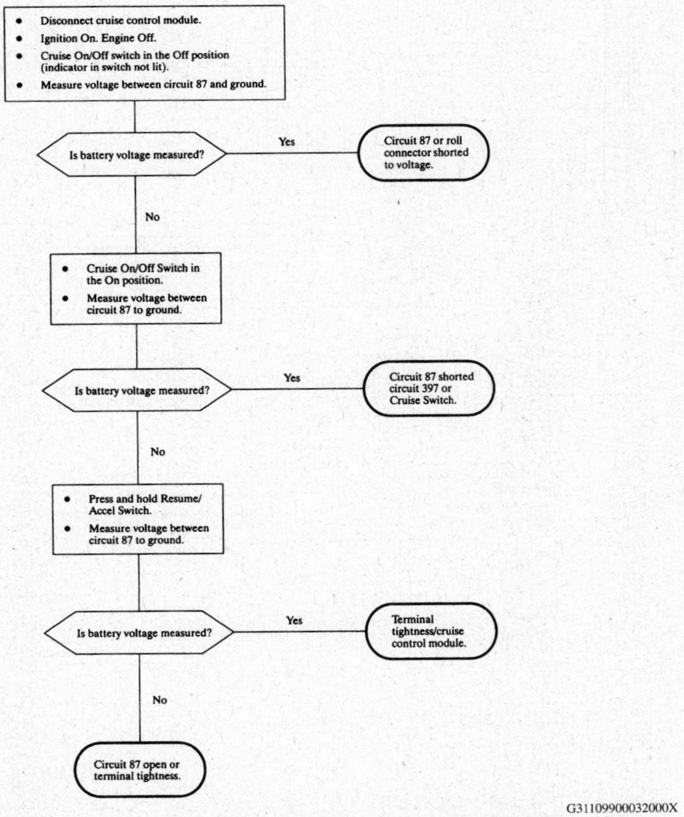

Fig. 13 Cruise System Does Not Resume/ Accelerate. 2000–01 L-Series w/2.2L Engine

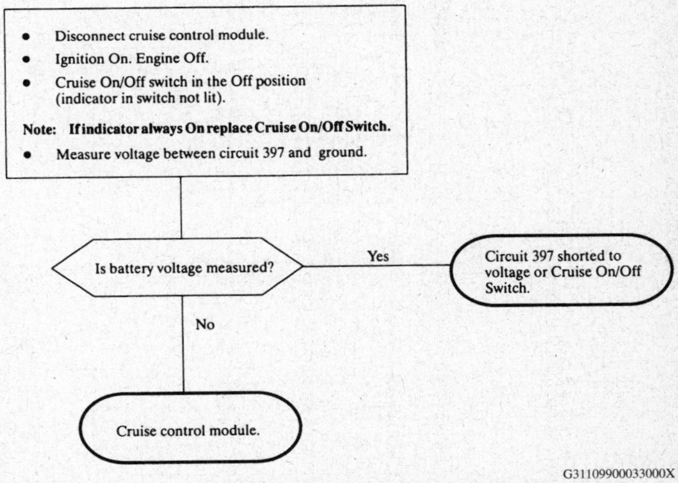

Fig. 14 Cruise System On/Off Input. 2000–01 L-Series w/2.2L Engine

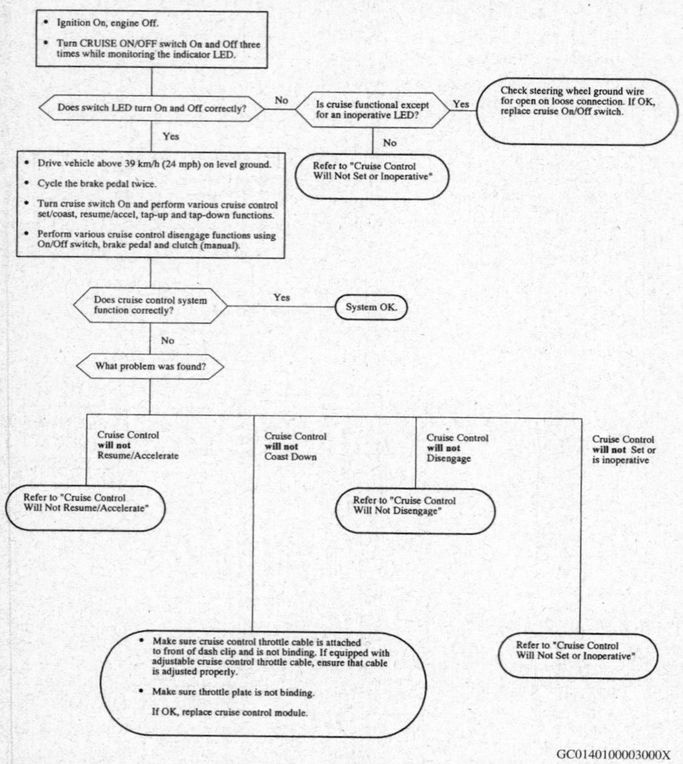

Fig. 15 System Check. 2002–04 L-Series w/2.2L Engine

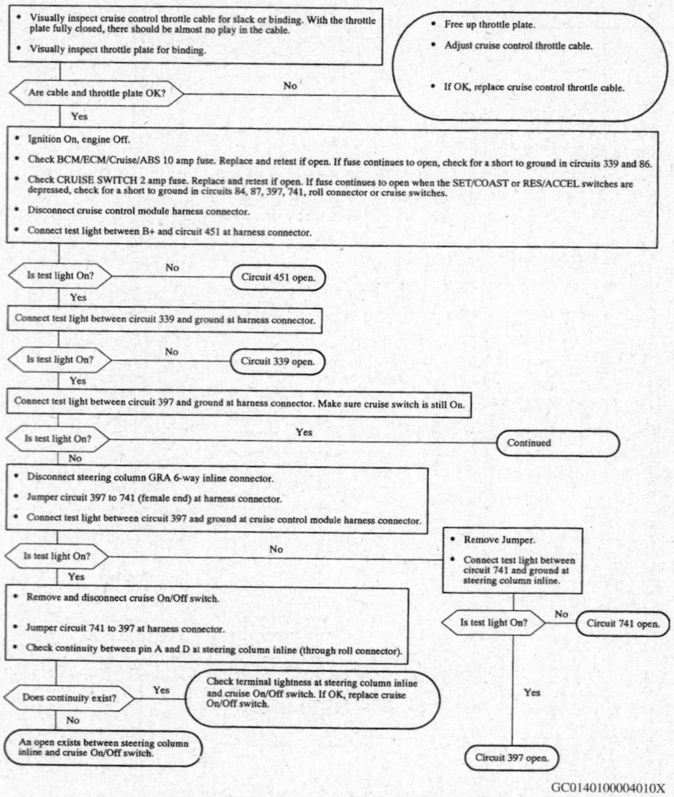

Fig. 16 Cruise Control Will Not Set Or Inoperative (Part 1 of 4). 2002–04 L-Series w/2.2L Engine

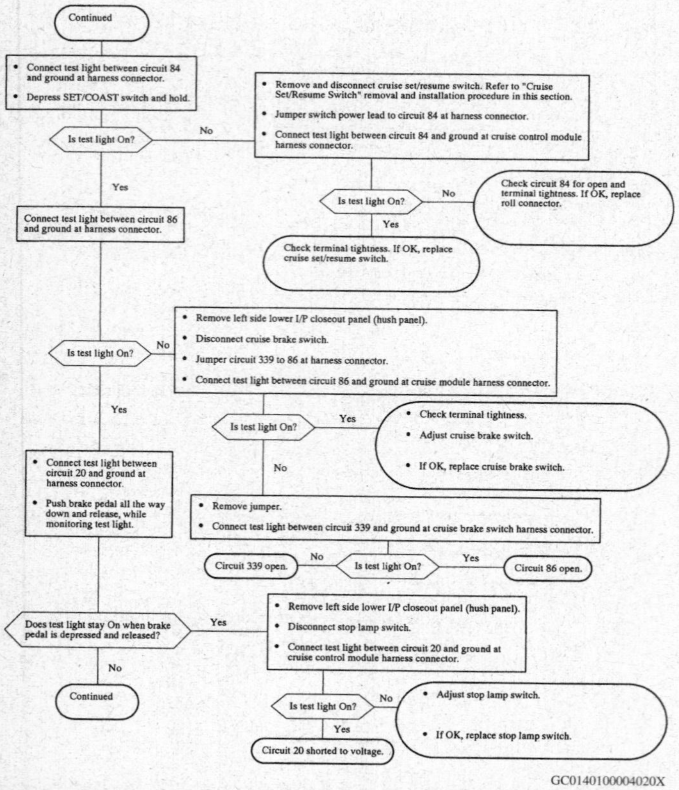

Fig. 16 Cruise Control Will Not Set Or Inoperative (Part 2 of 4). 2002–04 L-Series w/2.2L Engine

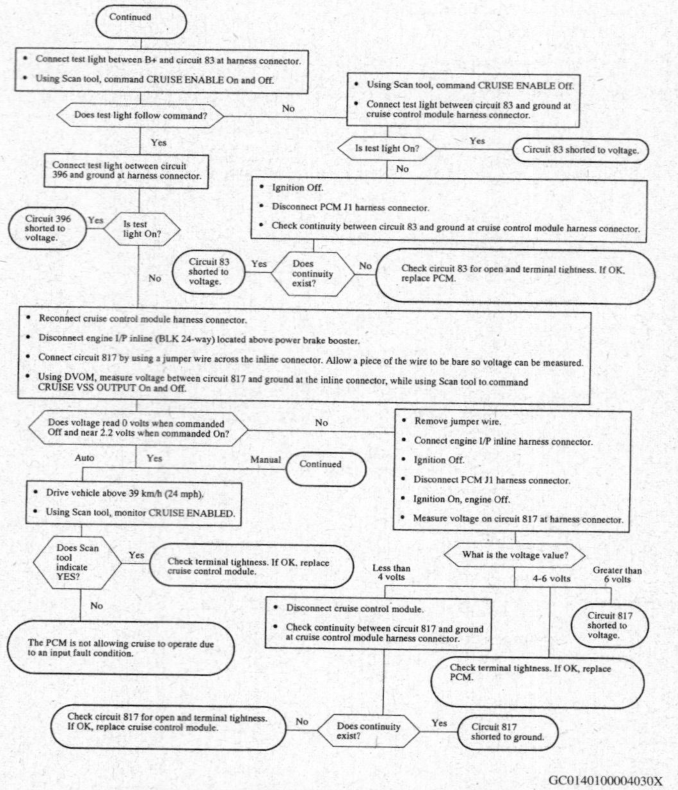

Fig. 16 Cruise Control Will Not Set Or Inoperative (Part 3 of 4). 2002–04 L-Series w/2.2L Engine

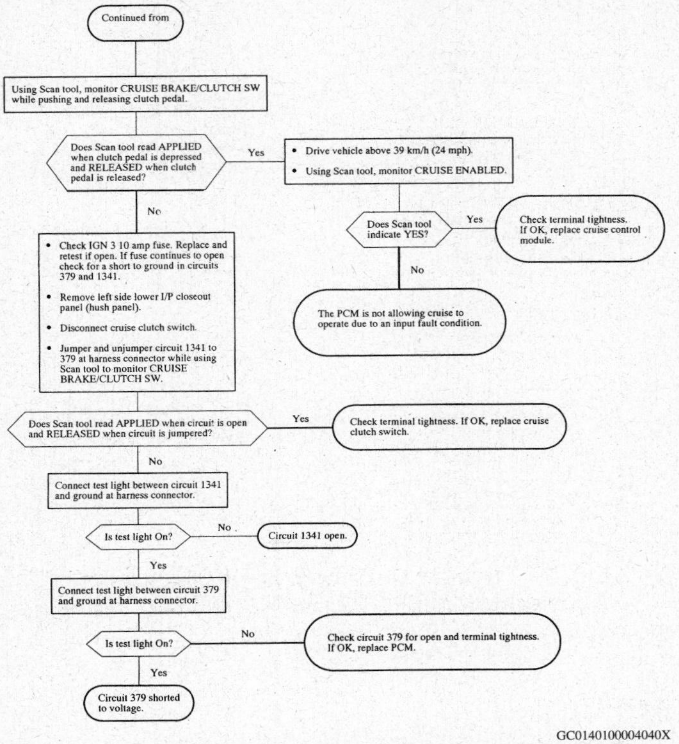

Fig. 16 Cruise Control Will Not Set Or Inoperative (Part 4 of 4). 2002–04 L-Series w/2.2L Engine

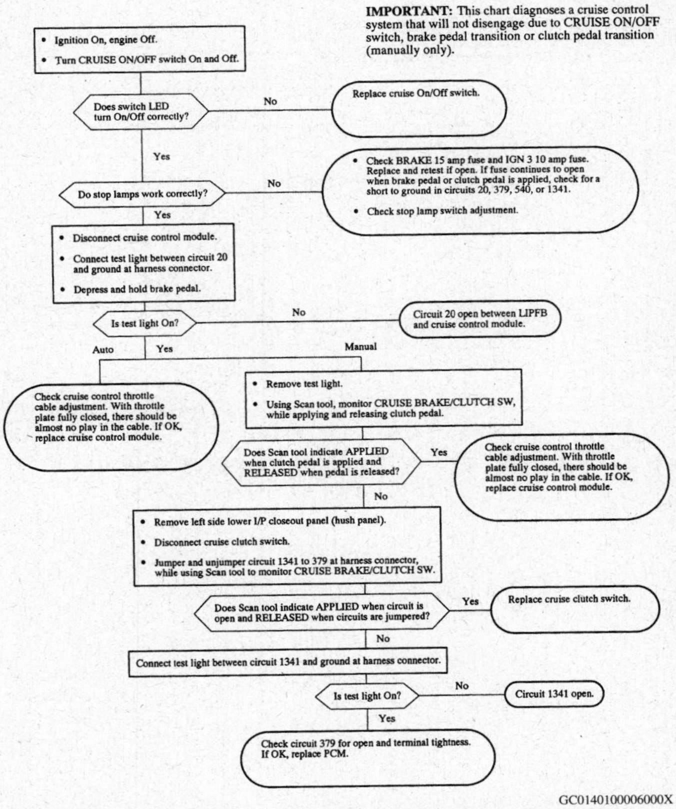

Fig. 18 Cruise Control Will Not Disengage. 2002–04 L-Series w/2.2L Engine

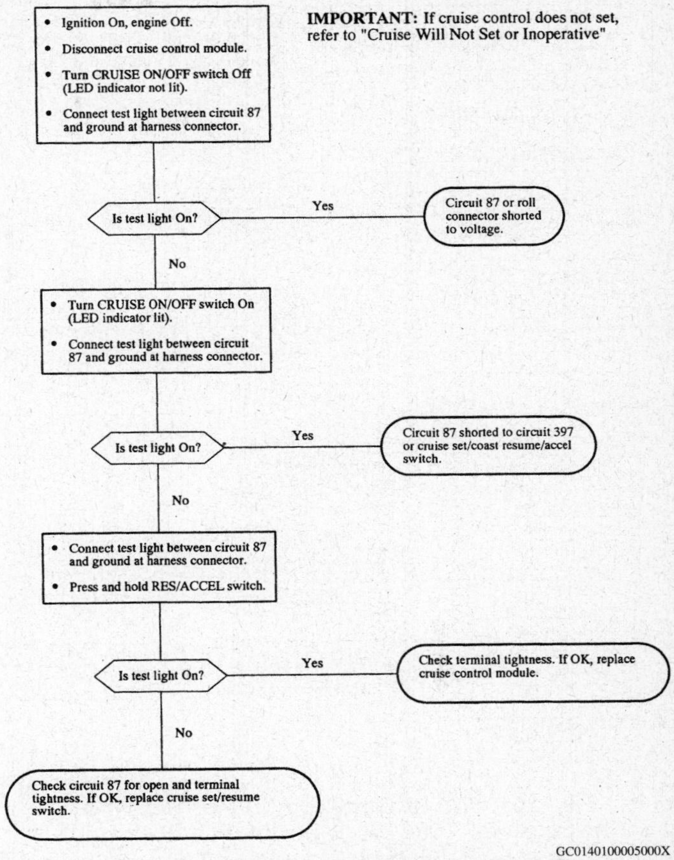

Fig. 17 Cruise Control Will Not Resume/Accelerate. 2002–04 L-Series w/2.2L Engine

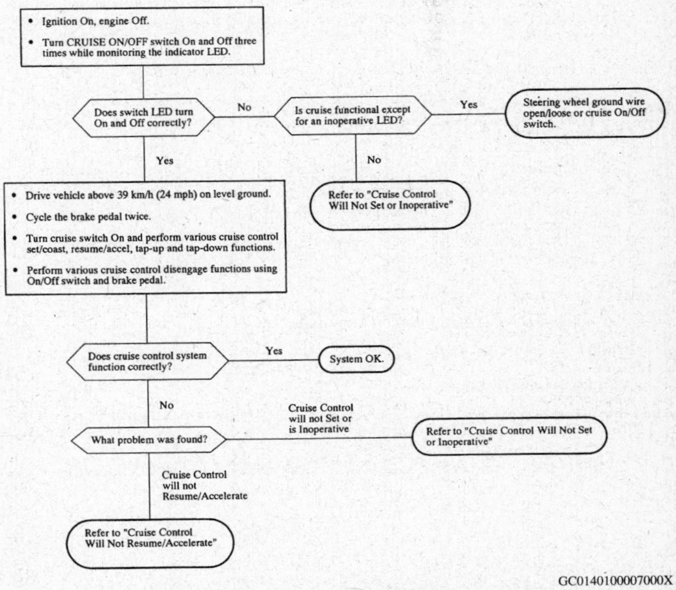

Fig. 19 System Check. 2002–04 L-Series w/3.0L Engine

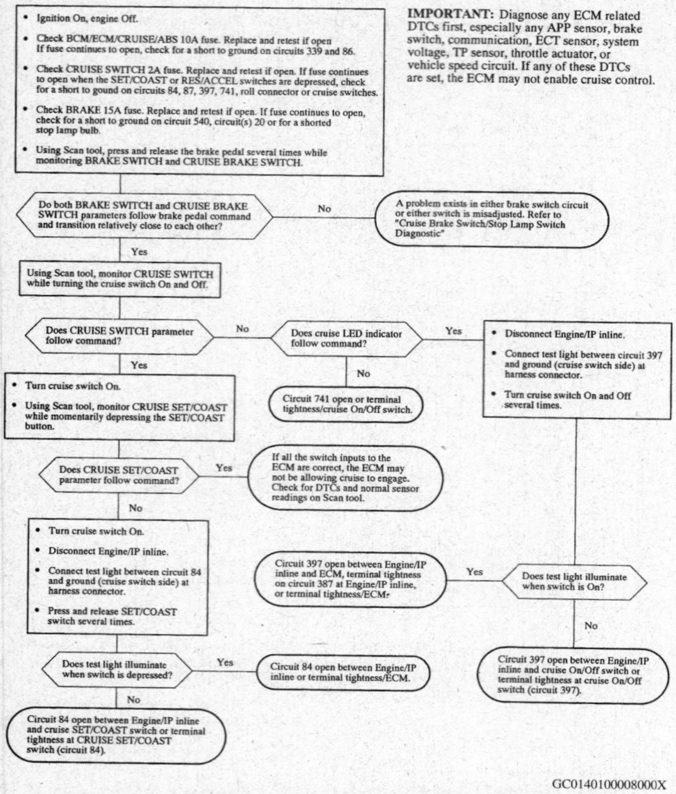

Fig. 20 Cruise Control Will Not Set Or Is Inoperative. 2002–04 L-Series w/3.0L Engine

Test Description

The numbers below refer to the step numbers on the diagnostic table.

2. Lack of communication may be due to a partial malfunction of the class 2 serial data circuit or due to a total malfunction of the class 2 serial data circuit. The specified procedure will determine the particular condition.

3. The symptom list in Symptoms will determine the correct diagnostic procedure to use.

Step	Action	Yes	No
1	Install a scan tool. Does the scan tool power up?	Go to Step 2	Diagnose Data Link Communications
2	1. Turn ON the ignition, with the engine OFF. 2. Attempt to establish communication with the Engine Control Module. Does the scan tool communicate with the Engine Control Module?	Go to Step 3	Diagnose Data Link Communications
3	Select the ECM display DTC function on the scan tool. Does the scan tool display any cruise control DTCs?	Diagnose Scan Tool	Go to Symptoms - Cruise Control

GC1100200866000X

Fig. 22 Cruise Control System Check. ION

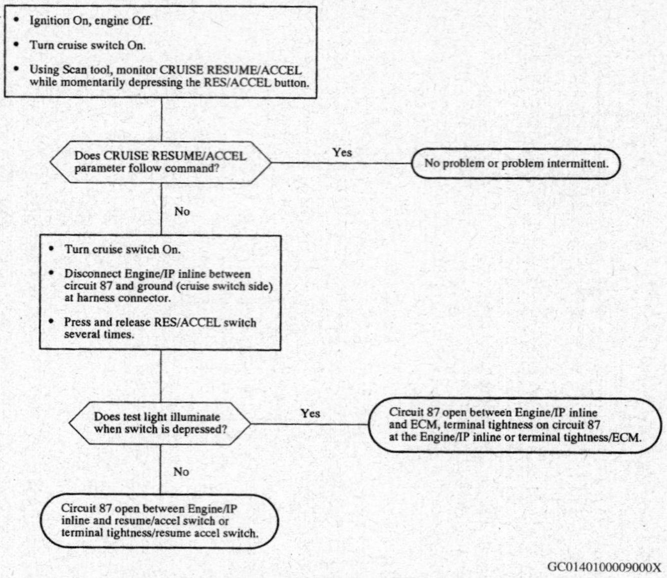

Fig. 21 Cruise Control Will Not Resume Or Accelerate. 2002–04 L-Series w/3.0L Engine

Diagnostic Aids

Important

Perform the following in order to avoid misdiagnosis.

- Inspect for proper operation of brake lamps and clutch switch, if equipped.
- Inspect throttle linkage for mechanical binding which could cause the system to malfunction.

Conditions for Enabling Cruise Control

The vehicle speed is greater than 40 km/h. (25 mph).

Step	Action	Value (s)	Yes	No
1	Did you perform the Cruise Control Diagnostic System Check?	--	Go to Step 2	Go to System Check -
2	1. Turn OFF the ignition. 2. Disconnect the cruise control module. 3. Turn ON the ignition, with the engine OFF. 4. Probe the ignition positive voltage circuit of the cruise control module with a test lamp that is connected to a good ground. Does the test lamp illuminate?	--	Go to Step 3	Go to Step 29
3	Probe the ignition positive voltage circuit of the cruise control module with a test lamp that is connected to the ground circuit of the cruise control module. Does the test lamp illuminate?	--	Go to Step 4	Go to Step 30

GC1100200867010X

Fig. 23 Cruise Control Inoperative/Fault (Part 1 of 5). ION

	1. Turn ON the ignition, with the engine OFF. 2. Turn OFF the cruise control switch. 3. Probe the cruise control on, set/coast, and the resume/accelerate signal circuits with a test lamp that is connected to a good ground. Does the test lamp illuminate on any of the circuits?	-	Go to Step 13	Go to Step 5
5	1. Probe the cruise control set/coast signal circuit with a test lamp that is connected to a good ground. 2. Press and hold the SET/COAST switch. Does the test lamp illuminate?	-	Go to Step 6	Go to Step 15
6	1. Probe the cruise control resume/accelerate signal circuit with a test lamp that is connected to a good ground. 2. Press and hold the RESUME/ACCEL switch. Does the test lamp illuminate?	-	Go to Step 7	Go to Step 16
7	Is the vehicle equipped with a manual transmission?	-	Go to Step 8	Go to Step 9
8	1. Turn OFF the ignition. 2. Disconnect the clutch pedal position (CPP) switch. 3. Turn ON the ignition, with the engine OFF. 4. Probe the CPP harness connector ignition positive voltage circuit with a test lamp connected to a good ground. Does the test lamp illuminate?	-	Go to Step 19	Go to Step 9
9	1. Turn OFF the ignition. 2. Disconnect the TCC/Brake switch. 3. Turn ON the ignition, with the engine OFF. 4. Probe the TCC/Brake switch harness connector ignition positive voltage circuit with a test lamp connected to a good ground. Does the test lamp illuminate?	-	Go to Step 17	Go to Step 23
10	Press the brake pedal while monitoring the test lamp. Does the test lamp illuminate?	-	Go to Step 20	Go to Step 11

GC1100200867020X

Fig. 23 Cruise Control Inoperative/Fault (Part 2 of 5). ION

11	Probe the stop lamp switch signal circuit with a test lamp that is connected to a good ground. Does the test lamp illuminate?	-	Go to Step 21	Go to Step 12
12	Press the brake pedal while monitoring the test lamp. Does the test lamp illuminate?	-	Go to Step 28	Go to Step 19
13	Test the circuit that illuminated the test lamp for a short to voltage. Did you find and correct the condition?	-	Go to Step 36	Go to Step 27
14	Test the ignition positive voltage circuit of the cruise control switch for an open or high resistance. Did you find and correct the condition?	-	Go to Step 36	Go to Step 27
15	Test the cruise control set/coast signal circuit for an open or a high resistance. Did you find and correct the condition?	-	Go to Step 36	Go to Step 27
16	Test the cruise control resume/accelerate signal circuit for an open or a high resistance. Did you find and correct the condition?	-	Go to Step 36	Go to Step 27
17	Check the TCC/Brake switch for proper adjustment. Did you find and correct the condition?	-	Go to Step 36	Go to Step 19
18	Check the stop lamp switch for proper adjustment. Did you find and correct the condition?	-	Go to Step 36	Go to Step 22
19	Test the TCC Brake switch signal circuit for an open or a high resistance. Did you find and correct the condition?	-	Go to Step 36	Go to Step 24
20	Test the TCC Brake switch signal circuit for a short to voltage. Did you find and correct the condition?	-	Go to Step 36	Go to Step 24

GC1100200867030X

Fig. 23 Cruise Control Inoperative/Fault (Part 3 of 5). ION

21	Test the stop lamp switch signal circuit for a short to voltage. Did you find and correct the condition?	-	Go to Step 36	Go to Step 24
22	Test the stop lamp switch signal circuit for an open or a high resistance. Did you find and correct the condition?	-	Go to Step 36	Go to Step 24
23	Test the ignition positive voltage circuit of the TCC/Brake switch for a open, a high resistance. Did you find and correct the condition?	-	Go to Step 36	Go to Step 24
24	Inspect for poor connections at the harness connector of the appropriate switch. Did you find and correct the condition?	-	Go to Step 36	Go to Step 31
25	Inspect for poor connections at the harness connector of the stop lamp switch. Did you find and correct the condition?	-	Go to Step 36	Go to Step 32
26	Inspect for poor connections at the harness connector of the ECM. Did you find and correct the condition?	-	Go to Step 36	Go to Step 33
27	Inspect for poor connections at the harness connector of the cruise control switch. Did you find and correct the condition?	-	Go to Step 36	Go to Step 34
28	Inspect for poor connections at the harness connector of the cruise control module. Did you find and correct the condition?	-	Go to Step 36	Go to Step 35

GC1100200867040X

Fig. 23 Cruise Control Inoperative/Fault (Part 4 of 5). ION

29	Repair the ignition positive voltage circuit of the cruise control module. Did you complete the repair?	-	Go to Step 36	--
30	Repair the ground circuit of the cruise control module. Did you complete the repair?	-	Go to Step 36	--
31	Replace the appropriate switch. Did you complete the replacement?	-	Go to Step 36	--
32	Replace the stop lamp switch. Did you complete the replacement?	-	Go to Step 36	--
33	**Important** The replacement ECM must be programmed. Replace the ECM. Did you complete the replacement?	-	Go to Step 36	--
34	Replace the cruise control switch. Did you complete the replacement?	-	Go to Step 36	--
35	Replace the cruise control module. Did you complete the replacement?	-	Go to Step 36	--
36	Operate the vehicle within the conditions for cruise control operation. Does the cruise control system operate correctly?	-	System OK	Go to Step 2

GC1100200867050X

Fig. 23 Cruise Control Inoperative/Fault (Part 5 of 5). ION

Cruise control will not be enabled unless the PCM detects a correct voltage level at the cruise control switch signal input. The Scan tool can be used to determine if this voltage is correct by verifying CRUISE SWITCH, CRUISE SET/COAST and CRUISE RESUME/ACCEL parameters read correctly when the switches are cycled with cruise switch On. The PCM also won't allow cruise control if any cruise control DTCs are active. Certain DTCs may set if the ignition voltage or ground to the cruise control module becomes interrupted. If the cruise control system circuits are intact, there still are specific vehicle operating parameters that must be met before the PCM will engage the cruise control clutch.

TEST DESCRIPTION

1. Check for any cruise control or cruise/brake DTCs. Diagnose those first as they are probably the cause of an inoperative cruise control system.
2. Verify power and ground circuit integrity at the cruise control module.
3. Verify that the PCM can recognize the CRUISE SWITCH On/Off, CRUISE SET/COAST and CRUISE RESUME/ACCEL switch transitions by cycling switches and monitoring the parameters on Scan tool.

   Note: The cruise switch must be On to read SET/COAST or RESUME/ACCEL switch inputs.
4. Verify the PCM can recognize the cruise/brake input by depressing the brake pedal. This can be read as BRAKE SWITCH on Scan tool.
5. Verify ignition voltage is present at the cruise control module on circuit 86 (cruise/brake input) when brake pedal is released.

DIAGNOSTIC AIDS

If the cruise control module ground circuit opens, DTC P1581, P1583 and P1587 will set when cruise clutch is commanded Off.

If the cruise control module ignition voltage circuit opens, DTC P1587 will set when cruise clutch is commanded Off.

The cruise control module uses the ignition voltage from the cruise/brake input to control the cruise control clutch high side driver. If this voltage is not present, ignition voltage to the cruise clutch will be lost.

On automatic transaxles, the PCM must detect a cruise/brake input transition (depressing the brake pedal) before it will allow cruise to operate. A rolling restart with no brake pedal input could result in an inoperative cruise control system.

G31109900020010X

Fig. 24 Cruise Control Inoperative (Part 1 of 3). S-Series

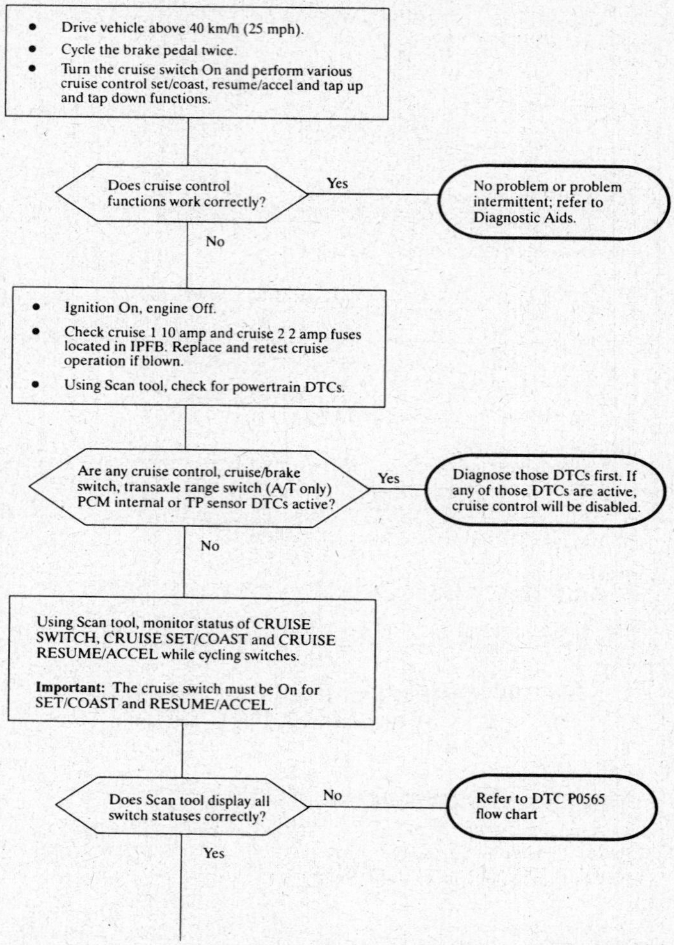

G31109900020020X

Fig. 24 Cruise Control Inoperative (Part 2 of 3). S-Series

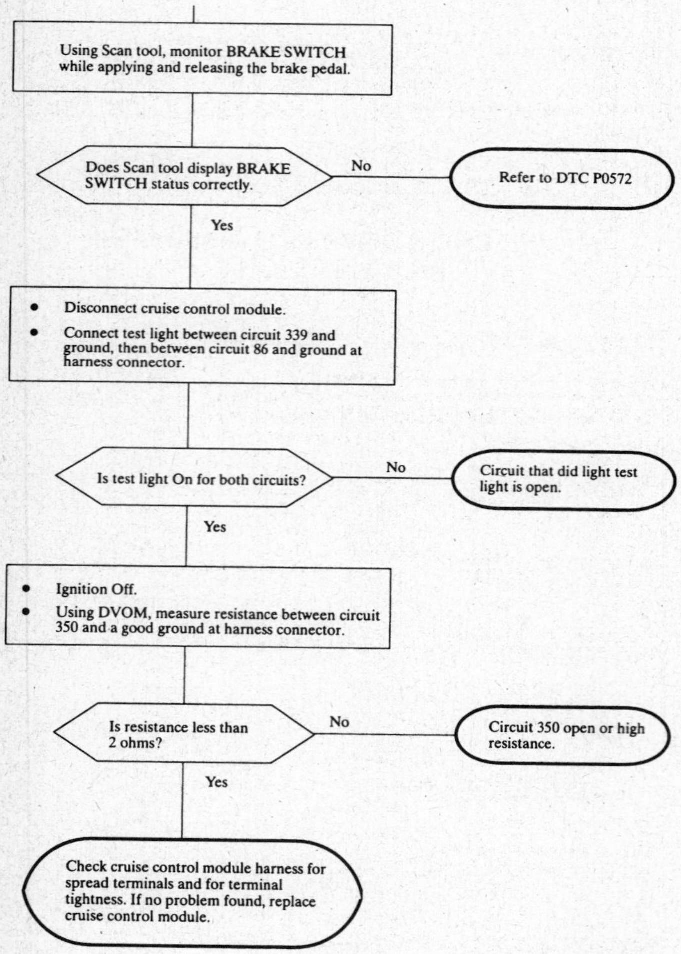

G31109900020030X

Fig. 24 Cruise Control Inoperative (Part 3 of 3). S-Series

The cruise control switches are used as inputs to the PCM to allow cruise On/Off, setting/resuming or increasing/decreasing vehicle cruise speed. Through a series of resistors in the cruise control switches and PCM, the PCM can determine if the cruise switch is On and if the SET/COAST or RES/ACCEL buttons are being depressed. The PCM cruise control input signal voltage level will change as these switches are cycled. The PCM will monitor the input signal for voltage levels that are out of range. If the input signal to the PCM is open or grounded, this fault acts as if the cruise switch is Off and no DTC will be set. DTC P0565 sets when the cruise control input signal voltage does not fall in a valid range.

DTC PARAMETERS

DTC P0565 will set if:

- Cruise switch is On and input voltage is less than 0.54 volts or greater than 0.87 volts.

OR

- RES/ACCEL switch is depressed (with cruise switch On) and input voltage is less than 1.20 volts or greater than 1.98 volts.

OR

- SET/COAST switch depressed (with cruise switch On) and input voltage is less than 2.7 volts or greater than 4.3 volts.

All voltage values are based on the range of 9-17 ignition volts.

DTC P0565 diagnostic runs continuously with engine running.

DTC P0565 is a type D DTC.

DIAGNOSTIC AIDS

An open, short to ground or short to voltage on circuit 1884 will disable cruise.

An open or short to ground in circuit 339 or 1884 should NOT set this DTC, as this looks like the cruise switch has been turned Off. A short to voltage on circuit 1884 will, however.

To locate an intermittent problem, use Scan tool to monitor CRUISE SWITCH, CRUISE RESUME/ACCEL and CRUISE SET/COAST while cycling the switches On and Off. Wiggling wires while monitoring Scan tool switch status may locate the problem.

G31109900021010X

Fig. 25 Code P0565: Cruise Switch Circuit Fault (Part 1 of 2). S-Series

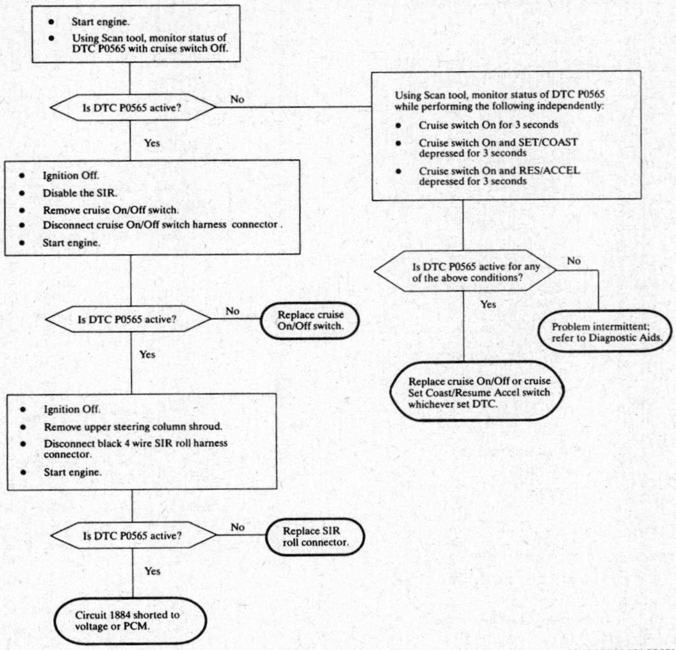

G31109900021020X

Fig. 25 Code P0565: Cruise Switch Circuit Fault (Part 2 of 2). S-Series

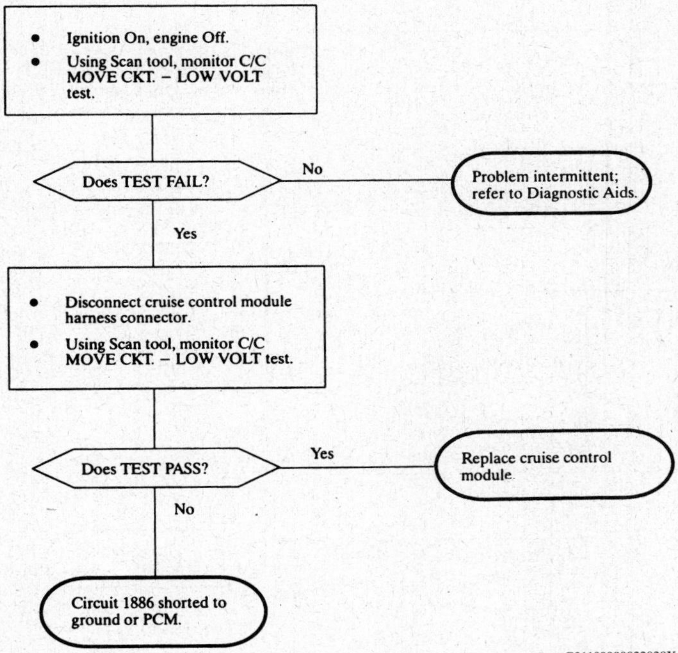

G31109900022020X

Fig. 26 Code P1580: Cruise Move Circuit Voltage Low (Part 2 of 2). S-Series

The cruise control move circuit is used to indicate to the cruise control module the amount of accelerator pedal movement needed to maintain cruise set speed. The PCM pulse width modulates (PWM) ignition voltage on the cruise control move circuit at a 100 ms PWM rate. When the cruise control clutch is commanded On, the PCM will begin to PWM the cruise control move circuit as needed. Very short On-time pulses indicate to the cruise control module to keep the accelerator pedal at the same position. The PCM monitors the cruise control move circuit for low and high voltage faults. DTC P1580 sets when the cruise control move circuit is commanded On (PWM On-time), and the feedback voltage at the PCM is low.

DTC PARAMETERS

DTC P1580 will set if cruise control move voltage is less than 2.5 volts when cruise control move is commanded On (PWM On-time).

DTC P1580 diagnostic runs continuously with engine running and cruise control move commanded On.

DTC P1580 is a type D DTC.

DIAGNOSTIC AIDS

To locate an intermittent problem, use Scan tool to monitoring the C/C MOVE CKT. – LOW VOLT test with ignition On, engine Off. When a fault (short to ground or open PCM driver) exists, the Scan tool will display TEST FAIL.

The test will fail only when the device is being commanded On and the voltage at the PCM is low. The test updates every 100 ms whenever the ignition is turned On and the device is being commanded On via the Scan tool or PCM.

The voltage measured with a DVOM on circuit 1886 with ignition On and cruise control module disconnected should read ignition voltage.

G31109900022010X

Fig. 26 Code P1580: Cruise Move Circuit Voltage Low (Part 1 of 2). S-Series

The cruise control move circuit is used to indicate to the cruise control module the amount of accelerator pedal movement needed to maintain cruise set speed. The PCM pulse width modulates (PWM) ignition voltage on the cruise control move circuit at a 100 ms PWM rate. When the cruise control clutch is commanded On, the PCM will begin to PWM the cruise control move circuit as needed. Very short On-time pulses indicate to the cruise control module to keep the accelerator pedal at the same position. The PCM monitors the cruise control move circuit for low and high voltage faults. DTC P1581 sets when the cruise control move circuit is commanded Off or PWM Off-time, and the feedback voltage at the PCM is high.

DTC PARAMETERS

DTC P1581 will set if cruise control move voltage is greater than 2.5 volts when cruise control move is commanded Off or PWM Off-time.

DTC P1581 diagnostic runs continuously with ignition On and cruise control move commanded Off.

DTC P1581 is a type D DTC.

DIAGNOSTIC AIDS

To locate an intermittent problem, use Scan tool to monitor the C/C MOVE CKT. – OPEN or C/C MOVE CKT. – HIGH VOLT test with ignition On, engine Off. When a fault (open or short to voltage) exists, the Scan tool will display TEST FAIL for both tests.

The tests will fail only when the device is being commanded Off and the voltage at the PCM is high. The tests update every 100 ms whenever the ignition is turned On and the device is being commanded Off via the Scan tool or PCM.

Loss of cruise control module ground can also set this DTC. If this condition exists, DTC P1583 and P1587 will also set.

G31109900023010X

Fig. 27 Code P1581: Cruise Move Circuit Voltage High (Part 1 of 2). S-Series

IMPORTANT: If DTCs P1583 and P1587 are also set, repair open in cruise module ground circuit 350.

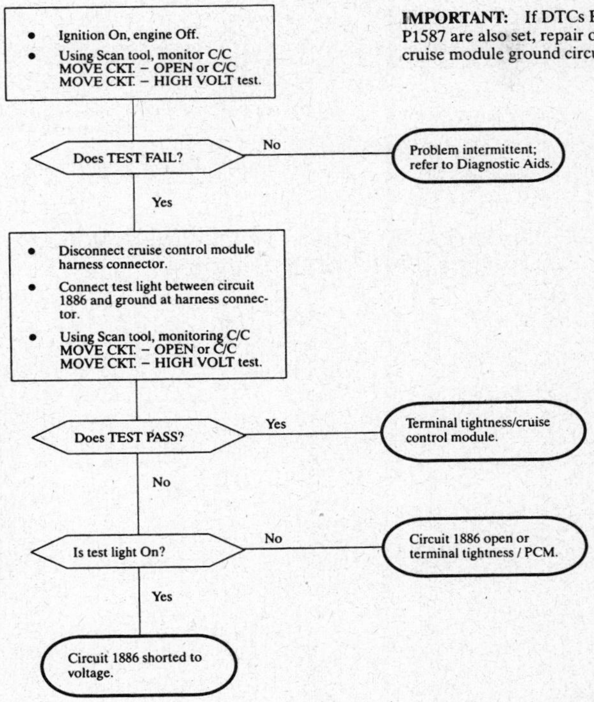

G31109900023020X

Fig. 27 Code P1581: Cruise Move Circuit Voltage High (Part 2 of 2). S-Series

The cruise control direction circuit is used to indicate to the cruise control module the direction of the accelerator pedal (toward wide-open-throttle [WOT] or toward idle) needed to maintain cruise set speed. The PCM supplies ignition voltage on the cruise control direction circuit during cruise control operation when the needed direction is toward WOT. After the cruise set speed has been met and the direction toward WOT is no longer needed, the PCM will open the driver and the cruise control direction input at the cruise control module will go low. Under steady cruise control when no pedal movement is needed, the PCM defaults to the idle direction. The PCM monitors the cruise control direction circuit for low and high voltage faults. DTC P1582 sets when the cruise control direction circuit is commanded On, and the voltage at the PCM is low.

DTC PARAMETERS

DTC P1582 will set if cruise control direction voltage is less than 2.5 volts when cruise control direction is commanded On.

DTC P1582 diagnostic runs continuously with engine running and cruise control direction commanded toward wide-open-throttle.

DTC P1582 is a type D DTC.

DIAGNOSTIC AIDS

To locate an intermittent problem, use Scan tool to perform CRUISE CONTROL CYCLE test. The accelerator pedal should go to 50% throttle and back to idle. If a fault (short to ground or open PCM driver) occurs, the accelerator will go back toward idle.

The C/C DIR. – LOW VOLT test parameter on Scan tool can also be used for intermittents. In cruise control mode, tap up the RES/ACCEL switch while monitoring the test. If a fault occurs, the Scan tool will display TEST FAIL.

The voltage measured with a DVOM on circuit 1887 with ignition On and cruise control module disconnected should read above 7 volts. This voltage should read ignition voltage when the CRUISE CONTROL CYCLE test is performed with Scan tool when accelerator pedal is toward W.O.T.

G31109900024010X

Fig. 28 Code P1582: Cruise Direction Circuit Voltage Low (Part 1 of 2). S-Series

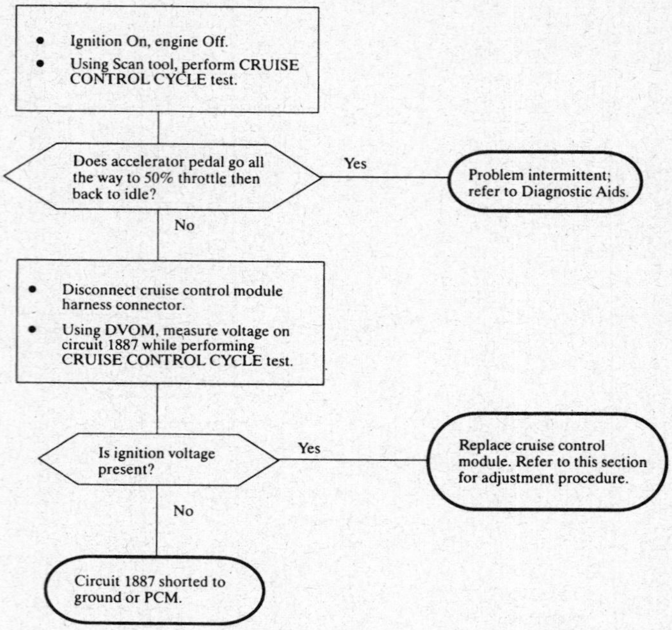

G31109900024020X

Fig. 28 Code P1582: Cruise Direction Circuit Voltage Low (Part 2 of 2). S-Series

The cruise control direction circuit is used to indicate to the cruise control module the direction of the accelerator pedal (toward wide-open-throttle [WOT] or toward idle) needed to maintain cruise set speed. The PCM supplies ignition voltage on the cruise control direction circuit during cruise control operation when the needed direction is toward WOT. After the cruise set speed has been met and the direction toward WOT is no longer needed, the PCM will open the driver and the cruise control direction input at the cruise control module will go low. Under steady cruise control when no pedal movement is needed, the PCM defaults to the idle direction. The PCM monitors the cruise control direction circuit for low and high voltage faults. DTC P1583 sets when the cruise control direction circuit is commanded Off, and the feedback voltage at the PCM is high.

DTC PARAMETERS

DTC P1583 will set if cruise control direction voltage is greater than 2.5 volts when cruise control direction is commanded Off.

DTC P1583 diagnostic runs continuously with ignition On and cruise control direction commanded Off.

DTC P1583 is a type D DTC.

DIAGNOSTIC AIDS

To locate an intermittent problem, use Scan tool to monitor the C/C DIR. CKT. – OPEN or C/C DIR. CKT. – HIGH VOLT test with ignition On, engine Off.. When a fault (open or short to voltage) exists, the Scan tool will display TEST FAIL for both tests.

The tests will fail only when the device is being commanded Off and the voltage at the PCM is high. The tests update every 100 ms whenever the ignition is turned On and the device is being commanded Off via the Scan tool or PCM.

Loss of cruise control module ground can also set this DTC. If this condition exists, DTC P1581 and P1587 will also set.

G31109900025010X

Fig. 29 Code P1583: Cruise Move Circuit Voltage High (Part 1 of 2). S-Series

IMPORTANT: If DTCs P1581 and P1587 are also set, repair open in cruise module ground circuit 350.

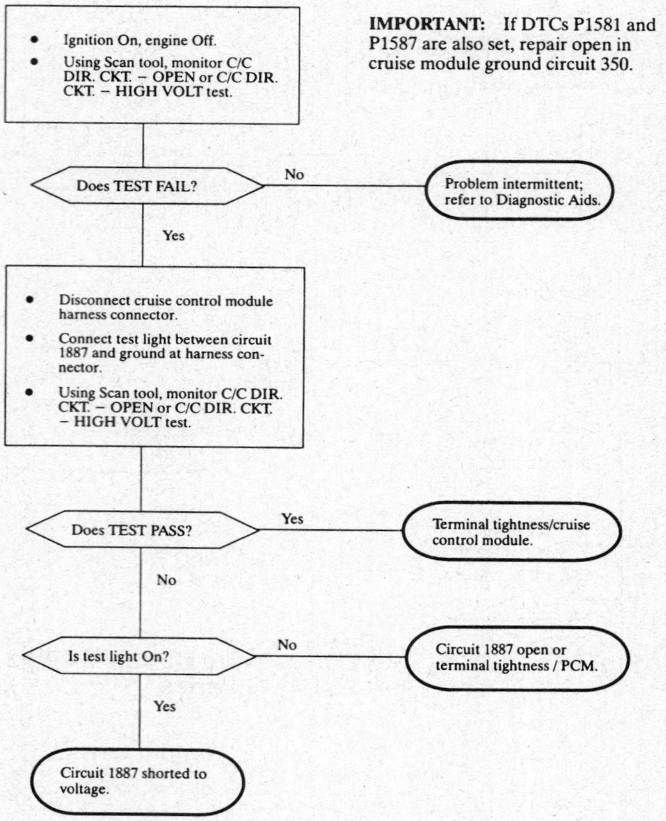

G31109900025020X

Fig. 29 Code P1583: Cruise Move Circuit Voltage High (Part 2 of 2). S-Series

The cruise control system can be disabled due to a number of conditions that may or may not set DTC P1584. Under a properly working cruise control system, normal driver commands such as turning the cruise control switch Off or depressing the brake pedal will NOT set this DTC. However, the driver may induce this DTC if the gear shift lever is placed in neutral while cruise is engaged. DTC P1584 sets when the PCM disables cruise control because any one of the following conditions listed under DTC parameters occurred while in cruise control mode.

DTC PARAMETERS

DTC P1584 will set if the PCM disables the cruise control clutch due to any of the following conditions occurring while in cruise control mode:

- Gear position is out of range (trans range switch indicates P, R, N, or 1st) A/T only
- Transaxle range switch position is invalid (A/T only)
- Cruise set speed is greater than 161 km/h (100 mph) or less than 40 km/h (25 mph)
- Vehicle speed is less than 32 km/h (20 mph)
- Engine speed is less than 950 RPM or greater than 6500 RPM
- Traction control is active
- Vehicle acceleration is greater than 16 km/h/second (10 mph/second)
- Vehicle deceleration is greater than 6.5 km/h/second (4 mph/second)
- Cruise set speed differs from actual vehicle speed by greater than 24 km/h (15 mph) for 10 seconds or greater than 32 km/h (20 mph) instantaneously
- Ignition voltage is less than 10 volts or greater than 16 volts
- Engine coolant temperature is greater than 118°C (244°F) (overheat condition)

DTC P1584 diagnostic runs continuously in cruise control mode.

DTC P1584 is a type D DTC.

DIAGNOSTIC AIDS

Use Scan tool Failure Record information to help diagnose driver induced cruise disable vs. cruise disable due to a system failure. Inspect the DISABLE BITS located toward the bottom of the Failure Record to determine the cause.

Make sure no transaxle range switch DTCs are present (A/T only). Diagnose those DTCs first if any are set.

Make sure VEHICLE SPEED reads correctly on Scan tool and that no VSS DTCs are present. Make sure SPEED NOISE = NO under the transmission data display table (A/T only) while the vehicle is driven. This will indicate if an intermittent vehicle speed sensor circuit fault is occurring.

G31109900026000X

Fig. 30 Code P1584: Cruise Control Disabled. S-Series

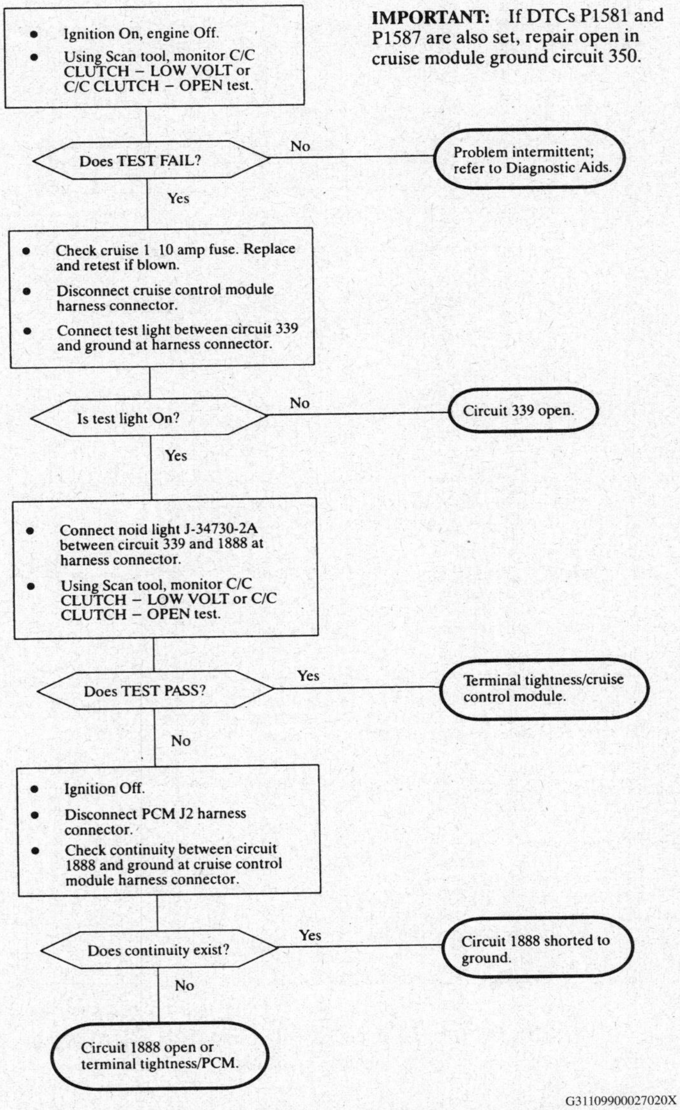

G31109900027020X

Fig. 31 Code P1587: Cruise Clutch Control Circuit Voltage Low (Part 2 of 2). S-Series

The cruise control clutch is used to engage the cruise control motor to the cruise control module attachment rod mechanism. The PCM controls the cruise control clutch by pulling the cruise control clutch circuit to ground. The cruise control module internally supplies the internal clutch ignition voltage through a driver circuit. In order for the driver circuit to supply ignition voltage to the clutch, ignition voltage must be present at the cruise/brake input of the cruise control module. When the brake pedal is depressed (switch opens, input goes low), the PCM opens the clutch ground circuit and the cruise control module opens the clutch ignition voltage circuit. The cruise control module also supplies ignition voltage on the cruise control clutch circuit through a resistor even when the brake pedal is depressed. This voltage cannot turn the clutch On, however. The PCM monitors the cruise control clutch circuit for low and high voltage faults. DTC P1587 sets when the cruise control clutch is commanded Off and the feedback voltage at the PCM is low.

DTC PARAMETERS

DTC P1587 will set if cruise control clutch voltage is less than 1.25 volts when cruise control clutch is commanded Off.

DTC P1587 diagnostic runs continuously with ignition On and cruise control clutch commanded Off.

DTC P1587 is a type D DTC.

DIAGNOSTIC AIDS

To locate an intermittent control problem, use Scan tool to monitor C/C CLUTCH – LOW VOLT or C/C CLUTCH – OPEN test with ignition On, engine Off. When a fault (open or short to ground) exists, the Scan tool will display TEST FAIL for both tests.

The tests will fail only when the device is being commanded Off and the voltage at the PCM is low. The tests update every 100 ms whenever the ignition is turn On and the device is being command Off via the Scan tool or PCM.

Loss of cruise control module ground can also set this DTC. If this condition exists, DTC P1581 and P1583 will also set.

Loss of cruise control module ignition voltage can also set this DTC.

G31109900027010X

Fig. 31 Code P1587: Cruise Clutch Control Circuit Voltage Low (Part 1 of 2). S-Series

The cruise control clutch is used to engage the cruise control motor to the cruise control module attachment rod mechanism. The PCM controls the cruise control clutch by pulling the cruise control clutch circuit to ground. The cruise control module internally supplies the internal clutch ignition voltage through a driver circuit. In order for the driver circuit to supply ignition voltage to the clutch, ignition voltage must be present at the cruise/brake input of the cruise control module. When the brake pedal is depressed (switch opens, input goes low), the PCM opens the clutch ground circuit and the cruise control module opens the clutch ignition voltage circuit. The cruise control module also supplies ignition voltage on the cruise control clutch circuit through a resistor even when the brake pedal is depressed. This voltage cannot turn the clutch On, however. The PCM monitors the cruise control clutch circuit for low and high voltage faults. DTC P1588 sets when the cruise control clutch is commanded On and the feedback voltage at the PCM is high.

DTC PARAMETERS

DTC P1588 will set if cruise control clutch voltage is greater than 1.25 volts when cruise control clutch is commanded On.

DTC P1588 diagnostic runs continuously with engine running and cruise control clutch commanded On.

DTC P1588 is a type D DTC.

DIAGNOSTIC AIDS

To locate an intermittent problem, use Scan tool to command CRUISE CONTROL CLUTCH On, while monitoring the C/C CLUTCH – HIGH VOLT test. When a fault (short to voltage or shorted cruise control clutch) exists, the Scan tool will display TEST FAIL.

The test will fail only when the device is being commanded On and the voltage at the PCM is high. The test updates every 100 ms whenever the ignition is turn On and the device is being command On via the Scan tool or PCM.

G31109900028010X

Fig. 32 Code P1588: Cruise Clutch Control Circuit Voltage High (Part 1 of 2). S-Series

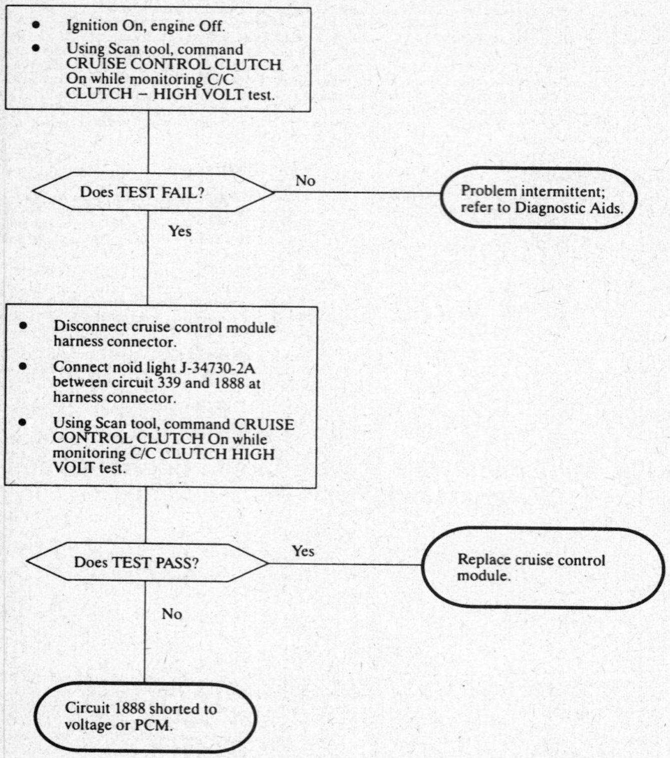

Fig. 32 Code P1588: Cruise Clutch Control Circuit Voltage High (Part 2 of 2). S-Series

Circuit Description

The cruise control switch is an input to the engine control module (ECM). The switch has 4 positions: On, Off, Resume/Accel, and Set/Coast. Switch voltage at the ECM varies depending on switch position. If the ECM detects a switch voltage that is out of range for longer than 3 seconds, DTC P0565 sets.

Conditions for Running the DTC

Continuously when engine is running.

Conditions for Setting the DTC

- The cruise switch is On and the input voltage is less than 0.47 volts or greater than 0.93 volts.
- The RES/ACCEL switch is depressed, with the cruise switch ON and the input voltage is less than 1.15 volts or greater than 2.0 volts.
- The SET/COAST switch depressed, with the cruise switch On and the input voltage is less than 2.63 volts or greater than 4.32 volts.

Action Taken When the DTC Sets

The ECM stores conditions which were present when the DTC set as Failure Records only. This information will not be stored as Freeze Frame Records.

Conditions for Clearing the MIL/DTC

- The DTC becomes history when the conditions for setting the DTC are no longer present.
- The history DTC clears after 40 malfunction free warm-up cycles.
- The ECM receives a clear code command from the scan tool.

Diagnostic Aids

Check for the following condition:

Open, short to ground or short to voltage on the Cruise Control Set/Coast and Resume/Accelerate Switch Signal circuit will disable cruise.

If DTC P0565 cannot be duplicated, the information included in the Failure Records data can be useful in determining how many ignition cycles have passed since the DTC was last set.

Test Description

The number below refers to the step number on the diagnostic table.

8. This vehicle is equipped with a ECM which utilizes an electrically erasable programmable read-only memory (EEPROM). When the ECM is replaced, the new ECM must be programmed.

Step	Action	Yes	No
1	Did you perform the Diagnostic System Check - Cruise Control?	Go to Step 2	System Check -

GC1100200868010X

Fig. 33 Code P0565: Cruise Switch Circuit (Part 1 of 3). ION

2	1. Install a scan tool. 2. Start the engine. 3. Cruise switch OFF. 4. With a scan tool, monitor the DTC information for DTC P0565 in the ECM. Is DTC P0565 active?	Go to Step 3	Go to Step 9
3	1. Turn OFF the ignition. 2. Disable the SIR system. 3. Remove Cruise On/Off switch. 4. Disconnect Cruise On/Off switch harness connector. 5. Start the engine. 6. With a scan tool, monitor the DTC information for DTC P0565 in the ECM. Is DTC P0565 active?	Go to Step 4	Go to Step 8
4	1. Turn OFF the ignition. 2. Disconnect SIR roll connector. 3. Start the engine. 4. With a scan tool, monitor the DTC information for DTC P0565 in the ECM. Is DTC P0565 active?	Go to Step 5	Go to Step 7
5	Test the Cruise Control Set/Coast and Resume/Accelerate Switch Signal circuit for a short to voltage. Did you find and correct the condition?	Go to Step 13	Go to Step 6
6	**Important** The replacement ECM must be programmed. Replace ECM. Did you complete the repair?	Go to Step 13	--
7	Replace the SIR roll connector. Did you complete the repair?	Go to Step 13	--

GC1100200868020X

Fig. 33 Code P0565: Cruise Switch Circuit (Part 2 of 3). ION

8	Replace cruise On/Off switch. Did you complete the repair?	Go to Step 13	--
9	1. Start the engine. 2. With a scan tool, monitor the DTC information for DTC P0565 in the ECM while holding cruise control switch ON for 3 seconds. Is DTC P0565 active?	Go to Step 8	Go to Step 10
10	1. Start the engine. 2. Cruise control switch ON. 3. With a scan tool, monitor the DTC information for DTC P0565 in the ECM while depressing SET/COAST for 3 seconds. Is DTC P0565 active?	Go to Step 12	Go to Step 11
11	1. Start the engine. 2. Cruise control switch ON. 3. With a scan tool, monitor the DTC information for DTC P0565 in the ECM while depressing RES/ACCEL for 3 seconds. Is DTC P0565 active?	Go to Step 12	Go to Diagnostic Aids
12	Replace the Set/Coast/Resume/Accel switch. in Cruise Control. Did you complete the replacement?	Go to Step 13	--
13	1. Use a scan tool in order to clear the DTC. 2. Operate the vehicle within the conditions for Running the DTC as specified in the supporting text. Does the DTC reset?	Go to Step 2	System OK

GC1100200868030X

Fig. 33 Code P0565: Cruise Switch Circuit (Part 3 of 3). ION

Circuit Description

The torque converter clutch (TCC)/Brake switch is a normally closed switch. When the TCC/Brake switch is closed, brake pedal released the engine control module (ECM) senses ignition voltage on the TCC/Brake Switch/Cruise Control Release Signal circuit. If the ECM senses a voltage on the TCC/Brake Switch/Cruise Control Release Signal circuit when the TCC/Brake switch should be open, this DTC sets.

Conditions for Running the DTC

- The vehicle has cycled from 0-60 km/h (0-37 mph) 3 times in 1 ignition cycle.
- Continuous once the previous criteria have been met.

Conditions for Setting the DTC

The ECM detects voltage on the TCC Brake Switch/Cruise Control Release Signal circuit when the switch should be open.

Action Taken When the DTC Sets

- The ECM stores the DTC information into memory when the diagnostic runs and fails.
- The malfunction indicator lamp (MIL) will not illuminate.
- The ECM records the operating conditions at the time the diagnostic fails. The ECM stores this information in the Failure Records.

Conditions for Clearing the DTC

- A last test failed, or current DTC, clears when the diagnostic runs and does not fail.
- A history DTC will clear after 40 consecutive warm-up cycles, if no failures are reported by this or any other non-emission related diagnostic.
- Use a scan tool in order to clear the DTC.

Diagnostic Aids

Important

- Verify that the TCC/Brake switch is adjusted properly. Refer to adjustment procedure.
- Test drive the vehicle if a switch or circuit condition cannot be located. An intermittent condition may be duplicated during a test drive.
- For an intermittent, Test for Intermittent and Poor Connections

Test Description

The number below refers to the step number on the diagnostic table.

2. This step determines if the fault is present.

GC1100200869010X

Fig. 34 Code P0572: Cruise Control Voltage Out Of Range (Part 1 of 3). ION

Step	Action	Yes	No
1	Did you perform the Diagnostic System Check -- Cruise Control?	Go to Step 2	Go to System Check -
2	1. Connect a scan tool. 2. Turn ON the ignition, with the engine OFF. 3. Monitor the Cruise Brake Switch parameter in the ECM data list. Does the Cruise Brake Switch parameter indicate Applied?	Go to Step 3	Go to Diagnostic Aids
3	1. Turn OFF the ignition. 2. Disconnect the Cruise Control Module harness connector. 3. Turn ON the ignition, with the engine OFF. 4. Observe the Cruise Brake Switch parameter in the Idle/Speed Control data list. Does the Cruise Control Brake switch parameter indicate Released?	Go to Step 10	Go to Step 4
4	1. Turn OFF the ignition. 2. Disconnect the TCC/Brake switch. 3. Connect a 3-amp fused jumper between Ignition Voltage and TCC Brake Switch/Cruise Control Release Signal circuit. 4. Turn ON the ignition, with the engine OFF. 5. Observe the Cruise Brake Switch parameter in the Idle/Speed Control data list. Does the Cruise Control Brake switch parameter indicate Released?	Go to Step 6	Go to Step 5
5	Inspect the Ignition Voltage and TCC Brake Switch/Cruise Control Release Signal circuits for an open or short to ground. Did you find and correct the problem?	Go to Step 12	Go to Step 8
6	Inspect the TCC/Brake switch for proper adjustment. Did you find and correct the condition?	Go to Step 12	Go to Step 7

GC1100200869020X

Fig. 34 Code P0572: Cruise Control Voltage Out Of Range (Part 2 of 3). ION

7	Inspect for poor connections at the harness connector of the TCC/Brake switch. Did you find and correct the condition?	Go to Step 12	Go to Step 9
8	Inspect for poor connections at the harness connector of the ECM. Did you find and correct the condition?	Go to Step 12	Go to Step 11
9	Replace the TCC/Brake switch. Did you complete the repair?	Go to Step 12	--
10	Replace the Cruise Control Module. Did you complete the repair?	Go to Step 12	--
11	**Important** The replacement ECM must be programmed. Replace the ECM. Is the action complete?	Go to Step 12	--
12	1. Use a scan tool in order to clear the DTCs. 2. Operate the vehicle within the Conditions for Running the DTC as specified in the supporting text.	Go to Step 2	System OK

GC1100200869030X

Fig. 34 Code P0572: Cruise Control Voltage Out Of Range (Part 3 of 3). ION

Circuit Description

The torque converter clutch (TCC)/Brake switch is a normally closed switch. When the TCC/Brake switch circuit is closed, brake pedal released, the engine control module (ECM) senses ignition voltage on the TCC Brake Switch/Cruise Control Release Signal circuit. If the ECM does not sense a voltage on the TCC Brake Switch/Cruise Control Release Signal circuit when the TCC/Brake switch should be closed, brake pedal released, this DTC sets.

Conditions for Running the DTC

- Vehicle has cycled from 0-60 km/h (0-37 mph) 3 times in 1 ignition cycle.
- Continuous once the previous criteria have been met.

Conditions for Setting the DTC

The ECM does not detect voltage on the TCC Brake Switch/Cruise Control Release Signal circuit when the switch should be closed, with the brake pedal released.

Action Taken When the DTC Sets

- The ECM stores the DTC information into memory when the diagnostic runs and fails.
- The malfunction indicator lamp (MIL) will not illuminate.
- The ECM records the operating conditions at the time the diagnostic fails. The ECM stores this information in the Failure Records.

Conditions for Clearing the DTC

- A last test failed, or current DTC, clears when the diagnostic runs and does not fail.
- A history DTC will clear after 40 consecutive warm-up cycles, if no failures are reported by this or any other non-emission related diagnostic.
- Use a scan tool in order to clear the DTC.

Diagnostic Aids

Important

- Verify that the TCC/Brake switch is adjusted properly. Refer to adjustment procedure.
- Test drive the vehicle if a switch or circuit condition cannot be located. An intermittent condition may be duplicated during a test drive.
- For an intermittent, Test for Intermittent and Poor Connections

Test Description

The number below refers to the step number on the diagnostic table.

2. This step determines if the fault is present.

GC1100200870010X

Fig. 35 Code P0573: No Cruise Control Voltage Detected (Part 1 of 2). ION

Step	Action	Yes	No
1	Did you perform the Diagnostic System Check -- Cruise Control?	Go to Step 2	Go to System Check -
2	1. Connect a scan tool. 2. Turn ON the ignition, with the engine OFF. 3. Monitor the Cruise Brake Switch parameter in the engine control module (ECM) data list while depressing the brake pedal. Does the Cruise Brake Switch parameter indicate Released?	Go to Step 3	Go to Diagnostic Aids
3	1. Turn OFF the ignition. 2. Disconnect the TCC/Brake switch harness connector. 3. Turn ON the ignition, with the engine OFF. 4. Observe the Cruise Brake Switch parameter in the Idle/Speed Control data list. Does the Cruise Control Brake switch parameter indicate Applied?	Go to Step 5	Go to Step 4
4	Inspect TCC Brake Switch/Cruise Control Release Signal circuit for a short to voltage. Did you find and correct the problem?	Go to Step 7	--
5	Inspect the TCC/Brake switch for proper adjustment. Did you find and correct the condition?	Go to Step 7	--
6	Replace the TCC/Brake switch. Did you complete the repair?	Go to Step 7	Go to Step 6
7	1. Use a scan tool in order to clear the DTCs. 2. Operate the vehicle within the Conditions for Running the DTC as specified in the supporting text. Does the DTC reset?	Go to Step 2	System OK

GC1100200870020X

Fig. 35 Code P0573: No Cruise Control Voltage Detected (Part 2 of 2). ION

Step	Action	Yes	No
1	Did you perform the Diagnostic System Check - Cruise Control?	Go to Step 2	Go to System Check -
2	1. Connect a scan tool. 2. Turn ON the ignition, with the engine OFF. 3. Monitor the Stop Lamp Switch parameter in the ECM data list. Does the Stop Lamp Switch parameter indicate Applied?	Go to Step 3	Go to Step 5
3	Verify that the stop lamp switch is adjusted correctly. Did you find and correct the problem?	Go to Step 15	Go to Step 5
4	Inspect the Stop Lamp Switch Signal circuits for a short to voltage. Did you find and correct the problem?	Go to Step 15	--
5	1. Connect a scan tool. 2. Turn ON the ignition, with the engine OFF. 3. Depress the brake pedal while monitoring the Stop Lamp Switch parameter in the ECM data list. Does the Stop Lamp Switch parameter indicate Released?	Go to Step 6	Go to Diagnostic Aids
6	Verify that the stop lamp switch is adjusted correctly. Did you find and correct the problem?	Go to Step 15	Go to Step 7
7	Do the stop lamps illuminate when the brake pedal is pressed?	Go to Step 11	Go to Step 8
8	Inspect for poor connections at the harness connector of the stop lamp switch. Did you find and correct the condition?	Go to Step 15	Go to Step 9
9	Inspect the Ignition voltage supply to the Stop Lamp Switch circuits for an open or short to ground. Did you find and correct the problem?	Go to Step 15	Go to Step 10

GC1100200871020X

Fig. 36 Code P1574: Stop Lamp Switch Out Of Range (Part 2 of 3). ION

Circuit Description

The stop lamp switch is a normally open switch. When the stop lamp switch is closed and the brake pedal is pressed, then the engine control module (ECM) senses ignition voltage on the Stop Lamp Switch Signal circuit. If the ECM senses voltage on the TCC Brake Switch/Cruise Control Release Signal circuit when the torque converter clutch (TCC)/Brake switch should be open, this DTC sets.

Conditions for Running the DTC

- Vehicle has cycled from 0-60 km/h (0-37 mph) 3 times in 1 ignition cycle.
- Continuous once the previous criteria have been met.

Conditions for Setting the DTC

The ECM does not detect a voltage state change on the Stop Lamp Switch Signal circuit after three stops. A high or low condition will set this code.

Action Taken When the DTC Sets

- The ECM stores the DTC information into memory when the diagnostic runs and fails.
- The malfunction indicator lamp (MIL) will not illuminate.
- The ECM records the operating conditions at the time the diagnostic fails. The ECM stores this information in the Failure Records.

Conditions for Clearing the DTC

- A last test failed, or current DTC, clears when the diagnostic runs and does not fail.
- A history DTC will clear after 40 consecutive warm-up cycles, if no failures are reported by this or any other non-emission related diagnostic.
- Use a scan tool in order to clear the DTC.

Diagnostic Aids

Important

- Verify that the stop lamp switch is adjusted properly.
- If any of the stop lamps are not operating correctly Diagnose in Lighting Systems.
- Test drive the vehicle if a switch or circuit condition cannot be located. An intermittent condition may be duplicated during a test drive.
- For an intermittent, refer to Testing for Intermittent and Poor Connections

Test Description

The number below refers to the step number on the diagnostic table.

2. This step determines if the fault is present.

GC1100200871010X

Fig. 36 Code P1574: Stop Lamp Switch Out Of Range (Part 1 of 3). ION

10	Inspect the Stop Lamp Switch Signal circuits for short to ground. Did you find and correct the problem?	Go to Step 15	Go to Step 12
11	Inspect for poor connections at the harness connector of the ECM. Did you find and correct the condition?	Go to Step 15	Go to Step 13
12	Replace the TCC/Brake switch. Did you complete the repair?	Go to Step 15	--
13	Inspect the Stop Lamp Switch Signal circuit for an open circuit in the branch between the integrated body control module (IBCM) and the ECM. Did you find and correct the condition?	Go to Step 15	Go to Step 14
14	**Important** The replacement ECM must be programmed. Replace the ECM. Is the action complete?	Go to Step 15	--
15	1. Use a scan tool in order to clear the DTCs. 2. Operate the vehicle within the Conditions for Running the DTC as specified in the supporting text. Does the DTC reset?	Go to Step 2	System OK

GC1100200871030X

Fig. 36 Code P1574: Stop Lamp Switch Out Of Range (Part 3 of 3). ION

Circuit Description

By pulse width modulating (PWM) the Cruise Control Servo Move Signal circuit the engine control module (ECM) indicates to the cruise control module how much accelerator pedal movement is necessary. The amount of pedal movement is determined by the duty cycle of the PWM signal, which is sent every 100 ms. DTC 1580 sets when Cruise Control Servo Move Signal circuit is commanded high, PWM is ON, and the voltage level at the ECM is low.

Conditions for Running the DTC

Continuously when the engine is running.

Conditions for Setting the DTC

- The ECM detects low feedback voltage when the Cruise Control Servo Move Signal circuit is commanded high.
- The condition exists for 500 ms.

Action Taken When the DTC Sets

- The ECM stores the DTC information into memory when the diagnostic runs and fails.
- The malfunction indicator lamp (MIL) will not illuminate.
- The ECM records the operating conditions at the time the diagnostic fails. The ECM stores this information in the Failure Records.

Conditions for Clearing the DTC

- A last test failed, or current DTC, clears when the diagnostic runs and does not fail.
- A history DTC will clear after 40 consecutive warm-up cycles, if no failures are reported by this or any other non-emission related diagnostic.
- Use a scan tool in order to clear the DTC.

Diagnostic Aids

Important

To locate an intermittent problem, use the scan tool to monitor the C/C MOVE CKT. -LOW VOLT test with the ignition ON, and the engine OFF. The scan tool will display Test Fail when a short to ground exists in the Cruise Control Servo Move Signal circuit.

Test Description

The number below refers to the step number on the diagnostic table.

2. This step determines if the fault is present.

GC1100200872010X

Fig. 37 Code P1580: Cruise Control Move Output Circuit Low Voltage (Part 1 of 2). ION

Step	Action	Yes	No
1	Did you perform the Diagnostic System Check - Cruise Control?	Go to Step 2	Go to System Check -
2	1. Connect a scan tool. 2. Turn ON the ignition, with the engine OFF. 3. Using scan tool monitor C/C Move Ckt.-Low Volt Test. Does the Test Fail?	Go to Step 3	Go to Diagnostic Aids
3	1. Turn OFF the ignition. 2. Disconnect the cruise control module at the harness connector. 3. Using scan tool monitor C/C Move Ckt.-Low Volt Test. Does the Test Fail?	Go to Step 4	Go to Step 5
4	Inspect Cruise Control Servo Move Signal circuit for short to ground. Did you find and correct the problem?	Go to Step 7	Go to Step 6
5	Replace the cruise control module. Did you complete the repair?	Go to Step 7	--
6	**Important** The replacement ECM must be programmed. Replace ECM. Did you complete the repair?	Go to Step 7	--
7	1. Use a scan tool in order to clear the DTCs. 2. Operate the vehicle within the Conditions for Running the DTC as specified in the supporting text. Does the DTC reset?	Go to Step 2	System OK

GC1100200872020X

Fig. 37 Code P1580: Cruise Control Move Output Circuit Low Voltage (Part 2 of 2). ION

Circuit Description

By pulse width modulating (PWM) the Cruise Control Servo Move Signal circuit the engine control module (ECM) indicates to the cruise control module how much accelerator pedal movement is necessary. The amount of pedal movement is determined by the duty cycle of the PWM signal, which is sent every 100 ms. DTC 1580 sets when Cruise Control Servo Move Signal circuit is commanded OFF (PWM is OFF) and the voltage level at the ECM is high.

Conditions for Running the DTC

Continuously when the engine is running.

Conditions for Setting the DTC

- The ECM detects low feedback voltage when the Cruise Control Servo Move Signal circuit is commanded OFF.
- The condition exists for 500 ms.

Action Taken When the DTC Sets

- The ECM stores the DTC information into memory when the diagnostic runs and fails.
- The malfunction indicator lamp (MIL) will not illuminate.
- The ECM records the operating conditions at the time the diagnostic fails. The ECM stores this information in the Failure Records.

Conditions for Clearing the DTC

- A last test failed, or current DTC, clears when the diagnostic runs and does not fail.
- A history DTC will clear after 40 consecutive warm-up cycles, if no failures are reported by this or any other non-emission related diagnostic.
- Use a scan tool in order to clear the DTC.

Diagnostic Aids

- To locate an intermittent problem, use the scan tool to monitor the C/C Move Ckt. -High Volt and C/C Move Ckt.-Open tests with ignition ON, engine OFF The scan tool will display Test Fail when a short to voltage or open exists in the Cruise Control Servo Move Signal circuit.
- Loss of ground for the cruise control module can cause this DTC to set. If this condition exists DTC P01583 and P1587 will also set.

Test Description

The number below refers to the step number on the diagnostic table.

2. This step determines if the fault is present.

GC1100200873010X

Fig. 38 Code P1581: Cruise Control Direction Output Circuit Low Voltage (Part 1 of 3). ION

Step	Action	Yes	No
1	Did you perform the Diagnostic System Check - Cruise Control?	Go to Step 2	Go to System Check -
2	1. Connect a scan tool. 2. Turn ON the ignition, with the engine OFF. 3. Using scan tool monitor C/C Move Ckt.-High Volt or C/C Move Ckt.-Open tests. Does the Test Fail?	Go to Step 3	Go to Diagnostic Aids
3	1. Turn OFF the ignition. 2. Connect a test light between the Cruise Control Servo Move Signal circuit and a good ground. 3. Using scan tool monitor C/C Move Ckt.-High Volt and C/C Move Ckt.-Open tests. Does the Test Pass?	Go to Step 7	Go to Step 4
4	Is the test light illuminated?	Go to Step 5	Go to Step 6
5	Inspect the Cruise Control Servo Move Signal circuit for short to voltage. Did you find and correct the problem?	Go to Step 9	--
6	Inspect the Cruise Control Servo Move Signal circuit for an open or high resistance. Did you find and correct the problem?	Go to Step 9	Go to Step 8

GC1100200873020X

Fig. 38 Code P1581: Cruise Control Direction Output Circuit Low Voltage (Part 2 of 3). ION

7	Replace the cruise control module. Did you complete the repair?	Go to Step 9	--
8	**Important** The replacement ECM must be programmed. Replace ECM. Did you complete the repair?	Go to Step 9	--
9	1. Use a scan tool in order to clear the DTCs. 2. Operate the vehicle within the Conditions for Running the DTC as specified in the supporting text. Does the DTC reset?	Go to Step 2	System OK

GC1100200873030X

Fig. 38 Code P1581: Cruise Control Direction Output Circuit Low Voltage (Part 3 of 3). ION

Step	Action	Yes	No
1	Did you perform the Diagnostic System Check -- Cruise Control?	Go to Step 2	Go to System Check -
2	1. Connect a scan tool. 2. Turn ON the ignition, with the engine OFF. 3. Using a scan tool perform Cruise Control Cycle special function. Does the throttle angle reach 50% then return to idle?	Go to Diagnostic Aids	Go to Step 3
3	1. Turn OFF the ignition. 2. Disconnect the cruise control module at the harness connector. 3. Turn ON the ignition. 4. Using a DMM measure voltage on Cruise Control Servo Move Direction Signal circuit while using the scan tool to perform Cruise Control Cycle special function. Is ignition voltage present?	Go to Step 5	Go to Step 4
4	Inspect Cruise Control Servo Move Signal circuit for short to ground. Did you find and correct the problem?	Go to Step 7	Go to Step 6
5	Replace the cruise control module. Did you complete the repair?	Go to Step 7	--
6	**Important** The replacement ECM must be programmed. Replace ECM. Did you complete the repair?	Go to Step 7	--
7	1. Use a scan tool in order to clear the DTCs. 2. Operate the vehicle within the Conditions for Running the DTC as specified in the supporting text. Does the DTC reset?	Go to Step 2	System OK

GC1100200874020X

Fig. 39 Code P1582: Cruise Control Move Output Circuit High Voltage (Part 2 of 2). ION

Circuit Description

To control which direction the cruise control module moves the accelerator pedal, the engine control module (ECM) commands the Cruise Control Servo Move Direction Signal circuit either high, wide open throttle (WOT) or low, idle. If the Cruise Servo Move Direction Signal circuit is commanded high and the ECM detects low feedback voltage, DTC P1582 will set.

Conditions for Running the DTC

Every time the Cruise Control Servo Move Direction Signal circuit is commanded high.

Conditions for Setting the DTC

- The ECM detects low feedback voltage when the Cruise Control Servo Move Direction Signal circuit is commanded high.
- The condition exists for 500 ms.

Action Taken When the DTC Sets

- The ECM stores the DTC information into memory when the diagnostic runs and fails.
- The malfunction indicator lamp (MIL) will not illuminate.
- The ECM records the operating conditions at the time the diagnostic fails. The ECM stores this information in the Failure Records.

Conditions for Clearing the DTC

- A last test failed, or current DTC, clears when the diagnostic runs and does not fail. A new ignition cycle must take place before a test passed can be reported.
- A history DTC will clear after 40 consecutive warm-up cycles, if no failures are reported by this or any other non-emission related diagnostic.
- Use a scan tool in order to clear the DTC.

Diagnostic Aids

Important

- To locate an intermittent problem, use a scan tool to perform the Cruise Control Cycle special function with the ignition ON, and the engine OFF. The accelerator pedal should move to 50 percent throttle and then return to idle. If a short to ground exists, the pedal will remain at rest or return to idle.
- C/C Dir. Ckt.-Low Volt test can be monitored to aid in diagnosing an intermittent fault. Monitor the test while tapping the Resume/Accel switch, this moves the throttle toward WOT. If a fault exists, the scan tool will display Test Fail.

Test Description

The number below refers to the step number on the diagnostic table.

2. This step determines if the fault is present.

GC1100200874010X

Fig. 39 Code P1582: Cruise Control Move Output Circuit High Voltage (Part 1 of 2). ION

Circuit Description

To control which direction the cruise control module moves the accelerator pedal the engine control module (ECM) commands the Cruise Control Servo Move Direction Signal circuit either high , wide open throttle (WOT) or low, idle. DTC P1582 will set if the ECM detects high feedback voltage when the Cruise Control Servo Move Direction Signal circuit should be low.

Conditions for Running the DTC

Every time the Cruise Control Servo Move Direction Signal circuit is commanded low, idle.

Conditions for Setting the DTC

- The ECM detects high feedback voltage when the Cruise Control Servo Move Direction Signal circuit is commanded high and the brake pedal is depressed.
- The ECM detects high feedback voltage when the Cruise Control Servo Move Direction Signal circuit is commanded low.
- The condition exists for 500 ms.

Action Taken When the DTC Sets

- The ECM stores the DTC information into memory when the diagnostic runs and fails.
- The malfunction indicator lamp (MIL) will not illuminate.
- The ECM records the operating conditions at the time the diagnostic fails. The ECM stores this information in the Failure Records.

Conditions for Clearing the DTC

- A last test failed, or current DTC, clears when the diagnostic runs and does not fail.
- A history DTC will clear after 40 consecutive warm-up cycles, if no failures are reported by this or any other non-emission related diagnostic.
- Use a scan tool in order to clear the DTC.

Diagnostic Aids

- To locate an intermittent problem, use a scan tool to perform Cruise Control Cycle special function with the ignition ON, engine OFF. The accelerator pedal should move to 50 percent throttle and then return to idle. If a short to ground exists the pedal will remain at rest or return to idle.
- C/C Dir. Ckt.-High Volt and C/C Dir. Ckt.-Open test can be monitored to aid in diagnosing intermittent fault. If a fault exists, the scan tool will display Test Fail.
- Loss of ground for the cruise control module can cause this DTC to set. If this condition exists DTC P01581 and P1587 will also set.

Test Description

The number below refers to the step number on the diagnostic table.

2. This step determines if the fault is present.

GC1100200875010X

Fig. 40 Code P1583: Cruise Control Direction Output Circuit High Voltage (Part 1 of 3). ION

Step	Action	Yes	No
1	Did you perform the Diagnostic System Check - Cruise Control?	Go to Step 2	Go to System Check -
2	1. Connect a scan tool. 2. Turn ON the ignition, with the engine OFF. 3. Using scan tool monitor C/C Dir. Ckt.-High Volt or C/C Dir. Ckt.-Open tests. Does the Test Fail?	Go to Step 3	Go to Diagnostic Aids
3	1. Turn OFF the ignition. 2. Disconnect the cruise control module at the harness connector. 3. Connect a test light between the Cruise Control Servo Move Direction Signal circuit and a good ground. 4. Using scan tool monitor C/C Dir. Ckt.-High Volt and C/C Dir. Ckt.-Open tests. Does the Test Pass?	Go to Step 7	Go to Step 4
4	Is test light illuminated?	Go to Step 5	Go to Step 6

GC1100200875020X

Fig. 40 Code P1583: Cruise Control Direction Output Circuit High Voltage (Part 2 of 3). ION

5	Inspect Cruise Control Servo Move Direction Signal circuit for short to voltage. Did you find and correct the problem?	Go to Step 9	--
6	Inspect Cruise Control Servo Move Direction Signal circuit for an open or high resistance. Did you find and correct the problem?	Go to Step 9	Go to Step 8
7	Replace the cruise control module. Did you complete the repair?	Go to Step 9	--
8	**Important** The replacement ECM must be programmed. Replace ECM. Did you complete the repair?	Go to Step 9	--
9	1. Use a scan tool in order to clear the DTCs. 2. Operate the vehicle within the Conditions for Running the DTC as specified in the supporting text. Does the DTC reset?	Go to Step 2	System OK

GC1100200875030X

Fig. 40 Code P1583: Cruise Control Direction Output Circuit High Voltage (Part 3 of 3). ION

Circuit Description

There are numerous conditions that can cause cruise control to be disabled. If the cruise control is engaged and any of the conditions listed in Condition for Setting the DTC occur, DTC P1584 will set.

Conditions for Running the DTC

Continuous with cruise control engaged.

Conditions for Setting the DTC

DTC P1584 will set if cruise control is engaged and 1 of the following conditions occur:

- The ignition voltage spikes to greater than 16 volts or drops below 10 volts.
- The traction control module (TCM) reports a transmission range switch error to the ECM.
- The TCM reports a gear ratio error to the ECM.
- The engine RPM is greater than 6,350 RPM or less than 950 RPM while in cruise accel or resume states.
- The vehicle acceleration greater than 16 km/h (10 mph).
- The vehicle deceleration greater than 8.7 km/h (5.4 mph).
- The traction control is active for more than 1 second.
- The cruise set speed is below 40 km/h (25 mph) or greater than 161 km/h (100 mph).
- The vehicle speed drops below 32 km/h (20 mph) or greater than 161 km/h (100 mph).
- The vehicle speed differs from cruise set speed by greater than 24 km/h (15 mph) for more than 10 seconds or greater than 32 km/h (20 mph) instantaneously.
- A severe misfire is present for more than 5 seconds.
- The park brake is applied.
- Low brake fluid is detected.
- Communication with the integrated brake control module (IBCM) or SDM is lost.
- The cruise control module is unable to move throttle towards idle or wide open throttle (WOT).
- A state transition is not detected on both the stop lamp switch and torque converter clutch (TCC)/Cruise Brake switch before the driver attempts to set the cruise set speed. Note: This will cause DTC P1584 to set before cruise is engaged.

Action Taken When the DTC Sets

- The engine control module (ECM) stores the diagnostic trouble code (DTC) information into memory when the diagnostic runs and fails.
- The malfunction indicator lamp (MIL) will not illuminate.
- The ECM records the operating conditions at the time the diagnostic fails. The ECM stores this information in the Failure Records.

Conditions for Clearing the DTC

- A last test failed, or current DTC, clears when the diagnostic runs and does not fail.
- A history DTC will clear after 40 consecutive warm-up cycles, if no failures are reported by this or any other non-emission related diagnostic.
- Use a scan tool in order to clear the DTC.

Diagnostic Aids

GC1100200876010X

Fig. 41 Code P1584: Cruise Control Disabled (Part 1 of 2). ION

- Any of the conditions listed in Conditions for Setting the DTC will cause cruise to be disabled. However, DTC P1584 will only set if cruise is engaged when the disabling condition occurs.
- View the failure record information for P1584. Cruise failure conditions will be listed, and a Yes will be displayed next to the condition that caused cruise to be disabled.
- Check cruise cable and throttle cable for proper connections and operation.
- Misadjusted brake switches will cause cruise to be disabled, and Cruise-No Brake Transition will display yes in the failure record.

Scan Tool Parameter	Normal Value	Description
Cruise-Volt Out Of Range	NO	Ignition voltage was out of range
Cruise-Trans Range Sw	NO	TCM reported a trans range switch fault
Cruise-Gear Out of Range	NO	TCM reported a gear ratio error
Cruise-VSS Out of Range	NO	Vehicle speed was detected out of range
Cruise-RPM Out of Range	NO	Engine RPM detected out of range
Cruise-Traction Active	NO	A traction control event was detected
Cruise-Off Brake	NO	--
Cruise- No Brake Transition	NO	A transition on both brake switches has not occurred

GC1100200876020X

Fig. 41 Code P1584: Cruise Control Disabled (Part 2 of 2). ION

Circuit Description

The cruise control clutch is used to engage and release the cruise control cable drive mechanism from the cruise control motor. To command the clutch ON, engaged, the engine control module (ECM) provides ground to the cruise control module via the Cruise Control Servo Clutch Control circuit. When the cruise control clutch is commanded OFF, disengaged, the feedback voltage at the ECM should be high. If the cruise control clutch is commanded OFF, and the feedback voltage on the Cruise Control Servo Clutch Control circuit is low, DTC P1587 will set indicating a short to ground or open exists.

Conditions for Running the DTC

Continuous when cruise control clutch commanded OFF, disengaged.

Conditions for Setting the DTC

- The ECM detects low feedback voltage when the cruise control clutch is commanded OFF.
- The condition exists for 500 ms.

Action Taken When the DTC Sets

- The ECM stores the DTC information into memory when the diagnostic runs and fails.
- The malfunction indicator lamp (MIL) will not illuminate.
- The ECM records the operating conditions at the time the diagnostic fails. The ECM stores this information in the Failure Records.

Conditions for Clearing the DTC

- A last test failed, or current DTC, clears when the diagnostic runs and does not fail.
- A history DTC will clear after 40 consecutive warm-up cycles, if no failures are reported by this or any other non-emission related diagnostic.
- Use a scan tool in order to clear the DTC.

Diagnostic Aids

- To locate an intermittent problem, use the scan tool to monitor the C/C Clutch-Low Volt and C/C Clutch-Open tests with ignition ON, engine OFF. The scan tool will display Test Fail when a short to ground or open exists in the Cruise Control Servo Clutch Control circuit.
- Loss of ground for the cruise control module can cause this DTC to set. If this condition exists DTC P01581 and P1583 will also set.
- Loss of ignition voltage for the cruise control module can also set this DTC.

Test Description

The number below refers to the step number on the diagnostic table.

2. This step determines if the fault is present.

GC1100200877010X

Fig. 42 Code P1587: Cruise Control Clutch Output Circuit Low Voltage (Part 1 of 3). ION

Step	Action	Yes	No
1	Did you perform the Diagnostic System Check - Cruise Control?	Go to Step 2	Go to System Check
2	1. Connect a scan tool. 2. Turn ON the ignition, with the engine OFF. 3. Using scan tool monitor C/C Clutch-Low Volt or C/C Clutch-Open tests. Does the Test Fail?	Go to Step 3	Go to Diagnostic Aids
3	1. Turn OFF the ignition. 2. Disconnect the cruise control module at the harness connector. 3. Connect a test light between the ignition 1 voltage and a good ground. Does the test light illuminate?	Go to Step 4	Go to Step 6
4	1. Connect noid light J 34730-2A Harness Test Lamp between the ignition 1 voltage and Cruise Control Servo Clutch Control circuits. 2. Using scan tool monitor C/C Clutch-Low Volt or C/C Clutch-Open tests. Does Test Fail?	Go to Step 5	Go to Step 7

GC1100200877020X

Fig. 42 Code P1587: Cruise Control Clutch Output Circuit Low Voltage (Part 2 of 3). ION

5	Inspect Cruise Control Servo Clutch Control circuit for short to ground or open circuit. Did you find and correct the problem?	Go to Step 9	Go to Step 8
6	Inspect the ignition 1 voltage circuit for an open or high resistance. Did you find and correct the problem?	Go to Step 9	--
7	Replace the cruise control module. Did you complete the repair?	Go to Step 9	--
8	**Important** The replacement ECM must be programmed. Replace ECM. Did you complete the repair?	Go to Step 9	--
9	1. Use a scan tool in order to clear the DTCs. 2. Operate the vehicle within the Conditions for Running the DTC as specified in the supporting text. Does the DTC reset?	Go to Step 2	System OK

GC1100200877030X

Fig. 42 Code P1587: Cruise Control Clutch Output Circuit Low Voltage (Part 3 of 3). ION

Circuit Description

The cruise control clutch is used to engage and release the cruise control cable drive mechanism from the cruise control motor. To command the clutch ON, engaged, the engine control module (ECM) provides ground to the cruise control module via the Cruise Control Servo Clutch Control circuit. When the cruise control clutch is commanded ON, engaged, the feedback voltage at the ECM should be low. If the cruise control clutch is commanded ON, and the feedback voltage on the Cruise Control Servo Clutch Control circuit is high, DTC P1587 will set indicating a short to voltage exists.

Conditions for Running the DTC

Continuous when cruise control clutch commanded on (engaged).

Conditions for Setting the DTC

- The ECM detects high feedback voltage when the cruise control clutch is commanded OFF.
- The condition exists for 500 ms.

Action Taken When the DTC Sets

- The ECM stores the DTC information into memory when the diagnostic runs and fails.
- The malfunction indicator lamp (MIL) will not illuminate.
- The ECM records the operating conditions at the time the diagnostic fails. The ECM stores this information in the Failure Records.

Conditions for Clearing the DTC

- A last test failed, or current DTC, clears when the diagnostic runs and does not fail.
- A history DTC will clear after 40 consecutive warm-up cycles, if no failures are reported by this or any other non-emission related diagnostic.
- Use a scan tool in order to clear the DTC.

Diagnostic Aids

To locate an intermittent problem, use the scan tool to command Cruise Clutch ON while monitoring C/C Clutch-High Volt test with ignition ON, engine OFF. The scan tool will display Test Fail when a short to voltage exists in the Cruise Control Servo Clutch Control circuit.

Test Description

The number below refers to the step number on the diagnostic table.

2. This step determines if the fault is present.

GC1100200878010X

Fig. 43 Code P1588: Cruise Control Clutch Output Circuit High Voltage (Part 1 of 2). ION

COMPONENT REPLACEMENT

Cruise Control Module (CCM)

L-SERIES

2.2L ENGINE

1. Remove cruise control module to bracket bolts leaving bracket attached to frame rail.
2. Pull module up behind brake booster and disconnect electrical connector.
3. Disconnect cruise control throttle cable tab from throttle body cam and release cruise control throttle cable adjuster.
4. Disconnect cruise throttle cable from module by rotating ¼ turn counterclockwise.
5. Remove cable from connecting strap and cruise control module.
6. Reverse procedure to install. Adjust cruise control throttle cable as outlined in "Adjustments."

ION

1. Disconnect cruise control module harness connector, then the cruise control cable from cruise control module by turning cable 1/4 turn counterclockwise.
2. Disconnect cruse control cable from accelerator pedal.
3. Remove nuts from cruise control module then the module.
4. Reverse procedure to install.

S-SERIES

1. Remove Connector Position Assurance (CPA) and disconnect cruise control electrical connector.
2. Disconnect cruise control cable or rod from accelerator pedal.
3. Remove mounting nuts and CCM.
4. Reverse procedure to install, noting the following:
   a. Adjust cruise control cable as outlined in "Adjustments."
   b. **Torque** module mounting nuts to 53 inch lbs.

Cruise Control Switch

L-SERIES

1. Remove steering wheel shroud and push switches out from rear of steering wheel. **Do not attempt to pry them out from front.**
2. Reverse procedure to install.

ION

1. Using a flat bladed tool, remove cruise switch from steering wheel.
2. Disconnect cruise switch electrical connector.
3. Reverse procedure to install.

S-SERIES

1. Pry switch from steering wheel using suitable small flat-blade screwdriver and disconnect electrical connector.
2. Remove driver's side air bag as outlined in "Passive Restraint Systems" chapter.
3. Remove integral connector lock device, disconnect electrical connector and remove air bag module.
4. Disconnect speed control switch, then remove two mounting screws and speed control switch.
5. Reverse procedure to install.

Step	Action	Yes	No
1	Did you perform the Diagnostic System Check - Cruise Control?	Go to Step 2	Go to System Check
2	1. Connect a scan tool. 2. Turn ON the ignition, with the engine OFF. 3. Using scan tool command Cruise Clutch ON while monitoring C/C Clutch-High Volt test. Does the Test Fail?	Go to Step 3	Go to Diagnostic Aids
3	1. Turn OFF the ignition. 2. Disconnect the cruise control module at the harness connector. 3. Connect noid light J 34730-2A Harness Test Lamp between the ignition 1 voltage and Cruise Control Servo Clutch Control circuits at harness connector. 4. Using a scan tool command Cruise Clutch ON. Does the test light illuminate?	Go to Step 5	Go to Step 4
4	Inspect Cruise Control Servo Clutch Control circuit for short to voltage. Did you find and correct the problem?	Go to Step 7	Go to Step 6
5	Replace the cruise control module. Did you complete the repair?	Go to Step 7	--
6	**Important** The replacement ECM must be programmed. Replace ECM. Did you complete the repair?	Go to Step 7	--
7	1. Use a scan tool in order to clear the DTCs. 2. Operate the vehicle within the Conditions for Running the DTC as specified in the supporting text. Does the DTC reset?	Go to Step 2	System OK

GC1100200878020X

Fig. 43 Code P1588: Cruise Control Clutch Output Circuit High Voltage (Part 2 of 2). ION

Brake & Clutch Switches

L-SERIES

2.2L ENGINE

1. Disconnect electrical connectors.
2. Remove brake switch by rotating it 180° and pulling out of bracket.
3. Remove clutch switch by sliding out locking collar and depress tabs on side of switch.
4. Reverse procedures to install. Adjust switches as outlined in "Adjustments."

3.0L ENGINE

1. Remove lefthand lower closeout panel and disconnect electrical connector.
2. Remove brake switch by rotating it 180° and pulling out of bracket.
3. Reverse procedures to install. Adjust switches as outlined in "Adjustments."

S-SERIES

1. Disconnect switch electrical connector.
2. Remove mounting bolt and switch.
3. Reverse procedure to install. **Torque** switch bolt to 96 inch lbs.

Cruise Release Switch

ION

1. Disconnect electrical connector from cruise control release switch.
2. Remove cruise control release switch from the bracket.
3. Reverse procedure to install. Adjust cruise release switch as outlined in "Adjustments."

Steering Column Slip Ring

1. Remove steering wheel as outlined in "Electrical" section of appropriate chassis chapter.
2. Remove upper steering column shroud.
3. Place ignition to ACC position.
4. Depress lock button and remove ignition cylinder.
5. Disconnect remaining slip ring electrical connectors.
6. Remove mounting screws and slip ring. If slip ring is rotated after removal, ensure alignment procedure is performed.
7. Reverse procedure to install. Align slip ring as follows:
   a. Rotate coil hub clockwise with tab removed until slight tension is felt.
   b. While counting number of revolutions, rotate hub counterclockwise until slight tension is felt.
   c. Rotate coil hub clockwise half number of turns counted in previous step and align tab.

WIPER SYSTEMS

TABLE OF CONTENTS

Application Chart

Model	System
Except Metro, Prizm & Saturn	Permanent Magnet Depressed Park System
Metro, Prizm & Vibe	One, Two & Three Speed Systems
Metro & Vibe	Rear Window Wiper Systems
Saturn	Saturn

Permanent Magnet Depressed Park System

NOTE: On Air Bag Equipped Models, Refer To "Air Bag System Precautions" Located In The Front Of This Manual For System Disarming & Arming Procedures.

NOTE: Refer To "Computer Relearn Procedures" Located In The Front Of This Manual When Battery Power To The Computer Has Been Interrupted.

NOTE: "Electrical Symbol & Wire Color Code Identification" Located In The Front Of This Manual May Be Used As An Aid When Using Wiring Circuits Found In This Section.

INDEX

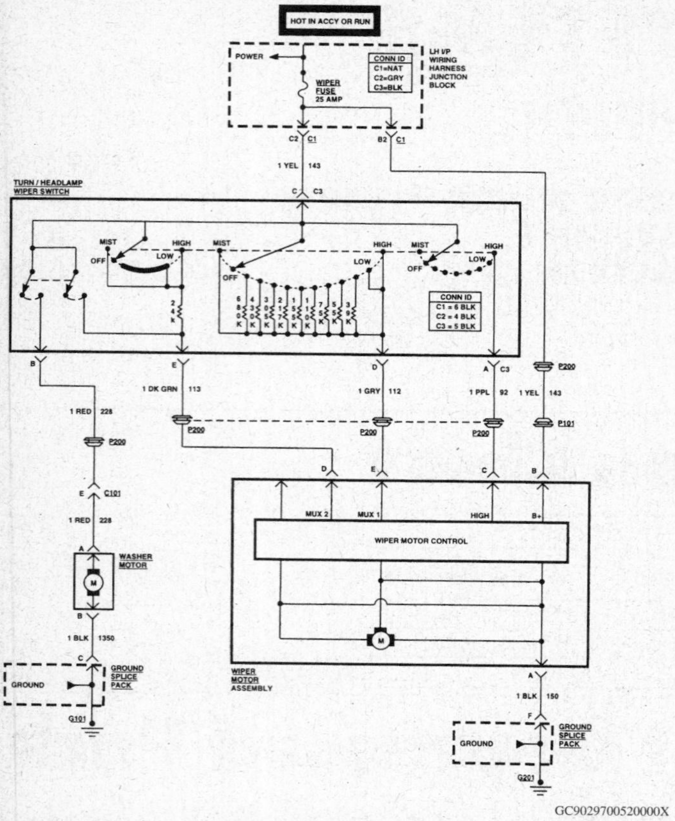

Fig. 1 Wiring diagram. Alero, Malibu & Grand Am

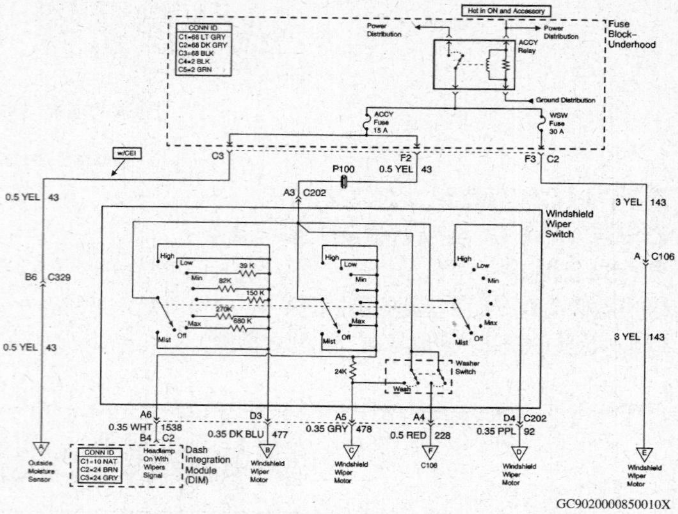

Fig. 2 Wiring diagram (Part 1 of 2). Aurora

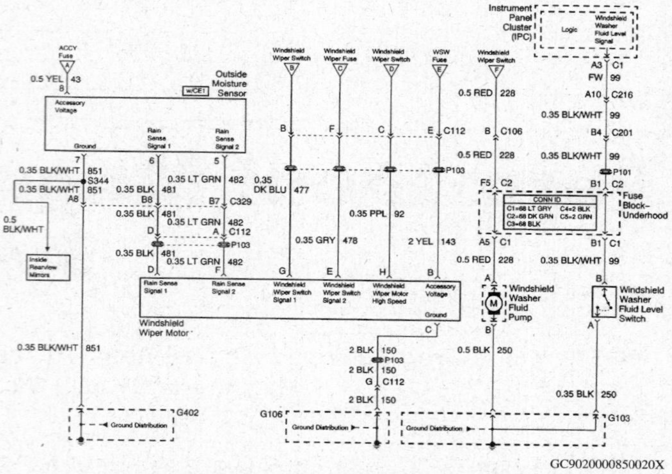

Fig. 2 Wiring diagram (Part 2 of 2). Aurora

PRECAUTIONS

Air Bag Systems

Refer to "Air Bag System Precautions" in the front of this manual for system disarming and arming procedures.

Battery Ground Cable

Prior to service, disconnect battery ground cable and isolate as required.

DESCRIPTION

The permanent magnet depressed park windshield wiper and remote washer pump system consists of a depressed park wiper motor and a washer pump mounted on the washer fluid reservoir.

Based on the type of control switch used and whether an optional electronic printed circuit board is attached in the wiper cover, the system can serve as either a pulse type wiper system or a standard type system. Pulse timing and demand functions are controlled electronically on pulse systems. The pulse system also uses the vehicle speed signal to adjust the wiper delay time. The faster the vehicle is traveling, the shorter delay time between wipe cycles.

Electronic logic circuits on the pulse wiper system's printed circuit board establish all timing and washer commands. If the WASH switch is pressed, a wash is performed for as long as the switch is depressed. The wash action is followed by six seconds of dry wipes before shutoff. With the control switch in the LO or HI speed position, the respective brush circuit is completed to the 12 volt DC source and the wiper motor runs at that particular speed setting.

Moving the switch to the PULSE mode operates the wiper motor intermittently. The intermittent delay can be varied by moving the switch back and forth in the delay mode. An instantaneous wipe can be obtained by moving the switch to the MIST position.

SYSTEM DIAGNOSIS & TESTING

Wiring Diagrams

Refer to **Figs. 1 through 16,** for wiring diagrams.

Connector Terminal Identification

Refer to **Figs. 17 through 30,** for connector terminal identification.

Diagnostic Tests

Inspect easily accessible or visible system components for obvious damage or conditions which may cause the symptom. Inspect the washer fluid reservoir for the proper fluid level.

Refer to **Figs. 31 through 144,** for symptom related tests.

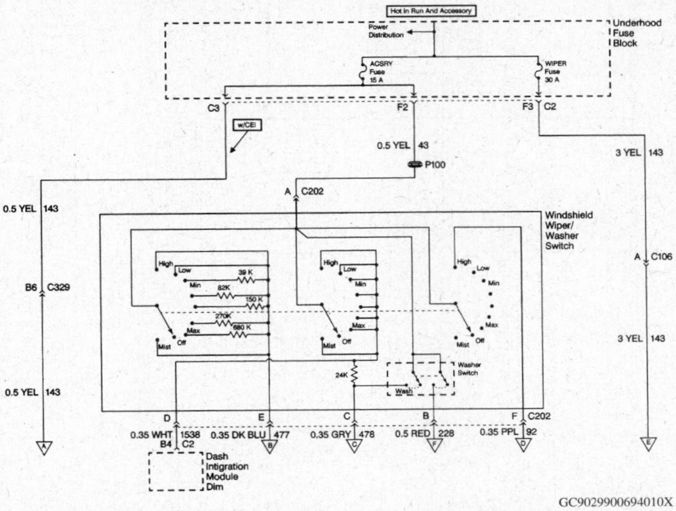

Fig. 3 Wiring diagram (Part 1 of 2). Bonneville & LeSabre

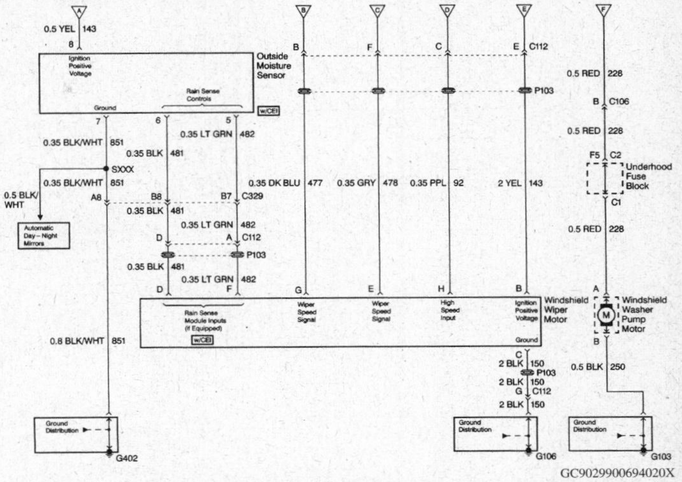

Fig. 3 Wiring diagram (Part 2 of 2). Bonneville & LeSabre

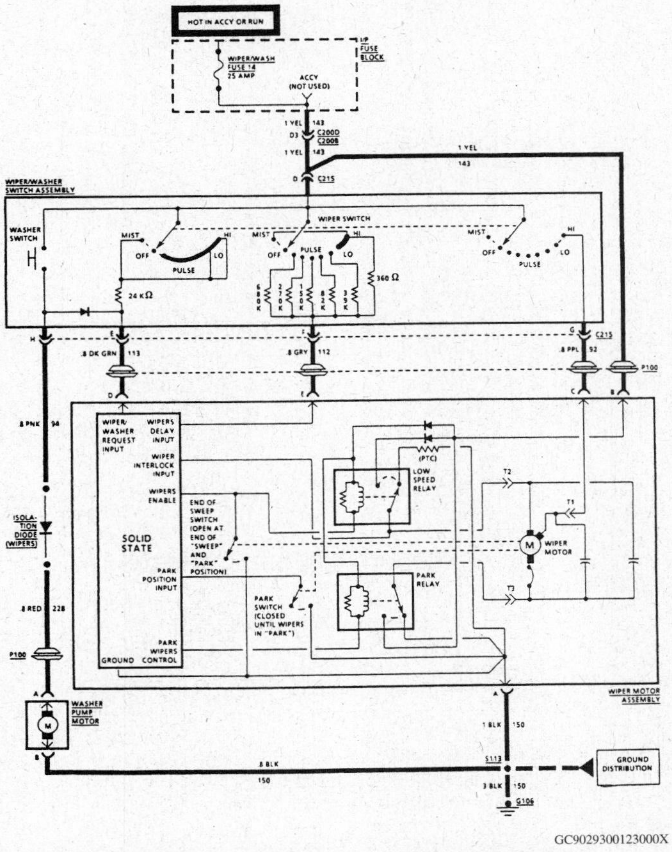

Fig. 4 Wiring diagram. Camaro & Firebird

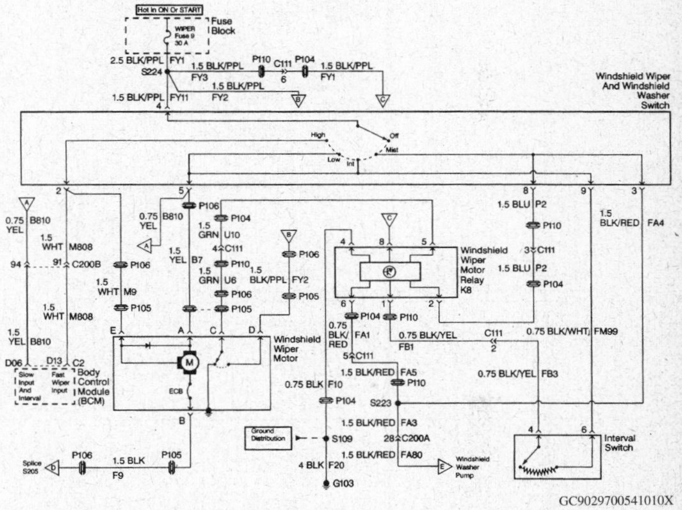

Fig. 5 Wiring diagram (Part 1 of 2). Catera

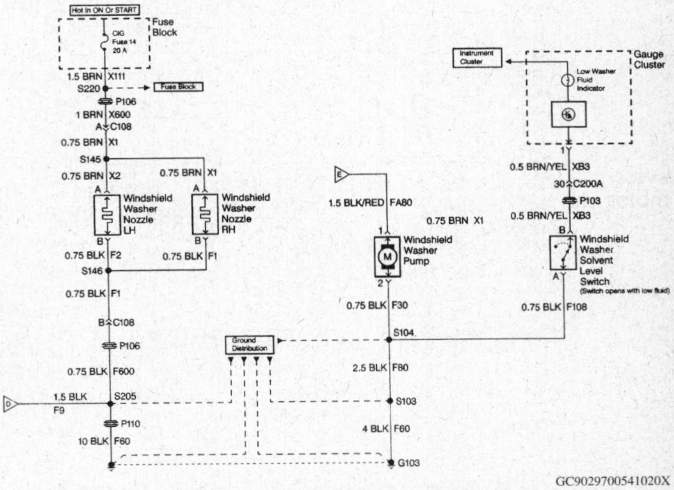

Fig. 5 Wiring diagram (Part 2 of 2). Catera

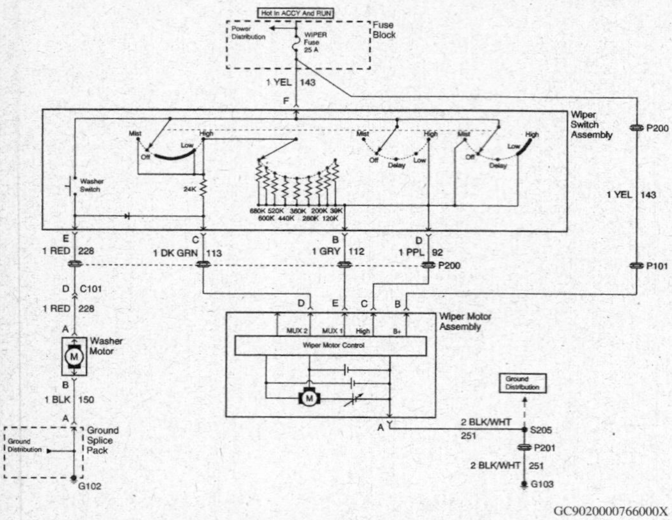

Fig. 6 Wiring diagram. Cavalier & Sunfire w/variable delay

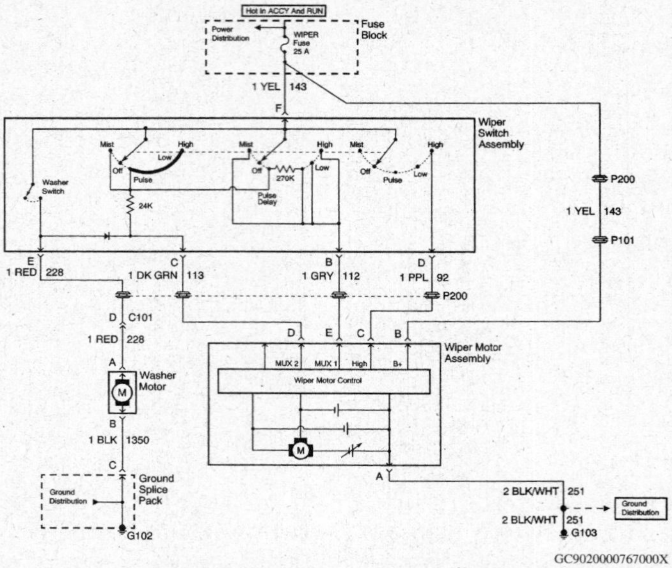

Fig. 7 Wiring diagram. Cavalier & Sunfire w/fixed delay

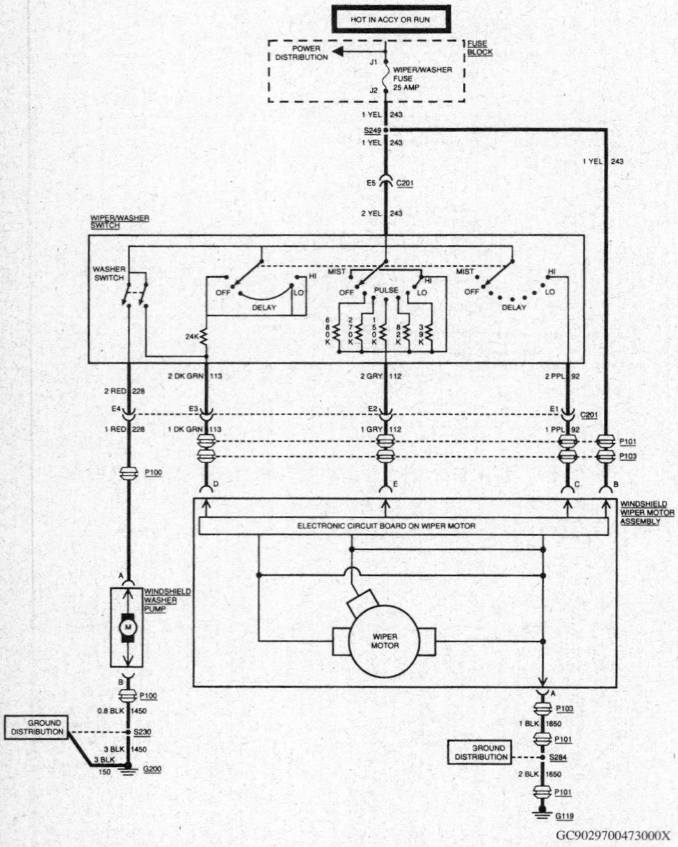

Fig. 8 Wiring diagram. Century, Grand Prix & Regal

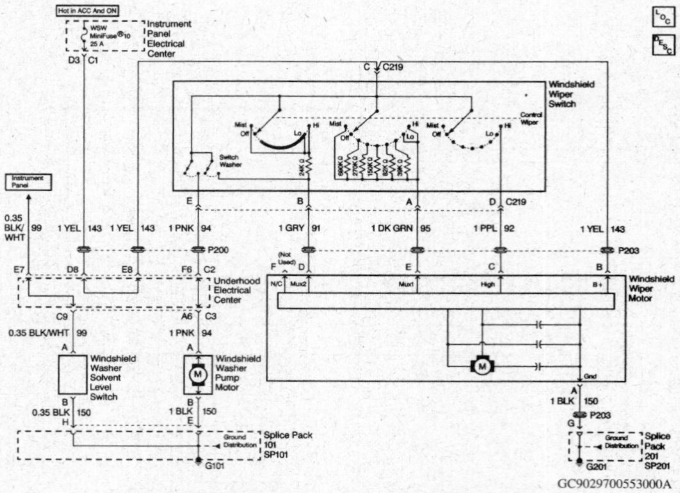

Fig. 9 Wiring diagram. Corvette

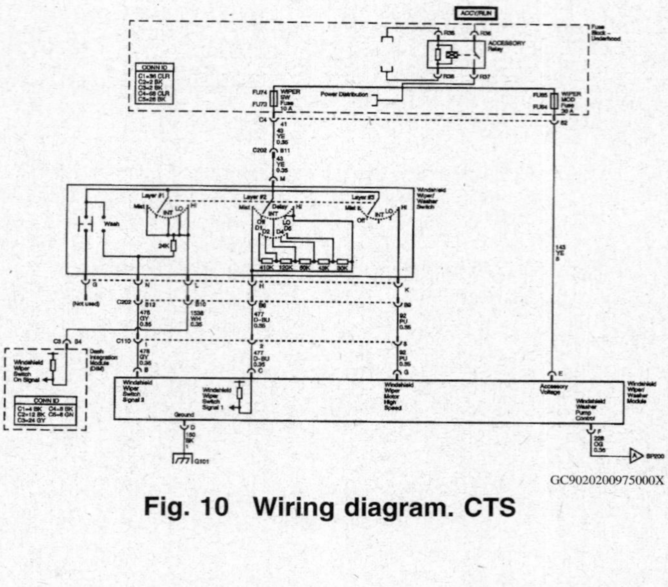

Fig. 10 Wiring diagram. CTS

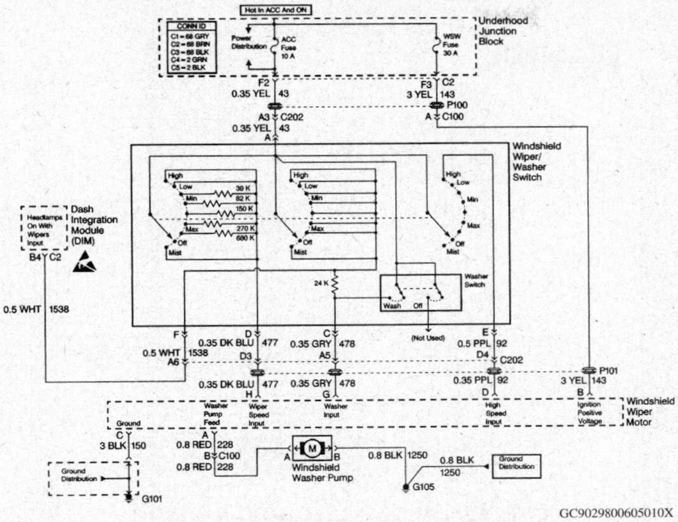

Fig. 11 Wiring diagram (Part 1 of 2). DeVille & Seville

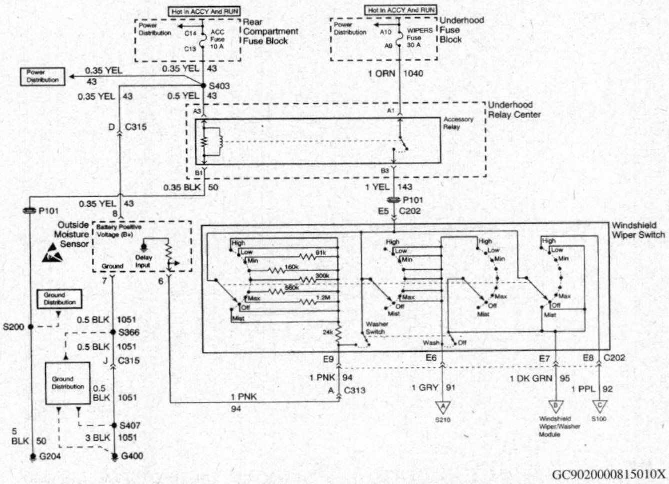

Fig. 12 Wiring diagram (Part 1 of 2). Eldorado

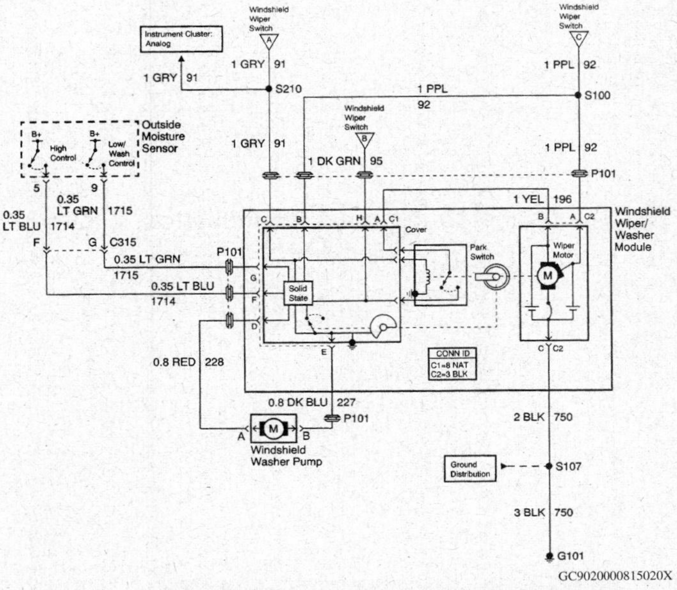

Fig. 12 Wiring diagram (Part 2 of 2). Eldorado

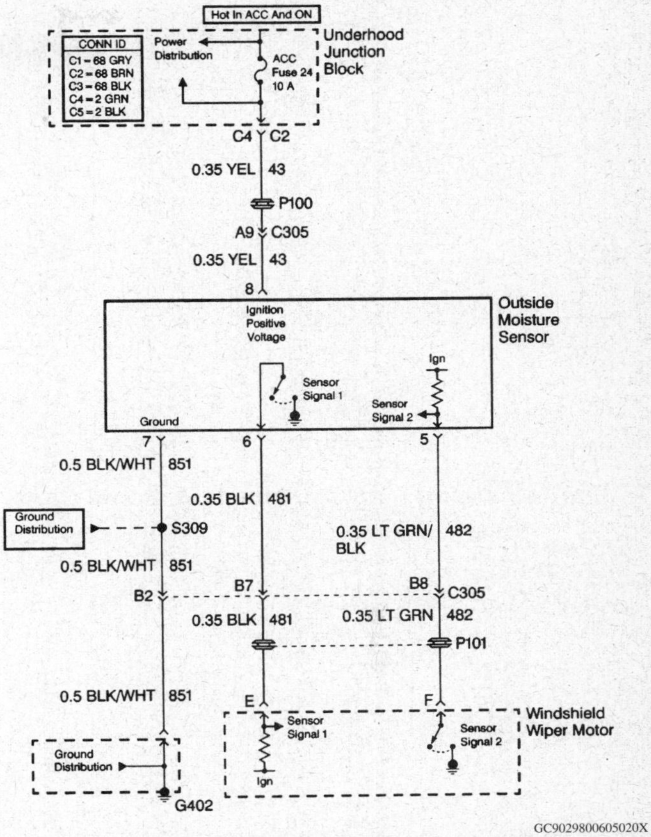

Fig. 11 Wiring diagram (Part 2 of 2). DeVille & Seville

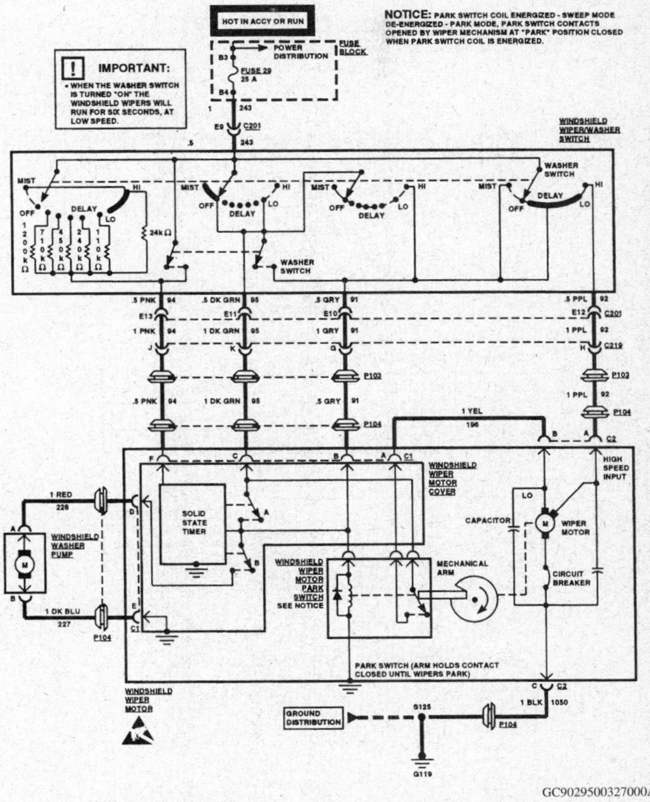

Fig. 13 Wiring diagram. Lumina

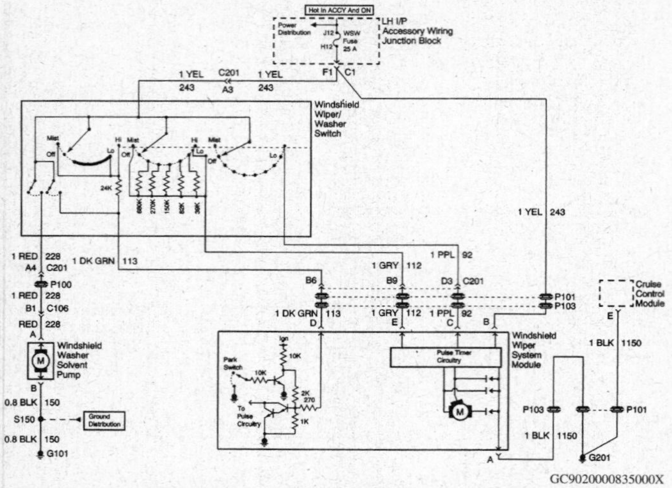

Fig. 14 Wiring Diagram. Impala & Monte Carlo

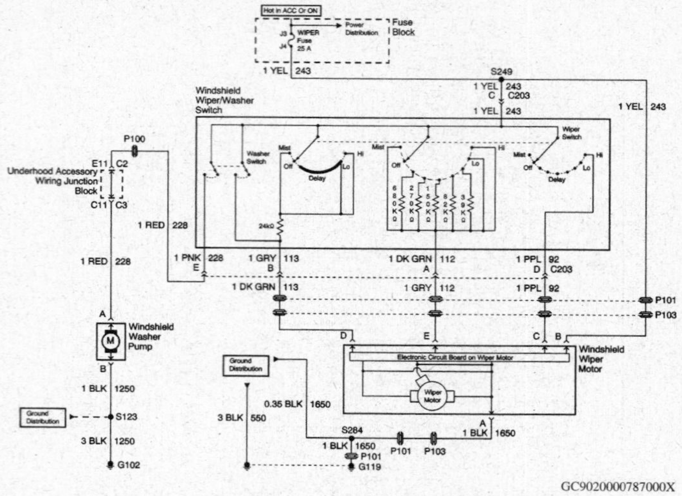

Fig. 15 Wiring diagram. Intrigue

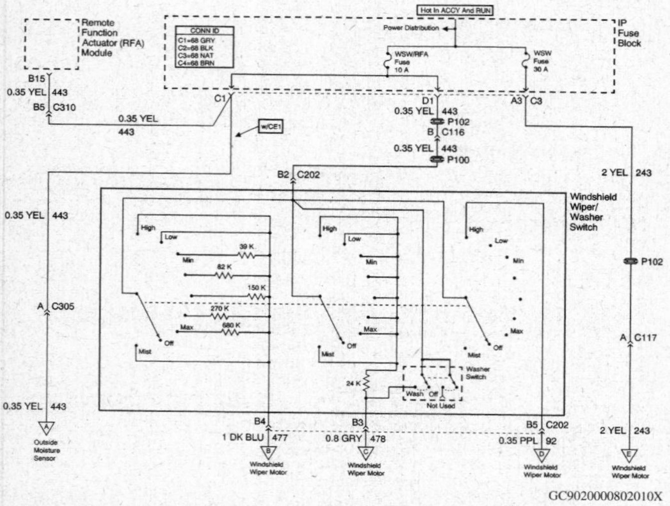

Fig. 16 Wiring diagram (Part 1 of 2). Park Avenue

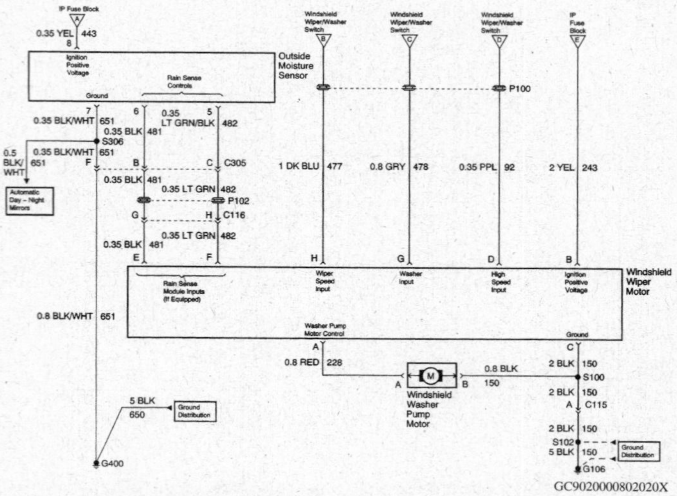

Fig. 16 Wiring diagram (Part 2 of 2). Park Avenue

Connector Part Information		
Pin	**Wire Color**	**Function**
A	BLK	Ground
B	YEL	Fuse Output, ACCY
C	PPL	Windshield Wiper Motor Feed (HIGH Speed)
D	DK GRN	Windshield Wiper Switch Signal (ON)
E	GRY	Windshield Wiper Switch Signal (LOW/PULSE)

GC9029900629000X

Fig. 17 Connector terminal identification. Alero & Grand Am

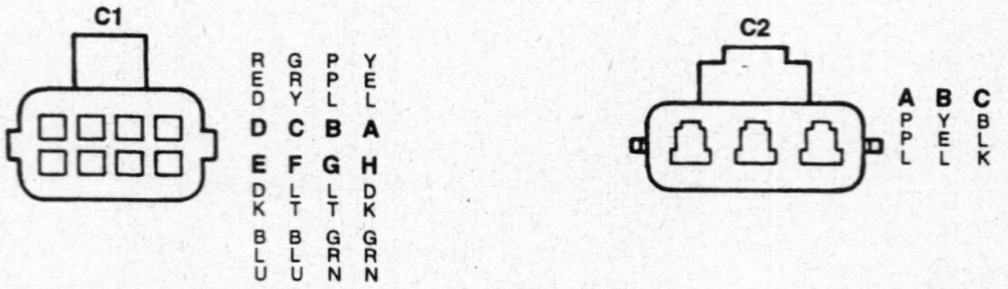

Fig. 18 Connector terminal identification. Lumina & Monte Carlo

Connector Part Information	• 12176334 • 7 Way F Metri-Pack 280 Series (NAT)		
Pin	Wire Color	Circuit No.	Function
A	—	—	Not Used – Cavity Plug
B	YEL	143	Fused Output (Accessory)
C	BLK	150	Ground
D	BLK	481	Rain Sense Signal 1
E	GRY	478	Rainsense Signal 2
F	LT GRN	482	Rainsense Signal 2
G	DK BLU	477	Windshield Wiper Switch Signal 1
H	PPL	92	Windshield Wiper Motor Feed – High Speed

GC9029900693000X

Fig. 19 Connector terminal identification. Bonneville & LeSabre

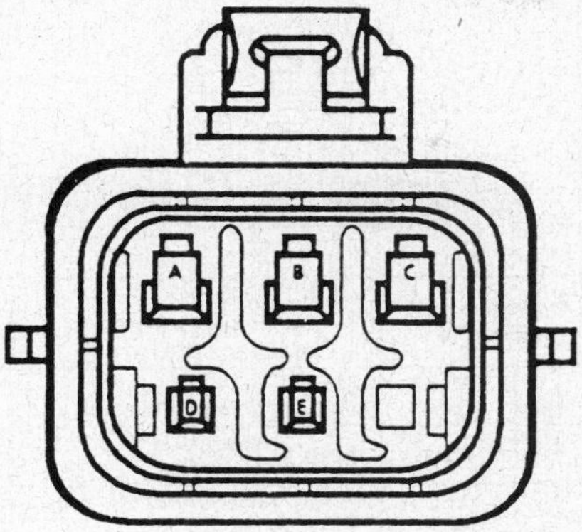

A BLK
B YEL
C PPL
D DK GRN
E GRY

GC9029300125000X

Fig. 20 Connector terminal identification. Camaro, Cavalier, Century, Firebird, Grand Prix, Intrigue, Malibu, Regal & Sunfire

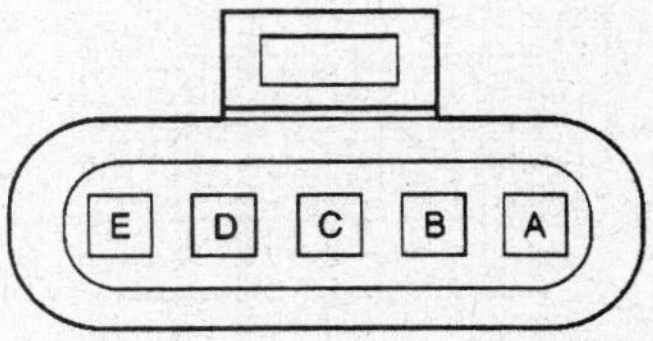

Connector Part Information		
Pin	Wire Color	Function
A	YEL	Speed Signal LO
B	BLK	Ground to G103
C	GRN	Interval Signal
D	BLK/PPL	B+ from fuse #9
E	WHT	Speed Signal HI

GC9029800630000X

Fig. 21 Wiper motor connector terminal identification. Catera

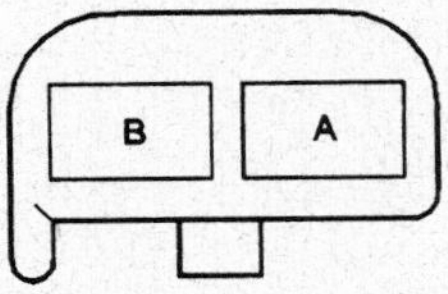

Connector Part Information		
Pin	Wire Color	Function
A	BRN	B+ from Fuse #14
B	BLK	Ground to G103

GC9029800631000X

Fig. 22 Washer nozzle connector terminal identification. Catera

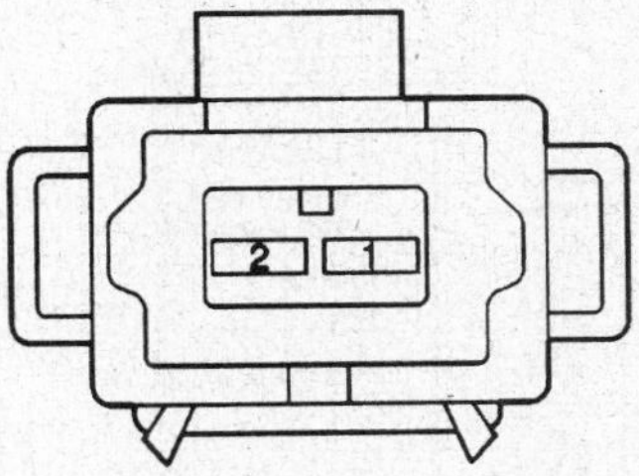

Connector Part Information		
Pin	Wire Color	Function
1	BLK/RED	Washer Pump Signal
2	BLK	Ground to G103

GC9029800632000X

Fig. 23 Windshield washer pump terminal identification. Catera

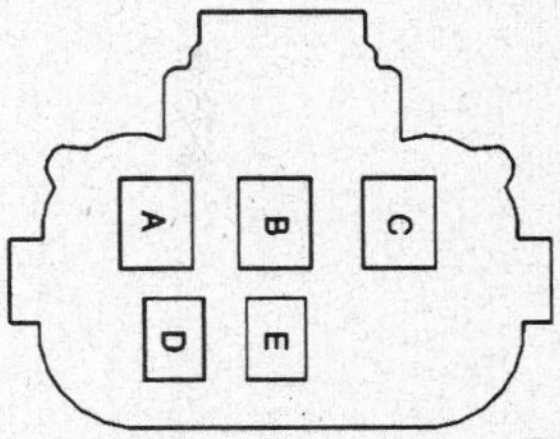

Connector Part Information		
Pin	Wire Color	Function
A	BLK	Ground
B	YEL	Fuse Output - Accessory - Type III Fuse
C	PPL	W/Shield Wiper Motor Feed - High Speed
D	GRY	W/Shield Wiper Relay Feed - Coil
E	DK GRN	W/Shield Wiper Motor Feed - Low Speed

GC9029700633000X

Fig. 24 Wiper motor connector terminal identification. Corvette

Connector Part Information	• 12176335 • 8-Way F Metri-Pack 280 Series		
Pin	Wire Color	Circuit Number	Function
A	--	--	Not Used
B	GY	478	Windshield Washer Switch Signal 2
C	D-BU	477	Windshield Washer Switch Signal 1
D	BK	150	Ground
E	YE	143	Accessory Voltage
F	OG	288	Windshield Washer Switch Control
G	PU	92	Windshield Wiper Motor High Speed
H	--	--	Not Used

GC9020200976000X

Fig. 25 Wiper & Washer Module connector terminal identification. CTS

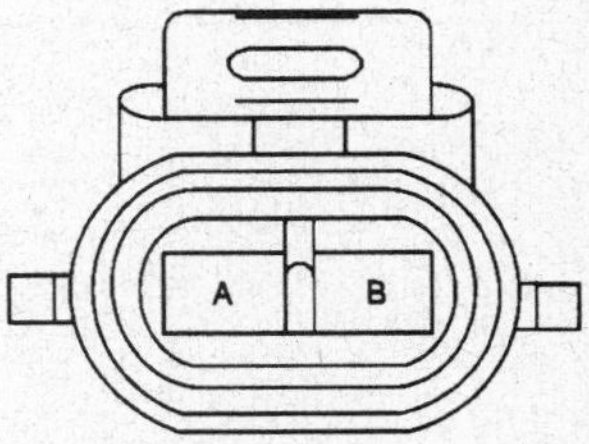

Connector Part Information		
Pin	Wire Color	Function
A	PNK	W/Shield Washer Switch Signal
B	BLK	Ground

GC9029700634000X

Fig. 26 Washer pump terminal connector identification. Corvette

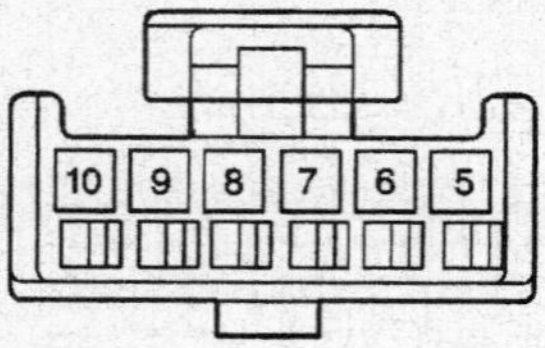

Connector Part Information	• 12064993 • 6 Way F Micro-Pack 100 Series (BLK)		
Pin	**Wire Color**	**Circuit No.**	**Function**
5	LT GRN	482	Sensor Signal -2
6	BLK	481	Sensor Signal -1
7	BLK/WHT	851	Ground
8	YEL	43	Ignition Positive Voltage
9- 10	—	—	Not Used

GC9020000846000X

Fig. 27 Outside moisture sensor terminal identification. DeVille & Seville w/rainsensor

Connector Part Information	• 12176335 • 8 Way F Metri-Pack 280 Series (NAT)		
Pin	**Wire Color**	**Circuit No.**	**Function**
A	RED	228	Windshield Washer Pump Motor Feed
B	YEL	143	Ignition Positive Voltage
C	BLK	150	Ground
D	BLK	481	Sensor Signal - 1
E	GRY	478	Washer Input
F	LT GRN	482	Sensor Signal - 2
G	DK BLU	477	Wiper Speed Input
H	PPL	92	Windshield Wiper Motor Feed - High Speed

GC9020000847000X

Fig. 28 Wiper motor connector terminal identification. DeVille

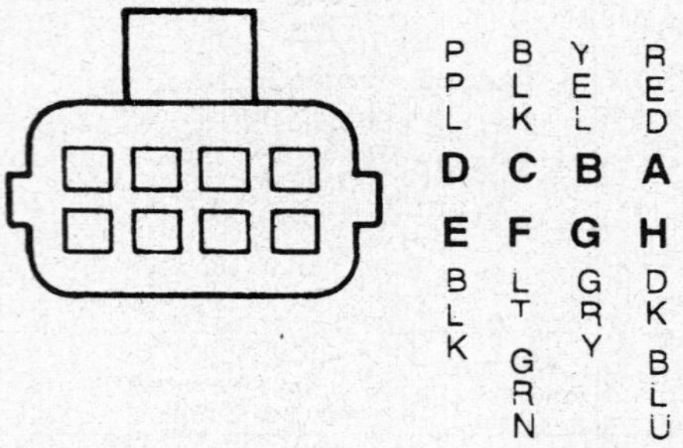

GC9029700519000X

Fig. 29 Connector terminal identification. Park Avenue

Connector Part Information	• 12176335 • 8 Way F Metri-Pack 280 Series (NAT)		
Pin	**Wire Color**	**Circuit No.**	**Function**
A	RED	228	Windshield Washer Pump Motor Feed
B	YEL	143	Ignition Positive Voltage
C	BLK	150	Ground
D	PPL	92	Windshield Wiper Motor Feed - High Speed
E	BLK	481	Sensor Signal - 1
F	LT GRN	482	Sensor Signal - 2
G	GRY	478	Washer Input
H	DK BLU	477	Wiper Speed Input

GC9020000848000X

Fig. 30 Wiper motor terminal identification. Seville

DIAGNOSTIC CHART INDEX

Continued

DIAGNOSTIC CHART INDEX—Continued

Continued

DIAGNOSTIC CHART INDEX—Continued

Step	Action	Yes	No
1	Did you review the Wiper/Washer System Description and Operation and perform the necessary inspections?	Go to *Step 2*	Go to *Symptoms -*
2	1. Turn ON the ignition, with the engine OFF 2. Drain the washer solvent container. 3. Wait one minute and observe the LOW WASHER FLUID indicator. 4. Fill the washer solvent container. 5. Wait one minute and observe the LOW WASHER FLUID indicator. Does the LOW WASHER FLUID indicator turn ON when the solvent container is empty and OFF when the solvent container is filled?	*Test for Intermittent and Poor Connections*	Go to *Step 3*
3	Does the Low Washer Fluid indicator remain ON when the washer solvent container is filled?	Go to *Step 4*	Go to *Step 6*
4	1. Disconnect the windshield washer solvent level switch. 2. Wait one minute. Did the Low Washer Fluid indicator turn OFF?	Go to *Step 9*	Go to *Step 5*
5	Test the low washer fluid indicator control circuit for a short to ground. Refer to *Circuit Testing* and *Wiring Repairs* in Wiring Systems. Did you find and correct the condition?	Go to *Step 11*	Go to *Step 10*
6	1. Disconnect the windshield washer solvent level switch. 2. Connect a fused jumper wire from the low washer fluid indicator control circuit to a good ground. 3. Wait one minute. Does the LOW WASHER FLUID indicator turn ON?	Go to *Step 8*	Go to *Step 7*

GC9020200977010X

Fig. 31 Test 1: Low Washer Fluid Indicator Fault (Part 1 of 2). Alero, Grand Am & Malibu

Step	Action	Yes	No
1	Did you review the Wiper/Washer System Description and Operation and perform the necessary inspections?	Go to *Step 2*	Go to *Symptoms -*
2	1. Turn ON the ignition, with the engine OFF. 2. Activate the windshield washer switch. Does the windshield washer operate properly?	*Test for Intermittent and Poor Connections*	Go to *Step 3*
3	1. Disconnect the windshield washer pump connector. 2. Connect a test lamp between the windshield washer pump control circuit and the windshield washer pump ground circuit. 3. Activate the windshield washer switch. Does the test lamp illuminate?	Go to *Step 7*	Go to *Step 4*
4	Test the windshield washer pump ground circuit for high resistance or an open. Did you find and correct the condition?	Go to *Step 8*	Go to *Step 5*
5	Test the windshield washer pump control circuit for high resistance, a short to ground or an open. Did you find and correct the condition?	Go to *Step 8*	Go to *Step 6*
6	Replace the wiper/washer switch. Did you complete the replacement?	Go to *Step 8*	—
7	Replace the windshield washer pump. Did you complete the replacement?	Go to *Step 8*	—
8	Operate the system in order to verify the repair. Did you correct the condition?	System OK	Go to *Step 3*

GC9020200978000X

Fig. 32 Test 2: Washer Inoperative. Alero, Grand Am & Malibu

Step	Action	Yes	No
1	Did you review the Wiper/Washer System Description and Operation and perform the necessary inspections?	Go to *Step 2*	Go to *Symptoms -*
2	1. Turn ON the ignition, with the engine OFF. 2. Turn the windshield wiper/washer switch through all the switch positions. Do the windshield wipers operate properly?	*Test for Intermittent and Poor Connections*	Go to *Step 3*
3	1. Disconnect the windshield wiper motor connector. 2. Connect a test lamp between the accessory voltage circuit and a good ground. Does the test lamp illuminate?	Go to *Step 4*	Go to *Step 7*
4	Connect a test lamp between the accessory voltage circuit and the ground circuit of the windshield wiper motor connector. Does the test lamp illuminate?	Go to *Step 5*	Go to *Step 8*
5	1. Connect a test lamp between the windshield wiper switch on signal circuit and a good ground. 2. Activate the windshield washer switch. Does the test lamp illuminate?	Go to *Step 10*	Go to *Step 6*
6	1. Disconnect the windshield wiper/washer switch connector. 2. Connect a test lamp between the accessory voltage circuit and a good ground. Does the test lamp illuminate?	Go to *Step 11*	Go to *Step 9*
7	Repair the open in the windshield wiper motor accessory voltage circuit. Did you complete the repair?	Go to *Step 12*	—

GC9020200980010X

Fig. 34 Test 4: Wiper Inoperative In All Modes (Part 1 of 2). Alero, Grand Am Malibu

Step	Action	Yes	No
7	Test the low washer fluid indicator control circuit for high resistance or an open. Did you find and correct the condition?	Go to *Step 11*	Go to *Step 10*
8	Test the ground circuit of the windshield washer solvent level switch for high resistance or an open. Did you find and correct the condition?	Go to *Step 11*	Go to *Step 9*
9	Replace the windshield solvent level sensor switch. Did you complete the replacement?	Go to *Step 11*	—
10	Replace the instrument panel cluster. Did you complete the replacement?	Go to *Step 11*	—
11	Operate the system in order to verify the repair. Did you correct the condition?	System OK	Go to *Step 3*

GC9020200977020X

Fig. 31 Test 1: Low Washer Fluid Indicator Fault (Part 2 of 2). Alero, Grand Am & Malibu

Step	Action	Yes	No
1	Did you review the Wiper/Washer System Description and Operation and perform the necessary inspections?	Go to *Step 2*	Go to *Symptoms -*
2	1. Turn ON the ignition, with the engine OFF. 2. Turn the wiper/washer switch to LO. 3. Turn the wiper/washer switch to HI. 4. Turn OFF the wiper/washer switch. Do the windshield wipers operate properly?	*Test for Intermittent and Poor Connections*	Go to *Step 3*
3	Disconnect the wiper/washer switch connector. Do the windshield wipers stop?	Go to *Step 5*	Go to *Step 4*
4	Test the following circuits for a short to voltage: • windshield wiper/washer switch on signal circuit. • windshield wiper switch low/pulse signal circuit • windshield wiper motor high speed circuit Did you find and correct the condition?	Go to *Step 7*	Go to *Step 6*
5	Replace the windshield wiper/washer switch. Did you complete the replacement?	Go to *Step 7*	—
6	Replace the wiper motor cover. Did you complete the replacement?	Go to *Step 7*	—
7	Operate the system in order to verify the repair. Did you correct the condition?	System OK	Go to *Step 3*

GC9020200979000X

Fig. 33 Test 3: Wiper Always On. Alero, Grand Am & Malibu

Step	Action	Yes	No
8	Repair the open in the windshield wiper motor ground circuit. Did you complete the repair?	Go to *Step 12*	—
9	Repair the open in the windshield wiper/washer switch accessory voltage circuit. Did you complete the repair?	Go to *Step 12*	—
10	Replace the windshield wiper motor. Did you complete the repair?	Go to *Step 12*	—
11	Replace the windshield wiper/washer switch. Did you complete the repair?	Go to *Step 12*	—
12	Operate the system in order to verify the repair. Did you correct the condition?	System OK	Go to *Step 3*

GC9020200980020X

Fig. 34 Test 4: Wiper Inoperative In All Modes (Part 2 of 2). Alero, Grand Am Malibu

Step	Action	Value(s)	Yes	No
1	Did you review the Wiper/Washer System Description and Operation and perform the necessary inspections?	—	Go to *Step 2*	Go to *Symptoms*
2	1. Turn ON the ignition, with the engine OFF. 2. Turn the windshield wiper/washer switch through all the switch positions. Do the windshield wipers operate properly in all modes?	—	*Test for Intermittent and Poor Connections*	Go to *Step 3*
3	1. Disconnect the windshield wiper/washer switch connector. 2. Measure the resistance between the accessory voltage circuit and the windshield wiper switch low/pulse signal circuit of the wiper/washer switch. 3. Turn the wiper/washer switch to the following positions: • MIST • LO • HI Does the resistance measure greater than the specified value?	2 Ω	Go to *Step 10*	Go to *Step 4*
4	1. Measure the resistance between the accessory voltage circuit and the windshield wiper switch low/pulse signal circuit of the wiper/washer switch. 2. Turn the wiper/washer switch through the DELAY range. Does the resistance measure within the specified values?	39K–680K Ω	Go to *Step 5*	Go to *Step 10*
5	1. Measure the resistance between the accessory voltage circuit and the windshield wiper switch on signal circuit of the wiper/washer switch. 2. Turn the wiper/washer switch to the following positions: • MIST • DELAY • LO • HI Does the resistance measure near the specified value?	24K Ω	Go to *Step 6*	Go to *Step 10*
6	1. Reconnect the windshield wiper/washer switch connector. 2. Turn the wiper/washer switch to HI. Do the windshield wipers operate properly in HI mode?	—	Go to *Step 7*	Go to *Step 9*

GC9020200981010X

Fig. 35 Test 5: Wipers Inoperative In One Or More Modes (Part 1 of 2). Alero, Grand Am & Malibu

Step	Action	Yes	No
1	Did you review the Wiper/Washer System Description and Operation and perform the necessary inspections?	Go to *Step 2*	Go to *Symptoms -*
2	1. Turn ON the ignition, with the engine OFF. 2. Turn the windshield wiper/washer switch to HI. 3. Turn the windshield wiper/washer switch to OFF. Do the wipers park properly?	*Test for Intermittent and Poor Connections*	Go to *Step 3*
3	Disconnect the windshield wiper/washer switch connector. Do the wipers park properly?	Go to *Step 4*	Go to *Step 5*
4	Replace the windshield wiper/washer switch. Did you complete the replacement?	Go to *Step 8*	—
5	Test the windshield wiper switch on signal circuit for a short to voltage. Did you find and correct the condition?	Go to *Step 8*	Go to *Step 6*
6	Test the windshield wiper switch low/pulse signal circuit for a short to voltage. Did you find and correct the condition?	Go to *Step 8*	Go to *Step 7*
7	Replace the wiper motor cover. Did you complete the replacement?	Go to *Step 8*	—
8	Operate the system in order to verify the repair. Did you correct the condition?	System OK	Go to *Step 3*

GC9020200982000X

Fig. 36 Test 6: Wiper Blades Do Not Park. Alero, Grand Am & Malibu

Step	Action	Value(s)	Yes	No
7	Test the windshield wiper switch low/pulse signal circuit for high resistance or an open. Did you find and correct the condition?	—	Go to *Step 13*	Go to *Step 8*
8	Test the windshield wiper switch on signal circuit for high resistance or an open. Did you find and correct the condition?	—	Go to *Step 13*	Go to *Step 11*
9	Test the windshield wiper motor high speed circuit for high resistance or an open. Did you find and correct the condition?	—	Go to *Step 13*	Go to *Step 12*
10	Replace the windshield wiper/washer switch. Did you complete the replacement?	—	Go to *Step 13*	—
11	Replace the windshield wiper motor cover. Did you complete the replacement?	—	Go to *Step 13*	—
12	Replace the windshield wiper motor. Did you complete the replacement?	—	Go to *Step 13*	—
13	Operate the wiper/washer system and inspect for proper operation. Did you correct the condition?	—	System OK	Go to *Step 3*

GC9020200981020X

Fig. 35 Test 5: Wipers Inoperative In One Or More Modes (Part 2 of 2). Alero, Grand Am & Malibu

Step	Action	Yes	No
1	Did you review the Wiper/Washer System Description and Operation and perform the necessary inspections?	Go to Step 2	Symptoms - Wiper/Washer Systems
2	1. Turn ON the ignition, with the engine OFF. 2. Turn the windshield wiper/washer switch through all the switch positions. Do the windshield wipers operate properly?	Test for Intermittent and Poor Connections	Go to Step 3
3	1. Disconnect the windshield wiper motor connector. 2. Connect a test lamp between the accessory voltage circuit and a good ground. Does the test lamp illuminate?	Go to Step 4	Go to Step 7
4	Connect a test lamp between the accessory voltage circuit and the ground circuit of the windshield wiper motor connector. Does the test lamp illuminate?	Go to Step 5	Go to Step 8
5	1. Connect a test lamp between the windshield wiper switch signal 2 circuit and a good ground. 2. Activate the windshield washer switch. Does the test lamp illuminate?	Go to Step 10	Go to Step 6
6	1. Disconnect the windshield wiper/washer switch connector. 2. Connect a test lamp between the accessory voltage circuit and a good ground. Does the test lamp illuminate?	Go to Step 11	Go to Step 9
7	Repair the open in the windshield wiper motor accessory voltage circuit. Did you complete the repair?	Go to Step 12	--
8	Repair the open in the windshield wiper motor ground circuit. Did you complete the repair?	Go to Step 12	--
9	Repair the open in the windshield wiper/washer switch accessory voltage circuit. Did you complete the repair?	Go to Step 12	--
10	Replace the windshield wiper motor. Did you complete the repair?	Go to Step 12	--
11	Replace the windshield wiper/washer switch. Did you complete the repair?	Go to Step 12	--
12	Operate the system in order to verify the repair. Did you correct the condition?	System OK	Go to Step 3

GC9020000851000X

Fig. 37 Test 1: Wipers Do Not Operate In Any Mode. Aurora

Step	Action	Value(s)	Yes	No
1	Did you review the Wiper/Washer System Description and Operation and perform the necessary inspections?	--	Go to Step 2	Go to Symptoms - Wiper/Washer Systems
2	1. Turn ON the ignition, with the engine OFF. 2. Turn the windshield wiper/washer switch through all the switch positions. Do the windshield wipers operate properly in all modes?	--	Go to Testing for Intermittent and Poor Connections	Go to Step 3
3	1. Disconnect the windshield wiper/washer switch connector. 2. Measure the resistance between the accessory voltage circuit and the windshield wiper switch signal 1 circuit of the wiper/washer switch. 3. Turn the wiper/washer switch to the following positions: o MIST o LO o HI Does the resistance measure greater than the specified value?	2 ohms	Go to Step 10	Go to Step 4
4	1. Measure the resistance between the accessory voltage circuit and the windshield wiper switch signal 1 circuit of the wiper/washer switch. 2. Turn the wiper/washer switch through the DELAY range. Does the resistance measure within the specified values?	39K-680K ohms	Go to Step 5	Go to Step 10
5	1. Measure the resistance between the accessory voltage circuit and the windshield wiper switch signal 2 circuit of the wiper/washer switch. 2. Turn the wiper/washer switch to the following positions: o MIST o DELAY o LO o HI Does the resistance measure near the specified value?	24K ohms	Go to Step 6	Go to Step 10
6	1. Reconnect the windshield wiper/washer switch connector. 2. Turn the windshield wiper/washer switch to HI. Do the windshield wipers operate properly in HI mode?	--	Go to Step 7	Go to Step 9
7	Test the windshield wiper switch signal 1 circuit for high resistance or an open. Did you find and correct the condition?	--	Go to Step 12	Go to Step 8

GC9020000852010X

Fig. 38 Test 2: Wipers Do Not Operate In One Or More Modes (Part 1 of 2). Aurora

Step	Action	Value(s)	Yes	No
8	Test the windshield wiper switch signal 2 circuit for high resistance or an open. Did you find and correct the condition?	--	Go to Step 12	Go to Step 11
9	Test the windshield wiper motor high speed circuit for high resistance or an open. Did you find and correct the condition?	--	Go to Step 12	Go to Step 11
10	Replace the windshield wiper/washer switch. in Steering Wheel and Column - Tilt. Did you complete the replacement?	--	Go to Step 12	--
11	Replace the windshield wiper motor. Did you complete the replacement?	--	Go to Step 12	--
12	Operate the wiper/washer system and inspect for proper operation. Did you correct the condition?	--	System OK	Go to Step 3

GC9020000852020X

Fig. 38 Test 2: Wipers Do Not Operate In One Or More Modes (Part 2 of 2). Aurora

Step	Action	Yes	No
1	Did you review the Wiper/Washer System Description and Operation and perform the necessary inspections?	Go to Step 2	Go to Symptoms - Wiper/Washer Systems
2	1. Turn ON the ignition, with the engine OFF. 2. Turn the windshield wiper/washer switch to LO. 3. Turn the windshield wiper/washer switch to HI. 4. Turn OFF the windshield wiper/washer switch. Do the windshield wipers operate properly?	Testing for Intermittent and Poor Connections	Go to Step 3
3	Disconnect the windshield wiper/washer switch connector. Do the windshield wipers stop?	Go to Step 5	Go to Step 4
4	Test the following circuits for a short to voltage: • windshield wiper switch signal 1 circuit. • windshield wiper switch signal 2 circuit • windshield wiper motor high speed circuit Did you find and correct the condition?	Go to Step 7	Go to Step 6
5	Replace the windshield wiper/washer switch. Did you complete the replacement?	Go to Step 7	--
6	Replace the windshield wiper motor. Did you complete the replacement?	Go to Step 7	--
7	Operate the system in order to verify the repair. Did you correct the condition?	System OK	Go to Step 3

GC9020000853000X

Fig. 39 Test 3: Wipers Always On. Aurora

Step	Action	Value (s)	Yes	No
1	Did you review the Wiper/Washer System Description and Operation and perform the necessary inspections?	--	Go to Step 2	Go to Symptoms - Wiper/Washer Systems
2	1. Turn the ignition ON, with the engine OFF. 2. Turn the windshield wiper/washer switch to LO. Do the windshield wipers stop for approximately 6 seconds and then operate for approximately 24 seconds repeatedly?	--	Go to Step 5	Go to Step 3
3	1. Turn OFF the windshield wiper/washer switch. 2. Disconnect the windshield wiper/washer switch connector. Do the windshield wipers park properly?	--	Go to Step 6	Go to Step 4
4	Test the following circuits for a short to voltage: • windshield wiper switch signal 1 circuit • windshield wiper switch signal 2 circuit Did you find and correct the condition?	10.5-15 V	Go to Step 7	Go to Step 5
5	Replace the wiper motor. Did you complete the replacement?	--	Go to Step 7	--
6	Replace the wiper/washer switch. Did you complete the replacement?	--	Go to Step 7	--
7	Operate the system in order to verify the repair. Did you correct the condition?	--	System OK	Go to Step 3

GC9020000854000X

Fig. 40 Test 4: Wiper Blades Do Not Park. Aurora

Step	Action	Yes	No
1	Did you review the Wiper/Washer System Description and Operation and perform the necessary inspections?	Go to Step 2	Check Symptoms Wiper/Washer Systems
2	1. Turn ON the ignition, with the engine OFF. 2. Observe the low washer fluid indicator. Does the low washer fluid indicator illuminate?	Go to Step 5	Go to Step 3
3	1. Disconnect the windshield washer solvent level sensor connector. 2. Connect a 3 amp fused jumper wire between the low washer fluid indicator control circuit and a good ground. 3. Wait for 2 ½ minutes. Does the low washer fluid indicator illuminate?	Go to Step 4	Go to Step 7
4	1. Connect a 3 amp fused jumper wire between the low washer fluid indicator control circuit and the windshield washer solvent level sensor ground circuit. 2. Wait for 2 ½ minutes. Does the low washer fluid indicator illuminate?	Go to Step 8	Go to Step 10
5	1. Disconnect the windshield washer solvent level sensor connector. 2. Wait for 2 ½ minutes. Did the low washer fluid indicator turn OFF?	Go to Step 8	Go to Step 6
6	Test the low washer fluid indicator signal circuit for a short to ground. Did you find and correct the condition?	Go to Step 13	Go to Step 9
7	Test the low washer fluid indicator signal circuit for an open or high resistance. Did you find and correct the condition?	Go to Step 13	Go to Step 9
8	Inspect for a poor connection at the windshield washer solvent level sensor. Did you find and correct the condition?	Go to Step 13	Go to Step 11
9	Inspect for a poor connection at the IPC connector. Did you find and correct the condition?	Go to Step 13	Go to Step 12
10	Repair the open or high resistance in the low washer fluid indicator ground circuit. Did you find and correct the condition?	Go to Step 13	--
11	Replace the windshield washer solvent level sensor. Did you complete the replacement?	Go to Step 13	--
12	Replace the IPC. Did you complete the replacement?	Go to Step 13	--
13	Operate the windshield wiper/washer system in order to verify the repair. Did you correct the condition?	System OK	Go to Step 3

GC9020000855000X

Fig. 41 Test 5: Low Washer Fluid Indicator Fault. Aurora

Step	Action	Yes	No
1	Did you review the Wiper/Washer System Description and Operation and perform the necessary inspections?	Go to Step 2	Check Symptoms Wiper/Washer Systems
2	1. Turn ON the ignition, with the engine OFF. 2. Activate the windshield washer switch. Does the windshield washer operate properly?	Test for Intermittent and Poor Connections	Go to Step 3
3	1. Disconnect the windshield washer pump connector. 2. Connect a test lamp between the windshield washer pump control circuit and the windshield washer pump ground circuit. 3. Activate the windshield washer switch. Does the test lamp illuminate?	Go to Step 7	Go to Step 4
4	Test the windshield washer pump ground circuit for high resistance or an open. Did you find and correct the condition?	Go to Step 8	Go to Step 5
5	Test the windshield washer pump control circuit for high resistance, a short to ground or an open. Did you find and correct the condition?	Go to Step 8	Go to Step 6
6	Replace the windshield wiper/washer switch. Did you complete the replacement?	Go to Step 8	--
7	Replace the windshield washer pump. Did you complete the replacement?	Go to Step 8	--
8	Operate the system in order to verify the repair. Did you correct the condition?	System OK	Go to Step 3

GC9020000857000X

Fig. 43 Test 7: Washer Inoperative. Aurora

Step	Action	Value (s)	Yes	No
1	Did you review the Wiper/Washer System Description and Operation and perform the necessary inspections?	--	Go to Step 2	Check Symptoms Wiper/Washer Systems
2	1. Turn ON the ignition, with the engine OFF. 2. Activate the windshield washer switch. Does the windshield washer operate properly?	--	Test for Intermittent and Poor Connections	Go to Step 3
3	Test for a short to voltage in the windshield washer pump control circuit. Did you find and correct the condition?	--	Go to Step 5	Go to Step 4
4	Replace the windshield wiper/washer switch. Did you complete the replacement?	--	Go to Step 5	--
5	Operate the system in order to verify the repair. Did you correct the condition?	--	System OK	Go to Step 3

GC9020000856000X

Fig. 42 Test 6: Washer Always On. Aurora

Step	Action	Value(s)	Yes	No
1	Did you review the Wiper/Washer System Description and Operation and perform the necessary inspections?	—	Go to *Step 2*	Go to *Symptoms*
2	1. Disconnect the wiper harness connector from the wiper motor. 2. Connect a test light between wiper motor connector (harness side) terminals B and C. Is the test light on?	—	Go to *Step 8*	Go to *Step 3*
3	Connect a test light between the wiper motor connector (harness side), terminal B, and ground. Is the test light on?	—	Go to *Step 7*	Go to *Step 4*
4	Check for an open WIPER fuse in the Underhood Junction Block. Is the fuse open?	—	Go to *Step 5*	Go to *Step 6*
5	1. Disconnect Underhood Junction Block connector C2. 2. Measure the resistance from Underhood Junction Block connector C2, terminal F3, to ground with a J 39200 DMM. Is the resistance measured less than the specified value?	0.5 Ω	Go to *Step 15*	Go to *Step 16*
6	Repair the open in CKT 143. Is the repair complete?	—	Go to *Step 17*	—
7	Repair the open in CKT 150. Is the repair complete?	—	Go to *Step 17*	—
8	1. Set the wiper switch to HI. 2. Connect a test light between wiper motor connector (harness side), terminal H, and ground. Is the test light on?	—	Go to *Step 14*	Go to *Step 9*
9	Check for an open ACSRY fuse in the Underhood Junction Block. Is the fuse open?	—	Go to *Step 10*	Go to *Step 11*
10	Replace the ACSRY fuse. Is the replacement complete?	—	Go to *Step 17*	—
11	Check for an open circuit condition in CKT 43 or CKT 477. Is an open circuit condition present?	—	Go to *Step 12*	Go to *Step 13*
12	Repair the open circuit condition in CKT 43 or CKT 477. Is the repair complete?	—	Go to *Step 17*	—

GC9029900695010X

Fig. 44 Test 1: Wipers All Modes Inoperative (Part 1 of 2). Bonneville & LeSabre

Step	Action	Value(s)	Yes	No
13	Replace the wiper/washer switch. Is the replacement complete?	—	Go to *Step 17*	—
14	Replace the wiper motor. Is the replacement complete?	—	Go to *Step 17*	—
15	Repair the short to ground in CKT 143. Is the repair complete?	—	Go to *Step 17*	—
16	Replace the WIPER fuse. Is the replacement complete?	—	Go to *Step 17*	—
17	Operate the system in order to verify the repair. Did you correct the condition?	—	System OK	Go to *Symptoms*

GC9029900695020X

Fig. 44 Test 1: Wipers All Modes Inoperative (Part 2 of 2). Bonneville & LeSabre

Step	Action	Value(s)	Yes	No
1	Did you review the Wiper/Washer System Description and Operation and perform the necessary inspections?	—	Go to *Step 2*	Go to *Symptoms*
2	1. Turn the ignition OFF. 2. Disconnect wiper/washer switch connector C202. 3. Set the wiper switch to DELAY. 4. Measure the resistance through connector C202 from terminal A3 to terminal D3 with a DMM set to the Ohms scale. 5. Move the wiper switch through the entire delay range. Does the resistance vary within the specified range?	39 kΩ to 680 kΩ	Go to *Step 4*	Go to *Step 3*
3	Replace the wiper/washer switch. Is the replacement complete?	—	Go to *Step 7*	—
4	1. Reconnect connector C202 to the wiper/washer switch connector. 2. Disconnect the harness connector from the wiper motor assembly. 3. Turn the ignition to ON. 4. Set the wiper switch to HI. 5. Measure the voltage from the wiper motor connector terminal H to ground with a DMM. Is voltage within the specified range?	10.5–15.5 V	Go to *Step 6*	Go to *Step 5*
5	Repair the open in CKT 477. Is the repair complete?	—	Go to *Step 7*	—
6	Replace the wiper motor. Is the replacement complete?	—	Go to *Step 7*	—
7	Operate the system in order to verify the repair. Did you correct the condition?	—	System OK	Go to *Symptoms*

GC9029900696000X

Fig. 45 Test 2: Wipers Delay Mode Inoperative. Bonneville & LeSabre Less Rainsensor

Step	Action	Value(s)	Yes	No
17	Check for unclean glass or a clouded rainsense module attachment. If windshield is clean and adhesive tape is not clouded, replace the rainsense module. Is the repair or replacement complete?	—	Go to *Step 21*	—
18	Move the wiper switch from the fourth highest sensitivity position to the fifth highest sensitivity position Does an instant wipe occur?	—	Go to *Step 20*	Go to *Step 19*
19	Replace the rainsense module. Is the replacement complete?	—	Go to *Step 21*	—
20	1. Check for an open in CKT 481. 2. If OK, replace the wiper motor. 3. If the problem persists replace the rainsense module. Is the replacement complete?	—	Go to *Step 21*	—
21	Operate the system in order to verify the repair. Did you correct the condition?	—	System OK	Go to *Symptoms*

GC9029900697020X

Fig. 46 Test 3: Wipers Delay Mode Inoperative (Part 2 of 2). Bonneville & LeSabre w/Rainsensor

Step	Action	Value(s)	Yes	No
1	Did you review the Wiper/Washer System Description and Operation and perform the necessary inspections?	—	Go to *Step 2*	Go to *Symptoms*
2	1. Disconnect the harness connector from the wiper motor. 2. Turn the ignition to RUN. 3. Set the wiper switch to HI. 4. Connect a test light from the wiper motor connector (harness side) terminal D to ground. Is the test light on?	—	Go to *Step 3*	Go to *Step 4*
3	Replace the wiper motor. Is the replacement complete?	—	Go to *Step 7*	—
4	Check for open in CKT 92. Is an open circuit condition present?	—	Go to *Step 5*	Go to *Step 6*
5	Repair the open in CKT 92. Is the repair complete?	—	Go to *Step 7*	—
6	Replace the wiper/washer switch. Is the replacement complete?	—	Go to *Step 7*	—
7	Operate the system in order to verify the repair. Did you correct the condition?	—	System OK	Go to *Symptoms*

GC9029900698000X

Fig. 47 Test 4: Wipers High Mode Inoperative, Low Mode Operates. Bonneville & LeSabre

Step	Action	Value(s)	Yes	No
1	Did you review the Wiper/Washer System Description and Operation and perform the necessary inspections?	—	Go to *Step 2*	Go to *Symptoms*
2	1. Turn the ignition to RUN. 2. Set the wiper switch to HI. Are the wipers operating?	—	Go to *Step 3*	Go to *Step 21*
3	Set the wiper switch to the middle AUTO DELAY position. Does the wiper system operate in delay mode?	—	Go to *Step 5*	Go to *Step 4*
4	Set the wiper switch to the next-higher sensitivity position (towards OFF). Does an instant wipe occur?	—	Go to *Step 6*	Go to *Step 21*
5	1. Set the wiper switch to the highest sensitivity level (towards OFF). 2. Move the wiper switch to the second highest sensitivity position (one position away from OFF). Does an instant wipe occur?	—	Go to *Step 7*	Go to *Step 14*
6	Replace the rainsense module. Is the replacement complete?	—	Go to *Step 21*	—
7	1. Disconnect the connector from the rainsense module. 2. Connect a test light between the rainsense module connector (harness side) terminals 7 and 8. Is the test light on?	—	Go to *Step 11*	Go to *Step 8*
8	Connect a test light between rainsense module connector (harness side), terminal 8, and ground. Is the test light on?	—	Go to *Step 9*	Go to *Step 10*
9	Repair the open in CKT 851. Is the repair complete?	—	Go to *Step 21*	—
10	Repair the open in CKT 143. Is the repair complete?	—	Go to *Step 21*	—
11	1. Disconnect the wiper motor connector. 2. Connect a DMM set to Ohms scale between wiper motor connector terminal F and rainsense module connector (harness side) terminal 5. Is there continuity?	—	Go to *Step 12*	Go to *Step 13*
12	Replace the rainsense module. Is the replacement complete?	—	Go to *Step 21*	—
13	Repair the open in CKT 482. Is the repair complete?	—	Go to *Step 21*	—
14	Move the wiper switch from the second highest sensitivity position to the third highest sensitivity position. Does an instant wipe occur?	—	Go to *Step 15*	Go to *Step 16*
15	Replace the rainsense module. Is the replacement complete?	—	Go to *Step 21*	—
16	Move the wiper switch from the third highest sensitivity position to the fourth highest sensitivity position Does an instant wipe occur?	—	Go to *Step 17*	Go to *Step 18*

GC9029900697010X

Fig. 46 Test 3: Wipers Delay Mode Inoperative (Part 1 of 2). Bonneville & LeSabre w/Rainsensor

Step	Action	Value(s)	Yes	No
1	Did you review the Wiper/Washer System Description and Operation and perform the necessary inspections?	—	Go to *Step 2*	Go to *Symptoms*
2	1. Disconnect the harness connector from the wiper motor. 2. Turn the ignition switch to RUN. 3. Set the wiper switch to LO. 4. Connect a test light between the wiper motor connector (harness side) terminal H and ground. Is the test light ON?	—	Go to *Step 6*	Go to *Step 3*
3	Check for an open in CKT 477. Is an open present?	—	Go to *Step 4*	Go to *Step 5*
4	Repair the open in CKT 477. Is the repair complete?	—	Go to *Step 7*	—
5	Replace the wiper/washer switch. Is the replacement complete?	—	Go to *Step 7*	—
6	Replace the wiper motor. Is the replacement complete?	—	Go to *Step 7*	—
7	Operate the system in order to verify the repair. Did you correct the condition?	—	System OK	Go to *Symptoms*

GC9029900699000X

Fig. 48 Test 5: Wipers Low Mode Inoperative, High Mode Operates. Bonneville & LeSabre

Step	Action	Value(s)	Yes	No
1	Did you review the Wiper/Washer System Description and Operation and perform the necessary inspections?	—	Go to *Step 2*	Go to *Symptoms*
2	1. Turn the ignition switch to RUN. 2. Move the wiper switch to all positions and then to OFF. 3. Disconnect connector C202 from the wiper/washer switch connector. Are the wipers still operating?	—	Go to *Step 6*	Go to *Step 3*
3	Test the pigtail wires leading to the wiper/washer switch for a short to voltage. Was a short to voltage found?	—	Go to *Step 4*	Go to *Step 5*
4	Repair the short to voltage in the wiper/washer switch pigtail wires. Is the repair complete?	—	Go to *Step 19*	—
5	Replace the wiper/washer switch. Is the replacement complete?	—	Go to *Step 19*	—
6	Turn the ignition OFF and then back to RUN. Are the wipers still operating?	—	Go to *Step 8*	Go to *Step 7*
7	Replace the wiper motor. Is the replacement complete?	—	Go to *Step 19*	—
8	Measure the voltage from connector C202 (vehicle side), terminal A5, to ground with a DMM. Is the voltage measured greater than the specified value?	1.0 V	Go to *Step 9*	Go to *Step 12*

GC9029900700010X

Fig. 49 Test 6: Wipers Always On (Part 1 of 2). Bonneville & LeSabre

Step	Action	Value(s)	Yes	No
9	1. Reconnect connector C202 to the wiper/washer switch connector. 2. Disconnect the harness connector from the wiper motor. 3. Measure the voltage from the wiper motor connector (vehicle side) terminal G to ground with the DMM. Is the voltage measured greater than the specified value?	1.0 V	Go to *Step 11*	Go to *Step 10*
10	Replace the wiper motor. Is the replacement complete?	—	Go to *Step 19*	—
11	Repair the short to voltage in CKT 478. Is the repair complete?	—	Go to *Step 19*	—
12	Measure the voltage from the connector C202 (vehicle side) terminal D3 to ground with a DMM. Is the voltage measured greater than the specified value?	1.0 V	Go to *Step 16*	Go to *Step 13*
13	1. Reconnect connector C202 to the wiper/washer switch connector. 2. Disconnect the harness connector from the wiper motor. 3. Measure the voltage from the wiper motor connector (harness side) terminal D to ground with a DMM. Is the voltage measured within the specified range?	10.5–15 V	Go to *Step 14*	Go to *Step 15*
14	Repair the short to voltage in CKT 92. Is the repair complete?	—	Go to *Step 19*	—
15	Replace the wiper motor. Is the replacement complete?	—	Go to *Step 19*	—
16	1. Reconnect wiper/washer switch connector C202. 2. Disconnect the harness connector from the wiper motor. 3. Measure the voltage from the wiper motor connector terminal H to ground with a DMM. Is the voltage measured greater than the specified value?	1.0 V	Go to *Step 17*	Go to *Step 18*
17	Repair the short to voltage in CKT 477. Is the repair complete?	—	Go to *Step 19*	—
18	Replace the wiper motor. Is the replacement complete?	—	Go to *Step 19*	—
19	Operate the system in order to verify the repair. Did you correct the condition?	—	System OK	Go to *Symptoms*

GC9029900700020X

Fig. 49 Test 6: Wipers Always On (Part 2 of 2). Bonneville & LeSabre

Step	Action	Value(s)	Yes	No
1	Did you review the Wiper/Washer System Description and Operation and perform the necessary inspections?	—	Go to *Step 2*	Go to *Symptoms*
2	Test for a short to voltage in CKT 228. Is a short to voltage found?	—	Go to *Step 3*	Go to *Step 4*
3	Repair the short to voltage in CKT 228. Is the repair complete?	—	Go to *Step 5*	—
4	Replace the wiper/washer switch. Is the replacement complete?	—	Go to *Step 5*	—
5	Operate the system in order to verify the repair. Did you correct the condition?	—	System OK	Go to *Symptoms*

GC9029900702000X

Fig. 51 Test 8: Washers Always On. Bonneville & LeSabre

Step	Action	Value(s)	Yes	No
1	Did you review the Wiper/Washer System Description and Operation and perform the necessary inspections?	—	Go to *Step 2*	Go to *Symptoms*
2	Check the washer solvent container fluid level. Is the washer solvent container filled?	—	Go to *Step 4*	Go to *Step 3*
3	Fill the washer solvent container. Is the washer solvent container filled?	—	Go to *Step 19*	—
4	Check the hoses to ensure that they are correctly attached and that they are not pinched or kinked. Are the hoses OK?	—	Go to *Step 6*	Go to *Step 5*
5	Repair the hoses. Are the hoses repaired?	—	Go to *Step 19*	—
6	Check for clogged windshield washer nozzles. Are the nozzles clogged?	—	Go to *Step 7*	Go to *Step 8*
7	Replace the clogged nozzles. Is the replacement complete?	—	Go to *Step 19*	—
8	Check for an open ACSRY fuse in the Underhood Junction Block. Is the fuse open?	—	Go to *Step 9*	Go to *Step 10*
9	Replace the open fuse. Is the replacement complete?	—	Go to *Step 19*	—
10	1. Disconnect the washer pump connector. 2. Turn the ignition switch to ON. 3. Connect a test light between terminals A and B of the washer pump connector (harness side). 4. Activate the washer switch while observing the test light. Is the test light on?	—	Go to *Step 11*	Go to *Step 14*
11	Check for a poor connection at the washer pump connector. Is a poor connection present?	—	Go to *Step 12*	Go to *Step 13*
12	Repair the poor connection. Is the repair complete?	—	Go to *Step 19*	—
13	Replace the washer pump. Is the replacement complete?	—	Go to *Step 19*	—

GC9029900703010X

Fig. 52 Test 9: Washers Inoperative. Bonneville & LeSabre

Step	Action	Value(s)	Yes	No
1	Did you review the Wiper/Washer System Description and Operation and perform the necessary inspections?	—	Go to *Step 2*	Go to *Symptoms*
2	1. Turn the ignition to RUN. 2. Set the wiper switch to LO. Do the wipers stop for approximately 6 seconds and then operate for approximately 24 seconds repeatedly?	—	Go to *Step 3*	Go to *Step 4*
3	Replace the wiper motor. Is the replacement complete?	—	Go to *Step 15*	—
4	1. Set the wiper switch to OFF. 2. Disconnect connector C202 from the wiper/washer switch connector. Do the wipers park properly?	—	Go to *Step 5*	Go to *Step 6*
5	Replace the wiper/washer switch. Is the replacement complete?	—	Go to *Step 15*	—
6	Measure the voltage from connector C202 (vehicle side) terminal A5 to ground. Is the voltage measured greater than the specified value?	1.0 V	Go to *Step 7*	Go to *Step 10*
7	1. Reconnect connector C202 to the wiper/washer switch connector. 2. Disconnect the harness connector from the wiper motor. 3. Measure the voltage from wiper motor connector (harness side) terminal G to ground. Is the voltage measured within the specified range?	10.5–15 V	Go to *Step 8*	Go to *Step 9*
8	Repair the short to voltage in CKT 478. Is the repair complete?	—	Go to *Step 15*	—
9	Replace the wiper motor. Is the replacement complete?	—	Go to *Step 15*	—
10	Measure the voltage from connector C202 (vehicle side) terminal D3 to ground. Is the voltage measured greater than the specified value?	1.0 V	Go to *Step 12*	Go to *Step 11*
11	Replace the wiper motor. Is the replacement complete?	—	Go to *Step 15*	—
12	1. Reconnect connector C202 to the wiper/washer switch connector. 2. Disconnect the harness connector from the wiper motor assembly. 3. Measure the voltage from the wiper motor connector (harness side) terminal H to ground. Is the voltage measured greater than the specified value?	1.0 V	Go to *Step 14*	Go to *Step 13*
13	Replace the wiper motor. Is the replacement complete?	—	Go to *Step 15*	—
14	Repair the short to voltage in CKT 477. Is the repair complete?	—	Go to *Step 15*	—
15	Operate the system in order to verify the repair. Did you correct the condition?	—	System OK	Go to *Symptoms*

GC9029900701000X

Fig. 50 Test 7: Wiper Blades Do Not Park w/Switch Off. Bonneville & LeSabre

Step	Action	Yes	No
1	Did you review the Wiper/Washer System Description and Operation and perform the necessary inspections?	Go to *Step 2*	Go to *Symptoms* -
2	1. Turn ON the ignition, with the engine OFF. 2. Activate the windshield washer switch. Does the windshield washer operate properly?	*Test for Intermittent and Poor Connections*	Go to *Step 3*
3	1. Disconnect the windshield washer pump connector. 2. Connect a test lamp between the windshield washer pump control circuit and the windshield washer pump ground circuit. 3. Activate the windshield washer switch. Does the test lamp illuminate?	Go to *Step 7*	Go to *Step 4*
4	1. Connect a test lamp between the windshield washer pump control circuit and a good ground. 2. Activate the windshield washer switch. Does the test lamp illuminate?	Go to *Step 8*	Go to *Step 5*
5	Test for a short to ground or an open in the following: • windshield washer pump control circuit • windshield washer switch signal circuit • windshield washer pump isolation diode Did you find and correct the condition?	Go to *Step 11*	Go to *Step 6*
6	Inspect for a poor connection at the windshield wiper/washer switch connector. Did you find and correct the condition?	Go to *Step 11*	Go to *Step 9*

GC9020200983010X

Fig. 53 Test 1: Washers Inoperative (Part 1 of 2). Camaro & Firebird

Step	Action	Yes	No
7	Inspect for a poor connection at the windshield washer pump motor. Did you find and correct the condition?	Go to *Step 11*	Go to *Step 10*
8	Repair the open in the windshield washer pump ground circuit. Did you complete the repair?	Go to *Step 11*	—
9	Replace the windshield wiper/washer switch. Did you complete the replacement?	Go to *Step 11*	—
10	Replace the windshield washer pump. Did you complete the replacement?	Go to *Step 11*	—
11	Operate the windshield wiper/washer system in order to verify the repair. Did you correct the condition?	System OK	Go to *Step 3*

GC9020200983020X

Fig. 53 Test 1: Washers Inoperative (Part 2 of 2). Camaro & Firebird

Step	Action	Yes	No
1	Did you review the Wiper/Washer System Description and Operation and perform the necessary inspections?	Go to *Step 2*	Go to *Symptoms* -
2	1. Turn ON the ignition, with the engine OFF. 2. Turn the windshield wiper/washer switch through all the switch positions. Do the windshield wipers operate properly?	*Test for Intermittent and Poor Connections*	Go to *Step 3*
3	1. Disconnect the windshield wiper motor connector. 2. Connect a test lamp between the accessory voltage circuit and a good ground. Does the test lamp illuminate?	Go to *Step 4*	Go to *Step 9*
4	Connect a test lamp between the accessory voltage circuit and the ground circuit of the windshield wiper motor connector. Does the test lamp illuminate?	Go to *Step 5*	Go to *Step 10*
5	1. Connect a test lamp between the windshield wiper switch on signal circuit and a good ground. 2. Activate the windshield washer/washer switch. Does the test lamp illuminate?	Go to *Step 7*	Go to *Step 6*
6	1. Disconnect the windshield wiper/washer switch connector. 2. Connect a test lamp between the accessory voltage circuit of the windshield wiper/washer switch connector and a good ground. Does the test lamp illuminate?	Go to *Step 8*	Go to *Step 11*
7	Inspect for a poor connection at the windshield wiper motor connector. Did you find and correct the condition?	Go to *Step 14*	Go to *Step 12*
8	Inspect for a poor connection at the windshield wiper/washer switch connector. Did you find and correct the condition?	Go to *Step 14*	Go to *Step 13*
9	Repair the open in the windshield wiper motor accessory voltage circuit. Did you complete the repair?	Go to *Step 14*	—
10	Repair the open in the windshield wiper motor ground circuit. Did you complete the repair?	Go to *Step 14*	—
11	Repair the open in the windshield wiper/washer switch accessory voltage circuit. Did you complete the repair?	Go to *Step 14*	—
12	Replace the windshield wiper motor. Did you complete the repair?	Go to *Step 14*	—
13	Replace the windshield wiper/washer switch. Did you complete the repair?	Go to *Step 14*	—
14	Operate the windshield wiper/washer system in order to verify the repair. Did you correct the condition?	System OK	Go to *Step 3*

GC9020200985000X

Fig. 55 Test 3: Wipers Inoperative In All Modes. Camaro & Firebird

Step	Action	Yes	No
1	Did you review the Wiper/Washer System Description and Operation and perform the necessary inspections?	Go to *Step 2*	Go to *Symptoms* -
2	1. Turn ON the ignition, with the engine OFF. 2. Turn the windshield wiper/washer switch to LO. 3. Turn the windshield wiper/washer switch to HI. 4. Turn OFF the windshield wiper/washer switch. Do the windshield wipers operate properly?	*Test for Intermittent and Poor Connections*	Go to *Step 3*
3	Disconnect the windshield wiper/washer switch connector. Do the windshield wipers stop?	Go to *Step 5*	Go to *Step 4*
4	Test the following circuits for a short to voltage: • windshield wiper switch on signal circuit • windshield wiper switch low/pulse signal circuit • windshield wiper motor high speed circuit Did you find and correct the condition?	Go to *Step 9*	Go to *Step 6*
5	Inspect for a poor connection at the windshield wiper/washer switch connector. Did you find and correct the condition?	Go to *Step 9*	Go to *Step 7*
6	Inspect for a poor connection at the windshield wiper motor connector. Did you find and correct the condition?	Go to *Step 9*	Go to *Step 8*
7	Replace the windshield wiper/washer switch. Did you complete the replacement?	Go to *Step 9*	—
8	Replace the windshield wiper motor cover. Did you complete the replacement?	Go to *Step 9*	—
9	Operate the windshield wiper/washer system in order to verify the repair. Did you correct the condition?	System OK	Go to *Step 3*

GC9020200984000X

Fig. 54 Test 2: Wipers Always On. Camaro & Firebird

Step	Action	Value(s)	Yes	No
1	Did you review the Wiper/Washer System Description and Operation and perform the necessary inspections?	—	Go to *Step 2*	Go to *Symptoms*
2	1. Turn ON the ignition, with the engine OFF. 2. Turn the windshield wiper/washer switch through all the switch positions. Do the windshield wipers operate properly in all modes?	—	*Test for Intermittent and Poor Connections*	Go to *Step 3*
3	Do the windshield wipers operate properly in HI mode?	—	Go to *Step 4*	Go to *Step 7*
4	1. Disconnect the windshield wiper motor connector. 2. Turn the windshield wiper/washer switch to LO. 3. Measure the voltage from the windshield wiper switch low/pulse signal circuit to a good ground. Does the voltage measure near the specified value?	B+	Go to *Step 5*	Go to *Step 8*
5	1. Measure the voltage from the windshield wiper switch low/pulse signal circuit to a good ground. 2. Turn the windshield wiper/washer switch through the entire DELAY range. Does the voltage measure near the specified value in each DELAY position?	B+	Go to *Step 6*	Go to *Step 13*
6	Measure the voltage from the windshield wiper switch on signal circuit to a good ground. Does the voltage measure near the specified value?	B+	Go to *Step 11*	Go to *Step 9*
7	1. Disconnect the windshield wiper motor connector. 2. Turn the windshield wiper/washer switch to HI. 3. Measure the voltage from the windshield wiper motor high speed circuit to a good ground. Does the voltage measure near the specified value?	B+	Go to *Step 12*	Go to *Step 10*
8	Test the windshield wiper switch low/pulse signal circuit for a short to ground or an open. Did you find and correct the condition?	—	Go to *Step 17*	Go to *Step 13*
9	Test the windshield wiper switch on signal circuit for short to ground or an open. Did you find and correct the condition?	—	Go to *Step 17*	Go to *Step 13*
10	Test the windshield wiper motor high speed circuit for short to ground or an open. Did you find and correct the condition?	—	Go to *Step 17*	Go to *Step 13*
11	Inspect for a poor connection at the windshield wiper motor connector. Did you find and correct the condition?	—	Go to *Step 17*	Go to *Step 14*
12	Inspect for a poor connection at the windshield wiper motor connector. Did you find and correct the condition?	—	Go to *Step 17*	Go to *Step 15*
13	Inspect for a poor connection at the windshield wiper/washer switch connector. Did you find and correct the condition?	Go to *Step 17*	Go to *Step 16*	

GC9020200986010X

Fig. 56 Test 4: Wipers Inoperative In One Or More Modes (Part 1 of 2). Camaro & Firebird

Step	Action	Value(s)	Yes	No
14	Replace the windshield wiper motor cover. Did you complete the replacement?	—	Go to *Step 17*	—
15	Replace the windshield wiper motor. Did you complete the replacement?	—	Go to *Step 17*	—
16	Replace the windshield wiper/washer switch. Did you complete the replacement?	—	Go to *Step 17*	—
17	Operate the windshield wiper/washer system in order to verify the repair. Did you correct the condition?	—	System OK	Go to *Step 3*

GC9020200986020X

Fig. 56 Test 4: Wipers Inoperative In One Or More Modes (Part 2 of 2). Camaro & Firebird

Step	Action	Value(s)	Yes	No
1	Did you review the Insrument Cluster Indicator Operation and perform the necessary inspections?	—	Go to *Step 2*	Check *Symptoms - Wiper/Washer Systems*
2	Turn the ignition on. Does the the low washer fluid indicator illuminate with the ignition on, engine off?	—	Go to *Step 4*	Go to *Step 3*
3	Inspect the low washer indicator lamp for an open and replace if necessary. Did you find and correct the condition?	—	Go to *Step 8*	Go to *Step 7*
4	1. Disconnect windshield washer fluid level switch connector. 2. Cycle the ignition switch off and on. Is the low washer fluid indicator on?	—	Go to *Step 5*	Go to *Step 6*
5	Test and repair the low washer fluid indicator control circuit for a short to ground. Did you find and correct the condition?	—	Go to *Step 8*	Go to *Step 7*
6	Replace the windshield washer fluid level switch. Is the repair complete?	—	Go to *Step 8*	—
7	Replace the instrument panel cluster. Is the repair complete?	—	Go to *Step 8*	—
8	Operate the system in order to verify the repair. Did you correct the condition?	—	System OK	Go to *Step 2*

GC9020000778000X

Fig. 58 Test 2: Low Washer Fluid Indicator Inoperative. Catera

Step	Action	Value(s)	Yes	No
1	Did you review the Wiper/Washer System Circuit Description and perform the necessary inspections?	—	Go to *Step 2*	Check *Symptoms - Wiper/Washer Systems*
2	1. Disconnect the windshield wiper motor relay K8. 2. Remove the WIPER fuse #9. 3. Connect a DMM from the wiper motor relay harness connector interval switch signal circuit terminal, to the accessory voltage circuit fuse terminal. 4. Turn the windshield wiper/washer switch to the delay position. 5. Measure the resistance through the delay and interval switches and circuits while rotating the interval switch through the adjustment range. Is the resistance within the specified values?	0.68K–5K Ω	Go to *Step 8*	Go to *Step 3*
3	1. Disconnect the windshield wiper/washer switch connector. 2. Turn the windshield wiper/washer switch to the delay position. 3. Measure the resistance through the delay switch. Is the resistance within the specified values.	0–2 Ω	Go to *Step 4*	Go to *Step 7*

GC9020000780010X

Fig. 60 Test 4: Wipers Delay Mode Inoperative (Part 1 of 2). Catera

Step	Action	Value(s)	Yes	No
4	1. Disconnect the interval switch connector. 2. Measure the resistance through the interval switch. 3. Rotate the interval switch through the adjustment range. Is the resistance within the specified values?	0.68K–5K Ω	Go to *Step 5*	Go to *Step 7*
5	Test and repair the delay switch signal circuit for an open or high resistance. Did you find and correct the condition?	—	Go to *Step 10*	Go to *Step 6*
6	Repair the open or high resistance in the interval switch signal circuit. Is the repair complete?	—	Go to *Step 10*	—
7	Replace the windshield wiper/washer switch. Is the repair complete?	—	Go to *Step 10*	—
8	Test and repair the accessory voltage circuit to the windshield wiper motor position switch for an open or high resistance. Did you find and correct the condition?	—	Go to *Step 10*	Go to *Step 9*
9	Replace the windshield wiper motor relay. Is the repair complete?	—	Go to *Step 10*	—
10	Operate the system in order to verify the repair. Did you correct the condition?	—	System OK	Go to *Step 2*

GC9020000780020X

Fig. 60 Test 4: Wipers Delay Mode Inoperative (Part 2 of 2). Catera

Step	Action	Value(s)	Yes	No
1	Did you review the Instrument Cluster Indicator Operation and perform the necessary inspections?	—	Go to *Step 2*	Check *Symptoms - Wiper/Washer Systems*
2	1. Inspect and fill the windshield washer fluid container as necessary. 2. Turn the ignition on. Is the low windshield washer fluid indicator on?	—	Go to *Step 3*	*Testing for Intermittent and Poor Connections*
3	1. Disconnect the windshield washer fluid level switch connector. 2. Connect a fused jumper wire from the low washer fluid indicator control circuit terminal to ground. 3. Turn the ignition switch off and on. Is the low washer fluid indicator illuminated?	—	Go to *Step 4*	Go to *Step 6*
4	Test and repair the low washer fluid indicator control circuit for an open or high resistance. Did you find and correct the condition?	—	Go to *Step 8*	Go to *Step 5*
5	Replace the instrument panel cluster. Is the repair complete?	—	Go to *Step 8*	—
6	Test and repair the windshield washer fluid level switch ground circuit for an open or high resistance. Did you find and correct the condition?	—	Go to *Step 8*	Go to *Step 7*
7	Replace the windshield washer fluid level switch. Is the repair complete?	—	Go to *Step 8*	—
8	Operate the system in order to verify the repair. Did you correct the condition?	—	System OK	Go to *Step 3*

GC9020000777000X

Fig. 57 Test 1: Low Washer Fluid Indicator Always On. Catera

Step	Action	Value(s)	Yes	No
1	Did you review the Wiper/Washer System Circuit Description and perform the necessary inspections?	—	Go to *Step 2*	Check *Symptoms - Wiper/Washer Systems*
2	1. Disconnect the windshield wiper motor connector. 2. Connect a test light from the high speed wiper motor supply circuit terminal to ground. 3. Turn the ignition on. 4. Turn the windshield wiper/washer switch to the high speed position. Does the test light illuminate?	—	Go to *Step 3*	Go to *Step 4*
3	Test and repair the windshield wiper motor ground circuit for an open or high resistance. Did you find and correct the condition?	—	Go to *Step 8*	Go to *Step 7*
4	1. Disconnect the windshield wiper/washer switch connector. 2. Connect a test light from the accessory voltage circuit terminal to ground. 3. Turn the ignition switch on. Does the test light illuminate?	—	Go to *Step 6*	Go to *Step 5*
5	Repair the open or high resistance in the accessory voltage circuit. Is the repair complete?	—	Go to *Step 8*	—
6	Replace the windshield wiper/washer switch. Is the repair complete?	—	Go to *Step 8*	—
7	Replace the windshield wiper motor. Is the repair complete?	—	Go to *Step 8*	—
8	Operate the system in order to verify the repair. Did you correct the condition?	—	System OK	Go to *Step 2*

GC9020000779000X

Fig. 59 Test 3: Wipers All Modes Inoperative. Catera

Step	Action	Value(s)	Yes	No
1	Did you review the Wiper/Washer System Circuit Description and perform the necessary inspections?	—	Go to *Step 2*	Check *Symptoms - Wiper/Washer Systems*
2	1. Disconnect the windshield wiper motor connector. 2. Connect a test light from the wiper motor high speed supply circuit in the wiper motor connector to ground. 3. Turn the ignition switch on. 4. Turn the windshield wiper/washer switch to the high speed position. Does the test light illuminate?	—	Go to *Step 5*	Go to *Step 3*
3	Test and repair the wiper motor high speed supply circuit for an open or high resistance. Did you find and correct the condition?	—	Go to *Step 6*	Go to *Step 4*
4	Replace the windshield wiper/washer switch. Is the repair complete?	—	Go to *Step 6*	—
5	1. Inspect for a faulty connection at the windshield wiper motor connector. 2. If the connection is OK, replace the windshield wiper motor. Is the repair complete?	—	Go to *Step 6*	—
6	Operate the system in order to verify the repair. Did you correct the condition?	—	System OK	Go to *Step 2*

GC9020000781000X

Fig. 61 Test 5: Wipers High Mode Inoperative. Catera

Step	Action	Value(s)	Yes	No
1	Did you review the Wiper/Washer System Circuit Description and perform the necessary inspections?	—	Go to *Step 2*	Check *Symptoms - Wiper/Washer Systems*
2	1. Disconnect the windshield wiper motor connector. 2. Connect a test light from the windshield wiper motor connector wiper motor low speed supply circuit terminal to ground. 3. Turn the ignition switch on. 4. Turn the windshield wiper/washer switch to the low speed position. Does the test light illuminate?	—	Go to *Step 5*	Go to *Step 3*
3	Test and repair the wiper motor low speed supply circuit for an open or high resistance. Did you find and correct the condition?	—	Go to *Step 6*	Go to *Step 4*
4	Replace the windshield wiper/washer switch. Is the repair complete?	—	Go to *Step 6*	—
5	1. Inspect for a faulty connection at the windshield wiper motor connector. 2. If the connection is OK, replace the windshield wiper motor. Is the repair complete?	—	Go to *Step 6*	—
6	Operate the system in order to verify the repair. Did you correct the condition?	—	System OK	Go to *Step 2*

GC9020000782000X

Fig. 62 Test 6: Wipers Low Mode Inoperative, High Mode Operates. Catera

Step	Action	Value(s)	Yes	No
6	Test and repair the following circuits for a short to voltage. • interval switch signal circuit • delay switch signal circuit Did you find and correct the condition?	—	*Go to Step 13*	*Go to Step 10*
7	Connect a test light from the washer switch signal circuit terminal in the wiper motor relay harness connector to ground. Does the test light illuminate?	—	*Go to Step 8*	*Go to Step 11*
8	Test and repair the washer switch signal circuit for a short to voltage. Did you find and correct the condition?	—	*Go to Step 13*	*Go to Step 10*
9	Test and repair the following circuits for a short to voltage. • wiper motor low speed supply circuit • wiper motor high speed supply circuit • wiper/washer switch relay functions supply circuit Did you find and correct the condition?	—	*Go to Step 13*	*Go to Step 10*
10	Replace the windshield wiper/washer switch. Is the repair complete?	—	*Go to Step 13*	—
11	Replace the windshield wiper motor relay K8. Is the repair complete?	—	*Go to Step 13*	—
12	Replace the windshield wiper motor. Is the repair complete?	—	*Go to Step 13*	—
13	Operate the system in order to verify the repair. Did you correct the condition?	—	System OK	*Go to Step 2*

GC9020000783020X

Fig. 63 Test 7: Wipers Always On (Part 2 of 2). Catera

Step	Action	Value(s)	Yes	No
1	Did you review the Wiper/Washer System Circuit Description and perform the necessary inspections?	—	*Go to Step 2*	Check *Symptoms - Wiper/Washer Systems*
2	Do the windshield wipers operate properly when the windshield wiper/washer switch is in the wash position?	—	*Go to Step 7*	*Go to Step 3*
3	1. Disconnect the windshield wiper motor relay K8. 2. Connect a test light from the washer switch signal circuit terminal in the wiper motor relay harness connector to ground. 3. Turn the ignition on. 4. Pull the windshield wiper washer switch to the wash position. Does the test light illuminate?	—	*Go to Step 6*	*Go to Step 4*
4	1. Disconnect the windshield wiper/washer switch connector. 2. Test and repair the washer switch signal circuit for an open or high resistance. Did you find and correct the condition?	—	*Go to Step 11*	*Go to Step 5*
5	Replace the windshield wiper/washer switch. Is the repair complete?	—	*Go to Step 11*	—
6	Replace the windshield wiper motor relay K8. Is the repair complete?	—	*Go to Step 11*	—
7	1. Disconnect the windshield washer pump connector. 2. Connect a test light from the washer switch signal circuit terminal in the washer pump connector to ground. 3. Turn the ignition on. 4. Pull the windshield wiper washer switch to the wash position. Does the test light illuminate?	—	*Go to Step 9*	*Go to Step 8*
8	Repair the windshield washer control circuit for an open or high resistance. Is the repair complete?	—	*Go to Step 11*	—
9	Test and repair the windshield washer pump ground circuit for an open or high resistance. Did you find and correct the condition?	—	*Go to Step 11*	*Go to Step 10*
10	Replace the windshield washer pump. Is the repair complete?	—	*Go to Step 11*	—
11	Operate the system in order to verify the repair. Did you correct the condition?	—	System OK	*Go to Step 2*

GC9020000785000X

Fig. 65 Test 9: Washers Inoperative (Wipers or Pump). Catera

Step	Action	Value(s)	Yes	No
1	Did you review the Wiper/Washer System Circuit Description and perform the necessary inspections?	—	Go to *Step 2*	Check *Symptoms - Wiper/Washer Systems*
2	1. Disconnect the windshield wiper motor relay K8. 2. Turn the ignition on. With the windshield wiper/washer switch in the OFF position are the windshield wipers on?	—	Go to *Step 9*	Go to *Step 3*
3	1. Connect a test light from the battery positive terminal to the wiper motor position switch signal circuit terminal in the wiper motor relay harness connector. 2. Turn the windshield wiper/washer switch to the low speed position. Does the test light flash every time the wiper arms are in the park position?	—	Go to *Step 5*	Go to *Step 4*
4	Test and repair the windshield wiper motor position switch signal circuit for an open or high resistance. Did you find and correct the condition?	—	*Go to Step 13*	*Go to Step 12*
5	1. Turn the windshield wiper/washer switch off. 2. Using a DMM measure for voltage at the windshield wiper motor relay harness connector interval switch signal circuit terminal. Is the voltage within the specified values?	0-0.1 volts	Go to *Step 7*	Go to *Step 6*

GC9020000783010X

Fig. 63 Test 7: Wipers Always On (Part 1 of 2). Catera

Step	Action	Value(s)	Yes	No
1	Did you review the Wiper/Washer System Circuit Description and perform the necessary inspections?	—	Go to *Step 2*	Check *Symptoms - Wiper/Washer Systems*
2	1. Disconnect the windshield wiper motor relay. 2. Connect a test light from the wiper motor position switch signal circuit terminal in the wiper motor relay harness connector to ground. 3. Turn the ignition switch on. 4. Turn the windshield wiper/washer switch to the low speed position. Does the test light illuminate while the wiper arms are up?	—	Go to *Step 3*	Go to *Step 4*
3	Replace the windshield wiper motor relay K8. Is the repair complete?	—	Go to *Step 6*	—
4	Test and repair the accessory voltage circuit to the wiper motor position switch for an open or high resistance. Did you find and correct the condition?	—	Go to *Step 6*	Go to *Step 5*
5	Replace the windshield wiper motor. Is the repair complete?	—	Go to *Step 6*	—
6	Operate the system in order to verify the repair. Did you correct the condition?	—	System OK	Go to *Step 2*

GC9020000784000X

Fig. 64 Test 8: Wipers Blades Do Not Park. Catera

Step	Action	Value(s)	Yes	No
1	Did you review the Wiper/Washer System Circuit Description and perform the necessary inspections?	—	*Go to Step 2*	Check *Symptoms - Wiper/Washer Systems*
2	1. Disconnect the inoperative windshield washer nozzle connector. 2. Connect a test light from the accessory voltage circuit terminal in the windshield washer nozzle connector to ground. 3. Turn the ignition switch on. Does the test light illuminate?	—	*Go to Step 4*	*Go to Step 3*
3	Repair the open or high resistance in the accessory voltage circuit to the windshield washer nozzle. Is the repair complete?	—	*Go to Step 7*	—
4	Connect a test light across the inoperative windshield washer nozzle connector terminals. Does the test light illuminate?	—	*Go to Step 6*	*Go to Step 5*
5	Repair the open or high resistance in the windshield washer nozzle ground circuit. Is the repair complete?	—	*Go to Step 7*	—
6	Replace the inoperative windshield washer nozzle. Is the replacement complete?	—	*Go to Step 7*	—
7	Operate the system in order to verify the repair. Did you correct the condition?	—	System OK	*Go to Step 2*

GC9020000786000X

Fig. 66 Test 10: Washers Inoperative (Washer Nozzles). Catera

Step	Action	Normal Result(s)	Abnormal Result(s)*
1	1. Turn the ignition switch to RUN. 2. Hold the washer switch in the ON position with the wiper switch OFF.	The wipers operate at low speed. The washer sprays the windshield as long as the washer switch is held ON. After releasing the switch, the washer stops and the wipers return to the park position after 3-5 sweeps.	• *Washers Inoperative.* • *Wipers Mist, Delay, and Low Modes Inoperative.*
2	Turn the wiper switch to DELAY (pulse mode).	The wipers make one complete sweep, then pause for 1-22 seconds before making the next sweep. The pause time is adjusted by turning the wiper switch through the delay range.	• *Wipers Delay Mode Inoperative.* • *Wipers Mist, Delay, and Low Modes Inoperative.*
3	1. Turn the wiper switch to the DELAY position. 2. Press the washer switch to ON.	The washer sprays the windshield as long as the washer switch is held ON. The wipers run at low speed during the spray period and continues for 3–5 sweeps after the washer switch is released. The wipers then return to pulse operation.	• *Washers Inoperative.* • *Wipers Delay Mode Inoperative.* • *Wipers Mist, Delay, and Low Modes Inoperative.*
4	Turn the wiper switch to LO.	The wipers run continuously at low speed.	*Wipers Mist, Delay, and Low Modes Inoperative.*
5	Turn the wiper switch to HI.	The wipers run continuously at high speed.	*Wipers High Mode Inoperative, Low Mode Operates.*
6	Turn the wiper switch to OFF.	The wipers return to the park position at low speed.	• *Wipers Blades Do Not Park.* • *Wipers Always On.*
7	Turn the wiper switch to MIST, then release.	The wipers make one complete sweep at low speed, then return to the park position.	*Wipers Mist, Delay, and Low Modes Inoperative.*

GC9020000768000X

Fig. 67 Wiper/Washer System Check. Cavalier & Sunfire

Step	Action	Value(s)	Yes	No
9	1. Disconnect the wiper motor connector. 2. Connect a J 34142 B from the wiper motor connector, terminal C, to ground. Is the test light on?	—	Go to *Step 11*	Go to *Step 10*
10	Repair the poor connection or the open in CKT 92. Is the repair complete?	—	Go to *Wiper/Washer System Check*	—
11	Connect a J 34142 B from the wiper motor connector, terminal C to terminal A. Is the test light on?	—	Go to *Step 13*	Go to *Step 12*
12	Repair the poor connection or the open in CKT 251. Is the repair complete?	—	Go to *Wiper/Washer System Check*	—
13	Check for a poor connection to the wiper motor. Is a poor connection present?	—	Go to *Step 15*	Go to *Step 14*
14	Replace the wiper motor. Is the replacement complete?	—	Go to *Wiper/Washer System Check*	—
15	Repair the poor connection to the wiper motor. Is the repair complete?	—	Go to *Wiper/Washer System Check*	—
16	Replace the wiper/washer switch. Is the replacement complete?	—	Go to *Wiper/Washer System Check*	—

GC9020000769020X

Fig. 68 Test 1: Wipers All Modes Inoperative (Part 2 of 2). Cavalier & Sunfire

Step	Action	Value(s)	Yes	No
5	Inspect for a poor connection or an open in CKT 112. Is a poor connection or an open present?	—	Go to *Step 6*	Go to *Step 7*
6	Repair the poor connection or the open in CKT 112. Is the repair complete?	—	Go to *Wiper/Washer System Check*	—
7	Replace the wiper motor cover. Is the replacement complete?	—	Go to *Wiper/Washer System Check*	—

GC9020000770020X

Fig. 69 Test 2: Wipers Delay Mode Inoperative (Part 2 of 2). Cavalier & Sunfire

Step	Action	Value(s)	Yes	No
1	Was the Wiper/Washer System Check performed?	—	Go to *Step 2*	Go to *Wiper/Washer System Check*
2	Inspect for an open WIPER fuse. Is the fuse open?	—	Go to *Step 3*	Go to *Step 4*
3	Replace the WIPER fuse. Is the replacement complete?	—	Go to *Wiper/Washer System Check*	—
4	1. Set the ignition switch to RUN. 2. Backprobe from the wiper/washer switch connector, terminal F, to ground using a J 34142 B. Is the test light on?	—	Go to *Step 6*	Go to *Step 5*
5	Repair the poor connection or open in CKT 143 to the wiper/washer switch. Is the repair complete?	—	Go to *Wiper/Washer System Check*	—
6	1. Set the wiper switch to HI. 2. Connect a J 34142 B from the wiper/washer switch connector, terminal D to ground. Is the test light on?	—	Go to *Step 9*	Go to *Step 7*
7	Check for a poor connection to the wiper/washer switch. Is a poor connection present?	—	Go to *Step 8*	Go to *Step 16*
8	Repair the poor connection to the wiper/washer switch. Is the repair complete?	—	Go to *Wiper/Washer System Check*	—

GC9020000769010X

Fig. 68 Test 1: Wipers All Modes Inoperative (Part 1 of 2). Cavalier & Sunfire

Step	Action	Value(s)	Yes	No
1	Was the Wiper/Washer System Check performed?	—	Go to *Step 2*	Go to *Wiper/Washer System Check*
2	1. Turn the ignition to OFF. 2. Disconnect wiper/washer switch connector. 3. Turn the wiper switch to DELAY. 4. Measure the resistance through the wiper/washer switch from switch terminal F to terminal B using a *J 39200* set to the ohm scale. 5. Move the wiper switch through the entire delay range, one notch at a time. Does the resistance vary within the specified range?	39 to 680 KΩ	Go to *Step 4*	Go to *Step 3*
3	Replace the wiper/washer switch. Is the replacement complete?	—	Go to *Wiper/Washer System Check*	—
4	1. Reconnect the wiper/washer switch connector. 2. Disconnect the wiper motor connector. 3. Turn the ignition switch to RUN. 4. Turn the wiper switch to DELAY. 5. Measure the voltage from the wiper motor connector, terminal E, to ground. Is the measurement within the specified values?	10.5–15 V	Go to *Step 7*	Go to *Step 5*

GC9020000770010X

Fig. 69 Test 2: Wipers Delay Mode Inoperative (Part 1 of 2). Cavalier & Sunfire

Step	Action	Value(s)	Yes	No
1	Was the Wiper/Washer System Check performed?	—	Go to *Step 2*	Go to *Wiper/Washer System Check*
2	Do the wipers operate at all with the wiper switch in HI?	—	Go to *Step 4*	Go to *Step 3*
3	Replace the wiper/washer switch. Is the replacement complete?	—	Go to *Wiper/Washer System Check*	—
4	1. Turn the ignition switch to RUN. 2. Turn the wiper switch to HI. 3. Backprobe from the wiper/washer switch connector, terminal D, to ground using a J 34142 B. Is the test light on?	—	Go to *Step 8*	Go to *Step 5*
5	Inspect for a poor connection at the wiper/washer switch connector, or for an open in the pigtail to the wiper/washer switch. Is a poor connection or open present?	—	Go to *Step 7*	Go to *Step 6*
6	Replace the wiper/washer switch. Is the replacement complete?	—	Go to *Wiper/Washer System Check*	—
7	Repair the poor connection or the open in the pigtail to the wiper/washer switch. Is the repair complete?	—	Go to *Wiper/Washer System Check*	—
8	1. Disconnect the wiper motor connector. 2. Connect a J 34142 B from the wiper motor connector, terminal C, to ground. Is the test light on?	—	Go to *Step 10*	Go to *Step 9*
9	Repair the open in CKT 92. Is the repair complete?	—	Go to *Wiper/Washer System Check*	—
10	Check for a poor connection to the wiper motor. Is a poor connection present?	—	Go to *Step 11*	Go to *Step 12*
11	Repair the poor connection to the wiper motor. Is the repair complete?	—	Go to *Wiper/Washer System Check*	—
12	Replace the wiper motor. Is the repair complete?	—	Go to *Wiper/Washer System Check*	—

GC9020000771000X

Fig. 70 Test 3: Wipers High Mode Inoperative, Low Mode Operates. Cavalier & Sunfire

Step	Action	Value(s)	Yes	No
1	Was the Wiper/Washer System Check performed?	—	Go to *Step 2*	Go to *Wiper/Washer System Check*
2	1. Turn the ignition switch to RUN. 2. Turn the wiper switch to LO. 3. Measure the voltage by backprobing from the wiper/washer switch connector, terminal C, to ground using a *J 39200.* Is the measurement greater than the specified value?	1 V	Go to *Step 6*	Go to *Step 3*
3	Check for a poor connection at the wiper/washer connector, or for an open in the pigtail wires to the wiper/washer switch. Is a poor connection or an open present?	—	Go to *Step 5*	Go to *Step 4*
4	Replace the wiper/washer switch. Is the replacement complete?	—	Go to *Wiper/Washer System Check*	—
5	Repair the poor connection or the open in the pigtail wires to the wiper/washer switch. Is the repair complete?	—	Go to *Wiper/Washer System Check*	—
6	Measure the voltage by backprobing from the wiper/washer switch connector, terminal B, to ground using a *J 39200.* Is the measurement greater than the specified value?	1 V	Go to *Step 7*	Go to *Step 3*
7	1. Disconnect the wiper motor connector. 2. Measure the voltage from the wiper motor connector, terminal D, to ground using a *J 39200.* Is the measurement greater than the specified value?	1 V	Go to *Step 9*	Go to *Step 8*
8	Repair the open in CKT 113. Is the repair complete?	—	Go to *Wiper/Washer System Check*	—
9	Measure the voltage from the wiper motor connector, terminal E, to ground using a *J 39200.* Is the measurement greater than the specified value?	1 V	Go to *Step 11*	Go to *Step 10*
10	Repair the open in CKT 112. Is the repair complete?	—	Go to *Wiper/Washer System Check*	—
11	Replace the wiper motor cover. Is the replacement complete?	—	Go to *Wiper/Washer System Check*	—

GC9020000772000X

Fig. 71 Test 4: Wipers Mist, Delay, & Low Modes Inoperative. Cavalier & Sunfire

Step	Action	Value(s)	Yes	No
1	Was the Wiper/Washer System Check performed?	—	Go to *Step 2*	Go to *Wiper/Washer System Check*
2	1. Turn the ignition switch to RUN. 2. Turn the wiper switch to OFF. 3. Disconnect the wiper/washer switch connector. Do the wipers park?	—	Go to *Step 3*	Go to *Step 4*
3	Replace the wiper/washer switch. Is the replacement complete?	—	Go to *Wiper/Washer System Check*	—
4	Measure the voltage from the wiper/washer switch connector (vehicle side), terminal C, to ground using a *J 39200.* Is the measurement greater than the specified value?	1 V	Go to *Step 10*	Go to *Step 5*
5	Measure the voltage from the wiper/washer switch connector (vehicle side), terminal B, to ground using a *J 39200.* Is the measurement greater than the specified value?	1 V	Go to *Step 7*	Go to *Step 6*
6	Replace the wiper motor cover. Is the replacement complete?	—	Go to *Wiper/Washer System Check*	—
7	1. Reconnect the wiper/washer switch connector. 2. Disconnect the wiper motor connector. 3. Measure the voltage from the wiper motor connector, terminal E, to ground using a *J 39200.* Is the measurement greater than the specified value?	1 V	Go to *Step 9*	Go to *Step 8*
8	Replace the wiper motor cover. Is the replacement complete?	—	Go to *Wiper/Washer System Check*	—
9	Repair the short circuit to battery voltage condition in CKT 112. Is the repair complete?	—	Go to *Wiper/Washer System Check*	—
10	1. Reconnect the wiper/washer switch connector. 2. Disconnect the wiper motor connector. 3. Measure the voltage from the wiper motor connector, terminal D, to ground using a *J 39200.* Is the measurement greater than the specified value?	1 V	Go to *Step 12*	Go to *Step 11*
11	Replace the wiper motor cover. Is the replacement complete?	—	Go to *Wiper/Washer System Check*	—
12	Repair the short to voltage in CKT 113. Is the repair complete?	—	Go to *Wiper/Washer System Check*	—

GC9020000774000X

Fig. 73 Test 6: Wiper Blades Do Not Park. Cavalier & Sunfire

Step	Action	Value(s)	Yes	No
1	Was the Wiper/Washer System Check performed?	—	Go to *Step 2*	Go to *Wiper/Washer System Check*
2	1. Set the ignition switch to RUN. 2. Set the wiper switch to OFF. 3. Disconnect the wiper/washer switch connector. Do the wipers keep running?	—	Go to *Step 6*	Go to *Step 3*
3	Check for a short to voltage in the pigtail wires to the wiper/washer switch. Is a short to voltage present?	—	Go to *Step 4*	Go to *Step 5*
4	Repair the short to voltage in the pigtail wires to the wiper/washer switch. Is the repair complete?	—	Go to *Wiper/Washer System Check*	—
5	Replace the wiper/washer switch. Is the replacement complete?	—	Go to *Wiper/Washer System Check*	—
6	Measure the voltage from the wiper/washer switch connector, terminal C, to ground using a *J 39200.* Is the measurement greater than the specified value?	1 V	Go to *Step 11*	Go to *Step 7*
7	Measure the voltage from the wiper/washer switch connector, terminal B, to ground using a *J 39200.* Is the measurement greater than the specified value?	1 V	Go to *Step 14*	Go to *Step 8*
8	1. Reconnect the wiper/washer switch connector. 2. Disconnect the wiper motor connector. 3. Measure the voltage from wiper motor connector, terminal C, to ground using a *J 39200.* Is the measurement within the specified values?	10.5–15 V	Go to *Step 9*	Go to *Step 10*
9	Repair the short to voltage in CKT 92. Is the repair complete?	—	Go to *Wiper/Washer System Check*	—
10	Replace the wiper motor cover. Is the replacement complete?	—	Go to *Wiper/Washer System Check*	—
11	1. Reconnect the wiper/washer switch connector. 2. Disconnect the wiper motor connector. 3. Measure the voltage from wiper motor connector terminal D to ground using a *J 39200.* Is the measurement greater than the specified value?	1 V	Go to *Step 13*	Go to *Step 12*
12	Replace the wiper motor cover. Is the replacement complete?	—	Go to *Wiper/Washer System Check*	—
13	Repair the short to voltage in CKT 113. Is the repair complete?	—	Go to *Wiper/Washer System Check*	—
14	1. Reconnect the wiper/washer switch connector. 2. Disconnect the wiper motor connector. 3. Measure the voltage from wiper motor connector, terminal E, to ground using a *J 39200.* Is the measurement within the specified values?	10.5–15 V	Go to *Step 16*	Go to *Step 15*
15	Replace the wiper motor cover. Is the replacement complete?	—	Go to *Wiper/Washer System Check*	—
16	Repair the short to voltage in CKT 112. Is the repair complete?	—	Go to *Wiper/Washer System Check*	—

GC9020000773000X

Fig. 72 Test 5: Wipers Always On. Cavalier & Sunfire

Step	Action	Value(s)	Yes	No
1	Was the Wiper/Washer System Check performed?	—	Go to *Step 2*	Go to *Wiper/Washer System Check*
2	Inspect the washer solvent container fluid level. Is the washer solvent container filled?	—	Go to *Step 4*	Go to *Step 3*
3	Fill the washer solvent container. Is the washer solvent container filled?	—	Go to *Wiper/Washer System Check*	—
4	Inspect the hoses to ensure that they are correctly attached and that they are not pinched or kinked. Are the hoses OK?	—	Go to *Step 6*	Go to *Step 5*
5	Repair the hoses. Are the hoses repaired?	—	Go to *Wiper/Washer System Check*	—
6	Inspect for clogged windshield washer nozzles. Are the nozzles clogged?	—	Go to *Step 7*	Go to *Step 8*
7	Clear the clogged nozzles. Are the nozzles clear?	—	Go to *Wiper/Washer System Check*	—
8	1. Disconnect the washer pump connector. 2. Turn the ignition switch to ON. 3. Connect a J 34142 B between terminal A and terminal B of the washer pump connector (harness side). 4. Activate the washer switch while observing the test light. Is the test light on?	—	Go to *Step 9*	Go to *Step 12*
9	Inspect for a poor connection at the washer pump connector. Is a poor connection present?	—	Go to *Step 10*	Go to *Step 11*
10	Repair the poor connection at the washer pump connector. Is the repair complete?	—	Go to *Wiper/Washer System Check*	—
11	Replace the washer pump. Is the replacement complete?	—	Go to *Wiper/Washer System Check*	—
12	1. Connect a J 34142 B from the washer pump connector (harness side), terminal A, to ground. 2. Activate the washer switch while observing the test light. Is the test light on?	—	Go to *Step 13*	Go to *Step 14*
13	Repair the poor connection or open in CKT 150. Is the repair complete?	—	Go to *Wiper/Washer System Check*	—
14	1. Backprobe the wiper/washer switch connector, terminal E, to ground using a J34142 B. 2. Activate the washer switch. Is the test light on?	—	Go to *Step 16*	Go to *Step 15*
15	Repair the poor connection or open in CKT 228. Is the repair complete?	—	Go to *Wiper/Washer System Check*	—
16	Replace the wiper/washer switch. Is the replacement complete?	—	Go to *Wiper/Washer System Check*	—

GC9020000775000X

Fig. 74 Test 7: Washers Inoperative. Cavalier & Sunfire

Step	Action	Yes	No
1	Did you review the Wiper/Washer System Description and Operation and perform the necessary inspections?	Go to *Step 2*	Go to *Symptoms -*
2	1. Turn ON the ignition, with the engine OFF. 2. Observe the low washer fluid indicator. Does the low washer fluid indicator illuminate?	Go to *Step 5*	Go to *Step 3*
3	1. Disconnect the windshield washer solvent level sensor connector. 2. Connect a 3-amp fused jumper wire between the low washer fluid indicator control circuit and a good ground. 3. Wait for 2 ½ minutes. Does the low washer fluid indicator illuminate?	Go to *Step 4*	Go to *Step 7*
4	1. Connect a 3-amp fused jumper wire between the low washer fluid indicator control circuit and the windshield washer solvent level sensor ground circuit. 2. Wait for 2 ½ minutes. Does the low washer fluid indicator illuminate?	Go to *Step 8*	Go to *Step 10*
5	1. Disconnect the windshield washer solvent level sensor connector. 2. Wait for 2 ½ minutes. Did the low washer fluid indicator turn OFF?	Go to *Step 8*	Go to *Step 6*
6	Test the low washer fluid indicator signal circuit for a short to ground. Did you find and correct the condition?	Go to *Step 13*	Go to *Step 9*

GC9020200987010X

Fig. 75 Test 1: Low Washer Fluid Indicator Fault (Part 1 of 2). Century, Grand Prix & Regal

Step	Action	Value(s)	Yes	No
1	Did you review the Wiper/Washer System Description and Operation and perform the necessary inspections?	—	Go to *Step 2*	Go to *Symptoms*
2	1. Turn ON the ignition, with the engine OFF. 2. Activate the windshield washer switch. Does the windshield washer operate properly?	—	*Test for Intermittent and Poor Connections*	Go to *Step 3*
3	Test for a short to voltage in the windshield washer pump control circuit. Did you find and correct the condition?	—	Go to *Step 5*	Go to *Step 4*
4	Replace the wiper/washer switch. Did you complete the replacement?	—	Go to *Step 5*	—
5	Operate the system in order to verify the repair. Did you correct the condition?	—	System OK	Go to *Step 3*

GC9020200988000X

Fig. 76 Test 2: Washer Always On. Century, Grand Prix & Regal

Step	Action	Yes	No
1	Did you review the Wiper/Washer System Description and Operation and perform the necessary inspections?	Go to *Step 2*	Go to *Symptoms -*
2	1. Turn ON the ignition, with the engine OFF. 2. Turn the wiper/washer switch to LO. 3. Turn the wiper/washer switch to HI. 4. Turn OFF the wiper/washer switch. Do the windshield wipers operate properly?	*Test for Intermittent and Poor Connections*	Go to *Step 3*
3	Disconnect the wiper/washer switch connector. Do the windshield wipers stop?	Go to *Step 5*	Go to *Step 4*
4	Test the following circuits for a short to voltage: • Windshield wiper/washer switch on signal circuit • Windshield wiper switch low/pulse signal circuit • Windshield wiper motor high speed circuit. Did you find and correct the condition?	Go to *Step 7*	Go to *Step 6*

GC9020200990010X

Fig. 78 Test 4: Wipers Always On (Part 1 of 2). Century, Grand Prix & Regal

Step	Action	Yes	No
5	Replace the windshield wiper/washer switch. Did you complete the replacement?	Go to *Step 7*	—
6	Replace the wiper motor cover. Did you complete the replacement?	Go to *Step 7*	—
7	Operate the system in order to verify the repair. Did you correct the condition?	System OK	Go to *Step 3*

GC9020200990020X

Fig. 78 Test 4: Wipers Always On (Part 2 of 2). Century, Grand Prix & Regal

Step	Action	Yes	No
7	Test the low washer fluid indicator signal circuit for an open or high resistance. Did you find and correct the condition?	Go to *Step 13*	Go to *Step 9*
8	Inspect for a poor connection at the windshield washer solvent level sensor. Did you find and correct the condition?	Go to *Step 13*	Go to *Step 11*
9	Inspect for a poor connection at the IPC connector. Did you find and correct the condition?	Go to *Step 13*	Go to *Step 12*
10	Repair the open or high resistance in the low washer fluid indicator ground circuit. Did you find and correct the condition?	Go to *Step 13*	—
11	Replace the windshield washer solvent level sensor. Did you complete the replacement?	Go to *Step 13*	—
12	Replace the IPC. Did you complete the replacement?	Go to *Step 13*	—
13	Operate the windshield wiper/washer system in order to verify the repair. Did you correct the condition?	System OK	Go to *Step 3*

GC9020200987020X

Fig. 75 Test 1: Low Washer Fluid Indicator Fault (Part 2 of 2). Century, Grand Prix & Regal

Step	Action	Yes	No
1	Did you review the Wiper/Washer System Description and Operation and perform the necessary inspections?	Go to *Step 2*	Go to *Symptoms -*
2	1. Turn ON the ignition, with the engine OFF. 2. Activate the windshield washer switch. Does the windshield washer operate properly?	*Test for Intermittent and Poor Connections*	Go to *Step 3*
3	1. Disconnect the windshield washer pump connector. 2. Connect a test lamp between the windshield washer pump control circuit and the windshield washer pump ground circuit. 3. Activate the windshield washer switch. Does the test lamp illuminate?	Go to *Step 7*	Go to *Step 4*
4	Test the windshield washer pump ground circuit for high resistance or an open. Did you find and correct the condition?	Go to *Step 8*	Go to *Step 5*
5	Test the windshield washer pump control circuit for high resistance, a short to ground or an open. Did you find and correct the condition?	Go to *Step 8*	Go to *Step 6*
6	Replace the wiper/washer switch. Did you complete the replacement?	Go to *Step 8*	—
7	Replace the windshield washer pump. Did you complete the replacement?	Go to *Step 8*	—
8	Operate the system in order to verify the repair. Did you correct the condition?	System OK	Go to *Step 3*

GC9020200989000X

Fig. 77 Test 3: Washer Inoperative. Century, Grand Prix & Regal

Step	Action	Yes	No
1	Did you review the Wiper/Washer System Description and Operation and perform the necessary inspections?	Go to *Step 2*	Go to *Symptoms -*
2	1. Turn ON the ignition, with the engine OFF. 2. Turn the windshield wiper/washer switch through all the switch positions. Do the windshield wipers operate properly?	*Test for Intermittent and Poor Connections*	Go to *Step 3*
3	1. Disconnect the windshield wiper motor connector. 2. Connect a test lamp between the accessory voltage circuit and a good ground. Does the test lamp illuminate?	Go to *Step 4*	Go to *Step 7*
4	Connect a test lamp between the accessory voltage circuit and the ground circuit of the windshield wiper motor connector. Does the test lamp illuminate?	Go to *Step 5*	Go to *Step 8*
5	1. Connect a test lamp between the windshield wiper switch on signal circuit and a good ground. 2. Activate the windshield washer switch. Does the test lamp illuminate?	Go to *Step 10*	Go to *Step 6*
6	1. Disconnect the windshield wiper/washer switch connector. 2. Connect a test lamp between the accessory voltage circuit and a good ground. Does the test lamp illuminate?	Go to *Step 11*	Go to *Step 9*
7	Repair the open in the windshield wiper motor accessory voltage circuit. Did you complete the repair?	Go to *Step 12*	—
8	Repair the open in the windshield wiper motor ground circuit. Did you complete the repair?	Go to *Step 12*	—
9	Repair the open in the windshield wiper/washer switch accessory voltage circuit. Did you complete the repair?	Go to *Step 12*	—
10	Replace the windshield wiper motor. Did you complete the repair?	Go to *Step 12*	—
11	Replace the windshield wiper/washer switch. Did you complete the repair?	Go to *Step 12*	—
12	Operate the system in order to verify the repair. Did you correct the condition?	System OK	Go to *Step 3*

GC9020200991000X

Fig. 79 Test 5: Wipers Inoperative. Century, Grand Prix & Regal

Step	Action	Value(s)	Yes	No
1	Did you review the Wiper/Washer System Description and Operation and perform the necessary inspections?	—	Go to *Step 2*	Go to *Symptoms*
2	1. Turn ON the ignition, with the engine OFF. 2. Turn the windshield wiper/washer switch through all the switch positions. Do the windshield wipers operate properly in all modes?	—	*Test for Intermittent and Poor Connections*	Go to *Step 3*
3	1. Disconnect the windshield wiper/washer switch connector. 2. Measure the resistance between the accessory voltage circuit and the windshield wiper switch low/pulse signal circuit of the wiper/washer switch. 3. Turn the wiper/washer switch to the following positions: • MIST • LO • HI Does the resistance measure greater than the specified value?	2 Ω	Go to *Step 10*	Go to *Step 4*
4	1. Measure the resistance between the accessory voltage circuit and the windshield wiper switch low/pulse signal circuit of the wiper/washer switch. 2. Turn the wiper/washer switch through the DELAY range. Does the resistance measure within the specified values?	39K–680K Ω	Go to *Step 5*	Go to *Step 10*
5	1. Measure the resistance between the accessory voltage circuit and the windshield wiper switch on signal circuit of the wiper/washer switch. 2. Turn the wiper/washer switch to the following positions: • MIST • DELAY • LO • HI Does the resistance measure near the specified value?	24K Ω	Go to *Step 6*	Go to *Step 10*
6	1. Reconnect the windshield wiper/washer switch connector. 2. Turn the wiper/washer switch to HI. Do the windshield wipers operate properly in HI mode?	—	Go to *Step 7*	Go to *Step 9*
7	Test the windshield wiper switch low/pulse signal circuit for high resistance or an open. Did you find and correct the condition?	—	Go to *Step 13*	Go to *Step 8*
8	Test the windshield wiper switch on signal circuit for high resistance or an open. Did you find and correct the condition?	—	Go to *Step 13*	Go to *Step 11*
9	Test the windshield wiper motor high speed circuit for high resistance or an open. Did you find and correct the condition?	—	Go to *Step 13*	Go to *Step 12*

GC9020200992010X

Fig. 80 Test 6: Wipers Inoperative In One Or More Modes (Part 1 of 2). Century, Grand Prix & Regal

Step	Action	Value(s)	Yes	No
1	Did you review the Wiper Washer System Circuit Description and perform the necessary inspections?	—	*Go to Step 2*	Go to *Symptoms*
2	1. Fill the windshield washer fluid container to the proper level. 2. Turn the ignition switch ON. 3. Wait 1 minute. Is the LOW WASHER FLUID message displayed on the driver information center?	—	*Go to Step 3*	*Go to Step 5*
3	1. Disconnect the windshield washer fluid level switch connector. 2. Turn the ignition switch ON. 3. Wait 1 minute. Is the LOW WASHER FLUID message displayed on the driver information center?	—	*Go to Step 4*	*Go to Step 6*
4	Test and repair the windshield washer fluid level switch signal circuit 99 for a short to ground. Did you find and correct the condition?	—	*Go to Step 11*	*Go to Step 9*
5	1. Disconnect the windshield washer fluid level switch connector. 2. Connect a fused jumper wire from the windshield washer fluid level switch connector terminal A to terminal B. 3. Turn the ignition switch ON. 4. Wait 1 minute. Is the LOW WASHER FLUID message displayed on the driver information center?	—	*Go to Step 6*	*Go to Step 7*
6	Replace the windshield wiper fluid level switch. Is the repair complete?	—	*Go to Step 11*	—

GC9020000796010X

Fig. 81 Test 1: Windshield Washer Fluid Low Message Inoperative (Part 1 of 2). Corvette

Step	Action	Value(s)	Yes	No
10	Replace the windshield wiper/washer switch. Did you complete the replacement?	—	Go to *Step 13*	—
11	Replace the windshield wiper motor cover. Did you complete the replacement?	—	Go to *Step 13*	—
12	Replace the windshield wiper motor. Did you complete the replacement?	—	Go to *Step 13*	—
13	Operate the wiper/washer system and inspect for proper operation. Did you correct the condition?	—	System OK	Go to *Step 3*

GC9020200992020X

Fig. 80 Test 6: Wipers Inoperative In One Or More Modes (Part 2 of 2). Century, Grand Prix & Regal

Step	Action	Value(s)	Yes	No
7	1. Connect a fused jumper wire from the windshield washer fluid level switch connector terminal A to ground. 2. Turn the ignition switch ON. 3. Wait 1 minute Is the LOW WASHER FLUID message displayed on the driver information center?	—	*Go to Step 8*	*Go to Step 9*
8	Repair the open or high resistance in the windshield washer fluid level switch ground circuit 150. Is the repair complete?	—	*Go to Step 11*	—
9	Test and repair the windshield washer fluid level switch signal circuit 99 for an open or high resistance. Did you find and correct the condition?	—	*Go to Step 11*	*Go to Step 10*
10	Replace the instrument cluster. Is the repair complete?	—	*Go to Step 11*	—
11	Operate the system in order to verify the repair. Did you correct the condition?	—	System OK	Go to *Symptoms*

GC9020000796020X

Fig. 81 Test 1: Windshield Washer Fluid Low Message Inoperative (Part 2 of 2). Corvette

Step	Action	Value(s)	Yes	No
1	Did you review the Wiper Washer System Circuit Description and perform the necessary inspections?	—	*Go to Step 2*	Check *Symptoms*
2	Inspect the WSW fuse #10 for an open. Is the fuse open?	—	*Go to Step 3*	*Go to Step 10*
3	1. Disconnect the windshield wiper motor connector. 2. Disconnect the washer pump connector. 3. Remove the WSW fuse #10. 4. Connect a DMM from the fuse terminal A in the instrument pannel electrical center to ground. 5. Measure the resistance to ground of circuit 143. Is circuit 143 shorted to ground?	—	*Go to Step 5*	*Go to Step 4*
4	1. With the DMM connected as in the previous step, the wiper motor, and washer pump connectors disconnected. 2. Operate all of the windshield wiper/washer switch functions while measuring the resistance to ground. Is a short to ground indicated during any of the windshield wiper/washer switch functions?	—	*Go to Step 6*	*Go to Step 7*
5	Repair the short to ground in circuit 143. Did you complete the repair?	—	*Go to Step 16*	—
6	Test and repair the following circuits for a short to ground: • circuit 91 • circuit 92 • circuit 94 • circuit 95 Did you complete the repair?	—	*Go to Step 16*	—
7	1. Install a good 25A fuse in the WSW fuse #10 location. 2. Connect the windshield washer pump motor connector. 3. Turn the ignition switch on. 4. Press the windshield washer switch. Does the WSW fuse #10 open?	—	*Go to Step 9*	*Go to Step 8*

GC9020000797010X

Fig. 82 Test 2: Wipers All Modes Inoperative (Part 1 of 2). Corvette

Step	Action	Value(s)	Yes	No
8	1. Connect the windshield wiper motor connector. 2. Operate the windshield wipers in all modes. Does the WSW fuse #10 open?	—	Go to Step 15	Testing for Electrical Intermittents
9	Replace the windshield washer pump motor. Did you complete the repair?	—	Go to Step 16	—
10	1. Disconnect the windshield wiper motor connector. 2. Turn the ignition switch on. 3. Connect a test light between the windshield wiper motor harness connector terminals A and B. Does the test light illuminate?	—	Go to Step 12	Go to Step 11
11	Test and repair the the following circuits for open or high resistance: • circuit 143 • windshield wiper motor ground circuit 150 Did you complete the repair?	—	Go to Step 16	—
12	1. Disconnect the windshield wiper/washer switch pigtail connector C219. 2. Turn the windshield wiper/washer switch to the high position. 3. Measure the resistance through the windshield wiper/washer switch from the following connector terminals: • terminal C to D (0-2Ω) • terminal C to A (0-2Ω) • terminal C to B (approximately 24K Ω) Are the resistance measurements within the values listed?	—	Go to Step 14	Go to Step 13
13	Replace the windshield wiper/washer switch. Is the repair complete?	—	Go to Step 16	—
14	Test and repair the following circuits for an open or high resistance between the windshield wiper/washer switch connector C219 and the windshield wiper motor connector: • circuit 91 • circuit 92 • circuit 95 Did you find and correct the condition?	—	Go to Step 16	Go to Step 15
15	1. Inspect and repair all wiper motor linkage for binding or damage. 2. If OK, replace the windshield wiper motor. Is the repair complete?	—	Go to Step 16	—
16	Operate the system in order to verify the repair. Did you correct the condition?	—	System OK	Check Symptoms

GC9020000797020X

Fig. 82 Test 2: Wipers All Modes Inoperative (Part 2 of 2). Corvette

Step	Action	Value(s)	Yes	No
1	Did you review the Wiper Washer System Circuit Description and perform the necessary inspections?	—	Go to Step 2	Check Symptoms
2	1. Disconnect the windshield wiper/washer switch pigtail connector C219. 2. Set the windshield wiper/washer switch to the LO position. 3. Measure the resistance through the windshield wiper/washer switch from the connector terminals C to A. Is the resistance within the specified values?	0–2 Ω	Go to Step 3	Go to Step 4
3	1. With the windshield wiper/washer switch set to the LO position. 2. Measure the resistance through the windshield wiper/washer switch from the connector terminals C to B. Is the resistance within the specified values?	23-25K Ω	Go to Step 5	Go to Step 4
4	Replace the windshield wiper/washer switch. Did you complete the repair?	—	Go to Step 7	—
5	Test and repair the following circuits for an open or high resistance between the windshield wiper/washer switch connector C219 and the windshield wiper motor connector: • circuit 91 • circuit 95 Did you find and correct the condition?	—	Go to Step 7	Go to Step 6
6	Replace the windshield wiper motor assembly. Is the repair complete?	—	Go to Step 7	—
7	Operate the system in order to verify the repair. Did you correct the condition?	—	System OK	Go to Symptoms

GC9020000799000X

Fig. 84 Test 4: Wipers Low Or Mist Inoperative. Corvette

Step	Action	Value(s)	Yes	No
5	Replace the windshield wiper motor assembly. Is the repair complete?	—	Go to Step 6	—
6	Operate the system in order to verify the repair. Did you correct the condition?	—	System OK	Check Symptoms

GC9020000800020X

Fig. 85 Test 5: Wipers Always On (Part 2 of 2). Corvette

Step	Action	Value(s)	Yes	No
DEFINITION: The wipers do not delay or the delay time is incorrect.				
1	Did you review the Wiper Washer System Circuit Description and perform the necessary inspections?	—	Go to Step 2	Go to Symptoms
2	1. Disconnect the windshield wiper/washer switch pigtail connector C219. 2. Set the windshield wiper/washer switch lever to the INT position. 3. Measure the resistance through the windshield wiper/washer switch from the connector terminals C to B. Is the resistance within the specified values?	23–25K Ω	Go to Step 3	Go to Step 4
3	1. With the windshield wiper/washer switch lever in the INT position. 2. Measure the resistance through the windshield wiper/washer switch from the connector terminals C to A. 3. Turn the INT ADJ band through the following 5 positions: • position 1 (39K Ω) • position 2 (82K Ω) • position 3 (150K Ω) • position 4 (270K Ω) • position 5 (680K Ω) Are the resistance measurements at or near the values listed?	—	Go to Step 5	Go to Step 4
4	Replace the windshield wiper/washer switch. Is the repair complete?	—	Go to Step 7	—
5	Test and repair the the following circuits for an open or high resistance between the windshield wiper/washer switch connector C219 and the windshield wiper motor connector: • circuit 91 • circuit 95 Did you find and correct the condition?	—	Go to Step 7	Go to Step 6
6	Replace the wiper motor assembly. Is the repair complete?	—	Go to Step 7	—
7	Operate the system in order to verify the repair. Did you correct the condition?	—	System OK	Check Symptoms

GC9020000798000X

Fig. 83 Test 3: Wipers Delay Mode Inoperative. Corvette

Step	Action	Value(s)	Yes	No
DEFINITION: The wiper motor continues to run, or does not PARK after the wiper switch is turned to the OFF position.				
1	Did you review the Wiper Washer System Circuit Description and perform the necessary inspections?	—	Go to Step 2	Check Symptoms
2	1. Turn the ignition switch to the ON position. 2. Turn the wiper switch OFF. 3. Disconnect the windshield wiper/washer switch pigtail connector C219. Do the windshild wipers stop and park?	—	Go to Step 3	Go to Step 4
3	Replace the windshield wiper/washer switch. Is the repair complete?	—	Go to Step 6	—
4	Test and repair the following circuits for a short to voltage between the windshield wiper/washer switch connector C219 and the windshield wiper motor connector: • circuit 91 • circuit 92 • circuit 95 Did you find and correct the condition?	—	Go to Step 6	Go to Step 5

GC9020000800010X

Fig. 85 Test 5: Wipers Always On (Part 1 of 2). Corvette

Step	Action	Value(s)	Yes	No
DEFINITION: The wiper washer is inoperative when the switch is activated. Wipers operate normally.				
1	Did you review the Wiper Washer System Circuit Description and perform the necessary inspections?	—	Go to Step 2	Check Symptoms
2	1. Disconnect the windshield washer pump connector. 2. Connect a test light between terminals A and B of the windshield washer pump harness connector. 3. Turn the ignition switch to the ON position. 4. Press the windshield washer switch. Does the test light illuminate?	—	Go to Step 3	Go to Step 5
3	Inspect and repair the washer pump lines, nozzles, and connections for any restrictions or leaks. Did you find and correct the condition?	—	Go to Step 8	Go to Step 4
4	Replace the windshield washer pump. Is the repair complete?	—	Go to Step 8	—
5	Test and repair the washer pump ground circuit 150 for an open or high resistance. Did you find and correct the condition?	—	Go to Step 8	Go to Step 6
6	Test and repair circuit 94 from the windshield wiper/washer switch connector C219 to the windshield washer pump connector for an open or high resistance. Did you find and correct the condition?	—	Go to Step 8	Go to Step 7
7	Replace the windshield wiper/washer switch. Is the repair complete?	—	Go to Step 8	—
8	Operate the system in order to verify the repair. Did you correct the condition?	—	System OK	Check Symptoms

GC9020000801000X

Fig. 86 Test 6: Washers Inoperative. Corvette

Test Description

The numbers below refer to the step numbers on the diagnostic table.

2. Lack of communication may be due to a partial malfunction of the class 2 serial data circuit or due to a total malfunction of the class 2 serial data circuit. The specified procedure will determine the particular condition.
3. This step tests for valid system power moding in all ignition switch positions
5. The presence of DTCs which begin with "U" indicate some other module is not communicating. The specified procedure will compile all the available information before tests are performed.

Step	Action	Yes	No
1	Install a scan tool. Does the scan tool power up?	Go to Step 2	Diagnose Data Link Communications
2	1. Turn the ignition ON. 2. Attempt to establish communication with the following systems: o Dash integration module o Radio Does the scan tool communicate with the systems listed?	Go to Step 3	Diagnose Data Link Communications
3	**Important** The engine may start during the following step. Turn OFF the engine as soon as you have observed the Crank power mode. 1. Access the Class 2 Power Mode parameter in the Diagnostic Circuit Check menu on the scan tool. 2. Rotate the ignition switch through all positions while observing the Class 2 Power Mode parameter. Does the Class 2 Power Mode parameter reading match the ignition switch position for all switch positions?	Go to Step 4	Go to Power Mode Mismatch

GC9020200993010X

Fig. 87 Wiper/Washer System Check (Part 1 of 2). CTS

4	Select the display the DTC function for the following systems: • Dash integration module • Radio Does the scan tool display any DTCs?	Go to Step 5	Go to Symptoms -
5	Does the scan tool display any DTCs which begin with a "U"?	Go to Scan Tool Does Not Communicate with Class 2 Device in Data Link Communications	Go to Step 6
6	Does the scan tool display DTCs B1000, B1004, B1007, or B1009?	Diagnose Body Control System	Go to Step 7
7	Does the scan tool display DTCs B1327 or B1328?	Diagnose Engine Electrical	Go to Symptoms -

GC9020200993020X

Fig. 87 Wiper/Washer System Check (Part 2 of 2). CTS

Step	Action	Yes	No
	DEFINITION: The check washer fluid message is always displayed or does not display with low washer fluid.		
1	Did you perform the Wiper/Washer Diagnostic System Check?	Go to Step 2	Go to System Check -
2	Verify the fault is present. Does the system operate normally?	Test for Intermittent and Poor Connections	Go to Step 3
3	1. Turn the ignition OFF. 2. Disconnect the washer fluid level switch connector. 3. Turn the ignition ON. Does the radio display the check washer fluid message?	Go to Step 7	Go to Step 4
4	1. Turn the ignition OFF. 2. Connect a fused jumper wire from the washer fluid level switch signal circuit terminal in the washer fluid level switch connector to a good ground. 3. Turn the ignition ON. Does the radio display the check washer fluid message?	Go to Step 6	Go to Step 5

GC9020200994010X

Fig. 88 Test 1: Low Washer Fluid Indicator Fault (Part 1 of 3). CTS

5	1. Install a scan tool. 2. Display the dash integration module inputs data list. Is the washer fluid level switch parameter displayed as low?	Go to Step 15	Go to Step 9
6	1. Turn the ignition OFF. 2. Connect a fused jumper wire across the washer fluid level switch harness connector terminals. 3. Turn the ignition ON. Does the radio display the check washer fluid message?	Go to Step 11	Go to Step 10
7	1. Install a scan tool. 2. Display the dash integration module inputs data list. Is the washer fluid level switch parameter displayed as low?	Go to Step 8	Go to Step 15
8	Test the washer fluid level switch signal circuit for a short to ground. Did you find and correct the condition?	Go to Step 17	Go to Step 13
9	Test the washer fluid level switch signal circuit for an open or high resistance. Did you find and correct the condition?	Go to Step 17	Go to Step 13
10	Repair the washer fluid level switch ground circuit for an open or high resistance. Is the repair complete?	Go to Step 17	--

GC9020200994020X

Fig. 88 Test 1: Low Washer Fluid Indicator Fault (Part 2 of 3). CTS

11	Inspect for poor connections at the washer fluid level switch. Did you find and correct the condition?	Go to Step 17	Go to Step 12
12	Replace the washer fluid level switch. Is the repair complete?	Go to Step 17	--
13	Inspect for poor connections at the dash integration module. Did you find and correct the condition?	Go to Step 17	Go to Step 14
14	**Important** Perform the programming or setup procedure for the dash integration module. Replace the dash integration module. Is the repair complete?	Go to Step 17	--
15	Inspect for poor connections at the radio. Did you find and correct the condition?	Go to Step 17	Go to Step 16
16	Replace the radio. Is the repair complete?	Go to Step 17	--
17	Operate the system in order to verify the repair. Did you correct the condition?	System OK	Go to Step 3

GC9020200994030X

Fig. 88 Test 1: Low Washer Fluid Indicator Fault (Part 3 of 3). CTS

Step	Action	Yes	No
1	Did you perform the Wiper/Washer Diagnostic System Check?	Go to Step 2	Go to Diagnostic System Check
2	Turn the ignition ON. Are the windshield washers always on?	Go to Step 3	Test for Intermittent and Poor Connections
3	Are the windshield wipers always on?	Go to Step 4	Go to Step 6
4	Remove the WPR SW 10A fuse. Are the windshield washers always on?	Go to Step 5	Go to Step 7
5	Test the windshield wiper switch signal 2 circuit for a short to voltage. Did you find and correct the condition?	Go to Step 11	Go to Step 9
6	Test the windshield washer pump control circuit for a short to voltage. Did you find and correct the condition?	Go to Step 11	Go to Step 9

GC9020200995010X

Fig. 89 Test 2: Washers Always On (Part 1 of 2). CTS

7	Inspect for poor connections at the windshield wiper/washer switch. Did you find and correct the condition?	Go to Step 11	Go to Step 8
8	Replace the windshield wiper/washer switch. Is the repair complete?	Go to Step 11	--
9	Inspect for poor connections at the windshield wiper motor. Did you find and correct the condition?	Go to Step 11	Go to Step 10
10	Replace the windshield wiper motor module. Is the repair complete?	Go to Step 11	--
11	Operate the system in order to verify the repair. Did you correct the condition?	System OK	Go to Step 3

GC9020200995020X

Fig. 89 Test 2: Washers Always On (Part 2 of 2). CTS

Step	Action	Yes	No
	Connector End View Reference: Wiper/Washer System Connector End Views		
1	Did you perform the Wiper/Washer Diagnostic System Check?	Go to Step 2	Go to Diagnostic System Check
2	1. Turn the ignition ON. 2. Press the windshield washer switch. Do the windshield washers operate normally?	Test for Intermittent and Poor Connections	Go to Step 3
3	While listening for washer pump operation press the windshield washer switch. Does the washer pump operate when the washer switch is pressed?	Go to Step 10	Go to Step 4
4	Do the windshield wipers operate when the washer switch is pressed?	Go to Step 5	Go to Step 8
5	1. Disconnect the windshield washer pump connector. 2. Connect a test lamp across the washer pump connector terminals. 3. Turn the ignition ON. 4. Press the windshield washer switch. Does the test lamp illuminate?	Go to Step 15	Go to Step 6

GC9020200996010X

Fig. 90 Test 3: Washer Inoperative (Part 1 of 4). CTS w/Heated Washer Nozzle

6	Test the windshield washer pump ground circuit for an open or high resistance. Did you find and correct the condition?	Go to Step 21	Go to Step 7
7	1. Disconnect the windshield wiper motor connector. 2. Test the windshield washer pump control circuit for an open or short to ground. Did you find and correct the condition?	Go to Step 21	Go to Step 17
8	1. Disconnect the windshield wiper motor connector. 2. Connect a test lamp from the windshield wiper switch signal 2 circuit terminal in the wiper motor harness connector to ground. 3. Turn the ignition ON. 4. Press the windshield washer switch. Does the test lamp illuminate?	Go to Step 17	Go to Step 9
9	Test the windshield wiper switch signal 2 circuit for high resistance. Did you find and correct the condition?	Go to Step 21	Go to Step 13
10	1. Disconnect an inoperative heated washer nozzle connector. 2. Connect a test lamp from the ignition 1 voltage circuit terminal in the harness connector to a good ground. 3. Turn the ignition ON. Does the test lamp illuminate?	Go to Step 12	Go to Step 11

GC9020200996020X

Fig. 90 Test 3: Washer Inoperative(Part 2 of 4). CTS w/Heated Washer Nozzle

11	Repair the ignition 1 voltage circuit for an open or short to ground. Is the repair complete?	Go to Step 21	--
12	Test the heated washer nozzle ground circuit for an open or high resistance. Did you find and correct the condition?	Go to Step 21	Go to Step 19
13	Inspect for poor connections at the windshield wiper/washer switch. Did you find and correct the condition?	Go to Step 21	Go to Step 14
14	Replace the windshield wiper/washer switch. Is the repair complete?	Go to Step 21	--
15	Inspect for poor connections at the windshield washer pump. Did you find and correct the condition?	Go to Step 21	Go to Step 16

GC9020200996030X

Fig. 90 Test 3: Washer Inoperative (Part 3 of 4). CTS w/Heated Washer Nozzle

16	Replace the windshield washer pump. Is the repair complete?	Go to Step 21	--
17	Inspect for poor connections at the windshield wiper motor. Did you find and correct the condition?	Go to Step 21	Go to Step 18
18	Replace the windshield wiper motor cover. Is the repair complete?	Go to Step 21	--
19	Inspect for poor connections at the heated washer nozzle. Did you find and correct the condition?	Go to Step 21	Go to Step 20
20	Replace the inoperative heated washer nozzle. Is the repair complete?	Go to Step 21	--
21	Operate the system in order to verify the repair. Did you correct the condition?	System OK	Go to Step 3

GC9020200996040X

Fig. 90 Test 3: Washer Inoperative (Part 4 of 4). CTS w/Heated Washer Nozzle

Step	Action	Yes	No
1	Did you perform the Wiper/Washer Diagnostic System Check?	Go to Step 2	Go to Diagnostic System Check -
2	1. Turn the ignition ON. 2. Press the windshield washer switch. Do the windshield washers operate normally?	Test for Intermittent and Poor Connections	Go to Step 3
3	Do the wipers operate when the windshield washer switch is pressed?	Go to Step 4	Go to Wipers Inoperative - One or More Modes
4	1. Turn OFF the ignition. 2. Disconnect the harness connector of the windshield washer pump. 3. Connect a test lamp between the control circuit and the ground circuit of the windshield washer pump. 4. Turn the ignition ON. 5. Press the windshield washer switch. Does the test lamp illuminate?	Go to Step 7	Go to Step 5
5	1. Connect a test lamp from the control circuit of the windshield washer pump to a good ground. 2. Press the windshield washer switch. Does the test lamp illuminate?	Go to Step 9	Go to Step 6
6	Test the control circuit of the windshield washer pump for an open or high resistance. Did you find and correct the condition?	Go to Step 12	Go to Step 8

GC9020200997010X

Fig. 91 Test 4: Washers Inoperative(Part 1 of 2). CTS Less Heated Water Nozzle

Step	Action	Yes	No
1	Did you perform the Wiper/Washer Diagnostic System Check?	Go to Step 2	Go to Diagnostic System Check -
2	1. Turn the ignition ON. 2. Turn the windshield wiper/washer switch OFF. Are the windshield wipers always on?	Test for Intermittent and Poor Connections	Go to Step 3
3	Remove the WPR SW 10A fuse. Are the windshield wipers always on?	Go to Step 4	Go to Step 7
4	1. Disconnect the windshield wiper motor connector. 2. Test the windshield wiper switch signal 1 circuit for a short to voltage. Did you find and correct the condition?	Go to Step 11	Go to Step 5
5	Test the windshield wiper switch signal 2 circuit for a short to voltage. Did you find and correct the condition?	Go to Step 11	Go to Step 6

GC9020200998010X

Fig. 92 Test 5: Wipers Always On (Part 1 of 2). CTS

7	Inspect for poor connections at the harness connector of the windshield washer pump. Did you find and correct the condition?	Go to Step 12	Go to Step 10
8	Inspect for poor connections at the harness connector of the windshield wiper motor. Did you find and correct the condition?	Go to Step 12	Go to Step 11
9	Repair an open or high resistance in the ground circuit of the windshield washer pump. Did you complete the repair?	Go to Step 12	--
10	Replace the windshield washer pump. Did you complete the replacement?	Go to Step 12	--
11	Replace the windshield wiper motor cover. Did you complete the replacement?	Go to Step 12	--
12	Operate the system in order to verify the repair. Did you correct the condition?	System OK	Go to Step 3

GC9020200997020X

Fig. 91 Test 4: Washers Inoperative (Part 2 of 2). CTS Less Heated Water Nozzle

6	Test the windshield wiper motor high speed circuit for a short to voltage. Did you find and correct the condition?	Go to Step 11	Go to Step 9
7	Inspect for poor connections at the windshield wiper/washer switch. Did you find and correct the condition?	Go to Step 11	Go to Step 8
8	Replace the windshield wiper/washer switch. Is the repair complete?	Go to Step 11	--
9	Inspect for poor connections at the windshield wiper motor. Did you find and correct the condition?	Go to Step 11	Go to Step 10
10	Replace the windshield wiper motor cover. Is the repair complete?	Go to Step 11	--
11	Operate the system in order to verify the repair. Did you correct the condition?	System OK	Go to Step 3

GC9020200998020X

Fig. 92 Test 5: Wipers Always On (Part 2 of 2). CTS

Step	Action	Yes	No
1	Did you perform the Wiper/Washer Diagnostic System Check?	Go to Step 2	Go to System Check -
2	1. Turn the ignition ON, with the engine OFF. 2. Turn the windshield wiper/washer switch through all the switch positions. Does the windshield wiper/washer system operate normally?	Test for Intermittent and Poor Connections	Go to Step 3
3	1. Turn OFF the ignition. 2. Disconnect the harness connector of the windshield wiper motor. 3. Turn the ignition ON, with the engine OFF. 4. Connect a test lamp from the accessory voltage circuit to the ground circuit of the windshield wiper motor. Does the test lamp illuminate?	Go to Step 5	Go to Step 4
4	Connect a test lamp from the accessory voltage circuit of the windshield wiper motor to a good ground. Does the test lamp illuminate?	Go to Step 15	Go to Step 7
5	1. Connect the test lamp from the windshield wiper switch signal 2 circuit to a good ground. 2. Press the windshield washer switch. Does the test lamp illuminate?	Go to Step 13	Go to Step 6

GC9020200999010X

Fig. 93 Test 6: Wipers Inoperative In All Modes (Part 1 of 3). CTS

12	Test the windshield wiper switch signal 2 circuit for a short to ground. Did you find and correct the condition?	Go to Step 18	Go to Step 13
13	Inspect for poor connections at the windshield wiper motor. Did you find and correct the condition?	Go to Step 18	Go to Step 16
14	Inspect for poor connections at the windshield wiper/washer switch. Did you find and correct the condition?	Go to Step 18	Go to Step 17
15	Repair the windshield wiper motor ground circuit for an open or high resistance. Did you complete the repair?	Go to Step 18	--
16	Replace the windshield wiper motor. Did you complete the replacement?	Go to Step 18	--
17	Replace the windshield wiper/washer switch. Did you complete the replacement?	Go to Step 18	--
18	Operate the system in order to verify the repair. Did you correct the condition?	System OK	Go to Step 3

GC9020200999030X

Fig. 93 Test 6: Wipers Inoperative In All Modes (Part 3 of 3). CTS

6	1. Turn OFF the ignition. 2. Disconnect the harness connector of the windshield wiper/washer switch. 3. Turn the ignition ON. 4. Connect a test lamp from the accessory voltage circuit of the windshield wiper/washer switch to a good ground. Does the test lamp illuminate?	Go to Step 14	Go to Step 9
7	Test the windshield wiper motor accessory voltage circuit for an open or short to ground. Did you find and correct the condition?	Go to Step 18	Go to Step 8
8	Test the windshield washer pump control circuit for a short to ground. Did you find and correct the condition?	Go to Step 18	Go to Step 13
9	Test the windshield wiper/washer switch accessory voltage circuit for an open or short to ground. Did you find and correct the condition?	Go to Step 18	Go to Step 10
10	Test the windshield wiper motor high speed circuit for a short to ground. Did you find and correct the condition?	Go to Step 18	Go to Step 11
11	Test the windshield wiper switch signal 1 circuit for a short to ground. Did you find and correct the condition?	Go to Step 18	Go to Step 12

GC9020200999020X

Fig. 93 Test 6: Wipers Inoperative In All Modes (Part 2 of 3). CTS

Test Description

The numbers below refer to the step numbers on the diagnostic table.

7. This step tests for continuity through the 24K ohms resistor in the windshield wiper/washer switch. The connector behind the instrument panel knee bolster is suitable for performing this step.

8. This step tests for continuity through the delay resistors in the windshield wiper/washer switch. The measured resistance will change in sequence from high to low as the delay speed is increased. The connector behind the instrument panel knee bolster is suitable for performing this step.

Step	Action	Values	Yes	No
1	Did you perform the Wiper/Washer Diagnostic System Check?	--	Go to Step 2	Go to System Check
2	1. Turn the ignition ON. 2. Operate the windshield wiper/washer switch through all the switch positions. Does the windshield wiper/washer system operate normally?	--	Test for Intermittent and Poor Connections	Go to Step 3
3	Do the windshield wipers operate in the high speed mode?	--	Go to Step 5	Go to Step 4
4	1. Disconnect the windshield wiper motor connector. 2. Connect a test lamp from the windshield wiper motor high speed circuit terminal to ground. 3. Turn the ignition ON. 4. Operate the windshield wiper/washer switch to the high speed position. Does the test lamp illuminate?	--	Go to Step 14	Go to Step 9

GC9020201000010X

Fig. 94 Test 7: Wipers Inoperative In One Or More Modes (Part 1 of 3). CTS

5	1. Disconnect the windshield wiper motor connector. 2. Connect a test lamp from the windshield wiper switch signal 2 circuit terminal to ground. 3. Turn the ignition ON. 4. Press the windshield washer switch. Does the test lamp illuminate?	--	Go to Step 6	Go to Step 10
6	1. Connect a test lamp from the windshield wiper switch signal 1 circuit terminal to ground. 2. Operate the windshield wiper/washer switch to the following positions: o MIST o LO o HI Does the test lamp illuminate in the listed switch positions?	--	Go to Step 7	Go to Step 11
7	1. Disconnect the windshield wiper/washer switch connector. 2. Measure the resistance through the windshield wiper/washer switch from the signal 2 circuit terminal to the accessory voltage circuit terminal of the wiper/washer switch. 3. Operate the windshield wiper/washer switch to the following positions: o MIST o INT o LO o HI Is the resistance at or near the specified value in all the listed switch positions?	24K ohms	Go to Step 8	Go to Step 12
8	1. Measure the resistance through the windshield wiper/washer switch from the signal 1 circuit terminal to the accessory voltage circuit terminal of the wiper/washer switch. 2. Operate the windshield wiper/washer switch through all of the delay positions. Does the resistance remain within the specified values from high to low as the delay speed is increased?	38K - 690K ohms	Go to Step 14	Go to Step 12
9	Test the windshield wiper motor high speed circuit for an open or high resistance. Did you find and correct the condition?	--	Go to Step 16	Go to Step 12
10	Test the windshield wiper switch signal 2 circuit for an open or short to ground. Did you find and correct the condition?	--	Go to Step 16	Go to Step 12

GC9020201000020X

Fig. 94 Test 7: Wipers Inoperative In One Or More Modes (Part 2 of 3). CTS

Step	Action	Value(s)	Yes	No
1	Did you review the Wiper/Washer System Description and Operation and perform the necessary inspections?	—	Go to *Step 2*	Go to *Symptoms*
2	1. Verify the windshield washer reservoir is full. 2. Turn the ignition on. 3. Wait one minute. Is the LOW WASHER FLUID message displayed on the driver information center?	—	Go to *Step 3*	*Test for Intermittent and Poor Connections*
3	1. Disconnect the windshield washer solvent level switch connector. 2. Turn the ignition on. 3. Wait one minute. Is the LOW WASHER FLUID message displayed on the driver information center?	—	Go to *Step 4*	Go to *Step 5*
4	Test and repair the windshield washer solvent level switch signal circuit for a short to ground. Did you find and correct the condition?	—	Go to *Step 7*	Go to *Step 6*
5	Replace the windshield washer solvent level switch. Is the repair complete?	—	Go to *Step 7*	—
6	Replace the instrument cluster. Is the repair complete?	—	Go to *Step 7*	—
7	Operate the system in order to verify the repair. Did you correct the condition?	—	System OK	Go to *Step 3*

GC9020201013000X

Fig. 95 Test 1: Low Washer Fluid Indicator Always On. DeVille & Seville

11	Test the windshield wiper switch signal 1 circuit for an open or short to ground. Did you find and correct the condition?	-	Go to Step 16	Go to Step 12
12	Inspect for poor connections at the windshield wiper/washer switch. Did you find and correct the condition?	-	Go to Step 16	Go to Step 13
13	Replace the windshield wiper/washer switch. Is the repair complete?	-	Go to Step 16	--
14	Inspect for poor connections at the windshield wiper motor. Did you find and correct the condition?	-	Go to Step 16	Go to Step 15
15	Replace the windshield wiper motor cover. Is the repair complete?	-	Go to Step 16	--
16	Operate the system in order to verify the repair. Did you correct the condition?	-	System OK	Go to Step 3

GC9020201000030X

Fig. 94 Test 7: Wipers Inoperative In One Or More Modes (Part 3 of 3). CTS

Step	Action	Value(s)	Yes	No
1	Did you review the Wiper/Washer System Description and Operation and perform the necessary inspections?	—	Go to *Step 2*	Go to *Symptoms*
2	1. Verify the windshield washer reservoir is at or near empty. 2. Turn the ignition on. 3. Wait one minute. Is the LOW WASHER FLUID message displayed on the driver information center?	—	*Test for Intermittent and Poor Connections*	Go to *Step 3*
3	1. Disconnect the windshield washer solvent level switch connector. 2. Connect a fused jumper wire from the windshield washer solvent level switch signal circuit terminal to ground. 3. Turn the ignition on. 4. Wait one minute. Is the LOW WASHER FLUID message displayed on the driver information center?	—	Go to *Step 5*	Go to *Step 4*
4	Test and repair the windshield washer solvent level switch signal circuit for an open or high resistance. Did you find and correct the condition?	—	Go to *Step 8*	Go to *Step 7*
5	Test and repair the windshield washer solvent level switch ground circuit for an open or high resistance. Did you find and correct the condition?	—	Go to *Step 8*	Go to *Step 6*
6	Replace the windshield washer solvent level switch. Is the repair complete?	—	Go to *Step 8*	—
7	Replace the instrument cluster. Is the repair complete?	—	Go to *Step 8*	—
8	Operate the system in order to verify the repair. Did you correct the condition?	—	System OK	Go to *Step 3*

GC9020201014000X

Fig. 96 Test 2: Low Washer Fluid Indicator Inoperative. DeVille & Seville

Step	Action	Value(s)	Yes	No
1	Did you review the Wiper/Washer System Description and Operation and perform the necessary inspections?	—	Go to *Step 2*	Go to *Symptoms*
2	1. Turn ON the ignition, with the engine OFF. 2. Activate the windshield washer switch. Does the windshield washer operate properly?	—	*Test for Intermittent and Poor Connections*	Go to *Step 3*
3	Test for a short to voltage in the windshield washer pump control circuit. Did you find and correct the condition?	—	Go to *Step 5*	Go to *Step 4*
4	Replace the windshield wiper/washer switch. Did you complete the replacement?	—	Go to *Step 5*	—
5	Operate the system in order to verify the repair. Did you correct the condition?	—	System OK	Go to *Step 3*

GC9020201015000X

Fig. 97 Test 3: Washer Always On. DeVille & Seville

Step	Action	Yes	No
1	Did you review the Wiper/Washer System Description and Operation and perform the necessary inspections?	Go to *Step 2*	Go to *Symptoms* -
2	1. Turn ON the ignition, with the engine OFF. 2. Activate the windshield washer switch. Does the windshield washer operate properly?	*Test for Intermittent and Poor Connections*	Go to *Step 3*
3	1. Disconnect the windshield washer pump connector. 2. Connect a test lamp between the windshield washer pump control circuit and the windshield washer pump ground circuit. 3. Activate the windshield washer switch. Does the test lamp illuminate?	Go to *Step 7*	Go to *Step 4*
4	Test the windshield washer pump ground circuit for high resistance or an open. Did you find and correct the condition?	Go to *Step 8*	Go to *Step 5*
5	Test the windshield washer pump control circuit for high resistance, a short to ground or an open. Did you find and correct the condition?	Go to *Step 8*	Go to *Step 6*
6	Replace the windshield wiper/washer switch. Did you complete the replacement?	Go to *Step 8*	—
7	Replace the windshield washer pump. Did you complete the replacement?	Go to *Step 8*	—
8	Operate the system in order to verify the repair. Did you correct the condition?	System OK	Go to *Step 3*

GC9020201016000X

Fig. 98 Test 4: Washer Inoperative. DeVille & Seville

Step	Action	Yes	No
6	Replace the windshield wiper motor. Did you complete the replacement?	Go to *Step 7*	—
7	Operate the system in order to verify the repair. Did you correct the condition?	System OK	Go to *Step 3*

GC9020201017020X

Fig. 99 Test 5: Wipers Always On (Part 2 of 2). DeVille & Seville

Step	Action	Value(s)	Yes	No
1	Did you review the Wiper/Washer System Description and Operation and perform the necessary inspections?	—	Go to *Step 2*	Go to *Symptoms*
2	1. Turn ON the ignition, with the engine OFF. 2. Turn the windshield wiper/washer switch through all the switch positions. Do the windshield wipers operate properly in all modes?	—	*Test for Intermittent and Poor Connections*	Go to *Step 3*
3	1. Disconnect the windshield wiper/washer switch connector. 2. Measure the resistance between the accessory voltage circuit and the windshield wiper switch signal 1 circuit of the wiper/washer switch. 3. Turn the wiper/washer switch to the following positions: • MIST • LO • HI Does the resistance measure greater than the specified value?	2 Ω	Go to *Step 10*	Go to *Step 4*
4	1. Measure the resistance between the accessory voltage circuit and the windshield wiper switch signal 1 circuit of the wiper/washer switch. 2. Turn the wiper/washer switch through the DELAY range. Does the resistance measure within the specified values?	39K–680K Ω	Go to *Step 5*	Go to *Step 10*
5	1. Measure the resistance between the accessory voltage circuit and the windshield wiper switch signal 2 circuit of the wiper/washer switch. 2. Turn the wiper/washer switch to the following positions: • MIST • DELAY • LO • HI Does the resistance measure near the specified value?	24K Ω	Go to *Step 6*	Go to *Step 10*
6	1. Reconnect the windshield wiper/washer switch connector. 2. Turn the windshield wiper/washer switch to HI. Do the windshield wipers operate properly in HI mode?	—	Go to *Step 7*	Go to *Step 9*
7	Test the windshield wiper switch signal 1 circuit for high resistance or an open. Did you find and correct the condition?	—	Go to *Step 12*	Go to *Step 8*
8	Test the windshield wiper switch signal 2 circuit for high resistance or an open. Did you find and correct the condition?	—	Go to *Step 12*	Go to *Step 11*
9	Test the windshield wiper motor high speed circuit for high resistance or an open. Did you find and correct the condition?	—	Go to *Step 12*	Go to *Step 11*

GC9020201019010X

Fig. 101 Test 7: Wipers Inoperative In One Or More Modes (Part 1 of 2). DeVille & Seville

Step	Action	Yes	No
1	Did you review the Wiper/Washer System Description and Operation and perform the necessary inspections?	Go to *Step 2*	Go to *Symptoms* -
2	1. Turn ON the ignition, with the engine OFF. 2. Turn the windshield wiper/washer switch to LO. 3. Turn the windshield wiper/washer switch to HI. 4. Turn OFF the windshield wiper/washer switch. Do the windshield wipers operate properly?	*Test for Intermittent and Poor Connections*	Go to *Step 3*
3	Disconnect the windshield wiper/washer switch connector. Do the windshield wipers stop?	Go to *Step 5*	Go to *Step 4*
4	Test the following circuits for a short to voltage: • Windshield wiper switch signal 1 circuit • Windshield wiper switch signal 2 circuit • Windshield wiper motor high speed circuit Did you find and correct the condition?	Go to *Step 7*	Go to *Step 6*
5	Replace the windshield wiper/washer switch. Did you complete the replacement?	Go to *Step 7*	—

GC9020201017010X

Fig. 99 Test 5: Wipers Always On (Part 1 of 2). DeVille & Seville

Step	Action	Yes	No
1	Did you review the Wiper/Washer System Description and Operation and perform the necessary inspections?	Go to *Step 2*	Go to *Symptoms* -
2	1. Turn ON the ignition, with the engine OFF. 2. Turn the windshield wiper/washer switch through all the switch positions. Do the windshield wipers operate properly?	*Test for Intermittent and Poor Connections*	Go to *Step 3*
3	1. Disconnect the windshield wiper motor connector. 2. Connect a test lamp between the accessory voltage circuit and a good ground. Does the test lamp illuminate?	Go to *Step 4*	Go to *Step 7*
4	Connect a test lamp between the accessory voltage circuit and the ground circuit of the windshield wiper motor connector. Does the test lamp illuminate?	Go to *Step 5*	Go to *Step 8*
5	1. Connect a test lamp between the windshield wiper switch signal 2 circuit and a good ground. 2. Activate the windshield washer switch. Does the test lamp illuminate?	Go to *Step 10*	Go to *Step 6*
6	1. Disconnect the windshield wiper/washer switch connector. 2. Connect a test lamp between the accessory voltage circuit and a good ground. Does the test lamp illuminate?	Go to *Step 11*	Go to *Step 9*
7	Repair the open in the windshield wiper motor accessory voltage circuit. Did you complete the repair?	Go to *Step 12*	—
8	Repair the open in the windshield wiper motor ground circuit. Did you complete the repair?	Go to *Step 12*	—
9	Repair the open in the windshield wiper/washer switch accessory voltage circuit. Did you complete the repair?	Go to *Step 12*	—
10	Replace the windshield wiper motor. Did you complete the repair?	Go to *Step 12*	—
11	Replace the windshield wiper/washer switch. Did you complete the repair?	Go to *Step 12*	—
12	Operate the system in order to verify the repair. Did you correct the condition?	System OK	Go to *Step 3*

GC9020201018000X

Fig. 100 Test 6: Wipers Inoperative In All Modes. DeVille & Seville

Step	Action	Value(s)	Yes	No
10	Replace the windshield wiper/washer switch. Did you complete the replacement?	—	Go to *Step 12*	—
11	Replace the windshield wiper motor. Did you complete the replacement?	—	Go to *Step 12*	—
12	Operate the wiper/washer system and inspect for proper operation. Did you correct the condition?	—	System OK	Go to *Step 3*

GC9020201019020X

Fig. 101 Test 7: Wipers Inoperative In One Or More Modes (Part 2 of 2). DeVille & Seville

Step	Action	Value(s)	Yes	No
1	Did you review the Wiper/Washer System Description and Operation and perform the necessary inspections?	—	Go to *Step 2*	Go to *Symptoms*
2	1. Turn the ignition ON, with the engine OFF. 2. Turn the windshield wiper/washer switch to LO. Do the windshield wipers stop for approximately 6 seconds and then operate for approximately 24 seconds repeatedly?	—	Go to *Step 9*	Go to *Step 3*
3	1. Turn OFF the windshield wiper/washer switch. 2. Disconnect the windshield wiper/washer switch connector. Do the windshield wipers park properly?	—	Go to *Step 8*	Go to *Step 4*
4	1. Reconnect the wiper/washer switch connector. 2. Disconnect the windshield wiper motor connector. 3. Measure the voltage from the windshield wiper switch signal 1 circuit to ground. Does the voltage measure greater than the specified value?	10.5–15 V	Go to *Step 6*	Go to *Step 5*
5	Measure the voltage from the windshield wiper switch signal 2 circuit to ground. Did the voltage measure greater than the specified value?	1.0 V	Go to *Step 7*	Go to *Step 9*
6	Repair the short to voltage in the windshield wiper switch signal 1 circuit. Did you complete the repair?	—	Go to *Step 10*	—
7	Repair the short to voltage in the windshield wiper switch signal 2 circuit. Did you complete the repair?	—	Go to *Step 10*	—
8	Replace the wiper/washer switch. Did you complete the replacement?	—	Go to *Step 10*	—
9	Replace the wiper motor. Is the replacement complete?	—	Go to *Step 10*	—
10	Operate the system in order to verify the repair. Did you correct the condition?	—	System OK	Go to *Symptoms*

GC9020201020000X

Fig. 102 Test 8: Wiper Blades Do Not Park. DeVille & Seville

Step	Action	Yes	No
1	Did you review the Wiper/Washer System Description and Operation and perform the necessary inspections?	Go to *Step 2*	Go to *Symptoms* -
2	1. Turn ON the ignition, with the engine OFF. 2. Observe the low washer fluid indicator. Does the low washer fluid indicator illuminate?	Go to *Step 5*	Go to *Step 3*
3	1. Disconnect the windshield washer solvent level sensor connector. 2. Connect a 3 amp fused jumper wire between the low washer fluid indicator control circuit and a good ground. 3. Wait for 2 ½ minutes. Does the low washer fluid indicator illuminate?	Go to *Step 4*	Go to *Step 7*
4	1. Connect a 3 amp fused jumper wire between the low washer fluid indicator control circuit and the windshield washer solvent level sensor ground circuit. 2. Wait for 2 ½ minutes. Does the low washer fluid indicator illuminate?	Go to *Step 8*	Go to *Step 10*
5	1. Disconnect the windshield washer solvent level sensor connector. 2. Wait for 2 ½ minutes. Did the low washer fluid indicator turn OFF?	Go to *Step 8*	Go to *Step 6*
6	Test the low washer fluid indicator signal circuit for a short to ground. Did you find and correct the condition?	Go to *Step 13*	Go to *Step 9*

GC9020201021010X

Fig. 103 Test 1: Low Washer Fluid Indicator Fault (Part 1 of 2). Eldorado

Step	Action	Yes	No
7	Test the low washer fluid indicator signal circuit for an open or high resistance. Did you find and correct the condition?	Go to *Step 13*	Go to *Step 9*
8	Inspect for a poor connection at the windshield washer solvent level sensor. Did you find and correct the condition?	Go to *Step 13*	Go to *Step 11*
9	Inspect for a poor connection at the IPC connector. Did you find and correct the condition?	Go to *Step 13*	Go to *Step 12*
10	Repair the open or high resistance in the low washer fluid indicator ground circuit. Did you find and correct the condition?	Go to *Step 13*	—
11	Replace the windshield washer solvent level sensor. Did you complete the replacement?	Go to *Step 13*	—
12	Replace the IPC. Did you complete the replacement?	Go to *Step 13*	—
13	Operate the windshield wiper/washer system in order to verify the repair. Did you correct the condition?	System OK	Go to *Step 3*

GC9020201021020X

Fig. 103 Test 1: Low Washer Fluid Indicator Fault (Part 2 of 2). Eldorado

Step	Action	Value(s)	Yes	No
1	Did you review the Wiper/Washer System Description and Operation and perform the necessary inspections?	—	Go to *Step 2*	Go to *Symptoms*
2	1. Turn ON the ignition, with the engine OFF. 2. Activate the windshield washer switch. Does the windshield washer operate properly?	—	*Test for Intermittent and Poor Connections*	Go to *Step 3*
3	1. Disconnect the wiper motor connector. 2. Connect a test lamp from the windshield washer switch signal circuit (w/o CE1) or the windshield wiper switch low signal circuit (w/CE1) to a good ground. 3. Momentarily activate the windshield washer switch. Does the test lamp stay illuminated after the windshield washer switch is released?	—	Go to *Step 4*	Go to *Step 6*
4	Test for a short to voltage in the windshield washer switch signal circuit (w/o CE1) or the windshield wiper switch low signal circuit (w/CE1). Did you find and correct the condition?	—	Go to *Step 7*	Go to *Step 5*
5	Replace the windshield wiper/washer switch. Did you complete the replacement?	—	Go to *Step 7*	—
6	Replace the wiper motor cover. Did you complete the replacement?	—	Go to *Step 7*	—
7	Operate the system in order to verify the repair. Did you correct the condition?	—	System OK	Go to *Step 3*

GC9020201022000X

Fig. 104 Test 2: Washer Always On. Eldorado

Step	Action	Yes	No
1	Did you review the Wiper/Washer System Description and Operation and perform the necessary inspections?	Go to *Step 2*	Go to *Symptoms* -
2	1. Turn ON the ignition, with the engine OFF. 2. Activate the windshield washer switch. Does the windshield washer operate properly?	*Test for Intermittent and Poor Connections*	Go to *Step 3*
3	1. Disconnect the windshield washer pump connector. 2. Connect a test lamp between the windshield washer pump control circuit and the windshield washer pump ground circuit. 3. Activate the windshield washer switch. Does the test lamp illuminate?	Go to *Step 9*	Go to *Step 4*
4	1. Connect a test lamp between the windshield washer pump control circuit and a good ground. 2. Activate the windshield washer switch. Does the test lamp illuminate?	Go to *Step 6*	Go to *Step 5*
5	1. Disconnect the windshield wiper motor connector. 2. Connect a test lamp from the windshield washer switch signal circuit (w/o CE1) or the windshield wiper switch low signal circuit (w/CE1) to a good ground. 3. Activate the windshield washer switch. Does the test lamp illuminate?	Go to *Step 7*	Go to *Step 8*
6	Test the windshield washer pump ground circuit for high resistance or an open. Did you find and correct the condition?	Go to *Step 12*	Go to *Step 10*
7	Test the windshield washer pump control circuit for high resistance, a short to ground or an open. Did you find and correct the condition?	Go to *Step 12*	Go to *Step 11*
8	Replace the windshield wiper/washer switch. Did you complete the replacement?	Go to *Step 12*	—
9	Replace the windshield washer pump. Did you complete the replacement?	Go to *Step 12*	—
10	Replace the wiper motor. Did you complete the replacement?	Go to *Step 12*	—
11	Replace the wiper motor cover. Did you complete the replacement?	Go to *Step 12*	—
12	Operate the system in order to verify the repair. Did you correct the condition?	System OK	Go to *Step 3*

GC9020201023000X

Fig. 105 Test 3: Washer Inoperative. Eldorado

Step	Action	Value(s)	Yes	No
1	Did you review the Wiper/Washer System Description and Operation and perform the necessary inspections?	—	Go to *Step 2*	Go to *Symptoms*
2	1. Turn ON the ignition, with the engine OFF. 2. Turn the windshield wiper/washer switch to LO. 3. Turn the windshield wiper/washer switch to HI. 4. Turn OFF the windshield wiper/washer switch. Do the windshield wipers operate properly?	—	*Test for Intermittent and Poor Connections*	Go to *Step 3*
3	1. Disconnect the windshield wiper motor connector C1. 2. Turn OFF the windshield wiper/washer switch. 3. Measure the voltage from the windshield wiper motor relay coil supply voltage circuit to a good ground. Does the voltage measure near the specified value?	10.5–15 V	Go to *Step 5*	Go to *Step 4*
4	1. Disconnect the windshield wiper motor connector C2. 2. Measure the voltage from the windshield wiper motor high speed circuit, terminal A, to a good ground. Does the voltage measure near the specified value?	10.5–15 V	Go to *Step 6*	Go to *Step 7*
5	Test the windshield wiper motor relay coil supply voltage circuit for a short to voltage. Did you find and correct the condition?	—	Go to *Step 10*	Go to *Step 8*
6	Test the windshield wiper motor high speed circuit for a short to voltage. Did you find and correct the condition?	—	Go to *Step 10*	Go to *Step 8*
7	Test the windshield wiper motor park switch signal circuit for a short to voltage. Did you find and correct the condition?	—	Go to *Step 10*	Go to *Step 9*
8	Replace the windshield wiper/washer switch. Did you complete the replacement?	—	Go to *Step 10*	—
9	Replace the wiper motor cover. Did you complete the replacement?	—	Go to *Step 10*	—
10	Operate the system in order to verify the repair. Did you correct the condition?	—	System OK	Go to *Step 3*

GC9020201024000X

Fig. 106 Test 4: Wipers Always On. Eldorado

Step	Action	Value(s)	Yes	No
4	1. Connect the windshield wiper switch connector. 2. Disconnect the windshield wiper motor connector C2. 3. Connect a test lamp between the windshield wiper motor ground circuit and battery voltage. Does the test lamp illuminate?	—	Go to *Step 5*	Go to *Step 16*
5	1. Disconnect the windshield wiper motor connector C1. 2. Connect a test lamp between the windshield wiper motor low speed circuit and a good ground. Does the test lamp illuminate?	—	Go to *Step 6*	Go to *Step 11*
6	1. Turn the windshield wiper switch to LO. 2. Connect a test lamp between the windshield wiper motor relay coil supply voltage circuit and a good ground. Does the test lamp illuminate?	—	Go to *Step 10*	Go to *Step 12*
7	1. Remove the windshield wiper accessory relay. 2. Connect a test lamp between the battery positive voltage circuit, terminal A1, and a good ground. Does the test lamp illuminate?	—	Go to *Step 8*	Go to *Step 14*
8	Connect a test lamp between the accessory voltage circuit, terminal A3, and a good ground. Does the test lamp illuminate?	—	Go to *Step 9*	Go to *Step 15*
9	Connect a test lamp between the accessory voltage circuit, terminal A3, and the ground circuit, terminal B1. Does the test lamp illuminate?	—	Go to *Step 13*	Go to *Step 17*
10	Test the windshield wiper motor park switch signal circuit for high resistance or an open. Did you find and correct the condition?	—	Go to *Step 21*	Go to *Step 20*
11	Test the windshield wiper motor low speed circuit for high resistance or an open. Did you find and correct the condition?	—	Go to *Step 21*	Go to *Step 19*
12	Test the windshield wiper motor relay coil supply voltage circuit for high resistance or an open. Did you find and correct the condition?	—	Go to *Step 21*	Go to *Step 19*
13	Test the windshield wiper accessory voltage circuit for high resistance or an open. Did you find and correct the condition?	—	Go to *Step 21*	Go to *Step 18*
14	Repair the open in the windshield wiper relay battery positive voltage circuit. Did you complete the repair?	—	Go to *Step 21*	—
15	Repair the open in the windshield wiper relay accessory voltage circuit. Did you complete the repair?	—	Go to *Step 21*	—
16	Repair the open in the windshield wiper motor ground circuit. Did you complete the repair?	—	Go to *Step 21*	—
17	Repair the open in the windshield wiper relay ground circuit. Did you complete the repair?	—	Go to *Step 21*	—
18	Replace the wiper motor accessory relay. Did you complete the replacement?	—	Go to *Step 21*	—

GC9020201025020X

Fig. 107 Test 5: Wipers Inoperative In All Modes (Part 2 of 3). Eldorado

Step	Action	Value(s)	Yes	No
1	Did you review the Wiper/Washer System Description and Operation and perform the necessary inspections?	—	Go to *Step 2*	Go to *Symptoms*
2	1. Turn ON the ignition, with the engine OFF. 2. Turn the windshield wiper switch to LO. 3. Turn the windshield wiper switch to HI. 4. Turn OFF the windshield wiper switch. Do the windshield wipers operate properly?	—	*Test for Intermittent and Poor Connections*	Go to *Step 3*
3	1. Disconnect the windshield wiper switch connector. 2. Connect a test lamp between the windshield wiper accessory voltage circuit and a good ground. Does the test lamp illuminate?	—	Go to *Step 4*	Go to *Step 7*

GC9020201025010X

Fig. 107 Test 5: Wipers Inoperative In All Modes (Part 1 of 3). Eldorado

Step	Action	Value(s)	Yes	No
19	Replace the windshield wiper/washer switch. Did you complete the replacement?	—	Go to *Step 21*	—
20	Replace the wiper motor cover. Did you complete the replacement?	—	Go to *Step 21*	—
21	Operate the system in order to verify the repair. Did you correct the condition?	—	System OK	Go to *Step 3*

GC9020201025030X

Fig. 107 Test 5: Wipers Inoperative In All Modes (Part 3 of 3). Eldorado

Step	Action	Value(s)	Yes	No
1	Did you review the Wiper/Washer System Description and Operation and perform the necessary inspections?	—	Go to *Step 2*	Go to *Symptoms*
2	1. Turn ON the ignition, with the engine OFF. 2. Turn the windshield wiper/washer switch through all the switch positions. Do the windshield wipers operate properly in all modes?	—	*Test for Intermittent and Poor Connections*	Go to *Step 3*
3	Do the wipers operate properly in HI?	—	Go to *Step 4*	Go to *Step 5*
4	Do the wipers operate properly in LO?	—	Go to *Step 12*	Go to *Step 7*
5	1. Disconnect wiper motor connector C2. 2. Turn the wiper switch to HI. 3. Connect a test lamp between the windshield wiper high speed circuit and a good ground. Does the test lamp illuminate?	—	Go to *Step 19*	Go to *Step 6*
6	Test the windshield wiper motor high speed circuit for an open. Did you find and correct the condition?	—	Go to *Step 23*	Go to *Step 17*
7	1. Disconnect wiper motor connector C1. 2. Turn the wiper switch to LO. 3. Connect a test lamp between the windshield wiper motor relay coil supply voltage circuit and a good ground. Does the test lamp illuminate?	—	Go to *Step 8*	Go to *Step 10*
8	Connect a test lamp between the windshield wiper motor low speed circuit and a good ground. Does the test lamp illuminate?	—	Go to *Step 9*	Go to *Step 11*
9	Test the windshield wiper motor park switch signal circuit for an open. Did you find and correct the condition?	—	Go to *Step 23*	Go to *Step 18*
10	Test the windshield wiper motor relay coil supply voltage circuit for an open. Did you find and correct the condition?	—	Go to *Step 23*	Go to *Step 17*
11	Test the windshield wiper motor low speed circuit for an open. Did you find and correct the condition?	—	Go to *Step 23*	Go to *Step 17*

GC9020201026010X

Fig. 108 Test 6: Wipers Inoperative In One Or More Modes (Part 1 of 2). Eldorado Less Moisture Sensitive Feature

Step	Action	Value(s)	Yes	No
12	1. Turn the ignition OFF. 2. Disconnect the windshield wiper switch connector. 3. Measure the resistance from the accessory voltage circuit of the windshield wiper switch to the windshield washer switch signal circuit of the windshield wiper switch. 4. Turn the windshield wiper switch through the DELAY range. Does the resistance measure within the specified values?	115K–1.2M Ω	Go to *Step 13*	Go to *Step 17*
13	1. Turn the windshield wiper switch to the DELAY position. 2. Measure the resistance from the accessory voltage circuit of the windshield wiper switch to the windshield wiper motor relay coil supply voltage circuit of the windshield wiper switch. Does the resistance measure less than the specified value?	3 Ω	Go to *Step 14*	Go to *Step 17*
14	Test the windshield wiper motor relay coil supply voltage circuit for an open. Did you find and correct the condition?	—	Go to *Step 23*	Go to *Step 15*
15	Test the windshield washer switch signal circuit for an open. Did you find and correct the condition?	—	Go to *Step 23*	Go to *Step 16*
16	1. Remove the wiper motor cover. 2. Inspect for a poor connection from the park switch terminals to the circuit board of the wiper motor cover. Did you find a poor connection?	—	Go to *Step 20*	Go to *Step 21*
17	Replace the windshield wiper/washer switch. Did you complete the replacement?	—	Go to *Step 23*	—
18	Replace the wiper motor cover. Did you complete the replacement?	—	Go to *Step 22*	—
19	Replace the wiper motor. Did you complete the replacement?	—	Go to *Step 23*	—
20	Replace the wiper motor park switch. Did you complete the replacement?	—	Go to *Step 23*	—
21	Replace the wiper motor cover. Did you complete the replacement?	—	Go to *Step 23*	—
22	Operate the system in order to verify the repair. Did you correct the condition?	—	System OK	Go to *Step 19*
23	Operate the system in order to verify the repair. Did you correct the condition?	—	System OK	Go to *Step 3*

GC9020201026020X

Fig. 108 Test 6: Wipers Inoperative In One Or More Modes (Part 2 of 2). Eldorado Less Moisture Sensitive Feature

Step	Action	Value(s)	Yes	No
15	1. Connect the rain sensor connector. 2. Measure the resistance from the accessory voltage circuit of the windshield wiper switch to the windshield washer switch signal circuit of the windshield wiper switch. 3. Turn the windshield wiper switch through the AUTO DELAY range. Does the resistance measure within the specified values?	115K–1.2M Ω	Go to *Step 16*	Go to *Step 23*
16	1. Turn the windshield wiper switch to the AUTO DELAY position. 2. Measure the resistance from the accessory voltage circuit of the windshield wiper switch to the windshield wiper motor relay coil supply voltage circuit of the windshield wiper switch. Does the resistance measure less than the specified value?	3 Ω	Go to *Step 17*	Go to *Step 23*
17	1. Disconnect wiper motor connector C1. 2. Measure the resistance in the windshield wiper switch high signal circuit. Does the resistance measure less than the specified value?	3 Ω	Go to *Step 18*	Go to *Step 21*
18	Measure the resistance in the windshield wiper switch low signal circuit. Does the resistance measure less than the specified value?	3 Ω	Go to *Step 26*	Go to *Step 22*
19	Repair the open in the rain sensor ground circuit. Did you complete the repair?	—	Go to *Step 30*	—
20	Repair the open in the rain sensor accessory voltage circuit. Did you complete the repair?	—	Go to *Step 30*	—
21	Repair the open in the windshield wiper switch high signal circuit. Did you complete the repair?	—	Go to *Step 30*	—
22	Repair the open in the windshield wiper switch low signal circuit. Did you complete the repair?	—	Go to *Step 30*	—
23	Replace the windshield wiper/washer switch. Did you complete the replacement?	—	Go to *Step 30*	—
24	Replace the wiper motor. Did you complete the replacement?	—	Go to *Step 30*	—
25	Replace the wiper motor cover. Did you complete the replacement?	—	Go to *Step 28*	—
26	Replace the wiper motor cover. Did you complete the replacement?	—	Go to *Step 29*	—
27	Replace the rain sensor. Did you complete the replacement?	—	Go to *Step 30*	—
28	Operate the system in order to verify the repair. Did you correct the condition?	—	System OK	Go to *Step 24*
29	Operate the system in order to verify the repair. Did you correct the condition?	—	System OK	Go to *Step 27*
30	Operate the system in order to verify the repair. Did you correct the condition?	—	System OK	Go to *Step 3*

GC9020201027020X

Fig. 109 Test 7: Wipers Inoperative In One Or More Modes (Part 2 of 2). Eldorado w/Moisture Sensitive Feature

Step	Action	Value(s)	Yes	No
1	Did you review the Wiper/Washer System Description and Operation and perform the necessary inspections?	—	Go to *Step 2*	Go to *Symptoms*
2	1. Turn ON the ignition, with the engine OFF. 2. Turn the windshield wiper/washer switch through all the switch positions. Do the windshield wipers operate properly in all modes?	—	*Test for Intermittent and Poor Connections*	Go to *Step 3*
3	Do the wipers operate properly in HI?	—	Go to *Step 4*	Go to *Step 5*
4	Do the wipers operate properly in LO?	—	Go to *Step 12*	Go to *Step 7*
5	1. Disconnect wiper motor connector C2. 2. Turn the wiper switch to HI. 3. Connect a test lamp between the windshield wiper high speed circuit and a good ground. Does the test lamp illuminate?	—	Go to *Step 24*	Go to *Step 6*
6	Test the windshield wiper motor high speed circuit for an open. Did you find and correct the condition?	—	Go to *Step 30*	Go to *Step 23*
7	1. Disconnect wiper motor connector C1. 2. Turn the wiper switch to LO. 3. Connect a test lamp between the windshield wiper motor relay coil supply voltage circuit and a good ground. Does the test lamp illuminate?	—	Go to *Step 8*	Go to *Step 10*
8	Connect a test lamp between the windshield wiper motor low speed circuit and a good ground. Does the test lamp illuminate?	—	Go to *Step 9*	Go to *Step 11*
9	Test the windshield wiper motor park switch signal circuit for an open. Did you find and correct the condition?	—	Go to *Step 30*	Go to *Step 25*
10	Test the windshield wiper motor relay coil supply voltage circuit for an open. Did you find and correct the condition?	—	Go to *Step 30*	Go to *Step 4*
11	Test the windshield wiper motor low speed circuit for an open. Did you find and correct the condition?	—	Go to *Step 30*	Go to *Step 23*
12	1. Disconnect the rain sensor connector. 2. Connect a test lamp between the accessory voltage circuit of the rain sensor and the ground circuit of the rain sensor. Does the test lamp illuminate?	—	Go to *Step 14*	Go to *Step 13*
13	Connect a test lamp between the accessory voltage circuit of the rain sensor and a good ground. Does the test lamp illuminate?	—	Go to *Step 19*	Go to *Step 20*
14	1. Disconnect the windshield wiper switch connector. 2. Test the windshield washer switch signal circuit for an open. Did you find and correct the condition?	—	Go to *Step 30*	Go to *Step 15*

GC9020201027010X

Fig. 109 Test 7: Wipers Inoperative In One Or More Modes (Part 1 of 2). Eldorado w/Moisture Sensitive Feature

Step	Action	Yes	No
1	Did you review the Wiper/Washer System Description and Operation and perform the necessary inspections?	Go to *Step 2*	Go to *Symptoms* -
2	1. Turn ON the ignition, with the engine OFF. 2. Turn the windshield wiper switch to LO. 3. Turn the windshield wiper switch to HI. 4. Turn OFF the windshield wiper switch. Do the windshield wipers park properly?	*Test for Intermittent and Poor Connections*	Go to *Step 3*
3	Do the wipers operate properly in LO?	Go to *Step 4*	Go to *Wipers Inoperative - One or More Modes (without CE1) or Wipers Inoperative - One or More Modes (with CE1)*
4	Replace the park switch. Did you complete the replacement?	Go to *Step 5*	—
5	1. Turn ON the ignition, with the engine OFF. 2. Turn the windshield wiper switch to LO. 3. Turn the windshield wiper switch to HI. 4. Turn OFF the windshield wiper switch. Do the windshield wipers park properly?	Go to *Step 7*	Go to *Step 6*
6	Replace the wiper motor. Did you complete the replacement?	Go to *Step 7*	—
7	Operate the system in order to verify the repair. Did you correct the condition?	System OK	Go to *Step 3*

GC9020201028000X

Fig. 110 Test 8: Wiper Blades Do Not Park. Eldorado

Step	Action	Normal Result(s)	Abnormal Result(s)*
1	1. Turn the ignition switch to ACCY or ON. 2. Hold the washer switch in the ON position for 1–2 seconds.	The washer sprays the windshield until the switch is released. The wipers run at low speed and continue to run for approximately 6 seconds after the wash cycle is complete, then return to the park position.	• *Washers Always On* • *Wipers Always On* • *Wipers All Modes Inoperative* • *Washers Inoperative*
2	1. Turn the wiper switch to DELAY (pulse mode). 2. Activate the delay time by turning the wiper switch.	The wipers make one complete sweep, then pause for 0–25 seconds before making the next sweep. The pause time is adjusted by turning the wiper switch through the delay range.	• *Wipers Delay Mode Inoperative* • *Wipers All Modes Inoperative*
3	1. Turn the wiper switch to DELAY. 2. Hold the washer switch ON for 1–2 seconds.	The washer sprays as long as the washer switch is held ON. The wipers run at low speed during the spray period and continue for approximately 6 seconds after the spray cycle. The wipers then return to pulse operation.	• *Wipers Delay Mode Inoperative* • *Wipers All Modes Inoperative* • *Washers Inoperative* • *Washers Always On*
4	Turn the wiper switch to LO.	The wipers run continuously at low speed.	• *Wipers Always On* • *Wipers All Modes Inoperative*
5	Turn the wiper switch to HI.	The wipers run continuously at high speed.	• *Wipers High Mode Inoperative, Low Mode Operates* • *Wipers All Modes Inoperative*
6	Turn the wiper switch to OFF.	The wipers return to the park position at low speed.	• *Wipers Blades Do Not Park with Switch Off* • *Wipers Always On*
7	Turn the wiper switch to MIST, then release.	The wipers make one complete sweep at low speed and park.	• *Wipers Always On* • *Wipers All Modes Inoperative*

GC9020201029000X

Fig. 111 Wiper/Washer System Check. Lumina

Step	Action	Value(s)	Yes	No
1	Was the Wiper/Washer System Check performed?	—	Go to *Step 2*	Go to *System Check*
2	Check the washer solvent container fluid level. Is the washer solvent container filled?	—	Go to *Step 4*	Go to *Step 3*
3	Fill the washer solvent container. Is the washer solvent container filled?	—	Go to *System Check*	—
4	Check the hoses to ensure that they are correctly attached and that they are not pinched or kinked. Are the hoses OK?	—	Go to *Step 6*	Go to *Step 5*
5	Repair the hoses. Is the repair complete?	—	Go to *System Check*	—
6	Check for clogged windshield washer nozzles. Are the nozzles clogged?	—	Go to *Step 7*	Go to *Step 8*
7	Repair the clogged nozzles. Is the repair complete?	—	Go to *System Check*	—
8	Check for a blown (open) wiper/washer fuse. Is the fuse blown (open)?	—	Go to *Step 9*	Go to *Step 10*
9	Replace the blown (open) fuse. Is the replacement complete?	—	Go to *System Check*	—
10	1. Disconnect the washer pump connector. 2. Turn the ignition switch to ON. 3. Connect a test light between terminals A and B of washer pump connector (harness side). 4. Activate the washer switch while observing the test light. Is the test light on?	—	Go to *Step 11*	Go to *Step 14*
11	Check for a poor connection condition at the washer pump connector. Is a poor connection condition present?	—	Go to *Step 12*	Go to *Step 13*
12	Repair the poor connection condition. Is the repair complete?	—	Go to *System Check*	—
13	Replace the washer pump. Is the replacement complete?	—	Go to *System Check*	—
14	1. Connect the test light between the washer pump connector terminal A (harness side) and ground. 2. Activate the washer switch while observing test light. Is the test light on?	—	Go to *Step 15*	Go to *Step 18*
15	Check for a poor connection condition or open circuit condition in CKT 227. Is a poor connection condition or open circuit condition present?	—	Go to *Step 16*	Go to *Step 17*
16	Repair the poor connection condition or open circuit condition Is the repair complete?	—	Go to *System Check*	—

GC9020201031010X

Fig. 113 Test 2: Washer Inoperative (Part 1 of 2). Lumina

Step	Action	Value(s)	Yes	No
1	Was the Wiper/Washer System Check performed?	—	Go to *Step 2*	Go to *System Check*
2	1. Set ignition switch to ON. 2. Set the wiper switch to LO. 3. Disconnect wiper motor connector C1. 4. Connect a test light from connector C1 terminal F, to ground. 5. Momentarily activate the washer switch while observing the test light. Is the test light on after the washer switch is released?	—	Go to *Step 4*	Go to *Step 3*
3	Replace the wiper motor cover. Is the replacement complete?	—	Go to *System Check*	—
4	Replace the wiper/washer switch. Is the replacement complete?	—	Go to *System Check*	—

GC9020201030000X

Fig. 112 Test 1: Washer Always On. Lumina

Step	Action	Value(s)	Yes	No
17	Replace the wiper motor (internal ground circuit open). Is the replacement complete?	—	Go to *System Check*	—
18	1. Backprobe the wiper motor connector C1, terminal D, to ground with a test light. 2. Activate the washer switch while observing the test light. Is the test light on?	—	Go to *Step 19*	Go to *Step 20*
19	Repair the poor connection condition or open circuit condition in CKT 228. Is the repair complete?	—	Go to *System Check*	—
20	1. Backprobe the wiper/washer switch connector C201, terminal E13, to ground with a DMM. 2. Activate the washer switch while observing the DMM Is the measurement within the specified range?	10.5 - 15 volts	Go to *Step 21*	Go to *Step 24*
21	Check for a poor connection at connectors C201 and C219, or for an open circuit condition in CKT 94. Is a poor connection condition or open circuit condition present?	—	Go to *Step 22*	Go to *Step 23*
22	Repair the poor connection condition or open circuit condition. Is the repair complete?	—	Go to *System Check*	—
23	Replace the wiper motor cover. Is the replacement complete?	—	Go to *System Check*	—
24	Replace the wiper/washer switch assembly. Is the replacement complete?	—	Go to *System Check*	—

GC9020201031020X

Fig. 113 Test 2: Washer Inoperative (Part 2 of 2). Lumina

Step	Action	Value(s)	Yes	No
1	Was the Wiper/Washer System Check performed?	—	Go to *Step 2*	Go to *System Check*
2	Check for a blown (open) wiper/washer fuse. Is the fuse blown (open)?	—	Go to *Step 3*	Go to *Step 4*
3	Replace the wiper/washer fuse. Is the replacement complete?	—	Go to *System Check*	—
4	1. Disconnect wiper/washer switch connector C201. 2. Set the ignition switch to ON. 3. Connect a test light from connector C201, terminal E9, to ground. Is the test light on?	—	Go to *Step 6*	Go to *Step 5*
5	Repair the open or poor connection in CKT 243. Is the repair complete?	—	Go to *System Check*	—
6	1. Disconnect the wiper motor connector C2. 2. Connect the test light from connector C2, terminal C, to battery voltage. Is the test light on?	—	Go to *Step 8*	Go to *Step 7*

GC9020201032010X

Fig. 114 Test 3: Wipers In All Modes Inoperative (Part 1 of 2). Lumina

Step	Action	Value(s)	Yes	No
7	Repair the open in CKT 1050. Is the repair complete?	—	Go to *System Check*	—
8	1. Reconnect the wiper/washer switch connector C201. 2. Disconnect the wiper motor connector C1. 3. Connect the test light from wiper motor connector C1, terminal C, to ground. Is the test light on?	—	Go to *Step 12*	Go to *Step 9*
9	Check for a poor connection or an open circuit condition in CKT 95. Is a poor connection or an open circuit condition present?	—	Go to *Step 10*	Go to *Step 11*
10	Repair the poor connection or open circuit condition in CKT 95. Is the repair complete?	—	Go to *System Check*	—
11	Replace the wiper/washer switch. Is the replacement complete?	—	Go to *System Check*	—
12	1. Set the wiper switch to LO. 2. Connect the test light from the wiper motor connector C1, terminal B, to ground. Is the test light on?	—	Go to *Step 15*	Go to *Step 13*
13	Check for a poor connection or an open circuit condition in CKT 91. Is a poor connection or an open circuit condition present?	—	Go to *Step 14*	Go to *Step 11*
14	Repair the poor connection or open circuit condition in CKT 91. Is the repair complete?	—	Go to *System Check*	—
15	Check for continuity between wiper motor connector C1, terminal A, and connector C2, terminal B. Is continuity present?	—	Go to *Step 16*	Go to *Step 19*
16	Check for a poor connection at wiper motor connectors C1 and C2. Is a poor connection condition present?	—	Go to *Step 18*	Go to *Step 17*
17	Replace the wiper motor. Is the replacement complete?	—	Go to *System Check*	—
18	Repair the poor connection condition. Is the repair complete?	—	Go to *System Check*	—
19	Repair the open circuit condition in CKT 196. Is the repair complete?	—	Go to *System Check*	—

GC9020201032020X

Fig. 114 Test 3: Wipers In All Modes Inoperative (Part 2 of 2). Lumina

Step	Action	Value(s)	Yes	No
1	Was the Wiper/Washer System Check performed?	—	Go to *Step 2*	Go to *System Check*
2	Does the wiper motor operate in LO?	—	Go to *Step 3*	Go to *Wipers Always On*
3	Replace the park switch. Is the problem corrected?	—	Go to *System Check*	Go to *Step 4*
4	Replace the wiper motor. Is the repair complete?	—	Go to *System Check*	—

GC9020201034000X

Fig. 116 Test 5: Wiper Blades Do Not Park w/Switch Off. Lumina

Step	Action	Value(s)	Yes	No
1	Was the Wiper/Washer System Check performed?	—	Go to *Step 2*	Go to *System Check*
2	1. Disconnect wiper motor connector C2. 2. Set the ignition switch to ON. 3. Set the wiper switch to HI. 4. Connect a test light from wiper motor connector C2, terminal A, to ground. Is the test light on?	—	Go to *Step 3*	Go to *Step 6*
3	Check for a poor connection at wiper motor connector C2, terminal A. Is a poor connection condition present?	—	Go to *Step 4*	Go to *Step 5*
4	Repair the poor connection condition. Is the repair complete?	—	Go to *System Check*	—
5	Replace the wiper motor. Is the replacement complete?	—	Go to *System Check*	—

GC9020201036010X

Fig. 118 Test 7: Wipers High Mode Inoperative, Low Mode Operates (Part 1 of 2). Lumina

Step	Action	Value(s)	Yes	No
1	Was the Wiper/Washer System Check performed?	—	Go to *Step 2*	Go to *System Check*
2	1. Disconnect wiper motor connector C1. 2. Set the ignition switch to ON. 3. Set the wiper switch to OFF. 4. Measure the voltage from wiper motor connector C1, terminal B, to ground with a DMM. Is the measurement within the specified range?	10.5 - 15 volts	Go to *Step 3*	Go to *Step 6*
3	Check for a short circuit to battery voltage condition in CKT 91. Is a short circuit condition present?	—	Go to *Step 4*	Go to *Step 5*
4	Repair the short circuit to battery condition in CKT 91. Is the repair complete?	—	Go to *System Check*	—
5	Replace the wiper/washer switch. Is the repair complete?	—	Go to *System Check*	—
6	1. Disconnect wiper motor connector C2. 2. Measure the voltage from wiper motor connector C2, terminal A, to ground with a DMM. Is the measurement within the specified range?	10.5 - 15 volts	Go to *Step 7*	Go to *Step 10*
7	Check for a short circuit to battery voltage condition in CKT 92. Is a short circuit condition present?	—	Go to *Step 8*	Go to *Step 9*
8	Repair the short circuit to battery condition in CKT 92. Is the repair complete?	—	Go to *System Check*	—
9	Replace the wiper/washer switch. Is the repair complete?	—	Go to *System Check*	—
10	Check for a short circuit to battery voltage condition in CKT 196. Is a short circuit condition present?	—	Go to *Step 11*	Go to *Step 12*
11	Repair the short circuit to battery condition in CKT 196. Is the repair complete?	—	Go to *System Check*	—
12	Replace the wiper motor. Is the repair complete?	—	Go to *System Check*	—

GC9020201033000X

Fig. 115 Test 4: Wipers Always On. Lumina

Step	Action	Value(s)	Yes	No
1	Was the Wiper/Washer System Check performed?	—	Go to *Step 2*	Go to *System Check*
2	1. Set the ignition switch to OFF. 2. Disconnect wiper/washer switch connector C201. 3. Set the wiper switch to DELAY. 4. Measure the resistance between wiper/washer switch connector C201, terminals E9 and E13, with a DMM 5. Move the wiper switch through the entire delay range. Does the resistance vary within the specified range?	110 KΩ to1200 KΩ	Go to *Step 4*	Go to *Step 3*
3	Replace the wiper/washer switch. Is the repair complete?	—	Go to *System Check*	—
4	Measure the resistance between wiper/washer switch connector C201, terminals E9 and E13, with a DMM. Is the resistance less than the specified value?	3 Ω	Go to *Step 6*	Go to *Step 5*
5	Replace the wiper/washer switch. Is the repair complete?	—	Go to *System Check*	—
6	Check for a poor connection condition or an open circuit condition in CKT 91 or CKT 94. Is a poor connection condition or an open circuit condition present?	—	Go to *Step 7*	Go to *Step 8*
7	Repair the poor connection condition or the open circuit condition in CKT 91 or CKT 94. Is the repair complete?	—	Go to *System Check*	—
8	Replace the wiper motor cover. Is the repair complete?	—	Go to *System Check*	—

GC9020201035000X

Fig. 117 Test 6: Wipers Delay Mode Inoperative. Lumina

Step	Action	Value(s)	Yes	No
6	Check for a poor connection condition or an open circuit condition CKT 92. Is a poor connection condition or an open circuit condition present?	—	Go to *Step 7*	Go to *Step 8*
7	Repair the poor connection condition or open circuit condition in CKT 92. Is the repair complete?	—	Go to *System Check*	—
8	Replace the wiper/washer switch. Is the replacement complete?	—	Go to *System Check*	—

GC9020201036020X

Fig. 118 Test 7: Wipers High Mode Inoperative, Low Mode Operates (Part 2 of 2). Lumina

Step	Action	Value(s)	Yes	No
1	Was the Wiper/Washer System Check performed?	—	Go to *Step 2*	Go to *System Check*
2	1. Disconnect wiper motor connector C1. 2. Set the ignition switch to ON. 3. Set the wiper switch to LO. 4. Connect a test light from wiper motor connector C1, terminal B, to ground. Is the test light on?	—	Go to *Step 6*	Go to *Step 3*
3	Check for an open circuit condition or poor connection condition in CKT 91. Is an open circuit condition or poor connection condition present?	—	Go to *Step 4*	Go to *Step 5*
4	Repair the open circuit condition or poor connection condition in CKT 91. Is the repair complete?	—	Go to *System Check*	—
5	Replace the wiper/washer switch. Is the replacement complete?	—	Go to *System Check*	—
6	Connect a test light from wiper motor connector C1, terminal C, to ground. Is the test light on?	—	Go to *Step 10*	Go to *Step 7*
7	Check for an open circuit condition or poor connection condition in CKT 95. Is an open circuit condition or poor connection condition present?	—	Go to *Step 9*	Go to *Step 8*
8	Repair the open circuit condition or the poor connection condition in CKT 95. Is the repair complete?	—	Go to *System Check*	—
9	Replace the wiper/washer switch. Is the replacement complete?	—	Go to *System Check*	—
10	Check for continuity between wiper motor connector C1, terminal A, and connector C2, terminal B, with a DMM. Is continuity present?	—	Go to *Step 12*	Go to *Step 11*
11	Repair the open circuit condition in CKT 196. Is the repair complete?	—	Go to *System Check*	—
12	Check for a poor connection condition to the wiper motor assembly at connector C1. Is a poor connection condition present?	—	Go to *Step 13*	Go to *Step 14*

GC9020201037010X

Fig. 119 Test 8: Wipers Low Mode Inoperative, High Mode Operates (Part 1 of 2). Lumina

Step	Action	Value(s)	Yes	No
1	Was the Wiper/Washer System Check performed?	—	Go to *Step 2*	Go to *System Check*
2	1. Remove the wiper fuse. 2. Connect an ammeter (0 - 30 amp) across the wiper fuse block terminals. 3. Set the ignition switch to ON. 4. Set the wiper switch to LO. 5. Observe the lowest current draw while the wipers are running on dry glass (current draw will fluctuate). 6. Set the wiper switch to OFF. Is the lowest current draw less than the specified value?	3.5 amps	Go to *Step 3*	Go to *Step 4*
3	Replace the wiper motor. Is the replacement complete?	—	Go to *System Check*	—
4	Is the lowest current draw greater than the specified value?	6.5 amps	Go to *Step 8*	Go to *Step 5*
5	Check for an intermittent poor connection or an open circuit condition in CKTs 293, 91, 92, 95, 196, and 1050. Is a poor connection condition or an open circuit condition present?	—	Go to *Step 6*	Go to *Step 7*
6	Repair the poor connection condition or the open circuit condition. Is the repair complete?	—	Go to *System Check*	—
7	Replace the wiper motor. Is the replacement complete?	—	Go to *System Check*	—
8	Replace the wiper blade elements. Is the replacement complete?	—	Go to *Step 9*	—
9	1. Set the wiper switch to LO. 2. Observe the ammeter for the lowest current draw while the wipers are running on dry glass (current draw will fluctuate). 3. Set the wiper switch to OFF. Is the lowest current draw greater than the specified value?	6.5 amps	Go to *Step 13*	Go to *Step 10*
10	Check for an intermittent poor connection or an open circuit condition in CKTs 91, 92, 93, 95, 150, and 196. Is a poor connection condition or an open circuit condition present?	—	Go to *Step 11*	Go to *Step 12*
11	Repair the poor connection condition or the open circuit condition. Is the repair complete?	—	Go to *System Check*	—

GC9020201038010X

Fig. 120 Test 9: Wipers Low Or High Modes Intermittent (Part 1 of 2). Lumina

Step	Action	Value(s)	Yes	No
13	Repair the poor connection condition at wiper motor connector C1. Is the repair complete?	—	Go to *System Check*	—
14	Replace the wiper motor. Is the replacement complete?	—	Go to *System Check*	—

GC9020201037020X

Fig. 119 Test 8: Wipers Low Mode Inoperative, High Mode Operates (Part 2 of 2). Lumina

Step	Action	Value(s)	Yes	No
12	Replace the wiper motor. Is the replacement complete?	—	Go to *System Check*	—
13	1. Disconnect the wiper transmission drive link from the wiper motor crank arm. 2. Set the wiper switch to LO. 3. Observe the ammeter for the lowest current draw while the wipers are running on dry glass (current draw will fluctuate). 4. Set the wiper switch to OFF. Is the lowest current draw greater than the specified value?	6.5 amps	Go to *Step 15*	Go to *Step 14*
14	The wiper transmission is binding. Repair or replace the wiper transmission. Is the repair or replacement complete?	—	Go to *System Check*	—
15	Replace the wiper motor. Is the replacement complete?	—	Go to *System Check*	—

GC9020201038020X

Fig. 120 Test 9: Wipers Low Or High Modes Intermittent (Part 2 of 2). Lumina

Step	Action	Normal Result(s)	Abnormal Result(s)*
1	1. Turn the ignition switch to RUN. 2. Hold the washer switch in the ON position.	• The wipers operate at LO speed. • The washer sprays the windshield as long as the washer switch is held in the ON position. • After releasing the switch, the washer stops and the wipers return to the park position after 2–4 sweeps.	• *Washers Inoperative* • *Wipers Mist, Delay, and Low Modes Inoperative*
2	Turn the wiper switch to DELAY (pulse mode).	• The wipers make one complete sweep, then pause for 1–22 seconds before making the next sweep. • The pause time is adjusted by turning the wiper switch through the delay range.	• *Wipers Delay Mode Inoperative* • *Wipers Mist, Delay, and Low Modes Inoperative*
3	1. Turn the wiper switch to DELAY. 2. Hold the wiper switch ON for 1–2 seconds.	• The washer sprays as long as the washer switch is held ON. • The wipers run at low speed during spray period and continue for 2–4 sweeps after the washer switch is released. • The wipers then return to pulse operation.	• *Washers Inoperative* • *Wipers Delay Mode Inoperative* • *Wipers Mist, Delay, and Low Modes Inoperative*
4	Turn the wiper switch to LO.	The wipers run continuously at low speed.	*Wipers Mist, Delay, and Low Modes Inoperative*
5	Turn the wiper switch to HI.	The wipers run continuously at high speed.	*Wipers High Mode Inoperative, Low Mode Operates*
6	Turn the wiper switch to OFF.	The wipers return to the park position at low speed.	• *Wipers Always On* • *Wipers Blades Do Not Park*
7	Turn the wiper switch to MIST, then release.	The wipers make one complete sweep, then return to the park position.	*Wipers Mist, Delay, and Low Modes Inoperative*

GC9020000836000X

Fig. 121 Wiper/Washer System Check. Impala & Monte Carlo

Step	Action	Value(s)	Yes	No
1	Did you review the system operation and perform the necessary inspections?	—	Go to *Step 2*	*Check Symptoms*
2	Turn ON the ignition, with the engine OFF. Does the instrument cluster (IPC) display the LOW WASHER FLUID message?	—	Go to *Step 3*	*Check for Intermittent and Poor Connections*
3	1. Turn OFF the ignition. 2. Disconnect the windshield washer solvent level switch. 3. Turn ON the ignition, with the engine OFF. 4. With a scan tool, observe the Washer Fluid Level parameter in the Instrument Panel Cluster data list. Does the scan tool display OK?	—	Go to *Step 5*	Go to *Step 4*
4	Test the signal circuit of the windshield washer solvent level switch for a short to ground. Did you find and correct the condition?	—	Go to *Step 7*	Go to *Step 6*
5	Replace the windshield washer solvent level switch. Did you complete the replacement?	—	Go to *Step 7*	—
6	Replace the IPC. Did you complete the replacement?	—	Go to *Step 7*	—
7	Operate the system in order to verify the repair. Did you correct the condition?	—	System Ok	Go to *Step 2*

GC9020000837000X

Fig. 122 Test 1: Low Washer Fluid Message Always On. Impala & Monte Carlo

Step	Action	Value(s)	Yes	No
1	Did you review the system operation and perform the necessary inspections?	—	Go to *Step 2*	*Check Symptoms*
2	1. Drain the windshield fluid. 2. Turn ON the ignition, with the engine OFF. Does the instrument cluster (IPC) display the LOW WASHER FLUID message?	—	*Test for Intermittent and Poor Connections*	Go to *Step 3*
3	1. Turn OFF the ignition. 2. Disconnect the windshield washer solvent level switch. 3. Connect a 3 amp fused jumper wire between the signal circuit of the windshield washer solvent level switch and a good ground. 4. Install a scan tool. 5. Turn ON the ignition, with the engine OFF. 6. With a scan tool, observe the Washer Fluid Level parameter in the Instrument Panel Cluster data list. Does the scan tool display LOW?	—	Go to *Step 5*	Go to *Step 4*
4	Test the signal circuit of the windshield washer solvent level switch for a high resistance or an open. Did you find and correct the condition?	—	Go to *Step 10*	Go to *Step 7*

GC9020000838010X

Fig. 123 Test 2: Low Washer Fluid Message Inoperative (Part 1 of 2). Impala & Monte Carlo

Step	Action	Value(s)	Yes	No
1	Did you review the system operation and perform the necessary inspections?	—	Go to *Step 2*	*Check Symptoms*
2	1. Turn the ignition to OFF. 2. Disconnect the wiper/washer switch connector. 3. Turn the wiper switch to DELAY. 4. Measure the resistance through the wiper/washer switch connector, terminal A3 to terminal B9. 5. Move the wiper switch through the entire delay range, one notch at a time. Does the resistance vary within the specified values?	39 KΩ to 680 KΩ	Go to *Step 4*	Go to *Step 3*
3	Replace the wiper/washer switch. Did you complete the replacement?	—	Go to *Step 7*	—
4	1. Reconnect the wiper/washer switch connector. 2. Disconnect the wiper motor connector. 3. Turn the ignition switch to RUN. 4. Turn the wiper switch to DELAY. 5. Measure the voltage from the wiper motor connector, terminal E, to ground. Does the voltage measure within the specified values?	10.5–15 V	Go to *Step 6*	Go to *Step 5*
5	Repair the open in CKT 112. Did you complete the repair?	—	Go to *Step 7*	—
6	Replace the wiper motor cover. Did you complete the replacement?	—	Go to *Step 7*	—
7	Operate the system in order to verify the repair. Did you correct the condition?	—	System OK	Go to *Step 2*

GC9020000839000X

Fig. 124 Test 3: Wipers Delay Mode Inoperative. Impala & Monte Carlo

Step	Action	Value(s)	Yes	No
9	Connect the *J 34142-B* from the wiper motor connector, terminal C to terminal A. Does the test lamp illuminate?	—	Go to *Step 11*	Go to *Step 10*
10	Repair the open in CKT 1150. Did you complete the repair?	—	Go to *Step 14*	—
11	Inspect for a poor connection to the wiper motor. Did you find and correct the condition?	—	Go to *Step 14*	Go to *Step 12*
12	Replace the wiper motor. Did you complete the replacement?	—	Go to *Step 14*	—
13	Replace the wiper/washer switch. Did you complete the replacement?	—	Go to *Step 14*	—
14	Operate the system in order to verify the repair. Did you correct the condition?	—	System OK	Go to *Step 2*

GC9020000840020X

Fig. 125 Test 4: Wipers All Modes Inoperative (Part 2 of 2). Impala & Monte Carlo

Step	Action	Value(s)	Yes	No
5	Test the ground circuit of the windshield washer solvent level switch for a high resistance or an open. Did you find and correct the condition?	—	Go to *Step 10*	Go to *Step 6*
6	Inspect for poor connections at the harness connector of the windshield washer solvent level switch. Did you find and correct the condition?	—	Go to *Step 10*	Go to *Step 8*
7	Inspect for poor connections at the harness connector of the IPC. Did you find and correct the condition?	—	Go to *Step 10*	Go to *Step 9*
8	Replace the windshield washer solvent level switch. Did you complete the replacement?	—	Go to *Step 10*	—
9	Replace the IPC. Did you complete the replacement?	—	Go to *Step 10*	—
10	Operate the system in order to verify the repair. Did you correct the condition?	—	System OK	Go to *Step 2*

GC9020000838020X

Fig. 123 Test 2: Low Washer Fluid Message Inoperative (Part 2 of 2). Impala & Monte Carlo

Step	Action	Value(s)	Yes	No
1	Did you review the system operation and perform the necessary inspections?	—	Go to *Step 2*	Go to *Symptoms*
2	Inspect for an open wiper fuse. Did you find and correct the condition?	—	Go to *Step 14*	Go to *Step 3*
3	1. Set ignition switch to RUN. 2. Backprobe from the wiper/washer switch connector, terminal A3, to ground using a *J 34142-B*. Does the test lamp illuminate?	—	Go to *Step 5*	Go to *Step 4*
4	Repair the open in CKT 243. Did you complete the repair?	—	Go to *Step 14*	—
5	1. Set the wiper switch to HI. 2. Connect the *J 34142-B* from the wiper/washer switch connector, terminal D3, to ground. Does the test lamp illuminate?	—	Go to *Step 7*	Go to *Step 6*
6	Test for high resistance or an open in CKTs 243 and 92. Did you find and correct the condition?	—	Go to *Step 14*	Go to *Step 13*
7	1. Disconnect the wiper motor connector. 2. Connect the *J 34142-B* from the wiper motor connector, terminal C, to ground. Does the test lamp illuminate?	—	Go to *Step 9*	Go to *Step 8*
8	Repair the open in CKT 92. Did you complete the repair?	—	Go to *Step 14*	—

GC9020000840010X

Fig. 125 Test 4: Wipers All Modes Inoperative (Part 1 of 2). Impala & Monte Carlo

Step	Action	Value(s)	Yes	No
1	Did you review the system operation and perform the necessary inspections?	—	Go to *Step 2*	*Check Symptoms*
2	Do the wipers operate at all with the wiper switch in HI?	—	Go to *Step 4*	Go to *Step 3*
3	Replace the wiper/washer switch. Did you complete the replacement?	—	Go to *Step 11*	—
4	1. Turn the ignition switch to RUN. 2. Turn the wiper switch to HI. 3. Backprobe from the wiper/washer switch connector, terminal D3, to ground using a *J 34142-B*. Does the test lamp illuminate?	—	Go to *Step 7*	Go to *Step 5*
5	Inspect for poor connections at the harness connector for the wiper/washer switch. Did you find and correct the condition?	—	Go to *Step 11*	Go to *Step 6*
6	Replace the wiper/washer switch. Did you complete the replacement?	—	Go to *Step 11*	—
7	1. Disconnect the wiper motor connector. 2. Connect the *J 34142-B* from the wiper motor connector, terminal C, to ground. Does the test lamp illuminate?	—	Go to *Step 9*	Go to *Step 8*
8	Repair the open in CKT 92. Did you complete the repair?	—	Go to *Step 11*	—
9	Inspect for a poor connection at the harness connector for the wiper motor. Did you find and correct the condition?	—	Go to *Step 11*	Go to *Step 10*
10	Replace the wiper motor. Did you complete the repair?	—	Go to *Step 11*	—
11	Operate the system in order to verify the repair. Did you correct the condition?	—	System OK	Go to *Step 2*

GC9020000841000X

Fig. 126 Test 5: Wipers High Mode Inoperative, Low Mode Operates. Impala & Monte Carlo

Step	Action	Value(s)	Yes	No
1	Did you review the system operation and perform the necessary inspections?	—	Go to *Step 2*	*Check Symptoms*
2	1. Turn the ignition switch to RUN. 2. Turn the wiper switch to LO. 3. Backprobe from the wiper/washer switch connector, terminal B6, to ground using a *J 39200.* Does the voltage measure greater than the specified value?	1.0 V	Go to *Step 5*	Go to *Step 3*
3	Inspect for poor connections at the harness connector for the wiper/washer switch. Did you find and correct the condition?	—	Go to *Step 13*	Go to *Step 4*
4	Replace the wiper/washer switch. Did you complete the replacement?	—	Go to *Step 13*	—
5	1. Disconnect the wiper motor connector. 2. Measure the voltage from the wiper motor connector, terminal D, to ground. Does the voltage measure greater than the specified value?	1.0 V	Go to *Step 7*	Go to *Step 6*
6	Repair the open in CKT 113. Did you complete the repair?	—	Go to *Step 13*	—
7	Backprobe from the wiper/washer switch connector, terminal B9, to ground, to ground using a *J 39200.* Does the voltage measure greater than the specified value?	1.0 V	Go to *Step 10*	Go to *Step 8*
8	Inspect for poor connections at the harness connector for the wiper/washer switch. Did you find and correct the condition?	—	Go to *Step 13*	Go to *Step 9*
9	Replace the wiper/washer switch. Did you complete the replacement?	—	Go to *Step 13*	—
10	Measure the voltage from the wiper motor connector, terminal E, to ground. Does the voltage measure greater than the specified value?	1.0 V	Go to *Step 12*	Go to *Step 11*
11	Repair the open in CKT 112. Did you complete the repair?	—	Go to *Step 13*	—
12	Replace the wiper motor cover. Did you complete the replacement?	—	Go to *Step 13*	—
13	Operate the system in order to verify the repair. Did you correct the condition?	—	System OK	Go to *Step 2*

GC9020000842000X

Fig. 127 Test 6: Wipers Mist, Delay & Low Modes Inoperative. Impala & Monte Carlo

Step	Action	Value(s)	Yes	No
1	Did you review the system operation and perform the necessary inspections?	—	Go to *Step 2*	Go to *Symptoms*
2	1. Turn the ignition switch to RUN. 2. Turn the wiper switch to OFF. 3. Disconnect the wiper/washer switch connector. Do the wipers park?	—	Go to *Step 3*	Go to *Step 4*
3	Replace the wiper/washer switch. Did you complete the replacement?	—	Go to *Step 9*	—
4	Measure the voltage from the wiper/washer switch connector (vehicle side), terminal B6, to ground. Does the voltage measure greater than the specified value?	1.0 V	Go to *Step 6*	Go to *Step 5*
5	Replace the wiper motor cover. Did you complete the replacement?	—	Go to *Step 9*	—
6	1. Reconnect the wiper/washer switch connector. 2. Disconnect the wiper motor connector. 3. Measure the voltage from the wiper motor connector, terminal D, to ground. Does the voltage measure greater than the specified value?	1.0 V	Go to *Step 8*	Go to *Step 7*
7	Replace the wiper motor cover. Did you complete the replacement?	—	Go to *Step 9*	—
8	Repair the short to voltage in CKT 113. Did you complete the repair?	—	Go to *Step 9*	—
9	Operate the system in order to verify the repair. Did you correct the condition?	—	System OK	Go to *Step 2*

GC9020000844000X

Fig. 129 Test 8: Wiper Blades Do Not Park. Impala & Monte Carlo

Step	Action	Value(s)	Yes	No
1	Did you review the system operation and perform the necessary inspections?	—	Go to *Step 2*	*Check Symptoms*
2	1. Set the ignition switch to RUN. 2. Set the wiper switch to OFF. 3. Disconnect the wiper/washer switch connector. Does the wiper keep running?	—	Go to *Step 5*	Go to *Step 3*
3	Test for a short to voltage in the pigtail wires to the wiper/washer switch. Did you find and correct the condition?	—	Go to *Step 12*	Go to *Step 4*
4	Replace the wiper/washer switch. Did you complete the replacement?	—	Go to *Step 12*	—
5	Measure the voltage from the wiper/washer switch connector (vehicle side), terminal B6, to ground. Does the voltage measure greater than the specified value?	1.0 V	Go to *Step 9*	Go to *Step 6*
6	1. Reconnect the wiper/washer switch connector. 2. Disconnect the wiper motor connector. 3. Measure the voltage from the wiper motor connector, terminal C, to ground. Does the voltage measure within the specified values?	10.5–15 V	Go to *Step 7*	Go to *Step 8*
7	Repair the short to voltage in CKT 92. Did you complete the repair?	—	Go to *Step 12*	—
8	Replace the wiper motor cover. Did you complete the replacement?	—	Go to *Step 12*	—
9	1. Reconnect the wiper/washer switch connector. 2. Disconnect the wiper motor connector. 3. Measure the voltage from the wiper motor connector, terminal D, to ground. Does the voltage measure greater than the specified value?	1.0 V	Go to *Step 11*	Go to *Step 10*
10	Replace the wiper motor cover. Did you complete the replacement?	—	Go to *Step 12*	—
11	Repair the short to voltage in CKT 113. Did you complete the repair?	—	Go to *Step 12*	—
12	Operate the system in order to verify the repair. Did you correct the condition?	—	System OK	Go to *Step 2*

GC9020000843000X

Fig. 128 Test 7: Wipers Always On. Impala & Monte Carlo

Step	Action	Value(s)	Yes	No
1	Did you review the system operation and perform the necessary inspections?	—	Go to *Step 2*	Go to *Symptoms*
2	Inspect the washer solvent container fluid level. Did you find and correct the condition?	—	Go to *Step 14*	Go to *Step 3*
3	Inspect the hoses to ensure that they are correctly attached and that they are not pinched or kinked. Did you find and correct the condition?	—	Go to *Step 14*	Go to *Step 4*
4	Inspect for clogged windshield washer nozzles. Did you find and correct the condition?	—	Go to *Step 14*	Go to *Step 5*
5	Inspect for an open wiper fuse. Did you find and correct the condition?	—	Go to *Step 14*	Go to *Step 6*
6	1. Disconnect the washer pump connector. 2. Turn the ignition switch to ON. 3. Connect a *J 34142-B* between terminals A and B of the washer pump connector (harness side). 4. Activate the washer switch while observing the test lamp. Does the test lamp illuminate?	—	Go to *Step 7*	Go to *Step 9*
7	Inspect for a poor connection at the washer pump connector. Did you find and correct the condition?	—	Go to *Step 14*	Go to *Step 8*
8	Replace the washer pump. Did you complete the replacement?	—	Go to *Step 14*	—
9	1. Connect the *J 34142-B* between the washer pump connector (harness side), terminal A, and ground. 2. Activate the washer switch while observing test lamp. Does the test lamp illuminate?	—	Go to *Step 10*	Go to *Step 11*
10	Repair the open in CKT 150. Did you complete the repair?	—	Go to *Step 14*	—
11	1. Backprobe the wiper/washer switch connector, terminal A4, to ground using a *J 34142-B.* 2. Activate the washer switch. Does the test lamp illuminate?	—	Go to *Step 13*	Go to *Step 12*
12	Repair the open in CKT 228. Did you complete the repair?	—	Go to *Step 14*	—
13	Replace the wiper/washer switch. Did you complete the replacement?	—	Go to *Step 14*	—
14	Operate the system in order to verify the repair. Did you correct the condition?	—	System OK	Go to *Step 2*

GC9020000845000X

Fig. 130 Test 9: Washers Inoperative. Impala & Monte Carlo

Step	Action	Yes	No
1	Did you review the Wiper/Washer System Description and Operation and perform the necessary inspections?	Go to *Step 2*	Go to *Symptoms - Systems*
2	1. Turn ON the ignition, with the engine OFF. 2. Observe the low washer fluid indicator. Does the low washer fluid indicator illuminate?	Go to *Step 5*	Go to *Step 3*
3	1. Disconnect the windshield washer solvent level sensor connector. 2. Connect a 3 amp fused jumper wire between the windshield washer fluid level signal circuit and a good ground. 3. Wait for 2 ½ minutes. Does the low washer fluid indicator illuminate?	Go to *Step 4*	Go to *Step 7*
4	1. Connect a 3 amp fused jumper wire between the windshield washer fluid level signal circuit and the windshield washer solvent level sensor ground circuit. 2. Wait for 2 ½ minutes. Does the low washer fluid indicator illuminate?	Go to *Step 8*	Go to *Step 10*
5	1. Disconnect the windshield washer solvent level sensor connector. 2. Wait for 2 ½ minutes. Did the low washer fluid indicator turn OFF?	Go to *Step 8*	Go to *Step 6*
6	Test the windshield washer fluid level signal circuit for a short to ground. Did you find and correct the condition?	Go to *Step 13*	Go to *Step 9*

GC9020201039010X

Fig. 131 Test 1: Low Washer Fluid Indicator Fault (Part 1 of 2). Intrigue

Step	Action	Yes	No
7	Test the windshield washer fluid level signal circuit for an open or high resistance. Did you find and correct the condition?	Go to *Step 13*	Go to *Step 9*
8	Inspect for a poor connection at the windshield washer solvent level sensor. Did you find and correct the condition?	Go to *Step 13*	Go to *Step 11*
9	Inspect for a poor connection at the IPC connector. Did you find and correct the condition?	Go to *Step 13*	Go to *Step 12*
10	Repair the open or high resistance in the low washer fluid indicator ground circuit. Did you find and correct the condition?	Go to *Step 13*	—
11	Replace the windshield washer solvent level sensor. Did you complete the replacement?	Go to *Step 13*	—
12	Replace the IPC. Did you complete the replacement?	Go to *Step 13*	—
13	Operate the windshield wiper/washer system in order to verify the repair. Did you correct the condition?	System OK	Go to *Step 3*

GC9020201039020X

Fig. 131 Test 1: Low Washer Fluid Indicator Fault (Part 2 of 2). Intrigue

Step	Action	Yes	No
1	Did you review the Wiper/Washer System Description and Operation and perform the necessary inspections?	Go to *Step 2*	Go to *Symptoms - Systems*
2	1. Turn ON the ignition, with the engine OFF. 2. Activate the windshield washer switch. Does the windshield washer operate properly?	*Test for Intermittent and Poor Connections*	Go to *Step 3*
3	Test for a short to voltage in the windshield washer pump control circuit. Did you find and correct the condition?	Go to *Step 5*	Go to *Step 4*
4	Replace the wiper/washer switch. Is the replacement complete?	Go to *Step 5*	—
5	Operate the system in order to verify the repair. Did you correct the condition?	System OK	Go to *Step 3*

GC9020201040000X

Fig. 132 Test 2: Washers Always On. Intrigue

Step	Action	Yes	No
1	Did you review the Wiper/Washer System Description and Operation and perform the necessary inspections?	Go to *Step 2*	Go to *Symptoms - Systems*
2	1. Turn ON the ignition, with the engine OFF. 2. Turn the windshield wiper/washer switch to LO. 3. Turn the windshield wiper/washer switch to HI. 4. Turn OFF the windshield wiper/washer switch. Do the windshield wipers operate properly?	*Test for Intermittent and Poor Connections*	Go to *Step 3*
3	Disconnect the windshield wiper/washer switch connector. Do the windshield wipers stop?	Go to *Step 5*	Go to *Step 4*
4	Test the following circuits for a short to voltage: • windshield wiper switch on signal circuit. • windshield wiper switch low/pulse signal circuit • windshield wiper motor high speed circuit Did you find and correct the condition?	Go to *Step 9*	Go to *Step 6*
5	Inspect for a poor connection at the windshield wiper/washer switch connector. Did you find and correct the condition?	Go to *Step 9*	Go to *Step 7*
6	Inspect for a poor connection at the windshield wiper motor connector. Did you find and correct the condition?	Go to *Step 9*	Go to *Step 8*
7	Replace the windshield wiper/washer switch. Did you complete the replacement?	Go to *Step 9*	—
8	Replace the windshield wiper motor cover. Refer to *Wiper Motor Cover Replacement.* Did you complete the replacement?	Go to *Step 9*	—
9	Operate the windshield wiper/washer system in order to verify the repair. Did you correct the condition?	System OK	Go to *Step 3*

GC9020201042000X

Fig. 134 Test 4: Wipers Always On. Intrigue

Step	Action	Yes	No
1	Did you review the Wiper/Washer System Description and Operation and perform the necessary inspections?	Go to *Step 2*	Go to *Symptoms - Systems*
2	1. Turn ON the ignition, with the engine OFF. 2. Activate the windshield washer switch. Does the windshield washer operate properly?	*Test for Intermittent and Poor Connections*	Go to *Step 3*
3	1. Disconnect the windshield washer pump connector. 2. Connect a test lamp between the windshield washer pump control circuit and the windshield washer pump ground circuit. 3. Activate the windshield washer switch. Does the test lamp illuminate?	Go to *Step 7*	Go to *Step 4*
4	1. Connect a test lamp between the windshield washer pump control circuit and a good ground. 2. Activate the windshield washer switch. Does the test lamp illuminate?	Go to *Step 8*	Go to *Step 5*
5	Test the windshield washer pump control circuit for a short to ground or an open. Did you find and correct the condition?	Go to *Step 11*	Go to *Step 6*
6	Inspect for a poor connection at the windshield wiper/washer switch connector. Did you find and correct the condition?	Go to *Step 11*	Go to *Step 9*
7	Inspect for a poor connection at the windshield washer pump motor. Did you find and correct the condition?	Go to *Step 11*	Go to *Step 10*
8	Repair the open in the windshield washer pump ground circuit. Did you complete the repair?	Go to *Step 11*	—
9	Replace the windshield wiper/washer switch. Did you complete the replacement?	Go to *Step 11*	—
10	Replace the windshield washer pump. Did you complete the replacement?	Go to *Step 11*	—
11	Operate the windshield wiper/washer system in order to verify the repair. Did you correct the condition?	System OK	Go to *Step 3*

GC9020201041000X

Fig. 133 Test 3: Washers Inoperative. Intrigue

Step	Action	Yes	No
1	Did you review the Wiper/Washer System Description and Operation and perform the necessary inspections?	Go to *Step 2*	Go to *Symptoms - Systems*
2	1. Turn ON the ignition, with the engine OFF. 2. Turn the windshield wiper/washer switch through all the switch positions. Do the windshield wipers operate properly?	*Test for Intermittent and Poor Connections*	Go to *Step 3*
3	1. Disconnect the windshield wiper motor connector. 2. Connect a test lamp between the accessory voltage circuit and a good ground. Does the test lamp illuminate?	Go to *Step 4*	Go to *Step 9*
4	Connect a test lamp between the accessory voltage circuit and the ground circuit of the windshield wiper motor connector. Does the test lamp illuminate?	Go to *Step 5*	Go to *Step 10*

GC9020201043010X

Fig. 135 Test 5: Wipers Inoperative In All Modes (Part 1 of 2). Intrigue

Step	Action	Yes	No
5	1. Connect a test lamp between the windshield wiper switch on signal circuit and a good ground. 2. Activate the windshield washer switch. Does the test lamp illuminate?	Go to *Step 7*	Go to *Step 6*
6	1. Disconnect the windshield wiper/washer switch connector. 2. Connect a test lamp between the accessory voltage circuit of the windshield wiper/washer switch connector and a good ground. Does the test lamp illuminate?	Go to *Step 8*	Go to *Step 11*
7	Inspect for a poor connection at the windshield wiper motor connector. Did you find and correct the condition?	Go to *Step 14*	Go to *Step 12*
8	Inspect for a poor connection at the windshield wiper/washer switch connector. Did you find and correct the condition?	Go to *Step 14*	Go to *Step 13*
9	Repair the open in the windshield wiper motor accessory voltage circuit. Did you complete the repair?	Go to *Step 14*	—
10	Repair the open in the windshield wiper motor ground circuit. Did you complete the repair?	Go to *Step 14*	—
11	Repair the open in the windshield wiper/washer switch accessory voltage circuit. Did you complete the repair?	Go to *Step 14*	—
12	Replace the windshield wiper motor. Did you complete the repair?	Go to *Step 14*	—
13	Replace the windshield wiper/washer switch. Did you complete the repair?	Go to *Step 14*	—
14	Operate the windshield wiper/washer system in order to verify the repair. Did you correct the condition?	System OK	Go to *Step 3*

GC9020201043020X

Fig. 135 Test 5: Wipers Inoperative In All Modes (Part 2 of 2). Intrigue

Step	Action	Value(s)	Yes	No
5	1. Measure the voltage from the windshield wiper switch low/pulse signal circuit to a good ground. 2. Turn the windshield wiper/washer switch through the entire DELAY range. Does the voltage measure near the specified value in each DELAY position?	B+	Go to *Step 6*	Go to *Step 13*
6	Measure the voltage from the windshield wiper switch on signal circuit to a good ground. Does the voltage measure near the specified value?	B+	Go to *Step 11*	Go to *Step 9*
7	1. Disconnect the windshield wiper motor connector. 2. Turn the windshield wiper/washer switch to HI. 3. Measure the voltage from the windshield wiper motor high speed circuit to a good ground. Does the voltage measure near the specified value?	B+	Go to *Step 12*	Go to *Step 10*
8	Test the windshield wiper switch low/pulse signal circuit for a short to ground or an open. Did you find and correct the condition?	—	Go to *Step 17*	Go to *Step 13*
9	Test the windshield wiper switch on signal circuit for short to ground or an open. Did you find and correct the condition?	—	Go to *Step 17*	Go to *Step 13*
10	Test the windshield wiper motor high speed circuit for short to ground or an open. Did you find and correct the condition?	—	Go to *Step 17*	Go to *Step 13*
11	Inspect for a poor connection at the windshield wiper motor connector. Did you find and correct the condition?	—	Go to *Step 17*	Go to *Step 14*
12	Inspect for a poor connection at the windshield wiper motor connector. Did you find and correct the condition?	—	Go to *Step 17*	Go to *Step 15*
13	Inspect for a poor connection at the windshield wiper/washer switch connector. Did you find and correct the condition?	—	Go to *Step 17*	Go to *Step 16*
14	Replace the windshield wiper motor cover. Did you complete the replacement?	—	Go to *Step 17*	—
15	Replace the windshield wiper motor. Did you complete the replacement?	—	Go to *Step 17*	—
16	Replace the windshield wiper/washer switch. Did you complete the replacement?	—	Go to *Step 17*	—
17	Operate the windshield wiper/washer system in order to verify the repair. Did you correct the condition?	—	System OK	Go to *Step 3*

GC9020201044020X

Fig. 136 Test 6: Wipers Inoperative In One Or More Modes (Part 2 of 2). Intrigue

Step	Action	Value(s)	Yes	No
1	Did you review the Wiper/Washer System Description and Operation and perform the necessary inspections?	—	Go to *Step 2*	Go to *Symptoms Systems*
2	1. Turn ON the ignition, with the engine OFF. 2. Turn the windshield wiper/washer switch through all the switch positions. Do the windshield wipers operate properly in all modes?	—	*Test for Intermittent and Poor Connections*	Go to *Step 3*
3	Do the windshield wipers operate properly in HI mode?	—	Go to *Step 4*	Go to *Step 7*
4	1. Disconnect the windshield wiper motor connector. 2. Turn the windshield wiper/washer switch to LO. 3. Measure the voltage from the windshield wiper switch low/pulse signal circuit to a good ground. Does the voltage measure near the specified value?	B+	Go to *Step 5*	Go to *Step 8*

GC9020201044010X

Fig. 136 Test 6: Wipers Inoperative In One Or More Modes (Part 1 of 2). Intrigue

Test Description

The number(s) below refer to the step number(s) on the diagnostic table.

2. Lack of communication may be due to a partial malfunction of the class 2 serial data circuit. The specified procedure will determine the particular condition.
4. The Symptom Table will determine the correct diagnostic procedure to use.
5. The presence of DTCs which begin with "U" indicate some other module is not communicating. The specified procedure will compile all the available information before tests are performed.

Step	Action	Yes	No
1	Install a scan tool. Does the scan tool power up?	Go to Step 2	Diagnose Data Link Communications
2	1. Turn ON the ignition, with the engine OFF. 2. Attempt to establish communication with the following: o The Instrument Panel Cluster (IPC) o The Body Control Module (BCM) Does the scan tool communicate with the modules?	Go to Step 3	Diagnose Data Link Communications
3	**Important** The engine may start during the following step. Turn OFF the engine as soon as you have observed the Crank power mode. 1. Access the Class 2 Power Mode parameter in the Diagnostic Circuit Check menu on the scan tool. 2. Rotate the ignition switch through all positions while observing the Class 2 Power Mode parameter. Does the Class 2 Power Mode parameter reading match the ignition switch position for all switch positions?	Go to Step 4	Go to Power Mode Mismatch

GC9020201045010X

Fig. 137 Wiper/Washer System Check (Part 1 of 2). Park Avenue

4	Select the display DTCs function on the scan tool for the following modules: • The IPC • The BCM Does the scan tool display any DTCs?	Go to Step 5	Go to Symptoms
5	Does the scan tool display DTCs that begin with "U"?	Diagnose Data Link Communications	Go to Step 6
6	Does the scan tool display DTCs B1656, B1657 or B1658?	Diagnose Body Control System	Go to Step 7
7	Does the scan tool display DTCs B1982 or B1983?	Diagnose Engine Electrical	Go to Symptoms

GC9020201045020X

Fig. 137 Wiper/Washer System Check (Part 2 of 2). Park Avenue

Step	Action	Yes	No
	Wiper/Washer System Connector End Views		
	DEFINITION: The windshield washer fluid low message is always displayed or does not display with low washer fluid.		
1	Did you review the Wiper/Washer Diagnoastic System Check?	Go to Step 2	Go to System Check -
2	Verify the fault is present. Does the system operate normally?	Test for Intermittent and Poor Connections	Go to Step 3
3	1. Turn the ignition OFF. 2. Disconnect the washer fluid level switch connector. 3. Turn the ignition ON. Is the windshield washer fluid low message displayed on the driver information center?	Go to Step 6	Go to Step 4

GC9020201046010X

Fig. 138 Test 1: Low Washer Fluid Indicator Fault (Part 1 of 3). Park Avenue

4	1. Turn the ignition OFF. 2. Connect a fused jumper wire from the washer fluid level switch signal circuit terminal in the washer fluid level switch connector to a good ground. 3. Turn the ignition ON. Is the windshield washer fluid low message displayed on the driver information center?	Go to Step 5	Go to Step 8
5	1. Turn the ignition OFF. 2. Connect a fused jumper wire across the washer fluid level switch harness connector terminals. 3. Turn the ignition ON. Is the windshield washer fluid low message displayed on the driver information center?	Go to Step 11	Go to Step 10
6	1. Install a scan tool. 2. Display the BCM Data List. With the washer fluid level switch disconnected is the Washer Fluid Level status OK?	Go to Step 13	Go to Step 7
7	Test the washer fluid level switch signal circuit for a short to ground. Did you find and correct the condition?	Go to Step 17	Go to Step 15

GC9020201046020X

Fig. 138 Test 1: Low Washer Fluid Indicator Fault (Part 2 of 3). Park Avenue

8	1. Install a scan tool. 2. Display the BCM Data List. With the washer fluid level switch signal circuit shorted to ground is the Washer Fluid Level status LOW?	Go to Step 13	Go to Step 9
9	Test the washer fluid level switch signal circuit for an open or high resistance. Did you find and correct the condition?	Go to Step 17	Go to Step 15
10	Repair the washer fluid level switch ground circuit for an open or high resistance. Is the repair complete?	Go to Step 17	--
11	Inspect for poor connections at the washer fluid level switch. Did you find and correct the condition?	Go to Step 17	Go to Step 12
12	Replace the washer fluid level switch. Is the repair complete?	Go to Step 17	--
13	Inspect for poor connections at the instrument panel cluster. Did you find and correct the condition?	Go to Step 17	Go to Step 14
14	Replace the instrument panel cluster. Is the repair complete?	Go to Step 17	--
15	Inspect for poor connections at the body control module. Did you find and correct the condition?	Go to Step 17	Go to Step 16
16	Replace the body control module. Is the repair complete?	Go to Step 17	--
17	Operate the system in order to verify the repair. Did you correct the condition?	System OK	Go to Step 3

GC9020201046030X

Fig. 138 Test 1: Low Washer Fluid Indicator Fault (Part 3 of 3). Park Avenue

Step	Action	Yes	No
	Wiper/Washer System Connector End Views		
1	Did you review the Wiper/Washer Diagnoastic System Check?	Go to Step 2	Go to System Check
2	Turn the ignition ON. Are the windshield washers always on?	Go to Step 3	Test for Intermittent and Poor Connections
3	Are the windshield washer wipers always on?	Go to Step 4	Go to Step 6
4	Disconnect the windshield wiper/washer switch connector. Are the windshield washers always on?	Go to Step 5	Go to Step 7
5	Test the windshield wiper switch signal 2 circuit for a short to voltage. Did you find and correct the condition?	Go to Step 9	Go to Step 8
6	Test the windshield washer pump control circuit for a short to voltage. Did you find and correct the condition?	Go to Step 9	Go to Step 8
7	Replace the windshield wiper/washer switch. Is the repair complete?	Go to Step 9	--
8	Replace the windshield wiper motor module. Is the repair complete?	Go to Step 9	--
9	Operate the system in order to verify the repair. Did you correct the condition?	System OK	Go to Step 3

GC9020201047000X

Fig. 139 Test 2: Washer Always On. Park Avenue

Step	Action	Yes	No
	Wiper/Washer System Connector End Views		
1	Did you review the Wiper/Washer Diagnostic System Check?	Go to Step 2	Go to System Check
2	1. Turn the ignition ON. 2. Press the windshield washer switch. Do the windshield washers operate normally?	Test for Intermittent and Poor Connections	Go to Step 3
3	1. Disconnect the windshield washer pump connector. 2. Connect a test lamp across the washer pump connector terminals. 3. Turn the ignition ON. 4. Press the windshield washer switch. Does the test lamp illuminate?	Go to Step 10	Go to Step 4
4	Test the windshield washer pump ground circuit for an open or high resistance. Did you find and correct the condition?	Go to Step 14	Go to Step 5
5	Test the windshield washer pump control circuit for an open or high resistance. Did you find and correct the condition?	Go to Step 14	Go to Step 6
6	1. Disconnect the windshield wiper motor connector. 2. Connect a test lamp from the windshield wiper switch signal 2 circuit terminal in the wiper motor harness connector to ground. 3. Turn the ignition ON. 4. Press the windshield washer switch. Does the test lamp illuminate?	Go to Step 12	Go to Step 7
7	Test the windshield wiper switch signal 2 circuit for high resistance. Did you find and correct the condition?	Go to Step 14	Go to Step 8

GC9020201048010X

Fig. 140 Test 3: Washers Inoperative (Part 1 of 2). Park Avenue

Step	Action	Yes	No
	Wiper/Washer System Connector End Views		
1	Did you review the Wiper/Washer Diagnostic System Check?	Go to Step 2	Go to System Check -
2	1. Turn the ignition ON. 2. Turn the windshield wiper/washer switch OFF. Are the windshield wipers always on?	Go to Step 3	Go to Testing for Intermittent and Poor Connections in Wiring Systems
3	Disconnect the windshield wiper/washer switch connector. Are the windshield wipers always on?	Go to Step 4	Go to Step 7
4	1. Disconnect the windshield wiper motor connector. 2. Test the windshield wiper switch signal 1 circuit for a short to voltage. Did you find and correct the condition?	Go to Step 11	Go to Step 5
5	Test the windshield wiper switch signal 2 circuit for a short to voltage. Did you find and correct the condition?	Go to Step 11	Go to Step 6
6	Test the windshield wiper motor high speed circuit for a short to voltage. Did you find and correct the condition?	Go to Step 11	Go to Step 9

GC9020201049010X

Fig. 141 Test 4: Wipers Always On (Part 1 of 2). Park Avenue

8	Inspect for poor connections at the windshield wiper/washer switch. Did you find and correct the condition?	Go to Step 14	Go to Step 9
9	Replace the windshield wiper/washer switch. Is the repair complete?	Go to Step 14	--
10	Inspect for poor connections at the windshield washer pump. Did you find and correct the condition?	Go to Step 14	Go to Step 11
11	Replace the windshield washer pump. Is the repair complete?	Go to Step 14	--
12	Inspect for poor connections at the windshield wiper motor. Did you find and correct the condition?	Go to Step 14	Go to Step 13
13	Replace the windshield wiper motor module. Is the repair complete?	Go to Step 14	--
14	Operate the system in order to verify the repair. Did you correct the condition?	System OK	Go to Step 3

GC9020201048020X

Fig. 140 Test 3: Washers Inoperative (Part 2 of 2). Park Avenue

7	Inspect for poor connections at the windshield wiper/washer switch. Did you find and correct the condition?	Go to Step 11	Go to Step 8
8	Replace the windshield wiper/washer switch. Is the repair complete?	Go to Step 11	--
9	Inspect for poor connections at the windshield wiper motor. Did you find and correct the condition?	Go to Step 11	Go to Step 10
10	Replace the windshield wiper motor module. Is the repair complete?	Go to Step 11	--
11	Operate the system in order to verify the repair. Did you correct the condition?	System OK	Go to Step 3

GC9020201049020X

Fig. 141 Test 4: Wipers Always On (Part 2 of 2). Park Avenue

Step	Action	Yes	No
1	Did you review the Wiper/Washer Diagnostic System Check?	Go to Step 2	Go to System Check -
2	1. Turn the ignition switch ON. 2. Turn the windshield wiper/washer switch through all the switch positions. Does the windshield wiper/washer system operate normally?	Test for Intermittent and Poor Connections	Go to Step 3
3	1. Disconnect the windshield wiper motor connector. 2. Connect a test lamp from the accessory voltage supply circuit terminal in the harness connector to ground. 3. Turn the ignition ON. Does the test lamp illuminate?	Go to Step 4	Go to Step 7
4	1. Connect a test lamp from the accessory voltage supply circuit terminal to the ground circuit terminal in the windshield wiper motor harness connector. 2. Turn the ignition ON. Does the test lamp illuminate?	Go to Step 5	Go to Step 8
5	1. Connect the test lamp from the windshield wiper switch signal 2 circuit terminal in the windshield wiper motor harness connector to ground. 2. Turn the ignition ON. 3. Press the windshield washer switch. Does the test lamp illuminate?	Go to Step 10	Go to Step 6
6	1. Disconnect the windshield wiper/washer switch connector. 2. Connect a test lamp from the accessory voltage supply circuit terminal in the windshield wiper/washer switch harness connector to ground. 3. Turn the ignition ON. Does the test lamp illuminate?	Go to Step 12	Go to Step 9

GC9020201050010X

Fig. 142 Test 5: Wipers Inoperative In All Modes (Part 1 of 2). Park Avenue

7	Repair the windshield wiper motor accessory voltage supply circuit for an open or short to ground. Is the repair complete?	Go to Step 14	--
8	Repair the windshield wiper motor ground circuit for an open or high resistance. Is the repair complete?	Go to Step 14	--
9	Repair the windshield wiper/washer switch accessory voltage supply circuit for an open or short to ground. Is the repair complete?	Go to Step 14	--
10	Inspect for poor connections at the windshield wiper motor. Did you find and correct the condition?	Go to Step 14	Go to Step 11
11	Replace the windshield wiper motor. Is the repair complete?	Go to Step 14	--
12	Inspect for poor connections at the windshield wiper/washer switch. Did you find and correct the condition?	Go to Step 14	Go to Step 13
13	Replace the windshield wiper/washer switch. Is the repair complete?	Go to Step 14	--
14	Operate the system in order to verify the repair. Did you correct the condition?	System OK	Go to Step 3

GC9020201050020X

Fig. 142 Test 5: Wipers Inoperative In All Modes (Part 2 of 2). Park Avenue

Test Description

The number(s) below refer to the step number(s) on the diagnostic table.

7. This step tests for continuity through the 24K ohms resistor in the windshield wiper/washer switch. The connector behind the instrument panel knee bolster is suitable for performing this step.

8. This step tests for continuity through the delay resistors in the windshield wiper/washer switch. The measured resistance will change in sequence from high to low as the delay speed is increased. The connector behind the instrument panel knee bolster is suitable for performing this step.

Step	Action	Value (s)	Yes	No
1	Did you review the Wiper/Washer Diagnostic System Check?	--	Go to Step 2	Go to System Check -
2	1. Turn the ignition ON. 2. Operate the windshield wiper/washer switch through all the switch positions. Does the windshield wiper/washer system operate normally?	--	Test for Intermittent and Poor Connections	Go to Step 3
3	Do the windshield wipers operate in the high speed mode?	--	Go to Step 5	Go to Step 4
4	1. Disconnect the windshield wiper motor connector. 2. Connect a test lamp from the wiper switch high speed signal circuit terminal to ground. 3. Turn the ignition ON. 4. Operate the windshield wiper/washer switch to the high speed position. Does the test lamp illuminate?	--	Go to Step 14	Go to Step 9

GC9020201051010X

Fig. 143 Test 6: Wipers Inoperative In One Or More Modes (Part 1 of 3). Park Avenue

5	1. Disconnect the windshield wiper motor connector. 2. Connect a test lamp from the wiper switch signal 2 circuit terminal to ground. 3. Turn the ignition ON. 4. Press the windshield washer switch. Does the test lamp illuminate?	--	Go to Step 6	Go to Step 10
6	1. Connect a test lamp from the wiper switch signal 1 circuit terminal to ground. 2. Operate the windshield wiper/washer switch to the following positions: o MIST o LO o HI Does the test lamp illuminate in the listed switch positions?	--	Go to Step 7	Go to Step 11
7	1. Disconnect the windshield wiper/washer switch connector. 2. Measure the resistance through the windshield wiper/washer switch from the signal 2 circuit terminal to the accessory voltage supply circuit terminal in the wiper/washer switch connector. 3. Operate the windshield wiper/washer switch to the following positions: o MIST o INT o LO o HI Is the resistance at or near the specified value in all the listed switch positions?	24K ohms	Go to Step 8	Go to Step 12
8	1. Measure the resistance through the windshield wiper/washer switch from the signal 1 circuit terminal to the accessory voltage supply circuit terminal in the wiper/washer switch connector. 2. Operate the windshield wiper/washer switch through all of the delay positions. Does the resistance remain within the specified values from high to low as the delay speed is increased?	38K - 690K ohms	Go to Step 14	Go to Step 12
9	Test the windshield wiper switch high speed signal circuit for an open or high resistance. Did you find and correct the condition?	--	Go to Step 16	Go to Step 12

GC9020201051020X

Fig. 143 Test 6: Wipers Inoperative In One Or More Modes (Part 2 of 3). Park Avenue

10	Test the windshield wiper switch signal 2 circuit for an open or short to ground. Did you find and correct the condition?	-	Go to Step 16	Go to Step 12
11	Test the windshield wiper switch signal 1 circuit for an open or short to ground. Did you find and correct the condition?	-	Go to Step 16	Go to Step 12
12	Inspect for poor connections at the windshield wiper/washer switch. Did you find and correct the condition?	-	Go to Step 16	Go to Step 13
13	Replace the windshield wiper/washer switch. Is the repair complete?	-	Go to Step 16	--
14	Inspect for poor connections at the windshield wiper motor. Did you find and correct the condition?	-	Go to Step 16	Go to Step 15
15	Replace the windshield wiper motor module. Is the repair complete?	-	Go to Step 16	--
16	Operate the system in order to verify the repair. Did you correct the condition?	-	System OK	Go to Step 3

GC9020201051030X

Fig. 143 Test 6: Wipers Inoperative In One Or More Modes (Part 3 of 3). Park Avenue

Step	Action	Yes	No
	Wiper/Washer System Connector End Views		
1	Did you review the Wiper/Washer Diagnoastic System Check?	Go to Step 2	Go to System Check -
2	Verify the fault is present. Does the system operate normally?	Test for Intermittent and Poor Connections	Go to Step 3
3	While the windshield wiper/washer system is in the automatic mode does the wiper motor operate at continuous delay intervals?	Go to Step 5	Go to Step 4
4	1. Turn the ignition ON. 2. Operate the windshield wiper/washer switch from the OFF position through all of the delay positions. Does the wiper motor cycle once and stop every time the switch is advanced to the next delay position?	Go to Step 11	Go to Wipers Inoperative - One or More Modes
5	1. Disconnect the moisture sensor connector. 2. Connect a test lamp from the accessory voltage supply circuit terminal in the harness connector to a good ground. Does the test lamp illuminate?	Go to Step 6	Go to Step 9
6	Connect a test lamp from the accessory voltage supply circuit terminal to the ground circuit terminal in the moisture sensor harness connector. Does the test lamp illuminate?	Go to Step 7	Go to Step 10
7	Test the moisture sensor signal 1 circuit for an open, short to ground, or short to voltage. Did you find and correct the condition?	Go to Step 13	Go to Step 8
8	Test the moisture sensor signal 2 circuit for an open, short to ground, or short to voltage. Did you find and correct the condition?	Go to Step 13	Go to Step 11

GC9020201052010X

Fig. 144 Test 7: Moisture Sensing Feature Inoperative (Part 1 of 2). Park Avenue

9	Repair the accessory voltage supply circuit to the moisture sensor for an open or high resistance. Is the repair complete?	Go to Step 13	--
10	Repair the moisture sensor ground circuit for an open or high resistance. Is the repair complete?	Go to Step 13	--
11	Inspect for poor connections at the moisture sensor. Did you find and correct the condition?	Go to Step 13	Go to Step 12
12	Replace the moisture sensor. — Is the repair complete?	Go to Step 13	--
13	Operate the system in order to verify the repair. Did you correct the condition?	System OK	Go to Step 2

GC9020201052020X

Fig. 144 Test 7: Moisture Sensing Feature Inoperative (Part 2 of 2). Park Avenue

One, Two & Three Speed Systems

NOTE: On Air Bag Equipped Models, Refer To "Air Bag System Precautions" Located In The Front Of This Manual For System Disarming & Arming Procedures.

NOTE: Refer To "Computer Relearn Procedures" Located In The Front Of This Manual When Battery Power To The Computer Has Been Interrupted.

NOTE: "Electrical Symbol & Wire Color Code Identification" Located In The Front Of This Manual May Be Used As An Aid When Using Wiring Circuits Found In This Section.

INDEX

PRECAUTIONS

Air Bag Systems

Refer to "Air Bag System Precautions" in the front of this manual for system disarming and arming procedures.

Battery Ground Cable

Prior to service, disconnect battery ground cable and isolate as required.

DESCRIPTION

Metro

STANDARD (NON-PULSE) WIPER OPERATION

When the wiper switch is on low, battery voltage is applied to the wiper motor through the blue wire. When the wiper switch is in high, battery voltage is applied directly to motor through the blue/red wire to the high speed brushes.

When the wiper switch is turned off, the run/park switch in the wiper motor is still in the Run position. Voltage is still applied to the wiper motor at the low speed brushes through the run/park switch, blue/white and blue wires.

PULSE WIPER OPERATION

When the wiper switch is in delay position, a shunt is applied to two of the inputs at the pulse wiper relay by the wiper switch to start the pulse operation. The pulse wiper relay momentarily supplies battery voltage to wiper switch to run wiper motor. The wiper blades make one sweep and reach park, the park/run switch opens. The wiper blades remain in park until the pulse wiper relay supplies battery voltage to start another sweep. The delay time between sweeps is determined by circuits in the pulse wiper relay.

Prizm

Windshield wiper operation is controlled by a dash or steering column mounted switch. The wiper feed circuit is protected by a fuse which is located in the fuse block on most models, or in an inline fuse holder on some models with pulse wipers. A circuit breaker, integral with the motor brush holder, protects the motor against overload. Pulse wipers, available on most models, use a variable resistor, a pulse control module, and/or a modified wiper motor to provide a delay wipe mode.

Vibe

The windshield wiper motor is a 2 speed motor and is operated at low speed in all modes except HIGH. The ignition positive voltage circuit to the windshield wiper/washer switch is used to supply the windshield wiper switch signal circuits. When the wiper/washer switch is in the LOW position voltage is supplied to the motor through the windshield wiper low speed circuit. The applied voltage causes the wiper motor to operate in the low speed mode.

SYSTEM DIAGNOSIS & TESTING

Wiring Diagrams

Refer to **Figs. 1 through 4,** for wiring diagrams.

Diagnostic Tests

METRO

Refer to **Figs. 5 through 14,** for symptom related tests.

PRIZM

Refer to **Figs. 15 through 23,** for symptom related tests.

VIBE

Refer to **Figs. 24 through 29,** for symptom related tests.

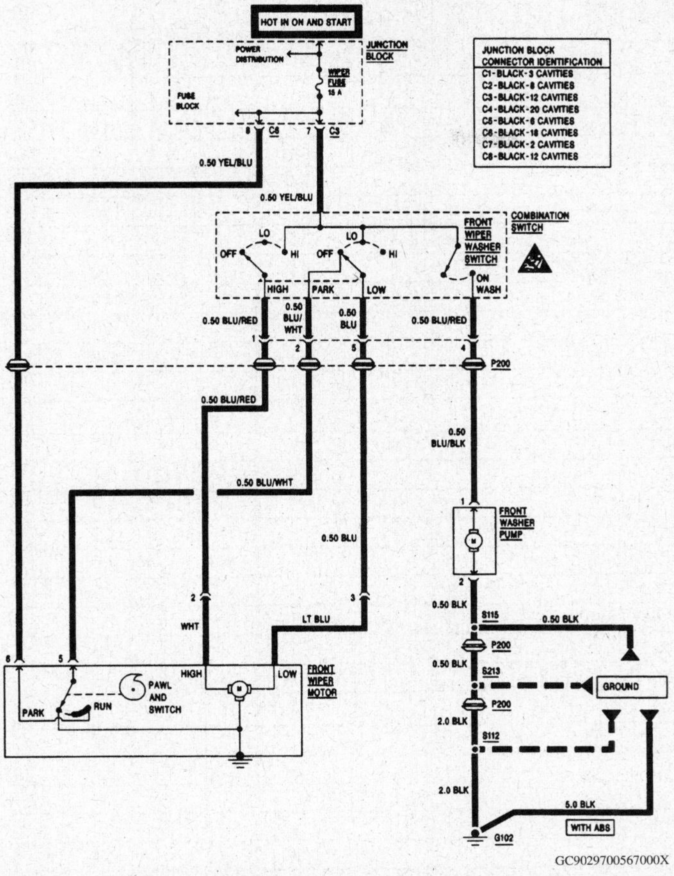

Fig. 1 Wiring diagram. Metro less pulse system

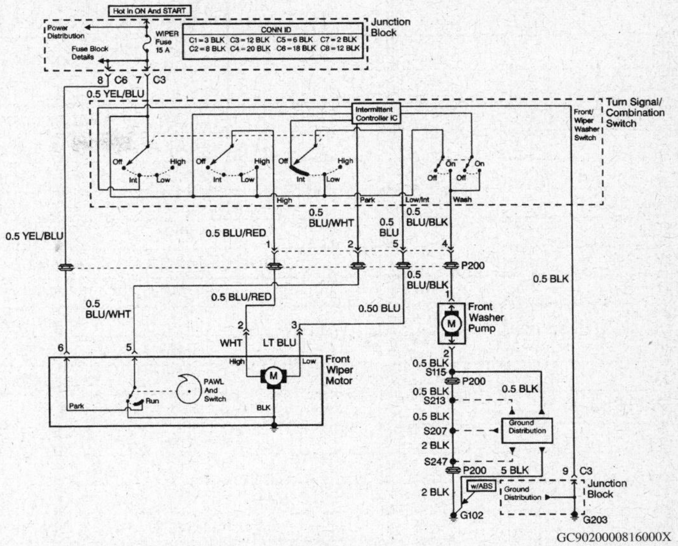

Fig. 2 Wiring diagram. Metro w/pulse wiper system

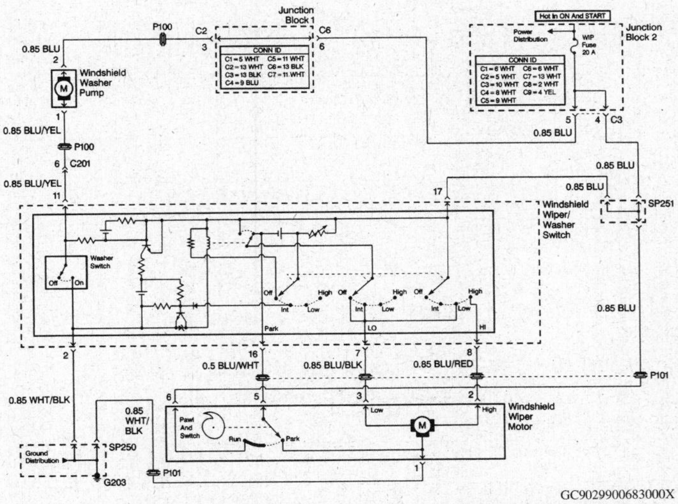

Fig. 3 Wiring diagram. Prizm w/pulse system

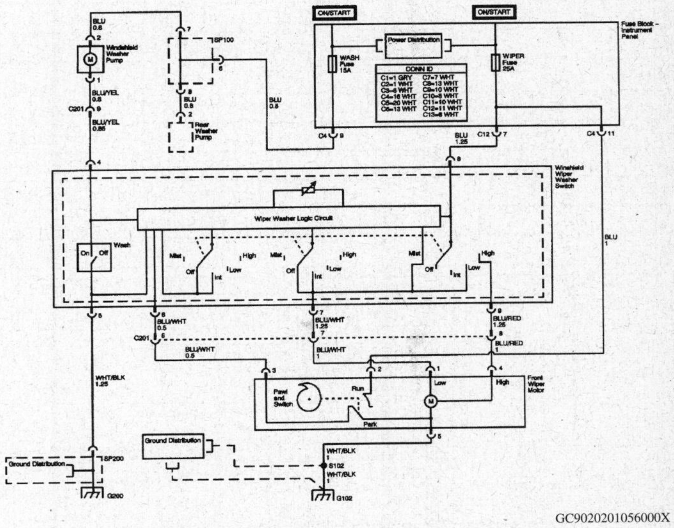

Fig. 4 Wiring diagram. Vibe

DIAGNOSTIC CHART INDEX

Step	Action	Normal Result(s)	Abnormal Result(s)*
1	1. Turn the ignition switch to the ON position. 2. Pull the front wiper/washer switch lever.	• The front washer pump operates. • The wipers operate at LOW speed.	• *Washers Inoperative* • *Wipers All Modes and Washer Inoperative*
2	Release the wiper/washer switch.	• The front washer pump stops. • The wipers complete the cycle and return to the PARK position.	*Wipers Blades Do Not Park*
3	Move the front wiper/washer switch lever to the LO position.	The wipers operate at LOW speed.	*Wipers High Mode Operates with Switch in Low*
4	Move the front wiper/washer switch lever to the HI position.	The wipers operate at HIGH speed.	• *Wipers Low Mode Operates with Switch in High* • *Wipers High Mode Inoperative*
5	Move the front wiper/washer lever to the INT position.	The wipers sweep once every 6 seconds.	*Wipers Delay Mode Inoperative*
6	Move the front wiper/washer switch lever to the OFF position.	The wipers complete the cycle and return to the PARK position.	• *Wipers Blades Do Not Park* • *Wipers Always On*
* Refer to the appropriate symptom diagnostic table for the applicable abnormal result.			

GC9020000834000X

Fig. 5 Test 1: Front Wiper/Washer System Check. Metro

Step	Action	Value(s)	Yes	No
1	Did you perform the system check?	—	Go to *Step 2*	Go to *Wiper/Washer System Check*
2	1. Turn the ignition switch to the ON position. 2. Backprobe the junction block connector C3 with a test lamp from cavity 7 to ground. Does the test lamp light?	—	Go to *Step 3*	Go to *Step 4*
3	Test for an open in the YEL/BLU wire between the junction block and the combination switch. Was an open found?	—	Go to *Step 6*	Go to *Step 5*
4	Replace the junction block. Is the repair complete?	—	Go to *Wiper/Washer System Check*	—
5	Replace the combination switch. Is the repair complete?	—	Go to *Wiper/Washer System Check*	—
6	Repair the open. Is the repair complete?	—	Go to *Wiper/Washer System Check*	—

GC9020000819000X

Fig. 6 Test 2: Wipers All Modes & Washer Inoperative. Metro

Step	Action	Value(s)	Yes	No
1	Did you perform the system check?	—	Go to *Step 2*	Go to *Wiper/Washer System Check*
2	Backprobe the junction block connector C3 with a test lamp from cavity 9 to B+. Does the test lamp light?	—	Go to *Step 3*	Go to *Step 4*
3	Replace the combination switch. Is the repair complete?	—	Go to *Wiper/Washer System Check*	—
4	Test for an open in the BLK wire between the combination switch and the junction block. Was an open found?	—	Go to *Step 6*	Go to *Step 5*
5	Replace the junction block. Is the repair complete?	—	Go to *Wiper/Washer System Check*	—
6	Repair the open. Is the repair complete?	—	Go to *Wiper/Washer System Check*	—

GC9020000820000X

Fig. 7 Test 3: Wipers Delay Mode Inoperative. Metro

Step	Action	Value(s)	Yes	No
1	Did you perform the system check?	—	Go to *Step 2*	Go to *Wiper/Washer System Check*
2	Backprobe the junction block connector C3 with a test lamp from cavity 9 to B+. Does the test lamp light?	—	Go to *Step 3*	Go to *Step 4*
3	Replace the combination switch. Is the repair complete?	—	Go to *Wiper/Washer System Check*	—
4	Test for an open in the BLK wire between the combination switch and the junction block. Was an open found?	—	Go to *Step 6*	Go to *Step 5*
5	Replace the junction block. Is the repair complete?	—	Go to *Wiper/Washer System Check*	—
6	Repair the open. Is the repair complete?	—	Go to *Wiper/Washer System Check*	—

GC9020000821000X

Fig. 8 Test 4: Wipers Mist, Delay & Low Modes Inoperative. Metro

Step	Action	Value(s)	Yes	No
1	Did you perform the system check?	—	Go to *Step 2*	Go to *Wiper/Washer System Check*
2	1. Turn the ignition switch to the ON position. 2. Move the front wiper/washer switch lever to the HI position. 3. Backprobe the front wiper motor connector with a test lamp from cavity 2 to ground. Does the test lamp light?	—	Go to *Step 4*	Go to *Step 3*
3	Test for an open in the BLU/RED wire between the combination switch and the front wiper motor. Was an open found?	—	Go to *Step 6*	Go to *Step 5*
4	Replace the front wiper motor. Is the repair complete?	—	Go to *Wiper/Washer System Check*	—
5	Replace the combination switch. Is the repair complete?	—	Go to *Wiper/Washer System Check*	—
6	Repair the open. Is the repair complete?	—	Go to *Wiper/Washer System Check*	—

GC9020000822000X

Fig. 9 Test 5: Wipers High Mode Inoperative. Metro

Step	Action	Value(s)	Yes	No
1	Did you perform the system check?	—	Go to *Step 2*	Go to *Wiper/Washer System Check*
2	1. Turn the ignition switch to the ON position. 2. Move the front wiper/washer lever to the LO position. 3. Backprobe the front wiper motor connector with a test lamp from cavity 2 to ground. Does the test lamp light?	—	Go to *Step 3*	Go to *Step 4*
3	Replace the combination switch. Is the repair complete?	—	Go to *Wiper/Washer System Check*	—
4	Replace the front wiper motor. Is the repair complete?	—	Go to *Wiper/Washer System Check*	—

GC9020000824000X

Fig. 11 Test 7: Wipers High Mode Operates w/Switch In Low. Metro

Step	Action	Value(s)	Yes	No
1	Did you perform the system check?	—	Go to *Step 2*	Go to *Wiper/Washer System Check*
2	1. Turn the ignition switch to the ON position. 2. Backprobe the front wiper motor connector with a test lamp from cavity 5 to ground. Does the test lamp light?	—	Go to *Step 3*	Go to *Step 4*
3	Test for an open in the BLU/WHT wire between the front wiper motor and combination switch. Was an open found?	—	Go to *Step 7*	Go to *Step 5*
4	Test for an open in the YEL/BLU wire between the junction block and front wiper motor. Was an open found?	—	Go to *Step 7*	Go to *Step 6*
5	Replace the combination switch. Is the repair complete?	—	Go to *Wiper/Washer System Check*	—
6	Replace the wiper motor. Is the repair complete?	—	Go to *Wiper/Washer System Check*	—
7	Repair the open. Is the repair complete?	—	Go to *Wiper/Washer System Check*	—

GC9020000826000X

Fig. 13 Test 9: Wiper Blades Do Not Park. Metro

Step	Action	Value(s)	Yes	No
1	Did you perform the system check?	—	Go to *Step 2*	Go to *Wiper/Washer System Check*
2	1. Turn the ignition switch to the ON position. 2. Backprobe the front washer pump connector with a test lamp from cavity 1 to ground. 3. Pull the front wiper/washer switch lever. Does the test lamp light?	—	Go to *Step 4*	Go to *Step 3*
3	Test for an open in the BLU/BLK wire between the combination switch and the front washer pump. Was an open found?	—	Go to *Step 5*	Go to *Step 6*
4	Test for an open in the BLK wire between the front washer pump and G102. Was an open found?	—	Go to *Step 5*	Go to *Step 7*
5	Repair the open. Is the repair complete?	—	Go to *Wiper/Washer System Check*	—
6	Replace the combination switch. Is the repair complete?	—	Go to *Wiper/Washer System Check*	—
7	Replace the front washer pump. Is the repair complete?	—	Go to *Wiper/Washer System Check*	—

GC9020000827000X

Fig. 14 Test 10: Washers Inoperative. Metro

Step	Action	Value(s)	Yes	No
1	Did you perform the system check?	—	Go to *Step 2*	Go to *Wiper/Washer System Check*
2	1. Turn the ignition switch to the ON position. 2. Move the front wiper/washer switch lever to the HI position. 3. Backprobe the front wiper motor connector with a digital multimeter from cavity 2 to ground. 4. Measure the voltage. Is the voltage greater than the specified value?	10V	Go to *Step 4*	Go to *Step 3*
3	Backprobe the front wiper motor connector with a test lamp from cavity 3 to ground. Does the test lamp light?	—	Go to *Step 6*	Go to *Step 5*
4	Replace the front wiper motor. Is the repair complete?	—	Go to *Wiper/Washer System Check*	—
5	1. Turn the ignition switch to the lock position. 2. Disconnect the front wiper/washer switch connector (switch still in HI position). 3. Disconnect the junction block connector C3. 4. Connect a digital multimeter from junction block connector C3 cavity 7 to the front wiper/washer switch connector terminal 1 (switch side). 5. Measure the resistance. Is the resistance greater than the specified value?	5Ω	Go to *Step 6*	Go to *Step 7*
6	Replace the combination switch. Is the repair complete?	—	Go to *Wiper/Washer System Check*	—
7	Test for an open or high resistance (more than 5.0 ohms) in the BLU/RED wire (including connectors) between the front wiper motor and the combination switch. Was high resistance found?	—	Go to *Step 8*	Go to *Step 4*
8	Repair the open/high resistance. Is the repair complete?	—	Go to *Wiper/Washer System Check*	—

GC9020000823000X

Fig. 10 Test 6: Wipers Low Mode Operates w/Switch In High. Metro

Step	Action	Value(s)	Yes	No
1	Did you perform the system check?	—	Go to *Step 2*	Go to *Wiper/Washer System Check*
2	1. Disconnect the junction block connector C6. 2. Turn the ignition switch to the ON position. Do the wipers stop?	—	Go to *Step 4*	Go to *Step 3*
3	Test for a short to voltage in the BLU wire or the BLU/RED wire between the combination switch and the front wiper motor. Was a short to voltage found?	—	Go to *Step 5*	Go to *Step 6*
4	Replace the front wiper motor. Is the repair complete?	—	Go to *Wiper/Washer System Check*	—
5	Repair the short. Is the repair complete?	—	Go to *Wiper/Washer System Check*	—
6	Replace the combination switch. Is the repair complete?	—	Go to *Wiper/Washer System Check*	—

GC9020000825000X

Fig. 12 Test 8: Wipers Always On. Metro

Step	Action	Normal Result(s)	Abnormal Result(s)*
1	1. Turn the ignition switch to the ON position. 2. Leave the windshield wiper/washer switch in the OFF position. 3. Pull the windshield wiper/washer switch for 2 to 4 seconds and release.	• Wipers operate at low speed. • Washer sprays windshield as long as washer switch is held in the ON position. • After releasing switch, washer stops and wipers return to park position after 1 to 4 sweeps.	• *Washers Inoperative* • *Wipers All Modes and Washer Inoperative* • *Washers Always On*
2	Move the windshield wiper/washer switch to the LO position.	Wipers run continuously at low speed.	• *Wipers Low Mode Inoperative, High Mode Operates* • *Wipers All Modes Inoperative*
3	Move the windshield wiper/washer switch to the HI position.	Wipers run continuously at high speed.	• *Wipers All Modes Inoperative* • *Wipers High Mode Inoperative, Low Mode Operates*
4	Move the windshield wiper/washer switch to the OFF position.	Wipers return to the park position at low speed.	*Wipers Always On*

* Refer to the appropriate symptom diagnostic table for the applicable abnormal result.

GC9020000849000X

Fig. 15 Wiper Wiper/Washer System Check. Prizm

Step	Action	Value(s)	Yes	No
1	Were you sent here from the Wiper/Washer System Check?	—	*Go to Step 2*	Go to *Wiper/Washer System Check*
2	1. Disconnect the windshield wiper/washer switch connector. 2. Disconnect the windshield washer pump connector. 3. Using a *J 39200* test for continuity from cavity 11 of the windshield wiper/washer switch connector and ground. Is there continuity to ground in the BLU/YEL wire?	—	*Go to Step 3*	*Go to Step 4*
3	Repair the short to ground condition in the BLU/YEL wire between cavity 11 of the windshield wiper/washer switch connector and cavity 1 of the windshield washer pump. Is the repair complete?	—	Go to *Wiper/Washer System Check*	—
4	Replace the windshield wiper/washer switch. Is the replacement complete??	—	Go to *Wiper/Washer System Check*	—

GC9029900684000X

Fig. 16 Test 1: Washers Always On. Prizm

Step	Action	Value(s)	Yes	No
1	Were you sent here from the Wiper/Washer System Check?	—	*Go to Step 2*	Go to *Wiper/Washer System Check*
2	Inspect the WIP fuse for continuity. Does the WIP fuse have continuity?	—	*Go to Step 3*	*Go to Step 6*
3	1. Turn the ignition switch to the on position. 2. Disconnect connector C3 of junction block 2. 3. Using a *J 39200*, test for B+ at cavity 4 of connector C3. Was B+ tested?	—	*Go to Step 4*	*Go to Step 5*
4	Replace the windshield wiper/washer switch. Is the repair complete?	—	Go to *Wiper/Washer System Check*	—
5	Repair/replace junction block 2. Is the repair complete?	—	Go to *Wiper/Washer System Check*	—
6	1. Disconnect connector C3 of junction block 2. 2. Turn the windshield wiper/washer switch to the off position. 3. Test for continuity using a *J 39200*, between cavity 4 of connector C3 of junction block 2 and ground. Is there continuity from cavity 4 to ground?	—	*Go to Step 7*	*Go to Step 8*
7	Repair the short to ground condition between cavity 4 of connector C3 of junction block 2 and the windshield wiper motor or the windshield wiper/washer switch. Is the repair complete?	—	Go to *Wiper/Washer System Check*	—
8	With connector C3 of junction block 2 still disconnected and the washer switch in the off position: Test for continuity using a *J 39200*, between cavity 5 of connector C3 of junction block 2 and ground. Is there continuity from cavity 5 to ground?	—	*Go to Step 10*	*Go to Step 9*
9	Replace the WIP fuse. Is the replacement complete?	—	Go to *Wiper/Washer System Check*	—
10	With connector C3 of junction block 2 still disconnected and the washer switch in the off position: 1. Disconnect the windshield washer pump connector. 2. Test for continuity using a *J 39200*, between cavity 5 of connector C3 of junction block 2 and ground. Is there continuity from cavity 5 to ground?	—	*Go to Step 11*	*Go to Step 12*
11	Repair the short to ground condition in the BLU wire between cavity 5 of connector C3 of junction block 2 and cavity 2 of the windshield washer pump connector. Is the repair complete?	—	Go to *Wiper/Washer System Check*	—
12	1. Disconnect the windshield wiper/washer switch connector. 2. Test for continuity using a *J 39200*, between cavity 11 of the windshield wiper/washer switch connector and ground. Is there continuity from cavity 11 to ground?	—	*Go to Step 13*	*Go to Step 4*
13	Repair the short to ground condition in the BLU/YEL wire between cavity 11 of the windshield wiper/washer switch connector and cavity 1 of the windshield washer pump connector. Is the repair complete?	—	Go to *Wiper/Washer System Check*	—

GC9029900686000X

Fig. 18 Test 3: Wipers All Modes & Washer Inoperative. Prizm

Step	Action	Value(s)	Yes	No
1	Were you sent here from the Wiper/Washer System Check?	—	*Go to Step 2*	Go to *Wiper/Washer System Check*
2	1. Turn the ignition switch to the ON position. 2. Disconnect the windshield washer pump connector. 3. Using a *J 39200*, test for B+ at cavity 2 (BLU wire) of the windshield washer pump connector. Was the voltage reading equal to B+?	—	*Go to Step 3*	*Go to Step 4*
3	With the windshield washer pump connector still disconnected: 1. Turn the washer switch to the on position. 2. Using a *J 39200*, test for continuity between cavity 1 (BLU/YEL wire) of the windshield washer pump connector and ground. Was continuity tested?	—	*Go to Step 7*	*Go to Step 8*
4	Using a *J 39200*, test for B+ at cavity 5 of connector C3 of junction block 2. Was the voltage reading equal to B+?	—	*Go to Step 5*	*Go to Step 6*
5	Repair the open condition in the BLU wire between cavity 2 of the windshield washer pump and cavity 5 of connector C3 of junction block 2. Is the repair complete?	—	Go to *Wiper/Washer System Check*	—
6	Repair the open in junction block 2. Is the repair complete?	—	Go to *Wiper/Washer System Check*	—
7	Replace the windshield washer pump. Is the repair complete?	—	Go to *Wiper/Washer System Check*	—
8	With the windshield washer pump connector still disconnected: 1. Disconnect the windshield wiper/washer switch connector. 2. Using a *J 39200*, test for continuity between cavity 1 (BLU/YEL wire) of the windshield washer pump connector and cavity 11 of the windshield wiper/washer switch connector. Was continuity tested?	—	*Go to Step 10*	*Go to Step 9*
9	Repair the open in the BLU/YEL wire between cavity 11 of the wiper/washer switch connector and cavity 1 of the windshield washer pump connector. is the repair complete?	—	Go to *Wiper/Washer System Check*	—
10	1. Place the windshield wiper/washer switch in the on position. 2. Using a *J 39200*, test for continuity between cavity 2 (BLU/YEL wire) and cavity 11 of the windshield wiper/washer switch. Was continuity tested?	—	*Go to Step 12*	*Go to Step 11*
11	Replace the windshield wiper/washer switch. Is the repair complete?	—	Go to *Wiper/Washer System Check*	—
12	Repair the open in the WHT/BLK wire between cavity 2 of the windshield wiper/washer switch connector and G203. is the repair complete?	—	Go to *Wiper/Washer System Check*	—

GC9029900685000X

Fig. 17 Test 2: Windshield Washer Pump Does Not Operate. Prizm

Step	Action	Value(s)	Yes	No
1	Were you sent here from the Wiper/Washer System Check?	—	*Go to Step 2*	Go to *Wiper/Washer System Check*
2	1. Disconnect connector C3 2. Turn the ignition switch to the ON position. 3. Using a *J 39200*, test for B+ at cavity 4 of junction block 2. Was the test result equal to B+?	—	*Go to Step 4*	*Go to Step 3*
3	Repair/replace junction block 2. Is the repair complete?	—	Go to *Wiper/Washer System Check*	—
4	1. Reconnect connector C3 to junction block 2 2. Disconnect the windshield wiper/washer switch connector. 3. Turn ignition to the on position. 4. Test for B+ at cavity 17 of the windshield wiper/washer switch connector using a *J 39200*. Was the test result equal to B+?	—	*Go to Step 6*	*Go to Step 5*
5	Repair the open in the BLU wire between the windshield wiper/washer switch connector cavity 17 and the junction block 2, connector C3 Cavity 4. Is the repair complete?	—	Go to *Wiper/Washer System Check*	—
6	1. Reconnect the windshield wiper/washer switch connector. 2. Disconnect the windshield wiper motor connector. 3. Turn the windshield wiper/washer switch to the HI position. 4. Turn the ignition switch to the on position. 5. Test for B+ at cavity 2 of the windshield wiper motor connector. Was the test result equal to B+?	—	*Go to Step 8*	*Go to Step 7*
7	Replace the windshield wiper/washer switch. Is the repair complete?	—	Go to *Wiper/Washer System Check*	—
8	Test for continuity between cavity 1 of the windshield wiper motor connector and ground using a *J 39200*. Is there continuity in the WHT/BLK wire?	—	*Go to Step 9*	*Go to Step 10*
9	Replace the windshield wiper motor. Is the repair complete?	—	Go to *Wiper/Washer System Check*	—
10	Repair the open in WHT/BLK wire between windshield wiper motor cavity 1 and G203. Is the repair complete?	—	Go to *Wiper/Washer System Check*	—

GC9029900687000X

Fig. 19 Test 4: Wipers Do Not Operate w/Windshield Wiper/Washer Switch in Any Position. Prizm

Step	Action	Value(s)	Yes	No
1	Were you sent here from the Wiper/Washer System Check?	—	*Go to Step 2*	Go to *Wiper/Washer System Check*
2	1. Disconnect the windshield wiper/washer switch connector. 2. Turn the ignition switch to the on position. Do the wipers continue to operate?	—	*Go to Step 4*	*Go to Step 3*
3	Replace the windshield wiper/washer switch. Is the repair complete?	—	Go to *Wiper/Washer System Check*	—
4	Replace the windshield wiper motor. Is the repair complete?	—	Go to *Wiper/Washer System Check*	—

GC9029900688000X

Fig. 20 Test 5: Wipers Continue To Operate w/Windshield Wiper/Washer Switch In Off Position. Prizm

Step	Action	Value(s)	Yes	No
1	Were you sent here from the Wiper/Washer System Check?	—	*Go to Step 2*	Go to *Wiper/Washer System Check*
2	1. Turn the ignition switch to the ON position. 2. Turn the windshield wiper/washer switch to the HIGH position. 3. Disconnect the windshield wiper motor connector. 4. Test for B+ at cavity 2 of the windshield wiper motor connector using a *J 39200*. Was the value tested equal to B+?	—	*Go to Step 3*	*Go to Step 4*
3	Replace the windshield wiper motor. Is the repair complete?	—	Go to *Wiper/Washer System Check*	—
4	1. Disconnect the windshield wiper/washer switch connector. 2. Test for continuity using a *J 39200* between cavity 8 of the windshield wiper/washer switch connector and cavity 2 of the windshield wiper motor connector. Is there continuity in the BLU/RED wire?	—	*Go to Step 5*	*Go to Step 6*
5	Replace the windshield wiper/washer switch. Is the repair complete?	—	Go to *Wiper/Washer System Check*	—
6	Repair the open in the BLU/RED wire between the windshield wiper motor connector cavity 2 and the windshield wiper/washer switch connector cavity 8. Is the repair complete?	—	Go to *Wiper/Washer System Check*	—

GC9029900690000X

Fig. 22 Test 7: Wipers High Mode Inoperative, Low Mode Operates. Prizm

Step	Action	Yes	No
1	Did you review the Wiper/Washer System Description and Operation and perform the necessary inspections?	Go to Step 2	Go to Diagnostic Starting Point -
2	1. Disconnect the wiper/washer switch connector. 2. Turn the ignition switch ON, engine OFF. Is the washer still on?	Go to Step 3	Go to Step 4
3	Repair the short to ground condition in the washer control circuit between the wiper/washer switch and the washer pump. Is the repair complete?	Go to Step 5	--
4	Replace the wiper/washer switch. Is the replacement complete?	Go to Step 5	--
5	1. Turn the ignition switch ON, engine OFF. 2. Operate the washer pump. Does the washer pump operate properly?	System OK	--

GC9020201057000X

Fig. 24 Test 1: Washer Always On. Vibe

Step	Action	Value(s)	Yes	No
1	Were you sent here from the Wiper/Washer System Check?	—	*Go to Step 2*	Go to *Wiper/Washer System Check*
2	1. Disconnect the windshield wiper motor connector. 2. Turn the ignition switch to the ON position. 3. Turn the windshield wiper/washer switch to the Off position. 4. Test for B+ at cavity 6 of the windshield wiper motor connector using a *J 39200*. Was the value tested equal to B+?	—	*Go to Step 3*	*Go to Step 6*
3	1. Disconnect the windshield wiper/washer switch connector. 2. Turn the windshield wiper/washer switch to the off position. 3. Test for continuity between cavity 16 and cavity 7 of the windshield wiper/washer switch using a *J 39200*. Is there continuity between cavity 16 and cavity 7?	—	*Go to Step 4*	*Go to Step 5*
4	Test for continuity between cavity 16 of the windshield wiper/washer switch connector and cavity 5 of the windshield wiper motor connector using a *J 39200*. Was there continuity in the BLU/WHT wire?	—	*Go to Step 7*	*Go to Step 8*
5	Replace the windshield wiper/washer switch. Is the repair complete?	—	Go to *Wiper/Washer System Check*	—
6	Repair the open in the BLU wire between the windshield wiper motor connector cavity 6 and SP251. Is the repair complete?	—	Go to *Wiper/Washer System Check*	—
7	Replace the windshield wiper motor. Is the repair complete?	—	Go to *Wiper/Washer System Check*	—
8	Repair the open in the BLU/WHT wire between cavity 16 of the windshield wiper/washer switch connector and cavity 5 of the windshield wiper motor connector. Is the repair complete?	—	Go to *Wiper/Washer System Check*	—

GC9029900689000X

Fig. 21 Test 6: Wipers Sweep But Do Not Return To Park Position. Prizm

Step	Action	Value(s)	Yes	No
1	Were you sent here from the Wiper/Washer System Check?	—	*Go to Step 2*	Go to *Wiper/Washer System Check*
2	1. Turn the ignition switch to the ON position. 2. Turn the windshield wiper/washer switch to the LO position. 3. Disconnect the windshield wiper motor connector. 4. Test for B+ at cavity 3 of the windshield wiper motor connector using a *J 39200*. Was the value tested equal to B+?	—	*Go to Step 3*	*Go to Step 4*
3	Replace the windshield wiper motor. Is the repair complete?	—	Go to *Wiper/Washer System Check*	—
4	1. Disconnect the windshield wiper/washer switch connector. 2. Test for continuity using a *J 39200* between cavity 7 of the windshield wiper/washer switch connector and cavity 3 of the windshield wiper motor connector. Is there continuity in the BLU/BLK wire?	—	*Go to Step 5*	*Go to Step 6*
5	Replace the windshield wiper/washer switch. Is the repair complete?	—	Go to *Wiper/Washer System Check*	—
6	Repair the open in the BLU/BLK wire between the windshield wiper motor connector cavity 3 and the windshield wiper/washer switch connector cavity 7. Is the repair complete?	—	Go to *Wiper/Washer System Check*	—

GC9029900691000X

Fig. 23 Test 8: Wipers Low Mode Inoperative, High Mode Operates. Prizm

Step	Action	Yes	No
	DEFINITION: This table diagnoses the washer pump inoperative and assumes that the wipers operate normally.		
1	Did you review the Wiper/Washer System Description and Operation and perform the necessary inspections?	Go to Step 2	Go to Diagnostic Starting Point -
2	1. Turn the ignition ON, engine OFF. 2. Place the washer switch in the wash position. Do the washers operate normally?	Test for Intermittent and Poor Connections	Go to Step 3
3	1. Disconnect the washer pump. 2. Turn ON the ignition with the engine OFF. 3. Connect a test lamp between washer pump control circuit and battery positive voltage. 4. Place the washer switch in the wash position. Does the test lamp illuminate when the washer switch is placed in the wash position?	Go to Step 5	Go to Step 4
4	1. Disconnect the wiper/washer switch connector. 2. Test for a high resistance or an open condition in the washer pump control circuit between the wiper/washer switch and the washer pump . Did you find and correct the condition?	Go to Step 10	Go to Step 6

GC9020201058010X

Fig. 25 Test 2: Washer Inoperative (Part 1 of 2). Vibe

	Test the washer pump feed circuit for a high resistance or an open condition. Did you find and correct the condition?	Go to Step 10	Go to Step 7
6	Inspect for poor connections at the harness connector of the wiper/washer switch. Did you find and correct the condition?	Go to Step 10	Go to Step 8
7	Inspect for poor connections at the harness connector of the washer pump. Did you find and correct the condition?	Go to Step 10	Go to Step 9
8	Replace the wiper/washer switch. Did you complete the replacement?	Go to Step 10	--
9	Replace the washer pump. Did you complete the replacement?	Go to Step 10	--
10	Operate the washers in order to verify the repair. Did you correct the condition?	System OK	Go to Step 3

GC9020201058020X

Fig. 25 Test 2: Washer Inoperative (Part 2 of 2). Vibe

5	Inspect for poor connections at the harness connector of the wiper/washer switch. Did you find and correct the condition?	Go to Step 10	Go to Step 8
6	Inspect for poor connections at the harness connector of the wiper motor. Did you find and correct the condition?	Go to Step 10	Go to Step 9
7	Repair the short to voltage condition. Did you complete the repair?	Go to Step 10	--
8	Replace the front wiper/washer switch. Did you complete the replacement?	Go to Step 10	--
9	Replace the front wiper motor. Did you complete the replacement?	Go to Step 10	--
10	Operate the system in order to verify the repair. Did you correct the condition?	Go to Step 10	--

GC9020201059020X

Fig. 26 Test 3: Wipers Always On (Part 2 of 2). Vibe

5	Test the ground circuit of the wiper motor for a high resistance or an open condition. Did you find and correct the condition?	Go to Step 10	Go to Step 7
6	Inspect for poor connections at the harness connector of the wiper/washer switch. Did you find and correct the condition?	Go to Step 10	Go to Step 8
7	Inspect for poor connections at the harness connector of the wiper motor. Did you find and correct the condition?	Go to Step 10	Go to Step 9
8	Replace the front wiper/washer switch. Did you complete the replacement?	Go to Step 10	--
9	Replace the front wiper motor. Did you complete the replacement?	Go to Step 10	--
10	Operate the system in order to verify the repair. Did you correct the condition?	System OK	Go to Step 3

GC9020201060020X

Fig. 27 Test 4: Wipers Inoperative In All Modes (Part 2 of 2). Vibe

Step	Action	Yes	No
DEFINITION: This table diagnoses the front wipers are always on when the wiper/washer switch is turned to the off position.			
1	Did you review the Wiper/Washer System Description and Operation and perform the necessary inspections?	Go to Step 2	Go to Diagnostic Starting Point
2	Verify that the front wipers are always on when the wiper/washer switch is turned to the OFF position. Do the front wipers operate normally?	Test for Intermittent and Poor Connections	Go to Step 3
3	1. Turn the front wiper switch to the OFF position. 2. Disconnect the front wiper motor connector. 3. Test the following circuits for a short to voltage condition at the wiper motor connector: o Run/Park o High o Low Did any of the circuits measure a short to voltage?	Go to Step 4	Go to Step 6
4	1. Disconnect the wiper/washer switch. 2. Retest the circuit that measured shorted to voltage at the wiper motor connector. Does the circuit still have a short to voltage condition?	Go to Step 7	Go to Step 5

GC9020201059010X

Fig. 26 Test 3: Wipers Always On (Part 1 of 2). Vibe

Step	Action	Yes	No
DEFINITION: This table diagnoses the front wipers inoperative in the LO, HI, and INT modes.			
1	Did you review the Wiper/Washer System Description and Operation and perform the necessary inspections?	Go to Step 2	Go to Diagnostic Starting Point -
2	1. Turn the ignition ON, engine OFF. 2. Operate the wiper switch in the LO, HI, and INT positions. Are the front wipers inoperative in all modes?	Go to Step 3	Test for Intermittent and Poor Connections
3	1. Disconnect the front wiper motor connector. 2. Turn the ignition ON, engine OFF. 3. Turn the front wiper switch to the HI position. 4. Test the High speed voltage supply circuit at the wiper motor connector. Did you measure ignition positive voltage at the wiper motor connector?	Go to Step 5	Go to Step 4
4	1. Disconnect the front wiper/washer switch connector. 2. Turn the ignition ON, engine OFF. 3. Test the voltage supply circuit at the front wiper/washer switch connector. Did you measure ignition positive voltage at the front wiper/washer switch connector?	Go to Step 10	Go to Step 6

GC9020201060010X

Fig. 27 Test 4: Wipers Inoperative In All Modes (Part 1 of 2). Vibe

Step	Action	Yes	No
1	Did you review the Wiper/Washer System Description and Operation and perform the necessary inspections?	Go to Step 2	Go to Diagnostic Starting Point -
2	1. Turn the ignition ON, engine OFF. 2. Turn the wiper switch to the LO, HI, and INT positions. Do the front wipers operate in the LO, HI, and INT positions?	Test for Intermittent and Poor Connections	Go to Step 3
3	Do the wipers operate in the LO and HI position, but not the INT position?	Go to Step 6	Go to Step 4
4	1. Disconnect the wiper motor. 2. Turn the ignition ON, engine OFF. 3. Turn the wiper switch to the affected speed. 4. With a test lamp connected to a good ground, test the corresponding voltage supply circuit at the wiper motor connector for ignition positive voltage. Does the test lamp illuminate?	Go to Step 7	Go to Step 5
5	1. Turn the wiper switch to the affected speed. 2. With a test lamp connected to a good ground, test the corresponding voltage supply circuit at the wiper/washer switch for ignition positive voltage. Does the test lamp illuminate?	Go to Step 8	Go to Step 6

GC9020201061010X

Fig. 28 Test 5: Wipers Inoperative In One Mode (Part 1 of 2). Vibe

6	Inspect for poor connections at the harness connector of the wiper/washer switch. Did you find and correct the condition?	Go to Step 11	Go to Step 9
7	Inspect for poor connections at the harness connector of the wiper motor. Did you find and correct the condition?	Go to Step 11	Go to Step 10
8	Repair the high resistance or open condition in the voltage supply circuit to the wiper motor. Did you complete the repair?	Go to Step 11	--
9	Replace the front wiper/washer switch. Did you complete the replacement?	Go to Step 11	--
10	Replace the front wiper motor. Did you complete the replacement?	Go to Step 11	--
11	Operate the system in order to verify the repair. Did you correct the condition?	System OK	Go to Step 3

GC9020201061020X

Fig. 28 Test 5: Wipers Inoperative In One Mode (Part 2 of 2). Vibe

Step	Action	Yes	No
DEFINITION: This table diagnoses the wipers operates normally but will not return to the park position when the wiper operation is cancelled.			
1	Did you review the Wiper/Washer System Description and Operation and perform the necessary inspections?	Go to Step 2	Go to Diagnostic Starting Point -
2	1. Turn the ignition ON, engine OFF. 2. Move the wiper switch to the LO position. 3. Move wiper switch to the OFF position. Do the front wipers advance to the park position?	Test for Intermittent and Poor Connections	Go to Step 3
3	1. Connect a test lamp between the park circuit and a good ground at the wiper motor connector. 2. Turn the ignition ON, engine OFF. 3. Move the wiper switch to the LO position. Does the test lamp flash on and off with each rotation of the wiper motor?	Go to Step 4	Go to Step 5
4	1. Connect a test lamp between the park circuit and a good ground at the wiper/washer switch connector. 2. Turn the ignition ON, engine OFF. 3. Move the wiper switch to the LO position. Does the test lamp flash on and off with each rotation of the wiper motor?	Go to Step 6	Go to Step 8
5	1. Connect a test lamp between the park switch supply circuit and a good ground at the wiper motor connector. 2. Turn the ignition ON, engine OFF. Does the test lamp illuminate?	Go to Step 7	Go to Step 9

GC9020201062010X

Fig. 29 Test 6: Wiper Blades Do Not Park (Part 1 of 2). Vibe

6	Inspect for poor connections at the harness connector of the wiper/washer switch. Did you find and correct the condition?	Go to Step 12	Go to Step 10
7	Inspect for poor connections at the harness connector of the wiper motor. Did you find and correct the condition?	Go to Step 12	Go to Step 11
8	Repair the open in the Run/Park circuit between the wiper motor connector and wiper/washer switch connector. Did you complete the repair?	Go to Step 12	--
9	Repair the open in the park switch supply circuit between the wiper motor connector and fuse block. Did you complete the repair?	Go to Step 12	--
10	Replace the front wiper/washer switch. Did you complete the replacement?	Go to Step 12	--
11	Replace the front wiper motor. Did you complete the replacement?	Go to Step 12	--
12	Operate the system in order to verify the repair. Did you correct the condition?	System OK	Go to Step 3

GC9020201062020X

Fig. 29 Test 6: Wiper Blades Do Not Park (Part 2 of 2). Vibe

Rear Window Wiper Systems

NOTE: On Air Bag Equipped Models, Refer To "Air Bag System Precautions" Located In The Front Of This Manual For System Disarming & Arming Procedures.

NOTE: Refer To "Computer Relearn Procedures" Located In The Front Of This Manual When Battery Power To The Computer Has Been Interrupted.

NOTE: "Electrical Symbol & Wire Color Code Identification" Located In The Front Of This Manual May Be Used As An Aid When Using Wiring Circuits Found In This Section.

INDEX

PRECAUTIONS

Air Bag Systems

Refer to "Air Bag System Precautions" in the front of this manual for system disarming and arming procedures.

Battery Ground Cable

Prior to service, disconnect battery ground cable and isolate as required.

DESCRIPTION

The rear wiper/washer system includes a wiper motor, wiper arm, wiper blade assembly, washer reservoir, nozzle and washer switch The rear wiper/washer switch controls the rear wiper/washer system. The rear wiper/washer switch is located on the lefthand garnish trim panel of the instrument panel. The rear wiper operates at 1 speed.

SYSTEM DIAGNOSIS & TESTING

Wiring Diagram

Refer to **Figs. 1 and 2,** for wiring diagram.

Symptom Related Tests

Refer to **Figs. 3 through 14,** for symptom related tests.

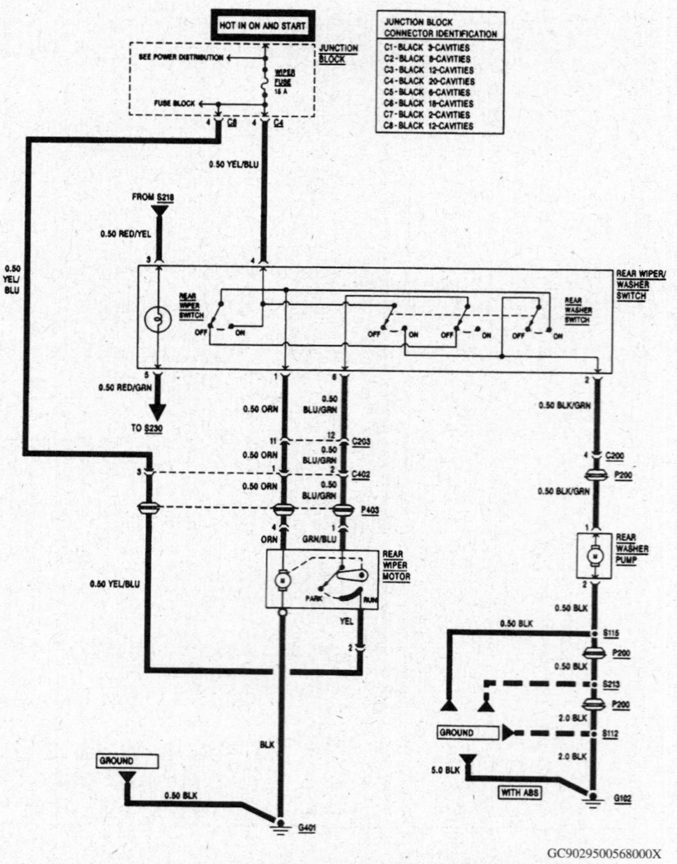

Fig. 1 Wiper system wiring diagram. Metro

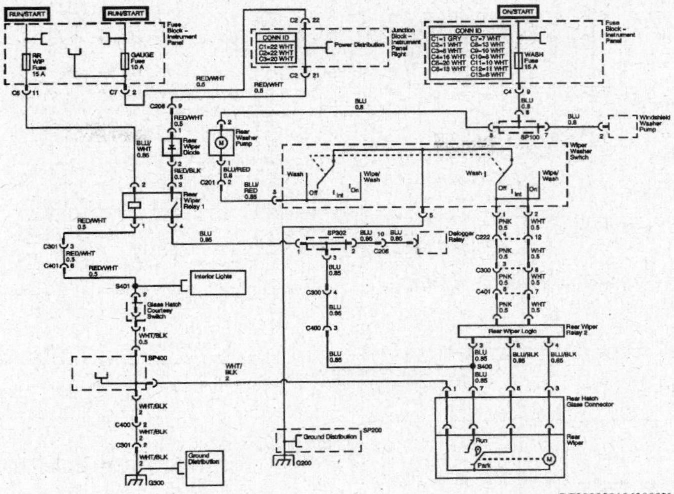

Fig. 2 Wiper system wiring diagram. Vibe

DIAGNOSTIC CHART INDEX

Test	Description	Page No.	Fig. No.
METRO			
1	Rear Wiper/Washer System Check	3-56	3
2	Rear Wiper Inoperative	3-56	4
3	Rear Wiper On Mode Inoperative	3-56	5
4	Rear Wiper Always On	3-56	6
5	Rear Wiper Blade Does Not Park	3-56	7
6	Rear Wiper Motor Runs, Blade Does Not Move	3-56	8
7	Rear Washer Inoperative	3-57	9
VIBE			
1	Rear Washer Always On	3-57	10
2	Rear Washer Inoperative	3-57	11
3	Rear Wiper Always On	3-57	12
4	Rear Wiper Inoperative	3-58	13
5	Rear Wiper Does Not Park	3-58	14

Step	Action	Normal Result(s)	Abnormal Result(s)*
1	1. Turn the ignition switch to the ON position. 2. Press and hold the rear wiper/washer switch.	1. The rear washer pump operates. 2. The rear wiper operates.	• *Wiper Inoperative - Rear* • *Washer Inoperative - Rear* • *Wipers On Mode Inoperative - Rear*
2	Release the rear washer switch.	The following components stop in the PARK position: • The washer pump • The rear wiper	• *Wiper Always On - Rear* • *Wiper Blade Does Not Park - Rear*
3	Press the rear wiper switch to the ON position.	The rear wiper operates.	*Wiper Inoperative - Rear*
4	Press the rear wiper switch to the OFF position.	The rear wiper completes the cycle and returns to the PARK position.	• *Wiper Always On - Rear* • *Wiper Blade Does Not Park - Rear*

* Refer to the appropriate symptom diagnostic table for the applicable abnormal result.

GC9020000818000X

Fig. 3 Test 1: Rear Wiper/Washer System Check. Metro

Step	Action	Value(s)	Yes	No
1	Did you perform the system check?	—	Go to *Step 2*	Go to *Wiper/Washer Rear System Check*
2	1. Turn the ignition switch to the ON position. 2. Backprobe the rear wiper/washer switch connector with a test lamp from cavity 4 to ground. Does the test lamp light?	—	Go to *Step 4*	Go to *Step 3*
3	Test for an open in the YEL/BLU wire between the junction block and the rear wiper/washer switch. Was an open found?	—	Go to *Step 5*	Go to *Step 6*
4	Replace the rear wiper/washer switch. Is the repair complete?	—	Go to *Wiper/Washer Rear System Check*	—
5	Repair the open. Is the repair complete?	—	Go to *Wiper/Washer Rear System Check*	—
6	Replace the junction block. Is the repair complete?	—	Go to *Wiper/Washer Rear System Check*	—

GC9020000829000X

Fig. 5 Test 3: Rear Wiper On Mode Inoperative. Metro

Step	Action	Value(s)	Yes	No
1	Did you perform the system check?	—	Go to *Step 2*	Go to *Wiper/Washer Rear System Check*
2	1. Turn the ignition switch to the ON position. 2. Backprobe the rear wiper motor connector with a test lamp from cavity 2 to ground. Does the test lamp light?	—	Go to *Step 3*	Go to *Step 4*
3	1. Manually move the rear wiper out of the PARK position. 2. Backprobe the rear wiper/washer switch connector with a test lamp from cavity 6 to ground. Does the test lamp light?	—	Go to *Step 6*	Go to *Step 5*
4	Test for an open in the YEL/BLU wire between the junction block and the rear wiper motor. Was an open found?	—	Go to *Step 8*	Go to *Step 9*
5	Test for an open in the BLU/GRN wire between the rear wiper/washer switch and the rear wiper motor. Was an open found?	—	Go to *Step 8*	Go to *Step 7*
6	Replace the rear wiper/washer switch. Is the repair complete?	—	Go to *Wiper/Washer Rear System Check*	—
7	Replace the rear wiper motor. Is the repair complete?	—	Go to *Wiper/Washer Rear System Check*	—
8	Repair the open. Systems. Is the repair complete?	—	Go to *Wiper/Washer Rear System Check*	—
9	Replace the junction block. Is the repair complete?	—	Go to *Wiper/Washer Rear System Check*	—

GC9020000831000X

Fig. 7 Test 5: Rear Wiper Blade Does Not Park. Metro

Step	Action	Value(s)	Yes	No
1	Did you perform the system check?	—	Go to *Step 2*	Go to *Wiper/Washer Rear System Check*
2	1. Turn the ignition switch to the ON position. 2. Press the rear wiper switch to the ON position. 3. Backprobe the rear wiper motor connector with a test lamp from cavity 4 to ground. Does the test lamp light?	—	Go to *Step 4*	Go to *Step 3*
3	Test for an open in the ORN wire between the rear wiper/washer switch and the rear wiper motor. Was an open found?	—	Go to *Step 7*	Go to *Step 5*
4	Test for an open in the BLK wire between the rear wiper motor and G401. Was an open found?	—	Go to *Step 7*	Go to *Step 6*
5	Replace the rear wiper/washer switch. Is the repair complete?	—	Go to *Wiper/Washer Rear System Check*	—
6	Replace the rear wiper motor. Is the repair complete?	—	Go to *Wiper/Washer Rear System Check*	—
7	Repair the open. Is the repair complete?	—	Go to *Wiper/Washer Rear System Check*	—

GC9020000828000X

Fig. 4 Test 2: Rear Wiper Inoperative. Metro

Step	Action	Value(s)	Yes	No
1	Did you perform the system check?	—	Go to *Step 2*	Go to *Wiper/Washer Rear System Check*
2	1. Disconnect the junction block connector C8. 2. Turn the ignition switch to the ON position. Does the rear wiper motor operate?	—	Go to *Step 3*	Go to *Step 4*
3	1. Turn the ignition switch to the LOCK position. 2. Disconnect the rear wiper/washer switch connector. 3. Turn the ignition switch to the ON position. Does the rear wiper motor operate?	—	Go to *Step 6*	Go to *Step 5*
4	Replace the rear wiper motor. Is the repair complete?	—	Go to *Wiper/Washer Rear System Check*	—
5	Test for a short to voltage in the BLU/GRN wire between the rear wiper/washer switch and rear wiper motor. Was a short to voltage found?	—	Go to *Step 8*	Go to *Step 7*
6	Repair a short to voltage in the ORN wire between the rear wiper/washer switch and the rear wiper motor. Is the repair complete?	—	Go to *Wiper/Washer Rear System Check*	—
7	Replace the rear wiper/washer switch. Is the repair complete?	—	Go to *Wiper/Washer Rear System Check*	—
8	Repair the short. Is the repair complete?	—	Go to *Wiper/Washer Rear System Check*	—

GC9020000830000X

Fig. 6 Test 4: Rear Wiper Always On. Metro

Step	Action	Value(s)	Yes	No
1	Did you perform the system check?	—	Go to *Step 2*	Go to *Wiper/Washer Rear System Check*
2	1. Turn the ignition switch to the ON position. 2. Press the rear wiper switch to the ON position. 3. Backprobe the rear wiper motor connector with a test lamp from cavity 4 to ground. Does the test lamp light?	—	Go to *Step 4*	Go to *Step 3*
3	Test for an open in the ORN wire between the rear wiper/washer switch and the rear wiper motor. Was an open found?	—	Go to *Step 7*	Go to *Step 5*
4	Test for an open in the BLK wire between the rear wiper motor and G401. Was an open found?	—	Go to *Step 7*	Go to *Step 6*
5	Replace the rear wiper/washer switch. Is the repair complete?	—	Go to *Wiper/Washer Rear System Check*	—
6	Replace the rear wiper motor. Is the repair complete?	—	Go to *Wiper/Washer Rear System Check*	—
7	Repair the open. Is the repair complete?	—	Go to *Wiper/Washer Rear System Check*	—

GC9020000832000X

Fig. 8 Test 6: Rear Wiper Motor Runs, Blade Does Not Move. Metro

Step	Action	Value(s)	Yes	No
1	Did you perform the system check?	—	Go to *Step 2*	Go to *Wiper/Washer Rear System Check*
2	1. Turn the ignition switch to the ON position. 2. Backprobe the rear washer pump connector with a test lamp from cavity 1 to ground. 3. Press and hold the rear washer switch. Does the test lamp light?	—	Go to *Step 4*	Go to *Step 3*
3	Test for an open in the BLK/GRN wire between the rear wiper/washer switch and the rear washer pump. Was an open found?	—	Go to *Step 5*	Go to *Step 6*
4	Test for an open in the BLK ground wire between the rear washer pump and G102. Was an open found?	—	Go to *Step 5*	Go to *Step 7*
5	Repair the open. Is the repair complete?	—	Go to *Wiper/Washer Rear System Check*	—
6	Replace the combination switch. Is the repair complete?	—	Go to *Wiper/Washer Rear System Check*	—
7	Replace the rear washer pump. Is the repair complete?	—	Go to *Wiper/Washer Rear System Check*	—

GC9020000833000X

Fig. 9 Test 7: Rear Washer Inoperative. Metro

Step	Action	Yes	No
DEFINITION: This table diagnoses the washer pump inoperative and assumes that the wipers operate normally.			
1	Did you review the Wiper/Washer System Description and Operation and perform the necessary inspections?	Go to Step 2	Go to Diagnostic Starting Point -
2	1. Turn the ignition ON, engine OFF. 2. Place the washer switch in the wash position. Do the washers operate normally?	Test for Intermittent and Poor Connections	Go to Step 3
3	1. Disconnect the washer pump. 2. Turn ON the ignition with the engine OFF. 3. Connect a test lamp between washer pump control circuit and battery positive voltage. 4. Place the washer switch in the wash position. Does the test lamp illuminate when the washer switch is placed in the wash position?	Go to Step 5	Go to Step 4
4	1. Disconnect the wiper/washer switch connector. 2. Test for a high resistance or an open condition in the washer pump control circuit between the wiper/washer switch and the washer pump . Did you find and correct the condition?	Go to Step 10	Go to Step 6

GC9020201065010X

Fig. 11 Test 2: Rear Washer Inoperative (Part 1 of 2). Vibe

Step	Action	Yes	No
DEFINITION: This table diagnoses the rear wipers are always on when the rear wiper/washer switch is in the OFF position.			
1	Did you review the Rear Wiper/Washer System Description and Operation and perform the necessary inspections?	Go to Step 2	Go to Symptoms -
2	1. Turn the ignition ON, engine OFF. 2. Verify that the rear wipers are always on when the wiper/washer switch is in the OFF position. Are the rear wipers always ON?	Go to Step 3	Test for Intermittent and Poor Connections
3	1. Turn the ignition OFF. 2. Disconnect the wiper/washer switch. 3. Turn the ignition ON, engine OFF. Are the rear wipers always ON?	Go to Step 4	Go to Step 7
4	1. Turn the ignition OFF. 2. Disconnect the rear wiper relay 2. 3. Turn the ignition ON, engine OFF. Are the rear wipers always ON?	Go to Step 5	Go to Step 8
5	1. Turn the ignition ON, engine OFF. 2. Test the wiper motor feed circuit for a short to voltage at the wiper motor connector. Does the circuit have a short to voltage condition?	Go to Step 9	Go to Step 6

GC9020201066010X

Fig. 12 Test 3: Rear Wiper Always On (Part 1 of 2). Vibe

Step	Action	Yes	No
1	Did you review the Wiper/Washer System Description and Operation and perform the necessary inspections?	Go to Step 2	Go to Diagnostic Starting Point -
2	1. Disconnect the wiper/washer switch connector. 2. Turn the ignition switch ON, engine OFF. Is the washer still on?	Go to Step 3	Go to Step 4
3	Repair the short to ground condition in the washer control circuit between the wiper/washer switch and the washer pump. Is the repair complete?	Go to Step 5	--
4	Replace the wiper/washer switch. Is the replacement complete?	Go to Step 5	--
5	1. Turn the ignition switch ON, engine OFF. 2. Operate the washer pump. Does the washer pump operate properly?	System OK	--

GC9020201064000X

Fig. 10 Test 1: Rear Washer Always On. Vibe

5	Test the washer pump feed circuit for a high resistance or an open condition. Did you find and correct the condition?	Go to Step 10	Go to Step 7
6	Inspect for poor connections at the harness connector of the wiper/washer switch. Did you find and correct the condition?	Go to Step 10	Go to Step 8
7	Inspect for poor connections at the harness connector of the washer pump. Did you find and correct the condition?	Go to Step 10	Go to Step 9
8	Replace the wiper/washer switch. Did you complete the replacement?	Go to Step 10	--
9	Replace the washer pump. Did you complete the replacement?	Go to Step 10	--
10	Operate the washers in order to verify the repair. Did you correct the condition?	System OK	Go to Step 3

GC9020201065020X

Fig. 11 Test 2: Rear Washer Inoperative (Part 2 of 2). Vibe

6	Replace the rear wiper motor. Did you complete the replacement?	Go to Step 13	--
7	Replace the rear wiper/washer switch. Did you complete the replacement?	Go to Step 13	--
8	1. Disconnect the rear wiper motor. 2. Turn the ignition ON, engine OFF. 3. Test the wiper motor feed circuit for a short to voltage at the wiper motor connector. Does the circuit have a short to voltage condition?	Go to Step 9	Go to Step 10
9	Repair the short to voltage condition. Did you complete the repair?	Go to Step 13	--
10	1. Turn the ignition OFF. 2. Test for a short to ground on the following circuits at the rear wiper relay connector: o Intermittent position circuit o Wiper relay ground circuit Does either circuit have a short to ground condition?	Go to Step 11	Go to Step 12
11	Repair the short to voltage condition. Did you complete the repair?	Go to Step 13	--
12	Replace the rear wiper relay 2. Did you complete the replacement?	Go to Step 13	--
13	Operate the system in order to verify the repair. Did you correct the condition?	System OK	Go to Step 3

GC9020201066020X

Fig. 12 Test 3: Rear Wiper Always On (Part 2 of 2). Vibe

Step	Action	Yes	No
1	Did you review the Rear Wiper/Washer System Description and Operation and perform the necessary inspections?	Go to Step 2	Go to Symptoms -
2	1. Ensure the rear hatch is closed. 2. Turn ON the ignition, with the engine OFF. 3. Turn the rear wiper switch to operate the rear wiper. Does the rear wiper operate normally?	Test for Intermittent and Poor Connections	Go to Step 3
3	1. Turn OFF the ignition. 2. Disconnect the rear wiper relay 2. 3. Connect a test lamp between the park control circuit of the rear wiper relay 2 and a good ground. 4. Turn ON the ignition, with the engine OFF. Does the test lamp illuminate?	Go to Step 4	Go to Step 5
4	1. Turn OFF the ignition. 2. Connect a fused jumper between the park control circuit and the wiper motor feed circuit of the rear wiper relay 2. 3. Turn ON the ignition, with the engine OFF. Does the rear wiper operate?	Go to Step 7	Go to Step 12
5	1. Turn OFF the ignition. 2. Disconnect the rear wiper relay 1. 3. Turn ON the ignition, with the engine OFF. 4. Probe the supply circuits of the rear wiper relay 1 with a test lamp that is connected to a good ground. Does the test lamp illuminate on both circuits?	Go to Step 17	Go to Step 6

GC9020201067010X

Fig. 13 Test 4: Rear Wiper Inoperative (Part 1 of 4). Vibe

6	Repair the open or short to ground in the relay supply circuit of the rear wiper relay 1. Did you complete the repair?	Go to Step 21	--
7	1. Turn OFF the ignition. 2. Reconnect the rear wiper relay 2. 3. Disconnect the wiper/washer switch connector. 4. Connect a fused jumper between the rear wiper control circuit of the wiper/washer switch and a good ground. 5. Turn ON the ignition, with the engine OFF. Does the rear wiper operate?	Go to Step 9	Go to Step 8
8	Test the rear wiper control circuit of the wiper/washer switch for a short to voltage or an open. Did you find and correct the condition?	Go to Step 21	Go to Step 10
9	Test the ground circuit of the wiper/washer switch for a short to voltage or an open. Did you find and correct the condition?	Go to Step 21	Go to Step 10
10	Inspect for poor connections at the harness connector of the wiper/washer switch. Did you find and correct the condition?	Go to Step 21	Go to Step 11
11	Replace the wiper/washer switch. Did you complete the replacement?	Go to Step 21	--

GC9020201067020X

Fig. 13 Test 4: Rear Wiper Inoperative (Part 2 of 4). Vibe

12	Replace the rear wiper relay 2. Did you complete the replacement?	Go to Step 21	--
13	1. Turn OFF the ignition. 2. Connect a fused jumper between battery positive voltage and the wiper motor feed circuit of the rear wiper relay 2. 3. Turn ON the ignition, with the engine OFF. Does the rear wiper operate?	Go to Step 14	Go to Step 15
14	Repair the open in the wiper motor feed circuit between the rear wiper motor and the rear wiper relay 2. Did you complete the repair?	Go to Step 21	--
15	Test the ground circuit of the rear wiper motor for a short to voltage or an open. Did you find and correct the condition?	Go to Step 21	Go to Step 16
16	Replace the rear wiper motor. Did you complete the replacement?	Go to Step 21	--
17	1. Connect a test lamp between the relay coil supply circuit and the relay coil control circuit of the rear wiper relay 1. 2. Turn ON the ignition, with the engine OFF. Does the test lamp illuminate?	Go to Step 18	Go to Step 20

GC9020201067030X

Fig. 13 Test 4: Rear Wiper Inoperative (Part 3 of 4). Vibe

18	Test the park control circuit between the rear wiper relay 1 and the rear wiper relay 2 for a short to ground or an open. Did you find and correct the condition?	Go to Step 21	Go to Step 19
19	Replace the rear wiper relay 1. Did you complete the replacement?	Go to Step 21	--
20	Repair the ground circuit between the rear wiper relay 1 and the glass hatch courtesy switch for a short to voltage or an open. Did you find and correct the condition?	Go to Step 21	--
21	Operate the system in order to verify the repair. Did you correct the condition?	System OK	Go to Step 3

GC9020201067040X

Fig. 13 Test 4: Rear Wiper Inoperative (Part 4 of 4). Vibe

Step	Action	Yes	No
DEFINITION: This table diagnoses the rear wiper operates normally but will not return to the park position when the rear wiper switch is turned to the OFF position.			
1	Did you review the Rear Wiper/Washer System Description and Operation and perform the necessary inspections?	Go to Step 2	Go to Symptoms -
2	Verify that the rear wiper will not park when the wiper switch is turned to OFF. Does the rear wiper park?	Test for Intermittent and Poor Connections	Go to Step 3
3	1. Disconnect the rear wiper motor connector. 2. Turn ON the ignition, with the engine OFF. 3. Test the park control circuit of the rear wiper motor for ignition positive voltage. Did you find and correct the condition?	Go to Step 10	Go to Step 4
4	1. Disconnect the rear wiper relay 2. 2. Test the park switch circuit for a short to voltage or an open condition between the rear wiper relay 2 and the rear wiper motor . Did you find and correct the condition?	Go to Step 10	Go to Step 5

GC9020201068000X

Fig. 14 Test 5: Rear Wiper Does Not Park. Vibe

Saturn

NOTE: On Air Bag Equipped Models, Refer To "Air Bag System Precautions" Located In The Front Of This Manual For System Disarming & Arming Procedures.

NOTE: Refer To "Computer Relearn Procedures" Located In The Front Of This Manual When Battery Power To The Computer Has Been Interrupted.

NOTE: "Electrical Symbol & Wire Color Code Identification" Located In The Front Of This Manual May Be Used As An Aid When Using Wiring Circuits Found In This Section.

INDEX

DESCRIPTION

On all models except Wagon, the wiper and washer system consists of a stalk mounted switch, a windshield wiper motor/control module, a two-speed front wiper motor and a washer pump motor. The wipers and washers operate with the ignition in the Run or Acc positions.

On Wagon models, the wiper and washer system consists of a stalk mounted switch, a windshield wiper motor/control module, a two-speed front wiper motor, one-speed rear wiper motor and front and rear washer pump motors. The wipers and washers operate with the ignition in the Run or Acc positions.

TROUBLESHOOTING

Refer to **Figs. 1 and 2,** for troubleshooting.

SYSTEM DIAGNOSIS & TESTING

Accessing Diagnostic Trouble Codes

L-SERIES & ION

Connect a suitably programmed scan tool to Data Link Connector (DLC), and follow manufacturer's instructions.

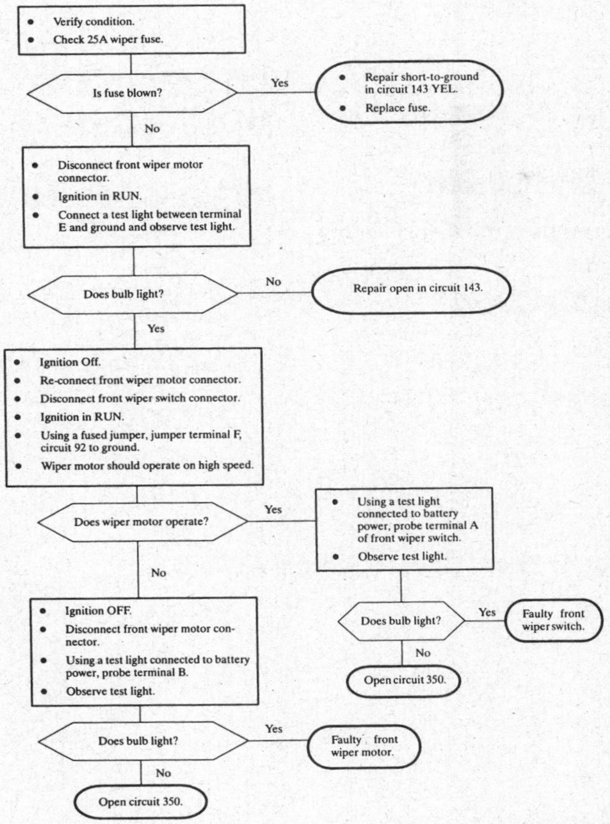

Fig. 1 Front wiper system troubleshooting chart (Part 1 of 4). S-Series

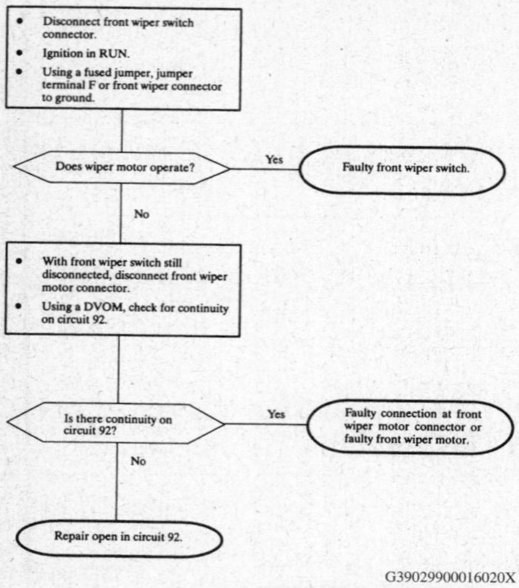

Fig. 1 Front wiper system troubleshooting chart (Part 2 of 4). S-Series

Diagnostic Trouble Code Interpretation

L-SERIES

Refer to **Fig. 3,** for Diagnostic Trouble Code (DTC) interpretation.

ION

Refer to "Diagnostic Trouble Code Index" for "Diagnostic Trouble Code Interpretation."

Wiring Diagrams

Refer to **Figs. 4 through 8,** for wiring diagrams.

Diagnostic Test

L-SERIES

Refer to **Figs. 9 through 16,** for diagnostic tests.

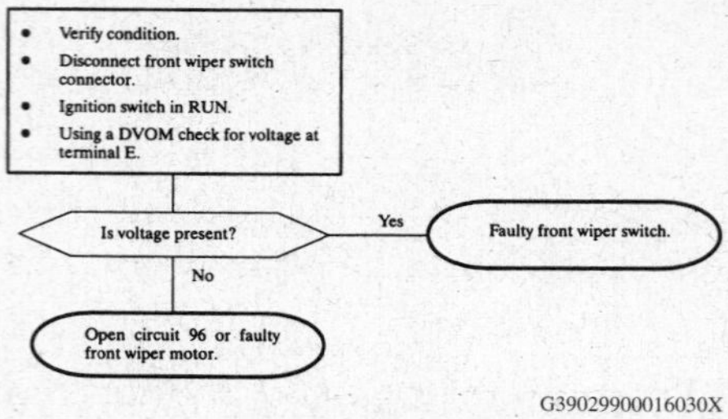

Fig. 1 Front wiper system troubleshooting chart (Part 3 of 4). S-Series

ION

Refer to **Figs. 17 through 23,** for diagnostic test.

S-SERIES

Refer to **Fig. 24,** for system performance test.

Clearing Diagnostic Trouble Codes

Connect a suitably programmed scan tool to Data Link Connector (DLC), and follow manufacturer's instructions.

COMPONENT DIAGNOSIS & TESTING

Wiper Module

1. Inspect wiper circuits, connectors and terminals.
2. Test wiper module in vehicle. It must be connected to windshield wiper switch to work properly.
3. Wiper module and motor are serviced as an assembly. Repair is by replacement only.

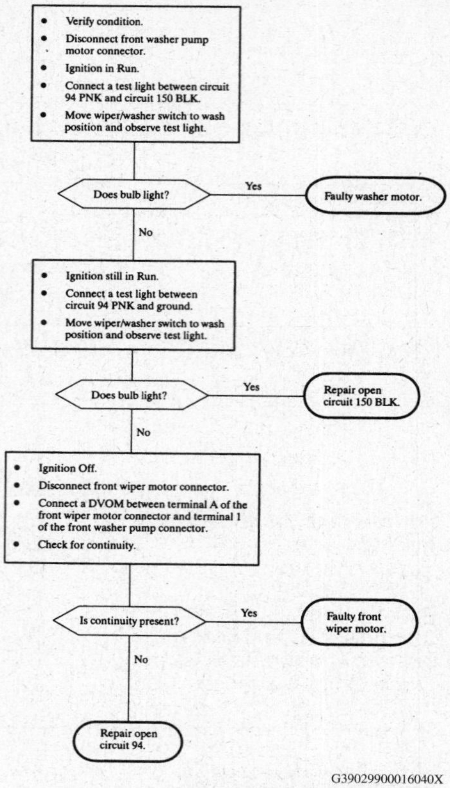

Fig. 1 Front wiper system troubleshooting chart (Part 4 of 4). S-Series

4. Inspect terminals and connections for damage and corrosion.

Wiper Switch

Test resistance between connector terminals, **Figs. 25 through 31.** Replace switch if results are not as specified.

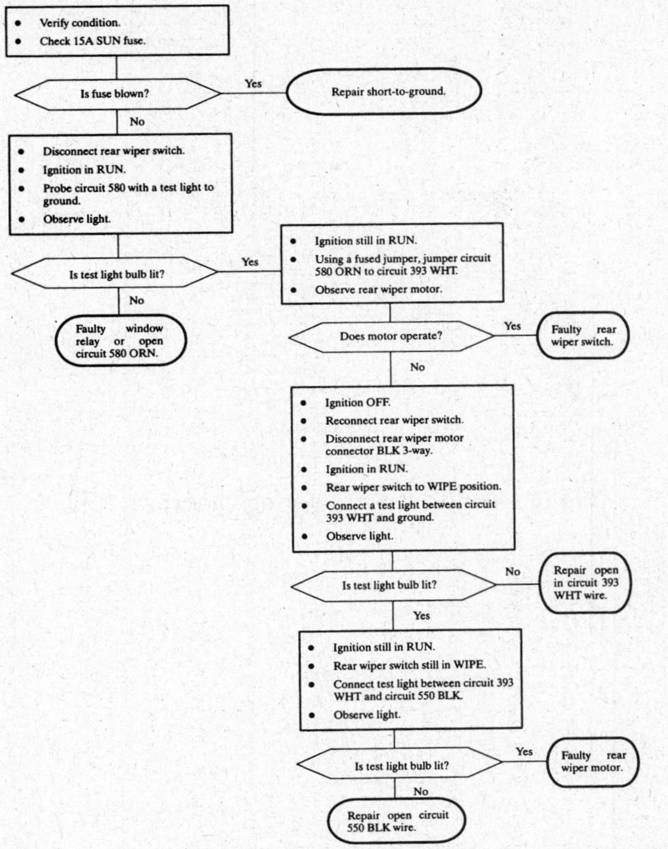

G39029900017010X

Fig. 2 Rear wiper system troubleshooting chart (Part 1 of 3). S-Series

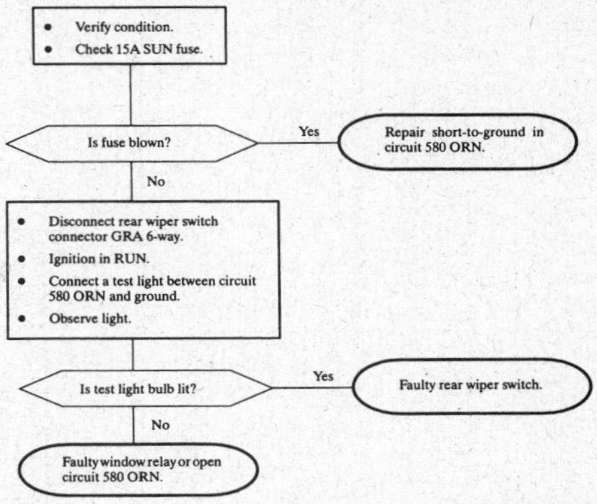

G39029900017020X

Fig. 2 Rear wiper system troubleshooting chart (Part 2 of 3). S-Series

DTC DESCRIPTIONS
Intermittent wiper delay input circuit low – B3702
Intermittent wiper delay input circuit high – B3703
Front washer motor input circuit high – B3708
Rear washer motor input circuit high – B3713
Front wiper relay drive circuit low – B3717
Front wiper relay drive circuit high – B3718
Rear wiper relay drive circuit low – B3722
Rear wiper relay drive circuit high – B3722

G39029900018000X

Fig. 3 DTC interpretation. L-Series

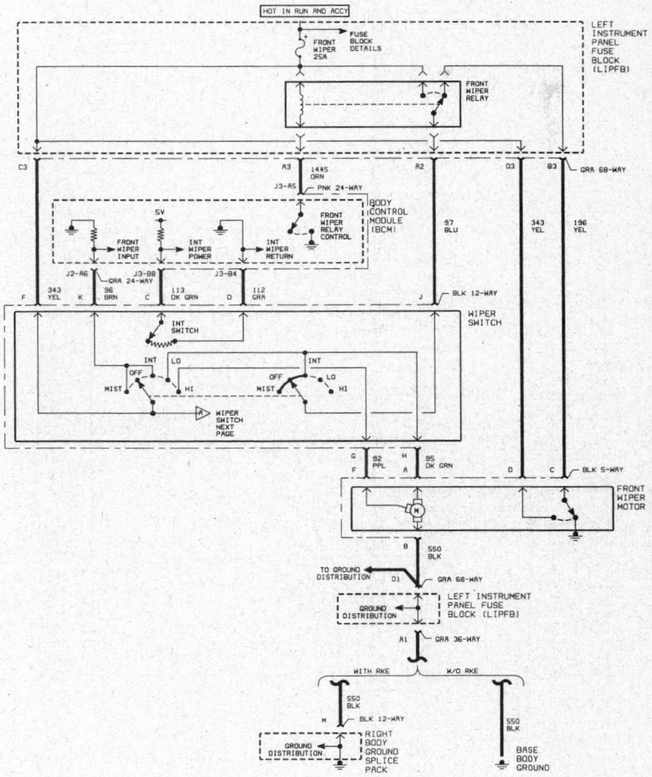

G39029900013000X

Fig. 4 Front wiper system wiring diagram. L-Series

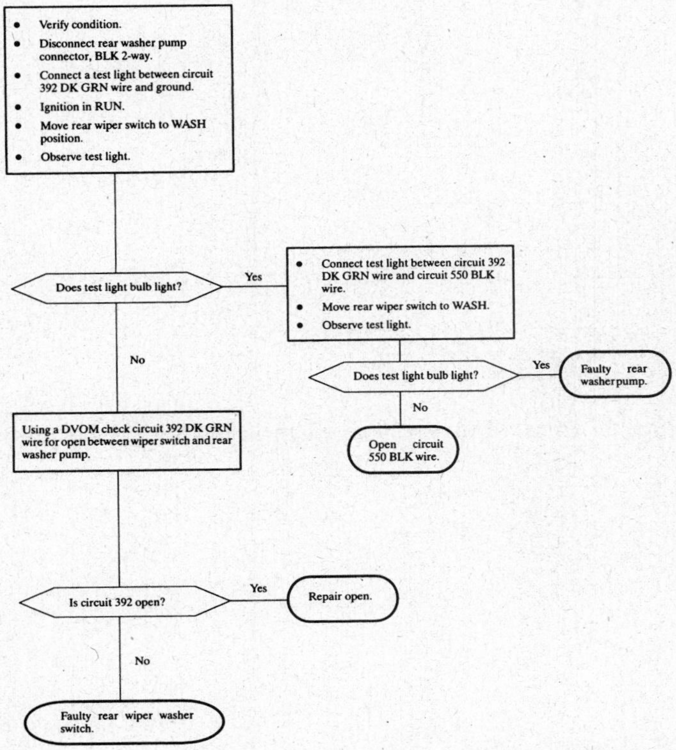

G39029900017030X

Fig. 2 Rear wiper system troubleshooting chart (Part 3 of 3). S-Series

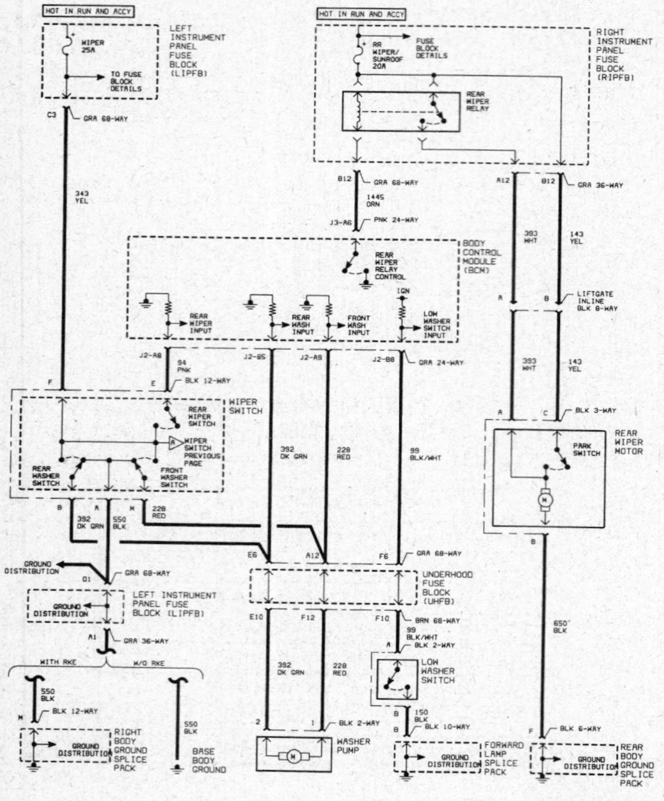

Fig. 5 Rear wiper system wiring diagram. L-Series

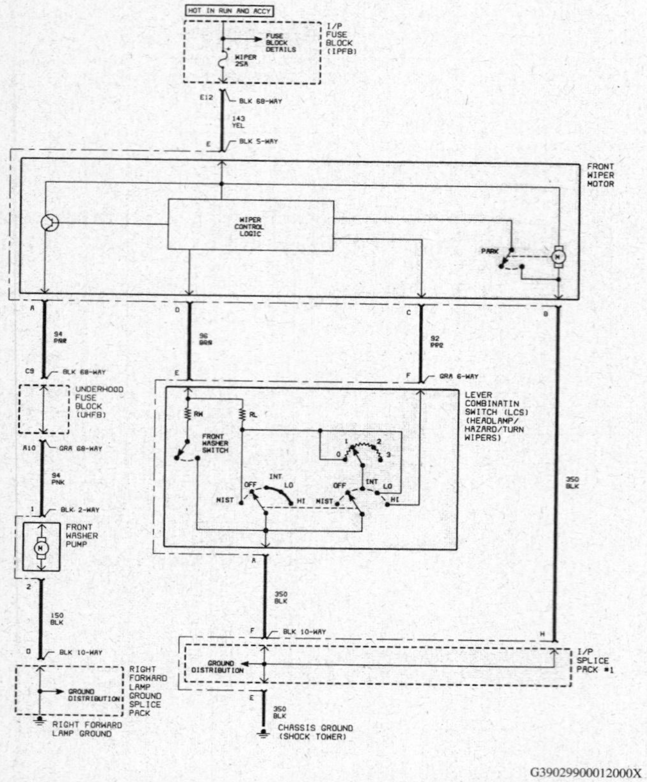

Fig. 7 Front wiper system wiring diagram. S-Series

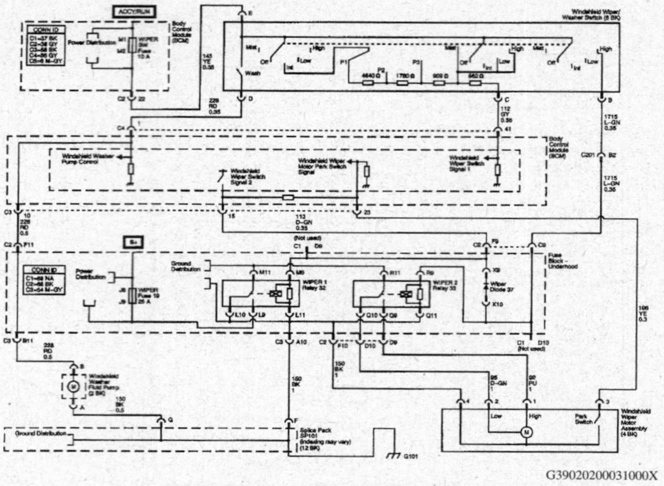

Fig. 6 Wiper system wiring diagram. ION

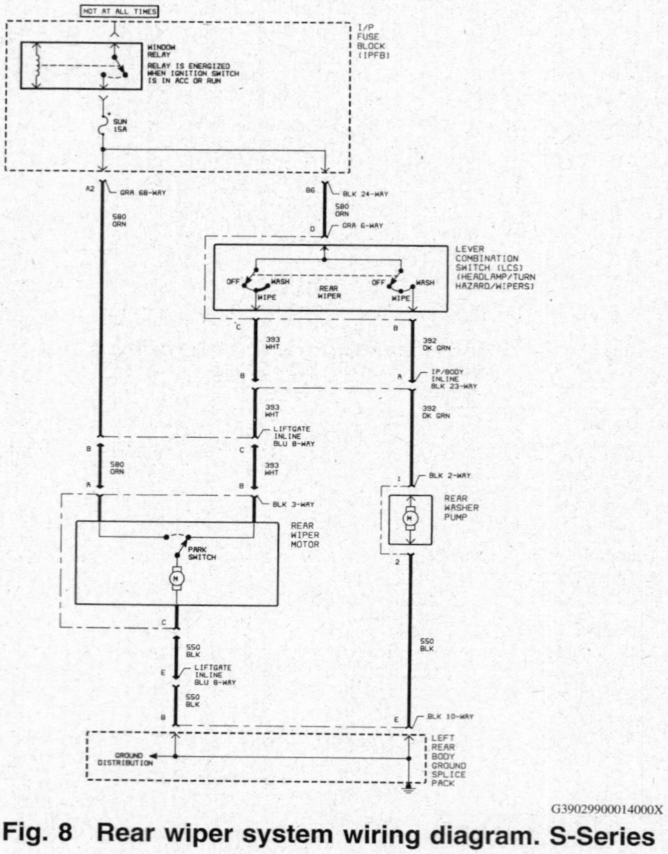

Fig. 8 Rear wiper system wiring diagram. S-Series

DIAGNOSTIC CHART INDEX

CIRCUIT DESCRIPTION

The intermittent wiper delay switch is a voltage divider connected across body control module (BCM) inputs circuit 113 and circuit 96. The wiper relay is energized by the BCM switching circuit 1445 to ground depending on delay switch position.

The intermittent wiper delay switch has three switch positions.

- Delay 1 (2000 ohms resistance, 1 swipe every 12 seconds)
- Delay 2 (1000 ohms resistance, 1 swipe every 7 seconds)
- Delay 3 (500 ohms resistance, 1 swipe every 2 seconds)

DTC SET CONDITIONS

- Ignition is in RUN or ACC position
- Circuit 113 shorted-to-ground

DIAGNOSTIC AIDS

- Inspect wiring harness for damage. Check for broken or chaffed insulation.
- If fault is suspected to be intermittent, wiggling harness wiring may help in locating fault.

G39029900019010X

Fig. 9 Code B3702: Intermittent Wiper Delay Input Circuit Low (Part 1 of 2). L-Series

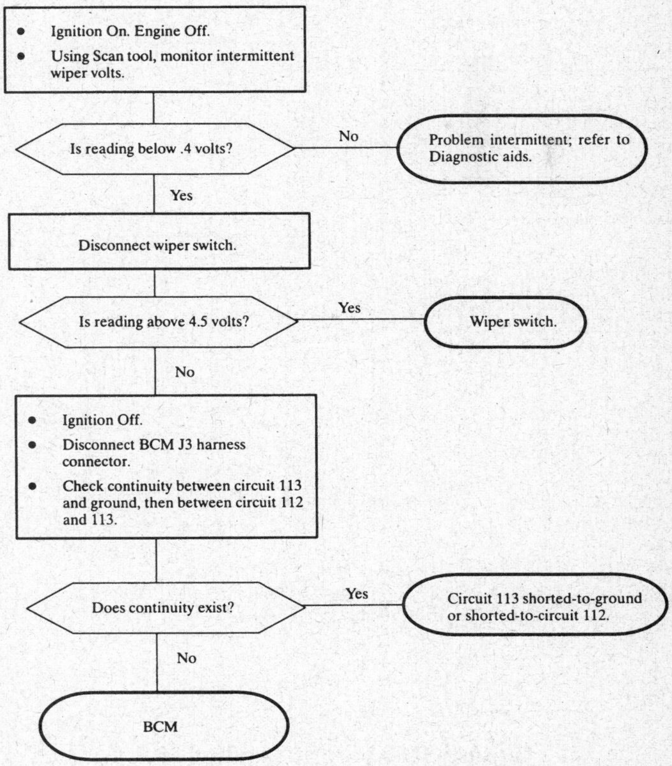

G39029900019020X

Fig. 9 Code B3702: Intermittent Wiper Delay Input Circuit Low (Part 2 of 2). L-Series

CIRCUIT DESCRIPTION

The intermittent wiper delay switch is a voltage divider connected across body control module (BCM) inputs circuit 113 and circuit 96. The wiper relay is energized by the BCM switching circuit 1445 to ground depending on delay switch position.

The intermittent wiper delay switch has three switch positions.

- Delay 1 (2000 ohms resistance, 1 swipe every 12 seconds)
- Delay 2 (1000 ohms resistance, 1 swipe every 7 seconds)
- Delay 3 (500 ohms resistance, 1 swipe every 2 seconds)

DTC SET CONDITIONS

- Ignition is in RUN or ACC position
- Circuit 113 greater than 5 volts

DIAGNOSTIC AIDS

- Inspect wiring harness for damage. Check for broken or chaffed insulation.
- If fault is suspected to be intermittent, wiggling harness wiring may help in locating fault.

G39029900020010X

Fig. 10 Code B3703: Intermittent Wiper Delay Input Circuit High (Part 1 of 2). L-Series

CIRCUIT DESCRIPTION

The body control module (BCM) monitors the front washer motor circuit 228. When a front windshield wash is requested for more than two minutes, circuit 228 at battery voltage, the BCM will turn OFF the front wiper motor if the front wiper is NOT requested by the wiper switch.

Power for the front washer motor (and rear washer motor when equipped) is supplied through the front wiper fuse and washer switch. Grounding for the front washer motor is through the circuit 550 or through the OFF position of the rear washer motor switch (when equipped).

DTC SET CONDITIONS

- Ignition in RUN or ACC
- Front washer circuit 228 at battery voltage for two minutes

DIAGNOSTIC AIDS

- Inspect wiring harness for damage. Check for broken or chaffed insulation.
- If fault is suspected to be intermittent, wiggling harness wiring may help in locating fault.

G39029900021010X

Fig. 11 Code B3708: Front Washer Motor Input Circuit High (Part 1 of 2). L-Series

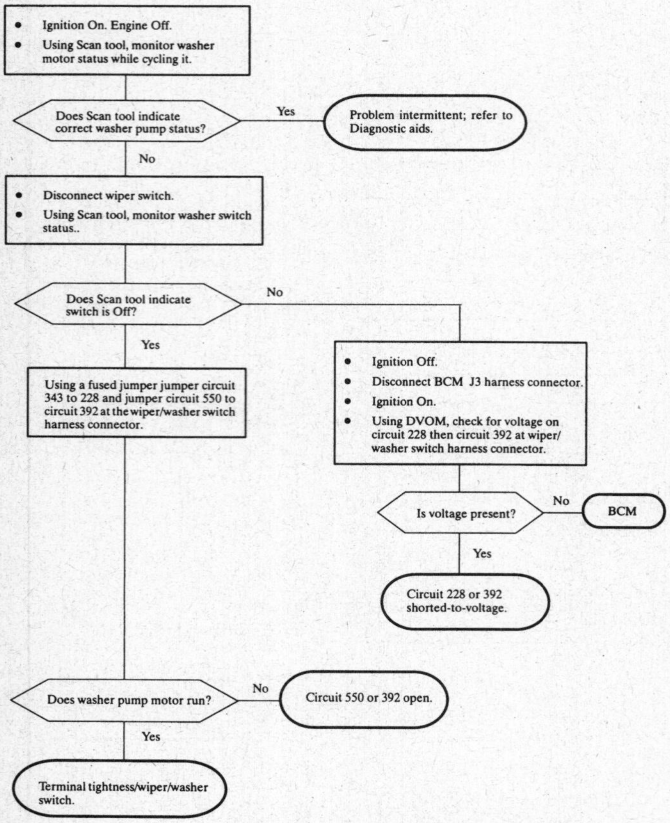

G39029900021020X

Fig. 11 Code B3708: Front Washer Motor Input Circuit High (Part 2 of 2). L-Series

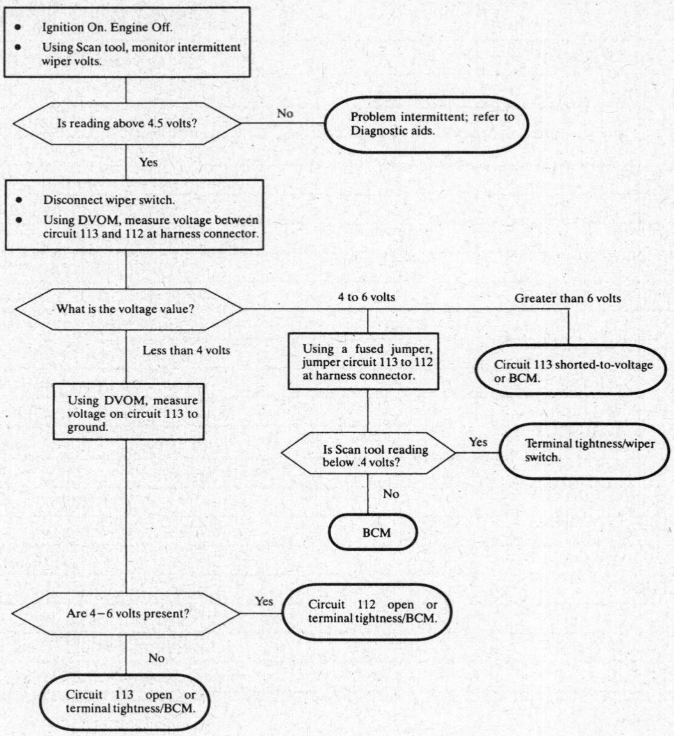

G39029900020020X

Fig. 10 Code B3703: Intermittent Wiper Delay Input Circuit High (Part 2 of 2). L-Series

CIRCUIT DESCRIPTION

The body control module (BCM) monitors the rear washer motor circuit 392. When a rear windshield wash is requested for more than two minutes, circuit 392 at battery voltage, the BCM will turn OFF the rear wiper motor if the rear wiper is NOT requested by the wiper switch.

Power for the rear washer motor is supplied through the front wiper fuse and rear washer switch. Grounding for the rear washer motor is through the OFF position of the front washer motor switch.

DTC SET CONDITIONS

- Ignition in RUN or ACC
- Rear washer circuit 392 at battery voltage for two minutes

DIAGNOSTIC AIDS

- Inspect wiring harness for damage. Check for broken or chaffed insulation.
- If fault is suspected to be intermittent, wiggling harness wiring may help in locating fault.

G39029900022010X

Fig. 12 Code B3713: Rear Washer Motor Input Circuit High (Part 1 of 2). L-Series

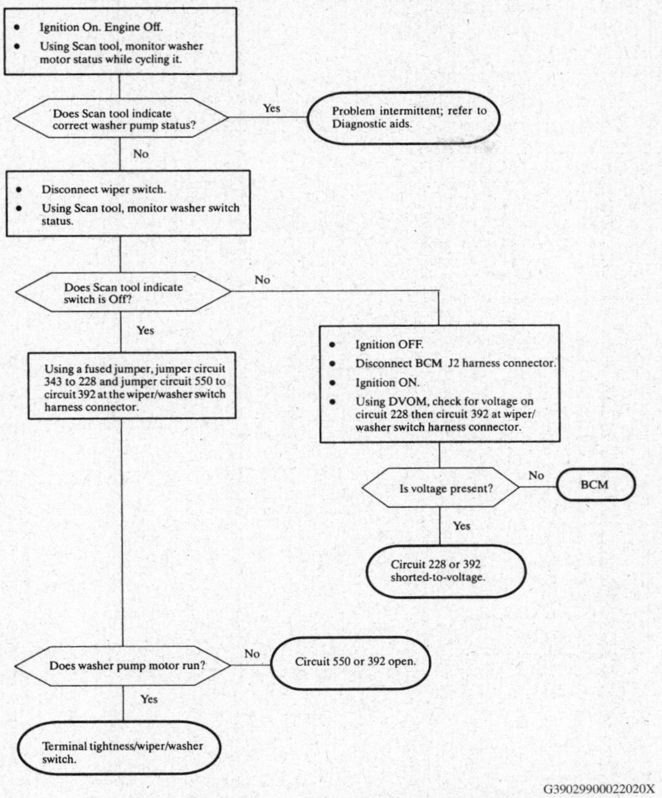

Fig. 12 Code B3713: Rear Washer Motor Input Circuit High (Part 2 of 2). L-Series

CIRCUIT DESCRIPTION

When intermittent or mist operation of the windshield wiper is selected, battery voltage from the wiper switch is applied to the front wiper input of the body control module (BCM). The BCM responds by switching circuit 1445 to ground. This action energizes the front wiper relay, providing low speed operation of the wiper motor during single swipes.

Control of the wiper during continuous LO or HI speed switch settings is direct wired from the wiper switch to the wiper motor and is not under the control of the BCM.

DTC SET CONDITIONS

- Ignition is in RUN or ACC position
- Circuit 1445, BCM is shorted-to-ground or open

DIAGNOSTIC AIDS

- Check for poor connection at the BCM. Inspect harness connectors for backed out terminals, improper terminal mating, broken connector locks, improperly formed or damaged terminals and poor terminal-to-wire connection (terminal crimped over wire insulation and not conductors).
- Inspect wiring harness for damage. Check for broken or chaffed insulation.
- If fault is suspected to be intermittent, wiggling harness wiring may help in locating fault.

G39029900023010X

Fig. 13 Code B3717: Front Wiper Relay Drive Circuit Low (Part 1 of 2). L-Series

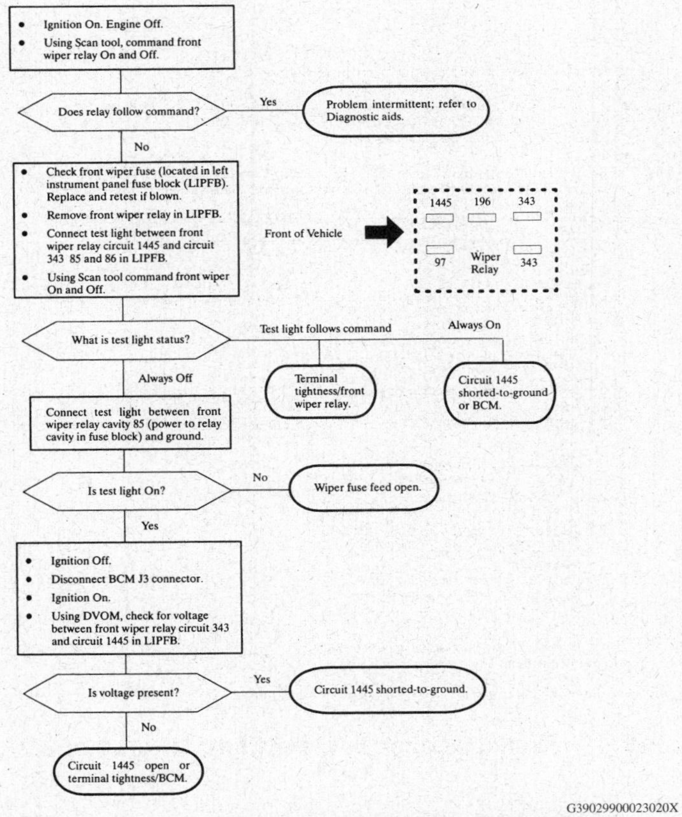

Fig. 13 Code B3717: Front Wiper Relay Drive Circuit Low (Part 2 of 2). L-Series

CIRCUIT DESCRIPTION

When intermittent or mist operation of the windshield wiper is selected, battery voltage from the wiper switch is applied to the front wiper input of the body control module (BCM) circuit 96. The BCM responds by switching circuit 1445 to ground. This action energizes the front wiper relay, providing low speed operation of the wiper motor during single swipes.

Control of the wiper during continuous LO or HI speed switch settings is direct wired from the wiper switch to the wiper motor and is not under the control of the BCM.

DTC SET CONDITIONS

- Ignition is in RUN or ACC position
- Mist or Intermittent wiper switch setting selected
- Circuit 1445 shorted-to-battery voltage

DIAGNOSTIC AIDS

- When a shorted-to-battery voltage condition exists in circuit 1445 and the BCM has been requested to activate the front wiper relay, the BCM will attempt to switch circuit 1445 to ground. High current flow will result and the BCM output will go into a protective state. The BCM output will not allow itself to be activated for as much as three minutes.
- Inspect wiring harness for damage. Check for broken or chaffed insulation.
- If fault is suspected to be intermittent, wiggling harness wiring may help in locating fault.

G39029900024010X

Fig. 14 Code B3718: Front Wiper Relay Drive Circuit High (Part 1 of 2). L-Series

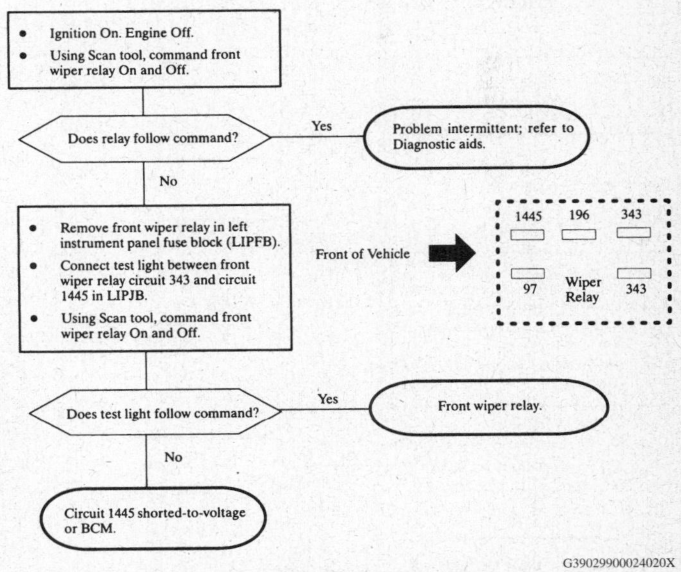

Fig. 14 Code B3718: Front Wiper Relay Drive Circuit High (Part 2 of 2). L-Series

CIRCUIT DESCRIPTION

When operation of the rear wiper is selected, battery voltage from the rear wiper switch is applied to the rear wiper input of the body control module (BCM) circuit 94. The BCM responds by switching circuit 1445 to ground. This action energizes the rear wiper relay, providing power to the rear wiper motor.

Control of the wiper during continuous LO or HI speed switch settings is direct wired from the wiper switch to the wiper motor and is not under the control of the BCM.

DTC SET CONDITIONS

- Ignition is in RUN or ACC position
- Circuit 1445 is shorted-to-ground or open

DIAGNOSTIC AIDS

- Check for poor connection at the BCM. Inspect harness connectors for backed out terminals, improper terminal mating, broken connector locks, improperly formed or damaged terminals and poor terminal-to-wire connection (terminal crimped over wire insulation and not conductors).
- Inspect wiring harness for damage. Check for broken or chaffed insulation.
- If fault is suspected to be intermittent, wiggling harness wiring may help in locating fault.

G39029900025010X

Fig. 15 Code B3722: Rear Wiper Relay Drive Circuit Low (Part 1 of 2). L-Series

CIRCUIT DESCRIPTION

When operation of the rear wiper is selected, battery voltage from the rear wiper switch is applied to the rear wiper input of the body control module (BCM) circuit 94. The BCM responds by switching circuit 1445 to ground. This action energizes the rear wiper relay, providing power to the rear wiper motor.

DTC SET CONDITIONS

- Ignition is in RUN or ACCY position
- Circuit 1445 shorted-to-battery voltage

DIAGNOSTIC AIDS

- When a shorted-to-battery voltage condition exists in circuit 1445 and the BCM has been requested to activate the front wiper relay, the BCM will attempt to switch circuit 1445 to ground. High current flow will result and the BCM output will go into a protective state. The BCM output will not allow itself to be activated for as much as three minutes.
- Check for poor connection at the BCM. Inspect harness connectors for backed out terminals, improper terminal mating, broken connector locks, improperly formed or damaged terminals and poor terminal-to-wire connection (terminal crimped over wire insulation and not conductors).
- Inspect wiring harness for damage. Check for broken or chaffed insulation.
- Review all fail information as this may assist in determining the conditions when the fault occurs.
- If fault is suspected to be intermittent, wiggling harness wiring may help in locating fault.

G39029900026010X

Fig. 16 Code B3723: Rear Wiper Relay Drive Circuit High (Part 1 of 2). L-Series

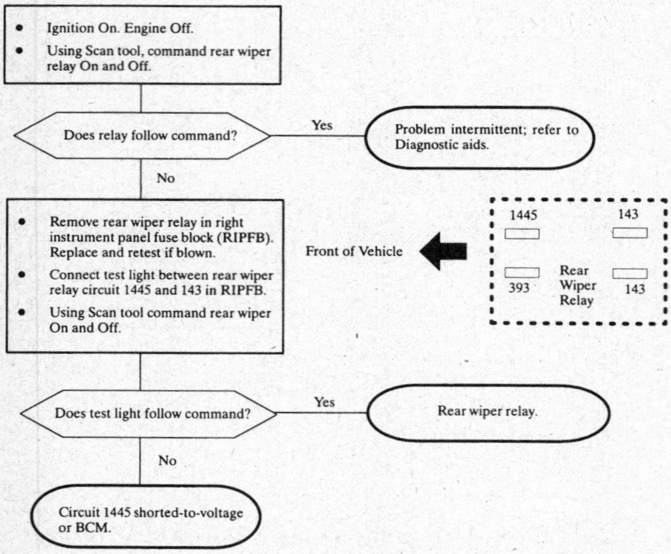

G39029900026020X

Fig. 16 Code B3723: Rear Wiper Relay Drive Circuit High (Part 2 of 2). L-Series

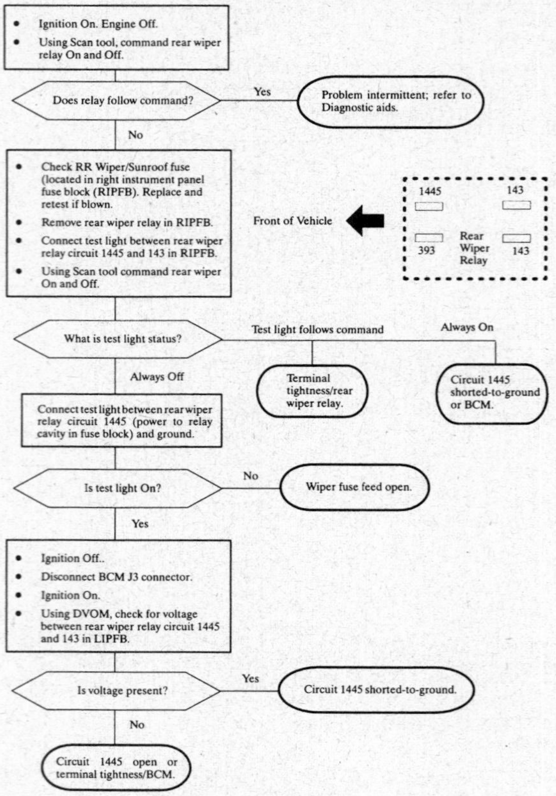

G39029900025020X

Fig. 15 Code B3722: Rear Wiper Relay Drive Circuit Low (Part 2 of 2). L-Series

Test Description

The numbers below refer to the step numbers on the diagnostic table.

2. Lack of communication may be due to a partial malfunction of the class 2 serial data circuit or due to a total malfunction of the class function of the class 2 serial data circuit. The specified procedure will determine the particular condition.

5. The presence of DTCs which began with U indicate some other module is not communicating. The specified procedure will compile all the available information before tests are performed.

Step	Action	Yes	No
1	Install a scan tool. Does the scan tool power up?	Go to Step 2	Diagnose Data Link Communications
2	1. Turn ON the ignition, with the engine OFF. 2. Attempt to establish communication with the body control module (BCM). Does the scan tool communicate with the body control module?	Go to Step 3	Diagnose Data Link Communications
3	**Important** The engine may start during the following step. Turn OFF the engine as soon as you have observed the Crank power mode. 1. Access the Class 2 Power Mode parameter in the Diagnostic Circuit Check menu on the scan tool. 2. Rotate the ignition switch through all positions while observing the Class 2 Power Mode parameter. Does the Class 2 Power Mode parameter reading match the ignition switch position for all switch positions?	Go to Step 4	Go to Power Mode Mismatch

G39020200032010X

Fig. 17 Wiper/Washer System Check (Part 1 of 2). ION

4	Select the display DTCs function on the scan tool for the BCM. Does the scan tool display any DTCs?	Go to Step 5	Go to Symptoms -
5	Does the scan tool display any DTCs which begin with a "U"?	Diagnose Data Link Communications	Go to Step 6
6	Does the scan tool display DTC B1000 or B1001?	Body Control System	Go to Step 7
7	Does the scan tool display DTC B1327 or B1328?	Diagnose Engine Electrical	Go to Diagnostic Trouble Code List

G39020200032020X

Fig. 17 Wiper/Washer System Check (Part 2 of 2). ION

7	Disconnect the Wiper 1 relay. Do the windshield wipers stop?	Go to Step 8	Go to Step 16
8	Connect a test lamp from the supply voltage circuit of the Wiper 1 relay coil to a good ground. Does the test lamp illuminate?	Go to Step 10	Go to Step 12
9	Test the signal circuit of the windshield wiper switch for a short to voltage. Did you find and correct the condition?	Go to Step 20	Go to Step 13
10	Test the supply voltage circuit of the Wiper 1 relay for a short to voltage. Did you find and correct the condition?	Go to Step 20	Go to Step 13
11	Inspect for poor connections at the windshield wiper/washer switch. Did you find and correct the condition?	Go to Step 20	Go to Step 17
12	Inspect for poor connections at the Wiper 1 relay. Did you find and correct the condition?	Go to Step 20	Go to Step 18

G39020200034020X

Fig. 18 Test 1: Washers Always On (Part 2 of 4). ION

13	Inspect for poor connections at the BCM. Did you find and correct the condition?	Go to Step 20	Go to Step 19
14	Repair a short to voltage on supply voltage circuit of the Wiper 2 relay coil. Did you complete the repair?	Go to Step 20	--
15	Repair a short to voltage on control circuit of the windshield washer pump. Did you complete the repair?	Go to Step 20	--
16	Repair a short to voltage on high speed circuit of the windshield wiper motor. Did you complete the repair?	Go to Step 20	--
17	Replace the windshield wiper/washer switch. Did you complete the replacement?	Go to Step 20	--
18	Replace the Wiper 1 relay. Did you complete the replacement?	Go to Step 20	--

G39020200034030X

Fig. 18 Test 1: Washers Always On (Part 3 of 4). ION

19	**Important** Perform the programming or set up procedure for the control module if required. Replace the BCM. Did you complete the replacement?	Go to Step 20	--
20	Operate the system in order to verify the repair. Did you correct the condition?	System OK	Go to Step 3

G39020200034040X

Fig. 18 Test 1: Washers Always On (Part 4 of 4). ION

Step	Action	Yes	No
	Wiper/Washer System Connector End Views		
1	Did you perform the Wiper/Washer Diagnostic System Check?	Go to Step 2	Go to System Check -
2	1. Turn the ignition ON. 2. Turn the windshield wiper/washer switch OFF. Do the windshield wipers remain in the park position?	Test for Intermittent and Poor Connections	Go to Step 3
3	Disconnect the harness connector of the windshield wiper/washer switch. Do the windshield wipers stop?	Go to Step 11	Go to Step 4
4	Connect a test lamp from the signal circuit of the windshield wiper/washer switch to a good ground. Does the test lamp illuminate?	Go to Step 9	Go to Step 5
5	Connect a test lamp from the supply voltage circuit of the Wiper 2 relay coil to a good ground. Does the test lamp illuminate?	Go to Step 14	Go to Step 6
6	Connect a test lamp from the control circuit of the windshield washer pump to a good ground. Does the test lamp illuminate?	Go to Step 15	Go to Step 7

G39020200034010X

Fig. 18 Test 1: Washers Always On (Part 1 of 4). ION

Step	Action	Yes	No
	Wiper/Washer System Connector End Views		
1	Did you perform the Wiper/Washer Diagnostic System Check?	Go to Step 2	Go to System Check -
2	1. Turn the ignition ON. 2. Press the windshield washer switch. Do the windshield washers operate normally?	Test for Intermittent and Poor Connections	Go to Step 3
3	1. Turn OFF the ignition. 2. Disconnect the harness connector of the windshield washer pump. 3. Turn the ignition ON, with the engine OFF. 4. Connect a test lamp from the control circuit to the ground circuit of the windshield washer pump. 5. Press the windshield washer switch. Does the test lamp illuminate?	Go to Step 10	Go to Step 4
4	1. Connect a test lamp from the control circuit of the windshield washer pump to a good ground. 2. Press the windshield washer switch. Does the test lamp illuminate?	Go to Step 15	Go to Step 5
5	1. Turn OFF the ignition. 2. Disconnect the harness connector of the windshield wiper/washer switch. 3. Turn the ignition ON, with the engine OFF. 4. Connect a test lamp from the accessory voltage circuit of the windshield wiper/washer switch to a good ground. Does the test lamp illuminate?	Go to Step 6	Go to Step 9
6	1. Connect the harness connector of the windshield washer pump. 2. Connect a 10-ampere fused jumper wire from the accessory voltage circuit of the windshield wiper/washer switch to the control circuit of the windshield washer pump. Do the windshield washers operate?	Go to Step 11	Go to Step 7

G39020200035010X

Fig. 19 Test 2: Washers Inoperative (Part 1 of 3). ION

7	1. Turn OFF the ignition. 2. Disconnect the harness connector C4 of the Body Control Module (BCM). 3. Turn the ignition ON, with the engine OFF. 4. Connect a test lamp from the control circuit of the windshield washer pump to a good ground. Does the test lamp illuminate?	Go to Step 8	Go to Step 14
8	1. Turn OFF the ignition. 2. Disconnect the harness connector C3 of the BCM. 3. Turn the ignition ON, with the engine OFF. 4. Connect a 10-ampere fused jumper wire from the control circuit of the windshield washer pump in the harness connector C3 to the control circuit of the windshield washer pump in the harness connector C4 of the BCM. Do the windshield washers operate?	Go to Step 12	Go to Step 14
9	Test the accessory voltage circuit of the windshield wiper/washer switch for an open or a short to ground. Did you find and correct the condition?	Go to Step 19	Go to Step 13
10	Inspect for poor connections at the windshield washer pump. Did you find and correct the condition?	Go to Step 19	Go to Step 16
11	Inspect for poor connections at the windshield wiper/washer switch. Did you find and correct the condition?	Go to Step 19	Go to Step 17
12	Inspect for poor connections at the BCM. Did you find and correct the condition?	Go to Step 19	Go to Step 18

G39020200035020X

Fig. 19 Test 2: Washers Inoperative (Part 2 of 3). ION

13	Repair a short to ground on the control circuit of the windshield washer pump. Did you complete the repair?	Go to Step 19	--
14	Repair an open or high resistance on the control circuit of the windshield washer pump. Did you complete the repair?	Go to Step 19	--
15	Repair an open or high resistance on the ground circuit of the windshield washer pump. Did you complete the repair?	Go to Step 19	--
16	Replace the windshield washer pump. Did you complete the replacement?	Go to Step 19	--
17	Replace the windshield wiper/washer switch. Did you complete the replacement?	Go to Step 19	--
18	**Important** Perform the programming or set up procedure for the control module if required. Replace the BCM. Did you complete the replacement?	Go to Step 19	--
19	Operate the system in order to verify the repair. Did you correct the condition?	System OK	Go to Step 3

G39020200035030X

Fig. 19 Test 2: Washers Inoperative (Part 3 of 3). ION

Step	Action	Yes	No
	Wiper/Washer System Connector End Views		
1	Did you perform the Wiper/Washer Diagnostic System Check?	Go to Step 2	Go to System Check
2	1. Turn the ignition ON. 2. Turn the windshield wiper/washer switch OFF. Do the windshield wipers remain in the park position?	Test for Intermittent and Poor Connections	Go to Step 3
3	Disconnect the harness connector of the windshield wiper/washer switch. Do the windshield wipers stop?	Go to Step 11	Go to Step 4
4	Connect a test lamp from the signal circuit of the windshield wiper/washer switch to a good ground. Does the test lamp illuminate?	Go to Step 9	Go to Step 5
5	Connect a test lamp from the supply voltage circuit of the Wiper 2 relay coil to a good ground. Does the test lamp illuminate?	Go to Step 14	Go to Step 6
6	Connect a test lamp from the control circuit of the windshield washer pump to a good ground. Does the test lamp illuminate?	Go to Step 15	Go to Step 7

G39020200036010X

Fig. 20 Test 3: Washers Always On (Part 1 of 3). ION

7	Disconnect the Wiper 1 relay. Do the windshield wipers stop?	Go to Step 8	Go to Step 16
8	Connect a test lamp from the supply voltage circuit of the Wiper 1 relay coil to a good ground. Does the test lamp illuminate?	Go to Step 10	Go to Step 12
9	Test the signal circuit of the windshield wiper switch for a short to voltage. Did you find and correct the condition?	Go to Step 20	Go to Step 13
10	Test the supply voltage circuit of the Wiper 1 relay for a short to voltage. Did you find and correct the condition?	Go to Step 20	Go to Step 13
11	Inspect for poor connections at the windshield wiper/washer switch. Did you find and correct the condition?	Go to Step 20	Go to Step 17
12	Inspect for poor connections at the Wiper 1 relay. Did you find and correct the condition?	Go to Step 20	Go to Step 18
13	Inspect for poor connections at the BCM. Did you find and correct the condition?	Go to Step 20	Go to Step 19

G39020200036020X

Fig. 20 Test 3: Washers Always On (Part 2 of 3). ION

14	Repair a short to voltage on supply voltage circuit of the Wiper 2 relay coil. Did you complete the repair?	Go to Step 20	--
15	Repair a short to voltage on control circuit of the windshield washer pump. Did you complete the repair?	Go to Step 20	--
16	Repair a short to voltage on high speed circuit of the windshield wiper motor. Did you complete the repair?	Go to Step 20	--
17	Replace the windshield wiper/washer switch. Did you complete the replacement?	Go to Step 20	--
18	Replace the Wiper 1 relay. Did you complete the replacement?	Go to Step 20	--
19	**Important** Perform the programming or set up procedure for the control module if required. Replace the BCM. Did you complete the replacement?	Go to Step 20	--
20	Operate the system in order to verify the repair. Did you correct the condition?	System OK	Go to Step 3

G39020200036030X

Fig. 20 Test 3: Washers Always On (Part 3 of 3). ION

6	Test accessory voltage circuit of the wiper/washer switch for an open or short to ground. Did you find and correct the condition?	Go to Step 16	Go to Step 7
7	Test supply voltage circuit of the Wiper 2 relay coil for a short to ground. Did you find and correct the condition?	Go to Step 16	Go to Step 8
8	Test the control circuit of the windshield washer pump for a short to ground. Did you find and correct the condition?	Go to Step 16	Go to Step 11
9	Inspect for poor connections at the harness connector of the windshield wiper motor. Did you find and correct the condition?	Go to Step 16	Go to Step 13
10	Inspect for poor connections at the harness connector of the windshield wiper/washer switch. Did you find and correct the condition?	Go to Step 16	Go to Step 14
11	Inspect for poor connections at the harness connector of the windshield washer pump. Did you find and correct the condition?	Go to Step 16	Go to Step 15
12	Repair an open or high resistance in the ground circuit of the windshield wiper motor. Did you complete the repair?	Go to Step 16	--

G39020200037020X

Fig. 21 Test 4: Wipers Inoperative In All Modes (Part 2 of 3). ION

Step	Action	Yes	No
	Wiper/Washer System Connector End Views		
1	Did you perform the Wiper/Washer Diagnostic System Check?	Go to Step 2	Go to System Check
2	1. Turn the ignition switch ON. 2. Operate the windshield wiper/washer switch through all the switch positions. Does the windshield wiper/washer system operate normally?	Test for Intermittent and Poor Connections	Go to Step 3
3	1. Turn OFF the ignition. 2. Disconnect the harness connector of the windshield wiper motor. 3. Turn the ignition ON, with the engine OFF. 4. Connect a test lamp from the low speed circuit to the ground circuit of the windshield wiper motor. 5. Press the windshield washer switch. Does the test lamp illuminate?	Go to Step 9	Go to Step 4
4	1. Connect a test lamp from the low speed circuit of the windshield wiper motor to a good ground. 2. Press the windshield washer switch. Does the test lamp illuminate?	Go to Step 12	Go to Step 5
5	1. Turn OFF the ignition. 2. Disconnect the harness connector of the windshield wiper/washer switch. 3. Turn the ignition ON, with the engine OFF. 4. Connect a test lamp from the accessory voltage circuit of the windshield wiper/washer switch to a good ground. Does the test lamp illuminate?	Go to Step 10	Go to Step 6

G39020200037010X

Fig. 21 Test 4: Wipers Inoperative In All Modes (Part 1 of 3). ION

13	Replace the windshield wiper motor. Did you complete the replacement?	Go to Step 16	--
14	Replace the windshield wiper/washer switch. Did you complete the replacement?	Go to Step 16	--
15	Replace the windshield washer pump. Did you complete the replacement?	Go to Step 16	--
16	Operate the system in order to verify the repair. Did you correct the condition?	System OK	Go to Step 3

G39020200037030X

Fig. 21 Test 4: Wipers Inoperative In All Modes (Part 3 of 3). ION

Step	Action	Values	Yes	No
1	Did you perform the Wiper/Washer System Check?	--	Go to Step 2	Go to System Check -
2	1. Turn the ignition ON, with the engine OFF. 2. Operate the windshield wiper/washer switch through all the switch positions. Does the windshield wiper/washer system operate normally?	--	Test for Intermittent and Poor Connections	Go to Step 3
3	Are the wipers only inoperative when the washer switch is depressed?	--	Go to Step 17	Go to Step 4
4	Are the windshield wipers only inoperative in the high speed mode?	--	Go to Step 12	Go to Step 5
5	1. With a scan tool, observe the Wiper Switch State data parameter in the Body Control Module (BCM) Wiper/Washer data list. 2. Operate the windshield wiper/washer switch through all the switch positions. Does the scan tool indicate that Off, Delay 1, Delay 2, Delay 3, and Mist/Hi/Lo is correctly displayed each wiper/washer switch position?	--	Go to Step 7	Go to Step 6
6	1. Turn OFF the ignition. 2. Disconnect the harness connector of the wiper/washer switch. 3. Turn ON the ignition, with the engine OFF. 4. Measure the resistance of the windshield wiper switch from the accessory voltage circuit to the signal circuit of the windshield wiper switch. 5. Operate the windshield wiper/washer switch through all the switch positions. Is the resistance within the specified range?	560-7900 ohms	Go to Step 18	Go to Step 26

G39020200038010X

Fig. 22 Test 5: Wipers Inoperative (Part 1 of 6). ION

13	1. Disconnect the Wiper 2 relay. 2. Connect a test lamp from the supply voltage circuit to the ground circuit of the Wiper 2 relay coil. 3. Place the wiper/washer switch in the high speed position. Does the test lamp illuminate?	-	Go to Step 25	Go to Step 14
14	Connect a test lamp from the supply voltage circuit of the Wiper 2 relay coil to a good ground. Does the test lamp illuminate?	-	Go to Step 29	Go to Step 22
15	1. Disconnect the Wiper 2 relay. 2. Connect a test lamp from the battery voltage circuit supplied from the Wiper 1 relay to the Wiper 2 relay switched input to a good ground. 3. Place the wiper/washer switch in the low speed position. Does the test lamp illuminate?	-	Go to Step 16	Go to Step 31
16	Connect a 10-ampere fused jumper wire from the Wiper 2 relay switched input to the relay switched output to the high speed circuit of the windshield wiper motor. Does the wiper motor operate at high speed?	-	Go to Step 25	Go to Step 23
17	1. Turn OFF the ignition. 2. Disconnect the harness connector of the wiper/washer switch. 3. Turn ON the ignition, with the engine OFF. 4. Connect a 10-ampere fused jumper wire from the accessory voltage circuit to the control circuit of the windshield washer pump. Do the windshield wipers operate?	-	Go to Step 26	Go to Step 24
18	Test the signal circuit of the wiper/washer switch for an open or a short to ground. Did you find and correct the condition?	-		Go to Step 28

G39020200038030X

Fig. 22 Test 5: Wipers Inoperative (Part 3 of 6). ION

7	Command the Wiper 1 relay ON and OFF by cycling the wiper/washer switch from the high to the low positions. Do you hear a click from the Wiper 1 relay in the underhood fuse block, when you command the relay ON and OFF?	-	Go to Step 10	Go to Step 8
8	1. Disconnect the Wiper 1 relay. 2. Connect a test lamp from the supply voltage circuit to the ground circuit of the Wiper 1 relay coil. 3. Place the wiper/washer switch in the low speed position. Does the test lamp illuminate?	-	Go to Step 25	Go to Step 9
9	Connect a test lamp from the supply voltage circuit of the Wiper 1 relay coil to a good ground. Does the test lamp illuminate?	-	Go to Step 29	Go to Step 19
10	1. Disconnect the Wiper 1 relay. 2. Connect a test lamp from the battery voltage circuit of the Wiper 1 relay switched input to a good ground. Does the test lamp illuminate?	-	Go to Step 11	Go to Step 20
11	Connect a 10-ampere fused jumper wire from the Wiper 1 relay switched input to the relay switched output to the low speed circuit of the windshield wiper motor. Does the wiper motor operate at low speed?	-	Go to Step 25	Go to Step 21
12	Command the Wiper 2 relay ON and OFF by cycling the wiper/washer switch from the high to the low positions. Do you hear a click from the Wiper 2 relay in the underhood fuse block, when you command the relay ON and OFF?	-	Go to Step 15	Go to Step 13

G39020200038020X

Fig. 22 Test 5: Wipers Inoperative (Part 2 of 6). ION

19	Test the supply voltage circuit of the Wiper 1 relay coil for an open or a short to ground. Did you find and correct the condition?	-	Go to Step 36	Go to Step 28
20	Test the battery voltage circuit of the Wiper 1 relay switched input for an open or high resistance. Did you find and correct the condition?	-	Go to Step 36	Go to Step 30
21	Test the low speed circuit of the windshield wiper motor for an open or high resistance. Did you find and correct the condition?	-	Go to Step 36	Go to Step 27
22	Test the supply voltage circuit of the Wiper 2 relay coil for an open or a short to ground. Did you find and correct the condition?	-	Go to Step 36	Go to Step 26
23	Test the high speed circuit of the windshield wiper motor for an open or high resistance. Did you find and correct the condition?	-	Go to Step 36	Go to Step 27
24	Test the control circuit of the windshield washer pump for an open or high resistance. Did you find and correct the condition?	-	Go to Step 36	Go to Step 28

G39020200038040X

Fig. 22 Test 5: Wipers Inoperative (Part 4 of 6). ION

25	Inspect for poor connections at the inoperative wiper relay. Did you find and correct the condition?	-	Go to Step 36	Go to Step 32
26	Inspect for poor connections at the harness connector of the windshield wiper/washer switch. Did you find and correct the condition?	-	Go to Step 36	Go to Step 33
27	Inspect for poor connections at the harness connector of the windshield wiper motor. Did you find and correct the condition?	-	Go to Step 36	Go to Step 34
28	Inspect for poor connections at the harness connector of the BCM. Did you find and correct the condition?	-	Go to Step 36	Go to Step 35
29	Repair an open or high resistance in the ground circuit of the inoperative wiper relay coil. Did you complete the repair?	-	Go to Step 36	--
30	Repair a short to ground on the low or high speed circuits of the windshield wiper motor. Did you complete the repair?	-	Go to Step 36	--
31	Repair an open or high resistance in the battery voltage circuit of the Wiper 2 relay switched input. Did you complete the repair?	-	Go to Step 36	

G39020200038050X

Fig. 22 Test 5: Wipers Inoperative (Part 5 of 6). ION

32	Replace the inoperative wiper relay. Did you complete the replacement?	-	Go to Step 36	--
33	Replace the windshield wiper/washer switch. Did you complete the replacement?	-	Go to Step 36	--
34	Replace the windshield wiper motor. Did you complete the replacement?	-	Go to Step 36	--
35	**Important** Perform the programming or set up procedure for the control module if required. Replace the BCM. Did you complete the replacement?	-	Go to Step 36	--
36	Operate the system in order to verify the repair. Did you correct the condition?	-	System OK	Go to Step 3

G39020200038060X

Fig. 22 Test 5: Wipers Inoperative (Part 6 of 6). ION

Circuit Description

The Body Control Module (BCM) monitors the voltage level on the supply voltage circuit of the Wiper 1 relay. The voltage level should be low while the Wiper 1 relay is de-energized. The voltage will be near system voltage when the BCM energizes the Wiper 1 relay. The supply voltage circuit of the Wiper 1 relay is shared with the signal circuit of the windshield wiper motor park switch internally in the BCM. The BCM monitors the signal circuit of the windshield wiper motor park switch to determine if the windshield wiper motor is operating when commanded. The voltage on the signal circuit of the windshield wiper motor park switch should be near system voltage while the wipers are active. This the result of the windshield wiper motor park switch being open. The voltage is pulled low when wipers are in or return to the PARK position. The windshield wiper motor park switch will be closed, pulling the circuit to ground.

Conditions for Running the DTC

- The ignition is ON.
- Automatic transmission shift lock control is active, if equipped.

Conditions for Setting the DTCs

The following conditions will cause these DTCs to set:

- B3715, the signal circuit of the windshield wiper motor park switch has not transition from a high to low state when the windshield wiper motor was commanded on.
- B3717 or B3719, the BCM detects a low voltage level on the supply circuit of the Wiper 1 relay when the relay is energized.

Action Taken When the DTC Sets

The windshield wipers will be disabled until the conditions mentioned above are no longer present.

Conditions for Clearing the DTC

- This DTC will change from current to history when the fault is no longer present.
- A history DTC will clear after 100 consecutive ignition cycles if the condition for the malfunction is no longer present.

Test Description

The numbers below refer to the step numbers on the diagnostic table.

10. Listen for an audible click when the Wiper 1 relay operates. Command both the ON and OFF states. Repeat the commands as necessary.
11. Verifies that the BCM is providing voltage to the Wiper 1 relay.

G39020200033010X

Fig. 23 Codes B3715, B3716, B3717, B3718 Or B3719: Low Voltage Level Detected (Part 1 of 8). ION

Step	Action	Values	Yes	No
	Wiper/Washer System Connector End Views			
1	Did you perform the Wiper/Washer Diagnostic System Check?	--	Go to Step 2	Go to System Check
2	1. Turn the ignition ON, with the engine OFF. 2. Operate the windshield wiper/washer switch through all the switch positions. Does the windshield wiper/washer system operate normally?	--	Test for Intermittent and Poor Connections	Go to Step 3
3	Are the wipers always on?	--	Go to Step 28	Go to Step 4
4	Operate the windshield wiper/washer switch through all the switch positions. Do the windshield wipers park correctly?	--	Go to Step 5	Go to Step 8
5	Turn the wiper/washer switch to the High position. Do the windshield wipers operate?	--	Go to Step 8	Go to Step 6
6	1. With a scan tool, observe the Wiper Switch State data parameter in the Body Control Module (BCM) Wiper/Washer data list. 2. Operate the windshield wiper/washer switch through all the switch positions. Does the scan tool indicate that Off, Delay 1, Delay 2, Delay 3, and Mist/Hi/Lo is correctly displayed each wiper/washer switch position?	--	Go to Step 10	Go to Step 7

G39020200033020X

Fig. 23 Codes B3715, B3716, B3717, B3718 Or B3719: Low Voltage Detected (Part 2 of 8). ION

7	1. Turn OFF the ignition. 2. Disconnect the harness connector of the wiper/washer switch. 3. Turn ON the ignition, with the engine OFF. 4. Measure the resistance of the windshield wiper switch from the accessory voltage circuit to the signal circuit of the windshield wiper switch. 5. Operate the windshield wiper/washer switch through all the switch positions. Is the resistance within the specified range?	560-7900 ohms	Go to Step 19	Go to Step 24
8	1. With a scan tool, observe the Wiper Park Switch data parameter from the BCM Wiper/Washer Data list. 2. Disconnect the harness connector of the windshield wiper motor. Does the Wiper Park Switch data parameter display Off?	--	Go to Step 20	Go to Step 9
9	While observing the Wiper Park Switch data parameter, connect a 3 ampere fused jumper wire from the signal circuit of the windshield wiper motor park switch to good ground. Does the Wiper Park Switch data parameter display On?	--	Go to Step 26	Go to Step 21
10	1. Select from miscellaneous test, the Wiper from the BCM output controls. 2. Place the wiper/washer switch in the low speed position. 3. With the scan tool, command the Wiper 1 relay ON and OFF. Do you hear a click from the Wiper 1 relay in the underhood fuse block, when you command the relay ON and OFF?	--	Go to Step 13	Go to Step 11

G39020200033030X

Fig. 23 Codes B3715, B3716, B3717, B3718 Or B3719: Low Voltage Detected (Part 3 of 8). ION

11	1. Turn OFF the ignition. 2. Disconnect the Wiper 1 relay. 3. Turn ON the ignition, with the engine OFF. 4. Connect a test lamp from the supply voltage circuit to the ground circuit of the Wiper 1 relay coil. 5. Place the wiper/washer switch in the low speed position. 6. With the scan tool, command the Wiper 1 relay ON. Does the test lamp illuminate?	-	Go to Step 25	Go to Step 12
12	1. Connect a test lamp from the supply voltage circuit of the Wiper 1 relay coil to a good ground. 2. Place the wiper/washer switch in the low speed position. 3. With the scan tool, command the Wiper 1 relay ON. Does the test lamp illuminate?	-	Go to Step 29	Go to Step 22
13	1. Turn OFF the ignition. 2. Disconnect the Wiper 1 relay. 3. Turn ON the ignition, with the engine OFF. 4. Connect a test lamp from the battery voltage circuit of the Wiper 1 relay switched input to a good ground. Does the test lamp illuminate?	-	Go to Step 14	Go to Step 23
14	Connect a 10-ampere fused jumper wire from the Wiper 1 relay switched input to the switched output to voltage circuit of the Wiper 2 relay switched input. Does the wiper motor operate at low speed?	-	Go to Step 25	Go to Step 15
15	1. Turn OFF the ignition. 2. Disconnect the Wiper 2 relay. 3. Turn ON the ignition, with the engine OFF. 4. Connect a test lamp from the battery voltage circuit supplied from the Wiper 1 relay to the Wiper 2 relay switched input to a good ground. Does the test lamp illuminate?	-	Go to Step 16	Go to Step 31

G39020200033040X

Fig. 23 Codes B3715, B3716, B3717, B3718 Or B3719: Low Voltage Detected (Part 4 of 8). ION

16	Connect a 10-ampere fused jumper wire from the Wiper 2 relay switched input to the relay switched output to the low speed circuit of the windshield wiper motor. Does the wiper motor operate?	-	Go to Step 25	Go to Step 17
17	1. Turn OFF the ignition. 2. Disconnect the harness connector of the wiper motor. 3. Turn ON the ignition, with the engine OFF. 4. Connect a test lamp from the low speed circuit to the ground circuit of the wiper motor. Does the test lamp illuminate?	-	Go to Step 26	Go to Step 18
18	Connect a test lamp from the low speed circuit of the wiper motor to a good ground. Does the test lamp illuminate?	-	Go to Step 33	Go to Step 32
19	Test the signal circuit of the wiper/washer switch for an open or a short to ground. Did you find and correct the condition?	-	Go to Step 38	Go to Step 27
20	Test the signal circuit of the wiper motor park switch for a short to ground. Did you find and correct the condition?	-	Go to Step 38	Go to Step 27
21	Test the signal circuit of the wiper motor park switch for an open or a short to voltage. Did you find and correct the condition?	-	Go to Step 38	Go to Step 27

G39020200033050X

Fig. 23 Codes B3715, B3716, B3717, B3718 Or B3719: Low Voltage Detected (Part 5 of 8). ION

22	Test the supply voltage circuit of the Wiper 1 relay coil for an open or a short to ground. Did you find and correct the condition?	-	Go to Step 38	Go to Step 27
23	Test the battery voltage circuit of the Wiper 1 relay switched input for an open or high resistance. Did you find and correct the condition?	-	Go to Step 38	Go to Step 30
24	Inspect for poor connections at the harness connector of the windshield wiper/washer switch. Did you find and correct the condition?	-	Go to Step 38	Go to Step 34
25	Inspect for poor connections at the inoperative wiper relay. Did you find and correct the condition?	-	Go to Step 38	Go to Step 35
26	Inspect for poor connections at the harness connector of the windshield wiper motor. Did you find and correct the condition?	-	Go to Step 38	Go to Step 36
27	Inspect for poor connections at the harness connector of the BCM. Did you find and correct the condition?	-	Go to Step 38	Go to Step 37

G39020200033060X

Fig. 23 Codes B3715, B3716, B3717, B3718 Or B3719: Low Voltage Detected (Part 6 of 8). ION

28	Repair a short to voltage in the supply voltage circuits of the Wiper 1 and Wiper 2 relay coils. Did you complete the repair?	-	Go to Step 38	-
29	Repair an open or high resistance in the ground circuit of the Wiper 1 relay coil. Did you complete the repair?	-	Go to Step 38	-
30	Repair a short to ground on the low or high speed circuit of the windshield wiper motor. Did you complete the repair?	-	Go to Step 38	-
31	Repair an open or high resistance in the battery voltage circuit of the Wiper 2 relay switched input. Did you complete the repair?	-	Go to Step 38	-
32	Repair an open or high resistance in the low speed circuit of the windshield wiper motor. Did you complete the repair?	-	Go to Step 38	

G39020200033070X

Fig. 23 Codes B3715, B3716, B3717, B3718 Or B3719: Low Voltage Detected (Part 7 of 8). ION

33	Repair an open or high resistance in the ground circuit of the windshield wiper motor. Did you complete the repair?	-	Go to Step 38	--
34	Replace the windshield wiper/washer switch. Did you complete the replacement?	-	Go to Step 38	--
35	Replace the inoperative wiper relay. Did you complete the replacement?	-	Go to Step 38	--
36	Replace the windshield wiper motor. Did you complete the replacement?	-	Go to Step 38	--
37	**Important** Perform the programming or set up procedure for the control module if required. Replace the BCM. Did you complete the replacement?	-	Go to Step 38	--
38	1. Use the scan tool to clear the DTCs. 2. Operate the vehicle within the Conditions for Running the DTC as specified in the supporting text. Does the DTC reset?	-	Go to Step 2	System OK

G39020200033080X

Fig. 23 Codes B3715, B3716, B3717, B3718 Or B3719: Low Voltage Detected (Part 8 of 8). ION

*Ignition switch must be in the RUN position for the entire system check.

Action	Normal Results
Pull the wiper lever toward you and release.	Windshield washer fluid will spray from the nozzles, and wipers will continue to wipe two or three times after the spray has stopped.
Move windshield wiper switch to the INT (intermittent) position, and rotate the INT switch to each position and let the wipers cycle.	Position 3 – One wipe per approximately 2 seconds. Position 2 – One wipe per approximately 7 seconds. Position 1 – One wipe per approximately 12 seconds.
Move INT switch to position 2, pull wiper lever toward you for 1–2 seconds.	Windshield washer fluid should spray the entire time the wiper lever is held back. Wipers should run at low speed, and continue to wipe two or three times after the spray has stopped.
Move windshield wiper switch to LOW (LO) position.	Windshield wiper will run at low speed.
Move windshield wiper switch to HIGH (HI) position.	Windshield wiper will run at high speed.
Move windshield wiper switch to OFF position.	Windshield wiper will run at slow speed, then park at the bottom of the windshield.
Move windshield wiper switch to the mist position.	Windshield wiper will wipe one time at slow speed and then return to park.

G39029900029000X

Fig. 24 System performance test chart. S Series

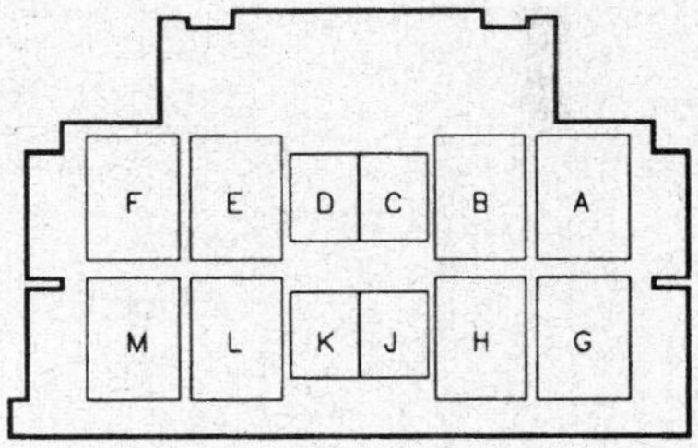

G39029900027000X

Fig. 25 Wiper switch connector terminal identification. L-Series

Windshield Wiper Switch	Wash Switch	Rear Wiper Switch	Cavity/Circuit Number (Black 12-way)												Valves
			A 550	B 392	C 343	D 112	E 94	F 343	G 228	H 95	J 97	K 96	L OPEN	M 228	
MIST	OFF														
OFF	OFF														
INT	OFF														
INT1															2000
INT2															1000
INT3															500
LOW	OFF														
HIGH	OFF														
	OFF														
	ON														
	OFF														
	ON														
	WASH														

This symbol indicates that the pins referenced are connected (less than one ohm resistance) when the switch is in the position indicated in the columns on the left side.

This symbol indicates that the pins referenced are connected (with resistance indicated) when the switch is in the position indicated in the columns on the left side of the chart. The resistance measurements should be within +/− 10 percent of the values shown.

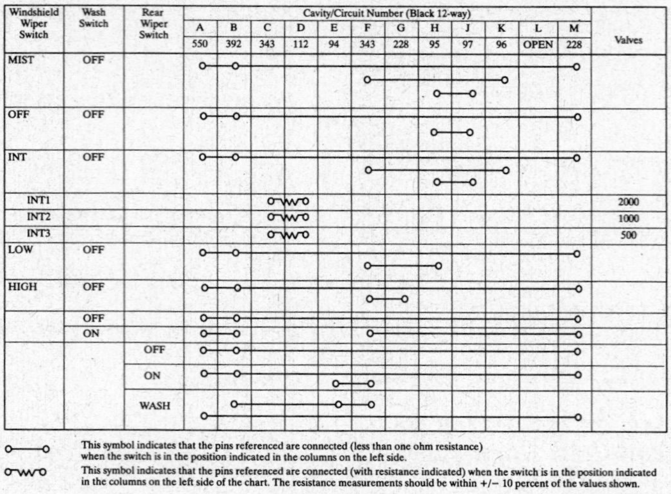

G39029900028000X

**Fig. 26 Wiper switch terminal resistance chart.
L-Series**

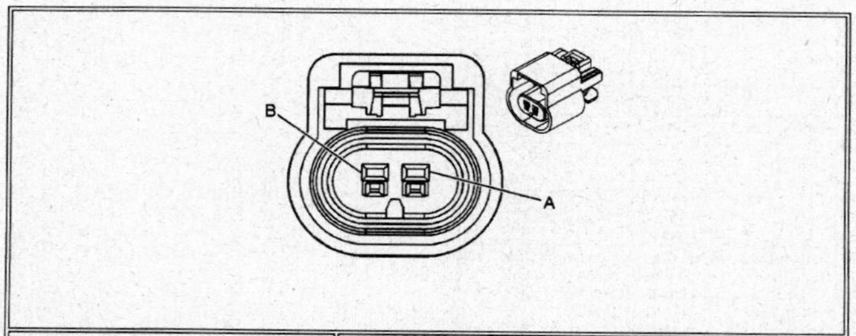

G39020200039000X

Fig. 27 Washer fluid pump connector terminal identification. ION

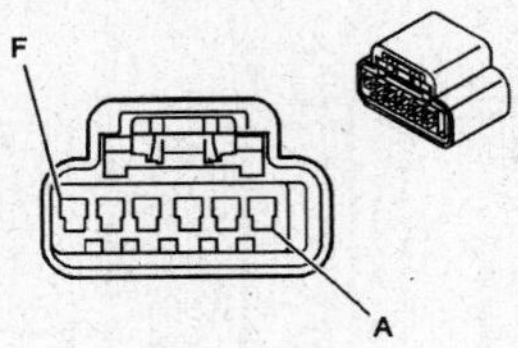

Connector Part Information	• 15332141 • 6-Way F GT 150 280 Sealed (BK)		
Pin	**Wire Color**	**Circuit No.**	**Function**
A	--	--	Not Used
B	L-GN	1715	Windshield Wiper Switch High Signal
C	GY	112	Windshield Wiper Switch Signal 1
D	RD	228	Windshield Washer Switch
E	YE	143	Accessory Voltage
F	--	--	Not Used

G39020200040000X

Fig. 28 Wiper & washer switch connector terminal identification. ION

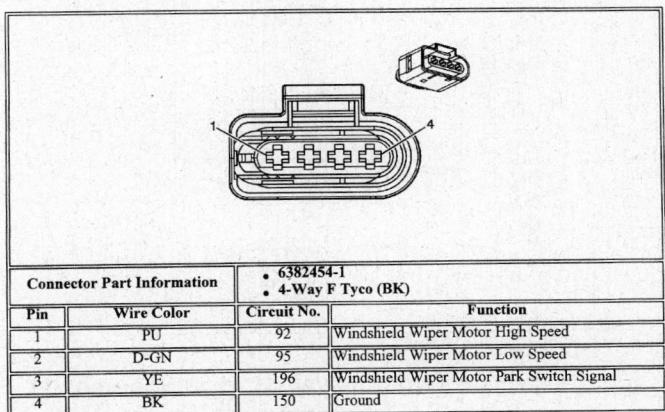

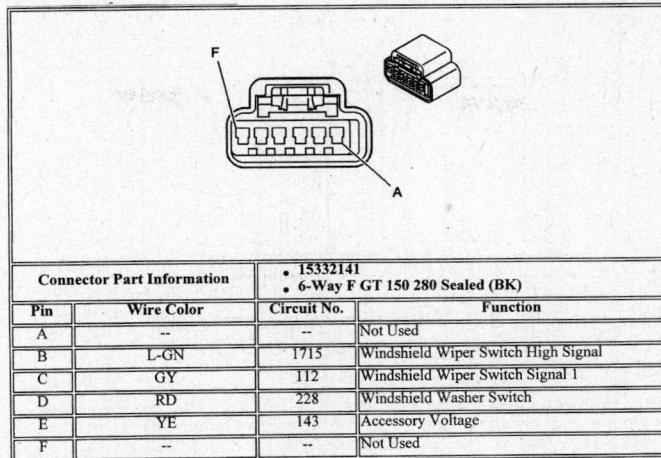

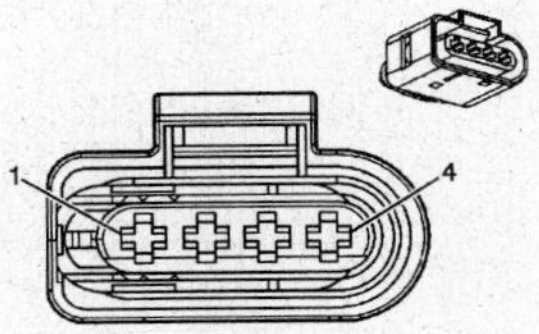

Connector Part Information	• 6382454-1 • 4-Way F Tyco (BK)		
Pin	**Wire Color**	**Circuit No.**	**Function**
1	PU	92	Windshield Wiper Motor High Speed
2	D-GN	95	Windshield Wiper Motor Low Speed
3	YE	196	Windshield Wiper Motor Park Switch Signal
4	BK	150	Ground

G39020200041000X

Fig. 29 Wiper motor connector terminal identification. ION

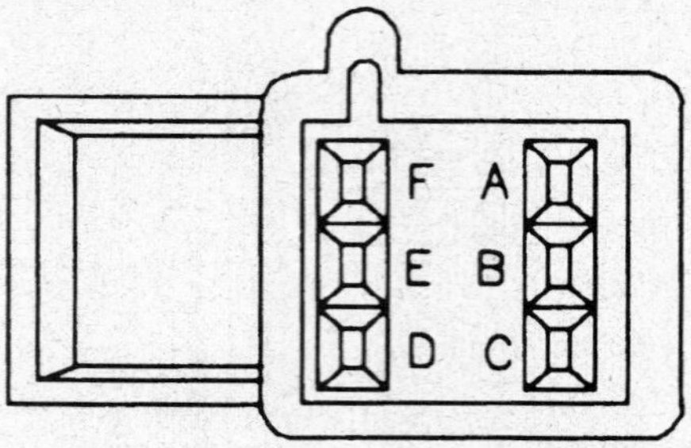

Fig. 30 Wiper switch connector terminal identification. S-Series

Harness Mating Connector Part NBR: 12064762 — * Wagon Only

Windshield Wiper Switch	Wash Switch	* Rear Wiper Switch	A 350F	B 392A	C 393A	D 580D	E 96	F 92	Ω Resistance
Mist	Off		o				o		300
Mist	On		o				o		91
Off	Off								
Off	On		o				o		130
INT 1	Off		o				o		2090
INT 1	On		o				o		122
INT 2	Off		o				o		990
INT 2	On		o				o		115
INT 3	Off		o				o		560
INT 3	On		o				o		106
Low	Off		o				o		300
Low	On		o				o		91
High	Off		o				o		300
High	On		o					o	0
High	On						o	o	91
			o				o		91
		Off			o	o			
		On		o	o	o			
		Wash							

G39029500009000X

Fig. 31 Wiper switch terminal resistance chart. S-Series

PASSIVE RESTRAINT SYSTEMS
Air Bag System

NOTE: Refer To "Computer Relearn Procedures" Located In The Front Of This Manual When Battery Power To The Computer Has Been Interrupted.

NOTE: Prior To Performing Any Service Operations Listed In This Section, Consult The "Technical Service Bulletins" Section For Related Information.

INDEX

AIR BAG SYSTEM DISARMING & ARMING

The Sensing and Diagnostic Module (SDM) can maintain enough voltage to cause air bag module deployment for up to 10 minutes after the ignition is turned Off and the battery is disconnected. Servicing the Supplemental Inflatable Restraint (SIR) system during this period may result in accidental deployment and personal injury.

Disarming

ALERO, MALIBU & GRAND AM

1. Ensure front wheels are pointed straight-ahead.
2. Turn ignition to Lock and remove key.
3. Remove AIR BAG fuse from instrument panel fuse junction block.
4. Remove lefthand sound insulator, then the courtesy lamp from sound insulator, if required.
5. Disconnect Connector Position Assurance (CPA) and driver's yellow two-way connector located above lefthand instrument panel wiring harness junction block.
6. Disconnect CPA and passenger's yellow two-way connector located above righthand instrument panel wiring harness junction block.

AURORA & BONNEVILLE

1. Ensure front wheels are pointed straight-ahead.
2. Turn ignition to Lock position and remove key.
3. Remove SIR fuse from rear fuse block located under rear seat.
4. Remove instrument panel lefthand sound insulator. **If required, remove courtesy lamp from sound insulator.**
5. Disconnect Connector Position Assurance (CPA) and driver's yellow two-way connector at base of steering column.
6. Remove righthand sound insulator.
7. Disconnect CPA and yellow two-way connector from passenger's inflator pigtail.
8. Remove CPA from driver's side air bag module electrical connector located under driver's seat.
9. Disconnect driver's side air bag module electrical connector.
10. Remove CPA from passenger's side air bag module electrical connector located under driver's seat.
11. Disconnect passenger's side air bag module electrical connector.

CAMARO & FIREBIRD

1. Ensure front wheels are pointed straight-ahead.
2. Turn ignition to Lock position and remove key.
3. Remove AIR BAG fuse from instrument panel fuse box.
4. Remove lefthand instrument panel insulator. **If required, remove courtesy lamp from sound insulator.**
5. Disconnect CPA and yellow two-way connector at base of steering column.
6. Remove righthand instrument panel insulator.
7. Disconnect CPA and yellow two-way connector from passenger's air bag module. This is located behind glove compartment.

CATERA

1. Turn steering wheel to straight-ahead position.
2. Turn ignition to Lock and remove key.
3. Wait one minute until SIR system energy reserve capacitors have discharged.
4. Remove steering column upper and lower covers.
5. Disconnect SRS coil assembly (clockspring) electrical connector from driver's air bag module.
6. Remove driver's air bag module.
7. Remove passenger's air bag module cover.
8. Remove CPA from passenger's air bag module electrical connector.
9. Disconnect passenger's air bag module electrical connector.
10. Remove driver's front seat track trim cover.
11. Disconnect driver's seat belt pretensioner two-way electrical connector from inline connector C315.
12. Remove CPA from lefthand side air bag module electrical connector.
13. Disconnect lefthand side air bag module electrical connector.
14. Remove passenger's front seat track trim cover.
15. Disconnect passenger's seat belt pretensioner two-way electrical connector from inline connector C316.
16. Remove CPA from righthand side air bag module electrical connector.
17. Disconnect righthand side air bag module electrical connector.
18. Disconnect battery ground cable. **If welding, body component replacement, painting or major electrical or mechanical service is to be performed, the Sensing and Diagnostic Module (SDM) should also be disconnected.**

CAVALIER & SUNFIRE

1. Ensure front wheels are pointed straight-ahead.
2. Turn ignition to Lock position and remove ignition key.
3. Remove AIR BAG fuse from instrument panel fuse block.
4. Remove CPA from steering wheel module coil connector.
5. Disconnect steering wheel module coil connector.
6. Remove instrument panel wiring harness junction panel.
7. Remove CPA from instrument panel module connector.

8. Disconnect instrument panel module connector.

CENTURY, GRAND PRIX, INTRIGUE, REGAL & VIBE

1. Ensure front wheels are pointed straight-ahead.
2. Move driver's seat as far rearward as possible.
3. Turn ignition to Lock position and remove ignition key.
4. Remove AIR BAG or SIR system fuse from instrument panel fuse block.
5. Remove lefthand underdash trim panel as required.
6. Disconnect CPA and yellow air bag connectors at base of steering column.
7. Disconnect passenger's CPA and yellow air bag connectors located to the righthand side of the steering column.
8. **On models equipped with side impact air bag module,** remove CPA from inflatable restraint side impact module located under driver seat.
9. **On all models,** disconnect side impact module connector.

CORVETTE

1. Place front wheels in straight-ahead position.
2. Turn ignition to Lock position and remove key.
3. Open up and remove front floor kick-up panel.
4. Remove SDM fuse from instrument panel fuse block.
5. Carefully pry courtesy lamp assembly from lefthand sound insulator panel.
6. Push on retaining nut from steering column bracket stud and twist rivets counterclockwise to disconnect from lower instrument panel support beam.
7. Insert courtesy lamp through panel.
8. Lower and remove the panel.
9. Remove both Connector Position Assurances (CPAs) and disconnect both yellow two-way SIR electrical connectors at base of steering column.

CTS

1. Place front wheels in the straight-ahead position.
2. Turn ignition to Lock position and remove key.
3. Remove rear seat cushion.
4. Remove SIR fuse from fuse block under rear seat.
5. Remove both CPA from driver side impact module and seat belt pretensioner yellow connector which is located under front of driver seat.
6. Disconnect lefthand front side impact module and pretensioner yellow connector from vehicle harness yellow connector.

DEVILLE

1. Place front wheels in the straight-ahead position.
2. Turn ignition to Lock position and remove key.
3. Remove rear seat cushion.
4. Remove SIR fuse from fuse block under rear seat.
5. Remove instrument panel lefthand sound insulator.
6. Disconnect CPA and yellow two-way SIR electrical connector at base of steering column.
7. Remove instrument panel righthand sound insulator.
8. Disconnect CPA and yellow two-way connector from passenger's air bag module pigtail above sound insulator.
9. Remove both CPAs from driver's seat air bag module and pretensioner yellow electrical connectors located under the seat.
10. Disconnect driver's seat air bag module and pretensioner yellow electrical connectors.
11. Remove both CPAs from passenger's front seat air bag module and pretensioner yellow electrical connectors located under the seat.
12. Disconnect passenger's front seat air bag module and pretensioner yellow electrical connectors.
13. **On models equipped with rear air bags (AW9),** proceed as follows:
    a. Remove rear seatback.
    b. Remove CPA from passenger's rear seat side air bag module yellow electrical connector.
    c. Disconnect passenger's rear seat side air bag module yellow electrical connector.
    d. Remove CPA from driver's rear seat side air bag module yellow electrical connector.
    e. Disconnect driver's rear seat side air bag module yellow electrical connector.

ELDORADO

1. Place front wheels in the straight-ahead position.
2. Turn ignition to Lock position and remove key.
3. Remove SIR fuse from trunk compartment fuse block.
4. Remove instrument panel lefthand sound insulator.
5. Disconnect CPA and both yellow two-way SIR electrical connectors at base of steering column.
6. Remove glove compartment.
7. Disconnect CPA and yellow two-way connector from passenger's inflator pigtail behind instrument panel.

IMPALA & MONTE CARLO

1. Ensure front wheels are pointed straight-ahead.
2. Turn ignition to Lock position and remove ignition key.
3. Remove instrument panel fuse access cover.
4. Remove SDM fuse from fuse block.
5. Remove instrument panel righthand access hole cover.
6. Unclip frontal air bags yellow 4-way electrical connector from metal rail.
7. Disconnect CPA and yellow air bag connector.
8. **On models equipped with driver's side air bag module,** remove CPA and disconnect yellow 2-way electrical connector located under driver's seat.

LESABRE

1. Ensure front wheels are pointed straight-ahead.
2. Turn ignition to Lock position and remove key.
3. Remove SIR fuse from rear fuse block located under rear seat.
4. Remove lefthand sound insulator.
5. Disconnect Connector Position Assurance (CPA) and driver's yellow two-way connector at base of steering column.
6. Remove righthand sound insulator.
7. Disconnect CPA and yellow two-way connector from passenger's front air bag module.
8. Disconnect CPA from yellow two-way connector located under driver's seat.
9. Disconnect driver's side air bag module yellow two-way connector from vehicle harness.
10. Disconnect CPA from yellow two-way connector located under front passenger's seat.
11. Disconnect passenger's side air bag module yellow two-way connector from vehicle harness.

LUMINA

1. Ensure front wheels are pointed straight-ahead.
2. Turn ignition to Lock position and remove ignition key.
3. Remove instrument panel fuse block door.
4. Remove Fuse 21 from fuse block.
5. Remove instrument panel lefthand sound insulator.
6. Disconnect CPA and yellow air bag electrical connectors at base of steering column.
7. Remove instrument panel righthand sound insulator.
8. Open glove compartment door.
9. Disconnect passenger's air bag module CPA and yellow electrical connector.

METRO

1. Ensure front wheels are pointed straight-ahead.
2. Turn ignition to Lock position.
3. Remove AIR BAG fuse from fuse block near steering wheel base.
4. Remove steering wheel side cap.
5. Remove CPA and disconnect yellow two-way electrical connector for driver's air bag module.
6. Pull glove compartment out while pushing inward on righthand and lefthand stoppers.
7. Remove CPA and disconnect passenger's air bag module electrical connector.

PARK AVENUE

1. Ensure front wheels are pointed straight-ahead.
2. Turn ignition to Lock position and remove key.
3. Remove SIR fuse from underhood fuse block.
4. Remove lefthand sound insulator. **If required, remove courtesy lamp from sound insulator.**

5. Disconnect Connector Position Assurance (CPA) and driver's yellow two-way connector at base of steering column.
6. Remove righthand sound insulator.
7. Remove the Connector Position Assurance (CPA) from I/P module yellow connector located above righthand side sound insulator.
8. Disconnect I/P module yellow connector from vehicle harness yellow connector.
9. Disconnect CPA and yellow two-way connector from passenger's air bag module wiring.
10. Disconnect CPA and yellow two-way connector from passenger's side air bag module electrical connector under front seat.
11. Remove the Connector Position Assurance (CPA) from lefthand side air bag yellow connector located under driver seat.
12. Disconnect the lefthand side air bag yellow connector from the vehicle harness yellow connector.
13. Remove the Connector Position Assurance (CPA) from the righthand side air bag yellow connector located under the passenger seat.
14. Disconnect the righthand side air bag yellow connector from the vehicle harness yellow connector.

PRIZM

1. Ensure front wheels are pointed straight-ahead.
2. Turn ignition to Lock position.
3. Remove IGN and CIG fuses from junction block No. 1 near base of steering column.
4. Remove steering column lower trim cover.
5. Remove CPA and disconnect yellow two-way electrical connector at base of steering column.
6. Remove glove compartment from instrument panel.
7. Remove CPA and disconnect yellow two-way connector from passenger's air bag module.
8. Release, unlock and disconnect driver and passenger front seat module electrical connectors.

SEVILLE

1. Place front wheels in the straight-ahead position.
2. Turn ignition to Lock position and remove key.
3. Remove rear seat cushion to access rear fuse block.
4. Remove SIR fuse from rear fuse block.
5. Remove instrument panel lefthand sound insulator.
6. Disconnect CPA and both yellow two-way SIR electrical connectors at base of steering column.
7. Remove instrument panel righthand sound insulator.
8. Disconnect CPA and yellow two-way connector from passenger's inflator pigtail above righthand sound insulator.
9. Disconnect CPA and side air bag/pretensioner yellow connector located under the driver's seat.
10. Disconnect CPA and side air bag/pretensioner yellow connector located under the front passenger's seat.

XLR

ZONE 1

1. Ensure that steering wheel is pointed in straight ahead position.
2. Ensure ignition is in Off position.
3. Remove kick panel to access I/P fuse block.
4. Remove SIR fuse (#16) from fuse block.
5. Open hood and remove air cleaner assembly.
6. Locate and remove lefthand and righthand electronic frontal sensors as indicated by numbers one and four in **Fig. 1.**
7. Remove lefthand and righthand CPA's from connecting EFS as indicated, **Fig. 1.**
8. Remove lefthand and righthand EFS connector from EFS.

ZONE 2

1. Ensure that steering wheel is pointed in straight ahead position.
2. Ensure ignition is in Off position.
3. Remove kick panel to access I/P fuse block.
4. Remove SIR fuse (#16) from fuse block.
5. Open lefthand and righthand doors, then remove door trim panels.
6. Locate and remove CPA from SIS connector, then the SIS connector from SIS, **Fig. 2.**

ZONE 3

1. Ensure that steering wheel is pointed in straight ahead position.
2. Ensure ignition is in Off position.
3. Remove kick panel to access I/P fuse block.
4. Remove SIR fuse (#16) from fuse block.
5. Remove lefthand driver side sound insulator from I/P.
6. Remove CPA from vehicle harness yellow connector.
7. Disconnect steering wheel module coil yellow connector from vehicle harness yellow connector, **Fig. 3.**

ZONE 4

1. Ensure that steering wheel is pointed in straight ahead position.
2. Ensure ignition is in Off position.
3. Remove kick panel to access I/P fuse block.
4. Remove SIR fuse (#16) from fuse block.
5. Remove righthand sound insulator from I/P.
6. Remove CPA from vehicle harness yellow connector.
7. Disconnect I/P module yellow connector from vehicle harness yellow connector, **Fig. 4.**
8. Remove both CPA's from righthand front passenger's side impact air bag module and seat belt pretensioner yellow connector under passenger's seat, **Fig. 5.**
9. Remove lefthand driver's side sound insulator from I/P.
10. Remove CPA from vehicle yellow harness from under steering column.
11. Disconnect steering wheel module coil yellow connector from vehicle harness yellow connector.
12. Remove both CPA's from lefthand front driver's side impact air bag module and pretenstioner yellow connector under driver's seat, **Fig. 6.**
13. Disconnect vehicle harness yellow connector from lefthand front side impact air bag module and pretensioner yellow connector.

ZONE 5

1. Ensure that steering wheel is pointed in straight ahead position.
2. Ensure ignition is in Off position.
3. Remove kick panel to access I/P fuse block.
4. Remove SIR fuse (#16) from fuse block.
5. Remove righthand passenger's side sound insulator panel.
6. Remove and disconnect CPA from vehicle harness yellow connector.

ZONE 6

1. Ensure that steering wheel is pointed in straight ahead position.
2. Ensure ignition is in Off position.
3. Remove kick panel to access I/P fuse block.
4. Remove SIR fuse (#16) from fuse block.
5. Open righthand side passenger door and remove door trim panel using suitable removal tool.
6. Remove CPA from SIS connector, then the SIS connector form SIS, **Fig. 7.**

ZONE 7

1. Ensure that steering wheel is pointed in straight ahead position.
2. Ensure ignition is in Off position.
3. Remove kick panel to access I/P fuse block.
4. Remove SIR fuse (#16) from fuse block.
5. Remove both CPA's from lefthand from driver's side impact air bag module and pretensioner yellow connector from under driver's seat, **Fig. 8.**

ZONE 9

1. Ensure that steering wheel is pointed in straight ahead position.
2. Ensure ignition is in Off position.
3. Remove kick panel to access I/P fuse block.
4. Remove SIR fuse (#16) from fuse block.
5. Remove and disconnect both CPA's from righthand front passenger's side impact air bag module and seat belt pretensioner yellow connector from under passenger's seat, **Fig. 9.**

L-SERIES

1. Place front wheels in straight-ahead position.
2. Turn ignition to Lock position and remove key.

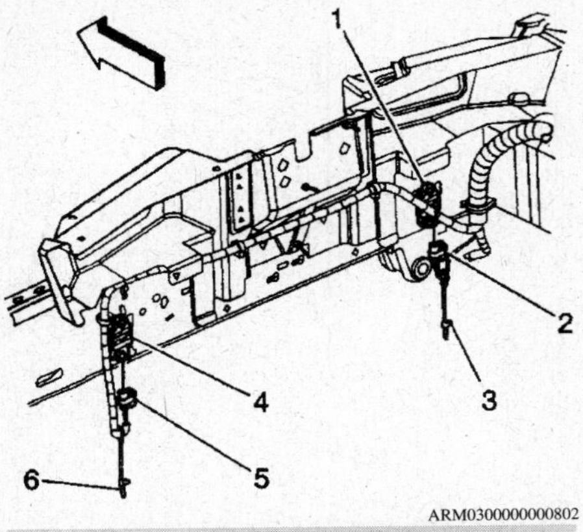

Fig. 1 Zone 1 component removal. XLR

3. Remove IGN1 mini-fuse from underhood fuse block.
4. Remove instrument panel lefthand lower closeout panel.
5. Push out clips securing yellow 2-way SIR connectors to instrument panel brace.
6. Disconnect SIR connectors.
7. **On models equipped with roof panel air bag,** remove lefthand and righthand side C-pillar trim panel as follows:
   a. Remove rear seat shoulder belt cover to expose fastener.
   b. Remove shoulder belt fastener and belt.
   c. Fold down rear seat back.
   d. Route shoulder belt out of C-pillar.
   e. Remove lefthand and righthand side C-pillar trim panel assembly.
   f. Disconnect lefthand and righthand side roof panel air bag yellow 2-way SIR connectors.

ION

1. Turn steering wheel so wheels are pointing straight ahead.
2. Turn ignition switch to OFF position, then remove key from ignition switch.
3. Locate body control module fuse center then remove fuse center cover.
4. Locate, Then remove AIR BAG fuse from body control module fuse center.
5. Remove coat hooks, then the trim panel from high mount stop lamp by pulling at clip locations.
6. Gently pull back on headliner to access lefthand pretensioner connector.
7. Remove CPA from lefthand side pretensioner, then disconnect lefthand pretensioner connector.
8. Remove garnish molding from upper lock pillar.
9. Remove CPA from left/driver roof rail module connector.
10. Disconnect lefthand roof rail module yellow connector from vehicle harness yellow connector.

S-SERIES

1. Place front wheels in straight-ahead position.
2. Turn ignition to Lock position and remove key.
3. Remove AIR BAG fuse from instrument panel fuse block.
4. Disconnect driver's air bag module 2-way yellow electrical connector clipped to steering column brace.
5. Reach under instrument panel on passenger's side and detach clip which retains yellow 2-way SIR electrical connector to metal brace near HVAC fan.
6. Disconnect passenger's SIR connector.
7. **On models equipped with roof panel air bag,** remove instrument panel upper trim panel as follows:
   a. Remove screws located under upper trim panel on passenger's side.
   b. Disengage clips at locations of upper trim panel and lifting up.
   c. Disengage hook and loop fastener attachments at rear of upper trim panel, lifting straight up.
   d. Raise upper trim panel up to clear VIN plate.
   e. Disconnect lefthand and righthand side roof panel air bag yellow 2-way SIR connectors.

Arming

ALERO, MALIBU & GRAND AM

1. Ensure front wheel are in the straight ahead position.
2. Place ignition in Lock position, then remove ignition key.
3. Connect yellow two-way connector to passenger's inflator pigtail and install CPA.
4. Connect yellow two-way SIR electrical connector and install CPA.
5. Install AIR BAG fuse into fuse block.
6. From a safe position at sides of or below air bag modules, turn ignition On.
7. Ensure SIR lamp flashes seven times and turns off. If lamp does not operate as specified a system fault is indicated.

AURORA & BONNEVILLE

1. Turn steering wheel to straight-ahead position.
2. Turn ignition to Lock position, then remove key.
3. Connect yellow two-way connector and CPA at passenger's side air bag module electrical connector under front seat.
4. Connect yellow two-way connector and CPA at driver's side air bag module electrical connector under front seat.
5. Connect yellow two-way connector to passenger's air bag module wiring and install CPA.
6. Install righthand sound insulator.
7. Connect yellow two-way SIR electrical connector at base of steering column and install CPA.
8. Install lefthand sound insulator. **Install courtesy lamp into sound insulator if required.**

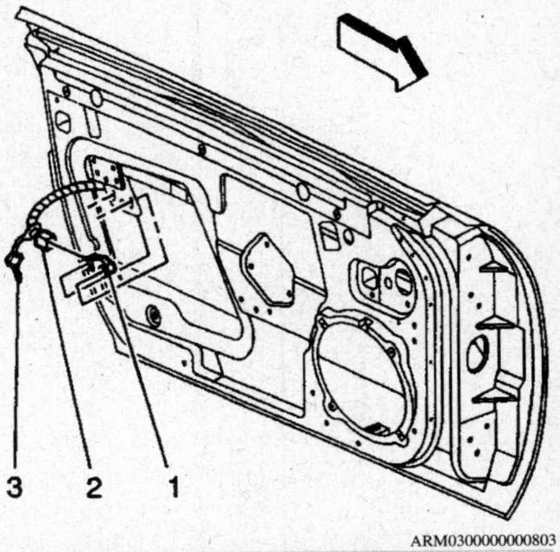

Fig. 2 Zone 2 component removal. XLR

9. Install SIR fuse into rear fuse block.
10. From a safe position at sides of or below air bag modules, turn ignition On.
11. Ensure SIR lamp flashes seven times, then turns off. If lamp does not operate a specified a system fault is indicated.

CAMARO & FIREBIRD

1. Turn ignition key to Lock and remove key.
2. Connect yellow two-way connector to passenger's air bag module, then install CPA.
3. Install righthand instrument panel insulator.
4. Connect driver's air bag yellow two-way SIR electrical connector.
5. Install CPA near base of steering column.
6. Install lefthand sound insulator. **Install courtesy lamp into sound insulator if required.**
7. Install AIR BAG fuse.
8. From a safe position at sides of or below air bag modules, turn ignition On.
9. Ensure SIR lamp flashes seven times, then turns off. If lamp does not operate as specified a system fault is indicated.

CATERA

1. Turn steering wheel to straight-ahead position.
2. Turn ignition to Lock position.
3. Connect SDM electrical connectors if required.
4. Connect passenger's side air bag module electrical connector and install CPA.
5. Connect passenger's seat belt pretensioner electrical connector.
6. Install passenger's front seat track trim cover.
7. Connect driver's side air bag module electrical connector and install CPA.
8. Connect driver's seat belt pretensioner electrical connector.
9. Install driver's front seat track trim cover.
10. Connect passenger's front air bag

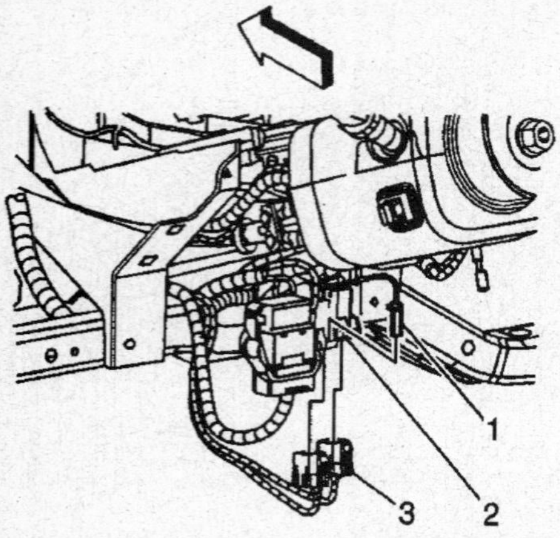

Fig. 3 Zone 3 component removal. XLR

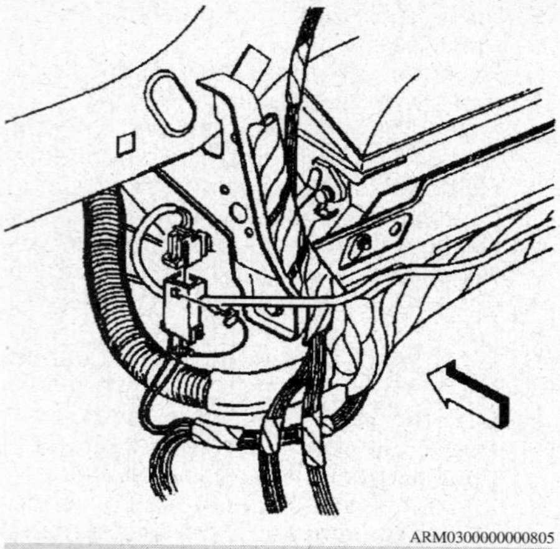

Fig. 4 Vehicle harness location. XLR

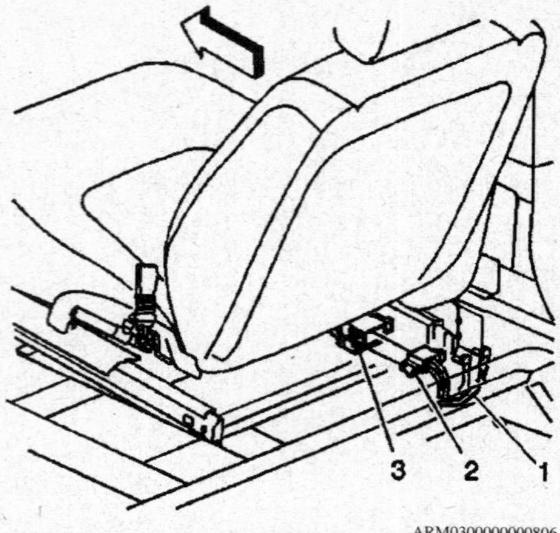

Fig. 5 Passenger's side impact air bag module connector. XLR

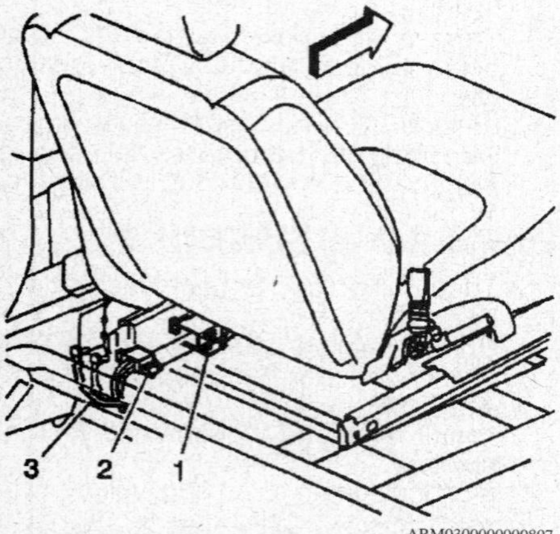

Fig. 6 Driver's seat electrical components. XLR

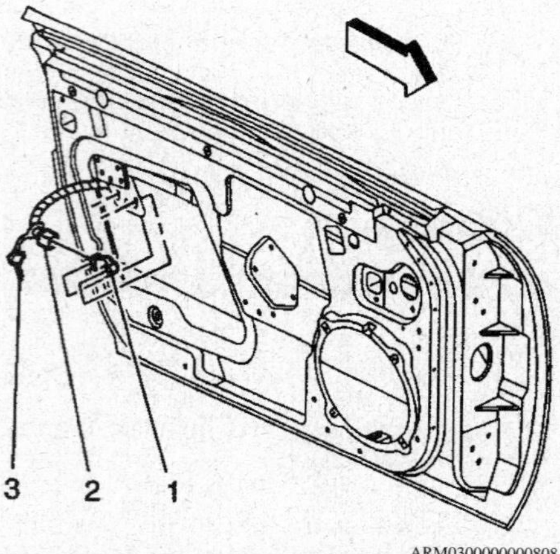

Fig. 7 Righthand side impact sensor removal. XLR

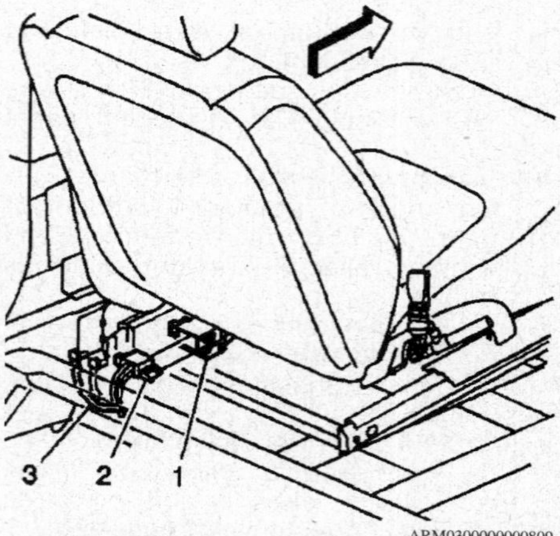

Fig. 8 Driver's side impact air bag module electrical connectors. XLR

module electrical connector and install CPA.

11. Install passenger's front air bag module cover.
12. Install driver's air bag module.
13. Connect driver's front air bag module electrical connector to SRS coil assembly (clockspring).
14. Install steering column lower and upper covers.
15. Connect battery ground cable.
16. From a safe position at sides of or below air bag modules, turn ignition On.
17. Ensure AIR BAG warning lamp flashes seven times, then turns off.
18. If lamp does not operate as specified a system fault is indicated.

CAVALIER & SUNFIRE

1. Turn ignition to Lock position and remove key.
2. Connect instrument panel module connector.
3. Install CPA to instrument panel module connector.
4. Install instrument panel wiring harness junction block.
5. Connect inflatable restraint steering wheel module coil connector.
6. Install CPA to steering wheel module coil connector.
7. Install AIR BAG fuse.
8. From a safe position at sides of or below air bag modules, turn ignition On.
9. Ensure AIR BAG warning lamp flashes seven times, then turns off. If lamp does not operate as specified a system fault is indicated.

CENTURY, GRAND PRIX, INTRIGUE, REGAL & VIBE

1. Ensure front wheels are in straight-ahead position and key is removed from ignition.
2. **On models equipped with side impact air bag module,** proceed as follows:
   a. Connect inflatable restraint side impact module connector.
   b. Install CPA to side impact module.
3. **On all models,** connect passenger's air bag module CPA and air bag yellow connectors located to the righthand side of steering column.
4. Connect driver's air bag module CPA and yellow air bag connectors at base of steering column.
5. Install AIR BAG or SIR fuse into fuse block.
6. From a safe position at sides of or below air bag modules, turn ignition On.
7. Ensure AIR BAG warning lamp lights and flashes seven times, then turns off. If lamp does not operate as specified a system fault is indicated.

CORVETTE

1. Turn ignition to Lock position and remove key.
2. Connect both yellow SIR connectors and install CPA.
3. Insert courtesy lamp through panel and install lefthand sound insulation panel.
4. Install push-on nut to steering column bracket stud and twist rivets clockwise to secure.
5. Align courtesy lamp and push into place.

6. Install SDM fuse into instrument panel fuse block.
7. Install front floor kick-up panel.
8. From a safe position at sides of or below air bag modules, turn ignition On.
9. Ensure AIR BAG warning lamp flashes seven times and turns off. If lamp does not operate as specified a system fault is indicated.

CTS

1. Turn ignition to Lock, then remove key.
2. Connect lefthand side impact module and pretensioner yellow connector to vehicle harness yellow connector.
3. Install both CPA locks to lefthand side impact module and pretensioner yellow connector.
4. Install SIR fuse into righthand rear fuse center, then the rear seat.
5. Use caution while reaching in, then turn ignition switch to the ON position. AIR BAG indicator will flash then turn OFF. If lamp does not operate as specified a system fault is indicated.

DEVILLE

1. Turn ignition to Lock, then remove key.
2. **On models equipped with rear air bags (AW9),** proceed as follows:
   a. Connect driver's rear seat side air bag module yellow electrical connector.
   b. Install CPA for driver's rear seat side air bag module yellow electrical connector.
   c. Connect passenger's rear seat side air bag module yellow electrical connector.
   d. Install CPA for passenger's rear seat side air bag module yellow electrical connector.
   e. Install rear seatback.
3. **On all models,** connect yellow two-way connector to passenger's inflator pigtail and install CPA.
4. Connect yellow two-way connector to driver's inflator pigtail and install CPA.
5. Connect yellow two-way SIR electrical connector at base of steering column and install CPA.
6. Install lefthand sound insulator.
7. Install SIR fuse into fuse block.
8. From a safe position at sides of or below air bag modules, turn ignition On.
9. Ensure SIR lamp flashes seven times, then turns off. If lamp does not operate as specified a system fault is indicated.

ELDORADO

1. Turn ignition to Lock position, then remove key.
2. Connect yellow two-way connector to passenger's inflator pigtail and install CPA.
3. Install glove compartment.
4. Connect yellow two-way SIR electrical connectors at base of steering column and install CPA.
5. Install lefthand sound insulator.
6. Install SIR fuse into fuse block.
7. From a safe position at sides of or below air bag modules, turn ignition On.

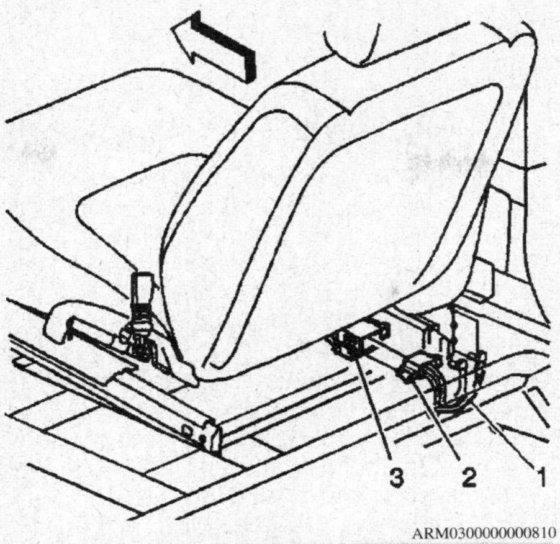

Fig. 9 Passenger's side impact air bag module electrical connectors. XLR

8. Ensure SIR lamp flashes seven times, then turns off. If lamp does not operate as specified a system fault is indicated.

IMPALA & MONTE CARLO

1. Ensure front wheels are in straight-ahead position and key is removed from ignition.
2. **On models equipped with driver's side air bag module,** connect yellow electrical connector under driver's seat and install CPA.
3. **On all models,** connect frontal air bag module CPA and yellow air bag connector.
4. Install instrument panel righthand access hole cover.
5. Install SDM fuse into fuse block.
6. Install instrument panel fuse access cover.
7. From a safe position at sides of or below air bag modules, turn ignition On.
8. Ensure AIR BAG warning lamp lights and flashes seven times, then turns off. If lamp does not operate as specified a system fault is indicated.

LESABRE

1. Ensure front wheels are pointed straight-ahead.
2. Ensure ignition is in Lock position, then remove key.
3. Connect passenger's side air bag module yellow two-way connector and CPA to vehicle harness.
4. Connect yellow two-way connector and CPA located under front passenger's seat.
5. Connect driver's side air bag module yellow two-way connector to vehicle harness.
6. Connect yellow two-way connector and CPA located under driver's seat.
7. Connect yellow two-way connector and CPA at passenger's front air bag module.
8. Install righthand sound insulator.
9. Connect driver's yellow two-way connector and CPA at base of steering column.
10. Install lefthand sound insulator.
11. Install SIR fuse into rear fuse block located under rear seat.
12. From a safe position at sides of or below air bag modules, turn ignition On.
13. Ensure AIR BAG lamp flashes seven times, then turns off. If lamp does not operate as specified a system fault is indicated.

LUMINA

1. Ensure front wheels are in straight-ahead position and key is removed from ignition.
2. Connect passenger's air bag module CPA and yellow air bag connector, then close glove compartment door.
3. Install righthand sound insulator.
4. Connect CPA and yellow air bag connectors at base of steering column.
5. Install lefthand sound insulator.
6. Install Fuse 21 into fuse block.
7. Install instrument panel fuse block door.
8. From a safe position at sides of or below air bag modules, turn ignition On.
9. Ensure AIR BAG warning lamp lights and flashes seven times, then turns off. If lamp does not operate as specified a system fault is indicated.

METRO

1. Turn ignition key to Lock position, then remove key.
2. Connect passenger's air bag module yellow electrical connector.
3. Install passenger's air bag module CPA and close glove compartment.
4. Connect yellow two-way electrical connector inside steering wheel air bag module housing.
5. Install driver's inflator CPA, then the steering wheel side cap.
6. Install AIR BAG fuse into Air Bag fuse block.
7. From a safe position at sides of or below air bag modules, turn ignition On.
8. Ensure AIR BAG lamp flashes seven times and turns off. If lamp does not operate as specified a system fault is indicated.

PARK AVENUE

1. Ensure front wheels are pointed straight-ahead.
2. Turn ignition to Lock position and remove key.
3. Connect righthand side air bag yellow connector to vehicle harness yellow connector located under passenger seat.
4. Install Connector Position Assurance (CPA) to righthand side air bag yellow connector.
5. Connect lefthand side air bag yellow connector to vehicle harness yellow connector located under driver seat.
6. Install Connector Position Assurance (CPA) to lefthand side air bag yellow connector.
7. Connect I/P module air bag yellow connector to vehicle harness yellow connector located above righthand

sound insulator.

8. Install Connector Position Assurance (CPA) to I/P module yellow connector.
9. Install the righthand sound insulator.
10. Connect steering wheel module air bag yellow connector to vehicle harness yellow connector located next to steering column.
11. Install Connector Position Assurance (CPA) to steering wheel module yellow connector.
12. Install lefthand sound insulator.
13. Install SIR fuse to underhood fuse block.
14. From a safe position at sides of or below air bag modules, turn ignition On.
15. Ensure AIR BAG lamp lights for approximately six seconds, then turns off. If lamp does not operate as specified a system fault is indicated.

PRIZM

1. Turn ignition to Lock position, then remove key.
2. Connect driver and passenger front seat module electrical connectors.
3. Connect passenger's air bag module yellow two-way connector and secure with CPA.
4. Install glove compartment.
5. Connect yellow two-way connector on lower steering column and secure with CPA.
6. Install steering column lower trim cover.
7. Install CIG and IGN fuses in junction block.
8. From a safe position at sides of or below air bag modules, turn ignition On.
9. Ensure AIR BAG lamp lights for approximately six seconds, then turns off. If lamp does not operate as specified a system fault is indicated.

SEVILLE

1. Turn ignition to Lock position, then remove key.
2. Connect side air bag/pretensioner yellow connector located under driver's seat, then install CPA.
3. Connect side air bag/pretensioner yellow connector located under front passenger's seat, then install CPA.
4. Connect yellow two-way connector to passenger's inflator pigtail and install CPA.
5. Install righthand sound insulator.
6. Connect yellow two-way SIR electrical connectors at base of steering column and install CPA.
7. Install lefthand sound insulator.
8. Install SIR fuse into rear fuse block.
9. Install rear seat cushion.
10. From a safe position at sides of or below air bag modules, turn ignition On.
11. Ensure SIR lamp flashes seven times, then turns off. If lamp does not operate as specified a system fault is indicated.

XLR

ZONE 1

Refer to "Disarming" procedure for component locations.

1. Ensure ignition is in Off position.
2. Connect lefthand and righthand EFS connector to appropriate sensor.
3. Connect lefthand and righthand CPA to appropriate EFS connector.
4. Install SIR fuse into fuse block.
5. Install block cover.
6. Use caution while placing ignition to On position from below or side.
7. The AIR BAG indicator will flash, then turn Off. Refer to "Diagnosis & Testing" in **MOTOR's "Air Bag Manual" or "Air Bag Diagnostics CD"** for information.

ZONE 2

Refer to "Disarming" procedure for component locations.

1. Ensure ignition is in Off position.
2. Connect SIS connector to SIS, then the CPA to SIS connector.
3. Install door trim panel.
4. Insatll SIR fuse into fuse block.
5. Install fuse block cover and kick panel to I/P.
6. Use caution while placing ignition to On position from below or side.
7. The AIR BAG indicator will flash, then turn Off. Refer to "Diagnosis & Testing" in **MOTOR's "Air Bag Manual" or "Air Bag Diagnostics CD"** for information.

ZONE 3

Refer to "Disarming" procedure for component locations.

1. Ensure ignition is in Off position.
2. Connect wheel module coil yellow connector to vehicle harness yellow connector.
3. Install CPA to vehicle harness yellow connector.
4. Install lefthand sound insulator to I/P.
5. Install SIR fuse into fuse block.
6. Install kick panel and cover to I/P.
7. Use caution while placing ignition to On position from below or side.
8. The AIR BAG indicator will flash, then turn Off. Refer to "Diagnosis & Testing" in **MOTOR's "Air Bag Manual" or "Air Bag Diagnostics CD"** for information.

ZONE 4

Refer to "Disarming" procedure for component locations.

1. Ensure ignition is in Off position.
2. Connect vehicle harness yellow connector to lefthand side impact air bag module and pretensioner yellow connector.
3. Install CPA's to lefthand side impact air bag module and pretensioner yellow connector.
4. Connect steering wheel module coil yellow connector to vehicle harness yellow connector.
5. Install CPA to harness yellow connector.
6. Install lefthand sound insulator panel to I/P.
7. Connect vehicle harness yellow connector to lefthand side impact air bag module and pretensioner yellow connector.
8. Install both CPA's to lefthand side imapct air bag module and pretensioner yellow connector.
9. Connect I/P module yellow connector to vehicle harness yellow connector.
10. Install CPA to vehicle harness yellow connector.
11. Install righthand sound insulator to I/P.
12. Install SIR fuse to fuse block.
13. Install kick panel to cover I/P.
14. Use caution while placing ignition to On position from below or side.
15. The AIR BAG indicator will flash, then turn Off. Refer to "Diagnosis & Testing" in **MOTOR's "Air Bag Manual" or "Air Bag Diagnostics CD"** for information.

ZONE 5

Refer to "Disarming" procedure for component locations.

1. Ensure ignition is in Off position.
2. Connect I/P module yellow connector to vehicle harness yellow connector.
3. Install CPA to vehicle harness yellow connector.
4. Install righthand sound insulator to I/P.
5. Install SIR fuse to fuse block.
6. Install I/P fuse block cover, then the kick panel to cover I/P fuse block.
7. Use caution while placing ignition to On position from below or side.
8. The AIR BAG indicator will flash, then turn Off. Refer to "Diagnosis & Testing" in **MOTOR's "Air Bag Manual" or "Air Bag Diagnostics CD"** for information.

ZONE 6

Refer to "Disarming" procedure for component locations.

1. Ensure ignition is in Off position.
2. Connect SIS connector to SIS, then the CPA to SIS connector.
3. Install door trim panel(s).
4. Install SIR fuse to fuse block.
5. Install kick panel and cover to I/P fuse block.
6. Use caution while placing ignition to On position from below or side.
7. The AIR BAG indicator will flash, then turn Off. Refer to "Diagnosis & Testing" in **MOTOR's "Air Bag Manual" or "Air Bag Diagnostics CD"** for information.

ZONE 7

Refer to "Disarming" procedure for component locations.

1. Ensure ignition is in Off position.
2. Connect vehicle harness yellow connector to lefthand side impact air bag module and pretensioner yellow connector.
3. Install both CPA's to lefthand side impact air bag module and pretensioner yellow connector.
4. Install SIR fuse into fuse block.
5. Install I/P fuse block cover, then the kick panel to cover I/P.

6. Use caution while placing ignition to On position from below or side.
7. The AIR BAG indicator will flash, then turn Off. Refer to "Diagnosis & Testing" in **MOTOR's "Air Bag Manual" or "Air Bag Diagnostics CD"** for information.

ZONE 9

Refer to "Disarming" procedure for component locations.

1. Ensure ignition is in Off position.
2. Connect and install vehicle harness yellow connector to righthand side impact air bag module and pretensioner yellow connector.
3. Install SIR fuse to I/P fuse block.
4. Install I/P fuse block cover, then the kick panel to I/P fuse block.
5. Use caution while placing ignition to On position from below or side.
6. The AIR BAG indicator will flash, then turn Off. Refer to "Diagnosis & Testing" in **MOTOR's "Air Bag Manual" or "Air Bag Diagnostics CD"** for information.

L-SERIES

1. Turn ignition to Lock position and remove key.
2. Connect lefthand and righthand side yellow 2-way SIR connectors.
3. **On models equipped with roof panel air bag,** install lefthand and righthand side C-pillar trim panel as follows:
   a. Install C-pillar trim, pushing at clip locations.
   b. Install rear shoulder belt to C-pillar.
   c. Install rear shoulder belt fastener cover.
   d. Route shoulder belt into C-pillar trim access slot.
   e. Fold up rear seat.
4. **On all models,** connect driver and passenger air bag module yellow 2-way connectors.
5. Fastener clips on yellow 2-way connectors to I/P panel brace.
6. Install IGN1 fuse in underhood fuse block.
7. From a safe position at sides of or below air bag modules, turn ignition On.
8. Ensure air bag lamp flashes seven times, then turns and remains off. If lamp does not operate as specified a system fault is indicated.

ION

1. Remove key from ignition switch.
2. Connect lefthand roof rail module yellow connector to harness yellow connector.
3. Install CPA to lefthand side roof rail module connector.
4. Install garnish molding to upper lock pillar.
5. Gently pull back on headliner to access lefthand pretensioner, then connect lefthand pretensioner connector and install connector position assurance.
6. Install trim panel to high mount stop lamp, then the coat hooks.
7. Install AIR BAG fuse into body control module fuse center, then the body control module fuse center cover.
8. Use caution while reaching in, then turn ignition switch to ON position. The AIR BAG indicator will flash then turn OFF. If lamp does not operate as specified a system fault is indicated.

S-SERIES

1. Turn ignition to Lock position and remove key.
2. Connect lefthand and righthand side yellow 2-way SIR connector.
3. **On models equipped with roof panel air bag,** install instrument panel upper trim panel as follows:
   a. Ensure hook and loop fastener attachments are correctly installed.
   b. Position upper trim panel on retainer assembly.
   c. Align tabs on sides of upper trim panel with windshield garnish molding.
   d. Align clips to clip locations.
   e. Install screws on underside of upper trim panel on passenger side.
4. **On all models,** reach under instrument panel on passenger's side and install clip which retains yellow 2-way SIR electrical connector to metal brace near HVAC fan.
5. Connect driver's air bag module 2-way yellow electrical connector clipped to steering column brace.
6. Install AIR BAG fuse into instrument panel fuse block.
7. From a safe position at sides of or below air bag modules, turn ignition On.
8. Ensure air bag lamp flashes seven times, then turns and remains off. If lamp does not operate as specified a system fault is indicated.

DESCRIPTION & OPERATION

Description

The Supplemental Inflatable Restraint (SIR) system helps supplement the protection offered by the driver and front passenger's seat belt by deploying an air bag module from the center of the steering wheel and from the top righthand side of the instrument panel.

The air bag module will deploy when the vehicle is involved in a frontal crash of sufficient force up to 30° off the longitudinal centerline of the vehicle.

The SIR system consists of the Sensing and Diagnostic Module (SDM) or Diagnostic Energy Reserve Module (DERM), arming sensor, forward discriminating sensor, passenger discriminating sensor, driver's air bag module, SIR coil assembly, passenger's air bag module and the AIR BAG or SIR warning lamp on the instrument cluster. The SDM/DERM, SIR coil assembly, driver's air bag module and connector wires make up the deployment loops. The function of the deployment loops is to supply current through the air bag modules. The air bag modules are only supplied with enough current to deploy when the SDM and forward discriminating sensor detect vehicle velocity changes severe enough to warrant deployment.

A roof panel air bag system is available on the S-Series. These modules are mounted on the C-pillars to the sides of the occupants and will deploy if the side impact sensors detect an crash force exceeding a predetermined level.

Operation

SYSTEM COMPONENTS

On models with SDM, the SDM contains a sensing device which converts vehicle velocity changes to an electrical signal. The electrical signal generated is processed by the SDM and then compared to a value stored in memory. When the generated signal exceeds the stored value, additional signals are compared to signals stored in memory. When two of the generated signals exceed the stored values or when one of the generated signals exceeds the stored value and the forward discriminating sensor closes, the SDM will cause current to flow through the air bag modules deploying the air bag modules.

On models with an arming sensor and DERM module, the arming sensor, air bag modules and discriminating sensors make up the deployment loop. The arming sensor switches power to the air bag module on high side (power side) of the deployment loop. Either of the discriminating sensors can supply ground to the air bag module on the low side (ground side) of the loop. The air bag module is only supplied sufficient current to deploy when the arming sensor and at least one of the two discriminating sensors are closed simultaneously. The DERM also supplies the deployment loop with a 36 volt reserve, this reserve is sufficient enough to deploy the air bag module if the ignition feed is lost during a frontal crash.

DIAGNOSTIC ENERGY RESERVE MODULE (DERM)

The Diagnostic Energy Reserve Module (DERM) performs several system functions. These functions include energy reserve, fault detection, fault recording, driver notification and frontal crash recording.

The DERM is connected to the SIR wiring harness by a multi-pin connector. This harness connector uses a shorting bar across certain terminals in the contact area. This shorting bar connects the AIR BAG warning lamp to ground when the DERM harness connector is disconnected. This will cause the AIR BAG warning lamp to come on steadily whenever the ignition is in the Run, Bulb Test or Start positions with the DERM disconnected.

SENSING & DIAGNOSTIC MODULE (SDM)

The Sensing and Diagnostic Module (SDM) performs several system functions. These functions include energy reserve, air bag module deployment, fault detection, fault diagnosis, driver notification, frontal crash detection and frontal crash recording.

The SDM is connected to the SIR wiring harness by a multi-pin connector. This harness connector uses a shorting bar across certain terminals in the contact area. This shorting bar connects the AIR BAG warning lamp to ground when the DERM harness connector is disconnected. This will cause the AIR BAG warning lamp to light steadily whenever the ignition is in the Run, Bulb Test or Start positions with the SDM disconnected.

AIR BAG WARNING LAMP

Voltage is supplied to the AIR BAG/SIR warning lamp when the ignition is in the Run, Bulb Test or Start position. The DERM/SDM controls the lamp by providing ground with a lamp driver. The AIR BAG warning lamp is used in the SIR system to verify lamp and DERM/SDM operation by flashing seven times whenever the ignition is turned On and to warn the driver of any SIR system faults.

DISCRIMINATING SENSORS & ARMING SENSORS

The discriminating and arming sensors are used by the SIR system to determine whether or not certain frontal crashes require deployment of the air bag modules. The sensor consists of a sensing element, normally open switch contacts and a diagnostic resistor. The sensing element closes the switch contacts when the vehicle velocity changes are severe enough to warrant air bag module deployment.

SIR COIL ASSEMBLY

The SIR coil assembly consists of two current carrying coils. They are attached to the steering column and allow rotation of the steering wheel while maintaining continuous contact of the driver deployment loop to the driver's air bag module.

AIR BAG MODULES

The air bag modules consist of an inflatable bag and an inflator (a canister of gas-generating material and an initiating device). When the vehicle is in a frontal crash of sufficient force, the SDM or arming sensor causes current to flow through the deployment loops. Current passing through the initiator ignites the material in the air bag module. The gas produced from this reaction rapidly inflates the air bag module.

DUAL STAGE AIR BAG MODULES

Some models are equipped with dual stage air bag modules containing a housing, inflatable air bag, two initiating devices, canister of gas generating material and, in some cases, stored compressed gas. The two initiators are part of the frontal deployment loop. The function of the frontal deployment loops are to supply current through the driver's and passenger's air bag modules to deploy the air bags.

The air bag modules have two stages of deployment, which varies the amount of restraint to the occupant according to the collision severity. For moderate frontal collisions the air bag modules deploy at less than full deployment (low deployment) which consists of stage 1 of the air bag module. For more severe frontal collisions a full deployment is initiated which consists of stage 1 and stage 2 of the air bag module. The current passing through the initiators ignites the material in the canister producing a rapid generation of gas and is some cases, the release of compressed gas. The gas produced from this reaction rapidly inflates the air bag. Once the air bag is inflated it quickly deflates through the air bag vent holes and/or the bag fabric.

Each dual stage air bag modules is equipped with a shorting bar located in the connector(s) of the module. The shorting bar shorts the air bag module deployment loop circuitry to prevent unwanted deployment of the air bag when it is disconnected.

INFLATABLE RESTRAINT SEAT BELT PRETENSIONER

The seat belt pretensioner modules contain a housing, an initiating device, and a canister of gas generating material. The initiator is part of the seat belt pretensioner deployment loop. When the vehicle is involved in a collision of sufficient force, the SDM will cause current to flow through the deployment loops to the initiator. Current passing through the initiator ignites the material in the canister producing a rapid generation of gas and the release of compressed gas, if present. The gas produced from this reaction rapidly shortens the seat belt buckle height.

Each seat belt pretensioner is equipped with a shorting bar located on the connector of the pretensioner. The shorting bar shorts the seat belt pretensioner deployment loop circuitry to prevent unwanted deployment of the pretensioner when servicing the seat belt pretensioner.

PRECAUTIONS

Battery Ground Cable

Prior to service, disconnect battery ground cable and isolate as required.

General Safety

EXCEPT SATURN

1. **Air bag modules should not be subjected to temperatures above 150°F.**
2. **Discriminating sensors, air bag modules, arming sensors or DERM/SDM should not be used if they have been dropped from a height of more than three feet.**
3. **When a discriminating sensor or arming sensor is replaced, it must be positioned with the arrow of the sensor pointing toward the front of the vehicle. It is important that the discriminating sensors and arming sensor are mounted flat on their mounting surfaces. It is also important that the sensor mounting surface be free of dirt or any other foreign substance.**
4. **Do not apply power to the SIR system unless all components are connected or a diagnostic chart requests it, as this will set a diagnostic trouble code.**
5. **When carrying a live air bag module, ensure bag opening is pointed away from the body. In case of accidental deployment, the bag will then deploy with a small chance of injury. Never carry an air bag module by the wires or connector on the underside of the module. When placing a live air bag module on a bench of other surface, always face the bag or trim cover up, away from the surface. Never rest a steering column assembly on the steering wheel with the air bag module face down and column vertical.**
6. **Failure to follow air bag module disposal procedures can result in air bag module deployment. Undeployed air bag modules must not be disposed of through normal channels. The undeployed air bag module contains substances that can cause severe illness or personal injury if the sealed container is damaged during disposal.**
7. **When troubleshooting the SIR system, do not use electrical test equipment such as a battery powered or AC powered voltmeter or ohmmeter, or any type of electrical equipment other than those that are specified. Do not use a non-powered probe type tester.**
8. **To avoid electrostatic discharge damage to air bag module and other system components, the technician should touch a suitable metal component prior to handling the component.**
9. **A deployed dual stage module looks the same whether one or both stages were used. Always assume a deployed dual stage module has an active stage 2. Both deployment loops must be energized to deploy the air bag.**

SATURN

Safe handling of live and deployed air bag modules requires adhering to the following procedures:

1. Before attempting service on or around SIR components or wiring, disarm SIR system as outlined in "Air Bag System Disarming & Arming."
2. **SDM maintains voltage after ignition is turned Off and battery is disconnected. Wait 10 minutes for this back-up power to discharge before performing any service on SIR system.**
3. Inspect SIR system components after an accident that may or may not involve air bag module deployment.
4. Use special electrical connector adapters when performing diagnostic tests.
5. Replace wiring terminals with special repair kits.

6. Never strike or jar a sensor in a way that could cause deployment.
7. Replace SDM if it has dropped from a height greater than two feet or shows any signs of damage.
8. Never power up SIR system when SDM is not rigidly attached to vehicle.
9. Avoid touching SDM terminals to prevent damage because of electrostatic discharge.

Handling Air Bag Modules

LIVE (UNDEPLOYED) AIR BAG MODULES

Special care is required when handling and storing a live (undeployed) air bag module. The rapid gas generation produced during deployment of the air bag module could cause the air bag module or an object in front of the air bag module to be thrown through the air.

When carrying a live air bag module, ensure the air bag module and trim cover are pointed away from you. Never carry the air bag module by the wires or by the connector on module. In case of accidental deployment, the air bag module will deploy with minimal chance of injury.

When placing air bag modules on a bench or other surface, always face the air bag module and trim cover away from the surface. Never rest a steering wheel with the inflator face down and the column vertical. A free space must be provided to allow for air bag module expansion in case of accidental deployment.

DEPLOYED AIR BAG MODULES

After the air bag module has been deployed, the surface of the air bag module may contain a powdery residue. This powder consists primarily of corn starch (used to lubricate the air bag module as it inflates) and by-products of the chemical reaction. Sodium hydroxide dust (similar to lye dust) is produced as a by-product of the deployment reaction. The sodium hydroxide then quickly reacts with atmospheric moisture and is converted to sodium carbonate and sodium bicarbonate (baking soda). Therefore, it is unlikely that sodium hydroxide will be present after deployment. Always wear safety glasses and gloves when handling a deployed module and wash hands with mild soap and water afterward.

AIR BAG MODULE DISPOSAL

When a deployed module has been removed from a vehicle, it may be disposed of with any other scrap material. Handle with gloves and safety glasses and wash hands after handling. **The air bag module must be deactivated prior to disposal. Failure to deactivate before disposing may result in personal injury since the module contains explosive material.**

WIRING & CIRCUIT DIAGRAMS

Refer to **MOTOR's "Air Bag Manual" or "Air Bag Diagnostics CD,"** for Wiring and Circuit Diagrams.

COMPONENT LOCATIONS

Refer to **MOTOR's "Air Bag Manual" or "Air Bag Diagnostics CD,"** for Component Locations.

DIAGNOSIS & TESTING

Refer to **MOTOR's "Air Bag Manual" or "Air Bag Diagnostics CD,"** for air bag system Diagnosis & Testing procedures.

COLLISION INSPECTION

Except Saturn

On vehicles which have experienced an air bag system deployment, certain air bag system components must be replaced. To determine which air bag system components require replacement, refer to MOTOR's "Air Bag Manual" or "Air Bag Diagnostics CD."

To ensure proper system operation on any vehicle involved in a collision, perform diagnosis and testing procedures outlined in **MOTOR's "Air Bag Manual" or "Air Bag Diagnostics CD."** All system components should be inspected for dents, cracks, exposure to excessive heat and other damage. All air bag system wiring should be inspected for chafing and interference with other vehicle components. The instrument panel should also be inspected. When repairing vehicle, system should be disarmed as outlined in "Air Bag System Disarming & Arming." Also, when performing service procedures, do not expose components or wiring to heat guns, welding or spray guns.

Proper operation of sensors and SIR system requires that any repairs to the vehicle structure must return it to the original production configuration. Deployment requires, at a minimum, replacement of the sensors in the area of accident damage, air bag module and dimensional inspection of the steering column. Any visible damage to the DERM or SDM mounting brackets requires replacement. Any visible damage to the sensors in the area of accident damage must be replaced and the steering column must be inspected whether deployment occurred or not.

1. If any system components are damaged, they must be replaced. If SIR component mounting points are damaged, they must be repaired or replaced.
2. Never use SIR components from another vehicle. This does not include remanufactured components available from General Motors Corporation.
3. Do not attempt to service discriminating sensors, arming sensor, DERM, SDM, SIR coil assembly or air bag module. Service of these items is by replacement only.
4. Verify part number of replacement air bag module. Some GM air bag modules look identical but contain different internal components.
5. After deployment has occurred, SIR diagnostic trouble codes must be cleared using scan tool Clear Codes command. This must be done to turn air bag warning lamp off.

Saturn

In all types of accidents, regardless of air bag module deployment, visually inspect the following components and their mounting points and replace as required:

1. Air bag modules
2. Steering wheel
3. SIR coil assembly
4. Steering column
5. Steering column foam energy absorber
6. Knee bolster and instrument panel mounting attachments
7. Driver's and passengers' seats and belts
8. SDM

If air bag modules deployment has occurred, the SIR coil assembly, SDM and the air bag module(s) must be replaced.

Inspect the SIR coil assembly wiring, steering wheel and righthand side dash panel for signs of scorching, melting or other damage because of excessive heat. If the coil assembly wiring or steering wheel is damaged, replace them. Inspect the steering column and wheel dimensions to determine if they are damaged.

Do not attempt to repair the SDM, the SIR coil assembly, the air bag modules, the steering wheel or the steering column. Service of these items is by replacement only. Verify the replacement part numbers.

Never use SIR components from another vehicle.

Proper operation of the SDM and the SIR system requires that any repairs to the vehicle structure return it to its original production configuration.

STEERING COLUMN POST-COLLISION INSPECTION

1. Inspect steering column assembly capsules. If capsules are not seated securely in bracket slots or if movement exceeds 1⁄16 inch, replace column.
2. **On L-Series,** inspect steering column jacket for collapse by measuring distance between end of bearing assembly and upper bracket lower edge. If distance is below 3.37 inches, replace jacket.
3. **On S-Series,** inspect steering column jacket for collapse by measuring distance between end of bearing assembly and upper bracket lower edge. If distance is below 4.76 inches, replace jacket.

4. **On all models,** remove driver's air bag module as outlined in "Component Service."
5. Remove steering wheel and combination switch as outlined in "Electrical" section of appropriate chassis chapter.
6. Remove Supplemental Inflatable Restraint (SIR) coil and intermediate shaft, then install dial indicator tool No. SA9179NE, or equivalent, with plunger resting against upper portion of steering shaft.
7. Rotate shaft and observe dial indicator. If runout exceeds 1/16 inch, replace steering column assembly.

COMPONENT SERVICE

Driver's Air Bag Module, Replace

ALERO & GRAND AM

1. Disarm air bag system as outlined in "Air Bag System Disarming & Arming."
2. Remove covers and two driver's air bag module mounting bolts from steering wheel rear.
3. Disconnect driver's air bag module electrical connector.
4. Remove air bag module.
5. Reverse procedure to install, noting the following:
   a. Ensure all wiring and electrical connectors are properly routed to avoid pinching.
   b. Arm air bag system as outlined in "Air Bag System Disarming & Arming."

AURORA

1. Disarm air bag system as outlined in "Air Bag System Disarming & Arming."
2. Rotate steering wheel 90° counterclockwise until two slots on rear side are facing straight up.
3. Insert driver's air bag module removal tool No. J-44298, or equivalent, into slots, **Fig. 10.**
4. Push handle back towards instrument panel while releasing two spring loaded fasteners.
5. Rotate steering wheel 180° clockwise until two slots on rear side are facing straight up.
6. Repeat previous removal steps.
7. Carefully pull air bag module away from steering wheel.
8. Record positioning and routing of all electrical connectors and wiring, then disconnect them, as required.
9. Reverse procedure to install, noting the following:
   a. Ensure all wiring and electrical connectors are properly routed to avoid pinching.
   b. Press air bag module firmly into steering column and ensure all its fasteners lock securely into place.
   c. Arm air bag system as outlined in "Air Bag System Disarming & Arming."

BONNEVILLE & LESABRE

1. Disarm air bag system as outlined in "Air Bag System Disarming & Arming."
2. Insert suitable flat-bladed screwdriver into one opening in back of steering wheel.
3. Turn screwdriver counterclockwise to disconnect wire from air bag module slot.
4. Repeat previous steps for three other holes.
5. Pull driver's air bag module gently away from steering wheel.
6. Remove CPA and disconnect driver's air bag module electrical connectors.
7. Remove horn grounded lead from threaded hole in steering wheel.
8. Rotate horn contact lead counterclockwise 1/4 turn and remove from steering column cam tower.
9. Remove driver's air bag module.
10. Reverse procedure to install noting the following:
    a. Ensure all wiring and electrical connectors are properly routed to avoid pinching.
    b. Arm air bag system as outlined in "Air Bag System Disarming & Arming."

CAMARO & FIREBIRD

1. Disarm air bag system as outlined in "Air Bag System Disarming & Arming."
2. Loosen driver's air bag module mounting bolts until module can be released from steering wheel.
3. Remove air bag module, then disconnect air bag module, horn lead and radio control switch electrical connectors.
4. Reverse procedure to install noting the following:
   a. Tighten mounting bolts to specifications.
   b. Arm air bag system as outlined in "Air Bag System Disarming & Arming."

CAVALIER & SUNFIRE

Refer to "Alero & Grand Am" for "Driver's Air Bag Module, Replace" procedure.

CATERA

1. Disable air bag as outlined in "Air Bag Disarming & Arming."
2. Remove driver's air bag module mounting screws from steering wheel rear.
3. Disconnect driver's air bag module electrical connector while removing air bag module.
4. Reverse procedure to install, noting the following:
   a. Tighten mounting bolts to specifications.
   b. Arm air bag system as outlined in "Air Bag System Disarming & Arming."

CENTURY, GRAND PRIX, INTRIGUE & REGAL

1. Disarm air bag system as outlined in "Air Bag System Disarming & Arming."
2. Release four retaining springs securing driver's air bag module to steering wheel rear side of steering wheel using suitable flat-bladed tool, **Fig. 11.**
3. Gently pull on air bag module while releasing leaf springs.
4. Disconnect driver's air bag module electrical connector.
5. Remove air bag module.
6. Reverse procedure to install, noting the following:
   a. Route all wiring and electrical connectors to avoid pinching.
   b. Ensure driver's air bag module snaps into place.
   c. Arm air bag system as outlined in "Air Bag System Disarming & Arming."

CORVETTE

1. Disarm air bag system as outlined in "Air Bag System Disarming & Arming."
2. Remove air bag module mounting screws from steering wheel rear.
3. Carefully lift air bag module.
4. Disconnect air bag module connector, horn wiring harness and ground wire.
5. Remove driver's air bag module.
6. Reverse procedure to install noting the following:
   a. Tighten driver's air bag module mounting screws to specifications, **Fig. 12.**
   b. Connect driver's air bag module electrical connector, then the horn and ground wires.
   c. Install air bag module by pushing on both lefthand and righthand sides until mounting screws snap into place.
   d. Arm air bag system as outlined in "Air Bag System Disarming & Arming."

MALIBU

Refer to "Alero & Grand Am" for "Driver's Air Bag Module, Replace" procedure.

CTS

Refer to "Aurora" for "Driver's Air Bag Module, Replace" procedure.

DEVILLE, ELDORADO & SEVILLE

1. Disarm air bag system as outlined in "Air Bag System Disarming & Arming."
2. Insert suitable flat-bladed screwdriver into one opening in back of steering wheel.
3. Turn screwdriver counterclockwise to disconnect wire from air bag module slot.
4. Repeat previous steps for three other holes.
5. Pull driver's air bag module gently away from steering wheel.
6. Remove CPA and disconnect driver's air bag module electrical connectors.
7. Remove horn grounded lead from threaded hole in steering wheel.
8. Rotate horn contact lead counterclockwise 1/4 turn and remove from steering column cam tower.
9. Remove driver's air bag module.
10. Reverse procedure to install noting the following:
    a. Ensure all wiring and electrical connectors are properly routed to avoid pinching.

b. Arm air bag system as outlined in "Air Bag System Disarming & Arming."

LUMINA

Refer to "Alero & Grand Am" for "Driver's Air Bag Module, Replace" procedure.

METRO

1. Disarm air bag system as outlined in "Air Bag System Disarming & Arming."
2. Remove steering wheel righthand side trim cover, then disconnect module and horn electrical connectors.
3. Remove mounting screws and driver's air bag module.
4. Reverse procedure to install, noting the following:
   a. Tighten mounting bolts to specifications.
   b. Arm air bag system as outlined in "Air Bag System Disarming & Arming."

MONTE CARLO & IMPALA

1. Disarm air bag system as outlined in "Air Bag System Disarming & Arming."
2. Insert suitable flat-bladed screwdriver into one opening in back of steering wheel.
3. Turn screwdriver counterclockwise to disconnect wire from air bag module slot.
4. Repeat previous steps for three other holes.
5. Pull driver's air bag module gently away from steering wheel.
6. Remove CPA and disconnect driver's air bag module electrical connectors.
7. Remove horn grounded lead from threaded hole in steering wheel.
8. Rotate horn contact lead counterclockwise 1/4 turn and remove from steering column cam tower.
9. Remove driver's air bag module.
10. Reverse procedure to install noting the following:
    a. Ensure all wiring and electrical connectors are properly routed to avoid pinching.
    b. Arm air bag system as outlined in "Air Bag System Disarming & Arming."

PARK AVENUE

Refer to "Century, Grand Prix, Intrigue & Regal" for "Driver's Air Bag Module, Replace" procedure.

PRIZM

1. Disarm system as outlined in "Air Bag System Disarming & Arming."
2. Remove steering column side trim panels.
3. Remove driver's air bag module mounting screws from rear of steering wheel.
4. Release CPA and disconnect driver's air bag module electrical connector.
5. Remove driver's air bag module.
6. Reverse procedure to install, noting the following:
   a. Ensure all wiring and electrical connectors are properly routed to avoid pinching.

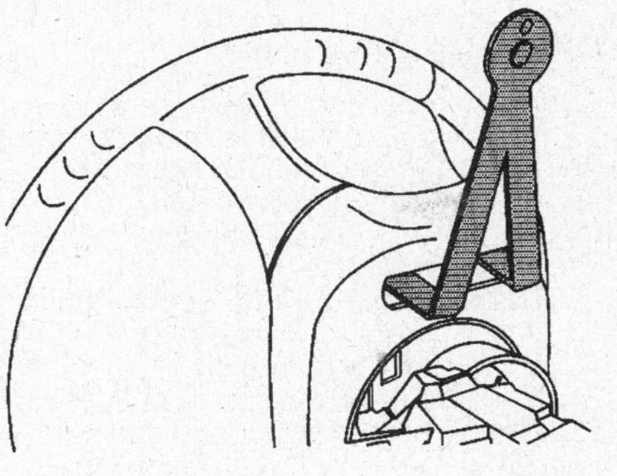

Fig. 10 Driver's air bag module removal. Aurora

   b. Tighten mounting bolts to specifications.
   c. Arm air bag system as outlined in "Air Bag System Disarming & Arming."

SATURN

L-SERIES & ION

1. Disarm air bag system as outlined in "Air Bag System Disarming & Arming."
2. Remove upper steering column shroud.
3. Turn steering wheel to 3 O'clock position.
4. Release spring fastener by inserting suitable flat bladed screwdriver into triangle hole in steering wheel rear cover, turn and lift on module corner nearest fastener.
5. Repeat previous for next fastener.
6. Turn steering wheel to 9 O'clock position.
7. Repeat previous until all spring fasteners are released.
8. Disconnect wiring and remove module.
9. Reverse procedure to install, noting the following:
   a. Ensure all electrical connectors and wiring are properly routed to avoid pinching.
   b. Align air bag studs with holes in steering wheel and press into position.
   c. Press each corner of air bag until all spring retainers snap into position.
   d. Arm air bag system as outlined in "Air Bag System Disarming & Arming."

S-SERIES

1. Disarm air bag system as outlined in "Air Bag System Disarming & Arming."
2. Remove steering column upper shroud.
3. Release spring fasteners by inserting suitable stubby flat-bladed screwdriver into triangle hole in steering wheel rear cover and lifting on corner of air bag closest to fastener
4. Repeat previous steps until all spring fasteners are released.
5. Disconnect electrical connector and remove air bag module.
6. Reverse procedure to install, noting the following:
   a. Ensure all electrical connectors and wiring are properly routed to avoid pinching.
   b. Align air bag studs with holes in steering wheel.
   c. Press each corner of air bag in until all spring retainers snap into position.
   d. Arm air bag system as outlined in "Air Bag System Disarming & Arming."

VIBE

Refer to "Camaro & Firebird" for "Driver's Air Bag Module, Replace" procedure.

XLR

1. Disarm air bag system as outlined in "Air Bag System Disarming & Arming."
2. Install tool No. J-44298, or equivalent, into one of three openings for removing steering wheel module, **Fig. 13.**
3. Seat air bag removal tool all the way in to perform properly, then pull handle air bag tool away from instrument panel releasing one of the spring loaded fasteners, repeat this process for other fasteners.
4. Pull driver's side air bag module away from steering wheel.
5. Remove CPA (4), horn contact (2) and electrical connector's from steering wheel module, **Fig. 14.**
6. Remove driver's side air bag module from steering wheel.
7. Reverse procedure to install, noting the following:
   a. Tighten mounting bolts and nuts to specifications.
   b. Arm air bag system as outlined in "Air Bag System Disarming & Arming."

Passenger's Air Bag Module, Replace

ALERO, GRAND AM & MALIBU

1. Disarm air bag system as outlined in "Air Bag System Disarming & Arming."
2. Unsnap glove compartment from instrument panel.
3. Remove CPA and disconnect air bag module electrical connector, **Fig. 15.**
4. Remove mounting bolts and passenger's air bag module.
5. Reverse procedure to install, noting the following:
   a. Tighten mounting bolts and nuts to specifications.
   b. Arm air bag system as outlined in "Air Bag System Disarming & Arming."

AURORA

1. Disarm air bag system as outlined in "Air Bag System Disarming & Arming."
2. Remove passenger's air bag module electrical connector from instrument panel bracket.
3. Remove instrument panel upper trim

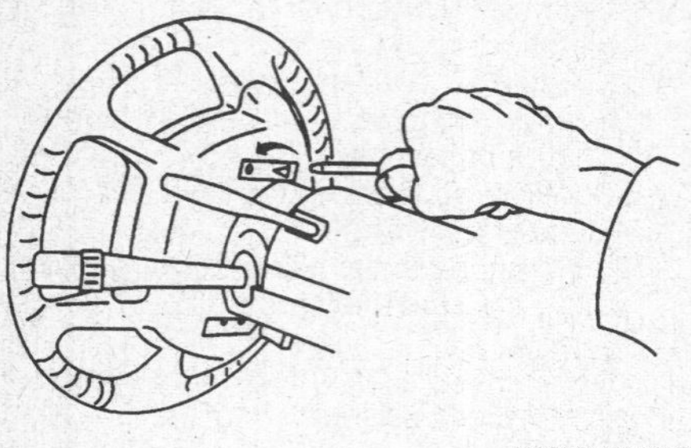
GC8019803083000X

Fig. 11 Releasing driver's air bag module retaining springs. Century, Grand Prix, Intrigue & Regal

pad as outlined in "Dash Panel Service" chapter.
4. Record air bag module wiring harness routing for installation.
5. Move air bag module yellow two-way electrical connector away from instrument panel.
6. Remove air bag module mounting bolts.
7. Carefully lift air bag module out of instrument panel, being careful to protect wiring pigtail.
8. Reverse procedure to install, noting the following:
   a. Ensure all electrical connectors and wiring are properly routed to avoid pinching.
   b. Arm air bag system as outlined in "Air Bag System Disarming & Arming."

BONNEVILLE

1. Disarm air bag system as outlined in "Air Bag System Disarming & Arming."
2. Remove righthand side insulator panel.
3. Remove CPA and disconnect air bag module electrical connector.
4. Remove upper trim pad. **Record passenger's air bag module wire harness routing position to aid installation.**
5. Push inflatable restraint passenger's air bag module yellow two-way connector back away from instrument panel.
6. Remove mounting bolts and passenger's air bag module.
7. Reverse procedure to install, noting the following:
   a. Ensure all wiring and electrical connectors are properly routed to avoid pinching.
   b. Arm air bag system as outlined in "Air Bag System Disarming & Arming."

CAMARO & FIREBIRD

1. Disarm air bag system as outlined in "Air Bag System Disarming & Arming."
2. Remove instrument panel as outlined in "Dash Panel Service" chapter.
3. Remove CPA and disconnect air bag module electrical connectors.
4. Remove mounting bolts and passenger's air bag module, **Fig. 16.**
5. Reverse procedure to install, then arm air bag system as outlined in "Air Bag System Disarming & Arming."

CATERA

1. Disable air bag system as outlined in "Air Bag System Disarming & Arming."
2. Remove righthand side air ducts.
3. Remove air bag trim cover.
4. Remove air bag module mounting bolts, **Fig. 17.**
5. Disconnect air bag electrical harness connector.
6. Remove air bag module.
7. Reverse procedure to install, then arm air bag system as outlined in "Air Bag System Disarming & Arming."

CAVALIER & SUNFIRE

1. Disarm system as outlined in "Air Bag System Disarming & Arming."
2. Remove instrument panel upper trim pad as outlined in "Dash Panel Service" chapter.
3. Remove CPA and disconnect air bag module electrical connector.
4. Remove mounting bolts and passenger's air bag module, **Fig. 18.**
5. Reverse procedure to install, noting the following:
   a. Ensure all wiring and electrical connectors are properly routed to avoid pinching.
   b. Arm air bag system as outlined in "Air Bag System Disarming & Arming."

CENTURY, GRAND PRIX, INTRIGUE & REGAL

1. Disarm air bag system as outlined in "Air Bag System Disarming & Arming" and apply parking brake.
2. Remove instrument panel as outlined in "Dash Panel Service" chapter.
3. Remove CPA and disconnect air bag module electrical connector.
4. Remove mounting bolts and passenger's air bag module, **Fig. 19.**
5. Reverse procedure to install, noting the following:
   a. Ensure all wiring and electrical connectors are properly routed to avoid pinching.
   b. Tighten mounting bolts and nuts to specifications.
   c. Arm air bag system as outlined in "Air Bag System Disarming & Arming."

CORVETTE

1. Disarm air bag system as outlined in "Air Bag System Disarming & Arming" and apply parking brake.
2. Remove instrument panel upper trim pad as in "Dash Panel Service" chapter.
3. Remove CPA and disconnect air bag module electrical connector.
4. Remove mounting nuts and passenger's air bag module, **Fig. 20.**
5. Reverse procedure to install, noting the following:
   a. Ensure all wiring and electrical connectors are properly routed to avoid pinching.
   b. Arm air bag system as outlined in

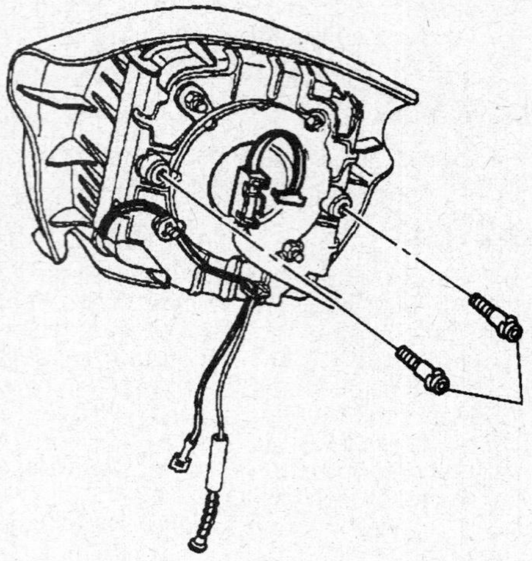
GC8019803084000X

Fig. 12 Installing mounting screws onto driver's air bag module. Corvette

"Air Bag System Disarming & Arming."

CTS

1. Disarm air bag system as outlined in "Air Bag System Disarming & Arming"
2. Remove instrument panel upper trim pad as in "Dash Panel Service" chapter.
3. Remove CPA and disconnect air bag module electrical connector.
4. Remove mounting nuts and passenger's air bag module.
5. Reverse procedure to install, noting the following:
   a. Ensure all wiring and electrical connectors are properly routed to avoid pinching.
   b. Arm air bag system as outlined in "Air Bag System Disarming & Arming."

DEVILLE & ELDORADO

1. Disarm air bag system as outlined in "Air Bag System Disarming & Arming."
2. Remove instrument panel upper trim pad as in "Dash Panel Service" chapter.
3. Remove mounting bolts and air bag module, **Fig. 21.**
4. Reverse procedure to install, noting the following:
   a. Ensure all wiring and electrical connectors are properly routed to avoid pinching.
   b. Arm air bag system as outlined in "Air Bag System Disarming & Arming."

IMPALA

1. Disarm system as outlined in "Air Bag System Disarming & Arming."
2. Remove instrument panel upper trim pad.
3. Remove CPA from passenger's air bag module yellow two-way wiring harness connector.
4. Disconnect passenger's air bag module yellow two-way wiring harness connector.

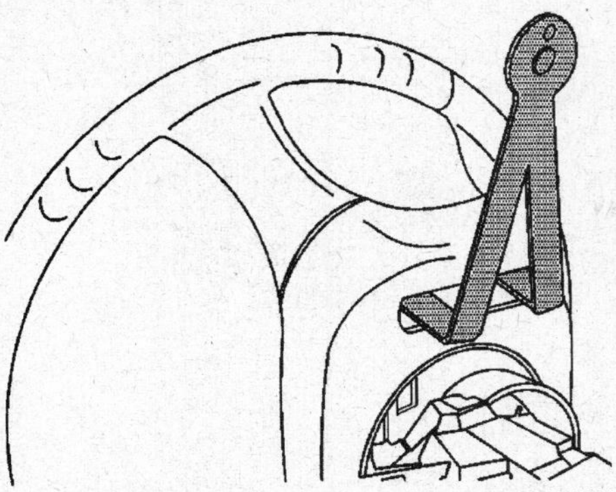

ARM0300000000811

Fig. 13 Driver's side air bag module removal. XLR

5. Remove passenger's air bag module mounting screws, **Fig. 22.**
6. Remove passenger's air bag module from cross-car beam.
7. Reverse procedure to install, noting the following:
   a. Tighten passenger's air bag module mounting screws to specifications.
   b. Arm air bag system as outlined in "Air Bag System Disarming & Arming."

LESABRE

1. Disarm air bag system as outlined in "Air Bag System Disarming & Arming."
2. Remove righthand insulator panel.
3. Remove passenger's air bag module yellow two-way electrical connector from instrument panel bracket.
4. Remove lefthand and righthand windshield garnish moldings.
5. Remove instrument panel as outlined in "Dash Panel Service" chapter.
6. Record electrical connector and wiring routing for installation.
7. Push yellow two-way electrical connector away from instrument panel.
8. Remove mounting bolts, nuts and passenger's air bag module. **Do not damage wiring pigtail.**
9. Reverse procedure to install, noting the following:
   a. Ensure electrical connectors and wiring are properly routed to avoid pinching.
   b. Arm air bag system as outlined in "Air Bag System Disarming & Arming."

PARK AVENUE

Refer to "LeSabre" for "Passenger's Air Bag Module, Replace" procedure.

LUMINA

1. Disarm system as outlined in "Air Bag System Disarming & Arming."
2. Lift up on front edge of passenger's air bag module trim cover and release front studs from retainers, **Fig. 23.**
3. Pull and lift to release passenger's air bag trim cover rear studs from retainers, then remove trim cover.
4. Remove CPA, and disconnect air bag module electrical connector.

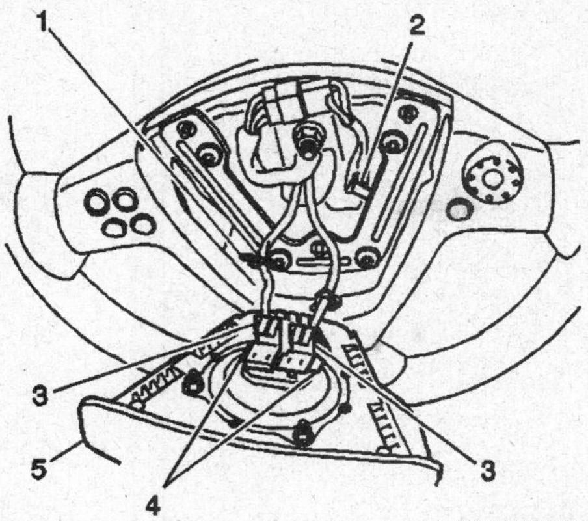

ARM0300000000812

Fig. 14 Driver's side air bag module electrical connector removal. XLR

5. Remove mounting bolts and air bag module.
6. Remove fasteners and cover tether.
7. Reverse procedure to install, noting the following:
   a. Ensure all wiring and electrical connectors are properly routed to avoid pinching.
   b. Arm air bag system as outlined in "Air Bag System Disarming & Arming."

METRO

1. Disarm system as outlined in "Air Bag System Disarming & Arming."
2. Remove glove compartment from instrument panel, as required.
3. Remove mounting bolts and passenger's air bag module, **Fig. 24.**
4. Reverse procedure to install, noting the following:
   a. Tighten mounting bolts and nuts to specifications.
   b. Arm air bag system as outlined in "Air Bag System Disarming & Arming."

MONTE CARLO

Refer to "Impala" for "Passenger's Air Bag Module, Replace" procedure.

PRIZM

1. Disarm air bag system as outlined in "Air Bag System Disarming & Arming."
2. Remove righthand front door sill plate.
3. Remove righthand lower instrument panel trim panel.
4. Remove mounting screws and glove compartment.
5. Disconnect passenger's air bag module electrical connector.
6. Remove mounting screws, nuts and passenger's air bag module, **Fig. 25.**
7. Reverse procedure to install, noting the following:
   a. Ensure all wiring and electrical connectors are properly routed to avoid pinching.
   b. Tighten mounting bolts and nuts to specifications.
   c. Arm air bag system as outlined in "Air Bag System Disarming & Arming."

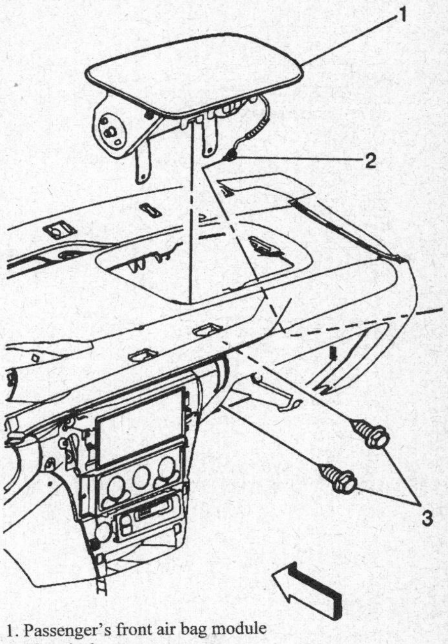

1. Passenger's front air bag module
2. Electrical connector
3. Bolts

GC8019803092000X

Fig. 15 Passenger's air bag module replacement. Alero, Grand Am & Malibu

SATURN

L-SERIES

1. Disarm air bag system as outlined in "Air Bag System Disarming & Arming."
2. Remove glove compartment.
3. Disconnect yellow two-way electrical connector from passenger's air bag module. **Harness on passenger's air bag module should not be removed.**
4. Remove mounting bolts, push air bag rearward and rotate round end downward.
5. Remove air bag through glove compartment opening.
6. Reverse procedure to install, noting the following:
   a. Ensure all wiring and electrical connectors are properly routed to avoid pinching.
   b. Arm air bag system as outlined in "Air Bag System Disarming & Arming."

ION

1. Disarm air bag system as outlined in "Air Bag System Disarming & Arming."
2. Remove the righthand instrument panel trim panel as outlined in "Dash Panel Service" chapter.
3. Remove air bag wire rosebud from instrument panel retainer bracket.
4. Remove air bag module bolts, then pull I/P air bag module out of retainer while depressing one of retaining tabs on retainer with a flat-bladed tool.
5. Reverse procedure to install, then arm air bag system as outlined in "Air Bag

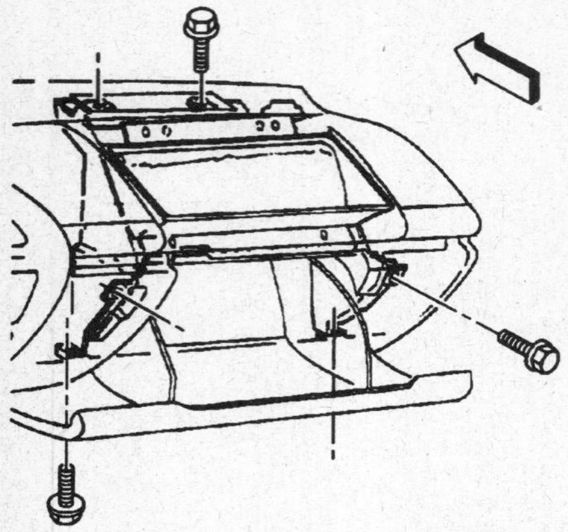

GC8019803095000X

Fig. 16 Passenger's air bag module replacement. Camaro & Firebird

System Disarming & Arming."

S-SERIES

1. Disarm air bag system as outlined in "Air Bag System Disarming & Arming."
2. Remove upper instrument panel trim panel and righthand instrument panel end cap as outlined in "Dash Panel Service" chapter.
3. Separate instrument panel bezel clips
4. Remove passenger's air bag module mounting screws, then the wiring harness from rosebud loop.
5. Remove glove compartment front retainers. Allow compartment bottom to hang on rear pins.
6. Remove passenger's air bag module mounting bolts through hole and opening in top of glove compartment.
7. Grasp air bag module, then pull gently while releasing plastic tabs at each end.
8. Reverse procedure to install, noting the following:
   a. Ensure all wiring and electrical connectors are properly routed to avoid pinching.
   b. Tighten bolts and screws to specifications.
   c. Arm air bag system as outlined in "Air Bag System Disarming & Arming."

SEVILLE

1. Disarm air bag system as outlined in "Air Bag System Disarming & Arming."
2. Remove instrument panel upper trim panel as outlined in "Dash Panel Service" chapter.
3. Disconnect passenger's air bag module electrical connector.
4. Remove four mounting bolts and passenger's air bag module, **Fig. 26.**
5. Reverse procedure to install, noting the following:
   a. Tighten mounting bolts and nuts to specifications.
   b. Arm air bag system as outlined in "Air Bag System Disarming & Arming."

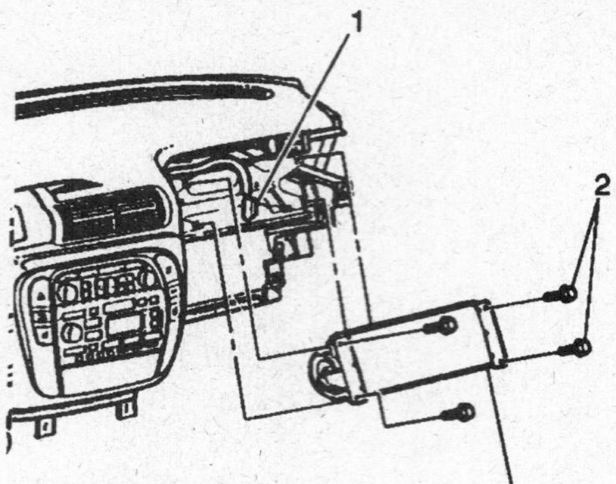

1. Harness pigtail
2. Mounting bolts
3. Passenger's front air bag module
4. Electrical connector

GC8019803096000X

Fig. 17 Passenger's air bag module replacement. Catera

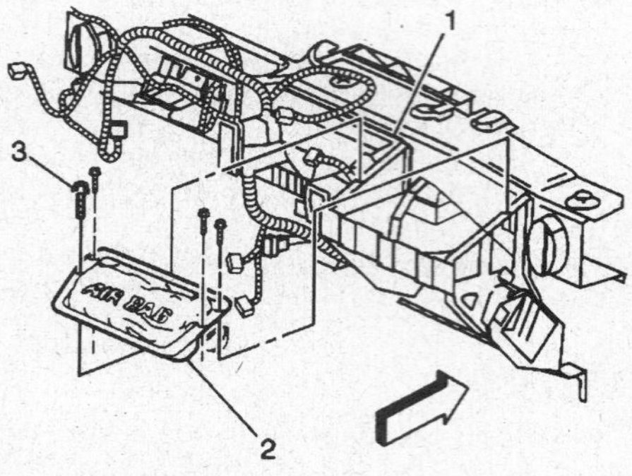

1. Instrument panel
2. Passenger's front air bag module
3. Mounting bolts

GC8019803098000X

Fig. 19 Passenger's air bag module replacement. Century, Grand Prix, Intrigue & Regal

VIBE

Refer to "Alero, Grand Am & Malibu" for "Passenger's Air Bag Module, Replace" procedure.

XLR

1. Disarm air bag system as outlined in "Air Bag System Disarming & Arming."
2. Remove shifter knob, then open center console door.
3. Remove hinge cover from console bin, then pull at rear of cover to disengage retainer.
4. Remove console cupholder, ashtray and trim plate.
5. Remove console retaining nuts.
6. Remove front of console to instrument panel carrier retaining bolts.
7. Lift rear of console slightly and pull rearward to release front of console from under instrument panel carrier.
8. Disconnect accessory plug electrical connector.
9. Remove accessory plug retainer from housing, then the housing from console.

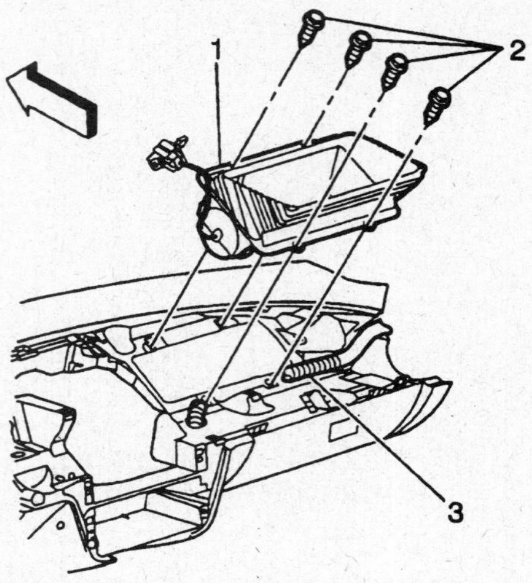

1. Passenger's front air bag module
2. Mounting bolts
3. Electrical connector

GC8019803097000X

Fig. 18 Passenger's air bag module replacement. Cavalier & Sunfire

10. Disengage lamp from retainer using a suitable flat-bladed tool.
11. Push lamp through hole in console bin, then remove console from vehicle.
12. Remove radio as outlined under "Radio, Replace" in "Electrical" section of appropriate chassis chapter.
13. Carefully pry instrument panel courtesy lamp assembly from right lower closeout panel.
14. Remove right lower closeout panel to instrument panel lower support beam push-in retainers.
15. Lower right lower closeout panel slightly, then carefully maneuver left side of closeout panel from above driveline tunnel.
16. Insert courtesy lamp assembly up through closeout panel opening.
17. Remove righthand closeout panel from instrument panel.
18. Pry fuel door and rear compartment lid release switch from knee bolster, then disconnect switch electrical connectors.
19. Remove driver knee bolster trim panel lower retaining screws.
20. Grasp knee bolster trim panel at side edges, then remove trim panel by pulling firmly to release locking tabs.
21. Carefully pry instrument panel courtesy lamp assembly from left lower closeout panel using a suitable flat-bladed tool.
22. Insert instrument panel courtesy lamp assembly up through opening in closeout panel.
23. Release notch in right forward edge of closeout panel from tab on accelerator pedal bracket, then remove lefthand closeout panel.
24. Open door on instrument panel compartment, then disconnect door dampener.

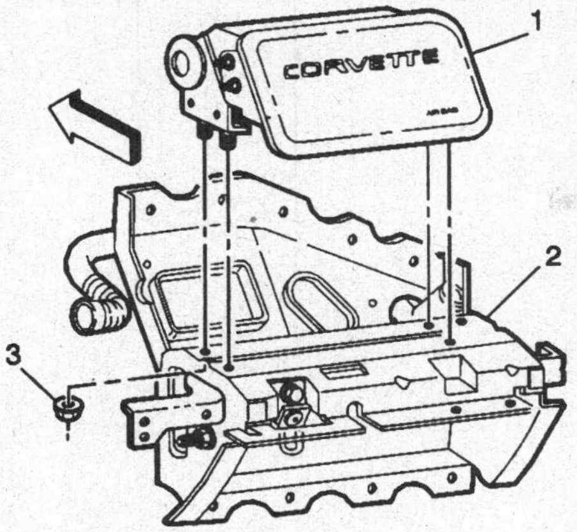

1. Passenger's front air bag module
2. Mounting bracket
3. Nuts

GC8019803099000X

Fig. 20 Passenger's air bag module replacement. Corvette

25. Disconnect instrument panel compartment lamp switch electrical connector.
26. With compartment open, depress both rear corners of compartment and swing compartment down towards floor.
27. Starting at outboard side, release compartment hinge from pin at bottom of door.
28. Slowly pull compartment far enough out of instrument panel to disconnect wiring harness connector from inflatable restraint module switch.
29. Remove instrument panel compartment.
30. Mark location of driver knee bolster bracket for installation reference.
31. Remove driver knee bolster bracket to steering column bracket retaining screws, then the driver knee bolster bracket from instrument panel.
32. Remove retaining screw from bottom of left trim panel.
33. Pull left trim panel outward to disengage retaining clips, then disconnect electrical connectors.
34. Remove fastener attaching top of upper trim panel and windshield side garnish molding to hinge pillar.
35. Unsnap hinge pillar upper trim from hinge pillar.
36. Remove lower hinge pillar trim.
37. Manually open folding top.
38. Pull windshield side garnish molding with its retainers from windshield frame.
39. Remove instrument panel trim pad retaining screws. Screws are located at each end of instrument panel, in center of instrument panel and behind DIC switch.
40. Pull up carefully on instrument panel trim pad to disengage retaining clips.
41. Disconnect sunload/twilight sensor from trim pad, then remove trim pad from vehicle.
42. Carefully lift HUD electrical harness from between instrument panel cluster and HUD.

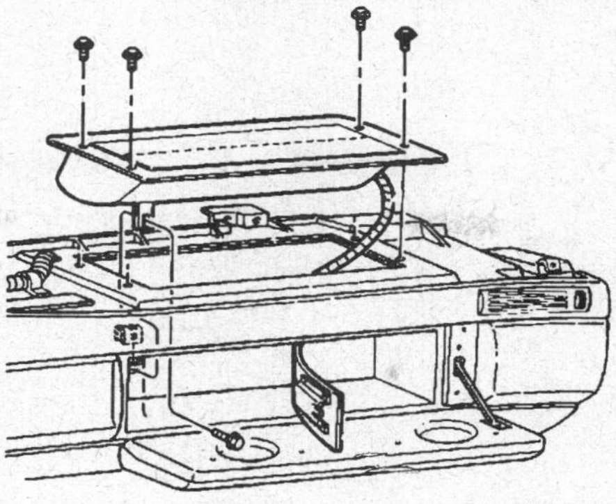

GC8019803100000X

Fig. 21 Passenger's air bag module replacement. DeVille & Eldorado

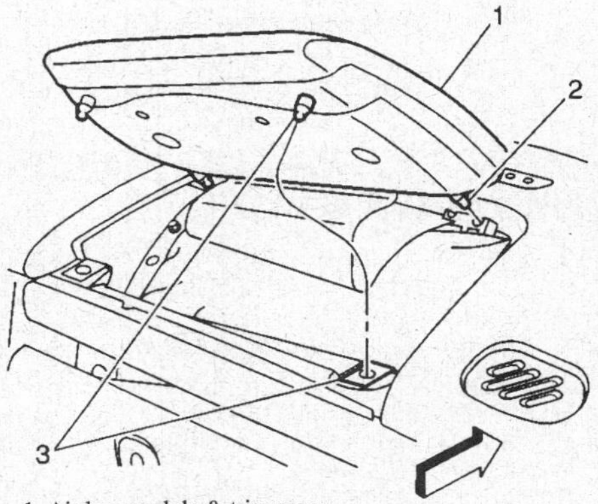

1. Air bag module & trim cover
2. Rear studs & retainers
3. Front studs & retainers

GC8019803082000X

Fig. 23 Passenger's air bag module cover replacement. Lumina

43. Disconnect HUD electrical connector from cluster.
44. Remove cluster to steering column bracket retaining screws.
45. Raise rear of cluster slightly, then disconnect cluster electrical connector.
46. Remove cluster from vehicle.
47. Remove speaker retaining screws from speakers, then lift the speaker out from instrument panel carrier.
48. Disconnect speaker wire harness.
49. Remove GPS antenna to instrument panel carrier plastic rivet retainers, then the GPS antenna with antenna lead from carrier.
50. Remove remote control door lock receiver retaining screws, then the receiver from carrier.
51. Remove steering wheel as outlined under "Steering Wheel, Replace" in "Electrical" section of appropriate chassis chapter.
52. Remove instrument panel carrier retaining bolts and nuts.
53. Remove carrier retaining bolts from lower beam behind compartment door.
54. Remove compartment striker from carrier.
55. Remove instrument panel carrier from

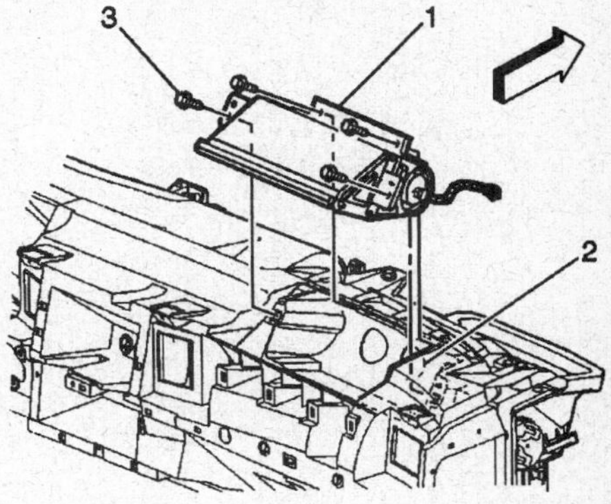

GC8010003838000X

Fig. 22 Passenger's air bag module replacement. Impala & Monte Carlo

mounting, then slowly route all wiring from carrier.

56. Remove instrument panel carrier from vehicle.
57. Remove CPA from I/P module harness connector, **Fig. 27.**
58. Disconnect pigatil connector from I/P.
59. Remove mounting fasteners from I/P, then the I/P module from bracket.
60. Reverse procedure to install, noting the following:
    a. Install new air bag module fasteners.
    b. Ensure all wiring and electrical connectors are properly routed to avoid pinching.
    c. Arm air bag system as outlined in "Air Bag System Disarming & Arming."

Side Impact Air Bag Module, Replace

AURORA

1. Move seat to full forward position.
2. Disarm air bag system as outlined in "Air Bag System Disarming & Arming."
3. Remove seat belt post rear cover from front section.
4. Reach under seat and unzip cushion cover from bottom to top.
5. Remove two outer side impact air bag module mounting nuts. **Do not remove center nut.**
6. Remove top and bottom push-in fasteners from side impact air bag module.
7. Carefully remove side impact air bag module from seat and disconnect electrical connector.
8. Reverse procedure to install, noting the following:
    a. Install new side impact air bag module fasteners.
    b. Ensure all wiring and electrical connectors are properly routed to avoid pinching.
    c. Arm air bag system as outlined in "Air Bag System Disarming & Arming."

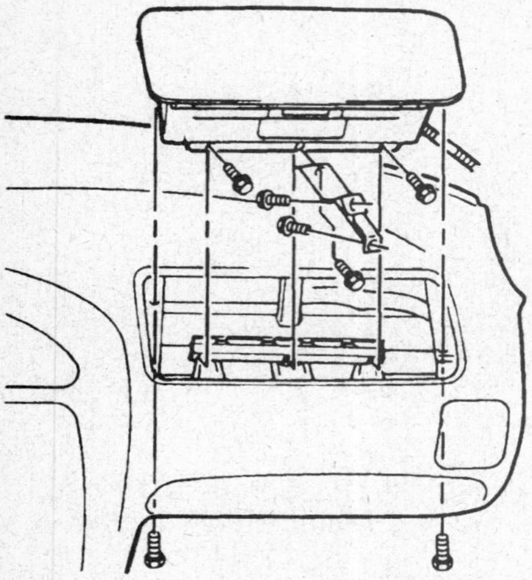

GC8019803081000X

Fig. 24 Passenger's air bag module replacement. Metro

BONNEVILLE & LESABRE

1. Move seat to full forward position.
2. Disarm air bag system as outlined in "Air Bag System Disarming & Arming."
3. Remove seat belt post rear cover from front section.
4. Reach under seat and unzip cushion cover from bottom to top.
5. Remove top and bottom side impact air bag module's outer fasteners. **Do not remove side impact air bag module's center fastener.**
6. Carefully remove side impact air bag module.
7. Remove CPA, and disconnect module electrical connector.
8. Reverse procedure to install, noting the following:
   a. Install new side impact air bag module fasteners.
   b. Ensure all electrical connectors and wiring are properly routed to avoid pinching.
   c. Tighten fasteners to specifications.
   d. Arm air bag system as outlined in "Air Bag System Disarming & Arming."

CATERA

1. Disable air bag as outlined in "Air Bag Disarming & Arming."
2. Position seat in full forward position.
3. Remove mounting screws and seat back panel.
4. Disconnect front seat side impact air bag module electrical connector.
5. Remove mounting nuts and front seat side impact air bag module from seat back.
6. Reverse procedure to install, noting the following:
   a. Ensure air bag module and wiring harness is properly positioned and secured.
   b. Ensure seat back cover is properly positioned.
   c. Install new seat back cover upholstery hooks.
   d. Arm air bag system as outlined in "Air Bag System Disarming & Arming."

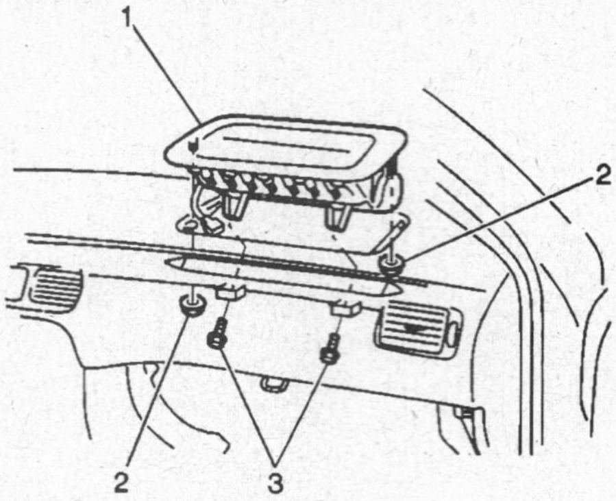

1. Passenger's front air bag module
2. Mounting nuts
3. Mounting bolts

GC8019803076000X

Fig. 25 Passenger's air bag module replacement. Prizm

"Air Bag System Disarming & Arming."

CENTURY, IMPALA, MONTE CARLO & REGAL

1. Disarm air bag system as outlined in "Air Bag System Disarming & Arming."
2. Remove seat.
3. Unclip J-clip along lower rear seatback.
4. Remove seatback cover.
5. Remove lefthand side impact air bag module retainers.
6. Remove lefthand side impact air bag module wiring harness and retaining clip attachments within seat.
7. Remove lefthand side impact air bag module wiring harness retaining clips from seat frame.
8. Gently pull pigtail harness up into seatback while guiding harness through wire triangle of seat frame.
9. Remove lefthand side impact air bag module from seat back frame.
10. Reverse procedure to install, noting the following:
    a. Tighten side impact air bag mounting screws to specifications.
    b. Arm air bag system as outlined in "Air Bag System Disarming & Arming."

CTS

Refer to "Aurora" for "Side Impact Air Bag Module, Replace" replacement procedure.

DEVILLE

1. Disarm air bag system as outlined in "Air Bag System Disarming & Arming."
2. Disconnect power window switch plate clip using suitable ½ inch wide flat-bladed tool.
3. Disconnect electrical connector and remove power window switch.
4. Carefully pry top upper edge of door bezel outward to disconnect three retaining clips.
5. Pull outward and upward to release tabs at bottom of door trim plate.
6. Disconnect electrical connectors, then remove trim plate and door lock switch.

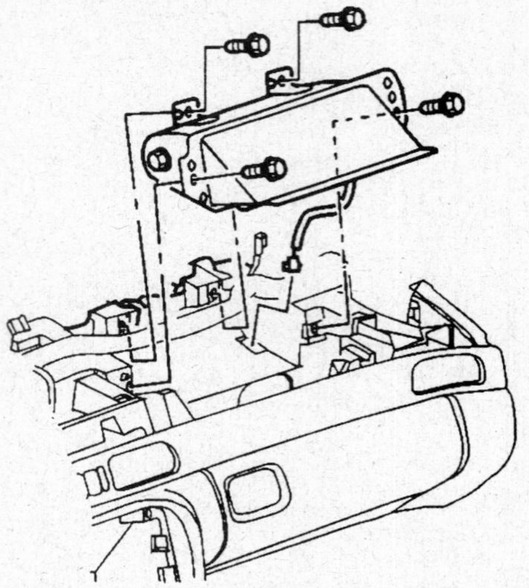

GC8019803080000X

Fig. 26 Passenger's air bag module replacement. Seville

7. Disconnect door trim panel fasteners retaining outside rear view mirror trim cover by gently pulling inboard.
8. Remove two door trim panel mounting screws from front and rear of arm rest.
9. Remove door trim panel by lifting upward and outward to disconnect hooks.
10. Disconnect electrical connectors and remove door trim panel.
11. Disconnect side impact air bag module electrical connector.
12. Remove mounting nuts and side impact air bag module, **Fig. 28.**
13. Reverse procedure to install, noting the following:
    a. Apply thread locking compound part No. 12345382, or equivalent to air bag module mounting stud threads.
    b. Ensure install side impact air bag module arrow faces toward front of vehicle.
    c. Tighten mounting nuts to specifications.
    d. Ensure air bag module and wiring harness is properly positioned and secured.
    e. Arm air bag system as outlined in "Air Bag System Disarming & Arming."

ELDORADO

1. Disarm air bag system as outlined in "Air Bag System Disarming & Arming."
2. Disconnect power window switch plate clip using suitable ½ inch wide flat-bladed tool.
3. Disconnect electrical connector and remove power window switch.
4. Carefully pull trim plate from trim panel.
5. Disconnect lock switch electrical connector and remove trim plate.
6. Remove one door trim panel mounting screw through switch opening.
7. Disconnect retainer behind shark fin using door trim pad clip remover tool No. J-38778, or equivalent.
8. Disconnect fastener using suitable

flat-bladed tool between upper rear corner of carpet and door trim panel. Fold back carpet.
9. Remove door trim panel screw located under carpet.
10. Remove door trim panel by lifting upward and outward to disconnect hooks.
11. Disconnect electrical connectors and remove door trim panel.
12. Disconnect side impact air bag module electrical connector.
13. Remove mounting nuts and side impact air bag module, **Fig. 28.**
14. Reverse procedure to install, noting the following:
    a. Apply thread locking compound part No. 12345382, or equivalent to air bag module mounting stud threads.
    b. Ensure install side impact air bag module arrow faces toward front of vehicle.
    c. Tighten mounting nuts to specifications.
    d. Ensure air bag module and wiring harness is properly positioned and secured.
    e. Arm air bag system as outlined in "Air Bag System Disarming & Arming."

PARK AVENUE

1. Disarm air bag system as outlined in "Air Bag System Disarming & Arming."
2. Move seat to full forward position.
3. Release hook retainers and remove seat back panel cover.
4. Remove seat back panel.
5. Remove side impact air bag top and bottom fasteners. **Do not remove side impact air bag module's center fastener.**
6. Remove side impact air bag.
7. Remove CPA and disconnect side impact air bag electrical connectors.
8. Reverse procedure to install, noting the following:
    a. Install new side impact air bag module fasteners.
    b. Ensure all electrical connectors and wiring are properly routed to avoid pinching.
    c. Tighten fasteners to specifications.
    d. Arm air bag system as outlined in "Air Bag System Disarming & Arming."

PRIZM

1. Disarm air bag system as outlined in "Air Bag System Disarming & Arming."
2. Remove covers and four front seat mounting bolts.
3. Disconnect side impact air bag electrical connector and remove front seat.
4. Remove seat headrest and recliner release handle.
5. Remove front seat cushion shields.
6. Remove side impact air bag wiring harness from protector.
7. Remove seat back cover upholstery rings.
8. Remove four mounting bolts and seat back.

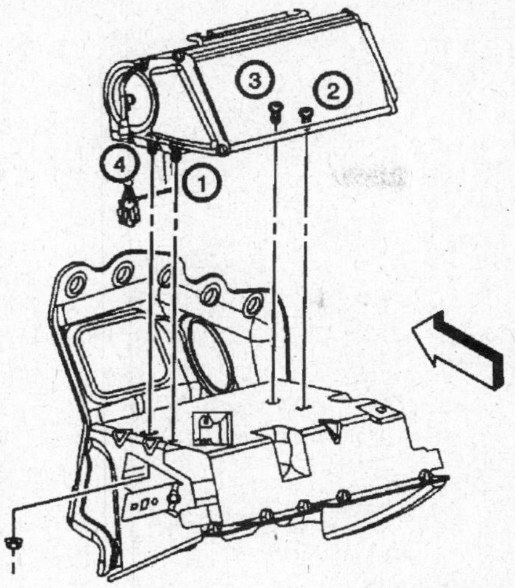

Fig. 27 Passenger's side air bag module removal. XLR

9. Remove seat back frame and two upholstery rings.
10. Remove headrest supports.
11. Remove seat back frame from seat back cover.
12. Remove two mounting nuts and side impact air bag module.
13. Reverse procedure to install, noting the following:
    a. Tighten mounting nuts to specifications.
    b. Ensure air bag module and wiring harness is properly positioned and secured.
    c. Ensure seat back cover is properly positioned.
    d. Install new upholstery hooks.
    e. Arm air bag system as outlined in "Air Bag System Disarming & Arming."

SEVILLE

1. Disarm air bag system as outlined in "Air Bag System Disarming & Arming."
2. Move front seat to full forward position.
3. Remove covers and rear seat track mounting bolts.
4. Move front seat to full rearward position.
5. Remove front seat track cover.
6. Recline front seat fully rearward, tilt seat forward and disconnect front mounting points.
7. Disconnect seat electrical connectors and remove seat.
8. Remove two fasteners and side impact air bag module.
9. Reverse procedure to install, noting the following:
    a. Tighten mounting fasteners to specifications.
    b. Ensure air bag module and wiring harness are properly positioned and secured.
    c. Arm air bag system as outlined in "Air Bag System Disarming & Arming."

VIBE

Refer to "Aurora" for "Side Impact Air Bag Module, Replace" replacement procedure.

XLR

1. Disarm air bag system as outlined in "Air Bag System Disarming & Arming."
2. Position seat rearward, remove push pins and covers from front of adjuster legs.
3. Remove nuts from front of adjuster legs, position seat forward.
4. Remove nuts attaching rear adjuster legs, then disconnect seat electrical connector.
5. Remove seatbelt retaining nut and seatbelt from anchor stud, then the seat.
6. Remove seat back insert, seat speaker grilles and seat speakers.
7. Remove J-hooks that secure seat back cover to bottom of seat back then the fir tree retainers that secure seat back cover to seat back frame.
8. Remove side impact air bag module electrical connectors and clips from seat frame.
9. Remove side impact air bag module.
10. Reverse procedure to install, noting the following:
    a. Tighten mounting fasteners to specifications.
    b. Ensure air bag module and wiring harness are properly positioned and secured.
    c. Arm air bag system as outlined in "Air Bag System Disarming & Arming."

Side Impact Sensing Module (SISM), Replace

DEVILLE & ELDORADO

1. Disarm air bag system as outlined in "Air Bag System Disarming & Arming."
2. Insert blade ¾ inch into door trim panel to disconnect power window switch plate clip using a suitable ½ inch wide flat-bladed tool. Pull tool upward while pressing firmly toward plate to remove switch from door trim panel. **Ensure tool has fully disconnected retaining clip before lifting switch plate upward.**
3. Disconnect power window switch electrical connector, then remove the switch.
4. **On DeVille models,** carefully pry top upper edge of door bezel outward to disconnect three retaining clips. Pull outward and upward to release tabs at bottom of door trim plate. Disconnect electrical connectors, then remove trim plate and door lock switch.
5. **On Eldorado models,** carefully pull trim plate from trim panel. Disconnect lock switch electrical connector, then remove trim plate.
6. **On DeVille models,** remove door trim

panel as follows:

a. Gently pull inboard to disconnect door trim panel fasteners retaining outside rear view mirror trim cover.
b. Remove two door trim panel mounting screws from front and rear of arm rest.
c. Remove door trim panel by lifting upward and outward to disconnect hooks from door.
d. Disconnect electrical connectors and remove door trim panel.

7. **On Eldorado models,** remove door trim panel as follows:
   a. Remove one door trim panel mounting screw through switch opening.
   b. Disconnect retainer behind shark fin using door trim pad clip remover tool No. J-38778, or equivalent.
   c. Insert suitable flat-bladed tool between upper rear corner of carpet attached to door trim panel to disconnect fastener and fold back carpet.
   d. Remove door trim panel screw located under carpet.
   e. Remove door trim panel by lifting upward and outward to disconnect hooks from door.
   f. Disconnect electrical connectors and remove door trim panel.
8. **On all models,** disconnect CPA and SISM connector.
9. Remove mounting fastener and SISM, **Fig. 28.**
10. Reverse procedure to install, noting the following:
    a. Ensure all wiring and electrical connectors are properly routed to avoid pinching.
    b. Tighten mounting nuts to specifications.
    c. Arm air bag system as outlined in "Air Bag System Disarming & Arming."

SEVILLE

1. Disable air bag as outlined in "Air Bag System Disarming & Arming."
2. Remove center pillar trim panel.
3. Disconnect CPA and SISM connector.
4. Remove mounting fastener and SISM.
5. Reverse procedure to install, noting the following:
   a. Tighten mounting nuts to specifications.
   b. Arm air bag system as outlined in "Air Bag System Disarming & Arming."

Side Impact Sensor (SIS), Replace

AURORA

1. Move front seat to full forward position.
2. Disarm air bag system as outlined in "Air Bag System Disarming & Arming."
3. Remove center pillar trim panel.
4. Disconnect SIS electrical connector.
5. Remove mounting bolts and SIS.
6. Reverse procedure to install, noting the following:
   a. Ensure all wiring and electrical connectors are properly routed to avoid pinching.
   b. Tighten mounting bolts to specifications.
   c. Arm air bag system as outlined in "Air Bag System Disarming & Arming."

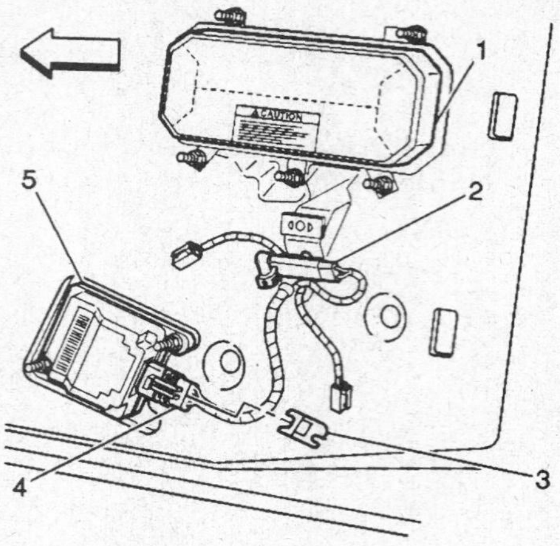

1. Side air bag module
2. Electrical connector
3. CPA
4. Electrical connector
5. SISDM

GC8019803078000X

Fig. 28 Passenger's air bag module replacement. DeVille & Eldorado

BONNEVILLE LESABRE & PARK AVENUE

Refer to "Aurora" for "Side Impact Sensor (SIS), Replace" replacement procedure.

CENTURY, IMPALA, MONTE CARLO & REGAL

Refer to "Aurora" for "Side Impact Sensor (SIS), Replace" replacement procedure.

CATERA

1. Disarm air bag system as outlined in "Air Bag System Disarming & Arming."
2. Remove tweeter speaker from front door trim panel.
3. Pry off assist handle front molding using suitable plastic tool.
4. Unsnap front door handle inside bezel.
5. Remove front door assist handle screws.
6. Remove front power door lock switch.
7. Disconnect power outside rear view mirror switch electrical connector.
8. Remove front door assist handle.
9. Remove front door trim panel courtesy lamp.
10. Remove front door trim panel mounting screws.
11. Remove the trim panel by lift it upward to release from clips.
12. Remove front door water deflector.
13. Disconnect SIS electrical connector.
14. Remove two mounting screws and SIS, **Fig. 29.**
15. Reverse procedure to install, noting the following:
    a. Tighten mounting screws to specifications.
    b. Arm air bag system as outlined in "Air Bag System Disarming & Arming."

CTS

Refer to "Aurora" for "Side Impact Sensor (SIS), Replace" replacement procedure.

DEVILLE, ELDORADO & SEVILLE

Refer to "Aurora" for "Side Impact Sensor (SIS), Replace" replacement procedure.

PRIZM

1. Disarm air bag system as outlined in "Air Bag System Disarming & Arming."
2. Remove front door sill plate.
3. Remove center pillar trim panel.
4. Disconnect SIS electrical connector.
5. Remove mounting screws and SIS, **Fig. 30.**
6. Reverse procedure to install, noting the following:
   a. Ensure all wiring and electrical connectors are properly routed to avoid pinching.
   b. Tighten mounting bolts and nuts to specifications.
   c. Arm air bag system as outlined in "Air Bag System Disarming & Arming."

SATURN

L-SERIES

1. Disarm air bag system as outlined in "Air Bag System Disarming & Arming."
2. Move front seat to forward position.
3. Remove carpet retains around center pillar lower molding.
4. Tape upper molding to center pillar and remove lower molding.
5. Remove mounting bolts and SIS. Disconnect electrical connector.
6. Reverse procedure to install, noting the following:
   a. Tighten mounting screws to specifications.
   b. Arm air bag system as outlined in "Air Bag System Disarming & Arming."

ION

Refer to "Saturn" "S-Series" for "Side Impact Sensor (SIS), Replace" replacement procedure.

S-SERIES

Coupe

1. Disarm air bag system as outlined in "Air Bag System Disarming & Arming."
2. Remove door inner trim panel.
3. Carefully peel back water deflector.
4. Disconnect SIS electrical connector.
5. Loosen mounting screws and remove SIS by sliding out of slotted holes.
6. Reverse procedure to install, noting the following:

a. Position SIS in slotted holes in door structure with screw heads facing outward.
b. Tighten mounting screws to specifications.
c. Arm air bag system as outlined in "Air Bag System Disarming & Arming."

Sedan & Wagon

1. Disarm air bag system as outlined in "Air Bag System Disarming & Arming."
2. Remove B-pillar trim.
3. Disconnect SIS electrical connector.
4. Remove mounting screws, then SIS bracket with sensor and pigtail.
5. Reverse procedure to install, noting the following:
   a. Tighten mounting screws to specifications.
   b. Arm air bag system as outlined in "Air Bag System Disarming & Arming."

VIBE

Refer to "Aurora" for "Side Impact Sensor (SIS), Replace" replacement procedure.

XLR

1. Disarm air bag system as outlined in "Air Bag System Disarming & Arming."
2. Remove side impact sensor retaining bolts, then the sensor from vehicle.
3. Reverse procedure to install, noting the following:
   a. Tighten mounting screws to specifications.
   b. Arm air bag system as outlined in "Air Bag System Disarming & Arming."

Sensing & Diagnostic Module (SDM), Replace

ALERO & GRAND AM

1. Move front seat to the full forward position.
2. Remove righthand front seat adjuster covers.
3. Remove righthand front seat track rear mounting bolts.
4. Disarm air bag system as outlined in "Air Bag System Disarming & Arming."
5. Tilt righthand front seat forward, disconnect floor pan hooks and remove seat.
6. Remove righthand carpet retainer.
7. Lift carpet and insulation up to access SDM.
8. Remove CPA and SDM electrical connector.
9. Remove mounting bolts and SDM.
10. Reverse procedure to install, noting the following:
    a. Install SDM with arrow facing toward front of vehicle.
    b. Arm air bag system as outlined in "Air Bag System Disarming & Arming."

AURORA

1. Move front seats to full forward and remove floor console rear mounting bolts.
2. Move front seats to full rearward and remove floor console front mounting bolts.
3. Disarm air bag system as outlined in "Air Bag System Disarming & Arming."
4. Remove floor console.
5. Roll back carpet at preformed slit to access SDM.
6. Remove CPA and disconnect SDM electrical connector.
7. Remove mounting nuts and SDM.
8. Reverse procedure to install, noting the following:
   a. Ensure all wiring and electrical connectors are properly routed to avoid pinching.
   b. Ensure SDM arrow points toward front of vehicle.
   c. Tighten mounting bolts to specifications.
   d. Arm air bag system as outlined in "Air Bag System Disarming & Arming."

BONNEVILLE & LESABRE

1. **On models equipped with bench seat,** proceed as follows:
   a. Move seat to full rearward and upward position.
   b. Remove track front fasteners.
   c. Move seat to full forward position.
   d. Remove track rear fasteners.
   e. Disarm air bag system as outlined in "Air Bag System Disarming & Arming."
   f. Disconnect seat electrical connectors and wiring.
   g. Remove seat.
   h. Remove rear carpet.
2. **On models equipped with bucket seats,** proceed as follows:
   a. Move both front seats to full forward position.
   b. Remove console rear mounting bolts.
   c. Move both front seats to full rearward position.
   d. Remove console front mounting bolts.
   e. Disarm air bag system as outlined in "Air Bag System Disarming & Arming."
   f. Remove floor console.
3. **On all models,** remove CPA and disconnect SDM electrical connector.
4. Remove mounting bolts and SDM.
5. Reverse procedure to install, noting the following:
   a. Ensure all wiring and electrical connectors are properly routed to avoid pinching.
   b. Tighten mounting bolts to specifications.
   c. Arm air bag system as outlined in "Air Bag System Disarming & Arming."

CAMARO & FIREBIRD

1. Disarm air bag system as outlined in "Air Bag System Disarming & Arming."
2. Apply parking brake.
3. Remove center floor console as outlined in "Dash Panel Service" chapter.
4. Remove CPA and disconnect SDM electrical connector.
5. Remove mounting bolts and SDM.
6. Reverse procedure to install, noting the following:
   a. Ensure SDM is mounted with electrical facing toward rear of vehicle.
   b. Arm air bag system as outlined in "Air Bag System Disarming & Arming."

CATERA

1. Disable air bag systems as outlined in "Air Bag System Disarming & Arming."
2. Remove center console as outlined in "Dash Panel Service" chapter.
3. Remove CPA and disconnect SDM harness connector.
4. Remove mounting bolts and SDM.
5. Reverse procedure to install, noting the following:
   a. Ensure SDM is mounted with arrow facing front of vehicle.
   b. Tighten SDM mounting bolts to specifications.
   c. Arm air bag system as outlined in "Air Bag System Disarming & Arming."

CAVALIER & SUNFIRE

1. Disarm system as outlined in "Air Bag System Disarming & Arming."
2. Pull upward and remove righthand front seat recliner cover.
3. Position righthand front seat forward to access and remove mounting nuts.
4. Position righthand front seat rearward to access and remove mounting nuts.
5. Remove righthand front seat.
6. Remove righthand front sill plate, then lift up carpet and insulation.
7. Remove CPA and disconnect SDM electrical connector.
8. Remove mounting bolts and SDM.
9. Reverse procedure to install, noting the following:
   a. Ensure SDM is mounted with arrow facing front of vehicle.
   b. Arm air bag system as outlined in "Air Bag System Disarming & Arming."

MALIBU

Refer to "Alero & Grand Am" for "Sensing & Diagnostic Module (SDM), Replace" replacement procedure.

CENTURY, GRAND PRIX, IMPALA, INTRIGUE, LUMINA, MONTE CARLO & REGAL

1. Position righthand front seat forward to access and remove seat track rear mounting nuts.
2. Position righthand front seat rearward to access and remove seat track front mounting nuts. Remove seat belt anchor nut or bolt, as required.
3. Disarm air bag system as outlined in "Air Bag System Disarming & Arming."
4. Disconnect power seat electrical connector.

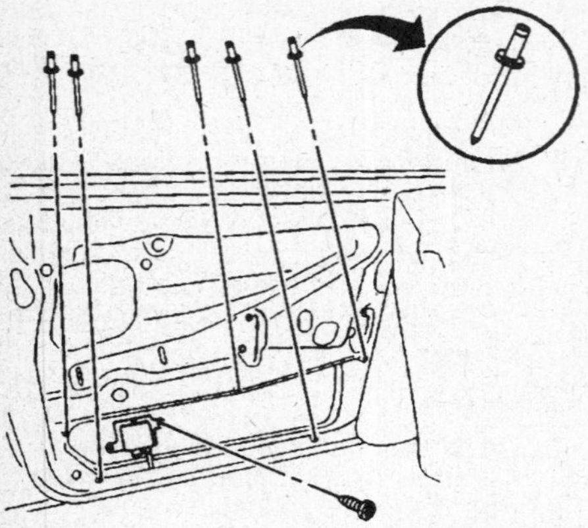

GC8019803079000X

Fig. 29 SIS replacement. Catera

5. Remove righthand front seat.
6. Remove righthand sill carpet retainers and roll carpet aside to access SDM.
7. Disconnect CPA and SDM connector.
8. Remove mounting nuts/bolts and SDM.
9. Reverse procedures to install, noting the following:
   a. Ensure SDM's arrow points forward.
   b. Arm air bag system as outlined in "Air Bag System Disarming & Arming."

CORVETTE

1. Disarm air bag system as outlined in "Air Bag System Disarming & Arming."
2. Remove console as outlined in "Dash Panel Service" chapter.
3. **On models equipped with manual transmission,** remove shift control boot from trim plate.
4. **On all models,** open cigarette lighter door and remove ashtray.
5. Remove instrument accessory panel trim plate grille. Release trim plate grille tab by prying gently at side edge with a suitable tool.
6. Remove trim plate mounting screws next to cigarette lighter and behind ashtray.
7. Remove trim plate mounting screw from grille opening.
8. Grasp sides of accessory trim panel near curve at base.
9. Pull trim panel rearward to release tabs, then lift trim plate to clear tunnel studs.
10. Disconnect electrical connector from cigarette lighter.
11. Lift accessory trim plate over shifter and remove.
12. Remove two A/C heater control assembly mounting screws.
13. Disconnect electrical and vacuum harness.
14. Remove CPA and disconnect SDM electrical connector.
15. Remove mounting bolts and SDM.
16. Reverse procedure to install, noting the following:
    a. Ensure all wiring and electrical connectors are properly routed to avoid pinching.
    b. Tighten mounting bolts to specifications.
    c. Arm air bag system as outlined in "Air Bag System Disarming & Arming."

CTS

Refer to "Aurora" for "Sensing & Diagnostic Module (SDM), Replace" replacement procedure.

DEVILLE & ELDORADO

1. Move driver's seat as far forward as possible.
2. Remove driver's side front seat mounting bolts.
3. Tilt seat forward and disconnect electrical connectors.
4. Disarm air bag system as outlined in "Air Bag System Disarming & Arming."
5. Pull seat rearward and disconnect front retaining hooks, then remove seat.
6. Remove door sill plate.
7. Lift carpet and insulation to access SDM.
8. Remove CPA and disconnect electrical connector.
9. Remove mounting bolts and SDM.
10. Reverse procedure to install, noting the following:
    a. Ensure all wiring and electrical connectors are properly routed to avoid pinching.
    b. Arm air bag system as outlined in "Air Bag System Disarming & Arming."

METRO

1. Disarm air bag system as outlined in "Air Bag System Disarming & Arming."
2. **On models equipped with manual transaxle,** remove gearshift lever upper boot.
3. **On all models,** remove six console mounting screws.
4. Remove console assembly.
5. Remove CPA and disconnect SDM electrical connector
6. Remove mounting bolts and SDM.
7. Reverse procedure to install, noting the following:
   a. Ensure SDM is mounted with arrow pointed toward front of vehicle.
   b. Arm air bag system as outlined in "Air Bag System Disarming & Arming."

PARK AVENUE

1. Move front seat to full forward position.
2. Remove righthand front seat track rear mounting bolts.
3. Remove rear support covers and move seat rearward.
4. Tilt righthand front seat forward and disconnect floor pan hooks.
5. Disarm air bag system as outlined in "Air Bag System Disarming & Arming."
6. Disconnect electrical connectors and remove seat.
7. Remove righthand side front sill plate.
8. Lift carpet and insulation up to gain access to SDM.
9. Remove CPA and disconnect SDM electrical connector.

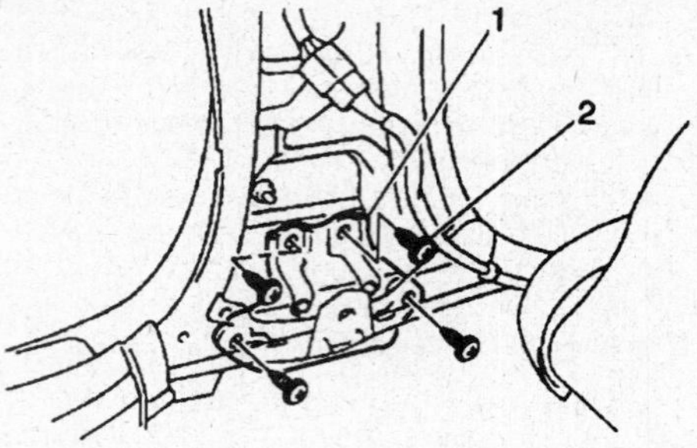

1. Side Impact Sensor
2. Screws

GC8019803077000X

Fig. 30 SIS replacement. Prizm

10. Remove mounting bolts and SDM.
11. Reverse procedure to install, noting the following:
    a. Install SDM with arrow facing toward front of vehicle.
    b. Arm air bag system as outlined in "Air Bag System Disarming & Arming."

PRIZM

1. Disarm air bag system as outlined in "Air Bag System Disarming & Arming."
2. Remove center console outlined in "Dash Panel Service" chapter.
3. Remove underseat duct.
4. Disconnect PCM electrical connectors.
5. Remove PCM fasteners and PCM.
6. Disconnect SDM connector.
7. Remove mounting bolts and SDM.
8. Reverse procedure to install, noting the following:
   a. Install SDM with electrical connector terminals facing toward rear of vehicle.
   b. Arm air bag system as outlined in "Air Bag System Disarming & Arming."

SATURN

L-SERIES

1. Disarm air bag system as outlined in "Air Bag System Disarming & Arming."
2. Remove console front and rear mounting screws.
3. Lift rear end of console.
4. Disconnect SDM electrical connectors.
5. Remove mounting bolts and SDM.
6. Reverse procedure to install, noting the following:
   a. Ensure SDM arrow faces front of vehicle.
   b. Ensure all electrical connectors are properly routed to avoid pinching.
   c. **Do not use any thread locking compounds on SDM mounting bolts. Doing so would interfere with ground path.**
   d. Arm air bag system as outlined in "Air Bag System Disarming & Arming."

ION

Refer to "L-Series" for "Sensing & Diagnostic Module (SDM), Replace" replacement procedure.

S-SERIES

Refer to "L-Series" for "Sensing & Diagnostic Module (SDM), Replace" replacement procedure.

SEVILLE

1. Move front seat to full forward position.
2. Remove righthand front seat track mounting bolt covers.
3. Remove righthand front seat track rear mounting bolts.
4. Move righthand front seat to full rearward position.
5. Remove righthand front seat track cover.
6. Recline righthand front seat fully rearward, tilt seat forward and disconnect front mounting points.
7. Disarm air bag system as outlined in "Air Bag System Disarming & Arming."
8. Disconnect seat electrical connectors and remove seat.
9. Remove righthand carpet retainer.
10. Lift carpet and insulation up to access SDM.
11. Remove CPA and disconnect SDM electrical connector.
12. Remove mounting bolts and SDM.
13. Reverse procedure to install, noting the following:
    a. Install SDM with arrow facing toward front of vehicle.
    b. Tighten mounting bolts to specifications.
    c. Arm air bag system as outlined in "Air Bag System Disarming & Arming."

VIBE

Refer to "Aurora" for "Sensing & Diagnostic Module (SDM), Replace" replacement procedure.

XLR

1. Disarm air bag system as outlined in "Air Bag System Disarming & Arming."
2. Remove instrument panel accessory trim plate.
3. Remove CPA from SDM harness connector.
4. Disconnect SDM harness connector, then remove mounting fasteners.
5. Remove SDM from I/P center suuport.
6. Reverse procedure to install, noting the following:
    a. Tighten to specifications.
    b. Arm air bag system as outlined in "Air Bag System Disarming & Arming."

Forward Discriminating Sensor, Replace

AURORA

1. Disarm air bag system as outlined in "Air Bag System Disarming & Arming."
2. Remove CPA and disconnect sensor electrical connectors.
3. Remove pigtail from mounting clips.
4. Remove mounting bolts and sensor.
5. Reverse procedure to install, noting the following:
    a. Tighten fasteners to specifications.
    b. Arm air bag system as outlined in "Air Bag System Disarming & Arming."

BONNEVILLE, LESABRE & PARK AVENUE

1. Disarm air bag system as outlined in "Air Bag System Disarming & Arming."
2. Remove CPA and disconnect sensor electrical connector.
3. Remove mounting bolts and sensor.
4. Reverse procedure to install, noting the following:
    a. Ensure all wiring and electrical connectors are properly routed to avoid pinching.
    b. Ensure arrow points toward front of vehicle.
    c. Tighten fasteners to specifications.
    d. Arm air bag system as outlined in "Air Bag System Disarming & Arming."

CORVETTE

1. Disarm system as outlined in "Air Bag System Disarming & Arming."
2. Remove air cleaner assembly.
3. Remove CPA and disconnect sensor electrical connector.
4. Remove mounting bolts and sensor.
5. Reverse procedure to install, noting the following:
    a. Ensure all wiring and electrical connectors are properly routed to avoid pinching.
    b. Ensure arrow points toward front of vehicle.
    c. Tighten fasteners to specifications.
    d. Arm air bag system as outlined in "Air Bag System Disarming & Arming."

CAVALIER, GRAND AM & SUNFIRE

1. Disarm air bag system as outlined in "Air Bag System Disarming & Arming."
2. Remove CPA and disconnect sensor electrical connector.
3. Remove mounting bolts and sensor.
4. Reverse procedure to install, noting the following:
    a. Ensure all wiring and electrical connectors are properly routed to avoid pinching.
    b. Ensure arrow points toward front of vehicle.
    c. Arm air bag system as outlined in "Air Bag System Disarming & Arming."

DEVILLE & ELDORADO

1. Disarm air bag system as outlined in "Air Bag System Disarming & Arming."
2. Remove radiator support cover.
3. Remove CPA and disconnect sensor electrical connector.
4. Remove mounting bolts and sensor. Sensor is located behind hood latch.
5. Reverse procedure to install, noting the following:
    a. Ensure sensor is mounted with arrow pointed toward front of vehicle.
    b. Arm air bag system as outlined in "Air Bag System Disarming & Arming."

METRO

1. Disarm air bag system as outlined in "Air Bag System Disarming & Arming."
2. Remove CPA and disconnect sensor electrical connector.
3. Remove mounting bolts and sensor.
4. Reverse procedure to install, noting the following:
    a. Ensure sensor is mounted with arrow pointed toward front of vehicle.
    b. Tighten sensor mounting bolts to specifications.
    c. Arm air bag system as outlined in "Air Bag System Disarming & Arming."

IMPALA & MONTE CARLO

1. Disarm air bag system as outlined in "Air Bag System Disarming & Arming."
2. Remove radiator upper air baffle retainers.
3. Tilt rear of air baffle upward, then slide baffle rearward and disengage clips from fascia support.
4. Remove radiator upper air baffle and deflector.
5. Remove Connector Position Assurance, (CPA), then disconnect sensor electrical connector.
6. Remove sensor attaching bolts, then the sensor from vehicle.
7. Reverse procedure to install, noting the following:
    a. Ensure sensor arrow is pointing toward front of vehicle.
    b. Arm air bag system as outlined in "Air Bag System Disarming & Arming."

PRIZM

LEFTHAND

1. Disarm air bag system as outlined in "Air Bag System Disarming & Arming."
2. Remove lefthand front engine splash shield.
3. Disconnect sensor electrical connector.
4. Remove two mounting nuts and sensor.
5. Reverse procedure to install, noting the following:
    a. Tighten sensor mounting bolts to specifications.
    b. Arm air bag system as outlined in "Air Bag System Disarming & Arming."

RIGHTHAND

1. Disarm air bag system as outlined in "Air Bag System Disarming & Arming."
2. Remove righthand turn signal lamp and headlamp.
3. Disconnect sensor electrical connector.
4. Remove two mounting bolts and sensor.
5. Reverse procedure to install, noting the following:
    a. Tighten sensor mounting bolts to specifications.

b. Arm air bag system as outlined in "Air Bag System Disarming & Arming."

VIBE

Refer to "Aurora" for "Forward Discriminating Sensor, Replace" replacement procedure.

SIR/SRS Coil Assembly, Replace

ALERO & GRAND AM

1. Place front wheels in straight-ahead position.
2. Disarm system as outlined in "Air Bag System Disarming & Arming."
3. Remove driver's air bag module as outlined in "Driver's Air Bag Module, Replace."
4. Remove steering wheel as outlined in "Electrical" section of appropriate chassis chapter.
5. Turn ignition to Lock.
6. Remove coil assembly retaining ring.
7. Remove lock plate, turn signal canceling cam and upper bearing spring, inner race seat and inner race.
8. Place turn signal lever in righthand turn position, then remove multi-function lever and hazard flasher warning knob.
9. Remove mounting screw and turn signal switch lever.
10. Remove mounting screws and allow turn signal switch to hang from wire.
11. Disconnect SIR coil connector from turn signal switch electrical connector.
12. Gently pull SIR coil wire through steering column using mechanic's wire.
13. Remove SIR coil assembly.
14. Reverse procedure to install, noting the following:
    a. Ensure wheels are in straight-ahead position.
    b. Ensure coil assembly is in centered position.
    c. Arm system as outlined in "Air Bag System Disarming & Arming."

AURORA

1. Place front wheels in straight-ahead position.
2. Disarm air bag system as outlined in "Air Bag System Disarming & Arming."
3. Remove driver's air bag module as outlined in "Driver's Air Bag Module, Replace."
4. Pull tilt wheel lever straight out from steering column.
5. Disconnect SIR and electrical connectors.
6. Remove upper and lower steering column covers, as required.
7. Remove retaining ring, SIR coil assembly and wave washer.
8. Reverse procedure to install, noting the following:
    a. New coil assemblies are pre-centered. If centering is required, follow instructions provided on coil assembly service label.
    b. Ensure SIR coil assembly is properly centered.
    c. Ensure all electrical connectors and wiring are properly routed to avoid pinching.
    d. Install tilt wheel lever by aligning it into column and sliding until it locks into position.
    e. Arm air bag system as outlined in "Air Bag System Disarming & Arming."

BONNEVILLE, LESABRE & PARK AVENUE

Refer to "Alero & Grand Am" for "SIR/SRS Coil Assembly, Replace" replacement procedure.

CAMARO & FIREBIRD

Refer to "Alero & Grand Am" for "SIR/SRS Coil Assembly, Replace" replacement procedure.

CATERA

1. Place front wheels in straight-ahead position.
2. Disarm air bag system as outlined in "Air Bag System Disarming & Arming."
3. Remove driver's air bag module as outlined in "Driver's Air Bag Module, Replace."
4. Remove steering wheel as outlined in "Electrical" section of appropriate chassis chapter.
5. Remove upper steering column covers.
6. Carefully thread out steering wheel tilt mechanism using suitable non-marring tool.
7. Remove lock cylinder rubber protective cover, mounting screws and lower steering column cover.
8. Disconnect electrical connector and remove SIR coil assembly.
9. Reverse procedure to install. Center SIR coil assembly as follows:
    a. Ensure front wheels are in straight-ahead position.
    b. New SIR coil are pre-centered.
    c. Holding outer casing, depress locking tab and carefully turn center counterclockwise until resistance is felt.
    d. Turn center 2½ turns clockwise, aligning arrows.

CAVALIER & SUNFIRE

Refer to "Alero & Grand Am" for "SIR/SRS Coil Assembly, Replace" replacement procedure.

CENTURY, GRAND PRIX, INTRIGUE & REGAL

1. Disarm system as outlined in "Air Bag System Disarming & Arming."
2. Remove driver's air bag module as outlined in "Driver's Air Bag Module, Replace."
3. Ensure wheels are in straight-ahead position, then remove steering wheel nut.
4. Remove steering wheel as outlined in "Electrical" section of appropriate chassis chapter.
5. Remove lefthand underdash panel and filler trim panel below steering column.
6. Remove lefthand knee bolster and disconnecting alarm system motion sensor, if equipped.
7. **On models equipped with tilt steering column,** pull tilt lever from column. Wriggle lever while pulling outward.
8. **On all models,** remove lower steering column cover mounting screws.
9. Tilt cover down and pull rearward to disconnect tabs from column.
10. While supporting steering column, remove upper and lower steering column mounting bolts.
11. Lower column onto suitable supports. **Do not allow column to hang from bolts or wiring.**
12. Remove upper steering column cover mounting screws.
13. Lift upper cover sufficiently to gain access to lock tumbler removal hole.
14. Turn and hold ignition in Start position.
15. Insert a 1⁄16 inch hex wrench into lock tumbler removal hole, press down with wrench and release ignition to Run position while pulling tumbler from ignition.
16. **On models equipped with ignition trim ring,** record position for assembly reference.
17. **On all models,** remove upper steering column cover.
18. Ensure block tooth centering mark of steering shaft is in 12 o'clock position.
19. Remove SIR coil retaining ring, SIR coil and wave washer. Discard retaining ring.
20. Remove wire straps and disconnect SIR coil wiring connectors.
21. Reverse procedure to install, noting the following:
    a. Ensure SIR coil is centered.
    b. Ensure block tooth centering mark of steering shaft is in 12 o'clock position.
    c. Install new SIR coil retaining ring.
    d. Ensure ignition assembly is in Run position when installing tumbler.
    e. **On models equipped with trim ring,** align as recorded during disassembly.

CORVETTE

1. Place front wheels in straight-ahead position.
2. Disarm air bag system as outlined in "Air Bag System Disarming & Arming."
3. Remove steering column upper and lower covers.
4. Remove driver's air bag module as outlined in "Driver's Air Bag Module, Replace."
5. Remove steering wheel as outlined in "Electrical" section of appropriate chassis chapter.
6. Remove wire harness straps from steering wheel column wire harness.
7. Remove retaining ring, SIR coil assembly and wave washer.
8. Reverse procedure to install, noting following:
    a. Center race and upper shaft assembly.
    b. Center SIR coil assembly.
    c. Ensure front wheels are in straight-ahead position.

d. Center block tooth and shaft assembly centering mark at 12 o'clock position.
e. Align coil with horn tower.

MALIBU

Refer to "Alero & Grand Am" for "SIR/SRS Coil Assembly, Replace" replacement procedure.

CTS

Refer to "Aurora" for "SIR/SRS Coil Assembly, Replace" replacement procedure.

DEVILLE, ELDORADO & SEVILLE

Refer to "Alero & Grand Am" for "SIR/SRS Coil Assembly, Replace" replacement procedure.

IMPALA

1. Disarm system as outlined in "Air Bag System Disarming & Arming."
2. Remove driver's air bag module as outlined in "Driver's Air Bag Module, Replace."
3. Remove steering column upper and lower shrouds.
4. Remove steering wheel as outlined in "Electrical" section of appropriate chassis chapter.
5. Disconnect eight-way inline connector located at base of steering column.
6. Remove tire wire harness straps from steering wheel column wire harness.
7. Remove retaining ring.
8. Remove steering wheel module coil.
9. Reverse procedure to install. Arm air bag system as outlined in "Air Bag System Disarming & Arming."

LUMINA

Refer to "Alero & Grand Am" for "SIR/SRS Coil Assembly, Replace" replacement procedure.

METRO

1. Place front wheels in straight-ahead position.
2. Disarm air bag system as outlined in "Air Bag System Disarming & Arming."
3. Remove driver's air bag module as outlined in "Driver's Air Bag Module, Replace."
4. Remove steering wheel as outlined in "Electrical" section of appropriate chassis chapter.
5. Remove steering column upper and lower covers.
6. Remove SRS coil and combination switch electrical wiring harness connectors and bands.
7. Remove mounting screws and SRS coil assembly.
8. Reverse procedure to install. Center SRS coil assembly as follows:
   a. Ensure front wheels are in straight-ahead position.
   b. Turn coil counterclockwise until stop is contacted.
   c. Turn coil assembly two and a half turns clockwise, aligning arrows.

MONTE CARLO

Refer to "Impala" for "SIR/SRS Coil Assembly, Replace" replacement procedure.

PRIZM

1. Place front wheels in straight-ahead position.
2. Disarm air bag system as outlined in "Air Bag System Disarming & Arming."
3. Remove driver's air bag module as outlined in "Driver's Air Bag Module, Replace."
4. Disconnect electrical connectors.
5. Remove steering wheel as outlined in "Electrical" section of appropriate chassis chapter.
6. Remove steering column upper and lower covers.
7. Remove lefthand front carpet retainer and disconnect hood release lever.
8. Remove trim caps, mounting bolts and knee bolster from instrument panel.
9. Remove tape holding SRS coil wiring harness to combination switch wiring harness and disconnect electrical connector.
10. Remove mounting screws and SRS coil assembly.
11. Reverse procedure to install. Center SRS coil assembly as follows:
    a. Ensure front wheels are in straight-ahead position.
    b. Turn coil counterclockwise until stop is contacted.
    c. Turn coil assembly three turns clockwise, aligning red marks.

SATURN

1. Place front wheels in straight-ahead position.
2. Disarm air bag system as outlined in "Air Bag System Disarming & Arming."
3. Remove driver's air bag module as outlined in "Driver's Air Bag Module, Replace."
4. Remove steering wheel as outlined in "Electrical" section of appropriate chassis chapter.
5. Remove steering column upper and lower shrouds.
6. Remove SIR coil assembly from lever control switch. **If coil is removed without wheels facing straight ahead and steering wheel has not been moved, original coil can be installed if coil hub also has not been rotated.**
7. Reverse procedure to install, noting the following:
   a. Route SIR coil pigtail down steering column and install SIR coil to lever control switch.
   b. Route wiring through steering wheel.
   c. Replacement SIR coil assemblies are equipped with yellow tab that is to be removed after steering wheel is installed. This tab must pass through steering wheel at pass-through hole.
   d. Arm air bag system as outlined in "Air Bag System Disarming & Arming."

VIBE

Refer to "Alero & Grand Am" for "SIR/SRS Coil Assembly, Replace" replacement procedure.

XLR

1. Disarm air bag system as outlined in "Air Bag System Disarming & Arming."
2. Remove steering wheel as outlined in "Electrical" section of chassis chapter.
3. **On models equipped with tilt steering column,** pull lever straight out from steering column.
4. **On all models,** remove lower and upper steering column shroud covers.
5. Remove wiring harness straps from column wiring harness.
6. Remove retaining ring, then the SIR coil from steering shaft, **Fig. 31.**
7. Reverse procedure to install. Center SRS coil assembly as follows:
   a. Ensure front wheels are in straight-ahead position.
   b. Align tooth and centering mark on race and upper shaft assembly at 12 o'clock position, **Fig. 32.**
   c. Ensure ignition switch is in Lock position.
   d. If front of SIR coil has a centering window, and back side has a spring service lock, perform following steps. Hold coil with face up while depressing spring service lock, rotate coil hub clockwise until coil ribbon stops.
   e. Rotate coil hub slowly, counterclockwise, until centering window appears yellow and both arrows line up. Release spring service lock between locking tab, SIR coil is now centered.
   f. Align centered SIR coil with horn tower and slide onto steering shaft assembly.
   g. If front of SIR coil has a centering window and back side has NO spring service lock, perform following steps. Hold coil with face up, rotate coil hub clockwise until coil ribbon stops. Rotate coil hub slowly, counterclockwise until centering window appears yellow and both arrows line up. This is the CENTER position.
   h. While holding coil hub in CENTER position, align coil with horn tower and slide coil onto steering shaft assembly.
   i. If no centering window is present on front side of SIR coil, but a spring service lock is on back side, perform the following steps. Hold coil with back side up, while depressing spring service lock, rotate coil hub in direction of arrow until coil ribbon stops. Still pressing spring service lock, rotate coil hub in opposite direction 2½ revolutions.
   j. Release spring service lock between locking tabs. The SIR coil is now centered. Align centered coil with horn tower and slide coil onto steering shaft assembly.

k. If no centering window appears on front side of SIR coil and no spring service lock exists on back side, perform the following steps. Hold coil with face up, rotate coil hub in direction of arrow until coil ribbon stops. Rotate coil hub, slowly, counterclockwise, for 2½ revolutions.
l. This is CENTER position. While maintaining coil hub in th CENTER position, align centered coil with horn tower and slide coil onto steering shaft assembly.
m. Install new clips and guides.
o. Arm air bag system as outlined in "Air Bag System Disarming & Arming."

Roof Panel Air Bag Module, Replace

CTS

Refer to "Saturn" "L-Series" for "Roof Panel Air Bag Module, Replace" replacement procedure.

SATURN

L-SERIES

1. Disarm air bag system as outlined in "Air Bag System Disarming & Arming."
2. Remove headliner and garnish molding.
3. Remove tabs, clips and roof panel air bag module.
4. Reverse procedure to install, noting the following:
   a. Install new clips and guides.
   b. Arm air bag system as outlined in "Air Bag System Disarming & Arming."

ION

Refer to "Saturn" "L-Series" for "Roof Panel Air Bag Module, Replace" replacement procedure.

S-SERIES

1. Disarm air bag system as outlined in "Air Bag System Disarming & Arming."
2. Record positioning of door weatherstrips over headliner.
3. Carefully remove headliner. **Do not bend.**
4. Loosen roof panel air bag module bolts.
5. Disconnect roof panel air bag module from cross-car beam by lifting.
6. Remove lower module fill tube and tether mounting bolt.
7. Remove upper fill tube mounting bolt.
8. Remove roof panel air bag module mounting bolts.
9. **On coupe models,** when replacing driver's air bag module, remove module from channel by disengaging straps.
10. **On all models,** disconnect module tether from Velcro location.
11. Remove remaining roof panel air bag module and tether bolts.
12. Remove roof panel air bag module.
13. Reverse procedure to install, noting the following:
    a. **On Coupe models,** position module into channel and fasten straps.
    b. **On all models,** tighten mounting bolts to specifications.
    c. Route tether below last roof panel air bag module bolt. **Ensure tether does not hang below edge of headliner.**
    d. Arm air bag system as outlined in "Air Bag System Disarming & Arming."

Air Bag Module Disposal

The air bag modules must be deactivated before disposal. The module contains explosive material. Failure to deactivate before disposing may result in personal injury.

When a deployed air bag module has been removed from a vehicle, it may be disposed of with any other scrap material. Handle with gloves and safety glasses, then wash hands after handling.

INSIDE VEHICLE

On models equipped with dual stage modules, they are used in both driver's and passenger's air bag modules. Both deployment loops must be energized to deploy the air bag. A deployed dual stage module looks the same whether one or both stages were used. Always assume a deployed dual stage module has an active stage 2.

Some vehicles with SIR systems that have live (undeployed) air bag modules may have to be scrapped because they have completed their useful life or have been severely damaged in a non-deployment type accident. The following procedure should be followed when scrapping a vehicle with an undeployed module:

1. Turn ignition switch to Off position and remove key.
2. Ensure steering wheel module is secured to steering wheel and that there is nobody in vehicle.
3. Remove all loose objects from vehicle.
4. Disconnect driver's air bag module coil connector.
5. **On models equipped with dual stage air bags,** the driver's and passenger's air bag modules will each have four wires.
6. **On all models,** cut lower steering column connector from vehicle harness leaving at least six inches of wire at connector.
7. **On models equipped with dual stage air bags,** twist high circuit wires from both stages together.
8. **On all models,** splice two 18 gauge (or thicker) wires, at least 30 feet long, into driver's air bag module circuit wiring.
9. Stretch wires out of lefthand side of vehicle to their full length.
10. Disconnect lefthand side impact air bag module connector.
11. Cut lefthand side impact air bag module connector out of vehicle leaving at least six inches of wire at connector.
12. Splice two 18 gauge (or thicker) wires, at least 30 feet long, into lefthand side impact air bag module circuit wiring.
13. Stretch wires out of lefthand side of vehicle to their full length.
14. Disconnect passenger's air bag module connector.
15. Cut passenger's module connector out of vehicle leaving at least six inches of wire at connector.
16. **On models equipped with dual stage air bags,** twist high circuit wires from both stages together.
17. **On all models,** splice two 18 gauge (or thicker) wires, at least 30 feet long, into passenger's air bag module circuit wiring.
18. Stretch wires out of righthand side of vehicle to their full length.
19. Completely cover windshield and front door openings with suitable drop cloth.
20. Deploy each deployment loop one at a time using fully charged battery, apply 12 volts across wires.
21. **Do not touch air bag modules for 20 minutes because of heat generated by deployment.**
22. Remove drop cloth.
23. Disconnect and discard harnesses.
24. **If one or more of air bag modules did not deploy, contact General Motors.**

OUTSIDE VEHICLE

On models equipped with dual stage modules, they are used in both driver's and passenger's air bag modules. Both deployment loops must be energized to deploy the air bag. A deployed dual stage module looks the same whether one or both stages were used. Always assume a deployed dual stage module has an active stage 2.

1. Disarm air bag system as outlined in "Air Bag System Disarming & Arming."
2. Remove air bag module, as follows:
   a. Remove driver's air bag module as outlined in "Driver's Air Bag Module, Replace."
   b. Remove passenger's air bag module as outlined in "Passenger's Air Bag Module, Replace."
   c. Remove side impact air bag module as outlined in "Side Impact Air Bag Module, Replace."
3. Position air bag module in secured paved outdoor location free of activity and clear in at least six-foot diameter. Ensure sufficient ventilation.
4. Position driver's air bag module in center of area with pad side facing upward.
5. If deploying passenger's or side impact air bag module, proceed as follows:
   a. Place deployment fixture tool No. J-39401-B, or equivalent, in center of cleared area.
   b. Fill plastic reservoir with water or sand.
   c. Mount arms tool No. J-39401-7A, or equivalent, to fixture using suitable carriage bolts and nuts.
   d. Mount air bag module into fixture with vinyl trim cover facing upwards. Secure in place using suitable nuts, bolts and washers.
6. Connect deployment harness tool No. J-38826, or equivalent, to air bag module.

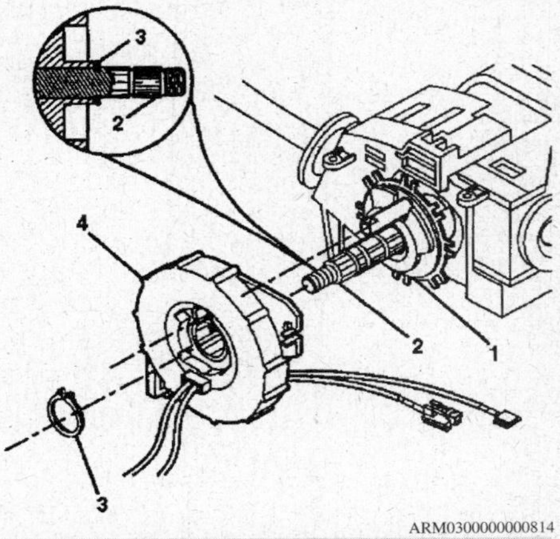

Fig. 31 SIR coil removal. XLR

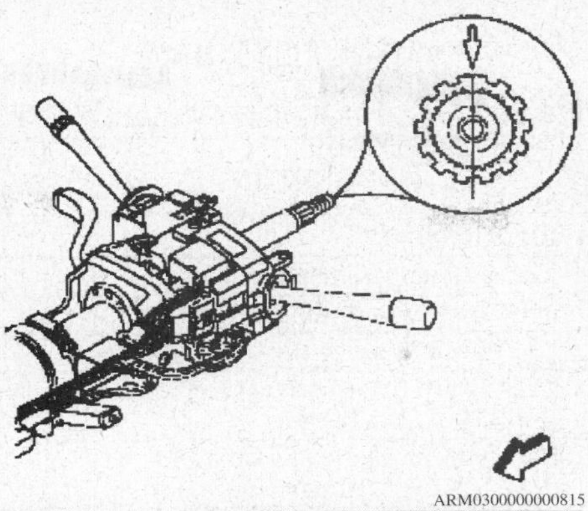

Fig. 32 SIR coil centering & alignment. XLR

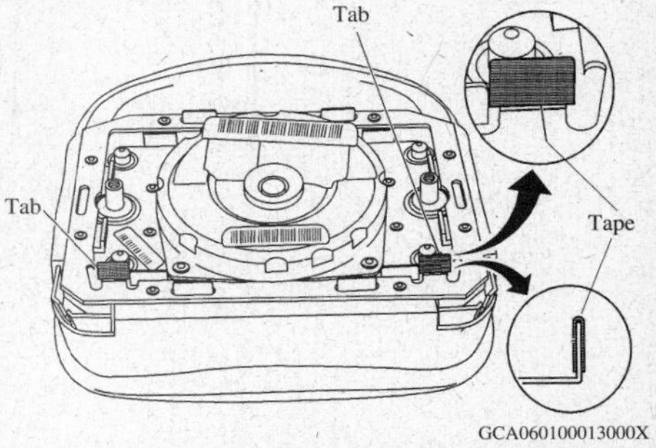

Fig. 33 Flocking tape installation. 2000–01 Camaro & Firebird

7. Stretch wires away from air bag module to their full length.
8. Ensure no people, animals or objects are in area of air bag unit.
9. Apply 12 volts across wires to deploy module using fully charged battery.
10. **Do not touch air bag module for 20 minutes, because of heat generated by deployment.**
11. **If air bag module fails to deploy, contact General Motors.**

TECHNICAL SERVICE BULLETINS

Steering Wheel Squeaks

2000–01 CAMARO & FIREBIRD

On some of these models built before Feb. 1, 2001, there may be a steering wheel squeak when turning.

This condition may be caused by air bag module mounting tabs contacting the inner steering wheel.

To correct this condition, proceed as follows:

1. Disarm air bag.
2. Remove mounting screws, air bag module and CPA.
3. Disconnect radio controls, as required.
4. Cut two pieces of adhesive flocking tape (part No. 12378189) to ⅝ by ¾ inch.
5. Clean mounting tabs using suitable dray shop rags.
6. Install tape on each tab, **Fig. 33.**
7. Connect and install air bag module. **Torque** mounting screws to 25 inch lbs.
8. Arm air bag.

TIGHTENING SPECIFICATIONS

Year	Component	Torque/Ft. Lbs.
ALERO		
2000–04	Driver's Air Bag Module	89①
	Front Seat Adjuster	30
	SDM	89①
	Steering Column Lower Cover	18①
	Steering Wheel	27
AURORA		
2001–04	Front Seat Anchor	22
	Passenger's Air Bag Module	80①
	Rear Seatback To Floor	30
	SDM	80①
	Side Impact Air Bag Module	80①
	Side Impact Air Bag Module Sensor	80①
	Steering Column Lower Shroud	31①
	Steering Column Upper Shroud	13①
	Steering Wheel	30
BONNEVILLE		
2000–04	Front Seat Anchor	22
	Passenger's Air Bag Module	89①
	SDM	80①
	Side Impact Air Bag Module	80①
	SIS	80①
	Steering Wheel	30

Continued

TIGHTENING SPECIFICATIONS—Continued

Year	Component	Torque/Ft. Lbs.
CAMARO & FIREBIRD		
2000–02	Driver's Air Bag Module	25①
	Floor Console	71①
	Passenger's Air Bag Module	28①
	Passenger's Air Bag Module Bracket, Lower	25①
	Passenger's Air Bag Module Bracket, Upper	53①
	SDM	71①
	Steering Wheel	32
CATERA		
2000–01	Driver's Air Bag Module	72①
	Front Seat Track	19
	Passenger's Air Bag Module	89①
	SDM	89①
	Seat Belt Pretensioner	26
	Side Impact Air Bag Module	45①
	SIS	45①
	Steering Wheel	21
CAVALIER & SUNFIRE		
2000–04	Driver's Air Bag Module	89①
	Front Seat Track	18
	Instrument Panel Trim Pad	18①
	Passenger's Air Bag Module	31①
	SDM	10
	Steering Wheel	27
CENTURY & REGAL		
2000–04	Floor Console	44①
	Front Seat Adjuster	18
	Instrument Panel Trim Pad	15
	Instrument Panel Trim Pad To Lower Hinge Pillar	15
	Passenger's Air Bag Module	89①
	SDM (After Modifications)	44①
	SDM (Original Fasteners)	89①
	Side Air Bag Module	89①
	SIS	89①
	Steering Column	18
	Steering Wheel	33
CORVETTE		
2000–04	Driver's Air Bag Module	54①
	Floor Console	89①
	Passenger's Air Bag Module	89①
	SDM	10
	Steering Wheel	30

Continued

TIGHTENING SPECIFICATIONS—Continued

Year	Component	Torque/Ft. Lbs.
CTS		
2003–04	Front Seat Anchor	22
	Passenger's Air Bag Module	80①
	Rear Seatback To Floor	30
	Roof Panel Air Bag Module	71①
	SDM	80①
	Side Impact Air Bag Module	80①
	Side Impact Air Bag Module Sensor	80①
	Steering Column Lower Shroud	31①
	Steering Column Upper Shroud	13①
	Steering Wheel	30
DEVILLE		
2000–04	Instrument Panel Upper Trim Pad	18①
	Passenger's Air Bag Module	16
	SDM	80①
	Seat Belt Pretensioner	30
	Side Impact Air Bag Module	80①
	SIS	80①
	Steering Column Shroud	13①
	Steering Wheel	30
ELDORADO		
2000–02	Driver's Air Bag Module	27①
	Forward Discriminating Sensor	98①
	Front Seat	24
	Instrument Panel Upper Trim Pad	18①
	Passenger's Air Bag Module	18①
	SDM (After Modifications)	12
	SDM (Original Fasteners)	80①
	SDM Ground (After Modifications)	12
	SDM Ground (Original Fasteners)	54①
	Side Air Bag Module	80①
	SISM	80①
	Steering Wheel	30
GRAND AM		
2000–04	Driver's Air Bag Module	89①
	Front Seat Adjuster	30
	SDM	89①
	Steering Column Lower Cover	18①
	Steering Wheel	27
GRAND PRIX & INTRIGUE		
2000–04	Front Bench Seat Adjuster	18
	Front Bucket Seat Anchor	31
	Passenger's Air Bag Module (Grand Prix)	106①
	Passenger's Air Bag Module (Intrigue)	89①
	SDM (After Modifications)	44①
	SDM (Original Fasteners)	89①
	Steering Column Bracket Bolts	18
	Steering Column Coupling Upper Pinch Bolt	35
	Steering Wheel	33

Continued

TIGHTENING SPECIFICATIONS—Continued

Year	Component	Torque/Ft. Lbs.
IMPALA		
2000–04	Driver's Seat Track To Floor Bolts	31
	Instrument Panel Cluster Trim Plate	18①
	Instrument Panel Upper Trim Pad, Horizontal	18①
	Instrument Panel Upper Trim Pad, Vertical	89①
	Passenger's Air Bag Module	89①
	SDM	89①
	Side Impact Air Bag Module	45①
	SIS	89①
	Steering Wheel	33
ION		
2003–04	Air Bag Module	71①
	Console	11①
	Instrument Panel Righthand Endcap	20①
	Instrument Panel Upper Trim Pad	53①
	Passenger's Air Bag Module	89①
	Passenger's Air Bag Module Cover	20①
	Passenger's Air Bag Module To Cross-Car Beam	71①
	Roof Panel Air Bag Module	71①
	SDM	89①
	Side Impact Air Bag Module Tether	71①
	Side Impact Air Bag Module Sensor	89①
	Steering Column Cover	35①
	Steering Wheel	26
L-SERIES		
2000–04	Air Bag Module	90①
	Console	11①
	Front Seat Frame	15
	Intermediate Shaft	33
	Passenger's Air Bag Module Bolts	89①
	SDM	11
	Steering Column, Lower	19
	Steering Column, Upper	26
	Steering Wheel	22
LESABRE		
2000–04	Front Bench Seat Track	22
	Instrument Panel Upper Trim Pad	18①
	Passenger's Air Bag Module	89①
	SDM	80①
	Side Impact Air Bag Module	80①
	SIS	80①
	Steering Column Shroud, Lower	31①
	Steering Column Shroud, Upper	13①
	Steering Wheel	30
LUMINA		
2000–01	Driver's Air Bag Module	25①
	Front Seat	18
	Passenger's Air Bag Module	62①
	Passenger's Air Bag Module Tether	53①
	SDM (After Modifications)	44①
	SDM (Original Fasteners)	53①
	Steering Wheel	33

Continued

TIGHTENING SPECIFICATIONS—Continued

Year	Component	Torque/Ft. Lbs.
MALIBU		
2000–04	Driver's Air Bag Module	89①
	Front Seat Adjuster	30
	SDM	89①
	Steering Column Lower Cover	18①
	Steering Wheel	27
METRO		
2000–01	Driver's Air Bag Module	17
	Forward Discriminating Sensor	49①
	Passenger's Air Bag Module, Bottom & Center	16.5
	Passenger's Air Bag Module, Upper	49①
	SDM	49①
	Steering Column	10
	Steering Wheel	24
MONTE CARLO		
2000–04	Driver's Seat Track	31
	Instrument Panel Cluster Trim Plate	18①
	Instrument Panel Upper Trim Pad, Horizontal	18①
	Instrument Panel Upper Trim Pad, Vertical	89①
	Passenger's Air Bag Module	89①
	SDM	89①
	Side Impact Air Bag Module	45①
	SIS	89①
	Steering Wheel Nut	33
PARK AVENUE		
2000–04	Front Seat Anchor	31
	Instrument Panel Upper Trim Pad	18①
	Passenger's Air Bag Module	80①
	SDM	80①
	Side Impact Air Bag Module	80①
	SISM	80①
	Steering Wheel	30
PRIZM		
2000–04	Driver's Air Bag Module	78①
	Forward Discriminating Sensor	14
	Front Seat Track	27
	Passenger's Air Bag Module	13
	PCM	11
	SDM	14
	Seat Belt Pretensioner, Lower	31
	Seat Belt Pretensioner, Upper	43①
	SIS	14
	Steering Wheel	25

Continued

TIGHTENING SPECIFICATIONS—Continued

Year	Component	Torque/Ft. Lbs.
SEVILLE		
2000–04	Floor Console, Front	18①
	Floor Console, Center & Rear	89①
	Front Seat	30
	Instrument Panel Upper Trim Pad, Side	44①
	Instrument Panel Upper Trim Pad, Upper	18①
	Passenger's Air Bag Module	80①
	SDM	80①
	Seat Belt Pretensioner	30
	Side Impact Air Bag Module	80①
	SISM	80①
	Steering Wheel	30
S-SERIES		
2000–04	Air Bag Module	71①
	Console	11①
	Instrument Panel Righthand Endcap	20①
	Instrument Panel Upper Trim Pad	53①
	Passenger's Air Bag Module	89①
	Passenger's Air Bag Module Cover	20①
	Passenger's Air Bag Module To Cross-Car Beam	71①
	Roof Panel Air Bag Module	71①
	SDM	89①
	Side Impact Air Bag Module Tether	71①
	Side Impact Air Bag Module Sensor	89①
	Steering Column Cover	35①
	Steering Wheel	26
VIBE		
2003–04	Driver Air Bag Module	78①
	Front End Discriminating Sensor	71①
	Passenger's Air Bag Module	15
	SDM	13
	Side Impact Air Bag Module Sensor	71①
	Steering Column Cover	35①
	Steering Wheel	26
XLR		
2004	I/P Module Mounting Fasteners	89①
	SDM	89①
	Side Impact Air Bag Module	89①
	Side Impact Air Bag Module Sensor	80①
	Steering Column Shroud Torx Bolts	13①
	Steering Wheel Nut	30

① — Inch lbs.

DASH PANEL SERVICE

NOTE: Refer To "Dash Gauges" Section For Related Information.

NOTE: On Air Bag Equipped Models, Refer To "Air Bag System Precautions" Located In The Front Of This Manual For System Disarming & Arming Procedures.

NOTE: Refer To "Computer Relearn Procedures" Located In The Front Of This Manual When Battery Power To The Computer Has Been Interrupted.

INDEX

PRECAUTIONS

Air Bag Systems

Refer to "Air Bag System Precautions" in the front of this manual for system disarming and arming procedures.

Battery Ground Cable

Prior to service, disconnect battery ground cable and isolate as required.

DASH PANEL

REPLACE

Alero

2000–02

1. Pull door weatherstrip from windshield side upper garnish molding, as required.
2. Remove windshield side upper garnish molding by disconnecting clips.
3. Remove defroster grill by disconnecting retainers using suitable small flat bladed tool.
4. Remove instrument panel endcaps by pulling outward.
5. Remove righthand sound insulator and disconnect heater hose from duct.
6. Remove mounting screws and lefthand sound insulator.
7. Remove mounting screws under glove compartment door and open door.
8. Remove pocket mounting screws and glove compartment. Disconnect compartment lamp electrical connector.
9. Remove passenger's air bag module as outlined in "Passive Restraint Systems" chapter.
10. Remove instrument panel accessory trim plate by pulling rearward to release retainers.
11. Remove mounting screws and HVAC control head.
12. Disconnect vacuum hose harness and two hose connectors, then the blower motor and rear defroster control electrical connectors.
13. Disconnect electrical connector and 12-volt power supply, as required.
14. Remove upper mounting screws and instrument panel cluster trim plate by pulling up and out to release lower retainers.
15. Disconnect electrical connector and remove trip reset switch using suitable small flat bladed tool, as required.
16. Remove mounting screws and instrument panel cluster. Disconnect electrical connector.
17. Remove mounting screws and radio. Disconnect instrument panel wiring harness and antenna cable connectors.
18. Remove driver's air bag module as outlined in "Passive Restraint Systems" chapter.
19. Remove steering wheel as outlined in "Electrical" section of appropriate chassis chapter.
20. Remove steering column as outlined in "Steering Columns" chapter.
21. Position front seats to most rearward position.
22. Position emergency brake lever to full up position.
23. Position gear selector to NEUTRAL position.
24. Remove gear selector knob retainer using suitable small flat bladed tool.
25. Remove gear selector knob by pulling upward.
26. Release console trim plate retainers using suitable flat bladed tool.
27. Remove trim plate.
28. Remove instrument panel accessory trim plate by pulling rearward to release retainers.
29. Lift up front floor console armrest and remove storage compartment rubber mat.
30. Remove storage compartment rear mounting bolts, **Fig. 1.**
31. Remove center bolts from console sides.
32. Remove covers using suitable small flat bladed tool at front edge, then the front mounting screws.
33. Release front retainers by pulling outward front sides of floor console.
34. Remove floor console by pulling up and rearward, guiding emergency brake lever boot over emergency brake lever.
35. Remove ignition switch mounting bolts. Position ignition switch for ease of removal.
36. Remove ignition switch mounting bolts and bracket.
37. Insert key and turn ignition switch lock cylinder to ACC position.
38. Depress retainer and remove transaxle park/lock cable.
39. Remove ignition switch lock cylinder

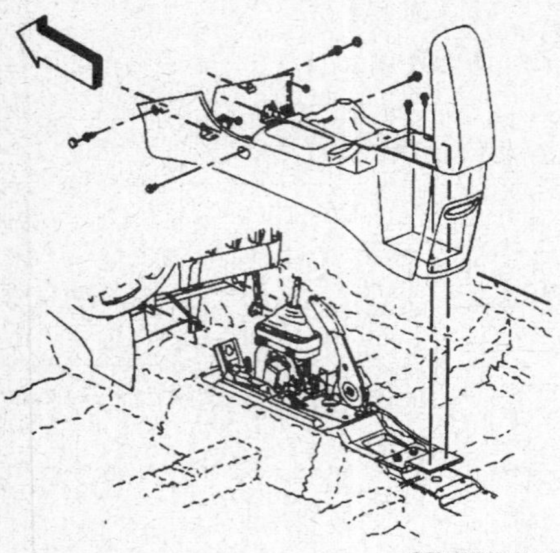

Fig. 1 Exploded view of console. Alero

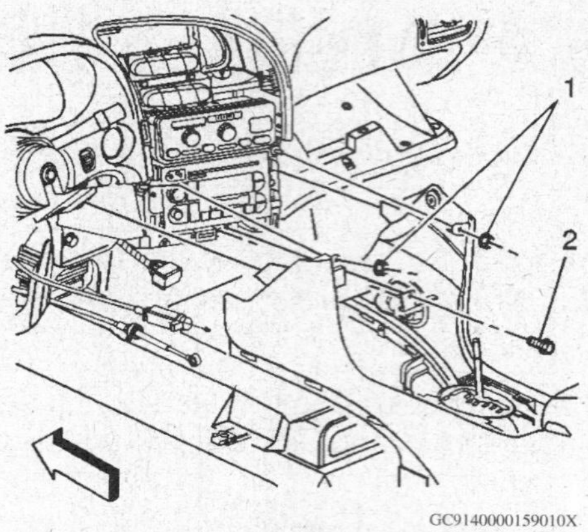

Fig. 2 Center Exploded view of console (Part 1 of 2). Aurora

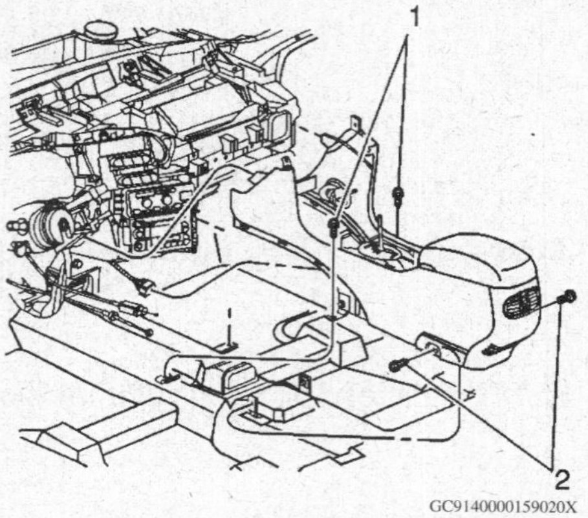

Fig. 2 Center Exploded view of console (Part 2 of 2). Aurora

by depressing retaining tab and pulling cylinder out with key.

40. Disconnect pass lock and ignition switch electrical connectors.
41. Remove ignition switch.
42. Remove fog lamp/dimmer switch/vent trim plate using suitable small flat bladed tool. Disconnect electrical connectors.
43. Remove fog lamp switch using suitable small flat bladed tool on back side to release retainer tabs.
44. Remove instrument panel upper bolt covers.
45. Disconnect electrical junction box electrical connections.
46. Remove instrument panel to cross car beam mounting screws.
47. Remove instrument panel.
48. Reverse procedure to install.

2003–04

1. Remove instrument panel endcaps by pulling outward.
2. Pull door weatherstrip from windshield side upper garnish molding.
3. Disconnect clips and remove windshield side upper garnish molding.
4. Disengage defroster grill retainers using suitable small flat bladed tool.
5. Remove righthand outboard sound insulator.
6. Remove mounting screws and wiring harness from opening on righthand inboard sound insulator.
7. Remove insulator from heater and A/C control, then the defroster duct from insulator.
8. Remove lefthand outboard sound insulator.
9. Remove mounting screws and disconnect defroster duct from lefthand inboard sound insulator.
10. Remove mounting screws under glove compartment door and open door.
11. Remove mounting screws and glove compartment.
12. Disconnect glove box lamp and pull through opening.
13. Remove passenger airbag module.
14. Remove instrument panel accessory trim plate by pulling rearward on bottom to release retainers.
15. Disconnect vacuum hoses; electrical connectors and 12–volt power supply from heater-A/C control.
16. Remove upper mounting screws, then the instrument panel cluster trim plate by pulling up and out to release lower retainers.
17. Disconnect electrical connector and remove trip reset switch.
18. Remove mounting screws and instrument panel cluster. Disconnect electrical connector.
19. Remove mounting screws and radio. Disconnect instrument panel wiring harness and antenna cable connectors.
20. Remove drivers airbag module as outlined in "Passive Restraint Systems" chapter.
21. Remove steering wheel.
22. Remove mounting screw and multifunction switch.
23. Move emergency brake lever to full upward position, then the gear selector to full rearward position.
24. Remove mounting screws and cupholder.
25. Remove mounting screws and floor console center support bracket.
26. Remove ignition switch mounting screws, then position switch for ease of removal.
27. Remove ignition switch mounting bolts and bracket.
28. Insert key and turn ignition switch to ON position.
29. Depress retainer and remove transaxle park/lock cable.
30. Remove ignition switch lock cylinder by depressing retaining tab and pulling cylinder out with key. **Remove lock cylinder before removing pass lock electrical connector.**
31. Disconnect pass lock and ignition switch electrical connectors.
32. Remove ignition switch.
33. Remove hazard warning switch trim plate using suitable flat bladed tool.
34. Release center air outlet retainer clips using a suitable flat bladed tool, then remove air outlet from opening.
35. Remove lefthand hazard warning switch bolt through instrument cluster opening.
36. Remove righthand and center lower bolts through center air outlet opening.
37. Disconnect hazard warning switch electrical connectors, then remove switch.
38. Remove lefthand side air outlet using suitable flat bladed tool.
39. Disconnect fog lamp switch electrical connectors, then remove fog lamp switch.
40. Disconnect electrical junction box connections.
41. Remove instrument panel to cross car beam mounting screws.
42. Remove instrument panel.
43. Reverse procedure to install.

Aurora

1. Remove left and righthand lower dash panel sound insulators.
2. Remove center instrument panel trim plate.
3. Remove center console trim plate screw, then pull up on rear of console trim plate to disconnect clips.
4. Disconnect electrical connectors and remove center console trim plate.
5. Remove console compartment.
6. Remove left and righthand console side trim panels.
7. Disconnect shift cable and park lock cable.
8. Disconnect console main wiring harness connector.
9. Open glove compartment and remove console mounting screw.
10. Remove mounting screws and console, **Fig. 2.**
11. Remove instrument panel endcaps.
12. Remove left and righthand windshield garnish moldings, then the defroster grille.
13. Remove righthand instrument panel trim panel and instrument cluster trim plate.
14. Remove carrier bolts and instrument panel upper trim pad, **Fig. 3.**
15. Remove steering column as outlined in "Steering Columns" chapter.
16. Remove steering column support.
17. Disconnect all electrical harnesses from instrument panel.
18. Remove instrument panel center support brackets.

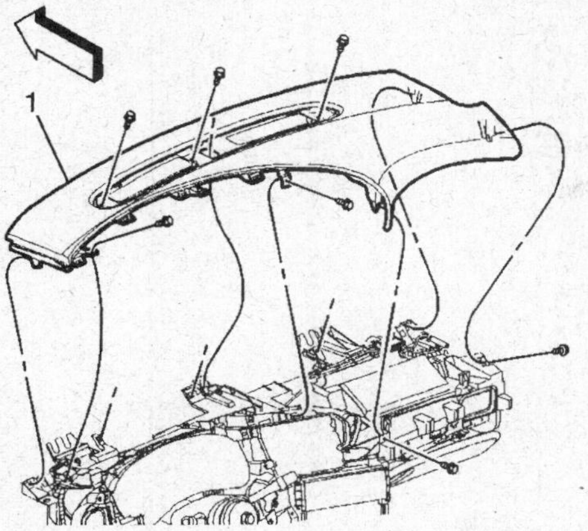

Fig. 3 Upper trim pad removal. Aurora

19. Remove brackets and instrument panel.
20. Reverse procedure to install.

Bonneville

1. Disconnect lefthand insulator panel from instrument panel by removing mounting screws at rear edge and prying out retainers to release.
2. Turn heater temperature sensor quarter turn to release and allow to remain connected to its wire.
3. Disconnect remaining electrical connectors, as required.
4. Remove insulator by sliding it rearward.
5. Repeat previous four steps to remove righthand insulator.
6. Remove defroster grilles by prying upward to release retainers.
7. Disconnect sensor from defroster grille.
8. Remove end cap by pulling it outward until rear edge retainers disconnects and slide tabs out on front edge.
9. Lower tilt steering column to lowest position.
10. Remove ignition cylinder bezel.
11. Remove Driver Information Center (DIC) switch by prying with suitable flat bladed tool at lower righthand corner and pull rearward. Disconnect electrical connector.
12. Remove push-in release fasteners and instrument panel cluster trim plate by pulling rearward to release clips.
13. Disconnect DIC switch electrical connector.
14. Disconnect Heads-Up Display (HUD) switch electrical connector, as required.
15. Remove instrument panel cluster trim panel.
16. Release five cluster pins, then pull cluster rearward and to right.
17. Remove left and righthand windshield garnish moldings.
18. Remove mounting screws and upper trim pad by lift pad upward to disconnect retainers.
19. Remove mounting screws and HUD module. Disconnect electrical connector.

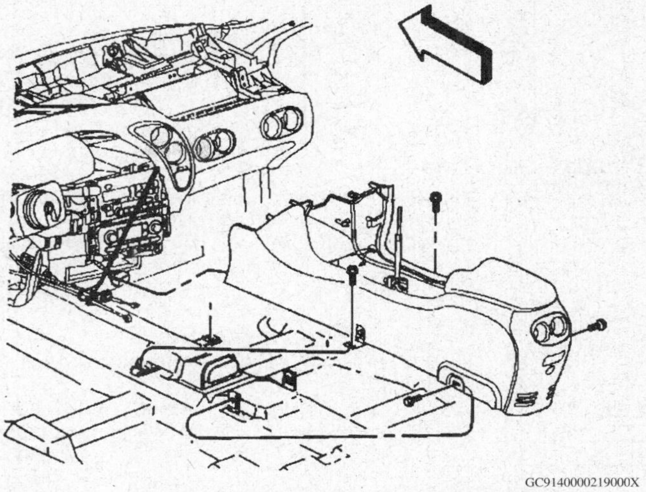

Fig. 4 Exploded view of console. Bonneville

20. Remove HUD bracket mounting screw to HVAC cross car duct.
21. Depress spring clip retainers at radio sides.
22. Pull radio straight out to remove.
23. Disconnect theft deterrent module electrical connector.
24. Pinch tabs and pull HVAC control head rearward.
25. Unsnap and pull knee bolster rearward.
26. Lower and support steering column.
27. Remove mounting bolts and upper steering column support.
28. Lower tilt steering column to lowest position.
29. Remove ignition cylinder bezel.
30. Remove push-in release fasteners and instrument panel cluster trim plate by pulling rearward to release clips.
31. Disconnect HIUD switch electrical connector, as required.
32. Remove front console storage compartment depress top tabs to release from instrument panel and console. Disconnect electrical connector.
33. Remove console shift knob.
34. Remove console upper trim plate.
35. Remove console trim plate by pulling upward to disconnect retainer clips. Disconnect electrical connectors, as required.
36. Disconnect shifter and shift lock cables.
37. Remove console main wiring harness connector.
38. Remove mounting bolts and console by sliding rearward and up, **Fig. 4.**
39. Open door, then remove glove compartment mounting screws and check strap.
40. Disconnect rear compartment release switch electrical connector.
41. Remove glove compartment by pulling toward rear.
42. Remove air outlet vent by using suitable flat blade tool to pry around edges and pull rearward.
43. Disconnect hazard warning lamp switch electrical connector.
44. Remove hazard warning lamp switch by depressing retaining tabs.
45. Remove retainer to carrier mounting bolts.
46. Disconnect two main wire harness connectors at top.
47. Disconnect flat wire harness connector from carrier tab.
48. Feed DIC wire through retainer opening.
49. Disconnect radio antenna extension cable by sliding cable connection upwards out of retainer.
50. Feed glove compartment wiring through retainer.
51. Remove air temperature sensors from HVAC ducts by turning quarter turn counterclockwise.
52. Disconnect fog lamp switch electrical connector.
53. Apply parking brake.
54. Insert ignition key and turn ignition switch to RUN position.
55. Depress and hold ignition lock cylinder retaining tab on righthand lower side of ignition switch using suitable flat bladed screwdriver or other suitable tool.
56. Remove cylinder by pulling on ignition cylinder.
57. Remove reader/exciter from ignition lock cylinder housing.
58. Release clips and slide reader/exciter off lock cylinder.
59. Remove ignition switch to retainer mounting screws.
60. Remove retainer from carrier.
61. Remove Data Link Connector (DLC) mounting bolts.
62. Remove passenger's air bag module as outlined in "Passive Restraint Systems" chapter.
63. Disconnect ignition switch electrical connectors.
64. Remove shift/park lock cable from ignition switch.
65. Disconnect body to instrument panel electrical connectors at upper righthand outside corner of carrier.
66. Remove HVAC aspirator tube.
67. Feed ignition switch wiring, shift/park lock cable and console wiring harness through carrier.
68. Release SIR harness retainer from carrier.

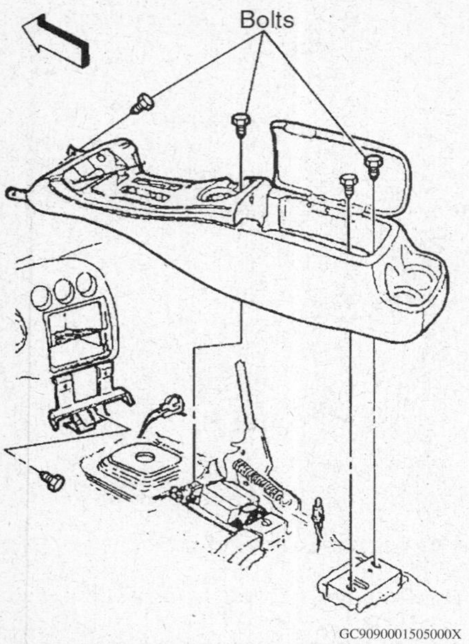

Fig. 5 Exploded view of console. Camaro & Firebird

69. Remove mounting bolts and carrier.
70. Reverse procedure to install.

Camaro & Firebird

1. Remove Heating, Ventilation and Air Conditioning (HVAC) module boss retainer.
2. Remove righthand insulator push-in retainers.
3. Slide HVAC module boss flange on insulator.
4. Unhook insulator flange from over kick panel.
5. Remove righthand insulator.
6. Remove lefthand insulator push-in retainers
7. Unhook lefthand insulator tab from dash mat retaining feature.
8. Lift lefthand insulator flange out of kick panel.
9. Remove T-tops, as required.
10. Open vehicle door.
11. **On models equipped with lift-off window panels,** remove lift-off window panel and remove garnish molding screws.
12. **On all models,** remove windshield upper garnish molding by pulling from inner side frame.
13. Gently lift trim pad to disconnect dual-lock fasteners.
14. Remove Daytime Running Lamp (DRL) ambient light sensor.
15. Remove security indicator lamp.
16. Remove upper trim panel.
17. Remove rear compartment lid release switch, as required.
18. Remove mounting bolts and knee bolster.
19. Remove mounting nuts and knee bolster deflector.
20. Open glove compartment, then remove hinge mounting screws and door.
21. Remove push-in retainers and disconnect insulator tab from dash mat retaining feature.
22. Lift insulator flange out of kick panel.
23. Disconnect electrical connector and remove stop lamp and TTC switch from bracket.
24. Disconnect accessory trim plate.
25. **On Camaro models,** disconnect switches' electrical connectors, as required.
26. **On all models,** remove bracket bolts and slide radio out.
27. Disconnect antenna cable and wiring harness connector.
28. Remove radio.
29. **On Camaro models,** proceed as follows:
    a. Loosen upper support nuts and lower steering column.
    b. Remove mounting screws and instrument cluster trim bezel.
30. **On Firebird models,** proceed as follows:
    a. Remove foam tape from around electrical connector.
    b. Disconnect fog lamp switch electrical connector.
    c. Remove fog lamp switch.
    d. Disconnect and remove instrument cluster trim bezel.
31. **On all models,** remove mounting bolts and instrument cluster. Gently pull cluster straight out to disconnect electrical connector.
32. **On Camaro model,** remove headlamp switch mounting bolts.
33. **On all models,** disconnect headlamp and dimmer switches connectors.
34. Remove mounting bolt and temperature control cable.
35. Disconnect retainer and remove from switch.
36. Push harness through instrument panel opening.
37. Remove mounting bolts and HVAC control.
38. Gently pull HVAC control out far enough to access vacuum electrical temperature cable.
39. Disconnect vacuum harness connector from vacuum selector valve.
40. Disconnect mode switch, control illumination, blower switch and rear defogger electrical connectors.
41. Remove temperature control cable from control. When releasing control cable clips, use suitable small screwdriver to gently pry cable from control.
42. Disconnect DRL module electrical connectors and remove DRL module.
43. Turn ignition key to RUN position.
44. Place shift lever in NEUTRAL position.
45. Remove shift control knob.
46. Open console armrest door and remove coin holder.
47. Unsnap switch plate and disconnect electrical connectors from switches, as required.
48. Remove console trim plate mounting bolts.
49. **On models equipped with automatic transmission,** disconnect PRNDL lamp connector.
50. **On models equipped with manual transmission,** lift trim plate up and disconnect ashtray lamp connector.

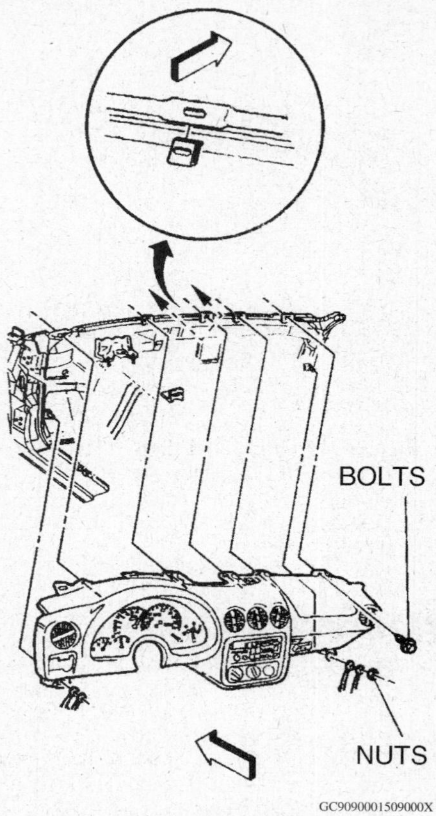

Fig. 6 Exploded view of Instrument panel carrier. Camaro & Firebird

51. **On all models,** disconnect cigarette lighter electrical connector.
52. Remove console trim plate.
53. Raise park brake handle as far as possible. If park brake handle cannot be pulled up far enough to remove console, proceed as follows:
    a. Release park brake handle.
    b. Hold adjuster pawl disconnected.
    c. Park brake handle can be pulled up further.
54. Remove floor console mounting bolts, **Fig. 5.**
55. Disconnect power outlet electrical connector.
56. Remove floor console.
57. Remove fuse block cover, mounting bolt and fuse block.
58. Remove mounting bolts and Data Link Connector (DLC).
59. Cut tie strap securing steering column branch to air distributor duct.
60. Unclip star connector from knee bolster bracket.
61. Remove instrument panel carrier mounting nuts.
62. Remove cross car and instrument panel harness grounds from mounting studs.
63. Remove instrument panel carrier mounting bolts.
64. Pull panel outward.
65. Remove three upper bolts starting at righthand side from air distribution duct.
66. Remove forward lamp harness and

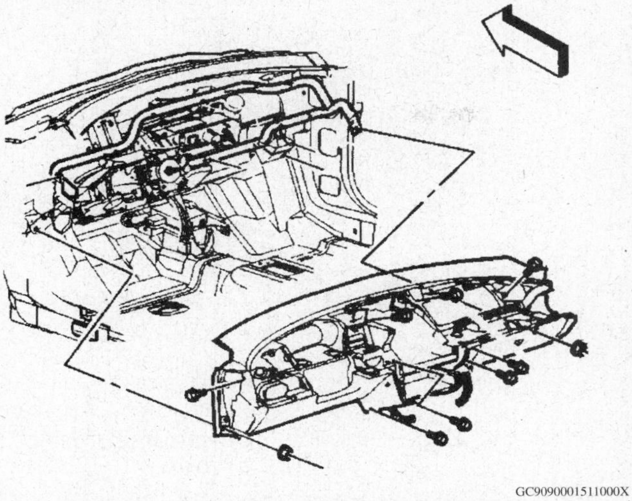

Fig. 7 Exploded view of instrument panel carrier. Cavalier & Sunfire

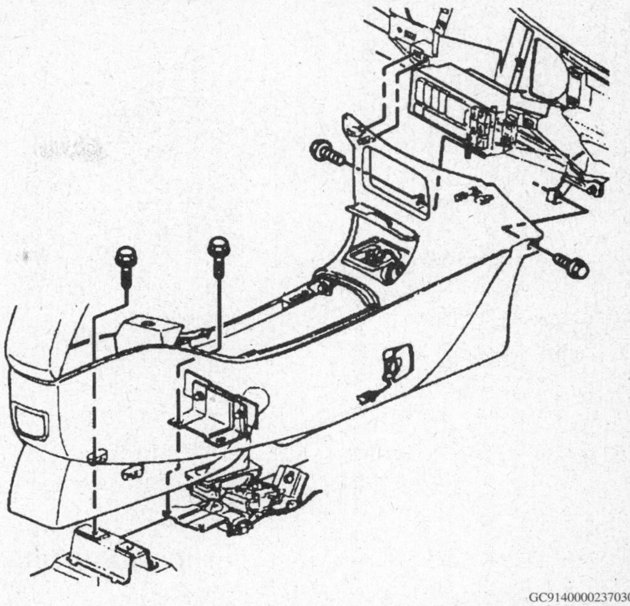

Fig. 8 Exploded view of console. Century & Regal

cross car harness.
67. Remove 48-way connector bolts and instrument panel connector.
68. Remove hatch release relay and blower motor relay.
69. Disconnect air conditioning resistor connector.
70. Unclip A/C resistor connector from instrument panel.
71. Remove rear fog lamp and convertible top relays, as required.
72. Disconnect rosebud connectors from tie bar.
73. Remove harness rosebuds.
74. Remove convertible top motor relay, as required.
75. Remove theft deterrent relay.
76. Remove harness branches from instrument panel openings.
77. Remove cluster connector.
78. Remove harness from retaining clips.
79. Disconnect harness rosebud.
80. Remove harness headlamp branch from opening.
81. Remove instrument panel carrier, **Fig. 6.**
82. Reverse procedure to install.

Catera

1. Remove driver's air bag module as outlined in "Passive Restraint Systems" chapter.
2. Remove SIR coil.
3. Remove ignition lock cylinder.
4. Disconnect and remove theft deterrent immobilizer.
5. Remove ignition switch, windshield washer switch and turn signal switch.
6. Remove driver's knee bolster and sound insulator.
7. Remove steering column as outlined in "Steering Columns" chapter.
8. Remove left and righthand assist handles, windshield pillar moldings and righthand side instrument panel access panel.
9. Remove mounting screw, righthand side air deflector outlet and duct.
10. Remove air bag module instrument panel cover.
11. Remove glove compartment.
12. Remove passenger's air bag module as outlined in "Passive Restraint Systems" chapter.
13. Remove upper and lower center console.
14. Remove mounting screw and center console air duct.
15. Remove radio trim plate bezel, climate control head and center air outlet deflector.
16. Remove mounting screw and center air deflector outlet housing.
17. Remove lefthand side access panel and air outlet deflector.
18. Remove mounting screw and lefthand side air deflector outlet housing.
19. Remove lefthand side lower outlet duct.
20. Remove headlamp switch and instrument cluster.
21. Remove mounting screws, then the fuse and relay panels.
22. Remove steering column support bracket nut and bolt.
23. Remove left and righthand instrument panel carrier bolts.
24. Remove headlamp automatic control ambient light sensor.
25. Disconnect wiring harness connectors from instrument panel. **Wiring harness cannot be removed with instrument panel.**
26. Remove instrument panel.
27. Reverse procedure to install.

Cavalier

1. Remove mounting screw and defroster grille using suitable small flat bladed tool.
2. Remove mounting screws and end caps.
3. Open glove compartment, then remove mounting screws and righthand instrument panel trim panel.
4. Remove mounting screws and instrument panel trim pad.
5. Remove mounting screws and lefthand side air distribution duct by moving to left disconnect from righthand side duct.
6. Move righthand side air distribution duct outlet towards self to release lock tabs.
7. Remove righthand duct through braces.
8. Remove passenger's air bag module as outlined in "Passive Restraint Systems" chapter.
9. Remove mounting screws and instrument panel trim plate by pulling rearward to disconnect retainers. Disconnect electrical connectors.
10. Remove mounting screws and instrument panel cluster by pulling rearward. Disconnect electrical connector.
11. Remove mounting screws and heater control.
12. Disconnect electrical connections, vacuum hoses and temperature blend cable.
13. Remove mounting screws and radio. Disconnect electrical connections and antenna coaxial cable.
14. Remove driver's air bag module as outlined in "Passive Restraint Systems" chapter.
15. Remove steering wheel as outlined in "Electrical" section of appropriate chassis chapter.
16. Remove tilt lever by turning counterclockwise.
17. Remove lower steering column trim cover mounting screws, then the upper column trim cover by tilting up and unsnapping from lower column trim cover hinges.
18. Remove lower column trim cover.
19. Remove mounting screws and multifunction switch. Disconnect electrical connectors.

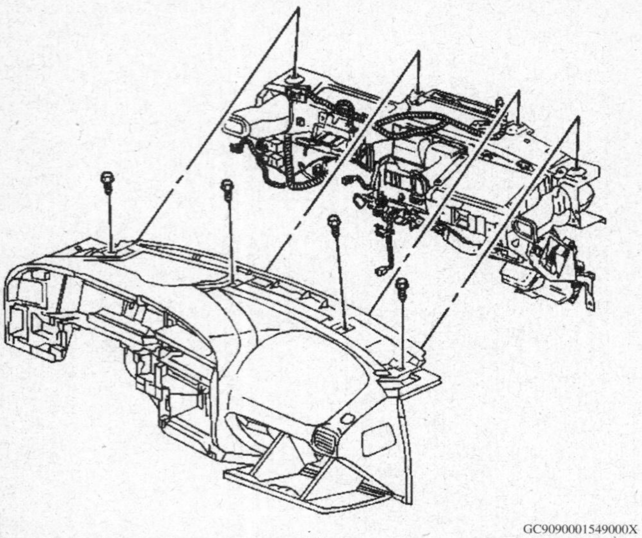

GC9090001549000X

Fig. 9 Exploded view of instrument panel. Century & Regal

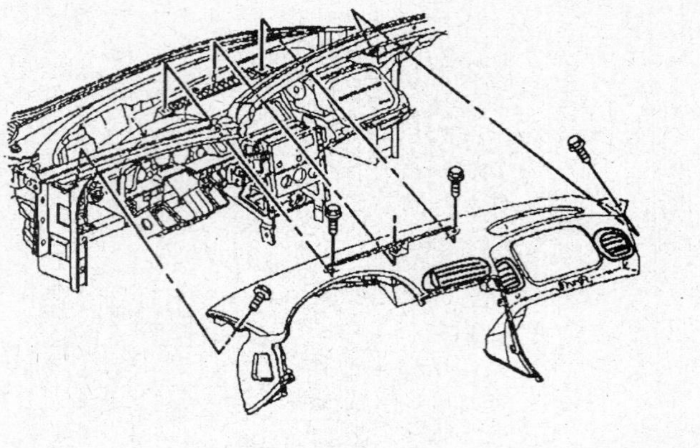

GC9149700137000X

Fig. 10 Exploded view of instrument panel (Part 1 of 2). Corvette

20. Remove steering wheel multi-function levers.
21. Remove mounting screw, disconnect electrical connector and remove windshield wiper switch.
22. Remove mounting screws and instrument carrier from cross car beam, **Fig. 7.**
23. Reverse procedure to install.

Century & Regal

1. Remove windshield side upper garnish moldings by pulling door weatherstrip from pinchweld flange to expose windshield garnish molding. Pull garnish molding to disconnect two clips.
2. Lift upper trim panel up approximately two inches and pull rearward to release retainers.
3. Remove ambient light sensor by rotating quarter turn counterclockwise.
4. Remove sun load sensor by rotating quarter turn counterclockwise, as required.
5. Remove upper trim panel. **Remove upper trim panel slowly. Retainer clips can fall into instrument panel.**
6. Apply parking brake and position transaxle shift lever to LOW position.
7. Remove trim plate starting at front and working back, pulling front upward to release retainers' tabs.
8. Disconnect traction control switch electrical connectors, as required.
9. Remove storage compartment rubber mat.
10. Remove storage compartment mounting bolts, **Fig. 8.**
11. Remove console bracket mounting bolts at rear of transaxle shift lever.
12. Remove left and righthand side mounting bolts.
13. Remove power accessory port or cigarette lighter fuse. Remove cigarette lighter element, as required.
14. Remove power accessory port or cigarette lighter socket by placing one side of T portion of cigarette lighter socket remover tool No. J-42059, or equivalent, into tab window and other should be angled into opposite tab window.
15. Pull power accessory port or cigarette lighter socket straight out.
16. Disconnect power accessory port or cigarette lighter electrical connector.
17. Remove power accessory port or cigarette lighter retainer.
18. Disconnect wiring harness.
19. Pull console front rearward to release instrument panel retainers.
20. Depress shifter trim plate front edge to pull back console.
21. Remove console.
22. Remove lefthand insulator retainers from steering column opening filler panel using door trim pad clip remover tool No. J-38778, or equivalent.
23. Disconnect courtesy lamp by turning quarter turn counterclockwise.
24. Remove lefthand insulator from accelerator pedal.
25. Remove righthand insulator retainers using door trim pad clip remover tool.
26. Adjust carpeting for access and disconnect courtesy turning quarter turn counterclockwise.
27. Remove righthand insulator.
28. Remove mounting bolts and steering column opening panel by pulling rearward and upward, releasing retaining clips.
29. Disconnect Driver Information Center (DIC) electrical connector, as required.
30. Remove mounting bolts to instrument panel and steering column support, then the knee bolster.
31. Remove driver's air bag module as outlined in "Passive Restraint Systems" chapter.
32. Remove steering wheel as outlined in "Electrical" section of appropriate chassis chapter.
33. Remove steering column as outlined in "Steering Columns" chapter.
34. Remove mounting bolts, cable and hood latch release handle bolts.
35. Remove mounting bolts and position Data Link Connector (DLC) harness aside.
36. Remove carpet retainer using door trim pad and garnish clip remover tool No. J-38778, or equivalent, to loosen retainer clips.
37. Remove bottom mounting screws and pull accessory trim plate rearward to release retaining clips.
38. Rotate accessory trim plate rearward and up to release two top edge tabs.
39. Disconnect ash tray harness electrical connector.
40. Remove accessory trim plate.
41. Remove instrument panel access opening covers and open glove compartment.
42. Remove righthand lower trim plate lower edge mounting screw.
43. Remove instrument panel righthand lower trim plate by pulling top, middle and bottom rearward to release top, middle and bottom retainers.
44. Remove instrument cluster trim plate righthand end mounting screw and release righthand end retainer tab.
45. Tilt steering column to lowest position.
46. Remove instrument cluster trim plate by pulling righthand edge and working towards left to release retaining clips.
47. Remove electrical connection and inside air temperature sensor by disconnecting it from aspirator duct.
48. Remove lefthand instrument panel access opening cover by pulling rearward edge outboard to release retainers using suitable plastic flat bladed, then release forward edge behind hinge pillar.
49. Remove mounting screws and headlamp switch by pulling outboard. Disconnect electrical connector.
50. Remove mounting screws and instrument cluster by rotating top and disconnect bottom locating pins. Disconnect electrical connector.
51. Remove mounting screws and radio. Disconnect electrical and coaxial cable connectors.
52. Remove mounting bolts and HVAC control module. Disconnect electrical and vacuum connectors.
53. Open glove compartment and release

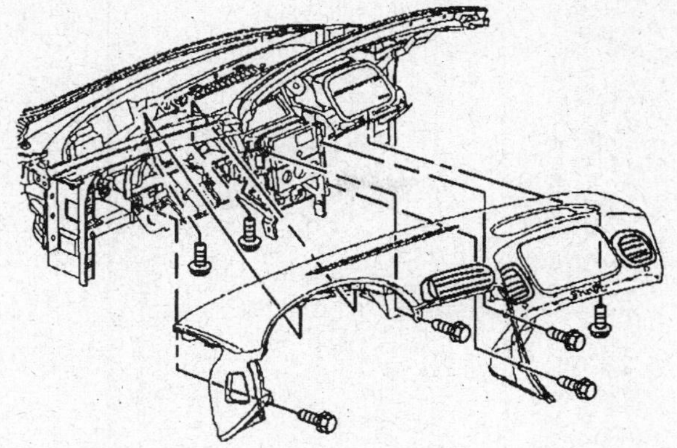

Fig. 10 Exploded view of instrument panel (Part 2 of 2). Corvette

damper cord loop.
54. Remove hinge mounting screws and glove compartment by pressing inward on both sides of housing, then rotating down and out.
55. Remove instrument panel righthand end, center and lower mounting bolts.
56. Remove lefthand end and upper mounting bolts, **Fig. 9.**
57. Position instrument panel wiring harness aside.
58. Remove instrument panel.
59. Reverse procedure to install.

Corvette

1. **On models equipped with convertible top,** proceed as follows:
   a. Open folding top stowage compartment lid.
   b. Remove extension panel lower sides and top mounting screws.
   c. Remove folding top stowage compartment lid extension panel upward from bracket.
2. **On all models,** open console door.
3. Release electronic traction control, ride control switch retaining clips by pulling up on rear. If switch does not release from trim plate, proceed as follows:
   a. Carefully insert suitable screwdriver into recess located at switch rear.
   b. Gently pull up switch rear.
4. Disconnect switch electrical connector.
5. Disconnect LED connector from wiring harness connector.
6. Remove switch.
7. Carefully remove console mounting nut covers using suitable small flat bladed screwdriver.
8. Remove console mounting nuts at rear, front and instrument panel accessory trim plate.
9. Lift console rear slightly and pull rearward to release front from under accessory trim plate.
10. Disconnect electrical accessory plug electrical connector.
11. Remove console electrical accessory plug retainer and accessory plug housing.
12. Disconnect electrical connector and remove fuel door release.
13. Turn console over and carefully insert suitable small flat bladed screwdriver to release switch tabs.
14. Remove console.
15. Apply parking brake for additional clearance around parking brake lever.
16. **On models equipped with automatic transmission,** shift transmission into SECOND.
17. **On models equipped with manual transmission,** proceed as follows:
   a. Shift transmission 4th.
   b. Grasp shift control boot and apply light pressure in toward shift control lever, to begin to release shift boot retaining tabs from instrument panel accessory trim plate.
   c. Continue to release remaining boot retaining tabs and lift boot from trim plate.
18. **On all models,** open cigarette lighter door and remove ashtray.
19. Remove instrument panel accessory trim plate grille. Pry gently at side edge with suitable flat bladed screwdriver to release tab.
20. Remove accessory trim plate mounting screws next to cigarette lighter and behind ashtray.
21. Remove accessory trim plate mounting screw in grille opening.
22. Grasp sides of accessory trim plate near curve at base and pull plate rearward to release locking tabs.
23. Lift rear of trim plate to clear driveline tunnel studs.
24. Disconnect cigarette lighter electrical connector.
25. **On models equipped with manual transmission,** rotate shift control boot and position one end down into shifter opening.
26. **On all models,** lift accessory trim plate over shifter and remove.
27. Remove fog lamp, rear compartment lid release switch by carefully prying at lower edge of switch to release locking tab. Disconnect electrical connector.
28. Remove driver's knee bolster trim panel mounting screw behind fog

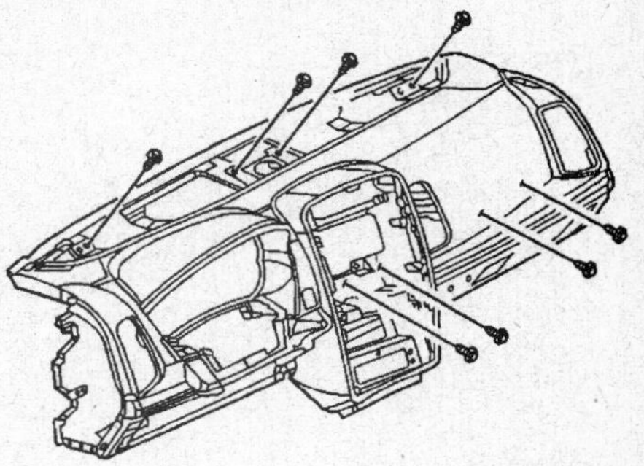

Fig. 11 Instrument panel carrier to retainer mounting screw locations (Part 1 of 2). CTS

lamp, rear compartment lid release switch.
29. Remove driver's knee bolster trim panel lower mounting screws.
30. Grasp trim panel at side edges and pull firmly rearward to release locking tabs.
31. Disconnect inside air temperature sensor electrical connector, as required.
32. Remove driver's knee bolster trim panel.
33. Open glove compartment door and disconnect lamp switch electrical connector.
34. Remove compartment door trim plugs from bottom. Reach behind compartment door and push plugs out using suitable flat bladed tool on front side to remove plugs, as required.
35. Remove compartment lower mounting bolts, side and upper mounting screws.
36. Slowly remove compartment enough to disconnect inflatable restraint module switch wiring harness connector.
37. Remove glove compartment.
38. Insert two suitable small flat bladed screwdrivers, or other tools, close to each other between rear edge of defroster grille and upper trim pad near one corner of grille.
39. Carefully pry grille up from trim pad. Work screwdrivers gradually to other corner of grille.
40. Lift grille and rotate to release DRL sensor from grille, as required.
41. Rotate to release sunload sensor from grille, as required.
42. Insert DRL and sunload sensors into nearest opening in windshield defroster duct to provide additional clearance to remove trim pad.
43. Remove windshield side garnish moldings.
44. Remove upper trim pad to defroster duct mounting screws, **Fig. 10.**
45. Remove upper trim pad to left and righthand hinge pillars mounting screws.
46. Remove instrument panel cluster bezel to upper trim pad mounting screws.
47. Remove upper trim pad to driver's knee bolster outer bracket and center support bracket mounting screws.
48. Remove trim pad to passenger's air bag module bracket mounting screw.

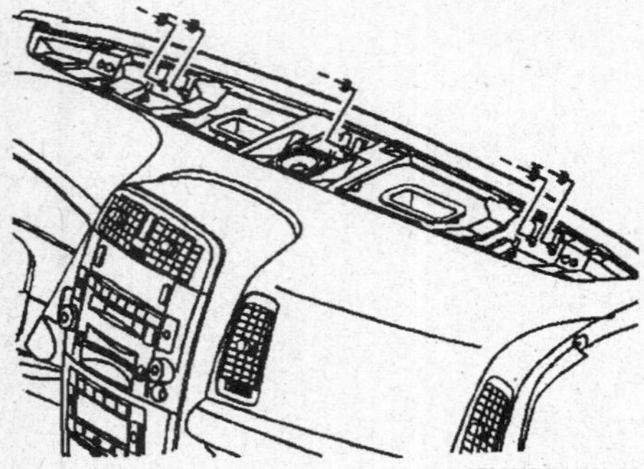

Fig. 11 Instrument panel carrier to retainer mounting screw locations (Part 2 of 2). CTS

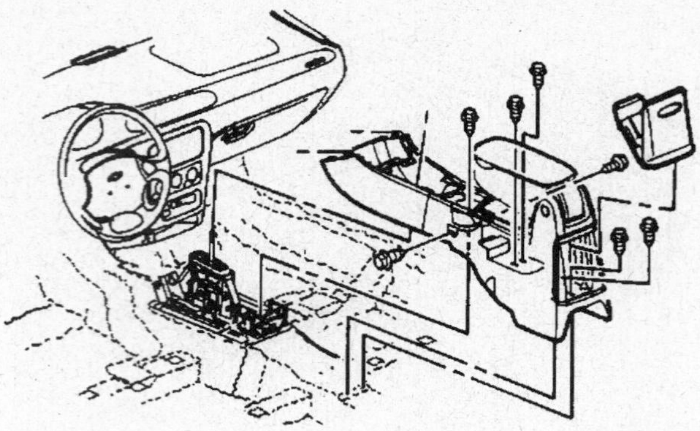

Fig. 12 Exploded view of console. Malibu

49. Tilt steering wheel to lowest position.
50. Lift upper trim pad rearward edge approximately two inches to provide clearance for air distribution duct.
51. Slowly pull upper trim pad from windshield while guiding tabs on side of trim pad past hinge pillars.
52. Disconnect hazard warning switch electrical connector.
53. Remove upper trim pad.
54. Reverse procedure to install.

CTS

1. Remove gearshift trim cover and disconnect electrical connector.
2. Remove console left and righthand trim panels.
3. Remove six mounting screws, then the console.
4. Remove upper A/C vents.
5. Remove mounting screws and radio, then disconnect electrical connectors and antenna lead.
6. Remove glove compartment.
7. Tilt steering column to lowest position.
8. Remove cluster trim cover by prying upward using a suitable small flat bladed tool.
9. Remove cluster mounting screws.
10. Pry cluster upward at top to release retainers, then pull out and disconnect electrical connectors.
11. Pry upward on defroster grille using suitable flat bladed tool to release retainers.
12. Disconnect sunload sensor connector, then remove defroster grille.
13. Remove lefthand insulator panel mounting screws. Disconnect courtesy lamp electrical connector.
14. Remove righthand insulator panel mounting screws and pull downward to release retainers. Disconnect courtesy lamp electrical connector.
15. Remove driver side airbag module as outlined in "Passive Restraint Systems" chapter.
16. Remove steering wheel as outlined in "Electrical" section of appropriate chassis chapter.
17. Remove steering column tilt lever.
18. Remove lower column trim cover mounting screws, then tilt downward and slide back to release retainers.
19. Remove upper column trim cover mounting screws, then the trim cover.
20. Remove mounting nuts, then lower steering column.
21. Remove lower retainer support bracket mounting bolts.
22. Remove mounting screws from side of instrument panel to carrier.
23. Remove mounting screws from lower center trim panel.
24. Remove instrument panel mounting screws from behind glove compartment.
25. Remove mounting screws and instrument panel, **Fig. 11.**
26. Reverse procedure to install.

Malibu

1. Remove windshield side upper garnish molding by pulling windshield side upper garnish molding rearward to release tabs.
2. Remove defroster grille by unsnapping and lifting upward.
3. Remove end caps pulling outward in finger pull area.
4. Remove mounting screws under glove compartment door.
5. Open door and remove mounting screws inside pocket.
6. Disconnect glove compartment lamp switch electrical connection.
7. Remove glove compartment.
8. Remove push pins and lefthand halve of lefthand side sound insulator.
9. Remove mounting bolts and righthand halve of lefthand side sound insulator.
10. Remove push pin and righthand side of righthand side sound insulator.
11. Remove mounting bolts and lefthand side of righthand side sound insulator.
12. Remove passenger's air bag module as outlined in "Passive Restraint Systems" chapter.
13. Remove driver's air bag module as outlined in "Passive Restraint Systems" chapter.
14. Remove steering wheel as outlined in "Electrical" section of appropriate chassis chapter.
15. Disconnect electrical connectors.
16. Remove mounting screw and multifunction switch, then disconnect electrical connectors.
17. Remove steering column stalks.
18. Remove mounting screws and instrument panel cluster trim plate by gently prying out using suitable small flat bladed tool.
19. Disconnect dimmer and hazard warning switches electrical connectors.
20. Remove ignition switch trim cover by prying off with suitable small flat bladed tool.
21. Remove accessory trim plate by gently prying with suitable small flat bladed tool to disconnect retainers.
22. Disconnect cigarette lighter electrical connector.
23. Remove cigarette lighter housing from trim plate.
24. Remove mounting screws and instrument cluster by pull rearward. Disconnect electrical connector.
25. Recover air conditioning refrigerant as outlined in "Air Conditioning" chapter.
26. Raise and support vehicle.
27. Drain engine coolant into suitable container.
28. Remove righthand wheel housing splash shield.
29. Remove evaporator hose nut from accumulator using suitable back-up wrench. Discard O-ring seal.
30. Remove mounting bolt and evaporator hose from condenser. Discard O-ring seal.
31. Remove mounting nut and evaporator hose from evaporator. Discard O-ring seal.
32. Unfasten two mounting clips and evaporator hose.
33. Lower vehicle.
34. Disconnect heater hose from heater pipe by squeezing quick-connect tabs.
35. Remove heater hose with quick-connect.
36. Remove heater hose and clamps from heater core.
37. Raise and support vehicle.
38. Remove evaporator block heater case plate drain tube elbow.
39. Remove mounting nuts, heater pipes' heater case plate and seals.
40. Remove mounting nuts, evaporator block heater case plate and seal.
41. Remove HVAC module bracket mounting nut.
42. Lower vehicle.
43. Remove mounting bolts and radio.
44. Disconnect radio electrical connectors and antenna lead.

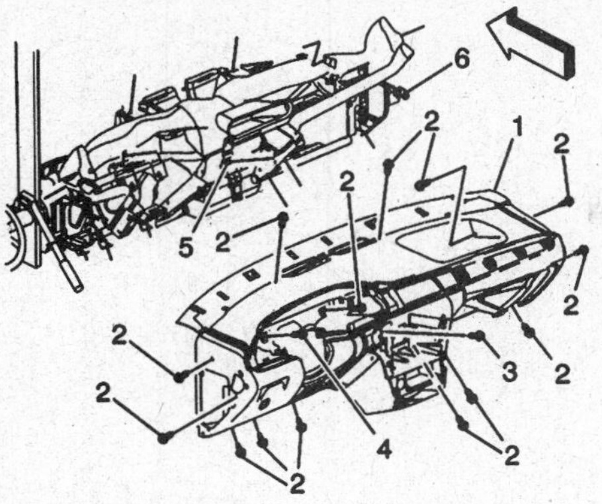

(1) Instrument Panel Assembly
(2) Screws (Tighten Last in Random Order)
(3) Screw (Tighten 1st)
(4) Screw (Tighten 2nd)
(5) Locator Pin
(6) Tie Bar Assembly

GC9149700134000X

Fig. 13 Exploded view of instrument panel. Malibu

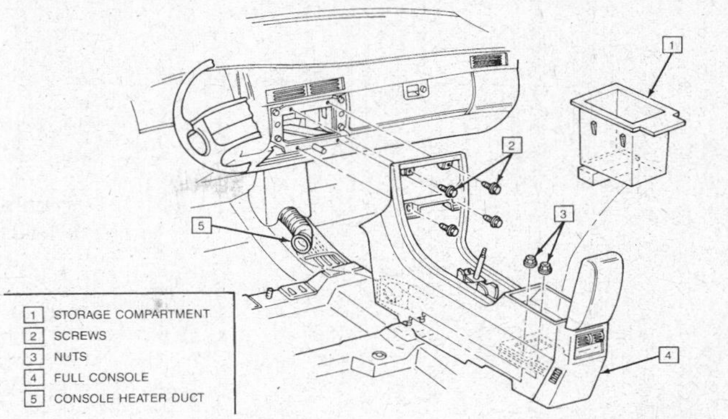

GC9140000186050X

Fig. 14 Exploded view of console. Eldorado & Seville

45. Remove mounting nuts and pull tape player out to access electrical connector.
46. Disconnect electrical connector and remove tape player.
47. Remove ignition switch mounting bolts and disconnect electrical connectors.
48. Insert key into ignition switch key cylinder, rotate key to RUN position.
49. Depress park lock cable tab and remove cable from ignition switch housing.
50. Press cylinder release plunger located at four o'clock position on ignition switch housing.
51. Pull cylinder from ignition switch housing using key.
52. Disconnect Pass Key electrical connector.
53. Remove ignition switch.
54. Position front seat forward and remove seat adjuster mounting bolts.
55. Disconnect lefthand side seat belt wiring harness.
56. Disconnect lefthand side power seat electrical connector, as required.
57. Manually tilt forward, disconnect floor pan hooks and remove front seats.
58. Fold console compartment up.
59. Remove gear shift lever handle by pulling retainer pin and upward on handle.
60. Remove console trim plate by gently pry upward to disconnect retainers.
61. Remove rear cupholder, **Fig. 12.**
62. Remove mounting screws and console.
63. Remove ashtray.
64. Remove instrument panel to tie bar mounting screws, **Fig. 13.**
65. Remove instrument panel.
66. Reverse procedure to install.

DeVille

1. Remove mounting screws, then the left and righthand closeout insulator panels by pulling down to disconnect push pin fasteners and sliding rearward. Ensure lefthand panel clears emergency brake bracket.
2. Remove lefthand knee bolster trim panel by grasping at top and bottom, then pulling rearward.
3. Disconnect night vision switch electrical connector, as required.
4. Remove four mounting screws and lefthand knee bolster.
5. Remove righthand knee bolster trim panel by grasping at top and bottom, then pulling rearward.
6. **On all models except DTS,** proceed as follows:
   a. Remove four center storage compartment mounting screws.
   b. Disconnect electrical connector, as required.
   c. Remove center storage compartment.
7. **On DTS models,** proceed as follows:
   a. Remove two mounting screws at bottom of center storage compartment.
   b. Open compartment door.
   c. Release upper retainers by pulling compartment, grasp inside.
   d. Disconnect electrical connector.
   e. Remove compartment.
8. **On all models,** set parking brake.
9. Grasp lefthand console side panel rear edge and pull out to disconnect rear retainers.
10. Push lefthand console side panel forward to disconnect from HVAC cover.
11. Remove lefthand console side panel.
12. Grasp righthand console side panel rear edge and pull out to disconnect retainers.
13. Remove righthand console side panel.
14. Shift transaxle into NEUTRAL position.
15. Disconnect four of six console trim plate clips by prying upward on rear edge using suitable thin bladed or hook tool.
16. Disconnect traction control switch electrical connector by lifting trim plate rear.
17. Disconnect front console trim panel clips by pushing down on console trim plate front and pulling towards rear.
18. Remove console trim plate by lifting over shift handle.
19. Remove lefthand knee bolster trim.
20. Remove transmission park/neutral position switch lever cable end cap.
21. Remove cable from bracket by prying lock button to unlocked position.
22. Remove shift control cable from floor shift.
23. **On models equipped with mobile phone connector,** proceed as follows:
   a. Open center console lid and disconnect cellular phone wiring, as required.
   b. Remove hinge mounting screws and center console tray.
   c. Remove four console tray insert mounting screws.
   d. Remove wiring junction box and disconnect wiring, as required.
   e. Remove console tray insert.
   f. Remove interface card and disconnect electrical connector.
   g. Remove rear HVAC control by prying using suitable flat bladed tool.
   h. Disconnect electrical connector.
   i. Remove mounting screws and center console endcap.
   j. Disconnect coil cord coaxial cable.
   k. Remove cellular phone wiring.
24. **On all models,** remove four console to instrument panel mounting bolts.
25. Adjust front seats rearward.
26. Remove two front console to floor mounting bolts.
27. Adjust front seats forward.
28. Remove two rear console to floor mounting bolts.
29. Move console rearward and disconnect electrical connectors.
30. Remove center console.
31. Release left and righthand instrument panel endcap by insert suitable flat bladed tool between panel and instrument panel, then pulling out while releasing retainer.
32. Slide instrument panel endcaps out of tabs on front edge of instrument panel.
33. Release defroster grilles' retaining clips by prying upward on rear using suitable flat bladed tool.
34. Disconnect sunload sensor electrical connector.
35. Remove defroster grille by pulling up on rear edge and then rearward.
36. Remove windshield pillar garnish molding by pulling from windshield pillar to disconnect clips.
37. **Air outlet vents are not interchangeable, record vent location during removal.**

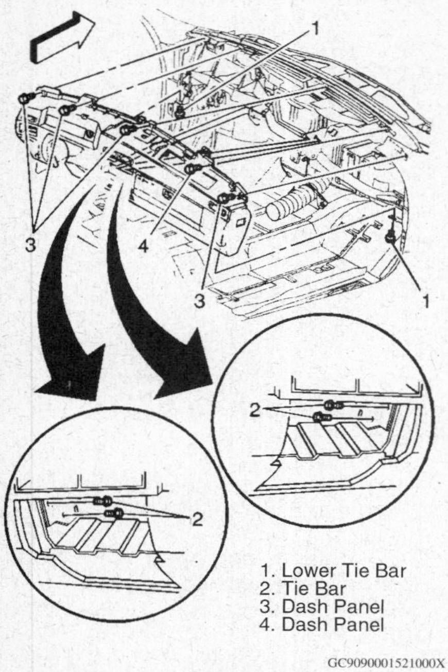

Fig. 15 Exploded view of instrument panel. Eldorado

38. Remove air outlet vents by grasp center, then release retainers on inside of vent at top and bottom of air outlet housing using suitable small flat bladed tool.
39. Remove four upper pad mounting screws inside vent outlet holes and three mounting bolts inside defroster grille outlet holes.
40. Lift upper instrument panel pad upward from rear edge of instrument panel cluster in disconnect instrument panel cluster retainers.
41. Disconnect electrical connectors, as required.
42. Remove instrument panel upper trim pad by lift padding on angle and slide rearward to disconnect retainers at front.
43. Disconnect body to instrument panel electrical connectors at top, outside corners.
44. Disconnect all other electrical connectors.
45. Remove steering column to body mounting bolts.
46. Remove transaxle park/neutral position switch lever cable end cap.
47. Remove cable from bracket by prying lock button to unlocked position.
48. Remove shift control cable from floor shift and disconnect from steering column.
49. Disconnect steering column to body connectors.
50. Remove instrument panel center support bracket to floor bracket mounting bolts.
51. Remove instrument panel carrier to cowl mounting nuts.
52. Remove left and righthand instrument panel carrier to hinge pillar mounting bolts and nuts.
53. Remove instrument panel and carrier.
54. Reverse procedure to install.

Eldorado

1. Lift armrest, then remove storage compartment by pulling up and out, **Fig. 14.**
2. Disconnect three electrical connectors on lefthand inner side of center console.
3. Block vehicle wheels.
4. Place shifter into NEUTRAL position.
5. Remove retaining clip and shifter handle.
6. Disconnect trim plate clips using suitable flat bladed tool.
7. Remove trim plate. Disconnect electrical connectors.
8. Remove two lower ashtray bracket mounting screws and pull ashtray box out.
9. Remove one lower hidden mounting screw and ashtray. Disconnect cigarette lighter electrical connector.
10. Pry out driver information display switch using suitable thin flat bladed tool on both sides.
11. Remove driver information display switch. Disconnect electrical connector.
12. Remove radio and heater/AC control mounting screws.
13. Disconnect electrical connectors and antenna coaxial cable.
14. Remove radio and heater/AC control.
15. Remove two console to floor mounting bolts.
16. Remove four console to instrument panel mounting bolts.
17. Disconnect console air supply duct. Turn to release.
18. Release tie band
19. Disconnect console electrical connectors.
20. Disconnect auto transaxle park lock cable from shift plate bracket.
21. Disconnect auto transaxle range selector lever cable from shift plate bracket.
22. Disconnect BTSI electrical connector.
23. Pull console rearward while lifting upward on rear of console.
24. Remove console.
25. Remove hinge pillar tie bar support brace support cover.
26. Remove mounting screws and disconnect insulator lower instrument panel.
27. Disconnect electrical connector.
28. Slide insulator panel rearward to clear emergency brake bracket.
29. Remove insulator panel.
30. Remove rear compartment fuse block RLY, IGN 1, IGN, O-BODY and CLUSTER fuses.
31. Remove front fuse block HAZARD and MIRROR fuses.
32. Pry defroster grill upward using suitable flat bladed tool.
33. Disconnect sunload and twilight sensors by turning quarter turn.
34. Disconnect windshield pillar garnish molding tabs from clips by pulling outward.
35. Remove garnish molding.
36. Remove four air outlet deflectors using suitable thin bladed tool.

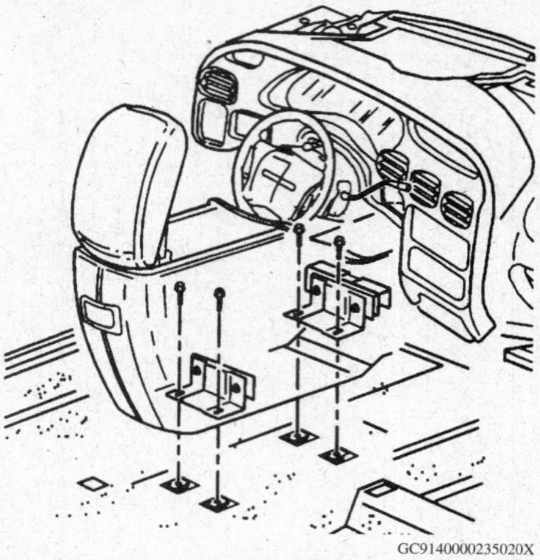

Fig. 16 Exploded view of console. Grand Prix

37. Release tab on inboard side of deflectors between deflector and deflector housing, while pulling air outlet deflectors out.
38. Close air outlet ducts. **Ensure air outlet ducts are closed to prevent upper trim pad fasteners from falling into HVAC ducts.**
39. Remove three upper trim panel mounting screws through defroster grille openings. Record fastener size and location.
40. Remove four upper trim panel mounting screws through air outlet deflector openings.
41. Press down on forward edge righthand side of trim panel while pulling upward and back on rear edge of trim panel.
42. Tilt steering wheel full downward.
43. Remove upper trim panel.
44. Disconnect instrument cluster top electrical connectors.
45. Remove four mounting screws and slide instrument cluster upward.
46. Grasp trim at front and rear edges edges, then pull filler trim downward.
47. Remove four mounting screws and steering column opening filler bracket.
48. Remove mounting screws, then disconnect left and righthand insulator panels from lower instrument panel.
49. Lower insulator panels and disconnect electrical connector.
50. Remove insulator panels.
51. Remove mounting screws and glove compartment. Disconnect electrical connectors.
52. Remove switches from instrument panel storage compartment, as required.
53. Disconnect retainers and remove glove compartment switch plate bezel.
54. Remove lamp, valet and traction control switches by squeezing retainers and prying out.
55. Disconnect aspirator tube.
56. Disconnect inside air temperature sensor electrical connector.
57. Remove passenger's air bag module as outlined in "Passive Restraint Systems" chapter.

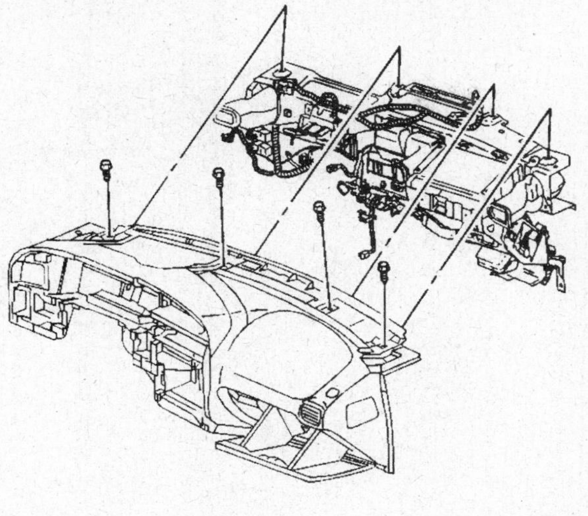

GC9149900151000X

Fig. 17 Exploded view of instrument panel. Grand Prix

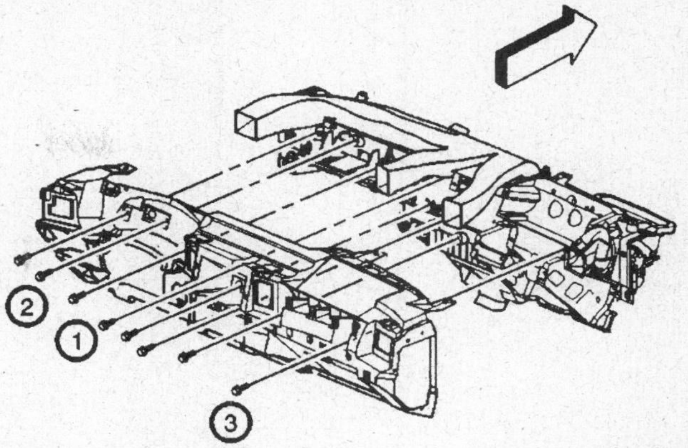

GC9090001545000X

Fig. 18 Exploded view of instrument panel. Impala & Monte Carlo

58. Remove two mounting screws and lefthand trim plate.
59. Remove two righthand trim panel end mounting screws.
60. Remove two righthand trim panel top center mounting screws.
61. Release hook and loop patch(s) from righthand trim panel back.
62. Remove trim panel.
63. Remove headlamp switch by depressing two tabs located to top left of switch knob and directly above fog lamp switch using suitable flat bladed tool.
64. Disconnect electrical connectors.
65. Remove hood latch release handle mounting screws.
66. Remove driver's air bag module as outlined in "Passive Restraint Systems" chapter.
67. Remove lefthand sound insulator by pulling downward.
68. Remove four mounting screws and steering column opening filler.
69. Disconnect ignition wiring, PASS key wiring and 48-way connectors.
70. Remove intermediate shaft pinch bolt.
71. Remove two mounting bolts and lower support bracket.
72. Remove two mounting bolts and upper column support.
73. Lower steering column.
74. Remove righthand instrument panel to hinge pillar tie bar mounting bolt.
75. Remove center instrument panel to hinge pillar tie bar mounting bolts each side of radio/climate control panel opening.
76. Remove lower instrument panel to bracket mounting bolts at each end, **Fig. 15.**
77. Remove instrument panel to dash panel mounting bolts.
78. Partially remove instrument panel.
79. Disconnect electrical connectors.
80. Push aspirator tube through instrument panel.
81. Remove instrument panel.
82. Reverse procedure to install.

Grand Am

1. Pull door weatherstrip from windshield side upper garnish molding, as required.
2. Remove windshield side upper garnish molding by disconnecting clips.
3. Remove defroster grill by disconnecting retainers using suitable small flat bladed tool.
4. Remove instrument panel endcaps by pulling outward.
5. Remove righthand sound insulator and disconnect heater hose form duct.
6. Remove mounting screws and lefthand sound insulator.
7. Remove mounting screws under glove compartment door and open door.
8. Remove pocket mounting screws and glove compartment. Disconnect compartment lamp electrical connector.
9. Remove passenger's air bag module as outlined in "Passive Restraint Systems" chapter.
10. Position front seats to most rearward position.
11. Position emergency brake lever to full up position.
12. Position gear selector to NEUTRAL position.
13. Release front floor console trim plate using suitable small flat bladed tool.
14. Remove trim plate by rotating 90° and guiding it over shift handle.
15. Position shift lever fully rearward.
16. Remove mounting screws and console cupholder.
17. Remove ignition switch bezel using suitable small flat blade tool.
18. Remove instrument panel accessory trim plate by pulling from storage compartment to release retainers.
19. Disconnect cigarette lighter and hazard warning switch electrical connectors.
20. Remove cigarette lighter fuse and element.
21. Remove cigarette lighter socket by placing one side of T portion of cigarette lighter socket remover tool No. J-42059, or equivalent, into tab window and then other should be angled into opposite tab window.
22. Pull lighter socket straight out and remove tool.
23. Disconnect cigarette lighter socket electrical connector.
24. Remove cigarette lighter retainer.
25. Remove mounting screws and hazard warning switch retainer bracket.
26. Remove flasher and switch from switch retainer bracket using suitable small flat bladed tool to depress and release flasher retainers, while pressing flasher and switch.
27. Remove flasher and switch from switch retainer bracket.
28. Remove lower steering column trim cover mounting screws.
29. Remove upper column trim cover by tilting up and unsnapping from lower column trim cover hinges.
30. Remove tilt steering wheel lever by pulling retaining pin and snapping out.
31. Remove lower column trim cover.
32. Remove lower and upper mounting screws, then the instrument panel cluster trim plate.
33. Remove mounting screws and instrument panel cluster. Disconnect electrical connector.
34. Remove mounting screws and radio. Disconnect instrument panel wiring harness and antenna cable connectors.
35. Remove steering wheel as outlined in "Electrical" section of appropriate chassis chapter.
36. Remove steering column as outlined in "Steering Columns" chapter.
37. Position shift lever fully rearward.
38. Remove mounting screws, then the cupholder by lifting up and rearward to clear storage compartment.
39. Disconnect storage compartment lamp from cupholder.
40. Lift up front floor console armrest and remove rubber mat from storage compartment.
41. Remove storage compartment rear mounting bolts.
42. Remove center bolts from console sides.

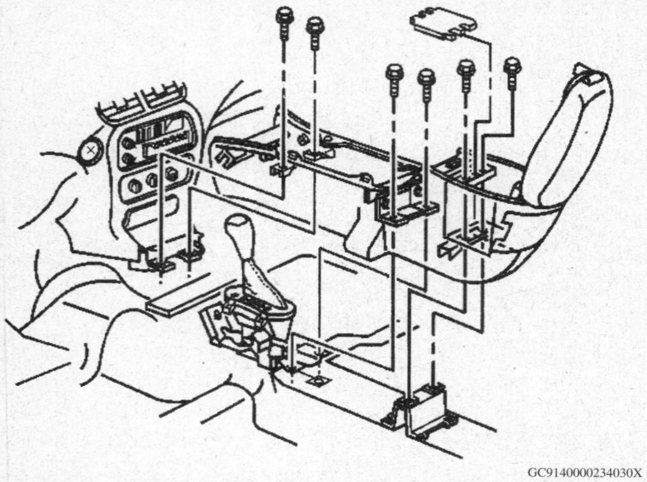

GC9140000234030X

Fig. 19 Exploded view of console. Intrigue

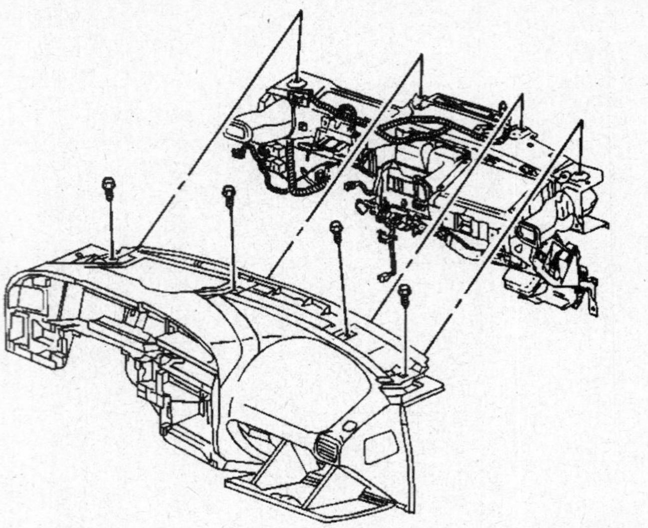

GC9090001543000X

Fig. 20 Exploded view of instrument panel. Intrigue

43. Remove covers using suitable small flat bladed tool at front edge, then the front mounting screws.
44. Remove bracket front mounting nuts.
45. Remove floor console by pulling up and rearward, guiding emergency brake lever boot over emergency brake lever.
46. Remove ignition switch mounting bolts. Position ignition switch for ease of removal.
47. Remove ignition switch mounting bolts and bracket.
48. Insert key and turn ignition switch lock cylinder to ACC position.
49. Depress retainer and remove transaxle park/lock cable.
50. Remove ignition switch lock cylinder by depressing retaining tab and pulling cylinder out with key.
51. Disconnect pass lock and ignition switch electrical connectors.
52. Remove ignition switch.
53. Remove fog lamp/dimmer switch/vent trim plate using suitable small flat bladed tool. Disconnect electrical connectors.
54. Remove fog lamp switch using suitable small flat bladed tool on back side to release retainer tabs.
55. Remove instrument panel upper bolt covers.
56. Disconnect electrical junction box electrical connections.
57. Remove instrument panel to cross car beam mounting screws.
58. Remove instrument panel.
59. Reverse procedure to install.

Grand Prix

1. Remove left and righthand insulator push-in retainers using door trim pad and garnish clip remover tool No. J-38778, or equivalent.
2. Rotate courtesy lamp socket counterclockwise to release. Remove bulb.
3. Remove left and righthand insulator by pulling rearward from accelerator pedal stud.
4. Remove carpet retainers using door trim pad and garnish clip remover tool No. 38778, or equivalent.
5. Remove mounting bolts, screws, then the windshield side upper garnish molding by disconnect tabs and clips.
6. Lift up upper trim panel approximately two inches and pull rearward to release retainers.
7. Remove sensor bezel by insert suitable small plastic flat bladed tool into rear edge slot and releasing retainer.
8. Remove security indicator lamp. Disconnect electrical connector.
9. Remove Daytime Running Lamp (DRL) ambient light sensor by turning counterclockwise. Disconnect electrical connector.
10. Remove sun load sensor. Disconnect electrical connector.
11. Remove upper trim panel. **Remove upper trim slowly to prevent retainer clips from falling into instrument panel.**
12. Remove rear storage compartment.
13. Position transaxle selector in low range.
14. Raise armrest, then remove storage compartment and mat.
15. Open cup holder and remove trim plate, starting at rear and pulling up, working forward to release retainers.
16. Disconnect driver's seat heater switch electrical connector, as required.
17. Remove shift control lever and indicator bezel.
18. Remove console rear mounting in rear storage compartment, **Fig. 16.**
19. Remove center mounting bolts at transaxle shift lever mounting bracket.
20. Remove console front mounting bolts.
21. Disconnect electrical connectors.
22. Remove console by pulling rearward to release from instrument panel guide pins.
23. Remove mounting bolts and steering column opening filler by pulling rearward and upward to unsnap.
24. Remove low tire reset switch connector, as required.
25. Remove mounting bolts from instrument panel and steering column support, then the knee bolster.
26. Remove driver's air bag module as outlined in "Passive Restraint Systems" chapter.
27. Remove steering wheel as outlined in "Electrical" section of appropriate chassis chapter.
28. Remove steering column as outlined in "Steering Columns" chapter.
29. Disconnect retainer clips by pulling trim plate and pull out.
30. Disconnect fog lamp switch electrical connector.
31. Remove instrument cluster trim plate.
32. Remove mounting screws and radio. Disconnect electrical/audio electrical and coaxial cable connectors.
33. Remove mounting bolts and HVAC control module. Disconnect electrical connectors and vacuum harness.
34. Remove mounting screws and rotate instrument cluster rearward and lift top up to disconnect locating pins. Disconnect electrical connectors.
35. Remove instrument cluster.
36. Remove headlamp switch by pulling to release retaining tabs. Disconnect electrical connector.
37. **On models equipped with Head Up Display (HUD),** proceed as follows:
    a. Remove HUD dimmer switch by unsnapping.
    b. Remove HUD dimmer switch electrical connectors.
    c. Remove HUD module mounting bolts.
    d. Disconnect HUD module electrical connector.
    e. Remove HUD module.
38. **On all models,** remove Driver Information Center (DIC) by unsnapping. Disconnect electrical connections.
39. Remove hinge mounting screws and open glove compartment.
40. Remove glove compartment housing by pressing inward on both sides, then rotating down and out.
41. Release glove compartment lamp by reaching behind support panel and depress retaining tabs.
42. Press glove compartment lamp switch

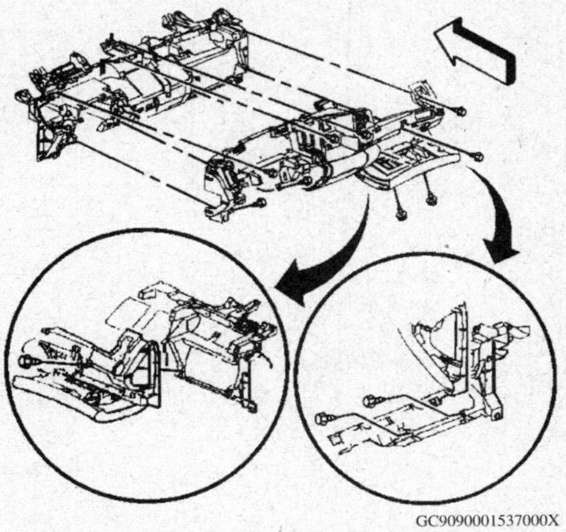

GC9090001537000X

Fig. 21 Exploded view of instrument panel. LeSabre

through opening. Disconnect electrical connector.

43. Disconnect electrical connector and remove inside air temperature sensor.
44. Remove trim pad mounting bolts at windshield and lower lefthand side, **Fig. 17.**
45. Remove cluster pocket trim pad mounting bolt.
46. Position wiring harness aside.
47. Remove trim pad.
48. Reverse procedure to install.

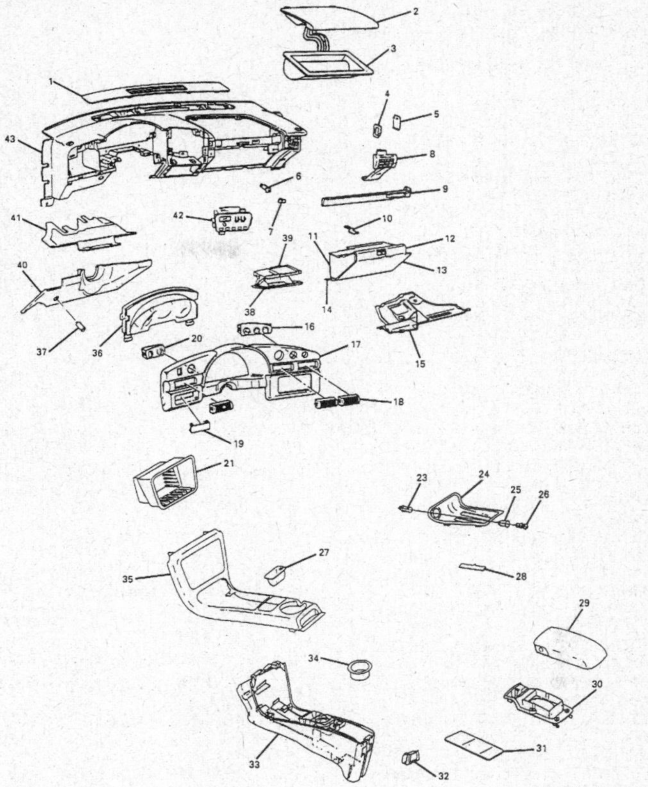

GC9090001547010X

Fig. 22 Exploded view of instrument panel. (Part 1 of 2). Lumina

Impala

1. Release lefthand insulator tabs.
2. Disconnect courtesy lamp by rotating counterclockwise.
3. Remove lefthand insulator by removing from accelerator pedal stud.
4. Remove righthand insulator push-in retainer using door trim pad clip remover tool No. J-38778, or equivalent.
5. Release tabs from retainers, pull rearward and lower righthand insulator.
6. Remove courtesy lamp by rotating counterclockwise.
7. Remove righthand insulator.
8. Remove lefthand instrument panel fuse block access opening cover.
9. Release lefthand instrument panel insulator tabs from lower trim pad retainers for access.
10. Remove mounting bolts and release steering column opening filler panel retainers.
11. Lower steering column opening filler panel, disconnect electrical connector and remove rear compartment release switch.
12. Remove steering column opening filler panel.
13. Remove driver's air bag module as outlined in "Passive Restraint Systems" chapter.
14. Remove steering wheel as outlined in "Electrical" section of appropriate chassis chapter.
15. Remove tilt lever by rocking it back and forth.
16. Remove mounting screws, steering column lower and upper trim covers.
17. Remove steering column wire harness retainer and two wire harness straps.
18. Remove steering column bulkhead connector from harness.
19. Disconnect multi-function turn signal lever steering column bulkhead connectors.
20. Remove mounting bolts and multi-function turn signal lever.
21. Remove righthand access opening cover.
22. Remove mounting screws and open glove compartment.
23. Remove glove compartment by disconnect damper cable and depressing side stops.
24. Apply parking brake and move automatic transaxle shift control indicator to 2 position.
25. Open storage compartment door and pry trim plate rear away console.
26. Pull trim plate towards rear to disconnect front.
27. Remove console shift control bezel.
28. Disconnect trim plate rear electrical connector.
29. Rotate trim plate 180°.
30. Lift trim plate over shift control handle.
31. Disconnect trim plate wiring harness retainers.
32. Disconnect ashtray lamp and wiring harness.
33. Disconnect cigarette lighter electrical connector.
34. Remove ashtray.
35. Remove front floor console trim plate.
36. Remove console mounting bolts near instrument panel, at transaxle shift control lever and under rear bin mat.
37. Pull console rearward to disconnect instrument panel clips.
38. Disconnect electrical connectors.
39. Remove console.
40. **On models equipped with column shift,** engage parking brake and move transaxle shift control indicator to 1 position. Key must remain in ignition switch cylinder.
41. **On all models,** remove ignition switch cylinder bezel using suitable small flat bladed tool.
42. Remove left and righthand instrument panel fuse block access opening covers, as required.
43. Remove instrument cluster trim plate mounting screws.
44. Release cluster trim plate retainers. Starting at righthand side, grasp plate and pull rearward, then continue working around.
45. Disconnect hazard switch and traction control switch electrical connectors, as required.
46. Remove instrument cluster trim plate.
47. Remove mounting bolts and lower ignition switch from carrier.
48. Insert key into ignition lock cylinder and turn it to RUN position.
49. Remove ignition lock cylinder by depress housing bottom detent. Disconnect ignition switch housing electrical connectors.
50. Remove mounting screws and radio. Disconnect instrument panel wiring harness and antenna cable connector.
51. Remove mounting bolts and HVAC control module. Disconnect electrical and vacuum connectors.

1 PANEL, INSTRUMENT PANEL UPPER TRIM
2 DOOR, INFLATABLE RESTRAINT INSTRUMENT PANEL MODULE
3 MODULE, INFLATABLE RESTRAINT INSTRUMENT PANEL
4 FUSE BOX, INSTRUMENT PANEL
5 DOOR, INSTRUMENT PANEL FUSE BOX
6 SWITCH, INSTRUMENT PANEL LOWER COMPARTMENT LIGHT
7 COVER, INSTRUMENT PANEL LOWER COMPARTMENT LIGHT SWITCH
8 OUTLET, HEATER AND AIR CONDITIONING
9 PLATE, INSTRUMENT PANEL TRIM
10 STRIKER, INSTRUMENT PANEL LOWER COMPARTMENT
11 BIN, INSTRUMENT PANEL LOWER COMPARTMENT
12 COMPARTMENT ASSEMBLY, INSTRUMENT PANEL LOWER
13 DOOR, INSTRUMENT PANEL LOWER COMPARTMENT
14 HINGE, INSTRUMENT PANEL LOWER COMPARTMENT
15 INSULATOR, INSTRUMENT PANEL RIGHT SOUND
16 CONTROL, HEATER AND AIR CONDITIONING
17 PLATE, INSTRUMENT PANEL CLUSTER TRIM
18 OUTLET, HEATER AND AIR CONDITIONING
19 PLUG, INSTRUMENT PANEL
20 SWITCH, HEADLAMP
21 COMPARTMENT, FRONT FLOOR CONSOLE FRONT
23 RETAINER, FRONT FLOOR CONSOLE
24 PLATE, FRONT FLOOR CONSOLE TRANSAXLE SHIFT OPENING TRIM
25 HOUSING, FRONT FLOOR CONSOLE LIGHTER ELEMENT
26 ELEMENT, FRONT FLOOR CONSOLE LIGHTER
27 ASHTRAY, FRONT FLOOR CONSOLE
28 LENS, FRONT FLOOR CONSOLE TRANSAXLE SHIFT OPENING TRIM PLATE
29 TRIM, FRONT FLOOR CONSOLE ARMREST
30 ARMREST, FRONT FLOOR CONSOLE
31 MAT, FRONT FLOOR CONSOLE
32 ASHTRAY, FRONT FLOOR CONSOLE REAR
33 CONSOLE, FRONT FLOOR
34 CUP HOLDER, FRONT FLOOR CONSOLE
35 PLATE, FRONT FLOOR CONSOLE TRIM
36 CLUSTER, INSTRUMENT
37 SWITCH, REAR COMPARTMENT LID RELEASE
38 ASHTRAY, INSTRUMENT PANEL
39 CUP HOLDER, INSTRUMENT PANEL
40 FILLER, INSTRUMENT PANEL STEERING COLUMN OPENING
41 INSULATOR, INSTRUMENT PANEL LEFT SOUND
42 AUDIO SYSTEM
43 INSTRUMENT PANEL ASSEMBLY

GC9090001547020X

Fig. 22 Exploded view of instrument panel. (Part 2 of 2). Lumina

52. Remove mounting screws and headlamp switch housing. Disconnect headlamp and foglamp switches' electrical connectors.
53. Remove foglamp switch using suitable small flat bladed tool.
54. Remove mounting bolts, cable and hood release handle.
55. Disconnect Data Link Connector (DLC).
56. Open lefthand seat belt guide loop cover, then remove mounting nut and seat belt guide loop from guide adjuster bracket.
57. Open righthand seat belt guide loop cover, then remove mounting nut and seat belt guide loop.
58. Remove upper center pillar trim panel.
59. Remove windshield garnish molding from upper side rail clip retainers, windshield pillar and front door carpet retainer by pulling up and back.
60. Remove defroster grille by lifting upwards starting at righthand side to release retainers. Continue working to left.
61. Disconnect Daytime Running Lamps (DRL) sensor.
62. Remove upper trim pad mounting screws.
63. Disconnect remote control door lock receiver retainers and electrical connectors.
64. Remove remote control door lock receiver.
65. Remove upper trim pad.
66. Remove mounting screws and instrument cluster. Disconnect electrical connector.
67. Remove passenger's air bag module as outlined in "Passive Restraint Systems" chapter.
68. Remove instrument panel mounting screws in sequence, **Fig. 18.**
69. Position wiring harness aside.
70. Remove instrument panel.
71. Reverse procedure to install.

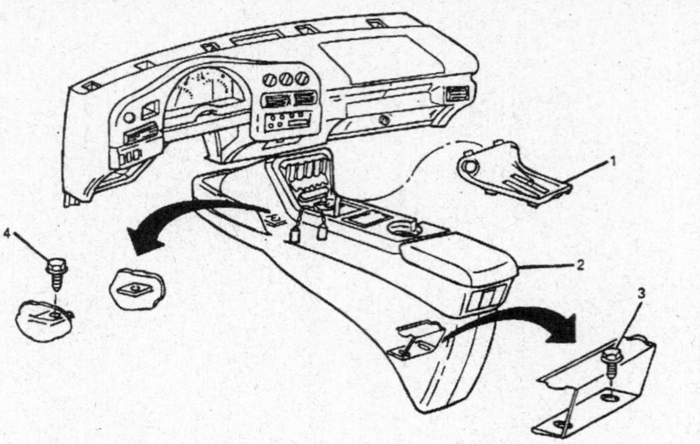

1 PLATE, FRONT FLOOR CONSOLE TRANSAXLE SHIFT OPENING TRIM
2 CONSOLE, FRONT FLOOR
3 BOLT/SCREW, FRONT FLOOR CONSOLE
4 BOLT/SCREW, FRONT FLOOR CONSOLE

GC9140000236020X

Fig. 23 Exploded view of console. Lumina

Intrigue

1. Remove end caps by pulling outward to disconnect retainers.
2. Remove lefthand insulator retainers from steering column opening filler panel using door trim pad clip remover tool No. J-38778, or equivalent.
3. Disconnect Data Link Connector (DLC).
4. Remove lefthand insulator retainers using door trim pad clip remover tool.
5. Disconnect courtesy lamp by turning quarter turn counterclockwise.
6. Remove accelerator pedal lefthand stud.
7. Remove lefthand insulator.
8. Adjust carpeting and disconnect courtesy lamp from righthand sound insulator by turning quarter turn counterclockwise.
9. Remove righthand insulator panel using door trim pad clip remover tool to disconnect retainers.
10. Remove left and righthand front pillar, lower trim panel using door trim pad clip remover tool.
11. Pull front door weatherstrip from pinchweld flange.
12. Remove windshield side upper garnish moldings by disconnecting.
13. Lift upper trim panel up approximately two inches and pull rearward to release retainers.
14. Remove Daytime Running Lamp (DRL) ambient light sensor by rotating counterclockwise to release from upper trim pad.
15. Disconnect sunload and DRL light sensors from defroster grille. Disconnect electrical connector.
16. Remove sunload sensor.
17. Remove upper trim panel.
18. Raise armrest and remove console trim plate mounting screws.
19. Open cupholder and pull up on trim plate.
20. Disconnect traction control switch wiring harness connector.
21. Remove traction control switch using suitable small flat bladed tool on back side of switch to release retaining clips.
22. Pull up on trim plate starting at rear and working forward to release retainer clips.
23. Remove front floor console trim plate lifting up and over transaxle shift lever.
24. Remove console shifter control trim plate bolts.
25. Disconnect electrical connectors, as required.
26. Remove console rear bracket mounting screws, **Fig. 19.**
27. Remove storage compartment mat.
28. Remove rear storage compartment bracket mounting screws.
29. Remove front mounting point screws.
30. Remove console by pulling rearward, up and out.
31. Remove steering column opening filler by unsnapping retainers.
32. Remove hood release handle base mounting bolts or screws.
33. Remove cable from hood release handle.
34. Remove hood release handle.
35. Remove SIR connector clip.
36. Remove mounting bolts and knee bolster bracket.
37. Remove lower steering column mounting bolts and upper steering column

mounting nuts.
38. Lower steering column.
39. Remove hood release handle.
40. Remove instrument cluster trim plate mounting screws.
41. Pull out instrument cluster trim plate to release from retainers.
42. Disconnect trip odometer and reset switch electrical connector.
43. Remove trip odometer and reset switch by releasing retainers using suitable small flat bladed tool.
44. Remove instrument cluster trim plate.
45. Remove mounting screws and instrument cluster. Disconnect electrical connector.
46. Remove accessory trim plate by releasing retainers.
47. Remove mounting bolts and pull radio out. Disconnect electrical/audio connector and coaxial cable.
48. Remove radio.
49. Remove mounting screws and HVAC control module. Disconnect electrical connector.
50. Remove mounting screws and instrument panel cluster. Disconnect electrical connector.
51. Remove ignition switch bezel using suitable small flat bladed tool.
52. Remove mounting bolts and position ignition switch to ease removal.
53. Insert key and turn ignition switch lock cylinder to ACC position.
54. Depress transaxle park/lock cable retainer to release and pull to remove park/lock cable from ignition switch.
55. Remove ignition switch lock cylinder by depressing retaining tab and pulling cylinder out with key.
56. Disconnect pass lock electrical connector.
57. Disconnect ignition switch electrical connectors.
58. Remove ignition switch through cluster opening.
59. Remove mounting bolts and bracket.
60. Release air outlet vent by inserting suitable small flat bladed tool to center upper position.
61. Remove vent by pulling out.
62. Remove hazard warning and cruise control switch from retainer by squeezing retainer Disconnect electrical connectors.
63. Remove hazard warning and cruise control switch bezel by using suitable small flat bladed tool to release retainers.
64. Remove switch bank mounting screws. Disconnect electrical connectors.
65. Open glove compartment, then remove hinge mounting bolts and screws.
66. Turn compartment door stops quarter turn and loosen damper string screw.
67. Remove damper string loop from screw and glove compartment.
68. Remove glove compartment lamp switch by using suitable small flat bladed tool to depress retainers.
69. Disconnect electrical connector and pull bulb from switch socket.
70. Position fuse block aside.

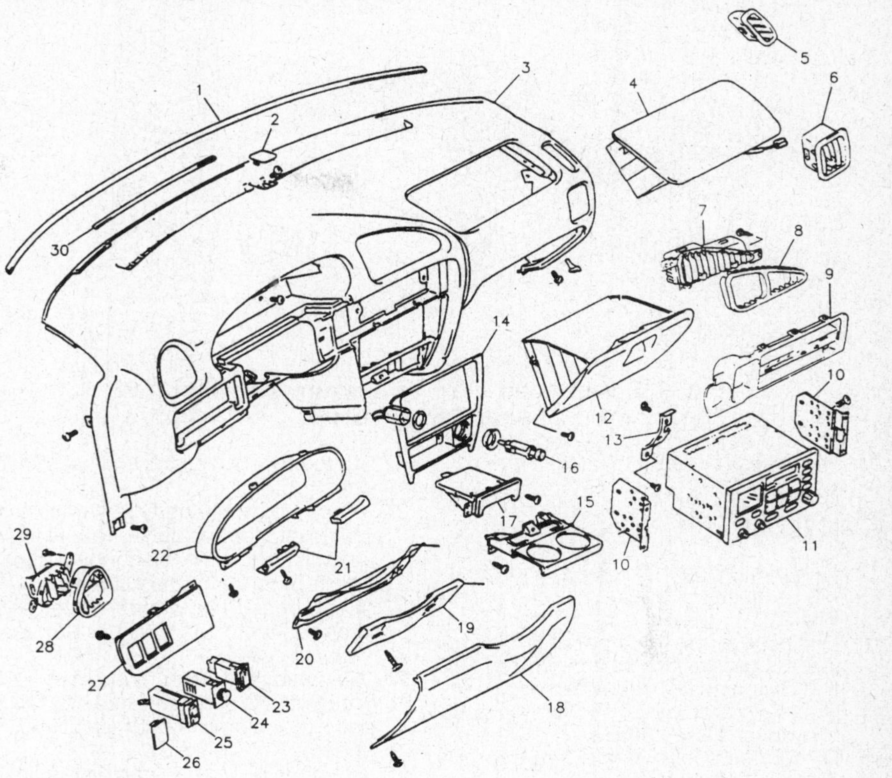

1 INSTRUMENT PANEL SEAL	11 RADIO	21 INSTRUMENT PANEL CLUSTER LOWER COVER
2 COVER	12 GLOVE BOX	22 INSTRUMENT PANEL BEZEL
3 INSTRUMENT PANEL ASSEMBLY	13 RADIO REAR BRACKET	23 REAR DEFOGGER SWITCH
4 PASSENGER INFLATOR MODULE	14 CENTER CONSOLE TRIM BEZEL	24 DIMMER SWITCH
5 SIDE DEMISTER NOZZLE	15 CUP HOLDER	25 REAR WIPER/WASHER SWITCH
6 SIDE VENT LOUVER	16 CIGAR LIGHTER	26 COVER
7 CENTER VENT LOUVER	17 ASHTRAY ASSEMBLY	27 LEFT GARNISH TRIM PANEL
8 CENTER VENT GARNISH	18 KNEE BOLSTER TRIM PANEL	28 SIDE VENT GARNISH
9 HEATER CONTROL PANEL	19 KNEE BOLSTER ABSORBER	29 SIDE VENT LOUVER
10 RADIO SIDE BRACKET	20 KNEE BOLSTER	30 DEFROSTER HOLE SEAL

GC9149500125000X

Fig. 24 Instrument panel replacement. Metro

71. Disconnect aspirator duct and position aside.
72. Disconnect electrical connector and remove inside air temperature sensor.
73. Remove instrument panel trim pad mounting screws, **Fig. 20.**
74. Position instrument panel wiring harness aside.
75. Remove trim pad.
76. Reverse procedure to install.

LeSabre

1. Disconnect lefthand sound insulator by removing mounting screw at rear edge.
2. Remove lefthand sound insulator by pushing in on snap tab retainers. Disconnect electrical connector.
3. Remove heater temperature sensor by turning quarter turn . Leave sensor connected to its wire.
4. Repeat previous three steps to remove righthand sound insulator.
5. Remove lefthand instrument panel accessory trim plate by pulling toward rear.
6. Disconnect headlamp and HUD switch electrical connectors.
7. Remove windshield pillar garnish molding by pulling it from pillar to disconnect retainer clips.
8. Remove lefthand endcap by pulling outward.
9. Open glove compartment door.
10. Remove righthand endcap by pulling outward to disconnect retainers.
11. Remove defroster grille by prying upward to release retainers.
12. Disconnect sensor electrical connector.
13. Remove sensor by twisting it counterclockwise.
14. Remove mounting screws and upper trim pad by lifting upward to disconnect retainers.
15. Disconnect body to instrument panel electrical connectors at top, righthand outside corner.
16. Disconnect center instrument panel to body harness electrical connector.
17. Remove instrument panel retainer.
18. Remove steering column as outlined in "Steering Column" chapter.
19. Remove mounting bolts and instrument panel carrier, **Fig. 21.**

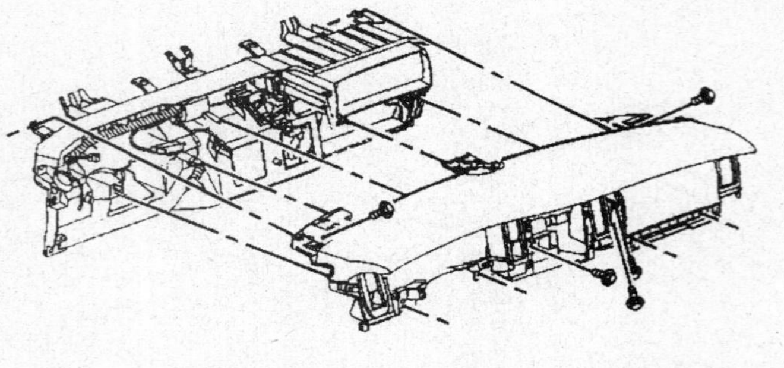

Fig. 25 Exploded view of instrument panel trim pad. Park Avenue

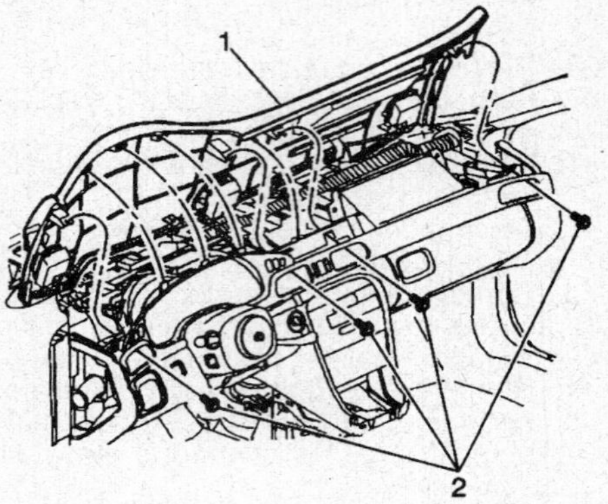

Fig. 26 Exploded view of upper trim pad. Seville

20. Reverse procedure to install.

Lumina

1. Remove mounting screws and steering column opening filler panel, **Fig. 22.**
2. Disconnect rear compartment lid release switch electrical connector.
3. Remove lefthand insulator.
4. Remove inner bracket mounting bolts and driver's knee bolster.
5. Disconnect driver's air bag module electrical connector.
6. Remove retainers using door trim pad and garnish clip remover tool No. J-38778, or equivalent, and righthand insulator.
7. Remove mounting screws and release door latch, then remove glove compartment.
8. Remove cover and disconnect glove compartment lamp.
9. Disconnect passenger's air bag module electrical connector.
10. Apply parking brake.
11. Remove storage tray by pulling tray toward to release retainers.
12. Remove storage compartment liner.
13. Remove console mounting screws, **Fig. 23.**
14. Remove clip and shift control handle.
15. Disconnect electrical connectors.
16. Adjust console shift control lever, as required.
17. Remove console.
18. Remove driver's air bag module as outlined in "Passive Restraint Systems" chapter.
19. Remove steering wheel as outlined in "Electrical" section of appropriate chassis chapter.
20. Remove steering column as outlined in "Steering Columns" chapter.
21. Remove two cross car beam bolts at brake pedal support bracket.
22. Remove lower brake pedal bracket brace bolts.
23. Remove cluster trim plate by disconnect retainers by pulling instrument cluster trim plate at one edge. Work way around entire cluster trim plate.
24. Remove mounting bolts and radio. Disconnect electrical connector.
25. Remove mounting and release retaining clip, then remove HVAC control. Disconnect electrical and vacuum connectors.
26. Remove mounting screws and instrument cluster by rotating rearward, then lifting bottom to disconnect locating pins. Slide instrument cluster out.
27. Disconnect instrument cluster electrical connector and wiring harness retaining clips.
28. Remove headlamp switch by pulling rearward to release retainers. Disconnect headlamp switch electrical connector.
29. Remove upper trim pad by prying front edge upward to disconnect retainers using suitable flat bladed tool.
30. Remove Daytime Running Lamp (DRL) sensor by turn it counterclockwise.
31. Remove passenger's air bag module as outlined in "Passive Restraint Systems" chapter.
32. Remove mounting screws and trim cover tether.
33. Remove name plate using suitable flat bladed tool.
34. Release righthand air outlet vent panel top retainer starting at righthand and pulling rearward.
35. Release middle retainer by pulling middle rearward.
36. Remove righthand air outlet by pulling bottom straight out.
37. Remove stop lamp handle, as required.
38. Disconnect windshield side upper garnish moldings retaining tabs and clips by pulling and using rocking motion.
39. Remove front door inside carpet retainers.
40. Remove mounting screws and Data Link Connector (DLC).
41. Remove lefthand front hinge A Pillar tie bar bolts.
42. Remove two trim pad mounting screws.
43. Remove righthand front hinge A pillar tie bar bolts.
44. Remove SIR connector.
45. Remove fuse block access opening cover.
46. Release retainers and position fuse block aside.
47. Remove glove compartment lamp switch.
48. Remove HVAC module to air duct tubes.
49. Remove wiring harness tie strap.
50. Disconnect retaining clips and wiring harness at cross car beam.
51. Remove instrument panel.
52. Remove mounting screws and main air distribution duct.
53. Remove lower tie bar, center support and lower trim panel mounting screws.
54. Remove cross car beam.
55. Reverse procedure to install.

Metro

1. Depress glove compartment stopper and pull rearward.
2. Remove mounting screws and glove compartment, **Fig. 24.**
3. Disconnect electrical connectors, then remove mounting screws and PCM.
4. **On models equipped with manual transaxle,** remove gearshift control lever upper boot.
5. **On all models,** remove six mounting screws and console.
6. Remove four mounting screws and center console trim bezel.
7. Remove cup holder and radio.
8. Disconnect cigar lighter electrical connector working through glove compartment opening.
9. Remove ashtray, heater control unit knobs and righthand dash panel cluster lower cover.
10. Gently pry heater face plate from dash panel, then remove heater face plate bulb socket and A/C switch.
11. Disconnect temperature, air mode and fresh/recirculation air control cables at heater and blower cases.
12. Remove heater control unit screws, push unit toward inside of dash panel and disconnect fan electrical connector.
13. Remove control unit through radio opening.
14. Remove mounting screws and lower hood release handle from dash panel.
15. Remove driver's air bag module as outlined in "Passive Restraint Systems" chapter.
16. Remove steering wheel as outlined in "Electrical" section of appropriate chassis chapter.

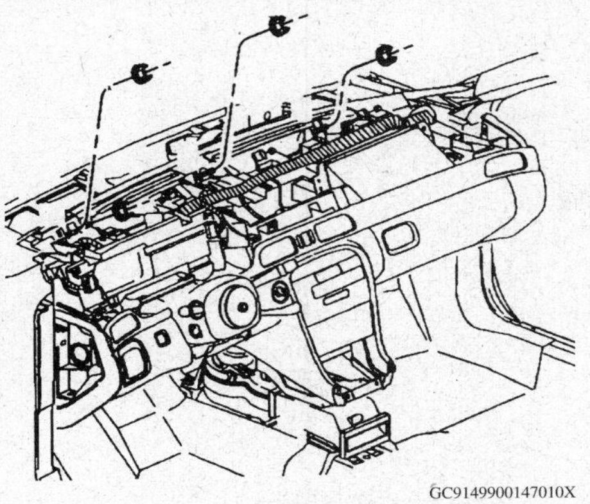

Fig. 27 Exploded view of instrument panel carrier. Seville

17. Remove lefthand dash panel cluster lower cover.
18. Remove cluster bezel to dash panel mounting screws.
19. Remove gauge cluster bezel, press on plastic tab and disconnect speedometer cable.
20. Remove gauge cluster mounting screws.
21. Disconnect electrical connectors and remove gauge cluster.
22. Remove passenger's air bag module as outlined in "Passive Restraint Systems" chapter.
23. Disconnect dome lamp, door speaker, blower motor, blower resistor, A/C amplifier and amplifier thermistor electrical connectors at righthand side of dash panel.
24. Disconnect main harness, fuse box and door speaker electrical connectors at lefthand side of dash panel, then the antenna cable hold-downs.
25. Remove A-pillar trim covers, then the seven dash panel brace bolts from door jamb A-pillar and steering column mounting areas.
26. Remove screws from upper center and lower dash panel corners, then the instrument panel.
27. Reverse procedure to install.

Monte Carlo

Refer to "Impala" for "Dash Panel, Replace" replacement procedure.

Park Avenue

1. Remove righthand sound insulator mounting screws.
2. Disconnect courtesy lamp, PSIR and heater temperature sensor connector.
3. Remove righthand sound insulator.
4. Remove left and righthand end cap by pulling outward to disconnect retainers.
5. Remove left and righthand instrument panel accessory trim plate by pulling rearward to disconnect retainers. Disconnect electrical connectors, as required.
6. Block wheels and place transaxle control lever into FIRST gear position.
7. Remove instrument cluster trim plate mounting screw lefthand end cap area.
8. Remove cluster trim plant by gently prying rearward to disconnect retainers. Disconnect electrical connectors.
9. Place suitable protective cloth on steering column.
10. Remove mounting screws and instrument cluster. Disconnect electrical connectors.
11. Remove data line mounting screws.
12. Remove mounting screws and lefthand sound insulator. Disconnect courtesy lamp, DSIR and heater temperature sensor connectors.
13. Remove righthand instrument panel trim plate mounting screw from righthand end cap area.
14. Remove righthand instrument panel trim plate by gently prying it rearward to disconnect retainers. Retainers are located on center most edge of trim plate.
15. Remove mounting bolts, nuts, screws and lower instrument panel trim panel. Disconnect electrical connectors.
16. Remove mounting screws, then the left and righthand side vent duct. Disconnect temperature sensors electrical connectors.
17. Remove mounting screws and radio. Disconnect electrical connectors and antenna lead.
18. Remove mounting screws and heater-A/C control. Disconnect electrical connectors.
19. Remove defroster grille by carefully prying upward to release retainers. Disconnect sensor.
20. Remove mounting screws and speaker. Disconnect electrical connector.
21. Remove windshield pillar garnish molding by pulling away to disconnect clips.
22. Remove mounting bolts and trim pad by pulling rearward slightly, **Fig. 25.**
23. Pull instrument panel trim pad rearward slightly.
24. Remove steering column as outlined in "Steering Columns" chapter.
25. Remove passenger's air bag module as outlined in "Passive Restraint Systems" chapter.
26. Remove steering column opening mounting studs.
27. Remove carrier to cowl and carrier to A-pillar mounting nuts.
28. Pull instrument panel carrier rearward slightly.
29. Disconnect body, righthand side body harness and lefthand side electrical connectors.
30. Remove instrument panel carrier.
31. Reverse procedure to install.

Prizm

2000

1. Remove body hinge pillar trim panels.
2. Remove instrument panel driver's knee bolster reinforcement.
3. Remove upper and lower steering column trim covers.
4. Remove driver's air bag module as outlined in "Passive Restraint Systems" chapter.

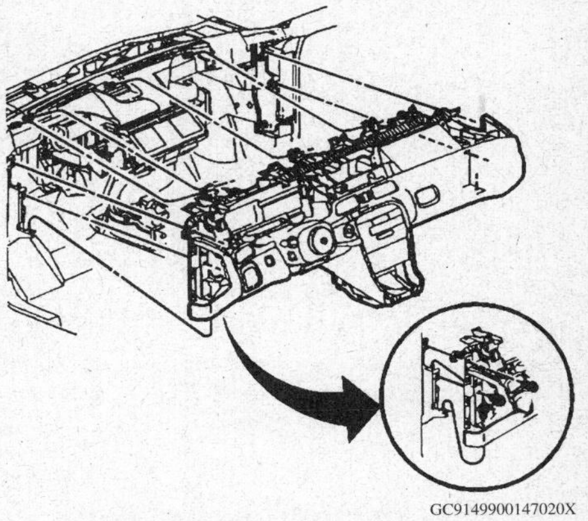

Fig. 28 Exploded view of instrument panel. Seville

5. Remove steering wheel as outlined in "Electrical" section of appropriate chassis chapter.
6. Unclip lefthand front carpet retainer, loosen mounting screws and disconnect hood release lever from knee bolster.
7. Remove trim caps and knee bolster to instrument panel mounting bolts.
8. Pull out instrument panel lefthand side ventilation duct.
9. Remove steering column as outlined in "Steering Columns" chapter.
10. Remove instrument cluster, instrument panel center trim plate and radio.
11. Remove glove compartment.
12. **On models equipped with manual transaxle,** remove manual transmission control lever boot and bezel from front floor console.
13. **On models equipped with automatic transaxle,** remove transaxle control opening cover bezel from front console by lightly prying on rear of bezel to release tabs.
14. **On all models,** remove two mounting screws and front floor front console by pulling front floor console rearward and up.
15. Remove Powertrain Control Module (PCM).
16. Remove two mounting screws and position junction block, as required.
17. Remove vent, temperature and mode control cables from heater case.
18. Disconnect and remove heater control with cables attached.
19. Remove two ground wires from instrument panel support braces.
20. Unclip and remove windshield side garnish moldings.
21. Gently pry and release four clips around instrument panel lamp dimmer/outside rearview mirror switch trim plate using suitable flat tipped screwdriver or prying tool.
22. Remove outside rearview mirror switch.
23. Gently pry and release three clips around instrument panel hazard warning/rear defogger switch trim plate using suitable flat tipped screwdriver or prying tool.
24. Remove rear defogger switch, hazard

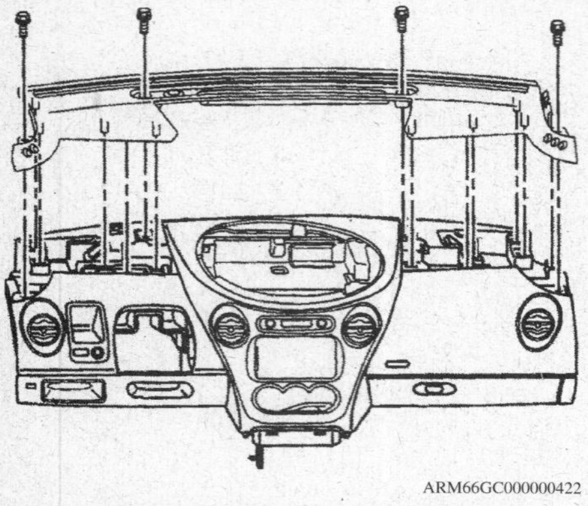

Fig. 29 Defroster grille replacement. ION

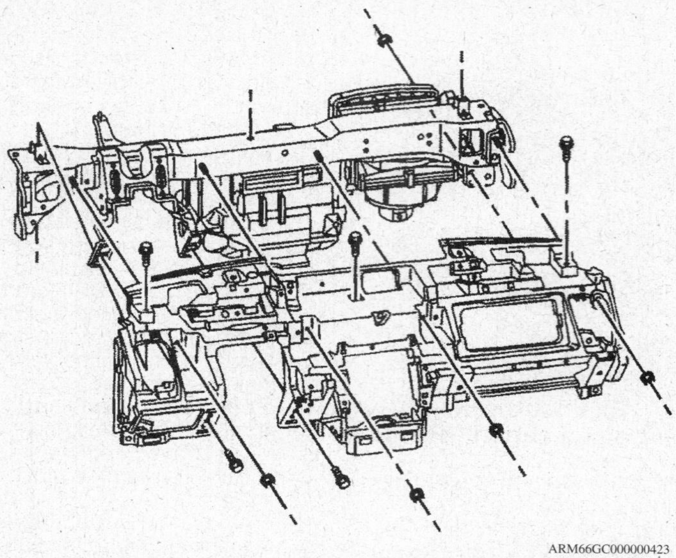

Fig. 30 Instrument panel replacement. ION

warning switch and ambient light sensor.
25. Remove righthand front door sill plate.
26. Remove righthand lower instrument panel trim panel.
27. Remove mounting screws and glove compartment.
28. Remove passenger's air bag module as outlined in "Passive Restraint Systems" chapter.
29. Remove instrument panel reinforcement and glove compartment striker bracket screw.
30. Disconnect park brake switch, oxygen sensor, Daytime Running Lamp (DRL) module, eight junction block connectors and connectors at right of instrument panel center support brace.
31. Disconnect three connectors located in connector cavity in lefthand body hinge pillar.
32. Remove instrument panel harness from wire harness retainers.
33. Remove two instrument panel to reinforcement mounting screws.
34. Remove instrument panel by lifting up on and pulling rearward, disengaging five clips.
35. Reverse procedure to install.

2001-02

1. Remove mounting nuts and body hinge pillar trim panels.
2. Remove instrument panel ashtray by depressing spring loaded tab and pulling rearward.
3. Remove accessory center trim plate using taped flat bladed tool to gently pry and release six retaining clips.
4. Disconnect two cigar lighter electrical connectors and ashtray bulb socket.
5. Remove cigarette lighter rear retainer, element housing and element by turning counterclockwise 90° and pushing on back of element housing.
6. Remove cigarette lighter lamp lens and ashtray housing, as required.
7. Remove four mounting screws and pull radio out.
8. Disconnect electrical connector and antenna lead.
9. Remove two lower mounting bolts and open glove compartment door.
10. Remove three upper mounting screws and glove compartment.
11. Remove two mounting bolts and position drivers knee bolster trim to gain access to reinforcement.
12. Remove two mounting bolts and drivers knee bolster reinforcement.
13. Remove steering column as outlined in "Steering Columns" chapter.
14. Remove two mounting screws and disconnect two instrument panel cluster trim plate lower clips.
15. Gently remove cluster trim plate.
16. Remove three instrument cluster mounting screws and disconnect four electrical connectors.
17. Remove instrument cluster.
18. Remove mounting screw from each side of front console.
19. Remove two rear compartment bolts.
20. Raise parking brake lever.
21. Remove rear floor console.
22. **On models equipped with manual transaxle,** remove control lever boot and front floor front console, as required.
23. **On models equipped with automatic transaxle,** remove control opening cover bezel by gently prying rear of bezel in order to release tabs, as required.
24. **On all models,** remove two mounting screws and front floor front console by pulling front floor console rearward and up.
25. Remove three Powertrain Control Module (PCM) mounting bolts and disconnect three PCM electrical connectors.
26. Remove PCM.
27. Remove mounting screw and position secures junction block No. 2, as required.
28. Remove heater case vent, temperature and mode control cables.
29. Remove two heater control mounting screws.
30. Disconnect blower motor and A/C switches from heater control.
31. Remove heater control with control cables attached.
32. Remove two ground wires mounting bolts from center support braces.
33. Unclip and remove windshield side garnish moldings.
34. Release four clips around instrument panel lamp dimmer/outside rearview mirror switch trim plate using suitable taped flat bladed tool to gently pry.
35. Disconnect instrument panel lamp dimmer and outside rearview mirror switch, as required.
36. Remove instrument panel lamp dimmer/outside rearview mirror switch.
37. Gently pry and release three clips around instrument panel hazard warning/rear defogger switch trim plate using suitable taped flat bladed tool.
38. Disconnect rear defogger, hazard warning and rear defogger switch/hazard warning switches.
39. Disconnect electrical connector and remove ambient light sensor.
40. Remove passenger's air bag module as outlined in "Passive Restraint Systems" chapter.
41. Remove two mounting bolts and glove compartment reinforcements.
42. Remove glove compartment door lock striker bracket screw.
43. Disconnect park brake switch electrical connector.
44. Disconnect oxygen sensor (H02S2) electrical connector.
45. Disconnect Daytime Running Lamp (DRL) control module electrical connector.
46. Disconnect eight connectors from Junction Block No. 2.
47. Disconnect connectors at righthand instrument panel center support brace.
48. Disconnect connectors at lefthand instrument panel center support brace.
49. Disconnect three connectors in connector cavity in lefthand body hinge pillar.
50. Disconnect automatic transaxle shift lock control module, shift lock park switch and four connectors from Junction Block No. 1.

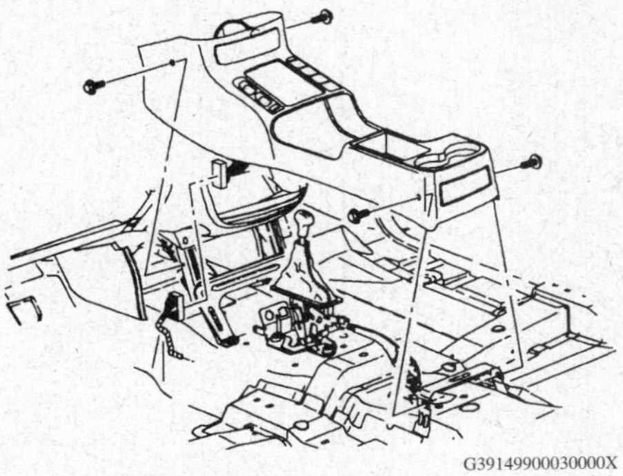

Fig. 31 Front console replacement. Saturn L-Series

51. Remove instrument panel wiring harness from all wire harness retainers.
52. Remove two reinforcement mounting screws and instrument panel by lifting up on and pulling rearward.
53. Disconnect five clips.
54. Reverse procedure to install.

Seville

1. Lift armrest, then remove storage compartment by pulling up and out, **Fig. 14.**
2. Disconnect three electrical connectors on lefthand inner side of center console.
3. Block vehicle wheels.
4. Place shifter into NEUTRAL position.
5. Remove retaining clip and shifter handle.
6. Disconnect trim plate clips using suitable flat bladed tool.
7. Remove trim plate. Disconnect electrical connectors.
8. Remove two lower ashtray bracket mounting screws and pull ashtray box out.
9. Remove one lower hidden mounting screw and ashtray. Disconnect cigarette lighter electrical connector.
10. Pry out driver information display switch using suitable thin flat bladed tool on both sides.
11. Remove driver information display switch. Disconnect electrical connector.
12. Remove radio and heater/AC control mounting screws.
13. Disconnect electrical connectors and antenna coaxial cable.
14. Remove radio and heater/AC control.
15. Remove two console to floor mounting bolts.
16. Remove four console to instrument panel mounting bolts.
17. Disconnect console air supply duct. Turn to release.
18. Release tie band
19. Disconnect console electrical connectors.
20. Disconnect auto transaxle park lock cable from shift plate bracket.
21. Disconnect auto transaxle range selector lever cable from shift plate bracket.
22. Disconnect BTSI electrical connector.
23. Pull console rearward while lifting upward on rear of console.

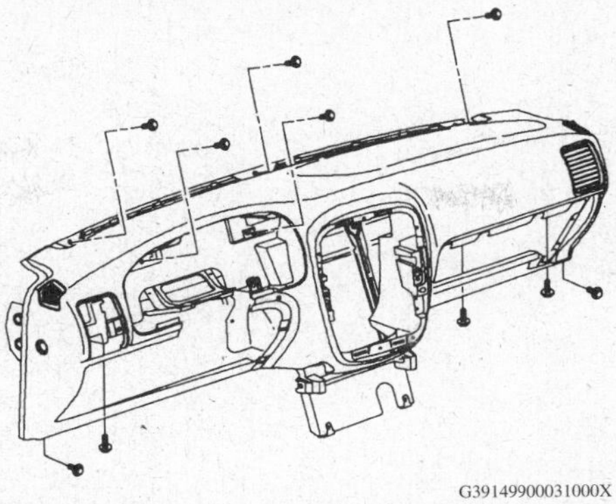

Fig. 32 Instrument panel pad & reinforcement replacement. Saturn L-Series

24. Remove console.
25. Remove left and righthand sound insulators mounting screws at rear edges.
26. Push in on insulators snap tab retainers to release.
27. Disconnect sound insulators' electrical connectors, as required.
28. Remove left and righthand sound insulators by sliding rearward.
29. Remove end caps by pulling outward to disconnect retainers at rear edge.
30. Remove windshield pillar garnish moldings by pulling from pillar to disconnect clips.
31. Remove air outlet deflectors using suitable flat bladed tool to release retainers on inside of outlet vents at top and bottom of housing.
32. Close air outlets to prevent upper trim pad mounting screws from falling into ducts.
33. Remove upper trim pad mounting screws inside of air outlet deflector openings, **Fig. 26.**
34. Lift upper trim pad upward from rear edge and over cluster to disconnect cluster trim plate retainers.
35. Lift pad on angle and slide rearward to disconnect front retainers. Push righthand front edge down to disconnect carrier retainer forward of passenger's air bag module.
36. Disconnect electrical connector and remove upper trim pad.
37. Remove defroster grille mounting screws.
38. Disconnect twilight sensor or solar sensor electrical connectors.
39. Remove sensors from defroster grill by twisting each sensor quarter turn.
40. Remove defroster grille.
41. Remove mounting bolts and knee bolster trim panel.
42. Slide Data Link Connector (DLC) from bracket.
43. Remove four mounting bolts and knee bolster bracket.
44. Disconnect two body-to-instrument panel electrical connectors at top outside corners of instrument panel.
45. Disconnect HVAC harness electrical connector near blower motor.
46. Disconnect radio antenna lead-in connector.

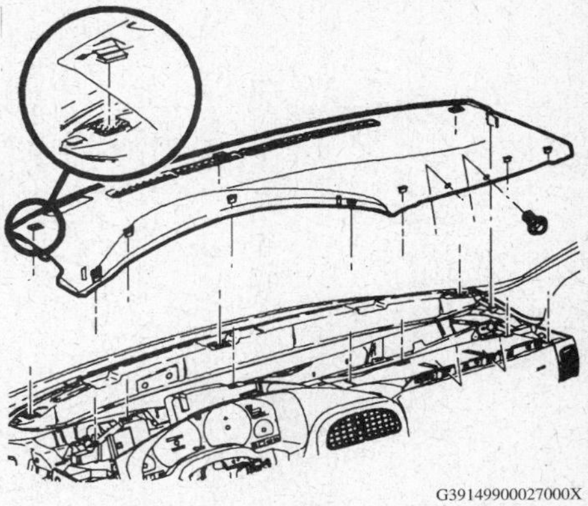

Fig. 33 Upper trim panel replacement. Saturn S-Series

47. Disconnect cigar lighter/ashtray lamp harness retainer push pin from bracket.
48. Remove driver's air bag module as outlined in "Passive Restraint Systems" chapter.
49. Remove steering wheel as outlined in "Electrical" section of appropriate chassis section.
50. Raise and support vehicle. **Ensure park brake pedal is in full returned position by pulling forward on emergency release lever.**
51. Relieve park brake cable tension by pulling down on front park brake cable.
52. Remove park brake cable from cable connector.
53. Lower vehicle.
54. Remove foot rest cover from by releasing tabs in top corners and sides using suitable small flat bladed tool.
55. Remove mounting bolts and foot rest base.
56. Pull back carpet, then remove floor pan grommet and park brake mounting nuts.
57. Disconnect electrical connector and remove front park brake cable from pedal.
58. Remove instrument panel center support bracket to floor bracket mounting bolts.
59. Remove steering column support bracket to instrument panel carrier mounting nuts, **Fig. 27.**
60. Remove instrument panel carrier to cowl mounting bolts.
61. Remove six instrument panel carrier to left and righthand hinge pillar mounting screws, **Fig. 28.**
62. Remove instrument panel carrier.
63. Reverse procedure to install.

Sunfire

1. Remove defroster grille using suitable small flat bladed tool.
2. Remove mounting screws and end caps.
3. Open glove compartment, then remove mounting screws and accessory trim plate.
4. Remove mounting screws and heater control.
5. Disconnect electrical connections,

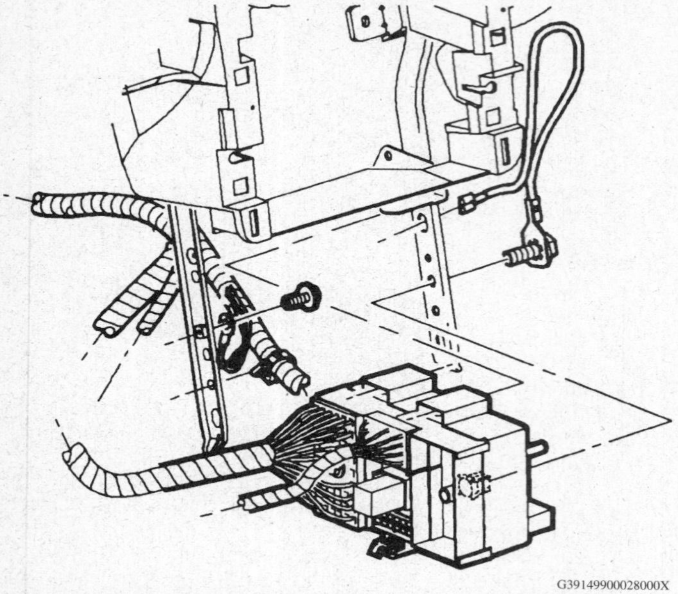

Fig. 34 Instrument panel fuse block replacement. Saturn S-Series

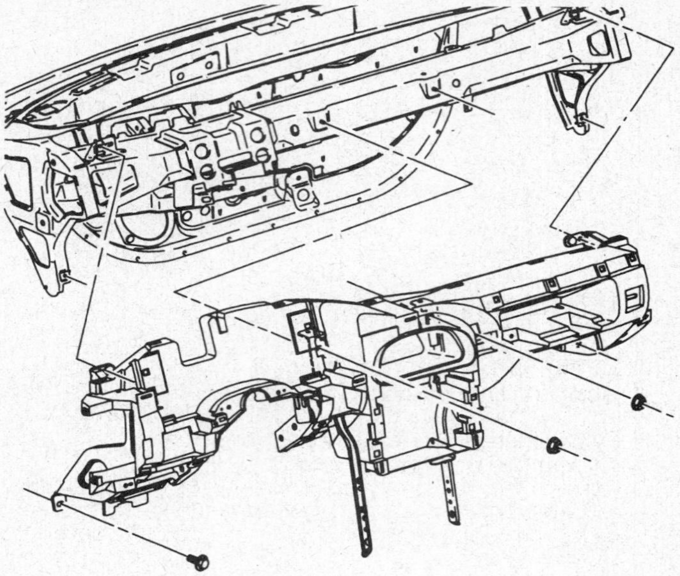

Fig. 35 Instrument panel pad & reinforcement replacement. Saturn S-Series

vacuum hoses and temperature blend cable.

6. Remove mounting screws and radio. Disconnect electrical connections and antenna coaxial cable.
7. Remove instrument panel valance by lifting upward to release retainers.
8. Open glove compartment, then remove mounting screws and righthand instrument panel trim panel.
9. Remove mounting screws and instrument panel trim pad.
10. Remove mounting screws and lefthand side air distribution duct by moving to left disconnect from righthand side duct.
11. Move righthand side air distribution duct outlet towards self to release lock tabs.
12. Remove righthand duct through braces.
13. Remove passenger's air bag module as outlined in "Passive Restraint Systems" chapter.
14. Remove driver's air bag module as outlined in "Passive Restraint Systems" chapter.
15. Remove steering wheel as outlined in "Electrical" section of appropriate chassis chapter.
16. Remove tilt lever by turning counterclockwise.
17. Remove lower steering column trim cover mounting screws, then the upper column trim cover by tilting up and unsnapping from lower column trim cover hinges.
18. Remove lower column trim cover.
19. Remove mounting screws and multifunction switch. Disconnect electrical connectors.
20. Remove steering wheel multi-function levers.
21. Remove mounting screw, disconnect electrical connector and remove windshield wiper switch.
22. Remove mounting screws and instrument carrier from cross car beam, **Fig. 7.**
23. Reverse procedure to install.

Saturn

ION

1. Apply parking brake.
2. **On models equipped with automatic or VTi transaxle,** place gearshift lever to neutral position.
3. **On all models,** remove console cupholder by carefully lifting up to release retainers.
4. **On models equipped with manual transaxle,** unsnap gearshift lever boot and slide through cupholder.
5. **On all models,** disconnect cigarette lighter electrical connector.
6. Remove left and righthand console side extension retainers by turning counterclockwise.
7. Remove left and righthand console side extensions by pulling rearward to release.
8. Remove center extension mounting screws from console, then carefully release retainers and remove extension.
9. Remove parking brake boot by unsnapping from console.
10. **On models equipped with armrest,** remove attaching screws and lift rear of armrest compartment to release retainers.
11. **On all models,** remove armrest compartment by lifting and pushing parking brake boot through opening, then slide over lever.
12. Disconnect electrical connector from rear power supply.
13. Remove attaching screws from front and rear of console, then the console by lifting over parking brake and gearshift levers.
14. Remove righthand center support bracket wiring harness retainer.
15. Remove righthand center support bracket and nuts by pulling back carpet at bottom.
16. Disconnect small and large body harness connectors, then the small and large instrument panel wiring harness connectors from Body Control Module (BCM).
17. **On models equipped with Onstar,** disconnect Onstar connector.
18. **On all models,** remove attaching nuts and BCM.
19. Remove end caps by pulling outward to release retainers, then sliding toward rear.
20. Disconnect door electrical connector.
21. Remove air bag electrical connector from outer instrument panel.
22. Remove accessory trim plate by pulling outward to release retainers, then disconnect electrical connectors.
23. Remove cluster trim plate attaching screw, then lift upward to release retainers.
24. Remove left and righthand windshield side upper garnish molding attaching screw trim covers and screws, then pull molding outward to release retainers and lift from bottom.
25. Remove defroster grille bolt covers, center attaching bolts and outer screws, **Fig. 29.**
26. Remove defroster grille by lifting upward to release retainers.
27. **On models equipped with ambient light sensor,** turn sensor body clockwise to remove from defroster grille.
28. **On all models,** remove defroster grille.
29. Open glove compartment door and remove attaching screws, then pull outward.
30. Remove righthand side upper trim pad mounting screws, then pull trim pad upward.
31. Remove steering column filler panel

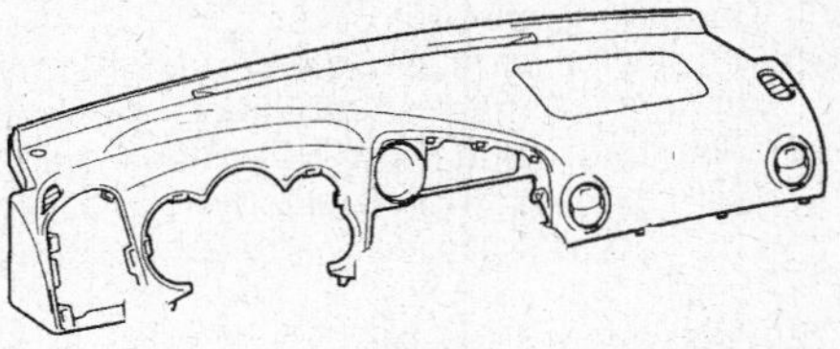
ARM66GC000000424

Fig. 36 Upper trim panel replacement. Vibe

attaching screws and pull panel outward to release, then disconnect rear compartment switch electrical connector.

32. Remove lower instrument panel compartment attaching screws and compartment.
33. Unsnap upper steering column trim cover.
34. Remove lower steering column trim cover attaching screws, then lower tilt lever.
35. Remove steering column lefthand and righthand lower trim covers.
36. Remove lefthand side instrument panel trim pad attaching screws and pull upward to release retainers.
37. Disconnect dimmer and fog lamp electrical connectors.
38. Remove instrument cluster attaching screws and instrument cluster, disconnect electrical connector.
39. Remove center instrument panel trim pad attaching screws and trim pad.
40. Remove radio retaining screws, then pull radio outward, disconnect electrical connector and antenna.
41. Disconnect mode and temperature cables, then the electrical connectors from heater-A/C control.
42. Remove attaching screws and heater-A/C control.
43. Remove attaching screws and center air outlet duct.
44. Remove accessory switch wire harness retainers.
45. Remove left and righthand outer air outlet duct attaching screws, then the ducts.
46. Remove defroster duct attaching screw.
47. Remove wire retainers and attaching bolts for passenger's side air bag. Pull air bag out while depressing one retaining tab with a suitable flat bladed tool.
48. Disconnect Data Link Connector (DLC) from instrument panel retainer.
49. Pull carpet retainer from behind hood release handle.
50. Place steering column in its' highest position, then remove rear steering column attaching bolts.
51. Remove instrumnent panel carrier nut from lower righthand side of instrument panel, then the remaining retainers, **Fig. 30.**
52. Remove instrument panel carrier by sliding along steering column support bracket and toward righthand side of vehicle until it clears steering wheel.
53. Reverse procedure to install. **Do not bend heater-A/C control cable when installing instrument panel carrier.**

L-SERIES

1. Remove left and righthand side console extensions by gently pulling.
2. Disconnect power window switch using suitable flat bladed tool.
3. Disconnect electrical connector and remove power window switch.
4. Squeeze console parking brake boot in while pulling upward, lift boot over parking brake lever and remove.
5. Pull front console tray upward to remove and disconnect console main body harness.
6. **On models equipped with automatic transaxle,** disconnect PRNDL cover by pulling it up.
7. **On models equipped with manual transaxle,** disconnect shifter boot by pulling it up.
8. **On all models,** move front seats to full forward position and remove console rear fasteners.
9. Move front seats to full rearward position and remove console front fasteners.
10. Gently lift console up and over shifter or PRNDL cover, then remove, **Fig. 31.**
11. Remove instrument panel floor pan bracket nuts and studs.
12. Disconnect center trim plate attaching clips and tilt trim plate sideways, then disconnect electrical connector and remove plate.
13. Remove mounting screws and pull radio from instrument panel. Disconnect electrical connector, antenna lead and ground strap connector.
14. Remove HVAC control fasteners, pull control out and disconnect electrical connector.
15. Remove driver's air bag module as outlined in "Passive Restraint Systems" chapter.
16. Remove steering wheel as outlined in "Electrical" section of appropriate chassis chapter.
17. Remove upper and lower steering column covers.
18. Remove ignition switch bezel and covers.
19. Remove wiper/washer and headlamp/turn signal switches.
20. Adjust steering column to its lowest position and cover top of column.
21. Remove lefthand side instrument panel lower closeout panel retainers and let closeout panel hang loose.
22. Remove lefthand side knee bolster, mounting screws and instrument panel cluster trim plate.
23. Remove instrument panel cluster mounting screws.
24. Pull rearward, disconnect electrical connector and remove cluster.
25. Remove lefthand side HVAC vent housing and disconnect electrical connectors.
26. Remove lefthand side lower air outlet duct and open glove compartment door.
27. Remove glove compartment lamp by pulling. Disconnect electrical connector.
28. Remove retainers and righthand side

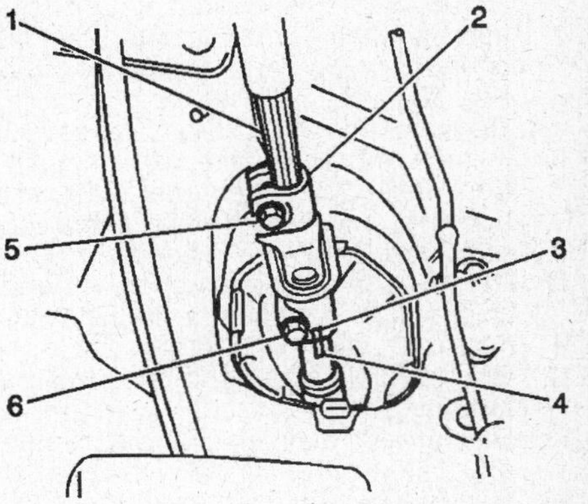

1. Steering Column Shaft
2. Upper Coupling
3. Lower Coupling
4. Lower Shaft
5 & 6. Pinch Bolts

ARM66GC000000426

Fig. 37 Steering column removal. Vibe

lower instrument panel closeout panel.

29. Remove righthand heater outlet duct, mounting screws and glove compartment door.
30. Remove fasteners and slowly remove glove compartment bin by tilting it downward to expose BCM located on top of compartment bin.
31. Slide BCM out of retaining slots and remove glove compartment bin. Let BCM hang on wiring harness.
32. Pull upward at vent locations and remove windshield defroster grille.
33. Unsnap hood release handle from instrument panel using suitable small screwdriver to disconnect retainer clips.
34. Remove Data Link Connector (DLC) by pulling downward at connector location.
35. Remove clips at lower steering column, instrument panel center outlet and glove compartment opening location.
36. Remove mounting screws and instrument panel, **Fig. 32.**
37. Reverse procedure to install.

S-SERIES

1. Apply parking brake, then lift window and mirror switch up with suitable screwdriver. Disconnect switch electrical connector.
2. Place gear selector in Neutral position and move front seats to fully forward.
3. Remove rear console mounting screws.
4. Move front seats fully rearward, then remove left and righthand lower trim panel extensions by pulling outward at dual lock locations.
5. Remove front console mounting screws.
6. Move console rearward to disconnect retainers and disconnect power outlet connector.
7. Lift rear of console and remove it.

8. Remove screws located under upper trim panel on righthand side, then disconnect clips and remove panel, **Fig. 33.**
9. Remove steering column filler screws.
10. Release hood release cable housing from its mount, then pull cable and housing downward until cable can pass through cutout in handle.
11. Remove hood release handle, steering column filler panel and Data Link Connector (DLC).
12. Remove left and righthand end cap mounting screws.
13. Disconnect retaining clips and remove end cap.
14. Remove wiring harness from door jamb switch and pry dimmer/traction switch from instrument panel.
15. Pry edges of ignition lock bezel and separate from lower steering column shroud.
16. Remove mounting screws and lower steering column shroud.
17. Lower steering column using adjusting handle, lift and remove upper steering column shroud.
18. Disconnect clips and remove instrument panel cluster trim bezel.
19. Remove instrument cluster mounting screws.
20. Pull rearward, disconnect electrical connector and remove cluster.
21. Remove mounting screws and pull radio put.
22. Disconnect electrical connector, antenna lead and ground strap connector.
23. Remove mounting screws and pull HVAC controller out.
24. Disconnect blower switch and control head connectors.
25. Squeeze locking tabs, then remove HVAC controller temperature and mode cables.
26. Disconnect door jamb switch wiring harness retainer, then remove lefthand and righthand wire harnesses from instrument panel retainer.
27. Disconnect dimmer/traction control switch wiring harness from retainer.
28. Remove mounting bolts and lower steering column onto front seat.
29. Open instrument panel compartment door, turn stops and remove door.
30. Disconnect antenna lead and remove H-brace to front bracket bolts.
31. Remove passenger's air bag module as outlined in "Passive Restraint Systems" chapter.
32. Remove instrument panel harness plastic retainer, screw and ground wire from H-brace.
33. Remove instrument panel fuse block from H-brace, **Fig. 34.**
34. Remove mounting screws, nuts and instrument panel, **Fig. 35.**
35. Reverse procedure to install.

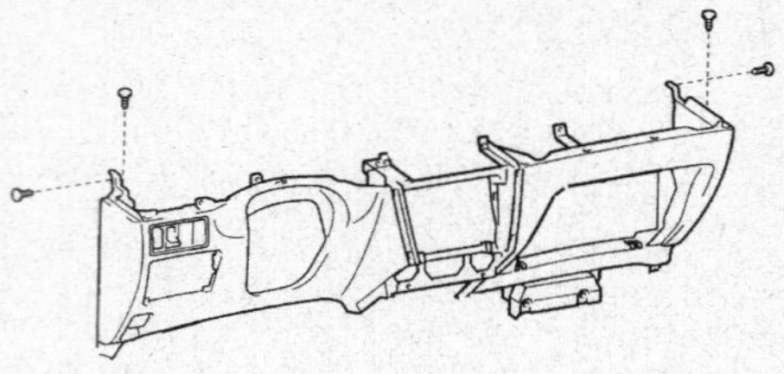

Fig. 38 Lower trim panel replacement. Vibe

Vibe

1. Remove center instrument panel trim plate using a suitable taped flat bladed tool to gently pry and release retainers.
2. Disconnect A/C, hazard warning, rear defogger and passenger's side seat belt indicator electrical connectors.
3. Remove mounting screws and disconnect bracket clamp to pull radio out.
4. Disconnect radio electrical connector and antenna lead.
5. **On models equipped with manual transaxle,** remove gearshift knob.
6. **On all models,** remove center A/C control knob and screw.
7. Remove front floor console trim plate using a suitable taped flat bladed tool to gently pry and release retainers.
8. Disconnect two cigarette lighters and accessory power receptacle electrical connectors.
9. Disconnect heater-A/C control electrical connector, then the mode, temperature and A/C cables.
10. Remove heater-A/C control.
11. Remove driver's air bag module as outlined in "Passive Restraint Systems" chapter.
12. Remove steering wheel as outlined in "Electrical" section of appropriate chassis chapter.
13. Remove three attaching screws, then the lower and upper steering column trim covers.
14. Disconnect electrical connectors, then remove turn signal/headlamp and wiper/washer switches.
15. Disconnect electrical connector and remove clockspring.
16. Remove passenger's airbag module as outlined in "Passive Restraint Systems" chapter.
17. Remove cluster trim plate using a suitable flat bladed tool to gently pry and release retainers.
18. **Ensure ignition switch is in OFF position.**
19. Remove mounting screw and release two lower retainers, then disconnect electrical connector.
20. Gently pry to remove left and righthand windshield garnish moldings.
21. Remove lefthand instrument panel trim plate using a suitable taped flat bladed tool to gently pry and release retainers.
22. Disconnect power mirror and dimmer switch electrical connectors.
23. Remove mounting screws and upper instrument panel by pulling rearward, **Fig. 36.**
24. **On models equipped with automatic transaxle,** proceed as follows:
    a. Insert and turn ignition key to ACC.
    b. Disconnect park lock cable by pushing release button.
    c. Remove ignition key and lock steering column in original position.
25. **On all models,** position insulator pad away from steering column.
26. Mark steering shaft coupling and shaft for installation alignment, **Fig. 37.**
27. Loosen upper coupling pinch bolt.
28. Remove lower pinch bolt and position coupling on to steering column shaft.
29. Disconnect steering column connectors and release wire harness retainers.
30. Remove mounting bolts and steering column.
31. Remove left and righthand door sill and kick panel trim plates.
32. Remove front floor console compartment door.
33. Remove mounting screws, then pull front floor console rearward and up.
34. Open door and remove glove compartment mounting screw.
35. Release upper tabs and remove glove compartment by pulling it out.
36. **On models equipped with automatic transaxle,** remove manual selector as follows:
    a. Disconnect cable from gearshift by pushing retainer clip in.
    b. Disconnect park lock cable from bracket using a suitable flat bladed tool.
    c. Disconnect shift cable from gearshift lever and plate.
    d. Disconnect electrical connectors and wire harness clip.
    e. Remove four mounting nuts and manual selector.
37. **On all models,** gently pry hood release handle from knee bolster trim.
38. Disconnect cable and remove hood release handle.
39. Remove eight mounting bolts and four retainers, then the wire harness clamps.
40. Remove lower instrument panel by pulling it rearward, **Fig. 38.**
41. Reverse procedure to install.

ANTI-LOCK BRAKES

TABLE OF CONTENTS

Application Chart

Model	Year	ABS System
BUICK		
Century	2000–04	DBC 7
LeSabre	2000–04	Delco/Bosch Type 5.3
Park Avenue	2000–04	Delco/Bosch Type 5.3
Regal	2000–04	DBC 7
CADILLAC		
Catera	2000–01	Bosch Type 5.3
CTS	2003–04	DBC 7
Deville	2000–04	Delco/Bosch Type 5.3
Eldorado	2000–02	Delco/Bosch Type 5
Seville	2000–04	Delco/Bosch Type 5.3
CHEVROLET		
Camero	2000–02	Bosch Type 5.3
Cavalier	2000–04	DBC7
Corvette	2000–04	Delco/Bosch Type 5
Impala	2000–04	DBC7
Lumina	2000–01	Delphi Type VI
Malibu	2000–02	DBC7
Monte Carlo	2000–03	DBC7
Metro	2000–01	Delphi Type VI
Prizm	2000–02	Lucas/Sumitomo
OLDSMOBILE		
Alero	2000	Delphi Type VI
	2001–04	DBC7
Aurora	2001–04	Delco/Bosch Type 5.3
Intrigue	2000–04	Bosch Type 5.3
PONTIAC		
Bonneville	2000–03	Delco/Bosch Type 5.3
Firebird	2000–02	Bosch Type 5.3
Grand Am	2000	Delphi Type VI
	2001–04	DBC7
Grand Prix	2000–04	Bosch Type 5.3
Sunfire	2000–04	DBC7
Vibe	2003–04	Lucas/Sumitomo

Delphi (Delco-Moraine) Type VI

NOTE: On Air Bag Equipped Models, Refer To "Air Bag System Precautions" Located In The Front Of This Manual For System Disarming & Arming Procedures.

NOTE: Refer To "Computer Relearn Procedures" Located In The Front Of This Manual When Battery Power To The Computer Has Been Interrupted.

NOTE: "Electrical Symbol & Wire Color Code Identification" Located In The Front Of This Manual May Be Used As An Aid When Using Wiring Circuits Found In This Section.

INDEX

PRECAUTIONS

Air Bag Systems

Refer to "Air Bag System Precautions" in the front of this manual for system disarming and arming procedures.

Battery Ground Cable

Prior to service, disconnect battery ground cable and isolate as required.

ABS Service

Before performing any repairs on the ABS system, note the following precautions:

1. Before using electric welding equipment, disconnect EBTCM.
2. Carefully note routing, position and mounting ABS and TCS wiring, connectors, clips and brackets. ABS and TCS are extremely sensitive to electromagnetic interference.
3. Do not use a fast charger when battery is connected. **Never disconnect battery from system with engine running.**
4. Ignition switch must be in Off position when disconnecting EBTCM.
5. Many ABS system components are non-serviceable and must be replaced as assemblies. **Do not disassemble non-serviceable components.**
6. Do not hang other components on wheel speed sensor cables.
7. Do not expose EBTCM to temperatures of more than 184°F.
8. Use DOT 3 brake fluid only. Do not use container that has been used with petroleum based fluids or is wet with water. Petroleum based fluids will damage system and water will lower boiling point. Keep fluid containers capped.
9. After replacing any ABS component, inspect system as outlined in "Diagnosis & Testing."

DESCRIPTION

System Operation

The function of the Anti-Lock Brake System (ABS) is to minimize wheel lock-up during heavy braking on most road surfaces. The system performs this function by monitoring wheel speed and controlling the brake fluid pressure to each front wheel and both rear wheels during braking. This allows the driver to retain directional stability and better steering capability.

System Components

Refer to **Fig. 1**, for system component locations.

ELECTRONIC BRAKE CONTROL MODULE/ ELECTRONIC BRAKE & TRACTION CONTROL MODULE

The ABS system is controlled by a microprocessor based Electronic Brake Control Module (EBCM). Inputs to the system include four wheel speed sensors, the brake switch, ignition switch and unswitched battery voltage. Outputs include three bidirectional motor controls, two solenoid controls and the system enable relay. A serial data line is provided for service diagnostic tools and assembly plant testing.

The EBCM monitors the speed of each wheel. If any wheel begins to approach lock-up and the brake switch is on, the EBCM controls the motors and solenoids to

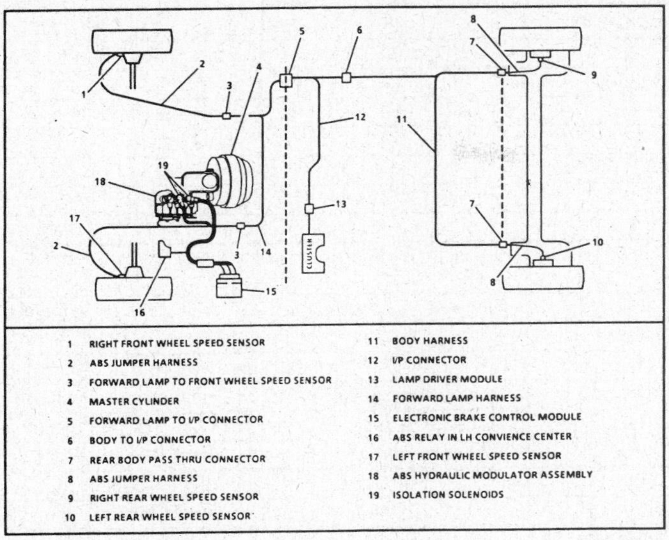

GC4029100648000A

Fig. 1 ABS components

Code	Description
C1211	ABS Warning Lamp Circuit Fault
C1213	ABS Active Lamp Circuit Fault
C1214	Brake Control Relay Contact Circuit Open
C1215	Brake Control Relay Contact Circuit Active
C1216	Brake Control Relay Coil Circuit Open
C1217	Brake Control Relay Coil Circuit Short To Ground
C1218	Brake Control Relay Coil Circuit Short To Voltage
C1221	Lefthand Front Wheel Speed Sensor Input Signal Is Zero
C1222	Righthand Front Wheel Speed Sensor Input Signal Is Zero
C1223	Lefthand Rear Wheel Speed Sensor Input Signal Is Zero
C1224	Righthand Rear Wheel Speed Sensor Input Signal Is Zero
C1225	Lefthand Front Wheel Speed Variation
C1226	Righthand Front Wheel Speed Variation
C1227	Lefthand Rear Wheel Speed Variation
C1228	Righthand Rear Wheel Speed Variation
C1232	Lefthand Front Wheel Circuit Open Or Shorted
C1233	Righthand Front Wheel Circuit Open Or Shorted
C1234	Lefthand Rear Wheel Circuit Open Or Shorted
C1235	Righthand Rear Wheel Circuit Open Or Shorted
C1236	Low System Supply Voltage
C1237	High System Supply Voltage

Fig. 2 DTC identification (Part 1 of 3)

reduce brake pressure to the wheel approaching lock-up. Once the wheel regains traction, brake pressure is increased until wheel begins to approach lock-up. This cycle repeats until either the vehicle comes to a stop, the brake is released or no wheels approach lock-up. Additionally, the EBCM monitors each input and each output for proper operation. If any system fault is detected, the EBCM will store a Diagnostic Trouble Code (DTC) in nonvolatile memory.

On an Electronic Brake and Traction Control Module (EBTCM), the ABS portion of the module operates the same as a EBCM. An EBTCM is used if the vehicle is equipped with either the Enhanced Traction System (ETS) or Traction Control System (TCS). The ETS or TCS portion of the EBTCM monitors wheel spin slip through the drive wheels speed sensors. If the wheels begin to slip, the EBTCM determines the desired wheel torque needed to minimize wheel slip. This information is sent to the Powertrain Control Module (PCM) through the serial data link. On models equipped with ETS, the PCM controls engine torque by ignition retard and transmission shifts. On models equipped with TCS, the PCM controls engine torque by ignition retard, transmission shifts and applies brakes several times until the vehicle regains traction. Once the vehicle regains traction, brake pressure is decreased and engine torque reduction is no longer requested. This cycle repeats until traction control is no longer required.

HYDRAULIC MODULATOR/ MOTOR PACK ASSEMBLY

The ABS hydraulic modulator/motor pack assembly controls hydraulic pressure to front and rear brakes by modulating hydraulic pressure to prevent wheel lock-up.

The basic ABS hydraulic modulator configuration consists of gear subassemblies, ball screws, nuts, pistons and hydraulic check valves. The ABS motor pack consists of three motors, three drive gears and three Expansion Spring Brakes (ESB's).

EXPANSION SPRING BRAKE

The Expansion Spring Brake (ESB) is used to hold the piston in the upper most or home position. An ESB is a spring that is retained in a housing at a close tolerance. One end of the spring is in contact with the motor drive dog and the other end is in contact with the pinion drive dog. In normal braking, brake pressure is present on the top of the piston, applying a downward force. The force applies a counterclockwise torque to the motor pinion which tries to rotate the spring counterclockwise. The counterclockwise torque expands the spring outward within the housing and prevents gear rotation. When the motor is turned on and tries to drive the ball screw nut, the end of the ESB in contact with the motor drive dog rotates inward causing the spring to contract in its housing allowing the motor to rotate the modulator gear.

WHEEL SPEED SENSORS

Wheel speed sensors are located on the front steering knuckles and in the integral wheel bearing on the rear wheels. An AC signal is generated by a rotating toothed ring near the sensor pole piece, which produces a magnetic field that increases and decreases in magnitude and frequency proportional to speed. This low voltage signal is sent to the EBCM/EBTCM.

ABS WARNING LAMP

The amber ABS warning light operates on a signal it receives from the EBCM/ EBTCM. If the EBCM/EBTCM detects a fault that does not interfere immediately with ABS operation, the ABS warning lamp will flash. However, ABS operation will continue. If the EBCM/EBTCM detects a fault that does interfere with ABS operation, the ABS warning lamp will stay lit and ABS operation will be suspended until the fault is repaired. In any case, the warning lamp indicates that the system requires serviced as soon as possible.

BRAKE WARNING LAMP

The red Brake warning lamp can be activated by a low brake fluid condition, a closed parking brake switch, a bulb test switch section of the ignition switch is closed or under the control of the EBCM/ EBTCM when certain ABS Diagnostic Trouble Codes (DTCs) are set.

TROUBLESHOOTING

DIAGNOSIS & TESTING

Accessing Diagnostic Trouble Codes

Diagnostic Trouble Codes (DTCs) may be read using a suitably programed scan tool. There are no provisions for flash code diagnostics.

1. Before beginning service, perform the following preliminary inspection:
   a. Inspect master cylinder for proper brake fluid level.
   b. Inspect hydraulic modulator for any leaks or wiring damage.

Code	Description
C1238	Lefthand Front ESB Does Not Hold Motor
C1241	Righthand Front ESB Does Not Hold Motor
C1242	Rear ESB Does Not Hold Motor
C1243	VES Steering Wheel Sensor Circuit Fault
C1244	Lefthand Front ABS Channel Does Not Move
C1245	Righthand Front ABS Channel Does Not Move
C1246	Rear ABS Channel Does Not Move
C1247	Lefthand Front ABS Motor Free Spins
C1248	Righthand Front ABS Motor Free Spins
C1251	Rear ABS Motor Free Spins
C1252	Lefthand Front ABS Channel In Release Too Long
C1253	Righthand Front ABS Channel In Release Too Long
C1254	Rear ABS Channel In Release Too Long
C1255	EBCM Internal Fault
C1256	Lefthand Front ABS Motor Circuit Open
C1257	Lefthand Front ABS Motor Circuit Short To Ground
C1258	Lefthand Front ABS Motor Circuit Short To Voltage
C1261	Righthand Front ABS Motor Circuit Open
C1262	Righthand Front ABS Motor Circuit Short To Ground
C1263	Righthand Front ABS Motor Circuit Short To Voltage
C1264	Rear ABS Motor Circuit Open

Fig. 2 DTC identification (Part 2 of 3)

Code	Description
C1265	Rear ABS Motor Circuit Short To Ground
C1266	Rear ABS Motor Circuit Short To Voltage
C1273	VES CKT Open/Short To Ground
C1274	VES CKT Short To Voltage
C1275	Serial Data Fault
C1276	Lefthand Front Solenoid Circuit Open/Short To Ground
C1277	Lefthand Front Solenoid Circuit Short To Voltage
C1278	Righthand Front Solenoid Circuit Open/Short To Ground
C1281	Righthand Front Solenoid Circuit Short To Voltage
C1282	Calibration Fault
C1286	EBCM Turned On Brake Warning Lamp
C1287	Brake Warning Lamp Circuit Open/Short To Voltage
C1291	Open Brake Lamp Switch Contacts During Decel
C1292	Open Brake Lamp Switch When ABS Required
C1293	Set Current/Previous Ignition Cycle
C1294	Brake Lamp Switch Always Active
C1295	Brake Lamp Switch Circuit Open
U1300	Brake Lamp Switch Circuit Open
U1301	Brake Lamp Switch Circuit Open

Fig. 2 DTC identification (Part 3 of 3)

c. Inspect brakes at all four wheels to ensure no drag exists and that brakes are operating normally.
d. Inspect wheel bearings for any excessive wear or damage.
e. Inspect wheel speed sensors for correct air gap, solid sensor attachment, damaged toothed ring or damaged wiring. Refer to "System Service."
f. Inspect CV joint for proper operation and alignment.

2. Turn ignition switch to Off position.
3. Connect suitably programmed scan tool connected to Data Link Connector (DLC), located on lefthand side of instrument panel below steering column.
4. Turn ignition switch to On position.
5. Select scan tool's Special Functions.
6. Select and run Automated Test.
7. Note Diagnostic Trouble Codes (DTCs).

Diagnostic Trouble Code Interpretation

Diagnostic Trouble Codes (DTCs) may be read using a suitably programmed scan tool. There is no provision for flash code diagnostics.

If there are no DTCs present, or if mechanical component DTCs are present, perform automated modulator test using the scan tool to isolate the cause of the problem. If the failure is intermittent and not reproducible, test drive vehicle while using the automatic snapshot feature of the scan tool. Perform normal acceleration, stopping and turning maneuvers. If this does not reproduce the fault, perform an ABS stop from approximately 30–50 mph while triggering an ABS DTC. If failure still will not reproduce, use enhanced diagnostic information found in CODE HISTORY to determine whether or not this failure should be further diagnosed.

Refer to **Fig. 2,** for Diagnostic Trouble Code (DTC) identification.

Wiring Diagrams

ALERO & MALIBU

Refer to **Fig. 3,** for wiring diagram.

CAVALIER & SUNFIRE

Refer to **Fig. 4,** for wiring diagrams.

INTRIGUE

Refer to **Fig. 5,** for wiring diagram.

LUMINA & MONTE CARLO

Refer **Fig. 6,** for wiring diagram.

METRO

Refer to **Fig. 7,** for wiring diagrams.

EBCM Connector Views

Refer to **Figs. 8 through 14,** for EBCM connector terminal identification.

Diagnostic Tests

Connector numbers, circuit numbers and wire codes for individual models may vary from those printed. Always refer to individual model's "Wiring Diagrams" before proceeding.

ALERO, GRAND AM & MALIBU

Refer to **Figs. 15 and 16,** for diagnostic system checks, **Figs. 17 through 76,** code diagnostic tests and **Figs. 77 through 87,** for system tests.

CAVALIER & SUNFIRE

Refer to **Fig. 88,** for diagnostic system check, **Figs. 89 through 141,** code diagnostic tests and **Figs. 142 through 147,** for system tests.

INTRIGUE, LUMINA, & MONTE CARLO

Refer to **Fig. 148,** for diagnostic system checks, **Figs. 149 through 201,** code diagnostic tests and **Figs. 202 through 208,** for system tests.

METRO

Refer to **Fig. 209,** for diagnostic system check, **Figs. 210 through 259,** for code diagnostic tests and **Figs. 260 through 265,** for system tests.

Clearing Diagnostic Trouble Codes

Diagnostic Trouble Codes (DTCs) cannot be cleared by disconnecting EBTCM or battery cables.

SCAN TOOL

Connect a suitably programmed scan tool to Data Link Connector (DLC), and follow manufacturer's instructions.

IGNITION CYCLE DEFAULT

If vehicle power is cycled 100 times without a particular fault reappearing, that particular DTC will be erased from the EBCM memory, and ignition cycle counter will be reset to zero.

Intermittents & Poor Connections

Intermittent failures in the anti-lock brake

system may be difficult to accurately diagnose. The ABS Diagnostic Trouble Codes (DTCs) which may be stored by the EBCM are not designated as Current or History DTCs. These DTCs can be helpful in diagnosing intermittent conditions.

If an intermittent condition is being diagnosed, the ABS system can be used in the following manner to help isolate the suspected circuit.

1. Display and clear any ABS DTCs present in EBCM.
2. Attempt to repeat failure condition, noting the following:
   a. Turn ignition switch to Off position.
   b. Disconnect scan tool. **If scan tool is installed, EBCM/EBTCM will not set DTCs and ABS/TCS functions may not be available.**
   c. Test drive vehicle.
3. After duplicating condition, stop vehicle and display any DTCs stored.
4. If no DTCs were stored refer to "Troubleshooting."
5. If a DTC was stored, inspect electrical connections and wiring for the following:
   a. Poor mating of connector halves.
   b. Terminals not fully seated in connector halves.
   c. Improperly formed, or damaged terminals. All connector terminals in a problem circuit should be carefully reformed to increase contact tension.
   d. Poor terminal to wire connection. In most cases, this will require removing wire from connector body.
6. If there is an intermittent warning lamp operation, the following EBCM circuits should be inspected:
   a. Low system voltage. If low voltage is detected at EBCM/EBTCM, Anti-lock lamp will illuminate until normal operating voltage is detected.
   b. Low brake fluid. This condition in Pressure Modulator Valve (PMV) reservoir will cause Brake and Anti-lock lamps to illuminate. When an acceptable fluid level is registered, lamps will no longer be illuminated.
7. Any condition which results in interruption of power to EBCM/EBTCM or hydraulic unit may cause warning lamps to turn on intermittently. These circuits include main relay, pump motor relay, fuses and related wiring.

Electromagnetic Interference Test

Due to the sensitivity of ABS components to electromagnetic interference, the following inspections should be performed if an intermittent fault is suspected.

1. Inspect for proper installation of wiring harnesses resulting from add on options.
2. Visually inspect wheel speed sensor and toothed sensor ring for looseness, damage, accumulation of foreign material and proper mounting. Replace damaged components, remove any foreign material and properly attach all components.
3. Inspect front wheel speed sensor wiring for proper routing away from spark plug wires.
4. Measure resistance of spark plug wires. If resistance is greater than 30,000 ohms for any wire, replace spark plug wires.
5. While test driving vehicle, monitor Tech 1 wheel speeds. If any wheel speed drops or displays an erratic speed, refer to appropriated wheel speed sensor DTC.

SYSTEM SERVICE

Brake System Bleed

Before bleeding the brakes, the front and rear displacement cylinder pistons must be returned to their top most position as outlined in "Rehome."

REHOME

SCAN TOOL

All Diagnostic Trouble Codes (DTCs) must be repaired and cleared before attempting to rehome displacement cylinder pistons. Connect a suitably programmed scan tool to Data Link Connector (DLC), and follow manufacturers instructions.

PRESSURE BLEED

On Metro models, refer to "Manual Bleed."

Pressure bleeding equipment must have a rubber diaphragm between air supply and brake fluid to prevent air, moisture and other contaminants from entering the system.

1. Clean reservoir cover and surrounding area.
2. Remove reservoir cover, inspect and fill reservoir completely with clean brake fluid.
3. Attach bleeding adapter tool No. J-35589, or equivalent, to brake fluid reservoir and pressure bleeding equipment.
4. Pressurize bleeding equipment to 5–10 psi and wait 30 seconds, ensure there are no leaks.
5. Pressurize equipment to 30–35 psi.
6. Attach clear plastic hose to rearward hydraulic modulator bleeder valve, then submerge other end of hose in clear container partially filled with brake fluid.
7. Slowly open bleeder valve and allow fluid to flow until no air is seen in fluid. **Use shop cloth to catch escaping brake fluid. Do not allow fluid to run down motor pack or on electrical connector. Bleeder hose is not used to bleed brake pipe connections.**
8. Close valve and repeat procedure until no air bubbles exist.
9. Repeat procedure on forward bleeder valve.
10. **Torque** bleeder valves to 84 inch lbs.
11. Slowly open hydraulic modulator forward brake pipe tube nut and allow air to escape, immediately after air stops flowing, **torque** nut to 18 ft. lbs.
12. Repeat procedure on remaining brake pipe connections, moving from front to back.
13. Raise and support vehicle.
14. Attach bleeder hose to righthand rear wheel bleeder valve, then submerge other end of hose in a clear container partially filled with brake fluid.
15. Slowly open bleeder valve and allow fluid to flow until no air bubbles are seen in fluid.
16. Close valve and repeat procedure until no air bubbles exist. **Torque** bleeder valves to 84 inch lbs.
17. Repeat procedure on lefthand rear, righthand front and lefthand front wheels, in turn.
18. Lower vehicle and remove bleeder adapter tool.
19. Inspect and fill reservoir with brake fluid.
20. Turn ignition switch to Run position and apply brake pedal with moderate force. If pedal feels firm and constant, and pedal travel is not excessive, proceed to next step. If pedal is soft or has excessive travel, repeat bleed procedure.
21. Start engine and apply brake pedal with moderate force. If pedal feels firm and constant, and pedal travel is not excessive, proceed to next step. If pedal is soft or has excessive travel, proceed as follows:
    a. Use scan tool to release and apply motors 2–3 times.
    b. Cycle solenoids 5–10 times.
    c. Apply front and rear motors to ensure pistons are at upper most position.
    d. Repeat bleed procedure.
22. Drive at six mph for five seconds, then stop vehicle and turn ignition switch off.
23. If pedal felt firm and constant during road test, proceed to next step. If pedal was soft or had excessive travel, repeat bleed procedure.
24. Road test vehicle, making several non-ABS stops at moderate speed to ensure proper braking function. Allow brakes to cool between stops.

MANUAL BLEED

Use suitable container and/or shop rags to catch fluid.

1. Clean reservoir cover and surrounding area.
2. Remove cover and fill reservoir with clean brake fluid, then install cover.
3. Attach a clear plastic hose to rearward hydraulic modulator bleeder valve, then submerge the other end of hose in a clear container, partially filled with brake fluid.
4. Slowly open bleeder valve ½–¾ turn, then press brake pedal and hold until fluid begins to flow.
5. Close valve when fluid flows without air bubbles, release brake pedal pressure.
6. Repeat procedure on forward bleeder valve.
7. Fill reservoir with fluid and install cover.
8. Raise and support vehicle.
9. Attach bleeder hose to righthand rear wheel bleeder valve, then submerge

other end of hose in a clear container partially filled with brake fluid.
10. Open bleeder valve and slowly press brake pedal until fluid begins to flow.
11. Close valve and release brake pedal pressure, then wait at least five seconds.
12. Press brake pedal and open bleeder valve, repeat steps until brake pedal feels firm at half travel and no air bubbles are observed.
13. Repeat procedure on lefthand rear, righthand front and lefthand front wheels, in turn.
14. Lower vehicle.
15. Fill fluid reservoir as required,
16. Attach clear plastic hose to rearward hydraulic modulator bleeder valve, then submerge other end of hose in a clean container, partially filled with brake fluid.
17. Slowly open bleeder valve ½–¾ turn.
18. Press brake pedal and hold until fluid begins to flow, then repeat until air bubbles do not exist.
19. Close valve and release brake pedal pressure.
20. Repeat procedure on forward bleeder valve.
21. Fill reservoir with fluid as required.
22. Turn ignition switch to the run position and apply brake pedal with moderate force. If pedal feels firm and constant, and pedal travel is not excessive, proceed to next step. If pedal is soft or has excessive travel, repeat bleed procedure.
23. Start engine and apply brake pedal with moderate force. If pedal feels firm and constant and travel is not excessive, proceed to next step. If pedal is soft or has excessive travel, proceed as follows:
    a. Use scan tool to release and apply motors 2–3 times.
    b. Cycle solenoids 5–10 times.
    c. Apply front and rear motors to ensure pistons are at upper most position.
    d. Repeat bleed procedure.
24. Drive vehicle at six mph for five seconds, then stop vehicle and turn ignition switch off.
25. If pedal felt firm and constant, and pedal travel was not excessive, proceed to next step. If pedal was soft or has excessive travel, repeat bleed procedure.
26. Road test vehicle and make several non-ABS stops at moderate speed to ensure proper braking function. Allow brakes to cool between stops.

HYDRAULIC SYSTEM FLUSH

If brake fluid is old, rusty or contaminated, or whenever new components are installed in hydraulic system, the system must be flushed. Bleed brakes, allowing at least one quart of clean brake fluid to pass through system. Any rubber components in hydraulic system which were exposed to contaminated fluid must be replaced.

PRESSURE FLUSH

Pressure bleeding equipment must have a rubber diaphragm between air supply and brake fluid to prevent air, moisture and other contaminants from entering system.

1. Clean reservoir cover and surrounding area.
2. Remove cover and reservoir fluid.
3. Fill reservoir with clean DOT 3 brake fluid.
4. Attach bleeding adapter tool No. J-35589, or equivalent, to brake fluid reservoir and pressure bleeding equipment.
5. Pressurize bleeding equipment to 5–10 psi and wait 30 seconds to ensure there are no leaks.
6. Pressurize equipment to 30–35 psi.
7. Attach clear plastic hose to rearward hydraulic modulator bleeder valve. Place other end in container to collect draining brake fluid. **Do not submerge hose end in fluid.**
8. Slowly open bleeder valve and allow fluid to flow until clean brake fluid flows, or until at least four ounces of fluid is collected.
9. Close valve and repeat procedure on forward bleeder valve.
10. **Torque** bleeder valves to 84 inch lbs.
11. Raise and support vehicle.
12. Attach bleeder hose to righthand rear wheel bleeder valve. Place other end in container to collect draining brake fluid. **Do not submerge hose end in fluid.**
13. Slowly open bleeder valve and allow fluid to flow until clean brake fluid flows, or until at least eight ounces of fluid is collected.
14. Close valve and repeat procedure on lefthand rear, righthand front and lefthand front wheels, in turn.
15. Lower vehicle and remove bleeder adapter tool.
16. Replace brake hose assemblies, master cylinder rubber components, brake caliper and wheel cylinder boots and seals, hydraulic modulator and ABS solenoids.
17. Repeat flushing procedure.
18. Inspect and correct reservoir fluid level.
19. Install reservoir cap and bleed system.

MANUAL FLUSH

Use suitable container and/or shop rags to catch fluid.

1. Clean reservoir cover and surrounding area.
2. Remove cover and reservoir fluid.
3. Fill reservoir with clean DOT 3 brake fluid.
4. Attach clear plastic hose to rearward hydraulic modulator bleeder valve, then place other end of hose in container to collect draining brake fluid. **Do not submerge hose end in fluid.**
5. Open bleeder valve ½–1 turn.
6. Press brake pedal until fluid begins to flow.
7. Close valve and release brake pedal pressure.
8. Repeat previous steps until at least four ounces of clear brake fluid is collected.
9. Close valve and repeat procedure on forward bleeder valve.
10. **Torque** bleeder valves to 84 inch lbs.
11. Inspect and correct reservoir fluid level.
12. Install reservoir cap and bleed system.
13. Raise and support vehicle.
14. Attach bleeder hose to righthand rear wheel bleeder valve, then place other end of hose in container to collect draining brake fluid. **Do not submerge hose end in fluid.**
15. Open bleeder valve and slowly press brake pedal until fluid begins to flow.
16. Close valve and release brake pedal pressure.
17. Repeat previous steps until at least eight ounces of clear brake fluid is collected.
18. Close valve and repeat procedure in the following order; lefthand rear, righthand front, lefthand front.
19. Lower vehicle.
20. Replace brake hose assemblies, master cylinder rubber components, brake caliper and wheel cylinder boots and seals, hydraulic modulator and ABS solenoids.
21. Repeat flushing procedure.
22. Inspect and correct reservoir fluid level.
23. Install reservoir cap and bleed system.

Component Replacement

BATTERY GROUND CABLE

Prior to service, disconnect battery ground cable and isolate as required.

HYDRAULIC MODULATOR SOLENOID

Hydraulic modulator solenoid cannot be repair. Complete unit must be replaced.

1. **On Malibu models,** remove battery and tray.
2. **On all models,** disconnect electrical connector, **Fig. 266.**
3. Remove mounting bolts.
4. Remove solenoid with seal attached.
5. Reverse procedure to install, noting the following:
    a. Lubricate lip seal with clean brake fluid.
    b. **Torque** mounting bolts to 40–44 inch lbs.
    c. Bleed hydraulic system as outlined in "Brake System Bleed."

HYDRAULIC MODULATOR ASSEMBLY

1. Attach suitably programmed scan tool and perform "Gear Tension Relief" function. **Failure to relieve gear tension could result in injury from a retained modulator assembly load.**
2. **On Malibu models,** remove battery, battery tray and upper radiator hose.
3. **On all models,** disconnect solenoid electrical connectors, **Fig. 267.**
4. Disconnect fluid level sensor and motor pack electrical connectors.
5. **On Cavalier and Sunfire models,** remove air cleaner cover and/or intake duct assembly.
6. **On all models,** place a shop cloth on

top of motor pack to catch any dripping hydraulic fluid.

7. Disconnect modulator hydraulic pipes and plug open lines.
8. Remove modulator assembly to brake booster mounting nuts. It may be required to remove vacuum check valve from booster to gain access to nut closest to check valve.
9. Remove modulator assembly.
10. Reverse procedure to install, noting the following:
    a. **Torque** modulator assembly to booster attaching nuts to 20 ft. lbs.
    b. **On Metro models, torque** mounting bolts to 48 inch lbs.
    c. **On all models, torque** hydraulic pipe nuts to 18 ft. lbs.
    d. Bleed hydraulic system as outlined in "Brake System Bleed."

ELECTRONIC BRAKE CONTROL MODULE(EBCM)/ ELECTRONIC BRAKE TRACTION CONTROL MODULE (EBTCM)

ALERO & GRAND AM

1. Disconnect electrical connectors, **Fig. 268.**
2. Remove mounting screws and EBCM from cowl panel.
3. Reverse procedure to install, noting the following:
    a. Ensure plastic grommets are located properly.
    b. **Torque** mounting screws to 17 inch lbs.
    c. Bleed brake system as outlined in "Brake System Bleed."

CAVALIER & SUNFIRE

1. Remove bracket mounting screw.
2. Remove EBCM from bracket.
3. Disconnect electrical connectors.
4. Reverse procedure to install, noting the following:
    a. **Torque** mounting screws to 20 inch lbs.
    b. Bleed brake system as outlined in "Brake System Bleed."

MALIBU

1. Remove lefthand front wheel and inner splash shield.
2. Disconnect EBCM connector, then the harness from bracket.
3. Remove mounting screws and EBCM.
4. Reverse procedure to install. **Torque** mounting screws to 96 inch lbs.

INTRIGUE, LUMINA & MONTE CARLO

1. Remove instrument panel sound panel from under lefthand side of instrument panel.
2. Release pressure tabs securing EBCM to bracket.
3. Disconnect EBCM electrical connectors and remove EBCM.
4. Reverse procedure to install.

METRO

1. Remove lefthand kick trim panel
2. Disconnect electrical connector, then remove mounting bolt and junction block.
3. Disconnect Lamp Driver Relay (LDR) and EBCM electrical connectors.
4. Remove mounting bolts, EBCM and LDR.
5. Reverse procedure to install. **Torque** mounting bolts to 72 inch lbs.

WHEEL SPEED SENSOR

FRONT

1. Raise and support vehicle.
2. Disconnect wheel sensor electrical connector, **Fig. 269.**
3. Remove sensor mounting bolt, then the sensor from mounting bracket.
4. If sensor will not slide out of knuckle, proceed as follows:
    a. Remove brake rotor.
    b. Use suitable blunt punch to push sensor from back side of knuckle.
5. If sensor locating pin breaks off and remains in knuckle, proceed as follows:
    a. Remove rotor.
    b. Use suitable blunt punch to remove broken pin.
    c. Use sandpaper wrapped around suitable screwdriver to clean hole.
    d. **Do not attempt to enlarge hole.**
6. Reverse procedure to install, noting the following:
    a. Ensure sensor is properly aligned and lays flat against knuckle bosses.
    b. **Torque** attaching bolt to 108 inch lbs.

REAR

Except Metro

The rear speed sensors and rings on these models are an integral part of the hub and bearing assembly. If speed sensors or rings are faulty, the entire assembly must be replaced as a unit. Refer to appropriate chassis section for hub replacement.

Metro

1. Raise and support vehicle. Remove rear wheel and tire.
2. Disconnect rear wheel speed sensor connector.
3. Remove mounting bolt and sensor from rear suspension knuckle.
4. Reverse procedure to install. **Torque** mounting bolt to 108 inch lbs.

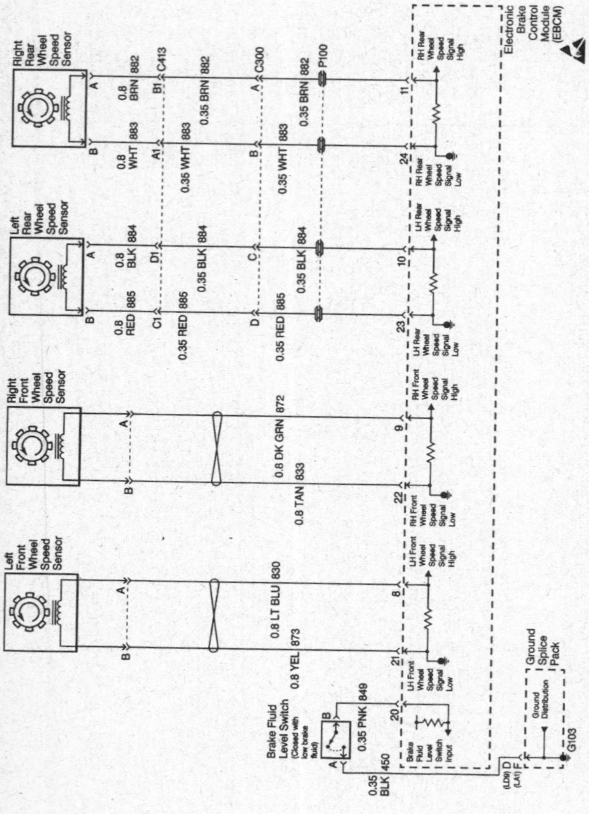

GC4029703048010X

Fig. 3 Wiring diagram (Part 1 of 4). Alero, Grand Am & Malibu

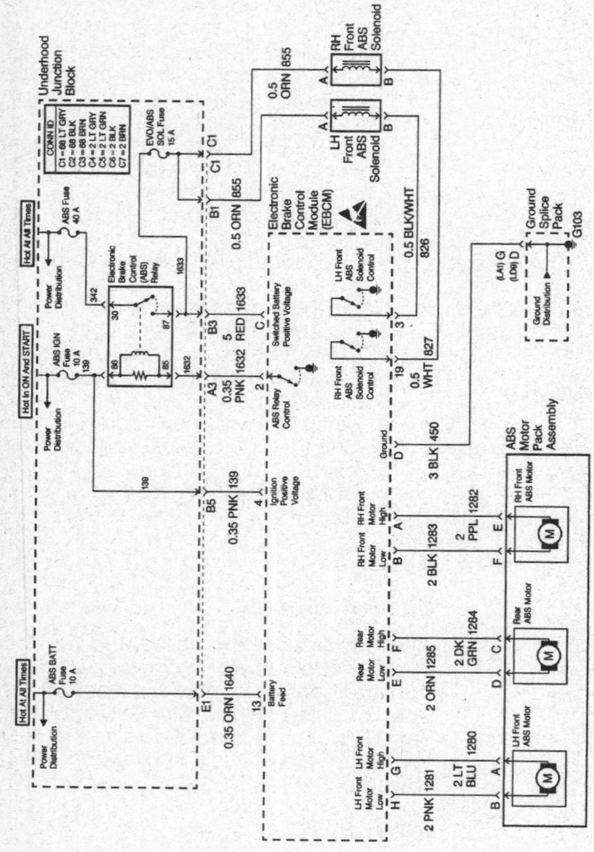

GC4029703048020X

Fig. 3 Wiring diagram (Part 2 of 4). Alero, Grand Am & Malibu

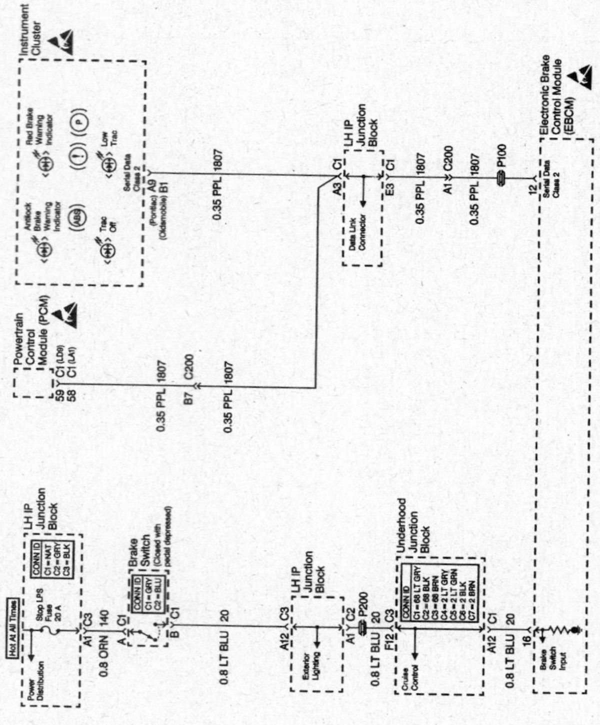

GC4029803048030X

Fig. 3 Wiring diagram (Part 3 of 4). Alero, Grand Am & Malibu

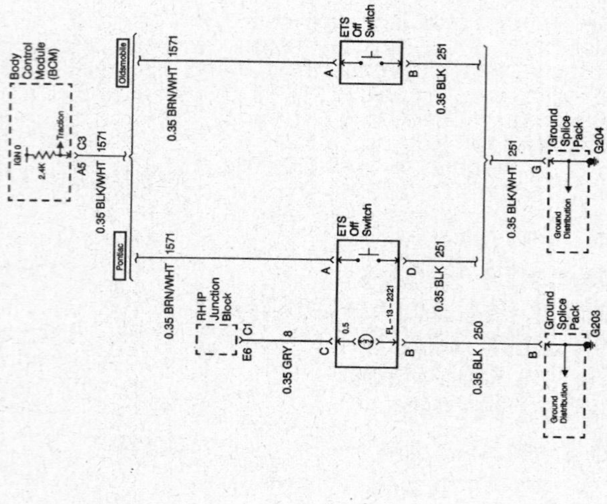

GC4029803048040X

Fig. 3 Wiring diagram (Part 4 of 4). Alero, Grand Am & Malibu

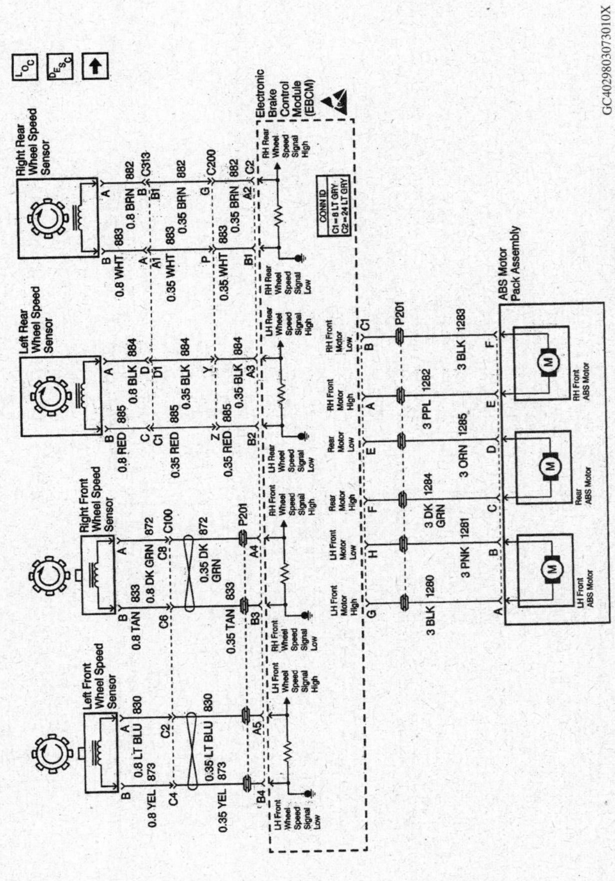

Fig. 4 Wiring diagram (Part 1 of 3). Cavalier & Sunfire

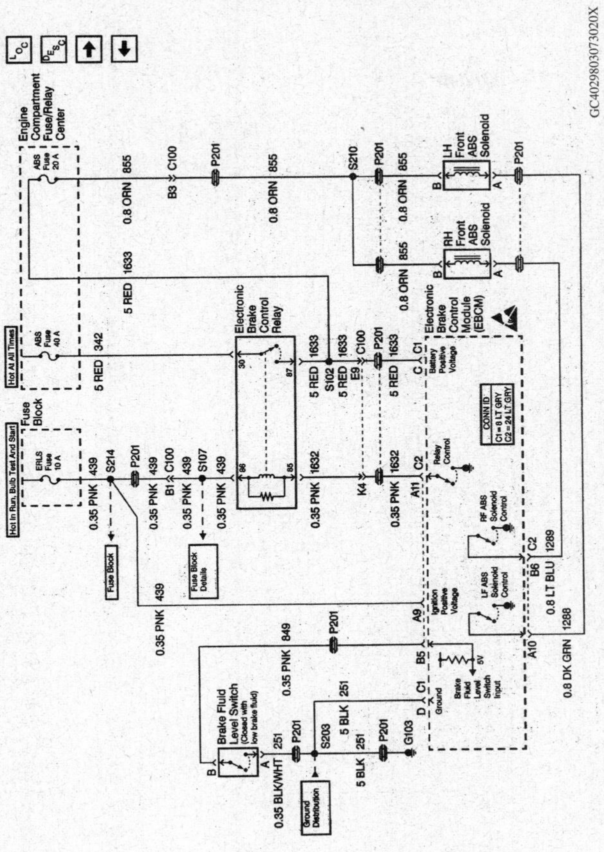

Fig. 4 Wiring diagram (Part 2 of 3). Cavalier & Sunfire

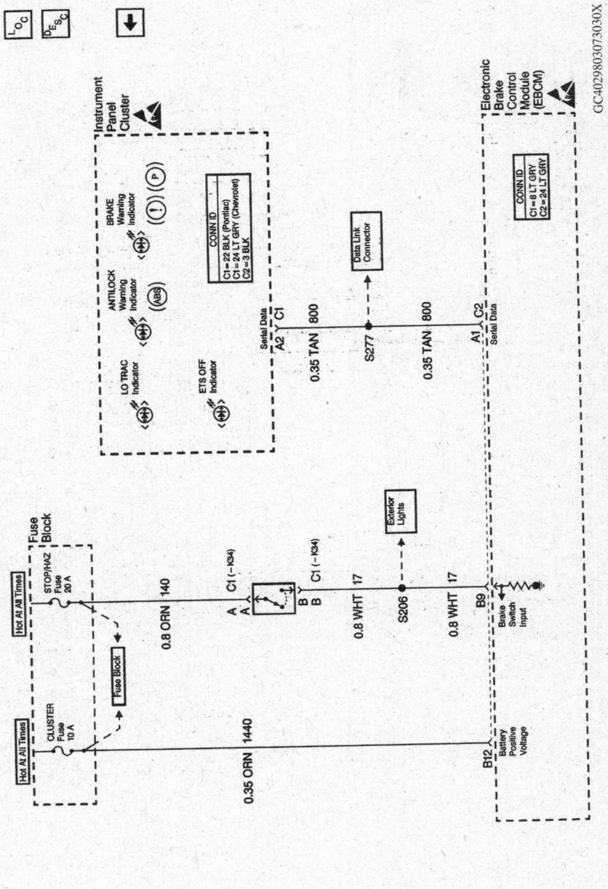

Fig. 4 Wiring diagram (Part 3 of 3). Cavalier & Sunfire

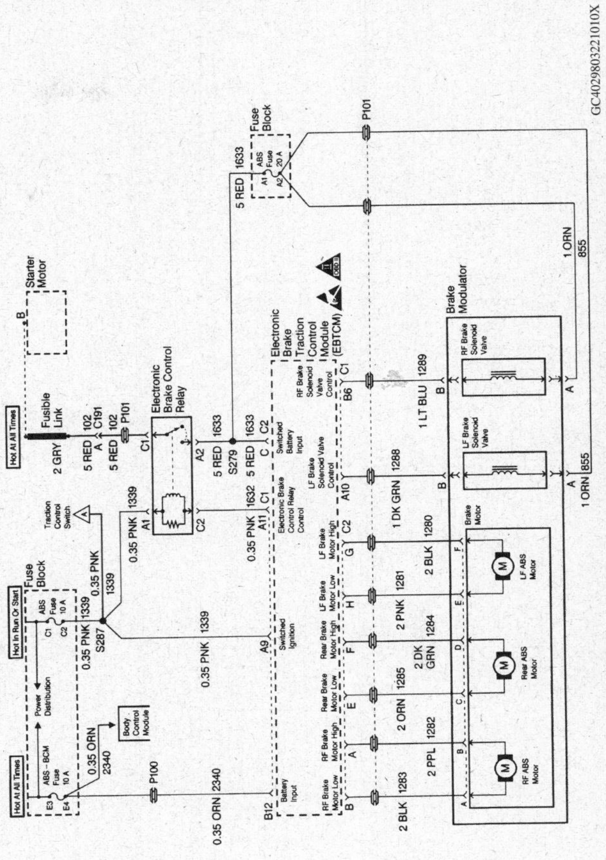

Fig. 5 Wiring diagram (Part 1 of 3). Intrigue

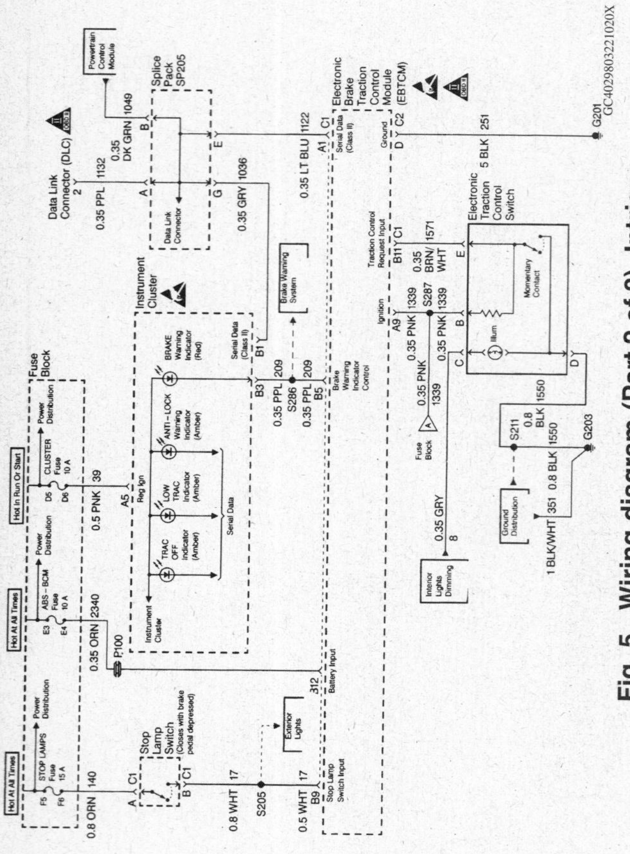

Fig. 5 Wiring diagram (Part 2 of 3). Intrigue

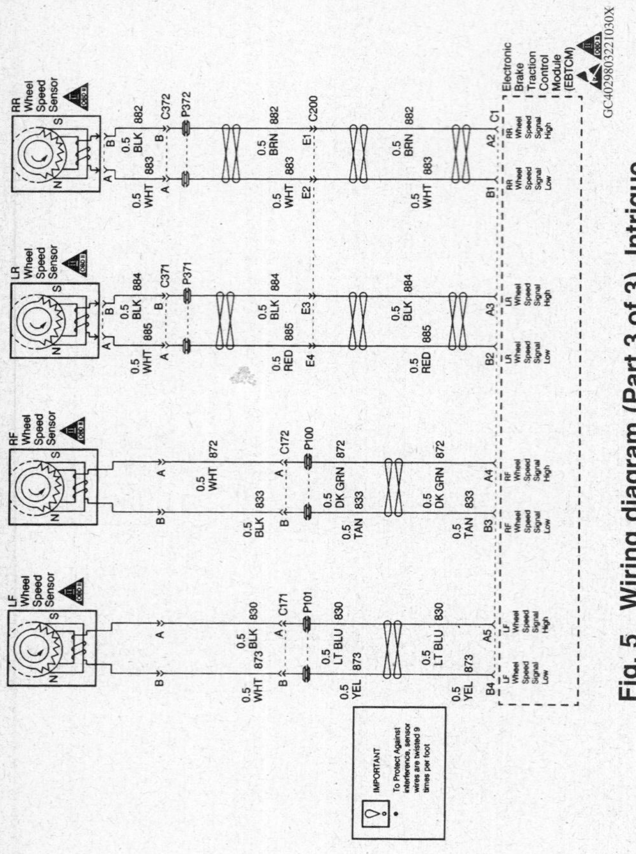

Fig. 5 Wiring diagram (Part 3 of 3). Intrigue

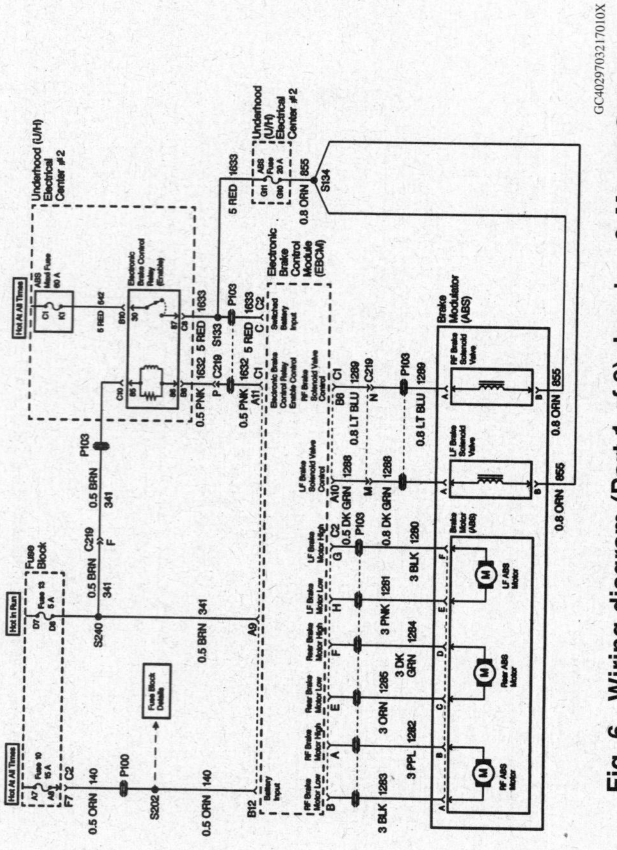

Fig. 6 Wiring diagram (Part 1 of 3). Lumina & Monte Carlo

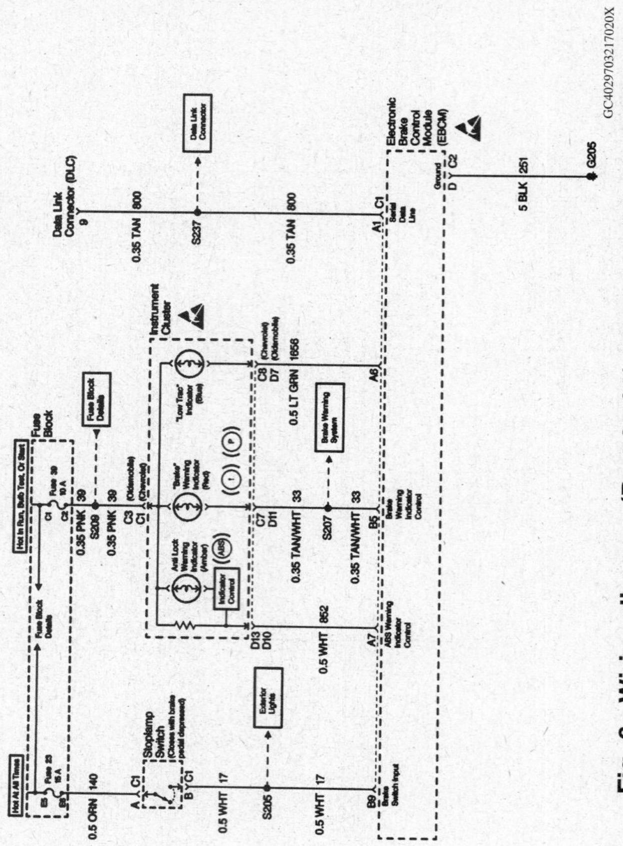

Fig. 6 Wiring diagram (Part 2 of 3). Lumina & Monte Carlo

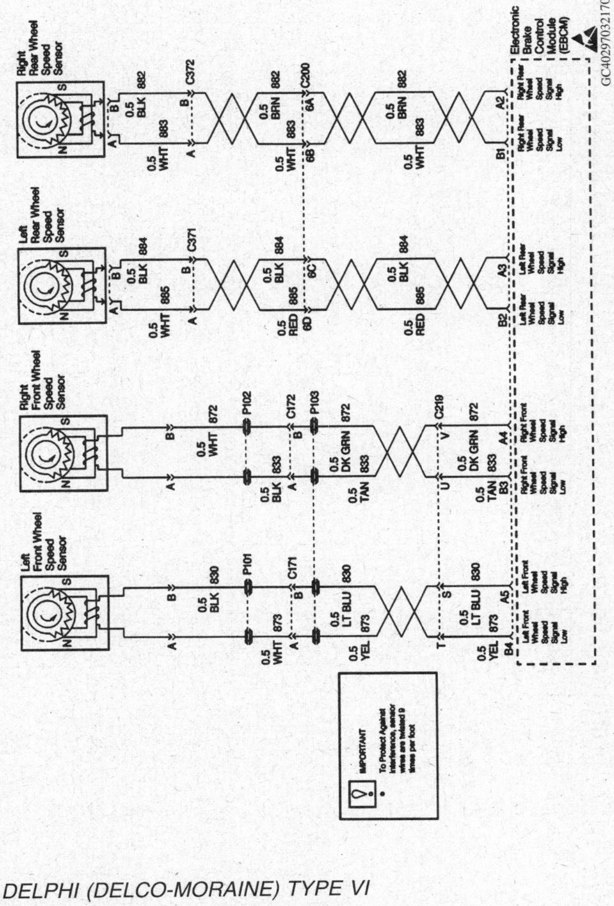

Fig. 6 Wiring diagram (Part 3 of 3). Lumina & Monte Carlo

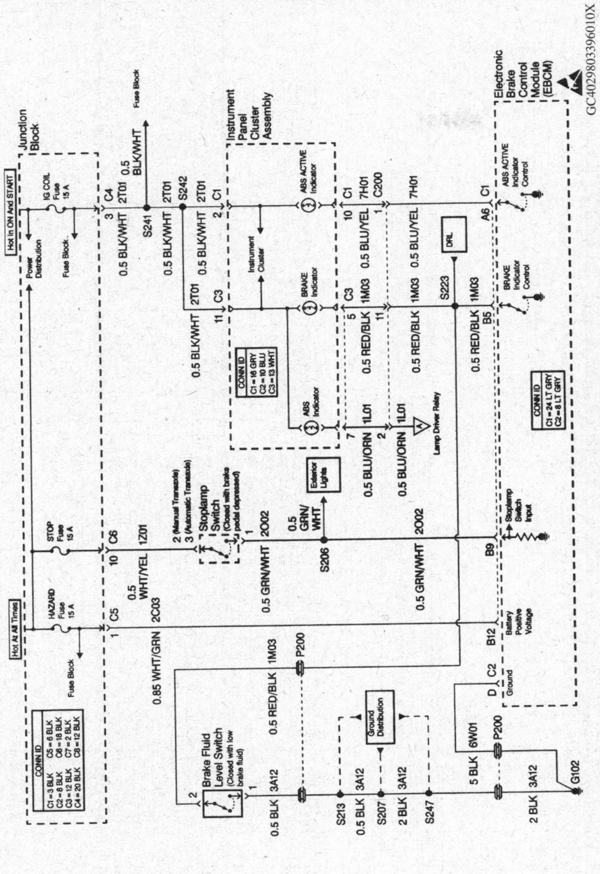

Fig. 7 Wiring diagram (Part 1 of 3). Metro

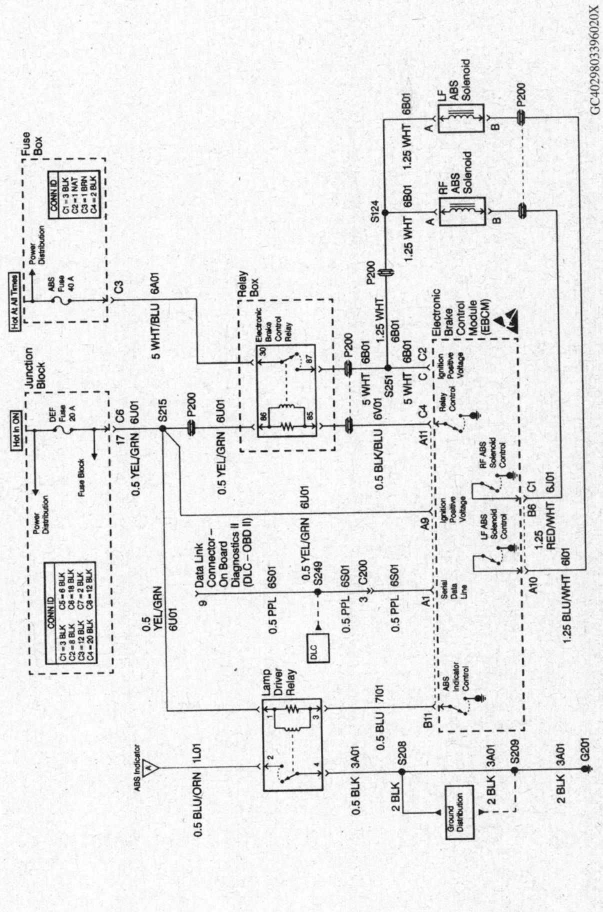

Fig. 7 Wiring diagram (Part 2 of 3). Metro

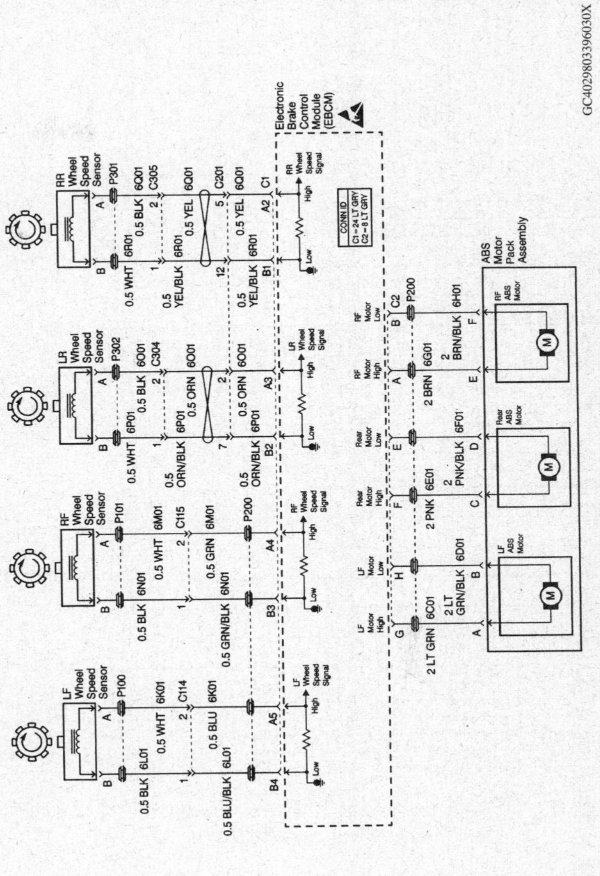

Fig. 7 Wiring diagram (Part 3 of 3). Metro

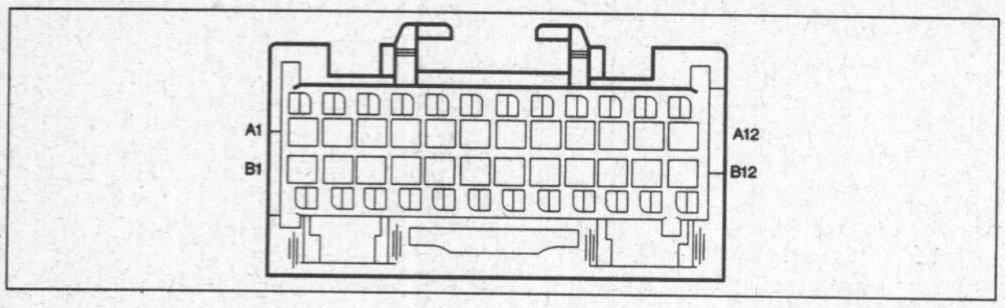

PIN	CIRCUIT NO.	COLOR	CIRCUIT
A1	800	TAN	SERIAL DATA
A2	882	BRN	RIGHT REAR WHEEL SPEED SENSOR HIGH
A3	884	BLK	LEFT REAR WHEEL SPEED SENSOR HIGH
A4	872	DK GRN	RIGHT FRONT WHEEL SPEED SENSOR HIGH
A5	830	LT BLU	LEFT FRONT WHEEL SPEED SENSOR HIGH
A6	OPEN		
A7	OPEN		
A8	OPEN		
A9	439	PNK	SWITCHED IGNITION
A10	1288	DK GRN	LEFT FRONT SOLENOID CONTROL
A11	1632	PNK	ABS RELAY CONTROL
A12	OPEN		
B1	883	WHT	RIGHT REAR WHEEL SPEED SENSOR LOW
B2	885	RED	LEFT REAR WHEEL SPEED SENSOR LOW
B3	833	TAN	RIGHT FRONT WHEEL SPEED SENSOR LOW
B4	873	YEL	LEFT FRONT WHEEL SPEED SENSOR LOW
B5	849	PNK	BRAKE FLUID LEVEL SWITCH INPUT
B6	1289	LT BLU	RIGHT FRONT SOLENOID CONTROL
B7	OPEN		
B8	OPEN		
B9	17	WHT	BRAKE SWITCH INPUT
B10	OPEN		
B11	OPEN		
B12	1440	ORN	BATTERY FEED

GC4029602027010X

Fig. 8 EBCM connector face views (Part 1 of 2). Cavalier & Sunfire

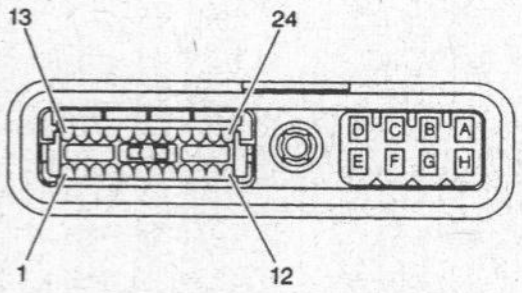

Connector Part Information	• 12160864 • 32-Way F Metri-Pack 280 Series (Black)		
Pin	**Wire Color**	**Circuit No.**	**Function**
1			
2	PNK	1632	ABS Relay Control
3	BLK/WHT	826	ABS Solenoid Control - Left Front
4	PNK	139	Fuse Output - Ignition 1 - Type III Fuse
5			

Connector Part Information	• 12160864 • 32-Way F Metri-Pack 280 Series (Black)		
Pin	**Wire Color**	**Circuit No.**	**Function**
6			
7			
8	LT BLU	830	Wheel Speed Sensor Signal - Left Front
9	DK GRN	872	Wheel Speed Sensor Signal - Right Front
10	BLK	884	Wheel Speed Sensor Signal - Left Rear
11	BRN	882	Wheel Speed Sensor Signal - Right Rear
12	PPL	1807	Serial Data Signal - Class B - 10400 Baud - Primary
13	ORN	1640	Fuse Output - Battery - Type III Fuse
14			
15			
16	LT BLU	20	Stoplamp Feed
17			
18			
19	WHT	827	ABS Solenoid Control - Right Front

Connector Part Information	• 12160864 • 32-Way F Metri-Pack 280 Series (Black)		
Pin	**Wire Color**	**Circuit No.**	**Function**
20	PNK	849	Brake Fluid Level Sensor Signal
21	YEL	873	Wheel Speed Sensor Return - Left Front
22	TAN	833	Wheel Speed Sensor Return - Right Front
23	RED	885	Wheel Speed Sensor Return - Left Rear
24	WHT	883	Wheel Speed Sensor Return - Right Rear
A	PPL	1282	ABS Motor Feed - Right Front
B	BLK	1283	ABS Motor Return - Right Front
C	RED	1633	ABS Relay Output
D	BLK	450	Ground
E	ORN	1285	ABS Motor Return - Rear
F	DK GRN	1284	ABS Motor Feed - Rear
G	LT BLU	1280	ABS Motor Feed - Left Front
H	PNK	1281	ABS Motor Return - Left Front

GC4029703050000X

Fig. 9 EBCM connector face view. Malibu

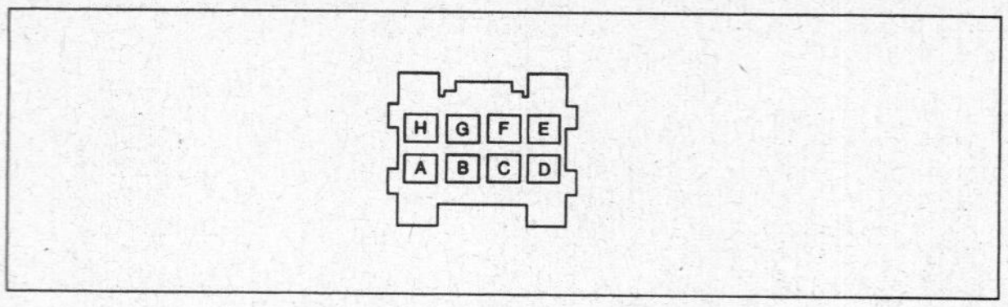

PIN	CIRCUIT NO.	COLOR	CIRCUIT
A	1282	PPL	RIGHT FRONT MOTOR HIGH
B	1283	BLK	RIGHT FRONT MOTOR LOW
C	1633	RED	SWITCHED BATTERY INPUT
D	251	BLK	GROUND
E	1285	ORN	REAR MOTOR LOW
F	1284	DK GRN	REAR MOTOR HIGH
G	1280	BLK	LEFT FRONT MOTOR HIGH
H	1281	PNK	LEFT FRONT MOTOR LOW

GC4029602027020X

Fig. 8 EBCM connector face views (Part 2 of 2). Cavalier & Sunfire

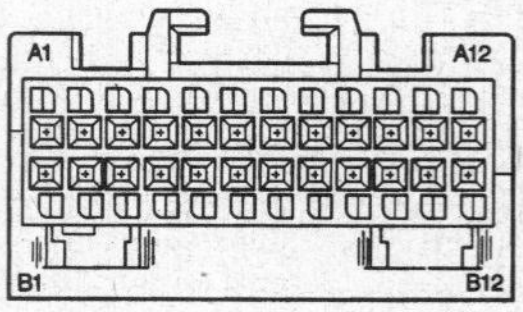

PIN	WIRE COLOR	CIRCUIT NO.	FUNCTION
A1	LT BLU	1122	SERIAL DATA LINE
A2	BRN	882	RIGHT REAR WHEEL SPEED SENSOR HIGH
A3	BLK	884	LEFT REAR WHEEL SPEED SENSOR HIGH
A4	DK GRN	872	RIGHT FRONT WHEEL SPEED SENSOR HIGH
A5	LT BLU	830	LEFT FRONT WHEEL SPEED SENSOR HIGH
A6	—	PLUGGED	NOT USED
A7	—	PLUGGED	NOT USED
A8	—	PLUGGED	NOT USED
A9	PNK	1339	SWITCHED IGNITION
A10	DK GRN	1288	LEFT FRONT BRAKE SOLENOID VALVE CONTROL
A11	PNK	1632	ELECTRONIC BRAKE CONTROL RELAY ENABLE CONTROL
A12	—	PLUGGED	NOT USED
B1	WHT	883	RIGHT REAR WHEEL SPEED SENSOR LOW
B2	RED	885	LEFT REAR WHEEL SPEED SENSOR LOW
B3	TAN	833	RIGHT FRONT WHEEL SPEED SENSOR LOW
B4	YEL	873	LEFT FRONT WHEEL SPEED SENSOR LOW
B5	PPL	209	BRAKE WARNING INDICATOR CONTROL
B6	LT BLU	1289	RIGHT FRONT BRAKE SOLENOID VALVE CONTROL
B7	WHT	345	MSVA LOW
B8	GRY	1787	MSVA HIGH
B9	WHT	17	BRAKE SWITCH INPUT
B10	LT GRN	1055	TIRE INFLATION MONITOR (TIM) RESET SWITCH SIGNAL
B11	BRN/WHT	1571	TCS MODE SWITCH INPUT
B12	ORN	2340	BATTERY INPUT

GC402970321801CX

Fig. 10 EBCM connector face views (Part 1 of 2). Intrigue

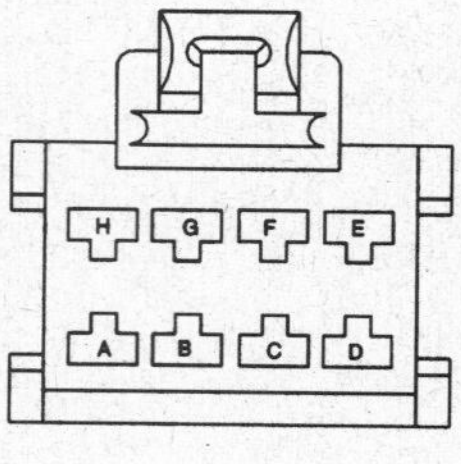

PIN	WIRE COLOR	CIRCUIT NO.	FUNCTION
A	PPL	1282	RIGHT FRONT BRAKE MOTOR HIGH
B	BLK	1283	RIGHT FRONT BRAKE MOTOR LOW
C	RED	1633	SWITCHED BATTERY INPUT
D	BLK	251	GROUND
E	ORN	1285	REAR BRAKE MOTOR LOW
F	DK GRN	1284	REAR BRAKE MOTOR HIGH
G	BLK	1280	LEFT FRONT BRAKE MOTOR HIGH
H	PNK	1281	LEFT FRONT BRAKE MOTOR LOW

GC4029703218020X

Fig. 10 EBCM connector face views (Part 2 of 2). Intrigue

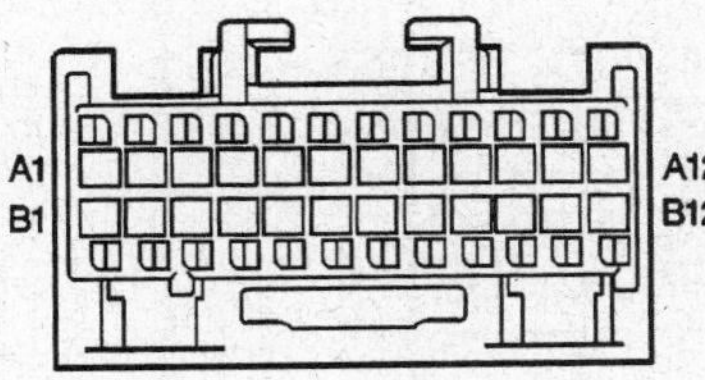

Connector Part Information	• 1211008 • 24-Way Micro-Pack F 100 Series (GRY)		
Pin	**Wire Color**	**Circuit No.**	**Function**
A1	TAN	800	Serial Data UART
A2	BRN	882	Wheel Speed Sensor-RR
A3	BLK	884	Wheel Speed Sensor-LR
A4	DK GRN	872	Wheel Speed Sensor-RF
A5	LT BLU	830	Wheel Speed Sensor-LF
A6	LT GRN	1652	Reverse Lockout Solenoid Output
A7	WHT	852	ABS Signal-ABS Failure

GC4029903823010X

Fig. 11 EBCM 24-way connector view (Part 1 of 2). Intrigue, Lumina & Monte Carlo

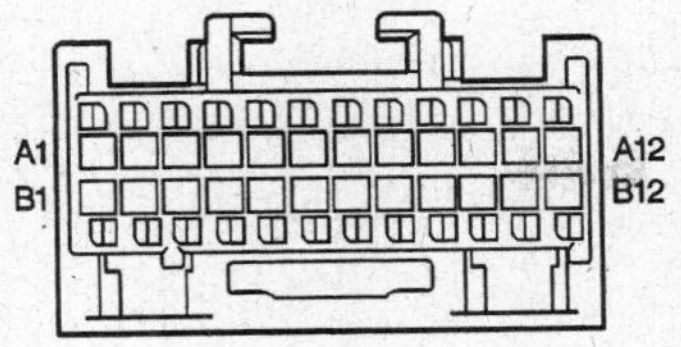

Connector Part Information	• 1211008 • 24-Way Micro-Pack F 100 Series (GRY)		
Pin	**Wire Color**	**Circuit No.**	**Function**
A8	—	—	Not Used
A9	BRN	341	Fused Output-IGN 3
A10	DK GRN	1288	ABS Isolated Solenoid Feed-LF
A11	PNK	1632	ABS Enable Relay Output-Coil
A12	—	—	Not Used
B1	WHT	883	Wheel Speed Sensor Retrun-RR
B2	RED	885	Wheel Speed Sensor Return-LR
B3	TAN	833	Wheel Speed Sensor Return-RF
B4	YEL	873	Wheel Speed Sensor Return-LF
B5	TAN/WHT	33	Brake Warning Indicator Lamp Output
B6	LT BLU	1289	ABS Isolation Solenoid Feed-RF
B7 - 8	—	—	Not Used
B9	WHT	17	Stop LAmp Switch Output
B10 - 11	—	—	Not Used
B12	ORN	640	Fused Output-Battery

GC4029903823020X

Fig. 11 EBCM 24-way connector view (Part 2 of 2) Intrigue, Lumina & Monte Carlo

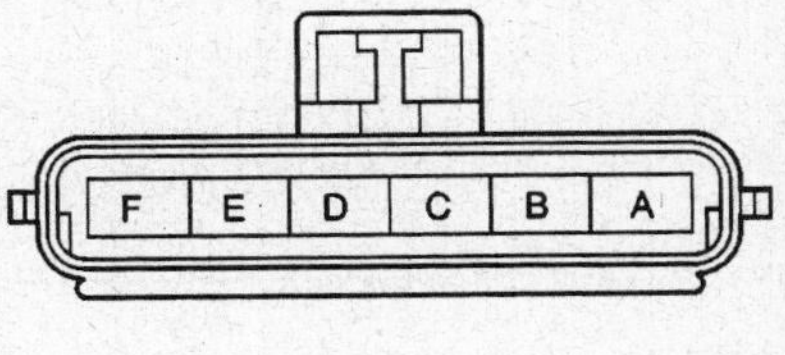

Connector Part Information	• 12110295 • 6-Way F Metric-Pack 280 Series, Sealed (GRY)		
Pin	**Wire Color**	**Circuit No.**	**Function**
A	BLK	1283	RF Brake Motor Low
B	PPL	1282	RF Brake Motor High
C	ORN	1285	Rear Brake Motor Low
D	DK GRN	1284	Rear Brake Motor High
E	PNK	1281	LF Brake Motor High
F	BLK	1280	LF Brake Motor Low

GC4029903822000X

Fig. 12 EBCM 8-way connector view. Intrigue, Lumina & Monte Carlo

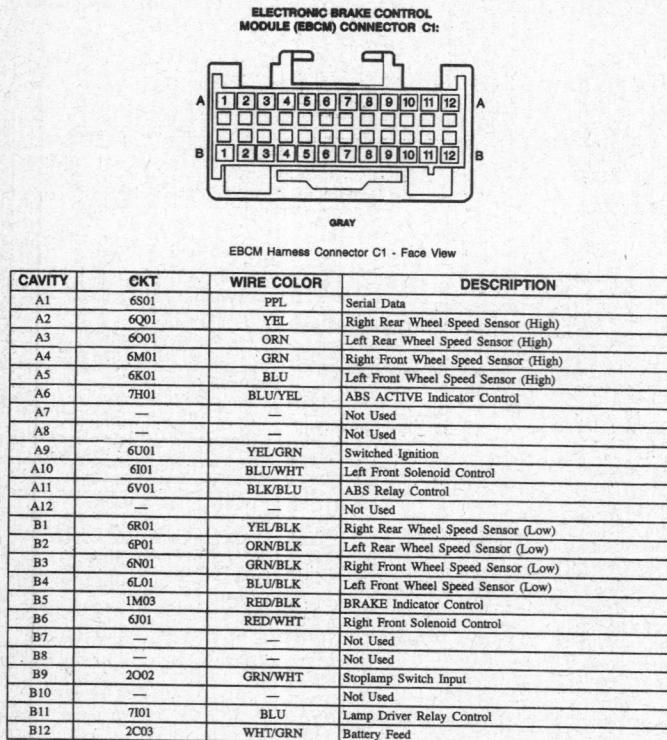

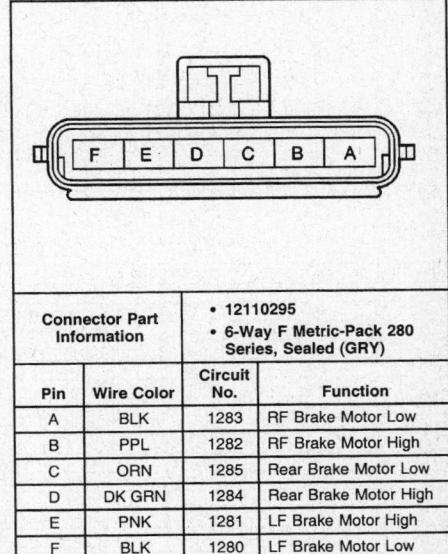

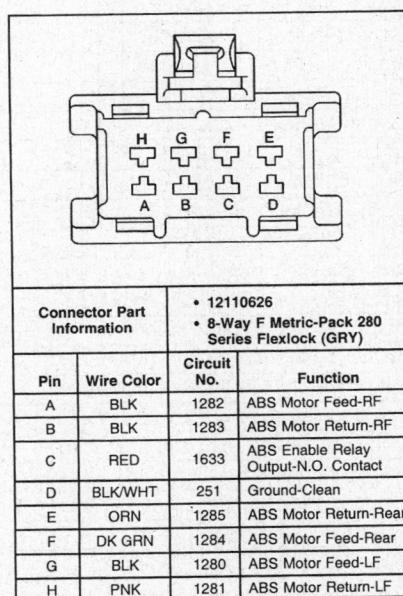

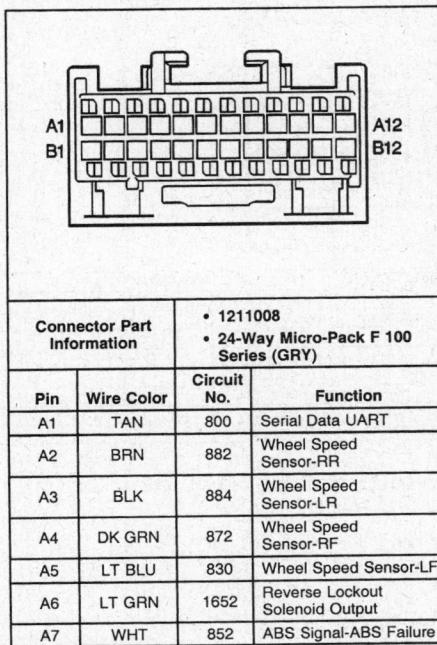

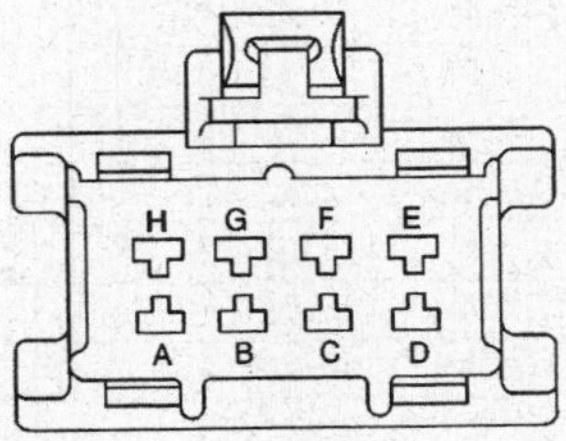

Connector Part Information	• 12110626 • 8-Way F Metric-Pack 280 Series Flexlock (GRY)		
Pin	**Wire Color**	**Circuit No.**	**Function**
A	BLK	1282	ABS Motor Feed-RF
B	BLK	1283	ABS Motor Return-RF
C	RED	1633	ABS Enable Relay Output-N.O. Contact
D	BLK/WHT	251	Ground-Clean
E	ORN	1285	ABS Motor Return-Rear
F	DK GRN	1284	ABS Motor Feed-Rear
G	BLK	1280	ABS Motor Feed-LF
H	PNK	1281	ABS Motor Return-LF

GC4029903824000X

Fig. 13 Brake motor connector view. Intrigue, Lumina & Monte Carlo

ELECTRONIC BRAKE CONTROL MODULE (EBCM) CONNECTOR C1:

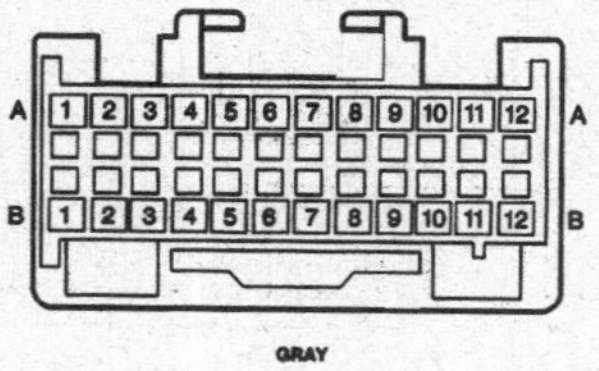

EBCM Harness Connector C1 - Face View

CAVITY	CKT	WIRE COLOR	DESCRIPTION
A1	6S01	PPL	Serial Data
A2	6Q01	YEL	Right Rear Wheel Speed Sensor (High)
A3	6O01	ORN	Left Rear Wheel Speed Sensor (High)
A4	6M01	GRN	Right Front Wheel Speed Sensor (High)
A5	6K01	BLU	Left Front Wheel Speed Sensor (High)
A6	7H01	BLU/YEL	ABS ACTIVE Indicator Control
A7	—	—	Not Used
A8	—	—	Not Used
A9	6U01	YEL/GRN	Switched Ignition
A10	6I01	BLU/WHT	Left Front Solenoid Control
A11	6V01	BLK/BLU	ABS Relay Control
A12	—	—	Not Used
B1	6R01	YEL/BLK	Right Rear Wheel Speed Sensor (Low)
B2	6P01	ORN/BLK	Left Rear Wheel Speed Sensor (Low)
B3	6N01	GRN/BLK	Right Front Wheel Speed Sensor (Low)
B4	6L01	BLU/BLK	Left Front Wheel Speed Sensor (Low)
B5	1M03	RED/BLK	BRAKE Indicator Control
B6	6J01	RED/WHT	Right Front Solenoid Control
B7	—	—	Not Used
B8	—	—	Not Used
B9	2O02	GRN/WHT	Stoplamp Switch Input
B10	—	—	Not Used
B11	7I01	BLU	Lamp Driver Relay Control
B12	2C03	WHT/GRN	Battery Feed

GC4029702837010X

Fig. 14 EBCM connector face views (Part 1 of 2). Metro

ELECTRONIC BRAKE CONTROL MODULE (EBCM) CONNECTOR C2:

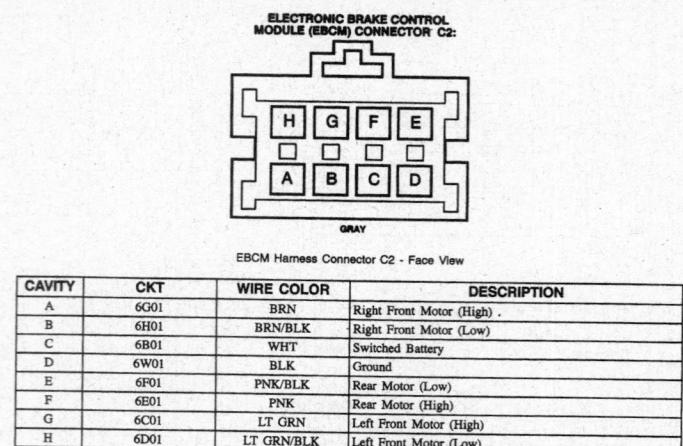

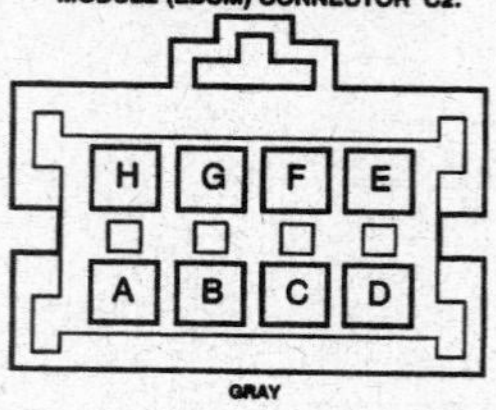

EBCM Harness Connector C2 - Face View

CAVITY	CKT	WIRE COLOR	DESCRIPTION
A	6G01	BRN	Right Front Motor (High) .
B	6H01	BRN/BLK	Right Front Motor (Low)
C	6B01	WHT	Switched Battery
D	6W01	BLK	Ground
E	6F01	PNK/BLK	Rear Motor (Low)
F	6E01	PNK	Rear Motor (High)
G	6C01	LT GRN	Left Front Motor (High)
H	6D01	LT GRN/BLK	Left Front Motor (Low)

GC4029702837020X

Fig. 14 EBCM connector face views (Part 2 of 2). Metro

DIAGNOSTIC CHART INDEX

Continued

DIAGNOSTIC CHART INDEX—Continued

Code/Test	Description	Page No.	Fig. No.
ALERO & GRAND AM			
Code C1236	Low System Supply Voltage	6-40	34
Code C1237	High System Supply Voltage	6-41	35
Code C1238	LH Front ESB Does Not Hold Motor	6-41	36
Code C1241	RH Front ESB Does Not Hold Motor	6-42	37
Code C1242	Rear ESB Does Not Hold Motor	6-43	38
Code C1243	VES Steering Wheel Sensor Circuit Fault	6-43	39
Code C1244	LH Front ABS Channel Does Not Move	6-45	40
Code C1245	RH Front ABS Channel Does Not Move	6-45	41
Code C1246	Rear ABS Channel Does Not Move	6-46	42
Code C1247	LH Front ABS Motor Free Spins	6-47	43
Code C1248	RH Front ABS Motor Free Spins	6-48	44
Code C1251	Rear ABS Motor Free Spins	6-49	45
Code C1252	LH Front ABS Channel In Release Too Long	6-51	46
Code C1253	RH Front ABS Channel In Release Too Long	6-51	47
Code C1254	Rear ABS Channel In Release Too Long	6-52	48
Code C1255	EBCM/EBTCM Internal Fault	6-53	49
Code C1256	LH Front ABS Motor Circuit Open	6-53	50
Code C1257	LH Front ABS Motor Circuit Shorted To Ground	6-54	51
Code C1258	LH Front ABS Motor Circuit Shorted To Voltage	6-54	52
Code C1261	RH Front ABS Motor Circuit Open	6-55	53
Code C1262	RH Front ABS Motor Circuit Shorted To Ground	6-55	54
Code C1263	RH Front ABS Motor Circuit Shorted To Voltage	6-56	55
Code C1264	Rear ABS Motor Circuit Open	6-57	56
Code C1265	Rear ABS Motor Circuit Shorted To Ground	6-57	57
Code C1266	Rear ABS Motor Circuit Shorted To Voltage	6-58	58
Code C1267	Code U1300 Previously Set	6-59	59
Code C1268	Code U1301 Previously Set	6-59	60
Code C1273	VES Circuit Open Or Shorted To Ground	6-59	61
Code C1274	VES Circuit Shorted To Voltage	6-60	62
Code C1275	PCM Requested ETS To Be Disabled	6-60	63
Code C1276	LH Front Solenoid Circuit Open Or Shorted To Ground	6-61	64
Code C1277	LH Front Solenoid Circuit Shorted To Voltage	6-62	65
Code C1278	RH Front Solenoid Circuit Open Or Shorted To Ground	6-62	66
Code C1281	RH Front Solenoid Circuit Shorted to Voltage	6-63	67
Code C1282	Calibration Fault	6-63	68
Code C1286	EBCM/EBTCM Turned On Brake Warning Lamp	6-64	69
Code C1291	Open Brake Lamp Switch Circuit During Decel	6-64	70
Code C1292	Open Brake Lamp Switch When ABS Required	6-65	71
Code C1293	Code C1291 Or C1292 Set In Current Or Previous Ignition Cycle	6-65	72
Code C1294	Brake Lamp Switch Circuit Always Active	6-66	73
Code C1295	Brake Lamp Switch Circuit Open	6-66	74
CAVALIER & SUNFIRE			
—	ABS Diagnostic System Check	6-73	88
—	No Communication With EBCM	6-114	142
—	ABS Indicator On No DTC Set	6-115	143
—	ABS Indicator Inoperative No DTC Set	6-115	144
—	ETS Off Indicator On w/No DTC Set	6-116	145
—	ETS Off Indicator Off w/No DTC Set	6-116	146
—	Scan Tool Displays Undefined DTC	6-116	147
Test A	ABS Lamp On w/No Code Set	6-67	77
Test B	ABS Lamp Off w/No Code Set	6-68	78
Test C	ETS Off Lamp On w/No Code Set	6-68	79
Code C1214	Brake Control Relay Contact Circuit Open	6-73	89
Code C1215	Brake Control Relay Contact Circuit Active	6-75	90
Code C1216	Brake Control Relay Coil Circuit Open	6-75	91
Code C1217	Brake Control Relay Coil Circuit Shorted To Ground	6-76	92

Continued

DIAGNOSTIC CHART INDEX—Continued

Code/Test	Description	Page No.	Fig. No.
CAVALIER & SUNFIRE			
Code C1218	Brake Control Relay Coil Circuit Shorted To Voltage	6-77	93
Code C1221	LH Front Wheel Speed Sensor Input Signal Is Zero	6-77	94
Code C1222	RH Front Wheel Speed Sensor Input Signal Is Zero	6-78	95
Code C1223	LH Rear Wheel Speed Sensor Input Signal Is Zero	6-79	96
Code C1224	RH Rear Wheel Speed Sensor Input Signal Is Zero	6-80	97
Code C1225	LH Front Excessive Wheel Speed Variation	6-81	98
Code C1226	RH Front Excessive Wheel Speed Variation	6-82	99
Code C1227	LH Rear Excessive Wheel Speed Variation	6-83	100
Code C1228	RH Rear Excessive Wheel Speed Variation	6-84	101
Code C1232	LH Front Wheel Speed Circuit Open Or Shorted	6-84	102
Code C1233	RH Front Wheel Speed Circuit Open Or Shorted	6-86	103
Code C1234	LH Rear Wheel Speed Circuit Open Or Shorted	6-87	104
Code C1235	RH Rear Wheel Speed Circuit Open Or Shorted	6-88	105
Code C1236	Low System Supply Voltage	6-89	106
Code C1237	High System Supply Voltage	6-90	107
Code C1238	LH Front ESB Does Not Hold Motor	6-91	108
Code C1241	RH Front ESB Does Not Hold Motor	6-91	109
Code C1242	Rear ESB Does Not Hold Motor	6-92	110
Code C1244	LH Front ABS Channel Does Not Move	6-93	111
Code C1245	RH Front ABS Channel Does Not Move	6-94	112
Code C1246	Rear ABS Channel Does Not Move	6-95	113
Code C1247	LH Front ABS Motor Free Spins	6-96	114
Code C1248	RH Front ABS Motor Free Spins	6-97	115
Code C1251	Rear ABS Motor Free Spins	6-98	116
Code C1252	LH Front ABS Channel In Release Too Long	6-99	117
Code C1253	RH Front ABS Channel In Release Too Long	6-100	118
Code C1254	Rear ABS Channel In Release Too Long	6-101	119
Code C1255	EBCM Internal Fault	6-101	120
Code C1256	LH Front ABS Motor Circuit Open	6-102	121
Code C1257	LH Front ABS Motor Circuit Shorted To Ground	6-102	122
Code C1258	LH Front ABS Motor Circuit Shorted To Voltage	6-103	123
Code C1261	RH Front ABS Motor Circuit Open	6-104	124
Code C1262	RH Front ABS Motor Circuit Shorted To Ground	6-104	125
Code C1263	RH Front ABS Motor Circuit Shorted To Voltage	6-105	126
Code C1264	Rear ABS Motor Circuit Open	6-106	127
Code C1265	Rear ABS Motor Circuit Shorted To Ground	6-106	128
Code C1266	Rear ABS Motor Circuit Shorted To Voltage	6-107	129
Code C1275	Serial Data Fault	6-108	130
Code C1276	LH Front Solenoid Circuit Open Or Shorted To Ground	6-108	131
Code C1277	LH Front Solenoid Circuit Shorted To Voltage	6-109	132
Code C1278	RH Front Solenoid Circuit Open Or Shorted To Ground	6-109	133
Code C1281	RH Front Solenoid Circuit Open Or Shorted To Voltage	6-110	134
Code C1282	Calibration Fault	6-111	135
Code C1286	EBCM Tuned On Brake Warning Lamp	6-111	136
Code C1291	Open Brake Lamp Switch Contact During Decel	6-111	137
Code C1292	Open Brake Lamp Switch When ABS Required	6-112	138
Code C1293	C1291 Or C1292 Set In Current Or Previous Ignition Cycle	6-113	139
Code C1294	Brake Lamp Switch Circuit Always Active	6-113	140
Code C1295	Brake Lamp Switch Circuit Open	6-114	141
MALIBU			
—	ABS Diagnostic System Check	6-23	16
Test A	ABS Warning Lamp On w/No Code Set	6-72	83
Test B	ABS Warning Lamp Inoperative	6-72	84
Test C	Scan Tool Displays Undefined Code	6-72	85
Code C1214	Brake Control Relay Contact Circuit Open	6-24	17
Code C1215	Brake Control Relay Contact Circuit Active	6-26	18

Continued

DIAGNOSTIC CHART INDEX—Continued

Continued

DIAGNOSTIC CHART INDEX—Continued

Code/Test	Description	Page No.	Fig. No.
INTRIGUE			
—	ABS Indicator On No DTC Set	6-159	205
—	Scan Tool Displays Undefined DTC	6-159	206
—	Low Traction Indicator Always On	6-159	207
—	Low Traction Indicator Inoperative	6-160	208
Code C1211	ABS Warning Lamp Circuit Fault	6-117	149
Code C1213	ABS Active Lamp Circuit Fault	6-118	150
Code C1214	Electronic Brake Control Relay Contact Circuit Open	6-118	151
Code C1215	Electronic Brake Control Relay Contact Circuit Always Active	6-120	152
Code C1216	Electronic Brake Control Relay Coil Circuit Open	6-120	153
Code C1217	Electronic Brake Control Relay Coil Circuit Shorted To Ground	6-121	154
Code C1218	Electronic Brake Control Relay Coil Circuit Shorted To Voltage	6-122	155
Code C1221	LH Front Wheel Speed Sensor Input Signal Is Zero	6-122	156
Code C1222	RH Front Wheel Speed Sensor Input Signal Is Zero	6-123	157
Code C1223	LH Rear Wheel Speed Sensor Input Signal Is Zero	6-124	158
Code C1224	RH Rear Wheel Speed Sensor Input Signal Is Zero	6-125	159
Code C1225	LH Front Excessive Wheel Speed Sensor Variation	6-126	160
Code C1226	RH Front Excessive Wheel Speed Sensor Variation	6-127	161
Code C1227	LH Rear Excessive Wheel Speed Sensor Variation	6-128	162
Code C1228	RH Rear Excessive Wheel Speed Sensor Variation	6-129	163
Code C1232	LH Front Wheel Speed Sensor Circuit Open Or Shorted	6-130	164
Code C1233	RH Front Wheel Speed Sensor Circuit Open Or Shorted	6-132	165
Code C1234	LH Rear Wheel Speed Sensor Circuit Open Or Shorted	6-133	166
Code C1235	RH Rear Wheel Speed Sensor Circuit Open Or Shorted	6-134	167
Code C1236	Low System Supply Voltage	6-135	168
Code C1237	High System Supply Voltage	6-136	169
Code C1238	LH Front ESB Will Not Hold Motor	6-137	170
Code C1241	RH Front ESB Will Not Hold Motor	6-137	171
Code C1242	Rear ESB Will Not Hold Motor	6-138	172
Code C1244	LH Front ABS Channel Will Not Move	6-138	173
Code C1245	RH Front ABS Channel Will Not Move	6-139	174
Code C1246	Rear ABS Channel Will Not Move	6-140	175
Code C1247	LH Front ABS Motor Free Spins	6-141	176
Code C1248	RH Front ABS Motor Free Spins	6-142	177
Code C1251	Rear ABS Motor Free Spins	6-143	178
Code C1252	LH Front ABS Channel In Release Too Long	6-144	179
Code C1253	RH Front ABS Channel In Release Too Long	6-145	180
Code C1254	Rear ABS Channel In Release Too Long	6-146	181
Code C1255	EBCM/EBTCM Internal Fault	6-146	182
Code C1256	LH Front ABS Motor Circuit Open	6-146	183
Code C1257	LH Front ABS Motor Circuit Shorted To Ground	6-147	184
Code C1258	LH Front ABS Motor Circuit Shorted To Voltage	6-148	185
Code C1261	RH Front ABS Motor Circuit Open	6-148	186
Code C1262	RH Front ABS Motor Circuit Shorted To Ground	6-149	187
Code C1263	RH Front ABS Motor Circuit Shorted To Voltage	6-149	188
Code C1264	Rear ABS Motor Circuit Open	6-150	189
Code C1265	Rear ABS Motor Circuit Shorted To Ground	6-150	190
Code C1266	Rear ABS Motor Circuit Shorted To Voltage	6-151	191
Code C1276	LH Front Solenoid Circuit Open Or Shorted To Ground	6-152	192
Code C1277	LH Front Solenoid Circuit Shorted To Voltage	6-153	193
Code C1278	RH Front Solenoid Circuit Open Or Shorted To Ground	6-153	194
Code C1281	RH Front Solenoid Circuit Shorted To Voltage	6-154	195
Code C1282	Calibration Fault	6-154	196
Code C1286	EBCM/EBTCM Turned On Brake Warning Lamp	6-154	197
Code C1287	Brake Warning Lamp Circuit Open Or Short To Voltage	6-155	198
Code C1291	Open Brake Lamp Switch During Decel	6-156	199
Code C1292	Open Brake Lamp Switch Circuit When ABS Was Required	6-157	200

Continued

DIAGNOSTIC CHART INDEX—Continued

Code/Test	Description	Page No.	Fig. No.
INTRIGUE			
Code C1295	Brake Lamp Switch Circuit Open	6-157	201
LUMINA			
—	ABS Diagnostic System Check	6-117	148
—	No Communication With EBCM	6-158	203
—	ABS Indicator Off No DTC Set	6-159	204
—	ABS Indicator On No DTC Set	6-159	205
—	Scan Tool Displays Undefined DTC	6-159	206
—	Low Traction Indicator Always On	6-159	207
—	Low Traction Indicator Inoperative	6-160	208
Test F	Scan Tool Displays Undefined Code	6-158	202
Code C1211	ABS Warning Lamp Circuit Fault	6-117	149
Code C1213	ABS Active Lamp Circuit Fault	6-118	150
Code C1214	Electronic Brake Control Relay Contact Circuit Open	6-118	151
Code C1215	Electronic Brake Control Relay Contact Circuit Always Active	6-120	152
Code C1216	Electronic Brake Control Relay Coil Circuit Open	6-120	153
Code C1217	Electronic Brake Control Relay Coil Circuit Shorted To Ground	6-121	154
Code C1218	Electronic Brake Control Relay Coil Circuit Shorted To Voltage	6-122	155
Code C1221	LH Front Wheel Speed Sensor Input Signal Is Zero	6-122	156
Code C1222	RH Front Wheel Speed Sensor Input Signal Is Zero	6-123	157
Code C1223	LH Rear Wheel Speed Sensor Input Signal Is Zero	6-124	158
Code C1224	RH Rear Wheel Speed Sensor Input Signal Is Zero	6-125	159
Code C1225	LH Front Excessive Wheel Speed Sensor Variation	6-126	160
Code C1226	RH Front Excessive Wheel Speed Sensor Variation	6-127	161
Code C1227	LH Rear Excessive Wheel Speed Sensor Variation	6-128	162
Code C1228	RH Rear Excessive Wheel Speed Sensor Variation	6-129	163
Code C1232	LH Front Wheel Speed Sensor Circuit Open Or Shorted	6-130	164
Code C1233	RH Front Wheel Speed Sensor Circuit Open Or Shorted	6-132	165
Code C1234	LH Rear Wheel Speed Sensor Circuit Open Or Shorted	6-133	166
Code C1235	RH Rear Wheel Speed Sensor Circuit Open Or Shorted	6-134	167
Code C1236	Low System Supply Voltage	6-135	168
Code C1237	High System Supply Voltage	6-136	169
Code C1238	LH Front ESB Will Not Hold Motor	6-137	170
Code C1241	RH Front ESB Will Not Hold Motor	6-137	171
Code C1242	Rear ESB Will Not Hold Motor	6-138	172
Code C1244	LH Front ABS Channel Will Not Move	6-138	173
Code C1245	RH Front ABS Channel Will Not Move	6-139	174
Code C1246	Rear ABS Channel Will Not Move	6-140	175
Code C1247	LH Front ABS Motor Free Spins	6-141	176
Code C1248	RH Front ABS Motor Free Spins	6-142	177
Code C1251	Rear ABS Motor Free Spins	6-143	178
Code C1252	LH Front ABS Channel In Release Too Long	6-144	179
Code C1253	RH Front ABS Channel In Release Too Long	6-145	180
Code C1254	Rear ABS Channel In Release Too Long	6-146	181
Code C1255	EBCM/EBTCM Internal Fault	6-146	182
Code C1256	LH Front ABS Motor Circuit Open	6-146	183
Code C1257	LH Front ABS Motor Circuit Shorted To Ground	6-147	184
Code C1258	LH Front ABS Motor Circuit Shorted To Voltage	6-148	185
Code C1261	RH Front ABS Motor Circuit Open	6-148	186
Code C1262	RH Front ABS Motor Circuit Shorted To Ground	6-149	187
Code C1263	RH Front ABS Motor Circuit Shorted To Voltage	6-149	188
Code C1264	Rear ABS Motor Circuit Open	6-150	189
Code C1265	Rear ABS Motor Circuit Shorted To Ground	6-150	190
Code C1266	Rear ABS Motor Circuit Shorted To Voltage	6-151	191
Code C1276	LH Front Solenoid Circuit Open Or Shorted To Ground	6-152	192
Code C1277	LH Front Solenoid Circuit Shorted To Voltage	6-153	193
Code C1278	RH Front Solenoid Circuit Open Or Shorted To Ground	6-153	194

Continued

DIAGNOSTIC CHART INDEX—Continued

Code/Test	Description	Page No.	Fig. No.
LUMINA			
Code C1281	RH Front Solenoid Circuit Shorted To Voltage	6-154	195
Code C1282	Calibration Fault	6-154	196
Code C1286	EBCM/EBTCM Turned On Brake Warning Lamp	6-154	197
Code C1287	Brake Warning Lamp Circuit Open Or Short To Voltage	6-155	198
Code C1291	Open Brake Lamp Switch During Decel	6-156	199
Code C1292	Open Brake Lamp Switch Circuit When ABS Was Required	6-157	200
Code C1295	Brake Lamp Switch Circuit Open	6-157	201
METRO			
—	ABS Diagnostic System Check	6-160	209
—	No Communication With EBCM	6-201	265
Test A	ABS Warning Lamp On w/No Code Set	6-199	260
Test B	ABS Warning Lamp Off w/No Code Set	6-199	261
Test C	ABS Active Lamp On w/No Code Set	6-200	262
Test D	ABS Active Lamp Inoperative w/No Code Set	6-200	263
Test E	Scan Tool Displays Undefined Code	6-201	264
Code C1214	Brake Control relay Contact Circuit Open	6-161	210
Code C1215	Brake Control Relay Contact Circuit Active	6-163	211
Code C1216	Bake Control Relay Coil Open	6-163	212
Code C1217	Brake Control Relay Coil Circuit Short To Ground	6-164	213
Code C1218	Brake Control Relay Coil Circuit Short To Voltage	6-164	214
Code C1221	LH Front Wheel Speed Sensor Input Signal Is Zero	6-165	215
Code C1222	RH Front Wheel Speed Sensor Input Signal Is Zero	6-166	216
Code C1223	LH Rear Wheel Speed Sensor Input Signal Is Zero	6-167	217
Code C1224	RH Rear Wheel Speed Sensor Input Signal Is Zero	6-168	218
Code C1225	LH Front Excessive Wheel Speed Variation	6-169	219
Code C1226	RH Front Excessive Wheel Speed Variation	6-170	220
Code C1227	LH Rear Excessive Wheel Speed Variation	6-171	221
Code C1228	RH Rear Excessive Wheel Speed Variation	6-172	222
Code C1232	LH Front Wheel Speed Circuit Open Or Shorted	6-172	223
Code C1233	RH Front Wheel Speed Circuit Open Or Shorted	6-174	224
Code C1234	LH Rear Wheel Speed Circuit Open Or Shorted	6-175	225
Code C1235	RH Rear Wheel Speed Circuit Open Or Shorted	6-176	226
Code C1236	Low System Supply Voltage	6-177	227
Code C1237	High System Supply Voltage	6-178	228
Code C1238	LH Front ESB Does Not Hold Motor	6-179	229
Code C1241	RH Front ESB Does Not Hold Motor	6-179	230
Code C1242	Rear ESB Does Not Hold Motor	6-180	231
Code C1244	LH Front ABS Channel Does Not Move	6-181	232
Code C1245	RH Front ABS Channel Does Not Move	6-182	233
Code C1246	Rear ABS Channel Does Not Move	6-183	234
Code C1247	LH Front ABS Motor Free Spins	6-184	235
Code C1248	RH Front ABS Motor Free Spins	6-185	236
Code C1251	Rear ABS Motor Free Spins	6-186	237
Code C1255	EBCM Internal Fault	6-187	238
Code C1256	LH Front ABS Motor Circuit Open	6-187	239
Code C1257	LH Front ABS Motor Circuit Short To Ground	6-188	240
Code C1258	LH Front ABS Motor Circuit Short To Voltage	6-189	241
Code C1261	RH Front ABS Motor Circuit Open	6-189	242
Code C1262	RH Front ABS Motor Circuit Short To Ground	6-190	243
Code C1263	RH Front ABS Motor Circuit Short To Voltage	6-190	244
Code C1264	Rear ABS Motor Circuit Open	6-191	245
Code C1265	Rear ABS Motor Circuit Short To Ground	6-192	246
Code C1266	Rear ABS Motor Circuit Short To Voltage	6-192	247
Code C1276	LH Front Solenoid Circuit Open/Short To Ground	6-193	248
Code C1277	LH Front Solenoid Circuit Short To Voltage	6-194	249
Code C1278	RH Front Solenoid Circuit Open/Short To Ground	6-194	250

Continued

DIAGNOSTIC CHART INDEX—Continued

Continued

DIAGNOSTIC CHART INDEX—Continued

System Description
The diagnostic system check is an organized method of identifying any problems caused by a malfunction in the ABS system.
The service technician must begin diagnosis of any ABS complaint with the diagnostic system check.
The diagnostic system check directs the service technician to the next logical step in diagnosing the complaint.

Diagnostic Process
Use the following ordered procedure when servicing the ABS.
Failure to use the following procedure may cause the loss of important diagnostic data.
Failure to use the following procedure may lead to difficult and time-consuming diagnosis procedures.

1. Use the following procedure to perform a vehicle preliminary diagnosis inspection:

- Inspect the brake master cylinder fluid reservoir:
  - Verify that the brake fluid level is correct.
  - Inspect the master cylinder for contamination.
- Inspect the brake modulator for the following conditions:
  - Leaks
  - Wiring damage
- Inspect the brake components of all four wheels:
  - Verify that no drag exists.
  - Verify that the brake apply operation is correct.
- Inspect for worn or damaged wheel bearings.
Worn or damaged wheel bearings may cause a wheel to "wobble".
- Inspect the wheel speed sensors and the wheel speed sensor wiring:
  - Verify that all of the sensors solidly attach.
  - Inspect for wiring damage, especially at vehicle attachment points.

GC402980346800AX

Fig. 15 ABS Diagnostic System Check (Part 1 of 4). Alero & Grand Am

- Inspect the outer CV joint:
  - Verify that the outer CV joint is aligned correctly.
  - Verify that the outer CV joint operates correctly.
- Inspect the tires. Verify that the tires meet legal trend depth requirements.

2. Perform the Diagnostic System Check.
If any DTCs are displayed, select DTC History.

   1. Determine which malfunction occurred the most recently.
   2. Diagnose and repair the most recent malfunction first.

3. Determine if the following conditions exist:

- No DTCs are present.
- There are malfunctions in the mechanical components.
- The failure is intermittent and cannot be reproduced.

4. If the above conditions exist, attempt to reproduce the malfunction:

   1. Use the automatic snapshot feature of the Scan Tool while test driving the vehicle. Perform normal acceleration, stopping, and turning maneuvers during the test drive.
   2. If the test drive does not reproduce the malfunction, perform an ABS stop:
      - Perform the stop on a low coefficient surface (such as gravel).
      - Perform the stop from a speed of 48-80 km/h (30-50 mph).
      - Trigger the snapshot mode on any ABS DTC while performing the stop.
   3. If the ABS stop does not reproduce the malfunction, use the enhanced diagnostic information in the DTC History in order to determine if further diagnosis is needed. This determination will be based on the frequency of failure.

5. Clear the ABS DTCs after all of the system malfunctions have been corrected.

Diagnostic Aids
Diagnosing DTCs in the correct order is very important. Failure to diagnose DTCs in the order specified may result in the following:

- Extended diagnostic time
- Incorrect diagnosis
- Incorrect parts replacement

GC402980346800BX

Fig. 15 ABS Diagnostic System Check (Part 2 of 4). Alero & Grand Am

Step	Action	Value(s)	Yes	No
1	1 Reconnect all previously disconnected components. 2 Cycle the Ignition switch from the OFF to ON position, engine OFF. 3 Plug the scan tool into the Data Link Connector (DLC), Does the Scan Tool communicate with the EBCM?	—	Go to Step 3	Go to Step 2
2	Does the scan tool communicate with other modules on the serial data line?	—	Go to No Communicatio with EBCM	Inspect Data Link Communicatio
3	With the scan tool read ABS DTCs. Are there any current Diagnostic Trouble Codes?	—	Go to Applicable DTC Table	Go to Step 4
4	Cycle the ignition switch from the OFF to ON position. Does the ABS Indicator come ON then go OFF after several seconds?	—	Go to Step 6	Go to Step 5
5	Does the ABS Warning Indicator come ON and stay ON?	—	Go to ABS Indicator On No DTC Set	Go to ABS Indicator Inoperative with no DTC Set

GC402980346800CX

Fig. 15 ABS Diagnostic System Check (Part 3 of 4). Alero & Grand Am

System Description

The diagnostic system check is an organized method of identifying any problems caused by a malfunction in the ABS system.

The service technician must begin diagnosis of any ABS complaint with the diagnostic system check.

The diagnostic system check directs the service technician to the next logical step in diagnosing the complaint.

The EBCM exchanges serial data through EBCM harness connector terminal 12.

Connector terminal 4 supplies the switched ignition voltage to the EBCM.

Connector terminal 13 supplies the battery voltage to the EBCM.

Connector terminal C supplies the switched battery voltage to the EBCM.

Connector Terminal D provides the ground for the EBCM.

Diagnostic Process

Use the following ordered procedure when servicing the ABS.

Failure to use the following procedure may cause the loss of important diagnostic data. Failure to use the following procedure may lead to difficult and time-consuming diagnosis procedures.

1. Use the following procedure to perform a vehicle preliminary diagnosis inspection:
   - Inspect the brake master cylinder fluid reservoir:
     - Verify that the brake fluid level is correct.
     - Inspect the master cylinder for contamination.
   - Inspect the brake modulator for the following conditions:
     - Leaks
     - Wiring damage

GC402980304900AX

Fig. 16 ABS Diagnostic System Check (Part 1 of 6). Malibu

- Inspect the brake components of all four wheels:
  - Verify that no drag exists.
  - Verify that the brake apply operation is correct.
- Inspect for worn or damaged wheel bearings.
  Worn or damaged wheel bearings may cause a wheel to "wobble".
- Inspect the wheel speed sensors and the wheel speed sensor wiring:
  - Verify that all of the sensors solidly attach.
  - Inspect for wiring damage, especially at vehicle attachment points.
- Inspect the outer CV joint.
  - Verify that the outer CV joint is aligned correctly.
  - Verify that the outer CV joint operates correctly.
- Inspect the tires. Verify that the tires meet legal trend depth requirements.

2. Perform the Diagnostic System Check.
   If any DTCs are displayed, select DTC History.
   2.1. Determine which malfunction occurred the most recently.
   2.2. Diagnose and repair the most recent malfunction first.
3. Determine if the following conditions exist:
   - No DTCs are present.
   - There are malfunctions in the mechanical components.
   - The failure is intermittent and cannot be reproduced.
4. If the above conditions exist, attempt to reproduce the malfunction:
   4.1. Use the automatic snapshot feature of the Scan Tool while test driving the vehicle.
   Perform normal acceleration, stopping, and turning maneuvers during the test drive.
   4.2. If the test drive does not reproduce the malfunction, perform an ABS stop:
   - Perform the stop on a low coefficient surface (such as gravel).
   - Perform the stop from a speed of 48–80 km/h (30–50 mph).
   - Trigger the snapshot mode on any ABS DTC while performing the stop.

   4.3. If the ABS stop does not reproduce the malfunction, use the enhanced diagnostic information in the DTC History in order to determine if further diagnosis is needed. This determination will be based on the frequency of failure.
5. Clear the ABS DTCs after all of the system malfunctions have been corrected.

Diagnostic Aids

Communication with the EBCM is not possible when excessive resistance exists in the following components:

- The ground
- The power supply circuits

If communication with the EBCM is not possible, perform the following actions:

- Verify that the EBCM ground connection is good.
- Verify that no excessive resistance exists in any of the power supply circuits.

Important: Zero the J 39200 test leads before making any resistance measurements.

GC402980304900BX

Fig. 16 ABS Diagnostic System Check (Part 2 of 6). Malibu

Step	Action	Value(s)	Yes	No
6	Are there any history DTCs?	—	Go to Step 7	System OK
7	1 Refer to the appropriate DTC table for the history DTC. 2 Read the diagnostic aids, and conditions for setting the DTC. 3 Carefully drive the vehicle above 24 Km/h (15 mph) for several minutes while monitoring a scan tool for ABS DTCs. Did the history DTC set as a current DTC while the vehicle was being driven?	—	Go to Applicable DTC Table	System OK

GC402980346800DX

Fig. 15 ABS Diagnostic System Check (Part 4 of 4). Alero & Grand Am

Step	Action	Value(s)	Yes	No
1	1. Verify that the EBCM connector is properly connected. 2. Install a Scan Tool. 3. Turn the ignition switch to the RUN position. Do not start the engine. 4. Select the ABS portion of the chassis application on the Scan Tool. 5. Select Data List on the Scan Tool. Is data being received from the EBCM?	—	*Go to Step 15*	*Go to Step 2*
2	Read the Scan Tool display. Does the Scan Tool display the message "No Communication With Vehicle. Check DLC Connector"?	—	Data Link Connector,	*Go to Step 3*
3	Verify the correct connection of the Scan Tool to the DLC. Is connection of the Scan Tool to the DLC correct?	—	*Go to Step 4*	*Go to Step 26*
4	1. Turn the ignition switch to the OFF position. 2. Remove and inspect the ICC BATT Fuse (10A). Is the fuse open?	—	*Go to Step 18*	*Go to Step 5*
5	1. Install the ICC BATT fuse (10A). 2. Remove the ICC IGN Fuse (10A). Is the fuse open?	—	*Go to Step 21*	*Go to Step 6*
6	1. Install the ICC IGN Fuse (10A). 2. Disconnect the EBCM connector. 3. Use the *J 39200* in order to measure the resistance between the EBCM connector terminal D and ground. Is the resistance within the specified range?	0–2 Ω	*Go to Step 7*	*Go to Step 27*
7	1. Disconnect the EBCM connector. 2. Use the *J 39200* in order to measure voltage between the EBCM connector terminal 13 and ground. Is the voltage equal to or greater than the specified voltage?	10 V	*Go to Step 8*	*Go to Step 28*
8	1. Turn the ignition switch to the RUN position. Do not start the engine. 2. Use the *J 39200* in order to measure voltage between the EBCM connector terminal 4 and ground. Is the voltage equal to or greater than the specified voltage?	10 V	*Go to Step 9*	*Go to Step 29*
9	1. Turn the ignition switch to the OFF position. 2. Disconnect the negative battery cable. 3. Disconnect the positive battery cable. 4. Use the *J 39200* in order to measure the resistance between the EBCM connector terminal D and the negative battery cable terminal. Is the resistance within the specified range?	0–2 Ω	*Go to Step 10*	*Go to Step 30*
10	Use the *J 39200* in order to measure the resistance between the EBCM connector terminal 13 and the positive battery cable terminal. Is the resistance within the specified range?	0–2 Ω	*Go to Step 11*	*Go to Step 31*

GC402980304900CX

Fig. 16 ABS Diagnostic System Check (Part 3 of 6). Malibu

Step	Action	Value(s)	Yes	No
11	1. Turn the ignition switch to the RUN position. Do not start the engine. 2. Use the *J 39200* in order to measure the resistance between the EBCM connector terminal 4 and the positive battery cable terminal. Is the resistance within the specified range?	0–2 Ω	*Go to Step 12*	*Go to Step 32*
12	1. Turn the ignition switch to the OFF position. 2. Use the *J 39200* in order to measure the resistance between the EBCM connector terminal 4 and the DLC terminal 9. Is the resistance within the specified range?	0–2 Ω	*Go to Step 13*	Data Link Connector
13	Use the *J 39200* in order to measure the resistance between the EBCM connector terminal 4 and ground. Is the resistance within the specified range?	OL (Infinite)	*Go to Step 14*	Data Link Connector,
14	1. Inspect the following components: • The EBCM connector • The negative battery cable • The positive battery cable 2. Inspect the components for the following conditions: • Poor terminal contact • Terminal corrosion • Damaged terminals Are there signs of poor terminal contact, terminal corrosion, or damaged terminals?	—	*Go to Step 33*	*Go to Step 39*
15	1. Connect the *Scan Tool.* 2. Select DTCs. Does the *Scan Tool* display any current DTCs?	—	Refer to the applicable DTC table.	*Go to Step 16*
16	1. Turn the ignition switch to the OFF position. 2. Wait for ten seconds. 3. Turn the ignition switch to the RUN position. Do not start the engine. 4. Observe the amber ABS warning indicator. Does the amber ABS warning indicator turn on for three seconds and then turn off?	—	*Go to Step 17*	Refer to the appropriate symptom table
17	1. Connect the *Scan Tool.* 2. Select DTC History. Does the *Scan Tool* display any history DTCs?	—	*Go to Step 40*	*Go to Step 41*
18	1. Replace the ICC BATT Fuse (10A) with a known good Fuse (10A). 2. Wait for ten seconds. 3. Remove and inspect the fuse. Is the fuse open?	—	*Go to Step 19*	*Go to Step 35*
19	1. Disconnect the EBCM connector. 2. Replace the ICC BATT Fuse (10A) with a known good Fuse (10A). 3. Wait for ten seconds. 4. Remove and inspect the ICC BATT Fuse (10A). Is the fuse open?	—	*Go to Step 34*	*Go to Step 20*

GC402980304900DX

Fig. 16 ABS Diagnostic System Check (Part 4 of 6). Malibu

Step	Action	Value(s)	Yes	No
20	1. Inspect CKT 1640 for physical damage. Physical damage may cause a short to ground with the EBCM connector connected. 2. Inspect the EBCM connector and the EBCM harness for physical damage. Physical damage may cause a short to ground with the EBCM connector connected. 3. Reconnect the EBCM connector. 4. Reinstall the ICC BATT Fuse (10A). 5. Wait for ten seconds. 6. Remove and inspect the ICC BATT Fuse (10A). Is the fuse open?	—	*Go to Step 25*	*Go to Step 38*
21	1. Replace the ICC IGN Fuse (10A) with a known good Fuse (10A). 2. Turn the ignition switch to the RUN position. Do not start the engine. 3. Wait for ten seconds. 4. Turn the ignition switch to the OFF position. 5. Remove and inspect the ICC IGN Fuse (10A). Is the fuse open?	—	*Go to Step 22*	*Go to Step 37*
22	1. Turn the ignition switch to the OFF position. 2. Disconnect the EBCM connector. 3. Replace the ICC IGN Fuse (10A) with a known good Fuse (10A). 4. Turn the ignition to the RUN position. Do not start the engine. 5. Wait for ten seconds. 6. Turn the ignition switch to the OFF position. 7. Remove and inspect the ICC IGN Fuse (10A). Is the fuse open?	—	*Go to Step 36*	*Go to Step 23*
23	1. Inspect CKT 139 for physical damage. Physical damage may cause a short to ground with the EBCM connector connected. 2. Reconnect the EBCM connector. 3. Reinstall the ICC IGN Fuse (10A). 4. Turn the engine to the RUN position. Do not start the engine. 5. Wait for ten seconds. 6. Turn the ignition switch to the OFF position. 7. Remove and inspect the ICC IGN Fuse (10A). Is the fuse open?	—	*Go to Step 24*	*Go to Step 38*
24	1. Replace the EBCM. 2. Replace the ICC IGN Fuse (10A) with a known good Fuse (10A). Is the repair complete?	—	*Go to Step 1*	—
25	1. Replace the EBCM. 2. Replace the ICC BATT Fuse (10A) with a known good Fuse (10A). Is the repair complete?	—	*Go to Step 1*	—

GC402980304900EX

Fig. 16 ABS Diagnostic System Check (Part 5 of 6). Malibu

Step	Action	Value(s)	Yes	No
26	Disconnect and reconnect the *Scan Tool* in order to ensure a good connection. Is the *Scan Tool* correctly connected?	—	*Go to Step 1*	—
27	Repair the open or high resistance in CKT 450. Is the repair complete?	—	*Go to Step 1*	—
28	Repair the open or high resistance in CKT 1640. Is the repair complete?	—	*Go to Step 1*	—
29	Repair the open or high resistance in CKT 139. Is the repair complete?	—	*Go to Step 1*	—
30	Repair the open or high resistance in any of the following components: • The negative battery cable • The negative battery cable terminals • The negative battery cable connections Is the repair complete?	—	*Go to Step 1*	—
31	Repair the high resistance in CKT 1640 or the voltage feed circuits for the ICC BATT Fuse (10A). Is the repair complete?	—	*Go to Step 1*	—
32	Repair the open or high resistance in one of the following circuits: • CKT 139 • CKT 3 • CKT 1 Is the repair complete?	—	*Go to Step 1*	—
33	Replace the terminals or the connectors that exhibit the following conditions: • Poor terminal contact • Terminal corrosion • Damaged terminals Is the repair complete?	—	*Go to Step 1*	—
34	Repair the short to ground in CKT 1640. Is the repair complete?	—	*Go to Step 18*	—
35	Reinstall the ICC BATT Fuse (10A). Is the installation complete?	—	*Go to Step 1*	—
36	Repair the short to ground in CKT 139. Is the repair complete?	—	*Go to Step 21*	—
37	Reinstall the ICC IGN Fuse (10A). Is the installation complete?	—	*Go to Step 1*	—
38	Is malfunction intermittent or not present at this time?	—	Refer to Diagnostic Process for more information.	—
39	Replace the EBCM. Is the repair complete?	—	*Go to Step 1*	—

GC402980304900FX

Fig. 16 ABS Diagnostic System Check (Part 6 of 6). Malibu

Circuit Description

Ignition voltage is supplied to terminal 86 of the Electronic Brake Control Relay. The above condition enables the EBCM to energize the pullin coil by completing the ground circuit at connector terminal 2 of the EBCM. The magnetic field created closes the Electronic Brake Control Relay contacts. The magnetic field also allows battery voltage and current through the Electronic Brake Control Relay terminal 30 to be supplied to the EBCM through connector terminal C. Connector terminal C supplies power to the EBCM, which supplies power to the motors and solenoids.

Conditions for Setting the DTC

DTC C1214 can set anytime after the EBCM commands the Electronic Brake Control Relay on. The command occurs during the three second bulb check.

DTC C1214 monitors the availability of current/voltage to the motors and solenoids.

The above malfunction indicates voltage is not available. The malfunction will not allow ABS operation.

Action Taken When the DTC Sets

- A malfunction DTC stores.
- ABS is disabled.
- The amber ABS warning indicator is turned on.

Conditions for Clearing the DTC

- The condition responsible for setting the DTC no longer exists and the Scan Tool Clear DTCs function is used.
- 100 drive cycles pass with no DTC(s) detected. A drive cycle consists of starting the vehicle, driving the vehicle over 16 km/h (10 mph), stopping and then turning the ignition OFF.

Diagnostic Aids

The following conditions may cause an intermittent malfunction:

- A poor connection
- Rubbed-through wire insulation
- A broken wire inside the insulation

Use the enhanced diagnostic function of the Scan Tool in order to measure the frequency of the malfunction.

Thoroughly inspect any circuitry that may be causing the intermittent complaint for the following conditions:

- Backed out terminals
- Improper mating
- Improperly formed or damaged terminals
- Poor terminal-to-wiring connections
- Physical damage to the wiring harness

Vibration and Temperature Effects

- Use the following procedure in order to inspect for vibration effects by performing the Relay Test function of the Scan Tool:
  1. With the Relay Test commanded on, lightly tap the top and sides of the Electronic Brake Control Relay while monitoring the Electronic Brake Control Relay voltage.
  2. If the Electronic Brake Control Relay voltage changes significantly, replace the Electronic Brake Control Relay.
- If DTC C1214 only sets when the vehicle is initially started in cold ambient conditions (temperature less than 0°C – 32°F), replace the Electronic Brake Control Relay.

Important: Zero the J 39200 test leads before making any resistance measurements. Refer to the J 39200 user's manual.

GC40298029920OAX

Fig. 17 Code C1214: Brake Control Relay Contact Circuit Open (Part 1 of 5). Alero, Grand Am & Malibu

Step	Action	Value(s)	Yes	No
1	Was the Diagnostic System Check performed?	—	Go to Step 2	Refer to *Diagnostic System Check*
2	1. Turn the ignition switch to the OFF position. 2. Install a *Scan Tool.* 3. Turn the ignition switch to the RUN position. Do not start the engine. 4. Use the *Scan Tool* in order to read the DTCs. Is DTC C1216 present (either as a current DTC or a history DTC)?	—	Refer to *DTC C1216 Brake Control Rly Coil CKT Open*	Go to Step 3
3	1. Select Data List on the *Scan Tool.* 2. Select and observe EBCM Battery Voltage. Is the voltage equal to or greater than the specified voltage?	10 V	Go to Step 25	Go to Step 4
4	1. Turn the ignition switch to the OFF position. 2. Disconnect the EBCM connector. 3. Connect a fused jumper wire (such as a *J 36169-A*) with a 3A fuse between the EBCM harness connector terminal 2 and ground. 4. Turn the ignition switch to the RUN position. Do not start the engine. 5. Use the *J 39200* in order to measure the voltage between the EBCM harness connector terminal C and ground. Is the voltage equal to or greater than the specified voltage?	10 V	Go to Step 5	Go to Step 10
5	1. Turn the ignition switch to the OFF position. 2. Disconnect the fused wire jumper. 3. Disconnect the Electronic Brake Control Relay. 4. Use the *J 39200* in order to measure the resistance between the Electronic Brake Control Relay connector terminal 87 and the EBCM harness connector terminal C. Is the resistance within the specified range?	0–2 Ω	Go to Step 6	Go to Step 19
6	1. Disconnect the negative battery cable. 2. Disconnect the positive battery cable. 3. Use the *J 39200* in order to measure the resistance between the positive battery cable terminal and the Electronic Brake Control Relay connector terminal 30. Is the resistance within the specified range?	0–2 Ω	Go to Step 7	Go to Step 20

GC402980299200BX

Fig. 17 Code C1214: Brake Control Relay Contact Circuit Open (Part 2 of 5). Alero, Grand Am & Malibu

Step	Action	Value(s)	Yes	No
7	1. Connect a jumper wire between the Electronic Brake Control Relay connector terminal 86 to ground. 2. Connect a fused jumper wire (such as a *J 36169-A*) with a 3A fuse between the Electronic Brake Control Relay terminal 85 and battery voltage. 3. Use the *J 39200* in order to measure the resistance between the Electronic Brake Control Relay terminal 30 and terminal 87. Is the resistance within the specified range?	0–2 Ω	Go to Step 8	Go to Step 22
8	1. Turn the ignition switch to the OFF position. 2. Inspect the following components: • The EBCM connector • The EBCM harness connector • The Electronic Brake Control Relay • The Electronic Brake Control Relay connector 3. Inspect the above components for signs of the following conditions: • Damage • Poor terminal contact • Terminal corrosion 4. Inspect the following components: • The positive battery terminal • The positive battery cable terminal • The negative battery terminal • The negative battery cable terminal 5. Inspect the above components for signs of the following conditions: • A poor connection • A poor terminal contact Are there signs of poor terminal contact, corrosion, or damaged terminal(s)?	—	Go to Step 17	Go to Step 9
9	1. Remove all of the jumpers. 2. Reconnect the EBCM connector. 3. Reconnect the Electronic Brake Control Relay 4. Reconnect the positive battery cable. 5. Reconnect the negative battery cable. 6. Turn the ignition switch to the RUN position. Do not start the engine. 7. Use the *Scan Tool* in order to look for current DTCs. Does DTC C1214 set as a current DTC?	—	Go to Step 24	Go to Step 25

GC402980299200CX

Fig. 17 Code C1214: Brake Control Relay Contact Circuit Open (Part 3 of 5). Alero, Grand Am & Malibu

Step	Action	Value(s)	Yes	No
10	1. Turn the ignition switch to the OFF position. 2. Disconnect the negative battery cable. 3. Disconnect the positive battery cable. 4. Turn the ignition switch to the RUN position. (This action completes the ignition circuit to the Electronic Brake Control Relay.) 5. Use the *J 39200* in order to measure the resistance between the EBCM harness connector terminal 2 and the positive battery cable terminal. Is the resistance within the specified range?	65–95 Ω	Go to Step 11	Go to Step 14
11	Use the *J 39200* in order to measure the voltage between the positive battery terminal and the negative battery terminal. Is the voltage equal to or greater than the specified voltage?	10 V	Go to Step 12	Go to Step 23
12	1. Turn the ignition switch to the OFF position. 2. Reconnect the positive battery cable. 3. Reconnect the negative battery cable. 4. Disconnect the Electronic Brake Control Relay. 5. Use the *J 39200* in order to measure the voltage between the Electronic Brake Control Relay connector terminal 30 and ground. Is the voltage equal to or greater than the specified voltage?	10 V	Go to Step 13	Go to Step 20
13	Use the *J 39200* in order to measure the resistance between the Electronic Brake Control Relay connector terminal 87 and the EBCM harness connector terminal C. Is the resistance within the specified range?	0–2 Ω	Go to Step 7	Go to Step 19
14	1. Disconnect the Electronic Brake Control Relay. 2. Use the *J 39200* in order to measure the resistance between the Electronic Brake Control Relay terminal 86 and the Electronic Brake Control Relay terminal 85. Is the resistance within the specified range?	60–95 Ω	Go to Step 15	Go to Step 22
15	Use the *J 39200* in order to measure the resistance between the Electronic Brake Control Relay connector terminal 85 and the EBCM harness connector terminal 2. Is the resistance within the specified range?	0–2 Ω	Go to Step 16	Go to Step 18
16	Use the *J 39200* in order to measure the resistance between the Electronic Brake Control Relay connector terminal 86 and the positive battery cable terminal. Is the resistance within the specified range?	0–2 Ω	Go to Step 8	Go to Step 21
17	Replace all of the terminals the connectors that exhibit signs of poor terminal contact, corrosion, or damaged terminal(s). Is the repair complete?	—	Refer to *Diagnostic System Check*	—
18	Repair the open or high resistance in CKT 1632. Is the repair complete?	—	Refer to *Diagnostic System Check*	—
19	Repair the open or high resistance in CKT 1633. Is the repair complete?	—	Refer to *Diagnostic System Check*	—

GC402980299200DX

Fig. 17 Code C1214: Brake Control Relay Contact Circuit Open (Part 4 of 5). Alero, Grand Am & Malibu

Step	Action	Value(s)	Yes	No
20	Repair the open or high resistance in CKT 342. Is the repair complete?	—	Refer to *Diagnostic System Check*	—
21	Repair the open or high resistance in the following components as necessary: • CKT 439 • CKT 3 • The ignition switch • The battery feed CKT 242 to the ignition switch Is the repair complete?	—	Refer to *Diagnostic System Check*	—
22	Replace the Electronic Brake Control Relay. Is the repair complete?	—	Refer to *Diagnostic System Check*	—
23	Repair the low voltage condition. Is the repair complete?	—	Refer to *Diagnostic System Check*	—
24	Replace the EBCM. Is the repair complete?	—	Refer to *Diagnostic System Check*	—
25	Malfunction is intermittent or not present at this time. Refer to Diagnostic Aids for more information.	—	—	—

GC402980299200EX

Fig. 17 Code C1214: Brake Control Relay Contact Circuit Open (Part 5 of 5). Alero, Grand Am & Malibu

Circuit Description

Ignition voltage is supplied to terminal 86 of the Electronic Brake Control Relay. The above condition enables the EBCM to energize the pullin coil by completing the ground circuit at connector terminal 2 of the EBCM. The magnetic field created closes the Electronic Brake Control Relay contacts. The magnetic field also allows battery voltage and current through the Electronic Brake Control Relay terminal 30 to be supplied to the EBCM through connector terminal C. Connector terminal C supplies power to the EBCM, which supplies power to the motors and solenoids.

Conditions for Setting the DTC

DTC C1215 can set only before the EBCM commands the Electronic Brake Control Relay on.

DTC C1215 determines if the Electronic Brake Control Relay energizes when the Electronic Brake Control Relay should not energize. The above malfunction will not allow the Electronic Brake Control Relay to remove power to the ABS system.

If a second malfunction occurs, that requires the Electronic Brake Control Relay to turn off, the second malfunction cannot be removed if the Electronic Brake Control Relay cannot be controlled. The DTC sets if the malfunction is present for three consecutive drive cycles.

Action Taken When the DTC Sets

- A malfunction DTC stores.
- The ABS does not disable.

Conditions for Clearing the DTC

- The condition responsible for setting the DTC no longer exists and the Scan Tool Clear DTCs function is used.
- 100 drive cycles pass with no DTC(s) detected. A drive cycle consists of starting the vehicle, driving the vehicle over 16 km/h (10 mph), stopping and then turning the ignition OFF.

Diagnostic Aids

A sticking or malfunctioning relay may cause an intermittent malfunction.

Use the enhanced diagnostic function of the Scan Tool in order to measure the frequency of the malfunction.

Clear the DTCs after completing the diagnosis. Test drive the vehicle for three drive cycles in order to verify that the DTC does not reset. Use the following procedure in order to complete one drive cycle:

1. Start the vehicle.
2. Drive the vehicle over 16 km/h (10 mph).
3. Stop the vehicle.
4. Turn the ignition switch to the OFF position.

Important: Zero the J 39200 test leads before making any resistance measurements. Refer to the J 39200 user's manual.

GC402980299300AX

Fig. 18 Code C1215: Brake Control Relay Contact Circuit Active (Part 1 of 3). Alero, Grand Am & Malibu

Step	Action	Value(s)	Yes	No
1	Was the Diagnostic System Check performed?	—	*Go to Step 2*	Refer to *Diagnostic System Check*
2	Are any other DTCs present?	—	Refer to the appropriate DTC table	*Go to Step 3*
3	1. Turn the ignition switch to the OFF position. 2. Install a *Scan Tool.* 3. Turn the ignition switch to the RUN position. Do not start the engine. 4. Use the Relay Test function of the Scan Tool to command the Electronic Brake Control Relay off. Does the Scan Tool indicate that the Electronic Brake Control Relay is off and the battery voltage less than or equal to the specified voltage?	5 V	*Go to Step 12*	*Go to Step 4*
4	1. Turn the ignition switch to the OFF position. 2. Disconnect the EBCM connector. 3. Turn the ignition switch to the RUN position. Do not start the engine. 4. Use the *J 39200* in order to measure the voltage between the EBCM harness connector terminal C and ground. Is the voltage within the specified voltage?	0–1 V	*Go to Step 6*	*Go to Step 5*
5	1. Turn the ignition switch to the OFF position. 2. Disconnect the Electronic Brake Control Relay. 3. Turn the ignition switch to the RUN position. Do not start the engine. 4. Use the *J 39200* in order to measure the voltage between the EBCM harness connector terminal C and ground. Is the voltage within the specified voltage?	0–1 V	*Go to Step 10*	*Go to Step 9*
6	1. Turn the ignition switch to the OFF position. 2. Inspect the following components: • The EBCM connector • EBCM harness connector 3. Inspect for the following conditions: • Poor terminal contact • Corrosion • Damaged terminals. The above conditions may cause a short to voltage. Is there a condition that may cause a short to voltage?	—	*Go to Step 8*	*Go to Step 7*

GC402980299300BX

Fig. 18 Code C1215: Brake Control Relay Contact Circuit Active (Part 2 of 3). Alero, Grand Am & Malibu

Step	Action	Value(s)	Yes	No
7	1. Reconnect the EBCM connector. 2. Turn the ignition switch to the RUN position. Do not start the engine. 3. Use the Relay Test function of the Scan Tool to command the Electronic Brake Control Relay off. Does the Scan Tool indicate that the Electronic Brake Control Relay is off and is the battery voltage less than or equal to the specified voltage?	5 V	*Go to Step 12*	*Go to Step 11*
8	Replace all of the terminals or the connectors that exhibit signs of poor terminal contact, corrosion, or damaged terminal(s). Is the repair complete?	—	Refer to *Diagnostic System Check*	—
9	Repair the short to voltage in CKT 1633. Is the repair complete?	—	Refer to *Diagnostic System Check*	—
10	Replace the Electronic Brake Control Relay. Is the repair complete?	—	Refer to *Diagnostic System Check*	—
11	Replace the EBCM. Is the repair complete?	—	Refer to *Diagnostic System Check*	—
12	The malfunction is intermittent or not present at this time. Refer to Diagnostic Aids for more information.	—	—	—

GC402980299300CX

Fig. 18 Code C1215: Brake Control Relay Contact Circuit Active (Part 3 of 3). Alero, Grand Am & Malibu

Circuit Description

Ignition voltage is supplied to terminal 86 of the Electronic Brake Control Relay. The above condition enables the EBCM to energize the pullin coil by completing the ground circuit at connector terminal 2 of the EBCM. The magnetic field created closes the Electronic Brake Control Relay contacts. The magnetic field also allows battery voltage and current through the Electronic Brake Control Relay terminal 30 to be supplied to the EBCM through connector terminal C. Connector terminal C supplies power to the EBCM, which supplies power to the motors and solenoids.

Conditions for Setting the DTC

DTC 1216 can set anytime after the Electronic Brake Control Relay is commanded ON. This test detects an open in the Electronic Brake Control Relay coil circuit. An open in this circuit will not allow the Electronic Brake Control Relay to be energized thus preventing power to the motors and solenoids.

A DTC C1286 will be set with DTC C1216 if the rear channel is not expected to be in the home position.

Action Taken When the DTC Sets

- A malfunction DTC stores.
- The ABS disables.
- The ABS warning indicator(s) turns on.

Conditions for Clearing the DTC

- The condition responsible for setting the DTC no longer exists and the Scan Tool Clear DTCs function is used.
- 100 drive cycles pass with no DTC(s) detected. A drive cycle consists of starting the vehicle, driving the vehicle over 16 km/h (10 mph), stopping and then turning the ignition switch to the OFF position.

Diagnostic Aids

The following conditions may cause an intermittent malfunction:

- A poor connection
- Rubbed-through wire insulation
- A broken wire inside the insulation

Use the enhanced diagnostic function of the Scan Tool in order to measure the frequency of the malfunction.

If the frequency of the malfunction is high, but is currently intermittent, inspect for high coil resistance. Use a *J 39200* in order to measure for high coil resistance by measuring between Electronic Brake Control Relay terminal 85 and terminal 86. If the resistance shows greater than 95 ohms, replace the Electronic Brake Control Relay.

Thoroughly inspect any circuitry that may be causing the intermittent complaint for the following conditions:

- Backed out terminals
- Improper mating
- Improperly formed or damaged terminals
- Poor terminal-to-wiring connections
- Physical damage to the wiring harness

Clear the DTCs after completing the diagnosis. Test drive the vehicle for three drive cycles in order to verify that the DTC does not reset. Use the following procedure in order to complete one drive cycle:

1. Start the vehicle.
2. Drive the vehicle over 16 km/h (10 mph).
3. Stop the vehicle.
4. Turn the ignition switch to the OFF position.

Important: Zero the J 39200 test leads before making any resistance measurements. Refer to the J 39200 user's manual.

GC402980299400AX

Fig. 19 Code C1216: Brake Control Relay Coil Circuit Open (Part 1 of 4). Alero, Grand Am & Malibu

Step	Action	Value(s)	Yes	No
1	Was the Diagnostic System Check performed?	—	*Go to Step 2*	Refer to *Diagnostic System Check*
2	1. Turn the ignition switch to the OFF position. 2. Install a *Scan Tool.* 3. Turn the ignition switch to the RUN position. Do not start the engine. 4. Use the Relay Test function of the *Scan Tool* in order to command the Electronic Brake Control Relay on. Does the Scan Tool indicate that the Electronic Brake Control Relay is on, and is the voltage equal to or greater than the specified voltage?	10 V	*Go to Step 23*	*Go to Step 3*
3	Use the *J 39200* in order to measure the voltage between the Electronic Brake Control Relay connector terminal 85 and ground. Is the voltage equal to or greater than the specified voltage?	10 V	*Go to Step 4*	*Go to Step 9*
4	Use the *J 39200* in order to measure the voltage between the Electronic Brake Control Relay connector terminal 86 and ground. Is the voltage equal to or greater than the specified voltage?	10 V	*Go to Step 5*	*Go to Step 13*
5	1. Turn the ignition switch to the OFF position. 2. Disconnect the EBCM connector. 3. Turn the ignition switch to the RUN position. Do not start the engine. 4. Use the *J 39200* in order to measure the voltage between the EBCM connector terminal 2 and ground. Is the voltage equal to or greater than the specified voltage?	10 V	*Go to Step 6*	*Go to Step 7*
6	1. Turn the ignition switch to the OFF position. 2. Inspect the following components: • The EBCM connector terminal 2 • The remaining terminals of the EBCM connector 3. Inspect the above components for the following conditions: • Damage • Poor terminal contact • Terminal corrosion Are there signs of poor terminal contact, corrosion, or damaged terminals?	—	*Go to Step 17*	*Go to Step 8*
7	1. Remove the Electronic Brake Control Relay. 2. Use the *J 39200* in order to measure the resistance between the EBCM connector terminal 2 and the Electronic Brake Control Relay connector terminal 85. Is the resistance within the specified range?	0–2 Ω	*Go to Step 8*	*Go to Step 18*

GC402980299400BX

Fig. 19 Code C1216: Brake Control Relay Coil Circuit Open (Part 2 of 4). Alero, Grand Am & Malibu

Step	Action	Value(s)	Yes	No
8	1. Reconnect the EBCM connector. 2. Reconnect the Electronic Brake Control Relay, if the Electronic Brake Control Relay is disconnected. 3. Turn the ignition switch to the RUN position. Do not start the engine. 4. Use the *Scan Tool* in order to read the DTCs. Does DTC C1216 set as current DTC?	—	*Go to Step 22*	*Go to Step 23*
9	1. Turn the ignition switch to the OFF position. 2. Remove the ERLS Fuse (20A) from the fuse block. 3. Turn the ignition switch to the RUN position. Do not start the engine. 4. Use the *J 39200* in order to measure the voltage between the fuse block terminal and ground. Is the voltage equal to or greater than the specified range?	10 V	*Go to Step 10*	*Go to Step 16*
10	Remove and inspect the ERLS Fuse (20A). Is the fuse open?	0–2 Ω	*Go to Step 12*	*Go to Step 11*
11	1. Turn the ignition switch to the OFF position. 2. Use the *J 39200* in order to measure the resistance between the Electronic Brake Control Relay connector terminal 86 and the fuse block terminal. Is the resistance within the specified range?	0–2 Ω	*Go to Step 23*	*Go to Step 15*
12	1. Turn the ignition switch to the OFF position. 2. Disconnect the EBCM connector. 3. Use the *J 39200* in order to measure the resistance between the EBCM harness connector terminal 4 and ground. Is the resistance within the specified range?	OL (Infinite)	*Go to Step 20*	*Go to Step 19*
13	1. Disconnect the Electronic Brake Control Relay. 2. Use the *J 39200* in order to measure the resistance between the Electronic Brake Control Relay terminal 85 and the Electronic Brake Control Relay terminal 86. Is the resistance within the specified range?	0–95 Ω	*Go to Step 14*	*Go to Step 21*
14	Inspect the Electronic Brake Control Relay connector for the following conditions: • Damage • Poor terminal contact • Terminal corrosion Are there signs of damage, poor terminal contact, or terminal corrosion?	—	*Go to Step 17*	*Go to Step 23*
15	Repair the open or high resistance in CKT 439. Is the repair complete?	—	Refer to *Diagnostic System Check*	—

GC402980299400CX

Fig. 19 Code C1216: Brake Control Relay Coil Circuit Open (Part 3 of 4). Alero, Grand Am & Malibu

Circuit Description

Ignition voltage is supplied to terminal 86 of the Electronic Brake Control Relay. The above condition enables the EBCM to energize the pullin coil by completing the ground circuit at connector terminal 2 of the EBCM. The magnetic field created closes the Electronic Brake Control Relay contacts. The magnetic field also allows battery voltage and current through the Electronic Brake Control Relay terminal 30 to be supplied to the EBCM through connector terminal C. Connector terminal C supplies power to the EBCM, which supplies power to the motors and solenoids.

Conditions for Setting the DTC

DTC C1217 can set before the EBCM commands the Electronic Brake Control Relay on.

DTC C1217 determines if the Electronic Brake Control Relay energizes when the Electronic Brake Control Relay should not energize. The above malfunction would not allow the Electronic Brake Control Relay to remove power to the ABS system.

If a second malfunction occurs, that requires the Electronic Brake Control Relay to turn off, the second malfunction cannot be removed if the Electronic Brake Control Relay cannot be controlled.

Action Taken When the DTC Sets

- A malfunction DTC stores.
- The ABS does not disable.

Conditions for Clearing the DTC

- The condition responsible for setting the DTC no longer exists and the Scan Tool Clear DTCs function is used.
- 100 drive cycles pass with no DTC(s) detected. A drive cycle consists of starting the vehicle, driving the vehicle over 16 km/h (10 mph), stopping and then turning the ignition OFF.

Diagnostic Aids

Use the enhanced diagnostic function of the Scan Tool in order to measure the frequency of the malfunction.

Clear the DTCs after completing the diagnosis.

Test drive the vehicle for three drive cycles in order to verify that the DTC does not reset.

Use the following procedure in order to complete one drive cycle:

1. Start the vehicle.
2. Drive the vehicle over 16 km/h (10 mph).
3. Stop the vehicle.
4. Turn the ignition switch to the OFF position.

Important: Zero the J 39200 test leads before making any resistance measurements. Refer to the J 39200 user's manual.

GC402980299500AX

Fig. 20 Code C1217: Brake Control Relay Coil Circuit Shorted To Ground (Part 1 of 3). Alero, Grand Am & Malibu

Step	Action	Value(s)	Yes	No
16	Repair the open or high resistance in the following circuits and components: • CKT 1 • CKT 3 • CKT 242 • The ignition switch • The IGN Fuse. Is the repair complete?	—	Refer to *Diagnostic System Check*	—
17	Replace all of the terminals that display signs of poor terminal contact, corrosion, or damaged terminal(s). If the Electronic Brake Control Relay displays signs of corrosion, replace the Electronic Brake Control Relay. Is the repair complete?	—	Refer to *Diagnostic System Check*	—
18	Repair the open or high resistance in CKT 1632. Is the repair complete?	—	Refer to *Diagnostic System Check*	—
19	Repair the short to ground in CKT 439. Is the repair complete?	—	*Go to Step 20*	—
20	Replace the fuse block ERLS Fuse (20A) with a known good fuse. Is the repair complete?	—	Refer to *Diagnostic System Check*	—
21	Replace the Electronic Brake Control Relay. Is the repair complete?	—	Refer to *Diagnostic System Check*	—
22	Replace the EBCM. Is the repair complete?	—	Refer to *Diagnostic System Check*	—
23	The malfunction is intermittent or is not present at this time. Refer to Diagnostic Aids for more information.	—	—	—

GC402980299400DX

Fig. 19 Code C1216: Brake Control Relay Coil Circuit Open (Part 4 of 4). Alero, Grand Am & Malibu

Step	Action	Value(s)	Yes	No
1	Was the Diagnostic System Check performed?	—	*Go to Step 2*	Refer to *Diagnostic System Check*
2	1. Turn the ignition switch to the OFF position. 2. Install a *Scan Tool.* 3. Turn the ignition switch to the RUN position. Do not start the engine. 4. Use the relay test function of the *Scan Tool* in order to command the Electronic Brake Control Relay off. Does the Scan Tool indicate that the Electronic Brake Control Relay is off, and is the voltage within the specified voltage?	0–5 V	*Go to Step 12*	*Go to Step 3*
3	1. Turn the ignition switch to the OFF position. 2. Disconnect the EBCM connector. 3. Turn the ignition switch to the RUN position. Do not start the engine. 4. Use the *J 39200* in order to measure the voltage between the EBCM connector terminal 2 and the battery voltage. Is the voltage within the specified voltage?	0–1 V	*Go to Step 4*	*Go to Step 7*
4	1. Turn the ignition switch to the OFF position. 2. Inspect the following components: • The EBCM connector terminal 2 • The remaining terminals of the EBCM connector 3. Inspect the above components for the following conditions: • Damage • Poor terminal contact • Terminal corrosion Are there signs of poor terminal contact, corrosion, or damaged terminals?	—	*Go to Step 8*	*Go to Step 5*
5	Use the *J 39200* in order to measure the resistance between the EBCM connector terminal 2 and ground. Is the resistance within the specified range?	OL (Infinite)	*Go to Step 6*	*Go to Step 9*
6	1. Reconnect the EBCM connector. 2. Turn the ignition switch to the RUN position. Do not start the engine. 3. Use the *Scan Tool* in order to look for DTCs. Does DTC C1217 set as a current DTC?	—	*Go to Step 11*	*Go to Step 12*

GC402980299500BX

Fig. 20 Code C1217: Brake Control Relay Coil Circuit Shorted To Ground (Part 2 of 3). Alero, Grand Am & Malibu

Step	Action	Value(s)	Yes	No
7	1. Turn the ignition switch to the OFF position. 2. Disconnect the Electronic Brake Control Relay. 3. Use the *J 39200* in order to measure the voltage between the Electronic Brake Control Relay connector terminal 85 and the battery voltage. Is the voltage less than or equal to the specified range?	0–1 V	*Go to Step 10*	*Go to Step 9*
8	Replace all of the terminals or connectors that exhibit signs of poor terminal contact, corrosion, or damaged terminal(s). Is the repair complete?	—	Refer to *Diagnostic System Check*	—
9	Repair the short to ground in CKT 1632. Is the repair complete?	—	Refer to *Diagnostic System Check*	—
10	Replace the Electronic Brake Control Relay. Is the repair complete?	—	Refer to *Diagnostic System Check*	—
11	Replace the EBCM. Is the repair complete?	—	Refer to *Diagnostic System Check*	—
12	The malfunction is intermittent or is not present at this time. Refer to Diagnostic Aids for more information.	—	—	—

GC402980299500CX

Fig. 20 Code C1217: Brake Control Relay Coil Circuit Shorted To Ground (Part 3 of 3). Alero, Grand Am & Malibu

Step	Action	Value(s)	Yes	No
1	Was the Diagnostic System Check performed?	—	*Go to Step 2*	Refer to *Diagnostic System Check*
2	1. Turn the ignition switch to the OFF position. 2. Install a *Scan Tool*. 3. Turn the ignition switch to the RUN position. Do not start the engine. 4. Use the Relay Test function of the *Scan Tool* in order to command the Electronic Brake Control Relay on. Does the Scan Tool indicate that the Electronic Brake Control Relay is off, and is the voltage equal to or greater than the specified voltage?	10 V	*Go to Step 12*	*Go to Step 3*
3	1. Turn the ignition switch to the OFF position. 2. Disconnect the Electronic Brake Control Relay. 3. Disconnect the EBCM connector. 4. Turn the ignition switch to the RUN position. Do not start the engine. 5. Use the *J 39200* in order to measure the voltage between the EBCM harness connector terminal 2 and ground. Is the voltage within the specified voltage?	0–1 V	*Go to Step 4*	*Go to Step 9*
4	1. Turn the ignition switch to the OFF position. 2. Use the *J 39200* in order to measure the resistance between the Electronic Brake Control Relay terminal 85 and the Electronic Brake Control Relay terminal 86. Is the resistance equal to or greater than the specified range?	65–95 Ω	*Go to Step 5*	*Go to Step 10*
5	Use the *J 39200* in order to measure the resistance between the Electronic Brake Control Relay terminal 30 and the Electronic Brake Control Relay terminal 87. Is the resistance within the specified range?	OL (Infinite)	*Go to Step 6*	*Go to Step 10*
6	1. Inspect the following components: • The EBCM connector terminal 2 • The remaining terminals of the EBCM connector 2. Inspect the above components for the following conditions: • Damage • Poor terminal contact • Terminal corrosion Are there signs of poor terminal contact, corrosion, or damaged terminals?	—	*Go to Step 8*	*Go to Step 7*

GC402980299600BX

Fig. 21 Code C1218: Brake Control Relay Coil Circuit Shorted To Voltage (Part 2 of 3). Alero, Grand Am & Malibu

Circuit Description

Ignition voltage is supplied to terminal 86 of the Electronic Brake Control Relay. The above enables the EBCM to energize the pullin coil by completing the ground circuit at connector terminal 2 of the EBCM. The magnetic field created closes the Electronic Brake Control Relay contacts. The magnetic field also allows battery voltage and current through the Electronic Brake Control Relay terminal 30 to be supplied to the EBCM through connector terminal C. Connector terminal C supplies power to the EBCM, which supplies power to the motors and solenoids.

Conditions for Setting the DTC

DTC C1218 can set after the EBCM commands the Electronic Brake Control Relay on.

This test monitors the availability of voltage to the EBCM.

DTC C1286 is set with DTC C1218 if the rear channel is not expected to be in the home position.

Action Taken When the DTC Sets

- A malfunction DTC stores.
- The ABS disables.
- The ABS warning indicator turns on.

Conditions for Clearing the DTC

- The condition responsible for setting the DTC no longer exists and the Scan Tool Clear DTCs function is used.
- 100 drive cycles pass with no DTC(s) detected. A drive cycle consists of starting the vehicle, driving the vehicle over 16 km/h (10 mph), stopping and then turning the ignition OFF.

Diagnostic Aids

Use the enhanced diagnostic function of the Scan Tool in order to measure the frequency of the malfunction.

Clear the DTCs after completing the diagnosis. Test drive the vehicle for three drive cycles in order to verify that the DTC does not reset. Use the following procedure in order to complete one drive cycle:

1. Start the vehicle.
2. Drive the vehicle over 16 km/h (10 mph).
3. Stop the vehicle.
4. Turn the ignition switch to the OFF position.

Important: Zero the J 39200 test leads before making any resistance measurements. Refer to the J 39200 user's manual.

GC402980299600AX

Fig. 21 Code C1218: Brake Control Relay Coil Circuit Shorted To Voltage (Part 1 of 3). Alero, Grand Am & Malibu

Step	Action	Value(s)	Yes	No
7	1. Reconnect the EBCM connector. 2. Reconnect the Electronic Brake Control Relay. 3. Turn the ignition switch to the RUN position. Do not start the engine. 4. Use the *Scan Tool* in order to look for DTCs. Does DTC C1218 set as a current DTC?	—	*Go to Step 11*	*Go to Step 12*
8	Replace all of the terminals or connectors that exhibit signs of poor terminal contact, corrosion, or damaged terminal(s). Is the repair complete?	—	Refer to *Diagnostic System Check*	—
9	Repair the short to voltage in CKT 1632. Is the repair complete?	—	Refer to *Diagnostic System Check*	—
10	Replace the Electronic Brake Control Relay. Is the repair complete?	—	Refer to *Diagnostic System Check*	—
11	Replace the EBCM. Is the repair complete?	—	Refer to *Diagnostic System Check*	—
12	The malfunction is intermittent or is not present at this time. Refer to Diagnostic Aids for more information.	—	—	—

GC402980299600CX

Fig. 21 Code C1218: Brake Control Relay Coil Circuit Shorted To Voltage (Part 3 of 3). Alero, Grand Am & Malibu

Circuit Description

As a toothed ring passes by the wheel speed sensor, changes in the electromagnetic field cause the wheel speed sensor to produce an AC voltage signal. The frequency of the AC voltage signal is proportional to the wheel speed. The amplitude of the AC voltage signal is directly related to wheel speed and the proximity of the wheel speed sensor to the toothed ring. The proximity of the wheel speed sensor to the toothed ring is also referred to as the air gap.

Conditions for Setting the DTC

DTC C1221 can set when the vehicle is not in an ABS stop.

A malfunction exists if both of the following conditions occur:

- The left front wheel speed sensor input signal equals zero.
- The vehicle's reference speed is greater than 8 km/h (5 mph)

Action Taken When the DTC Sets

- A malfunction DTC stores.
- The ABS disables.
- The ABS warning indicator turns on.

Conditions for Clearing the DTC

- The condition responsible for setting the DTC no longer exists and the Scan Tool Clear DTCs function is used.
- 100 drive cycles pass with no DTCs detected. A drive cycle consists of starting the vehicle, driving the vehicle over 16 km/h (10 mph), stopping and then turning the ignition switch to the OFF position.

Diagnostic Aids

The following conditions may cause an intermittent malfunction:

- A poor connection
- Rubbed-through wire insulation
- A broken wire inside the insulation

Use the enhanced diagnostic function of the Scan Tool in order to measure the frequency of the malfunction.

If the customer's comments reflect that the amber ABS warning indicator is on only during moist environmental changes (rain, snow, vehicle wash), inspect all the wheel speed sensor circuitry for signs of water intrusion. If the DTC is not current, clear all DTCs and simulate the effects of water intrusion by using the following procedure:

1. Spray the suspected area with a five percent saltwater solution.
   Add two teaspoons of salt to twelve ounces of water to make a five percent saltwater solution.
2. Test drive the vehicle over various road surfaces (bumps, turns, etc.) above 24 km/h (15 mph) for at least 30 seconds.
3. If the DTC returns, replace the suspected harness.

Thoroughly inspect any circuitry that may be causing the intermittent complaint for the following conditions:

- Backed out terminals
- Improper mating
- Broken locks
- Improperly formed or damaged terminals
- Poor terminal-to-wiring connections
- Physical damage to the wiring harness

GC402980305500AX

Fig. 22 Code C1221: LH Front Wheel Speed Sensor Input Signal Is Zero (Part 1 of 4). Alero, Grand Am & Malibu

Resistance of the wheel speed sensor will increase with an increase in sensor temperature.

Use the following procedure when replacing a wheel speed sensor or harness:

1. Inspect the wheel speed sensor terminals and harness connector for corrosion and/or water intrusion.
2. Replace the wheel speed sensor and jumper harness if evidence of corrosion or water intrusion exists.

Important: Zero the J 39200 test leads before making any resistance measurements. Refer to the J 39200 user's manual.

Important: Difficulty may occur when trying to locate the intermittent malfunctions in the wheel speed sensor circuit.

Do not disturb any of the electrical connections. Change electrical connections only when instructed to do so by a step in the diagnostic table.

Changing the electrical connections at the correct time will ensure that an intermittent electrical connection will not be corrected until the source of the malfunction is found.

Step	Action	Value(s)	Yes	No
1	Was the Diagnostic System Check performed?	—	Go to Step 2	Refer to *Diagnostic System Check*
2	1. Turn the ignition switch to the OFF position. 2. Inspect the left front wheel speed sensor and the left front wheel speed sensor harness connector for physical damage. Is there any physical damage?	—	Go to Step 16	Go to Step 3
3	Inspect the following components for physical damage: • The left front wheel speed sensor jumper harness • The left front wheel speed sensor jumper harness connectors Is there any physical damage?	—	Go to Step 15	Go to Step 4
4	1. Disconnect the left front wheel speed sensor directly at the left front wheel speed sensor connector. 2. Use the *J 39200* in order to measure the resistance between the left front wheel speed sensor connector terminal A and the left front wheel speed sensor connector terminal B. Is the resistance within the specified range?	950–1250 Ω	Go to Step 5	Go to Step 16
5	1. Select the A/C VOLTAGE scale on the *J 39200*. 2. Spin the left front wheel by hand while observing the voltage reading on the *J 39200*. Is the voltage equal to or greater than the specified voltage?	100 mV	Go to Step 6	Go to Step 16
6	1. Disconnect the EBCM connector. 2. Use the *J 39200* in order to measure the resistance between the EBCM terminal 8 and the EBCM terminal 21. Is the resistance within the specified range?	OL (Infinite)	Go to Step 7	Go to Step 8

GC402980305500BX

Fig. 22 Code C1221: LH Front Wheel Speed Sensor Input Signal Is Zero (Part 2 of 4). Alero, Grand Am & Malibu

Step	Action	Value(s)	Yes	No
16	Replace the left front wheel speed sensor Is the repair complete?	—	Refer to *Diagnostic System Check*	—
17	Replace the EBCM. Is the repair complete?	—	Refer to *Diagnostic System Check*	—
18	The malfunction is intermittent or is not present at this time. Refer to Diagnostic Aids for more information.	—	—	—

GC402980305500DX

Fig. 22 Code C1221: LH Front Wheel Speed Sensor Input Signal Is Zero (Part 4 of 4). Alero, Grand Am & Malibu

Circuit Description

As a toothed ring passes by the wheel speed sensor, changes in the electromagnetic field cause the wheel speed sensor to produce an AC voltage signal. The frequency of the AC voltage signal is proportional to the wheel speed. The amplitude of the AC voltage signal is directly related to wheel speed and the proximity of the wheel speed sensor to the toothed ring. The proximity of the wheel speed sensor to the toothed ring is also referred to as the air gap.

Conditions for Setting the DTC

DTC C1222 sets when the vehicle is not in an ABS stop.

A malfunction exists if both of the following conditions occur:

- The right front wheel speed sensor input signal equals zero.
- The vehicle's reference speed is greater than 8 km/h (5 mph)

Action Taken When the DTC Sets

- A malfunction DTC stores.
- The ABS disables.
- The ABS warning indicator turns on.

Conditions for Clearing the DTC

- The condition responsible for setting the DTC no longer exists and the Scan Tool Clear DTCs function is used.
- 100 drive cycles pass with no DTCs detected. A drive cycle consists of starting the vehicle, driving the vehicle over 16 km/h (10 mph), stopping and then turning the ignition switch to the OFF position.

Diagnostic Aids

The following conditions may cause an intermittent malfunction:

- A poor connection
- Rubbed-through wire insulation
- A broken wire inside the insulation

Use the enhanced diagnostic function of the Scan Tool in order to measure the frequency of the malfunction. Refer to the Scan Tool manual for the procedure.

If the customer's comments reflect that the amber ABS warning indicator is on only during moist environmental changes (rain, snow, vehicle wash), inspect all the wheel speed sensor circuitry for signs of water intrusion. If the DTC is not current, clear all DTCs and simulate the effects of water intrusion by using the following procedure:

1. Spray the suspected area with a five percent saltwater solution.

   Add two teaspoons of salt to twelve ounces of water to make a five percent saltwater solution.
2. Test drive the vehicle over various road surfaces (bumps, turns, etc.) above 24 km/h (15 mph) for at least 30 seconds.
3. If the DTC returns, replace the suspected harness.

Thoroughly inspect any circuitry that may be causing the intermittent complaint for the following conditions:

- Backed out terminals
- Improper mating
- Broken locks
- Improperly formed or damaged terminals
- Poor terminal-to-wiring connections
- Physical damage to the wiring harness

GC402980305600AX

Fig. 23 Code C1222: RH Front Wheel Speed Sensor Input Signal Is Zero (Part 1 of 4). Alero, Grand Am & Malibu

Step	Action	Value(s)	Yes	No
7	1. Inspect the EBCM connector for the following conditions: • Damage • Poor terminal contact • Terminal corrosion (Damage, poor terminal contact, and terminal corrosion may cause a short between the EBCM terminal 8 and the EBCM terminal 21. 2. Inspect the remaining terminals of the EBCM connector for the following conditions: • Damage • Poor terminal contact • Terminal corrosion Are there signs of poor terminal contact, corrosion, or damaged terminals?	—	Go to Step 12	Go to Step 8
8	Inspect the wiring of CKT 873 and CKT 830 for signs of damage that may cause a short between CKT 873 and CKT 830. Are there any signs of damaged wiring?	—	Go to Step 13	Go to Step 9
9	Inspect the harness connectors of CKT 873 and CKT 830 for signs of damage that may cause a short between CKT 873 and CKT 830. Are there any signs of damaged connectors?	—	Go to Step 14	Go to Step 10
10	1. Reconnect the EBCM harness connector. 2. Reconnect the left front wheel speed sensor harness connector. 3. Install a *Scan Tool*. 4. Test drive the vehicle at a speed above 24 km/h (15 mph) for at least 30 seconds. 5. Use the *Scan Tool* in order to read the DTCs. Does DTC C1221 set as a current DTC?	—	Go to Step 11	Go to Step 18
11	1. Select Data List on the *Scan Tool*. 2. Monitor the wheel speed sensor speeds. 3. Drive the vehicle in the following manner: 3.1. Slowly accelerate to 65 km/h (40 mph). 3.2. Slowly decelerate to 0 km/h (0 mph). Is the speed of the left front wheel speed sensor constantly higher than the speed of the three remaining wheel speed sensors?	—	Go to Step 15	Go to Step 17
12	Replace all of the terminals that exhibit signs of poor terminal contact, corrosion, or damaged terminal(s). Is the repair complete?	—	Refer to *Diagnostic System Check*	—
13	Replace the damaged wiring harness that causes the short between CKT 873 and CKT 830. Is the repair complete?	—	Refer to *Diagnostic System Check*	—
14	Replace the damaged wiring harness connectors that cause the short between CKT 873 and CKT 830. Is the repair complete?	—	Refer to *Diagnostic System Check*	—
15	Replace the left front wheel speed sensor jumper harness. Is the repair complete?	—	Refer to *Diagnostic System Check*	—

GC402980305500CX

Fig. 22 Code C1221: LH Front Wheel Speed Sensor Input Signal Is Zero (Part 3 of 4). Alero, Grand Am & Malibu

Step	Action	Value(s)	Yes	No
1	Was the Diagnostic System Check performed?	—	Go to Step 2	Refer to *Diagnostic System Check*
2	1. Turn the ignition switch to the OFF position. 2. Inspect the right front wheel speed sensor and the right front wheel speed sensor harness connector for physical damage. Is there any physical damage?	—	Go to Step 16	Go to Step 3
3	Inspect the following components for physical damage: • The right front wheel speed sensor jumper harness • The right front wheel speed sensor jumper harness connectors Is there any physical damage?	—	Go to Step 15	Go to Step 4
4	1. Disconnect the right front wheel speed sensor directly at the right front wheel speed sensor connector. 2. Use the *J 39200* in order to measure the resistance between the right front wheel speed sensor connector terminal A and the right front wheel speed sensor connector terminal B. Is the resistance within the specified range?	950–1250 Ω	Go to Step 5	Go to Step 16
5	1. Select the A/C VOLTAGE scale on the *J 39200*. 2. Spin the right front wheel by hand while observing the voltage reading on the *J 39200*. Is the voltage equal to or greater than the specified voltage?	100 mV	Go to Step 6	Go to Step 16
6	1. Disconnect the EBCM connector. 2. Use the *J 39200* in order to measure the resistance between the EBCM connector terminal 9 and the EBCM connector terminal 22. Is the resistance within the specified range?	OL (Infinite)	Go to Step 7	Go to Step 8

GC402980305600BX

Fig. 23 Code C1222: RH Front Wheel Speed Sensor Input Signal Is Zero (Part 2 of 4). Alero, Grand Am & Malibu

Step	Action	Value(s)	Yes	No
7	1. Inspect the EBCM connector for the following conditions: • Damage • Poor terminal contact • Terminal corrosion. Damage, poor terminal contact, and terminal corrosion may cause a short between the EBCM connector terminal 9 and the EBCM connector terminal 22. 2. Inspect the remaining terminals of the EBCM connector for the following conditions: • Damage • Poor terminal contact • Terminal corrosion. Are there signs of poor terminal contact, corrosion, or damaged terminals?	—	*Go to Step 12*	*Go to Step 8*
8	Inspect the wiring of CKT 872 and CKT 833 for signs of damage that may cause a short between CKT 872 and CKT 833. Are there any signs of damaged wiring?	—	*Go to Step 13*	*Go to Step 9*
9	Inspect the harness connectors of CKT 872 and CKT 833 for signs of damage that may cause a short between CKT 872 and CKT 833. Are there any signs of damaged connectors?	—	*Go to Step 14*	*Go to Step 10*
10	1. Reconnect the EBCM harness connector. 2. Reconnect the right front wheel speed sensor harness connector. 3. Install a *Scan Tool*. 4. Test drive the vehicle at a speed above 24 km/h (15 mph) for at least 30 seconds. 5. Use the *Scan Tool* in order to read the DTCs. Does DTC C1222 set as a current DTC?	—	*Go to Step 11*	*Go to Step 18*
11	1. Select Data List on the *Scan Tool*. 2. Monitor the wheel speed sensor speeds. 3. Use the following procedure when driving the vehicle in order to test the wheel speed sensor: 3.1. Slowly accelerate to 65 km/h (40 mph). 3.2. Slowly decelerate to 0 km/h (0 mph). Is the speed of the right front wheel speed sensor constantly higher than the speed of the three remaining wheel speed sensors?	—	*Go to Step 16*	*Go to Step 17*
12	Replace all of the terminals that exhibit signs of poor terminal contact, corrosion, or damaged terminal(s). Is the repair complete?	—	Refer to *Diagnostic System Check*	—
13	Replace the damaged wiring harness that causes the short between CKT 872 and CKT 833. Is the repair complete?	—	Refer to *Diagnostic System Check*	—
14	Replace the damaged wiring harness connectors that cause the short between CKT 872 and CKT 833. Is the repair complete?	—	Refer to *Diagnostic System Check*	—

GC402980305600CX

Fig. 23 Code C1222: RH Front Wheel Speed Sensor Input Signal Is Zero (Part 3 of 4). Alero, Grand Am & Malibu

Circuit Description

As a toothed ring passes by the wheel speed sensor, changes in the electromagnetic field cause the wheel speed sensor to produce an AC voltage signal. The frequency of the AC voltage signal is proportional to the wheel speed. The amplitude of the AC voltage signal is directly related to wheel speed and the proximity of the wheel speed sensor to the toothed ring. The proximity of the wheel speed sensor to the toothed ring is also referred to as the air gap.

Conditions for Setting the DTC

DTC C1223 can set when the vehicle is not in an ABS stop.

A malfunction exists if both of the following conditions occur:

- The left rear wheel speed sensor input signal equals zero.
- The vehicle's reference speed is greater than 8 km/h (5 mph)

Action Taken When the DTC Sets

- A malfunction DTC stores.
- The ABS disables.
- The ABS warning indicator turns on.

Conditions for Clearing the DTC

- The condition responsible for setting the DTC no longer exists and the Scan Tool Clear DTCs function is used.
- 100 drive cycles pass with no DTCs detected. A drive cycle consists of starting the vehicle, driving the vehicle over 16 km/h (10 mph), stopping and then turning the ignition switch to the OFF position.

Diagnostic Aids

The following conditions may cause an intermittent malfunction:

- A poor connection
- Rubbed-through wire insulation
- A broken wire inside the insulation

Use the enhanced diagnostic function of the Scan Tool in order to measure the frequency of the malfunction.

If the customer's comments reflect that the amber ABS warning indicator is on only during moist environmental changes (rain, snow, vehicle wash), inspect all the wheel speed sensor circuitry for signs of water intrusion. If the DTC is not current, clear all DTCs and simulate the effects of water intrusion by using the following procedure:

1. Spray the suspected area with a five percent saltwater solution.
   Add two teaspoons of salt to twelve ounces of water to make a five percent saltwater solution.
2. Test drive the vehicle over various road surfaces (bumps, turns, etc.) above 24 km/h (15 mph) for at least 30 seconds.
3. If the DTC returns, replace the suspected harness.

Thoroughly inspect any circuitry that may be causing the intermittent complaint for the following conditions:

- Backed out terminals
- Improper mating
- Broken locks
- Improperly formed or damaged terminals
- Poor terminal-to-wiring connections
- Physical damage to the wiring harness

GC402980305700AX

Fig. 24 Code C1223: LH Rear Wheel Speed Sensor Input Signal Is Zero (Part 1 of 4). Alero, Grand Am & Malibu

Step	Action	Value(s)	Yes	No
15	Replace the right front wheel speed sensor jumper harness. Is the repair complete?	—	Refer to *Diagnostic System Check*	—
16	Replace the right front wheel speed sensor. Is the repair complete?	—	Refer to *Diagnostic System Check*	—
17	Replace the EBCM. Is the repair complete?	—	Refer to *Diagnostic System Check*	—
18	The malfunction is intermittent or is not present at this time. Refer to Diagnostic Aids for more information.	—	—	—

GC402980305600DX

Fig. 23 Code C1222: RH Front Wheel Speed Sensor Input Signal Is Zero (Part 4 of 4). Alero, Grand Am & Malibu

Step	Action	Value(s)	Yes	No
1	Was the Diagnostic System Check performed?	—	*Go to Step 2*	Refer to *Diagnostic System Check*
2	1. Turn the ignition switch to the OFF position. 2. Inspect the left rear wheel speed sensor and the left rear wheel speed sensor harness connector for physical damage. Is there any physical damage?	—	*Go to Step 16*	*Go to Step 3*
3	Inspect the following components for physical damage: • The left rear wheel speed sensor jumper harness • The left rear wheel speed sensor jumper harness connectors. Is there any physical damage?	—	*Go to Step 15*	*Go to Step 4*
4	1. Disconnect the left rear wheel speed sensor directly at the left rear wheel speed sensor connector. 2. Use the *J 39200* in order to measure the resistance between the left rear wheel speed sensor connector terminal A and the left rear wheel speed sensor connector terminal B. Is the resistance within the specified range?	950–1250 Ω	*Go to Step 5*	*Go to Step 16*
5	1. Select the A/C VOLTAGE scale on the *J 39200*. 2. Spin the left rear wheel by hand while observing the voltage reading on the *J 39200*. Is the voltage equal to or greater than the specified voltage?	100 mV	*Go to Step 6*	*Go to Step 16*
6	1. Disconnect the EBCM connector. 2. Use the *J 39200* to measure the resistance between the EBCM connector terminal 10 and the EBCM connector terminal 23. Is the resistance within the specified range?	OL (Infinite)	*Go to Step 7*	*Go to Step 8*

GC402980305700BX

Fig. 24 Code C1223: LH Rear Wheel Speed Sensor Input Signal Is Zero (Part 2 of 4). Alero, Grand Am & Malibu

Step	Action	Value(s)	Yes	No
7	1. Inspect the EBCM connector for the following conditions: • Damage • Poor terminal contact • Terminal corrosion. (These conditions could result in a short between the EBCM connector terminal 10 and the EBCM connector terminal 23.) 2. Inspect the remaining terminals of the EBCM connector for the following conditions: • Damage • Poor terminal contact • Terminal corrosion. Are there signs of poor terminal contact, corrosion, or damaged terminals?	—	*Go to Step 12*	*Go to Step 8*
8	Inspect the wiring of CKT 885 and CKT 884 for signs of damage that may cause a short between CKT 885 and CKT 884. Are there any signs of damaged wiring?	—	*Go to Step 13*	*Go to Step 9*
9	Inspect the harness connectors of CKT 885 and CKT 884 for signs of damage that may cause a short between CKT 885 and CKT 884. Are there any signs of damaged connectors?	—	*Go to Step 14*	*Go to Step 10*
10	1. Reconnect the EBCM harness connector. 2. Reconnect the left rear wheel speed sensor harness connector. 3. Install a *Scan Tool*. 4. Test drive the vehicle at a speed above 24 km/h (15 mph) for at least 30 seconds. 5. Use the *Scan Tool* in order to read the DTCs. Does DTC C1223 set as a current DTC?	—	*Go to Step 11*	*Go to Step 18*
11	1. Select Data List on the *Scan Tool*. 2. Monitor the wheel speed sensor speeds. 3. Drive the vehicle in the following manner: 3.1. Slowly accelerate to 65 km/h (40 mph). 3.2. Slowly decelerate to 0 km/h (0 mph). Is the speed of the left rear wheel speed sensor constantly higher than the speed of the three remaining wheel speed sensors?	—	*Go to Step 16*	*Go to Step 17*
12	Replace all of the terminals that exhibit signs of poor terminal contact, corrosion, or damaged terminal(s). Is the repair complete?	—	Refer to *Diagnostic System Check*	—
13	Replace the damaged wiring harness that causes the short between CKT 885 and CKT 884. Is the repair complete?	—	Refer to *Diagnostic System Check*	—
14	Replace the damaged wiring harness connectors that cause the short between CKT 885 and CKT 884. Is the repair complete?	—	Refer to *Diagnostic System Check*	—
15	Replace the left rear wheel speed sensor jumper harness. Is the repair complete?	—	Refer to *Diagnostic System Check*	—

GC402980305700CX

Fig. 24 Code C1223: LH Rear Wheel Speed Sensor Input Signal Is Zero (Part 3 of 4). Alero, Grand Am & Malibu

Step	Action	Value(s)	Yes	No
16	Replace the left rear wheel speed sensor. Is the repair complete?	—	Refer to *Diagnostic System Check*	—
17	Replace the EBCM. Is the repair complete?	—	Refer to *Diagnostic System Check*	—
18	The malfunction is intermittent or is not present at this time. Refer to Diagnostic Aids for more information.	—	—	—

GC402980305700DX

Fig. 24 Code C1223: LH Rear Wheel Speed Sensor Input Signal Is Zero (Part 4 of 4). Alero, Grand Am & Malibu

Step	Action	Value(s)	Yes	No
1	Was the Diagnostic System Check performed?		*Go to Step 2*	Refer to *Diagnostic System Check*
2	1. Turn the ignition switch to the OFF position. 2. Inspect the right rear wheel speed sensor and the right rear wheel speed sensor harness connector for physical damage. Is there any physical damage?	—	*Go to Step 16*	*Go to Step 3*
3	Inspect the following components for physical damage: • The right rear wheel speed sensor jumper harness • The right rear wheel speed sensor jumper harness connectors Is there any physical damage?	—	*Go to Step 15*	*Go to Step 4*
4	1. Disconnect the right rear wheel speed sensor directly at the right rear wheel speed sensor connector. 2. Use the *J 39200* in order to measure the resistance between the right rear wheel speed sensor connector terminal A and the right rear wheel speed sensor connector terminal B. Is the resistance within the specified range?	950–1250 Ω	*Go to Step 5*	*Go to Step 16*
5	1. Select the A/C VOLTAGE scale on the *J 39200*. 2. Spin the right rear wheel by hand while observing the voltage reading on the *J 39200*. Is the voltage equal to or greater than the specified voltage?	100 mV	*Go to Step 6*	*Go to Step 16*
6	1. Disconnect the EBCM connector. 2. Use the *J 39200* in order to measure the resistance between the EBCM connector terminal 11 and the EBCM connector terminal 24. Is the resistance within the specified range?	OL (Infinite)	*Go to Step 7*	*Go to Step 8*

GC402980305800BX

Fig. 25 Code C1224: RH Rear Wheel Speed Sensor Input Signal Is Zero (Part 2 of 4). Alero, Grand Am & Malibu

Circuit Description

As a toothed ring passes by the wheel speed sensor, changes in the electromagnetic field cause the wheel speed sensor to produce an AC voltage signal. The frequency of the AC voltage signal is proportional to the wheel speed. The amplitude of the AC voltage signal is directly related to wheel speed and the proximity of the wheel speed sensor to the toothed ring. The proximity of the wheel speed sensor to the toothed ring is also referred to as the air gap.

Conditions for Setting the DTC

DTC C1224 can set when the vehicle is not in an ABS stop.

A malfunction exists if both of the following conditions occur:

- The right rear wheel speed sensor input signal equals zero.
- The vehicle's reference speed is greater than 8 km/h (5 mph)

Action Taken When the DTC Sets

- A malfunction DTC stores.
- The ABS disables.
- The ABS warning indicator turns on.

Conditions for Clearing the DTC

- The condition responsible for setting the DTC no longer exists and the Scan Tool Clear DTCs function is used.
- 100 drive cycles pass with no DTCs detected. A drive cycle consists of starting the vehicle, driving the vehicle over 16 km/h (10 mph), stopping and then turning the ignition OFF.

Diagnostic Aids

The following conditions may cause an intermittent malfunction:

- A poor connection
- Rubbed-through wire insulation
- A broken wire inside the insulation

Use the enhanced diagnostic function of the Scan Tool in order to measure the frequency of the malfunction.

If the customer's comments reflect that the amber ABS warning indicator is on only during moist environmental changes (rain, snow, vehicle wash), inspect all the wheel speed sensor circuitry for signs of water intrusion. If the DTC is not current, clear all DTCs and simulate the effects of water intrusion by using the following procedure:

1. Spray the suspected area with a five percent saltwater solution.
   Add two teaspoons of salt to twelve ounces of water to make a five percent saltwater solution.
2. Test drive the vehicle over various road surfaces (bumps, turns, etc.) above 24 km/h (15 mph) for at least 30 seconds.
3. If the DTC returns, replace the suspected harness.

Thoroughly inspect any circuitry that may be causing the intermittent complaint for the following conditions:

- Backed out terminals
- Improper mating
- Broken locks
- Improperly formed or damaged terminals
- Poor terminal-to-wiring connections
- Physical damage to the wiring harness

GC402980305800AX

Fig. 25 Code C1224: RH Rear Wheel Speed Sensor Input Signal Is Zero (Part 1 of 4). Alero, Grand Am & Malibu

Step	Action	Value(s)	Yes	No
7	1. Inspect the EBCM connector for the following conditions: • Damage • Poor terminal contact • Terminal corrosion Damage, poor terminal contact, and terminal corrosion may cause a short between the EBCM connector terminal 11 and the EBCM connector terminal 24. 2. Inspect the remaining terminals of the EBCM connector for the following conditions: • Damage • Poor terminal contact • Terminal corrosion Are there signs of poor terminal contact, corrosion, or damaged terminals?	—	*Go to Step 12*	*Go to Step 8*
8	Inspect the wiring of CKT 883 and CKT 882 for signs of damage that may cause a short between CKT 883 and CKT 882. Are there any signs of damaged wiring?	—	*Go to Step 13*	*Go to Step 9*
9	Inspect the harness connectors of CKT 883 and CKT 882 for signs of damage that may cause a short between CKT 883 and CKT 882. Are there any signs of damaged connectors?	—	*Go to Step 14*	*Go to Step 10*
10	1. Reconnect the EBCM harness connector. 2. Reconnect the right rear wheel speed sensor harness connector. 3. Install a *Scan Tool*. 4. Test drive the vehicle at a speed above 24 km/h (15 mph) for at least 30 seconds. 5. Use the *Scan Tool* in order to read the DTCs. Does DTC C1224 set as a current DTC?	—	*Go to Step 11*	*Go to Step 18*
11	1. Select Data List on the *Scan Tool*. 2. Monitor the wheel speed sensor speeds. 3. Drive the vehicle in the following manner: 3.1. Slowly accelerate to 65 km/h (40 mph). 3.2. Slowly decelerate to 0 km/h (0 mph). Is the speed of the right rear wheel speed sensor constantly higher than the speed of the three remaining wheel speed sensors?	—	*Go to Step 16*	*Go to Step 17*
12	Replace all of the terminals that exhibit signs of poor terminal contact, corrosion, or damaged terminal(s). Is the repair complete?	—	Refer to *Diagnostic System Check*	—
13	Replace the damaged wiring harness that causes the short between CKT 883 and CKT 882. Is the repair complete?	—	Refer to *Diagnostic System Check*	—
14	Replace the damaged wiring harness connectors that cause the short between CKT 883 and CKT 882. Is the repair complete?	—	Refer to *Diagnostic System Check*	—

GC402980305800CX

Fig. 25 Code C1224: RH Rear Wheel Speed Sensor Input Signal Is Zero (Part 3 of 4). Alero, Grand Am & Malibu

Step	Action	Value(s)	Yes	No
15	Replace the right rear wheel speed sensor jumper harness. Is the repair complete?	—	Refer to *Diagnostic System Check*	—
16	Replace the right rear wheel speed sensor. Is the repair complete?	—	Refer to *Diagnostic System Check*	—
17	Replace the EBCM. Is the repair complete?	—	Refer to *Diagnostic System Check*	—
18	Is malfunction intermittent or is not present at this time?	—	Refer to Diagnostic Aids for more information	—

GC402980305800DX

Fig. 25 Code C1224: RH Rear Wheel Speed Sensor Input Signal Is Zero (Part 4 of 4). Alero, Grand Am & Malibu

Step	Action	Value(s)	Yes	No
1	Was the Diagnostic System Check performed?	—	*Go to Step 2*	Refer to *Diagnostic System Check*
2	1. Turn the ignition switch to the OFF position. 2. Inspect the left front wheel speed sensor and the left front wheel speed sensor harness connector for physical damage. Is there any physical damage?	—	*Go to Step 16*	*Go to Step 3*
3	Inspect the following components for physical damage: • The left front wheel speed sensor jumper harness • The left front wheel speed sensor jumper harness connectors Is there any physical damage?	—	*Go to Step 15*	*Go to Step 4*
4	1. Disconnect the left front wheel speed sensor directly at the left front wheel speed sensor connector. 2. Use the *J 39200* in order to measure the resistance between the left front wheel speed sensor connector terminal A and the left front wheel speed sensor connector terminal B. Is the resistance within the specified range?	950–1250 Ω	*Go to Step 5*	*Go to Step 16*
5	1. Select the A/C VOLTAGE scale on the *J 39200.* 2. Spin the left front wheel by hand while observing the voltage reading on the *J 39200.* Is the voltage equal to or greater than the specified voltage?	100 mV	*Go to Step 6*	*Go to Step 16*
6	1. Disconnect the EBCM connector. 2. Use the *J 39200* in order to measure the resistance between the EBCM connector terminal 8 and the EBCM connector terminal 21. Is the resistance within the specified range?	OL (Infinite)	*Go to Step 7*	*Go to Step 8*
7	1. Inspect the EBCM connector for the following conditions: • Damage • Poor terminal contact • Terminal corrosion (These conditions could result in a short between the EBCM connector terminal 8 and the EBCM connector terminal 21.) 2. Inspect the remaining terminals of the connector for the following conditions: • Damage • Poor terminal contact • Terminal corrosion Are there signs of poor terminal contact, corrosion, or damaged terminals?	—	*Go to Step 12*	*Go to Step 8*

GC402980305900BX

Fig. 26 Code C1225: LH Front Excessive Wheel Speed Variation (Part 2 of 3). Alero, Grand Am & Malibu

Circuit Description

As a toothed ring passes by the wheel speed sensor, changes in the electromagnetic field cause the wheel speed sensor to produce an AC voltage signal. The frequency of the AC voltage signal is proportional to the wheel speed. The amplitude of the AC voltage signal is directly related to wheel speed and the proximity of the wheel speed sensor to the toothed ring. The proximity of the wheel speed sensor to the toothed ring is also referred to as the air gap.

Conditions for Setting the DTC

DTC C1225 can set when the brake is off.

DTC C1225 detects a situation in which the left front wheel acceleration or deceleration is beyond specified limits.

Action Taken When the DTC Sets

- A malfunction DTC stores.
- The ABS disables.
- The ABS warning indicator turns on.

Conditions for Clearing the DTC

- The condition responsible for setting the DTC no longer exists and the Scan Tool Clear DTCs function is used.
- 100 drive cycles pass with no DTCs detected. A drive cycle consists of starting the vehicle, driving the vehicle over 16 km/h (10 mph), stopping and then turning the ignition switch to the OFF position.

Diagnostic Aids

The following conditions may cause an intermittent malfunction:

- A poor connection
- Rubbed-through wire insulation
- A broken wire inside the insulation

Use the enhanced diagnostic function of the Scan Tool in order to measure the frequency of the malfunction.

If the customer's comments reflect that the amber ABS warning indicator is on only during moist environmental changes (rain, snow, vehicle wash), inspect all the wheel speed sensor circuitry for signs of water intrusion. If the DTC is not current, clear all DTCs and simulate the effects of water intrusion by using the following procedure:

1. Spray the suspected area with a five percent saltwater solution.
   Add two teaspoons of salt to twelve ounces of water to make a five percent saltwater solution.
2. Test drive the vehicle over various road surfaces (bumps, turns, etc.) above 24 km/h (15 mph) for at least 30 seconds.
3. If the DTC returns, replace the suspected harness.

Thoroughly inspect any circuitry that may be causing the intermittent complaint for the following conditions:

- Backed out terminals
- Improper mating
- Broken locks
- Improperly formed or damaged terminals
- Poor terminal-to-wiring connections
- Physical damage to the wiring harness

Resistance of the wheel speed sensor will increase with an increase in sensor temperature.

Use the following procedure when replacing a wheel speed sensor or harness:

1. Inspect the wheel speed sensor terminals and harness connector for corrosion and/or water intrusion.
2. Replace the wheel speed sensor and jumper harness if evidence of corrosion or water intrusion exists.

GC402980305900AX

Fig. 26 Code C1225: LH Front Excessive Wheel Speed Variation (Part 1 of 3). Alero, Grand Am & Malibu

Step	Action	Value(s)	Yes	No
8	Inspect the wiring of CKT 873 and CKT 830 for signs of damage that may cause a short between CKT 873 and CKT 830. Are there any signs of damaged wiring?	—	*Go to Step 13*	*Go to Step 9*
9	Inspect the harness connectors of CKT 873 and CKT 830 for signs of damage that may cause a short between CKT 873 and CKT 830. Are there any signs of damaged connectors?	—	*Go to Step 14*	*Go to Step 10*
10	1. Reconnect the EBCM harness connector. 2. Reconnect the left front wheel speed sensor harness connector. 3. Install a *Scan Tool.* 4. Test drive the vehicle at a speed above 24 km/h (15 mph) for at least 30 seconds. 5. Use the *Scan Tool* in order to read the DTCs. Does DTC C1225 set as a current DTC?	—	*Go to Step 11*	*Go to Step 18*
11	1. Select Data List on the *Scan Tool.* 2. Monitor the wheel speed sensor speeds. 3. Drive the vehicle in the following manner. 3.1. Slowly accelerate to 65 km/h (40 mph). 3.2. Slowly decelerate to 0 km/h (0 mph). Is the speed of the left front wheel speed sensor constantly higher than the speed of the three remaining wheel speed sensors?	—	*Go to Step 16*	*Go to Step 17*
12	Replace all of the terminals that exhibit signs of poor terminal contact, corrosion, or damaged terminal(s). Is the repair complete?	—	Refer to *Diagnostic System Check*	—
13	Replace the damaged wiring harness that causes the short between CKT 873 and CKT 830. Is the repair complete?	—	Refer to *Diagnostic System Check*	—
14	Replace the damaged wiring harness connectors that cause the short between CKT 873 and CKT 830. Is the repair complete?	—	Refer to *Diagnostic System Check*	—
15	Replace the left front wheel speed sensor harness. Is the repair complete?	—	Refer to *Diagnostic System Check*	—
16	Replace the left front wheel speed sensor. Is the repair complete?	—	Refer to *Diagnostic System Check*	—
17	Replace the EBCM. Is the repair complete?	—	Refer to *Diagnostic System Check*	—
18	Is malfunction intermittent or is not present at this time?	—	Refer to Diagnostic Aids for more information	—

GC402980305900CX

Fig. 26 Code C1225: LH Front Excessive Wheel Speed Variation (Part 3 of 3). Alero,, Grand Am & Malibu

Circuit Description

As a toothed ring passes by the wheel speed sensor, changes in the electromagnetic field cause the wheel speed sensor to produce an AC voltage signal. The frequency of the AC voltage signal is proportional to the wheel speed. The amplitude of the AC voltage signal is directly related to wheel speed and the proximity of the wheel speed sensor to the toothed ring. The proximity of the wheel speed sensor to the toothed ring is also referred to as the air gap.

Conditions for Setting the DTC

DTC C1226 can set when the brake is off.

DTC C1226 detects a situation in which the right front wheel acceleration or deceleration is beyond specified limits.

Action Taken When the DTC Sets

- A malfunction DTC stores.
- The ABS disables.
- The ABS warning indicator turns on.

Conditions for Clearing the DTC

- The condition responsible for setting the DTC no longer exists and the Scan Tool Clear DTCs function is used.
- 100 drive cycles pass with no DTCs detected. A drive cycle consists of starting the vehicle, driving the vehicle over 16 km/h (10 mph), stopping and then turning the ignition switch to the OFF position.

Diagnostic Aids

The following conditions may cause an intermittent malfunction:

- A poor connection
- Rubbed-through wire insulation
- A broken wire inside the insulation

Use the enhanced diagnostic function of the Scan Tool in order to measure the frequency of the malfunction.

If the customer's comments reflect that the amber ABS warning indicator is on only during moist environmental changes (rain, snow, vehicle wash), inspect all the wheel speed sensor circuitry for signs of water intrusion. If the DTC is not current, clear all DTCs and simulate the effects of water intrusion by using the following procedure:

1. Spray the suspected area with a five percent saltwater solution.
   Add two teaspoons of salt to twelve ounces of water to make a five percent saltwater solution.
2. Test drive the vehicle over various road surfaces (bumps, turns, etc.) above 24 km/h (15 mph) for at least 30 seconds.
3. If the DTC returns, replace the suspected harness.

Thoroughly inspect any circuitry that may be causing the intermittent complaint for the following conditions:

- Backed out terminals
- Improper mating
- Broken locks
- Improperly formed or damaged terminals
- Poor terminal-to-wiring connections
- Physical damage to the wiring harness

Resistance of the wheel speed sensor will increase with an increase in sensor temperature.

Use the following procedure when replacing a wheel speed sensor or harness:

1. Inspect the wheel speed sensor terminals and harness connector for corrosion and/or water intrusion.
2. Replace the wheel speed sensor and jumper harness if evidence of corrosion or water intrusion exists.

GC402980305903AX

Fig. 27 Code C1226: RH Front Excessive Wheel Speed Variation (Part 1 of 3). Alero, Grand Am & Malibu

Step	Action	Value(s)	Yes	No
1	Was the Diagnostic System Check performed?	—	*Go to Step 2*	Refer to *Diagnostic System Check*
2	1. Turn the ignition switch to the OFF position. 2. Inspect the right front wheel speed sensor and the right front wheel speed sensor harness connector for physical damage. Is there any physical damage?	—	*Go to Step 16*	*Go to Step 3*
3	Inspect the following components for physical damage: • The right front wheel speed sensor jumper harness • The right front wheel speed sensor jumper harness connectors. Is there any physical damage?	—	*Go to Step 15*	*Go to Step 4*
4	1. Disconnect the right front wheel speed sensor directly at the right front wheel speed sensor connector. 2. Use the *J 39200* in order to measure the resistance between the right front wheel speed sensor connector terminal A and the right front wheel speed sensor connector terminal B. Is the resistance within the specified range?	950–1250 Ω	*Go to Step 5*	*Go to Step 16*
5	1. Select the A/C VOLTAGE scale on the *J 39200*. 2. Spin the right front wheel by hand while observing the voltage reading on the *J 39200*. Is the voltage equal to or greater than the specified voltage?	100 mV	*Go to Step 6*	*Go to Step 16*
6	1. Disconnect the EBCM connector. 2. Use the *J 39200* in order to measure the resistance between the EBCM connector terminal 9 and the EBCM connector terminal 22. Is the resistance within the specified range?	OL (Infinite)	*Go to Step 7*	*Go to Step 8*
7	1. Inspect the EBCM connector for the following conditions: • Damage • Poor terminal contact • Terminal corrosion (These conditions may cause a short between the EBCM connector terminal 9 and the EBCM connector terminal 22. 2. Inspect the remaining terminals of the EBCM connector for the following conditions: • Damage • Poor terminal contact • Terminal corrosion. Are there signs of poor terminal contact, corrosion, or damaged terminals?	—	*Go to Step 12*	*Go to Step 8*

GC402980305903DX

Fig. 27 Code C1226: RH Front Excessive Wheel Speed Variation (Part 2 of 3). Alero, Grand Am & Malibu

Step	Action	Value(s)	Yes	No
8	Inspect the wiring of CKT 872 and CKT 833 for signs of damage that may cause a short between CKT 872 and CKT 833. Are there any signs of damaged wiring?	—	*Go to Step 13*	*Go to Step 9*
9	Inspect the harness connectors of CKT 872 and CKT 833 for signs of damage that may cause a short between CKT 872 and CKT 833. Are there any signs of damaged connectors?	—	*Go to Step 14*	*Go to Step 10*
10	1. Reconnect the EBCM harness connector. 2. Reconnect the right front wheel speed sensor harness connector. 3. Install a *Scan Tool*. 4. Test drive the vehicle at a speed above 24 km/h (15 mph) for at least 30 seconds. 5. Use the *Scan Tool* in order to read the DTCs. Does DTC C1226 set as a current DTC?	—	*Go to Step 11*	*Go to Step 18*
11	1. Select the Data List on the *Scan Tool*. 2. Monitor the wheel speed sensor speeds. 3. Use the following procedure to drive the vehicle when testing the wheel speed sensor: 3.1. Slowly accelerate to 65 km/h (40 mph) 3.2. Slowly decelerate to 0 km/h (0 mph). Is the speed of the right front wheel speed sensor constantly higher than the speed of the three remaining wheel speed sensors?	—	*Go to Step 16*	*Go to Step 17*
12	Replace all of the terminals that exhibit signs of poor terminal contact, corrosion, or damaged terminal(s). Is the repair complete?	—	Refer to *Diagnostic System Check*	—
13	Replace the damaged wiring harness that causes the short between CKT 872 and CKT 833. Is the repair complete?	—	Refer to *Diagnostic System Check*	—
14	Replace the damaged wiring harness connectors that cause the short between CKT 872 and CKT 833. Is the repair complete?	—	Refer to *Diagnostic System Check*	—
15	Replace the right front wheel speed sensor harness. Is the repair complete?	—	Refer to *Diagnostic System Check*	—
16	Replace the right front wheel speed sensor. Is the repair complete?	—	Refer to *Diagnostic System Check*	—
17	Replace the EBCM. Is the repair complete?	—	Refer to *Diagnostic System Check*	—
18	Is malfunction intermittent or is not present at this time?	—	Refer to Diagnostic Aids for more information	—

GC402980305900EX

Fig. 27 Code C1226: RH Front Excessive Wheel Speed Variation (Part 3 of 3). Alero, Grand Am & Malibu

Circuit Description

As a toothed ring passes by the wheel speed sensor, changes in the electromagnetic field cause the wheel speed sensor to produce an AC voltage signal. The frequency of the AC voltage signal is proportional to the wheel speed. The amplitude of the AC voltage signal is directly related to wheel speed and the proximity of the wheel speed sensor to the toothed ring. The proximity of the wheel speed sensor to the toothed ring is also referred to as the air gap.

Conditions for Setting the DTC

DTC C1227 can set when the brake is off.

DTC C1227 detects a situation in which the left rear wheel acceleration or deceleration is beyond specified limits.

Action Taken When the DTC Sets

- A malfunction DTC stores.
- The ABS disables.
- The ABS warning indicator turns on.

Conditions for Clearing the DTC

- The condition responsible for setting the DTC no longer exists and the Scan Tool Clear DTCs function is used.
- 100 drive cycles pass with no DTCs detected. A drive cycle consists of starting the vehicle, driving the vehicle over 16 km/h (10 mph), stopping and then turning the ignition switch to the OFF position.

Diagnostic Aids

The following conditions may cause an intermittent malfunction:

- A poor connection
- Rubbed-through wire insulation
- A broken wire inside the insulation

Use the enhanced diagnostic function of the Scan Tool in order to measure the frequency of the malfunction.

If the customer's comments reflect that the amber ABS warning indicator is on only during moist environmental changes (rain, snow, vehicle wash), inspect all the wheel speed sensor circuitry for signs of water intrusion. If the DTC is not current, clear all DTCs and simulate the effects of water intrusion by using the following procedure:

1. Spray the suspected area with a five percent saltwater solution.
   Add two teaspoons of salt to twelve ounces of water to make a five percent saltwater solution.
2. Test drive the vehicle over various road surfaces (bumps, turns, etc.) above 24 km/h (15 mph) for at least 30 seconds.
3. If the DTC returns, replace the suspected harness.

Thoroughly inspect any circuitry that may be causing the intermittent complaint for the following conditions:

- Backed out terminals
- Improper mating
- Broken locks
- Improperly formed or damaged terminals
- Poor terminal-to-wiring connections
- Physical damage to the wiring harness

Resistance of the wheel speed sensor will increase with an increase in sensor temperature.

Use the following procedure when replacing a wheel speed sensor or harness:

1. Inspect the wheel speed sensor terminals and harness connector for corrosion and/or water intrusion.
2. Replace the wheel speed sensor jumper harness if evidence of corrosion or water intrusion exists.

GC402980305902AX

Fig. 28 Code C1227: LH Rear Excessive Wheel Speed Variation (Part 1 of 3). Alero, Grand Am & Malibu

Step	Action	Value(s)	Yes	No
1	Was the Diagnostic System Check performed?	—	*Go to Step 2*	Refer to *Diagnostic System Check*
2	1. Turn the ignition switch to the OFF position. 2. Inspect the left rear wheel speed sensor and the left rear wheel speed sensor harness connector for physical damage. Is there any physical damage?	—	*Go to Step 16*	*Go to Step 3*
3	Inspect the following components for physical damage: • The left rear wheel speed sensor harness • The left rear wheel speed sensor harness connectors Is there any physical damage?	—	*Go to Step 15*	*Go to Step 4*
4	1. Disconnect the left rear wheel speed sensor directly at the left rear wheel speed sensor connector. 2. Use the *J 39200* in order to measure the resistance between the left rear wheel speed sensor connector terminal A and the left rear wheel speed sensor connector terminal B. Is the resistance within the specified range?	950–1250 Ω	*Go to Step 5*	*Go to Step 16*
5	1. Select the A/C VOLTAGE scale on the *J 39200*. 2. Spin the left rear wheel by hand while observing the voltage reading on the *J 39200*. Is the voltage equal to or greater than the specified voltage?	100 mV	*Go to Step 6*	*Go to Step 16*
6	1. Disconnect the EBCM connector. 2. Use the *J 39200* in order to measure the resistance between the EBCM connector terminal 10 and the EBCM connector terminal 23. Is the resistance within the specified range?	OL (Infinite)	*Go to Step 7*	*Go to Step 8*
7	1. Inspect the EBCM connector for the following conditions: • Damage • Poor terminal contact • Terminal corrosion Damage, poor terminal contact, and terminal corrosion may cause a short between the EBCM connector terminal 10 and the EBCM connector terminal 23. 2. Inspect the remaining terminals of the EBCM connector for the following conditions: • Damage • Poor terminal contact • Terminal corrosion Are there signs of poor terminal contact, corrosion, or damaged terminals?	—	*Go to Step 12*	*Go to Step 8*

GC402980305900FX

Fig. 28 Code C1227: LH Rear Excessive Wheel Speed Variation (Part 2 of 3). Alero, Grand Am & Malibu

Step	Action	Value(s)	Yes	No
8	Inspect the wiring of CKT 885 and CKT 884 for signs of damage that may cause a short between CKT 885 and CKT 884. Are there any signs of damaged wiring?	—	*Go to Step 13*	*Go to Step 9*
9	Inspect the harness connectors of CKT 885 and CKT 884 for signs of damage that may cause a short between CKT 885 and CKT 884. Are there any signs of damaged connectors?	—	*Go to Step 14*	*Go to Step 10*
10	1. Reconnect the EBCM harness connector. 2. Reconnect the left rear wheel speed sensor harness connector. 3. Install a *Scan Tool*. 4. Test drive the vehicle at a speed above 24 km/h (15 mph) for at least 30 seconds. 5. Use the *Scan Tool* in order to read the DTCs. Does DTC C1227 set as a current DTC?	—	*Go to Step 11*	*Go to Step 18*
11	1. Select Data List on the *Scan Tool*. 2. Monitor the wheel speed sensor speeds. 3. Use the following procedure to drive the vehicle when testing the wheel speed sensor: 3.1. Slowly accelerate to 65 km/h (40 mph). 3.2. Slowly decelerate to 0 km/h (0 mph). Is the speed of the left rear wheel speed sensor constantly higher or lower than the speed of the three remaining wheel speed sensors?	—	*Go to Step 16*	*Go to Step 17*
12	Replace all of the terminals that exhibit signs of poor terminal contact, corrosion, or damaged terminal(s). Is the repair complete?	—	Refer to *Diagnostic System Check*	—
13	Replace the damaged wiring harness that causes the short between CKT 885 and CKT 884. Is the repair complete?	—	Refer to *Diagnostic System Check*	—
14	Replace the damaged wiring harness connectors that cause the short between CKT 885 and CKT 884. Is the repair complete?	—	Refer to *Diagnostic System Check*	—
15	Replace the left rear wheel speed sensor harness. Is the repair complete?	—	Refer to *Diagnostic System Check*	—
16	Replace the left rear wheel speed sensor. Is the repair complete?	—	Refer to *Diagnostic System Check*	—
17	Replace the EBCM. Is the repair complete?	—	Refer to *Diagnostic System Check*	—
18	Is malfunction intermittent or is not present at this time?	—	Refer to Diagnostic Aids for more information	—

GC402980305900GX

Fig. 28 Code C1227: LH Rear Excessive Wheel Speed Variation (Part 3 of 3). Alero, Grand Am & Malibu

Circuit Description

As a toothed ring passes by the wheel speed sensor, changes in the electromagnetic field cause the wheel speed sensor to produce an AC voltage signal. The frequency of the AC voltage signal is proportional to the wheel speed. The amplitude of the AC voltage signal is directly related to wheel speed and the proximity of the wheel speed sensor to the toothed ring. The proximity of the wheel speed sensor to the toothed ring is also referred to as the air gap.

Conditions for Setting the DTC

DTC C1228 can set when the brake is off.

DTC C1228 detects a situation in which the right rear wheel acceleration or deceleration is beyond specified limits.

Action Taken When the DTC Sets

- A malfunction DTC stores.
- The ABS disables.
- The ABS warning indicator turns on.

Conditions for Clearing the DTC

- The condition responsible for setting the DTC no longer exists and the Scan Tool Clear DTCs function is used.
- 100 drive cycles pass with no DTCs detected. A drive cycle consists of starting the vehicle, driving the vehicle over 16 km/h (10 mph), stopping and then turning the ignition switch to the OFF position.

Diagnostic Aids

The following conditions may cause an intermittent malfunction:

- A poor connection
- Rubbed-through wire insulation
- A broken wire inside the insulation

Use the enhanced diagnostic function of the Scan Tool in order to measure the frequency of the malfunction.

If the customer's comments reflect that the amber ABS warning indicator is on only during moist environmental changes (rain, snow, vehicle wash), inspect all the wheel speed sensor circuitry for signs of water intrusion. If the DTC is not current, clear all DTCs and simulate the effects of water intrusion by using the following procedure:

1. Spray the suspected area with a five percent saltwater solution.
   Add two teaspoons of salt to twelve ounces of water to make a five percent saltwater solution.
2. Test drive the vehicle over various road surfaces (bumps, turns, etc.) above 24 km/h (15 mph) for at least 30 seconds.
3. If the DTC returns, replace the suspected harness.

Thoroughly inspect any circuitry that may be causing the intermittent complaint for the following conditions:

- Backed out terminals
- Improper mating
- Broken locks
- Improperly formed or damaged terminals
- Poor terminal-to-wiring connections
- Physical damage to the wiring harness

Resistance of the wheel speed sensor will increase with an increase in sensor temperature.

Use the following procedure when replacing a wheel speed sensor or harness:

1. Inspect the wheel speed sensor terminals and harness connector for corrosion and/or water intrusion.
2. Replace the wheel speed sensor and jumper harness if evidence of corrosion or water intrusion exists.

GC402980305901AX

Fig. 29 Code C1228: RH Rear Excessive Wheel Speed Variation (Part 1 of 3). Alero, Grand Am & Malibu

Step	Action	Value(s)	Yes	No
1	Was the Diagnostic System Check performed?	—	*Go to Step 2*	Refer to *Diagnostic System Check*
2	1. Turn the ignition switch to the OFF position. 2. Inspect the right rear wheel speed sensor and the rear axle harness connector for physical damage. Is there any physical damage?	—	*Go to Step 16*	*Go to Step 3*
3	Inspect the following components for physical damage: • The rear axle harness • The rear axle harness connectors Is there any physical damage?	—	*Go to Step 15*	*Go to Step 4*
4	1. Disconnect the right rear wheel speed sensor directly at the right rear wheel speed sensor connector. 2. Use the *J 39200* in order to measure the resistance between the right rear wheel speed sensor connector terminal A and the right rear wheel speed sensor connector terminal B. Is the resistance within the specified range?	950–1250 Ω	*Go to Step 5*	*Go to Step 16*
5	1. Select the A/C VOLTAGE scale on the *J 39200*. 2. Spin the right rear wheel by hand while observing the voltage reading on the *J 39200*. Is the voltage equal to or greater than the specified voltage?	100 mV	*Go to Step 6*	*Go to Step 16*
6	1. Disconnect the EBCM connector. 2. Use the *J 39200* in order to measure the resistance between the EBCM connector terminal 11 and the EBCM connector terminal 24. Is the resistance within the specified range?	OL (Infinite)	*Go to Step 7*	*Go to Step 8*
7	1. Inspect the EBCM connector for the following conditions: • Damage • Poor terminal contact • Terminal corrosion Damage, poor terminal contact may cause a short between the EBCM connector terminal 11 and the EBCM connector terminal 24. 2. Inspect the remaining terminals of the EBCM connector for the following conditions: • Damage • Poor terminal contact • Terminal corrosion Are there signs of poor terminal contact, corrosion, or damaged terminals?	—	*Go to Step 12*	*Go to Step 8*

GC402980305900HX

Fig. 29 Code C1228: RH Rear Excessive Wheel Speed Variation (Part 2 of 3). Alero, Grand Am & Malibu

Step	Action	Value(s)	Yes	No
8	Inspect the wiring of CKT 883 and CKT 882 for signs of damage that may cause a short between CKT 883 and CKT 882. Are there any signs of damaged wiring?	—	*Go to Step 13*	*Go to Step 9*
9	Inspect the harness connectors of CKT 883 and CKT 882 for signs of damage that may cause a short between CKT 883 and CKT 882. Are there any signs of damaged connectors?	—	*Go to Step 14*	*Go to Step 10*
10	1. Reconnect the EBCM harness connector. 2. Reconnect the right rear wheel speed sensor harness connector. 3. Install a *Scan Tool*. 4. Test drive the vehicle at a speed above 24 km/h (15 mph) for at least 30 seconds. 5. Use the *Scan Tool* in order to read the DTCs. Does DTC C1228 set as a current DTC?	—	*Go to Step 11*	*Go to Step 18*
11	1. Select Data List on the *Scan Tool*. 2. Monitor the wheel speed sensor speeds. 3. Use the following procedure to drive the vehicle when testing the wheel speed sensor: 3.1. Slowly accelerate to 65 km/h (40 mph). 3.2. Slowly decelerate to 0 km/h (0 mph). Is the speed of the right rear wheel speed sensor constantly higher or lower than the speed of the three remaining wheel speed sensors?	—	*Go to Step 16*	*Go to Step 17*
12	Replace all of the terminals that exhibit signs of poor terminal contact, corrosion, or damaged terminal(s). Is the repair complete?	—	Refer to *Diagnostic System Check*	—
13	Replace the damaged wiring harness that causes the short between CKT 883 and CKT 882. Is the repair complete?	—	Refer to *Diagnostic System Check*	—
14	Replace the damaged wiring harness connectors that cause the short between CKT 883 and CKT 882. Is the repair complete?	—	Refer to *Diagnostic System Check*	—
15	Replace the rear axle harness. Is the repair complete?	—	Refer to *Diagnostic System Check*	—
16	Replace the right rear wheel speed sensor. Is the repair complete?	—	Refer to *Diagnostic System Check*	—
17	Replace the EBCM. Is the repair complete?	—	Refer to *Diagnostic System Check*	—
18	Is malfunction intermittent or is not present at this time?	—	Refer to Diagnostic Aids for more information	—

GC402980305900IX

Fig. 29 Code C1228: RH Rear Excessive Wheel Speed Variation (Part 3 of 3). Alero, Grand Am & Malibu

Step	Action	Value(s)	Yes	No
1	Was the Diagnostic System Check performed?	—	*Go to Step 2*	Refer to *Diagnostic System Check*
2	1. Turn the ignition switch to the OFF position. 2. Make a 5 percent saltwater solution. 3. Thoroughly spray the left front wheel speed sensor harness with the saltwater solution. 4. Disconnect the EBCM harness connector. 5. Use the *J 39200* in order to measure the resistance between the EBCM harness connector terminal 8 and the EBCM harness connector terminal 21. Is the resistance within the specified range?	950–1250 Ω	*Go to Step 3*	*Go to Step 11*
3	Use the *J 39200* in order to measure the resistance between the EBCM harness connector terminal 21 and ground. Is the resistance within the specified range?	OL (Infinite)	*Go to Step 4*	*Go to Step 14*
4	1. Turn the ignition switch to the RUN position. Do not start the engine. 2. Use the *J 39200* in order to measure the voltage between the EBCM harness connector terminal 21 and ground. Is the voltage within the specified range?	0–1 V	*Go to Step 7*	*Go to Step 5*
5	1. Turn the ignition switch to the OFF position. 2. Disconnect the left front wheel speed sensor at the left front wheel speed sensor connector. 3. Turn the ignition switch to the RUN position. Do not start the engine. 4. Use the *J 39200* in order to measure the voltage between the EBCM harness connector terminal 21 and ground Is the voltage within the specified range?	0–1 V	*Go to Step 6*	*Go to Step 19*
6	Use the *J 39200* in order to measure the voltage between the EBCM harness connector terminal 8 and ground. Is the voltage within the specified range?	0–1 V	*Go to Step 31*	*Go to Step 20*

GC402980306000BX

Fig. 30 Code C1232: LH Front Wheel Speed Circuit Open Or Shorted (Part 2 of 5). Alero, Grand Am & Malibu

Circuit Description

As a toothed ring passes by the wheel speed sensor, changes in the electromagnetic field cause the wheel speed sensor to produce an AC voltage signal. The frequency of the AC voltage signal is proportional to the wheel speed. The amplitude of the AC voltage signal is directly related to wheel speed and the proximity of the wheel speed sensor to the toothed ring. The proximity of the wheel speed sensor to the toothed ring is also referred to as the air gap.

Conditions for Setting the DTC

DTC C1232 can set anytime after initialization.

A malfunction exists if either of the left front wheel speed sensor circuits are open or shorted to voltage or ground.

Action Taken When the DTC Sets

- A malfunction DTC stores.
- The ABS disables.
- The ABS warning indicator turns on.

Conditions for Clearing the DTC

- The condition responsible for setting the DTC no longer exists and the Scan Tool Clear DTCs function is used.
- 100 drive cycles pass with no DTCs detected. A drive cycle consists of starting the vehicle, driving the vehicle over 16 km/h (10 mph), stopping and then turning the ignition switch to the OFF position.

Diagnostic Aids

The following conditions may cause an intermittent malfunction:

- A poor connection
- Rubbed-through wire insulation
- A broken wire inside the insulation

Use the enhanced diagnostic function of the Scan Tool in order to measure the frequency of the malfunction.

If the customer's comments reflect that the amber ABS warning indicator is on only during moist environmental changes (rain, snow, vehicle wash), inspect all the wheel speed sensor circuitry for signs of water intrusion. If the DTC is not current, clear all DTCs and simulate the effects of water intrusion by using the following procedure:

1. Spray the suspected area with a five percent saltwater solution.
   Add two teaspoons of salt to twelve ounces of water to make a five percent saltwater solution.
2. Test drive the vehicle over various road surfaces (bumps, turns, etc.) above 24 km/h (15 mph) for at least 30 seconds.
3. If the DTC returns, replace the suspected harness.

Thoroughly inspect any circuitry that may be causing the intermittent complaint for the following conditions:

- Backed out terminals
- Improper mating
- Broken locks
- Improperly formed or damaged terminals
- Poor terminal-to-wiring connections
- Physical damage to the wiring harness

Resistance of the wheel speed sensor will increase with an increase in sensor temperature.

Use the following procedure when replacing a wheel speed sensor:

1. Inspect the wheel speed sensor terminals and harness connector for corrosion and/or water intrusion.
2. Replace the wheel speed sensor and jumper harness if evidence of corrosion or water intrusion exists.

GC402980306000AA

Fig. 30 Code C1232: LH Front Wheel Speed Circuit Open Or Shorted (Part 1 of 5). Alero, Grand Am & Malibu

Step	Action	Value(s)	Yes	No
7	1. Turn the ignition switch to the OFF position. 2. Inspect the following terminals: • The EBCM connector terminal 8 • The EBCM connector terminal 21 • The remaining terminals of the EBCM connector. 3. Inspect the above terminals for the following conditions: • Terminal damage • Poor terminal contact • Terminal corrosion Damage, terminal corrosion, and poor terminal contact may cause an open circuit, a short to voltage, or a short to ground. Are there signs of poor terminal contact, terminal corrosion, or damaged terminals?	—	*Go to Step 27*	*Go to Step 8*
8	Inspect the wiring of CKT 873 and CKT 830 for signs of wire damage. Wire damage may cause the following conditions in CKT 873 and CKT 830: • An open circuit • A short to voltage • A short to ground Are there signs of damaged wiring?	—	*Go to Step 21*	*Go to Step 9*
9	Inspect the harness connectors of CKT 873 and CKT 830 for signs of wire damage. Wire damage may cause the following conditions in CKT 873 and CKT 830: • An open circuit • A short to voltage • A short to ground Are there signs of damaged connectors?	—	*Go to Step 22*	*Go to Step 10*
10	1. Reconnect the EBCM connector. 2. Reconnect the left front wheel speed sensor harness connector. 3. Install a *Scan Tool*. 4. Test drive the vehicle at a speed above 24 km/h (15 mph) for at least 30 seconds. 5. Use the *Scan Tool* in order to read the DTCs. Does DTC C1232 set as a current DTC?	—	*Go to Step 30*	*Go to Step 31*
11	1. Disconnect the left front wheel speed sensor directly at the left front wheel speed sensor connector. 2. Use the *J 39200* in order to measure the resistance between the EBCM harness connector terminal 21 and the left front wheel speed sensor harness connector terminal B. Is the resistance within the specified range?	0–2 Ω	*Go to Step 12*	*Go to Step 23*
12	Use the *J 39200* in order to measure the resistance between the EBCM connector terminal 8 and the left front wheel speed sensor harness connector terminal A. Is the resistance within the specified range?	0–2 Ω	*Go to Step 13*	*Go to Step 24*

GC402980306000CX

Fig. 30 Code C1232: LH Front Wheel Speed Circuit Open Or Shorted (Part 3 of 5). Alero, Grand Am & Malibu

Step	Action	Value(s)	Yes	No
13	Use the *J 39200* in order to measure the resistance between the left front wheel speed sensor connector terminal A and the left front wheel speed sensor connector terminal B. Is the resistance within the specified range?	950–1250 Ω	*Go to Step 31*	*Go to Step 28*
14	Use the *J 39200* in order to measure the resistance between the EBCM connector terminal 21 and ground. Is the resistance within the specified range?	OL (Infinite)	*Go to Step 15*	*Go to Step 25*
15	Use the *J 39200* in order to measure the resistance between the EBCM connector terminal 8 and ground. Is the resistance within the specified range?	OL (Infinite)	*Go to Step 16*	*Go to Step 26*
16	1. Thoroughly respray the left front wheel speed sensor harness with the saltwater solution. 2. Disconnect the left front wheel speed sensor directly at the left front wheel speed sensor. 3. Use the *J 39200* in order to measure the resistance between the left front wheel speed sensor harness connector terminal A and ground. Is the resistance within the specified range?	OL (Infinite)	*Go to Step 17*	*Go to Step 29*
17	Use the *J 39200* in order to measure the resistance between the left front wheel speed sensor harness connector terminal B and ground. Is the resistance within the specified range?	OL (Infinite)	*Go to Step 18*	*Go to Step 29*
18	Use the *J 39200* in order to measure the resistance between the left front wheel speed sensor connector terminal A and ground. Is the resistance within the specified range?	OL (Infinite)	*Go to Step 31*	*Go to Step 28*
19	Repair the short to voltage in CKT 873. If the short to voltage is found in the left front wheel speed sensor harness, replace the left front wheel speed harness. Is the repair complete?	—	Refer to *Diagnostic System Check*	—
20	Repair the short to voltage in CKT 830. If the short to voltage is found in the left front wheel speed sensor harness, replace the left front wheel speed harness. Is the repair complete?	—	Refer to *Diagnostic System Check*	—
21	Repair the wiring damage in CKT 873 or CKT 830. If the wiring damage is found in the left front wheel speed sensor harness, replace the left front wheel speed jumper harness. Is the repair complete?	—	Refer to *Diagnostic System Check*	—
22	Repair the connector damage in CKT 873 or CKT 830. If the connector damage is found in the left front wheel speed sensor harness, replace the left front wheel speed harness. Is the repair complete?	—	Refer to *Diagnostic System Check*	—
23	Repair the open or high resistance in CKT 873. If the open or high resistance is found in the left front wheel speed sensor harness, replace the left front wheel speed sensor harness. Is the repair complete?	—	Refer to *Diagnostic System Check*	—

GC402980306000DX

Fig. 30 Code C1232: LH Front Wheel Speed Circuit Open Or Shorted (Part 4 of 5). Alero, Grand Am & Malibu

Step	Action	Value(s)	Yes	No
24	Repair the open or high resistance in CKT 830. If the open or high resistance is found in the left front wheel speed sensor harness, replace the left front wheel speed harness. Is the repair complete?	—	Refer to *Diagnostic System Check*	—
25	Repair the short to ground in CKT 873. If the short to ground is found in the left front wheel speed sensor harness, replace the left front wheel speed harness. Is the repair complete?	—	Refer to *Diagnostic System Check*	—
26	Repair the short to ground in CKT 830. If the short to ground is found in the left front wheel speed sensor harness, replace the left front wheel speed harness. Is the repair complete?	—	Refer to *Diagnostic System Check*	—
27	Replace all of the terminals and the connectors that exhibit signs of poor terminal contact, corrosion, or damaged terminals. Is the repair complete?	—	Refer to *Diagnostic System Check*	—
28	Replace the left front wheel speed sensor. Is the repair complete?	—	Refer to *Diagnostic System Check*	—
29	Replace the left front wheel speed sensor harness. Is the repair complete?	—	Refer to *Diagnostic System Check*	—
30	Replace the EBCM. Is the repair complete?	—	Refer to *Diagnostic System Check*	—
31	The malfunction is intermittent or not present at this time. Inspect all of the connectors and the harnesses for damage that could cause the following conditions: • An open or a high resistance • A short to ground • A short to voltage The sensor harness must be replaced if the sensor harness is damaged. Refer to Diagnostic Aids for more information.	—	—	—

GC402980306000QX

Fig. 30 Code C1232: LH Front Wheel Speed Circuit Open Or Shorted (Part 5 of 5). Alero, Grand Am & Malibu

Circuit Description

As a toothed ring passes by the wheel speed sensor, changes in the electromagnetic field cause the wheel speed sensor to produce an AC voltage signal. The frequency of the AC voltage signal is proportional to the wheel speed. The amplitude of the AC voltage signal is directly related to wheel speed and the proximity of the wheel speed sensor to the toothed ring. The proximity of the wheel speed sensor to the toothed ring is also referred to as the air gap.

Conditions for Setting the DTC

DTC C1233 can set anytime after initialization.

A malfunction exists if either of the right front wheel speed sensor circuits are open or shorted to voltage or ground.

Action Taken When the DTC Sets

- A malfunction DTC stores.
- The ABS disables.
- The ABS warning indicator turns on.

Conditions for Clearing the DTC

- The condition responsible for setting the DTC no longer exists and the Scan Tool Clear DTCs function is used.
- 100 drive cycles pass with no DTCs detected. A drive cycle consists of starting the vehicle, driving the vehicle over 16 km/h (10 mph), stopping and then turning the ignition switch to the OFF position.

Diagnostic Aids

The following conditions may cause an intermittent malfunction:

- A poor connection
- Rubbed-through wire insulation
- A broken wire inside the insulation

Use the enhanced diagnostic function of the Scan Tool in order to measure the frequency of the malfunction.

If the customer's comments reflect that the amber ABS warning indicator is on only during moist environmental changes (rain, snow, vehicle wash), inspect all the wheel speed sensor circuitry for signs of water intrusion. If the DTC is not current, clear all DTCs and simulate the effects of water intrusion by using the following procedure:

1. Spray the suspected area with a five percent saltwater solution.
   Add two teaspoons of salt to twelve ounces of water to make a five percent saltwater solution.
2. Test drive the vehicle over various road surfaces (bumps, turns, etc.) above 24 km/h (15 mph) for at least 30 seconds.
3. If the DTC returns, replace the suspected harness.

Thoroughly inspect any circuitry that may be causing the intermittent complaint for the following conditions:

- Backed out terminals
- Improper mating
- Broken locks
- Improperly formed or damaged terminals
- Poor terminal-to-wiring connections
- Physical damage to the wiring harness

Resistance of the wheel speed sensor will increase with an increase in sensor temperature.

Use the following procedure when replacing a wheel speed sensor:

1. Inspect the wheel speed sensor terminals and harness connector for corrosion and/or water intrusion.
2. Replace the wheel speed sensor and jumper harness if evidence of corrosion or water intrusion exists.

GC402980306001AX

Fig. 31 Code C1233: RH Front Wheel Speed Circuit Open Or Shorted (Part 1 of 5). Alero, Grand Am & Malibu

Step	Action	Value(s)	Yes	No
1	Was the Diagnostic System Check performed?	—	*Go to Step 2*	Refer to *Diagnostic System Check*
2	1. Turn the ignition switch to the OFF position. 2. Make a 5 percent saltwater solution. 3. Thoroughly spray the right front wheel speed sensor harness with the saltwater solution. 4. Disconnect the EBCM harness connector. 5. Use the *J 39200* in order to measure the resistance between the EBCM harness connector terminal 9 and the EBCM harness connector terminal 22. Is the resistance within the specified range?	950–1250 Ω	*Go to Step 3*	*Go to Step 11*
3	Use the *J 39200* in order to measure the resistance between the EBCM harness connector terminal 22 and ground. Is the resistance within the specified range?	OL (Infinite)	*Go to Step 4*	*Go to Step 14*
4	1. Turn the ignition switch to the RUN position. Do not start the engine. 2. Use the *J 39200* in order to measure the voltage between the EBCM harness connector terminal 22 and ground. Is the voltage within the specified range?	0–1 V	*Go to Step 7*	*Go to Step 5*
5	1. Turn the ignition switch to the OFF position. 2. Disconnect the right front wheel speed sensor at the right front wheel speed sensor connector. 3. Turn the ignition switch to the RUN position. Do not start the engine. 4. Use the *J 39200* in order to measure the voltage between the EBCM harness connector terminal 22 and ground. Is the voltage within the specified range?	0–1 V	*Go to Step 6*	*Go to Step 19*
6	Use the *J 39200* in order to measure the voltage between the EBCM harness connector terminal 9 and ground. Is the voltage within the specified range?	0–1 V	*Go to Step 31*	*Go to Step 20*

GC402980306000EX

Fig. 31 Code C1233: RH Front Wheel Speed Circuit Open Or Shorted (Part 2 of 5). Alero, Grand Am & Malibu

Step	Action	Value(s)	Yes	No
7	1. Turn the ignition switch to the OFF position. 2. Inspect the following terminals: • The EBCM connector terminal 9 • The EBCM connector terminal 22 • The remaining terminals of the EBCM connector. 3. Inspect the above terminals for the following conditions: • Terminal damage • Poor terminal contact • Terminal corrosion Terminal damage, terminal corrosion, and poor terminal contact may cause an open circuit, a short to voltage, or a short to ground. Are there signs of poor terminal contact, terminal corrosion, or damaged terminals?	—	*Go to Step 27*	*Go to Step 8*
8	Inspect the wiring of CKT 833 and CKT 872 for signs of wire damage. Wire damage may cause the following conditions in CKT 833 and CKT 872: • An open circuit • A short to voltage • A short to ground Are there signs of damaged wiring?	—	*Go to Step 21*	*Go to Step 9*
9	Inspect the harness connectors of CKT 833 and CKT 872 for signs of wire damage. Wire damage may cause the following conditions in CKT 833 and CKT 872: • An open circuit • A short to voltage • A short to ground Are there signs of damaged connectors?	—	*Go to Step 22*	*Go to Step 10*
10	1. Reconnect the EBCM connector. 2. Reconnect the right front wheel speed sensor harness connector. 3. Install a *Scan Tool*. 4. Test drive the vehicle at a speed above 24 km/h (15 mph) for at least 30 seconds. 5. Use the *Scan Tool* in order to read the DTCs. Does DTC C1233 set as a current DTC?	—	*Go to Step 30*	*Go to Step 31*
11	1. Disconnect the right front wheel speed sensor directly at the right front wheel speed sensor connector. 2. Use the *J 39200* in order to measure the resistance between the EBCM connector terminal 22 and the right front wheel speed sensor harness connector terminal B. Is the resistance within the specified range?	0–2 Ω	*Go to Step 12*	*Go to Step 23*
12	Use the *J 39200* in order to measure the resistance between the EBCM connector terminal 9 and the right front wheel speed sensor harness connector terminal A. Is the resistance within the specified range?	0–2 Ω	*Go to Step 13*	*Go to Step 24*

GC402980306000FX

Fig. 31 Code C1233: RH Front Wheel Speed Circuit Open Or Shorted (Part 3 of 5). Alero, Grand Am & Malibu

Step	Action	Value(s)	Yes	No
13	Use the *J 39200* in order to measure the resistance between the right front wheel speed sensor connector terminal A and the right front wheel speed sensor connector terminal B. Is the resistance within the specified range?	950–1250 Ω	*Go to Step 31*	*Go to Step 28*
14	Use the *J 39200* in order to measure the resistance between the EBCM connector terminal 22 and ground. Is the resistance within the specified range?	OL (Infinite)	*Go to Step 15*	*Go to Step 25*
15	Use the *J 39200* in order to measure the resistance between the EBCM connector terminal 9 and ground. Is the resistance within the specified range?	OL (Infinite)	*Go to Step 16*	*Go to Step 26*
16	1. Thoroughly respray the right front wheel speed sensor harness with the saltwater solution. 2. Disconnect the right front wheel speed sensor directly at the right front wheel speed sensor. 3. Use the *J 39200* in order to measure the resistance between the right front wheel speed sensor harness connector terminal A and ground. Is the resistance within the specified range?	OL (Infinite)	*Go to Step 17*	*Go to Step 29*
17	Use the *J 39200* in order to measure the resistance between the right front wheel speed sensor harness connector terminal B and ground. Is the resistance within the specified range?	OL (Infinite)	*Go to Step 18*	*Go to Step 29*
18	Use the *J 39200* in order to measure the resistance between the right front wheel speed sensor connector terminal A and ground. Is the resistance within the specified range?	OL (Infinite)	*Go to Step 31*	*Go to Step 28*
19	Repair the short to voltage in CKT 833. If the short to voltage is found in the right front wheel speed sensor harness, replace the right front wheel speed harness. Is the repair complete?	—	Refer to *Diagnostic System Check*	—
20	Repair the short to voltage in CKT 872. If the short to voltage is found in the right front wheel speed sensor harness, replace the right front wheel speed harness. Is the repair complete?	—	Refer to *Diagnostic System Check*	—
21	Repair the wiring damage in CKT 833 or CKT 872. If the wiring damage is found in the right front wheel speed sensor harness, replace the right front wheel speed harness. Is the repair complete?	—	Refer to *Diagnostic System Check*	—
22	Repair the connector damage in CKT 833 or CKT 872. If the connector damage is found in the right front wheel speed sensor harness, replace the right front wheel speed harness. Is the repair complete?	—	Refer to *Diagnostic System Check*	—
23	Repair the open or high resistance in CKT 833. If the open or high resistance is found in the right front wheel speed sensor harness, replace the right front wheel speed harness. Is the repair complete?	—	Refer to *Diagnostic System Check*	—

GC402980306000GX

Fig. 31 Code C1233: RH Front Wheel Speed Circuit Open Or Shorted (Part 4 of 5). Alero, Grand Am & Malibu

Step	Action	Value(s)	Yes	No
24	Repair the open or high resistance in CKT 872. If the open or high resistance is found in the right front wheel speed sensor harness, replace the right front wheel speed harness. Is the repair complete?	—	Refer to *Diagnostic System Check*	—
25	Repair the short to ground in CKT 833. If the short to ground is found in the right front wheel speed sensor harness, replace the right front wheel speed harness. Is the repair complete?	—	Refer to *Diagnostic System Check*	—
26	Repair the short to ground in CKT 872. If the short to ground is found in the right front wheel speed sensor harness, replace the right front wheel speed harness. Is the repair complete?	—	Refer to *Diagnostic System Check*	—
27	Replace all of the terminals and the connectors that exhibit signs of poor terminal contact, corrosion, or damaged terminals. Is the repair complete?	—	Refer to *Diagnostic System Check*	—
28	Replace the right front wheel speed sensor. Is the repair complete?	—	Refer to *Diagnostic System Check*	—
29	Replace the right front wheel speed sensor harness. Is the repair complete?	—	Refer to *Diagnostic System Check*	—
30	Replace the EBCM. Is the repair complete?	—	Refer to *Diagnostic System Check*	—
31	The malfunction is intermittent or not present at this time. Inspect all of the connectors and the harnesses for damage that may cause the following conditions: • An open or a high resistance • A short to ground • A short to voltage The wheel speed harness must be replaced if the harness is damaged. Refer to Diagnostic Aids for more information.	—	—	—

GC402980306000HX

Fig. 31 Code C1233: RH Front Wheel Speed Circuit Open Or Shorted (Part 5 of 5). Alero, Grand Am & Malibu

Circuit Description

As a toothed ring passes by the wheel speed sensor, changes in the electromagnetic field cause the wheel speed sensor to produce an AC voltage signal. The frequency of the AC voltage signal is proportional to the wheel speed. The amplitude of the AC voltage signal is directly related to wheel speed and the proximity of the wheel speed sensor to the toothed ring. The proximity of the wheel speed sensor to the toothed ring is also referred to as the air gap.

Conditions for Setting the DTC

DTC C1234 can set anytime after initialization.

A malfunction exists if either of the left rear wheel speed sensor circuits are open or shorted to voltage or ground.

Action Taken When the DTC Sets

- A malfunction DTC stores.
- The ABS disables.
- The ABS warning indicator turns on.

Conditions for Clearing the DTC

- The condition responsible for setting the DTC no longer exists and the Scan Tool Clear DTCs function is used.
- 100 drive cycles pass with no DTCs detected. A drive cycle consists of starting the vehicle, driving the vehicle over 16 km/h (10 mph), stopping and then turning the ignition switch to the OFF position.

Diagnostic Aids

The following conditions may cause an intermittent malfunction:

- A poor connection
- Rubbed-through wire insulation
- A broken wire inside the insulation

Use the enhanced diagnostic function of the Scan Tool in order to measure the frequency of the malfunction.

If the customer's comments reflect that the amber ABS warning indicator is on only during moist environmental changes (rain, snow, vehicle wash), inspect all the wheel speed sensor circuitry for signs of water intrusion. If the DTC is not current, clear all DTCs and simulate the effects of water intrusion by using the following procedure:

1. Spray the suspected area with a five percent saltwater solution.
   Add two teaspoons of salt to twelve ounces of water to make a five percent saltwater solution.
2. Test drive the vehicle over various road surfaces (bumps, turns, etc.) above 24 km/h (15 mph) for at least 30 seconds.
3. If the DTC returns, replace the suspected harness.

Thoroughly inspect any circuitry that may be causing the intermittent complaint for the following conditions:

- Backed out terminals
- Improper mating
- Broken locks
- Improperly formed or damaged terminals
- Poor terminal-to-wiring connections
- Physical damage to the wiring harness

Resistance of the wheel speed sensor will increase with an increase in sensor temperature.

Use the following procedure when replacing a wheel speed sensor or harness:

1. Inspect the wheel speed sensor terminals and harness connector for corrosion and/or water intrusion.
2. Replace the wheel speed sensor and jumper harness if evidence of corrosion or water intrusion exists.

GC402980306002AX

Fig. 32 Code C1234: LH Rear Wheel Speed Circuit Open Or Shorted (Part 1 of 5). Alero, Grand Am & Malibu

Step	Action	Value(s)	Yes	No
1	Was the Diagnostic System Check performed?	—	*Go to Step 2*	Refer to *Diagnostic System Check*
2	1. Turn the ignition switch to the OFF position. 2. Make a 5 percent saltwater solution. 3. Thoroughly spray the left rear wheel speed sensor harness with the saltwater solution. 4. Disconnect the EBCM harness connector. 5. Use the *J 39200* in order to measure the resistance between the EBCM harness connector terminal 10 and the EBCM harness connector terminal 23. Is the resistance within the specified range?	950–1250 Ω	*Go to Step 3*	*Go to Step 11*
3	Use the *J 39200* in order to measure the resistance between the EBCM harness connector terminal 23 and ground. Is the resistance within the specified range?	OL (Infinite)	*Go to Step 4*	*Go to Step 14*
4	1. Turn the ignition switch to the RUN position. Do not start the engine. 2. Use the *J 39200* in order to measure the voltage between the EBCM harness connector terminal 23 and ground. Is the voltage within the specified range?	0–1 V	*Go to Step 7*	*Go to Step 5*
5	1. Turn the ignition switch to the OFF position. 2. Disconnect the left rear wheel speed sensor at the left rear wheel speed sensor connector. 3. Turn the ignition switch to the RUN position. Do not start the engine. 4. Use the *J 39200* in order to measure the voltage between the EBCM harness connector terminal 23 and ground. Is the voltage within the specified range?	0–1 V	*Go to Step 6*	*Go to Step 19*
6	Use the *J 39200* in order to measure the voltage between the EBCM harness connector terminal 10 and ground. Is the voltage within the specified range?	0–1 V	*Go to Step 31*	*Go to Step 20*

GC402980306000IX

Fig. 32 Code C1234: LH Rear Wheel Speed Circuit Open Or Shorted (Part 2 of 5). Alero, Grand Am & Malibu

Step	Action	Value(s)	Yes	No
13	Use the *J 39200* in order to measure the resistance between the left rear wheel speed sensor connector terminal A and the left rear wheel speed sensor connector terminal B. Is the resistance within the specified range?	950–1250 Ω	*Go to Step 31*	*Go to Step 28*
14	1. Disconnect the connector C313. 2. Use the *J 39200* in order to measure the resistance between the EBCM connector terminal 23 and ground. Is the resistance within the specified range?	OL (Infinite)	*Go to Step 15*	*Go to Step 25*
15	Use the *J 39200* in order to measure the resistance between the EBCM connector terminal 10 and ground. Is the resistance within the specified range?	OL (Infinite)	*Go to Step 16*	*Go to Step 26*
16	1. Thoroughly respray the left rear wheel speed sensor harness with the saltwater solution. 2. Disconnect the left rear wheel speed sensor directly at the left rear wheel speed sensor. 3. Use the *J 39200* in order to measure the resistance between the left rear wheel speed sensor harness connector terminal A and ground. Is the resistance within the specified range?	OL (Infinite)	*Go to Step 17*	*Go to Step 29*
17	Use the *J 39200* in order to measure the resistance between the left rear wheel speed sensor harness connector terminal B and ground. Is the resistance within the specified range?	OL (Infinite)	*Go to Step 18*	*Go to Step 29*
18	Use the *J 39200* in order to measure the resistance between the left rear wheel speed sensor connector terminal A and ground. Is the resistance within the specified range?	OL (Infinite)	*Go to Step 31*	*Go to Step 28*
19	Repair the short to voltage in CKT 885. If the short to voltage is found in the left rear wheel speed sensor harness, replace the left rear wheel speed harness. Is the repair complete?	—	Refer to *Diagnostic System Check*	—
20	Repair the short to voltage in CKT 884. If the short to voltage is found in the left rear wheel speed sensor harness, replace the left rear wheel speed harness. Is the repair complete?	—	Refer to *Diagnostic System Check*	—
21	Repair the wiring damage in CKT 885 or CKT 884. If the wiring damage is found in the left rear wheel speed sensor harness, replace the left rear wheel speed harness. Is the repair complete?	—	Refer to *Diagnostic System Check*	—
22	Repair the connector damage in CKT 885 or CKT 884. If the connector damage is found in the left rear wheel speed sensor harness, replace the left rear wheel speed harness. Is the repair complete?	—	Refer to *Diagnostic System Check*	—
23	Repair the open or high resistance in CKT 885. If the open or high resistance is found in the left rear wheel speed sensor harness, replace the left rear wheel speed harness. Is the repair complete?	—	Refer to *Diagnostic System Check*	—

GC402980306000KX

Fig. 32 Code C1234: LH Rear Wheel Speed Circuit Open Or Shorted (Part 4 of 5). Alero, Grand Am & Malibu

Step	Action	Value(s)	Yes	No
7	1. Turn the ignition switch to the OFF position. 2. Inspect the following terminals: • The EBCM connector terminal 10 • The EBCM connector terminal 23 • The remaining terminals of the EBCM connector 3. Inspect the above terminals for the following conditions: • Terminal damage • Poor terminal contact • Terminal corrosion Terminal damage, terminal corrosion, and poor terminal contact may cause an open circuit, a short to voltage, or a short to ground. Are there signs of poor terminal contact, terminal corrosion, or damaged terminals?	—	*Go to Step 27*	*Go to Step 8*
8	Inspect the wiring of CKT 885 and CKT 884 for signs of wire damage. Wire damage may cause the following conditions in CKT 885 and CKT 884: • An open circuit • A short to voltage • A short to ground Are there signs of damaged wiring?	—	*Go to Step 21*	*Go to Step 9*
9	Inspect the harness connectors of CKT 885 and CKT 884 for signs of wire damage. Wire damage may cause the following conditions in CKT 885 and CKT 884: • An open circuit • A short to voltage • A short to ground Are there signs of damaged connectors?	—	*Go to Step 22*	*Go to Step 10*
10	1. Reconnect the EBCM connector. 2. Reconnect the left rear wheel speed sensor harness connector. 3. Install a *Scan Tool*. 4. Test drive the vehicle at a speed above 24 km/h (15 mph) for at least 30 seconds. 5. Use the *Scan Tool* in order to read the DTCs. Does DTC C1234 set as a current DTC?	—	*Go to Step 30*	*Go to Step 31*
11	1. Disconnect the left rear wheel speed sensor directly at the left rear wheel speed sensor connector. 2. Use the *J 39200* in order to measure the resistance between the EBCM connector terminal 23 and the left rear wheel speed sensor harness connector terminal B. Is the resistance within the specified range?	0–2 Ω	*Go to Step 12*	*Go to Step 23*
12	Use the *J 39200* in order to measure the resistance between the EBCM connector terminal 10 and the left rear wheel speed sensor harness connector terminal A. Is the resistance within the specified range?	0–2 Ω	*Go to Step 13*	*Go to Step 24*

GC402980306000JX

Fig. 32 Code C1234: LH Rear Wheel Speed Circuit Open Or Shorted (Part 3 of 5). Alero, Grand Am & Malibu

Step	Action	Value(s)	Yes	No
24	Repair the open or high resistance in CKT 884. If the open or high resistance is found in the left rear wheel speed sensor harness, replace the left rear wheel speed harness. Is the repair complete?	—	Refer to *Diagnostic System Check*	—
25	Repair the short to ground in CKT 885. If the short to ground is found in the left rear wheel speed sensor harness, replace the left rear wheel speed harness. Is the repair complete?	—	Refer to *Diagnostic System Check*	—
26	Repair the short to ground in CKT 884. If the short to ground is found in the left rear wheel speed sensor harness, replace the left rear wheel speed harness. Is the repair complete?	—	Refer to *Diagnostic System Check*	—
27	Replace all of the terminals and the connectors that exhibit signs of poor terminal contact, corrosion, or damaged terminals. Is the repair complete?	—	Refer to *Diagnostic System Check*	—
28	Replace the left rear wheel speed sensor. Is the repair complete?	—	Refer to *Diagnostic System Check*	—
29	Replace the left rear wheel speed sensor harness. Is the repair complete?	—	Refer to *Diagnostic System Check*	—
30	Replace the EBCM. Is the repair complete?	—	Refer to *Diagnostic System Check*	—
31	The malfunction is intermittent or not present at this time. Inspect all of the connectors and the harnesses for damage that may cause the following conditions: • An open or a high resistance • A short to ground • A short to voltage The wheel speed sensor harness must be replaced if the harness is damaged. Refer to Diagnostic Aids for more information.	—	—	—

GC402980306000LX

Fig. 32 Code C1234: LH Rear Wheel Speed Circuit Open Or Shorted (Part 5 of 5). Alero, Grand Am & Malibu

Circuit Description

As a toothed ring passes by the wheel speed sensor, changes in the electromagnetic field cause the wheel speed sensor to produce an AC voltage signal. The frequency of the AC voltage signal is proportional to the wheel speed. The amplitude of the AC voltage signal is directly related to wheel speed and the proximity of the wheel speed sensor to the toothed ring. The proximity of the wheel speed sensor to the toothed ring is also referred to as the air gap.

Conditions for Setting the DTC

DTC C1235 can set anytime after initialization.

A malfunction exists if either of the right rear wheel speed sensor circuits are open or shorted to voltage or ground.

Action Taken When the DTC Sets

- A malfunction DTC stores.
- The ABS disables.
- The ABS warning indicator turns on.

Conditions for Clearing the DTC

- The condition responsible for setting the DTC no longer exists and the Scan Tool Clear DTCs function is used.
- 100 drive cycles pass with no DTCs detected. A drive cycle consists of starting the vehicle, driving the vehicle over 16 km/h (10 mph), stopping and then turning the ignition switch to the OFF position.

Diagnostic Aids

The following conditions may cause an intermittent malfunction:

- A poor connection
- Rubbed-through wire insulation
- A broken wire inside the insulation

Use the enhanced diagnostic function of the Scan Tool in order to measure the frequency of the malfunction.

If the customer's comments reflect that the amber ABS warning indicator is on only during moist environmental changes (rain, snow, vehicle wash), inspect all the wheel speed sensor circuitry for signs of water intrusion. If the DTC is not current, clear all DTCs and simulate the effects of water intrusion by using the following procedure:

1. Spray the suspected area with a five percent saltwater solution.
   Add two teaspoons of salt to twelve ounces of water to make a five percent saltwater solution.
2. Test drive the vehicle over various road surfaces (bumps, turns, etc.) above 24 km/h (15 mph) for at least 30 seconds.
3. If the DTC returns, replace the suspected harness.

Thoroughly inspect any circuitry that may be causing the intermittent complaint for the following conditions:

- Backed out terminals
- Improper mating
- Broken locks
- Improperly formed or damaged terminals
- Poor terminal-to-wiring connections
- Physical damage to the wiring harness

Resistance of the wheel speed sensor will increase with an increase in sensor temperature.

Use the following procedure when replacing a wheel speed sensor or harness:

1. Inspect the wheel speed sensor terminals and harness connector for corrosion and/or water intrusion.
2. Replace the wheel speed sensor jumper harness if evidence of corrosion or water intrusion exists.

GC402980306003AX

Fig. 33 Code C1235: RH Rear Wheel Speed Circuit Open Or Shorted (Part 1 of 5). Alero, Grand Am & Malibu

Step	Action	Value(s)	Yes	No
1	Was the Diagnostic System Check performed?	—	*Go to Step 2*	Refer to *Diagnostic System Check*
2	1. Turn the ignition switch to the OFF position. 2. Make a 5 percent saltwater solution. 3. Thoroughly spray the rear axle harness with the saltwater solution. 4. Disconnect the EBCM harness connector. 5. Use the *J 39200* in order to measure the resistance between the EBCM harness connector terminal 11 and the EBCM harness connector terminal 24. Is the resistance within the specified range?	950–1250 Ω	*Go to Step 3*	*Go to Step 11*
3	Use the *J 39200* in order to measure the resistance between the EBCM harness connector terminal 24 and ground. Is the resistance within the specified range?	OL (Infinite)	*Go to Step 4*	*Go to Step 14*
4	1. Turn the ignition switch to the RUN position. Do not start the engine. 2. Use the *J 39200* in order to measure the voltage between the EBCM harness connector terminal 24 and ground. Is the voltage within the specified range?	0–1 V	*Go to Step 7*	*Go to Step 5*
5	1. Turn the ignition switch to the OFF position. 2. Disconnect the right rear wheel speed sensor at the right rear wheel speed sensor connector. 3. Turn the ignition switch to the RUN position. Do not start the engine. 4. Use the *J 39200* in order to measure the voltage between the EBCM harness connector terminal 24 and ground. Is the voltage within the specified range?	0–1 V	*Go to Step 6*	*Go to Step 19*
6	Use the *J 39200* in order to measure the voltage between the EBCM harness connector terminal 11 and ground. Is the voltage within the specified range?	0–1 V	*Go to Step 31*	*Go to Step 20*

GC402980306000MX

Fig. 33 Code C1235: RH Rear Wheel Speed Circuit Open Or Shorted (Part 2 of 5). Alero, Grand Am & Malibu

Step	Action	Value(s)	Yes	No
7	1. Turn the ignition switch to the OFF position. 2. Inspect the following terminals: • The EBCM connector terminal 11 • The EBCM connector terminal 24 • The remaining terminals of the EBCM connector 3. Inspect the above terminals for the following conditions: • Terminal damage • Poor terminal contact • Terminal corrosion Damage, terminal corrosion, and poor terminal contact may cause an open circuit, a short to voltage, or a short to ground. Are there signs of poor terminal contact, terminal corrosion, or damaged terminals?	—	*Go to Step 27*	*Go to Step 8*
8	Inspect the wiring of CKT 883 and CKT 882 for signs of wire damage. Wire damage may cause the following conditions in CKT 883 and CKT 882: • An open circuit • A short to voltage • A short to ground Are there signs of damaged wiring?	—	*Go to Step 21*	*Go to Step 9*
9	Inspect the harness connectors of CKT 883 and CKT 882 for signs of wire damage. Wire damage may cause the following conditions in CKT 883 and CKT 882: • An open circuit • A short to voltage • A short to ground Are there signs of damaged connectors?	—	*Go to Step 22*	*Go to Step 10*
10	1. Reconnect the EBCM connector. 2. Reconnect the rear axle harness connector. 3. Install a *Scan Tool*. 4. Test drive the vehicle at a speed above 24 km/h (15 mph) for at least 30 seconds. 5. Use the *Scan Tool* in order to read the DTCs. Does DTC C1235 set as a current DTC?	—	*Go to Step 30*	*Go to Step 31*
11	1. Disconnect the right rear wheel speed sensor directly at the right rear wheel speed sensor connector. 2. Use the *J 39200* in order to measure the resistance between the EBCM harness connector terminal 24 and the right rear wheel speed sensor harness connector terminal B. Is the resistance within the specified range?	0–2 Ω	*Go to Step 12*	*Go to Step 23*
12	Use the *J 39200* in order to measure the resistance between the EBCM harness connector terminal 11 and the right rear wheel speed sensor harness connector terminal A. Is the resistance within the specified range?	0–2 Ω	*Go to Step 13*	*Go to Step 24*

GC402980306000NX

Fig. 33 Code C1235: RH Rear Wheel Speed Circuit Open Or Shorted (Part 3 of 5). Alero, Grand Am & Malibu

Step	Action	Value(s)	Yes	No
13	Use the *J 39200* in order to measure the resistance between the right rear wheel speed sensor connector terminal A and the right rear wheel speed sensor connector terminal B. Is the resistance within the specified range?	950–1250 Ω	*Go to Step 31*	*Go to Step 28*
14	1. Disconnect the connector C313. 2. Use the *J 39200* in order to measure the resistance between the EBCM connector terminal 24 and ground. Is the resistance within the specified range?	OL (Infinite)	*Go to Step 15*	*Go to Step 25*
15	Use the *J 39200* in order to measure the resistance between the EBCM connector terminal 11 and ground. Is the resistance within the specified range?	OL (Infinite)	*Go to Step 16*	*Go to Step 26*
16	1. Thoroughly respray the rear axle harness with the saltwater solution. 2. Disconnect the right rear wheel speed sensor directly at the right rear wheel speed sensor. 3. Use the *J 39200* in order to measure the resistance between the rear axle harness connector terminal A and ground. Is the resistance within the specified range?	OL (Infinite)	*Go to Step 17*	*Go to Step 29*
17	Use the *J 39200* in order to measure the resistance between the rear axle harness connector terminal B and ground. Is the resistance within the specified range?	OL (Infinite)	*Go to Step 18*	*Go to Step 29*
18	Use the *J 39200* in order to measure the resistance between the rear axle harness connector terminal A and ground. Is the resistance within the specified range?	OL (Infinite)	*Go to Step 31*	*Go to Step 28*
19	Repair the short to voltage in CKT 883. If the short to voltage is found in the rear axle harness, replace the rear axle harness. Is the repair complete?	—	Refer to *Diagnostic System Check*	—
20	Repair the short to voltage in CKT 882. If the short to voltage is found in the rear axle harness, replace the rear axle harness. Is the repair complete?	—	Refer to *Diagnostic System Check*	—
21	Repair the wiring damage in CKT 882 or CKT 883. If the wiring damage is found in the rear axle harness, replace the rear axle harness. Is the repair complete?	—	Refer to *Diagnostic System Check*	—
22	Repair the connector damage in CKT 882 or CKT 883. If the connector damage is found in the rear axle harness, replace the rear axle harness. Is the repair complete?	—	Refer to *Diagnostic System Check*	—
23	Repair the open or high resistance in CKT 883. If the open or high resistance is found in the rear axle harness, replace the rear axle harness. Is the repair complete?	—	Refer to *Diagnostic System Check*	—

GC402980306000OX

Fig. 33 Code C1235: RH Rear Wheel Speed Circuit Open Or Shorted (Part 4 of 5). Alero, Grand Am & Malibu

Step	Action	Value(s)	Yes	No
24	Repair the open or high resistance in CKT 882. If the open or high resistance is found in the rear axle harness, replace the rear axle harness. Is the repair complete?	—	Refer to *Diagnostic System Check*	—
25	Repair the short to ground in CKT 883. If the short to ground is found in the rear axle harness, replace the rear axle harness. Is the repair complete?	—	Refer to *Diagnostic System Check*	—
26	Repair the short to ground in CKT 882. If the short to ground is found in the rear axle harness, replace the rear axle harness. Is the repair complete?	—	Refer to *Diagnostic System Check.*	—
27	Replace all of the terminals and the connectors that exhibit signs of poor terminal contact, corrosion, or damaged terminals. Is the repair complete?	—	Refer to *Diagnostic System Check*	—
28	Replace the right rear wheel speed sensor. Is the repair complete?	—	Refer to *Diagnostic System Check*	—
29	Replace the rear axle harness. Is the repair complete?	—	Refer to *Diagnostic System Check*	—
30	Replace the EBCM. Is the repair complete?	—	Refer to *Diagnostic System Check*	—
31	The malfunction is intermittent or not present at this time. Inspect all of the connectors and the harnesses for damage that may cause the following conditions: • An open or a high resistance • A short to ground • A short to voltage The rear axle harness must be replaced if the harness is damaged. Refer to Diagnostic Aids for more information.	—	—	—

GC402980306000PX

Fig. 33 Code C1235: RH Rear Wheel Speed Circuit Open Or Shorted (Part 5 of 5). Alero, Grand Am & Malibu

Step	Action	Value(s)	Yes	No
1	Was the Diagnostic System Check performed?	—	*Go to Step 2*	Refer to *Diagnostic System Check*
2	1. Turn the ignition switch to the RUN position. Do not start the engine. 2. Select Snapshot on the *Scan Tool.* 3. Select Single DTC on the *Scan Tool.* 4. Enter C1236 on the *Scan Tool.* 5. Drive the vehicle at a speed above 5 km/h (3 mph). Does DTC C1236 set as a current DTC?	—	*Go to Step 3*	*Go to Step 17*
3	1. Verify that the engine is running. 2. Turn the ignition switch to the RUN position. 3. Select Special Functions on the *Scan Tool.* 4. Use the *Scan Tool* in order to perform the Voltage Load test. Are the ignition voltage and the battery voltage equal to or greater than the specified range?	10 V	*Go to Step 4*	*Go to Step 10*
4	1. Turn the ignition switch to the OFF position. 2. Disconnect the EBCM connector. 3. Disconnect the Electronic Brake Control Relay. 4. Use the *J 39200* in order to measure the resistance between the Electronic Brake Control Relay connector terminal 87 and the EBCM connector terminal C. Is the resistance within the specified range?	0–2 Ω	*Go to Step 5*	*Go to Step 11*
5	1. Disconnect the negative battery cable. 2. Disconnect the positive battery cable. 3. Use the *J 39200* in order to measure the resistance between the positive battery terminal and the Electronic Brake Control Relay connector terminal 30. Is the resistance within the specified range?	0–2 Ω	*Go to Step 6*	*Go to Step 12*
6	1. Remove the fuse block ERLS Fuse (10A). 2. Use the *J 39200* in order to measure the resistance between the fuse block terminal (ERLS Fuse [10A]) and the EBCM connector terminal 4. Is the resistance within the specified range?	0–2 Ω	*Go to Step 7*	*Go to Step 13*
7	Use the *J 39200* in order to measure the resistance between the fuse block terminal (ERLS Fuse [10A]) and the EBCM connector terminal 4. Is the resistance within the specified range?	0–2 Ω	*Go to Step 8*	*Go to Step 14*

GC402980300900BX

Fig. 34 Code C1236: Low System Supply Voltage (Part 2 of 3). Alero, Grand Am & Malibu

Circuit Description

DTC C1236 monitors the voltage level available to the EBCM controller. If the voltage drops below 11.2 volts, full performance of the ABS system is not guaranteed. During ABS operation, there are several current requirements that will cause battery voltage at the EBCM to drop. As a result, voltage is monitored prior to an ABS event to indicate good charging system condition. Voltage is also monitored during an ABS event when voltage may drop significantly.

Conditions for Setting the DTC

DTC C1236 can set only if the vehicle's speed is greater than 5 km/h (3 mph).

A malfunction exists if the switched battery voltage is less than 11.4 volts without ABS being active or less than 8.4 volts during an ABS event.

Action Taken When the DTC Sets

- A malfunction DTC stores.
- The ABS disables.
- The ABS warning indicator turns on.

Conditions for Clearing the DTC

- The condition responsible for setting the DTC no longer exists and the Scan Tool Clear DTCs function is used.
- 100 drive cycles pass with no DTC(s) detected. A drive cycle consists of starting the vehicle, driving the vehicle over 16 km/h (10 mph), stopping and then turning the ignition off.

Diagnostic Aids

The following conditions may cause an intermittent malfunction:

- A poor connection
- Rubbed-through wire insulation
- A broken wire inside the insulation

Use the enhanced diagnostic function of the Scan Tool in order to measure the frequency of the malfunction.

Thoroughly inspect any circuitry that may be causing the intermittent complaint for the following conditions:

- Backed out terminals
- Improper mating
- Broken locks
- Improperly formed or damaged terminals
- Poor terminal-to-wiring connections
- Physical damage to the wiring harness

While performing a Voltage Load test, CKT 439 should be measured for high resistance or an open condition if it is noted that only the ignition voltage drops below acceptable voltage levels.

Ensure the starting and charging systems are in proper working order. The battery should be fully charged and in good condition before beginning the diagnostic table.

Important: Zero the J 39200 test leads before making any resistance measurements. Refer to the J 39200 user's manual.

GC402980300900AX

Fig. 34 Code C1236: Low System Supply Voltage (Part 1 of 3). Alero, Grand Am & Malibu

Step	Action	Value(s)	Yes	No
8	1. Inspect the following components: • The Electronic Brake Control Relay connector • The EBCM connector • The positive battery cable connections • The negative battery cable connections 2. Inspect the above components for the following conditions: • Terminal damage • Poor terminal contact • Terminal corrosion The above conditions may cause an open circuit. Are there signs of terminal damage, poor terminal contact, or terminal corrosion?	—	*Go to Step 15*	*Go to Step 9*
9	1. Reconnect the EBCM connector. 2. Reconnect the Electronic Brake Control Relay. 3. Reconnect the positive battery cable. 4. Reconnect the negative battery cable. 5. Drive the vehicle at a speed above 5 km/h (3 mph). Does DTC C1236 set as a current DTC?	—	*Go to Step 16*	*Go to Step 17*
10	Repair the low voltage condition. Is the low voltage condition repaired?	—	Refer to *Diagnostic System Check*	—
11	Repair the open or high resistance in CKT 1633. Is the repair complete?	—	Refer to *Diagnostic System Check*	—
12	Repair the open or high resistance in CKT 342. Is the repair complete?	—	Refer to *Diagnostic System Check*	—
13	Repair the open or high resistance in CKT 439. Is the repair complete?	—	Refer to *Diagnostic System Check*	—
14	Repair the open or high resistance in CKT 3 or CKT 1. Is the repair complete?	—	Refer to *Diagnostic System Check*	—
15	Replace all of the terminals or the connectors that exhibit signs of poor terminal contact, corrosion, or damaged terminals. Is the repair complete?	—	Refer to *Diagnostic System Check*	—
16	Replace the EBCM. Is the repair complete?	—	Refer to *Diagnostic System Check*	—
17	The malfunction is intermittent or is not present at this time. Refer to Diagnostic Aids for more information.	—	—	—

GC402980300900CX

Fig. 34 Code C1236: Low System Supply Voltage (Part 3 of 3). Alero, Grand Am & Malibu

Circuit Description

DTC C1237 detects high vehicle voltage levels prior to any required motor movement (initialization or ABS). Damage to the system may occur if excessive voltage exists.

Conditions for Setting the DTC

DTC C1237 can set only if the vehicle's speed is greater than 5 km/h (3 mph).

A malfunction exists if the switched battery voltage is greater than 17 volts.

Action Taken When the DTC Sets

- A malfunction DTC stores.
- The ABS disables.
- The ABS warning indicator turns on.

Conditions for Clearing the DTC

- The condition responsible for setting the DTC no longer exists and the Scan Tool Clear DTCs function is used.
- 100 drive cycles pass with no DTC(s) detected. A drive cycle consists of starting the vehicle, driving the vehicle over 16 km/h (10 mph), stopping and then turning the ignition off.

Diagnostic Aids

The following conditions may cause an intermittent malfunction:

- A poor connection
- Rubbed-through wire insulation
- A broken wire inside the insulation

Use the enhanced diagnostic function of the Scan Tool in order to measure the frequency of the malfunction.

Thoroughly inspect any circuitry that may be causing the intermittent complaint for the following conditions:

- Backed out terminals
- Improper mating
- Broken locks
- Improperly formed or damaged terminals
- Poor terminal-to-wiring connections
- Physical damage to the wiring harness

Important: Zero the J 39200 test leads before making any resistance measurements. Refer to the J 39200 user's manual.

GC402980301000AX

Fig. 35 Code C1237: High System Supply Voltage (Part 1 of 2). Alero, Grand Am & Malibu

Step	Action	Value(s)	Yes	No
1	Was the Diagnostic System Check performed?	—	*Go to Step 2*	Refer to *Diagnostic System Check*
2	1. Start the engine. 2. Install a *Scan Tool.* 3. Select Data List on the *Scan Tool.* 4. Select Battery Voltage on the *Scan Tool.* 5. Run the engine at approximately 2,000 RPM and monitor the voltage. Is the voltage less than or equal to the specified voltage?	16 V	*Go to Step 6*	*Go to Step 3*
3	1. Turn the ignition switch to the OFF position. 2. Disconnect the Electronic Brake Control Relay. 3. Start the engine. 4. Use the *J 39200* in order to measure the voltage between the Electronic Brake Control Relay connector terminal 30 and ground. 5. Run the engine at approximately 2,000 RPM and monitor the voltage. Is the voltage less than or equal to the specified range?	16 V	*Go to Step 4*	inspect charging system operation
4	1. Turn the ignition switch to the OFF position. 2. Reconnect the Electronic Brake Control Relay. 3. Drive the vehicle at a speed above 5 km/h (3 mph). 4. Use the *Scan Tool* in order to look for DTCs. Does DTC C1237 set as a current DTC?	—	*Go to Step 5*	*Go to Step 6*
5	Replace the EBCM. Is the repair complete?	—	Refer to *Diagnostic System Check*	—
6	The malfunction is intermittent or is not present at this time. Refer to Diagnostic Aids for more information.	—	—	—

GC402980301000BX

Fig. 35 Code C1237: High System Supply Voltage (Part 2 of 2). Alero, Grand Am & Malibu

Circuit Description

DTC C1238 detects a slipping left front ESB. During initialization and braking, the left front brake motor is rehomed. If the ESB slips, the motor/piston will move. During the next key to RUN initialization, a rehome of the motor verifies the motor/piston remained at the home position. If motor movement is detected, the ESB must be slipping.

If an ESB cannot hold a piston in the home position, the piston may be driven back when the brake pedal is applied. Then the brake pedal will drop.

Conditions for Setting the DTC

DTC C1238 can set during initialization at the following speeds:

- 0 km/h (0 mph) when the brake is off
- 5 km/h (3 mph) when the brake is on

A malfunction exists if the EBCM detects that the ESB could not hold the piston in the home position.

Action Taken When the DTC Sets

- A malfunction DTC stores.
- The ABS disables.
- The ABS warning indicator turns on.

Conditions for Clearing the DTC

- The condition responsible for setting the DTC no longer exists and the Scan Tool Clear DTCs function is used.
- 100 drive cycles pass with no DTCs detected. A drive cycle consists of starting the vehicle, driving the vehicle over 16 km/h (10 mph), stopping and then turning the ignition switch to the OFF position.

Diagnostic Aids

The following conditions may cause an intermittent malfunction if the conditions exist in a mechanical part of the system:

- Sticking
- Binding
- Slipping

Use the enhanced diagnostic function of the Scan Tool in order to measure the frequency of the malfunction.

Use the hydraulic control modulator test function of the Scan Tool in order to locate an intermittent malfunction associated with the ESB.

Clear the DTCs after completing the diagnosis. Test drive the vehicle for three drive cycles in order to verify that the DTC does not reset. Use the following procedure in order to complete one drive cycle:

1. Start the vehicle.
2. Drive the vehicle over 16 km/h (10 mph).
3. Stop the vehicle.
4. Turn the ignition to the OFF position.

Important: Zero the J 39200 test leads before making any resistance measurements.

GC402980301100AA

Fig. 36 Code C1238: LH Front ESB Does Not Hold Motor (Part 1 of 3). Alero, Grand Am & Malibu

Step	Action	Value(s)	Yes	No
1	Was the Diagnostic System Check performed?	—	*Go to Step 2*	Refer to *Diagnostic System Check*
2	Inspect the following connectors for the correct wire color/connector cavity combinations: • The 6-way ABS brake motor pack connector • The EBCM connector Are the correct wires located in the correct connector cavities?	—	*Go to Step 3*	*Go to Step 10*
3	1. Turn the ignition switch to the RUN position. Do not start the engine. 2. Pump the brake pedal until it is firm in order to deplete the brake booster vacuum reservoir. 3. Install a *Scan Tool.* 4. Select Special Functions on the *Scan Tool.* 5. Select the Manual Control function on the *Scan Tool.* 6. Select the ABS Motor Apply function of the left front ABS channel on the *Scan Tool.* 7. Use the *Scan Tool* in order to apply the left front ABS motor. 8. Wait for five seconds. 9. Apply firm pressure to the brake pedal. Does the brake pedal fall?	—	*Go to Step 9*	*Go to Step 4*
4	1. Use the *Scan Tool* in order to exit the Manual Control function. 2. Turn the ignition switch to the OFF position. 3. Disconnect the following connectors: • The 6-way ABS brake motor pack connector • The EBCM connector 4. Use the *J 39200* in order to measure the resistance between the 6-way ABS brake motor pack harness connector terminal A and the EBCM harness connector terminal G. Is the resistance within the specified range?	0–2 Ω	*Go to Step 5*	*Go to Step 11*
5	Use the *J 39200* in order to measure the resistance between the 6-way ABS brake motor pack harness connector terminal B and the EBCM harness connector terminal H. Is the resistance within the specified range?	0–2 Ω	*Go to Step 6*	*Go to Step 12*
6	Use the *J 39200* in order to measure the resistance between the 6-way ABS brake motor pack connector terminal A and the ABS brake motor pack connector terminal B. Is the resistance within the specified range?	0.2–1.5 Ω	*Go to Step 7*	*Go to Step 9*

GC402980301100BX

Fig. 36 Code C1238: LH Front ESB Does Not Hold Motor (Part 2 of 3). Alero, Grand Am & Malibu

Step	Action	Value(s)	Yes	No
7	1. Inspect the following connectors: • The 6-way ABS brake motor pack connector • The EBCM connector 2. Inspect the above connectors for the following conditions: • Poor terminal contact • Corrosion Are there signs of poor terminal contact or corrosion?	—	Go to Step 13	Go to Step 8
8	1. Turn the ignition switch to the OFF position. 2. Reconnect the EBCM connector. 3. Reconnect the 6-way ABS brake motor pack connector. 4. Start the engine. Do not depress the brake pedal while starting the engine. 5. Allow the engine to run for at least 10 seconds. 6. Repeat the above ignition cycle sequence at least two more times. 7. Use the *Scan Tool* in order to look for DTC's. Does the DTC C1238 set during the last three ignition cycles?	—	Go to Step 14	Go to Step 15
9	Replace the ABS brake motor pack. Is the repair complete?	—	Refer to Diagnostic System Check	—
10	Place the correct wires into the connector cavities. Is the repair complete?	—	Refer to Diagnostic System Check	—
11	Repair the open or high resistance in CKT 1280. Is the repair complete?	—	Refer to Diagnostic System Check	—
12	Repair the open or high resistance in CKT 1281. Is the repair complete?	—	Refer to Diagnostic System Check	—
13	Replace the terminals that exhibit signs of poor terminal contact or corrosion. Is the repair complete?	—	Refer to Diagnostic System Check	—
14	Replace the EBCM. Is the repair complete?	—	Refer to Diagnostic System Check	—
15	The malfunction is intermittent or is not present at this time. Refer to Diagnostic Aids for more information.	—	—	—

GC402980301100CX

Fig. 36 Code C1238: LH Front ESB Does Not Hold Motor (Part 3 of 3). Alero, Grand Am & Malibu

Step	Action	Value(s)	Yes	No
1	Was the Diagnostic System Check performed?	—	Go to Step 2	Refer to Diagnostic System Check
2	Inspect the following connectors for the correct wire color/connector cavity combinations: • The 6-way ABS brake motor pack connector • The EBCM connector Are the correct wires located in the correct connector cavities?	—	Go to Step 3	Go to Step 10
3	1. Turn the ignition switch to the RUN position. Do not start the engine. 2. Pump the brake pedal until it is firm in order to deplete the brake booster vacuum reservoir. 3. Install a *Scan Tool.* 4. Select the Special Functions on the *Scan Tool.* 5. Select the Manual Control function on the *Scan Tool.* 6. Select the ABS Motor Apply function of the left front ABS channel on the *Scan Tool.* 7. Use the *Scan Tool* in order to apply the left front ABS motor. 8. Wait for five seconds. 9. Apply firm pressure to the brake pedal. Does the brake pedal fall?	—	Go to Step 9	Go to Step 4
4	1. Use the *Scan Tool* in order to exit the Manual Control function. 2. Turn the ignition switch to the OFF position. 3. Disconnect the following connectors: • The 6-way ABS brake motor pack connector • The EBCM connector 4. Use the *J 39200* in order to measure the resistance between the 6-way ABS brake motor pack harness connector terminal E and the EBCM harness connector terminal A. Is the resistance within the specified range?	0–2 Ω	Go to Step 5	Go to Step 11
5	Use the *J 39200* in order to measure the resistance between the 6-way ABS brake motor pack harness connector terminal F and the EBCM harness connector terminal B. Is the resistance within the specified range?	0–2 Ω	Go to Step 6	Go to Step 12
6	Use the *J 39200* in order to measure the resistance between the 6-way ABS brake motor pack connector terminal E and the ABS brake motor pack connector terminal F. Is the resistance within the specified range?	0.2–1.5 Ω	Go to Step 7	Go to Step 9

GC402980301200BX

Fig. 37 Code C1241: RH Front ESB Does Not Hold Motor (Part 2 of 3). Alero, Grand Am & Malibu

Circuit Description

DTC C1241 detects a slipping right front ESB. During initialization and braking, the right front brake motor is rehomed. If the ESB slips, the motor/piston will move. During the next key to RUN initialization, a rehome of the motor verifies the motor/piston remained at the home position. If motor movement is detected, the ESB must be slipping.

If an ESB cannot hold a piston in the home position, the piston may be driven back when the brake pedal is applied. Then the brake pedal will drop.

Conditions for Setting the DTC

DTC C1241 can set during initialization at the following speeds:

- 0 km (0 mph) when the brake is off
- 5 km (3 mph) when the brake is on

A malfunction exists if the EBCM detects that the ESB could not hold the piston in the home position.

Action Taken When the DTC Sets

- A malfunction DTC stores.
- The ABS disables.
- The ABS warning indicator turns on.

Conditions for Clearing the DTC

- The condition responsible for setting the DTC no longer exists and the Scan Tool Clear DTCs function is used.
- 100 drive cycles pass with no DTCs detected. A drive cycle consists of starting the vehicle, driving the vehicle over 16 km/h (10 mph), stopping and then turning the ignition switch to the OFF position.

Diagnostic Aids

The following conditions may cause an intermittent malfunction if the conditions exist in a mechanical part of the system:

- Sticking
- Binding
- Slipping

Use the enhanced diagnostic function of the Scan Tool in order to measure the frequency of the malfunction.

Use the hydraulic control modulator test function of the Scan Tool in order to locate an intermittent malfunction associated with the ESB.

Clear the DTCs after completing the diagnosis. Test drive the vehicle for three drive cycles in order to verify that the DTC does not reset. Use the following procedure in order to complete one drive cycle:

1. Start the vehicle.
2. Drive the vehicle over 16 km/h (10 mph).
3. Stop the vehicle.
4. Turn the ignition to the OFF position.

Important: Zero the J 39200 test leads before making any resistance measurements.

GC402980301200AX

Fig. 37 Code C1241: RH Front ESB Does Not Hold Motor (Part 1 of 3). Alero, Grand Am & Malibu

Step	Action	Value(s)	Yes	No
7	1. Inspect the following connectors: • The 6-way ABS brake motor pack connector • The EBCM connector 2. Inspect the above connectors for the following conditions: • Poor terminal contact • Corrosion Are there signs of poor terminal contact or corrosion?	—	Go to Step 13	Go to Step 8
8	1. Turn the ignition switch to the OFF position. 2. Reconnect the EBCM connector. 3. Reconnect the 6-way ABS brake motor pack connector. 4. Start the engine. Do not depress the brake pedal while starting the engine. 5. Allow the engine to run for at least 10 seconds. 6. Repeat the above ignition cycle sequence at least two more times. 7. Use the *Scan Tool* in order to look for DTCs. Does the DTC C1241 set during the last three ignition cycles?	—	Go to Step 14	Go to Step 15
9	Replace the ABS brake motor pack. Is the repair complete?	—	Refer to Diagnostic System Check	—
10	Place the correct wires into the connector cavities. Is the repair complete?	—	Refer to Diagnostic System Check	—
11	Repair the open or high resistance in CKT 1282. Is the repair complete?	—	Refer to Diagnostic System Check	—
12	Repair the open or high resistance in CKT 1283. Is the repair complete?	—	Refer to Diagnostic System Check	—
13	Replace the terminals that exhibit signs of poor terminal contact or corrosion. Is the repair complete?	—	Refer to Diagnostic System Check	—
14	Replace the EBCM. Is the repair complete?	—	Refer to Diagnostic System Check	—
15	The malfunction is intermittent or is not present at this time. Refer to Diagnostic Aids for more information.	—	—	—

GC402980301200CX

Fig. 37 Code C1241: RH Front ESB Does Not Hold Motor (Part 3 of 3). Alero, Grand Am & Malibu

Circuit Description

DTC C1242 detects a slipping rear axle ESB. During initialization and braking, the rear motor is rehomed. If the ESB slips, the motor/piston will move. During the next key to RUN initialization, a rehome of the motor verifies the motor/piston remained at the home position. If motor movement is detected, the ESB must be slipping.

If an ESB cannot hold a piston in the home position, the piston may be driven back when the brake pedal is applied. Then the brake pedal will drop.

Conditions for Setting the DTC

DTC C1242 can set during initialization at the following speeds:

- 0 km/h (0 mph) when the brake is off
- 5 km/h (3 mph) when the brake is on

A malfunction exists if the EBCM detects that the ESB could not hold the piston in the home position.

DTC C1286 always sets with DTC C1242.

Action Taken When the DTC Sets

- A malfunction DTC stores.
- The ABS disables.
- The ABS warning indicator turns on.

Conditions for Clearing the DTC

- The condition responsible for setting the DTC no longer exists and the Scan Tool Clear DTCs function is used.
- 100 drive cycles pass with no DTCs detected. A drive cycle consists of starting the vehicle, driving the vehicle over 16 km/h (10 mph), stopping and then turning the ignition switch to the OFF position.

Diagnostic Aids

The following conditions may cause an intermittent malfunction if the conditions exist in a mechanical part of the system:

- Sticking
- Binding
- Slipping

Use the enhanced diagnostic function of the Scan Tool in order to measure the frequency of the malfunction.

Use the hydraulic control modulator test function of the Scan Tool in order to locate an intermittent malfunction associated with the ESB.

Clear the DTCs after completing the diagnosis. Test drive the vehicle for three drive cycles in order to verify that the DTC does not reset. Use the following procedure in order to complete one drive cycle:

1. Start the vehicle.
2. Drive the vehicle over 16 km/h (10 mph).
3. Stop the vehicle.
4. Turn the ignition switch to the OFF position.

Important: Zero the J 39200 test leads before making any resistance measurements.

GC402980301300AX

Fig. 38 Code C1242: Rear ESB Does Not Hold Motor (Part 1 of 3). Alero, Grand Am & Malibu

Step	Action	Value(s)	Yes	No
1	Was the Diagnostic System Check performed?	—	*Go to Step 2*	Refer to *Diagnostic System Check*
2	Inspect the following connectors for the correct wire color/connector cavity combinations: • The 6-way ABS brake motor pack connector • The EBCM connector Are the correct wires located in the correct connector cavities?	—	*Go to Step 3*	*Go to Step 10*
3	1. Turn the ignition switch to the RUN position. Do not start the engine. 2. Pump the brake pedal until it is firm in order to deplete the brake booster vacuum reservoir. 3. Raise and support the vehicle so that the rear wheels are approximately 6 inches off the floor. 4. Turn the ignition switch to the run position. 5. Install a *Scan Tool*. 6. Apply firm pressure to the brake pedal. 7. Select the Special Functions on the *Scan Tool*. 8. Select the Manual Control function on the *Scan Tool*. 9. Select the ABS Motor Apply function of the rear ABS channel on the *Scan Tool*. 10. Use the *Scan Tool* in order to apply the rear ABS motor. 11. Wait for five seconds. 12. Have an assistant try to spin the rear wheels by hand. Could the assistant spin the rear wheels?	—	*Go to Step 9*	*Go to Step 4*
4	1. Exit the Manual Control function. 2. Turn the ignition switch to the OFF position. 3. Disconnect the following connectors: • The 6-way ABS brake motor pack connector • The EBCM connector. 4. Use the *J 39200* in order to measure the resistance between the 6-way ABS brake motor pack harness connector terminal C and the EBCM harness connector terminal F. Is the resistance within the specified range?	0–2 Ω	*Go to Step 5*	*Go to Step 11*
5	Use the *J 39200* in order to measure the resistance between the 6-way ABS brake motor pack harness connector terminal D and the EBCM harness connector terminal E. Is the resistance within the specified range?	0–2 Ω	*Go to Step 6*	*Go to Step 12*
6	Use the *J 39200* in order to measure the resistance between the 6-way ABS brake motor pack connector terminal C and the ABS brake motor pack connector terminal D. Is the resistance within the specified range?	0.2–1.5 Ω	*Go to Step 7*	*Go to Step 9*

GC402980301300BX

Fig. 38 Code C1242: Rear ESB Does Not Hold Motor (Part 2 of 3). Alero, Grand Am & Malibu

Step	Action	Value(s)	Yes	No
7	1. Inspect the following connectors: • The 6-way ABS brake motor pack connector • The EBCM connector 2. Inspect the above connectors for the following conditions: • Poor terminal contact • Corrosion Are there signs of poor terminal contact or corrosion?	—	*Go to Step 13*	*Go to Step 8*
8	1. Turn the ignition switch to the OFF position. 2. Reconnect the EBCM connector. 3. Reconnect the 6-way ABS brake motor pack connector. 4. Start the engine. Do not depress the brake pedal while starting the engine. 5. Allow the engine to run for at least 10 seconds. 6. Repeat the above ignition cycle sequence at least two more times. 7. Use the *Scan Tool* in order to look for DTCs. Does the DTC C1242 set during the last three ignition cycles?	—	*Go to Step 14*	*Go to Step 15*
9	Replace the ABS brake motor pack. Is the repair complete?	—	Refer to *Diagnostic System Check*	—
10	Place the correct wires into the connector cavities. Is the repair complete?	—	Refer to *Diagnostic System Check*	—
11	Repair the open or high resistance in CKT 1284. Is the repair complete?	—	Refer to *Diagnostic System Check*	—
12	Repair the open or high resistance in CKT 1285. Is the repair complete?	—	Refer to *Diagnostic System Check*	—
13	Replace the terminals that exhibit signs of poor terminal contact or corrosion. Is the repair complete?	—	Refer to *Diagnostic System Check*	—
14	Replace the EBCM. Is the repair complete?	—	Refer to *Diagnostic System Check*	—
15	The malfunction is intermittent or is not present at this time. Refer to Diagnostic Aids for more information.	—	—	—

GC402980301300CX

Fig. 38 Code C1242: Rear ESB Does Not Hold Motor (Part 3 of 3). Alero, Grand Am & Malibu

Circuit Description

A 5.0 volt reference is supplied to the steering wheel position sensor through the EBCM connector terminal 1 to sensor terminal A. Steering wheel position input to the EBCM is provided through steering wheel position sensor terminal B to the EBCM terminal 17. Steering wheel position sensor ground is provided through the EBCM terminal 5.

Conditions for Setting the DTC

- DTC C1243 can set anytime.
- Steering wheel position sensor voltage is less than 0.4 volts or greater than 4.7 volts for 2 seconds or longer.
- Steering wheel position sensor voltage changes by more than 2.5 volts within 8.0 milliseconds.

Action Taken When the DTC Sets

- A malfunction DTC stores.
- VES is disabled and power steering returns to full assist.
- ABS remains functional.

Conditions for Clearing the DTC

- The condition responsible for setting the DTC no longer exists and the Scan Tool Clear DTCs function is used.
- 100 drive cycles pass with no DTCs detected. A drive cycle consists of starting the vehicle, driving the vehicle over 16 km/h (10 mph), stopping and then turning the ignition OFF.

Diagnostic Aids

The following conditions may cause an intermittent malfunction:

- A poor connection
- Rubbed-through wire insulation
- A broken wire inside the insulation
- Open or short in any of the sensor signal circuit wires
- Malfunctioning steering wheel position sensor

Use the Snapshot function of the Scan Tool to aid in monitoring steering wheel position sensor voltages.

Use the enhanced diagnostic function of the Scan Tool in order to measure the frequency of the malfunction.

Thoroughly inspect any circuitry that may be causing the intermittent complaint for the following conditions:

- Backed out terminals
- Improper mating
- Broken locks
- Improperly formed or damaged terminals
- Poor terminal-to-wiring connections
- Physical damage to the wiring harness

Ensure all ABS DTCs are diagnosed and corrected prior to clearing VES DTCs. Clearing VES DTCs will automatically clear ABS DTCs resulting in a loss of DTC history data.

GC4020052201010X

Fig. 39 Code C1243: VES Steering Wheel Sensor Circuit Fault (Part 1 of 5). Alero & Grand Am

Step	Action	Value(s)	Yes	No
	Important: Zero the J 39200 test leads before making any resistance measurements. Refer to the J 39200 user's manual. **Important:** Difficulty may occur when trying to locate intermittent malfunctions in the steering wheel position sensor circuit. Do not disturb any of the electrical connections. Change the electrical connections only when instructed to do so by a step in the diagnostic table.			
1	Was the ABS Diagnostic System Check performed?	—	Go to *Step 2*	Go to *A Diagnostic System Check - ABS*
2	1. Start the engine. 2. Using a scan tool, select DATA DISPLAY. 3. Select VES DATA. 4. Monitor the steering wheel sensor voltage while rotating the steering wheel from stop–to–stop. Does the voltage vary within the specified range?	0.4–4.7 V	Go to *Step 43*	Go to *Step 3*
3	Is the voltage from Step 2 less than the specified value?	0.4 V	Go to *Step 5*	Go to *Step 4*
4	Is the voltage from Step 2 greater than the specified value?	4.7 V	Go to *Step 14*	Go to *Step 21*
5	1. Turn the ignition switch to the OFF position. 2. Disconnect the steering wheel position sensor. 3. Disconnect the EBCM harness connector. 4. Using the *J 39200*, measure the resistance between the EBCM harness connector terminals 17 and 5. Is the resistance within the specified range?	OL (Infinite)	Go to *Step 6*	Go to *Step 29*
6	Using the *J 39200*, measure the resistance between the EBCM harness connector terminals 1 and 5. Is the resistance within the specified range?	OL (Infinite)	Go to *Step 7*	Go to *Step 30*
7	Using the *J 39200*, measure the resistance between the EBCM harness connector terminal 17 and ground. Is the resistance within the specified range?	OL (Infinite)	Go to *Step 8*	Go to *Step 31*
8	Using the *J 39200*, measure the resistance between the EBCM harness connector terminal 1 and ground. Is the resistance within the specified range?	OL (Infinite)	Go to *Step 9*	Go to *Step 32*
9	Using the *J 39200*, measure the resistance between the EBCM harness connector terminal 1 and the steering wheel position sensor harness connector terminal A. Is the resistance within the specified range?	0–2 Ω	Go to *Step 10*	Go to *Step 33*
10	Using the *J 39200*, measure the resistance between the EBCM harness connector terminal 17 and the steering wheel position sensor harness connector terminal B. Is the resistance within the specified range?	0–2 Ω	Go to *Step 11*	Go to *Step 34*
11	Inspect EBCM harness connector terminals 1 and 17 and all the steering wheel position sensor terminals for poor terminal contact. Is poor terminal contact evident?	—	Go to *Step 35*	Go to *Step 12*
12	1. Reconnect the EBCM harness connector. 2. Turn the ignition switch to the ON position. 3. Using the *J 39200*, measure the voltage between the steering wheel position sensor harness connector terminals A and C. Is the voltage greater than the specified value?	4.0 V	Go to *Step 41*	Go to *Step 13*

GC4020052201020X

Fig. 39 Code C1243: VES Steering Wheel Sensor Circuit Fault (Part 2 of 5). Alero & Grand Am

Step	Action	Value(s)	Yes	No
13	1. Turn the ignition switch to the OFF position. 2. Inspect CKTs 1056, 1059 and 556 for damage which may result in shorts between the circuits or shorts to ground. Repair damage if present. 3. Reconnect all connectors. 4. Turn the ignition switch to the ON position. Is DTC C1243 set as a current DTC?	—	Go to *Step 42*	Go to *A Diagnostic System Check - ABS*
14	1. Turn the ignition switch to the OFF position. 2. Disconnect the steering wheel position sensor. 3. Turn the ignition switch to the ON position. Does the scan tool display the steering wheel position sensor voltage within the specified range?	0–1.0 V	Go to *Step 15*	Go to *Step 16*
15	Using the *J 39200* measure the resistance between the steering wheel position sensor harness connector terminal C and ground. Is the resistance within the specified range?	0–5.0 Ω	Go to *Step 41*	Go to *Step 18*
16	1. Turn the ignition switch to the OFF position. 2. Disconnect the EBCM harness connector. 3. Turn the ignition switch to the ON position. 4. Using the *J 39200*, measure the voltage between the EBCM harness connector terminal 17 and ground. Is the voltage within the specified range?	0–1.0 V	Go to *Step 17*	Go to *Step 38*
17	1. Turn the ignition switch to the OFF position. 2. Inspect CKT 1059 for damage which may result in a short to voltage with all of the connectors connected. Repair damage if evident. 3. Reconnect all connectors. 4. Turn the ignition switch to the ON position. Is DTC C1243 set as a current DTC?	—	Go to *Step 42*	Go to *A Diagnostic System Check - ABS*
18	1. Turn the ignition switch to the OFF position. 2. Disconnect the EBCM harness connector. 3. Using the *J 39200*, measure the resistance between the steering wheel position sensor harness connector terminal C and the EBCM harness connector terminal 5. Is the resistance within the specified range?	0–2.0 Ω	Go to *Step 19*	Go to *Step 36*
19	1. Turn the ignition switch to the ON position. 2. Using the *J 39200*, measure the voltage between the EBCM harness connector terminal 5 and ground. Is the voltage within the specified range?	0–1.0 V	Go to *Step 20*	Go to *Step 37*
20	1. Turn the ignition switch to the OFF position. 2. Inspect the EBCM harness connector and the steering wheel position sensor terminals for poor terminal contact. Replace any terminals with poor terminal contact. 3. Inspect all the steering wheel position sensor circuits for damage which may result in a short to voltage or an open with all the connectors connected. Repair damage if present. 4. Reconnect all the connectors. 5. Turn the ignition switch to the ON position Is DTC C1243 set as a current DTC?	—	Go to *Step 42*	Go to *A Diagnostic System Check - ABS*

GC4020052201030X

Fig. 39 Code C1243: VES Steering Wheel Sensor Circuit Fault (Part 3 of 5). Alero & Grand Am

Step	Action	Value(s)	Yes	No
21	1. Turn the ignition switch to the ON position. 2. With the steering wheel position sensor connected, use the *J 39200* in order to measure the voltage between the steering wheel position sensor harness connector terminals A and C by backprobing the connector. Is the voltage greater than the specified value?	4.7 V	Go to *Step 22*	Go to *Step 23*
22	1. Turn the ignition switch to the OFF position. 2. Disconnect the steering wheel position sensor. 3. Turn the ignition switch to the ON position. 4. Using the *J 39200*, measure the resistance between the steering wheel position sensor harness connector terminals A and C. Is the voltage greater than the specified value?	4.7 V	Go to *Step 27*	Go to *Step 41*
23	1. Turn the ignition switch to the OFF position. 2. Disconnect the EBCM harness connector. 3. Disconnect the steering wheel position sensor harness connector. 4. Using the *J 39200*, measure the resistance between the EBCM harness connector terminals 1 and 17. Is the resistance within the specified range?	OL (Infinite)	Go to *Step 24*	Go to *Step 40*
24	Using the MIN/MAX function of the *J 39200*, measure the resistance between the steering wheel position sensor terminals A and B while rotating the steering wheel slowly from stop–to–stop. Is the resistance within the specified range?	390–12,000 Ω	Go to *Step 25*	Go to *Step 41*
25	1. Inspect CKTs 1056 and 1059 for damage which may result in a short between the two circuits with all the connectors connected. Repair damage if present. 2. Reconnect all connectors. 3. Being very careful not to move the steering wheel, turn the ignition switch to the ON position. Is DTC C1243 set as a current DTC?	—	Go to *Step 42*	Go to *Step 26*
26	Turn the steering wheel slowly from stop–to–stop. Is DTC C1243 set as a current DTC?	—	Go to *Step 41*	Go to *A Diagnostic System Check - ABS*
27	1. Turn the ignition switch to the OFF position. 2. Disconnect the EBCM harness connector. 3. Turn the ignition switch to the ON position. 4. Using the *J 39200*, measure the voltage between the EBCM harness connector terminal 1 and ground. Is the voltage greater than the specified voltage?	1.0 V	Go to *Step 39*	Go to *Step 28*
28	1. Turn the ignition switch to the OFF position. 2. Inspect CKT 1056 for damage which may result in a short to voltage with all the connectors connected. Repair damage if present. 3. Reconnect all the connectors. 4. Turn the ignition switch to the ON position. Is DTC C1243 set as a current DTC?	—	Go to *Step 42*	Go to *A Diagnostic System Check - ABS*
29	Repair the short between CKTs 1059 and 556. Is the repair complete?	—	Go to *A Diagnostic System Check - ABS*	—

GC4020052201040X

Fig. 39 Code C1243: VES Steering Wheel Sensor Circuit Fault (Part 4 of 5). Alero & Grand Am

Step	Action	Value(s)	Yes	No
30	Repair the short between CKTs 1056 and 556. Is the repair complete?	—	Go to *A Diagnostic System Check - ABS*	—
31	Repair the short to ground in CKT 1059. Is the repair complete?	—	Go to *A Diagnostic System Check - ABS*	—
32	Repair the short to ground in CKT 1056. Is the repair complete?	—	Go to *A Diagnostic System Check - ABS*	—
33	Repair the open or high resistance in CKT 1056. Is the repair complete?	—	Go to *A Diagnostic System Check - ABS*	—
34	Repair the open or high resistance in CKT 1059. Is the repair complete?	—	Go to *A Diagnostic System Check - ABS*	—
35	Replace the terminals that exhibit poor contact. Is the repair complete?	—	Go to *A Diagnostic System Check - ABS*	—
36	Repair the open or high resistance in CKT 556. Is the repair complete?	—	Go to *A Diagnostic System Check - ABS*	—
37	Repair the short to voltage in CKT 556. Is the repair complete?	—	Go to *A Diagnostic System Check - ABS*	—
38	Repair the short to voltage in CKT 1059. Is the repair complete?	—	Go to *A Diagnostic System Check - ABS*	—
39	Repair the short to voltage in CKT 1056. Is the repair complete?	—	Go to *A Diagnostic System Check - ABS*	—
40	Repair the short between CKTs 1056 and 1059. Is the repair complete?	—	Go to *A Diagnostic System Check - ABS*	—
41	Replace the Steering Wheel Position Sensor. Is the repair complete?	—	Go to *A Diagnostic System Check - ABS*	—
42	Replace the EBCM. Is the repair complete?	—	Go to *A Diagnostic System Check - ABS*	—
43	The malfunction is intermittent or not present at this time. Refer to Diagnostic Aids for more information. Is the action complete?	—	System OK	—

GC4020052201050X

Fig. 39 Code C1243: VES Steering Wheel Sensor Circuit Fault (Part 5 of 5). Alero & Grand Am

Circuit Description

DTC C1244 detects a bound-up ESB, a stuck ABS motor, or a seized brake modulator. When the release is commanded during initialization, the ESB should release the ABS motor, resulting in the sensed current being less than the commanded current (motor spins freely). If the ABS motor is not moving, sensed current will be equal to stall currents.

Conditions for Setting the DTC

DTC C1244 can set during brake motor initialization at the following speeds:

- 0 km/h (0 mph) when the brake is off
- 5 km/h (3 mph) when the brake is on

DTC C1244 can set during ABS stops

A malfunction exists if the EBCM detects a condition in which the EBCM cannot move the ABS motor in either direction.

Action Taken When the DTC Sets

- A malfunction DTC stores.
- The ABS disables.
- The ABS warning indicator turns on.

Conditions for Clearing the DTC

- The condition responsible for setting the DTC no longer exists and the Scan Tool Clear DTCs function is used.
- 100 drive cycles pass with no DTC(s) detected. A drive cycle consists of starting the vehicle, driving the vehicle over 16 km/h (10 mph), stopping and then turning the ignition off.

Diagnostic Aids

The following conditions may cause an intermittent malfunction if the conditions exist in a mechanical part of the system:

- Sticking
- Binding
- Slipping

Use the enhanced diagnostic function of the Scan Tool in order to measure the frequency of the malfunction. DTC C1244 may set after modulator disassembly if the modulator pistons are positioned at the bottom of the modulator piston bore.

Thoroughly inspect any circuitry that may be causing the intermittent complaint for the following conditions:

- Backed out terminals
- Improper mating
- Broken locks
- Improperly formed or damaged terminals
- Poor terminal-to-wiring connections
- Physical damage to the wiring harness

Clear the DTCs after completing the diagnosis. Test drive the vehicle for three drive cycles in order to verify that the DTC does not reset. Use the following procedure in order to complete one drive cycle:

1. Start the vehicle.
2. Drive the vehicle over 16 km/h (10 mph).
3. Stop the vehicle.
4. Turn the ignition to the OFF position.

Important: Zero the J 39200 test leads before making any resistance measurements. Refer to the J 39200 user's manual.

GC402980301500AX

Fig. 40 Code C1244: LH Front ABS Channel Does Not Move (Part 1 of 4). Alero, Grand Am & Malibu

Step	Action	Value(s)	Yes	No
6	1. Exit the Manual Control function on the *Scan Tool.* 2. Turn the ignition switch to the OFF position. 3. Disconnect the 6-way ABS brake motor pack connector. 4. Disconnect the EBCM connector 5. Use the *J 39200* in order to measure the resistance between the EBCM connector terminal G and the EBCM connector terminal H. Is the resistance within the specified range?	OL (Infinite)	*Go to Step 7*	*Go to Step 12*
7	Use the *J 39200* in order to measure the resistance between the ABS brake motor pack connector terminal A and the ABS brake motor pack connector terminal B. Is the resistance within the specified range?	0.2–1.5Ω	*Go to Step 8*	*Go to Step 13*
8	1. Inspect the following connectors: • The 6-way ABS motor pack connector • The EBCM connector 2. Inspect the connectors for the following conditions: • Poor terminal contact • Corrosion Do any of the terminals exhibit poor terminal contact or corrosion?	—	*Go to Step 15*	*Go to Step 9*
9	1. Turn the ignition switch to the OFF position. 2. Reconnect the EBCM connector. 3. Reconnect the ABS motor pack connector. 4. Start the engine. Do not depress the brake pedal. 5. Allow the engine to run for at least ten seconds. 6. Repeat the above ignition cycle sequence two more times. 7. Use the *Scan Tool* in order to inspect for DTCs. Does DTC C1244 set during the last three ignition cycles?	—	*Go to Step 16*	*Go to Step 17*
10	1. Select Special Functions on the *Scan Tool.* 2. Use the *Scan Tool* in order to perform the Gear Tension Relief function. 3. Turn the ignition switch to the OFF position. 4. Remove the brake modulator/master cylinder assembly from the vehicle. 5. Separate the ABS brake motor pack from the brake modulator. 6. Grasp the left front brake modulator gear and attempt to rotate the gear. (The ABS brake modulator left front gear is the gear that is closest to the front when the ABS brake modulator is mounted in the vehicle.) Is it possible to rotate the left front brake modulator gear at least 8.5 full revolutions from lock to lock?	—	*Go to Step 13*	*Go to Step 14*

GC402980301500CX

Fig. 40 Code C1244: LH Front ABS Channel Does Not Move (Part 3 of 4). Alero, Grand Am & Malibu

Step	Action	Value(s)	Yes	No
1	Was the Diagnostic System Check performed?	—	*Go to Step 2*	Refer to *Diagnostic System Check.*
2	Inspect the following connectors for the correct wire color/connector cavity combinations: • The 6-way ABS brake motor pack connector • The EBCM connector Are the correct wires located in the correct connector cavities?	—	*Go to Step 3*	*Go to Step 11*
3	1. Turn the ignition switch to the RUN position. Do not start the engine. 2. Pump the brake pedal until the brake pedal is firm in order to deplete the brake booster vacuum reservoir. 3. Install a *Scan Tool.* 4. Select Special Functions on the *Scan Tool.* 5. Select the Manual Control function on the *Scan Tool.* 6. Select the ABS Motor Apply function of the left front ABS channel on the *Scan Tool.* 7. Use the *Scan Tool* in order to apply the left front ABS motor. 8. Wait for five seconds. 9. Apply firm pressure to the brake pedal. 10. Select the left front ABS Motor Release function on the *Scan Tool.* 11. Use the *Scan Tool* in order to release the left front ABS motor. Does the brake pedal fall?	—	*Go to Step 4*	*Go to Step 5*
4	1. Continue to apply firm pressure on the brake pedal. 2. Select the left front ABS Motor Apply function on the *Scan Tool.* 3. Use the *Scan Tool* in order to apply the left front ABS motor. Does the brake pedal rise?	—	*Go to Step 17*	*Go to Step 5*
5	1. Remove the firm pressure from the brake pedal. 2. Select the left front ABS Motor Apply function on the *Scan Tool.* 3. Use the *Scan Tool* in order to apply the left front ABS motor. Carefully observe the following currents: • The left front ABS motor commanded current • The left front ABS motor feedback current. Did the left front ABS motor feedback current momentarily drop below the specified current?	8 A	*Go to Step 6*	*Go to Step 10*

GC402980301500BX

Fig. 40 Code C1244: LH Front ABS Channel Does Not Move (Part 2 of 4). Alero, Grand Am & Malibu

Step	Action	Value(s)	Yes	No
11	Place the wires into the correct connector cavities. Is the repair complete?	—	Refer to *Diagnostic System Check*	—
12	Repair the short between CKT 1280 and CKT 1281. Is the repair complete?	—	Refer to *Diagnostic System Check*	—
13	Replace the ABS motor pack. Is the repair complete?	—	Refer to *Diagnostic System Check*	—
14	Replace the brake modulator. Is the repair complete?	—	Refer to *Diagnostic System Check*	—
15	Replace the terminals that exhibit signs of poor terminal contact or corrosion. Is the repair complete?	—	Refer to *Diagnostic System Check*	—
16	Replace the EBCM. Is the repair complete?	—	Refer to *Diagnostic System Check*	—
17	The malfunction is intermittent or is not present at this time. Refer to Diagnostic Aids for more information.	—	—	—

GC402980301500DX

Fig. 40 Code C1244: LH Front ABS Channel Does Not Move (Part 4 of 4). Alero, Grand Am & Malibu

Circuit Description

DTC C1245 detects a bound-up ESB, a stuck ABS motor, or a seized brake modulator. When the release is commanded during initialization, the ESB should release the ABS motor, resulting in the feedback current being less than the commanded current (motor spins freely). If the ABS motor is not moving, feedback current will be equal to commanded current.

Conditions for Setting the DTC

DTC C1245 can set during brake motor initialization at the following speeds:

- 0 km (0 mph) when the brake is off
- 5 km (3 mph) when the brake is on

DTC C1245 can set during ABS stops

A malfunction exists if the EBCM detects a condition in which the EBCM cannot move the ABS motor in either direction.

Action Taken When the DTC Sets

- A malfunction DTC stores.
- The ABS disables.
- The ABS warning indicator turns on.

Conditions for Clearing the DTC

- The condition responsible for setting the DTC no longer exists and the Scan Tool Clear DTCs function is used.
- 100 drive cycles pass with no DTC(s) detected. A drive cycle consists of starting the vehicle, driving the vehicle over 16 km/h (10 mph), stopping and then turning the ignition off.

Diagnostic Aids

The following conditions may cause an intermittent malfunction if the conditions exist in a mechanical part of the system:

- Sticking
- Binding
- Slipping

Use the enhanced diagnostic function of the Scan Tool in order to measure the frequency of the malfunction. DTC C1245 may set after modulator disassembly if the modulator pistons are positioned at the bottom of the modulator piston bore.

Thoroughly inspect any circuitry that may be causing the intermittent complaint for the following conditions:

- Backed out terminals
- Improper mating
- Broken locks
- Improperly formed or damaged terminals
- Poor terminal-to-wiring connections
- Physical damage to the wiring harness

Clear the DTCs after completing the diagnosis. Test drive the vehicle for three drive cycles in order to verify that the DTC does not reset. Use the following procedure in order to complete one drive cycle:

1. Start the vehicle.
2. Drive the vehicle over 16 km/h (10 mph).
3. Stop the vehicle.
4. Turn the ignition to the OFF position.

Important: Zero the J 39200 test leads before making any resistance measurements. Refer to the J 39200 user's manual.

GC402980301600AX

Fig. 41 Code C1245: RH Front ABS Channel Does Not Move (Part 1 of 4). Alero, Grand Am & Malibu

Step	Action	Value(s)	Yes	No
1	Was the Diagnostic System Check performed?	—	Go to Step 2	Refer to Diagnostic System Check
2	Inspect the following connectors for the correct wire color/connector cavity combinations: • The 6-way ABS brake motor pack connector • The EBCM connector Are the correct wires located in the correct connector cavities?	—	Go to Step 3	Go to Step 11
3	1. Turn the ignition switch to the RUN position. Do not start the engine. 2. Pump the brake pedal until it is firm in order to deplete the brake booster vacuum reservoir. 3. Install a *Scan Tool.* 4. Select Special Functions on the *Scan Tool.* 5. Select the Manual Control function on the *Scan Tool.* 6. Select the ABS Motor Apply function of the right front ABS channel on the *Scan Tool.* 7. Use the *Scan Tool* to apply the right front ABS motor. 8. Wait for five seconds. 9. Apply firm pressure to the brake pedal. 10. Select the right front ABS Motor Release function on the *Scan Tool.* 11. Use the *Scan Tool* in order to release the right front ABS motor. Does the brake pedal fall?	—	Go to Step 4	Go to Step 5
4	1. Continue to apply firm pressure on the brake pedal. 2. Select the right front ABS Motor Apply function on the *Scan Tool.* 3. Use the *Scan Tool* in order to apply the right front ABS motor. Does the brake pedal rise?	—	Go to Step 17	Go to Step 5
5	1. Remove the firm pressure from the brake pedal. 2. Select the right front ABS Motor Apply function on the *Scan Tool.* 3. Use the *Scan Tool* in order to apply the right front ABS motor. Carefully observe the following currents: • The right front ABS motor commanded current • The right front ABS motor feedback current. Did the right front ABS motor feedback current Momentarily drop below the specified current?	8 A	Go to Step 6	Go to Step 10

GC402980301600BX

Fig. 41 Code C1245: RH Front ABS Channel Does Not Move (Part 2 of 4). Alero, Grand Am & Malibu

Step	Action	Value(s)	Yes	No
6	1. Exit the Manual Control function on the *Scan Tool.* 2. Turn the ignition switch to the OFF position. 3. Disconnect the 6-way ABS brake motor pack connector. 4. Disconnect the EBCM connector 5. Use the *J 39200* in order to measure the resistance between the EBCM connector terminal A and the EBCM connector terminal B. Is the resistance within the specified range?	OL (Infinite)	Go to Step 7	Go to Step 12
7	Use the *J 39200* in order to measure the resistance between the ABS brake motor pack connector terminal E and the ABS brake motor pack connector terminal F. Is the resistance within the specified range?	0.2–1.5Ω	Go to Step 8	Go to Step 13
8	1. Inspect the following connectors: • The 6-way ABS motor pack connector • The EBCM connector 2. Inspect the connectors for the following conditions: • Poor terminal contact • Corrosion Do any of the terminals exhibit poor terminal contact or corrosion?	—	Go to Step 15	Go to Step 9
9	1. Turn the ignition switch to the OFF position. 2. Reconnect the EBCM connector. 3. Reconnect the ABS motor pack connector. 4. Start the engine. Do not depress the brake pedal. 5. Allow the engine to run for at least ten seconds. 6. Repeat the above ignition cycle sequence two more times. 7. Use the *Scan Tool* in order to inspect for DTCs. Does DTC C1245 set during the last three ignition cycles?	—	Go to Step 16	Go to Step 17
10	1. Select Special Functions on the *Scan Tool.* 2. Use the *Scan Tool* in order to perform the Gear Tension Relief function. 3. Turn the ignition switch to the OFF position. 4. Remove the brake modulator/master cylinder assembly from the vehicle. 5. Separate the ABS brake motor pack from the brake modulator. 6. Grasp the right front brake modulator gear and attempt to rotate the gear. (The ABS brake modulator right front gear is the gear that is closest to the rear when the ABS brake modulator is mounted in the vehicle.) Is it possible to rotate the right front brake modulator gear at least 8.5 full revolutions from lock to lock?	—	Go to Step 13	Go to Step 14
11	Place the wires into the correct connector cavities. Is the repair complete?	—	Refer to Diagnostic System Check	—

GC402980301600CX

Fig. 41 Code C1245: RH Front ABS Channel Does Not Move (Part 3 of 4). Alero, Grand Am & Malibu

Step	Action	Value(s)	Yes	No
12	Repair the short between CKT 1282 and CKT 1283. Is the repair complete?	—	Refer to Diagnostic System Check	—
13	Replace the ABS motor pack. Is the repair complete?	—	Refer to Diagnostic System Check	—
14	Replace the brake modulator. Is the repair complete?	—	Refer to Diagnostic System Check	—
15	Replace the terminals that exhibit signs of poor terminal contact or corrosion. Is the repair complete?	—	Refer to Diagnostic System Check	—
16	Replace the EBCM. Is the repair complete?	—	Refer to Diagnostic System Check	—
17	The malfunction is intermittent or is not present at this time. Refer to Diagnostic Aids for more information.	—	—	—

GC402980301600DX

Fig. 41 Code C1245: RH Front ABS Channel Does Not Move (Part 4 of 4). Alero, Grand Am & Malibu

Circuit Description

DTC C1246 detects a bound-up ESB, a stuck ABS motor, or a seized brake modulator. When the release is commanded during initialization, the ESB should release the ABS motor, resulting in the feedback current being less than the commanded current (motor spins freely). If the ABS motor is not moving, feedback current will be equal to commanded current.

Conditions for Setting the DTC

DTC C1246 can set during brake motor initialization at the following speeds:

- 0 km (0 mph) when the brake is off
- 5 km (3 mph) when the brake is on

DTC C1246 can set during ABS stops

A malfunction exists if the EBCM detects a condition in which the EBCM cannot move the ABS motor in either direction.

Action Taken When the DTC Sets

- A malfunction DTC stores.
- The ABS disables.
- The ABS warning indicator turns on.

Conditions for Clearing the DTC

- The condition responsible for setting the DTC no longer exists and the Scan Tool Clear DTCs function is used.
- 100 drive cycles pass with no DTC(s) detected. A drive cycle consists of starting the vehicle, driving the vehicle over 16 km/h (10 mph), stopping and then turning the ignition off.

Diagnostic Aids

The following conditions may cause an intermittent malfunction if the conditions exist in a mechanical part of the system:

- Sticking
- Binding

Use the enhanced diagnostic function of the Scan Tool in order to measure the frequency of the malfunction. DTC C1246 may set after modulator disassembly if the modulator pistons are positioned at the bottom of the modulator piston bore. Depending on the frequency of the malfunction, a physical inspection of the mechanical parts suspected of causing the malfunction may be necessary.

Thoroughly inspect any circuitry that may be causing the intermittent complaint for the following conditions:

- Backed out terminals
- Improper mating
- Broken locks
- Improperly formed or damaged terminals
- Poor terminal-to-wiring connections
- Physical damage to the wiring harness

Clear the DTCs after completing the diagnosis. Test drive the vehicle for three drive cycles in order to verify that the DTC does not reset. Use the following procedure in order to complete one drive cycle:

1. Start the vehicle.
2. Drive the vehicle over 16 km/h (10 mph).
3. Stop the vehicle.
4. Turn the ignition to the OFF position.

Important: Zero the J 39200 test leads before making any resistance measurements. Refer to the J 39200 user's manual.

GC402980301700AX

Fig. 42 Code C1246: Rear ABS Channel Does Not Move (Part 1 of 4). Alero, Grand Am & Malibu

Step	Action	Value(s)	Yes	No
1	Was the Diagnostic System Check performed?	—	Go to Step 2	Refer to Diagnostic System Check
2	Inspect the following connectors for the correct wire color/connector cavity combinations: • The 6-way ABS brake motor pack connector • The EBCM connector Are the correct wires located in the correct connector cavities?	—	Go to Step 3	Go to Step 11
3	1. Raise and suitably support the vehicle. Verify that the rear wheels are approximately 15 cm (6 in) above the floor. 2. Turn the ignition switch to the RUN position. Do not start the engine. 3. Pump the brake pedal until it is firm in order to deplete the brake booster vacuum reservoir. 4. Install a *Scan Tool.* 5. Apply firm downward pressure on the brake pedal. 6. Select Special Functions on the *Scan Tool.* 7. Select the Manual Control function on the *Scan Tool.* 8. Select the Rear Axle Motor Apply function of the rear ABS channel on the *Scan Tool.* 9. Use the *Scan Tool* in order to apply the rear axle motor. 10. Have an assistant attempt to rotate the rear wheels by hand. Is it possible to rotate the rear wheels by hand?	—	Go to Step 5	Go to Step 4
4	1. Continue to apply firm downward pressure on the brake pedal. 2. Select the Rear Axle Motor Release function on the *Scan Tool.* 3. Use the *Scan Tool* in order to release the rear axle motor. Is it possible to rotate the rear wheels by hand?	—	Go to Step 17	Go to Step 5
5	1. Remove the firm pressure from the brake pedal. 2. Select the Rear Axle Motor Apply function on the *Scan Tool.* 3. Use the *Scan Tool* in order to apply the rear axle motor. Carefully observe the following currents: • The rear axle motor commanded current • The rear axle motor feedback current. Did the rear motor feedback current momentarily drop below the specified current?	8 A	Go to Step 6	Go to Step 10

GC402980301700BX

Fig. 42 Code C1246: Rear ABS Channel Does Not Move (Part 2 of 4). Alero, Grand Am & Malibu

Step	Action	Value(s)	Yes	No
6	1. Exit the Manual Control function on the *Scan Tool.* 2. Turn the ignition switch to the OFF position. 3. Disconnect the 6-way ABS brake motor pack connector. 4. Disconnect the EBCM connector. 5. Use the *J 39200* in order to measure the resistance between the EBCM connector terminal F and the EBCM connector terminal E. Is the resistance within the specified range?	OL (Infinite)	*Go to Step 7*	*Go to Step 12*
7	Use the *J 39200* in order to measure the resistance between the ABS brake motor pack connector terminal C and the ABS brake motor pack connector terminal D. Is the resistance within the specified range?	0.2–1.5 Ω	*Go to Step 8*	*Go to Step 13*
8	1. Inspect the following connectors: • The 6-way ABS motor pack connector • The EBCM connector 2. Inspect the connectors for the following conditions: • Poor terminal contact • Corrosion Do any of the terminals exhibit poor terminal contact or corrosion?	—	*Go to Step 15*	*Go to Step 9*
9	1. Turn the ignition switch to the OFF position. 2. Reconnect the EBCM connector. 3. Reconnect the ABS motor pack connector. 4. Start the engine. Do not depress the brake pedal. 5. Allow the engine to run for at least ten seconds. 6. Repeat the above ignition cycle sequence two more times. 7. Use the *Scan Tool* in order to inspect for DTCs. Does DTC C1246 set during the last three ignition cycles?	—	*Go to Step 16*	*Go to Step 17*
10	1. Select Special Functions on the *Scan Tool.* 2. Use the *Scan Tool* in order to perform the Gear Tension Relief function. 3. Turn the ignition switch to the OFF position. 4. Remove the hydraulic modulator/master cylinder assembly from the vehicle. 5. Separate the ABS brake motor pack from the hydraulic modulator. 6. Grasp the middle gear on the hydraulic modulator and attempt to rotate the gear. Is it possible to rotate the middle gear on the hydraulic modulator at least seven full revolutions from lock to lock?	—	*Go to Step 13*	*Go to Step 14*

GC402980301700CX

Fig. 42 Code C1246: Rear ABS Channel Does Not Move (Part 3 of 4). Alero, Grand Am & Malibu

Step	Action	Value(s)	Yes	No
11	Place the wires into the correct connector cavities. Is the repair complete?	—	Refer to *Diagnostic System Check*	—
12	Repair the short between CKT 1284 and CKT 1285. Is the repair complete?	—	Refer to *Diagnostic System Check*	—
13	Replace the ABS motor pack. Is the repair complete?	—	Refer to *Diagnostic System Check*	—
14	Replace the hydraulic modulator. Is the repair complete?	—	Refer to *Diagnostic System Check*	—
15	Replace the terminals that exhibit signs of poor terminal contact or corrosion. Is the repair complete?	—	Refer to *Diagnostic System Check*	—
16	Replace the EBCM. Is the repair complete?	—	Refer to *Diagnostic System Check*	—
17	The malfunction is intermittent or is not present at this time. Refer to Diagnostic Aids for more information.	—	—	—

GC402980301700DX

Fig. 42 Code C1246: Rear ABS Channel Does Not Move (Part 4 of 4). Alero, Grand Am & Malibu

Circuit Description

DTC C1247 detects a stripped nut or gear assembly during initialization. During the homing sequence, the piston should reach the top of the bore. Then the ABS motor stalls. If the ABS motor does not stall, the ABS motor must be spinning with little or no resistance. This indicates a nut/screw or gear malfunction.

Conditions for Setting the DTC

DTC C1247 can only set during initialization.

A malfunction exists if the feedback current is less than the command current for a specified period of time.

Action Taken When the DTC Sets

- A malfunction DTC stores.
- The ABS disables.
- The ABS warning indicator turns on.

Conditions for Clearing the DTC

- The condition responsible for setting the DTC no longer exists and the Scan Tool Clear DTCs function is used.
- 100 drive cycles pass with no DTCs detected. A drive cycle consists of starting the vehicle, driving the vehicle over 16 km/h (10 mph), stopping and then turning the ignition switch to the OFF position.

Diagnostic Aids

The following conditions may cause an intermittent malfunction if the conditions exist in a mechanical part of the system:

- Sticking
- Binding
- Slipping

Use the enhanced diagnostic function of the Scan Tool in order to measure the frequency of the malfunction. DTC C1247 may set after modulator disassembly if the modulator pistons are positioned at the bottom of the modulator piston bore. If DTC C1247 only occurs once and DTC C1256 also occurs, refer to DTC C1256. If intermittent and enhanced diagnostics shows this DTC occurs during ABS, refer to DTC C1256.

Depending on the frequency of the malfunction, a physical inspection of the mechanical parts suspected of causing the malfunction may be necessary.

Clear the DTCs after completing the diagnosis. Test drive the vehicle for three drive cycles in order to verify that the DTC does not reset. Use the following procedure in order to complete one drive cycle:

1. Start the vehicle.
2. Drive the vehicle over 16 km/h (10 mph).
3. Stop the vehicle.
4. Turn the ignition to the OFF position.

Important: Zero the J 39200 test leads before making any resistance measurements.

GC402980301800AA

Fig. 43 Code C1247: LH Front ABS Motor Free Spins (Part 1 of 5). Alero, Grand Am & Malibu

Step	Action	Value(s)	Yes	No
1	Was the Diagnostic System Check performed?	—	*Go to Step 2*	Refer to *Diagnostic System Check*
2	1. Turn the ignition switch to the RUN position. Do not start the engine. 2. Use the *Scan Tool* in order to read the DTCs. Does DTC C1256 also set as a current DTC?	—	Refer to *DTC C1256 Left Front ABS Motor Circuit Open*	*Go to Step 3*
3	1. Raise and suitably support the vehicle. Verify that the rear wheels are approximately 15 cm (6 in) above the floor. 2. Pump the brake pedal until it is firm in order to deplete the brake booster vacuum reservoir. 3. Install a *Scan Tool.* 4. Apply firm downward pressure on the brake pedal. 5. Select Special Functions on the *Scan Tool.* 6. Select the Manual Control function on the *Scan Tool.* 7. Select the ABS Motor Apply function on the *Scan Tool.* 8. Use the *Scan Tool* to apply the left front motor. Observe the following currents: • The left front ABS motor command current • The left front ABS motor feedback current Were the left front ABS motor command current and the left front ABS motor feedback current approximately the specified current?	10 A	*Go to Step 4*	*Go to Step 6*
4	1. Apply firm pressure to the brake pedal. 2. Select the left front ABS Motor Release function on the *Scan Tool.* 3. Use the *Scan Tool* in order to release the left front ABS motor. Observe the following currents: • The left front ABS motor command current • The left front ABS motor feedback current Have the following conditions been met? • The left front ABS motor command current and the left front ABS motor feedback current approximately the specified current • The brake pedal falls	6 A	*Go to Step 5*	*Go to Step 6*
5	1. Continue to apply firm pressure to the brake pedal. 2. Select the left front ABS Motor Apply function on the *Scan Tool.* 3. Use the *Scan Tool* in order to apply the left front ABS motor. Did the brake pedal rise?	—	*Go to Step 22*	*Go to Step 6*

GC402980301800BX

Fig. 43 Code C1247: LH Front ABS Motor Free Spins (Part 2 of 5). Alero, Grand Am & Malibu

Step	Action	Value(s)	Yes	No
6	1. Turn the ignition switch to the OFF position. 2. Disconnect the 6-way ABS brake motor pack connector. 3. Disconnect the EBCM connector 4. Use the *J 39200* in order to measure the resistance between the 6-way ABS brake motor pack connector terminal A and the EBCM connector terminal G. Is the resistance within the specified value?	0–2 Ω	*Go to Step 7*	*Go to Step 15*
7	Use the *J 39200* in order to measure the resistance between the 6-way ABS brake motor pack connector terminal B and the EBCM connector terminal H. Is the resistance within the specified range?	0–2 Ω	*Go to Step 8*	*Go to Step 16*
8	Use the *J 39200* in order to measure the resistance between the 6-way ABS brake motor pack connector terminal A and the 6-way ABS brake motor pack connector terminal B. Is the resistance within the specified range?	0.2–1.5Ω	*Go to Step 9*	*Go to Step 17*
9	1. Remove the ABS brake modulator/master cylinder assembly from the vehicle. 2. Remove the ABS brake modulator gear cover. 3. Inspect for a stripped ABS brake motor pack left front gear. (The ABS brake motor pack is the unit with the three small gears. The ABS brake motor pack left front gear is the gear closest to the front when the ABS brake modulator is mounted in the vehicle.) Is the ABS brake motor left front gear stripped?	—	*Go to Step 17*	*Go to Step 10*
10	Inspect for a stripped ABS brake modulator pack left front gear. (The ABS brake modulator unit is the unit with the three large gears. The ABS brake modulator left front gear is the gear closest to the front when the ABS brake modulator is mounted in the vehicle.) Is the ABS brake modulator left front gear stripped?	—	*Go to Step 18*	*Go to Step 11*

GC402980301800CX

Fig. 43 Code C1247: LH Front ABS Motor Free Spins (Part 3 of 5). Alero, Grand Am & Malibu

Step	Action	Value(s)	Yes	No
11	1. Reconnect the 6-way ABS brake motor pack connector. 2. Reconnect the EBCM connector. 3. Carefully secure the ABS brake modulator/master cylinder into the vehicle. Secure the assembly in a position that permits observation of the gears. 4. Turn the ignition switch to the RUN position. Do not start the engine. 5. Select the Manual Control function on the *Scan Tool.* 6. Select the left front ABS Motor Apply function on the *Scan Tool.* 7. Use the *Scan Tool* in order to apply the left front ABS motor while observing the ABS brake modulator left front gear set. (The ABS brake modulator left front gear is the gear closest to the front when the ABS brake modulator is mounted in the vehicle.) 8. Select the left front ABS Motor Release function on the *Scan Tool.* 9. Use the *Scan Tool* in order to release the left front ABS motor while observing the ABS brake modulator left front gear set. 10. Select the left front ABS Motor Apply function on the *Scan Tool.* 11. Use the *Scan Tool* in order to apply the left front ABS motor while observing the ABS brake modulator left front gear set. Does the ABS brake modulator left front gear set move at least one full revolution in both directions?	—	*Go to Step 12*	*Go to Step 17*
12	1. Use the *Scan Tool* in order to perform the Gear Tension Relief function. 2. Turn the ignition switch to the OFF position. 3. Separate the ABS brake motor pack from the ABS brake modulator. 4. Grasp the ABS brake modulator left front gear. 5. Rotate the ABS brake modulator left front gear. Does the ABS brake modulator left front gear rotate more than 13 full turns from lock to lock?	—	*Go to Step 19*	*Go to Step 13*
13	1. Disconnect the 6-way ABS brake motor pack connector. 2. Disconnect the EBCM connector. 3. Inspect the connectors for the following conditions: • Poor terminal contact • Corrosion Do any of the terminals exhibit poor terminal contact or corrosion?	—	*Go to Step 20*	*Go to Step 14*

GC402980301800DX

Fig. 43 Code C1247: LH Front ABS Motor Free Spins (Part 4 of 5). Alero, Grand Am & Malibu

Step	Action	Value(s)	Yes	No
14	1. Reinstall the ABS brake modulator gear cover. 2. Reinstall the ABS brake modulator/master cylinder assembly in the vehicle. 3. Reconnect the 6-way ABS brake motor pack connector. 4. Reconnect the EBCM connector. 5. Start the engine. Do not apply pressure to the brake pedal. 6. Let the engine run for at least 10 seconds. 7. Turn the ignition switch to the OFF position. 8. Repeat the above cycle (step 5 through step 7) two more times. 9. Use the *Scan Tool* in order to read the DTCs. Does DTC C1247 set as a current DTC?	—	*Go to Step 21*	*Go to Step 22*
15	Repair the high resistance in CKT 1280. Is the repair complete?	—	Refer to *Diagnostic System Check*	—
16	Repair the high resistance in CKT 1281. Is the repair complete?	—	Refer to *Diagnostic System Check*	—
17	Replace the ABS brake motor pack. Is the repair complete?	—	Refer to *Diagnostic System Check*	—
18	Replace the ABS brake modulator gear. Is the repair complete?	—	Refer to *Diagnostic System Check*	—
19	Replace the ABS brake modulator. Is the repair complete?	—	Refer to *Diagnostic System Check*	—
20	Replace the terminals that exhibit signs of poor terminal contact or corrosion. Is the repair complete?	—	Refer to *Diagnostic System Check*	—
21	Replace the EBCM. Is the repair complete?	—	Refer to *Diagnostic System Check*	—
22	The malfunction is intermittent or is not present at this time. Refer to Diagnostic Aids for more information.	—	—	—

GC402980301800EX

Fig. 43 Code C1247: LH Front ABS Motor Free Spins (Part 5 of 5). Alero, Grand Am & Malibu

Circuit Description

DTC C1248 detects a stripped nut or gear assembly during initialization. During the homing sequence, the piston should reach the top of the bore. Then the ABS motor stalls. If the ABS motor does not stall, the ABS motor must be spinning with little or no resistance. This indicates a nut/screw or gear malfunction.

Conditions for Setting the DTC

DTC C1248 can only set during initialization.

A malfunction exists if the feedback current is less than the command current for a specified period of time.

Action Taken When the DTC Sets

- A malfunction DTC stores.
- The ABS disables.
- The ABS warning indicator turns on.

Conditions for Clearing the DTC

- The condition responsible for setting the DTC no longer exists and the Scan Tool Clear DTCs function is used.
- 100 drive cycles pass with no DTCs detected. A drive cycle consists of starting the vehicle, driving the vehicle over 16 km/h (10 mph), stopping and then turning the ignition switch to the OFF position.

Diagnostic Aids

An intermittent malfunction in this DTC may result from a mechanical part of the system that slips, such as a backed off gear retaining nut.

Depending on the frequency of the malfunction, a physical inspection of the mechanical parts suspected of causing the malfunction may be necessary.

Important: Zero the J 39200 test leads before making any resistance measurements.

GC402980301900AX

Fig. 44 Code C1248: RH Front ABS Motor Free Spins (Part 1 of 5). Alero, Grand Am & Malibu

Step	Action	Value(s)	Yes	No
1	Was the Diagnostic System Check performed?	—	*Go to Step 2*	Refer to *Diagnostic System Check*
2	1. Turn the ignition switch to the RUN position. Do not start the engine. 2. Use the *Scan Tool* in order to read the DTCs. Does DTC C1261 also set as a current DTC?	—	Refer to *DTC C1261 Right Front ABS Motor Circuit Open*	*Go to Step 3*
3	1. Pump the brake pedal until it is firm in order to deplete the brake booster vacuum reservoir. 2. Select Special Functions on the *Scan Tool.* 3. Select the Manual Control function on the *Scan Tool.* 4. Select the right front Motor Apply function on the *Scan Tool.* 5. Use the *Scan Tool* in order to apply the right front motor. Observe the following currents: • The right front ABS motor command current • The right front ABS motor feedback current Were the right front ABS motor command current and the right front ABS motor feedback current approximately the specified current?	10 A	*Go to Step 4*	*Go to Step 6*
4	1. Apply firm pressure to the brake pedal. 2. Select the right front ABS Motor Release function on the *Scan Tool.* 3. Use the *Scan Tool* in order to release the right front ABS motor. Observe the following currents: • The right front ABS motor command current • The right front ABS motor feedback current 4. Release the right front ABS motor and observe the brake pedal height. Have the following conditions been met? • The right front ABS motor command current and the right front ABS motor feedback current approximately the specified current • The brake pedal falls	6 A	*Go to Step 5*	*Go to Step 6*
5	1. Continue to apply firm pressure to the brake pedal. 2. Select the right front ABS Motor Release function on the *Scan Tool.* 3. Use the *Scan Tool* in order to apply the right front ABS motor. Did the brake pedal rise?	—	*Go to Step 22*	*Go to Step 6*

GC402980301900BX

Fig. 44 Code C1248: RH Front ABS Motor Free Spins (Part 2 of 5). Alero, Grand Am & Malibu

Step	Action	Value(s)	Yes	No
6	1. Select Special Functions on the *Scan Tool*. 2. Use the *Scan Tool* in order to perform the Gear Tension Relief function. 3. Turn the ignition switch to the OFF position. 4. Disconnect the 6-way ABS brake motor pack connector. 5. Disconnect the EBCM connector 6. Use the *J 39200* in order to measure the resistance between the 6-way ABS brake motor pack connector terminal E and the EBCM connector terminal A. Is the resistance within the specified range?	0–2 Ω	*Go to Step 7*	*Go to Step 15*
7	Use the *J 39200* in order to measure the resistance between the 6-way ABS brake motor pack connector terminal F and the EBCM connector terminal B. Is the resistance within the specified range?	0–2 Ω	*Go to Step 8*	*Go to Step 16*
8	Use the *J 39200* in order to measure the resistance between the 6-way ABS brake motor pack connector terminal E and the 6-way ABS brake motor pack connector terminal F. Is the resistance within the specified range?	0.2–1.5 Ω	*Go to Step 9*	*Go to Step 17*
9	1. Remove the ABS brake modulator/master cylinder assembly from the vehicle. 2. Remove the ABS brake modulator gear cover. 3. Inspect for a stripped ABS brake motor pack right front gear. (The ABS brake motor pack is the unit with the three small gears. The ABS brake motor pack right front gear is the gear closest to the rear when the ABS brake modulator is mounted in the vehicle.) Is the ABS brake motor right front gear stripped?	—	*Go to Step 17*	*Go to Step 10*
10	Inspect for a stripped ABS brake modulator right front gear. (The ABS brake modulator unit is the unit with the three large gears. The ABS brake modulator right front gear is the gear closest to the rear when the ABS brake modulator is mounted in the vehicle.) Is the ABS brake modulator right front gear stripped?	—	*Go to Step 18*	*Go to Step 11*

GC402980301900CX

Fig. 44 Code C1248: RH Front ABS Motor Free Spins (Part 3 of 5). Alero, Grand Am & Malibu

Step	Action	Value(s)	Yes	No
11	1. Reconnect the 6-way ABS brake motor pack connector. 2. Reconnect the EBCM connector. 3. Carefully secure the ABS brake modulator/master cylinder in the vehicle. Secure the assembly in a position that permits observation of the gears. 4. Turn the ignition switch to the RUN position. Do not start the engine. 5. Select the Manual Control function on the *Scan Tool*. 6. Select the right front ABS Motor Apply function on the *Scan Tool*. 7. Use the *Scan Tool* in order to apply the right front ABS motor while observing the ABS brake modulator right front gear set. (The ABS brake modulator right front gear is the gear closest to the rear when the ABS brake modulator is mounted in the vehicle.) 8. Select the right front ABS Motor Release function on the *Scan Tool*. 9. Use the *Scan Tool* in order to release the right front ABS motor while observing the ABS brake modulator right front gear set. 10. Select the right front ABS Motor Apply function on the *Scan Tool*. 11. Use the *Scan Tool* in order to apply the right front ABS motor while observing the ABS brake modulator right front gear set. Does the ABS brake modulator right front gear set move at least one full revolution in both directions?	—	*Go to Step 12*	*Go to Step 17*
12	1. Use the *Scan Tool* in order to perform the Gear Tension Relief function. 2. Turn the ignition switch to the OFF position. 3. Separate the ABS brake motor pack from the ABS brake modulator. 4. Grasp the ABS brake modulator right front gear. 5. Rotate the ABS brake modulator right front gear. Does the ABS brake modulator right front gear rotate more than 13 full turns from lock to lock?	—	*Go to Step 19*	*Go to Step 13*
13	1. Disconnect the 6-way ABS brake motor pack connector. 2. Disconnect the EBCM connector. 3. Inspect the connectors for the following conditions: • Poor terminal contact • Corrosion Do any of the terminals exhibit poor terminal contact or corrosion?	—	*Go to Step 20*	*Go to Step 14*

GC402980301900DX

Fig. 44 Code C1248: RH Front ABS Motor Free Spins (Part 4 of 5). Alero, Grand Am & Malibu

Step	Action	Value(s)	Yes	No
14	1. Reinstall the ABS brake modulator gear cover. 2. Reinstall the ABS brake modulator/master cylinder assembly in the vehicle. 3. Reconnect the 6-way ABS brake motor pack connector. 4. Reconnect the EBCM connector. 5. Start the engine. Do not apply pressure to the brake pedal. 6. Let the engine run for at least 10 seconds. 7. Turn the ignition switch to the OFF position. 8. Repeat the above cycle (step 5 through step 7) two more times. 9. Use the *Scan Tool* in order to read the DTCs. Does DTC C1248 set as a current DTC?	—	*Go to Step 21*	*Go to Step 22*
15	Repair the high resistance in CKT 1282. Is the repair complete?	—	Refer to *Diagnostic System Check*	—
16	Repair the high resistance in CKT 1283. Is the repair complete?	—	Refer to *Diagnostic System Check*	—
17	Replace the ABS brake motor pack. Is the repair complete?	—	Refer to *Diagnostic System Check*	—
18	Replace the ABS brake modulator gear. Is the repair complete?	—	Refer to *Diagnostic System Check*	—
19	Replace the ABS brake modulator. Is the repair complete?	—	Refer to *Diagnostic System Check*	—
20	Replace the terminals that exhibit signs of poor terminal contact or corrosion. Is the repair complete?	—	Refer to *Diagnostic System Check*	—
21	Replace the EBCM. Is the repair complete?	—	Refer to *Diagnostic System Check*	—
22	The malfunction is intermittent or is not present at this time. Refer to Diagnostic Aids for more information.	—	—	—

GC402980301900EX

Fig. 44 Code C1248: RH Front ABS Motor Free Spins (Part 5 of 5). Alero, Grand Am & Malibu

Circuit Description

DTC C1251 detects a stripped nut or gear assembly during initialization. During the homing sequence, the piston should reach the top of the bore. Then the ABS motor stalls. If the ABS motor does not stall, the ABS motor must be spinning with little or no resistance. This indicates a nut/screw or gear malfunction.

Conditions for Setting the DTC

DTC C1251 can only set during initialization.

A malfunction exists if the feedback current is less than the command current for a specified period of time.

Action Taken When the DTC Sets

- A malfunction DTC stores. A corresponding DTC C1286 will also set.
- The ABS disables.
- The ABS warning indicator turns on.
- The red BRAKE warning indicator turns on.

Conditions for Clearing the DTC

- The condition responsible for setting the DTC no longer exists and the Scan Tool Clear DTCs function is used.
- 100 drive cycles pass with no DTCs detected. A drive cycle consists of starting the vehicle, driving the vehicle over 16 km/h (10 mph), stopping and then turning the ignition switch to the OFF position.

Diagnostic Aids

An intermittent malfunction in this DTC may result from a mechanical part of the system that slips, such as a stripped gear or a backed off gear retaining nut.

Depending on the frequency of the malfunction, a physical inspection of the mechanical parts suspected of causing the malfunction may be necessary.

Important: Zero the J 39200 test leads before making any resistance measurements.

GC402980302000AX

Fig. 45 Code C1251: Rear ABS Motor Free Spins (Part 1 of 5). Alero, Grand Am & Malibu

Step	Action	Value(s)	Yes	No
1	Was the Diagnostic System Check performed?	—	*Go to Step 2*	Refer to *Diagnostic System Check*
2	1. Turn the ignition switch to the RUN position. Do not start the engine. 2. Use the *Scan Tool* in order to read the DTCs. Does DTC C1264 also set as a current DTC?	—	Refer to *DTC C1264 Rear ABS Motor Circuit Open*	*Go to Step 3*
3	1. Pump the brake pedal until it is firm in order to deplete the brake booster vacuum reservoir. 2. Select Special Functions on the *Scan Tool*. 3. Select the Manual Control function on the *Scan Tool*. 4. Select the rear ABS Motor Apply function on the *Scan Tool*. 5. Use the *Scan Tool* in order to apply the rear ABS motor. Observe the following currents: • The rear ABS motor command current • The rear ABS motor feedback current Were the rear ABS motor command current and the rear ABS motor feedback current approximately the specified current?	10 A	*Go to Step 4*	*Go to Step 6*
4	1. Raise and support the vehicle so that the rear wheels are approximately 6 inches off the floor. 2. Turn the ignition switch to the run position. 3. Apply firm pressure to the brake pedal. 4. Select Special Functions on the *Scan Tool*. 5. Select Manual Control on the *Scan Tool*. 6. Use the *Scan Tool* in order to Apply the rear ABS motor. 7. Have an assistant try to spin the rear wheels by hand. Could the assistant spin the rear wheels?	—	*Go to Step 5*	*Go to Step 6*
5	1. Continue to apply firm pressure to the brake pedal. 2. Select the rear ABS Apply function on the *Scan Tool*. 3. Use the *Scan Tool* in order to apply the rear ABS motor. Could the assistant spin the rear wheels?	—	*Go to Step 22*	*Go to Step 6*

GC402980302000BX

Fig. 45 Code C1251: Rear ABS Motor Free Spins (Part 2 of 5). Alero, Grand Am & Malibu

Step	Action	Value(s)	Yes	No
6	1. Select Special Functions on the *Scan Tool*. 2. Use the *Scan Tool* in order to perform the Gear Tension Relief function. 3. Turn the ignition switch to the OFF position. 4. Disconnect the 6-way ABS brake motor pack connector. 5. Disconnect the EBCM connector 6. Use the *J 39200* in order to measure the resistance between the 6-way ABS brake motor pack connector terminal C and the EBCM connector terminal F. Is the resistance within the specified range?	0–2 Ω	*Go to Step 7*	*Go to Step 15*
7	Use the *J 39200* in order to measure the resistance between the 6-way ABS brake motor pack connector terminal D and the EBCM connector terminal E. Is the resistance less within the specified range?	0–2 Ω	*Go to Step 8*	*Go to Step 16*
8	Use the *J 39200* in order to measure the resistance between the 6-way ABS brake motor pack connector terminal C and the 6-way ABS brake motor pack connector terminal D. Is the resistance within the specified range?	0.2–1.5 Ω	*Go to Step 9*	*Go to Step 17*
9	1. Remove the ABS brake modulator/master cylinder assembly from the vehicle. 2. Remove the ABS brake modulator gear cover. 3. Inspect for a stripped ABS brake motor pack rear gear. (The ABS brake motor pack is the unit with the three small gears. The ABS brake motor pack rear gear is the middle gear when the ABS brake modulator is mounted in the vehicle.) Is the ABS brake motor rear gear stripped?	—	*Go to Step 17*	*Go to Step 10*
10	Inspect for a stripped ABS brake modulator rear gear. (The ABS brake modulator unit is the unit with the three large gears. The ABS brake modulator rear gear is the middle gear when the ABS brake modulator is mounted in the vehicle.) Is the ABS brake modulator rear gear stripped?	—	*Go to Step 18*	*Go to Step 11*

GC402980302000CX

Fig. 45 Code C1251: Rear ABS Motor Free Spins (Part 3 of 5). Alero, Grand Am & Malibu

Step	Action	Value(s)	Yes	No
11	1. Reconnect the 6-way ABS brake motor pack connector. 2. Reconnect the EBCM connector. 3. Carefully secure the ABS brake modulator/master cylinder in the vehicle. Secure the assembly in a position that permits observation of the gears. 4. Turn the ignition switch to the RUN position. Do not start the engine. 5. Select the Manual Control function on the *Scan Tool*. 6. Select the rear ABS Motor Apply function on the *Scan Tool*. 7. Use the *Scan Tool* in order to apply the rear ABS motor while observing the ABS brake modulator rear gear set. (The ABS brake modulator rear gear is the middle gear when the ABS brake modulator is mounted in the vehicle.) 8. Select the rear ABS Motor Release function on the *Scan Tool*. 9. Use the *Scan Tool* in order to release the rear ABS motor while observing the ABS brake modulator rear gear set. 10. Select the rear ABS Motor Apply function on the *Scan Tool*. 11. Use the *Scan Tool* in order to apply the rear ABS motor while observing the ABS brake modulator rear gear set. Does the ABS brake modulator rear gear set move at least one full revolution in both directions?	—	*Go to Step 12*	*Go to Step 17*
12	1. Use the *Scan Tool* in order to perform the Gear Tension Relief function. 2. Turn the ignition switch to the OFF position. 3. Separate the ABS brake motor pack from the ABS brake modulator. 4. Grasp the ABS brake modulator rear gear. 5. Rotate the ABS brake modulator rear gear. Does the ABS brake modulator rear gear rotate more than 3.5 full turns from lock to lock?	—	*Go to Step 19*	*Go to Step 13*
13	1. Disconnect the 6-way ABS brake motor pack connector. 2. Disconnect the EBCM connector. 3. Inspect the connectors for the following conditions: • Poor terminal contact • Corrosion Do any of the terminals exhibit poor terminal contact or corrosion?	—	*Go to Step 20*	*Go to Step 14*

GC402980302000DX

Fig. 45 Code C1251: Rear ABS Motor Free Spins (Part 4 of 5). Alero, Grand Am & Malibu

Step	Action	Value(s)	Yes	No
14	1. Reinstall the ABS brake modulator gear cover. 2. Reinstall the ABS brake modulator/master cylinder assembly in the vehicle. 3. Reconnect the 6-way ABS brake motor pack connector. 4. Reconnect the EBCM connector. 5. Start the engine. Do not apply pressure to the brake pedal. 6. Let the engine run for at least 10 seconds. 7. Turn the ignition switch to the OFF position. 8. Repeat the above cycle (steps 5 through 7) two more times. 9. Use the *Scan Tool* in order to read the DTCs. Does DTC C1251 set as a current DTC?	—	*Go to Step 21*	*Go to Step 22*
15	Repair the high resistance in CKT 1284. Is the repair complete?	—	Refer to *Diagnostic System Check*	—
16	Repair the high resistance in CKT 1285. Is the repair complete?	—	Refer to *Diagnostic System Check*	—
17	Replace the ABS brake motor pack. Is the repair complete?	—	Refer to *Diagnostic System Check*	—
18	Replace the ABS brake modulator gear. Is the repair complete?	—	Refer to *Diagnostic System Check*	—
19	Replace the ABS brake modulator. Is the repair complete?	—	Refer to *Diagnostic System Check*	—
20	Replace the terminals that exhibit signs of poor terminal contact or corrosion. Is the repair complete?	—	Refer to *Diagnostic System Check*	—
21	Replace the EBCM. Is the repair complete?	—	Refer to *Diagnostic System Check*	—
22	The malfunction is intermittent or is not present at this time. Refer to Diagnostic Aids for more information.	—	—	—

GC402980302000EX

Fig. 45 Code C1251: Rear ABS Motor Free Spins (Part 5 of 5). Alero, Grand Am & Malibu

Circuit Description

DTC C1252 diagnoses an ABS motor that energizes longer than expected. The following conditions may cause the longer period of being energized:

- A wheel speed sensor malfunctions.
- The left front brake solenoid valve mechanically fails open.
- The ABS brake motor wires are crossed.

Conditions for Setting the DTC

DTC C1252 can only set during an ABS stop.

A malfunction exists if the EBCM commands the left front ABS channel in release for greater than three seconds.

Action Taken When the DTC Sets

- A malfunction DTC stores.
- The ABS disables.
- The ABS warning indicator turns on.

Conditions for Clearing the DTC

- The condition responsible for setting the DTC no longer exists and the Scan Tool Clear DTCs function is used.
- 100 drive cycles pass with no DTCs detected. A drive cycle consists of starting the vehicle, driving the vehicle over 16 km/h (10 mph), stopping and then turning the ignition switch to the OFF position.

Diagnostic Aids

Use the enhanced diagnostic function of the Scan Tool in order to measure the frequency of the malfunction. DTC C1252 may occur if the vehicle is on ice and the steering wheel is turned to lock during braking. Use the scan tool hydraulic test to ensure the total brake system is functional.

Thoroughly inspect any circuitry that may be causing the intermittent complaint for the following conditions:

- Backed out terminals
- Improper mating
- Broken locks
- Improperly formed or damaged terminals
- Poor terminal-to-wiring connections
- Physical damage to the wiring harness

Clear the DTCs after completing the diagnosis. Test drive the vehicle for three drive cycles in order to verify that the DTC does not reset. Use the following procedure in order to complete one drive cycle:

1. Start the vehicle.
2. Drive the vehicle over 16 km/h (10 mph).
3. Stop the vehicle.
4. Turn the ignition to the OFF position.

Important: Zero the J 39200 test leads before making any resistance measurements. Refer to the J 39200 user's manual.

Important: Inspect for and correct the following conditions in the base brake or suspension system before proceeding with the DTC diagnosis:

- Excessive drag
- High resistance

GC402980302100AA

Fig. 46 Code C1252: LH Front ABS Channel In Release Too Long (Part 1 of 3). Alero, Grand Am & Malibu

Step	Action	Value(s)	Yes	No
1	Was the Diagnostic System Check performed?	—	*Go to Step 2*	Refer to *Diagnostic System Check*
2	1. Turn the ignition switch to the RUN position. Do not start the engine. 2. Install a *Scan Tool*. 3. Use the *Scan Tool* in order to read the DTCs. Are there any wheel speed sensor DTCs that set as current DTCs?	—	Refer to the appropriate DTC table.	*Go to Step 3*
3	1. Select Data List on the *Scan Tool*. 2. Drive the vehicle, slowly decelerating from 56 km/h to 0 km/h (35 mph to 0 mph). 3. Monitor all of the wheel speed sensor speeds while driving. Do any of the wheel speed sensors indicate erratic or intermittent operation?	—	Go to the Excessive Wheel Speed Sensor Variation DTC for the affected wheel	*Go to Step 4*
4	1. Turn the ignition switch to the RUN position. Do not start the engine. 2. Select Special Functions on the *Scan Tool*. 3. Select the Manual Control function on the *Scan Tool*. 4. Select the left front ABS Motor Apply function on the *Scan Tool*. 5. Use the *Scan Tool* in order to apply the left front ABS motor. 6. Apply firm pressure to the brake pedal. 7. Select the left front ABS Motor Release function on the *Scan Tool*. 8. Use the *Scan Tool* in order to release the left front ABS motor.	—	*Go to Step 5*	*Go to Step 8*
5	1. Remove the firm pressure from the brake pedal. 2. Select the Manual Control function on the *Scan Tool*. 3. Select the left front ABS Brake Solenoid Valve on the *Scan Tool*. 4. Use the *Scan Tool* in order to command the left front ABS brake solenoid valve on. 5. Apply firm pressure to the brake pedal. Does the brake pedal fall?	—	*Go to Step 7*	*Go to Step 6*
6	1. Continue to apply firm pressure to the brake pedal. 2. Use the *Scan Tool* in order to command the left front ABS brake solenoid valve off. Did the brake pedal fall?	—	*Go to Step 14*	*Go to Step 7*

GC402980302100BX

Fig. 46 Code C1252: LH Front ABS Channel In Release Too Long (Part 2 of 3). Alero, Grand Am & Malibu

Step	Action	Value(s)	Yes	No
7	1. Remove the firm pressure from the brake pedal. 2. Turn the ignition switch to the OFF position. 3. Remove the left front ABS brake solenoid valve. 4. Remove the right front ABS brake solenoid valve. 5. Reinstall the left front ABS brake solenoid valve to the right front ABS brake solenoid valve position. 6. Reinstall the right front ABS brake solenoid valve to the left front ABS brake solenoid valve position. 7. Turn the ignition switch to the RUN position. 8. Make sure that the engine is off. 9. Select the Manual Control function on the *Scan Tool*. 10. Select the left front ABS Brake Solenoid Valve on the *Scan Tool*. 11. Use the *Scan Tool* in order to command the left front ABS brake solenoid valve on. 12. Apply firm pressure to the brake pedal. Does the brake pedal fall?	—	*Go to Step 10*	*Go to Step 11*
8	Did the brake pedal rise?	—	*Go to Step 12*	*Go to Step 9*
9	1. Use the *Scan Tool* in order to perform the Gear Tension Relief function. 2. Turn the ignition switch to the OFF position. 3. Separate the ABS motor pack from the ABS brake modulator. 4. Grasp the ABS brake modulator left front gear. (The ABS brake modulator left front gear is the large gear that is the closest to the front when the ABS brake modulator is mounted in the vehicle.) 5. Attempt to rotate the ABS brake modulator left front gear in either direction. Is it possible to rotate the ABS brake modulator left front gear by hand?	—	*Go to Step 13*	*Go to Step 10*
10	Replace the ABS brake modulator. Is the repair complete?	—	Refer to *Diagnostic System Check*	—
11	Replace the ABS brake solenoid valve that was originally in the left front ABS brake solenoid valve position. Is the repair complete?	—	Refer to *Diagnostic System Check*	—
12	Repair the crossed wires to the left front ABS motor (CKT 1280 and CKT 1281). Is the repair complete?	—	Refer to *Diagnostic System Check*	—
13	Replace the ABS brake motor pack. Is the repair complete?	—	Refer to *Diagnostic System Check*	—
14	The malfunction is intermittent or is not present at this time. Refer to Diagnostic Aids for more information.	—	—	—

GC402980302100CX

Fig. 46 Code C1252: LH Front ABS Channel In Release Too Long (Part 3 of 3). Alero, Grand Am & Malibu

Circuit Description

DTC C1253 diagnoses an ABS motor that energizes longer than expected. The following conditions may cause the longer period of being energized:

- A wheel speed sensor malfunctions.
- The ABS motor does not turn.
- The right front brake solenoid valve mechanically fails open.
- The ABS brake motor wires are crossed.

Conditions for Setting the DTC

DTC C1253 can only set during an ABS stop.

A malfunction exists if the EBCM commands the right front ABS channel in release for greater than three seconds.

Action Taken When the DTC Sets

- A malfunction DTC stores.
- The ABS disables.
- The ABS warning indicator turns on.

Conditions for Clearing the DTC

- The condition responsible for setting the DTC no longer exists and the Scan Tool Clear DTCs function is used.
- 100 drive cycles pass with no DTCs detected. A drive cycle consists of starting the vehicle, driving the vehicle over 16 km/h (10 mph), stopping and then turning the ignition switch to the OFF position.

Diagnostic Aids

The following conditions may cause an intermittent malfunction if the conditions exist in a mechanical part of the system:

- Sticking
- Binding

Use the enhanced diagnostic function of the Scan Tool in order to measure the frequency of the malfunction. DTC C1253 may occur if the vehicle is on ice and the steering wheel is turned to lock during braking. Use the scan tool hydraulic test to ensure the total brake system is functional.

Thoroughly inspect any circuitry that may be causing the intermittent complaint for the following conditions:

- Backed out terminals
- Improper mating
- Broken locks
- Improperly formed or damaged terminals
- Poor terminal-to-wiring connections
- Physical damage to the wiring harness

Clear the DTCs after completing the diagnosis. Test drive the vehicle for three drive cycles in order to verify that the DTC does not reset. Use the following procedure in order to complete one drive cycle:

1. Start the vehicle.
2. Drive the vehicle over 16 km/h (10 mph).
3. Stop the vehicle.
4. Turn the ignition to the OFF position.

Important: Zero the J 39200 test leads before making any resistance measurements. Refer to the J 39200 user's manual.

Important: Inspect for and correct the following conditions in the base brake or suspension system before proceeding with the DTC diagnosis:

- Excessive drag
- High resistance

GC402980302200AX

Fig. 47 Code C1253: RH Front ABS Channel In Release Too Long (Part 1 of 3). Alero, Grand Am & Malibu

Step	Action	Value(s)	Yes	No
1	Was the Diagnostic System Check performed?	—	*Go to Step 2*	Refer to *Diagnostic System Check*
2	1. Turn the ignition switch to the RUN position. Do not start the engine. 2. Install a *Scan Tool*. 3. Use the *Scan Tool* in order to read the DTCs. Are there any wheel speed sensor DTCs that set as current DTCs?	—	Refer to the appropriate DTC table.	*Go to Step 3*
3	1. Select Data List on the *Scan Tool*. 2. Drive the vehicle, slowly decelerating from 56 km/h to 0 km/h (35 mph to 0 mph). 3. Monitor all of the wheel speed sensor speeds while driving. Do any of the wheel speed sensors indicate erratic or intermittent operation?	—	Go to the Excessive Wheel Speed Sensor Variation DTC for the affected wheel	*Go to Step 4*
4	1. Turn the ignition switch to the RUN position. Do not start the engine. 2. Select Special Functions on the *Scan Tool*. 3. Select the Manual Control function on the *Scan Tool*. 4. Select the right front ABS Motor Apply function on the *Scan Tool*. 5. Use the *Scan Tool* to apply the right front ABS motor. 6. Apply firm pressure to the brake pedal. 7. Select the right front ABS Motor Release function on the *Scan Tool*. 8. Use the *Scan Tool* in order to release the right front ABS motor. Did the brake pedal fall?	—	*Go to Step 5*	*Go to Step 8*
5	1. Remove the firm pressure from the brake pedal. 2. Select the Manual Control function on the *Scan Tool*. 3. Select the right front ABS Brake Solenoid Valve on the *Scan Tool*. 4. Use the *Scan Tool* in order to command the right front ABS brake solenoid valve on. 5. Apply firm pressure to the brake pedal. Did the brake pedal fall?	—	*Go to Step 7*	*Go to Step 6*
6	1. Continue to apply firm pressure to the brake pedal. 2. Use the *Scan Tool* in order to command the right front ABS brake solenoid valve off. Did the brake pedal fall?	—	*Go to Step 14*	*Go to Step 7*

GC402980302200BX

Fig. 47 Code C1253: RH Front ABS Channel In Release Too Long (Part 2 of 3). Alero, Grand Am & Malibu

Step	Action	Value(s)	Yes	No
7	1. Remove the firm pressure from the brake pedal. 2. Turn the ignition switch to the OFF position. 3. Remove the right front ABS brake solenoid valve. 4. Remove the left front ABS brake solenoid valve. 5. Reinstall the right front ABS brake solenoid valve to the left front ABS brake solenoid valve position. 6. Reinstall the left front ABS brake solenoid valve to the right front ABS brake solenoid valve position. 7. Turn the ignition switch to the RUN position. Do not start the engine. 8. Select the Manual Control function on the *Scan Tool*. 9. Select the right front ABS Brake Solenoid Valve on the *Scan Tool*. 10. Use the *Scan Tool* in order to command the right front ABS brake solenoid valve on. 11. Apply firm pressure to the brake pedal. Did the brake pedal fall?	—	*Go to Step 10*	*Go to Step 11*
8	Did the brake pedal rise?	—	*Go to Step 12*	*Go to Step 9*
9	1. Use the *Scan Tool* in order to perform the Gear Tension Relief function. 2. Turn the ignition switch to the OFF position. 3. Separate the ABS motor pack from the ABS brake modulator. 4. Grasp the ABS brake modulator right front gear. (The ABS brake modulator right front gear is the large gear that is the closest to the rear when the ABS brake modulator is mounted in the vehicle.) 5. Attempt to rotate the ABS brake modulator right front gear in either direction. Is it possible to rotate the ABS brake modulator right front gear by hand?	—	*Go to Step 13*	*Go to Step 10*
10	Replace the ABS brake modulator. Is the repair complete?	—	Refer to *Diagnostic System Check*	—
11	Replace the ABS brake solenoid valve that was originally in the right front ABS brake solenoid valve position. Is the repair complete?	—	Refer to *Diagnostic System Check*	—
12	Repair the crossed wires to the right front ABS motor (CKT 1282 and CKT 1283). Is the repair complete?	—	Refer to *Diagnostic System Check*	—
13	Replace the ABS brake motor pack. Is the repair complete?	—	Refer to *Diagnostic System Check*	—
14	The malfunction is intermittent or is not present at this time. Refer to Diagnostic Aids for more information.	—	—	—

GC402980302200CX

Fig. 47 Code C1253: RH Front ABS Channel In Release Too Long (Part 3 of 3). Alero, Grand Am & Malibu

Circuit Description

DTC C1254 diagnoses an ABS motor that energizes longer than expected. The following conditions may cause the longer period of being energized:

- A wheel speed sensor malfunctions.
- The ABS motor does not turn.
- The ABS brake motor wires cross.

Conditions for Setting the DTC

DTC C1254 can only set during an ABS stop.

A malfunction exists if the EBCM commands the rear ABS channel in release for greater than three seconds.

Action Taken When the DTC Sets

- A malfunction DTC stores.
- The ABS/TCS disables.
- The amber ABS/TCS warning indicator(s) turn on.

Conditions for Clearing the DTC

- The condition responsible for setting the DTC no longer exists and the Scan Tool Clear DTCs function is used.
- 100 drive cycles pass with no DTCs detected.

Diagnostic Aids

The following conditions may cause an intermittent malfunction if the conditions exist in a mechanical part of the system:

- Sticking
- Binding

Use the enhanced diagnostic function of the Scan Tool in order to measure the frequency of the malfunction. Use the Scan Tool hydraulic test in order to ensure the total brake system is functional.

Thoroughly inspect any circuitry that may be causing the intermittent complaint for the following conditions:

- Backed out terminals
- Improper mating
- Broken locks
- Improperly formed or damaged terminals
- Poor terminal-to-wiring connections
- Physical damage to the wiring harness

Clear the DTCs after completing the diagnosis. Test drive the vehicle for three drive cycles in order to verify that the DTC does not reset. Use the following procedure in order to complete one drive cycle:

1. Start the vehicle.
2. Drive the vehicle over 16 km/h (10 mph).
3. Stop the vehicle.
4. Turn the ignition to the OFF position.

Important: Zero the J 39200 test leads before making any resistance measurements. Refer to the J 39200 user's manual.

Important: Inspect for and correct the following conditions in the base brake or suspension system before proceeding with the DTC diagnosis:

- Excessive brake drag
- High resistance

GC402980302300AX

Fig. 48 Code C1254: Rear ABS Channel In Release Too Long (Part 1 of 3). Alero, Grand Am & Malibu

Step	Action	Value(s)	Yes	No
1	Was the Diagnostic System Check performed?	—	*Go to Step 2*	Refer to *Diagnostic System Check*
2	1. Turn the ignition switch to the RUN position. Do not start the engine. 2. Install a *Scan Tool*. 3. Use the *Scan Tool* in order to read the DTCs. Are there any wheel speed sensor DTCs that set as current DTCs?	—	Refer to the appropriate DTC table.	*Go to Step 3*
3	1. Select Data List on the *Scan Tool*. 2. Drive the vehicle, slowly decelerating from 56 km/h to 0 km/h (35 mph to 0 mph). 3. Monitor all of the wheel speed sensor speeds while driving. Do any of the wheel speed sensors indicate erratic or intermittent operation?	—	Go to the Excessive Wheel Speed Sensor Variation DTC for the affected wheel	*Go to Step 4*
4	1. Turn the ignition switch to the OFF position. 2. Raise and suitably support the rear of the vehicle. Make sure that the two rear wheels are off of the ground. 3. Spin each of the rear wheels by hand. Is it possible to spin each rear wheel freely by hand?	—	*Go to Step 5*	*Go to Step 11*
5	1. Turn the ignition switch to the RUN position. Do not start the engine. 2. Select the Manual Control function on the *Scan Tool*. 3. Select the rear axle ABS Motor Apply function on the *Scan Tool*. 4. Apply firm pressure to the brake pedal. 5. Use the *Scan Tool* in order to apply the rear axle ABS motor. 6. Spin each rear wheel by hand. Is it possible to freely spin each rear wheel?	—	*Go to Step 6*	*Go to Step 12*
6	1. Continue to apply firm pressure to the brake pedal. 2. Use the *Scan Tool* in order to command a Motor Release of the rear ABS motor. Is it possible to freely spin each rear wheel?	—	*Go to Step 7*	*Go to Step 9*

GC402980302300BX

Fig. 48 Code C1254: Rear ABS Channel In Release Too Long (Part 2 of 3). Alero, Grand Am & Malibu

Step	Action	Value(s)	Yes	No
7	1. Use the *Scan Tool* in order to perform the Gear Tension Relief function. 2. Turn the ignition switch to the OFF position. 3. Separate the ABS brake motor pack from the ABS brake modulator, if it is disconnected. 4. Turn the ignition switch to the RUN position. Do not start the engine. 5. Use the *Scan Tool* in order to perform a ABS brake motor pack motor test. Do all three of the ABS brake motor pack gears (small gears) spin freely when commanded?	—	*Go to Step 8*	*Go to Step 10*
8	Replace the ABS brake modulator. Is the repair complete?	—	Refer to *Diagnostic System Check*	—
9	Repair the crossed wires to the rear ABS motor (CKT 1284 and CKT 1285). Is the repair complete?	—	Refer to *Diagnostic System Check*	—
10	Replace the ABS brake motor pack. Is the repair complete?	—	Refer to *Diagnostic System Check*	—
11	Repair the source of resistance in the base brake system. Is the repair complete?	—	Refer to *Diagnostic System Check*	—
12	The malfunction is intermittent or is not present at this time. Refer to Diagnostic Aids for more information.	—	—	—

GC402980302300CX

Fig. 48 Code C1254: Rear ABS Channel In Release Too Long (Part 3 of 3). Alero, Grand Am & Malibu

Step	Action	Value(s)	Yes	No
1	Was the Diagnostic System Check performed?	—	*Go to Step 2*	Refer to *Diagnostic System Check*
2	1. Turn the ignition switch to the RUN position. Do not start the engine. 2. Install a *Scan Tool*. 3. Use the *Scan Tool* in order to read the DTCs. Is DTC C1255 set as a current DTC?	—	*Go to Step 3*	*Go to Step 5*
3	1. Use the *Scan Tool* in order to clear the DTCs. 2. Test drive the vehicle for three drive cycles. 3. Use the *Scan Tool* in order to look for DTCs. Does DTC C1255 set as a current DTC?	—	*Go to Step 4*	*Go to Step 5*
4	Replace the EBCM. Is the repair complete?	—	Refer to *Diagnostic System Check*	—
5	The malfunction is intermittent or is not present at this time. Refer to Diagnostic Aids for more information.	—	—	—

GC402980302400BX

Fig. 49 Code C1255: EBCM/EBTCM Internal Fault (Part 2 of 2). Alero, Grand Am & Malibu

Step	Action	Value(s)	Yes	No
1	Was the Diagnostic System Check performed?	—	*Go to Step 2*	Refer to *Diagnostic System Check*
2	Does DTC C1256 occur intermittently?	—	Refer to Diagnostic Aids	*Go to Step 3*
3	1. Turn the ignition switch to the OFF position. 2. Disconnect the 6-way ABS brake motor pack connector. 3. Use the *J 39200* in order to measure the resistance between the 6-way ABS brake motor pack connector terminal A and the 6-way ABS brake motor pack connector terminal B. Is the resistance within the specified range?	0.2–1.5 Ω	*Go to Step 4*	*Go to Step 8*
4	1. Disconnect the EBCM connector. 2. Use the *J 39200* in order to measure the resistance between the 6-way ABS brake motor pack harness connector terminal A and the EBCM harness connector terminal G. Is the resistance within the specified range?	0–2 Ω	*Go to Step 5*	*Go to Step 9*
5	Use the *J 39200* in order to measure the resistance between the 6-way ABS brake motor pack harness connector terminal B and the EBCM harness connector terminal H. Is the resistance within the specified range?	0–2 Ω	*Go to Step 6*	*Go to Step 10*
6	1. Inspect the following connectors: • The 6-way ABS brake motor pack connector • The 6-way ABS brake motor pack harness connector • The EBCM connector • The EBCM harness connector 2. Inspect the connectors for the following conditions: • Poor terminal contact • Corrosion Is there evidence of poor terminal contact and corrosion?	—	*Go to Step 11*	*Go to Step 7*
7	1. Reconnect the 6-way ABS brake motor pack connector. 2. Reconnect the EBCM connector. 3. Test drive the vehicle. Be sure to obtain a speed of at least 16 km/h (10 mph). 4. Turn the ignition switch to the OFF position. 5. Repeat the drive sequence two more times. 6. Use the *Scan Tool* in order to look for DTCs. Does DTC C1256 set as a current DTC during the last three drive cycles?	—	*Go to Step 12*	*Go to Step 13*

GC402980302500BX

Fig. 50 Code C1256: LH Front ABS Motor Circuit Open (Part 2 of 3). Alero, Grand Am & Malibu

Circuit Description

DTC C1255 identifies an internal malfunction detected by the EBCM ABS motor driver interface, custom integrated circuit.

Conditions for Setting the DTC

DTC C1255 is set when an internal EBCM malfunction exists.

Action Taken When the DTC Sets

- A malfunction DTC stores.
- The ABS disables.
- The ABS warning indicator turns on.
- The red BRAKE warning indicator turns on and DTC C1286 sets if the rear piston in the ABS brake motor pack is not in the home piston.

Conditions for Clearing the DTC

- The condition responsible for setting the DTC no longer exists and the Scan Tool Clear DTCs function is used.
- 100 drive cycles pass with no DTC(s) detected. A drive cycle consists of starting the vehicle, driving the vehicle over 16 km/h (10 mph), stopping and then turning the ignition off.

Diagnostic Aids

Use the enhanced diagnostic function of the Scan Tool in order to measure the frequency of the malfunction.

Clear the DTCs after completing the diagnosis. Test drive the vehicle for three drive cycles in order to verify that the DTC does not reset. Use the following procedure in order to complete one drive cycle:

1. Start the vehicle.
2. Drive the vehicle over 16 km/h (10 mph).
3. Stop the vehicle.
4. Turn the ignition to the OFF position.

GC402980302400AX

Fig. 49 Code C1255: EBCM/EBTCM Internal Fault (Part 1 of 2). Alero, Grand Am & Malibu

Circuit Description

DTC C1256 identifies an ABS motor that cannot energize due to an open in the ABS motor circuitry. The malfunction will not allow proper front ABS operation.

Conditions for Setting the DTC

DTC C1256 can only set when the motor is commanded off.

A malfunction exists if the EBCM detects an out of range voltage on either of the left front ABS motor circuits. The out of range voltage on either circuit indicates an open circuit exists.

Action Taken When the DTC Sets

- An open ABS motor will not activate.
- A malfunction DTC stores.
- The ABS disables.
- The ABS warning indicator turns on.

Conditions for Clearing the DTC

- The condition responsible for setting the DTC no longer exists and the Scan Tool Clear DTCs function is used.
- 100 drive cycles pass with no DTCs detected. A drive cycle consists of starting the vehicle, driving the vehicle over 16 km/h (10 mph), stopping and then turning the ignition off.

Diagnostic Aids

Use the Scan Tool Manual Control function in order to exercise ABS motor movement of affected channel in both directions while applying light pressure on the brake pedal.

An intermittent malfunction may be indicated if erratic or jumpy brake pedal movement is detected while performing an apply or release function of the ABS monitor.

The following conditions may cause an intermittent malfunction:

- A poor connection
- Rubbed-through wire insulation
- A broken wire inside the insulation

If the malfunction is not current, use the following procedure to pinpoint an intermittent malfunction in the motor circuitry or connections:

1. Wiggle the wires of the affected channel.
2. Inspect if the DTC resets.

Use the enhanced diagnostic function of the Scan Tool in order to measure the frequency of the malfunction.

Thoroughly inspect any circuitry that may be causing the intermittent complaint for the following conditions:

- Backed out terminals
- Improper mating
- Broken locks
- Improperly formed or damaged terminals
- Poor terminal-to-wiring connections
- Physical damage to the wiring harness

Clear the DTCs after completing the diagnosis. Test drive the vehicle for three drive cycles in order to verify that the DTC does not reset. Use the following procedure in order to complete one drive cycle:

1. Start the vehicle.
2. Drive the vehicle over 16 km/h (10 mph).
3. Stop the vehicle.
4. Turn the ignition to the OFF position.

Important: Zero the J 39200 test leads before making any resistance measurements.

GC402980302500AA

Fig. 50 Code C1256: LH Front ABS Motor Circuit Open (Part 1 of 3). Alero, Grand Am & Malibu

Step	Action	Value(s)	Yes	No
8	Replace the ABS brake motor pack. Is the repair complete?	—	Refer to *Diagnostic System Check*	—
9	Repair the open or high resistance in CKT 1280. Is the repair complete?	—	Refer to *Diagnostic System Check*	—
10	Repair the open or high resistance in CKT 1281. Is the repair complete?	—	Refer to *Diagnostic System Check*	—
11	Replace all of the terminals or the connectors that exhibit signs of poor terminal contact, corrosion, or damaged terminal(s). Is the repair complete?	—	Refer to *Diagnostic System Check*	—
12	Replace the EBCM. Is the repair complete?	—	Refer to *Diagnostic System Check*	—
13	The malfunction is intermittent or is not present at this time. Refer to Diagnostic Aids for more information.	—	—	—

GC402980302500CX

Fig. 50 Code C1256: LH Front ABS Motor Circuit Open (Part 3 of 3). Alero, Grand Am & Malibu

Circuit Description

DTC C1257 identifies an ABS motor circuit that shorts to ground. The malfunction will cause one of the following conditions to occur:

- The ABS motor will not be controlled at the commanded current rate.
- The driver circuit will allow current directly to the ground.

Conditions for Setting the DTC

DTC C1257 can set anytime.

A malfunction exists if The EBCM detects an out of range voltage on either of the left front ABS motor circuits.

An out of range voltage on either circuit indicates one of the following conditions:

- A circuit shorts to ground.
- An ABS brake motor shorts internally.

Action Taken When the DTC Sets

- A malfunction DTC stores.
- The ABS disables.
- The ABS warning indicator turns on.

Conditions for Clearing the DTC

- The condition responsible for setting the DTC no longer exists and the Scan Tool Clear DTCs function is used.
- 100 drive cycles pass with no DTCs detected. A drive cycle consists of starting the vehicle, driving the vehicle over 16 km/h (10 mph), stopping and then turning the ignition off.

Diagnostic Aids

Use the Scan Tool Manual Control function in order to exercise ABS motor movement of affected channel in both directions while applying light pressure on the brake pedal.

An intermittent malfunction may be indicated if erratic or jumpy brake pedal movement is detected while performing an apply or release function of the ABS monitor.

The following conditions may cause an intermittent malfunction:

- Rubbed-through wire insulation
- An internal motor short

If the malfunction is not current, use the following procedure to pinpoint an intermittent malfunction in the motor circuitry or connections:

1. Wiggle the wires of the affected channel.
2. Inspect if the DTC resets.

Use the enhanced diagnostic function of the Scan Tool in order to measure the frequency of the malfunction.

Clear the DTCs after completing the diagnosis. Test drive the vehicle for three drive cycles in order to verify that the DTC does not reset. Use the following procedure in order to complete one drive cycle:

1. Start the vehicle.
2. Drive the vehicle over 16 km/h (10 mph).
3. Stop the vehicle.
4. Turn the ignition to the OFF position.

Important: Zero the J 39200 test leads before making any resistance measurements.

GC402980302600AA

Fig. 51 Code C1257: LH Front ABS Motor Circuit Shorted To Ground (Part 1 of 3). Alero, Grand Am & Malibu

Step	Action	Value(s)	Yes	No
1	Was the Diagnostic System Check performed?	—	*Go to Step 2*	Refer to *Diagnostic System Check*
2	Does DTC C1257 occur intermittently?	—	Refer to Diagnostic Aids	*Go to Step 3*
3	1. Turn the ignition switch to the OFF position. 2. Disconnect the 6-way ABS brake motor pack connector. 3. Disconnect the EBCM connector 4. Use the *J 39200* in order to measure the resistance between the 6-way ABS brake motor pack harness connector terminal A and ground. Is the resistance within the specified range?	OL (Infinite)	*Go to Step 4*	*Go to Step 9*
4	Use *J 39200* in order to measure the resistance between the 6-way ABS brake motor pack harness connector terminal B and ground. Is the resistance within the specified range?	OL (Infinite)	*Go to Step 5*	*Go to Step 10*
5	Use the *J 39200* in order to measure the resistance between the 6-way ABS brake motor pack connector terminal A and ground. Is the resistance within the specified range?	OL (Infinite)	*Go to Step 6*	*Go to Step 8*
6	1. Inspect the following components for damage: • The 6-way ABS brake motor pack connector • The 6-way ABS brake motor pack harness connector Damage may cause a short to ground with the connector connected. 2. Inspect the following components for damage: • The EBCM connector • The EBCM harness connector Damage may cause a short to ground with the connector connected. 3. Inspect CKT 1280 and CKT 1281 for damage. Damage may cause a short to ground. Is there damage which may cause a short to ground?	—	*Go to Step 11*	*Go to Step 7*
7	1. Reconnect the 6-way ABS brake motor pack connector. 2. Reconnect the EBCM connector. 3. Test drive the vehicle obtaining a speed at least 16 km/h (10 mph). 4. Turn the ignition switch to the OFF position. 5. Repeat the drive sequence two additional times. 6. Use the *Scan Tool* in order to inspect for DTCs. Did DTC C1257 set as a current DTC in the last three drive cycles?	—	*Go to Step 12*	*Go to Step 13*

GC402980302600BX

Fig. 51 Code C1257: LH Front ABS Motor Circuit Shorted To Ground (Part 2 of 3). Alero, Grand Am & Malibu

Step	Action	Value(s)	Yes	No
8	Replace the ABS brake motor pack. Is the repair complete?	—	Refer to *Diagnostic System Check*	—
9	Repair the short to ground in CKT 1280. Is the repair complete?	—	Refer to *Diagnostic System Check*	—
10	Repair the short to ground in CKT 1281. Is the repair complete?	—	Refer to *Diagnostic System Check*	—
11	Replace all of the following components that exhibit signs of damage: • The terminals • The connectors • The wires Damage may cause a short to ground. Is the repair complete?	—	Refer to *Diagnostic System Check*	—
12	Replace the EBCM. Is the repair complete?	—	Refer to *Diagnostic System Check*	—
13	The malfunction is intermittent or not present at this time. Refer to Diagnostic Aids for more information.	—	—	—

GC402980302600CX

Fig. 51 Code C1257: LH Front ABS Motor Circuit Shorted To Ground (Part 3 of 3). Alero, Grand Am & Malibu

Circuit Description

DTC C1258 identifies an ABS motor circuit that shorts to voltage or an ABS motor that has low or no resistance. A short to voltage will not allow controlled ABS operation.

Conditions for Setting the DTC

DTC C1258 can set only when the ABS motor is commanded off.

A malfunction exists if The EBCM detects an out of range voltage on either of the left front ABS motor circuits.

An out of range voltage on either circuit indicates one of the following conditions:

- A circuit shorts to voltage.
- An ABS brake motor shorts internally.

Action Taken When the DTC Sets

- A malfunction DTC stores.
- The ABS disables.
- The ABS warning indicator turns on.

Conditions for Clearing the DTC

- The condition responsible for setting the DTC no longer exists and the Scan Tool Clear DTCs function is used.
- 100 drive cycles pass with no DTCs detected. A drive cycle consists of starting the vehicle, driving the vehicle over 16 km/h (10 mph), stopping and then turning the ignition off.

Diagnostic Aids

Use the Scan Tool Manual Control function in order to exercise ABS motor movement of affected channel in both directions while applying light pressure on the brake pedal.

An intermittent malfunction may be indicated if erratic or jumpy brake pedal movement is detected while performing an apply or release function of the ABS monitor.

If the malfunction is not current, use the following procedure to pinpoint an intermittent malfunction in the motor circuitry or connections:

1. Wiggle the wires of the affected channel.
2. Inspect if the DTC resets.

Use the enhanced diagnostic function of the Scan Tool in order to measure the frequency of the malfunction.

Thoroughly inspect any circuitry that may be causing the intermittent complaint for the following conditions:

Clear the DTCs after completing the diagnosis. Test drive the vehicle for three drive cycles in order to verify that the DTC does not reset. Use the following procedure in order to complete one drive cycle:

1. Start the vehicle.
2. Drive the vehicle over 16 km/h (10 mph).
3. Stop the vehicle.
4. Turn the ignition to the OFF position.

Important: Zero the J 39200 test leads before making any resistance measurements.

GC402980302700AA

Fig. 52 Code C1258: LH Front ABS Motor Circuit Shorted To Voltage (Part 1 of 3). Alero, Grand Am & Malibu

Step	Action	Value(s)	Yes	No
1	Was the Diagnostic System Check performed?	—	*Go to Step 2*	Refer to *Diagnostic System Check*
2	Does DTC C1258 occur intermittently?	—	Refer to Diagnostic Aids	*Go to Step 3*
3	1. Turn the ignition switch to the OFF position. 2. Disconnect the 6-way ABS brake motor pack connector. 3. Disconnect the EBCM connector 4. Use the *J 39200* in order to measure the voltage between the 6-way ABS brake motor pack harness connector terminal A and ground. Is the voltage within the specified range?	0–1 V	*Go to Step 4*	*Go to Step 10*
4	Use the *J 39200* in order to measure the voltage between the 6-way ABS brake motor pack harness connector terminal B and ground. Is the voltage within the specified range?	0–1 V	*Go to Step 5*	*Go to Step 11*
5	1. Turn the ignition switch to the OFF position. 2. Use the *J 39200* in order to measure the resistance between the 6-way ABS motor pack harness connector terminal A and the 6-way ABS motor pack harness connector terminal B. Is the resistance within the specified range?	OL (Infinite)	*Go to Step 6*	*Go to Step 12*
6	Use the *J 39200* in order to measure the resistance between the 6-way ABS motor pack connector terminal A and the 6-way ABS motor pack connector terminal B. Is the resistance within the specified range?	0.2–1.5 Ω	*Go to Step 7*	*Go to Step 9*
7	1. Inspect the following components for damage: • The 6-way ABS motor pack connector • The 6-way ABS motor pack harness connector Damage may cause a short to voltage with the connector connected. 2. Inspect the following components for damage: • The EBCM connector • The EBCM harness connector Damage may cause a short to voltage with the connector connected. 3. Inspect CKT 1280 and CKT 1281 for signs of damage. Damage may cause a short to voltage. Is there damage which may result in a short to voltage?	—	*Go to Step 13*	*Go to Step 8*
8	1. Reconnect the 6-way ABS motor pack connector. 2. Reconnect the EBCM connector. 3. Test drive the vehicle obtaining a speed of at least 16 km/h (10 mph). 4. Turn the ignition switch to the OFF position. 5. Repeat the drive sequence two additional times. 6. Use the *Scan Tool* in order to inspect for DTCs. Did DTC C1258 set as a current DTC in the last three drive cycles?	—	*Go to Step 14*	*Go to Step 15*

GC402980302700BX

Fig. 52 Code C1258: LH Front ABS Motor Circuit Shorted To Voltage (Part 2 of 3). Alero, Grand Am & Malibu

Step	Action	Value(s)	Yes	No
9	Replace the ABS motor pack. Is the repair complete?	—	Refer to *Diagnostic System Check*	—
10	Repair the short to voltage in CKT 1280. Is the repair complete?	—	Refer to *Diagnostic System Check*	—
11	Repair the short to voltage in CKT 1281. Is the repair complete?	—	Refer to *Diagnostic System Check*	—
12	Repair the short between CKT 1280 and CKT 1281. Is the repair complete?	—	Refer to *Diagnostic System Check*	—
13	Replace all of the following components that are damaged: • The terminals • The connectors • The wires Damage may cause a short to voltage. Is the repair complete?	—	Refer to *Diagnostic System Check*	—
14	Replace the EBCM. Is the repair complete?	—	Refer to *Diagnostic System Check*	—
15	The malfunction is intermittent or not present at this time. Refer to Diagnostic Aids for more information.	—	—	—

GC402980302700CX

Fig. 52 Code C1258: LH Front ABS Motor Circuit Shorted To Voltage (Part 3 of 3). Alero, Grand Am & Malibu

Step	Action	Value(s)	Yes	No
1	Was the Diagnostic System Check performed?	—	*Go to Step 2*	Refer to *Diagnostic System Check*
2	Does DTC C1261 occur intermittently?	—	Refer to Diagnostic Aids	*Go to Step 3*
3	1. Turn the ignition switch to the OFF position. 2. Disconnect the 6-way ABS brake motor pack connector. 3. Use the *J 39200* in order to measure the resistance between the 6-way ABS brake motor pack connector terminal E and 6-way ABS motor pack connector terminal F. Is the resistance within the specified range?	0.2–1.5 Ω	*Go to Step 4*	*Go to Step 8*
4	1. Disconnect the EBCM connector. 2. Use *J 39200* in order to measure the resistance between the 6-way ABS brake motor pack harness connector terminal E and the EBCM harness connector terminal A. Is the resistance within the specified range?	0–2 Ω	*Go to Step 5*	*Go to Step 9*
5	Use the *J 39200* in order to measure the resistance between the 6-way ABS brake motor pack harness connector terminal F and the EBCM harness connector terminal B. Is the resistance within the specified range?	0–2 Ω	*Go to Step 6*	*Go to Step 10*
6	1. Inspect the following components for poor terminal contact and corrosion: • The 6-way ABS brake motor pack connector • The 6-way ABS brake motor pack harness connector 2. Inspect the following components for poor terminal contact and corrosion: • The EBCM connector • The EBCM harness connector Damage that may cause an open with the connector connected. 3. Inspect CKT 1282 and CKT 1283 for damage. Damage may cause an open circuit. Is there poor terminal contact or corrosion?	—	*Go to Step 11*	*Go to Step 7*
7	1. Reconnect the 6-way ABS brake motor pack connector. 2. Reconnect the EBCM connector. 3. Test drive the vehicle obtaining a speed at least 16 km/h (10 mph). 4. Turn the ignition switch to the OFF position. 5. Repeat the drive sequence two additional times. 6. Use the *Scan Tool* in order to inspect for DTCs. Did DTC C1261 set as a current DTC in the last three drive cycles?	—	*Go to Step 12*	*Go to Step 13*

GC402980302800BX

Fig. 53 Code C1261: RH Front ABS Motor Circuit Open (Part 2 of 3). Alero, Grand Am & Malibu

Circuit Description

DTC C1261 identifies an ABS motor that cannot energize due to an open in the ABS motor circuitry. The malfunction will not allow proper front ABS operation.

Conditions for Setting the DTC

DTC C1261 can only set when the motor is commanded off.

A malfunction exists if the EBCM detects an out of range voltage on either of the right front ABS motor circuits. The out of range voltage on either circuit indicates an open circuit exists.

Action Taken When the DTC Sets

- An open ABS motor will not activate.
- A malfunction DTC stores.
- The ABS disables.
- The ABS warning indicator turns on.

Conditions for Clearing the DTC

- The condition responsible for setting the DTC no longer exists and the Scan Tool Clear DTCs function is used.
- 100 drive cycles pass with no DTCs detected. A drive cycle consists of starting the vehicle, driving the vehicle over 16 km/h (10 mph), stopping and then turning the ignition off.

Diagnostic Aids

Use the Scan Tool Manual Control function in order to exercise ABS motor movement of affected channel in both directions while applying light pressure on the brake pedal.

An intermittent malfunction may be indicated if erratic or jumpy brake pedal movement is detected while performing an apply or release function of the ABS monitor.

The following conditions may cause an intermittent malfunction:

- A poor connection
- Rubbed-through wire insulation
- A broken wire inside the insulation

If the malfunction is not current, use the following procedure to pinpoint an intermittent malfunction in the motor circuitry or connections:

1. Wiggle the wires of the affected channel.
2. Inspect if the DTC resets.

Use the enhanced diagnostic function of the Scan Tool in order to measure the frequency of the malfunction.

Thoroughly inspect any circuitry that may be causing the intermittent complaint for the following conditions:

- Backed out terminals
- Improper mating
- Broken locks
- Improperly formed or damaged terminals
- Poor terminal-to-wiring connections
- Physical damage to the wiring harness

Clear the DTCs after completing the diagnosis. Test drive the vehicle for three drive cycles in order to verify that the DTC does not reset. Use the following procedure in order to complete one drive cycle:

1. Start the vehicle.
2. Drive the vehicle over 16 km/h (10 mph).
3. Stop the vehicle.
4. Turn the ignition to the OFF position.

Important: Zero the J 39200 test leads before making any resistance measurements.

GC402980302800AX

Fig. 53 Code C1261: RH Front ABS Motor Circuit Open (Part 1 of 3). Alero, Grand Am & Malibu

Step	Action	Value(s)	Yes	No
8	Replace the ABS brake motor pack. Is the repair complete?	—	Refer to *Diagnostic System Check*	—
9	Repair the open in CKT 1282. Is the repair complete?	—	Refer to *Diagnostic System Check*	—
10	Repair the open in CKT 1283. Is the repair complete?	—	Refer to *Diagnostic System Check*	—
11	Replace all of the terminals and connectors that exhibit the following conditions: • Poor terminal contact • Corrosion • Damaged terminal(s) Is the repair complete?	—	Refer to *Diagnostic System Check*	—
12	Replace the EBCM. Is the repair complete?	—	Refer to *Diagnostic System Check*	—
13	The malfunction is intermittent or not present at this time. Refer to Diagnostic Aids for more information.	—	—	—

GC402980302800CX

Fig. 53 Code C1261: RH Front ABS Motor Circuit Open (Part 3 of 3). Alero, Grand Am & Malibu

Circuit Description

DTC C1262 identifies an ABS motor circuit that shorts to ground. The malfunction will cause one of the following conditions to occur:

- The ABS motor will not be controlled at the commanded current rate.
- The driver circuit will allow current directly to ground.

Conditions for Setting the DTC

DTC C1262 can set anytime.

A malfunction exists if The EBCM detects an out of range voltage on either of the right front ABS motor circuits.

An out of range voltage on either circuit indicates one of the following conditions:

- A circuit shorts to ground.
- An ABS brake motor internally shorts.

Action Taken When the DTC Sets

- A malfunction DTC stores.
- The ABS disables.
- The ABS warning indicator turns on.

Conditions for Clearing the DTC

- The condition responsible for setting the DTC no longer exists and the Scan Tool Clear DTCs function is used.
- 100 drive cycles pass with no DTCs detected. A drive cycle consists of starting the vehicle, driving the vehicle over 16 km/h (10 mph), stopping and then turning the ignition off.

Diagnostic Aids

Use the Scan Tool Manual Control function in order to exercise ABS motor movement of affected channel in both directions while applying light pressure on the brake pedal.

An intermittent malfunction may be indicated if erratic or jumpy brake pedal movement is detected while performing an apply or release function of the ABS monitor.

A rubbed-through wire may cause an intermittent malfunction:

If the malfunction is not current, use the following procedure to pinpoint an intermittent malfunction in the motor circuitry or connections:

1. Wiggle the wires of the affected channel.
2. Inspect if the DTC resets.

Use the enhanced diagnostic function of the Scan Tool in order to measure the frequency of the malfunction.

Clear the DTCs after completing the diagnosis. Test drive the vehicle for three drive cycles in order to verify that the DTC does not reset. Use the following procedure in order to complete one drive cycle:

1. Start the vehicle.
2. Drive the vehicle over 16 km/h (10 mph).
3. Stop the vehicle.
4. Turn the ignition to the OFF position.

Important: Zero the J 39200 test leads before making any resistance measurements.

GC402980302900AX

Fig. 54 Code C1262: RH Front ABS Motor Circuit Shorted To Ground (Part 1 of 3). Alero, Grand Am & Malibu

Step	Action	Value(s)	Yes	No
1	Was the Diagnostic System Check performed?	—	*Go to Step 2*	Refer to *Diagnostic System Check*
2	Does DTC C1262 occur intermittently?	—	Refer to Diagnostic Aids	*Go to Step 3*
3	1. Turn the ignition switch to the OFF position. 2. Disconnect the 6-way ABS brake motor pack connector. 3. Disconnect the EBCM connector 4. Use the *J 39200* in order to measure the resistance between the 6-way ABS brake motor pack harness connector terminal E and ground. Is the resistance within the specified range?	OL (Infinite)	*Go to Step 4*	*Go to Step 9*
4	Use *J 39200* in order to measure the resistance between the 6-way ABS brake motor pack harness connector terminal F and ground. Is the resistance within the specified range?	OL (Infinite)	*Go to Step 5*	*Go to Step 10*
5	Use the *J 39200* in order to measure the resistance between the 6-way ABS brake motor pack connector terminal E and ground. Is the resistance within the specified range?	OL (Infinite)	*Go to Step 6*	*Go to Step 8*
6	1. Inspect the following components for damage: • The 6-way ABS brake motor pack connector • The 6-way ABS brake motor pack harness connector Damage that may cause a short to ground with the connector connected. 2. Inspect the following components for damage: • The EBCM connector • The EBCM harness connector Damage that may cause a short to ground with the connector connected. 3. Inspect CKT 1282 and CKT 1283 for damage. Damage may cause a short to ground. Is there damage which may result in a short to ground?	—	*Go to Step 11*	*Go to Step 7*
7	1. Reconnect the 6-way ABS brake motor pack connector. 2. Reconnect the EBCM connector. 3. Test drive the vehicle obtaining a speed at least 16 km/h (10 mph). 4. Turn the ignition switch to the OFF position. 5. Repeat the drive sequence two additional times. 6. Use the *Scan Tool* in order to inspect for DTCs. Did DTC C1262 set as a current DTC in the last three drive cycles?	—	*Go to Step 12*	*Go to Step 13*

GC402980302900BX

Fig. 54 Code C1262: RH Front ABS Motor Circuit Shorted To Ground (Part 2 of 3). Alero, Grand Am & Malibu

Step	Action	Value(s)	Yes	No
8	Replace the ABS brake motor pack. Is the repair complete?	—	Refer to *Diagnostic System Check*	—
9	Repair the short to ground in CKT 1282. Is the repair complete?		Refer to *Diagnostic System Check*	—
10	Repair the short to ground in CKT 1283. Is the repair complete?	—	Refer to *Diagnostic System Check*	—
11	Replace all of the following components that exhibit signs of damage: • The terminals • The connectors • The wires Damage may cause a short to ground. Is the repair complete?	—	Refer to *Diagnostic System Check*	—
12	Replace the EBCM. Is the repair complete?	—	Refer to *Diagnostic System Check*	—
13	The malfunction is intermittent or not present at this time. Refer to Diagnostic Aids for more information.	—	—	—

GC402980302900CX

Fig. 54 Code C1262: RH Front ABS Motor Circuit Shorted To Ground (Part 3 of 3). Alero, Grand Am & Malibu

Circuit Description

DTC C1263 identifies an ABS motor circuit that is shorted shorts to voltage or an ABS motor that has low or no resistance.

Conditions for Setting the DTC

DTC C1263 can set only when the ABS motor is commanded off.

A malfunction exists if The EBCM detects an out of range voltage on either of the right front ABS motor circuits.

An out of range voltage on either circuit indicates one of the following conditions:

- A circuit shorts to voltage.
- An ABS brake motor shorts internally.

Action Taken When the DTC Sets

- A malfunction DTC stores.
- The ABS disables.
- The ABS warning indicator turns on.

Conditions for Clearing the DTC

- The condition responsible for setting the DTC no longer exists and the Scan Tool Clear DTCs function is used.
- 100 drive cycles pass with no DTCs detected. A drive cycle consists of starting the vehicle, driving the vehicle over 16 km/h (10 mph), stopping and then turning the ignition off.

Diagnostic Aids

Use the Scan Tool Manual Control function in order to exercise ABS motor movement of affected channel in both directions while applying light pressure on the brake pedal.

An intermittent malfunction may be indicated if erratic or jumpy brake pedal movement is detected while performing an apply or release function of the ABS monitor.

If the malfunction is not current, use the following procedure to pinpoint an intermittent malfunction in the motor circuitry or connections:

1. Wiggle the wires of the affected channel.
2. Inspect if the DTC resets.

Use the enhanced diagnostic function of the Scan Tool in order to measure the frequency of the malfunction.

Clear the DTCs after completing the diagnosis. Test drive the vehicle for three drive cycles in order to verify that the DTC does not reset. Use the following procedure in order to complete one drive cycle:

1. Start the vehicle.
2. Drive the vehicle over 16 km/h (10 mph).
3. Stop the vehicle.
4. Turn the ignition to the OFF position.

Important: Zero the J 39200 test leads before making any resistance measurements.

GC402980303000AX

Fig. 55 Code C1263: RH Front ABS Motor Circuit Shorted To Voltage (Part 1 of 3). Alero, Grand Am & Malibu

Step	Action	Value(s)	Yes	No
1	Was the Diagnostic System Check performed?	—	*Go to Step 2*	Refer to *Diagnostic System Check*
2	Does DTC C1263 occur intermittently?	—	Refer to Diagnostic Aids	*Go to Step 3*
3	1. Turn the ignition switch to the OFF position. 2. Disconnect the 6-way ABS brake motor pack connector. 3. Disconnect the EBCM connector 4. Turn the ignition switch to the RUN position. Do not start the engine. 5. Use the *J 39200* in order to measure the voltage between the 6-way ABS brake motor pack harness connector terminal E and ground. Is the voltage within the specified range?	0–1 V	*Go to Step 4*	*Go to Step 10*
4	Use the *J 39200* in order to measure the voltage between the 6-way ABS brake motor pack harness connector terminal F and ground. Is the voltage within the specified range?	0–1 V	*Go to Step 5*	*Go to Step 11*
5	1. Turn the ignition switch to the OFF position. 2. Use the *J 39200* in order to measure the resistance between the 6-way ABS motor pack harness connector terminal E and the 6-way ABS motor pack harness connector terminal F. Is the resistance within the specified range?	OL (Infinite)	*Go to Step 6*	*Go to Step 12*
6	Use the *J 39200* in order to measure the resistance between the 6-way ABS motor pack connector terminal E and the 6-way ABS motor pack connector terminal F. Is the resistance within the specified range?	0.2–1.5 Ω	*Go to Step 7*	*Go to Step 9*
7	1. Inspect the following components for damage: • The 6-way ABS motor pack connector • The 6-way ABS motor pack harness connector Damage that may cause a short to voltage with the connector connected. 2. Inspect the following components for damage: • The EBCM connector • The EBCM harness connector Damage may cause a short to voltage with the connector connected. 3. Inspect CKT 1282 and CKT 1283 for signs of damage. Damage may cause a short to voltage. Is there damage which may cause a short to voltage?	—	*Go to Step 13*	*Go to Step 8*

GC402980303000BX

Fig. 55 Code C1263: RH Front ABS Motor Circuit Shorted To Voltage (Part 2 of 3). Alero, Grand Am & Malibu

Step	Action	Value(s)	Yes	No
8	1. Reconnect the 6-way ABS motor pack connector. 2. Reconnect the EBCM connector. 3. Test drive the vehicle at a speed of at least 16 km/h (10 mph). 4. Turn the ignition switch to the OFF position. 5. Repeat the drive sequence two additional times. 6. Use the *Scan Tool* in order to inspect for DTCs. Did DTC C1263 set as a current DTC during the last three drive cycles?	—	*Go to Step 14*	*Go to Step 15*
9	Replace the ABS motor pack. Is the repair complete?	—	Refer to *Diagnostic System Check*	—
10	Repair the short to voltage in CKT 1282. Is the repair complete?	—	Refer to *Diagnostic System Check*	—
11	Repair the short to voltage in CKT 1283. Is the repair complete?	—	Refer to *Diagnostic System Check*	—
12	Repair the short between CKT 1282 and CKT 1283. Is the repair complete?	—	Refer to *Diagnostic System Check*	—
13	Replace all of the following components that are damaged: • The terminals • The connectors • The wires Damage may cause a short to voltage. Is the repair complete?	—	Refer to *Diagnostic System Check*	—
14	Replace the EBCM. Is the repair complete?	—	Refer to *Diagnostic System Check*	—
15	The malfunction is intermittent or is not present at this time. Refer to Diagnostic Aids for more information.	—	—	—

GC402980303000CX

Fig. 55 Code C1263: RH Front ABS Motor Circuit Shorted To Voltage (Part 3 of 3). Alero, Grand Am & Malibu

Step	Action	Value(s)	Yes	No
1	Was the Diagnostic System Check performed?	—	*Go to Step 2*	Refer to *Diagnostic System Check*
2	Does DTC C1264 occur intermittently?	—	Refer to Diagnostic Aids	*Go to Step 3*
3	1. Turn the ignition switch to the OFF position. 2. Disconnect the 6-way ABS brake motor pack connector. 3. Use the *J 39200* in order to measure the resistance between the 6-way ABS brake motor pack connector terminal D and 6-way ABS motor pack connector terminal C Is the resistance within the specified range?	0.2–1.5 Ω	*Go to Step 4*	*Go to Step 8*
4	1. Disconnect the EBCM connector. 2. Use the *J 39200* in order to measure the resistance between the 6-way ABS brake motor pack harness connector terminal C and the EBCM harness connector terminal F. Is the resistance within the specified range?	0–2 Ω	*Go to Step 5*	*Go to Step 9*
5	Use the *J 39200* in order to measure the resistance between the 6-way ABS brake motor pack harness connector terminal D and the EBCM harness connector terminal E. Is the resistance within the specified range?	0–2 Ω	*Go to Step 6*	*Go to Step 10*
6	1. Inspect the following components for poor terminal contact and corrosion: • The 6-way ABS brake motor pack connector • The 6-way ABS brake motor pack harness connector 2. Inspect the following components for poor terminal contact and corrosion: • The EBCM connector • The EBCM harness connector Damage may cause a short to ground with the connector connected. 3. Inspect CKT 1284 and CKT 1285 for damage. Damage may cause a short to ground. Is there poor terminal contact or corrosion?	—	*Go to Step 11*	*Go to Step 7*
7	1. Reconnect the 6-way ABS brake motor pack connector. 2. Reconnect the EBCM connector. 3. Test drive the vehicle at a speed of at least 16 km/h (10 mph). 4. Turn the ignition switch to the OFF position. 5. Repeat the drive sequence two additional times. 6. Use the *Scan Tool* in order to inspect for DTCs. Did DTC C1264 set as a current DTC in the last three drive cycles?	—	*Go to Step 12*	*Go to Step 13*

GC402980303100BX

Fig. 56 Code C1264: Rear ABS Motor Circuit Open (Part 2 of 3). Alero, Grand Am & Malibu

Circuit Description

DTC 1264 identifies an ABS motor that cannot energize due to an open in the ABS motor circuitry. The malfunction will not allow proper rear ABS operation.

Conditions for Setting the DTC

DTC C1264 can only set when the motor is commanded off.

A malfunction exists if the EBCM detects an out of range voltage on either of the rear ABS motor circuits. The out of range voltage on either circuit indicates an open circuit exists.

Action Taken When the DTC Sets

- An open ABS motor will not activate.
- A malfunction DTC stores.
- The ABS disables.
- The ABS warning indicator turns on.
- The red BRAKE warning indicator turns on and DTC C1286 also sets if the rear piston in the ABS brake motor pack is not in the home position.

Conditions for Clearing the DTC

- The condition responsible for setting the DTC no longer exists and the Scan Tool Clear DTCs function is used.
- 100 drive cycles pass with no DTCs detected. A drive cycle consists of starting the vehicle, driving the vehicle over 16 km/h (10 mph), stopping and then turning the ignition off.

Diagnostic Aids

Use the Scan Tool Manual Control function in order to exercise ABS motor movement of affected channel in both directions while applying light pressure on the brake pedal.

An intermittent malfunction may be indicated if erratic or jumpy brake pedal movement is detected while performing an apply or release function of the ABS monitor.

The following conditions may cause an intermittent malfunction:

- A poor connection
- Rubbed-through wire insulation
- A broken wire inside the insulation

If the malfunction is not current, use the following procedure to pinpoint an intermittent malfunction in the motor circuitry or connections:

1. Wiggle the wires of the affected channel.
2. Inspect if the DTC resets.

Use the enhanced diagnostic function of the Scan Tool in order to measure the frequency of the malfunction.

Thoroughly inspect any circuitry that may be causing the intermittent complaint for the following conditions:

- Backed out terminals
- Improper mating
- Broken locks
- Improperly formed or damaged terminals
- Poor terminal-to-wiring connections
- Physical damage to the wiring harness

Clear the DTCs after completing the diagnosis. Test drive the vehicle for three drive cycles in order to verify that the DTC does not reset. Use the following procedure in order to complete one drive cycle:

1. Start the vehicle.
2. Drive the vehicle over 16 km/h (10 mph).
3. Stop the vehicle.
4. Turn the ignition to the OFF position.

Important: Zero the J 39200 test leads before making any resistance measurements.

GC402980303100AX

Fig. 56 Code C1264: Rear ABS Motor Circuit Open (Part 1 of 3). Alero, Grand Am & Malibu

Step	Action	Value(s)	Yes	No
8	Replace the ABS brake motor pack. Is the repair complete?	—	Refer to *Diagnostic System Check*	—
9	Repair the short to ground in CKT 1284. Is the repair complete?	—	Refer to *Diagnostic System Check*	—
10	Repair the short to ground in CKT 1285. Is the repair complete?	—	Refer to *Diagnostic System Check*	—
11	Replace all of the terminals and connectors that exhibit the following conditions: • Poor terminal contact • Corrosion • Damaged terminal(s) Is the repair complete?	—	Refer to *Diagnostic System Check*	—
12	Replace the EBCM. Is the repair complete?	—	Refer to *Diagnostic System Check*	—
13	The malfunction is intermittent or is not present at this time. Refer to Diagnostic Aids for more information.	—	—	—

GC402980303100CX

Fig. 56 Code C1264: Rear ABS Motor Circuit Open (Part 3 of 3). Alero, Grand Am & Malibu

Circuit Description

DTC C1265 identifies an ABS motor circuit that shorts to ground. The malfunction will cause one of the following conditions to occur:

- The ABS motor will not be controlled at the commanded current rate.
- The driver circuit will allow current directly to the ground.

Conditions for Setting the DTC

DTC C1265 can set anytime.

A malfunction exists if The EBCM detects an out of range voltage on either of the rear ABS motor circuits.

An out of range voltage on either circuit indicates one of the following conditions:

- A circuit shorts to ground.
- An ABS brake motor is shorts internally.

Action Taken When the DTC Sets

- A malfunction DTC stores.
- The ABS disables.
- The ABS warning indicator turns on.
- The red BRAKE warning indicator turns on and DTC C1286 also sets if the rear piston in the ABS brake motor pack is not in the home position.

Conditions for Clearing the DTC

- The condition responsible for setting the DTC no longer exists and the Scan Tool Clear DTCs function is used.
- 100 drive cycles pass with no DTC(s) detected. A drive cycle consists of starting the vehicle, driving the vehicle over 16 km/h (10 mph), stopping and then turning the ignition off.

Diagnostic Aids

Use the Scan Tool Manual Control function in order to exercise ABS motor movement of affected channel in both directions while applying light pressure on the brake pedal.

An intermittent malfunction may be indicated if erratic or jumpy brake pedal movement is detected while performing an apply or release function of the ABS monitor.

If the malfunction is not current, use the following procedure to pinpoint an intermittent malfunction in the motor circuitry or connections:

1. Wiggle the wires of the affected channel.
2. Inspect if the DTC resets.

Use the enhanced diagnostic function of the Scan Tool in order to measure the frequency of the malfunction.

Clear the DTCs after completing the diagnosis. Test drive the vehicle for three drive cycles in order to verify that the DTC does not reset. Use the following procedure in order to complete one drive cycle:

1. Start the vehicle.
2. Drive the vehicle over 16 km/h (10 mph).
3. Stop the vehicle.
4. Turn the ignition to the OFF position.

Important: Zero the J 39200 test leads before making any resistance measurements.

GC402980303200AX

Fig. 57 Code C1265: Rear ABS Motor Circuit Shorted To Ground (Part 1 of 3). Alero, Grand Am & Malibu

Step	Action	Value(s)	Yes	No
1	Was the Diagnostic System Check performed?	—	*Go to Step 2*	Refer to *Diagnostic System Check*
2	Does DTC C1265 occur intermittently?	—	Refer to Diagnostic Aids	*Go to Step 3*
3	1. Turn the ignition switch to the OFF position. 2. Disconnect the 6-way ABS brake motor pack connector. 3. Disconnect the EBCM connector 4. Use the *J 39200* in order to measure the resistance between the 6-way ABS brake motor pack harness connector terminal C and ground. Is the resistance within the specified range?	OL (Infinite)	*Go to Step 4*	*Go to Step 9*
4	Use *J 39200* in order to measure the resistance between the 6-way ABS brake motor pack harness connector terminal D and ground. Is the resistance within the specified range?	OL (Infinite)	*Go to Step 5*	*Go to Step 10*
5	Use the *J 39200* in order to measure the resistance between the 6-way ABS brake motor pack connector terminal C and ground. Is the resistance within the specified range?	OL (Infinite)	*Go to Step 6*	*Go to Step 8*
6	1. Inspect the following components for damage: • The 6-way ABS brake motor pack connector • The 6-way ABS brake motor pack harness connector Damage that may cause a short to ground with the connector connected. 2. Inspect the following components for damage: • The EBCM connector • The EBCM harness connector Damage that may cause a short to ground with the connector connected. 3. Inspect the following circuits for damage: • CKT 1284 • CKT 1285 Damage may cause a short to ground. Is there damage which may cause a short to ground?	—	*Go to Step 11*	*Go to Step 7*
7	1. Reconnect the 6-way ABS brake motor pack connector. 2. Reconnect the EBCM connector. 3. Test drive the vehicle obtaining a speed at least 16 km/h (10 mph). 4. Turn the ignition switch to the OFF position. 5. Repeat the drive sequence two additional times. 6. Use the *Scan Tool* in order to inspect for DTCs. Did DTC C1265 set as a current DTC during the last three drive cycles?	—	*Go to Step 12*	*Go to Step 13*

GC402980303200BX

Fig. 57 Code C1265: Rear ABS Motor Circuit Shorted To Ground (Part 2 of 3). Alero, Grand Am & Malibu

Step	Action	Value(s)	Yes	No
8	Replace the ABS brake motor pack. Is the repair complete?	—	Refer to *Diagnostic System Check*	—
9	Repair the short to ground in CKT 1284. Is the repair complete?	—	Refer to *Diagnostic System Check*	—
10	Repair the short to ground in CKT 1285. Is the repair complete?	—	Refer to *Diagnostic System Check*	—
11	Replace all of the following components that exhibit signs of damage: • The terminals • The connectors • The wires Damage may cause a short to ground. Is the repair complete?	—	Refer to *Diagnostic System Check*	—
12	Replace the EBCM. Is the repair complete?	—	Refer to *Diagnostic System Check*	—
13	The malfunction is intermittent or is not present at this time. Refer to Diagnostic Aids for more information.	—	—	—

GC402980303200CX

Fig. 57 Code C1265: Rear ABS Motor Circuit Shorted To Ground (Part 3 of 3). Alero, Grand Am & Malibu

Circuit Description

DTC C1266 identifies an ABS motor circuit that shorts to voltage or an ABS motor that has low or zero resistance. The malfunction will cause one of the following conditions to occur:

- The ABS motor will not be controlled at the commanded current rate.
- The ABS motor will turn in the opposite direction or not at all.

Conditions for Setting the DTC

DTC C1266 can set only when the ABS motor is commanded off.

A malfunction exists if The EBCM detects an out of range voltage on either of the rear ABS motor circuits.

An out of range voltage on either circuit indicates one of the following conditions:

- A circuit shorts to voltage.
- An ABS brake motor shorts internally.

Action Taken When the DTC Sets

- A malfunction DTC stores.
- The ABS disables.
- The ABS warning indicator turns on.

Conditions for Clearing the DTC

- The condition responsible for setting the DTC no longer exists and the Scan Tool Clear DTCs function is used.
- 100 drive cycles pass with no DTCs detected. A drive cycle consists of starting the vehicle, driving the vehicle over 16 km/h (10 mph), stopping and then turning the ignition off.

Diagnostic Aids

Use the Scan Tool Manual Control function to exercise ABS motor movement of affected channel in both directions while applying light pressure on the brake pedal.

An intermittent malfunction may be indicated if erratic or jumpy brake pedal movement is detected while performing an apply or release function of the ABS monitor.

If the malfunction is not current, use the following procedure to pinpoint an intermittent malfunction in the motor circuitry or connections:

1. Wiggle the wires of the affected channel.
2. Inspect if the DTC resets.

Use the enhanced diagnostic function of the Scan Tool in order to measure the frequency of the malfunction.

Clear the DTCs after completing the diagnosis. Test drive the vehicle for three drive cycles in order to verify that the DTC does not reset. Use the following procedure in order to complete one drive cycle:

1. Start the vehicle.
2. Drive the vehicle over 16 km/h (10 mph).
3. Stop the vehicle.
4. Turn the ignition to the OFF position.

Important: Zero the J 39200 test leads before making any resistance measurements. Refer to the J 39200 user's manual.

GC402980303300AX

Fig. 58 Code C1266: Rear ABS Motor Circuit Shorted To Voltage (Part 1 of 3). Alero, Grand Am & Malibu

Step	Action	Value(s)	Yes	No
1	Was the Diagnostic System Check performed?	—	*Go to Step 2*	Refer to *Diagnostic System Check*
2	Does DTC C1266 occur intermittently?	—	Refer to Diagnostic Aids	*Go to Step 3*
3	1. Turn the ignition switch to the OFF position. 2. Disconnect the 6-way ABS brake motor pack connector. 3. Disconnect the EBCM connector 4. Turn the ignition switch to the RUN position. Do not start the engine. 5. Use the *J 39200* in order to measure the voltage between the 6-way ABS brake motor pack harness connector terminal C and ground. Is the voltage within the specified range?	0–1 V	*Go to Step 4*	*Go to Step 10*
4	Use the *J 39200* in order to measure the voltage between the 6-way ABS brake motor pack harness connector terminal D and ground. Is the voltage within the specified range?	0–1 V	*Go to Step 5*	*Go to Step 11*
5	1. Turn the ignition switch to the OFF position. 2. Use the *J 39200* in order to measure the resistance between the 6-way ABS motor pack harness connector terminal D and the 6-way ABS motor pack harness connector terminal C. Is the resistance within the specified range?	OL (Infinite)	*Go to Step 6*	*Go to Step 12*
6	Use the *J 39200* in order to measure the resistance between the 6-way ABS motor pack connector terminal D and the 6-way ABS motor pack connector terminal C. Is the resistance within the specified range?	0.2–1.5 Ω	*Go to Step 7*	*Go to Step 9*
7	1. Inspect the following components for damage: • The 6-way ABS motor pack connector • The 6-way ABS motor pack harness connector Damage that may cause a short to voltage with the connector connected. 2. Inspect the following components for damage: • The EBCM connector • The EBCM harness connector Damage that may cause a short to voltage with the connector connected. 3. Inspect CKT 1284 and CKT 1285 for damage. Damage may cause a short to voltage. Is there damage that may cause a short to voltage?	—	*Go to Step 13*	*Go to Step 8*

GC402980303300BX

Fig. 58 Code C1266: Rear ABS Motor Circuit Shorted To Voltage (Part 2 of 3). Alero, Grand Am & Malibu

Step	Action	Value(s)	Yes	No
8	1. Reconnect the 6-way ABS motor pack connector. 2. Reconnect the EBCM connector. 3. Test drive the vehicle at a speed of at least 16 km/h (10 mph). 4. Turn the ignition switch to the OFF position. 5. Repeat the drive sequence two additional times. 6. Use the *Scan Tool* in order to inspect for DTCs. Did DTC C1266 set as a current DTC in the last three drive cycles?	—	*Go to Step 14*	*Go to Step 15*
9	Replace the ABS motor pack. Is the repair complete?	—	Refer to *Diagnostic System Check*	—
10	Repair the short to voltage in CKT 1284. Is the repair complete?	—	Refer to *Diagnostic System Check*	—
11	Repair the short to voltage in CKT 1285. Is the repair complete?	—	Refer to *Diagnostic System Check*	—
12	Repair the short between CKT 1284 and CKT 1285. Is the repair complete?	—	Refer to *Diagnostic System Check*	—
13	Replace all of the following components that are damaged: • The terminals • The connectors • The wires Damage may cause a short to voltage. Is the repair complete?	—	Refer to *Diagnostic System Check*	—
14	Replace the EBCM. Is the repair complete?	—	Refer to *Diagnostic System Check*	—
15	The malfunction is intermittent or is not present at this time. Refer to Diagnostic Aids for more information.	—	—	—

GC402980303300CX

Fig. 58 Code C1266: Rear ABS Motor Circuit Shorted To Voltage (Part 3 of 3). Alero, Grand Am & Malibu

Step	Action	Value(s)	Yes	No
1	Was the ABS Diagnostic System Check performed?	—	Go to *Step 2*	Go to *A Diagnostic System Check - ABS*
2	1. Disconnect the LH I/P Wiring Harness Junction Block connector C1. 2. Disconnect the EBCM harness connector. 3. Use the *J 39200* to measure the resistance between the EBCM harness connector terminal 12 and ground. Is the measured resistance within the specified value?	OL (Infinite)	Data Link Communications	Go to *Step 3*
3	Repair short to ground in CKT 1807. Is the repair complete?	—	Go to *A Diagnostic System Check - ABS*	—

GC4020052202020X

Fig. 59 Code C1267: Code U1300 Previously Set (Part 2 of 2). Alero & Grand Am

Step	Action	Value(s)	Yes	No
1	Was the ABS Diagnostic System Check performed?	—	Go to *Step 2*	Go to *A Diagnostic System Check - ABS*
2	1. Disconnect the LH I/P Wiring Harness Junction Block connector C1. 2. Disconnect the EBCM harness connector. 3. Use the *J 39200* to measure the resistance between the EBCM harness connector terminal 12 and ground. Is the measured resistance within the specified value?	OL (Infinite)	Data Link Communications	Go to *Step 3*
3	Repair short to ground in CKT 1807. Is the repair complete?	—	Go to *A Diagnostic System Check - ABS*	—

GC4020052203020X

Fig. 60 Code C1268: Code U1301 Previously Set (Part 2 of 2). Alero & Grand Am

Circuit Description

The serial data link is a communication line between the PCM, Instrument Cluster and the EBCM.

Conditions for Setting the DTC

DTC C1267 sets along with DTC U1300.

DTC C1267 can be set any time the ignition is ON.

A malfunction exists if CKT 1807 is shorted to ground resulting in no communication to the PCM or any other controller.

Action Taken When the DTC Sets

- A malfunction DTC stores.
- ABS and ETS remain functional.
- No action towards the electronic brake control relay is taken.
- No action towards the ABS warning indicator is taken.

Conditions for Clearing the DTC

- The condition for DTC C1267 is no longer present.
- The use of the scan tool CLEAR DTCs function.
- DTC C1267 clears after 100 drive cycles with no DTCs detected. A drive cycle consists of starting the vehicle, driving the vehicle over 16 km/h (10 mph), stopping and then turning the ignition OFF.

Diagnostic Aids

- Perform the Powertrain OBD System Check before beginning this DTC table. This eliminates the PCM as a possible source of the malfunction.
- The following conditions may cause an intermittent malfunction:
  - Rubbed-through wire insulation.
- Use the enhanced diagnostic function of the scan tool in order to check the frequency of the malfunction.

The malfunction may be intermittent. Try performing the tests shown while "wiggling" wiring and connectors, this can often cause the malfunction to appear. PCM DTCs will likely be set along with DTC C1267.

DTC U1300 will only be able to be read as a history code since the scan tool uses the same serial data circuit. If CKT 1807 is shorted to ground, no communication with the scan tool will be possible.

GC4020052202010X

Fig. 59 Code C1267: Code U1300 Previously Set (Part 1 of 2). Alero & Grand Am

Circuit Description

The serial data link is a communication line between the PCM, Instrument Cluster and the EBCM.

Conditions for Setting the DTC

DTC C1268 sets along with DTC U1301.

DTC C1268 can be set any time the ignition is ON.

A malfunction exists if CKT 1807 is shorted to ground resulting in no communication to the PCM or any other controller.

Action Taken When the DTC Sets

- A malfunction DTC stores.
- ABS and ETS remain functional.
- No action towards the electronic brake control relay is taken.
- No action towards the ABS warning indicator is taken.

Conditions for Clearing the DTC

- The condition for DTC C1268 is no longer present.
- The use of the scan tool CLEAR DTCs function.
- DTC C1268 clears after 100 drive cycles with no DTCs detected. A drive cycle consists of starting the vehicle, driving the vehicle over 16 km/h (10 mph), stopping and then turning the ignition OFF.

Diagnostic Aids

- Perform the Powertrain OBD System Check before beginning this DTC table. This eliminates the PCM as a possible source of the malfunction.
- The following conditions may cause an intermittent malfunction:
  - Rubbed-through wire insulation.
- Use the enhanced diagnostic function of the scan tool in order to check the frequency of the malfunction.

The malfunction may be intermittent. Try performing the tests shown while wiggling wiring and connectors, this can often cause the malfunction to appear. PCM DTCs will likely be set along with DTC C1268.

DTC U1301 will only be able to be read as a history code since the scan tool uses the same serial data circuit. If CKT 1807 is shorted to ground, no communication with the scan tool will be possible.

GC4020052203010X

Fig. 60 Code C1268: Code U1301 Previously Set (Part 1 of 2). Alero & Grand Am

Circuit Description

Battery voltage is supplied to the power steering pump actuator terminal A when the EBCM commands the Electronic Brake Control Relay ON. Ground for the power steering pump actuator is provided through EBCM terminal 18 to actuator terminal B. The EBCM controls the amount of current supplied to the actuator based on input from the ABS wheel speed sensors and the steering wheel position sensor.

Conditions for Setting the DTC

- DTC C1273 can be set before ABS initialization or above 16 km/h (10 mph).
- The EBCM detects the power steering pump actuator control circuit is open or shorted to ground before ABS initialization.
- The actuator senses current less than half the command current when the vehicle is above 16 km/h (10 mph).

Action Taken When the DTC Sets

- A malfunction DTC stores.
- ABS/VES is disabled.
- The ABS warning indicator is turned ON and power steering returns to full assist.

Conditions for Clearing the DTC

- The condition responsible for setting the DTC no longer exists and the Scan Tool Clear DTCs function is used.
- 100 drive cycles pass with no ABS DTCs detected. A drive cycle consists of starting the vehicle, driving the vehicle over 16 km/h (10 mph), stopping and then turning the ignition OFF.

Diagnostic Aids

The following conditions may cause an intermittent malfunction:

- A poor connection
- Rubbed-through wire insulation
- A broken wire inside the insulation
- Open or short to ground in any of the EVO actuator circuit wires.
- Malfunctioning power steering pump actuator.

Use the enhanced diagnostic function of the scan tool in order to determine the frequency of the malfunction.

GC4020052204010X

Fig. 61 Code C1273: VES Circuit Open Or Shorted To Ground (Part 1 of 3). Alero & Grand Am

Thoroughly inspect any circuitry that may cause the intermittent complaint for the following conditions:
- Backed out terminals
- Improper mating
- Broken locks
- Improperly formed or damaged terminals
- Poor terminal-to-wiring connections
- Physical damage to the wiring harness

Diagnose and correct all ABS DTCs prior to clearing the VES DTCs. Clearing VES DTCs will automatically clear ABS DTCs resulting in a loss of DTC history data.

Step	Action	Value(s)	Yes	No
Important: Zero the J 39200 test leads before making any resistance measurements. Refer to the J 39200 user's manual.				
1	Was the ABS Diagnostic System Check performed?	—	Go to *Step 2*	Go to *A Diagnostic System Check - ABS*
2	1. Turn the ignition switch to the ON position. 2. Using the scan tool, select SPECIAL FUNCTIONS. 3. Select the VES ACTUATOR TEST function and command the power steering pump actuator ON. Is the feedback current greater than the specified value?	100 mA	Go to *Step 14*	Go to *Step 3*
3	1. Turn the ignition switch to the OFF position. 2. Disconnect the EBCM harness connector. 3. Disconnect the power steering pump actuator connector. 4. Using the *J 39200*, measure the resistance between the power steering pump actuator harness connector terminal B and the EBCM harness connector terminal 18. Is the resistance within the specified range?	0–2 Ω	Go to *Step 4*	Go to *Step 10*
4	Using the *J 39200*, measure the resistance between the EBCM harness connector terminal 18 and ground. Is the resistance within the specified range?	OL (Infinite)	Go to *Step 5*	Go to *Step 11*
5	Using the *J 39200*, measure the resistance between the actuator harness connector terminal A and the EBCM harness connector terminal C. Is the resistance within the specified range?	0–2 Ω	Go to *Step 6*	Go to *Step 12*
6	Using the *J 39200*, measure the resistance between the EBCM harness connector terminal C and ground. Is the resistance within the specified range?	OL (Infinite)	Go to *Step 7*	Go to *Step 13*
7	1. Reconnect the actuator connector. 2. Using the *J 39200*, measure the resistance between the EBCM harness connector terminal 18 and ground. Is the resistance within the specified range?	OL (Infinite)	Go to *Step 8*	Go to *Step 15*
8	Using the *J 39200*, measure the resistance between the EBCM harness connector terminals 18 and C. Is the resistance within the specified range?	7–19 Ω	Go to *Step 9*	Go to *Step 15*
9	1. Inspect the EBCM harness connector and the power steering pump actuator harness connector for poor terminal contact or corrosion. Replace any terminals with poor terminal contact or corrosion. 2. Inspect circuit 1295 for damage which may result in a short to ground or an open with all connectors connected. Repair the damage if present. 3. Reconnect all the connectors. 4. Turn the ignition switch to the ON position. Is DTC C1273 set as a current DTC?	—	Go to *Step 16*	Go to *Step 14*

GC4020052204020X

Fig. 61 Code C1273: VES Circuit Open Or Shorted To Ground (Part 2 of 3). Alero & Grand Am

Step	Action	Value(s)	Yes	No
10	Repair the open or high resistance in CKT 1295. Is the repair complete?	—	Go to *A Diagnostic System Check - ABS*	—
11	Repair the short to ground in CKT 1295. Is the repair complete?	—	Go to *A Diagnostic System Check - ABS*	—
12	Repair the open or high resistance in CKT 1633 or CKT 855. Is the repair complete?	—	Go to *A Diagnostic System Check - ABS*	—
13	1. Repair the short to ground in CKT 1633 or 855. 2. Replace the ABS Fuse. Is the repair complete?	—	Go to *A Diagnostic System Check - ABS*	—
14	The malfunction is intermittent. Is the action complete?	—	Go to *A Diagnostic System Check - ABS*	—
15	Replace the Power Steering Pump Actuator. Is the repair complete?	—	Go to *A Diagnostic System Check - ABS*	—
16	Replace the EBCM. Is the repair complete?	—	Go to *A Diagnostic System Check - ABS*	—

GC4020052204030X

Fig. 61 Code C1273: VES Circuit Open Or Shorted To Ground (Part 3 of 3). Alero & Grand Am

Circuit Description

Battery voltage is supplied to power steering pump actuator terminal A when the EBCM commands the Electronic Brake Control Relay ON. Ground for the actuator is provided through EBCM terminal 18 to actuator terminal B. The EBCM controls the amount of current supplied to the actuator based on input from the ABS wheel speed sensors and the steering wheel position sensor.

Conditions for Setting the DTC

- DTC C1274 can be set anytime after ABS initialization.
- Excessive voltage drop across the power steering pump actuator driver.

Action Taken When the DTC Sets

- A malfunction DTC stores.
- VES is disabled and power steering returns to full assist.
- ABS remains functional.

Conditions for Clearing the DTC

- The condition responsible for setting the DTC no longer exists and the scan tool CLEAR DTCs function is used.
- 100 drive cycles pass with no ABS DTCs detected. A drive cycle consists of starting the vehicle, driving the vehicle over 16 km/h (10 mph), stopping and then turning the ignition OFF.

Diagnostic Aids

The following conditions may cause an intermittent malfunction:
- A poor connection
- Rubbed-through wire insulation
- A broken wire inside the insulation
- Open or short in any of the steering wheel sensor signal circuit wires
- Malfunctioning power steering pump actuator.

Use the enhanced diagnostic function of the scan tool in order to determine the frequency of the malfunction.

Thoroughly inspect any circuitry that may be causing the intermittent complaint for the following conditions:
- Backed out terminals
- Improper mating
- Broken locks
- Improperly formed or damaged terminals
- Poor terminal-to-wiring connections
- Physical damage to the wiring harness

Diagnose and correct all ABS DTCs prior to clearing VES DTCs. Clearing VES DTCs will automatically clear ABS DTCs resulting in a loss of DTC history data.

GC4020052205010X

Fig. 62 Code C1274: VES Circuit Shorted To Voltage (Part 1 of 2). Alero & Grand Am

Step	Action	Value(s)	Yes	No
Important: Zero the J 39200 test leads before making any resistance measurements. Refer to the J 39200 user's manual.				
1	Was the ABS Diagnostic System Check performed?	—	Go to *Step 2*	Go to *A Diagnostic System Check - ABS*
2	1. Turn the ignition switch to the OFF position. 2. Disconnect the EBCM harness connector. 3. Turn the ignition switch to the ON position. 4. Using the *J 39200*, measure the voltage between the EBCM harness connector terminal 18 and ground. Is the voltage within the specified range?	0–1 V	Go to *Step 3*	Go to *Step 6*
3	1. Turn the ignition switch to the OFF position. 2. Using the *J 39200*, measure the resistance between the EBCM harness connector terminals 18 and C. Is the resistance within the specified range?	7–19 Ω	Go to *Step 4*	Go to *Step 5*
4	1. Inspect the EBCM harness connector and the power steering pump actuator harness connector for damage which may result in a short to voltage or an open with all the connectors connected. Repair the damage if present. 2. Reconnect all the connectors. 3. Start the engine. Wait 10 seconds. Does DTC C1274 set as a current DTC?	—	Go to *Step 10*	Go to *Step 8*
5	1. Disconnect the power steering pump actuator connector. 2. Using the *J 39200*, measure the resistance between the EBCM harness connector terminals 18 and C. Is the resistance within the specified range?	OL (Infinite)	Go to *Step 9*	Go to *Step 7*
6	Repair the short to voltage in CKT 1295. Is the repair complete?	—	Go to *A Diagnostic System Check - ABS*	—
7	Repair the short between CKTs 1295 and 1633/855. Is the repair complete?	—	Go to *A Diagnostic System Check - ABS*	—
8	The malfunction is intermittent. Is the action complete?	—	Go to *A Diagnostic System Check - ABS*	—
9	Replace the power steering pump actuator. Is the repair complete?	—	Go to *A Diagnostic System Check - ABS*	—
10	Replace the EBCM. Is the repair complete?	—	Go to *A Diagnostic System Check - ABS*	—

GC4020052205020X

Fig. 62 Code C1274: VES Circuit Shorted To Voltage (Part 2 of 2). Alero & Grand Am

Circuit Description

DTC C1275 will set if the EBCM receives a malfunction message from the PCM. The PCM sends this message to the EBCM because of a powertrain malfunction or a loss of class 2 communications from the EBCM to the PCM.

Conditions for Setting the DTC

When a malfunction is detected by the PCM, the PCM causes ETS to shutdown until the malfunction is corrected.

Action Taken When the DTC Sets

This DTC is an operational malfunction.

The following actions are taken when the DTC sets:
- A malfunction DTC is stored
- ETS is disabled
- The TRAC OFF indicator is turned ON

The ABS remains functional.

Conditions for Clearing the DTC

ETS will remain disabled until the EBCM receives a traction allowed message from the PCM. When the EBCM receives this message, it will re-enable the ETS and turn OFF the TRAC OFF indicator with the following drive cycle.

Diagnostic Aids

Check for PCM DTCs. If no PCM DTC is stored, DTC C1275 may have set due to a hot engine or a hot transaxle (both normal conditions). No repairs should be made to the Traction Control System.

Perform a thorough inspection of the wiring and the connectors.

Failure to carefully inspect wiring may result in a misdiagnosis. A misdiagnosis may result in replacing parts without repairing the malfunction.

GC4020052206010X

Fig. 63 Code C1275: PCM Requested ETS To Be Disabled (Part 1 of 2). Alero & Grand Am

Step	Action	Value(s)	Yes	No
1	Was the ABS Diagnostic System Check performed?	—	Go to *Step 2*	Go to *A Diagnostic System Check - ABS*
2	1. Turn the ignition switch to the ON position. 2. Use the Scan Tool in order to read the DTCs. Make note of the DTCs. Are any other ABS/ETS or PCM DTCs set?	—	Go to the appropriate DTC Table	Go to *Step 3*
3	1. Clear the DTCs. 2. Turn the ignition switch to the OFF position. 3. Turn the ignition switch to the ON position. Does DTC C1275 reset?	—	Go to *Step 5*	Go to *Step 4*
4	1. Start the engine and test drive the vehicle at a speed of at least 16 km/h (10 mph). 2. Repeat the above drive cycle sequence two more times. Did the DTC C1275 set in these last three drive cycles?	—	Go to *Step 5*	Go to *A Diagnostic System Check - ABS*
5	Perform a Powertrain OBD System Check. Did the vehicle pass the OBD system check?	—	Go to *Step 6*	—
6	Replace the EBCM. Is the repair complete?	—	Go to *A Diagnostic System Check - ABS*	—

GC4020052206020X

Fig. 63 Code C1275: PCM Requested ETS To Be Disabled (Part 2 of 2). Alero & Grand Am

Thoroughly inspect any circuitry that may cause the intermittent complaint for the following conditions:

- Backed out terminals
- Improper mating
- Broken locks
- Improperly formed or damaged terminals
- Poor terminal-to-wiring connections
- Physical damage to the wiring harness

Important: Zero the J 39200 test leads before making any resistance measurements. Refer to the J 39200 user's manual.

Step	Action	Value(s)	Yes	No
1	Was the Diagnostic System Check performed?	—	Go to *Step 2*	Refer to *Diagnostic System Check*
2	1. Turn the ignition switch to the OFF position. 2. Disconnect the EBCM connector. 3. Use the *J 39200* in order to measure the resistance between the EBCM harness connector terminal 3 and ground. Is the resistance within the specified range?	OL (Infinite)	Go to *Step 3*	Go to *Step 12*
3	1. Disconnect the left front brake solenoid valve connector. 2. Use the *J 39200* in order to measure the resistance between the EBCM harness connector terminal 3 and the left front brake solenoid valve harness connector terminal B. Is the resistance within the specified range?	0–2 Ω	Go to *Step 4*	Go to *Step 15*
4	Use the *J 39200* in order to measure the resistance between the left front ABS brake solenoid valve connector terminal A and the left front brake solenoid valve connector terminal B. Is the resistance within the specified range?	2–5 Ω	Go to *Step 5*	Go to *Step 16*
5	Use a *J 39200* in order to measure the resistance between the Electronic Brake Control Relay harness connector terminal 87 and the left front brake solenoid valve connector terminal A. Is the resistance within the specified range?	0–2 Ω	Go to *Step 6*	Go to *Step 9*
6	1. Inspect the EBCM connector and the EBCM harness connector for the following conditions: • Terminal damage • Poor terminal contact • Terminal corrosion 2. Inspect the left front brake solenoid valve connector and the left front brake solenoid valve harness connector for the following conditions: • Terminal damage • Poor terminal contact • Terminal corrosion Are terminal corrosion, damaged terminals, or poor terminal contact evident?	—	Go to *Step 17*	Go to *Step 7*

GC402980303700BX

Fig. 64 Code C1276: LH Front Solenoid Circuit Open Or Shorted To Ground (Part 2 of 4). Alero, Grand Am & Malibu

Circuit Description

DTC C1276 identifies a brake solenoid valve that cannot be energized. The malfunction may be caused by one of the following conditions:

- An open in the solenoid valve circuitry
- The solenoid valve is always energized due to a short to ground in the solenoid valve circuitry between the EBCM and the brake solenoid valve.

An open will not allow proper ABS operation, but the short to ground simply turns on the brake solenoid valve. A path for base brakes is still allowed once the motor rehomes and the check ball is lifted off its seat during key to RUN initialization.

Conditions for Setting the DTC

DTC C1276 can set only when the brake solenoid valve is commanded off while the Electronic Brake Control Relay is enabled.

A malfunction exists if the EBCM detects the left front brake solenoid valve control circuit voltage is not within specifications.

Action Taken When the DTC Sets

- A malfunction DTC stores.
- The ABS disables.
- The ABS warning indicator turns on.

Conditions for Clearing the DTC

- The condition responsible for setting the DTC no longer exists and the Scan Tool Clear DTCs function is used.
- 100 drive cycles pass with no DTC(s) detected. A drive cycle consists of starting the vehicle, driving the vehicle over 16 km/h (10 mph), stopping and then turning the ignition off.

Diagnostic Aids

The following conditions may cause an intermittent malfunction:

- A poor connection
- Rubbed-through wire insulation
- A broken wire inside the insulation

Use the enhanced diagnostic function of the Scan Tool in order to measure the frequency of the malfunction.

GC402980303700AX

Fig. 64 Code C1276: LH Front Solenoid Circuit Open Or Shorted To Ground (Part 1 of 4). Alero, Grand Am & Malibu

Step	Action	Value(s)	Yes	No
7	Inspect CKT 1288 for damage. Damage may cause a short to ground with all the connectors connected. Is there damage that may cause a short to ground with the connectors connected?	—	Go to *Step 18*	Go to *Step 8*
8	1. Reconnect the EBCM connector. 2. Reconnect the left front brake solenoid valve connector. 3. Turn the ignition switch to the RUN position. Do not start the engine. 4. Use the *Scan Tool* in order to inspect for DTCs. Does DTC C1276 set as a current DTC?	—	Go to *Step 22*	Go to *Step 23*
9	Remove and inspect the ABS Mini Fuse (20 A). Is the fuse open?	—	Go to *Step 19*	Go to *Step 10*
10	Use the *J 39200* in order to measure the resistance between the Electronic Brake Control Relay harness connector terminal 87 and the ABS Mini Fuse (20 A) terminal. Is the resistance within the specified range?	0–2 Ω	Go to *Step 11*	Go to *Step 20*
11	Use the *J 39200* in order to measure the resistance between the ABS Mini Fuse (20 A) terminal and the left front brake solenoid valve harness connector terminal A. Is the resistance within the specified range?	0–2 Ω	Go to *Step 13*	Go to *Step 21*
12	1. Disconnect the left front brake solenoid valve connector. 2. Use the *J 39200* in order to measure the resistance between the left front brake solenoid valve connector terminal B and ground. Is the resistance within the specified range?	OL (Infinite)	Go to *Step 14*	Go to *Step 16*
13	Replace the ABS Mini Fuse (20A) with a known good Fuse (20A). Is the replacement complete?	—	Go to *Step 8*	—
14	Repair the short to ground in CKT 1288. Is the repair complete?	—	Refer to *Diagnostic System Check*	—
15	Repair the open or high resistance in CKT 1288. Is the repair complete?	—	Refer to *Diagnostic System Check*	—
16	Replace the left front brake solenoid valve. Is the repair complete?	—	Refer to *Diagnostic System Check*	—
17	Replace all the terminals and connectors that exhibit the following conditions: • Poor terminal contact • Terminal corrosion • Damaged terminals Is the repair complete?	—	Refer to *Diagnostic System Check*	—

GC402980303700CX

Fig. 64 Code C1276: LH Front Solenoid Circuit Open Or Shorted To Ground (Part 3 of 4). Alero, Grand Am & Malibu

Step	Action	Value(s)	Yes	No
18	Repair the damage to CKT 1288. Is the repair complete?	—	Refer to *Diagnostic System Check*	—
19	Replace the fuse block ABS Mini Fuse (20A). Is the repair complete?	—	Refer to *Diagnostic System Check*	—
20	Repair the open or high resistance in CKT 1633. Is the repair complete?	—	Refer to *Diagnostic System Check*	—
21	Repair the open or high resistance in CKT 855. Is the repair complete?	—	Refer to *Diagnostic System Check*	—
22	Replace the EBCM. Is the repair complete?	—	Refer to *Diagnostic System Check*	—
23	Malfunction is intermittent or is not present at this time. Refer to Diagnostic Aids for more information.	—	—	—

GC402980303700DX

Fig. 64 Code C1276: LH Front Solenoid Circuit Open Or Shorted To Ground (Part 4 of 4). Alero, Grand Am & Malibu

Circuit Description

DTC C1277 identifies a solenoid that cannot be energized due to a short to voltage in the solenoid driver circuitry. The malfunction can affect ABS operation since the flow of brake fluid to the wheel cylinder cannot be stopped. The unstoppable flow of brake fluid to the wheel cylinder makes ABS operation for that channel impossible.

Conditions for Setting the DTC

DTC C1277 can set only when the brake solenoid valve is commanded on.

A malfunction exists if the EBCM detects the left front brake solenoid valve control circuit voltage is not within specifications.

Action Taken When the DTC Sets

- A malfunction DTC stores.
- The ABS disables.
- The ABS warning indicator turns on.

Conditions for Clearing the DTC

- The condition responsible for setting the DTC no longer exists and the Scan Tool Clear DTCs function is used.
- 100 drive cycles pass with no DTC(s) detected. A drive cycle consists of starting the vehicle, driving the vehicle over 16 km/h (10 mph), stopping and then turning the ignition off.

Diagnostic Aids

Use the enhanced diagnostic function of the Scan Tool in order to measure the frequency of the malfunction.

Any circuitry that is suspected of causing the intermittent complaint should be thoroughly checked for improper mating, improperly formed or damaged terminals, poor terminal to wiring connections, or physical damage to the wiring harness.

Important: Zero the J 39200 test leads before making any resistance measurements. Refer to the J 39200 user's manual.

GC402980303800AX

Fig. 65 Code C1277: LH Front Solenoid Circuit Shorted To Voltage (Part 1 of 3). Alero, Grand Am & Malibu

Step	Action	Value(s)	Yes	No
1	Was the Diagnostic System Check performed?	—	Go to Step 2	Refer to *Diagnostic System Check*
2	1. Turn the ignition switch to the OFF position. 2. Disconnect the left front solenoid valve connector 3. Turn the ignition switch to the RUN position. Do not start the engine. 4. Use the *J 39200* in order to measure the voltage between the left front brake solenoid valve connector terminal A and ground. Is the voltage within the specified range?	0.0–1.0 V	Go to Step 3	Go to Step 7
3	1. Turn the ignition switch to the OFF position. 2. Use the *J 39200* in order to measure the resistance between the following components: • The left front brake solenoid valve connector terminal B • The left front brake solenoid valve connector terminal A Is the resistance within the specified range?	2.5–5.0 Ω	Go to Step 4	Go to Step 7
4	1. Disconnect the EBCM connector. 2. Turn the ignition switch to the RUN position. Do not start the engine. 3. Use the *J 39200* in order to measure the voltage between the EBCM harness connector terminal 3 and ground. Is the voltage within the specified range?	0.0–1.0 V	Go to Step 5	Go to Step 8
5	1. Turn the ignition switch to the OFF position. 2. Inspect the left front brake solenoid valve connector for damage. Damage may cause a short to voltage with the left front brake solenoid valve connector connected. 3. Inspect CKT 1288 for damage. Damage that may cause a short to voltage. 4. Inspect the EBCM connector for damage. Damage may cause a short to voltage with the EBCM connector connected. Is there damage that may cause a short to voltage?	—	Go to Step 9	Go to Step 6
6	1. Reconnect the EBCM connector. 2. Reconnect the left front brake solenoid valve connector. 3. Start the engine with your foot off the brake. 4. Allow the engine to run for at least ten seconds. 5. Use the *Scan Tool* in order to inspect for DTCs. Does DTC C1277 set as a current DTC?	—	Go to Step 10	Go to Step 11

GC402980303800BX

Fig. 65 Code C1277: LH Front Solenoid Circuit Shorted To Voltage (Part 2 of 3). Alero, Grand Am & Malibu

Step	Action	Value(s)	Yes	No
7	Replace the left front brake solenoid valve. Is the repair complete?	—	Refer to *Diagnostic System Check*	—
8	Repair the short to voltage in CKT 1288. Is the repair complete?	—	Refer to *Diagnostic System Check*	—
9	Repair the damage that caused a short to voltage. Is the repair complete?	—	Refer to *Diagnostic System Check*	—
10	Replace the EBCM. Is the repair complete?	—	Refer to *Diagnostic System Check*	—
11	The malfunction is intermittent or is not present at this time. Refer to Diagnostic Aids for more information.	—	—	—

GC402980303800CX

Fig. 65 Code C1277: LH Front Solenoid Circuit Shorted To Voltage (Part 3 of 3). Alero, Grand Am & Malibu

Circuit Description

DTC C1278 identifies a brake solenoid valve that cannot be energized. The malfunction may be caused by one of the following conditions:

- An open in the solenoid valve circuitry
- The solenoid valve is always energized due to a short to ground in the solenoid valve circuitry between the driver and the brake solenoid valve.

An open will not allow proper ABS operation, but the short to ground simply turns on the brake solenoid valve. A path for base brakes is still allowed once the motor rehomes and the check ball is lifted off its seat during key to RUN initialization.

Conditions for Setting the DTC

DTC C1278 can set only when the solenoid is commanded off while the Electronic Brake Control Relay is enabled.

A malfunction exists if the EBCM detects the right front brake solenoid valve control circuit voltage is not within specifications.

Action Taken When the DTC Sets

- A malfunction DTC stores.
- The ABS disables.
- The ABS warning indicator turns on.

Conditions for Clearing the DTC

- The condition responsible for setting the DTC no longer exists and the Scan Tool Clear DTCs function is used.
- 100 drive cycles pass with no DTC(s) detected. A drive cycle consists of starting the vehicle, driving the vehicle over 16 km/h (10 mph), stopping and then turning the ignition off.

Diagnostic Aids

The following conditions may cause an intermittent malfunction:

- A poor connection
- Rubbed-through wire insulation
- A broken wire inside the insulation

Use the enhanced diagnostic function of the Scan Tool in order to measure the frequency of the malfunction.

Thoroughly inspect any circuitry that may cause the intermittent complaint for the following conditions:

- Backed out terminals
- Improper mating
- Broken locks
- Improperly formed or damaged terminals
- Poor terminal-to-wiring connections
- Physical damage to the wiring harness

GC402980303900AX

Fig. 66 Code C1278: RH Front Solenoid Circuit Open Or Shorted To Ground (Part 1 of 3). Alero, Grand Am & Malibu

Important: Zero the J 39200 test leads before making any resistance measurements. Refer to the J 39200 user's manual.

Step	Action	Value(s)	Yes	No
1	Was the Diagnostic System Check performed?	—	Go to Step 2	Refer to *Diagnostic System Check*
2	1. Turn the ignition switch to the OFF position. 2. Disconnect the EBCM connector. 3. Use the *J 39200* in order to measure the resistance between the EBCM harness connector terminal 19 and ground. Is the resistance within the specified range?	OL (Infinite)	Go to Step 3	Go to Step 12
3	1. Disconnect the right front brake solenoid valve connector. 2. Use the *J 39200* in order to measure the resistance between the EBCM harness connector terminal 19 and the right front brake solenoid valve harness connector terminal B. Is the resistance within the specified range?	0.0–2.0 Ω	Go to Step 4	Go to Step 15
4	Use the *J 39200* in order to measure the resistance between the right front ABS brake solenoid valve connector terminal A and the right front brake solenoid valve connector terminal B. Is the resistance within the specified range?	2.0–5.0 Ω	Go to Step 5	Go to Step 16
5	Use a *J 39200* in order to measure the resistance between the Electronic Brake Control Relay harness connector terminal 87 and the right front brake solenoid valve connector terminal A. Is the resistance within the specified range?	0.0–2.0 Ω	Go to Step 6	Go to Step 9
6	1. Inspect the EBCM connector and the EBCM harness connector for the following conditions: • Terminal damage • Poor terminal contact • Terminal corrosion 2. Inspect the right front brake solenoid valve connector and the right front brake solenoid valve harness connector for the following conditions: • Terminal damage • Poor terminal contact • Terminal corrosion Are terminal corrosion, damaged terminals, or poor terminal contact evident?	—	Go to Step 17	Go to Step 7
7	Inspect CKT 1289 for damage. Damage may cause a short to ground with all the connectors connected. Is there damage which may cause a short to ground with the connectors connected?	—	Go to Step 18	Go to Step 8
8	1. Reconnect the EBCM connector. 2. Reconnect the right front brake solenoid valve connector. 3. Turn the ignition switch to the RUN position. Do not start the engine. 4. Use the *Scan Tool* in order to inspect for DTCs. Does DTC C1278 set as a current DTC?	—	Go to Step 22	Go to Step 23

GC402980303900BX

Fig. 66 Code C1278: RH Front Solenoid Circuit Open Or Shorted To Ground (Part 2 of 3). Alero, Grand Am & Malibu

Step	Action	Value(s)	Yes	No
9	1. Remove the ABS Mini Fuse (20A) of the fuse block. 2. Inspect the ABS Mini Fuse (20A) of the fuse block. Is the fuse open?	—	*Go to Step 19*	*Go to Step 10*
10	Use the *J 39200* in order to measure the resistance between the Electronic Brake Control Relay harness connector terminal 87 and the ABS Mini Fuse (20A) in the fuse block. Is the resistance within the specified range?	0.0–2.0 Ω	*Go to Step 11*	*Go to Step 20*
11	Use the *J 39200* in order to measure the resistance between the fuse block terminal and the left front brake solenoid valve harness connector terminal B. Is the resistance within the specified range?	0.0–2.0 Ω	*Go to Step 13*	*Go to Step 21*
12	1. Disconnect the right front brake solenoid valve connector. 2. Use the *J 39200* in order to measure the resistance between the right front brake solenoid valve connector terminal B and ground. Is the resistance within the specified range?	OL (Infinite)	*Go to Step 14*	*Go to Step 16*
13	Replace the ABS Mini Fuse (20A) with a known good Fuse (20A). Is the replacement complete?	—	*Go to Step 8*	—
14	Repair the short to ground in CKT 1289. Is the repair complete?	—	Refer to *Diagnostic System Check*	—
15	Repair the open or high resistance in CKT 1289. Is the repair complete?	—	Refer to *Diagnostic System Check*	—
16	Replace the right front brake solenoid valve. Is the repair complete?	—	Refer to *Diagnostic System Check*	—
17	Replace all the terminals and connectors that exhibit the following conditions: • Poor terminal contact • Terminal corrosion • Damaged terminals Is the repair complete?	—	Refer to *Diagnostic System Check*	—
18	Repair the damage to CKT 1289. Is the repair complete?	—	Refer to *Diagnostic System Check*	—
19	Replace the fuse block ABS Mini Fuse (20A). Is the repair complete?	—	Refer to *Diagnostic System Check*	—
20	Repair the open or high resistance in CKT 1633. Is the repair complete?	—	Refer to *Diagnostic System Check*	—
21	Repair the open or high resistance in CKT 855. Is the repair complete?	—	Refer to *Diagnostic System Check*	—
22	Replace the EBCM. Is the repair complete?	—	Refer to *Diagnostic System Check*	—
23	The malfunction is intermittent or is not present at this time. Refer to Diagnostic Aids for more information.	—	—	—

GC402980303900CX

Fig. 66 Code C1278: RH Front Solenoid Circuit Open Or Shorted To Ground (Part 3 of 3). Alero, Grand Am & Malibu

Step	Action	Value(s)	Yes	No
1	Was the Diagnostic System Check performed?	—	*Go to Step 2*	Refer to *Diagnostic System Check*
2	1. Turn the ignition switch to the OFF position. 2. Disconnect the right front solenoid valve connector 3. Turn the ignition switch to the RUN position. Do not start the engine. 4. Use the *J 39200* in order to measure the voltage between the right front brake solenoid valve connector terminal A and ground. Is the voltage within the specified range?	0.0–1.0 V	*Go to Step 3*	*Go to Step 7*
3	1. Turn the ignition switch to the OFF position. 2. Use the *J 39200* in order to measure the resistance between the following components: • The right front brake solenoid valve connector terminal A • The right front brake solenoid valve connector terminal B Is the resistance within the specified range?	2.5–5.0 Ω	*Go to Step 4*	*Go to Step 7*
4	1. Disconnect the EBCM connector. 2. Turn the ignition switch to the RUN position. Do not start the engine. 3. Use the *J 39200* in order to measure the voltage between the EBCM harness connector terminal 19 and ground. Is the voltage within the specified range?	0.0–1.0 V	*Go to Step 5*	*Go to Step 8*
5	1. Turn the ignition switch to the OFF position. 2. Inspect the right front brake solenoid valve connector for damage. Damage may cause a short to voltage with the left front brake solenoid valve connector connected. 3. Inspect CKT 1289 for damage. Damage may cause a short to voltage. 4. Inspect the EBCM connector for damage. Damage may cause a short to voltage with the EBCM connector connected. Is there damage that may cause a short to voltage?	—	*Go to Step 9*	*Go to Step 6*
6	1. Reconnect the EBCM connector. 2. Reconnect the right front brake solenoid valve connector. 3. Start the engine with your foot off the brake. 4. Allow the engine to run for at least ten seconds. 5. Use the *Scan Tool* in order to inspect for DTCs. Does DTC C1281 set as a current DTC?	—	*Go to Step 10*	*Go to Step 11*

GC402980304000BX

Fig. 67 Code C1281: RH Front Solenoid Circuit Shorted to Voltage (Part 2 of 3). Alero, Grand Am & Malibu

Circuit Description

DTC C1281 identifies a solenoid that cannot be energized due to a short to voltage in the solenoid driver circuitry. The malfunction can affect ABS operation since the flow of brake fluid to the wheel cylinder cannot be stopped. The unstoppable flow of brake fluid to the wheel cylinder makes ABS operation for that channel impossible.

Conditions for Setting the DTC

DTC C1281 can set only when the brake solenoid is commanded on.

A malfunction exists if the EBCM detects the right front brake solenoid valve control circuit voltage is not within specifications.

Action Taken When the DTC Sets

- A malfunction DTC stores.
- The ABS disables.
- The ABS warning indicator turns on.

Conditions for Clearing the DTC

- The condition responsible for setting the DTC no longer exists and the Scan Tool Clear DTCs function is used.
- 100 drive cycles pass with no DTC(s) detected. A drive cycle consists of starting the vehicle, driving the vehicle over 16 km/h (10 mph), stopping and then turning the ignition off.

Diagnostic Aids

Use the enhanced diagnostic function of the Scan Tool in order to measure the frequency of the malfunction.

Any circuitry that is suspected of causing the intermittent complaint should be thoroughly checked for improper mating, improperly formed or damaged terminals, poor terminal to wiring connections, or physical damage to the wiring harness.

Important: Zero the J 39200 test leads before making any resistance measurements. Refer to the J 39200 user's manual.

GC402980304000AX

Fig. 67 Code C1281: RH Front Solenoid Circuit Shorted to Voltage (Part 1 of 3). Alero, Grand Am & Malibu

Step	Action	Value(s)	Yes	No
7	Replace the right front brake solenoid valve. Is the repair complete?	—	Refer to *Diagnostic System Check*	—
8	Repair the short to voltage in CKT 1289. Is the repair complete?	—	Refer to *Diagnostic System Check*	—
9	Repair the damage that caused a short to voltage. Is the repair complete?	—	Refer to *Diagnostic System Check*	—
10	Replace the EBCM. Is the repair complete?	—	Refer to *Diagnostic System Check*	—
11	The malfunction is intermittent or is not present at this time. Refer to Diagnostic Aids for more information.	—	—	—

GC402980304000CX

Fig. 67 Code C1281: RH Front Solenoid Circuit Shorted to Voltage (Part 3 of 3). Alero, Grand Am & Malibu

Circuit Description

DTC C1282 allows the EBCM to inspect for a calibration malfunction by comparing the calibration value to a known value.

DTC C1282 also acts as a security measure to prevent improper use of calibrations or changes to these calibrations. Improper calibrations may alter the designed function of ABS.

Conditions for Setting the DTC

DTC C1282 can be set at ABS initialization. A malfunction exists if the EBCM internal memory calibration is incorrect.

Action Taken When the DTC Sets

- A malfunction DTC stores.
- The ABS disables.
- The ABS warning indicator turns on.

Conditions for Clearing the DTC

- The condition responsible for setting the DTC no longer exists and the Scan Tool Clear DTCs function is used.
- 100 drive cycles pass with no DTC(s) detected. A drive cycle consists of starting the vehicle, driving the vehicle over 16 km/h (10 mph), stopping and then turning the ignition off.

Diagnostic Aids

An intermittent DTC C1282 is most likely caused by a malfunctioning EBCM that is sensitive to temperature changes. If DTC C1282 occurred more than once, but is intermittent, replace EBCM.

Use the enhanced diagnostic function of the Scan Tool in order to measure the frequency of the malfunction.

Step	Action	Value(s)	Yes	No
1	Was the Diagnostic System Check performed?	—	*Go to Step 2*	Refer to *Diagnostic System Check*
2	1. Turn the ignition switch to the RUN position. Do not start the engine. 2. Install a *Scan Tool*. 3. Use the *Scan Tool* in order to inspect for DTCs. Is DTC C1282 set as a current DTC?	—	*Go to Step 3*	*Go to Step 4*
3	Replace the EBCM. Is the repair complete?	—	Refer to *Diagnostic System Check*	—
4	The malfunction is intermittent or is not present at this time. Refer to Diagnostic Aids for more information.	—	—	—

GC402980304100X

Fig. 68 Code C1282: Calibration Fault. Alero, Grand Am & Malibu

Circuit Description

DTC C1286 is provided as an "information only" test and reflects the status of the command issued by the EBCM to illuminate the red BRAKE warning indicator.

Conditions for Setting the DTC

When another diagnostic DTC issues a command to illuminate the red BRAKE warning indicator, DTC C1286 will be stored in memory as a history DTC at the conclusion of the ignition cycle.

Action Taken When the DTC Sets

- A malfunction DTC stores.
- The ABS disables.
- The ABS warning indicator turns on.
- The red Brake warning indicator turns on.

Conditions for Clearing the DTC

- The condition responsible for setting the DTC no longer exists and the Scan Tool Clear DTCs function is used.
- 100 drive cycles pass with no DTC(s) detected. A drive cycle consists of starting the vehicle, driving the vehicle over 16 km/h (10 mph), stopping and then turning the ignition off.

Diagnostic Aids

The following ABS mechanical DTCs command the red BRAKE warning indicator to illuminate. The DTCs will also cause the EBCM to store DTC C1286 during shutdown:

- C1242
- C1246
- C1251

If the motors are not in their home position, the following electrical DTCs will also command the red BRAKE warning indicator on:

- C1214
- C1216
- C1218
- C1236
- C1255
- C1264
- C1265
- C1266

If any of the electrical DTCs are indicated along with DTC C1286, correct the electrical DTCs prior to addressing a DTC C1286 malfunction.

Step	Action	Value(s)	Yes	No
1	Was the Diagnostic System Check performed?	—	*Go to Step 2*	Refer to *Diagnostic System Check*
2	1. Turn the ignition switch to the RUN position. Do not start the engine. 2. Install the *Scan Tool*. 3. Use the *Scan Tool* in order to inspect for DTCs.	—	Refer to *Diagnostic System Check*	*Go to Step 3*
3	Use the *Scan Tool* in order to clear DTC C1286. Was DTC C1286 cleared?	—	Refer to *Diagnostic System Check*	—

GC4029803042000X

Fig. 69 Code C1286: EBCM/EBTCM Turned On Brake Warning Lamp. Alero, Grand Am & Malibu

Circuit Description

DTC C1291 detects an open brake switch. The EBCM looks for deceleration rates that may indicate braking action. The EBCM verifies braking action by repeating the method for finding deceleration rates that indicate braking action several times. In each case, the ABS will not be available because the EBCM does not see the brake switch input.

Conditions for Setting the DTC

DTC C1291 can set if three deceleration cycles within the specified rate occur during the current ignition cycle with the brake switch off.

Action Taken When the DTC Sets

- A malfunction DTC stores.
- The ABS disables.
- The ABS warning indicator turns on.

Conditions for Clearing the DTC

- The condition responsible for setting the DTC no longer exists and the Scan Tool Clear DTCs function is used.
- 100 drive cycles pass with no DTC(s) detected. A drive cycle consists of starting the vehicle, driving the vehicle over 16 km/h (10 mph), stopping and then turning the ignition off.

Diagnostic Aids

The following conditions may cause an intermittent malfunction:

- A poor connection
- Rubbed-through wire insulation
- A broken wire inside the insulation

Use the enhanced diagnostic function of the Scan Tool in order to measure the frequency of the malfunction.

Thoroughly inspect any circuitry that may cause the intermittent complaint for the following conditions:

- Backed out terminals
- Improper mating
- Broken locks
- Improperly formed or damaged terminals
- Poor terminal-to-wiring connections
- Physical damage to the wiring harness
- Sticking brake switch

Important: Zero the J 39200 test leads before making any resistance measurements. Refer to the J 39200 user's manual.

Step	Action	Value(s)	Yes	No
1	Was the Diagnostic System Check performed?	—	*Go to Step 2*	Refer to *Diagnostic System Check*
2	1. Turn the ignition switch to the RUN position. Do not start the engine. 2. Install a *Scan Tool*. 3. Use the *Scan Tool* in order to inspect for DTCs. Is DTC C1295 set as either a current and/or history DTC?	—	Refer to *DTC C1295 Brake Lamp Switch Circuit Open*	*Go to Step 3*

GC402980304300AX

Fig. 70 Code C1291: Open Brake Lamp Switch Circuit During Decel (Part 1 of 3). Alero, Grand Am & Malibu

Step	Action	Value(s)	Yes	No
3	1. Select Data List on the *Scan Tool*. 2. Select Brake Switch Position on the *Scan Tool*. 3. Apply light pressure to the brake pedal while monitoring the Brake Switch Position on the *Scan Tool*. Does the Scan Tool indicate that the brake switch is on within 25 mm (1.0 inch) of brake pedal travel?	—	*Go to Step 25*	*Go to Step 4*
4	1. Apply firm pressure to the brake pedal. 2. Observe the rear brake lamps. Are the rear brake lamps on?	—	*Go to Step 5*	*Go to Step 8*
5	1. Turn the ignition switch to the OFF position. 2. Disconnect the EBCM connector. 3. Turn the ignition switch to the RUN position. Do not start the engine. 4. Apply firm pressure to the brake pedal. 5. Use the *J 39200* in order to measure the voltage between the EBCM harness connector terminal 16 and ground. Is the voltage equal to or greater than the specified voltage?	10.0 V	*Go to Step 6*	*Go to Step 16*
6	Inspect the EBCM connector and the EBCM harness connector for the following conditions: • Terminal damage • Poor terminal contact • Terminal corrosion Is there poor terminal contact, terminal corrosion, or damaged terminals?	—	*Go to Step 17*	*Go to Step 7*
7	1. Reconnect the connector. 2. Test drive the vehicle and perform a brake stop from 32 km/h (20 mph) engaging the ABS. 3. Use the *Scan Tool* in order to inspect for DTCs. Does DTC C1291 and DTC Caw set as a current DTC?	—	*Go to Step 23*	*Go to Step 25*
8	Use the *J 39200* in order to measure the voltage between the stoplamp switch harness connector terminal A and ground. Is the voltage equal to or greater than the specified voltage?	10.0 V	*Go to Step 9*	*Go to Step 11*
9	1. Apply firm pressure to the brake pedal. 2. Use the *J 39200* in order to measure the voltage between the stoplamp switch harness connector terminal B and ground. Is the voltage equal to or greater than the specified voltage?	10.0 V	*Go to Step 16*	*Go to Step 10*
10	Inspect for proper adjustment of the stoplamp switch. Is the stoplamp switch adjusted correctly?	—	*Go to Step 18*	*Go to Step 19*
11	Remove and inspect the fuse block STOP-HZD Fuse (20A). Is the fuse open?	—	*Go to Step 13*	*Go to Step 12*

GC402980304300BX

Fig. 70 Code C1291: Open Brake Lamp Switch Circuit During Decel (Part 2 of 3). Alero, Grand Am & Malibu

Step	Action	Value(s)	Yes	No
12	1. Disconnect the stoplamp switch connector. 2. Use a *J 39200* in order to measure the resistance between the stoplamp switch harness connector terminal A and the STOP-HZD Fuse terminal of the fuse block. Is the resistance within the specified range?	0.0–2.0 Ω	*Go to Step 14*	*Go to Step 21*
13	1. Disconnect the EBCM connector. 2. Use the *J 39200* in order to measure the resistance between the EBCM harness connector terminal 16 and ground. Is the resistance within the specified range?	OL (Infinite)	*Go to Step 15*	*Go to Step 20*
14	Use the *J 39200* in order to measure the voltage between the STOP-HZD Fuse of the fuse block and ground. Is the voltage equal to or greater than the specified voltage?	10 V	*Go to Step 25*	***Inspect Wiring***
15	1. Disconnect the stoplamp switch connector. 2. Use the *J 39200* in order to measure the resistance between the stoplamp switch harness connector terminal A and ground. Is the resistance within the specified range?	OL (Infinite)	*Go to Step 24*	*Go to Step 22*
16	Repair the open in CKT 17. Is the repair complete?	—	Refer to *Diagnostic System Check*	—
17	Replace all the terminal or the connectors that exhibit the following conditions: • Poor terminal contact • Terminal corrosion • Damaged terminals Is the repair complete?	—	Refer to *Diagnostic System Check*	—
18	Replace the stoplamp switch. Is the repair complete?	—	Refer to *Diagnostic System Check*	—
19	Adjust the stoplamp switch. Is the repair complete?	—	Refer to *Diagnostic System Check*	—
20	1. Repair the short to ground in CKT 17. 2. Replace the STOP-HZD Fuse (20A) with a known good Fuse (20A). Is the repair complete?	—	Refer to *Diagnostic System Check*	—
21	Repair the open in CKT 140. Is the repair complete?	—	Refer to *Diagnostic System Check*	—
22	1. Repair the short to ground in CKT 140. 2. Replace the STOP-HZD Fuse (20A) with a known good Fuse (20A). Is the repair complete?	—	Refer to *Diagnostic System Check*	—
23	Replace the EBCM. Is the repair complete?	—	Refer to *Diagnostic System Check*	—
24	Replace the STOP-HZD Fuse (20A) with a known good Fuse (20A). Is the repair complete?	—	Refer to *Diagnostic System Check*	—
25	The malfunction is intermittent or is not present at this time. Refer to Diagnostic Aids for more information.	—	—	—

GC402980304300CX

Fig. 70 Code C1291: Open Brake Lamp Switch Circuit During Decel (Part 3 of 3). Alero, Grand Am & Malibu

Circuit Description

DTC C1292 determines the proper operation of the brake switch. Proper operation of the brake switch is important because the brake switch activates the ABS when the brake switch is on. If the brake switch is off, the ABS will never activate. This malfunction is only detected when ABS is required because it is difficult to detect the malfunction under normal braking conditions.

Conditions for Setting the DTC

DTC C1292 can set if the vehicle speed is greater than 8 km/h (5 mph).

A malfunction exists if the following conditions occur:

- The brake was not on.
- A release was required on two channels for 0.5 second.

Action Taken When the DTC Sets

- A malfunction DTC stores.
- The ABS disables.
- The ABS warning indicator turns on.

Conditions for Clearing the DTC

- The condition responsible for setting the DTC no longer exists and the Scan Tool Clear DTCs function is used.
- 100 drive cycles pass with no DTC(s) detected. A drive cycle consists of starting the vehicle, driving the vehicle over 16 km/h (10 mph), stopping and then turning the ignition off.

Diagnostic Aids

The following conditions may cause an intermittent malfunction:

- A poor connection
- Rubbed–through wire insulation
- A broken wire inside the insulation

Use the enhanced diagnostic function of the Scan Tool in order to measure the frequency of the malfunction.

Thoroughly inspect any circuitry that may cause the intermittent complaint for the following conditions:

- Backed out terminals
- Improper mating
- Broken locks
- Improperly formed or damaged terminals
- Poor terminal-to-wiring connections
- Physical damage to the wiring harness
- Sticking brake switch

Important: Zero the J 39200 test leads before making any resistance measurements. Refer to the J 39200 user's manual.

GC402980304400AX

Fig. 71 Code C1292: Open Brake Lamp Switch When ABS Required (Part 1 of 4). Alero, Grand Am & Malibu

Step	Action	Value(s)	Yes	No
1	Was the Diagnostic System Check performed?	—	*Go to Step 2*	Refer to *Diagnostic System Check*
2	1. Turn the ignition switch to the RUN position. Do not start the engine. 2. Install a *Scan Tool.* 3. Use the *Scan Tool* in order to inspect for DTCs. Is DTC C1295 set as either a current and/or history DTC?	—	Refer to *DTC C1295 Brake Lamp Switch Circuit Open*	*Go to Step 3*
3	1. Select Data List on the *Scan Tool.* 2. Select Brake Switch Position on the *Scan Tool.* 3. Apply light pressure to the brake pedal while monitoring the Brake Switch Position on the Scan Tool. Does the Scan Tool indicate that the brake switch is on within 25 mm (1.0 inch) of brake pedal travel?	—	*Go to Step 25*	*Go to Step 4*
4	1. Apply firm pressure to the brake pedal. 2. Observe the rear brake lamps. Are the rear brake lamps on?	—	*Go to Step 5*	*Go to Step 8*
5	1. Turn the ignition switch to the OFF position. 2. Disconnect the EBCM connector. 3. Turn the ignition switch to the RUN position. Do not start the engine. 4. Apply firm pressure to the brake pedal. 5. Use the *J 39200* in order to measure the voltage between the EBCM harness connector terminal 16 and ground. Is the voltage equal to or greater than the specified voltage?	10.0 V	*Go to Step 6*	*Go to Step 16*
6	Inspect the EBCM connector and the EBCM harness connector for the following conditions: • Terminal damage • Poor terminal contact • Terminal corrosion Is there poor terminal contact, terminal corrosion, or damaged terminals?	—	*Go to Step 17*	*Go to Step 7*
7	1. Reconnect the EBCM connector. 2. Test drive the vehicle and perform a brake stop from 32 km/h (20 mph) while engaging the ABS. 3. Use the *Scan Tool* in order to inspect for DTCs. Does DTC C1291 or DTC C1292 set as a current DTC?	—	*Go to Step 23*	*Go to Step 25*
8	Use the *J 39200* in order to measure the voltage between the stopplamp switch harness connector terminal A and ground. Is the voltage equal to or greater than the specified voltage?	10.0 V	*Go to Step 9*	*Go to Step 11*

GC402980304400BX

Fig. 71 Code C1292: Open Brake Lamp Switch When ABS Required (Part 2 of 4). Alero, Grand Am & Malibu

Step	Action	Value(s)	Yes	No
9	1. Apply firm pressure to the brake pedal. 2. Use the *J 39200* in order to measure the voltage between the stoplamp switch harness connector terminal B and ground. Is the voltage equal to or greater than the specified voltage?	10.0 V	*Go to Step 16*	*Go to Step 10*
10	Inspect for proper adjustment of the stoplamp switch. Is the stoplamp switch adjusted correctly?	—	*Go to Step 18*	*Go to Step 19*
11	1. Remove the fuse block STOP-HZD Fuse (20A). 2. Inspect the fuse block STOP-HZD Fuse (20A). Is the fuse open?	—	*Go to Step 13*	*Go to Step 12*
12	1. Disconnect the stoplamp switch connector. 2. Use a *J 39200* in order to measure the resistance between the stoplamp switch harness connector terminal A and the STOP-HZD Fuse terminal of the fuse block. Is the resistance within the specified range?	0.0–2.0 Ω	*Go to Step 14*	*Go to Step 21*
13	1. Disconnect the EBCM connector. 2. Use the *J 39200* in order to measure the resistance between the EBCM harness connector terminal 16 and ground. Is the resistance within the specified range?	OL (Infinite)	*Go to Step 15*	*Go to Step 20*
14	Use the *J 39200* in order to measure the voltage between the STOP-HZD Fuse terminal of the fuse block and ground. Is the voltage equal to or greater than the specified voltage?	10 V	*Go to Step 25*	Electrical Diagnosis
15	1. Disconnect the stoplamp switch connector. 2. Use the *J 39200* in order to measure the resistance between the stoplamp switch harness connector terminal A and ground. Is the resistance within the specified range?	OL (Infinite)	*Go to Step 24*	*Go to Step 22*
16	Repair the open in CKT 17. Is the repair complete?	—	Refer to *Diagnostic System Check*	—
17	Replace all the terminal or the connectors that exhibit the following conditions: • Poor terminal contact • Terminal corrosion • Damaged terminals Is the repair complete?	—	Refer to *Diagnostic System Check*	—
18	Replace the stoplamp switch. Is the repair complete?	—	Refer to *Diagnostic System Check*	—
19	Adjust the stoplamp switch. Is the repair complete?	—	Refer to *Diagnostic System Check*	—

GC402980304400CX

Fig. 71 Code C1292: Open Brake Lamp Switch When ABS Required (Part 3 of 4). Alero, Grand Am & Malibu

Step	Action	Value(s)	Yes	No
20	1. Repair the short to ground in CKT 17. 2. Replace the STOP-HZD Fuse (20A) with a known good fuse (20A). Is the repair complete?	—	Refer to *Diagnostic System Check*	—
21	Repair the open in CKT 140. Is the repair complete?	—	Refer to *Diagnostic System Check*	—
22	1. Repair the short to ground in CKT 140. 2. Replace the STOP-HZD Fuse (20A) with a known good fuse (20A). Is the repair complete?	—	Refer to *Diagnostic System Check*	—
23	Replace the EBCM. Is the repair complete?	—	Refer to *Diagnostic System Check*	—
24	Replace the STOP-HZD Fuse (20A) with a known good fuse (20A). Is the repair complete?	—	Refer to *Diagnostic System Check*	—
25	The malfunction is intermittent or is not present at this time. Refer to Diagnostic Aids for more information.	—	—	—

GC402980304400DX

Fig. 71 Code C1292: Open Brake Lamp Switch When ABS Required (Part 4 of 4). Alero, Grand Am & Malibu

Circuit Description

If DTC 1291 or DTC 1292 failed during the last ignition cycle, DTC C1293 becomes a current failure during the next ignition cycle. DTC C1293 failure keeps ABS/ETS disabled until identifying a brake switch on state. When identifying a change during an ignition cycle in which DTC C1293 is a current malfunction, DTC C1291 or DTC 1292 will clear itself at the end of the current ignition cycle. ABS/ETS will then enable itself at the start of the next ignition cycle. DTC C1293 alone indicates DTC C1291 or DTC C1292 failed previously, but is intermittent, or has been corrected.

Conditions for Setting the DTC

DTC C1293 alone indicates DTC C0091 or C0092 occurred previously, but is intermittent, or has been corrected.

Action Taken When the DTC Sets

- A malfunction DTC stores.
- ABS is disabled until the EBCM receives a valid input from the brake switch.
- The ABS warning indicator turns on.

Conditions for Clearing the DTC

- The condition responsible for setting the DTC no longer exists and the Scan Tool Clear DTCs function is used.
- When a change is seen during an ignition cycle in which DTC C1293 is a current malfunction, DTC C1291 or C1292 will clear itself at the end of the current ignition cycle and ABS will enable itself at the start of the next ignition cycle.

Diagnostic Aids

Use the Data List of the Scan Tool verify proper brake switch operation. The Data List should display the brake switch as the brake is applied within 25 mm (1.0 in) of brake pedal travel.

GC402980304500AX

Fig. 72 Code C1293: Code C1291 Or C1292 Set In Current Or Previous Ignition Cycle (Part 1 of 2). Alero, Grand Am & Malibu

Step	Action	Value(s)	Yes	No
1	Was the Diagnostic System Check performed?	—	Go to Step 2	Refer to Diagnostic System Check
2	1. Install a *Scan Tool*. 2. Use the *Scan Tool* to read the DTCs. Is DTC C1291 or DTC C1292 set as either a current and/or a history DTC?	—	Refer to *DTC C1291 Open Brake Lamp Sw Contacts During Decel* or *DTC C1292 Open Brake Lamp Sw When ABS Required*	Go to Step 3
3	1. Select DTC history on the *Scan Tool*. 2. Verify that the malfunction frequency was infrequent. 3. Use the *Scan Tool* in order to clear the DTCs. Did DTC C1293 clear?	—	Refer to Diagnostic System Check	Go to Step 4
4	Replace the EBCM. Is the repair complete?	—	Refer to Diagnostic System Check	—

GC402980304500BX

Fig. 72 Code C1293: Code C1291 Or C1292 Set In Current Or Previous Ignition Cycle (Part 2 of 2). Alero, Grand Am & Malibu

Step	Action	Value(s)	Yes	No
5	1. Disconnect the EBCM connector. 2. Turn the ignition switch to the RUN position. Do not start the engine. 3. Use the *J 39200* in order to measure the voltage between the EBCM connector terminal 16 and ground. Is the voltage within the specified range?	0–1 V	Go to Step 6	Go to Step 8
6	1. Turn the ignition switch to the OFF position. 2. Inspect the EBCM connector and the EBCM harness connector for the following conditions: • Terminal damage • Poor terminal contact • Terminal corrosion Is there evidence of poor terminal contact, terminal corrosion, or damaged terminals?	—	Go to Step 11	Go to Step 7
7	1. Reconnect the EBCM connector. 2. Install a *Scan Tool*. 3. Turn the ignition switch to the RUN position. Do not start the engine. 4. Start the engine. 5. Test drive the vehicle obtaining a speed at least 40 km/h (25 mph). 6. Repeat the drive cycle, and steps 3,4, and 5 at least two additional times. 7. Use the *Scan Tool* in order to inspect for DTCs. Does DTC C1294 set as a current DTC during the last three drive cycles?	—	Go to Step 12	Go to Step 13
8	Repair the short to voltage in CKT 17 or 20. Is the repair complete?	—	Refer to Diagnostic System Check	—
9	Adjust the stoplamp switch. Is the repair complete?	—	Refer to Diagnostic System Check	—
10	Replace the stoplamp switch. Is the repair complete?	—	Refer to Diagnostic System Check	—
11	Replace all of the terminals and connectors that exhibit the following conditions: • Poor terminal contact • Corrosion • Damaged terminal(s) Is repair complete?	—	Refer to Diagnostic System Check	—
12	Replace the EBCM. Is the repair complete?	—	Refer to Diagnostic System Check	—
13	The malfunction is intermittent or is not present at this time. Refer to Diagnostic Aids for more information.	—	—	—

GC402980304600BX

Fig. 73 Code C1294: Brake Lamp Switch Circuit Always Active (Part 2 of 2). Alero, Grand Am & Malibu

Circuit Description

DTC C1294 determines the proper operation of the brake switch. Proper operation of the brake switch is important because the brake switch activates the ABS and inhibits the ETS when the brake switch is on. The brake switch deactivates the ABS when the brake switch is off. The following conditions always occur when the brake switch is on:

- ABS operation is requested.
- ETS operation is inhibited.

Conditions for Setting the DTC

DTC C1294 can set if the vehicle's speed is greater than 40 km/h (25 mph).

A malfunction exists if the brake was always on during two consecutive drive cycles.

Action Taken When the DTC Sets

- A malfunction DTC stores.
- ABS operation remains.
- ETS operation is inhibited.

Conditions for Clearing the DTC

- The condition responsible for setting the DTC no longer exists and the Scan Tool Clear DTCs function is used.
- 100 drive cycles pass with no DTC(s) detected. A drive cycle consists of starting the vehicle, driving the vehicle over 16 km/h (10 mph), stopping and then turning the ignition off.

Diagnostic Aids

Use the enhanced diagnostic function of the Scan Tool in order to measure the frequency of the malfunction.

Important: Zero the J 39200 test leads before making any resistance measurements. Refer to the J 39200 user's manual.

Step	Action	Value(s)	Yes	No
1	Was the Diagnostic System Check performed?	—	Go to Step 2	Refer to Diagnostic System Check
2	1. Turn the ignition switch to the OFF position. 2. Verify that there is no pressure on the brake pedal. 3. Observe the rear brake lamps. Are the rear brake lamps on?	—	Go to Step 3	Go to Step 5
3	Disconnect the stoplamp switch connector. Are the rear brake lamps on?	—	Go to Step 8	Go to Step 4
4	Inspect the adjustment of the stoplamp switch. Is the stoplamp switch adjusted correctly?	—	Go to Step 10	Go to Step 9

GC402980304600AX

Fig. 73 Code C1294: Brake Lamp Switch Circuit Always Active (Part 1 of 2). Alero, Grand Am & Malibu

Circuit Description

DTC C1295 identifies open brake switch circuitry that prevents the brake switch input to the EBCM from changing states while applying the brake.

Conditions for Setting the DTC

DTC C1295 can set after initialization is complete.

A malfunction exists if the brake switch input voltage is out of specification for one second. An open circuit exists when the brake switch input voltage is out of specification.

Action Taken When the DTC Sets

- A malfunction DTC stores.
- ABS disables.
- The ABS warning indicator turns on.

Conditions for Clearing the DTC

- The condition responsible for setting the DTC no longer exists and the Scan Tool Clear DTCs function is used.
- 100 drive cycles pass with no DTC(s) detected. A drive cycle consists of starting the vehicle, driving the vehicle over 16 km/h (10 mph), stopping and then turning the ignition off.

Diagnostic Aids

The following conditions may cause an intermittent malfunction:

- A poor connection
- Rubbed-through wire insulation
- A broken wire inside the insulation

Use the enhanced diagnostic function of the Scan Tool in order to measure the frequency of the malfunction.

Thoroughly inspect any circuitry that may cause the intermittent complaint for the following conditions:

- Backed out terminals
- Improper mating
- Broken locks
- Improperly formed or damaged terminals
- Poor terminal-to-wiring connections
- Physical damage to the wiring harness

Important: Zero the J 39200 test leads before making any resistance measurements. Refer to the J 39200 user's manual.

Step	Action	Value(s)	Yes	No
1	Was the Diagnostic System Check performed?	—	Go to Step 2	Refer to Diagnostic System Check
2	1. Turn the ignition switch to the RUN position. Do not start the engine. 2. Install a *Scan Tool*. 3. Select Data List on the *Scan Tool*. 4. Select Brake Switch Position on the *Scan Tool*. Does the Scan Tool indicate that the brake switch circuit is open?	—	Go to Step 3	Go to Step 11

GC402980304700AX

Fig. 74 Code C1295: Brake Lamp Switch Circuit Open (Part 1 of 2). Alero, Grand Am & Malibu

Step	Action	Value(s)	Yes	No
3	Apply light pressure to the brake pedal while monitoring the Brake Switch Position on the *Scan Tool*. Does the Scan Tool indicate that the brake switch is on within 25 mm (1.0 inch) of the brake pedal travel?	—	*Go to Step 9*	*Go to Step 4*
4	1. Apply firm pressure to the brake pedal. 2. Observe the rear brake lamps. Are the rear brake lamps on?	—	*Go to Step 5*	*Go to Step 9*
5	1. Turn the ignition switch to the OFF position. 2. Disconnect the EBCM connector. 3. Turn the ignition switch to the RUN position. Do not start the engine. 4. Apply firm pressure to the brake pedal. 5. Use the *J 39200* in order to measure the voltage between the EBCM connector terminal 16 and ground. Is the voltage equal to or greater than the specified voltage?	10.0 V	*Go to Step 6*	*Go to Step 7*
6	Inspect the EBCM connector and the EBCM harness connector for the following conditions: • Terminal damage • Poor terminal contact • Terminal corrosion Are poor terminal contact, terminal corrosion or damaged terminals evident?	—	*Go to Step 8*	*Go to Step 10*
7	Repair the open in CKT 17 or 20. Is the repair complete?	—	Refer to *Diagnostic System Check*	—
8	Replace all the terminals or the connectors that exhibit the following conditions: • Poor terminal contact • Terminal corrosion • Damaged terminal(s). Is the repair complete?	—	Refer to *Diagnostic System Check*	—
9	Repair the open brake lamp circuit wiring. Is the repair complete?	—	Refer to *Diagnostic System Check*	—
10	Replace the EBCM. Is the repair complete?	—	Refer to *Diagnostic System Check*	—
11	The malfunction is intermittent or is not present at this time. Refer to Diagnostic Aids for more information.	—	—	—

GC402980304700BX

Fig. 74 Code C1295: Brake Lamp Switch Circuit Open (Part 2 of 2). Alero, Grand Am & Malibu

The scan tool Serial Data Link (SDL) monitor used in this diagnostic is within the body portion of the scan tool. This requires exiting from the chassis portion of the scan tool to the main menu and entering into the body portion of the scan tool and selecting SDL MONITOR.

With the SDL monitor (ABS to Instrument Cluster Mode), any message that is being transmitted on the serial data link can be observed

The malfunction may be intermittent. Try performing the tests shown while "wiggling" wiring and connectors, this can often cause the malfunction to appear. PCM and BFC DTCs will likely be set along with DTC U1300.

DTC U1300 will only be able to be read as a history code since the scan tool uses the same serial data circuit. If CKT 1807 is shorted to ground, no communication with the scan tool will be possible.

Step	Action	Value(s)	Yes	No
1	Was the Diagnostic System Check performed?	—	*Go to Step 2*	Go to *Diagnostic System Check*
2	1. Disconnect the LH I/P Wiring Harness Junction Block connector C1. 2. Disconnect the EBCM harness connector. 3. Use the *J 39200* to measure the resistance between the EBCM harness connector terminal 12 and ground. Is the measured resistance within the specified value?	OL (Infinite)	Data Link Connector (DLC)	*Go to Step 3*
3	Repair the short to ground in CKT 1807. Is the repair complete?	—	Go to *Diagnostic System Check*	—

GC402980306100BX

Fig. 75 Code U1300: Class 2 Circuit Shorted To Ground (Part 2 of 2). Malibu

The scan tool Serial Data Link (SDL) monitor used in this diagnostic is within the body portion of the scan tool. This requires exiting from the chassis portion of the scan tool to the main menu and entering into the body portion of the scan tool and selecting SDL MONITOR.

With the SDL monitor (ABS to Instrument Cluster Mode), any message that is being transmitted on the serial data link can be observed

The malfunction may be intermittent. Try performing the tests shown while "wiggling" wiring and connectors, this can often cause the malfunction to appear. PCM and BFC DTCs will likely be set along with DTC U1301.

DTC U1301 will only be able to be read as a history code since the scan tool uses the same serial data circuit. If CKT 1807 is shorted to voltage, no communication with the scan tool will be possible.

Step	Action	Value(s)	Yes	No
1	Was the Diagnostic System Check performed?	—	*Go to Step 2*	Go to *Diagnostic System Check*
2	1. Disconnect the LH I/P Wiring Harness Junction Block connector C1. 2. Disconnect the EBCM harness connector. 3. Turn the ignition switch to the ON Position. 4. Use the *J 39200* to measure the voltage between the EBCM harness connector terminal 12 and ground. Is the measured voltage within the specified value?	0–1 V	Inspect Data Link Connector (DLC)	*Go to Step 3*
3	Repair the short to voltage in CKT 1807. Is the repair complete?	—	Go to *Diagnostic System Check*	—

GC402980306200BX

Fig. 76 Code U1301: Class 2 Circuit Shorted To Battery (Part 2 of 2). Malibu

Circuit Description

The serial data link is a communication line between the PCM, EBCM, and the BFC.

Conditions for Setting the DTC

DTC U1300 can be set anytime the ignition is in RUN. A malfunction exists if CKT 1807 is shorted to ground resulting in no communication to the PCM or any other controller.

Action Taken When the DTC Sets

- A malfunction DTC stores.
- The ABS remains functional.
- No action towards the electronic brake control relay is taken.
- No action towards the ABS warning indicator is taken.

Conditions for Clearing the DTC

- The condition for DTC U1300 is no longer present.
- The use of the scan tool CLEAR DTCs function.
- DTC U1300 clears after 100 drive cycles with no DTCs detected. A drive cycle consists of starting the vehicle, driving the vehicle over 16 km/h (10 mph), stopping and then turning the ignition off.

Diagnostic Aids

- Perform the Powertrain OBD System Check before beginning this DTC table. This eliminates the PCM as a possible source of the malfunction.
- The following conditions may cause an intermittent malfunction:
  - A poor connection.
  - Rubbed-through wire insulation.
  - A broken wire inside the insulation within the serial data line.
- The use of the enhanced diagnostic function of the scan tool to check the frequency of the malfunction.
- Check all circuitry suspected of causing the intermittent complaint for the following conditions:
  - Check for backed-out terminals.
  - Check for improper mating.
  - Check for broken locks.
  - Check for improperly formed terminals.
  - Check for damaged terminals.
  - Check for poor terminal to wiring connections.
  - Check for physical damage to the wiring harness.

GC402980306100AX

Fig. 75 Code U1300: Class 2 Circuit Shorted To Ground (Part 1 of 2). Malibu

Circuit Description

The serial data link is a communication line between the BFC, PCM, and the EBCM.

Conditions for Setting the DTC

DTC U1301 can be set anytime the ignition is in RUN. A malfunction exists if CKT 1807 is shorted to voltage resulting in no communication to the PCM or any other controller.

Action Taken When the DTC Sets

- A malfunction DTC stores.
- The ABS remains functional.
- No action towards the electronic brake control relay is taken.
- No action towards the ABS warning indicator is taken.

Conditions for Clearing the DTC

- The condition for DTC U1300 is no longer present.
- The use of the scan tool CLEAR DTCs function.
- DTC U1300 clears after 100 drive cycles with no DTCs detected. A drive cycle consists of starting the vehicle, driving the vehicle over 16 km/h (10 mph), stopping and then turning the ignition off.

Diagnostic Aids

Perform the Powertrain OBD System Check before beginning this DTC table. This eliminates the PCM as a possible source of the malfunction.

The following conditions may cause an intermittent malfunction:

- A poor connection.
- Rubbed-through wire insulation.
- A broken wire inside the insulation within the serial data line.

The use of the enhanced diagnostic function of the scan tool to check the frequency of the malfunction.

Check all circuitry suspected of causing the intermittent complaint for the following conditions:

- Check for backed-out terminals.
- Check for improper mating.
- Check for broken locks.
- Check for improperly formed terminals.
- Check for damaged terminals.
- Check for damaged terminals.
- Check for poor terminal to wiring connections.
- Check for physical damage to the wiring harness.

GC402980306200AX

Fig. 76 Code U1301: Class 2 Circuit Shorted To Battery (Part 1 of 2). Malibu

Circuit Description

Two-way serial communication is sent back and forth between the EBCM and the IPC. A message from the IPC is sent to the EBCM within seven seconds after ABS initialization. A serial communication failure does not allow the proper warning indicator commands to be sent back to the IPC.

Diagnostic Aids

Use the Lamp Test function of the Scan Tool in order to turn the indicator on while looking for an intermittent malfunction in the ABS warning indicator circuitry.

Thoroughly inspect any circuitry that may cause the intermittent complaint for the following conditions:

- Backed out terminals
- Improper mating
- Broken locks
- Improperly formed or damaged terminals
- Poor terminal-to-wiring connections
- Physical damage to the wiring harness

GC402980347000AX

Fig. 77 Test A: ABS Lamp On w/No Code Set (Part 1 of 2). Alero, Cavalier, Grand Am & Sunfire

Step	Action	Value(s)	Yes	No
Important Zero the digital multimeter **test leads before making any resistance measurements.**				
1	Was the ABS Diagnostic System Check performed?	—	Go to Step 2	Go to **ABS Diagnostic System Check**
2	1 Turn the ignition switch to the OFF position. 2 Install a **scan tool** 3 Turn the ignition switch to the ON position. Do not start the engine. 4 Select the Body menu then IPC on the **scan tool** 5 Select Lamp Test on the **scan tool** 6 Use the **scan tool** in order to turn the warning indicators ON and OFF. Did the warning indicators turn ON and OFF?	—	Go to Step 6	Go to Step 3
3	Inspect all of the connectors and the terminals for the following conditions: • Poor terminal contact • Evidence of corrosion Is there evidence of poor terminal contact or corrosion?	—	Go to Step 4	Go to Step 5
4	Replace all of the terminals that exhibit signs of poor terminal contact or corrosion. Is the repair complete?	—	Go to **ABS Diagnostic System Check**	—
5	Repair the instrument panel cluster. Is the repair complete?	—	Go to **ABS Diagnostic System Check**	—
6	Replace the EBCM. Is the action complete?	—	Go to **ABS Diagnostic System Check**	—

GC402980347000BX

Fig. 77 Test A: ABS Lamp On w/No Code Set (Part 2 of 2). Alero, Cavalier, Grand Am & Sunfire

Step	Action	Value(s)	Yes	No
Important Zero the digital multimeter **test leads before making any resistance measurements.**				
1	Was the ABS Diagnostic System Check performed?	—	Go to Step 2	Go to **ABS Diagnostic System Check**
2	1 Turn the ignition switch to the OFF position. 2 Install a **scan tool** 3 Turn the ignition switch to the ON position. 4 Select Body menu then IPC on the **scan tool** 5 Select Lamp Test on the **scan tool** 6 Use the **scan tool** in order to flash the warning indicators ON and OFF. Did the warning indicators flash ON and OFF?	—	Go to Step 6	Go to Step 3
3	Inspect all of the connectors and the terminals for the following conditions: • Poor terminal contact • Evidence of corrosion Is there evidence of poor terminal contact or corrosion?	—	Go to Step 4	Go to Step 5
4	Replace all of the terminals that exhibit signs of poor terminal contact or corrosion. Is the repair complete?	—	Go to **ABS Diagnostic System Check**	—
5	Repair the instrument panel cluster. Is the repair complete?	—	Go to **ABS Diagnostic System Check**	—
6	Replace the EBCM. Is the repair complete?	—	Go to **ABS Diagnostic System Check**	—

GC402980346900BX

Fig. 78 Test B: ABS Lamp Off w/No Code Set (Part 2 of 2). Alero, Cavalier, Grand Am & Sunfire

Circuit Description

Two-way serial communication is sent back and forth between the EBCM and the IPC. A message from the IPC is sent to the EBCM within seven seconds after ABS initialization. A serial communication failure does not allow the proper warning indicator commands to be sent back to the IPC.

Diagnostic Aids

The following conditions may cause an intermittent malfunction:

- A poor connection
- Rubbed-through wire insulation
- A broken wire inside the insulation

Use the Lamp Test function of the Scan Tool in order to turn the indicator ON while looking for an intermittent malfunction in the ABS warning indicator circuitry.
Thoroughly inspect any circuitry that may cause the intermittent complaint for the following conditions:

- Backed out terminals
- Improper mating
- Broken locks
- Improperly formed or damaged terminals
- Poor terminal-to-wiring connections
- Physical damage to the wiring harness

GC402980346900AX

Fig. 78 Test B: ABS Lamp Off w/No Code Set (Part 1 of 2). Alero, Cavalier, Grand Am & Sunfire

Circuit Description

Four-way serial communication is sent back and forth between the EBCM, IPC, PCM, and the BCM. A message from the IPC is sent to the BCM within seven seconds after ABS initialization. A serial communication failure does not allow the proper warning indicator commands to be sent back to the IPC.

Diagnostic Aids

The ETS OFF indicator will be ON and the Enhanced Traction System will be disabled whenever the scan tool is connected to the DLC with the ignition switch is in the ON position.
Use the Lamp Test function of the Scan Tool in order to turn the indicator ON while looking for an intermittent malfunction in the ETS OFF warning indicator circuitry.
Thoroughly inspect any circuitry that may cause the intermittent complaint for the following conditions:

- Backed out terminals
- Improper mating
- Broken locks
- Improperly formed or damaged terminals
- Poor terminal-to-wiring connections
- Physical damage to the wiring harness

Test Description

2.This test determines if a Powertrain malfunction has turned the ETS Off indicator ON.
3.This test determines if the malfunction is caused by the IPC.
4.This test checks for an ETS Off switch stuck in the closed position.
5.This test checks for a short to ground in the switched input to the BCM.

ETS Off Indicator On No DTCs Set

GC402980347200AX

Fig. 79 Test C: ETS Off Lamp On w/No Code Set (Part 1 of 3). Alero, Cavalier, Grand Am & Sunfire

Step	Action	Value(s)	Yes	No
	Important Zero the digital multimeter test leads before making any resistance measurements.			
1	Was the ABS Diagnostic System Check performed?	—	Go to Step 2	Go to ABS Diagnostic System Check
2	1 Turn the ignition switch to the OFF position. 2 Connect a **scan tool** 3 Turn the ignition switch to the ON position. 4 Use the **scan tool** in order to check for any PCM DTCs. Are there any PCM DTCs?	—	**Inspect** Powertrain OBD System Check	Go to Step 3
3	1 Use the **scan tool** to select the BODY Menu. 2 Use the **scan tool** to select IPC then Lamp Test. 3 Use the **scan tool** to turn the warning indicators OFF. Did the warning indicators turn OFF?	—	Go to Step 4	**Inspect** Instrument Cluster Diagnostic
4	Disconnect the ETS Off switch connector. Does the ETS Off indicator turn OFF?	—	Go to Step 7	Go to Step 5
5	1 Disconnect the IPC connector C1. 2 Using the **J 39200** measure the resistance between the ETS Off switch harness connector terminal B and ground. Is the resistance within the specified range?	OL (Infinite)	Go to Step 6	Go to Step 8
6	1 Turn the ignition switch to the OFF position. 2 Inspect the following components: • The IPC connector C1 • The ETS Off connector 3 Inspect the above components for the following conditions: • Damage • Poor terminal contact • Terminal corrosion Are there signs of poor terminal contact, corrosion or damaged terminals?	—	Go to Step 9	Go to Step 10

GC402980347200BX

Fig. 79 Test C: ETS Off Lamp On w/No Code Set (Part 2 of 3). Alero, Cavalier, Grand Am & Sunfire

Circuit Description

Four-way serial communication is sent back and forth between the EBCM, IPC, PCM, and the BCM. A message from the IPC is sent to the BCM within seven seconds after ABS initialization. A serial communication failure does not allow the proper warning indicator commands to be sent back to the IPC.

Diagnostic Aids

The frequency of the malfunction can be checked by using the ENHANCED DIAGNOSTIC function of the scan tool.

The following conditions may cause an intermittent malfunction:

- A poor connection
- Rubbed-through wire insulation
- A broken wire inside the insulation

Use the Lamp Test function of the Scan Tool in order to turn the indicator on while looking for an intermittent malfunction in the ETS OFF warning indicator circuitry.

Thoroughly inspect any circuitry that may cause the intermittent complaint for the following conditions:

- Backed out terminals
- Improper mating
- Broken locks
- Improperly formed or damaged terminals
- Poor terminal-to-wiring connections
- Physical damage to the wiring harness

Test Description

2. This test determines if the malfunction is caused by the IPC.
3. This test determines if the malfunction is caused by the ETS Off switch.
4. This test checks for an open or high resistance in the ETS Off switch ground circuit.
5. This test checks for an open or high resistance in the switched input to the BCM.

GC402980347100AX

Fig. 80 Test D: ETS Off Lamp Off w/No Code Set (Part 1 of 3). Alero & Grand Am

7	Replace the ETS Off switch. Is the repair complete?	—	Go to ABS Diagnostic System Check	—
8	Repair short to ground in CKT 1571. Is the repair complete?	—	Go to ABS Diagnostic System Check	—
9	Replace all of the terminals or connectors that exhibit signs of poor terminal contact, corrosion or damaged terminal(s). Is the repair complete?	—	Go to ABS Diagnostic System Check	—
10	Replace the EBCM. Is the repair complete?	—	Go to ABS Diagnostic System Check	—

GC402980347200CX

Fig. 79 Test C: ETS Off Lamp On w/No Code Set (Part 3 of 3). Alero, Cavalier, Grand Am & Sunfire

Step	Action	Value(s)	Yes	No
	Important Zero the digital multimeter test leads before making any resistance measurements.			
1	Was the ABS Diagnostic System Check performed?	—	Go to Step 2	Go to **ABS Diagnostic System Check**
2	1 Turn the ignition switch to the OFF position. 2 Install a **scan tool** 3 Turn the ignition switch to the ON position. 4 Select Body menu then IPC on the **scan tool** 5 Select Lamp Test on the **scan tool** 6 Use the **scan tool** in order to turn the Warning Indicators ON. Did the amber ETS OFF warning indicator turn ON?	—	Go to Step 3	**Inspect** Instrument Cluster
3	1 Disconnect the ETS Off switch connector. 2 Using a fused jumper wire connect the ETS Off switch harness connector terminal A and terminal D (Pontiac) or terminal B (Olds). Does the ETS Off warning indicator turn ON?	—	Go to Step 7	Go to Step 4
4	Using the J 39200 measure the resistance between the ETS Off switch harness connector terminal D (Pontiac) or terminal B (Olds) and ground. Is the resistance within the specified range?	0–2Ω	Go to Step 5	Go to Step 8
5	1 Disconnect the BCM connector C3 2 Using the J 39200 measure the resistance between the BCM harness connector C3 terminal A5 and the ETS Off switch harness connector terminal A. Is the resistance within the specified range?	0–2Ω	Go to Step 6	Go to Step 9
6	Inspect all of the connectors and the terminals for the following conditions: • Poor terminal contact • Evidence of corrosion Is there evidence of poor terminal contact or corrosion?	—	Go to Step 10	Go to Step 11
7	Replace the ETS Off switch. Is the repair complete?	—	Go to ABS Diagnostic System Check	—

GC402980347100BX

Fig. 80 Test D: ETS Off Lamp Off w/No Code Set (Part 2 of 3). Alero & Grand Am

8	Repair the open or high resistance in CKT 251. Is the repair complete?	—	Go to ABS Diagnostic System Check	—
9	Repair the open or high resistance in CKT 1571. Is the repair complete?	—	Go to ABS Diagnostic System Check	—
10	Replace all of the terminals that exhibit signs of poor terminal contact or corrosion. Is the repair complete?	—	Go to ABS Diagnostic System Check	—
11	Replace the BCM. Is the repair complete?	—	Go to ABS Diagnostic System Check	—

GC402980347100CX

Fig. 80 Test D: ETS Off Lamp Off w/No Code Set (Part 3 of 3). Alero & Grand Am

Circuit Description

The EBCM exchanges serial data through EBCM harness connector terminal 12.
Connector terminal 4 supplies the switched ignition voltage to the EBCM.
Connector terminal 13 supplies the battery voltage to the EBCM.
Connector terminal C supplies the switched battery voltage to the EBCM.
Connector Terminal D provides the ground for the EBCM.

Diagnostic Aids

Communication with the EBCM is not possible when excessive resistance exists in the following components:

- The ground
- The power supply circuits

If communication with the EBCM is not possible, perform the following actions:

- Verify that the EBCM ground connection is good.
- Verify that no excessive resistance exists in any of the power supply circuits.

Test Description

2. This test determines if the EBCM is sending data.
3. This test checks for a serial data link malfunction.
7. This test checks for high resistance in the EBCM ground circuit.
8. This test checks for an open in the EBCM battery feed circuit.
9. This test checks for an open in the EBCM switched ignition circuit.
10. This test checks for an open or high resistance in the EBCM ground circuit.
11. This test checks for an open or high resistance in the EBCM battery feed circuit.
12. This test checks for an open or high resistance in the EBCM switched ignition circuit.
13. This test checks for an open or high resistance in the EBCM serial data circuit.
14. This test checks for a short to ground in the EBCM serial data circuit.
16. This test checks for a short to ground in the EBCM battery feed circuit.
17. This test isolates the short to ground to either the wiring or the EBCM.
19. This test checks for a short to ground in the EBCM switched ignition circuit.
20. This test isolates the short to ground to either the wiring or the EBCM.

GC402980347300AX

Fig. 82 Test F: No Communications w/EBCM (Part 1 of 6). Alero & Grand Am

Step	Action	Value(s)	Yes	No
1	Was the Diagnostic System Check performed?	—	*Go to Step 2*	Refer to *Diagnostic System Check*
2	1. Turn the ignition switch to the OFF position. 2. Install a *Scan Tool*. 3. Turn the ignition switch to the RUN position. Do not start the engine. 4. Use the *Scan Tool* in order to clear the DTCs. 5. Turn the ignition switch to the OFF position. 6. Turn the ignition switch to the RUN position. 7. Do not start the engine Does the undefined DTC(s) reset?	—	*Go to Step 3*	*Go to Step 4*
3	Replace the EBCM. Is the repair complete?	—	Go to *Diagnostic System Check*	—
4	The malfunction is not present at this time. Refer to Diagnostic Aids for more information.	—	—	—

GC4029802945000X

Fig. 81 Test E: Scan Tool Displays Undefined Code. Alero & Grand Am

Step	Action	Value(s)	Yes	No
Important **Zero the digital multimeter test leads before making any resistance measurements.**				
1	Was the ABS Diagnostic System Check performed?	—	Go to Step 2	Go to **ABS Diagnostic System Check**
2	1 Verify that the EBCM connector is properly connected. 2 Install a Scan Tool. 3 Turn the ignition switch to the ON position. Do not start the engine. 4 Select Data Display on the Scan Tool. 5 Select ABS Data. Is data being received from the EBCM?	—	Go to Step 36	Go to Step 3
3	Read the Scan Tool display. Does the Scan Tool display the message "No Communication With Vehicle. Check DLC Connector"?	—	**Inspect** Data Link Communication	Go to Step 4
4	Verify the correct connection of the Scan Tool to the DLC. Is connection of the Scan Tool to the DLC correct?	—	Go to Step 5	Go to Step 24
5	1 Turn the ignition switch to the OFF position. 2 Remove and inspect the ABS BATT Fuse (10A). Is the fuse open?	—	Go to Step 16	Go to Step 6
6	1 Install the ABS BATT fuse (10A). 2 Remove the ABS IGN Fuse (10A). Is the fuse open?	—	Go to Step 19	Go to Step 7
7	1 Install the ABS IGN Fuse (10A). 2 Disconnect the EBCM connector. 3 Use the **J 39200** in order to measure the resistance between the EBCM connector terminal D and ground. Is the resistance within the specified range?	0–2Ω	Go to Step 8	Go to Step 25
8	1 Disconnect the EBCM connector. 2 Use the **J 39200** in order to measure voltage between the EBCM connector terminal 13 and ground. Is the voltage equal to or greater than the specified voltage?	10 V	Go to Step 9	Go to Step 26
9	1 Turn the ignition switch to the ON position. Do not start the engine. 2 Use the **J 39200** in order to measure voltage between the EBCM connector terminal 4 and ground. Is the voltage equal to or greater than the specified voltage?	10 V	Go to Step 10	Go to Step 27

GC402980347300BX

Fig. 82 Test F: No Communications w/EBCM (Part 2 of 6). Alero & Grand Am

10	1 Turn the ignition switch to the OFF position. 2 Disconnect the negative battery cable. 3 Disconnect the positive battery cable. 4 Use the J 39200 in order to measure the resistance between the EBCM connector terminal D and the negative battery cable terminal. Is the resistance within the specified range?	0–2Ω	Go to Step 11	Go to Step 28
11	Use the J 39200 in order to measure the resistance between the EBCM connector terminal 13 and the positive battery cable terminal. Is the resistance within the specified range?	0–2Ω	Go to Step 12	Go to Step 29
12	1 Turn the ignition switch to the ON position. Do not start the engine. 2 Use the J 39200 in order to measure the resistance between the EBCM connector terminal 4 and the positive battery cable terminal. Is the resistance within the specified range?	0–2Ω	Go to Step 13	Go to Step 30
13	1 Turn the ignition switch to the OFF position. 2 Use the J 39200 in order to measure the resistance between the EBCM connector terminal 12 and the DLC terminal 9. Is the resistance within the specified range?	0–2Ω	Go to Step 14	**Inspect** Data Link Communication
14	Use the J 39200 in order to measure the resistance between the EBCM connector terminal 12 and ground. Is the resistance within the specified range?	OL (Infinite)	Go to Step 15	**Inspect** Data Link Communication
15	1 Inspect the following components: • The EBCM connector • The negative battery cable • The positive battery cable 2 Inspect the components for the following conditions: • Poor terminal contact • Terminal corrosion • Damaged terminals Are there signs of poor terminal contact, terminal corrosion, or damaged terminals?	—	Go to Step 31	Go to Step 37
16	1 Replace the ABS BATT Fuse (10A) with a known good fuse (10A). 2 Wait for ten seconds. 3 Remove and inspect the fuse. Is the fuse open?	—	Go to Step 17	Go to Step 33

GC402980347300CX

Fig. 82 Test F: No Communications w/EBCM (Part 3 of 6). Alero & Grand Am

17	1 Disconnect the EBCM connector. 2 Replace the ABS BATT Fuse (10A) with a known good fuse (10A). 3 Wait for ten seconds. 4 Remove and inspect the ABS BATT Fuse (10A). Is the fuse open?	—	Go to Step 32	Go to Step 18
18	1 Inspect CKT 1640 for physical damage. Physical damage may cause a short to ground with the EBCM connector connected. 2 Inspect the EBCM connector and the EBCM harness for physical damage. Physical damage may cause a short to ground with the EBCM connector connected. 3 Reconnect the EBCM connector. 4 Reinstall the ABS BATT Fuse (10A). 5 Wait for ten seconds. 6 Remove and inspect the ABS BATT Fuse (10A). Is the fuse open?	—	Go to Step 23	Go to Step 36
19	1 Replace the ABS IGN Fuse (10A) with a known good fuse (10A). 2 Turn the ignition switch to the ON position. Do not start the engine. 3 Wait for ten seconds. 4 Turn the ignition switch to the OFF position. 5 Remove and inspect the ABS IGN Fuse (10A). Is the fuse open?	—	Go to Step 20	Go to Step 35
20	1 Turn the ignition switch to the OFF position. 2 Disconnect the EBCM connector. 3 Replace the ABS IGN Fuse (10A) with a known good fuse (10A). 4 Turn the ignition to the ON position. Do not start the engine. 5 Wait for ten seconds. 6 Turn the ignition switch to the OFF position. 7 Remove and inspect the ABS IGN Fuse (10A). Is the fuse open?	—	Go to Step 34	Go to Step 21
21	1 Inspect CKT 139 for physical damage. Physical damage may cause a short to ground with the EBCM connector connected. 2 Reconnect the EBCM connector. 3 Reinstall the ABS IGN Fuse (10A). 4 Turn the engine to the ON position. Do not start the engine. 5 Wait for ten seconds. 6 Turn the ignition switch to the OFF position. 7 Remove and inspect the ABS IGN Fuse (10A). Is the fuse open?	—	Go to Step 22	Go to Step 36
22	1 Replace the EBCM. 2 Replace the ABS IGN Fuse (10A) with a known good fuse (10A). Is the repair complete?	—	Go to **ABS Diagnostic System Check**	—

GC402980347300DX

Fig. 82 Test F: No Communications w/EBCM (Part 4 of 6). Alero & Grand Am

23	1 Replace the EBCM. 2 Replace the ABS BATT Fuse (10A) with a known good fuse (10A). Is the repair complete?	—	Go to **ABS Diagnostic System Check**	—
24	Disconnect and reconnect the scan tool in order to ensure a good connection. Is the scan tool correctly connected?	—	Go to **ABS Diagnostic System Check**	—
25	Repair the open or high resistance in CKT 450. Is the repair complete?	—	Go to **ABS Diagnostic System Check**	—
26	Repair the open or high resistance in CKT 1640. Is the repair complete?	—	Go to **ABS Diagnostic System Check**	—
27	Repair the open or high resistance in CKT 139. Is the repair complete?	—	Go to **ABS Diagnostic System Check**	—
28	Repair the open or high resistance in any of the following components: • The negative battery cable • The negative battery cable terminals • The negative battery cable connections Is the repair complete?	—	Go to **ABS Diagnostic System Check**	—
29	Repair the high resistance in CKT 1640 or the voltage feed circuits for the ABS BATT Fuse (10A). Is the repair complete?	—	Go to **ABS Diagnostic System Check**	—
30	Repair the open or high resistance in one of the following circuits: • CKT 139 • CKT 3 • CKT 1 Is the repair complete?	—	Go to **ABS Diagnostic System Check**	—
31	Replace the terminals or the connectors that exhibit the following conditions: • Poor terminal contact • Terminal corrosion • Damaged terminals Is the repair complete?	—	Go to **ABS Diagnostic System Check**	—
32	Repair the short to ground in CKT 1640. Is the repair complete?	—	Go to **ABS Diagnostic System Check**	—
33	Reinstall the ABS BATT Fuse (10A). Is the installation complete?	—	Go to **ABS Diagnostic System Check**	—

GC402980347300EX

Fig. 82 Test F: No Communications w/EBCM (Part 5 of 6). Alero & Grand Am

34	Repair the short to ground in CKT 139. Is the repair complete?	—	Go to **ABS Diagnostic System Check**	—
35	Reinstall the ABS IGN Fuse (10A). Is the installation complete?	—	Go to **ABS Diagnostic System Check**	—
36	The malfunction is intermittent or not present at this time. Refer to Diagnostic Aids for more information. Is the action complete?	—	Go to **ABS Diagnostic System Check**	—
37	Replace the EBCM. Is the repair complete?	—	Go to **ABS Diagnostic System Check**	—

GC402980347300FX

Fig. 82 Test F: No Communications w/EBCM (Part 6 of 6). Alero & Grand Am

Circuit Description

Two way serial communication is sent back and forth between the EBCM, BFC, and the Instrument Cluster. A message from the Instrument Cluster is sent to the EBCM within seven seconds after ABS initialization. A serial communication failure does not allow the proper warning indicator commands to be sent back to the Instrument Cluster.

Diagnostic Aids

The scan tool Serial Data Link (SDL) monitor used in this diagnostic is within the body portion of the scan tool. This requires exiting from the chassis portion of the scan tool to the main menu and entering into the body portion of the scan tool menu and selecting SDL MONITOR.

With the SDL monitor (ABS to Instrument Cluster mode), any message that is being transmitted on the serial data link can be observed.

The frequency of the malfunction can be checked by using the ENHANCED DIAGNOSTIC function of the scan tool.

Any circuitry that is suspected of causing the intermittent complaint should be thoroughly checked for backed-out terminals, improper mating, improperly formed or damaged terminals, poor terminal to wiring connections, or physical damage to the wiring harness.

GC4029703052010X

Fig. 83 Test A: ABS Warning Lamp On w/No Code Set (Part 1 of 2). Malibu

Step	Action	Value(s)	Yes	No
1	Was the Diagnostic System Check performed?	—	Go to Step 2	Go to Diagnostic System Check
2	1. Turn the ignition switch to the OFF position. 2. Install a scan tool. 3. Turn the ignition switch to the RUN position. 4. Using the scan tool, select SPECIAL FUNCTIONS. 5. Select LAMP TEST. 6. Turn the ABS Warning indicator OFF. Did the ABS Warning indicator turn OFF?	—	Go to Step 3	Go to Step 4
3	1. Using the scan tool, select SPECIAL FUNCTIONS 2. Select LAMP TEST. 3. FLASH the ABS Warning indicator. Did the ABS Warning indicator FLASH?	—	Go to Step 7	Go to Step 4
4	Inspect all connectors and terminals for poor terminal contact and evidence of corrosion. Is there evidence of poor terminal contact or corrosion?	—	Go to Step 5	Go to Step 6
5	Replace all terminals that exhibit signs of poor terminal contact or corrosion. Is the repair complete?	—	Go to Diagnostic System Check	—
6	Repair the Instrument Cluster. Is the repair complete?	—	Go to Diagnostic System Check	—
7	Malfunction is not present at this time. Refer to Diagnostic Aids for more information.	—	—	—

GC4029703052020X

Fig. 83 Test A: ABS Warning Lamp On w/No Code Set (Part 2 of 2). Malibu

Circuit Description

Two way serial communication is sent back and forth between the EBCM, BFC, and the Instrument Cluster. A message from the Instrument Cluster is sent to the EBCM within seven seconds after ABS initialization. A serial communication failure does not allow the proper indicator commands to be sent back to the Instrument Cluster.

Diagnostic Aids

The scan tool Serial Data Link (SDL) monitor used in this diagnostic is within the body portion of the scan tool. This requires exiting from the chassis portion of the scan tool to the main menu and entering into the body portion of the scan tool menu and selecting SDL MONITOR.

With the SDL monitor (ABS to Instrument Cluster mode), any message that is being transmitted on the serial data link can be observed.

The frequency of the malfunction can be checked by using the ENHANCED DIAGNOSTIC function of the scan tool.

Any circuitry that is suspected of causing the intermittent complaint should be thoroughly checked for backed-out terminals, improper mating, improperly formed or damaged terminals, poor terminal to wiring connections, or physical damage to the wiring harness.

GC4029703053010X

Fig. 84 Test B: ABS Warning Lamp Inoperative (Part 1 of 2). Malibu

Step	Action	Value(s)	Yes	No
1	Was the Diagnostic System Check performed?	—	Go to Step 2	Go to Diagnostic System Check
2	1. Turn the ignition switch to the OFF position. 2. Install a scan tool. 3. Turn the ignition switch to the RUN position. 4. Using the scan tool, select SPECIAL FUNCTIONS. 5. Select LAMP TEST. 6. Turn the ABS Warning indicator ON. Did the ABS Warning indicator turn ON?	—	Go to Step 3	Go to Step 4
3	1. Using the scan tool, select SPECIAL FUNCTIONS. 2. Select LAMP TEST. 3. FLASH the ABS Warning indicator. Did the ABS Warning indicator FLASH?	—	Go to Step 7	Go to Step 4
4	Inspect all connectors and terminals for poor terminal contact and evidence of corrosion. Is there evidence of poor terminal contact or corrosion?	—	Go to Step 5	Go to Step 6
5	Replace all terminals that exhibit signs of poor terminal contact or corrosion. Is the repair complete?	—	Go to Diagnostic System Check	—
6	Repair the Instrument Cluster. Is the repair complete?	—	Go to Diagnostic System Check	—
7	Malfunction is not present at this time. Refer to Diagnostic Aids for more information.	—	—	—

GC4029703053020X

Fig. 84 Test B: ABS Warning Lamp Inoperative (Part 2 of 2). Malibu

Step	Action	Value(s)	Yes	No
1	Was the Diagnostic System Check performed?	—	Go to Step 2	Go to Diagnostic System Check
2	1. Turn the ignition switch to the OFF position. 2. Install a scan tool. 3. Turn the ignition switch to the RUN position. 4. Using the scan tool, clear any ABS DTCs. 5. Turn the ignition switch to the OFF position. 6. Turn the ignition switch to the RUN position. Does the undefined DTC or DTCs reset?	—	Go to Step 3	Go to Step 4
3	Replace the EBCM. Is the repair complete?	—	Go to Diagnostic System Check	—
4	Malfunction is not present at this time.	—	—	—

GC4029703054000X

Fig. 85 Test C: Scan Tool Displays Undefined Code. Malibu

Circuit Description

Four-way serial communication is sent back and forth between the EBCM, IPC, PCM, and the BCM. A message from the IPC is sent to the BCM within seven seconds after ABS initialization. A serial communication failure does not allow the proper warning indicator commands to be sent back to the IPC.

Diagnostic Aids

Use the Lamp Test function of the Scan Tool in order to turn the indicator ON and OFF while looking for an intermittent malfunction. Thoroughly inspect any circuitry that may cause the intermittent complaint for the following conditions:

- Backed out terminals
- Improper mating
- Broken locks
- Improperly formed or damaged terminals
- Poor terminal-to-wiring connections
- Physical damage to the wiring harness

Test Description

The numbers below refer to the step numbers on the diagnostic table.

2. This test ensures that the instrument cluster can operate the LOW TRAC indicator.

GC4020052207010X

Fig. 86 Low Traction Indicator Always On (Part 1 of 2). Alero & Grand Am

Step	Action	Value(s)	Yes	No
1	Did you perform the ABS Diagnostic System Check?	—	Go to *Step 2*	Go to *A Diagnostic System Check - ABS*
2	1. Turn OFF the ignition. 2. Install a scan tool. 3. Turn ON the ignition, with the engine OFF. 4. Select the Body menu and then IPC on the scan tool. 5. Select Lamp Test on the scan tool. 6. With the scan tool, turn the warning indicators ON and OFF. Does the LOW TRAC indicator turn ON and OFF?	—	Go to *Step 3*	Go to *Step 4*
3	Inspect for poor connections at the harness connector of the EBCM. Did you find and correct the condition?	—	Go to *Step 7*	Go to *Step 5*
4	Inspect for poor connections at the harness connector of the instrument cluster (IPC). Did you find and correct the condition?	—	Go to *Step 7*	Go to *Step 6*
5	Replace the EBCM. Did you complete the repair?	—	Go to *Step 7*	—
6	Replace the instrument cluster (IPC). Did you complete the repair?	—	Go to *Step 7*	—
7	Operate the system in order to verify the repair. Did you correct the condition?	—	System OK	Go to *Step 2*

GC4020052207020X

Fig. 86 Low Traction Indicator Always On (Part 2 of 2). Alero & Grand Am

Circuit Description

Four-way serial communication is sent back and forth between the EBCM, IPC, PCM, and the BCM. A message from the IPC is sent to the BCM within seven seconds after ABS initialization. A serial communication failure does not allow the proper warning indicator commands to be sent back to the IPC.

Diagnostic Aids

The following conditions may cause an intermittent malfunction:

- A poor connection
- Rubbed-through wire insulation
- A broken wire inside the insulation

Use the Lamp Test function of the Scan Tool in order to turn the indicator ON and OFF while looking for an intermittent malfunction.

Thoroughly inspect any circuitry that may cause the intermittent complaint for the following conditions:

- Backed out terminals
- Improper mating
- Broken locks
- Improperly formed or damaged terminals
- Poor terminal-to-wiring connections
- Physical damage to the wiring harness

Test Description

The numbers below refer to the step numbers on the diagnostic table.

2. This test ensures that the instrument cluster can operate the LOW TRAC indicator.

GC4020052208010X

Fig. 87 Low Traction Indicator Inoperative (Part 1 of 2). Alero & Grand Am

System Description

The diagnostic system check is an organized method of identifying any problems caused by a malfunction in either of the following systems:

- The Antilock Brake System (ABS)
- The Enhanced Traction System (ETS)

The service technician must begin diagnosis of any ABS or ABS/ETS complaint with the diagnostic system check.

The diagnostic system check directs the service technician to the next logical step in diagnosing the complaint.

Diagnostic Process

Use the following ordered procedure when servicing the ABS/ETS.

Failure to use the following procedure may cause the loss of important diagnostic data. Failure to use the following procedure may lead to difficult and time-consuming diagnosis procedures.

1. Use the following procedure to perform a vehicle preliminary diagnosis inspection:
   - Inspect the brake master cylinder fluid reservoir:
     - Verify that the brake fluid level is correct.
     - Inspect the master cylinder for contamination.
   - Inspect the brake modulator for the following conditions:
     - Leaks
     - Wiring damage
   - Inspect the brake components of all four wheels:
     - Verify that no drag exists.
     - Verify that the brake apply operation is correct.
   - Inspect for worn or damaged wheel bearings. Worn or damaged wheel bearings may cause a wheel to "wobble".
   - Inspect the wheel speed sensors and the wheel speed sensor wiring:
     - Verify that all of the sensors solidly attach.
     - Inspect for wiring damage, especially at vehicle attachment points.
   - Inspect the outer CV joint:
     - Verify that the outer CV joint is aligned correctly.
     - Verify that the outer CV joint operates correctly.
   - Inspect the tires. Verify that the tires meet legal trend depth requirements.

GC4029903847010X

Fig. 88 ABS Diagnostic System Check (Part 1 of 2). Cavalier & Sunfire

2. Perform the ABS Diagnostic System Check.
   If any DTCs are displayed, select DTC History.
   2.1. Determine which malfunction occurred most recently.
   2.2. Diagnose and repair the most recent malfunction first.
3. Determine if the following conditions exist:
   - No DTCs are present.
   - There are malfunctions in the mechanical components.
   - The failure is intermittent and cannot be reproduced.
4. If the above conditions exist, attempt to reproduce the malfunction:
   4.1. Use the automatic snapshot feature of the Scan Tool while test driving the vehicle.
   Perform normal acceleration, stopping, and turning maneuvers during the test drive.
   4.2. If the test drive does not reproduce the malfunction, perform an ABS stop:
   - Perform the stop on a low coefficient surface (such as gravel).
   - Perform the stop from a speed of 48–80 km/h (30–50 mph).
   - Trigger the snapshot mode on any ABS DTC while performing the stop.

   4.3. If the ABS stop does not reproduce the malfunction, use the enhanced diagnostic information in the DTC History in order to determine if further diagnosis is needed. This determination will be based on the frequency of failure.
5. Clear the ABS/ETS DTCs after all of the system malfunctions have been corrected.

Diagnostic Aids

Diagnosing DTCs in the correct order is very important. Failure to diagnose DTCs in the order specified may result in the following:

- Extended diagnostic time
- Incorrect diagnosis
- Incorrect parts replacement

Step	Action	Value(s)	Yes	No
1	1. Reconnect all previously disconnected components. 2. Cycle the Ignition switch from the OFF to RUN position, engine OFF. 3. Plug the *Scan Tool* into the Data Link Connector (DLC). Does the Scan Tool communicate with the EBCM?	—	*Go to Step 3*	*Go to Step 2*
2	Does the scan tool communicate with other modules on the serial data line?	—	Go to *No Communication with EBCM*	Go to *Data Link Communications System*
3	With the scan tool read ABS DTCs. Are there any current Diagnostic Trouble Codes?	--	Go to Applicable DTC Table	*Go to Step 4*
4	Cycle the ignition switch from the OFF to RUN position. Does the ABS Indicator come ON then go OFF after several seconds?	—	*Go to Step 6*	*Go to Step 5*
5	Does the ABS Warning Indicator come ON and stay ON?	—	Go to *ABS Indicator On No DTC Set*	Go to *ABS Indicator Inoperative with No DTC Set*
6	Are there any history DTCs?	—	*Go to Step 7*	System OK
7	1. Refer to the appropriate DTC table for the history DTC. 2. Read the diagnostic aids, and conditions for setting the DTC. 3. Carefully drive the vehicle above 24 Km/h (15 mph) for several minutes while monitoring a scan tool for ABS DTCs. Did the history DTC set as a current DTC while the vehicle was being driven?	—	Go to Applicable DTC Table	System OK

GC4029903847020X

Fig. 88 ABS Diagnostic System Check (Part 2 of 2). Cavalier & Sunfire

Step	Action	Value(s)	Yes	No
1	Did you perform the ABS Diagnostic System Check?	—	Go to *Step 2*	Go to *A Diagnostic System Check - ABS*
2	1. Turn OFF the ignition. 2. Install a scan tool. 3. Turn ON the ignition, with the engine OFF. 4. Select the Body menu and then IPC on the scan tool. 5. Select Lamp Test on the scan tool. 6. With the scan tool, turn the warning indicators ON and OFF Does the LOW TRAC indicator turn ON and OFF?	—	Go to *Step 3*	Go to *Step 4*
3	Inspect for poor connections at the harness connector of the EBCM. Did you find and correct the condition?	—	Go to *Step 7*	Go to *Step 5*
4	Inspect for poor connections at the harness connector of the instrument cluster (IPC). Did you find and correct the condition?	—	Go to *Step 7*	Go to *Step 6*
5	Replace the EBCM. Did you complete the repair?	—	Go to *Step 7*	—
6	Replace the instrument cluster (IPC). Did you complete the repair?	—	Go to *Step 7*	—
7	Operate the system in order to verify the repair. Did you correct the condition?	—	System OK	Go to *Step 2*

GC4020052208020X

Fig. 87 Low Traction Indicator Inoperative (Part 2 of 2). Alero & Grand Am

Circuit Description

Ignition voltage is supplied to terminal 86 of the Electronic Brake Control Relay. The above condition enables the EBCM to energize the pullin coil by completing the ground circuit at connector C1 terminal A11 of the EBCM. The magnetic field created closes the Electronic Brake Control Relay contacts. The magnetic field also allows battery voltage and current through the Electronic Brake Control Relay terminal 30 to be supplied to the EBCM through connector C2 terminal C. Connector C2 terminal C supplies power to the EBCM, which supplies power to the motors and solenoids.

Conditions for Setting the DTC

DTC C1214 can set anytime after the EBCM commands the Electronic Brake Control Relay on. The command occurs during the three second bulb check.

DTC C1214 monitors the availability of current/voltage to the motors and solenoids.

The above malfunction indicates voltage is not available. The malfunction will not allow ABS operation.

Action Taken When the DTC Sets

- A malfunction DTC stores.
- ABS is disabled.
- The amber ABS warning indicator is turned on.

Conditions for Clearing the DTC

- The condition responsible for setting the DTC no longer exists and the Scan Tool Clear DTCs function is used.
- 100 drive cycles pass with no DTCs detected. A drive cycle consists of starting the vehicle, driving the vehicle over 16 km/h (10 mph), stopping and then turning the ignition OFF.

Diagnostic Aids

The following conditions may cause an intermittent malfunction:

- A poor connection
- Rubbed-through wire insulation
- A broken wire inside the insulation

Use the enhanced diagnostic function of the Scan Tool in order to measure the frequency of the malfunction.

Thoroughly inspect any circuitry that may be causing the intermittent complaint for the following conditions:

- Backed out terminals
- Improper mating
- Improperly formed or damaged terminals
- Poor terminal-to-wiring connections
- Physical damage to the wiring harness

GC402980308000AX

Fig. 89 Code C1214: Brake Control Relay Contact Circuit Open (Part 1 of 5). Cavalier & Sunfire

Vibration and Temperature Effects

- Use the following procedure in order to inspect for vibration effects by performing the Relay Test function of the Scan Tool:
  1. With the Relay Test commanded on, lightly tap the top and sides of the Electronic Brake Control Relay while monitoring the Electronic Brake Control Relay voltage.
  2. If the Electronic Brake Control Relay voltage changes significantly, replace the Electronic Brake Control Relay.
- If DTC C1214 only sets when the vehicle is initially started in cold ambient conditions (temperature less than 0°C – 32°F), replace the Electronic Brake Control Relay.

Important: Zero the J 39200 test leads before making any resistance measurements. Refer to the J 39200 user's manual.

Step	Action	Value(s)	Yes	No
1	Was the Diagnostic System Check performed?	—	*Go to Step 2*	Refer to *Diagnostic System Check*
2	1. Turn the ignition switch to the OFF position. 2. Install a *Scan Tool.* 3. Turn the ignition switch to the RUN position. Do not start the engine. 4. Use the *Scan Tool* in order to read the DTCs. Is DTC C1216 present (either as a current DTC or a history DTC)?	—	Refer to *DTC C1216 Brake Control Rly Coil CKT Open*	*Go to Step 3*
3	1. Select Data List on the *Scan Tool.* 2. Select and observe EBCM Battery Voltage. Is the voltage equal to or greater than the specified voltage?	10 V	*Go to Step 25*	*Go to Step 4*
4	1. Turn the ignition switch to the OFF position. 2. Disconnect the 24-way EBCM connector C2. 3. Connect a fused jumper wire (such as a *J 36169-A*) with a 3A fuse between the 24-way EBCM harness connector C2 terminal A11 and ground. 4. Turn the ignition switch to the RUN position. Do not start the engine. 5. Use the *J 39200* in order to measure the voltage between the 8-way EBCM harness connector C1 terminal C and ground. Is the voltage equal to or greater than the specified voltage?	10 V	*Go to Step 5*	*Go to Step 10*
5	1. Turn the ignition switch to the OFF position. 2. Disconnect the fused wire jumper. 3. Disconnect the Electronic Brake Control Relay. 4. Use the *J 39200* in order to measure the resistance between the Electronic Brake Control Relay connector terminal 87 and the EBCM harness connector C1 terminal C. Is the resistance within the specified range?	0–2 Ω	*Go to Step 6*	*Go to Step 19*
6	1. Disconnect the negative battery cable. 2. Disconnect the positive battery cable. 3. Use the *J 39200* in order to measure the resistance between the positive battery cable terminal and the Electronic Brake Control Relay connector terminal 30. Is the resistance within the specified range?	0–2 Ω	*Go to Step 7*	*Go to Step 20*

GC402980308000BX

Fig. 89 Code C1214: Brake Control Relay Contact Circuit Open (Part 2 of 5). Cavalier & Sunfire

Step	Action	Value(s)	Yes	No
7	1. Connect a jumper wire between the Electronic Brake Control Relay connector terminal 86 to ground. 2. Connect a fused jumper wire (such as a *J 36169-A*) with a 3A fuse between the Electronic Brake Control Relay terminal 85 and battery voltage. 3. Use the *J 39200* in order to measure the resistance between the Electronic Brake Control Relay terminal 30 and terminal 87. Is the resistance within the specified range?	0–2 Ω	*Go to Step 8*	*Go to Step 22*
8	1. Turn the ignition switch to the OFF position. 2. Inspect the following components: • The 24-way EBCM connector C2 • The 8-way EBCM connector C1 • The 24-way EBCM harness connector C2 • The 8-way EBCM harness connector C1 • The Electronic Brake Control Relay • The Electronic Brake Control Relay connector 3. Inspect the above components for signs of the following conditions: • Damage • Poor terminal contact • Terminal corrosion 4. Inspect the following components: • The positive battery terminal • The positive battery cable terminal • The negative battery terminal • The negative battery cable terminal 5. Inspect the above components for signs of the following conditions: • A poor connection • Poor terminal contact Are there signs of poor terminal contact, corrosion, or damaged terminal(s)?	—	*Go to Step 17*	*Go to Step 9*
9	1. Remove all of the jumpers. 2. Reconnect the EBCM connector C1 and connector C2. 3. Reconnect the Electronic Brake Control Relay 4. Reconnect the positive battery cable. 5. Reconnect the negative battery cable. 6. Turn the ignition switch to the RUN position. Do not start the engine. 7. Use the *Scan Tool* in order to look for current DTCs. Does DTC C1214 set as a current DTC?	—	*Go to Step 24*	*Go to Step 25*

GC402980308000CX

Fig. 89 Code C1214: Brake Control Relay Contact Circuit Open (Part 3 of 5). Cavalier & Sunfire

Step	Action	Value(s)	Yes	No
10	1. Turn the ignition switch to the OFF position. 2. Disconnect the negative battery cable. 3. Disconnect the positive battery cable. 4. Turn the ignition switch to the RUN position. (This action completes the ignition circuit to the Electronic Brake Control Relay.) 5. Use the *J 39200* in order to measure the resistance between the 24-way EBCM harness connector C2 terminal A11 and the positive battery cable terminal. Is the resistance within the specified range?	65–95 Ω	*Go to Step 11*	*Go to Step 14*
11	Use the *J 39200* in order to measure the voltage between the positive battery terminal and the negative battery terminal. Is the voltage equal to or greater than the specified voltage?	10 V	*Go to Step 12*	*Go to Step 23*
12	1. Turn the ignition switch to the OFF position. 2. Reconnect the positive battery cable. 3. Reconnect the negative battery cable. 4. Disconnect the Electronic Brake Control Relay. 5. Use the *J 39200* in order to measure the voltage between the Electronic Brake Control Relay connector terminal 30 and ground. Is the voltage equal to or greater than the specified voltage?	10 V	*Go to Step 13*	*Go to Step 20*
13	Use the *J 39200* in order to measure the resistance between the Electronic Brake Control Relay connector terminal 87 and the 8-way EBCM harness connector C1 terminal C. Is the resistance within the specified range?	0–2 Ω	*Go to Step 7*	*Go to Step 19*
14	1. Disconnect the Electronic Brake Control Relay. 2. Use the *J 39200* in order to measure the resistance between the Electronic Brake Control Relay terminal 86 and the Electronic Brake Control Relay terminal 85. Is the resistance within the specified range?	65–95 Ω	*Go to Step 15*	*Go to Step 22*
15	Use the *J 39200* in order to measure the resistance between the Electronic Brake Control Relay connector terminal 85 and the 8-way EBCM/EBTCM harness connector C2 terminal A11. Is the resistance within the specified range?	0–2 Ω	*Go to Step 16*	*Go to Step 18*
16	Use the *J 39200* in order to measure the resistance between the Electronic Brake Control Relay connector terminal 86 and the positive battery cable terminal. Is the resistance within the specified range?	0–2 Ω	*Go to Step 8*	*Go to Step 21*
17	Replace all of the terminals the connectors that exhibit signs of poor terminal contact, corrosion, or damaged terminal(s). Is the repair complete?	—	Refer to *Diagnostic System Check*	—
18	Repair the open or high resistance in CKT 1632. Is the repair complete?	—	Refer to *Diagnostic System Check*	—

GC402980308000DX

Fig. 89 Code C1214: Brake Control Relay Contact Circuit Open (Part 4 of 5). Cavalier & Sunfire

Step	Action	Value(s)	Yes	No
19	Repair the open or high resistance in CKT 1633. Is the repair complete?	—	Refer to *Diagnostic System Check*	—
20	Repair the open or high resistance in CKT 342. Is the repair complete?	—	Refer to *Diagnostic System Check*	—
21	Repair the open or high resistance in the following components as necessary: • CKT 439 • CKT 3 • The ignition switch • The battery feed CKT 242 to the ignition switch Is the repair complete?	—	Refer to *Diagnostic System Check*	—
22	Replace the Electronic Brake Control Relay. Is the repair complete?	—	Refer to *Diagnostic System Check*	—
23	Repair the low voltage condition. Is the repair complete?	—	Refer to *Diagnostic System Check*	—
24	Replace the EBCM. Is the repair complete?	—	Refer to *Diagnostic System Check*	—
25	The malfunction is intermittent or is not present at this time. Refer to Diagnostic Aids for more information.	—	—	—

GC402980308000EX

Fig. 89 Code C1214: Brake Control Relay Contact Circuit Open (Part 5 of 5). Cavalier & Sunfire

Circuit Description

Ignition voltage is supplied to terminal 86 of the Electronic Brake Control Relay. The above condition enables the EBCM to energize the pullin coil by completing the ground circuit at connector C2 terminal A11 of the EBCM. The magnetic field created closes the Electronic Brake Control Relay contacts. The magnetic field also allows battery voltage and current through the Electronic Brake Control Relay terminal 30 to be supplied to the EBCM through connector C1 terminal C. Connector C1 terminal C supplies power to the EBCM, which supplies power to the motors and solenoids.

Conditions for Setting the DTC

DTC C1215 can set only before the EBCM commands the Electronic Brake Control Relay on.

DTC C1215 determines if the Electronic Brake Control Relay energizes when the Electronic Brake Control Relay should not energize. The above malfunction will not allow the Electronic Brake Control Relay to remove power to the ABS system.

If a second malfunction occurs, that requires the Electronic Brake Control Relay to turn off, the second malfunction cannot be removed if the Electronic Brake Control Relay cannot be controlled. The DTC sets if the malfunction is present for three consecutive drive cycles.

Action Taken When the DTC Sets

- A malfunction DTC stores.
- The ABS does not disable.

Conditions for Clearing the DTC

- The condition responsible for setting the DTC no longer exists and the Scan Tool Clear DTCs function is used.
- 100 drive cycles pass with no DTCs detected. A drive cycle consists of starting the vehicle, driving the vehicle over 16 km/h (10 mph), stopping and then turning the ignition OFF.

Diagnostic Aids

A sticking or malfunctioning relay may cause an intermittent malfunction.

Use the enhanced diagnostic function of the Scan Tool in order to measure the frequency of the malfunction.

Clear the DTCs after completing the diagnosis. Test drive the vehicle for three drive cycles in order to verify that the DTC does not reset. Use the following procedure in order to complete one drive cycle:

1. Start the vehicle.
2. Drive the vehicle over 16 km/h (10 mph).
3. Stop the vehicle.
4. Turn the ignition to the OFF position.

GC402980308100AX

Fig. 90 Code C1215: Brake Control Relay Contact Circuit Active (Part 1 of 3). Cavalier & Sunfire

Important: Zero the J 39200 test leads before making any resistance measurements. Refer to the J 39200 user's manual.

Step	Action	Value(s)	Yes	No
1	Was the Diagnostic System Check performed?	—	*Go to Step 2*	Refer to *Diagnostic System Check*
2	Are any other DTCs present?	—	Refer to the appropriate DTC table	*Go to Step 3*
3	1. Turn the ignition switch to the OFF position. 2. Install a *Scan Tool*. 3. Turn the ignition switch to the RUN position. Do not start the engine. 4. Use the Relay Test function of the Scan Tool to command the Electronic Brake Control Relay off. Does the Scan Tool indicate that the Electronic Brake Control Relay is off and the battery voltage less than or equal to the specified voltage?	5 V	*Go to Step 12*	*Go to Step 4*
4	1. Turn the ignition switch to the OFF position. 2. Disconnect the 24-way EBCM connector C2. 3. Disconnect the 8-way EBCM connector C1. 4. Turn the ignition switch to the RUN position. Do not start the engine. 5. Use the *J 39200* in order to measure the voltage between the 8-way EBCM harness connector C1 terminal C and ground. Is the voltage within the specified voltage?	0–1 V	*Go to Step 6*	*Go to Step 5*
5	1. Turn the ignition switch to the OFF position. 2. Disconnect the Electronic Brake Control Relay. 3. Turn the ignition switch to the RUN position. Do not start the engine. 4. Use the *J 39200* in order to measure the voltage between the 8-way EBCM harness connector C1 terminal C and ground. Is the voltage within the specified voltage?	0–1 V	*Go to Step 10*	*Go to Step 9*
6	1. Turn the ignition switch to the OFF position. 2. Inspect the following components: • The 8-way EBCM connector C1 • 24-way EBCM harness connector C2 3. Inspect for the following conditions: • Poor terminal contact • Corrosion • Damaged terminals. The above conditions may cause a short to voltage. Is there a condition that may cause a short to voltage?	—	*Go to Step 8*	*Go to Step 7*

GC402980308100BX

Fig. 90 Code C1215: Brake Control Relay Contact Circuit Active (Part 2 of 3). Cavalier & Sunfire

Step	Action	Value(s)	Yes	No
7	1. Reconnect the 24–way EBCM connector C2. 2. Reconnect the 8–way EBCM connector C1. 3. Turn the ignition switch to the RUN position. Do not start the engine. 4. Use the Relay Test function of the Scan Tool to command the Electronic Brake Control Relay off. Does the Scan Tool indicate that the Electronic Brake Control Relay is off and is the battery voltage less than or equal to the specified voltage?	5 V	*Go to Step 12*	*Go to Step 11*
8	Replace all of the terminals or the connectors that exhibit signs of poor terminal contact, corrosion, or damaged terminal(s). Is the repair complete?	—	Refer to *Diagnostic System Check*	—
9	Repair the short to voltage in CKT 1633. Is the repair complete?	—	Refer to *Diagnostic System Check*	—
10	Replace the Electronic Brake Control Relay. Is the repair complete?	—	Refer to *Diagnostic System Check*	—
11	Replace the EBCM. Is the repair complete?	—	Refer to *Diagnostic System Check*	—
12	The malfunction is intermittent or not present at this time. Refer to Diagnostic Aids for more information.	—	—	—

GC402980308100CX

Fig. 90 Code C1215: Brake Control Relay Contact Circuit Active (Part 3 of 3). Cavalier & Sunfire

Circuit Description

Ignition voltage is supplied to terminal 86 of the Electronic Brake Control Relay. The above condition enables the EBCM to energize the pullin coil by completing the ground circuit at connector C2 terminal A11 of the EBCM. The magnetic field created closes the Electronic Brake Control Relay contacts. The magnetic field also allows battery voltage and current through the Electronic Brake Control Relay terminal 30 to be supplied to the EBCM through connector C1 terminal C. Connector C1 terminal C supplies power to the EBCM, which supplies power to the motors and solenoids.

Conditions for Setting the DTC

DTC 1216 can set anytime after the Electronic Brake Control Relay is commanded ON. This test detects an open in the Electronic Brake Control Relay coil circuit. An open in this circuit will not allow the Electronic Brake Control Relay to be energized thus preventing power to the motors and solenoids.

A DTC C1286 will be set with DTC C1216 if the rear channel is not expected to be in the home position.

Action Taken When the DTC Sets

- A malfunction DTC stores.
- The ABS disables.
- The ABS warning indicator(s) turns on.

Conditions for Clearing the DTC

- The condition responsible for setting the DTC no longer exists and the Scan Tool Clear DTCs function is used.
- 100 drive cycles pass with no DTCs detected. A drive cycle consists of starting the vehicle, driving the vehicle over 16 km/h (10 mph), stopping and then turning the ignition OFF.

GC402980308200AX

Fig. 91 Code C1216: Brake Control Relay Coil Circuit Open (Part 1 of 4). Cavalier & Sunfire

Diagnostic Aids

The following conditions may cause an intermittent malfunction:

- A poor connection
- Rubbed-through wire insulation
- A broken wire inside the insulation

Use the enhanced diagnostic function of the Scan Tool in order to measure the frequency of the malfunction.

If the frequency of the malfunction is high, but is currently intermittent, inspect for high coil resistance. Use a *J 39200* in order to measure for high coil resistance by measuring between Electronic Brake Control Relay terminal 85 and terminal 86. If the resistance shows greater than 95 ohms, replace the Electronic Brake Control Relay.

Thoroughly inspect any circuitry that may be causing the intermittent complaint for the following conditions:

- Backed out terminals
- Improper mating
- Improperly formed or damaged terminals
- Poor terminal-to-wiring connections
- Physical damage to the wiring harness

Clear the DTCs after completing the diagnosis. Test drive the vehicle for three drive cycles in order to verify that the DTC does not reset. Use the following procedure in order to complete one drive cycle:

1. Start the vehicle.
2. Drive the vehicle over 16 km/h (10 mph).
3. Stop the vehicle.
4. Turn the ignition to the OFF position.

Important: Zero the J 39200 test leads before making any resistance measurements. Refer to the J 39200 user's manual.

Step	Action	Value(s)	Yes	No
1	Was the Diagnostic System Check performed?	—	*Go to Step 2*	Refer to *Diagnostic System Check*
2	1. Turn the ignition switch to the OFF position. 2. Install a *Scan Tool*. 3. Turn the ignition switch to the RUN position. Do not start the engine. 4. Use the Relay Test function of the *Scan Tool* in order to command the Electronic Brake Control Relay on. Does the Scan Tool indicate that the Electronic Brake Control Relay is on, and is the voltage equal to or greater than the specified voltage?	10 V	*Go to Step 23*	*Go to Step 3*
3	Use the *J 39200* in order to measure the voltage between the Electronic Brake Control Relay connector terminal 85 and ground. Is the voltage equal to or greater than the specified voltage?	10 V	*Go to Step 4*	*Go to Step 9*
4	Use the *J 39200* in order to measure the voltage between the Electronic Brake Control Relay connector terminal 86 and ground. Is the voltage equal to or greater than the specified voltage?	10 V	*Go to Step 5*	*Go to Step 13*
5	1. Turn the ignition switch to the OFF position. 2. Disconnect the 24-way EBCM connector C2. 3. Turn the ignition switch to the RUN position. Do not start the engine. 4. Use the *J 39200* in order to measure the voltage between the EBCM connector C2 terminal A11 and ground. Is the voltage equal to or greater than the specified voltage?	10 V	*Go to Step 6*	*Go to Step 7*

GC402980308200BX

Fig. 91 Code C1216: Brake Control Relay Coil Circuit Open (Part 2 of 4). Cavalier & Sunfire

Step	Action	Value(s)	Yes	No
6	1. Turn the ignition switch to the OFF position. 2. Inspect the following components: • The 24-way EBCM connector C2 terminal A11 • The remaining terminals of the 24-way EBCM connector C2 3. Inspect the above components for the following conditions: • Damage • Poor terminal contact • Terminal corrosion Are there signs of poor terminal contact, corrosion, or damaged terminals?	—	*Go to Step 17*	*Go to Step 8*
7	1. Remove the Electronic Brake Control Relay. 2. Use the *J 39200* in order to measure the resistance between the 24-way EBCM connector terminal A11 and the Electronic Brake Control Relay connector terminal 85. Is the resistance within the specified range?	0–2 Ω	*Go to Step 8*	*Go to Step 18*
8	1. Reconnect the 24-way EBCM connector C2. 2. Reconnect the Electronic Brake Control Relay, if the Electronic Brake Control Relay is disconnected. 3. Turn the ignition switch to the RUN position. Do not start the engine. 4. Use the *Scan Tool* in order to read the DTCs. Does DTC C1216 set as current DTC?	—	*Go to Step 22*	*Go to Step 23*
9	1. Turn the ignition switch to the OFF position. 2. Remove the ERLS Fuse (10A) from the fuse block. 3. Turn the ignition switch to the RUN position. Do not start the engine. 4. Use the *J 39200* in order to measure the voltage between the fuse block terminal and ground. Is the voltage equal to or greater than the specified range?	10 V	*Go to Step 10*	*Go to Step 16*
10	Remove and inspect the ERLS Fuse (10A). Is the fuse open?	0–2 Ω	*Go to Step 12*	*Go to Step 11*
11	1. Turn the ignition switch to the OFF position. 2. Use the *J 39200* in order to measure the resistance between the Electronic Brake Control Relay connector terminal 86 and the fuse block terminal. Is the resistance within the specified range?	0–2 Ω	*Go to Step 23*	*Go to Step 15*
12	1. Turn the ignition switch to the OFF position. 2. Disconnect the 24-way EBCM connector C2. 3. Use the *J 39200* in order to measure the resistance between the 24-way EBCM harness connector C2 terminal A9 and ground. Is the resistance within the specified range?	OL (Infinite)	*Go to Step 20*	*Go to Step 19*
13	1. Disconnect the Electronic Brake Control Relay. 2. Use the *J 39200* in order to measure the resistance between the Electronic Brake Control Relay terminal 85 and the Electronic Brake Control Relay terminal 86. Is the resistance within the specified range?	65–95 Ω	*Go to Step 14*	*Go to Step 21*

GC402980308200CX

Fig. 91 Code C1216: Brake Control Relay Coil Circuit Open (Part 3 of 4). Cavalier & Sunfire

Step	Action	Value(s)	Yes	No
14	Inspect the Electronic Brake Control Relay connector for the following conditions: • Damage • Poor terminal contact • Terminal corrosion Are there signs of damage, poor terminal contact, or terminal corrosion?	—	*Go to Step 17*	*Go to Step 23*
15	Repair the open or high resistance in CKT 439. Is the repair complete?	—	Refer to *Diagnostic System Check*	—
16	Repair the open or high resistance in the following circuits and components: • CKT 1 • CKT 3 • CKT 242 • The ignition switch • The IGN Fuse. Is the repair complete?	—	Refer to *Diagnostic System Check*	—
17	Replace all of the terminals that display signs of poor terminal contact, corrosion, or damaged terminal(s). If the Electronic Brake Control Relay displays signs of corrosion, replace the Electronic Brake Control Relay. Is the repair complete?	—	Refer to *Diagnostic System Check*	—
18	Repair the open or high resistance in CKT 1632. Is the repair complete?	—	Refer to *Diagnostic System Check*	—
19	Repair the short to ground in CKT 439. Is the repair complete?	—	*Go to Step 20*	—
20	Replace the fuse block ERLS Fuse (10A) with a known good fuse. Is the repair complete?	—	Refer to *Diagnostic System Check*	—
21	Replace the Electronic Brake Control Relay. Is the repair complete?	—	Refer to *Diagnostic System Check*	—
22	Replace the EBCM. Is the repair complete?	—	Refer to *Diagnostic System Check*	—
23	The malfunction is intermittent or is not present at this time. Refer to Diagnostic Aids for more information.	—	—	—

GC402980308200DX

Fig. 91 Code C1216: Brake Control Relay Coil Circuit Open (Part 4 of 4). Cavalier & Sunfire

Circuit Description

Ignition voltage is supplied to terminal 86 of the Electronic Brake Control Relay. The above condition enables the EBCM to energize the pullin coil by completing the ground circuit at connector C2 terminal A11 of the EBCM. The magnetic field created closes the Electronic Brake Control Relay contacts. The magnetic field also allows battery voltage and current through the Electronic Brake Control Relay terminal 30 to be supplied to the EBCM through connector C1 terminal C. Connector C1 terminal C supplies power to the EBCM, which supplies power to the motors and solenoids.

Conditions for Setting the DTC

DTC C1217 can set before the EBCM commands the Electronic Brake Control Relay on.

DTC C1217 determines if the Electronic Brake Control Relay energizes when the Electronic Brake Control Relay should not energize. The above malfunction would not allow the Electronic Brake Control Relay to remove power to the ABS system.

If a second malfunction occurs, that requires the Electronic Brake Control Relay to turn off, the second malfunction cannot be removed if the Electronic Brake Control Relay cannot be controlled.

Action Taken When the DTC Sets

- A malfunction DTC stores.
- The ABS does not disable.

Conditions for Clearing the DTC

- The condition responsible for setting the DTC no longer exists and the Scan Tool Clear DTCs function is used.
- 100 drive cycles pass with no DTCs detected. A drive cycle consists of starting the vehicle, driving the vehicle over 16 km/h (10 mph), stopping and then turning the ignition OFF.

Diagnostic Aids

Use the enhanced diagnostic function of the Scan Tool in order to measure the frequency of the malfunction.

Clear the DTCs after completing the diagnosis.

Test drive the vehicle for three drive cycles in order to verify that the DTC does not reset.

Use the following procedure in order to complete one drive cycle:

1. Start the vehicle.
2. Drive the vehicle over 16 km/h (10 mph).
3. Stop the vehicle.
4. Turn the ignition to the OFF position.

GC4029903848010X

Fig. 92 Code C1217: Brake Control Relay Coil Circuit Shorted To Ground (Part 1 of 3). Cavalier & Sunfire

Test Description

2. This test determines if the EBCM is capable of controlling the electronic brake control relay as commanded.
3. This test ensures that the electronic brake control relay or control circuit are not shorted to ground.
5. This test ensures that the electronic brake control relay or control circuit are not shorted to ground.
6. This test determines if the malfunction is due to the EBCM.

Step	Action	Value(s)	Yes	No
Important: Zero the J 39200 test leads before making any resistance measurements.				
1	Was the ABS Diagnostic System Check performed?	—	*Go to Step 2*	*Go to A Diagnostic System Check - ABS*
2	1. Turn the ignition switch to the OFF position. 2. Install a *Scan Tool*. 3. Turn the ignition switch to the RUN position. Do not start the engine. 4. Use the relay test function of the *Scan Tool* in order to command the Electronic Brake Control Relay OFF. Does the Scan Tool indicate that the Electronic Brake Control Relay is OFF, and is the voltage within the specified range?	0–5 V	*Go to Step 12*	*Go to Step 3*
3	1. Turn the ignition switch to the OFF position. 2. Disconnect the 24-way EBCM connector C2. 3. Turn the ignition switch to the RUN position. Do not start the engine. 4. Use the *J 39200* in order to measure the voltage between the 24-way EBCM harness connector C2 terminal A11 and the battery voltage. Is the voltage within the specified voltage?	0–1 V	*Go to Step 4*	*Go to Step 7*
4	1. Turn the ignition switch to the OFF position. 2. Inspect the following components: • The 24-way EBCM connector C2 terminal A11 • The remaining terminals of the 24-way EBCM connector C2 3. Inspect the above components for the following conditions: • Damage • Poor terminal contact • Terminal corrosion Are there signs of poor terminal contact, corrosion, or damaged terminals?	—	*Go to Step 8*	*Go to Step 5*
5	Use the *J 39200* in order to measure the resistance between the 24-way EBCM harness connector C2 terminal A11 and ground. Is the resistance within the specified range?	OL (Infinite)	*Go to Step 6*	*Go to Step 9*
6	1. Reconnect the 24-way EBCM connector C2. 2. Turn the ignition switch to the RUN position. Do not start the engine. 3. Use the *Scan Tool* in order to look for DTCs. Does DTC C1217 set as a current DTC?	—	*Go to Step 11*	*Go to Step 12*

GC4029903848020X

Fig. 92 Code C1217: Brake Control Relay Coil Circuit Shorted To Ground (Part 2 of 3). Cavalier & Sunfire

Step	Action	Value(s)	Yes	No
7	1. Turn the ignition switch to the OFF position. 2. Disconnect the Electronic Brake Control Relay. 3. Use the *J 39200* in order to measure the voltage between the Electronic Brake Control Relay connector terminal 85 and the battery voltage. Is the voltage within the specified range?	0–1 V	*Go to Step 10*	*Go to Step 9*
8	Replace all of the terminals or connectors that exhibit signs of poor terminal contact, corrosion, or damaged terminal(s). Is the repair complete?	—	Go to *A Diagnostic System Check - ABS*	—
9	Repair the short to ground in CKT 1632. Is the repair complete?	—	Go to *A Diagnostic System Check - ABS*	—
10	Replace the Electronic Brake Control Relay. Is the repair complete?	—	Go to *A Diagnostic System Check - ABS*	—
11	Replace the EBCM. Is the repair complete?	—	Go to *A Diagnostic System Check - ABS*	—
12	The malfunction is intermittent or is not present at this time. Refer to Diagnostic Aids for more information. Is the action complete?	—	System OK	—

GC4029903848030X

Fig. 92 Code C1217: Brake Control Relay Coil Circuit Shorted To Ground (Part 3 of 3). Cavalier & Sunfire

Step	Action	Value(s)	Yes	No
1	Was the Diagnostic System Check performed?	—	*Go to Step 2*	Refer to *Diagnostic System Check*
2	1. Turn the ignition switch to the OFF position. 2. Install a *Scan Tool.* 3. Turn the ignition switch to the RUN position. Do not start the engine. 4. Use the Relay Test function of the *Scan Tool* in order to command the Electronic Brake Control Relay on. Does the Scan Tool indicate that the Electronic Brake Control Relay is off, and is the voltage equal to or greater than the specified voltage?	10 V	*Go to Step 12*	*Go to Step 3*
3	1. Turn the ignition switch to the OFF position. 2. Disconnect the Electronic Brake Control Relay. 3. Disconnect the 24-way EBCM connector C2. 4. Turn the ignition switch to the RUN position. Do not start the engine. 5. Use the *J 39200* in order to measure the voltage between the 24-way EBCM harness connector C2 terminal A11 and ground. Is the voltage within the specified voltage?	0–1 V	*Go to Step 4*	*Go to Step 9*
4	1. Turn the ignition switch to the OFF position. 2. Use the *J 39200* in order to measure the resistance between the Electronic Brake Control Relay terminal 85 and the Electronic Brake Control Relay terminal 86. Is the resistance equal to or greater than the specified range?	65–95 Ω	*Go to Step 5*	*Go to Step 10*
5	Use the *J 39200* in order to measure the resistance between the Electronic Brake Control Relay terminal 30 and the Electronic Brake Control Relay terminal 87. Is the resistance within the specified range?	OL (Infinite)	*Go to Step 6*	*Go to Step 10*
6	1. Inspect the following components: • The 24-way EBCM connector C2 terminal A11 • The remaining terminals of the 24-way EBCM connector C2 2. Inspect the above components for the following conditions: • Damage • Poor terminal contact • Terminal corrosion Are there signs of poor terminal contact, corrosion, or damaged terminals?	—	*Go to Step 8*	*Go to Step 7*

GC402980308400BX

Fig. 93 Code C1218: Brake Control Relay Coil Circuit Shorted To Voltage (Part 2 of 3). Cavalier & Sunfire

Circuit Description

Ignition voltage is supplied to terminal 86 of the Electronic Brake Control Relay. The above enables the EBCM to energize the pullin coil by completing the ground circuit at connector C2 terminal A11 of the EBCM. The magnetic field created closes the Electronic Brake Control Relay contacts. The magnetic field also allows battery voltage and current through the Electronic Brake Control Relay terminal 30 to be supplied to the EBCM through connector C1 terminal C. Connector C1 terminal C supplies power to the EBCM, which supplies power to the motors and solenoids.

Conditions for Setting the DTC

DTC C1218 can set after the EBCM commands the Electronic Brake Control Relay on.

This test monitors the availability of voltage to the EBCM.

DTC C1286 is set with DTC C1218 if the rear channel is not expected to be in the home position.

Action Taken When the DTC Sets

- A malfunction DTC stores.
- The ABS disables.
- The ABS warning indicator turns on.

Conditions for Clearing the DTC

- The condition responsible for setting the DTC no longer exists and the Scan Tool Clear DTCs function is used.
- 100 drive cycles pass with no DTCs detected. A drive cycle consists of starting the vehicle, driving the vehicle over 16 km/h (10 mph), stopping and then turning the ignition OFF.

Diagnostic Aids

Use the enhanced diagnostic function of the Scan Tool in order to measure the frequency of the malfunction.

Clear the DTCs after completing the diagnosis. Test drive the vehicle for three drive cycles in order to verify that the DTC does not reset. Use the following procedure in order to complete one drive cycle:

1. Start the vehicle.
2. Drive the vehicle over 16 km/h (10 mph).
3. Stop the vehicle.
4. Turn the ignition to the OFF position.

Important: Zero the J 39200 test leads before making any resistance measurements. Refer to the J 39200 user's manual.

GC402980308400AX

Fig. 93 Code C1218: Brake Control Relay Coil Circuit Shorted To Voltage (Part 1 of 3). Cavalier & Sunfire

Step	Action	Value(s)	Yes	No
7	1. Reconnect the EBCM connector C2. 2. Reconnect the Electronic Brake Control Relay. 3. Turn the ignition switch to the RUN position. Do not start the engine. 4. Use the *Scan Tool* in order to look for DTCs. Does DTC C1218 set as a current DTC?	—	*Go to Step 11*	*Go to Step 12*
8	Replace all of the terminals or connectors that exhibit signs of poor terminal contact, corrosion, or damaged terminal(s). Is the repair complete?	—	Refer to *Diagnostic System Check*	—
9	Repair the short to voltage in CKT 1632. Is the repair complete?	—	Refer to *Diagnostic System Check*	—
10	Replace the Electronic Brake Control Relay. Is the repair complete?	—	Refer to *Diagnostic System Check*	—
11	Replace the EBCM. Is the repair complete?	—	Refer to *Diagnostic System Check*	—
12	The malfunction is intermittent or is not present at this time. Refer to Diagnostic Aids for more information.	—	—	—

GC402980308400CX

Fig. 93 Code C1218: Brake Control Relay Coil Circuit Shorted To Voltage (Part 3 of 3). Cavalier & Sunfire

Circuit Description

As a toothed ring passes by the wheel speed sensor, changes in the electromagnetic field cause the wheel speed sensor to produce an AC voltage signal. The frequency of the AC voltage signal is proportional to the wheel speed. The amplitude of the AC voltage signal is directly related to wheel speed and the proximity of the wheel speed sensor to the toothed ring. The proximity of the wheel speed sensor to the toothed ring is also referred to as the air gap.

Conditions for Setting the DTC

DTC C1221 can set when the vehicle is not in an ABS stop.

A malfunction exists if both of the following conditions occur:

- The left front wheel speed sensor input signal equals zero.
- The vehicle's reference speed is greater than 8 km/h (5 mph)

Action Taken When the DTC Sets

- A malfunction DTC stores.
- The ABS disables.
- The ABS warning indicator turns on.

Conditions for Clearing the DTC

- The condition responsible for setting the DTC no longer exists and the Scan Tool Clear DTCs function is used.
- 100 drive cycles pass with no DTCs detected. A drive cycle consists of starting the vehicle, driving the vehicle over 16 km/h (10 mph), stopping and then turning the ignition OFF.

Diagnostic Aids

The following conditions may cause an intermittent malfunction:

- A poor connection
- Rubbed-through wire insulation
- A broken wire inside the insulation

Use the enhanced diagnostic function of the Scan Tool in order to measure the frequency of the malfunction.

If the customer's comments reflect that the amber ABS warning indicator is on only during moist environmental changes (rain, snow, vehicle wash), inspect all the wheel speed sensor circuitry for signs of water intrusion. If the DTC is not current, clear all DTCs and simulate the effects of water intrusion by using the following procedure:

1. Spray the suspected area with a five percent saltwater solution.

   Add two teaspoons of salt to twelve ounces of water to make a five percent saltwater solution.
2. Test drive the vehicle over various road surfaces (bumps, turns, etc.) above 24 km/h (15 mph) for at least 30 seconds.
3. If the DTC returns, replace the suspected harness.

Thoroughly inspect any circuitry that may be causing the intermittent complaint for the following conditions:

- Backed out terminals
- Improper mating
- Broken locks
- Improperly formed or damaged terminals
- Poor terminal-to-wiring connections
- Physical damage to the wiring harness

GC402980308500AX

Fig. 94 Code C1221: LH Front Wheel Speed Sensor Input Signal Is Zero (Part 1 of 4). Cavalier & Sunfire

Resistance of the wheel speed sensor will increase with an increase in sensor temperature.

Use the following procedure when replacing a wheel speed sensor or harness:

1. Inspect the wheel speed sensor terminals and harness connector for corrosion and/or water intrusion.
2. Replace the wheel speed sensor and jumper harness if evidence of corrosion or water intrusion exists.

Important: Zero the J 39200 test leads before making any resistance measurements. Refer to the J 39200 user's manual.

Important: Difficulty may occur when trying to locate the intermittent malfunctions in the wheel speed sensor circuit.

Do not disturb any of the electrical connections. Change electrical connections only when instructed to do so by a step in the diagnostic table.

Changing the electrical connections at the correct time will ensure that an intermittent electrical connection will not be corrected until the source of the malfunction is found.

Step	Action	Value(s)	Yes	No
1	Was the Diagnostic System Check performed?	—	*Go to Step 2*	Refer to *Diagnostic System Check*
2	1. Turn the ignition switch to the OFF position. 2. Inspect the left front wheel speed sensor and the left front wheel speed sensor harness connector for physical damage. Is there any physical damage?	—	*Go to Step 16*	*Go to Step 3*
3	Inspect the following components for physical damage: • The left front wheel speed sensor jumper harness • The left front wheel speed sensor jumper harness connectors Is there any physical damage?	—	*Go to Step 15*	*Go to Step 4*
4	1. Disconnect the left front wheel speed sensor directly at the left front wheel speed sensor connector. 2. Use the *J 39200* in order to measure the resistance between the left front wheel speed sensor connector terminal A and the left front wheel speed sensor connector terminal B. Is the resistance within the specified range?	1530–1870 Ω	*Go to Step 5*	*Go to Step 16*
5	1. Select the A/C VOLTAGE scale on the *J 39200*. 2. Spin the left front wheel by hand while observing the voltage reading on the *J 39200*. Is the voltage equal to or greater than the specified voltage?	100 mV	*Go to Step 6*	*Go to Step 16*
6	1. Disconnect the 24-way EBCM connector C2. 2. Use the *J 39200* in order to measure the resistance between the 24-way EBCM connector C2 terminal A5 and the 24-way EBCM connector C2 terminal B4. Is the resistance within the specified range?	OL (Infinite)	*Go to Step 7*	*Go to Step 8*

GC402980308500BX

Fig. 94 Code C1221: LH Front Wheel Speed Sensor Input Signal Is Zero (Part 2 of 4). Cavalier & Sunfire

Step	Action	Value(s)	Yes	No
7	1. Inspect the 24-way EBCM connector C2 for the following conditions: • Damage • Poor terminal contact • Terminal corrosion (Damage, poor terminal contact, and terminal corrosion may cause a short between the 24-way EBCM connector C2 terminal A5 and the EBCM connector C2 terminal B4. 2. Inspect the remaining terminals of the 24-way EBCM connector C2 for the following conditions: • Damage • Poor terminal contact • Terminal corrosion Are there signs of poor terminal contact, corrosion, or damaged terminals?	—	*Go to Step 12*	*Go to Step 8*
8	Inspect the wiring of CKT 873 and CKT 830 for signs of damage that may cause a short between CKT 873 and CKT 830. Are there any signs of damaged wiring?	—	*Go to Step 13*	*Go to Step 9*
9	Inspect the harness connectors of CKT 873 and CKT 830 for signs of damage that may cause a short between CKT 873 and CKT 830. Are there any signs of damaged connectors?	—	*Go to Step 14*	*Go to Step 10*
10	1. Reconnect the 24-way EBCM harness connector C2. 2. Reconnect the left front wheel speed sensor harness connector. 3. Install a *Scan Tool*. 4. Test drive the vehicle at a speed above 24 km/h (15 mph) for at least 30 seconds. 5. Use the *Scan Tool* in order to read the DTCs. Does DTC C1221 set as a current DTC?	—	*Go to Step 11*	*Go to Step 18*
11	1. Select Data List on the *Scan Tool*. 2. Monitor the wheel speed sensor speeds. 3. Drive the vehicle in the following manner: 3.1. Slowly accelerate to 65 km/h (40 mph). 3.2. Slowly decelerate to 0 km/h (0 mph). Is the speed of the left front wheel speed sensor constantly higher than the speed of the three remaining wheel speed sensors?	—	*Go to Step 15*	*Go to Step 17*
12	Replace all of the terminals that exhibit signs of poor terminal contact, corrosion, or damaged terminal(s). Is the repair complete?	—	Refer to *Diagnostic System Check*	—
13	Replace the damaged wiring harness that causes the short between CKT 873 and CKT 830. Is the repair complete?	—	Refer to *Diagnostic System Check*	—

GC402980308500CX

Fig. 94 Code C1221: LH Front Wheel Speed Sensor Input Signal Is Zero (Part 3 of 4). Cavalier & Sunfire

Step	Action	Value(s)	Yes	No
14	Replace the damaged wiring harness connectors that cause the short between CKT 873 and CKT 830. Is the repair complete?	—	Refer to *Diagnostic System Check*	—
15	Replace the left front wheel speed sensor jumper harness. Is the repair complete?	—	Refer to *Diagnostic System Check*	—
16	Replace the left front wheel speed sensor. Is the repair complete?	—	Refer to *Diagnostic System Check*	—
17	Replace the EBCM. Is the repair complete?	—	Refer to *Diagnostic System Check*	—
18	The malfunction is intermittent or is not present at this time. Refer to Diagnostic Aids for more information.	—	—	—

GC402980308500DX

Fig. 94 Code C1221: LH Front Wheel Speed Sensor Input Signal Is Zero (Part 4 of 4). Cavalier & Sunfire

Circuit Description

As a toothed ring passes by the wheel speed sensor, changes in the electromagnetic field cause the wheel speed sensor to produce an AC voltage signal. The frequency of the AC voltage signal is proportional to the wheel speed. The amplitude of the AC voltage signal is directly related to wheel speed and the proximity of the wheel speed sensor to the toothed ring. The proximity of the wheel speed sensor to the toothed ring is also referred to as the air gap.

Conditions for Setting the DTC

DTC C1222 sets when the vehicle is not in an ABS stop.

A malfunction exists if both of the following conditions occur:

- The right front wheel speed sensor input signal equals zero.
- The vehicle's reference speed is greater than 8 km/h (5 mph)

Action Taken When the DTC Sets

- A malfunction DTC stores.
- The ABS disables.
- The ABS warning indicator turns on.

Conditions for Clearing the DTC

- The condition responsible for setting the DTC no longer exists and the Scan Tool Clear DTCs function is used.
- 100 drive cycles pass with no DTCs detected. A drive cycle consists of starting the vehicle, driving the vehicle over 16 km/h (10 mph), stopping and then turning the ignition OFF.

Diagnostic Aids

The following conditions may cause an intermittent malfunction:

- A poor connection
- Rubbed-through wire insulation
- A broken wire inside the insulation

Use the enhanced diagnostic function of the Scan Tool in order to measure the frequency of the malfunction. Refer to the Scan Tool manual for the procedure.

If the customer's comments reflect that the amber ABS warning indicator is on only during moist environmental changes (rain, snow, vehicle wash), inspect all the wheel speed sensor circuitry for signs of water intrusion. If the DTC is not current, clear all DTCs and simulate the effects of water intrusion by using the following procedure:

1. Spray the suspected area with a five percent saltwater solution.

   Add two teaspoons of salt to twelve ounces of water to make a five percent saltwater solution.
2. Test drive the vehicle over various road surfaces (bumps, turns, etc.) above 24 km/h (15 mph) for at least 30 seconds.
3. If the DTC returns, replace the suspected harness.

Thoroughly inspect any circuitry that may be causing the intermittent complaint for the following conditions:

- Backed out terminals
- Improper mating
- Broken locks
- Improperly formed or damaged terminals
- Poor terminal-to-wiring connections
- Physical damage to the wiring harness

GC402980308600AX

Fig. 95 Code C1222: RH Front Wheel Speed Sensor Input Signal Is Zero (Part 1 of 4). Cavalier & Sunfire

Resistance of the wheel speed sensor will increase with an increase in sensor temperature.

Use the following procedure when replacing a wheel speed sensor or harness:

1. Inspect the wheel speed sensor terminals and harness connector for corrosion and/or water intrusion.
2. Replace the wheel speed sensor and jumper harness if evidence of corrosion or water intrusion exists.

Important: Zero the J 39200 test leads before making any resistance measurements. Refer to the J 39200 user's manual.

Important: Difficulty may occur when trying to locate intermittent malfunctions in the wheel speed sensor circuit.

Do not disturb any of the electrical connections. Change electrical connections only when instructed to do so by a step in the diagnostic table.

Changing the electrical connections at the correct time will ensure that an intermittent electrical connection will not be corrected until the source of the malfunction is found.

Step	Action	Value(s)	Yes	No
1	Was the Diagnostic System Check performed?	—	*Go to Step 2*	Refer to *Diagnostic System Check*
2	1. Turn the ignition switch to the OFF position. 2. Inspect the right front wheel speed sensor and the right front wheel speed sensor harness connector for physical damage. Is there any physical damage?	—	*Go to Step 16*	*Go to Step 3*
3	Inspect the following components for physical damage: • The right front wheel speed sensor jumper harness • The right front wheel speed sensor jumper harness connectors Is there any physical damage?	—	*Go to Step 15*	*Go to Step 4*
4	1. Disconnect the right front wheel speed sensor directly at the right front wheel speed sensor connector. 2. Use the *J 39200* in order to measure the resistance between the right front wheel speed sensor connector terminal A and the right front wheel speed sensor connector terminal B. Is the resistance within the specified range?	1530–1870 Ω	*Go to Step 5*	*Go to Step 16*
5	1. Select the A/C VOLTAGE scale on the *J 39200*. 2. Spin the right front wheel by hand while observing the voltage reading on the *J 39200*. Is the voltage equal to or greater than the specified voltage?	100 mV	*Go to Step 6*	*Go to Step 16*
6	1. Disconnect the 24-way EBCM connector C2. 2. Use the *J 39200* in order to measure the resistance between the 24-way EBCM connector C2 terminal A4 and the 24-way EBCM connector C2 terminal B3. Is the resistance within the specified range?	OL (Infinite)	*Go to Step 7*	*Go to Step 8*

GC402980308600BX

Fig. 95 Code C1222: RH Front Wheel Speed Sensor Input Signal Is Zero (Part 2 of 4). Cavalier & Sunfire

Step	Action	Value(s)	Yes	No
7	1. Inspect the 24-way EBCM connector C1 for the following conditions: • Damage • Poor terminal contact • Terminal corrosion Damage, poor terminal contact, and terminal corrosion may cause a short between the 24-way EBCM connector C2 terminal A4 and the EBCM connector C2 terminal B3. 2. Inspect the remaining terminals of the 24-way EBCM connector C2 for the following conditions: • Damage • Poor terminal contact • Terminal corrosion Are there signs of poor terminal contact, corrosion, or damaged terminals?	—	*Go to Step 12*	*Go to Step 8*
8	Inspect the wiring of CKT 872 and CKT 833 for signs of damage that may cause a short between CKT 872 and CKT 833. Are there any signs of damaged wiring?	—	*Go to Step 13*	*Go to Step 9*
9	Inspect the harness connectors of CKT 872 and CKT 833 for signs of damage that may cause a short between CKT 872 and CKT 833. Are there any signs of damaged connectors?	—	*Go to Step 14*	*Go to Step 10*
10	1. Reconnect the 24-way EBCM harness connector C2. 2. Reconnect the right front wheel speed sensor harness connector. 3. Install a *Scan Tool*. 4. Test drive the vehicle at a speed above 24 km/h (15 mph) for at least 30 seconds. 5. Use the *Scan Tool* in order to read the DTCs. Does DTC C1222 set as a current DTC?	—	*Go to Step 11*	*Go to Step 18*
11	1. Select Data List on the *Scan Tool*. 2. Monitor the wheel speed sensor speeds. 3. Use the following procedure when driving the vehicle in order to test the wheel speed sensor: 3.1. Slowly accelerate to 65 km/h (40 mph). 3.2. Slowly decelerate to 0 km/h (0 mph). Is the speed of the right front wheel speed sensor constantly higher than the speed of the three remaining wheel speed sensors?	—	*Go to Step 16*	*Go to Step 17*
12	Replace all of the terminals that exhibit signs of poor terminal contact, corrosion, or damaged terminal(s). Is the repair complete?	—	Refer to *Diagnostic System Check*	—
13	Replace the damaged wiring harness that causes the short between CKT 872 and CKT 833. Is the repair complete?	—	Refer to *Diagnostic System Check*	—

GC402980308600CX

Fig. 95 Code C1222: RH Front Wheel Speed Sensor Input Signal Is Zero (Part 3 of 4). Cavalier & Sunfire

Step	Action	Value(s)	Yes	No
14	Replace the damaged wiring harness connectors that cause the short between CKT 872 and CKT 833. Is the repair complete?	—	Refer to *Diagnostic System Check*	—
15	Replace the right front wheel speed sensor jumper harness. Is the repair complete?	—	Refer to *Diagnostic System Check*	—
16	Replace the right front wheel speed sensor. Is the repair complete?	—	Refer to *Diagnostic System Check*	—
17	Replace the EBCM. Is the repair complete?	—	Refer to *Diagnostic System Check*	—
18	The malfunction is intermittent or is not present at this time. Refer to Diagnostic Aids for more information.	—	—	—

GC402980308600DX

Fig. 95 Code C1222: RH Front Wheel Speed Sensor Input Signal Is Zero (Part 4 of 4). Cavalier & Sunfire

Circuit Description

As a toothed ring passes by the wheel speed sensor, changes in the electromagnetic field cause the wheel speed sensor to produce an AC voltage signal. The frequency of the AC voltage signal is proportional to the wheel speed. The amplitude of the AC voltage signal is directly related to wheel speed and the proximity of the wheel speed sensor to the toothed ring. The proximity of the wheel speed sensor to the toothed ring is also referred to as the air gap.

Conditions for Setting the DTC

DTC C1223 can set when the vehicle is not in an ABS stop.

A malfunction exists if both of the following conditions occur:

- The left rear wheel speed sensor input signal equals zero.
- The vehicle's reference speed is greater than 8 km/h (5 mph)

Action Taken When the DTC Sets

- A malfunction DTC stores.
- The ABS disables.
- The ABS warning indicator turns on.

Conditions for Clearing the DTC

- The condition responsible for setting the DTC no longer exists and the Scan Tool Clear DTCs function is used.
- 100 drive cycles pass with no DTCs detected. A drive cycle consists of starting the vehicle, driving the vehicle over 16 km/h (10 mph), stopping and then turning the ignition OFF.

Diagnostic Aids

The following conditions may cause an intermittent malfunction:

- A poor connection
- Rubbed-through wire insulation
- A broken wire inside the insulation

Use the enhanced diagnostic function of the Scan Tool in order to measure the frequency of the malfunction.

If the customer's comments reflect that the amber ABS warning indicator is on only during moist environmental changes (rain, snow, vehicle wash), inspect all the wheel speed sensor circuitry for signs of water intrusion. If the DTC is not current, clear all DTCs and simulate the effects of water intrusion by using the following procedure:

1. Spray the suspected area with a five percent saltwater solution.
   Add two teaspoons of salt to twelve ounces of water to make a five percent saltwater solution.
2. Test drive the vehicle over various road surfaces (bumps, turns, etc.) above 24 km/h (15 mph) for at least 30 seconds.
3. If the DTC returns, replace the suspected harness.

Thoroughly inspect any circuitry that may be causing the intermittent complaint for the following conditions:

- Backed out terminals
- Improper mating
- Broken locks
- Improperly formed or damaged terminals
- Poor terminal-to-wiring connections
- Physical damage to the wiring harness

Resistance of the wheel speed sensor will increase with an increase in sensor temperature.

GC4029903849010X

Fig. 96 Code C1223: LH Rear Wheel Speed Sensor Input Signal Is Zero (Part 1 of 4). Cavalier & Sunfire

Use the following procedure when replacing a wheel speed sensor or harness:

1. Inspect the wheel speed sensor terminals and harness connector for corrosion and/or water intrusion.
2. Replace the wheel speed sensor and jumper harness if evidence of corrosion or water intrusion exists.

Test Description

4. This test checks the wheel speed sensor for the proper resistance value.
5. This test ensures that the wheel speed sensor generates the proper voltage.
6. This test checks for a short between the wheel speed sensor high and low circuits.
10. This test determines if a wheel speed sensor circuit could be shorted when the EBCM is connected.

Step	Action	Value(s)	Yes	No
	Important: Zero the J 39200 test leads before making any resistance measurements. **Important:** Difficulty may occur when trying to locate intermittent malfunctions in the wheel speed sensor circuit. Do not disturb any of the electrical connections. Change the electrical connections only when instructed to do so by a step in the diagnostic table. Changing the electrical connections at the correct time will ensure that an intermittent electrical connection will not be corrected until the source of the malfunction is found.			
1	Was the ABS Diagnostic System Check performed?	—	*Go to Step 2*	*Go to A Diagnostic System Check - ABS*
2	1. Turn the ignition switch to the OFF position. 2. Inspect the left rear wheel speed sensor and the left rear wheel speed sensor harness connector for physical damage. Is there any physical damage?	—	*Go to Step 16*	*Go to Step 3*
3	Inspect the following components for physical damage: • The left rear wheel speed sensor jumper harness • The left rear wheel speed sensor jumper harness connectors Is there any physical damage?	—	*Go to Step 15*	*Go to Step 4*
4	1. Disconnect the left rear wheel speed sensor directly at the left rear wheel speed sensor connector. 2. Use the *J 39200* in order to measure the resistance between the left rear wheel speed sensor connector terminal A and the left rear wheel speed sensor connector terminal B. Is the resistance within the specified range?	950–1250 Ω	*Go to Step 5*	*Go to Step 16*
5	1. Select the A/C VOLTAGE scale on the *J 39200*. 2. Spin the left rear wheel by hand while observing the voltage reading on the *J 39200*. Is the voltage equal to or greater than the specified voltage?	100 mV	*Go to Step 6*	*Go to Step 16*
6	1. Disconnect the 24-way EBCM connector C2. 2. Use the *J 39200* in order to measure the resistance between the 24-way EBCM harness connector C2 terminal A3 and the 24-way EBCM harness connector C2 terminal B2. Is the resistance within the specified range?	OL (Infinite)	*Go to Step 7*	*Go to Step 8*

GC4029903849020X

Fig. 96 Code C1223: LH Rear Wheel Speed Sensor Input Signal Is Zero (Part 2 of 4). Cavalier & Sunfire

Step	Action	Value(s)	Yes	No
7	1. Inspect the 24-way EBCM connector C2 for the following conditions: • Damage • Poor terminal contact • Terminal corrosion (These conditions could result in a short between the 24-way EBCM connector C2 terminal A3 and the EBCM connector C2 terminal B2. 2. Inspect the remaining terminals of the 24-way EBCM connector C2 for the following conditions: • Damage • Poor terminal contact • Terminal corrosion Are there signs of poor terminal contact, corrosion, or damaged terminals?	—	*Go to Step 12*	*Go to Step 8*
8	Inspect the wiring of CKT 885 and CKT 884 for signs of damage that may cause a short between CKT 885 and CKT 884. Are there any signs of damaged wiring?	—	*Go to Step 13*	*Go to Step 9*
9	Inspect the harness connectors of CKT 885 and CKT 884 for signs of damage that may cause a short between CKT 885 and CKT 884. Are there any signs of damaged connectors?	—	*Go to Step 14*	*Go to Step 10*
10	1. Reconnect the 24-way EBCM harness connector C2. 2. Reconnect the left rear wheel speed sensor harness connector. 3. Install a *Scan Tool.* 4. Test drive the vehicle at a speed above 24 km/h (15 mph) for at least 30 seconds. 5. Use the *Scan Tool* in order to read the DTCs. Does DTC C1223 set as a current DTC?	—	*Go to Step 11*	*Go to Step 18*
11	1. Select Data Display on the *Scan Tool.* 2. Select ABS Data. 3. Monitor the wheel speed sensor speeds. 4. Drive the vehicle in the following manner: 4.1. Slowly accelerate to 65 km/h (40 mph). 4.2. Slowly decelerate to 0 km/h (0 mph). Is the speed of the left rear wheel speed sensor constantly lower than the speed of the three remaining wheel speed sensors?	—	*Go to Step 16*	*Go to Step 17*
12	Replace all of the terminals that exhibit signs of poor terminal contact, corrosion, or damaged terminal(s). Is the repair complete?	—	Go to *A Diagnostic System Check - ABS*	—
13	Replace the damaged wiring harness that causes the short between CKT 885 and CKT 884. Is the repair complete?	—	Go to *A Diagnostic System Check - ABS*	—
14	Replace the damaged wiring harness connectors that cause the short between CKT 885 and CKT 884. Is the repair complete?	—	Go to *A Diagnostic System Check - ABS*	—
15	Replace the left rear wheel speed sensor jumper harness. Is the repair complete?	—	Go to *A Diagnostic System Check - ABS*	—

GC4029903849030X

Fig. 96 Code C1223: LH Rear Wheel Speed Sensor Input Signal Is Zero (Part 3 of 4). Cavalier & Sunfire

Circuit Description

As a toothed ring passes by the wheel speed sensor, changes in the electromagnetic field cause the wheel speed sensor to produce an AC voltage signal. The frequency of the AC voltage signal is proportional to the wheel speed. The amplitude of the AC voltage signal is directly related to wheel speed and the proximity of the wheel speed sensor to the toothed ring. The proximity of the wheel speed sensor to the toothed ring is also referred to as the air gap.

Conditions for Setting the DTC

DTC C1224 can set when the vehicle is not in an ABS stop.

A malfunction exists if both of the following conditions occur:

- The right rear wheel speed sensor input signal equals zero.
- The vehicle's reference speed is greater than 8 km/h (5 mph)

Action Taken When the DTC Sets

- A malfunction DTC stores.
- The ABS disables.
- The ABS warning indicator turns on.

Conditions for Clearing the DTC

- The condition responsible for setting the DTC no longer exists and the Scan Tool Clear DTCs function is used.
- 100 drive cycles pass with no DTCs detected. A drive cycle consists of starting the vehicle, driving the vehicle over 16 km/h (10 mph), stopping and then turning the ignition OFF.

Diagnostic Aids

The following conditions may cause an intermittent malfunction:

- A poor connection
- Rubbed-through wire insulation
- A broken wire inside the insulation

Use the enhanced diagnostic function of the Scan Tool in order to measure the frequency of the malfunction.

If the customer's comments reflect that the amber ABS warning indicator is on only during moist environmental changes (rain, snow, vehicle wash), inspect all the wheel speed sensor circuitry for signs of water intrusion. If the DTC is not current, clear all DTCs and simulate the effects of water intrusion by using the following procedure:

1. Spray the suspected area with a five percent saltwater solution.
   Add two teaspoons of salt to twelve ounces of water to make a five percent saltwater solution.
2. Test drive the vehicle over various road surfaces (bumps, turns, etc.) above 24 km/h (15 mph) for at least 30 seconds.
3. If the DTC returns, replace the suspected harness.

Thoroughly inspect any circuitry that may be causing the intermittent complaint for the following conditions:

- Backed out terminals
- Improper mating
- Broken locks
- Improperly formed or damaged terminals
- Poor terminal-to-wiring connections
- Physical damage to the wiring harness

Resistance of the wheel speed sensor will increase with an increase in sensor temperature.

GC4029903850010X

Fig. 97 Code C1224: RH Rear Wheel Speed Sensor Input Signal Is Zero (Part 1 of 4). Cavalier & Sunfire

Step	Action	Value(s)	Yes	No
16	Replace the left rear wheel speed sensor. Is the repair complete?	—	Go to *A Diagnostic System Check - ABS*	—
17	Replace the EBCM. Is the repair complete?	—	Go to *A Diagnostic System Check - ABS*	—
18	The malfunction is intermittent or is not present at this time. Refer to Diagnostic Aids for more information. Is the action complete?	—	System OK	—

GC4029903849040X

Fig. 96 Code C1223: LH Rear Wheel Speed Sensor Input Signal Is Zero (Part 4 of 4). Cavalier & Sunfire

Use the following procedure when replacing a wheel speed sensor or harness:

1. Inspect the wheel speed sensor terminals and harness connector for corrosion and/or water intrusion.
2. Replace the wheel speed sensor and jumper harness if evidence of corrosion or water intrusion exists.

Test Description

4. This test checks the wheel speed sensor for the proper resistance value.
5. This test ensures that the wheel speed sensor generates the proper voltage.
6. This test checks for a short between the wheel speed sensor high and low circuits.
10. This test determines if a wheel speed sensor circuit could be shorted when the EBCM is connected.

Step	Action	Value(s)	Yes	No
	Important: Zero the J 39200 test leads before making any resistance measurements. **Important:** Difficulty may occur in trying to locate intermittent malfunctions in the wheel speed sensor circuit. Do not disturb any of the electrical connections. Change electrical connections only when instructed to do so by a step in the diagnostic table. Changing electrical connections at the correct time will ensure that an intermittent electrical connection will not be corrected until the source of the malfunction is found.			
1	Was the ABS Diagnostic System Check performed?	—	*Go to Step 2*	Go to *A Diagnostic System Check - ABS*
2	1. Turn the ignition switch to the OFF position. 2. Inspect the right rear wheel speed sensor and the right rear wheel speed sensor harness connector for physical damage. Is there any physical damage?	—	*Go to Step 16*	*Go to Step 3*
3	Inspect the following components for physical damage: • The right rear wheel speed sensor jumper harness • The right rear wheel speed sensor jumper harness connectors Is there any physical damage?	—	*Go to Step 15*	*Go to Step 4*
4	1. Disconnect the right rear wheel speed sensor directly at the right rear wheel speed sensor connector. 2. Use the *J 39200* in order to measure the resistance between the right rear wheel speed sensor connector terminal A and the right rear wheel speed sensor connector terminal B. Is the resistance within the specified range?	950–1250 Ω	*Go to Step 5*	*Go to Step 16*
5	1. Select the A/C VOLTAGE scale on the *J 39200.* 2. Spin the right rear wheel by hand while observing the voltage reading on the *J 39200.* Is the voltage equal to or greater than the specified voltage?	100 mV	*Go to Step 6*	*Go to Step 16*
6	1. Disconnect the 24-way EBCM connector C2. 2. Use the *J 39200* in order to measure the resistance between the 24-way EBCM harness connector C2 terminal A2 and the 24-way EBCM harness connector C2 terminal B1. Is the resistance within the specified range?	OL (Infinite)	*Go to Step 7*	*Go to Step 8*

GC4029903850020X

Fig. 97 Code C1224: RH Rear Wheel Speed Sensor Input Signal Is Zero (Part 2 of 4). Cavalier & Sunfire

Step	Action	Value(s)	Yes	No
7	1. Inspect the 24-way EBCM connector C2 for the following conditions: • Damage • Poor terminal contact • Terminal corrosion Damage, poor terminal contact, and terminal corrosion may cause a short between the 24-way EBCM connector C2 terminal A2 and the EBCM connector C2 terminal B1. 2. Inspect the remaining terminals of the 24-way EBCM connector C2 for the following conditions: • Damage • Poor terminal contact • Terminal corrosion Are there signs of poor terminal contact, corrosion, or damaged terminals?	—	*Go to Step 12*	*Go to Step 8*
8	Inspect the wiring of CKT 883 and CKT 882 for signs of damage that may cause a short between CKT 883 and CKT 882. Are there any signs of damaged wiring?	—	*Go to Step 13*	*Go to Step 9*
9	Inspect the harness connectors of CKT 883 and CKT 882 for signs of damage that may cause a short between CKT 883 and CKT 882. Are there any signs of damaged connectors?	—	*Go to Step 14*	*Go to Step 10*
10	1. Reconnect the 24-way EBCM harness connector C2. 2. Reconnect the right rear wheel speed sensor harness connector. 3. Install a *Scan Tool*. 4. Test drive the vehicle at a speed above 24 km/h (15 mph) for at least 30 seconds. 5. Use the *Scan Tool* in order to read the DTCs. Does DTC C1224 set as a current DTC?	—	*Go to Step 11*	*Go to Step 18*
11	1. Select Data Display on the *Scan Tool*. 2. Select ABS Data. 3. Monitor the wheel speed sensor speeds. 4. Drive the vehicle in the following manner: 4.1. Slowly accelerate to 65 km/h (40 mph). 4.2. Slowly decelerate to 0 km/h (0 mph). Is the speed of the right rear wheel speed sensor constantly lower than the speed of the three remaining wheel speed sensors?	—	*Go to Step 16*	*Go to Step 17*
12	Replace all of the terminals that exhibit signs of poor terminal contact, corrosion, or damaged terminal(s). Is the repair complete?	—	Go to *A Diagnostic System Check - ABS*	—
13	Replace the damaged wiring harness that causes the short between CKT 883 and CKT 882. Is the repair complete?	—	Go to *A Diagnostic System Check - ABS*	—
14	Replace the damaged wiring harness connectors that cause the short between CKT 883 and CKT 882. Is the repair complete?	—	Go to *A Diagnostic System Check - ABS*	—

GC4029903850030X

Fig. 97 Code C1224: RH Rear Wheel Speed Sensor Input Signal Is Zero (Part 3 of 4). Cavalier & Sunfire

Circuit Description

As a toothed ring passes by the wheel speed sensor, changes in the electromagnetic field cause the wheel speed sensor to produce an AC voltage signal. The frequency of the AC voltage signal is proportional to the wheel speed. The amplitude of the AC voltage signal is directly related to wheel speed and the proximity of the wheel speed sensor to the toothed ring. The proximity of the wheel speed sensor to the toothed ring is also referred to as the air gap.

Conditions for Setting the DTC

DTC C1225 can set when the brake is off.

DTC C1225 detects a situation in which the left front wheel acceleration or deceleration is beyond specified limits.

Action Taken When the DTC Sets

- A malfunction DTC stores.
- The ABS disables.
- The ABS warning indicator turns on.

Conditions for Clearing the DTC

- The condition responsible for setting the DTC no longer exists and the Scan Tool Clear DTCs function is used.
- 100 drive cycles pass with no DTCs detected. A drive cycle consists of starting the vehicle, driving the vehicle over 16 km/h (10 mph), stopping and then turning the ignition OFF.

Diagnostic Aids

The following conditions may cause an intermittent malfunction:

- A poor connection
- Rubbed-through wire insulation
- A broken wire inside the insulation

Use the enhanced diagnostic function of the Scan Tool in order to measure the frequency of the malfunction.

If the customer's comments reflect that the amber ABS warning indicator is on only during moist environmental changes (rain, snow, vehicle wash), inspect all the wheel speed sensor circuitry for signs of water intrusion. If the DTC is not current, clear all DTCs and simulate the effects of water intrusion by using the following procedure:

1. Spray the suspected area with a five percent saltwater solution.
   Add two teaspoons of salt to twelve ounces of water to make a five percent saltwater solution.
2. Test drive the vehicle over various road surfaces (bumps, turns, etc.) above 24 km/h (15 mph) for at least 30 seconds.
3. If the DTC returns, replace the suspected harness.

Thoroughly inspect any circuitry that may be causing the intermittent complaint for the following conditions:

- Backed out terminals
- Improper mating
- Broken locks
- Improperly formed or damaged terminals
- Poor terminal-to-wiring connections
- Physical damage to the wiring harness

GC402980308900AX

Fig. 98 Code C1225: LH Front Excessive Wheel Speed Variation (Part 1 of 4). Cavalier & Sunfire

Step	Action	Value(s)	Yes	No
15	Replace the right rear wheel speed sensor jumper harness. Is the repair complete?	—	Go to *A Diagnostic System Check - ABS*	—
16	Replace the right rear wheel speed sensor. Is the repair complete?	—	Go to *A Diagnostic System Check - ABS*	—
17	Replace the EBCM. Is the repair complete?	—	Go to *A Diagnostic System Check - ABS*	—
18	The malfunction is intermittent or is not present at this time. Refer to Diagnostic Aids for more information. Is the action complete?	—	System OK	—

GC4029903850040X

Fig. 97 Code C1224: RH Rear Wheel Speed Sensor Input Signal Is Zero (Part 4 of 4). Cavalier & Sunfire

Step	Action	Value(s)	Yes	No
1	Was the Diagnostic System Check performed?	—	*Go to Step 2*	Refer to *Diagnostic System Check*
2	1. Turn the ignition switch to the OFF position. 2. Inspect the left front wheel speed sensor and the left front wheel speed sensor harness connector for physical damage. Is there any physical damage?	—	*Go to Step 16*	*Go to Step 3*
3	Inspect the following components for physical damage: • The left front wheel speed sensor jumper harness • The left front wheel speed sensor jumper harness connectors Is there any physical damage?	—	*Go to Step 15*	*Go to Step 4*
4	1. Disconnect the left front wheel speed sensor directly at the left front wheel speed sensor connector. 2. Use the *J 39200* in order to measure the resistance between the left front wheel speed sensor connector terminal A and the left front wheel speed sensor connector terminal B. Is the resistance within the specified range?	1530–1870 Ω	*Go to Step 5*	*Go to Step 16*
5	1. Select the A/C VOLTAGE scale on the *J 39200*. 2. Spin the left front wheel by hand while observing the voltage reading on the *J 39200*. Is the voltage equal to or greater than the specified voltage?	100 mV	*Go to Step 6*	*Go to Step 16*
6	1. Disconnect the 24-way EBCM connector C2. 2. Use the *J 39200* in order to measure the resistance between the 24-way EBCM connector C2 terminal A5 and the 24-way EBCM connector C2 terminal B4. Is the resistance within the specified range?	OL (Infinite)	*Go to Step 7*	*Go to Step 8*

GC402980308900BX

Fig. 98 Code C1225: LH Front Excessive Wheel Speed Variation (Part 2 of 4). Cavalier & Sunfire

Step	Action	Value(s)	Yes	No
7	1. Inspect the 24-way EBCM connector C2 for the following conditions: • Damage • Poor terminal contact • Terminal corrosion (These conditions could result in a short between the 24-way EBCM connector C2 terminal A5 and the EBCM connector C2 terminal B4.) 2. Inspect the remaining terminals of the 24-way EBCM connector C2 for the following conditions: • Damage • Poor terminal contact • Terminal corrosion Are there signs of poor terminal contact, corrosion, or damaged terminals?	—	*Go to Step 12*	*Go to Step 8*
8	Inspect the wiring of CKT 873 and CKT 830 for signs of damage that may cause a short between CKT 873 and CKT 830. Are there any signs of damaged wiring?	—	*Go to Step 13*	*Go to Step 9*
9	Inspect the harness connectors of CKT 873 and CKT 830 for signs of damage that may cause a short between CKT 873 and CKT 830. Are there any signs of damaged connectors?	—	*Go to Step 14*	*Go to Step 10*
10	1. Reconnect the 24-way EBCM harness connector C2. 2. Reconnect the left front wheel speed sensor harness connector. 3. Install a *Scan Tool*. 4. Test drive the vehicle at a speed above 24 km/h (15 mph) for at least 30 seconds. 5. Use the *Scan Tool* in order to read the DTCs. Does DTC C1225 set as a current DTC?	—	*Go to Step 11*	*Go to Step 18*
11	1. Select Data List on the *Scan Tool*. 2. Monitor the wheel speed sensor speeds. 3. Drive the vehicle in the following manner: 3.1. Slowly accelerate to 65 km/h (40 mph). 3.2. Slowly decelerate to 0 km/h (0 mph). Is the speed of the left front wheel speed sensor constantly higher than the speed of the three remaining wheel speed sensors?	—	*Go to Step 16*	*Go to Step 17*
12	Replace all of the terminals that exhibit signs of poor terminal contact, corrosion, or damaged terminal(s). Is the repair complete?	—	Refer to *Diagnostic System Check*	—
13	Replace the damaged wiring harness that causes the short between CKT 873 and CKT 830. Is the repair complete?	—	Refer to *Diagnostic System Check*	—

GC402980308900CX

Fig. 98 Code C1225: LH Front Excessive Wheel Speed Variation (Part 3 of 4). Cavalier & Sunfire

Step	Action	Value(s)	Yes	No
14	Replace the damaged wiring harness connectors that cause the short between CKT 873 and CKT 830. Is the repair complete?	—	Refer to *Diagnostic System Check*	—
15	Replace the left front wheel speed sensor harness. Is the repair complete?	—	Refer to *Diagnostic System Check*	—
16	Replace the left front wheel speed sensor. Is the repair complete?	—	Refer to *Diagnostic System Check*	—
17	Replace the EBCM. Is the repair complete?	—	Refer to *Diagnostic System Check*	—
18	The malfunction is intermittent or is not present at this time. Refer to Diagnostic Aids for more information.	—	—	—

GC402980308900DX

Fig. 98 Code C1225: LH Front Excessive Wheel Speed Variation (Part 4 of 4). Cavalier & Sunfire

Resistance of the wheel speed sensor will increase with an increase in sensor temperature.

Use the following procedure when replacing a wheel speed sensor or harness:

1. Inspect the wheel speed sensor terminals and harness connector for corrosion and/or water intrusion.
2. Replace the wheel speed sensor and jumper harness if evidence of corrosion or water intrusion exists.

Important: Zero the J 39200 test leads before making any resistance measurements. Refer to the J 39200 user's manual.

Important: Difficulty may occur when trying to locate intermittent malfunctions in the wheel speed sensor circuit.

Do not disturb any of the electrical connections. Change the electrical connections only when instructed to do so by a step in the diagnostic table.

Changing the electrical connections at the correct time will ensure that an intermittent electrical connection will not be corrected until the source of the malfunction is found.

Step	Action	Value(s)	Yes	No
1	Was the Diagnostic System Check performed?	—	*Go to Step 2*	Refer to *Diagnostic System Check*
2	1. Turn the ignition switch to the OFF position. 2. Inspect the right front wheel speed sensor and the right front wheel speed sensor harness connector for physical damage. Is there any physical damage?	—	*Go to Step 16*	*Go to Step 3*
3	Inspect the following components for physical damage: • The right front wheel speed sensor jumper harness • The right front wheel speed sensor jumper harness connectors Is there any physical damage?	—	*Go to Step 15*	*Go to Step 4*
4	1. Disconnect the right front wheel speed sensor directly at the right front wheel speed sensor connector. 2. Use the *J 39200* in order to measure the resistance between the right front wheel speed sensor connector terminal A and the right front wheel speed sensor connector terminal B. Is the resistance within the specified range?	1530–1870 Ω	*Go to Step 5*	*Go to Step 16*
5	1. Select the A/C VOLTAGE scale on the *J 39200*. 2. Spin the right front wheel by hand while observing the voltage reading on the *J 39200*. Is the voltage equal to or greater than the specified voltage?	100 mV	*Go to Step 6*	*Go to Step 16*
6	1. Disconnect the 24-way EBCM connector C2. 2. Use the *J 39200* in order to measure the resistance between the 24-way EBCM connector C2 terminal A4 and the 24-way EBCM connector C2 terminal B3. Is the resistance within the specified range?	OL (Infinite)	*Go to Step 7*	*Go to Step 8*

GC402980309000BX

Fig. 99 Code C1226: RH Front Excessive Wheel Speed Variation (Part 2 of 4). Cavalier & Sunfire

Circuit Description

As a toothed ring passes by the wheel speed sensor, changes in the electromagnetic field cause the wheel speed sensor to produce an AC voltage signal. The frequency of the AC voltage signal is proportional to the wheel speed. The amplitude of the AC voltage signal is directly related to wheel speed and the proximity of the wheel speed sensor to the toothed ring. The proximity of the wheel speed sensor to the toothed ring is also referred to as the air gap.

Conditions for Setting the DTC

DTC C1226 can set when the brake is off.

DTC C1226 detects a situation in which the right front wheel acceleration or deceleration is beyond specified limits.

Action Taken When the DTC Sets

- A malfunction DTC stores.
- The ABS disables.
- The ABS warning indicator turns on.

Conditions for Clearing the DTC

- The condition responsible for setting the DTC no longer exists and the Scan Tool Clear DTCs function is used.
- 100 drive cycles pass with no DTCs detected. A drive cycle consists of starting the vehicle, driving the vehicle over 16 km/h (10 mph), stopping and then turning the ignition off.

Diagnostic Aids

The following conditions may cause an intermittent malfunction:

- A poor connection
- Rubbed-through wire insulation
- A broken wire inside the insulation

Use the enhanced diagnostic function of the Scan Tool in order to measure the frequency of the malfunction.

If the customer's comments reflect that the amber ABS warning indicator is on only during moist environmental changes (rain, snow, vehicle wash), inspect all the wheel speed sensor circuitry for signs of water intrusion. If the DTC is not current, clear all DTCs and simulate the effects of water intrusion by using the following procedure:

1. Spray the suspected area with a five percent saltwater solution.
   Add two teaspoons of salt to twelve ounces of water to make a five percent saltwater solution.
2. Test drive the vehicle over various road surfaces (bumps, turns, etc.) above 24 km/h (15 mph) for at least 30 seconds.
3. If the DTC returns, replace the suspected harness.

Thoroughly inspect any circuitry that may be causing the intermittent complaint for the following conditions:

- Backed out terminals
- Improper mating
- Broken locks
- Improperly formed or damaged terminals
- Poor terminal-to-wiring connections
- Physical damage to the wiring harness

GC402980309000AX

Fig. 99 Code C1226: RH Front Excessive Wheel Speed Variation (Part 1 of 4). Cavalier & Sunfire

Step	Action	Value(s)	Yes	No
7	1. Inspect the 24-way EBCM connector C2 for the following conditions: • Damage • Poor terminal contact • Terminal corrosion (These conditions may cause a short between the 24-way EBCM connector C2 terminal A4 and the EBCM connector C2 terminal B3). 2. Inspect the remaining terminals of the 24-way EBCM connector C2 for the following conditions: • Damage • Poor terminal contact • Terminal corrosion Are there signs of poor terminal contact, corrosion, or damaged terminals?	—	*Go to Step 12*	*Go to Step 8*
8	Inspect the wiring of CKT 872 and CKT 833 for signs of damage that may cause a short between CKT 872 and CKT 833. Are there any signs of damaged wiring?	—	*Go to Step 13*	*Go to Step 9*
9	Inspect the harness connectors of CKT 872 and CKT 833 for signs of damage that may cause a short between CKT 872 and CKT 833. Are there any signs of damaged connectors?	—	*Go to Step 14*	*Go to Step 10*
10	1. Reconnect the 24-way EBCM harness connector C2. 2. Reconnect the right front wheel speed sensor harness connector. 3. Install a *Scan Tool*. 4. Test drive the vehicle at a speed above 24 km/h (15 mph) for at least 30 seconds. 5. Use the *Scan Tool* in order to read the DTCs. Does DTC C1226 set as a current DTC?	—	*Go to Step 11*	*Go to Step 18*
11	1. Select the Data List on the *Scan Tool*. 2. Monitor the wheel speed sensor speeds. 3. Use the following procedure to drive the vehicle when testing the wheel speed sensor: 3.1. Slowly accelerate to 65 km/h (40 mph). 3.2. Slowly decelerate to 0 km/h (0 mph). Is the speed of the right front wheel speed sensor constantly higher than the speed of the three remaining wheel speed sensors?	—	*Go to Step 16*	*Go to Step 17*
12	Replace all of the terminals that exhibit signs of poor terminal contact, corrosion, or damaged terminal(s). Is the repair complete?	—	Refer to *Diagnostic System Check*	—
13	Replace the damaged wiring harness that causes the short between CKT 872 and CKT 833. Is the repair complete?	—	Refer to *Diagnostic System Check*	—

GC402980309000CX

Fig. 99 Code C1226: RH Front Excessive Wheel Speed Variation (Part 3 of 4). Cavalier & Sunfire

Step	Action	Value(s)	Yes	No
14	Replace the damaged wiring harness connectors that cause the short between CKT 872 and CKT 833. Is the repair complete?	—	Refer to *Diagnostic System Check*	—
15	Replace the right front wheel speed sensor harness. Is the repair complete?	—	Refer to *Diagnostic System Check*	—
16	Replace the right front wheel speed sensor. Is the repair complete?	—	Refer to *Diagnostic System Check*	—
17	Replace the EBCM. Is the repair complete?	—	Refer to *Diagnostic System Check*	—
18	The malfunction is intermittent or is not present at this time. Refer to Diagnostic Aids for more information.	—	—	—

GC402980309000DX

Fig. 99 Code C1226: RH Front Excessive Wheel Speed Variation (Part 4 of 4). Cavalier & Sunfire

Circuit Description

As a toothed ring passes by the wheel speed sensor, changes in the electromagnetic field cause the wheel speed sensor to produce an AC voltage signal. The frequency of the AC voltage signal is proportional to the wheel speed. The amplitude of the AC voltage signal is directly related to wheel speed and the proximity of the wheel speed sensor to the toothed ring. The proximity of the wheel speed sensor to the toothed ring is also referred to as the air gap.

Conditions for Setting the DTC

DTC C1227 can set when the brake is off.

DTC C1227 detects a situation in which the left rear wheel acceleration or deceleration is beyond specified limits.

Action Taken When the DTC Sets

- A malfunction DTC stores.
- The ABS disables.
- The ABS warning indicator turns on.

Conditions for Clearing the DTC

- The condition responsible for setting the DTC no longer exists and the Scan Tool Clear DTCs function is used.
- 100 drive cycles pass with no DTCs detected. A drive cycle consists of starting the vehicle, driving the vehicle over 16 km/h (10 mph), stopping and then turning the ignition off.

Diagnostic Aids

The following conditions may cause an intermittent malfunction:

- A poor connection
- Rubbed-through wire insulation
- A broken wire inside the insulation

Use the enhanced diagnostic function of the Scan Tool in order to measure the frequency of the malfunction.

If the customer's comments reflect that the amber ABS warning indicator is on only during moist environmental changes (rain, snow, vehicle wash), inspect all the wheel speed sensor circuitry for signs of water intrusion. If the DTC is not current, clear all DTCs and simulate the effects of water intrusion by using the following procedure:

1. Spray the suspected area with a five percent saltwater solution.

   Add two teaspoons of salt to twelve ounces of water to make a five percent saltwater solution.
2. Test drive the vehicle over various road surfaces (bumps, turns, etc.) above 24 km/h (15 mph) for at least 30 seconds.
3. If the DTC returns, replace the suspected harness.

Thoroughly inspect any circuitry that may be causing the intermittent complaint for the following conditions:

- Backed out terminals
- Improper mating
- Broken locks
- Improperly formed or damaged terminals
- Poor terminal-to-wiring connections
- Physical damage to the wiring harness

Resistance of the wheel speed sensor will increase with an increase in sensor temperature.

Use the following procedure when replacing a wheel speed sensor or harness:

1. Inspect the wheel speed sensor terminals and harness connector for corrosion and/or water intrusion.
2. Replace the wheel speed sensor jumper harness if evidence of corrosion or water intrusion exists.

GC4029903851010X

Fig. 100 Code C1227: LH Rear Excessive Wheel Speed Variation (Part 1 of 3). Cavalier & Sunfire

Test Description

4. This test checks the wheel speed sensor for the proper resistance value.
5. This test ensures that the wheel speed sensor generates the proper voltage.
6. This test checks for a short between the wheel speed sensor high and low circuits.
10. This test determines if a wheel speed sensor circuit could be shorted when the EBCM is connected.

Step	Action	Value(s)	Yes	No
	Important: Zero the J 39200 test leads before making any resistance measurements. **Important:** Difficulty may occur when trying to locate intermittent malfunctions in the wheel speed sensor circuit. Do not disturb any of the electrical connections. Change the electrical connections only when instructed to do so by a step in the diagnostic table. Changing the electrical connections at the correct time will ensure that an intermittent electrical connection will not be corrected until the source of the malfunction is found.			
1	Was the ABS Diagnostic System Check performed?	—	*Go to Step 2*	*Go to A Diagnostic System Check - ABS*
2	1. Turn the ignition switch to the OFF position. 2. Inspect the left rear wheel speed sensor and the left rear wheel speed sensor harness connector for physical damage. Is there any physical damage?	—	*Go to Step 16*	*Go to Step 3*
3	Inspect the following components for physical damage: • The left rear wheel speed sensor harness • The left rear wheel speed sensor harness connectors Is there any physical damage?	—	*Go to Step 15*	*Go to Step 4*
4	1. Disconnect the left rear wheel speed sensor directly at the left rear wheel speed sensor connector. 2. Use the *J 39200* in order to measure the resistance between the left rear wheel speed sensor connector terminal A and the left rear wheel speed sensor connector terminal B. Is the resistance within the specified range?	950–1250 Ω	*Go to Step 5*	*Go to Step 16*
5	1. Select the A/C VOLTAGE scale on the *J 39200*. 2. Spin the left rear wheel by hand while observing the voltage reading on the *J 39200*. Is the voltage equal to or greater than the specified voltage?	100 mV	*Go to Step 6*	*Go to Step 16*
6	1. Disconnect the 24-way EBCM connector C2. 2. Use the *J 39200* in order to measure the resistance between the 24-way EBCM harness connector C2 terminal A3 and the 24-way EBCM harness connector C2 terminal B2. Is the resistance within the specified range?	OL (Infinite)	*Go to Step 7*	*Go to Step 8*
7	1. Inspect the 24-way EBCM connector C2 for the following conditions: • Damage • Poor terminal contact • Terminal corrosion Damage, poor terminal contact, and terminal corrosion may cause a short between the 24-way EBCM harness connector C2 terminal A3 and the EBCM harness connector C2 terminal B2. 2. Inspect the remaining terminals of the 24-way EBCM harness connector C2 for the following conditions: • Damage • Poor terminal contact • Terminal corrosion Are there signs of poor terminal contact, corrosion, or damaged terminals?	—	*Go to Step 12*	*Go to Step 8*

GC4029903851020X

Fig. 100 Code C1227: LH Rear Excessive Wheel Speed Variation (Part 2 of 3). Cavalier & Sunfire

Step	Action	Value(s)	Yes	No
8	Inspect the wiring of CKT 885 and CKT 884 for signs of damage that may cause a short between CKT 885 and CKT 884. Are there any signs of damaged wiring?	—	*Go to Step 13*	*Go to Step 9*
9	Inspect the harness connectors of CKT 885 and CKT 884 for signs of damage that may cause a short between CKT 885 and CKT 884. Are there any signs of damaged connectors?	—	*Go to Step 14*	*Go to Step 10*
10	1. Reconnect the 24-way EBCM harness connector C2. 2. Reconnect the left rear wheel speed sensor harness connector. 3. Install a *Scan Tool*. 4. Test drive the vehicle at a speed above 24 km/h (15 mph) for at least 30 seconds. 5. Use the *Scan Tool* in order to read the DTCs. Does DTC C1227 set as a current DTC?	—	*Go to Step 11*	*Go to Step 18*
11	1. Select Data Display on the *Scan Tool*. 2. Select ABS Data. 3. Monitor the wheel speed sensor speeds. 4. Use the following procedure to drive the vehicle when testing the wheel speed sensor: 4.1. Slowly accelerate to 65 km/h (40 mph). 4.2. Slowly decelerate to 0 km/h (0 mph). Is the speed of the left rear wheel speed sensor constantly higher or lower than the speed of the three remaining wheel speed sensors?	—	*Go to Step 16*	*Go to Step 17*
12	Replace all of the terminals that exhibit signs of poor terminal contact, corrosion, or damaged terminal(s). Is the repair complete?	—	*Go to A Diagnostic System Check - ABS*	—
13	Replace the damaged wiring harness that causes the short between CKT 885 and CKT 884. Is the repair complete?	—	*Go to A Diagnostic System Check - ABS*	—
14	Replace the damaged wiring harness connectors that cause the short between CKT 885 and CKT 884. Is the repair complete?	—	*Go to A Diagnostic System Check - ABS*	—
15	Replace the left rear wheel speed sensor harness. Is the repair complete?	—	*Go to A Diagnostic System Check - ABS*	—
16	Replace the left rear wheel speed sensor. Is the repair complete?	—	*Go to A Diagnostic System Check - ABS*	—
17	Replace the EBCM. Is the repair complete?	—	*Go to A Diagnostic System Check - ABS*	—
18	The malfunction is intermittent or is not present at this time. Refer to Diagnostic Aids for more information. Is the action complete?	—	System OK	—

GC4029903851030X

Fig. 100 Code C1227: LH Rear Excessive Wheel Speed Variation (Part 3 of 3). Cavalier & Sunfire

Circuit Description

As a toothed ring passes by the wheel speed sensor, changes in the electromagnetic field cause the wheel speed sensor to produce an AC voltage signal. The frequency of the AC voltage signal is proportional to the wheel speed. The amplitude of the AC voltage signal is directly related to wheel speed and the proximity of the wheel speed sensor to the toothed ring. The proximity of the wheel speed sensor to the toothed ring is also referred to as the air gap.

Conditions for Setting the DTC

DTC C1228 can set when the brake is off.

DTC C1228 detects a situation in which the right rear wheel acceleration or deceleration is beyond specified limits.

Action Taken When the DTC Sets

- A malfunction DTC stores.
- The ABS disables.
- The ABS warning indicator turns on.

Conditions for Clearing the DTC

- The condition responsible for setting the DTC no longer exists and the Scan Tool Clear DTCs function is used.
- 100 drive cycles pass with no DTCs detected. A drive cycle consists of starting the vehicle, driving the vehicle over 16 km/h (10 mph), stopping and then turning the ignition off.

Diagnostic Aids

The following conditions may cause an intermittent malfunction:

- A poor connection
- Rubbed-through wire insulation
- A broken wire inside the insulation

Use the enhanced diagnostic function of the Scan Tool in order to measure the frequency of the malfunction.

If the customer's comments reflect that the amber ABS warning indicator is on only during moist environmental changes (rain, snow, vehicle wash), inspect all the wheel speed sensor circuitry for signs of water intrusion. If the DTC is not current, clear all DTCs and simulate the effects of water intrusion by using the following procedure:

1. Spray the suspected area with a five percent saltwater solution.

   Add two teaspoons of salt to twelve ounces of water to make a five percent saltwater solution.
2. Test drive the vehicle over various road surfaces (bumps, turns, etc.) above 24 km/h (15 mph) for at least 30 seconds.
3. If the DTC returns, replace the suspected harness.

Thoroughly inspect any circuitry that may be causing the intermittent complaint for the following conditions:

- Backed out terminals
- Improper mating
- Broken locks
- Improperly formed or damaged terminals
- Poor terminal-to-wiring connections
- Physical damage to the wiring harness

Resistance of the wheel speed sensor will increase with an increase in sensor temperature.

Use the following procedure when replacing a wheel speed sensor or harness:

1. Inspect the wheel speed sensor terminals and harness connector for corrosion and/or water intrusion.
2. Replace the wheel speed sensor and jumper harness if evidence of corrosion or water intrusion exists.

GC4029903852010X

Fig. 101 Code C1228: RH Rear Excessive Wheel Speed Variation (Part 1 of 3). Cavalier & Sunfire

Test Description

4. This test checks the wheel speed sensor for the proper resistance value.
5. This test ensures that the wheel speed sensor generates the proper voltage.
6. This test checks for a short between the wheel speed sensor high and low circuits.
10. This test determines if a wheel speed sensor circuit could be shorted when the EBCM is connected.

Step	Action	Value(s)	Yes	No
	Important: Zero the J 39200 test leads before making any resistance measurements. **Important:** Difficulty may occur when trying to locate intermittent malfunctions in the wheel speed sensor circuit. Do not disturb any of the electrical connections. Change the electrical connections only when instructed to do so by a step in the diagnostic table. Changing the electrical connections at the correct time will ensure that an intermittent electrical connection will not be corrected until the source of the malfunction is found.			
1	Was the ABS Diagnostic System Check performed?	—	*Go to Step 2*	*Go to A Diagnostic System Check - ABS*
2	1. Turn the ignition switch to the OFF position. 2. Inspect the right rear wheel speed sensor and the rear axle harness connector for physical damage. Is there any physical damage?	—	*Go to Step 16*	*Go to Step 3*
3	Inspect the following components for physical damage: • The rear axle harness • The rear axle harness connectors Is there any physical damage?	—	*Go to Step 15*	*Go to Step 4*
4	1. Disconnect the right rear wheel speed sensor directly at the right rear wheel speed sensor connector. 2. Use the *J 39200* in order to measure the resistance between the right rear wheel speed sensor connector terminal A and the right rear wheel speed sensor connector terminal B. Is the resistance within the specified range?	950–1250 Ω	*Go to Step 5*	*Go to Step 16*
5	1. Select the A/C VOLTAGE scale on the *J 39200.* 2. Spin the right rear wheel by hand while observing the voltage reading on the *J 39200.* Is the voltage equal to or greater than the specified voltage?	100 mV	*Go to Step 6*	*Go to Step 16*
6	1. Disconnect the 24-way EBCM connector C2. 2. Use the *J 39200* in order to measure the resistance between the 24-way EBCM harness connector C2 terminal A2 and the 24-way EBCM harness connector C2 terminal B1. Is the resistance within the specified range?	OL (Infinite)	*Go to Step 7*	*Go to Step 8*
7	1. Inspect the 24-way EBCM harness connector C2 for the following conditions: • Damage • Poor terminal contact • Terminal corrosion Damage, poor terminal contact may cause a short between the 24-way EBCM harness connector C2 terminal A2 and the EBCM harness connector C2 terminal B1. 2. Inspect the remaining terminals of the 24-way EBCM harness connector C2 for the following conditions: • Damage • Poor terminal contact • Terminal corrosion Are there signs of poor terminal contact, corrosion, or damaged terminals?	—	*Go to Step 12*	*Go to Step 8*

GC4029903852020X

Fig. 101 Code C1228: RH Rear Excessive Wheel Speed Variation (Part 2 of 3). Cavalier & Sunfire

Step	Action	Value(s)	Yes	No
8	Inspect the wiring of CKT 883 and CKT 882 for signs of damage that may cause a short between CKT 883 and CKT 882. Are there any signs of damaged wiring?	—	*Go to Step 13*	*Go to Step 9*
9	Inspect the harness connectors of CKT 883 and CKT 882 for signs of damage that may cause a short between CKT 883 and CKT 882. Are there any signs of damaged connectors?	—	*Go to Step 14*	*Go to Step 10*
10	1. Reconnect the 24-way EBCM harness connector C2. 2. Reconnect the right rear wheel speed sensor harness connector. 3. Install a *Scan Tool.* 4. Test drive the vehicle at a speed above 24 km/h (15 mph) for at least 30 seconds. 5. Use the *Scan Tool* in order to read the DTCs. Does DTC C1228 set as a current DTC?	—	*Go to Step 11*	*Go to Step 18*
11	1. Select Data Display on the *Scan Tool.* 2. Select ABS Data. 3. Monitor the wheel speed sensor speeds. 4. Use the following procedure to drive the vehicle when testing the wheel speed sensor: 4.1. Slowly accelerate to 65 km/h (40 mph). 4.2. Slowly decelerate to 0 km/h (0 mph). Is the speed of the right rear wheel speed sensor constantly higher or lower than the speed of the three remaining wheel speed sensors?	—	*Go to Step 16*	*Go to Step 17*
12	Replace all of the terminals that exhibit signs of poor terminal contact, corrosion, or damaged terminal(s). Is the repair complete?	—	Go to *A Diagnostic System Check - ABS*	—
13	Replace the damaged wiring harness that causes the short between CKT 883 and CKT 882. Is the repair complete?	—	Go to *A Diagnostic System Check - ABS*	—
14	Replace the damaged wiring harness connectors that cause the short between CKT 883 and CKT 882. Is the repair complete?	—	Go to *A Diagnostic System Check - ABS*	—
15	Replace the rear axle harness. Is the repair complete?	—	Go to *A Diagnostic System Check - ABS*	—
16	Replace the right rear wheel speed sensor. Is the repair complete?	—	Go to *A Diagnostic System Check - ABS*	—
17	Replace the EBCM. Is the repair complete?	—	Go to *A Diagnostic System Check - ABS*	—
18	The malfunction is intermittent or is not present at this time. Refer to Diagnostic Aids for more information. Is the action complete?	—	System OK	—

GC4029903852030X

Fig. 101 Code C1228: RH Rear Excessive Wheel Speed Variation (Part 3 of 3). Cavalier & Sunfire

Circuit Description

As a toothed ring passes by the wheel speed sensor, changes in the electromagnetic field cause the wheel speed sensor to produce an AC voltage signal. The frequency of the AC voltage signal is proportional to the wheel speed. The amplitude of the AC voltage signal is directly related to wheel speed and the proximity of the wheel speed sensor to the toothed ring. The proximity of the wheel speed sensor to the toothed ring is also referred to as the air gap.

Conditions for Setting the DTC

DTC C1232 can set anytime after initialization.

A malfunction exists if either of the left front wheel speed sensor circuits are open or shorted to voltage or ground.

Action Taken When the DTC Sets

- A malfunction DTC stores.
- The ABS disables.
- The ABS warning indicator turns on.

Conditions for Clearing the DTC

- The condition responsible for setting the DTC no longer exists and the Scan Tool Clear DTCs function is used.
- 100 drive cycles pass with no DTCs detected. A drive cycle consists of starting the vehicle, driving the vehicle over 16 km/h (10 mph), stopping and then turning the ignition off.

Diagnostic Aids

The following conditions may cause an intermittent malfunction:

- A poor connection
- Rubbed-through wire insulation
- A broken wire inside the insulation

Use the enhanced diagnostic function of the Scan Tool in order to measure the frequency of the malfunction.

If the customer's comments reflect that the amber ABS warning indicator is on only during moist environmental changes (rain, snow, vehicle wash), inspect all the wheel speed sensor circuitry for signs of water intrusion. If the DTC is not current, clear all DTCs and simulate the effects of water intrusion by using the following procedure:

1. Spray the suspected area with a five percent saltwater solution.

   Add two teaspoons of salt to twelve ounces of water to make a five percent saltwater solution.
2. Test drive the vehicle over various road surfaces (bumps, turns, etc.) above 24 km/h (15 mph) for at least 30 seconds.
3. If the DTC returns, replace the suspected harness.

Thoroughly inspect any circuitry that may be causing the intermittent complaint for the following conditions:

- Backed out terminals
- Improper mating
- Broken locks
- Improperly formed or damaged terminals
- Poor terminal-to-wiring connections
- Physical damage to the wiring harness

Resistance of the wheel speed sensor will increase with an increase in sensor temperature.

Use the following procedure when replacing a wheel speed sensor or harness:

1. Inspect the wheel speed sensor terminals and harness connector for corrosion and/or water intrusion.
2. Replace the wheel speed sensor and jumper harness if evidence of corrosion or water intrusion exists.

GC4029903853010X

Fig. 102 Code C1232: LH Front Wheel Speed Circuit Open Or Shorted (Part 1 of 5). Cavalier & Sunfire

Test Description

2. This test checks the wheel speed sensor circuitry for proper resistance values at the EBCM.
3. This test checks for a short to ground in the wheel speed sensor circuit.
4. This test checks for a short to voltage in either the high or the low wheel speed sensor signal circuits.
5. This test determines if the wheel speed sensor signal low is shorted to voltage.
6. This test determines if the wheel speed sensor signal high is shorted to voltage.
10. This test determines if the malfunction is caused by the EBCM.
11. This test checks for an open or high resistance in the wheel speed sensor signal low circuit.
12. This test checks for an open or high resistance in the wheel speed sensor signal high circuit.
13. This test checks the wheel speed sensor for the proper resistance value.
14. This test checks for a short to ground in the wheel speed sensor signal low circuit.
15. This test checks for a short to ground in the wheel speed sensor signal high circuit.
16. This test checks for an intermittent short to ground in the wheel speed sensor signal high circuit.
17. This test checks for an intermittent short to ground in the wheel speed sensor signal low circuit.
18. This test checks for a short to ground in the wheel speed sensor.

Step	Action	Value(s)	Yes	No
	Important: Zero the J 39200 test leads before making any resistance measurements. **Important:** Difficulty may occur when trying to locate intermittent malfunctions in the wheel speed sensor circuit. Do not disturb any of the electrical connections. Change the electrical connections only when instructed to do so by a step in the diagnostic table. Changing the electrical connections at the correct time will ensure that an intermittent electrical connection will not be corrected until the source of the malfunction is found.			
1	Was the ABS Diagnostic System Check performed?	—	*Go to Step 2*	*Go to A Diagnostic System Check - ABS*
2	1. Turn the ignition switch to the OFF position. 2. Make a 5 percent saltwater solution. 3. Thoroughly spray the left front wheel speed sensor harness with the saltwater solution. 4. Disconnect the EBCM harness connector. 5. Use the *J 39200* in order to measure the resistance between the EBCM harness connector terminal A5 and the EBCM harness connector terminal B4. Is the resistance within the specified range?	1530–1870 Ω	*Go to Step 3*	*Go to Step 11*
3	Use the *J 39200* in order to measure the resistance between the EBCM harness connector terminal B4 and ground. Is the resistance within the specified range?	OL (Infinite)	*Go to Step 4*	*Go to Step 14*
4	1. Turn the ignition switch to the RUN position. Do not start the engine. 2. Use the *J 39200* in order to measure the voltage between the EBCM harness connector terminal B4 and ground. Is the voltage within the specified range?	0–1 V	*Go to Step 7*	*Go to Step 5*
5	1. Turn the ignition switch to the OFF position. 2. Disconnect the left front wheel speed sensor at the left front wheel speed sensor connector. 3. Turn the ignition switch to the RUN position. Do not start the engine. 4. Use the *J 39200* in order to measure the voltage between the EBCM harness connector terminal B4 and ground Is the voltage within the specified range?	0–1 V	*Go to Step 6*	*Go to Step 19*

GC4029903853020X

Fig. 102 Code C1232: LH Front Wheel Speed Circuit Open Or Shorted (Part 2 of 5). Cavalier & Sunfire

Step	Action	Value(s)	Yes	No
6	Use the *J 39200* in order to measure the voltage between the EBCM harness connector B4 terminal A5 and ground. Is the voltage within the specified range?	0–1 V	*Go to Step 31*	*Go to Step 20*
7	1. Turn the ignition switch to the OFF position. 2. Inspect the following terminals: • The EBCM harness connector terminal A4 • The EBCM harness connector terminal B4 • The remaining terminals of the EBCM harness connector 3. Inspect the above terminals for the following conditions: • Terminal damage • Poor terminal contact • Terminal corrosion Damage, terminal corrosion, and poor terminal contact may cause an open circuit, a short to voltage, or a short to ground. Are there signs of poor terminal contact, terminal corrosion, or damaged terminals?	—	*Go to Step 27*	*Go to Step 8*
8	Inspect the wiring of CKT 873 and CKT 830 for signs of wire damage. Wire damage may cause the following conditions in CKT 873 and CKT 830: • An open circuit • A short to voltage • A short to ground Are there signs of damaged wiring?	—	*Go to Step 21*	*Go to Step 9*
9	Inspect the harness connectors of CKT 873 and CKT 830 for signs of wire damage. Wire damage may cause the following conditions in CKT 873 and CKT 830: • An open circuit • A short to voltage • A short to ground Are there signs of damaged connectors?	—	*Go to Step 22*	*Go to Step 10*
10	1. Reconnect the EBCM connector. 2. Reconnect the left front wheel speed sensor harness connector. 3. Install a *Scan Tool.* 4. Test drive the vehicle at a speed above 24 km/h (15 mph) for at least 30 seconds. 5. Use the *Scan Tool* in order to read the DTCs. Does DTC C1232 set as a current DTC?	—	*Go to Step 30*	*Go to Step 31*
11	1. Disconnect the left front wheel speed sensor directly at the left front wheel speed sensor connector. 2. Use the *J 39200* in order to measure the resistance between the EBCM harness connector terminal B4 and the left front wheel speed sensor harness connector terminal B. Is the resistance within the specified range?	0–2 Ω	*Go to Step 12*	*Go to Step 23*
12	Use the *J 39200* in order to measure the resistance between the EBCM harness connector terminal A5 and the left front wheel speed sensor harness connector terminal A. Is the resistance within the specified range?	0–2 Ω	*Go to Step 13*	*Go to Step 24*

GC4029903853030X

Fig. 102 Code C1232: LH Front Wheel Speed Circuit Open Or Shorted (Part 3 of 5). Cavalier & Sunfire

Step	Action	Value(s)	Yes	No
13	Use the *J 39200* in order to measure the resistance between the left front wheel speed sensor connector terminal A and the left front wheel speed sensor connector terminal B. Is the resistance within the specified range?	1530–1870 Ω	*Go to Step 31*	*Go to Step 28*
14	1. Disconnect the connector C100. 2. Use the *J 39200* in order to measure the resistance between the EBCM harness connector terminal B4 and ground. Is the resistance within the specified range?	OL (Infinite)	*Go to Step 15*	*Go to Step 25*
15	Use the *J 39200* in order to measure the resistance between the EBCM harness connector terminal A5 and ground. Is the resistance within the specified range?	OL (Infinite)	*Go to Step 16*	*Go to Step 26*
16	1. Thoroughly respray the left front wheel speed sensor harness with the saltwater solution. 2. Disconnect the left front wheel speed sensor directly at the left front wheel speed sensor. 3. Use the *J 39200* in order to measure the resistance between the left front wheel speed sensor harness connector terminal A and ground. Is the resistance within the specified range?	OL (Infinite)	*Go to Step 17*	*Go to Step 29*
17	Use the *J 39200* in order to measure the resistance between the left front wheel speed sensor harness connector terminal B and ground. Is the resistance within the specified range?	OL (Infinite)	*Go to Step 18*	*Go to Step 29*
18	Use the *J 39200* in order to measure the resistance between the left front wheel speed sensor connector terminal A and ground. Is the resistance within the specified range?	OL (Infinite)	*Go to Step 31*	*Go to Step 28*
19	Repair the short to voltage in CKT 873. If the short to voltage is found in the left front wheel speed sensor harness, replace the left front wheel speed harness. Is the repair complete?	—	Go to *A Diagnostic System Check - ABS*	—
20	Repair the short to voltage in CKT 830. If the short to voltage is found in the left front wheel speed sensor harness, replace the left front wheel speed harness. Is the repair complete?	—	Go to *A Diagnostic System Check - ABS*	—
21	Repair the wiring damage in CKT 873 or CKT 830. If the wiring damage is found in the left front wheel speed sensor harness, replace the left front wheel speed jumper harness. Is the repair complete?	—	Go to *A Diagnostic System Check - ABS*	—
22	Repair the connector damage in CKT 873 or CKT 830. If the connector damage is found in the left front wheel speed sensor harness, replace the left front wheel speed harness. Is the repair complete?	—	Go to *A Diagnostic System Check - ABS*	—

GC4029903853040X

Fig. 102 Code C1232: LH Front Wheel Speed Circuit Open Or Shorted (Part 4 of 5). Cavalier & Sunfire

Step	Action	Value(s)	Yes	No
23	Repair the open or high resistance in CKT 873. If the open or high resistance is found in the left front wheel speed sensor harness, replace the left front wheel speed sensor harness. Is the repair complete?	—	Go to *A Diagnostic System Check - ABS*	—
24	Repair the open or high resistance in CKT 830. If the open or high resistance is found in the left front wheel speed sensor harness, replace the left front wheel speed harness. Is the repair complete?	—	Go to *A Diagnostic System Check - ABS*	—
25	Repair the short to ground in CKT 873. If the short to ground is found in the left front wheel speed sensor harness, replace the left front wheel speed harness. Is the repair complete?	—	Go to *A Diagnostic System Check - ABS*	—
26	Repair the short to ground in CKT 830. If the short to ground is found in the left front wheel speed sensor harness, replace the left front wheel speed harness. Is the repair complete?	—	Go to *A Diagnostic System Check - ABS*	—
27	Replace all of the terminals and the connectors that exhibit signs of poor terminal contact, corrosion, or damaged terminals. Is the repair complete?	—	Go to *A Diagnostic System Check - ABS*	—
28	Replace the left front wheel speed sensor. Is the repair complete?	—	Go to *A Diagnostic System Check - ABS*	—
29	Replace the left front wheel speed sensor harness. Is the repair complete?	—	Go to *A Diagnostic System Check - ABS*	—
30	Replace the EBCM. Is the repair complete?	—	Go to *A Diagnostic System Check - ABS*	—
31	The malfunction is intermittent or not present at this time. Inspect all of the connectors and the harnesses for damage that could cause the following conditions: • An open or a high resistance • A short to ground • A short to voltage The sensor harness must be replaced if the sensor harness is damaged. Refer to Diagnostic Aids for more information. Is the action complete?	—	System OK	—

GC4029903853050X

Fig. 102 Code C1232: LH Front Wheel Speed Circuit Open Or Shorted (Part 5 of 5). Cavalier & Sunfire

Circuit Description

As a toothed ring passes by the wheel speed sensor, changes in the electromagnetic field cause the wheel speed sensor to produce an AC voltage signal. The frequency of the AC voltage signal is proportional to the wheel speed. The amplitude of the AC voltage signal is directly related to wheel speed and the proximity of the wheel speed sensor to the toothed ring. The proximity of the wheel speed sensor to the toothed ring is also referred to as the air gap.

Conditions for Setting the DTC

DTC C1233 can set anytime after initialization.

A malfunction exists if either of the right front wheel speed sensor circuits are open or shorted to voltage or ground.

Action Taken When the DTC Sets

- A malfunction DTC stores.
- The ABS disables.
- The ABS warning indicator turns on.

Conditions for Clearing the DTC

- The condition responsible for setting the DTC no longer exists and the Scan Tool Clear DTCs function is used.
- 100 drive cycles pass with no DTCs detected. A drive cycle consists of starting the vehicle, driving the vehicle over 16 km/h (10 mph), stopping and then turning the ignition off.

Diagnostic Aids

The following conditions may cause an intermittent malfunction:

- A poor connection
- Rubbed-through wire insulation
- A broken wire inside the insulation

Use the enhanced diagnostic function of the Scan Tool in order to measure the frequency of the malfunction.

If the customer's comments reflect that the amber ABS warning indicator is on only during moist environmental changes (rain, snow, vehicle wash), inspect all the wheel speed sensor circuitry for signs of water intrusion. If the DTC is not current, clear all DTCs and simulate the effects of water intrusion by using the following procedure:

1. Spray the suspected area with a five percent saltwater solution.
   Add two teaspoons of salt to twelve ounces of water to make a five percent saltwater solution.
2. Test drive the vehicle over various road surfaces (bumps, turns, etc.) above 24 km/h (15 mph) for at least 30 seconds.
3. If the DTC returns, replace the suspected harness.

Thoroughly inspect any circuitry that may be causing the intermittent complaint for the following conditions:

- Backed out terminals
- Improper mating
- Broken locks
- Improperly formed or damaged terminals
- Poor terminal-to-wiring connections
- Physical damage to the wiring harness

GC402980309301AX

Fig. 103 Code C1233: RH Front Wheel Speed Circuit Open Or Shorted (Part 1 of 5). Cavalier & Sunfire

Resistance of the wheel speed sensor will increase with an increase in sensor temperature.

Use the following procedure when replacing a wheel speed sensor or harness:

1. Inspect the wheel speed sensor terminals and harness connector for corrosion and/or water intrusion.
2. Replace the wheel speed sensor and jumper harness if evidence of corrosion or water intrusion exists.

Important: Zero the J 39200 test leads before making any resistance measurements. Refer to the J 39200 user's manual.

Important: Difficulty may occur when trying to locate intermittent malfunctions in the wheel speed sensor circuit.

Do not disturb any of the electrical connections. Change the electrical connections only when instructed to do so by a step in the diagnostic table.

Changing the electrical connections at the correct time will ensure that an intermittent electrical connection will not be corrected until the source of the malfunction is found.

Step	Action	Value(s)	Yes	No
1	Was the Diagnostic System Check performed?	—	*Go to Step 2*	Refer to *Diagnostic System Check*
2	1. Turn the ignition switch to the OFF position. 2. Make a 5 percent saltwater solution. 3. Thoroughly spray the right front wheel speed sensor harness with the saltwater solution. 4. Disconnect the 24-way EBCM harness connector C2. 5. Use the *J 39200* in order to measure the resistance between the 24-way EBCM harness connector C2 terminal A4 and the 24-way EBCM harness connector C2 terminal B3. Is the resistance within the specified range?	1530–1870 Ω	*Go to Step 3*	*Go to Step 11*
3	Use the *J 39200* in order to measure the resistance between the 24-way EBCM harness connector C2 terminal B3 and ground. Is the resistance within the specified range?	OL (Infinite)	*Go to Step 4*	*Go to Step 14*
4	1. Turn the ignition switch to the RUN position. Do not start the engine. 2. Use the *J 39200* in order to measure the voltage between the 24-way EBCM harness connector C2 terminal B3 and ground. Is the voltage within the specified range?	0–1 V	*Go to Step 7*	*Go to Step 5*
5	1. Turn the ignition switch to the OFF position. 2. Disconnect the right front wheel speed sensor at the right front wheel speed sensor connector. 3. Turn the ignition switch to the RUN position. Do not start the engine. 4. Use the *J 39200* in order to measure the voltage between the 24-way EBCM harness connector C2 terminal B3 and ground. Is the voltage within the specified range?	0–1 V	*Go to Step 6*	*Go to Step 19*
6	Use the *J 39200* in order to measure the voltage between the 24-way EBCM harness connector C2 terminal A4 and ground. Is the voltage within the specified range?	0–1 V	*Go to Step 31*	*Go to Step 20*

GC402980309300FX

Fig. 103 Code C1233: RH Front Wheel Speed Circuit Open Or Shorted (Part 2 of 5). Cavalier & Sunfire

Step	Action	Value(s)	Yes	No
7	1. Turn the ignition switch to the OFF position. 2. Inspect the following terminals: • The 24-way EBCM connector C2 terminal A4 • The 24-way EBCM connector C2 terminal B3 • The remaining terminals of the 24-way EBCM connector C2 3. Inspect the above terminals for the following conditions: • Terminal damage • Poor terminal contact • Terminal corrosion Terminal damage, terminal corrosion, and poor terminal contact may cause an open circuit, a short to voltage, or a short to ground. Are there signs of poor terminal contact, terminal corrosion, or damaged terminals?	—	*Go to Step 27*	*Go to Step 8*
8	Inspect the wiring of CKT 833 and CKT 872 for signs of wire damage. Wire damage may cause the following conditions in CKT 833 and CKT 872: • An open circuit • A short to voltage • A short to ground Are there signs of damaged wiring?	—	*Go to Step 21*	*Go to Step 9*
9	Inspect the harness connectors of CKT 833 and CKT 872 for signs of wire damage. Wire damage may cause the following conditions in CKT 833 and CKT 872: • An open circuit • A short to voltage • A short to ground Are there signs of damaged connectors?	—	*Go to Step 22*	*Go to Step 10*
10	1. Reconnect the 24-way EBCM connector C2. 2. Reconnect the right front wheel speed sensor harness connector. 3. Install a *Scan Tool*. 4. Test drive the vehicle at a speed above 24 km/h (15 mph) for at least 30 seconds. 5. Use the *Scan Tool* in order to read the DTCs. Does DTC C1233 set as a current DTC?	—	*Go to Step 30*	*Go to Step 31*
11	1. Disconnect the right front wheel speed sensor directly at the right front wheel speed sensor connector. 2. Use the *J 39200* in order to measure the resistance between the 24-way EBCM connector C2 terminal B3 and the right front wheel speed sensor harness connector terminal B. Is the resistance within the specified range?	0–2 Ω	*Go to Step 12*	*Go to Step 23*

GC402980309300GX

Fig. 103 Code C1233: RH Front Wheel Speed Circuit Open Or Shorted (Part 3 of 5). Cavalier & Sunfire

Step	Action	Value(s)	Yes	No
12	Use the *J 39200* in order to measure the resistance between the 24-way EBCM connector C2 terminal A4 and the right front wheel speed sensor harness connector terminal A. Is the resistance within the specified range?	0–2 Ω	*Go to Step 13*	*Go to Step 24*
13	Use the *J 39200* in order to measure the resistance between the right front wheel speed sensor connector terminal A and the right front wheel speed sensor connector terminal B. Is the resistance within the specified range?	1530–1870 Ω	*Go to Step 31*	*Go to Step 28*
14	1. Disconnect the connector C100. 2. Use the *J 39200* in order to measure the resistance between the 24-way EBCM connector C2 terminal B3 and ground. Is the resistance within the specified range?	OL (Infinite)	*Go to Step 15*	*Go to Step 25*
15	Use the *J 39200* in order to measure the resistance between the 24-way EBCM connector C2 terminal A4 and ground. Is the resistance within the specified range?	OL (Infinite)	*Go to Step 16*	*Go to Step 26*
16	1. Thoroughly respray the right front wheel speed sensor harness with the saltwater solution. 2. Disconnect the right front wheel speed sensor directly at the right front wheel speed sensor. 3. Use the *J 39200* in order to measure the resistance between the right front wheel speed sensor harness connector terminal A and ground. Is the resistance within the specified range?	OL (Infinite)	*Go to Step 17*	*Go to Step 29*
17	Use the *J 39200* in order to measure the resistance between the right front wheel speed sensor harness connector terminal B and ground. Is the resistance within the specified range?	OL (Infinite)	*Go to Step 18*	*Go to Step 29*
18	Use the *J 39200* in order to measure the resistance between the right front wheel speed sensor connector terminal A and ground. Is the resistance within the specified range?	OL (Infinite)	*Go to Step 31*	*Go to Step 28*
19	Repair the short to voltage in CKT 833. If the short to voltage is found in the right front wheel speed sensor harness, replace the right front wheel speed harness. Is the repair complete?	—	Refer to *Diagnostic System Check*	—
20	Repair the short to voltage in CKT 872. If the short to voltage is found in the right front wheel speed sensor harness, replace the right front wheel speed harness. Is the repair complete?	—	Refer to *Diagnostic System Check*	—
21	Repair the wiring damage in CKT 833 or CKT 872. If the wiring damage is found in the right front wheel speed sensor harness, replace the right front wheel speed harness. Is the repair complete?	—	Refer to *Diagnostic System Check*	—

GC402980309300HX

Fig. 103 Code C1233: RH Front Wheel Speed Circuit Open Or Shorted (Part 4 of 5). Cavalier & Sunfire

Step	Action	Value(s)	Yes	No
22	Repair the connector damage in CKT 833 or CKT 872. If the connector damage is found in the right front wheel speed sensor harness, replace the right front wheel speed harness. Is the repair complete?	—	Refer to *Diagnostic System Check*	—
23	Repair the open or high resistance in CKT 833. If the open or high resistance is found in the right front wheel speed sensor harness, replace the right front wheel speed harness. Is the repair complete?	—	Refer to *Diagnostic System Check*	—
24	Repair the open or high resistance in CKT 872. If the open or high resistance is found in the right front wheel speed sensor harness, replace the right front wheel speed harness. Is the repair complete?	—	Refer to *Diagnostic System Check*	—
25	Repair the short to ground in CKT 833. If the short to ground is found in the right front wheel speed sensor harness, replace the right front wheel speed harness. Is the repair complete?	—	Refer to *Diagnostic System Check*	—
26	Repair the short to ground in CKT 872. If the short to ground is found in the right front wheel speed sensor harness, replace the right front wheel speed harness. Is the repair complete?	—	Refer to *Diagnostic System Check*	—
27	Replace all of the terminals and the connectors that exhibit signs of poor terminal contact, corrosion, or damaged terminals. Is the repair complete?	—	Refer to *Diagnostic System Check*	—
28	Replace the right front wheel speed sensor. Is the repair complete?	—	Refer to *Diagnostic System Check*	—
29	Replace the right front wheel speed sensor harness. Is the repair complete?	—	Refer to *Diagnostic System Check*	—
30	Replace the EBCM. Is the repair complete?	—	Refer to *Diagnostic System Check*	—
31	The malfunction is intermittent or not present at this time. Inspect all of the connectors and the harnesses for damage that may cause the following conditions: • An open or a high resistance • A short to ground • A short to voltage The wheel speed harness must be replaced if the harness is damaged. Refer to Diagnostic Aids for more information.	—	—	—

GC402980309300IX

Fig. 103 Code C1233: RH Front Wheel Speed Circuit Open Or Shorted (Part 5 of 5). Cavalier & Sunfire

Test Description

2. This test checks the wheel speed sensor circuitry for proper resistance values at the EBCM.
3. This test checks for a short to ground in the wheel speed sensor signal low circuitry
4. This test checks for a short to voltage in either the high or the low wheel speed sensor signal circuits.
5. This test determines if the wheel speed sensor signal low is shorted to voltage.
6. This test determines if the wheel speed sensor signal high is shorted to voltage.
10. This test determines if the malfunction is caused by the EBCM.
11. This test checks for an open or high resistance in the wheel speed sensor signal low circuitry.
12. This test checks for an open or high resistance in the wheel speed sensor signal high circuitry.
13. This test checks the wheel speed sensor for the proper resistance value.
16. This test checks for an intermittent short to ground in the wheel speed sensor signal high circuitry.
17. This test checks for an intermittent short to ground in the wheel speed sensor signal low circuitry.
18. This test checks for a short to ground in the wheel speed sensor.

Step	Action	Value(s)	Yes	No
	Important: Zero the J 39200 test leads before making any resistance measurements. **Important:** Difficulty may occur when trying to locate intermittent malfunctions in the wheel speed sensor circuit. Do not disturb any of the electrical connections. Change the electrical connections only when instructed to do so by a step in the diagnostic table. Changing the electrical connections at the correct time will ensure that an intermittent electrical connection will not be corrected until the source of the malfunction is found.			
1	Was the ABS Diagnostic System Check performed?	—	*Go to Step 2*	*Go to A Diagnostic System Check - ABS*
2	1. Turn the ignition switch to the OFF position. 2. Make a 5 percent saltwater solution. 3. Thoroughly spray the left rear wheel speed sensor harness with the saltwater solution. 4. Disconnect the 24-way EBCM harness connector C2. 5. Use the *J 39200* in order to measure the resistance between the 24-way EBCM harness connector C2 terminal A3 and the 24-way EBCM harness connector C2 terminal B2. Is the resistance within the specified range?	950–1250 Ω	*Go to Step 3*	*Go to Step 11*
3	Use the *J 39200* in order to measure the resistance between the 24-way EBCM harness connector C2 terminal B2 and ground. Is the resistance within the specified range?	OL (Infinite)	*Go to Step 4*	*Go to Step 14*
4	1. Turn the ignition switch to the RUN position. Do not start the engine. 2. Use the *J 39200* in order to measure the voltage between the 24-way EBCM harness connector C2 terminal B2 and ground. Is the voltage within the specified range?	0–1 V	*Go to Step 7*	*Go to Step 5*
5	1. Turn the ignition switch to the OFF position. 2. Disconnect the left rear wheel speed sensor at the left rear wheel speed sensor connector. 3. Turn the ignition switch to the RUN position. Do not start the engine. 4. Use the *J 39200* in order to measure the voltage between the 24-way EBCM harness connector C2 terminal B2 and ground Is the voltage within the specified range?	0–1 V	*Go to Step 6*	*Go to Step 19*

GC4029903854020X

Fig. 104 Code C1234: LH Rear Wheel Speed Circuit Open Or Shorted (Part 2 of 5). Cavalier & Sunfire

Circuit Description

As a toothed ring passes by the wheel speed sensor, changes in the electromagnetic field cause the wheel speed sensor to produce an AC voltage signal. The frequency of the AC voltage signal is proportional to the wheel speed. The amplitude of the AC voltage signal is directly related to wheel speed and the proximity of the wheel speed sensor to the toothed ring. The proximity of the wheel speed sensor to the toothed ring is also referred to as the air gap.

Conditions for Setting the DTC

DTC C1234 can set anytime after initialization.

A malfunction exists if either of the left rear wheel speed sensor circuits are open or shorted to voltage or ground.

Action Taken When the DTC Sets

- A malfunction DTC stores.
- The ABS disables.
- The ABS warning indicator turns on.

Conditions for Clearing the DTC

- The condition responsible for setting the DTC no longer exists and the Scan Tool Clear DTCs function is used.
- 100 drive cycles pass with no DTCs detected. A drive cycle consists of starting the vehicle, driving the vehicle over 16 km/h (10 mph), stopping and then turning the ignition off.

Diagnostic Aids

The following conditions may cause an intermittent malfunction:

- A poor connection
- Rubbed-through wire insulation
- A broken wire inside the insulation

Use the enhanced diagnostic function of the Scan Tool in order to measure the frequency of the malfunction.

If the customer's comments reflect that the amber ABS warning indicator is on only during moist environmental changes (rain, snow, vehicle wash), inspect all the wheel speed sensor circuitry for signs of water intrusion. If the DTC is not current, clear all DTCs and simulate the effects of water intrusion by using the following procedure:

1. Spray the suspected area with a five percent saltwater solution.

   Add two teaspoons of salt to twelve ounces of water to make a five percent saltwater solution.
2. Test drive the vehicle over various road surfaces (bumps, turns, etc.) above 24 km/h (15 mph) for at least 30 seconds.
3. If the DTC returns, replace the suspected harness.

Thoroughly inspect any circuitry that may be causing the intermittent complaint for the following conditions:

- Backed out terminals
- Improper mating
- Broken locks
- Improperly formed or damaged terminals
- Poor terminal-to-wiring connections
- Physical damage to the wiring harness

Resistance of the wheel speed sensor will increase with an increase in sensor temperature.

Use the following procedure when replacing a wheel speed sensor or harness:

1. Inspect the wheel speed sensor terminals and harness connector for corrosion and/or water intrusion.
2. Replace the wheel speed sensor and jumper harness if evidence of corrosion or water intrusion exists.

GC4029903854010X

Fig. 104 Code C1234: LH Rear Wheel Speed Circuit Open Or Shorted (Part 1 of 5). Cavalier & Sunfire

Step	Action	Value(s)	Yes	No
6	Use the *J 39200* in order to measure the voltage between the 24-way EBCM harness connector C2 terminal A3 and ground. Is the voltage within the specified range?	0–1 V	*Go to Step 31*	*Go to Step 20*
7	1. Turn the ignition switch to the OFF position. 2. Inspect the following terminals: • The 24-way EBCM harness connector C2 terminal A3 • The 24-way EBCM harness connector C2 terminal B2 • The remaining terminals of the 24-way EBCM harness connector C2 3. Inspect the above terminals for the following conditions: • Terminal damage • Poor terminal contact • Terminal corrosion Terminal damage, terminal corrosion, and poor terminal contact may cause an open circuit, a short to voltage, or a short to ground. Are there signs of poor terminal contact, terminal corrosion, or damaged terminals?	—	*Go to Step 27*	*Go to Step 8*
8	Inspect the wiring of CKT 885 and CKT 884 for signs of wire damage. Wire damage may cause the following conditions in CKT 885 and CKT 884: • An open circuit • A short to voltage • A short to ground Are there signs of damaged wiring?	—	*Go to Step 21*	*Go to Step 9*
9	Inspect the harness connectors of CKT 885 and CKT 884 for signs of wire damage. Wire damage may cause the following conditions in CKT 885 and CKT 884: • An open circuit • A short to voltage • A short to ground Are there signs of damaged connectors?	—	*Go to Step 22*	*Go to Step 10*
10	1. Reconnect the 24-way EBCM connector C1. 2. Reconnect the left rear wheel speed sensor harness connector. 3. Install a *Scan Tool*. 4. Test drive the vehicle at a speed above 24 km/h (15 mph) for at least 30 seconds. 5. Use the *Scan Tool* in order to read the DTCs. Does DTC C1234 set as a current DTC?	—	*Go to Step 30*	*Go to Step 31*
11	1. Disconnect the left rear wheel speed sensor directly at the left rear wheel speed sensor connector. 2. Use the *J 39200* in order to measure the resistance between the 24-way EBCM harness connector C2 terminal B2 and the left rear wheel speed sensor harness connector terminal B. Is the resistance within the specified range?	0–2 Ω	*Go to Step 12*	*Go to Step 23*

GC4029903854030X

Fig. 104 Code C1234: LH Rear Wheel Speed Circuit Open Or Shorted (Part 3 of 5). Cavalier & Sunfire

Step	Action	Value(s)	Yes	No
12	Use the *J 39200* in order to measure the resistance between the 24-way EBCM harness connector C2 terminal A3 and the left rear wheel speed sensor harness connector terminal A. Is the resistance within the specified range?	0–2 Ω	*Go to Step 13*	*Go to Step 24*
13	Use the *J 39200* in order to measure the resistance between the left rear wheel speed sensor connector terminal A and the left rear wheel speed sensor connector terminal B. Is the resistance within the specified range?	950–1250 Ω	*Go to Step 31*	*Go to Step 28*
14	1. Disconnect the connector C313. 2. Use the *J 39200* in order to measure the resistance between the 24-way EBCM harness connector C2 terminal B2 and ground. Is the resistance within the specified range?	OL (Infinite)	*Go to Step 15*	*Go to Step 25*
15	Use the *J 39200* in order to measure the resistance between the 24-way EBCM harness connector C2 terminal A3 and ground. Is the resistance within the specified range?	OL (Infinite)	*Go to Step 16*	*Go to Step 26*
16	1. Thoroughly respray the left rear wheel speed sensor harness with the saltwater solution. 2. Disconnect the left rear wheel speed sensor directly at the left rear wheel speed sensor. 3. Use the *J 39200* in order to measure the resistance between the left rear wheel speed sensor harness connector terminal A and ground. Is the resistance within the specified range?	OL (Infinite)	*Go to Step 17*	*Go to Step 29*
17	Use the *J 39200* in order to measure the resistance between the left rear wheel speed sensor harness connector terminal B and ground. Is the resistance within the specified range?	OL (Infinite)	*Go to Step 18*	*Go to Step 29*
18	Use the *J 39200* in order to measure the resistance between the left rear wheel speed sensor connector terminal A and ground. Is the resistance within the specified range?	OL (Infinite)	*Go to Step 31*	*Go to Step 28*
19	Repair the short to voltage in CKT 885. If the short to voltage is found in the left rear wheel speed sensor harness, replace the left rear wheel speed harness. Is the repair complete?	—	Go to *A Diagnostic System Check - ABS*	—
20	Repair the short to voltage in CKT 884. If the short to voltage is found in the left rear wheel speed sensor harness, replace the left rear wheel speed harness. Is the repair complete?	—	Go to *A Diagnostic System Check - ABS*	—
21	Repair the wiring damage in CKT 885 or CKT 884. If the wiring damage is found in the left rear wheel speed sensor harness, replace the left rear wheel speed harness. Is the repair complete?	—	Go to *A Diagnostic System Check - ABS*	—

GC4029903854040X

Fig. 104 Code C1234: LH Rear Wheel Speed Circuit Open Or Shorted (Part 4 of 5). Cavalier & Sunfire

Step	Action	Value(s)	Yes	No
22	Repair the connector damage in CKT 885 or CKT 884. If the connector damage is found in the left rear wheel speed sensor harness, replace the left rear wheel speed harness. Is the repair complete?	—	Go to *A Diagnostic System Check - ABS*	—
23	Repair the open or high resistance in CKT 885. If the open or high resistance is found in the left rear wheel speed sensor harness, replace the left rear wheel speed harness. Is the repair complete?	—	Go to *A Diagnostic System Check - ABS*	—
24	Repair the open or high resistance in CKT 884. If the open or high resistance is found in the left rear wheel speed sensor harness, replace the left rear wheel speed harness. Is the repair complete?	—	Go to *A Diagnostic System Check - ABS*	—
25	Repair the short to ground in CKT 885. If the short to ground is found in the left rear wheel speed sensor harness, replace the left rear wheel speed harness. Is the repair complete?	—	Go to *A Diagnostic System Check - ABS*	—
26	Repair the short to ground in CKT 884. If the short to ground is found in the left rear wheel speed sensor harness, replace the left rear wheel speed harness. Is the repair complete?	—	Go to *A Diagnostic System Check - ABS*	—
27	Replace all of the terminals and the connectors that exhibit signs of poor terminal contact, corrosion, or damaged terminals. Is the repair complete?	—	Go to *A Diagnostic System Check - ABS*	—
28	Replace the left rear wheel speed sensor. Is the repair complete?	—	Go to *A Diagnostic System Check - ABS*	—
29	Replace the left rear wheel speed sensor harness. Is the repair complete?	—	Go to *A Diagnostic System Check - ABS*	—
30	Replace the EBCM. Is the repair complete?	—	Go to *A Diagnostic System Check - ABS*	—
31	The malfunction is intermittent or not present at this time. Inspect all of the connectors and the harnesses for damage that may cause the following conditions: • An open or a high resistance • A short to ground • A short to voltage The wheel speed sensor harness must be replaced if the harness is damaged. Refer to Diagnostic Aids for more information. Is the action complete?	—	System OK	—

GC4029903854050X

Fig. 104 Code C1234: LH Rear Wheel Speed Circuit Open Or Shorted (Part 5 of 5). Cavalier & Sunfire

Circuit Description

As a toothed ring passes by the wheel speed sensor, changes in the electromagnetic field cause the wheel speed sensor to produce an AC voltage signal. The frequency of the AC voltage signal is proportional to the wheel speed. The amplitude of the AC voltage signal is directly related to wheel speed and the proximity of the wheel speed sensor to the toothed ring. The proximity of the wheel speed sensor to the toothed ring is also referred to as the air gap.

Conditions for Setting the DTC

DTC C1235 can set anytime after initialization.

A malfunction exists if either of the right rear wheel speed sensor circuits are open or shorted to voltage or ground.

Action Taken When the DTC Sets

- A malfunction DTC stores.
- The ABS disables.
- The ABS warning indicator turns on.

Conditions for Clearing the DTC

- The condition responsible for setting the DTC no longer exists and the Scan Tool Clear DTCs function is used.
- 100 drive cycles pass with no DTCs detected. A drive cycle consists of starting the vehicle, driving the vehicle over 16 km/h (10 mph), stopping and then turning the ignition off.

Diagnostic Aids

The following conditions may cause an intermittent malfunction:

- A poor connection
- Rubbed-through wire insulation
- A broken wire inside the insulation

Use the enhanced diagnostic function of the Scan Tool in order to measure the frequency of the malfunction.

If the customer's comments reflect that the amber ABS warning indicator is on only during moist environmental changes (rain, snow, vehicle wash), inspect all the wheel speed sensor circuitry for signs o water intrusion. If the DTC is not current, clear all DTCs and simulate the effects of water intrusion by using the following procedure:

1. Spray the suspected area with a five percent saltwater solution.

   Add two teaspoons of salt to twelve ounces of water to make a five percent saltwater solution.
2. Test drive the vehicle over various road surfaces (bumps, turns, etc.) above 24 km/h (15 mph) for at least 30 seconds.
3. If the DTC returns, replace the suspected harness

Thoroughly inspect any circuitry that may be causing the intermittent complaint for the following conditions:

- Backed out terminals
- Improper mating
- Broken locks
- Improperly formed or damaged terminals
- Poor terminal-to-wiring connections
- Physical damage to the wiring harness

Resistance of the wheel speed sensor will increase with an increase in sensor temperature.

Use the following procedure when replacing a wheel speed sensor or harness:

1. Inspect the wheel speed sensor terminals and harness connector for corrosion and/or water intrusion.
2. Replace the wheel speed sensor jumper harness if evidence of corrosion or water intrusion exists.

GC4029903855010X

Fig. 105 Code C1235: RH Rear Wheel Speed Circuit Open Or Shorted (Part 1 of 5). Cavalier & Sunfire

Test Description

2. This test checks the wheel speed sensor circuitry for proper resistance values at the EBCM.
3. This test checks for a short to ground in the wheel speed sensor signal low circuitry
4. This test checks for a short to voltage in either the high or the low wheel speed sensor signal circuits.
5. This test determines if the wheel speed sensor signal low is shorted to voltage.
6. This test determines if the wheel speed sensor signal high is shorted to voltage.
10. This test determines if the malfunction is caused by the EBCM.
11. This test checks for an open or high resistance in the wheel speed sensor signal low circuitry.
12. This test checks for an open or high resistance in the wheel speed sensor signal high circuitry.
13. This test checks the wheel speed sensor for the proper resistance value.
16. This test checks for an intermittent short to ground in the wheel speed sensor signal high circuitry.
17. This test checks for an intermittent short to ground in the wheel speed sensor signal low circuitry.
18. This test checks for a short to ground in the wheel speed sensor.

Step	Action	Value(s)	Yes	No
	Important: Zero the J 39200 test leads before making any resistance measurements. **Important:** Difficulty may occur when trying to locate intermittent malfunctions in the wheel speed sensor circuit. Do not disturb any of the electrical connections. Change the electrical connections only when instructed to do so by a step in the diagnostic table. Changing the electrical connections at the correct time will ensure that an intermittent electrical connection will not be corrected until the source of the malfunction is found.			
1	Was the ABS Diagnostic System Check performed?	—	*Go to Step 2*	Go to *A Diagnostic System Check - ABS*
2	1. Turn the ignition switch to the OFF position. 2. Make a 5 percent saltwater solution. 3. Thoroughly spray the rear axle harness with the saltwater solution. 4. Disconnect the 24-way EBCM harness connector C2. 5. Use the *J 39200* in order to measure the resistance between the 24-way EBCM harness connector C2 terminal A2 and the 24-way EBCM harness connector C2 terminal B1. Is the resistance within the specified range?	950–1250 Ω	*Go to Step 3*	*Go to Step 11*
3	Use the *J 39200* in order to measure the resistance between the 24-way EBCM harness connector C2 terminal B1 and ground. Is the resistance within the specified range?	OL (Infinite)	*Go to Step 4*	*Go to Step 14*
4	1. Turn the ignition switch to the RUN position. Do not start the engine. 2. Use the *J 39200* in order to measure the voltage between the 24-way EBCM harness connector C2 terminal B1 and ground. Is the voltage within the specified range?	0–1 V	*Go to Step 7*	*Go to Step 5*
5	1. Turn the ignition switch to the OFF position. 2. Disconnect the right rear wheel speed sensor at the right rear wheel speed sensor connector. 3. Turn the ignition switch to the RUN position. Do not start the engine. 4. Use the *J 39200* in order to measure the voltage between the 24-way EBCM harness connector C2 terminal B1 and ground Is the voltage within the specified range?	0–1 V	*Go to Step 6*	*Go to Step 19*

GC4029903855020X

Fig. 105 Code C1235: RH Rear Wheel Speed Circuit Open Or Shorted (Part 2 of 5). Cavalier & Sunfire

Step	Action	Value(s)	Yes	No
6	Use the *J 39200* in order to measure the voltage between the 24-way EBCM harness connector C2 terminal A2 and ground. Is the voltage within the specified range?	0–1 V	*Go to Step 31*	*Go to Step 20*
7	1. Turn the ignition switch to the OFF position. 2. Inspect the following terminals: • The 24-way EBCM harness connector C2 terminal A2 • The 24-way EBCM harness connector C2 terminal B1 • The remaining terminals of the 24-way EBCM harness connector C2 3. Inspect the above terminals for the following conditions: • Terminal damage • Poor terminal contact • Terminal corrosion Damage, terminal corrosion, and poor terminal contact may cause an open circuit, a short to voltage, or a short to ground. Are there signs of poor terminal contact, terminal corrosion, or damaged terminals?	—	*Go to Step 27*	*Go to Step 8*
8	Inspect the wiring of CKT 883 and CKT 882 for signs of wire damage. Wire damage may cause the following conditions in CKT 883 and CKT 882: • An open circuit • A short to voltage • A short to ground Are there signs of damaged wiring?	—	*Go to Step 21*	*Go to Step 9*
9	Inspect the harness connectors of CKT 883 and CKT 882 for signs of wire damage. Wire damage may cause the following conditions in CKT 883 and CKT 882: • An open circuit • A short to voltage • A short to ground Are there signs of damaged connectors?	—	*Go to Step 22*	*Go to Step 10*
10	1. Reconnect the 24-way EBCM connector C2. 2. Reconnect the rear axle harness connector. 3. Install a *Scan Tool.* 4. Test drive the vehicle at a speed above 24 km/h (15 mph) for at least 30 seconds. 5. Use the *Scan Tool* in order to read the DTCs. Does DTC C1235 set as a current DTC?	—	*Go to Step 30*	*Go to Step 31*
11	1. Disconnect the right rear wheel speed sensor directly at the right rear wheel speed sensor connector. 2. Use the *J 39200* in order to measure the resistance between the 24-way EBCM harness connector C2 terminal B1 and the right rear wheel speed sensor harness connector terminal B. Is the resistance within the specified range?	0–2 Ω	*Go to Step 12*	*Go to Step 23*
12	Use the *J 39200* in order to measure the resistance between the 24-way EBCM harness connector C2 terminal A2 and the right rear wheel speed sensor harness connector terminal A. Is the resistance within the specified range?	0–2 Ω	*Go to Step 13*	*Go to Step 24*

GC4029903855030X

Fig. 105 Code C1235: RH Rear Wheel Speed Circuit Open Or Shorted (Part 3 of 5). Cavalier & Sunfire

Step	Action	Value(s)	Yes	No
13	Use the *J 39200* in order to measure the resistance between the right rear wheel speed sensor connector terminal A and the right rear wheel speed sensor connector terminal B. Is the resistance within the specified range?	950–1250 Ω	*Go to Step 31*	*Go to Step 28*
14	1. Disconnect the connector C313. 2. Use the *J 39200* in order to measure the resistance between the 24-way EBCM harness connector C2 terminal B1 and ground. Is the resistance within the specified range?	OL (Infinite)	*Go to Step 15*	*Go to Step 25*
15	Use the *J 39200* in order to measure the resistance between the 24-way EBCM harness connector C2 terminal A2 and ground. Is the resistance within the specified range?	OL (Infinite)	*Go to Step 16*	*Go to Step 26*
16	1. Thoroughly respray the rear axle harness with the saltwater solution. 2. Disconnect the right rear wheel speed sensor directly at the right rear wheel speed sensor. 3. Use the *J 39200* in order to measure the resistance between the rear axle harness connector terminal A and ground. Is the resistance within the specified range?	OL (Infinite)	*Go to Step 17*	*Go to Step 29*
17	Use the *J 39200* in order to measure the resistance between the rear axle harness connector terminal B and ground. Is the resistance within the specified range?	OL (Infinite)	*Go to Step 18*	*Go to Step 29*
18	Use the *J 39200* in order to measure the resistance between the rear axle harness connector terminal A and ground. Is the resistance within the specified range?	OL (Infinite)	*Go to Step 31*	*Go to Step 28*
19	Repair the short to voltage in CKT 883. If the short to voltage is found in the rear axle harness, replace the rear axle harness. Is the repair complete?	—	Go to *A Diagnostic System Check - ABS*	—
20	Repair the short to voltage in CKT 882. If the short to voltage is found in the rear axle harness, replace the rear axle harness. Is the repair complete?	—	Go to *A Diagnostic System Check - ABS*	—
21	Repair the wiring damage in CKT 883 or CKT 882. If the wiring damage is found in the rear axle harness, replace the rear axle harness. Is the repair complete?	—	Go to *A Diagnostic System Check - ABS*	—
22	Repair the connector damage in CKT 883 or CKT 882. If the connector damage is found in the rear axle harness, replace the rear axle harness. Is the repair complete?	—	Go to *A Diagnostic System Check - ABS*	—

GC4029903855040X

Fig. 105 Code C1235: RH Rear Wheel Speed Circuit Open Or Shorted (Part 4 of 5). Cavalier & Sunfire

Step	Action	Value(s)	Yes	No
23	Repair the open or high resistance in CKT 883. If the open or high resistance is found in the rear axle harness, replace the rear axle harness. Is the repair complete?	—	Go to *A Diagnostic System Check - ABS*	—
24	Repair the open or high resistance in CKT 882. If the open or high resistance is found in the rear axle harness, replace the rear axle harness. Is the repair complete?	—	Go to *A Diagnostic System Check - ABS*	—
25	Repair the short to ground in CKT 883. If the short to ground is found in the rear axle harness, replace the rear axle harness. Is the repair complete?	—	Go to *A Diagnostic System Check - ABS*	—
26	Repair the short to ground in CKT 882. If the short to ground is found in the rear axle harness, replace the rear axle harness. Is the repair complete?	—	Go to *A Diagnostic System Check - ABS*	—
27	Replace all of the terminals and the connectors that exhibit signs of poor terminal contact, corrosion, or damaged terminals. Is the repair complete?	—	Go to *A Diagnostic System Check - ABS*	—
28	Replace the right rear wheel speed sensor. Is the repair complete?	—	Go to *A Diagnostic System Check - ABS*	—
29	Replace the rear axle harness. Is the repair complete?	—	Go to *A Diagnostic System Check - ABS*	—
30	Replace the EBCM. Is the repair complete?	—	Go to *A Diagnostic System Check - ABS*	—
31	The malfunction is intermittent or not present at this time. Inspect all of the connectors and the harnesses for damage that may cause the following conditions: • An open or a high resistance • A short to ground • A short to voltage The rear axle harness must be replaced if the harness is damaged. Refer to Diagnostic Aids for more information. Is the action complete?	—	System OK	—

GC4029903855050X

Fig. 105 Code C1235: RH Rear Wheel Speed Circuit Open Or Shorted (Part 5 of 5). Cavalier & Sunfire

Circuit Description

DTC C1236 monitors the voltage level available to the EBCM controller. If the voltage drops below 11.2 volts, full performance of the ABS system is not guaranteed. During ABS operation, there are several current requirements that will cause battery voltage at the EBCM to drop. As a result, voltage is monitored prior to an ABS event to indicate good charging system condition. Voltage is also monitored during an ABS event when voltage may drop significantly.

Conditions for Setting the DTC

DTC C1236 can set only if the vehicle's speed is greater than 5 km/h (3 mph).

A malfunction exists if the switched battery voltage is less than 11.4 volts without ABS being active or less than 8.4 volts during an ABS event.

Action Taken When the DTC Sets

- A malfunction DTC stores.
- The ABS disables.
- The ABS warning indicator turns on.

Conditions for Clearing the DTC

- The condition responsible for setting the DTC no longer exists and the Scan Tool Clear DTCs function is used.
- 100 drive cycles pass with no DTCs detected. A drive cycle consists of starting the vehicle, driving the vehicle over 16 km/h (10 mph), stopping and then turning the ignition off.

Diagnostic Aids

The following conditions may cause an intermittent malfunction:

- A poor connection
- Rubbed-through wire insulation
- A broken wire inside the insulation

Use the enhanced diagnostic function of the Scan Tool in order to measure the frequency of the malfunction.

GC402980309400AX

Fig. 106 Code C1236: Low System Supply Voltage (Part 1 of 3). Cavalier & Sunfire

Thoroughly inspect any circuitry that may be causing the intermittent complaint for the following conditions:

- Backed out terminals
- Improper mating
- Broken locks
- Improperly formed or damaged terminals
- Poor terminal-to-wiring connections
- Physical damage to the wiring harness

While performing a Voltage Load test, CKT 439 should be measured for high resistance or an open condition if it is noted that only the ignition voltage drops below acceptable voltage levels.

Ensure the starting and charging systems are in proper working order. The battery should be fully charged and in good condition before beginning the diagnostic table.

Important: Zero the J 39200 test leads before making any resistance measurements. Refer to the J 39200 user's manual.

Step	Action	Value(s)	Yes	No
1	Was the Diagnostic System Check performed?	—	*Go to Step 2*	Refer to *Diagnostic System Check*
2	1. Turn the ignition switch to the RUN position. Do not start the engine. 2. Select Snapshot on the *Scan Tool.* 3. Select Single DTC on the *Scan Tool.* 4. Enter C1236 on the *Scan Tool.* 5. Drive the vehicle at a speed above 5 km/h (3 mph). Does DTC C1236 set as a current DTC?	—	*Go to Step 3*	*Go to Step 17*
3	1. Verify that the engine is running. 2. Turn the ignition switch to the RUN position. 3. Select Special Functions on the *Scan Tool.* 4. Use the *Scan Tool* in order to perform the Voltage Load test. Are the ignition voltage and the battery voltage equal to or greater than the specified range?	10 V	*Go to Step 4*	*Go to Step 10*
4	1. Turn the ignition switch to the OFF position. 2. Disconnect the 24-way EBCM connector C2. 3. Disconnect the 8-way EBCM connector C1. 4. Disconnect the Electronic Brake Control Relay. 5. Use the *J 39200* in order to measure the resistance between the Electronic Brake Control Relay connector terminal 87 and the 8-way EBCM connector C1 terminal C. Is the resistance within the specified range?	0–2 Ω	*Go to Step 5*	*Go to Step 11*
5	1. Disconnect the negative battery cable. 2. Disconnect the positive battery cable. 3. Use the *J 39200* in order to measure the resistance between the positive battery terminal and the Electronic Brake Control Relay connector terminal 30. Is the resistance within the specified range?	0–2 Ω	*Go to Step 6*	*Go to Step 12*
6	1. Remove the fuse block ERLS Fuse (10A). 2. Use the *J 39200* in order to measure the resistance between the fuse block terminal (ERLS Fuse [10A]) and the 24-way EBCM connector C2 terminal A9. Is the resistance within the specified range?	0–2 Ω	*Go to Step 7*	*Go to Step 13*

GC402980309400BX

Fig. 106 Code C1236: Low System Supply Voltage (Part 2 of 3). Cavalier & Sunfire

Step	Action	Value(s)	Yes	No
7	Use the *J 39200* in order to measure the resistance between the fuse block terminal (ERLS Fuse [10A]) and the 24-way EBCM connector C2 terminal A9. Is the resistance within the specified range?	0–2 Ω	*Go to Step 8*	*Go to Step 14*
8	1. Inspect the following components: • The Electronic Brake Control Relay connector • The 24-way EBCM connector C2 • The 8-way EBCM connector C1 • The positive battery cable connections • The negative battery cable connections 2. Inspect the above components for the following conditions: • Terminal damage • Poor terminal contact • Terminal corrosion The above conditions may cause an open circuit. Are there signs of terminal damage, poor terminal contact, or terminal corrosion?	—	*Go to Step 15*	*Go to Step 9*
9	1. Reconnect the 24-way EBCM connector C2. 2. Reconnect the 8-way EBCM connector C1. 3. Reconnect the Electronic Brake Control Relay. 4. Reconnect the positive battery cable. 5. Reconnect the negative battery cable. 6. Drive the vehicle at a speed above 5 km/h (3 mph). Does DTC C1236 set as a current DTC?	—	*Go to Step 16*	*Go to Step 17*
10	Repair the low voltage condition. Is the low voltage condition repaired?	—	Refer to *Diagnostic System Check*	—
11	Repair the open or high resistance in CKT 1633. Is the repair complete?	—	Refer to *Diagnostic System Check*	—
12	Repair the open or high resistance in CKT 342. Is the repair complete?	—	Refer to *Diagnostic System Check*	—
13	Repair the open or high resistance in CKT 439. Is the repair complete?	—	Refer to *Diagnostic System Check*	—
14	Repair the open or high resistance in CKT 3 or CKT 1. Is the repair complete?	—	Refer to *Diagnostic System Check*	—
15	Replace all of the terminals or the connectors that exhibit signs of poor terminal contact, corrosion, or damaged terminals. Is the repair complete?	—	Refer to *Diagnostic System Check*	—
16	Replace the EBCM. Is the repair complete?	—	Refer to *Diagnostic System Check*	—
17	The malfunction is intermittent or is not present at this time. Refer to Diagnostic Aids for more information.	—	—	—

GC402980309400CX

Fig. 106 Code C1236: Low System Supply Voltage (Part 3 of 3). Cavalier & Sunfire

Circuit Description

DTC C1237 detects high vehicle voltage levels prior to any required motor movement (initialization or ABS). Damage to the system may occur if excessive voltage exists.

Conditions for Setting the DTC

DTC C1237 can set only if the vehicle's speed is greater than 5 km/h (3 mph).

A malfunction exists if the switched battery voltage is greater than 17 volts.

Action Taken When the DTC Sets

- A malfunction DTC stores.
- The ABS disables.
- The ABS warning indicator turns on.

Conditions for Clearing the DTC

- The condition responsible for setting the DTC no longer exists and the Scan Tool Clear DTCs function is used.
- 100 drive cycles pass with no DTC(s) detected. A drive cycle consists of starting the vehicle, driving the vehicle over 16 km/h (10 mph), stopping and then turning the ignition off.

Diagnostic Aids

The following conditions may cause an intermittent malfunction:

- A poor connection
- Rubbed-through wire insulation
- A broken wire inside the insulation

Use the enhanced diagnostic function of the Scan Tool in order to measure the frequency of the malfunction.

Thoroughly inspect any circuitry that may be causing the intermittent complaint for the following conditions:

- Backed out terminals
- Improper mating
- Broken locks
- Improperly formed or damaged terminals
- Poor terminal-to-wiring connections
- Physical damage to the wiring harness

Important: Zero the J 39200 test leads before making any resistance measurements. Refer to the J 39200 user's manual.

GC402980309500AX

Fig. 107 Code C1237: High System Supply Voltage (Part 1 of 2). Cavalier & Sunfire

Step	Action	Value(s)	Yes	No
1	Was the Diagnostic System Check performed?	—	*Go to Step 2*	Refer to *Diagnostic System Check*
2	1. Start the engine. 2. Install a *Scan Tool.* 3. Select Data List on the *Scan Tool.* 4. Select Battery Voltage on the *Scan Tool.* 5. Run the engine at approximately 2000 RPM and monitor the voltage. Is the voltage less than or equal to the specified voltage?	16 V	*Go to Step 6*	*Go to Step 3*
3	1. Turn the ignition switch to the OFF position. 2. Disconnect the Electronic Brake Control Relay. 3. Start the engine. 4. Use the *J 39200* in order to measure the voltage between the Electronic Brake Control Relay connector terminal 30 and ground. 5. Run the engine at approximately 2000 RPM and monitor the voltage. Is the voltage less than or equal to the specified range?	16 V	*Go to Step 4*	Charging System
4	1. Turn the ignition switch to the OFF position. 2. Reconnect the Electronic Brake Control Relay. 3. Drive the vehicle at a speed above 5 km/h (3 mph). 4. Use the *Scan Tool* in order to look for DTCs. Does DTC C1237 set as a current DTC?	—	*Go to Step 5*	*Go to Step 6*
5	Replace the EBCM. Is the repair complete?	—	Refer to *Diagnostic System Check*	—
6	The malfunction is intermittent or is not present at this time. Refer to Diagnostic Aids for more information.	—	—	—

GC402980309500BX

Fig. 107 Code C1237: High System Supply Voltage (Part 2 of 2). Cavalier & Sunfire

Circuit Description

DTC C1238 detects a slipping left front ESB. During initialization and braking, the left front brake motor is rehomed. If the ESB slips, the motor/piston will move. During the next key to RUN initialization, a rehome of the motor verifies the motor/piston remained at the home position. If motor movement is detected, the ESB must be slipping.

If an ESB cannot hold a piston in the home position, the piston may be driven back when the brake pedal is applied. Then the brake pedal will drop.

Conditions for Setting the DTC

DTC C1238 can set during initialization at the following speeds:

- 0 km/h (0 mph) when the brake is off
- 5 km/h (3 mph) when the brake is on

A malfunction exists if the EBCM detects that the ESB could not hold the piston in the home position.

Action Taken When the DTC Sets

- A malfunction DTC stores.
- The ABS disables.
- The ABS warning indicator turns on.

Conditions for Clearing the DTC

- The condition responsible for setting the DTC no longer exists and the Scan Tool Clear DTCs function is used.
- 100 drive cycles pass with no DTCs detected. A drive cycle consists of starting the vehicle, driving the vehicle over 16 km/h (10 mph), stopping and then turning the ignition off.

Diagnostic Aids

The following conditions may cause an intermittent malfunction if the conditions exist in a mechanical part of the system:

- Sticking
- Binding
- Slipping

Use the enhanced diagnostic function of the Scan Tool in order to measure the frequency of the malfunction.

Use the hydraulic control modulator test function of the Scan Tool in order to locate an intermittent malfunction associated with the ESB.

Clear the DTCs after completing the diagnosis. Test drive the vehicle for three drive cycles in order to verify that the DTC does not reset. Use the following procedure in order to complete one drive cycle:

1. Start the vehicle.
2. Drive the vehicle over 16 km/h (10 mph).
3. Stop the vehicle.
4. Turn the ignition to the OFF position.

Important: Zero the J 39200 test leads before making any resistance measurements. Refer to the J 39200 user's manual.

GC402980309600AA

Fig. 108 Code C1238: LH Front ESB Does Not Hold Motor (Part 1 of 3). Cavalier & Sunfire

Step	Action	Value(s)	Yes	No
1	Was the Diagnostic System Check performed?	—	*Go to Step 2*	Refer to *Diagnostic System Check*
2	Inspect the following connectors for the correct wire color/connector cavity combinations: • The 6-way ABS brake motor pack connector • The 8-way EBCM connector C1 Are the correct wires located in the correct connector cavities?	—	*Go to Step 3*	*Go to Step 10*
3	1. Turn the ignition switch to the RUN position. Do not start the engine. 2. Pump the brake pedal until it is firm in order to deplete the brake booster vacuum reservoir. 3. Install a *Scan Tool.* 4. Select Special Functions on the *Scan Tool.* 5. Select the Manual Control function on the *Scan Tool.* 6. Select the ABS Motor Apply function of the left front ABS channel on the *Scan Tool.* 7. Use the *Scan Tool* in order to apply the left front ABS motor. 8. Wait for five seconds. 9. Apply firm pressure to the brake pedal. Does the brake pedal fall?	—	*Go to Step 9*	*Go to Step 4*
4	1. Use the *Scan Tool* in order to exit the Manual Control function. 2. Turn the ignition switch to the OFF position. 3. Disconnect the following connectors: • The 6-way ABS brake motor pack connector • The 8-way EBCM connector C1 4. Use the *J 39200* in order to measure the resistance between the 6-way ABS brake motor pack harness connector terminal A and the 8-way EBCM harness connector C1 terminal G. Is the resistance within the specified range?	0–2 Ω	*Go to Step 5*	*Go to Step 11*
5	Use the *J 39200* in order to measure the resistance between the 6-way ABS brake motor pack harness connector terminal B and the 8-way EBCM harness connector C1 terminal H. Is the resistance within the specified range?	0–2 Ω	*Go to Step 6*	*Go to Step 12*
6	Use the *J 39200* in order to measure the resistance between the 6-way ABS brake motor pack connector terminal A and the ABS brake motor pack connector terminal B. Is the resistance within the specified range?	0.2–1.5 Ω	*Go to Step 7*	*Go to Step 9*

GC402980309600BX

Fig. 108 Code C1238: LH Front ESB Does Not Hold Motor (Part 2 of 3). Cavalier & Sunfire

Step	Action	Value(s)	Yes	No
7	1. Inspect the following connectors: • The 6-way ABS brake motor pack connector • The 8-way EBCM connector C1 2. Inspect the above connectors for the following conditions: • Poor terminal contact • Corrosion Are there signs of poor terminal contact or corrosion?	—	*Go to Step 13*	*Go to Step 8*
8	1. Turn the ignition switch to the OFF position. 2. Reconnect the 8-way EBCM connector C1 3. Reconnect the 6-way ABS brake motor pack connector 4. Start the engine. Do not depress the brake pedal while starting the engine. 5. Allow the engine to run for at least 10 seconds. 6. Repeat the above ignition cycle sequence at least two more times. 7. Use the *Scan Tool* in order to look for DTCs. Does the DTC C1238 set during the last three ignition cycles?	—	*Go to Step 14*	*Go to Step 15*
9	Replace the ABS brake motor pack. Is the repair complete?	—	Refer to *Diagnostic System Check*	—
10	Place the correct wires into the connector cavities. Is the repair complete?	—	Refer to *Diagnostic System Check*	—
11	Repair the open or high resistance in CKT 1280. Is the repair complete?	—	Refer to *Diagnostic System Check*	—
12	Repair the open or high resistance in CKT 1281. Is the repair complete?	—	Refer to *Diagnostic System Check*	—
13	Replace the terminals that exhibit signs of poor terminal contact or corrosion. Is the repair complete?	—	Refer to *Diagnostic System Check*	—
14	Replace the EBCM. Is the repair complete?	—	Refer to *Diagnostic System Check*	—
15	The malfunction is intermittent or is not present at this time. Refer to Diagnostic Aids for more information.	—	—	—

GC402980309600CX

Fig. 108 Code C1238: LH Front ESB Does Not Hold Motor (Part 3 of 3). Cavalier & Sunfire

Circuit Description

DTC C1241 detects a slipping right front ESB. During initialization and braking, the right front brake motor is rehomed. If the ESB slips, the motor/piston will move. During the next key to RUN initialization, a rehome of the motor verifies the motor/piston remained at the home position. If motor movement is detected, the ESB must be slipping.

If an ESB cannot hold a piston in the home position, the piston may be driven back when the brake pedal is applied. Then the brake pedal will drop.

Conditions for Setting the DTC

DTC C1241 can set during initialization at the following speeds:

- 0 km/h (0 mph) when the brake is off
- 5 km/h (3 mph) when the brake is on

A malfunction exists if the EBCM detects that the ESB could not hold the piston in the home position.

Action Taken When the DTC Sets

- A malfunction DTC stores.
- The ABS disables.
- The ABS warning indicator turns on.

Conditions for Clearing the DTC

- The condition responsible for setting the DTC no longer exists and the Scan Tool Clear DTCs function is used.
- 100 drive cycles pass with no DTCs detected. A drive cycle consists of starting the vehicle, driving the vehicle over 16 km/h (10 mph), stopping and then turning the ignition off.

Diagnostic Aids

The following conditions may cause an intermittent malfunction if the conditions exist in a mechanical part of the system:

- Sticking
- Binding
- Slipping

Use the enhanced diagnostic function of the Scan Tool in order to measure the frequency of the malfunction.

Use the hydraulic control modulator test function of the Scan Tool in order to locate an intermittent malfunction associated with the ESB.

Clear the DTCs after completing the diagnosis. Test drive the vehicle for three drive cycles in order to verify that the DTC does not reset. Use the following procedure in order to complete one drive cycle:

1. Start the vehicle.
2. Drive the vehicle over 16 km/h (10 mph).
3. Stop the vehicle.
4. Turn the ignition to the OFF position.

Important: Zero the J 39200 test leads before making any resistance measurements. Refer to the J 39200 user's manual.

GC402980309602AX

Fig. 109 Code C1241: RH Front ESB Does Not Hold Motor (Part 1 of 3). Cavalier & Sunfire

Step	Action	Value(s)	Yes	No
1	Was the Diagnostic System Check performed?	—	*Go to Step 2*	Refer to *Diagnostic System Check*
2	Inspect the following connectors for the correct wire color/connector cavity combinations: • The 6-way ABS brake motor pack connector • The 8-way EBCM connector C1 Are the correct wires located in the correct connector cavities?	—	*Go to Step 3*	*Go to Step 10*
3	1. Turn the ignition switch to the RUN position. Do not start the engine. 2. Pump the brake pedal until it is firm in order to deplete the brake booster vacuum reservoir. 3. Install a *Scan Tool*. 4. Select the Special Functions on the *Scan Tool*. 5. Select the Manual Control function on the *Scan Tool*. 6. Select the ABS Motor Apply function of the left front ABS channel on the *Scan Tool*. 7. Use the *Scan Tool* in order to apply the left front ABS motor. 8. Wait for five seconds. 9. Apply firm pressure to the brake pedal. Does the brake pedal fall?	—	*Go to Step 9*	*Go to Step 4*
4	1. Use the *Scan Tool* in order to exit the Manual Control function. 2. Turn the ignition switch to the OFF position. 3. Disconnect the following connectors: • The 6-way ABS brake motor pack connector • The 8-way EBCM connector C1 4. Use the *J 39200* in order to measure the resistance between the 6-way ABS brake motor pack harness connector terminal E and the 8-way EBCM harness connector C1 terminal A. Is the resistance within the specified range?	0–2 Ω	*Go to Step 5*	*Go to Step 11*
5	Use the *J 39200* in order to measure the resistance between the 6-way ABS brake motor pack harness connector terminal F and the 8-way EBCM harness connector C1 terminal B. Is the resistance within the specified range?	0–2 Ω	*Go to Step 6*	*Go to Step 12*
6	Use the *J 39200* in order to measure the resistance between the 6-way ABS brake motor pack connector terminal E and the ABS brake motor pack connector terminal F. Is the resistance within the specified range?	0.2–1.5 Ω	*Go to Step 7*	*Go to Step 9*

GC402980309600DX

Fig. 109 Code C1241: RH Front ESB Does Not Hold Motor (Part 2 of 3). Cavalier & Sunfire

Step	Action	Value(s)	Yes	No
7	1. Inspect the following connectors: • The 6-way ABS brake motor pack connector • The 8-way EBCM connector C1 2. Inspect the above connectors for the following conditions: • Poor terminal contact • Corrosion Refer to Checking Terminal Contact in the service manual. Are there signs of poor terminal contact or corrosion?	—	*Go to Step 13*	*Go to Step 8*
8	1. Turn the ignition switch to the OFF position. 2. Reconnect the 8-way EBCM connector C1 3. Reconnect the 6-way ABS brake motor pack connector 4. Start the engine. Do not depress the brake pedal while starting the engine. 5. Allow the engine to run for at least 10 seconds. 6. Repeat the above ignition cycle sequence at least two more times. 7. Use the *Scan Tool* in order to look for DTCs. Does the DTC C1241 set during the last three ignition cycles?	—	*Go to Step 14*	*Go to Step 15*
9	Replace the ABS brake motor pack. Is the repair complete?	—	Refer to *Diagnostic System Check*	—
10	Place the correct wires into the connector cavities. Is the repair complete?	—	Refer to *Diagnostic System Check*	—
11	Repair the open or high resistance in CKT 1282. Is the repair complete?	—	Refer to *Diagnostic System Check*	—
12	Repair the open or high resistance in CKT 1283. Is the repair complete?	—	Refer to *Diagnostic System Check*	—
13	Replace the terminals that exhibit signs of poor terminal contact or corrosion. Is the repair complete?	—	Refer to *Diagnostic System Check*	—
14	Replace the EBCM. Is the repair complete?	—	Refer to *Diagnostic System Check*	—
15	The malfunction is intermittent or is not present at this time. Refer to Diagnostic Aids for more information.	—	—	—

GC402980309600EX

Fig. 109 Code C1241: RH Front ESB Does Not Hold Motor (Part 3 of 3). Cavalier & Sunfire

Circuit Description

DTC C1242 detects a slipping rear axle ESB. During initialization and braking, the rear motor is rehomed. If the ESB slips, the motor/piston will move. During the next key to RUN initialization, a rehome of the motor verifies the motor/piston remained at the home position. If motor movement is detected, the ESB must be slipping.

If an ESB cannot hold a piston in the home position, the piston may be driven back when the brake pedal is applied. Then the brake pedal will drop.

Conditions for Setting the DTC

DTC C1242 can set during initialization at the following speeds:

- 0 km/h (0 mph) when the brake is off
- 5 km/h (3 mph) when the brake is on

A malfunction exists if the EBCM detects that the ESB could not hold the piston in the home position.

DTC C1286 always sets with DTC C1242.

Action Taken When the DTC Sets

- A malfunction DTC stores.
- The ABS disables.
- The ABS warning indicator turns on.

Conditions for Clearing the DTC

- The condition responsible for setting the DTC no longer exists and the Scan Tool Clear DTCs function is used.
- 100 drive cycles pass with no DTCs detected. A drive cycle consists of starting the vehicle, driving the vehicle over 16 km/h (10 mph), stopping and then turning the ignition off.

Diagnostic Aids

The following conditions may cause an intermittent malfunction if the conditions exist in a mechanical part of the system:

- Sticking
- Binding
- Slipping

Use the enhanced diagnostic function of the Scan Tool in order to measure the frequency of the malfunction.

Use the hydraulic control modulator test function of the Scan Tool in order to locate an intermittent malfunction associated with the ESB.

Clear the DTCs after completing the diagnosis. Test drive the vehicle for three drive cycles in order to verify that the DTC does not reset. Use the following procedure in order to complete one drive cycle:

1. Start the vehicle.
2. Drive the vehicle over 16 km/h (10 mph).
3. Stop the vehicle.
4. Turn the ignition to the OFF position.

Important: Zero the J 39200 test leads before making any resistance measurements.

GC402980309601AX

Fig. 110 Code C1242: Rear ESB Does Not Hold Motor (Part 1 of 3). Cavalier & Sunfire

Step	Action	Value(s)	Yes	No
1	Was the Diagnostic System Check performed?	—	*Go to Step 2*	Refer to *Diagnostic System Check*
2	Inspect the following connectors for the correct wire color/connector cavity combinations: • The 6-way ABS brake motor pack connector • The 8-way EBCM connector C1 Are the correct wires located in the correct connector cavities?	—	*Go to Step 3*	*Go to Step 10*
3	1. Turn the ignition switch to the RUN position. Do not start the engine. 2. Pump the brake pedal until it is firm in order to deplete the brake booster vacuum reservoir. 3. Raise and support the vehicle so that the rear wheels are approximately 6 inches off the floor. 4. Turn the ignition switch to the run position. 5. Install a *Scan Tool*. 6. Apply firm pressure to the brake pedal. 7. Select the Special Functions on the *Scan Tool*. 8. Select the Manual Control function on the *Scan Tool*. 9. Select the ABS Motor Apply function of the rear ABS channel on the *Scan Tool*. 10. Use the *Scan Tool* in order to apply the rear ABS motor. 11. Wait for five seconds. 12. Have an assistant try to spin the rear wheels by hand. Could the assistant spin the rear wheels?	—	*Go to Step 9*	*Go to Step 4*
4	1. Exit the Manual Control function. 2. Turn the ignition switch to the OFF position. 3. Disconnect the following connectors: • The 6-way ABS brake motor pack connector • The 8-way EBCM connector C1 4. Use the *J 39200* in order to measure the resistance between the 6-way ABS brake motor pack harness connector terminal C and the 8-way EBCM harness connector C1 terminal F. Is the resistance within the specified range?	0–2 Ω	*Go to Step 5*	*Go to Step 11*
5	Use the *J 39200* in order to measure the resistance between the 6-way ABS brake motor pack harness connector terminal D and the 8-way EBCM harness connector C1 terminal E. Is the resistance within the specified range?	0–2 Ω	*Go to Step 6*	*Go to Step 12*
6	Use the *J 39200* in order to measure the resistance between the 6-way ABS brake motor pack connector terminal C and the ABS brake motor pack connector terminal D. Is the resistance within the specified range?	0.2–1.5 Ω	*Go to Step 7*	*Go to Step 9*

GC402980309600FX

Fig. 110 Code C1242: Rear ESB Does Not Hold Motor (Part 2 of 3). Cavalier & Sunfire

Step	Action	Value(s)	Yes	No
7	1. Inspect the following connectors: • The 6-way ABS brake motor pack connector • The 8-way EBCM connector C1 2. Inspect the above connectors for the following conditions: • Poor terminal contact • Corrosion Refer to Checking Terminal Contact in the service manual. Are there signs of poor terminal contact or corrosion?	—	Go to Step 13	Go to Step 8
8	1. Turn the ignition switch to the OFF position. 2. Reconnect the 8-way EBCM connector C1 3. Reconnect the 6-way ABS brake motor pack connector 4. Start the engine. Do not depress the brake pedal while starting the engine. 5. Allow the engine to run for at least 10 seconds. 6. Repeat the above ignition cycle sequence at least two more times. 7. Use the *Scan Tool* in order to look for DTCs. Does the DTC C1242 set during the last three ignition cycles?	—	Go to Step 14	Go to Step 15
9	Replace the ABS brake motor pack. Is the repair complete?	—	Refer to *Diagnostic System Check*	—
10	Place the correct wires into the connector cavities. Is the repair complete?	—	Refer to *Diagnostic System Check*	—
11	Repair the open or high resistance in CKT 1284. Is the repair complete?	—	Refer to *Diagnostic System Check*	—
12	Repair the open or high resistance in CKT 1285. Is the repair complete?	—	Refer to *Diagnostic System Check*	—
13	Replace the terminals that exhibit signs of poor terminal contact or corrosion. Is the repair complete?	—	Refer to *Diagnostic System Check*	—
14	Replace the EBCM. Is the repair complete?	—	Refer to *Diagnostic System Check*	—
15	The malfunction is intermittent or is not present at this time. Refer to Diagnostic Aids for more information.	—	—	—

GC402980309600GX

Fig. 110 Code C1242: Rear ESB Does Not Hold Motor (Part 3 of 3). Cavalier & Sunfire

Step	Action	Value(s)	Yes	No
1	Was the Diagnostic System Check performed?	—	Go to Step 2	Refer to *Diagnostic System Check.*
2	Inspect the following connectors for the correct wire color/connector cavity combinations: • The 6-way ABS brake motor pack connector • The 8-way EBCM connector C1 Are the correct wires located in the correct connector cavities?	—	Go to Step 3	Go to Step 11
3	1. Turn the ignition switch to the RUN position. Do not start the engine. 2. Pump the brake pedal until the brake pedal is firm in order to deplete the brake booster vacuum reservoir. 3. Install a *Scan Tool.* 4. Select Special Functions on the *Scan Tool.* 5. Select the Manual Control function on the *Scan Tool.* 6. Select the ABS Motor Apply function of the left front ABS channel on the *Scan Tool.* 7. Use the *Scan Tool* in order to apply the left front ABS motor. 8. Wait for five seconds. 9. Apply firm pressure to the brake pedal. 10. Select the left front ABS Motor Release function on the *Scan Tool.* 11. Use the *Scan Tool* in order to release the left front ABS motor. Does the brake pedal fall?	—	Go to Step 4	Go to Step 5
4	1. Continue to apply firm pressure on the brake pedal. 2. Select the left front ABS Motor Apply function on the *Scan Tool.* 3. Use the *Scan Tool* in order to apply the left front ABS motor. Does the brake pedal rise?	—	Go to Step 17	Go to Step 5
5	1. Remove the firm pressure from the brake pedal. 2. Select the left front ABS Motor Apply function on the *Scan Tool.* 3. Use the *Scan Tool* in order to apply the left front ABS motor. 4. Carefully observe the following currents: • The left front ABS motor commanded current • The left front ABS motor feedback current. Did the left front ABS motor feedback current momentarily drop below the specified current?	8 A	Go to Step 6	Go to Step 10

GC402980309800BX

Fig. 111 Code C1244: LH Front ABS Channel Does Not Move (Part 2 of 4). Cavalier & Sunfire

Circuit Description

DTC C1244 detects a bound-up ESB, a stuck ABS motor, or a seized brake modulator. When the release is commanded during initialization, the ESB should release the ABS motor, resulting in the sensed current being less than the commanded current (motor spins freely). If the ABS motor is not moving, sensed current will be equal to stall currents.

Conditions for Setting the DTC

DTC C1244 can set during brake motor initialization at the following speeds:

- 0 km/h (0 mph) when the brake is off
- 5 km/h (3 mph) when the brake is on

DTC C1244 can set during ABS stops

A malfunction exists if the EBCM detects a condition in which the EBCM cannot move the ABS motor in either direction.

Action Taken When the DTC Sets

- A malfunction DTC stores.
- The ABS disables.
- The ABS warning indicator turns on.

Conditions for Clearing the DTC

- The condition responsible for setting the DTC no longer exists and the Scan Tool Clear DTCs function is used.
- 100 drive cycles pass with no DTCs detected. A drive cycle consists of starting the vehicle, driving the vehicle over 16 km/h (10 mph), stopping and then turning the ignition off.

Diagnostic Aids

The following conditions may cause an intermittent malfunction if the conditions exist in a mechanical part of the system:

- Sticking
- Binding
- Slipping

Use the enhanced diagnostic function of the Scan Tool in order to measure the frequency of the malfunction. DTC C1244 may set after modulator disassembly if the modulator pistons are positioned at the bottom of the modulator piston bore.

Thoroughly inspect any circuitry that may be causing the intermittent complaint for the following conditions:

- Backed out terminals
- Improper mating
- Broken locks
- Improperly formed or damaged terminals
- Poor terminal-to-wiring connections
- Physical damage to the wiring harness

Clear the DTCs after completing the diagnosis. Test drive the vehicle for three drive cycles in order to verify that the DTC does not reset. Use the following procedure in order to complete one drive cycle:

1. Start the vehicle.
2. Drive the vehicle over 16 km/h (10 mph).
3. Stop the vehicle.
4. Turn the ignition to the OFF position.

Important: Zero the J 39200 test leads before making any resistance measurements.

GC402980309800AX

Fig. 111 Code C1244: LH Front ABS Channel Does Not Move (Part 1 of 4). Cavalier & Sunfire

Step	Action	Value(s)	Yes	No
6	1. Exit the Manual Control function on the *Scan Tool.* 2. Turn the ignition switch to the OFF position. 3. Disconnect the 6-way ABS brake motor pack connector. 4. Disconnect the 8-way EBCM connector C1 5. Use the *J 39200* in order to measure the resistance between the 8-way EBCM connector C1 terminal G and the 8-way EBCM connector C1 terminal H. Is the resistance within the specified range?	OL (Infinite)	Go to Step 7	Go to Step 12
7	Use the *J 39200* in order to measure the resistance between the ABS brake motor pack connector terminal A and the ABS brake motor pack connector terminal B. Is the resistance within the specified range?	0.2–1.5Ω	Go to Step 8	Go to Step 13
8	1. Inspect the following connectors: • The 6-way ABS motor pack connector • The 8-way EBCM connector C1 2. Inspect the connectors for the following conditions: • Poor terminal contact • Corrosion Do any of the terminals exhibit poor terminal contact or corrosion?	—	Go to Step 15	Go to Step 9
9	1. Turn the ignition switch to the OFF position. 2. Reconnect the 8-way EBCM connector C1. 3. Reconnect the ABS motor pack connector. 4. Start the engine. Do not depress the brake pedal. 5. Allow the engine to run for at least ten seconds. 6. Repeat the above ignition cycle sequence two more times. 7. Use the *Scan Tool* in order to inspect for DTCs. Does DTC C1244 set during the last three ignition cycles?	—	Go to Step 16	Go to Step 17
10	1. Select Special Functions on the *Scan Tool.* 2. Use the *Scan Tool* in order to perform the Gear Tension Relief function. 3. Turn the ignition switch to the OFF position. 4. Remove the brake modulator/master cylinder assembly from the vehicle. 5. Separate the ABS brake motor pack from the brake modulator. 6. Grasp the left front brake modulator gear and attempt to rotate the gear. (The ABS brake modulator left front gear is the gear that is closest to the front when the ABS brake modulator is mounted in the vehicle.) Is it possible to rotate the left front brake modulator gear at least 8.5 full revolutions from lock to lock?	—	Go to Step 13	Go to Step 14

GC402980309800CX

Fig. 111 Code C1244: LH Front ABS Channel Does Not Move (Part 3 of 4). Cavalier & Sunfire

Step	Action	Value(s)	Yes	No
11	Place the wires into the correct connector cavities. Is the repair complete?	—	Refer to *Diagnostic System Check*	—
12	Repair the short between CKT 1280 and CKT 1281. Is the repair complete?	—	Refer to *Diagnostic System Check*	—
13	Replace the ABS motor pack. Is the repair complete?	—	Refer to *Diagnostic System Check*	—
14	Replace the brake modulator. Is the repair complete?	—	Refer to *Diagnostic System Check*	—
15	Replace the terminals that exhibit signs of poor terminal contact or corrosion. Is the repair complete?	—	Refer to *Diagnostic System Check*	—
16	Replace the EBCM. Is the repair complete?	—	Refer to *Diagnostic System Check*	—
17	The malfunction is intermittent or is not present at this time. Refer to Diagnostic Aids for more information.	—	—	—

GC402980309800DX

Fig. 111 Code C1244: LH Front ABS Channel Does Not Move (Part 4 of 4). Cavalier & Sunfire

Step	Action	Value(s)	Yes	No
1	Was the Diagnostic System Check performed?	—	*Go to Step 2*	Refer to *Diagnostic System Check*
2	Inspect the following connectors for the correct wire color/connector cavity combinations: • The 6-way ABS brake motor pack connector • The 8-way EBCM connector C1 Are the correct wires located in the correct connector cavities?	—	*Go to Step 3*	*Go to Step 11*
3	1. Turn the ignition switch to the RUN position. Do not start the engine. 2. Pump the brake pedal until it is firm in order to deplete the brake booster vacuum reservoir. 3. Install a *Scan Tool.* 4. Select Special Functions on the *Scan Tool.* 5. Select the Manual Control function on the *Scan Tool.* 6. Select the ABS Motor Apply function of the right front ABS channel on the *Scan Tool.* 7. Use the *Scan Tool* to apply the right front ABS motor. 8. Wait for five seconds. 9. Apply firm pressure to the brake pedal. 10. Select the right front ABS Motor Release function on the *Scan Tool.* 11. Use the *Scan Tool* in order to release the right front ABS motor. Does the brake pedal fall?	—	*Go to Step 4*	*Go to Step 5*
4	1. Continue to apply firm pressure on the brake pedal. 2. Select the right front ABS Motor Apply function on the *Scan Tool.* 3. Use the *Scan Tool* in order to apply the right front ABS motor. Does the brake pedal rise?	—	*Go to Step 17*	*Go to Step 5*
5	1. Remove the firm pressure from the brake pedal. 2. Select the right front ABS Motor Apply function on the *Scan Tool.* 3. Use the *Scan Tool* in order to apply the right front ABS motor. 4. Carefully observe the following currents: • The right front ABS motor commanded current • The right front ABS motor feedback current. Did the right front ABS motor feedback current Momentarily drop below the specified current?	8 A	*Go to Step 6*	*Go to Step 10*

GC402980309900BX

Fig. 112 Code C1245: RH Front ABS Channel Does Not Move (Part 2 of 4). Cavalier & Sunfire

Circuit Description

DTC C1245 detects a bound-up ESB, a stuck ABS motor, or a seized brake modulator. When the release is commanded during initialization, the ESB should release the ABS motor, resulting in the feedback current being less than the commanded current (motor spins freely). If the ABS motor is not moving, feedback current will be equal to commanded current.

Conditions for Setting the DTC

DTC C1245 can set during brake motor initialization at the following speeds:

- 0 km/h (0 mph) when the brake is off
- 5 km/h (3 mph) when the brake is on

DTC C1245 can set during ABS stops

A malfunction exists if the EBCM detects a condition in which the EBCM cannot move the ABS motor in either direction.

Action Taken When the DTC Sets

- A malfunction DTC stores.
- The ABS disables.
- The ABS warning indicator turns on.

Conditions for Clearing the DTC

- The condition responsible for setting the DTC no longer exists and the Scan Tool Clear DTCs function is used.
- 100 drive cycles pass with no DTCs detected. A drive cycle consists of starting the vehicle, driving the vehicle over 16 km/h (10 mph), stopping and then turning the ignition off.

Diagnostic Aids

The following conditions may cause an intermittent malfunction if the conditions exist in a mechanical part of the system:

- Sticking
- Binding
- Slipping

Use the enhanced diagnostic function of the Scan Tool in order to measure the frequency of the malfunction. DTC C1245 may set after modulator disassembly if the modulator pistons are positioned at the bottom of the modulator piston bore.

Thoroughly inspect any circuitry that may be causing the intermittent complaint for the following conditions:

- Backed out terminals
- Improper mating
- Broken locks
- Improperly formed or damaged terminals
- Poor terminal-to-wiring connections
- Physical damage to the wiring harness

Clear the DTCs after completing the diagnosis. Test drive the vehicle for three drive cycles in order to verify that the DTC does not reset. Use the following procedure in order to complete one drive cycle:

1. Start the vehicle.
2. Drive the vehicle over 16 km/h (10 mph).
3. Stop the vehicle.
4. Turn the ignition to the OFF position.

Important: Zero the J 39200 test leads before making any resistance measurements. Refer to the J 39200 user's manual.

GC402980309900AX

Fig. 112 Code C1245: RH Front ABS Channel Does Not Move (Part 1 of 4). Cavalier & Sunfire

Step	Action	Value(s)	Yes	No
6	1. Exit the Manual Control function on the *Scan Tool.* 2. Turn the ignition switch to the OFF position. 3. Disconnect the 6-way ABS brake motor pack connector. 4. Disconnect the 8-way EBCM connector C1 5. Use the *J 39200* in order to measure the resistance between the 8-way EBCM connector C1 terminal A and the 8-way EBCM connector C1 terminal B. Is the resistance within the specified range?	OL (Infinite)	*Go to Step 7*	*Go to Step 12*
7	Use the *J 39200* in order to measure the resistance between the ABS brake motor pack connector terminal E and the ABS brake motor pack connector terminal F. Is the resistance within the specified range?	0.2–1.5Ω	*Go to Step 8*	*Go to Step 13*
8	1. Inspect the following connectors: • The 6-way ABS motor pack connector • The 8-way EBCM connector C1 2. Inspect the connectors for the following conditions: • Poor terminal contact • Corrosion Do any of the terminals exhibit poor terminal contact or corrosion?	—	*Go to Step 15*	*Go to Step 9*
9	1. Turn the ignition switch to the OFF position. 2. Reconnect the 8-way EBCM connector C1. 3. Reconnect the ABS motor pack connector. 4. Start the engine. Do not depress the brake pedal. 5. Allow the engine to run for at least ten seconds. 6. Repeat the above ignition cycle sequence two more times. 7. Use the *Scan Tool* in order to inspect for DTCs. Does DTC C1245 set during the last three ignition cycles?	—	*Go to Step 16*	*Go to Step 17*
10	1. Select Special Functions on the *Scan Tool.* 2. Use the *Scan Tool* in order to perform the Gear Tension Relief function. 3. Turn the ignition switch to the OFF position. 4. Remove the brake modulator/master cylinder assembly from the vehicle. 5. Separate the ABS brake motor pack from the brake modulator. 6. Grasp the right front brake modulator gear and attempt to rotate the gear. (The ABS brake modulator right front gear is the gear that is closest to the rear when the ABS brake modulator is mounted in the vehicle.) Is it possible to rotate the right front brake modulator gear at least 8.5 full revolutions from lock to lock?	—	*Go to Step 13*	*Go to Step 14*

GC402980309900CX

Fig. 112 Code C1245: RH Front ABS Channel Does Not Move (Part 3 of 4). Cavalier & Sunfire

Step	Action	Value(s)	Yes	No
11	Place the wires into the correct connector cavities. Is the repair complete?	—	Refer to *Diagnostic System Check*	—
12	Repair the short between CKT 1282 and CKT 1283. Is the repair complete?	—	Refer to *Diagnostic System Check*	—
13	Replace the ABS motor pack. Is the repair complete?	—	Refer to *Diagnostic System Check*	—
14	Replace the brake modulator. Is the repair complete?	—	Refer to *Diagnostic System Check*	—
15	Replace the terminals that exhibit signs of poor terminal contact or corrosion. Is the repair complete?	—	Refer to *Diagnostic System Check*	—
16	Replace the EBCM. Is the repair complete?	—	Refer to *Diagnostic System Check*	—
17	The malfunction is intermittent or is not present at this time. Refer to Diagnostic Aids for more information.	—	—	—

GC402980309900DX

Fig. 112 Code C1245: RH Front ABS Channel Does Not Move (Part 4 of 4). Cavalier & Sunfire

Step	Action	Value(s)	Yes	No
1	Was the Diagnostic System Check performed?	—	*Go to Step 2*	Refer to *Diagnostic System Check*
2	Inspect the following connectors for the correct wire color/connector cavity combinations: • The 6-way ABS brake motor pack connector • The 8-way EBCM connector C1 Are the correct wires located in the correct connector cavities?	—	*Go to Step 3*	*Go to Step 11*
3	1. Raise and suitably support the vehicle. Verify that the rear wheels are approximately 15 cm (six in) above the floor. Refer to Vehicle Lifting and Jacking in General Information. 2. Turn the ignition switch to the RUN position. Do not start the engine. 3. Pump the brake pedal until it is firm in order to deplete the brake booster vacuum reservoir. 4. Install a *Scan Tool*. 5. Apply firm downward pressure on the brake pedal. 6. Select Special Functions on the *Scan Tool*. 7. Select the Manual Control function on the *Scan Tool*. 8. Select the Rear Axle Motor Apply function of the rear ABS channel on the *Scan Tool*. 9. Use the *Scan Tool* in order to apply the rear axle motor. 10. Have an assistant attempt to rotate the rear wheels by hand. Is it possible to rotate the rear wheels by hand?	—	*Go to Step 5*	*Go to Step 4*
4	1. Continue to apply firm downward pressure on the brake pedal. 2. Select the Rear Axle Motor Release function on the *Scan Tool*. 3. Use the *Scan Tool* in order to release the rear axle motor. Is it possible to rotate the rear wheels by hand?	—	*Go to Step 17*	*Go to Step 5*
5	1. Remove the firm pressure from the brake pedal. 2. Select the Rear Axle Motor Apply function on the *Scan Tool*. 3. Use the *Scan Tool* in order to apply the rear axle motor. 4. Carefully observe the following currents: • The rear axle motor commanded current • The rear axle motor feedback current. Did the rear motor feedback current momentarily drop below the specified current?	8 A	*Go to Step 6*	*Go to Step 10*

GC402980310000BX

Fig. 113 Code C1246: Rear ABS Channel Does Not Move (Part 2 of 4). Cavalier & Sunfire

Circuit Description

DTC C1246 detects a bound-up ESB, a stuck ABS motor, or a seized brake modulator. When the release is commanded during initialization, the ESB should release the ABS motor, resulting in the feedback current being less than the commanded current (motor spins freely). If the ABS motor is not moving, feedback current will be equal to commanded current.

Conditions for Setting the DTC

DTC C1246 can set during brake motor initialization at the following speeds:

- 0 km/h (0 mph) when the brake is off
- 5 km/h (3 mph) when the brake is on

DTC C1246 can set during ABS stops

A malfunction exists if the EBCM detects a condition in which the EBCM cannot move the ABS motor in either direction.

Action Taken When the DTC Sets

- A malfunction DTC stores.
- The ABS disables.
- The ABS warning indicator turns on.

Conditions for Clearing the DTC

- The condition responsible for setting the DTC no longer exists and the Scan Tool Clear DTCs function is used.
- 100 drive cycles pass with no DTCs detected. A drive cycle consists of starting the vehicle, driving the vehicle over 16 km/h (10 mph), stopping and then turning the ignition off.

Diagnostic Aids

The following conditions may cause an intermittent malfunction if the conditions exist in a mechanical part of the system:

- Sticking
- Binding

Use the enhanced diagnostic function of the Scan Tool in order to measure the frequency of the malfunction. DTC C1246 may set after modulator disassembly if the modulator pistons are positioned at the bottom of the modulator piston bore. Depending on the frequency of the malfunction, a physical inspection of the mechanical parts suspected of causing the malfunction may be necessary.

Thoroughly inspect any circuitry that may be causing the intermittent complaint for the following conditions:

- Backed out terminals
- Improper mating
- Broken locks
- Improperly formed or damaged terminals
- Poor terminal-to-wiring connections
- Physical damage to the wiring harness

Clear the DTCs after completing the diagnosis. Test drive the vehicle for three drive cycles in order to verify that the DTC does not reset. Use the following procedure in order to complete one drive cycle:

1. Start the vehicle.
2. Drive the vehicle over 16 km/h (10 mph).
3. Stop the vehicle.
4. Turn the ignition to the OFF position.

Important: Zero the J 39200 test leads before making any resistance measurements. Refer to the J 39200 user's manual.

GC402980310000AX

Fig. 113 Code C1246: Rear ABS Channel Does Not Move (Part 1 of 4). Cavalier & Sunfire

Step	Action	Value(s)	Yes	No
6	1. Exit the Manual Control function on the *Scan Tool*. 2. Turn the ignition switch to the OFF position. 3. Disconnect the 6-way ABS brake motor pack connector. 4. Disconnect the 8-way EBCM connector C1 5. Use the *J 39200* in order to measure the resistance between the 8-way EBCM connector C1 terminal F and the 8-way EBCM connector C1 terminal E. Is the resistance within the specified range?	OL (Infinite)	*Go to Step 7*	*Go to Step 12*
7	Use the *J 39200* in order to measure the resistance between the ABS brake motor pack connector terminal C and the ABS brake motor pack connector terminal D. Is the resistance within the specified range?	0.2–1.5 Ω	*Go to Step 8*	*Go to Step 13*
8	1. Inspect the following connectors: • The 6-way ABS motor pack connector • The 8-way EBCM connector C1 2. Inspect the connectors for the following conditions: • Poor terminal contact • Corrosion Do any of the terminals exhibit poor terminal contact or corrosion?	—	*Go to Step 15*	*Go to Step 9*
9	1. Turn the ignition switch to the OFF position. 2. Reconnect the 8-way EBCM connector C1. 3. Reconnect the ABS motor pack connector. 4. Start the engine. Do not depress the brake pedal. 5. Allow the engine to run for at least ten seconds. 6. Repeat the above ignition cycle sequence two more times. 7. Use the *Scan Tool* in order to inspect for DTCs. Does DTC C1246 set during the last three ignition cycles?	—	*Go to Step 16*	*Go to Step 17*
10	1. Select Special Functions on the *Scan Tool*. 2. Use the *Scan Tool* in order to perform the Gear Tension Relief function. 3. Turn the ignition switch to the OFF position. 4. Remove the hydraulic modulator/master cylinder assembly from the vehicle. 5. Separate the ABS brake motor pack from the hydraulic modulator. 6. Grasp the middle gear on the hydraulic modulator and attempt to rotate the gear. Is it possible to rotate the middle gear on the hydraulic modulator at least seven full revolutions from lock to lock?	—	*Go to Step 13*	*Go to Step 14*
11	Place the wires into the correct connector cavities. Is the repair complete?	—	Refer to *Diagnostic System Check*	—

GC402980310000CX

Fig. 113 Code C1246: Rear ABS Channel Does Not Move (Part 3 of 4). Cavalier & Sunfire

Step	Action	Value(s)	Yes	No
12	Repair the short between CKT 1284 and CKT 1285. Is the repair complete?	—	Refer to *Diagnostic System Check*	—
13	Replace the ABS motor pack. Is the repair complete?	—	Refer to *Diagnostic System Check*	—
14	Replace the hydraulic modulator. Is the repair complete?	—	Refer to *Diagnostic System Check*	—
15	Replace the terminals that exhibit signs of poor terminal contact or corrosion. Is the repair complete?	—	Refer to *Diagnostic System Check*	—
16	Replace the EBCM. Is the repair complete?	—	Refer to *Diagnostic System Check*	—
17	The malfunction is intermittent or is not present at this time. Refer to Diagnostic Aids for more information.	—	—	—

GC402980310000DX

Fig. 113 Code C1246: Rear ABS Channel Does Not Move (Part 4 of 4). Cavalier & Sunfire

Step	Action	Value(s)	Yes	No
1	Was the Diagnostic System Check performed?	—	*Go to Step 2*	Refer to *Diagnostic System Check*
2	1. Turn the ignition switch to the RUN position. Do not start the engine. 2. Use the *Scan Tool* in order to read the DTCs. Does DTC C1256 also set as a current DTC?	—	Refer to *DTC C1256 Left Front ABS Motor Circuit Open*	*Go to Step 3*
3	1. Raise and suitably support the vehicle. Verify that the rear wheels are approximately 15 cm (six in) above the floor. 2. Pump the brake pedal until it is firm in order to deplete the brake booster vacuum reservoir. 3. Install a *Scan Tool.* 4. Apply firm downward pressure on the brake pedal. 5. Select Special Functions on the *Scan Tool.* 6. Select the Manual Control function on the *Scan Tool.* 7. Select the ABS Motor Apply function on the *Scan Tool.* 8. Use the *Scan Tool* to apply the left front motor. 9. Observe the following currents: • The left front ABS motor command current • The left front ABS motor feedback current. Were the left front ABS motor command current and the left front ABS motor feedback current approximately the specified current?	10 A	*Go to Step 4*	*Go to Step 6*
4	1. Apply firm pressure to the brake pedal. 2. Select the left front ABS Motor Release function on the *Scan Tool.* 3. Use the *Scan Tool* in order to release the left front ABS motor. 4. Observe the following currents: • The left front ABS motor command current • The left front ABS motor feedback current. Have the following conditions been met? • The left front ABS motor command current and the left front ABS motor feedback current approximately the specified current • The brake pedal falls	6 A	*Go to Step 5*	*Go to Step 6*
5	1. Continue to apply firm pressure to the brake pedal. 2. Select the left front ABS Motor Apply function on the *Scan Tool.* 3. Use the *Scan Tool* in order to apply the left front ABS motor. Did the brake pedal rise?	—	*Go to Step 22*	*Go to Step 6*

GC402980310100BX

Fig. 114 Code C1247: LH Front ABS Motor Free Spins (Part 2 of 5). Cavalier & Sunfire

Circuit Description

DTC detects a stripped nut or gear assembly during initialization. During the homing sequence, the piston should reach the top of the bore. Then the ABS motor stalls. If the ABS motor does not stall, the ABS motor must be spinning with little or no resistance. This indicates a nut/screw or gear malfunction.

Conditions for Setting the DTC

DTC C1247 can only set during initialization.

A malfunction exists if the feedback current is less than the command current for a specified period of time.

Action Taken When the DTC Sets

- A malfunction DTC stores.
- The ABS disables.
- The ABS warning indicator turns on.

Conditions for Clearing the DTC

- The condition responsible for setting the DTC no longer exists and the Scan Tool Clear DTCs function is used.
- 100 drive cycles pass with no DTC(s) detected. A drive cycle consists of starting the vehicle, driving the vehicle over 16 km/h (10 mph), stopping and then turning the ignition off.

Diagnostic Aids

The following conditions may cause an intermittent malfunction if the conditions exist in a mechanical part of the system:

- Sticking
- Binding
- Slipping

Use the enhanced diagnostic function of the Scan Tool in order to measure the frequency of the malfunction. DTC C1247 may set after modulator disassembly if the modulator pistons are positioned at the bottom ot the modulator piston bore. If DTC C1247 only occurs once and DTC C1256 also occurs, refer to DTC C1256. If intermittent and enhanced diagnostics shows this DTC occurs during ABS, refer to DTC C1256.

Depending on the frequency of the malfunction, a physical inspection of the mechanical parts suspected of causing the malfunction may be necessary.

Clear the DTCs after completing the diagnosis. Test drive the vehicle for three drive cycles in order to verify that the DTC does not reset. Use the following procedure in order to complete one drive cycle:

1. Start the vehicle.
2. Drive the vehicle over 16 km/h (10 mph).
3. Stop the vehicle.
4. Turn the ignition to the OFF position.

Important: Zero the J 39200 test leads before making any resistance measurements. Refer to the J 39200 user's manual.

GC402980310100AA

Fig. 114 Code C1247: LH Front ABS Motor Free Spins (Part 1 of 5). Cavalier & Sunfire

Step	Action	Value(s)	Yes	No
6	1. Turn the ignition switch to the OFF position. 2. Disconnect the 6-way ABS brake motor pack connector. 3. Disconnect the 8-way EBCM connector C1 4. Use the *J 39200* in order to measure the resistance between the 6-way ABS brake motor pack connector terminal A and the 8-way EBCM connector C1 terminal G. Is the resistance within the specified range?	0–2 Ω	*Go to Step 7*	*Go to Step 15*
7	Use the *J 39200* in order to measure the resistance between the 6-way ABS brake motor pack connector terminal B and the 8-way EBCM connector C1 terminal H. Is the resistance withine the specified range?	0–2 Ω	*Go to Step 8*	*Go to Step 16*
8	Use the *J 39200* in order to measure the resistance between the 6-way ABS brake motor pack connector terminal A and the 6-way ABS brake motor pack connector terminal B. Is the resistance withine the specified range?	0.2–1.5Ω	*Go to Step 9*	*Go to Step 17*
9	1. Remove the ABS brake modulator/master cylinder assembly from the vehicle. 2. Remove the ABS brake modulator gear cover. 3. Inspect for a stripped ABS brake motor pack left front gear. (The ABS brake motor pack is the unit with the three small gears. The ABS brake motor pack left front gear is the gear closest to the front when the ABS brake modulator is mounted in the vehicle.) Is the ABS brake motor left front gear stripped?	—	*Go to Step 17*	*Go to Step 10*
10	Inspect for a stripped ABS brake modulator pack left front gear. (The ABS brake modulator unit is the unit with the three large gears. The ABS brake modulator left front gear is the gear closest to the front when the ABS brake modulator is mounted in the vehicle.) Is the ABS brake modulator left front gear stripped?	—	*Go to Step 18*	*Go to Step 11*

GC402980310100CX

Fig. 114 Code C1247: LH Front ABS Motor Free Spins (Part 3 of 5). Cavalier & Sunfire

Step	Action	Value(s)	Yes	No
11	1. Reconnect the 6-way ABS brake motor pack connector. 2. Reconnect the 8-way EBCM connector C1. 3. Carefully secure the ABS brake modulator/master cylinder into the vehicle. Secure the assembly in a position that permits observation of the gears. 4. Turn the ignition switch to the RUN position. Do not start the engine. 5. Select the Manual Control function on the *Scan Tool.* 6. Select the left front ABS Motor Apply function on the *Scan Tool.* 7. Use the *Scan Tool* in order to apply the left front ABS motor while observing the ABS brake modulator left front gear set. (The ABS brake modulator left front gear is the gear closest to the front when the ABS brake modulator is mounted in the vehicle.) 8. Select the left front ABS Motor Release function on the *Scan Tool.* 9. Use the *Scan Tool* in order to release the left front ABS motor while observing the ABS brake modulator left front gear set. 10. Select the left front ABS Motor Apply function on the *Scan Tool.* 11. Use the *Scan Tool* in order to apply the left front ABS motor while observing the ABS brake modulator left front gear set. Does the ABS brake modulator left front gear set move at least one full revolution in both directions?	—	*Go to Step 12*	*Go to Step 17*
12	1. Use the *Scan Tool* in order to perform the Gear Tension Relief function. 2. Turn the ignition switch to the OFF position. 3. Separate the ABS brake motor pack from the ABS brake modulator. 4. Grasp the ABS brake modulator left front gear. 5. Rotate the ABS brake modulator left front gear. Does the ABS brake modulator left front gear rotate more than 13 full turns from lock to lock?	—	*Go to Step 19*	*Go to Step 13*
13	1. Disconnect the 6-way ABS brake motor pack connector. 2. Disconnect the 8-way EBCM connector C1. 3. Inspect the connectors for the following conditions: • Poor terminal contact • Corrosion Do any of the terminals exhibit poor terminal contact or corrosion?	—	*Go to Step 20*	*Go to Step 14*

GC402980310100DX

Fig. 114 Code C1247: LH Front ABS Motor Free Spins (Part 4 of 5). Cavalier & Sunfire

Step	Action	Value(s)	Yes	No
14	1. Reinstall the ABS brake modulator gear cover. 2. Reinstall the ABS brake modulator/master cylinder assembly in the vehicle. 3. Reconnect the 6-way ABS brake motor pack connector. 4. Reconnect the 8-way EBCM connector C1. 5. Start the engine. Do not apply pressure to the brake pedal. 6. Let the engine run for at least 10 seconds. 7. Turn the ignition switch to the OFF position. 8. Repeat the above cycle (step 5 through step 7) two more times. 9. Use the *Scan Tool* in order to read the DTCs. Does DTC C1247 set as a current DTC?	—	*Go to Step 21*	*Go to Step 22*
15	Repair the high resistance in CKT 1280. Is the repair complete?	—	Refer to *Diagnostic System Check*	—
16	Repair the high resistance in CKT 1281. Is the repair complete?	—	Refer to *Diagnostic System Check*	—
17	Replace the ABS brake motor pack. Is the repair complete?	—	Refer to *Diagnostic System Check*	—
18	Replace the ABS brake modulator gear. Is the repair complete?	—	Refer to *Diagnostic System Check*	—
19	Replace the ABS brake modulator. Is the repair complete?	—	Refer to *Diagnostic System Check*	—
20	Replace the terminals that exhibit signs of poor terminal contact or corrosion. Is the repair complete?	—	Refer to *Diagnostic System Check*	—
21	Replace the EBCM. Is the repair complete?	—	Refer to *Diagnostic System Check*	—
22	The malfunction is intermittent or is not present at this time. Refer to Diagnostic Aids for more information.	—	—	—

GC402980310100EX

Fig. 114 Code C1247: LH Front ABS Motor Free Spins (Part 5 of 5). Cavalier & Sunfire

Circuit Description

DTC C1248 detects a stripped nut or gear assembly during initialization. During the homing sequence, the piston should reach the top of the bore. Then the ABS motor stalls. If the ABS motor does not stall, the ABS motor must be spinning with little or no resistance. This indicates a nut/screw or gear malfunction.

Conditions for Setting the DTC

DTC C1248 can only set during initialization.

A malfunction exists if the feedback current is less than the command current for a specified period of time.

Action Taken When the DTC Sets

- A malfunction DTC stores.
- The ABS disables.
- The ABS warning indicator turns on.

Conditions for Clearing the DTC

- The condition responsible for setting the DTC no longer exists and the Scan Tool Clear DTCs function is used.
- 100 drive cycles pass with no DTC(s) detected. A drive cycle consists of starting the vehicle, driving the vehicle over 16 km/h (10 mph), stopping and then turning the ignition off.

Diagnostic Aids

An intermittent malfunction in this DTC may result from a mechanical part of the system that slips, such as a backed off gear retaining nut.

Depending on the frequency of the malfunction, a physical inspection of the mechanical parts suspected of causing the malfunction may be necessary.

Important: Zero the J 39200 test leads before making any resistance measurements.

GC402980310101AX

Fig. 115 Code C1248: RH Front ABS Motor Free Spins (Part 1 of 5). Cavalier & Sunfire

Step	Action	Value(s)	Yes	No
1	Was the Diagnostic System Check performed?	—	*Go to Step 2*	Refer to *Diagnostic System Check*
2	1. Turn the ignition switch to the RUN position. Do not start the engine. 2. Use the *Scan Tool* in order to read the DTCs. Does DTC C1261 also set as a current DTC?	—	Refer to *DTC C1261 Right Front ABS Motor Circuit Open*	*Go to Step 3*
3	1. Pump the brake pedal until it is firm in order to deplete the brake booster vacuum reservoir. 2. Select Special Functions on the *Scan Tool.* 3. Select the Manual Control function on the *Scan Tool.* 4. Select the right front Motor Apply function on the *Scan Tool.* 5. Use the *Scan Tool* in order to apply the right front motor. 6. Observe the following currents: • The right front ABS motor command current • The right front ABS motor feedback current Were the right front ABS motor command current and the right front ABS motor feedback current approximately the specified current?	10 A	*Go to Step 4*	*Go to Step 6*
4	1. Apply firm pressure to the brake pedal. 2. Select the right front ABS Motor Release function on the *Scan Tool.* 3. Use the *Scan Tool* in order to release the right front ABS motor. 4. Observe the following currents: • The right front ABS motor command current • The right front ABS motor feedback current 5. Release the right front ABS motor and observe the brake pedal height. Have the following conditions been met? • The right front ABS motor command current and the right front ABS motor feedback current approximately the specified current • The brake pedal falls	6 A	*Go to Step 5*	*Go to Step 6*
5	1. Continue to apply firm pressure to the brake pedal. 2. Select the right front ABS Motor Release function on the *Scan Tool.* 3. Use the *Scan Tool* in order to apply the right front ABS motor. Did the brake pedal rise?	—	*Go to Step 22*	*Go to Step 6*

GC402980310100FX

Fig. 115 Code C1248: RH Front ABS Motor Free Spins (Part 2 of 5). Cavalier & Sunfire

Step	Action	Value(s)	Yes	No
6	1. Select Special Functions on the *Scan Tool.* 2. Use the *Scan Tool* in order to perform the Gear Tension Relief function. 3. Turn the ignition switch to the OFF position. 4. Disconnect the 6-way ABS brake motor pack connector. 5. Disconnect the 8-way EBCM connector C1 6. Use the *J 39200* in order to measure the resistance between the 6-way ABS brake motor pack connector terminal E and the 8-way EBCM connector C1 terminal A. Is the resistance within the specified range?	0–2 Ω	*Go to Step 7*	*Go to Step 15*
7	Use the *J 39200* in order to measure the resistance between the 6-way ABS brake motor pack connector terminal F and the 8-way EBCM connector C1 terminal B. Is the resistance within the specified range?	0–2 Ω	*Go to Step 8*	*Go to Step 16*
8	Use the *J 39200* in order to measure the resistance between the 6-way ABS brake motor pack connector terminal E and the 6-way ABS brake motor pack connector terminal F. Is the resistance within the specified range?	0.2–1.5 Ω	*Go to Step 9*	*Go to Step 17*
9	1. Remove the ABS brake modulator/master cylinder assembly from the vehicle. 2. Remove the ABS brake modulator gear cover. 3. Inspect for a stripped ABS brake motor pack right front gear. (The ABS brake motor pack is the unit with the three small gears. The ABS brake motor pack right front gear is the gear closest to the rear when the ABS brake modulator is mounted in the vehicle.) Is the ABS brake motor right front gear stripped?	—	*Go to Step 17*	*Go to Step 10*
10	Inspect for a stripped ABS brake modulator right front gear. (The ABS brake modulator unit is the unit with the three large gears. The ABS brake modulator right front gear is the gear closest to the rear when the ABS brake modulator is mounted in the vehicle.) Is the ABS brake modulator right front gear stripped?	—	*Go to Step 18*	*Go to Step 11*

GC402980310100GX

Fig. 115 Code C1248: RH Front ABS Motor Free Spins (Part 3 of 5). Cavalier & Sunfire

Step	Action	Value(s)	Yes	No
14	1. Reinstall the ABS brake modulator gear cover. 2. Reinstall the ABS brake modulator/master cylinder assembly in the vehicle. 3. Reconnect the 6-way ABS brake motor pack connector. 4. Reconnect the 8-way EBCM connector C1. 5. Start the engine. Do not apply pressure to the brake pedal. 6. Let the engine run for at least 10 seconds. 7. Turn the ignition switch to the OFF position. 8. Repeat the above cycle (step 5 through step 7) two more times. 9. Use the *Scan Tool* in order to read the DTCs. Does DTC C1248 set as a current DTC?	—	*Go to Step 21*	*Go to Step 22*
15	Repair the high resistance in CKT 1282. Is the repair complete?	—	Refer to *Diagnostic System Check*	—
16	Repair the high resistance in CKT 1283. Is the repair complete?	—	Refer to *Diagnostic System Check*	—
17	Replace the ABS brake motor pack. Is the repair complete?	—	Refer to *Diagnostic System Check*	—
18	Replace the ABS brake modulator gear. Is the repair complete?	—	Refer to *Diagnostic System Check*	—
19	Replace the ABS brake modulator. Is the repair complete?	—	Refer to *Diagnostic System Check*	—
20	Replace the terminals that exhibit signs of poor terminal contact or corrosion. Is the repair complete?	—	Refer to *Diagnostic System Check*	—
21	Replace the EBCM. Is the repair complete?	—	Refer to *Diagnostic System Check*	—
22	The malfunction is intermittent or is not present at this time. Refer to Diagnostic Aids for more information.	—	—	—

GC402980310100IX

Fig. 115 Code C1248: RH Front ABS Motor Free Spins (Part 5 of 5). Cavalier & Sunfire

Step	Action	Value(s)	Yes	No
11	1. Reconnect the 6-way ABS brake motor pack connector. 2. Reconnect the 8-way EBCM connector C1. 3. Carefully secure the ABS brake modulator/master cylinder in the vehicle. Secure the assembly in a position that permits observation of the gears. 4. Turn the ignition switch to the RUN position. Do not start the engine. 5. Select the Manual Control function on the *Scan Tool.* 6. Select the right front ABS Motor Apply function on the *Scan Tool.* 7. Use the *Scan Tool* in order to apply the right front ABS motor while observing the ABS brake modulator right front gear set. (The ABS brake modulator right front gear is the gear closest to the rear when the ABS brake modulator is mounted in the vehicle.) 8. Select the right front ABS Motor Release function on the *Scan Tool.* 9. Use the *Scan Tool* in order to release the right front ABS motor while observing the ABS brake modulator right front gear set. 10. Select the right front ABS Motor Apply function on the *Scan Tool.* 11. Use the *Scan Tool* in order to apply the right front ABS motor while observing the ABS brake modulator right front gear set. Does the ABS brake modulator right front gear set move at least one full revolution in both directions?	—	*Go to Step 12*	*Go to Step 17*
12	1. Use the *Scan Tool* in order to perform the Gear Tension Relief function. 2. Turn the ignition switch to the OFF position. 3. Separate the ABS brake motor pack from the ABS brake modulator. 4. Grasp the ABS brake modulator right front gear. 5. Rotate the ABS brake modulator right front gear. Does the ABS brake modulator right front gear rotate more than 13 full turns from lock to lock?	—	*Go to Step 19*	*Go to Step 13*
13	1. Disconnect the 6-way ABS brake motor pack connector. 2. Disconnect the 8-way EBCM connector C1. 3. Inspect the connectors for the following conditions: • Poor terminal contact • Corrosion Do any of the terminals exhibit poor terminal contact or corrosion?	—	*Go to Step 20*	*Go to Step 14*

GC402980310100HX

Fig. 115 Code C1248: RH Front ABS Motor Free Spins (Part 4 of 5). Cavalier & Sunfire

Circuit Description

DTC C1251 detects a stripped nut or gear assembly during initialization. During the homing sequence, the piston should reach the top of the bore. Then the ABS motor stalls. If the ABS motor does not stall, the ABS motor must be spinning with little or no resistance. This indicates a nut/screw or gear malfunction.

Conditions for Setting the DTC

DTC C1251 can only set during initialization.

A malfunction exists if the feedback current is less than the command current for a specified period of time.

Action Taken When the DTC Sets

- A malfunction DTC stores. A corresponding DTC C1286 will also set.
- The ABS disables.
- The ABS warning indicator turns on.
- The red BRAKE warning indicator turns on.

Conditions for Clearing the DTC

- The condition responsible for setting the DTC no longer exists and the Scan Tool Clear DTCs function is used.
- 100 drive cycles pass with no DTC(s) detected. A drive cycle consists of starting the vehicle, driving the vehicle over 16 km/h (10 mph), stopping and then turning the ignition off.

Diagnostic Aids

An intermittent malfunction in this DTC may result from a mechanical part of the system that slips, such as a stripped gear or a backed off gear retaining nut.

Depending on the frequency of the malfunction, a physical inspection of the mechanical parts suspected of causing the malfunction may be necessary.

Important: Zero the J 39200 test leads before making any resistance measurements. Refer to the J 39200 user's manual.

GC402980310102AX

Fig. 116 Code C1251: Rear ABS Motor Free Spins (Part 1 of 5). Cavalier & Sunfire

Step	Action	Value(s)	Yes	No
1	Was the Diagnostic System Check performed?	—	*Go to Step 2*	Refer to *Diagnostic System Check*
2	1. Turn the ignition switch to the RUN position. Do not start the engine. 2. Use the *Scan Tool* in order to read the DTCs. Does DTC C1264 also set as a current DTC?	—	Refer to *DTC C1264 Rear ABS Motor Circuit Open*	*Go to Step 3*
3	1. Pump the brake pedal until it is firm in order to deplete the brake booster vacuum reservoir. 2. Select Special Functions on the *Scan Tool.* 3. Select the Manual Control function on the *Scan Tool.* 4. Select the rear ABS Motor Apply function on the *Scan Tool.* 5. Use the *Scan Tool* in order to apply the rear ABS motor. 6. Observe the following currents: • The rear ABS motor command current • The rear ABS motor feedback current Were the rear ABS motor command current and the rear ABS motor feedback current approximately the specified current?	10 A	*Go to Step 4*	*Go to Step 6*
4	1. Raise and support the vehicle so that the rear wheels are approximately 6 inches off the floor. 2. Turn the ignition switch to the run position. 3. Apply firm pressure to the brake pedal. 4. Select Special Functions on the *Scan Tool.* 5. Select Manual Control on the *Scan Tool.* 6. Use the *Scan Tool* in order to Apply the rear ABS motor. 7. Have an assistant try to spin the rear wheels by hand. Could the assistant spin the rear wheels?	—	*Go to Step 5*	*Go to Step 6*
5	1. Continue to apply firm pressure to the brake pedal. 2. Select the rear ABS Apply function on the *Scan Tool.* 3. Use the *Scan Tool* in order to apply the rear ABS motor. Could the assistant spin the rear wheels?	—	*Go to Step 22*	*Go to Step 6*
6	1. Select Special Functions on the *Scan Tool.* 2. Use the *Scan Tool* in order to perform the Gear Tension Relief function. 3. Turn the ignition switch to the OFF position. 4. Disconnect the 6-way ABS brake motor pack connector. 5. Disconnect the 8-way EBCM connector C1 6. Use the *J 39200* in order to measure the resistance between the 6-way ABS brake motor pack connector terminal C and the 8-way EBCM connector C2 terminal F. Is the resistance within the specified range?	0–2 Ω	*Go to Step 7*	*Go to Step 15*

GC402980310100JX

Fig. 116 Code C1251: Rear ABS Motor Free Spins (Part 2 of 5). Cavalier & Sunfire

Step	Action	Value(s)	Yes	No
11	1. Reconnect the 6-way ABS brake motor pack connector. 2. Reconnect the 8-way EBCM connector C1. 3. Carefully secure the ABS brake modulator/master cylinder in the vehicle. Secure the assembly in a position that permits observation of the gears. 4. Turn the ignition switch to the RUN position. Do not start the engine. 5. Select the Manual Control function on the *Scan Tool.* 6. Select the rear ABS Motor Apply function on the *Scan Tool.* 7. Use the *Scan Tool* in order to apply the rear ABS motor while observing the ABS brake modulator rear gear set. (The ABS brake modulator rear gear is the middle gear when the ABS brake modulator is mounted in the vehicle.) 8. Select the rear ABS Motor Release function on the *Scan Tool.* 9. Use the *Scan Tool* in order to release the rear ABS motor while observing the ABS brake modulator rear gear set. 10. Select the rear ABS Motor Apply function on the *Scan Tool.* 11. Use the *Scan Tool* in order to apply the rear ABS motor while observing the ABS brake modulator rear gear set. Does the ABS brake modulator rear gear set move at least one full revolution in both directions?	—	*Go to Step 12*	*Go to Step 17*
12	1. Use the *Scan Tool* in order to perform the Gear Tension Relief function. 2. Turn the ignition switch to the OFF position. 3. Separate the ABS brake motor pack from the ABS brake modulator. 4. Grasp the ABS brake modulator rear gear. 5. Rotate the ABS brake modulator rear gear. Does the ABS brake modulator rear gear rotate more than 3.5 full turns from lock to lock?	—	*Go to Step 19*	*Go to Step 13*
13	1. Disconnect the 6-way ABS brake motor pack connector. 2. Disconnect the 8-way EBCM connector C2. 3. Inspect the connectors for the following conditions: • Poor terminal contact • Corrosion Do any of the terminals exhibit poor terminal contact or corrosion?	—	*Go to Step 20*	*Go to Step 14*

GC402980310100LX

Fig. 116 Code C1251: Rear ABS Motor Free Spins (Part 4 of 5). Cavalier & Sunfire

Step	Action	Value(s)	Yes	No
7	Use the *J 39200* in order to measure the resistance between the 6-way ABS brake motor pack connector terminal D and the 8-way EBCM connector C1 terminal E. Is the resistance within the specified range?	0–2 Ω	*Go to Step 8*	*Go to Step 16*
8	Use the *J 39200* in order to measure the resistance between the 6-way ABS brake motor pack connector terminal C and the 6-way ABS brake motor pack connector terminal D. Is the resistance within the specified range?	0.2–1.5 Ω	*Go to Step 9*	*Go to Step 17*
9	1. Remove the ABS brake modulator/master cylinder assembly from the vehicle. 2. Remove the ABS brake modulator gear cover. 3. Inspect for a stripped ABS brake motor pack rear gear. (The ABS brake motor pack is the unit with the three small gears. The ABS brake motor pack rear gear is the middle gear when the ABS brake modulator is mounted in the vehicle.) Is the ABS brake motor rear gear stripped?	—	*Go to Step 17*	*Go to Step 10*
10	Inspect for a stripped ABS brake modulator rear gear. (The ABS brake modulator unit is the unit with the three large gears. The ABS brake modulator rear gear is the middle gear when the ABS brake modulator is mounted in the vehicle.) Is the ABS brake modulator rear gear stripped?	—	*Go to Step 18*	*Go to Step 11*

GC402980310100KX

Fig. 116 Code C1251: Rear ABS Motor Free Spins (Part 3 of 5). Cavalier & Sunfire

Step	Action	Value(s)	Yes	No
14	1. Reinstall the ABS brake modulator gear cover. 2. Reinstall the ABS brake modulator/master cylinder assembly in the vehicle. 3. Reconnect the 6-way ABS brake motor pack connector. 4. Reconnect the 8-way EBCM connector C1. 5. Start the engine. Do not apply pressure to the brake pedal. 6. Let the engine run for at least 10 seconds. 7. Turn the ignition switch to the OFF position. 8. Repeat the above cycle (steps 5 through 7) two more times. 9. Use the *Scan Tool* in order to read the DTCs. Does DTC C1251 set as a current DTC?	—	*Go to Step 21*	*Go to Step 22*
15	Repair the high resistance in CKT 1284. Is the repair complete?	—	Refer to *Diagnostic System Check*	—
16	Repair the high resistance in CKT 1285. Is the repair complete?	—	Refer to *Diagnostic System Check*	—
17	Replace the ABS brake motor pack. Is the repair complete?	—	Refer to *Diagnostic System Check*	—
18	Replace the ABS brake modulator gear. Is the repair complete?	—	Refer to *Diagnostic System Check*	—
19	Replace the ABS brake modulator. Is the repair complete?	—	Refer to *Diagnostic System Check*	—
20	Replace the terminals that exhibit signs of poor terminal contact or corrosion. Is the repair complete?	—	Refer to *Diagnostic System Check*	—
21	Replace the EBCM. Is the repair complete?	—	Refer to *Diagnostic System Check*	—
22	The malfunction is intermittent or is not present at this time. Refer to Diagnostic Aids for more information.	—	—	—

GC402980310100MX

Fig. 116 Code C1251: Rear ABS Motor Free Spins (Part 5 of 5). Cavalier & Sunfire

Circuit Description

DTC diagnoses an ABS motor that energizes longer than expected. The following conditions may cause the longer period of being energized:

- A wheel speed sensor malfunctions.
- The left front brake solenoid valve mechanically fails open.
- The ABS brake motor wires are crossed.

Conditions for Setting the DTC

DTC can only set during an ABS stop.

A malfunction exists if the EBCM commands the ABS channel in release for greater than three seconds.

Action Taken When the DTC Sets

- A malfunction DTC stores.
- The ABS disables.
- The ABS warning indicator turns on.

Conditions for Clearing the DTC

- The condition responsible for setting the DTC no longer exists and the Scan Tool Clear DTCs function is used.
- 100 drive cycles pass with no DTC(s) detected. A drive cycle consists of starting the vehicle, driving the vehicle over 16 km/h (10 mph), stopping and then turning the ignition off.

Diagnostic Aids

Use the enhanced diagnostic function of the Scan Tool in order to measure the frequency of the malfunction. DTC C1252 may occur if the vehicle is on ice and the steering wheel is turned to lock during braking. Use the scan tool hydraulic test to ensure the total brake system is functional.

Thoroughly inspect any circuitry that may be causing the intermittent complaint for the following conditions:

- Backed out terminals
- Improper mating
- Broken locks
- Improperly formed or damaged terminals
- Poor terminal-to-wiring connections
- Physical damage to the wiring harness

Clear the DTCs after completing the diagnosis. Test drive the vehicle for three drive cycles in order to verify that the DTC does not reset. Use the following procedure in order to complete one drive cycle:

1. Start the vehicle.
2. Drive the vehicle over 16 km/h (10 mph).
3. Stop the vehicle.
4. Turn the ignition to the OFF position.

Important: Zero the J 39200 test leads before making any resistance measurements. Refer to the J 39200 user's manual.

Important: Inspect for and correct the following conditions in the base brake or suspension system before proceeding with the DTC diagnosis:

- Excessive drag
- High resistance

GC402980310200AA

Fig. 117 Code C1252: LH Front ABS Channel In Release Too Long (Part 1 of 3). Cavalier & Sunfire

Step	Action	Value(s)	Yes	No
1	Was the Diagnostic System Check performed?	—	*Go to Step 2*	Refer to *Diagnostic System Check*
2	1. Turn the ignition switch to the RUN position. Do not start the engine. 2. Install a *Scan Tool.* 3. Use the *Scan Tool* in order to read the DTCs. Are there any wheel speed sensor DTCs that set as current DTCs?	—	Refer to the appropriate DTC table.	*Go to Step 3*
3	1. Select Data List on the *Scan Tool.* 2. Drive the vehicle, slowly decelerating from 56 km/h to 0 km/h (35 mph to 0 mph). 3. Monitor all of the wheel speed sensor speeds while driving. Do any of the wheel speed sensors indicate erratic or intermittent operation?	—	Go to the Excessive Wheel Speed Sensor Variation DTC for the affected wheel	*Go to Step 4*
4	1. Turn the ignition switch to the RUN position. Do not start the engine. 2. Select Special Functions on the *Scan Tool.* 3. Select the Manual Control function on the *Scan Tool.* 4. Select the left front ABS Motor Apply function on the *Scan Tool.* 5. Use the *Scan Tool* in order to apply the left front ABS motor. 6. Apply firm pressure to the brake pedal. 7. Select the left front ABS Motor Release function on the *Scan Tool.* 8. Use the *Scan Tool* in order to release the left front ABS motor.	—	*Go to Step 5*	*Go to Step 8*
5	1. Remove the firm pressure from the brake pedal. 2. Select the Manual Control function on the *Scan Tool.* 3. Select the left front ABS Brake Solenoid Valve on the *Scan Tool.* 4. Use the *Scan Tool* in order to command the left front ABS brake solenoid valve on. 5. Apply firm pressure to the brake pedal. Does the brake pedal fall?	—	*Go to Step 7*	*Go to Step 6*
6	1. Continue to apply firm pressure to the brake pedal. 2. Use the *Scan Tool* in order to command the left front ABS brake solenoid valve off. Did the brake pedal fall?	—	*Go to Step 14*	*Go to Step 7*

GC402980310200BX

Fig. 117 Code C1252: LH Front ABS Channel In Release Too Long (Part 2 of 3). Cavalier & Sunfire

Step	Action	Value(s)	Yes	No
7	1. Remove the firm pressure from the brake pedal. 2. Turn the ignition switch to the OFF position. 3. Remove the left front ABS brake solenoid valve. 4. Remove the right front ABS brake solenoid valve. 5. Reinstall the left front ABS brake solenoid valve to the right front ABS brake solenoid valve position. 6. Reinstall the right front ABS brake solenoid valve to the left front ABS brake solenoid valve position. 7. Turn the ignition switch to the RUN position. 8. Make sure that the engine is off. 9. Select the Manual Control function on the *Scan Tool.* 10. Select the left front ABS Brake Solenoid Valve on the *Scan Tool.* 11. Use the *Scan Tool* in order to command the left front ABS brake solenoid valve on. 12. Apply firm pressure to the brake pedal. Does the brake pedal fall?	—	*Go to Step 10*	*Go to Step 11*
8	Did the brake pedal rise?	—	*Go to Step 12*	*Go to Step 9*
9	1. Use the *Scan Tool* in order to perform the Gear Tension Relief function. 2. Turn the ignition switch to the OFF position. 3. Separate the ABS motor pack from the ABS brake modulator. 4. Grasp the ABS brake modulator left front gear. (The ABS brake modulator left front gear is the large gear that is the closest to the front when the ABS brake modulator is mounted in the vehicle.) 5. Attempt to rotate the ABS brake modulator left front gear in either direction. Is it possible to rotate the ABS brake modulator left front gear by hand?	—	*Go to Step 13*	*Go to Step 10*
10	Replace the ABS brake modulator. Is the repair complete?	—	Refer to *Diagnostic System Check*	—
11	Replace the ABS brake solenoid valve that was originally in the left front ABS brake solenoid valve position. Is the repair complete?	—	Refer to *Diagnostic System Check*	—
12	Repair the crossed wires to the left front ABS motor (CKT 1280 and CKT 1281). Is the repair complete?	—	Refer to *Diagnostic System Check*	—
13	Replace the ABS brake motor pack. Is the repair complete?	—	Refer to *Diagnostic System Check*	—
14	The malfunction is intermittent or is not present at this time. Refer to Diagnostic Aids for more information.	—	—	—

GC402980310200CX

Fig. 117 Code C1252: LH Front ABS Channel In Release Too Long (Part 3 of 3). Cavalier & Sunfire

Circuit Description

DTC C1253 diagnoses an ABS motor that energizes longer than expected. The following conditions may cause the longer period of being energized:

- A wheel speed sensor malfunctions.
- The ABS motor does not turn.
- The right front brake solenoid valve mechanically fails open.
- The ABS brake motor wires are crossed.

Conditions for Setting the DTC

DTC C1253 can only set during an ABS stop.

A malfunction exists if the EBCM commands the right front ABS channel in release for greater than three seconds.

Action Taken When the DTC Sets

- A malfunction DTC stores.
- The ABS disables.
- The ABS warning indicator turns on.

Conditions for Clearing the DTC

- The condition responsible for setting the DTC no longer exists and the Scan Tool Clear DTCs function is used.
- 100 drive cycles pass with no DTC(s) detected. A drive cycle consists of starting the vehicle, driving the vehicle over 16 km/h (10 mph), stopping and then turning the ignition off.

Diagnostic Aids

The following conditions may cause an intermittent malfunction if the conditions exist in a mechanical part of the system:

- Sticking
- Binding

Use the enhanced diagnostic function of the Scan Tool in order to measure the frequency of the malfunction. DTC C1253 may occur if the vehicle is on ice and the steering wheel is turned to lock during braking. Use the scan tool hydraulic test to ensure the total brake system is functional.

Thoroughly inspect any circuitry that may be causing the intermittent complaint for the following conditions:

- Backed out terminals
- Improper mating
- Broken locks
- Improperly formed or damaged terminals
- Poor terminal-to-wiring connections
- Physical damage to the wiring harness

Clear the DTCs after completing the diagnosis. Test drive the vehicle for three drive cycles in order to verify that the DTC does not reset. Use the following procedure in order to complete one drive cycle:

1. Start the vehicle.
2. Drive the vehicle over 16 km/h (10 mph).
3. Stop the vehicle.
4. Turn the ignition to the OFF position.

Important: Zero the J 39200 test leads before making any resistance measurements. Refer to the J 39200 user's manual.

Important: Inspect for and correct the following conditions in the base brake or suspension system before proceeding with the DTC diagnosis:

- Excessive drag
- High resistance

GC402980310201AX

Fig. 118 Code C1253: RH Front ABS Channel In Release Too Long (Part 1 of 3). Cavalier & Sunfire

Step	Action	Value(s)	Yes	No
1	Was the Diagnostic System Check performed?	—	*Go to Step 2*	Refer to *Diagnostic System Check*
2	1. Turn the ignition switch to the RUN position. Do not start the engine. 2. Install a *Scan Tool.* 3. Use the *Scan Tool* in order to read the DTCs. Are there any wheel speed sensor DTCs that set as current DTCs?	—	Refer to DTC table.	*Go to Step 3*
3	1. Select Data List on the *Scan Tool.* 2. Drive the vehicle, slowly decelerating from 56 km/h to 0 km/h (35 mph to 0 mph). 3. Monitor all of the wheel speed sensor speeds while driving. Do any of the wheel speed sensors indicate erratic or intermittent operation?	—	Diagnose Wheel Speed Sensor	*Go to Step 4*
4	1. Turn the ignition switch to the RUN position. Do not start the engine. 2. Select Special Functions on the *Scan Tool.* 3. Select the Manual Control function on the *Scan Tool.* 4. Select the right front ABS Motor Apply function on the *Scan Tool.* 5. Use the *Scan Tool* to apply the right front ABS motor. 6. Apply firm pressure to the brake pedal. 7. Select the right front ABS Motor Release function on the *Scan Tool.* 8. Use the *Scan Tool* in order to release the right front ABS motor. Did the brake pedal fall?	—	*Go to Step 5*	*Go to Step 8*
5	1. Remove the firm pressure from the brake pedal. 2. Select the Manual Control function on the *Scan Tool.* 3. Select the right front ABS Brake Solenoid Valve on the *Scan Tool.* 4. Use the *Scan Tool* in order to command the right front ABS brake solenoid valve on. 5. Apply firm pressure to the brake pedal. Did the brake pedal fall?	—	*Go to Step 7*	*Go to Step 6*
6	1. Continue to apply firm pressure to the brake pedal. 2. Use the *Scan Tool* in order to command the right front ABS brake solenoid valve off. Did the brake pedal fall?	—	*Go to Step 14*	*Go to Step 7*

GC402980310201BX

Fig. 118 Code C1253: RH Front ABS Channel In Release Too Long (Part 2 of 3). Cavalier & Sunfire

Step	Action	Value(s)	Yes	No
7	1. Remove the firm pressure from the brake pedal. 2. Turn the ignition switch to the OFF position. 3. Remove the right front ABS brake solenoid valve. 4. Remove the left front ABS brake solenoid valve. 5. Reinstall the right front ABS brake solenoid valve to the left front ABS brake solenoid valve position. 6. Reinstall the left front ABS brake solenoid valve to the right front ABS brake solenoid valve position. 7. Turn the ignition switch to the RUN position. Do not start the engine. 8. Select the Manual Control function on the *Scan Tool.* 9. Select the right front ABS Brake Solenoid Valve on the *Scan Tool.* 10. Use the *Scan Tool* in order to command the right front ABS brake solenoid valve on. 11. Apply firm pressure to the brake pedal. Did the brake pedal fall?	—	*Go to Step 10*	*Go to Step 11*
8	Did the brake pedal rise?	—	*Go to Step 12*	*Go to Step 9*
9	1. Use the *Scan Tool* in order to perform the Gear Tension Relief function. 2. Turn the ignition switch to the OFF position. 3. Separate the ABS motor pack from the ABS brake modulator. 4. Grasp the ABS brake modulator right front gear. (The ABS brake modulator right front gear is the large gear that is the closest to the rear when the ABS brake modulator is mounted in the vehicle.) 5. Attempt to rotate the ABS brake modulator right front gear in either direction. Is it possible to rotate the ABS brake modulator right front gear by hand?	—	*Go to Step 13*	*Go to Step 10*
10	Replace the ABS brake modulator. Is the repair complete?	—	Refer to *Diagnostic System Check*	—
11	Replace the ABS brake solenoid valve that was originally in the right front ABS brake solenoid valve position. Is the repair complete?	—	Refer to *Diagnostic System Check*	—
12	Repair the crossed wires to the right front ABS motor (CKT 1282 and CKT 1283). Is the repair complete?	—	Refer to *Diagnostic System Check*	—
13	Replace the ABS brake motor pack. Is the repair complete?	—	Refer to *Diagnostic System Check*	—
14	The malfunction is intermittent or is not present at this time. Refer to Diagnostic Aids for more information.	—	—	—

GC402980310201CX

Fig. 118 Code C1253: RH Front ABS Channel In Release Too Long (Part 3 of 3). Cavalier & Sunfire

Step	Action	Value(s)	Yes	No
	Important: Zero the J 39200 test leads before making any resistance measurements. Refer to the J 39200 user's manual. **Important:** Inspect for and correct the following conditions in the base brake or suspension system before proceeding with the DTC diagnosis: • Excessive brake drag • High resistance			
1	Was the Diagnostic System Check performed?	—	*Go to Step 2*	Go to *A Diagnostic System Check*
2	1. Turn the ignition switch to the RUN position. Do not start the engine. 2. Install a *Scan Tool.* 3. Use the *Scan Tool* in order to read the DTCs. Are there any wheel speed sensor DTCs that set as current DTCs?	—	Go to the appropriate DTC table.	*Go to Step 3*
3	1. Select Data List on the *Scan Tool.* 2. Drive the vehicle, slowly decelerating from 56 km/h to 0 km/h (35 mph to 0 mph). 3. Monitor all of the wheel speed sensor speeds while driving. Do any of the wheel speed sensors indicate erratic or intermittent operation?	—	Go to the Excessive Wheel Speed Sensor Variation DTC for the affected wheel	*Go to Step 4*
4	1. Turn the ignition switch to the OFF position. 2. Raise and suitably support the rear of the vehicle. Make sure that the two rear wheels are off of the ground. 3. Spin each of the rear wheels by hand. Is it possible to spin each rear wheel freely by hand?	—	*Go to Step 5*	*Go to Step 11*
5	1. Turn the ignition switch to the RUN position. Do not start the engine. 2. Select the Manual Control function on the *Scan Tool.* 3. Select the rear axle ABS Motor Apply function on the *Scan Tool.* 4. Apply firm pressure to the brake pedal. 5. Use the *Scan Tool* in order to apply the rear axle ABS motor. 6. Spin each rear wheel by hand. Is it possible to freely spin each rear wheel?	—	*Go to Step 6*	*Go to Step 12*
6	1. Continue to apply firm pressure to the brake pedal. 2. Use the *Scan Tool* in order to command a Motor Release of the rear ABS motor. Is it possible to freely spin each rear wheel?	—	*Go to Step 7*	*Go to Step 9*

GC402980310200GX

Fig. 119 Code C1254: Rear ABS Channel In Release Too Long (Part 2 of 3). Cavalier & Sunfire

Circuit Description

DTC C1254 diagnoses an ABS motor that energizes longer than expected. The following conditions may cause the longer period of being energized:

- A wheel speed sensor malfunctions.
- The ABS motor does not turn.
- The ABS brake motor wires cross.

Conditions for Setting the DTC

DTC C1254 can only set during an ABS stop.

A malfunction exists if the EBCM commands the rear ABS channel in release for greater than three seconds.

Action Taken When the DTC Sets

- A malfunction DTC stores.
- The ABS disables.
- The amber ABS warning indicator turns on.

Conditions for Clearing the DTC

- The condition responsible for setting the DTC no longer exists and the Scan Tool Clear DTCs function is used.
- 100 drive cycles pass with no DTCs detected. A drive cycle consists of starting the vehicle, driving the vehicle over 16 km/h (10 mph), stopping and then turning the ignition off.

Diagnostic Aids

The following conditions may cause an intermittent malfunction if the conditions exist in a mechanical part of the system:

- Sticking
- Binding

Use the enhanced diagnostic function of the Scan Tool in order to measure the frequency of the malfunction. Use the Scan Tool hydraulic test in order to ensure the total brake system is functional.

Thoroughly inspect any circuitry that may be causing the intermittent complaint for the following conditions:

- Backed out terminals
- Improper mating
- Broken locks
- Improperly formed or damaged terminals
- Poor terminal-to-wiring connections
- Physical damage to the wiring harness

Clear the DTCs after completing the diagnosis. Test drive the vehicle for three drive cycles in order to verify that the DTC does not reset. Use the following procedure in order to complete one drive cycle:

1. Start the vehicle.
2. Drive the vehicle over 16 km/h (10 mph).
3. Stop the vehicle.
4. Turn the ignition to the OFF position.

Important: Zero the J 39200 test leads before making any resistance measurements. Refer to the J 39200 user's manual.

Important: Inspect for and correct the following conditions in the base brake or suspension system before proceeding with the DTC diagnosis:

- Excessive brake drag
- High resistance

GC402980310202AX

Fig. 119 Code C1254: Rear ABS Channel In Release Too Long (Part 1 of 3). Cavalier & Sunfire

Step	Action	Value(s)	Yes	No
7	1. Use the *Scan Tool* in order to perform the Gear Tension Relief function. 2. Turn the ignition switch to the OFF position. 3. Separate the ABS brake motor pack from the ABS brake modulator, if it is disconnected. 4. Turn the ignition switch to the RUN position. Do not start the engine. 5. Use the *Scan Tool* in order to perform a ABS brake motor pack motor test. Do all three of the ABS brake motor pack gears (small gears) spin freely when commanded?	—	*Go to Step 8*	*Go to Step 10*
8	Replace the ABS brake modulator. Is the repair complete?	—	Go to *A Diagnostic System Check*	—
9	Repair the crossed wires to the rear ABS motor (CKT 1284 and CKT 1285). Is the repair complete?	—	Go to *A Diagnostic System Check*	—
10	Replace the ABS brake motor pack. Is the repair complete?	—	Go to *A Diagnostic System Check*	—
11	Repair the source of resistance in the base brake system. Is the repair complete?	—	Go to *A Diagnostic System Check*	—
12	The malfunction is intermittent or is not present at this time. Refer to Diagnostic Aids for more information. Is the action complete?	—	System OK	—

GC402980310200FX

Fig. 119 Code C1254: Rear ABS Channel In Release Too Long (Part 3 of 3). Cavalier & Sunfire

Circuit Description

DTC C1255 identifies an internal malfunction detected by the EBCM ABS motor driver interface, custom integrated circuit.

Conditions for Setting the DTC

DTC C1255 is set when an internal EBCM malfunction exists.

Action Taken When the DTC Sets

- A malfunction DTC stores.
- The ABS disables.
- The ABS warning indicator turns on.
- The red BRAKE warning indicator turns on and DTC C1286 sets if the rear piston in the ABS brake motor pack is not in the home piston.

Conditions for Clearing the DTC

- The condition responsible for setting the DTC no longer exists and the Scan Tool Clear DTCs function is used.
- 100 drive cycles pass with no DTC(s) detected. A drive cycle consists of starting the vehicle, driving the vehicle over 16 km/h (10 mph), stopping and then turning the ignition off.

Diagnostic Aids

Use the enhanced diagnostic function of the Scan Tool in order to measure the frequency of the malfunction.

Clear the DTCs after completing the diagnosis. Test drive the vehicle for three drive cycles in order to verify that the DTC does not reset. Use the following procedure in order to complete one drive cycle:

1. Start the vehicle.
2. Drive the vehicle over 16 km/h (10 mph).
3. Stop the vehicle.
4. Turn the ignition to the OFF position.

GC402980310300AX

Fig. 120 Code C1255: EBCM Internal Fault (Part 1 of 2). Cavalier & Sunfire

Step	Action	Value(s)	Yes	No
1	Was the Diagnostic System Check performed?	—	*Go to Step 2*	Refer to *Diagnostic System Check*
2	1. Turn the ignition switch to the RUN position. Do not start the engine. 2. Install a *Scan Tool.* 3. Use the *Scan Tool* in order to read the DTCs. Is DTC C1255 set as a current DTC?	—	*Go to Step 3*	*Go to Step 5*
3	1. Use the *Scan Tool* in order to clear the DTCs. 2. Test drive the vehicle for three drive cycles. 3. Use the *Scan Tool* in order to look for DTCs. Does DTC C1255 set as a current DTC?	—	*Go to Step 4*	*Go to Step 5*
4	Replace the EBCM. Is the repair complete?	—	Refer to *Diagnostic System Check*	—
5	The malfunction is intermittent or is not present at this time. Refer to Diagnostic Aids for more information.	—	—	—

GC402980310300BX

Fig. 120 Code C1255: EBCM Internal Fault (Part 2 of 2). Cavalier & Sunfire

Step	Action	Value(s)	Yes	No
1	Was the Diagnostic System Check performed?	—	*Go to Step 2*	Refer to *Diagnostic System Check*
2	Does DTC C1256 occur intermittently?	—	Refer to Diagnostic Aids	*Go to Step 3*
3	1. Turn the ignition switch to the OFF position. 2. Disconnect the 6-way ABS brake motor pack connector. 3. Use the *J 39200* in order to measure the resistance between the 6-way ABS brake motor pack connector terminal A and the 6-way ABS brake motor pack connector terminal B. Is the resistance within the specified range?	0.2–1.5 Ω	*Go to Step 4*	*Go to Step 8*
4	1. Disconnect the 8-way EBCM connector C1. 2. Use the *J 39200* in order to measure the resistance between the 6-way ABS brake motor pack harness connector terminal A and the 8-way EBCM harness connector C1 terminal G. Is the resistance within the specified range?	0–2 Ω	*Go to Step 5*	*Go to Step 9*
5	Use the *J 39200* in order to measure the resistance between the 6-way ABS brake motor pack harness connector terminal B and the 8-way EBCM harness connector C1 terminal H. Is the resistance within the specified range?	0–2 Ω	*Go to Step 6*	*Go to Step 10*
6	1. Inspect the following connectors: • The 6-way ABS brake motor pack connector • The 6-way ABS brake motor pack harness connector • The 8-way EBCM connector • The 8-way EBCM harness connector 2. Inspect the connectors for the following conditions: • Poor terminal contact • Corrosion Is there evidence of poor terminal contact and corrosion?	—	*Go to Step 11*	*Go to Step 7*
7	1. Reconnect the 6-way ABS brake motor pack connector. 2. Reconnect the 8-way EBCM connector C1. 3. Test drive the vehicle. Be sure to obtain a speed of at least 16 km/h (10 mph). 4. Turn the ignition switch to the OFF position. 5. Repeat the drive sequence two more times. 6. Use the *Scan Tool* in order to look for DTCs. Does DTC C1256 set as a current DTC during the last three drive cycles?	—	*Go to Step 12*	*Go to Step 13*

GC402980310400BX

Fig. 121 Code C1256: LH Front ABS Motor Circuit Open (Part 2 of 3). Cavalier & Sunfire

Circuit Description

DTC identifies an ABS motor that cannot energize due to an open in the ABS motor circuitry. The malfunction will not allow proper front ABS operation.

Conditions for Setting the DTC

DTC C1256 can only set when the motor is commanded off.

A malfunction exists if the EBCM detects an out of range voltage on either of the ABS motor circuits. The out of range voltage on either circuit indicates an open circuit exists.

Action Taken When the DTC Sets

- An open ABS motor will not activate.
- A malfunction DTC stores.
- The ABS disables.
- The ABS warning indicator turns on.

Conditions for Clearing the DTC

- The condition responsible for setting the DTC no longer exists and the Scan Tool Clear DTCs function is used.
- 100 drive cycles pass with no DTC(s) detected. A drive cycle consists of starting the vehicle, driving the vehicle over 16 km/h (10 mph), stopping and then turning the ignition off.

Diagnostic Aids

Use the Scan Tool Manual Control function in order to exercise ABS motor movement of affected channel in both directions while applying light pressure on the brake pedal.

An intermittent malfunction may be indicated if erratic or jumpy brake pedal movement is detected while performing an apply or release function of the ABS monitor.

The following conditions may cause an intermittent malfunction:

- A poor connection
- Rubbed-through wire insulation
- A broken wire inside the insulation

If the malfunction is not current, use the following procedure to pinpoint an intermittent malfunction in the motor circuitry or connections:

1. Wiggle the wires of the affected channel.
2. Inspect if the DTC resets.

Use the enhanced diagnostic function of the Scan Tool in order to measure the frequency of the malfunction.

Thoroughly inspect any circuitry that may be causing the intermittent complaint for the following conditions:

- Backed out terminals
- Improper mating
- Broken locks
- Improperly formed or damaged terminals
- Poor terminal-to-wiring connections
- Physical damage to the wiring harness

Clear the DTCs after completing the diagnosis. Test drive the vehicle for three drive cycles in order to verify that the DTC does not reset. Use the following procedure in order to complete one drive cycle:

1. Start the vehicle.
2. Drive the vehicle over 16 km/h (10 mph).
3. Stop the vehicle.
4. Turn the ignition to the OFF position.

Important: Zero the J 39200 test leads before making any resistance measurements. Refer to the J 39200 user's manual.

GC402980310400AA

Fig. 121 Code C1256: LH Front ABS Motor Circuit Open (Part 1 of 3). Cavalier & Sunfire

Step	Action	Value(s)	Yes	No
8	Replace the ABS brake motor pack. Is the repair complete?	—	Refer to *Diagnostic System Check*	—
9	Repair the open or high resistance in CKT 1280. Is the repair complete?	—	Refer to *Diagnostic System Check*	—
10	Repair the open or high resistance in CKT 1281. Is the repair complete?	—	Refer to *Diagnostic System Check*	—
11	Replace all of the terminals or the connectors that exhibit signs of poor terminal contact, corrosion, or damaged terminal(s). Is the repair complete?	—	Refer to *Diagnostic System Check*	—
12	Replace the EBCM. Is the repair complete?	—	Refer to *Diagnostic System Check*	—
13	The malfunction is intermittent or is not present at this time. Refer to Diagnostic Aids for more information.	—	—	—

GC402980310400CX

Fig. 121 Code C1256: LH Front ABS Motor Circuit Open (Part 3 of 3). Cavalier & Sunfire

Circuit Description

DTC identifies an ABS motor circuit that shorts to ground. The malfunction will cause one of the following conditions to occur:

- The ABS motor will not be controlled at the commanded current rate.
- The driver circuit will allow current directly to ground.

Conditions for Setting the DTC

DTC can set anytime.

A malfunction exists if the EBCM detects an out of range voltage on either of the ABS motor circuits.

An out of range voltage on either circuit indicates one of the following conditions:

- A circuit shorts to ground.
- An ABS brake motor shorts internally.

Action Taken When the DTC Sets

- A malfunction DTC stores.
- The ABS disables.
- The ABS warning indicator turns on.

Conditions for Clearing the DTC

- The condition responsible for setting the DTC no longer exists and the Scan Tool Clear DTCs function is used.
- 100 drive cycles pass with no DTCs detected. A drive cycle consists of starting the vehicle, driving the vehicle over 16 km/h (10 mph), stopping and then turning the ignition off.

Diagnostic Aids

Use the Scan Tool Manual Control function in order to exercise ABS motor movement of affected channel in both directions while applying light pressure on the brake pedal.

An intermittent malfunction may be indicated if erratic or jumpy brake pedal movement is detected while performing an apply or release function of the ABS monitor.

The following conditions may cause an intermittent malfunction:

- Rubbed-through wire insulation
- An internal motor short

If the malfunction is not current, use the following procedure to pinpoint an intermittent malfunction in the motor circuitry or connections:

1. Wiggle the wires of the affected channel.
2. Inspect if the DTC resets.

Use the enhanced diagnostic function of the Scan Tool in order to measure the frequency of the malfunction.

Clear the DTCs after completing the diagnosis. Test drive the vehicle for three drive cycles in order to verify that the DTC does not reset. Use the following procedure in order to complete one drive cycle:

1. Start the vehicle.
2. Drive the vehicle over 16 km/h (10 mph).
3. Stop the vehicle.
4. Turn the ignition to the OFF position.

Important: Zero the J 39200 test leads before making any resistance measurements. Refer to the J 39200 user's manual.

GC402980310500AA

Fig. 122 Code C1257: LH Front ABS Motor Circuit Shorted To Ground (Part 1 of 3). Cavalier & Sunfire

Step	Action	Value(s)	Yes	No
1	Was the Diagnostic System Check performed?	—	*Go to Step 2*	Refer to *Diagnostic System Check*
2	Does DTC C1257 occur intermittently?	—	Refer to Diagnostic Aids	*Go to Step 3*
3	1. Turn the ignition switch to the OFF position. 2. Disconnect the 6-way ABS brake motor pack connector. 3. Disconnect the 8-way EBCM connector C1 4. Use the *J 39200* in order to measure the resistance between the 6-way ABS brake motor pack harness connector terminal A and ground. Is the resistance within the specified range?	OL (Infinite)	*Go to Step 4*	*Go to Step 9*
4	Use *J 39200* in order to measure the resistance between the 6-way ABS brake motor pack harness connector terminal B and ground. Is the resistance within the specified range?	OL (Infinite)	*Go to Step 5*	*Go to Step 10*
5	Use the *J 39200* in order to measure the resistance between the 6-way ABS brake motor pack connector terminal A and ground. Is the resistance within the specified range?	OL (Infinite)	*Go to Step 6*	*Go to Step 8*
6	1. Inspect the following components for damage: • The 6-way ABS brake motor pack connector • The 6-way ABS brake motor pack harness connector Damage may cause a short to ground with the connector connected. 2. Inspect the following components for damage: • The 8-way EBCM connector C1 • The 8-way EBCM harness connector C1 Damage may cause a short to ground with the connector connected. 3. Inspect CKT 1280 and CKT 1281 for damage. Damage may cause a short to ground. Is there damage which may cause a short to ground?	—	*Go to Step 11*	*Go to Step 7*
7	1. Reconnect the 6-way ABS brake motor pack connector. 2. Reconnect the 8-way EBCM connector C1. 3. Test drive the vehicle obtaining a speed at least 16 km/h (10 mph). 4. Turn the ignition switch to the OFF position. 5. Repeat the drive sequence two additional times. 6. Use the *Scan Tool* in order to inspect for DTCs. Did DTC C1257 set as a current DTC in the last three drive cycles?	—	*Go to Step 12*	*Go to Step 13*

GC402980310500BX

Fig. 122 Code C1257: LH Front ABS Motor Circuit Shorted To Ground (Part 2 of 3). Cavalier & Sunfire

Step	Action	Value(s)	Yes	No
8	Replace the ABS brake motor pack. Is the repair complete?	—	Refer to *Diagnostic System Check*	—
9	Repair the short to ground in CKT 1280. Is the repair complete?	—	Refer to *Diagnostic System Check*	—
10	Repair the short to ground in CKT 1281. Is the repair complete?	—	Refer to *Diagnostic System Check*	—
11	Replace all of the following components that exhibit signs of damage: • The terminals • The connectors • The wires Damage may cause a short to ground. Is the repair complete?	—	Refer to *Diagnostic System Check*	—
12	Replace the EBCM. Is the repair complete?	—	Refer to *Diagnostic System Check*	—
13	The malfunction is intermittent or not present at this time. Refer to Diagnostic Aids for more information.	—	—	—

GC402980310500CX

Fig. 122 Code C1257: LH Front ABS Motor Circuit Shorted To Ground (Part 3 of 3). Cavalier & Sunfire

Circuit Description

DTC identifies an ABS motor circuit that shorts to voltage or an ABS motor that has low or no resistance. A short to voltage will not allow controlled ABS operation.

Conditions for Setting the DTC

DTC can set only when the ABS motor is commanded off.

A malfunction exists if the EBCM detects an out of range voltage on either of the ABS motor circuits.

An out of range voltage on either circuit indicates one of the following conditions:

- A circuit shorts to voltage.
- An ABS brake motor shorts internally.

Action Taken When the DTC Sets

- A malfunction DTC stores.
- The ABS disables.
- The ABS warning indicator turns on.

Conditions for Clearing the DTC

- The condition responsible for setting the DTC no longer exists and the Scan Tool Clear DTCs function is used.
- 100 drive cycles pass with no DTCs detected. A drive cycle consists of starting the vehicle, driving the vehicle over 16 km/h (10 mph), stopping and then turning the ignition off.

Diagnostic Aids

Use the Scan Tool Manual Control function in order to exercise ABS motor movement of affected channel in both directions while applying light pressure on the brake pedal.

An intermittent malfunction may be indicated if erratic or jumpy brake pedal movement is detected while performing an apply or release function of the ABS monitor.

If the malfunction is not current, use the following procedure to pinpoint an intermittent malfunction in the motor circuitry or connections:

1. Wiggle the wires of the affected channel.
2. Inspect if the DTC resets.

Use the enhanced diagnostic function of the Scan Tool in order to measure the frequency of the malfunction.

Thoroughly inspect any circuitry that may be causing the intermittent complaint for the following conditions:

Clear the DTCs after completing the diagnosis. Test drive the vehicle for three drive cycles in order to verify that the DTC does not reset. Use the following procedure in order to complete one drive cycle:

1. Start the vehicle.
2. Drive the vehicle over 16 km/h (10 mph).
3. Stop the vehicle.
4. Turn the ignition to the OFF position.

Important: Zero the J 39200 test leads before making any resistance measurements. Refer to the J 39200 user's manual.

GC402980310600AA

Fig. 123 Code C1258: LH Front ABS Motor Circuit Shorted To Voltage (Part 1 of 3). Cavalier & Sunfire

Step	Action	Value(s)	Yes	No
1	Was the Diagnostic System Check performed?	—	*Go to Step 2*	Refer to *Diagnostic System Check*
2	Does DTC C1258 occur intermittently?	—	Refer to Diagnostic Aids	*Go to Step 3*
3	1. Turn the ignition switch to the OFF position. 2. Disconnect the 6-way ABS brake motor pack connector. 3. Disconnect the 8-way EBCM connector C1 4. Use the *J 39200* in order to measure the voltage between the 6-way ABS brake motor pack harness connector terminal A and ground. Is the voltage within the specified range?	0–1 V	*Go to Step 4*	*Go to Step 10*
4	Use the *J 39200* in order to measure the voltage between the 6-way ABS brake motor pack harness connector terminal B and ground. Is the voltage within the specified range?	0–1 V	*Go to Step 5*	*Go to Step 11*
5	1. Turn the ignition switch to the OFF position. 2. Use the *J 39200* in order to measure the resistance between the 6-way ABS motor pack harness connector terminal A and the 6-way ABS motor pack harness connector terminal B. Is the resistance within the specified range?	OL (Infinite)	*Go to Step 6*	*Go to Step 12*
6	Use the *J 39200* in order to measure the resistance between the 6-way ABS motor pack connector terminal A and the 6-way ABS motor pack connector terminal B. Is the resistance within the specified range?	0.2–1.5 Ω	*Go to Step 7*	*Go to Step 9*
7	1. Inspect the following components for damage: • The 6-way ABS motor pack connector • The 6-way ABS motor pack harness connector Damage may cause a short to voltage with the connector connected. 2. Inspect the following components for damage: • The 8-way EBCM connector C1 • The 8-way EBCM harness connector C1 Damage may cause a short to voltage with the connector connected. 3. Inspect CKT 1280 and CKT 1281 for signs of damage. Damage may cause a short to voltage. Is there damage which may result in a short to voltage?	—	*Go to Step 13*	*Go to Step 8*
8	1. Reconnect the 6-way ABS motor pack connector. 2. Reconnect the 8-way EBCM connector C1. 3. Test drive the vehicle obtaining a speed of at least 16 km/h (10 mph). 4. Turn the ignition switch to the OFF position. 5. Repeat the drive sequence two additional times. 6. Use the *Scan Tool* in order to inspect for DTCs. Did DTC C1258 set as a current DTC in the last three drive cycles?	—	*Go to Step 14*	*Go to Step 15*

GC402980310600BX

Fig. 123 Code C1258: LH Front ABS Motor Circuit Shorted To Voltage (Part 2 of 3). Cavalier & Sunfire

Step	Action	Value(s)	Yes	No
9	Replace the ABS motor pack. Is the repair complete?	—	Refer to *Diagnostic System Check*	—
10	Repair the short to voltage in CKT 1280. Is the repair complete?	—	Refer to *Diagnostic System Check*	—
11	Repair the short to voltage in CKT 1281. Is the repair complete?	—	Refer to *Diagnostic System Check*	—
12	Repair the short between CKT 1280 and CKT 1281. Is the repair complete?	—	Refer to *Diagnostic System Check*	—
13	Replace all of the following components that are damaged: • The terminals • The connectors • The wires Damage may cause a short to voltage. • Is the repair complete?	—	Refer to *Diagnostic System Check*	—
14	Replace the EBCM. Is the repair complete?	—	Refer to *Diagnostic System Check*	—
15	The malfunction is intermittent or not present at this time. Refer to Diagnostic Aids for more information.	—	—	—

GC402980310600CX

Fig. 123 Code C1258: LH Front ABS Motor Circuit Shorted To Voltage (Part 3 of 3). Cavalier & Sunfire

Step	Action	Value(s)	Yes	No
1	Was the Diagnostic System Check performed?	—	*Go to Step 2*	Refer to *Diagnostic System Check*
2	Does DTC C1261 occur intermittently?	—	Refer to Diagnostic Aids	*Go to Step 3*
3	1. Turn the ignition switch to the OFF position. 2. Disconnect the 6-way ABS brake motor pack connector. 3. Use the *J 39200* in order to measure the resistance between the 6-way ABS brake motor pack connector terminal E and 6-way ABS motor pack connector terminal F Is the resistance within the specified range?	0.2–1.5 Ω	*Go to Step 4*	*Go to Step 8*
4	1. Disconnect the 8-way EBCM connector C1. 2. Use *J 39200* in order to measure the resistance between the 6-way ABS brake motor pack harness connector terminal E and the 8-way EBCM harness connector C1 terminal A. Is the resistance within the specified range?	0–2 Ω	*Go to Step 5*	*Go to Step 9*
5	Use the *J 39200* in order to measure the resistance between the 6-way ABS brake motor pack harness connector terminal F and the 8-way EBCM harness connector C1 terminal B. Is the resistance within the specified range?	0–2 Ω	*Go to Step 6*	*Go to Step 10*
6	1. Inspect the following components for poor terminal contact and corrosion: • The 6-way ABS brake motor pack connector • The 6-way ABS brake motor pack harness connector 2. Inspect the following components for poor terminal contact and corrosion: • The 8-way EBCM connector • The 8-way EBCM harness connector C1 Damage that may cause an open with the connector connected. 3. Inspect CKT 1282 and CKT 1283 for damage. Damage may cause an open circuit. Is there poor terminal contact or corrosion?	—	*Go to Step 11*	*Go to Step 7*
7	1. Reconnect the 6-way ABS brake motor pack connector. 2. Reconnect the 8-way EBCM connector C1. 3. Test drive the vehicle obtaining a speed at least 16 km/h (10 mph). 4. Turn the ignition switch to the OFF position. 5. Repeat the drive sequence two additional times. 6. Use the *Scan Tool* in order to inspect for DTCs. Did DTC C1261 set as a current DTC in the last three drive cycles?	—	*Go to Step 12*	*Go to Step 13*

GC402980310400DX

Fig. 124 Code C1261: RH Front ABS Motor Circuit Open (Part 2 of 3). Cavalier & Sunfire

Circuit Description

DTC C1261 identifies an ABS motor that cannot energize due to an open in the ABS motor circuitry. The malfunction will not allow proper front ABS operation.

Conditions for Setting the DTC

DTC C1261 can only set when the motor is commanded off.

A malfunction exists if the EBCM detects an out of range voltage on either of the right front ABS motor circuits. The out of range voltage on either circuit indicates an open circuit exists.

Action Taken When the DTC Sets

- An open ABS motor will not activate.
- A malfunction DTC stores.
- The ABS disables.
- The ABS warning indicator turns on.

Conditions for Clearing the DTC

- The condition responsible for setting the DTC no longer exists and the Scan Tool Clear DTCs function is used.
- 100 drive cycles pass with no DTC(s) detected. A drive cycle consists of starting the vehicle, driving the vehicle over 16 km/h (10 mph), stopping and then turning the ignition off.

Diagnostic Aids

Use the Scan Tool Manual Control function in order to exercise ABS motor movement of affected channel in both directions while applying light pressure on the brake pedal.

An intermittent malfunction may be indicated if erratic or jumpy brake pedal movement is detected while performing an apply or release function of the ABS monitor.

The following conditions may cause an intermittent malfunction:

- A poor connection
- Rubbed-through wire insulation
- A broken wire inside the insulation

If the malfunction is not current, use the following procedure to pinpoint an intermittent malfunction in the motor circuitry or connections:

1. Wiggle the wires of the affected channel.
2. Inspect if the DTC resets.

Use the enhanced diagnostic function of the Scan Tool in order to measure the frequency of the malfunction.

Thoroughly inspect any circuitry that may be causing the intermittent complaint for the following conditions:

- Backed out terminals
- Improper mating
- Broken locks
- Improperly formed or damaged terminals
- Poor terminal-to-wiring connections
- Physical damage to the wiring harness

Clear the DTCs after completing the diagnosis. Test drive the vehicle for three drive cycles in order to verify that the DTC does not reset. Use the following procedure in order to complete one drive cycle:

1. Start the vehicle.
2. Drive the vehicle over 16 km/h (10 mph).
3. Stop the vehicle.
4. Turn the ignition to the OFF position.

Important: Zero the J 39200 test leads before making any resistance measurements. Refer to the J 39200 user's manual.

GC402980310601AX

Fig. 124 Code C1261: RH Front ABS Motor Circuit Open (Part 1 of 3). Cavalier & Sunfire

Step	Action	Value(s)	Yes	No
8	Replace the ABS brake motor pack. Is the repair complete?	—	Refer to *Diagnostic System Check*	—
9	Repair the open in CKT 1282. Is the repair complete?	—	Refer to *Diagnostic System Check*	—
10	Repair the open in CKT 1283. Is the repair complete?	—	Refer to *Diagnostic System Check*	—
11	Replace all of the terminals and connectors that exhibit the following conditions: • Poor terminal contact • Corrosion • Damaged terminal(s) • Is the repair complete?	—	Refer to *Diagnostic System Check*	—
12	Replace the EBCM. Is the repair complete?	—	Refer to *Diagnostic System Check*	—
13	The malfunction is intermittent or not present at this time. Refer to Diagnostic Aids for more information.	—	—	—

GC402980310400EX

Fig. 124 Code C1261: RH Front ABS Motor Circuit Open (Part 3 of 3). Cavalier & Sunfire

Circuit Description

DTC C1262 identifies an ABS motor circuit that shorts to ground. The malfunction will cause one of the following conditions to occur:

- The ABS motor will not be controlled at the commanded current rate.
- The driver circuit will allow current directly to ground.

Conditions for Setting the DTC

DTC C1262 can set anytime.

A malfunction exists if the EBCM detects an out of range voltage on either of the right front ABS motor circuits.

An out of range voltage on either circuit indicates one of the following conditions:

- A circuit shorts to ground.
- An ABS brake motor internally shorts.

Action Taken When the DTC Sets

- A malfunction DTC stores.
- The ABS disables.
- The ABS warning indicator turns on.

Conditions for Clearing the DTC

- The condition responsible for setting the DTC no longer exists and the Scan Tool Clear DTCs function is used.
- 100 drive cycles pass with no DTCs detected. A drive cycle consists of starting the vehicle, driving the vehicle over 16 km/h (10 mph), stopping and then turning the ignition off.

Diagnostic Aids

Use the Scan Tool Manual Control function in order to exercise ABS motor movement of affected channel in both directions while applying light pressure on the brake pedal.

An intermittent malfunction may be indicated if erratic or jumpy brake pedal movement is detected while performing an apply or release function of the ABS monitor.

A rubbed-through wire may cause an intermittent malfunction.

If the malfunction is not current, use the following procedure to pinpoint an intermittent malfunction in the motor circuitry or connections:

1. Wiggle the wires of the affected channel.
2. Inspect if the DTC resets.

Use the enhanced diagnostic function of the Scan Tool in order to measure the frequency of the malfunction.

Clear the DTCs after completing the diagnosis. Test drive the vehicle for three drive cycles in order to verify that the DTC does not reset. Use the following procedure in order to complete one drive cycle:

1. Start the vehicle.
2. Drive the vehicle over 16 km/h (10 mph).
3. Stop the vehicle.
4. Turn the ignition to the OFF position.

Important: Zero the J 39200 test leads before making any resistance measurements. Refer to the J 39200 user's manual.

GC402980310502AX

Fig. 125 Code C1262: RH Front ABS Motor Circuit Shorted To Ground (Part 1 of 3). Cavalier & Sunfire

Step	Action	Value(s)	Yes	No
1	Was the Diagnostic System Check performed?	—	*Go to Step 2*	Refer to *Diagnostic System Check*
2	Does DTC C1262 occur intermittently?	—	Refer to Diagnostic Aids	*Go to Step 3*
3	1. Turn the ignition switch to the OFF position. 2. Disconnect the 6-way ABS brake motor pack connector. 3. Disconnect the 8-way EBCM connector C1 4. Use the *J 39200* in order to measure the resistance between the 6-way ABS brake motor pack harness connector terminal E and ground. Is the resistance within the specified range?	OL (Infinite)	*Go to Step 4*	*Go to Step 9*
4	Use *J 39200* in order to measure the resistance between the 6-way ABS brake motor pack harness connector terminal F and ground. Is the resistance within the specified range?	OL (Infinite)	*Go to Step 5*	*Go to Step 10*
5	Use the *J 39200* in order to measure the resistance between the 6-way ABS brake motor pack connector terminal E and ground. Is the resistance within the specified range?	OL (Infinite)	*Go to Step 6*	*Go to Step 8*
6	1. Inspect the following components for damage: • The 6-way ABS brake motor pack connector • The 6-way ABS brake motor pack harness connector Damage that may cause a short to ground with the connector connected. 2. Inspect the following components for damage: • The 8-way EBCM connector C1 • The 8-way EBCM harness connector C1 Damage that may cause a short to ground with the connector connected. 3. Inspect CKT 1282 and CKT 1283 for damage. Damage may cause a short to ground. Is there damage which may result in a short to ground?	—	*Go to Step 11*	*Go to Step 7*
7	1. Reconnect the 6-way ABS brake motor pack connector. 2. Reconnect the 8-way EBCM connector C1. 3. Test drive the vehicle obtaining a speed at least 16 km/h (10 mph). 4. Turn the ignition switch to the OFF position. 5. Repeat the drive sequence two additional times. 6. Use the *Scan Tool* in order to inspect for DTCs. Did DTC C1262 set as a current DTC in the last three drive cycles?	—	*Go to Step 12*	*Go to Step 13*

GC402980310500DX

Fig. 125 Code C1262: RH Front ABS Motor Circuit Shorted To Ground (Part 2 of 3). Cavalier & Sunfire

Circuit Description

DTC C1263 identifies an ABS motor circuit that is shorted shorts to voltage or an ABS motor that has low or no resistance.

Conditions for Setting the DTC

DTC C1263 can set only when the ABS motor is commanded off.

A malfunction exists if the EBCM detects an out of range voltage on either of the right front ABS motor circuits.

An out of range voltage on either circuit indicates one of the following conditions:

- A circuit shorts to voltage.
- An ABS brake motor shorts internally.

Action Taken When the DTC Sets

- A malfunction DTC stores.
- The ABS disables.
- The ABS warning indicator turns on.

Conditions for Clearing the DTC

- The condition responsible for setting the DTC no longer exists and the Scan Tool Clear DTCs function is used.
- 100 drive cycles pass with no DTCs detected. A drive cycle consists of starting the vehicle, driving the vehicle over 16 km/h (10 mph), stopping and then turning the ignition off.

Diagnostic Aids

Use the Scan Tool Manual Control function in order to exercise ABS motor movement of affected channel in both directions while applying light pressure on the brake pedal.

An intermittent malfunction may be indicated if erratic or jumpy brake pedal movement is detected while performing an apply or release function of the ABS monitor.

If the malfunction is not current, use the following procedure to pinpoint an intermittent malfunction in the motor circuitry or connections:

1. Wiggle the wires of the affected channel.
2. Inspect if the DTC resets.

Use the enhanced diagnostic function of the Scan Tool in order to measure the frequency of the malfunction.

Clear the DTCs after completing the diagnosis. Test drive the vehicle for three drive cycles in order to verify that the DTC does not reset. Use the following procedure in order to complete one drive cycle:

1. Start the vehicle.
2. Drive the vehicle over 16 km/h (10 mph).
3. Stop the vehicle.
4. Turn the ignition to the OFF position.

Important: Zero the J 39200 test leads before making any resistance measurements. Refer to the J 39200 user's manual.

GC402980310603AX

Fig. 126 Code C1263: RH Front ABS Motor Circuit Shorted To Voltage (Part 1 of 3). Cavalier & Sunfire

Step	Action	Value(s)	Yes	No
8	Replace the ABS brake motor pack. Is the repair complete?	—	Refer to *Diagnostic System Check*	—
9	Repair the short to ground in CKT 1282. Is the repair complete?	—	Refer to *Diagnostic System Check*	—
10	Repair the short to ground in CKT 1283. Is the repair complete?	—	Refer to *Diagnostic System Check*	—
11	Replace all of the following components that exhibit signs of damage: • The terminals • The connectors • The wires Damage may cause a short to ground. Is the repair complete?	—	Refer to *Diagnostic System Check*	—
12	Replace the EBCM. Is the repair complete?	—	Refer to *Diagnostic System Check*	—
13	The malfunction is intermittent or not present at this time. Refer to Diagnostic Aids for more information.	—	—	—

GC402980310500EX

Fig. 125 Code C1262: RH Front ABS Motor Circuit Shorted To Ground (Part 3 of 3). Cavalier & Sunfire

Step	Action	Value(s)	Yes	No
1	Was the Diagnostic System Check performed?	—	*Go to Step 2*	Refer to *Diagnostic System Check*
2	Does DTC C1263 occur intermittently?	—	Refer to Diagnostic Aids	*Go to Step 3*
3	1. Turn the ignition switch to the OFF position. 2. Disconnect the 6-way ABS brake motor pack connector. 3. Disconnect the 8-way EBCM connector C1 4. Turn the ignition switch to the RUN position. Do not start the engine. 5. Use the *J 39200* in order to measure the voltage between the 6-way ABS brake motor pack harness connector terminal E and ground. Is the voltage within the specified range?	0–1 V	*Go to Step 4*	*Go to Step 10*
4	Use the *J 39200* in order to measure the voltage between the 6-way ABS brake motor pack harness connector terminal F and ground. Is the voltage within the specified range?	0–1 V	*Go to Step 5*	*Go to Step 11*
5	1. Turn the ignition switch to the OFF position. 2. Use the *J 39200* in order to measure the resistance between the 6-way ABS motor pack harness connector terminal E and the 6-way ABS motor pack harness connector terminal F. Is the resistance within the specified range?	OL (Infinite)	*Go to Step 6*	*Go to Step 12*
6	Use the *J 39200* in order to measure the resistance between the 6-way ABS motor pack connector terminal E and the 6-way ABS motor pack connector terminal F. Is the resistance within the specified range?	0.2–1.5 Ω	*Go to Step 7*	*Go to Step 9*
7	1. Inspect the following components for damage: • The 6-way ABS motor pack connector • The 6-way ABS motor pack harness connector Damage that may cause a short to voltage with the connector connected. 2. Inspect the following components for damage: • The 8-way EBCM connector • The 8-way EBCM harness connector C1 Damage may cause a short to voltage with the connector connected. 3. Inspect CKT 1282 and CKT 1283 for signs of damage. Damage may cause a short to voltage. Is there damage which may cause a short to voltage?	—	*Go to Step 13*	*Go to Step 8*

GC402980310600DX

Fig. 126 Code C1263: RH Front ABS Motor Circuit Shorted To Voltage (Part 2 of 3). Cavalier & Sunfire

Step	Action	Value(s)	Yes	No
8	1. Reconnect the 6-way ABS motor pack connector. 2. Reconnect the 8-way EBCM connector C1. 3. Test drive the vehicle at a speed of at least 16 km/h (10 mph). 4. Turn the ignition switch to the OFF position. 5. Repeat the drive sequence two additional times. 6. Use the *Scan Tool* in order to inspect for DTCs. Did DTC C1263 set as a current DTC during the last three drive cycles?	—	*Go to Step 14*	*Go to Step 15*
9	Replace the ABS motor pack. Is the repair complete?	—	Refer to *Diagnostic System Check*	—
10	Repair the short to voltage in CKT 1282. Is the repair complete?	—	Refer to *Diagnostic System Check*	—
11	Repair the short to voltage in CKT 1283. Is the repair complete?	—	Refer to *Diagnostic System Check*	—
12	Repair the short between CKT 1282 and CKT 1283. Is the repair complete?	—	Refer to *Diagnostic System Check*	—
13	Replace all of the following components that are damaged: • The terminals • The connectors • The wires Damage may cause a short to voltage. Is the repair complete?	—	Refer to *Diagnostic System Check*	—
14	Replace the EBCM. Is the repair complete?	—	Refer to *Diagnostic System Check*	—
15	The malfunction is intermittent or is not present at this time. Refer to Diagnostic Aids for more information.	—	—	—

GC402980310600EX

Fig. 126 Code C1263: RH Front ABS Motor Circuit Shorted To Voltage (Part 3 of 3). Cavalier & Sunfire

Step	Action	Value(s)	Yes	No
1	Was the Diagnostic System Check performed?	—	*Go to Step 2*	Refer to *Diagnostic System Check*
2	Does DTC C1264 occur intermittently?	—	Refer to Diagnostic Aids	*Go to Step 3*
3	1. Turn the ignition switch to the OFF position. 2. Disconnect the 6-way ABS brake motor pack connector. 3. Use the *J 39200* in order to measure the resistance between the 6-way ABS brake motor pack connector terminal D and 6-way ABS motor pack connector terminal C Is the resistance within the specified range?	0.2–1.5 Ω	*Go to Step 4*	*Go to Step 8*
4	1. Disconnect the 8-way EBCM connector C1. 2. Use the *J 39200* in order to measure the resistance between the 6-way ABS brake motor pack harness connector terminal C and the 8-way EBCM harness connector C1 terminal F. Is the resistance within the specified range?	0–2 Ω	*Go to Step 5*	*Go to Step 9*
5	Use the *J 39200* in order to measure the resistance between the 6-way ABS brake motor pack harness connector terminal D and the 8-way EBCM harness connector C1 terminal E. Is the resistance within the specified range?	0–2 Ω	*Go to Step 6*	*Go to Step 10*
6	1. Inspect the following components for poor terminal contact and corrosion: • The 6-way ABS brake motor pack connector • The 6-way ABS brake motor pack harness connector 2. Inspect the following components for poor terminal contact and corrosion: • The 8-way EBCM connector • The 8-way EBCM harness connector C1 Damage may cause a short to ground with the connector connected. 3. Inspect CKT 1284 and CKT 1285 for damage. Damage may cause a short to ground. Is there poor terminal contact or corrosion?	—	*Go to Step 11*	*Go to Step 7*
7	1. Reconnect the 6-way ABS brake motor pack connector. 2. Reconnect the 8-way EBCM harness connector C1. 3. Test drive the vehicle at a speed at least 16 km/h (10 mph). 4. Turn the ignition switch to the OFF position. 5. Repeat the drive sequence two additional times. 6. Use the *Scan Tool* in order to inspect for DTCs. Did DTC C1264 set as a current DTC in the last three drive cycles?	—	*Go to Step 12*	*Go to Step 13*

GC402980310400FX

Fig. 127 Code C1264: Rear ABS Motor Circuit Open (Part 2 of 3). Cavalier & Sunfire

Circuit Description

DTC 1264 identifies an ABS motor that cannot energize due to an open in the ABS motor circuitry. The malfunction will not allow proper rear ABS operation.

Conditions for Setting the DTC

DTC C1264 can only set when the motor is commanded off.

A malfunction exists if the EBCM detects an out of range voltage on either of the rear ABS motor circuits. The out of range voltage on either circuit indicates an open circuit exists.

Action Taken When the DTC Sets

- An open ABS motor will not activate.
- A malfunction DTC stores.
- The ABS disables.
- The ABS warning indicator turns on.
- The red BRAKE warning indicator turns on and DTC C1286 also sets if the rear piston in the ABS brake motor pack is not in the home position.

Conditions for Clearing the DTC

- The condition responsible for setting the DTC no longer exists and the Scan Tool Clear DTCs function is used.
- 100 drive cycles pass with no DTC(s) detected. A drive cycle consists of starting the vehicle, driving the vehicle over 16 km/h (10 mph), stopping and then turning the ignition off.

Diagnostic Aids

Use the Scan Tool Manual Control function in order to exercise ABS motor movement of affected channel in both directions while applying light pressure on the brake pedal.

An intermittent malfunction may be indicated if erratic or jumpy brake pedal movement is detected while performing an apply or release function of the ABS monitor.

The following conditions may cause an intermittent malfunction:

- A poor connection
- Rubbed-through wire insulation
- A broken wire inside the insulation

If the malfunction is not current, use the following procedure to pinpoint an intermittent malfunction in the motor circuitry or connections:

1. Wiggle the wires of the affected channel.
2. Inspect if the DTC resets.

Use the enhanced diagnostic function of the Scan Tool in order to measure the frequency of the malfunction.

Thoroughly inspect any circuitry that may be causing the intermittent complaint for the following conditions:

- Backed out terminals
- Improper mating
- Broken locks
- Improperly formed or damaged terminals
- Poor terminal-to-wiring connections
- Physical damage to the wiring harness

Clear the DTCs after completing the diagnosis. Test drive the vehicle for three drive cycles in order to verify that the DTC does not reset. Use the following procedure in order to complete one drive cycle:

1. Start the vehicle.
2. Drive the vehicle over 16 km/h (10 mph).
3. Stop the vehicle.
4. Turn the ignition to the OFF position.

Important: Zero the J 39200 test leads before making any resistance measurements. Refer to the J 39200 user's manual.

GC402980310404AX

Fig. 127 Code C1264: Rear ABS Motor Circuit Open (Part 1 of 3). Cavalier & Sunfire

Step	Action	Value(s)	Yes	No
8	Replace the ABS brake motor pack. Is the repair complete?	—	Refer to *Diagnostic System Check*	—
9	Repair the short to ground in CKT 1284. Is the repair complete?	—	Refer to *Diagnostic System Check*	—
10	Repair the short to ground in CKT 1285. Is the repair complete?	—	Refer to *Diagnostic System Check*	—
11	Replace all of the terminals and connectors that exhibit the following conditions: • Poor terminal contact • Corrosion • Damaged terminal(s) • Is the repair complete?	—	Refer to *Diagnostic System Check*	—
12	Replace the EBCM. Is the repair complete?	—	Refer to *Diagnostic System Check*	—
13	The malfunction is intermittent or is not present at this time. Refer to Diagnostic Aids for more information.	—	—	—

GC402980310400GX

Fig. 127 Code C1264: Rear ABS Motor Circuit Open (Part 3 of 3). Cavalier & Sunfire

Circuit Description

DTC C1265 identifies an ABS motor circuit that shorts to ground. The malfunction will cause one of the following conditions to occur:

- The ABS motor will not be controlled at the commanded current rate.
- The driver circuit will allow current directly to ground.

Conditions for Setting the DTC

DTC C1265 can set anytime.

A malfunction exists if the EBCM detects an out of range voltage on either of the rear ABS motor circuits.

An out of range voltage on either circuit indicates one of the following conditions:

- A circuit shorts to ground.
- An ABS brake motor is shorts internally.

Action Taken When the DTC Sets

- A malfunction DTC stores.
- The ABS disables.
- The ABS warning indicator turns on.
- The red BRAKE warning indicator turns on and DTC C1286 also sets if the rear piston in the ABS brake motor pack is not in the home position.

Conditions for Clearing the DTC

- The condition responsible for setting the DTC no longer exists and the Scan Tool Clear DTCs function is used.
- 100 drive cycles pass with no DTCs detected. A drive cycle consists of starting the vehicle, driving the vehicle over 16 km/h (10 mph), stopping and then turning the ignition off.

Diagnostic Aids

Use the Scan Tool Manual Control function in order to exercise ABS motor movement of affected channel in both directions while applying light pressure on the brake pedal.

An intermittent malfunction may be indicated if erratic or jumpy brake pedal movement is detected while performing an apply or release function of the ABS monitor.

If the malfunction is not current, use the following procedure to pinpoint an intermittent malfunction in the motor circuitry or connections:

1. Wiggle the wires of the affected channel.
2. Inspect if the DTC resets.

Use the enhanced diagnostic function of the Scan Tool in order to measure the frequency of the malfunction.

Clear the DTCs after completing the diagnosis. Test drive the vehicle for three drive cycles in order to verify that the DTC does not reset. Use the following procedure in order to complete one drive cycle:

1. Start the vehicle.
2. Drive the vehicle over 16 km/h (10 mph).
3. Stop the vehicle.
4. Turn the ignition to the OFF position.

Important: Zero the J 39200 test leads before making any resistance measurements. Refer to the J 39200 user's manual.

GC402980310505AX

Fig. 128 Code C1265: Rear ABS Motor Circuit Shorted To Ground (Part 1 of 3). Cavalier & Sunfire

Step	Action	Value(s)	Yes	No
1	Was the Diagnostic System Check performed?	—	*Go to Step 2*	Refer to *Diagnostic System Check*
2	Does DTC C1265 occur intermittently?	—	Refer to Diagnostic Aids	*Go to Step 3*
3	1. Turn the ignition switch to the OFF position. 2. Disconnect the 6-way ABS brake motor pack connector. 3. Disconnect the 8-way EBCM connector C1. 4. Use the *J 39200* in order to measure the resistance between the 6-way ABS brake motor pack harness connector terminal C and ground. Is the resistance within the specified range?	OL (Infinite)	*Go to Step 4*	*Go to Step 9*
4	Use *J 39200* in order to measure the resistance between the 6-way ABS brake motor pack harness connector terminal D and ground. Is the resistance within the specified range?	OL (Infinite)	*Go to Step 5*	*Go to Step 10*
5	Use the *J 39200* in order to measure the resistance between the 6-way ABS brake motor pack connector terminal C and ground. Is the resistance within the specified range?	OL (Infinite)	*Go to Step 6*	*Go to Step 8*
6	1. Inspect the following components for damage: • The 6-way ABS brake motor pack connector • The 6-way ABS brake motor pack harness connector Damage that may cause a short to ground with the connector connected. 2. Inspect the following components for damage: • The 8-way EBCM connector • The 8-way EBCM harness connector C1 Damage that may cause a short to ground with the connector connected. 3. Inspect the following circuits for damage: • CKT 1284 • CKT 1285 Damage may cause a short to ground. Is there damage which may cause a short to ground?	—	*Go to Step 11*	*Go to Step 7*
7	1. Reconnect the 6-way ABS brake motor pack connector. 2. Reconnect the 8-way EBCM connector C1. 3. Test drive the vehicle obtaining a speed at least 16 km/h (10 mph). 4. Turn the ignition switch to the OFF position. 5. Repeat the drive sequence two additional times. 6. Use the *Scan Tool* in order to inspect for DTCs. Did DTC C1265 set as a current DTC during the last three drive cycles?	—	*Go to Step 12*	*Go to Step 13*

GC402980310500FX

Fig. 128 Code C1265: Rear ABS Motor Circuit Shorted To Ground (Part 2 of 3). Cavalier & Sunfire

Circuit Description

DTC C1266 identifies an ABS motor circuit that shorts to voltage or an ABS motor that has low or zero resistance. The malfunction will cause one of the following conditions to occur:

- The ABS motor will not be controlled at the commanded current rate.
- The ABS motor will turn in the opposite direction or not at all.

Conditions for Setting the DTC

DTC C1266 can set only when the ABS motor is commanded off.

A malfunction exists if the EBCM detects an out of range voltage on either of the rear ABS motor circuits.

An out of range voltage on either circuit indicates one of the following conditions:

- A circuit shorts to voltage.
- An ABS brake motor shorts internally.

Action Taken When the DTC Sets

- A malfunction DTC stores.
- The ABS disables.
- The ABS warning indicator turns on.

Conditions for Clearing the DTC

- The condition responsible for setting the DTC no longer exists and the Scan Tool Clear DTCs function is used.
- 100 drive cycles pass with no DTCs detected. A drive cycle consists of starting the vehicle, driving the vehicle over 16 km/h (10 mph), stopping and then turning the ignition off.

Diagnostic Aids

Use the Scan Tool Manual Control function to exercise ABS motor movement of affected channel in both directions while applying light pressure on the brake pedal.

An intermittent malfunction may be indicated if erratic or jumpy brake pedal movement is detected while performing an apply or release function of the ABS monitor.

If the malfunction is not current, use the following procedure to pinpoint an intermittent malfunction in the motor circuitry or connections:

1. Wiggle the wires of the affected channel.
2. Inspect if the DTC resets.

Use the enhanced diagnostic function of the Scan Tool in order to measure the frequency of the malfunction.

Clear the DTCs after completing the diagnosis. Test drive the vehicle for three drive cycles in order to verify that the DTC does not reset. Use the following procedure in order to complete one drive cycle:

1. Start the vehicle.
2. Drive the vehicle over 16 km/h (10 mph).
3. Stop the vehicle.
4. Turn the ignition to the OFF position.

Important: Zero the J 39200 test leads before making any resistance measurements. Refer to the J 39200 user's manual.

GC402980310606AX

Fig. 129 Code C1266: Rear ABS Motor Circuit Shorted To Voltage (Part 1 of 3). Cavalier & Sunfire

Step	Action	Value(s)	Yes	No
8	Replace the ABS brake motor pack. Is the repair complete?	—	Refer to *Diagnostic System Check*	—
9	Repair the short to ground in CKT 1284. Is the repair complete?	—	Refer to *Diagnostic System Check*	—
10	Repair the short to ground in CKT 1285. Is the repair complete?	—	Refer to *Diagnostic System Check*	—
11	Replace all of the following components that exhibit signs of damage: • The terminals • The connectors • The wires Damage may cause a short to ground. Is the repair complete?	—	Refer to *Diagnostic System Check*	—
12	Replace the EBCM. Is the repair complete?	—	Refer to *Diagnostic System Check*	—
13	The malfunction is intermittent or is not present at this time. Refer to Diagnostic Aids for more information.	—	—	—

GC402980310500GX

Fig. 128 Code C1265: Rear ABS Motor Circuit Shorted To Ground (Part 3 of 3). Cavalier & Sunfire

Step	Action	Value(s)	Yes	No
1	Was the Diagnostic System Check performed?	—	*Go to Step 2*	Refer to *Diagnostic System Check*
2	Does DTC C1266 occur intermittently?	—	Refer to Diagnostic Aids	*Go to Step 3*
3	1. Turn the ignition switch to the OFF position. 2. Disconnect the 6-way ABS brake motor pack connector. 3. Disconnect the 8-way EBCM connector C1 4. Turn the ignition switch to the RUN position. Do not start the engine. 5. Use the *J 39200* in order to measure the voltage between the 6-way ABS brake motor pack harness connector terminal C and ground. Is the voltage within the specified range?	0–1 V	*Go to Step 4*	*Go to Step 10*
4	Use the *J 39200* in order to measure the voltage between the 6-way ABS brake motor pack harness connector terminal D and ground. Is the voltage within the specified range?	0–1 V	*Go to Step 5*	*Go to Step 11*
5	1. Turn the ignition switch to the OFF position. 2. Use the *J 39200* in order to measure the resistance between the 6-way ABS motor pack harness connector terminal D and the 6-way ABS motor pack harness connector terminal C. Is the resistance within the specified range?	OL (Infinite)	*Go to Step 6*	*Go to Step 12*
6	Use the *J 39200* in order to measure the resistance between the 6-way ABS motor pack connector terminal D and the 6-way ABS motor pack connector terminal C. Is the resistance within the specified range?	0.2–1.5 Ω	*Go to Step 7*	*Go to Step 9*
7	1. Inspect the following components for damage: • The 6-way ABS motor pack connector • The 6-way ABS motor pack harness connector Damage that may cause a short to voltage with the connector connected. 2. Inspect the following components for damage: • The 8-way EBCM connector • The 8-way EBCM harness connector C1 Damage that may cause a short to voltage with the connector connected. 3. Inspect CKT 1284 and CKT 1285 for damage. Damage may cause a short to voltage. Is there damage that may cause a short to voltage?	—	*Go to Step 13*	*Go to Step 8*
8	1. Reconnect the 6-way ABS motor pack connector. 2. Reconnect the 8-way EBCM connector C1. 3. Test drive the vehicle at a speed of at least 16 km/h (10 mph). 4. Turn the ignition switch to the OFF position. 5. Repeat the drive sequence two additional times. 6. Use the *Scan Tool* in order to inspect for DTCs. Did DTC C1266 set as a current DTC in the last three drive cycles?	—	*Go to Step 14*	*Go to Step 15*

GC402980310600FX

Fig. 129 Code C1266: Rear ABS Motor Circuit Shorted To Voltage (Part 2 of 3). Cavalier & Sunfire

Step	Action	Value(s)	Yes	No
9	Replace the ABS motor pack. Is the repair complete?	—	Refer to *Diagnostic System Check*	—
10	Repair the short to voltage in CKT 1284. Is the repair complete?	—	Refer to *Diagnostic System Check*	—
11	Repair the short to voltage in CKT 1285. Is the repair complete?	—	Refer to *Diagnostic System Check*	—
12	Repair the short between CKT 1284 and CKT 1285. Is the repair complete?	—	Refer to *Diagnostic System Check*	—
13	Replace all of the following components that are damaged: • The terminals • The connectors • The wires Damage may cause a short to voltage. Is the repair complete?	—	Refer to *Diagnostic System Check*	—
14	Replace the EBCM. Is the repair complete?	—	Refer to *Diagnostic System Check*	—
15	The malfunction is intermittent or is not present at this time. Refer to Diagnostic Aids for more information.	—	—	—

GC402980310600GX

Fig. 129 Code C1266: Rear ABS Motor Circuit Shorted To Voltage (Part 3 of 3). Cavalier & Sunfire

Circuit Description

The serial data communications circuit (CKT 800) transmits messages from one electronic control module to another when interface between systems is necessary. The ABS VI systems depend on information to and from the PCM and IPC for proper operation.

Conditions for Setting the DTC

DTC C1275 will set if either of the following conditions occurs:

- The vehicle speed is greater than 5 km/h (3 mph) and a malfunction exists in the serial data circuit.
- The PCM has not broadcasted a serial message for at least 10 seconds.

Action Taken When the DTC Sets

A serial communication failure does not allow the proper warning indicator commands to be sent to the IPC. A malfunction DTC is stored.

Conditions for Clearing the DTC

- The condition responsible for setting the DTC no longer exists and the Scan Tool Clear DTCs function is used.
- 100 drive cycles pass with no DTC(s) detected. A drive cycle consists of starting the vehicle, driving the vehicle over 16 km/h (10 mph), stopping and then turning the ignition off.

Diagnostic Aids

When DTC C1275 is current (malfunction in CKT 800), no communication can be established with the scan tool. When the malfunction is removed, DTC C1275 will be stored in system memory.

The following conditions may cause an intermittent malfunction:

- A poor connection
- Rubbed-through wire insulation
- A broken wire inside the insulation

Use the enhanced diagnostic function of the Scan Tool to measure the frequency of the malfunction.

Thoroughly inspect any circuitry that may cause the intermittent complaint for the following conditions:

- Backed out terminals
- Improper mating
- Broken locks
- Improperly formed or damaged terminals
- Poor terminal-to-wiring connections
- Physical damage to the wiring harness

Important: Zero the J 39200 test leads before making any resistance measurements. Refer to the J 39200 user's manual.

GC402980310700AX

Fig. 130 Code C1275: Serial Data Fault (Part 1 of 2). Cavalier & Sunfire

Step	Action	Value(s)	Yes	No
1	Was the Diagnostic System Check performed?	—	*Go to Step 2*	Refer to *Diagnostic System Check*
2	1. Using the *J 39200*, exit back to the Application Menu. 2. Select the Body portion of the menu. 3. Select the SDL Monitor Mode. 4. Select the IPC To ABS Mode. 5. Engage the parking brake. Is the *J 39200* displaying BRAKE T/T ON?	—	*Go to Step 3*	Refer to Instrument Panel for diagnosis
3	1. Disconnect the brake fluid level switch harness connector. 2. Connect a jumper wire such as the J 36169, between brake switch connector terminals A and B. Is the *J 39200* displaying BRAKE T/T ON?	—	*Go to Step 5*	*Go to Step 4*
4	Replace the EBCM. Is the repair complete?	—	Refer to *Diagnostic System Check*	—
5	The malfunction is intermittent or is not present at this time. Refer to Diagnostic Aids for more information.	—	—	—

GC402980310700BX

Fig. 130 Code C1275: Serial Data Fault (Part 2 of 2). Cavalier & Sunfire

Circuit Description

DTC identifies a brake solenoid valve that cannot be energized. The malfunction may be caused by one of the following conditions:

- An open in the solenoid valve circuitry.
- The solenoid valve is always energized due to a short to ground in the solenoid valve circuitry between the EBCM and the brake solenoid valve.

An open will not allow proper ABS operation, but the short to ground simply turns on the brake solenoid valve. A path for base brakes is still allowed once the motor rehomes and the check ball is lifted off its seat during key to RUN initialization.

Conditions for Setting the DTC

DTC can set only when the brake solenoid valve is commanded off while the Electronic Brake Control Relay is enabled.

A malfunction exists if the EBCM detects the brake solenoid valve control circuit voltage is not within specifications.

Action Taken When the DTC Sets

- A malfunction DTC stores.
- The ABS disables.
- The ABS warning indicator turns on.

Conditions for Clearing the DTC

- The condition responsible for setting the DTC no longer exists and the Scan Tool Clear DTCs function is used.
- 100 drive cycles pass with no DTCs detected. A drive cycle consists of starting the vehicle, driving the vehicle over 16 km/h (10 mph), stopping and then turning the ignition off.

GC402980310800AX

Fig. 131 Code C1276: LH Front Solenoid Circuit Open Or Shorted To Ground (Part 1 of 4). Cavalier & Sunfire

Diagnostic Aids

The following conditions may cause an intermittent malfunction:

- A poor connection
- Rubbed-through wire insulation
- A broken wire inside the insulation

Use the enhanced diagnostic function of the Scan Tool in order to measure the frequency of the malfunction.

Thoroughly inspect any circuitry that may cause the intermittent complaint for the following conditions:

- Backed out terminals
- Improper mating
- Broken locks
- Improperly formed or damaged terminals
- Poor terminal-to-wiring connections
- Physical damage to the wiring harness

Important: Zero the J 39200 test leads before making any resistance measurements. Refer to the J 39200 user's manual.

Step	Action	Value(s)	Yes	No
1	Was the Diagnostic System Check performed?	—	*Go to Step 2*	Refer to *Diagnostic System Check*
2	1. Turn the ignition switch to the OFF position. 2. Disconnect the 24-way EBCM connector C2. 3. Use the *J 39200* in order to measure the resistance between the 24-way EBCM harness connector C2 terminal A10 and ground. Is the resistance within the specified range?	OL (Infinite)	*Go to Step 3*	*Go to Step 12*
3	1. Disconnect the left front brake solenoid valve connector. 2. Use the *J 39200* in order to measure the resistance between the 24-way EBCM harness connector C2 terminal A10 and the left front brake solenoid valve harness connector terminal A. Is the resistance within the specified range?	0–2 Ω	*Go to Step 4*	*Go to Step 15*
4	Use the *J 39200* in order to measure the resistance between the left front ABS brake solenoid valve connector terminal A and the left front brake solenoid valve connector terminal B. Is the resistance within the specified range?	2–5 Ω	*Go to Step 5*	*Go to Step 16*
5	Use a *J 39200* in order to measure the resistance between the Electronic Brake Control Relay harness connector terminal 87 and the left front brake solenoid valve connector terminal B. Is the resistance within the specified range?	0–2 Ω	*Go to Step 6*	*Go to Step 9*
6	1. Inspect the 24-way EBCM connector and the 24-way EBCM harness connector C2 for the following conditions: • Terminal damage • Poor terminal contact • Terminal corrosion 2. Inspect the left front brake solenoid valve connector and the left front brake solenoid valve harness connector for the following conditions: • Terminal damage • Poor terminal contact • Terminal corrosion Are terminal corrosion, damaged terminals, or poor terminal contact evident?	—	*Go to Step 17*	*Go to Step 7*

GC402980310800BX

Fig. 131 Code C1276: LH Front Solenoid Circuit Open Or Shorted To Ground (Part 2 of 4). Cavalier & Sunfire

Step	Action	Value(s)	Yes	No
7	Inspect CKT 1288 for damage. Damage may cause a short to ground with all the connectors connected. Is there damage that may cause a short to ground with the connectors connected?	—	*Go to Step 18*	*Go to Step 8*
8	1. Reconnect the 24-way EBCM connector C2. 2. Reconnect the left front brake solenoid valve connector. 3. Turn the ignition switch to the RUN position. Do not start the engine. 4. Use the *Scan Tool* in order to inspect for DTCs. Does DTC C1276 set as a current DTC?	—	*Go to Step 22*	*Go to Step 23*
9	Remove and inspect the ABS Mini Fuse (20 A). Is the fuse open?	—	*Go to Step 19*	*Go to Step 10*
10	Use the *J 39200* in order to measure the resistance between the Electronic Brake Control Relay harness connector terminal 87 and the ABS Mini Fuse (20 A) terminal. Is the resistance within the specified range?	0–2 Ω	*Go to Step 11*	*Go to Step 20*
11	Use the *J 39200* in order to measure the resistance between the ABS Mini Fuse (20 A) terminal and the left front brake solenoid valve harness connector terminal B. Is the resistance within the specified range?	0–2 Ω	*Go to Step 13*	*Go to Step 21*
12	1. Disconnect the left front brake solenoid valve connector. 2. Use the *J 39200* in order to measure the resistance between the left front brake solenoid valve connector terminal B and ground. Is the resistance within the specified range?	OL (Infinite)	*Go to Step 14*	*Go to Step 16*
13	Replace the ABS Mini Fuse (20A) with a known good Fuse (20A). Is the replacement complete?	—	*Go to Step 8*	—
14	Repair the short to ground in CKT 1288. Is the repair complete?	—	Refer to *Diagnostic System Check*	—
15	Repair the open or high resistance in CKT 1288. Is the repair complete?	—	Refer to *Diagnostic System Check*	—
16	Replace the left front brake solenoid valve. Is the repair complete?	—	Refer to *Diagnostic System Check*	—
17	Replace all the terminals and connectors that exhibit the following conditions: • Poor terminal contact • Terminal corrosion • Damaged terminals Is the repair complete?	—	Refer to *Diagnostic System Check*	—
18	Repair the damage to CKT 1288. Is the repair complete?	—	Refer to *Diagnostic System Check*	—

GC402980310800CX

Fig. 131 Code C1276: LH Front Solenoid Circuit Open Or Shorted To Ground (Part 3 of 4). Cavalier & Sunfire

Step	Action	Value(s)	Yes	No
19	Replace the fuse block ABS Mini Fuse (20A). Is the repair complete?	—	Refer to *Diagnostic System Check*	—
20	Repair the open or high resistance in CKT 1633. Is the repair complete?	—	Refer to *Diagnostic System Check*	—
21	Repair the open or high resistance in CKT 855. Is the repair complete?	—	Refer to *Diagnostic System Check*	—
22	Replace the EBCM. Is the repair complete?	—	Refer to *Diagnostic System Check*	—
23	Malfunction is intermittent or is not present at this time. Refer to Diagnostic Aids for more information.	—	—	—

GC402980310800DX

Fig. 131 Code C1276: LH Front Solenoid Circuit Open Or Shorted To Ground (Part 4 of 4). Cavalier & Sunfire

Circuit Description

DTC C1277 identifies a solenoid that cannot be energized due to a short to voltage in the solenoid driver circuitry. The malfunction can affect ABS operation since the flow of brake fluid to the wheel cylinder cannot be stopped. The unstoppable flow of brake fluid to the wheel cylinder makes ABS operation for that channel impossible.

Conditions for Setting the DTC

DTC C1277 can set only when the brake solenoid valve is commanded on.

A malfunction exists if the EBCM detects the left front brake solenoid valve control circuit voltage is not within specifications.

Action Taken When the DTC Sets

- A malfunction DTC stores.
- The ABS disables.
- The ABS warning indicator turns on.

Conditions for Clearing the DTC

- The condition responsible for setting the DTC no longer exists and the Scan Tool Clear DTCs function is used.
- 100 drive cycles pass with no DTC(s) detected. A drive cycle consists of starting the vehicle, driving the vehicle over 16 km/h (10 mph), stopping and then turning the ignition off.

Diagnostic Aids

Use the enhanced diagnostic function of the Scan Tool in order to measure the frequency of the malfunction.

Any circuitry that is suspected of causing the intermittent complaint should be thoroughly checked for improper mating, improperly formed or damaged terminals, poor terminal to wiring connections, or physical damage to the wiring harness.

Test Description

2. This test checks the solenoid for the proper resistance value.
3. This test checks for a short to voltage in the solenoid circuit.
5. This test determines if the malfunction is caused by the EBCM.

GC4029903856010X

Fig. 132 Code C1277: LH Front Solenoid Circuit Shorted To Voltage (Part 1 of 2). Cavalier & Sunfire

Step	Action	Value(s)	Yes	No
Important: Zero the J 39200 test leads before making any resistance measurements.				
1	Was the ABS Diagnostic System Check performed?	—	*Go to Step 2*	Go to *A Diagnostic System Check - ABS*
2	1. Turn the ignition switch to the OFF position. 2. Use the *J 39200* in order to measure the resistance between the following components: • The left front brake solenoid valve connector terminal B • The left front brake solenoid valve connector terminal A Is the resistance within the specified range?	2.5–5.0 Ω	*Go to Step 3*	*Go to Step 6*
3	1. Disconnect the 24-way EBCM connector C2. 2. Turn the ignition switch to the RUN position. Do not start the engine. 3. Use the *J 39200* in order to measure the voltage between the 24-way EBCM harness connector C2 terminal A10 and ground. Is the voltage within the specified range?	0–1 V	*Go to Step 4*	*Go to Step 7*
4	1. Turn the ignition switch to the OFF position. 2. Inspect the left front brake solenoid valve connector for damage. Damage may cause a short to voltage with the left front brake solenoid valve connector connected. 3. Inspect CKT 1288 for damage. Damage may cause a short to voltage. 4. Inspect the 24-way EBCM harness connector C2 for damage. Damage may cause a short to voltage with the 24-way EBCM connector C2 connected. Is there damage that may cause a short to voltage?	—	*Go to Step 8*	*Go to Step 5*
5	1. Reconnect the 24-way EBCM connector C2. 2. Reconnect the left front brake solenoid valve connector. 3. Start the engine with your foot off the brake. 4. Allow the engine to run for at least 10 seconds. 5. Use the *Scan Tool* in order to inspect for DTCs. Does DTC C1277 set as a current DTC?	—	*Go to Step 9*	*Go to Step 10*
6	Replace the left front brake solenoid valve. Is the repair complete?	—	Go to *A Diagnostic System Check - ABS*	—
7	Repair the short to voltage in CKT 1288. Is the repair complete?	—	Go to *A Diagnostic System Check - ABS*	—
8	Repair the damage that caused a short to voltage. Is the repair complete?	—	Go to *A Diagnostic System Check - ABS*	—
9	Replace the EBCM. Is the repair complete?	—	Go to *A Diagnostic System Check - ABS*	—
10	The malfunction is intermittent or is not present at this time. Refer to Diagnostic Aids for more information. Is the action complete?	—	System OK	—

GC4029903856020X

Fig. 132 Code C1277: LH Front Solenoid Circuit Shorted To Voltage (Part 2 of 2). Cavalier & Sunfire

Circuit Description

DTC C1278 identifies a brake solenoid valve that cannot be energized. The malfunction may be caused by one of the following conditions:

- An open in the solenoid valve circuitry
- The solenoid valve is always energized due to a short to ground in the solenoid valve circuitry between the driver and the brake solenoid valve.

An open will not allow proper ABS operation, but the short to ground simply turns on the brake solenoid valve. A path for base brakes is still allowed once the motor rehomes and the check ball is lifted off its seat during key to RUN initialization.

Conditions for Setting the DTC

DTC C1278 can set only when the solenoid is commanded off while the Electronic Brake Control Relay is enabled.

A malfunction exists if the EBCM detects the right front brake solenoid valve control circuit voltage is not within specifications.

Action Taken When the DTC Sets

- A malfunction DTC stores.
- The ABS disables.
- The ABS warning indicator turns on.

Conditions for Clearing the DTC

- The condition responsible for setting the DTC no longer exists and the Scan Tool Clear DTCs function is used.
- 100 drive cycles pass with no DTC(s) detected. A drive cycle consists of starting the vehicle, driving the vehicle over 16 km/h (10 mph), stopping and then turning the ignition off.

GC402980311000AX

Fig. 133 Code C1278: RH Front Solenoid Circuit Open Or Shorted To Ground (Part 1 of 4). Cavalier & Sunfire

Diagnostic Aids

The following conditions may cause an intermittent malfunction:

- A poor connection
- Rubbed-through wire insulation
- A broken wire inside the insulation

Use the enhanced diagnostic function of the Scan Tool in order to measure the frequency of the malfunction.

Thoroughly inspect any circuitry that may cause the intermittent complaint for the following conditions:

- Backed out terminals
- Improper mating
- Broken locks
- Improperly formed or damaged terminals
- Poor terminal-to-wiring connections
- Physical damage to the wiring harness

Important: Zero the J 39200 test leads before making any resistance measurements. Refer to the J 39200 user's manual.

Step	Action	Value(s)	Yes	No
1	Was the Diagnostic System Check performed?	—	*Go to Step 2*	Refer to *Diagnostic System Check*
2	1. Turn the ignition switch to the OFF position. 2. Disconnect the 24-way EBCM connector C2. 3. Use the *J 39200* in order to measure the resistance between the 24-way EBCM harness connector C2 terminal B6 and ground. Is the resistance within the specified range?	OL (Infinite)	*Go to Step 3*	*Go to Step 12*
3	1. Disconnect the right front brake solenoid valve connector. 2. Use the *J 39200* in order to measure the resistance between the 24-way EBCM harness connector C2 terminal B6 and the right front brake solenoid valve harness connector terminal A. Is the resistance within the specified range?	0.0–2.0 Ω	*Go to Step 4*	*Go to Step 15*
4	Use the *J 39200* in order to measure the resistance between the right front ABS brake solenoid valve connector terminal A and the right front brake solenoid valve connector terminal B. Is the resistance within the specified range?	2.0–5.0 Ω	*Go to Step 5*	*Go to Step 16*
5	Use a *J 39200* in order to measure the resistance between the Electronic Brake Control Relay harness connector terminal 87 and the right front brake solenoid valve connector terminal B. Is the resistance within the specified range?	0.0–2.0 Ω	*Go to Step 6*	*Go to Step 9*
6	1. Inspect the 24-way EBCM connector and the 24-way EBCM harness connector C2 for the following conditions: • Terminal damage • Poor terminal contact • Terminal corrosion 2. Inspect the right front brake solenoid valve connector and the right front brake solenoid valve harness connector for the following conditions: • Terminal damage • Poor terminal contact • Terminal corrosion Are terminal corrosion, damaged terminals, or poor terminal contact evident?	—	*Go to Step 17*	*Go to Step 7*

GC402980311000BX

Fig. 133 Code C1278: RH Front Solenoid Circuit Open Or Shorted To Ground (Part 2 of 4). Cavalier & Sunfire

Step	Action	Value(s)	Yes	No
7	Inspect CKT 1289 for damage. Damage may cause a short to ground with all the connectors connected. Is there damage which may cause a short to ground with the connectors connected?	—	*Go to Step 18*	*Go to Step 8*
8	1. Reconnect the 24-way EBCM connector C2. 2. Reconnect the right front brake solenoid valve connector. 3. Turn the ignition switch to the RUN position. Do not start the engine. 4. Use the *Scan Tool* in order to inspect for DTCs. Does DTC C1278 set as a current DTC?	—	*Go to Step 22*	*Go to Step 23*
9	1. Remove the ABS Mini Fuse (20A) of the fuse block. 2. Inspect the ABS Mini Fuse (20A) of the fuse block. Is the fuse open?	—	*Go to Step 19*	*Go to Step 10*
10	Use the *J 39200* in order to measure the resistance between the Electronic Brake Control Relay harness connector terminal 87 and the ABS Mini Fuse (20A) in the fuse block. Is the resistance within the specified range?	0.0–2.0 Ω	*Go to Step 11*	*Go to Step 20*
11	Use the *J 39200* in order to measure the resistance between the fuse block terminal and the left front brake solenoid valve harness connector terminal B. Is the resistance within the specified range?	0.0–2.0 Ω	*Go to Step 13*	*Go to Step 21*
12	1. Disconnect the right front brake solenoid valve connector. 2. Use the *J 39200* in order to measure the resistance between the right front brake solenoid valve connector terminal B and ground. Is the resistance within the specified range?	OL (Infinite)	*Go to Step 14*	*Go to Step 16*
13	Replace the ABS Mini Fuse (20A) with a known good Fuse (20A). Is the replacement complete?	—	*Go to Step 8*	—
14	Repair the short to ground in CKT 1289. Is the repair complete?	—	Refer to *Diagnostic System Check*	—
15	Repair the open or high resistance in CKT 1289. Is the repair complete?	—	Refer to *Diagnostic System Check*	—
16	Replace the right front brake solenoid valve. Is the repair complete?	—	Refer to *Diagnostic System Check*	—
17	Replace all the terminals and connectors that exhibit the following conditions: • Poor terminal contact • Terminal corrosion • Damaged terminals Is the repair complete?	—	Refer to *Diagnostic System Check*	—
18	Repair the damage to CKT 1289. Is the repair complete?	—	Refer to *Diagnostic System Check*	—

GC402980311000CX

Fig. 133 Code C1278: RH Front Solenoid Circuit Open Or Shorted To Ground (Part 3 of 4). Cavalier & Sunfire

Step	Action	Value(s)	Yes	No
19	Replace the fuse block ABS Mini Fuse (20A). Is the repair complete?	—	Refer to *Diagnostic System Check*	—
20	Repair the open or high resistance in CKT 1633. Is the repair complete?	—	Refer to *Diagnostic System Check*	—
21	Repair the open or high resistance in CKT 855. Is the repair complete?	—	Refer to *Diagnostic System Check*	—
22	Replace the EBCM. Is the repair complete?	—	Refer to *Diagnostic System Check*	—
23	The malfunction is intermittent or is not present at this time. Refer to Diagnostic Aids for more information.	—	—	—

GC402980311000DX

Fig. 133 Code C1278: RH Front Solenoid Circuit Open Or Shorted To Ground (Part 4 of 4). Cavalier & Sunfire

Circuit Description

DTC C1281 identifies a solenoid that cannot be energized due to a short to voltage in the solenoid driver circuitry. The malfunction can affect ABS operation since the flow of brake fluid to the wheel cylinder cannot be stopped. The unstoppable flow of brake fluid to the wheel cylinder makes ABS operation for that channel impossible.

Conditions for Setting the DTC

DTC C1281 can set only when the brake solenoid is commanded on.

A malfunction exists if the EBCM detects the right front brake solenoid valve control circuit voltage is not within specifications.

Action Taken When the DTC Sets

- A malfunction DTC stores.
- The ABS disables.
- The ABS warning indicator turns on.

Conditions for Clearing the DTC

- The condition responsible for setting the DTC no longer exists and the Scan Tool Clear DTCs function is used.
- 100 drive cycles pass with no DTC(s) detected. A drive cycle consists of starting the vehicle, driving the vehicle over 16 km/h (10 mph), stopping and then turning the ignition off.

Diagnostic Aids

Use the enhanced diagnostic function of the Scan Tool in order to measure the frequency of the malfunction.

Any circuitry that is suspected of causing the intermittent complaint should be thoroughly checked for improper mating, improperly formed or damaged terminals, poor terminal to wiring connections, or physical damage to the wiring harness.

Test Description

2. This test checks the solenoid for the proper resistance value.
3. This test checks for a short to voltage in the solenoid circuit.
5. This test determines if the malfunction is caused by the EBCM.

GC4029903857010X

Fig. 134 Code C1281: RH Front Solenoid Circuit Open Or Shorted To Voltage (Part 1 of 2). Cavalier & Sunfire

Step	Action	Value(s)	Yes	No
Important: Zero the J 39200 test leads before making any resistance measurements. Refer to the J 39200 user's manual.				
1	Was the ABS Diagnostic System Check performed?	—	*Go to Step 2*	Go to *A Diagnostic System Check - ABS*
2	1. Turn the ignition switch to the OFF position. 2. Use the *J 39200* in order to measure the resistance between the following components: • The right front brake solenoid valve connector terminal A • The right front brake solenoid valve connector terminal B Is the resistance within the specified range?	2.5–5.0 Ω	*Go to Step 3*	*Go to Step 6*
3	1. Disconnect the 24-way EBCM connector C2. 2. Turn the ignition switch to the RUN position. Do not start the engine. 3. Use the *J 39200* in order to measure the voltage between the 24-way EBCM harness connector C2 terminal B6 and ground. Is the voltage within the specified range?	0–1 V	*Go to Step 4*	*Go to Step 7*
4	1. Turn the ignition switch to the OFF position. 2. Inspect the right front brake solenoid valve connector for damage. Damage may cause a short to voltage with the left front brake solenoid valve connector connected. 3. Inspect CKT 1289 for damage. Damage may cause a short to voltage. 4. Inspect the 24-way EBCM harness connector C2 for damage. Damage may cause a short to voltage with the 24-way EBCM connector C2 connected. Is there damage that may cause a short to voltage?	—	*Go to Step 8*	*Go to Step 5*
5	1. Reconnect the 24-way EBCM connector C2. 2. Reconnect the right front brake solenoid valve connector. 3. Start the engine with your foot off the brake. 4. Allow the engine to run for at least ten seconds. 5. Use the *Scan Tool* in order to inspect for DTCs. Does DTC C1281 set as a current DTC?	—	*Go to Step 9*	*Go to Step 10*
6	Replace the right front brake solenoid valve. Is the repair complete?	—	Go to *A Diagnostic System Check - ABS*	—
7	Repair the short to voltage in CKT 1289. Is the repair complete?	—	Go to *A Diagnostic System Check - ABS*	—
8	Repair the damage that caused a short to voltage. Is the repair complete?	—	Go to *A Diagnostic System Check - ABS*	—
9	Replace the EBCM. Is the repair complete?	—	Go to *A Diagnostic System Check - ABS*	—
10	The malfunction is intermittent or is not present at this time. Refer to Diagnostic Aids for more information. Is the action complete?	—	System OK	—

GC4029903857020X

Fig. 134 Code C1281: RH Front Solenoid Circuit Open Or Shorted To Voltage (Part 2 of 2). Cavalier & Sunfire

Circuit Description

DTC C1286 is provided as an information only test and reflects the status of the command issued by the EBCM to illuminate the red BRAKE warning indicator.

Conditions for Setting the DTC

When another diagnostic DTC issues a command to illuminate the red BRAKE warning indicator, DTC C1286 will be stored in memory as a history DTC at the conclusion of the ignition cycle.

Action Taken When the DTC Sets

- A malfunction DTC stores.
- The ABS disables.
- The ABS warning indicator turns on.
- The red Brake warning indicator turns on.

Conditions for Clearing the DTC

- The condition responsible for setting the DTC no longer exists and the Scan Tool Clear DTCs function is used.
- 100 drive cycles pass with no DTC(s) detected. A drive cycle consists of starting the vehicle, driving the vehicle over 16 km/h (10 mph), stopping and then turning the ignition off.

Diagnostic Aids

The following ABS mechanical DTCs command the red BRAKE warning indicator to illuminate. The DTCs will also cause the EBCM to store DTC C1286 during shutdown:

- C1242
- C1246
- C1251

If the motors are not in their home position, the following electrical DTCs will also command the red BRAKE warning indicator on:

- C1214
- C1216
- C1218
- C1236
- C1255
- C1264
- C1265
- C1266

If any of the electrical DTCs are indicated along with DTC C1286, correct the electrical DTCs prior to addressing a DTC C1286 malfunction.

GC402980311200AX

Fig. 136 Code C1286: EBCM Tuned On Brake Warning Lamp (Part 1 of 2). Cavalier & Sunfire

Circuit Description

DTC C1282 allows the EBCM to inspect for a calibration malfunction by comparing the calibration value to a known value.

DTC C1282 also acts as a security measure to prevent improper use of calibrations or changes to these calibrations. Improper calibrations may alter the designed function of ABS.

Conditions for Setting the DTC

DTC C1282 can be set at ABS initialization. A malfunction exists if the EBCM internal memory calibration is incorrect.

Action Taken When the DTC Sets

- A malfunction DTC stores.
- The ABS disables.
- The ABS warning indicator turns on.

Conditions for Clearing the DTC

- The condition responsible for setting the DTC no longer exists and the Scan Tool Clear DTCs function is used.
- 100 drive cycles pass with no DTC(s) detected. A drive cycle consists of starting the vehicle, driving the vehicle over 16 km/h (10 mph), stopping and then turning the ignition off.

Diagnostic Aids

An intermittent DTC C1282 is most likely caused by a malfunctioning EBCM that is sensitive to temperature changes. If DTC C1282 occurred more than once, but is intermittent, replace EBCM.

Use the enhanced diagnostic function of the Scan Tool in order to measure the frequency of the malfunction.

Step	Action	Value(s)	Yes	No
1	Was the Diagnostic System Check performed?	—	*Go to Step 2*	Refer to *Diagnostic System Check*
2	1. Turn the ignition switch to the RUN position. Do not start the engine. 2. Install a *Scan Tool*. 3. Use the *Scan Tool* in order to inspect for DTCs. Is DTC C1282 set as a current DTC?	—	*Go to Step 3*	*Go to Step 4*
3	Replace the EBCM. Is the repair complete?	—	Refer to *Diagnostic System Check*	—
4	The malfunction is intermittent or is not present at this time. Refer to Diagnostic Aids for more information.	—	—	—

GC4029803111000X

Fig. 135 Code C1282: Calibration Fault. Cavalier & Sunfire

Step	Action	Value(s)	Yes	No
1	Was the Diagnostic System Check performed?	—	*Go to Step 2*	Refer to *Diagnostic System Check*
2	1. Turn the ignition switch to the RUN position. Do not start the engine. 2. Install the *Scan Tool*. 3. Use the *Scan Tool* in order to inspect for DTCs.	—	Refer to *Diagnostic System Check*	*Go to Step 3*
3	Use the *Scan Tool* in order to clear DTC C1286. Was DTC C1286 cleared?	—	Refer to *Diagnostic System Check*	—

GC402980311200BX

Fig. 136 Code C1286: EBCM Tuned On Brake Warning Lamp (Part 2 of 2). Cavalier & Sunfire

Circuit Description

DTC C1291 detects an open brake switch. The EBCM looks for deceleration rates that may indicate braking action. The EBCM verifies braking action by repeating the method for finding deceleration rates that indicate braking action several times. In each case, the ABS will not be available because the EBCM does not see the brake switch input.

Conditions for Setting the DTC

DTC C1291 can set if three deceleration cycles within the specified rate occur during the current ignition cycle with the brake switch off.

Action Taken When the DTC Sets

- A malfunction DTC stores.
- The ABS disables.
- The ABS warning indicator turns on.

Conditions for Clearing the DTC

- The condition responsible for setting the DTC no longer exists and the Scan Tool Clear DTCs function is used.
- 100 drive cycles pass with no DTC(s) detected. A drive cycle consists of starting the vehicle, driving the vehicle over 16 km/h (10 mph), stopping and then turning the ignition off.

Diagnostic Aids

The following conditions may cause an intermittent malfunction:

- A poor connection
- Rubbed-through wire insulation
- A broken wire inside the insulation

Use the enhanced diagnostic function of the Scan Tool in order to measure the frequency of the malfunction.

Thoroughly inspect any circuitry that may cause the intermittent complaint for the following conditions:

- Backed out terminals
- Improper mating
- Broken locks
- Improperly formed or damaged terminals
- Poor terminal-to-wiring connections
- Physical damage to the wiring harness
- Sticking brake switch

Important: Zero the J 39200 test leads before making any resistance measurements. Refer to the J 39200 user's manual.

Step	Action	Value(s)	Yes	No
1	Was the Diagnostic System Check performed?	—	*Go to Step 2*	Refer to *Diagnostic System Check*
2	1. Turn the ignition switch to the RUN position. Do not start the engine. 2. Install a *Scan Tool*. 3. Use the *Scan Tool* in order to inspect for DTCs. Is DTC C1295 set as either a current and/or history DTC?	—	Refer to *DTC C1295 Brake Lamp Switch Circuit Open*	*Go to Step 3*

GC402980311300AX

Fig. 137 Code C1291: Open Brake Lamp Switch Contact During Decel (Part 1 of 3). Cavalier & Sunfire

Step	Action	Value(s)	Yes	No
3	1. Select Data List on the *Scan Tool.* 2. Select Brake Switch Position on the *Scan Tool.* 3. Apply light pressure to the brake pedal while monitoring the Brake Switch Position on the *Scan Tool.* Does the Scan Tool indicate that the brake switch is on within 25 mm (1.0 in) of brake pedal travel?	—	*Go to Step 25*	*Go to Step 4*
4	1. Apply firm pressure to the brake pedal. 2. Observe the rear brake lamps. Are the rear brake lamps on?	—	*Go to Step 5*	*Go to Step 8*
5	1. Turn the ignition switch to the OFF position. 2. Disconnect the 24-way EBCM connector C2. 3. Turn the ignition switch to the RUN position. Do not start the engine. 4. Apply firm pressure to the brake pedal. 5. Use the *J 39200* in order to measure the voltage between the 24-way EBCM harness connector C2 terminal B9 and ground. Is the voltage equal to or greater than the specified voltage?	10.0 V	*Go to Step 6*	*Go to Step 16*
6	Inspect the 24-way EBCM connector and the 24-way EBCM harness connector C2 for the following conditions: • Terminal damage • Poor terminal contact • Terminal corrosion Is there poor terminal contact, terminal corrosion, or damaged terminals?	—	*Go to Step 17*	*Go to Step 7*
7	1. Reconnect the 24-way EBCM connector C2. 2. Test drive the vehicle and perform a brake stop from 32 km/h (20 mph) engaging the ABS. 3. Use the *Scan Tool* in order to inspect for DTCs. Does DTC C1291 or DTC C1292 set as a current DTC?	—	*Go to Step 23*	*Go to Step 25*
8	Use the *J 39200* in order to measure the voltage between the stoplamp switch harness connector terminal A and ground. Is the voltage equal to or greater than the specified voltage?	10.0 V	*Go to Step 9*	*Go to Step 11*
9	1. Apply firm pressure to the brake pedal. 2. Use the *J 39200* in order to measure the voltage between the stoplamp switch harness connector terminal B and ground. Is the voltage equal to or greater than the specified voltage?	10.0 V	*Go to Step 16*	*Go to Step 10*
10	Inspect for proper adjustment of the stoplamp switch. Is the stoplamp switch adjusted correctly?	—	*Go to Step 18*	*Go to Step 19*
11	Remove and inspect the fuse block STOP-HAZ Fuse (15A). Is the fuse open?	—	*Go to Step 13*	*Go to Step 12*

GC402980311300BX

Fig. 137 Code C1291: Open Brake Lamp Switch Contact During Decel (Part 2 of 3). Cavalier & Sunfire

Circuit Description

DTC C1292 determines the proper operation of the brake switch. Proper operation of the brake switch is important because the brake switch activates the ABS when the brake switch is on. If the brake switch is off, the ABS will never activate. This malfunction is only detected when ABS is required because it is difficult to detect the malfunction under normal braking conditions.

Conditions for Setting the DTC

DTC C1292 can set if the vehicle speed is greater than 8 km/h (5 mph).

A malfunction exists if the following conditions occur:

- The brake was not on.
- A release was required on two channels for 0.5 second.

Action Taken When the DTC Sets

- A malfunction DTC stores.
- The ABS disables.
- The ABS warning indicator turns on.

Conditions for Clearing the DTC

- The condition responsible for setting the DTC no longer exists and the Scan Tool Clear DTCs function is used.
- 100 drive cycles pass with no DTC(s) detected. A drive cycle consists of starting the vehicle, driving the vehicle over 16 km/h (10 mph), stopping and then turning the ignition off.

Diagnostic Aids

The following conditions may cause an intermittent malfunction:

- A poor connection
- Rubbed-through wire insulation
- A broken wire inside the insulation

Use the enhanced diagnostic function of the Scan Tool in order to measure the frequency of the malfunction.

Thoroughly inspect any circuitry that may cause the intermittent complaint for the following conditions:

- Backed out terminals
- Improper mating
- Broken locks
- Improperly formed or damaged terminals
- Poor terminal-to-wiring connections
- Physical damage to the wiring harness
- Sticking brake switch

Important: Zero the J 39200 test leads before making any resistance measurements. Refer to the J 39200 user's manual.

GC402980311400AX

Fig. 138 Code C1292: Open Brake Lamp Switch When ABS Required (Part 1 of 4). Cavalier & Sunfire

Step	Action	Value(s)	Yes	No
12	1. Disconnect the stoplamp switch connector. 2. Use a *J 39200* in order to measure the resistance between the stoplamp switch harness connector terminal A and the STOP-HAZ Fuse terminal of the fuse block. Is the resistance within the specified range?	0.0–2.0 Ω	*Go to Step 14*	*Go to Step 21*
13	1. Disconnect the 24-way EBCM connector C2. 2. Use the *J 39200* in order to measure the resistance between the 24-way EBCM harness connector C2 terminal B9 and ground. Is the resistance within the specified range?	OL (Infinite)	*Go to Step 15*	*Go to Step 20*
14	Use the *J 39200* in order to measure the voltage between the STOP-HAZ Fuse of the fuse block and ground. Is the voltage equal to or greater than the specified voltage?	10 V	*Go to Step 25*	Refer to wiring diagram
15	1. Disconnect the stoplamp switch connector. 2. Use the *J 39200* in order to measure the resistance between the stoplamp switch harness connector terminal A and ground. Is the resistance within the specified range?	OL (Infinite)	*Go to Step 24*	*Go to Step 22*
16	Repair the open in CKT 17. Is the repair complete?	—	Refer to *Diagnostic System Check*	—
17	Replace all the terminal or the connectors that exhibit the following conditions: • Poor terminal contact • Terminal corrosion • Damaged terminals Is the repair complete?	—	Refer to *Diagnostic System Check*	—
18	Replace the stoplamp switch. Is the repair complete?	—	Refer to *Diagnostic System Check*	—
19	Adjust the stoplamp switch. Is the repair complete?	—	Refer to *Diagnostic System Check*	—
20	1. Repair the short to ground in CKT 17. 2. Replace the STOP-HAZ Fuse (20A) with a known good Fuse (20A). Is the repair complete?	—	Refer to *Diagnostic System Check*	—
21	Repair the open in CKT 140. Is the repair complete?	—	Refer to *Diagnostic System Check*	—
22	1. Repair the short to ground in CKT 140. 2. Replace the STOP-HAZ Fuse (20A) with a known good Fuse (20A). Is the repair complete?	—	Refer to *Diagnostic System Check*	—
23	Replace the EBCM. Is the repair complete?	—	Refer to *Diagnostic System Check*	—
24	Replace the STOP-HAZ Fuse (20A) with a known good Fuse (20A). Is the repair complete?	—	Refer to *Diagnostic System Check*	—
25	The malfunction is intermittent or is not present at this time. Refer to Diagnostic Aids for more information.	—	—	—

GC402980311300CX

Fig. 137 Code C1291: Open Brake Lamp Switch Contact During Decel (Part 3 of 3). Cavalier & Sunfire

Step	Action	Value(s)	Yes	No
1	Was the Diagnostic System Check performed?	—	*Go to Step 2*	Refer to *Diagnostic System Check*
2	1. Turn the ignition switch to the RUN position. Do not start the engine. 2. Install a *Scan Tool.* 3. Use the *Scan Tool* in order to inspect for DTCs. Is DTC C1295 set as either a current and/or history DTC?	—	Refer to *DTC C1295 Brake Lamp Switch Circuit Open*	*Go to Step 3*
3	1. Select Data List on the *Scan Tool.* 2. Select Brake Switch Position on the *Scan Tool.* 3. Apply light pressure to the brake pedal while monitoring the Brake Switch Position on the Scan Tool. Does the Scan Tool indicate that the brake switch is on within 25 mm (1.0 in) of brake pedal travel?	—	*Go to Step 25*	*Go to Step 4*
4	1. Apply firm pressure to the brake pedal. 2. Observe the rear brake lamps. Are the rear brake lamps on?	—	*Go to Step 5*	*Go to Step 8*
5	1. Turn the ignition switch to the OFF position. 2. Disconnect the 24-way EBCM connector C2. 3. Turn the ignition switch to the RUN position. Do not start the engine. 4. Apply firm pressure to the brake pedal. 5. Use the *J 39200* in order to measure the voltage between the 24-way EBCM harness connector C2 terminal B9 and ground. Is the voltage equal to or greater than the specified voltage?	10.0 V	*Go to Step 6*	*Go to Step 16*
6	Inspect the 24-way EBCM connector and the 24-way EBCM harness connector C2 for the following conditions: • Terminal damage • Poor terminal contact • Terminal corrosion Is there poor terminal contact, terminal corrosion, or damaged terminals?	—	*Go to Step 17*	*Go to Step 7*
7	1. Reconnect the 24-way EBCM connector C2. 2. Test drive the vehicle and perform a brake stop from 32 km/h (20 mph) while engaging the ABS. 3. Use the *Scan Tool* in order to inspect for DTCs. Does DTC C1291 or DTC C1292 set as a current DTC?	—	*Go to Step 23*	*Go to Step 25*
8	Use the *J 39200* in order to measure the voltage between the stoplamp switch harness connector terminal A and ground. Is the voltage equal to or greater than the specified voltage?	10.0 V	*Go to Step 9*	*Go to Step 11*
9	1. Apply firm pressure to the brake pedal. 2. Use the *J 39200* in order to measure the voltage between the stoplamp switch harness connector terminal B and ground. Is the voltage equal to or greater than the specified voltage?	10.0 V	*Go to Step 16*	*Go to Step 10*

GC402980311400BX

Fig. 138 Code C1292: Open Brake Lamp Switch When ABS Required (Part 2 of 4). Cavalier & Sunfire

Step	Action	Value(s)	Yes	No
10	Inspect for proper adjustment of the stoplamp switch. Is the stoplamp switch adjusted correctly?	—	Go to Step 18	Go to Step 19
11	1. Remove the fuse block STOP-HAZ Fuse (20A). 2. Inspect the fuse block STOP-HAZ Fuse (20A). Is the fuse open?	—	Go to Step 13	Go to Step 12
12	1. Disconnect the stoplamp switch connector. 2. Use a *J 39200* in order to measure the resistance between the stoplamp switch harness connector terminal A and the STOP-HAZ Fuse terminal of the fuse block. Is the resistance within the specified range?	0.0–2.0 Ω	Go to Step 14	Go to Step 21
13	1. Disconnect the 24-way EBCM connector C2. 2. Use the *J 39200* in order to measure the resistance between the 24-way EBCM harness connector C2 terminal B9 and ground. Is the resistance within the specified range?	OL (Infinite)	Go to Step 15	Go to Step 20
14	Use the *J 39200* in order to measure the voltage between the STOP-HAZ Fuse terminal of the fuse block and ground. Is the voltage equal to or greater than the specified voltage?	10 V	Go to Step 25	
15	1. Disconnect the stoplamp switch connector. 2. Use the *J 39200* in order to measure the resistance between the stoplamp switch harness connector terminal A and ground. Is the resistance within the specified range?	OL (Infinite)	Go to Step 24	Go to Step 22
16	Repair the open in CKT 17. Is the repair complete?	—	Refer to Diagnostic System Check	—
17	Replace all the terminal or the connectors that exhibit the following conditions: • Poor terminal contact • Terminal corrosion • Damaged terminals Is the repair complete?	—	Refer to Diagnostic System Check	—
18	Replace the stoplamp switch. Is the repair complete?	—	Refer to Diagnostic System Check	—
19	Adjust the stoplamp switch. Is the repair complete?	—	Refer to Diagnostic System Check	—
20	1. Repair the short to ground in CKT 17. 2. Replace the STOP-HAZ Fuse (20A) with a known good fuse (20A). Is the repair complete?	—	Refer to Diagnostic System Check	—
21	Repair the open in CKT 140. Is the repair complete?	—	Refer to Diagnostic System Check	—

GC402980311400CX

Fig. 138 Code C1292: Open Brake Lamp Switch When ABS Required (Part 3 of 4). Cavalier & Sunfire

Circuit Description

If DTC 1291 or DTC 1292 failed during the last ignition cycle, DTC C1293 becomes a current failure during the next ignition cycle. DTC C1293 failure keeps ABS/ETS disabled until identifying a Brake Switch On state. When identifying a change during an ignition cycle in which DTC C1293 is a current malfunction, DTC C1291 or DTC 1292 will clear itself at the end of the current ignition cycle. ABS/ETS will then enable itself at the start of the next ignition cycle. DTC C1293 alone indicates DCT C1291 or DTC C1292 failed previously, but is intermittent, or has been corrected.

Conditions for Setting the DTC

DTC C1293 alone indicates DTC C0091 or C0092 occurred previously, but is intermittent, or has been corrected.

Action Taken When the DTC Sets

- A malfunction DTC stores.
- ABS is disabled until the EBCM receives a valid input from the brake switch.
- The ABS warning indicator turns on.

Conditions for Clearing the DTC

- The condition responsible for setting the DTC no longer exists and the Scan Tool Clear DTCs function is used.
- When a change is seen during an ignition cycle in which DTC C1293 is a current malfunction, DTC C1291 or C1292 will clear itself at the end of the current ignition cycle and ABS will enable itself at the start of the next ignition cycle.

Diagnostic Aids

Use the Data List of the Scan Tool to verify proper brake switch operation. The Data List should display the brake switch as the brake is applied within 25 mm (1.0 in) of brake pedal travel.

GC402980311500AX

Fig. 139 Code C1293: Code C1291 Or C1292 Set In Current Or Previous Ignition Cycle (Part 1 of 2). Cavalier & Sunfire

Step	Action	Value(s)	Yes	No
22	1. Repair the short to ground in CKT 140. 2. Replace the STOP-HAZ Fuse (20A) with a known good fuse (20A). Is the repair complete?	—	Refer to Diagnostic System Check	—
23	Replace the EBCM. Is the repair complete?	—	Refer to Diagnostic System Check	—
24	Replace the STOP-HAZ Fuse (20A) with a known good fuse (20A). Is the repair complete?	—	Refer to Diagnostic System Check	—
25	The malfunction is intermittent or is not present at this time. Refer to Diagnostic Aids for more information.	—	—	—

GC402980311400DX

Fig. 138 Code C1292: Open Brake Lamp Switch When ABS Required (Part 4 of 4). Cavalier & Sunfire

Step	Action	Value(s)	Yes	No
1	Was the Diagnostic System Check performed?	—	Go to Step 2	Refer to Diagnostic System Check
2	1. Install a *Scan Tool*. 2. Use the *Scan Tool* to read the DTCs. Is DTC C1291 or DTC C1292 set as either a current and/or a history DTC?	—	Refer to *DTC C1291 Open Brake Lamp Sw Contacts During Decel* or *DTC C1292 Open Brake Lamp Sw When ABS Required*	Go to Step 3
3	1. Select DTC history on the *Scan Tool*. 2. Verify that the malfunction frequency was infrequent. 3. Use the *Scan Tool* in order to clear the DTCs. Did DTC C1293 clear?	—	Refer to Diagnostic System Check	Go to Step 4
4	Replace the EBCM. Is the repair complete?	—	Refer to Diagnostic System Check	—

GC402980311500BX

Fig. 139 Code C1293: Code C1291 Or C1292 Set In Current Or Previous Ignition Cycle (Part 2 of 2). Cavalier & Sunfire

Circuit Description

DTC C1294 determines the proper operation of the brake switch. Proper operation of the brake switch is important because the brake switch activates the ABS and inhibits the ETS when the brake switch is on. The brake switch deactivates the ABS when the brake switch is off. The following conditions always occur when the brake switch is on:

- ABS operation is requested.
- ETS operation is inhibited.

Conditions for Setting the DTC

DTC C1294 can set if the vehicle's speed is greater than 40 km/h (25 mph).

A malfunction exists if the brake was always on during two consecutive drive cycles.

Action Taken When the DTC Sets

- A malfunction DTC stores.
- ABS operation remains.
- ETS operation is inhibited.

Conditions for Clearing the DTC

- The condition responsible for setting the DTC no longer exists and the Scan Tool Clear DTCs function is used.
- 100 drive cycles pass with no DTC(s) detected. A drive cycle consists of starting the vehicle, driving the vehicle over 16 km/h (10 mph), stopping and then turning the ignition off.

Diagnostic Aids

Use the enhanced diagnostic function of the Scan Tool in order to measure the frequency of the malfunction.

Important: Zero the J 39200 test leads before making any resistance measurements. Refer to the J 39200 user's manual.

Step	Action	Value(s)	Yes	No
1	Was the Diagnostic System Check performed?	—	Go to Step 2	Refer to Diagnostic System Check
2	1. Turn the ignition switch to the OFF position. 2. Verify that there is no pressure on the brake pedal. 3. Observe the rear brake lamps. Are the rear brake lamps on?	—	Go to Step 3	Go to Step 5
3	Disconnect the stoplamp switch connector. Are the rear brake lamps on?	—	Go to Step 8	Go to Step 4
4	Inspect the adjustment of the stoplamp switch. Is the stoplamp switch adjusted correctly?	—	Go to Step 10	Go to Step 9

GC402980311600AX

Fig. 140 Code C1294: Brake Lamp Switch Circuit Always Active (Part 1 of 2). Cavalier & Sunfire

Step	Action	Value(s)	Yes	No
5	1. Disconnect the 24-way EBCM connector C2. 2. Turn the ignition switch to the RUN position. Do not start the engine. 3. Use the *J 39200* in order to measure the voltage between the 24-way EBCM connector C2 terminal B9 and ground. Is the voltage within the specified range?	0–1 V	*Go to Step 6*	*Go to Step 8*
6	1. Turn the ignition switch to the OFF position. 2. Inspect the 24-way EBCM connector and the 24-way EBCM harness connector C2 for the following conditions: • Terminal damage • Poor terminal contact • Terminal corrosion Is there evidence of poor terminal contact, terminal corrosion, or damaged terminals?	—	*Go to Step 11*	*Go to Step 7*
7	1. Reconnect the 24-way EBCM connector C2. 2. Install a *Scan Tool.* 3. Turn the ignition switch to the RUN position. Do not start the engine. 4. Start the engine. 5. Test drive the vehicle obtaining a speed at least 40 km/h (25 mph). 6. Repeat the drive cycle, and steps 3,4, and 5 at least two additional times. 7. Use the *Scan Tool* in order to inspect for DTCs. Does DTC C1294 set as a current DTC during the last three drive cycles?	—	*Go to Step 12*	*Go to Step 13*
8	Repair the short to voltage in CKT 17 or 140. Is the repair complete?	—	Refer to *Diagnostic System Check*	—
9	Adjust the stoplamp switch. Is the repair complete?	—	Refer to *Diagnostic System Check*	—
10	Replace the stoplamp switch. Is the repair complete?	—	Refer to *Diagnostic System Check*	—
11	Replace all of the terminals and connectors that exhibit the following conditions: • Poor terminal contact • Corrosion • Damaged terminal(s) Is the repair complete?	—	Refer to *Diagnostic System Check*	—
12	Replace the EBCM. Is the repair complete?	—	Refer to *Diagnostic System Check*	—
13	The malfunction is intermittent or is not present at this time. Refer to Diagnostic Aids for more information.	—	—	—

GC402980311600BX

Fig. 140 Code C1294: Brake Lamp Switch Circuit Always Active (Part 2 of 2). Cavalier & Sunfire

Step	Action	Value(s)	Yes	No
3	Apply light pressure to the brake pedal while monitoring the Brake Switch Position on the *Scan Tool.* Does the Scan Tool indicate that the brake switch is on within 25 mm (1.0 in) of the brake pedal travel?	—	*Go to Step 9*	*Go to Step 4*
4	1. Apply firm pressure to the brake pedal. 2. Observe the rear brake lamps. Are the rear brake lamps on?	—	*Go to Step 5*	*Go to Step 9*
5	1. Turn the ignition switch to the OFF position. 2. Disconnect the 24-way EBCM connector C2. 3. Turn the ignition switch to the RUN position. Do not start the engine. 4. Apply firm pressure to the brake pedal. 5. Use the *J 39200* in order to measure the voltage between the 24-way EBCM connector C2 terminal B9 and ground. Is the voltage equal to or greater than the specified voltage?	10.0 V	*Go to Step 6*	*Go to Step 7*
6	Inspect the 24-way EBCM connector and the 24-way EBCM harness connector C2 for the following conditions: • Terminal damage • Poor terminal contact • Terminal corrosion Are poor terminal contact, terminal corrosion or damaged terminals evident?	—	*Go to Step 8*	*Go to Step 10*
7	Repair the open in CKT 17 or 140 Is the repair complete?	—	Refer to *Diagnostic System Check*	—
8	Replace all the terminals or the connectors that exhibit the following conditions: • Poor terminal contact • Terminal corrosion • Damaged terminal(s). Is the repair complete?	—	Refer to *Diagnostic System Check*	—
9	Repair the open brake lamp circuit wiring. Is the repair complete?	—	Refer to *Diagnostic System Check*	—
10	Replace the EBCM. Is the repair complete?	—	Refer to *Diagnostic System Check*	—
11	The malfunction is intermittent or is not present at this time. Refer to Diagnostic Aids for more information.	—	—	—

GC402980311700BX

Fig. 141 Code C1295: Brake Lamp Switch Circuit Open (Part 2 of 2). Cavalier & Sunfire

Circuit Description

DTC C1295 identifies open brake switch circuitry that prevents the brake switch input to the EBCM from changing states while applying the brake.

Conditions for Setting the DTC

DTC C1295 can set after initialization is complete.

A malfunction exists if the brake switch input voltage is out of specification for one second. An open circuit exists when the brake switch input voltage is out of specification.

Action Taken When the DTC Sets

- A malfunction DTC stores.
- ABS disables.
- The ABS warning indicator turns on.

Conditions for Clearing the DTC

- The condition responsible for setting the DTC no longer exists and the Scan Tool Clear DTCs function is used.
- 100 drive cycles pass with no DTC(s) detected. A drive cycle consists of starting the vehicle, driving the vehicle over 16 km/h (10 mph), stopping and then turning the ignition off.

Diagnostic Aids

The following conditions may cause an intermittent malfunction:

- A poor connection
- Rubbed-through wire insulation
- A broken wire inside the insulation

Use the enhanced diagnostic function of the Scan Tool in order to measure the frequency of the malfunction.

Thoroughly inspect any circuitry that may cause the intermittent complaint for the following conditions:

- Backed out terminals
- Improper mating
- Broken locks
- Improperly formed or damaged terminals
- Poor terminal-to-wiring connections
- Physical damage to the wiring harness

Important: Zero the J 39200 test leads before making any resistance measurements. Refer to the J 39200 user's manual.

Step	Action	Value(s)	Yes	No
1	Was the Diagnostic System Check performed?	—	*Go to Step 2*	Refer to *Diagnostic System Check*
2	1. Turn the ignition switch to the RUN position. Do not start the engine. 2. Install a *Scan Tool.* 3. Select Data List on the *Scan Tool.* 4. Select Brake Switch Position on the *Scan Tool.* Does the Scan Tool indicate that the brake switch circuit is open?	—	*Go to Step 3*	*Go to Step 11*

GC402980311700AX

Fig. 141 Code C1295: Brake Lamp Switch Circuit Open (Part 1 of 2). Cavalier & Sunfire

Circuit Description

The EBCM exchanges serial data through the connector C2 terminal A1.

Connector C2 terminal A9 supplies the switched ignition voltage to the EBCM.

Connector C2 terminal B12 supplies the battery voltage to the EBCM.

Connector C1 terminal C supplies the switched battery voltage to the EBCM.

Connector C1 Terminal D provides the ground for the EBCM.

Diagnostic Aids

Communication with the EBCM is not possible when excessive resistance exists in the following components:

- The ground
- The power supply circuits

If communication with the EBCM is not possible, perform the following actions:

- Verify that the EBCM ground connection is good.
- Verify that no excessive resistance exists in any of the power supply circuits.

Test Description

5. This test checks for high resistance in the EBCM ground circuit.
6. This test checks for an open in the EBCM battery feed circuit.
7. This test checks for an open or high resistance in the EBCM switched ignition circuit.
8. This test checks for an open or high resistance in the EBCM serial data circuit.
9. This test checks for a short to ground in the EBCM serial data circuit.
11. This test checks for a short to ground in the EBCM battery feed circuit.
12. This test checks for a short to ground in the EBCM switched ignition circuit.

GC4029903858010X

Fig. 142 No Communication With EBCM (Part 1 of 3). Cavalier & Sunfire

Step	Action	Value(s)	Yes	No
Important: Zero the J 39200 test leads before making any resistance measurements.				
1	Was the ABS Diagnostic System Check performed?	—	Go to *Step 2*	Go to *A Diagnostic System Check - ABS*
2	Verify the correct connection of the Scan Tool to the DLC. Is connection of the Scan Tool to the DLC correct?	—	Go to *Step 3*	Go to *Step 13*
3	1. Turn the ignition switch to the OFF position. 2. Remove and inspect the ABS Fuse (20A). Is the fuse open?	—	Go to *Step 11*	Go to *Step 4*
4	1. Install the ABS fuse (20A). 2. Remove the ERLS Fuse (10A). Is the fuse open?	—	Go to *Step 12*	Go to *Step 5*
5	1. Install the ERLS Fuse (10A). 2. Disconnect the EBCM connector. 3. Use the *J 39200* in order to measure the resistance between the EBCM connector terminal D and ground. Is the resistance within the specified range?	0–2 Ω	Go to *Step 6*	Go to *Step 18*
6	1. Disconnect the EBCM connector. 2. Use the *J 39200* in order to measure voltage between the EBCM connector terminal C and ground. Is the voltage equal to or greater than the specified voltage?	10 V	Go to *Step 7*	Go to *Step 19*
7	1. Turn the ignition switch to the ON position. Do not start the engine. 2. Use the *J 39200* in order to measure voltage between the EBCM connector terminal A9 and ground. Is the voltage equal to or greater than the specified voltage?	10 V	Go to *Step 8*	Go to *Step 20*
8	1. Turn the ignition switch to the OFF position. 2. Use the *J 39200* in order to measure the resistance between the EBCM connector terminal A1 and the DLC terminal 9. Is the resistance within the specified range?	0–2 Ω	Go to *Step 9*	Go to *Step 21*
9	Use the *J 39200* in order to measure the resistance between the EBCM connector terminal A1 and ground. Is the resistance within the specified range?	OL (Infinite)	Go to *Step 10*	Go to *Step 22*
10	Inspect the EBCM connector for the following conditions: • Poor terminal contact • Terminal corrosion • Damaged terminals Are there signs of poor terminal contact, terminal corrosion, or damaged terminals?	—	Go to *Step 23*	Go to *Step 24*
11	1. Disconnect the EBCM connector. 2. Use the *J 39200* in order to measure the resistance between the EBCM connector terminal C and ground. Is the resistance within the specified range?	OL (Infinite)	Go to *Step 14*	Go to *Step 15*
12	1. Disconnect the EBCM connector. 2. Use the *J 39200* in order to measure the resistance between the EBCM connector terminal A9 and ground. Is the resistance within the specified range?	OL (Infinite)	Go to *Step 16*	Go to *Step 17*

GC4029903858020X

Fig. 142 No Communication With EBCM (Part 2 of 3). Cavalier & Sunfire

Step	Action	Value(s)	Yes	No
13	Disconnect and reconnect the *Scan Tool* in order to ensure a good connection. Is the *Scan Tool* correctly connected?	—	Go to *A Diagnostic System Check - ABS*	—
14	Replace the ABS Fuse. Is the repair complete?	—	Go to *A Diagnostic System Check - ABS*	—
15	Repair the short to ground in CKT 1633 and replace the ABS Fuse. Is the repair complete?	—	Go to *A Diagnostic System Check - ABS*	—
16	Replace the ERLS Fuse. Is the repair complete?	—	Go to *A Diagnostic System Check - ABS*	—
17	Repair the short to ground in CKT 439 and replace the ERLS Fuse. Is the repair complete?	—	Go to *A Diagnostic System Check - ABS*	—
18	Repair the open or high resistance in CKT 251. Is the repair complete?	—	Go to *A Diagnostic System Check - ABS*	—
19	Repair the open or high resistance in CKT 1633. Is the repair complete?	—	Go to *A Diagnostic System Check - ABS*	—
20	Repair the open or high resistance in CKT 439. Is the repair complete?	—	Go to *A Diagnostic System Check - ABS*	—
21	Repair the open or high resistance in CKT 800. Is the repair complete?	—	Go to *A Diagnostic System Check - ABS*	—
22	Repair the short to ground in CKT 800. Is the repair complete?	—	Go to *A Diagnostic System Check - ABS*	—
23	Replace the terminals or the connectors that exhibit the following conditions: • Poor terminal contact • Terminal corrosion • Damaged terminals Is the repair complete?	—	Go to *A Diagnostic System Check - ABS*	—
24	Replace the EBCM. Is the repair complete?	—	Go to *A Diagnostic System Check - ABS*	—

GC4029903858030X

Fig. 142 No Communication With EBCM (Part 3 of 3). Cavalier & Sunfire

Circuit Description

Two-way serial communication is sent back and forth between the EBCM and the IPC. A message from the IPC is sent to the EBCM within seven seconds after ABS initialization. A serial communication failure does not allow the proper warning indicator commands to be sent back to the IPC.

Diagnostic Aids

Use the Lamp Test function of the Scan Tool in order to turn the indicator on while looking for an intermittent malfunction in the ABS warning indicator circuitry.

Thoroughly inspect any circuitry that may cause the intermittent complaint for the following conditions:

- Backed out terminals
- Improper mating
- Broken locks
- Improperly formed or damaged terminals
- Poor terminal-to-wiring connections
- Physical damage to the wiring harness

GC4029903859010X

Fig. 143 ABS Indicator On No DTC Set (Part 1 of 2). Cavalier & Sunfire

Step	Action	Value(s)	Yes	No
Important: Zero the J 39200 test leads before making any resistance measurements.				
1	Was the ABS Diagnostic System Check performed?	—	Go to *Step 2*	Go to *A Diagnostic System Check - ABS*
2	1. Turn the ignition switch to the OFF position. 2. Install a *Scan Tool.* 3. Turn the ignition switch to the RUN position. Do not start the engine. 4. Select the Body menu then IPC on the *Scan Tool.* 5. Select Lamp Test on the *Scan Tool.* 6. Use the *Scan Tool* in order to flash the warning indicators ON and OFF. Did the warning indicators flash ON and OFF?	—	Go to *Step 6*	Go to *Step 3*
3	Inspect all of the connectors and the terminals for the following conditions: • Poor terminal contact • Evidence of corrosion Is there evidence of poor terminal contact or corrosion?	—	Go to *Step 4*	Go to *Step 5*
4	Replace all of the terminals that exhibit signs of poor terminal contact or corrosion. Is the repair complete?	—	Go to *A Diagnostic System Check - ABS*	—
5	Repair the instrument panel cluster. Is the repair complete?	—	Go to *A Diagnostic System Check - ABS*	—
6	The malfunction is not present at this time. Refer to Diagnostic Aids for more information. Is the action complete?	—	System OK	—

GC4029903859020X

Fig. 143 ABS Indicator On No DTC Set (Part 2 of 2). Cavalier & Sunfire

Circuit Description

Two-way serial communication is sent back and forth between the EBCM and the IPC. A message from the IPC is sent to the EBCM within seven seconds after ABS initialization. A serial communication failure does not allow the proper warning indicator commands to be sent back to the IPC.

Diagnostic Aids

The following conditions may cause an intermittent malfunction:

- A poor connection
- Rubbed-through wire insulation
- A broken wire inside the insulation

Use the Lamp Test function of the Scan Tool in order to turn the indicator on while looking for an intermittent malfunction in the ABS warning indicator circuitry.

Thoroughly inspect any circuitry that may cause the intermittent complaint for the following conditions:

- Backed out terminals
- Improper mating
- Broken locks
- Improperly formed or damaged terminals
- Poor terminal-to-wiring connections
- Physical damage to the wiring harness

GC4029903860010X

Fig. 144 ABS Indicator Inoperative No DTC Set (Part 1 of 2). Cavalier & Sunfire

Step	Action	Value(s)	Yes	No
Important: Zero the J 39200 test leads before making any resistance measurements.				
1	Was the ABS Diagnostic System Check performed?	—	*Go to Step 2*	*Go to A Diagnostic System Check - ABS*
2	1. Turn the ignition switch to the OFF position. 2. Install a *J 39200.* 3. Turn the ignition switch to the RUN position. 4. Select the Body menu then IPC on the *Scan Tool.* 5. Select Lamp Test on the *Scan Tool.* 6. Use the *Scan Tool* in order to turn the warning indicators ON and OFF. Did the warning indicators turn ON and OFF?	—	*Go to Step 6*	*Go to Step 3*
3	Inspect all of the connectors and the terminals for the following conditions: • Poor terminal contact • Evidence of corrosion Is there evidence of poor terminal contact or corrosion?	—	*Go to Step 4*	*Go to Step 5*
4	Replace all of the terminals that exhibit signs of poor terminal contact or corrosion. Is the repair complete?	—	Go to *A Diagnostic System Check - ABS*	—
5	Repair the instrument panel cluster. Is the repair complete?	—	Go to *A Diagnostic System Check - ABS*	—
6	The malfunction is not present at this time. Refer to Diagnostic Aids for more information. Is the action complete?	—	System OK	—

GC4029903860020X

Fig. 144 ABS Indicator Inoperative No DTC Set (Part 2 of 2). Cavalier & Sunfire

Step	Action	Value(s)	Yes	No
Important: Zero the J 39200 test leads before making any resistance measurements.				
1	Was the ABS Diagnostic System Check performed?	—	Go to *Step 2*	Go to *A Diagnostic System Check - ABS*
2	1. Turn the ignition switch to the OFF position. 2. Connect a *Scan Tool.* 3. Turn the ignition switch to the ON position. 4. Use the *Scan Tool* in order to check for any PCM DTCs. Are there any PCM DTCs?	—	Go to Engine Controls	Go to *Step 3*
3	1. Use the *Scan Tool* to select the BODY Menu. 2. Use the *Scan Tool* to select IPC then Lamp Test. 3. Use the *Scan Tool* to turn the warning indicators OFF. Did the warning indicators turn OFF?	—	Go to *Step 4*	*Diagnose Instrument Cluster*
4	Disconnect the ETS Off switch connector. Does the ETS Off indicator turn OFF?	—	Go to *Step 7*	Go to *Step 5*
5	1. Disconnect the IPC connector C1. 2. Using the *J 39200* measure the resistance between the ETS Off switch harness connector terminal B and ground. Is the resistance within the specified range?	OL (Infinite)	Go to *Step 6*	Go to *Step 8*
6	1. Turn the ignition switch to the OFF position. 2. Inspect the following components: • The IPC connector C1 • The ETS Off connector 3. Inspect the above components for the following conditions: • Damage • Poor terminal contact • Terminal corrosion Are there signs of poor terminal contact, corrosion or damaged terminals?	—	Go to *Step 9*	Go to *Step 10*
7	Replace the ETS Off switch. Is the repair complete?	—	Go to *A Diagnostic System Check - ABS*	—
8	Repair short to ground in CKT 1571. Is the repair complete?	—	Go to *A Diagnostic System Check - ABS*	—
9	Replace all of the terminals or connectors that exhibit signs of poor terminal contact, corrosion or damaged terminal(s). Is the repair complete?	—	Go to *A Diagnostic System Check - ABS*	—
10	Replace the EBCM. Is the repair complete?	—	Go to *A Diagnostic System Check - ABS*	—

GC4029903861020X

Fig. 145 ETS Off Indicator On w/No DTC Set (Part 2 of 2). Cavalier & Sunfire

Circuit Description

Two-way serial communication is sent back and forth between the EBCM and the IPC. A message from the IPC is sent to the EBCM within seven seconds after ABS initialization. A serial communication failure does not allow the proper warning indicator commands to be sent back to the IPC.

Diagnostic Aids

The ETS OFF indicator will be ON and the Enhanced Traction System will be disabled whenever the scan tool is connected to the DLC with the ignition switch is in the RUN position.

Use the Lamp Test function of the Scan Tool in order to turn the indicator on while looking for an intermittent malfunction in the ETS OFF warning indicator circuitry.

Thoroughly inspect any circuitry that may cause the intermittent complaint for the following conditions:

- Backed out terminals
- Improper mating
- Broken locks
- Improperly formed or damaged terminals
- Poor terminal-to-wiring connections
- Physical damage to the wiring harness

Test Description

2. This test determines if a Powertrain malfunction has turned the ETS Off indicator ON.
3. This test determines if the malfunction is caused by the IPC.
4. This test checks for an ETS Off switch stuck in the closed position.
5. This test checks for a short to ground in the ETS OFF switch input to the IPC.

GC4029903861010X

Fig. 145 ETS Off Indicator On w/No DTC Set (Part 1 of 2). Cavalier & Sunfire

Circuit Description

Two-way serial communication is sent back and forth between the EBCM and the IPC. A message from the IPC is sent to the EBCM within seven seconds after ABS initialization. A serial communication failure does not allow the proper warning indicator commands to be sent back to the IPC.

Diagnostic Aids

The frequency of the malfunction can be checked by using the ENHANCED DIAGNOSTIC function of the scan tool.

The following conditions may cause an intermittent malfunction:

- A poor connection
- Rubbed-through wire insulation
- A broken wire inside the insulation

Use the Lamp Test function of the Scan Tool in order to turn the indicator on while looking for an intermittent malfunction in the ETS OFF warning indicator circuitry.

Thoroughly inspect any circuitry that may cause the intermittent complaint for the following conditions:

- Backed out terminals
- Improper mating
- Broken locks
- Improperly formed or damaged terminals
- Poor terminal-to-wiring connections
- Physical damage to the wiring harness

GC4029903862010X

Fig. 146 ETS Off Indicator Off w/No DTC Set (Part 1 of 2). Cavalier & Sunfire

Step	Action	Value(s)	Yes	No
Important: Zero the J 39200 test leads before making any resistance measurements.				
1	Was the ABS Diagnostic System Check performed?	—	*Go to Step 2*	*Go to A Diagnostic System Check - ABS*
2	1. Turn the ignition switch to the OFF position. 2. Install a *Scan Tool.* 3. Turn the ignition switch to the RUN position. 4. Select the Body menu then IPC on the *Scan Tool.* 5. Select Lamp Test on the *Scan Tool.* 6. Use the *Scan Tool* in order to flash the warning indicators ON and OFF. Did the warning indicators flash ON and OFF?	—	*Go to Step 6*	*Go to Step 3*
3	Inspect all of the connectors and the terminals for the following conditions: • Poor terminal contact • Evidence of corrosion Is there evidence of poor terminal contact or corrosion?	—	*Go to Step 4*	*Go to Step 5*
4	Replace all of the terminals that exhibit signs of poor terminal contact or corrosion. Is the repair complete?	—	Go to *A Diagnostic System Check - ABS*	—
5	Repair the instrument panel cluster. Is the repair complete?	—	Go to *A Diagnostic System Check - ABS*	—
6	The malfunction is not present at this time. Refer to Diagnostic Aids for more information. Is the action complete?	—	System OK	—

GC4029903862020X

Fig. 146 ETS Off Indicator Off w/No DTC Set (Part 2 of 2). Cavalier & Sunfire

Step	Action	Value(s)	Yes	No
1	Was the ABS Diagnostic System Check performed?	—	*Go to Step 2*	Go to *A Diagnostic System Check - ABS*
2	1. Turn the ignition switch to the OFF position. 2. Install a *Scan Tool.* 3. Turn the ignition switch to the RUN position. Do not start the engine. 4. Use the *Scan Tool* in order to clear the DTCs. 5. Turn the ignition switch to the OFF position. 6. Turn the ignition switch to the RUN position. 7. Do not start the engine Does the undefined DTC(s) reset?	—	*Go to Step 3*	*Go to Step 4*
3	Replace the EBCM. Is the repair complete?	—	Go to *A Diagnostic System Check - ABS*	—
4	The malfunction is not present at this time. Is the action complete?	—	System OK	—

GC4029903863000X

Fig. 147 Scan Tool Displays Undefined DTC. Cavalier & Sunfire

Circuit Description

The EBCM Diagnostic System Check is an organized approach to identify problems associated with the EBCM. This check must be the starting point for any EBCM complaint, and will direct you to the next logical step in diagnosing the complaint. The EBCM is a very reliable component and is not likely the cause of the malfunction. Most system complaints are linked to faulty wiring, connectors, and occasionally to components. Understanding the ABS (Antilock Brake System which is standard for this vehicle) system and using the tables correctly will reduce diagnostic time and prevent unnecessary parts replacement.

The Diagnostic system check directs the service technician to the next logical step in diagnosing the complaint. The following connectors/terminals will give you a better understanding on what each terminal performs.

- Connector C1 terminal A1 exchanges serial data to and from the EBCM.
- Connector C1 terminal A9 supplies the switched ignition voltage to the EBCM.
- Connector C1 terminal B12 supplies the battery voltage to the EBCM.
- Connector C2 terminal C supplies the switched battery voltage to the EBCM.
- Connector C2 terminal D provides the ground for the EBCM.

Diagnostic Aids

- An intermittent failure in the electronic system may be very difficult to detect and to accurately diagnose. The EBCM tests for different malfunctions under different vehicle conditions. For this reason, a thorough test drive is often needed in order to repeat a malfunction. If the system malfunction is not repeated during the test drive, a good description of the complaint may be very useful in locating an intermittent malfunction. Faulty electrical connections or wiring causes most intermitting problems. When an intermittent condition is suspected, check the suspected circuits for the following conditions:
  - Poor mating of connector halves or backed out terminals
  - Improperly formed or damaged terminals
  - Wiring damage, especially at vehicle attachment points
  - Poor wire to terminal connections
  - Dirty or corroded terminals
  - Damage to connector bodies

GC4029903825010X

Fig. 148 ABS Diagnostic System Check (Part 1 of 2). Intrigue, Lumina & Monte Carlo

- If the DTC is a history DTC, the problem may be intermittent. Perform the tests shown while moving related wiring and connectors. This can often cause the malfunction to occur.

Perform a thorough inspection of all related wiring and connectors pertaining to the history DTC stored.

Step	Action	Value(s)	Yes	No
1	1. Turn the ignition switch from the OFF to ON position, do not start engine. 2. Plug a scan tool into the Diagnostic Link Connector (DLC). Does the scan tool communicate with the EBCM?	—	*Go to Step 3*	*Go to Step 2*
2	Does the scan tool communicate with other modules on the UART serial data line?	—	*Go to Step 3*	Go to *Data Link Communications System*
3	1. Disconnect the scan tool. 2. Turn the ignition switch from the OFF to the ON position, do not start engine. 3. Carefully road test the vehicle for several minutes over different road surfaces and with several turns above 24 km/h (15 mph). 4. Plug a scan tool into the Diagnostic Link Connector (DLC). 5. With the scan tool read ABS DTCs. Are there any current Diagnostic Trouble Codes?	—	Go to *DTC List* for the Applicable DTC	*Go to Step 4*
4	1. Remove the scan tool from the DLC. 2. Turn the ignition switch from the OFF to ON position, do not start engine. Does the ABS Indicator turn on then turn off after several seconds?	—	*Go to Step 8*	*Go to Step 6*
5	Turn the ignition switch from the OFF to ON position, do not start engine. Does the Low Traction Indicator turn on then turn off after several seconds?	—	*Go to Step 6*	*Go to Step 7*
6	Does the ABS Indicator stay on?	—	Go to *ABS Indicator On No DTC Set*	Go to *ABS Indicator Off No DTC Set*
7	Does the Low Traction indicator stay on	—	Go to *Low Traction Indicator Always On*	Go to *Low Traction Indicator Inoperative*
8	Are there any history DTCs?	—	*Go to Step 9*	System OK
9	1. Refer to the appropriate DTC table for the history DTC. 2. Read the diagnostic aids and the conditions for setting the DTC. 3. Unplug the scan tool from the DLC if not already removed. 4. Carefully drive the vehicle above 24 Km/h (15 mph) for several minutes. 5. Leave the vehicle running and plug the scan tool into the DLC. 6. With the scan tool read ABS DTCs. Did the history DTC set as a current DTC while the vehicle was being driven?	—	Go to *DTC List* for the Applicable DTC	System OK

GC4029903825020X

Fig. 148 ABS Diagnostic System Check (Part 2 of 2). Intrigue, Lumina & Monte Carlo

Circuit Description

This DTC checks the state of the ABS warning indicator to identify a situation in which the driver could not be warned of a system malfunction by the ABS warning indicator, or the ABS warning indicator is always on. Due to an integral lamp driver module within the instrument panel cluster, the EBCM/EBTCM must provide a ground to turn the amber ABS warning indicator off. Because of the circuitry in the integral Lamp Driver Module (LDM), only external malfunctions can be detected. As a result, the integral LDM itself is not diagnosable, only the control line to the EBCM/EBTCM can be diagnosed. In the event of an open CKT 867, the ABS warning indicator will be on at all times, due to the loss of ground at the integral LDM input. If the control line is shorted to ground, the ABS warning indicator is kept off, due to the integral LDM input being grounded.

Conditions for Setting the DTC

DTC C1211 can be set only during the three second bulb check or when the amber ABS warning indicator is commanded on. If the EBCM/EBTCM cannot control the ABS warning indicator for two seconds, a malfunction exists.

Action Taken When the DTC Sets

A malfunction DTC is stored. However, ABS/ETS is not disabled.

Conditions for Clearing DTC

Condition for DTC is no longer present and the Scan Tool (CLEAR DTCs) function is used, or 100 drive cycles have passed with no DTCs detected.

Diagnostic Aids

An intermittent malfunction may be caused by a poor connection, rubbed-through wire insulation, or a wire that is broken inside the insulation.

The lamp test function of the Scan Tool may be used to command the lamp on while looking for an intermittent malfunction in the ABS warning indicator circuitry.

The frequency of the malfunction can be checked by using the enhanced diagnostic function of the Scan Tool, as described in Scan Tool Diagnostics in this section.

Any circuitry that is suspected of causing the intermittent complaint should be thoroughly checked for backed-out terminals, improper mating, broken locks, improperly formed or damaged terminals, poor terminal to wiring connections, or physical damage to the wiring harness.

Important

- J 39200 test leads must be zeroed prior to making any resistance measurements. Refer to J 39200 user's manual.

GC402970323400AX

Fig. 149 Code C1211: ABS Warning Lamp Circuit Fault (Part 1 of 4). Intrigue, Lumina & Monte Carlo

Step	Action	Value(s)	Yes	No
1	Was the Diagnostic System Check performed?	—	Go to Step 2	Go to Diagnostic System Check
2	1. Turn the ignition switch to the OFF position. 2. Install a Scan Tool. 3. Turn the ignition switch to the RUN position, engine off. 4. Using the Scan Tool, select MISC TESTS. 5. With the Scan Tool, then select LAMP TEST and attempt to turn on and flash the amber ABS warning indicator. Can the amber ABS warning indicator be both turned on and flashed?	—	Go to Step 23	Go to Step 3
3	1. Turn the ignition switch to the OFF position. 2. Turn the ignition switch to the RUN position, engine off. Does the amber ABS warning indicator turn on and stay on?	—	Go to Step 4	Go to Step 10
4	1. Turn the ignition switch to the OFF position. 2. Turn the ignition switch to the RUN position, engine off. 3. Using the Scan Tool, check for other DTCs. Are any other DTCs present?	—	Go to Applicable DTC Table	Go to Step 5
5	1. Turn the ignition switch to the OFF position. 2. Disconnect the 24-way EBCM/EBTCM connector C1. 3. Connect a fused jumper wire, such as J 36169, with a 3A fuse between the 24-way EBCM/EBTCM harness connector C1 terminal A7 and ground. 4. Turn the ignition switch to the RUN position, engine off. Is the amber ABS warning indicator on?	—	Go to Step 6	Go to Step 8
6	1. Turn the ignition switch to the OFF position. 2. Remove the fused jumper wire. 3. Disconnect the instrument panel cluster connector C1. 4. Using J 39200 measure the resistance between the 24-way EBCM/EBTCM harness connector C1 terminal A7 and the instrument panel cluster harness connector C1 terminal E. Is the resistance within the specified range?	0-2 Ω	Go to Step 7	Go to Step 20
7	1. Turn the ignition switch to the RUN position, engine off. 2. Using J 39200 measure the voltage between the 24-way EBCM/EBTCM harness connector C1 terminal A7 and ground. Is the voltage within the specified range?	0-2V	Electrical Diagnosis	Go to Step 21

GC402970323400BX

Fig. 149 Code C1211: ABS Warning Lamp Circuit Fault (Part 2 of 4). Intrigue, Lumina & Monte Carlo

Step	Action	Value(s)	Yes	No
8	1. Turn the ignition switch to the OFF position. 2. Inspect the 24-way EBCM/EBTCM connector C1 terminal A7 for signs of damage, poor terminal contact, or terminal corrosion. 3. Inspect the remaining terminals of the 24-way EBCM/EBTCM connector C1 for signs of damage, poor terminal contact, or terminal corrosion. Are there signs of poor terminal contact, corrosion, or damaged terminal?	—	Go to Step 19	Go to Step 9
9	1. Reconnect the 24-way EBCM/EBTCM harness connector C1 and if disconnected, the instrument panel cluster harness connector C1. 2. Install a Scan Tool. 3. Turn the ignition switch to the RUN position, engine off. 4. Using the scan tool, read DTCs. Does DTC C1211 reset?	—	Go to Step 22	Go to Diagnostic System Check
10	1. Perform an instrument panel cluster bulb check. 2. Observe the remaining instrument panel cluster warning indicators. Do the remaining instrument panel cluster warning indicators operate properly?	—	Go to Step 11	Go to Step 13
11	1. Turn the ignition switch to the OFF position. 2. Disconnect the 24-way EBCM/EBTCM connector C1. 3. Turn the ignition switch to the RUN position, engine off. Does the amber ABS warning indicator turn on?	—	Go to Step 8	Go to Step 12
12	1. Turn the ignition switch to the OFF position. 2. Disconnect the instrument panel cluster connector C1. 3. Using J 39200 measure the resistance between the 24-way EBCM/EBTCM harness connector C1 terminal A7 and ground. Is the resistance within the specified range?	OL (Infinite)	Electrical Diagnosis	Go to Step 18
13	1. Turn the ignition switch to the OFF position. 2. Remove the fuse block I/P-IGN 10A fuse. 3. Inspect the fuse block I/P-IGN 10A fuse. Is the fuse open?	—	Go to Step 14	Go to Step 16
14	Using J 39200 measure the resistance between CKT 39and ground. Is the resistance within the specified range?	0-2 Ω	Go to Step 15	Go to Step 17
15	Repair short to ground in CKT 39. Is the repair complete?	—	Go to Step 17	—
16	Repair the open in CKT 39. Is the repair complete?	—	Go to Diagnostic System Check	—
17	Replace the fuse block I/P-IGN 10A fuse with a known good 10A fuse. Is the repair complete?	—	Go to Diagnostic System Check	—
18	Repair short to ground in CKT 867. Is the repair complete?	—	Go to Diagnostic System Check	—

GC402970323400CX

Fig. 149 Code C1211: ABS Warning Lamp Circuit Fault (Part 3 of 4). Intrigue, Lumina & Monte Carlo

Step	Action	Value(s)	Yes	No
19	Repair the 24-way EBCM/EBTCM connector C1. Is the repair complete?	—	Go to Step 9	—
20	Repair the open, or high resistance in CKT 867. Is the repair complete?	—	Go to Diagnostic System Check	—
21	Repair the short to voltage in CKT 867. Is the repair complete?	—	Go to Diagnostic System Check	—
22	Replace the EBCM/EBTCM. Is the repair complete?	—	Go to Diagnostic System Check	—
23	Malfunction is intermittent or not present at this time. Refer to Diagnostic Aids for more information.	—	—	—

GC402970323400DX

Fig. 149 Code C1211: ABS Warning Lamp Circuit Fault (Part 4 of 4). Intrigue, Lumina & Monte Carlo

Step	Action	Value(s)	Yes	No
1	Was the Diagnostic System Check performed?	—	Go to Step 2	Go to Diagnostic System Check
2	1. Turn the ignition switch to the OFF position. 2. Install a Scan Tool. 3. Turn the ignition switch to the RUN position, engine off. 4. Using the Scan Tool, select MISC TESTS. 5. With the Scan Tool, then select LAMP TEST and attempt to turn on then off the ABS active indicator. Can the ABS active indicator (LOW TRAC) be both turned on and off?	—	Go to Step 21	Go to Step 3
3	1. Turn the ignition switch to the OFF position. 2. Remove the scan tool. 3. Turn the ignition switch to the RUN position, engine off. Does the ABS active indicator turn on and stay on?	—	Go to Step 4	Go to Step 7
4	1. Turn the ignition switch to the OFF position. 2. Disconnect the 24-way EBCM/EBTCM connector C1. 3. Turn the ignition switch to the RUN position, engine off. Does the ABS active indicator turn on?	—	Go to Step 16	Go to Step 5
5	1. Turn the ignition switch to the OFF position. 2. Inspect the 24-way EBCM/EBTCM connector C1 terminal A6 for signs of damage, poor terminal contact, or terminal corrosion. 3. Inspect the remaining terminals of the 24-way EBCM/EBTCM connector C1 for signs of damage, poor terminal contact, or terminal corrosion. Are there signs of poor terminal contact, corrosion, or damaged terminal(s)?	—	Go to Step 17	Go to Step 6
6	1. Reconnect the 24-way EBCM/EBTCM harness connector C1 and if disconnected, the Driver Information Display (base) harness connector or if equipped the Trip Calculator (optional) harness connector. 2. Install a Scan Tool. 3. Turn the ignition switch to the RUN position, engine off. 4. Using the scan tool, read DTCs. Does DTC C1213 reset?	—	Go to Step 20	Go to Diagnostic System Check

GC402970323500BX

Fig. 150 Code C1213: ABS Active Lamp Circuit Fault (Part 2 of 4). Intrigue, Lumina & Monte Carlo

Step	Action	Value(s)	Yes	No
15	Replace the fuse block I/P IGN 10A fuse with a known good 10A fuse. Is the repair complete?	—	Go to Diagnostic System Check	—
16	Repair the short to ground in CKT 1656. Is the repair complete?	—	Go to Diagnostic System Check	—
17	Repair the 24-way EBCM/EBTCM connector C1. Is the repair complete?	—	Go to Step 6	—
18	Repair the open, or high resistance in CKT 1656. Is the repair complete?	—	Go to Diagnostic System Check	—
19	Repair the short to voltage in CKT 1656. Is the repair complete?	—	Go to Diagnostic System Check	—
20	Replace the EBCM/EBTCM. Is the repair complete?	—	Go to Diagnostic System Check	—
21	Malfunction is intermittent or not present at this time. Refer to Diagnostic Aids for more information.	—	—	—

GC402970323500DX

Fig. 150 Code C1213: ABS Active Lamp Circuit Fault (Part 4 of 4). Intrigue, Lumina & Monte Carlo

Circuit Description

This DTC checks the state of the ABS/ETS (LOW TRAC) active indicator to identify a situation in which the driver could not be warned of a low traction event by the ABS/ETS active indicator, or the ABS/ETS active indicator is always on. The EBCM/EBTCM provides a ground through CKT 1656 to turn the ABS/ETS active indicator on. If the control line, CKT 1656 is open or shorted to voltage the ABS/ETS active indicator will always be off. If the control line, CKT 1656 is shorted to ground, the ABS/ETS active indicator is on when the ignition is in the RUN position.

Conditions for Setting the DTC

DTC C1213 only can be set during the three second bulb check or when the indicator is commanded on. If the EBCM/EBTCM cannot control the ABS/ETS active (LOW TRAC) indicator for two seconds, a malfunction exists.

Action Taken When the DTC Sets

A malfunction DTC is stored. However, ABS/ETS is not disabled.

Conditions for Clearing DTC

Condition for DTC is no longer present and the Scan Tool (CLEAR DTCs) function is used, or 100 drive cycles have passed with no DTCs detected.

Diagnostic Aids

An intermittent malfunction may be caused by a poor connection, rubbed-through wire insulation, or a wire that is broken inside the insulation.

The lamp test function of the scan tool may be used to command the indicator on while looking for an intermittent malfunction in the ABS/ETS active (LOW TRAC) indicator circuitry.

The frequency of the malfunction can be checked by using the enhanced diagnostic function of the scan tool, as described in Scan Tool Diagnostics in this section.

Any circuitry that is suspected of causing the intermittent complaint should be thoroughly checked for backed-out terminals, improper mating, broken locks, improperly formed or damaged terminals, poor terminal to wiring connections, or physical damage to the wiring harness.

Important

- J 39200 test leads must be zeroed prior to making any resistance measurements. Refer to J 39200 user's manual.

GC402970323500AX

Fig. 150 Code C1213: ABS Active Lamp Circuit Fault (Part 1 of 4). Intrigue, Lumina & Monte Carlo

Step	Action	Value(s)	Yes	No
7	1. Turn the ignition switch to the OFF position. 2. Turn the ignition switch to the RUN position, engine off. 3. Observe the (CHECK TIRE PRESS) and (TRAC OFF) indicators. Do the (CHECK TIRE PRESS) and (TRAC OFF) indicators turn on then off?	—	Go to Step 8	Go to Step 11
8	1. Turn the ignition switch to the OFF position. 2. Disconnect the 24-way EBCM/EBTCM connector C1. 3. Connect a fused jumper wire, such as J 36169, with a 3A fuse between the 24-way EBCM/EBTCM harness connector C1 terminal A6 and ground. 4. Turn the ignition switch to the RUN position, engine off. Does the ABS active indicator turn on?	—	Go to Step 5	Go to Step 9
9	1. Turn the ignition switch to the OFF position. 2. Remove the jumper wire. 3. Disconnect the Driver Information Display (base) connector or if equipped the Trip Calculator (optional) connector. 4. Using J 39200 measure the resistance between the 24-way EBCM/EBTCM harness connector C1 terminal A6 and the Driver Information Display (base) harness connector, terminal H or if equipped the Trip Calculator (optional) harness connector, terminal A3. Is the resistance within the specified range?	0-2 Ω	Go to Step 10	Go to Step 18
10	1. Turn the ignition switch to the RUN position, engine off. 2. Using J 39200 measure the voltage between the 24-way EBCM/EBTCM harness connector C1 terminal A6 and ground. Is the voltage within the specified range?	0-2V	Electrical Diagnosis	Go to Step 19
11	1. Turn the ignition switch to the OFF position. 2. Remove the fuse block I/P IGN 10A fuse. 3. Inspect the fuse block I/P IGN 10A fuse. Is the fuse block I/P IGN 10A fuse open?	—	Go to Step 12	Go to Step 14
12	Using J 39200 measure the resistance between the fuse block terminal D6 and ground. Is the resistance within the specified range?	0-2 Ω	Go to Step 13	Go to Step 15
13	Repair the short to ground in CKT 39. Is the repair complete?	—	Go to Step 15	—
14	Repair the open in CKT 39. Is the repair complete?	—	Go to Diagnostic System Check	—

GC402970323500CX

Fig. 150 Code C1213: ABS Active Lamp Circuit Fault (Part 3 of 4). Intrigue, Lumina & Monte Carlo

Circuit Description

Ignition voltage is supplied through terminal C10 of the Electronic Brake Control Relay. The above condition enables the EBCM to energize the pull-in coil by completing the ground circuit at connector C1 terminal A11 of the EBCM. The magnetic field created closes the Electronic Brake Control Relay contacts. The magnetic field also allows battery voltage and current through the Electronic Brake Control Relay terminal B10 to be supplied to the EBCM through connector C2 terminal C and to the brake solenoid valves through S133.

Conditions for Setting the DTC

DTC C 1214 can set anytime after the EBCM commands the Electronic Brake Control Relay on. The command occurs during the three second bulb check.

DTC C 1214 monitors the availability of current/voltage to the motors and solenoids.

The above malfunction indicates voltage is not available. The malfunction will not allow ABS operation.

Action Taken When the DTC Sets

- A malfunction DTC stores.
- The ABS disables.
- The amber ABS warning indicators turn on.
- The red BRAKE warning indicator turns on if the rear piston in the ABS brake motor pack is not in the home position.

Conditions for Clearing the DTC

- The condition responsible for setting the DTC no longer exists and the Scan Tool Clear DTCs function is used.
- 100 drive cycles pass with no DTCs detected.

Diagnostic Aids

The following conditions may cause an intermittent malfunction:

- A poor connection
- Rubbed-through wire insulation
- A broken wire inside the insulation

Use the enhanced diagnostic function of the Scan Tool in order to measure the frequency of the malfunction.

GC4029903826010X

Fig. 151 Code C1214: Electronic Brake Control Relay Contact Circuit Open (Part 1 of 5). Intrigue, Lumina & Monte Carlo

Thoroughly inspect any circuitry that may be causing the intermittent complaint for the following conditions:

- Backed out terminals
- Improper mating
- Improperly formed or damaged terminals
- Poor terminal-to-wiring connections
- Physical damage to the wiring harness

Vibration and Temperature Effects

- Use the following procedure in order to inspect for vibration effects by performing the Relay Test function of the Scan Tool:
  1. With the Relay Test commanded on, lightly tap the top and sides of the Electronic Brake Control Relay while monitoring the Electronic Brake Control Relay voltage.
  2. If the Electronic Brake Control Relay voltage changes significantly, replace the Electronic Brake Control Relay.
- If DTC C1214 only sets when the vehicle is initially started in cold ambient conditions (temperature less than 0° F – 32° F), replace the Electronic Brake Control Relay.

Important: Zero the *J 39200* test leads before making any resistance measurements.

Step	Action	Value(s)	Yes	No
1	Was the Diagnostic System Check performed?	—	*Go to Step 2*	*Go to ABS Diagnostic System*
2	1. Turn the ignition switch to the OFF position. 2. Install a scan tool. 3. Turn the ignition switch to the ON position. Do not start the engine. Use the scan tool in order to read the DTCs. Is DTC C1216 present (either as a current DTC or a history DTC)?	—	*Go to DTC C1216 Brake Control Relay Coil Circuit Open*	*Go to Step 3*
3	1. Select Data List on the scan tool. 2. Select and observe EBCM Battery Voltage. Is the voltage equal to or greater than the specified voltage?	10 V	*Go to Step 4*	*Charging System Check*
4	1. Turn the ignition switch to the OFF position. 2. Disconnect the 24-way EBCM connector C1. 3. Connect a fused jumper wire (such as a *J 36169-A*) with a 3A fuse between the 24-way EBCM harness connector C1 terminal A11 and ground. 4. Turn the ignition switch to the ON position. Do not start the engine. 5. Use the *J 39200* in order to measure the voltage between the 8-way EBCM harness connector C2 terminal C and ground. Is the voltage equal to or greater than the specified voltage?	10 V	*Go to Step 5*	*Go to Step 10*
5	1. Turn the ignition switch to the OFF position. 2. Disconnect the fused wire jumper. 3. Disconnect the Electronic Brake Control Relay. 4. Use the *J 39200* in order to measure the resistance between the Electronic Brake Control Relay harness connector terminal C8 and the EBCM harness connector C2 terminal C. Is the resistance within the specified range?	0–2 Ω	*Go to Step 6*	*Go to Step 19*

GC4029903826020X

Fig. 151 Code C1214: Electronic Brake Control Relay Contact Circuit Open (Part 2 of 5). Intrigue, Lumina & Monte Carlo

Step	Action	Value(s)	Yes	No
6	1. Disconnect the negative battery cable. 2. Remove ABS MaxiFuse (60A) from Engine Wiring Harness Junction Block 2. 3. Use the *J 39200* in order to measure the resistance between the ABS MaxiFuse terminal K1 and the Electronic Brake Control Relay harness connector terminal B10. Is the resistance within the specified range?	0–2 Ω	*Go to Step 7*	*Go to Step 20*
7	1. Connect a jumper wire between the Electronic Brake Control Relay harness connector terminal B10 to the ground. 2. Connect a fused jumper wire (such as a *J 36169-A*) with a 3A fuse between the Electronic Brake Control Relay terminal C10 and the battery voltage. 3. Use the *J 39200* in order to measure the resistance between the Electronic Brake Control Relay terminal B10 and terminal C8. Is the resistance within the specified range?	0–2 Ω	*Go to Step 8*	*Go to Step 22*
8	1. Turn the ignition switch to the OFF position. 2. Inspect the following components: • The 24-way EBCM connector C1 • The 8-way EBCM connector C2 • The 24-way EBTCM harness connector C1 • The 8-way EBCM harness connector C2 • The Electronic Brake Control Relay and Harness Connector 3. Inspect the following components: • The positive and negative battery terminals • The positive and negative battery cable terminals 4. Inspect all of the above components for signs of the following conditions: • Damage • Poor connection • Poor terminal contact Are there signs of poor terminal contact, corrosion, or damaged terminals?	—	*Go to Step 17*	*Go to Step 9*
9	1. Remove all of the jumpers. 2. Reconnect the EBCM connector C1 and connector C2. 3. Reconnect the Electronic Brake Control Relay 4. Reconnect the positive battery cable. 5. Reconnect the ABS MaxiFuse (60A). 6. Turn the ignition switch to the ON position. Do not start the engine. 7. Use the scan tool in order to look for current DTCs. Does DTC C1214 set as a current DTC?	—	*Go to Step 24*	Go to Diagnostic Aids

GC4029903826030X

Fig. 151 Code C1214: Electronic Brake Control Relay Contact Circuit Open (Part 3 of 5). Intrigue, Lumina & Monte Carlo

Step	Action	Value(s)	Yes	No
10	1. Turn the ignition switch to the OFF position. 2. Disconnect the negative battery cable. 3. Disconnect the positive battery cable. 4. Turn the ignition switch to the ON position. (This action completes the ignition circuit to the Electronic Brake Control Relay.) 5. Use the *J 39200* in order to measure the resistance between the 24-way EBCM harness connector C1 terminal A11 and the positive battery cable terminal. Is the resistance within the specified range?	70–95 Ω	*Go to Step 11*	*Go to Step 14*
11	Use the *J 39200* in order to measure the voltage between the positive battery terminal and the negative battery terminal. Is the voltage equal to or greater than the specified voltage?	10 V	*Go to Step 12*	*Go to Step 23*
12	1. Turn the ignition switch to the OFF position. 2. Reconnect the positive battery cable. 3. Reconnect the negative battery cable. 4. Disconnect the Electronic Brake Control Relay. 5. Use the *J 39200* in order to measure the voltage between the Electronic Brake Control Relay harness connector terminal B10 and ground. Is the voltage equal to or greater than the specified voltage?	10 V	*Go to Step 13*	*Go to Step 20*
13	Use the *J 39200* in order to measure the resistance between the Electronic Brake Control Relay harness connector terminal C8 and the 8-way EBCM harness connector C2 terminal C. Is the resistance within the specified range?	0–2 Ω	*Go to Step 7*	*Go to Step 19*
14	1. Disconnect the Electronic Brake Control Relay. 2. Use the *J 39200* in order to measure the resistance between the Electronic Brake Control Relay terminal C10 and the Electronic Brake Control Relay terminal B8. Is the resistance within the specified range?	70–95 Ω	*Go to Step 15*	*Go to Step 22*
15	Use the *J 39200* in order to measure the resistance between the Electronic Brake Control Relay harness connector terminal B8 and the 24-way EBCM harness connector C1 terminal A11. Is the resistance within the specified range?	0–2 Ω	*Go to Step 16*	*Go to Step 18*
16	Use the *J 39200* in order to measure the resistance between the Electronic Brake Control Relay harness connector terminal C10 and the positive battery cable terminal. Is the resistance within the specified range?	0–2 Ω	*Go to Step 8*	*Go to Step 21*
17	Replace all of the terminals the connectors that exhibit signs of poor terminal contact, corrosion, or damaged terminals. Is the repair complete?	—	Go to *ABS Diagnostic System Check*	—
18	Repair the open or high resistance in CKT 1632. Is the repair complete?	—	Go to *ABS Diagnostic System Check*	—
19	Repair the open or high resistance in CKT 1633. Is the repair complete?	—	Go to *ABS Diagnostic System Check*	—

GC4029903826040X

Fig. 151 Code C1214: Electronic Brake Control Relay Contact Circuit Open (Part 4 of 5). Intrigue, Lumina & Monte Carlo

Step	Action	Value(s)	Yes	No
20	Repair the open or high resistance in CKT 542. Is the repair complete?	—	Go to *ABS Diagnostic System Check*	—
21	Repair the open or high resistance in the following components as necessary: • CKT 341 • CKT 300 • The ignition switch • The battery feed CKT 142 to the ignition switch Is the repair complete?	—	Go to *ABS Diagnostic System Check*	—
22	Replace the Electronic Brake Control Relay. Is the repair complete?	—	Go to *ABS Diagnostic System Check*	—
23	Repair the low voltage condition. Is the repair complete?	—	Go to *ABS Diagnostic System Check*	—
24	Replace the EBCM. Is the repair complete?	—	Go to *ABS Diagnostic System Check*	—

GC4029903826050X

Fig. 151 Code C1214: Electronic Brake Control Relay Contact Circuit Open (Part 5 of 5). Intrigue, Lumina & Monte Carlo

Circuit Description

Ignition voltage is supplied through terminal A1 of the electronic brake control relay. The EBTCM then is able to energize the pull-in coil by completing the ground circuit at connector C1 terminal A11 of the EBTCM. The magnetic field created closes the electronic brake control relay contacts and allows battery voltage and current through the electronic brake control relay terminal C1 to be supplied to the EBTCM through connector C2 terminal C, which supplies power to the motors and solenoids.

Conditions for Setting the DTC

DTC C1215 can be set only before the EBTCM commands the electronic brake control relay on. This test determines if the electronic brake control relay is energized when it should not be. This malfunction would not allow the electronic brake control relay to remove power to the ABS/TCS system. If a second malfunction were to occur that requires the electronic brake control relay to be turned off, that malfunction cannot be removed if the electronic brake control relay cannot be controlled. The malfunction must be present for three consecutive drive cycles before the DTC is set.

Action Taken When the DTC Sets

A malfunction DTC is stored. ABS/TCS is not disabled.

Conditions for Clearing DTC

Condition for DTC is no longer present and the scan tool (CLEAR DTCs) function is used, or 100 drive cycles have passed with no DTCs detected.

Diagnostic Aids:

An intermittent malfunction may be caused by a poor connection, rubbed-through wire insulation, or a wire that is broken inside the insulation.

The frequency of the malfunction can be checked by using the enhanced diagnostic function of the Scan Tool, as described in Scan Tool Diagnostics in this section.

Any circuitry that is suspected of causing the intermittent complaint should be thoroughly checked for backed-out terminals, improper mating, broken locks, improperly formed or damaged terminals, poor terminal to wiring connections, or physical damage to the wiring harness.

Important

- J 39200 test leads must be zeroed prior to making any resistance measurements. Refer to J 39200 user's manual.

After diagnosis is complete, clear the DTCs and test drive the vehicle for three drive cycles to verify that the DTC does not reset. A drive cycle consists of starting the vehicle, driving the vehicle over 16 km/h (10 mph), stopping the vehicle and then turning the ignition to the OFF position.

GC402970323700AX

Fig. 152 Code C1215: Electronic Brake Control Relay Contact Circuit Always Active (Part 1 of 3). Intrigue, Lumina & Monte Carlo

Step	Action	Value(s)	Yes	No
1	Was the Diagnostic System Check performed?	—	Go to Step 2	Go to Diagnostic System Check
2	Are any other DTCs present?	—	Go to Applicable DTC Table	Go to Step 3
3	1. Turn the ignition switch to the OFF position. 2. Install a scan tool. 3. Turn the ignition switch to the RUN position, engine off. 4. Using the relay test function of the scan tool, command the electronic brake control relay off. Does the scan tool indicate that the electronic brake control relay is off and the battery voltage equal to or less than the specified voltage?	5V	Go to Step 12	Go to Step 4
4	1. Turn the ignition switch to the OFF position. 2. Disconnect the 24-way EBTCM connector C1. 3. Disconnect the 8-way EBTCM connector C2. 4. Turn the ignition switch to the RUN position, engine off. 5. Using J 39200, measure the voltage between the 8-way EBTCM harness connector C2 terminal C and ground. Is the voltage equal to or less than the specified voltage?	2V	Go to Step 6	Go to Step 5
5	1. Turn the ignition switch to the OFF position. 2. Disconnect the electronic brake control relay. 3. Turn the ignition switch to the RUN position, engine off. 4. Using J 39200, measure the voltage between the 8-way EBTCM harness connector C2 terminal C and ground. Is the voltage equal to or less than the specified voltage?	2V	Go to Step 10	Go to Step 9
6	1. Turn the ignition switch to the OFF position. 2. Inspect the 8-way EBTCM connector C2 and the 8-way EBTCM harness connector C2 for signs of poor terminal contact, corrosion, or damaged terminal(s) atwould result in a short to voltage. Is there a condition that would result in a short to voltage?	—	Go to Step 8	Go to Step 7
7	1. Reconnect the 24-way EBTCM connector C1. 2. Reconnect the 8-way EBTCM connector C2. 3. Turn the ignition switch to the RUN position, engine off. 4. Using the relay test function of the scan tool, command the electronic brake control relay off. Does the scan tool indicate that the electronic brake control relay is off and the battery voltage equal to or less than the specified voltage?	5V	Go to Step 12	Go to Step 11

GC402970323700BX

Fig. 152 Code C1215: Electronic Brake Control Relay Contact Circuit Always Active (Part 2 of 3). Intrigue, Lumina & Monte Carlo

Step	Action	Value(s)	Yes	No
8	Replace all terminals or connectors that exhibit signs of poor terminal contact, corrosion, or damaged terminal(s). Is the repair complete?	—	Go to Diagnostic System Check	—
9	Repair short to voltage in CKT 1633. Is the repair complete?	—	Go to Diagnostic System Check	—
10	Replace the electronic brake control relay. Is the repair complete?	—	Go to Diagnostic System Check	—
11	Replace the EBTCM. Is the repair complete?	—	Go to Diagnostic System Check	—
12	Malfunction is intermittent or not present at this time.	—	—	—

GC402970323700CX

Fig. 152 Code C1215: Electronic Brake Control Relay Contact Circuit Always Active (Part 3 of 3). Intrigue, Lumina & Monte Carlo

Circuit Description

Ignition voltage is supplied through terminal C10 of the Electronic Brake Control Relay. The above condition enables the EBCM to energize the pullin coil by completing the ground circuit at terminal B8 of Brake Relay connector, by the EBCM through circuit 1632. The magnetic field created closes the Electronic Brake Control Relay contacts. The magnetic field also allows battery voltage and current through the Electronic Brake Control Relay terminal B10 to be supplied to the EBTCM through connector C2 terminal C and to the brake solenoid valves through S133.

Conditions for Setting the DTC

DTC 1216 can set anytime.

DTC C1216 detects an open in the Electronic Brake Control Relay coil circuit. An open in the above circuit will not allow the Electronic Brake Control Relay to energize. If the Electronic Brake Control Relay cannot energize, voltage/current fails to reach the motors and solenoids.

DTC C1216 sets alone if the above malfunction exists and the ignition is turned off before reaching 5 km/h (3 mph).

Action Taken When the DTC Sets

- A malfunction DTC stores.
- The ABS disables.
- The amber ABS warning indicators turns on.
- The red BRAKE warning indicator turns on if the rear piston in the ABS brake motor pack is not in the home position.

Conditions for Clearing the DTC

- The condition responsible for setting the DTC no longer exists and the Scan Tool Clear DTCs function is used.
- 100 drive cycles pass with no DTCs detected.

Diagnostic Aids

The following conditions may cause an intermittent malfunction:

- A poor connection
- Rubbed-through wire insulation
- A broken wire inside the insulation

Use the enhanced diagnostic function of the Scan Tool in order to measure the frequency of the malfunction.

If the frequency of the malfunction is high, but is currently intermittent, inspect for high coil resistance. Use a *J 39200* in order to measure for high coil resistance by measuring between Electronic Brake Control Relay terminal C10 and terminal B8. If the resistance shows greater than 95 ohms, replace the Electronic Brake Control Relay.

GC4029903827010X

Fig. 153 Code C1216: Electronic Brake Control Relay Coil Circuit Open (Part 1 of 4). Intrigue, Lumina & Monte Carlo

Thoroughly inspect any circuitry that may be causing the intermittent complaint for the following conditions:

- Backed out terminals
- Improper mating
- Improperly formed or damaged terminals
- Poor terminal-to-wiring connections
- Physical damage to the wiring harness

Clear the DTCs after completing the diagnosis. Test drive the vehicle for three drive cycles in order to verify that the DTC does not reset. Use the following procedure in order to complete one drive cycle:

1. Start the vehicle.
2. Drive the vehicle over 16 km/h (10 mph).
3. Stop the vehicle.
4. Turn the ignition to the OFF position.

Important: Zero the *J 39200* test leads before making any resistance measurements.

Step	Action	Value(s)	Yes	No
1	Was the Diagnostic System Check performed?	—	*Go to Step 2*	*Go to ABS Diagnostic System Check*
2	1. Turn the ignition switch to the OFF position. 2. Install a scan tool. 3. Turn the ignition switch to the ON position. Do not start the engine. 4. Use the relay test function of the scan tool in order to view the Electronic Brake Control (ABS) Relay command. Does the scan tool indicate that the Electronic Brake Control (ABS) Relay is on, and is the voltage equal to or greater than the specified voltage?	10 V	*Go to Step 23*	*Go to Step 3*
3	Use the *J 39200* in order to measure the voltage between the Electronic Brake Control Relay connector terminal B8 and ground. Is the voltage equal to or greater than the specified voltage?	10 V	*Go to Step 4*	*Go to Step 9*
4	Use the *J 39200* in order to measure the voltage between the Electronic Brake Control Relay connector terminal C10 and ground. Is the voltage equal to or greater than the specified voltage?	10 V	*Go to Step 5*	*Go to Step 13*
5	1. Turn the ignition switch to the OFF position. 2. Disconnect the 24-way EBCM connector C1. 3. Turn the ignition switch to the ON position. Do not start the engine. 4. Use the *J 39200* in order to measure the voltage between the EBCM connector C1 terminal A11 and ground. Is the voltage equal to or greater than the specified voltage?	10 V	*Go to Step 6*	*Go to Step 7*
6	1. Turn the ignition switch to the OFF position. 2. Inspect the following components: • The 24-way EBCM connector C1 terminal A11 • The remaining terminals of the 24-way EBCM connector C1 3. Inspect the above components for the following conditions: • Damage • Poor terminal contact • Terminal corrosion Are there signs of poor terminal contact, corrosion, or damaged terminals?	—	*Go to Step 17*	*Go to Step 8*

GC4029903827020X

Fig. 153 Code C1216: Electronic Brake Control Relay Coil Circuit Open (Part 2 of 4). Intrigue, Lumina & Monte Carlo

Step	Action	Value(s)	Yes	No
7	1. Remove the Electronic Brake Control Relay. 2. Use the *J 39200* in order to measure the resistance between the 24-way EBCM connector terminal A11 and the Electronic Brake Control Relay connector terminal B8. Is the resistance within the specified range?	0–2 Ω	*Go to Step 8*	*Go to Step 18*
8	1. Reconnect the 24-way EBCM connector C1. 2. Reconnect the Electronic Brake Control Relay. 3. Turn the ignition switch to the ON position. Do not start the engine. 4. Use the scan tool in order to read the DTCs. Does DTC C1216 set as current DTC?	—	*Go to Step 22*	*Go to Step 23*
9	1. Turn the ignition switch to the OFF position. 2. Remove the ABS Fuse (5A) from the fuse block. 3. Turn the ignition switch to the ON position. Do not start the engine. 4. Use the *J 39200* in order to measure the voltage between the fuse block terminal B10 and ground. Is the voltage equal to or greater than the specified range?	10 V	*Go to Step 10*	*Go to Step 16*
10	Use the *J 39200* in order to measure the resistance between the ABS Fuse (10A) terminals. Is the resistance within the specified range?	0–2 Ω	*Go to Step 11*	*Go to Step 12*
11	1. Turn the ignition switch to the OFF position. 2. Use the *J 39200* in order to measure the resistance between the Electronic Brake Control Relay connector terminal C10 and the fuse block terminal D8. Is the resistance within the specified range?	0–2 Ω	*Go to Step 23*	*Go to Step 15*
12	1. Turn the ignition switch to the OFF position. 2. Remove the 24-way EBCM connector C1. 3. Use the *J 39200* in order to measure the resistance between the 24-way EBCM harness connector C1 terminal A9 and ground. Is the resistance within the specified range?	OL (Infinite)	*Go to Step 20*	*Go to Step 19*
13	1. Disconnect the Electronic Brake Control Relay. 2. Use the *J 39200* in order to measure the resistance between the Electronic Brake Control Relay terminal 85 and the Electronic Brake Control Relay terminal 86. Is the resistance within the specified range?	70–95 Ω	*Go to Step 14*	*Go to Step 21*
14	Inspect the Electronic Brake Control Relay connector for the following conditions: • Damage • Poor terminal contact corrosion • Terminal corrosion Are there signs of damage, poor terminal contact, or terminal corrosion?	—	*Go to Step 17*	*Go to Step 23*
15	Repair the open or high resistance in CKT 341. Is the repair complete?	—	Go to *ABS Diagnostic System Check*	—

GC4029903827030X

Fig. 153 Code C1216: Electronic Brake Control Relay Coil Circuit Open (Part 3 of 4). Intrigue, Lumina & Monte Carlo

Step	Action	Value(s)	Yes	No
16	Repair the open or high resistance in the following Circuits and components: • CKT 1 • CKT 542 Is the repair complete?	—	Go to *ABS Diagnostic System Check*	—
17	Replace all of the terminals that display signs of poor terminal contact, corrosion, or damaged terminals. Is the repair complete?	—	Go to *ABS Diagnostic System Check*	—
18	Repair the open or high resistance in CKT 1632. Is the repair complete?	—	Go to *ABS Diagnostic System Check*	—
19	Repair the short to ground in CKT 341. Is the repair complete?	—	*Go to Step 20*	—
20	Replace the fuse block ABS Fuse (10A) with a known good fuse. Is the repair complete?	—	Go to *ABS Diagnostic System Check*	—
21	Replace the Electronic Brake Control Relay. Is the repair complete?	—	Go to *ABS Diagnostic System Check*	—
22	Replace the EBCM. Is the repair complete?	—	Go to *ABS Diagnostic System Check*	—
23	Is the malfunction intermittent or is not present at this time?	—	Go to Diagnostic Aids	—

GC4029903827040X

Fig. 153 Code C1216: Electronic Brake Control Relay Coil Circuit Open (Part 4 of 4). Intrigue, Lumina & Monte Carlo

Circuit Description

Ignition voltage is supplied through terminal C10 of the Electronic Brake Control Relay. The above condition enables the EBCM to energize the pullin coil by completing the ground circuit at connector C1 terminal A11 of the EBCM. The magnetic field created closes the Electronic Brake Control Relay contacts. The magnetic field also allows battery voltage and current through the Electronic Brake Control Relay terminal C8 to be supplied to the EBCM through connector C2 terminal C and to the brake solenoid valves through S133.

Conditions for Setting the DTC

DTC C1217 can set before the EBCM commands the Electronic Brake Control Relay on.

DTC C1217 determines if the Electronic Brake Control Relay energizes when the Electronic Brake Control Relay should not energize. The above malfunction would not allow the Electronic Brake Control Relay to remove power to the ABS system.

If a second malfunction occurs, that requires the Electronic Brake Control Relay to turn off, the second malfunction cannot be removed if the Electronic Brake Control Relay cannot be controlled.

Action Taken When the DTC Sets

- A malfunction DTC stores.
- The ABS does not disable.

Conditions for Clearing the DTC

- The condition responsible for setting the DTC no longer exists and the Scan Tool Clear DTCs function is used.
- 100 drive cycles pass with no DTCs detected.

Diagnostic Aids

The following conditions may cause an intermittent malfunction:

- A poor connection
- Rubbed-through wire insulation
- A broken wire inside the insulation

Use the enhanced diagnostic function of the Scan Tool in order to measure the frequency of the malfunction.

Thoroughly inspect any circuitry that may be causing the intermittent complaint for the following conditions:

- Backed out terminals
- Improper mating
- Improperly formed or damaged terminals
- Poor terminal-to-wiring connections
- Physical damage to the wiring harness

Clear the DTCs after completing the diagnosis.

Test drive the vehicle for three drive cycles in order to verify that the DTC does not reset.

GC4029903828010X

Fig. 154 Code C1217: Electronic Brake Control Relay Coil Circuit Shorted To Ground (Part 1 of 3). Intrigue, Lumina & Monte Carlo

Use the following procedure in order to complete one drive cycle:

1. Start the vehicle.
2. Drive the vehicle over 16 km/h (10 mph).
3. Stop the vehicle.
4. Turn the ignition to the OFF position.

Important: Zero the *J 39200* test leads before making any resistance measurements.

Step	Action	Value(s)	Yes	No
1	Was the Diagnostic System Check performed?	—	*Go to Step 2*	Go to *ABS Diagnostic System Check*
2	1. Turn the ignition switch to the OFF position. 2. Install a scan tool. 3. Turn the ignition switch to the ON position. Do not start the engine. 4. Use the relay test function of the scan tool in order to view the Electronic Brake Control (ABS) Relay command. Does the scan tool indicate that the Electronic Brake Control (ABS) Relay is off?	—	Go to Diagnostic Aids	*Go to Step 3*
3	1. Turn the ignition switch to the OFF position. 2. Disconnect the 24-way EBCM connector C1. 3. Turn the ignition switch to the ON position. Do not start the engine. 4. Use the *J 39200* in order to measure the voltage between the 24-way EBCM connector C1 terminal A11 and the battery voltage. Is the voltage less than the specified voltage?	10 V	*Go to Step 4*	*Go to Step 7*
4	1. Turn the ignition switch to the OFF position. 2. Inspect the following components: • The 24-way EBCM connector C1 terminal A11 • The remaining terminals of the 24-way EBCM connector C1 3. Inspect the above components for the following conditions: • Damage • Poor terminal contact • Terminal corrosion Are there signs of poor terminal contact, corrosion, or damaged terminals?	—	*Go to Step 8*	*Go to Step 5*
5	Use the *J 39200* to measure the resistance between the 24-way EBCM connector C1 terminal A11 and ground. Is the resistance within the specified range?	OL (Infinite)	*Go to Step 6*	*Go to Step 9*
6	1. Reconnect the 24-way EBCM connector C1. 2. Turn the ignition switch to the ON position. Do not start the engine. 3. Use the scan tool in order to look for DTCs. Does DTC C1217 set as a current DTC?	—	*Go to Step 11*	Go to Diagnostic Aids
7	1. Turn the ignition switch to the OFF position. 2. Disconnect the Electronic Brake Control Relay. 3. Use the *J 39200* in order to measure the voltage between the Electronic Brake Control Relay connector terminal C2 and the battery voltage. Is the voltage less than or equal to the specified range?	0–2 V	*Go to Step 10*	*Go to Step 9*

GC4029903828020X

Fig. 154 Code C1217: Electronic Brake Control Relay Coil Circuit Shorted To Ground (Part 2 of 3). Intrigue, Lumina & Monte Carlo

Step	Action	Value(s)	Yes	No
8	Replace all of the terminals or connectors that exhibit signs of poor terminal contact, corrosion, or damaged terminals. Is the repair complete?	—	Go to *ABS Diagnostic System Check*	—
9	Repair the short to ground in CKT 1632. Is the repair complete?	—	Go to *ABS Diagnostic System Check*	—
10	Replace the Electronic Brake Control Relay. Is the repair complete?	—	Go to *ABS Diagnostic System Check*	—
11	Replace the EBCM. Is the repair complete?	—	Go to *ABS Diagnostic System Check*	—

GC4029903828030X

Fig. 154 Code C1217: Electronic Brake Control Relay Coil Circuit Shorted To Ground (Part 3 of 3). Intrigue, Lumina & Monte Carlo

Clear the DTCs after completing the diagnosis. Test drive the vehicle for three drive cycles in order to verify that the DTC does not reset. Use the following procedure in order to complete one drive cycle:

1. Start the vehicle.
2. Drive the vehicle over 16 km/h (10 mph).
3. Stop the vehicle.
4. Turn the ignition to the OFF position.

Important: Zero the *J 39200* test leads before making any resistance measurements.

Step	Action	Value(s)	Yes	No
1	Was the Diagnostic System Check performed?	—	*Go to Step 2*	Go to *ABS Diagnostic System Check*
2	1. Turn the ignition switch to the OFF position. 2. Install a scan tool. 3. Turn the ignition switch to the ON position. Do not start the engine. 4. Use the Relay Test function of the scan tool in order to view the Electronic Brake Control (ABS) Relay command. Does the scan tool indicate that the Electronic Brake Control (ABS) Relay is off?	—	Go to Diagnostic Aids	*Go to Step 3*
3	1. Turn the ignition switch to the OFF position. 2. Disconnect the Electronic Brake Control Relay. 3. Disconnect the 24-way EBCM connector C1. 4. Turn the ignition switch to the ON position. Do not start the engine. 5. Use the *J 39200* in order to measure the voltage between the 24-way EBCM harness connector C1 terminal A11 and ground. Is the voltage less than or equal to the specified voltage?	0–2 V	*Go to Step 4*	*Go to Step 9*
4	1. Turn the ignition switch to the OFF position. 2. Use the *J 39200* to measure the resistance between the Electronic Brake Control Relay terminal C10 and the Electronic Brake Control Relay terminal B8. Is the resistance equal to or greater than the specified range?	40 Ω	*Go to Step 5*	*Go to Step 10*
5	Use the *J 39200* in order to measure the resistance between the Electronic Brake Control Relay terminal B10 and the Electronic Brake Control Relay terminal C8. Is the resistance within the specified range?	OL (Infinite)	*Go to Step 6*	*Go to Step 10*
6	1. Inspect the following components: • The 24-way EBCM connector C1 terminal A11 • The remaining terminals of the 24-way EBCM connector C1 2. Inspect the above components for the following conditions: • Damage • Poor terminal contact • Terminal corrosion Are there signs of poor terminal contact, corrosion, or damaged terminals?	—	*Go to Step 8*	*Go to Step 7*

GC4029903829020X

Fig. 155 Code C1218: Electronic Brake Control Relay Coil Circuit Shorted To Voltage (Part 2 of 3). Intrigue, Lumina & Monte Carlo

Circuit Description

Ignition voltage is supplied through terminal C10 of the Electronic Brake Control Relay. The above enables the EBCM to energize the pullin coil by completing the ground circuit at connector C1 terminal A11 of the EBCM. The magnetic field created closes the Electronic Brake Control Relay contacts. The magnetic field also allows battery voltage and current through the Electronic Brake Control Relay terminal B10 to be supplied to the EBCM through connector C2 terminal C and to the brake solenoid valves through S133.

Conditions for Setting the DTC

DTC C1218 can set after the EBCM commands the Electronic Brake Control Relay on.

The test monitors the availability of current/voltage to the motors and solenoids.

The above malfunction indicates voltage is not available to the motors and solenoids. The malfunction may not allow ABS operation.

Action Taken When the DTC Sets

- A malfunction DTC stores.
- The ABS disables.
- The amber ABS warning indicators turn on.
- The red BRAKE warning indicator turns on if the rear piston in the ABS brake motor pack is not in the home position.

Conditions for Clearing the DTC

- The condition responsible for setting the DTC no longer exists and the Scan Tool Clear DTCs function is used.
- 100 drive cycles pass with no DTCs detected.

Diagnostic Aids

The following conditions may cause an intermittent malfunction:

- A poor connection
- Rubbed-through wire insulation
- A broken wire inside the insulation

Use the enhanced diagnostic function of the Scan Tool in order to measure the frequency of the malfunction.

Thoroughly inspect any circuitry that may be causing the intermittent complaint for the following conditions:

- Backed out terminals
- Improper mating
- Improperly formed or damaged terminals
- Poor terminal-to-wiring connections
- Physical damage to the wiring harness

GC4029903829010X

Fig. 155 Code C1218: Electronic Brake Control Relay Coil Circuit Shorted To Voltage (Part 1 of 3). Intrigue, Lumina & Monte Carlo

Step	Action	Value(s)	Yes	No
7	1. Reconnect the EBCM connector C1. 2. Reconnect the Electronic Brake Control Relay. 3. Turn the ignition switch to the ON position. Do not start the engine. 4. Use the scan tool in order to look for DTCs. Does DTC C1218 set as a current DTC?	—	*Go to Step 11*	Go to Diagnostic Aids
8	Replace all of the terminals or connectors that exhibit signs of poor terminal contact, corrosion, or damaged terminals. Is the repair complete?	—	Go to *ABS Diagnostic System Check*	—
9	Repair the short to voltage in CKT 1632. Is the repair complete?	—	Go to *ABS Diagnostic System Check*	—
10	Replace the Electronic Brake Control Relay. Is the repair complete?	—	Go to *ABS Diagnostic System Check*	—
11	Replace the EBCM. Is the repair complete?	—	Go to *ABS Diagnostic System Check*	—

GC4029903829030X

Fig. 155 Code C1218: Electronic Brake Control Relay Coil Circuit Shorted To Voltage (Part 3 of 3). Intrigue, Lumina & Monte Carlo

Circuit Description

As a toothed ring passes by the wheel speed sensor, changes in the electromagnetic field cause the wheel speed sensor to produce a sinusoidal (AC) voltage signal whose frequency is proportional to wheel speed. The magnitude of this signal is directly related to wheel speed and the proximity of the wheel speed sensor to the toothed ring, often referred to as the air gap.

Conditions for Setting the DTC

DTC C1221 can be set when the vehicle is not in an ABS stop. If the left front wheel speed sensor input signal = 0 and the vehicle's reference speed is greater than 8 km/h (5 mph), a malfunction exists.

Action Taken When the DTC Sets

A malfunction DTC is stored, ABS/TCS is disabled and the amber ABS warning indicator is turned on.

Conditions for Clearing DTC

Condition for DTC is no longer present and the scan tool (CLEAR DTCs) function is used, or 100 drive cycles have passed with no DTCs detected.

Diagnostic Aids

An intermittent malfunction may be caused by a poor connection, rubbed-through wire insulation, or a wire that is broken inside the insulation.

The frequency of the malfunction can be checked by using the enhanced diagnostic function of the Scan Tool, as described in Scan Tool Diagnostics in this section.

If the customer's comments reflect that the amber ABS warning indicator is on only during moist environmental changes (rain, snow, vehicle wash), all wheel speed sensor circuitry should be thoroughly inspected for signs of water intrusion. If DTC is not current, clear DTCs and simulate the effects of water intrusion. Use the following procedure. Spray the suspected area with a 5 percent salt water solution (two teaspoons of salt to 355 ml [12 ounces] of water). Test drive vehicle over various road surfaces (bumps, turns, etc.) above 24 km/h (15 mph) for at least 30 seconds. If DTC returns, replace suspected harness.

Any circuitry that is suspected of causing the intermittent complaint should be thoroughly checked for backed-out terminals, improper mating, broken locks, improperly formed or damaged terminals, poor terminal to wiring connections, or physical damage to the wiring harness.

Resistance of the wheel speed sensor will increase with an increase in sensor temperature.

When replacing a wheel speed sensor, inspect the sensor terminals and harness connector for corrosion and/or water intrusion. If evidence of corrosion, or water intrusion exists, replace wheel speed sensor jumper harness. Likewise, if replacing a wheel speed sensor jumper harness, inspect sensor terminals. If evidence of corrosion, or water intrusion exists, replace wheel speed sensor.

GC402970324100AX

Fig. 156 Code C1221: LH Front Wheel Speed Sensor Input Signal Is Zero (Part 1 of 4). Intrigue, Lumina & Monte Carlo

Important

- J 39200 test leads must be zeroed prior to making any resistance measurements. Refer to J 39200 user's manual.

Important

- Wheel speed sensor intermittent malfunctions may be difficult to locate. Care should be taken not to disturb any electrical connections prior to an indicated step of the diagnosis table. This will ensure that an intermittent condition will not be corrected before the source of the malfunction is found.

FRONT WHEEL SPEED SENSOR RESISTANCE

This table contains resistance values for the front wheel speed sensors at varying temperatures for use in diagnosis. The values are approximate and should be used as a guideline for diagnosis.

TEMP. (°C)	TEMP. (°F)	RESISTANCE (OHMS)
-34 to 4	-30 to 40	804 to 1066
5 to 43	41 to 110	956 to 1240
44 to 93	111 to 200	1112 to 1463

Step	Action	Value(s)	Yes	No
1	Was the Diagnostic System Check performed?	—	Go to Step 2	Go to Diagnostic System Check
2	1. Turn the ignition switch to the OFF position. 2. Inspect the left front wheel speed sensor and the left front wheel speed sensor harness connector for physical damage. Is there any physical damage evident?	—	Go to Step 16	Go to Step 3
3	Inspect the left front wheel speed sensor jumper harness and the left front wheel speed sensor jumper harness connectors for physical damage. Is there any physical damage evident?	—	Go to Step 15	Go to Step 4
4	1. Disconnect the left front wheel speed sensor directly at the left front wheel speed sensor connector. 2. Using J 39200, measure the resistance between the left front wheel speed sensor connector terminal A and the left front wheel speed sensor connector terminal B. Is the resistance within the specified range?	1020-1137 Ω at 20°C (68°F)	Go to Step 5	Go to Step 16
5	1. Select the A/C VOLTAGE scale on J 39200. 2. Spin the left front wheel by hand while observing voltage reading on J 39200. Is the voltage equal to or greater than the specified voltage?	100mV	Go to Step 6	Go to Step 16

GC402970324100BX

Fig. 156 Code C1221: LH Front Wheel Speed Sensor Input Signal Is Zero (Part 2 of 4). Intrigue, Lumina & Monte Carlo

Step	Action	Value(s)	Yes	No
6	1. Disconnect the 24-way EBTCM connector C1. 2. Using J 39200, measure the resistance between the 24-way EBTCM connector C1 terminal A5 and the 24-way EBTCM connector C1 terminal B4. Is the resistance within the specified range?	OL (Infinite)	Go to Step 7	Go to Step 8
7	1. Inspect the 24-way EBTCM connector C1 for signs of damage, poor terminal contact or terminal corrosion that would result in a short between the 24-way EBTCM connector C1 terminal A5 and the 24-way EBTCM connector C1 terminal B4. 2. Inspect the remaining terminals of the 24-way EBTCM connector C1 for signs of damage, poor terminal contact or terminal corrosion. Are there signs of poor terminal contact, corrosion, or damaged terminals?	—	Go to Step 12	Go to Step 8
8	Inspect the wiring for CKT 873 and CKT 830 for signs of damage that would result in a short between CKT 873 and CKT 830. Are there any signs of damaged wiring?	—	Go to Step 13	Go to Step 9
9	Inspect the harness connectors for CKT 873 and CKT 830 for signs of damage that would result in a short between CKT 873 and CKT 830. Are there any signs of damaged connectors?	—	Go to Step 14	Go to Step 10
10	1. Reconnect the 24-way EBTCM connector C1. 2. Reconnect the left front wheel speed sensor harness connector. 3. Install a scan tool. 4. Test drive the vehicle above 24 km/h (15 mph) for at least 30 seconds. 5. Using the scan tool, read the DTCs. Does DTC C1221 set as a current DTC?	—	Go to Step 10	Go to Step 18
11	1. Using the scan tool, select DATA LIST. 2. Monitor wheel speed sensor speeds. 3. Slowly accelerate to 65 km/h (40 mph) and slowly decelerate to 0 km/h (0 mph). Is the left front wheel speed sensor speed constantly higher than the three remaining wheel speed sensor speeds?	—	Go to Step 16	Go to Step 17
12	Replace all terminals or connectors that exhibit signs of poor terminal contact, corrosion, or damaged terminal(s). Is the repair complete?	—	Go to Diagnostic System Check	—
13	Replace the damaged wiring harness that caused the short between CKT 873 and CKT 830. Is the repair complete?	—	Go to Diagnostic System Check	—

GC402970324100CX

Fig. 156 Code C1221: LH Front Wheel Speed Sensor Input Signal Is Zero (Part 3 of 4). Intrigue, Lumina & Monte Carlo

Step	Action	Value(s)	Yes	No
14	Repair the damaged wiring harness connectors that caused the short between CKT 873 and CKT 830. Is the repair complete?	—	Go to Diagnostic System Check	—
15	Replace the left front wheel speed sensor jumper harness. Is the repair complete?	—	Go to Diagnostic System Check	—
16	Replace left front wheel speed sensor. Is the repair complete?	—	Go to Diagnostic System Check	—
17	Replace the EBTCM. Is the repair complete?	—	Go to Diagnostic System Check	—
18	Malfunction is intermittent or not present at this time. Refer to Diagnostic Aids for more information.	—	—	—

GC402970324100DX

Fig. 156 Code C1221: LH Front Wheel Speed Sensor Input Signal Is Zero (Part 4 of 4). Intrigue, Lumina & Monte Carlo

Circuit Description

As a toothed ring passes by the wheel speed sensor, changes in the electromagnetic field cause the wheel speed sensor to produce a sinusoidal (AC) voltage signal whose frequency is proportional to wheel speed. The magnitude of this signal is directly related to wheel speed and the proximity of the wheel speed sensor to the toothed ring, often referred to as the air gap.

Conditions for Setting the DTC

DTC C1222 can be set when the vehicle is not in an ABS stop. If the right front wheel speed sensor input signal = 0 and the vehicle's reference speed is greater than 8 km/h (5 mph), a malfunction exists.

Action Taken When the DTC Sets

A malfunction DTC is stored, ABS/TCS is disabled and the amber ABS warning indicator is turned on.

Conditions for Clearing DTC

Condition for DTC is no longer present and the scan tool (CLEAR DTCs) function is used, or 100 drive cycles have passed with no DTCs detected.

Diagnostic Aids

An intermittent malfunction may be caused by a poor connection, rubbed-through wire insulation, or a wire that is broken inside the insulation.

The frequency of the malfunction can be checked by using the enhanced diagnostic function of the Scan Tool, as described in Scan Tool Diagnostics in this section.

If the customer's comments reflect that the amber ABS warning indicator is on only during moist environmental changes (rain, snow, vehicle wash), all wheel speed sensor circuitry should be thoroughly inspected for signs of water intrusion. If DTC is not current, clear DTCs and simulate the effects of water intrusion. Use the following procedure. Spray the suspected area with a 5 percent salt water solution (two teaspoons of salt to 355 ml [12 ounces] of water). Test drive vehicle over various road surfaces (bumps, turns, etc.) above 24 km/h (15 mph) for at least 30 seconds. If DTC returns, replace suspected harness.

Any circuitry that is suspected of causing the intermittent complaint should be thoroughly checked for backed-out terminals, improper mating, broken locks, improperly formed or damaged terminals, poor terminal to wiring connections, or physical damage to the wiring harness.

Resistance of the wheel speed sensor will increase with an increase in sensor temperature.

When replacing a wheel speed sensor, inspect the sensor terminals and harness connector for corrosion and/or water intrusion. If evidence of corrosion, or water intrusion exists, replace wheel speed sensor jumper harness. Likewise, if replacing a wheel speed sensor jumper harness, inspect sensor terminals. If evidence of corrosion, or water intrusion exists, replace wheel speed sensor.

GC402970324200AX

Fig. 157 Code C1222: RH Front Wheel Speed Sensor Input Signal Is Zero (Part 1 of 4). Intrigue, Lumina & Monte Carlo

Important

- J 39200 test leads must be zeroed prior to making any resistance measurements. Refer to J 39200 user's manual.

Important

- Wheel speed sensor intermittent malfunctions may be difficult to locate. Care should be taken not to disturb any electrical connections prior to an indicated step of the diagnosis table. This will ensure that an intermittent condition will not be corrected before the source of the malfunction is found.

FRONT WHEEL SPEED SENSOR RESISTANCE

This table contains resistance values for the front wheel speed sensors at varying temperatures for use in diagnosis. The values are approximate and should be used as a guideline for diagnosis.

TEMP. (°C)	TEMP. (°F)	RESISTANCE (OHMS)
-34 to 4	-30 to 40	804 to 1066
5 to 43	41 to 110	956 to 1240
44 to 93	111 to 200	1112 to 1463

Step	Action	Value(s)	Yes	No
1	Was the Diagnostic System Check performed?	—	Go to Step 2	Go to Diagnostic System Check
2	1. Turn the ignition switch to the OFF position. 2. Inspect the right front wheel speed sensor and the right front wheel speed sensor harness connector for physical damage. Is there any physical damage evident?	—	Go to Step 16	Go to Step 3
3	Inspect the right front wheel speed sensor jumper harness and the right front wheel speed sensor jumper harness connectors for physical damage. Is there any physical damage evident?	—	Go to Step 15	Go to Step 4
4	1. Disconnect the right front wheel speed sensor directly at the right front wheel speed sensor connector. 2. Using J 39200, measure the resistance between the right front wheel speed sensor connector terminal A and the right front wheel speed sensor connector terminal B. Is the resistance within the specified range?	1020-1137 Ω at 20°C (68°F)	Go to Step 5	Go to Step 16
5	1. Select the A/C VOLTAGE scale on J 39200. 2. Spin the right front wheel by hand while observing voltage reading on J 39200. Is the voltage equal to or greater than the specified voltage?	100mV	Go to Step 6	Go to Step 16

GC402970324200BX

Fig. 157 Code C1222: RH Front Wheel Speed Sensor Input Signal Is Zero (Part 2 of 4). Intrigue, Lumina & Monte Carlo

Step	Action	Value(s)	Yes	No
6	1. Disconnect the 24-way EBTCM connector C1. 2. Using J 39200, measure the resistance between the 24-way EBTCM connector C1 terminal A4 and the 24-way EBTCM connector C1 terminal B3. Is the resistance within the specified range?	OL (Infinite)	Go to Step 7	Go to Step 8
7	1. Inspect the 24-way EBTCM connector C1 for signs of damage, poor terminal contact or terminal corrosion that would result in a short between the 24-way EBTCM connector C1 terminal A4 and the 24-way EBTCM connector C1 terminal B3. 2. Inspect the remaining terminals of the 24-way EBTCM connector C1 for signs of damage, poor terminal contact or terminal corrosion. Are there signs of poor terminal contact, corrosion, or damaged terminals?	—	Go to Step 12	Go to Step 8
8	Inspect the wiring for CKT 872 and CKT 833 for signs of damage that would result in a short between CKT 872 and CKT 833. Are there any signs of damaged wiring?	—	Go to Step 13	Go to Step 9
9	Inspect the harness connectors for CKT 872 and CKT 833 for signs of damage that would result in a short between CKT 872 and CKT 833. Are there any signs of damaged connectors?	—	Go to Step 14	Go to Step 10
10	1. Reconnect the 24-way EBTCM connector C1. 2. Reconnect the right front wheel speed sensor harness connector. 3. Install a scan tool. 4. Test drive the vehicle above 24 km/h (15 mph) for at least 30 seconds. 5. Using the scan tool, read the DTCs. Does DTC C1222 set as a current DTC?	—	Go to Step 10	Go to Step 18
11	1. Using the scan tool, select DATA LIST. 2. Monitor wheel speed sensor speeds. 3. Slowly accelerate to 65 km/h (40 mph) and slowly decelerate to 0 km/h (0 mph). Is the right front wheel speed sensor speed constantly higher than the three remaining wheel speed sensor speeds?	—	Go to Step 16	Go to Step 17
12	Replace all terminals or connectors that exhibit signs of poor terminal contact, corrosion, or damaged terminal(s). Is the repair complete?	—	Go to Diagnostic System Check	—
13	Replace the damaged wiring harness that caused the short between CKT 872 and CKT 833. Is the repair complete?	—	Go to Diagnostic System Check	—

GC402970324200CX

Fig. 157 Code C1222: RH Front Wheel Speed Sensor Input Signal Is Zero (Part 3 of 4). Intrigue, Lumina & Monte Carlo

Step	Action	Value(s)	Yes	No
14	Repair the damaged wiring harness connectors that caused the short between CKT 872 and CKT 833. Is the repair complete?	—	Go to Diagnostic System Check	—
15	Replace the right front wheel speed sensor jumper harness. Is the repair complete?	—	Go to Diagnostic System Check	—
16	Replace right front wheel speed sensor. Is the repair complete?	—	Go to Diagnostic System Check	—
17	Replace the EBTCM. Is the repair complete?	—	Go to Diagnostic System Check	—
18	Malfunction is intermittent or not present at this time. Refer to Diagnostic Aids for more information.	—	—	—

GC402970324200DX

Fig. 157 Code C1222: RH Front Wheel Speed Sensor Input Signal Is Zero (Part 4 of 4). Intrigue, Lumina & Monte Carlo

Circuit Description

As a toothed ring passes by the wheel speed sensor, changes in the electromagnetic field cause the wheel speed sensor to produce a sinusoidal (AC) voltage signal whose frequency is proportional to wheel speed. The magnitude of this signal is directly related to wheel speed and the proximity of the wheel speed sensor to the toothed ring, often referred to as the air gap.

Conditions for Setting the DTC

DTC C1223 can be set when the vehicle is not in an ABS stop. If the left rear wheel speed sensor input signal = 0 and the vehicle's reference speed is greater than 8 km/h (5 mph), a malfunction exists.

Action Taken When the DTC Sets

A malfunction DTC is stored, ABS/TCS is disabled and the amber ABS warning indicator is turned on.

Conditions for Clearing DTC

Condition for DTC is no longer present and the scan tool (CLEAR DTCs) function is used, or 100 drive cycles have passed with no DTCs detected.

Diagnostic Aids:

An intermittent malfunction may be caused by a poor connection, rubbed-through wire insulation, or a wire that is broken inside the insulation.

The frequency of the malfunction can be checked by using the enhanced diagnostic function of the Scan Tool, as described in Scan Tool Diagnostics in this section.

If the customer's comments reflect that the ABS/TCS warning indicator is on only during moist environmental changes (rain, snow, vehicle wash), all wheel speed sensor circuitry should be thoroughly inspected for signs of water intrusion. If DTC is not current, clear DTCs and simulate the effects of water intrusion. Use the following procedure. Spray the suspected area with a 5 percent salt water solution (two teaspoons of salt to 355 ml [12 ounces] of water). Test drive vehicle over various road surfaces (bumps, turns, etc.) above 24 km/h (15 mph) for at least 30 seconds. If DTC returns, replace suspected harness.

Any circuitry that is suspected of causing the intermittent complaint should be thoroughly checked for backed-out terminals, improper mating, broken locks, improperly formed or damaged terminals, poor terminal to wiring connections, or physical damage to the wiring harness.

Resistance of the wheel speed sensor will increase with an increase in sensor temperature.

When replacing a wheel speed sensor, inspect the sensor terminals and harness connector for corrosion and/or water intrusion. If evidence of corrosion, or water intrusion exists, replace wheel speed sensor jumper harness. Likewise, if replacing a wheel speed sensor jumper harness, inspect sensor terminals. If evidence of corrosion, or water intrusion exists, replace wheel speed sensor.

Important

- J 39200 test leads must be zeroed prior to making any resistance measurements. Refer to J 39200 user's manual.

GC402970324300AX

Fig. 158 Code C1223: LH Rear Wheel Speed Sensor Input Signal Is Zero (Part 1 of 4). Intrigue, Lumina & Monte Carlo

Important

- Wheel speed sensor intermittent malfunctions may be difficult to locate. Care should be taken not to disturb any electrical connections prior to an indicated step of the diagnosis table. This will ensure that an intermittent condition will not be corrected before the source of the malfunction is found.

REAR WHEEL SPEED SENSOR RESISTANCE

This table contains resistance values for the rear wheel speed sensors at varying temperatures for use in diagnosis. The values are approximate and should be used as a guideline for diagnosis.

TEMP. (°C)	TEMP. (°F)	RESISTANCE (OHMS)
-34 to 4	-30 to 40	800 to 1100
5 to 43	41 to 110	950 to 1300
44 to 93	111 to 200	1100 to 1600

Step	Action	Value(s)	Yes	No
1	Was the Diagnostic System Check performed?	—	Go to Step 2	Go to Diagnostic System Check
2	1. Turn the ignition switch to the OFF position. 2. Inspect the left rear wheel speed sensor and the left rear wheel speed sensor harness connector for physical damage. Is there any physical damage evident?	—	Go to Step 16	Go to Step 3
3	Inspect the left rear wheel speed sensor jumper harness and the left rear wheel speed sensor jumper harness connectors for physical damage. Is there any physical damage evident?	—	Go to Step 15	Go to Step 4
4	1. Disconnect the left rear wheel speed sensor directly at the left rear wheel speed sensor connector. 2. Using J 39200, measure the resistance between the left rear wheel speed sensor connector terminal A and the left rear wheel speed sensor connector terminal B. Is the resistance within the specified range?	1030-1180 Ω at 20°C (68°F)	Go to Step 5	Go to Step 16
5	1. Select the A/C VOLTAGE scale on J 39200. 2. Spin the left rear wheel by hand while observing voltage reading on J 39200. Is the voltage equal to or greater than the specified voltage?	100mV	Go to Step 6	Go to Step 16

GC402970324300BX

Fig. 158 Code C1223: LH Rear Wheel Speed Sensor Input Signal Is Zero (Part 2 of 4). IIntrigue, Lumina & Monte Carlo

Step	Action	Value(s)	Yes	No
14	Repair the damaged wiring harness connectors that caused the short between CKT 885 and CKT 884. Is the repair complete?	—	Go to Diagnostic System Check	—
15	Replace the left rear wheel speed sensor jumper harness. Is the repair complete?	—	Go to Diagnostic System Check	—
16	Replace left rear wheel speed sensor. Is the repair complete?	—	Go to Diagnostic System Check	—
17	Replace the EBTCM. Is the repair complete?	—	Go to Diagnostic System Check	—
18	Malfunction is intermittent or not present at this time. Refer to Diagnostic Aids for more information.	—	—	—

GC402970324300DX

Fig. 158 Code C1223: LH Rear Wheel Speed Sensor Input Signal Is Zero (Part 4 of 4). Intrigue, Lumina & Monte Carlo

Step	Action	Value(s)	Yes	No
6	1. Disconnect the 24-way EBTCM connector C1. 2. Using J 39200, measure the resistance between the 24-way EBTCM connector C1 terminal A3 and the 24-way EBTCM connector C1 terminal B2. Is the resistance within the specified range?	OL (Infinite)	Go to Step 7	Go to Step 8
7	1. Inspect the 24-way EBTCM connector C1 for signs of damage, poor terminal contact or terminal corrosion that would result in a short between the 24-way EBTCM connector C1 terminal A3 and the 24-way EBTCM connector C1 terminal B2. 2. Inspect the remaining terminals of the 24-way EBTCM connector C1 for signs of damage, poor terminal contact or terminal corrosion. Are there signs of poor terminal contact, corrosion, or damaged terminals?	—	Go to Step 12	Go to Step 8
8	Inspect the wiring for CKT 885 and CKT 884 for signs of damage that would result in a short between CKT 885 and CKT 884. Are there any signs of damaged wiring?	—	Go to Step 13	Go to Step 9
9	Inspect the harness connectors for CKT 885 and CKT 884 for signs of damage that would result in a short between CKT 885 and CKT 884. Are there any signs of damaged connectors?	—	Go to Step 14	Go to Step 10
10	1. Reconnect the 24-way EBTCM connector C1. 2. Reconnect the left rear wheel speed sensor harness connector. 3. Install a scan tool. 4. Test drive the vehicle above 24 km/h (15 mph) for at least 30 seconds. 5. Using the scan tool, read the DTCs. Does DTC C1223 set as a current DTC?	—	Go to Step 10	Go to Step 18
11	1. Using the scan tool, select DATA LIST. 2. Monitor wheel speed sensor speeds. 3. Slowly accelerate to 65 km/h (40 mph) and slowly decelerate to 0 km/h (0 mph). Is the left rear wheel speed sensor speed constantly higher than the three remaining wheel speed sensor speeds?	—	Go to Step 16	Go to Step 17
12	Replace all terminals or connectors that exhibit signs of poor terminal contact, corrosion, or damaged terminal(s). Is the repair complete?	—	Go to Diagnostic System Check	—
13	Replace the damaged wiring harness that caused the short between CKT 885 and CKT 884. Is the repair complete?	—	Go to Diagnostic System Check	—

GC402970324300CX

Fig. 158 Code C1223: LH Rear Wheel Speed Sensor Input Signal Is Zero (Part 3 of 4). Intrigue, Lumina & Monte Carlo

Circuit Description

As a toothed ring passes by the wheel speed sensor, changes in the electromagnetic field cause the wheel speed sensor to produce a sinusoidal (AC) voltage signal whose frequency is proportional to wheel speed. The magnitude of this signal is directly related to wheel speed and the proximity of the wheel speed sensor to the toothed ring, often referred to as the air gap.

Conditions for Setting the DTC

DTC C1224 can be set when the vehicle is not in an ABS stop. If the right rear wheel speed sensor input signal = 0 and the vehicle's reference speed is greater than 8 km/h (5 mph), a malfunction exists.

Action Taken When the DTC Sets

A malfunction DTC is stored, ABS/TCS is disabled and the amber ABS warning indicator is turned on.

Conditions for Clearing DTC

Condition for DTC is no longer present and the scan tool (CLEAR DTCs) function is used, or 100 drive cycles have passed with no DTCs detected.

Diagnostic Aids

An intermittent malfunction may be caused by a poor connection, rubbed-through wire insulation, or a wire that is broken inside the insulation.

The frequency of the malfunction can be checked by using the enhanced diagnostic function of the Scan Tool, as described in Scan Tool Diagnostics in this section.

If the customer's comments reflect that the ABS/TCS warning indicator is on only during moist environmental changes (rain, snow, vehicle wash), all wheel speed sensor circuitry should be thoroughly inspected for signs of water intrusion. If DTC is not current, clear DTCs and simulate the effects of water intrusion. Use the following procedure. Spray the suspected area with a 5 percent salt water solution (two teaspoons of salt to 355 ml [12 ounces] of water). Test drive vehicle over various road surfaces (bumps, turns, etc.) above 24 km/h (15 mph) for at least 30 seconds. If DTC returns, replace suspected harness.

Any circuitry that is suspected of causing the intermittent complaint should be thoroughly checked for backed-out terminals, improper mating, broken locks, improperly formed or damaged terminals, poor terminal to wiring connections, or physical damage to the wiring harness.

Resistance of the wheel speed sensor will increase with an increase in sensor temperature.

When replacing a wheel speed sensor, inspect the sensor terminals and harness connector for corrosion and/or water intrusion. If evidence of corrosion, or water intrusion exists, replace wheel speed sensor jumper harness. Likewise, if replacing a wheel speed sensor jumper harness, inspect sensor terminals. If evidence of corrosion, or water intrusion exists, replace wheel speed sensor.

Important

- J 39200 test leads must be zeroed prior to making any resistance measurements. Refer to J 39200 user's manual.

GC402970324400AX

Fig. 159 Code C1224: RH Rear Wheel Speed Sensor Input Signal Is Zero (Part 1 of 4). Intrigue, Lumina & Monte Carlo

Important

- Wheel speed sensor intermittent malfunctions may be difficult to locate. Care should be taken not to disturb any electrical connections prior to an indicated step of the diagnosis table. This will ensure that an intermittent condition will not be corrected before the source of the malfunction is found.

REAR WHEEL SPEED SENSOR RESISTANCE

This table contains resistance values for the rear wheel speed sensors at varying temperatures for use in diagnosis. The values are approximate and should be used as a guideline for diagnosis.

TEMP. (°C)	TEMP. (°F)	RESISTANCE (OHMS)
-34 to 4	-30 to 40	800 to 1100
5 to 43	41 to 110	950 to 1300
44 to 93	111 to 200	1100 to 1600

Step	Action	Value(s)	Yes	No
1	Was the Diagnostic System Check performed?	—	Go to Step 2	Go to Diagnostic System Check
2	1. Turn the ignition switch to the OFF position. 2. Inspect the right rear wheel speed sensor and the right rear wheel speed sensor harness connector for physical damage. Is there any physical damage evident?	—	Go to Step 16	Go to Step 3
3	Inspect the right rear wheel speed sensor jumper harness and the right rear wheel speed sensor jumper harness connectors for physical damage. Is there any physical damage evident?	—	Go to Step 15	Go to Step 4
4	1. Disconnect the right rear wheel speed sensor directly at the right rear wheel speed sensor connector. 2. Using J 39200, measure the resistance between the right rear wheel speed sensor connector terminal A and the right rear wheel speed sensor connector terminal B. Is the resistance within the specified range?	1030-1180 Ω at 20°C (68°F)	Go to Step 5	Go to Step 16
5	1. Select the A/C VOLTAGE scale on J 39200. 2. Spin the right rear wheel by hand while observing voltage reading on J 39200. Is the voltage equal to or greater than the specified voltage?	100mV	Go to Step 6	Go to Step 16

GC402970324400BX

Fig. 159 Code C1224: RH Rear Wheel Speed Sensor Input Signal Is Zero (Part 2 of 4). Intrigue, Lumina & Monte Carlo

Step	Action	Value(s)	Yes	No
14	Repair the damaged wiring harness connectors that caused the short between CKT 883 and CKT 882. Is the repair complete?	—	Go to Diagnostic System Check	—
15	Replace the right rear wheel speed sensor jumper harness. Is the repair complete?	—	Go to Diagnostic System Check	—
16	Replace right rear wheel speed sensor. Is the repair complete?	—	Go to Diagnostic System Check	—
17	Replace the EBTCM. Is the repair complete?	—	Go to Diagnostic System Check	—
18	Malfunction is intermittent or not present at this time. Refer to Diagnostic Aids for more information.	—	—	—

GC402970324400DX

Fig. 159 Code C1224: RH Rear Wheel Speed Sensor Input Signal Is Zero (Part 4 of 4). Intrigue, Lumina & Monte Carlo

Step	Action	Value(s)	Yes	No
6	1. Disconnect the 24-way EBTCM connector C1. 2. Using J 39200, measure the resistance between the 24-way EBTCM connector C1 terminal A2 and the 24-way EBTCM connector C1 terminal B1. Is the resistance within the specified range?	OL (Infinite)	Go to Step 7	Go to Step 8
7	1. Inspect the 24-way EBTCM connector C1 for signs of damage, poor terminal contact or terminal corrosion that would result in a short between the 24-way EBTCM connector C1 terminal A2 and the 24-way EBTCM connector C1 terminal B1. 2. Inspect the remaining terminals of the 24-way EBTCM connector C1 for signs of damage, poor terminal contact or terminal corrosion. Are there signs of poor terminal contact, corrosion, or damaged terminals?	—	Go to Step 12	Go to Step 8
8	Inspect the wiring for CKT 883 and CKT 882 for signs of damage that would result in a short between CKT 883 and CKT 882. Are there any signs of damaged wiring?	—	Go to Step 13	Go to Step 9
9	Inspect the harness connectors for CKT 883 and CKT 882 for signs of damage that would result in a short between CKT 883 and CKT 882. Are there any signs of damaged connectors?	—	Go to Step 14	Go to Step 10
10	1. Reconnect the 24-way EBTCM connector C1. 2. Reconnect the right rear wheel speed sensor harness connector. 3. Install a scan tool. 4. Test drive the vehicle above 24 km/h (15 mph) for at least 30 seconds. 5. Using the scan tool, read the DTCs. Does DTC C1224 set as a current DTC?	—	Go to Step 10	Go to Step 18
11	1. Using the scan tool, select DATA LIST. 2. Monitor wheel speed sensor speeds. 3. Slowly accelerate to 65 km/h (40 mph) and slowly decelerate to 0 km/h (0 mph). Is the right rear wheel speed sensor speed constantly higher than the three remaining wheel speed sensor speeds?	—	Go to Step 16	Go to Step 17
12	Replace all terminals or connectors that exhibit signs of poor terminal contact, corrosion, or damaged terminal(s). Is the repair complete?	—	Go to Diagnostic System Check	—
13	Replace the damaged wiring harness that caused the short between CKT 883 and CKT 882. Is the repair complete?	—	Go to Diagnostic System Check	—

GC402970324400CX

Fig. 159 Code C1224: RH Rear Wheel Speed Sensor Input Signal Is Zero (Part 3 of 4). Intrigue, Lumina & Monte Carlo

Circuit Description

As a toothed ring passes by the wheel speed sensor, changes in the electromagnetic field cause the wheel speed sensor to produce a sinusoidal (AC) voltage signal whose frequency is proportional to wheel speed. The magnitude of this signal is directly related to wheel speed and the proximity of the wheel speed sensor to the toothed ring, often referred to as the air gap.

Conditions for Setting the DTC

DTC C1225 can be set when the brake is off. The purpose of this test is to detect a situation in which the left front wheel acceleration or deceleration is beyond specified limits.

Action Taken When the DTC Sets

A malfunction DTC is stored, ABS/TCS is disabled and the amber ABS warning indicator is turned on.

Conditions for Clearing DTC

Condition for DTC is no longer present and the scan tool (CLEAR DTCs) function is used, or 100 drive cycles have passed with no DTCs detected.

Diagnostic Aids

An intermittent malfunction may be caused by a poor connection, rubbed-through wire insulation, or a wire that is broken inside the insulation.

The frequency of the malfunction can be checked by using the enhanced diagnostic function of the Scan Tool.

If the customer's comments reflect that the amber ABS warning indicator is on only during moist environmental changes (rain, snow, vehicle wash), all wheel speed sensor circuitry should be thoroughly inspected for signs of water intrusion. If DTC is not current, clear DTCs and simulate the effects of water intrusion. Use the following procedure. Spray the suspected area with a 5 percent salt water solution (two teaspoons of salt to 355 ml [12 ounces] of water). Test drive vehicle over various road surfaces (bumps, turns, etc.) above 24 km/h (15 mph) for at least 30 seconds. If DTC returns, replace suspected harness.

Any circuitry that is suspected of causing the intermittent complaint should be thoroughly checked for backed-out terminals, improper mating, broken locks, improperly formed or damaged terminals, poor terminal to wiring connections, or physical damage to the wiring harness.

Resistance of the wheel speed sensor will increase with an increase in sensor temperature.

When replacing a wheel speed sensor, inspect the sensor terminals and harness connector for corrosion and/or water intrusion. If evidence of corrosion, or water intrusion exists, replace wheel speed sensor jumper harness. Likewise, if replacing a wheel speed sensor jumper harness, inspect sensor terminals. If evidence of corrosion, or water intrusion exists, replace wheel speed sensor.

GC402970324500AX

Fig. 160 Code C1225: LH Front Excessive Wheel Speed Sensor Variation (Part 1 of 4). Intrigue, Lumina & Monte Carlo

Important

- J 39200 test leads must be zeroed prior to making any resistance measurements. Refer to J 39200 user's manual.

Important

- Wheel speed sensor intermittent malfunctions may be difficult to locate. Care should be taken not to disturb any electrical connections prior to an indicated step of the diagnosis table. This will ensure that an intermittent condition will not be corrected before the source of the malfunction is found.

FRONT WHEEL SPEED SENSOR RESISTANCE

This table contains resistance values for the front wheel speed sensors at varying temperatures for use in diagnosis. The values are approximate and should be used as a guideline for diagnosis.

TEMP. (°C)	TEMP. (°F)	RESISTANCE (OHMS)
-34 to 4	-30 to 40	804 to 1066
5 to 43	41 to 110	956 to 1240
44 to 93	111 to 200	1112 to 1463

Step	Action	Value(s)	Yes	No
1	Was the Diagnostic System Check performed?	—	Go to Step 2	Go to Diagnostic System Check
2	1. Turn the ignition switch to the OFF position. 2. Inspect the left front wheel speed sensor and the left front wheel speed sensor harness connector for physical damage. Is there any physical damage evident?	—	Go to Step 16	Go to Step 3
3	Inspect the left front wheel speed sensor jumper harness and the left front wheel speed sensor jumper harness connectors for physical damage. Is there any physical damage evident?	—	Go to Step 15	Go to Step 4
4	1. Disconnect the left front wheel speed sensor directly at the left front wheel speed sensor connector. 2. Using J 39200, measure the resistance between the left front wheel speed sensor connector terminal A and the left front wheel speed sensor connector terminal B. Is the resistance within the specified range?	1020-1137 Ω at 20°C (68°F)	Go to Step 5	Go to Step 16
5	1. Seleot the A/C VOLTAGE scale on J 39200. 2. Spin the left front wheel by hand while observing voltage reading on J 39200. Is the voltage equal to or greater than the specified voltage?	100mV	Go to Step 6	Go to Step 16

GC402970324500BX

Fig. 160 Code C1225: LH Front Excessive Wheel Speed Sensor Variation (Part 2 of 4). Intrigue, Lumina & Monte Carlo

Step	Action	Value(s)	Yes	No
14	Repair the damaged wiring harness connectors that caused the short between CKT 873 and CKT 830. Is the repair complete?	—	Go to Diagnostic System Check	—
15	Replace the left front wheel speed sensor jumper harness. Is the repair complete?	—	Go to Diagnostic System Check	—
16	Replace left front wheel speed sensor. Is the repair complete?	—	Go to Diagnostic System Check	—
17	Replace the EBTCM. Is the repair complete?	—	Go to Diagnostic System Check	—
18	Malfunction is intermittent or not present at this time. Refer to Diagnostic Aids for more information.	—	—	—

GC402970324500DX

Fig. 160 Code C1225: LH Front Excessive Wheel Speed Sensor Variation (Part 4 of 4). Intrigue, Lumina & Monte Carlo

Step	Action	Value(s)	Yes	No
6	1. Disconnect the 24-way EBTCM connector C1. 2. Using J 39200, measure the resistance between the 24-way EBTCM connector C1 terminal A5 and the 24-way EBTCM connector C1 terminal B4. Is the resistance within the specified range?	OL (Infinite)	Go to Step 7	Go to Step 8
7	1. Inspect the 24-way EBTCM connector C1 for signs of damage, poor terminal contact or terminal corrosion that would result in a short between the 24-way EBTCM connector C1 terminal A5 and the 24-way EBTCM connector C1 terminal B4. 2. Inspect the remaining terminals of the 24-way EBTCM connector C1 for signs of damage, poor terminal contact or terminal corrosion. Are there signs of poor terminal contact, corrosion, or damaged terminals?	—	Go to Step 12	Go to Step 8
8	Inspect the wiring for CKT 873 and CKT 830 for signs of damage that would result in a short between CKT 873 and CKT 830. Are there any signs of damaged wiring?	—	Go to Step 13	Go to Step 9
9	Inspect the harness connectors for CKT 873 and CKT 830 for signs of damage that would result in a short between CKT 873 and CKT 830. Are there any signs of damaged connectors?	—	Go to Step 14	Go to Step 10
10	1. Reconnect the 24-way EBTCM connector C1. 2. Reconnect the left front wheel speed sensor harness connector. 3. Install a scan tool. 4. Test drive the vehicle above 24 km/h (15 mph) for at least 30 seconds. 5. Using the scan tool, read the DTCs. Does DTC C1225 set as a current DTC?	—	Go to Step 10	Go to Step 18
11	1. Using the scan tool, select DATA LIST. 2. Monitor wheel speed sensor speeds. 3. Slowly accelerate to 65 km/h (40 mph) and slowly decelerate to 0 km/h (0 mph). Is the left front wheel speed sensor speed constantly higher than the three remaining wheel speed sensor speeds?	—	Go to Step 16	Go to Step 17
12	Replace all terminals or connectors that exhibit signs of poor terminal contact, corrosion, or damaged terminal(s). Is the repair complete?	—	Go to Diagnostic System Check	—
13	Replace the damaged wiring harness that caused the short between CKT 873 and CKT 830. Is the repair complete?	—	Go to Diagnostic System Check	—

GC402970324500CX

Fig. 160 Code C1225: LH Front Excessive Wheel Speed Sensor Variation (Part 3 of 4). Intrigue, Lumina & Monte Carlo

Circuit Description

As a toothed ring passes by the wheel speed sensor, changes in the electromagnetic field cause the wheel speed sensor to produce a sinusoidal (AC) voltage signal whose frequency is proportional to wheel speed. The magnitude of this signal is directly related to wheel speed and the proximity of the wheel speed sensor to the toothed ring, often referred to as the air gap.

Conditions for Setting the DTC

DTC C1226 can be set when the brake is off. The purpose of this test is to detect a situation in which the right front wheel acceleration or deceleration is beyond specified limits.

Action Taken When the DTC Sets

A malfunction DTC is stored, ABS/TCS is disabled and the amber ABS warning indicator is turned on.

Conditions for Clearing DTC

Condition for DTC is no longer present and the scan tool (CLEAR DTCs) function is used, or 100 drive cycles have passed with no DTCs detected.

Diagnostic Aids

An intermittent malfunction may be caused by a poor connection, rubbed-through wire insulation, or a wire that is broken inside the insulation.

The frequency of the malfunction can be checked by using the enhanced diagnostic function of the Scan Tool

If the customer's comments reflect that the amber ABS warning indicator is on only during moist environmental changes (rain, snow, vehicle wash), all wheel speed sensor circuitry should be thoroughly inspected for signs of water intrusion. If DTC is not current, clear DTCs and simulate the effects of water intrusion. Use the following procedure. Spray the suspected area with a 5 percent salt water solution (two teaspoons of salt to 355 ml [12 ounces] of water). Test drive vehicle over various road surfaces (bumps, turns, etc.) above 24 km/h (15 mph) for at least 30 seconds. If DTC returns, replace suspected harness.

Any circuitry that is suspected of causing the intermittent complaint should be thoroughly checked for backed-out terminals, improper mating, broken locks, improperly formed or damaged terminals, poor terminal to wiring connections, or physical damage to the wiring harness.

Resistance of the wheel speed sensor will increase with an increase in sensor temperature.

When replacing a wheel speed sensor, inspect the sensor terminals and harness connector for corrosion and/or water intrusion. If evidence of corrosion, or water intrusion exists, replace wheel speed sensor jumper harness. Likewise, if replacing a wheel speed sensor jumper harness, inspect sensor terminals. If evidence of corrosion, or water intrusion exists, replace wheel speed sensor.

GC402970324600AX

Fig. 161 Code C1226: RH Front Excessive Wheel Speed Sensor Variation (Part 1 of 4). Intrigue, Lumina & Monte Carlo

Important

- J 39200 test leads must be zeroed prior to making any resistance measurements. Refer to J 39200 user's manual.

Important

- Wheel speed sensor intermittent malfunctions may be difficult to locate. Care should be taken not to disturb any electrical connections prior to an indicated step of the diagnosis table. This will ensure that an intermittent condition will not be corrected before the source of the malfunction is found.

FRONT WHEEL SPEED SENSOR RESISTANCE

This table contains resistance values for the front wheel speed sensors at varying temperatures for use in diagnosis. The values are approximate and should be used as a guideline for diagnosis.

TEMP. (°C)	TEMP. (°F)	RESISTANCE (OHMS)
-34 to 4	-30 to 40	804 to 1066
5 to 43	41 to 110	956 to 1240
44 to 93	111 to 200	1112 to 1463

Step	Action	Value(s)	Yes	No
1	Was the Diagnostic System Check performed?	—	Go to Step 2	Go to Diagnostic System Check
2	1. Turn the ignition switch to the OFF position. 2. Inspect the right front wheel speed sensor and the right front wheel speed sensor harness connector for physical damage. Is there any physical damage evident?	—	Go to Step 16	Go to Step 3
3	Inspect the right front wheel speed sensor jumper harness and the right front wheel speed sensor jumper harness connectors for physical damage. Is there any physical damage evident?	—	Go to Step 15	Go to Step 4
4	1. Disconnect the right front wheel speed sensor directly at the right front wheel speed sensor connector. 2. Using J 39200, measure the resistance between the right front wheel speed sensor connector terminal A and the right front wheel speed sensor connector terminal B. Is the resistance within the specified range?	1020-1137 Ω at 20°C (68°F)	Go to Step 5	Go to Step 16
5	1. Select the A/C VOLTAGE scale on J 39200. 2. Spin the right front wheel by hand while observing voltage reading on J 39200. Is the voltage equal to or greater than the specified voltage?	100mV	Go to Step 6	Go to Step 16

GC402970324600BX

Fig. 161 Code C1226: RH Front Excessive Wheel Speed Sensor Variation (Part 2 of 4). Intrigue, Lumina & Monte Carlo

Step	Action	Value(s)	Yes	No
14	Repair the damaged wiring harness connectors that caused the short between CKT 872 and CKT 833. Is the repair complete?	—	Go to Diagnostic System Check	—
15	Replace the right front wheel speed sensor jumper harness. Is the repair complete?	—	Go to Diagnostic System Check	—
16	Replace right front wheel speed sensor. Is the repair complete?	—	Go to Diagnostic System Check	—
17	Replace the EBTCM. Is the repair complete?	—	Go to Diagnostic System Check	—
18	Malfunction is intermittent or not present at this time. Refer to Diagnostic Aids for more information.	—	—	—

GC402970324600DX

Fig. 161 Code C1226: RH Front Excessive Wheel Speed Sensor Variation (Part 4 of 4). Intrigue, Lumina & Monte Carlo

Step	Action	Value(s)	Yes	No
6	1. Disconnect the 24-way EBTCM connector C1. 2. Using J 39200, measure the resistance between the 24-way EBTCM connector C1 terminal A4 and the 24-way EBTCM connector C1 terminal B3. Is the resistance within the specified range?	OL (Infinite)	Go to Step 7	Go to Step 8
7	1. Inspect the 24-way EBTCM connector C1 for signs of damage, poor terminal contact or terminal corrosion that would result in a short between the 24-way EBTCM connector C1 terminal A4 and the 24-way EBTCM connector C1 terminal B3. 2. Inspect the remaining terminals of the 24-way EBTCM connector C1 for signs of damage, poor terminal contact or terminal corrosion. Are there signs of poor terminal contact, corrosion, or damaged terminals?	—	Go to Step 12	Go to Step 8
8	Inspect the wiring for CKT 872 and CKT 833 for signs of damage that would result in a short between CKT 872 and CKT 833. Are there any signs of damaged wiring?	—	Go to Step 13	Go to Step 9
9	Inspect the harness connectors for CKT 872 and CKT 833 for signs of damage that would result in a short between CKT 872 and CKT 833. Are there any signs of damaged connectors?	—	Go to Step 14	Go to Step 10
10	1. Reconnect the 24-way EBTCM connector C1. 2. Reconnect the right front wheel speed sensor harness connector. 3. Install a scan tool. 4. Test drive the vehicle above 24 km/h (15 mph) for at least 30 seconds. 5. Using the scan tool, read the DTCs. Does DTC C1226 set as a current DTC?	—	Go to Step 10	Go to Step 18
11	1. Using the scan tool, select DATA LIST. 2. Monitor wheel speed sensor speeds. 3. Slowly accelerate to 65 km/h (40 mph) and slowly decelerate to 0 km/h (0 mph). Is the right front wheel speed sensor speed constantly higher than the three remaining wheel speed sensor speeds?	—	Go to Step 16	Go to Step 17
12	Replace all terminals or connectors that exhibit signs of poor terminal contact, corrosion, or damaged terminal(s). Is the repair complete?	—	Go to Diagnostic System Check	—
13	Replace the damaged wiring harness that caused the short between CKT 872 and CKT 833. Is the repair complete?	—	Go to Diagnostic System Check	—

GC402970324600CX

Fig. 161 Code C1226: RH Front Excessive Wheel Speed Sensor Variation (Part 3 of 4). Intrigue, Lumina & Monte Carlo

Circuit Description

As a toothed ring passes by the wheel speed sensor, changes in the electromagnetic field cause the wheel speed sensor to produce a sinusoidal (AC) voltage signal whose frequency is proportional to wheel speed. The magnitude of this signal is directly related to wheel speed and the proximity of the wheel speed sensor to the toothed ring, often referred to as the air gap.

Conditions for Setting the DTC

DTC C1227 can be set when the brake is off. The purpose of this test is to detect a situation in which the left rear wheel acceleration or deceleration is beyond specified limits.

Action Taken When the DTC Sets

A malfunction DTC is stored, ABS/TCS is disabled and the amber ABS warning indicator is turned on.

Conditions for Clearing DTC

Condition for DTC is no longer present and the scan tool (CLEAR DTCs) function is used, or 100 drive cycles have passed with no DTCs detected.

Diagnostic Aids

An intermittent malfunction may be caused by a poor connection, rubbed-through wire insulation, or a wire that is broken inside the insulation.

The frequency of the malfunction can be checked by using the enhanced diagnostic function of the Scan Tool

If the customer's comments reflect that the amber ABS warning indicator is on only during moist environmental changes (rain, snow, vehicle wash), all wheel speed sensor circuitry should be thoroughly inspected for signs of water intrusion. If DTC is not current, clear DTCs and simulate the effects of water intrusion. Use the following procedure. Spray the suspected area with a 5 percent salt water solution (two teaspoons of salt to 355 ml [12 ounces] of water). Test drive vehicle over various road surfaces (bumps, turns, etc.) above 24 km/h (15 mph) for at least 30 seconds. If DTC returns, replace suspected harness.

Any circuitry that is suspected of causing the intermittent complaint should be thoroughly checked for backed-out terminals, improper mating, broken locks, improperly formed or damaged terminals, poor terminal to wiring connections, or physical damage to the wiring harness.

Resistance of the wheel speed sensor will increase with an increase in sensor temperature.

When replacing a wheel speed sensor, inspect the sensor terminals and harness connector for corrosion and/or water intrusion. If evidence of corrosion, or water intrusion exists, replace wheel speed sensor jumper harness. Likewise, if replacing a wheel speed sensor jumper harness, inspect sensor terminals. If evidence of corrosion, or water intrusion exists, replace wheel speed sensor.

Important

- J 39200 test leads must be zeroed prior to making any resistance measurements. Refer to J 39200 user's manual.

GC402970324700AX

Fig. 162 Code C1227: LH Rear Excessive Wheel Speed Sensor Variation (Part 1 of 4). Intrigue, Lumina & Monte Carlo

Important

- Wheel speed sensor intermittent malfunctions may be difficult to locate. Care should be taken not to disturb any electrical connections prior to an indicated step of the diagnosis table. This will ensure that an intermittent condition will not be corrected before the source of the malfunction is found.

REAR WHEEL SPEED SENSOR RESISTANCE

This table contains resistance values for the rear wheel speed sensors at varying temperatures for use in diagnosis. The values are approximate and should be used as a guideline for diagnosis.

TEMP. (°C)	TEMP. (°F)	RESISTANCE (OHMS)
-34 to 4	-30 to 40	800 to 1100
5 to 43	41 to 110	950 to 1300
44 to 93	111 to 200	1100 to 1600

Step	Action	Value(s)	Yes	No
1	Was the Diagnostic System Check performed?	—	Go to Step 2	Go to Diagnostic System Check
2	1. Turn the ignition switch to the OFF position. 2. Inspect the left rear wheel speed sensor and the left rear wheel speed sensor harness connector for physical damage. Is there any physical damage evident?	—	Go to Step 16	Go to Step 3
3	Inspect the left rear wheel speed sensor jumper harness and the left rear wheel speed sensor jumper harness connectors for physical damage. Is there any physical damage evident?	—	Go to Step 15	Go to Step 4
4	1. Disconnect the left rear wheel speed sensor directly at the left rear wheel speed sensor connector. 2. Using J 39200, measure the resistance between the left rear wheel speed sensor connector terminal A and the left rear wheel speed sensor connector terminal B. Is the resistance within the specified range?	1030-1180 Ω at 20°C (68°F)	Go to Step 5	Go to Step 16
5	1. Select the A/C VOLTAGE scale on J 39200. 2. Spin the left rear wheel by hand while observing voltage reading on J 39200. Is the voltage equal to or greater than the specified voltage?	100mV	Go to Step 6	Go to Step 16

GC402970324700BX

Fig. 162 Code C1227: LH Rear Excessive Wheel Speed Sensor Variation (Part 2 of 4). Intrigue, Lumina & Monte Carlo

Step	Action	Value(s)	Yes	No
6	1. Disconnect the 24-way EBTCM connector C1. 2. Using J 39200, measure the resistance between the 24-way EBTCM connector C1 terminal A3 and the 24-way EBTCM connector C1 terminal B2. Is the resistance within the specified range?	OL (Infinite)	Go to Step 7	Go to Step 8
7	1. Inspect the 24-way EBTCM connector C1 for signs of damage, poor terminal contact or terminal corrosion that would result in a short between the 24-way EBTCM connector C1 terminal A3 and the 24-way EBTCM connector C1 terminal B2. 2. Inspect the remaining terminals of the 24-way EBTCM connector C1 for signs of damage, poor terminal contact or terminal corrosion. Are there signs of poor terminal contact, corrosion, or damaged terminals?	—	Go to Step 12	Go to Step 8
8	Inspect the wiring for CKT 885 and CKT 884 for signs of damage that would result in a short between CKT 885 and CKT 884. Are there any signs of damaged wiring?	—	Go to Step 13	Go to Step 9
9	Inspect the harness connectors for CKT 885 and CKT 884 for signs of damage that would result in a short between CKT 885 and CKT 884. Are there any signs of damaged connectors?	—	Go to Step 14	Go to Step 10
10	1. Reconnect the 24-way EBTCM connector C1. 2. Reconnect the left rear wheel speed sensor harness connector. 3. Install a scan tool. 4. Test drive the vehicle above 24 km/h (15 mph) for at least 30 seconds. 5. Using the scan tool, read the DTCs. Does DTC C1227 set as a current DTC?	—	Go to Step 11	Go to Step 18
11	1. Using the scan tool, select DATA LIST. 2. Monitor wheel speed sensor speeds. 3. Slowly accelerate to 65 km/h (40 mph) and slowly decelerate to 0 km/h (0 mph). Is the left rear wheel speed sensor speed constantly higher than the three remaining wheel speed sensor speeds?	—	Go to Step 16	Go to Step 17
12	Replace all terminals or connectors that exhibit signs of poor terminal contact, corrosion, or damaged terminal(s). Is the repair complete?	—	Go to Diagnostic System Check	—
13	Replace the damaged wiring harness that caused the short between CKT 885 and CKT 884. Is the repair complete?	—	Go to Diagnostic System Check	—

GC402970324700CX

Fig. 162 Code C1227: LH Rear Excessive Wheel Speed Sensor Variation (Part 3 of 4). Intrigue, Lumina & Monte Carlo

Step	Action	Value(s)	Yes	No
14	Repair the damaged wiring harness connectors that caused the short between CKT 885 and CKT 884. Is the repair complete?	—	Go to Diagnostic System Check	—
15	Replace the left rear wheel speed sensor jumper harness. Is the repair complete?	—	Go to Diagnostic System Check	—
16	Replace left rear wheel speed sensor. Is the repair complete?	—	Go to Diagnostic System Check	—
17	Replace the EBTCM. Is the repair complete?	—	Go to Diagnostic System Check	—
18	Malfunction is intermittent or not present at this time. Refer to Diagnostic Aids for more information.	—	—	—

GC402970324700DX

Fig. 162 Code C1227: LH Rear Excessive Wheel Speed Sensor Variation (Part 4 of 4). Intrigue, Lumina & Monte Carlo

Circuit Description

As a toothed ring passes by the wheel speed sensor, changes in the electromagnetic field cause the wheel speed sensor to produce a sinusoidal (AC) voltage signal whose frequency is proportional to wheel speed. The magnitude of this signal is directly related to wheel speed and the proximity of the wheel speed sensor to the toothed ring, often referred to as the air gap.

Conditions for Setting the DTC

DTC C1228 can be set when the brake is off. The purpose of this test is to detect a situation in which the right rear wheel acceleration or deceleration is beyond specified limits.

Action Taken When the DTC Sets

A malfunction DTC is stored, ABS/TCS is disabled and the amber ABS warning indicator is turned on.

Conditions for Clearing DTC

Condition for DTC is no longer present and the scan tool (CLEAR DTCs) function is used, or 100 drive cycles have passed with no DTCs detected.

Diagnostic Aids

An intermittent malfunction may be caused by a poor connection, rubbed-through wire insulation, or a wire that is broken inside the insulation.

The frequency of the malfunction can be checked by using the enhanced diagnostic function of the Scan Tool.

If the customer's comments reflect that the amber ABS warning indicator is on only during moist environmental changes (rain, snow, vehicle wash), all wheel speed sensor circuitry should be thoroughly inspected for signs of water intrusion. If DTC is not current, clear DTCs and simulate the effects of water intrusion. Use the following procedure. Spray the suspected area with a 5 percent salt water solution (two teaspoons of salt to 355 ml [12 ounces] of water). Test drive vehicle over various road surfaces (bumps, turns, etc.) above 24 km/h (15 mph) for at least 30 seconds. If DTC returns, replace suspected harness.

Any circuitry that is suspected of causing the intermittent complaint should be thoroughly checked for backed-out terminals, improper mating, broken locks, improperly formed or damaged terminals, poor terminal to wiring connections, or physical damage to the wiring harness.

Resistance of the wheel speed sensor will increase with an increase in sensor temperature.

When replacing a wheel speed sensor, inspect the sensor terminals and harness connector for corrosion and/or water intrusion. If evidence of corrosion, or water intrusion exists, replace wheel speed sensor jumper harness. Likewise, if replacing a wheel speed sensor jumper harness, inspect sensor terminals. If evidence of corrosion, or water intrusion exists, replace wheel speed sensor.

GC402970324800AX

Fig. 163 Code C1228: RH Rear Excessive Wheel Speed Sensor Variation (Part 1 of 4). Intrigue, Lumina & Monte Carlo

Important

- J 39200 test leads must be zeroed prior to making any resistance measurements. Refer to J 39200 user's manual.

Important

- Wheel speed sensor intermittent malfunctions may be difficult to locate. Care should be taken not to disturb any electrical connections prior to an indicated step of the diagnosis table. This will ensure that an intermittent condition will not be corrected before the source of the malfunction is found.

REAR WHEEL SPEED SENSOR RESISTANCE

This table contains resistance values for the rear wheel speed sensors at varying temperatures for use in diagnosis. The values are approximate and should be used as a guideline for diagnosis.

TEMP. (°C)	TEMP. (°F)	RESISTANCE (OHMS)
-34 to 4	-30 to 40	800 to 1100
5 to 43	41 to 110	950 to 1300
44 to 93	111 to 200	1100 to 1600

Step	Action	Value(s)	Yes	No
1	Was the Diagnostic System Check performed?	—	Go to Step 2	Go to Diagnostic System Check
2	1. Turn the ignition switch to the OFF position. 2. Inspect the right rear wheel speed sensor and the right rear wheel speed sensor harness connector for physical damage. Is there any physical damage evident?	—	Go to Step 16	Go to Step 3
3	Inspect the right rear wheel speed sensor jumper harness and the right rear wheel speed sensor jumper harness connectors for physical damage. Is there any physical damage evident?	—	Go to Step 15	Go to Step 4
4	1. Disconnect the right rear wheel speed sensor directly at the right rear wheel speed sensor connector. 2. Using J 39200, measure the resistance between the right rear wheel speed sensor connector terminal A and the right rear wheel speed sensor connector terminal B. Is the resistance within the specified range?	1030-1180 Ω at 20°C (68°F)	Go to Step 5	Go to Step 16
5	1. Select the A/C VOLTAGE scale on J 39200. 2. Spin the right rear wheel by hand while observing voltage reading on J 39200. Is the voltage equal to or greater than the specified voltage?	100mV	Go to Step 6	Go to Step 16

GC402970324800BX

Fig. 163 Code C1228: RH Rear Excessive Wheel Speed Sensor Variation (Part 2 of 4). Intrigue, Lumina & Monte Carlo

Step	Action	Value(s)	Yes	No
14	Repair the damaged wiring harness connectors that caused the short between CKT 883 and CKT 882. Is the repair complete?	—	Go to Diagnostic System Check	—
15	Replace the right rear wheel speed sensor jumper harness. Is the repair complete?	—	Go to Diagnostic System Check	—
16	Replace right rear wheel speed sensor. Is the repair complete?	—	Go to Diagnostic System Check	—
17	Replace the EBTCM. Is the repair complete?	—	Go to Diagnostic System Check	—
18	Malfunction is intermittent or not present at this time. Refer to Diagnostic Aids for more information.	—	—	—

GC402970324800DX

Fig. 163 Code C1228: RH Rear Excessive Wheel Speed Sensor Variation (Part 4 of 4). Intrigue, Lumina & Monte Carlo

Step	Action	Value(s)	Yes	No
6	1. Disconnect the 24-way EBTCM connector C1. 2. Using J 39200, measure the resistance between the 24-way EBTCM connector C1 terminal A2 and the 24-way EBTCM connector C1 terminal B1 Is the resistance within the specified range?	OL (Infinite)	Go to Step 7	Go to Step 8
7	1. Inspect the 24-way EBTCM connector C1 for signs of damage, poor terminal contact or terminal corrosion that would result in a short between the 24-way EBTCM connector C1 terminal A2 and the 24-way EBTCM connector C1 terminal B1. 2. Inspect the remaining terminals of the 24-way EBTCM connector C1 for signs of damage, poor terminal contact or terminal corrosion. Are there signs of poor terminal contact, corrosion, or damaged terminals?	—	Go to Step 12	Go to Step 8
8	Inspect the wiring for CKT 883 and CKT 882 for signs of damage that would result in a short between CKT 883 and CKT 882. Are there any signs of damaged wiring?	—	Go to Step 13	Go to Step 9
9	Inspect the harness connectors for CKT 883 and CKT 882 for signs of damage that would result in a short between CKT 883 and CKT 882. Are there any signs of damaged connectors?	—	Go to Step 14	Go to Step 10
10	1. Reconnect the 24-way EBTCM connector C1. 2. Reconnect the right rear wheel speed sensor harness connector. 3. Install a scan tool. 4. Test drive the vehicle above 24 km/h (15 mph) for at least 30 seconds. 5. Using the scan tool, read the DTCs. Does DTC C1228 set as a current DTC?	—	Go to Step 10	Go to Step 18
11	1. Using the scan tool, select DATA LIST. 2. Monitor wheel speed sensor speeds. 3. Slowly accelerate to 65 km/h (40 mph) and slowly decelerate to 0 km/h (0 mph). Is the right rear wheel speed sensor speed constantly higher than the three remaining wheel speed sensor speeds?	—	Go to Step 16	Go to Step 17
12	Replace all terminals or connectors that exhibit signs of poor terminal contact, corrosion, or damaged terminal(s). Is the repair complete?	—	Go to Diagnostic System Check	—
13	Replace the damaged wiring harness that caused the short between CKT 883 and CKT 882. Is the repair complete?	—	Go to Diagnostic System Check	—

GC402970324800CX

Fig. 163 Code C1228: RH Rear Excessive Wheel Speed Sensor Variation (Part 3 of 4). Intrigue, Lumina & Monte Carlo

Circuit Description

As a toothed ring passes by the wheel speed sensor, changes in the electromagnetic field cause the wheel speed sensor to produce a sinusoidal (AC) voltage signal whose frequency is proportional to wheel speed. The magnitude of this signal is directly related to wheel speed and the proximity of the wheel speed sensor to the toothed ring, often referred to as the air gap.

Conditions for Setting the DTC

DTC C1232 can be set anytime after initialization. If either of the left front wheel speed sensor circuits are open or shorted to voltage or ground, a malfunction exists.

Action Taken When the DTC Sets

A malfunction DTC is stored and ABS/ETS is disabled, and the amber ABS warning indicator is turned on.

Conditions for Clearing DTC

The condition for the DTC is no longer present and the scan tool CLEAR DTCs function is used, or 100 drive cycles have passed with no DTCs detected.

Diagnostic Aids

An intermittent malfunction may be caused by a poor connection, rubbed-through wire insulation, or a wire that is broken inside the insulation.

The frequency of the malfunction can be checked by using the enhanced diagnostic function of the scan tool, as described in Scan Tool Diagnostics in this section.

If the customer's comments reflect that the amber ABS warning indicator is on only during moist environmental changes (rain, snow, vehicle wash), all wheel speed sensor circuitry should be thoroughly inspected for signs of water intrusion. If DTC is not current, clear DTCs and simulate the effects of water intrusion. Use the following procedure. Spray the suspected area with a 5 percent salt water solution (two teaspoons of salt to 355 ml[12 ounces] of water). Test drive vehicle over various road surfaces (bumps, turns, etc.) above 24 km/h (15 mph) for at least 30 seconds. If DTC returns, replace suspected harness.

Any circuitry that is suspected of causing the intermittent complaint should be thoroughly checked for backed-out terminals, improper mating, broken locks, improperly formed or damaged terminals, poor terminal to wiring connections, or physical damage to the wiring harness.

Resistance of the wheel speed sensor will increase with an increase in sensor temperature.

When replacing a wheel speed sensor, inspect the sensor terminals and harness connector for corrosion and/or water intrusion. If evidence of corrosion or water intrusion exists, replace wheel speed sensor jumper harness. Likewise, if replacing a wheel speed sensor jumper harness, inspect sensor terminals. If evidence of corrosion or water intrusion exists, replace wheel speed sensor.

GC402970324900AA

Fig. 164 Code C1232: LH Front Wheel Speed Sensor Circuit Open Or Shorted (Part 1 of 5). Intrigue, Lumina & Monte Carlo

Important

- J 39200 test leads must be zeroed prior to making any resistance measurements. Refer to J 39200 user's manual.

Important

- Wheel speed sensor intermittent malfunctions may be difficult to locate. Care should be taken not to disturb any electrical connections prior to an indicated step of the diagnosis table. This will ensure that an intermittent condition will not be corrected before the source of the malfunction is found.

FRONT WHEEL SPEED SENSOR RESISTANCE

This table contains resistance values for the front wheel speed sensors at varying temperatures for use in diagnosis. The values are approximate and should be used as a guideline for diagnosis.

TEMP. (°C)	TEMP. (°F)	RESISTANCE (OHMS)
-34 to 4	-30 to 40	804 to 1066
5 to 43	41 to 110	956 to 1240
44 to 93	111 to 200	1112 to 1463

Step	Action	Value(s)	Yes	No
1	Was the Diagnostic System Check performed?	—	Go to Step 2	Go to Diagnostic System Check
2	1. Turn the ignition switch to the OFF position. 2. Using a 5 percent salt water solution (two teaspoons of salt to 355 ml [12 ounces] of water), thoroughly spray the left front wheel speed sensor jumper harness. 3. Disconnect the 24-way EBTCM harness connector C1. 4. Using J 39200, measure the resistance between the 24-way EBTCM harness connector C1 terminal A5 and the 24-way EBTCM harness connector C1 terminal B4. Is the resistance within the specified range?	1020-1137 Ω at 20°C (68°F)	Go to Step 3	Go to Step 11
3	Using J 39200, measure the resistance between the 24-way EBTCM harness connector C1 terminal B4 and ground. Is the resistance within the specified range?	OL (Infinite)	Go to Step 4	Go to Step 14
4	1. Turn the ignition switch to the RUN position, engine off. 2. Using J 39200, measure the voltage between the 24-way EBTCM harness connector C1 terminal B4 and ground. Is the voltage within the specified range?	0-1V	Go to Step 7	Go to Step 5
5	1. Turn the ignition switch to the OFF position. 2. Disconnect the left front wheel speed sensor at the left front wheel speed sensor connector. 3. Turn the ignition switch to the RUN position, engine off. 4. Using J 39200, measure the voltage between the 24-way EBTCM harness connector C1 terminal B4 and ground. Is the voltage within the specified range?	0-1V	Go to Step 6	Go to Step 19

GC402970324900BX

Fig. 164 Code C1232: LH Front Wheel Speed Sensor Circuit Open Or Shorted (Part 2 of 5). Intrigue, Lumina & Monte Carlo

Step	Action	Value(s)	Yes	No
15	Using J 39200, measure the resistance between the 24-way EBTCM connector C1 terminal A5 and ground. Is the resistance within the specified range?	OL (Infinite)	Go to Step 16	Go to Step 26
16	1. Thoroughly re-spray the left front wheel speed sensor jumper harness with the salt water solution. 2. Disconnect the left front wheel speed sensor directly at the left front wheel speed sensor. 3. Using J 39200, measure the resistance between the left front wheel speed sensor jumper harness connector terminal A and ground. Is the resistance within the specified range?	OL (Infinite)	Go to Step 17	Go to Step 29
17	Using J 39200, measure the resistance between the left front wheel speed sensor jumper harness connector terminal B and ground. Is the resistance within the specified range?	OL (Infinite)	Go to Step 18	Go to Step 29
18	Using J 39200, measure the resistance between the left front wheel speed sensor connector terminal A and ground. Is the resistance within the specified range?	OL (Infinite)	Go to Step 31	Go to Step 28
19	Repair the short to voltage in CKT 873. If the short to voltage is found in the left front wheel speed sensor jumper harness the left front wheel speed jumper harness must be replaced. Is the repair complete?	-	Go to Diagnostic System Check	—
20	Repair the short to voltage in CKT 830. If the short to voltage is found in the left front wheel speed sensor jumper harness the left front wheel speed jumper harness must be replaced. Is the repair complete?	—	Go to Diagnostic System Check	—
21	Repair the wiring damage in CKT 873 or CKT 830. If the wiring damage is found in the left front wheel speed sensor jumper harness the left front wheel speed jumper harness must be replaced. Is the repair complete?	—	Go to Diagnostic System Check	—
22	Repair the connector damage in CKT 873 or CKT 830. If the connector damage is found in the left front wheel speed sensor jumper harness the left front wheel speed jumper harness must be replaced. Is the repair complete?	—	Go to Diagnostic System Check	—
23	Repair the open or high resistance in CKT 873. If the open or high resistance is found in the left front wheel speed sensor jumper harness the left front wheel speed jumper harness must be replaced. Is the repair complete?	—	Go to Diagnostic System Check	—
24	Repair the open or high resistance in CKT 830. If the open or high resistance is found in the left front wheel speed sensor jumper harness the left front wheel speed jumper harness must be replaced. Is the repair complete?	—	Go to Diagnostic System Check	—
25	Repair the short to ground in CKT 873. If the short to ground is found in the left front wheel speed sensor jumper harness the left front wheel speed jumper harness must be replaced. Is the repair complete?	—	Go to Diagnostic System Check	—

GC402970324900DX

Fig. 164 Code C1232: LH Front Wheel Speed Sensor Circuit Open Or Shorted (Part 4 of 5). Intrigue, Lumina & Monte Carlo

Step	Action	Value(s)	Yes	No
6	Using J 39200, measure the voltage between the 24-way EBTCM harness connector C1 terminal A5 and ground. Is the voltage within the specified range?	0-1V	Go to Step 31	Go to Step 20
7	1. Turn the ignition switch to the OFF position. 2. Inspect the 24-way EBTCM connector C1 terminal A5 and the 24-way EBTCM connector C1 terminal B4 for signs of terminal damage, poor terminal contact or terminal corrosion that would result in an open circuit, a short to voltage or a short to ground. 3. Inspect the remaining terminals of the 24-way EBTCM connector C1 for signs of terminal damage, poor terminal contact or terminal corrosion. Are there signs of poor terminal contact, terminal corrosion, or damaged terminals?	—	Go to Step 27	Go to Step 8
8	Inspect the wiring for CKT 873 and CKT 830 for signs of wire damage that would result in an open circuit, a short to voltage or a short to ground on CKT 873 and CKT 830. Are there any signs of damaged wiring?	—	Go to Step 21	Go to Step 9
9	Inspect the harness connectors for CKT 873 and CKT 830 for signs of damage that would result in an open circuit, a short to voltage or a short to ground on CKT 873 and CKT 830. Are there any signs of damaged connectors?	—	Go to Step 22	Go to Step 10
10	1. Reconnect the 24-way EBTCM connector C1. 2. Reconnect the left front wheel speed sensor harness connector. 3. Install a scan tool. 4. Test drive the vehicle above 24 km/h (15 mph) for at least 30 seconds. 5. Using the scan tool, read the DTCs. Does DTC C1232 set as a current DTC?	—	Go to Step 30	Go to Step 31
11	1. Disconnect the left front wheel speed sensor directly at left front wheel speed sensor connector. 2. Using J 39200, measure the resistance between the 24-way EBTCM connector C1 terminal B4 and the left front wheel speed sensor harness connector terminal B. Is the resistance within the specified range?	0-2 Ω	Go to Step 12	Go to Step 23
12	Using J 39200, measure the resistance between the 24-way EBTCM connector C1 terminal A5 and the left front wheel speed sensor harness connector terminal A. Is the resistance within the specified range?	0-2 Ω	Go to Step 13	Go to Step 24
13	Using J 39200, measure the resistance between the left front wheel speed sensor connector terminal A and the left front wheel speed sensor connector terminal B. Is the resistance within the specified range?	1020-1137 Ω at 20°C (68°F)	Go to Step 31	Go to Step 28
14	1. Disconnect connector C171. 2. Using J 39200, measure the resistance between the 24-way EBTCM connector C1 terminal B4 and ground. Is the resistance within the specified range?	OL (Infinite)	Go to Step 15	Go to Step 25

GC402970324900CX

Fig. 164 Code C1232: LH Front Wheel Speed Sensor Circuit Open Or Shorted (Part 3 of 5). Intrigue, Lumina & Monte Carlo

Step	Action	Value(s)	Yes	No
26	Repair the short to ground in CKT 830. If the short to ground is found in the left front wheel speed sensor jumper harness the left front wheel speed jumper harness must be replaced. Is the repair complete?	—	Go to Diagnostic System Check	—
27	Replace all terminals or connectors that exhibit signs of poor terminal contact, corrosion, or damaged terminal(s). Is the repair complete?	—	Go to Diagnostic System Check	—
28	Replace the left front wheel speed sensor. Is the repair complete?	—	Go to Diagnostic System Check	—
29	Replace the left front wheel speed sensor jumper harness. Is the repair complete?	—	Go to Diagnostic System Check	—
30	Replace EBTCM. Is the repair complete?	—	Go to Diagnostic System Check	—
31	Malfunction is intermittent or not present at this time. Inspect all connectors and harnesses for damage that may result in an open or high resistance, short to ground or short to voltage. Jumper harness must be replaced if damaged. Refer to Diagnostic Aids for more information.	—	—	—

GC402970324900EX

Fig. 164 Code C1232: LH Front Wheel Speed Sensor Circuit Open Or Shorted (Part 5 of 5). Intrigue, Lumina & Monte Carlo

Circuit Description

As a toothed ring passes by the wheel speed sensor, changes in the electromagnetic field cause the wheel speed sensor to produce a sinusoidal (AC) voltage signal whose frequency is proportional to wheel speed. The magnitude of this signal is directly related to wheel speed and the proximity of the wheel speed sensor to the toothed ring, often referred to as the air gap.

Conditions for Setting the DTC

DTC C1233 can be set anytime after initialization. If either of the right front wheel speed sensor circuits are open or shorted to voltage or ground, a malfunction exists.

Action Taken When the DTC Sets

A malfunction DTC is stored and ABS/ETS is disabled, and the amber ABS warning indicator is turned on.

Conditions for Clearing DTC

The condition for the DTC is no longer present and the scan tool CLEAR DTCs function is used, or 100 drive cycles have passed with no DTCs detected.

Diagnostic Aids

An intermittent malfunction may be caused by a poor connection, rubbed-through wire insulation, or a wire that is broken inside the insulation.

The frequency of the malfunction can be checked by using the enhanced diagnostic function of the scan tool, as described in Scan Tool Diagnostics in this section.

If the customer's comments reflect that the amber ABS warning indicator is on only during moist environmental changes (rain, snow, vehicle wash), all wheel speed sensor circuitry should be thoroughly inspected for signs of water intrusion. If DTC is not current, clear DTCs and simulate the effects of water intrusion. Use the following procedure. Spray the suspected area with a 5 percent salt water solution (two teaspoons of salt to 355 ml[12 ounces] of water). Test drive vehicle over various road surfaces (bumps, turns, etc.) above 24 km/h (15 mph) for at least 30 seconds. If DTC returns, replace suspected harness.

Any circuitry that is suspected of causing the intermittent complaint should be thoroughly checked for backed-out terminals, improper mating, broken locks, improperly formed or damaged terminals, poor terminal to wiring connections, or physical damage to the wiring harness.

Resistance of the wheel speed sensor will increase with an increase in sensor temperature.

When replacing a wheel speed sensor, inspect the sensor terminals and harness connector for corrosion and/or water intrusion. If evidence of corrosion or water intrusion exists, replace wheel speed sensor jumper harness. Likewise, if replacing a wheel speed sensor jumper harness, inspect sensor terminals. If evidence of corrosion or water intrusion exists, replace wheel speed sensor.

GC402970324901AX

Fig. 165 Code C1233: RH Front Wheel Speed Sensor Circuit Open Or Shorted (Part 1 of 5). Intrigue, Lumina & Monte Carlo

Important

- J 39200 test leads must be zeroed prior to making any resistance measurements. Refer to J 39200 user's manual.

Important

- Wheel speed sensor intermittent malfunctions may be difficult to locate. Care should be taken not to disturb any electrical connections prior to an indicated step of the diagnosis table. This will ensure that an intermittent condition will not be corrected before the source of the malfunction is found.

FRONT WHEEL SPEED SENSOR RESISTANCE

This table contains resistance values for the front wheel speed sensors at varying temperatures for use in diagnosis. The values are approximate and should be used as a guideline for diagnosis.

TEMP. (°C)	TEMP. (°F)	RESISTANCE (OHMS)
-34 to 4	-30 to 40	804 to 1066
5 to 43	41 to 110	956 to 1240
44 to 93	111 to 200	1112 to 1463

Step	Action	Value(s)	Yes	No
1	Was the Diagnostic System Check performed?	—	Go to Step 2	Go to Diagnostic System Check
2	1. Turn the ignition switch to the OFF position. 2. Using a 5 percent salt water solution (two teaspoons of salt to 355 ml [12 ounces] of water), thoroughly spray the right front wheel speed sensor jumper harness. 3. Disconnect the 24-way EBTCM harness connector C1. 4. Using J 39200, measure the resistance between the 24-way EBTCM harness connector C1 terminal A4 and the 24-way EBTCM harness connector C1 terminal B3. Is the resistance within the specified range?	1020-1137 Ω at 20°C (68°F)	Go to Step 3	Go to Step 11
3	Using J 39200, measure the resistance between the 24-way EBTCM harness connector C1 terminal B3 and ground. Is the resistance within the specified range?	OL (Infinite)	Go to Step 4	Go to Step 14
4	1. Turn the ignition switch to the RUN position, engine off. 2. Using J 39200, measure the voltage between the 24-way EBTCM harness connector C1 terminal B3 and ground. Is the voltage within the specified range?	0-1V	Go to Step 7	Go to Step 5
5	1. Turn the ignition switch to the OFF position. 2. Disconnect the right front wheel speed sensor at the right front wheel speed sensor connector. 3. Turn the ignition switch to the RUN position, engine off. 4. Using J 39200, measure the voltage between the 24-way EBTCM harness connector C1 terminal B3 and ground. Is the voltage within the specified range?	0-1V	Go to Step 6	Go to Step 19

GC402970324900FX

Fig. 165 Code C1233: RH Front Wheel Speed Sensor Circuit Open Or Shorted (Part 2 of 5). Intrigue, Lumina & Monte Carlo

Step	Action	Value(s)	Yes	No
6	Using J 39200, measure the voltage between the 24-way EBTCM harness connector C1 terminal A4 and ground. Is the voltage within the specified range?	0-1V	Go to Step 31	Go to Step 20
7	1. Turn the ignition switch to the OFF position. 2. Inspect the 24-way EBTCM connector C1 terminal A4 and the 24-way EBTCM connector C1 terminal B3 for signs of terminal damage, poor terminal contact or terminal corrosion that would result in an open circuit, a short to voltage or a short to ground. 3. Inspect the remaining terminals of the 24-way EBTCM connector C1 for signs of terminal damage, poor terminal contact or terminal corrosion. Are there signs of poor terminal contact, terminal corrosion, or damaged terminals?	—	Go to Step 27	Go to Step 8
8	Inspect the wiring for CKT 833 and CKT 872 for signs of wire damage that would result in an open circuit, a short to voltage or a short to ground on CKT 833 and CKT 872. Are there any signs of damaged wiring?	—	Go to Step 21	Go to Step 9
9	Inspect the harness connectors for CKT 833 and CKT 872 for signs of damage that would result in an open circuit, a short to voltage or a short to ground on CKT 833 and CKT 872. Are there any signs of damaged connectors?	—	Go to Step 22	Go to Step 10
10	1. Reconnect the 24-way EBTCM connector C1. 2. Reconnect the right front wheel speed sensor harness connector. 3. Install a scan tool. 4. Test drive the vehicle above 24 km/h (15 mph) for at least 30 seconds. 5. Using the scan tool, read the DTCs. Does DTC C1233 set as a current DTC?	—	Go to Step 30	Go to Step 31
11	1. Disconnect the right front wheel speed sensor directly at right front wheel speed sensor connector. 2. Using J 39200, measure the resistance between the 24-way EBTCM connector C1 terminal B3 and the right front wheel speed sensor harness connector terminal B. Is the resistance within the specified range?	0-2 Ω	Go to Step 12	Go to Step 23
12	Using J 39200, measure the resistance between the 24-way EBTCM connector C1 terminal A4 and the right front wheel speed sensor harness connector terminal A. Is the resistance within the specified range?	0-2 Ω	Go to Step 13	Go to Step 24
13	Using J 39200, measure the resistance between the right front wheel speed sensor connector terminal A and the right front wheel speed sensor connector terminal B. Is the resistance within the specified range?	1020-1137 Ω at 20°C (68°F)	Go to Step 31	Go to Step 28
14	1. Disconnect connector C172. 2. Using J 39200, measure the resistance between the 24-way EBTCM connector C1 terminal B3 and ground. Is the resistance within the specified range?	OL (Infinite)	Go to Step 15	Go to Step 25

GC402970324900GX

Fig. 165 Code C1233: RH Front Wheel Speed Sensor Circuit Open Or Shorted (Part 3 of 5). Intrigue, Lumina & Monte Carlo

Step	Action	Value(s)	Yes	No
15	Using J 39200, measure the resistance between the 24-way EBTCM connector C1 terminal A4 and ground. Is the resistance within the specified range?	OL (Infinite)	Go to Step 16	Go to Step 26
16	1. Thoroughly re-spray the right front wheel speed sensor jumper harness with the salt water solution. 2. Disconnect the right front wheel speed sensor directly at the right front wheel speed sensor. 3. Using J 39200, measure the resistance between the right front wheel speed sensor jumper harness connector terminal A and ground. Is the resistance within the specified range?	OL (Infinite)	Go to Step 17	Go to Step 29
17	Using J 39200, measure the resistance between the right front wheel speed sensor jumper harness connector terminal B and ground. Is the resistance within the specified range?	OL (Infinite)	Go to Step 18	Go to Step 29
18	Using J 39200, measure the resistance between the right front wheel speed sensor connector terminal A and ground. Is the resistance within the specified range?	OL (Infinite)	Go to Step 31	Go to Step 28
19	Repair the short to voltage in CKT 833. If the short to voltage is found in the right front wheel speed sensor jumper harness the right front wheel speed jumper harness must be replaced. Is the repair complete?	—	Go to Diagnostic System Check	—
20	Repair the short to voltage in CKT 872. If the short to voltage is found in the right front wheel speed sensor jumper harness the right front wheel speed jumper harness must be replaced. Is the repair complete?	—	Go to Diagnostic System Check	—
21	Repair the wiring damage in CKT 833 or CKT 872. If the wiring damage is found in the right front wheel speed sensor jumper harness the right front wheel speed jumper harness must be replaced. Is the repair complete?	—	Go to Diagnostic System Check	—
22	Repair the connector damage in CKT 833 or CKT 872. If the connector damage is found in the right front wheel speed sensor jumper harness the right front wheel speed jumper harness must be replaced. Is the repair complete?	—	Go to Diagnostic System Check	—
23	Repair the open or high resistance in CKT 833. If the open or high resistance is found in the right front wheel speed sensor jumper harness the right front wheel speed jumper harness must be replaced. Is the repair complete?	—	Go to Diagnostic System Check	—
24	Repair the open or high resistance in CKT 872. If the open or high resistance is found in the right front wheel speed sensor jumper harness the right front wheel speed jumper harness must be replaced. Is the repair complete?	—	Go to Diagnostic System Check	—
25	Repair the short to ground in CKT 833. If the short to ground is found in the right front wheel speed sensor jumper harness the right front wheel speed jumper harness must be replaced. Is the repair complete?	—	Go to Diagnostic System Check	—

GC402970324900HX

Fig. 165 Code C1233: RH Front Wheel Speed Sensor Circuit Open Or Shorted (Part 4 of 5). Intrigue, Lumina & Monte Carlo

Step	Action	Value(s)	Yes	No
26	Repair the short to ground in CKT 872. If the short to ground is found in the right front wheel speed sensor jumper harness the right front wheel speed jumper harness must be replaced. Is the repair complete?	—	Go to Diagnostic System Check	—
27	Replace all terminals or connectors that exhibit signs of poor terminal contact, corrosion, or damaged terminal(s). Is the repair complete?	—	Go to Diagnostic System Check	—
28	Replace the right front wheel speed sensor. Is the repair complete?	—	Go to Diagnostic System Check	—
29	Replace the right front wheel speed sensor jumper harness. Is the repair complete?	—	Go to Diagnostic System Check	—
30	Replace EBTCM. Is the repair complete?	—	Go to Diagnostic System Check	—
31	Malfunction is intermittent or not present at this time. Inspect all connectors and harnesses for damage that may result in an open or high resistance, short to ground or short to voltage. Jumper harness must be replaced if damaged. Refer to Diagnostic Aids for more information.	—	—	—

GC402970324900IX

Fig. 165 Code C1233: RH Front Wheel Speed Sensor Circuit Open Or Shorted (Part 5 of 5). Intrigue, Lumina & Monte Carlo

Circuit Description

As a toothed ring passes by the wheel speed sensor, changes in the electromagnetic field cause the wheel speed sensor to produce a AC voltage signal. The frequency of the sinusoidal (AC) voltage signal is proportional to the wheel speed. The amplitude of the AC voltage signal is directly related to wheel speed and the proximity of the wheel speed sensor to the toothed ring. The proximity of the wheel speed sensor to the toothed ring is also referred to as the air gap.

Conditions for Setting the DTC

DTC C1234 can set anytime after initialization.

A malfunction exists if either of the left rear wheel speed sensor circuits are open or shorted to voltage or ground.

Action Taken When the DTC Sets

- A malfunction DTC stores.
- The ABS disables.
- The amber ABS warning indicators turn on.

Conditions for Clearing the DTC

- The condition responsible for setting the DTC no longer exists and the Scan Tool Clear DTCs function is used.
- 100 drive cycles pass with no DTCs detected.

Diagnostic Aids

The following conditions may cause an intermittent malfunction:

- A poor connection
- Rubbed-through wire insulation
- A broken wire inside the insulation

Use the enhanced diagnostic function of the Scan Tool in order to measure the frequency of the malfunction.

If the customer's comments reflect that the amber ABS warning indicator is on only during moist environmental changes (rain, snow, vehicle wash), inspect all the wheel speed sensor circuitry for signs of water intrusion. If the DTC is not current, clear all DTCs and simulate the effects of water intrusion by using the following procedure:

1. Spray the suspected area with a five percent saltwater solution.
   Add two teaspoons of salt to twelve ounces of water to make a five percent saltwater solution.
2. Test drive the vehicle over various road surfaces (bumps, turns, etc.) above 24 km/h (15 mph) for at least 30 seconds.
3. If the DTC returns, replace the suspected harness.

GC4029903830010X

Fig. 166 Code C1234: LH Rear Wheel Speed Sensor Circuit Open Or Shorted (Part 1 of 5). Intrigue, Lumina & Monte Carlo

Thoroughly inspect any circuitry that may be causing the intermittent complaint for the following conditions:

- Backed out terminals
- Improper mating
- Broken locks
- Improperly formed or damaged terminals
- Poor terminal-to-wiring connections
- Physical damage to the wiring harness

Resistance of the wheel speed sensor will increase with an increase in sensor temperature.

Use the following procedure in order to replace a wheel speed sensor:

1. Inspect the wheel speed sensor terminals and harness connector for corrosion and/or water intrusion.
2. Replace the wheel speed sensor if evidence of corrosion or water intrusion exists.

Use the following procedure in order to replace the wheel speed sensor jumper harness:

1. Inspect the wheel speed sensor jumper harness terminals for corrosion and/or water intrusion.
2. Replace the wheel speed sensor jumper harness if evidence of corrosion or water intrusion exists.

Rear Wheel Speed Sensor Resistance

The following table contains resistance values for the rear wheel speed sensors at varying temperatures for use in diagnosis. The values are approximate and should be used as a guideline for diagnosis.

Temperature (°C)	Temperature (°F)	Resistance (Ohms)
-34 to 4	-30 to 40	800 to 1100
5 to 43	41 to 110	950 to 1300
44 to 93	111 to 200	1100 to 1600

Important: Zero the *J 39200* test leads before making any resistance measurements.

Important: Difficulty may occur when trying to locate intermittent malfunctions in the wheel speed sensor.

Do not disturb any of the electrical connections. Change the electrical connections only when instructed to do so by a step in the diagnostic table.

Changing the electrical connections at the correct time will ensure that an intermittent electrical connection will not be corrected until the source of the malfunction is found.

Step	Action	Value(s)	Yes	No
1	Was the Diagnostic System Check performed?	—	*Go to Step 2*	Go to *ABS Diagnostic System Check*
2	1. Turn the ignition switch to the OFF position. 2. Make a 5 percent saltwater solution. 3. Thoroughly spray the left rear wheel speed sensor jumper harness with the saltwater solution. 4. Disconnect the 24-way EBCM harness connector C1. 5. Use the *J 39200* in order to measure the resistance between the 24-way EBCM harness connector C1 terminal A3 and terminal B2. Is the resistance within the specified range?	1020–1137 Ω at 20°C (68°F)	*Go to Step 3*	*Go to Step 11*
3	Use the *J 39200* in order to measure the resistance between the 24-way EBCM harness connector C1 terminal B2 and ground. Is the resistance within the specified range?	OL (Infinite)	*Go to Step 4*	*Go to Step 14*
4	1. Turn the ignition switch to the ON position. Do not start the engine. 2. Use the *J 39200* in order to measure the voltage between the 24-way EBCM harness connector C1 terminal B2 and ground. Is the voltage within the specified range?	0–1 V	*Go to Step 7*	*Go to Step 5*

GC4029903830020X

Fig. 166 Code C1234: LH Rear Wheel Speed Sensor Circuit Open Or Shorted (Part 2 of 5). Intrigue, Lumina & Monte Carlo

Step	Action	Value(s)	Yes	No
5	1. Turn the ignition switch to the OFF position. 2. Disconnect the left rear wheel speed sensor at the left front wheel speed sensor connector. 3. Turn the ignition switch to the ON position. Do not start the engine. 4. Use the *J 39200* in order to measure the voltage between the 24-way EBCM harness connector C1 terminal B2 and ground. Is the voltage within the specified range?	0–1 V	*Go to Step 6*	*Go to Step 19*
6	Use the *J 39200* in order to measure the voltage between the 24-way EBCM harness connector C1 terminal A3 and ground. Is the voltage within the specified range?	0–1 V	*Go to Step 28*	*Go to Step 19*
7	1. Turn the ignition switch to the OFF position. 2. Inspect the following terminals: • The 24-way EBCM connector C1 terminal A3 and terminal B2 • The all of the remaining terminals of the 24-way EBCM connector C1 3. Inspect the above terminals for the following conditions: • Terminal damage • Poor terminal contact • Terminal corrosion. Damage, terminal corrosion, and poor terminal contact may cause an open circuit, a short to voltage, or a short to ground. Are there signs of poor terminal contact, terminal corrosion, or damaged terminals?	—	*Go to Step 24*	*Go to Step 8*
8	Inspect the wiring of CKT 884 and CKT 885 for signs of wire damage. Wire damage may cause the following conditions in CKT 884 and CKT 885: • An open circuit • A short to voltage • A short to ground. Are there signs of damaged wiring?	—	*Go to Step 20*	*Go to Step 9*
9	Inspect the harness connectors of CKT 884 and CKT 885 for signs of wire damage. Wire damage may cause the following conditions in CKT 884 and CKT 885: • An open circuit • A short to voltage • A short to ground. Are there signs of damaged connectors?	—	*Go to Step 21*	*Go to Step 10*
10	1. Reconnect the 24-way EBCM connector C1. 2. Reconnect the left rear wheel speed sensor harness connector. 3. Install a scan tool. 4. Test drive the vehicle at a speed above 24 km/h (15 mph) for at least 30 seconds. 5. Use the scan tool in order to read the DTCs. Does DTC C1234 set as a current DTC?	—	*Go to Step 27*	*Go to Step 28*

GC4029903830030X

Fig. 166 Code C1234: LH Rear Wheel Speed Sensor Circuit Open Or Shorted (Part 3 of 5). Intrigue, Lumina & Monte Carlo

Step	Action	Value(s)	Yes	No
11	1. Disconnect the left rear wheel speed sensor directly at the left rear wheel speed sensor connector. 2. Use the *J 39200* in order to measure the resistance between the 24-way EBCM connector C1 terminal B2 and the rear wheel speed sensor harness connector terminal A. Is the resistance within the specified range?	0–2 Ω	*Go to Step 12*	*Go to Step 22*
12	Use the *J 39200* in order to measure the resistance between the 24-way EBCM connector C1 terminal A3 and the rear wheel speed sensor harness connector terminal B. Is the resistance within the specified range?	0–2 Ω	*Go to Step 13*	*Go to Step 22*
13	Use the *J 39200* in order to measure the resistance between the left rear wheel speed sensor connector terminal A and the rear wheel speed sensor connector terminal B. Is the resistance within the specified range?	1020–1137 Ω at 20°C (68°F)	*Go to Step 28*	*Go to Step 25*
14	1. Disconnect the connector C200. 2. Use the *J 39200* in order to measure the resistance between the 24-way EBCM connector C1 terminal B2 and ground. Is the resistance within the specified range?	OL (Infinite)	*Go to Step 15*	*Go to Step 23*
15	Use the *J 39200* in order to measure the resistance between the 24-way EBCM connector C1 terminal A3 and ground. Is the resistance within the specified range?	OL (Infinite)	*Go to Step 16*	*Go to Step 23*
16	1. Thoroughly respray the left rear wheel speed sensor jumper harness with the saltwater solution. 2. Disconnect the left rear wheel speed sensor directly at the left rear wheel speed sensor. 3. Use the *J 39200* in order to measure the resistance between the left rear wheel speed sensor jumper harness connector terminal A and ground. Is the resistance within the specified range?	OL (Infinite)	*Go to Step 17*	*Go to Step 26*
17	Use the *J 39200* in order to measure the resistance between the left rear wheel speed sensor jumper harness connector terminal B and ground. Is the resistance within the specified range?	OL (Infinite)	*Go to Step 18*	*Go to Step 26*
18	Use the *J 39200* in order to measure the resistance between the left rear wheel speed sensor jumper connector terminal A and ground. Is the resistance within the specified range?	OL (Infinite)	*Go to Step 28*	*Go to Step 26*
19	Repair the short to voltage in CKT 884 or CKT 885. If the short to voltage is found in the left rear wheel speed sensor jumper harness, replace the rear wheel speed jumper harness. Is the repair complete?	—	Go to *ABS Diagnostic System Check*	—
20	Repair the wiring damage in CKT 884 or CKT 885. If the wiring damage is found in the left rear wheel speed sensor jumper harness, replace the rear wheel speed jumper harness. Is the repair complete?	—	Go to *ABS Diagnostic System Check*	—

GC4029903830040X

Fig. 166 Code C1234: LH Rear Wheel Speed Sensor Circuit Open Or Shorted (Part 4 of 5). Intrigue, Lumina & Monte Carlo

Step	Action	Value(s)	Yes	No
21	Repair the connector damage in CKT 884 or CKT 885. If the connector damage is found in the left rear wheel speed sensor jumper harness, replace the rear wheel speed jumper harness. Is the repair complete?	—	Go to *ABS Diagnostic System Check*	—
22	Repair the open or high resistance in CKT 884 or CKT 885. If the open or high resistance is found in the left rear wheel speed sensor jumper harness, replace the rear wheel speed jumper harness. Is the repair complete?	—	Go to *ABS Diagnostic System Check*	—
23	Repair the short to ground in CKT 884 or CKT 885. If the short to ground is found in the left rear wheel speed sensor jumper harness, replace the rear wheel speed jumper harness. Is the repair complete?	—	Go to *ABS Diagnostic System Check*	—
24	Replace all of the terminals and the connectors that exhibit signs of poor terminal contact, corrosion, or damaged terminals. Is the repair complete?	—	Go to *ABS Diagnostic System Check*	—
25	Replace the left rear wheel speed sensor. Is the repair complete?	—	Go to *ABS Diagnostic System Check*	—
26	Replace the rear wheel speed sensor jumper harness. Is the repair complete?	—	Go to *ABS Diagnostic System Check*	—
27	Replace the EBCM. Is the repair complete?	—	Go to *ABS Diagnostic System Check*	—
28	Is the malfunction intermittent or not present at this time?	—	Go to Diagnostic Aids	—

GC4029903830050X

Fig. 166 Code C1234: LH Rear Wheel Speed Sensor Circuit Open Or Shorted (Part 5 of 5). Intrigue, Lumina & Monte Carlo

Circuit Description

As a toothed ring passes by the wheel speed sensor, changes in the electromagnetic field cause the wheel speed sensor to produce a AC voltage signal. The frequency of the sinusoidal (AC) voltage signal is proportional to the wheel speed. The amplitude of the AC voltage signal is directly related to wheel speed and the proximity of the wheel speed sensor to the toothed ring. The proximity of the wheel speed sensor to the toothed ring is also referred to as the air gap.

Conditions for Setting the DTC

DTC C1235 can set anytime after initialization.

A malfunction exists if either of the right rear wheel speed sensor circuits are open or shorted to voltage or ground.

Action Taken When the DTC Sets

- A malfunction DTC stores.
- The ABS disables.
- The amber ABS warning indicators turn on.

Conditions for Clearing the DTC

- The condition responsible for setting the DTC no longer exists and the Scan Tool Clear DTCs function is used.
- 100 drive cycles pass with no DTCs detected.

Diagnostic Aids

The following conditions may cause an intermittent malfunction:

- A poor connection
- Rubbed-through wire insulation
- A broken wire inside the insulation

Use the enhanced diagnostic function of the Scan Tool in order to measure the frequency of the malfunction.

If the customer's comments reflect that the amber ABS warning indicator is on only during moist environmental changes (rain, snow, vehicle wash), inspect all the wheel speed sensor circuitry for signs of water intrusion. If the DTC is not current, clear all DTCs and simulate the effects of water intrusion by using the following procedure:

1. Spray the suspected area with a five percent saltwater solution.

   Add two teaspoons of salt to twelve ounces of water to make a five percent saltwater solution.
2. Test drive the vehicle over various road surfaces (bumps, turns, etc.) above 24 km/h (15 mph) for at least 30 seconds.
3. If the DTC returns, replace the suspected harness.

Thoroughly inspect any circuitry that may be causing the intermittent complaint for the following conditions:

- Backed out terminals
- Improper mating
- Broken locks
- Improperly formed or damaged terminals
- Poor terminal-to-wiring connections
- Physical damage to the wiring harness

Resistance of the wheel speed sensor will increase with an increase in sensor temperature.

Use the following procedure in order to replace a wheel speed sensor:

1. Inspect the wheel speed sensor terminals and harness connector for corrosion and/or water intrusion.
2. Replace the wheel speed sensor if evidence of corrosion or water intrusion exists.

Use the following procedure in order to replace the wheel speed sensor jumper harness:

1. Inspect the wheel speed sensor jumper harness terminals for corrosion and/or water intrusion.
2. Replace the wheel speed sensor jumper harness if evidence of corrosion or water intrusion exists.

Rear Wheel Speed Sensor Resistance

The following table contains resistance values for the rear wheel speed sensors at varying temperatures for use in diagnosis. The values are approximate and should be used as a guideline for diagnosis.

Temperature (°C)	Temperature (°F)	Resistance (Ohms)
−34 to 4	−30 to 40	800 to 1100
5 to 43	41 to 110	950 to 1300
44 to 93	111 to 200	1100 to 1600

Important: Zero the *J 39200* test leads before making any resistance measurements.

Important: Difficulty may occur when trying to locate intermittent malfunctions in the wheel speed sensor.

Do not disturb any of the electrical connections. Change the electrical connections only when instructed to do so by a step in the diagnostic table.

Changing the electrical connections at the correct time will ensure that an intermittent electrical connection will not be corrected until the source of the malfunction is found.

GC4029903831010X

Fig. 167 Code C1235: RH Rear Wheel Speed Sensor Circuit Open Or Shorted (Part 1 of 5). Intrigue, Lumina & Monte Carlo

Step	Action	Value(s)	Yes	No
1	Was the Diagnostic System Check performed?	—	*Go to Step 2*	Go to *ABS Diagnostic System Check*
2	1. Turn the ignition switch to the OFF position. 2. Make a 5 percent saltwater solution. 3. Thoroughly spray the right rear wheel speed sensor jumper harness with the saltwater solution. 4. Disconnect the 24-way EBCM harness connector C1. 5. Use the *J 39200* in order to measure the resistance between the 24-way EBCM harness connector C1 terminal A2 and terminal B1. Is the resistance within the specified range?	1020–1137 Ω at 20°C (68°F)	*Go to Step 3*	*Go to Step 11*
3	Use the *J 39200* in order to measure the resistance between the 24-way EBCM harness connector C1 terminal B1 and ground. Is the resistance within the specified range?	OL (Infinite)	*Go to Step 4*	*Go to Step 14*
4	1. Turn the ignition switch to the ON position. Do not start the engine. 2. Use the *J 39200* in order to measure the voltage between the 24-way EBCM harness connector C1 terminal B1 and ground. Is the voltage within the specified range?	0–1 V	*Go to Step 7*	*Go to Step 5*

GC4029903831020X

Fig. 167 Code C1235: RH Rear Wheel Speed Sensor Circuit Open Or Shorted (Part 2 of 5). Intrigue, Lumina & Monte Carlo

Step	Action	Value(s)	Yes	No
5	1. Turn the ignition switch to the OFF position. 2. Disconnect the right rear wheel speed sensor at the right rear wheel speed sensor connector. 3. Turn the ignition switch to the ON position. Do not start the engine. 4. Use the *J 39200* in order to measure the voltage between the 24-way EBCM harness connector C1 terminal B1 and ground Is the voltage within the specified range?	0–1 V	*Go to Step 6*	*Go to Step 19*
6	Use the *J 39200* in order to measure the voltage between the 24-way EBCM harness connector C1 terminal A2 and ground. Is the voltage within the specified range?	0–1 V	*Go to Step 28*	*Go to Step 19*
7	1. Turn the ignition switch to the OFF position. 2. Inspect the following terminals: • The 24-way EBCM connector C1 terminal A2 and terminal B1 • The all of the remaining terminals of the 24-way EBCM connector C1 3. Inspect the above terminals for the following conditions: • Terminal damage • Poor terminal contact • Terminal corrosion Damage, terminal corrosion, and poor terminal contact may cause an open circuit, a short to voltage, or a short to ground. Are there signs of poor terminal contact, terminal corrosion, or damaged terminals?	—	*Go to Step 24*	*Go to Step 8*
8	Inspect the wiring of CKT 882 and CKT 883 for signs of wire damage. Wire damage may cause the following conditions in CKT 882 and CKT 883: • An open circuit • A short to voltage • A short to ground Are there signs of damaged wiring?	—	*Go to Step 20*	*Go to Step 9*
9	Inspect the harness connectors of CKT 882 and CKT 883 for signs of wire damage. Wire damage may cause the following conditions in CKT 882 and CKT 883: • An open circuit • A short to voltage • A short to ground Are there signs of damaged connectors?	—	*Go to Step 21*	*Go to Step 10*
10	1. Reconnect the 24-way EBCM connector C1. 2. Reconnect the right rear wheel speed sensor harness connector. 3. Install a scan tool. 4. Test drive the vehicle at a speed above 24 km/h (15 mph) for at least 30 seconds. 5. Use the scan tool in order to read the DTCs. Does DTC C1235 set as a current DTC?	—	*Go to Step 27*	*Go to Step 28*

GC4029903831030X

Fig. 167 Code C1235: RH Rear Wheel Speed Sensor Circuit Open Or Shorted (Part 3 of 5). Intrigue, Lumina & Monte Carlo

Step	Action	Value(s)	Yes	No
11	1. Disconnect the right rear wheel speed sensor directly at the right rear wheel speed sensor connector. 2. Use the *J 39200* in order to measure the resistance between the 24-way EBCM connector C1 terminal B1 and the rear wheel speed sensor harness connector terminal A. Is the resistance within the specified range?	0–2 Ω	*Go to Step 12*	*Go to Step 22*
12	Use the *J 39200* in order to measure the resistance between the 24-way EBCM connector C1 terminal A2 and the rear wheel speed sensor harness connector terminal B. Is the resistance within the specified range?	0–2 Ω	*Go to Step 13*	*Go to Step 22*
13	Use the *J 39200* in order to measure the resistance between the right rear wheel speed sensor connector terminal A and the rear wheel speed sensor connector terminal B. Is the resistance within the specified range?	1020–1137 Ω at 20°C (68°F)	*Go to Step 28*	*Go to Step 25*
14	1. Disconnect the connector C200. 2. Use the *J 39200* in order to measure the resistance between the 24-way EBCM connector C1 terminal B1 and ground. Is the resistance within the specified range?	OL (Infinite)	*Go to Step 15*	*Go to Step 23*
15	Use the *J 39200* in order to measure the resistance between the 24-way EBCM connector C1 terminal A2 and ground. Is the resistance within the specified range?	OL (Infinite)	*Go to Step 16*	*Go to Step 23*
16	1. Thoroughly respray the right rear wheel speed sensor jumper harness with the saltwater solution. 2. Disconnect the right rear wheel speed sensor directly at the right rear wheel speed sensor. 3. Use the *J 39200* in order to measure the resistance between the right rear wheel speed sensor jumper harness connector terminal A and ground. Is the resistance within the specified range?	OL (Infinite)	*Go to Step 17*	*Go to Step 26*
17	Use the *J 39200* in order to measure the resistance between the right rear wheel speed sensor jumper harness connector terminal B and ground. Is the resistance within the specified range?	OL (Infinite)	*Go to Step 18*	*Go to Step 26*
18	Use the *J 39200* in order to measure the resistance between the right rear wheel speed sensor jumper connector terminal A and ground. Is the resistance within the specified range?	OL (Infinite)	*Go to Step 28*	*Go to Step 26*
19	Repair the short to voltage in CKT 882 or CKT 883. If the short to voltage is found in the right rear wheel speed sensor jumper harness, replace the rear wheel speed jumper harness. Is the repair complete?	—	Go to *ABS Diagnostic System Check*	—
20	Repair the wiring damage in CKT 882 or CKT 883. If the wiring damage is found in the right rear wheel speed sensor jumper harness, replace the rear wheel speed jumper harness. Is the repair complete?	—	Go to *ABS Diagnostic System Check*	—

GC4029903831040X

Fig. 167 Code C1235: RH Rear Wheel Speed Sensor Circuit Open Or Shorted (Part 4 of 5). Intrigue, Lumina & Monte Carlo

Step	Action	Value(s)	Yes	No
21	Repair the connector damage in CKT 882 or CKT 883. If the connector damage is found in the right rear wheel speed sensor jumper harness, replace the rear wheel speed jumper harness. Is the repair complete?	—	Go to *ABS Diagnostic System Check*	—
22	Repair the open or high resistance in CKT 882 or CKT 883. If the open or high resistance is found in the right rear wheel speed sensor jumper harness, replace the rear wheel speed jumper harness. Is the repair complete?	—	Go to *ABS Diagnostic System Check*	—
23	Repair the short to ground in CKT 882 or CKT 883. If the short to ground is found in the right rear wheel speed sensor jumper harness, replace the rear wheel speed jumper harness. Is the repair complete?	—	Go to *ABS Diagnostic System Check*	—
24	Replace all of the terminals and the connectors that exhibit signs of poor terminal contact, corrosion, or damaged terminals. Is the repair complete?	—	Go to *ABS Diagnostic System Check*	—
25	Replace the right rear wheel speed sensor. Is the repair complete?	—	Go to *ABS Diagnostic System Check*	—
26	Replace the rear wheel speed sensor jumper harness. Is the repair complete?	—	Go to *ABS Diagnostic System Check*	—
27	Replace the EBCM. Is the repair complete?	—	Go to *ABS Diagnostic System Check*	—
28	Is the malfunction intermittent or not present at this time?	—	Go to Diagnostic Aids	—

GC4029903831050X

Fig. 167 Code C1235: RH Rear Wheel Speed Sensor Circuit Open Or Shorted (Part 5 of 5). Intrigue, Lumina & Monte Carlo

Circuit Description

DTC C1236 monitors the voltage level available to the EBCM controller. If the voltage drops below 11.4 volts, full performance of the ABS system is not guaranteed. During ABS operation, there are several current requirements that will cause battery voltage at the EBCM to drop. As a result, voltage is monitored prior to an ABS event to indicate good charging system condition. Voltage is also monitored during an ABS event when voltage may drop significantly.

Conditions for Setting the DTC

DTC C1236 can set only if the vehicle's speed is greater than 5 km/h (3 mph).

A malfunction exists if the switched battery voltage is less than 11.4 volts during a non-ABS event or less than 8.4 volts during an ABS event.

Action Taken When the DTC Sets

- A malfunction DTC stores.
- The ABS disables.
- The amber ABS warning indicators turn on.
- The red BRAKE warning indicator turns on if the rear piston in the ABS brake motor pack is not in the home position.

Conditions for Clearing the DTC

- The condition responsible for setting the DTC no longer exists and the Scan Tool Clear DTCs function is used.
- 100 drive cycles pass with no DTCs detected.

Diagnostic Aids

The following conditions may cause an intermittent malfunction:

- A poor connection
- Rubbed-through wire insulation
- A broken wire inside the insulation

Use the enhanced diagnostic function of the Scan Tool in order to measure the frequency of the malfunction.

Thoroughly inspect any circuitry that may be causing the intermittent complaint for the following conditions:

- Backed out terminals
- Improper mating
- Improperly formed or damaged terminals
- Poor terminal-to-wiring connections
- Physical damage to the wiring harness

GC4029903832010X

Fig. 168 Code C1236: Low System Supply Voltage (Part 1 of 3). Intrigue, Lumina & Monte Carlo

While performing a Voltage Load test, CKT 341 should be measured for high resistance or an open condition if it is noted that only the ignition voltage drops below acceptable voltage levels.

Important: Zero the *J 39200* test leads before making any resistance measurements.

Step	Action	Value(s)	Yes	No
1	Was the Diagnostic System Check performed?	—	*Go to Step 2*	Go to *ABS Diagnostic System Check*
2	1. Turn the ignition switch to the ON position. Do not start the engine. 2. Select Snapshot on the scan tool. 3. Select Single DTC on the scan tool. 4. Enter C1236 on the scan tool. 5. Drive the vehicle at a speed above 5 km/h (3 mph). Does DTC C1236 set as a current DTC?	—	*Go to Step 9*	*Go to Step 3*
3	1. Turn the ignition switch to the ON position. 2. Select Special Functions on the scan tool. 3. Use the scan tool in order to perform the Voltage Load test. Are the ignition voltage and the battery voltage equal to or greater than the specified range?	10 V	*Go to Step 4*	*Go to Step 9*
4	1. Turn the ignition switch to the OFF position. 2. Disconnect the 24-way EBCM connector C1. 3. Disconnect the 8-way EBCM connector C2. 4. Disconnect the Electronic Brake Control Relay. 5. Use the *J 39200* in order to measure the resistance between the Electronic Brake Control Relay harness connector terminal C8 and the 8-way EBCM connector C2 terminal C. Is the resistance within the specified range?	0–2 Ω	*Go to Step 5*	*Go to Step 10*
5	1. Disconnect the negative battery cable. 2. Disconnect the ABS Fuse (60A), located in the Engine Wiring Harness Junction Block 2. 3. Use the *J 39200* in order to measure the resistance between the ABS Fuse (60A) terminal K1 and the Electronic Brake Control Relay Harness connector terminal B10. Is the resistance within the specified range?	0–2 Ω	*Go to Step 6*	*Go to Step 11*
6	1. Remove the fuse block ABS Fuse (5A). 2. Use the *J 39200* in order to measure the resistance between the fuse block terminal D8 (ABS Fuse 5A) and the 24-way EBCM connector C1 terminal A9. Is the resistance within the specified range?	0–2 Ω	*Go to Step 7*	*Go to Step 12*

GC4029903832020X

Fig. 168 Code C1236: Low System Supply Voltage (Part 2 of 3). Intrigue, Lumina & Monte Carlo

Step	Action	Value(s)	Yes	No
7	1. Inspect the following components: • The Electronic Brake Control Relay harness connector • The 24-way EBCM connector C1 • The 8-way EBCM connector C2 • The positive battery cable connections • The negative battery cable connections 2. Inspect the above components for the following conditions: • Terminal damage • Poor terminal contact • Terminal corrosion The above conditions may cause an open circuit. Are there signs of terminal damage, poor terminal contact, or terminal corrosion?	—	*Go to Step 13*	*Go to Step 8*
8	1. Reconnect the 24-way EBCM connector C1. 2. Reconnect the 8-way EBCM connector C2. 3. Reconnect the Electronic Brake Control Relay. 4. Reconnect the negative battery cable. 5. Drive the vehicle at a speed above 5 km/h (3 mph). Does DTC C1236 set as a current DTC?	—	*Go to Step 14*	*Go to Step 15*
9	Repair the low voltage condition. Is the low voltage condition repaired?	—	Go to *ABS Diagnostic System Check*	—
10	Repair the open or high resistance in CKT 1633. Is the repair complete?	—	Go to *ABS Diagnostic System Check*	—
11	Repair the open or high resistance in CKT 542. Is the repair complete?	—	Go to *ABS Diagnostic System Check*	—
12	Repair the open or high resistance in CKT 341. Is the repair complete?	—	Go to *ABS Diagnostic System Check*	—
13	Replace all of the terminals or the connectors that exhibit signs of poor terminal contact, corrosion, or damaged terminals. Is the repair complete?	—	Go to *ABS Diagnostic System Check*	—
14	Replace the EBCM. Is the repair complete?	—	Go to *ABS Diagnostic System Check*	—
15	Is the malfunction intermittent or is not present at this time?	—	Go to Diagnostic Aids	—

GC4029903832030X

Fig. 168 Code C1236: Low System Supply Voltage (Part 3 of 3). Intrigue, Lumina & Monte Carlo

Circuit Description

This DTC is designed to detect high vehicle voltage levels prior to any required motor movement (initialization or ABS/TCS). If excessive voltage exists, demagnetization of the motor magnets may occur, which would eventually affect or eliminate ABS/TCS performance.

Conditions for Setting the DTC

DTC C1237 can only be set if the vehicle's speed is greater than 5 km/h (3 mph). If the switched battery voltage is greater than 17.1 volts, a malfunction exists.

Action Taken When the DTC Sets

A malfunction DTC is stored, ABS/TCS is disabled and the amber ABS warning indicator is turned on.

Conditions for Clearing DTC

Condition for DTC is no longer present and the scan tool (CLEAR DTCs) function is used, or 100 drive cycles have passed with no DTCs detected.

Diagnostic Aids

An intermittent malfunction may be caused by a poor connection, rubbed-through wire insulation, or a wire that is broken inside the insulation.

The frequency of the malfunction can be checked by using the enhanced diagnostic function of the Scan Tool.

Any circuitry that is suspected of causing the intermittent complaint should be thoroughly checked for backed-out terminals, improper mating, broken locks, improperly formed or damaged terminals, poor terminal to wiring connections, or physical damage to the wiring harness.

Important

- J 39200 test leads must be zeroed prior to making any resistance measurements. Refer to J 39200 user's manual.

GC402970325100AX

Fig. 169 Code C1237: High System Supply Voltage (Part 1 of 2). Intrigue, Lumina & Monte Carlo

Step	Action	Value(s)	Yes	No
1	Was the Diagnostic System Check performed?	—	Go to Step 2	Go to Diagnostic System Check
2	1. Start the engine. 2. Install a scan tool. 3. Using the scan tool, select DATA LIST. 4. Using the scan tool, select (BATTERY VOLTAGE). 5. While running engine at approximately 2000 RPM monitor the battery voltage. Is the voltage equal to or less than the specified voltage.	16V	Go to Step 6	Go to Step 3
3	1. Turn the ignition switch to the OFF position. 2. Disconnect the electronic brake control relay. 3. Start the engine. 4. Using J 39200, measure the voltage between the electronic brake control relay harness connector terminal C1 and ground. 5. While running engine at approximately 2000 RPM monitor the voltage. Is the voltage equal to or less than the specified voltage.	16V	Go to Step 4	Check Charging System Operation
4	1. Turn the ignition switch to the OFF position. 2. Reconnect the electronic brake control relay. 3. Drive the vehicle above 5 km/h (3 mph). 4. Using the scan tool, check for DTCs. Does DTC C1237 set as a current DTC?	—	Go to Step 5	Go to Step 6
5	Replace the EBTCM. Is the repair complete.	—	Go to Diagnostic System Check	—
6	Malfunction is intermittent or not present at this time. Refer to Diagnostic Aids for more information.	—	—	—

GC402970325100BX

Fig. 169 Code C1237: High System Supply Voltage (Part 2 of 2). Intrigue, Lumina & Monte Carlo

Circuit Description

This DTC is designed to detect a slipping left front ESB. During initialization and braking, the left front brake motor is rehomed. If the ESB slips, the motor/piston will move. During the next key-to-RUN initialization, a rehome of the motor verifies the motor/piston remained at the home position. If motor movement is detected, the ESB must be slipping.

Conditions for Setting the DTC

DTC C1238 can be set during brake motor initialization at 0 km/h (0 mph) with the brake off. DTC C1238 can also be set during brake motor initialization at 5 km/h (3 mph) with the brake on. If the EBTCM detects that the ESB could not hold the piston in the home position, a malfunction exists. DTC C1286 is always set with DTC C1238.

Action Taken When the DTC Sets

If an ESB cannot hold a piston in the home position, the piston may be back-driven when the brake pedal is applied, causing the brake pedal to drop. A malfunction DTC is stored and ABS/ETS is disabled, the amber ABS warning indicator and the red BRAKE warning indicator are turned on.

Conditions for Clearing DTC

The condition for the DTC is no longer present and the scan tool CLEAR DTCs function is used, or 100 drive cycles have passed with no DTCs detected.

Diagnostic Aids

An intermittent malfunction in this DTC may result from a mechanical part of the system that sticks, binds, or slips.

The frequency of the malfunction can be checked by using the enhanced diagnostic function of the scan tool, as described in Scan Tool Diagnostics in this section.

The hydraulic control modulator test function of the scan tool may be used to locate an intermittent malfunction associated with the ESB.

Important

- J 39200 test leads must be zeroed prior to making any resistance measurements. Refer to J 39200 user's manual.

After diagnosis is complete, clear the DTCs and test drive the vehicle for three drive cycles to verify that the DTC does not reset. A drive cycle consists of starting the vehicle, driving the vehicle over 16 km/h (10 mph), stopping, and then turning the ignition off.

GC402970325201AA

Fig. 170 Code C1238: LH Front ESB Will Not Hold Motor (Part 1 of 3). Intrigue, Lumina & Monte Carlo

Step	Action	Value(s)	Yes	No
1	Was the Diagnostic System Check performed?	—	Go to Step 2	Go to Diagnostic System Check
2	1. Turn the ignition switch to the RUN position, engine off. 2. Pump the brake pedal until firm to deplete the brake booster vacuum reservoir. 3. Install a scan tool. 4. Using the scan tool, select MISC TESTS. 5. Using the scan tool, select manual control function. 6. Using the scan tool, select ABS motor apply function of the left front ABS channel. 7. Using the scan tool, apply the left front ABS motor. 8. Wait five seconds. 9. Apply firm pressure to the brake pedal. Did the brake pedal fall?	—	Go to Step 9	Go to Step 3
3	Visually inspect the 6-way ABS brake motor pack connector and the 8-way EBTCM connector C2 for proper wire color/connector cavity combination. Are the proper wires located in the proper connector cavities?	—	Go to Step 4	Go to Step 10
4	1. Using the scan tool, exit the scan tool manual control function. 2. Turn the ignition switch to the OFF position. 3. Disconnect the 6-way ABS brake motor pack connector and the 8-way EBTCM connector C2. 4. Using J 39200, measure the resistance between the 6-way ABS brake motor pack harness connector terminal F and the 8-way EBTCM harness connector C2 terminal G. Is the resistance measured within the specified range?	0 - 1.5 Ω	Go to Step 5	Go to Step 11
5	Using J 39200, measure the resistance between the 6-way ABS brake motor pack harness connector terminal E and the 8-way EBTCM harness connector C2 terminal H. Is the resistance measured within the specified range?	0 - 1.5 Ω	Go to Step 6	Go to Step 12
6	Using J 39200, measure the resistance between the ABS brake motor pack connector terminal E and the ABS brake motor pack connector terminal F. Is the resistance measured within the specified range?	0.2 - 1.5 Ω	Go to Step 7	Go to Step 9
7	Inspect the 6-way ABS brake motor pack connector and the 8-way EBTCM connector C2 for poor terminal contact or corrosion. Do any of the terminals exhibit poor contact or evidence of corrosion?	—	Go to Step 13	Go to Step 8

GC402970325200BX

Fig. 170 Code C1238: LH Front ESB Will Not Hold Motor (Part 2 of 3). Intrigue, Lumina & Monte Carlo

Step	Action	Value(s)	Yes	No
8	1. Turn the ignition switch to the OFF position. 2. Reconnect the 8-way EBTCM connector C2. 3. Reconnect the ABS brake motor pack connector. 4. Start the engine with foot off the brake pedal. 5. Allow the engine to run for at least 10 seconds. 6. Repeat the above ignition cycle sequence two more times. 7. Using the scan tool, check for DTCs. Did DTC C1238 set in the last three ignition cycles?	—	Go to Step 14	Go to Step 15
9	Replace the ABS brake motor pack. Is the repair complete?	—	Go to Diagnostic System Check	—
10	Using the circuit diagram, place the proper wires into the proper connector cavities. Is the repair complete?	—	Go to Diagnostic System Check	—
11	Repair the open or high resistance in CKT 1280. Is the repair complete?	—	Go to Diagnostic System Check	—
12	Repair the open or high resistance in CKT 1281. Is the repair complete?	—	Go to Diagnostic System Check	—
13	Replace the terminals that exhibit poor terminal contact or evidence of corrosion. Is the repair complete?	—	Go to Diagnostic System Check	—
14	Replace the EBTCM. Is the repair complete?	—	Go to Diagnostic System Check	—
15	Malfunction is intermittent or not present at this time. Refer to Diagnostic Aids for more information.	—	—	—

GC402970325200CX

Fig. 170 Code C1238: LH Front ESB Will Not Hold Motor (Part 3 of 3). Intrigue, Lumina & Monte Carlo

Circuit Description

This DTC is designed to detect a slipping right front ESB. During initialization and braking, the right front motor is rehomed. If the ESB slips, the motor/piston will move. During the next key-to-RUN initialization, a rehome of the motor verifies the motor/piston remained at the home position. If motor movement is detected, the ESB must be slipping.

Conditions for Setting the DTC

DTC C1241 can be set during brake motor initialization at 0 km/h (0 mph) with the brake off. DTC C1241 can also be set during brake motor initialization at 5 km/h (3 mph) with the brake on. If the EBTCM detects that the ESB could not hold the piston in the home position, a malfunction exists. DTC C1286 is always set with DTC C1241.

Action Taken When the DTC Sets

If an ESB cannot hold a piston in the home position, the piston may be back-driven when the brake pedal is applied, causing the brake pedal to drop. A malfunction DTC is stored and ABS/ETS is disabled, the amber ABS warning indicator and the red BRAKE warning indicator are turned on.

Conditions for Clearing DTC

The condition for the DTC is no longer present and the scan tool CLEAR DTCs function is used, or 100 drive cycles have passed with no DTCs detected.

Diagnostic Aids

An intermittent malfunction in this DTC may result from a mechanical part of the system that sticks, binds, or slips.

The frequency of the malfunction can be checked by using the enhanced diagnostic function of the scan tool, as described in Scan Tool Diagnostics in this section.

The hydraulic control modulator test function of the scan tool may be used to locate an intermittent malfunction associated with the ESB.

Important

- J 39200 test leads must be zeroed prior to making any resistance measurements. Refer to J 39200 user's manual.

After diagnosis is complete, clear the DTCs and test drive the vehicle for three drive cycles to verify that the DTC does not reset. A drive cycle consists of starting the vehicle, driving the vehicle over 16 km/h (10 mph), stopping, and then turning the ignition off.

GC402970325202AX

Fig. 171 Code C1241: RH Front ESB Will Not Hold Motor (Part 1 of 3). Intrigue, Lumina & Monte Carlo

Step	Action	Value(s)	Yes	No
1	Was the Diagnostic System Check performed?	—	*Go to Step 2*	Refer to *Diagnostic System Check*
2	Inspect the following connectors for the correct wire color/connector cavity combinations: • The 6-way ABS brake motor pack connector • The 8-way EBCM/EBTCM connector C2 Are the correct wires located in the correct connector cavities?	—	*Go to Step 3*	*Go to Step 10*
3	1. Turn the ignition switch to the RUN position. Do not start the engine. 2. Pump the brake pedal until it is firm in order to deplete the brake booster vacuum reservoir. 3. Install a *Scan Tool*. 4. Select the Special Functions on the *Scan Tool*. 5. Select the Manual Control function on the *Scan Tool*. 6. Select the ABS Motor Apply function of the left front ABS channel on the *Scan Tool*. 7. Use the *Scan Tool* in order to apply the left front ABS motor. 8. Wait for five seconds. 9. Apply firm pressure to the brake pedal. Does the brake pedal fall?	—	*Go to Step 9*	*Go to Step 4*
4	1. Use the *Scan Tool* in order to exit the Manual Control function. 2. Turn the ignition switch to the OFF position. 3. Disconnect the following connectors: • The 6-way ABS brake motor pack connector • The 8-way EBCM/EBTCM connector C2 4. Use the *J 39200* in order to measure the resistance between the 6-way ABS brake motor pack harness connector terminal B and the 8-way EBCM/EBTCM harness connector C2 terminal A. Is the resistance within the specified range?	0–1.5 Ω	*Go to Step 5*	*Go to Step 11*

GC402970325200DX

Fig. 171 Code C1241: RH Front ESB Will Not Hold Motor (Part 2 of 3). Intrigue, Lumina & Monte Carlo

Step	Action	Value(s)	Yes	No
5	Use the *J 39200* in order to measure the resistance between the 6-way ABS brake motor pack harness connector terminal A and the 8-way EBCM/EBTCM harness connector C2 terminal B. Is the resistance within the specified range?	0–1.5 Ω	*Go to Step 6*	*Go to Step 12*
6	Use the *J 39200* in order to measure the resistance between the 6-way ABS brake motor pack connector terminal A and the ABS brake motor pack connector terminal B. Is the resistance within the specified range?	0.2–1.5 Ω	*Go to Step 7*	*Go to Step 9*
7	Inspect the following connectors: • The 6-way ABS brake motor pack connector • The 8-way EBCM/EBTCM connector C2 Inspect the above connectors for the following conditions: • Poor terminal contact • Corrosion Are there signs of poor terminal contact or corrosion?	—	*Go to Step 13*	*Go to Step 8*
8	1. Turn the ignition switch to the OFF position. 2. Reconnect the 8-way EBCM/EBTCM connector C2 3. Reconnect the 6-way ABS brake motor pack connector 4. Start the engine. Do not depress the brake pedal while starting the engine. 5. Allow the engine to run for at least 10 seconds. 6. Repeat the above ignition cycle sequence at least two more times. 7. Use the *Scan Tool* in order to look for DTCs. Does the DTC C1241 set during the last three ignition cycles?	—	*Go to Step 14*	*Go to Step 15*
9	Replace the ABS brake motor pack. Is the repair complete?	—	Refer to *Diagnostic System Check*	—
10	Place the correct wires into the connector cavities. Is the repair complete?	—	Refer to *Diagnostic System Check*	—
11	Repair the open or high resistance in CKT 1282. Is the repair complete?	—	Refer to *Diagnostic System Check*	—
12	Repair the open or high resistance in CKT 1283. Is the repair complete?	—	Refer to *Diagnostic System Check*	—
13	Replace the terminals that exhibit signs of poor terminal contact or corrosion. Is the repair complete?	—	Refer to *Diagnostic System Check*	—
14	Replace the EBCM/EBTCM. Is the repair complete?	—	Refer to *Diagnostic System Check*	—
15	Is the malfunction intermittent or not present at this time?	—	Refer to Diagnostic Aids	—

GC402970325200EX

Fig. 171 Code C1241: RH Front ESB Will Not Hold Motor (Part 3 of 3). Intrigue, Lumina & Monte Carlo

Clear the DTCs after completing the diagnosis. Test drive the vehicle for three drive cycles in order to verify that the DTC does not reset. Use the following procedure in order to complete one drive cycle:

1. Start the vehicle.
2. Drive the vehicle over 16 km/h (10 mph).
3. Stop the vehicle.
4. Turn the ignition to the OFF position.

Important: Zero the *J 39200* test leads before making any resistance measurements.

Step	Action	Value(s)	Yes	No
1	Was the Diagnostic System Check performed?	—	*Go to Step 2*	Go to *ABS Diagnostic System Check*
2	Inspect the following connectors for the correct wire color/connector cavity combinations: • The 6-way ABS brake motor pack connector • The 8-way EBCM connector C2 Are the correct wires located in the correct connector cavities?	—	*Go to Step 3*	*Go to Step 10*
3	1. Turn the ignition switch to the ON position. Do not start the engine. 2. Pump the brake pedal until it is firm in order to deplete the brake booster vacuum reservoir. 3. Install a scan tool. 4. Select the Special Functions on the scan tool. 5. Select the Manual Control function on the scan tool. 6. Select the ABS Motor Apply function of the left front ABS channel on the scan tool. 7. Use the scan tool in order to apply the left front ABS motor. 8. Wait for five seconds. 9. Apply firm pressure to the brake pedal. Does the brake pedal fall?	—	*Go to Step 9*	*Go to Step 4*
4	1. Use the scan tool in order to exit the Manual Control function. 2. Turn the ignition switch to the OFF position. 3. Disconnect the following connectors: • The 6-way ABS brake motor pack connector • The 8-way EBCM connector C2 4. Use the *J 39200* in order to measure the resistance between the 6-way ABS brake motor pack harness connector terminal D and the 8-way EBCM harness connector C2 terminal F. Is the resistance within the specified range?	0.2 – 1.5 Ω	*Go to Step 5*	*Go to Step 11*
5	Use the *J 39200* in order to measure the resistance between the 6-way ABS brake motor pack harness connector terminal C and the 8-way EBCM harness connector C2 terminal E. Is the resistance within the specified range?	0.2–1.5 Ω	*Go to Step 6*	*Go to Step 12*
6	Use the *J 39200* in order to measure the resistance between the 6-way ABS brake motor pack connector terminal C and the ABS brake motor pack connector terminal D. Is the resistance within the specified range?	0.2–1.5 Ω	*Go to Step 7*	*Go to Step 9*

GC4029903833020X

Fig. 172 Code C1242: Rear ESB Will Not Hold Motor (Part 2 of 3). Intrigue, Lumina & Monte Carlo

Circuit Description

DTC C1242 detects a slipping rear wheels ESB. During initialization and braking, the rear motor is rehomed. If the ESB slips, the motor/piston will move. During the next key to RUN initialization, a rehome of the motor verifies the motor/piston remained at the home position. If motor movement is detected, the ESB must be slipping.

If an ESB cannot hold a piston in the home position, the piston may be driven back when the brake pedal is applied. Then the brake pedal will drop.

Conditions for Setting the DTC

DTC C1242 can set during initialization at the following speeds:

- 0 km (0 mph) when the brake is off
- 5 km (3 mph) when the brake is on

A malfunction exists if the EBCM detects that the ESB could not hold the piston in the home position.

DTC C1286 EBCM Turned On Brake Warning Indicator always sets with DTC C1242.

Action Taken When the DTC Sets

- A malfunction DTC stores.
- The ABS disables.
- The amber ABS warning indicators turn on.
- The red BRAKE warning indicator turns on.

Conditions for Clearing the DTC

- The condition responsible for setting the DTC no longer exists and the Scan Tool Clear DTCs function is used.
- 100 drive cycles pass with no DTCs detected.

Diagnostic Aids

The following conditions may cause an intermittent malfunction if the conditions exist in a mechanical part of the system:

- Sticking
- Binding
- Slipping

Use the enhanced diagnostic function of the Scan Tool in order to measure the frequency of the malfunction.

Use the hydraulic control modulator test function of the Scan Tool in order to locate an intermittent malfunction associated with the ESB.

GC4029903833010X

Fig. 172 Code C1242: Rear ESB Will Not Hold Motor (Part 1 of 3). Intrigue, Lumina & Monte Carlo

Step	Action	Value(s)	Yes	No
7	1. Inspect the following connectors: • The 6-way ABS brake motor pack connector • The 8-way EBCM connector C2 2. Inspect the above connectors for the following conditions: • Poor terminal contact • Corrosion Are there signs of poor terminal contact or corrosion?	—	*Go to Step 13*	*Go to Step 8*
8	1. Turn the ignition switch to the OFF position. 2. Reconnect the 8-way EBCM connector C2 3. Reconnect the 6-way ABS brake motor pack connector 4. Start the engine. Do not depress the brake pedal while starting the engine. 5. Allow the engine to run for at least 10 seconds. 6. Repeat the above ignition cycle sequence at least two more times. 7. Use the scan tool in order to look for DTCs. Does the DTC C1242 set during the last three ignition cycles?	—	*Go to Step 14*	*Go to Step 15*
9	Replace the ABS brake motor pack. Is the repair complete?	—	Go to *ABS Diagnostic System Check*	—
10	Place the correct wires into the connector cavities. Is the repair complete?	—	Go to *ABS Diagnostic System Check*	—
11	Repair the open or high resistance in CKT 1284. Is the repair complete?	—	Go to *ABS Diagnostic System Check*	—
12	Repair the open or high resistance in CKT 1285. Is the repair complete?	—	Go to *ABS Diagnostic System Check*	—
13	Replace the terminals that exhibit signs of poor terminal contact or corrosion. Is the repair complete?	—	Go to *ABS Diagnostic System Check*	—
14	Replace the EBCM. Is the repair complete?	—	Go to *ABS Diagnostic System Check*	—
15	Is the malfunction intermittent or is not present at this time?	—	Go to Diagnostic Aids	—

GC4029903833030X

Fig. 172 Code C1242: Rear ESB Will Not Hold Motor (Part 3 of 3). Intrigue, Lumina & Monte Carlo

Circuit Description

This DTC is designed to detect a bound-up ESB, a stuck ABS motor, or a seized brake modulator. When the release is commanded during initialization, the ESB should release the ABS motor, resulting in sensed current being less than commanded current (motor is spinning freely). If the ABS motor is not moving, sensed current will be equal to stall current.

Conditions for Setting the DTC

DTC C1244 can be set during brake motor initialization at 0 km/h (0 mph) with the brake off or DTC C1244 can be set during brake motor initialization at 5 km/h (3 mph) with the brake on. DTC C1244 can also be set during ABS stops. If the EBTCM detects a condition in which it cannot move the ABS motor in either direction, a malfunction exists.

Action Taken When the DTC Sets

This malfunction indicates the channel cannot be moved properly. A malfunction DTC is stored, ABS/TCS is disabled and the amber ABS warning indicator is turned on.

Conditions for Clearing DTC

Condition for DTC is no longer present and the scan tool (CLEAR DTCs) function is used, or 100 drive cycles have passed with no DTCs detected.

Diagnostic Aids

An intermittent malfunction in this DTC may result from a mechanical part of the system that sticks, binds, or slips.

The frequency of the malfunction can be checked by using the enhanced diagnostic function of the Scan Tool

DTC C1244 may set after modulator disassembly if the modulator pistons are positioned at the bottom of their bore.

Any circuitry that is suspected of causing the intermittent complaint should be thoroughly checked for backed-out terminals, improper mating, broken locks, improperly formed or damaged terminals, poor terminal to wiring connections, or physical damage to the wiring harness.

Important

- J 39200 test leads must be zeroed prior to making any resistance measurements. Refer to J 39200 user's manual.

After diagnosis is complete, clear the DTCs and test drive the vehicle for three drive cycles to verify that the DTC does not reset. A drive cycle consists of starting the vehicle, driving the vehicle over 16 km/h (10 mph), stopping, and then turning the ignition off.

GC402970325300AX

Fig. 173 Code C1244: LH Front ABS Channel Will Not Move (Part 1 of 4). Intrigue, Lumina & Monte Carlo

Step	Action	Value(s)	Yes	No
1	Was the Diagnostic System Check performed?	—	Go to Step 2	Go to Diagnostic System Check
2	Visually inspect the 6-way ABS brake motor pack connector and the 8-way EBTCM connector C2 for proper wire color/connector cavity combination. Are the proper wires located in the proper connector cavities?	—	Go to Step 3	Go to Step 11
3	1. Turn the ignition switch to the RUN position, engine off. 2. Pump the brake pedal until firm to deplete the brake booster vacuum reservoir. 3. Install a scan tool. 4. Using the scan tool, select MISC TESTS. 5. Using the scan tool, select manual control function. 6. Using the scan tool, select ABS motor apply function of the left front ABS channel. 7. Using the scan tool, apply the left front ABS motor. 8. Wait five seconds. 9. Apply firm pressure to the brake pedal. 10. Using the scan tool, select the left front ABS motor release function. 11. Using the scan tool, release the left front ABS motor. Did the brake pedal fall?	—	Go to Step 4	Go to Step 5
4	1. Keep the firm pressure on the brake pedal. 2. Using the scan tool, select the left front ABS motor release function. 3. Using the scan tool, apply the left front ABS motor. Did the brake pedal rise?	—	Go to Step 17	Go to Step 5
5	1. Remove the firm pressure from the brake pedal. 2. Using the scan tool, select the left front ABS motor release function. 3. Using the scan tool, apply the left front ABS motor while carefully observing the left front ABS motor commanded current and the left front ABS motor feedback current. Was the left front ABS motor feedback current equal to or less than the specified current?	8A	Go to Step 6	Go to Step 10

GC402970325300BX

Fig. 173 Code C1244: LH Front ABS Channel Will Not Move (Part 2 of 4). Intrigue, Lumina & Monte Carlo

Step	Action	Value(s)	Yes	No
12	Repair the short between CKT 1280 and CKT 1281. Is the repair complete?	—	Go to Diagnostic System Check	—
13	Replace the ABS brake motor pack. Is the repair complete?	—	Go to Diagnostic System Check	—
14	Replace the brake modulator. Is the repair complete?	—	Go to Diagnostic System Check	—
15	Replace the terminals that exhibit poor terminal contact or evidence of corrosion. Is the repair complete?	—	Go to Diagnostic System Check	—
16	Replace the EBTCM. Is the repair complete?	—	Go to Diagnostic System Check	—
17	Malfunction is intermittent or not present at this time. Refer to Diagnostic Aids for more information.	—	—	—

GC402970325300DX

Fig. 173 Code C1244: LH Front ABS Channel Will Not Move (Part 4 of 4). Intrigue, Lumina & Monte Carlo

Circuit Description

This DTC is designed to detect a bound-up ESB, a stuck ABS motor, or a seized brake modulator. When the release is commanded during initialization, the ESB should release the ABS motor, resulting in sensed current being less than commanded current (motor is spinning freely). If the ABS motor is not moving, sensed current will be equal to stall current.

Conditions for Setting the DTC

DTC C1245 can be set during brake motor initialization at 0 km/h (0 mph) with the brake off or DTC C1245 can be set during brake motor initialization at 5 km/h (3 mph) with the brake on. DTC C1245 can also be set during ABS stops. If the EBTCM detects a condition in which it cannot move the ABS motor in either direction, a malfunction exists.

Action Taken When the DTC Sets

This malfunction indicates the channel cannot be moved properly. A malfunction DTC is stored, ABS/TCS is disabled and the amber ABS warning indicator is turned on.

Conditions for Clearing DTC

Condition for DTC is no longer present and the scan tool (CLEAR DTCs) function is used, or 100 drive cycles have passed with no DTCs detected.

Diagnostic Aids

An intermittent malfunction in this DTC may result from a mechanical part of the system that sticks, binds, or slips.

The frequency of the malfunction can be checked by using the enhanced diagnostic function of the Scan Tool

DTC C1245 may set after modulator disassembly if the modulator pistons are positioned at the bottom of their bore.

Any circuitry that is suspected of causing the intermittent complaint should be thoroughly checked for backed-out terminals, improper mating, broken locks, improperly formed or damaged terminals, poor terminal to wiring connections, or physical damage to the wiring harness.

[!] Important

- J 39200 test leads must be zeroed prior to making any resistance measurements. Refer to J 39200 user's manual.

After diagnosis is complete, clear the DTCs and test drive the vehicle for three drive cycles to verify that the DTC does not reset. A drive cycle consists of starting the vehicle, driving the vehicle over 16 km/h (10 mph), stopping, and then turning the ignition off.

GC402970325400AX

Fig. 174 Code C1245: RH Front ABS Channel Will Not Move (Part 1 of 4). Intrigue, Lumina & Monte Carlo

Step	Action	Value(s)	Yes	No
6	1. Using the scan tool, exit the scan tool manual control function. 2. Turn the ignition switch to the OFF position. 3. Disconnect the 6-way ABS brake motor pack connector. 4. Disconnect the 8-way EBTCM connector C2. 5. Using J 39200, measure the resistance between the 8-way EBTCM harness connector C2 terminal G and the 8-way EBTCM harness connector C2 terminal H. Is the resistance measured within the specified range?	OL (Infinite)	Go to Step 7	Go to Step 12
7	Using J 39200, measure the resistance between the ABS brake motor pack connector terminal E and the ABS brake motor pack connector terminal F. Is the resistance measured equal to or greater than the specified resistance?	0.2 Ω	Go to Step 8	Go to Step 13
8	1. Inspect the 6-way ABS brake motor pack connector for poor terminal contact or evidence of corrosion. 2. Inspect the 8-way EBTCM connector C2 for poor terminal contact or evidence of corrosion. Do any of the terminals exhibit poor terminal contact or evidence of corrosion?	—	Go to Step 15	Go to Step 9
9	1. Turn the ignition switch to the OFF position. 2. Reconnect the 8-way EBTCM connector C2. 3. Reconnect the ABS brake motor pack connector. 4. Start the engine with foot off the brake pedal. 5. Allow the engine to run for at least 10 seconds. 6. Repeat the above ignition cycle sequence two more times. 7. Using the scan tool, check for DTCs. Did DTC C1244 set in the last three ignition cycles?	—	Go to Step 16	Go to Step 17
10	1. Using the scan tool, select MISC TESTS. 2. Using the scan tool, perform the gear tension relief function. 3. Turn the ignition switch to the OFF position. 4. Remove the brake modulator/master cylinder assembly from the vehicle. 5. Separate the ABS brake motor pack from the brake modulator. 6. Grasp the left front brake modulator gear and attempt to rotate the gear. (The ABS brake modulator left front gear is the gear furthest forward when the ABS brake modulator is mounted in the vehicle.) Can the left front brake modulator gear be rotated at least 10 full revolutions lock to lock?	—	Go to Step 13	Go to Step 14
11	Using the circuit diagram, place the proper wires into the proper connector cavities. Is the repair complete?	—	Go to Diagnostic System Check	—

GC402970325300CX

Fig. 173 Code C1244: LH Front ABS Channel Will Not Move (Part 3 of 4). Intrigue, Lumina & Monte Carlo

Step	Action	Value(s)	Yes	No
1	Was the Diagnostic System Check performed?	—	Go to Step 2	Go to Diagnostic System Check
2	Visually inspect the 6-way ABS brake motor pack connector and the 8-way EBTCM connector C2 for proper wire color/connector cavity combination. Are the proper wires located in the proper connector cavities?	—	Go to Step 3	Go to Step 11
3	1. Turn the ignition switch to the RUN position, engine off. 2. Pump the brake pedal until firm to deplete the brake booster vacuum reservoir. 3. Install a scan tool. 4. Using the scan tool, select MISC TESTS. 5. Using the scan tool, select manual control function. 6. Using the scan tool, select ABS motor apply function of the right front ABS channel. 7. Using the scan tool, apply the right front ABS motor. 8. Wait five seconds. 9. Apply firm pressure to the brake pedal. 10. Using the scan tool, select the right front ABS motor release function. 11. Using the scan tool, release the right front ABS motor. Did the brake pedal fall?	—	Go to Step 4	Go to Step 5
4	1. Keep the firm pressure on the brake pedal. 2. Using the scan tool, select the right front ABS motor release function. 3. Using the scan tool, apply the right front ABS motor. Did the brake pedal rise?	—	Go to Step 17	Go to Step 5
5	1. Remove the firm pressure from the brake pedal. 2. Using the scan tool, select the right front ABS motor release function. 3. Using the scan tool, apply the right front ABS motor while carefully observing the right front ABS motor commanded current and the right front ABS motor feedback current. Was the right front ABS motor feedback current equal to or less than the specified current?	8A	Go to Step 6	Go to Step 10

GC402970325400BX

Fig. 174 Code C1245: RH Front ABS Channel Will Not Move (Part 2 of 4). Intrigue, Lumina & Monte Carlo

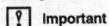

Step	Action	Value(s)	Yes	No
6	1. Using the scan tool, exit the scan tool manual control function. 2. Turn the ignition switch to the OFF position. 3. Disconnect the 6-way ABS brake motor pack connector. 4. Disconnect the 8-way EBTCM connector C2. 5. Using J 39200, measure the resistance between the 8-way EBTCM harness connector C2 terminal A and the 8-way EBTCM harness connector C2 terminal B. Is the resistance measured within the specified range?	OL (Infinite)	Go to Step 7	Go to Step 12
7	Using J 39200, measure the resistance between the ABS brake motor pack connector terminal A and the ABS brake motor pack connector terminal B. Is the resistance measured equal to or greater than the specified resistance?	0.2 Ω	Go to Step 8	Go to Step 13
8	1. Inspect the 6-way ABS brake motor pack connector for poor terminal contact or evidence of corrosion. 2. Inspect the 8-way EBTCM connector C2 for poor terminal contact or evidence of corrosion. Do any of the terminals exhibit poor terminal contact or evidence of corrosion?	—	Go to Step 15	Go to Step 9
9	1. Turn the ignition switch to the OFF position. 2. Reconnect the 8-way EBTCM connector C2. 3. Reconnect the ABS brake motor pack connector. 4. Start the engine with foot off the brake pedal. 5. Allow the engine to run for at least 10 seconds. 6. Repeat the above ignition cycle sequence two more times. 7. Using the scan tool, check for DTCs. Did DTC C1245 set in the last three ignition cycles?	—	Go to Step 16	Go to Step 17
10	1. Using the scan tool, select MISC TESTS. 2. Using the scan tool, perform the gear tension relief function. 3. Turn the ignition switch to the OFF position. 4. Remove the brake modulator/master cylinder assembly from the vehicle. 5. Separate the ABS brake motor pack from the brake modulator. 6. Grasp the right front brake modulator gear and attempt to rotate the gear. (The ABS brake modulator right front gear is the gear furthest rearward when the ABS brake modulator is mounted in the vehicle.) Can the brake modulator gear be rotated at least 10 full revolutions lock to lock?	—	Go to Step 13	Go to Step 14
11	Using the circuit diagram, place the proper wires into the proper connector cavities. Is the repair complete?	—	Go to Diagnostic System Check	—

GC402970325400CX

Fig. 174 Code C1245: RH Front ABS Channel Will Not Move (Part 3 of 4). Intrigue, Lumina & Monte Carlo

Step	Action	Value(s)	Yes	No
12	Repair the short between CKT 1282 and CKT 1283. Is the repair complete?	—	Go to Diagnostic System Check	—
13	Replace the ABS brake motor pack. Is the repair complete?	—	Go to Diagnostic System Check	—
14	Replace the brake modulator. Is the repair complete?	—	Go to Diagnostic System Check	—
15	Replace the terminals that exhibit poor terminal contact or evidence of corrosion. Is the repair complete?	—	Go to Diagnostic System Check	—
16	Replace the EBTCM. Is the repair complete?	—	Go to Diagnostic System Check	—
17	Malfunction is intermittent or not present at this time. Refer to Diagnostic Aids for more information.	—	—	—

GC402970325400DX

Fig. 174 Code C1245: RH Front ABS Channel Will Not Move (Part 4 of 4). Intrigue, Lumina & Monte Carlo

Circuit Description

This DTC is designed to detect a bound-up ESB, a stuck ABS motor, or a seized brake modulator. When the release is commanded during initialization, the ESB should release the ABS motor, resulting in sensed current being less than commanded current (motor is spinning freely). If the ABS motor is not moving, sensed current will be equal to stall current.

Conditions for Setting the DTC

DTC C1246 can be set during brake motor initialization at 0 km/h (0 mph) with the brake off or DTC C1246 can be set during brake motor initialization at 5 km/h (3 mph) with the brake on. DTC C1246 can also be set during ABS stops. If the EBTCM detects a condition in which it cannot move the ABS motor in either direction, a malfunction exists.

Action Taken When the DTC Sets

This malfunction indicates the channel cannot be moved properly. A malfunction DTC is stored, ABS/TCS is disabled, the amber ABS warning indicator and the red BRAKE warning indicator are turned on.

Conditions for Clearing DTC

Condition for DTC is no longer present and the scan tool (CLEAR DTCs) function is used, or 100 drive cycles have passed with no DTCs detected.

Diagnostic Aids

An intermittent malfunction in this DTC may result from a mechanical part of the system that sticks or binds.

The frequency of the malfunction can be checked by using the enhanced diagnostic function of the Scan Tool

DTC C1246 may set after modulator disassembly if the modulator pistons are positioned at the bottom of their bore. Depending on the frequency of the malfunction, a physical inspection of the mechanical parts suspected may be necessary.

Any circuitry that is suspected of causing the intermittent complaint should be thoroughly checked for backed-out terminals, improper mating, broken locks, improperly formed or damaged terminals, poor terminal to wiring connections, or physical damage to the wiring harness.

Important

- J 39200 test leads must be zeroed prior to making any resistance measurements. Refer to J 39200 user's manual.

After diagnosis is complete, clear the DTCs and test drive the vehicle for three drive cycles to verify that the DTC does not reset. A drive cycle consists of starting the vehicle, driving the vehicle over 16 km/h (10 mph), stopping, and then turning the ignition off.

GC402970325500AX

Fig. 175 Code C1246: Rear ABS Channel Will Not Move (Part 1 of 4). Intrigue, Lumina & Monte Carlo

Step	Action	Value(s)	Yes	No
1	Was the Diagnostic System Check performed?	—	Go to Step 2	—
2	Visually inspect the 6-way ABS motor pack connector and the 8-way EBTCM connector C2 for proper wire color/connector cavity combination. Are the proper wires located in the proper connector cavities?	—	Go to Step 3	Go to Step 11
3	1. Raise and support the vehicle on a suitable hoist so that the rear wheels are approximately 15 cm (six inches) off the floor. Refer to SECTION 0A. 2. Turn the ignition switch to the RUN position, engine off. 3. Pump the brake pedal until firm to deplete the brake booster vacuum reservoir. 4. Install a scan tool. 5. Apply firm downward pressure on the brake pedal. 6. Using the scan tool, select MISC TESTS. 7. Using the scan tool, select the MANUAL CONTROL function. 8. Using the scan tool, select the REAR AXLE MOTOR APPLY function. 9. Using the scan tool, apply the rear axle motor. 10. Have a assistant attempt to rotate the rear wheels by hand. Could the assistant rotate the rear wheels?	—	Go to Step 5	Go to Step 4
4	1. Keep the firm downward pressure on the brake pedal. 2. Using the scan tool, select the REAR AXLE MOTOR RELEASE function. 3. Using the scan tool, release the rear axle motor. 4. Have a assistant attempt to rotate the rear wheels by hand. Could the assistant rotate the rear wheels?	—	Go to Step 17	Go to Step 5
5	1. Remove the firm pressure from the brake pedal. 2. Using the scan tool, select the REAR AXLE MOTOR APPLY function. 3. Using the scan tool, apply the rear axle motor while carefully observing the rear axle motor commanded current and the rear axle motor feedback current. Was the rear axle motor feedback current equal to or less than the specified current?	8A	Go to Step 6	Go to Step 10

GC402970325500BX

Fig. 175 Code C1246: Rear ABS Channel Will Not Move (Part 2 of 4). Intrigue, Lumina & Monte Carlo

Step	Action	Value(s)	Yes	No
6	1. Using the scan tool, exit the scan tool MANUAL CONTROL function. 2. Turn the ignition switch to OFF position. 3. Disconnect the 6-way ABS motor pack connector. 4. Disconnect the 8-way EBTCM connector C2. 5. Using J 39200, measure the resistance between the 8-way EBTCM harness connector C2 terminal F and the 8-way EBTCM harness connector C2 terminal E. Is the resistance measured within the specified range?	OL (Infinite)	Go to Step 7	Go to Step 12
7	Using J 39200, measure the resistance between the ABS motor pack connector terminal C and the ABS motor pack connector terminal D. Is the resistance measured equal to or greater than the specified resistance?	0.2 Ω	Go to Step 8	Go to Step 13
8	1. Inspect the 6-way ABS motor pack connector for damage, poor terminal contact or evidence of corrosion. 2. Inspect the 8-way EBTCM connector C2 for damage, poor terminal contact or evidence of corrosion. Do any of the terminals exhibit damage, poor terminal contact or evidence of corrosion?	—	Go to Step 15	Go to Step 9
9	1. Turn the ignition switch to OFF position. 2. Reconnect the 8-way EBTCM connector C2. 3. Reconnect the ABS motor pack connector 4. Start the engine with foot off the brake pedal. 5. Allow the engine to run for at least 10 seconds. 6. Repeat the above ignition cycle sequence two more times. 7. Using the scan tool, check for DTCs. Did DTC C1246 set in the last three ignition cycles?	—	Go to Step 16	Go to Step 17
10	1. Using the scan tool, select MISC TESTS. 2. Using the scan tool, perform the GEAR TENSION RELIEF function. 3. Turn the ignition switch to OFF position. 4. Remove the hydraulic modulator/master cylinder assembly from the vehicle. 5. Separate the ABS motor pack from the hydraulic modulator. 6. Grasp the middle gear on the hydraulic modulator and attempt to rotate the gear. Can the middle gear on the hydraulic modulator be rotated at least 7 full revolutions lock to lock?	—	Go to Step 13	Go to Step 14
11	Using the circuit diagram, place the proper wires into the proper connector cavities. Is the repair complete?	—	Go to Diagnostic System Check	—

GC402970325500CX

Fig. 175 Code C1246: Rear ABS Channel Will Not Move (Part 3 of 4). Intrigue, Lumina, Monte Carlo, Century & Regal

Step	Action	Value(s)	Yes	No
12	Repair the short between CKT 1284 and CKT 1285. Is the repair complete?	—	Go to Diagnostic System Check	—
13	Replace the ABS motor pack. Is the repair complete?	—	Go to Diagnostic System Check	—
14	Replace the hydraulic modulator. Is the repair complete?	—	Go to Diagnostic System Check	—
15	Replace the terminals that exhibit damage, poor terminal contact or evidence of corrosion. Is the repair complete?	—	Go to Diagnostic System Check	—
16	Replace the EBTCM. Is the repair complete?	—	Go to Diagnostic System Check	—
17	Malfunction is intermittent or not present at this time. Refer to Diagnostic Aids for more information.	—	—	—

GC402970325500DX

Fig. 175 Code C1246: Rear ABS Channel Will Not Move (Part 4 of 4). Intrigue, Lumina & Monte Carlo

Circuit Description

This DTC is designed to detect a stripped nut or gear assembly during initialization. During the homing sequence, the piston should reach the top of the bore resulting in a stalled ABS motor. If this does not occur, the ABS motor must be spinning with little or no resistance, indicating a nut/screw or gear malfunction.

Conditions for Setting the DTC

DTC C1247 can only be set during initialization. If the feedback current is less than the command current for a specified period of time, a malfunction exists.

Action Taken When the DTC Sets

A malfunction DTC is stored and ABS/ETS is disabled, and the amber ABS warning indicator is turned on.

Conditions for Clearing DTC

The condition for the DTC is no longer present and the scan tool CLEAR DTCs function is used, or 100 drive cycles have passed with no DTCs detected.

Diagnostic Aids

An intermittent malfunction in this DTC may result from a mechanical part of the system that sticks, binds, or slips.

The frequency of the malfunction can be checked by using the enhanced diagnostic function of the scan tool, as described in Scan Tool Diagnostics in this section. If the DTC only occurs once and DTC C1256 also occurs, refer to DTC C1256. If intermittent and enhanced diagnostics shows this DTC occurs during ABS, refer to DTC C1256.

Depending on the frequency of the malfunction, a physical inspection of the suspected mechanical parts may be necessary.

Important

- J 39200 test leads must be zeroed prior to making any resistance measurements. Refer to J 39200 user's manual.

After diagnosis is complete, clear the DTCs and test drive the vehicle for three drive cycles to verify that the DTC does not reset. A drive cycle consists of starting the vehicle, driving the vehicle over 16 km/h (10 mph), stopping, and then turning the ignition off.

GC402970325601AX

Fig. 176 Code C1247: LH Front ABS Motor Free Spins (Part 1 of 5). Intrigue, Lumina & Monte Carlo

Step	Action	Value(s)	Yes	No
1	Was the Diagnostic System Check performed?	—	Go to Step 2	Go to Diagnostic System Check
2	1. Turn the ignition switch to the RUN position, engine off. 2. Install a scan tool. 3. Using the scan tool, read the DTCs. Is DTC C1256 also set as a current DTC?	—	Go to DTC C1256	Go to Step 3
3	1. Pump the brake pedal until firm to deplete the brake booster vacuum reservoir. 2. Using the scan tool, select MISC TEST. 3. Using the scan tool, select the manual control function. 4. Using the scan tool, select the left front ABS motor apply function. 5. Using the scan tool, apply the left front ABS motor while observing the left front ABS motor command current and the left front ABS motor feedback current. Were both the left front ABS motor command current and the left front ABS motor feedback current approximately the specified current?	10A	Go to Step 4	Go to Step 5
4	1. Apply firm pressure to the brake pedal. 2. Using the scan tool, select the left front ABS release function. 3. Using the scan tool, release the left front ABS motor while observing the left front ABS motor command current and the left front ABS motor feedback current. 4. While releasing the left front ABS motor observe brake pedal height. Were both the left front ABS motor command current and the left front ABS motor feedback current approximately the specified current and did the brake pedal fall?	6A	Go to Step 5	Go to Step 6
5	1. Keep firm pressure on the brake pedal. 2. Using the scan tool, select the left front ABS apply function. 3. Using the scan tool, apply the left front ABS motor. Did the brake pedal rise?	—	Go to Step 22	Go to Step 6
6	1. Using the scan tool, select MISC TESTS. 2. Using the scan tool, perform the gear tension relief function. 3. Turn the ignition switch to the OFF position. 4. Disconnect the 6-way ABS brake motor pack connector. 5. Disconnect the 8-way EBTCM connector C2. 6. Using J 39200, measure the resistance between the 6-way ABS brake motor pack connector terminal F and the 8-way EBTCM connector C2 terminal G. Is the resistance measured equal to or less than the specified resistance?	1.5 Ω	Go to Step 7	Go to Step 15

GC402970325600BX

Fig. 176 Code C1247: LH Front ABS Motor Free Spins (Part 2 of 5). Intrigue, Lumina & Monte Carlo

Step	Action	Value(s)	Yes	No
7	Using J 39200, measure the resistance between the 6-way ABS brake motor pack connector terminal E and the 8-way EBTCM connector C2 terminal H. Is the resistance measured equal to or less than the specified resistance?	1.5 Ω	Go to Step 8	Go to Step 16
8	Using J 39200, measure the resistance between the 6-way ABS brake motor pack connector terminal E and the 6-way ABS brake motor pack connector terminal F. Is the resistance measured equal to or less than the specified resistance?	1.5 Ω	Go to Step 9	Go to Step 17
9	1. Remove the ABS brake modulator/master cylinder assembly from the vehicle. 2. Remove the ABS brake modulator gear cover. 3. Check for a stripped ABS brake motor pack left front gear. (The ABS brake motor pack is the unit with the three small gears. The ABS brake motor pack left front gear is the gear furthest forward when the ABS brake modulator is mounted in the vehicle.) Is the ABS brake motor pack left front gear stripped?	—	Go to Step 17	Go to Step 10
10	Check for a stripped ABS brake modulator left front gear. (The ABS brake modulator is the unit with the three large gears. The ABS brake modulator left front gear is the gear furthest forward when the ABS brake modulator is mounted in the vehicle.) Is the ABS brake modulator left front gear stripped?	—	Go to Step 18	Go to Step 11
11	1. Reconnect the 6-way ABS brake motor pack connector. 2. Reconnect the 8-way EBTCM connector C2. 3. Carefully secure the ABS brake modulator/master cylinder assembly in the vehicle in a position to observe the gears. 4. Turn the ignition switch to the RUN position, engine off. 5. Using the scan tool, select the manual control function. 6. Using the scan tool, select the left front ABS motor apply function. 7. Using the scan tool, apply the left front ABS motor while observing the ABS brake modulator left front gear set. (The ABS brake modulator left front gear is the gear furthest forward when the ABS brake modulator is mounted in the vehicle.) 8. Using the scan tool, select the left front ABS release function. 9. Using the scan tool, release the left front ABS motor while observing the ABS brake modulator left front gear set. 10. Using the scan tool, select the left front ABS motor apply function. 11. Using the scan tool, apply the left front ABS motor while observing the ABS brake modulator left front gear set. Did the ABS brake modulator left front gear set move in both directions at least one full revolution?	—	Go to Step 12	Go to Step 17

GC402970325600CX

Fig. 176 Code C1247: LH Front ABS Motor Free Spins (Part 3 of 5). Intrigue, Lumina & Monte Carlo

Step	Action	Value(s)	Yes	No
12	1. Using the scan tool, perform the gear tension relief function. 2. Turn the ignition switch to the OFF position. 3. Separate the ABS brake motor pack from the ABS brake modulator. 4. Grasp the ABS brake modulator left front gear and rotate the ABS brake modulator left front gear. Does the ABS brake modulator left front gear rotate more than 13 full turns lock to lock?	—	Go to Step 19	Go to Step 13
13	1. Disconnect the 6-way ABS brake motor pack connector. 2. Disconnect the 8-way EBTCM connector C2. 3. Inspect the 6-way ABS brake motor pack connector for poor terminal contact or evidence of corrosion. 4. Inspect the 8-way EBTCM connector C2 for poor terminal contact or evidence of corrosion. Do any of the terminals exhibit poor terminal contact or evidence of corrosion?	—	Go to Step 20	Go to Step 14
14	1. Reinstall the ABS brake modulator gear cover. 2. Reinstall the ABS brake modulator/master cylinder assembly in the vehicle. 3. Reconnect the 6-way ABS brake motor pack connector. 4. Reconnect the 8-way EBTCM connector C2. 5. Start the engine with no pressure applied to the brake pedal. 6. Let engine run for at least 10 seconds. 7. Turn the ignition switch to the OFF position. 8. Repeat step 5 through step 7 two more times. 9. Using the scan tool, read the DTCs. Does DTC C1247 set as a current DTC.	—	Go to Step 21	Go to Step 22
15	Repair high resistance in CKT 1280. Is the repair complete?	—	Go to Diagnostic System Check	—
16	Repair high resistance in CKT 1281. Is the repair complete?	—	Go to Diagnostic System Check	—
17	Replace the ABS brake motor pack. Is the repair complete?	—	Go to Diagnostic System Check	—
18	Replace the ABS brake modulator gear. Is the repair complete?	—	Go to Diagnostic System Check	—

GC402970325600DX

Fig. 176 Code C1247: LH Front ABS Motor Free Spins (Part 4 of 5). Intrigue, Lumina & Monte Carlo

Step	Action	Value(s)	Yes	No
19	Replace the ABS brake modulator. Is the repair complete?	—	Go to Diagnostic System Check	—
20	Replace the terminals that exhibit poor terminal contact or evidence of corrosion. Is the repair complete?	—	Go to Diagnostic System Check	—
21	Replace the EBTCM. Is the repair complete?	—	Go to Diagnostic System Check	—
22	Malfunction is intermittent or not present at this time. Refer to Diagnostic Aids for more information.	—	—	—

GC402970325600EX

Fig. 176 Code C1247: LH Front ABS Motor Free Spins (Part 5 of 5). Intrigue, Lumina & Monte Carlo

Circuit Description

This DTC is designed to detect a stripped nut or gear assembly during initialization. During the homing sequence, the piston should reach the top of the bore resulting in a stalled ABS motor. If this does not occur, the ABS motor must be spinning with little or no resistance, indicating a nut/screw or gear malfunction.

Conditions for Setting the DTC

DTC C1248 can only be set during initialization. If the feedback current is less than the command current for a specified period of time, a malfunction exists.

Action Taken When the DTC Sets

A malfunction DTC is stored and ABS/ETS is disabled, and the amber ABS warning indicator is turned on.

Conditions for Clearing DTC

The condition for the DTC is no longer present and the scan tool CLEAR DTCs function is used, or 100 drive cycles have passed with no DTCs detected.

Diagnostic Aids

An intermittent malfunction in this DTC may result from a mechanical part of the system that sticks, binds, or slips.

The frequency of the malfunction can be checked by using the enhanced diagnostic function of the scan tool, as described in Scan Tool Diagnostics in this section. If the DTC only occurs once and DTC C1261 also occurs, refer to DTC C1261. If intermittent and enhanced diagnostics shows this DTC occurs during ABS, refer to DTC C1261.

Depending on the frequency of the malfunction, a physical inspection of the suspected mechanical parts may be necessary.

Important

- J 39200 test leads must be zeroed prior to making any resistance measurements. Refer to J 39200 user's manual.

After diagnosis is complete, clear the DTCs and test drive the vehicle for three drive cycles to verify that the DTC does not reset. A drive cycle consists of starting the vehicle, driving the vehicle over 16 km/h (10 mph), stopping, and then turning the ignition off.

GC402970325602AX

Fig. 177 Code C1248: RH Front ABS Motor Free Spins (Part 1 of 5). Intrigue, Lumina & Monte Carlo

Step	Action	Value(s)	Yes	No
1	Was the Diagnostic System Check performed?	—	Go to Step 2	Go to Diagnostic System Check
2	1. Turn the ignition switch to the RUN position, engine off. 2. Install a scan tool. 3. Using the scan tool, read the DTCs. Is DTC C1261 also set as a current DTC?	—	Go to DTC C1261	Go to Step 3
3	1. Pump the brake pedal until firm to deplete the brake booster vacuum reservoir. 2. Using the scan tool, select MISC TEST. 3. Using the scan tool, select the manual control function. 4. Using the scan tool, select the right front ABS motor apply function. 5. Using the scan tool, apply the right front ABS motor while observing the right front ABS motor command current and the right front ABS motor feedback current. Were both the right front ABS motor command current and the right front ABS motor feedback current approximately the specified current?	10A	Go to Step 4	Go to Step 5
4	1. Apply firm pressure to the brake pedal. 2. Using the scan tool, select the right front ABS release function. 3. Using the scan tool, release the right front ABS motor while observing the right front ABS motor command current and the right front ABS motor feedback current. 4. While releasing the right front ABS motor observe brake pedal height. Were both the right front ABS motor command current and the right front ABS motor feedback current approximately the specified current and did the brake pedal fall?	6A	Go to Step 5	Go to Step 6
5	1. Keep firm pressure on the brake pedal. 2. Using the scan tool, select the right front ABS apply function. 3. Using the scan tool, apply the right front ABS motor. Did the brake pedal rise?	—	Go to Step 22	Go to Step 6
6	1. Using the scan tool, select MISC TESTS. 2. Using the scan tool, perform the gear tension relief function. 3. Turn the ignition switch to the OFF position. 4. Disconnect the 6-way ABS brake motor pack connector. 5. Disconnect the 8-way EBTCM connector C2. 6. Using J 39200, measure the resistance between the 6-way ABS brake motor pack connector terminal B and the 8-way EBTCM connector C2 terminal A. Is the resistance measured equal to or less than the specified resistance?	1.5 Ω	Go to Step 7	Go to Step 15

GC402970325600FX

Fig. 177 Code C1248: RH Front ABS Motor Free Spins (Part 2 of 5). Intrigue, Lumina & Monte Carlo

Step	Action	Value(s)	Yes	No
7	Using J 39200, measure the resistance between the 6-way ABS brake motor pack connector terminal A and the 8-way EBTCM connector C2 terminal B. Is the resistance measured equal to or less than the specified resistance?	1.5 Ω	Go to Step 8	Go to Step 16
8	Using J 39200, measure the resistance between the 6-way ABS brake motor pack connector terminal A and the 6-way ABS brake motor pack connector terminal B. Is the resistance measured equal to or less than the specified resistance?	1.5 Ω	Go to Step 9	Go to Step 17
9	1. Remove the ABS brake modulator/master cylinder assembly from the vehicle. 2. Remove the ABS brake modulator gear cover. 3. Check for a stripped ABS brake motor pack right front gear. (The ABS brake motor pack is the unit with the three small gears. The ABS brake motor pack right front gear is the gear furthest rearward when the ABS brake modulator is mounted in the vehicle.) Is the ABS brake motor pack right front gear stripped?	—	Go to Step 17	Go to Step 10
10	Check for a stripped ABS brake modulator right front gear. (The ABS brake modulator is the unit with the three large gears. The ABS brake modulator right front gear is the gear furthest rearward when the ABS brake modulator is mounted in the vehicle.) Is the ABS brake modulator right front gear stripped?	—	Go to Step 18	Go to Step 11
11	1. Reconnect the 6-way ABS brake motor pack connector. 2. Reconnect the 8-way EBTCM connector C2. 3. Carefully secure the ABS brake modulator/master cylinder assembly in the vehicle in a position to observe the gears. 4. Turn the ignition switch to the RUN position, engine off. 5. Using the scan tool, select the manual control function. 6. Using the scan tool, select the right front ABS motor apply function. 7. Using the scan tool, apply the right front ABS motor while observing the ABS brake modulator right front gear set. (The ABS brake modulator right front gear is the gear furthest rearward when the ABS brake modulator is mounted in the vehicle.) 8. Using the scan tool, select the right front ABS release function. 9. Using the scan tool, release the right front ABS motor while observing the ABS brake modulator right front gear set. 10. Using the scan tool, select the right front ABS motor apply function. 11. Using the scan tool, apply the right front ABS motor while observing the ABS brake modulator right front gear set. Did the ABS brake modulator right front gear set move in both directions at least one full revolution?	—	Go to Step 12	Go to Step 17

GC402970325600GX

Fig. 177 Code C1248: RH Front ABS Motor Free Spins (Part 3 of 5). Intrigue, Lumina & Monte Carlo

Step	Action	Value(s)	Yes	No
12	1. Using the scan tool, perform the gear tension relief function. 2. Turn the ignition switch to the OFF position. 3. Separate the ABS brake motor pack from the ABS brake modulator. 4. Grasp the ABS brake modulator right front gear and rotate the ABS brake modulator right front gear. Does the ABS brake modulator right front gear rotate more than 13 full turns lock to lock?	—	Go to Step 19	Go to Step 13
13	1. Disconnect the 6-way ABS brake motor pack connector. 2. Disconnect the 8-way EBTCM connector C2. 3. Inspect the 6-way ABS brake motor pack connector for poor terminal contact or evidence of corrosion. 4. Inspect the 8-way EBTCM connector C2 for poor terminal contact or evidence of corrosion. Do any of the terminals exhibit poor terminal contact or evidence of corrosion?	—	Go to Step 20	Go to Step 14
14	1. Reinstall the ABS brake modulator gear cover. 2. Reinstall the ABS brake modulator/master cylinder assembly in the vehicle. 3. Reconnect the 6-way ABS brake motor pack connector. 4. Reconnect the 8-way EBTCM connector C2. 5. Start the engine with no pressure applied to the brake pedal. 6. Let engine run for at least 10 seconds. 7. Turn the ignition switch to the OFF position. 8. Repeat step 5 through step 7 two more times. 9. Using the scan tool, read the DTCs. Does DTC C1248 set as a current DTC.	—	Go to Step 21	Go to Step 22
15	Repair high resistance in CKT 1282. Is the repair complete?	—	Go to Diagnostic System Check	—
16	Repair high resistance in CKT 1283. Is the repair complete?	—	Go to Diagnostic System Check	—
17	Replace the ABS brake motor pack. Is the repair complete?	—	Go to Diagnostic System Check	—
18	Replace the ABS brake modulator gear. Is the repair complete?	—	Go to Diagnostic System Check	—

GC402970325600HX

Fig. 177 Code C1248: RH Front ABS Motor Free Spins (Part 4 of 5). Intrigue, Lumina & Monte Carlo

Step	Action	Value(s)	Yes	No
19	Replace the ABS brake modulator. Is the repair complete?	—	Go to Diagnostic System Check	—
20	Replace the terminals that exhibit poor terminal contact or evidence of corrosion. Is the repair complete?	—	Go to Diagnostic System Check	—
21	Replace the EBCM/EBTCM. Is the repair complete?	—	Go to Diagnostic System Check	—
22	Malfunction is intermittent or not present at this time. Refer to Diagnostic Aids for more information.	—	—	—

GC402970325600IX

Fig. 177 Code C1248: RH Front ABS Motor Free Spins (Part 5 of 5). Intrigue, Lumina & Monte Carlo

Circuit Description

This DTC is designed to detect a stripped nut or gear assembly during initialization. During the homing sequence, the piston should reach the top of the bore resulting in a stalled ABS motor. If this does not occur, the ABS motor must be spinning with little or no resistance, indicating a nut/screw or gear malfunction.

Conditions for Setting the DTC

DTC C1251 can be set during initialization. If the feedback current is less than the command current for a specified period of time, a malfunction exists.

Action Taken When the DTC Sets

A malfunction DTC is stored and ABS/ETS is disabled, the amber ABS warning indicator and the red BRAKE warning indicator are turned on.

Conditions for Clearing DTC

The condition for the DTC is no longer present and the scan tool CLEAR DTCs function is used, or 100 drive cycles have passed with no DTCs detected.

Diagnostic Aids

An intermittent malfunction in this DTC may result from a mechanical part of the system that sticks, binds, or slips.

The frequency of the malfunction can be checked by using the enhanced diagnostic function of the scan tool, as described in Scan Tool Diagnostics in this section. If the DTC only occurs once and DTC C1264 also occurs, refer to DTC C1264. If intermittent and enhanced diagnostics show this DTC occurs during ABS, refer to DTC C1264.

Depending on the frequency of the malfunction, a physical inspection of the suspected mechanical parts may be necessary.

Important

- J 39200 test leads must be zeroed prior to making any resistance measurements. Refer to J 39200 user's manual.

After diagnosis is complete, clear the DTCs and test drive the vehicle for three drive cycles to verify that the DTC does not reset. A drive cycle consists of starting the vehicle, driving the vehicle over 16 km/h (10 mph), stopping, and then turning the ignition off.

GC402970325603AX

Fig. 178 Code C1251: Rear ABS Motor Free Spins (Part 1 of 4). Intrigue, Lumina & Monte Carlo

Step	Action	Value(s)	Yes	No
1	Was the Diagnostic System Check performed?	—	Go to Step 2	Go to Diagnostic System Check
2	1. Turn the ignition switch to the RUN position, engine off. 2. Install a scan tool. 3. Using the scan tool, read the DTCs. Is DTC C1264 also set as a current DTC?	—	Go to DTC C1264	Go to Step 3
3	1. Pump the brake pedal until firm to deplete the brake booster vacuum reservoir. 2. Using the scan tool, select MISC TEST. 3. Using the scan tool, select the manual control function. 4. Using the scan tool, select the rear ABS motor apply function. 5. Using the scan tool, apply the rear ABS motor while observing the rear ABS motor command current and the rear ABS motor feedback current. Were both the rear ABS motor command current and the rear ABS motor feedback current approximately the specified current?	10A	Go to Step 4	Go to Step 5
4	1. Apply firm pressure to the brake pedal. 2. Using the scan tool, select the rear ABS release function. 3. Using the scan tool, release the rear ABS motor while observing the rear ABS motor command current and the rear ABS motor feedback current. 4. While releasing the rear ABS motor observe brake pedal height. Were both the rear ABS motor command current and the rear ABS motor feedback current approximately the specified current and did the brake pedal fall?	6A	Go to Step 5	Go to Step 6
5	1. Keep firm pressure on the brake pedal. 2. Using the scan tool, select the rear ABS apply function. 3. Using the scan tool, apply the rear ABS motor. Did the brake pedal rise?	—	Go to Step 22	Go to Step 6
6	1. Using the scan tool, select MISC TESTS. 2. Using the scan tool, perform the gear tension relief function. 3. Turn the ignition switch to the OFF position. 4. Disconnect the 6-way ABS brake motor pack connector. 5. Disconnect the 8-way EBTCM connector C2. 6. Using J 39200, measure the resistance between the 6-way ABS brake motor pack connector terminal D and the 8-way EBTCM connector C2 terminal F. Is the resistance measured equal to or less than the specified resistance?	1.5 Ω	Go to Step 7	Go to Step 15

GC402970325700JX

Fig. 178 Code C1251: Rear ABS Motor Free Spins (Part 2 of 4). Intrigue, Lumina & Monte Carlo

Step	Action	Value(s)	Yes	No
7	Using J 39200, measure the resistance between the 6-way ABS brake motor pack connector terminal C and the 8-way EBTCM connector C2 terminal E. Is the resistance measured equal to or less than the specified resistance?	1.5 Ω	Go to Step 8	Go to Step 16
8	Using J 39200, measure the resistance between the 6-way ABS brake motor pack connector terminal C and the 6-way ABS brake motor pack connector terminal D. Is the resistance measured equal to or less than the specified resistance?	1.5 Ω	Go to Step 9	Go to Step 17
9	1. Remove the ABS brake modulator/master cylinder assembly from the vehicle. 2. Remove the ABS brake modulator gear cover. 3. Check for a stripped ABS brake motor pack rear gear. (The ABS brake motor pack is the unit with the three small gears. The ABS brake motor pack rear gear is the middle gear when the ABS brake modulator is mounted in the vehicle.) Is the ABS brake motor pack rear gear stripped?	—	Go to Step 17	Go to Step 10
10	Check for a stripped ABS brake modulator rear gear. (The ABS brake modulator is the unit with the three large gears. The ABS brake modulator rear gear is the middle gear when the ABS brake modulator is mounted in the vehicle.) Is the ABS brake modulator rear gear stripped?	—	Go to Step 18	Go to Step 11
11	1. Reconnect the 6-way ABS brake motor pack connector. 2. Reconnect the 8-way EBTCM connector C2. 3. Carefully secure the ABS brake modulator/master cylinder assembly in the vehicle in a position to observe the gears. 4. Turn the ignition switch to the RUN position, engine off. 5. Using the scan tool, select the manual control function. 6. Using the scan tool, select the rear ABS motor apply function. 7. Using the scan tool, apply the rear ABS motor while observing the ABS brake modulator rear gear set. (The ABS brake modulator rear gear is the middle gear when the ABS brake modulator is mounted in the vehicle.) 8. Using the scan tool, select the rear ABS release function. 9. Using the scan tool, release the rear ABS motor while observing the ABS brake modulator rear gear set. 10. Using the scan tool, select the rear ABS motor apply function. 11. Using the scan tool, apply the rear ABS motor while observing the ABS brake modulator rear gear set. Did the ABS brake modulator rear gear set move in both directions at least one full revolution?	—	Go to Step 12	Go to Step 17
12	1. Using the scan tool, perform the gear tension relief function. 2. Turn the ignition switch to the OFF position. 3. Separate the ABS brake motor pack from the ABS brake modulator. 4. Grasp the ABS brake modulator rear gear and rotate the ABS brake modulator rear gear. Does the ABS brake modulator rear gear rotate more than 13 full turns lock to lock?	—	Go to Step 19	Go to Step 13

GC402970325600KX

Fig. 178 Code C1251: Rear ABS Motor Free Spins (Part 3 of 4). Intrigue, Lumina & Monte Carlo

Step	Action	Value(s)	Yes	No
13	1. Disconnect the 6-way ABS brake motor pack connector. 2. Disconnect the 8-way EBTCM connector C2. 3. Inspect the 6-way ABS brake motor pack connector for poor terminal contact or evidence of corrosion. 4. Inspect the 8-way EBTCM connector C2 for poor terminal contact or evidence of corrosion. Do any of the terminals exhibit poor terminal contact or evidence of corrosion?	—	Go to Step 20	Go to Step 14
14	1. Reinstall the ABS brake modulator gear cover. 2. Reinstall the ABS brake modulator/master cylinder assembly in the vehicle. 3. Reconnect the 6-way ABS brake motor pack connector. 4. Reconnect the 8-way EBTCM connector C2. 5. Start the engine with no pressure applied to the brake pedal. 6. Let engine run for at least 10 seconds. 7. Turn the ignition switch to the OFF position. 8. Repeat step 5 through step 7 two more times. 9. Using the scan tool, read the DTCs. Does DTC C1251 set as a current DTC.	—	Go to Step 21	Go to Step 22
15	Repair high resistance in CKT 1284. Is the repair complete?	—	Go to Diagnostic System Check	—
16	Repair high resistance in CKT 1285. Is the repair complete?	—	Go to Diagnostic System Check	—
17	Replace the ABS brake motor pack. Is the repair complete?	—	Go to Diagnostic System Check	—
18	Replace the ABS brake modulator gear. Is the repair complete?	—	Go to Diagnostic System Check	—
19	Replace the ABS brake modulator. Is the repair complete?	—	Go to Diagnostic System Check	—
20	Replace the terminals that exhibit poor terminal contact or evidence of corrosion. Is the repair complete?	—	Go to Diagnostic System Check	—
21	Replace the EBTCM. Is the repair complete?	—	Go to Diagnostic System Check	—
22	Malfunction is intermittent or not present at this time. Refer to Diagnostic Aids for more information.	—	—	—

GC402970325600LX

Fig. 178 Code C1251: Rear ABS Motor Free Spins (Part 4 of 4). Intrigue, Lumina & Monte Carlo

Circuit Description

This DTC will diagnose an ABS motor that is energized longer than expected. This could occur if a wheel speed sensor is malfunctioning, the ABS motor does not turn, the left front brake solenoid valve mechanically fails open, or the ABS brake motor wires are crossed.

Conditions for Setting the DTC

DTC C1252 can be set only during an ABS stop. If the EBTCM commands the left front ABS channel in release for greater than three seconds a malfunction exists.

Action Taken When the DTC Sets

A malfunction DTC is stored and ABS/ETS is disabled, and the amber ABS warning indicator is turned on.

Conditions for Clearing DTC

The condition for the DTC is no longer present and the scan tool CLEAR DTCs function is used, or 100 drive cycles have passed with no DTCs detected.

Diagnostic Aids

An intermittent malfunction may be caused by a mechanical part of the system that sticks or binds.

The frequency of the malfunction can be checked by using the enhanced diagnostic function of the scan tool, as described in Scan Tool Diagnostics in this section. DTC C1252 may occur if on ice and steering wheel is turned to lock during braking. Using the Scan Tool, perform hydraulic test to ensure total brake system is functional.

Any circuitry that is suspected of causing the intermittent complaint should be thoroughly checked for backed-out terminals, improper mating, broken locks, improperly formed or damaged terminals, poor terminal to wiring connections, or physical damage to the wiring harness.

Important

- J 39200 test leads must be zeroed prior to making any resistance measurements. Refer to J 39200 user's manual.

After diagnosis is complete, clear the DTCs and test drive the vehicle for three drive cycles to verify that the DTC does not reset. A drive cycle consists of starting the vehicle, driving the vehicle over 16 km/h (10 mph), stopping, and then turning the ignition off.

Important

- Excessive drag or high resistance in the base brake or suspension system must be inspected and corrected before proceeding with DTC diagnosis.

GC402970325701AX

Fig. 179 Code C1252: LH Front ABS Channel In Release Too Long (Part 1 of 3). Intrigue, Lumina & Monte Carlo

Step	Action	Value(s)	Yes	No
1	Was the Diagnostic System Check performed?	—	Go to Step 2	Go to Diagnostic System Check
2	1. Turn the ignition switch to the RUN position, engine off. 2. Install a scan tool. 3. Using the scan tool, read the DTCs. Are there any wheel speed sensor DTCs set as current DTCs?	—	Go to Applicable DTC Table First	Go to Step 3
3	1. Using the scan tool, select DATA LIST. 2. Drive the vehicle and test the vehicle during a steady deceleration condition from 56 km/h to 0 km/h (35 mph to 0 mph) while monitoring all wheel speed sensor speeds. Do any of the wheel speed sensors indicate erratic or intermittent operation?	—	Go to Excessive Wheel Speed Sensor Variation DTC for Affected Wheel Speed Sensor	Go to Step 4
4	1. Turn the ignition switch to the RUN position, engine off. 2. Using the scan tool, select MISC TEST. 3. Using the scan tool, select the manual control function. 4. Using the scan tool, select the left front ABS motor apply function. 5. Using the scan tool, apply the left front ABS motor. 6. Apply firm pressure to the brake pedal. 7. Using the scan tool, select the left front ABS release function. 8. Using the scan tool, release the left front ABS motor. Did the brake pedal fall?	—	Go to Step 5	Go to Step 8
5	1. Remove the firm pressure from the brake pedal. 2. Using the scan tool, select the manual control function. 3. Using the scan tool, select the left front ABS brake solenoid valve. 4. Using the scan tool, command the left front ABS brake solenoid valve on. 5. Apply firm pressure to the brake pedal. Did the brake pedal fall?	—	Go to Step 7	Go to Step 6
6	1. Keep firm pressure applied to the brake pedal. 2. Using the scan tool, command the left front ABS brake solenoid valve off. Did the brake pedal fall?	—	Go to Step 14	Go to Step 7

GC402970325700BX

Fig. 179 Code C1252: LH Front ABS Channel In Release Too Long (Part 2 of 3). Intrigue, Lumina & Monte Carlo

Step	Action	Value(s)	Yes	No
7	1. Remove the firm pressure from the brake pedal. 2. Turn the ignition switch to the OFF position. 3. Remove the left front ABS brake solenoid valve. 4. Remove the right front ABS brake solenoid valve. 5. Reinstall the left front ABS brake solenoid valve to the right front ABS brake solenoid valve position. 6. Reinstall the right front ABS brake solenoid valve to the left front ABS brake solenoid valve position. 7. Turn the ignition switch to the RUN position, engine off. 8. Using the scan tool, select the manual control function. 9. Using the scan tool, select the left front ABS brake solenoid valve. 10. Using the scan tool, command the left front ABS brake solenoid valve on. 11. Apply firm pressure to the brake pedal. Did the brake pedal fall?	—	Go to Step 10	Go to Step 11
8	Did the brake pedal rise?	—	Go to Step 12	Go to Step 9
9	1. Using the scan tool, perform the gear tension relief function. 2. Turn the ignition switch to the OFF position. 3. Separate the ABS brake motor pack from the ABS brake modulator. 4. Grasp the ABS brake modulator left front gear. (The ABS brake modulator left front gear is the large gear furthest forward when the ABS brake modulator is mounted in the vehicle.) 5. Attempt to rotate the ABS brake modulator left front gear in either direction. Can the ABS brake modulator left front gear be rotated by hand?	—	Go to Step 13	Go to Step 10
10	Replace the ABS brake modulator. Is the repair complete?	—	Go to Diagnostic System Check	—
11	Replace the ABS brake solenoid valve that was originally in the left front ABS brake solenoid valve position. Is the repair complete?	—	Go to Diagnostic System Check	—
12	Repair the crossed wires to the left front ABS motor (CKT 1280 and CKT 1281). Is the repair complete?	—	Go to Diagnostic System Check	—
13	Replace the ABS brake motor pack. Is the repair complete?	—	Go to Diagnostic System Check	—
14	Malfunction is intermittent or not present at this time. Refer to Diagnostic Aids for more information.	—	—	—

GC402970325700CX

Fig. 179 Code C1252: LH Front ABS Channel In Release Too Long (Part 3 of 3). Intrigue, Lumina & Monte Carlo

Step	Action	Value(s)	Yes	No
1	Was the Diagnostic System Check performed?	—	Go to Step 2	Go to Diagnostic System Check
2	1. Turn the ignition switch to the RUN position, engine off. 2. Install a scan tool. 3. Using the scan tool, read the DTCs. Are there any wheel speed sensor DTCs set as current DTCs?	—	Go to Applicable DTC Table First	Go to Step 3
3	1. Using the scan tool, select DATA LIST. 2. Drive the vehicle and test the vehicle during a steady deceleration condition from 56 km/h to 0 km/h (35 mph to 0 mph) while monitoring all wheel speed sensor speeds. Do any of the wheel speed sensors indicate erratic or intermittent operation?	—	Go to Excessive Wheel Speed Sensor Variation DTC for Affected Wheel Speed Sensor	Go to Step 4
4	1. Turn the ignition switch to the RUN position, engine off. 2. Using the scan tool, select MISC TEST. 3. Using the scan tool, select the manual control function. 4. Using the scan tool, select the right front ABS motor apply function. 5. Using the scan tool, apply the right front ABS motor. 6. Apply firm pressure to the brake pedal. 7. Using the scan tool, select the right front ABS release function. 8. Using the scan tool, release the right front ABS motor. Did the brake pedal fall?	—	Go to Step 5	Go to Step 8
5	1. Remove the firm pressure from the brake pedal. 2. Using the scan tool, select the manual control function. 3. Using the scan tool, select the right front ABS brake solenoid valve. 4. Using the scan tool, command the right front ABS brake solenoid valve on. 5. Apply firm pressure to the brake pedal. Did the brake pedal fall?	—	Go to Step 7	Go to Step 6
6	1. Keep firm pressure applied to the brake pedal. 2. Using the scan tool, command the right front ABS brake solenoid valve off. Did the brake pedal fall?	—	Go to Step 14	Go to Step 7

GC402970325700DX

Fig. 180 Code C1253: RH Front ABS Channel In Release Too Long (Part 2 of 3). Intrigue, Lumina & Monte Carlo

Circuit Description

This DTC will diagnose an ABS motor that is energized longer than expected. This could occur if a wheel speed sensor is malfunctioning, the ABS motor does not turn, the right front solenoid mechanically fails open, or the ABS motor wires are crossed.

Conditions for Setting the DTC

DTC C1253 can be set only during an ABS stop. If the EBTCM commands the right front channel in release for greater than three seconds a malfunction exists.

Action Taken When the DTC Sets

A malfunction DTC is stored and ABS/ETS is disabled, and the amber ABS warning indicator is turned on.

Conditions for Clearing DTC

The condition for the DTC is no longer present and the scan tool CLEAR DTCs function is used, or 100 drive cycles have passed with no DTCs detected.

Diagnostic Aids

An intermittent malfunction may be caused by a mechanical part of the system that sticks or binds.

The frequency of the malfunction can be checked by using the enhanced diagnostic function of the scan tool, as described in Scan Tool Diagnostics in this section. DTC C1253 may occur on ice if steering wheel is turned to lock during braking. Using the Scan Tool perform hydraulic test to ensure total brake system is functional.

Any circuitry that is suspected of causing the intermittent complaint should be thoroughly checked for backed-out terminals, improper mating, broken locks, improperly formed or damaged terminals, poor terminal to wiring connections, or physical damage to the wiring harness.

Important

- J 39200 test leads must be zeroed prior to making any resistance measurements. Refer to J 39200 user's manual.

After diagnosis is complete, clear the DTCs and test drive the vehicle for three drive cycles to verify that the DTC does not reset. A drive cycle consists of starting the vehicle, driving the vehicle over 16 km/h (10 mph), stopping, and then turning the ignition off.

Important

- Excessive drag or high resistance in the base brake or suspension system must be inspected and corrected before proceeding with DTC diagnosis.

GC402970325702AX

Fig. 180 Code C1253: RH Front ABS Channel In Release Too Long (Part 1 of 3). Intrigue, Lumina & Monte Carlo

Step	Action	Value(s)	Yes	No
7	1. Remove the firm pressure from the brake pedal. 2. Turn the ignition switch to the OFF position. 3. Remove the right front ABS brake solenoid valve. 4. Remove the left front ABS brake solenoid valve. 5. Reinstall the right front ABS brake solenoid valve to the left front ABS brake solenoid valve position. 6. Reinstall the left front ABS brake solenoid valve to the right front ABS brake solenoid valve position. 7. Turn the ignition switch to the RUN position, engine off. 8. Using the scan tool, select the manual control function. 9. Using the scan tool, select the right front ABS brake solenoid valve. 10. Using the scan tool, command the right front ABS brake solenoid valve on. 11. Apply firm pressure to the brake pedal. Did the brake pedal fall?	—	Go to Step 10	Go to Step 11
8	Did the brake pedal rise?	—	Go to Step 12	Go to Step 9
9	1. Using the scan tool, perform the gear tension relief function. 2. Turn the ignition switch to the OFF position. 3. Separate the ABS brake motor pack from the ABS brake modulator. 4. Grasp the ABS brake modulator right front gear. (The ABS brake modulator right front gear is the large gear furthest rearward when the ABS brake modulator is mounted in the vehicle.) 5. Attempt to rotate the ABS brake modulator right front gear in either direction. Can the ABS brake modulator right front gear be rotated by hand?	—	Go to Step 13	Go to Step 10
10	Replace the ABS brake modulator. Is the repair complete?	—	Go to Diagnostic System Check	—
11	Replace the ABS brake solenoid valve that was originally in the right front ABS brake solenoid valve position. Is the repair complete?	—	Go to Diagnostic System Check	—
12	Repair the crossed wires to the right front ABS motor (CKT 1282 and CKT 1283). Is the repair complete?	—	Go to Diagnostic System Check	—
13	Replace the ABS brake motor pack. Is the repair complete?	—	Go to Diagnostic System Check	—
14	Malfunction is intermittent or not present at this time. Refer to Diagnostic Aids for more information.	—	—	—

GC402970325700EX

Fig. 180 Code C1253: RH Front ABS Channel In Release Too Long (Part 3 of 3). Intrigue, Lumina & Monte Carlo

Circuit Description

This DTC will diagnose an ABS motor that is energized longer than expected. This could occur if a wheel speed sensor is malfunctioning, the ABS motor does not turn, or the ABS motor wires are crossed.

Conditions for Setting the DTC

DTC C1254 can be set only during an ABS stop. A malfunction exists if the EBTCM commands the rear channel in release for greater than three seconds, and a difference of greater than 11 km/h (7 mph) exists between the vehicle reference speed and the maximum rear axle wheel speed. A malfunction exists if the EBTCM commands the rear channel in release for greater than four seconds, and a difference of less than 11 km/h (7 mph) exists between the vehicle reference speed and the maximum rear axle wheel speed.

Action Taken When the DTC Sets

A malfunction DTC is stored and ABS/ETS is disabled, and the amber ABS warning indicator is turned on.

Conditions for Clearing DTC

The condition for the DTC is no longer present and the scan tool CLEAR DTCs function is used, or 100 drive cycles have passed with no DTCs detected.

Diagnostic Aids

An intermittent malfunction may be caused by a mechanical part of the system that sticks or binds.

The frequency of the malfunction oan be checked by using the enhanced diagnostic function of the scan tool, as described in Scan Tool Diagnostics in this section. Using the Scan Tool, perform hydraulic test to ensure total brake system is functional.

Any circuitry that is suspected of causing the intermittent complaint should be thoroughly checked for backed-out terminals, improper mating, broken locks, improperly formed or damaged terminals, poor terminal to wiring connections, or physical damage to the wiring harness.

Important

- J 39200 test leads must be zeroed prior to making any resistance measurements. Refer to J 39200 user's manual.

After diagnosis is complete, clear the DTCs and test drive the vehicle for three drive cycles to verify that the DTC does not reset. A drive cycle consists of starting the vehicle, driving the vehicle over 16 km/h (10 mph), stopping, and then turning the ignition off.

Important

- Excessive drag or high resistance in the base brake or suspension system must be inspected and corrected before proceeding with DTC diagnosis.

GC402970325703AX

Fig. 181 Code C1254: Rear ABS Channel In Release Too Long (Part 1 of 3). Intrigue, Lumina & Monte Carlo

Step	Action	Value(s)	Yes	No
8	Replace the ABS brake modulator. Is the repair complete?	—	Go to Diagnostic System Check	—
9	Repair the crossed wires to the rear ABS motor (CKT 1284 and CKT 1285). Is the repair complete?	—	Go to Diagnostic System Check	—
10	Replace the ABS brake motor pack. Is the repair complete?	—	Go to Diagnostic System Check	—
11	Repair source of resistance in the base brake system. Is the repair complete?	—	Go to Diagnostic System Check	—
12	Malfunction is intermittent or not present at this time. Refer to Diagnostic Aids for more information.	—	—	—

GC402970325700GX

Fig. 181 Code C1254: Rear ABS Channel In Release Too Long (Part 3 of 3). Intrigue, Lumina & Monte Carlo

Step	Action	Value(s)	Yes	No
1	Was the Diagnostic System Check performed?	—	Go to Step 2	Go to Diagnostic System Check
2	1. Turn the ignition switch to the RUN position, engine off. 2. Install a scan tool. 3. Using the scan tool, read the DTCs. Is DTC C1255 set as a current DTC?	—	Go to Step 3	Go to Step 5
3	1. Using the scan tool, clear the DTCs. 2. Test drive the vehicle for three drive cycles. 3. Using the scan tool, check for DTCs. Does DTC C1255 set as a current DTC?	—	Go to Step 4	Go to Step 5
4	Replace the EBTCM. Is the repair complete?	—	Go to Diagnostic System Check	—
5	Malfunction is intermittent or not present at this time. Refer to Diagnostic Aids for additional information.	—	—	—

GC402970325800BX

Fig. 182 Code C1255: EBCM/EBTCM Internal Fault (Part 2 of 2). Intrigue, Lumina & Monte Carlo

Step	Action	Value(s)	Yes	No
1	Was the Diagnostic System Check performed?	—	Go to Step 2	Go to Diagnostic System Check
2	1. Turn the ignition switch to the RUN position, engine off. 2. Install a scan tool. 3. Using the scan tool, read the DTCs. Are there any wheel speed sensor DTCs set as current DTCs?	—	Go to Applicable DTC Table First	Go to Step 3
3	1. Using the scan tool, select DATA LIST. 2. Drive the vehicle and test the vehicle during a steady deceleration condition from 56 km/h to 0 km/h (35 mph to 0 mph) while monitoring all wheel speed sensor speeds. Do any of the wheel speed sensors indicate erratic or intermittent operation?	—	Go to Excessive Wheel Speed Sensor Variation DTC for Affected Wheel Speed Sensor	Go to Step 4
4	1. Turn the ignition switch to the OFF position. 2. Raise the rear of the vehicle until both rear wheels are off the ground. 3. Spin each rear wheel by hand. Can each rear wheel be spun freely by hand?	—	Go to Step 5	Go to Step 11
5	1. Turn the ignition switch to the RUN position, engine off. 2. Using the scan tool, select MISC TEST. 3. Using the scan tool, select the manual control function. 4. Using the scan tool, select the rear axle ABS motor apply function. 5. Apply firm pressure to the brake pedal. 6. Using the scan tool, apply the rear axle ABS motor. 7. Spin each rear wheel by hand. Can each rear wheel be spun freely by hand?	—	Go to Step 6	Go to Step 12
6	1. Keep firm pressure applied to the brake pedal. 2. Using the scan tool, command a release of the rear axle ABS motor. Can each rear wheel be spun freely by hand?	—	Go to Step 7	Go to Step 9
7	1. Using the scan tool, perform the gear tension relief function. 2. Turn the ignition switch to the OFF position. 3. Separate the ABS brake motor pack from the ABS brake modulator. 4. Reconnect the ABS brake motor pack connector if disconnected. 5. Turn the ignition switch to the RUN position, engine off. 6. Using the scan tool, perform a ABS brake motor pack motor test. Do all three ABS brake motor pack gears (small gears) spin freely?	—	Go to Step 8	Go to Step 10

GC402970325700FX

Fig. 181 Code C1254: Rear ABS Channel In Release Too Long (Part 2 of 3). Intrigue, Lumina & Monte Carlo

Circuit Description

This DTC identifies an internal malfunction detected by the EBTCM ABS motor driver interface, custom integrated circuit.

Action Taken When the DTC Sets

A malfunction DTC is stored, ABS/TCS is disabled and the amber ABS/TCS warning indicator(s) are turned on. The red BRAKE warning indicator is turned on if the rear piston in the ABS brake motor pack is not in the home position. The red BRAKE warning indicator is also turned on if the TCS motors are not in the home position.

Conditions for Clearing DTC

Condition for DTC is no longer present and the scan tool (CLEAR DTCs) function is used, or 100 drive cycles have passed with no DTCs detected.

Diagnostic Aids

An intermittent malfunction may be caused by a poor connection, rubbed-through wire insulation, or a wire that is broken inside the insulation.

The frequency of the malfunction can be checked by using the enhanced diagnostic function of the scan tool, as described in the Scan Tool manual.

Any circuitry that is suspected of causing the intermittent complaint should be thoroughly checked for backed out terminals, improper mating, broken locks, improperly formed or damaged terminals, poor terminal to wiring connections or physical damage to the wiring harness.

After diagnosis is complete, clear the DTCs and test drive the vehicle for three drive cycles to verify that the DTC does not reset. A drive cycle consists of starting the vehicle, driving the vehicle over 16 km/h (10 mph), stopping, and then turning the ignition to the OFF position.

GC402970325800AX

Fig. 182 Code C1255: EBCM/EBTCM Internal Fault (Part 1 of 2). Intrigue, Lumina & Monte Carlo

Circuit Description

This DTC identifies an ABS motor that cannot be energized due to an open in its circuitry. This malfunction will not allow proper front ABS operation.

Conditions for Setting the DTC

DTC C1256 can be set only when the motor is commanded off. If the EBTCM detects an out of range voltage on either of the left front ABS motor circuits indicating an open circuit, a malfunction exists.

Action Taken When the DTC Sets

An open ABS motor will not activate when requested. A malfunction DTC is stored and ABS/ETS is disabled, and the amber ABS warning indicator is turned on.

Conditions for Clearing DTC

The condition for the DTC is no longer present and the scan tool CLEAR DTCs function is used, or 100 drive cycles have passed with no DTCs detected.

Diagnostic Aids

Using the scan tool, select manual control function, and exercise ABS motor movement of the affected channel in both directions while applying light pressure on the brake pedal.

If erratic or jumpy brake pedal movement is detected while performing an apply or release function of the ABS motor, an intermittent malfunction may be indicated.

An intermittent malfunction may be caused by a poor connection, rubbed-through wire insulation, or a wire that is broken inside the insulation.

If the malfunction is not current, wiggle the wires of the affected channel and check if the DTC resets. This will help to pinpoint an intermittent malfunction in the motor circuitry or connections.

The frequency of the malfunction can be checked by using the enhanced diagnostic function of the scan tool, as described in Scan Tool Diagnostics in this section.

Any circuitry that is suspected of causing the intermittent complaint should be thoroughly checked for backed-out terminals, improper mating, broken locks, improperly formed or damaged terminals, poor terminal to wiring connections, or physical damage to the wiring harness.

Important

- J 39200 test leads must be zeroed prior to making any resistance measurements. Refer to J 39200 user's manual.

After diagnosis is complete, clear the DTCs and test drive the vehicle for three drive cycles to verify that the DTC does not reset. A drive cycle consists of starting the vehicle, driving the vehicle over 16 km/h (10 mph), stopping, and then turning the ignition to off.

GC402970325901AX

Fig. 183 Code C1256: LH Front ABS Motor Circuit Open (Part 1 of 3). Intrigue, Lumina & Monte Carlo

Step	Action	Value(s)	Yes	No
1	Was the Diagnostic System Check performed?	—	Go to Step 2	Go to Diagnostic System Check
2	Does DTC C1256 occur intermittently?	—	Go to Diagnostic Aids	Go to Step 3
3	1. Turn the ignition switch to the OFF position. 2. Disconnect the 6-way ABS brake motor pack connector. 3. Using J 39200, measure the resistance between the 6-way ABS brake motor pack connector terminal E and the 6-way ABS brake motor pack connector terminal F. Is the resistance measured within the specified range?	0.2-1.5 Ω	Go to Step 4	Go to Step 8
4	1. Disconnect the 8-way EBTCM connector C2. 2. Using J 39200, measure the resistance between the 6-way ABS brake motor pack harness connector terminal F and the 8-way EBTCM harness connector C2 terminal G. Is the resistance measured within the specified range?	0-2 Ω	Go to Step 5	Go to Step 9
5	Using J 39200, measure the resistance between the 6-way ABS brake motor pack harness connector terminal E and the 8-way EBTCM harness connector C2 terminal H. Is the resistance measured within the specified range?	0-2 Ω	Go to Step 6	Go to Step 10
6	1. Inspect the 6-way ABS brake motor pack connector and the 6-way ABS brake motor pack harness connector for signs of poor terminal contact and evidence of corrosion. 2. Inspect the 8-way EBTCM connector C2 and the 8-way EBTCM harness connector C2 for signs of poor terminal contact and evidence of corrosion. Are there signs of poor terminal contact and evidence of corrosion?	—	Go to Step 11	Go to Step 7
7	1. Reconnect the 6-way ABS brake motor pack connector. 2. Reconnect the 8-way EBTCM connector C2. 3. Test drive the vehicle obtaining a speed at least 16 km/h (10 mph). 4. Turn the ignition switch to the OFF position. 5. Repeat the drive sequence two additional times. 6. Using the scan tool, check for DTCs. Did DTC C1256 set as a current DTC in the last three drive cycles?	—	Go to Step 12	Go to Step 13
8	Replace the ABS brake motor pack. Is the repair complete?	—	Go to Diagnostic System Check	—
9	Repair the open or high resistance in CKT 1280. Is the repair complete?	—	Go to Diagnostic System Check	—

GC402970325900BX

Fig. 183 Code C1256: LH Front ABS Motor Circuit Open (Part 2 of 3). Intrigue, Lumina & Monte Carlo

Circuit Description

This DTC identifies an ABS motor circuit that is shorted to ground. This malfunction will not allow the ABS motor to be controlled at the commanded current rate or will cause the driver circuit to allow current directly to ground.

Conditions for Setting the DTC

DTC C1257 can be set anytime. If the EBTCM detects an out of range voltage on either of the left front ABS motor circuits indicating a circuit shorted to ground or a ABS brake motor internally shorted, a malfunction exists.

Action Taken When the DTC Sets

A malfunction DTC is stored and ABS/ETS is disabled, and the amber ABS warning indicator is turned on.

Conditions for Clearing DTC

The condition for the DTC is no longer present and the scan tool CLEAR DTCs function is used, or 100 drive cycles have passed with no DTCs detected.

Diagnostic Aids

Using the scan tool, select manual control function, and exercise ABS motor movement of the affected channel in both directions while applying light pressure on the brake pedal.

If erratic or jumpy brake pedal movement is detected while performing an apply or release function of the ABS motor, an intermittent malfunction may be indicated.

An intermittent malfunction may be caused by a poor connection, rubbed-through wire insulation, or a wire that is broken inside the insulation.

If the malfunction is not current, wiggle the wires of the affected channel and check if the DTC resets. This will help to pinpoint an intermittent malfunction in the motor circuitry or connections.

The frequency of the malfunction can be checked by using the enhanced diagnostic function of the scan tool, as described in Scan Tool Diagnostics in this section.

Any circuitry that is suspected of causing the intermittent complaint should be thoroughly checked for backed-out terminals, improper mating, broken locks, improperly formed or damaged terminals, poor terminal to wiring connections, or physical damage to the wiring harness.

Important

- J 39200 test leads must be zeroed prior to making any resistance measurements. Refer to J 39200 user's manual.

After diagnosis is complete, clear the DTCs and test drive the vehicle for three drive cycles to verify that the DTC does not reset. A drive cycle consists of starting the vehicle, driving the vehicle over 16 km/h (10 mph), stopping, and then turning the ignition to off.

GC402970326001AX

Fig. 184 Code C1257: LH Front ABS Motor Circuit Shorted To Ground (Part 1 of 3). Intrigue, Lumina & Monte Carlo

Step	Action	Value(s)	Yes	No
10	Repair the open or high resistance in CKT 1281. Is the repair complete?	—	Go to Diagnostic System Check	—
11	Replace all the terminals or the connectors that exhibit signs of poor terminal contact, corrosion, or damaged terminal(s). Is the repair complete?	—	Go to Diagnostic System Check	—
12	Replace the EBTCM. Is the repair complete?	—	Go to Diagnostic System Check	—
13	Malfunction is intermittent or not present at this time. Refer to Diagnostic Aids for more information.	—	—	—

GC402970325900CX

Fig. 183 Code C1256: LH Front ABS Motor Circuit Open (Part 3 of 3). Intrigue, Lumina & Monte Carlo

Step	Action	Value(s)	Yes	No
1	Was the Diagnostic System Check performed?	—	Go to Step 2	Go to Diagnostic System Check
2	Does DTC C1257 occur intermittently?	—	Go to Diagnostic Aids	Go to Step 3
3	1. Turn the ignition switch to the OFF position. 2. Disconnect the 6-way ABS brake motor pack connector. 3. Disconnect the 8-way EBTCM connector C2. 4. Using J 39200, measure the resistance between the 6-way ABS brake motor pack harness connector terminal F and ground. Is the resistance measured within the specified range?	OL (Infinite)	Go to Step 4	Go to Step 9
4	Using J 39200, measure the resistance between the 6-way ABS brake motor pack harness connector terminal E and ground. Is the resistance measured within the specified range?	OL (Infinite)	Go to Step 5	Go to Step 10
5	Using J 39200, measure the resistance between the 6-way ABS brake motor pack connector terminal F and ground. Is the resistance measured within the specified range?	OL (Infinite)	Go to Step 6	Go to Step 8
6	1. Inspect the 6-way ABS brake motor pack connector and the 6-way ABS brake motor pack harness connector for signs of damage which may result in a short to ground with the connector connected. 2. Inspect the 8-way EBTCM connector C2 and the 8-way EBTCM harness connector C2 for signs of damage which may result in a short to ground with the connector connected. 3. Inspect CKT 1280 and CKT 1281 for signs of damage which may result in a short to ground. Are there signs of damage which may result in a short to ground?	—	Go to Step 11	Go to Step 7
7	1. Reconnect the 6-way ABS brake motor pack connector. 2. Reconnect the 8-way EBTCM connector C2. 3. Test drive the vehicle obtaining a speed at least 16 km/h (10 mph). 4. Turn the ignition switch to the OFF position. 5. Repeat the drive sequence two additional times. 6. Using the scan tool, check for DTCs. Did DTC C1257 set as a current DTC in the last three drive cycles?	—	Go to Step 12	Go to Step 13
8	Replace the ABS brake motor pack. Is the repair complete?	—	Go to Diagnostic System Check	—
9	Repair the short to ground in CKT 1280. Is the repair complete?	—	Go to Diagnostic System Check	—

GC402970326000BX

Fig. 184 Code C1257: LH Front ABS Motor Circuit Shorted To Ground (Part 2 of 3). Intrigue, Lumina, Monte Carlo, Century & Regal

Step	Action	Value(s)	Yes	No
10	Repair the short to ground in CKT 1281. Is the repair complete?	—	Go to Diagnostic System Check	—
11	Replace all the terminals, the connectors or the wires that exhibit signs of damage which may result in a short to ground. Is the repair complete?	—	Go to Diagnostic System Check	—
12	Replace the EBTCM. Is the repair complete?	—	Go to Diagnostic System Check	—
13	Malfunction is intermittent or not present at this time. Refer to Diagnostic Aids for more information.	—	—	—

GC402970326000CX

Fig. 184 Code C1257: LH Front ABS Motor Circuit Shorted To Ground (Part 3 of 3). Intrigue, Lumina & Monte Carlo

Circuit Description

This DTC identifies an ABS motor circuit that is shorted to voltage or an ABS motor that has low or no resistance. This malfunction will not allow the ABS motor to be controlled at the commanded current rate or will cause the ABS motor to turn in the opposite direction, or not at all.

Conditions for Setting the DTC

DTC C1258 can be set only when the ABS motor is commanded off. If the EBTCM detects an out of range voltage on either of the left front ABS motor circuits indicating a circuit shorted to voltage or an ABS motor internally shorted, a malfunction exists.

Action Taken When the DTC Sets

A malfunction DTC is stored and ABS/ETS is disabled, and the amber ABS warning indicator is turned on.

Conditions for Clearing DTC

The condition for the DTC is no longer present and the scan tool CLEAR DTCs function is used, or 100 drive cycles have passed with no DTCs detected.

Diagnostic Aids

Using the scan tool, select manual control function, and exercise ABS motor movement of the affected channel in both directions while applying light pressure on the brake pedal.

If erratic or jumpy brake pedal movement is detected while performing an apply or release function of the ABS motor, an intermittent malfunction may be indicated.

An intermittent malfunction may be caused by a poor connection, rubbed-through wire insulation, or a wire that is broken inside the insulation.

If the malfunction is not current, wiggle the wires of the affected channel and check if the DTC resets. This will help to pinpoint an intermittent malfunction in the motor circuitry or connections.

The frequency of the malfunction can be checked by using the enhanced diagnostic function of the scan tool, as described in Scan Tool Diagnostics in this section. Any circuitry that is suspected of causing the intermittent complaint should be thoroughly checked for backed-out terminals, improper mating, broken locks, improperly formed or damaged terminals, poor terminal to wiring connections, or physical damage to the wiring harness.

Important

- J 39200 test leads must be zeroed prior to making any resistance measurements. Refer to J 39200 user's manual.

After diagnosis is complete, clear the DTCs and test drive the vehicle for three drive cycles to verify that the DTC does not reset. A drive cycle consists of starting the vehicle, driving the vehicle over 16 km/h (10 mph), stopping, and then turning the ignition to off.

GC402970326101AX

Fig. 185 Code C1258: LH Front ABS Motor Circuit Shorted To Voltage (Part 1 of 3). Intrigue, Lumina & Monte Carlo

Step	Action	Value(s)	Yes	No
1	Was the Diagnostic System Check performed?	—	Go to Step 2	Go to Diagnostic System Check
2	Does DTC C1258 occur intermittently?	—	Go to Diagnostic Aids	Go to Step 3
3	1. Turn the ignition switch to the OFF position. 2. Disconnect the 6-way ABS motor pack connector. 3. Disconnect the 8-way EBTCM connector C2. 4. Turn the ignition switch to the RUN position, engine off. 5. Using J 39200, measure the voltage between the 6-way ABS motor pack harness connector terminal F and ground. Is the voltage measured within the specified range?	0-1V	Go to Step 4	Go to Step 10
4	Using J 39200, measure the voltage between the 6-way ABS motor pack harness connector terminal E and ground. Is the voltage measured within the specified range?	0-1V	Go to Step 5	Go to Step 11
5	1. Turn the ignition switch to the OFF position. 2. Using J 39200, measure the resistance between the 6-way ABS motor pack harness connector terminal F and the 6-way ABS motor pack harness connector terminal E. Is the resistance measured within the specified range?	OL (Infinite)	Go to Step 6	Go to Step 12
6	Using J 39200, measure the resistance between the 6-way ABS motor pack connector terminal F and the 6-way ABS motor pack connector terminal E. Is the resistance measured equal to or greater than the specified resistance?	0.2 Ω	Go to Step 7	Go to Step 9
7	1. Inspect the 6-way ABS motor pack connector and the 6-way ABS motor pack harness connector for signs of damage which may result in a short to voltage with the connector connected. 2. Inspect the 8-way EBTCM connector C2 and the 8-way EBTCM harness connector C2 for signs of damage which may result in a short to voltage with the connector connected. 3. Inspect CKT 1280 and CKT 1281 for signs of damage which may result in a short to voltage. Are there signs of damage which may result in a short to voltage?	—	Go to Step 13	Go to Step 8
8	1. Reconnect the 6-way ABS motor pack connector. 2. Reconnect the 8-way EBTCM connector C2. 3. Test drive the vehicle obtaining a speed at least 16 km/h (10 mph). 4. Turn the ignition switch to the OFF position. 5. Repeat the drive sequence two additional times. 6. Using the scan tool, check for DTCs. Did DTC C1258 set as a current DTC in the last three drive cycles?	—	Go to Step 14	Go to Step 15

GC402970326100BX

Fig. 185 Code C1258: LH Front ABS Motor Circuit Shorted To Voltage (Part 2 of 3). Intrigue, Lumina & Monte Carlo

Step	Action	Value(s)	Yes	No
9	Replace the ABS motor pack. Is the repair complete?	—	Go to Diagnostic System Check	—
10	Repair the short to voltage in CKT 1280. Is the repair complete?	—	Go to Diagnostic System Check	—
11	Repair the short to voltage in CKT 1281. Is the repair complete?	—	Go to Diagnostic System Check	—
12	Repair the short between CKT 1280 and CKT 1281. Is the repair complete?	—	Go to Diagnostic System Check	—
13	Replace all the terminals, the connectors or the wires that exhibit signs of damage which may result in a short to voltage. Is the repair complete?	—	Go to Diagnostic System Check	—
14	Replace the EBTCM. Is the repair complete?	—	Go to Diagnostic System Check	—
15	Malfunction is intermittent or not present at this time. Refer to Diagnostic Aids for more information.	—	—	—

GC402970326100CX

Fig. 185 Code C1258: LH Front ABS Motor Circuit Shorted To Voltage (Part 3 of 3). Intrigue, Lumina & Monte Carlo

Circuit Description

This DTC identifies an ABS motor that cannot be energized due to an open in its circuitry. This malfunction will not allow proper front ABS operation.

Conditions for Setting the DTC

DTC C1261 can be set only when the ABS motor is commanded off. If the EBTCM detects an out of range voltage on either of the right front ABS motor circuits indicating an open circuit, a malfunction exists.

Action Taken When the DTC Sets

An open ABS motor will not activate when requested. A malfunction DTC is stored, ABS is disabled, and the amber ABS warning indicator is turned on.

Conditions for Clearing DTC

The condition for the DTC is no longer present and the scan tool CLEAR DTCs function is used, or 100 drive cycles have passed with no DTCs detected.

Diagnostic Aids

Using the scan tool, select manual control function, and exercise ABS motor movement of the affected channel in both directions while applying light pressure on the brake pedal.

If erratic or jumpy brake pedal movement is detected while performing an apply or release function of the ABS motor, an intermittent malfunction may be indicated.

An intermittent malfunction may be caused by a poor connection, rubbed-through wire insulation, or a wire that is broken inside the insulation.

If the malfunction is not current, wiggle the wires of the affected channel and check if the DTC resets. This will help to pinpoint an intermittent malfunction in the motor circuitry or connections.

The frequency of the malfunction can be checked by using the enhanced diagnostic function of the scan tool, as described in Scan Tool Diagnostics in this section.

Any circuitry that is suspected of causing the intermittent complaint should be thoroughly checked for backed-out terminals, improper mating, broken locks, improperly formed or damaged terminals, poor terminal to wiring connections, or physical damage to the wiring harness.

Important

- J 39200 test leads must be zeroed prior to making any resistance measurements. Refer to J 39200 user's manual.

After diagnosis is complete, clear the DTCs and test drive the vehicle for three drive cycles to verify that the DTC does not reset. A drive cycle consists of starting the vehicle, driving the vehicle over 16 km/h (10 mph), stopping, and then turning the ignition to off.

GC402970325902AX

Fig. 186 Code C1261: RH Front ABS Motor Circuit Open (Part 1 of 3). Intrigue, Lumina & Monte Carlo

Step	Action	Value(s)	Yes	No
1	Was the Diagnostic System Check performed?	—	Go to Step 2	Go to Diagnostic System Check
2	Does DTC C1261 occur intermittently?	—	Go to Diagnostic Aids	Go to Step 3
3	1. Turn the ignition switch to the OFF position. 2. Disconnect the 6-way ABS brake motor pack connector. 3. Using J 39200, measure the resistance between the 6-way ABS brake motor pack connector terminal A and the 6-way ABS brake motor pack connector terminal B. Is the resistance measured within the specified range?	0.2-1.5 Ω	Go to Step 4	Go to Step 8
4	1. Disconnect the 8-way EBTCM connector C2. 2. Using J 39200, measure the resistance between the 6-way ABS brake motor pack harness connector terminal B and the 8-way EBTCM harness connector C2 terminal A. Is the resistance measured within the specified range?	0-2 Ω	Go to Step 5	Go to Step 9
5	Using J 39200, measure the resistance between the 6-way ABS brake motor pack harness connector terminal A and the 8-way EBTCM harness connector C2 terminal B. Is the resistance measured within the specified range?	0-2 Ω	Go to Step 6	Go to Step 10
6	1. Inspect the 6-way ABS brake motor pack connector and the 6-way ABS brake motor pack harness connector for signs of poor terminal contact and evidence of corrosion. 2. Inspect the 8-way EBTCM connector C2 and the 8-way EBTCM harness connector C2 for signs of poor terminal contact and evidence of corrosion. Are there signs of poor terminal contact and evidence of corrosion?	—	Go to Step 11	Go to Step 7
7	1. Reconnect the 6-way ABS brake motor pack connector. 2. Reconnect the 8-way EBTCM connector C2. 3. Test drive the vehicle obtaining a speed at least 16 km/h (10 mph). 4. Turn the ignition switch to the OFF position. 5. Repeat the drive sequence two additional times. 6. Using the scan tool, check for DTCs. Did DTC C1261 set as a current DTC in the last three drive cycles?	—	Go to Step 12	Go to Step 13
8	Replace the ABS brake motor pack. Is the repair complete?	—	Go to Diagnostic System Check	—
9	Repair the open or high resistance in CKT 1282. Is the repair complete?	—	Go to Diagnostic System Check	—

GC402970325900DX

Fig. 186 Code C1261: RH Front ABS Motor Circuit Open (Part 2 of 3). Intrigue, Lumina & Monte Carlo

Step	Action	Value(s)	Yes	No
10	Repair the open or high resistance in CKT 1283. Is the repair complete?	—	Go to Diagnostic System Check	—
11	Replace all the terminals or the connectors that exhibit signs of poor terminal contact, corrosion, or damaged terminal(s). Is the repair complete?	—	Go to Diagnostic System Check	—
12	Replace the EBTCM. Is the repair complete?	—	Go to Diagnostic System Check	—
13	Malfunction is intermittent or not present at this time. Refer to Diagnostic Aids for more information.	—	—	—

GC402970325900EX

Fig. 186 Code C1261: RH Front ABS Motor Circuit Open (Part 3 of 3). Intrigue, Lumina & Monte Carlo

Step	Action	Value(s)	Yes	No
1	Was the Diagnostic System Check performed?	—	Go to Step 2	Go to Diagnostic System Check
2	Does DTC C1262 occur intermittently?	—	Go to Diagnostic Aids	Go to Step 3
3	1. Turn the ignition switch to the OFF position. 2. Disconnect the 6-way ABS brake motor pack connector. 3. Disconnect the 8-way EBTCM connector C2. 4. Using J 39200, measure the resistance between the 6-way ABS brake motor pack harness connector terminal B and ground. Is the resistance measured within the specified range?	OL (Infinite)	Go to Step 4	Go to Step 9
4	Using J 39200, measure the resistance between the 6-way ABS brake motor pack harness connector terminal A and ground. Is the resistance measured within the specified range?	OL (Infinite)	Go to Step 5	Go to Step 10
5	Using J 39200, measure the resistance between the 6-way ABS brake motor pack connector terminal B and ground. Is the resistance measured within the specified range?	OL (Infinite)	Go to Step 6	Go to Step 8
6	1. Inspect the 6-way ABS brake motor pack connector and the 6-way ABS brake motor pack harness connector for signs of damage which may result in a short to ground with the connector connected. 2. Inspect the 8-way EBTCM connector C2 and the 8-way EBTCM harness connector C2 for signs of damage which may result in a short to ground with the connector connected. 3. Inspect CKT 1282 and CKT 1283 for signs of damage which may result in a short to ground. Are there signs of damage which may result in a short to ground?	—	Go to Step 11	Go to Step 7
7	1. Reconnect the 6-way ABS brake motor pack connector. 2. Reconnect the 8-way EBTCM connector C2. 3. Test drive the vehicle obtaining a speed at least 16 km/h (10 mph). 4. Turn the ignition switch to the OFF position. 5. Repeat the drive sequence two additional times. 6. Using the scan tool, check for DTCs. Did DTC C1262 set as a current DTC in the last three drive cycles?	—	Go to Step 12	Go to Step 13
8	Replace the ABS brake motor pack. Is the repair complete?	—	Go to Diagnostic System Check	—
9	Repair the short to ground in CKT 1282. Is the repair complete?	—	Go to Diagnostic System Check	—

GC402970326000DX

Fig. 187 Code C1262: RH Front ABS Motor Circuit Shorted To Ground (Part 2 of 3). Intrigue, Lumina & Monte Carlo

Circuit Description

This DTC identifies an ABS motor circuit that is shorted to voltage or an ABS motor that has low or no resistance. This malfunction will not allow the ABS motor to be controlled at the commanded current rate or will cause the ABS motor to turn in the opposite direction or not at all.

Conditions for Setting the DTC

DTC C1263 can be set only when the ABS motor is commanded off. If the EBTCM detects an out of range voltage on either of the right front ABS motor circuits indicating a circuit shorted to voltage or an ABS motor shorted, a malfunction exists.

Action Taken When the DTC Sets

A malfunction DTC is stored, ABS is disabled, and the amber ABS warning indicator is turned on.

Conditions for Clearing DTC

The condition for the DTC is no longer present and the scan tool CLEAR DTCs function is used, or 100 drive cycles have passed with no DTCs detected.

Diagnostic Aids

Using the scan tool, select manual control function, and exercise ABS motor movement of the affected channel in both directions while applying light pressure on the brake pedal.

If erratic or jumpy brake pedal movement is detected while performing an apply or release function of the ABS motor, an intermittent malfunction may be indicated.

An intermittent malfunction may be caused by a poor connection, rubbed-through wire insulation, or a wire that is broken inside the insulation.

If the malfunction is not current, wiggle the wires of the affected channel and check if the DTC resets. This will help to pinpoint an intermittent malfunction in the motor circuitry or connections.

The frequency of the malfunction can be checked by using the enhanced diagnostic function of the scan tool, as described in Scan Tool Diagnostics in this section.

Any circuitry that is suspected of causing the intermittent complaint should be thoroughly checked for backed-out terminals, improper mating, broken locks, improperly formed or damaged terminals, poor terminal to wiring connections, or physical damage to the wiring harness.

Important

- J 39200 test leads must be zeroed prior to making any resistance measurements.

After diagnosis is complete, clear the DTCs and test drive the vehicle for three drive cycles to verify that the DTC does not reset. A drive cycle consists of starting the vehicle, driving the vehicle over 16 km/h (10 mph), stopping, and then turning the ignition to off.

GC402970326102AX

Fig. 188 Code C1263: RH Front ABS Motor Circuit Shorted To Voltage (Part 1 of 3). Intrigue, Lumina & Monte Carlo

Circuit Description

This DTC identifies an ABS motor circuit that is shorted to ground. This malfunction will not allow the ABS motor to be controlled at the commanded current rate or will cause the ABS motor driver circuit to allow current directly to ground.

Conditions for Setting the DTC

DTC C1262 can be set anytime. If the EBTCM detects an out of range voltage on either of the right front ABS motor circuits indicating a circuit shorted to ground or an ABS brake motor internally shorted, a malfunction exists.

Action Taken When the DTC Sets

A malfunction DTC is stored, ABS is disabled, and the amber ABS warning indicator is turned on.

Conditions for Clearing DTC

The condition for the DTC is no longer present and the scan tool CLEAR DTCs function is used, or 100 drive cycles have passed with no DTCs detected.

Diagnostic Aids

Using the scan tool, select manual control function, and exercise ABS motor movement of the affected channel in both directions while applying light pressure on the brake pedal.

If erratic or jumpy brake pedal movement is detected while performing an apply or release function of the ABS motor, an intermittent malfunction may be indicated.

An intermittent malfunction may be caused by a poor connection, rubbed-through wire insulation, or a wire that is broken inside the insulation.

If the malfunction is not current, wiggle the wires of the affected channel and check if the DTC resets. This will help to pinpoint an intermittent malfunction in the motor circuitry or connections.

The frequency of the malfunction can be checked by using the enhanced diagnostic function of the scan tool, as described in Scan Tool Diagnostics in this section.

Any circuitry that is suspected of causing the intermittent complaint should be thoroughly checked for backed-out terminals, improper mating, broken locks, improperly formed or damaged terminals, poor terminal to wiring connections, or physical damage to the wiring harness.

Important

- J 39200 test leads must be zeroed prior to making any resistance measurements. Refer to J 39200 user's manual.

After diagnosis is complete, clear the DTCs and test drive the vehicle for three drive cycles to verify that the DTC does not reset. A drive cycle consists of starting the vehicle, driving the vehicle over 16 km/h (10 mph), stopping, and then turning the ignition to off.

GC402970326002AX

Fig. 187 Code C1262: RH Front ABS Motor Circuit Shorted To Ground (Part 1 of 3). Intrigue, Lumina & Monte Carlo

Step	Action	Value(s)	Yes	No
10	Repair the short to ground in CKT 1283. Is the repair complete?	—	Go to Diagnostic System Check	—
11	Replace all the terminals, the connectors or the wires that exhibit signs of damage which may result in a short to ground. Is the repair complete?	—	Go to Diagnostic System Check	—
12	Replace the EBTCM. Is the repair complete?	—	Go to Diagnostic System Check	—
13	Malfunction is intermittent or not present at this time. Refer to Diagnostic Aids for more information.	—	—	—

GC402970326000EX

Fig. 187 Code C1262: RH Front ABS Motor Circuit Shorted To Ground (Part 3 of 3). IIntrigue, Lumina & Monte Carlo

Step	Action	Value(s)	Yes	No
1	Was the Diagnostic System Check performed?	—	Go to Step 2	Go to Diagnostic System Check
2	Does DTC C1263 occur intermittently?	—	Go to Diagnostic Aids	Go to Step 3
3	1. Turn the ignition switch to the OFF position. 2. Disconnect the 6-way ABS brake motor pack connector. 3. Disconnect the 8-way EBTCM connector C2. 4. Turn the ignition switch to the RUN position, engine off. 5. Using J 39200, measure the voltage between the 6-way ABS brake motor pack harness connector terminal B and ground. Is the voltage measured within the specified range?	0-1V	Go to Step 4	Go to Step 10
4	Using J 39200, measure the voltage between the 6-way ABS brake motor pack harness connector terminal A and ground. Is the voltage measured within the specified range?	0-1V	Go to Step 5	Go to Step 11
5	1. Turn the ignition switch to the OFF position. 2. Using J 39200, measure the resistance between the 6-way ABS brake motor pack harness connector terminal B and the 6-way ABS brake motor pack harness connector terminal A. Is the resistance measured within the specified range?	OL (Infinite)	Go to Step 6	Go to Step 12
6	Using J 39200, measure the resistance between the 6-way ABS brake motor pack connector terminal B and the 6-way ABS brake motor pack connector terminal A. Is the resistance measured equal to or greater than the specified resistance?	0.2 Ω	Go to Step 7	Go to Step 9
7	1. Inspect the 6-way ABS brake motor pack connector and the 6-way ABS brake motor pack harness connector for signs of damage which may result in a short to voltage with the connector connected. 2. Inspect the 8-way EBTCM connector C2 and the 8-way EBTCM harness connector C2 for signs of damage which may result in a short to voltage with the connector connected. 3. Inspect CKT 1282 and CKT 1283 for signs of damage which may result in a short to voltage. Are there signs of damage which may result in a short to voltage?	—	Go to Step 13	Go to Step 8

GC402970326100DX

Fig. 188 Code C1263: RH Front ABS Motor Circuit Shorted To Voltage (Part 2 of 3). Intrigue, Lumina & Monte Carlo

Step	Action	Value(s)	Yes	No
8	1. Reconnect the 6-way ABS brake motor pack connector. 2. Reconnect the 8-way EBTCM connector C2. 3. Test drive the vehicle obtaining a speed of at least 16 km/h (10 mph). 4. Turn the ignition switch to the OFF position. 5. Repeat the drive sequence two additional times. 6. Using the scan tool, check for DTCs. Did DTC C1263 set as a current DTC in the last three drive cycles?	—	Go to Step 14	Go to Step 15
9	Replace the ABS brake motor pack. Is the repair complete?	—	Go to Diagnostic System Check	—
10	Repair the short to voltage in CKT 1282. Is the repair complete?	—	Go to Diagnostic System Check	—
11	Repair the short to voltage in CKT 1283. Is the repair complete?	—	Go to Diagnostic System Check	—
12	Repair the short between CKT 1282 and CKT 1283. Is the repair complete?	—	Go to Diagnostic System Check	—
13	Replace all the terminals, the connectors or the wires that exhibit signs of damage which may result in a short to voltage. Is the repair complete?	—	Go to Diagnostic System Check	—
14	Replace the EBTCM. Is the repair complete?	—	Go to Diagnostic System Check	—
15	Malfunction is intermittent or not present at this time. Refer to Diagnostic Aids for more information.	—	—	—

GC402970326100EX

Fig. 188 Code C1263: RH Front ABS Motor Circuit Shorted To Voltage (Part 3 of 3). Intrigue, Lumina & Monte Carlo

Step	Action	Value(s)	Yes	No
1	Was the Diagnostic System Check performed?	—	Go to Step 2	Go to Diagnostic System Check
2	Does DTC C1264 occur intermittently?	—	Go to Diagnostic Aids	Go to Step 3
3	1. Turn the ignition switch to the OFF position. 2. Disconnect the 6-way ABS brake motor pack connector. 3. Using J 39200, measure the resistance between the 6-way ABS brake motor pack connector terminal D and the 6-way ABS brake motor pack connector terminal C. Is the resistance measured within the specified range?	0.2-1.5 Ω	Go to Step 4	Go to Step 8
4	1. Disconnect the 8-way EBTCM connector C2. 2. Using J 39200, measure the resistance between the 6-way ABS brake motor pack harness connector terminal D and the 8-way EBTCM harness connector C2 terminal F. Is the resistance measured within the specified range?	0-2 Ω	Go to Step 5	Go to Step 9
5	Using J 39200, measure the resistance between the 6-way ABS brake motor pack harness connector terminal C and the 8-way EBTCM harness connector C2 terminal E. Is the resistance measured within the specified range?	0-2 Ω	Go to Step 6	Go to Step 10
6	1. Inspect the 6-way ABS brake motor pack connector and the 6-way ABS brake motor pack harness connector for signs of poor terminal contact and evidence of corrosion. 2. Inspect the 8-way EBTCM connector C2 and the 8-way EBTCM harness connector C2 for signs of poor terminal contact and evidence of corrosion. Are there signs of poor terminal contact and evidence of corrosion?	—	Go to Step 11	Go to Step 7
7	1. Reconnect the 6-way ABS brake motor pack connector. 2. Reconnect the 8-way EBTCM connector C2. 3. Test drive the vehicle obtaining a speed at least 16 km/h (10 mph). 4. Turn the ignition switch to the OFF position. 5. Repeat the drive sequence two additional times. 6. Using the scan tool, check for DTCs. Did DTC C1264 set as a current DTC in the last three drive cycles?	—	Go to Step 12	Go to Step 13
8	Replace the ABS brake motor pack. Is the repair complete?	—	Go to Diagnostic System Check	—
9	Repair the open or high resistance in CKT 1284. Is the repair complete?	—	Go to Diagnostic System Check	—

GC402970325900FX

Fig. 189 Code C1264: Rear ABS Motor Circuit Open (Part 2 of 3). Intrigue, Lumina & Monte Carlo

Circuit Description

This DTC identifies an ABS motor that cannot be energized due to an open in its circuitry. This malfunction will not allow proper rear ABS operation.

Conditions for Setting the DTC

DTC C1264 can be set only when the ABS motor is commanded off. If the EBTCM detects an out of range voltage on either of the rear ABS motor circuits indicating an open circuit, a malfunction exists.

Action Taken When the DTC Sets

An open motor will not activate when requested. A malfunction DTC is stored and ABS/ETS is disabled, and the amber ABS warning indicator is turned on. The red BRAKE warning indicator is turned on if the rear piston in the ABS brake motor pack is not in the home position.

Conditions for Clearing DTC

The condition for the DTC is no longer present and the scan tool CLEAR DTCs function is used, or 100 drive cycles have passed with no DTCs detected.

Diagnostic Aids

Using the scan tool, select manual control function, and exercise ABS motor movement of the affected channel in both directions while applying light pressure on the brake pedal.

If erratic or jumpy brake pedal movement is detected while performing an apply or release function of the ABS motor, an intermittent malfunction may be indicated.

An intermittent malfunction may be caused by a poor connection, rubbed-through wire insulation, or a wire that is broken inside the insulation.

If the malfunction is not current, wiggle the wires of the affected channel and check if the DTC resets. This will help to pinpoint an intermittent malfunction in the motor circuitry or connections.

The frequency of the malfunction can be checked by using the enhanced diagnostic function of the scan tool, as described in Scan Tool Diagnostics in this section.

Any circuitry that is suspected of causing the intermittent complaint should be thoroughly checked for backed-out terminals, improper mating, broken locks, improperly formed or damaged terminals, poor terminal to wiring connections, or physical damage to the wiring harness.

! Important

- J 39200 test leads must be zeroed prior to making any resistance measurements. Refer to J 39200 user's manual.

After diagnosis is complete, clear the DTCs and test drive the vehicle for three drive cycles to verify that the DTC does not reset. A drive cycle consists of starting the vehicle, driving the vehicle over 16 km/h (10 mph), stopping, and then turning the ignition to off.

GC402970325903AX

Fig. 189 Code C1264: Rear ABS Motor Circuit Open (Part 1 of 3). Intrigue, Lumina & Monte Carlo

Step	Action	Value(s)	Yes	No
10	Repair the open or high resistance in CKT 1285. Is the repair complete?	—	Go to Diagnostic System Check	—
11	Replace all the terminals or the connectors that exhibit signs of poor terminal contact, corrosion, or damaged terminal(s). Is the repair complete?	—	Go to Diagnostic System Check	—
12	Replace the EBTCM. Is the repair complete?	—	Go to Diagnostic System Check	—
13	Malfunction is intermittent or not present at this time. Refer to Diagnostic Aids for more information.	—	—	—

GC402970325900GX

Fig. 189 Code C1264: Rear ABS Motor Circuit Open (Part 3 of 3). Intrigue, Lumina & Monte Carlo

Circuit Description

This DTC identifies an ABS motor circuit that is shorted to ground. This malfunction will not allow the ABS motor to be controlled at the commanded current rate or will cause the driver circuit to allow current directly to ground.

Conditions for Setting the DTC

DTC C1265 can be set anytime. If the EBTCM detects an out of range voltage on either of the rear ABS motor circuits indicating a circuit shorted to ground or an ABS brake motor internally shorted, a malfunction exists.

Action Taken When the DTC Sets

An open motor will not activate when requested. A malfunction DTC is stored and ABS/ETS is disabled, and the amber ABS warning indicator is turned on. The red BRAKE warning indicator is turned on if the rear piston in the ABS brake motor pack is not in the home position.

Conditions for Clearing DTC

The condition for the DTC is no longer present and the scan tool CLEAR DTCs function is used, or 100 drive cycles have passed with no DTCs detected.

Diagnostic Aids

Using the scan tool, select manual control function, and exercise ABS motor movement of the affected channel in both directions while applying light pressure on the brake pedal.

If erratic or jumpy brake pedal movement is detected while performing an apply or release function of the ABS motor, an intermittent malfunction may be indicated.

An intermittent malfunction may be caused by a poor connection, rubbed-through wire insulation, or a wire that is broken inside the insulation.

If the malfunction is not current, wiggle the wires of the affected channel and check if the DTC resets. This will help to pinpoint an intermittent malfunction in the motor circuitry or connections.

The frequency of the malfunction can be checked by using the enhanced diagnostic function of the scan tool, as described in Scan Tool Diagnostics in this section.

Any circuitry that is suspected of causing the intermittent complaint should be thoroughly checked for backed-out terminals, improper mating, broken locks, improperly formed or damaged terminals, poor terminal to wiring connections, or physical damage to the wiring harness.

! Important

- J 39200 test leads must be zeroed prior to making any resistance measurements.

After diagnosis is complete, clear the DTCs and test drive the vehicle for three drive cycles to verify that the DTC does not reset. A drive cycle consists of starting the vehicle, driving the vehicle over 16 km/h (10 mph), stopping, and then turning the ignition to off.

GC402970326003AX

Fig. 190 Code C1265: Rear ABS Motor Circuit Shorted To Ground (Part 1 of 3). Intrigue, Lumina & Monte Carlo

Step	Action	Value(s)	Yes	No
1	Was the Diagnostic System Check performed?	—	Go to Step 2	Go to Diagnostic System Check
2	Does DTC C1265 occur intermittently?	—	Go to Diagnostic Aids	Go to Step 3
3	1. Turn the ignition switch to the OFF position. 2. Disconnect the 6-way ABS brake motor pack connector. 3. Disconnect the 8-way EBTCM connector C2. 4. Using J 39200, measure the resistance between the 6-way ABS brake motor pack harness connector terminal D and ground. Is the resistance measured within the specified range?	OL (Infinite)	Go to Step 4	Go to Step 9
4	Using J 39200, measure the resistance between the 6-way ABS brake motor pack harness connector terminal C and ground. Is the resistance measured within the specified range?	OL (Infinite)	Go to Step 5	Go to Step 10
5	Using J 39200, measure the resistance between the 6-way ABS brake motor pack connector terminal D and ground. Is the resistance measured within the specified range?	OL (Infinite)	Go to Step 6	Go to Step 8
6	1. Inspect the 6-way ABS brake motor pack connector and the 6-way ABS brake motor pack harness connector for signs of damage which may result in a short to ground with the connector connected. 2. Inspect the 8-way EBTCM connector C2 and the 8-way EBTCM harness connector C2 for signs of damage which may result in a short to ground with the connector connected. 3. Inspect CKT 1284 and CKT 1285 for signs of damage which may result in a short to ground. Are there signs of damage which may result in a short to ground?	—	Go to Step 11	Go to Step 7
7	1. Reconnect the 6-way ABS brake motor pack connector. 2. Reconnect the 8-way EBTCM connector C2. 3. Test drive the vehicle obtaining a speed of at least 16 km/h (10 mph). 4. Turn the ignition switch to the OFF position. 5. Repeat the drive sequence two additional times. 6. Using the scan tool, check for DTCs. Did DTC C1265 set as a current DTC in the last three drive cycles?	—	Go to Step 12	Go to Step 13
8	Replace the ABS brake motor pack. Is the repair complete?	—	Go to Diagnostic System Check	—
9	Repair the short to ground in CKT 1284. Is the repair complete?	—	Go to Diagnostic System Check	—

GC402970326000FX

Fig. 190 Code C1265: Rear ABS Motor Circuit Shorted To Ground (Part 2 of 3). Intrigue, Lumina & Monte Carlo

Circuit Description

This DTC identifies an ABS motor circuit that is shorted to voltage or an ABS motor that has low or zero resistance. This malfunction will not allow the ABS motor to be controlled at the commanded current rate or will cause the ABS motor to turn in the opposite direction or not turn at all.

Conditions for Setting the DTC

DTC C1266 can be set only when the ABS motor is commanded off. If the EBTCM detects an out of range voltage on either of the rear ABS motor circuits indicating a circuit shorted to voltage or an ABS motor shorted, a malfunction exists.

Action Taken When the DTC Sets

A malfunction DTC is stored and ABS/ETS is disabled, and the amber ABS warning indicator is turned on. If the rear axle motor is not in home position then the red BRAKE warning indicator is turned on.

Conditions for Clearing DTC

The condition for the DTC is no longer present and the scan tool CLEAR DTCs function is used, or 100 drive cycles have passed with no DTCs detected.

Diagnostic Aids

Using the scan tool, select manual control function, and exercise ABS motor movement of the affected channel in both directions while applying light pressure on the brake pedal.

If erratic or jumpy brake pedal movement is detected while performing an apply or release function of the ABS motor, an intermittent malfunction may be indicated.

An intermittent malfunction may be caused by a poor connection, rubbed-through wire insulation, or a wire that is broken inside the insulation.

If the malfunction is not current, wiggle the wires of the affected channel and check if the DTC resets. This will help to pinpoint an intermittent malfunction in the motor circuitry or connections.

The frequency of the malfunction can be checked by using the enhanced diagnostic function of the scan tool, as described in Scan Tool Diagnostics in this section.

Any circuitry that is suspected of causing the intermittent complaint should be thoroughly checked for backed-out terminals, improper mating, broken locks, improperly formed or damaged terminals, poor terminal to wiring connections, or physical damage to the wiring harness.

Important

- J 39200 test leads must be zeroed prior to making any resistance measurements.

After diagnosis is complete, clear the DTCs and test drive the vehicle for three drive cycles to verify that the DTC does not reset. A drive cycle consists of starting the vehicle, driving the vehicle over 16 km/h (10 mph), stopping, and then turning the ignition to off.

GC402970326103AX

Fig. 191 Code C1266: Rear ABS Motor Circuit Shorted To Voltage (Part 1 of 3). Intrigue, Lumina & Monte Carlo

Step	Action	Value(s)	Yes	No
10	Repair the short to ground in CKT 1285. Is the repair complete?	—	Go to Diagnostic System Check	—
11	Replace all the terminals, the connectors or the wires that exhibit signs of damage which may result in a short to ground. Is the repair complete?	—	Go to Diagnostic System Check	—
12	Replace the EBTCM. Is the repair complete?	—	Go to Diagnostic System Check	—
13	Malfunction is intermittent or not present at this time. Refer to Diagnostic Aids for more information.	—	—	—

GC402970326000GX

Fig. 190 Code C1265: Rear ABS Motor Circuit Shorted To Ground (Part 3 of 3). Intrigue, Lumina & Monte Carlo

Step	Action	Value(s)	Yes	No
1	Was the Diagnostic System Check performed?	—	Go to Step 2	Go to Diagnostic System Check
2	Does DTC C1266 occur intermittently?	—	Go to Diagnostic Aids	Go to Step 3
3	1. Turn the ignition switch to the OFF position. 2. Disconnect the 6-way ABS motor pack connector. 3. Disconnect the 8-way EBTCM connector C2. 4. Turn the ignition switch to the RUN position, engine off. 5. Using J 39200, measure the voltage between the 6-way ABS motor pack harness connector terminal D and ground. Is the voltage measured within the specified range?	0-1V	Go to Step 4	Go to Step 10
4	Using J 39200, measure the voltage between the 6-way ABS motor pack harness connector terminal C and ground. Is the voltage measured within the specified range?	0-1V	Go to Step 5	Go to Step 11
5	1. Turn the ignition switch to the OFF position. 2. Using J 39200, measure the resistance between the 6-way ABS motor pack harness connector terminal D and the 6-way ABS motor pack harness connector terminal C. Is the resistance measured within the specified range?	OL (Infinite)	Go to Step 6	Go to Step 12
6	Using J 39200, measure the resistance between the 6-way ABS motor pack connector terminal D and the 6-way ABS motor pack connector terminal C. Is the resistance measured equal to or greater than the specified resistance?	0.2 Ω	Go to Step 7	Go to Step 9
7	1. Inspect the 6-way ABS motor pack connector and the 6-way ABS motor pack harness connector for signs of damage which may result in a short to voltage with the connector connected. 2. Inspect the 8-way EBTCM connector C2 and the 8-way EBTCM harness connector C2 for signs of damage which may result in a short to voltage with the connector connected. 3. Inspect CKT 1284 and CKT 1285 for signs of damage which may result in a short to voltage. Are there signs of damage which may result in a short to voltage?	—	Go to Step 13	Go to Step 8
8	1. Reconnect the 6-way ABS motor pack connector. 2. Reconnect the 8-way EBTCM connector C2. 3. Test drive the vehicle obtaining a speed of at least 16 km/h (10 mph). 4. Turn the ignition switch to the OFF position. 5. Repeat the drive sequence two additional times. 6. Using the scan tool, check for DTCs. Did DTC C1266 set as a current DTC in the last three drive cycles?	—	Go to Step 14	Go to Step 15

GC402970326100FX

Fig. 191 Code C1266: Rear ABS Motor Circuit Shorted To Voltage (Part 2 of 3). Intrigue, Lumina & Monte Carlo

Step	Action	Value(s)	Yes	No
9	Replace the ABS motor pack. Is the repair complete?	—	Go to Diagnostic System Check	—
10	Repair the short to voltage in CKT 1284. Is the repair complete?	—	Go to Diagnostic System Check	—
11	Repair the short to voltage in CKT 1285. Is the repair complete?	—	Go to Diagnostic System Check	—
12	Repair the short between CKT 1284 and CKT 1285. Is the repair complete?	—	Go to Diagnostic System Check	—
13	Replace all the terminals, the connectors or the wires that exhibit signs of damage which may result in a short to voltage. Is the repair complete?	—	Go to Diagnostic System Check	—
14	Replace the EBTCM. Is the repair complete?	—	Go to Diagnostic System Check	—
15	Malfunction is intermittent or not present at this time. Refer to Diagnostic Aids for more information.	—	—	—

GC402970326100GX

Fig. 191 Code C1266: Rear ABS Motor Circuit Shorted To Voltage (Part 3 of 3). Intrigue, Lumina & Monte Carlo

Step	Action	Value(s)	Yes	No
1	Was the Diagnostic System Check performed?	—	*Go to Step 2*	Go to *A Diagnostic System Check - ABS*
2	1. Turn the ignition switch to the OFF position. 2. Disconnect the 24-way EBTCM connector C1. 3. Use the *J 39200* in order to measure the resistance between the 24-way EBTCM harness connector C1 terminal A10 and ground. Is the resistance within the specified range?	OL (Infinite)	*Go to Step 3*	*Go to Step 12*
3	1. Disconnect the left front brake solenoid valve connector. 2. Use the *J 39200* in order to measure the resistance between the 24-way EBTCM harness connector C1 terminal A10 and the left front brake solenoid valve harness connector terminal B. Is the resistance within the specified range?	0.0–2.0 Ω	*Go to Step 4*	*Go to Step 15*
4	Use the *J 39200* in order to measure the resistance between the left front ABS brake solenoid valve connector terminal A and the left front brake solenoid valve connector terminal B. Is the resistance within the specified range?	2.0–5.0 Ω	*Go to Step 5*	*Go to Step 16*
5	Use a *J 39200* in order to measure the resistance between the Electronic Brake Control Relay harness connector terminal A2 and the left front brake solenoid valve connector terminal A. Is the resistance within the specified range?	0.0–2.0 Ω	*Go to Step 6*	*Go to Step 9*
6	1. Inspect the 24-way EBTCM connector C1 and the 24-way EBTCM harness connector C1 for the following conditions: • Terminal damage • Poor terminal contact • Terminal corrosion 2. Inspect the left front brake solenoid valve connector and the right front brake solenoid valve harness connector for the following conditions: • Terminal damage • Poor terminal contact • Terminal corrosion Are terminal corrosion, damaged terminals, or poor terminal contact evident?	—	*Go to Step 17*	*Go to Step 7*
7	Inspect CKT 1288 for damage. Damage may cause a short to ground with all the connectors connected. Is there damage that may cause a short to ground with the connectors connected?	—	*Go to Step 18*	*Go to Step 8*
8	1. Reconnect the 24-way EBTCM connector C1. 2. Reconnect the left front brake solenoid valve connector. 3. Turn the ignition switch to the RUN position. Do not start the engine. 4. Use the scan tool in order to inspect for DTCs. Does DTC C1276 set as a current DTC?	—	*Go to Step 22*	*Go to Step 23*
9	1. Remove the ABS Fuse (20A) from the engine wiring harness junction block 2. 2. Use the *J 39200* in order to measure the resistance between the terminals of the ABS Fuse (20A). Is the resistance within the specified range?	0.0–2.0 Ω	*Go to Step 10*	*Go to Step 19*

GC4029903834020X

Fig. 192 Code C1276: LH Front Solenoid Circuit Open Or Shorted To Ground (Part 2 of 3). Intrigue, Lumina & Monte Carlo

Circuit Description

DTC 1276 identifies a brake solenoid valve that cannot be energized. The malfunction may be caused by one of the following conditions:

- An open in the solenoid valve circuitry
- The solenoid valve is always energized due to a short to ground in the solenoid valve circuitry between the driver and the brake solenoid valve.

An open will not allow proper ABS operation, but the short to ground simply turns on the brake solenoid valve. A path for base brakes is still allowed once the motor rehomes and the check ball is lifted off its seat during key to RUN initialization.

Conditions for Setting the DTC

DTC C1276 can set only when the brake solenoid valve is commanded off while the Electronic Brake Control Relay is enabled.

A malfunction exists if the EBTCM detects the left front brake solenoid valve control circuit voltage is not within specifications.

Action Taken When the DTC Sets

- A malfunction DTC stores.
- The ABS/ETS disables.
- The amber ABS/ETS warning indicators turn on.

Conditions for Clearing the DTC

- The condition responsible for setting the DTC no longer exists and the Scan Tool Clear DTCs function is used.
- 100 drive cycles pass with no DTCs detected.

Diagnostic Aids

If the malfunction is not current, use wiggle test on the wiring harness to pinpoint an intermittent malfunction in the motor circuitry or connections. Thoroughly inspect any circuitry that may be causing the intermittent complaint for the following conditions:

- Backed out terminals
- Improper mating
- Improperly formed or damaged terminals
- Poor terminal-to-wiring connections
- Physical damage to the wiring harness
- Rubbed-through wire insulation
- A broken wire inside the insulation

GC4029903834010X

Fig. 192 Code C1276: LH Front Solenoid Circuit Open Or Shorted To Ground (Part 1 of 3). Intrigue, Lumina & Monte Carlo

Step	Action	Value(s)	Yes	No
10	Use the *J 39200* in order to measure the resistance between the Electronic Brake Control Relay harness connector terminal A2 and the fuse block terminal A1. Is the resistance within the specified range?	0.0–2.0 Ω	*Go to Step 11*	*Go to Step 20*
11	Use the *Scan Tool* in order to measure the resistance between the fuse block terminal A2 and the left front brake solenoid valve harness connector terminal A. Is the resistance within the specified range?	0.0–2.0 Ω	*Go to Step 13*	*Go to Step 21*
12	1. Disconnect the left front brake solenoid valve connector. 2. Use the *J 39200* in order to measure the resistance between the left front brake solenoid valve connector terminal A and ground. Is the resistance within the specified range?	OL (Infinite)	*Go to Step 14*	*Go to Step 16*
13	Replace the ABS Fuse (20A) with a known good fuse (20A). Is the replacement complete?	—	*Go to Step 8*	—
14	Repair the short to ground in CKT 1288. Is the repair complete?	—	Go to *A Diagnostic System Check - ABS*	—
15	Repair the open or high resistance in CKT 1288. Is the repair complete?	—	Go to *A Diagnostic System Check - ABS*	—
16	Replace the left front brake solenoid valve. Is the repair complete?	—	Go to *A Diagnostic System Check - ABS*	—
17	Replace all the terminals and connectors that exhibit the following conditions: • Poor terminal contact • Terminal corrosion • Damaged terminals Is the repair complete?	—	Go to *A Diagnostic System Check - ABS*	—
18	Repair the damage to CKT 1288. Is the repair complete?	—	Go to *A Diagnostic System Check - ABS*	—
19	Replace the fuse block ABS engine wiring harness junction block 2 Fuse (20A). Is the repair complete?	—	Go to *A Diagnostic System Check - ABS*	—
20	Repair the open or high resistance in CKT 1633. Is the repair complete?	—	Go to *A Diagnostic System Check - ABS*	—
21	Repair the open or high resistance in CKT 855. Is the repair complete?	—	Go to *A Diagnostic System Check - ABS*	—
22	Replace the EBTCM. Is the repair complete?	—	Go to *A Diagnostic System Check - ABS*	—
23	Is the malfunction intermittent or is not present at this time?	—	Go to Diagnostic Aids	—

GC4029903834030X

Fig. 192 Code C1276: LH Front Solenoid Circuit Open Or Shorted To Ground (Part 3 of 3). Intrigue, Lumina & Monte Carlo

Circuit Description

DTC C1277 identifies a solenoid that cannot be energized due to a short to voltage in the solenoid driver circuitry. The malfunction can affect ABS operation since the flow of brake fluid to the wheel cylinder cannot be stopped. The unstoppable flow of brake fluid to the wheel cylinder makes ABS operation for that channel impossible.

Conditions for Setting the DTC

DTC C1277 can set only when the brake solenoid valve is commanded on.

A malfunction exists if the EBCM detects the left front brake solenoid valve control circuit voltage is not within specifications.

Action Taken When the DTC Sets

- A malfunction DTC stores.
- The ABS disables.
- The amber ABS warning indicators turn on.

Conditions for Clearing the DTC

- The condition responsible for setting the DTC no longer exists and the Scan Tool Clear DTCs function is used.
- 100 drive cycles pass with no DTCs detected.

Diagnostic Aids

The following conditions may cause an intermittent malfunction:

- A poor connection
- Rubbed-through wire insulation
- A broken wire inside the insulation

Use the enhanced diagnostic function of the Scan Tool in order to measure the frequency of the malfunction.

Thoroughly inspect any circuitry that may cause the intermittent complaint for the following conditions:

- Backed out terminals
- Improper mating
- Improperly formed or damaged terminals
- Poor terminal-to-wiring connections
- Physical damage to the wiring harness

Important: Zero the *J 39200* test leads before making any resistance measurements.

GC4029703835010X

Fig. 193 Code C1277: LH Front Solenoid Circuit Shorted To Voltage (Part 1 of 2). Intrigue, Lumina & Monte Carlo

Circuit Description

DTC C1278 identifies a brake solenoid valve that cannot be energized. The malfunction may be caused by one of the following conditions:

- An open in the solenoid valve circuitry
- The solenoid valve is always energized due to a short to ground in the solenoid valve circuitry between the driver and the brake solenoid valve.

An open will not allow proper ABS operation, but the short to ground simply turns on the brake solenoid valve. A path for base brakes is still allowed once the motor rehomes and the check ball is lifted off its seat during key to RUN initialization.

Conditions for Setting the DTC

DTC C1278 can set only when the solenoid is commanded off while the Electronic Brake Control Relay is enabled.

A malfunction exists if the EBCM detects the right front brake solenoid valve control circuit voltage is not within specifications.

Action Taken When the DTC Sets

- A malfunction DTC stores.
- The ABS disables.
- The amber ABS warning indicators turn on.

Conditions for Clearing the DTC

- The condition responsible for setting the DTC no longer exists and the Scan Tool Clear DTCs function is used.
- 100 drive cycles pass with no DTCs detected.

Diagnostic Aids

The following conditions may cause an intermittent malfunction:

- A poor connection
- Rubbed-through wire insulation
- A broken wire inside the insulation

Use the enhanced diagnostic function of the Scan Tool in order to measure the frequency of the malfunction.

Thoroughly inspect any circuitry that may cause the intermittent complaint for the following conditions:

- Backed out terminals
- Improper mating
- Improperly formed or damaged terminals
- Poor terminal-to-wiring connections
- Physical damage to the wiring harness

Important: Zero the *J 39200* test leads before making any resistance measurements.

GC4029903836010X

Fig. 194 Code C1278: RH Front Solenoid Circuit Open Or Shorted To Ground (Part 1 of 3). Intrigue, Lumina & Monte Carlo

Step	Action	Value(s)	Yes	No
1	Was the Diagnostic System Check performed?	—	*Go to Step 2*	Go to *ABS Diagnostic System Check*
2	1. Turn the ignition switch to the OFF position. 2. Disconnect the left front solenoid valve connector 3. Turn the ignition switch to the ON position. Do not start the engine. 4. Use the *J 39200* in order to measure the voltage between the left front brake solenoid valve connector terminal A and ground. Is the voltage within the specified range?	0.0–1.0 V	*Go to Step 3*	*Go to Step 7*
3	1. Turn the ignition switch to the OFF position. 2. Use the *J 39200* in order to measure the resistance between the following components: • The left front brake solenoid valve connector terminal A • The left front brake solenoid valve connector terminal B Is the resistance within the specified range?	2.5–5.0 Ω	*Go to Step 4*	*Go to Step 7*
4	1. Disconnect the 24-way EBCM connector C1. 2. Turn the ignition switch to the ON position. Do not start the engine. 3. Use the *J 39200* in order to measure the voltage between the 24-way EBCM harness connector C1 terminal A10 and ground. Is the voltage within the specified range?	0.0–1.0 V	*Go to Step 5*	*Go to Step 8*
5	1. Turn the ignition switch to the OFF position. 2. Inspect the left front brake solenoid valve connector for damage. Damage may cause a short to voltage with the left front brake solenoid valve connector connected. 3. Inspect CKT 1288 for damage. Damage may cause a short to voltage. 4. Inspect the 24-way EBCM connector C1 for damage. Damage may cause a short to voltage with the 24-way EBCM connector C1 connected. Is there damage that may cause a short to voltage?	—	*Go to Step 9*	*Go to Step 6*
6	1. Reconnect the 24-way EBCM connector C1. 2. Reconnect the left front brake solenoid valve connector. 3. Start the engine with your foot off the brake. 4. Allow the engine to run for at least ten seconds. 5. Use the scan tool in order to inspect for DTCs. Does DTC C1277 set as a current DTC?	—	*Go to Step 10*	*Go to Step 11*
7	Replace the left front brake solenoid valve. Is the repair complete?	—	Go to *ABS Diagnostic System Check*	—
8	Repair the short to voltage in CKT 1288. Is the repair complete?	—	Go to *ABS Diagnostic System Check*	—
9	Repair the damage that caused a short to voltage. Is the repair complete?	—	Go to *ABS Diagnostic System Check*	—
10	Replace the EBCM. Is the repair complete?	—	Go to *ABS Diagnostic System Check*	—
11	Is the malfunction intermittent or is not present at this time?	—	Go to Diagnostic Aids	—

GC4029703835020X

Fig. 193 Code C1277: LH Front Solenoid Circuit Shorted To Voltage (Part 2 of 2). Intrigue, Lumina & Monte Carlo

Step	Action	Value(s)	Yes	No
1	Was the Diagnostic System Check performed?	—	*Go to Step 2*	Go to *ABS Diagnostic System Check*
2	1. Turn the ignition switch to the OFF position. 2. Disconnect the 24-way EBCM connector C1. 3. Use the *J 39200* in order to measure the resistance between the 24-way EBCM harness connector C1 terminal B6 and ground. Is the resistance within the specified range?	OL (Infinite)	*Go to Step 3*	*Go to Step 12*
3	1. Disconnect the right front brake solenoid valve connector. 2. Use the *J 39200* in order to measure the resistance between the 24-way EBCM harness connector C1 terminal B6 and the right front brake solenoid valve harness connector terminal A. Is the resistance within the specified range?	0.0–2.0 Ω	*Go to Step 4*	*Go to Step 15*
4	Use the *J 39200* in order to measure the resistance between the right front ABS brake solenoid valve connector terminal A and the right front brake solenoid valve connector terminal B. Is the resistance within the specified range?	2.0–5.0 Ω	*Go to Step 5*	*Go to Step 16*
5	Use a *J 39200* in order to measure the resistance between the Electronic Brake Control Relay harness connector terminal C8 and the right front brake solenoid valve connector terminal B. Is the resistance within the specified range?	0.0–2.0 Ω	*Go to Step 6*	*Go to Step 9*
6	1. Inspect the 24-way EBCM connector C1 and the 24-way EBCM harness connector C1 for the following conditions: • Terminal damage • Poor terminal contact • Terminal corrosion 2. Inspect the right front brake solenoid valve connector and the right front brake solenoid valve harness connector for the following conditions: • Terminal damage • Poor terminal contact • Terminal corrosion Are terminal corrosion, damaged terminals, or poor terminal contact evident?	—	*Go to Step 17*	*Go to Step 7*
7	Inspect CKT 1289 for damage. Damage may cause a short to ground with all the connectors connected. Is there damage which may cause a short to ground with the connectors connected?	—	*Go to Step 18*	*Go to Step 8*
8	1. Reconnect the 24-way EBCM connector C1. 2. Reconnect the right front brake solenoid valve connector. 3. Turn the ignition switch to the ON position. Do not start the engine. 4. Use the scan tool in order to inspect for DTCs. Does DTC C1278 set as a current DTC?	—	*Go to Step 22*	*Go to Step 23*

GC4029903836020X

Fig. 194 Code C1278: RH Front Solenoid Circuit Open Or Shorted To Ground (Part 2 of 3). Intrigue, Lumina & Monte Carlo

Step	Action	Value(s)	Yes	No
9	1. Remove the ABS Fuse (20A) from the engine wiring harness junction block 2. 2. Use the *J 39200* in order to measure the resistance between the terminals of the ABS Fuse (20A). Is the resistance within the specified range?	0.0–2.0 Ω	*Go to Step 10*	*Go to Step 19*
10	Use the *J 39200* in order to measure the resistance between the Electronic Brake Control Relay harness connector terminal C8 and the terminal G11 of junction block 2. Is the resistance within the specified range?	0.0–2.0 Ω	*Go to Step 11*	*Go to Step 20*
11	Use the *J 39200* in order to measure the resistance between the terminal G10 and the left front brake solenoid valve harness connector terminal B. Is the resistance within the specified range?	0.0–2.0 Ω	*Go to Step 13*	*Go to Step 21*
12	1. Disconnect the right front brake solenoid valve connector. 2. Use the *J 39200* in order to measure the resistance between the right front brake solenoid valve connector terminal B and ground. Is the resistance within the specified range?	OL (Infinite)	*Go to Step 14*	*Go to Step 16*
13	Replace the ABS Fuse (20A) with a known good Fuse (20A). Is the replacement complete?	—	*Go to Step 8*	—
14	Repair the short to ground in CKT 1289. Is the repair complete?	—	Go to *ABS Diagnostic System Check*	—
15	Repair the open or high resistance in CKT 1289. Is the repair complete?	—	Go to *ABS Diagnostic System Check*	—
16	Replace the right front brake solenoid valve. Is the repair complete?	—	Go to *ABS Diagnostic System Check*	—
17	Replace all the terminals and connectors that exhibit the following conditions: • Poor terminal contact • Terminal corrosion • Damaged terminals Is the repair complete?	—	Go to *ABS Diagnostic System Check*	—
18	Repair the damage to CKT 1289. Is the repair complete?	—	Go to *ABS Diagnostic System Check*	—
19	Replace the fuse block ABS Fuse (20A). Is the repair complete?	—	Go to *ABS Diagnostic System Check*	—
20	Repair the open or high resistance in CKT 1633. Is the repair complete?	—	Go to *ABS Diagnostic System Check*	—
21	Repair the open or high resistance in CKT 855. Is the repair complete?	—	Go to *ABS Diagnostic System Check*	—
22	Replace the EBCM. Is the repair complete?	—	Go to *ABS Diagnostic System Check*	—
23	Is the malfunction intermittent or is not present at this time?	—	Go to Diagnostic Aids	—

GC4029903836030X

Fig. 194 Code C1278: RH Front Solenoid Circuit Open Or Shorted To Ground (Part 3 of 3). Intrigue, Lumina & Monte Carlo

Step	Action	Value(s)	Yes	No
1	Was the Diagnostic System Check performed?	—	*Go to Step 2*	Go to *ABS Diagnostic System Check*
2	1. Turn the ignition switch to the OFF position. 2. Disconnect the right front solenoid valve connector 3. Turn the ignition switch to the ON position. Do not start the engine. 4. Use the *J 39200* in order to measure the voltage between the right front brake solenoid valve connector terminal B and ground. Is the voltage within the specified range?	0.0–1.0 V	*Go to Step 3*	*Go to Step 7*
3	1. Turn the ignition switch to the OFF position. 2. Use the *J 39200* in order to measure the resistance between the following components: • The right front brake solenoid valve connector terminal B • The right front brake solenoid valve connector terminal A Is the resistance within the specified range?	2.5–5.0 Ω	*Go to Step 4*	*Go to Step 7*
4	1. Disconnect the 24-way EBCM connector C1. 2. Turn the ignition switch to the ON position. Do not start the engine. 3. Use the *J 39200* in order to measure the voltage between the 24-way EBCM harness connector C1 terminal B6 and ground. Is the voltage within the specified range?	0.0–1.0 V	*Go to Step 5*	*Go to Step 8*
5	1. Turn the ignition switch to the OFF position. 2. Inspect the right front brake solenoid valve connector for damage. Damage may cause a short to voltage with the right front brake solenoid valve connector connected. 3. Inspect CKT 1289 for damage. Damage may cause a short to voltage. 4. Inspect the 24-way EBCM connector C1 for damage. Damage may cause a short to voltage with the 24-way EBCM connector C1 connected. Is there damage that may cause a short to voltage?	—	*Go to Step 9*	*Go to Step 6*
6	1. Reconnect the 24-way EBCM connector C1. 2. Reconnect the right front brake solenoid valve connector. 3. Start the engine with your foot off the brake. 4. Allow the engine to run for at least ten seconds. 5. Use the scan tool in order to inspect for DTCs. Does DTC C1281 set as a current DTC?	—	*Go to Step 10*	*Go to Step 11*
7	Replace the right front brake solenoid valve. Is the repair complete?	—	Go to *ABS Diagnostic System Check*	—
8	Repair the short to voltage in CKT 1289. Is the repair complete?	—	Go to *ABS Diagnostic System Check*	—
9	Repair the damage that caused a short to voltage. Is the repair complete?	—	Go to *ABS Diagnostic System Check*	—
10	Replace the EBCM. Is the repair complete?	—	Go to *ABS Diagnostic System Check*	—
11	Is the malfunction intermittent or is not present at this time?	—	Go to Diagnostic Aids	—

GC4029703837020X

Fig. 195 Code C1281: RH Front Solenoid Circuit Shorted To Voltage (Part 2 of 2). Intrigue, Lumina & Monte Carlo

Circuit Description

DTC C1281 identifies a solenoid that cannot be energized due to a short to voltage in the solenoid driver circuitry. The malfunction can affect ABS operation since the flow of brake fluid to the wheel cylinder cannot be stopped. The unstoppable flow of brake fluid to the wheel cylinder makes ABS operation for that channel impossible.

Conditions for Setting the DTC

DTC C1281 can set only when the brake solenoid is commanded on.

A malfunction exists if the EBCM detects the right front brake solenoid valve control circuit voltage is not within specifications.

Action Taken When the DTC Sets

- A malfunction DTC stores.
- The ABS disables.
- The amber ABS warning indicators turn on.

Conditions for Clearing the DTC

- The condition responsible for setting the DTC no longer exists and the Scan Tool Clear DTCs function is used.
- 100 drive cycles pass with no DTCs detected.

Diagnostic Aids

The following conditions may cause an intermittent malfunction:

- A poor connection
- Rubbed-through wire insulation
- A broken wire inside the insulation

Use the enhanced diagnostic function of the Tcan Tool in order to measure the frequency of the malfunction.

Thoroughly inspect any circuitry that may cause the intermittent complaint for the following conditions:

- Backed out terminals
- Improper mating
- Improperly formed or damaged terminals
- Poor terminal-to-wiring connections
- Physical damage to the wiring harness

Important: Zero the *J 39200* test leads before making any resistance measurements.

GC4029703837010X

Fig. 195 Code C1281: RH Front Solenoid Circuit Shorted To Voltage (Part 1 of 2). Intrigue, Lumina & Monte Carlo

Circuit Description

This DTC allows the EBTCM to check for a calibration malfunction by comparing the calibration value to a known value checksum stored in the EEPROM.

This DTC is also used as a security measure to prevent improper use of calibrations or changes to these calibrations that may alter the designed function of ABS/TCS.

Conditions for Setting the DTC

DTC C1282 can be set any time after the ignition is turned to the RUN position. If the program identifier is incorrect or the memory checksum is incorrect, a malfunction exists.

Action Taken When the DTC Sets

A malfunction DTC is stored, ABS/TCS is disabled and the amber ABS warning indicator is turned on.

Conditions for Clearing DTC

Condition for DTC is no longer present and the scan tool (CLEAR DTCs) function is used, or 100 drive cycles have passed with no DTCs detected.

Diagnostic Aids

An intermittent DTC C1282 may be caused by a bad cell in the EEPROM that is sensitive to temperature changes. If DTC C1282 has set more than once, but is intermittent, replace EBTCM.

The frequency of the malfunction can be checked by using the enhanced diagnostic function of the Scan Tool

GC402970326500AX

Fig. 196 Code C1282: Calibration Fault (Part 1 of 2). Intrigue, Lumina & Monte Carlo

Step	Action	Value(s)	Yes	No
1	Was the Diagnostic System Check performed?	—	Go to Step 2	Go to Diagnostic System Check
2	1. Turn the ignition switch to the RUN position, engine off. 2. Install a scan tool. 3. Using the scan tool, check for DTCs. Is DTC C1282 set as a current DTC?	—	Go to Step 3	Go to Step 4
3	Replace the EBTCM. Is the repair complete?	—	Go to Diagnostic System Check	—
4	Malfunction is intermittent or not present at this time. Refer to Diagnostic Aids for more information.	—	—	—

GC402970326500BX

Fig. 196 Code C1282: Calibration Fault (Part 2 of 2). Intrigue, Lumina & Monte Carlo

Circuit Description

This DTC is provided as an information only DTC and reflects the status of the command issued by the EBTCM to illuminate the red BRAKE warning indicator. If another DTC issues a command to illuminate the red BRAKE warning indicator, DTC C1286 will be stored in EEPROM as a history DTC at the conclusion of the ignition cycle.

Conditions for Clearing DTC

Condition for DTC is no longer present and the scan tool (CLEAR DTCs) function is used, or 100 drive cycles have passed with no DTCs detected.

Diagnostic Aids

Any ABS mechanical DTC that issues a command to illuminate the red BRAKE warning indicator will also result in DTC C1286 being stored in EEPROM during shutdown. These mechanical DTCs are: C1238, C1241, C1242, C1246, and C1251. If the motors are not in their home position, certain electrical DTCs will also command the red BRAKE warning indicator on. These electrical DTCs are: C1214, C1216, C1218, C1255, C1256, C1257, C1258, C1261, C1262, C1263, C1264, C1265, and C1266.

If any of these DTCs are indicated along with DTC C1286, they must be corrected prior to addressing a DTC C1286 malfunction.

GC402970326600AX

Fig. 197 Code C1286: EBCM/EBTCM Turned On Brake Warning Lamp (Part 1 of 2). Intrigue, Lumina & Monte Carlo

Step	Action	Value(s)	Yes	No
1	Was the Diagnostic System Check performed?	—	Go to Step 2	Go to Diagnostic System Check
2	1. Turn the ignition switch to the RUN position, engine off. 2. Install a scan tool. 3. Using the scan tool, check for DTCs. Are any other DTCs set with DTC C1286 as a current or history DTC?	—	Go Diagnostic Aids	Go to Step 3
3	Using the scan tool, clear DTC C1286. Was DTC C1286 cleared?	—	Go to Diagnostic System Check	—

GC402970326600BX

Fig. 197 Code C1286: EBCM/EBTCM Turned On Brake Warning Lamp (Part 2 of 2). Intrigue, Lumina & Monte Carlo

Thoroughly inspect any circuitry that may cause the intermittent complaint for the following conditions:

- Backed out terminals
- Improper mating
- Improperly formed or damaged terminals
- Poor terminal-to-wiring connections
- Physical damage to the wiring harness

Important: Zero the *J 39200* test leads before making any resistance measurements.

Step	Action	Value(s)	Yes	No
1	as the Diagnostic System Check performed?	—	*Go to Step 2*	*Go to ABS Diagnostic System Check*
2	1. Turn the ignition switch to the OFF position. 2. Disconnect the 24-way EBCM connector. 3. Disconnect the instrument panel harness connector C1. 4. Turn the ignition switch to the ON position. Do not start the engine. 5. Use the *J 39200* in order to measure the voltage between the 24-way EBCM harness connector C1 terminal B5 and ground. Is the voltage within the specified range?	0.0–1.0 V	*Go to Step 3*	*Go to Step 11*
3	1. Turn the ignition switch to the OFF position. 2. Reconnect the instrument panel harness connector. 3. Use a fused jumper (such as a *J 36169-A*) with a 3A fuse in order to connect the 24-way EBCM connector C1 terminal B5 to ground. 4. Turn the ignition switch to the ON position. Do not start the engine. Is the red BRAKE warning indicator on?	—	*Go to Step 4*	*Go to Step 9*
4	Inspect the master cylinder brake fluid level. Is the brake master cylinder fluid full?	—	*Go to Step 5*	*Go to Step 18*
5	1. Turn the ignition switch to the OFF position. 2. Remove the fused jumper. 3. Apply parking Brake. 4. Turn the ignition switch to the ON position. Do not start the engine. 5. Use the *J 39200* in order to measure the voltage between the 24-way EBCM harness connector C1 terminal B5 and ground. Is the voltage within the specified range?	0.0–2.0 V	*Go to Step 6*	*Go to Step 19*
6	1. Release the park brake. 2. Turn the ignition switch to the OFF position. 3. Disconnect the brake fluid level indicator sensor connector. 4. Inspect the 24-way EBCM connector C1 terminal B5 for the following conditions: • Poor terminal contact • Terminal corrosion • Terminal damage 5. Inspect the brake fluid level indicator sensor connector for the following conditions: • Poor terminal contact • Terminal corrosion • Terminal damage Is there poor terminal contact, terminal corrosion, or terminal damage?	—	*Go to Step 20*	*Go to Step 7*

GC4029903838020X

Fig. 198 Code C1287: Brake Warning Lamp Circuit Open Or Short To Voltage (Part 2 of 4). Intrigue, Lumina & Monte Carlo

Circuit Description

DTC C1287 identifies one of the following conditions:

- An open or short to voltage between the EBCM and the red BRAKE warning indicator.
- An open driver that does not allow the EBCM to illuminate the red BRAKE warning indicator.

DTC C1287 will only occur if an ABS malfunction is detected that may degrade base brake operation.

A short to ground in the circuit cannot be detected because the EBCM is not the only device controling the red BRAKE warning indicator. The following components may also turn on the red BRAKE warning indicator:

- The parking brake indicator switch
- The brake fluid level indicator sensor

Conditions for Setting the DTC

DTC C1287 can set during the three second bulb check and after completing initialization.

A malfunction exists if the red BRAKE warning indicator circuit voltage is out of specification. If the circuit voltage is out of specification, an open circuit or a short to voltage exists.

Action Taken When the DTC Sets

- A malfunction DTC stores.
- The ABS does not disable.
- The amber ABS warning indicator will flash to indicate a serious problem if the following conditions occur:
  1. The EBCM commands the red BRAKE warning indicator on due to an ABS malfunction that may degrade base brake operation.
  2. The red BRAKE warning indicator cannot turn on.

Conditions for Clearing the DTC

- The condition responsible for setting the DTC no longer exists and the Scan Tool Clear DTCs function is used.
- 100 drive cycles pass with no DTCs detected.

Diagnostic Aids

The following conditions may cause an intermittent malfunction:

- A poor connection
- Rubbed-through wire insulation
- A broken wire inside the insulation

Use the enhanced diagnostic function of the Scan Tool in order to measure the frequency of the malfunction.

If the Scan Tool is not available, lift the parking brake handle in order to verify proper indicator operation and continuity of CKT 33 and CKT 39.

GC4029903838010X

Fig. 198 Code C1287: Brake Warning Lamp Circuit Open Or Short To Voltage (Part 1 of 4). Intrigue, Lumina & Monte Carlo

Step	Action	Value(s)	Yes	No
7	1. Reconnect the 24-way EBCM connector C1. 2. Start the engine. 3. Use the scan tool in order to inspect for DTCs. Does DTC C1287 set as a current DTC?	—	*Go to Step 26*	*Go to Step 8*
8	1. Turn the ignition switch to the OFF position. 2. Reconnect the brake fluid level indicator sensor connector. 3. Start the engine. 4. Allow the engine to run for at least 10 seconds. 5. Use the scan tool in order to inspect for DTCs. Does DTC C1287 set as a current DTC?	—	*Go to Step 21*	*Go to Step 27*
9	1. Turn the ignition switch to the OFF position. 2. Remove the instrument panel cluster. Is the red BRAKE warning indicator lamp open?	—	*Instrument Cluster System Check*	*Go to Step 10*
10	Use the *J 39200* in order to measure the resistance between the instrument panel cluster connector C1 terminal C7 and the 24-way EBCM connector C1 terminal B5. Is the resistance within the specified range?	0.0–2.0 Ω	*Instrument Cluster System Check*	*Go to Step 25*
11	1. Turn the ignition switch to the OFF position. 2. Reconnect the instrument panel harness connector C1. 3. Turn the ignition switch to the ON position. Do not start the engine. 4. Observe the red BRAKE warning indicator. Is the red BRAKE warning indicator on?	—	*Go to Step 12*	*Go to Step 14*
12	Install the scan tool in order to inspect for DTCs. Is DTC C1286 set as either a current and/or history DTC?	—	*Go to DTC C1286 EBCM Turned On Brake Warning Indicator*	*Go to Step 13*
13	1. Release the park brake. 2. Disconnect the park brake indicator switch connector. 3. Use the *J 39200* in order to measure the resistance between the park brake indicator switch terminal A and ground. Is the resistance within the specified range?	OL (Infinite)	*Go to Step 27*	*Go to Step 22*
14	1. Reconnect the 24-way EBCM connector C1. 2. Install a scan tool. 3. Select Special Functions on the scan tool. 4. Select the Lamp Test on the scan tool. 5. Use the scan tool in order to command the red BRAKE warning indicator on. Is the red BRAKE warning indicator on?	—	*Go to Step 27*	*Go to Step 15*
15	1. Turn the ignition switch to the OFF position 2. Remove the fuse block Cluster Fuse (10A). 3. Disconnect the 24-way EBCM connector C1. 4. Turn the ignition switch to the ON position. Do not start the engine. 5. Use *J 39200* in order to measure the voltage between the 24-way EBCM connector C1 terminal C7 and ground. Is the voltage within the specified range?	0.0–1.0 V	*Go to Step 16*	*Go to Step 23*

GC4029903838030X

Fig. 198 Code C1287: Brake Warning Lamp Circuit Open Or Short To Voltage (Part 3 of 4). Intrigue, Lumina & Monte Carlo

Step	Action	Value(s)	Yes	No
16	1. Turn the ignition switch to the OFF position. 2. Inspect CKT 33 and the 24-way EBCM connector C1 for damage. Damage may result in a short to voltage with the 24-way EBCM connector C1 connected. Is there any damage to CKT 33 or the 24-way EBCM connector C1 which may cause a short to voltage?	—	Go to Step 24	Go to Step 17
17	1. Reconnect the 24-way EBCM connector C1. 2. Turn the ignition switch to the ON position. 3. Verify that the engine is off. 4. Use the scan tool in order to inspect for DTCs. Does DTC C1287 set as a current DTC?	—	Go to Step 26	Go to Step 27
18	Fill the brake master cylinder with approved brake fluid such as SUPREME 11 (GM Brand) or equivalent DOT 3 brake fluid. Is the brake master cylinder full?	—	Go to Step 5	—
19	Repair the open or the high resistance in the park brake wiring. Is the repair complete?	—	Go to ABS Diagnostic System Check	—
20	Replace all the terminals or the connectors that exhibit any of the following conditions: • Poor terminal contact • Terminal corrosion • Damaged terminals Is the repair complete?	—	Go to ABS Diagnostic System Check	—
21	Repair the open or the high resistance in the master cylinder brake fluid level indicator sensor. Is the repair complete?	—	Go to ABS Diagnostic System Check	—
22	Replace the park brake indicator switch. Is the repair complete?	—	Go to ABS Diagnostic System Check	—
23	Repair the short to voltage in CKT 39 or CKT 33. Is the repair complete?	—	Go to ABS Diagnostic System Check	—
24	Repair the damage to CKT 33 or the 24-way EBCM connector C1. The damage may cause a short to voltage. Is the repair complete?	—	Go to ABS Diagnostic System Check	—
25	Repair the open or the high resistance in CKT 33 between the following components: • The instrument panel cluster connector C2 terminal C7 • The 24-way EBCM connector C1 terminal C7 Is the repair complete?	—	Go to ABS Diagnostic System Check	—
26	Replace the EBCM. Is the repair complete?	—	Go to ABS Diagnostic System Check	—
27	Is the malfunction intermittent or is not present at this time?	—	Go to Diagnostic Aids	—

GC4029903838040X

Fig. 198 Code C1287: Brake Warning Lamp Circuit Open Or Short To Voltage (Part 4 of 4). Intrigue, Lumina & Monte Carlo

Step	Action	Value(s)	Yes	No
1	Was the Diagnostic System Check performed?	—	Go to Step 2	Go to ABS Diagnostic System Check
2	1. Turn the ignition switch to the ON position. Do not start the engine. 2. Install a scan tool. 3. Use the scan tool in order to inspect for DTCs. Is DTC C1295 set as either a current and/or history DTC?	—	Go to DTC C1293 DTC C1291/C1292 Set in Current or Previous Ignition Cycle	Go to Step 3
3	1. Select Data List on the scan tool. 2. Select Brake Switch Position on the scan tool. 3. Apply light pressure to the brake pedal while monitoring the Brake Switch Position on the scan tool. Does the scan tool indicate that the brake switch is on within 25 mm (1.0 inch) of brake pedal travel?	—	Go to Step 25	Go to Step 4
4	1. Apply firm pressure to the brake pedal. 2. Observe the rear brake lamps. Are the rear brake lamps on?	—	Go to Step 5	Go to Step 8
5	1. Turn the ignition switch to the OFF position. 2. Disconnect the 24-way EBCM connector C1. 3. Turn the ignition switch to the ON position. Do not start the engine. 4. Apply firm pressure to the brake pedal. 5. Use the *J 39200* in order to measure the voltage between the 24-way EBCM harness connector C1 terminal B9 and ground. Is the voltage equal to or greater than the specified voltage?	10.0 V	Go to Step 6	Go to Step 16
6	Inspect the 24-way EBCM connector C1 and the 24-way EBCM harness connector C1 for the following conditions: • Terminal damage • Poor terminal contact • Terminal corrosion Is there poor terminal contact, terminal corrosion, or damaged terminals?	—	Go to Step 17	Go to Step 7
7	1. Reconnect the 24-way ECM connector C1. 2. Test drive the vehicle and perform a brake stop from 32 km/h (20 mph) while engaging the ABS. 3. Use the scan tool in order to inspect for DTCs. Does DTC C1291 or DTC C1292 set as a current DTC?	—	Go to Step 23	Go to Step 25
8	Use the *J 39200* in order to measure the voltage between the stoplamp switch harness connector C1 terminal A and ground. Is the voltage equal to or greater than the specified voltage?	10.0 V	Go to Step 9	Go to Step 11
9	1. Apply firm pressure to the brake pedal. 2. Use the *J 39200* in order to measure the voltage between the stoplamp switch harness connector C1 terminal B and ground. Is the voltage equal to or greater than the specified voltage?	10.0 V	Go to Step 16	Go to Step 10

GC4029903839020X

Fig. 199 Code C1291: Open Brake Lamp Switch During Decel (Part 2 of 4). Intrigue, Lumina & Monte Carlo

Circuit Description

DTC C1291 detects an open brake switch in the non-ABS mode. The EBCM looks for deceleration rates that may indicate braking action. The EBCM verifies braking action by repeating the method for finding deceleration rates that indicate braking action several times. In each case, the ABS will not be available because the EBCM does not see the brake switch input.

Conditions for Setting the DTC

DTC C1291 can set if three deceleration cycles within the specified rate occur during the current ignition cycle with the brake switch off.

Action Taken When the DTC Sets

- A malfunction DTC stores.
- The ABS disables.
- The amber ABS warning indicators turns on.

Conditions for Clearing the DTC

- The condition responsible for setting the DTC no longer exists and the Scan Tool Clear DTCs function is used.
- 100 drive cycles pass with no DTCs detected.

Diagnostic Aids

The following conditions may cause an intermittent malfunction:

- A poor connection
- Rubbed-through wire insulation
- A broken wire inside the insulation

Use the enhanced diagnostic function of the Scan Tool in order to measure the frequency of the malfunction.

Thoroughly inspect any circuitry that may cause the intermittent complaint for the following conditions:

- Backed out terminals
- Improper mating
- Improperly formed or damaged terminals
- Poor terminal-to-wiring connections
- Physical damage to the wiring harness

Important: Zero the *J 39200* test leads before making any resistance measurements.

GC4029903839010X

Fig. 199 Code C1291: Open Brake Lamp Switch During Decel (Part 1 of 4). Intrigue, Lumina & Monte Carlo

Step	Action	Value(s)	Yes	No
10	Inspect for proper adjustment of the stoplamp switch. Is the stoplamp switch adjusted correctly?	—	Go to Step 18	Go to Step 19
11	1. Remove the fuse block STOPLAMP Fuse (15A). 2. Use the *J 39200* in order to measure the resistance between the STOPLAMP Fuse (15A) terminals. Is the resistance within the specified range?	0.0–2.0 Ω	Go to Step 12	Go to Step 13
12	1. Disconnect the stoplamp switch connector C1. 2. Use a *J 39200* in order to measure the resistance between the stoplamp switch harness connector C1 terminal A and the fuse block terminal E6. Is the resistance within the specified range?	0.0–2.0 Ω	Go to Step 14	Go to Step 21
13	1. Disconnect the 24-way EBCM connector C1. 2. Use the *J 39200* in order to measure the resistance between the 24-way EBCM connector C1 terminal B9 and ground. Is the resistance within the specified range?	OL (Infinite)	Go to Step 15	Go to Step 20
14	Use the *J 39200* in order to measure the voltage between the fuse block terminal E5 and ground. Is the voltage equal to or greater than the specified voltage?	10 V	Go to Step 25	Go to Power Distribution
15	1. Disconnect the stoplamp switch connector C1. 2. Use the *J 39200* in order to measure the resistance between the stoplamp switch harness connector C1 terminal A and ground. Is the resistance within the specified range?	OL (Infinite)	Go to Step 24	Go to Step 22
16	Repair the open in CKT 17. Is the repair complete?	—	Go to ABS Diagnostic System Check	—
17	Replace all the terminal or the connectors that exhibit the following conditions: • Poor terminal contact • Terminal corrosion • Damaged terminals Is the repair complete?	—	Go to ABS Diagnostic System Check	—
18	Replace the stoplamp switch. Is the repair complete?	—	Go to ABS Diagnostic System Check	—
19	Adjust the stoplamp switch. Is the repair complete?	—	Go to ABS Diagnostic System Check	—
20	1. Repair the short to ground in CKT 17. 2. Replace the STOPLAMP Fuse (15A) with a known good fuse (15A). Is the repair complete?	—	Go to ABS Diagnostic System Check	—
21	Repair the open in CKT 140. Is the repair complete?	—	Go to ABS Diagnostic System Check	—
22	1. Repair the short to ground in CKT 140. 2. Replace the STOPLAMP Fuse (15A) with a known good fuse (15A). Is the repair complete?	—	Go to ABS Diagnostic System Check	—

GC4029903839030X

Fig. 199 Code C1291: Open Brake Lamp Switch During Decel (Part 3 of 4). Intrigue, Lumina & Monte Carlo

Step	Action	Value(s)	Yes	No
23	Replace the EBCM. Is the repair complete?	—	Go to ABS Diagnostic System Check	—
24	Replace the STOPLAMP Fuse (15A) with a known good fuse (15A). Is the repair complete?	—	Go to ABS Diagnostic System Check	—
25	Is the malfunction intermittent or is not present at this time?	—	Go to Diagnostic Aids	—

GC4029903839040X

Fig. 199 Code C1291: Open Brake Lamp Switch During Decel (Part 4 of 4). Intrigue, Lumina & Monte Carlo

Circuit Description

DTC C1292 determines the proper operation of the brake switch. Proper operation of the brake switch is important because the brake switch activates the ABS when the brake switch is on. If the brake switch is off, the ABS will never activate. This malfunction is only detected when ABS is required because it is difficult to detect the malfunction under normal braking conditions.

Conditions for Setting the DTC

DTC C1292 can set if the vehicle speed is greater than 8 km/h (5 mph).

A malfunction exists if the following conditions occur:

- The brake was not ON.
- A release was required on two channels for 0.5 second.

Action Taken When the DTC Sets

- A malfunction DTC stores.
- The ABS disables.
- The amber ABS warning indicators turns on.

Conditions for Clearing the DTC

- The condition responsible for setting the DTC no longer exists and the Scan Tool Clear DTCs function is used.
- 100 drive cycles pass with no DTCs detected.

Diagnostic Aids

- The following conditions may cause an intermittent malfunction:
  - A poor connection
  - Rubbed-through wire insulation
  - A broken wire inside the insulation
- Use the enhanced diagnostic function of the Scan Tool in order to measure the frequency of the malfunction.
- Thoroughly inspect any circuitry that may cause the intermittent complaint for the following conditions:
  - Backed out terminals
  - Improper mating
  - Improperly formed or damaged terminals
  - Poor terminal-to-wiring connections
  - Physical damage to the wiring harness

Important: Zero the *J 39200* test leads before making any resistance measurements.

GC4029903840010X

Fig. 200 Code C1292: Open Brake Lamp Switch Circuit When ABS Was Required (Part 1 of 4). Intrigue, Lumina & Monte Carlo

Step	Action	Value(s)	Yes	No
1	Was the Diagnostic System Check performed?	—	*Go to Step 2*	*Go to ABS Diagnostic System Check*
2	1. Turn the ignition switch to the ON position. Do not start the engine. 2. Install a scan tool. 3. Use the scan tool in order to inspect for DTCs. Is DTC C1295 set as either a current and/or history DTC?	—	*Go to DTC C1293 DTC C1291/C1292 Set in Current or Previous Ignition Cycle*	*Go to Step 3*
3	1. Select Data List on the scan tool. 2. Select Brake Switch Position on the scan tool. 3. Apply light pressure to the brake pedal while monitoring the Brake Switch Position on the scan tool. Does the scan tool indicate that the brake switch is on within 25 mm (1.0 inch) of brake pedal travel?	—	*Go to Step 25*	*Go to Step 4*
4	1. Apply firm pressure to the brake pedal. 2. Observe the rear brake lamps. Are the rear brake lamps on?	—	*Go to Step 5*	*Go to Step 8*
5	1. Turn the ignition switch to the OFF position. 2. Disconnect the 24-way EBCM connector C1. 3. Turn the ignition switch to the ON position. Do not start the engine. 4. Apply firm pressure to the brake pedal. 5. Use the *J 39200* in order to measure the voltage between the 24-way EBCM harness connector C1 terminal B9 and ground. Is the voltage equal to or greater than the specified voltage?	10.0 V	*Go to Step 6*	*Go to Step 16*
6	Inspect the 24-way EBCM connector C1 and the 24-way EBCM harness connector C1 for the following conditions: • Terminal damage • Poor terminal contact • Terminal corrosion Is there poor terminal contact, terminal corrosion, or damaged terminals?	—	*Go to Step 17*	*Go to Step 7*
7	1. Reconnect the 24-way EBCM connector C1. 2. Test drive the vehicle and perform a brake stop from 32 km/h (20 mph) while engaging the ABS. 3. Use the scan tool in order to inspect for DTCs. Does DTC C1291 or DTC C1292 set as a current DTC?	—	*Go to Step 23*	*Go to Step 25*
8	Use the *J 39200* in order to measure the voltage between the stoplamp switch harness connector C1 terminal A and ground. Is the voltage equal to or greater than the specified voltage?	10.0 V	*Go to Step 9*	*Go to Step 11*
9	1. Apply firm pressure to the brake pedal. 2. Use the *J 39200* in order to measure the voltage between the stoplamp switch harness connector C1 terminal B and ground. Is the voltage equal to or greater than the specified voltage?	10.0 V	*Go to Step 16*	*Go to Step 10*

GC4029903840020X

Fig. 200 Code C1292: Open Brake Lamp Switch Circuit When ABS Was Required (Part 2 of 4). Intrigue, Lumina & Monte Carlo

Step	Action	Value(s)	Yes	No
10	Inspect for proper adjustment of the stoplamp switch. Is the stoplamp switch adjusted correctly?	—	*Go to Step 18*	*Go to Step 19*
11	1. Remove the fuse block STOPLAMP Fuse (15A). 2. Use the *J 39200* in order to measure the resistance between the STOPLAMP Fuse (15A) terminals. Is the resistance within the specified range?	0.0–2.0 Ω	*Go to Step 12*	*Go to Step 13*
12	1. Disconnect the stoplamp switch connector C1. 2. Use a *J 39200* in order to measure the resistance between the stoplamp switch harness connector C1 terminal A and the fuse block terminal E6. Is the resistance within the specified range?	0.0–2.0 Ω	*Go to Step 14*	*Go to Step 21*
13	1. Disconnect the 24-way EBCM connector C1. 2. Use the *J 39200* in order to measure the resistance between the 24-way EBCM connector C1 terminal B9 and ground. Is the resistance within the specified range?	OL (Infinite)	*Go to Step 15*	*Go to Step 20*
14	Use the *J 39200* in order to measure the voltage between the fuse block terminal E5 and ground. Is the voltage equal to or greater than the specified voltage?	10 V	*Go to Step 25*	*Go to Power Distribution*
15	1. Disconnect the stoplamp switch connector C1. 2. Use the *J 39200* in order to measure the resistance between the stoplamp switch harness connector C1 terminal A and ground. Is the resistance within the specified range?	OL (Infinite)	*Go to Step 24*	*Go to Step 22*
16	Repair the open in CKT 17. Is the repair complete?	—	*Go to ABS Diagnostic System Check*	—
17	Replace all the terminal or the connectors that exhibit the following conditions: • Poor terminal contact • Terminal corrosion • Damaged terminals Is the repair complete?	—	*Go to ABS Diagnostic System Check*	—
18	Replace the stoplamp switch. Is the repair complete?	—	*Go to ABS Diagnostic System Check*	—
19	Adjust the stoplamp switch. Is the repair complete?	—	*Go to ABS Diagnostic System Check*	—
20	1. Repair the short to ground in CKT 17. 2. Replace the STOPLAMP Fuse (15A) with a known good fuse (15A). Is the repair complete?	—	*Go to ABS Diagnostic System Check*	—
21	Repair the open in CKT 140. Is the repair complete?	—	*Go to ABS Diagnostic System Check*	—
22	1. Repair the short to ground in CKT 140. 2. Replace the STOPLAMP Fuse (15A) with a known good fuse (15A). Is the repair complete?	—	*Go to ABS Diagnostic System Check*	—

GC4029903840030X

Fig. 200 Code C1292: Open Brake Lamp Switch Circuit When ABS Was Required (Part 3 of 4). Intrigue, Lumina & Monte Carlo

Step	Action	Value(s)	Yes	No
23	Replace the EBCM. Is the repair complete?	—	*Go to ABS Diagnostic System Check*	—
24	Replace the STOPLAMP Fuse (15A) with a known good fuse (15A). Is the repair complete?	—	*Go to ABS Diagnostic System Check*	—
25	Is the malfunction intermittent or is not present at this time?	—	*Go to Diagnostic Aids*	—

GC4029903840040X

Fig. 200 Code C1292: Open Brake Lamp Switch Circuit When ABS Was Required (Part 4 of 4). Intrigue, Lumina & Monte Carlo

Circuit Description

DTC C1295 identifies open brake switch circuitry that prevents the brake switch input to the EBCM from changing states while applying the brake. DTC C1295 is used in conjunction with DTC C1291 and DTC C1292 to determine the cause of an open brake switch malfunction.

Conditions for Setting the DTC

DTC C1295 can set after initialization is complete.

A malfunction exists if the brake switch input voltage is out of specification for one second. An open circuit exists when the brake switch input voltage is out of specification.

Action Taken When the DTC Sets

- A malfunction DTC stores.
- ABS disables.
- The amber ABS warning indicators turns on.

Conditions for Clearing the DTC

- The condition responsible for setting the DTC no longer exists and the Scan Tool Clear DTCs function is used.
- 100 drive cycles pass with no DTCs detected.

Diagnostic Aids

The following conditions may cause an intermittent malfunction:

- A poor connection
- Rubbed-through wire insulation
- A broken wire inside the insulation

Use the enhanced diagnostic function of the Scan Tool in order to measure the frequency of the malfunction.

Thoroughly inspect any circuitry that may cause the intermittent complaint for the following conditions:

- Backed out terminals
- Improper mating
- Improperly formed or damaged terminals
- Poor terminal-to-wiring connections
- Physical damage to the wiring harness

GC4029903841010X

Fig. 201 Code C1295: Brake Lamp Switch Circuit Open (Part 1 of 2). Intrigue, Lumina & Monte Carlo

Step	Action	Value(s)	Yes	No
1	Was the Diagnostic System Check performed?	—	Go to Step 2	Go to ABS Diagnostic System Check
2	1. Turn the ignition switch to the ON position. Do not start the engine. 2. Install a scan tool. 3. Select Data List on the scan tool. 4. Select Brake Switch Position on the scan tool. Does the scan tool indicate that the brake switch circuit is open?	—	Go to Step 3	Go to Step 11
3	Apply light pressure to the brake pedal while monitoring the Brake Switch Position on the scan tool. Does the scan tool indicate that the brake switch is on within 25 mm (1.0 inch) of the brake pedal travel?	—	Go to Step 9	Go to Step 4
4	1. Apply firm pressure to the brake pedal. 2. Observe the rear brake lamps. Are the rear brake lamps on?	—	Go to Step 5	Go to Step 9
5	1. Turn the ignition switch to the OFF position. 2. Disconnect the 24-way EBCM connector C1. 3. Turn the ignition switch to the ON position. Do not start the engine. 4. Apply firm pressure to the brake pedal. 5. Use the *J 39200* in order to measure the voltage between the 24-way EBCM connector C1 terminal B9 and ground. Is the voltage equal to or greater than the specified voltage?	10.0 V	Go to Step 6	Go to Step 7
6	Inspect the 24-way EBCM connector C1 and the 24-way EBCM harness connector C1 for the following conditions: • Terminal damage • Poor terminal contact • Terminal corrosion Are poor terminal contact, terminal corrosion or damaged terminals evident?	—	Go to Step 8	Go to Step 10
7	Repair the open in CKT 17. Is the repair complete?	—	Go to ABS Diagnostic System Check	—
8	Replace all the terminals or the connectors that exhibit the following conditions: • Poor terminal contact • Terminal corrosion • Damaged terminals. Is the repair complete?	—	Go to ABS Diagnostic System Check	—
9	Repair the open brake lamp circuit wiring. Is the repair complete?	—	Go to ABS Diagnostic System Check	—
10	Replace the EBCM. Is the repair complete?	—	Go to ABS Diagnostic System Check	—
11	Is the malfunction intermittent or is not present at this time?	—	Go to Diagnostic Aids	—

GC4029903841020X

Fig. 201 Code C1295: Brake Lamp Switch Circuit Open (Part 2 of 2). Intrigue, Lumina & Monte Carlo

Step	Action	Value(s)	Yes	No
1	Was the Diagnostic System Check performed?	—	Go to Step 2	Go to Diagnostic System Check
2	1. Turn the ignition switch to the OFF position. 2. Install a Scan Tool. 3. Turn the ignition switch to the RUN position. 4. Using the Scan Tool clear DTCs. 5. Turn the ignition switch to the OFF position. 6. Turn the ignition switch to the RUN position. Does the undefined DTC(s) reset?	—	Go to Step 3	Go to Step 4
3	Replace the EBCM/EBTCM. Is the repair complete?	—	Go to Diagnostic System Check	—
4	Malfunction is not present at this time. Refer to Diagnostic Aids.	—	—	—

GC402970323100BX

Fig. 202 Test F: Scan Tool Displays Undefined Code (Part 2 of 2). Intrigue, Lumina & Monte Carlo

Circuit Description

This symptom table identifies undefined DTCs which are caused by an internal malfunction in the EBCM/EBTCM.

Diagnostic Aids

An intermittent malfunction may be caused by a poor connection, rubbed-through wire insulation, or a wire that is broken inside the insulation.

Any circuitry that is suspected of causing the intermittent complaint should be thoroughly checked for backed-out terminals, improper mating, broken locks, improperly formed or damaged terminals, poor terminal to wiring connections, or physical damage to the wiring harness.

GC402970323100AX

Fig. 202 Test F: Scan Tool Displays Undefined Code (Part 1 of 2). Intrigue, Lumina & Monte Carlo

Circuit Description

The UART serial data link allows information to be exchanged from module to module as needed. This is done by the PCM, the PCM requests and sends all the information that is transmitted on the UART line. When a scan tool is connected to the UART line it takes over for the PCM and sends and requests the needed information.

Diagnostic Aids

- Thoroughly inspect the wiring and the connectors. Failure to carefully and fully inspect the wiring and the connectors can result in misdiagnosis. Misdiagnosis may cause replacement of parts without repairing the malfunction.

GC4029903842010X

Fig. 203 No Communication With EBCM (Part 1 of 2). Intrigue, Lumina & Monte Carlo

Step	Action	Value(s)	Yes	No
DEFINITION: Scan tool can not communicate with the EBCM.				
1	Was the Diagnostic System Check performed?	—	Go to Step 2	Go to ABS Diagnostic System Check
2	Turn the Ignition switch to the ON position with the engine off. Connect a scan tool, can the scan tool communicate with other modules on the UART serial data line, such as the PCM?	—	Go to Step 3	Data Link Communications System Check
3	1. Turn the ignition switch to the OFF position. 2. Disconnect the EBCM connector C1. 3. Using *J 39200* DMM, measure the resistance between connector C1 terminal A1 and the DLC (Data Link Connector) terminal 9. Is the resistance within the range specified in the values column?	0.2 - 5 Ω	Go to Step 5	Go to Step 4
4	Repair CKT 800 for an open or high resistance. Is the repair complete?	—	ABS Diagnostic System Check	—
5	1. Turn the ignition switch to the OFF position. 2. Inspect the ABS fuse located in I/P Fuse Block 3. Disconnect the EBCM connector C1. 4. Turn the ignition switch to the ON position, engine off. 5. Using *J 39200* DMM, measure the voltage between connector C1 terminal A9 and a good ground. Is the voltage within the range specified within the values column?	Battery Voltage	Go to Step 7	Go to Step 6
6	Repair CKT 341 for a short to ground or open. Is the repair complete?	—	Go to Step 7	—
7	1. Turn the ignition switch to the OFF position. 2. Reconnect C1 to EBCM. 3. Disconnect the EBCM C2. 4. Using *J 39200* DMM, measure the resistance between connector C2 terminal D and a good ground. Is the resistance within the range specified within the values column?	0.2–10 Ω	Go to Step 8	Go to *Wiring*
8	Replace the EBCM. Is the repair complete?	—	ABS Diagnostic System Check	—

GC4029903842020X

Fig. 203 No Communication With EBCM (Part 2 of 2). Intrigue, Lumina & Monte Carlo

Circuit Description

This symptom table test the state of the ABS warning indicator in order to identify either of the following conditions:

- The ABS warning indicator could not warn the driver of a system malfunction
- The ABS warning indicator is always off

The EBCM must provide a ground in order to turn the amber ABS warning indicator off because of an integral lamp driver module within the instrument panel cluster.

Because of the circuitry in the integral Lamp Driver Module (LDM),only external malfunctions can be detected. As a result, the integral LDM is not diagnosable.

If CKT 852 is open, the ABS warning indicator will remain on due to the loss of ground at the integral LDM input.

If the control line is shorted to ground, the ABS warning indicator will remain off. The ABS indicator will remain off because the integral LDM input will be grounded.

DTC C1211 will set if nay of the following conditions exist:

- An open in CKT 852
- A short to ground on CKT 852
- A short to voltage in CKT 852

Diagnostic Aids

Use the lamp test function of the scan tool in order to command the indicator ON while looking for an malfunction in the ABS indicator.

The following conditions may cause an intermittent malfunction:

- A poor connection
- Rubbed-through wire insulation
- A broken wire inside the insulation

Use the Lamp Test function of the Scan Tool in order to turn the indicator on while looking for an intermittent malfunction in the ABS warning indicator circuitry.

Thoroughly inspect any circuitry that may cause the intermittent complaint for the following conditions:

- Backed out terminals
- Improper mating
- Improperly formed or damaged terminals
- Poor terminal-to-wiring connections
- Physical damage to the wiring harness

GC4029903843010X

Fig. 204 ABS Indicator Off No DTC Set (Part 1 of 2). Intrigue, Lumina & Monte Carlo

Circuit Description

This symptom table test the state of the ABS warning indicator in order to identify either of the following conditions:

- The ABS warning indicator could not warn the driver of a system malfunction
- The ABS warning indicator is always off

The EBCM must provide a ground in order to turn the amber ABS warning indicator off because of an integral lamp driver module within the instrument panel cluster.

Because of the circuitry in the integral Lamp Driver Module (LDM),only external malfunctions can be detected. As a result, the integral LDM is not diagnosable.

If CKT 852 is open, the ABS warning indicator will remain on due to the loss of ground at the integral LDM input.

If the control line is shorted to ground, the ABS warning indicator will remain off. The ABS indicator will remain off because the integral LDM input will be grounded.

DTC C1211 will set if nay of the following conditions exist:

- An open in CKT 852
- A short to ground on CKT 852
- A short to voltage in CKT 852

Diagnostic Aids

The lamp test function of the scan tool may be used to command the indicator ON while looking for an intermittent malfunction in the ABS warning indicator.

The following conditions may cause an intermittent malfunction:

- A poor connection
- Rubbed-through wire insulation
- A broken wire inside the insulation

Use the Lamp Test function of the Scan Tool in order to turn the indicator on while looking for an intermittent malfunction in the ABS warning indicator circuitry.

GC4029903844010X

Fig. 205 ABS Indicator On No DTC Set (Part 1 of 2). Intrigue, Lumina & Monte Carlo

Step	Action	Value(s)	Yes	No
1	Was the Diagnostic System Check performed?	—	*Go to Step 2*	Go to *A Diagnostic System Check - ABS*
2	1. Turn the ignition switch to the OFF position. 2. Install a Scan Tool. 3. Turn the ignition switch to the ON position, engine off. 4. Use the Scan Tool in order to clear DTCs. 5. Turn the ignition switch to the OFF position. 6. Turn the ignition switch to the ON position, engine off. Does the undefined DTC or DTCs reset?	—	*Go to Step 3*	*Go to Step 4*
3	Replace the EBCM. Is the repair complete?	—	Go to *A Diagnostic System Check - ABS*	—
4	Is the malfunction intermittent or not present at this time?	—	Refer to Diagnostic Aids	—

GC4020052210000X

Fig. 206 Scan Tool Displays Undefined DTC. Intrigue, Lumina & Monte Carlo

Step	Action	Value(s)	Yes	No
1	Was the Diagnostic System Check performed?	—	*Go to Step 2*	Go to *ABS Diagnostic System Check*
2	1. Turn the ignition switch to the OFF position. 2. Install a Scan Tool. 3. Turn the ignition switch to the ON position. 4. Use the Scan Tool in order to select SPECIAL FUNCTIONS. 5. Use the Scan Tool in order to select LAMP TEST. 6. Use the Scan Tool in order to turn the amber ABS indicator on. Did the amber ABS warning indicator turn on?	—	*Go to Step 3*	*Go to Step 4*
3	1. Use the Scan Tool in order to select SPECIAL FUNCTIONS. 2. Use the Scan Tool in order to select LAMP TEST. 3. Use the Scan Tool in order to flash the amber ABS warning indicator. Did the amber ABS warning indicator flash?	—	System OK	*Go to Step 4*
4	Repair the instrument panel cluster. Is the repair complete?	—	Go to *ABS Diagnostic System Check*	—

GC4029903843020X

Fig. 204 ABS Indicator Off No DTC Set (Part 2 of 2). Intrigue, Lumina & Monte Carlo

Thoroughly inspect any circuitry that may cause the intermittent complaint for the following conditions:

- Backed out terminals
- Improper mating
- Improperly formed or damaged terminals
- Poor terminal-to-wiring connections
- Physical damage to the wiring harness

ABS Indicator On No DTC Set

Step	Action	Value(s)	Yes	No
1	Was the Diagnostic System Check performed?	—	*Go to Step 2*	Go to *ABS Diagnostic System Check*
2	1. Turn the ignition switch to the OFF position. 2. Install a Scan Tool. 3. Turn the ignition switch to the ON position, engine off. 4. Use the Scan Tool in order to select SPECIAL FUNCTIONS. 5. Use the Scan Tool in order to select LAMP TEST. 6. Use the Scan Tool in order to turn the amber ABS warning indicator on. Did the amber ABS warning indicator turn on?	—	*Go to Step 3*	*Go to Step 4*
3	1. Use the Scan Tool in order to select SPECIAL FUNCTIONS. 2. Use the Scan Tool in order to select LAMP TEST. 3. Use the Scan Tool in order to flash the amber ABS warning indicator. Did the amber ABS warning indicator flash?	—	*Go to Step 5*	*Go to Step 4*
4	Repair the instrument panel cluster. Is the repair complete?	—	Go to *ABS Diagnostic System Check*	—
5	Is the malfunction intermittent or not present at this time?	—	Go to Diagnostic Aids	—

GC4029903844020X

Fig. 205 ABS Indicator On No DTC Set (Part 2 of 2). Intrigue, Lumina & Monte Carlo

Circuit Description

The LOW TRAC Indicator is controlled by the EBCM. The LOW TRAC Indicator is activated during a traction control event only. When the EBCM detects a low traction condition it supplies a ground for CKT 1656 turning on the LOW TRAC Indicator.

Diagnostic Aids

- It is very important that a thorough inspection of the wiring and connectors be performed. Failure to carefully and fully inspect wiring and connectors may result in misdiagnosis, causing part replacement with reappearance of the malfunction.
- Thoroughly inspect any circuitry that may be causing the complaint for the following conditions:
  - Backed out terminals
  - Improper mating
  - Improperly formed or damaged terminals
  - Poor terminal-to-wiring connections
  - Physical damage to the wiring harness
- The following conditions may cause an intermittent malfunction:
  - A poor connection
  - Rubbed-through wire insulation
  - Dirty or corroded terminals
  - A broken wire inside the insulation
- Zero the *J 39200* test leads before making any resistance measurements.

GC4029903845010X

Fig. 207 Low Traction Indicator Always On (Part 1 of 2). Intrigue, Lumina & Monte Carlo

Step	Action	Value(s)	Yes	No
1	Was the Diagnostic System Check performed?	—	*Go to Step 2*	*Go to ABS Diagnostic System Check*
2	1. Observe the amber ABS active indicator Low Trac. 2. Turn the ignition switch to the OFF position. Did the amber ABS indicator LOW TRAC stay turn on?	—	*Go to Step 3*	*Go to Step 4*
3	Repair a short to voltage in CKT 1656. Is the repair complete?	—	*Go to ABS Diagnostic System Check*	—
4	1. Inspect EBCM connectors and EBCM harness connectors C1 and C2 for poor terminal contact, damage or evidence of corrosion. 2. Inspect the Instrument panel connectors and terminals for poor terminal contact, damage or evidence of corrosion. Is there evidence of poor terminal contact or corrosion?	—	*Go to Step 5*	*Go to Step 6*
5	1. Replace all terminals that exhibit signs of poor terminal contact or corrosion. 2. Reconnect EBCM connectors and instrument panel connector. 3. Turn the ingition switch to ON position, engine off. Did the LOW TRAC Indicator comes on for approximate 3 seconds then turn OFF?	—	SYSTEM OK	*Go to Step 6*
6	Replace the EBCM. Is the repair complete?	—	*Go to ABS Diagnostic System Check*	—

GC4029903845020X

Fig. 207 Low Traction Indicator Always On (Part 2 of 2). Intrigue, Lumina & Monte Carlo

Step	Action	Value(s)	Yes	No
1	Was the Diagnostic System Check performed?	—	*Go to Step 2*	*Go to ABS Diagnostic System Check*
2	1. Turn the ignition switch to the ON position, engine off. 2. Amber Low Trac indicator will be turned on for approximate 3 seconds, then indicator should turn off. Did the amber ABS indicator LOW TRAC turn on?	—	*Go to ABS Diagnostic System Check*	*Go to Step 3*
3	1. Turn the ignition switch to the OFF position. 2. Disconnect the 24–way EBCM connector C1. 3. Connect a fused jumper wire between EBCM connector C1 terminal A6 and a good known ground. 4. Turn the ignition switch to the ON position, engine off. Does the Amber Low Trac indicator come on?	—	*Go to Step 7*	*Go to Step 4*
4	1. Turn the ignition switch to the OFF position. 2. Disconnect the instrument panel connector. 3. Using *J 39200* DMM, measure the resistance between 24–way EBCM connector C1 terminal A6 and Instrument cluster connector terminal C8. Is the resistance within the range specified in the values column?	0.2–10 Ω	*Go to Step 6*	*Go to Step 5*
5	Repair a short to voltage in CKT 1656. Is the repair complete?	—	*Go to Step 6*	—
6	1. Replace all terminals that exhibit signs of poor terminal contact or corrosion. 2. Reconnect EBCM connectors C1 and C2 and instrument panel connector. 3. Turn the ingition switch to ON position. Did the LOW TRAC Indicator comes on for approximate 3 seconds then turn OFF?	—	SYSTEM OK	*Go to Step 7*
7	Replace the EBCM. Is the repair complete?	—	*Go to ABS Diagnostic System Check*	—

GC4029903846020X

Fig. 208 Low Traction Indicator Inoperative (Part 2 of 2). Intrigue, Lumina & Monte Carlo

Step	Action	Value(s)	Yes	No
1	1. Verify that the EBCM connector is properly connected. 2. Install a Scan Tool. 3. Turn the ignition switch to the ON position. Do not start the engine. 4. Select the ABS portion of the chassis application on the Scan Tool. 5. Select Data List on the Scan Tool. Is data being received from the EBCM?	—	*Go to Step 15*	*Go to Step 2*
2	Read the Scan Tool display. Does the Scan Tool display the message "No Communication With Vehicle. Check DLC Connector"?	—	Data Link Connector,	*Go to Step 3*
3	Verify the correct connection of the Scan Tool to the DLC. Is connection of the Scan Tool to the DLC correct?	—	*Go to Step 4*	*Go to Step 26*
4	1. Turn the ignition switch to the OFF position. 2. Remove and inspect the fuse block HAZARD Fuse (15A). Is the fuse open?	—	*Go to Step 18*	*Go to Step 5*

GC402980339701AX

Fig. 209 ABS Diagnostic System Check (Part 1 of 5). Metro

Circuit Description

The LOW TRAC Indicator is controlled by the EBCM. The LOW TRAC Indicator is activated during a traction control event only. When the EBCM detects a low traction condition it supplies a ground for CKT 1656 turning on the LOW TRAC Indicator.

Diagnostic Aids

- It is very important that a thorough inspection of the wiring and connectors be performed. Failure to carefully and fully inspect wiring and connectors may result in misdiagnosis, causing part replacement with reappearance of the malfunction.
- Thoroughly inspect any circuitry that may be causing the complaint for the following conditions:
  - Backed out terminals
  - Improper mating
  - Improperly formed or damaged terminals
  - Poor terminal-to-wiring connections
  - Physical damage to the wiring harness
- The following conditions may cause an intermittent malfunction:
  - A poor connection
  - Rubbed-through wire insulation
  - Dirty or corroded terminals
  - A broken wire inside the insulation
- Zero the *J 39200* test leads before making any resistance measurements.

GC4029903846010X

Fig. 208 Low Traction Indicator Inoperative (Part 1 of 2). Intrigue, Lumina & Monte Carlo

Step	Action	Value(s)	Yes	No
5	1. Install the fuse block HAZARD Fuse (15A). 2. Remove the fuse block DEF Fuse (20A). Is the fuse open?	—	*Go to Step 21*	*Go to Step 6*
6	1. Install the fuse block DEF Fuse (20A). 2. Disconnect the EBCM connector. 3. Use the *J 39200* in order to measure the resistance between the EBCM connector terminal D and ground. Is the resistance within the specified range?	0–2 Ω	*Go to Step 7*	*Go to Step 27*
7	1. Disconnect the EBCM connector. 2. Use the *J 39200* in order to measure voltage between the EBCM connector terminal B12 and ground. Is the voltage equal to or greater than the specified voltage?	10 V	*Go to Step 8*	*Go to Step 28*
8	1. Turn the ignition switch to the ON position. Do not start the engine. 2. Use the *J 39200* in order to measure voltage between the EBCM connector terminal A9 and ground. Is the voltage equal to or greater than the specified voltage?	10 V	*Go to Step 9*	*Go to Step 29*
9	1. Turn the ignition switch to the OFF position. 2. Disconnect the negative battery cable. 3. Disconnect the positive battery cable. 4. Use the *J 39200* in order to measure the resistance between the EBCM connector terminal D and the negative battery cable terminal. Is the resistance within the specified range?	0–2 Ω	*Go to Step 10*	*Go to Step 30*
10	Use the *J 39200* in order to measure the resistance between the EBCM connector terminal B12 and the positive battery cable terminal. Is the resistance within the specified range?	0–2 Ω	*Go to Step 11*	*Go to Step 31*
11	1. Turn the ignition switch to the ON position. Do not start the engine. 2. Use the *J 39200* in order to measure the resistance between the EBCM connector terminal A9 and the positive battery cable terminal. Is the resistance within the specified range?	0–2 Ω	*Go to Step 12*	*Go to Step 32*
12	1. Turn the ignition switch to the OFF position. 2. Use the *J 39200* in order to measure the resistance between the EBCM connector terminal A9 and the DLC terminal 9. Is the resistance within the specified range?	0–2 Ω	*Go to Step 13*	Data Link Connector
13	Use the *J 39200* in order to measure the resistance between the EBCM connector terminal A9 and ground. Is the resistance within the specified range?	OL (Infinite)	*Go to Step 14*	Data Link Connector

GC402980339701BX

Fig. 209 ABS Diagnostic System Check (Part 2 of 5). Metro

Step	Action	Value(s)	Yes	No
14	1. Inspect the following components: • The EBCM connector • The negative battery cable • The positive battery cable 2. Inspect the components for the following conditions: • Poor terminal contact • Terminal corrosion • Damaged terminals Are there signs of poor terminal contact, terminal corrosion, or damaged terminals?	—	*Go to Step 33*	*Go to Step 39*
15	1. Connect the *Scan Tool*. 2. Select DTCs. Does the *Scan Tool* display any current DTCs?	—	Refer to the applicable DTC table	*Go to Step 16*
16	1. Turn the ignition switch to the OFF position. 2. Wait for ten seconds. 3. Turn the ignition switch to the ON position. Do not start the engine. 4. Observe the amber ABS warning indicator. Does the amber ABS warning indicator turn on for three seconds and then turn off?	—	*Go to Step 17*	Refer to the appropriate symptom table
17	1. Connect the *Scan Tool*. 2. Select DTC History. Does the *Scan Tool* display any history DTCs?	—	*Go to Step 40*	*Go to Step 41*
18	1. Replace the fuse block HAZARD Fuse (15A) with a known good fuse (20A). 2. Wait for ten seconds. 3. Remove and inspect the fuse. Is the fuse open?	—	*Go to Step 19*	*Go to Step 35*
19	1. Disconnect the EBCM connector. 2. Replace the fuse block HAZARD Fuse (15A) with a known good fuse (20A). 3. Wait for ten seconds. 4. Remove and inspect the fuse block HAZARD Fuse (15A). Is the fuse open?	—	*Go to Step 34*	*Go to Step 20*
20	1. Inspect CKT 2C03 for physical damage. Physical damage may cause a short to ground with the EBCM connector connected. 2. Inspect the EBCM connector and the EBCM harness for physical damage. Physical damage may cause a short to ground with the EBCM connector connected. 3. Reconnect the EBCM connector. 4. Reinstall the fuse block HAZARD Fuse (15A). 5. Wait for ten seconds. 6. Remove and inspect the fuse block HAZARD Fuse (15A). Is the fuse open?	—	*Go to Step 25*	*Go to Step 38*

GC402980339702AX

Fig. 209 ABS Diagnostic System Check (Part 3 of 5). Metro

Step	Action	Value(s)	Yes	No
21	1. Replace the fuse block DEF Fuse (20A) with a known good Fuse (20A). 2. Turn the ignition switch to the ON position. Do not start the engine. 3. Wait for ten seconds. 4. Turn the ignition switch to the OFF position. 5. Remove and inspect the DEF Fuse (20A). Is the fuse open?	—	*Go to Step 22*	*Go to Step 37*
22	1. Turn the ignition switch to the OFF position. 2. Disconnect the EBCM connector. 3. Replace the fuse block DEF Fuse (20A) with a known good fuse (20A). 4. Turn the ignition to the ON position. Do not start the engine. 5. Wait for ten seconds. 6. Turn the ignition switch to the OFF position. 7. Remove and inspect the DEF Fuse (20A). Is the fuse open?	—	*Go to Step 36*	*Go to Step 23*
23	1. Inspect CKT 6U01 for physical damage. Physical damage may cause a short to ground with the EBCM connector connected. 2. Reconnect the EBCM connector. 3. Reinstall the fuse block DEF Fuse (20A). 4. Turn the engine to the ON position. Do not start the engine. 5. Wait for ten seconds. 6. Turn the ignition switch to the OFF position. 7. Remove and inspect the fuse block DEF Fuse (20A). Is the fuse open?	—	*Go to Step 24*	*Go to Step 38*
24	1. Replace the EBCM. 2. Replace the fuse block DEF Fuse (20A) with a known good fuse (20A).. Is the repair complete?	—	*Go to Step 1*	—
25	1. Replace the EBCM. 2. Replace the fuse block HAZARD Fuse (15A) with a known good fuse (15A). Is the repair complete?	—	*Go to Step 1*	—
26	Disconnect and reconnect the *Scan Tool* in order to ensure a good connection. Is the *Scan Tool* correctly connected?	—	*Go to Step 1*	—
27	Repair the open or high resistance in CKT 6W01. Is the repair complete?	—	*Go to Step 1*	—
28	Repair the open or high resistance in CKT 2C03. Is the repair complete?	—	*Go to Step 1*	—
29	Repair the open or high resistance in CKT 6U01. Is the repair complete?	—	*Go to Step 1*	—

GC402980339702BX

Fig. 209 ABS Diagnostic System Check (Part 4 of 5). Metro

Step	Action	Value(s)	Yes	No
30	Repair the open or high resistance in any of the following components: • The negative battery cable • The negative battery cable terminals • The negative battery cable connections Is the repair complete?	—	*Go to Step 1*	—
31	Repair the high resistance in CKT 2C03 or the voltage feed circuits for the fuse block HAZARD Fuse (15A). Is the repair complete?	—	*Go to Step 1*	—
32	Repair the open or high resistance in one of the following circuits: • CKT 6U01 • The power feed circuits to the fuse block. Is the repair complete?	—	*Go to Step 1*	—
33	Replace the terminals or the connectors that exhibit the following conditions: • Poor terminal contact • Terminal corrosion • Damaged terminals Is the repair complete?	—	*Go to Step 1*	—
34	Repair the short to ground in CKT 2C03. Is the repair complete?	—	*Go to Step 18*	—
35	Reinstall the fuse block HAZARD Fuse (15A). Is the installation complete?	—	*Go to Step 1*	—
36	Repair the short to ground in CKT 6U01. Is the repair complete?	—	*Go to Step 21*	—
37	Reinstall the fuse block DEF Fuse (20A). Is the installation complete?	—	*Go to Step 1*	—
38	The malfunction is intermittent or not present at this time. Is the action complete?	—	System OK	—
39	Replace the EBCM. Is the repair complete?	—	*Go to Step 1*	—
40	Review the Enhanced Diagnostics information in the Scan Tool manual. Is the action complete?	—	*Go to Step 1*	—
41	The system is good. Is the action complete?	—	*Go to Step 1*	—

GC4029803397030X

Fig. 209 ABS Diagnostic System Check (Part 5 of 5). Metro

Circuit Description

Ignition voltage is supplied to terminal 86 of the Electronic Brake Control Relay. The above condition enables the EBCM to energize the pullin coil by completing the ground circuit at connector terminal A11 of the EBCM. The magnetic field created closes the Electronic Brake Control Relay contacts. The magnetic field also allows battery voltage and current through the Electronic Brake Control Relay terminal 30 to be supplied to the EBCM through connector terminal C. Connector terminal C supplies power to the EBCM, which supplies power to the motors.

Conditions for Setting the DTC

DTC C1214 can set anytime after the EBCM commands the Electronic Brake Control Relay ON. The command occurs during the three second bulb check.

DTC C1214 monitors the availability of current/voltage to the motors.

The above malfunction indicates voltage is not available. The malfunction will not allow ABS operation.

Action Taken When the DTC Sets

- A malfunction DTC stores.
- ABS is disabled.
- The amber ABS warning indicator is turned ON.

Conditions for Clearing the DTC

- The condition responsible for setting the DTC no longer exists and the Scan Tool Clear DTCs function is used.
- 100 drive cycles pass with no DTCs detected. A drive cycle consists of starting the vehicle, driving the vehicle over 16 km/h (10 mph), stopping and then turning the ignition OFF.

Diagnostic Aids

The following conditions may cause a malfunction:

- A poor connection
- Rubbed-through wire insulation
- A broken wire inside the insulation
- Open ABS fuse
- Malfunctioning Electronic Brake Control Relay (contacts open/high resistance)
- Poor terminal contacts from the relay box to the Electronic Brake Control Relay (look for spread terminals)
- Malfunctioning electrical circuits (open or high resistance) between the Electronic Brake Control Relay and the EBCM (CKT 6B01) and/or between the fuse box and the Electronic Brake Control Relay (CKT 6A01)

Use the enhanced diagnostic function of the Scan Tool in order to measure the frequency of the malfunction.

GC402980341800AX

Fig. 210 Code C1214: Brake Control relay Contact Circuit Open (Part 1 of 5). Metro

Thoroughly inspect any circuitry that may be causing the intermittent complaint for the following conditions:

- Backed out terminals
- Improper mating
- Improperly formed or damaged terminals
- Poor terminal-to-wiring connections
- Physical damage to the wiring harness

Vibration and Temperature Effects

- Use the following procedure in order to inspect for vibration effects by performing the Relay Test function of the Scan Tool:
  1. With the Relay Test commanded on, lightly tap the top and sides of the Electronic Brake Control Relay while monitoring the Electronic Brake Control Relay voltage.
  2. If the Electronic Brake Control Relay voltage changes significantly, replace the Electronic Brake Control Relay.
- If DTC C1214 only sets when the vehicle is initially started in cold ambient conditions (temperature less than 0°C – 32°F), replace the Electronic Brake Control Relay.

Important: Zero the J 39200 test leads before making any resistance measurements.

Step	Action	Value(s)	Yes	No
1	Was the Diagnostic System Check performed?	—	*Go to Step 2*	Refer to *Diagnostic System Check*
2	1. Turn the ignition switch to the OFF position. 2. Install a *Scan Tool*. 3. Turn the ignition switch to the ON position. Do not start the engine. 4. Use the *Scan Tool* in order to read the DTCs. Is DTC C1216 present (either as a current DTC or a history DTC)?	—	Refer to *DTC C1216 Brake Control Rly Coil CKT Open*	*Go to Step 3*
3	1. Select Data List on the *Scan Tool*. 2. Select and observe EBCM Battery Voltage. Is the voltage equal to or greater than the specified voltage?	10 V	*Go to Step 25*	*Go to Step 4*
4	1. Turn the ignition switch to the OFF position. 2. Disconnect the EBCM connector. 3. Connect a fused jumper wire (such as a *J 36169-A*) with a 3A fuse between the EBCM harness connector terminal A11 and ground. 4. Turn the ignition switch to the ON position. Do not start the engine. 5. Use the *J 39200* in order to measure the voltage between the EBCM harness connector terminal C and ground. Is the voltage equal to or greater than the specified voltage?	10 V	*Go to Step 5*	*Go to Step 10*
5	1. Turn the ignition switch to the OFF position. 2. Disconnect the fused wire jumper. 3. Disconnect the Electronic Brake Control Relay. 4. Use the *J 39200* in order to measure the resistance between the Electronic Brake Control Relay connector terminal 87 and the EBCM harness connector terminal C. Is the resistance within the specified range?	0–2 Ω	*Go to Step 6*	*Go to Step 19*

GC402980341800BX

Fig. 210 Code C1214: Brake Control relay Contact Circuit Open (Part 2 of 5). Metro

Step	Action	Value(s)	Yes	No
10	1. Turn the ignition switch to the OFF position. 2. Disconnect the negative battery cable. 3. Disconnect the positive battery cable. 4. Turn the ignition switch to the ON position. (This action completes the ignition circuit to the Electronic Brake Control Relay.) 5. Use the *J 39200* in order to measure the resistance between the EBCM harness connector terminal A11 and the positive battery cable terminal. Is the resistance within the specified range?	65–95 Ω	*Go to Step 11*	*Go to Step 14*
11	Use the *J 39200* in order to measure the voltage between the positive battery terminal and the negative battery terminal. Is the voltage equal to or greater than the specified voltage?	10 V	*Go to Step 12*	*Go to Step 23*
12	1. Turn the ignition switch to the OFF position. 2. Reconnect the positive battery cable. 3. Reconnect the negative battery cable. 4. Disconnect the Electronic Brake Control Relay. 5. Use the *J 39200* in order to measure the voltage between the Electronic Brake Control Relay connector terminal 30 and ground. Is the voltage equal to or greater than the specified voltage?	10 V	*Go to Step 13*	*Go to Step 20*
13	Use the *J 39200* in order to measure the resistance between the Electronic Brake Control Relay connector terminal 87 and the EBCM harness connector terminal C. Is the resistance within the specified range?	0–2 Ω	*Go to Step 7*	*Go to Step 19*
14	1. Disconnect the Electronic Brake Control Relay. 2. Use the *J 39200* in order to measure the resistance between the Electronic Brake Control Relay terminal 86 and the Electronic Brake Control Relay terminal 85. Is the resistance within the specified range?	65–95 Ω	*Go to Step 15*	*Go to Step 22*
15	Use the *J 39200* in order to measure the resistance between the Electronic Brake Control Relay connector terminal 85 and the EBCM harness connector terminal A11. Is the resistance within the specified range?	0–2 Ω	*Go to Step 16*	*Go to Step 18*
16	Use the *J 39200* in order to measure the resistance between the Electronic Brake Control Relay connector terminal 86 and the positive battery cable terminal. Is the resistance within the specified range?	0–2 Ω	*Go to Step 8*	*Go to Step 21*
17	Replace all of the terminals the connectors that exhibit signs of poor terminal contact, corrosion, or damaged terminal(s). Is the repair complete?	—	Refer to *Diagnostic System Check*	—
18	Repair the open or high resistance in CKT 6V01. Is the repair complete?	—	Refer to *Diagnostic System Check*	—
19	Repair the open or high resistance in CKT 6B01. Is the repair complete?	—	Refer to *Diagnostic System Check*	—

GC402980341800DX

Fig. 210 Code C1214: Brake Control relay Contact Circuit Open (Part 4 of 5). Metro

Step	Action	Value(s)	Yes	No
6	1. Disconnect the negative battery cable. 2. Disconnect the positive battery cable. 3. Use the *J 39200* in order to measure the resistance between the positive battery cable terminal and the Electronic Brake Control Relay connector terminal 30. Is the resistance within the specified range?	0–2 Ω	*Go to Step 7*	*Go to Step 20*
7	1. Connect a jumper wire between the Electronic Brake Control Relay connector terminal 86 to ground. 2. Connect a fused jumper wire (such as a *J 36169-A*) with a 3A fuse between the Electronic Brake Control Relay terminal 85 and battery voltage. 3. Use the *J 39200* in order to measure the resistance between the Electronic Brake Control Relay terminal 30 and terminal 87. Is the resistance within the specified range?	0–2 Ω	*Go to Step 8*	*Go to Step 22*
8	1. Turn the ignition switch to the OFF position. 2. Inspect the following components: • The EBCM connector • The EBCM harness connector • The Electronic Brake Control Relay • The Electronic Brake Control Relay connector 3. Inspect the above components for signs of the following conditions: • Damage • Poor terminal contact • Terminal corrosion 4. Inspect the following components: • The positive battery terminal • The positive battery cable terminal • The negative battery terminal • The negative battery cable terminal 5. Inspect the above components for signs of the following conditions: • A poor connection • Poor terminal contact Are there signs of poor terminal contact, corrosion, or damaged terminal(s)?	—	*Go to Step 17*	*Go to Step 9*
9	1. Remove all of the jumpers. 2. Reconnect the EBCM connector. 3. Reconnect the Electronic Brake Control Relay 4. Reconnect the positive battery cable. 5. Reconnect the negative battery cable. 6. Turn the ignition switch to the ON position. Do not start the engine. 7. Use the *Scan Tool* in order to look for current DTCs. Does DTC C1214 set as a current DTC?	—	*Go to Step 24*	*Go to Step 25*

GC402980341800CX

Fig. 210 Code C1214: Brake Control relay Contact Circuit Open (Part 3 of 5). Metro

Step	Action	Value(s)	Yes	No
20	Repair the open or high resistance in CKT 6A01. Is the repair complete?	—	Refer to *Diagnostic System Check*	—
21	Repair the open or high resistance in the following components as necessary: • CKT 439 • CKT 3 • The ignition switch • The battery feed circuit to the ignition switch Is the repair complete?	—	Refer to *Diagnostic System Check*	—
22	Replace the Electronic Brake Control Relay. Is the repair complete?	—	Refer to *Diagnostic System Check*	—
23	Repair the low voltage condition. Is the repair complete?	—	Refer to *Diagnostic System Check*	—
24	Replace the EBCM. Is the repair complete?	—	Refer to *Diagnostic System Check*	—
25	The malfunction is intermittent or is not present at this time. Refer to Diagnostic Aids for more information. Is the action complete?	—	System OK	—

GC402980341800EX

Fig. 210 Code C1214: Brake Control relay Contact Circuit Open (Part 5 of 5). Metro

Circuit Description

Ignition voltage is supplied to terminal 86 of the Electronic Brake Control Relay. The above condition enables the EBCM to energize the pullin coil by completing the ground circuit at connector terminal A11 of the EBCM. The magnetic field created closes the Electronic Brake Control Relay contacts. The magnetic field also allows battery voltage and current through the Electronic Brake Control Relay terminal 30 to be supplied to the EBCM through connector terminal C. Connector terminal C supplies power to the EBCM, which supplies power to the motors.

Conditions for Setting the DTC

- DTC C1215 can set only before the EBCM commands the Electronic Brake Control Relay ON.
- DTC C1215 determines if the Electronic Brake Control Relay energizes when the Electronic Brake Control Relay should not energize. The above malfunction will not allow the Electronic Brake Control Relay to remove power to the ABS system.
- If a second malfunction occurs, that requires the Electronic Brake Control Relay to turn OFF, the second malfunction cannot be removed if the Electronic Brake Control Relay cannot be controlled. The DTC sets if the malfunction is present for three consecutive drive cycles.

Action Taken When the DTC Sets

- A malfunction DTC stores.
- The ABS does not disable.

Conditions for Clearing the DTC

- The condition responsible for setting the DTC no longer exists and the Scan Tool Clear DTCs function is used.
- 100 drive cycles pass with no DTCs detected. A drive cycle consists of starting the vehicle, driving the vehicle over 16 km/h (10 mph), stopping and then turning the ignition OFF.

Diagnostic Aids

A sticking or malfunctioning relay may cause an intermittent malfunction.

Use the enhanced diagnostic function of the Scan Tool in order to measure the frequency of the malfunction.

Clear the DTCs after completing the diagnosis. Test drive the vehicle for three drive cycles in order to verify that the DTC does not reset. Use the following procedure in order to complete one drive cycle:

1. Start the vehicle.
2. Drive the vehicle over 16 km/h (10 mph).
3. Stop the vehicle.
4. Turn the ignition to the OFF position.

Important: Zero the J 39200 test leads before making any resistance measurements.

GC402980341900AX

Fig. 211 Code C1215: Brake Control Relay Contact Circuit Active (Part 1 of 3). Metro

Step	Action	Value(s)	Yes	No
1	Was the Diagnostic System Check performed?	—	*Go to Step 2*	Refer to *Diagnostic System Check*
2	Are any other DTCs present?	—	Refer to the appropriate DTC table	*Go to Step 3*
3	1. Turn the ignition switch to the OFF position. 2. Install a *Scan Tool*. 3. Turn the ignition switch to the ON position. Do not start the engine. 4. Use the Relay Test function of the Scan Tool to command the Electronic Brake Control Relay OFF. Does the Scan Tool indicate that the Electronic Brake Control Relay is OFF and the battery voltage less than or equal to the specified voltage?	5 V	*Go to Step 12*	*Go to Step 4*
4	1. Turn the ignition switch to the OFF position. 2. Disconnect the EBCM connector. 3. Turn the ignition switch to the ON position. Do not start the engine. 4. Use the *J 39200* in order to measure the voltage between the EBCM harness connector terminal C and ground. Is the voltage within the specified range?	0–1 V	*Go to Step 6*	*Go to Step 5*
5	1. Turn the ignition switch to the OFF position. 2. Disconnect the Electronic Brake Control Relay. 3. Turn the ignition switch to the ON position. Do not start the engine. 4. Use the *J 39200* in order to measure the voltage between the EBCM harness connector terminal C and ground. Is the voltage within the specified range?	0–1 V	*Go to Step 10*	*Go to Step 9*
6	1. Turn the ignition switch to the OFF position. 2. Inspect the following components: • The EBCM connector • EBCM harness connector 3. Inspect for the following conditions: • Poor terminal contact • Corrosion • Damaged terminals. The above conditions may cause a short to voltage. Is there a condition that may cause a short to voltage?	—	*Go to Step 8*	*Go to Step 7*
7	1. Reconnect the EBCM connector. 2. Turn the ignition switch to the ON position. Do not start the engine. 3. Use the Relay Test function of the Scan Tool to command the Electronic Brake Control Relay OFF. Does the Scan Tool indicate that the Electronic Brake Control Relay is OFF and is the battery voltage less than or equal to the specified voltage?	5 V	*Go to Step 12*	*Go to Step 11*

GC402980341900BX

Fig. 211 Code C1215: Brake Control Relay Contact Circuit Active (Part 2 of 3). Metro

Step	Action	Value(s)	Yes	No
8	Replace all of the terminals or the connectors that exhibit signs of poor terminal contact, corrosion, or damaged terminal(s). Is the repair complete?	—	Refer to *Diagnostic System Check*	—
9	Repair the short to voltage in CKT 6B01. Is the repair complete?	—	Refer to *Diagnostic System Check*	—
10	Replace the Electronic Brake Control Relay. Is the repair complete?	—	Refer to *Diagnostic System Check*	—
11	Replace the EBCM. Is the repair complete?	—	Refer to *Diagnostic System Check*	—
12	The malfunction is intermittent or not present at this time. Refer to Diagnostic Aids for more information. Is the action complete?	—	System OK	—

GC402980341900CX

Fig. 211 Code C1215: Brake Control Relay Contact Circuit Active (Part 3 of 3). Metro

Circuit Description

Ignition voltage is supplied to terminal 86 of the Electronic Brake Control Relay. The above condition enables the EBCM to energize the pullin coil by completing the ground circuit at connector terminal A11 of the EBCM. The magnetic field created closes the Electronic Brake Control Relay contacts. The magnetic field also allows battery voltage and current through the Electronic Brake Control Relay terminal 30 to be supplied to the EBCM through connector terminal C. Connector terminal C supplies power to the EBCM, which supplies power to the motors.

Conditions for Setting the DTC

DTC 1216 can set anytime after the Electronic Brake Control Relay is commanded ON. This test detects an open in the Electronic Brake Control Relay coil circuit. An open in this circuit will not allow the Electronic Brake Control Relay to be energized thus preventing power to the motors and solenoids.

A DTC C1286 will be set with DTC C1216 if the rear channel is not expected to be in the home position.

Action Taken When the DTC Sets

- A malfunction DTC stores.
- The ABS disables.
- The ABS warning indicator(s) turns ON.

Note: DTC C1214 will also set with this DTC. If DTC C1214 is set as current DTC, follow the diagnostic table for this DTC first.

Conditions for Clearing the DTC

- The condition responsible for setting the DTC no longer exists and the Scan Tool Clear DTCs function is used.
- 100 drive cycles pass with no DTCs detected. A drive cycle consists of starting the vehicle, driving the vehicle over 16 km/h (10 mph), stopping and then turning the ignition OFF.

Diagnostic Aids

The following conditions may cause an intermittent malfunction:

- A poor connection
- Rubbed-through wire insulation
- A broken wire inside the insulation

Use the enhanced diagnostic function of the Scan Tool in order to measure the frequency of the malfunction.

GC402980342000AX

Fig. 212 Code C1216: Bake Control Relay Coil Open (Part 1 of 4). Metro

If the frequency of the malfunction is high, but is currently intermittent, inspect for high coil resistance. Use a *J 39200* in order to measure for high coil resistance by measuring between Electronic Brake Control Relay terminal 85 and terminal 86. If the resistance shows greater than 95 ohms, replace the Electronic Brake Control Relay.

Thoroughly inspect any circuitry that may be causing the intermittent complaint for the following conditions:

- Backed out terminals
- Improper mating
- Improperly formed or damaged terminals
- Poor terminal-to-wiring connections
- Physical damage to the wiring harness

Clear the DTCs after completing the diagnosis. Test drive the vehicle for three drive cycles in order to verify that the DTC does not reset. Use the following procedure in order to complete one drive cycle:

1. Start the vehicle.
2. Drive the vehicle over 16 km/h (10 mph).
3. Stop the vehicle.
4. Turn the ignition to the OFF position.

Important: Zero the J 39200 test leads before making any resistance measurements.

Step	Action	Value(s)	Yes	No
1	Was the Diagnostic System Check performed?	—	*Go to Step 2*	Refer to *Diagnostic System Check*
2	1. Turn the ignition switch to the OFF position. 2. Install a *Scan Tool*. 3. Turn the ignition switch to the ON position. Do not start the engine. 4. Use the Relay Test function of the *Scan Tool* in order to command the Electronic Brake Control Relay ON. Does the Scan Tool indicate that the Electronic Brake Control Relay is ON, and is the voltage equal to or greater than the specified voltage?	10 V	*Go to Step 23*	*Go to Step 3*
3	Use the *J 39200* in order to measure the voltage between the Electronic Brake Control Relay connector terminal 85 and ground. Is the voltage equal to or greater than the specified voltage?	10 V	*Go to Step 4*	*Go to Step 9*
4	Use the *J 39200* in order to measure the voltage between the Electronic Brake Control Relay connector terminal 86 and ground. Is the voltage equal to or greater than the specified voltage?	10 V	*Go to Step 5*	*Go to Step 13*
5	1. Turn the ignition switch to the OFF position. 2. Disconnect the EBCM connector. 3. Turn the ignition switch to the ON position. Do not start the engine. 4. Use the *J 39200* in order to measure the voltage between the EBCM connector terminal A11 and ground. Is the voltage equal to or greater than the specified voltage?	10 V	*Go to Step 6*	*Go to Step 7*

GC402980342000BX

Fig. 212 Code C1216: Bake Control Relay Coil Open (Part 2 of 4). Metro

Step	Action	Value(s)	Yes	No
6	1. Turn the ignition switch to the OFF position. 2. Inspect the following components: • The EBCM connector terminal A11 • The remaining terminals of the EBCM connector 3. Inspect the above components for the following conditions: • Damage • Poor terminal contact • Terminal corrosion Are there signs of poor terminal contact, corrosion, or damaged terminals?	—	*Go to Step 17*	*Go to Step 8*
7	1. Remove the Electronic Brake Control Relay. 2. Use the *J 39200* in order to measure the resistance between the EBCM connector terminal A11 and the Electronic Brake Control Relay connector terminal 85. Is the resistance within the specified range?	0–2 Ω	*Go to Step 8*	*Go to Step 18*
8	1. Reconnect the EBCM connector. 2. Reconnect the Electronic Brake Control Relay, if the Electronic Brake Control Relay is disconnected. 3. Turn the ignition switch to the ON position. Do not start the engine. 4. Use the *Scan Tool* in order to read the DTCs. Does DTC C1216 set as current DTC?	—	*Go to Step 22*	*Go to Step 23*
9	1. Turn the ignition switch to the OFF position. 2. Remove the DEF Fuse (20A) from the fuse block. 3. Turn the ignition switch to the ON position. Do not start the engine. 4. Use the *J 39200* in order to measure the voltage between the fuse block terminal and ground. Is the voltage equal to or greater than the specified voltage?	10 V	*Go to Step 10*	*Go to Step 16*
10	Remove and inspect the DEF Fuse (20A). Is the fuse open?	0–2 Ω	*Go to Step 12*	*Go to Step 11*
11	1. Turn the ignition switch to the OFF position. 2. Use the *J 39200* in order to measure the resistance between the Electronic Brake Control Relay connector terminal 86 and the fuse block terminal. Is the resistance within the specified range?	0–2 Ω	*Go to Step 23*	*Go to Step 15*
12	1. Turn the ignition switch to the OFF position. 2. Disconnect the EBCM connector. 3. Use the *J 39200* in order to measure the resistance between the EBCM harness connector terminal A9 and ground. Is the resistance within the specified range?	OL (Infinite)	*Go to Step 20*	*Go to Step 19*
13	1. Disconnect the Electronic Brake Control Relay. 2. Use the *J 39200* in order to measure the resistance between the Electronic Brake Control Relay terminal 85 and the Electronic Brake Control Relay terminal 86. Is the resistance within the specified range?	65–95 Ω	*Go to Step 14*	*Go to Step 21*

GC402980342000CX

Fig. 212 Code C1216: Bake Control Relay Coil Open (Part 3 of 4). Metro

Step	Action	Value(s)	Yes	No
14	Inspect the Electronic Brake Control Relay connector for the following conditions: • Damage • Poor terminal contact • Terminal corrosion Are there signs of damage, poor terminal contact, or terminal corrosion?	—	*Go to Step 17*	*Go to Step 23*
15	Repair the open or high resistance in CKT 6U01. Is the repair complete?	—	Refer to *Diagnostic System Check*	—
16	Repair the open or high resistance in the following circuits and components: • The power feed circuits to the fuse block. • The ignition switch • The DEF Fuse. Is the repair complete?	—	Refer to *Diagnostic System Check*	—
17	Replace all of the terminals that display signs of poor terminal contact, corrosion, or damaged terminal(s). If the Electronic Brake Control Relay displays signs of corrosion, replace the Electronic Brake Control Relay. Is the repair complete?	—	Refer to *Diagnostic System Check*	—
18	Repair the open or high resistance in CKT 6V01. Is the repair complete?	—	Refer to *Diagnostic System Check*	—
19	Repair the short to ground in CKT 6U01. Is the repair complete?	—	*Go to Step 20*	—
20	Replace the fuse block DEF Fuse (20A) with a known good fuse. Is the repair complete?	—	Refer to *Diagnostic System Check*	—
21	Replace the Electronic Brake Control Relay. Is the repair complete?	—	Refer to *Diagnostic System Check*	—
22	Replace the EBCM. Is the repair complete?	—	Refer to *Diagnostic System Check*	—
23	The malfunction is intermittent or is not present at this time. Refer to Diagnostic Aids for more information. Is the action complete?	—	System OK	—

GC402980342000DX

Fig. 212 Code C1216: Bake Control Relay Coil Open (Part 4 of 4). Metro

Circuit Description

Ignition voltage is supplied to terminal 86 of the Electronic Brake Control Relay. The above condition enables the EBCM to energize the pullin coil by completing the ground circuit at connector terminal A11 of the EBCM. The magnetic field created closes the Electronic Brake Control Relay contacts. The magnetic field also allows battery voltage and current through the Electronic Brake Control Relay terminal 30 to be supplied to the EBCM through connector terminal C. Connector terminal C supplies power to the EBCM, which supplies power to the motors and solenoids.

Conditions for Setting the DTC

DTC C1217 can set before the EBCM commands the Electronic Brake Control Relay ON.

DTC C1217 determines if the Electronic Brake Control Relay energizes when the Electronic Brake Control Relay should not energize. The above malfunction would not allow the Electronic Brake Control Relay to remove power to the ABS system. If a second malfunction occurs, that requires the Electronic Brake Control Relay to turn OFF, the second malfunction cannot be removed if the Electronic Brake Control Relay cannot be controlled.

Action Taken When the DTC Sets

- A malfunction DTC stores.
- The ABS does not disable.

Conditions for Clearing the DTC

- The condition responsible for setting the DTC no longer exists and the Scan Tool Clear DTCs function is used.
- 100 drive cycles pass with no DTCs detected. A drive cycle consists of starting the vehicle, driving the vehicle over 16 km/h (10 mph), stopping and then turning the ignition OFF.

Diagnostic Aids

Use the enhanced diagnostic function of the Scan Tool in order to measure the frequency of the malfunction.

Clear the DTCs after completing the diagnosis.

Test drive the vehicle for three drive cycles in order to verify that the DTC does not reset.

Use the following procedure in order to complete one drive cycle:

1. Start the vehicle.
2. Drive the vehicle over 16 km/h (10 mph).
3. Stop the vehicle.
4. Turn the ignition to the OFF position.

Important: Zero the J 39200 test leads before making any resistance measurements.

GC402980342100AX

Fig. 213 Code C1217: Brake Control Relay Coil Circuit Short To Ground (Part 1 of 3). Metro

Circuit Description

This DTC is designed to detect a slipping rear ESB. During initialization, the rear motor is rehomed. If the ESB slips, the motor will move. During the next initialization, a rehome of the motor verifies the motor remained at the home position. If motor movement is detected, the ESB must be slipping.

Conditions for Setting the DTC

This DTC will set when the following conditions are met:

- Forward movement of the rear motor is detected (motor feedback current is less than the motor stall current [12A]).
- This test checks if rear hydraulic modulator pistons are in the home position during initialization.
- This DTC can be set during initialization. DTC C1286 is always set with this DTC.

Action Taken When the DTC Sets

If the ESB cannot hold the motor, the motor may be back driven when the brake pedal is applied causing the rear hydraulic modulator pistons to be away from home position. A malfunction DTC is stored, ABS is disabled and both the amber ABS indicator lamp and the red BRAKE warning lamp are turned ON.

Conditions for Clearing the DTC

- Conditions for the malfunction are no longer present and the Tech 2 scan tool Clear DTC Information function is used.
- One hundred drive cycles have passed with no malfunctions detected.

Diagnostic Aids

The following list contains items that need to be inspected when diagnosing this system:

- Faulty motor pack.
- Faulty hydraulic modulator (rear pistons sticking and not returning to home position).

An intermittent malfunction in this DTC may result from a mechanical part of the system that sticks, binds, or slips.

The frequency of the malfunction can be checked by using the Enhanced Diagnostic function of the Tech 2 scan tool

Test Description

The numbers below refer to step numbers on the diagnostic table.

2. Checks the ability of the ESB to hold the motor. A broken or faulty ESB would result in the rear piston being back driven by hydraulic pressure; therefore the rear wheels would move.
3. Releases the tension of the motor pack prior to its removal from the hydraulic modulator.

GC402980342100BX

Fig. 213 Code C1217: Brake Control Relay Coil Circuit Short To Ground (Part 2 of 3). Metro

Step	Action	Value(s)	Yes	No
9	Repair the short to ground in CKT 6V01. Is the repair complete?	—	Refer to *Diagnostic System Check*	—
10	Replace the Electronic Brake Control Relay. Is the repair complete?	—	Refer to *Diagnostic System Check*	—
11	Replace the EBCM. Is the repair complete?	—	Refer to *Diagnostic System Check*	—
12	The malfunction is intermittent or is not present at this time. Refer to Diagnostic Aids for more information. Is the action complete?	—	System OK	—

GC402980342100CX

Fig. 213 Code C1217: Brake Control Relay Coil Circuit Short To Ground (Part 3 of 3). Metro

Circuit Description

Ignition voltage is supplied to terminal 86 of the Electronic Brake Control Relay. The above enables the EBCM to energize the pullin coil by completing the ground circuit at connector terminal A11 of the EBCM. The magnetic field created closes the Electronic Brake Control Relay contacts. The magnetic field also allows battery voltage and current through the Electronic Brake Control Relay terminal 30 to be supplied to the EBCM through connector terminal C. Connector terminal C supplies power to the EBCM, which supplies power to the motors and solenoids.

Conditions for Setting the DTC

- DTC C1218 can set after the EBCM commands the Electronic Brake Control Relay ON.
- This test monitors the availability of voltage to the EBCM.
- DTC C1286 is set with DTC C1218 if the rear channel is not expected to be in the home position.

Action Taken When the DTC Sets

- A malfunction DTC stores.
- The ABS disables.
- The ABS warning indicator turns ON.

Conditions for Clearing the DTC

- The condition responsible for setting the DTC no longer exists and the Scan Tool Clear DTCs function is used.
- 100 drive cycles pass with no DTCs detected. A drive cycle consists of starting the vehicle, driving the vehicle over 16 km/h (10 mph), stopping and then turning the ignition OFF.

Diagnostic Aids

Use the enhanced diagnostic function of the Scan Tool in order to measure the frequency of the malfunction.

Clear the DTCs after completing the diagnosis. Test drive the vehicle for three drive cycles in order to verify that the DTC does not reset. Use the following procedure in order to complete one drive cycle:

1. Start the vehicle.
2. Drive the vehicle over 16 km/h (10 mph).
3. Stop the vehicle.
4. Turn the ignition to the OFF position.

Important: Zero the J 39200 test leads before making any resistance measurements.

GC402980342200AX

Fig. 214 Code C1218: Brake Control Relay Coil Circuit Short To Voltage (Part 1 of 3). Metro

Step	Action	Value(s)	Yes	No
1	Was the Diagnostic System Check performed?	—	*Go to Step 2*	Refer to *Diagnostic System Check*
2	1. Turn the ignition switch to the OFF position. 2. Install a *Scan Tool.* 3. Turn the ignition switch to the RUN position. Do not start the engine. 4. Use the Relay Test function of the *Scan Tool* in order to command the Electronic Brake Control Relay ON. Does the Scan Tool indicate that the Electronic Brake Control Relay is OFF, and is the voltage equal to or greater than the specified voltage?	0–10 V	*Go to Step 12*	*Go to Step 3*
3	1. Turn the ignition switch to the OFF position. 2. Disconnect the Electronic Brake Control Relay. 3. Disconnect the EBCM connector. 4. Turn the ignition switch to the RUN position. Do not start the engine. 5. Use the *J 39200* in order to measure the voltage between the EBCM harness connector terminal 2 and ground. Is the voltage within the specified voltage?	0–2 V	*Go to Step 4*	*Go to Step 9*
4	1. Turn the ignition switch to the OFF position. 2. Use the *J 39200* in order to measure the resistance between the Electronic Brake Control Relay terminal 85 and the Electronic Brake Control Relay terminal 86. Is the resistance equal to or greater than the specified range?	65–95 Ω	*Go to Step 5*	*Go to Step 10*
5	Use the *J 39200* in order to measure the resistance between the Electronic Brake Control Relay terminal 30 and the Electronic Brake Control Relay terminal 87. Is the resistance within the specified range?	OL (Infinite)	*Go to Step 6*	*Go to Step 10*
6	1. Inspect the following components: • The EBCM connector terminal 2 • The remaining terminals of the EBCM connector 2. Inspect the above components for the following conditions: • Damage • Poor terminal contact • Terminal corrosion Are there signs of poor terminal contact, corrosion, or damaged terminals?	—	*Go to Step 8*	*Go to Step 7*
7	1. Reconnect the EBCM connector. 2. Reconnect the Electronic Brake Control Relay. 3. Turn the ignition switch to the RUN position. Do not start the engine. 4. Use the *Scan Tool* in order to look for DTCs. Does DTC C1218 set as a current DTC?	—	*Go to Step 11*	*Go to Step 12*

GC402980342200BX

Fig. 214 Code C1218: Brake Control Relay Coil Circuit Short To Voltage (Part 2 of 3). Metro

Step	Action	Value(s)	Yes	No
8	Replace all of the terminals or connectors that exhibit signs of poor terminal contact, corrosion, or damaged terminal(s). Is the repair complete?	—	Refer to *Diagnostic System Check*	—
9	Repair the short to voltage in CKT 1632. Is the repair complete?	—	Refer to *Diagnostic System Check*	—
10	Replace the Electronic Brake Control Relay. Is the repair complete?	—	Refer to *Diagnostic System Check*	—
11	Replace the EBCM. Is the repair complete?	—	Refer to *Diagnostic System Check*	—
12	The malfunction is intermittent or is not present at this time. Refer to Diagnostic Aids for more information. Is the action complete?	—	System OK	—

GC402980342200CX

Fig. 214 Code C1218: Brake Control Relay Coil Circuit Short To Voltage (Part 3 of 3). Metro

Circuit Description

As a toothed ring passes by the wheel speed sensor, changes in the electromagnetic field cause the wheel speed sensor to produce an AC voltage signal. The frequency of the AC voltage signal is proportional to the wheel speed. The amplitude of the AC voltage signal is directly related to wheel speed and the proximity of the wheel speed sensor to the toothed ring. The proximity of the wheel speed sensor to the toothed ring is also referred to as the air gap.

Conditions for Setting the DTC

DTC C1221 can set when the vehicle is not in an ABS stop.

A malfunction exists if both of the following conditions occur:

- The left front wheel speed sensor input signal equals zero.
- The vehicle's reference speed is greater than 8 km/h (5 mph)

Action Taken When the DTC Sets

- A malfunction DTC stores.
- The ABS disables.
- The ABS warning indicator turns ON.

Conditions for Clearing the DTC

- The condition responsible for setting the DTC no longer exists and the Scan Tool Clear DTCs function is used.
- 100 drive cycles pass with no DTCs detected. A drive cycle consists of starting the vehicle, driving the vehicle over 16 km/h (10 mph), stopping and then turning the ignition OFF.

Diagnostic Aids

The following conditions may cause a malfunction:

- A poor connection
- Rubbed-through wire insulation
- A broken wire inside the insulation
- Wheel speed sensor physically damaged
- Wheel speed sensor input circuits shorted together
- Missing speed sensor ring
- Excessive wheel speed sensor gap

Use the enhanced diagnostic function of the Scan Tool in order to measure the frequency of the malfunction.

If the customer's comments reflect that the amber ABS warning indicator is ON only during moist environmental changes (rain, snow, vehicle wash), inspect all the wheel speed sensor circuitry for signs of water intrusion.

Thoroughly inspect any circuitry that may be causing the intermittent complaint for the following conditions:

- Backed out terminals
- Improper mating
- Broken locks
- Improperly formed or damaged terminals
- Poor terminal-to-wiring connections
- Physical damage to the wiring harness

Resistance of the wheel speed sensor will increase with an increase in sensor temperature.

Use the following procedure when replacing a wheel speed sensor or harness:

1. Inspect the wheel speed sensor terminals and harness connector for corrosion and/or water intrusion.

GC402980342300AX

Fig. 215 Code C1221: LH Front Wheel Speed Sensor Input Signal Is Zero (Part 1 of 4). Metro

2. Replace the wheel speed sensor and jumper harness if evidence of corrosion or water intrusion exists.

Important: Zero the J 39200 test leads before making any resistance measurements. Refer to the J 39200 user's manual.

Important: Difficulty may occur when trying to locate the intermittent malfunctions in the wheel speed sensor circuit.

Do not disturb any of the electrical connections. Change electrical connections only when instructed to do so by a step in the diagnostic table.

Changing the electrical connections at the correct time will ensure that an intermittent electrical connection will not be corrected until the source of the malfunction is found.

Step	Action	Value(s)	Yes	No
1	Was the Diagnostic System Check performed?	—	*Go to Step 2*	Refer to *Diagnostic System Check*
2	1. Turn the ignition switch to the OFF position. 2. Inspect the left front wheel speed sensor and the left front wheel speed sensor harness connector for physical damage. Is there any physical damage?	—	*Go to Step 16*	*Go to Step 3*
3	Inspect the following components for physical damage: • The left front wheel speed sensor jumper harness • The left front wheel speed sensor jumper harness connectors Is there any physical damage?	—	*Go to Step 15*	*Go to Step 4*
4	1. Disconnect the left front wheel speed sensor directly at the left front wheel speed sensor connector. 2. Use the *J 39200* in order to measure the resistance between the left front wheel speed sensor connector terminal A and the left front wheel speed sensor connector terminal B. Is the resistance within the specified range?	920–1220 Ω	*Go to Step 5*	*Go to Step 16*
5	1. Select the A/C VOLTAGE scale on the *J 39200.* 2. Spin the left front wheel by hand while observing the voltage reading on the *J 39200.* Is the voltage equal to or greater than the specified voltage?	100 mV	*Go to Step 6*	*Go to Step 16*
6	1. Disconnect the EBCM connector. 2. Use the *J 39200* in order to measure the resistance between the EBCM terminal A5 and the EBCM terminal B4. Is the resistance within the specified range?	OL (Infinite)	*Go to Step 7*	*Go to Step 8*

GC402980342300BX

Fig. 215 Code C1221: LH Front Wheel Speed Sensor Input Signal Is Zero (Part 2 of 4). Metro

Step	Action	Value(s)	Yes	No
7	1. Inspect the EBCM connector for the following conditions: • Damage • Poor terminal contact • Terminal corrosion (Damage, poor terminal contact, and terminal corrosion may cause a short between the EBCM terminal A5 and the EBCM terminal B4. 2. Inspect the remaining terminals of the EBCM connector for the following conditions: • Damage • Poor terminal contact • Terminal corrosion Are there signs of poor terminal contact, corrosion, or damaged terminals?	—	*Go to Step 12*	*Go to Step 8*
8	Inspect the wiring of CKT 6L01 and CKT 6K01 for signs of damage that may cause a short between CKT 6L01 and CKT 6K01. Are there any signs of damaged wiring?	—	*Go to Step 13*	*Go to Step 9*
9	Inspect the harness connectors of CKT 6L01 and CKT 6K01 for signs of damage that may cause a short between CKT 6L01 and CKT 6K01. Are there any signs of damaged connectors?	—	*Go to Step 14*	*Go to Step 10*
10	1. Reconnect the EBCM harness connector. 2. Reconnect the left front wheel speed sensor harness connector. 3. Install a *Scan Tool.* 4. Test drive the vehicle at a speed above 24 km/h (15 mph) for at least 30 seconds. 5. Use the *Scan Tool* in order to read the DTCs. Does DTC C1221 set as a current DTC?	—	*Go to Step 11*	*Go to Step 18*
11	1. Select Data List on the *Scan Tool.* 2. Monitor the wheel speed sensor speeds. 3. Drive the vehicle in the following manner: 3.1. Slowly accelerate to 65 km/h (40 mph). 3.2. Slowly decelerate to 0 km/h (0 mph). Is the speed of the left front wheel speed sensor constantly higher than the speed of the three remaining wheel speed sensors?	—	*Go to Step 15*	*Go to Step 17*
12	Replace all of the terminals that exhibit signs of poor terminal contact, corrosion, or damaged terminal(s). Is the repair complete?	—	Refer to *Diagnostic System Check*	—
13	Replace the damaged wiring harness that causes the short between CKT 6L01 and CKT 6K01. Is the repair complete?	—	Refer to *Diagnostic System Check*	—
14	Replace the damaged wiring harness connectors that cause the short between CKT 6L01 and CKT 6K01. Is the repair complete?	—	Refer to *Diagnostic System Check*	—
15	Replace the left front wheel speed sensor jumper harness. Is the repair complete?	—	Refer to *Diagnostic System Check*	—

GC402980342300CX

Fig. 215 Code C1221: LH Front Wheel Speed Sensor Input Signal Is Zero (Part 3 of 4). Metro

Step	Action	Value(s)	Yes	No
16	Replace the left front wheel speed sensor. Is the repair complete?	—	Refer to *Diagnostic System Check*	—
17	Replace the EBCM. Is the repair complete?	—	Refer to *Diagnostic System Check*	—
18	The malfunction is intermittent or is not present at this time. Refer to Diagnostic Aids for more information. Is the action complete?	—	System OK	—

GC402980342300DX

Fig. 215 Code C1221: LH Front Wheel Speed Sensor Input Signal Is Zero (Part 4 of 4). Metro

Circuit Description

As a toothed ring passes by the wheel speed sensor, changes in the electromagnetic field cause the wheel speed sensor to produce an AC voltage signal. The frequency of the AC voltage signal is proportional to the wheel speed. The amplitude of the AC voltage signal is directly related to wheel speed and the proximity of the wheel speed sensor to the toothed ring. The proximity of the wheel speed sensor to the toothed ring is also referred to as the air gap.

Conditions for Setting the DTC

DTC C1222 sets when the vehicle is not in an ABS stop.

A malfunction exists if both of the following conditions occur:

- The right front wheel speed sensor input signal equals zero
- The vehicle's reference speed is greater than 8 km/h (5 mph)
- This DTC will not set if DTC C1233 has already failed

Action Taken When the DTC Sets

- A malfunction DTC stores.
- The ABS disables.
- The ABS warning indicator turns ON.

Conditions for Clearing the DTC

- The condition responsible for setting the DTC no longer exists and the Scan Tool Clear DTCs function is used.
- 100 drive cycles pass with no DTCs detected. A drive cycle consists of starting the vehicle, driving the vehicle over 16 km/h (10 mph), stopping and then turning the ignition OFF.

Diagnostic Aids

The following conditions may cause a malfunction:

- A poor connection
- Rubbed-through wire insulation
- A broken wire inside the insulation
- Wheel speed sensor physically damaged
- Wheel speed sensor input circuits shorted together
- Missing speed sensor ring
- Excessive wheel speed sensor gap

Use the enhanced diagnostic function of the Scan Tool in order to measure the frequency of the malfunction. Refer to the Scan Tool manual for the procedure.

If the customer's comments reflect that the amber ABS warning indicator is ON only during moist environmental changes (rain, snow, vehicle wash), inspect all the wheel speed sensor circuitry for signs of water intrusion.

Thoroughly inspect any circuitry that may be causing the intermittent complaint for the following conditions:

- Backed out terminals
- Improper mating
- Broken locks
- Improperly formed or damaged terminals
- Poor terminal-to-wiring connections
- Physical damage to the wiring harness

Resistance of the wheel speed sensor will increase with an increase in sensor temperature.

Use the following procedure when replacing a wheel speed sensor or harness:

1. Inspect the wheel speed sensor terminals and harness connector for corrosion and/or water intrusion.
2. Replace the wheel speed sensor and jumper harness if evidence of corrosion or water intrusion exists.

Important: Zero the J 39200 test leads before making any resistance measurements. Refer to the J 39200 user's manual.

Important: Difficulty may occur when trying to locate the intermittent malfunctions in the wheel speed sensor circuit.

Do not disturb any of the electrical connections. Change electrical connections only when instructed to do so by a step in the diagnostic table.

Changing the electrical connections at the correct time will ensure that an intermittent electrical connection will not be corrected until the source of the malfunction is found.

GC402980342400AX

Fig. 216 Code C1222: RH Front Wheel Speed Sensor Input Signal Is Zero (Part 1 of 4). Metro

Step	Action	Value(s)	Yes	No
1	Was the Diagnostic System Check performed?	—	*Go to Step 2*	Refer to *Diagnostic System Check*
2	1. Turn the ignition switch to the OFF position. 2. Inspect the left front wheel speed sensor and the left front wheel speed sensor harness connector for physical damage. Is there any physical damage?	—	*Go to Step 16*	*Go to Step 3*
3	Inspect the following components for physical damage: • The left front wheel speed sensor jumper harness • The left front wheel speed sensor jumper harness connectors Is there any physical damage?	—	*Go to Step 15*	*Go to Step 4*
4	1. Disconnect the left front wheel speed sensor directly at the left front wheel speed sensor connector. 2. Use the *J 39200* in order to measure the resistance between the left front wheel speed sensor connector terminal A and the left front wheel speed sensor connector terminal B. Is the resistance within the specified range?	920–1220 Ω	*Go to Step 5*	*Go to Step 16*
5	1. Select the A/C VOLTAGE scale on the *J 39200.* 2. Spin the left front wheel by hand while observing the voltage reading on the *J 39200.* Is the voltage equal to or greater than the specified voltage?	100 mV	*Go to Step 6*	*Go to Step 16*
6	1. Disconnect the EBCM connector. 2. Use the *J 39200* in order to measure the resistance between the EBCM terminal A5 and the EBCM terminal B4. Is the resistance within the specified range?	OL (Infinite)	*Go to Step 7*	*Go to Step 8*

GC402980342400BX

Fig. 216 Code C1222: RH Front Wheel Speed Sensor Input Signal Is Zero (Part 2 of 4). Metro

Step	Action	Value(s)	Yes	No
7	1. Inspect the EBCM connector for the following conditions: • Damage • Poor terminal contact • Terminal corrosion (Damage, poor terminal contact, and terminal corrosion may cause a short between the EBCM terminal A5 and the EBCM terminal B4. 2. Inspect the remaining terminals of the EBCM connector for the following conditions: • Damage • Poor terminal contact • Terminal corrosion Are there signs of poor terminal contact, corrosion, or damaged terminals?	—	*Go to Step 12*	*Go to Step 8*
8	Inspect the wiring of CKT 6L01 and CKT 6K01 for signs of damage that may cause a short between CKT 60L1 and CKT 6K01. Are there any signs of damaged wiring?	—	*Go to Step 13*	*Go to Step 9*
9	Inspect the harness connectors of CKT 6L01 and CKT 6K01 for signs of damage that may cause a short between CKT 6L01 and CKT 6K01. Are there any signs of damaged connectors?	—	*Go to Step 14*	*Go to Step 10*
10	1. Reconnect the EBCM harness connector. 2. Reconnect the left front wheel speed sensor harness connector. 3. Install a *Scan Tool.* 4. Test drive the vehicle at a speed above 24 km/h (15 mph) for at least 30 seconds. 5. Use the *Scan Tool* in order to read the DTCs. Does DTC C1221 set as a current DTC?	—	*Go to Step 11*	*Go to Step 18*
11	1. Select Data List on the *Scan Tool.* 2. Monitor the wheel speed sensor speeds. 3. Drive the vehicle in the following manner: 3.1. Slowly accelerate to 65 km/h (40 mph). 3.2. Slowly decelerate to 0 km/h (0 mph). Is the speed of the left front wheel speed sensor constantly higher than the speed of the three remaining wheel speed sensors?	—	*Go to Step 15*	*Go to Step 17*
12	Replace all of the terminals that exhibit signs of poor terminal contact, corrosion, or damaged terminal(s). Is the repair complete?	—	Refer to *Diagnostic System Check*	—
13	Replace the damaged wiring harness that causes the short between CKT 6L01 and CKT 6K01. Is the repair complete?	—	Refer to *Diagnostic System Check*	—
14	Replace the damaged wiring harness connectors that cause the short between CKT 6L01 and CKT 6K01. Is the repair complete?	—	Refer to *Diagnostic System Check*	—
15	Replace the left front wheel speed sensor jumper harness. Is the repair complete?	—	Refer to *Diagnostic System Check*	—

GC402980342400CX

Fig. 216 Code C1222: RH Front Wheel Speed Sensor Input Signal Is Zero (Part 3 of 4). Metro

Step	Action	Value(s)	Yes	No
16	Replace the left front wheel speed sensor. Is the repair complete?	—	Refer to *Diagnostic System Check*	—
17	Replace the EBCM. Is the repair complete?	—	Refer to *Diagnostic System Check*	—
18	The malfunction is intermittent or is not present at this time. Refer to Diagnostic Aids for more information. Is the action complete?	—	System OK	—

GC402980342400DX

Fig. 216 Code C1222: RH Front Wheel Speed Sensor Input Signal Is Zero (Part 4 of 4). Metro

Circuit Description

As a toothed ring passes by the wheel speed sensor, changes in the electromagnetic field cause the wheel speed sensor to produce an AC voltage signal. The frequency of the AC voltage signal is proportional to the wheel speed. The amplitude of the AC voltage signal is directly related to wheel speed and the proximity of the wheel speed sensor to the toothed ring. The proximity of the wheel speed sensor to the toothed ring is also referred to as the air gap.

Conditions for Setting the DTC

DTC C1223 can set when the vehicle is not in an ABS stop.

A malfunction exists if both of the following conditions occur:

- The left rear wheel speed sensor input signal equals zero.
- The vehicle's reference speed is greater than 8 km/h (5 mph)

Action Taken When the DTC Sets

- A malfunction DTC stores.
- The ABS disables.
- The ABS warning indicator turns ON.

Conditions for Clearing the DTC

- The condition responsible for setting the DTC no longer exists and the Scan Tool Clear DTCs function is used.
- 100 drive cycles pass with no DTCs detected. A drive cycle consists of starting the vehicle, driving the vehicle over 16 km/h (10 mph), stopping and then turning the ignition OFF.

Diagnostic Aids

The following conditions may cause a malfunction:

- A poor connection
- Rubbed-through wire insulation
- A broken wire inside the insulation
- Wheel speed sensor physically damaged
- Wheel speed sensor input circuits shorted together
- Missing speed sensor ring
- Excessive wheel speed sensor gap

Use the enhanced diagnostic function of the Scan Tool in order to measure the frequency of the malfunction.

Two separate wheel speed = 0 DTCs will be set if two wheel speeds are 0 km/h (0 mph) for greater than 20 seconds while the remaining wheel speed(s) are greater than 16 km/h (10 mph) and within 11 km/h (6.8\ mph).

If the customer's comments reflect that the amber ABS warning indicator is ON only during moist environmental changes (rain, snow, vehicle wash), inspect all the wheel speed sensor circuitry for signs of water intrusion.

Thoroughly inspect any circuitry that may be causing the intermittent complaint for the following conditions:

- Backed out terminals
- Improper mating
- Broken locks
- Improperly formed or damaged terminals
- Poor terminal-to-wiring connections
- Physical damage to the wiring harness

GC402980342500AX

Fig. 217 Code C1223: LH Rear Wheel Speed Sensor Input Signal Is Zero (Part 1 of 4). Metro

Resistance of the wheel speed sensor will increase with an increase in sensor temperature.

Use the following procedure when replacing a wheel speed sensor or harness:

1. Inspect the wheel speed sensor terminals and harness connector for corrosion and/or water intrusion.
2. Replace the wheel speed sensor and jumper harness if evidence of corrosion or water intrusion exists.

Important: Zero the J 39200 test leads before making any resistance measurements. Refer to the J 39200 user's manual.

Important: Difficulty may occur when trying to locate intermittent malfunctions in the wheel speed sensor circuit.

Do not disturb any of the electrical connections. Change the electrical connections only when instructed to do so by a step in the diagnostic table.

Changing the electrical connections at the correct time will ensure that an intermittent electrical connection will not be corrected until the source of the malfunction is found.

Step	Action	Value(s)	Yes	No
1	Was the Diagnostic System Check performed?	—	*Go to Step 2*	Refer to *Diagnostic System Check*
2	1. Turn the ignition switch to the OFF position. 2. Inspect the left rear wheel speed sensor and the left rear wheel speed sensor harness connector for physical damage. Is there any physical damage?	—	*Go to Step 16*	*Go to Step 3*
3	Inspect the following components for physical damage: • The left rear wheel speed sensor jumper harness • The left rear wheel speed sensor jumper harness connectors Is there any physical damage?	—	*Go to Step 15*	*Go to Step 4*
4	1. Disconnect the left rear wheel speed sensor directly at the left rear wheel speed sensor connector. 2. Use the *J 39200* in order to measure the resistance between the left rear wheel speed sensor connector terminal A and the left rear wheel speed sensor connector terminal B. Is the resistance within the specified range?	1050–1450 Ω	*Go to Step 5*	*Go to Step 16*
5	1. Select the A/C VOLTAGE scale on the *J 39200.* 2. Spin the left rear wheel by hand while observing the voltage reading on the *J 39200.* Is the voltage equal to or greater than the specified voltage?	100 mV	*Go to Step 6*	*Go to Step 16*
6	1. Disconnect the EBCM connector. 2. Use the *J 39200* to measure the resistance between the EBCM connector terminal A3 and the EBCM connector terminal B2. Is the resistance within the specified range?	OL (Infinite)	*Go to Step 7*	*Go to Step 8*

GC402980342500BX

Fig. 217 Code C1223: LH Rear Wheel Speed Sensor Input Signal Is Zero (Part 2 of 4). Metro

Step	Action	Value(s)	Yes	No
7	1. Inspect the EBCM connector for the following conditions: • Damage • Poor terminal contact • Terminal corrosion (These conditions could result in a short between the EBCM connector terminal A3 and the EBCM connector terminal B2.) 2. Inspect the remaining terminals of the EBCM connector for the following conditions: • Damage • Poor terminal contact • Terminal corrosion Are there signs of poor terminal contact, corrosion, or damaged terminals?	—	*Go to Step 12*	*Go to Step 8*
8	Inspect the wiring of CKT 6P01 and CKT 6O01 for signs of damage that may cause a short between CKT 6P01 and CKT 6O01. Are there any signs of damaged wiring?	—	*Go to Step 13*	*Go to Step 9*
9	Inspect the harness connectors of CKT 6P01 and CKT 6O01 for signs of damage that may cause a short between CKT 6P01 and CKT 6O01. Are there any signs of damaged connectors?	—	*Go to Step 14*	*Go to Step 10*
10	1. Reconnect the EBCM harness connector. 2. Reconnect the left rear wheel speed sensor harness connector. 3. Install a *Scan Tool.* 4. Test drive the vehicle at a speed above 24 km/h (15 mph) for at least 30 seconds. 5. Use the *Scan Tool* in order to read the DTCs. Does DTC C1223 set as a current DTC?	—	*Go to Step 11*	*Go to Step 18*
11	1. Select Data List on the *Scan Tool.* 2. Monitor the wheel speed sensor speeds. 3. Drive the vehicle in the following manner: 3.1. Slowly accelerate to 65 km/h (40 mph). 3.2. Slowly decelerate to 0 km/h (0 mph). Is the speed of the left rear wheel speed sensor constantly higher than the speed of the three remaining wheel speed sensors?	—	*Go to Step 16*	*Go to Step 17*
12	Replace all of the terminals that exhibit signs of poor terminal contact, corrosion, or damaged terminal(s). Is the repair complete?	—	Refer to *Diagnostic System Check*	—
13	Replace the damaged wiring harness that causes the short between CKT 6P01 and CKT 6O01. Is the repair complete?	—	Refer to *Diagnostic System Check*	—
14	Replace the damaged wiring harness connectors that cause the short between CKT 6P01 and CKT 6O01. Is the repair complete?	—	Refer to *Diagnostic System Check*	—
15	Replace the left rear wheel speed sensor jumper harness. Is the repair complete?	—	Refer to *Diagnostic System Check*	—

GC402980342500CX

Fig. 217 Code C1223: LH Rear Wheel Speed Input Sensor Signal Is Zero (Part 3 of 4). Metro

Circuit Description

As a toothed ring passes by the wheel speed sensor, changes in the electromagnetic field cause the wheel speed sensor to produce an AC voltage signal. The frequency of the AC voltage signal is proportional to the wheel speed. The amplitude of the AC voltage signal is directly related to wheel speed and the proximity of the wheel speed sensor to the toothed ring. The proximity of the wheel speed sensor to the toothed ring is also referred to as the air gap.

Conditions for Setting the DTC

DTC C1224 can set when the vehicle is not in an ABS stop.

A malfunction exists if both of the following conditions occur:

- The right rear wheel speed sensor input signal equals zero
- The vehicle's reference speed is greater than 8 km/h (5 mph)
- This DTC will not set if DTC C1235 has already failed

Action Taken When the DTC Sets

- A malfunction DTC stores.
- The ABS disables.
- The ABS warning indicator turns ON.

Conditions for Clearing the DTC

- The condition responsible for setting the DTC no longer exists and the Scan Tool Clear DTCs function is used.
- 100 drive cycles pass with no DTCs detected. A drive cycle consists of starting the vehicle, driving the vehicle over 16 km/h (10 mph), stopping and then turning the ignition OFF.

Diagnostic Aids

The following conditions may cause a malfunction:

- A poor connection
- Rubbed-through wire insulation
- A broken wire inside the insulation
- Wheel speed sensor physically damaged
- Wheel speed sensor input circuits shorted together
- Missing speed sensor ring
- Excessive wheel speed sensor gap

Use the enhanced diagnostic function of the Scan Tool in order to measure the frequency of the malfunction.

If the customer's comments reflect that the amber ABS warning indicator is ON only during moist environmental changes (rain, snow, vehicle wash), inspect all the wheel speed sensor circuitry for signs of water intrusion.

Thoroughly inspect any circuitry that may be causing the intermittent complaint for the following conditions:

- Backed out terminals
- Improper mating
- Broken locks
- Improperly formed or damaged terminals
- Poor terminal-to-wiring connections
- Physical damage to the wiring harness

Resistance of the wheel speed sensor will increase with an increase in sensor temperature.

Use the following procedure when replacing a wheel speed sensor or harness:

1. Inspect the wheel speed sensor terminals and harness connector for corrosion and/or water intrusion.

GC402980342600AX

Fig. 218 Code C1224: RH Rear Wheel Speed Sensor Input Signal Is Zero (Part 1 of 4). Metro

Step	Action	Value(s)	Yes	No
16	Replace the left rear wheel speed sensor. Is the repair complete?	—	Refer to *Diagnostic System Check*	—
17	Replace the EBCM. Is the repair complete?	—	Refer to *Diagnostic System Check*	—
18	The malfunction is intermittent or is not present at this time. Refer to Diagnostic Aids for more information. Is the action complete?	—	System OK	—

GC402980342500DX

Fig. 217 Code C1223: LH Rear Wheel Speed Input Sensor Signal Is Zero (Part 4 of 4). Metro

2. Replace the wheel speed sensor and jumper harness if evidence of corrosion or water intrusion exists.

Two separate wheel speed = 0 DTCs will be set if two wheel speeds are 0 km/h (0 mph) for greater than 20 seconds while the remaining wheel speed(s) are greater than 16 km/h (10 mph) and within 11 km/h (6.8 mph).

Important: Zero the J 39200 test leads before making any resistance measurements. Refer to the J 39200 user's manual.

Important: Difficulty may occur in trying to locate intermittent malfunctions in the wheel speed sensor circuit.

Do not disturb any of the electrical connections. Change electrical connections only when instructed to do so by a step in the diagnostic table.

Changing electrical connections at the correct time will ensure that an intermittent electrical connection will not be corrected until the source of the malfunction is found.

Step	Action	Value(s)	Yes	No
1	Was the Diagnostic System Check performed?	—	*Go to Step 2*	Refer to *Diagnostic System Check*
2	1. Turn the ignition switch to the OFF position. 2. Inspect the right rear wheel speed sensor and the right rear wheel speed sensor harness connector for physical damage. Is there any physical damage?	—	*Go to Step 16*	*Go to Step 3*
3	Inspect the following components for physical damage: • The right rear wheel speed sensor jumper harness • The right rear wheel speed sensor jumper harness connectors Is there any physical damage?	—	*Go to Step 15*	*Go to Step 4*
4	1. Disconnect the right rear wheel speed sensor directly at the right rear wheel speed sensor connector. 2. Use the *J 39200* in order to measure the resistance between the right rear wheel speed sensor connector terminal A and the right rear wheel speed sensor connector terminal B. Is the resistance within the specified range?	1050–1450 Ω	*Go to Step 5*	*Go to Step 16*
5	1. Select the A/C VOLTAGE scale on the *J 39200.* 2. Spin the right rear wheel by hand while observing the voltage reading on the *J 39200.* Is the voltage equal to or greater than the specified voltage?	100 mV	*Go to Step 6*	*Go to Step 16*
6	1. Disconnect the EBCM connector. 2. Use the *J 39200* in order to measure the resistance between the EBCM connector terminal A2 and the EBCM connector terminal B1. Is the resistance within the specified range?	OL (Infinite)	*Go to Step 7*	*Go to Step 8*

GC402980342600BX

Fig. 218 Code C1224: RH Rear Wheel Speed Sensor Input Signal Is Zero (Part 2 of 4). Metro

Step	Action	Value(s)	Yes	No
7	1. Inspect the EBCM connector for the following conditions: • Damage • Poor terminal contact • Terminal corrosion Damage, poor terminal contact, and terminal corrosion may cause a short between the EBCM connector terminal A2 and the EBCM connector terminal B11. 2. Inspect the remaining terminals of the EBCM connector for the following conditions: • Damage • Poor terminal contact • Terminal corrosion Are there signs of poor terminal contact, corrosion, or damaged terminals?	—	*Go to Step 12*	*Go to Step 8*
8	Inspect the wiring of CKT 6R01 and CKT 6Q01 for signs of damage that may cause a short between CKT 6R01 and CKT 6Q01. Are there any signs of damaged wiring?	—	*Go to Step 13*	*Go to Step 9*
9	Inspect the harness connectors of CKT 6R01 and CKT 6Q01 for signs of damage that may cause a short between CKT 6R01 and CKT 6Q01. Are there any signs of damaged connectors?	—	*Go to Step 14*	*Go to Step 10*
10	1. Reconnect the EBCM harness connector. 2. Reconnect the right rear wheel speed sensor harness connector. 3. Install a *Scan Tool.* 4. Test drive the vehicle at a speed above 24 km/h (15 mph) for at least 30 seconds. 5. Use the *Scan Tool* in order to read the DTCs. Does DTC C1224 set as a current DTC?	—	*Go to Step 11*	*Go to Step 18*
11	1. Select Data List on the *Scan Tool.* 2. Monitor the wheel speed sensor speeds. 3. Drive the vehicle in the following manner: 3.1. Slowly accelerate to 65 km/h (40 mph). 3.2. Slowly decelerate to 0 km/h (0 mph). Is the speed of the right rear wheel speed sensor constantly higher than the speed of the three remaining wheel speed sensors?	—	*Go to Step 16*	*Go to Step 17*
12	Replace all of the terminals that exhibit signs of poor terminal contact, corrosion, or damaged terminal(s). Is the repair complete?	—	Refer to *Diagnostic System Check*	—
13	Replace the damaged wiring harness that causes the short between CKT 6R01 and CKT 6Q01. Is the repair complete?	—	Refer to *Diagnostic System Check*	—
14	Replace the damaged wiring harness connectors that cause the short between CKT 6R01 and CKT 6Q01. Is the repair complete?	—	Refer to *Diagnostic System Check*	—
15	Replace the right rear wheel speed sensor jumper harness. Is the repair complete?	—	Refer to *Diagnostic System Check*	—

GC402980342600CX

Fig. 218 Code C1224: RH Rear Wheel Speed Sensor Input Signal Is Zero (Part 3 of 4). Metro

Step	Action	Value(s)	Yes	No
16	Replace the right rear wheel speed sensor. Is the repair complete?	—	Refer to *Diagnostic System Check*	—
17	Replace the EBCM. Is the repair complete?	—	Refer to *Diagnostic System Check*	—
18	The malfunction is intermittent or is not present at this time. Refer to Diagnostic Aids for more information. Is the action complete?	—	System OK	—

GC402980342600DX

Fig. 218 Code C1224: RH Rear Wheel Speed Sensor Input Signal Is Zero (Part 4 of 4). Metro

Circuit Description

As a toothed ring passes by the wheel speed sensor, changes in the electromagnetic field cause the wheel speed sensor to produce an AC voltage signal. The frequency of the AC voltage signal is proportional to the wheel speed. The amplitude of the AC voltage signal is directly related to wheel speed and the proximity of the wheel speed sensor to the toothed ring. The proximity of the wheel speed sensor to the toothed ring is also referred to as the air gap.

Conditions for Setting the DTC

- DTC C1225 can set when the brake is OFF.
- DTC C1225 detects a situation in which the left front wheel acceleration or deceleration is beyond specified limits.
- This DTC will not set if DTC C1232 has already failed.

Action Taken When the DTC Sets

- A malfunction DTC stores.
- The ABS disables.
- The ABS warning indicator turns ON.

Conditions for Clearing the DTC

- The condition responsible for setting the DTC no longer exists and the Scan Tool Clear DTCs function is used.
- 100 drive cycles pass with no DTCs detected. A drive cycle consists of starting the vehicle, driving the vehicle over 16 km/h (10 mph), stopping and then turning the ignition OFF.

Diagnostic Aids

The following conditions may cause a malfunction:

- A poor connection
- Rubbed-through wire insulation
- A broken wire inside the insulation
- Loose wheel speed sensor
- Worn suspension/drivetrain components
- Wheel speed sensor physically damaged
- Wheel speed sensor ring damaged

Use the enhanced diagnostic function of the Scan Tool in order to measure the frequency of the malfunction.

If the customer's comments reflect that the amber ABS warning indicator is ON only during moist environmental changes (rain, snow, vehicle wash), inspect all the wheel speed sensor circuitry for signs of water intrusion.

Thoroughly inspect any circuitry that may be causing the intermittent complaint for the following conditions:

- Backed out terminals
- Improper mating
- Broken locks
- Improperly formed or damaged terminals
- Poor terminal-to-wiring connections
- Physical damage to the wiring harness

Resistance of the wheel speed sensor will increase with an increase in sensor temperature.

Use the following procedure when replacing a wheel speed sensor or harness:

1. Inspect the wheel speed sensor terminals and harness connector for corrosion and/or water intrusion.
2. Replace the wheel speed sensor and jumper harness if evidence of corrosion or water intrusion exists.

Important: Zero the J 39200 test leads before making any resistance measurements. Refer to the J 39200 user's manual.

Important: Difficulty may occur when trying to locate intermittent malfunctions in the wheel speed sensor.

Do not disturb any of the electrical connections. Change the electrical connections only when instructed to do so by a step in the diagnostic table. Changing the electrical connections at the correct time will ensure that an intermittent electrical connection will not be corrected until the source of the malfunction is found.

GC402980342700AX

Fig. 219 Code C1225: LH Front Excessive Wheel Speed Variation (Part 1 of 4). Metro

Step	Action	Value(s)	Yes	No
1	Was the Diagnostic System Check performed?	—	*Go to Step 2*	Refer to *Diagnostic System Check*
2	1. Turn the ignition switch to the OFF position. 2. Inspect the left front wheel speed sensor and the left front wheel speed sensor harness connector for physical damage. Is there any physical damage?	—	*Go to Step 16*	*Go to Step 3*
3	Inspect the following components for physical damage: • The left front wheel speed sensor jumper harness • The left front wheel speed sensor jumper harness connectors Is there any physical damage?	—	*Go to Step 15*	*Go to Step 4*
4	1. Disconnect the left front wheel speed sensor directly at the left front wheel speed sensor connector. 2. Use the *J 39200* in order to measure the resistance between the left front wheel speed sensor connector terminal A and the left front wheel speed sensor connector terminal B. Is the resistance within the specified range?	920–1220 Ω	*Go to Step 5*	*Go to Step 16*
5	1. Select the A/C VOLTAGE scale on the *J 39200.* 2. Spin the left front wheel by hand while observing the voltage reading on the *J 39200.* Is the voltage equal to or greater than the specified voltage?	100 mV	*Go to Step 6*	*Go to Step 16*
6	1. Disconnect the EBCM connector. 2. Use the *J 39200* in order to measure the resistance between the EBCM connector terminal A5 and the EBCM connector terminal B4. Is the resistance within the specified range?	OL (Infinite)	*Go to Step 7*	*Go to Step 8*

GC402980342700BX

Fig. 219 Code C1225: LH Front Excessive Wheel Speed Variation (Part 2 of 4). Metro

Step	Action	Value(s)	Yes	No
7	1. Inspect the EBCM connector for the following conditions: • Damage • Poor terminal contact • Terminal corrosion (These conditions could result in a short between the EBCM connector terminal A5 and the EBCM connector terminal B4.) 2. Inspect the remaining terminals of the EBCM connector for the following conditions: • Damage • Poor terminal contact • Terminal corrosion Are there signs of poor terminal contact, corrosion, or damaged terminals?	—	*Go to Step 12*	*Go to Step 8*
8	Inspect the wiring of CKT 6L01 and CKT 6K01 for signs of damage that may cause a short between CKT 6L01 and CKT 6K01. Are there any signs of damaged wiring?	—	*Go to Step 13*	*Go to Step 9*
9	Inspect the harness connectors of CKT 6L01 and CKT 6K01 for signs of damage that may cause a short between CKT 6L01 and CKT 6K01. Are there any signs of damaged connectors?	—	*Go to Step 14*	*Go to Step 10*
10	1. Reconnect the EBCM harness connector. 2. Reconnect the left front wheel speed sensor harness connector. 3. Install a *Scan Tool.* 4. Test drive the vehicle at a speed above 24 km/h (15 mph) for at least 30 seconds. 5. Use the *Scan Tool* in order to read the DTCs. Does DTC C1225 set as a current DTC?	—	*Go to Step 11*	*Go to Step 18*
11	1. Select Data List on the *Scan Tool.* 2. Monitor the wheel speed sensor speeds. 3. Drive the vehicle in the following manner: 3.1. Slowly accelerate to 65 km/h (40 mph). 3.2. Slowly decelerate to 0 km/h (0 mph). Is the speed of the left front wheel speed sensor constantly higher than the speed of the three remaining wheel speed sensors?	—	*Go to Step 16*	*Go to Step 17*
12	Replace all of the terminals that exhibit signs of poor terminal contact, corrosion, or damaged terminal(s). Is the repair complete?	—	Refer to *Diagnostic System Check*	—
13	Replace the damaged wiring harness that causes the short between CKT 6L01 and CKT 6K01. Is the repair complete?	—	Refer to *Diagnostic System Check*	—
14	Replace the damaged wiring harness connectors that cause the short between CKT 6L01 and CKT 6K01. Is the repair complete?	—	Refer to *Diagnostic System Check*	—
15	Replace the left front wheel speed sensor harness. Is the repair complete?	—	Refer to *Diagnostic System Check*	—

GC402980342700CX

Fig. 219 Code C1225: LH Front Excessive Wheel Speed Variation (Part 3 of 4). Metro

Step	Action	Value(s)	Yes	No
16	Replace the left front wheel speed sensor. Is the repair complete?	—	Refer to *Diagnostic System Check*	—
17	Replace the EBCM. Is the repair complete?	—	Refer to *Diagnostic System Check*	—
18	The malfunction is intermittent or is not present at this time. Refer to Diagnostic Aids for more information. Is the action complete?	—	System OK	—

GC402980342700DX

Fig. 219 Code C1225: LH Front Excessive Wheel Speed Variation (Part 4 of 4). Metro

Circuit Description

As a toothed ring passes by the wheel speed sensor, changes in the electromagnetic field cause the wheel speed sensor to produce an AC voltage signal. The frequency of the AC voltage signal is proportional to the wheel speed. The amplitude of the AC voltage signal is directly related to wheel speed and the proximity of the wheel speed sensor to the toothed ring. The proximity of the wheel speed sensor to the toothed ring is also referred to as the air gap.

Conditions for Setting the DTC

- DTC C1226 can set when the brake is OFF.
- DTC C1226 detects a situation in which the right front wheel acceleration or deceleration is beyond specified limits.
- This DTC will not set if DTC C1233 has already set.

Action Taken When the DTC Sets

- A malfunction DTC stores.
- The ABS disables.
- The ABS warning indicator turns ON.

Conditions for Clearing the DTC

- The condition responsible for setting the DTC no longer exists and the Scan Tool Clear DTCs function is used.
- 100 drive cycles pass with no DTCs detected. A drive cycle consists of starting the vehicle, driving the vehicle over 16 km/h (10 mph), stopping and then turning the ignition OFF.

Diagnostic Aids

The following conditions may cause a malfunction:

- A poor connection
- Rubbed-through wire insulation
- A broken wire inside the insulation
- Loose wheel speed sensor
- Worn suspension/drivetrain components
- Wheel speed sensor physically damaged
- Wheel speed sensor ring damaged

Use the enhanced diagnostic function of the Scan Tool in order to measure the frequency of the malfunction.

If the customer's comments reflect that the amber ABS warning indicator is ON only during moist environmental changes (rain, snow, vehicle wash), inspect all the wheel speed sensor circuitry for signs of water intrusion.

Thoroughly inspect any circuitry that may be causing the intermittent complaint for the following conditions:

- Backed out terminals
- Improper mating
- Broken locks
- Improperly formed or damaged terminals
- Poor terminal-to-wiring connections
- Physical damage to the wiring harness

Resistance of the wheel speed sensor will increase with an increase in sensor temperature.

Use the following procedure when replacing a wheel speed sensor or harness:

1. Inspect the wheel speed sensor terminals and harness connector for corrosion and/or water intrusion.
2. Replace the wheel speed sensor and jumper harness if evidence of corrosion or water intrusion exists.

Important: Zero the J 39200 test leads before making any resistance measurements.

GC402980342800AX

Fig. 220 Code C1226: RH Front Excessive Wheel Speed Variation (Part 1 of 3). Metro

Important: Difficulty may occur when trying to locate intermittent malfunctions in the wheel speed sensor circuit.

Do not disturb any of the electrical connections. Change the electrical connections only when instructed to do so by a step in the diagnostic table.

Changing the electrical connections at the correct time will ensure that an intermittent electrical connection will not be corrected until the source of the malfunction is found.

Step	Action	Value(s)	Yes	No
1	Was the Diagnostic System Check performed?	—	*Go to Step 2*	Refer to *Diagnostic System Check*
2	1. Turn the ignition switch to the OFF position. 2. Inspect the right front wheel speed sensor and the right front wheel speed sensor harness connector for physical damage. Is there any physical damage?	—	*Go to Step 16*	*Go to Step 3*
3	Inspect the following components for physical damage: • The right front wheel speed sensor jumper harness • The right front wheel speed sensor jumper harness connectors Is there any physical damage?	—	*Go to Step 15*	*Go to Step 4*
4	1. Disconnect the right front wheel speed sensor directly at the right front wheel speed sensor connector. 2. Use the *J 39200* in order to measure the resistance between the right front wheel speed sensor connector terminal A and the right front wheel speed sensor connector terminal B. Is the resistance within the specified range?	920–1220 Ω	*Go to Step 5*	*Go to Step 16*
5	1. Select the A/C VOLTAGE scale on the *J 39200.* 2. Spin the right front wheel by hand while observing the voltage reading on the *J 39200.* Is the voltage equal to or greater than the specified voltage?	100 mV	*Go to Step 6*	*Go to Step 16*
6	1. Disconnect the EBCM connector. 2. Use the *J 39200* in order to measure the resistance between the EBCM connector terminal A4 and the EBCM connector terminal B3. Is the resistance within the specified range?	OL (Infinite)	*Go to Step 7*	*Go to Step 8*
7	1. Inspect the EBCM connector for the following conditions: • Damage • Poor terminal contact • Terminal corrosion (These conditions may cause a short between the EBCM connector terminal A4 and the EBCM connector terminal B3.) 2. Inspect the remaining terminals of the EBCM connector for the following conditions: • Damage • Poor terminal contact • Terminal corrosion Are there signs of poor terminal contact, corrosion, or damaged terminals?	—	*Go to Step 12*	*Go to Step 8*

GC402980342800BX

Fig. 220 Code C1226: RH Front Excessive Wheel Speed Variation (Part 2 of 3). Metro

Step	Action	Value(s)	Yes	No
8	Inspect the wiring of CKT 6M01 and CKT 6N01 for signs of damage that may cause a short between CKT 6M01 and CKT 6N01. Are there any signs of damaged wiring?	—	*Go to Step 13*	*Go to Step 9*
9	Inspect the harness connectors of CKT 6M01 and CKT 6N01 for signs of damage that may cause a short between CKT 6M01 and CKT 6N01. Are there any signs of damaged connectors?	—	*Go to Step 14*	*Go to Step 10*
10	1. Reconnect the EBCM harness connector. 2. Reconnect the right front wheel speed sensor harness connector. 3. Install a *Scan Tool*. 4. Test drive the vehicle at a speed above 24 km/h (15 mph) for at least 30 seconds. 5. Use the *Scan Tool* in order to read the DTCs. Does DTC C1226 set as a current DTC?	—	*Go to Step 11*	*Go to Step 18*
11	1. Select the Data List on the *Scan Tool*. 2. Monitor the wheel speed sensor speeds. 3. Use the following procedure to drive the vehicle when testing the wheel speed sensor: 3.1. Slowly accelerate to 65 km/h (40 mph). 3.2. Slowly decelerate to 0 km/h (0 mph). Is the speed of the right front wheel speed sensor constantly higher than the speed of the three remaining wheel speed sensors?	—	*Go to Step 16*	*Go to Step 17*
12	Replace all of the terminals that exhibit signs of poor terminal contact, corrosion, or damaged terminal(s). Is the repair complete?	—	Refer to *Diagnostic System Check*	—
13	Replace the damaged wiring harness that causes the short between CKT 6M01 and CKT 6N01. Is the repair complete?	—	Refer to *Diagnostic System Check*	—
14	Replace the damaged wiring harness connectors that cause the short between CKT 6M01 and CKT 6N01. Is the repair complete?	—	Refer to *Diagnostic System Check*	—
15	Replace the right front wheel speed sensor harness. Is the repair complete?	—	Refer to *Diagnostic System Check*	—
16	Replace the right front wheel speed sensor. Is the repair complete?	—	Refer to *Diagnostic System Check*	—
17	Replace the EBCM. Is the repair complete?	—	Refer to *Diagnostic System Check*	—
18	The malfunction is intermittent or is not present at this time. Refer to Diagnostic Aids for more information. Is the action complete?	—	System OK	—

GC402980342800CX

Fig. 220 Code C1226: RH Front Excessive Wheel Speed Variation (Part 3 of 3). Metro

Important: Difficulty may occur when trying to locate the intermittent malfunctions in the wheel speed sensor circuit.

Do not disturb any of the electrical connections. Change electrical connections only when instructed to do so by a step in the diagnostic table.

Changing the electrical connections at the correct time will ensure that an intermittent electrical connection will not be corrected until the source of the malfunction is found.

Step	Action	Value(s)	Yes	No
1	Was the Diagnostic System Check performed?	—	*Go to Step 2*	Refer to *Diagnostic System Check*
2	1. Turn the ignition switch to the OFF position. 2. Inspect the left front wheel speed sensor and the left front wheel speed sensor harness connector for physical damage. Is there any physical damage?	—	*Go to Step 16*	*Go to Step 3*
3	Inspect the following components for physical damage: • The left front wheel speed sensor jumper harness • The left front wheel speed sensor jumper harness connectors Is there any physical damage?	—	*Go to Step 15*	*Go to Step 4*
4	1. Disconnect the left front wheel speed sensor directly at the left front wheel speed sensor connector. 2. Use the *J 39200* in order to measure the resistance between the left front wheel speed sensor connector terminal A and the left front wheel speed sensor connector terminal B. Is the resistance within the specified range?	1050–1450 Ω	*Go to Step 5*	*Go to Step 16*
5	1. Select the A/C VOLTAGE scale on the *J 39200*. 2. Spin the left front wheel by hand while observing the voltage reading on the *J 39200*. Is the voltage equal to or greater than the specified voltage?	100 mV	*Go to Step 6*	*Go to Step 16*
6	1. Disconnect the EBCM connector. 2. Use the *J 39200* in order to measure the resistance between the EBCM terminal A5 and the EBCM terminal B4. Is the resistance within the specified range?	OL (Infinite)	*Go to Step 7*	*Go to Step 8*
7	1. Inspect the EBCM connector for the following conditions: • Damage • Poor terminal contact • Terminal corrosion (Damage, poor terminal contact, and terminal corrosion may cause a short between the EBCM terminal A5 and the EBCM terminal B4. 2. Inspect the remaining terminals of the EBCM connector for the following conditions: • Damage • Poor terminal contact • Terminal corrosion Are there signs of poor terminal contact, corrosion, or damaged terminals?	—	*Go to Step 12*	*Go to Step 8*

GC402980342900BX

Fig. 221 Code C1227: LH Rear Excessive Wheel Speed Variation (Part 2 of 3). Metro

Circuit Description

As a toothed ring passes by the wheel speed sensor, changes in the electromagnetic field cause the wheel speed sensor to produce an AC voltage signal. The frequency of the AC voltage signal is proportional to the wheel speed. The amplitude of the AC voltage signal is directly related to wheel speed and the proximity of the wheel speed sensor to the toothed ring. The proximity of the wheel speed sensor to the toothed ring is also referred to as the air gap.

Conditions for Setting the DTC

- DTC C1227 can set when the brake is OFF.
- DTC C1227 detects a situation in which the left rear wheel acceleration or deceleration is beyond specified limits.
- This DTC will not set if DTC C1234 has already set.

Action Taken When the DTC Sets

- A malfunction DTC stores.
- The ABS disables.
- The ABS warning indicator turns ON.

Conditions for Clearing the DTC

- The condition responsible for setting the DTC no longer exists and the Scan Tool Clear DTCs function is used.
- 100 drive cycles pass with no DTCs detected. A drive cycle consists of starting the vehicle, driving the vehicle over 16 km/h (10 mph), stopping and then turning the ignition OFF.

Diagnostic Aids

The following conditions may cause an intermittent malfunction:

- A poor connection
- Rubbed-through wire insulation
- A broken wire inside the insulation
- Loose wheel speed sensor
- Worn suspension components
- Wheel speed sensor physically damaged
- Wheel speed sensor ring damaged

Use the enhanced diagnostic function of the Scan Tool in order to measure the frequency of the malfunction.

If the customer's comments reflect that the amber ABS warning indicator is ON only during moist environmental changes (rain, snow, vehicle wash), inspect all the wheel speed sensor circuitry for signs of water intrusion.

Thoroughly inspect any circuitry that may be causing the intermittent complaint for the following conditions:

- Backed out terminals
- Improper mating
- Broken locks
- Improperly formed or damaged terminals
- Poor terminal-to-wiring connections
- Physical damage to the wiring harness

Resistance of the wheel speed sensor will increase with an increase in sensor temperature.

Use the following procedure when replacing a wheel speed sensor or harness:

1. Inspect the wheel speed sensor terminals and harness connector for corrosion and/or water intrusion.
2. Replace the wheel speed sensor jumper harness if evidence of corrosion or water intrusion exists.

Important: Zero the J 39200 test leads before making any resistance measurements.

GC402980342900AX

Fig. 221 Code C1227: LH Rear Excessive Wheel Speed Variation (Part 1 of 3). Metro

Step	Action	Value(s)	Yes	No
8	Inspect the wiring of CKT 6L01 and CKT 6K01 for signs of damage that may cause a short between CKT 6L01 and CKT 6K01. Are there any signs of damaged wiring?	—	*Go to Step 13*	*Go to Step 9*
9	Inspect the harness connectors of CKT 6L01 and CKT 6K01 for signs of damage that may cause a short between CKT 6L01 and CKT 6K01. Are there any signs of damaged connectors?	—	*Go to Step 14*	*Go to Step 10*
10	1. Reconnect the EBCM harness connector. 2. Reconnect the left front wheel speed sensor harness connector. 3. Install a *Scan Tool*. 4. Test drive the vehicle at a speed above 24 km/h (15 mph) for at least 30 seconds. 5. Use the *Scan Tool* in order to read the DTCs. Does DTC C1221 set as a current DTC?	—	*Go to Step 11*	*Go to Step 18*
11	1. Select Data List on the *Scan Tool*. 2. Monitor the wheel speed sensor speeds. 3. Drive the vehicle in the following manner: 3.1. Slowly accelerate to 65 km/h (40 mph). 3.2. Slowly decelerate to 0 km/h (0 mph). Is the speed of the left front wheel speed sensor constantly higher than the speed of the three remaining wheel speed sensors?	—	*Go to Step 15*	*Go to Step 17*
12	Replace all of the terminals that exhibit signs of poor terminal contact, corrosion, or damaged terminal(s). Is the repair complete?	—	Refer to *Diagnostic System Check*	—
13	Replace the damaged wiring harness that causes the short between CKT 6L01 and CKT 6K01. Is the repair complete?	—	Refer to *Diagnostic System Check*	—
14	Replace the damaged wiring harness connectors that cause the short between CKT 6L01 and CKT 6K01. Is the repair complete?	—	Refer to *Diagnostic System Check*	—
15	Replace the left front wheel speed sensor jumper harness. Is the repair complete?	—	Refer to *Diagnostic System Check*	—
16	Replace the left front wheel speed sensor. Is the repair complete?	—	Refer to *Diagnostic System Check*	—
17	Replace the EBCM. Is the repair complete?	—	Refer to *Diagnostic System Check*	—
18	The malfunction is intermittent or is not present at this time. Refer to Diagnostic Aids for more information. Is the repair complete?	—	System OK	—

GC402980342900CX

Fig. 221 Code C1227: LH Rear Excessive Wheel Speed Variation (Part 3 of 3). Metro

Circuit Description

As a toothed ring passes by the wheel speed sensor, changes in the electromagnetic field cause the wheel speed sensor to produce an AC voltage signal. The frequency of the AC voltage signal is proportional to the wheel speed. The amplitude of the AC voltage signal is directly related to wheel speed and the proximity of the wheel speed sensor to the toothed ring. The proximity of the wheel speed sensor to the toothed ring is also referred to as the air gap.

Conditions for Setting the DTC

- DTC C1228 can set when the brake is OFF.
- DTC C1228 detects a situation in which the right rear wheel acceleration or deceleration is beyond specified limits.
- This DTC will not set if DTC C1235 has already set.

Action Taken When the DTC Sets

- A malfunction DTC stores.
- The ABS disables.
- The ABS warning indicator turns ON.

Conditions for Clearing the DTC

- The condition responsible for setting the DTC no longer exists and the Scan Tool Clear DTCs function is used.
- 100 drive cycles pass with no DTCs detected. A drive cycle consists of starting the vehicle, driving the vehicle over 16 km/h (10 mph), stopping and then turning the ignition OFF.

Diagnostic Aids

The following conditions may cause a malfunction:

- A poor connection
- Rubbed-through wire insulation
- A broken wire inside the insulation
- Loose wheel speed sensor
- Worn suspension components
- Wheel speed sensor physically damaged
- Wheel speed sensor ring damaged

Use the enhanced diagnostic function of the Scan Tool in order to measure the frequency of the malfunction.

If the customer's comments reflect that the amber ABS warning indicator is ON only during moist environmental changes (rain, snow, vehicle wash), inspect all the wheel speed sensor circuitry for signs of water intrusion.

Thoroughly inspect any circuitry that may be causing the intermittent complaint for the following conditions:

- Backed out terminals
- Improper mating
- Broken locks
- Improperly formed or damaged terminals
- Poor terminal-to-wiring connections
- Physical damage to the wiring harness

Resistance of the wheel speed sensor will increase with an increase in sensor temperature.

Use the following procedure when replacing a wheel speed sensor or harness:

1. Inspect the wheel speed sensor terminals and harness connector for corrosion and/or water intrusion.
2. Replace the wheel speed sensor and jumper harness if evidence of corrosion or water intrusion exists.

Important: Zero the J 39200 test leads before making any resistance measurements.

GC402980343000AX

Fig. 222 Code C1228: RH Rear Excessive Wheel Speed Variation (Part 1 of 3). Metro

Important: Difficulty may occur when trying to locate intermittent malfunctions in the wheel speed sensor circuit.

Do not disturb any of the electrical connections. Change the electrical connections only when instructed to do so by a step in the diagnostic table.

Changing the electrical connections at the correct time will ensure that an intermittent electrical connection will not be corrected until the source of the malfunction is found.

Step	Action	Value(s)	Yes	No
1	Was the Diagnostic System Check performed?	—	*Go to Step 2*	Refer to *Diagnostic System Check*
2	1. Turn the ignition switch to the OFF position. 2. Inspect the right rear wheel speed sensor and the rear axle harness connector for physical damage. Is there any physical damage?	—	*Go to Step 16*	*Go to Step 3*
3	Inspect the following components for physical damage: • The rear axle harness • The rear axle harness connectors Is there any physical damage?	—	*Go to Step 15*	*Go to Step 4*
4	1. Disconnect the right rear wheel speed sensor directly at the right rear wheel speed sensor connector. 2. Use the *J 39200* in order to measure the resistance between the right rear wheel speed sensor connector terminal A and the right rear wheel speed sensor connector terminal B. Is the resistance within the specified range?	1050–1450 Ω	*Go to Step 5*	*Go to Step 16*
5	1. Select the A/C VOLTAGE scale on the *J 39200.* 2. Spin the right rear wheel by hand while observing the voltage reading on the *J 39200.* Is the voltage equal to or greater than the specified voltage?	100 mV	*Go to Step 6*	*Go to Step 16*
6	1. Disconnect the EBCM connector. 2. Use the *J 39200* in order to measure the resistance between the EBCM connector terminal A2 and the EBCM connector terminal B1. Is the resistance within the specified range?	OL (Infinite)	*Go to Step 7*	*Go to Step 8*
7	1. Inspect the EBCM connector for the following conditions: • Damage • Poor terminal contact • Terminal corrosion Damage, poor terminal contact may cause a short between the EBCM connector terminal A2 and the EBCM connector terminal B1. 2. Inspect the remaining terminals of the EBCM connector for the following conditions: • Damage • Poor terminal contact • Terminal corrosion Are there signs of poor terminal contact, corrosion, or damaged terminals?	—	*Go to Step 12*	*Go to Step 8*

GC402980343000BX

Fig. 222 Code C1228: RH Rear Excessive Wheel Speed Variation (Part 2 of 3). Metro

Step	Action	Value(s)	Yes	No
8	Inspect the wiring of CKT 6R01 and CKT 6Q01 for signs of damage that may cause a short between CKT 6R01 and CKT 6Q01. Are there any signs of damaged wiring?	—	*Go to Step 13*	*Go to Step 9*
9	Inspect the harness connectors of CKT 6R01 and CKT 6Q01 for signs of damage that may cause a short between CKT 6R01 and CKT 6Q01. Are there any signs of damaged connectors?	—	*Go to Step 14*	*Go to Step 10*
10	1. Reconnect the EBCM harness connector. 2. Reconnect the right rear wheel speed sensor harness connector. 3. Install a *Scan Tool.* 4. Test drive the vehicle at a speed above 24 km/h (15 mph) for at least 30 seconds. 5. Use the *Scan Tool* in order to read the DTCs. Does DTC C1228 set as a current DTC?	—	*Go to Step 11*	*Go to Step 18*
11	1. Select Data List on the *Scan Tool.* 2. Monitor the wheel speed sensor speeds. 3. Use the following procedure to drive the vehicle when testing the wheel speed sensor: 3.1. Slowly accelerate to 65 km/h (40 mph). 3.2. Slowly decelerate to 0 km/h (0 mph). Is the speed of the right rear wheel speed sensor constantly higher or lower than the speed of the three remaining wheel speed sensors?	—	*Go to Step 16*	*Go to Step 17*
12	Replace all of the terminals that exhibit signs of poor terminal contact, corrosion, or damaged terminal(s). Is the repair complete?	—	Refer to *Diagnostic System Check*	—
13	Replace the damaged wiring harness that causes the short between CKT 6R01 and CKT 6Q01. Is the repair complete?	—	Refer to *Diagnostic System Check*	—
14	Replace the damaged wiring harness connectors that cause the short between CKT 6R01 and CKT 6Q01. Is the repair complete?	—	Refer to *Diagnostic System Check*	—
15	Replace the rear axle harness. Is the repair complete?	—	Refer to *Diagnostic System Check*	—
16	Replace the right rear wheel speed sensor. Is the repair complete?	—	Refer to *Diagnostic System Check*	—
17	Replace the EBCM. Is the repair complete?	—	Refer to *Diagnostic System Check*	—
18	The malfunction is intermittent or is not present at this time. Refer to Diagnostic Aids for more information. Is the action complete?	—	System OK	—

GC402980343000CX

Fig. 222 Code C1228: RH Rear Excessive Wheel Speed Variation (Part 3 of 3). Metro

Circuit Description

As a toothed ring passes by the wheel speed sensor, changes in the electromagnetic field cause the wheel speed sensor to produce an AC voltage signal. The frequency of the AC voltage signal is proportional to the wheel speed. The amplitude of the AC voltage signal is directly related to wheel speed and the proximity of the wheel speed sensor to the toothed ring. The proximity of the wheel speed sensor to the toothed ring is also referred to as the air gap.

Conditions for Setting the DTC

DTC C1232 can set anytime after initialization.

A malfunction exists if either of the left front wheel speed sensor circuits are open or shorted to voltage or ground.

Action Taken When the DTC Sets

- A malfunction DTC stores.
- The ABS disables.
- The ABS warning indicator turns ON.

Conditions for Clearing the DTC

- The condition responsible for setting the DTC no longer exists and the Scan Tool Clear DTCs function is used.
- 100 drive cycles pass with no DTCs detected. A drive cycle consists of starting the vehicle, driving the vehicle over 16 km/h (10 mph), stopping and then turning the ignition OFF.

Diagnostic Aids

The following conditions may cause a malfunction:

- A poor connection
- Rubbed-through wire insulation
- A broken wire inside the insulation
- Faulty electrical circuits (open/high resistance, short to voltage or ground) between the LF wheel speed sensor and the EBCM
- Malfunctioning wheel speed sensor (high resistance)

Use the enhanced diagnostic function of the Scan Tool in order to measure the frequency of the malfunction.

If the customer's comments reflect that the amber ABS warning indicator is ON only during moist environmental changes (rain, snow, vehicle wash), inspect all the wheel speed sensor circuitry for signs of water intrusion. If the DTC is not current, clear all DTCs and simulate the effects of water intrusion by using the following procedure:

1. Spray the suspected area with a five percent saltwater solution.
   Add two teaspoons of salt to twelve ounces of water to make a five percent saltwater solution.
2. Test drive the vehicle over various road surfaces (bumps, turns, etc.) above 24 km/h (15 mph) for at least 30 seconds.
3. If the DTC returns, replace the suspected harness.

Thoroughly inspect any circuitry that may be causing the intermittent complaint for the following conditions:

- Backed out terminals
- Improper mating
- Broken locks
- Improperly formed or damaged terminals
- Poor terminal-to-wiring connections
- Physical damage to the wiring harness

Resistance of the wheel speed sensor will increase with an increase in sensor temperature.

Use the following procedure when replacing a wheel speed sensor or harness:

1. Inspect the wheel speed sensor terminals and harness connector for corrosion and/or water intrusion.
2. Replace the wheel speed sensor and jumper harness if evidence of corrosion or water intrusion exists.

GC402980343100AX

Fig. 223 Code C1232: LH Front Wheel Speed Circuit Open Or Shorted (Part 1 of 5). Metro

Important: Zero the J 39200 test leads before making any resistance measurements.

Important: Difficulty may occur when trying to locate intermittent malfunctions in the wheel speed sensor circuit.

Do not disturb any of the electrical connections. Change the electrical connections only when instructed to do so by a step in the diagnostic table. Changing the electrical connections at the correct time will ensure that an intermittent electrical connection will not be corrected until the source of the malfunction is found.

Step	Action	Value(s)	Yes	No
1	Was the Diagnostic System Check performed?	—	*Go to Step 2*	Refer to *Diagnostic System Check*
2	1. Turn the ignition switch to the OFF position. 2. Make a 5 percent saltwater solution. 3. Thoroughly spray the left front wheel speed sensor harness with the saltwater solution. 4. Disconnect the EBCM harness connector. 5. Use the *J 39200* in order to measure the resistance between the EBCM harness connector terminal A5 and the EBCM harness connector terminal B4. Is the resistance within the specified range?	920–1220 Ω	*Go to Step 3*	*Go to Step 11*
3	Use the *J 39200* in order to measure the resistance between the EBCM harness connector terminal B4 and ground. Is the resistance within the specified range?	OL (Infinite)	*Go to Step 4*	*Go to Step 14*
4	1. Turn the ignition switch to the ON position. Do not start the engine. 2. Use the *J 39200* in order to measure the voltage between the EBCM harness connector terminal B4 and ground. Is the voltage within the specified range?	0–1 V	*Go to Step 7*	*Go to Step 5*
5	1. Turn the ignition switch to the OFF position. 2. Disconnect the left front wheel speed sensor at the left front wheel speed sensor connector. 3. Turn the ignition switch to the ON position. Do not start the engine. 4. Use the *J 39200* in order to measure the voltage between the EBCM harness connector terminal B4 and ground Is the voltage within the specified range?	0–1 V	*Go to Step 6*	*Go to Step 19*
6	Use the *J 39200* in order to measure the voltage between the EBCM harness connector terminal A5 and ground. Is the voltage within the specified range?	0–1 V	*Go to Step 31*	*Go to Step 20*

GC402980343100BX

Fig. 223 Code C1232: LH Front Wheel Speed Circuit Open Or Shorted (Part 2 of 5). Metro

Step	Action	Value(s)	Yes	No
7	1. Turn the ignition switch to the OFF position. 2. Inspect the following terminals: • The EBCM connector terminal A5 • The EBCM connector terminal B4 • The remaining terminals of the EBCM connector. 3. Inspect the above terminals for the following conditions: • Terminal damage • Poor terminal contact • Terminal corrosion Damage, terminal corrosion, and poor terminal contact may cause an open circuit, a short to voltage, or a short to ground. Are there signs of poor terminal contact, terminal corrosion, or damaged terminals?	—	*Go to Step 27*	*Go to Step 8*
8	Inspect the wiring of CKT 6L01 and CKT 6K01 for signs of wire damage. Wire damage may cause the following conditions in CKT 6L01 and CKT 6K01: • An open circuit • A short to voltage • A short to ground Are there signs of damaged wiring?	—	*Go to Step 21*	*Go to Step 9*
9	Inspect the harness connectors of CKT 6L01 and CKT 6K01 for signs of wire damage. Wire damage may cause the following conditions in CKT 6L01 and CKT 6K01: • An open circuit • A short to voltage • A short to ground Are there signs of damaged connectors?	—	*Go to Step 22*	*Go to Step 10*
10	1. Reconnect the EBCM connector. 2. Reconnect the left front wheel speed sensor harness connector. 3. Install a *Scan Tool.* 4. Test drive the vehicle at a speed above 24 km/h (15 mph) for at least 30 seconds. 5. Use the *Scan Tool* in order to read the DTCs. Does DTC C1232 set as a current DTC?	—	*Go to Step 30*	*Go to Step 31*
11	1. Disconnect the left front wheel speed sensor directly at the left front wheel speed sensor connector. 2. Use the *J 39200* in order to measure the resistance between the EBCM harness connector terminal B4 and the left front wheel speed sensor harness connector terminal B. Is the resistance within the specified range?	0–2 Ω	*Go to Step 12*	*Go to Step 23*
12	Use the *J 39200* in order to measure the resistance between the EBCM connector terminal A5 and the left front wheel speed sensor harness connector terminal A. Is the resistance within the specified range?	0–2 Ω	*Go to Step 13*	*Go to Step 24*

GC402980343100CX

Fig. 223 Code C1232: LH Front Wheel Speed Circuit Open Or Shorted (Part 3 of 5). Metro

Step	Action	Value(s)	Yes	No
13	Use the *J 39200* in order to measure the resistance between the left front wheel speed sensor connector terminal A and the left front wheel speed sensor connector terminal B. Is the resistance within the specified range?	920–1220 Ω	*Go to Step 31*	*Go to Step 28*
14	Use the *J 39200* in order to measure the resistance between the EBCM connector terminal B4 and ground. Is the resistance within the specified range?	OL (Infinite)	*Go to Step 15*	*Go to Step 25*
15	Use the *J 39200* in order to measure the resistance between the EBCM connector terminal A5 and ground. Is the resistance within the specified range?	OL (Infinite)	*Go to Step 16*	*Go to Step 26*
16	1. Thoroughly respray the left front wheel speed sensor harness with the saltwater solution. 2. Disconnect the left front wheel speed sensor directly at the left front wheel speed sensor. 3. Use the *J 39200* in order to measure the resistance between the left front wheel speed sensor harness connector terminal A and ground. Is the resistance within the specified range?	OL (Infinite)	*Go to Step 17*	*Go to Step 29*
17	Use the *J 39200* in order to measure the resistance between the left front wheel speed sensor harness connector terminal B and ground. Is the resistance within the specified range?	OL (Infinite)	*Go to Step 18*	*Go to Step 29*
18	Use the *J 39200* in order to measure the resistance between the left front wheel speed sensor connector terminal A and ground. Is the resistance within the specified range?	OL (Infinite)	*Go to Step 31*	*Go to Step 28*
19	Repair the short to voltage in CKT 6L01. If the short to voltage is found in the left front wheel speed sensor harness, replace the left front wheel speed harness. Is the repair complete?	—	Refer to *Diagnostic System Check*	—
20	Repair the short to voltage in CKT 6K01. If the short to voltage is found in the left front wheel speed sensor harness, replace the left front wheel speed harness. Is the repair complete?	—	Refer to *Diagnostic System Check*	—
21	Repair the wiring damage in CKT 6L01 or CKT 6K01. If the wiring damage is found in the left front wheel speed sensor harness, replace the left front wheel speed jumper harness. Is the repair complete?	—	Refer to *Diagnostic System Check*	—
22	Repair the connector damage in CKT 6L01 or CKT 6K01. If the connector damage is found in the left front wheel speed sensor harness, replace the left front wheel speed harness. Is the repair complete?	—	Refer to *Diagnostic System Check*	—
23	Repair the open or high resistance in CKT 6L01. If the open or high resistance is found in the left front wheel speed sensor harness, replace the left front wheel speed sensor harness. Is the repair complete?	—	Refer to *Diagnostic System Check*	—

GC402980343100DX

Fig. 223 Code C1232: LH Front Wheel Speed Circuit Open Or Shorted (Part 4 of 5). Metro

Step	Action	Value(s)	Yes	No
24	Repair the open or high resistance in CKT 6K01. If the open or high resistance is found in the left front wheel speed sensor harness, replace the left front wheel speed harness. Is the repair complete?	—	Refer to *Diagnostic System Check*	—
25	Repair the short to ground in CKT 6L01. If the short to ground is found in the left front wheel speed sensor harness, replace the left front wheel speed harness. Is the repair complete?	—	Refer to *Diagnostic System Check*	—
26	Repair the short to ground in CKT 6K01. If the short to ground is found in the left front wheel speed sensor harness, replace the left front wheel speed harness. Is the repair complete?	—	Refer to *Diagnostic System Check*	—
27	Replace all of the terminals and the connectors that exhibit signs of poor terminal contact, corrosion, or damaged terminals. Is the repair complete?	—	Refer to *Diagnostic System Check*	—
28	Replace the left front wheel speed sensor. Is the repair complete?	—	Refer to *Diagnostic System Check*	—
29	Replace the left front wheel speed sensor harness. Is the repair complete?	—	Refer to *Diagnostic System Check*	—
30	Replace the EBCM. Is the repair complete?	—	Refer to *Diagnostic System Check*	—
31	The malfunction is intermittent or not present at this time. Inspect all of the connectors and the harnesses for damage that could cause the following conditions: • An open or a high resistance • A short to ground • A short to voltage The sensor harness must be replaced if the sensor harness is damaged. Refer to Diagnostic Aids for more information. Is the action complete?	—	System OK	—

GC402980343100EX

Fig. 223 Code C1232: LH Front Wheel Speed Circuit Open Or Shorted (Part 5 of 5). Metro

Circuit Description

As a toothed ring passes by the wheel speed sensor, changes in the electromagnetic field cause the wheel speed sensor to produce an AC voltage signal. The frequency of the AC voltage signal is proportional to the wheel speed. The amplitude of the AC voltage signal is directly related to wheel speed and the proximity of the wheel speed sensor to the toothed ring. The proximity of the wheel speed sensor to the toothed ring is also referred to as the air gap.

Conditions for Setting the DTC

- DTC C1233 can set anytime after initialization.
- A malfunction exists if either of the right front wheel speed sensor circuits are open or shorted to voltage or ground.

Action Taken When the DTC Sets

- A malfunction DTC stores.
- The ABS disables.
- The ABS warning indicator turns ON.

Conditions for Clearing the DTC

- The condition responsible for setting the DTC no longer exists and the Scan Tool Clear DTCs function is used.
- 100 drive cycles pass with no DTCs detected. A drive cycle consists of starting the vehicle, driving the vehicle over 16 km/h (10 mph), stopping and then turning the ignition OFF.

Diagnostic Aids

The following conditions may cause a malfunction:

- A poor connection
- Rubbed-through wire insulation
- A broken wire inside the insulation
- Faulty electrical circuits (open/high resistance, short to voltage or ground) between the RF wheel speed sensor and the EBCM
- Malfunctioning wheel speed sensor (high resistance)

Use the enhanced diagnostic function of the Scan Tool in order to measure the frequency of the malfunction.

If the customer's comments reflect that the amber ABS warning indicator is ON only during moist environmental changes (rain, snow, vehicle wash), inspect all the wheel speed sensor circuitry for signs of water intrusion. If the DTC is not current, clear all DTCs and simulate the effects of water intrusion by using the following procedure:

1. Spray the suspected area with a five percent saltwater solution.

   Add two teaspoons of salt to twelve ounces of water to make a five percent saltwater solution.
2. Test drive the vehicle over various road surfaces (bumps, turns, etc.) above 24 km/h (15 mph) for at least 30 seconds.
3. If the DTC returns, replace the suspected harness.

Thoroughly inspect any circuitry that may be causing the intermittent complaint for the following conditions:

- Backed out terminals
- Improper mating
- Broken locks
- Improperly formed or damaged terminals
- Poor terminal-to-wiring connections
- Physical damage to the wiring harness

GC402980343200AX

Fig. 224 Code C1233: RH Front Wheel Speed Circuit Open Or Shorted (Part 1 of 5). Metro

Resistance of the wheel speed sensor will increase with an increase in sensor temperature.

Use the following procedure when replacing a wheel speed sensor or harness:

1. Inspect the wheel speed sensor terminals and harness connector for corrosion and/or water intrusion.
2. Replace the wheel speed sensor and jumper harness if evidence of corrosion or water intrusion exists.

Important: Difficulty may occur when trying to locate intermittent malfunctions in the wheel speed sensor circuit.

Do not disturb any of the electrical connections. Change the electrical connections only when instructed to do so by a step in the diagnostic table.

Changing the electrical connections at the correct time will ensure that an intermittent electrical connection will not be corrected until the source of the malfunction is found.

Important: Zero the J 39200 test leads before making any resistance measurements. Refer to the J 39200 user's manual.

Step	Action	Value(s)	Yes	No
1	Was the Diagnostic System Check performed?	—	*Go to Step 2*	Refer to *Diagnostic System Check*
2	1. Turn the ignition switch to the OFF position. 2. Make a 5 percent saltwater solution. 3. Thoroughly spray the right front wheel speed sensor harness with the saltwater solution. 4. Disconnect the EBCM harness connector. 5. Use the *J 39200* in order to measure the resistance between the EBCM harness connector terminal A4 and the EBCM harness connector terminal B3. Is the resistance within the specified range?	920–1220 Ω	*Go to Step 3*	*Go to Step 11*
3	Use the *J 39200* in order to measure the resistance between the EBCM harness connector terminal B3 and ground. Is the resistance within the specified range?	OL (Infinite)	*Go to Step 4*	*Go to Step 14*
4	1. Turn the ignition switch to the ON position. Do not start the engine. 2. Use the *J 39200* in order to measure the voltage between the EBCM harness connector terminal B3 and ground. Is the voltage within the specified range?	0–1 V	*Go to Step 7*	*Go to Step 5*
5	1. Turn the ignition switch to the OFF position. 2. Disconnect the right front wheel speed sensor at the right front wheel speed sensor connector. 3. Turn the ignition switch to the ON position. Do not start the engine. 4. Use the *J 39200* in order to measure the voltage between the EBCM harness connector terminal B3 and ground. Is the voltage within the specified range?	0–1 V	*Go to Step 6*	*Go to Step 19*
6	Use the *J 39200* in order to measure the voltage between the EBCM harness connector terminal A4 and ground. Is the voltage within the specified range?	0–1 V	*Go to Step 31*	*Go to Step 20*

GC402980343200BX

Fig. 224 Code C1233: RH Front Wheel Speed Circuit Open Or Shorted (Part 2 of 5). Metro

Step	Action	Value(s)	Yes	No
7	1. Turn the ignition switch to the OFF position. 2. Inspect the following terminals: • The EBCM connector terminal A4 • The EBCM connector terminal B3 • The remaining terminals of the EBCM connector. 3. Inspect the above terminals for the following conditions: • Terminal damage • Poor terminal contact • Terminal corrosion Terminal damage, terminal corrosion, and poor terminal contact may cause an open circuit, a short to voltage, or a short to ground. Are there signs of poor terminal contact, terminal corrosion, or damaged terminals?	—	*Go to Step 27*	*Go to Step 8*
8	Inspect the wiring of CKT 6N01 and CKT 6M01 for signs of wire damage. Wire damage may cause the following conditions in CKT 6N01 and CKT 6M01: • An open circuit • A short to voltage • A short to ground Are there signs of damaged wiring?	—	*Go to Step 21*	*Go to Step 9*
9	Inspect the harness connectors of CKT 6N01 and CKT 6M01 for signs of wire damage. Wire damage may cause the following conditions in CKT 6N01 and CKT 6M01: • An open circuit • A short to voltage • A short to ground Are there signs of damaged connectors?	—	*Go to Step 22*	*Go to Step 10*
10	1. Reconnect the EBCM connector. 2. Reconnect the right front wheel speed sensor harness connector. 3. Install a *Scan Tool.* 4. Test drive the vehicle at a speed above 24 km/h (15 mph) for at least 30 seconds. 5. Use the *Scan Tool* in order to read the DTCs. Does DTC C1233 set as a current DTC?	—	*Go to Step 30*	*Go to Step 31*
11	1. Disconnect the right front wheel speed sensor directly at the right front wheel speed sensor connector. 2. Use the *J 39200* in order to measure the resistance between the EBCM connector terminal B3 and the right front wheel speed sensor harness connector terminal B. Is the resistance within the specified range?	0–2 Ω	*Go to Step 12*	*Go to Step 23*
12	Use the *J 39200* in order to measure the resistance between the EBCM connector terminal A4 and the right front wheel speed sensor harness connector terminal A. Is the resistance within the specified range?	0–2 Ω	*Go to Step 13*	*Go to Step 24*

GC402980343200CX

Fig. 224 Code C1233: RH Front Wheel Speed Circuit Open Or Shorted (Part 3 of 5). Metro

Step	Action	Value(s)	Yes	No
13	Use the *J 39200* in order to measure the resistance between the right front wheel speed sensor connector terminal A and the right front wheel speed sensor connector terminal B. Is the resistance within the specified range?	920–1220 Ω	*Go to Step 31*	*Go to Step 28*
14	Use the *J 39200* in order to measure the resistance between the EBCM connector terminal B3 and ground. Is the resistance within the specified range?	OL (Infinite)	*Go to Step 15*	*Go to Step 25*
15	Use the *J 39200* in order to measure the resistance between the EBCM connector terminal A4 and ground. Is the resistance within the specified range?	OL (Infinite)	*Go to Step 16*	*Go to Step 26*
16	1. Thoroughly respray the right front wheel speed sensor harness with the saltwater solution. 2. Disconnect the right front wheel speed sensor directly at the right front wheel speed sensor. 3. Use the *J 39200* in order to measure the resistance between the right front wheel speed sensor harness connector terminal A and ground. Is the resistance within the specified range?	OL (Infinite)	*Go to Step 17*	*Go to Step 29*
17	Use the *J 39200* in order to measure the resistance between the right front wheel speed sensor harness connector terminal B and ground. Is the resistance within the specified range?	OL (Infinite)	*Go to Step 18*	*Go to Step 29*
18	Use the *J 39200* in order to measure the resistance between the right front wheel speed sensor connector terminal A and ground. Is the resistance within the specified range?	OL (Infinite)	*Go to Step 31*	*Go to Step 28*
19	Repair the short to voltage in CKT 833. If the short to voltage is found in the right front wheel speed sensor harness, replace the right front wheel speed harness. Is the repair complete?	—	Refer to *Diagnostic System Check*	—
20	Repair the short to voltage in CKT 6M01. If the short to voltage is found in the right front wheel speed sensor harness, replace the right front wheel speed harness. Is the repair complete?	—	Refer to *Diagnostic System Check*	—
21	Repair the wiring damage in CKT 6N01 or CKT 6M01. If the wiring damage is found in the right front wheel speed sensor harness, replace the right front wheel speed harness. Is the repair complete?	—	Refer to *Diagnostic System Check*	—
22	Repair the connector damage in CKT 6N01 or CKT 6M01. If the connector damage is found in the right front wheel speed sensor harness, replace the right front wheel speed harness. Is the repair complete?	—	Refer to *Diagnostic System Check*	—
23	Repair the open or high resistance in CKT 6N01. If the open or high resistance is found in the right front wheel speed sensor harness, replace the right front wheel speed harness. Is the repair complete?	—	Refer to *Diagnostic System Check*	—

GC402980343200DX

Fig. 224 Code C1233: RH Front Wheel Speed Circuit Open Or Shorted (Part 4 of 5). Metro

Step	Action	Value(s)	Yes	No
24	Repair the open or high resistance in CKT 6M01. If the open or high resistance is found in the right front wheel speed sensor harness, replace the right front wheel speed harness. Is the repair complete?	—	Refer to *Diagnostic System Check*	—
25	Repair the short to ground in CKT 6N01. If the short to ground is found in the right front wheel speed sensor harness, replace the right front wheel speed harness. Is the repair complete?	—	Refer to *Diagnostic System Check*	—
26	Repair the short to ground in CKT 6M01. If the short to ground is found in the right front wheel speed sensor harness, replace the right front wheel speed harness. Is the repair complete?	—	Refer to *Diagnostic System Check*	—
27	Replace all of the terminals and the connectors that exhibit signs of poor terminal contact, corrosion, or damaged terminals. Is the repair complete?	—	Refer to *Diagnostic System Check*	—
28	Replace the right front wheel speed sensor. Is the repair complete?	—	Refer to *Diagnostic System Check*	—
29	Replace the right front wheel speed sensor harness. Is the repair complete?	—	Refer to *Diagnostic System Check*	—
30	Replace the EBCM. Is the repair complete?	—	Refer to *Diagnostic System Check*	—
31	The malfunction is intermittent or not present at this time. Inspect all of the connectors and the harnesses for damage that may cause the following conditions: • An open or a high resistance • A short to ground • A short to voltage The wheel speed harness must be replaced if the harness is damaged. Refer to Diagnostic Aids for more information. Is the action complete?	—	System OK	—

GC402980343200EX

Fig. 224 Code C1233: RH Front Wheel Speed Circuit Open Or Shorted (Part 5 of 5). Metro

Resistance of the wheel speed sensor will increase with an increase in sensor temperature.

Use the following procedure when replacing a wheel speed sensor or harness:

1. Inspect the wheel speed sensor terminals and harness connector for corrosion and/or water intrusion.
2. Replace the wheel speed sensor and jumper harness if evidence of corrosion or water intrusion exists.

Important: Difficulty may occur when trying to locate intermittent malfunctions in the wheel speed sensor circuit.

Do not disturb any of the electrical connections. Change the electrical connections only when instructed to do so by a step in the diagnostic table.

Changing the electrical connections at the correct time will ensure that an intermittent electrical connection will not be corrected until the source of the malfunction is found.

Important: Zero the J 39200 test leads before making any resistance measurements.

Step	Action	Value(s)	Yes	No
1	Was the Diagnostic System Check performed?	—	*Go to Step 2*	Refer to *Diagnostic System Check*
2	1. Turn the ignition switch to the OFF position. 2. Make a 5 percent saltwater solution. 3. Thoroughly spray the left rear wheel speed sensor harness with the saltwater solution. 4. Disconnect the EBCM harness connector. 5. Use the *J 39200* in order to measure the resistance between the EBCM harness connector terminal A3 and the EBCM harness connector terminal B2. Is the resistance within the specified range?	1050–1450 Ω	*Go to Step 3*	*Go to Step 11*
3	Use the *J 39200* in order to measure the resistance between the EBCM harness connector terminal B2 and ground. Is the resistance within the specified range?	OL (Infinite)	*Go to Step 4*	*Go to Step 14*
4	1. Turn the ignition switch to the ON position. Do not start the engine. 2. Use the *J 39200* in order to measure the voltage between the EBCM harness connector terminal B2 and ground. Is the voltage within the specified range?	0–1 V	*Go to Step 7*	*Go to Step 5*
5	1. Turn the ignition switch to the OFF position. 2. Disconnect the left rear wheel speed sensor at the left rear wheel speed sensor connector. 3. Turn the ignition switch to the ON position. Do not start the engine. 4. Use the *J 39200* in order to measure the voltage between the EBCM harness connector terminal B2 and ground. Is the voltage within the specified range?	0–1 V	*Go to Step 6*	*Go to Step 19*
6	Use the *J 39200* in order to measure the voltage between the EBCM harness connector terminal A3 and ground. Is the voltage within the specified range?	0–1 V	*Go to Step 31*	*Go to Step 20*

GC402980343300BX

Fig. 225 Code C1234: LH Rear Wheel Speed Circuit Open Or Shorted (Part 2 of 5). Metro

Circuit Description

As a toothed ring passes by the wheel speed sensor, changes in the electromagnetic field cause the wheel speed sensor to produce an AC voltage signal. The frequency of the AC voltage signal is proportional to the wheel speed. The amplitude of the AC voltage signal is directly related to wheel speed and the proximity of the wheel speed sensor to the toothed ring. The proximity of the wheel speed sensor to the toothed ring is also referred to as the air gap.

Conditions for Setting the DTC

- DTC C1234 can set anytime after initialization.
- A malfunction exists if either of the left rear wheel speed sensor circuits are open or shorted to voltage or ground.

Action Taken When the DTC Sets

- A malfunction DTC stores.
- The ABS disables.
- The ABS warning indicator turns ON.

Conditions for Clearing the DTC

- The condition responsible for setting the DTC no longer exists and the Scan Tool Clear DTCs function is used.
- 100 drive cycles pass with no DTCs detected. A drive cycle consists of starting the vehicle, driving the vehicle over 16 km/h (10 mph), stopping and then turning the ignition OFF.

Diagnostic Aids

The following conditions may cause a malfunction:

- A poor connection
- Rubbed-through wire insulation
- A broken wire inside the insulation
- Faulty electrical circuits (open/high resistance, short to voltage or ground) between the LR wheel speed sensor and the EBCM
- Malfunctioning wheel speed sensor (high resistance)

Use the enhanced diagnostic function of the Scan Tool in order to measure the frequency of the malfunction.

If the customer's comments reflect that the amber ABS warning indicator is ON only during moist environmental changes (rain, snow, vehicle wash), inspect all the wheel speed sensor circuitry for signs of water intrusion. If the DTC is not current, clear all DTCs and simulate the effects of water intrusion by using the following procedure:

1. Spray the suspected area with a five percent saltwater solution.
   Add two teaspoons of salt to twelve ounces of water to make a five percent saltwater solution.
2. Test drive the vehicle over various road surfaces (bumps, turns, etc.) above 24 km/h (15 mph) for at least 30 seconds.
3. If the DTC returns, replace the suspected harness.

Thoroughly inspect any circuitry that may be causing the intermittent complaint for the following conditions:

- Backed out terminals
- Improper mating
- Broken locks
- Improperly formed or damaged terminals
- Poor terminal-to-wiring connections
- Physical damage to the wiring harness

GC402980343300AX

Fig. 225 Code C1234: LH Rear Wheel Speed Circuit Open Or Shorted (Part 1 of 5). Metro

Step	Action	Value(s)	Yes	No
7	1. Turn the ignition switch to the OFF position. 2. Inspect the following terminals: • The EBCM connector terminal A3 • The EBCM connector terminal B2 • The remaining terminals of the EBCM connector 3. Inspect the above terminals for the following conditions: • Terminal damage • Poor terminal contact • Terminal corrosion Terminal damage, terminal corrosion, and poor terminal contact may cause an open circuit, a short to voltage, or a short to ground. Are there signs of poor terminal contact, terminal corrosion, or damaged terminals?	—	*Go to Step 27*	*Go to Step 8*
8	Inspect the wiring of CKT 6P01 and CKT 6O01 for signs of wire damage. Wire damage may cause the following conditions in CKT 6P01 and CKT 6O01: • An open circuit • A short to voltage • A short to ground Are there signs of damaged wiring?	—	*Go to Step 21*	*Go to Step 9*
9	Inspect the harness connectors of CKT 6P01 and CKT 6O01 for signs of wire damage. Wire damage may cause the following conditions in CKT 6P01 and CKT 6O01: • An open circuit • A short to voltage • A short to ground Are there signs of damaged connectors?	—	*Go to Step 22*	*Go to Step 10*
10	1. Reconnect the EBCM connector. 2. Reconnect the left rear wheel speed sensor harness connector. 3. Install a *Scan Tool.* 4. Test drive the vehicle at a speed above 24 km/h (15 mph) for at least 30 seconds. 5. Use the *Scan Tool* in order to read the DTCs. Does DTC C1234 set as a current DTC?	—	*Go to Step 30*	*Go to Step 31*
11	1. Disconnect the left rear wheel speed sensor directly at the left rear wheel speed sensor connector. 2. Use the *J 39200* in order to measure the resistance between the EBCM connector terminal B2 and the left rear wheel speed sensor harness connector terminal B. Is the resistance within the specified range?	0–2 Ω	*Go to Step 12*	*Go to Step 23*
12	Use the *J 39200* in order to measure the resistance between the EBCM connector terminal A3 and the left rear wheel speed sensor harness connector terminal A. Is the resistance within the specified range?	0–2 Ω	*Go to Step 13*	*Go to Step 24*

GC402980343300CX

Fig. 225 Code C1234: LH Rear Wheel Speed Circuit Open Or Shorted (Part 3 of 5). Metro

Step	Action	Value(s)	Yes	No
13	Use the *J 39200* in order to measure the resistance between the left rear wheel speed sensor connector terminal A and the left rear wheel speed sensor connector terminal B. Is the resistance within the specified range?	1050–1450Ω	*Go to Step 31*	*Go to Step 28*
14	1. Disconnect the connector C305. 2. Use the *J 39200* in order to measure the resistance between the EBCM connector terminal B2 and ground. Is the resistance within the specified range?	OL (Infinite)	*Go to Step 15*	*Go to Step 25*
15	Use the *J 39200* in order to measure the resistance between the EBCM connector terminal A3 and ground. Is the resistance within the specified range?	OL (Infinite)	*Go to Step 16*	*Go to Step 26*
16	1. Thoroughly respray the left rear wheel speed sensor harness with the saltwater solution. 2. Disconnect the left rear wheel speed sensor directly at the left rear wheel speed sensor. 3. Use the *J 39200* in order to measure the resistance between the left rear wheel speed sensor harness connector terminal A and ground. Is the resistance within the specified range?	OL (Infinite)	*Go to Step 17*	*Go to Step 29*
17	Use the *J 39200* in order to measure the resistance between the left rear wheel speed sensor harness connector terminal B and ground. Is the resistance within the specified range?	OL (Infinite)	*Go to Step 18*	*Go to Step 29*
18	Use the *J 39200* in order to measure the resistance between the left rear wheel speed sensor connector terminal A and ground. Is the resistance within the specified range?	OL (Infinite)	*Go to Step 31*	*Go to Step 28*
19	Repair the short to voltage in CKT 6P01. If the short to voltage is found in the left rear wheel speed sensor harness, replace the left rear wheel speed harness. Is the repair complete?	—	Refer to *Diagnostic System Check*	—
20	Repair the short to voltage in CKT 6O01. If the short to voltage is found in the left rear wheel speed sensor harness, replace the left rear wheel speed harness. Is the repair complete?	—	Refer to *Diagnostic System Check*	—
21	Repair the wiring damage in CKT 6P01 or CKT 6O01. If the wiring damage is found in the left rear wheel speed sensor harness, replace the left rear wheel speed harness. Is the repair complete?	—	Refer to *Diagnostic System Check*	—
22	Repair the connector damage in CKT 6P01 or CKT 6O01. If the connector damage is found in the left rear wheel speed sensor harness, replace the left rear wheel speed harness. Is the repair complete?	—	Refer to *Diagnostic System Check*	—
23	Repair the open or high resistance in CKT 6P01. If the open or high resistance is found in the left rear wheel speed sensor harness, replace the left rear wheel speed harness. Is the repair complete?	—	Refer to *Diagnostic System Check*	—

GC402980343300DX

Fig. 225 Code C1234: LH Rear Wheel Speed Circuit Open Or Shorted (Part 4 of 5). Metro

Circuit Description

As a toothed ring passes by the wheel speed sensor, changes in the electromagnetic field cause the wheel speed sensor to produce an AC voltage signal. The frequency of the AC voltage signal is proportional to the wheel speed. The amplitude of the AC voltage signal is directly related to wheel speed and the proximity of the wheel speed sensor to the toothed ring. The proximity of the wheel speed sensor to the toothed ring is also referred to as the air gap.

Conditions for Setting the DTC

- DTC C1235 can set anytime after initialization.
- A malfunction exists if either of the right rear wheel speed sensor circuits are open or shorted to voltage or ground.

Action Taken When the DTC Sets

- A malfunction DTC stores.
- The ABS disables.
- The ABS warning indicator turns ON.

Conditions for Clearing the DTC

- The condition responsible for setting the DTC no longer exists and the Scan Tool Clear DTCs function is used.
- 100 drive cycles pass with no DTCs detected. A drive cycle consists of starting the vehicle, driving the vehicle over 16 km/h (10 mph), stopping and then turning the ignition OFF.

Diagnostic Aids

The following conditions may cause a malfunction:

- A poor connection
- Rubbed-through wire insulation
- A broken wire inside the insulation
- Faulty electrical circuits (open/high resistance, short to voltage or ground) between the RR wheel speed sensor and the EBCM
- Malfunctioning wheel speed sensor (high resistance)

Use the enhanced diagnostic function of the Scan Tool in order to measure the frequency of the malfunction.

If the customer's comments reflect that the amber ABS warning indicator is ON only during moist environmental changes (rain, snow, vehicle wash), inspect all the wheel speed sensor circuitry for signs of water intrusion. If the DTC is not current, clear all DTCs and simulate the effects of water intrusion by using the following procedure:

1. Spray the suspected area with a five percent saltwater solution.
   Add two teaspoons of salt to twelve ounces of water to make a five percent saltwater solution.
2. Test drive the vehicle over various road surfaces (bumps, turns, etc.) above 24 km/h (15 mph) for at least 30 seconds.
3. If the DTC returns, replace the suspected harness.

Thoroughly inspect any circuitry that may be causing the intermittent complaint for the following conditions:

- Backed out terminals
- Improper mating
- Broken locks
- Improperly formed or damaged terminals
- Poor terminal-to-wiring connections
- Physical damage to the wiring harness

GC402980343400AX

Fig. 226 Code C1235: RH Rear Wheel Speed Circuit Open Or Shorted (Part 1 of 5). Metro

Step	Action	Value(s)	Yes	No
24	Repair the open or high resistance in CKT 6O01. If the open or high resistance is found in the left rear wheel speed sensor harness, replace the left rear wheel speed harness. Is the repair complete?	—	Refer to *Diagnostic System Check*	—
25	Repair the short to ground in CKT 6P01. If the short to ground is found in the left rear wheel speed sensor harness, replace the left rear wheel speed harness. Is the repair complete?	—	Refer to *Diagnostic System Check*	—
26	Repair the short to ground in CKT 6O01. If the short to ground is found in the left rear wheel speed sensor harness, replace the left rear wheel speed harness. Is the repair complete?	—	Refer to *Diagnostic System Check*	—
27	Replace all of the terminals and the connectors that exhibit signs of poor terminal contact, corrosion, or damaged terminals. Is the repair complete?	—	Refer to *Diagnostic System Check*	—
28	Replace the left rear wheel speed sensor. Is the repair complete?	—	Refer to *Diagnostic System Check*	—
29	Replace the left rear wheel speed sensor harness. Is the repair complete?	—	Refer to *Diagnostic System Check*	—
30	Replace the EBCM. Is the repair complete?	—	Refer to *Diagnostic System Check*	—
31	The malfunction is intermittent or not present at this time. Inspect all of the connectors and the harnesses for damage that may cause the following conditions: • An open or a high resistance • A short to ground • A short to voltage The wheel speed sensor harness must be replaced if the harness is damaged. Refer to Diagnostic Aids for more information. Is the action complete?	—	System OK	—

GC402980343300EX

Fig. 225 Code C1234: LH Rear Wheel Speed Circuit Open Or Shorted (Part 5 of 5). Metro

Resistance of the wheel speed sensor will increase with an increase in sensor temperature.

Use the following procedure when replacing a wheel speed sensor or harness:

1. Inspect the wheel speed sensor terminals and harness connector for corrosion and/or water intrusion.
2. Replace the wheel speed sensor and jumper harness if evidence of corrosion or water intrusion exists.

Important: Zero the J 39200 test leads before making any resistance measurements. Refer to the J 39200 user's manual.

Important: Difficulty may occur when trying to locate intermittent malfunctions in the wheel speed sensor circuit.

Do not disturb any of the electrical connections. Change the electrical connections only when instructed to do so by a step in the diagnostic table.

Changing the electrical connections at the correct time will ensure that an intermittent electrical connection will not be corrected until the source of the malfunction is found.

Step	Action	Value(s)	Yes	No
1	Was the Diagnostic System Check performed?	—	*Go to Step 2*	Refer to *Diagnostic System Check*
2	1. Turn the ignition switch to the OFF position. 2. Make a 5 percent saltwater solution. 3. Thoroughly spray the rear wheel speed sensor harness with the saltwater solution. 4. Disconnect the EBCM harness connector. 5. Use the *J 39200* in order to measure the resistance between the EBCM harness connector terminal A2 and the EBCM harness connector terminal B1. Is the resistance within the specified range?	1050–1450 Ω	*Go to Step 3*	*Go to Step 11*
3	Use the *J 39200* in order to measure the resistance between the EBCM harness connector terminal B1 and ground. Is the resistance within the specified range?	OL (Infinite)	*Go to Step 4*	*Go to Step 14*
4	1. Turn the ignition switch to the ON position. Do not start the engine. 2. Use the *J 39200* in order to measure the voltage between the EBCM harness connector terminal B1 and ground. Is the voltage within the specified range?	0–1 V	*Go to Step 7*	*Go to Step 5*
5	1. Turn the ignition switch to the OFF position. 2. Disconnect the right rear wheel speed sensor at the right rear wheel speed sensor connector. 3. Turn the ignition switch to the ON position. Do not start the engine. 4. Use the *J 39200* in order to measure the voltage between the EBCM harness connector terminal B1 and ground Is the voltage within the specified range?	0–1 V	*Go to Step 6*	*Go to Step 19*
6	Use the *J 39200* in order to measure the voltage between the EBCM harness connector terminal A2 and ground. Is the voltage within the specified range?	0–1 V	*Go to Step 31*	*Go to Step 20*

GC402980343400BX

Fig. 226 Code C1235: RH Rear Wheel Speed Circuit Open Or Shorted (Part 2 of 5). Metro

Step	Action	Value(s)	Yes	No
7	1. Turn the ignition switch to the OFF position. 2. Inspect the following terminals: • The EBCM connector terminal A1 • The EBCM connector terminal B1 • The remaining terminals of the EBCM connector 3. Inspect the above terminals for the following conditions: • Terminal damage • Poor terminal contact • Terminal corrosion Damage, terminal corrosion, and poor terminal contact may cause an open circuit, a short to voltage, or a short to ground. Are there signs of poor terminal contact, terminal corrosion, or damaged terminals?	—	*Go to Step 27*	*Go to Step 8*
8	Inspect the wiring of CKT 6R01 and CKT 6Q01 for signs of wire damage. Wire damage may cause the following conditions in CKT 6R01 and CKT 6Q01: • An open circuit • A short to voltage • A short to ground Are there signs of damaged wiring?	—	*Go to Step 21*	*Go to Step 9*
9	Inspect the harness connectors of CKT 6R01 and CKT 6Q01 for signs of wire damage. Wire damage may cause the following conditions in CKT 6R01 and CKT 6Q01: • An open circuit • A short to voltage • A short to ground Are there signs of damaged connectors?	—	*Go to Step 22*	*Go to Step 10*
10	1. Reconnect the EBCM connector. 2. Reconnect the rear wheel speed sensor harness connector. 3. Install a *Scan Tool*. 4. Test drive the vehicle at a speed above 24 km/h (15 mph) for at least 30 seconds. 5. Use the *Scan Tool* in order to read the DTCs. Does DTC C1235 set as a current DTC?	—	*Go to Step 30*	*Go to Step 31*
11	1. Disconnect the right rear wheel speed sensor directly at the right rear wheel speed sensor connector. 2. Use the *J 39200* in order to measure the resistance between the EBCM harness connector terminal B1 and the right rear wheel speed sensor harness connector terminal B. Is the resistance within the specified range?	0–2 Ω	*Go to Step 12*	*Go to Step 23*
12	Use the *J 39200* in order to measure the resistance between the EBCM harness connector terminal A2 and the right rear wheel speed sensor harness connector terminal A. Is the resistance within the specified range?	0–2 Ω	*Go to Step 13*	*Go to Step 24*

GC402980343400CX

Fig. 226 Code C1235: RH Rear Wheel Speed Circuit Open Or Shorted (Part 3 of 5). Metro

Step	Action	Value(s)	Yes	No
13	Use the *J 39200* in order to measure the resistance between the right rear wheel speed sensor connector terminal A and the right rear wheel speed sensor connector terminal B. Is the resistance within the specified range?	1050–1450 Ω	*Go to Step 31*	*Go to Step 28*
14	1. Disconnect the connector C301. 2. Use the *J 39200* in order to measure the resistance between the EBCM connector terminal B1 and ground. Is the resistance within the specified range?	OL (Infinite)	*Go to Step 15*	*Go to Step 25*
15	Use the *J 39200* in order to measure the resistance between the EBCM connector terminal A2 and ground. Is the resistance within the specified range?	OL (Infinite)	*Go to Step 16*	*Go to Step 26*
16	1. Thoroughly respray the rear wheel speed sensor harness with the saltwater solution. 2. Disconnect the right rear wheel speed sensor directly at the right rear wheel speed sensor. 3. Use the *J 39200* in order to measure the resistance between the rear wheel speed sensor harness connector terminal A and ground. Is the resistance within the specified range?	OL (Infinite)	*Go to Step 17*	*Go to Step 29*
17	Use the *J 39200* in order to measure the resistance between the rearwheel speed sensor harness connector terminal B and ground. Is the resistance within the specified range?	OL (Infinite)	*Go to Step 18*	*Go to Step 29*
18	Use the *J 39200* in order to measure the resistance between the rear wheel speed sensor harness connector terminal A and ground. Is the resistance within the specified range?	OL (Infinite)	*Go to Step 31*	*Go to Step 28*
19	Repair the short to voltage in CKT 6R01. If the short to voltage is found in the rear wheel speed sensor harness, replace the rear wheel speed sensor harness. Is the repair complete?	—	Refer to *Diagnostic System Check*	—
20	Repair the short to voltage in CKT 6Q01. If the short to voltage is found in the rear wheel speed sensor harness, replace the rear wheel speed sensor harness. Is the repair complete?	—	Refer to *Diagnostic System Check*	—
21	Repair the wiring damage in CKT 6R01 or CKT 6Q01. If the wiring damage is found in the rear wheel speed sensor harness, replace the rear wheel speed sensor harness. Is the repair complete?	—	Refer to *Diagnostic System Check*	—
22	Repair the connector damage in CKT 6R01 or CKT 6Q01. If the connector damage is found in the rear wheel speed sensor harness, replace the rear wheel speed sensor harness. Is the repair complete?	—	Refer to *Diagnostic System Check*	—

GC402980343400DX

Fig. 226 Code C1235: RH Rear Wheel Speed Circuit Open Or Shorted (Part 4 of 5). Metro

Step	Action	Value(s)	Yes	No
23	Repair the open or high resistance in CKT 6R01. If the open or high resistance is found in the rear wheel speed sensor harness, replace the rear wheel speed sensor harness. Is the repair complete?	—	Refer to *Diagnostic System Check*	—
24	Repair the open or high resistance in CKT 6Q01. If the open or high resistance is found in the rear wheel speed sensor harness, replace the rear wheel speed sensor harness. Is the repair complete?	—	Refer to *Diagnostic System Check*	—
25	Repair the short to ground in CKT 6R01. If the short to ground is found in the rear wheel speed sensor harness, replace the rear wheel speed sensor harness. Is the repair complete?	—	Refer to *Diagnostic System Check*	—
26	Repair the short to ground in CKT 6Q01. If the short to ground is found in the rear wheel speed sensor harness, replace the rear wheel speed sensor harness. Is the repair complete?	—	Refer to *Diagnostic System Check*	—
27	Replace all of the terminals and the connectors that exhibit signs of poor terminal contact, corrosion, or damaged terminals. Is the repair complete?	—	Refer to *Diagnostic System Check*	—
28	Replace the right rear wheel speed sensor. Is the repair complete?	—	Refer to *Diagnostic System Check*	—
29	Replace the rear wheel speed sensor harness. Is the repair complete?	—	Refer to *Diagnostic System Check*	—
30	Replace the EBCM. Is the repair complete?	—	Refer to *Diagnostic System Check*	—
31	The malfunction is intermittent or not present at this time. Inspect all of the connectors and the harnesses for damage that may cause the following conditions: • An open or a high resistance • A short to ground • A short to voltage The rear axle harness must be replaced if the harness is damaged. Refer to Diagnostic Aids for more information. Is the action complete?	—	System OK	—

GC402980343400EX

Fig. 226 Code C1235: RH Rear Wheel Speed Circuit Open Or Shorted (Part 5 of 5). Metro

Circuit Description

DTC C1236 monitors the voltage level available to the EBCM controller. If the voltage drops below 11.2 volts, full performance of the ABS system is not guaranteed. During ABS operation, there are several current requirements that will cause battery voltage at the EBCM to drop. As a result, voltage is monitored prior to an ABS event to indicate good charging system condition. Voltage is also monitored during an ABS event when voltage may drop significantly.

Conditions for Setting the DTC

- DTC C1236 can set only if the vehicle's speed is greater than 5 km/h (3 mph).
- A malfunction exists if both the switched battery (CKT 6B01) and switched ignition (CKT 6U01) voltages are less than 11 volts during non-ABS event, or less than 9 volts during an ABS event.

Action Taken When the DTC Sets

- A malfunction DTC stores.
- The ABS disables.
- The ABS warning indicator turns ON.

Conditions for Clearing the DTC

- The condition responsible for setting the DTC no longer exists and the Scan Tool Clear DTCs function is used.
- 100 drive cycles pass with no DTCs detected. A drive cycle consists of starting the vehicle, driving the vehicle over 16 km/h (10 mph), stopping and then turning the ignition OFF.

Diagnostic Aids

The following conditions may cause a malfunction:

- A poor connection
- Rubbed-through wire insulation
- A broken wire inside the insulation
- Vehicle's charging system is not operating properly (low generator output, faulty battery)
- High resistance in CKT 6U01, 6B01 or 6W01
- Poor G102

Use the enhanced diagnostic function of the Scan Tool in order to measure the frequency of the malfunction.

GC402980343500AX

Fig. 227 Code C1236: Low System Supply Voltage (Part 1 of 3). Metro

Thoroughly inspect any circuitry that may be causing the intermittent complaint for the following conditions:

- Backed out terminals
- Improper mating
- Broken locks
- Improperly formed or damaged terminals
- Poor terminal-to-wiring connections
- Physical damage to the wiring harness

While performing a Voltage Load test, CKT 6U01 should be measured for high resistance or an open condition if it is noted that only the ignition voltage drops below acceptable voltage levels.

Ensure the starting and charging systems are in proper working order. The battery should be fully charged and in good condition before beginning the diagnostic table.

Important: Zero the J 39200 test leads before making any resistance measurements.

Step	Action	Value(s)	Yes	No
1	Was the Diagnostic System Check performed?	—	*Go to Step 2*	Refer to *Diagnostic System Check*
2	1. Turn the ignition switch to the ON position. Do not start the engine. 2. Select Snapshot on the *Scan Tool*. 3. Select Single DTC on the *Scan Tool*. 4. Enter C1236 on the *Scan Tool*. 5. Drive the vehicle at a speed above 5 km/h (3 mph). Does DTC C1236 set as a current DTC?	—	*Go to Step 3*	*Go to Step 17*
3	1. Verify that the engine is running. 2. Turn the ignition switch to the ON position. 3. Select Special Functions on the *Scan Tool*. 4. Use the *Scan Tool* in order to perform the Voltage Load test. Are the ignition voltage and the battery voltage equal to or greater than the specified voltage?	10 V	*Go to Step 4*	*Go to Step 10*
4	1. Turn the ignition switch to the OFF position. 2. Disconnect the EBCM connector. 3. Disconnect the Electronic Brake Control Relay. 4. Use the *J 39200* in order to measure the resistance between the Electronic Brake Control Relay connector terminal 87 and the EBCM connector terminal C. Is the resistance within the specified range?	0–2 Ω	*Go to Step 5*	*Go to Step 11*
5	1. Disconnect the negative battery cable. 2. Disconnect the positive battery cable. 3. Use the *J 39200* in order to measure the resistance between the positive battery terminal and the Electronic Brake Control Relay connector terminal 30. Is the resistance within the specified range?	0–2 Ω	*Go to Step 6*	*Go to Step 12*
6	1. Remove the fuse block DEF Fuse (20A). 2. Use the *J 39200* in order to measure the resistance between the fuse block terminal (DEF Fuse [20A]) and the EBCM connector terminal A9. Is the resistance within the specified range?	0–2 Ω	*Go to Step 7*	*Go to Step 13*

GC402980343500BX

Fig. 227 Code C1236: Low System Supply Voltage (Part 2 of 3). Metro

Step	Action	Value(s)	Yes	No
7	Use the *J 39200* in order to measure the resistance between the fuse block terminal (DEF Fuse [20A]) and the EBCM connector terminal A9. Is the resistance within the specified range?	0–2 Ω	*Go to Step 8*	*Go to Step 14*
8	1. Inspect the following components: • The Electronic Brake Control Relay connector • The EBCM connector • The positive battery cable connections • The negative battery cable connections 2. Inspect the above components for the following conditions: • Terminal damage • Poor terminal contact • Terminal corrosion The above conditions may cause an open circuit. Are there signs of terminal damage, poor terminal contact, or terminal corrosion?	—	*Go to Step 15*	*Go to Step 9*
9	1. Reconnect the EBCM connector. 2. Reconnect the Electronic Brake Control Relay. 3. Reconnect the positive battery cable. 4. Reconnect the negative battery cable. 5. Drive the vehicle at a speed above 5 km/h (3 mph). Does DTC C1236 set as a current DTC?	—	*Go to Step 16*	*Go to Step 17*
10	Repair the low voltage condition. Is the low voltage condition repaired?	—	Refer to *Diagnostic System Check*	—
11	Repair the open or high resistance in CKT 6B01. Is the repair complete?	—	Refer to *Diagnostic System Check*	—
12	Repair the open or high resistance in CKT 6A01. Is the repair complete?	—	Refer to *Diagnostic System Check*	—
13	Repair the open or high resistance in CKT 6U01. Is the repair complete?	—	Refer to *Diagnostic System Check*	—
14	Repair the open or high resistance in the power feed circuits to the fuse block. Is the repair complete?	—	Refer to *Diagnostic System Check*	—
15	Replace all of the terminals or the connectors that exhibit signs of poor terminal contact, corrosion, or damaged terminals. Is the repair complete?	—	Refer to *Diagnostic System Check*	—
16	Replace the EBCM. Is the repair complete?	—	Refer to *Diagnostic System Check*	—
17	The malfunction is intermittent or is not present at this time. Refer to Diagnostic Aids for more information. Is the action complete?	—	System OK	—

GC402980343500CX

Fig. 227 Code C1236: Low System Supply Voltage (Part 3 of 3). Metro

Circuit Description

DTC C1237 detects high vehicle voltage levels prior to any required motor movement (initialization or ABS). Damage to the system may occur if excessive voltage exists.

Conditions for Setting the DTC

- DTC C1237 can set only if the vehicle's speed is greater than 5 km/h (3 mph).
- A malfunction exists if the switched battery voltage is greater than 17 volts.

Action Taken When the DTC Sets

- A malfunction DTC stores.
- The ABS disables.
- The ABS warning indicator turns ON.

Conditions for Clearing the DTC

- The condition responsible for setting the DTC no longer exists and the Scan Tool Clear DTCs function is used.
- 100 drive cycles pass with no DTCs detected. A drive cycle consists of starting the vehicle, driving the vehicle over 16 km/h (10 mph), stopping and then turning the ignition OFF.

Diagnostic Aids

Use the enhanced diagnostic function of the Scan Tool in order to measure the frequency of the malfunction.

Ensure the vehicle's charging system is working properly.

Important: Zero the J 39200 test leads before making any resistance measurements.

GC402980343600AX

Fig. 228 Code C1237: High System Supply Voltage (Part 1 of 2). Metro

Step	Action	Value(s)	Yes	No
1	Was the Diagnostic System Check performed?	—	*Go to Step 2*	Refer to *Diagnostic System Check*
2	1. Start the engine. 2. Install a *Scan Tool*. 3. Select Data List on the *Scan Tool*. 4. Select Battery Voltage on the *Scan Tool*. 5. Run the engine at approximately 2,000 RPM and monitor the voltage. Is the voltage less than or equal to the specified voltage?	16 V	*Go to Step 6*	*Go to Step 3*
3	1. Turn the ignition switch to the OFF position. 2. Disconnect the Electronic Brake Control Relay. 3. Start the engine. 4. Use the *J 39200* in order to measure the voltage between the Electronic Brake Control Relay connector terminal 30 and ground. 5. Run the engine at approximately 2,000 RPM and monitor the voltage. Is the voltage less than or equal to the specified range?	16 V	*Go to Step 4*	Charging System
4	1. Turn the ignition switch to the OFF position. 2. Reconnect the Electronic Brake Control Relay. 3. Drive the vehicle at a speed above 5 km/h (3 mph). 4. Use the *Scan Tool* in order to look for DTCs. Does DTC C1237 set as a current DTC?	—	*Go to Step 5*	*Go to Step 6*
5	Replace the EBCM. Is the repair complete?	—	Refer to *Diagnostic System Check*	—
6	The malfunction is intermittent or is not present at this time. Refer to Diagnostic Aids for more information. Is the action complete?	—	System OK	—

GC402980343600BX

Fig. 228 Code C1237: High System Supply Voltage (Part 2 of 2). Metro

Circuit Description

DTC C1238 detects a slipping left front ESB. During initialization and braking, the left front brake motor is rehomed. If the ESB slips, the motor/piston will move. During the next key to RUN initialization, a rehome of the motor verifies the motor/piston remained at the home position. If motor movement is detected, the ESB must be slipping.

If an ESB cannot hold a piston in the home position, the piston may be driven back when the brake pedal is applied. Then the brake pedal will drop.

Conditions for Setting the DTC

DTC C1238 can set during initialization at the following speeds:

- 0 km/h (0 mph) when the brake is OFF
- 5 km/h (3 mph) when the brake is ON

A malfunction exists if the EBCM detects that the ESB could not hold the piston in the home position.

Action Taken When the DTC Sets

- A malfunction DTC stores.
- The ABS disables.
- The ABS warning indicator turns ON.

Conditions for Clearing the DTC

- The condition responsible for setting the DTC no longer exists and the Scan Tool Clear DTCs function is used.
- 100 drive cycles pass with no DTCs detected. A drive cycle consists of starting the vehicle, driving the vehicle over 16 km/h (10 mph), stopping and then turning the ignition OFF.

Diagnostic Aids

The following conditions may cause an intermittent malfunction if the conditions exist in a mechanical part of the system:

- Sticking
- Binding
- Slipping

Use the enhanced diagnostic function of the Scan Tool in order to measure the frequency of the malfunction.

Use the hydraulic control modulator test function of the Scan Tool in order to locate an intermittent malfunction associated with the ESB.

Clear the DTCs after completing the diagnosis. Test drive the vehicle for three drive cycles in order to verify that the DTC does not reset. Use the following procedure in order to complete one drive cycle:

1. Start the vehicle.
2. Drive the vehicle over 16 km/h (10 mph).
3. Stop the vehicle.
4. Turn the ignition to the OFF position.

Important: Zero the J 39200 test leads before making any resistance measurements. Refer to the J 39200 user's manual.

GC402980343700AX

Fig. 229 Code C1238: LH Front ESB Does Not Hold Motor (Part 1 of 3). Metro

Step	Action	Value(s)	Yes	No
1	Was the Diagnostic System Check performed?	—	*Go to Step 2*	Refer to *Diagnostic System Check*
2	Inspect the following connectors for the correct wire color/connector cavity combinations: • The 6-way ABS brake motor pack connector • The EBCM connector Are the correct wires located in the correct connector cavities?	—	*Go to Step 3*	*Go to Step 10*
3	1. Turn the ignition switch to the ON position. Do not start the engine. 2. Pump the brake pedal until it is firm in order to deplete the brake booster vacuum reservoir. 3. Install a *Scan Tool.* 4. Select Special Functions on the *Scan Tool.* 5. Select the Manual Control function on the *Scan Tool.* 6. Select the ABS Motor Apply function of the left front ABS channel on the *Scan Tool.* 7. Use the *Scan Tool* in order to apply the left front ABS motor. 8. Wait for five seconds. 9. Apply firm pressure to the brake pedal. Does the brake pedal fall?	—	*Go to Step 9*	*Go to Step 4*
4	1. Use the *Scan Tool* in order to exit the Manual Control function. 2. Turn the ignition switch to the OFF position. 3. Disconnect the following connectors: • The 6-way ABS brake motor pack connector • The EBCM connector 4. Use the *J 39200* in order to measure the resistance between the 6-way ABS brake motor pack harness connector terminal A and the EBCM harness connector terminal G. Is the resistance within the specified range?	0–2 Ω	*Go to Step 5*	*Go to Step 11*
5	Use the *J 39200* in order to measure the resistance between the 6-way ABS brake motor pack harness connector terminal B and the EBCM harness connector terminal H. Is the resistance within the specified range?	0–2 Ω	*Go to Step 6*	*Go to Step 12*
6	Use the *J 39200* in order to measure the resistance between the 6-way ABS brake motor pack connector terminal A and the ABS brake motor pack connector terminal B. Is the resistance within the specified range?	0.2–1.5 Ω	*Go to Step 7*	*Go to Step 9*

GC402980343700BX

Fig. 229 Code C1238: LH Front ESB Does Not Hold Motor (Part 2 of 3). Metro

Step	Action	Value(s)	Yes	No
7	1. Inspect the following connectors: • The 6-way ABS brake motor pack connector • The EBCM connector 2. Inspect the above connectors for the following conditions: • Poor terminal contact • Corrosion Are there signs of poor terminal contact or corrosion?	—	*Go to Step 13*	*Go to Step 8*
8	1. Turn the ignition switch to the OFF position. 2. Reconnect the EBCM connector 3. Reconnect the 6-way ABS brake motor pack connector 4. Start the engine. Do not depress the brake pedal while starting the engine. 5. Allow the engine to run for at least 10 seconds. 6. Repeat the above ignition cycle sequence at least two more times. 7. Use the *Scan Tool* in order to look for DTCs. Does the DTC C1238 set during the last three ignition cycles?	—	*Go to Step 14*	*Go to Step 15*
9	Replace the ABS brake motor pack. Is the repair complete?	—	Refer to *Diagnostic System Check*	—
10	Place the correct wires into the connector cavities. Is the repair complete?	—	Refer to *Diagnostic System Check*	—
11	Repair the open or high resistance in CKT 6C01. Is the repair complete?	—	Refer to *Diagnostic System Check*	—
12	Repair the open or high resistance in CKT 6D01. Is the repair complete?	—	Refer to *Diagnostic System Check*	—
13	Replace the terminals that exhibit signs of poor terminal contact or corrosion. Is the repair complete?	—	Refer to *Diagnostic System Check*	—
14	Replace the EBCM. Is the repair complete?	—	Refer to *Diagnostic System Check*	—
15	The malfunction is intermittent or is not present at this time. Refer to Diagnostic Aids for more information. Is the action complete?	—	System OK	—

GC402980343700CX

Fig. 229 Code C1238: LH Front ESB Does Not Hold Motor (Part 3 of 3). Metro

Circuit Description

DTC C1241 detects a slipping right front ESB. During initialization and braking, the right front brake motor is rehomed. If the ESB slips, the motor/piston will move. During the next key to RUN initialization, a rehome of the motor verifies the motor/piston remained at the home position. If motor movement is detected, the ESB must be slipping.

If an ESB cannot hold a piston in the home position, the piston may be driven back when the brake pedal is applied. Then the brake pedal will drop.

Conditions for Setting the DTC

DTC C1241 can set during initialization at the following speeds:

- 0 km/h (0 mph) when the brake is OFF
- 5 km/h (3 mph) when the brake is ON

A malfunction exists if the EBCM detects that the ESB could not hold the piston in the home position.

DTC C1286 is always set with this DTC.

Action Taken When the DTC Sets

- A malfunction DTC stores.
- The ABS disables.
- The ABS warning indicator turns ON.

Conditions for Clearing the DTC

- The condition responsible for setting the DTC no longer exists and the Scan Tool Clear DTCs function is used.
- 100 drive cycles pass with no DTCs detected. A drive cycle consists of starting the vehicle, driving the vehicle over 16 km/h (10 mph), stopping and then turning the ignition OFF.

Diagnostic Aids

The following conditions may cause an intermittent malfunction if the conditions exist in a mechanical part of the system:

- Sticking
- Binding
- Slipping

Use the enhanced diagnostic function of the Scan Tool in order to measure the frequency of the malfunction.

Use the hydraulic control modulator test function of the Scan Tool in order to locate an intermittent malfunction associated with the ESB.

Clear the DTCs after completing the diagnosis. Test drive the vehicle for three drive cycles in order to verify that the DTC does not reset. Use the following procedure in order to complete one drive cycle:

1. Start the vehicle.
2. Drive the vehicle over 16 km/h (10 mph).
3. Stop the vehicle.
4. Turn the ignition to the OFF position.

Important: Zero the J 39200 test leads before making any resistance measurements.

GC402980343800AX

Fig. 230 Code C1241: RH Front ESB Does Not Hold Motor (Part 1 of 3). Metro

Step	Action	Value(s)	Yes	No
1	Was the Diagnostic System Check performed?	—	*Go to Step 2*	Refer to *Diagnostic System Check*
2	Inspect the following connectors for the correct wire color/connector cavity combinations: • The 6-way ABS brake motor pack connector • The EBCM connector Are the correct wires located in the correct connector cavities?	—	*Go to Step 3*	*Go to Step 10*
3	1. Turn the ignition switch to the ON position. Do not start the engine. 2. Pump the brake pedal until it is firm in order to deplete the brake booster vacuum reservoir. 3. Install a *Scan Tool*. 4. Select the Special Functions on the *Scan Tool*. 5. Select the Manual Control function on the *Scan Tool*. 6. Select the ABS Motor Apply function of the left front ABS channel on the *Scan Tool*. 7. Use the *Scan Tool* in order to apply the left front ABS motor. 8. Wait for five seconds. 9. Apply firm pressure to the brake pedal. Does the brake pedal fall?	—	*Go to Step 9*	*Go to Step 4*
4	1. Use the *Scan Tool* in order to exit the Manual Control function. 2. Turn the ignition switch to the OFF position. 3. Disconnect the following connectors: • The 6-way ABS brake motor pack connector • The EBCM connector 4. Use the *J 39200* in order to measure the resistance between the 6-way ABS brake motor pack harness connector terminal E and the EBCM harness connector terminal A. Is the resistance within the specified range?	0–2 Ω	*Go to Step 5*	*Go to Step 11*
5	Use the *J 39200* in order to measure the resistance between the 6-way ABS brake motor pack harness connector terminal F and the EBCM harness connector terminal B. Is the resistance within the specified range?	0–2 Ω	*Go to Step 6*	*Go to Step 12*
6	Use the *J 39200* in order to measure the resistance between the 6-way ABS brake motor pack connector terminal E and the 6-way ABS brake motor pack connector terminal F. Is the resistance within the specified range?	0.2–1.5 Ω	*Go to Step 7*	*Go to Step 9*

GC402980343800BX

Fig. 230 Code C1241: RH Front ESB Does Not Hold Motor (Part 2 of 3). Metro

Circuit Description

DTC C1242 detects a slipping rear axle ESB. During initialization and braking, the rear motor is rehomed. If the ESB slips, the motor/piston will move. During the next key to RUN initialization, a rehome of the motor verifies the motor/piston remained at the home position. If motor movement is detected, the ESB must be slipping.

If an ESB cannot hold a piston in the home position, the piston may be driven back when the brake pedal is applied. Then the brake pedal will drop.

DTC C1286 is always set with this DTC.

Conditions for Setting the DTC

DTC C1242 can set during initialization at the following speeds:

- 0 km/h (0 mph) when the brake is OFF
- 5 km/h (3 mph) when the brake is ON

A malfunction exists if the EBCM detects that the ESB could not hold the piston in the home position.

DTC C1286 always sets with DTC C1242.

Action Taken When the DTC Sets

- A malfunction DTC stores.
- The ABS disables.
- The ABS warning indicator turns ON.

Conditions for Clearing the DTC

- The condition responsible for setting the DTC no longer exists and the Scan Tool Clear DTCs function is used.
- 100 drive cycles pass with no DTCs detected. A drive cycle consists of starting the vehicle, driving the vehicle over 16 km/h (10 mph), stopping and then turning the ignition OFF.

Diagnostic Aids

The following conditions may cause an intermittent malfunction if the conditions exist in a mechanical part of the system:

- Sticking
- Binding
- Slipping

Use the enhanced diagnostic function of the Scan Tool in order to measure the frequency of the malfunction.

Use the hydraulic control modulator test function of the Scan Tool in order to locate an intermittent malfunction associated with the ESB.

Clear the DTCs after completing the diagnosis. Test drive the vehicle for three drive cycles in order to verify that the DTC does not reset. Use the following procedure in order to complete one drive cycle:

1. Start the vehicle.
2. Drive the vehicle over 16 km/h (10 mph).
3. Stop the vehicle.
4. Turn the ignition to the OFF position.

Important: Zero the J 39200 test leads before making any resistance measurements.

GC402980343900AX

Fig. 231 Code C1242: Rear ESB Does Not Hold Motor (Part 1 of 3). Metro

Step	Action	Value(s)	Yes	No
7	1. Inspect the following connectors: • The 6-way ABS brake motor pack connector • The EBCM connector 2. Inspect the above connectors for the following conditions: • Poor terminal contact • Corrosion Are there signs of poor terminal contact or corrosion?	—	*Go to Step 13*	*Go to Step 8*
8	1. Turn the ignition switch to the OFF position. 2. Reconnect the EBCM connector. 3. Reconnect the 6-way ABS brake motor pack connector. 4. Start the engine. Do not depress the brake pedal while starting the engine. 5. Allow the engine to run for at least 10 seconds. 6. Repeat the above ignition cycle sequence at least two more times. 7. Use the *Scan Tool* in order to look for DTCs. Does the DTC C1241 set during the last three ignition cycles?	—	*Go to Step 14*	*Go to Step 15*
9	Replace the ABS brake motor pack. Is the repair complete?	—	Refer to *Diagnostic System Check*	—
10	Place the correct wires into the connector cavities. Is the repair complete?	—	Refer to *Diagnostic System Check*	—
11	Repair the open or high resistance in CKT 6G01. Is the repair complete?	—	Refer to *Diagnostic System Check*	—
12	Repair the open or high resistance in CKT 6H01. Is the repair complete?	—	Refer to *Diagnostic System Check*	—
13	Replace the terminals that exhibit signs of poor terminal contact or corrosion. Is the repair complete?	—	Refer to *Diagnostic System Check*	—
14	Replace the EBCM. Is the repair complete?	—	Refer to *Diagnostic System Check*	—
15	The malfunction is intermittent or is not present at this time. Refer to Diagnostic Aids for more information. Is the action complete?	—	System OK	—

GC402980343800CX

Fig. 230 Code C1241: RH Front ESB Does Not Hold Motor (Part 3 of 3). Metro

Step	Action	Value(s)	Yes	No
1	Was the Diagnostic System Check performed?	—	*Go to Step 2*	Refer to *Diagnostic System Check*
2	Inspect the following connectors for the correct wire color/connector cavity combinations: • The 6-way ABS brake motor pack connector • The EBCM connector Are the correct wires located in the correct connector cavities?	—	*Go to Step 3*	*Go to Step 10*
3	1. Turn the ignition switch to the ON position. Do not start the engine. 2. Pump the brake pedal until it is firm in order to deplete the brake booster vacuum reservoir. 3. Raise and support the vehicle so that the rear wheels are approximately 6 inches off the floor. 4. Turn the ignition switch to the ON position. 5. Install a *Scan Tool*. 6. Apply firm pressure to the brake pedal. 7. Select the Special Functions on the *Scan Tool*. 8. Select the Manual Control function on the *Scan Tool*. 9. Select the ABS Motor Apply function of the rear ABS channel on the *Scan Tool*. 10. Use the *Scan Tool* in order to apply the rear ABS motor. 11. Wait for five seconds. 12. Have an assistant try to spin the rear wheels by hand. Could the assistant spin the rear wheels?	—	*Go to Step 9*	*Go to Step 4*
4	1. Exit the Manual Control function. 2. Turn the ignition switch to the OFF position. 3. Disconnect the following connectors: • The 6-way ABS brake motor pack connector • The EBCM connector 4. Use the *J 39200* in order to measure the resistance between the 6-way ABS brake motor pack harness connector terminal C and the EBCM harness connector terminal F. Is the resistance within the specified range?	0–2 Ω	*Go to Step 5*	*Go to Step 11*
5	Use the *J 39200* in order to measure the resistance between the 6-way ABS brake motor pack harness connector terminal D and the EBCM harness connector terminal E. Is the resistance within the specified range?	0–2 Ω	*Go to Step 6*	*Go to Step 12*
6	Use the *J 39200* in order to measure the resistance between the 6-way ABS brake motor pack connector terminal C and the 6-way ABS brake motor pack connector terminal D. Is the resistance within the specified range?	0.2–1.5 Ω	*Go to Step 7*	*Go to Step 9*

GC402980343900BX

Fig. 231 Code C1242: Rear ESB Does Not Hold Motor (Part 2 of 3). Metro

Step	Action	Value(s)	Yes	No
7	1. Inspect the following connectors: • The 6-way ABS brake motor pack connector • The EBCM connector 2. Inspect the above connectors for the following conditions: • Poor terminal contact • Corrosion Are there signs of poor terminal contact or corrosion?	—	*Go to Step 13*	*Go to Step 8*
8	1. Turn the ignition switch to the OFF position. 2. Reconnect the EBCM connector 3. Reconnect the 6-way ABS brake motor pack connector 4. Start the engine. Do not depress the brake pedal while starting the engine. 5. Allow the engine to run for at least 10 seconds. 6. Repeat the above ignition cycle sequence at least two more times. 7. Use the *Scan Tool* in order to look for DTCs. Does the DTC C1242 set during the last three ignition cycles?	—	*Go to Step 14*	*Go to Step 15*
9	Replace the ABS brake motor pack. Is the repair complete?	—	Refer to *Diagnostic System Check*	—
10	Place the correct wires into the connector cavities. Is the repair complete?	—	Refer to *Diagnostic System Check*	—
11	Repair the open or high resistance in CKT 6E01. Is the repair complete?	—	Refer to *Diagnostic System Check*	—
12	Repair the open or high resistance in CKT 6F01. Is the repair complete?	—	Refer to *Diagnostic System Check*	—
13	Replace the terminals that exhibit signs of poor terminal contact or corrosion. Is the repair complete?	—	Refer to *Diagnostic System Check*	—
14	Replace the EBCM. Is the repair complete?	—	Refer to *Diagnostic System Check*	—
15	The malfunction is intermittent or is not present at this time. Refer to Diagnostic Aids for more information. Is the action complete?	—	System OK	—

GC402980343900CX

Fig. 231 Code C1242: Rear ESB Does Not Hold Motor (Part 3 of 3). Metro

Step	Action	Value(s)	Yes	No
1	Was the Diagnostic System Check performed?	—	*Go to Step 2*	Refer to *Diagnostic System Check*
2	Inspect the following connectors for the correct wire color/connector cavity combinations: • The 6-way ABS brake motor pack connector • The EBCM connector Are the correct wires located in the correct connector cavities?	—	*Go to Step 3*	*Go to Step 11*
3	1. Turn the ignition switch to the ON position. Do not start the engine. 2. Pump the brake pedal until the brake pedal is firm in order to deplete the brake booster vacuum reservoir. 3. Install a *Scan Tool.* 4. Select Special Functions on the *Scan Tool.* 5. Select the Manual Control function on the *Scan Tool.* 6. Select the ABS Motor Apply function of the left front ABS channel on the *Scan Tool.* 7. Use the *Scan Tool* in order to apply the left front ABS motor. 8. Wait for five seconds. 9. Apply firm pressure to the brake pedal. 10. Select the left front ABS Motor Release function on the *Scan Tool.* 11. Use the *Scan Tool* in order to release the left front ABS motor. Does the brake pedal fall?	—	*Go to Step 4*	*Go to Step 5*
4	1. Continue to apply firm pressure on the brake pedal. 2. Select the left front ABS Motor Apply function on the *Scan Tool.* 3. Use the *Scan Tool* in order to apply the left front ABS motor. Does the brake pedal rise?	—	*Go to Step 17*	*Go to Step 5*
5	1. Remove the firm pressure from the brake pedal. 2. Select the left front ABS Motor Apply function on the *Scan Tool.* 3. Use the *Scan Tool* in order to apply the left front ABS motor. 4. Carefully observe the following currents: • The left front ABS motor commanded current • The left front ABS motor feedback current. Did the left front ABS motor feedback current momentarily drop below the specified current?	8 A	*Go to Step 6*	*Go to Step 10*
6	1. Exit the Manual Control function on the *Scan Tool.* 2. Turn the ignition switch to the OFF position. 3. Disconnect the 6-way ABS brake motor pack connector. 4. Disconnect the EBCM connector 5. Use the *J 39200* in order to measure the resistance between the EBCM connector terminal G and the EBCM connector terminal H. Is the resistance within the specified range?	OL (Infinite)	*Go to Step 7*	*Go to Step 12*

GC402980344000BX

Fig. 232 Code C1244: LH Front ABS Channel Does Not Move (Part 2 of 4). Metro

Circuit Description

DTC C1244 detects a bound-up ESB, a stuck ABS motor, or a seized brake modulator. When the release is commanded during initialization, the ESB should release the ABS motor, resulting in the sensed current being less than the commanded current (motor spins freely). If the ABS motor is not moving, sensed current will be equal to stall currents.

Conditions for Setting the DTC

DTC C1244 can set during brake motor initialization at the following speeds:

- 0 km/h (0 mph) when the brake is OFF
- 5 km/h (3 mph) when the brake is ON

DTC C1244 can set during ABS stops

A malfunction exists if the EBCM detects a condition in which the EBCM cannot move the ABS motor in either direction.

If the motor pack was removed from the hydraulic modulator without performing the scan tool's Gear Tension Relief function, this DTC may set after motor pack-to-hydraulic modulator reassembly.

Action Taken When the DTC Sets

- A malfunction DTC stores.
- The ABS disables.
- The ABS warning indicator turns ON.
- The red BRAKE warning indicator turns ON.

Conditions for Clearing the DTC

- The condition responsible for setting the DTC no longer exists and the Scan Tool Clear DTCs function is used.
- 100 drive cycles pass with no DTCs detected. A drive cycle consists of starting the vehicle, driving the vehicle over 16 km/h (10 mph), stopping and then turning the ignition OFF.

Diagnostic Aids

The following conditions may cause an intermittent malfunction if the conditions exist in a mechanical part of the system:

- Sticking
- Binding
- Slipping

Use the enhanced diagnostic function of the Scan Tool in order to measure the frequency of the malfunction. DTC C1244 may set after modulator disassembly if the modulator pistons are positioned at the bottom of the modulator piston bore.

Thoroughly inspect any circuitry that may be causing the intermittent complaint for the following conditions:

- Backed out terminals
- Improper mating
- Broken locks
- Improperly formed or damaged terminals
- Poor terminal-to-wiring connections
- Physical damage to the wiring harness

Clear the DTCs after completing the diagnosis. Test drive the vehicle for three drive cycles in order to verify that the DTC does not reset. Use the following procedure in order to complete one drive cycle:

1. Start the vehicle.
2. Drive the vehicle over 16 km/h (10 mph).
3. Stop the vehicle.
4. Turn the ignition to the OFF position.

Important: Zero the J 39200 test leads before making any resistance measurements.

GC402980344000AX

Fig. 232 Code C1244: LH Front ABS Channel Does Not Move (Part 1 of 4). Metro

Step	Action	Value(s)	Yes	No
7	Use the *J 39200* in order to measure the resistance between the 6-way ABS brake motor pack connector terminal A and the 6-way ABS brake motor pack connector terminal B. Is the resistance within the specified range?	0.2–1.5 Ω	*Go to Step 8*	*Go to Step 13*
8	1. Inspect the following connectors: • The 6-way ABS motor pack connector • The EBCM connector 2. Inspect the connectors for the following conditions: • Poor terminal contact • Corrosion Do any of the terminals exhibit poor terminal contact or corrosion?	—	*Go to Step 15*	*Go to Step 9*
9	1. Turn the ignition switch to the OFF position. 2. Reconnect the EBCM connector. 3. Reconnect the ABS motor pack connector. 4. Start the engine. Do not depress the brake pedal. 5. Allow the engine to run for at least ten seconds. 6. Repeat the above ignition cycle sequence two more times. 7. Use the *Scan Tool* in order to inspect for DTCs. Does DTC C1244 set during the last three ignition cycles?	—	*Go to Step 16*	*Go to Step 17*
10	1. Select Special Functions on the *Scan Tool.* 2. Use the *Scan Tool* in order to perform the Gear Tension Relief function. 3. Turn the ignition switch to the OFF position. 4. Remove the brake modulator assembly from the vehicle. 5. Separate the ABS brake motor pack from the brake modulator. 6. Grasp the left front brake modulator gear and attempt to rotate the gear. (The ABS brake modulator left front gear is the gear that is closest to the front when the ABS brake modulator is mounted in the vehicle.) Is it possible to rotate the left front brake modulator gear at least 8.5 full revolutions from lock to lock?	—	*Go to Step 13*	*Go to Step 14*
11	Place the wires into the correct connector cavities. Is the repair complete?	—	Refer to *Diagnostic System Check*	—
12	Repair the short between CKT 6C01 and CKT 6D01. Is the repair complete?	—	Refer to *Diagnostic System Check*	—
13	Replace the ABS motor pack. Is the repair complete?	—	Refer to *Diagnostic System Check*	—
14	Replace the brake modulator. Is the repair complete?	—	Refer to *Diagnostic System Check*	—

GC402980344000CX

Fig. 232 Code C1244: LH Front ABS Channel Does Not Move (Part 3 of 4). Metro

Step	Action	Value(s)	Yes	No
15	Replace the terminals that exhibit signs of poor terminal contact or corrosion. Is the repair complete?	—	Refer to *Diagnostic System Check*	—
16	Replace the EBCM. Is the repair complete?	—	Refer to *Diagnostic System Check*	—
17	The malfunction is intermittent or is not present at this time. Refer to Diagnostic Aids for more information. Is the action complete?	—	System OK	—

GC402980344000DX

Fig. 232 Code C1244: LH Front ABS Channel Does Not Move (Part 4 of 4). Metro

Step	Action	Value(s)	Yes	No
1	Was the Diagnostic System Check performed?	—	*Go to Step 2*	Refer to *Diagnostic System Check*
2	Inspect the following connectors for the correct wire color/connector cavity combinations: • The 6-way ABS brake motor pack connector • The EBCM connector Are the correct wires located in the correct connector cavities?	—	*Go to Step 3*	*Go to Step 11*
3	1. Turn the ignition switch to the ON position. Do not start the engine. 2. Pump the brake pedal until it is firm in order to deplete the brake booster vacuum reservoir. 3. Install a *Scan Tool*. 4. Select Special Functions on the *Scan Tool*. 5. Select the Manual Control function on the *Scan Tool*. 6. Select the ABS Motor Apply function of the right front ABS channel on the *Scan Tool*. 7. Use the *Scan Tool* to apply the right front ABS motor. 8. Wait for five seconds. 9. Apply firm pressure to the brake pedal. 10. Select the right front ABS Motor Release function on the *Scan Tool*. 11. Use the *Scan Tool* in order to release the right front ABS motor. Does the brake pedal fall?	—	*Go to Step 4*	*Go to Step 5*
4	1. Continue to apply firm pressure on the brake pedal. 2. Select the right front ABS Motor Apply function on the *Scan Tool*. 3. Use the *Scan Tool* in order to apply the right front ABS motor. Does the brake pedal rise?	—	*Go to Step 17*	*Go to Step 5*
5	1. Remove the firm pressure from the brake pedal. 2. Select the right front ABS Motor Apply function on the *Scan Tool*. 3. Use the *Scan Tool* in order to apply the right front ABS motor. 4. Carefully observe the following currents: • The right front ABS motor commanded current • The right front ABS motor feedback current. Did the right front ABS motor feedback current Momentarily drop below the specified current?	8 A	*Go to Step 6*	*Go to Step 10*
6	1. Exit the Manual Control function on the *Scan Tool*. 2. Turn the ignition switch to the OFF position. 3. Disconnect the 6-way ABS brake motor pack connector. 4. Disconnect the EBCM connector 5. Use the *J 39200* in order to measure the resistance between the EBCM connector terminal A and the EBCM connector terminal B. Is the resistance within the specified range?	OL (Infinite)	*Go to Step 7*	*Go to Step 12*

GC402980344100BX

Fig. 233 Code C1245: RH Front ABS Channel Does Not Move (Part 2 of 4). Metro

Circuit Description

DTC C1245 detects a bound-up ESB, a stuck ABS motor, or a seized brake modulator. When the release is commanded during initialization, the ESB should release the ABS motor, resulting in the feedback current being less than the commanded current (motor spins freely). If the ABS motor is not moving, feedback current will be equal to commanded current.

Conditions for Setting the DTC

DTC C1245 can set during brake motor initialization at the following speeds:

- 0 km/h (0 mph) when the brake is OFF
- 5 km/h (3 mph) when the brake is ON

DTC C1245 can set during ABS stops

A malfunction exists if the EBCM detects a condition in which the EBCM cannot move the ABS motor in either direction.

If the motor pack was removed from the hydraulic modulator without performing the scan tool's Gear Tension Relief function, this DTC may set after motor pack-to-hydraulic modulator reassembly.

Action Taken When the DTC Sets

- A malfunction DTC stores.
- The ABS disables.
- The ABS warning indicator turns ON.

Conditions for Clearing the DTC

- The condition responsible for setting the DTC no longer exists and the Scan Tool Clear DTCs function is used.
- 100 drive cycles pass with no DTCs detected. A drive cycle consists of starting the vehicle, driving the vehicle over 16 km/h (10 mph), stopping and then turning the ignition OFF.

Diagnostic Aids

The following conditions may cause an intermittent malfunction if the conditions exist in a mechanical part of the system:

- Sticking
- Binding
- Slipping

Use the enhanced diagnostic function of the Scan Tool in order to measure the frequency of the malfunction. DTC C1245 may set after modulator disassembly if the modulator pistons are positioned at the bottom of the modulator piston bore.

Thoroughly inspect any circuitry that may be causing the intermittent complaint for the following conditions:

- Backed out terminals
- Improper mating
- Broken locks
- Improperly formed or damaged terminals
- Poor terminal-to-wiring connections
- Physical damage to the wiring harness

Clear the DTCs after completing the diagnosis. Test drive the vehicle for three drive cycles in order to verify that the DTC does not reset. Use the following procedure in order to complete one drive cycle:

1. Start the vehicle.
2. Drive the vehicle over 16 km/h (10 mph).
3. Stop the vehicle.
4. Turn the ignition to the OFF position.

Important: Zero the J 39200 test leads before making any resistance measurements.

GC402980344100AX

Fig. 233 Code C1245: RH Front ABS Channel Does Not Move (Part 1 of 4). Metro

Step	Action	Value(s)	Yes	No
7	Use the *J 39200* in order to measure the resistance between the ABS brake motor pack connector terminal E and the ABS brake motor pack connector terminal F. Is the resistance within the specified range?	0.2–1.5 Ω	*Go to Step 8*	*Go to Step 13*
8	1. Inspect the following connectors: • The 6-way ABS motor pack connector • The EBCM connector 2. Inspect the connectors for the following conditions: • Poor terminal contact • Corrosion Do any of the terminals exhibit poor terminal contact or corrosion?	—	*Go to Step 15*	*Go to Step 9*
9	1. Turn the ignition switch to the OFF position. 2. Reconnect the EBCM connector. 3. Reconnect the ABS motor pack connector. 4. Start the engine. Do not depress the brake pedal. 5. Allow the engine to run for at least ten seconds. 6. Repeat the above ignition cycle sequence two more times. 7. Use the *Scan Tool* in order to inspect for DTCs. Does DTC C1245 set during the last three ignition cycles?	—	*Go to Step 16*	*Go to Step 17*
10	1. Select Special Functions on the *Scan Tool*. 2. Use the *Scan Tool* in order to perform the Gear Tension Relief function. 3. Turn the ignition switch to the OFF position. 4. Remove the brake modulator assembly from the vehicle. 5. Separate the ABS brake motor pack from the brake modulator. 6. Grasp the right front brake modulator gear and attempt to rotate the gear. (The ABS brake modulator right front gear is the gear that is closest to the rear when the ABS brake modulator is mounted in the vehicle.) Is it possible to rotate the right front brake modulator gear at least 8.5 full revolutions from lock to lock?	—	*Go to Step 13*	*Go to Step 14*
11	Place the wires into the correct connector cavities. Is the repair complete?	—	Refer to *Diagnostic System Check*	—
12	Repair the short between CKT 6G01 and CKT 6H01. Is the repair complete?	—	Refer to *Diagnostic System Check*	—
13	Replace the ABS motor pack. Is the repair complete?	—	Refer to *Diagnostic System Check*	—

GC402980344100CX

Fig. 233 Code C1245: RH Front ABS Channel Does Not Move (Part 3 of 4). Metro

Step	Action	Value(s)	Yes	No
14	Replace the brake modulator. Is the repair complete?	—	Refer to *Diagnostic System Check*	—
15	Replace the terminals that exhibit signs of poor terminal contact or corrosion. Is the repair complete?	—	Refer to *Diagnostic System Check*	—
16	Replace the EBCM. Is the repair complete?	—	Refer to *Diagnostic System Check*	—
17	The malfunction is intermittent or is not present at this time. Refer to Diagnostic Aids for more information. Is the action complete?	—	System OK	—

GC402980344100DX

Fig. 233 Code C1245: RH Front ABS Channel Does Not Move (Part 4 of 4). Metro

Step	Action	Value(s)	Yes	No
1	Was the Diagnostic System Check performed?	—	*Go to Step 2*	Refer to *Diagnostic System Check*
2	Inspect the following connectors for the correct wire color/connector cavity combinations: • The 6-way ABS brake motor pack connector • The EBCM connector Are the correct wires located in the correct connector cavities?	—	*Go to Step 3*	*Go to Step 11*
3	1. Raise and suitably support the vehicle. Verify that the rear wheels are approximately 15 cm (six inches) above the floor. 2. Turn the ignition switch to the ON position. Do not start the engine. 3. Pump the brake pedal until it is firm in order to deplete the brake booster vacuum reservoir. 4. Install a *Scan Tool.* 5. Apply firm downward pressure on the brake pedal. 6. Select Special Functions on the *Scan Tool.* 7. Select the Manual Control function on the *Scan Tool.* 8. Select the Rear Motor Apply function of the rear ABS channel on the *Scan Tool.* 9. Use the *Scan Tool* in order to apply the rear motor. 10. Have an assistant attempt to rotate the rear wheels by hand. Is it possible to rotate the rear wheels by hand?	—	*Go to Step 5*	*Go to Step 4*
4	1. Continue to apply firm downward pressure on the brake pedal. 2. Select the Rear Motor Release function on the *Scan Tool.* 3. Use the *Scan Tool* in order to release the rear motor. Is it possible to rotate the rear wheels by hand?	—	*Go to Step 17*	*Go to Step 5*
5	1. Remove the firm pressure from the brake pedal. 2. Select the Rear Motor Apply function on the *Scan Tool.* 3. Use the *Scan Tool* in order to apply the rear axle motor. 4. Carefully observe the following currents: • The rear motor commanded current • The rear motor feedback current. Did the rear motor feedback current momentarily drop below the specified current?	8 A	*Go to Step 6*	*Go to Step 10*

GC402980344200BX

Fig. 234 Code C1246: Rear ABS Channel Does Not Move (Part 2 of 4). Metro

Circuit Description

DTC C1246 detects a bound-up ESB, a stuck ABS motor, or a seized brake modulator. When the release is commanded during initialization, the ESB should release the ABS motor, resulting in the feedback current being less than the commanded current (motor spins freely). If the ABS motor is not moving, feedback current will be equal to commanded current.

Conditions for Setting the DTC

DTC C1246 can set during brake motor initialization at the following speeds:

- 0 km/h (0 mph) when the brake is OFF
- 5 km/h (3 mph) when the brake is ON

DTC C1246 can set during ABS stops

A malfunction exists if the EBCM detects a condition in which the EBCM cannot move the ABS motor in either direction.

If the motor pack was removed from the hydraulic modulator without performing the scan tool's Gear Tension Relief function, this DTC may set after motor pack-to-hydraulic modulator reassembly.

Action Taken When the DTC Sets

- A malfunction DTC stores.
- The ABS disables.
- The ABS warning indicator turns ON.

Conditions for Clearing the DTC

- The condition responsible for setting the DTC no longer exists and the Scan Tool Clear DTCs function is used.
- 100 drive cycles pass with no DTCs detected. A drive cycle consists of starting the vehicle, driving the vehicle over 16 km/h (10 mph), stopping and then turning the ignition OFF.

Diagnostic Aids

The following conditions may cause an intermittent malfunction if the conditions exist in a mechanical part of the system:

- Sticking
- Binding

Use the enhanced diagnostic function of the Scan Tool in order to measure the frequency of the malfunction. DTC C1246 may set after modulator disassembly if the modulator pistons are positioned at the bottom of the modulator piston bore. Depending on the frequency of the malfunction, a physical inspection of the mechanical parts suspected of causing the malfunction may be necessary.

Thoroughly inspect any circuitry that may be causing the intermittent complaint for the following conditions:

- Backed out terminals
- Improper mating
- Broken locks
- Improperly formed or damaged terminals
- Poor terminal-to-wiring connections
- Physical damage to the wiring harness

Clear the DTCs after completing the diagnosis. Test drive the vehicle for three drive cycles in order to verify that the DTC does not reset. Use the following procedure in order to complete one drive cycle:

1. Start the vehicle.
2. Drive the vehicle over 16 km/h (10 mph).
3. Stop the vehicle.
4. Turn the ignition to the OFF position.

Important: Zero the J 39200 test leads before making any resistance measurements.

GC402980344200AX

Fig. 234 Code C1246: Rear ABS Channel Does Not Move (Part 1 of 4). Metro

Step	Action	Value(s)	Yes	No
6	1. Exit the Manual Control function on the *Scan Tool.* 2. Turn the ignition switch to the OFF position. 3. Disconnect the 6-way ABS brake motor pack connector. 4. Disconnect the EBCM connector. 5. Use the *J 39200* in order to measure the resistance between the EBCM connector terminal F and the EBCM connector terminal E. Is the resistance within the specified range?	OL (Infinite)	*Go to Step 7*	*Go to Step 12*
7	Use the *J 39200* in order to measure the resistance between the ABS brake motor pack connector terminal C and the ABS brake motor pack connector terminal D. Is the resistance within the specified range?	0.2–1.5 Ω	*Go to Step 8*	*Go to Step 13*
8	1. Inspect the following connectors: • The 6-way ABS motor pack connector • The EBCM connector 2. Inspect the connectors for the following conditions: • Poor terminal contact • Corrosion Do any of the terminals exhibit poor terminal contact or corrosion?	—	*Go to Step 15*	*Go to Step 9*
9	1. Turn the ignition switch to the OFF position. 2. Reconnect the EBCM connector. 3. Reconnect the ABS motor pack connector. 4. Start the engine. Do not depress the brake pedal. 5. Allow the engine to run for at least ten seconds. 6. Repeat the above ignition cycle sequence two more times. 7. Use the *Scan Tool* in order to inspect for DTCs. Does DTC C1246 set during the last three ignition cycles?	—	*Go to Step 16*	*Go to Step 17*
10	1. Select Special Functions on the *Scan Tool.* 2. Use the *Scan Tool* in order to perform the Gear Tension Relief function. 3. Turn the ignition switch to the OFF position. 4. Remove the hydraulic modulator assembly from the vehicle. 5. Separate the ABS brake motor pack from the hydraulic modulator. 6. Grasp the middle gear on the hydraulic modulator and attempt to rotate the gear. Is it possible to rotate the middle gear on the hydraulic modulator at least seven full revolutions from lock to lock?	—	*Go to Step 13*	*Go to Step 14*
11	Place the wires into the correct connector cavities. Is the repair complete?	—	Refer to *Diagnostic System Check*	—
12	Repair the short between CKT 6E01 and CKT 6F01. Is the repair complete?	—	Refer to *Diagnostic System Check*	—
13	Replace the ABS motor pack. Is the repair complete?	—	Refer to *Diagnostic System Check*	—

GC402980344200CX

Fig. 234 Code C1246: Rear ABS Channel Does Not Move (Part 3 of 4). Metro

Step	Action	Value(s)	Yes	No
14	Replace the hydraulic modulator. Is the repair complete?	—	Refer to *Diagnostic System Check*	—
15	Replace the terminals that exhibit signs of poor terminal contact or corrosion. Is the repair complete?	—	Refer to *Diagnostic System Check*	—
16	Replace the EBCM. Is the repair complete?	—	Refer to *Diagnostic System Check*	—
17	The malfunction is intermittent or is not present at this time. Refer to Diagnostic Aids for more information. Is the action complete?	—	System OK	—

GC402980344200DX

Fig. 234 Code C1246: Rear ABS Channel Does Not Move (Part 4 of 4). Metro

Step	Action	Value(s)	Yes	No
1	Was the Diagnostic System Check performed?	—	*Go to Step 2*	Refer to *Diagnostic System Check*
2	1. Turn the ignition switch to the ON position. Do not start the engine. 2. Use the *Scan Tool* in order to read the DTCs. Does DTC C1256 also set as a current DTC?	—	Refer to *DTC C1256 Left Front ABS Motor Circuit Open*	*Go to Step 3*
3	1. Raise and suitably support the vehicle. Verify that the rear wheels are approximately 15 cm (6 in) above the floor. 2. Pump the brake pedal until it is firm in order to deplete the brake booster vacuum reservoir. 3. Install a *Scan Tool*. 4. Apply firm downward pressure on the brake pedal. 5. Select Special Functions on the *Scan Tool*. 6. Select the Manual Control function on the *Scan Tool*. 7. Select the ABS Motor Apply function on the *Scan Tool*. 8. Use the *Scan Tool* to apply the left front motor. 9. Observe the following currents: • The left front ABS motor command current • The left front ABS motor feedback current Were the left front ABS motor command current and the left front ABS motor feedback current approximately the specified current?	10 A	*Go to Step 4*	*Go to Step 6*
4	1. Apply firm pressure to the brake pedal. 2. Select the left front ABS Motor Release function on the *Scan Tool*. 3. Use the *Scan Tool* in order to release the left front ABS motor. 4. Observe the following currents: • The left front ABS motor command current • The left front ABS motor feedback current Have the following conditions been met? • The left front ABS motor command current and the left front ABS motor feedback current approximately the specified current • The brake pedal falls	6 A	*Go to Step 5*	*Go to Step 6*
5	1. Continue to apply firm pressure to the brake pedal. 2. Select the left front ABS Motor Apply function on the *Scan Tool*. 3. Use the *Scan Tool* in order to apply the left front ABS motor. Did the brake pedal rise?	—	*Go to Step 22*	*Go to Step 6*

GC402980344300BX

Fig. 235 Code C1247: LH Front ABS Motor Free Spins (Part 2 of 5). Metro

Circuit Description

DTC C1247 detects a stripped nut or gear assembly during initialization. During the homing sequence, the piston should reach the top of the bore. Then the ABS motor stalls. If the ABS motor does not stall, the ABS motor must be spinning with little or no resistance. This indicates a nut/screw or gear malfunction.

Conditions for Setting the DTC

- DTC C1247 can only set during initialization.
- A malfunction exists if the feedback current is less than the command current for a specified period of time.

Action Taken When the DTC Sets

- A malfunction DTC stores.
- The ABS disables.
- The ABS warning indicator turns ON.

Conditions for Clearing the DTC

- The condition responsible for setting the DTC no longer exists and the Scan Tool Clear DTCs function is used.
- 100 drive cycles pass with no DTCs detected. A drive cycle consists of starting the vehicle, driving the vehicle over 16 km/h (10 mph), stopping and then turning the ignition OFF.

Diagnostic Aids

The following conditions may cause an intermittent malfunction if the conditions exist in a mechanical part of the system:

- Sticking
- Binding
- Slipping

Use the enhanced diagnostic function of the Scan Tool in order to measure the frequency of the malfunction. DTC C1247 may set after modulator disassembly if the modulator pistons are positioned at the bottom of the modulator piston bore. If DTC C1247 only occurs once and DTC C1256 also occurs, refer to DTC C1256. If intermittent and enhanced diagnostics shows this DTC occurs during ABS, refer to DTC C1256.

Depending on the frequency of the malfunction, a physical inspection of the mechanical parts suspected of causing the malfunction may be necessary.

Clear the DTCs after completing the diagnosis. Test drive the vehicle for three drive cycles in order to verify that the DTC does not reset. Use the following procedure in order to complete one drive cycle:

1. Start the vehicle.
2. Drive the vehicle over 16 km/h (10 mph).
3. Stop the vehicle.
4. Turn the ignition to the OFF position.

Important: Zero the J 39200 test leads before making any resistance measurements.

GC402980344300AX

Fig. 235 Code C1247: LH Front ABS Motor Free Spins (Part 1 of 5). Metro

Step	Action	Value(s)	Yes	No
6	1. Turn the ignition switch to the OFF position. 2. Disconnect the 6-way ABS brake motor pack connector. 3. Disconnect the EBCM connector 4. Use the *J 39200* in order to measure the resistance between the 6-way ABS brake motor pack connector terminal A and the EBCM connector terminal G. Is the resistance within the specified range?	0–2 Ω	*Go to Step 7*	*Go to Step 15*
7	Use the *J 39200* in order to measure the resistance between the 6-way ABS brake motor pack connector terminal B and the EBCM connector terminal H. Is the resistance within the specified range?	0–2 Ω	*Go to Step 8*	*Go to Step 16*
8	Use the *J 39200* in order to measure the resistance between the 6-way ABS brake motor pack connector terminal A and the 6-way ABS brake motor pack connector terminal B. Is the resistance within the specified range?	0.2–1.5 Ω	*Go to Step 9*	*Go to Step 17*
9	1. Remove the ABS brake modulator assembly from the vehicle. 2. Remove the ABS brake modulator gear cover. 3. Inspect for a stripped ABS brake motor pack left front gear. (The ABS brake motor pack is the unit with the three small gears. The ABS brake motor pack left front gear is the gear closest to the front when the ABS brake modulator is mounted in the vehicle.) Is the ABS brake motor left front gear stripped?	—	*Go to Step 17*	*Go to Step 10*
10	Inspect for a stripped ABS brake modulator pack left front gear. (The ABS brake modulator unit is the unit with the three large gears. The ABS brake modulator left front gear is the gear closest to the front when the ABS brake modulator is mounted in the vehicle.) Is the ABS brake modulator left front gear stripped?	—	*Go to Step 18*	*Go to Step 11*

GC402980344300CX

Fig. 235 Code C1247: LH Front ABS Motor Free Spins (Part 3 of 5). Metro

Step	Action	Value(s)	Yes	No
11	1. Reconnect the 6-way ABS brake motor pack connector. 2. Reconnect the EBCM connector. 3. Carefully secure the ABS brake modulator into the vehicle. Secure the assembly in a position that permits observation of the gears. 4. Turn the ignition switch to the ON position. Do not start the engine. 5. Select the Manual Control function on the *Scan Tool*. 6. Select the left front ABS Motor Apply function on the *Scan Tool*. 7. Use the *Scan Tool* in order to apply the left front ABS motor while observing the ABS brake modulator left front gear set. (The ABS brake modulator left front gear is the gear closest to the front when the ABS brake modulator is mounted in the vehicle.) 8. Select the left front ABS Motor Release function on the *Scan Tool*. 9. Use the *Scan Tool* in order to release the left front ABS motor while observing the ABS brake modulator left front gear set. 10. Select the left front ABS Motor Apply function on the *Scan Tool*. 11. Use the *Scan Tool* in order to apply the left front ABS motor while observing the ABS brake modulator left front gear set. Does the ABS brake modulator left front gear set move at least one full revolution in both directions?	—	*Go to Step 12*	*Go to Step 17*
12	1. Use the *Scan Tool* in order to perform the Gear Tension Relief function. 2. Turn the ignition switch to the OFF position. 3. Separate the ABS brake motor pack from the ABS brake modulator. 4. Grasp the ABS brake modulator left front gear. 5. Rotate the ABS brake modulator left front gear. Does the ABS brake modulator left front gear rotate more than 13 full turns from lock to lock?	—	*Go to Step 19*	*Go to Step 13*
13	1. Disconnect the 6-way ABS brake motor pack connector. 2. Disconnect the EBCM connector. 3. Inspect the connectors for the following conditions: • Poor terminal contact • Corrosion Do any of the terminals exhibit poor terminal contact or corrosion?	—	*Go to Step 20*	*Go to Step 14*

GC402980344300DX

Fig. 235 Code C1247: LH Front ABS Motor Free Spins (Part 4 of 5). Metro

Step	Action	Value(s)	Yes	No
14	1. Reinstall the ABS brake modulator gear cover. 2. Reinstall the ABS brake modulator assembly in the vehicle. 3. Reconnect the 6-way ABS brake motor pack connector. 4. Reconnect the EBCM connector. 5. Start the engine. Do not apply pressure to the brake pedal. 6. Let the engine run for at least 10 seconds. 7. Turn the ignition switch to the OFF position. 8. Repeat the above cycle (step 5 through step 7) two more times. 9. Use the *Scan Tool* in order to read the DTCs. Does DTC C1247 set as a current DTC?	—	*Go to Step 21*	*Go to Step 22*
15	Repair the high resistance in CKT 6C01. Is the repair complete?	—	Refer to *Diagnostic System Check*	—
16	Repair the high resistance in CKT 6D01. Is the repair complete?	—	Refer to *Diagnostic System Check*	—
17	Replace the ABS brake motor pack. Is the repair complete?	—	Refer to *Diagnostic System Check*	—
18	Replace the ABS brake modulator gear. Is the repair complete?	—	Refer to *Diagnostic System Check*	—
19	Replace the ABS brake modulator. Is the repair complete?	—	Refer to *Diagnostic System Check*	—
20	Replace the terminals that exhibit signs of poor terminal contact or corrosion. Is the repair complete?	—	Refer to *Diagnostic System Check*	—
21	Replace the EBCM. Is the repair complete?	—	Refer to *Diagnostic System Check*	—
22	The malfunction is intermittent or is not present at this time. Refer to Diagnostic Aids for more information. Is the action complete?	—	System OK	—

GC402980344300EX

Fig. 235 Code C1247: LH Front ABS Motor Free Spins (Part 5 of 5). Metro

Circuit Description

DTC C1248 detects a stripped nut or gear assembly during initialization. During the homing sequence, the piston should reach the top of the bore. Then the ABS motor stalls. If the ABS motor does not stall, the ABS motor must be spinning with little or no resistance. This indicates a nut/screw or gear malfunction.

Conditions for Setting the DTC

- DTC C1248 can only set during initialization.
- A malfunction exists if the feedback current is less than the command current for a specified period of time.

Action Taken When the DTC Sets

- A malfunction DTC stores.
- The ABS disables.
- The ABS warning indicator turns ON.

Conditions for Clearing the DTC

- The condition responsible for setting the DTC no longer exists and the Scan Tool Clear DTCs function is used.
- 100 drive cycles pass with no DTCs detected. A drive cycle consists of starting the vehicle, driving the vehicle over 16 km/h (10 mph), stopping and then turning the ignition OFF.

Diagnostic Aids

An intermittent malfunction in this DTC may result from a mechanical part of the system that slips, such as a backed off gear retaining nut.

Depending on the frequency of the malfunction, a physical inspection of the mechanical parts suspected of causing the malfunction may be necessary.

Important: Zero the J 39200 test leads before making any resistance measurements. J 39200 user's manual.

GC402980344400AX

Fig. 236 Code C1248: RH Front ABS Motor Free Spins (Part 1 of 5). Metro

Step	Action	Value(s)	Yes	No
1	Was the Diagnostic System Check performed?	—	*Go to Step 2*	Refer to *Diagnostic System Check*
2	1. Turn the ignition switch to the ON position. Do not start the engine. 2. Use the *Scan Tool* in order to read the DTCs. Does DTC C1261 also set as a current DTC?	—	Refer to *DTC C1261 Right Front ABS Motor Circuit Open*	*Go to Step 3*
3	1. Pump the brake pedal until it is firm in order to deplete the brake booster vacuum reservoir. 2. Select Special Functions on the *Scan Tool*. 3. Select the Manual Control function on the *Scan Tool*. 4. Select the right front Motor Apply function on the *Scan Tool*. 5. Use the *Scan Tool* in order to apply the right front motor. 6. Observe the following currents: • The right front ABS motor command current • The right front ABS motor feedback current Were the right front ABS motor command current and the right front ABS motor feedback current approximately the specified current?	10 A	*Go to Step 4*	*Go to Step 6*
4	1. Apply firm pressure to the brake pedal. 2. Select the right front ABS Motor Release function on the *Scan Tool*. 3. Use the *Scan Tool* in order to release the right front ABS motor. 4. Observe the following currents: • The right front ABS motor command current • The right front ABS motor feedback current 5. Release the right front ABS motor and observe the brake pedal height. Have the following conditions been met? • The right front ABS motor command current and the right front ABS motor feedback current approximately the specified current • The brake pedal falls	6 A	*Go to Step 5*	*Go to Step 6*
5	1. Continue to apply firm pressure to the brake pedal. 2. Select the right front ABS Motor Release function on the *Scan Tool*. 3. Use the *Scan Tool* in order to apply the right front ABS motor. Did the brake pedal rise?	—	*Go to Step 22*	*Go to Step 6*

GC402980344400BX

Fig. 236 Code C1248: RH Front ABS Motor Free Spins (Part 2 of 5). Metro

Step	Action	Value(s)	Yes	No
6	1. Select Special Functions on the *Scan Tool.* 2. Use the *Scan Tool* in order to perform the Gear Tension Relief function. 3. Turn the ignition switch to the OFF position. 4. Disconnect the 6-way ABS brake motor pack connector. 5. Disconnect the EBCM connector 6. Use the *J 39200* in order to measure the resistance between the 6-way ABS brake motor pack connector terminal E and the EBCM connector terminal A. Is the resistance within the specified range?	0–2 Ω	*Go to Step 7*	*Go to Step 15*
7	Use the *J 39200* in order to measure the resistance between the 6-way ABS brake motor pack connector terminal F and the EBCM connector terminal B. Is the resistance within the specified range?	0–2 Ω	*Go to Step 8*	*Go to Step 16*
8	Use the *J 39200* in order to measure the resistance between the 6-way ABS brake motor pack connector terminal E and the 6-way ABS brake motor pack connector terminal F. Is the resistance within the specified range?	0.2–1.5 Ω	*Go to Step 9*	*Go to Step 17*
9	1. Remove the ABS brake modulator assembly from the vehicle. 2. Remove the ABS brake modulator gear cover. 3. Inspect for a stripped ABS brake motor pack right front gear. (The ABS brake motor pack is the unit with the three small gears. The ABS brake motor pack right front gear is the gear closest to the rear when the ABS brake modulator is mounted in the vehicle.) Is the ABS brake motor right front gear stripped?	—	*Go to Step 17*	*Go to Step 10*
10	Inspect for a stripped ABS brake modulator right front gear. (The ABS brake modulator unit is the unit with the three large gears. The ABS brake modulator right front gear is the gear closest to the rear when the ABS brake modulator is mounted in the vehicle.) Is the ABS brake modulator right front gear stripped?	—	*Go to Step 18*	*Go to Step 11*

GC402980344400CX

Fig. 236 Code C1248: RH Front ABS Motor Free Spins (Part 3 of 5). Metro

Step	Action	Value(s)	Yes	No
11	1. Reconnect the 6-way ABS brake motor pack connector. 2. Reconnect the EBCM connector. 3. Carefully secure the ABS brake modulator in the vehicle. Secure the assembly in a position that permits observation of the gears. 4. Turn the ignition switch to the ON position. Do not start the engine. 5. Select the Manual Control function on the *Scan Tool.* 6. Select the right front ABS Motor Apply function on the *Scan Tool.* 7. Use the *Scan Tool* in order to apply the right front ABS motor while observing the ABS brake modulator right front gear set. (The ABS brake modulator right front gear is the gear closest to the rear when the ABS brake modulator is mounted in the vehicle.) 8. Select the right front ABS Motor Release function on the *Scan Tool.* 9. Use the *Scan Tool* in order to release the right front ABS motor while observing the ABS brake modulator right front gear set. 10. Select the right front ABS Motor Apply function on the *Scan Tool.* 11. Use the *Scan Tool* in order to apply the right front ABS motor while observing the ABS brake modulator right front gear set. Does the ABS brake modulator right front gear set move at least one full revolution in both directions?	—	*Go to Step 12*	*Go to Step 17*
12	1. Use the *Scan Tool* in order to perform the Gear Tension Relief function. 2. Turn the ignition switch to the OFF position. 3. Separate the ABS brake motor pack from the ABS brake modulator. 4. Grasp the ABS brake modulator right front gear. 5. Rotate the ABS brake modulator right front gear. Does the ABS brake modulator right front gear rotate more than 13 full turns from lock to lock?	—	*Go to Step 19*	*Go to Step 13*
13	1. Disconnect the 6-way ABS brake motor pack connector. 2. Disconnect the EBCM connector. 3. Inspect the connectors for the following conditions: • Poor terminal contact • Corrosion Do any of the terminals exhibit poor terminal contact or corrosion?	—	*Go to Step 20*	*Go to Step 14*

GC402980344400DX

Fig. 236 Code C1248: RH Front ABS Motor Free Spins (Part 4 of 5). Metro

Step	Action	Value(s)	Yes	No
14	1. Reinstall the ABS brake modulator gear cover. 2. Reinstall the ABS brake modulator/master cylinder assembly in the vehicle. 3. Reconnect the 6-way ABS brake motor pack connector. 4. Reconnect the EBCM connector. 5. Start the engine. Do not apply pressure to the brake pedal. 6. Let the engine run for at least 10 seconds. 7. Turn the ignition switch to the OFF position. 8. Repeat the above cycle (step 5 through step 7) two more times. 9. Use the *Scan Tool* in order to read the DTCs. Does DTC C1248 set as a current DTC?	—	*Go to Step 21*	*Go to Step 22*
15	Repair the high resistance in CKT 6G01. Is the repair complete?	—	Refer to *Diagnostic System Check*	—
16	Repair the high resistance in CKT 6H01. Is the repair complete?	—	Refer to *Diagnostic System Check*	—
17	Replace the ABS brake motor pack. Is the repair complete?	—	Refer to *Diagnostic System Check*	—
18	Replace the ABS brake modulator gear. Is the repair complete?	—	Refer to *Diagnostic System Check*	—
19	Replace the ABS brake modulator. Is the repair complete?	—	Refer to *Diagnostic System Check*	—
20	Replace the terminals that exhibit signs of poor terminal contact or corrosion. Is the repair complete?	—	Refer to *Diagnostic System Check*	—
21	Replace the EBCM. Is the repair complete?	—	Refer to *Diagnostic System Check*	—
22	The malfunction is intermittent or is not present at this time. Refer to Diagnostic Aids for more information. Is the action complete?	—	System OK	—

GC402980344400EX

Fig. 236 Code C1248: RH Front ABS Motor Free Spins (Part 5 of 5). Metro

Circuit Description

DTC C1251 detects a stripped nut or gear assembly during initialization. During the homing sequence, the piston should reach the top of the bore. Then the ABS motor stalls. If the ABS motor does not stall, the ABS motor must be spinning with little or no resistance. This indicates a nut/screw or gear malfunction.

Conditions for Setting the DTC

- DTC C1251 can only set during initialization.
- A malfunction exists if the feedback current is less than the command current for a specified period of time.
- This DTC can be set during motor re-home.

Action Taken When the DTC Sets

- A malfunction DTC stores. A corresponding DTC C1286 will also set.
- The ABS disables.
- The ABS warning indicator turns ON.
- The red BRAKE warning indicator turns ON.

Conditions for Clearing the DTC

- The condition responsible for setting the DTC no longer exists and the Scan Tool Clear DTCs function is used.
- 100 drive cycles pass with no DTCs detected. A drive cycle consists of starting the vehicle, driving the vehicle over 16 km/h (10 mph), stopping and then turning the ignition OFF.

Diagnostic Aids

An intermittent malfunction in this DTC may result from a mechanical part of the system that slips, such as a stripped gear or a backed off gear retaining nut.

Depending on the frequency of the malfunction, a physical inspection of the mechanical parts suspected of causing the malfunction may be necessary.

Important: Zero the J 39200 test leads before making any resistance measurements. Refer to the J 39200 user's manual.

GC402980344500AX

Fig. 237 Code C1251: Rear ABS Motor Free Spins (Part 1 of 5). Metro

Step	Action	Value(s)	Yes	No
1	Was the Diagnostic System Check performed?	—	*Go to Step 2*	Refer to *Diagnostic System Check*
2	1. Turn the ignition switch to the ON position. Do not start the engine. 2. Use the *Scan Tool* in order to read the DTCs. Does DTC C1264 also set as a current DTC?	—	Refer to *DTC C1264 Rear ABS Motor Circuit Open*	*Go to Step 3*
3	1. Pump the brake pedal until it is firm in order to deplete the brake booster vacuum reservoir. 2. Select Special Functions on the *Scan Tool.* 3. Select the Manual Control function on the *Scan Tool.* 4. Select the rear ABS Motor Apply function on the *Scan Tool.* 5. Use the *Scan Tool* in order to apply the rear ABS motor. 6. Observe the following currents: • The rear ABS motor command current • The rear ABS motor feedback current Were the rear ABS motor command current and the rear ABS motor feedback current approximately the specified current?	10 A	*Go to Step 4*	*Go to Step 6*
4	1. Raise and support the vehicle so that the rear wheels are approximately 6 inches off the floor. 2. Turn the ignition switch to the ON position. 3. Apply firm pressure to the brake pedal. 4. Select Special Functions on the *Scan Tool.* 5. Select Manual Control on the *Scan Tool.* 6. Use the *Scan Tool* in order to Apply the rear ABS motor. 7. Have an assistant try to spin the rear wheels by hand. Could the assistant spin the rear wheels?	—	*Go to Step 5*	*Go to Step 6*
5	1. Continue to apply firm pressure to the brake pedal. 2. Select the rear ABS Apply function on the *Scan Tool.* 3. Use the *Scan Tool* in order to apply the rear ABS motor. Could the assistant spin the rear wheels?	—	*Go to Step 22*	*Go to Step 6*
6	1. Select Special Functions on the *Scan Tool.* 2. Use the *Scan Tool* in order to perform the Gear Tension Relief function. 3. Turn the ignition switch to the OFF position. 4. Disconnect the 6-way ABS brake motor pack connector. 5. Disconnect the EBCM connector 6. Use the *J 39200* in order to measure the resistance between the 6-way ABS brake motor pack connector terminal C and the EBCM connector terminal F. Is the resistance within the specified range?	0–2 Ω	*Go to Step 7*	*Go to Step 15*
7	Use the *J 39200* in order to measure the resistance between the 6-way ABS brake motor pack connector terminal D and the EBCM connector terminal E. Is the resistance within the specified range?	0–2 Ω	*Go to Step 8*	*Go to Step 16*

GC402980344500BX

Fig. 237 Code C1251: Rear ABS Motor Free Spins (Part 2 of 5). Metro

Step	Action	Value(s)	Yes	No
8	Use the *J 39200* in order to measure the resistance between the 6-way ABS brake motor pack connector terminal C and the 6-way ABS brake motor pack connector terminal D. Is the resistance within the specified range?	0.2–1.5 Ω	*Go to Step 9*	*Go to Step 17*
9	1. Remove the ABS brake modulator assembly from the vehicle. 2. Remove the ABS brake modulator gear cover. 3. Inspect for a stripped ABS brake motor pack rear gear. (The ABS brake motor pack is the unit with the three small gears. The ABS brake motor pack rear gear is the middle gear when the ABS brake modulator is mounted in the vehicle.) Is the ABS brake motor rear gear stripped?	—	*Go to Step 17*	*Go to Step 10*
10	Inspect for a stripped ABS brake modulator rear gear. (The ABS brake modulator unit is the unit with the three large gears. The ABS brake modulator rear gear is the middle gear when the ABS brake modulator is mounted in the vehicle.) Is the ABS brake modulator rear gear stripped?	—	*Go to Step 18*	*Go to Step 11*
11	1. Reconnect the 6-way ABS brake motor pack connector. 2. Reconnect the EBCM connector. 3. Carefully secure the ABS brake modulator in the vehicle. Secure the assembly in a position that permits observation of the gears. 4. Turn the ignition switch to the ON position. Do not start the engine. 5. Select the Manual Control function on the *Scan Tool*. 6. Select the rear ABS Motor Apply function on the *Scan Tool*. 7. Use the *Scan Tool* in order to apply the rear ABS motor while observing the ABS brake modulator rear gear set. (The ABS brake modulator rear gear is the middle gear when the ABS brake modulator is mounted in the vehicle.) 8. Select the rear ABS Motor Release function on the *Scan Tool*. 9. Use the *Scan Tool* in order to release the rear ABS motor while observing the ABS brake modulator rear gear set. 10. Select the rear ABS Motor Apply function on the *Scan Tool*. 11. Use the *Scan Tool* in order to apply the rear ABS motor while observing the ABS brake modulator rear gear set. Does the ABS brake modulator rear gear set move at least one full revolution in both directions?	—	*Go to Step 12*	*Go to Step 17*

GC402980344500CX

Fig. 237 Code C1251: Rear ABS Motor Free Spins (Part 3 of 5). Metro

Step	Action	Value(s)	Yes	No
20	Replace the terminals that exhibit signs of poor terminal contact or corrosion. Is the repair complete?	—	Refer to *Diagnostic System Check*	—
21	Replace the EBCM. Is the repair complete?	—	Refer to *Diagnostic System Check*	—
22	The malfunction is intermittent or is not present at this time. Refer to Diagnostic Aids for more information. Is the action complete?	—	System OK	—

GC402980344500EX

Fig. 237 Code C1251: Rear ABS Motor Free Spins (Part 5 of 5). Metro

Step	Action	Value(s)	Yes	No
1	Was the Diagnostic System Check performed?	—	*Go to Step 2*	Refer to *Diagnostic System Check*
2	1. Turn the ignition switch to the ON position. Do not start the engine. 2. Install a *Scan Tool*. 3. Use the *Scan Tool* in order to read the DTCs. Is DTC C1255 set as a current DTC?	—	*Go to Step 3*	*Go to Step 5*
3	1. Use the *Scan Tool* in order to clear the DTCs. 2. Test drive the vehicle for three drive cycles. 3. Use the *Scan Tool* in order to look for DTCs. Does DTC C1255 set as a current DTC?	—	*Go to Step 4*	*Go to Step 5*
4	Replace the EBCM. Is the repair complete?	—	Refer to *Diagnostic System Check*	—
5	The malfunction is intermittent or is not present at this time. Refer to Diagnostic Aids for more information. Is the action complete?	—	System OK	—

GC402980344600BX

Fig. 238 Code C1255: EBCM Internal Fault (Part 2 of 2). Metro

Step	Action	Value(s)	Yes	No
12	1. Use the *Scan Tool* in order to perform the Gear Tension Relief function. 2. Turn the ignition switch to the OFF position. 3. Separate the ABS brake motor pack from the ABS brake modulator. 4. Grasp the ABS brake modulator rear gear. 5. Rotate the ABS brake modulator rear gear. Does the ABS brake modulator rear gear rotate more than 3.5 full turns from lock to lock?	—	*Go to Step 19*	*Go to Step 13*
13	1. Disconnect the 6-way ABS brake motor pack connector. 2. Disconnect the EBCM connector. 3. Inspect the connectors for the following conditions: • Poor terminal contact • Corrosion Do any of the terminals exhibit poor terminal contact or corrosion?	—	*Go to Step 20*	*Go to Step 14*
14	1. Reinstall the ABS brake modulator gear cover. 2. Reinstall the ABS brake modulator assembly in the vehicle. 3. Reconnect the 6-way ABS brake motor pack connector. 4. Reconnect the EBCM connector. 5. Start the engine. Do not apply pressure to the brake pedal. 6. Let the engine run for at least 10 seconds. 7. Turn the ignition switch to the OFF position. 8. Repeat the above cycle (steps 5 through 7) two more times. 9. Use the *Scan Tool* in order to read the DTCs. Does DTC C1251 set as a current DTC?	—	*Go to Step 21*	*Go to Step 22*
15	Repair the high resistance in CKT 6E01. Is the repair complete?	—	Refer to *Diagnostic System Check*	—
16	Repair the high resistance in CKT 6F01. Is the repair complete?	—	Refer to *Diagnostic System Check*	—
17	Replace the ABS brake motor pack. Is the repair complete?	—	Refer to *Diagnostic System Check*	—
18	Replace the ABS brake modulator gear. Is the repair complete?	—	Refer to *Diagnostic System Check*	—
19	Replace the ABS brake modulator. Is the repair complete?	—	Refer to *Diagnostic System Check*	—

GC402980344500DX

Fig. 237 Code C1251: Rear ABS Motor Free Spins (Part 4 of 5). Metro

Circuit Description

DTC C1255 identifies an internal malfunction detected by the EBCM.

Conditions for Setting the DTC

DTC C1255 is set when an internal EBCM malfunction exists.

Action Taken When the DTC Sets

- A malfunction DTC stores.
- The ABS disables.
- The ABS warning indicator turns ON.
- The red BRAKE warning indicator turns ON and DTC C1286 sets if the rear piston in the ABS brake motor pack is not in the home piston.

Conditions for Clearing the DTC

- The condition responsible for setting the DTC no longer exists and the Scan Tool Clear DTCs function is used.
- 100 drive cycles pass with no DTCs detected. A drive cycle consists of starting the vehicle, driving the vehicle over 16 km/h (10 mph), stopping and then turning the ignition OFF.

Diagnostic Aids

Use the enhanced diagnostic function of the Scan Tool in order to measure the frequency of the malfunction.

Clear the DTCs after completing the diagnosis. Test drive the vehicle for three drive cycles in order to verify that the DTC does not reset. Use the following procedure in order to complete one drive cycle:

1. Start the vehicle.
2. Drive the vehicle over 16 km/h (10 mph).
3. Stop the vehicle.
4. Turn the ignition to the OFF position.

GC402980344600AX

Fig. 238 Code C1255: EBCM Internal Fault (Part 1 of 2). Metro

Circuit Description

DTC C1256 identifies an ABS motor that cannot energize due to an open in the ABS motor circuitry. The malfunction will not allow proper front ABS operation.

Conditions for Setting the DTC

- DTC C1256 can only set when the motor is commanded off.
- A malfunction exists if the EBCM detects an out of range voltage on either of the left front ABS motor circuits. The out of range voltage on either circuit indicates an open circuit exists.

Action Taken When the DTC Sets

- An open ABS motor will not activate.
- A malfunction DTC stores.
- The ABS disables.
- The ABS warning indicator turns ON.

Conditions for Clearing the DTC

- The condition responsible for setting the DTC no longer exists and the Scan Tool Clear DTCs function is used.
- 100 drive cycles pass with no DTCs detected. A drive cycle consists of starting the vehicle, driving the vehicle over 16 km/h (10 mph), stopping and then turning the ignition OFF.

Diagnostic Aids

Use the Scan Tool Manual Control function in order to exercise ABS motor movement of affected channel in both directions while applying light pressure on the brake pedal.

An intermittent malfunction may be indicated if erratic or jumpy brake pedal movement is detected while performing an apply or release function of the ABS monitor.

The following conditions may cause a malfunction:

- A poor connection
- Rubbed-through wire insulation
- A broken wire inside the insulation
- Open or high resistance in CKT 6C01 or CKT 6D01 between the left front motor and the EBCM
- Malfunctioning motor pack (left front motor armature winding open)

If the malfunction is not current, use the following procedure to pinpoint an intermittent malfunction in the motor circuitry or connections:

1. Wiggle the wires of the affected channel.
2. Inspect if the DTC resets.

Use the enhanced diagnostic function of the Scan Tool in order to measure the frequency of the malfunction.

Thoroughly inspect any circuitry that may be causing the intermittent complaint for the following conditions:

- Backed out terminals
- Improper mating
- Broken locks
- Improperly formed or damaged terminals
- Poor terminal-to-wiring connections
- Physical damage to the wiring harness

GC402980344700AX

Fig. 239 Code C1256: LH Front ABS Motor Circuit Open (Part 1 of 3). Metro

Step	Action	Value(s)	Yes	No
1	Was the Diagnostic System Check performed?	—	*Go to Step 2*	Refer to *Diagnostic System Check*
2	Does DTC C1256 occur intermittently?	—	Refer to Diagnostic Aids	*Go to Step 3*
3	1. Turn the ignition switch to the OFF position. 2. Disconnect the 6-way ABS brake motor pack connector. 3. Use the *J 39200* in order to measure the resistance between the 6-way ABS brake motor pack connector terminal A and the 6-way ABS brake motor pack connector terminal B. Is the resistance within the specified range?	0.2–1.5 Ω	*Go to Step 4*	*Go to Step 8*
4	1. Disconnect the EBCM connector. 2. Use the *J 39200* in order to measure the resistance between the 6-way ABS brake motor pack harness connector terminal A and the EBCM harness connector terminal G. Is the resistance within the specified range?	0–2 Ω	*Go to Step 5*	*Go to Step 9*
5	Use the *J 39200* in order to measure the resistance between the 6-way ABS brake motor pack harness connector terminal B and the EBCM harness connector terminal H. Is the resistance within the specified range?	0–2 Ω	*Go to Step 6*	*Go to Step 10*
6	1. Inspect the following connectors: • The 6-way ABS brake motor pack connector • The 6-way ABS brake motor pack harness connector • The EBCM connector • The EBCM harness connector 2. Inspect the connectors for the following conditions: • Poor terminal contact • Corrosion Is there evidence of poor terminal contact and corrosion?	—	*Go to Step 11*	*Go to Step 7*
7	1. Reconnect the 6-way ABS brake motor pack connector. 2. Reconnect the EBCM connector. 3. Test drive the vehicle. Be sure to obtain a speed of at least 16 km/h (10 mph). 4. Turn the ignition switch to the OFF position. 5. Repeat the drive sequence two more times. 6. Use the *Scan Tool* in order to look for DTCs. Does DTC C1256 set as a current DTC during the last three drive cycles?	—	*Go to Step 12*	*Go to Step 13*

GC402980344700BX

Fig. 239 Code C1256: LH Front ABS Motor Circuit Open (Part 2 of 3). Metro

Step	Action	Value(s)	Yes	No
8	Replace the ABS brake motor pack. Is the repair complete?	—	Refer to *Diagnostic System Check*	—
9	Repair the open or high resistance in CKT 6C01. Is the repair complete?	—	Refer to *Diagnostic System Check*	—
10	Repair the open or high resistance in CKT 6D01. Is the repair complete?	—	Refer to *Diagnostic System Check*	—
11	Replace all of the terminals or the connectors that exhibit signs of poor terminal contact, corrosion, or damaged terminal(s). Is the repair complete?	—	Refer to *Diagnostic System Check*	—
12	Replace the EBCM. Is the repair complete?	—	Refer to *Diagnostic System Check*	—
13	The malfunction is intermittent or is not present at this time. Refer to Diagnostic Aids for more information. Is the action complete?	—	System OK	—

GC402980344700CX

Fig. 239 Code C1256: LH Front ABS Motor Circuit Open (Part 3 of 3). Metro

Circuit Description

This DTC identifies a motor circuit that is shorted to ground. A motor shorted to ground will not allow controlled ABS operation.

Conditions for Setting the DTC

- DTC C1257 can set anytime.
- A malfunction exists if the EBCM detects an out of range voltage on either of the left front ABS motor circuits.
- An out of range voltage on either circuit indicates one of the following conditions:
  - A circuit shorts to ground.
  - An ABS brake motor shorts internally.

Action Taken When the DTC Sets

- A malfunction DTC stores.
- The ABS disables.
- The ABS warning indicator turns ON.

Conditions for Clearing the DTC

- The condition responsible for setting the DTC no longer exists and the Scan Tool Clear DTCs function is used.
- 100 drive cycles pass with no DTCs detected. A drive cycle consists of starting the vehicle, driving the vehicle over 16 km/h (10 mph), stopping and then turning the ignition OFF.

Diagnostic Aids

Use the Scan Tool Manual Control function in order to exercise ABS motor movement of affected channel in both directions while applying light pressure on the brake pedal.

An intermittent malfunction may be indicated if erratic or jumpy brake pedal movement is detected while performing an apply or release function of the ABS monitor.

The following conditions may cause a malfunction:

- Rubbed-through wire insulation
- An internal motor short
- Short to ground between the left front motor and the EBCM (CKT 6C01 and/or CKT 6D01)
- Left front motor armature winding grounded (low resistance to ground)

If the malfunction is not current, use the following procedure to pinpoint an intermittent malfunction in the motor circuitry or connections:

1. Wiggle the wires of the affected channel.
2. Inspect if the DTC resets.

Use the enhanced diagnostic function of the Scan Tool in order to measure the frequency of the malfunction.

Clear the DTCs after completing the diagnosis. Test drive the vehicle for three drive cycles in order to verify that the DTC does not reset. Use the following procedure in order to complete one drive cycle:

1. Start the vehicle.
2. Drive the vehicle over 16 km/h (10 mph).
3. Stop the vehicle.
4. Turn the ignition to the OFF position.

Important: Zero the J 39200 test leads before making any resistance measurements.

GC402980344800AX

Fig. 240 Code C1257: LH Front ABS Motor Circuit Short To Ground (Part 1 of 3). Metro

Step	Action	Value(s)	Yes	No
1	Was the Diagnostic System Check performed?	—	*Go to Step 2*	Refer to *Diagnostic System Check*
2	Does DTC C1257 occur intermittently?	—	Refer to Diagnostic Aids	*Go to Step 3*
3	1. Turn the ignition switch to the OFF position. 2. Disconnect the 6-way ABS brake motor pack connector. 3. Disconnect the EBCM connector 4. Use the *J 39200* in order to measure the resistance between the 6-way ABS brake motor pack harness connector terminal A and ground. Is the resistance within the specified range?	OL (Infinite)	*Go to Step 4*	*Go to Step 9*
4	Use *J 39200* in order to measure the resistance between the 6-way ABS brake motor pack harness connector terminal B and ground. Is the resistance within the specified range?	OL (Infinite)	*Go to Step 5*	*Go to Step 10*
5	Use the *J 39200* in order to measure the resistance between the 6-way ABS brake motor pack connector terminal A and ground. Is the resistance within the specified range?	OL (Infinite)	*Go to Step 6*	*Go to Step 8*
6	1. Inspect the following components for damage: • The 6-way ABS brake motor pack connector • The 6-way ABS brake motor pack harness connector Damage may cause a short to ground with the connector connected. 2. Inspect the following components for damage: • The EBCM connector • The EBCM harness connector Damage may cause a short to ground with the connector connected. 3. Inspect CKT 6C01 and CKT 6D01 for damage. Damage may cause a short to ground. Is there damage which may cause a short to ground?	—	*Go to Step 11*	*Go to Step 7*
7	1. Reconnect the 6-way ABS brake motor pack connector. 2. Reconnect the EBCM connector. 3. Test drive the vehicle obtaining a speed at least 16 km/h (10 mph). 4. Turn the ignition switch to the OFF position. 5. Repeat the drive sequence two additional times. 6. Use the *Scan Tool* in order to inspect for DTCs. Did DTC C1257 set as a current DTC in the last three drive cycles?	—	*Go to Step 12*	*Go to Step 13*
8	Replace the ABS brake motor pack. Is the repair complete?	—	Refer to *Diagnostic System Check*	—
9	Repair the short to ground in CKT 6C01. Is the repair complete?	—	Refer to *Diagnostic System Check*	—

GC402980344800BX

Fig. 240 Code C1257: LH Front ABS Motor Circuit Short To Ground (Part 2 of 3). Metro

Step	Action	Value(s)	Yes	No
10	Repair the short to ground in CKT 6D01. Is the repair complete?	—	Refer to *Diagnostic System Check*	—
11	Replace all of the following components that exhibit signs of damage: • The terminals • The connectors • The wires Damage may cause a short to ground. Is the repair complete?	—	Refer to *Diagnostic System Check*	—
12	Replace the EBCM. Is the repair complete?	—	Refer to *Diagnostic System Check*	—
13	The malfunction is intermittent or not present at this time. Refer to Diagnostic Aids for more information. Is the action complete?	—	System OK	—

GC402980344800CX

Fig. 240 Code C1257: LH Front ABS Motor Circuit Short To Ground (Part 3 of 3). Metro

Circuit Description

DTC C1258 identifies an ABS motor circuit that shorts to voltage or an ABS motor that has low or no resistance. A short to voltage will not allow controlled ABS operation.

Conditions for Setting the DTC

- DTC C1258 can set only when the ABS motor is commanded off.
- A malfunction exists if the EBCM detects an out of range voltage on either of the left front ABS motor circuits.

Action Taken When the DTC Sets

- A malfunction DTC stores.
- The ABS disables.
- The ABS warning indicator turns ON.

Conditions for Clearing the DTC

- The condition responsible for setting the DTC no longer exists and the Scan Tool Clear DTCs function is used.
- 100 drive cycles pass with no DTCs detected. A drive cycle consists of starting the vehicle, driving the vehicle over 16 km/h (10 mph), stopping and then turning the ignition OFF.

Diagnostic Aids

Use the Scan Tool Manual Control function in order to exercise ABS motor movement of affected channel in both directions while applying light pressure on the brake pedal.

An intermittent malfunction may be indicated if erratic or jumpy brake pedal movement is detected while performing an apply or release function of the ABS monitor.

If the malfunction is not current, use the following procedure to pinpoint an intermittent malfunction in the motor circuitry or connections:

1. Wiggle the wires of the affected channel.
2. Inspect if the DTC resets.

Use the enhanced diagnostic function of the Scan Tool in order to measure the frequency of the malfunction.

Thoroughly inspect any circuitry that may be causing the intermittent complaint for the following conditions:

Clear the DTCs after completing the diagnosis. Test drive the vehicle for three drive cycles in order to verify that the DTC does not reset. Use the following procedure in order to complete one drive cycle:

1. Start the vehicle.
2. Drive the vehicle over 16 km/h (10 mph).
3. Stop the vehicle.
4. Turn the ignition to the OFF position.

Important: Zero the J 39200 test leads before making any resistance measurements.

GC402980344900AX

Fig. 241 Code C1258: LH Front ABS Motor Circuit Short To Voltage (Part 1 of 3). Metro

Step	Action	Value(s)	Yes	No
1	Was the Diagnostic System Check performed?	—	*Go to Step 2*	Refer to *Diagnostic System Check*
2	Does DTC C1258 occur intermittently?	—	Refer to Diagnostic Aids	*Go to Step 3*
3	1. Turn the ignition switch to the OFF position. 2. Disconnect the 6-way ABS brake motor pack connector. 3. Disconnect the EBCM connector 4. Use the *J 39200* in order to measure the voltage between the 6-way ABS brake motor pack harness connector terminal A and ground. Is the voltage within the specified range?	0–1 V	*Go to Step 4*	*Go to Step 10*
4	Use the *J 39200* in order to measure the voltage between the 6-way ABS brake motor pack harness connector terminal B and ground. Is the voltage within the specified range?	0–1 V	*Go to Step 5*	*Go to Step 11*
5	1. Turn the ignition switch to the OFF position. 2. Use the *J 39200* in order to measure the resistance between the 6-way ABS motor pack harness connector terminal A and the 6-way ABS motor pack harness connector terminal B. Is the resistance within the specified range?	OL (Infinite)	*Go to Step 6*	*Go to Step 12*
6	Use the *J 39200* in order to measure the resistance between the 6-way ABS motor pack connector terminal A and the 6-way ABS motor pack connector terminal B. Is the resistance within the specified range?	0.2–1.5 Ω	*Go to Step 7*	*Go to Step 9*
7	1. Inspect the following components for damage: • The 6-way ABS motor pack connector • The 6-way ABS motor pack harness connector Damage may cause a short to voltage with the connector connected. 2. Inspect the following components for damage: • The EBCM connector • The EBCM harness connector Damage may cause a short to voltage with the connector connected. 3. Inspect CKT 6C01 and CKT 6D01 for signs of damage. Damage may cause a short to voltage. Is there damage which may result in a short to voltage?	—	*Go to Step 13*	*Go to Step 8*
8	1. Reconnect the 6-way ABS motor pack connector. 2. Reconnect the EBCM connector. 3. Test drive the vehicle obtaining a speed of at least 16 km/h (10 mph). 4. Turn the ignition switch to the OFF position. 5. Repeat the drive sequence two additional times. 6. Use the *Scan Tool* in order to inspect for DTCs. Did DTC C1258 set as a current DTC in the last three drive cycles?	—	*Go to Step 14*	*Go to Step 15*
9	Replace the ABS motor pack. Is the repair complete?	—	Refer to *Diagnostic System Check*	—

GC402980344900BX

Fig. 241 Code C1258: LH Front ABS Motor Circuit Short To Voltage (Part 2 of 3). Metro

Step	Action	Value(s)	Yes	No
10	Repair the short to voltage in CKT 6C01. Is the repair complete?	—	Refer to *Diagnostic System Check*	—
11	Repair the short to voltage in CKT 6D01. Is the repair complete?	—	Refer to *Diagnostic System Check*	—
12	Repair the short between CKT 6C01 and CKT 6D01. Is the repair complete?	—	Refer to *Diagnostic System Check*	—
13	Replace all of the following components that are damaged: • The terminals • The connectors • The wires Damage may cause a short to voltage. Is the repair complete?	—	Refer to *Diagnostic System Check*	—
14	Replace the EBCM. Is the repair complete?	—	Refer to *Diagnostic System Check*	—
15	The malfunction is intermittent or not present at this time. Refer to Diagnostic Aids for more information. Is the action complete?	—	System OK	—

GC402980344900CX

Fig. 241 Code C1258: LH Front ABS Motor Circuit Short To Voltage (Part 3 of 3). Metro

Circuit Description

DTC C1261 identifies an ABS motor that cannot energize due to an open in the ABS motor circuitry. The malfunction will not allow proper front ABS operation.

Conditions for Setting the DTC

- DTC C1261 can only set when the motor is commanded off.
- A malfunction exists if the EBCM detects an out of range voltage on either of the right front ABS motor circuits. The out of range voltage on either circuit indicates an open circuit exists.

Action Taken When the DTC Sets

- An open ABS motor will not activate.
- A malfunction DTC stores.
- The ABS disables.
- The ABS warning indicator turns ON.

Conditions for Clearing the DTC

- The condition responsible for setting the DTC no longer exists and the Scan Tool Clear DTCs function is used.
- 100 drive cycles pass with no DTCs detected. A drive cycle consists of starting the vehicle, driving the vehicle over 16 km/h (10 mph), stopping and then turning the ignition OFF.

Diagnostic Aids

Use the Scan Tool Manual Control function in order to exercise ABS motor movement of affected channel in both directions while applying light pressure on the brake pedal.

An intermittent malfunction may be indicated if erratic or jumpy brake pedal movement is detected while performing an apply or release function of the ABS monitor.

The following conditions may cause an intermittent malfunction:

- A poor connection
- Rubbed-through wire insulation
- A broken wire inside the insulation

If the malfunction is not current, use the following procedure to pinpoint an intermittent malfunction in the motor circuitry or connections:

1. Wiggle the wires of the affected channel.
2. Inspect if the DTC resets.

Use the enhanced diagnostic function of the Scan Tool in order to measure the frequency of the malfunction.

Thoroughly inspect any circuitry that may be causing the intermittent complaint for the following conditions:

- Backed out terminals
- Improper mating
- Broken locks
- Improperly formed or damaged terminals
- Poor terminal-to-wiring connections
- Physical damage to the wiring harness

Clear the DTCs after completing the diagnosis. Test drive the vehicle for three drive cycles in order to verify that the DTC does not reset. Use the following procedure in order to complete one drive cycle:

1. Start the vehicle.
2. Drive the vehicle over 16 km/h (10 mph).
3. Stop the vehicle.
4. Turn the ignition to the OFF position.

Important: Zero the J 39200 test leads before making any resistance measurements.

GC402980345000AX

Fig. 242 Code C1261: RH Front ABS Motor Circuit Open (Part 1 of 3). Metro

Step	Action	Value(s)	Yes	No
1	Was the Diagnostic System Check performed?	—	*Go to Step 2*	Refer to *Diagnostic System Check*
2	Does DTC C1261 occur intermittently?	—	Refer to Diagnostic Aids	*Go to Step 3*
3	1. Turn the ignition switch to the OFF position. 2. Disconnect the 6-way ABS brake motor pack connector. 3. Use the *J 39200* in order to measure the resistance between the 6-way ABS brake motor pack connector terminal E and 6-way ABS motor pack connector terminal F. Is the resistance within the specified range?	0.2–1.5 Ω	*Go to Step 4*	*Go to Step 8*
4	1. Disconnect the EBCM connector. 2. Use *J 39200* in order to measure the resistance between the 6-way ABS brake motor pack harness connector terminal E and the EBCM harness connector terminal A. Is the resistance within the specified range?	0–2 Ω	*Go to Step 5*	*Go to Step 9*
5	Use the *J 39200* in order to measure the resistance between the 6-way ABS brake motor pack harness connector terminal F and the EBCM harness connector terminal B. Is the resistance within the specified range?	0–2 Ω	*Go to Step 6*	*Go to Step 10*
6	1. Inspect the following components for poor terminal contact and corrosion: • The 6-way ABS brake motor pack connector • The 6-way ABS brake motor pack harness connector 2. Inspect the following components for poor terminal contact and corrosion: • The EBCM connector • The EBCM harness connector Damage that may cause an open with the connector connected. 3. Inspect CKT 6G01 and CKT 6H01 for damage. Damage may cause an open circuit. Is there poor terminal contact or corrosion?	—	*Go to Step 11*	*Go to Step 7*
7	1. Reconnect the 6-way ABS brake motor pack connector. 2. Reconnect the EBCM connector. 3. Test drive the vehicle obtaining a speed at least 16 km/h (10 mph). 4. Turn the ignition switch to the OFF position. 5. Repeat the drive sequence two additional times. 6. Use the *Scan Tool* in order to inspect for DTCs. Did DTC C1261 set as a current DTC in the last three drive cycles?	—	*Go to Step 12*	*Go to Step 13*
8	Replace the ABS brake motor pack. Is the repair complete?	—	Refer to *Diagnostic System Check*	—

GC402980345000BX

Fig. 242 Code C1261: RH Front ABS Motor Circuit Open (Part 2 of 3). Metro

Step	Action	Value(s)	Yes	No
9	Repair the open in CKT 6G01. Is the repair complete?	—	Refer to *Diagnostic System Check*	—
10	Repair the open in CKT 6H01. Is the repair complete?	—	Refer to *Diagnostic System Check*	—
11	Replace all of the terminals and connectors that exhibit the following conditions: • Poor terminal contact • Corrosion • Damaged terminal(s) Is the repair complete?	—	Refer to *Diagnostic System Check*	—
12	Replace the EBCM. Is the repair complete?	—	Refer to *Diagnostic System Check*	—
13	The malfunction is intermittent or not present at this time. Refer to Diagnostic Aids for more information. Is the action complete?	—	System OK	—

GC402980345000CX

Fig. 242 Code C1261: RH Front ABS Motor Circuit Open (Part 3 of 3). Metro

Step	Action	Value(s)	Yes	No
1	Was the Diagnostic System Check performed?	—	*Go to Step 2*	Refer to *Diagnostic System Check*
2	Does DTC C1262 occur intermittently?	—	Refer to Diagnostic Aids	*Go to Step 3*
3	1. Turn the ignition switch to the OFF position. 2. Disconnect the 6-way ABS brake motor pack connector. 3. Disconnect the EBCM connector. 4. Use the *J 39200* in order to measure the resistance between the 6-way ABS brake motor pack harness connector terminal E and ground. Is the resistance within the specified range?	OL (Infinite)	*Go to Step 4*	*Go to Step 9*
4	Use *J 39200* in order to measure the resistance between the 6-way ABS brake motor pack harness connector terminal F and ground. Is the resistance within the specified range?	OL (Infinite)	*Go to Step 5*	*Go to Step 10*
5	Use the *J 39200* in order to measure the resistance between the 6-way ABS brake motor pack connector terminal E and ground. Is the resistance within the specified range?	OL (Infinite)	*Go to Step 6*	*Go to Step 8*
6	1. Inspect the following components for damage: • The 6-way ABS brake motor pack connector • The 6-way ABS brake motor pack harness connector Damage that may cause a short to ground with the connector connected. 2. Inspect the following components for damage: • The EBCM connector • The EBCM harness connector Damage that may cause a short to ground with the connector connected. 3. Inspect CKT 6G01 and CKT 6H01 for damage. Damage may cause a short to ground. Is there damage which may result in a short to ground?	—	*Go to Step 11*	*Go to Step 7*
7	1. Reconnect the 6-way ABS brake motor pack connector. 2. Reconnect the EBCM connector. 3. Test drive the vehicle obtaining a speed at least 16 km/h (10 mph). 4. Turn the ignition switch to the OFF position. 5. Repeat the drive sequence two additional times. 6. Use the *Scan Tool* in order to inspect for DTCs. Did DTC C1262 set as a current DTC in the last three drive cycles?	—	*Go to Step 12*	*Go to Step 13*
8	Replace the ABS brake motor pack. Is the repair complete?	—	Refer to *Diagnostic System Check*	—
9	Repair the short to ground in CKT 6G01. Is the repair complete?	—	Refer to *Diagnostic System Check*	—

GC402980345100BX

Fig. 243 Code C1262: RH Front ABS Motor Circuit Short To Ground (Part 2 of 3). Metro

Circuit Description

This DTC identifies a motor circuit that is shorted to ground. A short to ground will not allow controlled ABS operation.

Conditions for Setting the DTC

- DTC C1262 can set anytime.
- A malfunction exists if the EBCM detects an out of range voltage on either of the right front ABS motor circuits.
- An out of range voltage on either circuit indicates one of the following conditions:
  - CKT 6G01 and/or CKT 6H01 shorts to ground.
  - An ABS brake motor internally shorts.

Action Taken When the DTC Sets

- A malfunction DTC stores.
- The ABS disables.
- The ABS warning indicator turns ON.

Conditions for Clearing the DTC

- The condition responsible for setting the DTC no longer exists and the Scan Tool Clear DTCs function is used.
- 100 drive cycles pass with no DTCs detected. A drive cycle consists of starting the vehicle, driving the vehicle over 16 km/h (10 mph), stopping and then turning the ignition OFF.

Diagnostic Aids

Use the Scan Tool Manual Control function in order to exercise ABS motor movement of affected channel in both directions while applying light pressure on the brake pedal.

An intermittent malfunction may be indicated if erratic or jumpy brake pedal movement is detected while performing an apply or release function of the ABS monitor.

A rubbed-through wire may cause an intermittent malfunction:

If the malfunction is not current, use the following procedure to pinpoint an intermittent malfunction in the motor circuitry or connections:

1. Wiggle the wires of the affected channel.
2. Inspect if the DTC resets.

Use the enhanced diagnostic function of the Scan Tool in order to measure the frequency of the malfunction.

Clear the DTCs after completing the diagnosis. Test drive the vehicle for three drive cycles in order to verify that the DTC does not reset. Use the following procedure in order to complete one drive cycle:

1. Start the vehicle.
2. Drive the vehicle over 16 km/h (10 mph).
3. Stop the vehicle.
4. Turn the ignition to the OFF position.

Important: Zero the J 39200 test leads before making any resistance measurements.

GC402980345100AX

Fig. 243 Code C1262: RH Front ABS Motor Circuit Short To Ground (Part 1 of 3). Metro

Step	Action	Value(s)	Yes	No
10	Repair the short to ground in CKT 6H01. Is the repair complete?	—	Refer to *Diagnostic System Check*	—
11	Replace all of the following components that exhibit signs of damage: • The terminals • The connectors • The wires Damage may cause a short to ground. Is the repair complete?	—	Refer to *Diagnostic System Check*	—
12	Replace the EBCM. Is the repair complete?	—	Refer to *Diagnostic System Check*	—
13	The malfunction is intermittent or not present at this time. Refer to Diagnostic Aids for more information. Is the action complete?	—	System OK	—

GC402980345100CX

Fig. 243 Code C1262: RH Front ABS Motor Circuit Short To Ground (Part 3 of 3). Metro

Circuit Description

DTC C1263 identifies an ABS motor circuit that is shorted to voltage or an ABS motor that has low or no resistance.

Conditions for Setting the DTC

- DTC C1263 can set only when the ABS motor is commanded off.
- A malfunction exists if the EBCM detects an out of range voltage on either of the right front ABS motor circuits.
- An out of range voltage on either circuit indicates one of the following conditions:
  - A circuit shorts to voltage.
  - An ABS brake motor shorts internally.

Action Taken When the DTC Sets

- A malfunction DTC stores.
- The ABS disables.
- The ABS warning indicator turns ON.

Conditions for Clearing the DTC

- The condition responsible for setting the DTC no longer exists and the Scan Tool Clear DTCs function is used.
- 100 drive cycles pass with no DTCs detected. A drive cycle consists of starting the vehicle, driving the vehicle over 16 km/h (10 mph), stopping and then turning the ignition OFF.

Diagnostic Aids

Use the Scan Tool Manual Control function in order to exercise ABS motor movement of affected channel in both directions while applying light pressure on the brake pedal.

An intermittent malfunction may be indicated if erratic or jumpy brake pedal movement is detected while performing an apply or release function of the ABS monitor.

If the malfunction is not current, use the following procedure to pinpoint an intermittent malfunction in the motor circuitry or connections:

1. Wiggle the wires of the affected channel.
2. Inspect if the DTC resets.

Use the enhanced diagnostic function of the Scan Tool in order to measure the frequency of the malfunction.

Clear the DTCs after completing the diagnosis. Test drive the vehicle for three drive cycles in order to verify that the DTC does not reset. Use the following procedure in order to complete one drive cycle:

1. Start the vehicle.
2. Drive the vehicle over 16 km/h (10 mph).
3. Stop the vehicle.
4. Turn the ignition to the OFF position.

Important: Zero the J 39200 test leads before making any resistance measurements.

GC402980345200AX

Fig. 244 Code C1263: RH Front ABS Motor Circuit Short To Voltage (Part 1 of 3). Metro

Step	Action	Value(s)	Yes	No
1	Was the Diagnostic System Check performed?	—	*Go to Step 2*	Refer to *Diagnostic System Check*
2	Does DTC C1263 occur intermittently?	—	Refer to Diagnostic Aids	*Go to Step 3*
3	1. Turn the ignition switch to the OFF position. 2. Disconnect the 6-way ABS brake motor pack connector. 3. Disconnect the EBCM connector 4. Turn the ignition switch to the ON position. Do not start the engine. 5. Use the *J 39200* in order to measure the voltage between the 6-way ABS brake motor pack harness connector terminal E and ground. Is the voltage within the specified range?	0–1 V	*Go to Step 4*	*Go to Step 10*
4	Use the *J 39200* in order to measure the voltage between the 6-way ABS brake motor pack harness connector terminal F and ground. Is the voltage within the specified range?	0–1 V	*Go to Step 5*	*Go to Step 11*
5	1. Turn the ignition switch to the OFF position. 2. Use the *J 39200* in order to measure the resistance between the 6-way ABS motor pack harness connector terminal E and the 6-way ABS motor pack harness connector terminal F. Is the resistance within the specified range?	OL (Infinite)	*Go to Step 6*	*Go to Step 12*
6	Use the *J 39200* in order to measure the resistance between the 6-way ABS motor pack connector terminal E and the 6-way ABS motor pack connector terminal F. Is the resistance within the specified range?	0.2–1.5 Ω	*Go to Step 7*	*Go to Step 9*
7	1. Inspect the following components for damage: • The 6-way ABS motor pack connector • The 6-way ABS motor pack harness connector Damage that may cause a short to voltage with the connector connected. 2. Inspect the following components for damage: • The EBCM connector • The EBCM harness connector Damage may cause a short to voltage with the connector connected. 3. Inspect CKT 6G01 and CKT 6H01 for signs of damage. Damage may cause a short to voltage. Is there damage which may cause a short to voltage?	—	*Go to Step 13*	*Go to Step 8*
8	1. Reconnect the 6-way ABS motor pack connector. 2. Reconnect the EBCM connector. 3. Test drive the vehicle at a speed of at least 16 km/h (10 mph). 4. Turn the ignition switch to the OFF position. 5. Repeat the drive sequence two additional times. 6. Use the *Scan Tool* in order to inspect for DTCs. Did DTC C1263 set as a current DTC during the last three drive cycles?	—	*Go to Step 14*	*Go to Step 15*

GC402980345200BX

Fig. 244 Code C1263: RH Front ABS Motor Circuit Short To Voltage (Part 2 of 3). Metro

Circuit Description

DTC 1264 identifies an ABS motor that cannot energize due to an open in the ABS motor circuitry. The malfunction will not allow proper rear ABS operation.

Conditions for Setting the DTC

- DTC C1264 can only set when the motor is commanded off.
- A malfunction exists if the EBCM detects an out of range voltage on either of the rear ABS motor circuits. The out of range voltage on either circuit indicates an open circuit exists.

Action Taken When the DTC Sets

- An open ABS motor will not activate.
- A malfunction DTC stores.
- The ABS disables.
- The ABS warning indicator turns ON.
- The red BRAKE warning indicator turns ON and DTC C1286 also sets if the rear piston in the ABS brake motor pack is not in the home position.

Conditions for Clearing the DTC

- The condition responsible for setting the DTC no longer exists and the Scan Tool Clear DTCs function is used.
- 100 drive cycles pass with no DTCs detected. A drive cycle consists of starting the vehicle, driving the vehicle over 16 km/h (10 mph), stopping and then turning the ignition OFF.

Diagnostic Aids

Use the Scan Tool Manual Control function in order to exercise ABS motor movement of affected channel in both directions while applying light pressure on the brake pedal.

An intermittent malfunction may be indicated if erratic or jumpy brake pedal movement is detected while performing an apply or release function of the ABS monitor.

The following conditions may cause an intermittent malfunction:

- A poor connection
- Rubbed-through wire insulation
- A broken wire inside the insulation

If the malfunction is not current, use the following procedure to pinpoint an intermittent malfunction in the motor circuitry or connections:

1. Wiggle the wires of the affected channel.
2. Inspect if the DTC resets.

Use the enhanced diagnostic function of the Scan Tool in order to measure the frequency of the malfunction.

Thoroughly inspect any circuitry that may be causing the intermittent complaint for the following conditions:

- Backed out terminals
- Improper mating
- Broken locks
- Improperly formed or damaged terminals
- Poor terminal-to-wiring connections
- Physical damage to the wiring harness

Clear the DTCs after completing the diagnosis. Test drive the vehicle for three drive cycles in order to verify that the DTC does not reset. Use the following procedure in order to complete one drive cycle:

1. Start the vehicle.
2. Drive the vehicle over 16 km/h (10 mph).
3. Stop the vehicle.
4. Turn the ignition to the OFF position.

Important: Zero the J 39200 test leads before making any resistance measurements.

GC402980345300AX

Fig. 245 Code C1264: Rear ABS Motor Circuit Open (Part 1 of 3). Metro

Step	Action	Value(s)	Yes	No
9	Replace the ABS motor pack. Is the repair complete?	—	Refer to *Diagnostic System Check*	—
10	Repair the short to voltage in CKT 6G01. Is the repair complete?	—	Refer to *Diagnostic System Check*	—
11	Repair the short to voltage in CKT 6H01. Is the repair complete?	—	Refer to *Diagnostic System Check*	—
12	Repair the short between CKT 6G01 and CKT 6H01. Is the repair complete?	—	Refer to *Diagnostic System Check*	—
13	Replace all of the following components that are damaged: • The terminals • The connectors • The wires Damage may cause a short to voltage. Is the repair complete?	—	Refer to *Diagnostic System Check*	—
14	Replace the EBCM. Is the repair complete?	—	Refer to *Diagnostic System Check*	—
15	The malfunction is intermittent or is not present at this time. Refer to Diagnostic Aids for more information. Is the action complete?	—	System OK	—

GC402980345200CX

Fig. 244 Code C1263: RH Front ABS Motor Circuit Short To Voltage (Part 3 of 3). Metro

Step	Action	Value(s)	Yes	No
1	Was the Diagnostic System Check performed?	—	*Go to Step 2*	Refer to *Diagnostic System Check*
2	Does DTC C1264 occur intermittently?	—	Refer to Diagnostic Aids	*Go to Step 3*
3	1. Turn the ignition switch to the OFF position. 2. Disconnect the 6-way ABS brake motor pack connector. 3. Use the *J 39200* in order to measure the resistance between the 6-way ABS brake motor pack connector terminal D and 6-way ABS motor pack connector terminal C. Is the resistance within the specified range?	0.2–1.5 Ω	*Go to Step 4*	*Go to Step 8*
4	1. Disconnect the EBCM connector. 2. Use the *J 39200* in order to measure the resistance between the 6-way ABS brake motor pack harness connector terminal C and the EBCM harness connector terminal F. Is the resistance within the specified range?	0–2 Ω	*Go to Step 5*	*Go to Step 9*
5	Use the *J 39200* in order to measure the resistance between the 6-way ABS brake motor pack harness connector terminal D and the EBCM harness connector terminal E. Is the resistance within the specified range?	0–2 Ω	*Go to Step 6*	*Go to Step 10*
6	1. Inspect the following components for poor terminal contact and corrosion: • The 6-way ABS brake motor pack connector • The 6-way ABS brake motor pack harness connector 2. Inspect the following components for poor terminal contact and corrosion: • The EBCM connector • The EBCM harness connector Damage may cause a short to ground with the connector connected. 3. Inspect CKT 6E01 and CKT 6F01 for damage. Damage may cause a short to ground. Is there poor terminal contact or corrosion?	—	*Go to Step 11*	*Go to Step 7*
7	1. Reconnect the 6-way ABS brake motor pack connector. 2. Reconnect the EBCM connector. 3. Test drive the vehicle at a speed at least 16 km/h (10 mph). 4. Turn the ignition switch to the OFF position. 5. Repeat the drive sequence two additional times. 6. Use the *Scan Tool* in order to inspect for DTCs. Did DTC C1264 set as a current DTC in the last three drive cycles?	—	*Go to Step 12*	*Go to Step 13*
8	Replace the ABS brake motor pack. Is the repair complete?	—	Refer to *Diagnostic System Check*	—

GC402980345300BX

Fig. 245 Code C1264: Rear ABS Motor Circuit Open (Part 2 of 3). Metro

Step	Action	Value(s)	Yes	No
9	Repair the short to ground in CKT 6E01. Is the repair complete?	—	Refer to *Diagnostic System Check*	—
10	Repair the short to ground in CKT 6F01. Is the repair complete?	—	Refer to *Diagnostic System Check*	—
11	Replace all of the terminals and connectors that exhibit the following conditions: • Poor terminal contact • Corrosion • Damaged terminal(s) Is the repair complete?	—	Refer to *Diagnostic System Check*	—
12	Replace the EBCM. Is the repair complete?	—	Refer to *Diagnostic System Check*	—
13	The malfunction is intermittent or is not present at this time. Refer to Diagnostic Aids for more information. Is the action complete?	—	System OK	—

GC402980345300CX

Fig. 245 Code C1264: Rear ABS Motor Circuit Open (Part 3 of 3). Metro

Step	Action	Value(s)	Yes	No
1	Was the Diagnostic System Check performed?	—	*Go to Step 2*	Refer to *Diagnostic System Check*
2	Does DTC C1265 occur intermittently?	—	Refer to Diagnostic Aids	*Go to Step 3*
3	1. Turn the ignition switch to the OFF position. 2. Disconnect the 6-way ABS brake motor pack connector. 3. Disconnect the EBCM connector 4. Use the *J 39200* in order to measure the resistance between the 6-way ABS brake motor pack harness connector terminal C and ground. Is the resistance within the specified range?	OL (Infinite)	*Go to Step 4*	*Go to Step 9*
4	Use *J 39200* in order to measure the resistance between the 6-way ABS brake motor pack harness connector terminal D and ground. Is the resistance within the specified range?	OL (Infinite)	*Go to Step 5*	*Go to Step 10*
5	Use the *J 39200* in order to measure the resistance between the 6-way ABS brake motor pack connector terminal C and ground. Is the resistance within the specified range?	OL (Infinite)	*Go to Step 6*	*Go to Step 8*
6	1. Inspect the following components for damage: • The 6-way ABS brake motor pack connector • The 6-way ABS brake motor pack harness connector Damage that may cause a short to ground with the connector connected. 2. Inspect the following components for damage: • The EBCM connector • The EBCM harness connector Damage that may cause a short to ground with the connector connected. 3. Inspect the following circuits for damage: • CKT 6E01 • CKT 6F01 Damage may cause a short to ground. Is there damage which may cause a short to ground?	—	*Go to Step 11*	*Go to Step 7*
7	1. Reconnect the 6-way ABS brake motor pack connector. 2. Reconnect the EBCM connector. 3. Test drive the vehicle obtaining a speed at least 16 km/h (10 mph). 4. Turn the ignition switch to the OFF position. 5. Repeat the drive sequence two additional times. 6. Use the *Scan Tool* in order to inspect for DTCs. Did DTC C1265 set as a current DTC during the last three drive cycles?	—	*Go to Step 12*	*Go to Step 13*
8	Replace the ABS brake motor pack. Is the repair complete?	—	Refer to *Diagnostic System Check*	—

GC402980345400BX

Fig. 246 Code C1265: Rear ABS Motor Circuit Short To Ground (Part 2 of 3). Metro

Circuit Description

DTC C1265 identifies an ABS motor circuit that shorts to ground.

Conditions for Setting the DTC

- DTC C1265 can set anytime.
- A malfunction exists if the EBCM detects an out of range voltage on either of the rear ABS motor circuits.
- An out of range voltage on either circuit indicates one of the following conditions:
  - CKT 6E01 and/or CKT 6F01 shorts to ground.
  - An ABS brake motor is shorts internally.

Action Taken When the DTC Sets

- A malfunction DTC stores.
- The ABS disables.
- The ABS warning indicator turns ON.
- The red BRAKE warning indicator turns ON and DTC C1286 also sets if the rear piston in the ABS brake motor pack is not in the home position.

Conditions for Clearing the DTC

- The condition responsible for setting the DTC no longer exists and the Scan Tool Clear DTCs function is used.
- 100 drive cycles pass with no DTCs detected. A drive cycle consists of starting the vehicle, driving the vehicle over 16 km/h (10 mph), stopping and then turning the ignition OFF.

Diagnostic Aids

Use the Scan Tool Manual Control function in order to exercise ABS motor movement of affected channel in both directions while applying light pressure on the brake pedal.

An intermittent malfunction may be indicated if erratic or jumpy brake pedal movement is detected while performing an apply or release function of the ABS monitor.

If the malfunction is not current, use the following procedure to pinpoint an intermittent malfunction in the motor circuitry or connections:

1. Wiggle the wires of the affected channel.
2. Inspect if the DTC resets.

Use the enhanced diagnostic function of the Scan Tool in order to measure the frequency of the malfunction.

Clear the DTCs after completing the diagnosis. Test drive the vehicle for three drive cycles in order to verify that the DTC does not reset. Use the following procedure in order to complete one drive cycle:

1. Start the vehicle.
2. Drive the vehicle over 16 km/h (10 mph).
3. Stop the vehicle.
4. Turn the ignition to the OFF position.

Important: Zero the J 39200 test leads before making any resistance measurements.

GC402980345400AX

Fig. 246 Code C1265: Rear ABS Motor Circuit Short To Ground (Part 1 of 3). Metro

Step	Action	Value(s)	Yes	No
9	Repair the short to ground in CKT 6E01. Is the repair complete?	—	Refer to *Diagnostic System Check*	—
10	Repair the short to ground in CKT 6F01. Is the repair complete?	—	Refer to *Diagnostic System Check*	—
11	Replace all of the following components that exhibit signs of damage: • The terminals • The connectors • The wires Damage may cause a short to ground. Is the repair complete?	—	Refer to *Diagnostic System Check*	—
12	Replace the EBCM. Is the repair complete?	—	Refer to *Diagnostic System Check*	—
13	The malfunction is intermittent or is not present at this time. Refer to Diagnostic Aids for more information. Is the action complete?	—	System OK	—

GC402980345400CX

Fig. 246 Code C1265: Rear ABS Motor Circuit Short To Ground (Part 3 of 3). Metro

Circuit Description

DTC C1266 identifies an ABS motor circuit that shorts to voltage or an ABS motor that has low or zero resistance.

Conditions for Setting the DTC

- DTC C1266 can set only when the ABS motor is commanded off.
- A malfunction exists if the EBCM detects an out of range voltage on either of the rear ABS motor circuits.
- An out of range voltage on either circuit indicates one of the following conditions:
  - CKT 6E01 and/or CKT 6F01 is shorted to voltage.
  - An ABS brake motor shorts internally.

Action Taken When the DTC Sets

- A malfunction DTC stores.
- The ABS disables.
- The ABS warning indicator turns ON.

Conditions for Clearing the DTC

- The condition responsible for setting the DTC no longer exists and the Scan Tool Clear DTCs function is used.
- 100 drive cycles pass with no DTCs detected. A drive cycle consists of starting the vehicle, driving the vehicle over 16 km/h (10 mph), stopping and then turning the ignition OFF.

Diagnostic Aids

Use the Scan Tool Manual Control function to exercise ABS motor movement of affected channel in both directions while applying light pressure on the brake pedal.

An intermittent malfunction may be indicated if erratic or jumpy brake pedal movement is detected while performing an apply or release function of the ABS monitor.

If the malfunction is not current, use the following procedure to pinpoint an intermittent malfunction in the motor circuitry or connections:

1. Wiggle the wires of the affected channel.
2. Inspect if the DTC resets.

Use the enhanced diagnostic function of the Scan Tool in order to measure the frequency of the malfunction.

Clear the DTCs after completing the diagnosis. Test drive the vehicle for three drive cycles in order to verify that the DTC does not reset. Use the following procedure in order to complete one drive cycle:

1. Start the vehicle.
2. Drive the vehicle over 16 km/h (10 mph).
3. Stop the vehicle.
4. Turn the ignition to the OFF position.

Important: Zero the J 39200 test leads before making any resistance measurements.

GC402980345500AX

Fig. 247 Code C1266: Rear ABS Motor Circuit Short To Voltage (Part 1 of 3). Metro

Step	Action	Value(s)	Yes	No
1	Was the Diagnostic System Check performed?	—	*Go to Step 2*	Refer to *Diagnostic System Check*
2	Does DTC C1266 occur intermittently?	—	Refer to Diagnostic Aids	*Go to Step 3*
3	1. Turn the ignition switch to the OFF position. 2. Disconnect the 6-way ABS brake motor pack connector. 3. Disconnect the EBCM connector 4. Turn the ignition switch to the ON position. Do not start the engine. 5. Use the *J 39200* in order to measure the voltage between the 6-way ABS brake motor pack harness connector terminal C and ground. Is the voltage within the specified range?	0–1 V	*Go to Step 4*	*Go to Step 10*
4	Use the *J 39200* in order to measure the voltage between the 6-way ABS brake motor pack harness connector terminal D and ground. Is the voltage within the specified range?	0–1 V	*Go to Step 5*	*Go to Step 11*
5	1. Turn the ignition switch to the OFF position. 2. Use the *J 39200* in order to measure the resistance between the 6-way ABS motor pack harness connector terminal D and the 6-way ABS motor pack harness connector terminal C. Is the resistance within the specified range?	OL (Infinite)	*Go to Step 6*	*Go to Step 12*
6	Use the *J 39200* in order to measure the resistance between the 6-way ABS motor pack connector terminal D and the 6-way ABS motor pack connector terminal C. Is the resistance within the specified range?	0.2–1.5 Ω	*Go to Step 7*	*Go to Step 9*
7	1. Inspect the following components for damage: • The 6-way ABS motor pack connector • The 6-way ABS motor pack harness connector Damage that may cause a short to voltage with the connector connected. 2. Inspect the following components for damage: • The EBCM connector • The EBCM harness connector Damage that may cause a short to voltage with the connector connected. 3. Inspect CKT 6E01 and CKT 6F01 for damage. Damage may cause a short to voltage. Is there damage that may cause a short to voltage?	—	*Go to Step 13*	*Go to Step 8*
8	1. Reconnect the 6-way ABS motor pack connector. 2. Reconnect the EBCM connector. 3. Test drive the vehicle at a speed of at least 16 km/h (10 mph). 4. Turn the ignition switch to the OFF position. 5. Repeat the drive sequence two additional times. 6. Use the *Scan Tool* in order to inspect for DTCs. Did DTC C1266 set as a current DTC in the last three drive cycles?	—	*Go to Step 14*	*Go to Step 15*

GC402980345500BX

Fig. 247 Code C1266: Rear ABS Motor Circuit Short To Voltage (Part 2 of 3). Metro

Step	Action	Value(s)	Yes	No
9	Replace the ABS motor pack. Is the repair complete?	—	Refer to *Diagnostic System Check*	—
10	Repair the short to voltage in CKT 6E01. Is the repair complete?	—	Refer to *Diagnostic System Check*	—
11	Repair the short to voltage in CKT 6F01. Is the repair complete?	—	Refer to *Diagnostic System Check*	—
12	Repair the short between CKT 6E01 and CKT 6F01. Is the repair complete?	—	Refer to *Diagnostic System Check*	—
13	Replace all of the following components that are damaged: • The terminals • The connectors • The wires Damage may cause a short to voltage. Is the repair complete?	—	Refer to *Diagnostic System Check*	—
14	Replace the EBCM. Is the repair complete?	—	Refer to *Diagnostic System Check*	—
15	The malfunction is intermittent or is not present at this time. Refer to Diagnostic Aids for more information. Is the action complete?	—	System OK	—

GC402980345500CX

Fig. 247 Code C1266: Rear ABS Motor Circuit Short To Voltage (Part 3 of 3). Metro

Circuit Description

This DTC identifies a solenoid that cannot be energized due to an open in its circuitry, or a solenoid that is always energized due to a short to ground in its circuitry between the EBCM and the solenoid.

An open will not allow proper ABS operation, but the short to ground simply turns ON the solenoid. A path for base brakes is still allowed once the motor rehomes and the check valve is lifted off its seat when the ignition switch is turned to ON.

Conditions for Setting the DTC

DTC C1276 can set only when the brake solenoid valve is commanded off while the Electronic Brake Control Relay is enabled.

A malfunction exists if the EBCM detects the left front brake solenoid valve control circuit voltage is not within specifications.

Action Taken When the DTC Sets

- A malfunction DTC stores.
- The ABS disables.
- The ABS warning indicator turns ON.

Conditions for Clearing the DTC

- The condition responsible for setting the DTC no longer exists and the Scan Tool Clear DTCs function is used.
- 100 drive cycles pass with no DTCs detected. A drive cycle consists of starting the vehicle, driving the vehicle over 16 km/h (10 mph), stopping and then turning the ignition OFF.

Diagnostic Aids

The following conditions may cause an intermittent malfunction:

- A poor connection
- Rubbed-through wire insulation
- A broken wire inside the insulation

Use the enhanced diagnostic function of the Scan Tool in order to measure the frequency of the malfunction.

Thoroughly inspect any circuitry that may cause the intermittent complaint for the following conditions:

- Backed out terminals
- Improper mating
- Broken locks
- Improperly formed or damaged terminals
- Poor terminal-to-wiring connections
- Physical damage to the wiring harness

Important: Zero the J 39200 test leads before making any resistance measurements.

GC402980345600AX

Fig. 248 Code C1276: LH Front Solenoid Circuit Open/Short To Ground (Part 1 of 3). Metro

Step	Action	Value(s)	Yes	No
1	Was the Diagnostic System Check performed?	—	*Go to Step 2*	Refer to *Diagnostic System Check*
2	1. Turn the ignition switch to LOCK. 2. Disconnect the EBCM connector C1. 3. Using *J 39200* measure the resistance between the EBCM harness connector C1 terminal A10 and ground. Is the resistance within the specified range?	OL (Infinite)	*Go to Step 3*	*Go to Step 4*
3	1. Disconnect the left front brake solenoid valve connector. 2. Using *J 39200* measure the resistance between the EBCM harness connector C1 terminal A10 and the left front brake solenoid valve harness connector terminal B. Is the resistance within the specified range?	0–2 Ω	*Go to Step 5*	*Go to Step 9*
4	1. Disconnect the LF ABS solenoid connector. 2. Using *J 39200* measure the resistance between the left front ABS brake solenoid valve connector terminal B and ground. Is the resistance within the specified range?	OL (Infinite)	*Go to Step 8*	*Go to Step 11*
5	1. Disconnect the EBCM harness connector C2. 2. Using *J 39200* measure the resistance between the EBCM harness connector C2 terminal C and the left front ABS solenoid valve harness connector terminal A. Is the resistance within the specified range?	0–2 Ω	*Go to Step 6*	*Go to Step 10*
6	Using *J 39200* measure the resistance between the LF ABS solenoid terminals A and B. Is the resistance within the specified range?	2.5–5.0 Ω	*Go to Step 7*	*Go to Step 11*
7	1. Inspect the LF ABS solenoid and connectors for poor terminal contact or corrosion. 2. Inspect CKT 6I01 and 6B01 for damage which may result in a short to ground with all connectors connected. 3. Reconnect all connectors. 4. Start the engine. 5. Drive the vehicle at 16 km/h (10 mph) for 10 seconds. 6. Stop the vehicle and turn the ignition switch to LOCK. 7. Repeat the drive cycle (steps 4, 5 and 6). 8. Turn the ignition switch to ON. 9. Using the scan tool, check for DTCs. Did DTC C1276 set in the past three ignition cycles?	—	*Go to Step 12*	Refer to *Diagnostic System Check*
8	Repair the short to ground in CKT 6I01. Is the repair complete?	—	*Go to Step 6*	—

GC402980345600BX

Fig. 248 Code C1276: LH Front Solenoid Circuit Open/Short To Ground (Part 2 of 3). Metro

Step	Action	Value(s)	Yes	No
9	Repair the open or high resistance in CKT 6I01. Is the repair complete?	—	Refer to *Diagnostic System Check*	—
10	Repair the open or high resistance in CKT 6B01. Is the repair complete?	—	Refer to *Diagnostic System Check*	—
11	Replace the LF ABS solenoid. Is the repair complete?	—	Refer to *Diagnostic System Check*	—
12	Replace the EBCM Is the replacement complete?	—	Refer to *Diagnostic System Check*	—

GC402980345600CX

Fig. 248 Code C1276: LH Front Solenoid Circuit Open/Short To Ground (Part 3 of 3). Metro

Step	Action	Value(s)	Yes	No
1	Was the Diagnostic System Check performed?	—	*Go to Step 2*	Refer to *Diagnostic System Check*
2	1. Turn the ignition switch to LOCK. 2. Disconnect the EBCM harness connector C1. 3. Turn the ignition switch to ON. 4. Using *J 39200* measure the voltage between the EBCM harness connector C2 terminal A10 and ground. Is the voltage within the specified range?	0–1 V	*Go to Step 3*	*Go to Step 5*
3	1. Turn the ignition switch to LOCK. 2. Disconnect the left front ABS solenoid valve connector. 3. Using *J 39200* measure the resistance between the left front solenoid valve terminals A and B. Is the resistance within the specified range?	2.5–5.0 Ω	*Go to Step 4*	*Go to Step 6*
4	1. Inspect CKT 6I01, LF solenoid, and the EBCM connector C1 for damage which may result in a short to voltage with all connectors connected. 2. Reconnect connector(s). 3. Start the engine. 4. Drive vehicle at 16 km/h (10 mph) for 10 seconds. 5. Stop vehicle and turn ignition to LOCK. 6. Repeat drive cycle (steps 3, 4 and 5). 7. Turn the ignition switch ON. 8. Using a scan tool, check for DTCs. Did DTC C1277 set during the past three ignition cycles?	—	*Go to Step 7*	Refer to *Diagnostic System Check*
5	Repair the short to voltage in CKT 6I01. Is the repair complete?	—	Refer to *Diagnostic System Check*	—
6	Replace the LF ABS solenoid. Is the repair complete?	—	Refer to *Diagnostic System Check*	—
7	Replace the EBCM. Is the repair complete?	—	Refer to *Diagnostic System Check*	—

GC402980345700BX

Fig. 249 Code C1277: LH Front Solenoid Circuit Short To Voltage (Part 2 of 2). Metro

Circuit Description

This DTC identifies a solenoid that cannot be energized due to an open in its circuitry or a solenoid that is always energized due to a short to ground in its circuitry between the EBCM and the solenoid.

An open will not allow proper ABS operation, but the short to ground simply turns ON the solenoid. A path for base brakes is still allowed once the motor rehomes and the check valve is lifted off its seat when the ignition switch is turned to ON.

Conditions for Setting the DTC

- DTC C1278 can set only when the solenoid is commanded off while the Electronic Brake Control Relay is enabled.
- A malfunction exists if the EBCM detects the right front brake solenoid valve control circuit voltage is not within specifications.

Action Taken When the DTC Sets

- A malfunction DTC stores.
- The ABS disables.
- The ABS warning indicator turns ON.

Conditions for Clearing the DTC

- The condition responsible for setting the DTC no longer exists and the Scan Tool Clear DTCs function is used.
- 100 drive cycles pass with no DTCs detected. A drive cycle consists of starting the vehicle, driving the vehicle over 16 km/h (10 mph), stopping and then turning the ignition OFF.

Diagnostic Aids

The following conditions may cause an intermittent malfunction:

- A poor connection
- Rubbed-through wire insulation
- A broken wire inside the insulation

Use the enhanced diagnostic function of the Scan Tool in order to measure the frequency of the malfunction.

Thoroughly inspect any circuitry that may cause the intermittent complaint for the following conditions:

- Backed out terminals
- Improper mating
- Broken locks
- Improperly formed or damaged terminals
- Poor terminal-to-wiring connections
- Physical damage to the wiring harness

Important: Zero the J 39200 test leads before making any resistance measurements.

GC402980345800AX

Fig. 250 Code C1278: RH Front Solenoid Circuit Open/Short To Ground (Part 1 of 3). Metro

Circuit Description

DTC C1277 identifies a solenoid that cannot be energized due to a short to voltage in the solenoid circuitry. The malfunction can affect ABS operation since the flow of brake fluid to the wheel cylinder cannot be stopped. The unstoppable flow of brake fluid to the wheel cylinder makes ABS operation for that channel impossible.

Conditions for Setting the DTC

- DTC C1277 can set only when the brake solenoid valve is commanded on.
- A malfunction exists if the EBCM detects the left front brake solenoid valve control circuit voltage is not within specifications.

Action Taken When the DTC Sets

- A malfunction DTC stores.
- The ABS disables.
- The ABS warning indicator turns ON.

Conditions for Clearing the DTC

- The condition responsible for setting the DTC no longer exists and the Scan Tool Clear DTCs function is used.
- 100 drive cycles pass with no DTCs detected. A drive cycle consists of starting the vehicle, driving the vehicle over 16 km/h (10 mph), stopping and then turning the ignition OFF.

Diagnostic Aids

Use the enhanced diagnostic function of the Scan Tool in order to measure the frequency of the malfunction.

Any circuitry that is suspected of causing the intermittent complaint should be thoroughly checked for improper mating, improperly formed or damaged terminals, poor terminal to wiring connections, or physical damage to the wiring harness.

Important: Zero the J 39200 test leads before making any resistance measurements. Refer to the J 39200 user's manual.

Important: Difficulty may occur when trying to locate the intermittent malfunctions in the wheel speed sensor circuit.

Do not disturb any of the electrical connections. Change electrical connections only when instructed to do so by a step in the diagnostic table.

Changing the electrical connections at the correct time will ensure that an intermittent electrical connection will not be corrected until the source of the malfunction is found.

GC402980345700AX

Fig. 249 Code C1277: LH Front Solenoid Circuit Short To Voltage (Part 1 of 2). Metro

Step	Action	Value(s)	Yes	No
1	Was the Diagnostic System Check performed?	—	*Go to Step 2*	Refer to *Diagnostic System Check*
2	1. Turn the ignition switch to LOCK. 2. Disconnect the EBCM connector C1. 3. Using *J 39200* measure the resistance between the EBCM harness connector C1 terminal B6 and ground. Is the resistance within the specified range?	OL (Infinite)	*Go to Step 3*	*Go to Step 4*
3	1. Disconnect the RF ABS solenoid connector. 2. Using *J 39200* measure the resistance between the EBCM harness connector C1 terminal B6 and the right front ABS solenoid valve harness connector terminal B. Is the resistance within the specified range?	0.0–2.0 Ω	*Go to Step 5*	*Go to Step 9*
4	1. Disconnect the RF ABS solenoid connector. 2. Using *J 39200* measure the resistance between the right front ABS brake solenoid connector terminal B and ground. Is the resistance within the specified range?	OL (Infinite)	*Go to Step 8*	*Go to Step 11*
5	1. Disconnect the EBCM harness connector C2. 2. Using *J 39200* measure the resistance between the EBCM harness connector C2 terminal C and the right front ABS solenoid valve connector terminal A. Is the resistance within the specified range?	0.0–2.0 Ω	*Go to Step 6*	*Go to Step 10*
6	Using *J 39200* set to ohms, measure the resistance between the RF ABS solenoid terminals A and B. Is the resistance within the specified range?	—	*Go to Step 7*	*Go to Step 11*
7	1. Inspect the RF ABS solenoid and connectors for poor terminal contact or corrosion. 2. Inspect CKT 6J01 and 6B01 for damage which may result in a short to ground with all connectors connected. 3. Reconnect all connectors. 4. Start the engine. 5. Drive the vehicle at 16 km/h (10 mph) for 10 seconds. 6. Stop the vehicle and turn the ignition switch to LOCK. 7. Repeat drive cycle (steps 4, 5 and 6). 8. Turn the ignition switch to ON. 9. Using a scan tool, check for DTCs. Did DTC C1278 set in the past three ignition cycles?	—	*Go to Step 12*	Refer to *Diagnostic System Check*
8	Repair the short to ground in CKT 6J01. Is the repair complete?	—	*Go to Step 6*	—

GC402980345800BX

Fig. 250 Code C1278: RH Front Solenoid Circuit Open/Short To Ground (Part 2 of 3). Metro

Step	Action	Value(s)	Yes	No
9	Repair the open or high resistance in CKT 6J01. Is the repair complete?	—	Refer to *Diagnostic System Check*	—
10	Repair the open or high resistance in CKT 6B01. Is the repair complete?	—	Refer to *Diagnostic System Check*	—
11	Replace the RF ABS solenoid. Is the repair complete?	—	Refer to *Diagnostic System Check*	—
12	Replace the EBCM. Is the repair complete?	—	Refer to *Diagnostic System Check*	—

GC402980345800CX

Fig. 250 Code C1278: RH Front Solenoid Circuit Open/Short To Ground (Part 3 of 3). Metro

Step	Action	Value(s)	Yes	No
1	Was the Diagnostic System Check performed?	—	*Go to Step 2*	Refer to *Diagnostic System Check*
2	1. Turn the ignition switch to LOCK. 2. Disconnect the EBCM harness connector C1. 3. Turn the ignition switch to ON. 4. Using *J 39200* measure the voltage between the EBCM harness connector C1 terminal B6 and ground. Is the voltage within the specified range?	0–1 V	*Go to Step 3*	*Go to Step 5*
3	1. Turn the ignition switch to LOCK. 2. Disconnect the right front ABS solenoid valve connector. 3. Using *J 39200* measure the resistance between the right front solenoid valve terminals A and B. Is the resistance within the specified range?	2.5–5.0 Ω	*Go to Step 4*	*Go to Step 6*
4	1. Inspect CKT 6J01, RF solenoid, and the EBCM connector C1 for damage which may result in a short to voltage with all the connectors connected. 2. Reconnect connector(s). 3. Start the engine. 4. Drive the vehicle at 16 km/h (10 mph). 5. Stop the vehicle and turn the ignition switch to LOCK. 6. Repeat drive cycle (steps 3, 4 and 5). 7. Turn the ignition switch to ON. 8. Using a scan tool, check for DTCs. Did DTC C1281 set during the past three ignition cycles?	—	*Go to Step 7*	Refer to *Diagnostic System Check*
5	Repair the short to voltage in CKT 6J01. Is the repair complete?	—	Refer to *Diagnostic System Check*	—
6	Replace the RF ABS solenoid. Is the repair complete?	—	Refer to *Diagnostic System Check*	—
7	Replace the EBCM. Is the repair complete?	—	Refer to *Diagnostic System Check*	—

GC402980345900BX

Fig. 251 Code C1281: RH Front Solenoid Circuit Short To Voltage (Part 2 of 2). Metro

Step	Action	Value(s)	Yes	No
1	Was the Diagnostic System Check performed?	—	*Go to Step 2*	Refer to *Diagnostic System Check*
2	1. Turn the ignition switch to the ON position. Do not start the engine. 2. Install a *Scan Tool*. 3. Use the *Scan Tool* in order to inspect for DTCs. Is DTC C1282 set as a current DTC?	—	*Go to Step 3*	*Go to Step 4*
3	Replace the EBCM. Is the repair complete?	—	Refer to *Diagnostic System Check*	—
4	The malfunction is intermittent or is not present at this time. Refer to Diagnostic Aids for more information. Is the action complete?	—	System OK	—

GC402980346000BX

Fig. 252 Code C1282: Calibration Fault (Part 2 of 2). Metro

Step	Action	Value(s)	Yes	No
1	Was the Diagnostic System Check performed?	—	*Go to Step 2*	Refer to *Diagnostic System Check*
2	1. Turn the ignition switch to the ON position. Do not start the engine. 2. Install the *Scan Tool*. 3. Use the *Scan Tool* in order to inspect for DTCs.	—	Refer to *Diagnostic System Check*	*Go to Step 3*
3	Use the *Scan Tool* in order to clear DTC C1286. Was DTC C1286 cleared?	—	Refer to *Diagnostic System Check*	—

GC402980346100BX

Fig. 253 Code C1286: EBCM Turned On Brake Warning Lamp (Part 2 of 2). Metro

Circuit Description

DTC C1281 identifies a solenoid that cannot be energized due to a short to voltage in the solenoid circuitry. The malfunction can affect ABS operation since the flow of brake fluid to the wheel cylinder cannot be stopped. The unstoppable flow of brake fluid to the wheel cylinder makes ABS operation for that channel impossible.

Conditions for Setting the DTC

- DTC C1281 can set only when the brake solenoid is commanded ON.
- A malfunction exists if the EBCM detects the right front brake solenoid valve control circuit voltage is not within specifications.

Action Taken When the DTC Sets

- A malfunction DTC stores.
- The ABS disables.
- The ABS warning indicator turns ON.

Conditions for Clearing the DTC

- The condition responsible for setting the DTC no longer exists and the Scan Tool Clear DTCs function is used.
- 100 drive cycles pass with no DTCs detected. A drive cycle consists of starting the vehicle, driving the vehicle over 16 km/h (10 mph), stopping and then turning the ignition OFF.

Diagnostic Aids

Use the enhanced diagnostic function of the Scan Tool in order to measure the frequency of the malfunction.

Any circuitry that is suspected of causing the intermittent complaint should be thoroughly checked for improper mating, improperly formed or damaged terminals, poor terminal to wiring connections, or physical damage to the wiring harness.

Important: Zero the J 39200 test leads before making any resistance measurements. Refer to the J 39200 user's manual.

Important: Difficulty may occur when trying to locate the intermittent malfunctions in the wheel speed sensor circuit.

Do not disturb any of the electrical connections. Change electrical connections only when instructed to do so by a step in the diagnostic table.

Changing the electrical connections at the correct time will ensure that an intermittent electrical connection will not be corrected until the source of the malfunction is found.

GC402980345900AX

Fig. 251 Code C1281: RH Front Solenoid Circuit Short To Voltage (Part 1 of 2). Metro

Circuit Description

DTC C1282 allows the EBCM to inspect for a calibration malfunction by comparing the calibration value to a known value stored in the EBCM's memory.

DTC C1282 also acts as a security measure to prevent improper use of calibrations or changes to these calibrations. Improper calibrations may alter the designed function of ABS.

Conditions for Setting the DTC

DTC C1282 can be set at ABS initialization. A malfunction exists if the EBCM internal memory calibration is incorrect.

Action Taken When the DTC Sets

- A malfunction DTC stores.
- The ABS disables.
- The ABS warning indicator turns ON.

Conditions for Clearing the DTC

- The condition responsible for setting the DTC no longer exists and the Scan Tool Clear DTCs function is used.
- 100 drive cycles pass with no DTC(s) detected. A drive cycle consists of starting the vehicle, driving the vehicle over 16 km/h (10 mph), stopping and then turning the ignition OFF.

Diagnostic Aids

An intermittent DTC C1282 is most likely caused by a malfunctioning EBCM that is sensitive to temperature changes. If DTC C1282 occurred more than once, but is intermittent, replace EBCM.

Use the enhanced diagnostic function of the Scan Tool in order to measure the frequency of the malfunction.

GC402980346000AX

Fig. 252 Code C1282: Calibration Fault (Part 1 of 2). Metro

Circuit Description

DTC C1286 is provided as an "information only" test and reflects the status of the command issued by the EBCM to illuminate the red BRAKE warning indicator.

Conditions for Setting the DTC

When another diagnostic DTC issues a command to illuminate the red BRAKE warning indicator, DTC C1286 will be stored in memory as a history DTC at the conclusion of the ignition cycle.

Action Taken When the DTC Sets

- A malfunction DTC stores.
- The ABS disables.
- The ABS warning indicator turns ON.
- The red Brake warning indicator turns ON.

Conditions for Clearing the DTC

- The condition responsible for setting the DTC no longer exists and the Scan Tool Clear DTCs function is used.
- 100 drive cycles pass with no DTCs detected. A drive cycle consists of starting the vehicle, driving the vehicle over 16 km/h (10 mph), stopping and then turning the ignition OFF.

Diagnostic Aids

The following ABS mechanical DTCs command the red BRAKE warning indicator to illuminate. The DTCs will also cause the EBCM to store DTC C1286 during shutdown:

- C1242
- C1246
- C1251

If the motors are not in their home position, the following electrical DTCs will also command the red BRAKE warning indicator ON:

- C1214
- C1216
- C1218
- C1236
- C1255
- C1264
- C1265
- C1266
- C1282

If any of the electrical DTCs are indicated along with DTC C1286, correct the electrical DTCs prior to addressing a DTC C1286 malfunction.

GC402980346100AX

Fig. 253 Code C1286: EBCM Turned On Brake Warning Lamp (Part 1 of 2). Metro

Circuit Description

This DTC identifies an open or short to voltage between the EBCM and the red BRAKE warning indicator, or an open driver that does not allow the red BRAKE warning indicator to be illuminated by the EBCM.

This will only occur if an ABS malfunction is detected that may degrade base brake operation. Because the EBCM is not the only device controlling the red BRAKE warning indicator (parking brake and the brake fluid level switch may also turn on the red BRAKE warning indicator), a short to ground in this circuit cannot be detected.

Conditions for Setting the DTC

This DTC will set when the following conditions are met:

- The EBCM detects a short to voltage in the red BRAKE warning indicator control circuit during the three second bulb check.
- The EBCM detects a short to voltage in the red BRAKE warning indicator control circuit when the red BRAKE warning lamp is commanded ON with a scan tool (output for the red BRAKE warning lamp control circuit is greater than 3.43 volts).
- The EBCM detects an open or high resistance in the red BRAKE warning indicator control circuit at above 5 km/h (3 mph) with red BRAKE warning lamp turned OFF (output for the red BRAKE warning lamp control circuit is between 3.35 volts and 5.23 volts).

Action Taken When the DTC Sets

- A malfunction DTC stores.
- ABS remains functional.
- If the EBCM commands the red BRAKE warning indicator ON due to an ABS malfunction that may degrade base brake operation and cannot do so, the amber ABS indicator lamp will flash to indicate the serious nature of the problem.

Conditions for Clearing the DTC

- The condition responsible for setting the DTC no longer exists and the Scan Tool Clear DTCs function is used.
- 100 drive cycles pass with no DTCs detected. A drive cycle consists of starting the vehicle, driving the vehicle over 16 km/h (10 mph), stopping and then turning the ignition OFF.

GC402980346200AX

Fig. 254 Code C1287: Brake Warning Lamp Circuit Open/Short To Voltage (Part 1 of 5). Metro

Step	Action	Value(s)	Yes	No
1	Was the Diagnostic System Check performed?	—	*Go to Step 2*	Refer to *Diagnostic System Check*
2	1. Turn the ignition switch to LOCK. 2. Disconnect EBCM connector C1. 3. Disconnect the I/P cluster connector C3. 4. Turn the ignition switch to ON. 5. Using *J 39200* measure the voltage between EBCM connector C1 terminal B5 and ground. Is the voltage within the specified range?	0–1 V	*Go to Step 3*	*Go to Step 11*
3	1. Turn the ignition switch to LOCK. 2. Reconnect the I/P cluster connector C3. 3. Using a fused jumper such as J 36169 with a 3A fuse, connect the EBCM connector C1 terminal B5 to ground. 4. Turn the ignition switch to ON. Is the red BRAKE warning indicator ON?	—	*Go to Step 4*	*Go to Step 9*
4	Check the master cylinder brake fluid level. Is the brake fluid level below the LOW mark?	—	*Go to Step 18*	*Go to Step 5*
5	1. Turn the ignition switch to LOCK. 2. Remove the fused jumper (from step 3). 3. Apply the parking brake. 4. Turn the ignition switch to ON. 5. Using *J 39200* measure the voltage between the EBCM connector C1, terminal B5 and ground. Is the voltage within the specified range?	0–2 V	*Go to Step 6*	*Go to Step 19*

GC402980346200BX

Fig. 254 Code C1287: Brake Warning Lamp Circuit Open/Short To Voltage (Part 2 of 5). Metro

Step	Action	Value(s)	Yes	No
15	1. Turn the ignition to LOCK. 2. Remove the IG COIL fuse at the junction block. 3. Disconnect the EBCM connector C1. 4. Turn the ignition switch to ON. 5. Using *J 39200* measure the voltage between the EBCM connector C1 terminal B5 and ground. Is the voltage measured within the specified range?	0.1 V	*Go to Step 16*	*Go to Step 24*
16	1. Turn the ignition switch to LOCK. 2. Inspect CKT 1M03 and the EBCM connector C1 terminal B5 for damage which may result in a short to voltage with the EBCM connector C1 connected. Is there any damage as described?	—	*Go to Step 25*	*Go to Step 17*
17	1. Reconnect the EBCM connector C1. 2. Turn the ignition switch to ON. 3. Using the *Scan Tool*, check for DTCs. Does DTC 1287 set as current DTC?	—	*Go to Step 27*	*Go to Step 28*
18	Fill the brake master cylinder with approved brake fluid such as Delco Supreme 11® Brake Fluid, GM P/N 1052542, or equivalent DOT 3 brake fluid to the FULL mark. Is the action complete?	—	*Go to Step 5*	—
19	Repair the open or high resistance in the parking brake switch wiring. Is the repair complete?	—	Refer to *Diagnostic System Check*	—
20	Replace all the terminals or the connectors that exhibit signs of poor terminal contact, corrosion or damage terminal(s). Is the repair complete?	—	Refer to *Diagnostic System Check*	—
21	Repair the open or high resistance in the master cylinder brake fluid level sensor. Is the repair complete?	—	Refer to *Diagnostic System Check*	—
22	Replace the red Brake warning indicator lamp bulb. Is the repair complete?	—	Refer to *Diagnostic System Check*	—
23	Replace the parking brake switch. Is the repair complete?	—	Refer to *Diagnostic System Check*	—
24	Repair the short to voltage in CKT 1M03 or 2T01. Is the repair complete?	—	Refer to *Diagnostic System Check*	—
25	Repair the damage to CKT 1M03 or the EBCM connector C1 which may result in a short to voltage. Is the repair complete?	—	Refer to *Diagnostic System Check*	—

GC402980346200DX

Fig. 254 Code C1287: Brake Warning Lamp Circuit Open/Short To Voltage (Part 4 of 5). Metro

Step	Action	Value(s)	Yes	No
6	1. Release the parking brake. 2. Turn the ignition switch to LOCK. 3. Disconnect the brake fluid level sensor connector. 4. Inspect the brake fluid level sensor connector and the EBCM connector C1 for poor terminal contact, corrosion or damage. Are there signs of poor terminal contact, corrosion or damage?	—	*Go to Step 20*	*Go to Step 7*
7	1. Reconnect the EBCM connector C1. 2. Turn the ignition switch to ON. 3. Using a *Scan Tool*, check for DTCs. Does DTC C1287 set as current DTC?	—	*Go to Step 27*	*Go to Step 8*
8	1. Turn the ignition switch to LOCK. 2. Reconnect the brake fluid level sensor connector. 3. Turn the ignition switch to ON. 4. Using a *Scan Tool*, check for DTCs. Does DTC C1287 set as current DTC?	—	*Go to Step 21*	*Go to Step 28*
9	1. Turn the ignition switch to LOCK. 2. Remove the I/P cluster. 3. Remove the red BRAKE warning indicator lamp. Is the red BRAKE warning indicator lamp bulb filament open?	—	*Go to Step 22*	*Go to Step 10*
10	Using *J 39200* measure the resistance between the I/P cluster connector C1 terminal B5. Is the resistance measured within the specified range?	0–2 Ω	*Go to Step 29*	*Go to Step 26*
11	1. Turn the ignition switch to LOCK. 2. Reconnect the I/P cluster connector C3. 3. Turn the ignition switch to ON. 4. Observe the red BRAKE warning indicator. Is the red BRAKE warning indicator ON?	—	*Go to Step 12*	*Go to Step 14*
12	1. Install a *Scan Tool*. 2. Using the *Scan Tool*, check for DTCs. Does DTC C1286 set as either current and/or history DTC?	—	*Go to DTC C1286 EBCM Turned On Brake Warning Indicator*	*Go to Step 13*
13	1. Release the parking brake. 2. Disconnect the parking brake switch connector. 3. Using *J 39200* measure the resistance between the parking brake switch connector and ground. Is the resistance measured within the specified range?	Infinite	*Go to Step 28*	*Go to Step 23*
14	1. Install a *Scan Tool*. 2. Select Lamp Test. 3. Using the *Scan Tool*, command the red BRAKE warning indicator ON. Is the red BRAKE warning indicator ON?	—	*Go to Step 28*	*Go to Step 15*

GC402980346200CX

Fig. 254 Code C1287: Brake Warning Lamp Circuit Open/Short To Voltage (Part 3 of 5). Metro

Step	Action	Value(s)	Yes	No
26	Repair the open or high resistance in CKT 1M03. Is the repair complete?	—	Refer to *Diagnostic System Check*	—
27	Replace the EBCM. Is the repair complete?	—	Refer to *Diagnostic System Check*	—
28	Malfunction is intermittent of not present at this time. Refer to Diagnostic Aids for more information. Is the action complete?	—	Refer to *Diagnostic System Check*	—
29	Refer to Instrument Cluster. Is the action complete?	—	Refer to *Diagnostic System Check*	—

GC402980346200EX

Fig. 254 Code C1287: Brake Warning Lamp Circuit Open/Short To Voltage (Part 5 of 5). Metro

Circuit Description

DTC C1291 detects an open brake switch. The EBCM looks for deceleration rates that may indicate braking action. The EBCM verifies braking action by repeating the method for finding deceleration rates that indicate braking action several times. In each case, the ABS will not be available because the EBCM does not see the brake switch input.

Conditions for Setting the DTC

DTC C1291 can set if three deceleration cycles within the specified rate occur during the current ignition cycle with the brake switch off.

Action Taken When the DTC Sets

- A malfunction DTC stores.
- The ABS disables.
- The ABS warning indicator turns ON.

Conditions for Clearing the DTC

- The condition responsible for setting the DTC no longer exists and the Scan Tool Clear DTCs function is used.
- 100 drive cycles pass with no DTCs detected. A drive cycle consists of starting the vehicle, driving the vehicle over 16 km/h (10 mph), stopping and then turning the ignition OFF.

Diagnostic Aids

The following conditions may cause an intermittent malfunction:

- A poor connection
- Rubbed-through wire insulation
- A broken wire inside the insulation

Use the enhanced diagnostic function of the Scan Tool in order to measure the frequency of the malfunction.

Thoroughly inspect any circuitry that may cause the intermittent complaint for the following conditions:

- Backed out terminals
- Improper mating
- Broken locks
- Improperly formed or damaged terminals
- Poor terminal-to-wiring connections
- Physical damage to the wiring harness
- Sticking brake switch

Important: Zero the J 39200 test leads before making any resistance measurements.

GC402980346300AX

Fig. 255 Code C1291: Open Brake Lamp Switch Contacts During Decel (Part 1 of 4). Metro

Step	Action	Value(s)	Yes	No
1	Was the Diagnostic System Check performed?	—	*Go to Step 2*	*Refer to Diagnostic System Check*
2	1. Turn the ignition switch to the ON position. Do not start the engine. 2. Install a *Scan Tool*. 3. Use the *Scan Tool* in order to inspect for DTCs. Is DTC C1295 set as either a current and/or history DTC?	—	Refer to *DTC C1295 Brake Lamp Switch Circuit Open*	*Go to Step 3*
3	1. Select Data List on the *Scan Tool*. 2. Select Brake Switch Position on the *Scan Tool*. 3. Apply light pressure to the brake pedal while monitoring the Brake Switch Position on the *Scan Tool*. Does the Scan Tool indicate that the brake switch is on within 25 mm (1.0 in) of brake pedal travel?	—	*Go to Step 25*	*Go to Step 4*
4	1. Apply firm pressure to the brake pedal. 2. Observe the rear brake lamps. Are the rear brake lamps on?	—	*Go to Step 5*	*Go to Step 8*
5	1. Turn the ignition switch to the OFF position. 2. Disconnect the EBCM connector. 3. Turn the ignition switch to the ON position. Do not start the engine. 4. Apply firm pressure to the brake pedal. 5. Use the *J 39200* in order to measure the voltage between the EBCM harness connector terminal B9 and ground. Is the voltage equal to or greater than the specified voltage?	10.0 V	*Go to Step 6*	*Go to Step 16*
6	Inspect the EBCM connector and the EBCM harness connector for the following conditions: • Terminal damage • Poor terminal contact • Terminal corrosion Is there poor terminal contact, terminal corrosion, or damaged terminals?	—	*Go to Step 17*	*Go to Step 7*
7	1. Reconnect the connector. 2. Test drive the vehicle and perform a brake stop from 32 km/h (20 mph) engaging the ABS. 3. Use the *Scan Tool* in order to inspect for DTCs. Does DTC C1291 or DTC C1292 set as a current DTC?	—	*Go to Step 23*	*Go to Step 25*
8	Use the *J 39200* in order to measure the voltage between the stoplamp switch harness connector terminal 2 (MANUAL) or 3 (AUTO) and ground. Is the voltage equal to or greater than the specified voltage?	10.0 V	*Go to Step 9*	*Go to Step 11*
9	1. Apply firm pressure to the brake pedal. 2. Use the *J 39200* in order to measure the voltage between the stoplamp switch harness connector terminal 1 and ground. Is the voltage equal to or greater than the specified voltage?	10.0 V	*Go to Step 16*	*Go to Step 10*

GC402980346300BX

Fig. 255 Code C1291: Open Brake Lamp Switch Contacts During Decel (Part 2 of 4). Metro

Step	Action	Value(s)	Yes	No
10	Inspect for proper adjustment of the stoplamp switch. Is the stoplamp switch adjusted correctly?	—	*Go to Step 18*	*Go to Step 19*
11	Remove and inspect the fuse block STOP Fuse (15A). Is the fuse open?	—	*Go to Step 13*	*Go to Step 12*
12	1. Disconnect the stoplamp switch connector. 2. Use a *J 39200* in order to measure the resistance between the stoplamp switch harness connector terminal 2 (MANUAL), 3 (AUTO) and the STOP Fuse terminal of the fuse block. Is the resistance within the specified range?	0.0–2.0 Ω	*Go to Step 14*	*Go to Step 21*
13	1. Disconnect the EBCM connector. 2. Use the *J 39200* in order to measure the resistance between the EBCM harness connector terminal B9 and ground. Is the resistance within the specified range?	OL (Infinite)	*Go to Step 15*	*Go to Step 20*
14	Use the *J 39200* in order to measure the voltage between the STOP Fuse (15A) of the fuse block and ground. Is the voltage equal to or greater than the specified voltage?	10 V	*Go to Step 25*	—
15	1. Disconnect the stoplamp switch connector. 2. Use the *J 39200* in order to measure the resistance between the stoplamp switch harness connector terminal 2 (MANUAL), 3 (AUTO) and ground. Is the resistance within the specified range?	OL (Infinite)	*Go to Step 24*	*Go to Step 22*
16	Repair the open in CKT 2O02. Is the repair complete?	—	Refer to *Diagnostic System Check*	—
17	Replace all the terminal or the connectors that exhibit the following conditions: • Poor terminal contact • Terminal corrosion • Damaged terminals Is the repair complete?	—	Refer to *Diagnostic System Check*	—
18	Replace the stoplamp switch. Is the repair complete?	—	Refer to *Diagnostic System Check*	—
19	Adjust the stoplamp switch. Is the repair complete?	—	Refer to *Diagnostic System Check*	—
20	1. Repair the short to ground in CKT 2O02. 2. Replace the STOP Fuse (15A) with a known good fuse (20A). Is the repair complete?	—	Refer to *Diagnostic System Check*	—
21	Repair the open in CKT 1Z01. Is the repair complete?	—	Refer to *Diagnostic System Check*	—
22	1. Repair the short to ground in CKT 1Z01. 2. Replace the STOP Fuse (15A) with a known good fuse (15A). Is the repair complete?	—	Refer to *Diagnostic System Check*	—

GC402980346300CX

Fig. 255 Code C1291: Open Brake Lamp Switch Contacts During Decel (Part 3 of 4). Metro

Step	Action	Value(s)	Yes	No
23	Replace the EBCM. Is the repair complete?	—	Refer to *Diagnostic System Check*	—
24	Replace the STOP Fuse (15A) with a known good fuse (15A). Is the repair complete?	—	Refer to *Diagnostic System Check*	—
25	The malfunction is intermittent or is not present at this time. Refer to Diagnostic Aids for more information. Is the action complete?	—	System OK	—

GC402980346300DX

Fig. 255 Code C1291: Open Brake Lamp Switch Contacts During Decel (Part 4 of 4). Metro

Circuit Description

DTC C1292 determines the proper operation of the brake switch. Proper operation of the brake switch is important because the brake switch activates the ABS when the brake switch is on. If the brake switch is off, the ABS will never activate. This malfunction is only detected when ABS is required because it is difficult to detect the malfunction under normal braking conditions.

Conditions for Setting the DTC

DTC C1292 can set if the vehicle speed is greater than 8 km/h (5 mph).

A malfunction exists when the following conditions occur:

- The brake was not ON.
- A release was required on two channels for 0.5 second.

Action Taken When the DTC Sets

- A malfunction DTC stores.
- The ABS disables.
- The ABS warning indicator turns ON.

Conditions for Clearing the DTC

- The condition responsible for setting the DTC no longer exists and the Scan Tool Clear DTCs function is used.
- 100 drive cycles pass with no DTCs detected. A drive cycle consists of starting the vehicle, driving the vehicle over 16 km/h (10 mph), stopping and then turning the ignition OFF.

Diagnostic Aids

- The following conditions may cause a malfunction:
  - Faulty stoplamp switch (contacts open all the time)
  - Loss of two wheel speed sensors at the same time
- Use the enhanced diagnostic function of the Scan Tool in order to measure the frequency of the malfunction.

Thoroughly inspect any circuitry that may cause the intermittent complaint for the following conditions:

- Backed out terminals
- Improper mating
- Broken locks
- Improperly formed or damaged terminals
- Poor terminal-to-wiring connections
- Physical damage to the wiring harness
- Sticking brake switch

Important: Zero the J 39200 test leads before making any resistance measurements. Refer to the J 39200 user's manual.

GC402980346400AX

Fig. 256 Code C1292: Open Brake Lamp Switch When ABS Required (Part 1 of 4). Metro

Step	Action	Value(s)	Yes	No
1	Was the Diagnostic System Check performed?	—	*Go to Step 2*	*Refer to Diagnostic System Check*
2	1. Turn the ignition switch to the ON position. Do not start the engine. 2. Install a *Scan Tool*. 3. Use the *Scan Tool* in order to inspect for DTCs. Is DTC C1295 set as either a current and/or history DTC?	—	Refer to *DTC C1295 Brake Lamp Switch Circuit Open*	*Go to Step 3*
3	1. Select Data List on the *Scan Tool*. 2. Select Brake Switch Position on the *Scan Tool*. 3. Apply light pressure to the brake pedal while monitoring the Brake Switch Position on the Scan Tool. Does the Scan Tool indicate that the brake switch is on within 25 mm (1.0 in) of brake pedal travel?	—	*Go to Step 25*	*Go to Step 4*
4	1. Apply firm pressure to the brake pedal. 2. Observe the rear brake lamps. Are the rear brake lamps ON?	—	*Go to Step 5*	*Go to Step 8*
5	1. Turn the ignition switch to the OFF position. 2. Disconnect the EBCM connector. 3. Turn the ignition switch to the ON position. Do not start the engine. 4. Apply firm pressure to the brake pedal. 5. Use the *J 39200* in order to measure the voltage between the EBCM harness connector terminal B9 and ground. Is the voltage equal to or greater than the specified voltage?	10.0 V	*Go to Step 6*	*Go to Step 16*
6	Inspect the EBCM connector and the EBCM harness connector for the following conditions: • Terminal damage • Poor terminal contact • Terminal corrosion Is there poor terminal contact, terminal corrosion, or damaged terminals?	—	*Go to Step 17*	*Go to Step 7*
7	1. Reconnect the EBCM connector. 2. Test drive the vehicle and perform a brake stop from 32 km/h (20 mph) while engaging the ABS. 3. Use the *Scan Tool* in order to inspect for DTCs. Does DTC C1291 or DTC C1292 set as a current DTC?	—	*Go to Step 23*	*Go to Step 25*
8	Use the *J 39200* in order to measure the voltage between the stoplamp switch harness connector terminal 2 (MANUAL), 3 (AUTO) and ground. Is the voltage equal to or greater than the specified voltage?	10.0 V	*Go to Step 9*	*Go to Step 11*
9	1. Apply firm pressure to the brake pedal. 2. Use the *J 39200* in order to measure the voltage between the stoplamp switch harness connector terminal 1 and ground. Is the voltage equal to or greater than the specified voltage?	10.0 V	*Go to Step 16*	*Go to Step 10*

GC402980346400BX

Fig. 256 Code C1292: Open Brake Lamp Switch When ABS Required (Part 2 of 4). Metro

Step	Action	Value(s)	Yes	No
10	Inspect for proper adjustment of the stoplamp switch. Is the stoplamp switch adjusted correctly?	—	*Go to Step 18*	*Go to Step 19*
11	1. Remove the fuse block STOP Fuse (15A). 2. Inspect the fuse block STOP Fuse (15A). Is the fuse open?	—	*Go to Step 13*	*Go to Step 12*
12	1. Disconnect the stoplamp switch connector. 2. Use a *J 39200* in order to measure the resistance between the stoplamp switch harness connector terminal 2 (MANUAL), 3 (AUTO) and the STOP Fuse terminal of the fuse block. Is the resistance within the specified range?	0.0–2.0 Ω	*Go to Step 14*	*Go to Step 21*
13	1. Disconnect the EBCM connector. 2. Use the *J 39200* in order to measure the resistance between the EBCM harness connector terminal B9 and ground. Is the resistance within the specified range?	OL (Infinite)	*Go to Step 15*	*Go to Step 20*
14	Use the *J 39200* in order to measure the voltage between the STOP Fuse terminal of the fuse block and ground. Is the voltage equal to or greater than the specified voltage?	10 V	*Go to Step 25*	Electrical Diagnosis
15	1. Disconnect the stoplamp switch connector. 2. Use the *J 39200* in order to measure the resistance between the stoplamp switch harness connector terminal 2 (MANUAL), 3 (AUTO) and ground. Is the resistance within the specified range?	OL (Infinite)	*Go to Step 24*	*Go to Step 22*
16	Repair the open in CKT 2O02. Is the repair complete?	—	Refer to *Diagnostic System Check*	—
17	Replace all the terminal or the connectors that exhibit the following conditions: • Poor terminal contact • Terminal corrosion • Damaged terminals Is the repair complete?	—	Refer to *Diagnostic System Check*	—
18	Replace the stoplamp switch. Is the repair complete?	—	Refer to *Diagnostic System Check*	—
19	Adjust the stoplamp switch. Is the repair complete?	—	Refer to *Diagnostic System Check*	—
20	1. Repair the short to ground in CKT 2O02. 2. Replace the STOP Fuse (15A) with a known good fuse (15A). Is the repair complete?	—	Refer to *Diagnostic System Check*	—
21	Repair the open in CKT 1Z01. Is the repair complete?	—	Refer to *Diagnostic System Check*	—
22	1. Repair the short to ground in CKT 1Z01. 2. Replace the STOP Fuse (15A) with a known good fuse (15A). Is the repair complete?	—	Refer to *Diagnostic System Check*	—

GC402980346400CX

Fig. 256 Code C1292: Open Brake Lamp Switch When ABS Required (Part 3 of 4). Metro

Circuit Description

This DTC is the second portion of DTC C1291 and C1292. If DTCs C1291 or C1292 occurred during the last drive cycle, DTC C1293 becomes a current malfunction during the next ignition cycle, keeping ABS disabled until a Stoplamp Switch ON state is seen.

Conditions for Setting the DTC

DTC C1293 alone indicates DTC C0091 or C0092 occurred previously, but is intermittent, or has been corrected.

Action Taken When the DTC Sets

- A malfunction DTC stores.
- ABS is disabled until the EBCM receives a valid input from the brake switch.

Conditions for Clearing the DTC

- The condition responsible for setting the DTC no longer exists and the Scan Tool Clear DTCs function is used.
- When a change is seen during an ignition cycle in which DTC C1293 is a current malfunction, DTC C1291 or C1292 will clear itself at the end of the current ignition cycle and ABS will enable itself at the start of the next ignition cycle.

Diagnostic Aids

Use the Data List of the Scan Tool to verify proper brake switch operation. The Data List should display the brake switch as the brake is applied within 25 mm (1.0 in) of brake pedal travel.

GC402980346500AX

Fig. 257 Code C1293: Codes C1291/C1292 Set Current Or Previous Ignition Cycle (Part 1 of 2). Metro

Circuit Description

This DTC is run to determine the proper operation of the stoplamp switch, which detects that the stoplamp switch is closed at all times or there is a short to voltage in the stoplamp switch input circuit to the EBCM.

Conditions for Setting the DTC

- DTC C1294 can set if the vehicle's speed is greater than 40 km/h (25 mph).
- A malfunction exists if the brake was always on during two consecutive drive cycles.

Action Taken When the DTC Sets

- A malfunction DTC stores.
- ABS operation remains functional.

Conditions for Clearing the DTC

- The condition responsible for setting the DTC no longer exists and the Scan Tool Clear DTCs function is used.
- 100 drive cycles pass with no DTCs detected. A drive cycle consists of starting the vehicle, driving the vehicle over 16 km/h (10 mph), stopping and then turning the ignition OFF.

Diagnostic Aids

Inspect for the following when diagnosing this system:

- Stoplamp switch out-of-adjustment
- Faulty stoplamp switch (contacts always closed)
- Stoplamp switch input circuit shorted to battery (CKT 2O02)

Use the enhanced diagnostic function of the Scan Tool in order to measure the frequency of the malfunction.

Important: Zero the J 39200 test leads before making any resistance measurements.

GC402980346600AX

Fig. 258 Code C1294: Brake Lamp Switch Circuit Always Active (Part 1 of 3). Metro

Step	Action	Value(s)	Yes	No
23	Replace the EBCM. Is the repair complete?	—	Refer to *Diagnostic System Check*	—
24	Replace the STOP Fuse (15A) with a known good fuse (15A). Is the repair complete?	—	Refer to *Diagnostic System Check*	—
25	The malfunction is intermittent or is not present at this time. Refer to Diagnostic Aids for more information. Is the action complete?	—	System OK	—

GC402980346400DX

Fig. 256 Code C1292: Open Brake Lamp Switch When ABS Required (Part 4 of 4). Metro

Step	Action	Value(s)	Yes	No
1	Was the Diagnostic System Check performed?	—	*Go to Step 2*	Refer to *Diagnostic System Check*
2	1. Install a *Scan Tool.* 2. Use the *Scan Tool* to read the DTCs. Is DTC C1291 or DTC C1292 set as either a current and/or a history DTC?	—	Refer to *DTC C1291 Open Brake Lamp Sw Contacts During Decel* or *DTC C1292 Open Brake Lamp Sw When ABS Required*	*Go to Step 3*
3	1. Select DTC history on the *Scan Tool.* 2. Verify that the malfunction frequency was infrequent. 3. Use the *Scan Tool* in order to clear the DTCs. Did DTC C1293 clear?	—	Refer to *Diagnostic System Check*	*Go to Step 4*
4	Replace the EBCM. Is the repair complete?	—	Refer to *Diagnostic System Check*	—

GC402980346500BX

Fig. 257 Code C1293: Codes C1291/C1292 Set Current Or Previous Ignition Cycle (Part 2 of 2). Metro

Step	Action	Value(s)	Yes	No
1	Was the Diagnostic System Check performed?	—	*Go to Step 2*	Refer to *Diagnostic System Check*
2	1. Turn the ignition switch to the OFF position. 2. Verify that there is no pressure on the brake pedal. 3. Observe the rear brake lamps. Are the rear brake lamps on?	—	*Go to Step 3*	*Go to Step 5*
3	Disconnect the stoplamp switch connector. Are the rear brake lamps on?	—	*Go to Step 8*	*Go to Step 4*
4	Inspect the adjustment of the stoplamp switch. Is the stoplamp switch adjusted correctly?	—	*Go to Step 10*	*Go to Step 9*
5	1. Disconnect the EBCM connector. 2. Turn the ignition switch to the ON position. Do not start the engine. 3. Use the *J 39200* in order to measure the voltage between the EBCM connector terminal B9 and ground. Is the voltage within the specified range?	0–1 V	*Go to Step 6*	*Go to Step 8*
6	1. Turn the ignition switch to the OFF position. 2. Inspect the EBCM connector and the EBCM harness connector for the following conditions: • Terminal damage • Poor terminal contact • Terminal corrosion Is there evidence of poor terminal contact, terminal corrosion, or damaged terminals?	—	*Go to Step 11*	*Go to Step 7*
7	1. Reconnect the EBCM connector. 2. Install a *Scan Tool.* 3. Turn the ignition switch to the ON position. Do not start the engine. 4. Start the engine. 5. Test drive the vehicle obtaining a speed at least 40 km/h (25 mph). 6. Repeat the drive cycle, and steps 3,4, and 5 at least two additional times. 7. Use the *Scan Tool* in order to inspect for DTCs. Does DTC C1294 set as a current DTC during the last three drive cycles?	—	*Go to Step 12*	*Go to Step 13*
8	Repair the short to voltage in CKT 2O02 or 1Z01. Is the repair complete?	—	Refer to *Diagnostic System Check*	—
9	Adjust the stoplamp switch. Is the repair complete?	—	Refer to *Diagnostic System Check*	—
10	Replace the stoplamp switch. Is the repair complete?	—	Refer to *Diagnostic System Check*	—

GC402980346600BX

Fig. 258 Code C1294: Brake Lamp Switch Circuit Always Active (Part 2 of 3). Metro

Step	Action	Value(s)	Yes	No
11	Replace all of the terminals and connectors that exhibit the following conditions: • Poor terminal contact • Corrosion • Damaged terminal(s) Is the repair complete?	—	Refer to *Diagnostic System Check*	—
12	Replace the EBCM. Is the repair complete?	—	Refer to *Diagnostic System Check*	—
13	The malfunction is intermittent or is not present at this time. Refer to Diagnostic Aids for more information. Is the action complete?	—	System OK	—

GC402980346600CX

Fig. 258 Code C1294: Brake Lamp Switch Circuit Always Active (Part 3 of 3). Metro

Step	Action	Value(s)	Yes	No
1	Was the Diagnostic System Check performed?	—	*Go to Step 2*	Refer to *Diagnostic System Check*
2	1. Turn the ignition switch to the ON position. Do not start the engine. 2. Install a *Scan Tool*. 3. Select Data List on the *Scan Tool*. 4. Select Brake Switch Position on the *Scan Tool*. Does the Scan Tool indicate that the brake switch circuit is open?	—	*Go to Step 3*	*Go to Step 11*
3	Apply light pressure to the brake pedal while monitoring the Brake Switch Position on the *Scan Tool*. Does the Scan Tool indicate that the brake switch is on within 25 mm (1.0 in) of the brake pedal travel?	—	*Go to Step 9*	*Go to Step 4*
4	1. Apply firm pressure to the brake pedal. 2. Observe the rear brake lamps. Are the rear brake lamps ON?	—	*Go to Step 5*	*Go to Step 9*
5	1. Turn the ignition switch to the OFF position. 2. Disconnect the EBCM connector. 3. Turn the ignition switch to the ON position. Do not start the engine. 4. Apply firm pressure to the brake pedal. 5. Use the *J 39200* in order to measure the voltage between the EBCM connector terminal B9 and ground. Is the voltage equal to or greater than the specified voltage?	10.0 V	*Go to Step 6*	*Go to Step 7*
6	Inspect the EBCM connector and the EBCM harness connector for the following conditions: • Terminal damage • Poor terminal contact • Terminal corrosion Are poor terminal contact, terminal corrosion or damaged terminals evident?	—	*Go to Step 8*	*Go to Step 10*
7	Repair the open in CKT 2O02 or 1Z01. Is the repair complete?	—	Refer to *Diagnostic System Check*	—
8	Replace all the terminals or the connectors that exhibit the following conditions: • Poor terminal contact • Terminal corrosion • Damaged terminal(s). Is the repair complete?	—	Refer to *Diagnostic System Check*	—
9	Repair the open brake lamp circuit wiring. Is the repair complete?	—	Refer to *Diagnostic System Check*	—
10	Replace the EBCM. Is the repair complete?	—	Refer to *Diagnostic System Check*	—
11	The malfunction is intermittent or is not present at this time. Refer to Diagnostic Aids for more information. Is the action complete?	—	System OK	—

GC402980346700BX

Fig. 259 Code C1295: Brake Lamp Switch Circuit Open (Part 2 of 2). Metro

Step	Action	Value(s)	Yes	No
1	Was the Diagnostic System Check performed?	—	*Go to Step 2*	Refer to *Diagnostic System Check*
2	1. Turn the ignition switch to the OFF position. 2. Install a *Scan Tool*. 3. Turn the ignition switch to the ON position. Do not start the engine. 4. Select Special Functions on the *Scan Tool*. 5. Select Lamp Test on the *Scan Tool*. 6. Use the *Scan Tool* in order to turn the amber ABS warning indicator OFF. Did the amber ABS warning indicator turn OFF?	—	*Go to Step 3*	*Go to Step 4*
3	1. Select Special Functions on the *Scan Tool*. 2. Select Lamp Test on the *Scan Tool*. 3. Use the *Scan Tool* in order to flash the amber ABS warning indicator. Did the amber ABS warning indicator flash?	—	*Go to Step 7*	*Go to Step 4*
4	Inspect all of the connectors and the terminals for the following conditions: • Poor terminal contact • Evidence of corrosion Is there evidence of poor terminal contact or corrosion?	—	*Go to Step 5*	*Go to Step 6*
5	Replace all of the terminals that exhibit signs of poor terminal contact or corrosion. Is the repair complete?	—	Refer to *Diagnostic System Check*	—
6	Repair the instrument panel cluster. Is the repair complete?	—	Refer to *Diagnostic System Check*	—
7	The malfunction is not present at this time. Refer to Diagnostic Aids for more information. Is the action complete?	—	System OK	—

GC402980339901BX

Fig. 260 Test A: ABS Warning Lamp On w/No Code Set (Part 2 of 2). Metro

Circuit Description

DTC C1295 identifies open brake switch circuitry that prevents the brake switch input to the EBCM from changing states while applying the brake.

This DTC is used in conjunction with DTCs C1291 and C1292 to determine the cause of an open stoplamp switch malfunction.

Conditions for Setting the DTC

- DTC C1295 can set after initialization is complete.
- A malfunction exists if the brake switch input voltage is out of specification for one second. An open circuit exists when the brake switch input voltage is out of specification.

Action Taken When the DTC Sets

- A malfunction DTC stores.
- ABS disables.
- The ABS warning indicator turns ON.

Conditions for Clearing the DTC

- The condition responsible for setting the DTC no longer exists and the Scan Tool Clear DTCs function is used.
- 100 drive cycles pass with no DTCs detected. A drive cycle consists of starting the vehicle, driving the vehicle over 16 km/h (10 mph), stopping and then turning the ignition OFF.

Diagnostic Aids

The following conditions may cause a malfunction:

- A poor connection
- Rubbed-through wire insulation
- A broken wire inside the insulation
- Faulty (open) stoplamp switch electrical circuit
- All brake lamp bulbs are open
- Faulty stoplamp bulb electrical circuit (open/high resistance to ground)

Use the enhanced diagnostic function of the Scan Tool in order to measure the frequency of the malfunction.

Thoroughly inspect any circuitry that may cause the intermittent complaint for the following conditions:

- Backed out terminals
- Improper mating
- Broken locks
- Improperly formed or damaged terminals
- Poor terminal-to-wiring connections
- Physical damage to the wiring harness

Important: Zero the J 39200 test leads before making any resistance measurements.

GC402980346700AX

Fig. 259 Code C1295: Brake Lamp Switch Circuit Open (Part 1 of 2). Metro

Circuit Description

The Electronic Brake Control Module (EBCM) controls the operation of the amber ABS indicator lamp by means of a lamp driver relay.

The amber ABS indicator lamp is connected to the IG COIL fuse through CKT 2T01. This circuit is hot in ON and START ignition switch positions.

When the lamp driver relay is in the OFF state (CKT 7I01 is open), the lamp driver relay grounds the amber ABS indicator lamp through CKT 1L01. This causes the amber ABS indicator lamp to turn ON.

When the EBCM commands OFF the ABS indicator, the EBCM turns ON the lamp driver relay by grounding CKT 7I01. This causes the lamp driver relay to open the path to ground in CKT 1L01, turning OFF the amber ABS indicator lamp.

When the ignition switch is turned to the ON position, the EBCM turns ON the ABS indicator for 3 seconds for a bulb check. Whenever a malfunction is detected within the ABS system, the EBCM tuns ON the ABS indicator, notifying the driver that ABS needs to be serviced. If the EBCM commands the red BRAKE warning indicator ON due to an ABS malfunction that may degrade base braking operation and cannot do so, the ABS indicator will flash to indicate the serious nature of the problem.

Diagnostic Aids

The following conditions may cause a malfunction:

- Short to ground between the lamp driver relay and the amber ABS indicator lamp (CKT 1L01)
- Open circuit or high resistance between the EBCM and the lamp driver relay (CKT 7I01)
- Open DEF fuse
- Open coil or constantly closed contacts of the lamp driver relay

Use the Lamp Test function of the Scan Tool in order to turn the indicator on while looking for an intermittent malfunction in the ABS warning indicator circuitry.

Thoroughly inspect any circuitry that may cause the intermittent complaint for the following conditions:

- Backed out terminals
- Improper mating
- Broken locks
- Improperly formed or damaged terminals
- Poor terminal-to-wiring connections
- Physical damage to the wiring harness

Important: Zero the J 39200 test leads before making any resistance measurements. Refer to the J 39200 user's manual.

GC402980339901AX

Fig. 260 Test A: ABS Warning Lamp On w/No Code Set (Part 1 of 2). Metro

Circuit Description

The Electronic Brake Control Module (EBCM) controls the operation of the amber ABS indicator lamp by means of a lamp driver relay.

The amber ABS indicator lamp is connected to the IG COIL fuse through CKT 2T01. This circuit is hot in ON and START ignition switch positions.

When the lamp driver relay is in the OFF state (CKT 7I01 is open), the lamp driver relay grounds the amber ABS indicator lamp through CKT 1L01. This causes to turn ON the amber ABS indicator lamp.

When the EBCM commands OFF the ABS indicator, the EBCM turns ON the lamp driver relay by grounding CKT 7I01. This causes the lamp driver relay to open the path to ground in CKT 1L01, turning OFF the amber ABS indicator lamp.

When the ignition switch is turned to the ON position, the EBCM turns ON the ABS indicator for 3 seconds for a bulb check. Whenever a malfunction is detected within the ABS system, the EBCM tuns ON the ABS indicator, notifying the driver that ABS needs to be serviced. If the EBCM commands the red BRAKE warning indicator ON due to an ABS malfunction that may degrade base braking operation and cannot do so, the ABS indicator will flash to indicate the serious nature of the problem.

Diagnostic Aids

The following conditions may cause a malfunction:

- A poor connection
- Rubbed-through wire insulation
- A broken wire inside the insulation
- Open IG COIL fuse
- Open bulb filament
- Open or poor G201
- Short to ground in lamp driver relay control circuit (CKT 7I01)
- Open within I/P gage printed circuit
- Faulty lamp driver relay (open contacts)

Use the Lamp Test function of the Scan Tool in order to turn the indicator on while looking for an intermittent malfunction in the ABS warning indicator circuitry.

GC402980339801AX

Fig. 261 Test B: ABS Warning Lamp Off w/No Code Set (Part 1 of 2). Metro

Thoroughly inspect any circuitry that may cause the intermittent complaint for the following conditions:

- Backed out terminals
- Improper mating
- Broken locks
- Improperly formed or damaged terminals
- Poor terminal-to-wiring connections
- Physical damage to the wiring harness

Important: Zero the J 39200 test leads before making any resistance measurements. Refer to the J 39200 user's manual.

ABS Indicator Off No DTC Set

Step	Action	Value(s)	Yes	No
1	Was the Diagnostic System Check performed?	—	*Go to Step 2*	Refer to *Diagnostic System Check*
2	1. Turn the ignition switch to the OFF position. 2. Install a *Scan Tool*. 3. Turn the ignition switch to the ON position. 4. Select Special Functions on the *Scan Tool*. 5. Select Lamp Test on the *Scan Tool*. 6. Use the *Scan Tool* in order to turn the amber ABS warning indicator on. Did the amber ABS warning indicator turn ON?	—	*Go to Step 3*	*Go to Step 4*
3	1. Select Special Functions on the *Scan Tool*. 2. Select Lamp Test on the *Scan Tool*. 3. Use the *Scan Tool* in order to flash the amber ABS warning indicator. Did the amber ABS warning indicator flash?	—	*Go to Step 7*	*Go to Step 4*
4	Inspect all of the connectors and the terminals for the following conditions: • Poor terminal contact • Evidence of corrosion Is there evidence of poor terminal contact or corrosion?	—	*Go to Step 5*	*Go to Step 6*
5	Replace all of the terminals that exhibit signs of poor terminal contact or corrosion. Is the repair complete?	—	Refer to *Diagnostic System Check*	—
6	Repair the instrument panel cluster. Is the repair complete?	—	Refer to *Diagnostic System Check*	—
7	The malfunction is not present at this time. Refer to Diagnostic Aids for more information. Is the action complete?	—	System OK	—

GC402980339801BX

Fig. 261 Test B: ABS Warning Lamp Off w/No Code Set (Part 2 of 2). Metro

Step	Action	Value(s)	Yes	No
1	Was the Diagnostic System Check performed?	—	*Go to Step 2*	Refer to *Diagnostic System Check*
2	1. Turn the ignition switch to the OFF position. 2. Install a *Scan Tool*. 3. Turn the ignition switch to the ON position. 4. Select Special Functions on the *Scan Tool*. 5. Select Lamp Test on the *Scan Tool*. 6. Use the *Scan Tool* in order to turn the amber ABS warning indicator ON. Did the amber ABS warning indicator turn ON?	—	*Go to Step 3*	*Go to Step 4*
3	1. Select Special Functions on the *Scan Tool*. 2. Select Lamp Test on the *Scan Tool*. 3. Use the *Scan Tool* in order to flash the amber ABS warning indicator. Did the amber ABS warning indicator flash?	—	*Go to Step 7*	*Go to Step 4*
4	Inspect all of the connectors and the terminals for the following conditions: • Poor terminal contact • Evidence of corrosion Is there evidence of poor terminal contact or corrosion?	—	*Go to Step 5*	*Go to Step 6*
5	Replace all of the terminals that exhibit signs of poor terminal contact or corrosion. Is the repair complete?	—	Refer to *Diagnostic System Check*	—
6	Repair the instrument panel cluster. Is the repair complete?	—	Refer to *Diagnostic System Check*	—
7	The malfunction is not present at this time. Refer to Diagnostic Aids for more information. Is the action complete?	—	System OK	—

GC402980340001BX

Fig. 262 Test C: ABS Active Lamp On w/No Code Set (Part 2 of 2). Metro

Circuit Description

The ABS ACTIVE indicator lamp is connected to the IG COIL fuse through CKT 2T01. This circuit is hot in ON and START ignition switch positions. The Electronic Brake Control Module (EBCM) turns ON the ABS ACTIVE by ground CKT 7H01.

When the ignition switch is turned to the ON position, the EBCM turns ON the ABS ACTIVE indicator for 3 seconds for a bulb check. Whenever the vehicle is involved in an ABS event, the EBCM tuns ON the ABS ACTIVE indicator for the duration of the event (and 1-2 seconds after an ABS event), notifying the driver that ABS is in operation.

Diagnostic Aids

The following list contains items that need to be inspected when diagnosing this system:

- Short to ground between EBCM and the ABS ACTIVE indicator lamp (CKT 7H01)
- EBCM connector C1
- C200
- I/P cluster C1

Use the Lamp Test function of the Scan Tool in order to turn the indicator on while looking for an intermittent malfunction in the ABS warning indicator circuitry.

Thoroughly inspect any circuitry that may cause the intermittent complaint for the following conditions:

- Backed out terminals
- Improper mating
- Broken locks
- Improperly formed or damaged terminals
- Poor terminal-to-wiring connections
- Physical damage to the wiring harness

Important: Zero the J 39200 test leads before making any resistance measurements. Refer to the J 39200 user's manual.

GC402980340001AX

Fig. 262 Test C: ABS Active Lamp On w/No Code Set (Part 1 of 2). Metro

Circuit Description

The ABS ACTIVE indicator lamp is connected to the IG COIL fuse through CKT 2T01. This circuit is hot in ON and START ignition switch positions. The Electronic Brake Control Module (EBCM) turns ON the ABS ACTIVE by ground CKT 7H01.

When the ignition switch is turned to the ON position, the EBCM turns ON the ABS ACTIVE indicator for 3 seconds for a bulb check. Whenever the vehicle is involved in an ABS event, the EBCM tuns ON the ABS ACTIVE indicator for the duration of the event (and 1–2 seconds after the event), notifying the driver that ABS is in operation.

Diagnostic Aids

The following conditions may cause a malfunction:

- A poor connection
- Rubbed-through wire insulation
- A broken wire inside the insulation
- Open IG COIL fuse
- Open bulb filament
- Open within I/P gage printed circuit

Use the Lamp Test function of the Scan Tool in order to turn the indicator on while looking for an intermittent malfunction in the ABS warning indicator circuitry.

Thoroughly inspect any circuitry that may cause the intermittent complaint for the following conditions:

- Backed out terminals
- Improper mating
- Broken locks
- Improperly formed or damaged terminals
- Poor terminal-to-wiring connections
- Physical damage to the wiring harness

Important: Zero the J 39200 test leads before making any resistance measurements. Refer to the J 39200 user's manual.

GC402980340101AX

Fig. 263 Test D: ABS Active Lamp Inoperative w/No Code Set (Part 1 of 2). Metro

Step	Action	Value(s)	Yes	No
1	Was the Diagnostic System Check performed?	—	*Go to Step 2*	Refer to *Diagnostic System Check*
2	1. Turn the ignition switch to the OFF position. 2. Install a *Scan Tool*. 3. Turn the ignition switch to the ON position. Do not start the engine. 4. Select Special Functions on the *Scan Tool*. 5. Select Lamp Test on the *Scan Tool*. 6. Use the *Scan Tool* in order to turn the amber ABS warning indicator OFF. Did the amber ABS warning indicator turn OFF?	—	*Go to Step 3*	*Go to Step 4*
3	1. Select Special Functions on the *Scan Tool*. 2. Select Lamp Test on the *Scan Tool*. 3. Use the *Scan Tool* in order to flash the amber ABS warning indicator. Did the amber ABS warning indicator flash?	—	*Go to Step 7*	*Go to Step 4*
4	Inspect all of the connectors and the terminals for the following conditions: • Poor terminal contact • Evidence of corrosion Is there evidence of poor terminal contact or corrosion?	—	*Go to Step 5*	*Go to Step 6*
5	Replace all of the terminals that exhibit signs of poor terminal contact or corrosion. Is the repair complete?	—	Refer to *Diagnostic System Check*	—
6	Repair the instrument panel cluster. Is the repair complete?	—	Refer to *Diagnostic System Check*	—
7	The malfunction is not present at this time. Refer to Diagnostic Aids for more information. Is the action complete?	—	System OK	—

GC402980340101BX

Fig. 263 Test D: ABS Active Lamp Inoperative w/No Code Set (Part 2 of 2). Metro

Step	Action	Value(s)	Yes	No
1	Was the Diagnostic System Check performed?	—	Go to Step 2	Refer to *Diagnostic System Check*
2	1. Turn the ignition switch to the OFF position. 2. Install a *Scan Tool.* 3. Turn the ignition switch to the RUN position. Do not start the engine. 4. Use the *Scan Tool* in order to clear the DTCs. 5. Turn the ignition switch to the OFF position. 6. Turn the ignition switch to the RUN position. 7. Do not start the engine Does the undefined DTC(s) reset?	—	*Go to Step 3*	*Go to Step 4*
3	Replace the EBCM. Is the repair complete?	—	Go to *Diagnostic System Check*	—
4	The malfunction is not present at this time. Refer to Diagnostic Aids for more information.	—	—	—

GC4029702844AAAX

Fig. 264 Test E: Scan Tool Displays Undefined Code. Metro

Step	Action	Value(s)	Yes	No
Important: Zero the J 39200 test leads before making any resistance measurements. Refer to the J 39200 user's manual.				
1	Was the ABS Diagnostic System Check performed?	—	Go to *Step 2*	Go to *A Diagnostic System Check - ABS*
2	Verify the correct connection of the Scan Tool to the DLC. Is connection of the Scan Tool to the DLC correct?	—	Go to *Step 3*	Go to *Step 13*
3	1. Turn the ignition switch to the OFF position. 2. Remove and inspect the HAZARD Fuse (15A). Is the fuse open?	—	Go to *Step 11*	Go to *Step 4*
4	1. Install the HAZARD fuse (15A). 2. Remove the DEF Fuse (20A). Is the fuse open?	—	Go to *Step 12*	Go to *Step 5*
5	1. Install the DEF Fuse (20A). 2. Disconnect the EBCM connector. 3. Use the *J 39200* in order to measure the resistance between the EBCM connector terminal D and ground. Is the resistance within the specified range?	0–2 Ω	Go to *Step 6*	Go to *Step 18*
6	1. Disconnect the EBCM connector. 2. Use the *J 39200* in order to measure voltage between the EBCM connector terminal B12 and ground. Is the voltage equal to or greater than the specified voltage?	10 V	Go to *Step 7*	Go to *Step 19*
7	1. Turn the ignition switch to the ON position. Do not start the engine. 2. Use the *J 39200* in order to measure voltage between the EBCM connector terminal A9 and ground. Is the voltage equal to or greater than the specified voltage?	10 V	Go to *Step 8*	Go to *Step 20*
8	1. Turn the ignition switch to the OFF position. 2. Use the *J 39200* in order to measure the resistance between the EBCM connector terminal A1 and the DLC terminal 9. Is the resistance within the specified range?	0–2 Ω	Go to *Step 9*	Go to *Step 21*
9	Use the *J 39200* in order to measure the resistance between the EBCM connector terminal A1 and ground. Is the resistance within the specified range?	OL (Infinite)	Go to *Step 10*	Go to *Step 22*
10	Inspect the EBCM connector for the following conditions: • Poor terminal contact • Terminal corrosion • Damaged terminals Are there signs of poor terminal contact, terminal corrosion, or damaged terminals?	—	Go to *Step 23*	Go to *Step 24*
11	1. Disconnect the EBCM connector. 2. Use the *J 39200* in order to measure the resistance between the EBCM connector terminal B12 and ground. Is the resistance within the specified range?	OL (Infinite)	Go to *Step 14*	Go to *Step 15*
12	1. Disconnect the EBCM connector. 2. Use the *J 39200* in order to measure the resistance between the EBCM connector terminal A9 and ground. Is the resistance within the specified range?	OL (Infinite)	Go to *Step 16*	Go to *Step 17*

GC4020052209020X

Fig. 265 No Communication With EBCM (Part 2 of 3). Metro

Circuit Description

Serial data is transmitted/received by the EBCM through terminal A1. The EBCM is supplied switched ignition voltage through connector C1 terminal A9 and battery feed voltage through connector C1 terminal B12. The EBCM ground is provided through connector C2 terminal D.

Diagnostic Aids

Communication with the EBCM is not possible when excessive resistance exists in the following components:

- The ground
- The power supply circuits

If communication with the EBCM is not possible, perform the following actions:

- Verify that the EBCM ground connection is good.
- Verify that no excessive resistance exists in any of the power supply circuits

Test Description

5. This test checks for high resistance in the EBCM ground circuit.
6. This test checks for an open in the EBCM battery feed circuit.
7. This test checks for an open or high resistance in the EBCM switched ignition circuit.
8. This test checks for an open or high resistance in the EBCM serial data circuit.
9. This test checks for a short to ground in the EBCM serial data circuit.
11. This test checks for a short to ground in the EBCM battery feed circuit.
12. This test checks for a short to ground in the EBCM switched ignition circuit.

GC4020052209010X

Fig. 265 No Communication With EBCM (Part 1 of 3). Metro

Step	Action	Value(s)	Yes	No
13	Disconnect and reconnect the *Scan Tool* in order to ensure a good connection. Is the *Scan Tool* correctly connected?	—	Go to *A Diagnostic System Check - ABS*	—
14	Replace the HAZARD Fuse. Is the repair complete?	—	Go to *A Diagnostic System Check - ABS*	—
15	Repair the short to ground in the WHT/GRN wire between the junction block and the EBCM and replace the HAZARD Fuse. Is the repair complete?	—	Go to *A Diagnostic System Check - ABS*	—
16	Replace the DEF Fuse. Is the repair complete?	—	Go to *A Diagnostic System Check - ABS*	—
17	Repair the short to ground in the YEL/GRN wire between the junction block and the EBCM and replace the DEF Fuse. Is the repair complete?	—	Go to *A Diagnostic System Check - ABS*	—
18	Repair the open or high resistance in the BLK wire between the EBCM and G102. Is the repair complete?	—	Go to *A Diagnostic System Check - ABS*	—
19	Repair the open or high resistance in the WHT/GRN wire between the junction block and the EBCM. Is the repair complete?	—	Go to *A Diagnostic System Check - ABS*	—
20	Repair the open or high resistance in the YEL/GRN wire between the junction block and the EBCM. Is the repair complete?	—	Go to *A Diagnostic System Check - ABS*	—
21	Repair the open or high resistance in the PPL wire between the Data Link Connector (DLC) and the EBCM. Is the repair complete?	—	Go to *A Diagnostic System Check - ABS*	—
22	Repair the short to ground in the PPL wire between the Data Link Connector (DLC) and the EBCM. Is the repair complete?	—	Go to *A Diagnostic System Check - ABS*	—
23	Replace the terminals or the connectors that exhibit the following conditions: • Poor terminal contact • Terminal corrosion • Damaged terminals Is the repair complete?	—	Go to *A Diagnostic System Check - ABS*	—
24	Replace the EBCM. Is the repair complete?	—	Go to *A Diagnostic System Check - ABS*	—

GC4020052209030X

Fig. 265 No Communication With EBCM (Part 3 of 3). Metro

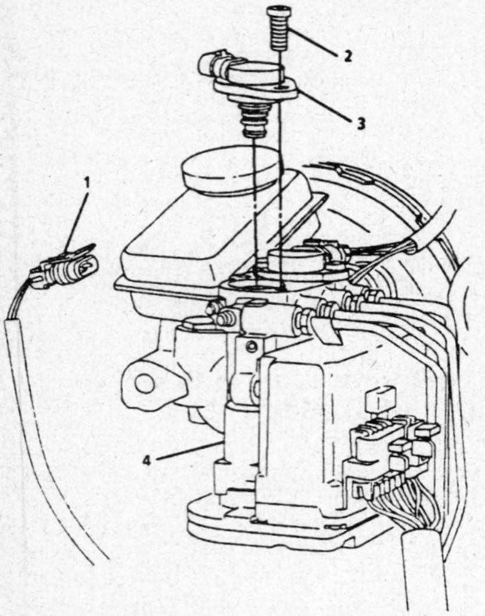

1 SOLENOID ELECTRICAL CONNECTOR
2 TORX® HEAD BOLTS
3 SOLENOID ASSEMBLY
4 ABS HYDRAULIC MODULATOR

GC4029100845000X

Fig. 266 Hydraulic modulator solenoid replacement

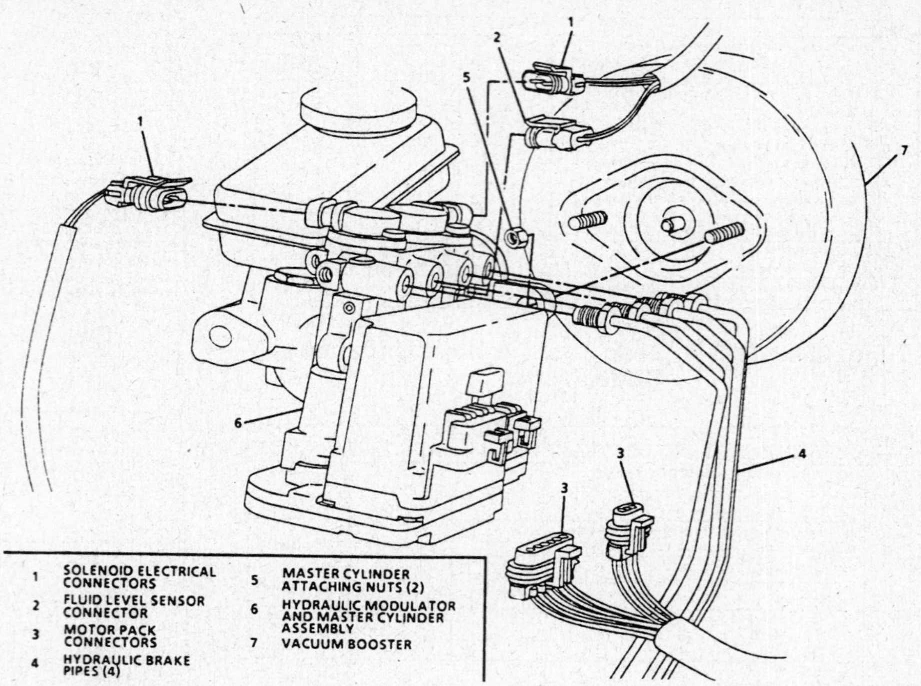

1 SOLENOID ELECTRICAL CONNECTORS
2 FLUID LEVEL SENSOR CONNECTOR
3 MOTOR PACK CONNECTORS
4 HYDRAULIC BRAKE PIPES (4)
5 MASTER CYLINDER ATTACHING NUTS (2)
6 HYDRAULIC MODULATOR AND MASTER CYLINDER ASSEMBLY
7 VACUUM BOOSTER

GC4029100850000X

Fig. 267 ABS hydraulic modulator assembly replacement

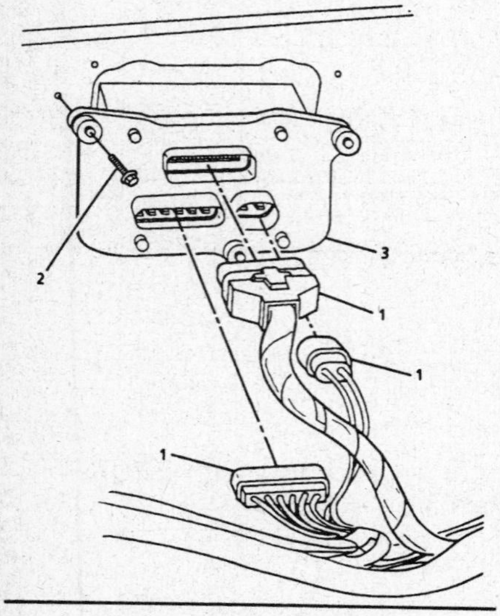

1 EBCM ELECTRICAL CONNECTORS
2 HEX HEAD SCREWS
3 EBCM

GC4029100846000X

Fig. 268 EBCM assembly replacement. Alero & Grand Am

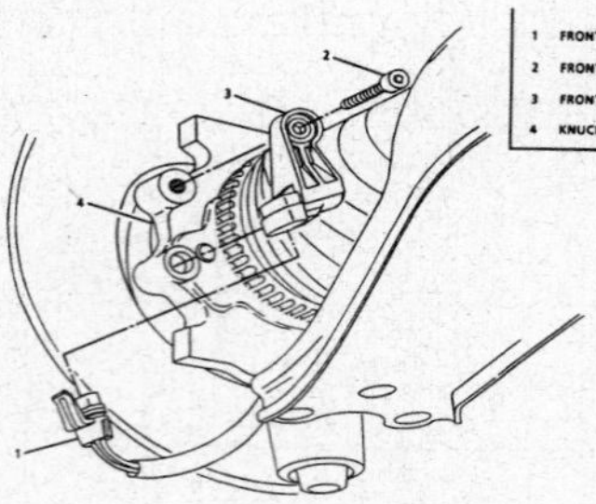

1 FRONT SENSOR ELECTRICAL CONNECTOR
2 FRONT SENSOR ATTACHING BOLT
3 FRONT SENSOR
4 KNUCKLE

GC4029100848000X

Fig. 269 Front wheel speed sensor replacement.

Bosch Type 5.3

NOTE: On Air Bag Equipped Models, Refer To "Air Bag System Precautions" Located In The Front Of This Manual For System Disarming & Arming Procedures.

NOTE: Refer To "Computer Relearn Procedures" Located In The Front Of This Manual When Battery Power To The Computer Has Been Interrupted.

NOTE: "Electrical Symbol & Wire Color Code Identification" Located In The Front Of This Manual May Be Used As An Aid When Using Wiring Circuits Found In This Section.

INDEX

PRECAUTIONS

Air Bag Systems

Refer to "Air Bag System Precautions" in the front of this manual for system disarming and arming procedures.

Battery Ground Cable

Prior to service, disconnect battery ground cable and isolate as required.

ABS Service

Before performing any repairs on the ABS system, note the following precautions:

1. Before using electric welding equipment, disconnect EBTCM.
2. Carefully note routing, position and mounting ABS and TCS wiring, connectors, clips and brackets. ABS and TCS are extremely sensitive to electromagnetic interference.
3. Do not use a fast charger when battery is connected. **Never disconnect battery from system with engine running.**
4. Ignition switch must be in Off position when disconnecting EBTCM.
5. Do not hang other components on wheel speed sensor cables.
6. Do not force wheel speed sensors into place.
7. Do not expose EBTCM to temperatures of more than 203°F. Do not expose EBTCM to temperatures of more than 184°F for more than two hours.
8. Many ABS system components are non-serviceable and must be replaced as assemblies. **Do not disassemble non-serviceable components.**
9. Use DOT 3 brake fluid only. Do not use container that has been used with petroleum based fluids or is wet with water. Petroleum based fluids will damage system and water will lower boiling point. Keep fluid containers capped.
10. After replacing any ABS component, inspect system as outlined in "Diagnosis & Testing."
11. Do not use lubricated compressed air on brake components. Lubricate brake components with clean brake fluid.
12. If hydraulic components are removed or disconnected, bleed system as outlined in "System Service."
13. Ensure working area is clean and free of mineral oils.

DESCRIPTION

System Operation

The Bosch Anti-Lock Brake System (ABS) with Traction Control System (TCS) minimizes wheel lock-up during heavy braking on most road surfaces to improve driver control. ABS monitors each wheel's speed and controls brake fluid pressure to each front wheel independently and both rear wheels simultaneously.

A separate hydraulic line and solenoid valve for each front wheel, and one hydraulic line and solenoid valve for both rear wheels allow hydraulic pressure to be modulated, preventing wheel lock-up. The ABS can decrease, hold or increase hydraulic pressure.

The system continuously monitors all components, uses several methods to determine faults and notify the driver of faults. When the engine is started, the ABS electrical circuitry is functionally inspected. As the vehicle reaches four mph, the Brake Pressure Modulator Valve (BPMV) is functionally inspected. The driver is informed of faults when the system illuminates either or both the Brake and/or ABS lamps.

If the Brake warning lamp is lit, brake system conditions may result in reduced braking ability. If the ABS indicator lamp is lit, an ABS fault has been detected and the anti-lock and traction control functions are turned off. If the ABS indicator lamp only is on, normal braking with full power assist is available without anti-lock. If both lamps are on, there may be a hydraulic brake system problem.

The system also monitors rear wheel speed and compares it to front wheel speed. If rear speed is more than the front wheel speed, the Electronic Brake Traction Control Module (EBTCM) will signal the Engine Control Module (ECM) to reduce engine torque by retarding timing, turning off one or more fuel injectors and preventing transmission down shifting to improve traction and stability. This function may to turned on or off by the driver. The TC indicator lamp flashes when the system is active. If the lamp is on steady, a problem has been found and the TCS disabled. When the driver turns the TCS off, the lamp will also be turned off.

System Components

ELECTRONIC BRAKE TRACTION CONTROL MODULE

The Electronic Brake Traction Control Module (EBTCM) is a microprocessor which monitors wheel speeds and Brake Pressure Modulator Valve (BPMV) electrical status. It is located between the BPMV and master cylinder, on the lefthand front side of the engine compartment.

The EBTCM detects wheel locking tendencies and rotating speed differences, controls anti-lock brake operations, commands traction control torque reduction and monitors system electrical operations, in addition to controlling Diagnostic Trouble Code (DTC) displays.

BRAKE PRESSURE MODULATOR VALVE

Mounted on the lefthand front side of the engine compartment, the Brake Pressure Modulator Valve (BPMV) modulates front and rear wheel brake circuits. The BPMV is not serviceable.

WHEEL SPEED SENSORS

Wheel speed sensors transmit wheel speed information to the EBTCM with voltage generated by magnetic induction caused by a passing toothed sensor ring.

The front wheel speed sensors are mounted in the front steering knuckles and are not adjustable.

The rear wheel speed sensors are mounted at each end of the differential housing and are not adjustable.

PUMP MOTOR

This small pump is part of the BPMV and circulate brake fluid back to the master cylinder during anti-lock operations. The pump cannot be serviced.

SOLENOID VALVES

The solenoid valves are part of the BPMV and cannot be serviced. They increase, decrease or maintain brake fluid pressure to the individual circuits as commanded by the EBTCM.

PUMP MOTOR & SOLENOID RELAYS

Both relays are integral components of the EBTCM and cannot be serviced.

DIAGNOSIS & TESTING

Accessing Diagnostic Trouble Codes

Diagnostic Trouble Codes (DTCs) can be accessed with a suitably programmed scan tool connected to the Data Link Connector (DLC), located to the left of the steering column on the instrument panel carrier. Follow the tool manufacturers instructions.

Diagnostic Trouble Code Interpretation

Refer to **Figs. 1 and 2,** for Diagnostic Trouble Code (DTC) identification.

Wiring Diagrams

CAMARO & FIREBIRD

Refer to **Figs. 3 through 5,** for wiring diagrams.

CATERA

Refer to **Fig. 6,** for wiring diagrams.

GRAND PRIX

Refer to **Fig. 7,** for wiring diagrams.

INTRIGUE

Refer to **Fig. 8,** for wiring diagrams.

EBCM/EBTCM Connector Views

Refer to **Figs. 9 through 13,** for EBCM/EBTCM connector terminal identification.

Diagnostic Tests

CAMARO & FIREBIRD

Refer to **Figs. 14 through 43** for diagnostic tests.

CATERA

Refer to **Figs. 44 through 79,** for diagnostic tests.

GRAND PRIX & INTRIGUE

2000

Refer to **Figs. 80 through 133,** for diagnostic tests.

2001-04

Refer to **Figs. 134 through 177,** for diagnostic tests.

Clearing Diagnostic Trouble Codes

Diagnostic Trouble Codes (DTCs) cannot be cleared by disconnecting EBTCM or battery cables.

SCAN TOOL

Connect a suitably programmed scan tool to Data Link Connector (DLC), and follow manufacturer's instructions.

IGNITION CYCLE DEFAULT

If vehicle power is cycled 100 times without a particular fault reappearing, that particular DTC will be erased from the EBCM memory, and ignition cycle counter will be reset to zero.

Intermittents & Poor Connections

Intermittent failures in the anti-lock brake system may be difficult to accurately diagnose. The ABS Diagnostic Trouble Codes (DTCs) which may be stored by the EBCM are not designated as Current or History DTCs. These DTCs can be helpful in diagnosing intermittent conditions.

If an intermittent condition is being diagnosed, the ABS system can be used in the following manner to help isolate the suspected circuit.

1. Display and clear any ABS DTCs present in EBCM.
2. Attempt to repeat failure condition, noting following:
   a. Turn ignition switch to Off position.
   b. Disconnect scan tool. **If scan tool is installed, EBCM/EBTCM will not set DTCs and ABS/TCS functions may not be available.**
   c. Test drive vehicle.
3. After duplicating condition, stop vehicle and display any DTCs stored.
4. If no DTCs were stored refer to "Troubleshooting."
5. If a DTC was stored, inspect electrical connections and wiring for the following:
   a. Poor mating of connector halves.
   b. Terminals not fully seated in connector halves.
   c. Improperly formed, or damaged terminals. All connector terminals in a problem circuit should be carefully reformed to increase contact tension.
   d. Poor terminal to wire connection. In most cases, this will require removing wire from connector body.
6. If there is an intermittent warning lamp operation, the following EBCM circuits should be inspected:
   a. Low system voltage. If low voltage is detected at EBCM/EBTCM, Anti-lock lamp will illuminate until normal operating voltage is detected.
   b. Low brake fluid. This condition in

Code	Description
C0035	Lefthand Front Wheel Circuit Fault
C0036	Lefthand Front Wheel Circuit Range/Performance
C0040	Righthand Front Wheel Circuit Fault
C0041	Righthand Front Wheel Circuit Range/Performance
C0045	Lefthand Rear Wheel Circuit Fault
C0046	Lefthand Rear Wheel Circuit Range/Performance
C0050	Righthand Rear Wheel Circuit Fault
C0051	Righthand Rear Wheel Circuit Range/Performance
C0055	Rear Wheel Speed Circuit Fault
C0056	Rear Wheel Speed Circuit Range/Performance
C0060	Lefthand Front ABS Solenoid No. 1 Circuit Fault
C0065	Lefthand Front ABS Solenoid No. 2 Circuit Fault
C0070	Righthand Front ABS Solenoid No. 1 Circuit Fault
C0075	Righthand Front ABS Solenoid No. 2 Circuit Fault
C0080	Lefthand Rear ABS Solenoid No. 1 Circuit Fault
C0085	Lefthand Rear ABS Solenoid No. 2 Circuit Fault

Fig. 1 DTC identification (Part 1 of 2). Camaro, Firebird, Grand Prix & Intrigue

Code	Description
C0090	Righthand Rear ABS Solenoid No. 1 Circuit Fault
C0095	Righthand Rear ABS Solenoid No. 2 Circuit Fault
C0100	Rear ABS Solenoid No. 1 Circuit Fault
C0105	Rear ABS Solenoid No. 2 Circuit Fault
C0110	Pump Motor Circuit Fault
C0121	Valve Relay Circuit Fault
C0161	ABS/TCS Brake Switch Circuit Fault
C0171	TCS Pilot Valve Circuit Fault
C0181	Throttle Reduction Motor Circuit Fault
C0182	Throttle Reduction Motor Circuit Range/Performance
C0236	TCS RPM Signal Circuit Fault
C0237	TCS Throttle Position Signal Fault
C0238	TCS Throttle Position Sensor Comparison Fault
C0239	TCS Spark Retard Monitoring Fault
C0240	PCM Traction Control Not Allowed
C0241	PCM Indicated Requested Torque Fault
C0245	Wheel Speed Sensor Frequency Error
C0550	ECU Fault
C0896	Device Voltage Range Performance
C0901	Device No. 2 Voltage Low
U1304	Lost Communication With UART System

Fig. 1 DTC identification (Part 2 of 2). Camaro, Firebird, Grand Prix & Intrigue

Pressure Modulator Valve (PMV) reservoir will cause Brake and Anti-lock lamps to illuminate. When an acceptable fluid level is registered, lamps will no longer be illuminated.

7. Any condition which results in interruption of power to EBCM/EBTCM or hydraulic unit may cause warning lamps to turn on intermittently. These circuits include main relay, pump motor relay, fuses and related wiring.

Electromagnetic Interference Test

Due to the sensitivity of ABS components to electromagnetic interference, the following inspections should be performed is an intermittent fault is suspected.

1. Inspect for proper installation of wiring harnesses resulting from add on options.
2. Visually inspect wheel speed sensor and toothed sensor ring for looseness, damage, accumulation of foreign material and proper mounting. Replace damaged components, remove any foreign material and properly attach all components.
3. Inspect front wheel speed sensor wiring for proper routing away from spark plug wires.
4. Measure resistance of spark plug wires. If resistance is greater than 30,000 ohms for any wire, replace spark plug wire.
5. While test driving vehicle, monitor Tech 1 or equivalent scan tool, wheel speeds. If any wheel speed drops or displays an erratic speed, refer to appropriated wheel speed sensor DTC.

SYSTEM SERVICE

Brake System Bleed

MANUAL BLEED

Pressure bleeding is recommended for all hydraulic systems. However, if a pressure bleeder is unavailable, use the following procedure. **Brake fluid damages painted surfaces. Immediately clean any spilled fluid.**

1. Remove vacuum reserve by pumping brakes several times with engine off.
2. Fill master cylinder reservoir with clean brake fluid. Inspect fluid level often during bleeding procedure, do not let reservoir fall below half full.
3. If required, bleed master cylinder as follows:
   a. Disconnect front EBTCM pipe fitting at master cylinder.
   b. Allow fluid to fill master cylinder body bore until it flows from front pipe fitting port.
   c. Connect EBTCM pipe and tighten.
   d. Instruct an assistant to slowly depress brake pedal one time and hold.
   e. Loosen front EBTCM pipe fitting and purge air from cylinder.
   f. Tighten connection and slowly release brake pedal.
   g. Wait 15 seconds and repeat until all air is purged.
   h. **Torque** pipe fitting to 12 ft. lbs.
4. Loosen and slightly tighten bleeder valves at all four wheels. Repair any broken, stripped or frozen valves at this time.
5. Bleed all front and rear brake calipers in following order: righthand rear, lefthand rear, righthand front and lefthand front.
6. Place transparent tube over bleeder valve and allow tube to hang down into transparent container. Ensure end of tube is submerged in clean brake fluid.
7. Slowly depress brake pedal one time and hold, then loosen bleeder valve and purge air. Tighten bleeder screw and slowly release pedal, then wait 15 seconds and repeat this step until all air is bled from system.
8. **Torque** bleed valves to 7 ft. lbs.

HYDRAULIC SYSTEM FLUSH

If brake fluid is old, rusty or contaminated, or whenever new components are installed in hydraulic system, the system must be flushed. Bleed brakes, allowing at least one quart of clean brake fluid to pass through system. Any rubber components in hydraulic system which were exposed to contaminated fluid must be replaced.

Component Replacement

BRAKE PRESSURE MODULATOR VALVE (BPMV)

The Brake Pressure Modulator Valve (BPMV) cannot be repaired. The complete unit must be replaced. **If the BPMV screws**

are loosened it will not be possible to get brake circuits leak tight.

CATERA

1. Turn ignition switch to Off position.
2. Remove power steering fluid reservoir mounting screw and set reservoir aside.
3. Remove upper radiator hose from engine and set aside.
4. Remove relay center cover and Engine Control Module (ECM). Set ECM harness aside.
5. Disconnect EBTCM harness connector.
6. Note brake pipe locations for installation reference, then remove and plug brake pipes.
7. Remove BPMV pump motor ground cable and slide heat shield front off front insulator stud.
8. Remove bracket nuts and BPMV.
9. Reverse procedure to install, noting the following:
   a. **Torque** mounting nuts and screws to 96 inch lbs.
   b. **Torque** brake pipe fittings to 11 ft. lbs.
   c. Fill and bleed hydraulic system.

GRAND PRIX & INTRIGUE

1. Turn ignition switch to OFF position.
2. Pull lock tab from Electronic Brake Traction Control Module (EBTCM) harness connector.
3. Disconnect EBTCM harness connector.
4. Disconnect wheel cylinder and master cylinder brake hydraulic pipes from BPMV. Note location of brake pipes for installation reference.
5. Remove two BPMV to BPMV bracket retaining nuts.
6. Remove BPMV and EBTCM module as an assembly from bracket.
7. Remove EBTCM to BPMV mounting screws, then separate EBTCM from BPMV.
8. Reverse procedure to install, noting the following:
   a. **Torque** EBTCM to BPMV mounting screws to 26 inch lbs.
   b. **Torque** BPMV to BPMV bracket retaining nuts to 96 inch lbs.
   c. **Torque** hydraulic brake pipe fittings to 11 ft. lbs.

ELECTRONIC BRAKE CONTROL MODULE (EBCM)

CAMARO & FIREBIRD

1. Turn ignition switch to Off position.
2. Pull EBCM/EBTCM harness connector tab lock out and disconnect connector.
3. Disconnect pump motor connector.
4. Remove mounting screws and separate EBCM/EBTCM from BPMV. **Do not damage seal or solenoid valves. Do not use pry tool to separate EBCM/EBTCM and BPMV.**
5. Remove wave spring(s).
6. Reverse procedure to install. **Torque** mounting screws to 26 inch lbs., tighten top screws in X pattern.

DTC	Definition
C0035 (High or Low)	DTC C0035 LF Wheel Speed Circuit Malfunction (High or Low)
C0035 (No Signal)	DTC C0035 LF Wheel Speed Circuit Malfunction (No Signal)
C0040 (High or Low)	DTC C0040 RF Wheel Speed Circuit Malfunction (High or Low)
C0040 (No Signal)	DTC C0040 RF Wheel Speed Circuit Malfunction (No Signal)
C0045 (High or Low)	DTC C0045 LR Wheel Speed Circuit Malfunction (High or Low)
C0045 (No Signal)	DTC C0045 LR Wheel Speed Circuit Malfunction (No Signal)
C0050 (High or Low)	DTC C0050 RR Wheel Speed Circuit Malfunction (High or Low)
C0050 (No Signal)	DTC C0050 RR Wheel Speed Circuit Malfunction (No Signal)
C0060	DTC C0060 LF ABS Solenoid #1 Circuit Malfunction
C0065	DTC C0065 LF ABS Solenoid #2 Circuit Malfunction
C0070	DTC C0070 RF ABS Solenoid #1 Circuit Malfunction
C0075	DTC C0075 RF ABS Solenoid #2 Circuit Malfunction
C0080	DTC C0080 LR ABS Solenoid #1 Circuit Malfunction
C0085	DTC C0085 LR ABS Solenoid #2 Circuit Malfunction

DTC	Definition
C0090	DTC C0090 RR ABS Solenoid #1 Circuit Malfunction
C0095	DTC C0095 RR ABS Solenoid #2 Circuit Malfunction
C0110	DTC C0110 Pump Motor Circuit Malfunction
C0121	DTC C0121 Valve Relay Circuit Malfunction
C0141	DTC C0141 Left TCS Solenoid #1 Circuit Malfunction
C0146	DTC C0146 Left TCS Solenoid #2 Circuit Malfunction
C0151	DTC C0151 Right TCS Solenoid #1 CKT Malfunction
C0156	DTC C0156 Right TCS Solenoid #2 CKT Malfunction
C0161	DTC C0161 ABS/TCS Brake Switch Circuit Malfunction
C0236	DTC C0236 TCS RPM Signal Circuit Malfunction
C0241	DTC C0241 PCM Indicated Requested Torque Malf
C0244	DTC C0244 PWM Delivered Torque Malfunction
C0245	DTC C0245 Wheel Speed Sensor Frequency Error
C0550	DTC C0550 ECU Malfunction
C0551	DTC C0551 Option Configuration Error
C0800	DTC C0800 Device Power #1 Circuit Malfunction

GC4029802954000X

Fig. 2 DTC identification. Catera

ELECTRONIC BRAKE TRACTION CONTROL MODULE (EBTCM)

CATERA

1. Turn ignition switch to Off position and remove relay center cover.
2. Remove Engine Control Module (ECM) and set ECM harness aside.
3. Remove lower radiator hose from engine and set aside.
4. Pull tab and disconnect EBTCM connector.
5. Remove pump motor connector and EBTCM to BPMV mounting screws.
6. Separate EBTCM from BPMV. **Do not damage seal or use pry apart with a tool.**
7. Note position and orientation of wave springs, remove and discard.
8. Remove power steering fluid reservoir mounting screw and set reservoir aside.
9. Remove mounting screw and EBTCM cover.
10. Reverse procedure to install. **Torque** mounting screws to 26 inch lbs.

GRAND PRIX & INTRIGUE

1. Turn ignition switch to OFF position.
2. Pull lock tab from Electronic Brake Traction Control Module (EBTCM) harness connector.
3. Disconnect EBTCM harness connector.
4. Remove EBTCM to BPMV retaining screws.
5. Gently pull EBTCM away from BPMV.
6. **On models equipped with Enhanced Traction System (ETS),** remove one wave spring between EBTCM and BPMV and discard.
7. **On models equipped with Traction Control System (TCS),** remove two wave springs between EBTCM and BPMV and discard.
8. **On all models,** reverse procedure to install. **Torque** retaining screws to 26 inch lbs.

WHEEL SPEED SENSOR

FRONT

Camaro & Firebird

The front speed sensors and rings on these models are an integral part of the hub and bearing assembly. If speed sensors or rings are faulty, the entire assembly must be replaced as a unit. Refer to "Camaro & Firebird" chassis section for hub replacement.

Catera

1. Raise and support vehicle.
2. Remove mounting bolt and wheel speed sensor from steering knuckle, **Fig. 178.**
3. Remove cable from spring strut and wheel housing clips.
4. Disconnect connector from wiring harness, then remove speed sensor.
5. Reverse procedure to install. **Torque** mounting bolt to 6 ft. lbs. **Do not force sensor into position.**

Grand Prix & Intrigue

1. Raise and support vehicle.
2. Disconnect wheel sensor electrical connector, **Fig. 179.**
3. Remove sensor mounting bolt, then the sensor from mounting bracket.
4. If sensor will not slide out of knuckle, proceed as follows:
   a. Remove brake rotor.
   b. Use suitable blunt punch to push sensor from back side of knuckle.
5. If sensor locating pin breaks off and remains in knuckle, proceed as follows:
   a. Remove rotor.
   b. Use suitable blunt punch to remove broken pin.
   c. Use sandpaper wrapped around suitable screwdriver to clean hole.
   d. **Do not attempt to enlarge hole.**
6. Reverse procedure to install. Ensure sensor is properly aligned and lays flat against knuckle bosses.

REAR

Camaro & Firebird

1. Raise and support vehicle.
2. Remove speed sensor connector and sensor mounting bolt.
3. Remove sensor from backing plate.
4. Reverse procedure to install. **Torque** mounting bolt to 7 ft. lbs.

Catera

1. Raise and support vehicle.
2. Remove mounting bolt, then the wheel speed sensor from differential housing, **Fig. 180.**
3. Disconnect wiring harness connector for underbody clip and wheel speed sensor connector from wiring harness.
4. Reverse procedure to install. **Torque** mounting bolt to 72 inch lbs. **Do not force sensor into position.**

Grand Prix & Intrigue

The rear speed sensors and rings on these models are an integral part of the hub and bearing assembly. If speed sensors or rings are faulty, the entire assembly must be replaced as a unit. Refer to appropriate chassis section for hub replacement.

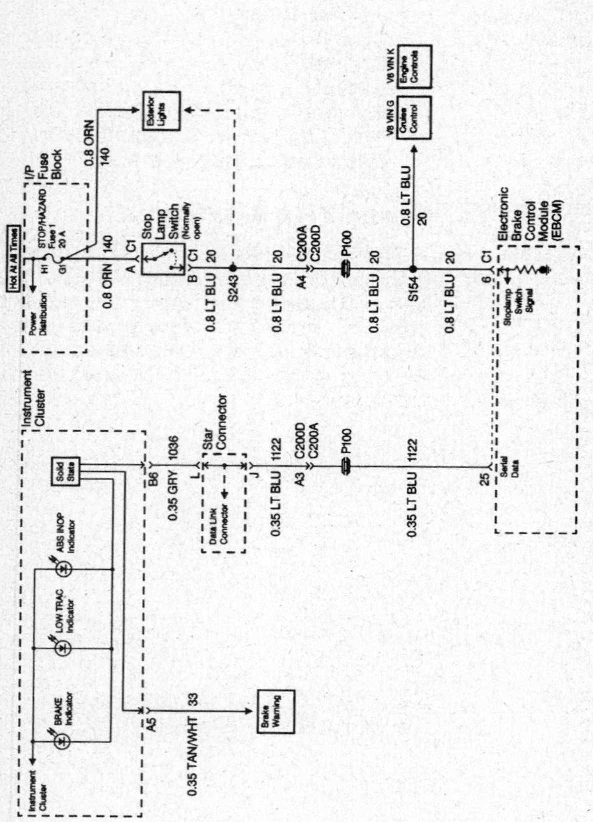

GC402980352302 0X

Fig. 3 ABS wiring circuit (Part 2 of 3). Camaro & Firebird less traction control

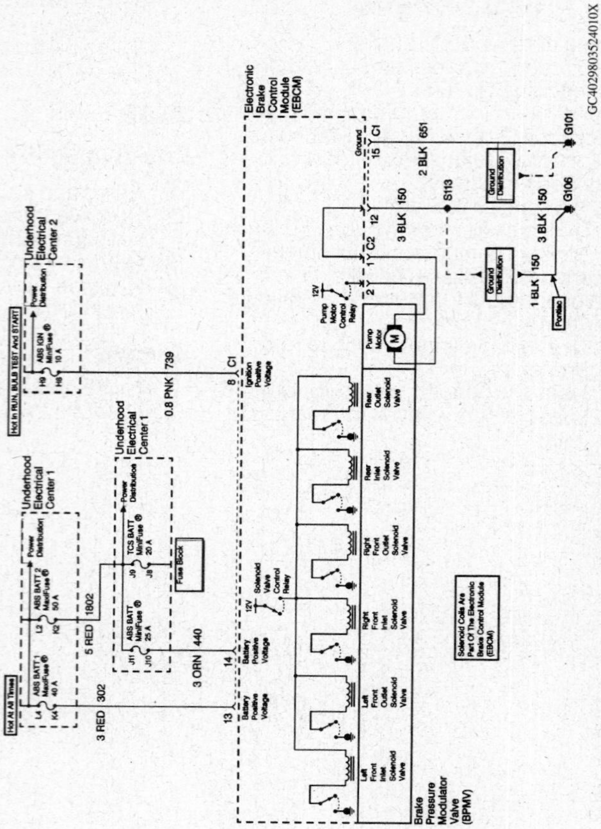

GC402980352401 0X

Fig. 4 ABS wiring circuit (Part 1 of 4). Camaro & Firebird w/3.8L engine & traction control

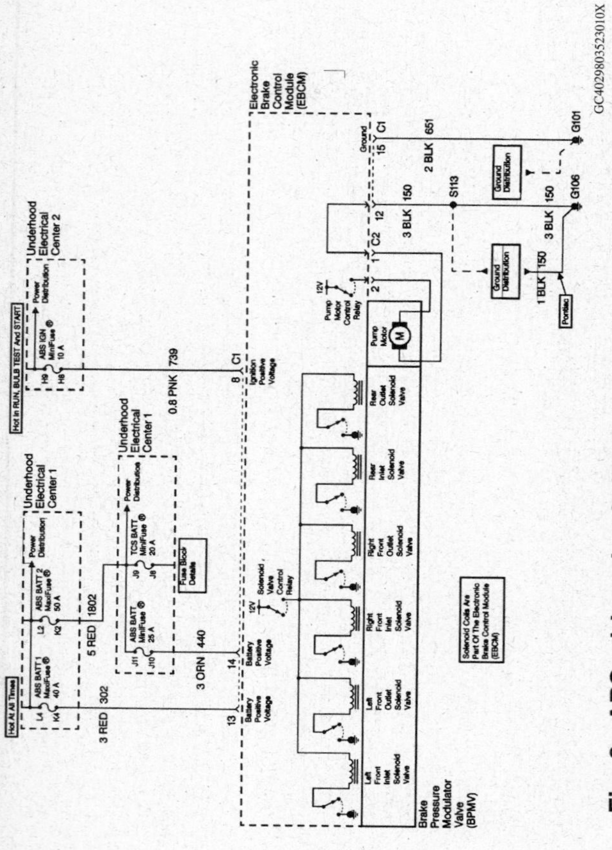

GC402980352301 0X

Fig. 3 ABS wiring circuit (Part 1 of 3). Camaro & Firebird less traction control

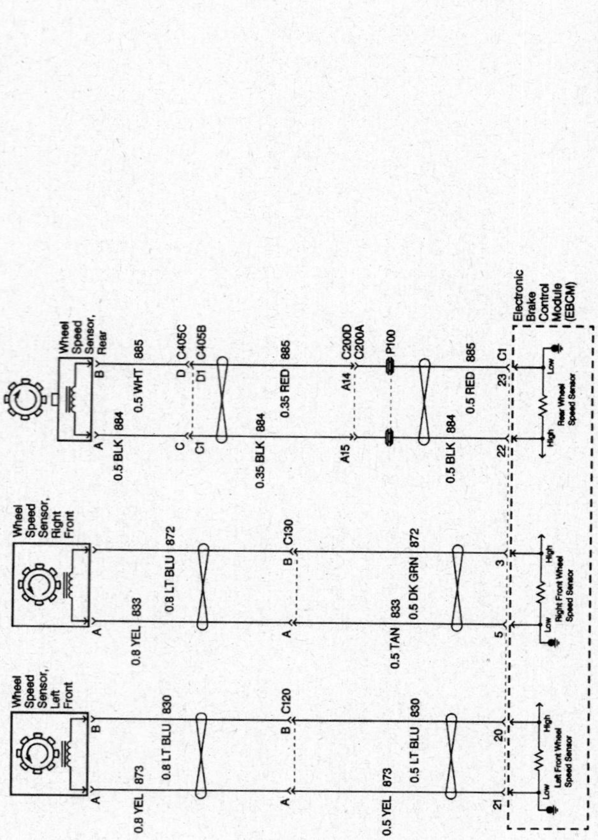

GC402980352303 0X

Fig. 3 ABS wiring circuit (Part 3 of 3). Camaro & Firebird less traction control

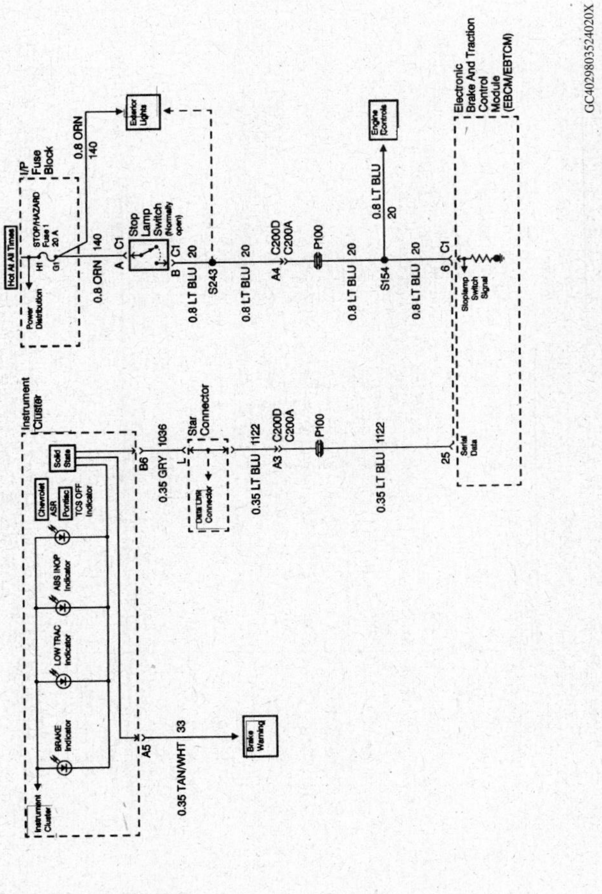

Fig. 4 ABS wiring circuit (Part 2 of 4). Camaro & Firebird w/3.8L engine & traction control

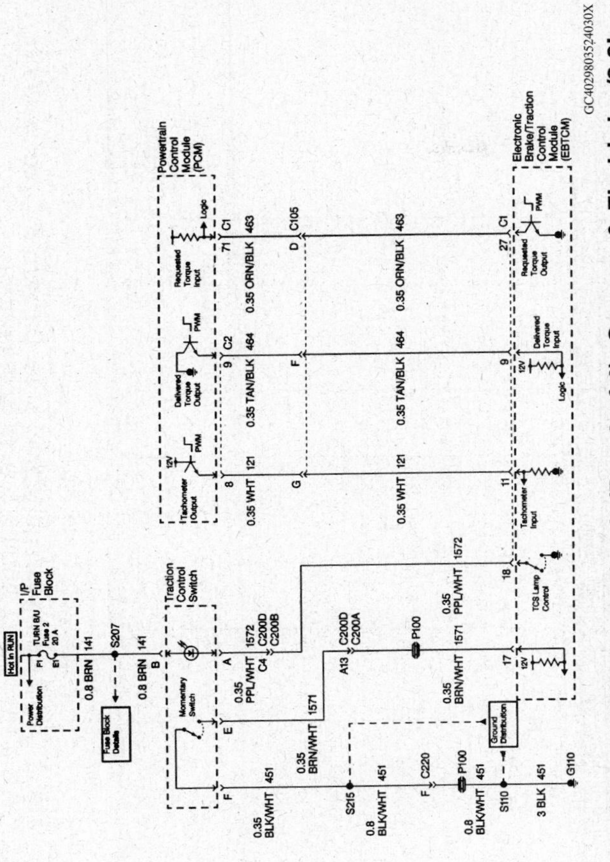

Fig. 4 ABS wiring circuit (Part 3 of 4). Camaro & Firebird w/3.8L engine & traction control

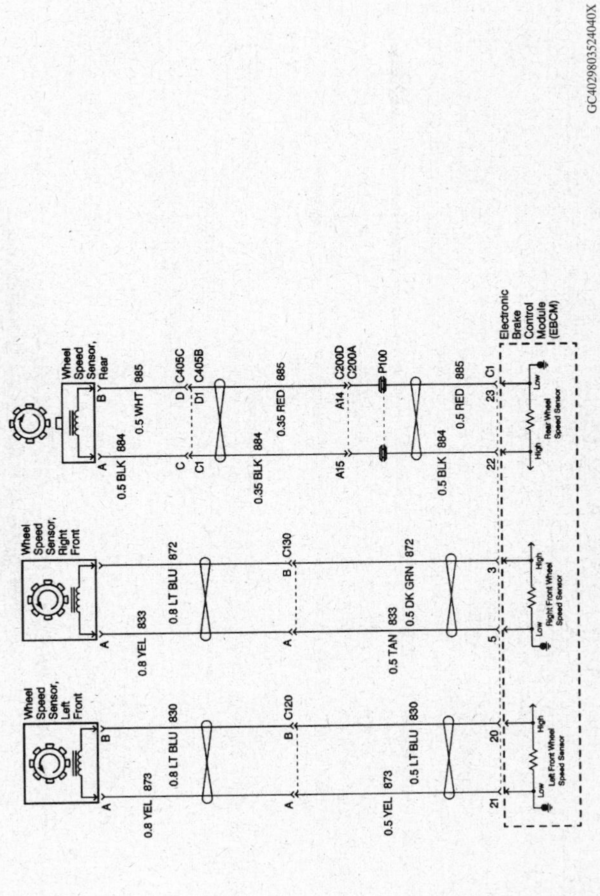

Fig. 4 ABS wiring circuit (Part 4 of 4). Camaro & Firebird w/3.8L engine & traction control

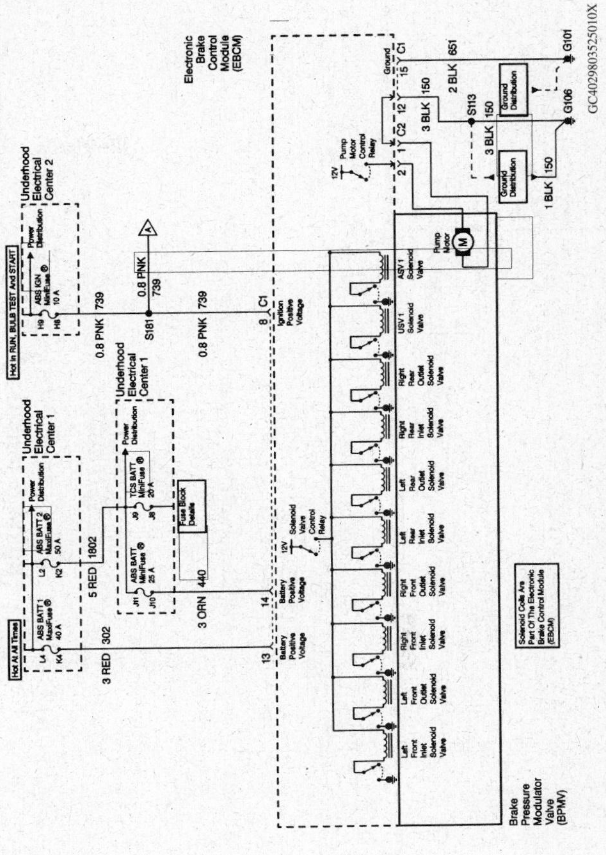

Fig. 5 ABS wiring circuit (Part 1 of 5). Camaro & Firebird w/5.7L engine & tractional control

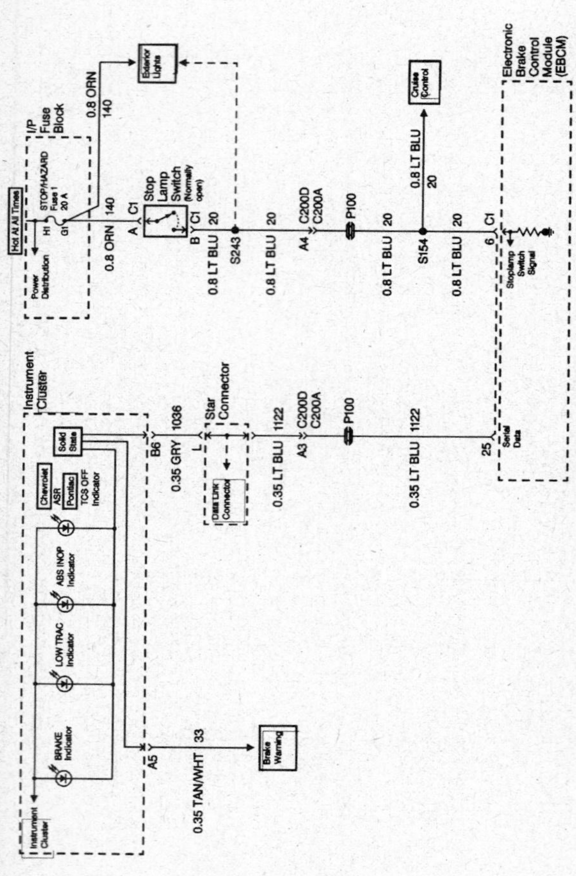

GC4029803525020X

Fig. 5 ABS wiring circuit (Part 2 of 5). Camaro & Firebird w/5.7L engine & tractional control

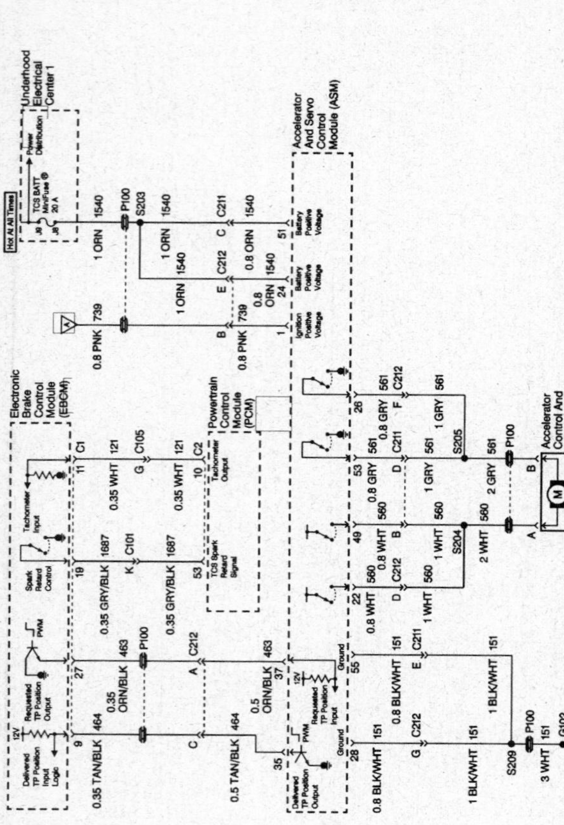

GC4029803525030X

Fig. 5 ABS wiring circuit (Part 3 of 5). Camaro & Firebird w/5.7L engine & tractional control

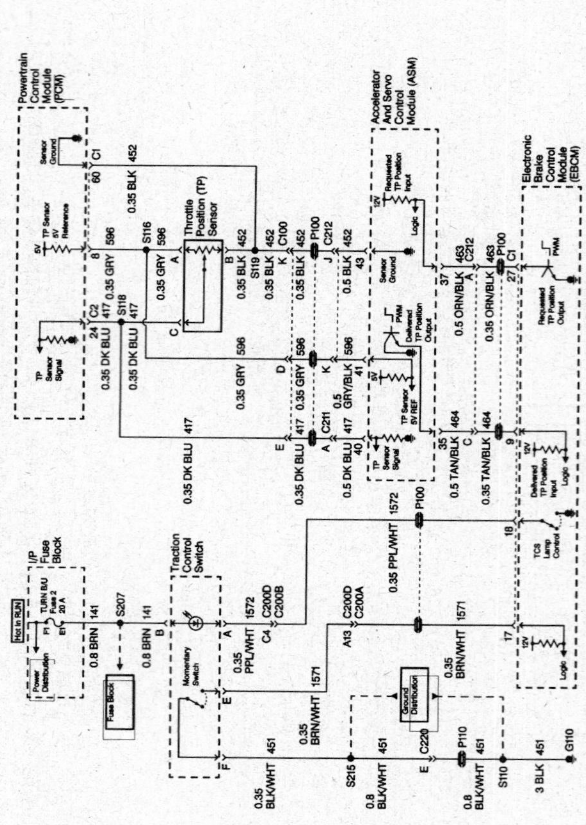

GC4029803525040X

Fig. 5 ABS wiring circuit (Part 4 of 5). Camaro & Firebird w/5.7L engine & tractional control

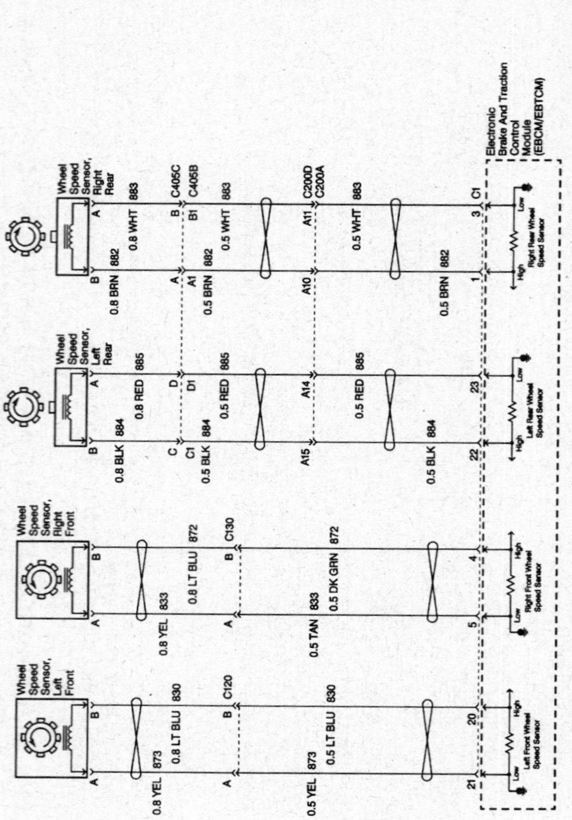

GC4029803525050X

Fig. 5 ABS wiring circuit (Part 5 of 5). Camaro & Firebird w/5.7L engine & tractional control

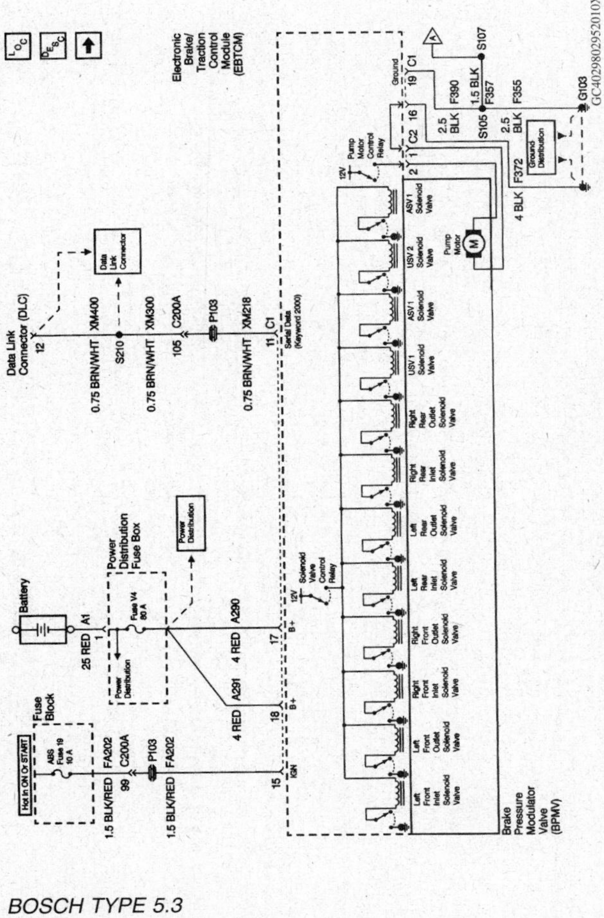

Fig. 6 ABS wiring circuits (Part 1 of 4). Catera

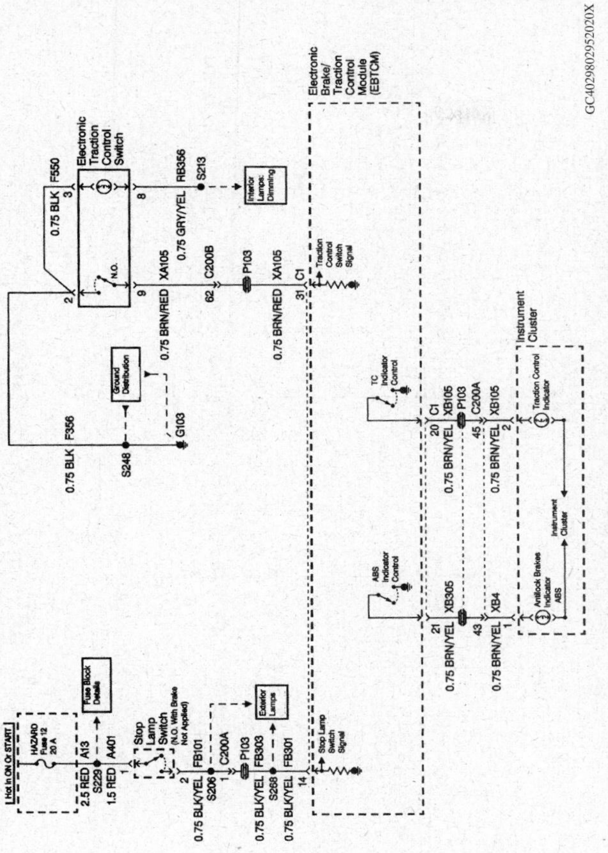

Fig. 6 ABS wiring circuits (Part 2 of 4). Catera

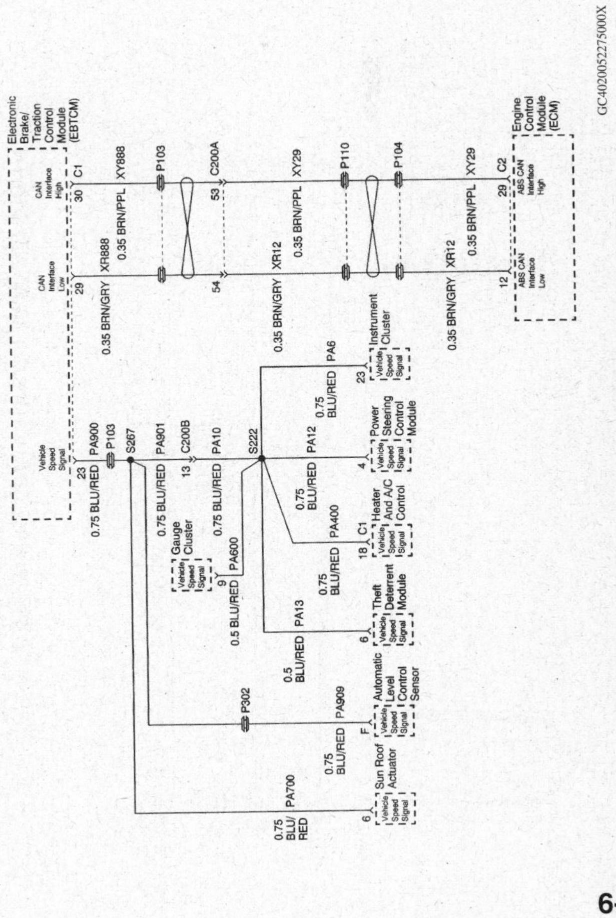

Fig. 6 ABS wiring circuits (Part 3 of 4). Catera

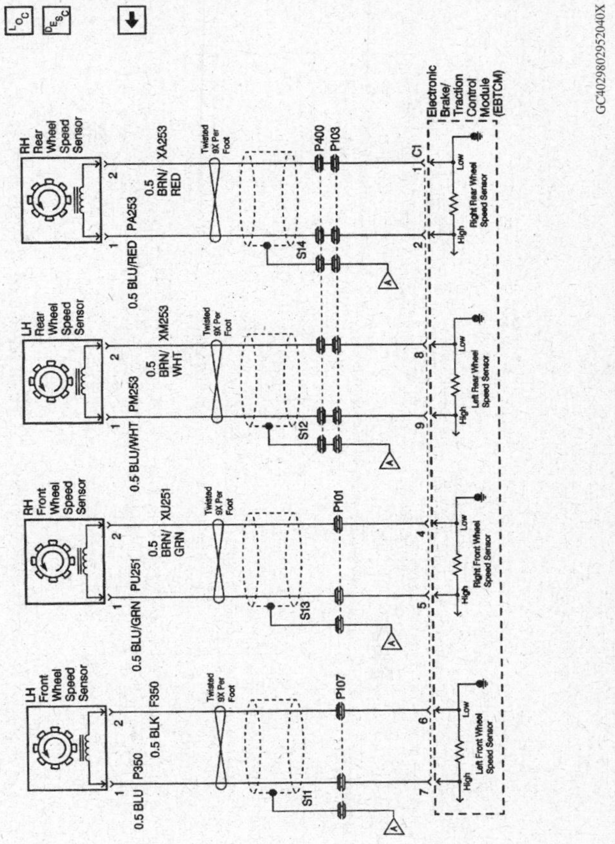

Fig. 6 ABS wiring circuits (Part 4 of 4). Catera

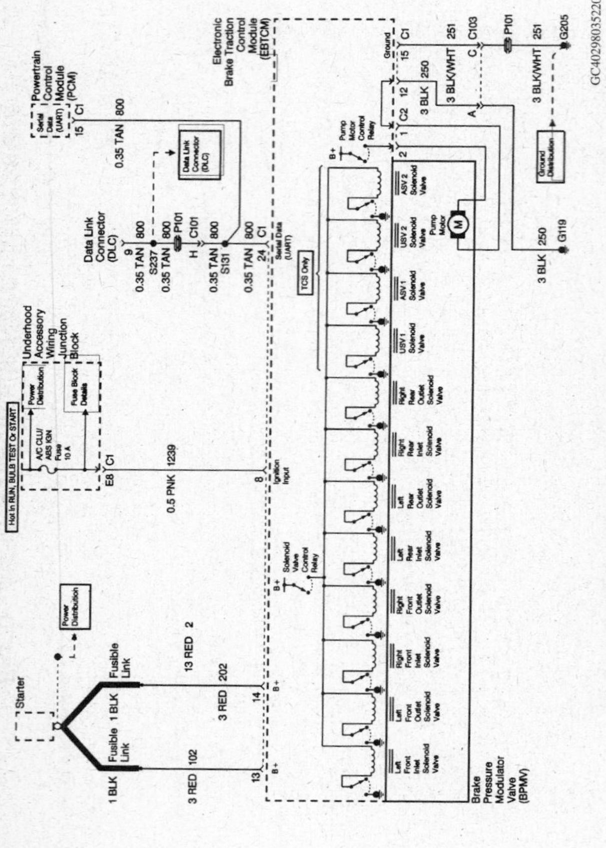

Fig. 7 ABS wiring circuit (Part 1 of 4). Grand Prix

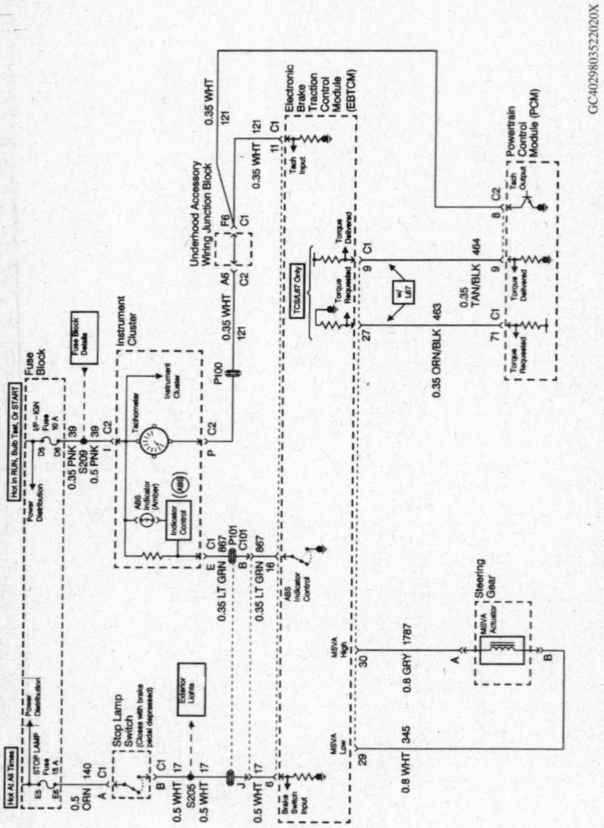

Fig. 7 ABS wiring circuit (Part 2 of 4). Grand Prix

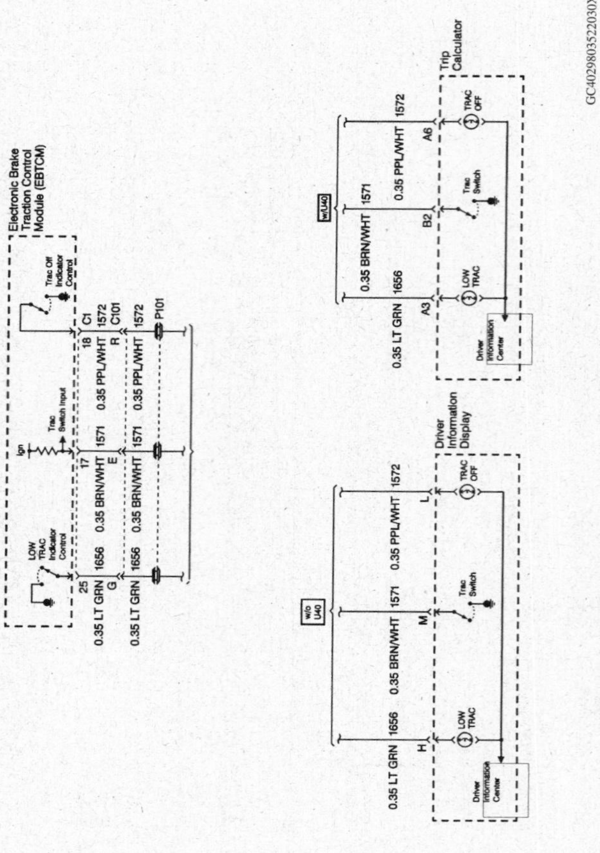

Fig. 7 ABS wiring circuit (Part 3 of 4). Grand Prix

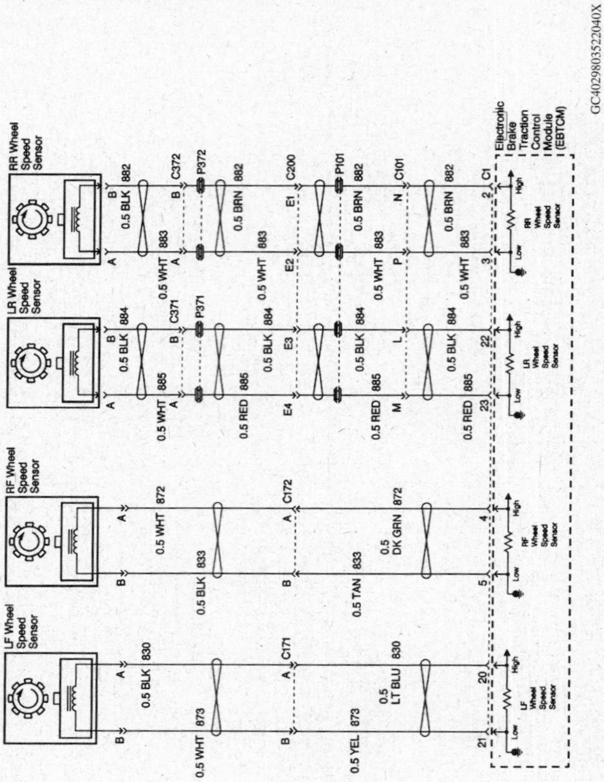

Fig. 7 ABS wiring circuit (Part 4 of 4). Grand Prix

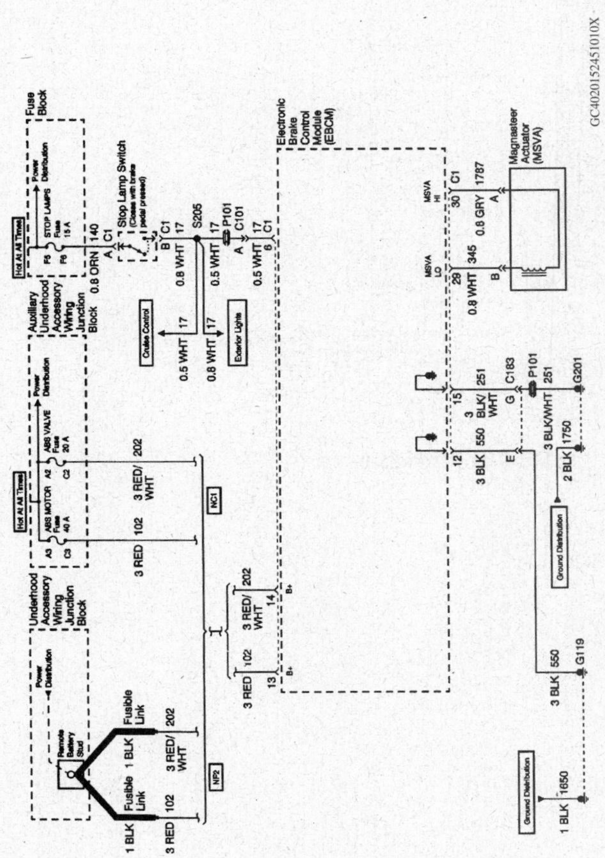

Fig. 8 ABS wiring circuit (Part 1 of 6). Intrigue

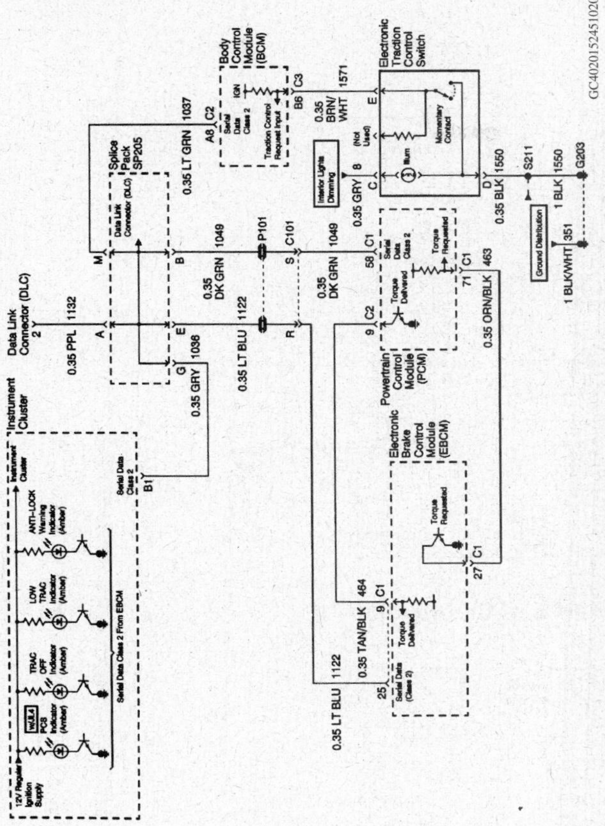

Fig. 8 ABS wiring circuit (Part 2 of 6). Intrigue

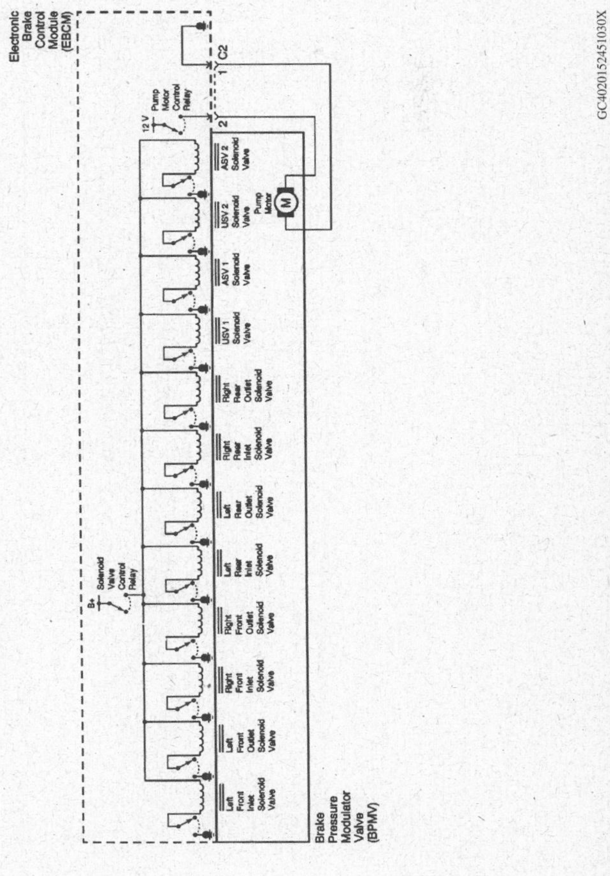

Fig. 8 ABS wiring circuit (Part 3 of 6). Intrigue

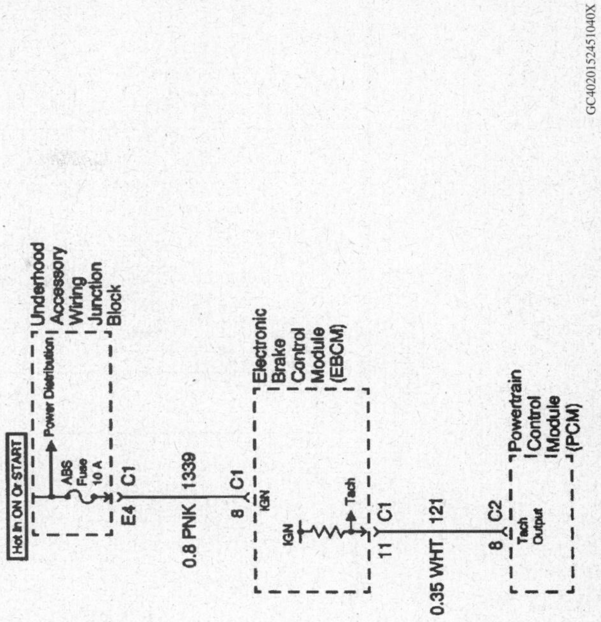

Fig. 8 ABS wiring circuit (Part 4 of 6). Intrigue

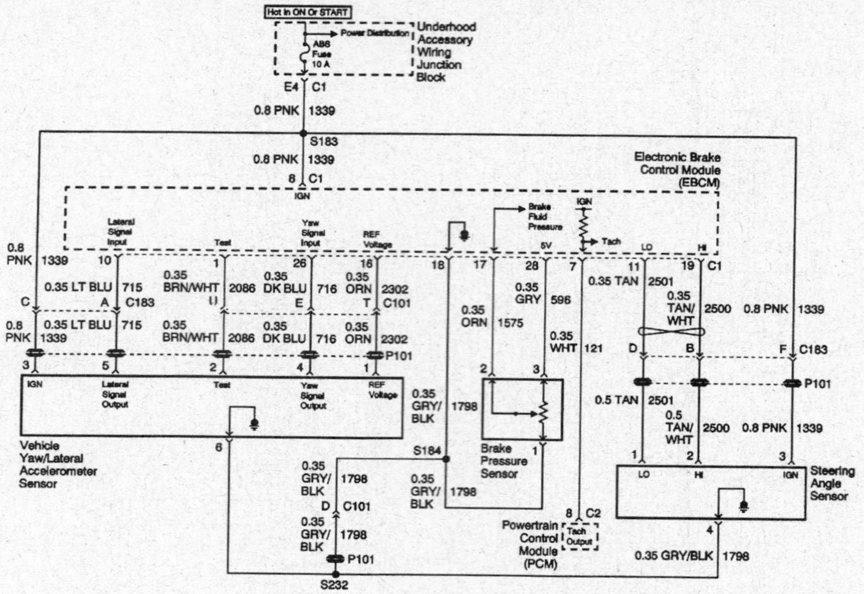

Fig. 8 ABS wiring circuit (Part 5 of 6). Intrigue

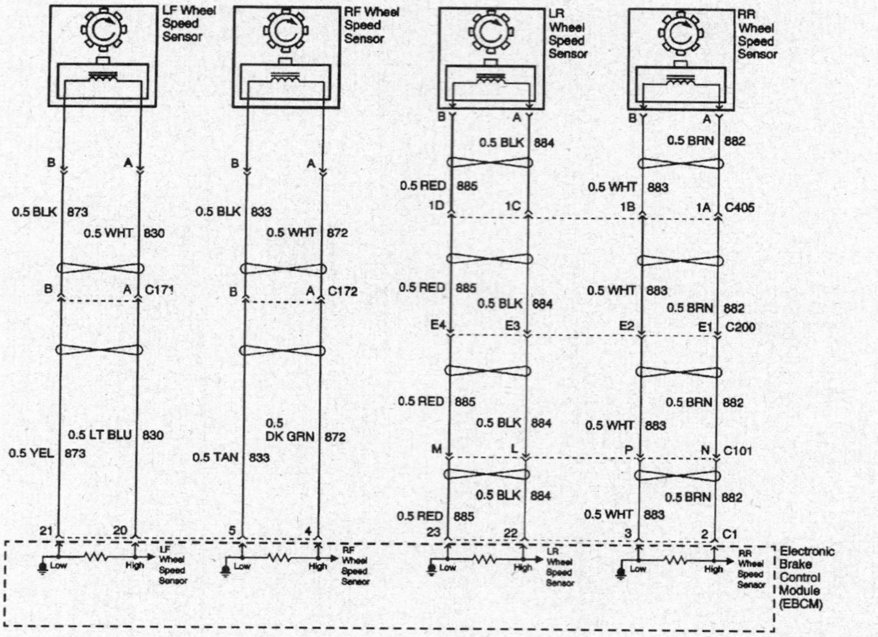

Fig. 8 ABS wiring circuit (Part 6 of 6). Intrigue

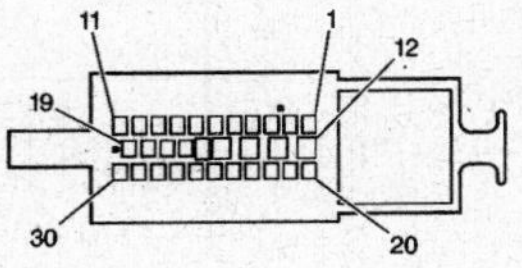

Connector Part Information	• 1532-6390 • 30 Way F GT 150 Series Sealed (BLK)		
Pin	Wire Color	Circuit No.	Function
1	BRN	882	Right rear wheel speed sensor signal (LS1 with NW9)
2	—	—	Not used
3	DK GRN	872	Right front wheel speed sensor signal (LS1 without NW9 and L36)
3	WHT	883	Right rear wheel speed sensor low reference
4	DK GRN	872	Right front wheel speed sensor signal (LSI with NW9)
5	TAN	833	Right front wheel speed sensor low reference
6	LT BLU	20	Stop lamp supply voltage
7	—	—	Not used
8	PNK	739	Ignition 1 voltage
9	TAN/BLK	464	Delivered torque signal (with NW9)
10	—	—	Not used
11	WHT	121	Engine speed signal (with NW9)
12	BLK	150	Ground
13	RED	302	Battery positive voltage
14	ORN	440	Battery positive voltage
15	BLK	651	Ground
16	—	—	Not used
17	BRN/WHT	1571	Traction control switch signal (with NW9)

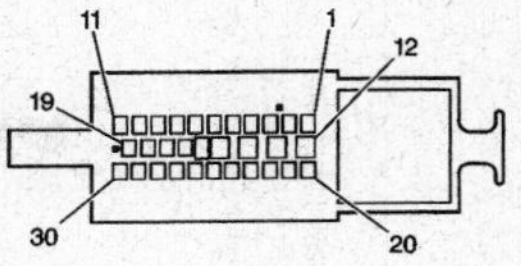

Connector Part Information	• 1532-6390 • 30 Way F GT 150 Series Sealed (BLK)		
Pin	Wire Color	Circuit No.	Function
18	PPL/WHT	1572	Service traction system indicator control
19	GRY/BLK	1687	Ignition retard signal (LS1 with NW9)
20	LT BLU	830	Left front wheel speed sensor signal
21	YEL	873	Left front wheel speed sensor low reference
22	BLK	884	Rear wheel speed sensor signal (LS1 without NW9 and L36)
22	BLK	884	Left rear wheel speed sensor signal (LS1 with NW9)
23	RED	885	Rear wheel speed sensor low reference (LS1 without NW9 and L36)
23	RED	885	Left rear wheel speed sensor low reference (LS1 with NW9)
24	—	—	Not used
25	LT BLU	1122	ABS/TCS Class 2 serial data
26	—	—	Not used
27	ORN/BLK	463	Requested torque signal (with NW9)
28-30	—	—	Not used

GC4020152452000X

Fig. 9 EBTCM connector face view. Camaro & Firebird

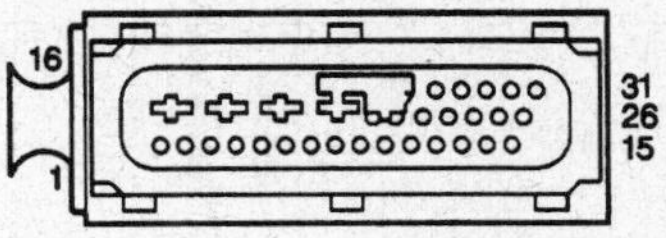

Connector Part Information	ZFW 31-1		
Pin	Wire Color	Circuit No.	Function
1	BRN/RED	XA253	RH rear speed sensor LOW
2	BLU/RED	PA253	RH rear speed sensor HIGH
3	—	—	NOT USED
4	BRN/GRN	XU251	RH front speed sensor LOW
5	BLU/GRN	PU251	RH front speed sensor HIGH
6	BLK	F350	LH front speed sensor LOW
7	BLU	P350	LH front speed sensor HIGH
8	BRN/WHT	XM253	LH rear speed sensor LOW
9	BLU/WHT	PM253	LH rear speed sensor HIGH
10	—	—	NOT USED
11	BRN/WHT	XM218	Serial Data (Keyword 2000)
12	—	—	NOT USED
13	GRY	R40	Requested engine torque output
14	BLK/YEL	FB301	Stop lamp switch signal input
15	BLK/RED	FA202	IGN

GC4029803527010X

Fig. 10 EBTCM connector face view (Part 1 of 2). Catera

Connector Part Information	ZFW 31-1		
Pin	Wire Color	Circuit No.	Function
16	BLK	F372	Ground to G103
17	RED	A290	B+ from fuse V4
18	RED	A291	B+ from fuse V4
19	BLK	F390	Ground to G103
20	BRN/YEL	XB105	TC indicator control
21	BRN/YEL	XB305	ABS indicator control
22			NOT USED
23	BLU/RED	PA900	Vehicle speed signal
24-26			NOT USED
27	GRY	R830	Delivered engine torque input
28-29			NOT USED
30	GRN	U102	Tach input
31	BRN/RED	XA105	Traction control switch input

GC4029803527020X

Fig. 10 EBTCM connector face view (Part 2 of 2). Catera

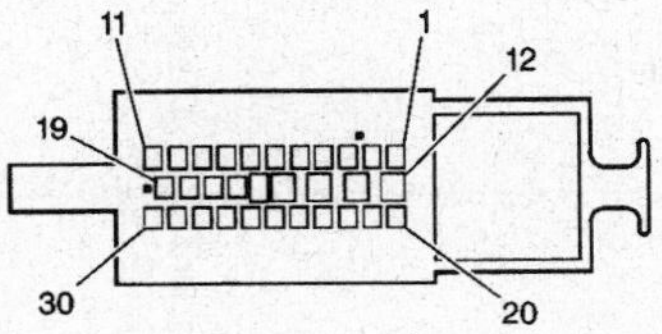

Connector Part Information	• 15326390 • 30-Way F GT Mixed Series Sealed (BLK)		
Pin	Wire Color	Circuit No.	Function
1	—	—	Not Used
2	BRN	882	Wheel Speed Sensor-RR
3	WHT	883	Wheel Speed Sensor Return-RR
4	DK GRN	872	Wheel Speed Sensor Signal-RF
5	TAN	833	Wheel Speed Sensor Return-RF
6	WHT	17	Stop Lamp Switch Output
7	—	—	Not Used
8	PNK	1239	Fused Output-IGN 1
9	TAN/BLK	464	Manifold Absolute Temperature Sensor Return
10	—	—	Not Used
11	WHT	121	Tachometer Signal
12	BLK	250	Ground
13	RED	102	Fused Output-Battery
14	RED	202	Fused Output-Battery
15	BLK/WHT	251	Ground-Clean
16	LT GRN	867	ABS Failure Indicator Lamp Output
17	BRN//WHT	1571	Traction Control System Switch Signal

GC4029903877010X

Fig. 11 EBCM connector face views (Part 1 of 2). Grand Prix

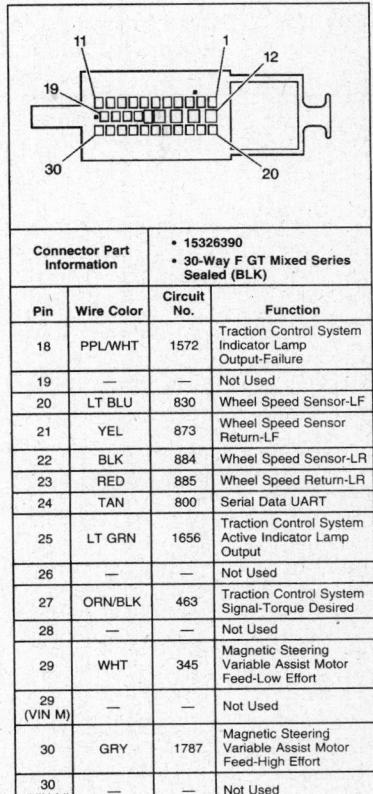

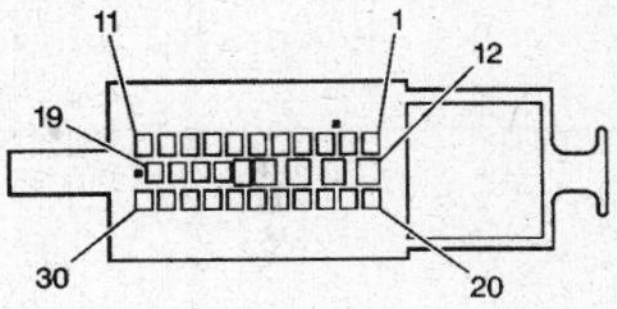

Connector Part Information	• 15326390 • 30-Way F GT Mixed Series Sealed (BLK)		
Pin	Wire Color	Circuit No.	Function
18	PPL/WHT	1572	Traction Control System Indicator Lamp Output-Failure
19	—	—	Not Used
20	LT BLU	830	Wheel Speed Sensor-LF
21	YEL	873	Wheel Speed Sensor Return-LF
22	BLK	884	Wheel Speed Sensor-LR
23	RED	885	Wheel Speed Return-LR
24	TAN	800	Serial Data UART
25	LT GRN	1656	Traction Control System Active Indicator Lamp Output
26	—	—	Not Used
27	ORN/BLK	463	Traction Control System Signal-Torque Desired
28	—	—	Not Used
29	WHT	345	Magnetic Steering Variable Assist Motor Feed-Low Effort
29 (VIN M)	—	—	Not Used
30	GRY	1787	Magnetic Steering Variable Assist Motor Feed-High Effort
30 (VIN M)	—	—	Not Used

GC4029903877020X

Fig. 11 EBCM connector face views (Part 2 of 2). Grand Prix

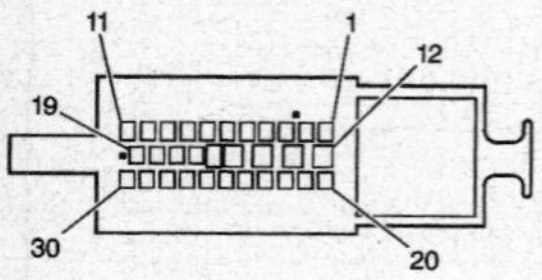

Connector Part Information	• 15326390 • 30-Way F GT Mixed (BLK)		
Pin	Wire Color	Circuit No.	Function
1	BRN/WHT	2086	Test Signal
2	BRN	882	Right Rear Wheel Speed Sensor Signal
3	WHT	883	Right Rear Wheel Speed Sensor Low Reference
4	DK GRN	872	Right Front Wheel Speed Sensor Signal
5	TAN	833	Right Front Wheel Speed Sensor Low Reference
6	WHT	17	Stop Lamp Switch Signal
7	WHT	121	Engine Speed Signal

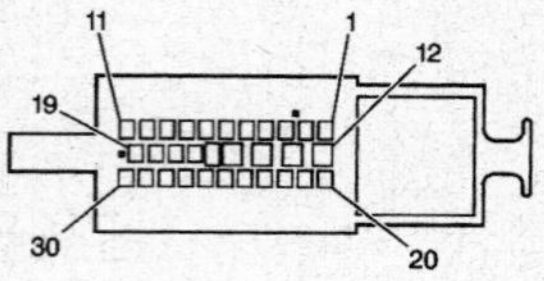

Connector Part Information	• 15326390 • 30-Way F GT Mixed (BLK)		
Pin	Wire Color	Circuit No.	Function
8	PNK	1339	Ignition 1 Voltage
9	TAN/BLK	464	Delivered Torque Signal
10	LT BLU	715	Lateral Accelerometer Signal
11	TAN	2501	CAN Serial Data Low
12	BLK	550	Ground
13	RED	102	Battery Positive Voltage
14	RED/WHT	202	Battery Positive Voltage
15	BLK/WHT	251	Ground
16	ORN	2302	Reference Voltage Feed to Vehicle Yaw/Lateral Accelerometer Sensor
17	ORN	1575	Brake Fluid Pressure Signal
18	GRY/BLK	1798	Ground
19	TAN/WHT	2500	CAN Serial Data Low
20	LT BLU	830	Left Front Wheel Speed Sensor Signal
21	YEL	873	Left Front Wheel Speed Sensor Low Reference
22	BLK	884	Left Rear Wheel Speed Sensor Signal
23	RED	885	Left Rear Wheel Speed Sensor Low Reference
24	—	—	Not Used
25	LT BLU	1122	ABS/TCS Class 2 Serial Data
26	DK BLU	716	Yaw Rate Sensor Signal
27	ORN/BLK	463	Requested Torque Signal
28	GRY	596	5 Volt Reference
29	WHT	345	Variable Effort Steering Actuator Low Effort Control
30	GRY	1787	Variable Effort Steering Actuator High Effort Control

GC4020152453000X

Fig. 12 EBCM connector face views. Intrigue w/control active brake

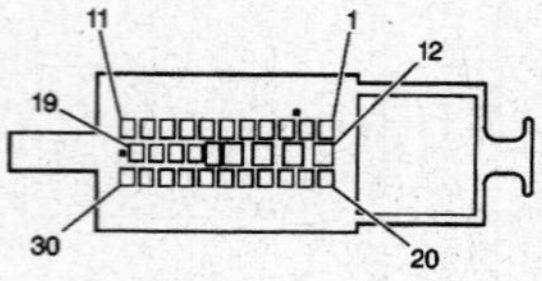

Connector Part Information	• 15326390 • 30-Way F GT Mixed (BLK)		
Pin	Wire Color	Circuit No.	Function
1	—	—	Not Used
2	BRN	882	Right Rear Wheel Speed Sensor Signal
3	WHT	883	Right Rear Wheel Speed Sensor Low Reference
4	DK GRN	872	Right Front Wheel Speed Sensor Signal
5	TAN	833	Right Front Wheel Speed Sensor Low Reference
6	WHT	17	Stop Lamp Switch Signal
7	—	—	Not Used
8	PNK	1339	Ignition 1 Voltage
9	TAN/WHT	464	Delivered Torque Signal
10	—	—	Not Used
11	WHT	121	Engine Speed Signal
12	BLK	550	Ground
13	RED	102	Battery Positive Voltage
14	RED/WHT	202	Battery Positive Voltage
15	BLK/WHT	251	Ground
16-19	—	—	Not Used
20	LT BLU	830	Left Front Wheel Speed Sensor Signal
21	YEL	873	Left Front Wheel Speed Sensor Low Reference
22	BLK	884	Left Rear Wheel Speed Sensor Signal
23	RED	885	Left Rear Wheel Speed Sensor Low Reference
24	—	—	Not Used
25	DK BLU	1122	ABS/TCS Class 2 Serial Data

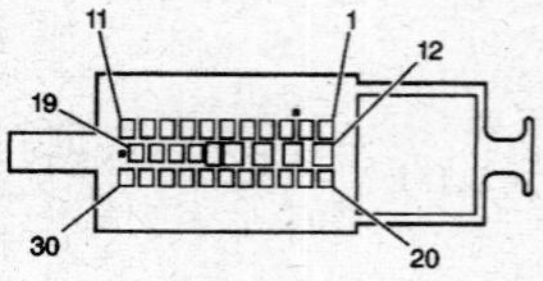

Connector Part Information	• 15326390 • 30-Way F GT Mixed (BLK)		
Pin	Wire Color	Circuit No.	Function
26	—	—	Not Used
27	ORN/BLK	463	Requested Torque Signal
28	—	—	Not Used
29	WHT	345	Variable Effort Steering Actuator Low Effort Control
30	GRY	1787	Variable Effort Steering Actuator High Effort Control

GC4020152454000X

Fig. 13 EBCM connector face views. Intrigue less control active brake

DIAGNOSTIC CHART INDEX

Code/Test	Description	Page No.	Fig. No.
CAMARO & FIREBIRD			
—	ABS Diagnostic System Check	6-222	14
—	ABS Symptoms	6-230	35
—	ABS Indicator Always On	6-230	36
—	ABS Indicator Inoperative	6-231	37
—	ASR Indicator Always On	6-231	38
—	ASR Indicator Inoperative	6-231	39
—	Low Traction Indicator Always On	6-232	40
—	Low Traction Indicator Inoperative	6-232	41
—	Traction Off Indicator Always On	6-232	42
—	Traction Off Indicator Inoperative	6-233	43
C0035	Wheel Speed Sensor Circuit Fault	6-222	15
C0036	Wheel Speed Sensor Circuit Fault	6-222	15
C0040	Wheel Speed Sensor Circuit Fault	6-222	15
C0041	Wheel Speed Sensor Circuit Fault	6-222	15
C0045	Wheel Speed Sensor Circuit Fault	6-222	15
C0046	Wheel Speed Sensor Circuit Fault	6-222	15
C0050	Wheel Speed Sensor Circuit Fault	6-222	15
C0051	Wheel Speed Sensor Circuit Fault	6-222	15
C0060	ABS Solenoid Circuit Fault	6-223	16
C0065	ABS Solenoid Circuit Fault	6-223	16
C0070	ABS Solenoid Circuit Fault	6-223	16
C0075	ABS Solenoid Circuit Fault	6-223	16
C0080	ABS Solenoid Circuit Fault	6-223	16
C0085	ABS Solenoid Circuit Fault	6-223	16
C0090	ABS Solenoid Circuit Fault	6-223	16
C0095	ABS Solenoid Circuit Fault	6-223	16
C0100	ABS Solenoid Circuit Fault	6-223	17
C0105	ABS Solenoid Circuit Fault	6-223	17
C0110	Pump Motor Circuit Fault	6-223	18
C0121	Valve Relay Circuit Fault	6-224	19
C0161	ABS/TCS Brake Switch Circuit Fault	6-224	20
C0166	TCS Priming Line Valve Circuit Fault	6-225	21
C0171	TCS Priming Line Valve Circuit Fault	6-225	21
C0181	Throttle Reduction Motor Circuit Fault	6-225	22
C0182	Throttle Reduction Motor Circuit Range Performance	6-225	23
C0235	TCS RPM Signal Circuit Fault	6-226	24
C0236	TCS RPM Signal Circuit Fault	6-226	24
C0237	TCS RPM Signal Circuit Fault	6-226	24
C0238	TCS Throttle Position Sensor Comparison Fault	6-226	25
C0239	TCS Spark Retard Monitoring Fault	6-226	26
C0240	PCM Traction Control Not Allowed	6-227	27
C0241	PCM Indicated Requested Torque Fault	6-227	28
C0244	PWM Delivered Torque Fault	6-228	29
C0245	Wheel Speed Sensor Frequency Error	6-228	30
C0266	ADS Controller Fault	6-229	31
C0550	ECU Fault	6-229	32
C0896	Device Voltage Range/Performance	6-229	33
C0901	Device No	6-230	34
CATERA			
—	ABS Diagnostic System Check	6-233	44
A	ABS Lamp On w/No Code Set	6-247	75
B	ABS Lamp Off w/No Code Set	6-247	76
C	TC Lamp On w/No Code Set	6-247	77
D	TC Lamp Off w/No Code Set	6-248	78
E	No Communication w/EBTCM	6-248	79

Continued

DIAGNOSTIC CHART INDEX—Continued

Code/Test	Description	Page No.	Fig. No.
CATERA			
C0035	LH Front Wheel Speed Circuit Fault, High Or Low	6-234	45
	LH Front Wheel Speed Circuit Fault, No Signal	6-234	46
C0040	RH Front Wheel Speed Circuit Fault, High Or Low	6-235	47
	RH Front Wheel Speed Circuit Fault, No Signal	6-236	48
C0045	LH Rear Wheel Speed Circuit Fault, High Or Low	6-236	49
	LH Rear Wheel Speed Circuit Fault, No Signal	6-237	50
C0050	RH Rear Wheel Speed Circuit Fault, High Or Low	6-238	51
	RH Rear Wheel Speed Circuit Fault, No Signal	6-238	52
C0060	LH Front ABS Solenoid Circuit No. 1 Fault	6-239	53
C0065	LH Front ABS Solenoid Circuit No. 2 Fault	6-239	54
C0070	RH Front ABS Solenoid Circuit No. 1 Fault	6-239	55
C0075	RH Front ABS Solenoid Circuit No. 2 Fault	6-239	56
C0080	LH Rear ABS Solenoid Circuit No. 1 Fault	6-239	57
C0085	LH Rear ABS Solenoid Circuit No. 2 Fault	6-240	58
C0090	LH Rear ABS Solenoid Circuit No. 1 Fault	6-240	59
C0095	LH Rear ABS Solenoid Circuit No. 2 Fault	6-240	60
C0110	Pump Motor Circuit Fault	6-240	61
C0121	Valve Relay Circuit Fault	6-241	62
C0141	LH TCS Solenoid Circuit No. 1 Fault	6-242	63
C0146	LH TCS Solenoid Circuit No. 2 Fault	6-242	64
C0151	RH TCS Solenoid Circuit No. 1 Fault	6-242	65
C0156	RH TCS Solenoid Circuit No. 2 Fault	6-242	66
C0161	ABS/TCS Brake Switch Circuit Fault	6-243	67
C0236	TCS RPM Signal Circuit Fault	6-243	68
C0241	PCM Indicated Requested Torque Fault	6-244	69
C0244	PWM Delivered Torque Fault	6-244	70
C0245	Wheel Speed Sensor Frequency Error	6-205	71
C0550	ECU Fault	6-205	72
C0551	Option Configuration Error	6-205	73
C0800	Device Power No 1 Circuit Fault.	6-205	74
2000 GRAND PRIX			
—	ABS Diagnostic System Check	6-249	80
—	Traction Off Indicator On With No DTC Set	6-269	118
—	Traction Off Indicator Inoperative With No DTC Set	6-269	119
—	No Communication With EBTCM	6-270	120
—	ABS Indicator Off No DTC Set	6-270	121
—	ABS Indicator On No DTC Set	6-270	122
—	Low Traction Indicator Always On	6-271	123
—	Low Traction Indicator Inoperative	6-271	124
C0035	LH Front Wheel Speed Circuit Fault	6-249	81
C0036	LH Front Wheel Speed Circuit Range/Performance	6-250	82
C0040	RH Front Wheel Speed Circuit Fault	6-251	83
C0041	RH Front Wheel Speed Circuit Range/Performance	6-251	84
C0045	LH Rear Wheel Speed Circuit Fault	6-252	85
C0046	LH Rear Wheel Speed Circuit Range/Performance	6-253	86
C0050	RH Rear Wheel Speed Circuit Fault	6-253	87
C0051	RH Rear Wheel Speed Circuit Range/Performance	6-254	88
C0060	ABS Solenoid Circuit Fault	6-255	89
C0065	ABS Solenoid Circuit Fault	6-255	89
C0070	ABS Solenoid Circuit Fault	6-255	89
C0075	ABS Solenoid Circuit Fault	6-255	89
C0080	ABS Solenoid Circuit Fault	6-255	89
C0085	ABS Solenoid Circuit Fault	6-255	89
C0090	ABS Solenoid Circuit Fault	6-255	89
C0095	ABS Solenoid Circuit Fault	6-255	89
C0110	Pump Motor Circuit Fault	6-255	90

Continued

DIAGNOSTIC CHART INDEX—Continued

Code/Test	Description	Page No.	Fig. No.
2000 GRAND PRIX			
C0121	Valve Relay Circuit Fault	6-256	92
C0141	TCS Solenoid Circuit Fault	6-258	96
C0146	TCS Solenoid Circuit Fault	6-258	96
C0151	TCS Solenoid Circuit Fault	6-258	96
C0156	TCS Solenoid Circuit Fault	6-258	96
C0161	ABS/TCS Brake Switch Circuit Fault	6-259	97
C0236	TCS RPM Signal Circuit Fault	6-262	102
C0240	PCM Traction Control Not Allowed	6-263	104
C0244	PWM Delivered Torque Fault	6-263	106
C0245	Wheel Speed Sensor Frequency Error	6-264	107
C0252	Active Brake Control Sensors Uncorrelated	6-265	108
C0253	Centering Fault	6-265	109
C0550	ECU Fault	6-266	110
C0710	Steering Position Signal Fault	6-266	111
C0870	Device Voltage Reference Output No	6-266	112
C0875	Device Voltage Reference Input No	6-267	113
C0896	Device Voltage Range/Performance	6-267	114
U1304	Lost Communication w/UART System	6-268	115
U1650	Chassis System Dedicated Bus Controller Fault	6-268	116
U1651	Chassis System Dedicated Bus Sensor No	6-268	117
2001–04 GRAND PRIX			
—	ABS Diagnostic System Check	6-274	134
—	ABS Symptoms	6-287	163
—	ABS Indicator Always On	6-287	164
—	ABS Indicator Inoperative	6-288	165
—	Low Traction Indicator Always On	6-288	166
—	Low Traction Indicator Inoperative	6-288	167
—	Traction Off Indicator Always On	6-288	168
—	Traction Off Indicator Inoperative	6-289	169
—	ABS Indicator Always On	6-289	170
C0035	Wheel Speed Circuit Fault	6-275	136
C0036	Wheel Speed Circuit Fault	6-275	136
C0040	Wheel Speed Circuit Fault	6-275	136
C0041	Wheel Speed Circuit Fault	6-275	136
C0045	Wheel Speed Circuit Fault	6-275	136
C0046	Wheel Speed Circuit Fault	6-275	136
C0050	Wheel Speed Circuit Fault	6-275	136
C0051	Wheel Speed Circuit Fault	6-275	136
C0060	ABS Solenoid Circuit Fault	6-275	137
C0065	ABS Solenoid Circuit Fault	6-275	137
C0070	ABS Solenoid Circuit Fault	6-275	137
C0075	ABS Solenoid Circuit Fault	6-275	137
C0080	ABS Solenoid Circuit Fault	6-275	137
C0085	ABS Solenoid Circuit Fault	6-275	137
C0090	ABS Solenoid Circuit Fault	6-275	137
C0095	ABS Solenoid Circuit Fault	6-275	137
C0110	Pump Motor Circuit Fault	6-276	138
C0121	Value Relay Circuit Fault	6-276	139
C0141	TCS Solenoid Circuit Fault	6-278	142
C0146	TCS Solenoid Circuit Fault	6-278	142
C0151	TCS Solenoid Circuit Fault	6-278	142
C0156	TCS Solenoid Circuit Fault	6-278	142
C0161	ABS/TCS Brake Switch Circuit Fault	6-278	143
C0235	TCS RPM Signal Circuit Fault	6-281	148
C0236	TCS RPM Signal Circuit Fault	6-281	148
C0237	TCS RPM Signal Circuit Fault	6-281	148

Continued

DIAGNOSTIC CHART INDEX—Continued

Code/Test	Description	Page No.	Fig. No.
2001–04 GRAND PRIX			
C0240	PCM Traction Control Not Allowed	6-281	149
C0241	PCM Indicated Requested Torque Fault	6-282	150
C0244	PWM Delivered Torque Fault	6-282	151
C0245	Wheel Speed Sensor Frequency Error	6-283	152
C0550	ECU Fault	6-284	155
2000 INTRIGUE			
—	PCS Indicator Always On	6-272	125
—	PCS Indicator Inoperative	6-272	126
—	Traction Off Indicator On With No DTC Set	6-272	127
—	Traction Off Indicator Inoperative	6-273	128
—	No Communication With EBTCM	6-273	129
—	ABS Indicator Off No DTC Set	6-274	130
—	ABS Indicator On No DTC Set	6-274	131
—	Low Traction Indicator Always On	6-274	132
—	Low Traction Indicator Inoperative	6-274	133
—	ABS Diagnostic System Check	6-249	80
C0035	LH Front Wheel Speed Circuit Fault	6-249	81
C0036	LH Front Wheel Speed Circuit Range/Performance	6-250	82
C0040	RH Front Wheel Speed Circuit Fault	6-251	83
C0041	RH Front Wheel Speed Circuit Range/Performance	6-251	84
C0045	LH Rear Wheel Speed Circuit Fault	6-252	85
C0046	LH Rear Wheel Speed Circuit Range/Performance	6-253	86
C0050	RH Rear Wheel Speed Circuit Fault	6-253	87
C0051	RH Rear Wheel Speed Circuit Range/Performance	6-254	88
C0060	ABS Solenoid Circuit Fault	6-255	89
C0065	ABS Solenoid Circuit Fault	6-255	89
C0070	ABS Solenoid Circuit Fault	6-255	89
C0075	ABS Solenoid Circuit Fault	6-255	89
C0080	ABS Solenoid Circuit Fault	6-255	89
C0085	ABS Solenoid Circuit Fault	6-255	89
C0090	ABS Solenoid Circuit Fault	6-255	89
C0095	ABS Solenoid Circuit Fault	6-255	89
C0110	Pump Motor Circuit Fault	6-256	91
C0121	Valve Relay Circuit Fault	6-257	93
C0131	ABS/TCS System Pressure Circuit Fault	6-257	94
C0132	ABS/TCS System Pressure Circuit Range/Performance	6-258	95
C0141	TCS Solenoid Circuit Fault	6-258	96
C0146	TCS Solenoid Circuit Fault	6-258	96
C0151	TCS Solenoid Circuit Fault	6-258	96
C0156	TCS Solenoid Circuit Fault	6-258	96
C0161	ABS/TCS Brake Switch Circuit Fault	6-259	97
C0186	Lateral Accelerometer Circuit Fault	6-259	98
C0187	Lateral Accelerometer Circuit Range/Performance	6-260	99
C0196	Yaw Rate Circuit Fault	6-260	100
C0197	Yaw Rate Circuit Range/Performance	6-261	101
C0236	TCS RPM Signal Circuit Fault	6-262	103
C0240	PCM Traction Control Not Allowed	6-263	104
C0241	PCM Indicated Requested Torque Fault	6-263	105
C0244	PWM Delivered Torque Fault	6-263	106
C0245	Wheel Speed Sensor Frequency Error	6-264	107
C0252	Active Brake Control Sensors Uncorrelated	6-265	108
C0253	Centering Fault	6-265	109
C0550	ECU Fault	6-266	110
C0710	Steering Position Signal Fault	6-266	111
C0870	Device Voltage Reference Output No	6-266	112
C0875	Device Voltage Reference Input No	6-267	113

Continued

DIAGNOSTIC CHART INDEX—Continued

Code/Test	Description	Page No.	Fig. No.
2000 INTRIGUE			
C0896	Device Voltage Range/Performance	6-267	114
U1650	Chassis System Dedicated Bus Controller Fault	6-268	116
U1651	Chassis System Dedicated Bus Sensor No	6-268	117
2001–02 INTRIGUE			
—	ABS Diagnostic System Check	6-275	135
—	ABS Symptoms	6-287	162
—	ABS Indicator Always On	6-289	170
—	ABS Indicator Inoperative	6-289	171
—	Low Traction Indicator Always On	6-290	172
—	Low Traction Indicator Inoperative	6-290	173
—	PCS Indicator Always On	6-290	174
—	PCS Indicator Inoperative	6-290	175
—	Traction Off Indicator Always On	6-291	176
—	Traction Off Indicator Inoperative	6-291	177
C0035	Wheel Speed Circuit Fault	6-275	136
C0036	Wheel Speed Circuit Fault	6-275	136
C0040	Wheel Speed Circuit Fault	6-275	136
C0041	Wheel Speed Circuit Fault	6-275	136
C0045	Wheel Speed Circuit Fault	6-275	136
C0046	Wheel Speed Circuit Fault	6-275	136
C0050	Wheel Speed Circuit Fault	6-275	136
C0051	Wheel Speed Circuit Fault	6-275	136
C0060	ABS Solenoid Circuit Fault	6-275	137
C0065	ABS Solenoid Circuit Fault	6-275	137
C0070	ABS Solenoid Circuit Fault	6-275	137
C0075	ABS Solenoid Circuit Fault	6-275	137
C0080	ABS Solenoid Circuit Fault	6-275	137
C0085	ABS Solenoid Circuit Fault	6-275	137
C0090	ABS Solenoid Circuit Fault	6-275	137
C0095	ABS Solenoid Circuit Fault	6-275	137
C0110	Pump Motor Circuit Fault	6-276	138
C0121	Value Relay Circuit Fault	6-276	139
C0131	ABS/TCS System Pressure Circuit Fault	6-276	140
C0132	ABS/TCS System Pressure Circuit Range/Performance	6-277	141
C0141	TCS Solenoid Circuit Fault	6-278	142
C0146	TCS Solenoid Circuit Fault	6-278	142
C0151	TCS Solenoid Circuit Fault	6-278	142
C0156	TCS Solenoid Circuit Fault	6-278	142
C0161	ABS/TCS Brake Switch Circuit Fault	6-278	143
C0186	Lateral Accelerometer Circuit Fault	6-278	144
C0187	Lateral Accelerometer Circuit Range/Performance	6-279	145
C0196	Yaw Rate Circuit Fault	6-280	146
C0197	Yaw Rate Circuit Range/Performance	6-280	147
C0235	TCS RPM Signal Circuit Fault	6-281	148
C0236	TCS RPM Signal Circuit Fault	6-281	148
C0237	TCS RPM Signal Circuit Fault	6-281	148
C0240	PCM Traction Control Not Allowed	6-281	149
C0241	PCM Indicated Requested Torque Fault	6-282	150
C0244	PWM Delivered Torque Fault	6-282	151
C0245	Wheel Speed Sensor Frequency Error	6-283	152
C0252	Active Brake Control Sensor Uncorrelated	6-283	153
C0253	Centering Fault	6-284	154
C0550	ECU Fault	6-284	155
C0710	Steering Position Signal Fault	6-284	156
C0870	Device Voltage Reference Output No. 1 Circuit Fault	6-284	157
C0875	Device Voltage Reference Input No. 2	6-285	158

Continued

DIAGNOSTIC CHART INDEX—Continued

Code/Test	Description	Page No.	Fig. No.
2001–02 INTRIGUE			
C0896	Device Voltage Range/Performance	6-285	159
U1650	Chassis System Dedicated Bus Controller Fault	6-286	160
U1651	Chassis System Dedicated Bus Sensor No. 1 Fault	6-286	161

Diagnostic System Check - ABS

Circuit Description

The ABS Diagnostic System Check is an organized approach to identify problems associated with the EBCM. This check must be the starting point for any EBCM complaint, and will direct you to the next logical step in diagnosing the complaint. The EBCM is a very reliable component and is not likely the cause of the malfunction. Most system complaints are linked to faulty wiring, connectors, and occasionally to components. Understanding the ABS system and using the tables correctly will reduce diagnostic time and prevent unnecessary parts replacement.

Test Description

The numbers below refer to the step numbers on the diagnostic table.

2. Lack of communication may be due to a partial malfunction of the serial data circuit or due to a total malfunction of the serial data circuit. The specified procedure will determine the particular condition.
4. The presence of DTCs which begin with "U" indicate some other module is not communication. The specified procedure will compile all the available information before tests are performed.

Diagnostic System Check - ABS

Step	Action	Value(s)	Yes	No
1	Install a scan tool. Does the scan tool power up?	—	Go to *Step 2*	Go to *Scan Tool Does Not Power Up* In Data Link Communications
2	1. Turn ON the ignition, with the engine OFF. 2. Attempt to establish communications with the following control modules: • Electronic brake control module (EBCM) • Instrument panel module (IPC) • Powertrain control module (PCM) Does the scan tool communicate with the control modules?	—	Go to *Step 3*	Go to *Scan Tool Does Not Communicate with Class 2 Device* In Data Link Communications
3	Select the display DTCs function on the scan tool for the following control modules: • Electronic brake control module (EBCM) • Instrument panel module (IPC) • Powertrain control module (PCM) Does the scan tool display any DTCs?	—	Go to *Step 4*	Go to *Symptoms - Antilock Brake System*
4	Does the scan tool display any DTCs which begin with a U (i.e. DTC U1000, U1016 or U1300, U1301)?	—	Go to *Scan Tool Does Not Communicate with Class 2 Device*	Go to *Diagnostic Trouble Code (DTC) List* For The Applicable DTC

Scan Tool Output Controls

Scan Tool Output Control	Additional Menu Selection(s)	Description
ABS Warning Lamp	—	Commands the ABS indicator ON and OFF.
Left Front Solenoid	—	Commands the solenoid ON and OFF.
Left Rear Solenoid	—	Commands the solenoid ON and OFF.
Pump Motor	—	Commands the pump motor ON and OFF.
LF Inlet Solenoid	Solenoid Test	Commands the solenoid ON and OFF.
LF Outlet Solenoid	Solenoid Test	Commands the solenoid ON and OFF.
LR Inlet Solenoid	Solenoid Test	Commands the solenoid ON and OFF.
LR Outlet Solenoid	Solenoid Test	Commands the solenoid ON and OFF.
LF Master Cylinder Isolation Solenoid	Solenoid Test	Commands the solenoid ON and OFF.
LF Prime Solenoid	Solenoid Test	Commands the solenoid ON and OFF.
TCS On/Off test	—	Commands the traction control system ON and OFF. Performs the same function as the traction control switch.

GC4020152455000X

Fig. 14 Diagnostic System Check. Camaro & Firebird

Circuit Description

As the wheel spins, the wheel speed sensor produces an AC signal. The EBCM uses the frequency of the AC signal to calculate the wheel speed.

Conditions for Running the DTC

C0035 C0040 C0045 C0050

The ignition is ON.

C0036 C0041 C0046 C0051

- Vehicle speed is over 40 km/h (25 mph).
- The brake pedal is not pressed.
- The ABS is not active.

Conditions for Setting the DTC

C0035 C0040 C0045 C0050

One of the following conditions exists for 0.02 seconds:

- A short to voltage - the wheel speed sensor signal circuit greater than 4.25 volts.
- An open - the wheel speed sensor signal circuit voltage is greater than 4.25 volts and wheel speed sensor return circuit voltage is less than 0.75 volts.

C0036 C0041 C0046 C0051

All of the following conditions exists for 10 ms:

- The suspect wheel speed equals zero.
- The other wheel speeds are greater than 40 km/h (25 mph) for 0.01 seconds.
- The suspect wheel equals zero during drive off, and the other wheels are greater than 12 km/h (7.5 mph).
- A short to ground - the wheel speed sensor signal circuit is shorted to ground.
- A deviation of two wheel speeds at either side of the vehicle greater than 6 km/h (4 mph), or at the front axle greater than 10 km/h (6 mph) for a time period of 10 to 20 seconds.

Action Taken When the DTC Sets

If equipped, the following actions occur:

- The EBCM disables the ABS/TCS for the duration of the ignition cycle.
- The ABS indicator turns ON.
- The Traction Off indicator turns ON.
- The Red BRAKE Warning indicator could turn on.

Conditions for Clearing the DTC

- The condition for the DTC is no longer present (the DTC is not current) and you used the scan tool Clear DTC function.
- The EBCM automatically clears the history DTC when a current DTC is not detected in 100 consecutive drive cycles.

Diagnostic Aids

C0035 C0040 C0045 C0050

If the customer comments that the ABS indicator is ON only during moist environmental conditions (rain, snow, vehicle wash, etc.), inspect the wheel speed sensor wiring for signs of water intrusion. If the DTC is not current, clear all DTCs and simulate the effects of water intrusion by using the following procedure:

1. Spray the suspected area with a 5 percent saltwater solution. To create a 5 percent saltwater solution, add 2 teaspoons of salt to 354 ml (12 oz) of water.
2. Test drive the vehicle over various road surfaces (bumps, turns, etc.) above 40 km/h (25 mph) for at least 30 seconds.
3. If the DTC returns, replace the suspected wheel speed sensor or repair the wheel speed sensor wiring.
4. Rinse the are thoroughly when completed.

C0036 C0041 C0046 C0051

Under the following conditions, 2 Wheel Speed Sensor Input is 0 DTCs are set:

- The 2 suspect wheel speeds equal zero for 10–20 seconds.
- The other wheel speeds are greater than 16 km/h (10 mph).
- The other wheel speeds are within 11 km/h (7 mph) of each other.

Diagnose each wheel speed sensor individually.

C0036 C0041 C0046 C0051

A possible cause of this DTC is electrical noise on the wheel speed sensor harness wiring. Electrical noise could result from the wheel speed sensor wires being routed to close to high energy ignition system components, such as spark plug wires.

Test Description

The numbers below refer to the step numbers on the diagnostic table.

4. This step tests the wheel speed sensor for the proper resistance value.
5. This step ensures that the wheel speed sensor generates the proper voltage.

GC4020152456010X

Fig. 15 Codes C0035-C0051: Wheel Speed Sensor Circuit Fault (Part 1 of 2). Camaro & Firebird

Step	Action	Value(s)	Yes	No
Schematic Reference: *ABS Schematics*				
1	Did you perform the ABS Diagnostic System Check?	—	Go to *Step 2*	Go to *Diagnostic System Check - ABS*
2	1. Install a scan tool. 2. Turn ON the ignition. 3. Set up the scan tool snap shot feature to trigger for this DTC. 4. Drive the vehicle at a speed greater than the specified value. Does the scan tool indicate that this wheel speed DTC set?	8 km/h (5 mph)	Go to *Step 3*	Go to Diagnostic Aids
3	1. Raise and support the vehicle. Refer to *Lifting and Jacking the Vehicle* in General Information. 2. Disconnect the wheel speed sensor connector. 3. Measure the resistance across the wheel speed sensor. Does the resistance measure within the specified range?	800–1600 Ω	Go to *Step 4*	Go to *Step 8*
4	1. Spin the wheel. 2. Measure the AC voltage across the wheel speed sensor. Does the AC voltage measure greater than the specified value?	100 mV	Go to *Step 5*	Go to *Step 8*
5	Inspect for poor connections at the harness connector of the wheel speed sensor. Refer to *Testing for Intermittent and Poor Connections* and *Connector Repairs* in Wiring Systems. Did you find and correct the condition?	—	Go to *Step 10*	Go to *Step 6*
6	1. Disconnect the EBCM harness connector. 2. Install the *J 39700* using *J 39700-530* to the EBCM harness connector only. 3. Test the wheel speed sensor circuits for the following: • An open • A short to ground • A short to voltage • Shorted together Refer to *Testing for Intermittent and Poor Connections* and *Wiring Repairs* in Wiring Systems. Did you find and correct the condition?	—	Go to *Step 10*	Go to *Step 7*
7	Inspect for poor connections at the harness connector for the EBCM. Refer *Testing for Intermittent and Poor Connections* and *Connector Repairs* in Wiring Systems. Did you find and correct the condition?	—	Go to *Step 10*	Go to *Step 9*
8	Replace the wheel speed sensor. Refer to *Wheel Bearing/Hub Replacement - Front* or *Wheel Speed Sensor Replacement - Rear (Without Traction Control)* or *Wheel Speed Sensor Replacement - Rear (With Traction Control)* in Rear Suspension. Did you complete the replacement?	—	Go to *Step 10*	—
9	Replace the EBCM. Refer to *Electronic Brake Control Module (EBCM) Replacement.* Did you complete the repair?	—	Go to *Step 10*	—
10	1. Use the scan tool in order to clear the DTCs. 2. Operate the vehicle within the Conditions for Running the DTC as specified in the supporting text. Does the DTC reset?	—	Go to *Step 2*	System OK

GC4020152456020X

Fig. 15 Codes C0035-C0051: Wheel Speed Sensor Circuit Fault (Part 2 of 2). Camaro & Firebird

Circuit Description

The inlet and outlet valve solenoid circuits are supplied with battery power when the ignition is in the ON position. The EBCM controls the valve functions by grounding the circuit when necessary.

Conditions for Running the DTC

- The DTC can set anytime the ignition switch is in the ON position.
- The DTC can set when the vehicle speed is greater then 6 km/h (4 mph) and the brake pedal is not applied.
- The DTC can set when the vehicle speed is greater then 15 km/h (9 mph) and the brake pedal is applied.

Conditions for Setting the DTC

The DTC will set when the EBCM detects one of the following internal to the EBCM only:

- An open in the solenoid coil or circuit.
- A short to ground in the solenoid coil or circuit.
- A short to voltage in the solenoid coil or circuit.

Action Taken When the DTC Sets

If equiped, the following actions occur:

- A malfunction DTC is stored.
- ABS/TCS is disabled.
- The ABS/TCS indicators are turned on.

Conditions for Clearing the DTC

- The condition for the DTC is no longer present (the DTC is not current) and you used the scan tool Clear DTC function.
- The EBCM automatically clears the history DTC when a current DTC is not detected in 100 consecutive drive cycles.

Diagnostic Aids

The solenoid valve circuit and the solenoid coil are internal to the EBCM. No part of the solenoid circuit is diagnosable external to the EBCM. The DTC sets when there is a malfunction in the solenoid circuit internal to the EBCM only.

Test Description

The numbers below refer to step numbers on the Diagnostic Table.

2. This step determines if the DTC is current.

Step	Action	Yes	No
Schematic Reference: *ABS Schematics*			
1	Did you perform the Diagnostic System Check?	Go to *Step 2*	Go to *Diagnostic System Check - ABS*
2	1. Using a scan tool clear the DTC. 2. Remove the scan tool from the DLC. 3. Carefully drive the vehicle above 12 km/h (8 mph) for several minutes. 4. Turn the ignition switch to the OFF position. 5. Install a scan tool. 6. Turn the ignition switch to the ON position, engine off. 7. Using the scan tool in Diagnostic Trouble Codes, check for DTCs. Did any one of the DTCs C0060-C0095 reset as a current DTC?	Go to *Step 3*	Go to *Testing for Intermittent and Poor Connections*
3	Replace the EBCM. Refer to *Electronic Brake Control Module (EBCM) Replacement.* Is the repair complete?	Go to *Step 4*	—
4	1. Use the scan tool in order to clear the DTCs. 2. Operate the vehicle within the Conditions for Running the DTC as specification in the supporting text. Does the DTC reset?	Go to *Step 2*	System OK

GC4020152458000X

Fig. 17 Codes C0100 Or C0105: ABS solenoid Circuit Fault. Camaro & Firebird

Circuit Description

The inlet and outlet valve solenoid circuits are supplied with battery power when the ignition is in the ON position. The EBCM controls the valve functions by grounding the circuit when necessary.

Conditions for Running the DTC

- The DTC can set anytime the ignition switch is in the ON position.
- The DTC can set when the vehicle speed is greater then 6 km/h (4 mph) and the brake pedal is not applied.
- The DTC can set when the vehicle speed is greater then 15 km/h (9 mph) and the brake pedal is applied.

Conditions for Setting the DTC

The DTC will set when the EBCM detects one of the following internal to the EBCM only:

- An open in the solenoid coil or circuit.
- A short to ground in the solenoid coil or circuit.
- A short to voltage in the solenoid coil or circuit.

Action Taken When the DTC Sets

If equiped, the following actions occur:

- A malfunction DTC is stored.
- ABS/TCS is disabled.
- The ABS/TCS indicators are turned on.

Conditions for Clearing the DTC

- The condition for the DTC is no longer present (the DTC is not current) and you used the scan tool Clear DTC function.
- The EBCM automatically clears the history DTC when a current DTC is not detected in 100 consecutive drive cycles.

Diagnostic Aids

The solenoid valve circuit and the solenoid coil are internal to the EBCM. No part of the solenoid circuit is diagnosable external to the EBCM. The DTC sets when there is a malfunction in the solenoid circuit internal to the EBCM only.

Test Description

The numbers below refer to step numbers on the Diagnostic Table.

2. This step determines if the DTC is current.

DTC C0060-C0095

Step	Action	Yes	No
Schematic Reference: *ABS Schematics*			
1	Did you perform the Diagnostic System Check?	Go to *Step 2*	Go to *Diagnostic System Check - ABS*
2	1. Using a scan tool clear the DTC. 2. Remove the scan tool from the DLC. 3. Carefully drive the vehicle above 12 km/h (8 mph) for several minutes. 4. Turn the ignition switch to the OFF position. 5. Install a scan tool. 6. Turn the ignition switch to the ON position, engine off. 7. Using the scan tool in Diagnostic Trouble Codes, check for DTCs. Did any one of the DTCs C0060-C0095 reset as a current DTC?	Go to *Step 3*	Go to *Testing for Intermittent and Poor Connections*
3	Replace the EBCM. Refer to *Electronic Brake Control Module (EBCM) Replacement.* Is the repair complete?	Go to *Step 4*	—
4	1. Use the scan tool in order to clear the DTCs. 2. Operate the vehicle within the Conditions for Running the DTC as specification in the supporting text. Does the DTC reset?	Go to *Step 2*	System OK

GC4020152457000X

Fig. 16 Codes C0060-C0095: ABS solenoid Circuit Fault. Camaro & Firebird

Circuit Description

The pump motor is an integral part of the BPMV, while the pump motor relay is integral to the EBCM. The pump motor relay is not engaged during normal system operation. When ABS or TCS operation is required the EBCM activates the pump motor relay and battery power is provided to the pump motor.

Conditions for Running the DTC

- The ignition switch is in the ON position.
- Initialization is complete.

Conditions for Setting the DTC

- Pump motor voltage is not present 60 milliseconds after activation of the pump motor relay.
- Pump motor voltage is present for more than 2.5 seconds with no activation of the pump motor relay.
- Pump motor voltage is not present for 40 milliseconds after the pump motor relay is commanded off.

Action Taken When the DTC Sets

If equiped, the following actions occur:

- A malfunction DTC stores.
- The ABS/TCS disables.
- The amber ABS/TCS indicator(s) turn on.
- The Brake Warning indicator turns on.

Conditions for Clearing the DTC

- The condition for the DTC is no longer present (the DTC is not current) and you used the scan tool Clear DTC function.
- The EBCM automatically clears the history DTC when a current DTC is not detected in 100 consecutive drive cycles.

Diagnostic Aids

- It is very important that a thorough inspection of the wiring and connectors be performed. Failure to carefully and fully inspect wiring and connectors may result in misdiagnosis, causing part replacement with reappearance of the malfunction.
- Thoroughly inspect any circuitry that may be causing the complaint for the following conditions:
  - Backed out terminals
  - Improper mating
  - Broken locks
  - Improperly formed or damaged terminals
  - Poor terminal-to-wiring connections
  - Physical damage to the wiring harness
- The following conditions may cause an intermittent malfunction:
  - A poor connection
  - Rubbed-through wire insulation
  - A broken wire inside the insulation
- If an intermittent malfunction exists, refer to *Testing for Intermittent and Poor Connections* in Wiring Systems.

Test Description

The number below refers to the step number on the diagnostic table.

3. Tests the pump motor circuits of the BPMV for a short to the housing of the BPMV. The wiring from the BPMV to the EBCM should not be repaired.

GC4020152459010X

Fig. 18 Code C0110: Pump Motor Circuit Fault (Part 1 of 2). Camaro & Firebird

Step	Action	Value(s)	Yes	No
Schematic Reference: *ABS Schematics*				
1	Did you perform the ABS Diagnostic System Check?	—	Go to *Step 2*	Go to *Diagnostic System Check - ABS*
2	1. Disconnect the EBCM harness connector 2. Connect the *J 39700* universal pinout box using the *J 39700-530* cable adapter to the EBCM harness connector only. 3. Test both ground circuits of the EBCM including the EBCM ground for a high resistance or an open. Refer to *Circuit Testing* and *Wiring Repairs* in Wiring Systems. 4. Test the Battery Positive Voltage circuits for an open, high resistance, or a short to ground. Refer to *Circuit Testing* and *Wiring Repairs* in Wiring Systems. Did you find and correct the condition?	—	Go to *Step 8*	Go to *Step 3*
3	1. Disconnect the pump motor harness pigtail connector of the BPMV. 2. Measure the resistance between each pump motor control circuit and the housing of the BPMV at the pump motor harness pigtail connector of the BPMV. Does the resistance measure less than the specified value?	5 Ω	Go to *Step 4*	Go to *Step 5*
4	Inspect for poor connections at the pump motor harness pigtail connector of the BPMV. Refer to *Testing for Intermittent and Poor Connections* and *Connector Repairs* in Wiring Systems. Did you find and correct the condition?	—	Go to *Step 8*	Go to *Step 6*
5	Inspect for poor connections at the harness connector of the EBCM. Refer to *Testing for Intermittent and Poor Connections* and *Connector Repairs* in Wiring Systems. Did you find and correct the condition?	—	Go to *Step 8*	Go to *Step 7*
6	Replace the BPMV. Refer to *Brake Pressure Modulator Valve (BPMV) Replacement.* Did you complete the repair?	—	Go to *Step 8*	—
7	Replace the EBCM. Refer to *Electronic Brake Control Module (EBCM) Replacement.* Did you complete the repair?	—	Go to *Step 8*	—
8	1. Use the scan tool in order to clear the DTCs. 2. Operate the vehicle within the conditions for Running the DTC as specified in the supporting text Does the DTC reset?	—	Go to *Step 2*	System OK

GC4020152459020X

Fig. 18 Code C0110: Pump Motor Circuit Fault (Part 2 of 2). Camaro & Firebird

Circuit Description

The Stoplamp Switch is a normally open switch, when the brake pedal is depressed the EBCM will sense battery voltage. This allows the EBCM to determine the state of the brake lamps.

Conditions for Running the DTC

- The ignition switch is ON.
- The DTC can be set after system initialization.

Conditions for Setting the DTC

- EBCM detects battery voltage at all times.
- EBCM never detects battery voltage from CKT 17.
- Both brake lamps are faulty.

Action Taken When the DTC Sets

If equiped, the following actions occur:

- The EBCM disables the ABS/TCS for the duration of the ignition cycle.
- A malfunction DTC will set.
- The ANTI-LOCK indicator turns ON.
- The TRAC Off indicator turns ON.
- The Red BRAKE Warning indicator could turn on.

Conditions for Clearing the DTC

- The condition for the DTC is no longer present (the DTC is not current) and you used the scan tool Clear DTC function.
- The EBCM automatically clears the history DTC when a current DTC is not detected in 100 consecutive drive cycles.

Diagnostic Aids

- It is very important that a thorough inspection of the wiring and connectors be performed. Failure to carefully and fully inspect wiring and connectors may result in misdiagnosis, causing part replacement with reappearance of the malfunction.
- Thoroughly inspect any circuitry that may be causing the complaint for the following conditions:
  - Backed out terminals
  - Improper mating
  - Broken locks
  - Improperly formed or damaged terminals
  - Poor terminal-to-wiring connections
  - Physical damage to the wiring harness
- The following conditions may cause an intermittent malfunction:
  - A poor connection
  - Rubbed-through wire insulation
  - A broken wire inside the insulation
- If an intermittent malfunction exists refer to *Testing for Intermittent and Poor Connections* in Wiring Systems.

Test Description

The numbers below refer to the step numbers on the diagnostic table.

3. This DTC detects an open stoplamp switch signal circuit from the stoplamp side of the splice to the EBCM.
4. The EBCM sources 5 volts on the stoplamp switch signal circuit. This small voltage has a ground path through the stoplamp bulbs. This DTC sets if the path to ground is open.
7. With the scan tool, Test for the current state of the brake lamp switch parameter.
10. Test the stoplamp signal circuit for a short to voltage.

DTC C0161

Step	Action	Yes	No
Schematic Reference: *ABS Schematics*			
1	Did you perform the ABS Diagnostic System Check?	Go to *Step 2*	Go to *Diagnostic System Check - ABS*
2	1. Press the brake pedal. 2. With the scan tool, observe the Brake Switch Status parameter in the ABS data list. Does the Brake Switch Status parameter display Applied?	Go to *Step 4*	Go to *Step 3*
3	Test the signal circuit of the stoplamp switch for an open. Refer to *Circuit Testing* and *Wiring Repairs* in Wiring Systems. Did you find and correct the condition?	Go to *Step 15*	Go to *Step 11*
4	Press the brake pedal. Are all of the stoplamps OFF?	Go to *Step 5*	Go to *Step 7*

GC4020152461010X

Fig. 20 Code C0161: ABS/TCS Brake Switch Circuit Fault (Part 1 of 2). Camaro & Firebird

Circuit Description

The solenoid valve relay supplies power to the solenoid valve coils in the EBCM. The solenoid valve relay, located in the EBCM, is activated whenever the ignition switch is in the RUN position and no faults are present. The solenoid valve relay remains engaged until the ignition is turned OFF or a failure is detected.

Conditions for Running the DTC

The ignition switch is in the ON position.

Conditions for Setting the DTC

- DTC C0121 will set anytime the solenoid valve relay is commanded on and the EBCM does not see battery voltage at the solenoid valves.
- DTC C0121 will set anytime the EBCM commands the solenoid valve relay off and battery voltage is still present at the solenoid valves.

Action Taken When the DTC Sets

If equiped, the following actions occur:

- A malfunction DTC stores.
- The ABS/TCS disables.
- The amber ABS/TCS indicator(s) turn on.
- The Brake warning indicator turns on.

Conditions for Clearing the DTC

- The condition for the DTC is no longer present (the DTC is not current) and you used the scan tool Clear DTC function.
- The EBCM automatically clears the history DTC when a current DTC is not detected in 100 consecutive drive cycles.

Diagnostic Aids

- It is very important that a thorough inspection of the wiring and connectors be performed. Failure to carefully and fully inspect wiring and connectors may result in misdiagnosis, causing part replacement with reappearance of the malfunction.
- Thoroughly inspect any circuitry that may be causing the complaint for the following conditions:
  - Backed out terminals
  - Improper mating
  - Broken locks
  - Improperly formed or damaged terminals
  - Poor terminal-to-wiring connections
  - Physical damage to the wiring harness
- The following conditions may cause an intermittent malfunction:
  - A poor connection
  - Rubbed-through wire insulation
  - A broken wire inside the insulation
- If an intermittent malfunction exists, refer to *Testing for Intermittent and Poor Connections* in Wiring Systems.
- The solenoid valve relay is an integral part of the EBCM and is not serviced separately.

Test Description

The number below refers to step number on the Diagnostic Table.

2. This step determines if the DTC is current.

Step	Action	Yes	No
Schematic Reference: *ABS Schematics*			
1	Did you perform the Diagnostic System Check?	Go to *Step 2*	Go to *Diagnostic System Check - ABS*
2	1. Install a scan tool. 2. Turn ON the ignition, with the engine OFF. 3. Use the scan tool in order to clear the DTCs. Does the DTC reset?	Go to *Step 3*	Go to Diagnostic Aids
3	1. Connect the *J 39700* universal pinout box using the *J 39700-530* cable adapter to the EBCM harness connector only. 2. Test the battery positive voltage circuit for an open, high resistance, or a short to ground. Refer to *Circuit Testing* and *Wiring Repairs* in Wiring Systems. Did you find and correct the condition?	Go to *Step 5*	Go to *Step 4*
4	Replace the Electronic Brake Control Module (EBCM). Refer to *Electronic Brake Control Module (EBCM) Replacement.* Did you complete the replacement?	Go to *Step 5*	—
5	1. Use the scan tool in order to clear the DTCs. 2. Operate the vehicle within the Conditions for Running the DTC as specified in the supporting text. Does the DTC reset?	Go to *Step 2*	System OK

GC4020152460000X

Fig. 19 Code C0121: Valve Relay Circuit Fault. Camaro & Firebird

Step	Action	Yes	No
5	Test the feed circuit of the stoplamps for an open or high resistance. Refer to *Circuit Testing* and *Wiring Repairs* in Wiring Systems. Did you find and correct the condition?	Go to *Step 15*	Go to *Step 6*
6	Test the ground circuit of the stoplamps for an open or high resistance. Refer to *Circuit Testing* and *Wiring Repairs* in Wiring Systems. Did you find and correct the condition?	Go to *Step 15*	Go to Diagnostic Aids
7	1. Press the brake pedal. 2. With a scan tool, observe the Brake Switch Status parameter. Does the Brake Switch Status parameter change state?	Go to Diagnostic Aids	Go to *Step 8*
8	1. Turn OFF the ignition. 2. Inspect the stoplamp switch and adjust and/or calibrate if needed. Did you find and correct the condition?	Go to *Step 15*	Go to *Step 9*
9	1. Turn OFF the ignition switch. 2. Disconnect the stoplamp switch connector. 3. Turn ON the ignition, with the engine OFF. 4. With a scan tool, observe the Brake Switch Status parameter. Does the scan tool display Released?	Go to *Step 11*	Go to *Step 10*
10	Test the stoplamp signal circuit for a short to voltage. Refer to *Circuit Testing* and *Wiring Repairs* in Wiring Systems. Did you find and correct the condition?	Go to *Step 15*	Go to *Step 12*
11	Inspect for poor connections at the harness connector of the stoplamp switch. Refer to *Testing for Intermittent and Poor Connections* and *Connector Repairs* in Wiring Systems. Did you find and correct the condition?	Go to *Step 15*	Go to *Step 13*
12	Inspect for poor connections at the harness connector of the EBCM. Refer to *Testing for Intermittent and Poor Connections* and *Connector Repairs* in Wiring Systems. Did you find and correct the condition?	Go to *Step 15*	Go to *Step 14*
13	Replace the stoplamp switch. Refer to *Stoplamp Switch Replacement* in Park Brakes. Did you complete the repair?	Go to *Step 15*	—
14	Replace the EBCM. Refer to *Electronic Brake Control Module (EBCM) Replacement.* Did you complete the replacement?	Go to *Step 15*	—
15	1. Use the scan tool in order to clear the DTCs. 2. Operate the vehicle within the Conditions for Running the DTC as specified in the supporting text. Does the DTC reset?	Go to *Step 2*	System OK

GC4020152461020X

Fig. 20 Code C0161: ABS/TCS Brake Switch Circuit Fault (Part 2 of 2). Camaro & Firebird

Circuit Description

The Master Cylinder Isolation valve, or TCS Prime valve solenoid circuits are supplied with battery power when the ignition is in the RUN position. The EBCM controls the valve functions by grounding the circuit when necessary.

Conditions for Setting the DTC

The EBCM senses a discrepancy such as an open, short to ground, or short to voltage in the circuit.

Action Taken When the DTC Sets

- A malfunction DTC is stored.
- ABS/TCS disabled
- ABS/TCS Indicators are turned on.
- The Red BRAKE Warning Indicator turns on.

Conditions for Clearing the DTC

- Condition for DTC is no longer present and scan tool clear DTC function is used.
- 100 ignition cycles pass with no DTC detected.

Test Description

The numbers below refer to step numbers on the Diagnostic Table.

2. This step determines if the DTC is current.

Step	Action	Value(s)	Yes	No
Schematic Reference: *ABS Schematics*				
1	Did you perform the ABS Diagnostic System Check?	—	*Go to Step 2*	Go to *Diagnostic System Check - ABS*
2	1. Using a scan tool clear the DTC. 2. Remove the scan tool from the DLC. 3. Carefully drive the vehicle above 12 km/h (8 mph) for several minutes. 4. Turn the ignition switch to the OFF position. 5. Install a scan tool. 6. Turn the ignition switch to the ON position, engine off. 7. Using the scan tool in Diagnostic Trouble Codes, check for DTCs. Did any on of the DTCs C0060-C0095 reset as a current DTC?	—	*Go to Step 3*	Go to *Diagnostic System Check - ABS*
3	Replace the EBCM. Refer to *Electronic Brake Control Module (EBCM) Replacement.* Is the repair complete?	—	*Go to Step 4*	—
4	1. Use the scan tool in order to clear the DTCs. 2. Operate the vehicle within the conditions for Running the DTC as specified in the supporting text. Dose the DTC reset?	—	*Go to Step 2*	System OK

GC4020152462000X

Fig. 21 Codes C0166 Or C0171: TCS Priming Line Valve Circuit Fault. Camaro & Firebird

Step	Action	Value(s)	Yes	No
7	Repair the Accelerator Control and Adjuster ground for a short to ground. Refer to *Wiring Repairs* in Wiring Systems. Is the repair complete?	—	*Go to Step 19*	—
8	Using the *J 39200* DMM, measure the resistance between the ASM harness connector terminal 22 and the Accelerator Adjuster harness connector terminal A. Is the resistance within the range specified in the value(s) column?	0–5 Ω	*Go to Step 10*	*Go to Step 9*
9	Repair the Accelerator Control and Adjuster Supply voltage for an open. Refer to *Wiring Repairs* in Wiring Systems. Is the repair complete?	—	*Go to Step 19*	—
10	Using the *J 39200* DMM, measure the resistance between the ASM harness connector terminal 49 and the Accelerator Adjuster harness connector terminal A. Is the resistance within the range specified in the value(s) column?	0–5 Ω	*Go to Step 11*	*Go to Step 9*
11	Using the *J 39200* DMM, measure the resistance between the ASM harness connector terminal 26 and the Accelerator Adjuster harness connector terminal B. Is the resistance within the range specified in the value(s) column?	0–5 Ω	*Go to Step 13*	*Go to Step 12*
12	Repair the Accelerator Control and Adjuster Ground for an open. Refer to *Wiring Repairs* in Wiring Systems Is the repair complete?	—	*Go to Step 19*	—
13	Using the *J 39200* DMM, measure the resistance between the ASM harness connector terminal 53 and the Accelerator Adjuster harness connector terminal B. Is the resistance within the range specified in the value(s) column?	0–5 Ω	*Go to Step 14*	*Go to Step 12*
14	1. Turn the ignition switch to the RUN position, engine off. 2. Using the *J 39200* DMM, measure the voltage at the ASM harness connector terminal 22. Is the voltage within the range specified in the value(s) column?	Above 1 V	*Go to Step 15*	*Go to Step 16*
15	Repair the Accelerator Control and Adjuster Supply voltage for a short to voltage. Refer to *Wiring Repairs* in Wiring Systems. Is the repair complete?	—	*Go to Step 19*	—
16	Using the *J 39200* DMM, measure the voltage at the ASM harness connector terminal 26. Is the voltage within the range specified in the value(s) column?	Above 1 V	*Go to Step 17*	*Go to Step 18*
17	Repair the Accelerator Control and Adjuster Ground for a short to voltage. Refer to *Wiring Repairs* in Wiring Systems. Is the repair complete?	—	*Go to Step 19*	—
18	Replace the ASM. Refer to *Accelerator and Servo Control Module (ASM) Replacement.* Is the replacement complete?	—	*Go to Step 19*	—
19	1. Use the scan tool in order to clear the DTCs. 2. Operate the vehicle within the Conditions for Running the DTC as specified in the supporting text.	—	*Go to Step 2*	System OK

GC4020152463020X

Fig. 22 Code C0181: Throttle Reduction Motor Circuit Fault (Part 2 of 2). Camaro & Firebird

Circuit Description

Identifies an adjuster assembly motor circuit that is shorted to ground, shorted to voltage, or an open circuit. This malfunction will not allow the adjuster assembly motor to be controlled at the commanded current rate or will cause the driver circuit to allow current directly to ground.

Conditions for Setting the DTC

DTC C0181 can set anytime the ignition switch is in the RUN position and the EBCM detects an open, short to ground, or a short to voltage.

Action Taken When the DTC Sets

- A malfunction DTC stores
- The TCS disables
- The amber TCS indicator turns on

Conditions for Clearing the DTC

- The condition responsible for setting the DTC no longer exists and the scan tool Clear DTCs function is used.
- 100 ignition cycles pass with no DTCs detected.

Diagnostic Aids

Thoroughly inspect any circuitry that may be causing the complaint for the following conditions:

- Backed out terminals
- Improper mating
- Broken locks
- Improperly formed or damaged terminals
- Poor terminal-to-wiring connections
- Physical damage to the wiring harness

The following conditions may cause an intermittent malfunction:

- A poor connection
- Rubbed-through wire insulation
- A broken wire inside the insulation

If an intermittent malfunction exists, refer to *Testing for Intermittent and Poor Connections* in Wiring Systems.

Test Description

The number(s) below refer to the step number(s) on the diagnostic table.

4. This step checks for a short to ground.
8. This step checks for an open.
14. This step checks for a short to voltage.

Step	Action	Value(s)	Yes	No
Schematic Reference: *ABS Schematics*				
1	Did you perform the Diagnostic System Check?	—	*Go to Step 2*	Go to *Diagnostic System Check - ABS*
2	1. Turn the ignition switch to the OFF position. 2. Disconnect the Accelerator Control and Adjuster connector. 3. Disconnect all cables from the Accelerator Control and Adjuster. 4. Rotate Adjuster by hand fully, then release and allow to return to the stop. Repeat this procedure three times. 5. Zero the leads on the *J 39200* DMM. 6. Using *J 39200* DMM, measure the resistance between the Accelerator Control and Adjuster connector terminals A and B. Is the resistance within the range specified in the value(s) column?	0.5–10 Ω	*Go to Step 4*	*Go to Step 3*
3	Replace the Accelerator Control and Adjuster. Is the repair complete?	—	*Go to Step 19*	—
4	1. Disconnect the ASM harness connector. 2. Using *J 39200* DMM measure the resistance between the ASM harness connector terminals 22 and 28. Is the resistance within the range specified in the value(s) column?	OL	*Go to Step 6*	*Go to Step 5*
5	Repair the Accelerator Control and Adjuster Supply Voltage for a short to ground. Refer to *Wiring Repairs* in Wiring Systems. Is the repair complete?	—	*Go to Step 19*	—
6	Using *J 39200* DMM measure the resistance between the ASM harness connector terminals 26 and 28. Is the resistance within the range specified in the value(s) column?	OL	*Go to Step 8*	*Go to Step 7*

GC4020152463010X

Fig. 22 Code C0181: Throttle Reduction Motor Circuit Fault (Part 1 of 2). Camaro & Firebird

Circuit Description

The throttle position signal is used by the ASM to control the actual throttle position that is requested by the EBCM. The EBCM compares the Delivered throttle position sensor value that is sent from the ASM to the throttle position sensor value sent from the PCM over the Class 2 serial data line.

Conditions for Setting the DTC

DTC C0182 will set if the ASM delivers current greater than 18 amps to the Accelerator Control and Adjuster for more than three seconds without the cable adjuster reaching its desired position.

Action Taken When the DTC Sets

- A malfunction DTC is stored.
- The TCS is disabled.

Conditions for Clearing the DTC

- Condition for DTC is no longer present and scan tool clear DTC function is used.
- 100 ignition cycles have passed with no DTCs detected.

Diagnostic Aids

If an intermittent malfunction exists, refer to *Testing for Intermittent and Poor Connections* in Wiring Systems.

Test Description

The number(s) below refer to the step number(s) on the diagnostic table.

4. This step checks if DTC C0181 is the cause for DTC C0182 for setting.
5. This step checks if DTC C0182 is a current fault.

Step	Action	Yes	No
Schematic Reference: *ABS Schematics*			
1	Did you perform the Diagnostic System Check?	*Go to Step 2*	Go to *Diagnostic System Check - ABS*
2	Inspect all Accelerator Control and Adjuster cables and linkages for any obvious problems that could cause binding or sticking. Were any problems found?	*Go to Step 3*	*Go to Step 4*
3	Repair as necessary. Is the repair complete?	*Go to Step 7*	—
4	Is DTC C0181 also set as a current DTC?	Go to *DTC C0182*	*Go to Step 5*
5	1. Using a scan tool clear DTC C0182. 2. Raise the rear of the vehicle so that both rear wheel are approximately 6 inches off the floor. 3. Start the engine. 4. Using a scan tool in TCS Data List monitor the Throttle Angle 5. Press the brake pedal. 6. Put vehicle in gear. 7. Release the brake pedal. 8. Depress and hold the Accelerator pedal between 15 degrees and 45 degrees for at least four seconds. Did DTC C0182 reset as a current DTC?	*Go to Step 6*	Go to *Diagnostic System Check - ABS*
6	Replace the Accelerator Control and Adjuster. Is the replacement complete?	*Go to Step 7*	—
7	1. Use the scan tool in order to clear the DTCs. 2. Operate the vehicle within the Conditions for Running the DTC as specified in the supporting text. Does the DTC reset?	*Go to Step 2*	System OK

GC4020152464000X

Fig. 23 Code C0182: Throttle Reduction Motor Circuit Range Performance. Camaro & Firebird

Circuit Description

The RPM signal circuit provides the EBCM with an indication of engine RPM to help determine TCS control methods and rates when a TCS event takes place.

Conditions for Running the DTC

- The ignition switch is ON and the engine running.
- After 2 seconds starting, and if there is a undervoltage condition.

Conditions for Setting the DTC

The EBCM does not received an RPM input signal after 1 second, after the engine has been started.

Action Taken When the DTC Sets

If equiped, the following actions occur:

- A malfunction DTC is stored.
- The TRAC OFF indicator is turned on.
- The TCS is disabled. ABS remains functional.

Conditions for Clearing the DTC

- The condition for DTC is no longer present and the scan tool Clear DTCs function is used.
- 100 ignition cycles have passed with no DTC(s) detected.

Diagnostic Aids

Perform a thorough inspection of the wiring. Perform a thorough inspection of the connectors. Failure to carefully and fully inspect the wiring and the connectors may result in misdiagnosis. Misdiagnosis causes part replacement with reappearance of the malfunction.

Test Description

The number(s) below refer to the step number(s) on the diagnostic table.

2. If the instrument panel tachometer is working properly, the cause of the malfunction is most likely between the PCM and the EBCM, or the EBCM itself.
9. At this point, the PCM is likely causing the malfunction. Refer to the OBD system check.

Step	Action	Value(s)	Yes	No
Schematic Reference: *ABS Schematics*				
1	Did you perform the Diagnostic System Check?	—	Go to *Step 2*	Go to *Diagnostic System Check - ABS*
2	1. Start the engine. 2. Vary the engine RPM with the throttle while observing the IP tachometer. Does the IP tachometer work properly as the engine RPM changes?	—	Go to *Step 3*	Go to *Step 9*
3	1. Turn the ignition switch to the OFF position. 2. Disconnect the PCM connector C2 from the PCM. 3. Disconnect the EBCM connector from the EBCM. 4. Install the *J 39700* with the *J 39700-530* cable adapter to the EBCM harness only. 5. Use a *J 39200* to measure the resistance between the PCM harness connector tach signal circuit, and the universal breakout box terminal 11. Is the resistance within the specified range?	0–5 Ω	Go to *Step 4*	Go to *Step 10*
4	Use a *J 39200* to measure the resistance between the universal breakout box terminal 11 and a good ground. Is the resistance within the specified range?	OL	Go to *Step 5*	Go to *Step 11*
5	1. Turn the ignition switch to the ON position 2. Use a *J 39200* to measure the voltage between the universal breakout box terminal 11 and a good ground. Is the voltage within the specified range?	0–2 V	Go to *Step 6*	Go to *Step 12*

GC4020152465010X

Fig. 24 Codes C0235-C0237: TCS RPM Signal Circuit Fault (Part 1 of 2). Camaro & Firebird

Step	Action	Value(s)	Yes	No
6	1. Inspect the PCM connector C2 for the following: • Inspect for damage. • Inspect for poor terminal contact. • Inspect for corrosion. 2. Inspect the EBCM connector for the following: • Inspect for damage. • Inspect for poor terminal contact. • Inspect for corrosion. 3. Ensure both the PCM connector C2 and the EBCM connector are properly retained when connected. Are the following signs present on either connector: • Is poor terminal contact present? • Is corrosion present? • Is damaged terminals present?	—	Go to *Step 13*	Go to *Step 7*
7	1. Reconnect all the connectors. 2. Using the scan tool clear the DTC. 3. Disconnect the scan tool from the DLC. 4. Start the engine. Did DTC C0236 reset?	—	Go to *Step 8*	Go to *Diagnostic System Check - ABS*
8	Replace the EBCM. Is the repair complete?	—	Go to *Step 14*	—
9	Check the PCM. Is the repair complete?	—	Go to *Step 14*	—
10	Repair an open between PCM and EBCM tach signal circuit. Is the repair complete?	—	Go to *Step 14*	—
11	Repair a short to ground in tach signal circuit. Is the repair complete?	—	Go to *Step 14*	—
12	Repair a short to voltage in TACH signal circuit. Is the repair complete?	—	Go to *Step 14*	—
13	Replace all the terminals or replace the connectors that exhibit signs of the following: • That exhibit signs of poor terminal contact. • That exhibit signs of corrosion. • That exhibit signs of damaged terminals. Is the repair complete?	—	Go to *Step 14*	—
14	1. Use the scan tool in order to clear the DTCs. 2. Operate the vehicle within the Conditions for Running the DTC as specified in the supporting text. Dose the DTC reset?	—	Go to *Step 2*	System OK

GC4020152465020X

Fig. 24 Codes C0235-C0237: TCS RPM Signal Circuit Fault (Part 2 of 2). Camaro & Firebird

Circuit Description

The throttle position signal is used by the ASM to control the actual throttle position that is requested by the EBCM. The EBCM compares the Delivered throttle position sensor value that is sent from the ASM to the throttle position sensor value sent from the PCM over the Class 2 serial data line.

Conditions for Setting the DTC

DTC C0238 will set if the EBCM detects a difference between the PCM throttle position and the throttle position sent from the ASM.

Action Taken When the DTC Sets

- A malfunction DTC is stored.
- The TCS is disabled.

Conditions for Clearing the DTC

- Condition for DTC is no longer present and scan tool clear DTC function is used.
- 100 ignition cycles have passed with no DTCs detected.

Diagnostic Aids

- It is very important that a thorough inspection of the wiring and connectors be performed. Failure to carefully and fully inspect wiring and connectors may result in misdiagnosis, causing part replacement with reappearance of the malfunction.
- If an intermittent malfunction exists refer to *Testing for Intermittent and Poor Connections* in Wiring Systems.

Test Description

The number(s) below refer to the step number(s) on the diagnostic table.

2. This step checks if the PCM detected a fault.

Step	Action	Value(s)	Yes	No
1	Did you perform the Diagnostic System Check?	—	*Go to Step 2*	Go to *Diagnostic System Check - ABS*
2	Are any PCM TPS DTCs set?	—	*Diagnose In Engine Controls*	*Go to Step 3*
3	1. Using a scan tool clear the DTC. 2. Turn the ignition switch to the OFF position. 3. Disconnect the scan tool. 4. Turn the ignition switch to the RUN position, engine off. Does DTC C0238 reset as a current DTC?	—	*Go to Step 4*	Go to *Diagnostic System Check - ABS*
4	Replace the EBCM. Is the replacement complete?	—	*Go to Step 5*	—
5	1. Use the scan tool in order to clear the DTCs. 2. Operate the vehicle within the Conditions for Running the DTC as specified in the supporting text. Does the DTC reset?	—	*Go to Step 2*	System OK

GC4020152466000X

Fig. 25 Code C0238: TCS Throttle Position Sensor Comparison Fault. Camaro & Firebird

Circuit Description

The vehicle stability enhancement system (VSES) is activated by the EBCM calculating the desired yaw rate and comparing it to the actual yaw rate input. The desired yaw rate is calculated from measured steering wheel position, vehicle speed, and lateral acceleration. The difference between the desired yaw rate and actual yaw rate is the yaw rate error, which is a measurement of oversteer or understeer. If the yaw rate error becomes too large, the EBCM will attempt to correct the vehicle's yaw motion by applying differential braking to the wheels.

To correct for oversteer, differential braking is used on the left front or right front wheel brake. To correct for understeer, differential braking is used on the left rear or right rear wheel brake.

Conditions for Running the DTC

- The ignition is ON.
- The vehicle speed is greater than 40 km/h (25 mph).

Conditions for Setting the DTC

The EBCM performs different tests to detect a DTC condition. A malfunction is detected when the yaw rate sensor signal input voltage is less than 0.225 volts or greater than 4.775 volts for more than 100 milliseconds.

Action Taken When the DTC Sets

If equiped, the following actions occur:

- The EBCM disables theTCS/VSES for the duration of the ignition cycle.
- A malfunction DTC is set.
- The ANTI-LOCK indicator turns ON.
- The TRAC Off indicator turns ON.
- The PCS indicator turns ON.

Conditions for Clearing the DTC

- Using a scan tool.
- The DTC will clear after 100 consecutive ignition cycles if the condition for the malfunction is no longer present.

Diagnostic Aids

The following conditions may cause a malfunction:

- Open in the yaw rate signal circuit
- Short to ground in the yaw rate signal circuit
- Short to voltage in the yaw rate signal circuit
- Open in the yaw rate ground circuit
- Open in ignition voltage circuit
- Malfunctioning vehicle yaw/lateral accelerometer sensor
- Malfunctioning EBCM

Test Description

The number(s) below refer to the step number(s) on the diagnostic table.

2. Tests for specified voltage on the yaw rate signal circuit.
3. Checks the voltage between the ignition and ground circuit for a specified value.
4. Checks the voltage between the ignition and ground circuit for a specified value.
5. Checks to see if voltage was above specified voltage.
6. Checks to see if voltage was below specified voltage.
7. Checks to see if EBCM 5 volt reference signal is within specified limit.
8. Checks to see if voltage was above specified voltage.
9. Checks to see if resistance of ground circuit is less than 5 ohms.
10. Tests for a short to voltage on the 5 volt reference circuit.
11. Tests for a short to ground, a high resistance, or an open in the 5 volt reference circuit.
12. Tests for a short to voltage in the yaw rate signal circuit.
13. Tests for a short to ground, a high resistance, or an open in the yaw rate signal circuit.
14. Tests for a high resistance or an open in the ground circuit.
15. Checks the EBCM connector for poor connections.
16. Checks the yaw/lateral accelerometer sensor connector for poor connections.

GC4020152467010X

Fig. 26 Code C0239: TCS Spark Retard Monitoring Fault (Part 1 of 2). Camaro & Firebird

Step	Action	Value(s)	Yes	No
Schematic Reference: *ABS Schematics*				
1	Did you perform the ABS Diagnostic System Check?	—	Go to *Step 2*	Go to *Diagnostic System Check - ABS*
2	1. Turn OFF the ignition. 2. Disconnect the EBCM. 3. Install the *J 39700* universal pinout box with the *J 39700-530* cable adapter between the EBCM and the EBCM harness connector. 4. Turn ON the ignition, with the engine OFF. 5. Using the DMM, measure the voltage between pin 26 and pin 15 of the *J 39700* universal pinout box. Is the voltage within the specified value?	0.225 V - 4.775 V	Go to Diagnostic Aids	Go to *Step 3*
3	1. Turn OFF the ignition. 2. Disconnect the yaw/lateral accelerometer sensor. 3. Turn ON the ignition, with the engine OFF. 4. Using the DMM, measure the voltage between the ignition and ground circuits of the yaw/lateral accelerometer sensor. Is the voltage in the specified value?	B+	Go to *Step 5*	Go to *Step 4*
4	Test the ignition circuit of the yaw/lateral accelerometer sensor for high resistance or an open. Did you find and correct the condition?	—	Go to *Step 18*	*Power Distribution*
5	1. Reconnect the yaw/lateral accelerometer sensor. 2. Using the DMM, measure the voltage between pin 26 and pin 15 of the *J 39700* universal pinout box. Is the voltage less than the specified value?	4.775 V	Go to *Step 6*	Go to *Step 13*
6	Using the DMM, measure the voltage between pin 26 and pin 15 of the *J 39700* universal pinout box. Is the voltage greater than the specified value?	0.225 V	Go to *Step 7*	Go to *Step 12*
7	Using a DMM, measure the voltage between the 5 volt reference circuit pin 16 and the ground circuit pin 15 of the *J 39700* universal pinout box. Does the voltage measure below the specified value?	2 V	Go to *Step 11*	Go to *Step 8*
8	Using a DMM, measure the voltage between the 5 volt reference circuit pin 16 and ground pin 15 of the *J 39700* universal pinout box. Does the voltage measure above the specified value?	3 V	Go to *Step 10*	Go to *Step 9*
9	1. Turn OFF the engine. 2. Disconnect the negative battery cable. 3. Measure the resistance from the ground circuit of the yaw/lateral accelerometer sensor to a good ground. Does the resistance measure less than the specified value?	5 Ω	Go to *Step 16*	Go to *Step 14*
10	Test the 5 volt reference circuit of the yaw/lateral accelerometer sensor for a short to voltage. Did you find and correct the condition?	—	Go to *Step 19*	Go to *Step 15*

GC4020152467020X

Fig. 26 Code C0239: TCS Spark Retard Monitoring Fault (Part 2 of 2). Camaro & Firebird

Circuit Description

The EBCM and the PCM simultaneously control the traction control. The EBCM sends a Requested Torque message via a pulse width modulated (PWM) signal to the PCM. The duty cycle of the signal is used to determine how much engine torque the EBCM is requesting the PCM to deliver. Normal values are between 10 and 90 percent duty cycle. The signal should be at 90 percent when traction control is not active and at lower values during traction control activations. The PCM supplies the pull up voltage that the EBCM switches to ground to create the signal.

Conditions for Running the DTC

The ignition is ON.

Conditions for Setting the DTC

The PCM diagnoses the requested torque PWM signal circuit and sends a class 2 serial data message to the EBCM indicating a fault is present. A fault exists in the circuit if the PCM detects one of the following conditions:

- The requested torque PWM signal is less than 5 percent duty cycle or greater than 95 percent duty cycle.
- The requested torque PWM signal is not present for 10 seconds.

Action Taken When the DTC Sets

If equiped, the following actions occur:

- The EBCM disables the TCS for the duration of the ignition cycle.
- The TRAC OFFindicator turns ON.
- The ABS remains functional.

Conditions for Clearing the DTC

- The condition for the DTC is no longer present (the DTC is not current) and you used the scan tool Clear DTC function.
- The EBCM automatically clears the history DTC when a current DTC is not detected in 100 consecutive drive cycles.

Test Description

The numbers below refer to the step numbers on the diagnostic table.

3. Use the scan tool in order to determine if the requested torque signal has a valid duty cycle.
4. Measure the requested torque signal in order to determine if the signal has a valid duty cycle.
5. Measure the requested torque signal in order to determine if the signal has a valid frequency.
11. This vehicle is equipped with a PCM which uses an Electrically Erasable Programmable Read Only Memory (EEPROM). When replacing the PCM, the replacement PCM must be programmed.

Step	Action	Value(s)	Yes	No
Schematic Reference: *ABS Schematics*				
1	Did you perform the ABS Diagnostic System Check?	—	Go to *Step 2*	Go to *Diagnostic System Check - ABS*
2	Inspect the EBCM ground and PCM ground, making sure each ground is clean and torqued to the proper specification. Did you find and correct the condition?	—	Go to *Step 13*	Go to *Step 3*
3	1. Install a scan tool. 2. Start the engine. 3. With the scan tool, observe the Torque Request Signal parameter in the Powertrain Control Module data list. Does the scan tool display less than the specified value?	100%	*Test for Intermittent and Poor Connections*	Go to *Step 4*
4	1. Turn OFF the ignition. 2. Disconnect the EBCM harness connector. 3. Install the *J 39700* universal breakout box using the *J 39700-530* cable adapter to the EBCM harness connector and the EBCM connector. 4. Start the engine. 5. Measure the DC duty cycle between the requested torque signal circuit and a good ground. Is the duty cycle within the specified range?	5–95%	Go to *Step 5*	Go to *Step 6*
5	Measure the DC Hz between the requested torque signal circuit and a good ground. Does the frequency measure within the specified range?	121–134 Hz	Go to *Step 8*	Go to *Step 6*

GC4020152469010X

Fig. 28 Code C0241: PCM Indicated Requested Torque Fault (Part 1 of 2). Camaro & Firebird

Circuit Description

The PCM monitors various parameters and will not allow traction control operation if any parameter falls below a specified value.

Conditions for Running the DTC

The ignition is ON.

Conditions for Setting the DTC

The PCM detects a malfunction and then causes TCS shut down until the malfunction has been corrected.

Action Taken When the DTC Sets

If equiped, the following actions occur:

- A DTC C0240 is stored
- The TCS is disabled
- The TRAC OFF indicator is turned on
- If the TCS is again allowed to function, the indicator will be turned off but the DTC will be stored

Conditions for Clearing the DTC

- The condition for the DTC is no longer present (the DTC is not current) and you used the scan tool Clear DTC function.
- The EBCM automatically clears the history DTC when a current DTC is not detected in 100 consecutive drive cycles.

Test Description

The numbers below refer to the step numbers on the diagnostic table.

4. This step checks if DTC C0240 resets.

Step	Action	Value(s)	Yes	No
1	Did you perform the Diagnostic System Check?	—	Go to *Step 2*	Go to *Diagnostic System Check*
2	1. Turn the ignition switch to the RUN position with the engine off. 2. Using a Scan Tool, read the ABS/TCS DTCs. Are any other DTCs set?	—	Go to *Diagnostic Trouble Code (DTC) List* for the appropriate DTC table	Go to *Step 3*
3	Is DTC C0240 set as a current code?	—	Go to *Step 5*	Go to *Step 4*
4	1. Using the scan tool clear the DTC. 2. Remove the scan tool from the DLC. 3. Carefully drive the vehicle above 12 Km/h (8 mph) for several minutes. Did DTC C0240 set as a current DTC?	—	Go to *Step 5*	Go to *Diagnostic System Check - ABS*
5	Perform the Powertrain OBD System Check. Did the vehicle pass the OBD System Check?	—	Go to *Step 6*	*Diagnose* Engine Controls
6	1. Use the scan tool in order to clear the DTCs. 2. Operate the vehicle within the Conditions for Running the DTC as specified in the supporting text. Does the DTC reset?	—	Go to *Step 2*	System OK

GC4020152468000X

Fig. 27 Code C0240: PCM Traction Control Not Allowed. Camaro & Firebird

Step	Action	Value(s)	Yes	No
6	1. Turn OFF the ignition. 2. Disconnect the cable adapter from the EBCM connector. **Important:** Disconnecting the EBCM connector and turning ON the ignition could cause other modules to set loss of communication DTCs (Uxxxx). Once the EBCM is reconnected, the EBCM may set DTC C0241. 3. Turn ON the ignition, with the engine OFF. 4. Measure the voltage from the requested torque signal circuit to a good ground. Does the voltage measure within the specified range?	4 – 6 V	Go to *Step 10*	Go to *Step 7*
7	1. Turn OFF the ignition. 2. Disconnect the powertrain control module (PCM) harness connector. 3. Test the requested torque signal circuit for the following conditions: • A short to voltage • A short to ground Did you find and correct the condition?	—	Go to *Step 13*	Go to *Step 10*
8	1. Turn OFF the ignition. 2. Disconnect the powertrain control module (PCM) harness connector. 3. Test the requested torque signal circuit for the following conditions: • An open • A high resistance Did you find and correct the condition?	—	Go to *Step 13*	Go to *Step 9*
9	Inspect for poor connections the harness connector of the PCM. Did you find and correct the condition?	—	Go to *Step 13*	Go to *Step 11*
10	Inspect for poor connections the harness connector of the EBCM. Did you find and correct the condition?	—	Go to *Step 13*	Go to *Step 12*
11	**Important:** The replacement PCM must be programmed. Replace the PCM. Did you complete the repair?	—	Go to *Step 13*	—
12	Replace the EBCM. Did you complete the repair?	—	Go to *Step 13*	—
13	1. Use the scan tool in order to clear the DTCs. 2. Operate the vehicle within the Conditions for Running the DTC as specified in the supporting text. Does the DTC reset?	—	Go to *Step 2*	System OK

GC4020152469020X

Fig. 28 Code C0241: PCM Indicated Requested Torque Fault (Part 2 of 2). Camaro & Firebird

Circuit Description

Traction Control is simultaneously controlled by the EBCM and the PCM. The PCM sends a DELIVERED TORQUE message via a Pulse Width Modulated (PWM) signal to the EBCM confirming the delivered torque level for proper Traction Control system operation. The EBCM supplies the pull up voltage.

Conditions for Running the DTC

- The ignition switch is ON.
- The DTC can be set after system initialization.

Conditions for Setting the DTC

DTC C0244 can be set anytime when ignition voltage is present. A malfunction exists if the PWM signal is out of range or no signal is received for a period of 2 seconds.

Action Taken When the DTC Sets

If equiped, the following actions occur:

- A malfunction DTC is stored.
- The TCS is disabled.
- The TRAC OFF indicator is turned on. The ABS remains functional.

Conditions for Clearing the DTC

- The condition for the DTC is no longer present (the DTC is not current) and you used the scan tool Clear DTC function.
- The EBCM automatically clears the history DTC when a current DTC is not detected in 100 consecutive drive cycles.

Diagnostic Aids

- It is very important that a thorough inspection of the wiring and connectors be performed. Failure to carefully and fully inspect wiring and connectors may result in misdiagnosis, causing part replacement with reappearance of the malfunction.
- Possible causes for DTC C0244 to set:
  - Open in CKT 464.
  - CKT 464 shorted to ground or voltage.
  - Communication frequency problem.
  - Communication duty cycle problem.
  - CKT 464 has a wiring problem, terminal corrosion, or poor connections.
  - EBCM not receiving information from the PCM.

Test Description

The numbers below refer to the step numbers on the diagnostic table.

3. Use the scan tool in order to determine if the delivered torque signal has a valid duty cycle.
9. This vehicle is equipped with a PCM which uses an Electrically Erasable Programmable Read Only Memory (EEPROM). When replacing the PCM, the replacement PCM must be programmed.

Step	Action	Value(s)	Yes	No
Schematic Reference: *ABS Schematics*				
1	Did you perform the ABS Diagnostic System Check?	—	Go to *Step 2*	Go to *Diagnostic System Check - ABS*
2	Inspect the EBCM ground and PCM ground, making sure each ground is clean and torqued to the proper specification. Did you find and correct the condition?	—	Go to *Step 11*	Go to *Step 3*
3	1. Install a scan tool. 2. Start the engine. 3. With a scan tool, observe the PCM to EBCM Delivered parameter in the Engine Control data list. Does the scan tool display the specified value?	90%	Go to *Step 4*	*Intermittent and Poor Connections*

GC4020152470010X

Fig. 29 Code C0244: PWM Delivered Torque Fault (Part 1 of 2). Camaro & Firebird

Step	Action	Value(s)	Yes	No
4	1. Turn OFF the ignition. 2. Disconnect the EBCM harness connector. 3. Install the *J 39700* universal breakout box using the *J 39700-530* cable adapter to the EBCM harness connector and the EBCM connector. 4. Disconnect the powertrain control module (PCM) harness connector. 5. Turn ON the ignition, with the engine OFF. 6. Measure the voltage from the delivered torque signal circuit to a good ground. Does the voltage measure near the specified value?	B+	Go to *Step 5*	Go to *Step 6*
5	1. Turn OFF the ignition. 2. Disconnect the cable adapter from the EBCM connector. 3. Turn ON the ignition, with the engine OFF. 4. Test the delivered torque signal circuit for a short to voltage. Did you find and correct the condition?	—	Go to *Step 11*	Go to *Step 7*
6	1. Turn OFF the ignition. 2. Disconnect the cable adapter from the EBCM connector. 3. Test the delivered torque signal circuit for the following conditions: • An open • A short to ground • A high resistance. Did you find and correct the condition?	—	Go to *Step 11*	Go to *Step 8*
7	Inspect for poor connections the harness connector of the PCM. Did you find and correct the condition?	—	Go to *Step 11*	Go to *Step 9*
8	Inspect for poor connections the harness connector of the EBCM. Did you find and correct the condition?	—	Go to *Step 11*	Go to *Step 10*
9	**Important:** The replacement PCM must be programmed. Replace the PCM. Did you complete the repair?	—	Go to *Step 11*	—
10	Replace the EBCM. Did you complete the repair?	—	Go to *Step 11*	—
11	1. Use the scan tool in order to clear the DTCs. 2. Operate the vehicle within the Conditions for Running the DTC as specified in the supporting text. Does the DTC reset?	—	Go to *Step 2*	System OK

GC4020152470020X

Fig. 29 Code C0244: PWM Delivered Torque Fault (Part 2 of 2). Camaro & Firebird

Circuit Description

The speed sensors used on the front of this vehicle are multiple pole and the rear uses a single pole magnetic pickup. This sensor produces an AC signal that the EBCM uses the frequency from to calculate the wheel speed.

Conditions for Running the DTC

- The ignition switch is ON.
- The DTC can be set after system initialization.

Conditions for Setting the DTC

- The EBCM detects a deviation between the left and right rear wheel speeds of greater than 6 km/h (3.75 mph) at a vehicle speed of less than 100 km/h (62 mph) on vehicles equipped with TCS.
- The EBCM detects a deviation between the left and right front wheel speeds of greater than 10 km/h (6.25 mph) at a vehicle speed of less than 100 km/h (62 mph).
- The EBCM detects a deviation between the left and right rear wheel speeds of greater than 6 percent of the vehicle speed at greater than 100 km/h (62 mph) on vehicles equipped with TCS.
- The EBCM detects a deviation between the left and right front wheel speeds of greater than 4 km/h plus 6 percent of the vehicle speed at greater than 100 km/h (62 mph).

This DTC will set when the EBCM cannot specifically identify which wheel speed sensor is causing the malfunction. If the EBCM can identify the specific wheel speed sensor causing the malfunction, DTC C0245 will become a history DTC, and the DTC associated with the sensor (DTC C0036, DTC C0041, DTC C0046, DTC C0051, or DTC C0056) will be set concurrent with DTC C0245.

Action Taken When the DTC Sets

If equiped, the following actions occur:

- A malfunction DTC stores.
- The ABS/TCS disables.
- The amber ABS/TCS indicator(s) turn on.
- The Red BRAKE Warning indicator turn on.

Conditions for Clearing the DTC

- The condition for the DTC is no longer present (the DTC is not current) and you used the scan tool Clear DTC function.
- The EBCM automatically clears the history DTC when a current DTC is not detected in 100 consecutive drive cycles.

Diagnostic Aids

- It is very important that a thorough inspection of the wiring and connectors be performed. Failure to carefully and fully inspect wiring and connectors may result in misdiagnosis, causing part replacement with reappearance of the malfunction.
- Thoroughly inspect any circuitry that may be causing the complaint for the following conditions:
  - Backed out terminals
  - Improper mating
  - Broken locks
  - Improperly formed or damaged terminals
  - Poor terminal-to-wiring connections
  - Physical damage to the wiring harness
- The following conditions may cause an intermittent malfunction:
  - A poor connection
  - Rubbed-through wire insulation
  - A broken wire inside the insulation
- If the customer's comments reflect that the amber ABS/TCS indicator is on only during moist environmental conditions (rain, snow, vehicle wash), inspect all the wheel speed sensor circuitry for signs of water intrusion. If the DTC is not current, clear all DTCs and simulate the effects of water intrusion by using the following procedure:
  1. Spray the suspected area with a five percent saltwater solution.
     Add two teaspoons of salt to twelve ounces of water to make a five percent saltwater solution.
  2. Test drive the vehicle over various road surfaces (bumps, turns, etc.) above 40 km/h (25 mph) for at least 30 seconds.
  3. If the DTC returns, replace the suspected harness.
- If an intermittent malfunction exists *Testing for Intermittent and Poor Connections*

Test Description

The numbers below refer to step numbers on the diagnostic table.

2. If DTC C0245 is a history code, this step checks if a specific Wheel Speed Circuit Malfunction DTC is set concurrently with DTC C0245.
7. This step checks if the wheel speed sensor harness is routed in close proximity to the spark plug wires.
9. In this step, if the scan tool can record any erroneous wheel speed sensor signals, diagnose that sensor(s) first.

GC4020152471010X

Fig. 30 Code C0245: Wheel Speed Sensor Frequency Error (Part 1 of 3). Camaro & Firebird

Step	Action	Yes	No
Schematic Reference: *ABS Schematics*			
1	Did you perform the diagnostic system check?	Go to *Step 2*	Go to *Diagnostic System Check - ABS*
2	Is the following DTC(s) set concurrently with a history DTC C0245? • DTC C0036 • DTC C0041 • DTC C0046 • DTC C0051 • DTC C0056	Go to DTC *Diagnostic Trouble Code (DTC) List*	Go to *Step 3*
3	Inspect the WSS for physical damage. Is physical damage of the WSS evident?	Go to *Step 4*	Go to *Step 5*
4	Replace the WSS. Is the replacement complete?	Go to *Step 14*	—
5	Inspect the jumper harness for physical damage. Is physical damage of the jumper harness evident?	Go to *Step 6*	Go to *Step 7*
6	Replace the jumper harness. Is the replacement complete?	Go to *Step 14*	—
7	1. Check for Proper routing of the wheel speed sensor harness. 2. Check that the wheel speed sensor harness is routed away from the spark plug wires. Is the wheel speed sensor harness properly routed?	Go to *Step 9*	Go to *Step 8*
8	Reroute the wheel speed sensor harness away from the spark plug wires. Is the reroute complete?	Go to *Step 14*	—
9	1. Install a scan tool. 2. Turn the ignition switch to the RUN position. 3. Set the scan tool to Snap Shot Auto Trigger mode and monitor the wheel speed sensors. 4. Carefully drive the vehicle above 12 km/h (8 mph) for several minutes. Did the scan tool trigger on any of the wheel speed sensors?	Go to *Step 10*	Go to *Step 11*
10	Note which wheel speed sensor triggered the scan tool. Follow the appropriate Wheel Speed Sensor Malfunction DTC table for the wheel speed sensor that triggered. Is the repair complete?	Go to *Step 14*	—

GC4020152471020X

Fig. 30 Code C0245: Wheel Speed Sensor Frequency Error (Part 2 of 3). Camaro & Firebird

Step	Action	Yes	No
11	1. Reconnect all previously disconnected components. 2. Using a scan tool clear the DTC. 3. Remove the scan tool from the DLC. 4. Carefully drive the vehicle above 12 km/h (8 mph) for several minutes. Does the DTC reset as a current DTC?	Go to *Step 13*	Go to *Step 12*
12	Malfunction is intermittent. Inspect all connectors and harnesses for damage that may result in an open or high resistance when connected. Is the repair complete?	Go to *Diagnostic System Check - ABS*	—
13	Replace the EBCM. Is the replacement complete?	Go to *Step 14*	—
14	1. Use the scan tool in order to clear the DTCs. 2. Operate the vehicle within the conditions for running the DTC as specified in the supporting text. Does the DTC reset?	Go to *Step 2*	System OK

GC4020152471030X

Fig. 30 Code C0245: Wheel Speed Sensor Frequency Error (Part 3 of 3). Camaro & Firebird

Step	Action	Value(s)	Yes	No
9	Replace the ASM. Is the replacement complete?	—	Go to *Step 16*	—
10	1. Turn the ignition switch to the OFF position. 2. Disconnect the EBCM connector C1. 3. Install the *J 39700* Universal Pinout Box using the *J 39700-530* to the EBCM harness connector C1 only. 4. Using *J 39200* DMM, measure the resistance between terminals 9 and 15 of *J 39700.* Is the resistance within the range specified in the value(s) column?	OL (infinite)	Go to *Step 12*	Go to *Step 11*
11	Repair the delivered torque signal circuit for a short to ground. Is the circuit repair complete?	—	Go to *Step 16*	—
12	Using *J 39200* DMM, measure the resistance between terminal 9 of *J 39700* and terminal 35 of the ASM harness connector. Is the resistance within the range specified in the value(s) column?	0–5 Ω	Go to *Step 14*	Go to *Step 13*
13	Repair the open or high resistance in the delivered torque signal circuit. Is the circuit repair complete?	—	Go to *Step 16*	—
14	1. Turn the ignition switch to the RUN position, engine off. 2. Using *J 39200* DMM, measure the voltage at terminal 9 of *J 39700.* Is the voltage within the range specified in the value(s) column?	Above 1 V	Go to *Step 15*	Go to *Step 9*
15	Repair the delivered torque signal circuit for a short to voltage Is the circuit repair complete?	—	Go to *Step 16*	—
16	1. Use the scan tool in order to clear the DTCs. 2. Operate the vehicle within the Conditions for Running the DTC as specified in the supporting text. Does the DTC reset?	—	Go to *Step 2*	System OK

GC4020152472020X

Fig. 31 Code C0266: ADS Controller Fault (Part 2 of 2). Camaro & Firebird

Circuit Description
This DTC identifies a malfunction within the EBCM.

Conditions for Running the DTC
The ignition switch is in the ON position.

Conditions for Setting the DTC
DTC C0550 is set when an internal EBCM malfunction exists.

Action Taken When the DTC Sets
If equiped, the following actions occur:

- The EBCM disables the ABS/TCS and MSVA for the duration of the ignition cycle.
- A malfunction DTC will set.
- The ABS indicator turns on.
- The TCS indicator turns on.
- The Red BRAKE Warning indicator turns on.

Conditions for Clearing the DTC
- The condition for the DTC is no longer present (the DTC is not current) and you used the scan tool Clear DTC function.
- The EBCM automatically clears the history DTC when a current DTC is not detected in 100 consecutive drive cycles.

DTC C0550

Step	Action	Yes	No
Schematic Reference: *ABS Schematics*			
1	Did you perform the Diagnostic System Check?	Go to *Step 2*	Go to *Diagnostic System Check - ABS*
2	Are any other DTC(s) present besides C0550?	Go to *Diagnostic Trouble Code (DTC) List*	Go to *Step 3*
3	Replace the EBCM. Is the replacement complete?	Go to*Step 4*	—
4	1. Use the scan tool in order to clear the DTCs. 2. Operate the vehicle within the Conditions for Running the DTC as specified in the supporting text. Does the DTC reset?	Go to *Step 2*	System OK

GC4020152473000X

Fig. 32 Code C0550: ECU Fault. Camaro & Firebird

Circuit Description
This circuit monitors the Delivered Trottle Position Input for proper operation.

Conditions for Setting the DTC
DTC C0266 can set anytime the ignition is in the RUN position and the EBCM does not recieve a Delivered Throttle Position Input.

Action Taken When the DTC Sets
- The TCS is disabled
- The traction control indicator is turned on

Conditions for Clearing the DTC
- The condition for the DTC is no longer present and the scan tool clear DTC function is used
- 100 ignition cycles have passed with no DTCs detected

Diagnostic Aids
- Thoroughly inspect the wiring and the connectors. Failure to carefully and fully inspect the wiring and the connectors can result in misdiagnosis. Misdiagnosis may cause replacement of parts without repairing the malfunction.

Test Description
The numbers below refer to the step numbers on the diagnostic table.

3. This step checks for a good ground.
5. This step checks for proper voltage.

Step	Action	Value(s)	Yes	No
Schematic Reference: *ABS Schematics*				
1	Did you perform the Diagnostic System Check?	—	Go to *Step 2*	Go to *Diagnostic System Check - ABS*
2	1. Turn the ignition switch to the OFF position. 2. Disconnect the ASM harness connector. 3. Inspect the ASM harness connector and the connector for damage or corrosion. Is there any evidence of damage or corrosion?	—	Go to *Step 7*	Go to *Step 3*
3	Using the *J 39200* DMM, measure the resistance between the ASM harness connector terminal 28 and a good ground. Is the resistance within specifications?	0-5 Ω	Go to *Step 4*	Go to *Step 8*
4	Using the *J 39200* DMM, measure the resistance between the ASM harness connector terminal 55 and a good ground. s the resistance within specifications?	0-5 Ω	Go to *Step 5*	Go to *Step 8*
5	1. Turn the ignition switch to the RUN position with the engine off. 2. Measure the voltage between the ASM harness connector terminals 1 and 28. Is the voltage within specifications?	B+	Go to *Step 10*	Go to *Step 6*
6	Repair the Ignition 1 circuit for an open or high resistance. Is the circuit repair complete?	—	Go to *Step 16*	—
7	Repair the harness connector as necessary. Are the repairs complete?	—	Go to *Step 16*	—
8	Repair the open or high resistance in the ground circuit. Is the circuit repair complete?	—	Go to *Step 16*	—

GC4020152472010X

Fig. 31 Code C0266: ADS Controller Fault (Part 1 of 2). Camaro & Firebird

Circuit Description
The EBCM is required to operate within a specified range of voltage to function properly. During ABS and TCS operation, there are current requirements that will cause the voltage to drop. Because of this, voltage is monitored out of ABS/TCS control to indicate a good charging system condition, and also during ABS/TCS control when voltage may drop significantly. The EBCM also monitors for high voltage conditions which could damage the EBCM.

Conditions for Running the DTC
- The ignition switch is ON.
- The DTC can be set after system initialization.

Conditions for Setting the DTC
- The EBCM operating voltage falls below 9.4 volts out of ABS/TCS control, or 8.8 volts during ABS/TCS control.
- The EBCM operating voltage rises above 17.4 volts.
- The low voltage or the high voltage is detected for more than 500 milliseconds with the vehicle speed above 6 km/h (3.6 mph).

Action Taken When the DTC Sets
If equiped, the following actions occur:

- A malfunction DTC is stored.
- The ABS and the Traction Control indicators are turned on.
- The ABS/TCS is disabled.
- The Brake warning indicator turns on.

Conditions for Clearing the DTC
- The condition for the DTC is no longer present (the DTC is not current) and you used the scan tool Clear DTC function.
- The EBCM automatically clears the history DTC when a current DTC is not detected in 100 consecutive drive cycles.

Diagnostic Aids
- It is very important that a thorough inspection of the wiring and connectors be performed. Failure to carefully and fully inspect wiring and connectors may result in misdiagnosis, causing part replacement with reappearance of the malfunction.
- Thoroughly inspect any circuitry that may be causing the complaint for the following conditions:
  - Backed out terminals
  - Improper mating
  - Broken locks
  - Improperly formed or damaged terminals
  - Poor terminal-to-wiring connections
  - Physical damage to the wiring harness
- The following conditions may cause an intermittent malfunction:
  - A poor connection
  - Rubbed-through wire insulation
  - A broken wire inside the insulation

Test Description
The number(s) below refer to the step number(s) on the diagnostic table.

2. This step checks if the voltage is above the maximum of the range.
4. Step 4 checks if the voltage is below the minimum of the range.
6. This step checks for the integrity of the ground circuit.

GC4020152474010X

Fig. 33 Code C0896: Device Voltage Range/ Performance (Part 1 of 2). Camaro & Firebird

Step	Action	Value(s)	Yes	No
Schematic Reference: *ABS Schematics*				
1	Did you perform the Diagnostic System Check?	—	Go to *Step 2*	Go to *Diagnostic System Check - ABS*
2	1. Turn all the accessories off. 2. Install a scan tool. 3. Start the engine. 4. Use the scan tool to monitor the battery voltage while running the engine at approximately 2000 RPM. Is the monitored battery voltage within the specified range?	0–17.4 V	Go to *Step 4*	Go to *Step 3*
3	Use a *J 39200 DMM to measure the voltage between the battery positive terminal and ground.* Is the voltage within the specified range?	0–17.4 V	Go to *Step 5*	*Diagnose* Engine Electrical
4	Continue to monitor the battery voltage with the scan tool while running the engine at approximately 2000 RPM. Is the monitored battery voltage within the specified range?	0–9.4 V	Go to *Step 6*	Go to *Step 5*
5	1. Turn the ignition switch to the OFF position. 2. Disconnect the scan tool if still connected. 3. Test drive the vehicle above 6 km/h (3.5 mph). Did DTC C0896 reset?	—	Go to *Step 10*	Go to *Diagnostic System Check - ABS*
6	1. Turn the ignition switch to the OFF position. 2. Disconnect the EBCM connector. 3. Install the *J 39700* with the *J 39700-530* to the EBCM harness connector only. 4. Use a *J 39200 DMM to measure the resistance between the J 39700* terminal 15 and a good ground. Is the resistance within the specified range?	0-5 Ω	Go to *Step 8*	Go to *Step 7*
7	Repair open or high resistance in the ground circuit. Is the repair complete?	—	Go to *Step 11*	—
8	1. Turn the ignition switch to the RUN position. 2. Use a *J 39200 DMM to measure the voltage between the J 39700* terminal 8 and 15. Is the voltage within the specified range?	Above 9.4 V	Go to *Step 9*	*Diagnose* Engine Electrical
9	1. Turn the ignition switch to the OFF position. 2. Reconnect the EBCM connector. 3. Disconnect the scan tool if the scan tool is still connected. 4. Test drive the vehicle above 6 km/h (3.5 mph). Did DTC C0896 reset?	—	Go to*Step 10*	Go to *Step 11*
10	Replace the EBCM. Is the repair complete?	—	Go to *Step 11*	—
11	1. Use the scan tool in order to clear clear the DTCs. 2. Operate the vehicle within the Conditions for Running the DTC as specified in the supporting text. Does the DTC reset?	—	Go to*Step 2*	System OK

GC4020152474020X

Fig. 33 Code C0896: Device Voltage Range/ Performance (Part 2 of 2). Camaro & Firebird

Step	Action	Value(s)	Yes	No
6	1. Turn the ignition switch to the RUN position with the engine off. 2. Measure the voltage between the ASM harness connector terminals 1 and 28. Is the voltage within specifications?	More than 7.5 V	Go to *Step 9*	*Battery Charging*
7	Repair the harness connector as necessary. Are the repairs complete?	—	Go to *Step 10*	—
8	Repair the open or high resistance in the ground circuit. Is the circuit repair complete?	—	Go to *Step 10*	—
9	Replace the EBCM. Is the replacement complete?	—	Go to *Step 10*	—
10	1. Use the scan tool in order to clear the DTCs. 2. Operate the vehicle within the Conditions for Running the DTC as specified in the supporting text. Does the DTC reset?	—	Go to *Step 2*	System OK

GC4020152475020X

Fig. 34 Code C0901: Device No. 2 Voltage Low (Part 2 of 2). Camaro & Firebird

Symptoms - Antilock Brake System

Important: The following steps must be completed before using the symptom tables.

1. Perform the *Diagnostic System Check - ABS* before using the Symptom Tables in order to verify that all of the following are true:
   - There are no DTCs set.
   - The control module(s) can communicate via the serial data link.
2. Review the system operation in order to familiarize yourself with the system functions.

Visual/Physical Inspection

- Inspect for aftermarket devices which could affect the operation of the antilock brake system.
- Inspect the easily accessible or visible system components for obvious damage or conditions which could cause the symptom.
- Inspect the master cylinder reservoir for the proper fluid level.

Intermittent

Faulty electrical connections or wiring may be the cause of intermittent conditions.

Symptom List

Refer to a symptom diagnostic procedure from the following list in order to diagnose the symptom:

- *ABS Indicator Always On*
- *ABS Indicator Inoperative*
- *Low Traction Indicator Always On*
- *Low Traction Indicator Inoperative*
- *Traction Off Indicator Always On*
- *Traction Off Indicator Inoperative*

GC4020152476000X

Fig. 35 ABS Symptoms. Camaro & Firebird

Circuit Description

This circuit monitors the voltage level available to the ASM. If the voltage drops below 7.5 volts, full performance of the traction control system cannot be guaranteed.

Conditions for Setting the DTC

DTC C0901 can set anytime the ignition is in the RUN position and ignition voltage is less than 7.5 volts

Action Taken When the DTC Sets

- The TCS is disabled
- The traction control indicator is turned on

Conditions for Clearing the DTC

- The condition for the DTC is no longer present and the scan tool clear DTC function is used
- 100 ignition cycles have passed with no DTCs detected

Diagnostic Aids

- Thoroughly inspect the wiring and the connectors. Failure to carefully and fully inspect the wiring and the connectors can result in misdiagnosis. Misdiagnosis may cause replacement of parts without repairing the malfunction.
- Inspect for other low voltage conditions.
- Test the charging system.
- The following conditions are other possible causes of low system voltage:
  – A charging system malfunction
  – Excessive parasitic drain
  – A weak battery
  – A faulty system ground

Test Description

The numbers below refer to the step numbers on the diagnostic table.

4. This step checks for a good ground.
6. This step checks for proper voltage voltage.

Step	Action	Value(s)	Yes	No
Schematic Reference: *ABS Schematics*				
1	Did you perform the Diagnostic System Check?	—	Go to *Step 2*	Go to *Diagnostic System Check - ABS*
2	Check the Charging System. Is the charging system OK?	—	Go to *Step 3*	*Diagnose* Engine Electrical
3	1. Turn the ignition switch to the OFF position. 2. Disconnect the ASM harness connector. 3. Inspect the ASM harness connector and the connector for damage or corrosion. Is there any evidence of damage or corrosion?	—	Go to *Step 7*	Go to *Step 4*
4	Using the *J 39200* DMM, measure the resistance between the ASM harness connector terminal 28 and a good ground. Is the resistance within specifications?	0-5 Ω	Go to *Step 5*	Go to *Step 8*
5	Using the *J 39200* DMM, measure the resistance between the ASM harness connector terminal 55 and a good ground. s the resistance within specifications?	0-5 Ω	Go to *Step 6*	Go to *Step 8*

GC4020152475010X

Fig. 34 Code C0901: Device No. 2 Voltage Low (Part 1 of 2). Camaro & Firebird

Circuit Description

The Instrument Panel Cluster (IPC) turns the ABS Indicator on during the IPC bulb check for approximately 3 seconds when the ignition switch is turned to the ON position. If the EBCM sets a Diagnostic Trouble Code (DTC) the EBCM sends a class 2 message to the IPC to command the ABS Indicator on.

Diagnostic Aids

- It is very important that a thorough inspection of the wiring and connectors be performed. Failure to carefully and fully inspect wiring and connectors may result in misdiagnosis, causing part replacement with reappearance of the malfunction.
- Thoroughly inspect any circuitry that may be causing the complaint for the following conditions:
  – Backed out terminals
  – Improper mating
  – Broken locks
  – Improperly formed or damaged terminals
  – Poor terminal-to-wiring connections
  – Physical damage to the wiring harness
- The following conditions may cause an intermittent malfunction:
  – A poor connection
  – Rubbed-through wire insulation
  – A broken wire inside the insulation

Test Description

The number(s) below refer to the step number(s) on the diagnostic table.

2. Checks if the scan tool can turn on and off all the indicator lamps in the instrument cluster.
4. Checks if the circuits going to the instrument cluster or the cluster is at fault.

Step	Action	Yes	No
Schematic Reference: *ABS Schematics*			
1	Did you perform the Diagnostic System Check?	Go to *Step 2*	Go to *Diagnostic System Check - ABS*
2	1. Using a scan tool, select the Instrument Panel Cluster Special Functions mode. 2. Go to Displays Test in Output Control. 3. In the Displays Test mode you can turn on or off the instrument panel indicators. All indicators will turn ON when commanded on. Does the ABS indicator turn on then off?	Go to *Step 3*	Go to *Step 4*
3	Replace the EBCM. Is the replacement complete?	Go to *Diagnostic System Check - ABS*	—
4	1. Disconnect the Instrument Cluster and connect a Test Light across the appropriate power and ground terminals. 2. Test Light OFF, repair open in power or ground circuit to cluster 3. Test Light ON, check connector for poor connection to cluster. 4. If OK, replace the Instrument Cluster. Is the Instrument Cluster replacement complete?	Go to *Diagnostic System Check - ABS*	—

GC4020152477000X

Fig. 36 ABS Indicator Always On. Camaro & Firebird

Circuit Description

The Instrument Panel Cluster (IPC) turns the ABS Indicator on during the IPC bulb check for approximately 3 seconds when the ignition switch is turned to the ON position. If the EBCM sets a Diagnostic Trouble Code (DTC) the EBCM sends a class 2 message to the IPC to command the ABS Indicator on.

Diagnostic Aids

- It is very important that a thorough inspection of the wiring and connectors be performed. Failure to carefully and fully inspect wiring and connectors may result in misdiagnosis, causing part replacement with reappearance of the malfunction.
- Thoroughly inspect any circuitry that may be causing the complaint for the following conditions:
  - Backed out terminals
  - Improper mating
  - Broken locks
  - Improperly formed or damaged terminals
  - Poor terminal-to-wiring connections
  - Physical damage to the wiring harness
- The following conditions may cause an intermittent malfunction:
  - A poor connection
  - Rubbed-through wire insulation
  - A broken wire inside the insulation

Test Description

The number(s) below refer to the step number(s) on the diagnostic table.

2. Checks if the scan tool can turn on and off all the indicator lamps in the instrument cluster.
4. Checks if the circuits going to the instrument Cluster or the cluster is at fault.

Step	Action	Yes	No
Schematic Reference: *ABS Schematics*			
1	Did you perform the Diagnostic System Check?	Go to *Step 2*	Go to *Diagnostic System Check - ABS*
2	1. Using a scan tool, select the Instrument Panel Cluster Special Functions mode. 2. Go to Displays Test in Output Control. 3. In the Displays Test mode you can turn on or off the instrument panel indicators. All indicators will turn ON when commanded on. Does the ABS Indicator turn on then off?	Go to *Step 3*	Go to*Step 4*
3	Replace the EBCM. Is the replacement complete?	Go to *Diagnostic System Check - ABS*	—
4	1. Disconnect the Instrument Cluster and connect a Test Light across the appropriate power and ground terminals. 2. Test Light OFF, repair open in power or ground circuit to cluster. 3. Test Light ON, check connector for poor connection to the cluster. 4. If OK, replace the Instrument Cluster. Is the instrument cluster replacement complete?	Go to *Diagnostic System Check - ABS*	—

GC4020152478000X

Fig. 37 ABS Indicator Inoperative. Camaro & Firebird

Step	Action	Value(s)	Yes	No
Schematic Reference: *ABS Schematics*				
1	Did you perform the Diagnostic System Check?	—	*Go to Step 2*	Go to *Diagnostic System Check - ABS*
2	1. Turn the ignition switch to the RUN position, engine off. 2. Using a scan tool enter TCS Data List. 3. While monitoring the ASR On/Off switch status, press and release the ASR On/Off switch. Does the switch status change from pressed to released as the ASR switch is pressed and released?	—	*Go to Step 3*	*Go to Step 5*
3	1. Using a scan tool in the instrument Pannel Cluster Special Function. 2. Go to Displays Test in Output Control. 3. In the Displays Test mode you can turn on or off the instrument panel indicators. 4. All indicators will turn ON when commanded on. Does the ASR OFF indicator turn on then off?	—	*Go to Step 9*	*Go to Step 4*
4	1. Disconnect the instrument cluster and connect a Test light across the appropraiate power and ground terminals. 2. Test light OFF, repair open in power or ground circuit to cluster. 3. Test light ON, check connector for poor connection to the cluster. 4. If OK, replace the instrument cluster. Is the instrument cluster replacement complete?	—	Go to Step *Diagnostic System Check - ABS*	—
5	1. Remove the ASR Switch and disconnect the connector. 2. Using a scan tool in ABS/TC Data List read the TCS Switch Status. 3. With the ASR Switch disconnected. Does the TCS switch status read released?	—	*Go to Step 6*	*Go to Step 7*
6	Replace the ASR Switch. Is the replacement complete?	—	Go to *Diagnostic System Check - ABS*	—
7	1. Turn the ignition switch to the OFF position. 2. Using *J 39200* DMM, measure the resistance between the ASR switch harness connector terminal E and a known good ground. Is the resistance within the range specified in the value(s) column?	OL (Infinite)	*Go to Step 9*	*Go to Step 8*
8	Repair the traction control switch signal circuit for a short to ground. Is the repair complete?	—	Go to *Diagnostic System Check - ABS*	—
9	Replace the EBCM. Is the replacement complete?	—	Go to *Diagnostic System Check - ABS*	—

GC4020152479020X

Fig. 38 ASR Indicator Always On (Part 2 of 2). Camaro & Firebird

Circuit Description

The ASR OFF Indicator is controlled by the EBCM by sending class 2 messages to the Instrument Panel Cluster (IPC). It is turned on when the EBCM sets a DTC that turns on the ASR OFF indicator. It is also turned on or off when the Accelerator Slip Regulation (ASR) Switch is pressed. The Electronic Brake Control Module (EBCM) supplies 12 volts to the ASR Switch, when the ASR switch is depressed the EBCM sees the voltage go low, and that the ASR switch state has changed. When the EBCM receives that a switch state has changed it turns on or off the ASR and sends a message to the IPC to turn on or off the ASR OFF indicator depending on its previous state.

Diagnostic Aids

- It is very important that a thorough inspection of the wiring and connectors be performed. Failure to carefully and fully inspect wiring and connectors may result in misdiagnosis, causing part replacement with reappearance of the malfunction.
- Thoroughly inspect any circuitry that may be causing the complaint for the following conditions:
  - Backed out terminals
  - Improper mating
  - Broken locks
  - Improperly formed or damaged terminals
  - Poor terminal-to-wiring connections
  - Physical damage to the wiring harness
- The following conditions may cause an intermittent malfunction:
  - A poor connection
  - Rubbed-through wire insulation
  - A broken wire inside the insulation

Test Description

The number(s) below refer to the step number(s) on the diagnostic table.

2. Checks if EBCM is receiving a ASR Switch message from the switch.
3. Checks if the scan tool can turn on and off all the indicator lamps in the instrument cluster.
5. Checks if the EBCM or ASR Switch is at fault.

GC4020152479010X

Fig. 38 ASR Indicator Always On (Part 1 of 2). Camaro & Firebird

Circuit Description

The ASR OFF Indicator is controlled by the EBCM by sending class 2 messages to the Instrument Panel Cluster (IPC). It is turned on when the EBCM sets a DTC that turns on the ASR OFF indicator. It is also turned on or off when the Accelerator Slip Regulation (ASR) Switch is pressed. The Electronic Brake Control Module (EBCM) supplies 12 volts to the ASR Switch, when the ASR switch is depressed the EBCM sees the voltage go low, and that the ASR switch state has changed. When the EBCM receives that a switch state has changed it turns on or off the ASR and sends a message to the IPC to turn on or off the ASR OFF indicator depending on its previous state.

Diagnostic Aids

- It is very important that a thorough inspection of the wiring and connectors be performed. Failure to carefully and fully inspect wiring and connectors may result in misdiagnosis, causing part replacement with reappearance of the malfunction.
- Thoroughly inspect any circuitry that may be causing the complaint for the following conditions:
  - Backed out terminals
  - Improper mating
  - Broken locks
  - Improperly formed or damaged terminals
  - Poor terminal-to-wiring connections
  - Physical damage to the wiring harness
- The following conditions may cause an intermittent malfunction:
  - A poor connection
  - Rubbed-through wire insulation
  - A broken wire inside the insulation

Test Description

The number(s) below refer to the step number(s) on the diagnostic table.

2. Checks if EBCM is receiving a ASR switch message from the switch.
3. Check if the scan tool can turn on and off the indicator lamps in the instrument cluster.
5. Checks if the EBCM or ASR Switch is at fault.

Step	Action	Value(s)	Yes	No
Schematic Reference: *ABS Schematics*				
1	Did you perform the Diagnostic System Check?	—	*Go to Step 2*	Go to *Diagnostic System Check - ABS*
2	1. Turn the ignition switch to the RUN position, engine off. 2. Using a scan tool enter TCS Data List. 3. While monitoring the TCS On/Off switch status, press and release the ASR On/Off switch. Does the switch status change from pressed to released as the ASR switch is pressed and released?	—	*Go to Step 3*	*Go to Step 5*
3	1. Using a scan tool in the Instrument Pannel Cluster Special Function. 2. Go to Displays Test in Output Control. 3. In the Displays Testmode you can turn on or off the instrument panel indicators. 4. All indicators will turn ON when commanded on. Does the ASR OFF indicator turn on then off?	—	*Go to Step 11*	*Go to Step 4*

GC4020152480010X

Fig. 39 ASR Indicator Inoperative (Part 1 of 2). Camaro & Firebird

Step	Action	Value(s)	Yes	No
4	1. Disconnect instrument cluster and connect a test light across the appropraiate power and ground terminals. 2. Test light OFF, repair open in power or ground circuit to cluster. 3. Test light ON, check connector for poor connection to Cluster. 4. If OK, replace the instrument cluster. Is the instrument cluster replacement complete?	—	Go to Step *Diagnostic System Check - ABS*	—
5	1. Remove the ASR switch and disconnect the connector. 2. Using a scan tool in ABS/TC Data List read the TCS switch status. 3. Connect a jumper wire between terminals E and F of the ASR Switch harness connector. Does the TCS switch status read pressed with the jumper wire connected?	—	*Go to Step 6*	*Go to Step 7*
6	Replace the ASR switch. Is the replacement complete?	—	Go to *Diagnostic System Check - ABS*	—
7	1. Turn the ignition switch to the OFF position. 2. Using *J 39200* DMM, measure the resistance between the ASR switch harness connector terminal F and a known good ground. Is the resistance within the range specified in the value(s) column?	0-5 Ω	*Go to Step 9*	*Go to Step 8*
8	Repair the ground circuit for a open or high resistance. Is the repair complete?	—	Go to *Diagnostic System Check - ABS*	—
9	1. Disconnect the EBCM Connector C1. 2. Install the *J 39700* Universal Pinout box using the *J 39700-25* cable adapter to connector C1 only. 3. Using DMM, measure the resistance between the ASR switch harness connector terminal E and 17 of *J 39700*. 4. Is the resistace within the range specified in the value(s) column?	0-5 Ω	*Go to Step 11*	*Go to Step 10*
10	Repair traction control switch signal circuit for an open or high resistance. Is the repair complete?	—	Go to *Diagnostic System Check - ABS*	—
11	Replace the EBCM. Is the replacement complete?	—	Go to *Diagnostic System Check - ABS*	—

GC4020152480020X

Fig. 39 ASR Indicator Inoperative (Part 2 of 2). Camaro & Firebird

Circuit Description

The Instrument Panel Cluster (IPC) turns the LOW TRAC Indicator on during the IPC bulb check for approximately 3 seconds when the ignition switch is turned to the ON position. If the EBCM sets a Diagnostic Trouble Code (DTC) the EBCM sends the IPC the command to turn the LOW TRAC Indicator on.

Diagnostic Aids

- It is very important that a thorough inspection of the wiring and connectors be performed. Failure to carefully and fully inspect wiring and connectors may result in misdiagnosis, causing part replacement with reappearance of the malfunction.
- Thoroughly inspect any circuitry that may be causing the complaint for the following conditions:
  - Backed out terminals
  - Improper mating
  - Broken locks
  - Improperly formed or damaged terminals
  - Poor terminal-to-wiring connections
  - Physical damage to the wiring harness
- The following conditions may cause an intermittent malfunction:
  - A poor connection
  - Rubbed-through wire insulation
  - A broken wire inside the insulation

Test Description

The number(s) below refer to the step number(s) on the diagnostic table.

2. Checks if the scan tool can turn on and off all the indicator lamps in the instrument cluster.
4. Checks if the circuits going to the instrument cluster or the cluster is at fault.

Low Traction Indicator Always On

Step	Action	Yes	No
Schematic Reference: *ABS Schematics*			
1	Did you perform the Diagnostic System Check?	Go to *Step 2*	Go to *Diagnostic System Check - ABS*
2	1. Using a scan tool, select the Instrument Panel Cluster Special Functions mode. 2. Go to Displays Test in Output Control. 3. In the Displays Test mode you can turn on or off the instrument panel indicators. All indicators will turn ON when commanded on. Does the LOW TRAC Indicator turn on then off?	Go to *Step 3*	Go to *Step 4*
3	Replace the EBCM. Is the replacement complete?	Go to *Diagnostic System Check - ABS*	—
4	1. Disconnect the instrument cluster and connect a Test Light across the appropriate power and ground terminals. 2. Test Light OFF, repair open in power or ground circuit to cluster 3. Test Light ON, check connector for poor connection to cluster. 4. If OK, replace the instrument cluster. Is the instrument cluster replacement complete?	Go to *Diagnostic System Check - ABS*	—

GC4020152481000X

Fig. 40 Low Traction Indicator Always On. Camaro & Firebird

Circuit Description

The Instrument Panel Cluster (IPC) turns the LOW TRAC Indicator on during the IPC bulb check for approximately 3 seconds when the ignition switch is turned to the ON position. If the EBCM sets a Diagnostic Trouble Code (DTC) the EBCM sends the IPC the command to turn the LOW TRAC Indicator on.

Diagnostic Aids

- It is very important that a thorough inspection of the wiring and connectors be performed. Failure to carefully and fully inspect wiring and connectors may result in misdiagnosis, causing part replacement with reappearance of the malfunction.
- Thoroughly inspect any circuitry that may be causing the complaint for the following conditions:
  - Backed out terminals
  - Improper mating
  - Broken locks
  - Improperly formed or damaged terminals
  - Poor terminal-to-wiring connections
  - Physical damage to the wiring harness
- The following conditions may cause an intermittent malfunction:
  - A poor connection
  - Rubbed-through wire insulation
  - A broken wire inside the insulation

Test Description

The number(s) below refer to the step number(s) on the diagnostic table.

2. Checks if the scan tool can turn on and off all the indicator lamps in the instrument cluster.
4. Checks if the circuits going to the instrument Cluster or the cluster is at fault.

Step	Action	Yes	No
Schematic Reference: *ABS Schematics*			
1	Did you perform the Diagnostic System Check?	Go to *Step 2*	Go to *Diagnostic System Check - ABS*
2	1. Using a scan tool, select the Instrument Panel Cluster Special Functions mode. 2. Go to Displays Test in Output Control. 3. In the Displays Test mode you can turn on or off the instrument panel indicators. All indicators will turn ON when commanded on. Does the LOW TRAC Indicator turn on then off?	Go to *Step 3*	Go to *Step 4*
3	Replace the EBCM. Is the replacement complete?	Go to *Diagnostic System Check - ABS*	—
4	1. Disconnect the Instrument Cluster and connect a Test Light across the Appropriate power and ground terminals. 2. Test Light OFF, repair open in power or ground circuit to cluster. 3. Test Light ON, check connector for poor connection to the cluster. 4. If OK, replace the Instrument Cluster. Is the instrument cluster replacement complete?	Go to *Diagnostic System Check - ABS*	—

GC4020152482000X

Fig. 41 Low Traction Indicator Inoperative. Camaro & Firebird

Circuit Description

The TRAC OFF indicator is controlled by the instrument cluster via class 2 serial data messages from the EBCM. When the body control module (BCM) sees the traction control switch input grounded through the momentary traction control switch, it sends a class 2 message to the EBCM that tells the EBCM that the traction control switch has been pressed. The EBCM then disables traction control and sends a message to the instrument cluster to turn the TRAC OFF indicator ON. Each time the ignition is cycled from OFF to ON, the traction control system is enabled.

The following conditions will cause the TRAC OFF indicator to illuminate:

- The EBCM has disabled the TCS due to a DTC.
- The driver manually disabling the TCS via the traction control switch.
- The instrument cluster bulb check. When the ignition switch is turned to ON, the TRAC OFF indicator will turn on for approximately 3 seconds and then turn OFF.

Diagnostic Aids

- It is very important that a thorough inspection of the wiring and connectors be performed. Failure to carefully and fully inspect wiring and connectors may result in misdiagnosis, causing part replacement with reappearance of the malfunction.
- Thoroughly inspect any circuitry that may be causing the complaint for the following conditions:
  - Backed out terminals
  - Improper mating
  - Broken locks
  - Improperly formed or damaged terminals
  - Poor terminal-to-wiring connections
  - Physical damage to the wiring harness
- The following conditions may cause an intermittent malfunction:
  - A poor connection
  - Rubbed-through wire insulation
  - A broken wire inside the insulation

GC4020152483010X

Fig. 42 Traction Off Indicator Always On (Part 1 of 2). Camaro & Firebird

Step	Action	Yes	No
Schematic Reference: *ABS Schematics*			
1	Did you perform the ABS Diagnostic System Check?	Go to *Step 2*	Go to *Diagnostic System Check - ABS*
2	1. Install a scan tool. 2. Turn ON the ignition, with the engine OFF. 3. With a scan tool, observe the Traction Switch parameter in the Body Control Module data list. Does the scan tool display Off?	Go to *Step 3*	Go to *Step 4*
3	1. Activate the traction control switch. 2. With the scan tool, observe the Traction Switch parameter. Does the Traction Switch parameter change state?	*Intermittent and Poor Connections*	Go to *Step 4*
4	1. Turn OFF the ignition. 2. Disconnect the traction control switch connector. 3. Turn ON the ignition, with the engine OFF. 4. With a scan tool, observe the Traction Switch parameter. Does the scan tool display Off?	Go to *Step 7*	Go to *Step 5*
5	Test the signal circuit of the traction control switch for a short to ground. Did you find and correct the condition?	Go to *Step 10*	Go to *Step 6*
6	Inspect for poor connections at the harness connector of the body control module (BCM). Did you find and correct the condition?	Go to *Step 10*	Go to *Step 8*
7	Inspect for poor connections at the harness connector of the traction control switch. Did you find and correct the condition?	Go to *Step 10*	Go to *Step 9*
8	Replace the body control module (BCM). Did you complete the replacement?	Go to *Step 10*	—
9	Replace the traction control switch. Did you complete the replacement?	Go to *Step 10*	—
10	Operate the system in order to verify the repair. Did you correct the condition?	System OK	Go to *Step 2*

GC4020152483020X

Fig. 42 Traction Off Indicator Always On (Part 2 of 2). Camaro & Firebird

Step	Action	Yes	No
Schematic Reference: *ABS Schematics*			
1	Did you perform the ABS Diagnostic System Check?	Go to *Step 2*	Go to *Diagnostic System Check - ABS*
2	1. Install a scan tool. 2. Turn ON the ignition, with the engine OFF. 3. With a scan tool, observe the Traction Switch parameter in the Body Control Module data list. 4. Activate the traction control switch. Does the Traction Switch parameter change state?	*Test for Intermittent and Poor Connections*	Go to *Step 3*
3	1. Turn OFF the ignition. 2. Disconnect the traction control switch connector. 3. Connect a fused jumper from the signal circuit of the traction control switch harness connector to a good ground. 4. Turn ON the ignition, with the engine OFF. 5. With a scan tool, observe the Traction Switch parameter. Does the scan tool display On?	Go to *Step 5*	Go to *Step 4*
4	Test the signal circuit of the traction control switch for an open or high resistance. Did you find and correct the condition?	Go to *Step 10*	Go to *Step 6*
5	Test the ground circuit of the traction control switch for an open or high resistance. Did you find and correct the condition?	Go to *Step 10*	Go to *Step 7*
6	Inspect for poor connections at the harness connector of the body control module (BCM). Did you find and correct the condition?	Go to *Step 10*	Go to *Step 8*
7	Inspect for poor connections at the harness connector of the traction control switch. Did you find and correct the condition?	Go to *Step 10*	Go to *Step 9*
8	Replace the body control module (BCM). Did you complete the replacement?	Go to *Step 10*	—
9	Replace the traction control switch. Did you complete the replacement?	Go to *Step 10*	—
10	Operate the system in order to verify the repair. Did you correct the condition?	System OK	Go to *Step 2*

GC4020152484020X

Fig. 43 Traction Off Indicator Inoperative (Part 2 of 2). Camaro & Firebird

Circuit Description

The TRAC OFF indicator is controlled by the instrument cluster via class 2 serial data messages from the EBCM. When the body control module (BCM) sees the traction control switch input grounded through the momentary traction control switch, it sends a class 2 message to the EBCM that tells the EBCM that the traction control switch has been pressed. The EBCM then disables traction control and sends a message to the instrument cluster to turn the TRAC OFF indicator ON. Each time the ignition is cycled from OFF to ON, the traction control system is enabled.

The following conditions will cause the TRAC OFF indicator to illuminate:

- The EBCM has disabled the TCS due to a DTC.
- The driver manually disabling the TCS via the traction control switch.
- The instrument cluster bulb check. When the ignition switch is turned to ON, the TRAC OFF indicator will turn on for approximately 3 seconds and then turn OFF.

Diagnostic Aids

- It is very important that a thorough inspection of the wiring and connectors be performed. Failure to carefully and fully inspect wiring and connectors may result in misdiagnosis, causing part replacement with reappearance of the malfunction.
- Thoroughly inspect any circuitry that may be causing the complaint for the following conditions:
  - Backed out terminals
  - Improper mating
  - Broken locks
  - Improperly formed or damaged terminals
  - Poor terminal-to-wiring connections
  - Physical damage to the wiring harness
- The following conditions may cause an intermittent malfunction:
  - A poor connection
  - Rubbed-through wire insulation
  - A broken wire inside the insulation

GC4020152484010X

Fig. 43 Traction Off Indicator Inoperative (Part 1 of 2). Camaro & Firebird

Circuit Description

The EBTCM Diagnostic System Check is an organized approach to identify problems associated with the EBTCM. This check must be the starting point for any EBTCM complaint, and will direct you to the next logical step in diagnosing the complaint. The EBTCM is a very reliable component and is not likely the cause of the malfunction. Most system complaints are linked to faulty wiring, connectors, and occasionally to components. Understanding the ABS system and using the tables correctly will reduce diagnostic time and prevent unnecessary parts replacement.

Diagnostic Aids

- An intermittent failure in the electronic system may be very difficult to detect and to accurately diagnose. The EBTCM tests for different malfunctions under different vehicle conditions. For this reason, a thorough test drive is often needed in order to repeat a malfunction. If the system malfunction is not repeated during the test drive, a good description of the complaint may be very useful in locating an intermittent malfunction. Faulty electrical connections or wiring causes most intermitting problems. Wher an intermittent condition is suspected, check th suspected circuits for the following conditions:
  - Poor mating of connector halves or backed out terminals
  - Improperly formed or damaged terminals
  - Wire chafing
  - Poor wire to terminal connections
  - Dirty or corroded terminals
  - Damage to connector bodies
- If the DTC is a history DTC, the problem may be intermittent. Perform the tests shown while moving related wiring and connectors. This car often cause the malfunction to occur. Perform thorough inspection of all related wiring and connectors pertaining to the history DTC store

GC402980295300AX

Fig. 44 ABS Diagnostic System Check (Part 1 of 2). Catera

Step	Action	Value(s)	Yes	No
1	1. Reconnect all previously disconnected components. 2. Turn the ignition switch from the OFF to RUN position, engine off. 3. Plug a scan tool into the Diagnostic Link Connector (DLC). Does the scan tool communicate with the EBTCM?	—	*Go to Step 3*	*Go to Step 2*
2	Does the scan tool communicate with other modules on the Keyword 2000 serial data line?	—	Go to *No Communication with EBTCM*	*Data Link Connector System Check*
3	1. Disconnect the scan tool. 2. Turn the ignition switch from the OFF to Run position. 3. Carefully road test the vehicle for several minutes over different road surfaces and with several turns above 24 km/h (12 mph). 4. Plug a scan tool into the Diagnostic Link Connector (DLC). 5. With the scan tool read ABS/TCS DTC(s). Are there any current Diagnostic Trouble Codes?	—	Go to *DTC List* for the Applicable DTC Table	*Go to Step 4*
4	1. Remove the scan tool from the DLC 2. Turn the ignition switch from the OFF to RUN position, engine off. Does the ABS Indicator turn on then turn off after several seconds?	—	*Go to Step 5*	*Go to Step 6*
5	Turn the ignition switch from the OFF to RUN position, engine off. Does the TC Indicator turn on then turn off after several seconds?	—	*Go to Step 8*	*Go to Step 7*
6	Does the ABS Indicator stay on?	—	Go to *ABS Indicator On No DTC Set*	Go to *ABS Indicator Off No DTC Set*
7	Does the TC Indicator stay on?		Go to *Traction Control Indicator Always On No DTC*	Go to *Traction Control Indicator Always Off No DTC*
8	Are there any history DTC(s)?	—	*Go to Step 9*	System OK
9	1. Refer to the appropriate DTC table for the history DTC. 2. Read the diagnostic aids, and the conditions for setting the DTC. 3. Unplug the scan tool from the DLC if not already removed. 4. Turn the ignition switch from the OFF to RUN position. 5. Carefully drive the vehicle above 24 Km/h (15 mph) for several minutes. 6. Leave the vehicle running and plug the scan tool into the DLC. 7. With the scan tool read ABS/TCS DTC(s). Did the history DTC set as a current DTC while the vehicle was being driven?	—	Go to *DTC List* for the Applicable DTC Table	System OK

GC402980295300BX

Fig. 44 ABS Diagnostic System Check (Part 2 of 2). Catera

Circuit Description

The speed sensor used on this vehicle is a single point magnetic pickup. This sensor produces an AC signal that the EBTCM uses the frequency from to calculate the wheel speed.

Conditions for Setting the DTC

The DTC can be set any time the ignition is in the RUN position and the EBTCM detects an open or a short to voltage.

Action Taken When the DTC Sets

- A malfunction DTC stores.
- The ABS/TCS disables.
- The amber ABS/TC indicator(s) turn on.

Conditions for Clearing the DTC

- The condition responsible for setting the DTC no longer exists and the scan tool Clear DTCs function is used.
- 100 ignition cycles pass with no DTC(s) detected.

Diagnostic Aids

- It is very important that a thorough inspection of the wiring and connectors be performed. Failure to carefully and fully inspect wiring and connectors may result in misdiagnosis, causing part replacement with reappearance of the malfunction.
- Thoroughly inspect any circuitry that may be causing the complaint for the following conditions:
  - Backed out terminals
  - Improper mating
  - Broken locks
  - Improperly formed or damaged terminals
  - Poor terminal-to-wiring connections
  - Physical damage to the wiring harness
- The following conditions may cause an intermittent malfunction:
  - A poor connection
  - Rubbed-through wire insulation
  - A broken wire inside the insulation
- If the customer's comments reflect that the amber ABS/TCS indicator is on only during moist environmental conditions (rain, snow, vehicle wash), inspect all the wheel speed sensor circuitry for signs of water intrusion. If the DTC is not current, clear all DTCs and simulate the effects of water intrusion by using the following procedure:
  1. Spray the suspected area with a five percent saltwater solution.

     Add two teaspoons of salt to twelve ounces of water to make a five percent saltwater solution.
  2. Test drive the vehicle over various road surfaces (bumps, turns, etc.) above 40 km/h (25 mph) for at least 30 seconds.
  3. If the DTC returns, replace the suspected harness.

GC402980295500AX

Fig. 45 Code C0035: LH Front Wheel Speed Circuit Fault, High Or Low (Part 1 of 3). Catera

Step	Action	Value(s)	Yes	No
1	Was the Diagnostic System Check performed?	—	*Go to Step 2*	Go to *ABS Diagnostic System Check*
2	Inspect the WSS for physical damage. Is physical damage of the WSS evident?	—	*Go to Step 3*	*Go to Step 4*
3	Replace the WSS. Is the replacement complete?	—	*Go to Step 16*	—
4	1. Turn the ignition switch to the OFF position. 2. Disconnect the EBTCM. 3. Install the *J 39700* Universal Pinout Box using the J 39700-280 cable adapter to the EBTCM harness connector only. 4. Using *J 39200* DMM, measure the resistance between terminals 7 and 6 of *J 39700.* Is the resistance within the range specified in the value(s) column?	800–1700Ω	*Go to Step 11*	*Go to Step 5*
5	1. Disconnect the Wheel Speed Sensor. 2. Using *J 39200* DMM, measure the resistance between terminals 1 and 2 of the Wheel Speed Sensor Connector. Is the resistance within the range specified in the value(s) column?	800–1700Ω	*Go to Step 6*	*Go to Step 3*
6	Using *J 39200* DMM, measure the resistance between terminal 7 of *J 39700* and terminal 1 of the WSS harness connector. Is the resistance within the range specified in the value(s) column?	0-5Ω	*Go to Step 8*	*Go to Step 7*
7	Repair CKT P350 for an open or high resistance. Is the repair complete?	—	*Go to Step 16*	—
8	Using *J 39200* DMM, measure the resistance between terminal 6 of *J 39700* and terminal 2 of the WSS harness connector. Is the resistance within the range specified in the value(s) column?	0-5Ω	*Go to Step 10*	*Go to Step 9*

GC402980295500BX

Fig. 45 Code C0035: LH Front Wheel Speed Circuit Fault, High Or Low (Part 2 of 3). Catera

Step	Action	Value(s)	Yes	No
9	Repair CKT F350 for an open or high resistance. Is the repair complete?	—	*Go to Step 16*	—
10	Malfunction is intermittent. Inspect all connectors and harnesses for damage that may result in an open or high resistance when connected. Is the repair complete?	—	*Go to Step 16*	—
11	1. Disconnect the Wheel Speed Sensor. 2. Turn the ignition switch to the RUN position, engine off. 3. Using *J 39200* DMM, measure the voltage at terminal 7 of *J 39700.* Is the voltage within the range specified in the value(s) column?	Above 1V	*Go to Step 12*	*Go to Step 13*
12	Repair CKT P350 for a short to voltage. Is the repair complete?	—	*Go to Step 16*	—
13	Using *J 39200* DMM, measure the voltage at terminal 6 of *J 39700.* Is the voltage within the range specified in the value(s) column?	Above 1V	*Go to Step 14*	*Go to Step 15*
14	Repair CKT F350 for a short to voltage. Is the repair complete?	—	*Go to Step 16*	—
15	Replace the EBTCM. Is the replacement complete?	—	Go to *ABS Diagnostic System Check*	—
16	1. Reconnect all previously disconnected components. 2. Using a scan tool clear the DTC. 3. Remove the scan tool from the DLC. 4. Carefully drive the vehicle above 12 Km/h (8 mph) for several minutes. Does the DTC reset as a current DTC?	—	*Go to Step 2*	Go to *ABS Diagnostic System Check*

GC402980295500CX

Fig. 45 Code C0035: LH Front Wheel Speed Circuit Fault, High Or Low (Part 3 of 3). Catera

Circuit Description

The speed sensor used on this vehicle is a single point magnetic pickup. This sensor produces an AC signal that the EBTCM uses the frequency from to calculate the wheel speed.

Conditions for Setting the DTC

- The DTC will set if one wheel speed = 0 and the other WSS are greater than 40 Km/h (25 mph) for 10 ms.
- The DTC will set if during drive off, one wheel speed = 0, and the other WSS are greater than 12 Km/h (7.5 mph).
- The EBTCM detects a short to ground.

Action Taken When the DTC Sets

- A malfunction DTC stores.
- The ABS/TCS disables.
- The amber ABS/TCS indicator(s) turn on.

Conditions for Clearing the DTC

- The condition responsible for setting the DTC no longer exists and the scan tool Clear DTCs function is used.
- 100 ignition cycles pass with no DTC(s) detected.

Diagnostic Aids

- It is very important that a thorough inspection of the wiring and connectors be performed. Failure to carefully and fully inspect wiring and connectors may result in misdiagnosis, causing part replacement with reappearance of the malfunction.
- Thoroughly inspect any circuitry that may be causing the complaint for the following conditions:
  - Backed out terminals
  - Improper mating
  - Broken locks
  - Improperly formed or damaged terminals
  - Poor terminal-to-wiring connections
  - Physical damage to the wiring harness
- The following conditions may cause an intermittent malfunction:
  - A poor connection
  - Rubbed-through wire insulation
  - A broken wire inside the insulation
- If the customer's comments reflect that the amber ABS/TCS indicator is on only during moist environmental conditions (rain, snow, vehicle wash), inspect all the wheel speed sensor circuitry for signs of water intrusion. If the DTC is not current, clear all DTCs and simulate the effects of water intrusion by using the following procedure:
  1. Spray the suspected area with a five percent saltwater solution.

     Add two teaspoons of salt to twelve ounces of water to make a five percent saltwater solution.
  2. Test drive the vehicle over various road surfaces (bumps, turns, etc.) above 40 km/h (25 mph) for at least 30 seconds.
  3. If the DTC returns, replace the suspected harness.

GC402980315600AX

Fig. 46 Code C0035: LH Front Wheel Speed Circuit Fault, No Signal (Part 1 of 3). Catera

Test Description

The number(s) below refer to the step number(s) on the diagnostic table.

4. This step checks for the proper resistance in the WSS.
5. This step checks for the proper WSS output.

Step	Action	Value(s)	Yes	No
1	Was the Diagnostic System Check performed?	—	*Go to Step 2*	Go to *ABS Diagnostic System Check*
2	Inspect the WSS for physical damage. Is physical damage of the WSS evident?	—	*Go to Step 3*	*Go to Step 4*
3	Replace the WSS. Is the replacement complete?	—	*Go to Step 14*	—
4	1. Disconnect the WSS connector directly at the WSS. 2. Using *J 39200* DMM, measure the resistance between terminals 1 and 2 of the WSS. Is the resistance within the range specified in the value(s) column?	800–1700 Ω	*Go to Step 5*	*Go to Step 3*
5	1. With the *J 39200* DMM still connected to the WSS select the mV AC scale. 2. Spin the wheel at approximately 1 revolution per second by hand while monitoring the AC output. Is the AC voltage within the range specified in the value(s) column?	Above 30 mV	*Go to Step 6*	*Go to Step 3*
6	Using *J 39200* DMM, measure the resistance between the WSS terminal 1 and ground. Is the resistance within the range specified in the value(s) column?	OL (infinite)	*Go to Step 7*	*Go to Step 3*
7	1. Disconnect the EBTCM harness connector. 2. Install the *J 39700* Universal Pinout Box using the J 39700-280 cable adapter to the EBTCM harness connector only. 3. Using *J 39200* DMM, measure the resistance between terminals 7 and 6 of *J 39700*. Is the resistance within the range specified in the values column?	OL (infinite)	*Go to Step 9*	*Go to Step 8*
8	Repair short between CKT(s) P350 and F350. Is the repair complete?	—	*Go to Step 14*	—
9	Using *J 39200* DMM, measure the resistance between terminals 7 and 19 of *J 39700*. Is the resistance within the range specified in the values column?	OL (infinite)	*Go to Step 11*	*Go to Step 10*

GC402980315600BX

Fig. 46 Code C0035: LH Front Wheel Speed Circuit Fault, No Signal (Part 2 of 3). Catera

Step	Action	Value(s)	Yes	No
10	Repair CKT P350 for a short to ground. Is the repair complete?	—	*Go to Step 14*	—
11	Using *J 39200* DMM, measure the resistance between terminals 6 and 19 of *J 39700*. Is the resistance within the range specified in the values column?	OL (infinite)	*Go to Step 13*	*Go to Step 12*
12	Repair CKT F350 for a short to ground. Is the repair complete?	—	*Go to Step 14*	—
13	Replace the EBTCM. Is the replacement complete?	—	Go to *ABS Diagnostic System Check*	—
14	1. Reconnect all previously disconnected components. 2. Using a scan tool clear the DTC. 3. Remove the scan tool from the DLC. 4. Carefully drive vehicle above 12 Km/h (8 mph) for several minutes. Does the DTC reset as a current DTC?	—	*Go to Step 2*	Go to *ABS Diagnostic System Check*

GC402980295600CX

Fig. 46 Code C0035: LH Front Wheel Speed Circuit Fault, No Signal (Part 3 of 3). Catera

Circuit Description

The speed sensor used on this vehicle is a single point magnetic pickup. This sensor produces an AC signal that the EBTCM uses the frequency from to calculate the wheel speed.

Conditions for Setting the DTC

The DTC can be set any time the ignition is in the RUN position and the EBTCM detects an open or a short to voltage.

Action Taken When the DTC Sets

- A malfunction DTC stores.
- The ABS/TCS disables.
- The amber ABS/TC indicator(s) turn on.

Conditions for Clearing the DTC

- The condition responsible for setting the DTC no longer exists and the scan tool Clear DTCs function is used.
- 100 ignition cycles pass with no DTC(s) detected.

Diagnostic Aids

- It is very important that a thorough inspection of the wiring and connectors be performed. Failure to carefully and fully inspect wiring and connectors may result in misdiagnosis, causing part replacement with reappearance of the malfunction.
- Thoroughly inspect any circuitry that may be causing the complaint for the following conditions:
  - Backed out terminals
  - Improper mating
  - Broken locks
  - Improperly formed or damaged terminals
  - Poor terminal-to-wiring connections
  - Physical damage to the wiring harness
- The following conditions may cause an intermittent malfunction:
  - A poor connection
  - Rubbed-through wire insulation
  - A broken wire inside the insulation
- If the customer's comments reflect that the amber ABS/TCS indicator is on only during moist environmental conditions (rain, snow, vehicle wash), inspect all the wheel speed sensor circuitry for signs of water intrusion. If the DTC is not current, clear all DTCs and simulate the effects of water intrusion by using the following procedure:
  1. Spray the suspected area with a five percent saltwater solution.

     Add two teaspoons of salt to twelve ounces of water to make a five percent saltwater solution.
  2. Test drive the vehicle over various road surfaces (bumps, turns, etc.) above 40 km/h (25 mph) for at least 30 seconds.
  3. If the DTC returns, replace the suspected harness.

Test Description

The numbers below refer to step numbers on the diagnostic table.

4. This step checks for an open in the WSS or WSS CKT.
11. Checks for a short to voltage in the WSS CKT.
13. Checks for a short to voltage in the WSS CKT.

GC402980295700AX

Fig. 47 Code C0040: RH Front Wheel Speed Circuit Fault, High Or Low (Part 1 of 3). Catera

Step	Action	Value(s)	Yes	No
1	Was the Diagnostic System Check performed?	—	*Go to Step 2*	Go to *ABS Diagnostic System Check*
2	Inspect the WSS for physical damage. Is physical damage of the WSS evident?	—	*Go to Step 3*	*Go to Step 4*
3	Replace the WSS. Is the replacement complete?	—	*Go to Step 16*	—
4	1. Turn the ignition switch to the OFF position. 2. Disconnect the EBTCM. 3. Install the *J 39700* Universal Pinout Box using the J 39700-280 cable adapter to the EBTCM harness connector only. 4. Using *J 39200* DMM, measure the resistance between terminals 5 and 4 of *J 39700*. Is the resistance within the range specified in the value(s) column?	800–1700Ω	*Go to Step 11*	*Go to Step 5*
5	1. Disconnect the Wheel Speed Sensor. 2. Using *J 39200* DMM, measure the resistance between terminals 1 and 2 of the Wheel Speed Sensor Connector. Is the resistance within the range specified in the value(s) column?	800–1700Ω	*Go to Step 6*	*Go to Step 3*
6	Using *J 39200* DMM, measure the resistance between terminal 5 of *J 39700* and terminal 1 of the WSS harness connector. Is the resistance within the range specified in the value(s) column?	0-5Ω	*Go to Step 8*	*Go to Step 7*
7	Repair CKT PU251 for an open or high resistance. Is the repair complete?	—	*Go to Step 16*	—
8	Using *J 39200* DMM, measure the resistance between terminal 4 of *J 39700* and terminal 2 of the WSS harness connector. Is the resistance within the range specified in the value(s) column?	0-5Ω	*Go to Step 10*	*Go to Step 9*
9	Repair CKT XU251 for an open or high resistance. Is the repair complete?	—	*Go to Step 16*	—
10	Malfunction is intermittent. Inspect all connectors and harnesses for damage that may result in an open or high resistance when connected. Is the repair complete?	—	*Go to Step 16*	—

GC402980295700BX

Fig. 47 Code C0040: RH Front Wheel Speed Circuit Fault, High Or Low (Part 2 of 3). Catera

Step	Action	Value(s)	Yes	No
11	1. Disconnect the Wheel Speed Sensor. 2. Turn the ignition switch to the RUN position, engine off. 3. Using *J 39200* DMM, measure the voltage at terminal 5 of *J 39700.* Is the voltage within the range specified in the value(s) column?	Above 1V	*Go to Step 12*	*Go to Step 13*
12	Repair CKT PU251 for a short to voltage. Is the repair complete?	—	*Go to Step 16*	—
13	Using *J 39200* DMM, measure the voltage at terminal 4 of *J 39700.* Is the voltage within the range specified in the value(s) column?	Above 1V	*Go to Step 14*	*Go to Step 15*
14	Repair CKT XU251 for a short to voltage. Is the repair complete?	—	*Go to Step 16*	—
15	Replace the EBTCM. Is the replacement complete?	—	*Go to ABS Diagnostic System Check*	—
16	1. Reconnect all previously disconnected components. 2. Using a scan tool clear the DTC. 3. Remove the scan tool from the DLC. 4. Carefully drive the vehicle above 12 Km/h (8 mph) for several minutes. Does the DTC reset as a current DTC?	—	*Go to Step 2*	*Go to ABS Diagnostic System Check*

GC402980295700CX

Fig. 47 Code C0040: RH Front Wheel Speed Circuit Fault, High Or Low (Part 3 of 3). Catera

Circuit Description

The speed sensor used on this vehicle is a single point magnetic pickup. This sensor produces an AC signal that the EBTCM uses the frequency from to calculate the wheel speed.

Conditions for Setting the DTC

- The DTC will set if one wheel speed = 0 and the other WSS are greater than 40 Km/h (25 mph) for 10 ms.
- The DTC will set if during drive off, one wheel speed = 0, and the other WSS are greater than 12 Km/h (7.5 mph).
- The EBTCM detects a short to ground.

Action Taken When the DTC Sets

- A malfunction DTC stores.
- The ABS/TCS disables.
- The amber ABS/TCS indicator(s) turn on.

Conditions for Clearing the DTC

- The condition responsible for setting the DTC no longer exists and the scan tool Clear DTCs function is used.
- 100 ignition cycles pass with no DTC(s) detected.

Diagnostic Aids

- It is very important that a thorough inspection of the wiring and connectors be performed. Failure to carefully and fully inspect wiring and connectors may result in misdiagnosis, causing part replacement with reappearance of the malfunction.
- Thoroughly inspect any circuitry that may be causing the complaint for the following conditions:
  - Backed out terminals
  - Improper mating
  - Broken locks
  - Improperly formed or damaged terminals
  - Poor terminal-to-wiring connections
  - Physical damage to the wiring harness
- The following conditions may cause an intermittent malfunction:
  - A poor connection
  - Rubbed-through wire insulation
  - A broken wire inside the insulation
- If the customer's comments reflect that the amber ABS/TCS indicator is on only during moist environmental conditions (rain, snow, vehicle wash), inspect all the wheel speed sensor circuitry for signs of water intrusion. If the DTC is not current, clear all DTCs and simulate the effects of water intrusion by using the following procedure:
  1. Spray the suspected area with a five percent saltwater solution.
     Add two teaspoons of salt to twelve ounces of water to make a five percent saltwater solution.
  2. Test drive the vehicle over various road surfaces (bumps, turns, etc.) above 40 km/h (25 mph) for at least 30 seconds.
  3. If the DTC returns, replace the suspected harness.

Test Description

The number(s) below refer to the step number(s) on the diagnostic table.

4. This step checks for the proper resistance in the WSS.
5. This step checks for the proper WSS output.

GC402980295800AX

Fig. 48 Code C0040: RH Front Wheel Speed Circuit Fault, No Signal (Part 1 of 3). Catera

Step	Action	Value(s)	Yes	No
1	Was the Diagnostic System Check performed?	—	*Go to Step 2*	Go to *ABS Diagnostic System Check*
2	Inspect the WSS for physical damage. Is physical damage of the WSS evident?	—	*Go to Step 3*	*Go to Step 4*
3	Replace the WSS. Is the replacement complete?	—	*Go to Step 14*	—
4	1. Disconnect the WSS connector directly at the WSS. 2. Using *J 39200* DMM, measure the resistance between terminals 1 and 2 of the WSS. Is the resistance within the range specified in the value(s) column?	800–1700 Ω	*Go to Step 5*	*Go to Step 3*
5	1. With the *J 39200* DMM still connected to the WSS select the mV AC scale. 2. Spin the wheel at approximately 1 revolution per second by hand while monitoring the AC output. Is the AC voltage within the range specified in the value(s) column?	Above 30 mV	*Go to Step 6*	*Go to Step 3*
6	Using *J 39200* DMM, measure the resistance between the WSS terminal 1 and ground. Is the resistance within the range specified in the value(s) column?	OL (infinite)	*Go to Step 7*	*Go to Step 3*
7	1. Disconnect the EBTCM harness connector. 2. Install the *J 39700* Universal Pinout Box using the J 39700-280 cable adapter to the EBTCM harness connector only. 3. Using *J 39200* DMM, measure the resistance between terminals 5 and 4 of *J 39700.* Is the resistance within the range specified in the values column?	OL (infinite)	*Go to Step 9*	*Go to Step 8*
8	Repair short between CKT(s) PU251 and XU251. Is the repair complete?	—	*Go to Step 14*	—
9	Using *J 39200* DMM, measure the resistance between terminals 5 and 19 of *J 39700.* Is the resistance within the range specified in the values column?	OL (infinite)	*Go to Step 11*	*Go to Step 10*
10	Repair CKT PU251 for a short to ground. Is the repair complete?	—	*Go to Step 14*	—

GC402980295800BX

Fig. 48 Code C0040: RH Front Wheel Speed Circuit Fault, No Signal (Part 2 of 3). Catera

Step	Action	Value(s)	Yes	No
11	Using *J 39200* DMM, measure the resistance between terminals 4 and 19 of *J 39700.* Is the resistance within the range specified in the values column?	OL (infinite)	*Go to Step 13*	*Go to Step 12*
12	Repair CKT XU251 for a short to ground. Is the repair complete?	—	*Go to Step 14*	—
13	Replace the EBTCM. Is the replacement complete?	—	Go to *ABS Diagnostic System Check*	—
14	1. Reconnect all previously disconnected components. 2. Using a scan tool clear the DTC. 3. Remove the scan tool from the DLC. 4. Carefully drive vehicle above 12 Km/h (8 mph) for several minutes. Does the DTC reset as a current DTC?	—	*Go to Step 2*	Go to *ABS Diagnostic System Check*

GC402980295800CX

Fig. 48 Code C0040: RH Front Wheel Speed Circuit Fault, No Signal (Part 3 of 3). Catera

Circuit Description

The speed sensor used on this vehicle is a single point magnetic pickup. This sensor produces an AC signal that the EBTCM uses the frequency from to calculate the wheel speed.

Conditions for Setting the DTC

The DTC can be set any time the ignition is in the RUN position and the EBTCM detects an open or a short to voltage.

Action Taken When the DTC Sets

- A malfunction DTC stores.
- The ABS/TCS disables.
- The amber ABS/TC indicator(s) turn on.

Conditions for Clearing the DTC

- The condition responsible for setting the DTC no longer exists and the scan tool Clear DTCs function is used.
- 100 ignition cycles pass with no DTC(s) detected.

Diagnostic Aids

- It is very important that a thorough inspection of the wiring and connectors be performed. Failure to carefully and fully inspect wiring and connectors may result in misdiagnosis, causing part replacement with reappearance of the malfunction.
- Thoroughly inspect any circuitry that may be causing the complaint for the following conditions:
  - Backed out terminals
  - Improper mating
  - Broken locks
  - Improperly formed or damaged terminals
  - Poor terminal-to-wiring connections
  - Physical damage to the wiring harness
- The following conditions may cause an intermittent malfunction:
  - A poor connection
  - Rubbed-through wire insulation
  - A broken wire inside the insulation
- If the customer's comments reflect that the amber ABS/TCS indicator is on only during moist environmental conditions (rain, snow, vehicle wash), inspect all the wheel speed sensor circuitry for signs of water intrusion. If the DTC is not current, clear all DTCs and simulate the effects of water intrusion by using the following procedure:
  1. Spray the suspected area with a five percent saltwater solution.
     Add two teaspoons of salt to twelve ounces of water to make a five percent saltwater solution.
  2. Test drive the vehicle over various road surfaces (bumps, turns, etc.) above 40 km/h (25 mph) for at least 30 seconds.
  3. If the DTC returns, replace the suspected harness.

Test Description

The numbers below refer to step numbers on the diagnostic table.

4. This step checks for an open in the WSS or WSS CKT.
11. Checks for a short to voltage in the WSS CKT.
13. Checks for a short to voltage in the WSS CKT.

GC402980315900AX

Fig. 49 Code C0045: LH Rear Wheel Speed Circuit Fault, High Or Low (Part 1 of 3). Catera

Step	Action	Value(s)	Yes	No
1	Was the Diagnostic System Check performed?	—	Go to Step 2	Go to ABS Diagnostic System Check
2	Inspect the WSS for physical damage. Is physical damage of the WSS evident?	—	Go to Step 3	Go to Step 4
3	Replace the WSS. Is the replacement complete?	—	Go to Step 16	—
4	1. Turn the ignition switch to the OFF position. 2. Disconnect the EBTCM. 3. Install the *J 39700* Universal Pinout Box using the J 39700-280 cable adapter to the EBTCM harness connector only. 4. Using *J 39200* DMM, measure the resistance between terminals 9 and 8 of *J 39700*. Is the resistance within the range specified in the value(s) column?	800–1700Ω	Go to Step 11	Go to Step 5
5	1. Disconnect the Wheel Speed Sensor. 2. Using *J 39200* DMM, measure the resistance between terminals 1 and 2 of the Wheel Speed Sensor Connector. Is the resistance within the range specified in the value(s) column?	800–1700Ω	Go to Step 6	Go to Step 3
6	Using *J 39200* DMM, measure the resistance between terminal 9 of *J 39700* and terminal 1 of the WSS harness connector. Is the resistance within the range specified in the value(s) column?	0-5Ω	Go to Step 8	Go to Step 7
7	Repair CKT PM253 for an open or high resistance. Is the repair complete?	—	Go to Step 16	—
8	Using *J 39200* DMM, measure the resistance between terminal 8 of *J 39700* and terminal 2 of the WSS harness connector. Is the resistance within the range specified in the value(s) column?	0-5Ω	Go to Step 10	Go to Step 9
9	Repair CKT XM253 for an open or high resistance. Is the repair complete?	—	Go to Step 16	—
10	Malfunction is intermittent. Inspect all connectors and harnesses for damage that may result in an open or high resistance when connected. Is the repair complete?	—	Go to Step 16	—
11	1. Disconnect the Wheel Speed Sensor. 2. Turn the ignition switch to the RUN position, engine off. 3. Using *J 39200* DMM, measure the voltage at terminal 9 of *J 39700*. Is the voltage within the range specified in the value(s) column?	Above 1V	Go to Step 12	Go to Step 13

GC402980315900BX

Fig. 49 Code C0045: LH Rear Wheel Speed Circuit Fault, High Or Low (Part 2 of 3). Catera

Circuit Description

The speed sensor used on this vehicle is a single point magnetic pickup. This sensor produces an AC signal that the EBTCM uses the frequency from to calculate the wheel speed.

Conditions for Setting the DTC

- The DTC will set if one wheel speed = 0 and the other WSS are greater than 40 Km/h (25 mph) for 10 ms.
- The DTC will set if during drive off, one wheel speed = 0, and the other WSS are greater than 12 Km/h (7.5 mph).
- The EBTCM detects a short to ground.

Action Taken When the DTC Sets

- A malfunction DTC stores.
- The ABS/TCS disables.
- The amber ABS/TCS indicator(s) turn on.

Conditions for Clearing the DTC

- The condition responsible for setting the DTC no longer exists and the scan tool Clear DTCs function is used.
- 100 ignition cycles pass with no DTC(s) detected.

Diagnostic Aids

- It is very important that a thorough inspection of the wiring and connectors be performed. Failure to carefully and fully inspect wiring and connectors may result in misdiagnosis, causing part replacement with reappearance of the malfunction.
- Thoroughly inspect any circuitry that may be causing the complaint for the following conditions:
  - Backed out terminals
  - Improper mating
  - Broken locks
  - Improperly formed or damaged terminals
  - Poor terminal-to-wiring connections
  - Physical damage to the wiring harness
- The following conditions may cause an intermittent malfunction:
  - A poor connection
  - Rubbed-through wire insulation
  - A broken wire inside the insulation
- If the customer's comments reflect that the amber ABS/TCS indicator is on only during moist environmental conditions (rain, snow, vehicle wash), inspect all the wheel speed sensor circuitry for signs of water intrusion. If the DTC is not current, clear all DTCs and simulate the effects of water intrusion by using the following procedure:
  1. Spray the suspected area with a five percent saltwater solution.
     Add two teaspoons of salt to twelve ounces of water to make a five percent saltwater solution.
  2. Test drive the vehicle over various road surfaces (bumps, turns, etc.) above 40 km/h (25 mph) for at least 30 seconds.
  3. If the DTC returns, replace the suspected harness.

Test Description

The number(s) below refer to the step number(s) on the diagnostic table.

4. This step checks for the proper resistance in the WSS.
5. This step checks for the proper WSS output.

GC402980296000AX

Fig. 50 Code C0045: LH Rear Wheel Speed Circuit Fault, No Signal (Part 1 of 3). Catera

Step	Action	Value(s)	Yes	No
12	Repair CKT PM253 for a short to voltage. Is the repair complete?	—	Go to Step 16	—
13	Using *J 39200* DMM, measure the voltage at terminal 8 of *J 39700*. Is the voltage within the range specified in the value(s) column?	Above 1V	Go to Step 14	Go to Step 15
14	Repair CKT XM253 for a short to voltage. Is the repair complete?	—	Go to Step 16	—
15	Replace the EBTCM. Is the replacement complete?	—	Go to ABS Diagnostic System Check	—
16	1. Reconnect all previously disconnected components. 2. Using a scan tool clear the DTC. 3. Remove the scan tool from the DLC. 4. Carefully drive the vehicle above 12 Km/h (8 mph) for several minutes. Does the DTC reset as a current DTC?	—	Go to Step 2	Go to ABS Diagnostic System Check

GC402980295900CX

Fig. 49 Code C0045: LH Rear Wheel Speed Circuit Fault, High Or Low (Part 3 of 3). Catera

Step	Action	Value(s)	Yes	No
1	Was the Diagnostic System Check performed?	—	Go to Step 2	Go to ABS Diagnostic System Check
2	Inspect the WSS for physical damage. Is physical damage of the WSS evident?	—	Go to Step 3	Go to Step 4
3	Replace the WSS. Is the replacement complete?	—	Go to Step 14	—
4	1. Disconnect the WSS connector directly at the WSS. 2. Using *J 39200* DMM, measure the resistance between terminals 1 and 2 of the WSS. Is the resistance within the range specified in the value(s) column?	800–1700 Ω	Go to Step 5	Go to Step 3
5	1. With the *J 39200* DMM still connected to the WSS select the mV AC scale. 2. Spin the wheel at approximately 1 revolution per second by hand while monitoring the AC output. Is the AC voltage within the range specified in the value(s) column?	Above 30 mV	Go to Step 6	Go to Step 3
6	Using *J 39200* DMM, measure the resistance between the WSS terminal 1 and ground. Is the resistance within the range specified in the value(s) column?	OL (infinite)	Go to Step 7	Go to Step 3
7	1. Disconnect the EBTCM harness connector. 2. Install the *J 39700* Universal Pinout Box using the J 39700-280 cable adapter to the EBTCM harness connector only. 3. Using *J 39200* DMM, measure the resistance between terminals 9 and 8 of *J 39700*. Is the resistance within the range specified in the values column?	OL (infinite)	Go to Step 9	Go to Step 8
8	Repair short between CKT(s) PM253 and XM253. Is the repair complete?	—	Go to Step 14	—
9	Using *J 39200* DMM, measure the resistance between terminals 9 and 19 of *J 39700*. Is the resistance within the range specified in the values column?	OL (infinite)	Go to Step 11	Go to Step 10
10	Repair CKT PM253 for a short to ground. Is the repair complete?	—	Go to Step 14	—

GC402980296000BX

Fig. 50 Code C0045: LH Rear Wheel Speed Circuit Fault, No Signal (Part 2 of 3). Catera

Step	Action	Value(s)	Yes	No
11	Using *J 39200* DMM, measure the resistance between terminals 8 and 19 of *J 39700*. Is the resistance within the range specified in the values column?	OL (infinite)	Go to Step 13	Go to Step 12
12	Repair CKT XM253 for a short to ground. Is the repair complete?	—	Go to Step 14	—
13	Replace the EBTCM. Is the replacement complete?	—	Go to ABS Diagnostic System Check	—
14	1. Reconnect all previously disconnected components. 2. Using a scan tool clear the DTC. 3. Remove the scan tool from the DLC. 4. Carefully drive vehicle above 12 Km/h (8 mph) for several minutes. Does the DTC reset as a current DTC?	—	Go to Step 2	Go to ABS Diagnostic System Check

GC402980296000CX

Fig. 50 Code C0045: LH Rear Wheel Speed Circuit Fault, No Signal (Part 3 of 3). Catera

Circuit Description

The speed sensor used on this vehicle is a single point magnetic pickup. This sensor produces an AC signal that the EBTCM uses the frequency from to calculate the wheel speed.

Conditions for Setting the DTC

The DTC can be set any time the ignition is in the RUN position and the EBTCM detects an open or a short to voltage.

Action Taken When the DTC Sets

- A malfunction DTC stores.
- The ABS/TCS disables.
- The amber ABS/TC indicator(s) turn on.

Conditions for Clearing the DTC

- The condition responsible for setting the DTC no longer exists and the scan tool Clear DTCs function is used.
- 100 ignition cycles pass with no DTC(s) detected.

Diagnostic Aids

- It is very important that a thorough inspection of the wiring and connectors be performed. Failure to carefully and fully inspect wiring and connectors may result in misdiagnosis, causing part replacement with reappearance of the malfunction.
- Thoroughly inspect any circuitry that may be causing the complaint for the following conditions:
  - Backed out terminals
  - Improper mating
  - Broken locks
  - Improperly formed or damaged terminals
  - Poor terminal-to-wiring connections
  - Physical damage to the wiring harness
- The following conditions may cause an intermittent malfunction:
  - A poor connection
  - Rubbed-through wire insulation
  - A broken wire inside the insulation
- If the customer's comments reflect that the amber ABS/TCS indicator is on only during moist environmental conditions (rain, snow, vehicle wash), inspect all the wheel speed sensor circuitry for signs of water intrusion. If the DTC is not current, clear all DTCs and simulate the effects of water intrusion by using the following procedure:
  1. Spray the suspected area with a five percent saltwater solution.

     Add two teaspoons of salt to twelve ounces of water to make a five percent saltwater solution.
  2. Test drive the vehicle over various road surfaces (bumps, turns, etc.) above 40 km/h (25 mph) for at least 30 seconds.
  3. If the DTC returns, replace the suspected harness.

Test Description

The numbers below refer to step numbers on the diagnostic table.

4. This step checks for an open in the WSS or WSS CKT.
11. Checks for a short to voltage in the WSS CKT.
13. Checks for a short to voltage in the WSS CKT.

GC402980316100AX

Fig. 51 Code C0050: RH Rear Wheel Speed Circuit Fault, High Or Low (Part 1 of 3). Catera

The scan tool Serial Data Link (SDL) monitor used in this diagnostic is within the body portion of the scan tool. This requires exiting from the chassis portion of the scan tool to the main menu and entering into the body portion of the scan tool and selecting SDL MONITOR.

With the SDL monitor (ABS to Instrument Cluster Mode), any message that is being transmitted on the serial data link can be observed

The malfunction may be intermittent. Try performing the tests shown while "wiggling" wiring and connectors, this can often cause the malfunction to appear. PCM and BFC DTCs will likely be set along with DTC U1300.

DTC U1300 will only be able to be read as a history code since the scan tool uses the same serial data circuit. If CKT 1807 is shorted to ground, no communication with the scan tool will be possible.

Step	Action	Value(s)	Yes	No
1	Was the Diagnostic System Check performed?	—	Go to Step 2	Go to *Diagnostic System Check*
2	1. Disconnect the LH I/P Wiring Harness Junction Block connector C1. 2. Disconnect the EBCM harness connector. 3. Use the *J 39200* to measure the resistance between the EBCM harness connector terminal 12 and ground. Is the measured resistance within the specified value?	OL (Infinite)	Inspect Data Link Connector (DLC)	Go to Step 3
3	Repair the short to ground in CKT 1807. Is the repair complete?	—	Go to *Diagnostic System Check*	—

GC402980316100BX

Fig. 51 Code C0050: RH Rear Wheel Speed Circuit Fault, High Or Low (Part 2 of 3). Catera

Step	Action	Value(s)	Yes	No
12	Repair CKT PA253 for a short to voltage. Is the repair complete?	—	Go to Step 16	—
13	Using *J 39200* DMM, measure the voltage at terminal 1 of *J 39700.* Is the voltage within the range specified in the value(s) column?	Above 1V	Go to Step 14	Go to Step 15
14	Repair CKT XA253 for a short to voltage. Is the repair complete?	—	Go to Step 16	—
15	Replace the EBTCM. Is the replacement complete?	—	Go to *ABS Diagnostic System Check*	—
16	1. Reconnect all previously disconnected components. 2. Using a scan tool clear the DTC. 3. Remove the scan tool from the DLC. 4. Carefully drive the vehicle above 12 Km/h (8 mph) for several minutes. Does the DTC reset as a current DTC?	—	Go to Step 2	Go to *ABS Diagnostic System Check*

GC402980296100CX

Fig. 51 Code C0050: RH Rear Wheel Speed Circuit Fault, High Or Low (Part 3 of 3). Catera

Circuit Description

The speed sensor used on this vehicle is a single point magnetic pickup. This sensor produces an AC signal that the EBTCM uses the frequency from to calculate the wheel speed.

Conditions for Setting the DTC

- The DTC will set if one wheel speed = 0 and the other WSS are greater than 40 Km/h (25 mph) for 10 ms.
- The DTC will set if during off, one wheel speed = 0, and the other WSS are greater than 12 Km/h (7.5 mph).
- The EBTCM detects a short to ground.

Action Taken When the DTC Sets

- A malfunction DTC stores.
- The ABS/TCS disables.
- The amber ABS/TCS indicator(s) turn on.

Conditions for Clearing the DTC

- The condition responsible for setting the DTC no longer exists and the scan tool Clear DTCs function is used.
- 100 ignition cycles pass with no DTC(s) detected.

Diagnostic Aids

- It is very important that a thorough inspection of the wiring and connectors be performed. Failure to carefully and fully inspect wiring and connectors may result in misdiagnosis, causing part replacement with reappearance of the malfunction.
- Thoroughly inspect any circuitry that may be causing the complaint for the following conditions:
  - Backed out terminals
  - Improper mating
  - Broken locks
  - Improperly formed or damaged terminals
  - Poor terminal-to-wiring connections
  - Physical damage to the wiring harness
- The following conditions may cause an intermittent malfunction:
  - A poor connection
  - Rubbed-through wire insulation
  - A broken wire inside the insulation
- If the customer's comments reflect that the amber ABS/TCS indicator is on only during moist environmental conditions (rain, snow, vehicle wash), inspect all the wheel speed sensor circuitry for signs of water intrusion. If the DTC is not current, clear all DTCs and simulate the effects of water intrusion by using the following procedure:
  1. Spray the suspected area with a five percent saltwater solution.

     Add two teaspoons of salt to twelve ounces of water to make a five percent saltwater solution.
  2. Test drive the vehicle over various road surfaces (bumps, turns, etc.) above 40 km/h (25 mph) for at least 30 seconds.
  3. If the DTC returns, replace the suspected harness.

Test Description

The number(s) below refer to the step number(s) on the diagnostic table.

4. This step checks for the proper resistance in the WSS.
5. This step checks for the proper WSS output.

GC402980296200AX

Fig. 52 Code C0050: RH Rear Wheel Speed Circuit Fault, No Signal (Part 1 of 3). Catera

Step	Action	Value(s)	Yes	No
1	Was the Diagnostic System Check performed?	—	Go to Step 2	Go to *ABS Diagnostic System Check*
2	Inspect the WSS for physical damage. Is physical damage of the WSS evident?	—	Go to Step 3	Go to Step 4
3	Replace the WSS. Is the replacement complete?	—	Go to Step 14	—
4	1. Disconnect the WSS connector directly at the WSS. 2. Using *J 39200* DMM, measure the resistance between terminals 1 and 2 of the WSS. Is the resistance within the range specified in the value(s) column?	800–1700 Ω	Go to Step 5	Go to Step 3
5	1. With the *J 39200* DMM still connected to the WSS select the mV AC scale. 2. Spin the wheel at approximately 1 revolution per second by hand while monitoring the AC output. Is the AC voltage within the range specified in the value(s) column?	Above 30 mV	Go to Step 6	Go to Step 3
6	Using *J 39200* DMM, measure the resistance between the WSS terminal 1 and ground. Is the resistance within the range specified in the value(s) column?	OL (infinite)	Go to Step 7	Go to Step 3
7	1. Disconnect the EBTCM harness connector. 2. Install the *J 39700* Universal Pinout Box using the J 39700-280 cable adapter to the EBTCM harness connector only. 3. Using *J 39200* DMM, measure the resistance between terminals 2 and 1 of *J 39700.* Is the resistance within the range specified in the values column?	OL (infinite)	Go to Step 9	Go to Step 8
8	Repair short between CKT(s) PA253 and XA253. Is the repair complete?	—	Go to Step 14	—
9	Using *J 39200* DMM, measure the resistance between terminals 2 and 19 of *J 39700.* Is the resistance within the range specified in the values column?	OL (infinite)	Go to Step 11	Go to Step 10
10	Repair CKT PA253 for a short to ground. Is the repair complete?	—	Go to Step 14	—

GC402980296200BX

Fig. 52 Code C0050: RH Rear Wheel Speed Circuit Fault, No Signal (Part 2 of 3). Catera

Step	Action	Value(s)	Yes	No
11	Using *J 39200* DMM, measure the resistance between terminals 1 and 19 of *J 39700*. Is the resistance within the range specified in the values column?	OL (infinite)	*Go to Step 13*	*Go to Step 12*
12	Repair CKT XA253 for a short to ground. Is the repair complete?	—	*Go to Step 14*	—
13	Replace the EBTCM. Is the replacement complete?	—	*Go to ABS Diagnostic System Check*	—
14	1. Reconnect all previously disconnected components. 2. Using a scan tool clear the DTC. 3. Remove the scan tool from the DLC. 4. Carefully drive vehicle above 12 Km/h (8 mph) for several minutes. Does the DTC reset as a current DTC?	—	*Go to Step 2*	*Go to ABS Diagnostic System Check*

GC402980296200CX

Fig. 52 Code C0050: RH Rear Wheel Speed Circuit Fault, No Signal (Part 3 of 3). Catera

Step	Action	Value(s)	Yes	No
1	Was the Diagnostic System Check performed?	—	*Go to Step 2*	*Go to ABS Diagnostic System Check*
2	1. Turn the ignition switch to the OFF position. 2. Install a scan tool. 3. Turn the ignition switch to the RUN position, engine off. 4. Using the scan tool run the Automated test. Does DTC C0060 reset as a current DTC?	—	*Go to Step 3*	*Go to ABS Diagnostic System Check*
3	Replace the EBTCM. Is the repair complete?	—	*Go to ABS Diagnostic System Check*	—

GC402980296300BX

Fig. 53 Code C0060: LH Front ABS Solenoid Circuit No. 1 Fault (Part 2 of 2). Catera

Step	Action	Value(s)	Yes	No
1	Was the Diagnostic System Check performed?	—	*Go to Step 2*	*Go to ABS Diagnostic System Check*
2	1. Turn the ignition switch to the OFF position. 2. Install a scan tool. 3. Turn the ignition switch to the RUN position, engine off. 4. Using the scan tool run the Automated test. Does DTC C0065 reset as a current DTC?	—	*Go to Step 3*	*Go to ABS Diagnostic System Check*
3	Replace the EBTCM. Is the repair complete?	—	*Go to ABS Diagnostic System Check*	—

GC402980296400BX

Fig. 54 Code C0065: LH Front ABS Solenoid Circuit No. 2 Fault (Part 2 of 2). Catera

Step	Action	Value(s)	Yes	No
1	Was the Diagnostic System Check performed?	—	*Go to Step 2*	*Go to ABS Diagnostic System Check*
2	1. Turn the ignition switch to the OFF position. 2. Install a scan tool. 3. Turn the ignition switch to the RUN position, engine off. 4. Using the scan tool run the Automated test. Does DTC C0070 reset as a current DTC?	—	*Go to Step 3*	*Go to ABS Diagnostic System Check*
3	Replace the EBTCM. Is the repair complete?	—	*Go to ABS Diagnostic System Check*	—

GC402980296500BX

Fig. 55 Code C0070: RH Front ABS Solenoid Circuit No. 1 Fault (Part 2 of 2). Catera

Step	Action	Value(s)	Yes	No
1	Was the Diagnostic System Check performed?	—	*Go to Step 2*	*Go to ABS Diagnostic System Check*
2	1. Turn the ignition switch to the OFF position. 2. Install a scan tool. 3. Turn the ignition switch to the RUN position, engine off. 4. Using the scan tool run the Automated test. Does DTC C0085 reset as a current DTC?	—	*Go to Step 3*	*Go to ABS Diagnostic System Check*
3	Replace the EBTCM. Is the repair complete?	—	*Go to ABS Diagnostic System Check*	—

GC402980296600BX

Fig. 56 Code C0075: RH Front ABS Solenoid Circuit No. 2 Fault (Part 2 of 2). Catera

Circuit Description

The outlet valve solenoid circuits are supplied with battery power when the ignition is in the run position. The EBTCM controls the valve functions by grounding the circuit when necessary.

Conditions for Setting the DTC

The EBTCM senses a discrepancy such as an open, short to ground, or short to voltage in the circuit.

Action Taken When the DTC Sets

- A malfunction DTC is stored.
- ABS/TCS is disabled.
- The ABS and TC Indicators are turned on.

Conditions for Clearing the DTC

- Condition for DTC is no longer present and scan tool clear DTC function is used.
- 100 ignition cycles pass with no DTC(s) detected.

Diagnostic Aids

The solenoid valve circuit and the solenoid coil are internal to the EBTCM. No part of the solenoid circuit is diagnosable external to the EBTCM. The DTC sets when there is a malfunction in the solenoid circuit internal to the EBTCM only.

Test Description

The numbers below refer to step numbers on the Diagnostic Table.

2. This step determines if the DTC is current.

GC402980296300AX

Fig. 53 Code C0060: LH Front ABS Solenoid Circuit No. 1 Fault (Part 1 of 2). Catera

Circuit Description

The inlet valve solenoid circuits are supplied with battery power when the ignition is in the run position. The EBTCM controls the valve functions by grounding the circuit when necessary.

Conditions for Setting the DTC

The EBTCM senses a discrepancy such as an open, short to ground, or short to voltage in the circuit.

Action Taken When the DTC Sets

- A malfunction DTC is stored.
- ABS/TCS is disabled.
- The ABS and TC Indicators are turned on.

Conditions for Clearing the DTC

- Condition for DTC is no longer present and scan tool clear DTC function is used.
- 100 ignition cycles pass with no DTC(s) detected.

Diagnostic Aids

The solenoid valve circuit and the solenoid coil are internal to the EBTCM. No part of the solenoid circuit is diagnosable external to the EBTCM. The DTC sets when there is a malfunction in the solenoid circuit internal to the EBTCM only.

Test Description

The numbers below refer to step numbers on the Diagnostic Table.

2. This step determines if the DTC is current.

GC402980296400AX

Fig. 54 Code C0065: LH Front ABS Solenoid Circuit No. 2 Fault (Part 1 of 2). Catera

Circuit Description

The outlet valve solenoid circuits are supplied with battery power when the ignition is in the run position. The EBTCM controls the valve functions by grounding the circuit when necessary.

Conditions for Setting the DTC

The EBTCM senses a discrepancy such as an open, short to ground, or short to voltage in the circuit.

Action Taken When the DTC Sets

- A malfunction DTC is stored.
- ABS/TCS is disabled.
- The ABS and TC Indicators are turned on.

Conditions for Clearing the DTC

- Condition for DTC is no longer present and scan tool clear DTC function is used.
- 100 ignition cycles pass with no DTC(s) detected.

Diagnostic Aids

The solenoid valve circuit and the solenoid coil are internal to the EBTCM. No part of the solenoid circuit is diagnosable external to the EBTCM. The DTC sets when there is a malfunction in the solenoid circuit internal to the EBTCM only.

Test Description

The numbers below refer to step numbers on the Diagnostic Table.

2. This step determines if the DTC is current.

GC402980296500AX

Fig. 55 Code C0070: RH Front ABS Solenoid Circuit No. 1 Fault (Part 1 of 2). Catera

Circuit Description

The inlet valve solenoid circuits are supplied with battery power when the ignition is in the run position. The EBTCM controls the valve functions by grounding the circuit when necessary.

Conditions for Setting the DTC

The EBTCM senses a discrepancy such as an open, short to ground, or short to voltage in the circuit.

Action Taken When the DTC Sets

- A malfunction DTC is stored.
- ABS/TCS is disabled.
- The ABS and TC Indicators are turned on.

Conditions for Clearing the DTC

- Condition for DTC is no longer present and scan tool clear DTC function is used.
- 100 ignition cycles pass with no DTC(s) detected.

Diagnostic Aids

The solenoid valve circuit and the solenoid coil are internal to the EBTCM. No part of the solenoid circuit is diagnosable external to the EBTCM. The DTC sets when there is a malfunction in the solenoid circuit internal to the EBTCM only.

Test Description

The numbers below refer to step numbers on the Diagnostic Table.

2. This step determines if the DTC is current.

GC402980296600AX

Fig. 56 Code C0075: RH Front ABS Solenoid Circuit No. 2 Fault (Part 1 of 2). Catera

Circuit Description

The outlet valve solenoid circuits are supplied with battery power when the ignition is in the run position. The EBTCM controls the valve functions by grounding the circuit when necessary.

Conditions for Setting the DTC

The EBTCM senses a discrepancy such as an open, short to ground, or short to voltage in the circuit.

Action Taken When the DTC Sets

- A malfunction DTC is stored.
- ABS/TCS is disabled.
- The ABS and TC Indicators are turned on.

Conditions for Clearing the DTC

- Condition for DTC is no longer present and scan tool clear DTC function is used.
- 100 ignition cycles pass with no DTC(s) detected.

Diagnostic Aids

The solenoid valve circuit and the solenoid coil are internal to the EBTCM. No part of the solenoid circuit is diagnosable external to the EBTCM. The DTC sets when there is a malfunction in the solenoid circuit internal to the EBTCM only.

Test Description

The numbers below refer to step numbers on the Diagnostic Table.

2. This step determines if the DTC is current.

GC402980296700AX

Fig. 57 Codes C0080: LH Rear ABS Solenoid Circuit No. 1 Fault (Part 1 of 2). Catera

Step	Action	Value(s)	Yes	No
1	Was the Diagnostic System Check performed?	—	Go to Step 2	Go to ABS Diagnostic System Check
2	1. Turn the ignition switch to the OFF position. 2. Install a scan tool. 3. Turn the ignition switch to the RUN position, engine off. 4. Using the scan tool run the Automated test. Does DTC C0080 reset as a current DTC?	—	Go to Step 3	Go to ABS Diagnostic System Check
3	Replace the EBTCM. Is the repair complete?	—	Go to ABS Diagnostic System Check	—

GC402980296700BX

Fig. 57 Codes C0080: LH Rear ABS Solenoid Circuit No. 1 Fault (Part 2 of 2). Catera

Step	Action	Value(s)	Yes	No
1	Was the Diagnostic System Check performed?	—	Go to Step 2	Go to ABS Diagnostic System Check
2	1. Turn the ignition switch to the OFF position. 2. Install a scan tool. 3. Turn the ignition switch to the RUN position, engine off. 4. Using the scan tool run the Automated test. Does DTC C0085 reset as a current DTC?	—	Go to Step 3	Go to ABS Diagnostic System Check
3	Replace the EBTCM. Is the repair complete?	—	Go to ABS Diagnostic System Check	—

GC402980296800BX

Fig. 58 Code C0085: LH Rear ABS Solenoid Circuit No. 2 Fault (Part 2 of 2). Catera

Step	Action	Value(s)	Yes	No
1	Was the Diagnostic System Check performed?	—	Go to Step 2	Go to ABS Diagnostic System Check
2	1. Turn the ignition switch to the OFF position. 2. Install a scan tool. 3. Turn the ignition switch to the RUN position, engine off. 4. Using the scan tool run the Automated test. Does DTC C0090 reset as a current DTC?	—	Go to Step 3	Go to ABS Diagnostic System Check
3	Replace the EBTCM. Is the repair complete?	—	Go to ABS Diagnostic System Check	—

GC402980296900BX

Fig. 59 Code C0090: LH Rear ABS Solenoid Circuit No. 1 Fault (Part 2 of 2). Catera

Step	Action	Value(s)	Yes	No
1	Was the Diagnostic System Check performed?	—	Go to Step 2	Go to ABS Diagnostic System Check
2	1. Turn the ignition switch to the OFF position. 2. Install a scan tool. 3. Turn the ignition switch to the RUN position, engine off. 4. Using the scan tool run the Automated test. Does DTC C0095 reset as a current DTC?	—	Go to Step 3	Go to ABS Diagnostic System Check
3	Replace the EBTCM. Is the repair complete?	—	Go to ABS Diagnostic System Check	—

GC402980297000BX

Fig. 60 Code C0095: LH Rear ABS Solenoid Circuit No. 2 Fault (Part 2 of 2). Catera

Circuit Description

The inlet valve solenoid circuits are supplied with battery power when the ignition is in the run position. The EBTCM controls the valve functions by grounding the circuit when necessary.

Conditions for Setting the DTC

The EBTCM senses a discrepancy such as an open, short to ground, or short to voltage in the circuit.

Action Taken When the DTC Sets

- A malfunction DTC is stored.
- ABS/TCS is disabled.
- The ABS and TC Indicators are turned on.

Conditions for Clearing the DTC

- Condition for DTC is no longer present and scan tool clear DTC function is used.
- 100 ignition cycles pass with no DTC(s) detected.

Diagnostic Aids

The solenoid valve circuit and the solenoid coil are internal to the EBTCM. No part of the solenoid circuit is diagnosable external to the EBTCM. The DTC sets when there is a malfunction in the solenoid circuit internal to the EBTCM only.

Test Description

The numbers below refer to step numbers on the Diagnostic Table.

2. This step determines if the DTC is current.

GC402980296800AX

Fig. 58 Code C0085: LH Rear ABS Solenoid Circuit No. 2 Fault (Part 1 of 2). Catera

Circuit Description

The outlet valve solenoid circuits are supplied with battery power when the ignition is in the run position. The EBTCM controls the valve functions by grounding the circuit when necessary.

Conditions for Setting the DTC

The EBTCM senses a discrepancy such as an open, short to ground, or short to voltage in the circuit.

Action Taken When the DTC Sets

- A malfunction DTC is stored.
- ABS/TCS is disabled.
- The ABS and TC Indicators are turned on.

Conditions for Clearing the DTC

- Condition for DTC is no longer present and scan tool clear DTC function is used.
- 100 ignition cycles pass with no DTC(s) detected.

Diagnostic Aids

The solenoid valve circuit and the solenoid coil are internal to the EBTCM. No part of the solenoid circuit is diagnosable external to the EBTCM. The DTC sets when there is a malfunction in the solenoid circuit internal to the EBTCM only.

Test Description

The numbers below refer to step numbers on the Diagnostic Table.

2. This step determines if the DTC is current.

GC402980296900AX

Fig. 59 Code C0090: LH Rear ABS Solenoid Circuit No. 1 Fault (Part 1 of 2). Catera

Circuit Description

The inlet valve solenoid circuits are supplied with battery power when the ignition is in the run position. The EBTCM controls the valve functions by grounding the circuit when necessary.

Conditions for Setting the DTC

The EBTCM senses a discrepancy such as an open, short to ground, or short to voltage in the circuit.

Action Taken When the DTC Sets

- A malfunction DTC is stored.
- ABS/TCS is disabled.
- The ABS and TC Indicators are turned on.

Conditions for Clearing the DTC

- Condition for DTC is no longer present and scan tool clear DTC function is used.
- 100 ignition cycles pass with no DTC(s) detected.

Diagnostic Aids

The solenoid valve circuit and the solenoid coil are internal to the EBTCM. No part of the solenoid circuit is diagnosable external to the EBTCM. The DTC sets when there is a malfunction in the solenoid circuit internal to the EBTCM only.

Test Description

The numbers below refer to step numbers on the Diagnostic Table.

2. This step determines if the DTC is current.

GC402980297000AX

Fig. 60 Code C0095: LH Rear ABS Solenoid Circuit No. 2 Fault (Part 1 of 2). Catera

Circuit Description

The pump motor is an integral part of the BPMV, while the pump motor relay is integral to the EBTCM. The pump motor relay is not engaged during normal system operation. When ABS or TCS operation is required, the EBTCM activates the pump motor relay and battery power is provided to the pump motor.

Conditions for Setting the DTC

- Pump motor voltage is not present 60 milliseconds after activation of the pump motor relay.
- Pump motor voltage is present for more than 2.5 seconds with no activation of the pump motor relay.
- Pump motor voltage is not present for at least 40 milliseconds after the pump motor relay is commanded off.

Action Taken When the DTC Sets

- A malfunction DTC stores.
- The ABS/TCS disables.
- The amber ABS/TCS indicator(s) turn on.

Conditions for Clearing the DTC

- The condition responsible for setting the DTC no longer exists and the scan tool Clear DTCs function is used.
- 100 ignition cycles pass with no DTC(s) detected.

Diagnostic Aids

- It is very important that a thorough inspection of the wiring and connectors be performed. Failure to carefully and fully inspect wiring and connectors may result in misdiagnosis, causing part replacement with reappearance of the malfunction.
- Thoroughly inspect any circuitry that may be causing the complaint for the following conditions:
  - Backed out terminals
  - Improper mating
  - Broken locks
  - Improperly formed or damaged terminals
  - Poor terminal-to-wiring connections
  - Physical damage to the wiring harness

GC402980297100AX

Fig. 61 Code C0110: Pump Motor Circuit Fault (Part 1 of 3). Catera

- The following conditions may cause an intermittent malfunction:
  - A poor connection
  - Rubbed-through wire insulation
  - A broken wire inside the insulation

A disconnected pump motor connector will cause this malfunction.

Test Description

The numbers below refer to step numbers on the diagnostic table.

4. This step checks for a short to ground in CKT 302.
10. This step checks for an open in CKT 302.
14. This step checks for a mechanical malfunction with the pump motor or the pump. This step also cleans the commutator and brushes of the pump motor prior to the resistance check in step 15.

Step	Action	Value(s)	Yes	No
1	Was the Diagnostic System Check performed?	—	*Go to Step 2*	Go to *ABS Diagnostic System Check*
2	Inspect the 80A Fuse V4 Maxifuse®, in the Power Distribution Fuse Box. Is the fuse OK?	—	*Go to Step 7*	*Go to Step 3*
3	1. Install a new 80A Fuse V4 Maxifuse®. 2. Turn the ignition switch from the OFF to RUN position, engine OFF. 3. Using a scan tool in ABS/TCS Special Functions attempt to run the Automated test. 4. Recheck the 80A Fuse V4 Maxifuse®. Is the fuse OK?	—	*Go to Step 16*	*Go to Step 4*
4	1. Turn the Ignition switch to the OFF position. 2. Remove the 80A Fuse V4 Maxifuse®. 3. Disconnect the EBTCM connector C1. 4. Connect the *J 39700* Universal Pinout Box using the J 39700-280 cable adapter to the EBTCM harness connector only. 5. Using *J 39200* DMM, measure the resistance between terminals 18 and 19 of *J 39700*. Is the resistance within the range specified in the value(s) column?	OL (infinite)	*Go to Step 5*	*Go to Step 12*
5	1. Disconnect the EBTCM pump motor connector C2. 2. Connect a 10A fused jumper wire between the pump motor connector C2 terminal 2 and battery voltage. 3. Connect a jumper wire between the pump motor connector C2 terminal 1 and ground. Only attempt to run the pump motor for 5 seconds. 4. Disconnect the jumper wires. 5. Inspect the 10A fuse in the jumper wire. Is the fuse OK?	—	*Go to Step 11*	*Go to Step 6*
6	Replace the BPMV. Is the replacement complete?	—	*Go to Step 16*	—

GC402980297100BX

Fig. 61 Code C0110: Pump Motor Circuit Fault (Part 2 of 3). Catera

Step	Action	Value(s)	Yes	No
7	1. Turn the Ignition switch to the OFF position. 2. Disconnect the EBTCM connector C1. 3. Connect *J 39700* Universal Pinout Box using the J 39700-280 cable adaptor to the EBTCM harness connector C1 only. 4. Using *J 39200* DMM, measure the resistance between terminals 16 and 19 of *J 39700*. Is the resistance within the range specified in the value(s) column?	0–5 Ω	*Go to Step 9*	*Go to Step 8*
8	Repair CKT F372 for an open or high resistance. Is the repair complete?	—	*Go to Step 16*	—
9	1. Install the fuse if removed. 2. Using *J 39200* DMM, measure the voltage at the 80A Fuse V4 Maxifuse® by probing between the fuse test terminals and a good ground. Is the voltage within the range specified in the value(s) column?	Battery volts	*Go to Step 10*	Inspect Power Distribution
10	Using *J 39200* DMM, measure the voltage at terminal 18 and terminal 17 of *J 39700*. Is the voltage within the range specified in the value(s) column at both terminals?	Battery volts	*Go to Step 14*	*Go to Step 13*
11	Replace EBTCM. Is the replacement complete?	—	Go to *ABS Diagnostic System Check*	—
12	Repair short to ground in CKT A291 or A290. Is the repair complete?	—	*Go to Step 16*	—
13	Repair open in CKT A291 and A290. Is the repair complete?	—	*Go to Step 16*	—
14	1. Disconnect the EBTCM pump motor connector C2. 2. Connect a 10A fused jumper wire between the pump motor connector C2 terminal 2 and battery voltage. 3. Connect a jumper wire between the pump motor connector C2 terminal 1 and ground. Only attempt to run the pump motor for 5 seconds. 4. Disconnect the jumper wires. 5. Inspect the 10A fuse in the jumper wire. Is the fuse OK?	—	*Go to Step 15*	*Go to Step 6*
15	1. Zero the *J 39200* DMM leads. 2. Using *J 39200* DMM, measure the resistance between terminals 1 and 2 of the pump motor connector C2. Is the resistance within the range specified in the value(s) column?	0–4 Ω	*Go to Step 11*	*Go to Step 6*
16	1. Reconnect all previously disconnected components. 2. Using a scan tool clear the DTC. 3. Remove the scan tool from the DLC. 4. Carefully drive the vehicle above 12 Km/h (8 mph) for several minutes. Does the DTC reset as a current DTC?	—	*Go to Step 2*	Go to *ABS Diagnostic System Check*

GC402980297100CX

Fig. 61 Code C0110: Pump Motor Circuit Fault (Part 3 of 3). Catera

Circuit Description

The solenoid valve relay supplies power to the solenoid valve coils in the EBTCM. The solenoid valve relay, located in the EBTCM, is activated whenever the ignition switch is in the RUN position and no faults are present. The solenoid valve relay remains engaged until the ignition is turned OFF or a failure is detected.

Conditions for Setting the DTC

- DTC C0121 will set anytime the solenoid valve relay is commanded on and the EBTCM does not see battery voltage at the solenoid valves.
- DTC C0121 will set anytime the EBTCM commands the solenoid valve relay off and battery voltage is still present at the solenoid valves.

Action Taken When the DTC Sets

- A malfunction DTC stores.
- The ABS/TCS disables.
- The amber ABS/TCS indicator(s) turn on.

Conditions for Clearing the DTC

- The condition responsible for setting the DTC no longer exists and the scan tool Clear DTCs function is used.
- 100 ignition cycles pass with no DTC(s) detected.

Diagnostic Aids

- It is very important that a thorough inspection of the wiring and connectors be performed. Failure to carefully and fully inspect wiring and connectors may result in misdiagnosis, causing part replacement with reappearance of the malfunction.
- Thoroughly inspect any circuitry that may be causing the complaint for the following conditions:
  - Backed out terminals
  - Improper mating
  - Broken locks
  - Improperly formed or damaged terminals
  - Poor terminal-to-wiring connections
  - Physical damage to the wiring harness

GC402980297200AX

Fig. 62 Code C0121: Valve Relay Circuit Fault (Part 1 of 3). Catera

- The following conditions may cause an intermittent malfunction:
  - A poor connection
  - Rubbed-through wire insulation
  - A broken wire inside the insulation
- The solenoid valve relay is an integral part of the EBTCM and is not serviced separately.

Test Description

The numbers below refer to step numbers on the diagnostic table.

4. This step checks for a short to ground in CKTs A291 or A290.
6. This step checks for an open in CKTs A291 and A290.

Step	Action	Value(s)	Yes	No
1	Was the Diagnostic System Check performed?	—	*Go to Step 2*	Go to *ABS Diagnostic System Check*
2	Inspect the 80A Fuse V4 Maxifuse® in the Power Distribution Fuse Box. Is the fuse OK?	—	*Go to Step 5*	*Go to Step 3*
3	1. Install a new 80A Fuse V4 Maxifuse®. 2. Turn the ignition switch from the OFF to RUN position, engine OFF. 3. Using a scan tool in ABS/TCS Special Functions attempt to run the AUTOMATED test. 4. Recheck the fuse. Is the fuse OK?	—	*Go to Step 10*	*Go to Step 4*
4	1. Turn the Ignition switch to the OFF position. 2. Remove the Fuse V4 Maxifuse®. 3. Disconnect the EBTCM connector C1. 4. Connect the *J 39700* Universal Pinout Box using the J 39700-280 cable adapter to the EBTCM harness connector only. 5. Using *J 39200* DMM, measure the resistance between terminals 18 and 19 of *J 39700*. Is the resistance within the range specified in the value(s) column?	OL (infinite)	*Go to Step 7*	*Go to Step 8*
5	1. Replace the Fuse V4 Maxifuse®. 2. Using *J 39200* DMM, measure the voltage between the Fuse V4 test terminals and a good ground. Is the voltage within the range specified in the value(s) column?	Battery volts	*Go to Step 6*	**Inspect** Power Distribution
6	Using *J 39200* DMM, measure the voltage at terminal 18 and 17 of *J 39700*. Is the voltage within the range specified in the value(s) column at both terminals?	Battery volts	*Go to Step 7*	*Go to Step 9*

GC402980297200CX

Fig. 62 Code C0121: Valve Relay Circuit Fault (Part 2 of 3). Catera

Step	Action	Value(s)	Yes	No
7	1. Turn the ignition switch to the OFF position. 2. Disconnect the EBTCM connector C1. 3. Connect *J 39700* Universal Pinout Box using the J 39700-280 cable adaptor to the EBTCM harness connector C1 only. 4. Using *J 39200* DMM, measure the resistance between terminals 16 and 19 of *J 39700*. Is the resistance within the range specified in the value(s) column?	0–5 Ω	*Go to Step 9*	*Go to Step 8*
8	Repair CKT F372 for an open or high resistance. Is the repair complete?	—	*Go to Step 16*	—
9	1. Install the fuse if removed. 2. Using *J 39200* DMM, measure the voltage at the 80A Fuse V4 Maxifuse® by probing between the fuse test terminals and a good ground. Is the voltage within the range specified in the value(s) column?	Battery volts	*Go to Step 10*	Inspect Power Distribution
10	Using *J 39200* DMM, measure the voltage at terminal 18 and terminal 17 of *J 39700*. Is the voltage within the range specified in the value(s) column at both terminals?	Battery volts	*Go to Step 14*	*Go to Step 13*
11	Replace EBTCM. Is the replacement complete?	—	Go to *ABS Diagnostic System Check*	—
12	Repair short to ground in CKT A291 or A290. Is the repair complete?	—	*Go to Step 16*	—
13	Repair open in CKT A291 and A290. Is the repair complete?	—	*Go to Step 16*	—
14	1. Disconnect the EBTCM pump motor connector C2. 2. Connect a 10A fused jumper wire between the pump motor connector C2 terminal 2 and battery voltage. 3. Connect a jumper wire between the pump motor connector C2 terminal 1 and ground. Only attempt to run the pump motor for 5 seconds. 4. Disconnect the jumper wires. 5. Inspect the 10A fuse in the jumper wire. Is the fuse OK?	—	*Go to Step 15*	*Go to Step 6*
15	1. Zero the *J 39200* DMM leads. 2. Using *J 39200* DMM, measure the resistance between terminals 1 and 2 of the pump motor connector C2. Is the resistance within the range specified in the value(s) column?	0–4 Ω	*Go to Step 11*	*Go to Step 6*
16	1. Reconnect all previously disconnected components. 2. Using a scan tool clear the DTC. 3. Remove the scan tool from the DLC. 4. Carefully drive the vehicle above 12 Km/h (8 mph) for several minutes. Does the DTC reset as a current DTC?	—	*Go to Step 2*	Go to *ABS Diagnostic System Check*

GC402980297200BX

Fig. 62 Code C0121: Valve Relay Circuit Fault (Part 3 of 3). Catera

Step	Action	Value(s)	Yes	No
1	Was the Diagnostic System Check performed?	—	*Go to Step 2*	Go to *ABS Diagnostic System Check*
2	1. Turn the ignition switch to the OFF position. 2. Install a scan tool. 3. Turn the ignition switch to the RUN position, engine off. 4. Using the scan tool run the Automated test. Does DTC C00141 reset as a current DTC?	—	*Go to Step 3*	Go to *ABS Diagnostic System Check*
3	Replace the EBTCM. Is the repair complete?	—	Go to *ABS Diagnostic System Check*	—

GC402980297300BX

Fig. 63 Code C0141: LH TCS Solenoid Circuit No. 1 Fault (Part 2 of 2). Catera

Step	Action	Value(s)	Yes	No
1	Was the Diagnostic System Check performed?	—	*Go to Step 2*	Go to *ABS Diagnostic System Check*
2	1. Turn the ignition switch to the OFF position. 2. Install a scan tool. 3. Turn the ignition switch to the RUN position, engine off. 4. Using the scan tool run the Automated test. Does DTC C00146 reset as a current DTC?	—	*Go to Step 3*	Go to *ABS Diagnostic System Check*
3	Replace the EBTCM. Is the repair complete?	—	Go to *ABS Diagnostic System Check*	—

GC402980297400BX

Fig. 64 Code C0146: LH TCS Solenoid Circuit No. 2 Fault (Part 2 of 2). Catera

Circuit Description

The prime valve solenoid circuits are supplied with battery power when the ignition is in the run position. The EBTCM controls the valve functions by grounding the circuit when necessary.

Conditions for Setting the DTC

The EBTCM senses a discrepancy such as an open, short to ground, or short to voltage in the circuit.

Action Taken When the DTC Sets

- A malfunction DTC is stored.
- ABS/TCS is disabled.
- The ABS and TC Indicators are turned on.

Conditions for Clearing the DTC

- Condition for DTC is no longer present and scan tool clear DTC function is used.
- 100 ignition cycles pass with no DTC(s) detected.

Diagnostic Aids

The solenoid valve circuit and the solenoid coil are internal to the EBTCM. No part of the solenoid circuit is diagnosable external to the EBTCM. The DTC sets when there is a malfunction in the solenoid circuit internal to the EBTCM only.

Test Description

The numbers below refer to step numbers on the Diagnostic Table.

2. This step determines if the DTC is current.

GC402980297300AX

Fig. 63 Code C0141: LH TCS Solenoid Circuit No. 1 Fault (Part 1 of 2). Catera

Circuit Description

The isolation valve solenoid circuits are supplied with battery power when the ignition is in the run position. The EBTCM controls the valve functions by grounding the circuit when necessary.

Conditions for Setting the DTC

The EBTCM senses a discrepancy such as an open, short to ground, or short to voltage in the circuit.

Action Taken When the DTC Sets

- A malfunction DTC is stored.
- ABS/TCS is disabled.
- The ABS and TC Indicators are turned on.

Conditions for Clearing the DTC

- Condition for DTC is no longer present and scan tool clear DTC function is used.
- 100 ignition cycles pass with no DTC(s) detected.

Diagnostic Aids

The solenoid valve circuit and the solenoid coil are internal to the EBTCM. No part of the solenoid circuit is diagnosable external to the EBTCM. The DTC sets when there is a malfunction in the solenoid circuit internal to the EBTCM only.

Test Description

The numbers below refer to step numbers on the Diagnostic Table.

2. This step determines if the DTC is current.

GC402980297400AX

Fig. 64 Code C0146: LH TCS Solenoid Circuit No. 2 Fault (Part 1 of 2). Catera

Circuit Description

The prime valve solenoid circuits are supplied with battery power when the ignition is in the run position. The EBTCM controls the valve functions by grounding the circuit when necessary.

Conditions for Setting the DTC

The EBTCM senses a discrepancy such as an open, short to ground, or short to voltage in the circuit.

Action Taken When the DTC Sets

- A malfunction DTC is stored.
- ABS/TCS is disabled.
- The ABS and TC Indicators are turned on.

Conditions for Clearing the DTC

- Condition for DTC is no longer present and scan tool clear DTC function is used.
- 100 ignition cycles pass with no DTC(s) detected.

Diagnostic Aids

The solenoid valve circuit and the solenoid coil are internal to the EBTCM. No part of the solenoid circuit is diagnosable external to the EBTCM. The DTC sets when there is a malfunction in the solenoid circuit internal to the EBTCM only.

Test Description

The numbers below refer to step numbers on the Diagnostic Table.

2. This step determines if the DTC is current.

GC402980297500AX

Fig. 65 Code C0151: RH TCS Solenoid Circuit No. 1 Fault (Part 1 of 2). Catera

Step	Action	Value(s)	Yes	No
1	Was the Diagnostic System Check performed?	—	*Go to Step 2*	Go to *ABS Diagnostic System Check*
2	1. Turn the ignition switch to the OFF position. 2. Install a scan tool. 3. Turn the ignition switch to the RUN position, engine off. 4. Using the scan tool run the Automated test. Does DTC C00151 reset as a current DTC?	—	*Go to Step 3*	Go to *ABS Diagnostic System Check*
3	Replace the EBTCM. Is the repair complete?	—	Go to *ABS Diagnostic System Check*	—

GC402980297500BX

Fig. 65 Code C0151: RH TCS Solenoid Circuit No. 1 Fault (Part 2 of 2). Catera

Circuit Description

The isolation valve solenoid circuits are supplied with battery power when the ignition is in the run position. The EBTCM controls the valve functions by grounding the circuit when necessary.

Conditions for Setting the DTC

The EBTCM senses a discrepancy such as an open, short to ground, or short to voltage in the circuit.

Action Taken When the DTC Sets

- A malfunction DTC is stored.
- ABS/TCS is disabled.
- The ABS and TC Indicators are turned on.

Conditions for Clearing the DTC

- Condition for DTC is no longer present and scan tool clear DTC function is used.
- 100 ignition cycles pass with no DTC(s) detected.

Diagnostic Aids

The solenoid valve circuit and the solenoid coil are internal to the EBTCM. No part of the solenoid circuit is diagnosable external to the EBTCM. The DTC sets when there is a malfunction in the solenoid circuit internal to the EBTCM only.

Test Description

The numbers below refer to step numbers on the Diagnostic Table.

2. This step determines if the DTC is current.

GC402980297600AX

Fig. 66 Code C0156: RH TCS Solenoid Circuit No. 2 Fault (Part 1 of 2). Catera

Step	Action	Value(s)	Yes	No
1	Was the Diagnostic System Check performed?	—	Go to Step 2	Go to ABS Diagnostic System Check
2	1. Turn the ignition switch to the OFF position. 2. Install a scan tool. 3. Turn the ignition switch to the RUN position, engine off. 4. Using the scan tool run the Automated test. Does DTC C00156 reset as a current DTC?	—	Go to Step 3	Go to ABS Diagnostic System Check
3	Replace the EBTCM. Is the repair complete?	—	Go to ABS Diagnostic System Check	—

GC402980297600BX

Fig. 66 Code C0156: RH TCS Solenoid Circuit No. 2 Fault (Part 2 of 2). Catera

Circuit Description

The Stoplamp Switch is a normally open switch, when the brake pedal is depressed, the EBTCM senses battery voltage. This allows the EBTCM to determine the state of the brake lamps.

Conditions for Setting the DTC

- EBTCM detects battery voltage at all times.
- EBTCM never detects battery voltage from the stoplamp switch input circuit.
- Both brake lamps are faulty.

Action Taken When the DTC Sets

- DTC C0161 is set.
- ABS and TCS remains active.

Conditions for Clearing the DTC

- The condition responsible for setting the DTC no longer exists and the scan tool Clear DTCs function is used.
- 100 ignition cycles pass with no DTC(s) detected.

Diagnostic Aids

- It is very important that a thorough inspection of the wiring and connectors be performed. Failure to carefully and fully inspect wiring and connectors may result in misdiagnosis, causing part replacement with reappearance of the malfunction.
- Thoroughly inspect any circuitry that may be causing the complaint for the following conditions:
  - Backed out terminals
  - Improper mating
  - Broken locks
  - Improperly formed or damaged terminals
  - Poor terminal-to-wiring connections
  - Physical damage to the wiring harness
- The following conditions may cause an intermittent malfunction:
  - A poor connection
  - Rubbed-through wire insulation
  - A broken wire inside the insulation

Test Description

The numbers below refer to the step numbers on the diagnostic table.

5. This step checks for voltage at the EBTCM.
11. This step checks the Stoplamp switch.

GC402980297700AX

Fig. 67 Code C0161: ABS/TCS Brake Switch Circuit Fault (Part 1 of 3). Catera

Step	Action	Value(s)	Yes	No
1	Was the Diagnostic System Check performed?	—	Go to Step 2	Go to ABS Diagnostic System Check
2	Observe the rear brake lamps. Are the brake lamps off?	—	Go to Step 4	Go to Step 3
3	Disconnect the Stoplamp Switch connector. Are the brake lamps on?	—	Go to Step 18	Go to Step 12
4	Press the brake pedal. Do the brake lights come on?	—	Go to Step 5	Go to Step 8
5	1. Turn the ignition switch to the OFF position. 2. Disconnect the EBTCM connector C1. 3. Install the *J 39700* Universal Pinout Box using the J 39700-280 cable adapter to the EBTCM harness connector only. 4. Using the *J 39200* DMM, measure the voltage at the *J 39700* terminal 14 while an assistant presses the brake pedal. Is the voltage within specifications?	Battery voltage	Go to Step 6	Go to Step 7
6	Replace the EBTCM. Is the replacement complete?	—	Go to ABS Diagnostic System Check	—
7	Repair the open or high resistance in the stoplamp switch input circuit. Is the circuit repair complete?	—	Go to ABS Diagnostic System Check	—
8	Check the HAZARD FUSE 12 in the Fuse Block. Is the fuse OK?	—	Go to Step 9	Go to Step 13
9	1. Disconnect the Stoplamp Switch connector. 2. Using the *J 39200* DMM, measure the voltage at the Stoplamp Switch harness connector terminal 1. Is the voltage within specifications?	Battery voltage	Go to Step 11	Go to Step 10
10	Repair the open in the stoplamp CKT between the stoplamp switch and the HAZARD FUSE 12. Is the circuit repair complete?	—	Go to ABS Diagnostic System Check	—
11	Connect a fused jumper wire between the Stoplamp Switch harness connector terminals 1 and 2. Do the brake lamps come on?	—	Go to Step 12	Go to Step 7
12	Adjust or replace the Stoplamp Switch as necessary. Is the repair complete?	—	Go to ABS Diagnostic System Check	—

GC402980297700BX

Fig. 67 Code C0161: ABS/TCS Brake Switch Circuit Fault (Part 2 of 3). Catera

Step	Action	Value(s)	Yes	No
13	1. Replace the HAZARD FUSE 12. (Do not press the brake pedal.) 2. Check the fuse. Is the fuse OK?	—	Go to Step 15	Go to Step 14
14	Repair the short to ground in the stoplamp circuit between the stoplamp switch and the HAZARD FUSE 12. Is the circuit repair complete?	—	Go to ABS Diagnostic System Check	—
15	1. Press the brake pedal. 2. Check the HAZARD FUSE 12. Is the fuse OK?	—	Go to ABS Diagnostic System Check	Go to Step 16
16	1. Turn the ignition switch to the OFF position. 2. Disconnect the EBTCM. 3. Replace the fuse. 4. Depress the brake pedal. 5. Check the HAZARD FUSE 12. Is the fuse OK?	—	Go to Step 6	Go to Step 17
17	Repair the short to ground in the stoplamp switch input circuit. Is the circuit repair complete?	—	Go to ABS Diagnostic System Check	—
18	Repair the stoplamp switch circuit for a short to voltage. Is the repair complete?	—	Go to ABS Diagnostic System Check	—

GC402980297800CX

Fig. 67 Code C0161: ABS/TCS Brake Switch Circuit Fault (Part 3 of 3). Catera

Circuit Description

The RPM signal circuit provides the EBTCM with an indication of engine RPM to help determine TCS control methods and rates when a TCS event takes place.

Conditions for Setting the DTC

The EBTCM does not received an RPM input signal after 1 second, after the engine has been started.

Action Taken When the DTC Sets

- A malfunction DTC is stored.
- The TC indicator is turned on.
- The TCS is disabled. ABS remains functional.

Conditions for Clearing the DTC

- The condition for DTC is no longer present and the scan tool Clear DTCs function is used.
- 100 ignition cycles have passed with no DTC(s) detected.

Diagnostic Aids

Perform a thorough inspection of the wiring. Perform a thorough inspection of the connectors. Failure to carefully and fully inspect the wiring and the connectors may result in misdiagnosis. Misdiagnosis causes part replacement with reappearance of the malfunction.

Test Description

The number(s) below refer to the step number(s) on the diagnostic table.

2. If the instrument panel tachometer is working properly, the cause of the malfunction is most likely between splice S228 and the EBTCM, or the EBTCM itself.
10. At this point, the ECM is likely causing the malfunction.

GC402980298000AX

Fig. 68 Code C0236: TCS RPM Signal Circuit Fault (Part 1 of 3). Catera

Step	Action	Value(s)	Yes	No
1	Was the Diagnostic System Check performed?	—	Go to Step 2	Go to ABS Diagnostic System Check
2	1. Start the engine. 2. Vary the engine RPM with the throttle while observing the I/P tachometer. Does the I/P tachometer work properly as the engine RPM changes?	—	Go to Step 3	Go to Step 4
3	1. Turn the ignition switch to the OFF position. 2. Disconnect the ECM connector from the ECM. 3. Disconnect the EBTCM connector from the EBTCM. 4. Install the *J 39700* Universal Breakout Box with the J 39700-280 Cable Adapter to the EBTCM harness only. 5. Use a *J 39200* DMM to measure the resistance between the ECM harness connector terminal 80 and the *J 39700* Universal Breakout Box terminal 30. Is the resistance within the specified range?	0–5 Ω	Go to Step 9	Go to Step 11
4	1. Turn the ignition switch to the OFF position. 2. Disconnect the ECM connector from the ECM. 3. Disconnect the EBTCM connector from the EBTCM. 4. Install the *J 39700* Universal Breakout Box with the J 39700-280 Cable Adapter to the EBTCM harness only. 5. Use a *J 39200* DMM to measure the resistance between the ECM harness connector terminal 80 and the *J 39700* Universal Breakout Box terminal 30. Is the resistance within the specified range?	0–5 Ω	Go to Step 5	Go to Step 12
5	Use a *J 39200* DMM to measure the resistance between the *J 39700* Universal Breakout Box terminal 30 and terminal 19. Is the resistance within the specified range?	OL (Infinite)	Go to Step 6	Go to Step 13
6	1. Turn the ignition switch to the RUN position 2. Use a *J 39200* DMM to measure the voltage between the *J 39700* Universal Breakout Box terminal 30 and terminal 19. Is the voltage within the specified range?	0–2 V	Go to Step 7	Go to Step 14
7	1. Inspect the ECM connector for the following: • Inspect for damage. • Inspect for poor terminal contact. • Inspect for corrosion. 2. Inspect the EBTCM connector for the following: • Inspect for damage. • Inspect for poor terminal contact. • Inspect for corrosion. 3. Ensure both the ECM connector and the EBTCM connector are properly retained when connected. Are the following signs present on either connector: • Is poor terminal contact present? • Is corrosion present? • Is damaged terminals present?	—	Go to Step 15	Go to Step 8

GC402980298000BX

Fig. 68 Code C0236: TCS RPM Signal Circuit Fault (Part 2 of 3). Catera

Step	Action	Value(s)	Yes	No
8	1. Reconnect all the connectors. 2. Using the scan tool clear the DTC. 3. Disconnect the scan tool from the DLC. 4. Start the engine. Did DTC C0236 reset?	—	Go to Step 10	Go to ABS Diagnostic System Check
9	Replace the EBTCM. Is the repair complete?	—	Go to ABS Diagnostic System Check	—
10	Suspect ECM. Is the repair complete?	—	Go to ABS Diagnostic System Check	—
11	Repair an open between splice S228 and the EBTCM harness connector terminal 30. Is the repair complete?	—	Go to ABS Diagnostic System Check	—
12	Repair an open between splice S228 and the ECM harness connector terminal 80. Is the repair complete?	—	Go to ABS Diagnostic System Check	—
13	Repair a short to ground in the Tach input circuit. Is the repair complete?	—	Go to ABS Diagnostic System Check	—
14	Repair a short to voltage in the Tach input circuit. Is the repair complete?	—	Go to ABS Diagnostic System Check	—
15	Replace all the terminals or replace the connectors that exhibit signs of the following: • That exhibit signs of poor terminal contact. • That exhibit signs of corrosion. • That exhibit signs of damaged terminals. Is the repair complete?	—	Go to ABS Diagnostic System Check	—

GC402980298000CX

Fig. 68 Code C0236: TCS RPM Signal Circuit Fault (Part 3 of 3). Catera

Test Description

The numbers below refer to step numbers on the diagnostic table.

4. Step 4 checks for the proper requested torque value.
5. Step 5 checks if the ECM is sending back a PWM signal of 95–97 % via the delivered engine torque circuit indicating a defective requested torque signal. If the ECM is sending this signal, after the requested torque checks OK with the scan tool in step 4, the ECM is suspect.
7. Step 7 checks for the presence of a pull-up voltage from the EBTCM.

Step	Action	Value(s)	Yes	No
1	Was the Diagnostic System Check performed?	—	Go to Step 2	Go to ABS Diagnostic System Check
2	Check that ground, G103 is clean, tight and free of damage. Were any loose, damaged, or corroded grounds found?	—	Go to Step 3	Go to Step 4
3	Repair ground as necessary. Is the repair complete?	—	Go to ABS Diagnostic System Check	—
4	1. Turn the ignition switch to the OFF position. 2. Install the scan tool. 3. Turn the ignition switch to the RUN position, engine off. 4. Use the scan tool to select Engine Data Display in Powertrain. 5. Using the scan tool, observe the TC Torque Request. Is the requested torque within the range specified in the value(s) column?	6–10 %	Go to Step 5	Go to Step 7
5	1. Using the scan tool, select ABS/TCS Data Display. 2. Observe the Delivered Engine Torque. Is the delivered torque within the range specified in the value(s) column?	95–97 %	Go to Step 13	Go to Step 6
6	Replace the EBTCM. Is the replacement complete?	—	Go to ABS Diagnostic System Check	—
7	1. Turn the ignition switch to the OFF position. 2. Disconnect the ECM connector. 3. Disconnect the TCM Connector. 4. Disconnect the EBTCM connector. 5. Install J 39700 Universal Pinout Box using the J 39700-280 cable adapter to the EBTCM harness connector and the EBTCM connector. 6. Turn the ignition switch to the RUN position, engine off. 7. Using J 39200 DMM, measure the voltage between terminals 13 and 19 of J 39700. Is the voltage within the range specified in the value(s) column?	Above 8 V	Go to Step 8	Go to Step 10

GC402980298100BX

Fig. 69 Code C0241: PCM Indicated Requested Torque Fault (Part 2 of 3). Catera

Circuit Description

Traction Control is simultaneously controlled by the EBTCM and the ECM. The EBTCM sends a requested torque message via a Pulse Width Modulated (PWM) signal to the ECM requesting a desired engine torque level for proper Traction Control system operation. The EBTCM supplies the pull up voltage.

Conditions for Setting the DTC

- If a defective requested torque signal is detected by the ECM, a PWM signal outside the normal range (95–97 %) is sent back to the EBTCM via the delivered torque circuit. The DTC will set if the EBTCM receives the out of range signal for 30 milliseconds continuously.
- DTC C0241 can be set anytime when ignition voltage is present and the EBTCM detects an engine RPM greater than 480 RPM.

Action Taken When the DTC Sets

- A malfunction DTC is stored.
- The TCS is disabled.
- The TC indicator is turned on. The ABS remains functional.

Conditions for Clearing the DTC

- Condition for DTC is no longer present and scan tool clear DTC function is used.
- 100 ignition cycles have passed with no DTC(s) detected.

Diagnostic Aids

- It is very important that a thorough inspection of the wiring and connectors be performed. Failure to carefully and fully inspect wiring and connectors may result in misdiagnosis, causing part replacement with reappearance of the malfunction.
- Possible causes for DTC C0241 to set:
  - Open in the requested torque circuit.
  - Requested torque circuit shorted to ground or voltage.
  - Communication problem.
  - Requested torque circuit has a wiring problem, terminal corrosion, or poor connections.
  - ECM not receiving information from the EBTCM.

GC402980298100AX

Fig. 69 Code C0241: PCM Indicated Requested Torque Fault (Part 1 of 3). Catera

Step	Action	Value(s)	Yes	No
8	1. Turn the ignition switch to the OFF position. 2. Disconnect the J 39700-25 cable adapter from the EBTCM leaving the cable adapter connected to the EBTCM harness only. 3. Turn the ignition switch to the RUN position, engine off. 4. Using J 39200 DMM, measure the voltage between terminals 13 and 19 of J 39700. Is the voltage within the range specified in the value(s) column?	Greater than 1V	Go to Step 9	Go to Step 12
9	Repair the requested engine torque circuit for a short to voltage. Is the repair complete?	—	Go to ABS Diagnostic System Check	—
10	1. Turn the ignition switch to the OFF position. 2. Using J 39200 DMM, measure the resistance between J 39700 terminals 13 and 19. Is the resistance within the range specified in the value(s) column?	OL (infinite)	Go to Step 6	Go to Step 11
11	Repair the requested engine torque circuit for a short to ground. Is the repair complete?	—	Go to ABS Diagnostic System Check	—
12	1. Turn the ignition switch to the OFF position. 2. Using J 39200 DMM, measure the resistance between terminal 13 of J 39700 and the ECM connector terminal 48. Is the resistance within the range specified in the value(s) column?	0–2 Ω	Go to Step 6	Go to Step 14
13	Suspect ECM. Is the Repair complete?	—	Go to ABS Diagnostic System Check	—
14	Repair the requested torque circuit for an open. Is the repair complete?	—	Go to ABS Diagnostic System Check	—

GC402980298100CX

Fig. 69 Code C0241: PCM Indicated Requested Torque Fault (Part 3 of 3). Catera

Circuit Description

Traction Control is simultaneously controlled by the EBTCM and the ECM. The PCM sends a Delivered Torque message via a Pulse Width Modulated (PWM) signal to the EBTCM confirming the delivered torque level for proper Traction Control system operation. The EBTCM supplies the pull up voltage.

Conditions for Setting the DTC

DTC C0244 can be set anytime when ignition voltage is present. A malfunction exists if the PWM signal is out of range or no signal is received for a period of 2 seconds.

Action Taken When the DTC Sets

- A malfunction DTC is stored.
- The TCS is disabled.
- The TC indicator is turned on. The ABS remains functional.

Conditions for Clearing the DTC

- Condition for DTC is no longer present and scan tool clear DTC function is used.
- 100 ignition cycles have passed with no DTC(s) detected.

Diagnostic Aids

- It is very important that a thorough inspection of the wiring and connectors be performed. Failure to carefully and fully inspect wiring and connectors may result in misdiagnosis, causing part replacement with reappearance of the malfunction.
- Possible causes for DTC C0244 to set:
  - Open in the delivered torque circuit.
  - The delivered torque circuit shorted to ground or voltage.
  - Communication frequency problem.
  - Communication duty cycle problem.
  - The delivered torque circuit has a wiring problem, terminal corrosion, or poor connections.
  - EBTCM not receiving information from the ECM.

Test Description

The numbers below refer to step numbers on the diagnostic table.

4. Checks for proper delivered torque value.
6. Checks for the presence of a pull-up voltage from the EBTCM.

GC402980298200AX

Fig. 70 Code C0244: PWM Delivered Torque Fault (Part 1 of 3). Catera

Step	Action	Value(s)	Yes	No
1	Was the Diagnostic System Check performed?	—	Go to Step 2	Go to ABS Diagnostic System Check
2	Check that ground G103 is clean, tight and free of damage. Were any loose, damaged, or corroded grounds found?	—	Go to Step 3	Go to Step 4
3	Repair ground as necessary. Is the repair complete?	—	Go to ABS Diagnostic System Check	—
4	1. Turn the ignition switch to the OFF position. 2. Install the scan tool. 3. Start the engine. 4. Using the scan tool, observe the ECM to EBTCM delivered engine torque. 5. With the engine running, momentarily press the accelerator while observing the delivered engine torque. Did the delivered engine torque fluctuate within the range specified in the value(s) column?	20–60 %	Go to Step 5	Go to Step 6
5	Replace the EBTCM. Is the replacement complete?	—	Go to ABS Diagnostic System Check	—
6	1. Turn the ignition switch to the OFF position. 2. Disconnect the ECM connector. 3. Disconnect the TCM connector. 4. Disconnect the EBTCM connector. 5. Install J 39700 Universal Pinout Box using the J 39700-280 cable adapter to the EBTCM harness connector and the EBTCM connector. 6. Turn the ignition switch to the RUN position, engine off. 7. Using J 39200 DMM, measure the voltage between terminals 27 and 19 of J 39700. Is the voltage within the range specified in the value(s) column?	Above 10V	Go to Step 7	Go to Step 9
7	1. Turn the ignition switch to the OFF position. 2. Disconnect the J 39700-25 cable adapter from the EBTCM leaving the cable adapter connected to the EBTCM harness only. 3. Turn the ignition switch to the RUN position, engine off. 4. Using J 39200 DMM, measure the voltage between terminals 27 and 19 of J 39700. Is the voltage within the range specified in the value(s) column?	Greater than 1V	Go to Step 8	Go to Step 11

GC402980298200BX

Fig. 70 Code C0244: PWM Delivered Torque Fault (Part 2 of 3). Catera

Step	Action	Value(s)	Yes	No
8	Repair the delivered torque circuit for a short to voltage. Refer to Wiring. Is the repair complete?	—	Go to ABS Diagnostic System Check	—
9	1. Turn the ignition switch to the OFF position. 2. Using J 39200 DMM, measure the resistance between J 39700 terminals 27 and 19. Is the resistance within the range specified in the value(s) column?	OL (infinite)	Go to Step 5	Go to Step 10
10	Repair the delivered torque circuit for a short to ground. Is the repair complete?	—	Go to ABS Diagnostic System Check	—
11	1. Turn the ignition switch to the OFF position. 2. Using J 39200 DMM, measure the resistance between terminal 27 of J 39700 and the ECM connector terminal 83. Is the resistance within the range specified in the value(s) column?	0–2 Ω	Go to Step 12	Go to Step 13
12	Suspect ECM. I Is the Repair complete?	—	Go to ABS Diagnostic System Check	—
13	Repair the delivered torque circuit for an open. Is the repair complete?	—	Go to ABS Diagnostic System Check	—

GC402980298200CX

Fig. 70 Code C0244: PWM Delivered Torque Fault (Part 3 of 3). Catera

Circuit Description

The speed sensor used on this vehicle is a single point magnetic pickup. This sensor produces an AC signal that the EBTCM uses the frequency from to calculate the wheel speed.

Conditions for Setting the DTC

- The EBTCM detects a deviation between the left and right rear wheel speeds of greater than 6 km/h (3.75 mph) at a vehicle speed of less than 100Km/h (62 mph).
- The EBTCM detects a deviation between the left and right front wheel speeds of greater than 10 Km/h (6.25 mph) at a vehicle speed of less than 100Km/h (62 mph).
- The EBTCM detects a deviation between the left and right rear wheel speeds of greater than 6% of the vehicle speed at greater than 100 km/h (62 mph).
- The EBTCM detects a deviation between the left and right front wheel speeds of greater than 4 km/h (2.5 mph) plus 6 % of the vehicle speed at greater than 100 km/h (62 mph).

This DTC will set when the EBTCM cannot specifically identify which wheel speed sensor is causing the malfunction. If the EBTCM can identify a specific wheel speed sensor causing the malfunction, the DTC associated with the sensor (DTC C0035, DTC C0040, DTC C0045, or DTC C0050) will be set.

Action Taken When the DTC Sets

- A malfunction DTC stores.
- The ABS/TCS disables.
- The amber ABS/TCS indicator(s) turn on.

GC402980298300AX

Fig. 71 Code C0245: Wheel Speed Sensor Frequency Error (Part 1 of 3). Catera

Conditions for Clearing the DTC

- The condition responsible for setting the DTC no longer exists and the scan tool Clear DTCs function is used.
- 100 ignition cycles pass with no DTC(s) detected.

Diagnostic Aids

- It is very important that a thorough inspection of the wiring and connectors be performed. Failure to carefully and fully inspect wiring and connectors may result in misdiagnosis, causing part replacement with reappearance of the malfunction.
- Thoroughly inspect any circuitry that may be causing the complaint for the following conditions:
  - Backed out terminals
  - Improper mating
  - Broken locks
  - Improperly formed or damaged terminals
  - Poor terminal-to-wiring connections
  - Physical damage to the wiring harness
- The following conditions may cause an intermittent malfunction:
  - A poor connection
  - Rubbed-through wire insulation
  - A broken wire inside the insulation
- If the customer's comments reflect that the amber ABS/TCS indicator is on only during moist environmental conditions (rain, snow, vehicle wash), inspect all the wheel speed sensor circuitry for signs of water intrusion. If the DTC is not current, clear all DTCs and simulate the effects of water intrusion by using the following procedure:
  1. Spray the suspected area with a five percent saltwater solution. Add two teaspoons of salt to twelve ounces of water to make a five percent saltwater solution.
  2. Test drive the vehicle over various road surfaces (bumps, turns, etc.) above 40 km/h (25 mph) for at least 30 seconds.
  3. If the DTC returns, replace the suspected harness.

Possible causes for DTC C0245 to set:

- Damaged or missing teeth on one or more if the wheel speed sensor rings.
- Large grooves or gouges, or buildup of foreign material in the gaps between the wheel speed sensor ring teeth.
- A worn front hub bearing assembly, or worn inner axle bearing which could allow the sensor to toothed ring gap to change excessively.

Test Description

The numbers below refer to step numbers on the diagnostic table.

2. If DTC C0245 is a history code, this step checks if a specific wheel speed Circuit DTC is set concurrently with DTC C0245.
5. This step checks if the wheel speed sensor harness is routed in close proximity to the spark plug wires.
7. In this step, if the scan tool can record any erroneous wheel speed sensor signals, diagnose that sensor(s) first.

Step	Action	Value(s)	Yes	No
1	Was the Diagnostic System Check performed?	—	Go to Step 2	Go to ABS Diagnostic System Check
2	Is the following DTC(s) set concurrently with a history DTC C0245? • DTC C0035 • DTC C0040 • DTC C0045 • DTC C0050	—	Go to DTC List for the Appropriate DTC Table	Go to Step 3
3	Inspect all of the WSS and WSS rings for physical damage. Is physical damage of any WSS or WSS ring evident?	—	Go to Step 4	Go to Step 5

GC402980298300BX

Fig. 71 Code C0245: Wheel Speed Sensor Frequency Error (Part 2 of 3). Catera

Step	Action	Value(s)	Yes	No
4	Replace the WSS or WSS ring. Is the replacement complete?	—	Go to Step 12	—
5	Check for Proper routing of the wheel speed sensor harnesses. Check that the wheel speed sensor harnesses are routed away from the spark plug wires. Are the wheel speed sensor harnesses properly routed?	—	Go to Step 7	Go to Step 6
6	Reroute the wheel speed sensor harness away from the spark plug wires. Is the repair complete?	—	Go to Step 12	—
7	1. Install a scan tool. 2. Turn the ignition switch to the RUN position. 3. Set the scan tool to Snap Shot Auto Trigger mode and monitor the wheel speed sensors. 4. Carefully drive the vehicle above 12 Km/h (8 mph) for several minute. Did the scan tool trigger on any of the wheel speed sensors?	—	Go to Step 8	Go to Step 9
8	Note which wheel speed sensor triggered the scan tool. Follow the appropriate Wheel Speed Sensor DTC table for the wheel speed sensor that triggered. Is the repair complete?	—	Go to ABS Diagnostic System Check	—
9	1. Reconnect all previously disconnected components. 2. Using a scan tool clear the DTC. 3. Remove the scan tool from the DLC. 4. Carefully drive the vehicle above 12 Km/h (8 mph) for several minutes. Does the DTC reset as a current DTC?	—	Go to Step 11	Go to Step 10
10	Malfunction is intermittent. Inspect all connectors and harnesses for damage that may result in an open or high resistance when connected. I Is the repair complete?	—	Go to ABS Diagnostic System Check	—
11	Replace the EBTCM. Is the replacement complete?	—	Go to ABS Diagnostic System Check	—
12	1. Reconnect all previously disconnected components. 2. Using a scan tool clear the DTC. 3. Remove the scan tool from the DLC. 4. Carefully drive the vehicle above 12 Km/h (8 mph) for several minutes. Does the DTC reset as a current DTC?	—	Go to Step 2	Go to ABS Diagnostic System Check

GC402980298300CX

Fig. 71 Code C0245: Wheel Speed Sensor Frequency Error (Part 3 of 3). Catera

23036:

Circuit Description

Replacement EBTCMs require programming of the EBTCM memory. Program the EBTCM if a new EBTCM is installed in a vehicle. The programming is performed with the scan tool. When ABS Programming is performed with the scan tool, the engine type and the transmission type are coded into the EBTCM memory. The EBTCM requires the engine and transmission coding for TCS operation.

Conditions for Setting the DTC

The coding has not been programmed into the EBTCM.

Action Taken When the DTC Sets

- A malfunction DTC is stored.
- The TC indicator lamp is turned on.
- The TCS will be disabled.
- The ABS remains functional.

Conditions for Clearing the DTC

- The condition for the DTC is no longer present.
- The scan tool Clear DTCs function is used.
- 100 drive cycles have passed with no DTC(s) detected.

Diagnostic Aids

In the most unfavorable circumstances, incorrect programming can lead to minor driveability problems.

Test Description

The number(s) below refer to the step number(s) on the diagnostic table.

2. If DTC C0551 is set as a current DTC, perform the ABS Programming in ABS diagnostics of the scan tool.

GC402980298500AX

Fig. 73 Code C0551: Option Configuration Error (Part 1 of 2). Catera

Circuit Description

The EBTCM is required to operate within a specified range of voltage to function properly. During ABS and TCS operation, there are current requirements that will cause the voltage to drop. Because of this, voltage is monitored out of ABS/TCS control to indicate a good charging system condition, and also during ABS/TCS control when voltage may drop significantly. The EBTCM also monitors for high voltage conditions which could damage the EBTCM.

Conditions for Setting the DTC

- The EBTCM ignition operating voltage at terminal 15 falls below 9.4 volts out of ABS/TCS control, or 8.8 volts during ABS/TCS control.
- The EBTCM ignition operating voltage at terminal 15 rises above 17.4 volts.
- The low voltage or the high voltage is detected for more than 500 milliseconds with the vehicle speed above 6 km/h (3.6 mph).

Action Taken When the DTC Sets

- A malfunction DTC is stored.
- The ABS and the TC indicator lamps are turned on.

The ABS/TCS is disabled.

Conditions for Clearing the DTC

- The condition for the DTC is no longer present, the scan tool Clear DTCs function is used.
- 100 ignition cycles have passed with no DTC(s) detected.

Diagnostic Aids

- It is very important that a thorough inspection of the wiring and connectors be performed. Failure to carefully and fully inspect wiring and connectors may result in misdiagnosis, causing part replacement with reappearance of the malfunction.
- Thoroughly inspect any circuitry that may be causing the complaint for the following conditions:
  - Backed out terminals
  - Improper mating
  - Broken locks
  - Improperly formed or damaged terminals
  - Poor terminal-to-wiring connections
  - Physical damage to the wiring harness

GC402980298600AX

Fig. 74 Code C0800: Device Power No. 1 Circuit Fault (Part 1 of 3). Catera

Circuit Description

This DTC identifies a malfunction within the EBTCM.

Conditions for Setting the DTC

DTC C0550 is set when an internal EBTCM malfunction exists.

Action Taken When the DTC Sets

A malfunction DTC is stored, ABS/TCS is disabled and the ABS and Traction Control Indicators are turned on.

Conditions for Clearing the DTC

- Condition for DTC is no longer present and scan tool clear DTC function is used.
- 100 ignition cycles pass with no DTC(s) detected.

Step	Action	Value(s)	Yes	No
1	Was the Diagnostic System Check performed?	—	Go to Step 2	Go to ABS Diagnostic System Check
2	Are any other DTC(s) present besides C0550?	—	Go to DTC List for the Applicable DTC Table	Go to Step 3
3	Replace the EBTCM. Is the replacement complete?	—	Go to ABS Diagnostic System Check	—

GC4029802984000X

Fig. 72 Code C0550: ECU Fault. Catera

Step	Action	Value(s)	Yes	No
1	Was the Diagnostic System Check performed?	—	Go to Step 2	Go to ABS Diagnostic System Check
2	The EBTCM requires ABS Programming. Perform the following step: 1. Use a scan tool to select ABS Diagnostics. 2. Select and run ABS Programming in ABS Diagnostics. Is the programming complete?	—	Go to Step 3	—
3	1. Install the scan tool. 2. Turn the ignition switch to the RUN position with the engine off. 3. Use the scan tool to read the DTCs. Did DTC C0551 set as a current DTC?	—	Go to Step 4	Go to ABS Diagnostic System Check
4	Replace the EBTCM. Is the repair complete?	—	Go to ABS Diagnostic System Check	—

GC402980298500BX

Fig. 73 Code C0551: Option Configuration Error (Part 2 of 2). Catera

- The following conditions may cause an intermittent malfunction:
  - A poor connection
  - Rubbed-through wire insulation
  - A broken wire inside the insulation

Test Description

The number(s) below refer to the step number(s) on the diagnostic table.

2. This step checks if the voltage is above the maximum of the range.
4. This step checks if the voltage is below the minimum of the range.
6. This step checks for the integrity of the ground circuit.

Step	Action	Value(s)	Yes	No
1	Was a Diagnostic System Check performed?	—	Go to Step 2	Go to ABS Diagnostic System Check
2	1. Turn all the accessories off. 2. Install a scan tool. 3. Start the engine. 4. Use the scan tool to monitor the battery voltage while running the engine at approximately 2000 RPM. Is the monitored battery voltage within the specified range?	0–17.4 V	Go to Step 4	Go to Step 3
3	Use a J 39200 DMM to measure the voltage between the battery positive terminal and ground. Is the voltage within the specified range?	0–17.4 V	Go to Step 5	Inspect Starting System Check
4	Continue to monitor the battery voltage with the scan tool while running the engine at approximately 2000 RPM. Is the monitored battery voltage within the specified range?	0–9.4 V	Go to Step 6	Go to Step 5
5	1. Turn the ignition switch to the OFF position. 2. Disconnect the scan tool if still connected. 3. Test drive the vehicle above 6 km/h (3.5 mph). Did DTC C0800 reset?	—	Go to Step 12	Go to ABS Diagnostic System Check
6	1. Disconnect the EBTCM connector from the EBTCM. 2. Install the J 39700 Universal Pinout Box with the J 39700-280 Cable Adapter to the EBTCM harness only. 3. Use a J 39200 DMM to measure the resistance between the J 39700 terminal 19 and a good ground. Is the resistance within the specified range?	0-5Ω	Go to Step 8	Go to Step 7
7	Repair open or high resistance in the ground circuit. Is the repair complete?	—	Go to ABS Diagnostic System Check	—

GC402980298600BX

Fig. 74 Code C0800: Device Power No. 1 Circuit Fault (Part 2 of 3). Catera

Step	Action	Value(s)	Yes	No
8	1. Turn the ignition switch to the RUN position with the engine off. 2. Use a *J 39200* DMM to measure the voltage between the *J 39700* terminal 15 and 19. Is the voltage within the specified range?	Above 9.4 Volts	*Go to Step 11*	*Go to Step 9*
9	1. Remove ABS Fuse 19 from the Fuse Block. 2. Use a *J 39200* DMM to measure the resistance between the fuse block test terminal on the EBTCM side and the *J 39700* terminal 15. Is the resistance within the specified range?	0-5Ω	*Inspect Starting System*	*Go to Step 10*
10	Repair high resistance in CKT FA202. Is the repair complete?	—	*Go to ABS Diagnostic System Check*	—
11	1. Turn the ignition switch to the OFF position. 2. Reconnect the EBTCM connector. 3. Disconnect the scan tool if the scan tool is still connected. 4. Test drive the vehicle above 6 km/h (3.5 mph). Did DTC C0800 reset?	—	*Go to Step 12*	*Go to ABS Diagnostic System Check*
12	Replace the EBTCM. Is the repair complete?	—	*Go to ABS Diagnostic System Check*	—

GC402980298600CX

Fig. 74 Code C0800: Device Power No. 1 Circuit Fault (Part 3 of 3). Catera

Step	Action	Value(s)	Yes	No
DEFINITION: ABS Indicator is On with no DTC(s).				
1	Was the Diagnostic System Check performed?	—	*Go to Step 2*	*Go to ABS Diagnostic System Check*
2	1. Turn the ignition switch to the OFF position. 2. Disconnect the EBTCM connector C1. 3. Install the *J 39700* Universal Pinout Box using the J 39700-280 cable adapter to connector C1 only. 4. Turn the ignition switch to the RUN position. Is the ABS Indicator off?	—	*Go to Step 3*	*Go to Step 4*
3	Replace the EBTCM. Is the replacement complete?	—	*Go to ABS Diagnostic System Check*	—
4	1. Disconnect the Instrument panel connector. 2. Using *J 39200* DMM, measure the resistance between terminals 21 and 19 of *J 39700.* Is the resistance within the range specified in the value(s) column?	OL(Infinite)	*Go to Step 6*	*Go to Step 5*
5	Repair the ABS indicator circuit for a short to ground. Is the repair complete?	—	*Go to ABS Diagnostic System Check*	—
6	Suspect the instrument cluster. Is the repair complete?	—	*Go to ABS Diagnostic System Check*	—

GC402980298900BX

Fig. 75 Test A: ABS Lamp On w/No Code Set (Part 2 of 2). Catera

Step	Action	Value(s)	Yes	No
DEFINITION: ABS Indicator never comes on.				
1	Was the Diagnostic System Check performed?	—	*Go to Step 2*	*Go to ABS Diagnostic System Check*
2	1. Turn the ignition switch to the OFF position. 2. Disconnect the EBTCM connector C1. 3. Install the *J 39700* Universal Pinout Box using the J 39700-280 cable adapter to connector C1 only. 4. Connect a fused jumper wire between terminals 21 and 19 of *J 39700.* 5. Turn the ignition switch to the RUN position. Does the ABS Indicator come on?	—	*Go to Step 3*	*Go to Step 4*
3	Replace the EBTCM. Is the replacement complete?	—	*Go to ABS Diagnostic System Check*	—
4	1. Turn the ignition switch to the OFF position. 2. Disconnect the Instrument Cluster connector. 3. Using *J 39200* DMM, measure the resistance between terminals 21 of *J 39700* and the Instrument Cluster harness connector terminal 1. Is the resistance within the range specified in the value(s) column?	0–5Ω	*Go to Step 6*	*Go to Step 5*
5	Repair the ABS Indicator circuit for an open or high resistance. Is the repair complete?	—	*Go to ABS Diagnostic System Check*	—
6	Suspect the Instrument Cluster. Is the repair complete?	—	*Go to ABS Diagnostic System Check*	—

GC402980298800BX

Fig. 76 Test B: ABS Lamp Off w/No Code Set (Part 2 of 2). Catera

Circuit Description

The ABS indicator is controlled by the EBTCM. The EBTCM supplies the ground to the ABS indicator circuit to turn the indicator on. When the ABS indicator circuit is not grounded at the EBTCM, the ABS indicator remains off. The EBTCM harness connector contains a shorting bar for the ABS indicator circuit. When the EBTCM connector is disconnected from the EBTCM, the shorting bar shorts the ABS indicator terminal to ground turning on the indicator.

Diagnostic Aids

If the EBTCM harness connector is not securely connected to the EBTCM, the shorting bar in the harness connector may turn on the ABS indicator. Make sure the EBTCM harness connector is securely connected to the EBTCM.

- It is very important that a thorough inspection of the wiring and connectors be performed. Failure to carefully and fully inspect wiring and connectors may result in misdiagnosis, causing part replacement with reappearance of the malfunction.
- Thoroughly inspect any circuitry that may be causing the complaint for the following conditions:
  - Backed out terminals
  - Improper mating
  - Broken locks
  - Improperly formed or damaged terminals
  - Poor terminal-to-wiring connections
  - Physical damage to the wiring harness
- The following conditions may cause an intermittent malfunction:
  - A poor connection
  - Rubbed-through wire insulation
  - A broken wire inside the insulation

Test Description

The number(s) below refer to the step number(s) on the diagnostic table.

2. This step checks for an internal EBTCM short. You must install the pinout box and cable adapter to the harness connector at this point to prevent the shorting bar in the harness connector from grounding the circuit and turning on the indicator.
4. This step checks for a short to ground in the ABS indicator circuit.

GC402980298900AX

Fig. 75 Test A: ABS Lamp On w/No Code Set (Part 1 of 2). Catera

Circuit Description

The ABS indicator is controlled by the EBTCM. The EBTCM supplies the ground to the ABS indicator circuit to turn the indicator on. When the ABS indicator circuit is not grounded at the EBTCM, the ABS indicator remains off. The EBTCM harness connector contains a shorting bar for the ABS indicator circuit. When the EBTCM connector is disconnected from the EBTCM, the shorting bar shorts the ABS indicator terminal to ground turning on the indicator.

Diagnostic Aids

- It is very important that a thorough inspection of the wiring and connectors be performed. Failure to carefully and fully inspect wiring and connectors may result in misdiagnosis, causing part replacement with reappearance of the malfunction.
- Thoroughly inspect any circuitry that may be causing the complaint for the following conditions:
  - Backed out terminals
  - Improper mating
  - Broken locks
  - Improperly formed or damaged terminals
  - Poor terminal-to-wiring connections
  - Physical damage to the wiring harness
- The following conditions may cause an intermittent malfunction:
  - A poor connection
  - Rubbed-through wire insulation
  - A broken wire inside the insulation

Test Description

The number(s) below refer to the step number(s) o the diagnostic table.

2. This step checks for an internal EBTCM malfunction.
4. This step checks for an open in the ABS indicator circuit.

GC402980298800AX

Fig. 76 Test B: ABS Lamp Off w/No Code Set (Part 1 of 2). Catera

Circuit Description

The TC indicator is controlled by the EBTCM. The EBTCM supplies the ground to the TC indicator circuit to turn the indicator on. When the TC indicator circuit is not grounded at the EBTCM, the TC indicator remains off. When the EBTCM sees the traction control switch voltage go low, it turns the TC indicator on and disables traction control. The EBTCM harness connector contains a shorting bar for the TC indicator circuit. When the EBTCM connector is disconnected from the EBTCM, the shorting bar shorts the TC indicator terminal to ground turning on the indicator.

Diagnostic Aids

If the EBTCM harness connector is not securely connected to the EBTCM, the shorting bar in the harness connector may turn on the TC indicator. Make sure the EBTCM harness connector is securely connected to the EBTCM.

- It is very important that a thorough inspection of the wiring and connectors be performed. Failure to carefully and fully inspect wiring and connectors may result in misdiagnosis, causing part replacement with reappearance of the malfunction.
- Thoroughly inspect any circuitry that may be causing the complaint for the following conditions:
  - Backed out terminals
  - Improper mating
  - Broken locks
  - Improperly formed or damaged terminals
  - Poor terminal-to-wiring connections
  - Physical damage to the wiring harness
- The following conditions may cause an intermittent malfunction:
  - A poor connection
  - Rubbed-through wire insulation
  - A broken wire inside the insulation

GC402980299000AX

Fig. 77 Test C: TC Lamp On w/No Code Set (Part 1 of 2). Catera

Step	Action	Value(s)	Yes	No
1	Was the Diagnostic System Check performed?	—	*Go to Step 2*	Go to *Diagnostic System Check*
2	1. Inspect the WSS wiring and connectors for damage. 2. Inspect the WSS for looseness or damage. Is physical damage of sensor evident?	—	*Go to Step 3*	*Go to Step 4*
3	Repair as necessary. Is the repair complete?	—	Go to *Diagnostic System Check*	—
4	1. Turn the ignition switch to the OFF position. 2. Disconnect the EBTCM. 3. Install the *J 39700* Universal Pinout Box using the *J 39700-25* cable adapter to the EBTCM harness connector only. 4. Using *J 39200* DMM, measure the resistance between terminals 13 and 29 of *J 39700*. Is the resistance within the range specified in the value(s) column?	850-1350Ω	*Go to Step 12*	*Go to Step 5*
5	1. Disconnect the RR Wheel Speed Sensor. 2. Using *J 39200* DMM, measure the resistance between terminals A and B of the Wheel Speed Sensor Connector. Is the resistance within the range specified in the value(s) column?	850-1350Ω	*Go to Step 6*	*Go to Step 11*
6	Using *J 39200* DMM, measure the resistance between terminals 29 of *J 39700* and A of the RR Wheel Speed Sensor harness connector. Is the resistance within the range specified in the value(s) column?	0-5Ω	*Go to Step 8*	*Go to Step 7*
7	Repair CKT 882 for an open or high resistance. Is the repair complete?	—	Go to *Diagnostic System Check*	—
8	Using *J 39200* DMM, measure the resistance between terminals 13 of *J 39700* and B of the RR Wheel Speed Sensor harness connector. Is the resistance within the range specified in the value(s) column?	0-5Ω	*Go to Step 10*	*Go to Step 9*
9	Repair CKT 883 for an open or high resistance. Is the repair complete?	—	Go to *Diagnostic System Check*	—
10	Malfunction is intermittent. Inspect all connectors and harnesses for damage that may result in an open or high resistance when connected. Is the repair complete?	—	Go to *Diagnostic System Check*	—
11	Replace the Wheel Speed Sensor. Is the replacement complete?	—	Go to *Diagnostic System Check*	—

GC402980299000BX

Fig. 77 Test C: TC Lamp On w/No Code Set (Part 2 of 2). Catera

Step	Action	Value(s)	Yes	No
DEFINITION: TC indicator is inoperative when attempting to disable traction control.				
1	Was the Diagnostic System Check performed?	—	*Go to Step 2*	Go to *ABS Diagnostic System Check*
2	1. Turn the ignition switch to the RUN position, engine off. 2. Using a scan tool enter ABS/TCS Data List. 3. While monitoring the TCS On/Off switch status, press and release the TCS On/Off switch. Does the switch status change from pressed to released as the TCS switch is pressed and released?	—	*Go to Step 3*	*Go to Step 8*
3	1. Turn the ignition switch to the OFF position. 2. Disconnect the EBTCM connector C1. 3. Install the *J 39700* Universal Pinout Box using the J 39700-280 cable adapter to connector C1 only. 4. Connect a fused jumper wire between terminals 20 and 19 of *J 39700*. 5. Turn the ignition switch to the RUN position, engine off. Does the TC Indicator turn on?	—	*Go to Step 4*	*Go to Step 5*
4	Replace the EBTCM. **Is the repair complete?**	—	Go to *ABS Diagnostic System Check*	—
5	1. Turn the ignition switch to the OFF position. 2. Disconnect the Instrument Cluster connector. 3. Using *J 39200* DMM, measure the resistance between terminal 20 of *J 39700* and the Instrument Cluster harness connector terminal 2. Is the resistance within the range specified in the value(s) column?	0–5Ω	*Go to Step 7*	*Go to Step 6*
6	Repair CKT XB105 for an open or high resistance. Is the repair complete?	—	Go to *ABS Diagnostic System Check*	—
7	Suspect the Instrument Cluster. Is the repair complete?	—	Go to *ABS Diagnostic System Check*	—
8	1. Turn the ignition switch to the OFF position. 2. Disconnect the EBTCM connector C1. 3. Install the *J 39700* Universal Pinout Box using the J 39700-280 cable adapter to connector C1 only. 4. Using *J 39200* DMM, measure the resistance between terminals 31 and 19 of *J 39700* while an assistant presses the TCS On/Off switch. Is the resistance within the range specified in the value(s) column?	0-5Ω	*Go to Step 4*	*Go to Step 9*
9	Repair CKT XA105 for an open or high resistance, being sure to check the traction control switch for an open. Is the repair complete?	—	Go to *ABS Diagnostic System Check*	—

GC402980299100BX

Fig. 78 Test D: TC Lamp Off w/No Code Set (Part 2 of 2). Catera

Circuit Description

The TC indicator is controlled by the EBTCM. The EBTCM supplies the ground to the TC indicator circuit to turn the indicator on. When the TC indicator circuit is not grounded at the EBTCM, the TC indicator remains off. When the EBTCM sees the traction control switch voltage go low, it turns the TC indicator on and disables traction control. The EBTCM harness connector contains a shorting bar for the TC indicator circuit. When the EBTCM connector is disconnected from the EBTCM, the shorting bar shorts the TC indicator terminal to ground turning on the indicator.

Diagnostic Aids

- It is very important that a thorough inspection of the wiring and connectors be performed. Failure to carefully and fully inspect wiring and connectors may result in misdiagnosis, causing part replacement with reappearance of the malfunction.
- Thoroughly inspect any circuitry that may be causing the complaint for the following conditions:
  - Backed out terminals
  - Improper mating
  - Broken locks
  - Improperly formed or damaged terminals
  - Poor terminal-to-wiring connections
  - Physical damage to the wiring harness
- The following conditions may cause an intermittent malfunction:
  - A poor connection
  - Rubbed-through wire insulation
  - A broken wire inside the insulation

Test Description

The number(s) below refer to the step number(s) of the diagnostic table.

3. This step checks for an internal EBTCM malfunction.
5. This step checks for an open in CKT XB105.

GC402980299100AX

Fig. 78 Test D: TC Lamp Off w/No Code Set (Part 1 of 2). Catera

Circuit Description

The Keyword 2000 serial data link allows information to be exchanged from module to module as needed. This is done by the PCM, the PCM requests and sends all the information that is transmitted on the Keyword 2000 line. When a scan tool is connected to the Keyword line it takes over for the PCM and sends and requests the needed information.

Diagnostic Aids

- Thoroughly inspect the wiring and the connectors. Failure to carefully and fully inspect the wiring and the connectors can result in misdiagnosis. Misdiagnosis may cause replacement of parts without repairing the malfunction.

Step	Action	Value(s)	Yes	No
DEFINITION: Scan tool can not communicate with the EBTCM.				
1	Was the Diagnostic System Check performed?	—	*Go to Step 2*	Go to *ABS Diagnostic System Check*
2	Turn the Ignition switch to the RUN position with the engine off. Can the scan tool communicate with other modules on the Keyword 2000 serial data line, such as the PCM?	—	*Go to Step 3*	Inspect *Data Link Connector System Check*
3	Inspect the 10A ABS Fuse 19 in the Fuse Block. Is the fuse OK?	—	*Go to Step 4*	*Go to Step 6*

GC402980298700AX

Fig. 79 Test E: No Communication w/EBTCM (Part 1 of 3). Catera

Step	Action	Value(s)	Yes	No
4	1. Install the fuse if removed. 2. Turn the ignition switch to the RUN position, engine off. 3. Using *J 39200* DMM, measure the voltage at the 10A ABS Fuse 19 by probing between the fuse test terminals and a good ground. Is the voltage within the range specified within the value(s) column?	Battery Volts	*Go to Step 5*	Inspect *Power Distribution Schematics*
5	1. Turn the ignition switch to the OFF position. 2. Disconnect the EBTCM connector C1. 3. Connect the *J 39700* Universal Pinout Box using the J 39700-280 cable adapter to the EBTCM harness connector C1 only. 4. Using *J 39200* DMM, measure the resistance between *J 39700* terminal 19 and a good ground. Is the resistance within the range specified in the value(s) column?	0 - 5Ω	*Go to Step 10*	*Go to Step 9*
6	1. Install a new 10A ABS Fuse 19. 2. Turn the ignition switch from the OFF to RUN position, engine off. 3. Recheck the fuse. Is the fuse OK?	—	Go to *ABS Diagnostic System Check*	*Go to Step 7*
7	1. Turn the ignition switch to the OFF position. 2. Remove the 10A ABS Fuse 19. 3. Disconnect the EBTCM connector C1. 4. Connect the *J 39700* Universal Pinout Box using the J 39700-280 cable adapter to the EBTCM harness connector C1 only. 5. Using *J 39200* DMM, measure the resistance between terminals 15 and 19 of *J 39700*. Is the resistance within the range specified in the value(s) column?	OL (infinite)	*Go to Step 12*	*Go to Step 8*
8	Repair CKT FA202 for a short to ground. Is the repair complete?	—	Go to *ABS Diagnostic System Check*	—
9	Repair the ground circuit or G103 for an open or high resistance. Is the repair complete?	—	Go to *ABS Diagnostic System Check*	—

GC402980298700BX

Fig. 79 Test E: No Communication w/EBTCM (Part 2 of 3). Catera

Step	Action	Value(s)	Yes	No
10	1. Turn the ignition switch to the RUN position, engine off. 2. Using *J 39200* DMM, measure the voltage between *J 39700* terminals 15 and 19. Is the voltage within the range specified in the value(s) column?	Battery Volts	*Go to Step 13*	*Go to Step 11*
11	Repair CKT FA202 for an open or high resistance. Is the repair complete?	—	Go to *ABS Diagnostic System Check*	—
12	Replace the EBTCM. Is the replacement complete?	—	Go to *ABS Diagnostic System Check*	—
13	1. Turn the ignition switch to the OFF position. 2. Using *J 39200* DMM, measure the resistance between the *J 39700* terminal 11 and the DLC terminal 12. Is the resistance within the range specified in the values column?	0–5Ω	*Go to Step 12*	*Go to Step 14*
14	Repair the Keyword 2000 serial data circuit for an open or high resistance. Is the repair complete?	—	Go to *ABS Diagnostic System Check*	—

GC402980298700CX

Fig. 79 Test E: No Communication w/EBTCM (Part 3 of 3). Catera

Step	Action	Value(s)	Yes	No
1	1. Reconnect all previously disconnected components. 2. Turn the ignition switch from the OFF to RUN position, engine off. 3. Plug a scan tool into the Diagnostic Link Connector (DLC). Does the scan tool communicate with the EBTCM?	—	*Go to Step 3*	*Go to Step 2*
2	Does the scan tool communicate with other modules on the UART serial data line?	—	Go to *No Communication with EBTCM*	*Data Link Communications System*
3	1. Disconnect the scan tool. 2. Turn the ignition switch from the OFF to Run position. 3. Carefully road test the vehicle for several minutes over different road surfaces and with several turns above 24 km/h (12 mph). 4. Plug a scan tool into the Diagnostic Link Connector (DLC). 5. With the scan tool read ABS/TCS DTC(s). Are there any current Diagnostic Trouble Codes?	—	Go to *DTC List* for the Applicable DTC Table	*Go to Step 4*
4	1. Remove the scan tool from the DLC. 2. Turn the ignition switch from the OFF to RUN position, engine off. Does the ABS Indicator turn on then turn off after several seconds?	—	*Go to Step 5*	*Go to Step 7*
5	Turn the ignition switch from the OFF to RUN position, engine off. Does the LOW TRAC Indicator turn on then turn off after several seconds?	—	*Go to Step 6*	*Go to Step 9*
6	Turn the ignition switch from the OFF to RUN position, engine off. Does the TRAC OFF Indicator turn on then turn off after several seconds?	—	*Go to Step 10*	*Go to Step 8*
7	Does the ABS Indicator stay on?	—	Go to *ABS Indicator On No DTC Set*	Go to *ABS Indicator Off No DTC Set*
8	Does the TRAC OFF Indicator stay on?	—	Go to *Traction Off Indicator On with No DTC Set*	Go to *Traction Off Indicator Inoperative with No DTC Set*
9	Does the LOW TRAC Indicator stay on?	—	Go to *Low Traction Indicator Always On*	Go to *Low Traction Indicator Inoperative*
10	Are there any history DTC(s)?	—	*Go to Step 11*	System OK
11	1. Refer to the appropriate DTC table for the history DTC. 2. Read the diagnostic aids and the conditions for setting the DTC. 3. Unplug the scan tool from the DLC if not already removed. 4. Turn the ignition switch from the OFF to RUN position. 5. Carefully drive the vehicle above 24 Km/h (15 mph) for several minutes. 6. Leave the vehicle running and plug the scan tool into the DLC. 7. With the scan tool read ABS/TCS DTC(s). Did the history DTC set as a current DTC while the vehicle was being driven?	—	Go to *DTC List* for the Applicable DTC Table	System OK

GC4029903878020X

Fig. 80 ABS Diagnostic System Check (Part 2 of 2). 2000 Grand Prix & Intrigue

Circuit Description

The EBTCM Diagnostic System Check is an organized approach to identify problems associated with the EBTCM. This check must be the starting point for any EBTCM complaint, and will direct you to the next logical step in diagnosing the complaint. The EBTCM is a very reliable component and is not likely the cause of the malfunction. Most system complaints are linked to faulty wiring, connectors, and occasionally to components. Understanding the ABS system and using the tables correctly will reduce diagnostic time and prevent unnecessary parts replacement.

Diagnostic Aids

- An intermittent failure in the electronic system may be very difficult to detect and to accurately diagnose. The EBTCM tests for different malfunctions under different vehicle conditions. For this reason, a thorough test drive is often needed in order to repeat a malfunction. If the system malfunction is not repeated during the test drive, a good description of the complaint may be very useful in locating an intermittent malfunction. Faulty electrical connections or wiring causes most intermitting problems. When an intermittent condition is suspected, check the suspected circuits for the following conditions:
  - Poor mating of connector halves or backed out terminals
  - Improperly formed or damaged terminals
  - Wire chafing
  - Poor wire to terminal connections
  - Dirty or corroded terminals
  - Damage to connector bodies
- If there is a history DTC stored, the problem may be intermittent. Perform the tests shown while moving related wiring and connectors. This can often cause the malfunction to occur. Perform a thorough inspection of all related wiring and connectors pertaining to the history DTC stored.

GC4029903878010X

Fig. 80 ABS Diagnostic System Check (Part 1 of 2). 2000 Grand Prix & Intrigue

Circuit Description

The speed sensor used on this vehicle is a multiple pole magnetic pickup. This sensor produces an AC signal that the EBCM uses the frequency from to calculate the wheel speed.

Conditions for Setting the DTC

The DTC can be set any time the ignition is in the ON position and the EBCM detects an open or a short to voltage.

Action Taken When the DTC Sets

- A malfunction DTC stores.
- The ABS/TCS disables.
- The amber ABS/TCS indicator(s) turn on.

Conditions for Clearing the DTC

- The condition responsible for setting the DTC no longer exists and the scan tool Clear DTCs function is used.
- 100 ignition cycles pass with no DTC(s) detected.

Diagnostic Aids

- It is very important that a thorough inspection of the wiring and connectors be performed. Failure to carefully and fully inspect wiring and connectors may result in misdiagnosis, causing part replacement with reappearance of the malfunction.
- Thoroughly inspect any circuitry that may be causing the complaint for the following conditions:
  - Backed out terminals
  - Improper mating
  - Broken locks
  - Improperly formed or damaged terminals
  - Poor terminal-to-wiring connections
  - Physical damage to the wiring harness
- The following conditions may cause an intermittent malfunction:
  - A poor connection
  - Rubbed-through wire insulation
  - A broken wire inside the insulation
- If the customer's comments reflect that the amber ABS/TCS indicator is on only during moist environmental conditions (rain, snow, vehicle wash), inspect all the wheel speed sensor circuitry for signs of water intrusion. If the DTC is not current, clear all DTCs and simulate the effects of water intrusion by using the following procedure:
  1. Spray the suspected area with a five percent saltwater solution.

     Add two teaspoons of salt to twelve ounces of water to make a five percent saltwater solution.
  2. Test drive the vehicle over various road surfaces (bumps, turns, etc.) above 40 km/h (25 mph) for at least 30 seconds.
  3. If the DTC returns, replace the suspected harness.

GC4020052001010X

Fig. 81 Code C0035: LH Front Wheel Speed Circuit Fault (Part 1 of 3). 2000 Grand Prix & Intrigue

Front Wheel Speed Sensor Resistance

The following table contains resistance values for the front wheel speed sensors at varying sensor temperatures for use in diagnosis. The values are approximate and should be used as a guideline for diagnosis.

Sensor Temperature (°C)	Sensor Temperature (°F)	Sensor Resistance (Ohms)
-34 to 4	-30 to 40	800 to 1100
5 to 43	41 to 110	950 to 1300
44 to 93	111 to 200	1100 to 1600

Test Description

The numbers below refer to step numbers on the diagnostic table.

6. This step checks for an open in the WSS or WSS CKT.
13. Checks for a short to voltage in the WSS CKT.
15. Checks for a short to voltage in the WSS CKT.

Step	Action	Value(s)	Yes	No
1	Was the Diagnostic System Check performed?	—	*Go to Step 2*	Go to *A Diagnostic System Check - ABS*
2	Inspect the WSS for physical damage. Is physical damage of the WSS evident?	—	*Go to Step 3*	*Go to Step 4*
3	Replace the WSS. Is the replacement complete?	—	*Go to Step 18*	—
4	Inspect the jumper harness for physical damage. Is physical damage of the jumper harness evident?	—	*Go to Step 5*	*Go to Step 6*
5	Replace the jumper harness. Is the replacement complete?	—	*Go to Step 18*	—
6	1. Turn the ignition switch to the OFF position. 2. Disconnect the EBTCM. 3. Install the *J 39700* universal pinout box using the *J 39700-530* cable adapter to the EBCM harness connector only. 4. Using DMM, measure the resistance between terminals 20 and 21 of the *J 39700* universal pinout box Is the resistance within the range specified in the value(s) column?	800–1600 Ω	*Go to Step 13*	*Go to Step 7*
7	1. Disconnect the wheel speed sensor. 2. Using DMM, measure the resistance between terminals A and B of the wheel speed sensor connector. Is the resistance within the range specified in the value(s) column?	800–1600 Ω	*Go to Step 8*	*Go to Step 3*
8	Using DMM, measure the resistance between terminal 20 of the *J 39700* universal pinout box and terminal A of the WSS harness connector. Is the resistance within the range specified in the value(s) column?	0-5 Ω	*Go to Step 10*	*Go to Step 9*
9	Repair CKT 830 for an open or high resistance. If open or high resistance is found in the jumper harness, replace the jumper harness. Is the repair complete?	—	*Go to Step 18*	—

GC4020052001020X

Fig. 81 Code C0035: LH Front Wheel Speed Circuit Fault (Part 2 of 3). 2000 Grand Prix & Intrigue

Step	Action	Value(s)	Yes	No
10	Using DMM, measure the resistance between terminal 21 of the *J 39700* universal pinout box and terminal B of the WSS harness connector. Is the resistance within the range specified in the value(s) column?	0-5 Ω	*Go to Step 12*	*Go to Step 11*
11	Repair CKT 873 for an open or high resistance. If open or high resistance is found in the jumper harness, replace the jumper harness. Is the repair complete?	—	*Go to Step 18*	—
12	Malfunction is intermittent. Inspect all connectors and harnesses for damage that may result in an open or high resistance when connected. Is the repair complete?	—	*Go to Step 18*	—
13	1. Disconnect the wheel speed sensor. 2. Turn the ignition switch to the ON position, engine off. 3. Using DMM, measure the voltage at terminal 20 of the *J 39700* universal pinout box. Is the voltage above the value specified in the value(s) column?	0 V	*Go to Step 14*	*Go to Step 15*
14	Repair CKT 830 for a short to voltage. If short to voltage is found in the jumper harness, replace the jumper harness. Is the repair complete?	—	*Go to Step 18*	—
15	Using DMM, measure the voltage at terminal 21 of the *J 39700* universal pinout box. Is the voltage above the value specified in the value(s) column?	0 V	*Go to Step 16*	*Go to Step 17*
16	Repair CKT 873 for a short to voltage. If short to voltage is found in the jumper harness, replace the jumper harness. Is the repair complete?	—	*Go to Step 18*	—
17	Replace the EBCM. Is the replacement complete?	—	*Go to A Diagnostic System Check - ABS*	—
18	1. Reconnect all previously disconnected components. 2. Using a scan tool clear the DTC. 3. Remove the scan tool from the DLC. 4. Carefully drive the vehicle above 12 km/h (8 mph) for several minutes. Does the DTC reset as a current DTC?	—	*Go to Step 2*	*Go to A Diagnostic System Check - ABS*

GC4020052001030X

Fig. 81 Code C0035: LH Front Wheel Speed Circuit Fault (Part 3 of 3). 2000 Grand Prix & Intrigue

Front Wheel Speed Sensor Resistance

The following table contains resistance values for the front wheel speed sensors at varying sensor temperatures for use in diagnosis. The values are approximate and should be used as a guideline for diagnosis.

Sensor Temperature (°C)	Sensor Temperature (°F)	Sensor Resistance (Ohms)
-34 to 4	-30 to 40	800 to 1100
5 to 43	41 to 110	950 to 1300
44 to 93	111 to 200	1100 to 1600

Test Description

The number(s) below refer to the step number(s) on the diagnostic table.

6. This step checks for the proper resistance in the WSS.
7. This step checks for the proper WSS output.

Step	Action	Value(s)	Yes	No
1	Was the Diagnostic System Check performed?	—	*Go to Step 2*	*Go to Diagnostic System Check*
2	Inspect the WSS for physical damage. Is physical damage of the WSS evident?	—	*Go to Step 3*	*Go to Step 4*
3	Replace the WSS. Is the replacement complete?	—	*Go to Step 16*	—
4	Inspect the jumper harness for physical damage. Is physical damage of the jumper harness evident?	—	*Go to Step 5*	*Go to Step 6*
5	Replace the jumper harness. Is the replacement complete?	—	*Go to Step 16*	—
6	1. Disconnect the WSS connector directly at the WSS. 2. Using *J 39200* DMM, measure the resistance between terminals A and B of the WSS. Is the resistance within the range specified in the value(s) column?	800–1600 Ω	*Go to Step 7*	*Go to Step 3*
7	1. With the *J 39200* DMM still connected to the WSS select the mV AC scale. 2. Spin the wheel as fast as you can by hand while monitoring the AC output. Is the AC voltage within the range specified in the value(s) column?	Above 100 mV	*Go to Step 8*	*Go to Step 3*
8	Using *J 39200* DMM, measure the resistance between the WSS terminal A and ground. Is the resistance within the range specified in the value(s) column?	OL (infinite)	*Go to Step 9*	*Go to Step 3*
9	1. Disconnect the EBTCM harness connector. 2. Install the *J 39700* Universal Pinout Box using the J 39700-530 cable adapter to the EBTCM harness connector only. 3. Using *J 39200* DMM, measure the resistance between terminals 20 and 21 of *J 39700*. Is the resistance within the range specified in the values column?	OL (infinite)	*Go to Step 11*	*Go to Step 10*

GC402980329900BX

Fig. 82 Code C0036: LH Front Wheel Speed Circuit Range/Performance (Part 2 of 3). 2000 Grand Prix & Intrigue

Circuit Description

The speed sensor used on this vehicle is a multiple pole magnetic pickup. This sensor produces an AC signal that the EBTCM uses the frequency from to calculate the wheel speed.

Conditions for Setting the DTC

- The DTC will set if one wheel speed = 0 and the other WSS are greater than 40 Km/h (25 mph) for 10 ms.
- The DTC will set if during drive off, one wheel speed = 0, and the other WSS are greater than 12 Km/h (7.5 mph).
- The EBTCM detects a short to ground.

Action Taken When the DTC Sets

- A malfunction DTC stores.
- The ABS/TCS disables.
- The amber ABS/TCS indicator(s) turn on.

Conditions for Clearing the DTC

- The condition responsible for setting the DTC no longer exists and the scan tool Clear DTCs function is used.
- 100 ignition cycles pass with no DTC(s) detected.

Diagnostic Aids

- It is very important that a thorough inspection of the wiring and connectors be performed. Failure to carefully and fully inspect wiring and connectors may result in misdiagnosis, causing part replacement with reappearance of the malfunction.
- Thoroughly inspect any circuitry that may be causing the complaint for the following conditions:
  - Backed out terminals
  - Improper mating
  - Broken locks
  - Improperly formed or damaged terminals
  - Poor terminal-to-wiring connections
  - Physical damage to the wiring harness
- The following conditions may cause an intermittent malfunction:
  - A poor connection
  - Rubbed-through wire insulation
  - A broken wire inside the insulation
- If the customer's comments reflect that the amber ABS/TCS indicator is on only during moist environmental conditions (rain, snow, vehicle wash), inspect all the wheel speed sensor circuitry for signs of water intrusion. If the DTC is not current, clear all DTCs and simulate the effects of water intrusion by using the following procedure:
  1. Spray the suspected area with a five percent saltwater solution.
     Add two teaspoons of salt to twelve ounces of water to make a five percent saltwater solution.
  2. Test drive the vehicle over various road surfaces (bumps, turns, etc.) above 40 km/h (25 mph) for at least 30 seconds.
  3. If the DTC returns, replace the suspected harness.
- If an intermittent malfunction exists refer to Troubleshooting Electrical Diagnosis

GC402980329900AX

Fig. 82 Code C0036: LH Front Wheel Speed Circuit Range/Performance (Part 1 of 3). 2000 Grand Prix & Intrigue

Step	Action	Value(s)	Yes	No
10	Repair short between CKT(s) 830 and 873. If short between wheel speed sensor circuits is found in the jumper harness, replace the jumper harness. Is the repair complete?	—	*Go to Step 16*	—
11	Using *J 39200* DMM, measure the resistance between terminals 20 and 15 of *J 39700*. Is the resistance within the range specified in the values column?	OL (infinite)	*Go to Step 13*	*Go to Step 12*
12	Repair CKT 830 for a short to ground. If short to ground is found in the jumper harness, replace the jumper harness. Is the repair complete?	—	*Go to Step 16*	—
13	Using *J 39200* DMM, measure the resistance between terminals 21 and 15 of *J 39700*. Is the resistance within the range specified in the values column?	OL (infinite)	*Go to Step 15*	*Go to Step 14*
14	Repair CKT 873 for a short to ground. If short to ground is found in the jumper harness, replace the jumper harness. Is the repair complete?	—	*Go to Step 16*	—
15	Replace the EBTCM. Is the replacement complete?	—	*Go to Diagnostic System Check*	—
16	1. Reconnect all previously disconnected components. 2. Using a scan tool clear the DTC. 3. Remove the scan tool from the DLC. 4. Carefully drive vehicle above 12 Km/h (8 mph) for several minutes. Does the DTC reset as a current DTC?	—	*Go to Step 2*	*Go to Diagnostic System Check*

GC402980329900CX

Fig. 82 Code C0036: LH Front Wheel Speed Circuit Range/Performance (Part 3 of 3). 2000 Grand Prix & Intrigue

Circuit Description

The speed sensor used on this vehicle is a multiple pole magnetic pickup. This sensor produces an AC signal that the EBCM uses the frequency from to calculate the wheel speed.

Conditions for Setting the DTC

The DTC can be set any time the ignition is in the ON position and the EBCM detects an open or a short to voltage.

Action Taken When the DTC Sets

- A malfunction DTC stores.
- The ABS/TCS disables.
- The amber ABS/TCS indicator(s) turn on.

Conditions for Clearing the DTC

- The condition responsible for setting the DTC no longer exists and the scan tool Clear DTCs function is used.
- 100 ignition cycles pass with no DTC(s) detected.

Diagnostic Aids

- It is very important that a thorough inspection of the wiring and connectors be performed. Failure to carefully and fully inspect wiring and connectors may result in misdiagnosis, causing part replacement with reappearance of the malfunction.
- Thoroughly inspect any circuitry that may be causing the complaint for the following conditions:
  - Backed out terminals
  - Improper mating
  - Broken locks
  - Improperly formed or damaged terminals
  - Poor terminal-to-wiring connections
  - Physical damage to the wiring harness
- The following conditions may cause an intermittent malfunction:
  - A poor connection
  - Rubbed-through wire insulation
  - A broken wire inside the insulation
- If the customer's comments reflect that the amber ABS/TCS indicator is on only during moist environmental conditions (rain, snow, vehicle wash), inspect all the wheel speed sensor circuitry for signs of water intrusion. If the DTC is not current, clear all DTCs and simulate the effects of water intrusion by using the following procedure:
  1. Spray the suspected area with a five percent saltwater solution.

     Add two teaspoons of salt to twelve ounces of water to make a five percent saltwater solution.
  2. Test drive the vehicle over various road surfaces (bumps, turns, etc.) above 40 km/h (25 mph) for at least 30 seconds.
  3. If the DTC returns, replace the suspected harness.

GC4020052002010X

Fig. 83 Code C0040: RH Front Wheel Speed Circuit Fault (Part 1 of 3). 2000 Grand Prix & Intrigue

Front Wheel Speed Sensor Resistance

The following table contains resistance values for the front wheel speed sensors at varying sensor temperatures for use in diagnosis. The values are approximate and should be used as a guideline for diagnosis.

Sensor Temperature (°C)	Sensor Temperature (°F)	Sensor Resistance (Ohms)
-34 to 4	-30 to 40	800 to 1100
5 to 43	41 to 110	950 to 1300
44 to 93	111 to 200	1100 to 1600

Test Description

The numbers below refer to step numbers on the diagnostic table.

6. This step checks for an open in the WSS or WSS CKT.
13. Checks for a short to voltage in the WSS CKT.
15. Checks for a short to voltage in the WSS CKT.

Step	Action	Value(s)	Yes	No
1	Was the Diagnostic System Check performed?	—	*Go to Step 2*	*Go to A Diagnostic System Check - ABS*
2	Inspect the WSS for physical damage. Is physical damage of the WSS evident?	—	*Go to Step 3*	*Go to Step 4*
3	Replace the WSS. Is the replacement complete?	—	*Go to Step 18*	—
4	Inspect the jumper harness for physical damage. Is physical damage of the jumper harness evident?	—	*Go to Step 5*	*Go to Step 6*
5	Replace the jumper harness. Is the replacement complete?	—	*Go to Step 18*	—
6	1. Turn the ignition switch to the OFF position. 2. Disconnect the EBCM. 3. Install the *J 39700* universal pinout box using the *J 39700-530* cable adapter to the EBCM harness connector only. 4. Using DMM, measure the resistance between terminals 4 and 5 of the universal pinout box. Is the resistance within the range specified in the value(s) column?	800–1600 Ω	*Go to Step 13*	*Go to Step 7*
7	1. Disconnect the wheel speed sensor. 2. Using DMM, measure the resistance between terminals A and B of the wheel speed sensor connector. Is the resistance within the range specified in the value(s) column?	800–1600 Ω	*Go to Step 8*	*Go to Step 3*
8	Using DMM, measure the resistance between terminal 4 of the *J 39700* universal pinout box and terminal A of the WSS harness connector. Is the resistance within the range specified in the value(s) column?	0-5 Ω	*Go to Step 10*	*Go to Step 9*
9	Repair CKT 872 for an open or high resistance. Refer to *Wiring Repairs* in Wiring Systems. If open or high resistance is found in the jumper harness, replace the jumper harness. Is the repair complete?	—	*Go to Step 18*	—

GC4020052002020X

Fig. 83 Code C0040: RH Front Wheel Speed Circuit Fault (Part 2 of 3). 2000 Grand Prix & Intrigue

Step	Action	Value(s)	Yes	No
10	Using DMM, measure the resistance between terminal 5 of the *J 39700* universal pinout box and terminal B of the WSS harness connector. Is the resistance within the range specified in the value(s) column?	0-5 Ω	*Go to Step 12*	*Go to Step 11*
11	Repair CKT 833 for an open or high resistance. If open or high resistance is found in the jumper harness, replace the jumper harness. Is the repair complete?	—	*Go to Step 18*	—
12	Malfunction is intermittent. Inspect all connectors and harnesses for damage that may result in an open or high resistance when connected. Is the repair complete?	—	*Go to Step 18*	—
13	1. Disconnect the wheel speed sensor. 2. Turn the ignition switch to the ON position, engine off. 3. Using DMM, measure the voltage at terminal 4 of the *J 39700* universal pinout box. Is the voltage above the value specified in the value(s) column?	0 V	*Go to Step 14*	*Go to Step 15*
14	Repair CKT 872 for a short to voltage. If short to voltage is found in the jumper harness, replace the jumper harness. Is the repair complete?	—	*Go to Step 18*	—
15	Using DMM, measure the voltage at terminal 5 of the *J 39700* universal pinout box. Is the voltage above the value specified in the value(s) column?	0 V	*Go to Step 16*	*Go to Step 17*
16	Repair CKT 833 for a short to voltage. If short to voltage is found in the jumper harness, replace the jumper harness. Is the repair complete?	—	*Go to Step 18*	—
17	Replace the EBCM. Is the replacement complete?	—	*Go to A Diagnostic System Check - ABS*	—
18	1. Reconnect all previously disconnected components. 2. Using a scan tool clear the DTC. 3. Remove the scan tool from the DLC. 4. Carefully drive the vehicle above 12 km/h (8 mph) for several minutes. Does the DTC reset as a current DTC?	—	*Go to Step 2*	*Go to A Diagnostic System Check - ABS*

GC4020052002030X

Fig. 83 Code C0040: RH Front Wheel Speed Circuit Fault (Part 3 of 3). 2000 Grand Prix & Intrigue

Circuit Description

The speed sensor used on this vehicle is a multiple pole magnetic pickup. This sensor produces an AC signal that the EBCM uses the frequency from to calculate the wheel speed.

Conditions for Setting the DTC

- The DTC will set if one wheel speed = 0 and the other WSS are greater than 40 km/h (25 mph) for 10 ms.
- The DTC will set if during drive off, one wheel speed = 0, and the other WSS are greater than 12 km/h (7.5 mph).
- The EBCM detects a short to ground.

Action Taken When the DTC Sets

- A malfunction DTC stores.
- The ABS/TCS disables.
- The amber ABS/TCS indicator(s) turn on.

Conditions for Clearing the DTC

- The condition responsible for setting the DTC no longer exists and the scan tool Clear DTCs function is used.
- 100 ignition cycles pass with no DTC(s) detected.

Diagnostic Aids

- It is very important that a thorough inspection of the wiring and connectors be performed. Failure to carefully and fully inspect wiring and connectors may result in misdiagnosis, causing part replacement with reappearance of the malfunction.
- Thoroughly inspect any circuitry that may be causing the complaint for the following conditions:
  - Backed out terminals
  - Improper mating
  - Broken locks
  - Improperly formed or damaged terminals
  - Poor terminal-to-wiring connections
  - Physical damage to the wiring harness
- The following conditions may cause an intermittent malfunction:
  - A poor connection
  - Rubbed-through wire insulation
  - A broken wire inside the insulation
- If the customer's comments reflect that the amber ABS/TCS indicator is on only during moist environmental conditions (rain, snow, vehicle wash), inspect all the wheel speed sensor circuitry for signs of water intrusion. If the DTC is not current, clear all DTCs and simulate the effects of water intrusion by using the following procedure:
  1. Spray the suspected area with a five percent saltwater solution.

     Add two teaspoons of salt to twelve ounces of water to make a five percent saltwater solution.
  2. Test drive the vehicle over various road surfaces (bumps, turns, etc.) above 40 km/h (25 mph) for at least 30 seconds.
  3. If the DTC returns, replace the suspected harness.

GC4020052003010X

Fig. 84 Code C0041: RH Front Wheel Speed Circuit Range/Performance (Part 1 of 3). 2000 Grand Prix & Intrigue

Front Wheel Speed Sensor Resistance

The following table contains resistance values for the front wheel speed sensors at varying sensor temperatures for use in diagnosis. The values are approximate and should be used as a guideline for diagnosis.

Sensor Temperature (°C)	Sensor Temperature (°F)	Sensor Resistance (Ohms)
-34 to 4	-30 to 40	800 to 1100
5 to 43	41 to 110	950 to 1300
44 to 93	111 to 200	1100 to 1600

Test Description

The number(s) below refer to the step number(s) on the diagnostic table.

6. This step checks for the proper resistance in the WSS.
7. This step checks for the proper WSS output.

Step	Action	Value(s)	Yes	No
1	Was the Diagnostic System Check performed?	—	*Go to Step 2*	Go to *A Diagnostic System Check - ABS*
2	Inspect the WSS for physical damage. Is physical damage of the WSS evident?	—	*Go to Step 3*	*Go to Step 4*
3	Replace the WSS. Is the replacement complete?	—	*Go to Step 16*	—
4	Inspect the jumper harness for physical damage. Is physical damage of the jumper harness evident?	—	*Go to Step 5*	*Go to Step 6*
5	Replace the jumper harness. Is the replacement complete?	—	*Go to Step 16*	—
6	1. Disconnect the WSS connector directly at the WSS. 2. Using DMM, measure the resistance between terminals A and B of the WSS. Is the resistance within the range specified in the value(s) column?	800–1600 Ω	*Go to Step 7*	*Go to Step 3*
7	1. With the DMM still connected to the WSS select the mV AC scale. 2. Spin the wheel as fast as you can by hand while monitoring the AC output. Is the AC voltage above the value specified in the value(s) column?	100 mV	*Go to Step 8*	*Go to Step 3*
8	Using DMM, measure the resistance between the WSS terminal A and ground. Is the resistance within the range specified in the value(s) column?	OL (infinite)	*Go to Step 9*	*Go to Step 3*
9	1. Disconnect the EBCM harness connector. 2. Install the *J 39700* universal pinout box using the *J 39700-530* cable adapter to the EBCM harness connector only. 3. Using DMM, measure the resistance between terminals 4 and 5 of the universal pinout box. Is the resistance within the range specified in the values column?	OL (infinite)	*Go to Step 11*	*Go to Step 10*
10	Repair short between CKT(s) 872 and 833. If short between wheel speed sensor circuits is found in the jumper harness, replace the jumper harness. Is the repair complete?	—	*Go to Step 16*	—

GC4020052003020X

Fig. 84 Code C0041: RH Front Wheel Speed Circuit Range/Performance (Part 2 of 3). 2000 Grand Prix & Intrigue

Circuit Description

The speed sensor used on this vehicle is a multiple pole magnetic pickup. This sensor produces an AC signal that the EBCM uses the frequency from to calculate the wheel speed.

Conditions for Setting the DTC

The DTC can be set any time the ignition is in the ON position and the EBCM detects an open or a short to voltage.

Action Taken When the DTC Sets

- A malfunction DTC stores.
- The ABS/TCS disables.
- The amber ABS/TCS indicator(s) turn on.

Conditions for Clearing the DTC

- The condition responsible for setting the DTC no longer exists and the scan tool Clear DTCs function is used.
- 100 ignition cycles pass with no DTC(s) detected.

Diagnostic Aids

- It is very important that a thorough inspection of the wiring and connectors be performed. Failure to carefully and fully inspect wiring and connectors may result in misdiagnosis, causing part replacement with reappearance of the malfunction.
- Thoroughly inspect any circuitry that may be causing the complaint for the following conditions:
  - Backed out terminals
  - Improper mating
  - Broken locks
  - Improperly formed or damaged terminals
  - Poor terminal-to-wiring connections
  - Physical damage to the wiring harness
- The following conditions may cause an intermittent malfunction:
  - A poor connection
  - Rubbed-through wire insulation
  - A broken wire inside the insulation
- If the customer's comments reflect that the amber ABS/TCS indicator is on only during moist environmental conditions (rain, snow, vehicle wash), inspect all the wheel speed sensor circuitry for signs of water intrusion. If the DTC is not current, clear all DTCs and simulate the effects of water intrusion by using the following procedure:
  1. Spray the suspected area with a five percent saltwater solution.

     Add two teaspoons of salt to twelve ounces of water to make a five percent saltwater solution.
  2. Test drive the vehicle over various road surfaces (bumps, turns, etc.) above 40 km/h (25 mph) for at least 30 seconds.
  3. If the DTC returns, replace the suspected harness.

GC4020052004010X

Fig. 85 Code C0045: LH Rear Wheel Speed Circuit Fault (Part 1 of 3). 2000 Grand Prix & Intrigue

Step	Action	Value(s)	Yes	No
11	Using DMM, measure the resistance between terminals 4 and 15 of the *J 39700* universal pinout box. Is the resistance within the range specified in the values column?	OL (infinite)	*Go to Step 13*	*Go to Step 12*
12	Repair CKT 872 for a short to ground. If short to ground is found in the jumper harness, replace the jumper harness. Is the repair complete?	—	*Go to Step 16*	—
13	Using DMM, measure the resistance between terminals 5 and 15 of the *J 39700* universal pinout box. Is the resistance within the range specified in the values column?	OL (infinite)	*Go to Step 15*	*Go to Step 14*
14	Repair CKT 833 for a short to ground. If short to ground is found in the jumper harness, replace the jumper harness. Is the repair complete?	—	*Go to Step 16*	—
15	Replace the EBCM. Is the replacement complete?	—	Go to *A Diagnostic System Check - ABS*	—
16	1. Reconnect all previously disconnected components. 2. Using a scan tool clear the DTC. 3. Remove the scan tool from the DLC. 4. Carefully drive vehicle above 12 km/h (8 mph) for several minutes. Does the DTC reset as a current DTC?	—	*Go to Step 2*	Go to *A Diagnostic System Check - ABS*

GC4020052003030X

Fig. 84 Code C0041: RH Front Wheel Speed Circuit Range/Performance (Part 3 of 3). 2000 Grand Prix & Intrigue

Rear Wheel Speed Sensor Resistance

The following table contains resistance values for the rear wheel speed sensors at varying sensor temperatures for use in diagnosis. The values are approximate and should be used as a guideline for diagnosis.

Sensor Temperature (°C)	Sensor Temperature (°F)	Sensor Resistance (Ohms)
-34 to 4	-30 to 40	800 to 1100
5 to 43	41 to 110	950 to 1300
44 to 93	111 to 200	1100 to 1600

Test Description

The numbers below refer to step numbers on the diagnostic table.

6. This step checks for an open in the WSS or WSS CKT.
13. Checks for a short to voltage in the WSS CKT.
15. Checks for a short to voltage in the WSS CKT.

Step	Action	Value(s)	Yes	No
1	Was the Diagnostic System Check performed?	—	*Go to Step 2*	Go to *A Diagnostic System Check - ABS*
2	Inspect the WSS for physical damage. Is physical damage of the WSS evident?	—	*Go to Step 3*	*Go to Step 4*
3	Replace the WSS. Is the replacement complete?	—	*Go to Step 18*	—
4	Inspect the jumper harness for physical damage. Is physical damage of the jumper harness evident?	—	*Go to Step 5*	*Go to Step 6*
5	Replace the jumper harness. Is the replacement complete?	—	*Go to Step 18*	—
6	1. Turn the ignition switch to the OFF position. 2. Disconnect the EBCM. 3. Install the *J 39700* universal pinout box using the *J 39700-530* cable adapter to the EBCM harness connector only. 4. Using DMM, measure the resistance between terminals 22 and 23 of the universal pinout box. Is the resistance within the range specified in the value(s) column?	800–1600 Ω	*Go to Step 13*	*Go to Step 7*
7	1. Disconnect the wheel speed sensor. 2. Using DMM, measure the resistance between terminals A and B of the wheel speed sensor connector. Is the resistance within the range specified in the value(s) column?	800–1600 Ω	*Go to Step 8*	*Go to Step 3*
8	Using DMM, measure the resistance between terminal 22 of the *J 39700* universal pinout box and terminal B of the WSS harness connector. Is the resistance within the range specified in the value(s) column?	0-5 Ω	*Go to Step 10*	*Go to Step 9*
9	Repair CKT 884 for an open or high resistance. If open or high resistance is found in the jumper harness, replace the jumper harness. Is the repair complete?	—	*Go to Step 18*	—

GC4020052004020X

Fig. 85 Code C0045: LH Rear Wheel Speed Circuit Fault (Part 2 of 3). 2000 Grand Prix & Intrigue

Step	Action	Value(s)	Yes	No
10	Using DMM, measure the resistance between terminal 23 of the *J 39700* universal pinout box and terminal A of the WSS harness connector. Is the resistance within the range specified in the value(s) column?	0-5 Ω	*Go to Step 12*	*Go to Step 11*
11	Repair CKT 885 for an open or high resistance. If open or high resistance is found in the jumper harness, replace the jumper harness. Is the repair complete?	—	*Go to Step 18*	—
12	Malfunction is intermittent. Inspect all connectors and harnesses for damage that may result in an open or high resistance when connected. Is the repair complete?	—	*Go to Step 18*	—
13	1. Disconnect the wheel speed sensor. 2. Turn the ignition switch to the ON position, engine off. 3. Using DMM, measure the voltage at terminal 22 of the *J 39700* universal pinout box. Is the voltage above the value specified in the value(s) column?	0 V	*Go to Step 14*	*Go to Step 15*
14	Repair CKT 884 for a short to voltage. If short to voltage is found in the jumper harness, replace the jumper harness. Is the repair complete?	—	*Go to Step 18*	—
15	Using DMM, measure the voltage at terminal 23 of the *J 39700* universal pinout box. Is the voltage above the value specified in the value(s) column?	0 V	*Go to Step 16*	*Go to Step 17*
16	Repair CKT 885 for a short to voltage. If short to voltage is found in the jumper harness, replace the jumper harness. Is the repair complete?	—	*Go to Step 18*	—
17	Replace the EBCM. Is the replacement complete?	—	*Go to A Diagnostic System Check - ABS*	—
18	1. Reconnect all previously disconnected components. 2. Using a scan tool clear the DTC. 3. Remove the scan tool from the DLC. 4. Carefully drive the vehicle above 12 km/h (8 mph) for several minutes. Does the DTC reset as a current DTC?	—	*Go to Step 2*	*Go to A Diagnostic System Check - ABS*

GC4020052004030X

Fig. 85 Code C0045: LH Rear Wheel Speed Circuit Fault (Part 3 of 3). 2000 Grand Prix & Intrigue

Rear Wheel Speed Sensor Resistance

The following table contains resistance values for the rear wheel speed sensors at varying sensor temperatures for use in diagnosis. The values are approximate and should be used as a guideline for diagnosis.

Sensor Temperature (°C)	Sensor Temperature (°F)	Sensor Resistance (Ohms)
-34 to 4	-30 to 40	800 to 1100
5 to 43	41 to 110	950 to 1300
44 to 93	111 to 200	1110 to 1600

Test Description

The number(s) below refer to the step number(s) on the diagnostic table.

6. This step checks for the proper resistance in the WSS.
7. This step checks for the proper WSS output.

DTC C0046 LR Wheel Speed Circuit Range/Performance

Step	Action	Value(s)	Yes	No
1	Was the Diagnostic System Check performed?	—	*Go to Step 2*	*Go to A Diagnostic System Check - ABS*
2	Inspect the WSS for physical damage. Is physical damage of the WSS evident?	—	*Go to Step 3*	*Go to Step 4*
3	Replace the WSS. Is the replacement complete?	—	*Go to Step 16*	—
4	Inspect the jumper harness for physical damage. Is physical damage of the jumper harness evident?	—	*Go to Step 5*	*Go to Step 6*
5	Replace the jumper harness. Is the replacement complete?	—	*Go to Step 16*	—
6	1. Disconnect the WSS connector directly at the WSS. 2. Using DMM, measure the resistance between terminals A and B of the WSS. Is the resistance within the range specified in the value(s) column?	800–1600 Ω	*Go to Step 7*	*Go to Step 3*
7	1. With the DMM still connected to the WSS select the mV AC scale. 2. Spin the wheel as fast as you can by hand while monitoring the AC output. Is the AC voltage above the value specified in the value(s) column?	100 mV	*Go to Step 8*	*Go to Step 3*
8	Using DMM, measure the resistance between the WSS terminal A and ground. Is the resistance within the range specified in the value(s) column?	OL (infinite)	*Go to Step 9*	*Go to Step 3*
9	1. Disconnect the EBCM harness connector. 2. Install the *J 39700* universal pinout box using the *J 39700-530* cable adapter to the EBTCM harness connector only. 3. Using DMM, measure the resistance between terminals 22 and 23 of the universal pinout box. Is the resistance within the range specified in the values column?	OL (infinite)	*Go to Step 11*	*Go to Step 10*
10	Repair short between CKT(s) 884 and 885. If short between wheel speed sensor circuits is found in the jumper harness, replace the jumper harness. Is the repair complete?	—	*Go to Step 16*	—

GC4020052005020X

Fig. 86 Code C0046: LH Rear Wheel Speed Circuit Range/Performance (Part 2 of 3). 2000 Grand Prix & Intrigue

Circuit Description

The speed sensor used on this vehicle is a multiple pole magnetic pickup. This sensor produces an AC signal that the EBCM uses the frequency from to calculate the wheel speed.

Conditions for Setting the DTC

- The DTC will set if one wheel speed = 0 and the other WSS are greater than 40 km/h (25 mph) for 10 ms.
- The DTC will set if during drive off, one wheel speed = 0, and the other WSS are greater than 12 km/h (7.5 mph).
- The EBCM detects a short to ground.

Action Taken When the DTC Sets

- A malfunction DTC stores.
- The ABS/TCS disables.
- The amber ABS/TCS indicator(s) turn on.

Conditions for Clearing the DTC

- The condition responsible for setting the DTC no longer exists and the scan tool Clear DTCs function is used.
- 100 ignition cycles pass with no DTC(s) detected.

Diagnostic Aids

- It is very important that a thorough inspection of the wiring and connectors be performed. Failure to carefully and fully inspect wiring and connectors may result in misdiagnosis, causing part replacement with reappearance of the malfunction.
- Thoroughly inspect any circuitry that may be causing the complaint for the following conditions:
  - Backed out terminals
  - Improper mating
  - Broken locks
  - Improperly formed or damaged terminals
  - Poor terminal-to-wiring connections
  - Physical damage to the wiring harness
- The following conditions may cause an intermittent malfunction:
  - A poor connection
  - Rubbed-through wire insulation
  - A broken wire inside the insulation
- If the customer's comments reflect that the amber ABS/TCS indicator is on only during moist environmental conditions (rain, snow, vehicle wash), inspect all the wheel speed sensor circuitry for signs of water intrusion. If the DTC is not current, clear all DTCs and simulate the effects of water intrusion by using the following procedure:
  1. Spray the suspected area with a five percent saltwater solution.

     Add two teaspoons of salt to twelve ounces of water to make a five percent saltwater solution.
  2. Test drive the vehicle over various road surfaces (bumps, turns, etc.) above 40 km/h (25 mph) for at least 30 seconds.
  3. If the DTC returns, replace the suspected harness.

GC4020052005010X

Fig. 86 Code C0046: LH Rear Wheel Speed Circuit Range/Performance (Part 1 of 3). 2000 Grand Prix & Intrigue

Step	Action	Value(s)	Yes	No
11	Using DMM, measure the resistance between terminals 22 and 15 of the *J 39700* universal pinout box. Is the resistance within the range specified in the values column?	OL (infinite)	*Go to Step 13*	*Go to Step 12*
12	Repair CKT 884 for a short to ground. If short to ground is found in the jumper harness, replace the jumper harness. Is the repair complete?	—	*Go to Step 16*	—
13	Using DMM, measure the resistance between terminals 23 and 15 of the *J 39700* universal pinout box. Is the resistance within the range specified in the values column?	OL (infinite)	*Go to Step 15*	*Go to Step 14*
14	Repair CKT 885 for a short to ground. If short to ground is found in the jumper harness, replace the jumper harness. Is the repair complete?	—	*Go to Step 16*	—
15	Replace the EBCM. Is the replacement complete?	—	*Go to A Diagnostic System Check - ABS*	—
16	1. Reconnect all previously disconnected components. 2. Using a scan tool clear the DTC. 3. Remove the scan tool from the DLC. 4. Carefully drive vehicle above 12 km/h (8 mph) for several minutes. Does the DTC reset as a current DTC?	—	*Go to Step 2*	*Go to A Diagnostic System Check - ABS*

GC4020052005030X

Fig. 86 Code C0046: LH Rear Wheel Speed Circuit Range/Performance (Part 3 of 3). 2000 Grand Prix & Intrigue

Circuit Description

The speed sensor used on this vehicle is a multiple pole magnetic pickup. This sensor produces an AC signal that the EBCM uses the frequency from to calculate the wheel speed.

Conditions for Setting the DTC

The DTC can be set any time the ignition is in the ON position and the EBCM detects an open or a short to voltage.

Action Taken When the DTC Sets

- A malfunction DTC stores.
- The ABS/TCS disables.
- The amber ABS/TCS indicator(s) turn on.

Conditions for Clearing the DTC

- The condition responsible for setting the DTC no longer exists and the scan tool Clear DTCs function is used.
- 100 ignition cycles pass with no DTC(s) detected.

Diagnostic Aids

- It is very important that a thorough inspection of the wiring and connectors be performed. Failure to carefully and fully inspect wiring and connectors may result in misdiagnosis, causing part replacement with reappearance of the malfunction.
- Thoroughly inspect any circuitry that may be causing the complaint for the following conditions:
  - Backed out terminals
  - Improper mating
  - Broken locks
  - Improperly formed or damaged terminals
  - Poor terminal-to-wiring connections
  - Physical damage to the wiring harness
- The following conditions may cause an intermittent malfunction:
  - A poor connection
  - Rubbed-through wire insulation
  - A broken wire inside the insulation
- If the customer's comments reflect that the amber ABS/TCS indicator is on only during moist environmental conditions (rain, snow, vehicle wash), inspect all the wheel speed sensor circuitry for signs of water intrusion. If the DTC is not current, clear all DTCs and simulate the effects of water intrusion by using the following procedure:
  1. Spray the suspected area with a five percent saltwater solution.

     Add two teaspoons of salt to twelve ounces of water to make a five percent saltwater solution.
  2. Test drive the vehicle over various road surfaces (bumps, turns, etc.) above 40 km/h (25 mph) for at least 30 seconds.
  3. If the DTC returns, replace the suspected harness.

GC4020052006010X

Fig. 87 Code C0050: RH Rear Wheel Speed Circuit Fault (Part 1 of 3). 2000 Grand Prix & Intrigue

Rear Wheel Speed Sensor Resistance

The following table contains resistance values for the rear wheel speed sensors at varying sensor temperatures for use in diagnosis. The values are approximate and should be used as a guideline for diagnosis.

Sensor Temperature (°C)	Sensor Temperature (°F)	Sensor Resistance (Ohms)
-34 to 4	-30 to 40	800 to 1100
5 to 43	41 to 110	950 to 1300
44 to 93	111 to 200	1100 to 1600

Test Description

The numbers below refer to step numbers on the diagnostic table.

6. This step checks for an open in the WSS or WSS CKT.
13. Checks for a short to voltage in the WSS CKT.
15. Checks for a short to voltage in the WSS CKT.

Step	Action	Value(s)	Yes	No
1	Was the Diagnostic System Check performed?	—	*Go to Step 2*	*Go to A Diagnostic System Check - ABS*
2	Inspect the WSS for physical damage. Is physical damage of the WSS evident?	—	*Go to Step 3*	*Go to Step 4*
3	Replace the WSS. Is the replacement complete?	—	*Go to Step 18*	—
4	Inspect the jumper harness for physical damage. Is physical damage of the jumper harness evident?	—	*Go to Step 5*	*Go to Step 6*
5	Replace the jumper harness. Is the replacement complete?	—	*Go to Step 18*	—
6	1. Turn the ignition switch to the OFF position. 2. Disconnect the EBCM. 3. Install the *J 39700* universal pinout box using the *J 39700-530* cable adapter to the EBTCM harness connector only. 4. Using DMM, measure the resistance between terminals 2 and 3 of the universal pinout box. Is the resistance within the range specified in the value(s) column?	800–1600 Ω	*Go to Step 13*	*Go to Step 7*
7	1. Disconnect the wheel speed sensor. 2. Using DMM, measure the resistance between terminals A and B of the wheel speed sensor connector. Is the resistance within the range specified in the value(s) column?	800–1600 Ω	*Go to Step 8*	*Go to Step 3*
8	Using DMM, measure the resistance between terminal 2 of the *J 39700* universal pinout box and terminal B of the WSS harness connector. Is the resistance within the range specified in the value(s) column?	0-5 Ω	*Go to Step 10*	*Go to Step 9*
9	Repair CKT 882 for an open or high resistance. If open or high resistance is found in the jumper harness, replace the jumper harness. Is the repair complete?	—	*Go to Step 18*	—

GC4020052006020X

Fig. 87 Code C0050: RH Rear Wheel Speed Circuit Fault (Part 2 of 3). 2000 Grand Prix & Intrigue

Step	Action	Value(s)	Yes	No
10	Using DMM, measure the resistance between terminal 3 of the *J 39700* universal pinout box and terminal A of the WSS harness connector. Is the resistance within the range specified in the value(s) column?	0-5 Ω	*Go to Step 12*	*Go to Step 11*
11	Repair CKT 883 for an open or high resistance. If open or high resistance is found in the jumper harness, replace the jumper harness. Is the repair complete?	—	*Go to Step 18*	—
12	Malfunction is intermittent. Inspect all connectors and harnesses for damage that may result in an open or high resistance when connected. Is the repair complete?	—	*Go to Step 18*	—
13	1. Disconnect the wheel speed sensor. 2. Turn the ignition switch to the ON position, engine off. 3. Using DMM, measure the voltage at terminal 2 of the *J 39700* universal pinout box. Is the voltage above the value specified in the value(s) column?	0 V	*Go to Step 14*	*Go to Step 15*
14	Repair CKT 882 for a short to voltage. If short to voltage is found in the jumper harness, replace the jumper harness. Is the repair complete?	—	*Go to Step 18*	—
15	Using DMM, measure the voltage at terminal 3 of the *J 39700* universal pinout box. Is the voltage above the value specified in the value(s) column?	0 V	*Go to Step 16*	*Go to Step 17*
16	Repair CKT 883 for a short to voltage. If short to voltage is found in the jumper harness, replace the jumper harness. Is the repair complete?	—	*Go to Step 18*	—
17	Replace the EBCM. Is the replacement complete?	—	*Go to A Diagnostic System Check - ABS*	—
18	1. Reconnect all previously disconnected components. 2. Using a scan tool clear the DTC. 3. Remove the scan tool from the DLC. 4. Carefully drive the vehicle above 12 km/h (8 mph) for several minutes. Does the DTC reset as a current DTC?	—	*Go to Step 2*	*Go to A Diagnostic System Check - ABS*

GC4020052006030X

Fig. 87 Code C0050: RH Rear Wheel Speed Circuit Fault (Part 3 of 3). 2000 Grand Prix & Intrigue

Circuit Description

The speed sensor used on this vehicle is a multiple pole magnetic pickup. This sensor produces an AC signal that the EBTCM uses the frequency from to calculate the wheel speed.

Conditions for Setting the DTC

- The DTC will set if one wheel speed = 0 and the other WSS are greater than 40 Km/h (25 mph) for 10 ms.
- The DTC will set if during drive off, one wheel speed = 0, and the other WSS are greater than 12 Km/h (7.5 mph).
- The EBTCM detects a short to ground.

Action Taken When the DTC Sets

- A malfunction DTC stores.
- The ABS/TCS disables.
- The amber ABS/TCS indicator(s) turn on.

Conditions for Clearing the DTC

- The condition responsible for setting the DTC no longer exists and the scan tool Clear DTCs function is used.
- 100 ignition cycles pass with no DTC(s) detected.

Diagnostic Aids

- It is very important that a thorough inspection of the wiring and connectors be performed. Failure to carefully and fully inspect wiring and connectors may result in misdiagnosis, causing part replacement with reappearance of the malfunction.
- Thoroughly inspect any circuitry that may be causing the complaint for the following conditions:
  - Backed out terminals
  - Improper mating
  - Broken locks
  - Improperly formed or damaged terminals
  - Poor terminal-to-wiring connections
  - Physical damage to the wiring harness
- The following conditions may cause an intermittent malfunction:
  - A poor connection
  - Rubbed-through wire insulation
  - A broken wire inside the insulation
- If the customer's comments reflect that the amber ABS/TCS indicator is on only during moist environmental conditions (rain, snow, vehicle wash), inspect all the wheel speed sensor circuitry for signs of water intrusion. If the DTC is not current, clear all DTCs and simulate the effects of water intrusion by using the following procedure:
  1. Spray the suspected area with a five percent saltwater solution.

     Add two teaspoons of salt to twelve ounces of water to make a five percent saltwater solution.
  2. Test drive the vehicle over various road surfaces (bumps, turns, etc.) above 40 km/h (25 mph) for at least 30 seconds.
  3. If the DTC returns, replace the suspected harness.

GC402980329904AX

Fig. 88 Code C0051: RH Rear Wheel Speed Circuit Range/Performance (Part 1 of 3). 2000 Grand Prix & Intrigue

Rear Wheel Speed Sensor Resistance

The following table contains resistance values for the rear wheel speed sensors at varying sensor temperatures for use in diagnosis. The values are approximate and should be used as a guideline for diagnosis.

Test Description

The number(s) below refer to the step number(s) on the diagnostic table.

6. This step checks for the proper resistance in the WSS.
7. This step checks for the proper WSS output.

Sensor Temperature (°C)	Sensor Temperature (°F)	Sensor Resistance (Ohms)
-34 to 4	-30 to 40	800 to 1100
5 to 43	41 to 110	950 to 1300
44 to 93	111 to 200	1110 to 1600

Step	Action	Value(s)	Yes	No
1	Was the Diagnostic System Check performed?	—	*Go to Step 2*	Go to *Diagnostic System Check*
2	Inspect the WSS for physical damage. Is physical damage of the WSS evident?	—	*Go to Step 3*	*Go to Step 4*
3	Replace the WSS. Is the replacement complete?	—	*Go to Step 16*	—
4	Inspect the jumper harness for physical damage. Is physical damage of the jumper harness evident?	—	*Go to Step 5*	*Go to Step 6*
5	Replace the jumper harness. Is the replacement complete?	—	*Go to Step 16*	—
6	1. Disconnect the WSS connector directly at the WSS. 2. Using *J 39200* DMM, measure the resistance between terminals A and B of the WSS. Is the resistance within the range specified in the value(s) column?	800–1600 Ω	*Go to Step 7*	*Go to Step 3*
7	1. With the *J 39200* DMM still connected to the WSS select the mV AC scale. 2. Spin the wheel as fast as you can by hand while monitoring the AC output. Is the AC voltage within the range specified in the value(s) column?	Above 100 mV	*Go to Step 8*	*Go to Step 3*
8	Using *J 39200* DMM, measure the resistance between the WSS terminal A and ground. Is the resistance within the range specified in the value(s) column?	OL (infinite)	*Go to Step 9*	*Go to Step 3*
9	1. Disconnect the EBTCM harness connector. 2. Install the *J 39700* Universal Pinout Box using the J 39700-530 cable adapter to the EBTCM harness connector only. 3. Using *J 39200* DMM, measure the resistance between terminals 2 and 3 of *J 39700*. Is the resistance within the range specified in the values column?	OL (infinite)	*Go to Step 11*	*Go to Step 10*

GC402980329900HX

Fig. 88 Code C0051: RH Rear Wheel Speed Circuit Range/Performance (Part 2 of 3). 2000 Grand Prix & Intrigue

Step	Action	Value(s)	Yes	No
10	Repair short between CKT(s) 882 and 883. If short between wheel speed sensor circuits is found in the jumper harness, replace the jumper harness. Is the repair complete?	—	*Go to Step 16*	—
11	Using *J 39200* DMM, measure the resistance between terminals 2 and 15 of *J 39700.* Is the resistance within the range specified in the values column?	OL (infinite)	*Go to Step 13*	*Go to Step 12*
12	Repair CKT 882 for a short to ground. If short to ground is found in the jumper harness, replace the jumper harness. Is the repair complete?	—	*Go to Step 16*	—
13	Using *J 39200* DMM, measure the resistance between terminals 3 and 15 of *J 39700.* Is the resistance within the range specified in the values column?	OL (infinite)	*Go to Step 15*	*Go to Step 14*
14	Repair CKT 883 for a short to ground. If short to ground is found in the jumper harness, replace the jumper harness. Is the repair complete?	—	*Go to Step 16*	—
15	Replace the EBTCM. Is the replacement complete?	—	Go to *Diagnostic System Check*	—
16	1. Reconnect all previously disconnected components. 2. Using a scan tool clear the DTC. 3. Remove the scan tool from the DLC. 4. Carefully drive vehicle above 12 Km/h (8 mph) for several minutes. Does the DTC reset as a current DTC?	—	*Go to Step 2*	Go to *Diagnostic System Check*

GC402980329900IX

Fig. 88 Code C0051: RH Rear Wheel Speed Circuit Range/Performance (Part 3 of 3). 2000 Grand Prix & Intrigue

Step	Action	Value(s)	Yes	No
1	Was the Diagnostic System Check performed?	—	*Go to Step 2*	Go to *Diagnostic System Check*
2	1. Turn the ignition switch to the OFF position. 2. Install a scan tool. 3. Turn the ignition switch to the RUN position, engine off. 4. Using the scan tool, run the Automated test. Does DTC reset as a current DTC?	—	*Go to Step 3*	Go to *Diagnostic System Check*
3	Replace the EBTCM. Is the repair complete?	—	Go to *Diagnostic System Check*	—

GC402980330000BX

Fig. 89 Codes C0060, C0065, C0070, C0075, C0080, C0085, C0090 & C0095: ABS Solenoid Circuit Fault (Part 2 of 2). 2000 Grand Prix & Intrigue

Circuit Description

The pump motor is an integral part of the BPMV, while the pump motor relay is integral to the EBTCM. The pump motor relay is not engaged during normal system operation. When ABS or TCS operation is required the EBTCM activates the pump motor relay and battery power is provided to the pump motor.

Conditions for Setting the DTC

- Pump motor voltage is not present 60 milliseconds after activation of the pump motor relay.
- Pump motor voltage is present for more than 2.5 seconds with no activation of the pump motor relay.
- Pump motor voltage is not present for at least 40 milliseconds after the pump motor relay is commanded off.

Action Taken When the DTC Sets

- A malfunction DTC stores.
- The ABS/TCS disables.
- The amber ABS/TCS indicator(s) turn on.

Conditions for Clearing the DTC

- The condition responsible for setting the DTC no longer exists and the scan tool Clear DTCs function is used.
- 100 ignition cycles pass with no DTC(s) detected.

Diagnostic Aids

- It is very important that a thorough inspection of the wiring and connectors be performed. Failure to carefully and fully inspect wiring and connectors may result in misdiagnosis, causing part replacement with reappearance of the malfunction.
- Thoroughly inspect any circuitry that may be causing the complaint for the following conditions:
  - Backed out terminals
  - Improper mating
  - Broken locks
  - Improperly formed or damaged terminals
  - Poor terminal-to-wiring connections
  - Physical damage to the wiring harness
- The following conditions may cause an intermittent malfunction:
  - A poor connection
  - Rubbed-through wire insulation
  - A broken wire inside the insulation
- If an intermittent malfunction exists refer to Troubleshooting Electrical Diagnosis

A disconnected pump motor connector will cause this malfunction.

GC402980330100AX

Fig. 90 Code C0110: Pump Motor Circuit Fault (Part 1 of 3). 2000 Grand Prix

Circuit Description

The inlet valve solenoid circuits are supplied with battery power when the ignition is in the run position. The EBTCM controls the valve functions by grounding the circuit when necessary.

Conditions for Setting the DTC

The EBTCM senses a discrepancy such as an open, short to ground, or short to voltage in the circuit.

Action Taken When the DTC Sets

- A malfunction DTC is stored.
- ABS/TCS is disabled.
- The ABS and ETS/TRAC OFF Indicators are turned on.

Conditions for Clearing the DTC

- Condition for DTC is no longer present and scan tool clear DTC function is used.
- 100 ignition cycles pass with no DTC(s) detected.

Diagnostic Aids

The solenoid valve circuit and the solenoid coil are internal to the EBTCM. No part of the solenoid circuit is diagnosable external to the EBTCM. The DTC sets when there is a malfunction in the solenoid circuit internal to the EBTCM only.

Test Description

The numbers below refer to step numbers on the Diagnostic Table.

2. This step determines if the DTC is current.

GC402980330000AX

Fig. 89 Codes C0060, C0065, C0070, C0075, C0080, C0085, C0090 & C0095: ABS Solenoid Circuit Fault (Part 1 of 2). 2000 Grand Prix & Intrigue

Test Description

The numbers below refer to step numbers on the diagnostic table.

4. This step checks for a short to ground in CKT 102.
10. This step checks for an open in CKT 102.
14. This step checks for a mechanical malfunction with the pump motor, and also cleans the motor contacts for the measurement in step 15.

Step	Action	Value(s)	Yes	No
1	Was the Diagnostic System Check performed?	—	*Go to Step 2*	Go to *Diagnostic System Check*
2	Inspect the fusible link supplying voltage to CKT 102. Is the fusible link OK?	—	*Go to Step 7*	*Go to Step 3*
3	1. Install a new fusible link. 2. Turn the ignition switch from the OFF to RUN position, engine OFF. 3. Using a scan tool in ABS/TCS Special Functions attempt to run the AUTOMATED test. 4. Recheck the fusible link. Is the fusible link OK?	—	*Go to Step 16*	*Go to Step 4*
4	1. Turn the Ignition switch to the OFF position. 2. Disconnect the fusible link from the starter. 3. Disconnect the EBTCM connector C1. 4. Connect the *J 39700* Universal Pinout Box using the J 39700-530 cable adapter to the EBTCM harness connector only. 5. Using *J 39200* DMM, measure the resistance between terminals 13 and 15 of *J 39700.* Is the resistance within the range specified in the value(s) column?	OL (infinite)	*Go to Step 5*	*Go to Step 12*
5	1. Disconnect the EBTCM pump motor connector C2. 2. Connect a 10A fused jumper wire between the pump motor connector C2 terminal 1 and battery voltage. 3. Connect a jumper wire between the pump motor connector C2 terminal 2 and ground. Only attempt to run the pump motor for 5 seconds. 4. Disconnect the jumper wires. 5. Inspect the 10A fuse in the jumper wire. Is the fuse OK?	—	*Go to Step 11*	*Go to Step 6*
6	Replace the BPMV. Is the replacement complete?	—	*Go to Step 16*	—
7	1. Turn the Ignition switch to the OFF position. 2. Disconnect the EBTCM connector C1. 3. Connect *J 39700* Universal Pinout Box using the J 39700-530 cable adaptor to the EBTCM harness connector C1 only. 4. Using *J 39200* DMM, measure the resistance between terminals 12 and 15 of *J 39700.* Is the resistance within the range specified in the value(s) column?	0–5 Ω	*Go to Step 9*	*Go to Step 8*

GC402980330100BX

Fig. 90 Code C0110: Pump Motor Circuit Fault (Part 2 of 3). 2000 Grand Prix

Step	Action	Value(s)	Yes	No
8	Repair CKT 250 for an open or high resistance. Is the repair complete?	—	*Go to Step 16*	—
9	1. Reconnect the fusible link to the starter if disconnected. 2. Using *J 39200* DMM, measure the voltage between the starter and a good ground. Is the voltage within the range specified in the value(s) column?	Battery volts	*Go to Step 10*	Power Distribution Diagnosis
10	Using *J 39200* DMM, measure the voltage at terminal 13 of *J 39700*. Is the voltage within the range specified in the value(s) column?	Battery volts	*Go to Step 14*	*Go to Step 13*
11	Replace EBTCM. Is the replacement complete?	—	Go to *Diagnostic System Check*	—
12	Repair short to ground in CKT 102. Is the repair complete?	—	*Go to Step 16*	—
13	Repair open in CKT 102. Is the repair complete?	—	*Go to Step 16*	—
14	1. Disconnect the EBTCM pump motor connector C2. 2. Connect a 10A fused jumper wire between the pump motor connector C2 terminal 1 and battery voltage. 3. Connect a jumper wire between the pump motor connector C2 terminal 2 and ground. Only attempt to run the pump motor for 5 seconds. 4. Disconnect the jumper wires. 5. Inspect the 10A fuse in the jumper wire. Is the fuse OK?	—	*Go to Step 15*	*Go to Step 6*
15	1. Zero the *J 39200* DMM leads. 2. Using *J 39200* DMM, measure the resistance between terminals 1 and 2 of the pump motor connector C2. Is the resistance within the range specified in the value(s) column?	0–4 Ω	*Go to Step 11*	*Go to Step 6*
16	1. Reconnect all previously disconnected components. 2. Using a scan tool clear the DTC. 3. Remove the scan tool from the DLC. 4. Carefully drive the vehicle above 12 Km/h (8 mph) for several minutes. Does the DTC reset as a current DTC?	—	*Go to Step 2*	Go to *Diagnostic System Check*

GC402980330100CX

Fig. 90 Code C0110: Pump Motor Circuit Fault (Part 3 of 3). 2000 Grand Prix

Test Description

The numbers below refer to step numbers on the diagnostic table.

4. This step checks for a short to ground in CKT 102A.
10. This step checks for an open in CKT 102A.
14. This step checks for a mechanical malfunction with the pump motor, and also cleans the motor contacts for the measurement in step 15.

Step	Action	Value(s)	Yes	No
1	Was the Diagnostic System Check performed?	—	*Go to Step 2*	Go to *A Diagnostic System Check - ABS*
2	Inspect the fusible link supplying voltage to CKT 102A. Is the fusible link OK?	—	*Go to Step 7*	*Go to Step 3*
3	1. Install a new fusible link. 2. Carefully drive the vehicle above 12 Km/h (8 mph) for several minutes. 3. Recheck the fusible link. Is the fusible link OK?	—	*Go to Step 16*	*Go to Step 4*
4	1. Turn the Ignition switch to the OFF position. 2. Disconnect the fusible link from the remote battery stud. 3. Disconnect the EBTCM connector C1. 4. Connect the *J 39700* Universal Pinout Box using the J 39700-530 cable adapter to the EBTCM harness connector only. 5. Using *J 39200* DMM, measure the resistance between terminals 13 and 15 of *J 39700*. Is the resistance within the range specified in the value(s) column?	OL (infinite)	*Go to Step 5*	*Go to Step 12*
5	1. Disconnect the EBTCM pump motor connector C2. 2. Connect a 10A fused jumper wire between the pump motor connector C2 terminal 2 and battery voltage. 3. Connect a jumper wire between the pump motor connector C2 terminal 1 and ground. Only attempt to run the pump motor for 5 seconds. 4. Disconnect the jumper wires. 5. Inspect the 10A fuse in the jumper wire. Is the fuse OK?	—	*Go to Step 11*	*Go to Step 6*
6	Replace the BPMV. Is the replacement complete?	—	*Go to Step 16*	—
7	1. Turn the Ignition switch to the OFF position. 2. Disconnect the EBTCM connector C1. 3. Connect *J 39700* Universal Pinout Box using the J 39700-530 cable adaptor to the EBTCM harness connector C1 only. 4. Using *J 39200* DMM, measure the resistance between terminals 12 and 15 of *J 39700*. Is the resistance within the range specified in the value(s) column?	0–5 Ω	*Go to Step 9*	*Go to Step 8*
8	Repair CKT 550 for an open or high resistance. Is the repair complete?	—	*Go to Step 16*	—

GC4029903865020X

Fig. 91 Code C0110: Pump Motor Circuit Fault (Part 2 of 3). 2000 Intrigue

Circuit Description

The pump motor is an integral part of the BPMV, while the pump motor relay is integral to the EBTCM. The pump motor relay is not engaged during normal system operation. When ABS or TCS operation is required, the EBTCM activates the pump motor relay and battery power is provided to the pump motor.

Conditions for Setting the DTC

- Pump motor voltage is not present 60 milliseconds after activation of the pump motor relay.
- Pump motor voltage is present for more than 2.5 seconds with no activation of the pump motor relay.
- Pump motor voltage is not present for at least 40 milliseconds after the pump motor relay is commanded off.

Action Taken When the DTC Sets

- A malfunction DTC stores.
- The ABS/TCS disables.
- The amber ABS/TCS indicator(s) turn on.

Conditions for Clearing the DTC

- The condition responsible for setting the DTC no longer exists and the scan tool Clear DTCs function is used.
- 100 ignition cycles pass with no DTC(s) detected.

Diagnostic Aids

- It is very important that a thorough inspection of the wiring and connectors be performed. Failure to carefully and fully inspect wiring and connectors may result in misdiagnosis, causing part replacement with reappearance of the malfunction.
- Thoroughly inspect any circuitry that may be causing the complaint for the following conditions:
  - Backed out terminals
  - Improper mating
  - Broken locks
  - Improperly formed or damaged terminals
  - Poor terminal-to-wiring connections
  - Physical damage to the wiring harness
- The following conditions may cause an intermittent malfunction:
  - A poor connection
  - Rubbed-through wire insulation
  - A broken wire inside the insulation

A disconnected pump motor connector will cause this malfunction.

GC4029903865010X

Fig. 91 Code C0110: Pump Motor Circuit Fault (Part 1 of 3). 2000 Intrigue

Step	Action	Value(s)	Yes	No
9	1. Reconnect the fusible link to the remote battery stud if disconnected. 2. Using *J 39200* DMM, measure the voltage between the remote battery stud and a good ground. Is the voltage within the range specified in the value(s) column?	Battery volts	*Go to Step 10*	*Power Distribution*
10	Using *J 39200* DMM, measure the voltage at terminal 13 of *J 39700*. Is the voltage within the range specified in the value(s) column?	Battery volts	*Go to Step 14*	*Go to Step 13*
11	Replace EBTCM. Is the replacement complete?	—	Go to *A Diagnostic System Check - ABS*	—
12	Repair short to ground in CKT 102A. Is the repair complete?	—	*Go to Step 16*	—
13	Repair open in CKT 102A. Is the repair complete?	—	*Go to Step 16*	—
14	1. Disconnect the EBTCM pump motor connector C2. 2. Connect a 10A fused jumper wire between the pump motor connector C2 terminal 2 and battery voltage. 3. Connect a jumper wire between the pump motor connector C2 terminal 1 and ground. Only attempt to run the pump motor for 5 seconds. 4. Disconnect the jumper wires. 5. Inspect the 10A fuse in the jumper wire. Is the fuse OK?	—	*Go to Step 15*	*Go to Step 6*
15	1. Zero the *J 39200* DMM leads. 2. Using *J 39200* DMM, measure the resistance between terminals 1 and 2 of the pump motor connector C2. Is the resistance within the range specified in the value(s) column?	0–4 Ω	*Go to Step 11*	*Go to Step 6*
16	1. Reconnect all previously disconnected components. 2. Using a scan tool clear the DTC. 3. Remove the scan tool from the DLC. 4. Carefully drive the vehicle above 12 Km/h (8 mph) for several minutes. Does the DTC reset as a current DTC?	—	*Go to Step 2*	Go to *A Diagnostic System Check - ABS*

GC4029903865030X

Fig. 91 Code C0110: Pump Motor Circuit Fault (Part 3 of 3). 2000 Intrigue

Circuit Description

The solenoid valve relay supplies power to the solenoid valve coils in the EBTCM. The solenoid valve relay, located in the EBTCM, is activated whenever the ignition switch is in the RUN position and no faults are present. The solenoid valve relay remains engaged until the ignition is turned OFF or a failure is detected.

Conditions for Setting the DTC

- DTC C0121 will set anytime the solenoid valve relay is commanded on and the EBTCM does not see battery voltage at the solenoid valves.
- DTC C0121 will set anytime the EBTCM commands the solenoid valve relay off and battery voltage is still present at the solenoid valves.

Action Taken When the DTC Sets

- A malfunction DTC stores.
- The ABS/TCS disables.
- The amber ABS/TCS indicator(s) turn on.

Conditions for Clearing the DTC

- The condition responsible for setting the DTC no longer exists and the scan tool Clear DTCs function is used.
- 100 ignition cycles pass with no DTC(s) detected.

Diagnostic Aids

- It is very important that a thorough inspection of the wiring and connectors be performed. Failure to carefully and fully inspect wiring and connectors may result in misdiagnosis, causing part replacement with reappearance of the malfunction.
- Thoroughly inspect any circuitry that may be causing the complaint for the following conditions:
  - Backed out terminals
  - Improper mating
  - Broken locks
  - Improperly formed or damaged terminals
  - Poor terminal-to-wiring connections
  - Physical damage to the wiring harness
- The following conditions may cause an intermittent malfunction:
  - A poor connection
  - Rubbed-through wire insulation
  - A broken wire inside the insulation
- If an intermittent malfunction exists refer to Troubleshooting
- The solenoid valve relay is an integral part of the EBTCM and is not serviced separately.

GC402980330200AX

Fig. 92 Code C0121: Valve Relay Circuit Fault (Part 1 of 2). 2000 Grand Prix

Step	Action	Value(s)	Yes	No
1	Was the Diagnostic System Check performed?	—	Go to *Step 2*	Go to *Diagnostic System Check*
2	Check the fusible link feeding CKT 202. Is the fusible link OK?	—	Go to *Step 5*	Go to *Step 3*
3	1. Install a new fusible link. 2. Turn the ignition switch from the OFF to RUN position, engine OFF. 3. Using a scan tool in ABS/TCS Special Functions attempt to run the AUTOMATED test. 4. Recheck the fusible link. Is the fuse OK?	—	Go to *Step 10*	Go to *Step 4*
4	1. Turn the Ignition switch to the OFF position. 2. Disconnect the fusible link from the starter. 3. Disconnect the EBTCM connector C1. 4. Connect the *J 39700* Universal Pinout Box using the J 39700-530 cable adapter to the EBTCM harness connector only. 5. Using *J 39200* DMM, measure the resistance between terminals 14 and 15 of *J 39700.* Is the resistance within the range specified in the value(s) column?	OL (infinite)	Go to *Step 7*	Go to *Step 8*
5	1. Reconnect the fusible link to the starter if disconnected. 2. Using *J 39200* DMM, measure the voltage between the starter and a good ground. Is the voltage within the range specified in the value(s) column?	Battery volts	Go to *Step 6*	Power Distribution
6	Using *J 39200* DMM, measure the voltage at terminal 14 of *J 39700.* Is the voltage within the range specified in the value(s) column?	Battery volts	Go to *Step 7*	Go to *Step 9*
7	Replace EBTCM. Is the replacement complete?	—	Go to *Diagnostic System Check*	—
8	Repair short to ground in CKT 202. Is the repair complete?	—	Go to *Step 10*	—
9	Repair open in CKT 202. Is the repair complete?	—	Go to *Step 10*	—
10	1. Reconnect all previously disconnected components. 2. Using a scan tool clear the DTC. 3. Remove the scan tool from the DLC. 4. Carefully drive the vehicle above 12 Km/h (8 mph) for several minutes. Does the DTC reset as a current DTC?	—	Go to *Step 2*	Go to *Diagnostic System Check.*

GC402980330200BX

Fig. 92 Code C0121: Valve Relay Circuit Fault (Part 2 of 2). 2000 Grand Prix

Test Description

The numbers below refer to step numbers on the diagnostic table.

4. This step checks for a short to ground in CKT 202A.
6. This step checks for an open in CKT 202A.

Step	Action	Value(s)	Yes	No
1	Was the Diagnostic System Check performed?	—	Go to *Step 2*	Go to *A Diagnostic System Check - ABS*
2	Check the fusible link feeding CKT 202A. Is the fusible link OK?	—	Go to *Step 5*	Go to *Step 3*
3	1. Install a new fusible link. 2. Carefully drive the vehicle above 12 Km/h (8 mph) for several minutes. 3. Recheck the fusible link. Is the fuse OK?	—	Go to *Step 10*	Go to *Step 4*
4	1. Turn the Ignition switch to the OFF position. 2. Disconnect the fusible link from the remote battery stud. 3. Disconnect the EBTCM connector C1. 4. Connect the *J 39700* Universal Pinout Box using the J 39700-530 cable adapter to the EBTCM harness connector only. 5. Using *J 39200* DMM, measure the resistance between terminals 14 and 15 of *J 39700.* Is the resistance within the range specified in the value(s) column?	OL (infinite)	Go to *Step 7*	Go to *Step 8*
5	1. Reconnect the fusible link to the remote battery stud if disconnected. 2. Using *J 39200* DMM, measure the voltage between the remote battery stud and a good ground. Is the voltage within the range specified in the value(s) column?	Battery volts	Go to *Step 6*	*Power Distribution*
6	Using *J 39200* DMM, measure the voltage at terminal 14 of *J 39700.* Is the voltage within the range specified in the value(s) column?	Battery volts	Go to *Step 7*	Go to *Step 9*
7	Replace EBTCM. Is the replacement complete?	—	Go to *A Diagnostic System Check - ABS*	—
8	Repair short to ground in CKT 202A. Is the repair complete?	—	Go to *Step 10*	—
9	Repair open in CKT 202A. Is the repair complete?	—	Go to *Step 10*	—
10	1. Reconnect all previously disconnected components. 2. Using a scan tool clear the DTC. 3. Remove the scan tool from the DLC. 4. Carefully drive the vehicle above 12 Km/h (8 mph) for several minutes. Does the DTC reset as a current DTC?	—	Go to *Step 2*	Go to *A Diagnostic System Check - ABS*

GC4029903866020X

Fig. 93 Code C0121: Valve Relay Circuit Fault (Part 2 of 2). 2000 Intrigue

Circuit Description

The solenoid valve relay supplies power to the solenoid valve coils in the EBTCM. The solenoid valve relay, located in the EBTCM, is activated whenever the ignition switch is in the ON position and no faults are present. The solenoid valve relay remains engaged until the ignition is turned OFF or a failure is detected.

Conditions for Setting the DTC

- DTC C0121 will set anytime the solenoid valve relay is commanded on and the EBTCM does not see battery voltage at the solenoid valves.
- DTC C0121 will set anytime the EBTCM commands the solenoid valve relay off and battery voltage is still present at the solenoid valves.

Action Taken When the DTC Sets

- A malfunction DTC stores.
- The ABS/TCS disables.
- The amber ABS/TCS indicator(s) turn on.

Conditions for Clearing the DTC

- The condition responsible for setting the DTC no longer exists and the scan tool Clear DTCs function is used.
- 100 ignition cycles pass with no DTC(s) detected.

Diagnostic Aids

- It is very important that a thorough inspection of the wiring and connectors be performed. Failure to carefully and fully inspect wiring and connectors may result in misdiagnosis, causing part replacement with reappearance of the malfunction.
- Thoroughly inspect any circuitry that may be causing the complaint for the following conditions:
  - Backed out terminals
  - Improper mating
  - Broken locks
  - Improperly formed or damaged terminals
  - Poor terminal-to-wiring connections
  - Physical damage to the wiring harness
- The following conditions may cause an intermittent malfunction:
  - A poor connection
  - Rubbed-through wire insulation
  - A broken wire inside the insulation
- The solenoid valve relay is an integral part of the EBTCM and is not serviced separately.

GC4029903866010X

Fig. 93 Code C0121: Valve Relay Circuit Fault (Part 1 of 2). 2000 Intrigue

Circuit Description

The EBCM uses input from the brake pressure sensor for more accurate control during a vehicle stability enhancement system (VSES) event.

Conditions for Running the DTC

- DTC C0870 is not set.
- The ignition is ON.
- The vehicle speed is greater than 40 km/h (24 mph).

Conditions for Setting the DTC

Voltage at the pressure sensor signal output to the EBCM falls outside the 0.25 V – 4.75 V range for more than 100 milliseconds.

Action Taken When the DTC Sets

- A malfunction DTC is set
- ABS, TCS and VSES are disabled
- ABS, TCS, SERVICE VEHICLE SOON and PCS lamp indicators turn on

Conditions for Clearing the DTC

- The condition for the DTC is no longer present.
- A history DTC will clear after 124 consecutive ignition cycles if the condition for the malfunction is no longer present.
- Using a scan tool.

Diagnostic Aids

- A thorough inspection of the wiring system and connectors should be performed. Failure to carefully and fully inspect the wiring system and connectors may result in misdiagnosis which may result in replacing good parts and the reappearance of the malfunction.
- Inspection for poor connections, broken insulation, or a wire that is broken inside the insulation.

GC4020052007010X

Fig. 94 Code C0131: ABS/TCS System Pressure Circuit Fault (Part 1 of 3). 2000 Intrigue

Test Description

The number(s) below refer to the step number(s) on the diagnostic table.

2. Tests for specified voltage on the brake pressure signal circuit.
3. Checks to see if voltage was below specified voltage.
4. Checks to see if voltage was below specified voltage.
5. Checks to see if voltage was above specified voltage of 5 volt reference.
6. Tests for a short to ground in the 5 volt reference circuit.
7. Tests for a short to voltage in the 5 volt reference circuit.
8. Tests for a short to ground, a high resistance, or an open in the 5 volt reference circuit.
9. Tests for a short to voltage, a high resistance, or an open in the brake pressure sensor signal circuit.
10. Tests for a high resistance or an open in the ground circuit of the brake pressure sensor.
11. Checks the brake pressure sensor connector for poor connections.
12. Checks the EBCM connector for poor connections.

Step	Action	Value(s)	Yes	No
1	Did you perform the ABS Diagnostic System Check?	—	Go to *Step 2*	Go to *A Diagnostic System Check - ABS*
2	1. Turn OFF the ignition. 2. Disconnect the EBCM. 3. Install the *J 39700* universal pinout box with the *J 39700-530* cable adapter between the EBCM and the EBCM harness connector. 4. Turn ON the ignition, with the engine OFF. 5. Using the DMM, measure the voltage between pin 17 and pin 15 of the *J 39700* universal pinout box. Is the voltage within the specified value?	0.25 V - 4.75 V	Go to Diagnostic Aids	Go to *Step 3*
3	1. Turn OFF the ignition. 2. Disconnect the brake pressure sensor. 3. Turn ON the ignition with the engine OFF. 4. Using the DMM, measure the voltage between pin 17 and pin 15 of the *J 39700* universal pinout box. Is the voltage greater than the specified value?	5 V	Go to *Step 4*	Go to *Step 8*
4	1. Turn OFF the ignition. 2. Connect a 3 amp fused jumper wire between the signal circuit of the brake pressure sensor and the ground circuit of the brake pressure sensor. 3. Turn ON the ignition, with the engine OFF. 4. Using the DMM, measure the voltage between pin 17 and pin 15 of the *J 39700* universal pinout box. Is the voltage less than the specified value?	0.25 V	Go to *Step 5*	Go to *Step 9*
5	1. Turn OFF the ignition. 2. Disconnect the fused jumper wire. 3. Connect a 3 amp fused jumper wire between the 5 volt reference circuit of the brake pressure sensor and the signal circuit of the brake pressure sensor. 4. Measure the voltage between the 5 volt reference circuit of the brake pressure sensor and the signal circuit of the brake pressure sensor. Is the voltage measured greater than the specified value?	5 V	Go to *Step 7*	Go to *Step 6*
6	Test the 5 volt reference circuit of the brake pressure sensor for a short to ground. Did you find and correct the condition?	—	Go to *Step 15*	Go to *Step 12*

GC4020052007020X

Fig. 94 Code C0131: ABS/TCS System Pressure Circuit Fault (Part 2 of 3). 2000 Intrigue

Step	Action	Value(s)	Yes	No
7	Test the 5 volt reference circuit of the brake pressure sensor for a short to voltage. Did you find and correct the condition?	—	Go to *Step 15*	Go to *Step 11*
8	Test the signal circuit of the brake pressure sensor for a short to ground, a high resistance, or an open. Did you find and correct the condition?	—	Go to *Step 15*	Go to *Step 12*
9	Test the signal circuit of the brake pressure sensor for a short to voltage, a high resistance, or an open. Did you find and correct the condition?	—	Go to *Step 15*	Go to *Step 10*
10	Test the ground circuit of the brake pressure sensor for a high resistance or an open. Did you find and correct the condition?	—	Go to *Step 15*	Go to *Step 12*
11	Inspect for poor connections at the harness connector of the brake pressure sensor. Did you find and correct the condition?	—	Go to *Step 15*	Go to *Step 13*
12	Inspect for poor connections at the harness connector of the EBCM. Did you find and correct the condition?	—	Go to *Step 15*	Go to *Step 14*
13	Replace the brake pressure sensor. Did you complete the replacement?	—	Go to *Step 15*	—
14	Replace the EBCM. Did you complete the replacement?	—	Go to *Step 15*	—
15	1. Use the scan tool in order to clear the DTCs. 2. Operate the vehicle within the Conditions for Running the DTC as specified in the supporting text. Does the DTC reset?	—	Go to *Step 2*	System OK

GC4020052007030X

Fig. 94 Code C0131: ABS/TCS System Pressure Circuit Fault (Part 3 of 3). 2000 Intrigue

Test Description

The number(s) below refer to the step number(s) on the diagnostic table.

2. Tests for specified voltage on the brake pressure signal circuit.
3. Checks to see if voltage was below specified voltage.
4. Checks to see if voltage was above specified voltage.
5. Checks to see if voltage was above specified voltage of 5 volt reference.
6. Checks to see if 5 volt reference from EBCM is 5 volts.
7. Checks to see if resistance of ground circuit is less than 5 ohms.
8. Tests for short to voltage in the 5 volt reference circuit.
9. Tests for a short to ground, a high resistance or an open in the 5 volt reference circuit.
10. Tests for a short to voltage in the brake pressure sensor signal circuit.
11. Tests for a high resistance or an open in the ground circuit.
12. Checks to brake pressure sensor connector for poor connections.
13. Checks to EBCM connector for poor connections.

Step	Action	Value(s)	Yes	No
1	Did you perform the ABS Diagnostic System Check?	—	Go to *Step 2*	Go to *A Diagnostic System Check - ABS*
2	1. Turn OFF the ignition. 2. Disconnect the EBCM. 3. Install the *J 39700* universal pinout box with the *J 39700-530* cable adapter between the EBCM and the EBCM harness connector. 4. Turn ON the ignition, with the engine OFF. 5. Using the DMM, measure the voltage between pin 17 and pin 15 of the *J 39700* universal pinout box. Is the voltage within the specified value?	0.25 V - 4.75 V	Go to Diagnostic Aids	Go to *Step 3*
3	1. Turn OFF the ignition. 2. Disconnect the brake pressure sensor. 3. Turn ON the ignition with the engine OFF. 4. Using the DMM, measure the voltage between pin 17 and pin 15 of the *J 39700* universal pinout box. Is the voltage less than the specified value?	4.75 V	Go to *Step 4*	Go to *Step 10*
4	1. Turn OFF the ignition. 2. Connect a 3 amp fused jumper wire between the 5 volt reference circuit of the brake pressure sensor and the signal circuit of the brake pressure sensor. 3. Turn ON the ignition, with the engine OFF. 4. Using the DMM, measure the voltage between pin 17 and pin 15 of the *J 39700* universal pinout box. Is the voltage greater than the specified value?	0.25 V	Go to *Step 5*	Go to *Step 8*
5	1. Disconnect the fused jumper wire. 2. Measure the voltage between the 5 volt reference circuit of the brake pressure sensor and the ground circuit of the brake pressure sensor. Does the voltage measure less than the specified value?	5 V	Go to *Step 6*	Go to *Step 7*
6	1. Turn OFF the ignition. 2. Disconnect the negative battery cable. 3. Measure the resistance from the ground circuit of the brake pressure sensor to a good ground. Does the resistance measure less than the specified value?	5 Ω	Go to *Step 12*	Go to *Step 11*

GC4020052008020X

Fig. 95 Code C0132: ABS/TCS System Pressure Circuit Range/Performance (Part 2 of 3). 2000 Intrigue

Circuit Description

During calibration of the offset of the pressure sensor signal, the pressure sensor signal offset value must be in the range of +/- 217.5 psi (15 Bar).

The pressure sensor is also monitored for sensitivity via a correlation between estimated vehicle deceleration and the pressure sensor signal. This is monitored over the course of numerous straight line non ABS braking stops.

Conditions for Running the DTC

- The ignition is ON.
- The vehicle speed is greater than 40 km/h (25 mph).

Conditions for Setting the DTC

- The sensor signal offset value is out of range for more than 1 second.
- The brake pedal is applied.
- The ABS pump is not on.
- The pressure sensor sensitivity is outside a predetermined range.

Action Taken When the DTC Sets

- A malfunction DTC is set
- ABS, TCS and PCS are disabled
- ABS, TCS, SERVICE ENGINE SOON and PCS lamp indicators turn on
- ABS braking distance increases

Conditions for Clearing the DTC

- The condition for the DTC is no longer present.
- A history DTC will clear after 124 consecutive ignition cycles if the condition for the malfunction is no longer present.
- Using a scan tool.

Diagnostic Aids

- A malfunctioning pressure sensor.
- A malfunctioning EBCM.

GC4020052008010X

Fig. 95 Code C0132: ABS/TCS System Pressure Circuit Range/Performance (Part 1 of 3). 2000 Intrigue

Step	Action	Value(s)	Yes	No
7	Test the 5 volt reference circuit of the brake pressure sensor for a short to voltage. Did you find and correct the condition?	—	Go to *Step 16*	Go to *Step 13*
8	Test the 5 volt reference circuit of the brake pressure sensor for a short to ground, a high resistance, or an open. Did you find and correct the condition?	—	Go to *Step 16*	Go to *Step 9*
9	Test the signal circuit of the brake pressure sensor for a short to ground, a high resistance, or an open. Did you find and correct the condition?	—	Go to *Step 16*	Go to *Step 13*
10	Test the signal circuit of the brake pressure sensor for a short to voltage. Did you find and correct the condition?	—	Go to *Step 16*	Go to *Step 13*
11	1. Disconnect the EBCM. 2. Test the ground circuit of the brake pressure sensor for a high resistance or an open. Did you find and correct the condition?	—	Go to *Step 16*	Go to *Step 13*
12	Inspect for poor connections at the harness connector of the brake pressure sensor. Did you find and correct the condition?	—	Go to *Step 16*	Go to *Step 14*
13	Inspect for poor connections at the harness connector of the EBCM. Did you find and correct the condition?	—	Go to *Step 16*	Go to *Step 15*
14	Replace the brake pressure sensor. Did you complete the replacement?	—	Go to *Step 16*	—
15	Replace the EBCM. Did you complete the replacement?	—	Go to *Step 16*	—
16	1. Use the scan tool in order to clear the DTCs. 2. Operate the vehicle within the Conditions for Running the DTC as specified in the supporting text. Does the DTC reset?	—	Go to *Step 2*	System OK

GC4020052008030X

Fig. 95 Code C0132: ABS/TCS System Pressure Circuit Range/Performance (Part 3 of 3). 2000 Intrigue

Circuit Description

The prime valve solenoid circuits are supplied with battery power when the ignition is in the run position. The EBTCM controls the valve functions by grounding the circuit when necessary.

Conditions for Setting the DTC

The EBTCM senses a discrepancy such as an open, short to ground, or short to voltage in the circuit.

Action Taken When the DTC Sets

- A malfunction DTC is stored.
- ABS/TCS is disabled.
- The ABS and ETS/TRAC OFF Indicators are turned on.

Conditions for Clearing the DTC

- Condition for DTC is no longer present and scan tool clear DTC function is used.
- 100 ignition cycles pass with no DTC(s) detected.

Diagnostic Aids

The solenoid valve circuit and the solenoid coil are internal to the EBTCM. No part of the solenoid circuit is diagnosable external to the EBTCM. The DTC sets when there is a malfunction in the solenoid circuit internal to the EBTCM only.

Test Description

The numbers below refer to step numbers on the Diagnostic Table.

2. This step determines if the DTC is current.

GC402980330300AX

Fig. 96 Codes C0141, C0146, C0151 & C0156: TCS Solenoid Circuit Fault (Part 1 of 2). 2000 Grand Prix & Intrigue

Step	Action	Value(s)	Yes	No
1	Was the Diagnostic System Check performed?	—	*Go to Step 2*	Go to *Diagnostic System Check*
2	1. Turn the ignition switch to the OFF position. 2. Install a scan tool. 3. Turn the ignition switch to the RUN position, engine off. 4. Using the scan tool run the Automated test. Does DTC reset as a current DTC?	—	*Go to Step 3*	Go to *Diagnostic System Check*
3	Replace the EBTCM. Is the repair complete?	—	Go to *Diagnostic System Check*	—

GC402980330300BX

Fig. 96 Codes C0141, C0146, C0151 & C0156: TCS Solenoid Circuit Fault (Part 2 of 2). 2000 Grand Prix & Intrigue

Step	Action	Value(s)	Yes	No
1	Was the Diagnostic System Check performed?	—	*Go to Step 2*	Go to *Diagnostic System Check*
2	Observe the rear brake lamps. Are the brake lamps off?	—	*Go to Step 4*	*Go to Step 3*
3	Disconnect the Stoplamp Switch connector C1. Are the brake lamps on?	—	*Go to Step 18*	*Go to Step 12*
4	Press the brake pedal. Do the brake lights come on?	—	*Go to Step 5*	*Go to Step 8*
5	1. Turn the ignition switch to the OFF position. 2. Disconnect the EBTCM connector C1. 3. Install the *J 39700* Universal Pinout Box using the J 39700-530 cable adapter to the EBTCM harness connector only. 4. Using the *J 39200* DMM, measure the voltage at the *J 39700* terminal 6 while an assistant presses the brake pedal. Is the voltage within specifications?	Battery voltage	*Go to Step 6*	*Go to Step 7*
6	Replace the EBTCM. Is the replacement complete?	—	Go to *Diagnostic System Check*	—
7	Repair the open or high resistance in CKT 17. Is the circuit repair complete?	—	Go to *Diagnostic System Check*	—
8	Check the STOPLAMP fuse in the I/P Fuse Block. Is the fuse OK?	—	*Go to Step 9*	*Go to Step 13*
9	1. Disconnect the Stoplamp Switch connector C1. 2. Using the *J 39200* DMM, measure the voltage at the Stoplamp Switch harness connector terminal A. Is the voltage within specifications?	Battery voltage	*Go to Step 11*	*Go to Step 10*
10	Repair the open in CKT 140. Is the circuit repair complete?	—	Go to *Diagnostic System Check*	—
11	Connect a fused jumper wire between the Stoplamp Switch harness connector terminals A and B. Do the brake lamps come on?	—	*Go to Step 12*	*Go to Step 7*
12	Adjust or replace the Stoplamp Switch as necessary. Is the repair complete?	—	Go to *Diagnostic System Check*	—
13	1. Replace the STOPLAMP fuse. (Do not press the brake pedal.) 2. Check the STOPLAMP fuse. Is the fuse OK?	—	*Go to Step 15*	*Go to Step 14*
14	Repair the short to ground in CKT 140. Is the circuit repair complete?	—	Go to *Diagnostic System Check*	—
15	1. Press the brake pedal. 2. Check the STOPLAMP fuse. Is the fuse OK?	—	Go to *Diagnostic System Check*	*Go to Step 16*

GC402980330400BX

Fig. 97 Code C0161: ABS/TCS Brake Switch Circuit Fault (Part 2 of 3). 2000 Grand Prix & Intrigue

Circuit Description

The vehicle stability enhancement system (VSES) uses the lateral accelerometer input when calculating the desired yaw rate. The usable output voltage range for the lateral accelerometer is 0.25–4.75 volts. The lateral accelerometer sensor bias compensates for sensor mounting alignment errors and electronic signal errors.

Conditions for Running the DTC

- The ignition is ON.
- The vehicle speed is greater than 40 km/h (25 mph).

Conditions for Setting the DTC

Voltage at the lateral accelerometer signal output to the EBCM falls outside the 0.25 V – 4.75 V range for more than 100 milliseconds.

Action Taken When the DTC Sets

- A malfunction DTC is set
- TCS and VSES are disabled
- TCS, SERVICE VEHICLE SOON and PCS lamp indicators turn on

Conditions for Clearing the DTC

- The condition for the DTC is no longer present
- A history DTC will clear after 124 consecutive ignition cycles if the condition for the malfunction is no longer present.
- Using a scan tool.

Diagnostic Aids

- A thorough inspection of the wiring system and connectors be performed. Failure to carefully and fully inspect the wiring system and connectors may result in misdiagnosis which may result in replacing good parts and the reappearance of the malfunction.
- Inspection for poor connections, broken insulation, or a wire that is broken inside the insulation.

GC4020052009010X

Fig. 98 Code C0186: Lateral Accelerometer Circuit Fault (Part 1 of 3). 2000 Intrigue

Circuit Description

The Stoplamp Switch is a normally open switch, when the brake pedal is depressed the EBTCM senses battery voltage. This allows the EBTCM to determine the state of the brake lamps.

Conditions for Setting the DTC

- EBTCM detects battery voltage at all times.
- EBTCM never detects battery voltage from CKT 17.
- Both brake lamps are faulty.

Action Taken When the DTC Sets

- DTC C0161 is set.
- ABS and TCS remains active.

Conditions for Clearing the DTC

- The condition responsible for setting the DTC no longer exists and the scan tool Clear DTCs function is used.
- 100 ignition cycles pass with no DTC(s) detected.

Diagnostic Aids

- It is very important that a thorough inspection of the wiring and connectors be performed. Failure to carefully and fully inspect wiring and connectors may result in misdiagnosis, causing part replacement with reappearance of the malfunction.
- Thoroughly inspect any circuitry that may be causing the complaint for the following conditions:
  - Backed out terminals
  - Improper mating
  - Broken locks
  - Improperly formed or damaged terminals
  - Poor terminal-to-wiring connections
  - Physical damage to the wiring harness
- The following conditions may cause an intermittent malfunction:
  - A poor connection
  - Rubbed-through wire insulation
  - A broken wire inside the insulation
- If an intermittent malfunction exists refer to Troubleshooting Electrical Diagnosis

Test Description

The numbers below refer to the step numbers on the diagnostic table.

5. This step checks for voltage at the EBTCM.
11. This step checks the Stoplamp switch.

GC402980330400AX

Fig. 97 Code C0161: ABS/TCS Brake Switch Circuit Fault (Part 1 of 3). 2000 Grand Prix & Intrigue

Step	Action	Value(s)	Yes	No
16	1. Turn the ignition switch to the OFF position. 2. Disconnect the EBTCM. 3. Replace the fuse. 4. Depress the brake pedal. 5. Check the STOPLAMP fuse. Is the fuse OK?	—	*Go to Step 6*	*Go to Step 17*
17	Repair the short to ground in CKT 17. Is the circuit repair complete?	—	Go to *Diagnostic System Check*	—
18	Repair CKT 17 for a short to voltage. Is the repair complete?	—	Go to *Diagnostic System Check*	—

GC402980330400CX

Fig. 97 Code C0161: ABS/TCS Brake Switch Circuit Fault (Part 3 of 3). 2000 Grand Prix & Intrigue

Test Description

The number(s) below refer to the step number(s) on the diagnostic table.

2. Tests for specified voltage on the lateral accelerometer signal circuit.
3. Tests for B+ voltage on yaw/lateral accelerometer sensor.
4. Tests the ignition circuit for a high resistance or open.
5. Checks to see if voltage was below or above specified voltage.
6. Checks to see if voltage was above specified voltage.
7. Checks to see if voltage was below specified voltage.
8. Checks to see if voltage was above specified voltage.
9. Checks to see if resistance of ground circuit is less than 5 ohms.
10. Tests for a short to voltage on the 5 volt reference circuit.
11. Tests for a short to ground, a high resistance, or an open in the 5 volt reference circuit.
12. Tests for a short to ground, a high resistance, or an open in the lateral accelerometer signal circuit.
13. Tests for a short to voltage in the lateral accelerometer signal circuit.
14. Tests for a high resistance or an open in the ground circuit.
15. Checks the yaw/lateral accelerometer sensor connector for poor connections.
16. Checks the EBCM connector for poor connections.

Step	Action	Value(s)	Yes	No
1	Did you perform the ABS Diagnostic System Check?	—	Go to *Step 2*	Go to *A Diagnostic System Check - ABS*
2	1. Turn OFF the ignition. 2. Disconnect the EBCM. 3. Install the *J 39700* universal pinout box with the *J 39700-530* cable adapter between the EBCM and the EBCM harness connector. 4. Turn ON the ignition, with the engine OFF. 5. Using the DMM, measure the voltage between pin 10 and pin 15 of the *J 39700* universal pinout box. Is the voltage within the specified value?	0.25 V – 4.75 V	Go to Diagnostic Aids	Go to *Step 3*
3	1. Turn OFF the ignition. 2. Disconnect the yaw/lateral accelerometer sensor. 3. Turn ON the ignition, with the engine OFF. 4. Using a DMM, measure the voltage between the ignition and ground circuits of the yaw/lateral accelerometer sensor. Is the voltage in the specified value?	B+	Go to *Step 5*	Go to *Step 4*
4	Test the ignition circuit of the yaw/lateral accelerometer sensor for high resistance or an open. Did you find and correct the condition?	—	Go to *Step 19*	Power Distribution
5	1. Reconnect the yaw/lateral accelerometer sensor. 2. Using a DMM, measure the voltage between pin 10 and pin 15 of the *J 39700* universal pinout box. Is the voltage less than the specified value?	4.75 V	Go to *Step 6*	Go to *Step 13*
6	Using a DMM, measure the voltage between pin 10 and pin 15 of the *J 39700* universal pinout box. Is the voltage greater than the specified value?	0.25 V	Go to *Step 7*	Go to *Step 12*
7	Using a DMM, measure the voltage between the 5 volt reference circuit pin 16 and the ground circuit pin 15 on the *J 39700* universal pinout box. Does the voltage measure less than the specified value?	2 V	Go to *Step 11*	Go to *Step 8*

GC4020052009020X

Fig. 98 Code C0186: Lateral Accelerometer Circuit Fault (Part 2 of 3). 2000 Intrigue

Step	Action	Value(s)	Yes	No
8	Using a DMM, measure the voltage between the 5 volt reference circuit pin 16 and ground circuit pin 15 on the *J 39700* universal pinout box. Does the voltage measure greater than the specified voltage?	3 V	Go to *Step 10*	Go to *Step 9*
9	1. Turn OFF the ignition. 2. Disconnect the negative battery cable. 3. Measure the resistance from the ground circuit of the yaw/lateral accelerometer to a good ground. Does the resistance measure less than the specified value?	5 Ω	Go to *Step 16*	Go to *Step 14*
10	Test the 5 volt reference circuit of the yaw/lateral accelerometer sensor for a short to voltage. Did you find and correct the condition?	—	Go to *Step 19*	Go to *Step 15*
11	Test the 5 volt reference circuit of the yaw/lateral accelerometer sensor for a short to ground, a high resistance, or an open. Did you find and correct the condition?	—	Go to *Step 19*	Go to *Step 12*
12	Test the lateral accelerometer signal circuit of the yaw/lateral accelerometer sensor for a short to ground, a high resistance, or an open. Did you find and correct the condition?	—	Go to *Step 19*	Go to *Step 15*
13	Test the lateral accelerometer signal circuit of the yaw/lateral accelerometer sensor for a short to voltage. Did you find and correct the condition?	—	Go to *Step 19*	Go to *Step 15*
14	1. Disconnect the EBCM. 2. Test the ground circuit of the yaw/lateral accelerometer sensor for a high resistance or an open. Did you find and correct the condition?	—	Go to *Step 19*	Go to *Step 15*
15	Inspect for poor connections at the harness connector of the yaw/lateral accelerometer sensor. Did you find and correct the condition?	—	Go to *Step 19*	Go to *Step 17*
16	Inspect for poor connections at the harness connector of the EBCM. Did you find and correct the condition?	—	Go to *Step 19*	Go to *Step 18*
17	Replace the vehicle yaw/lateral accelerometer sensor. Did you complete the replacement?	—	Go to *Step 19*	—
18	Replace the EBCM. Did you complete the replacement?	—	Go to *Step 19*	—
19	1. Use the scan tool in order to clear the DTCs. 2. Operate the vehicle within the Conditions for Running the DTC Does the DTC reset?	—	Go to *Step 2*	System OK

GC4020052009030X

Fig. 98 Code C0186: Lateral Accelerometer Circuit Fault (Part 3 of 3). 2000 Intrigue

Conditions for Clearing the DTC

- The condition for the DTC is no longer present
- A history DTC will clear after 124 consecutive ignition cycles if the condition for the malfunction is no longer present.
- Using a scan tool.

Diagnostic Aids

- Find out from the customer under what condition was the DTC set. This information will help to duplicate the failure.
- Check the vehicle for proper alignment. The car should not pull in either direction while driving straight on a level surface.
- During diagnosis, park the vehicle on a level surface.
- Check for malfunctioning EBCM and lateral accelerometer.
- The snapshot function on the scan tool can help find an intermittent DTC.

Test Description

The number(s) below refer to the step number(s) on the diagnostic table.

2. Checks to see if steering angle sensor is centered.
3. Checks for specified voltage on the lateral accelerometer signal circuit.
4. Checks for specified voltage on the yaw rate signal circuit.

Step	Action	Value(s)	Yes	No
1	Did you perform the ABS Diagnostic System Check?	—	Go to *Step 2*	Go to *A Diagnostic System Check - ABS*
2	Perform the steering angle sensor centering procedure. Did you successfully complete the centering procedure?	—	Go to *Step 3*	Go to *Step 7*
3	1. Turn OFF the ignition. 2. Disconnect the EBCM connector. 3. Install the *J 39700* universal pinout box with the *J 39700-530* cable adapter between the EBCM and the EBCM harness connector. 4. Turn the ignition ON, with the engine OFF. 5. Using the DMM, measure the voltage between pin 10 and pin 15 of the *J 39700* universal pinout box. Is the voltage within the specified value?	2.3 V – 2.7 V	Go to *Step 4*	Go to *Step 8*
4	Using the DMM, measure the voltage between pin 26 and pin 15 of the *J 39700* universal pinout box. Is the voltage within the specified value?	2.3 V – 2.7 V	Go to *Step 5*	Go to *Step 8*
5	1. Use the scan tool in order to clear the DTCs. 2. Perform the Diagnostic Test Drive. Does the DTC reset?	—	Go to *Step 6*	Go to Diagnostic Aids
6	Replace the EBCM. Did you complete the replacement?	—	Go to *Step 9*	—
7	Replace the steering angle sensor. Did you complete the replacement?	—	Go to *Step 9*	–
8	Replace the vehicle yaw/lateral accelerometer sensor. Did you complete the repair?	—	Go to *Step 9*	–
9	1. Use the scan tool in order to clear the DTCs. 2. Operate the vehicle within the Conditions for Running the DTC Does the DTC reset?	—	Go to *Step 2*	System OK

GC4020052010020X

Fig. 99 Code C0187: Lateral Accelerometer Circuit Range/Performance (Part 2 of 2). 2000 Intrigue

Circuit Description

The vehicle stability enhancement system (VSES) uses the lateral accelerometer input when calculating the desired yaw rate. The usable output voltage range for the lateral accelerometer 0.25 – 4.75 volts. The scan tool will report zero lateral acceleration as 2.5 volts with no sensor bias present.

The lateral accelerometer sensor bias compensates for sensor mounting alignment errors and electronic signal errors.

Conditions for Running the DTC

- The ignition is ON.
- The vehicle speed is greater than 40 km/h (25 mph).

Conditions for Setting the DTC

- A reference lateral acceleration from the data of the yaw rate sensor, wheel speed sensors, and steering angle sensor is used to test the lateral accelerometer signal. If during stable driving conditions, the lateral accelerometer signal becomes larger than 0.26 g, the EBCM controller will disregard the signal so that a false EBCM intervention is prevented. A malfunction is detected if this condition continues for more than two seconds.
- Under normal driving conditions, the long time filtered driving direction is straight ahead. The long time filtered lateral accelerometer value is called the offset. If the offset value is higher than 0.23 g, a malfunction is detected. Malfunction time depends on driving distance, vehicle speed and the amount of malfunctioning later accelerometer signal.
- The lateral accelerometer signal is limited to an electrical stop of 1.8 g. If the lateral accelerometer signal is greater than 1.5 g for more than 500 milliseconds, a malfunction is detected.
- At a standstill, the range of the lateral accelerometer signal is less than 0.7 g. If the lateral accelerometer signal is greater than 0.7 g at standstill, a malfunction is detected.
- Lateral accelerometer signal cannot change rapidly under normal driving conditions. If the lateral accelerometer signal is changing faster than 55 g per second, a malfunction is detected.

Action Taken When the DTC Sets

- A malfunction DTC is set
- VSES is disabled for the duration of the ignition cycle
- ABS remains functional
- TCS, SERVICE ENGINE SOON and PCS lamp indicators turn on

GC4020052010010X

Fig. 99 Code C0187: Lateral Accelerometer Circuit Range/Performance (Part 1 of 2). 2000 Intrigue

Circuit Description

The vehicle stability enhancement system (VSES) is activated by the EBCM calculating the desired yaw rate and comparing it to the actual yaw rate input. The desired yaw rate is calculated from measured steering wheel position, vehicle speed, and lateral acceleration. The difference between the desired yaw rate and actual yaw rate is the yaw rate error, which is a measurement of oversteer or understeer. If the yaw rate error becomes too large, the EBCM will attempt to correct the vehicle's yaw motion by applying differential braking to the wheels.

To correct for oversteer, differential braking is used on the left front or right front wheel brake. To correct for understeer, differential braking is used on the left rear or right rear wheel brake.

Conditions for Running the DTC

- The ignition is ON.
- The vehicle speed is greater than 40 km/h (25 mph).

Conditions for Setting the DTC

The EBCM performs different tests to detect a DTC condition. A malfunction is detected when the yaw rate sensor signal input voltage is less than 0.225 volts or greater than 4.775 volts for more than 100 milliseconds.

Action Taken When the DTC Sets

- A malfunction DTC is set
- TCS and VSES are disabled
- TCS, SERVICE VEHICLE SOON and PCS lamp indicators turn on

Conditions for Clearing the DTC

- Using a scan tool.
- The DTC will clear after 124 consecutive ignition cycles if the condition for the malfunction is no longer present.

Diagnostic Aids

The following conditions may cause a malfunction:

- Open in the yaw rate signal circuit
- Short to ground in the yaw rate signal circuit
- Short to voltage in the yaw rate signal circuit
- Open in the yaw rate ground circuit
- Open in ignition voltage circuit
- Malfunctioning vehicle yaw/lateral accelerometer sensor
- Malfunctioning EBCM

GC4020052011010X

Fig. 100 Code C0196: Yaw Rate Circuit Fault (Part 1 of 3). 2000 Intrigue

Test Description

The number(s) below refer to the step number(s) on the diagnostic table.

2. Tests for specified voltage on the yaw rate signal circuit.
3. Checks the voltage between the ignition and ground circuit for a specified value.
4. Checks the voltage between the ignition and ground circuit for a specified value.
5. Checks to see if voltage was above specified voltage.
6. Checks to see if voltage was below specified voltage.
7. Checks to see if EBCM 5 volt reference signal is within specified limit.
8. Checks to see if voltage was above specified voltage.
9. Checks to see if resistance of ground circuit is less than 5 ohms.
10. Tests for a short to voltage on the 5 volt reference circuit.
11. Tests for a short to ground, a high resistance, or an open in the 5 volt reference circuit.
12. Tests for a short to voltage in the yaw rate signal circuit.
13. Tests for a short to ground, a high resistance, or an open in the yaw rate signal circuit.
14. Tests for a high resistance or an open in the ground circuit.
15. Checks the EBCM connector for poor connections.
16. Checks the yaw/lateral accelerometer sensor connector for poor connections.

Step	Action	Value(s)	Yes	No
1	Did you perform the ABS Diagnostic System Check?	—	Go to *Step 2*	Go to *A Diagnostic System Check - ABS*
2	1. Turn OFF the ignition. 2. Disconnect the EBCM. 3. Install the *J 39700* universal pinout box with the *J 39700-530* cable adapter between the EBCM and the EBCM harness connector. 4. Turn ON the ignition, with the engine OFF. 5. Using the DMM, measure the voltage between pin 26 and pin 15 of the *J 39700* universal pinout box. Is the voltage within the specified value?	0.225 V - 4.775 V	Go to Diagnostic Aids	Go to *Step 3*
3	1. Turn OFF the ignition. 2. Disconnect the yaw/lateral accelerometer sensor. 3. Turn ON the ignition, with the engine OFF. 4. Using the DMM, measure the voltage between the ignition and ground circuits of the yaw/lateral accelerometer sensor. Is the voltage in the specified value?	B+	Go to *Step 5*	Go to *Step 4*
4	Test the ignition circuit of the yaw/lateral accelerometer sensor for high resistance or an open. Did you find and correct the condition?	—	Go to *Step 18*	Power Distribution
5	1. Reconnect the yaw/lateral accelerometer sensor. 2. Using the DMM, measure the voltage between pin 26 and pin 15 of the *J 39700* universal pinout box. Is the voltage less than the specified value?	4.775 V	Go to *Step 6*	Go to *Step 13*
6	Using the DMM, measure the voltage between pin 26 and pin 15 of the *J 39700* universal pinout box. Is the voltage greater than the specified value?	0.225 V	Go to *Step 7*	Go to *Step 12*
7	Using a DMM, measure the voltage between the 5 volt reference circuit pin 16 and the ground circuit pin 15 of the *J 39700* universal pinout box. Does the voltage measure below the specified value?	2 V	Go to *Step 11*	Go to *Step 8*

GC4020052011020X

Fig. 100 Code C0196: Yaw Rate Circuit Fault (Part 2 of 3). 2000 Intrigue

Step	Action	Value(s)	Yes	No
8	Using a DMM, measure the voltage between the 5 volt reference circuit pin 16 and ground pin 15 of the *J 39700* universal pinout box. Does the voltage measure above the specified value?	3 V	Go to *Step 10*	Go to *Step 9*
9	1. Turn OFF the engine. 2. Disconnect the negative battery cable. 3. Measure the resistance from the ground circuit of the yaw/lateral accelerometer sensor to a good ground. Does the resistance measure less than the specified value?	5 Ω	Go to *Step 16*	Go to *Step 14*
10	Test the 5 volt reference circuit of the yaw/lateral accelerometer sensor for a short to voltage. Did you find and correct the condition?	—	Go to *Step 19*	Go to *Step 15*
11	Test the 5 volt reference circuit of the yaw/lateral accelerometer sensor for a short to ground, a high resistance, or an open. Did you find and correct the condition?	—	Go to *Step 19*	Go to *Step 12*
12	Test the yaw rate signal circuit of the yaw/lateral accelerometer sensor for a short to ground, a high resistance, or an open. Did you find and correct the condition?	—	Go to *Step 19*	Go to *Step 15*
13	Test the yaw rate signal circuit of the yaw/lateral accelerometer sensor for a short to voltage. Did you find and correct the condition?	—	Go to *Step 19*	Go to *Step 15*
14	1. Disconnect the EBCM. 2. Test the ground circuit of the yaw/lateral accelerometer sensor for a high resistance or an open. Did you find and correct the condition?	—	Go to *Step 19*	Go to *Step 15*
15	Inspect for poor connections at the harness connector of the yaw/lateral accelerometer sensor. Did you find and correct the condition?	—	Go to *Step 19*	Go to *Step 17*
16	Inspect for poor connections at the harness connector of the EBCM. Did you find and correct the condition?	—	Go to *Step 19*	Go to *Step 18*
17	Replace the vehicle yaw/lateral accelerometer sensor. Did you complete the replacement?	—	Go to *Step 19*	—
18	Replace the EBCM. Did you complete the replacement?	—	Go to *Step 19*	—
19	1. Use the scan tool in order to clear the DTCs. 2. Operate the vehicle within the Conditions for Running the DTC as specified in the supporting text. Does the DTC reset?	—	Go to *Step 2*	System OK

GC4020052011030X

Fig. 100 Code C0196: Yaw Rate Circuit Fault (Part 3 of 3). 2000 Intrigue

Circuit Description

The EBCM triggers a yaw rate sensor test every 40 milliseconds and switches the sensor into test mode. The EBCM sends a test signal to the sensor via the test circuit. When the test is run, the measured yaw rate from the sensor to the EBCM must be in the range of 25° per second +/- 7° per second. At standstill, the vehicle yaw rate is zero. The yaw rate signal at standstill is called the offset. If calibration at standstill is not possible, a quick calibration during driving is done. The measured yaw rate is calibrated to a calculated reference yaw rate signal. Yaw rate sensor sensitivity is estimated by comparison of the reference yaw rate and the measured yaw rate during cornering.

Steering angle centering is the process by which the EBCM calibrates the steering sensor output so that the output reads zero when the steering wheel is centered. The PCS steering angle sensor centering process is performed manually.

Conditions for Running the DTC

- The ignition is ON.
- The vehicle speed is greater than 40 km/h (25 mph).

Conditions for Setting the DTC

A malfunction is detected if one or more of the following conditions exist:

- The yaw rate sensor signal is out of range for 220–420 milliseconds.
- The yaw rate sensor signal at standstill which is called the offset is outside the allowed range of +/- 8° per second.
- The sensor sensitivity which is estimated by comparing the reference yaw rate and the measured yaw rate during cornering, is outside a predetermined range.
- The yaw rate is changing at a rate greater than 6–23° per second per 40 milliseconds.

Action Taken When the DTC Sets

- A malfunction DTC is set
- TCS and VSES are disabled
- TCS, SERVICE VEHICLE SOON and PCS lamp indicators turn on

GC4020052012010X

Fig. 101 Code C0197: Yaw Rate Circuit Range/ Performance (Part 1 of 2). 2000 Intrigue

Conditions for Clearing the DTC

- The condition for the DTC is no longer present
- A history DTC will clear after 124 consecutive ignition cycles if the condition for the malfunction is no longer present.
- Using a scan tool.

Diagnostic Aids

The following conditions may cause a malfunction:

- Malfunctioning lateral accelerometer
- Malfunctioning EBCM

Test Description

The number(s) below refer to the step number(s) on the diagnostic table.

2. Checks to see if steering angle sensor is centered.
3. Checks for specified voltage on the lateral accelerometer signal circuit.
4. Checks for specified voltage on the yaw rate signal circuit.

Step	Action	Value(s)	Yes	No
1	Did you perform the ABS Diagnostic System Check?	—	Go to *Step 2*	Go to *A Diagnostic System Check - ABS*
2	Perform the steering angle sensor centering procedure. Did you successfully complete the centering procedure?	—	Go to *Step 3*	Go to *Step 7*
3	1. Turn OFF the ignition. 2. Disconnect the EBCM connector. 3. Install the *J 39700* universal pinout box with the *J 39700-530* cable adapter between the EBCM and the EBCM harness connector. 4. Turn the ignition ON, with the engine OFF. 5. Using the DMM, measure the voltage between pin 10 and pin 15 of the *J 39700* universal pinout box. Is the voltage within the specified value?	2.3 V – 2.7 V	Go to *Step 4*	Go to *Step 8*
4	Using the DMM, measure the voltage between pin 26 and pin 15 of the *J 39700* universal pinout box. Is the voltage within the specified value?	2.3 V – 2.7 V	Go to *Step 5*	Go to *Step 8*
5	1. Use the scan tool in order to clear the DTCs. 2. Perform the Diagnostic Test Drive. Does the DTC reset?	—	Go to *Step 6*	Go to Diagnostic Aids
6	Replace the EBCM. Did you complete the replacement?	—	Go to *Step 9*	—
7	Replace the steering angle sensor. Did you complete the replacement?	—	Go to *Step 9*	—
8	Replace the vehicle yaw/lateral accelerometer sensor. Did you complete the repair?	—	Go to *Step 9*	—
9	1. Use the scan tool in order to clear the DTCs. 2. Operate the vehicle within the Conditions for Running the DTC Does the DTC reset?	—	Go to *Step 2*	System OK

GC4020052012020X

Fig. 101 Code C0197: Yaw Rate Circuit Range/ Performance (Part 2 of 2). 2000 Intrigue

Circuit Description

The RPM signal circuit provides the EBTCM with an indication of engine RPM to help determine TCS control methods and rates when a TCS event takes place.

Conditions for Setting the DTC

The EBTCM does not received an RPM input signal after 1 second, after the engine has been started.

Action Taken When the DTC Sets

- A malfunction DTC is stored.
- The ETC/Trac off indicator is turned on.
- The TCS is disabled. ABS remains functional.

Conditions for Clearing the DTC

- The condition for DTC is no longer present and the scan tool Clear DTCs function is used.
- 100 ignition cycles have passed with no DTC(s) detected.

Diagnostic Aids

Perform a thorough inspection of the wiring. Perform a thorough inspection of the connectors. Failure to carefully and fully inspect the wiring and the connectors may result in misdiagnosis. Misdiagnosis causes part replacement with reappearance of the malfunction.

Test Description

The number(s) below refer to the step number(s) on the diagnostic table.

2. If the instrument panel tachometer is working properly, the cause of the malfunction is most likely between the underhood accessory wiring junction block and the EBTCM, or the EBTCM itself.
10. At this point, the PCM is likely causing the malfunction. Refer to the appropriate OBD system check.

GC402980330500AX

Fig. 102 Code C0236: TCS RPM Signal Circuit Fault (Part 1 of 3). 2000 Grand Prix

Step	Action	Value(s)	Yes	No
8	1. Reconnect all the connectors. 2. Using the scan tool clear the DTC. 3. Disconnect the scan tool from the DLC. 4. Start the engine. Did DTC C0236 reset?	—	*Go to Step 10*	Go to *Diagnostic System Check*
9	Replace the EBTCM. Is the repair complete?	—	Go to *Diagnostic System Check*	—
10	Suspect PCM. *Powertrain OBD System Check* Is the repair complete?	—	Go to *Diagnostic System Check*	—
11	Repair an open between underhood accessory wiring junction block and the EBTCM harness connector terminal 11. Is the repair complete?	—	Go to *Diagnostic System Check*	—
12	Repair an open between underhood accessory wiring junction block and the PCM harness connector C2 terminal 8. Is the repair complete?	—	Go to *Diagnostic System Check*	—
13	Repair a short to ground in CKT 121. Is the repair complete?	—	Go to *Diagnostic System Check*	—
14	Repair a short to voltage in CKT 121. Is the repair complete?	—	Go to *Diagnostic System Check*	—
15	Replace all the terminals or replace the connectors that exhibit signs of the following: • That exhibit signs of poor terminal contact. • That exhibit signs of corrosion. • That exhibit signs of damaged terminals. Is the repair complete?	—	Go to *Diagnostic System Check*	—

GC402980330500CX

Fig. 102 Code C0236: TCS RPM Signal Circuit Fault (Part 3 of 3). 2000 Grand Prix

Step	Action	Value(s)	Yes	No
1	Was the Diagnostic System Check performed?	—	*Go to Step 2*	Go to *A Diagnostic System Check - ABS*
2	1. Start the engine. 2. Vary the engine RPM with the throttle while observing the I/P tachometer. Does the I/P tachometer work properly as the engine RPM changes?	—	*Go to Step 3*	*Go to Step 9*
3	1. Turn the ignition switch to the OFF position. 2. Disconnect the PCM connector C2 from the PCM. 3. Disconnect the EBTCM connector from the EBTCM. 4. Install the *J 39700* Universal Breakout Box with the J 39700-530 Cable Adapter to the EBTCM harness only. 5. Use a *J 39200* DMM to measure the resistance between the PCM harness connector C2 terminal 8 and the *J 39700* Universal Breakout Box terminal 11. Is the resistance within the specified range?	0–5 Ω	*Go to Step 5*	*Go to Step 10*
4	Use a *J 39200* DMM to measure the resistance between the *J 39700* Universal Breakout Box terminal 11 and terminal 15. Is the resistance within the specified range?	OL (Infinite)	*Go to Step 5*	*Go to Step 11*
5	1. Turn the ignition switch to the ON position 2. Use a *J 39200* DMM to measure the voltage between the *J 39700* Universal Breakout Box terminal 11 and terminal 15. Is the voltage within the specified range?	0–2 V	*Go to Step 6*	*Go to Step 12*
6	1. Inspect the PCM connector C2 for the following: • Inspect for damage. • Inspect for poor terminal contact. • Inspect for corrosion. 2. Inspect the EBTCM connector for the following: • Inspect for damage. • Inspect for poor terminal contact. • Inspect for corrosion. 3. Ensure both the PCM connector C2 and the EBTCM connector are properly retained when connected. Are the following signs present on either connector: • Is poor terminal contact present? • Is corrosion present? • Is damaged terminals present?	—	*Go to Step 13*	*Go to Step 7*
7	1. Reconnect all the connectors. 2. Using the scan tool clear the DTC. 3. Disconnect the scan tool from the DLC. 4. Start the engine. Did DTC C0236 reset?	—	*Go to Step 8*	Go to *A Diagnostic System Check - ABS*
8	Replace the EBTCM. Is the repair complete?	—	Go to *A Diagnostic System Check - ABS*	—

GC4029903867020X

Fig. 103 Code C0236: TCS RPM Signal Circuit Fault (Part 2 of 3). 2000 Intrigue

Step	Action	Value(s)	Yes	No
1	Was the Diagnostic System Check performed?	—	*Go to Step 2*	Go to *Diagnostic System Check*
2	1. Start the engine. 2. Vary the engine RPM with the throttle while observing the I/P tachometer. Does the I/P tachometer work properly as the engine RPM changes?	—	*Go to Step 3*	*Go to Step 4*
3	1. Turn the ignition switch to the OFF position. 2. Disconnect the PCM connector C2 from the PCM. 3. Disconnect the EBTCM connector from the EBTCM. 4. Install the *J 39700* Universal Breakout Box with the J 39700-530 Cable Adapter to the EBTCM harness only. 5. Use a *J 39200* DMM to measure the resistance between the PCM harness connector C2 terminal 8 and the *J 39700* Universal Breakout Box terminal 11. Is the resistance within the specified range?	0–5 Ω	*Go to Step 9*	*Go to Step 11*
4	1. Turn the ignition switch to the OFF position. 2. Disconnect the PCM connector C2 from the PCM. 3. Disconnect the EBTCM connector from the EBTCM. 4. Install the *J 39700* Universal Breakout Box with the J 39700-530 Cable Adapter to the EBTCM harness only. 5. Use a *J 39200* DMM to measure the resistance between the PCM harness connector C2 terminal 8 and the *J 39700* Universal Breakout Box terminal 11. Is the resistance within the specified range?	0–5 Ω	*Go to Step 5*	*Go to Step 12*
5	Use a *J 39200* DMM to measure the resistance between the *J 39700* Universal Breakout Box terminal 11 and terminal 15. Is the resistance within the specified range?	OL (Infinite)	*Go to Step 6*	*Go to Step 13*
6	1. Turn the ignition switch to the RUN position 2. Use a *J 39200* DMM to measure the voltage between the *J 39700* Universal Breakout Box terminal 11 and terminal 15. Is the voltage within the specified range?	0–2 V	*Go to Step 7*	*Go to Step 14*
7	1. Inspect the PCM connector C2 for the following: • Inspect for damage. • Inspect for poor terminal contact. • Inspect for corrosion. 2. Inspect the EBTCM connector for the following: • Inspect for damage. • Inspect for poor terminal contact. • Inspect for corrosion. 3. Ensure both the PCM connector C2 and the EBTCM connector are properly retained when connected. Are the following signs present on either connector: • Is poor terminal contact present? • Is corrosion present? • Is damaged terminals present?	—	*Go to Step 15*	*Go to Step 8*

GC402980330500BX

Fig. 102 Code C0236: TCS RPM Signal Circuit Fault (Part 2 of 3). 2000 Grand Prix

Circuit Description

The RPM signal circuit provides the EBTCM with an indication of engine RPM to help determine TCS control methods and rates when a TCS event takes place.

Conditions for Setting the DTC

The EBTCM does not received an RPM input signal after 1 second, after the engine has been started.

Action Taken When the DTC Sets

- A malfunction DTC is stored.
- The TRAC OFF indicator is turned on.
- The TCS is disabled. ABS remains functional.

Conditions for Clearing the DTC

- The condition for DTC is no longer present and the scan tool Clear DTCs function is used.
- 100 ignition cycles have passed with no DTC(s) detected.

Diagnostic Aids

Perform a thorough inspection of the wiring. Perform a thorough inspection of the connectors. Failure to carefully and fully inspect the wiring and the connectors may result in misdiagnosis. Misdiagnosis causes part replacement with reappearance of the malfunction.

Test Description

The number(s) below refer to the step number(s) on the diagnostic table.

2. If the instrument panel tachometer is working properly, the cause of the malfunction is most likely between the PCM and the EBTCM, or the EBTCM itself.
9. At this point, the PCM is likely causing the malfunction.

GC4029903867010X

Fig. 103 Code C0236: TCS RPM Signal Circuit Fault (Part 1 of 3). 2000 Intrigue

Step	Action	Value(s)	Yes	No
9	Suspect PCM. Is the repair complete?	—	Go to *A Diagnostic System Check - ABS*	—
10	Repair an open between PCM connector C2, terminal 8 and the EBTCM harness connector terminal 11. Is the repair complete?	—	Go to *A Diagnostic System Check - ABS*	—
11	Repair a short to ground in CKT 121. Is the repair complete?	—	Go to *A Diagnostic System Check - ABS*	—
12	Repair a short to voltage in CKT 121. Is the repair complete?	—	Go to *A Diagnostic System Check - ABS*	—
13	Replace all the terminals or replace the connectors that exhibit signs of the following: • That exhibit signs of poor terminal contact. • That exhibit signs of corrosion. • That exhibit signs of damaged terminals. Is the repair complete?	—	Go to *A Diagnostic System Check - ABS*	—

GC4029903867030X

Fig. 103 Code C0236: TCS RPM Signal Circuit Fault (Part 3 of 3). 2000 Intrigue

Circuit Description
The PCM monitors various parameters and will not allow traction control operation if any parameter falls below a specified value.

Conditions for Setting the DTC
The PCM detects a malfunction and then causes TCS shut down until the malfunction has been corrected.

Action Taken When the DTC Sets
- A DTC C0240 is stored
- The TCS is disabled
- The ETS/Trac off indicator is turned on
- If the TCS is again allowed to function, the indicator will be turned off but the DTC will be stored.

Conditions for Clearing the DTC
- The condition for the DTC is no longer present and the scan tool clear DTC function is used
- 100 ignition cycles have passed with no DTCs detected

Diagnostic Aids
This code is primarily for information only. As an aid to the technician, this code indicates that there are no problems in the ABS/TCS system if it is a history code. If it is a current code, there may be a suspect PCM.

Test Description
The numbers below refer to the step numbers on the diagnostic table.
4. This step checks if DTC C0240 resets.

Step	Action	Value(s)	Yes	No
1	Was the Diagnostic System Check performed?	—	*Go to Step 2*	Go to *Diagnostic System Check*
2	1. Turn the ignition switch to the RUN position with the engine off. 2. Using a Scan Tool, read the ABS/TCS DTCs. Are any other DTCs set?	—	Go to *DTC List* for the appropriate DTC table	*Go to Step 3*
3	Is DTC C0240 set as a current code?	—	*Go to Step 5*	*Go to Step 4*
4	1. Using the scan tool clear the DTC. 2. Remove the scan tool from the DLC. 3. Carefully drive the vehicle above 12 Km/h (8 mph) for several minutes. Did DTC C0240 set as a current DTC?	—	*Go to Step 5*	Go to *Diagnostic System Check*
5	Perform the Powertrain OBD System Check. Did the vehicle pass the OBD System Check?	—	Go to Diagnostic Aids	Engine Controls Diagnosis

GC4029803306000X

Fig. 104 Code C0240: PCM Traction Control Not Allowed. 2000 Grand Prix & Intrigue

Step	Action	Value(s)	Yes	No
1	Was the Diagnostic System Check performed?	—	*Go to Step 2*	Go to *A Diagnostic System Check - ABS*
2	Check that ground, G201 is clean, tight and free of damage. Were any loose, damaged, or corroded grounds found?	—	*Go to Step 3*	*Go to Step 4*
3	Repair ground as necessary. Is the repair complete?	—	Go to *A Diagnostic System Check - ABS*	—
4	1. Turn the ignition switch to the OFF position. 2. Install the scan tool. 3. Start the engine. 4. Use the scan tool to select Engine 2 Data Display in, Powertrain. 5. Using the scan tool, observe the Traction Control Desired Torque. Is the desired torque within the range specified in the value(s) column?	80–95 %	*Go to Step 5*	*Go to Step 7*
5	1. Turn the engine off. 2. Turn the ignition switch to the ON position, engine off. 3. Using the scan tool, select ABS/TCS Data Display. 4. Observe the EBTCM to PCM Requested Torque. Is the requested torque within the range specified in the value(s) column?	0 N·m	*Go to Step 13*	*Go to Step 6*
6	Replace the EBTCM. Is the replacement complete?	—	Go to *A Diagnostic System Check - ABS*	—
7	1. Turn the ignition switch to the OFF position. 2. Disconnect the EBTCM connector. 3. Install *J 39700* Universal Pinout Box using the J 39700-530 cable adapter to the EBTCM harness connector. 4. Turn the ignition switch to the ON position, engine off. 5. Using *J 39200* DMM, measure the voltage between terminals 27 and 15 of *J 39700.* Is the voltage within the range specified in the value(s) column?	4.5-5.5 V	*Go to Step 6*	*Go to Step 10*
8	1. Turn the ignition switch to the OFF position. 2. Disconnect the PCM connector C1. 3. Turn the ignition switch to the ON position, engine off. 4. Using *J 39200* DMM, measure the voltage between terminals 27 and 15 of *J 39700.* Is the voltage within the range specified in the value(s) column?	Greater than 1V	*Go to Step 9*	*Go to Step 10*
9	Repair CKT 463 for a short to voltage. Is the repair complete?	—	Go to *A Diagnostic System Check - ABS*	—
10	1. Turn the ignition switch to the OFF position. 2. Using *J 39200* DMM, measure the resistance between *J 39700* terminals 27 and 15. Is the resistance within the range specified in the value(s) column?	OL (infinite)	*Go to Step 12*	*Go to Step 11*

GC4029903868020X

Fig. 105 Code C0241: PCM Indicated Requested Torque Fault (Part 2 of 3). 2000 Intrigue

Circuit Description
Traction Control is simultaneously controlled by the EBTCM and the ECM. The EBTCM sends a requested torque message via a Pulse Width Modulated (PWM) signal to the ECM requesting a desired engine torque level for proper Traction Control system operation. The PCM supplies the pull up voltage.

Conditions for Setting the DTC
- If a defective requested torque signal is detected by the PCM, a message is broadcasted back to the EBTCM via class 2.
- DTC C0241 can be set anytime when ignition voltage is present and the EBTCM detects the first class 2 message of a defective requested torque signal from the PCM.

Action Taken When the DTC Sets
- A malfunction DTC is stored.
- The TCS is disabled.
- The TRAC OFF indicator is turned on. The ABS remains functional.

Conditions for Clearing the DTC
- Condition for DTC is no longer present and scan tool clear DTC function is used.
- 100 ignition cycles have passed with no DTC(s) detected.

Diagnostic Aids
- It is very important that a thorough inspection of the wiring and connectors be performed. Failure to carefully and fully inspect wiring and connectors may result in misdiagnosis, causing part replacement with reappearance of the malfunction.
- Possible causes for DTC C0241 to set:
  - Open in the circuit 463.
  - Circuit 463 shorted to ground or voltage.
  - Communication problem.
  - Circuit 463 has a wiring problem, terminal corrosion, or poor connections.
  - PCM not receiving information from the EBTCM.

Test Description
The numbers below refer to step numbers on the diagnostic table.
4. Step 4 checks for the proper requested torque value received at the PCM. This value is in percent of torque.
5. Step 5 checks for the proper requested torque value sent from the EBTCM. This value is in newton meters of torque.
7. Step 7 checks for the presence of a pull-up voltage from the PCM.

GC4029903868010X

Fig. 105 Code C0241: PCM Indicated Requested Torque Fault (Part 1 of 3). 2000 Intrigue

Step	Action	Value(s)	Yes	No
11	Repair CKT 463 for a short to ground. Is the repair complete?	—	Go to *A Diagnostic System Check - ABS*	—
12	1. Turn the ignition switch to the OFF position. 2. Using *J 39200* DMM, measure the resistance between terminal 27 of *J 39700* and the PCM connector C2 terminal 71. Is the resistance within the range specified in the value(s) column?	0–2 Ω	*Go to Step 13*	*Go to Step 14*
13	Suspect PCM. Is the Repair complete?	—	Go to *A Diagnostic System Check - ABS*	—
14	Repair CKT 463 for an open. Is the repair complete?	—	Go to *A Diagnostic System Check - ABS*	—

GC4029903868030X

Fig. 105 Code C0241: PCM Indicated Requested Torque Fault (Part 3 of 3). 2000 Intrigue

Circuit Description
Traction Control is simultaneously controlled by the EBTCM and the PCM. The PCM sends a DELIVERED TORQUE message via a Pulse Width Modulated (PWM) signal to the EBTCM confirming the delivered torque level for proper Traction Control system operation. The EBTCM supplies the pull up voltage.

Conditions for Setting the DTC
DTC C0244 can be set anytime when ignition voltage is present. A malfunction exists if the PWM signal is out of range or no signal is received for a period of 2 seconds.

Action Taken When the DTC Sets
- A malfunction DTC is stored.
- The TCS is disabled.
- The Trac off indicator is turned on. The ABS remains functional.

Conditions for Clearing the DTC
- Condition for DTC is no longer present and scan tool clear DTC function is used.
- 100 ignition cycles have passed with no DTC(s) detected.

Diagnostic Aids
- It is very important that a thorough inspection of the wiring and connectors be performed. Failure to carefully and fully inspect wiring and connectors may result in misdiagnosis, causing part replacement with reappearance of the malfunction.
- If an intermittent malfunction exists Electrical Diagnosis.
- Possible causes for DTC C0244 to set:
  - Open in CKT 464.
  - CKT 464 shorted to ground or voltage.
  - Communication frequency problem.
  - Communication duty cycle problem.
  - CKT 464 has a wiring problem, terminal corrosion, or poor connections.
  - EBTCM not receiving information from the PCM.

Test Description
The numbers below refer to step numbers on the diagnostic table.
4. Checks for proper torque value in N.m.
6. Checks for the presence of a pull-up voltage from the EBTCM.

GC402980330700AX

Fig. 106 Code C0244: PWM Delivered Torque Fault (Part 1 of 3). 2000 Grand Prix & Intrigue

Step	Action	Value(s)	Yes	No
1	Was the Diagnostic System Check performed?	—	*Go to Step 2*	Go to *Diagnostic System Check*
2	Check the following grounds, G113 and G205 making sure each ground is clean, tight and free of damage. Were any loose, damaged, or corroded grounds found?	—	*Go to Step 3*	*Go to Step 4*
3	Repair ground as necessary. Is the repair complete?	—	Go to *Diagnostic System Check*	—
4	1. Turn the ignition switch to the OFF position. 2. Install the scan tool. 3. Turn the ignition switch to the ON position, engine off. 4. Using the scan tool, observe the PCM to EBTCM delivered torque. Is the delivered torque within the range specified in the value(s) column?	0N·m	*Go to Step 5*	*Go to Step 6*
5	Replace the EBTCM. Is the replacement complete?	—	Go to *Diagnostic System Check*	—
6	1. Turn the ignition switch to the OFF position. 2. Disconnect the PCM connector C2. 3. Disconnect the EBTCM connector. 4. Install *J 39700* Universal Pinout Box using the J 39700-530 cable adapter to the EBTCM harness connector and the EBTCM connector. 5. Turn the ignition switch to the ON position, engine off. 6. Using *J 39200* DMM, measure the voltage between terminals 9 and 15 of *J 39700*. Is the voltage within the range specified in the value(s) column?	Battery Volts	*Go to Step 7*	*Go to Step 9*
7	1. Turn the ignition switch to the OFF position. 2. Disconnect the *J 39700-25* cable adapter from the EBTCM leaving the cable adapter connected to the EBTCM harness only. 3. Turn the ignition switch to the ON position, engine off. 4. Using *J 39200* DMM, measure the voltage between terminals 9 and 15 of *J 39700*. Is the voltage within the range specified in the value(s) column?	Greater than 1V	*Go to Step 8*	*Go to Step 11*
8	Repair CKT 464 for a short to voltage. Is the repair complete?	—	Go to *Diagnostic System Check*	—
9	1. Turn the ignition switch to the OFF position. 2. Using *J 39200* DMM, measure the resistance between *J 39700* terminals 9 and 15. Is the resistance within the range specified in the value(s) column?	OL (infinite)	*Go to Step 5*	*Go to Step 10*
10	Repair CKT 464 for a short to ground. Is the repair complete?	—	Go to *Diagnostic System Check*	—

GC402980330700BX

Fig. 106 Code C0244: PWM Delivered Torque Fault (Part 2 of 3). 2000 Grand Prix & Intrigue

Step	Action	Value(s)	Yes	No
11	1. Turn the ignition switch to the OFF position. 2. Using *J 39200* DMM, measure the resistance between terminal 9 of *J 39700* and the PCM connector C2 terminal 9. Is the resistance within the range specified in the value(s) column?	0–2 Ω	*Go to Step 12*	*Go to Step 13*
12	Suspect PCM. PCM *Powertrain OBD System Check* Is the Repair complete?	—	Go to *Diagnostic System Check*	—
13	Repair CKT 464 for an open. Is the repair complete?	—	Go to *Diagnostic System Check*	—

GC402980330700CX

Fig. 106 Code C0244: PWM Delivered Torque Fault (Part 3 of 3). 2000 Grand Prix & Intrigue

Circuit Description

The speed sensor used on this vehicle is a multiple pole magnetic pickup. This sensor produces an AC signal that the EBTCM uses the frequency from to calculate the wheel speed.

Conditions for Setting the DTC

- The EBTCM detects a deviation between the left and right rear wheel speeds of greater than 6 km/h (3.75 mph) at a vehicle speed of less than 100 Km/h (62 mph).
- The EBTCM detects a deviation between the left and right front wheel speeds of greater than 10 Km/h (6.25 mph) at a vehicle speed of less than 100Km/h (62 mph).
- The EBTCM detects a deviation between the left and right rear wheel speeds of greater than 6 % of the vehicle speed at greater than 100 km/h (62 mph).
- The EBTCM detects a deviation between the left and right front wheel speeds of greater than 4 km/h (2.5 mph) plus 6 % of the vehicle speed at greater than 100 km/h (62 mph).

This DTC will set when the EBTCM cannot specifically identify which wheel speed sensor is causing the malfunction. If the EBTCM can identify a specific wheel speed sensor causing the malfunction, the DTC associated with the sensor (DTC C0036, DTC C0041, DTC C0046, or DTC C0051) will be set.

GC402980330800AX

Fig. 107 Code C0245: Wheel Speed Sensor Frequency Error (Part 1 of 3). 2000 Grand Prix & Intrigue

Action Taken When the DTC Sets

- A malfunction DTC stores.
- The ABS/TCS disables.
- The amber ABS/TCS indicator(s) turn on.

Conditions for Clearing the DTC

- The condition responsible for setting the DTC no longer exists and the scan tool Clear DTCs function is used.
- 100 ignition cycles pass with no DTC(s) detected.

Diagnostic Aids

- It is very important that a thorough inspection of the wiring and connectors be performed. Failure to carefully and fully inspect wiring and connectors may result in misdiagnosis, causing part replacement with reappearance of the malfunction.
- Thoroughly inspect any circuitry that may be causing the complaint for the following conditions:
  - Backed out terminals
  - Improper mating
  - Broken locks
  - Improperly formed or damaged terminals
  - Poor terminal-to-wiring connections
  - Physical damage to the wiring harness
- The following conditions may cause an intermittent malfunction:
  - A poor connection
  - Rubbed-through wire insulation
  - A broken wire inside the insulation
- If the customer's comments reflect that the amber ABS/TCS indicator is on only during moist environmental conditions (rain, snow, vehicle wash), inspect all the wheel speed sensor circuitry for signs of water intrusion. If the DTC is not current, clear all DTCs and simulate the effects of water intrusion by using the following procedure:
  1. Spray the suspected area with a five percent saltwater solution.

     Add two teaspoons of salt to twelve ounces of water to make a five percent saltwater solution.
  2. Test drive the vehicle over various road surfaces (bumps, turns, etc.) above 40 km/h (25 mph) for at least 30 seconds.
  3. If the DTC returns, replace the suspected harness.
- If an intermittent malfunction exists refer to Troubleshooting Electrical Diagnosis

Test Description

The numbers below refer to step numbers on the diagnostic table.

2. If DTC C0245 is a history code, this step checks if a specific Wheel Speed Circuit Range/Performance DTC is set concurrently with DTC C0245.
7. This step checks if the wheel speed sensor harness is routed in close proximity to the spark plug wires.
9. In this step, if the scan tool can record any erroneous wheel speed sensor signals, diagnose that sensor(s) first.

Step	Action	Value(s)	Yes	No
1	Was the Diagnostic System Check performed?	—	*Go to Step 2*	Go to *Diagnostic System Check*
2	Is the following DTC(s) set concurrently with a history DTC C0245? • DTC C0036 • DTC C0041 • DTC C0046 • DTC C0051	—	Go to *DTC List* for the Appropriate DTC Table	*Go to Step 3*
3	Inspect all of the WSS for physical damage. Is physical damage of any WSS evident?	—	*Go to Step 4*	*Go to Step 5*
4	Replace the WSS. Is the replacement complete?	—	*Go to Step 14*	—
5	Inspect all of the jumper harnesses for physical damage. Is physical damage of any jumper harness evident?	—	*Go to Step 6*	*Go to Step 7*

GC402980330800BX

Fig. 107 Code C0245: Wheel Speed Sensor Frequency Error (Part 2 of 3). 2000 Grand Prix & Intrigue

Step	Action	Value(s)	Yes	No
6	Replace the jumper harness. Is the replacement complete?	—	*Go to Step 14*	—
7	Check for Proper routing of the wheel speed sensor harnesses. Check that the wheel speed sensor harnesses are routed away from the spark plug wires. Are the wheel speed sensor harnesses properly routed?	—	*Go to Step 9*	*Go to Step 8*
8	Reroute the wheel speed sensor harness away from the spark plug wires.	—	*Go to Step 14*	—
9	1. Install a scan tool. 2. Turn the ignition switch to the RUN position. 3. Set the scan tool to Snap Shot Auto Trigger mode and monitor the wheel speed sensors. 4. Carefully drive the vehicle above 12 Km/h (8 mph) for several minutes Did the scan tool trigger on any of the wheel speed sensors?	—	*Go to Step 10*	*Go to Step 11*
10	Note which wheel speed sensor triggered the scan tool. Follow the appropriate Wheel Speed Sensor Range/Performance DTC table for the wheel speed sensor that triggered. Is the repair complete?	—	Go to *Diagnostic System Check*	—
11	1. Reconnect all previously disconnected components. 2. Using a scan tool clear the DTC. 3. Remove the scan tool from the DLC. 4. Carefully drive the vehicle above 12 Km/h (8 mph) for several minutes. Does the DTC reset as a current DTC?	—	*Go to Step 13*	*Go to Step 12*
12	Malfunction is intermittent. Inspect all connectors and harnesses for damage that may result in an open or high resistance when connected. Is the repair complete?	—	Go to *Diagnostic System Check*	—
13	Replace the EBTCM. Is the replacement complete?	—	Go to *Diagnostic System Check*	—
14	1. Reconnect all previously disconnected components. 2. Using a scan tool clear the DTC. 3. Remove the scan tool from the DLC. 4. Carefully drive the vehicle above 12 Km/h (8 mph) for several minutes. Does the DTC reset as a current DTC?	—	*Go to Step 2*	Go to *Diagnostic System Check*

GC402980330800CX

Fig. 107 Code C0245: Wheel Speed Sensor Frequency Error (Part 3 of 3). 2000 Grand Prix & Intrigue

Step	Action	Value(s)	Yes	No
1	Did you perform the ABS Diagnostic System Check?	—	Go to *Step 2*	Go to *A Diagnostic System Check - ABS*
2	1. Turn OFF the ignition. 2. Install a scan tool. 3. Turn ON the ignition, with the engine OFF. 4. Select the ABS DTC display function. Does the scan tool display any DTC other than DTC C0252?	—	Go to *Diagnostic Trouble Code (DTC) List*	Go to *Step 3*
3	1. Use the scan tool in order to clear the DTC. 2. Perform the *Diagnostic Test Drive*. 3. Use the scan tool to select the ABS DTC display function. Does the DTC reset?	—	Go to *Step 4*	Go to Diagnostic Aids
4	1. Use the scan tool to select the VSES data list. 2. Compare data to the typical values located in the EBCM scan tool data list under VSES Data List. Refer to *Scan Tool Data List*. Are all parameters correct?	—	Go to *Step 5*	Go to *Intermittents*
5	Check the wiring harness connectors for the following: • EBCM • Brake pressure sensor • Steering angle sensor • Yaw/lateral accelerometer sensor • LF wheel speed sensor • RF wheel speed sensor • RF wheel speed sensor • RR wheel speed sensor Did you find and correct the condition?	—	Go to *Step 6*	Go to *Intermittents*
6	1. Reconnect previously disconnected components and connectors. 2. Use the scan tool in order to clear the DTCs. Did you complete the action?	—	Go to *Step 2*	System OK

GC4020052024020X

Fig. 108 Code C0252: Active Brake Control Sensors Uncorrelated (Part 2 of 2). 2000 Grand Prix & Intrigue

Circuit Description

The vehicle stability enhancement system (VSES) is activated by the EBCM calculating the desired yaw rate and comparing it to the actual yaw rate input. The desired yaw rate is calculated from measured steering wheel position, vehicle speed, and lateral acceleration. The difference between the desired yaw rate and actual yaw rate is the yaw rate error, which is a measurement of oversteer or understeer. If the yaw rate error becomes too large, the EBCM will attempt to correct the vehicle's yaw motion by applying differential braking to the left or right wheels..

Conditions for Running the DTC

- The steer angle has been centered.
- The VSES is active.
- The direction (understeer or oversteer) of the yaw rate error has not changed.
- The lateral acceleration is less than 0.5 g.

Conditions for Setting the DTC

One of the following conditions occur:

- The VSES is engaged for 10 seconds with the yaw rate error always in either understeer or oversteer. Under this condition, this DTC will set by itself.
- The yaw rate error is greater than 10 degrees/second for 5 seconds.

Action Taken When the DTC Sets

- A malfunction DTC is set.
- VSES is disabled.
- ABS, TCS, SERVICE VEHICLE SOON and PCS indicator lamps are on.

Conditions for Clearing the DTC

- The condition for the DTC is no longer present (the DTC is not current) and you used the scan tool Clear DTC function.
- The EBCM automatically clears the history DTC when a current DTC is not detected in 124 consecutive drive cycles.

Diagnostic Aids

- During diagnosis, park the vehicle on a level surface.
- Check the vehicle for proper alignment. The car should not pull in either direction while driving straight on a level surface.
- Find out from the customer the conditions under which the DTC was set. This information will help to duplicate the failure.
- The Snapshot function on the scan tool can help find an intermittent DTC.

Test Description

The numbers below refer to the step numbers on the diagnostic table.

2. This checks to see if DTC C0252 is set.
3. This step checks to see if the DTC C0252 resets.
4. This step checks to see if VSES data list parameters are correct.
5. This step checks the components harness connectors for poor connections.

GC4020052024010X

Fig. 108 Code C0252: Active Brake Control Sensors Uncorrelated (Part 1 of 2). 2000 Grand Prix & Intrigue

Circuit Description

Steer angle centering is the process by which the EBCM calibrates the steering sensor output so that the output reads zero when the steering wheel is centered.

Conditions for Running the DTC

- The ignition is ON.
- The vehicle speed is greater than 40 km/h (25 mph).

Conditions for Setting the DTC

If the steering angle sensor CAN message or the EBCM indicates an uncentered sensor.

Action Taken When the DTC Sets

- A malfunction DTC is set
- ABS and VSES are disabled
- TCS, SERVICE VEHICLE SOON and PCS lamp indicators turn on

Conditions for Clearing the DTC

- The condition for the DTC is no longer present.
- A history DTC will clear after 124 consecutive ignition cycles if the condition for the malfunction is no longer present.
- Using a scan tool.
- The EBCM automatically clears the history DTC when a current DTC is not detected in 124 consecutive drive cycles.

Diagnostic Aids

Perform the steering angle sensor centering procedure.

Test Description

The number(s) below refer to the step number(s) on the diagnostic table.

2. Checks to see if other DTC is set.
3. Checks to see if steering angle sensor is centered.

GC4020052013010X

Fig. 109 Code C0253: Centering Fault (Part 1 of 2). 2000 Grand Prix & Intrigue

Step	Action	Value(s)	Yes	No
1	Did you perform the ABS Diagnostic System Check?	—	Go to *Step 2*	Go to *A Diagnostic System Check - ABS*
2	1. Turn OFF the ignition. 2. Install a scan tool. 3. Turn ON the ignition, with the engine OFF. 4. Select the ABS DTC display function. Does the scan tool display any DTC other than DTC C0253?	—	Go to *Diagnostic Trouble Code (DTC) List*	Go to *Step 3*
3	Perform the steering angle sensor centering procedure. Did you successfully complete the centering procedure?	—	Go to *Step 4*	Go to *Step 5*
4	1. Use the scan tool in order to clear the DTCs. 2. Test drive the vehicle. Did DTC C0253 reset?	—	Go to *Step 6*	Go to Diagnostic Aids
5	Replace the steering angle sensor. Did you complete the replacement?	—	Go to *Step 7*	—
6	Replace the EBCM. Did you complete the replacement?	—	Go to *Step 7*	—
7	1. Use the scan tool in order to clear the DTCs. 2. Operate the vehicle within the Conditions for Running the DTC Does the DTC reset?	—	Go to *Step 2*	System OK

GC4020052013020X

Fig. 109 Code C0253: Centering Fault (Part 2 of 2). 2000 Grand Prix & Intrigue

Circuit Description

This DTC identifies a malfunction within the EBTCM.

Conditions for Setting the DTC

DTC C0550 is set when an internal EBTCM malfunction exists.

Action Taken When the DTC Sets

A malfunction DTC is stored, ABS/TCS is disabled and the ABS and Traction Control Indicators are turned on.

Conditions for Clearing the DTC

- Condition for DTC is no longer present and scan tool clear DTC function is used.
- 100 ignition cycles pass with no DTC(s) detected.

Step	Action	Value(s)	Yes	No
1	Was the Diagnostic System Check performed?	—	Go to *Step 2*	Go to *Diagnostic System Check*
2	Are any other DTC(s) present besides C0550?	—	Go to *DTC List* for the Applicable DTC Table	Go to *Step 3*
3	Replace the EBTCM. Is the replacement complete?	—	Go to *Diagnostic System Check*	—

GC4029803309000X

Fig. 110 Code C0550: ECU Fault. 2000 Grand Prix & Intrigue

Circuit Description

Under normal driving conditions, the EBCM monitors the steering angle sensor inputs to see if the steering wheel is moving. If the steering wheel is not moving for a set period of time, the EBCM assumes the vehicle is going in a straight line. At this point, the EBCM looks at the steering angle sensor inputs and considers the degree angle to be zero. This is called the offset value.

Steer angle centering is the process by which the EBCM calibrates the steering sensor output so that the output reads zero when the steering wheel is centered.

Conditions for Running the DTC

- The ignition is ON.
- The vehicle speed is greater than 40 km/h (25 mph).

Conditions for Setting the DTC

A malfunction is detected if one or more of the following conditions exist:

- The steering angle sensor detects an internal malfunction and sends a CAN message to the EBCM.
- If the offset value is higher than 15 degrees, a malfunction is detected. Malfunction time depends on driving distance, vehicle speed and the amount of malfunctioning steering angle signal.
- Rapid changes of the steering angle sensor signal cannot occur under normal driving conditions. If the signal change is higher than 2000 degrees per second or steering angle acceleration is higher than 37500 degrees per second squared, a malfunction is detected.
- A reference steering angle signal based on a vehicle model is used to check the actual steering angle. If the measured steering angle varies from the reference steering angle by more than a predetermined value, a malfunction is detected.

Action Taken When the DTC Sets

- A malfunction DTC is set
- TCS and VSES are disabled
- TCS, SERVICE VEHICLE SOON and PCS lamp indicators turn on

Conditions for Clearing the DTC

- The condition for the DTC is no longer present.
- A history DTC will clear after 124 consecutive ignition cycles if the condition for the malfunction is no longer present.
- Using a scan tool.
- The EBCM automatically clears the history DTC when a current DTC is not detected in 100 consecutive drive cycles.

GC4020052014010X

Fig. 111 Code C0710: Steering Position Signal Fault (Part 1 of 2). 2000 Grand Prix & Intrigue

Diagnostic Aids

Perform the steering angle sensor centering procedure.

Test Description

The number(s) below refer to the step number(s) on the diagnostic table.

2. Checks to see if any other DTC is set.
3. Checks to see if steering angle sensor is centered.

Step	Action	Value(s)	Yes	No
1	Did you perform the ABS Diagnostic System Check?	—	Go to *Step 2*	Go to *A Diagnostic System Check - ABS*
2	1. Turn OFF the ignition. 2. Install a scan tool. 3. Turn ON the ignition, with the engine OFF. 4. Select the ABS DTC display function. Does the scan tool display any DTC other than DTC C0710?	—	Go to *Diagnostic Trouble Code (DTC) List*	Go to *Step 3*
3	Perform the steering angle sensor centering procedure. Did you successfully complete the centering procedure?	—	Go to *Step 4*	Go to *Step 5*
4	1. Use the scan tool in order to clear the DTCs. 2. Test drive the vehicle. Did DTC C0710 reset?	—	Go to *Step 6*	Go to Diagnostic Aids
5	Replace the steering angle sensor. Did you complete the replacement?	—	Go to *Step 7*	—
6	Replace the EBCM. Did you complete the replacement?	—	Go to *Step 7*	—
7	1. Use the scan tool in order to clear the DTCs. 2. Operate the vehicle within the Conditions for Running the DTC Does the DTC reset?	—	Go to *Step 2*	System OK

GC4020052014020X

Fig. 111 Code C0710: Steering Position Signal Fault (Part 2 of 2). 2000 Grand Prix & Intrigue

Circuit Description

The brake pressure sensor reference voltage is monitored for an over or under voltage condition.

Conditions for Running the DTC

- The ignition is ON.
- The vehicle speed is greater than 40 km/h (25 mph).

Conditions for Setting the DTC

A malfunction is detected if the supply voltage is above 5.6 volts or below 4.4 volts for more than 60 milliseconds.

Action Taken When the DTC Sets

- A malfunction DTC is set
- ABS, TCS and VSES are disabled
- ABS, TCS, SERVICE VEHICLE SOON and PCS lamp indicators are ON

Conditions for Clearing the DTC

- The condition for the DTC is no longer present.
- A history DTC will clear after 124 consecutive ignition cycles if the condition for the malfunction is no longer present.
- Using a scan tool.
- The EBCM automatically clears the history DTC when a current DTC is not detected in 124 consecutive drive cycles.

Diagnostic Aids

Possible causes of this DTC are the following conditions:

- An open in the pressure sensor supply voltage circuit
- A short to ground in the pressure sensor supply voltage circuit
- A short to B+ in the pressure sensor supply voltage circuit

Test Description

The number(s) below refer to the step number(s) on the diagnostic table.

2. Tests for specified voltage on the brake pressure signal circuit.
3. Checks to see if the brake pressure signal circuit voltage was below specified voltage.
4. Checks to see if the brake pressure signal circuit voltage was above specified voltage.
5. Tests for a short to ground in the 5 volt reference circuit of the brake pressure sensor.

GC4020052015010X

Fig. 112 Code C0870: Device Voltage Reference Output No. 1 Circuit Fault (Part 1 of 2). 2000 Grand Prix & Intrigue

6. Tests for a short to voltage in the 5 volt reference circuit of the brake pressure sensor.
7. Tests for a high resistance or an open in the ground circuit of the brake pressure sensor.
8. Checks the brake pressure sensor connector for poor connections.
9. Checks the EBCM connector for poor connections.

Step	Action	Value(s)	Yes	No
1	Did you perform the ABS Diagnostic System Check?	—	Go to *Step 2*	Go to *A Diagnostic System Check - ABS*
2	1. Turn OFF the ignition. 2. Disconnect the EBCM. 3. Install the *J 39700* universal pinout box with the *J 39700-530* cable adapter between the EBCM and the EBCM harness connector. 4. Turn ON the ignition, with the engine OFF. 5. Using the DMM, measure the voltage between pin 17 and pin 15 of the *J 39700* universal pinout box. Is the voltage within the specified value?	4.4 V – 5.6–V	Go to Diagnostic Aids	Go to *Step 3*
3	1. Turn OFF the ignition. 2. Disconnect the brake pressure sensor. 3. Turn ON the ignition, with the engine OFF. 4. Using the DMM, measure the voltage between pin 17 and pin 15 of the *J 39700* universal pinout box. Is the voltage greater than the specified value?	4.4 V	Go to *Step 4*	Go to *Step 5*
4	Using the DMM, measure the voltage between pin 17 and pin 15 of the *J 39700* universal pinout box. Is the voltage less than the specified value?	5.6 V	Go to *Step 8*	Go to *Step 6*
5	Test the 5 volt reference circuit of the brake pressure sensor for a short to ground. Did you find and correct the condition?	—	Go to *Step 12*	Go to *Step 9*
6	Test the 5 volt reference circuit of the brake pressure sensor for a short to voltage. Did you find and correct the condition?	—	Go to *Step 12*	Go to *Step 7*
7	Test the ground circuit of the brake pressure sensor for a high resistance or an open. Did you find and correct the condition?	—	Go to *Step 12*	Go to *Step 9*
8	Inspect for poor connections at the harness connector of the brake pressure sensor. Did you find and correct the condition?	—	Go to *Step 12*	Go to *Step 10*
9	Inspect for poor connections at the harness connector of the EBCM. Did you find and correct the condition?	—	Go to *Step 12*	Go to *Step 11*
10	Replace the brake pressure sensor. Did you complete the replacement?	—	Go to *Step 12*	—
11	Replace the EBCM. Did you complete the replacement?	—	Go to *Step 12*	—
12	1. Use the scan tool in order to clear the DTCs. 2. Operate the vehicle within the Conditions for Running the DTC as specified in the supporting test. Does the DTC reset?	—	Go to *Step 2*	System OK

GC4020052015020X

Fig. 112 Code C0870: Device Voltage Reference Output No. 1 Circuit Fault (Part 2 of 2). 2000 Grand Prix & Intrigue

Circuit Description

The yaw rate sensor reference voltage is monitored for an over or under voltage condition.

Conditions for Running the DTC

- The ignition is ON.
- The vehicle speed is greater than 40 km/h (25 mph).

Conditions for Setting the DTC

A malfunction is detected if the supply voltage is above 2.9 volts or below 2.1 volts for more than 200 milliseconds.

Action Taken When the DTC Sets

- A malfunction DTC is set
- TCS and VSES are disabled
- TCS, PCS and SERVICE VEHICLE SOON lamp indicators are ON

Conditions for Clearing the DTC

- The condition for the DTC is no longer present.
- A history DTC will clear after 124 consecutive ignition cycles if the condition for the malfunction is no longer present.
- Using a scan tool.
- The EBCM automatically clears the history DTC when a current DTC is not detected in 124 consecutive drive cycles.

Diagnostic Aids

Possible causes of this DTC are the following conditions:

- An open in the yaw rate sensor supply voltage circuit
- A short to ground in the yaw rate sensor supply voltage circuit
- A short to B+ in the yaw rate sensor supply voltage circuit

Test Description

The number(s) below refer to the step number(s) on the diagnostic table.

2. Tests for specified voltage on the 5 volt reference signal circuit.
3. Checks to see if voltage was below specified voltage.
4. Checks to see if voltage was above specified voltage.
5. Tests for a short to ground in the 5 volt reference circuit of the yaw/lateral accelerometer sensor.

GC4020052016010X

Fig. 113 Code C0875: Device Voltage Reference Input No. 2 Circuit Fault (Part 1 of 2). 2000 Grand Prix & Intrigue

6. Tests for a short to voltage in the 5 volt reference circuit of the yaw/lateral accelerometer sensor.
7. Tests for a high resistance or an open in the ground circuit of the yaw/lateral accelerometer sensor.
8. Checks the yaw/lateral accelerometer sensor connector for poor connections.
9. Checks the EBCM connector for poor connections.

Step	Action	Value(s)	Yes	No
1	Did you perform the ABS Diagnostic System Check?	—	Go to *Step 2*	Go to *A Diagnostic System Check - ABS*
2	1. Turn OFF the ignition. 2. Disconnect the EBCM. 3. Install the *J 39700* universal pinout box with the *J 39700-530* cable adapter between the EBCM and the EBCM harness connector. 4. Turn ON the ignition, with the engine OFF. 5. Using the DMM, measure the voltage between pin 16 and pin 15 of the *J 39700* universal pinout box. Is the voltage within the specified value?	2.1 V – 2.9 V	Go to Diagnostic Aids	Go to *Step 3*
3	1. Turn OFF the ignition. 2. Disconnect the yaw/lateral accelerometer sensor. 3. Turn ON the ignition, with the engine OFF. 4. Using the DMM, measure the voltage between pin 16 and pin 15 of the *J 39700* universal pinout box. Is the voltage greater than the specified value?	2.1 V	Go to *Step 4*	Go to *Step 5*
4	Using the DMM, measure the voltage between pin 16 and pin 15 of the *J 39700* universal pinout box. Is the voltage less than the specified value?	2.9 V	Go to *Step 8*	Go to *Step 6*
5	Test the 5 volt reference circuit of the yaw/lateral accelerometer sensor for a short to ground. Did you find and correct the condition?	—	Go to *Step 12*	Go to *Step 9*
6	Test the 5 volt reference circuit of the yaw/lateral accelerometer sensor for a short to voltage. Did you find and correct the condition?	—	Go to *Step 12*	Go to *Step 7*
7	Test the ground circuit of the yaw/lateral accelerometer sensor for a high resistance or an open. Did you find and correct the condition?	—	Go to *Step 12*	Go to *Step 9*
8	Inspect for poor connections at the harness connector of the yaw/lateral accelerometer sensor. Did you find and correct the condition?	—	Go to *Step 12*	Go to *Step 10*
9	Inspect for poor connections at the harness connector of the EBCM. Did you find and correct the condition?	—	Go to *Step 12*	Go to *Step 11*
10	Replace the yaw/lateral accelerometer sensor. Did you complete the replacement?	—	Go to *Step 12*	—
11	Replace the EBCM. Did you complete the replacement?	—	Go to *Step 12*	—
12	1. Use the scan tool in order to clear the DTCs. 2. Operate the vehicle within the Conditions for Running the DTC as specified in the supporting test. Does the DTC reset?	—	Go to *Step 2*	System OK

GC4020052016020X

Fig. 113 Code C0875: Device Voltage Reference Input No. 2 Circuit Fault (Part 2 of 2). 2000 Grand Prix & Intrigue

Circuit Description

The EBTCM is required to operate within a specified range of voltage to function properly. During ABS and TCS operation, there are current requirements that will cause the voltage to drop. Because of this, voltage is monitored out of ABS/TCS control to indicate a good charging system condition, and also during ABS/TCS control when voltage may drop significantly. The ECM also monitors for high voltage conditions which could damage the EBCM.

Conditions for Setting the DTC

- The EBCM operating voltage at terminal 8 falls below 9.4 volts out of ABS/TCS control, or 8.8 volts during ABS/TCS control.
- The EBCM operating voltage at terminal 8 rises above 17.4 volts.
- The low voltage or the high voltage is detected for more than 500 milliseconds with the vehicle speed above 6 km/h (3.6 mph).

Action Taken When the DTC Sets

- A malfunction DTC is stored.
- The ABS and the TRAC OFF indicator lamps are turned on.
- The ABS/TCS is disabled.

Conditions for Clearing the DTC

- The condition for the DTC is no longer present, the scan tool Clear DTCs function is used.
- 100 ignition cycles have passed with no DTC(s) detected.

Diagnostic Aids

- It is very important that a thorough inspection of the wiring and connectors be performed. Failure to carefully and fully inspect wiring and connectors may result in misdiagnosis, causing part replacement with reappearance of the malfunction.
- Thoroughly inspect any circuitry that may be causing the complaint for the following conditions:
  - Backed out terminals
  - Improper mating
  - Broken locks
  - Improperly formed or damaged terminals
  - Poor terminal-to-wiring connections
  - Physical damage to the wiring harness
- The following conditions may cause an intermittent malfunction:
  - A poor connection
  - Rubbed-through wire insulation
  - A broken wire inside the insulation

Test Description

The number(s) below refer to the step number(s) on the diagnostic table.

2. This step checks if the voltage is above the maximum of the range.
4. This step checks if the voltage is below the minimum of the range.
6. This step checks for the integrity of the ground circuit.

Step	Action	Value(s)	Yes	No
1	Was a Diagnostic System Check performed?	—	*Go to Step 2*	Go to *A Diagnostic System Check - ABS*
2	1. Turn all the accessories off. 2. Install a scan tool. 3. Start the engine. 4. Use the scan tool to monitor the battery voltage while running the engine at approximately 2000 RPM. Is the monitored battery voltage within the specified range?	0–17.4 V	*Go to Step 4*	*Go to Step 3*
3	Use a DMM to measure the voltage between the battery positive terminal and ground. Is the voltage within the specified range?	0–17.4 V	*Go to Step 5*	Go to *Charging System*

GC4020052017010X

Fig. 114 Code C0896: Device Voltage Range/ Performance (Part 1 of 2). 2000 Grand Prix & Intrigue

Step	Action	Value(s)	Yes	No
4	Continue to monitor the battery voltage with the scan tool while running the engine at approximately 2000 RPM. Is the monitored battery voltage within the specified range?	0–9.4 V	*Go to Step 6*	*Go to Step 5*
5	1. Turn the ignition switch to the OFF position. 2. Disconnect the scan tool if still connected. 3. Test drive the vehicle above 6 km/h (3.5 mph). Did DTC C0896 reset?	—	*Go to Step 12*	Go to *A Diagnostic System Check - ABS*
6	1. Disconnect the EBCM connector from the EBCM. 2. Install the *J 39700* universal pinout box with the *J 39700-530* cable adapter to the EBCM harness only. 3. Use a DMM to measure the resistance between the *J 39700* universal pinout box terminal 15 and a good ground. Is the resistance within the specified range?	0-5 Ω	*Go to Step 8*	*Go to Step 7*
7	Repair open or high resistance in CKT 251. Is the repair complete?	—	Go to *A Diagnostic System Check - ABS*	—
8	1. Turn the ignition switch to the ON position with the engine off. 2. Use a DMM to measure the voltage between the *J 39700* universal pinout box terminal 8 and 15. Is the voltage above the specified value?	9.4 Volts	*Go to Step 11*	*Go to Step 9*
9	1. Remove the 10 A TRANS/ABS fuse 26 from the underhood accessory wiring junction block. 2. Use a DMM to measure the resistance between the underhood accessory wiring junction block connector C 1 terminal B 7 and the *J 39700* universal pinout box terminal 8. Is the resistance within the specified range?	0-5 Ω	Go to *Charging System*	*Go to Step 10*
10	Repair high resistance in CKT 1039. Is the repair complete?	—	Go to *A Diagnostic System Check - ABS*	—
11	1. Turn the ignition switch to the OFF position. 2. Reconnect the EBCM connector. 3. Disconnect the scan tool if the scan tool is still connected. 4. Test drive the vehicle above 6 km/h (3.5 mph). Did DTC C0896 reset?	—	*Go to Step 12*	Go to *A Diagnostic System Check - ABS*
12	Replace the EBCM. Is the repair complete?	—	Go to *A Diagnostic System Check - ABS*	—

GC4020052017020X

Fig. 114 Code C0896: Device Voltage Range/ Performance (Part 2 of 2). 2000 Grand Prix & Intrigue

Circuit Description

The UART serial data line allows information to be exchanged from module to module as needed. This is done by the PCM, the PCM requests and sends all the information that is transmitted on the UART line.

Conditions for Setting the DTC

DTC U1304 can be set anytime the ignition is in the RUN position and the EBTCM does not receive a $90 message from the PCM for 6 seconds.

Action Taken When the DTC Sets

- A malfunction DTC stores.
- The TCS is disabled.
- The amber TCS indicator is turned on.

Conditions for Clearing the DTC

- The condition responsible for setting the DTC no longer exists and the scan tool Clear DTCs function is used.
- 100 ignition cycles pass with no DTC(s) detected.

Diagnostic Aids

- It is very important that a thorough inspection of the wiring and connectors be performed. Failure to carefully and fully inspect wiring and connectors may result in misdiagnosis, causing part replacement with reappearance of the malfunction.
- Thoroughly inspect any circuitry that may be causing the complaint for the following conditions:
  - Backed out terminals
  - Improper mating
  - Broken locks
  - Improperly formed or damaged terminals
  - Poor terminal-to-wiring connections
  - Physical damage to the wiring harness
- The following conditions may cause an intermittent malfunction:
  - A poor connection
  - Rubbed-through wire insulation
  - A broken wire inside the insulation
- If an intermittent malfunction exists refer to Troubleshooting Electrical Diagnosis

Test Description

The number(s) below refer to the step number(s) on the diagnostic table.

2. This step checks for a short to ground in CKT 800.
4. This step checks for a short to battery voltage in CKT 800.
6. This step checks for an open in CKT 800.

GC402980331100AX

Fig. 115 Code U1304: Lost Communication w/UART System (Part 1 of 2). 2000 Grand Prix

Step	Action	Value(s)	Yes	No
1	Was the Diagnostic System Check performed?	—	Go to *Step 2*	Go to *Diagnostic System Check*
2	1. Turn the ignition switch to the OFF position. 2. Disconnect the EBTCM connector C1. 3. Install the *J 39700* Universal Pinout Box using the J 39700-530 cable adapter to the EBTCM harness connector C1 only. 4. Using *J 39200* DMM, measure the resistance between terminals 24 and 15 of *J 39700.* Is the resistance within the range specified in the value(s) column?	OL (infinite)	Go to *Step 4*	Go to *Step 3*
3	Repair CKT 800 for a short to ground. Is the repair complete?	—	Go to *Diagnostic System Check*	—
4	1. Turn the ignition switch to the RUN position, engine off. 2. Using *J 39200* DMM, measure the voltage at terminal 24 of *J 39700.* Is the voltage within the range specified in the value(s) column?	Battery voltage	Go to *Step 5*	Go to *Step 6*
5	Repair CKT 800 for a short to battery voltage. Is the repair complete?	—	Go to *Diagnostic System Check*	—
6	1. Turn the ignition switch to the OFF position. 2. Disconnect the PCM connector C1. 3. Using *J 39200* DMM measure the resistance between the *J 39700* terminal 24 and the PCM terminal 15. Is the resistance within the range specified in the values column?	0–5 Ω	Go to *Step 8*	Go to *Step 7*
7	Repair CKT 800 for an open. Is the repair complete?	—	Go to *Diagnostic System Check*	—
8	Replace the EBTCM. Is the replacement complete?	—	Go to *Diagnostic System Check*	—

GC402980331100BX

Fig. 115 Code U1304: Lost Communication w/UART System (Part 2 of 2). 2000 Grand Prix

Circuit Description

The Controller Area Network (CAN) serial data circuit is a high speed serial data bus used to communicate information between the steering angle sensor and the EBCM. When the ignition switch is turned to the ON position, the module and the steering angle sensor begin to transmit data between each other.

The CAN bus circuit is monitored continuously after the ignition switch is turned to the ON position.

Conditions for Running the DTC

- The ignition is ON.
- The vehicle speed is greater than 40 km/h (25 mph).

Conditions for Setting the DTC

Line interruptions are detected by CAN message monitor.

Action Taken When the DTC Sets

- A malfunction DTC is set
- TCS and VSES are disabled
- TCS, SERVICE VEHICLE SOON and PCS lamp indicators turn on

Conditions for Clearing the DTC

- The condition for the DTC is no longer present.
- Using a scan tool.
- The EBCM automatically clears the history DTC when a current DTC is not detected in 124 consecutive drive cycles.

Diagnostic Aids

Possible causes of this DTC are as follows:

- CAN HI and CAN LO circuits shorted together.
- CAN HI or CAN LO circuit shorted to ground.
- CAN HI or CAN LO circuit shorted to voltage.

Test Description

The number(s) below refer to the step number(s) on the diagnostic table.

2. Tests for a short to ground between the CAN HI and CAN LO circuits.
3. Tests the CAN HI and CAN LO circuits for a short together.
4. Checks to see if steering angle sensor is centered.

GC4020052018010X

Fig. 116 Code U1650: Chassis System Dedicated Bus Controller Fault (Part 1 of 2). 2000 Grand Prix & Intrigue

Step	Action	Value(s)	Yes	No
1	Did you perform the ABS Diagnostic System Check?	—	Go to *Step 2*	Go to *A Diagnostic System Check - ABS*
2	1. Turn OFF the ignition. 2. Disconnect the EBCM. 3. Install the *J 39700* universal pinout box with the *J 39700-530* cable adapter to the EBCM harness connector only. 4. Disconnect the steering angle sensor. 5. Using the DMM, test the CAN HI and CAN LO circuits for a short to ground between the steering angle sensor and the EBCM. Did you find and correct the condition?	—	Go to *Step 8*	Go to *Step 3*
3	Using the DMM, test the CAN HI and CAN LO circuits between the steering angle sensor and the EBCM for being shorted together. Did you find and correct the condition?	—	Go to *Step 8*	Go to *Step 4*
4	Perform the steering angle sensor centering procedure. Did you successfully complete the centering procedure?	—	Go to *Step 5*	Go to *Step 6*
5	1. Use the scan tool in order to clear the DTCs. 2. Test drive the vehicle. Did DTC C1650 reset?	—	Go to *Step 7*	Go to *Step 8*
6	Replace the steering angle sensor. Did you complete the replacement?	—	Go to *Step 8*	—
7	Replace the EBCM. Did you complete the replacement?	—	Go to *Step 8*	—
8	1. Use the scan tool in order to clear the DTCs. 2. Operate the vehicle within the Conditions for Running the DTC as specified in the supporting test. Does the DTC reset?	—	Go to *Step 2*	System OK

GC4020052018020X

Fig. 116 Code U1650: Chassis System Dedicated Bus Controller Fault (Part 2 of 2). 2000 Grand Prix & Intrigue

Circuit Description

The EBCM monitors the received messages from the steering angle sensor for corruption or for missing messages.

Conditions for Running the DTC

- The ignition is ON.
- The vehicle speed is greater than 40 km/h (25 mph).

Conditions for Setting the DTC

The EBCM receives a corrupt or a missing message after 100 milliseconds.

Action Taken When the DTC Sets

- A malfunction DTC is set
- TCS and VSES are disabled
- TCS, SERVICE VEHICLE SOON and PCS lamp indicators turn on

Conditions for Clearing the DTC

- The condition for the DTC is no longer present.
- Using a scan tool.
- The EBCM automatically clears the history DTC when a current DTC is not detected in 124 consecutive drive cycles.

Diagnostic Aids

Possible causes of this DTC are as follows:

- An open in the CAN HI or CAN LO circuit.
- An open in the ignition circuit.
- An open in the ground circuit.
- Malfunctioning steering angle sensor.
- Malfunctioning EBCM.

Test Description

The number(s) below refer to the step number(s) on the diagnostic table.

2. Tests the ignition circuit for an open.
3. Checks the ground circuit for an open.
4. Tests the CAN HI circuit for an open.
5. Tests the CAN LO circuit for an open.
6. Checks the steering angle sensor connector for poor connections.

GC4020052019010X

Fig. 117 Code U1651: Chassis System Dedicated Bus Sensor No. 1 Fault (Part 1 of 2). 2000 Grand Prix & Intrigue

Step	Action	Value(s)	Yes	No
1	Did you perform the ABS Diagnostic System Check?	—	Go to *Step 2*	Go to *A Diagnostic System Check - ABS*
2	1. Turn OFF the ignition. 2. Disconnect the steering angle sensor harness connector. 3. Using a DMM, check the ignition circuit for an open. Did you find and correct the condition?	—	Go to *Step 12*	Go to *Step 3*
3	1. Disconnect the EBCM harness connector. 2. Install the *J 39700* universal pinout box with the *J 39700-530* cable adapter between the EBCM and the EBCM harness connector. 3. Disconnect the steering angle sensor. 4. Using a DMM, check the ground circuit for an open. Did you find and correct the condition?	—	Go to *Step 12*	Go to *Step 4*
4	Using a DMM, check the CAN HI circuit for an open. Did you find and correct the condition?	—	Go to *Step 12*	Go to *Step 5*
5	Using a DMM, check the CAN LO circuit for an open. Did you find and correct the condition?	—	Go to *Step 12*	Go to *Step 6*
6	Inspect for poor connections at the harness connector of the steering angle sensor. Did you find and correct the condition?	—	Go to *Step 12*	Go to *Step 7*
7	Inspect for poor connections at the harness connector of the EBCM. Did you find and correct the condition?	—	Go to *Step 12*	Go to *Step 8*
8	Perform the steering angle sensor centering procedure. Did you successfully complete the centering procedure?	—	Go to *Step 9*	Go to *Step 10*
9	1. Use the scan tool in order to clear the DTCs. 2. Test drive the vehicle. Did DTC C1651 reset?	—	Go to *Step 11*	Go to *Step 12*
10	Replace the steering angle sensor. Did you complete the replacement?	—	Go to *Step 12*	—
11	Replace the EBCM. Did you complete the replacement?	—	Go to *Step 12*	—
12	1. Use the scan tool in order to clear the DTCs. 2. Operate the vehicle within the Conditions for Running the DTC Does the DTC reset?	—	Go to *Step 2*	System OK

GC4020052019020X

Fig. 117 Code U1651: Chassis System Dedicated Bus Sensor No. 1 Fault (Part 2 of 2). 2000 Grand Prix & Intrigue

Step	Action	Value(s)	Yes	No
DEFINITION: TRAC OFF indicator is on and traction control was not turned off. There are no DTC(s) set.				
1	Was the Diagnostic System Check performed?	—	Go to *Step 2*	Go to *A Diagnostic System Check - ABS*
2	1. Turn the ignition switch to the RUN position, engine off. 2. Using a scan tool enter ABS/TCS Data List. 3. While monitoring the TRAC On/Off switch status, press and release the TRAC On/Off switch. Does the switch status change from pressed to released as the TRAC switch is pressed and released?	—	Go to *Step 3*	Go to *Step 8*
3	1. Turn the ignition switch to the OFF position. 2. Disconnect the EBTCM connector C1. 3. Turn the ignition switch to the RUN position, engine off. Does the TRAC OFF Indicator turn off?	—	Go to *Step 4*	Go to *Step 5*
4	Replace the EBTCM. Is the replacement complete?	—	Go to *A Diagnostic System Check - ABS*	—
5	1. Turn the ignition switch to the OFF position. 2. Disconnect the EBTCM connector C1. 3. Install the *J 39700* Universal Pinout Box using the J 39700-530 cable adapter to connector C1 only. 4. Disconnect the Driver Information Display (Base) or Trip Computer (Up Level) connector. 5. Using *J 39200* DMM, measure the resistance between terminals 18 and 15 of *J 39700.* Is the resistance within the range specified in the value(s) column?	OL (infinite)	Go to *Step 7*	Go to *Step 6*
6	Repair CKT 1572 for a short to ground. Is the repair complete?	—	Go to *A Diagnostic System Check - ABS*	—
7	Suspect the Driver Information Display (Base) or Trip Computer (Up Level). Is the repair complete?	—	Go to *A Diagnostic System Check - ABS*	—
8	1. Turn the ignition switch to the OFF position. 2. Disconnect the EBTCM connector C1. 3. Install the *J 39700* Universal Pinout Box using the J 39700-530 cable adapter to connector C1 only. 4. Using *J 39200* DMM, measure the resistance between terminals 17 and 15 of *J 39700.* Is the resistance within the range specified in the value(s) column?	OL (Infinite)	Go to *Step 4*	Go to *Step 9*
9	Repair CKT 1571 for an Short to Ground, being sure to check the traction control switch for an short. Is the repair complete?	—	Go to *A Diagnostic System Check - ABS*	—

GC4029903879020X

Fig. 118 Traction Off Indicator On With No DTC Set (Part 2 of 2). 2000 Grand Prix

Circuit Description

The TRAC OFF indicator is controlled by the EBTCM. The EBTCM supplies the ground to CKT 1572 to turn the indicator on. When CKT 1572 is not grounded at the EBTCM, the TRAC OFF indicator remains off. When the EBTCM sees the traction control switch voltage go low, it turns the TRAC OFF indicator on and disables traction control.

Diagnostic Aids

- It is very important that a thorough inspection of the wiring and connectors be performed. Failure to carefully and fully inspect wiring and connectors may result in misdiagnosis, causing part replacement with reappearance of the malfunction.
- Thoroughly inspect any circuitry that may be causing the complaint for the following conditions:
  - Backed out terminals
  - Improper mating
  - Broken locks
  - Improperly formed or damaged terminals
  - Poor terminal-to-wiring connections
  - Physical damage to the wiring harness
- The following conditions may cause an intermittent malfunction:
  - A poor connection
  - Rubbed-through wire insulation
  - A broken wire inside the insulation

Test Description

The number(s) below refer to the step number(s) on the diagnostic table.

3. This step checks for an internal EBTCM malfunction.
5. This step checks for a short to ground in CKT 1572.

GC4029903879010X

Fig. 118 Traction Off Indicator On With No DTC Set (Part 1 of 2). 2000 Grand Prix

Circuit Description

The TRAC OFF indicator is controlled by the EBTCM. The EBTCM supplies the ground to CKT 1572 to turn the indicator on. When CKT 1572 is not grounded at the EBTCM, the TRAC OFF indicator remains off. When the EBTCM sees the traction control switch voltage go low, it turns the TRAC OFF indicator on and disables traction control.

Diagnostic Aids

- It is very important that a thorough inspection of the wiring and connectors be performed. Failure to carefully and fully inspect wiring and connectors may result in misdiagnosis, causing part replacement with reappearance of the malfunction.
- Thoroughly inspect any circuitry that may be causing the complaint for the following conditions:
  - Backed out terminals
  - Improper mating
  - Broken locks
  - Improperly formed or damaged terminals
  - Poor terminal-to-wiring connections
  - Physical damage to the wiring harness
- The following conditions may cause an intermittent malfunction:
  - A poor connection
  - Rubbed-through wire insulation
  - A broken wire inside the insulation

Test Description

The number(s) below refer to the step number(s) on the diagnostic table.

3. This step checks for an internal EBTCM malfunction.
5. This step checks for an open in CKT 1572.

GC4029903880010X

Fig. 119 Traction Off Indicator Inoperative With No DTC Set (Part 1 of 2). 2000 Grand Prix

Step	Action	Value(s)	Yes	No
DEFINITION: TRAC OFF indicator is inoperative when attempting to disable traction control.				
1	Was the Diagnostic System Check performed?	—	Go to *Step 2*	Go to *A Diagnostic System Check - ABS*
2	1. Turn the ignition switch to the RUN position, engine off. 2. Using a scan tool enter ABS/TCS Data List. 3. While monitoring the TRAC On/Off switch status, press and release the TRAC On/Off switch. Does the switch status change from pressed to released as the TRAC switch is pressed and released?	—	Go to *Step 3*	Go to *Step 8*
3	1. Turn the ignition switch to the OFF position. 2. Disconnect the EBTCM connector C1. 3. Install the *J 39700* Universal Pinout Box using the J 39700-530 cable adapter to connector C1 only. 4. Connect a fused jumper wire between terminals 18 and 15 of *J 39700.* 5. Turn the ignition switch to the RUN position, engine off. Does the TRAC OFF Indicator turn on?	—	Go to *Step 4*	Go to *Step 5*
4	Replace the EBTCM. Is the replacement complete?	—	Go to *A Diagnostic System Check - ABS*	—
5	1. Turn the ignition switch to the OFF position. 2. Disconnect the Driver Information Display (Base) or Trip Computer (Up Level) connector. 3. Using *J 39200* DMM, measure the resistance between terminals 18 of *J 39700* and the Driver Information Display (Base) or Trip Computer (Up Level) harness connector terminal L (Driver Information Display) or A6 (Trip Computer). Is the resistance within the range specified in the value(s) column?	0–5Ω	Go to *Step 7*	Go to *Step 6*
6	Repair CKT 1572 for an open or high resistance. Is the repair complete?	—	Go to *A Diagnostic System Check - ABS*	—
7	Suspect the Driver Information Display (Base) or Trip Computer (Up Level). Is the repair complete?	—	Go to *A Diagnostic System Check - ABS*	—
8	1. Turn the ignition switch to the OFF position. 2. Disconnect the EBTCM connector C1. 3. Install the *J 39700* Universal Pinout Box using the J 39700-530 cable adapter to connector C1 only. 4. Using *J 39200* DMM, measure the resistance between terminals 17 and 15 of *J 39700* while an assistant presses the TRAC On/Off switch. Is the resistance within the range specified in the value(s) column?	0-5Ω	Go to *Step 4*	Go to *Step 9*
9	Repair CKT 1571 for an open or high resistance, being sure to check the traction control switch for an open. Is the repair complete?	—	Go to *A Diagnostic System Check - ABS*	—

GC4029903880020X

Fig. 119 Traction Off Indicator Inoperative With No DTC Set (Part 2 of 2). 2000 Grand Prix

Circuit Description

The UART serial data link allows information to be exchanged from module to module as needed. This is done by the PCM, the PCM requests and sends all the information that is transmitted on the UART line. When a scan tool is connected to the UART line it takes over for the PCM and sends and requests the needed information.

Diagnostic Aids

- It is very important to start with the ABS Diagnostic System Check before performing the No Communications with EBTCM diagnosis. The ABS Diagnostic System Check will direct you to the Data Link Communications Diagnostic System Check in Data Link Communications to diagnose a malfunction that effects the entire serial data circuit. The No Communications with EBTCM diagnostic table will diagnose a malfunction with the power or ground circuits and the UART circuit to the EBTCM only.
- Thoroughly inspect the wiring and the connectors. Failure to carefully and fully inspect the wiring and the connectors can result in misdiagnosis. Misdiagnosis may cause replacement of parts without repairing the malfunction.

GC4029903881010X

Fig. 120 No Communication With EBTCM (Part 1 of 3). 2000 Grand Prix

Step	Action	Value(s)	Yes	No
10	1. Turn the ignition switch to the RUN position, engine off. 2. Using *J 39200* DMM, measure the voltage between *J 39700* terminals 8 and 15. Is the voltage within the range specified in the value(s) column?	Battery Volts	*Go to Step 13*	*Go to Step 11*
11	Repair CKT 1239 for an open or high resistance. Is the repair complete?	—	Go to *A Diagnostic System Check - ABS*	—
12	Replace the EBTCM. Is the replacement complete?	—	Go to *A Diagnostic System Check - ABS*	—
13	1. Turn the ignition switch to the OFF position. 2. Using *J 39200* DMM, measure the resistance between the *J 39700* terminal 24 and the DLC terminal 9. Is the resistance within the range specified in the values column?	0-5Ω	*Go to Step 12*	*Go to Step 14*
14	Repair CKT 800 for an open or high resistance. Is the repair complete?	—	Go to *A Diagnostic System Check - ABS*	—

GC4029903881030X

Fig. 120 No Communication With EBTCM (Part 3 of 3). 2000 Grand Prix

Step	Action	Value(s)	Yes	No
DEFINITION: ABS Indicator never comes on.				
1	Was the Diagnostic System Check performed?	—	*Go to Step 2*	Go to *A Diagnostic System Check - ABS*
2	1. Turn the ignition switch to the OFF position. 2. Disconnect the EBTCM connector C1. 3. Turn the ignition switch to the RUN position. Does the ABS Indicator come on?	—	*Go to Step 3*	*Go to Step 4*
3	Replace the EBTCM. Is the replacement complete?	—	Go to *A Diagnostic System Check - ABS*	—
4	1. Turn the ignition switch to the OFF position. 2. Install the *J 39700* Universal Pinout Box using the J 39700-530 cable adapter to connector C1 only. 3. Disconnect the Instrument Cluster connector C1. 4. Using *J 39200* DMM, measure the resistance between terminals 16 and 15 of *J 39700*. Is the resistance within the range specified in the value(s) column?	OL (infinite)	*Go to Step 6*	*Go to Step 5*
5	Repair CKT 867 for a short to ground. Is the repair complete?	—	Go to *A Diagnostic System Check - ABS*	—
6	1. Turn the ignition switch to the OFF position 2. Check the ABS indicator bulb. Is the ABS Indicator bulb OK?	—	*Go to Step 8*	*Go to Step 7*
7	Replace the ABS Indicator Bulb. Is the replacement complete?	—	Go to *A Diagnostic System Check - ABS*	—
8	Replace the Instrument Panel Cluster. Is the replacement complete?	—	Go to *A Diagnostic System Check - ABS*	—

GC4029903882020X

Fig. 121 ABS Indicator Off No DTC Set (Part 2 of 2). 2000 Grand Prix

Step	Action	Value(s)	Yes	No
DEFINITION: Scan tool can not communicate with the EBTCM.				
1	Was the Diagnostic System Check performed?	—	*Go to Step 2*	Go to *A Diagnostic System Check - ABS*
2	Turn the Ignition switch to the RUN position with the engine off. Can the scan tool communicate with other modules on the UART serial data line, such as the PCM?	—	*Go to Step 3*	Go to *Data Link Communications System*
3	Inspect the 10A A/C CLU / ABS IGN fuse in the Underhood Accessory Wiring Junction Block. Is the fuse OK?	—	*Go to Step 4*	*Go to Step 6*
4	1. Install the fuses if removed. 2. Turn the ignition switch to the RUN position, engine off. 3. Using *J 39200* DMM, measure the voltage at the 10A A/C / CLU / ABS IGN fuse by probing between the fuse test terminals and a good ground. Is the voltage within the range specified within the value(s) column?	Battery Volts	*Go to Step 5*	Go to *Power Distribution*
5	1. Turn the ignition switch to the OFF position. 2. Disconnect the EBTCM connector C1. 3. Connect the *J 39700* Universal Pinout Box using the J 39700-530 cable adapter to the EBTCM harness connector C1 only. 4. Using *J 39200* DMM, measure the resistance between *J 39700* terminal 15 and a good ground. Is the resistance within the range specified in the value(s) column?	0 - 5Ω	*Go to Step 10*	*Go to Step 9*
6	1. Install a new 10A A/C / CLU / ABS IGN fuse. 2. Turn the ignition switch from the OFF to RUN position, engine off. 3. Recheck the fuse. Is the fuse OK?	—	Go to *A Diagnostic System Check - ABS*	*Go to Step 7*
7	1. Turn the ignition switch to the OFF position. 2. Remove the 10A A/C / CLU / ABS IGN fuse. 3. Disconnect the EBTCM connector C1. 4. Connect the *J 39700* Universal Pinout Box using the J 39700-530 cable adapter to the EBTCM harness connector C1 only. 5. Using *J 39200* DMM, measure the resistance between terminals 8 and 15 of *J 39700*. Is the resistance within the range specified in the value(s) column?	OL (infinite)	*Go to Step 12*	*Go to Step 8*
8	Repair CKT 1239 for a short to ground. Is the repair complete?	—	Go to *A Diagnostic System Check - ABS*	—
9	Repair CKT 251 or G205 for an open or high resistance. Is the repair complete?	—	Go to *A Diagnostic System Check - ABS*	—

GC4029903881020X

Fig. 120 No Communication With EBTCM (Part 2 of 3). 2000 Grand Prix

Circuit Description

The ABS indicator is controlled by the EBTCM. The EBTCM supplies the ground to CKT 867 in order to keep the indicator off. When CKT 867 looses ground at the EBTCM, the ABS indicator turns on.

Diagnostic Aids

- It is very important that a thorough inspection of the wiring and connectors be performed. Failure to carefully and fully inspect wiring and connectors may result in misdiagnosis, causing part replacement with reappearance of the malfunction.
- Thoroughly inspect any circuitry that may be causing the complaint for the following conditions:
  - Backed out terminals
  - Improper mating
  - Broken locks
  - Improperly formed or damaged terminals
  - Poor terminal-to-wiring connections
  - Physical damage to the wiring harness
- The following conditions may cause an intermittent malfunction:
  - A poor connection
  - Rubbed-through wire insulation
  - A broken wire inside the insulation

Test Description

The number(s) below refer to the step number(s) on the diagnostic table.

2. This step checks for an internal EBTCM malfunction.
4. This step checks for a short to ground in CKT 867.

GC4029903882010X

Fig. 121 ABS Indicator Off No DTC Set (Part 1 of 2). 2000 Grand Prix

Circuit Description

The ABS indicator is controlled by the EBTCM. The EBTCM supplies the ground to CKT 867 in order to keep the indicator off. When CKT 867 looses ground at the EBTCM, the ABS indicator turns on.

Diagnostic Aids

- It is very important that a thorough inspection of the wiring and connectors be performed. Failure to carefully and fully inspect wiring and connectors may result in misdiagnosis, causing part replacement with reappearance of the malfunction.
- Thoroughly inspect any circuitry that may be causing the complaint for the following conditions:
  - Backed out terminals
  - Improper mating
  - Broken locks
  - Improperly formed or damaged terminals
  - Poor terminal-to-wiring connections
  - Physical damage to the wiring harness
- The following conditions may cause an intermittent malfunction:
  - A poor connection
  - Rubbed-through wire insulation
  - A broken wire inside the insulation

Test Description

The number(s) below refer to the step number(s) on the diagnostic table.

2. This step checks for an internal EBTCM malfunction.
4. This step checks for an open in CKT 867.

GC4029903883010X

Fig. 122 ABS Indicator On No DTC Set (Part 1 of 2). 2000 Grand Prix

Step	Action	Value(s)	Yes	No
DEFINITION: ABS Indicator is on with no DTC(s).				
1	Was the Diagnostic System Check performed?	—	*Go to Step 2*	Go to *A Diagnostic System Check - ABS*
2	1. Turn the ignition switch to the OFF position. 2. Disconnect the EBTCM connector C1. 3. Install the *J 39700* Universal Pinout Box using the J 39700-530 cable adapter to connector C1 only. 4. Connect a fused jumper wire between terminals 16 and 15 of *J 39700*. 5. Turn the ignition switch to the RUN position. Does the ABS Indicator turn off?	—	*Go to Step 3*	*Go to Step 4*
3	Replace the EBTCM. Is the replacement complete?	—	Go to *A Diagnostic System Check - ABS*	—
4	1. Turn the ignition switch to the OFF position. 2. Disconnect the Instrument Cluster connector C1. 3. Using *J 39200* DMM, measure the resistance between terminals 16 of *J 39700* and the Instrument Cluster harness connector C1 terminal E. Is the resistance within the range specified in the value(s) column?	0–5Ω	*Go to Step 6*	*Go to Step 5*
5	Repair CKT 867 for an open or high resistance. Is the repair complete?	—	Go to *A Diagnostic System Check - ABS*	—
6	Replace the Instrument Panel. Is the repair complete?	—	Go to *A Diagnostic System Check - ABS*	—

GC4029903883020X

Fig. 122 ABS Indicator On No DTC Set (Part 2 of 2). 2000 Grand Prix

Step	Action	Value(s)	Yes	No
DEFINITION: LOW TRAC Indicator On without a low traction condition.				
1	Was the Diagnostic System Check performed?	—	*Go to Step 2*	Go to *A Diagnostic System Check - ABS*
2	1. Turn the ignition switch to the OFF position. 2. Disconnect the EBTCM connector C1. 3. Turn the ignition switch to the RUN position. Is the LOW TRAC Indicator off?	—	*Go to Step 3*	*Go to Step 4*
3	Replace the EBTCM. Is the replacement complete?	—	Go to *A Diagnostic System Check - ABS*	—
4	1. Install the *J 39700* Universal Pinout Box using the J 39700-530 cable adapter to connector C1 only. 2. Disconnect the Driver Information Display (Base) or Trip Calculator (Up Level) connector. 3. Using *J 39200* DMM, measure the resistance between terminals 25 and 15 of *J 39700*. Is the resistance within the range specified in the value(s) column?	0–5Ω Infinite	*Go to Step 6*	*Go to Step 5*
5	Repair CKT 1656 for a short to ground. Is the repair complete?	—	Go to *A Diagn stic System Check - ABS*	—
6	Suspect the Driver Information Display (Base) or Trip Calculator (Up Level). Is the repair complete?	—	Go to *A Diagn ostic System Check - ABS*	—

GC4029903884020X

Fig. 123 Low Traction Indicator Always On (Part 2 of 2). 2000 Grand Prix

Circuit Description

The LOW TRAC Indicator is controlled by the EBTCM. The LOW TRAC Indicator is activated during a traction control event only. When the EBTCM detects a low traction condition it supplies a ground for CKT 1656 turning on the LOW TRAC Indicator.

Diagnostic Aids

- It is very important that a thorough inspection of the wiring and connectors be performed. Failure to carefully and fully inspect wiring and connectors may result in misdiagnosis, causing part replacement with reappearance of the malfunction.
- Thoroughly inspect any circuitry that may be causing the complaint for the following conditions:
  - Backed out terminals
  - Improper mating
  - Broken locks
  - Improperly formed or damaged terminals
  - Poor terminal-to-wiring connections
  - Physical damage to the wiring harness
- The following conditions may cause an intermittent malfunction:
  - A poor connection
  - Rubbed-through wire insulation
  - A broken wire inside the insulation

Test Description

The number(s) below refer to the step number(s) on the diagnostic table.

2. This step checks for an internal EBTCM short.
4. This step checks for a short to ground in CKT 1656

GC4029903884010X

Fig. 123 Low Traction Indicator Always On (Part 1 of 2). 2000 Grand Prix

Circuit Description

The LOW TRAC Indicator is controlled by the EBTCM. The LOW TRAC Indicator is activated during a traction control event only. When the EBTCM detects a low traction condition it supplies a ground for CKT 1656 turning on the LOW TRAC Indicator.

Diagnostic Aids

- It is very important that a thorough inspection of the wiring and connectors be performed. Failure to carefully and fully inspect wiring and connectors may result in misdiagnosis, causing part replacement with reappearance of the malfunction.
- Thoroughly inspect any circuitry that may be causing the complaint for the following conditions:
  - Backed out terminals
  - Improper mating
  - Broken locks
  - Improperly formed or damaged terminals
  - Poor terminal-to-wiring connections
  - Physical damage to the wiring harness
- The following conditions may cause an intermittent malfunction:
  - A poor connection
  - Rubbed-through wire insulation
  - A broken wire inside the insulation

Test Description

The number(s) below refer to the step number(s) on the diagnostic table.

2. This step checks for an internal EBTCM malfunction.
4. This step checks for an open in CKT 1656.

GC4029903885010X

Fig. 124 Low Traction Indicator Inoperative (Part 1 of 2). 2000 Grand Prix

Step	Action	Value(s)	Yes	No
DEFINITION: LOW TRAC Indicator never comes on.				
1	Was the Diagnostic System Check performed?	—	*Go to Step 2*	Go to *A Diagnostic System Check - ABS*
2	1. Turn the ignition switch to the OFF position. 2. Disconnect the EBTCM connector C1. 3. Install the *J 39700* Universal Pinout Box using the J 39700-530 cable adapter to connector C1 only. 4. Connect a fused jumper wire between terminals 25 and 15 of *J 39700*. 5. Turn the ignition switch to the RUN position. Does the LOW TRAC Indicator come on?	—	*Go to Step 3*	*Go to Step 4*
3	Replace the EBTCM. Is the replacement complete?	—	Go to *A Diagnostic System Check - ABS*	—
4	1. Turn the ignition switch to the OFF position. 2. Disconnect the Driver Information Display (Base) or Trip Calculator (Up Level) connector. 3. Using *J 39200* DMM, measure the resistance between terminals 25 of *J 39700* and the Driver Information Display (Base) or Trip Calculator (Up Level) harness connector terminal H (Driver Information Display) or A3 (Trip Calculator). Is the resistance within the range specified in the value(s) column?	0–5Ω	*Go to Step 6*	*Go to Step 5*
5	Repair CKT 1656 for an open or high resistance. Is the repair complete?	—	Go to *A Diagnostic System Check - ABS*	—
6	Suspect the Driver Information Display (Base) or Trip Calculator (Up Level). Is the repair complete?	—	Go to *A Diagnostic System Check - ABS*	—

GC4029903885020X

Fig. 124 Low Traction Indicator Inoperative (Part 2 of 2). 2000 Grand Prix

Circuit Description

The PCS On indicator is controlled by the instrument cluster via class 2 serial data messages from the EBCM. When the instrument cluster sees the PCS signal input grounded, it sends a class 2 message to the EBCM that tells the EBCM that the PCS is malfunctioning. The EBCM then disables PCS and TCS and sends a message to the instrument cluster to turn the PCS and TCS indicators ON. Each time the ignition is cycled from OFF to ON, the PCS is enabled.

The following conditions will cause the PCS/TCS indicators to illuminate:

- The EBCM has disabled the PCS/TCS due to a DTC.
- The instrument cluster bulb check. When the ignition switch is turned to ON, the PCS/TCS indicators will turn on for approximately 3 seconds and then turn OFF.

Test Description

The numbers below refer to the step numbers on the diagnostic table.

3. This test uses the scan tool to check the normal state of the ABS indicator control circuit.
4. This test ensures that the instrument cluster can operate the ABS indicator.

GC4020052021010X

Fig. 125 PCS Indicator Always On (Part 1 of 2). 2000 Intrigue

Step	Action	Value(s)	Yes	No
1	Did you perform the ABS Diagnostic System Check?	—	Go to *Step 2*	Go to *A Diagnostic System Check - ABS*
2	Inspect the EBCM ground, making sure the ground is clean and torqued to the proper specification. Did you find and correct the condition?	—	Go to *Step 9*	Go to *Step 3*
3	With a scan tool, observe the PCS Warning Indicator parameter in the ABS/TCS/PCS/VSES data list. Does the scan tool display Off?	—	Go to *Step 4*	Go to *Step 5*
4	1. Turn OFF the ignition. 2. Turn ON the ignition, with the engine OFF. 3. Observe the PCS indicator on the instrument cluster (IPC) during the bulb check. Does the PCS indicator illuminate during the bulb check and then turn OFF?	—	Go to *Step 5*	Go to *Step 6*
5	Inspect for poor connections at the harness connector of the EBCM. Did you find and correct the condition?	—	Go to *Step 9*	Go to *Step 7*
6	Inspect for poor connections at the harness connector of the instrument cluster (IPC). Did you find and correct the condition?	—	Go to *Step 9*	Go to *Step 8*
7	**Important:** Perform the setup procedure for the EBCM. An unprogrammed EBCM will result in the following conditions: • Inoperative or poorly functioning ABS/TCS/PCS/VSES/VES • Turns the PCS Warning Indicator On • EBCM Internal Malfunction Replace the EBCM. Did you complete the repair?	—	Go to *Step 9*	—
8	Replace the instrument cluster (IPC). Did you complete the repair?	—	Go to *Step 9*	—
9	Operate the system in order to verify the repair. Did you correct the condition?	—	System OK	Go to *Step 2*

GC4020052021020X

Fig. 125 PCS Indicator Always On (Part 2 of 2). 2000 Intrigue

Circuit Description

The PCS On indicator is controlled by the instrument cluster via class 2 serial data messages from the EBCM. When the instrument cluster sees that the PCS signal input is grounded, it sends a class 2 message to the EBCM that tells the EBCM that the PCS is malfunctioning. The EBCM then disables PCS and TCS and sends a message to the instrument cluster to turn the PCS and TCS indicators ON. Each time the ignition is cycled from OFF to ON, the PCS is enabled.

The following conditions will cause the PCS indicator not to illuminate:

- No signal received from the EBCM.
- The instrument cluster PCS indicator bulb is blown.
- Harness connector malfunctioned.

Test Description

The numbers below refer to the step numbers on the diagnostic table.

3. This test uses the scan tool to check the normal state of the ABS indicator control circuit.
4. This test ensures that the instrument cluster can operate the ABS indicator.

GC4020052022010X

Fig. 126 PCS Indicator Inoperative (Part 1 of 2). 2000 Intrigue

Step	Action	Value(s)	Yes	No
1	Did you perform the ABS Diagnostic System Check?	—	Go to *Step 2*	Go to *A Diagnostic System Check - ABS*
2	Inspect the EBCM ground, making sure the ground is clean and torqued to the proper specification. Did you find and correct the condition?	—	Go to *Step 9*	Go to *Step 3*
3	With a scan tool, observe the PCS Warning Indicator parameter in the ABS/TCS/PCS/VSES data list. Does the scan tool display Off?	—	Go to *Step 4*	Go to *Step 5*
4	1. Turn OFF the ignition. 2. Turn ON the ignition, with the engine OFF. 3. Observe the PCS indicator on the instrument cluster (IPC) during the bulb check. Does the PCS indicator illuminate during the bulb check and then turn OFF?	—	Go to *Step 5*	Go to *Step 6*
5	Inspect for poor connections at the harness connector of the EBCM. Did you find and correct the condition?	—	Go to *Step 9*	Go to *Step 7*
6	Inspect for poor connections at the harness connector of the instrument cluster (IPC). Did you find and correct the condition?	—	Go to *Step 9*	Go to *Step 8*
7	**Important:** Perform the setup procedure for the EBCM. An unprogrammed EBCM will result in the following conditions: • Inoperative or poorly functioning ABS/TCS/PCS/VSES/VES • Turns the PCS Warning Indicator On • EBCM Internal Malfunction Replace the EBCM. Did you complete the repair?	—	Go to *Step 9*	—
8	Replace the instrument cluster (IPC). Gauges and Console. Did you complete the repair?	—	Go to *Step 9*	—
9	Operate the system in order to verify the repair. Did you correct the condition?	—	System OK	Go to *Step 2*

GC4020052022020X

Fig. 126 PCS Indicator Inoperative (Part 2 of 2). 2000 Intrigue

Circuit Description

The TRAC OFF Indicator is controlled by the EBTCM by sending class 2 messages to the Instrument Panel Cluster (IPC). It is turned on when the EBTCM sets a DTC that turns on the TRAC OFF indicator. It is also turned on or off when the Traction Control Switch is pressed. The Body Control Module (BCM) receives the input from the Traction Control Switch, the BCM then sends a class 2 message to the EBTCM telling the EBTCM the state of the switch. The BCM supplies 12 volts to the TCS switch, when the TCS switch is pressed the BCM sees the voltage go low and sends the EBTCM the message that the TCS switch state has changed.

When the EBTCM receives the message from the BCM that the switch state has changed, the EBTCM turns on or off Traction Control and sends a message to the IPC to turn on or off the TRAC OFF indicator depending on its previous state.

Test Description

The numbers below refer to step numbers on the diagnostic table.

2. Checks if the Instrument Panel Cluster has the ability to turn the TRAC OFF indicator off or if the EBTCM is sending an incorrect command to turn the TRAC OFF indicator on.

GC4029903870010X

Fig. 127 Traction Off Indicator On With No DTC Set (Part 1 of 2). 2000 Intrigue

Step	Action	Value(s)	Yes	No
DEFINITION: The TRAC OFF indicator does not turn off after the Instrument Panel Cluster (IPC) bulb check or after the Traction control Switch is pressed to turn the Traction Control on after it was disabled.				
1	Was the ABS Diagnostic System Check performed?	—	Go to *Step 2*	Go to *A Diagnostic System Check - ABS*
2	Using a scan tool in the Instrument Panel Cluster Special Functions attempt to turn off the TRAC OFF indicator. Did the TRAC Off indicator Turn off?	—	Go to *Step 3*	Go to *Step 4*
3	Replace the EBTCM. Is the Replacement complete?	—	Go to *A Diagnostic System Check - ABS*	—
4	Replace the Instrument Panel Cluster. Is the Replacement complete?	—	Go to *A Diagnostic System Check - ABS*	—

GC4029903870020X

Fig. 127 Traction Off Indicator On With No DTC Set (Part 2 of 2). 2000 Intrigue

Circuit Description

The TRAC OFF indicator is controlled by the EBCM by sending class 2 messages to the instrument panel cluster (IPC). It is turned on when the EBCM sets a DTC that turns on the TRAC OFF indicator. It is also turned on or off when the traction control switch is pressed. The body control module (BCM) receives the input from the traction control switch, the BCM then sends a class 2 message to the EBCM telling the EBCM the state of the switch. The BCM supplies 12 volts to the TCS switch, when the TCS switch is pressed the BCM sees the voltage go low and sends the EBCM the message that the TCS switch state has changed. When the EBCM receives the message from the BCM that the switch state has changed, the EBCM turns on or off traction control and sends a message to the IPC to turn on or off the TRAC OFF indicator depending on its previous state.

Test Description

The numbers below refer to step numbers on the diagnostic table.

2. Checks if the body control module is receiving a traction control switch input.
3. Checks if the EBTCM is receiving a traction control switch message from the body control module.
9. Checks if the body control module or the traction control switch is at fault.

GC4020052020010X

Fig. 128 Traction Off Indicator Inoperative (Part 1 of 3). 2000 Intrigue

Step	Action	Value(s)	Yes	No
DEFINITION: The TRAC OFF indicator does not come on when the traction control switch is pressed to disable the traction control system.				
1	Was the ABS Diagnostic System Check performed?	—	*Go to Step 2*	*Go to A Diagnostic System Check - ABS*
2	1. Turn the ignition switch to the ON position, engine off. 2. Using a scan tool in the Body Control Module Data Display read the TCS Switch state as you press and release the TCS switch. Does the TCS switch state change properly as the switch is pressed and released?	—	*Go to Step 3*	*Go to Step 9*
3	Using a scan tool in ABS/TCS Data Display, read the TCS Switch Status as you press and release the TCS Switch. Does the TCS Switch state change properly as the switch is pressed and released?	—	*Go to Step 5*	*Go to Step 4*
4	Replace the EBCM. Is the replacement complete?	—	*Go to A Diagnostic System Check - ABS*	—
5	Using a scan tool in the Instrument Panel (IPC) Special Functions attempt to turn the TRAC OFF indicator on. Did the TRAC OFF indicator turn on?	—	*Go to Step 4*	*Go to Step 6*
6	1. Turn the ignition switch to the OFF position. 2. Check the TRAC OFF indicator bulb. Is the TRAC OFF indicator bulb OK?	—	*Go to Step 8*	*Go to Step 7*
7	Replace the TRAC OFF Indicator bulb. Is the replacement complete?	—	*Go to A Diagnostic System Check - ABS*	—
8	Replace the instrument panel cluster. Is the replacement complete?	—	*Go to A Diagnostic System Check - ABS*	—
9	1. Remove the traction control switch and disconnect the connector. 2. Using a scan tool in the Body Control Module Data Display read the TCS switch status. 3. Connect a jumper wire between terminals E and D of the traction control switch harness connector. Does the TCS switch status read pressed with the jumper wire connected?	—	*Go to Step 10*	*Go to Step 11*
10	Replace the traction control switch. Is the replacement complete?	—	*Go to A Diagnostic System Check - ABS*	—

GC4020052020020X

Fig. 128 Traction Off Indicator Inoperative (Part 2 of 3). 2000 Intrigue

Step	Action	Value(s)	Yes	No
11	1. Turn the ignition switch to the OFF position. 2. Using DMM, measure the resistance between the traction control switch harness connector terminal D and ground. Is the resistance within the range specified in the value(s) column?	0–5 Ω	*Go to Step 13*	*Go to Step 12*
12	Repair CKT 1550 for an open or high resistance. Is the repair complete?	—	*Go to A Diagnostic System Check - ABS*	—
13	1. Disconnect the body control module connector C 2. 2. Using DMM, measure the resistance between the traction control switch harness connector terminal E and the body control module connector C2 terminal A11. Is the resistance within the range specified in the value(s) column?	0–5 Ω	*Go to Step 15*	*Go to Step 14*
14	Repair CKT 1571 for an open or high resistance. Is the repair complete?	—	*Go to A Diagnostic System Check - ABS*	—
15	Replace the body control module. Is the replacement complete?	—	*Go to A Diagnostic System Check - ABS*	—

GC4020052020030X

Fig. 128 Traction Off Indicator Inoperative (Part 3 of 3). 2000 Intrigue

Circuit Description

The Class 2 serial data line allows all the modules on the line to transmit information to each other as needed. Each module is assigned an ID and all the information sent out on the line is assigned a priority by which it is received. When the ignition switch is turned to the run position each module begins to send and receive information. Each module on the Class 2 serial data line knows what information it needs to send out and what information it should be receiving. What the modules do not know is which module is supposed to send them the information. This information is only learned after the module has received the information it needs along with the ID of the module that sent the information. This information is then remembered until the ignition switch is turned off.

Diagnostic Aids

- It is very important to start with the ABS Diagnostic System Check before performing the No Communications with EBCM diagnosis. The ABS Diagnostic System Check will direct you to the Data Link Communications Diagnostic System Check in Data Link Communications to diagnose a malfunction that effects the entire serial data circuit. The No Communication with EBTCM diagnostic table will diagnose a malfunction with the power and ground circuits and the Class 2 circuit to the EBCM only. For diagnosis of the entire Class 2 serial data circuit, refer to A Diagnostic System Check - Data Link Communications in Data Link Communications.
- It is very important that a thorough inspection of the wiring and connectors be performed. Failure to carefully and fully inspect wiring and connectors may result in misdiagnosis, causing part replacement with reappearance of the malfunction.
- Thoroughly inspect any circuitry that may be causing the complaint for the following conditions:
  - Backed out terminals
  - Improper mating
  - Broken locks
  - Improperly formed or damaged terminals
  - Poor terminal-to-wiring connections
  - Physical damage to the wiring harness
- The following conditions may cause an intermittent malfunction:
  - A poor connection
  - Rubbed-through wire insulation
  - A broken wire inside the insulation

Step	Action	Value(s)	Yes	No
DEFINITION: Scan tool can not communicate with the EBTCM.				
1	Was the ABS Diagnostic System Check performed?	—	*Go to Step 2*	*Go to A Diagnostic System Check - ABS*
2	Turn the ignition switch to the ON position with the engine off. Can the scan tool communicate with other modules on the Class 2 serial data line, such as the PCM?	—	*Go to Step 3*	*Scan Tool Does Not Communicate with Class 2 Device*
3	Inspect the 10A Trans / ABS fuse 26 in the underhood accessory wiring junction block. Is the fuse OK?	—	*Go to Step 4*	*Go to Step 6*
4	1. Install the fuse if removed. 2. Turn the ignition switch to the ON position, engine off. 3. Using DMM, measure the voltage at the 10A Trans / ABS fuse 26 by probing between the fuse test terminals and a good ground. Is the voltage within the range specified within the value(s) column?	Battery Volts	*Go to Step 5*	*Power Distribution*

GC4020052023010X

Fig. 129 No Communication With EBTCM (Part 1 of 2). 2000 Intrigue

Step	Action	Value(s)	Yes	No
5	1. Turn the ignition switch to the OFF position. 2. Disconnect the EBCM connector C1. 3. Connect the *J 39700* universal pinout box using the *J 39700-530* cable adapter to the EBCM harness connector C1 only. 4. Using DMM, measure the resistance between the *J 39700* universal pinout box terminal 15 and a good ground. Is the resistance within the range specified in the value(s) column?	0 - 5 Ω	*Go to Step 10*	*Go to Step 9*
6	1. Install a new 10A Trans / ABS fuse 26. 2. Turn the ignition switch from the OFF to ON position, engine off. 3. Recheck the fuse. Is the fuse OK?	—	*Go to A Diagnostic System Check - ABS*	*Go to Step 7*
7	1. Turn the ignition switch to the OFF position. 2. Remove the 10A Trans / ABS fuse 26. 3. Disconnect the EBCM connector C1. 4. Connect the *J 39700* universal pinout box using the *J 39700-530* cable adapter to the EBCM harness connector C1 only. 5. Using DMM, measure the resistance between terminals 8 and 15 of the *J 39700* universal pinout box. Is the resistance within the range specified in the value(s) column?	OL (infinite)	*Go to Step 12*	*Go to Step 8*
8	Repair CKT 1039 for a short to ground. Is the repair complete?	—	*Go to A Diagnostic System Check - ABS*	—
9	Repair CKT 251 or G201 for an open or high resistance. Is the repair complete?	—	*Go to A Diagnostic System Check - ABS*	—
10	1. Turn the ignition switch to the ON position, engine off. 2. Using DMM, measure the voltage between the *J 39700* universal pinout box terminals 8 and 15. Is the voltage within the range specified in the value(s) column?	Battery Volts	*Go to Step 13*	*Go to Step 11*
11	Repair CKT 1039 for an open or high resistance. Is the repair complete?	—	*Go to A Diagnostic System Check - ABS*	—
12	Replace the EBCM. Is the replacement complete?	—	*Go to A Diagnostic System Check - ABS*	—
13	1. Turn the ignition switch to the OFF position. 2. Remove the bus bar from the splice pack SP 205. 3. Using DMM, measure the resistance between the *J 39700* universal pinout box terminal 25 and the splice pack terminal E. Is the resistance within the range specified in the values column?	0-5 Ω	*Go to Step 12*	*Go to Step 14*
14	Repair CKT 1122 for an open or high resistance. Is the repair complete?	—	*Go to A Diagnostic System Check - ABS*	—

GC4020052023020X

Fig. 129 No Communication With EBTCM (Part 2 of 2). 2000 Intrigue

Circuit Description

The Instrument Panel Cluster (IPC) turns the ABS Indicator on during the IPC bulb check for approximately 3 seconds when the ignition switch is turned to the ON position. If the EBTCM sets a Diagnostic Trouble Code (DTC) the EBTCM sends the IPC the command to turn the ABS Indicator on.

Test Description

The numbers below refer to step numbers on the diagnostic table.

2. Checks if the IPC has the ability to turn the ABS Indicator on.

GC4029903873010X

Fig. 130 ABS Indicator Off No DTC Set (Part 1 of 2). 2000 Intrigue

Circuit Description

The Instrument Panel Cluster (IPC) turns the ABS Indicator on during the IPC bulb check for approximately 3 seconds when the ignition switch is turned to the ON position. If the EBTCM sets a Diagnostic Trouble Code (DTC) the EBTCM sends the IPC the command to turn the ABS Indicator on.

Test Description

The numbers below refer to step numbers on the diagnostic table.

2. Checks if the Instrument Panel Cluster has the ability to turn the ABS indicator off or if the EBTCM is sending an incorrect command to turn the ABS indicator on.

GC4029903874010X

Fig. 131 ABS Indicator On No DTC Set (Part 1 of 2). 2000 Intrigue

Circuit Description

The Instrument Panel Cluster (IPC) turns the LOW TRAC Indicator on during the IPC bulb check for approximately 3 seconds when the ignition switch is turned to the ON position. The LOW TRAC Indicator is activated during a traction control event only. If the EBTCM detects a low traction condition, the EBTCM sends the IPC the command to turn the LOW TRAC Indicator on.

Test Description

The numbers below refer to step numbers on the diagnostic table.

2. Checks if the Instrument Panel Cluster has the ability to turn the LOW TRAC indicator off or if the EBTCM is sending an incorrect command to turn the LOW TRAC indicator on.

GC4029903875010X

Fig. 132 Low Traction Indicator Always On (Part 1 of 2). 2000 Intrigue

Circuit Description

The Instrument Panel Cluster (IPC) turns the LOW TRAC Indicator on during the IPC bulb check for approximately 3 seconds when the ignition switch is turned to the ON position. The LOW TRAC Indicator is activated during a traction control event only. If the EBTCM detects a low traction condition, the EBTCM sends the IPC the command to turn the LOW TRAC Indicator on.

Test Description

The numbers below refer to step numbers on the diagnostic table.

2. Checks if the IPC has the ability to turn the LOW TRAC indicator on.

GC4029903876010X

Fig. 133 Low Traction Indicator Inoperative (Part 1 of 2). 2000 Intrigue

Step	Action	Value(s)	Yes	No
DEFINITION: The LOW TRAC indicator does not come on during the IPC bulb check or during a traction control event.				
1	Was the ABS Diagnostic System Check performed?	—	Go to Step 2	Go to A Diagnostic System Check - ABS
2	Using a scan tool in the Instrument Panel (IPC) Special Functions attempt to turn the LOW TRAC indicator on. Did the LOW TRAC indicator turn on?	—	Go to Step 3	Go to Step 4
3	Replace the EBTCM. Is the replacement complete?	—	Go to A Diagnostic System Check - ABS	—
4	1. Turn the ignition switch to the OFF position. 2. Check the LOW TRAC indicator bulb. Is the LOW TRAC Indicator bulb OK?	—	Go to Step 6	Go to Step 5
5	Replace the LOW TRAC indicator bulb. Is the replacement complete?	—	Go to A Diagnostic System Check - ABS	—
6	Replace the Instrument Panel Cluster. Is the replacement complete?	—	Go to A Diagnostic System Check - ABS	—

GC4029903876020X

Fig. 133 Low Traction Indicator Inoperative (Part 2 of 2). 2000 Intrigue

Step	Action	Value(s)	Yes	No
DEFINITION: The ABS Indicator does not come on during the IPC bulb check.				
1	Was the ABS Diagnostic System Check performed?	—	Go to Step 2	Go to A Diagnostic System Check - ABS
2	Using a scan tool in the Instrument Panel (IPC) Special Functions attempt to turn the ABS Indicator on. Did the ABS Indicator turn on?	—	Go to Step 3	Go to Step 4
3	Replace the EBTCM. Is the replacement complete?	—	Go to A Diagnostic System Check - ABS	—
4	1. Turn the ignition switch to the OFF position. 2. Check the ABS indicator bulb. Is the ABS Indicator bulb OK?	—	Go to Step 6	Go to Step 5
5	Replace the ABS Indicator bulb. Is the replacement complete?	—	Go to A Diagnostic System Check - ABS	—
6	Replace the Instrument Panel Cluster. Is the replacement complete?	—	Go to A Diagnostic System Check - ABS	—

GC4029903873020X

Fig. 130 ABS Indicator Off No DTC Set (Part 2 of 2). 2000 Intrigue

Step	Action	Value(s)	Yes	No
DEFINITION: The ABS Indicator does not turn off after the Instrument Panel Cluster (IPC) bulb check and no ABS/TCS DTC(s) set.				
1	Was the ABS Diagnostic System Check performed?	—	Go to Step 2	Go to A Diagnostic System Check - ABS
2	Using a scan tool in the Instrument Panel Cluster Special Functions attempt to turn off the ABS Indicator. Did the ABS Indicator Turn off?	—	Go to Step 3	Go to Step 4
3	Replace the EBTCM. Is the Replacement complete?	—	Go to A Diagnostic System Check - ABS	—
4	Replace the Instrument Panel Cluster. Is the Replacement complete?	—	Go to A Diagnostic System Check - ABS	—

GC4029903874020X

Fig. 131 ABS Indicator On No DTC Set (Part 2 of 2). 2000 Intrigue

Step	Action	Value(s)	Yes	No
DEFINITION: The LOW TRAC Indicator does not turn off after the Instrument Panel Cluster (IPC) bulb check and there is not a low traction condition.				
1	Was the ABS Diagnostic System Check performed?	—	Go to Step 2	Go to A Diagnostic System Check - ABS
2	Using a scan tool in the Instrument Panel Cluster Special Functions attempt to turn off the LOW TRAC Indicator. Did the LOW TRAC Indicator Turn off?	—	Go to Step 3	Go to Step 4
3	Replace the EBTCM. Is the Replacement complete?	—	Go to A Diagnostic System Check - ABS	—
4	Replace the Instrument Panel Cluster. Is the Replacement complete?	—	Go to A Diagnostic System Check - ABS	—

GC4029903875020X

Fig. 132 Low Traction Indicator Always On (Part 2 of 2). 2000 Intrigue

Circuit Description

The ABS Diagnostic System Check is an organized approach to identify problems associated with the EBCM. This check must be the starting point for any EBCM complaint, and will direct you to the next logical step in diagnosing the complaint. The EBCM is a very reliable component and is not likely the cause of the malfunction. Most system complaints are linked to faulty wiring, connectors, and occasionally to components. Understanding the ABS system and using the tables correctly will reduce diagnostic time and prevent unnecessary parts replacement.

Test Description

The numbers below refer to the step numbers on the diagnostic table.

2. Lack of communication may be due to a partial malfunction of the Class 2 or UART serial data circuit or due to a total malfunction of the Class 2 or UART serial data circuit. The specified procedure will determine the particular condition.
6. The presence of DTCs which begin with "U" indicate some other module is not communicating. The specified procedure will compile all the available information before tests are performed.

Step	Action	Yes	No
1	Install a scan tool. Does the scan tool power up?	Go to Step 2	Diagnose Data Link Communications
2	Turn ON the ignition, with the engine OFF. Attempt to establish communication with the following control module. Electronic brake control module (EBCM). Does the scan tool communicate with the control module?	Go to Step 3	Diagnose Data Link Communications
3	Turn ON the ignition, with the engine OFF. Attempt to establish communication with the following control module. Powertrain control module. Does the scan tool communicate with the control module?	Go to Step 4	Diagnose Data Link Communications
4	Select the display DTCs function on the scan tool for the following control modules: • Electronic brake control module (EBCM). • Powertrain control module (PCM). Does the scan tool display any DTCs?	Go to Step 5	Go to Symptoms - Antilock Brake System
5	Does the scan tool display any DTCs which begin with a U (i.e. DTC U1001, U1254, U1304)?	Diagnose Communications	Go to Step 6
6	Does the scan tool display any DTCs which begin with a P (i.e. DTC P1571, P1573, P1689)?	Diagnose Engine Controls	Go to Diagnostic Trouble Code (DTC) List For The Applicable DTC

GC4020152485000X

Fig. 134 Diagnostic System Check. 2001–04 Grand Prix

Diagnostic System Check - ABS

Circuit Description

The ABS Diagnostic System Check is an organized approach to identify problems associated with the EBCM. This check must be the starting point for any EBCM complaint, and will direct you to the next logical step in diagnosing the complaint. The EBCM is a very reliable component and is not likely the cause of the malfunction. Most system complaints are linked to faulty wiring, connectors, and occasionally to components. Understanding the ABS system and using the tables correctly will reduce diagnostic time and prevent unnecessary parts replacement.

Test Description

The numbers below refer to the step numbers on the diagnostic table.

2. Lack of communication may be due to a partial malfunction of the class 2 serial data circuit or due to a total malfunction of the class 2 serial data circuit. The specified procedure will determine the particular condition.
4. The presence of DTCs which begin with "U" indicate some other module is not communicating. The specified procedure will compile all the available information before tests are performed.

Step	Action	Yes	No
1	Install a scan tool. Does the scan tool power up?	Go to *Step 2*	*Diagnose* Data Link Communications
2	1. Turn ON the ignition, with the engine OFF. 2. Attempt to establish communications with the following control modules. • Electronic brake control module (EBCM) • Powertrain control module (PCM) Does the scan tool communicate with all control modules?	Go to *Step 3*	*Diagnose* Data Link Communications
3	Select the display DTCs function on the scan tool for the following control modules: • Electronic brake control module (EBCM) • Powertrain control module (PCM) Does the scan tool display any DTCs?	Go to *Step 4*	Go to *Symptoms - Antilock Brake System*
4	Does the scan tool display any DTCs which begin with a "U"?	*Diagnose* Data Link Communications	Go to *Step 5*
5	Does the scan tool display DTCs which begin with a "B"?	*Diagnose* Body Control System	Go to *Step 6*
6	Does the scan tool display DTCs which begin with a "P"?	*Diagnose* Engine Electrical	*Diagnose Trouble Code (DTC) List*

GC4020152486000X

Fig. 135 Diagnostic System Check. 2001–02 Intrigue

Circuit Description

As the wheel spins, the wheel speed sensor produces an AC signal. The EBCM uses the frequency of the AC signal to calculate the wheel speed.

Conditions for Running the DTC

C0035 C0040 C0045 C0050

The ignition is ON.

C0036 C0041 C0046 C0051

- Vehicle speed is over 40 km/h (25 mph).
- The brake pedal is not pressed.
- The ABS is not active.

Conditions for Setting the DTC

C0035 C0040 C0045 C0050

One of the following conditions exists for 0.02 seconds:

- A short to voltage - in the wheel speed sensor signal circuit.
- An open - in the wheel speed sensor signal circuit.

C0036 C0041 C0046 C0051

All of the following conditions exists for.01 seconds:

- The suspect wheel speed equals zero.
- The other wheel speeds are greater than 40 km/h (25 mph) for 0.01 seconds.
- The suspect wheel equals zero during drive off, and the other wheels are greater than 18 km/h (11 mph).
- A short to ground - the wheel speed sensor signal circuit is shorted to ground.
- A deviation of two wheel speeds at either side of the vehicle greater than 6 km/h (4 mph), or at the front axle greater than 10 km/h (6 mph) for a time period of 10 to 20 seconds.

Action Taken When the DTC Sets

If equipped, the following actions occur:

- The EBCM disables the ABS/TCS/VSES for the duration of the ignition cycle.
- A DTC malfunction will set.
- The ANTI-LOCK indicator turns ON.
- The TRAC Off indicator turns ON.
- The PCS indicator turns ON.
- The Red BRAKE Warning indicator could turn on.

Conditions for Clearing the DTC

- The condition for the DTC is no longer present (the DTC is not current) and you used the scan tool Clear DTC function.
- The EBCM automatically clears the history DTC when a current DTC is not detected in 100 consecutive drive cycles.

Diagnostic Aids

C0035 C0040 C0045 C0050

If the customer comments that the ABS indicator is ON only during moist environmental conditions (rain, snow, vehicle wash, etc.), inspect the wheel speed sensor wiring for signs of water intrusion. If the DTC is not current, clear all DTCs and simulate the effects of water intrusion by using the following procedure:

1. Spray the suspected area with a 5 percent saltwater solution. To create a 5 percent saltwater solution, add 2 teaspoons of salt to 354 ml (12 oz) of water.
2. Test drive the vehicle over various road surfaces (bumps, turns, etc.) above 40 km/h (25 mph) for at least 30 seconds.
3. If the DTC returns, replace the suspected wheel speed sensor or repair the wheel speed sensor wiring.
4. Rinse the are thoroughly when completed.

C0036 C0041 C0046 C0051

Under the following conditions, 2 Wheel Speed Sensor Input is 0 DTCs are set:

- The 2 suspect wheel speeds equal zero for 10–20 seconds.
- The other wheel speeds are greater than 16 km/h (10 mph).
- The other wheel speeds are within 11 km/h (7 mph) of each other.

Diagnose each wheel speed sensor individually.

C0036 C0041 C0046 C0051

A possible cause of this DTC is electrical noise on the wheel speed sensor harness wiring. Electrical noise could result from the wheel speed sensor wires being routed to close to high energy ignition system components, such as spark plug wires.

Test Description

The numbers below refer to the step numbers on the diagnostic table.

3. This step tests the wheel speed sensor for the proper resistance value.
4. This step ensures that the wheel speed sensor generates the proper voltage.

GC4020152487010X

Fig. 136 Codes C0035–C0051: Wheel Speed Circuit Fault (Part 1 of 2). 2001–04 Grand Prix & 2001–02 Intrigue

Step	Action	Value(s)	Yes	No
Schematic Reference: *ABS Schematics*				
1	Did you perform the ABS Diagnostic System Check?	—	Go to *Step 2*	Go to *Diagnostic System Check - ABS*
2	1. Install a scan tool. 2. Turn ON the ignition. 3. Set up the scan tool snap shot feature to trigger for this DTC. 4. Drive the vehicle at a speed greater than the specified value. Does the scan tool indicate that this wheel speed DTC set?	8 km/h (5 mph)	Go to *Step 3*	Go to Diagnostic Aids
3	1. Raise and support the vehicle. 2. Disconnect the wheel speed sensor connector. 3. Measure the resistance across the wheel speed sensor. Does the resistance measure within the specified range?	800–1600 Ω	Go to *Step 4*	Go to *Step 8*
4	1. Spin the wheel. 2. Measure the AC voltage across the wheel speed sensor. Does the AC voltage measure greater than the specified value?	100 mV	Go to *Step 5*	Go to *Step 8*
5	Inspect for poor connections at the harness connector of the wheel speed sensor. Did you find and correct the condition?	—	Go to *Step 10*	Go to *Step 6*
6	1. Disconnect the EBCM harness connector. 2. Install the *J 39700* using *J 39700-530* to the EBCM harness connector only. 3. Test the wheel speed sensor circuits for the following: • An open • A short to ground • A short to voltage • Shorted together Did you find and correct the condition?	—	Go to *Step 10*	Go to *Step 7*
7	Inspect for poor connections at the harness connector for the EBCM. Did you find and correct the condition?	—	Go to *Step 10*	Go to *Step 9*
8	Replace the wheel speed sensor. Did you complete the replacement?	—	Go to *Step 10*	—
9	Replace the EBCM. Did you complete the repair?	—	Go to *Step 10*	—
10	1. Use the scan tool in order to clear the DTCs. 2. Operate the vehicle within the Conditions for Running the DTC as specified in the supporting text. Does the DTC reset?	—	Go to *Step 2*	System OK

GC4020152487020X

Fig. 136 Codes C0035–C0051: Wheel Speed Circuit Fault (Part 2 of 2). 2001–04 Grand Prix & 2001–02 Intrigue

Circuit Description

The inlet and outlet valve solenoid circuits are supplied with battery power when the ignition is in the ON position. The EBCM controls the valve functions by grounding the circuit when necessary.

Conditions for Running the DTC

- The DTC can set anytime the ignition switch is in the ON position.
- The DTC can set when the vehicle speed is greater then 6 Km/h (4 mph) and the brake pedal is not applied.
- The DTC can set when the vehicle speed is greater then 15 Km/h (9 mph) and the brake pedal is applied.

Conditions for Setting the DTC

The DTC will set when the EBCM detects one of the following internal to the EBCM only:

- An open in the solenoid coil or circuit.
- A short to ground in the solenoid coil or circuit.
- A short to voltage in the solenoid coil or circuit.

Action Taken When the DTC Sets

If equiped, the following actions occur:

- The EBCM disables the ABS/TCS/VSES/DRP for the duration of the ignition cycle.
- A malfunction DTC will set.
- The ANTI-LOCK indicator turns ON.
- The TRAC Off indicator turns ON.
- The PCS indicator turns ON.
- The Red BRAKE Warning indicator could turn on.

Conditions for Clearing the DTC

- The condition for the DTC is no longer present (the DTC is not current) and you used the scan tool Clear DTC function.
- The EBCM automatically clears the history DTC when a current DTC is not detected in 100 consecutive drive cycles.

Diagnostic Aids

The solenoid valve circuit and the solenoid coil are internal to the EBCM. No part of the solenoid circuit is diagnosable external to the EBCM. The DTC sets when there is a malfunction in the solenoid circuit internal to the EBCM only.

Test Description

The numbers below refer to step numbers on the Diagnostic Table.

2. This step determines if the DTC is current.

Step	Action	Yes	No
Schematic Reference: *ABS Schematics*			
1	Did you perform the Diagnostic System Check?	Go to*Step 2*	Go to *Diagnostic System Check - ABS*
2	1. Using a scan tool clear the DTC. 2. Remove the scan tool from the DLC. 3. Carefully drive the vehicle above 12 km/h (8 mph) for several minutes. 4. Turn the ignition switch to the OFF position. 5. Install a scan tool. 6. Turn the ignition switch to the ON position, engine off. 7. Using the scan tool in Diagnostic Trouble Codes, check for DTCs. Did any one of the DTCs C0060-C0095 reset as a current DTC?	Go to*Step 3*	*Intermittent and Poor Connections*
3	Replace the EBCM. Is the repair complete?	Go to*Step 4*	—
4	1. Use the scan tool in order to clear the DTCs. 2. Operate the vehicle within the Conditions for Running the DTC as specification in the supporting text. Does the DTC reset?	Go to*Step 2*	System OK

GC4020152488000X

Fig. 137 Codes C0060-C0095: ABS Solenoid Circuit Fault. 2001–04 Grand Prix & 2001–02 Intrigue

Circuit Description

The pump motor is an integral part of the BPMV, while the pump motor relay is integral to the EBCM. The pump motor relay is not engaged during normal system operation. When ABS or TCS operation is required the EBCM activates the pump motor relay and battery power is provided to the pump motor.

Conditions for Running the DTC

- The ignition switch is in the ON position.
- Initialization is complete.

Conditions for Setting the DTC

- Pump motor voltage is not present 60 milliseconds after activation of the pump motor relay.
- Pump motor voltage is present for more than 2.5 seconds with no activation of the pump motor relay.
- Pump motor voltage is not present for 40 milliseconds after the pump motor relay is commanded off.

Action Taken When the DTC Sets

If equiped, the following actions occur:

- The EBCM disables the ABS/TCS/VSES for the duration of the ignition cycle.
- A malfunction DTC will set.
- The ANTI-LOCK indicator turns ON.
- The TRAC Off indicator turns ON.
- The PCS indicator turns ON.
- The Red BRAKE Warning indicator could turn on.

Conditions for Clearing the DTC

- The condition for the DTC is no longer present (the DTC is not current) and you used the scan tool Clear DTC function.
- The EBCM automatically clears the history DTC when a current DTC is not detected in 100 consecutive drive cycles.

Diagnostic Aids

- It is very important that a thorough inspection of the wiring and connectors be performed. Failure to carefully and fully inspect wiring and connectors may result in misdiagnosis, causing part replacement with reappearance of the malfunction.
- Thoroughly inspect any circuitry that may be causing the complaint for the following conditions:
  - Backed out terminals
  - Improper mating
  - Broken locks
  - Improperly formed or damaged terminals
  - Poor terminal-to-wiring connections
  - Physical damage to the wiring harness
- The following conditions may cause an intermittent malfunction:
  - A poor connection
  - Rubbed-through wire insulation
  - A broken wire inside the insulation
- If an intermittent malfunction exists refer to Testing for Intermittent and Poor Connections

Test Description

The number below refers to the step number on the diagnostic table.

3. Tests the pump motor circuits of the BPMV for a short to the housing of the BPMV. The wiring from the BPMV to the EBCM should not be repaired.

GC4020152489010X

Fig. 138 Code C0110: Pump Motor Circuit Fault (Part 1 of 2). 2001–04 Grand Prix & 2001–02 Intrigue

Step	Action	Value(s)	Yes	No
Schematic Reference: *ABS Schematics*				
1	Did you perform the ABS Diagnostic System Check?	—	Go to *Step 2*	Go to *Diagnostic System Check - ABS*
2	1. Disconnect the EBCM harness connector 2. Connect the *J 39700* universal pinout box using the *J 39700-530* cable adapter to the EBCM harness connector only. 3. Test both ground circuits of the EBCM including the EBCM ground for a high resistance or an open. 4. Test the Battery Positive Voltage circuits for an open, high resistance, or a short to ground. Did you find and correct the condition?	—	Go to *Step 8*	Go to *Step 3*
3	1. Disconnect the pump motor harness pigtail connector of the BPMV. 2. Measure the resistance between each pump motor control circuit and the housing of the BPMV at the pump motor harness pigtail connector of the BPMV. Does the resistance measure less than the specified value?	5 Ω	Go to *Step 4*	Go to *Step 5*
4	Inspect for poor connections at the pump motor harness pigtail connector of the BPMV. Did you find and correct the condition?	—	Go to *Step 8*	Go to *Step 6*
5	Inspect for poor connections at the harness connector of the EBCM. Did you find and correct the condition?	—	Go to *Step 8*	Go to *Step 7*
6	Replace the BPMV. Did you complete the repair?	—	Go to *Step 8*	—
7	Replace the EBCM. Did you complete the repair?	—	Go to *Step 8*	—
8	1. Use the scan tool in order to clear the DTCs. 2. Operate the vehicle within the conditions for Running the DTC as specified in the supporting text Does the DTC reset?	—	Go to *Step 2*	System OK

GC4020152489020X

Fig. 138 Code C0110: Pump Motor Circuit Fault (Part 2 of 2). 2001–04 Grand Prix & 2001–02 Intrigue

Circuit Description

The solenoid valve relay supplies power to the solenoid valve coils in the EBCM. The solenoid valve relay, located in the EBCM, is activated whenever the ignition switch is in the RUN position and no faults are present. The solenoid valve relay remains engaged until the ignition is turned OFF or a failure is detected.

Conditions for Running the DTC

The ignition switch is in the ON position.

Conditions for Setting the DTC

- DTC C0121 will set anytime the solenoid valve relay is commanded on and the EBCM does not see battery voltage at the solenoid valves.
- DTC C0121 will set anytime the EBCM commands the solenoid valve relay off and battery voltage is still present at the solenoid valves.

Action Taken When the DTC Sets

If equiped, the following actions occur:

- The EBCM disables the ABS/TCS/VSES/DRP for the duration of the ignition cycle.
- A malfunction DTC is set.
- The ANTI-LOCK indicator turns ON.
- The TRAC Off indicator turns ON.
- The PCS indicator turns ON.
- The Red BRAKE Warning indicator could turn on.

Conditions for Clearing the DTC

- The condition for the DTC is no longer present (the DTC is not current) and you used the scan tool Clear DTC function.
- The EBCM automatically clears the history DTC when a current DTC is not detected in 100 consecutive drive cycles.

Diagnostic Aids

- It is very important that a thorough inspection of the wiring and connectors be performed. Failure to carefully and fully inspect wiring and connectors may result in misdiagnosis, causing part replacement with reappearance of the malfunction.
- Thoroughly inspect any circuitry that may be causing the complaint for the following conditions:
  - Backed out terminals
  - Improper mating
  - Broken locks
  - Improperly formed or damaged terminals
  - Poor terminal-to-wiring connections
  - Physical damage to the wiring harness
- The following conditions may cause an intermittent malfunction:
  - A poor connection
  - Rubbed-through wire insulation
  - A broken wire inside the insulation
- If an intermittent malfunction exists refer to Testing for Intermittent and Poor Connections
- The solenoid valve relay is an integral part of the EBCM and is not serviced separately.

Test Description

The number below refers to step number on the Diagnostic Table.

2. This step determines if the DTC is current.

DTC C0121

Step	Action	Value(s)	Yes	No
Schematic Reference: *ABS Schematics*				
1	Did you perform the Diagnostic System Check?	—	Go to *Step 2*	Go to *Diagnostic System Check - ABS*
2	1. Install a scan tool. 2. Turn ON the ignition, with the engine OFF. 3. Use the scan tool in order to clear the DTCs. Does the DTC reset?	—	Go to *Step 3*	Go to Diagnostic Aids
3	1. Connect the *J 39700* universal pinout box using the *J 39700-530* cable adapter to the EBCM harness connector only. 2. Test the battery positive voltage circuit for an open, high resistance, or a short to ground. Did you find and correct the condition?	—	Go to *Step 5*	Go to *Step 4*
4	Replace the Electronic Brake Control Module (EBCM). Did you complete the replacement?	—	Go to *Step 5*	—
5	1. Use the scan tool in order to clear the DTCs. 2. Operate the vehicle within the Conditions for Running the DTC as specified in the supporting text. Does the DTC reset?	—	Go to *Step 2*	System OK

GC4020152490000X

Fig. 139 Code C0121: Value Relay Circuit Fault. 2001–04 Grand Prix & 2001–02 Intrigue

Circuit Description

The EBCM uses input from the brake pressure sensor for more accurate control during a vehicle stability enhancement system (VSES) event.

Conditions for Running the DTC

- DTC C0870 is not set.
- The ignition is ON.
- The vehicle speed is greater than 40 km/h (24 mph).

Conditions for Setting the DTC

Voltage at the pressure sensor signal output to the EBCM falls outside the 0.25 V – 4.75 V range for more than 100 milliseconds.

Action Taken When the DTC Sets

If equiped, the following actions occur:

- The EBCM disables the ABS/TCS/VSES for the duration of the ignition cycle.
- A malfunction DTC will set.
- The ANTI-LOCK indicator turns ON.
- The TRAC Off indicator turns ON.
- The PCS indicator turns ON.
- The Red BRAKE Warning indicator could turn on.

Conditions for Clearing the DTC

- The condition for the DTC is no longer present
- A history DTC will clear after 100 consecutive ignition cycles if the condition for the malfunction is no longer present.
- Using a scan tool.

Diagnostic Aids

- A thorough inspection of the wiring system and connectors should be performed. Failure to carefully and fully inspect the wiring system and connectors may result in misdiagnosis which may result in replacing good parts and the reappearance of the malfunction.
- Inspection for poor connections, broken insulation, or a wire that is broken inside the insulation.
- If an intermittent malfunction exists refer to *Testing for Intermittent and Poor Connections*

Test Description

The number(s) below refer to the step number(s) on the diagnostic table.

2. Tests for specified voltage on the brake pressure signal circuit.
3. Checks to see if voltage was below specified voltage.
4. Checks to see if voltage was below specified voltage.
5. Checks to see if voltage was above specified voltage of 5 volt reference.
6. Tests for a short to ground in the 5 volt reference circuit.
7. Tests for a short to voltage in the 5 volt reference circuit.
8. Tests for a short to ground, a high resistance, or an open in the 5 volt reference circuit.
9. Tests for a short to voltage, a high resistance, or an open in the brake pressure sensor signal circuit.
10. Tests for a high resistance or an open in the ground circuit of the brake pressure sensor.
11. Checks the brake pressure sensor connector for poor connections.
12. Checks the EBCM connector for poor connections.

DTC C0131

Step	Action	Value(s)	Yes	No
Schematic Reference: *ABS Schematics*				
1	Did you perform the ABS Diagnostic System Check?	—	Go to *Step 2*	Go to *Diagnostic System Check - ABS*
2	1. Turn OFF the ignition. 2. Disconnect the EBCM. 3. Install the *J 39700* universal pinout box with the *J 39700-530* cable adapter between the EBCM and the EBCM harness connector. 4. Turn ON the ignition, with the engine OFF. 5. Using the DMM, measure the voltage between pin 17 and pin 15 of the *J 39700* universal pinout box. Is the voltage within the specified value?	0.25 V - 4.75 V	Go to Diagnostic Aids	Go to *Step 3*
3	1. Turn OFF the ignition. 2. Disconnect the brake pressure sensor. 3. Turn ON the ignition with the engine OFF. 4. Using the DMM, measure the voltage between pin 17 and pin 15 of the *J 39700* universal pinout box. Is the voltage greater than the specified value?	5 V	Go to *Step 4*	Go to *Step 8*

GC4020152491010X

Fig. 140 Code C0131: ABS/TCS System Pressure Circuit Fault (Part 1 of 2). 2001–02 Intrigue

Step	Action	Value(s)	Yes	No
4	1. Turn OFF the ignition. 2. Connect a 3 amp fused jumper wire between the signal circuit of the brake pressure sensor and the ground circuit of the brake pressure sensor. 3. Turn ON the ignition, with the engine OFF. 4. Using the DMM, measure the voltage between pin 17 and pin 15 of the *J 39700* universal pinout box. Is the voltage less than the specified value?	0.25 V	Go to *Step 5*	Go to *Step 9*
5	1. Turn OFF the ignition. 2. Disconnect the fused jumper wire. 3. Connect a 3 amp fused jumper wire between the 5 volt reference circuit of the brake pressure sensor and the signal circuit of the brake pressure sensor. 4. Measure the voltage between the 5 volt reference circuit of the brake pressure sensor and the signal circuit of the brake pressure sensor. Is the voltage measured greater than the specified value?	5 V	Go to *Step 7*	Go to *Step 6*
6	Test the 5 volt reference circuit of the brake pressure sensor for a short to ground. Did you find and correct the condition?	—	Go to *Step 15*	Go to *Step 12*
7	Test the 5 volt reference circuit of the brake pressure sensor for a short to voltage. Did you find and correct the condition?	—	Go to *Step 15*	Go to *Step 11*
8	Test the signal circuit of the brake pressure sensor for a short to ground, a high resistance, or an open. Did you find and correct the condition?	—	Go to *Step 15*	Go to *Step 12*
9	Test the signal circuit of the brake pressure sensor for a short to voltage, a high resistance, or an open. Did you find and correct the condition?	—	Go to *Step 15*	Go to *Step 10*
10	Test the ground circuit of the brake pressure sensor for a high resistance or an open. Did you find and correct the condition?	—	Go to *Step 15*	Go to *Step 12*
11	Inspect for poor connections at the harness connector of the brake pressure sensor. Did you find and correct the condition?	—	Go to *Step 15*	Go to *Step 13*
12	Inspect for poor connections at the harness connector of the EBCM. Did you find and correct the condition?	—	Go to *Step 15*	Go to *Step 14*
13	Replace the brake pressure sensor. Did you complete the replacement?	—	Go to *Step 15*	—
14	Replace the EBCM. Did you complete the replacement?	—	Go to *Step 15*	—
15	1. Use the scan tool in order to clear the DTCs. 2. Operate the vehicle within the Conditions for Running the DTC as specified in the supporting text. Does the DTC reset?	—	Go to *Step 2*	System OK

GC4020152491020X

Fig. 140 Code C0131: ABS/TCS System Pressure Circuit Fault (Part 2 of 2). 2001–02 Intrigue

Step	Action	Value(s)	Yes	No
Schematic Reference: *ABS Schematics*				
1	Did you perform the ABS Diagnostic System Check?	—	Go to *Step 2*	Go to *Diagnostic System Check - ABS*
2	1. Turn OFF the ignition. 2. Disconnect the EBCM. 3. Install the *J 39700* universal pinout box with the *J 39700-530* cable adapter between the EBCM and the EBCM harness connector. 4. Turn ON the ignition, with the engine OFF. 5. Using the DMM, measure the voltage between pin 17 and pin 15 of the *J 39700* universal pinout box. Is the voltage within the specified value?	0.25 V - 4.75 V	Go to Diagnostic Aids	Go to *Step 3*
3	1. Turn OFF the ignition. 2. Disconnect the brake pressure sensor. 3. Turn ON the ignition with the engine OFF. 4. Using the DMM, measure the voltage between pin 17 and pin 15 of the *J 39700* universal pinout box. Is the voltage less than the specified value?	4.75 V	Go to *Step 4*	Go to *Step 10*
4	1. Turn OFF the ignition. 2. Connect a 3 amp fused jumper wire between the 5 volt reference circuit of the brake pressure sensor and the signal circuit of the brake pressure sensor. 3. Turn ON the ignition, with the engine OFF. 4. Using the DMM, measure the voltage between pin 17 and pin 15 of the *J 39700* universal pinout box. Is the voltage greater than the specified value?	0.25 V	Go to *Step 5*	Go to *Step 8*
5	1. Disconnect the fused jumper wire. 2. Measure the voltage between the 5 volt reference circuit of the brake pressure sensor and the ground circuit of the brake pressure sensor. Does the voltage measure less than the specified value?	5 V	Go to *Step 6*	Go to *Step 7*
6	1. Turn OFF the ignition. 2. Disconnect the negative battery cable. 3. Measure the resistance from the ground circuit of the brake pressure sensor to a good ground. Does the resistance measure less than the specified value?	5 Ω	Go to *Step 12*	Go to *Step 11*
7	Test the 5 volt reference circuit of the brake pressure sensor for a short to voltage. Did you find and correct the condition?	—	Go to *Step 16*	Go to *Step 13*
8	Test the 5 volt reference circuit of the brake pressure sensor for a short to ground, a high resistance, or an open. Did you find and correct the condition?	—	Go to *Step 16*	Go to *Step 9*

GC4020152492020X

Fig. 141 Code C0132: ABS/TCS System Pressure Circuit Range/Performance (Part 2 of 3). 2001–02 Intrigue

Circuit Description

During calibration of the offset of the pressure sensor signal, the pressure sensor signal offset value must be in the range of +/- 217.5 psi (15 Bar).

The pressure sensor is also monitored for sensitivity via a correlation between estimated vehicle deceleration and the pressure sensor signal. This is monitored over the course of numerous straight line non ABS braking stops.

Conditions for Running the DTC

- The ignition is ON.
- The vehicle speed is greater than 40 km/h (25 mph).

Conditions for Setting the DTC

- The sensor signal offset value is out of range for more than 1 second.
- The brake pedal is applied.
- The ABS pump is not on.
- The pressure sensor sensitivity is outside a predetermined range.

Action Taken When the DTC Sets

If equiped, the following actions occur:

- The EBCM disables the ABS/TCS/VSES for the duration of the ignition cycle.
- A malfunction DTC will set.
- The ANTI-LOCK indicator turns ON.
- The TRAC Off indicator turns ON.
- The PCS indicator turns ON.
- The Red BRAKE Warning indicator could turn on.

Conditions for Clearing the DTC

- The condition for the DTC is no longer present.
- A history DTC will clear after 100 consecutive ignition cycles if the condition for the malfunction is no longer present.
- Using a scan tool.

Diagnostic Aids

- A malfunctioning pressure sensor.
- A malfunctioning EBCM.

Test Description

The number(s) below refer to the step number(s) on the diagnostic table.

2. Tests for specified voltage on the brake pressure signal circuit.
3. Checks to see if voltage was below specified voltage.
4. Checks to see if voltage was above specified voltage.
5. Checks to see if voltage was above specified voltage of 5 volt reference.
6. Checks to see if 5 volt reference from EBCM is 5 volts.
7. Checks to see if resistance of ground circuit is less than 5 ohms.
8. Tests for short to voltage in the 5 volt reference circuit.
9. Tests for a short to ground, a high resistance or an open in the 5 volt reference circuit.
10. Tests for a short to voltage in the brake pressure sensor signal circuit.
11. Tests for a high resistance or an open in the ground circuit.
12. Checks to brake pressure sensor connector for poor connections.
13. Checks to EBCM connector for poor connections.

GC4020152492010X

Fig. 141 Code C0132: ABS/TCS System Pressure Circuit Range/Performance (Part 1 of 3). 2001–02 Intrigue

Step	Action	Value(s)	Yes	No
9	Test the signal circuit of the brake pressure sensor for a short to ground, a high resistance, or an open. Did you find and correct the condition?	—	Go to *Step 16*	Go to *Step 13*
10	Test the signal circuit of the brake pressure sensor for a short to voltage. Did you find and correct the condition?	—	Go to *Step 16*	Go to *Step 13*
11	1. Disconnect the EBCM. 2. Test the ground circuit of the brake pressure sensor for a high resistance or an open. Did you find and correct the condition?	—	Go to *Step 16*	Go to *Step 13*
12	Inspect for poor connections at the harness connector of the brake pressure sensor. Did you find and correct the condition?	—	Go to *Step 16*	Go to *Step 14*
13	Inspect for poor connections at the harness connector of the EBCM. Did you find and correct the condition?	—	Go to *Step 16*	Go to *Step 15*
14	Replace the brake pressure sensor Did you complete the replacement?	—	Go to *Step 16*	—
15	Replace the EBCM. Did you complete the replacement?	—	Go to *Step 16*	—
16	1. Use the scan tool in order to clear the DTCs. 2. Operate the vehicle within the Conditions for Running the DTC as specified in the supporting text. Does the DTC reset?	—	Go to *Step 2*	System OK

GC4020152492030X

Fig. 141 Code C0132: ABS/TCS System Pressure Circuit Range/Performance (Part 3 of 3). 2001–02 Intrigue

Circuit Description

The isolation and prime valve solenoid circuits are supplied with battery power when the ignition is in the ON position. The EBCM controls the valve functions by grounding the circuit when necessary.

Conditions for Running the DTC

- The ignition switch is in the ON position.
- The DTC can be set after system initialization.

Conditions for Setting the DTC

The DTC will set when the EBCM detects one of the following internal to the EBCM only:

- An open in the solenoid coil or circuit.
- A short to ground in the solenoid coil or circuit.
- A short to voltage in the solenoid coil or circuit.

Action Taken When the DTC Sets

If equiped, the following actions occur:

- The EBCM disables the ABS/TCS/VSES/DRP for the duration of the ignition cycle.
- A malfunction DTC is set.
- The ANTI-LOCK indicator turns ON.
- The TRAC Off indicator turns ON.
- The PCS indicator turns ON.
- The Red BRAKE Warning indicator could turn on.

Conditions for Clearing the DTC

- Condition for DTC is no longer present and scan tool clear DTC function is used.
- 100 ignition cycles pass with no DTC(s) detected.

Diagnostic Aids

The solenoid valve circuit and the solenoid coil are internal to the EBCM. No part of the solenoid circuit is diagnosable external to the EBCM. The DTC sets when there is a malfunction in the solenoid circuit internal to the EBCM only.

Test Description

The numbers below refer to step numbers on the Diagnostic Table.

2. This step determines if the DTC is current.

DTC C0141-C0156

Step	Action	Yes	No
Schematic Reference: *ABS Schematics*			
1	Did you perform the Diagnostic System Check?	Go to *Step 2*	Go to *Diagnostic System Check - ABS*
2	1. Using a scan tool clear the DTC. 2. Remove the scan tool from the DLC. 3. Carefully drive the vehicle above 12 km/h (8 mph) for several minutes. 4. Turn the ignition switch to the OFF position. 5. Install a scan tool. 6. Turn the ignition switch to the ON position, engine off. 7. Using the scan tool in Diagnostic Trouble Codes, check for DTCs. Did any one of the DTCs C0141-C0151 reset as a current DTC?	Go to *Step 3*	Go to Diagnostic Aids
3	Replace the EBCM. Is the repair complete?	Go to *Step 4*	—
4	1. Use the scan tool in order to clear the DTCs. 2. Operate the vehicle within the Conditions for Running the DTC as specified in the supporting text. Does the DTC reset?	Go to *Step 2*	System OK

GC4020152493000X

Fig. 142 Codes C0141-C0156: TCS Solenoid Circuit Fault. 2001–04 Grand Prix & 2001–02 Intrigue

Step	Action	Yes	No
Schematic Reference: *ABS Schematics*			
1	Did you perform the ABS Diagnostic System Check?	Go to *Step 2*	Go to *Diagnostic System Check - ABS*
2	1. Press the brake pedal. 2. With the scan tool, observe the Brake Switch Status parameter in the ABS data list. Does the Brake Switch Status parameter display Applied?	Go to *Step 4*	Go to *Step 3*
3	Test the signal circuit of the stoplamp switch for an open. Did you find and correct the condition?	Go to *Step 15*	Go to *Step 11*
4	Press the brake pedal. Are all of the stoplamps OFF?	Go to *Step 5*	Go to *Step 7*
5	Test the feed circuit of the stoplamps for an open or high resistance. Did you find and correct the condition?	Go to *Step 15*	Go to *Step 6*
6	Test the ground circuit of the stoplamps for an open or high resistance. Did you find and correct the condition?	Go to *Step 15*	Go to Diagnostic Aids
7	1. Press the brake pedal. 2. With a scan tool, observe the Brake Switch Status parameter. Does the Brake Switch Status parameter change state?	Go to Diagnostic Aids	Go to *Step 8*
8	1. Turn OFF the ignition. 2. Inspect the stoplamp switch and adjust and/or calibrate if needed. Did you find and correct the condition?	Go to *Step 15*	Go to *Step 9*
9	1. Turn OFF the ignition switch. 2. Disconnect the stoplamp switch connector. 3. Turn ON the ignition, with the engine OFF. 4. With a scan tool, observe the Brake Switch Status parameter. Does the scan tool display Released?	Go to *Step 11*	Go to *Step 10*
10	Test the stoplamp signal circuit for a short to voltage. Did you find and correct the condition?	Go to *Step 15*	Go to *Step 12*
11	Inspect for poor connections at the harness connector of the stoplamp switch. Did you find and correct the condition?	Go to *Step 15*	Go to *Step 13*
12	Inspect for poor connections at the harness connector of the EBCM. Did you find and correct the condition?	Go to *Step 15*	Go to *Step 14*
13	Replace the stoplamp switch. Did you complete the repair?	Go to *Step 15*	—
14	Replace the EBCM. Did you complete the replacement?	Go to *Step 15*	—
15	1. Use the scan tool in order to clear the DTCs. 2. Operate the vehicle within the Conditions for Running the DTC as specified in the supporting text. Does the DTC reset?	Go to *Step 2*	System OK

GC4020152494020X

Fig. 143 Code C0161: ABS/TCS Brake Switch Circuit Fault (Part 2 of 2). 2001–04 Grand Prix & 2001–02 Intrigue

Circuit Description

The Stoplamp Switch is a normally open switch, when the brake pedal is depressed the EBCM will sense battery voltage. This allows the EBCM to determine the state of the brake lamps.

Conditions for Running the DTC

- The ignition switch is ON.
- The DTC can be set after system initialization.

Conditions for Setting the DTC

- EBCM detects battery voltage at all times.
- EBCM never detects battery voltage from CKT 17.
- Both brake lamps are faulty.

Action Taken When the DTC Sets

If equiped, the following actions occur:

- The EBCM disables the ABS/TCS/VSES for the duration of the ignition cycle.
- A malfunction DTC will set.
- The ANTI-LOCK indicator turns ON.
- The TRAC Off indicator turns ON.
- The PCS indicator turns ON.
- The Red BRAKE Warning indicator could turn on.

Conditions for Clearing the DTC

- The condition for the DTC is no longer present (the DTC is not current) and you used the scan tool Clear DTC function.
- The EBCM automatically clears the history DTC when a current DTC is not detected in 100 consecutive drive cycles.

Diagnostic Aids

- It is very important that a thorough inspection of the wiring and connectors be performed. Failure to carefully and fully inspect wiring and connectors may result in misdiagnosis, causing part replacement with reappearance of the malfunction.
- Thoroughly inspect any circuitry that may be causing the complaint for the following conditions:
  - Backed out terminals
  - Improper mating
  - Broken locks
  - Improperly formed or damaged terminals
  - Poor terminal-to-wiring connections
  - Physical damage to the wiring harness
- The following conditions may cause an intermittent malfunction:
  - A poor connection
  - Rubbed-through wire insulation
  - A broken wire inside the insulation

Test Description

The numbers below refer to the step numbers on the diagnostic table.

3. This DTC detects an open stoplamp switch signal circuit from the stoplamp side of the splice to the EBCM.
4. The EBCM sources 5 volts on the stoplamp switch signal circuit. This small voltage has a ground path through the stoplamp bulbs. This DTC sets if the path to ground is open.
7. With the scan tool, Test for the current state of the brake lamp switch parameter.
10. Test the stoplamp signal circuit for a short to voltage.

GC4020152494010X

Fig. 143 Code C0161: ABS/TCS Brake Switch Circuit Fault (Part 1 of 2). 2001–04 Grand Prix & 2001–02 Intrigue

Circuit Description

The vehicle stability enhancement system (VSES) uses the lateral accelerometer input when calculating the desired yaw rate. The usable output voltage range for the lateral accelerometer is 0.25–4.75 volts.

The lateral accelerometer sensor bias compensates for sensor mounting alignment errors and electronic signal errors.

Conditions for Running the DTC

- The ignition is ON.
- The vehicle speed is greater than 40 km/h (25 mph).

Conditions for Setting the DTC

Voltage at the lateral accelerometer signal output to the EBCM falls outside the 0.25 V – 4.75 V range for more than 100 milliseconds.

Action Taken When the DTC Sets

If equiped, the following actions occur:

- The EBCM disables the TCS/VSES for the duration of the ignition cycle.
- A malfunction DTC is set.
- The ANTI-LOCK indicator turns ON.
- The TRAC Off indicator turns ON.
- The PCS indicator turns ON.

Conditions for Clearing the DTC

- The condition for the DTC is no longer present
- A history DTC will clear after 100 consecutive ignition cycles if the condition for the malfunction is no longer present.
- Using a scan tool.

Diagnostic Aids

- A thorough inspection of the wiring system and connectors be performed. Failure to carefully and fully inspect the wiring system and connectors may result in misdiagnosis which may result in replacing good parts and the reappearance of the malfunction.
- Inspection for poor connections, broken insulation, or a wire that is broken inside the insulation.
- If an intermittent malfunction exists refer to *Testing for Intermittent and Poor Connections*

Test Description

The number(s) below refer to the step number(s) on the diagnostic table.

2. Tests for specified voltage on the lateral accelerometer signal circuit.
3. Tests for B+ voltage on yaw/lateral accelerometer sensor.
4. Tests the ignition circuit for a high resistance or open.
5. Checks to see if voltage was below or above specified voltage.
6. Checks to see if voltage was above specified voltage.
7. Checks to see if voltage was below specified voltage.
8. Checks to see if voltage was above specified voltage.
9. Checks to see if resistance of ground circuit is less than 5 ohms.
10. Tests for a short to voltage on the 5 volt reference circuit.
11. Tests for a short to ground, a high resistance, or an open in the 5 volt reference circuit.
12. Tests for a short to ground, a high resistance, or an open in the lateral accelerometer signal circuit.
13. Tests for a short to voltage in the lateral accelerometer signal circuit.
14. Tests for a high resistance or an open in the ground circuit.
15. Checks the yaw/lateral accelerometer sensor connector for poor connections.
16. Checks the EBCM connector for poor connections.

GC4020152495010X

Fig. 144 Code C0186: Lateral Accelerometer Circuit Fault (Part 1 of 3). 2001–02 Intrigue

Step	Action	Value(s)	Yes	No
Schematic Refererence: *ABS Schematics*				
1	Did you perform the ABS Diagnostic System Check?	—	Go to *Step 2*	Go to *Diagnostic System Check - ABS*
2	1. Turn OFF the ignition. 2. Disconnect the EBCM. 3. Install the *J 39700* universal pinout box with the *J 39700-530* cable adapter between the EBCM and the EBCM harness connector. 4. Turn ON the ignition, with the engine OFF. 5. Using the DMM, measure the voltage between pin 10 and pin 15 of the *J 39700* universal pinout box. Is the voltage within the specified value?	0.25 V – 4.75 V	Go to Diagnostic Aids	Go to *Step 3*
3	1. Turn OFF the ignition. 2. Disconnect the yaw/lateral accelerometer sensor. 3. Turn ON the ignition, with the engine OFF. 4. Using a DMM, measure the voltage between the ignition and ground circuits of the yaw/lateral accelerometer sensor. Is the voltage in the specified value?	B+	Go to *Step 5*	Go to *Step 4*
4	Test the ignition circuit of the yaw/lateral accelerometer sensor for high resistance or an open. Did you find and correct the condition?	—	Go to *Step 19*	*Diagnose* Wiring Systems
5	1. Reconnect the yaw/lateral accelerometer sensor. 2. Using a DMM, measure the voltage between pin 10 and pin 15 of the *J 39700* universal pinout box. Is the voltage less than the specified value?	4.75 V	Go to *Step 6*	Go to *Step 13*
6	Using a DMM, measure the voltage between pin 10 and pin 15 of the *J 39700* universal pinout box. Is the voltage greater than the specified value?	0.25 V	Go to *Step 7*	Go to *Step 12*
7	Using a DMM, measure the voltage between the 5 volt reference circuit pin 16 and the ground circuit pin 15 on the *J 39700* universal pinout box. Does the voltage measure less than the specified value?	2 V	Go to *Step 11*	Go to *Step 8*
8	Using a DMM, measure the voltage between the 5 volt reference circuit pin 16 and ground circuit pin 15 on the *J 39700* universal pinout box. Does the voltage measure greater than the specified voltage?	3 V	Go to *Step 10*	Go to *Step 9*
9	1. Turn OFF the ignition. 2. Disconnect the negative battery cable. 3. Measure the resistance from the ground circuit of the yaw/lateral accelerometer to a good ground. Does the resistance measure less than the specified value?	5 Ω	Go to *Step 16*	Go to *Step 14*
10	Test the 5 volt reference circuit of the yaw/lateral accelerometer sensor for a short to voltage. Did you find and correct the condition?	—	Go to *Step 19*	Go to *Step 15*

GC4020152495020X

Fig. 144 Code C0186: Lateral Accelerometer Circuit Fault (Part 2 of 3). 2001–02 Intrigue

Step	Action	Value(s)	Yes	No
11	Test the 5 volt reference circuit of the yaw/lateral accelerometer sensor for a short to ground, a high resistance, or an open. Did you find and correct the condition?	—	Go to *Step 19*	Go to *Step 12*
12	Test the lateral accelerometer signal circuit of the yaw/lateral accelerometer sensor for a short to ground, a high resistance, or an open. Did you find and correct the condition?	—	Go to *Step 19*	Go to *Step 15*
13	Test the lateral accelerometer signal circuit of the yaw/lateral accelerometer sensor for a short to voltage. Did you find and correct the condition?	—	Go to *Step 19*	Go to *Step 15*
14	1. Disconnect the EBCM. 2. Test the ground circuit of the yaw/lateral accelerometer sensor for a high resistance or an open. Did you find and correct the condition?	—	Go to *Step 19*	Go to *Step 15*
15	Inspect for poor connections at the harness connector of the yaw/lateral accelerometer sensor. Did you find and correct the condition?	—	Go to *Step 19*	Go to *Step 17*
16	Inspect for poor connections at the harness connector of the EBCM. Did you find and correct the condition?	—	Go to *Step 19*	Go to *Step 18*
17	Replace the vehicle yaw/lateral accelerometer sensor. Did you complete the replacement?	—	Go to *Step 19*	—
18	Replace the EBCM. Did you complete the replacement?	—	Go to *Step 19*	—
19	1. Use the scan tool in order to clear the DTCs. 2. Operate the vehicle within the Conditions for Running the DTC as specified in the supporting text. Does the DTC reset?	—	Go to *Step 2*	System OK

GC4020152495030X

Fig. 144 Code C0186: Lateral Accelerometer Circuit Fault (Part 3 of 3). 2001–02 Intrigue

Circuit Description

The vehicle stability enhancement system (VSES) uses the lateral accelerometer input when calculating the desired yaw rate. The usable output voltage range for the lateral accelerometer 0.25 – 4.75 volts. The scan tool will report zero lateral acceleration as 2.5 volts with no sensor bias present.

The lateral accelerometer sensor bias compensates for sensor mounting alignment errors and electronic signal errors.

Conditions for Running the DTC

- The ignition is ON.
- The vehicle speed is greater than 40 km/h (25 mph).

Conditions for Setting the DTC

- A reference lateral acceleration from the data of the yaw rate sensor, wheel speed sensors, and steering angle sensor is used to test the lateral accelerometer signal. If during stable driving conditions, the lateral accelerometer signal becomes larger than 0.26 g, the EBCM controller will disregard the signal so that a false EBCM intervention is prevented. A malfunction is detected if this condition continues for more than two seconds.
- Under normal driving conditions, the long time filtered driving direction is straight ahead. The long time filtered lateral accelerometer value is called the offset. If the offset value is higher than 0.23 g, a malfunction is detected. Malfunction time depends on driving distance, vehicle speed and the amount of malfunctioning later accelerometer signal.
- The lateral accelerometer signal is limited to an electrical stop of 1.8 g. If the lateral accelerometer signal is greater than 1.5 g for more than 500 milliseconds, a malfunction is detected.
- At a standstill, the range of the lateral accelerometer signal is less than 0.7 g. If the lateral accelerometer signal is greater than 0.7 g at standstill, a malfunction is detected.
- Lateral accelerometer signal cannot change rapidly under normal driving conditions. If the lateral accelerometer signal is changing faster than 55 g per second, a malfunction is detected.

Action Taken When the DTC Sets

If equiped, the following actions occur:

- The EBCM disables the TCS/VSES for the duration of the ignition cycle.
- A malfunction DTC will set.
- The ANTI-LOCK indicator turns ON.
- The TRAC Off indicator turns ON.
- The PCS indicator turns ON.

Conditions for Clearing the DTC

- The condition for the DTC is no longer present
- A history DTC will clear after 100 consecutive ignition cycles if the condition for the malfunction is no longer present.
- Using a scan tool.

Diagnostic Aids

- Find out from the customer under what condition was the DTC set. This information will help to duplicate the failure.
- Check the vehicle for proper alignment. The car should not pull in either direction while driving straight on a level surface.
- During diagnosis, park the vehicle on a level surface.
- Check for malfunctioning EBCM and lateral accelerometer.
- The snapshot function on the scan tool can help find an intermittent DTC.

Test Description

The number(s) below refer to the step number(s) on the diagnostic table.

2. Checks to see if steering angle sensor is centered.
3. Checks for specified voltage on the lateral accelerometer signal circuit.
4. Checks for specified voltage on the yaw rate signal circuit.

GC4020152496010X

Fig. 145 Code C0187: Lateral Accelerometer Circuit Range/Performance (Part 1 of 2). 2001–02 Intrigue

Step	Action	Value(s)	Yes	No
Schematic Reference: *ABS Schematics*				
1	Did you perform the ABS Diagnostic System Check?	—	Go to *Step 2*	Go to *Diagnostic System Check - ABS*
2	Perform the steering angle sensor centering procedure. Did you successfully complete the centering procedure?	—	Go to *Step 3*	Go to *Step 7*
3	1. Turn OFF the ignition. 2. Disconnect the EBCM connector. 3. Install the *J 39700* universal pinout box with the *J 39700-530* cable adapter between the EBCM and the EBCM harness connector. 4. Turn the ignition ON, with the engine OFF. 5. Using the DMM, measure the voltage between pin 10 and pin 15 of the *J 39700* universal pinout box. Is the voltage within the specified value?	2.3 – 2.7 V	Go to *Step 4*	Go to *Step 8*
4	Using the DMM, measure the voltage between pin 26 and pin 15 of the *J 39700* universal pinout box. Is the voltage within the specified value?	2.3 – 2.7 V	Go to *Step 5*	Go to *Step 8*
5	1. Use the scan tool in order to clear the DTCs. 2. Perform the Diagnostic Test Drive. Does the DTC reset?	—	Go to *Step 6*	Go to Diagnostic Aids
6	Replace the EBCM. Did you complete the replacement?	—	Go to *Step 9*	—
7	Replace the steering angle sensor. Did you complete the replacement?	—	Go to *Step 9*	–
8	Replace the vehicle yaw/lateral accelerometer sensor. Did you complete the repair?	—	Go to *Step 9*	–
9	1. Use the scan tool in order to clear the DTCs. 2. Operate the vehicle within the Conditions for Running the DTC as specified in the supporting text. Does the DTC reset?	—	Go to *Step 2*	System OK

GC4020152496020X

Fig. 145 Code C0187: Lateral Accelerometer Circuit Range/Performance (Part 2 of 2). 2001–02 Intrigue

Circuit Description

The vehicle stability enhancement system (VSES) is activated by the EBCM calculating the desired yaw rate and comparing it to the actual yaw rate input. The desired yaw rate is calculated from measured steering wheel position, vehicle speed, and lateral acceleration. The difference between the desired yaw rate and actual yaw rate is the yaw rate error, which is a measurement of oversteer or understeer. If the yaw rate error becomes too large, the EBCM will attempt to correct the vehicle's yaw motion by applying differential braking to the wheels.

To correct for oversteer, differential braking is used on the left front or right front wheel brake. To correct for understeer, differential braking is used on the left rear or right rear wheel brake.

Conditions for Running the DTC

- The ignition is ON.
- The vehicle speed is greater than 40 km/h (25 mph).

Conditions for Setting the DTC

The EBCM performs different tests to detect a DTC condition. A malfunction is detected when the yaw rate sensor signal input voltage is less than 0.225 volts or greater than 4.775 volts for more than 100 milliseconds.

Action Taken When the DTC Sets

If equiped, the following actions occur:

- The EBCM disables theTCS/VSES for the duration of the ignition cycle.
- A malfunction DTC is set.
- The ANTI-LOCK indicator turns ON.
- The TRAC Off indicator turns ON.
- The PCS indicator turns ON.

Conditions for Clearing the DTC

- Using a scan tool.
- The DTC will clear after 100 consecutive ignition cycles if the condition for the malfunction is no longer present.

Diagnostic Aids

The following conditions may cause a malfunction:

- Open in the yaw rate signal circuit
- Short to ground in the yaw rate signal circuit
- Short to voltage in the yaw rate signal circuit
- Open in the yaw rate ground circuit
- Open in ignition voltage circuit
- Malfunctioning vehicle yaw/lateral accelerometer sensor
- Malfunctioning EBCM

Test Description

The number(s) below refer to the step number(s) on the diagnostic table.

2. Tests for specified voltage on the yaw rate signal circuit.
3. Checks the voltage between the ignition and ground circuit for a specified value.
4. Checks the voltage between the ignition and ground circuit for a specified value.
5. Checks to see if voltage was above specified voltage.
6. Checks to see if voltage was below specified voltage.
7. Checks to see if EBCM 5 volt reference signal is within specified limit.
8. Checks to see if voltage was above specified voltage.
9. Checks to see if resistance of ground circuit is less than 5 ohms.
10. Tests for a short to voltage on the 5 volt reference circuit.
11. Tests for a short to ground, a high resistance, or an open in the 5 volt reference circuit.
12. Tests for a short to voltage in the yaw rate signal circuit.
13. Tests for a short to ground, a high resistance, or an open in the yaw rate signal circuit.
14. Tests for a high resistance or an open in the ground circuit.
15. Checks the EBCM connector for poor connections.
16. Checks the yaw/lateral accelerometer sensor connector for poor connections.

GC4020152497010X

Fig. 146 Code C0196: Yaw Rate Circuit Fault (Part 1 of 3). 2001–02 Intrigue

Step	Action	Value(s)	Yes	No
Schematic Reference: *ABS Schematics*				
1	Did you perform the ABS Diagnostic System Check?	—	Go to *Step 2*	Go to *Diagnostic System Check - ABS*
2	1. Turn OFF the ignition. 2. Disconnect the EBCM. 3. Install the *J 39700* universal pinout box with the *J 39700-530* cable adapter between the EBCM and the EBCM harness connector. 4. Turn ON the ignition, with the engine OFF. 5. Using the DMM, measure the voltage between pin 26 and pin 15 of the *J 39700* universal pinout box. Is the voltage within the specified value?	0.225 V - 4.775 V	Go to Diagnostic Aids	Go to *Step 3*
3	1. Turn OFF the ignition. 2. Disconnect the yaw/lateral accelerometer sensor. 3. Turn ON the ignition, with the engine OFF. 4. Using the DMM, measure the voltage between the ignition and ground circuits of the yaw/lateral accelerometer sensor. Is the voltage in the specified value?	B+	Go to *Step 5*	Go to *Step 4*
4	Test the ignition circuit of the yaw/lateral accelerometer sensor for high resistance or an open. Did you find and correct the condition?	—	Go to *Step 18*	Go to *Power Distribution Schematics* in Wiring Systems
5	1. Reconnect the yaw/lateral accelerometer sensor. 2. Using the DMM, measure the voltage between pin 26 and pin 15 of the *J 39700* universal pinout box. Is the voltage less than the specified value?	4.775 V	Go to *Step 6*	Go to *Step 13*
6	Using the DMM, measure the voltage between pin 26 and pin 15 of the *J 39700* universal pinout box. Is the voltage greater than the specified value?	0.225 V	Go to *Step 7*	Go to *Step 12*
7	Using a DMM, measure the voltage between the 5 volt reference circuit pin 16 and the ground circuit pin 15 of the *J 39700* universal pinout box. Does the voltage measure below the specified value?	2 V	Go to *Step 11*	Go to *Step 8*
8	Using a DMM, measure the voltage between the 5 volt reference circuit pin 16 and ground pin 15 of the *J 39700* universal pinout box. Does the voltage measure above the specified value?	3 V	Go to *Step 10*	Go to *Step 9*
9	1. Turn OFF the engine. 2. Disconnect the negative battery cable. 3. Measure the resistance from the ground circuit of the yaw/lateral accelerometer sensor to a good ground. Does the resistance measure less than the specified value?	5 Ω	Go to *Step 16*	Go to *Step 14*
10	Test the 5 volt reference circuit of the yaw/lateral accelerometer sensor for a short to voltage. Did you find and correct the condition?	—	Go to *Step 19*	Go to *Step 15*

GC4020152497020X

Fig. 146 Code C0196: Yaw Rate Circuit Fault (Part 2 of 3). 2001–02 Intrigue

Step	Action	Value(s)	Yes	No
11	Test the 5 volt reference circuit of the yaw/lateral accelerometer sensor for a short to ground, a high resistance, or an open. Did you find and correct the condition?	—	Go to *Step 19*	Go to *Step 12*
12	Test the yaw rate signal circuit of the yaw/lateral accelerometer sensor for a short to ground, a high resistance, or an open. Did you find and correct the condition?	—	Go to *Step 19*	Go to *Step 15*
13	Test the yaw rate signal circuit of the yaw/lateral accelerometer sensor for a short to voltage. Did you find and correct the condition?	—	Go to *Step 19*	Go to *Step 15*
14	1. Disconnect the EBCM. 2. Test the ground circuit of the yaw/lateral accelerometer sensor for a high resistance or an open. Did you find and correct the condition?	—	Go to *Step 19*	Go to *Step 15*
15	Inspect for poor connections at the harness connector of the yaw/lateral accelerometer sensor. Did you find and correct the condition?	—	Go to *Step 19*	Go to *Step 17*
16	Inspect for poor connections at the harness connector of the EBCM. Did you find and correct the condition?	—	Go to *Step 19*	Go to *Step 18*
17	Replace the vehicle yaw/lateral accelerometer sensor. Did you complete the replacement?	—	Go to *Step 19*	—
18	Replace the EBCM. Did you complete the replacement?	—	Go to *Step 19*	—
19	1. Use the scan tool in order to clear the DTCs. 2. Operate the vehicle within the Conditions for Running the DTC as specified in the supporting text. Does the DTC reset?	—	Go to *Step 2*	System OK

GC4020152497030X

Fig. 146 Code C0196: Yaw Rate Circuit Fault (Part 3 of 3). 2001–02 Intrigue

Circuit Description

The EBCM triggers a yaw rate sensor test every 40 milliseconds and switches the sensor into test mode. The EBCM sends a test signal to the sensor via the test circuit. When the test is run, the measured yaw rate from the sensor to the EBCM must be in the range of 25 degrees per second +/- 7 degrees per second. At standstill, the vehicle yaw rate is zero. The yaw rate signal at standstill is called the offset. If calibration at standstill is not possible, a quick calibration during driving is done. The measured yaw rate is calibrated to a calculated reference yaw rate signal. Yaw rate sensor sensitivity is estimated by comparison of the reference yaw rate and the measured yaw rate during cornering.

Steering angle centering is the process by which the EBCM calibrates the steering sensor output so that the output reads zero when the steering wheel is centered. The PCS steering angle sensor centering process is performed manually.

Conditions for Running the DTC

- The ignition is ON.
- The vehicle speed is greater than 40 km/h (25 mph).

Conditions for Setting the DTC

A malfunction is detected if one or more of the following conditions exist:

- The yaw rate sensor signal is out of range for 220–420 milliseconds.
- The yaw rate sensor signal at standstill which is called the offset is outside the allowed range of +/- 8 degrees per second.
- The sensor sensitivity which is estimated by comparing the reference yaw rate and the measured yaw rate during cornering, is outside a predetermined range.
- The yaw rate is changing at a rate greater than 6–23 degrees per second per 40 milliseconds.

Action Taken When the DTC Sets

If equiped, the following actions occur:

- The EBCM disables the TCS/VSES for the duration of the ignition cycle.
- A malfunction DTC is set.
- The ANTI-LOCK indicator turns ON.
- The TRAC Off indicator turns ON.
- The PCS indicator turns ON.

Conditions for Clearing the DTC

- The condition for the DTC is no longer present
- A history DTC will clear after 100 consecutive ignition cycles if the condition for the malfunction is no longer present.
- Using a scan tool.

Diagnostic Aids

The following conditions may cause a malfunction:

- Malfunctioning lateral accelerometer
- Malfunctioning EBCM

Test Description

The number(s) below refer to the step number(s) on the diagnostic table.

2. Checks to see if steering angle sensor is centered.
3. Checks for specified voltage on the lateral accelerometer signal circuit.
4. Checks for specified voltage on the yaw rate signal circuit.

GC4020152498010X

Fig. 147 Code C0197: Yaw Rate Circuit Range/ Performance (Part 1 of 2). 2001–02 Intrigue

Step	Action	Value(s)	Yes	No
Schematic Reference: *ABS Schematics*				
1	Did you perform the ABS Diagnostic System Check?	—	Go to *Step 2*	Go to *Diagnostic System Check - ABS*
2	Perform the steering angle sensor centering procedure. Did you successfully complete the centering procedure?	—	Go to *Step 3*	Go to *Step 7*
3	1. Turn OFF the ignition. 2. Disconnect the EBCM connector. 3. Install the *J 39700* universal pinout box with the *J 39700-530* cable adapter between the EBCM and the EBCM harness connector. 4. Turn the ignition ON, with the engine OFF. 5. Using the DMM, measure the voltage between pin 10 and pin 15 of the *J 39700* universal pinout box. Is the voltage within the specified value?	2.3 V – 2.7 V	Go to *Step 4*	Go to *Step 8*
4	Using the DMM, measure the voltage between pin 26 and pin 15 of the *J 39700* universal pinout box. Is the voltage within the specified value?	2.3 V – 2.7 V	Go to *Step 5*	Go to *Step 8*
5	1. Use the scan tool in order to clear the DTCs. 2. Perform the Diagnostic Test Drive. Does the DTC reset?	—	Go to *Step 6*	Go to Diagnostic Aids
6	Replace the EBCM. Did you complete the replacement?	—	Go to *Step 9*	—
7	Replace the steering angle sensor. Did you complete the replacement?	—	Go to *Step 9*	—
8	Replace the vehicle yaw/lateral accelerometer sensor. Did you complete the repair?	—	Go to *Step 9*	—
9	1. Use the scan tool in order to clear the DTCs. 2. Operate the vehicle within the Conditions for Running the DTC as specified in the supporting text. Does the DTC reset?	—	Go to *Step 2*	System OK

GC4020152498020X

Fig. 147 Code C0197: Yaw Rate Circuit Range/ Performance (Part 2 of 2). 2001–02 Intrigue

Step	Action	Value(s)	Yes	No
6	1. Inspect the PCM connector C2 for the following: • Inspect for damage. • Inspect for poor terminal contact. • Inspect for corrosion. 2. Inspect the EBCM connector for the following: • Inspect for damage. • Inspect for poor terminal contact. • Inspect for corrosion. 3. Ensure both the PCM connector C2 and the EBCM connector are properly retained when connected. Are the following signs present on either connector: • Is poor terminal contact present? • Is corrosion present? • Is damaged terminals present?	—	Go to *Step 13*	Go to *Step 7*
7	1. Reconnect all the connectors. 2. Using the scan tool clear the DTC. 3. Disconnect the scan tool from the DLC. 4. Start the engine. Did DTC C0236 reset?	—	Go to *Step 8*	Go to *Diagnostic System Check - ABS*
8	Replace the EBCM. Is the repair complete?	—	Go to *Step 14*	—
9	Check the PCM. Is the repair complete?	—	Go to *Step 14*	—
10	Repair an open between PCM and EBCM tach signal circuit. Is the repair complete?	—	Go to *Step 14*	—
11	Repair a short to ground in tach signal circuit. Is the repair complete?	—	Go to *Step 14*	—
12	Repair a short to voltage in TACH signal circuit. Is the repair complete?	—	Go to *Step 14*	—
13	Replace all the terminals or replace the connectors that exhibit signs of the following: • That exhibit signs of poor terminal contact. • That exhibit signs of corrosion. • That exhibit signs of damaged terminals. Is the repair complete?	—	Go to *Step 14*	—
14	1. Use the scan tool in order to clear the DTCs. 2. Operate the vehicle within the Conditions for Running the DTC as specified in the supporting text. Dose the DTC reset?	—	Go to *Step 2*	System OK

GC4020152499020X

Fig. 148 Codes C0235-C0237: TCS RPM Signal Circuit Fault (Part 2 of 2). 2001–04 Grand Prix & 2001–02 Intrigue

Circuit Description

The RPM signal circuit provides the EBCM with an indication of engine RPM to help determine TCS control methods and rates when a TCS event takes place.

Conditions for Running the DTC

- The ignition switch is ON and the engine running.
- After 2 seconds starting, and if there is a undervoltage condition.

Conditions for Setting the DTC

The EBCM does not received an RPM input signal after 1 second, after the engine has been started.

Action Taken When the DTC Sets

If equiped, the following actions occur:

- A malfunction DTC will set.
- The TRAC OFF indicator is turned on.
- The TCS is disabled. ABS remains functional.

Conditions for Clearing the DTC

- The condition for DTC is no longer present and the scan tool Clear DTCs function is used.
- 100 ignition cycles have passed with no DTC(s) detected.

Diagnostic Aids

Perform a thorough inspection of the wiring. Perform a thorough inspection of the connectors. Failure to carefully and fully inspect the wiring and the connectors may result in misdiagnosis. Misdiagnosis causes part replacement with reappearance of the malfunction.

Test Description

The number(s) below refer to the step number(s) on the diagnostic table.

2. If the instrument panel tachometer is working properly, the cause of the malfunction is more likely between the PCM and the EBCM, or the EBCM itself.
9. At this point, the PCM is likely causing the malfunction. Refer to the OBD system check.

Step	Action	Value(s)	Yes	No
Schematic Reference: *ABS Schematics*				
1	Did you perform the Diagnostic System Check?	—	Go to *Step 2*	Go to *Diagnostic System Check - ABS*
2	1. Start the engine. 2. Vary the engine RPM with the throttle while observing the IP tachometer. Does the IP tachometer work properly as the engine RPM changes?	—	Go to *Step 3*	Go to *Step 9*
3	1. Turn the ignition switch to the OFF position. 2. Disconnect the PCM connector C2 from the PCM. 3. Disconnect the EBCM connector from the EBCM. 4. Install the *J 39700* with the J 39700-530 cable adapter to the EBTCM harness only. 5. Use a *J 39200* to measure the resistance between the PCM harness connector tach signal circuit, and the universal breakout box terminal 11. Is the resistance within the specified range?	0–5 Ω	Go to *Step 4*	Go to *Step 10*
4	Use a *J 39200* to measure the resistance between the universal breakout box terminal 11 and a good ground. Is the resistance within the specified range?	OL	Go to *Step 5*	Go to *Step 11*
5	1. Turn the ignition switch to the ON position 2. Use a *J 39200* to measure the voltage between the universal breakout box terminal 11 and a good ground. Is the voltage within the specified range?	0–2 V	Go to *Step 6*	Go to *Step 12*

GC4020152499010X

Fig. 148 Codes C0235-C0237: TCS RPM Signal Circuit Fault (Part 1 of 2). 2001–04 Grand Prix & 2001–02 Intrigue

Circuit Description

The PCM monitors various parameters and will not allow traction control operation if any parameter falls below a specified value.

Conditions for Running the DTC

The ignition is ON.

Conditions for Setting the DTC

The PCM detects a malfunction and then causes TCS shut down until the malfunction has been corrected

Action Taken When the DTC Sets

If equiped, the following actions occur:

- The EBCM disables the TCS/VSES for the duration of the ignition cycle.
- A DTC C0240 is stored
- The TCS is disabled
- The TRAC OFF indicator is turned on
- The PCS indicator is turned on.
- If the TCS is again allowed to function, the indicator will be turned off but the DTC will be stored

Conditions for Clearing the DTC

- The condition for the DTC is no longer present (the DTC is not current) and you used the scan tool Clear DTC function.
- The EBCM automatically clears the history DTC when a current DTC is not detected in 100 consecutive drive cycles.

Test Description

The numbers below refer to the step numbers on the diagnostic table.

4. This step checks if DTC C0240 resets.

Step	Action	Yes	No
Schematic Reference: *ABS Schematics*			
1	Did you perform the Diagnostic System Check?	Go to *Step 2*	Go to *Diagnostic System Check - ABS*
2	1. Turn the ignition switch to the RUN position with the engine off. 2. Using a Scan Tool, read the ABS/TCS DTCs. Are any other DTCs set?	Go to *Diagnostic Trouble Code (DTC) List* for the appropriate DTC table	Go to *Step 3*
3	Is DTC C0240 set as a current code?	Go to *Step 5*	Go to *Step 4*
4	1. Using the scan tool clear the DTC. 2. Remove the scan tool from the DLC. 3. Carefully drive the vehicle above 12 km/h (8 mph) for several minutes. Did DTC C0240 set as a current DTC?	Go to *Step 5*	*Diagnose* Go to *Diagnostic System Check - ABS*
5	Perform the Powertrain OBD System Check. Did the vehicle pass the OBD System Check?	Go to *Step 6*	Engine Controls
6	1. Use the scan tool in order to clear the DTCs. 2. Operate the vehicle within the Conditions for Running the DTC as specified in the supporting text. Does the DTC reset?	Go to *Step 2*	System OK

GC4020152500000X

Fig. 149 Code C0240: PCM Traction Control Not Allowed. 2001–04 Grand Prix & 2001–02 Intrigue

Circuit Description

The EBCM and the PCM simultaneously control the traction control. The EBCM sends a Requested Torque message via a pulse width modulated (PWM) signal to the PCM. The duty cycle of the signal is used to determine how much engine torque the EBCM is requesting the PCM to deliver. Normal values are between 10 and 90 percent duty cycle. The signal should be at 90 percent when traction control is not active and at lower values during traction control activations. The PCM supplies the pull up voltage that the EBCM switches to ground to create the signal.

Conditions for Running the DTC

The ignition is ON.

Conditions for Setting the DTC

The PCM diagnoses the requested torque PWM signal circuit and sends a class 2 serial data message to the EBCM indicating a fault is present. A fault exists in the circuit if the PCM detects one of the following conditions:

- The requested torque PWM signal is less than 5 percent duty cycle or greater than 95 percent duty cycle.
- The requested torque PWM signal is not present for 10 seconds.

Action Taken When the DTC Sets

If equiped, the following actions occur:

- The EBCM disables the TCS/VSES for the duration of the ignition cycle.
- A malfunction DTC will set.
- The TRAC OFF indicator turns ON.
- The PCS indicator turns ON.
- The ABS remains functional.

Conditions for Clearing the DTC

- The condition for the DTC is no longer present (the DTC is not current) and you used the scan tool Clear DTC function.
- The EBCM automatically clears the history DTC when a current DTC is not detected in 100 consecutive drive cycles.

Test Description

The numbers below refer to the step numbers on the diagnostic table.

3. Use the scan tool in order to determine if the requested torque signal has a valid duty cycle.
4. Measure the requested torque signal in order to determine if the signal has a valid duty cycle.
5. Measure the requested torque signal in order to determine if the signal has a valid frequency.
11. This vehicle is equipped with a PCM which uses an Electrically Erasable Programmable Read Only Memory (EEPROM). When replacing the PCM, the replacement PCM must be programmed.

DTC C0241 or P1571

Step	Action	Value(s)	Yes	No
Schematic Reference: *ABS Schematics*				
1	Did you perform the ABS Diagnostic System Check?	—	Go to *Step 2*	Go to *Diagnostic System Check - ABS*
2	Inspect the EBCM ground and PCM ground, making sure each ground is clean and torqued to the proper specification. Did you find and correct the condition?	—	Go to *Step 13*	Go to *Step 3*
3	1. Install a scan tool. 2. Start the engine. 3. With the scan tool, observe the Torque Request Signal parameter in the Powertrain Control Module data list. Does the scan tool display less than the specified value?	100%	*Test for Intermittent and Poor Connections*	Go to *Step 4*
4	1. Turn OFF the ignition. 2. Disconnect the EBCM harness connector. 3. Install the *J 39700* universal breakout box using the *J 39700-530* cable adapter to the EBCM harness connector and the EBCM connector. 4. Start the engine. 5. Measure the DC duty cycle between the requested torque signal circuit and a good ground. Is the duty cycle within the specified range?	5–95%	Go to *Step 5*	Go to *Step 6*

GC4020152501010X

Fig. 150 Code C0241: PCM Indicated Requested Torque Fault (Part 1 of 2). 2001–04 Grand Prix & 2001–02 Intrigue

Step	Action	Value(s)	Yes	No
5	Measure the DC Hz between the requested torque signal circuit and a good ground. Does the frequency measure within the specified range?	121–134 Hz	Go to *Step 8*	Go to *Step 6*
6	1. Turn OFF the ignition. 2. Disconnect the cable adapter from the EBCM connector. **Important:** Disconnecting the EBCM connector and turning ON the ignition could cause other modules to set loss of communication DTCs (Uxxxx). Once the EBCM is reconnected, the EBCM may set DTC C0241. 3. Turn ON the ignition, with the engine OFF. 4. Measure the voltage from the requested torque signal circuit to a good ground. Does the voltage measure within the specified range?	4 – 6 V	Go to *Step 10*	Go to *Step 7*
7	1. Turn OFF the ignition. 2. Disconnect the powertrain control module (PCM) harness connector. 3. Test the requested torque signal circuit for the following conditions: • A short to voltage • A short to ground Did you find and correct the condition?	—	Go to *Step 13*	Go to *Step 10*
8	1. Turn OFF the ignition. 2. Disconnect the powertrain control module (PCM) harness connector. 3. Test the requested torque signal circuit for the following conditions: • An open • A high resistance Did you find and correct the condition?	—	Go to *Step 13*	Go to *Step 9*
9	Inspect for poor connections at the harness connector of the PCM. Did you find and correct the condition?	—	Go to *Step 13*	Go to *Step 11*
10	Inspect for poor connections at the harness connector of the EBCM. Did you find and correct the condition?	—	Go to *Step 13*	Go to *Step 12*
11	**Important:** The replacement PCM must be programmed. Replace the PCM. Did you complete the repair?	—	Go to *Step 13*	—
12	Replace the EBCM. Did you complete the repair?	—	Go to *Step 13*	—
13	1. Use the scan tool in order to clear the DTCs. 2. Operate the vehicle within the Conditions for Running the DTC as specified in the supporting text. Does the DTC reset?	—	Go to *Step 2*	System OK

GC4020152501020X

Fig. 150 Code C0241: PCM Indicated Requested Torque Fault (Part 2 of 2). 2001–04 Grand Prix & 2001–02 Intrigue

Circuit Description

Traction Control is simultaneously controlled by the EBCM and the PCM. The PCM sends a DELIVERED TORQUE message via a Pulse Width Modulated (PWM) signal to the EBCM confirming the delivered torque level for proper Traction Control system operation. The EBCM supplies the pull up voltage.

Conditions for Running the DTC

- The ignition switch is ON.
- The DTC can be set after system initialization.

Conditions for Setting the DTC

DTC C0244 can be set anytime when ignition voltage is present. A malfunction exists if the PWM signal is out of range or no signal is received for a period of 2 seconds.

Action Taken When the DTC Sets

If equiped, the following actions occur:

- The EBCM disables the TCS/VSES for the duration of the ignition cycle.
- A malfunction DTC will set.
- The TRAC OFF indicator is turned on. The ABS remains functional.
- The PCS indicator is turned on.

Conditions for Clearing the DTC

- The condition for the DTC is no longer present (the DTC is not current) and you used the scan tool Clear DTC function.
- The EBCM automatically clears the history DTC when a current DTC is not detected in 100 consecutive drive cycles.

Diagnostic Aids

- It is very important that a thorough inspection of the wiring and connectors be performed. Failure to carefully and fully inspect wiring and connectors may result in misdiagnosis, causing part replacement with reappearance of the malfunction.
- Possible causes for DTC C0244 to set:
  - Open in CKT 464.
  - CKT 464 shorted to ground or voltage.
  - Communication frequency problem.
  - Communication duty cycle problem.
  - CKT 464 has a wiring problem, terminal corrosion, or poor connections.
  - EBCM not receiving information from the PCM.

Test Description

The numbers below refer to the step numbers on the diagnostic table.

3. Use the scan tool in order to determine if the delivered torque signal has a valid duty cycle.
9. This vehicle is equipped with a PCM which uses an Electrically Erasable Programmable Read Only Memory (EEPROM). When replacing the PCM, the replacement PCM must be programmed.

DTC C0244 or P1689

Step	Action	Value(s)	Yes	No
Schematic Reference: *ABS Schematics*				
1	Did you perform the ABS Diagnostic System Check?	—	Go to *Step 2*	Go to *Diagnostic System Check - ABS*
2	Inspect the EBCM ground and PCM ground, making sure each ground is clean and torqued to the proper specification. Did you find and correct the condition?	—	Go to *Step 11*	Go to *Step 3*
3	1. Install a scan tool. 2. Start the engine. 3. With a scan tool, observe the PCM to EBTCM Delivered parameter in the Powertrain Control Module data list. Does the scan tool display the specified value?	90%	Go to *Step 4*	*Test for Intermittent and Poor Connections*

GC4020152502010X

Fig. 151 Code C0244: PWM Delivered Torque Fault (Part 1 of 2). 2001–04 Grand Prix & 2001–02 Intrigue

Step	Action	Value(s)	Yes	No
4	1. Turn OFF the ignition. 2. Disconnect the EBCM harness connector. 3. Install the *J 39700* universal breakout box using the *J 39700-530* cable adapter to the EBCM harness connector and the EBCM connector. 4. Disconnect the powertrain control module (PCM) harness connector. 5. Turn ON the ignition, with the engine OFF. 6. Measure the voltage from the delivered torque signal circuit to a good ground. Does the voltage measure near the specified value?	B+	Go to *Step 5*	Go to *Step 6*
5	1. Turn OFF the ignition. 2. Disconnect the cable adapter from the EBCM connector. 3. Turn ON the ignition, with the engine OFF. 4. Test the delivered torque signal circuit for a short to voltage. Did you find and correct the condition?	—	Go to *Step 11*	Go to *Step 7*
6	1. Turn OFF the ignition. 2. Disconnect the cable adapter from the EBCM connector. 3. Test the delivered torque signal circuit for the following conditions: • An open • A short to ground • A high resistance Did you find and correct the condition?	—	Go to *Step 11*	Go to *Step 8*
7	Inspect for poor connections at the harness connector of the PCM. Did you find and correct the condition?	—	Go to *Step 11*	Go to *Step 9*
8	Inspect for poor connections at the harness connector of the EBCM. Did you find and correct the condition?	—	Go to *Step 11*	Go to *Step 10*
9	**Important:** The replacement PCM must be programmed. Replace the PCM. Did you complete the repair?	—	Go to *Step 11*	—
10	Replace the EBCM. Did you complete the repair?	—	Go to *Step 11*	—
11	1. Use the scan tool in order to clear the DTCs. 2. Operate the vehicle within the Conditions for Running the DTC as specified in the supporting text. Does the DTC reset?	—	Go to *Step 2*	System OK

GC4020152502020X

Fig. 151 Code C0244: PWM Delivered Torque Fault (Part 2 of 2). 2001–04 Grand Prix & 2001–02 Intrigue

Circuit Description

The speed sensors used on the front of this vehicle are multiple pole and the rear uses a single pole magnetic pickup. This sensor produces an AC signal that the EBCM uses the frequency from to calculate the wheel speed.

Conditions for Running the DTC

- The ignition switch is ON.
- The DTC can be set after system initialization.

Conditions for Setting the DTC

- The EBCM detects a deviation between the left and right rear wheel speeds of greater than 6 km/h (3.75 mph) at a vehicle speed of less than 100 km/h (62 mph) on vehicles equipped with TCS.
- The EBCM detects a deviation between the left and right front wheel speeds of greater than 10 km/h (6.25 mph) at a vehicle speed of less than 100 km/h (62 mph).
- The EBCM detects a deviation between the left and right rear wheel speeds of greater than 6 percent of the vehicle speed at greater than 100 km/h (62 mph) on vehicles equipped with TCS.
- The EBCM detects a deviation between the left and right front wheel speeds of greater than 4 km/h plus 6 percent of the vehicle speed at greater than 100 km/h (62 mph).

This DTC will set when the EBCM cannot specifically identify which wheel speed sensor is causing the malfunction. If the EBCM can identify the specific wheel speed sensor causing the malfunction, DTC C0245 will become a history DTC, and the DTC associated with the sensor (DTC C0036, DTC C0041, DTC C0046, DTC C0051, or DTC C0056) will be set concurrent with DTC C0245.

Action Taken When the DTC Sets

If equiped, the following actions occur:

- The EBCM disables the ABS/TCS/VSES/DRP and MSVA for the duration of the ignition cycle.
- A malfunction DTC will set.
- The ABS indicator turns on.
- The TCS indicator turns on.
- The PCS indicator turns on.
- The Red BRAKE Warning indicator turns on.

Conditions for Clearing the DTC

- The condition for the DTC is no longer present (the DTC is not current) and you used the scan tool Clear DTC function.
- The EBCM automatically clears the history DTC when a current DTC is not detected in 100 consecutive drive cycles.

Diagnostic Aids

- It is very important that a thorough inspection of the wiring and connectors be performed. Failure to carefully and fully inspect wiring and connectors may result in misdiagnosis, causing part replacement with reappearance of the malfunction.
- Thoroughly inspect any circuitry that may be causing the complaint for the following conditions:
  - Backed out terminals
  - Improper mating
  - Broken locks
  - Improperly formed or damaged terminals
  - Poor terminal-to-wiring connections
  - Physical damage to the wiring harness
- The following conditions may cause an intermittent malfunction:
  - A poor connection
  - Rubbed-through wire insulation
  - A broken wire inside the insulation
- If the customer's comments reflect that the amber ABS/TCS indicator is on only during moist environmental conditions (rain, snow, vehicle wash), inspect all the wheel speed sensor circuitry for signs of water intrusion. If the DTC is not current, clear all DTCs and simulate the effects of water intrusion by using the following procedure:
  1. Spray the suspected area with a five percent saltwater solution.

     Add two teaspoons of salt to twelve ounces of water to make a five percent saltwater solution.
  2. Test drive the vehicle over various road surfaces (bumps, turns, etc.) above 40 km/h (25 mph) for at least 30 seconds.
  3. If the DTC returns, replace the suspected harness.
- If an intermittent malfunction exists refer to Testing for Intermittent and Poor Connections

Test Description

The numbers below refer to step numbers on the diagnostic table.

2. If DTC C0245 is a history code, this step checks if a specific Wheel Speed Circuit Malfunction DTC is set concurrently with DTC C0245.
7. This step checks if the wheel speed sensor harness is routed in close proximity to the spark plug wires.
9. In this step, if the scan tool can record any erroneous wheel speed sensor signals, diagnose that sensor(s) first.

GC4020152503010X

Fig. 152 Code C0245: Wheel Speed Sensor Frequency Error (Part 1 of 2). 2001–04 Grand Prix & 2001–02 Intrigue

Step	Action	Yes	No
Schematic Reference: *ABS Schematics*			
1	Did you perform the diagnostic system check?	Go to *Step 2*	Go to *Diagnostic System Check - ABS*
2	Is the following DTC(s) set concurrently with a history DTC C0245? • DTC C0036 • DTC C0041 • DTC C0046 • DTC C0051 • DTC C0056	Go to DTC *Diagnostic Trouble Code (DTC) List*	Go to *Step 3*
3	Inspect the WSS for physical damage. Is physical damage of the WSS evident?	Go to *Step 4*	Go to *Step 5*
4	Replace the WSS. Is the replacement complete?	Go to *Step 14*	—
5	Inspect the wiring harness for physical damage. Is physical damage of the wiring harness evident?	Go to *Step 6*	Go to *Step 7*
6	Repair the wiring harness. Is the replacement complete?	Go to *Step 14*	—
7	Check for Proper routing of the wheel speed sensor harness. Check that the wheel speed sensor harness is routed away from the spark plug wires. Is the wheel speed sensor harness properly routed?	Go to *Step 9*	Go to *Step 8*
8	Reroute the wheel speed sensor harness away from the spark plug wires. Is the reroute complete?	Go to *Step 14*	—
9	1. Install a scan tool. 2. Turn the ignition switch to the RUN position. 3. Set the scan tool to Snap Shot Auto Trigger mode and monitor the wheel speed sensors. 4. Carefully drive the vehicle above 12 km/h (8 mph) for several minutes Did the scan tool trigger on any of the wheel speed sensors?	Go to *Step 10*	Go to *Step 11*
10	Note which wheel speed sensor triggered the scan tool. Follow the appropriate Wheel Speed Sensor Malfunction DTC table for the wheel speed sensor that triggered. Is the repair complete?	Go to *Step 14*	—
11	1. Reconnect all previously disconnected components. 2. Using a scan tool clear the DTC. 3. Remove the scan tool from the DLC. 4. Carefully drive the vehicle above 12 km/h (8 mph) for several minutes. Does the DTC reset as a current DTC?	Go to *Step 13*	Go to *Step 12*
12	Malfunction is intermittent. Inspect all connectors and harnesses for damage that may result in an open or high resistance when connected. Is the repair complete?	Go to *Step 14*	—
13	Replace the EBCM. Is the replacement complete?	Go to *Step 14*	—
14	1. Use the scan tool in order to clear the DTCs. 2. Operate the vehicle within the conditions for running the DTC as specified in the supporting text. Does the DTC reset?	Go to *Step 2*	System OK

GC4020152503020X

Fig. 152 Code C0245: Wheel Speed Sensor Frequency Error (Part 2 of 2). 2001–04 Grand Prix & 2001–02 Intrigue

Circuit Description

The vehicle stability enhancement system (VSES) is activated by the EBCM calculating the desired yaw rate and comparing it to the actual yaw rate input. The desired yaw rate is calculated from measured steering wheel position, vehicle speed, and lateral acceleration. The difference between the desired yaw rate and actual yaw rate is the yaw rate error, which is a measurement of oversteer or understeer. If the yaw rate error becomes too large, the EBCM will attempt to correct the vehicle's yaw motion by applying differential braking to the left or right wheels.

Conditions for Running the DTC

- The steer angle has been centered.
- The VSES is active.
- The direction (understeer or oversteer) of the yaw rate error has not changed.
- The lateral acceleration is less than 0.5 g.

Conditions for Setting the DTC

One of the following conditions occur:

- The VSES is engaged for 10 seconds with the yaw rate error always in either understeer or oversteer. Under this condition, this DTC will set by itself.
- The yaw rate error is greater than 10 degrees/second for 5 seconds.

Action Taken When the DTC Sets

If equiped, the following actions occur:

- The EBCM disables the ABS/TCS/VSES and for the duration of the ignition cycle.
- A malfunction DTC will set.
- The ABS indicator turns on.
- The TCS indicator turns on.
- The PCS indicator turns on.

Conditions for Clearing the DTC

- The condition for the DTC is no longer present (the DTC is not current) and you used the scan tool Clear DTC function.
- The EBCM automatically clears the history DTC when a current DTC is not detected in 100 consecutive drive cycles.

Diagnostic Aids

- During diagnosis, park the vehicle on a level surface.
- Check the vehicle for proper alignment. The car should not pull in either direction while driving straight on a level surface.
- Find out from the customer the conditions under which the DTC was set. This information will help to duplicate the failure.
- The Snapshot function on the scan tool can help find an intermittent DTC.

Test Description

The numbers below refer to the step numbers on the diagnostic table.

2. This checks to see if DTC C0252 is set.
3. This step checks to see if the DTC C0252 resets.
4. This step checks to see if VSES data list parameters are correct.
5. This step checks the components harness connectors for poor connections.

GC4020152504010X

Fig. 153 Code C0252: Active Brake Control Sensor Uncorrelated (Part 1 of 2). 2001–02 Intrigue

Step	Action	Yes	No
Schematic Reference: *ABS Schematics*			
1	Did you perform the ABS Diagnostic System Check?	Go to *Step 2*	Go to *Diagnostic System Check - ABS*
2	1. Turn OFF the ignition. 2. Install a scan tool. 3. Turn ON the ignition, with the engine OFF. 4. Select the ABS DTC display function. Does the scan tool display any DTC other than DTC C0252?	Go to *Diagnostic Trouble Code (DTC) List*	Go to *Step 3*
3	1. Use the scan tool in order to clear the DTC. 2. Perform the *Diagnostic Test Drive*. 3. Use the scan tool to select the ABS DTC display function. Does the DTC reset?	Go to *Step 4*	Go to Diagnostic Aids
4	1. Use the scan tool to select the VSES data list. 2. Compare data to the typical values located in the EBCM scan tool data list under VSES Data List. Are all parameters correct?	Go to *Step 5*	*Test for Intermittent and Poor Connections*
5	Check the wiring harness connectors for the following: • EBCM • Brake pressure sensor • Steering angle sensor • Yaw/lateral accelerometer sensor • LF wheel speed sensor • RF wheel speed sensor • RF wheel speed sensor • RR wheel speed sensor Did you find and correct the condition?	Go to *Step 6*	*Test for Intermittent and Poor Connections*
6	1. Use the scan tool in order to clear the DTCs. 2. Operate the vehicle within the Conditions for Running the DTC as specified in the supporting text. Does the DTC reset?	Go to *Step 2*	System OK

GC4020152504020X

Fig. 153 Code C0252: Active Brake Control Sensor Uncorrelated (Part 2 of 2). 2001–02 Intrigue

Circuit Description

Steer angle centering is the process by which the EBCM calibrates the steering sensor output so that the output reads zero when the steering wheel is centered.

Conditions for Running the DTC

- The ignition is ON.
- The vehicle speed is greater than 40 km/h (25 mph).

Conditions for Setting the DTC

If the steering angle sensor CAN message or the EBCM indicates an uncentered sensor.

Action Taken When the DTC Sets

If equiped, the following actions occur:

- The EBCM disables the ABS/TCS/VSES and for the duration of the ignition cycle.
- A malfunction DTC will set.
- The ABS indicator turns on.
- The TCS indicator turns on.
- The PCS indicator turns on.

Conditions for Clearing the DTC

- The condition for the DTC is no longer present.
- A history DTC will clear after 100 consecutive ignition cycles if the condition for the malfunction is no longer present.
- Using a scan tool.
- The EBCM automatically clears the history DTC when a current DTC is not detected in 100 consecutive drive cycles.

Diagnostic Aids

Perform the steering angle sensor centering procedure.

Test Description

The number(s) below refer to the step number(s) on the diagnostic table.

2. Checks to see if other DTC is set.
3. Checks to see if steering angle sensor is centered.

DTC C0253

Step	Action	Yes	No
Schematic Reference: *ABS Schematics*			
1	Did you perform the ABS Diagnostic System Check?	Go to *Step 2*	Go to *Diagnostic System Check - ABS*
2	1. Turn OFF the ignition. 2. Install a scan tool. 3. Turn ON the ignition, with the engine OFF. 4. Select the ABS DTC display function. Does the scan tool display any DTC other than DTC C0253?	Go to *Diagnostic Trouble Code (DTC) List*	Go to *Step 3*
3	Perform the steering angle sensor centering procedure. Did you successfully complete the centering procedure?	Go to *Step 4*	Go to *Step 5*
4	1. Use the scan tool in order to clear the DTCs. 2. Test drive the vehicle. Did DTC C0253 reset?	Go to *Step 6*	Go to Diagnostic Aids
5	Replace the steering angle sensor. Did you complete the replacement?	Go to *Step 7*	—
6	Replace the EBCM. Did you complete the replacement?	Go to *Step 7*	—
7	1. Use the scan tool in order to clear the DTCs. 2. Operate the vehicle within the Conditions for Running the DTC as specified in the supporting test. Does the DTC reset?	Go to *Step 2*	System OK

GC4020152505000X

Fig. 154 Code C0253: Centering Fault. 2001–02 Intrigue

Circuit Description

Under normal driving conditions, the EBCM monitors the steering angle sensor inputs to see if the steering wheel is moving. If the steering wheel is not moving for a set period of time, the EBCM assumes the vehicle is going in a straight line. At this point, the EBCM looks at the steering angle sensor inputs and considers the degree angle to be zero. This is called the offset value.

Steer angle centering is the process by which the EBCM calibrates the steering sensor output so that the output reads zero when the steering wheel is centered.

Conditions for Running the DTC

- The ignition is ON.
- The vehicle speed is greater than 40 km/h (25 mph).

Conditions for Setting the DTC

A malfunction is detected if one or more of the following conditions exist:

- The steering angle sensor detects an internal malfunction and sends a CAN message to the EBCM.
- If the offset value is higher than 15 degrees, a malfunction is detected. Malfunction time depends on driving distance, vehicle speed and the amount of malfunctioning steering angle signal.
- Rapid changes of the steering angle sensor signal cannot occur under normal driving conditions. If the signal change is higher than 2000 degrees per second or steering angle acceleration is higher than 37500 degrees per second squared, a malfunction is detected.
- A reference steering angle signal based on a vehicle model is used to check the actual steering angle. If the measured steering angle varies from the reference steering angle by more than a predetermined value, a malfunction is detected.

Action Taken When the DTC Sets

If equiped, the following actions occur:

- The EBCM disables theTCS/VSES and for the duration of the ignition cycle.
- A malfunction DTC will set.
- The TCS indicator turns on.
- The PCS indicator turns on.

Conditions for Clearing the DTC

- The condition for the DTC is no longer present.
- A history DTC will clear after 100 consecutive ignition cycles if the condition for the malfunction is no longer present.
- Using a scan tool.
- The EBCM automatically clears the history DTC when a current DTC is not detected in 100 consecutive drive cycles.

Diagnostic Aids

Perform the steering angle sensor centering procedure.

Test Description

The number(s) below refer to the step number(s) on the diagnostic table.

2. Checks to see if any other DTC is set.
3. Checks to see if steering angle sensor is centered.

DTC C0710

Step	Action	Yes	No
Schematic Reference: *ABS Schematics*			
1	Did you perform the ABS Diagnostic System Check?	Go to *Step 2*	Go to *Diagnostic System Check - ABS*
2	1. Turn OFF the ignition. 2. Install a scan tool. 3. Turn ON the ignition, with the engine OFF. 4. Select the ABS DTC display function. Does the scan tool display any DTC other than DTC C0710?	Go to *Diagnostic Trouble Code (DTC) List*	Go to *Step 3*
3	Perform the steering angle sensor centering procedure. Did you successfully complete the centering procedure?	Go to *Step 4*	Go to *Step 5*
4	1. Use the scan tool in order to clear the DTCs. 2. Test drive the vehicle. Did DTC C0710 reset?	Go to *Step 6*	Go to Diagnostic Aids
5	Replace the steering angle sensor. Did you complete the replacement?	Go to *Step 7*	—
6	Replace the EBCM. Did you complete the replacement?	Go to *Step 7*	—
7	1. Use the scan tool in order to clear the DTCs. 2. Operate the vehicle within the Conditions for Running the DTC as specified in the supporting test. Does the DTC reset?	Go to *Step 2*	System OK

GC4020152507000X

Fig. 156 Code C0710: Steering Position Signal Fault. 2001–02 Intrigue

Circuit Description

This DTC identifies a malfunction within the EBCM.

Conditions for Running the DTC

The ignition switch is in the ON position.

Conditions for Setting the DTC

DTC C0550 is set when an internal EBCM malfunction exists.

Action Taken When the DTC Sets

If equiped, the following actions occur:

- The EBCM disables the ABS/TCS/VSES and MSVA for the duration of the ignition cycle.
- A malfunction DTC will set.
- The ABS indicator turns on.
- The TCS indicator turns on.
- The PCS indicator turns on.
- The Red BRAKE Warning indicator turns on.

Conditions for Clearing the DTC

- The condition for the DTC is no longer present (the DTC is not current) and you used the scan tool Clear DTC function.
- The EBCM automatically clears the history DTC when a current DTC is not detected in 100 consecutive drive cycles.

DTC C0550

Step	Action	Yes	No
Schematic Reference: *ABS Schematics*			
1	Did you perform the Diagnostic System Check?	Go to *Step 2*	Go to *Diagnostic System Check - ABS*
2	Are any other DTC(s) present besides C0550?	Go to *Diagnostic Trouble Code (DTC) List*	Go to *Step 3*
3	Replace the EBCM. Is the replacement complete?	Go to*Step 4*	—
4	1. Use the scan tool in order to clear the DTCs. 2. Operate the vehicle within the Conditions for Running the DTC as specified in the supporting text. Does the DTC reset?	Go to *Step 2*	System OK

GC4020152506000X

Fig. 155 Code C0550: ECU Fault. 2001–04 Grand Prix & 2001–02 Intrigue

Circuit Description

The brake pressure sensor reference voltage is monitored for an over or under voltage condition.

Conditions for Running the DTC

- The ignition is ON.
- The vehicle speed is greater than 40 km/h (25 mph).

Conditions for Setting the DTC

A malfunction is detected if the supply voltage is above 5.6 volts or below 4.4 volts for more than 60 milliseconds.

Action Taken When the DTC Sets

- A malfunction DTC is set
- ABS, TCS and VSES are disabled
- ABS, TCS, SERVICE VEHICLE SOON and PCS lamp indicators are ON

Conditions for Clearing the DTC

- The condition for the DTC is no longer present.
- A history DTC will clear after 100 consecutive ignition cycles if the condition for the malfunction is no longer present.
- Using a scan tool.
- The EBCM automatically clears the history DTC when a current DTC is not detected in 100 consecutive drive cycles.

Diagnostic Aids

Possible causes of this DTC are the following conditions:

- An open in the pressure sensor supply voltage circuit
- A short to ground in the pressure sensor supply voltage circuit
- A short to B+ in the pressure sensor supply voltage circuit

Test Description

The number(s) below refer to the step number(s) on the diagnostic table.

2. Tests for specified voltage on the brake pressure signal circuit.
3. Checks to see if the brake pressure signal circuit voltage was below specified voltage.
4. Checks to see if the brake pressure signal circuit voltage was above specified voltage.
5. Tests for a short to ground in the 5 volt reference circuit of the brake pressure sensor.
6. Tests for a short to voltage in the 5 volt reference circuit of the brake pressure sensor.
7. Tests for a high resistance or an open in the ground circuit of the brake pressure sensor.
8. Checks the brake pressure sensor connector for poor connections.
9. Checks the EBCM connector for poor connections.

GC4020152508010X

Fig. 157 Code C0870: Device Voltage Reference Output No. 1 Circuit Fault (Part 1 of 2). 2001–02 Intrigue

Step	Action	Value(s)	Yes	No
Schematic Reference: *ABS Schematics*				
1	Did you perform the ABS Diagnostic System Check?	—	Go to *Step 2*	Go to *Diagnostic System Check - ABS*
2	1. Turn OFF the ignition. 2. Disconnect the EBCM. 3. Install the *J 39700* universal pinout box with the *J 39700-530* cable adapter between the EBCM and the EBCM harness connector. 4. Turn ON the ignition, with the engine OFF. 5. Using the DMM, measure the voltage between pin 17 and pin 15 of the *J 39700* universal pinout box. Is the voltage within the specified value?	4.4 V – 5.6 V	Go to Diagnostic Aids	Go to *Step 3*
3	1. Turn OFF the ignition. 2. Disconnect the brake pressure sensor. 3. Turn ON the ignition, with the engine OFF. 4. Using the DMM, measure the voltage between pin 17 and pin 15 of the *J 39700* universal pinout box. Is the voltage greater than the specified value?	4.4 V	Go to *Step 4*	Go to *Step 5*
4	Using the DMM, measure the voltage between pin 17 and pin 15 of the *J 39700* universal pinout box. Is the voltage less than the specified value?	5.6 V	Go to *Step 8*	Go to *Step 6*
5	Test the 5 volt reference circuit of the brake pressure sensor for a short to ground. Did you find and correct the condition?	—	Go to *Step 12*	Go to *Step 9*
6	Test the 5 volt reference circuit of the brake pressure sensor for a short to voltage. Did you find and correct the condition?	—	Go to *Step 12*	Go to *Step 7*
7	Test the ground circuit of the brake pressure sensor for a high resistance or an open. Did you find and correct the condition?	—	Go to *Step 12*	Go to *Step 9*
8	Inspect for poor connections at the harness connector of the brake pressure sensor. Did you find and correct the condition?	—	Go to *Step 12*	Go to *Step 10*
9	Inspect for poor connections at the harness connector of the EBCM. Did you find and correct the condition?	—	Go to *Step 12*	Go to *Step 11*
10	Replace the brake pressure sensor. Did you complete the replacement?	—	Go to *Step 12*	—
11	Replace the EBCM. Did you complete the replacement?	—	Go to *Step 12*	—
12	1. Use the scan tool in order to clear the DTCs. 2. Operate the vehicle within the Conditions for Running the DTC as specified in the supporting test. Does the DTC reset?	—	Go to *Step 2*	System OK

GC4020152508020X

Fig. 157 Code C0870: Device Voltage Reference Output No. 1 Circuit Fault (Part 2 of 2). 2001–02 Intrigue

Step	Action	Value(s)	Yes	No
Schematic Reference: *ABS Schematics*				
1	Did you perform the ABS Diagnostic System Check?	—	Go to *Step 2*	Go to *Diagnostic System Check - ABS*
2	1. Turn OFF the ignition. 2. Disconnect the EBCM. 3. Install the *J 39700* universal pinout box with the *J 39700-530* cable adapter between the EBCM and the EBCM harness connector. 4. Turn ON the ignition, with the engine OFF. 5. Using the DMM, measure the voltage between pin 16 and pin 15 of the *J 39700* universal pinout box. Is the voltage within the specified value?	2.1 V – 2.9 V	Go to Diagnostic Aids	Go to *Step 3*
3	1. Turn OFF the ignition. 2. Disconnect the yaw/lateral accelerometer sensor. 3. Turn ON the ignition, with the engine OFF. 4. Using the DMM, measure the voltage between pin 16 and pin 15 of the *J 39700* universal pinout box. Is the voltage greater than the specified value?	2.1 V	Go to *Step 4*	Go to *Step 5*
4	Using the DMM, measure the voltage between pin 16 and pin 15 of the *J 39700* universal pinout box. Is the voltage less than the specified value?	2.9 V	Go to *Step 8*	Go to *Step 6*
5	Test the 5 volt reference circuit of the yaw/lateral accelerometer sensor for a short to ground. Did you find and correct the condition?	—	Go to *Step 12*	Go to *Step 9*
6	Test the 5 volt reference circuit of the yaw/lateral accelerometer sensor for a short to voltage. Did you find and correct the condition?	—	Go to *Step 12*	Go to *Step 7*
7	Test the ground circuit of the yaw/lateral accelerometer sensor for a high resistance or an open. Did you find and correct the condition?	—	Go to *Step 12*	Go to *Step 9*
8	Inspect for poor connections at the harness connector of the yaw/lateral accelerometer sensor. Did you find and correct the condition?	—	Go to *Step 12*	Go to *Step 10*
9	Inspect for poor connections at the harness connector of the EBCM. Did you find and correct the condition?	—	Go to *Step 12*	Go to *Step 11*
10	Replace the yaw/lateral accelerometer sensor. Did you complete the replacement?	—	Go to *Step 12*	—
11	Replace the EBCM. Did you complete the replacement?	—	Go to *Step 12*	—
12	1. Use the scan tool in order to clear the DTCs. 2. Operate the vehicle within the Conditions for Running the DTC as specified in the supporting test. Does the DTC reset?	—	Go to *Step 2*	System OK

GC4020152509020X

Fig. 158 Code C0875: Device Voltage Reference Input No. 2 (Part 2 of 2). 2001–02 Intrigue

Circuit Description

The yaw rate sensor reference voltage is monitored for an over or under voltage condition.

Conditions for Running the DTC

- The ignition is ON.
- The vehicle speed is greater than 40 km/h (25 mph).

Conditions for Setting the DTC

A malfunction is detected if the supply voltage is above 2.9 volts or below 2.1 volts for more than 200 milliseconds.

Action Taken When the DTC Sets

- A malfunction DTC is set.
- TCS and VSES are disabled.
- TCS, PCS and SERVICE VEHICLE SOON lamp indicators are ON.

Conditions for Clearing the DTC

- The condition for the DTC is no longer present.
- A history DTC will clear after 100 consecutive ignition cycles if the condition for the malfunction is no longer present.
- Using a scan tool.
- The EBCM automatically clears the history DTC when a current DTC is not detected in 100 consecutive drive cycles.

Diagnostic Aids

Possible causes of this DTC are the following conditions:

- An open in the yaw rate sensor supply voltage circuit
- A short to ground in the yaw rate sensor supply voltage circuit
- A short to B+ in the yaw rate sensor supply voltage circuit

Test Description

The number(s) below refer to the step number(s) on the diagnostic table.

2. Tests for specified voltage on the 5 volt reference signal circuit.
3. Checks to see if voltage was below specified voltage.
4. Checks to see if voltage was above specified voltage.
5. Tests for a short to ground in the 5 volt reference circuit of the yaw/lateral accelerometer sensor.
6. Tests for a short to voltage in the 5 volt reference circuit of the yaw/lateral accelerometer sensor.
7. Tests for a high resistance or an open in the ground circuit of the yaw/lateral accelerometer sensor.
8. Checks the yaw/lateral accelerometer sensor connector for poor connections.
9. Checks the EBCM connector for poor connections.

GC4020152509010X

Fig. 158 Code C0875: Device Voltage Reference Input No. 2 (Part 1 of 2). 2001–02 Intrigue

Circuit Description

The EBCM is required to operate within a specified range of voltage to function properly. During ABS and TCS operation, there are current requirements that will cause the voltage to drop. Because of this, voltage is monitored out of ABS/TCS control to indicate a good charging system condition, and also during ABS/TCS control when voltage may drop significantly. The ECM also monitors for high voltage conditions which could damage the EBCM.

Conditions for Running the DTC

- The ignition is ON.
- The vehicle speed is greater than 5 km/h (3 mph).

Conditions for Setting the DTC

- The EBCM operating voltage at terminal 8 falls below 9.4 volts out of ABS/TCS control, or 8.8 volts during ABS/TCS control.
- The EBCM operating voltage at terminal 8 rises above 17.4 volts.
- The low voltage or the high voltage is detected for more than 500 milliseconds with the vehicle speed above 6 km/h (3.6 mph).

Action Taken When the DTC Sets

If equipped, the following actions occur:

- The EBCM disables the ABS/TCS/VSES and for the duration of the ignition cycle.
- A malfunction DTC will set.
- The ABS indicator turns on.
- The TCS indicator turns on.
- The PCS indicator turns on.

Conditions for Clearing the DTC

- The condition for the DTC is no longer present, the scan tool Clear DTCs function is used.
- 100 ignition cycles have passed with no DTC(s) detected.

Diagnostic Aids

- It is very important that a thorough inspection of the wiring and connectors be performed. Failure to carefully and fully inspect wiring and connectors may result in misdiagnosis, causing part replacement with reappearance of the malfunction.
- Thoroughly inspect any circuitry that may be causing the complaint for the following conditions:
  - Backed out terminals
  - Improper mating
  - Broken locks
  - Improperly formed or damaged terminals
  - Poor terminal-to-wiring connections
  - Physical damage to the wiring harness
- The following conditions may cause an intermittent malfunction:
  - A poor connection
  - Rubbed-through wire insulation
  - A broken wire inside the insulation

Test Description

The number(s) below refer to the step number(s) on the diagnostic table.

2. This step checks if the voltage is above the maximum of the range.
4. This step checks if the voltage is below the minimum of the range.
6. This step checks for the integrity of the ground circuit.

DTC C0896

Step	Action	Value(s)	Yes	No
Schematic Reference: *ABS Schematics*				
1	Did you perform the Diagnostic System Check?	—	Go to *Step 2*	Go to *Diagnostic System Check - ABS*
2	1. Turn all the accessories off. 2. Install a scan tool. 3. Start the engine. 4. Use the scan tool to monitor the battery voltage while running the engine at approximately 2000 RPM. Is the monitored battery voltage within the specified range?	0–17.4 V	Go to *Step 4*	Go to *Step 3*
3	Use a DMM to measure the voltage between the battery positive terminal and ground. Is the voltage within the specified range?	0–17.4 V	Go to *Step 5*	*Diagnose Charging System*

GC4020152510010X

Fig. 159 Code C0896: Device Voltage Range/ Performance (Part 1 of 2). 2001–02 Intrigue

Step	Action	Value(s)	Yes	No
4	Continue to monitor the battery voltage with the scan tool while running the engine at approximately 2000 RPM. Is the monitored battery voltage within the specified range?	0–9.4 V	Go to *Step 6*	Go to *Step 5*
5	1. Turn the ignition switch to the OFF position. 2. Disconnect the scan tool if still connected. 3. Test drive the vehicle above 5 km/h (3 mph). Did DTC C0896 reset?	—	Go to *Step 12*	Go to *Diagnostic System Check - ABS*
6	1. Disconnect the EBCM connector from the EBCM. 2. Install the *J 39700* universal pinout box with the *J 39700-530* cable adapter to the EBCM harness only. 3. Use a DMM to measure the resistance between the *J 39700* universal pinout box terminal 15 and a good ground. Is the resistance within the specified range?	0-5 Ω	Go to *Step 8*	Go to *Step 7*
7	Repair open or high resistance in EBCM ground circuit. Is the repair complete?	—	Go to *Step 13*	—
8	1. Turn the ignition switch to the ON position with the engine off. 2. Use a DMM to measure the voltage between the *J 39700* universal pinout box terminal 8 and 15. Is the voltage above the specified value?	9.4 Volts	Go to *Step 11*	Go to *Step 9*
9	1. Remove the 10 A ABS fuse from the underhood accessory wiring junction block. 2. Use a DMM to measure the resistance between the underhood accessory wiring junction block connector C 1 terminal E 4 and the *J 39700* universal pinout box terminal 8. Is the resistance within the specified range?	0-5 Ω	*Diagnose Charging System*	Go to *Step 10*
10	Repair high resistance or open in the IGN circuit. Is the repair complete?	—	Go to *Step 13*	—
11	1. Turn the ignition switch to the OFF position. 2. Reconnect the EBCM connector. 3. Disconnect the scan tool if the scan tool is still connected. 4. Test drive the vehicle above 5 km/h (3 mph). Did DTC C0896 reset?	—	Go to *Step 12*	Go to *Step 13*
12	Replace the EBCM. Is the repair complete?	—	Go to *Step 13*	—
13	1. Use the scan tool in order to clear the DTCs. 2. Operate the vehicle within the Conditions for Running the DTC as specified in the supporting text. Does the DTC reset?	—	Go to *Step 2*	System OK

GC4020152510020X

Fig. 159 Code C0896: Device Voltage Range/ Performance (Part 2 of 2). 2001–02 Intrigue

Step	Action	Yes	No
Schematic Reference: *ABS Schematics*			
1	Did you perform the ABS Diagnostic System Check?	Go to *Step 2*	Go to *Diagnostic System Check - ABS*
2	1. Turn OFF the ignition. 2. Disconnect the EBCM. 3. Install the *J 39700* universal pinout box with the *J 39700-530* cable adapter to the EBCM harness connector only. 4. Disconnect the steering angle sensor. 5. Using the DMM, test the CAN HI and CAN LO circuits for a short to ground between the steering angle sensor and the EBCM. Did you find and correct the condition?	Go to *Step 8*	Go to *Step 3*
3	Using the DMM, test the CAN HI and CAN LO circuits between the steering angle sensor and the EBCM for being shorted together. Did you find and correct the condition?	Go to *Step 8*	Go to *Step 4*
4	Perform the steering angle sensor centering procedure. Did you successfully complete the centering procedure?	Go to *Step 5*	Go to *Step 6*
5	1. Use the scan tool in order to clear the DTCs. 2. Test drive the vehicle. Did DTC C1650 reset?	Go to *Step 7*	Go to *Step 8*
6	Replace the steering angle sensor. Did you complete the replacement?	Go to *Step 8*	—
7	Replace the EBCM. Did you complete the replacement?	Go to *Step 8*	—
8	1. Use the scan tool in order to clear the DTCs. 2. Operate the vehicle within the Conditions for Running the DTC as specified in the supporting test. Does the DTC reset?	Go to *Step 2*	System OK

GC4020152511020X

Fig. 160 Code U1650: Chassis System Dedicated Bus Controller Fault (Part 2 of 2). 2001–02 Intrigue

Circuit Description

The Controller Area Network (CAN) serial data circuit is a high speed serial data bus used to communicate information between the steering angle sensor and the EBCM. When the ignition switch is turned to the ON position, the module and the steering angle sensor begin to transmit data between each other.

The CAN bus circuit is monitored continuously after the ignition switch is turned to the ON position.

Conditions for Running the DTC

- The ignition is ON.
- The vehicle speed is greater than 40 km/h (25 mph).

Conditions for Setting the DTC

Line interruptions are detected by CAN message monitor.

Action Taken When the DTC Sets

If equiped, the following actions occur:

- The EBCM disables theTCS/VSES and for the duration of the ignition cycle.
- A malfunction DTC will set.
- The TCS indicator turns on.
- The PCS indicator turns on.

Conditions for Clearing the DTC

- The condition for the DTC is no longer present.
- Using a scan tool.
- The EBCM automatically clears the history DTC when a current DTC is not detected in 100 consecutive drive cycles.

Diagnostic Aids

Possible causes of this DTC are as follows:

- CAN HI and CAN LO circuits shorted together.
- CAN HI or CAN LO circuit shorted to ground.
- CAN HI or CAN LO circuit shorted to voltage.

Test Description

The number(s) below refer to the step number(s) on the diagnostic table.

2. Tests for a short to ground between the CAN HI and CAN LO circuits.
3. Tests the CAN HI and CAN LO circuits for a short together.
4. Checks to see if steering angle sensor is centered.

GC4020152511010X

Fig. 160 Code U1650: Chassis System Dedicated Bus Controller Fault (Part 1 of 2). 2001–02 Intrigue

Circuit Description

The EBCM monitors the received messages from the steering angle sensor for corruption or for missing messages.

Conditions for Running the DTC

- The ignition is ON.
- The vehicle speed is greater than 40 km/h (25 mph).

Conditions for Setting the DTC

The EBCM receives a corrupt or a missing message after 100 milliseconds.

Action Taken When the DTC Sets

If equiped, the following actions occur:

- The EBCM disables theTCS/VSES and for the duration of the ignition cycle.
- A malfunction DTC will set.
- The TCS indicator turns on.
- The PCS indicator turns on.

Conditions for Clearing the DTC

- The condition for the DTC is no longer present.
- Using a scan tool.
- The EBCM automatically clears the history DTC when a current DTC is not detected in 100 consecutive drive cycles.

Diagnostic Aids

Possible causes of this DTC are as follows:

- An open in the CAN HI or CAN LO circuit.
- An open in the ignition circuit.
- An open in the ground circuit.
- Malfunctioning steering angle sensor.
- Malfunctioning EBCM.

Test Description

The number(s) below refer to the step number(s) on the diagnostic table.

2. Tests the ignition circuit for an open.
3. Checks the ground circuit for an open.
4. Tests the CAN HI circuit for an open.
5. Tests the CAN LO circuit for an open.
6. Checks the steering angle sensor connector for poor connections.

DTC U1651

Step	Action	Yes	No
Schematic Reference: *ABS Schematics*			
1	Did you perform the ABS Diagnostic System Check?	Go to *Step 2*	Go to *Diagnostic System Check - ABS*
2	1. Turn OFF the ignition. 2. Disconnect the steering angle sensor harness connector. 3. Using a DMM, check the ignition circuit for an open. Did you find and correct the condition?	Go to *Step 12*	Go to *Step 3*
3	1. Disconnect the EBCM harness connector. 2. Install the *J 39700* universal pinout box with the *J 39700-530* cable adapter between the EBCM and the EBCM harness connector. 3. Disconnect the steering angle sensor. 4. Using a DMM, check the ground circuit for an open. Did you find and correct the condition?	Go to *Step 12*	Go to *Step 4*
4	Using a DMM, check the CAN HI circuit for an open. Did you find and correct the condition?	Go to *Step 12*	Go to *Step 5*
5	Using a DMM, check the CAN LO circuit for an open. Did you find and correct the condition?	Go to *Step 12*	Go to *Step 6*

GC4020152512010X

Fig. 161 Code U1651: Chassis System Dedicated Bus Sensor No. 1 Fault (Part 1 of 2). 2001–02 Intrigue

Step	Action	Yes	No
6	Inspect for poor connections at the harness connector of the steering angle sensor. Did you find and correct the condition?	Go to *Step 12*	Go to *Step 7*
7	Inspect for poor connections at the harness connector of the EBCM. Did you find and correct the condition?	Go to *Step 12*	Go to *Step 8*
8	Perform the steering angle sensor centering procedure. Did you successfully complete the centering procedure?	Go to *Step 9*	Go to *Step 10*
9	1. Use the scan tool in order to clear the DTCs. 2. Test drive the vehicle. Did DTC C1651 reset?	Go to *Step 11*	Go to *Step 12*
10	Replace the steering angle sensor. Did you complete the replacement?	Go to *Step 12*	—
11	Replace the EBCM. Did you complete the replacement?	Go to *Step 12*	—
12	1. Use the scan tool in order to clear the DTCs. 2. Operate the vehicle within the Conditions for Running the DTC as specified in the supporting test. Does the DTC reset?	Go to *Step 2*	System OK

GC4020152512020X

Fig. 161 Code U1651: Chassis System Dedicated Bus Sensor No. 1 Fault (Part 2 of 2). 2001–02 Intrigue

Symptoms - Antilock Brake System

Important: The following steps must be completed before using the symptom tables.

1. Perform the *Diagnostic System Check - ABS* before using the Symptom Tables in order to verify that all of the following are true:
   - There are no DTCs set.
   - The control module(s) can communicate via the serial data link.
2. Review the system operation in order to familiarize yourself with the system functions.

Visual/Physical Inspection

- Inspect for aftermarket devices which could affect the operation of the antilock brake system.
- Inspect the easily accessible or visible system components for obvious damage or conditions which could cause the symptom.
- Inspect the master cylinder reservoir for the proper brake fluid level.

Intermittent

Faulty electrical connections or wiring may be the cause of intermittent conditions.

Symptom List

Refer to a symptom diagnostic procedure from the following list in order to diagnose the symptom:

- *ABS Indicator Always On*
- *ABS Indicator Inoperative*
- *Low Traction Indicator Always On*
- *Low Traction Indicator Inoperative*
- *PCS Indicator Always On*
- *PCS Indicator Inoperative*
- *Traction Off Indicator Always On*
- *Traction Off Indicator Inoperative*

GC4020152513000X

Fig. 162 ABS Symptoms. 2001–02 Intrigue

Symptoms - Antilock Brake System

Important: The following steps must be completed before using the symptom tables.

1. Perform the *Diagnostic System Check - ABS* before using the Symptom Tables in order to verify that all of the following are true:
   - There are no DTCs set.
   - The control module(s) can communicate via the serial data link.
2. Review the system operation in order to familiarize yourself with the system functions.

Visual/Physical Inspection

- Inspect for aftermarket devices which could affect the operation of the antilock brake system.
- Inspect the easily accessible or visible system components for obvious damage or conditions which could cause the symptom.
- Inspect the master cylinder reservoir for the proper fluid level.

Intermittent

Faulty electrical connections or wiring may be the cause of intermittent conditions.

Symptom List

Refer to a symptom diagnostic procedure from the following list in order to diagnose the symptom:

- *ABS Indicator Always On*
- *ABS Indicator Inoperative*
- *Low Traction Indicator Always On*
- *Low Traction Indicator Inoperative*
- *Traction Off Indicator Always On*
- *Traction Off Indicator Inoperative*

GC4020152514000X

Fig. 163 ABS Symptoms. 2001–04 Grand Prix

Circuit Description

The ABS indicator is controlled by the EBCM. The EBCM supplies the ground to ABS indicator control circuit in order to keep the indicator off. When ABS indicator control circuit looses ground at the EBCM, the ABS indicator turns on.

Diagnostic Aids

- It is very important that a thorough inspection of the wiring and connectors be performed. Failure to carefully and fully inspect wiring and connectors may result in misdiagnosis, causing part replacement with reappearance of the malfunction.
- Thoroughly inspect any circuitry that may be causing the complaint for the following conditions:
  - Backed out terminals
  - Improper mating
  - Broken locks
  - Improperly formed or damaged terminals
  - Poor terminal-to-wiring connections
  - Physical damage to the wiring harness
- The following conditions may cause an intermittent malfunction:
  - A poor connection
  - Rubbed-through wire insulation
  - A broken wire inside the insulation
- If an intermittent malfunction exists refer to *General Electrical Diagnosis Procedures* in Wiring Systems for further diagnosis.

Test Description

The number(s) below refer to the step number(s) on the diagnostic table.

2. This step checks for an internal EBCM malfunction.
4. This step checks for an open in ABS indicator control circuit.

Step	Action	Value(s)	Yes	No
Schematic Reference: *ABS Schematics*				
1	Was the Diagnostic System Check performed?	—	Go to *Step 2*	Go to *Diagnostic System Check - ABS*
2	1. Turn the ignition switch to the OFF position. 2. Disconnect the EBCM connector C1. 3. Install the Universal Pinout Box *J 39700* using the cable adapter *J 39700-530* to connector C1 only. 4. Connect a fused jumper wire between terminals 16 and 15 of the Universal Pinout Box. 5. Turn the ignition switch to the RUN position. Does the ABS Indicator turn off?	—	Go to *Step 3*	Go to *Step 4*
3	Replace the EBCM. Is the replacement complete?	—	Go to *Step 7*	—
4	1. Turn the ignition switch to the OFF position. 2. Disconnect the Instrument Cluster connector C1. 3. Using the DMM, measure the resistance between terminals 16 of the Universal Pinout Box and the Instrument Cluster harness connector C1 terminal E. Is the resistance within the range specified in the value(s) column?	0–5Ω	Go to *Step 6*	Go to *Step 5*
5	Repair the ABS indicator control circuit for an open or high resistance. Is the repair complete?	—	Go to *Step 7*	—
6	Replace the Instrument Panel. Is the repair complete?	—	Go to *Step 7*	—
7	Operate the system in order to verify the repair. Did you correct the condition?	—	System OK	Go to *Step 2*

GC4020152515000X

Fig. 164 ABS Indicator Always On. 2001–04 Grand Prix

Circuit Description

The ABS indicator is controlled by the EBCM. The EBCM supplies the ground to ABS indicator control circuit in order to keep the indicator off. When ABS indicator control circuit looses ground at the EBCM, the ABS indicator turns on.

Diagnostic Aids

- It is very important that a thorough inspection of the wiring and connectors be performed. Failure to carefully and fully inspect wiring and connectors may result in misdiagnosis, causing part replacement with reappearance of the malfunction.
- Thoroughly inspect any circuitry that may be causing the complaint for the following conditions:
  - Backed out terminals
  - Improper mating
  - Broken locks
  - Improperly formed or damaged terminals
  - Poor terminal-to-wiring connections
  - Physical damage to the wiring harness
- The following conditions may cause an intermittent malfunction:
  - A poor connection
  - Rubbed-through wire insulation
  - A broken wire inside the insulation
- If an intermittent malfunction exists refer to *General Electrical Diagnosis Procedures* in Wiring Systems for further diagnosis.

Test Description

The number(s) below refer to the step number(s) on the diagnostic table.

2. This step checks for an internal EBCM malfunction.
4. This step checks for a short to ground in ABS indicator control circuit.

Step	Action	Value(s)	Yes	No
Schematic Reference: *ABS Schematics*				
1	Was the Diagnostic System Check performed?	—	Go to *Step 2*	Go to *Diagnostic System Check - ABS*
2	1. Turn the ignition switch to the OFF position. 2. Disconnect the EBCM connector C1. 3. Turn the ignition switch to the RUN position. Does the ABS Indicator come on?	—	Go to *Step 3*	Go to *Step 4*
3	Replace the EBCM. Is the replacement complete?	—	Go to *Step 9*	—
4	1. Turn the ignition switch to the OFF position. 2. Install the *J 39700* Universal Pinout Box using the *J 39700-530* cable adapter to connector C1 only. 3. Disconnect the Instrument Cluster connector C1. 4. Using *J 39200* DMM, measure the resistance between terminals 16 and 15 of *J 39700*. Is the resistance within the range specified in the value(s) column?	OL (infinite)	Go to *Step 6*	Go to *Step 5*
5	Repair ABS indicator control circuit for a short to ground. Is the repair complete?	—	Go to *Step 9*	—
6	1. Turn the ignition switch to the OFF position 2. Check the ABS indicator bulb. Is the ABS Indicator bulb OK?	—	Go to *Step 8*	Go to *Step 7*
7	Replace the ABS Indicator Bulb. Is the replacement complete?	—	Go to *Step 9*	—
8	Replace the Instrument Panel Cluster. Is the replacement complete?	—	Go to *Step 9*	—
9	Operate the system in order to verify the repair. Did you correct the condition?	—	System OK	Go to *Step 2*

GC4020152516000X

Fig. 165 ABS Indicator Inoperative. 2001–04 Grand Prix

Circuit Description

The LOW TRAC Indicator is controlled by the EBCM. The LOW TRAC Indicator is activated during a traction control event only. When the EBCM detects a low traction condition it supplies a ground for the LOW TRAC indicator control circuit turning on the LOW TRAC Indicator.

Diagnostic Aids

- It is very important that a thorough inspection of the wiring and connectors be performed. Failure to carefully and fully inspect wiring and connectors may result in misdiagnosis, causing part replacement with reappearance of the malfunction.
- Thoroughly inspect any circuitry that may be causing the complaint for the following conditions:
  - Backed out terminals
  - Improper mating
  - Broken locks
  - Improperly formed or damaged terminals
  - Poor terminal-to-wiring connections
  - Physical damage to the wiring harness
- The following conditions may cause an intermittent malfunction:
  - A poor connection
  - Rubbed-through wire insulation
  - A broken wire inside the insulation

Test Description

The number(s) below refer to the step number(s) on the diagnostic table.

2. This step checks for an internal EBCM short.
4. This step checks for a short to ground in the LOW TRAC indicator control circuit.

Step	Action	Value(s)	Yes	No
Schematic Reference: *ABS Schematics*				
1	Was the Diagnostic System Check performed?	—	Go to *Step 2*	Go to *Diagnostic System Check - ABS*
2	1. Turn the ignition switch to the OFF position. 2. Disconnect the EBCM connector C1. 3. Turn the ignition switch to the RUN position. Is the LOW TRAC Indicator off?	—	Go to *Step 3*	Go to *Step 4*
3	Replace the EBCM. Is the replacement complete?	—	Go to *Step 7*	—
4	1. Install the Universal Pinout Box *J 39700* using the *J 39700-530* cable adapter to connector C1 only. 2. Disconnect the Driver Information Display (Base) or Trip Calculator (Up Level) connector. 3. Using the DMM, measure the resistance between terminals 25 and 15 of the Universal Pinout Box. Is the resistance within the range specified in the value(s) column?	OL (Infinite)	Go to *Step 6*	Go to *Step 5*
5	Repair Traction Active indicator control circuit for a short to ground. Is the repair complete?	—	Go to *Step 7*	—
6	Suspect the Driver Information Display (Base) or Trip Calculator (Up Level). Is the repair complete?	—	Go to *Step 7*	—
7	Operate the system in order to verify the repair. Did you correct the condition?	—	System OK	Go to *Step 2*

GC4020152517000X

Fig. 166 Low Traction Indicator Always On. 2001–04 Grand Prix

Circuit Description

The LOW TRAC Indicator is controlled by the EBCM. The LOW TRAC Indicator is activated during a traction control event only. When the EBCM detects a low traction condition it supplies a ground for the LOW TRAC indicator control circuit turning on the LOW TRAC Indicator.

Diagnostic Aids

- It is very important that a thorough inspection of the wiring and connectors be performed. Failure to carefully and fully inspect wiring and connectors may result in misdiagnosis, causing part replacement with reappearance of the malfunction.
- Thoroughly inspect any circuitry that may be causing the complaint for the following conditions:
  - Backed out terminals
  - Improper mating
  - Broken locks
  - Improperly formed or damaged terminals
  - Poor terminal-to-wiring connections
  - Physical damage to the wiring harness
- The following conditions may cause an intermittent malfunction:
  - A poor connection
  - Rubbed-through wire insulation
  - A broken wire inside the insulation
- If an intermittent malfunction exists refer to *General Electrical Diagnosis Procedures* in Wiring Systems for further diagnosis.

Test Description

The number(s) below refer to the step number(s) on the diagnostic table.

2. This step checks for an internal EBCM malfunction.
4. This step checks for an open in LOW TRAC indicator control circuit.

Step	Action	Value(s)	Yes	No
Schematic Reference: *ABS Schematics*				
1	Was the Diagnostic System Check performed?	—	Go to *Step 2*	Go to *Diagnostic System Check - ABS*
2	1. Turn the ignition switch to the OFF position. 2. Disconnect the EBCM connector C1. 3. Install the *J 39700* Universal Pinout Box using *J 39700-530* cable adapter to connector C1 only. 4. Connect a fused jumper wire between terminals 25 and 15 of *J 39700*. 5. Turn the ignition switch to the RUN position. Does the LOW TRAC Indicator come on?	—	Go to *Step 3*	Go to *Step 4*
3	Replace the EBCM. Is the replacement complete?	—	Go to *Step 7*	—
4	1. Turn the ignition switch to the OFF position. 2. Disconnect the Driver Information Display (Base) or Trip Calculator (Up Level) connector. 3. Using *J 39200* DMM, measure the resistance between terminals 25 of and the Driver Information Display (Base) or Trip Calculator (Up Level) harness connector terminal H (Driver Information Display) or A3 (Trip Calculator). Is the resistance within the range specified in the value(s) column?	0–5Ω	Go to *Step 6*	Go to *Step 5*
5	Repair Traction Active indicator control circuit for an open or high resistance. Is the repair complete?	—	Go to *Step 7*	—
6	Suspect the Driver Information Display (Base) or Trip Calculator (Up Level). Is the repair complete?	—	Go to *Step 7*	—
7	Operate the system in order to verify the repair. Did you correct the condition?	—	System OK	Go to *Step 2*

GC4020152518000X

Fig. 167 Low Traction Indicator Inoperative. 2001–04 Grand Prix

Circuit Description

The TRAC OFF indicator is controlled by the EBCM. The EBCM supplies the ground to the Trac Off indicator control circuit to turn the indicator on. When the Trac Off indicator control circuit is not grounded at the EBCM, the TRAC OFF indicator remains off. When the EBCM sees the traction control switch voltage go low, it turns the TRAC OFF indicator on and disables traction control.

Diagnostic Aids

- It is very important that a thorough inspection of the wiring and connectors be performed. Failure to carefully and fully inspect wiring and connectors may result in misdiagnosis, causing part replacement with reappearance of the malfunction.
- Thoroughly inspect any circuitry that may be causing the complaint for the following conditions:
  - Backed out terminals
  - Improper mating
  - Broken locks
  - Improperly formed or damaged terminals
  - Poor terminal-to-wiring connections
  - Physical damage to the wiring harness
- The following conditions may cause an intermittent malfunction:
  - A poor connection
  - Rubbed-through wire insulation
  - A broken wire inside the insulation

Test Description

The number(s) below refer to the step number(s) on the diagnostic table.

3. This step checks for an internal EBCM malfunction.
5. This step checks for an open in the Trac Off indicator control circuit.

Step	Action	Value(s)	Yes	No
Schematic Reference: *ABS Schematics*				
1	Was the Diagnostic System Check performed?	—	Go to *Step 2*	Go to *Diagnostic System Check - ABS*
2	1. Turn the ignition switch to the RUN position, engine off. 2. Using a scan tool enter ABS/TCS Data List. 3. While monitoring the TRAC On/Off switch status, press and release the TRAC On/Off switch. Does the switch status change from pressed to released as the TRAC switch is pressed and released?	—	Go to *Step 3*	Go to *Step 8*
3	1. Turn the ignition switch to the OFF position. 2. Disconnect the EBCM connector C1. 3. Install the Universal Pinout Box *J 39700* using the *J 39700-530* cable adapter to connector C1 only. 4. Connect a fused jumper wire between terminals 18 and 15 of the Universal Pinout Box 5. Turn the ignition switch to the RUN position, engine off. Does the TRAC OFF Indicator turn on?	—	Go to *Step 4*	Go to *Step 5*
4	Replace the EBCM. Is the replacement complete?	—	Go to *Step 10*	—

GC4020152519010X

Fig. 168 Traction Off Indicator Always On (Part 1 of 2). 2001–04 Grand Prix

Step	Action	Value(s)	Yes	No
5	1. Turn the ignition switch to the OFF position. 2. Disconnect the Driver Information Display (Base) or Trip Computer (Up Level) connector. 3. Using the DMM, measure the resistance between terminals 18 of the Universal Pinout Box and the Driver Information Display (Base) or Trip Computer (Up Level) harness connector terminal L (Driver Information Display) or A6 (Trip Computer). Is the resistance within the range specified in the value(s) column?	0–5Ω	Go to *Step 7*	Go to *Step 6*
6	Repair Traction Indicator control circuit for an open or high resistance. Is the repair complete?	—	Go to *Step 10*	—
7	Suspect the Driver Information Display (Base) or Trip Computer (Up Level). Is the repair complete?	—	Go to *Step 10*	—
8	1. Turn the ignition switch to the OFF position. 2. Disconnect the EBCM connector C1. 3. Install the Universal Pinout Box *J 39700* using the *J 39700-530* cable adapter to connector C1 only. 4. Using the DMM, measure the resistance between terminals 17 and 15 of the Universal Pinout Box while an assistant presses the TRAC On/Off switch. Is the resistance within the range specified in the value(s) column?	0-5Ω	Go to *Step 4*	Go to *Step 9*
9	Repair Traction Control switch signal circuit for an open or high resistance, being sure to check the traction control switch for an open. Is the repair complete?	—	Go to *Step 10*	—
10	Operate the system in order to verify the repair. Did you correct the condition?	—	System OK	Go to *Step 2*

GC4020152519020X

Fig. 168 Traction Off Indicator Always On (Part 2 of 2). 2001–04 Grand Prix

Step	Action	Value(s)	Yes	No
5	1. Turn the ignition switch to the OFF position. 2. Disconnect the Driver Information Display (Base) or Trip Computer (Up Level) connector. 3. Using the DMM, measure the resistance between terminals 18 of the Universal Pinout Box and the Driver Information Display (Base) or Trip Computer (Up Level) harness connector terminal L (Driver Information Display) or A6 (Trip Computer). Is the resistance within the range specified in the value(s) column?	0–5Ω	Go to *Step 7*	Go to *Step 6*
6	Repair Traction Indicator control circuit for an open or high resistance. Is the repair complete?	—	Go to *Step 10*	—
7	Suspect the Driver Information Display (Base) or Trip Computer (Up Level). Is the repair complete?	—	Go to *Step 10*	—
8	1. Turn the ignition switch to the OFF position. 2. Disconnect the EBCM connector C1. 3. Install the Universal Pinout Box *J 39700* using the *J 39700-530* cable adapter to connector C1 only. 4. Using the DMM, measure the resistance between terminals 17 and 15 of the Universal Pinout Box while an assistant presses the TRAC On/Off switch. Is the resistance within the range specified in the value(s) column?	0-5Ω	Go to *Step 4*	Go to *Step 9*
9	Repair Traction Control switch signal circuit for an open or high resistance, being sure to check the traction control switch for an open. Is the repair complete?	—	Go to *Step 10*	—
10	Operate the system in order to verify the repair. Did you correct the condition?	—	System OK	Go to *Step 2*

GC4020152520020X

Fig. 169 Traction Off Indicator Inoperative (Part 2 of 2). 2001–04 Grand Prix

Circuit Description

The TRAC OFF indicator is controlled by the EBCM. The EBCM supplies the ground to the Trac Off indicator control circuit to turn the indicator on. When the Trac Off indicator control circuit is not grounded at the EBCM, the TRAC OFF indicator remains off. When the EBCM sees the traction control switch voltage go low, it turns the TRAC OFF indicator on and disables traction control.

Diagnostic Aids

- It is very important that a thorough inspection of the wiring and connectors be performed. Failure to carefully and fully inspect wiring and connectors may result in misdiagnosis, causing part replacement with reappearance of the malfunction.
- Thoroughly inspect any circuitry that may be causing the complaint for the following conditions:
  - Backed out terminals
  - Improper mating
  - Broken locks
  - Improperly formed or damaged terminals
  - Poor terminal-to-wiring connections
  - Physical damage to the wiring harness
- The following conditions may cause an intermittent malfunction:
  - A poor connection
  - Rubbed-through wire insulation
  - A broken wire inside the insulation

Test Description

The number(s) below refer to the step number(s) on the diagnostic table.

3. This step checks for an internal EBCM malfunction.
5. This step checks for an open in the Trac Off indicator control circuit.

Step	Action	Value(s)	Yes	No
Schematic Reference: *ABS Schematics*				
1	Was the Diagnostic System Check performed?	—	Go to *Step 2*	Go to *Diagnostic System Check - ABS*
2	1. Turn the ignition switch to the RUN position, engine off. 2. Using a scan tool enter ABS/TCS Data List. 3. While monitoring the TRAC On/Off switch status, press and release the TRAC On/Off switch. Does the switch status change from pressed to released as the TRAC switch is pressed and released?	—	Go to *Step 3*	Go to *Step 8*
3	1. Turn the ignition switch to the OFF position. 2. Disconnect the EBCM connector C1. 3. Install the Universal Pinout Box *J 39700* using the *J 39700-530* cable adapter to connector C1 only. 4. Connect a fused jumper wire between terminals 18 and 15 of the Universal Pinout Box 5. Turn the ignition switch to the RUN position, engine off. Does the TRAC OFF Indicator turn on?	—	Go to *Step 4*	Go to *Step 5*
4	Replace the EBCM. Is the replacement complete?	—	Go to *Step 10*	—

GC4020152520010X

Fig. 169 Traction Off Indicator Inoperative (Part 1 of 2). 2001–04 Grand Prix

Circuit Description

The instrument panel cluster (IPC) turns the ABS Indicator on during the IPC bulb check for approximately 3 seconds when the ignition switch is turned to the ON position. If the EBCM sets a diagnostic trouble code (DTC) the EBCM sends the IPC the command to turn the ABS indicator on.

Test Description

The numbers below refer to step numbers on the diagnostic table.

2. Checks if the instrument panel cluster has the ability to turn the ABS indicator off or if the EBCM is sending an incorrect command to turn the ABS indicator on.

Step	Action	Yes	No
Schematic Reference: *ABS Schematics*			
1	Was the ABS Diagnostic System Check performed?	Go to *Step 2*	Go to *Diagnostic System Check - ABS*
2	Using a scan tool in the Instrument Panel Cluster Special Functions attempt to turn off the ABS indicator. Did the ABS indicator turn off?	Go to *Step 3*	Go to *Step 4*
3	Replace the EBCM. Is the replacement complete?	Go to *Diagnostic System Check - ABS*	—
4	Replace the instrument panel cluster. Is the replacement complete?	Go to *Diagnostic System Check - ABS*	—

GC4020152521000X

Fig. 170 ABS Indicator Always On. 2001–02 Intrigue

Circuit Description

The instrument panel cluster (IPC) turns the ABS Indicator on during the IPC bulb check for approximately 3 seconds when the ignition switch is turned to the ON position. If the EBCM sets a diagnostic trouble code (DTC) the EBCM sends the IPC the command to turn the ABS indicator on.

Test Description

The numbers below refer to step numbers on the diagnostic table.

2. Checks if the IPC has the ability to turn the ABS Indicator on.

Step	Action	Yes	No
Schematic Reference: *ABS Schematics*			
1	Was the ABS Diagnostic System Check performed?	Go to *Step 2*	Go to *Diagnostic System Check - ABS*
2	Using a scan tool in the Instrument Panel (IPC) Special Functions attempt to turn the ABS indicator on. Did the ABS indicator turn on?	Go to *Step 3*	Go to *Step 4*
3	Replace the EBCM. Is the replacement complete?	Go to *Diagnostic System Check - ABS*	—
4	1. Turn the ignition switch to the OFF position. 2. Check the ABS indicator bulb. Is the ABS Indicator bulb OK?	Go to *Step 6*	Go to *Step 5*
5	Replace the ABS Indicator bulb. Is the replacement complete?	Go to *Diagnostic System Check - ABS*	—
6	Replace the Instrument Panel Cluster. Is the replacement complete?	Go to *Diagnostic System Check - ABS*	—

GC4020152522000X

Fig. 171 ABS Indicator Inoperative. 2001–02 Intrigue

Circuit Description

The instrument panel cluster (IPC) turns the LOW TRAC Indicator on during the IPC bulb check for approximately 3 seconds when the ignition switch is turned to the ON position. The LOW TRAC Indicator is activated during a traction control event only. If the EBCM detects a low traction condition, the EBCM sends the IPC the command to turn the LOW TRAC indicator on.

Test Description

The numbers below refer to step numbers on the diagnostic table.

2. Checks if the instrument panel cluster has the ability to turn the LOW TRAC indicator off or if the EBTCM is sending an incorrect command to turn the LOW TRAC indicator on.

Step	Action	Yes	No
Schematic Reference: *ABS Schematics*			
1	Was the ABS Diagnostic System Check performed?	Go to *Step 2*	Go to *Diagnostic System Check - ABS*
2	Using a scan tool in the Instrument Panel Cluster Special Functions attempt to turn off the LOW TRAC indicator. Did the LOW TRAC indicator turn off?	Go to *Step 3*	Go to *Step 4*
3	Replace the EBCM. Is the replacement complete?	Go to *Diagnostic System Check - ABS*	—
4	Replace the instrument panel cluster. Is the replacement complete?	Go to *Diagnostic System Check - ABS*	—

GC4020152523000X

Fig. 172 Low Traction Indicator Always On. 2001–02 Intrigue

Circuit Description

The instrument panel cluster (IPC) turns the LOW TRAC indicator on during the IPC bulb check for approximately 3 seconds when the ignition switch is turned to the ON position. The LOW TRAC Indicator is activated during a traction control event only. If the EBCM detects a low traction condition, the EBCM sends the IPC the command to turn the LOW TRAC Indicator on.

Test Description

The numbers below refer to step numbers on the diagnostic table.

2. Checks if the IPC has the ability to turn the LOW TRAC indicator on.

Step	Action	Yes	No
Schematic Reference: *ABS Schematics*			
1	Was the ABS Diagnostic System Check performed?	Go to *Step 2*	Go to *Diagnostic System Check - ABS*
2	Using a scan tool in the Instrument Panel (IPC) Special Functions attempt to turn the LOW TRAC indicator on. Did the LOW TRAC indicator turn on?	Go to *Step 3*	Go to *Step 4*
3	Replace the EBCM. Is the replacement complete?	Go to *Diagnostic System Check - ABS*	—
4	1. Turn the ignition switch to the OFF position. 2. Check the LOW TRAC indicator bulb. Is the LOW TRAC Indicator bulb OK?	Go to *Step 6*	Go to *Step 5*
5	Replace the LOW TRAC indicator bulb. Is the replacement complete?	Go to *Diagnostic System Check - ABS*	—
6	Replace the Instrument Panel Cluster. Is the replacement complete?	Go to *Diagnostic System Check - ABS*	—

GC4020152524000X

Fig. 173 Low Traction Indicator Inoperative. 2001–02 Intrigue

Circuit Description

The PCS On indicator is controlled by the instrument cluster via class 2 serial data messages from the EBCM. When the instrument cluster sees the PCS signal input grounded, it sends a class 2 message to the EBCM that tells the EBCM that the PCS is malfunctioning. The EBCM then disables PCS and TCS and sends a message to the instrument cluster to turn the PCS and TCS indicators ON. Each time the ignition is cycled from OFF to ON, the PCS is enabled.

The following conditions will cause the PCS/TCS indicators to illuminate:

- The EBCM has disabled the PCS/TCS due to a DTC.
- The instrument cluster bulb check. When the ignition switch is turned to ON, the PCS/TCS indicators will turn on for approximately 3 seconds and then turn OFF.

Test Description

The numbers below refer to the step numbers on the diagnostic table.

3. This test uses the scan tool to check the normal state of the ABS indicator control circuit.
4. This test ensures that the instrument cluster can operate the ABS indicator.

Step	Action	Yes	No
Schematic Reference: *ABS Schematics*			
1	Did you perform the ABS Diagnostic System Check?	Go to *Step 2*	Go to *Diagnostic System Check - ABS*
2	Inspect the EBCM ground, making sure the ground is clean and torqued to the proper specification. Did you find and correct the condition?	Go to *Step 9*	Go to *Step 3*
3	With a scan tool, observe the PCS Warning Indicator parameter in the ABS/TCS/PCS/VSES data list. Does the scan tool display Off?	Go to *Step 4*	Go to *Step 5*
4	1. Turn OFF the ignition. 2. Turn ON the ignition, with the engine OFF. 3. Observe the PCS indicator on the instrument cluster (IPC) during the bulb check. Does the PCS indicator illuminate during the bulb check and then turn OFF?	Go to *Step 5*	Go to *Step 6*
5	Inspect for poor connections at the harness connector of the EBCM. Did you find and correct the condition?	Go to *Step 9*	Go to *Step 7*
6	Inspect for poor connections at the harness connector of the instrument cluster (IPC). Did you find and correct the condition?	Go to *Step 9*	Go to *Step 8*
7	**Important:** Perform the setup procedure for the EBCM. An unprogrammed EBCM will result in the following conditions: • Inoperative or poorly functioning ABS/TCS/PCS/VSES/VES • Turns the PCS Warning Indicator On • EBCM Internal Malfunction. Replace the EBCM. Did you complete the repair?	Go to *Step 9*	—
8	Replace the instrument cluster (IPC). Did you complete the repair?	Go to *Step 9*	—
9	Operate the system in order to verify the repair. Did you correct the condition?	System OK	Go to *Step 2*

GC4020152525000X

Fig. 174 PCS Indicator Always On. 2001–02 Intrigue

Circuit Description

The PCS On indicator is controlled by the instrument cluster via class 2 serial data messages from the EBCM. When the instrument cluster sees that the PCS signal input is grounded, it sends a class 2 message to the EBCM that tells the EBCM that the PCS is malfunctioning. The EBCM then disables PCS and TCS and sends a message to the instrument cluster to turn the PCS and TCS indicators ON. Each time the ignition is cycled from OFF to ON, the PCS is enabled.

The following conditions will cause the PCS indicator not to illuminate:

- No signal received from the EBCM.
- The instrument cluster PCS indicator bulb is blown.
- Harness connector malfunctioned.

Test Description

The numbers below refer to the step numbers on the diagnostic table.

3. This test uses the scan tool to check the normal state of the ABS indicator control circuit.
4. This test ensures that the instrument cluster can operate the ABS indicator.

Step	Action	Yes	No
Schematic Reference: *ABS Schematics*			
1	Did you perform the ABS Diagnostic System Check?	Go to *Step 2*	Go to *Diagnostic System Check - ABS*
2	Inspect the EBCM ground, making sure the ground is clean and torqued to the proper specification. Did you find and correct the condition?	Go to *Step 9*	Go to *Step 3*
3	With a scan tool, observe the PCS Warning Indicator parameter in the ABS/TCS/PCS/VSES data list. Does the scan tool display Off?	Go to *Step 4*	Go to *Step 5*
4	1. Turn OFF the ignition. 2. Turn ON the ignition, with the engine OFF. 3. Observe the PCS indicator on the instrument cluster (IPC) during the bulb check. Does the PCS indicator illuminate during the bulb check and then turn OFF?	Go to *Step 5*	Go to *Step 6*
5	Inspect for poor connections at the harness connector of the EBCM. Did you find and correct the condition?	Go to *Step 9*	Go to *Step 7*
6	Inspect for poor connections at the harness connector of the instrument cluster (IPC). Did you find and correct the condition?	Go to *Step 9*	Go to *Step 8*
7	**Important:** Perform the setup procedure for the EBCM. An unprogrammed EBCM will result in the following conditions: • Inoperative or poorly functioning ABS/TCS/PCS/VSES/VES • Turns the PCS Warning Indicator On • EBCM Internal Malfunction. Replace the EBCM. Did you complete the repair?	Go to *Step 9*	—
8	Replace the instrument cluster (IPC). Did you complete the repair?	Go to *Step 9*	—
9	Operate the system in order to verify the repair. Did you correct the condition?	System OK	Go to *Step 2*

GC4020152526000X

Fig. 175 PCS Indicator Inoperative. 2001–02 Intrigue

Circuit Description

The TRAC OFF indicator is controlled by the instrument cluster via class 2 serial data messages from the EBCM. When the body control module (BCM) sees the traction control switch input grounded through the momentary traction control switch, it sends a class 2 message to the EBCM that tells the EBCM that the traction control switch has been pressed. The EBCM then disables traction control and sends a message to the instrument cluster to turn the TRAC OFF indicator ON. Each time the ignition is cycled from OFF to ON, the traction control system is enabled.

The following conditions will cause the TRAC OFF indicator to illuminate:

- The EBCM has disabled the TCS due to a DTC.
- The driver manually disabling the TCS via the traction control switch.
- The instrument cluster bulb check. When the ignition switch is turned to ON, the TRAC OFF indicator will turn on for approximately 3 seconds and then turn OFF.

Diagnostic Aids

- It is very important that a thorough inspection of the wiring and connectors be performed. Failure to carefully and fully inspect wiring and connectors may result in misdiagnosis, causing part replacement with reappearance of the malfunction.
- Thoroughly inspect any circuitry that may be causing the complaint for the following conditions:
  - Backed out terminals
  - Improper mating
  - Broken locks
  - Improperly formed or damaged terminals
  - Poor terminal-to-wiring connections
  - Physical damage to the wiring harness
- The following conditions may cause an intermittent malfunction:
  - A poor connection
  - Rubbed-through wire insulation
  - A broken wire inside the insulation

GC4020152527010X

Fig. 176 Traction Off Indicator Always On (Part 1 of 2). 2001–02 Intrigue

Step	Action	Yes	No
Schematic Reference: *ABS Schematics*			
1	Did you perform the ABS Diagnostic System Check?	Go to *Step 2*	Go to *Diagnostic System Check - ABS*
2	1. Install a scan tool. 2. Turn ON the ignition, with the engine OFF. 3. With a scan tool, observe the Traction Switch parameter in the Body Control Module data list. Does the scan tool display Off?	Go to *Step 3*	Go to *Step 4*
3	1. Activate the traction control switch. 2. With the scan tool, observe the Traction Switch parameter. Does the Traction Switch parameter change state?	*Intermittent and Poor Connections*	Go to *Step 4*
4	1. Turn OFF the ignition. 2. Disconnect the traction control switch connector. 3. Turn ON the ignition, with the engine OFF. 4. With a scan tool, observe the Traction Switch parameter. Does the scan tool display Off?	Go to *Step 7*	Go to *Step 5*
5	Test the signal circuit of the traction control switch for a short to ground. Did you find and correct the condition?	Go to *Step 10*	Go to *Step 6*
6	Inspect for poor connections at the harness connector of the body control module (BCM). Did you find and correct the condition?	Go to *Step 10*	Go to *Step 8*
7	Inspect for poor connections at the harness connector of the traction control switch. Did you find and correct the condition?	Go to *Step 10*	Go to *Step 9*
8	Replace the body control module (BCM). Did you complete the replacement?	Go to *Step 10*	—
9	Replace the traction control switch. Did you complete the replacement?	Go to *Step 10*	—
10	Operate the system in order to verify the repair. Did you correct the condition?	System OK	Go to *Step 2*

GC4020152527020X

Fig. 176 Traction Off Indicator Always On (Part 2 of 2). 2001–02 Intrigue

Circuit Description

The TRAC OFF indicator is controlled by the instrument cluster via class 2 serial data messages from the EBCM. When the body control module (BCM) sees the traction control switch input grounded through the momentary traction control switch, it sends a class 2 message to the EBCM that tells the EBCM that the traction control switch has been pressed. The EBCM then disables traction control and sends a message to the instrument cluster to turn the TRAC OFF indicator ON. Each time the ignition is cycled from OFF to ON, the traction control system is enabled.

The following conditions will cause the TRAC OFF indicator to illuminate:

- The EBCM has disabled the TCS due to a DTC.
- The driver manually disabling the TCS via the traction control switch.
- The instrument cluster bulb check. When the ignition switch is turned to ON, the TRAC OFF indicator will turn on for approximately 3 seconds and then turn OFF.

Diagnostic Aids

- It is very important that a thorough inspection of the wiring and connectors be performed. Failure to carefully and fully inspect wiring and connectors may result in misdiagnosis, causing part replacement with reappearance of the malfunction.
- Thoroughly inspect any circuitry that may be causing the complaint for the following conditions:
  - Backed out terminals
  - Improper mating
  - Broken locks
  - Improperly formed or damaged terminals
  - Poor terminal-to-wiring connections
  - Physical damage to the wiring harness
- The following conditions may cause an intermittent malfunction:
  - A poor connection
  - Rubbed-through wire insulation
  - A broken wire inside the insulation

GC4020152528010X

Fig. 177 Traction Off Indicator Inoperative (Part 1 of 2). 2001–02 Intrigue

Step	Action	Yes	No
Schematic Reference: *ABS Schematics*			
1	Did you perform the ABS Diagnostic System Check?	Go to *Step 2*	Go to *Diagnostic System Check - ABS*
2	1. Install a scan tool. 2. Turn ON the ignition, with the engine OFF. 3. With a scan tool, observe the Traction Switch parameter in the Body Control Module data list. 4. Activate the traction control switch. Does the Traction Switch parameter change state?	*Intermittent and Poor Connections*	Go to *Step 3*
3	1. Turn OFF the ignition. 2. Disconnect the traction control switch connector. 3. Connect a fused jumper from the signal circuit of the traction control switch harness connector to a good ground. 4. Turn ON the ignition, with the engine OFF. 5. With a scan tool, observe the Traction Switch parameter. Does the scan tool display On?	Go to *Step 5*	Go to *Step 4*
4	Test the signal circuit of the traction control switch for an open or high resistance. Did you find and correct the condition?	Go to *Step 10*	Go to *Step 6*
5	Test the ground circuit of the traction control switch for an open or high resistance. Did you find and correct the condition?	Go to *Step 10*	Go to *Step 7*
6	Inspect for poor connections at the harness connector of the body control module (BCM). Did you find and correct the condition?	Go to *Step 10*	Go to *Step 8*
7	Inspect for poor connections at the harness connector of the traction control switch.- Did you find and correct the condition?	Go to *Step 10*	Go to *Step 9*
8	Replace the body control module (BCM). Did you complete the replacement?	Go to *Step 10*	—
9	Replace the traction control switch. Did you complete the replacement?	Go to *Step 10*	—
10	Operate the system in order to verify the repair. Did you correct the condition?	System OK	Go to *Step 2*

GC4020152528020X

Fig. 177 Traction Off Indicator Inoperative (Part 2 of 2). 2001–02 Intrigue

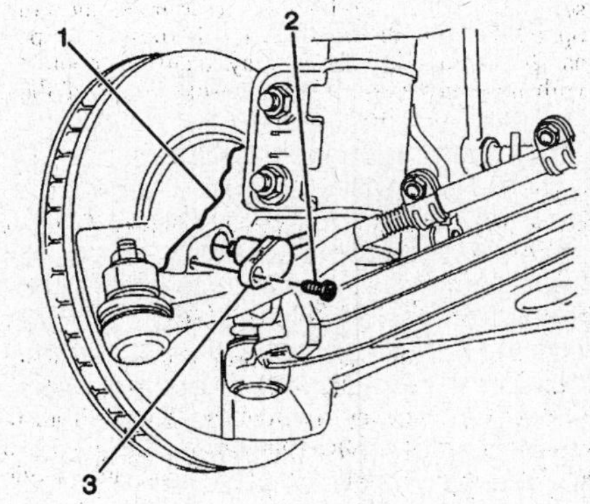

(1) Steering Knuckle
(2) Wheel Speed Sensor Bolt/Screw
(3) Wheel Speed Sensor

GC4029702625000X

Fig. 178 Front wheel speed sensor replacement. Catera

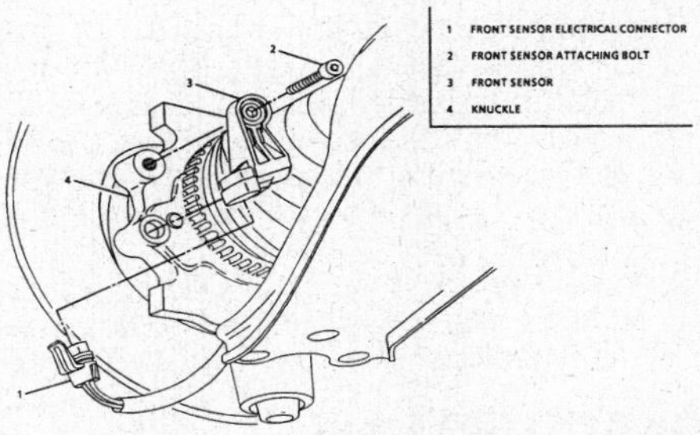

GC4029100848000X

Fig. 179 Front wheel speed sensor replacement. Grand Prix & Intrigue

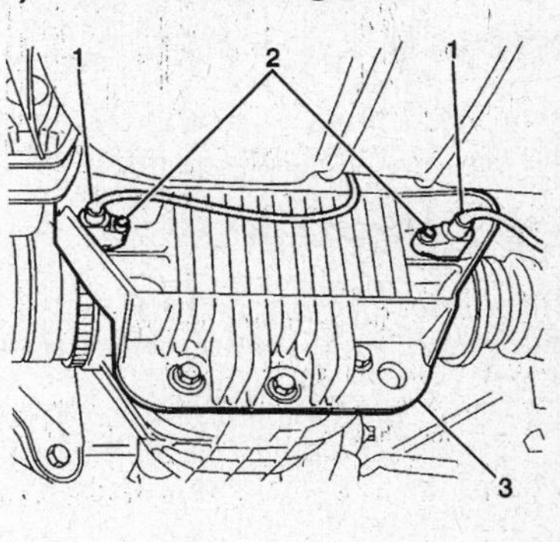

(1) Rear Wheel Speed Sensors
(2) Rear Wheel Speed Sensor Screws
(3) Differential Housing

GC4029702626000X

Fig. 180 Rear wheel speed sensor replacement. Catera

Delco/Bosch Type 5

NOTE: On Air Bag Equipped Models, Refer To "Air Bag System Precautions" Located In The Front Of This Manual For System Disarming & Arming Procedures.

NOTE: Refer To "Computer Relearn Procedures" Located In The Front Of This Manual When Battery Power To The Computer Has Been Interrupted.

NOTE: "Electrical Symbol & Wire Color Code Identification" Located In The Front Of This Manual May Be Used As An Aid When Using Wiring Circuits Found In This Section.

INDEX

PRECAUTIONS

Air Bag Systems

Refer to "Air Bag System Precautions" in the front of this manual for system disarming and arming procedures.

Battery Ground Cable

Prior to service, disconnect battery ground cable and isolate as required.

ABS Service

Before performing any repairs on the ABS system, note the following precautions:

1. Before using electric welding equipment, disconnect EBTCM.
2. Carefully note routing, position and mounting ABS and TCS wiring, connectors, clips and brackets. ABS and TCS are extremely sensitive to electromagnetic interference.
3. Do not use a fast charger when battery is connected. **Never disconnect battery from system with engine running.**
4. Ignition switch must be in Off position when disconnecting EBTCM.
5. Many ABS system components are non-serviceable and must be replaced as assemblies. **Do not disassemble non-serviceable components.**
6. Do not hang other components on wheel speed sensor cables.
7. Do not expose EBTCM to temperatures of more than 184°F .
8. Use DOT 3 brake fluid only. Do not use container that has been used with petroleum based fluids or is wet with water. Petroleum based fluids will damage system and water will lower boiling point. Keep fluid containers capped.
9. After replacing any ABS component, inspect system as outlined in "Diagnosis & Testing."

DESCRIPTION

System Operation

The Anti-Lock Brake System (ABS) minimizes wheel lock-up during heavy braking. The ABS monitors each wheel's speed and controls brake fluid pressure to each wheel independently, **Figs. 1 through 3.** A separate hydraulic line and solenoid valve for each wheel allows hydraulic pressure to be modulated, preventing wheel lock-up. The ABS can decrease, hold or increase hydraulic pressure.

The system continuously monitors all components, uses several methods to determine faults and notify the driver of faults. When the engine is started, the ABS electrical circuitry is functionally inspected. As the vehicle reaches four mph, the Brake Pressure Modulator Valve (BPMV) is functionally inspected. The driver is informed of faults when the system illuminates either or both the Brake and/or ABS lamps.

If the Brake warning lamp is lit, brake system conditions may result in reduced braking ability. If the ABS indicator lamp is lit, an ABS fault has been detected and the anti-lock and traction control functions are turned off. If the ABS indicator lamp only is on, normal braking with full power assist is available without anti-lock. If both lamps are on, there may be a hydraulic brake system problem.

The Traction Control System (TCS) system also monitors rear wheel speed and compares it to front wheel speed. On rear wheel drive models, if rear speed is excessive, the TCS will activate. On front wheel drive models, if either front wheel speed is excessive, the TCS will activate. When the TCS activates, it signals the Powertrain

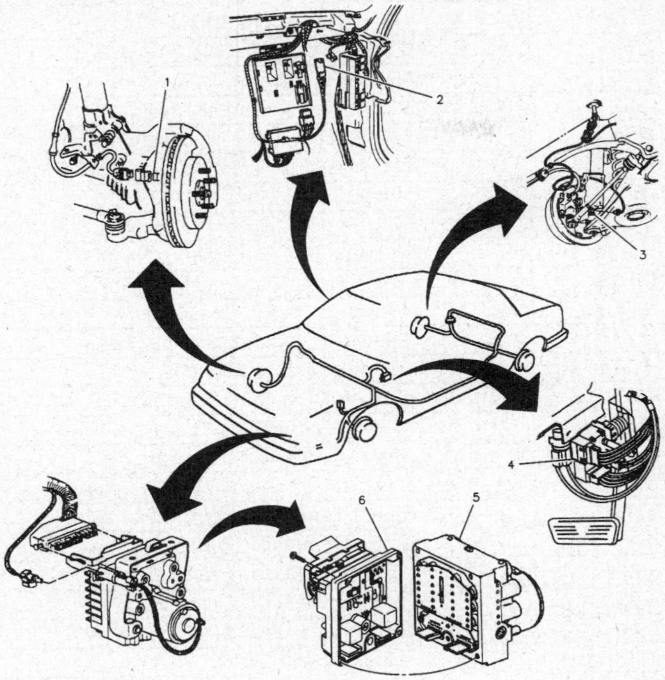

1 FRONT WHEEL SPEED SENSOR
2 ELECTRONIC BRAKE LAMP DRIVER MODULE (LDM)
3 REAR WHEEL SPEED SENSOR
4 BRAKE EXTENDED TRAVEL SWITCH
5 BRAKE PRESSURE MODULATOR VALVE (BPMV)
6 ELECTRONIC BRAKE TRACTION CONTROL MODULE (EBTCM)

GC4029601852000X

Fig. 1 Anti-lock components. Bonneville, LeSabre & Park Avenue

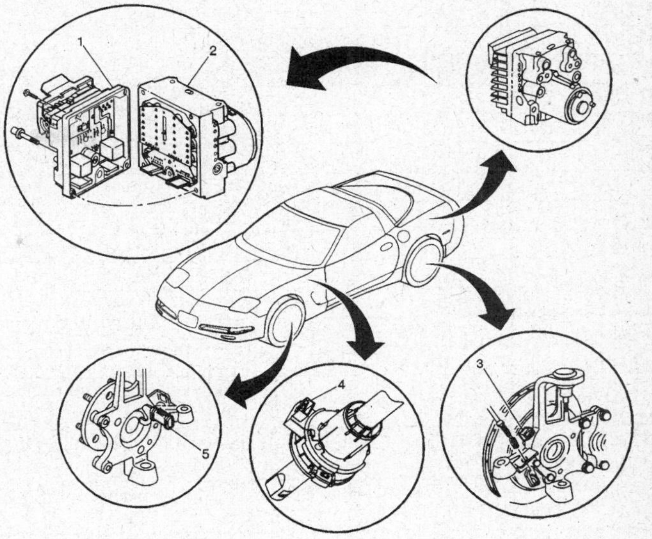

(1) EBTCM
(2) BPMV
(3) Rear Wheel Speed Sensor
(4) Steering Wheel Position Sensor
(5) Front Wheel Speed Sensor

GC4029702631000X

Fig. 2 ABS components. Corvette

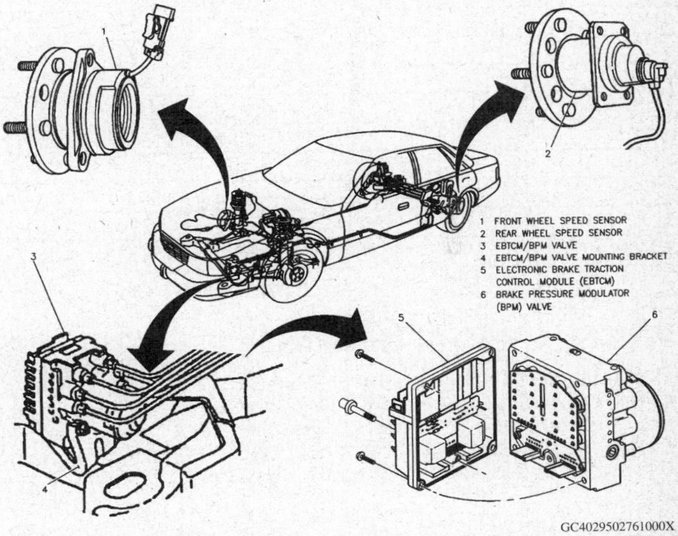

GC4029502761000X

Fig. 3 ABS components. DeVille, Eldorado & Seville

Control Module (PCM) to retard timing, selectively turn off fuel injectors and/or apply rear brakes of rear drive vehicles, or front brakes and front wheel drive models to reduce drive wheel torque, and improve traction and stability. This function may to turned on or off by the driver.

System Components

BRAKE PRESSURE MODULATOR VALVE

The Brake Pressure Modulator Valve (BPMV), mounted on the lefthand side of the engine compartment, provides brake fluid modulation for individual wheel circuits during anti-lock operations. The BPMV can also apply the rear brakes during traction control mode.

The BPMV is not serviceable. The BPMV contains a small pump motor to circulate brake fluid back to the master cylinder. Also integrated into the BPMV are the solenoid valves which can increase, decrease or hold hydraulic pressure. There are also two non-serviceable relays in the BPMV for the pump motor and solenoid valve.

ELECTRONIC BRAKE CONTROL MODULE/ ELECTRONIC BRAKE TRACTION CONTROL MODULE

The Electronic Brake Traction Control Module (EBTCM) is a microprocessor which monitors wheel speeds and Brake Pressure Modulator Valve (BPMV) electrical status. It is located between the BPMV and master cylinder, on the lefthand front side of the engine compartment.

The EBTCM detects wheel locking tendencies and rotating speed differences, controls anti-lock brake operations, commands traction control torque reduction and monitors system electrical operations, in addition to controlling Diagnostic Trouble Code (DTC) displays.

Code	Description
C1211	ABS Lamp Circuit Fault
C1214	Solenoid Valve Relay Contact Or Coil Circuit Open
C1216	Brake Control Relay Circuit Open
C1217	BPMV Pump Motor Relay Contact Circuit Open
C1221	LH Front Wheel Speed Sensor Signal Is Zero
C1222	RH Front Wheel Speed Sensor Signal Is Zero
C1223	LH Rear Wheel Speed Sensor Signal Is Zero
C1224	RH Rear Wheel Speed Sensor Signal Is Zero
C1225	LH Front Excessive Wheel Speed Variation
C1226	RH Front Excessive Wheel Speed Variation
C1227	LH Rear Excessive Wheel Speed Variation
C1228	RH Rear Excessive Wheel Speed Variation
C1232	LH Front Wheel Speed Sensor Circuit Open Or Shorted
C1233	RH Front Wheel Speed Sensor Circuit Open Or Shorted
C1234	LH Rear Wheel Speed Sensor Circuit Open Or Shorted
C1235	RH Rear Wheel Speed Sensor Circuit Open Or Shorted
C1236	Low System Supply Voltage
C1237	High System Supply Voltage
C1238	Brake Thermal Model Exceeded
C1241	Magnasteer Circuit Fault
C1242	BPMV Pump Motor Ground Circuit Open
C1243	BPMV Pump Motor Stalled
C1251	RSS Steering Sensor Data Fault
C1252	ICCS 2 Data Link Left Fault
C1253	ICCS 2 Data Link Right Fault
C1255	EBTCM Internal Fault
C1256	EBTCM Internal Fault
C1261	LH Front Inlet Valve Solenoid Fault
C1262	LH Front Outlet Valve Solenoid Fault
C1263	RH Front Inlet Valve Solenoid Fault
C1264	RH Front Outlet Valve Solenoid Fault

Fig. 4 DTC identification (Part 1 of 2)

Code	Description
C1265	LH Rear Inlet Valve Solenoid Fault
C1266	LH Rear Outlet Valve Solenoid Fault
C1267	RH Rear Inlet Valve Solenoid Fault
C1268	RH Rear Outlet Valve Solenoid Fault
C1271	LH Front TCS Master Cylinder Isolation Valve Fault
C1272	LH Front TCS Prima Valve Fault
C1273	RH Front TCS Master Cylinder Isolation Valve Fault
C1274	RH Front TCS Prima Valve Fault
C1275	Serial Data Fault
C1276	Delivered Torque Circuit Fault
C1277	Requested Torque Signal Circuit Fault
C1278	TCS Temporarily Inhibited By PCM
C1281	Steering Or ABC Sensors Uncorrelated Fault
C1282	Yaw Rate Sensor Bias Circuit Fault
C1283	Excessive Time To Center Steering
C1284	Lateral Accelerator Sensor Self Test Fault
C1285	Lateral Accelerator Sensor Circuit Fault
C1286	Steering Sensor Bias Fault
C1287	Steering Sensor Rate Fault
C1288	Steering Sensor Circuit Fault
C1291	Open Brake Lamp Switch Circuit Always Active
C1292	Brake Lamp Switch Circuit
C1293	Code C1291 Or C1292 Set In Previous Ignition Cycle
C1294	Brake Lamp Switch Circuit Always Active
C1295	Brake Lamp Switch Circuit Open
C1298	PCM Class 2 Serial Data Link Fault
U1016	Loss Of Communications w/PCM
U1255	Generic Loss Of Communications
U1256	Loss Of Communications w/CVRSS
U1300	Class 2 Short To Ground
U1301	Class 2 Circuit Short To Battery

Fig. 4 DTC identification (Part 2 of 2)

WHEEL SPEED SENSORS

Wheel speed sensors transmit wheel speed information to the EBTCM with voltage generated by magnetic induction caused by a passing toothed sensor ring. The wheel speed sensors are not adjustable.

FRONT

The front wheel speed sensors are mounted in the front steering knuckles.

REAR

The rear wheel speed sensors are mounted in the rear spindles.

DIAGNOSIS & TESTING

Accessing Diagnostic Trouble Codes

1. Turn ignition switch to Off position.
2. Connect suitably programmed scan tool connected to Data Link Connector (DLC), located on lefthand side of instrument panel below steering column.
3. Turn ignition switch to On position.
4. Select scan tool's Special Functions.
5. Select and run Automated Test.
6. Note Diagnostic Trouble Codes (DTCs).

Diagnostic Trouble Code Interpretation

Refer to **Fig. 4,** for Diagnostic Trouble Code (DTC) identification and description.

Wiring Diagrams

BONNEVILLE & LESABRE

Refer to **Figs. 5 through 9,** for wiring diagrams.

CORVETTE

Refer to **Fig. 10 through 14,** for wiring diagrams.

DEVILLE, ELDORADO & SEVILLE

Refer to **Figs. 15 through 21,** for wiring diagrams.

PARK AVENUE

Refer to **Figs. 22 through 25,** for wiring diagram.

EBCM/EBTCM Connector Views

Refer to **Figs. 26 through 31,** for EBCM/EBTCM connector views.

Diagnostic Tests

BONNEVILLE, LESABRE & PARK AVENUE

Refer to **Figs. 32 through 109,** for diagnostic tests.

CORVETTE

Refer to **Figs. 110 through 177,** for diagnostic tests.

DEVILLE, ELDORADO & SEVILLE

Refer to **Figs. 178 through 333,** for diagnostic tests.

Clearing Diagnostic Trouble Codes

Diagnostic Trouble Codes (DTCs) cannot be cleared by disconnecting EBTCM or battery cables.

SCAN TOOL

Connect a suitably programmed scan tool to Data Link Connector (DLC), and follow manufacturer's instructions.

Intermittents & Poor Connections

Intermittent failures in the anti-lock brake system may be difficult to accurately diagnose. The ABS Diagnostic Trouble Codes (DTCs) which may be stored by the EBCM are not designated as Current or History DTCs. These DTCs can be helpful in diagnosing intermittent conditions.

If an intermittent condition is being diagnosed, the ABS system can be used in the following manner to help isolate the suspected circuit.

1. Display and clear any ABS DTCs present in EBCM.
2. Attempt to repeat failure condition, noting following:
   a. Turn ignition switch to Off position.
   b. Disconnect scan tool. **If scan tool is installed, EBCM/EBTCM will not set DTCs and ABS/TCS functions may not be available.**
   c. Test drive vehicle.
3. After duplicating condition, stop vehicle and display any DTCs stored.
4. If a DTC was stored, inspect electrical connections and wiring for the following:
   a. Poor mating of connector halves.
   b. Terminals not fully seated in connector halves.
   c. Improperly formed, or damaged terminals. All connector terminals in a problem circuit should be carefully reformed to increase contact tension.
   d. Poor terminal to wire connection. In most cases, this will require removing wire from connector body.
5. If there is an intermittent warning lamp operation, the following EBCM circuits should be inspected:
   a. Low system voltage. If low voltage is detected at EBCM/EBTCM, Anti-lock lamp will illuminate until normal operating voltage is detected.
   b. Low brake fluid. This condition in Pressure Modulator Valve (PMV) reservoir will cause Brake and Anti-lock lamps to illuminate. When an acceptable fluid level is registered, lamps will no longer be On.
6. Any condition which results in interruption of power to EBCM/EBTCM or hydraulic unit may cause warning lamps to turn on intermittently. These circuits include main relay, pump motor relay, fuses and related wiring.

Ignition Cycle Default

If vehicle power is cycled 100 times without a particular fault reappearing, that particular DTC will be erased from the EBCM memory, and ignition cycle counter will be reset to zero.

Electromagnetic Interference Test

Due to the sensitivity of ABS components to electromagnetic interference, the following inspects should be performed is an intermittent fault is suspected.

1. Inspect for proper installation of wiring harnesses resulting from add on options.
2. Visually inspect wheel speed sensor and toothed sensor ring for looseness, damage, accumulation of foreign material and proper mounting. Replace damaged components, remove any foreign material and properly attach all components.
3. Inspect front wheel speed sensor wiring for proper routing away from spark plug wires.
4. Measure resistance of spark plug wires. If resistance is greater than 30,000 ohms for any wire, replace spark plug wires.
5. While test driving vehicle, monitor Tech 1 wheel speeds. If any wheel speed drops or displays an erratic speed, refer to appropriated wheel speed sensor DTC.

SYSTEM SERVICE

Brake System Bleed

AUTO BLEED

Perform manual or pressure bleeding as outlined in "Manual Bleed" or "Pressure Bleed" before auto bleeding system.

1. Turn ignition switch to Off position.
2. Raise and support vehicle, then remove tire and wheel assemblies.
3. Inspect brake system for leaks and damage.
4. Connect a suitably programmed scan tool to Data Link Connector (DLC), DLC is located in lefthand side of instrument panel below steering column.
5. Turn ignition switch to On position. Do not start engine.
6. Establish scan tool communications by selecting ABS/TCS, Special Functions and Automate Bleed Procedure.
7. Bleed system as outlined in "Manual Bleed" or "Pressure Bleed."
8. Follow scan tool instructions until desired brake pedal height is obtained. Inspect pedal for firmness.

MANUAL BLEED

Brake fluid damages painted surfaces. Immediately clean any spilled fluid.

1. Remove vacuum reserve by pumping brakes several times with engine off.
2. Fill master cylinder reservoir with clean brake fluid. Inspect fluid level often during bleeding procedure; do not let reservoir fall below half full.
3. If required, bleed master cylinder as follows:
   a. Disconnect master cylinder forward brake line connection.
   b. Allow brake fluid to fill master cylinder until it flow from forward port.
   c. Connect and tighten brake line.
   d. Slowly depress brake pedal one time and hold.
   e. Loosen front brake line connection and purge air.
   f. Tighten connection and slowly release brake pedal.
   g. Wait 15 seconds and repeat until all air is purged.
   h. Repeat procedure on rearward (nearest cowl) brake line connection.
4. Loosen and slightly tighten bleeder valves at all four wheels.
5. Bleed calipers in following order: righthand rear, lefthand rear, righthand front and lefthand front.
6. Place transparent tube over bleeder valve and allow tube to hang down into a transparent container. Ensure end of tube is submerged in clean brake fluid.
7. Slowly depress brake pedal one time and hold.
8. Loosen bleeder valve and purge air from cylinder, then tighten bleeder screw and slowly release pedal. Wait 15 seconds and repeat this step until all air is bled from system.
9. **Torque** bleed screws to 108 inch lbs.
10. If brake pedal is spongy, auto bleed modulator as outlined in "Auto Bleed" and repeat this bleeding procedure.

PRESSURE BLEED

1. Loosen and slightly tighten bleeder valves at all four wheels. Repair any broken, stripped or frozen valves at this time.
2. Replace master cylinder reservoir cap with suitable pressure bleeding adapter.
3. Charge suitable bleeder to 20–25 psi and connect hose to adapter.
4. Raise and support vehicle.
5. Bleed calipers in following order: righthand rear, lefthand rear, righthand front and lefthand front.
6. Place one end of a transparent tube over bleeder valve and allow other end of tube to hang down into a transparent container. Ensure end of tube is submerged in clean brake fluid.
7. Open bleed screw at least ¾ turn and allow fluid to flow until no air is seen. Pump brake pedal while pressure bleeding
8. Close bleed screw and **torque** to 108 inch lbs.
9. If brake pedal is spongy, auto bleed modulator as outlined in "Auto Bleed" and repeat this bleeding procedure.

HYDRAULIC SYSTEM FLUSH

If brake fluid is old, rusty or contaminated, or whenever new components are installed in hydraulic system, the system must be flushed. Bleed brakes, allowing at least one quart of clean brake fluid to pass through system. Any rubber components in hydraulic system which were exposed to contaminated fluid must be replaced.

Component Replacement

BRAKE PRESSURE MODULATOR VALVE (BPMV)

Brake Pressure Modulator Valve (BPMV) cannot be repair. Complete unit must be replaced. **If BPMV screws are loosened it will not be possible to get brake circuits leak tight.**

BONNEVILLE, DEVILLE, ELDORADO, LESABRE, PARK AVENUE & SEVILLE

1. Turn ignition switch to Off position.
2. Remove air cleaner assembly and Powertrain Control Module (PCM) cover.
3. Disconnect EBCM/EBTCM wiring harness and BPMV motor ground cable.
4. Remove brake pipe fittings. Note locations for installation reference.
5. Remove EBCM/EBTCM bracket and mounting bolt, then the upper bracket and EBCM/BPMV assembly.
6. Remove mounting bolts and separate EBCM/EBTCM from BPMV.
7. Reverse procedure to install, noting the following:
   a. **Torque** mounting bolts to 40 inch lbs.
   b. **Torque** center bracket bolt to 10 ft. lbs.
   c. **Torque** frame rail bracket bolts to 9 ft. lbs.
   d. **Torque** brake pipe fittings to 13 ft. lbs.

CORVETTE

EBTCM

1. Turn ignition switch to the OFF position.
2. Disconnect EBTCM harness connector.
3. Remove brake hydraulic lines from BPMV. Note location for installation reference.
4. Disconnect BPMV pump motor ground wire.
5. Remove EBTCM/BPMV retaining nuts, then the EBTCM/BPMV from vehicle.
6. Remove EBTCM insulator bolt, then the EBTCM to BPMV attaching bolts.
7. Separate EBTCM from BPMV.
8. Reverse procedure to install, noting the following:
   a. **Torque** EBTCM to BPMV attaching bolts to 53 inch lbs.
   b. **Torque** EBTCM insulator bolt to 10 ft. lbs.
   c. **Torque** EBTCM/BPMV retaining nuts to 89 inch lbs.
   d. **Torque** brake hydraulic line fittings to 12 ft. lbs.

ELECTRONIC BRAKE TRACTION CONTROL MODULE

BONNEVILLE, DEVILLE, ELDORADO, LESABRE, PARK AVENUE & SEVILLE

1. Remove air cleaner assembly and Powertrain Control Module (PCM) cover.
2. Disconnect EBCM/EBTCM wiring harness and BPMV motor ground cable.
3. Remove EBCM/EBTCM bracket.
4. Remove bolts and separate EBCM/EBTCM from BPMV.
5. Reverse procedure to install, noting the following:
   a. **Torque** mounting bolts to 40 inch lbs.
   b. **Torque** center bracket bolt to 10 ft. lbs.
   c. **Torque** bracket nuts to 80 inch lbs.

CORVETTE

Refer to "Brake Pressure Modulator Valve (BPMV)" for EBTCM replacement procedure.

WHEEL SPEED SENSOR

BONNEVILLE, DEVILLE, ELDORADO, LESABRE, PARK AVENUE & SEVILLE

Front

1. Disconnect wheel speed sensor connector.
2. Remove hub and bearing assembly.
3. Pry wheel speed sensor slinger off.
4. Pry wheel speed sensor from bearing assembly.
5. Reverse procedure to install, noting the following:
   a. Apply Loctite 620, or equivalent, to bearing hub outer diameter.
   b. Use front wheel speed sensor installer tool No. J-38764-1A, or equivalent, to install sensor.

Rear

1. Disconnect wheel speed sensor connector.
2. Lower strut mounting nuts and bolts.
3. Remove mounting screws and sensor.
4. Reverse procedure to install, noting the following:
   a. Lubricate new sensor O-ring.
   b. **Torque** mounting screws to 25 inch lbs.
   c. **Torque** strut mounting nuts and bolts to 140 ft. lbs.

CORVETTE

Front wheel speed sensors are part of the hub/bearing assembly. Rear wheel speed sensors are mounted in the bearing assembly. They are not adjustable, and are removed and installed with the assemblies.

LATERAL ACCELERATOR

CORVETTE

1. Turn ignition switch to the OFF position.
2. Remove passenger seat.
3. Disconnect lateral accelerator connector.
4. Remove accelerator retaining nuts, then the accelerator.
5. Reverse procedure to install.

YAW RATE SENSOR

CORVETTE

1. Turn ignition switch to the OFF position.
2. Remove instrument panel accessory trim plate from center of instrument panel.
3. Disconnect yaw rate sensor electrical connector.
4. Remove yaw rate sensor retaining nuts, then the sensor, **Fig. 334.**
5. Reverse procedure to install.

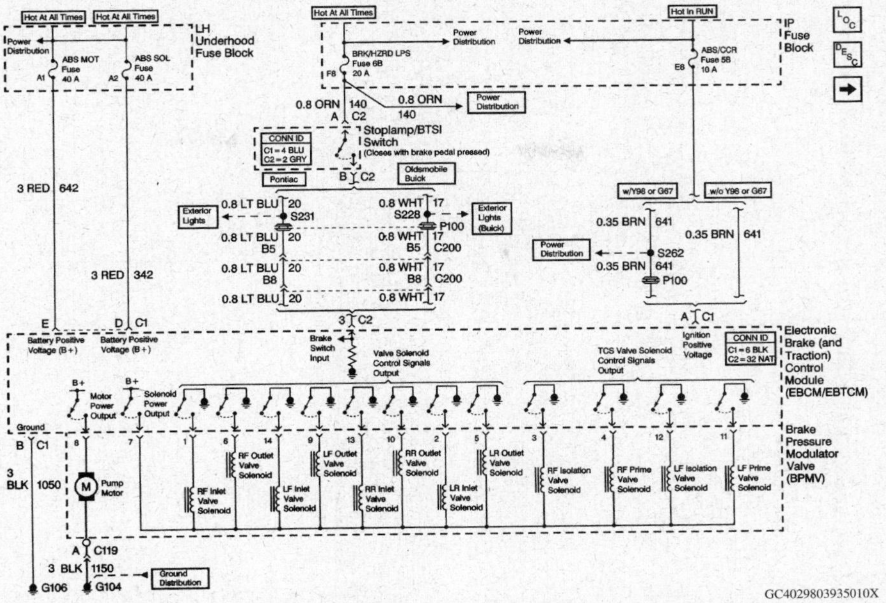

Fig. 5 Wiring diagram (Ground, Power & Stop Lamp). Bonneville & LeSabre

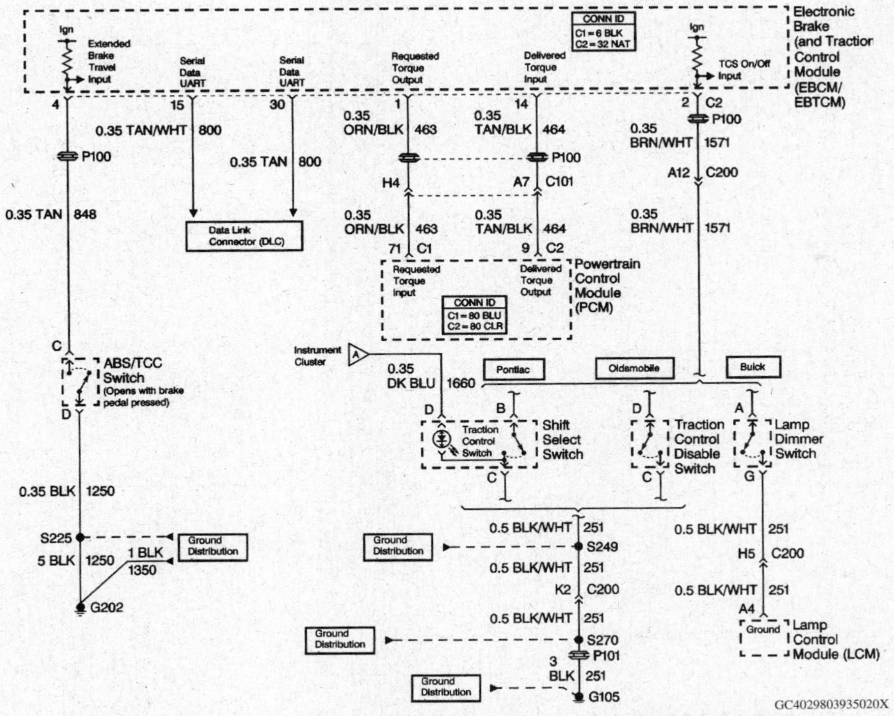

Fig. 6 Wiring diagram (ABS/TCS Switch, PCM & UART Data Line). Bonneville & LeSabre

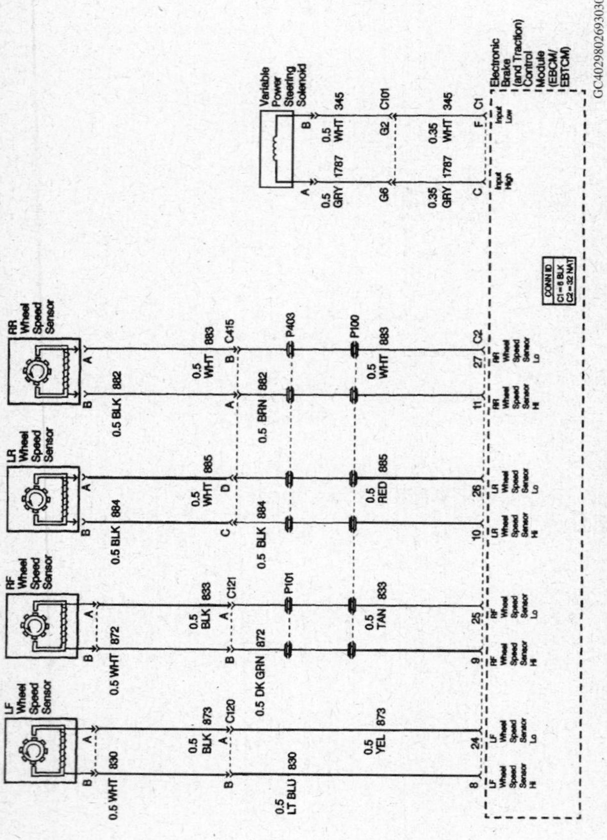

GC4029802693030X

Fig. 7 Wiring diagram (Variable Power Steering Actuator & Wheel Speed Sensors). Bonneville & LeSabre

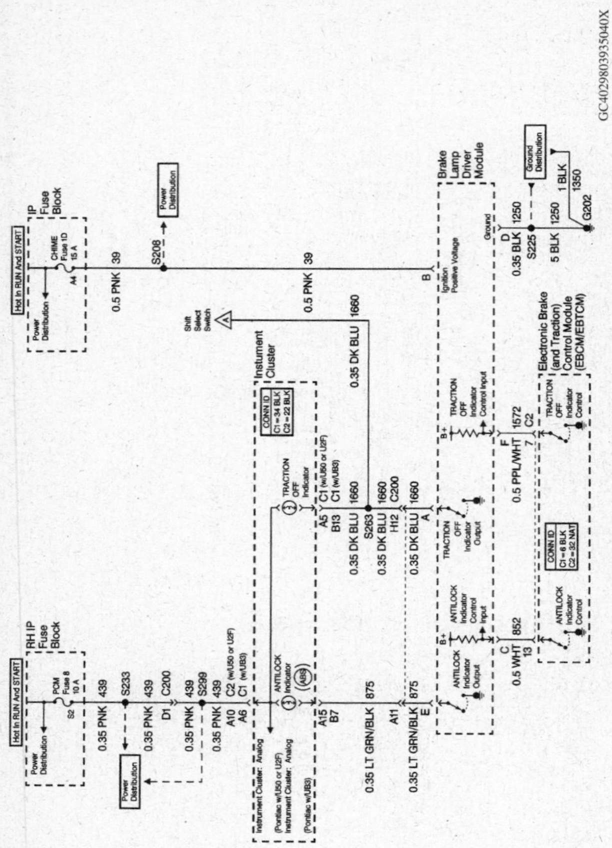

GC4029803935040X

Fig. 8 Wiring diagram (Indicators). Bonneville

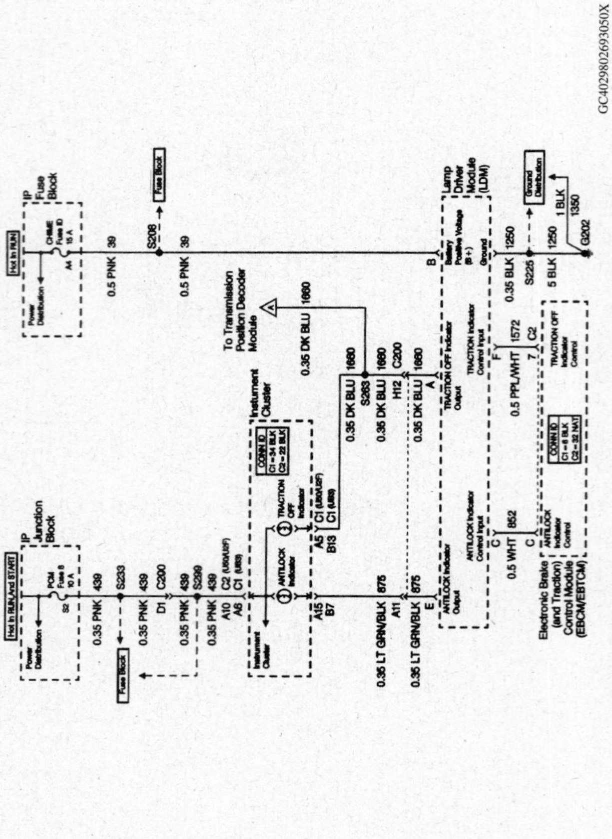

GC4029802693050X

Fig. 9 Wiring diagram (Indicators). LeSabre

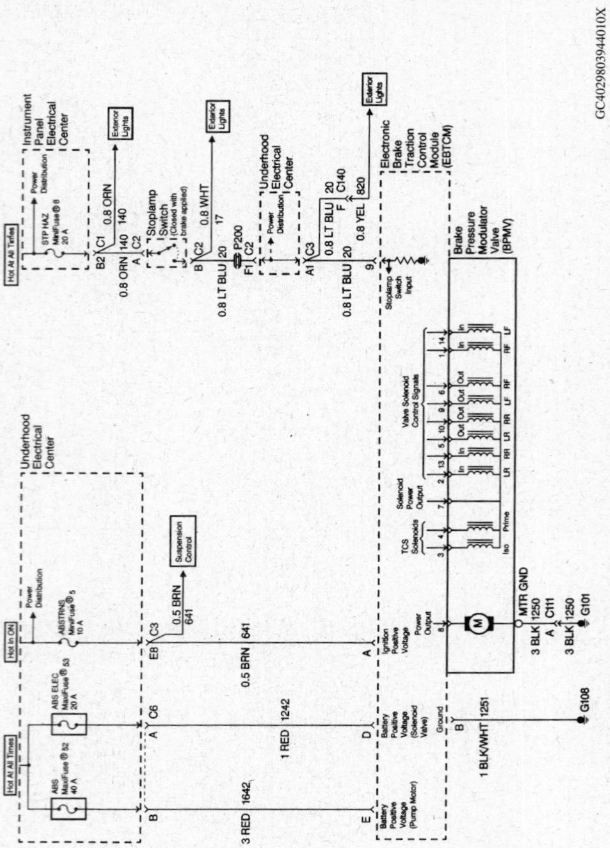

GC4029803944010X

Fig. 10 Wiring diagram (Ground & Power). Corvette

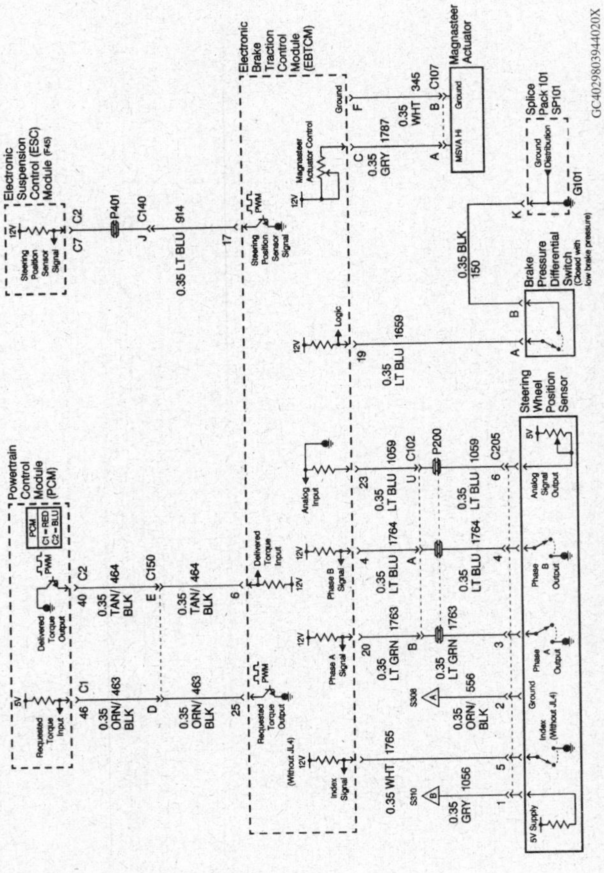

Fig. 11 Wiring diagram (Magnasteer System). Corvette

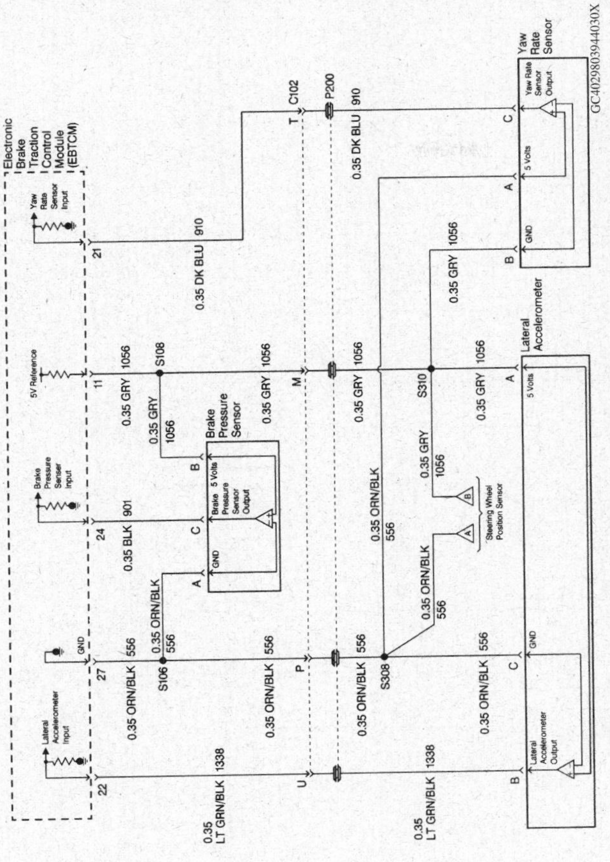

Fig. 12 Wiring diagram (Sensor Inputs). Corvette

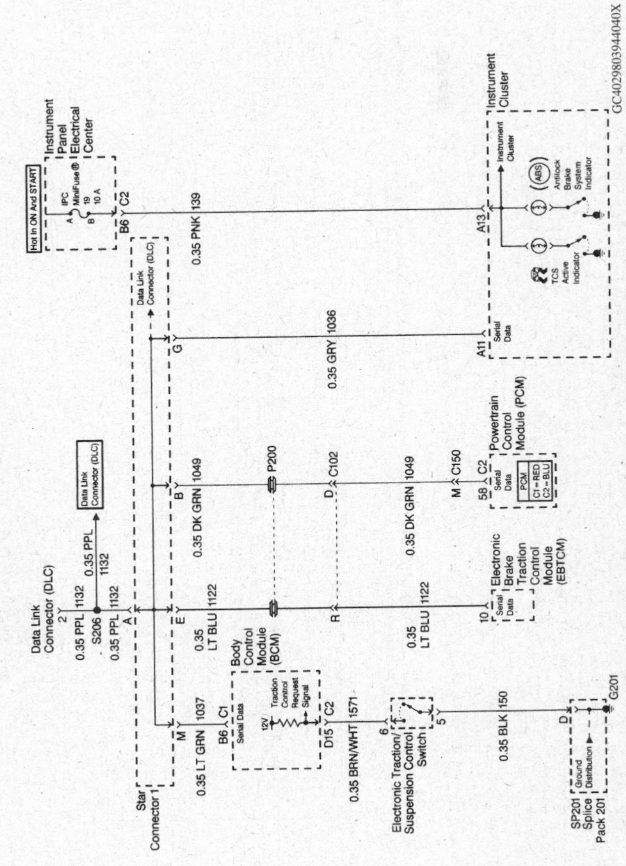

Fig. 13 Wiring diagram (Data Link Connector). Corvette

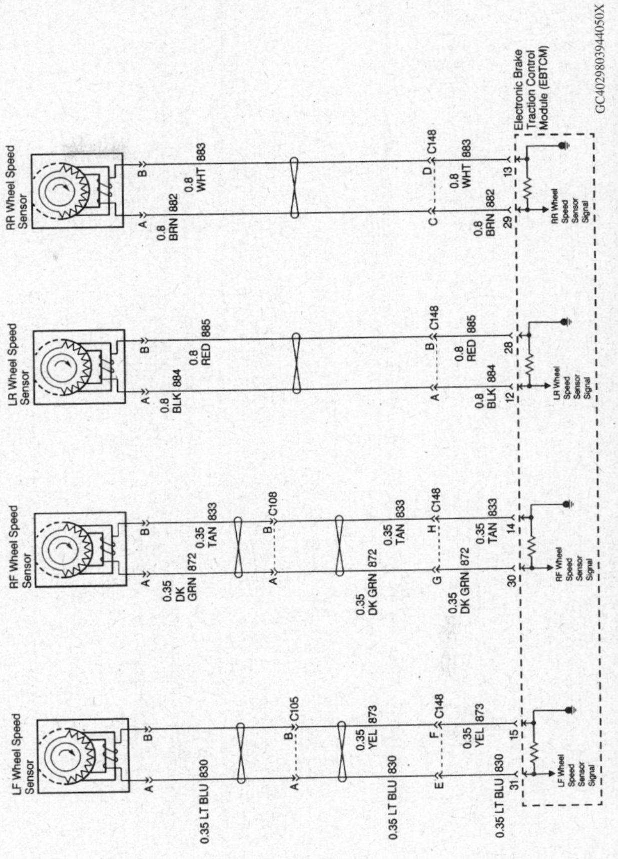

Fig. 14 Wiring diagram (Wheel Speed Sensors). Corvette

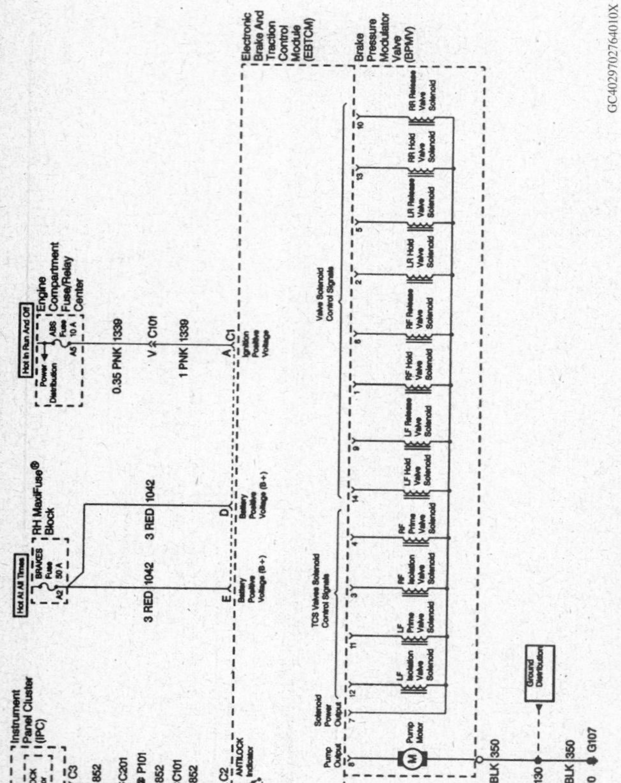

Fig. 15 Wiring diagram (Part 1 of 4). DeVille

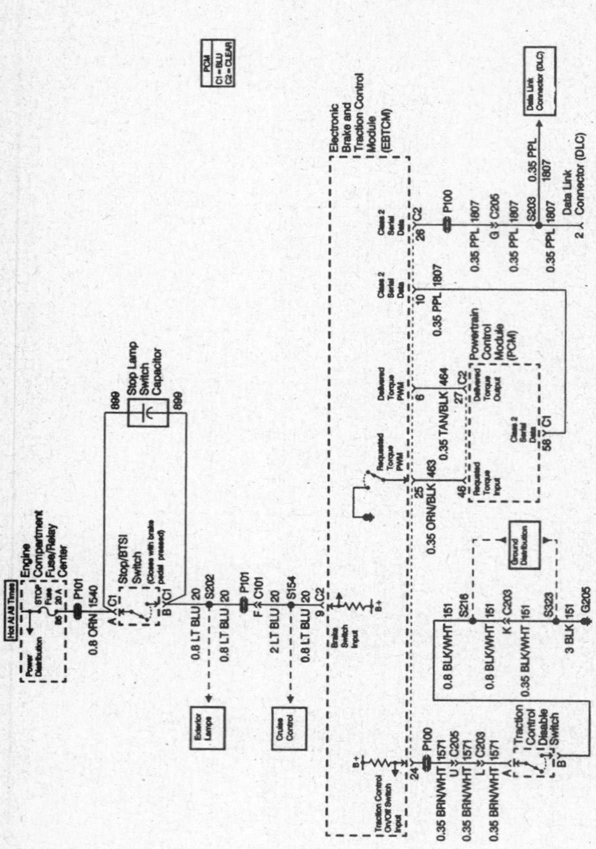

Fig. 15 Wiring diagram (Part 2 of 4). DeVille

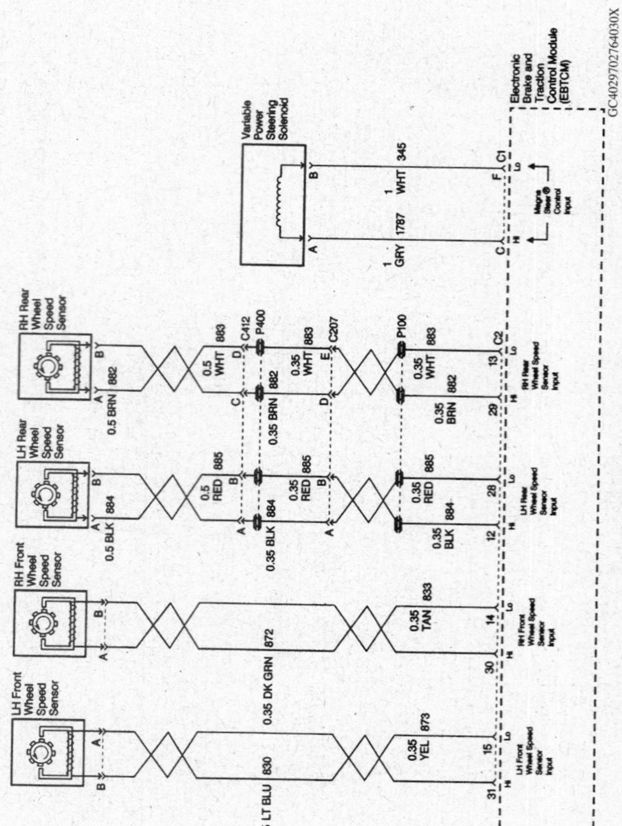

Fig. 15 Wiring diagram (Part 3 of 4). DeVille

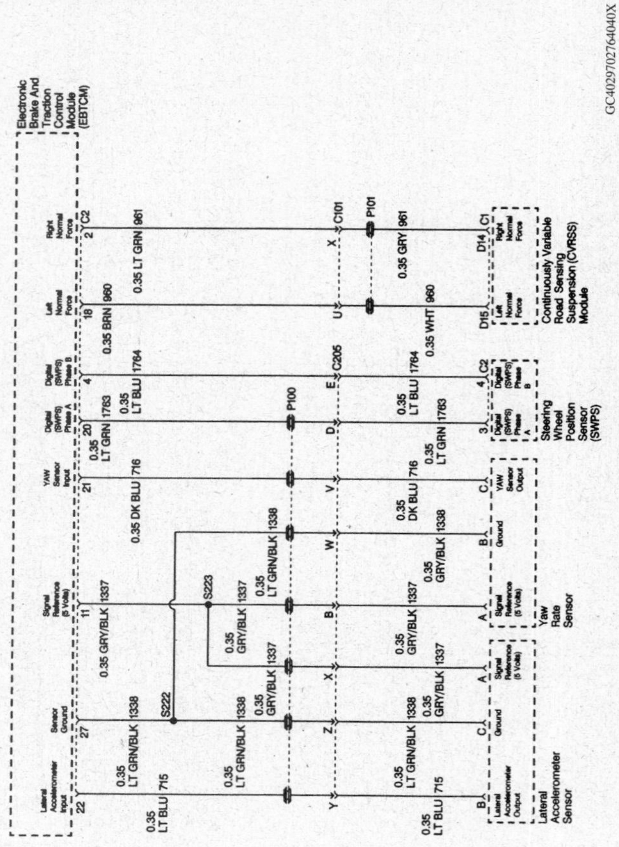

Fig. 15 Wiring diagram (Part 4 of 4). DeVille

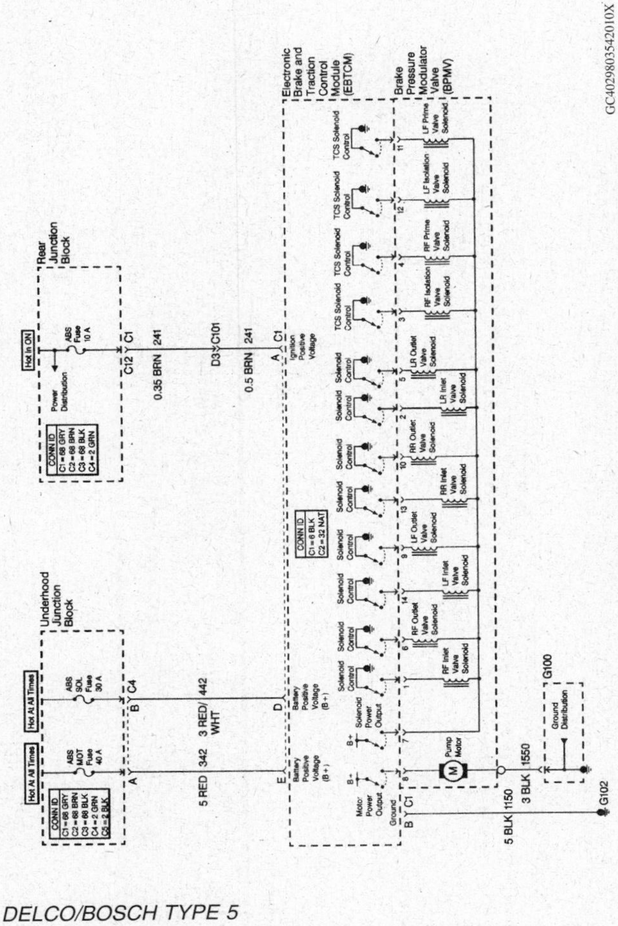

GC402980354201OX

Fig. 16 Wiring diagram (Part 1 of 6). Seville

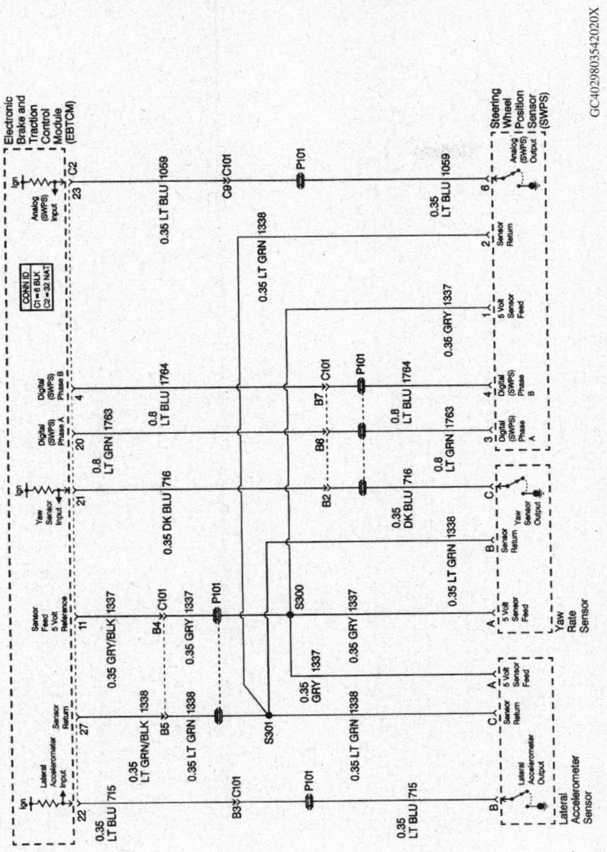

GC402980354202OX

Fig. 16 Wiring diagram (Part 2 of 6). Seville

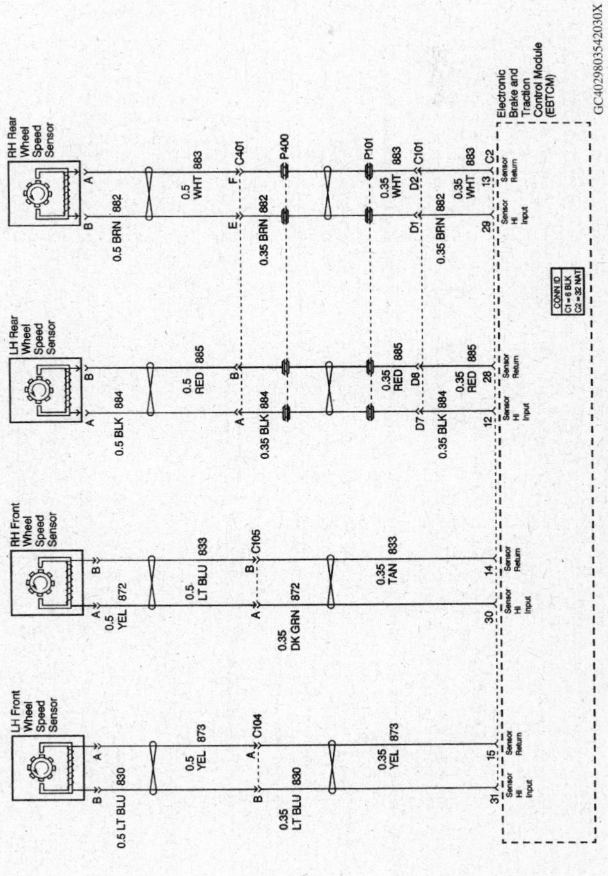

GC402980354203OX

Fig. 16 Wiring diagram (Part 3 of 6). Seville

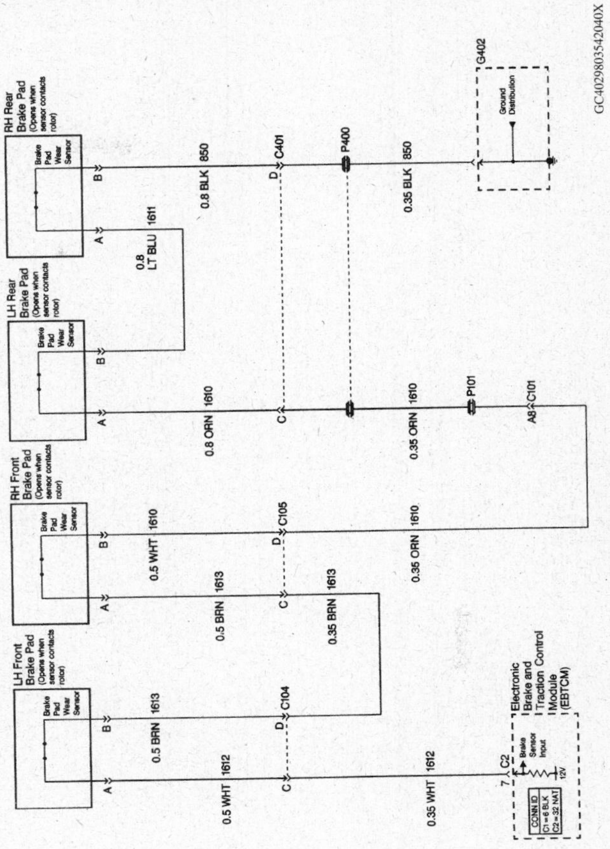

GC402980354204OX

Fig. 16 Wiring diagram (Part 4 of 6). Seville

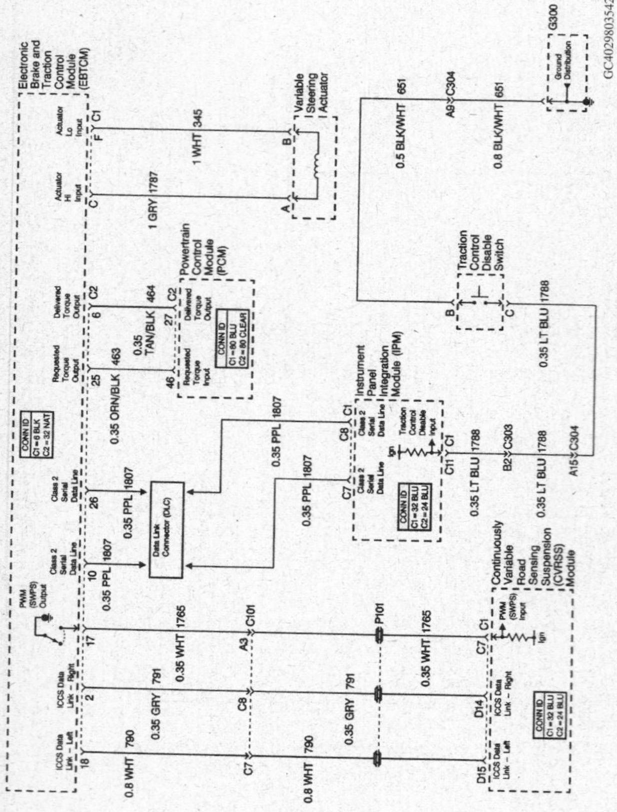

Fig. 16 Wiring diagram (Part 5 of 6). Seville

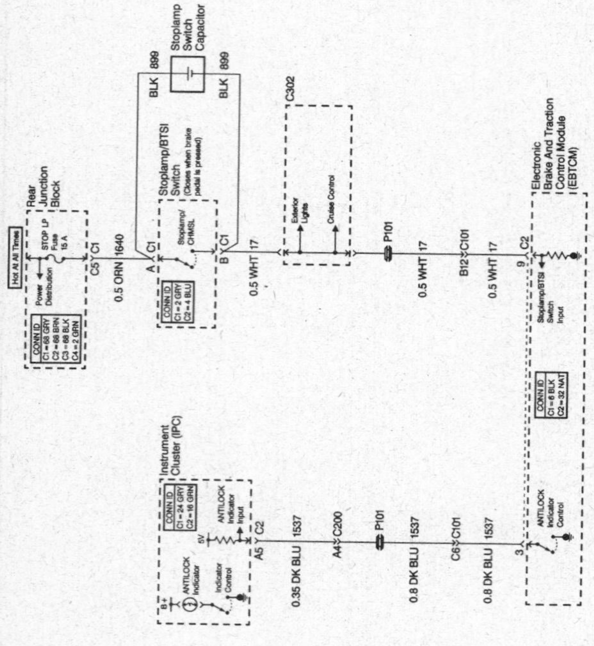

Fig. 16 Wiring diagram (Part 6 of 6). Seville

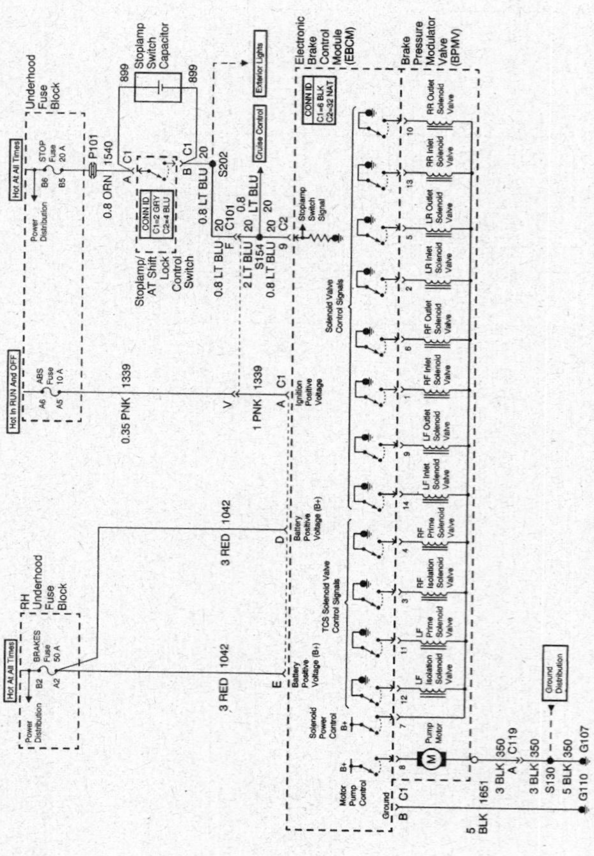

Fig. 17 Wiring diagram (Ground, Power, Pump Motor, Solenoid Valves & Stop Lamp Switch). Eldorado

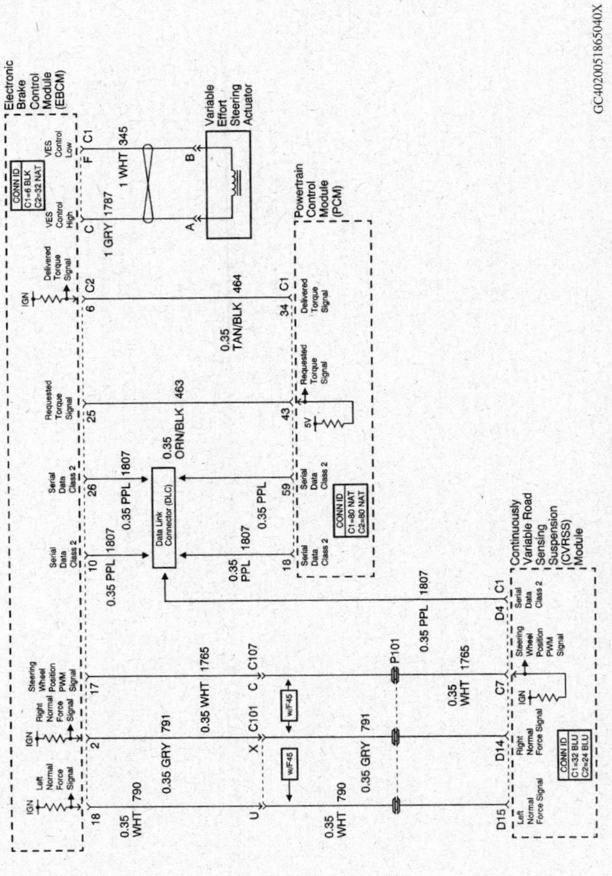

Fig. 18 Wiring diagram (Suspension Inputs, Traction Control & Variable Effort Steering). Eldorado

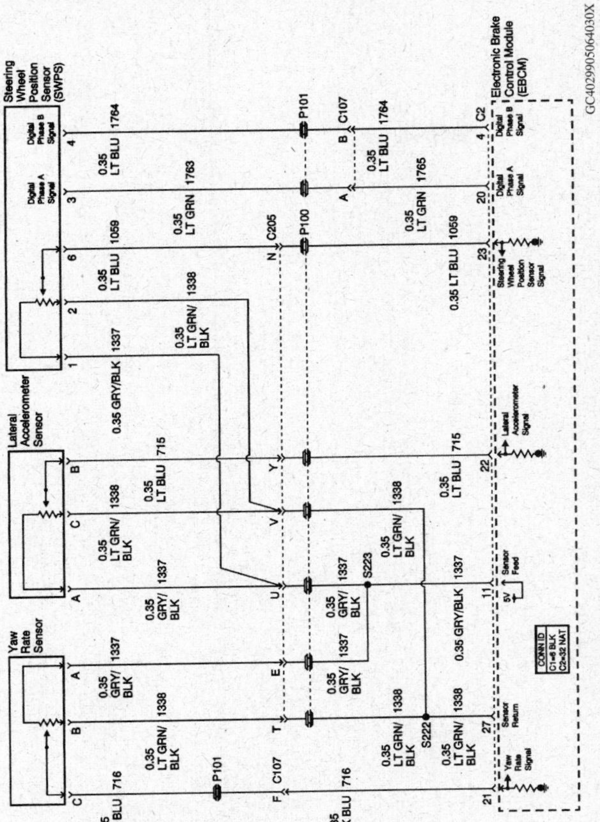

Fig. 19 Wiring diagram (Vehicle Stability Enhancement System). Eldorado

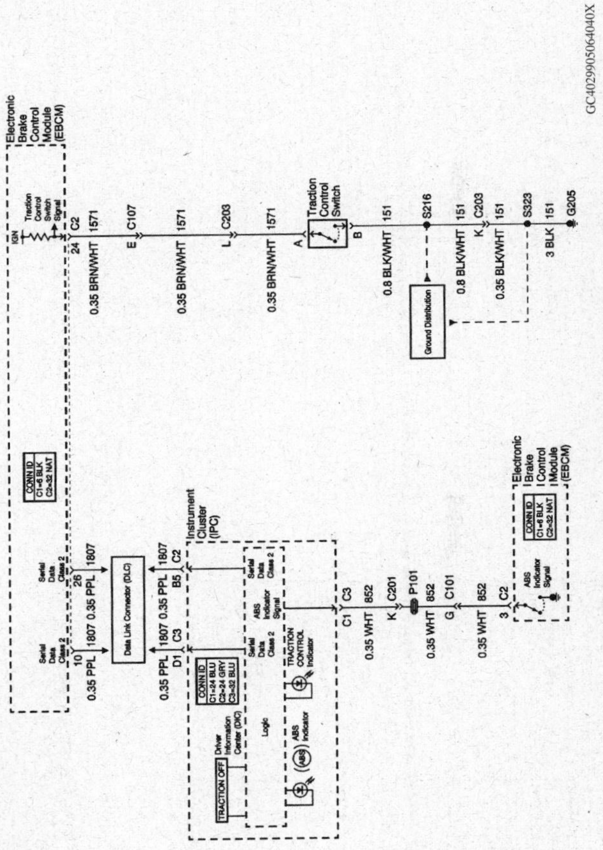

Fig. 20 Wiring diagram (Indicators & Traction Control Switch). Eldorado

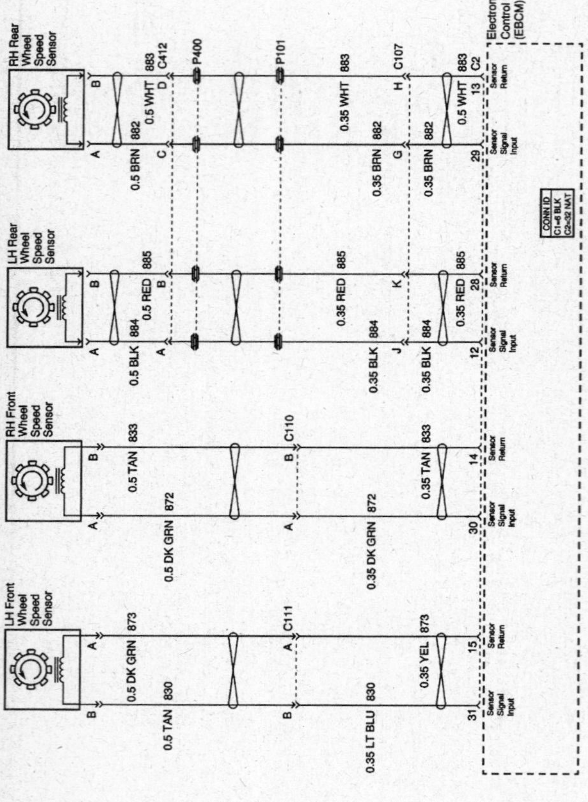

Fig. 21 Wiring diagram (Wheel Speed Sensors). Eldorado

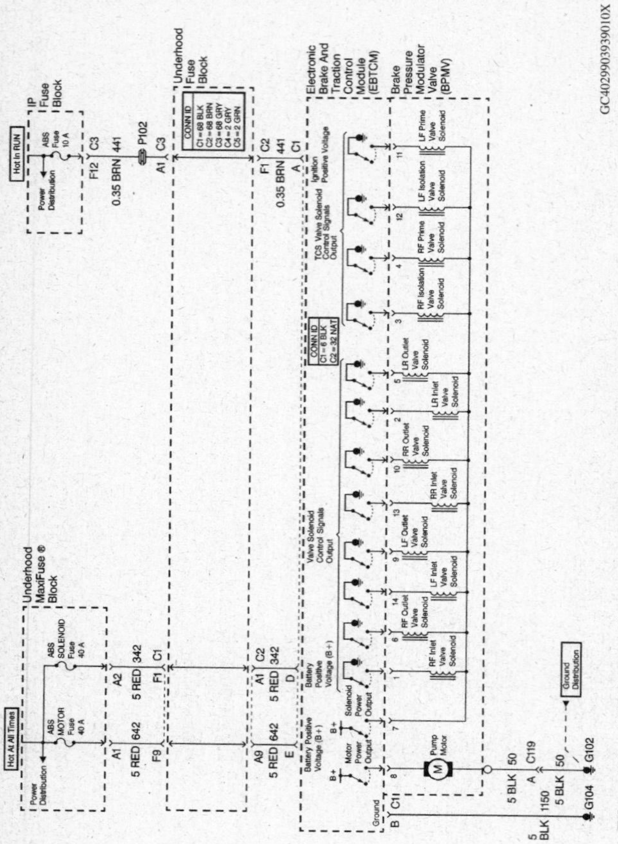

Fig. 22 Wiring diagram (BPMV, EBCM/EBTCM, Ground & Power). Park Avenue

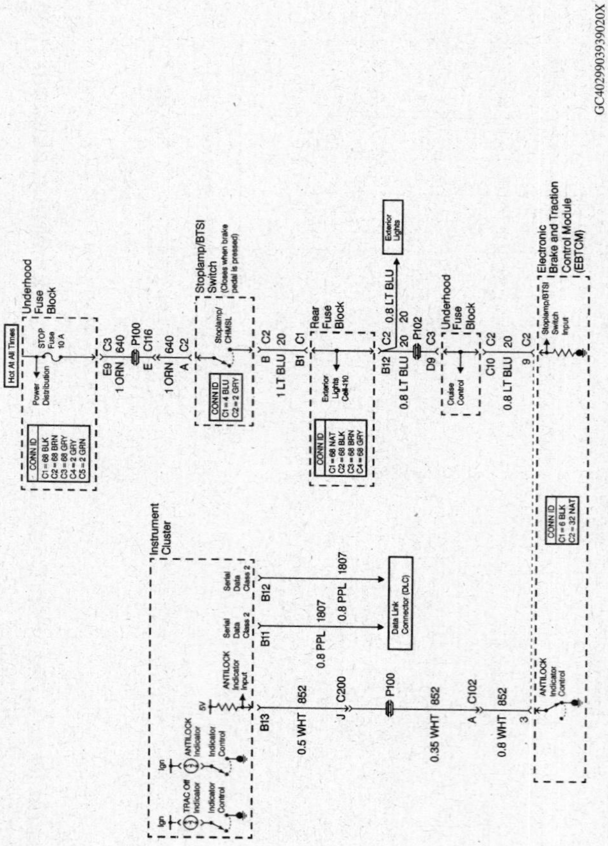

Fig. 23 Wiring diagram (Indicators & Stop Lamp Switch). Park Avenue

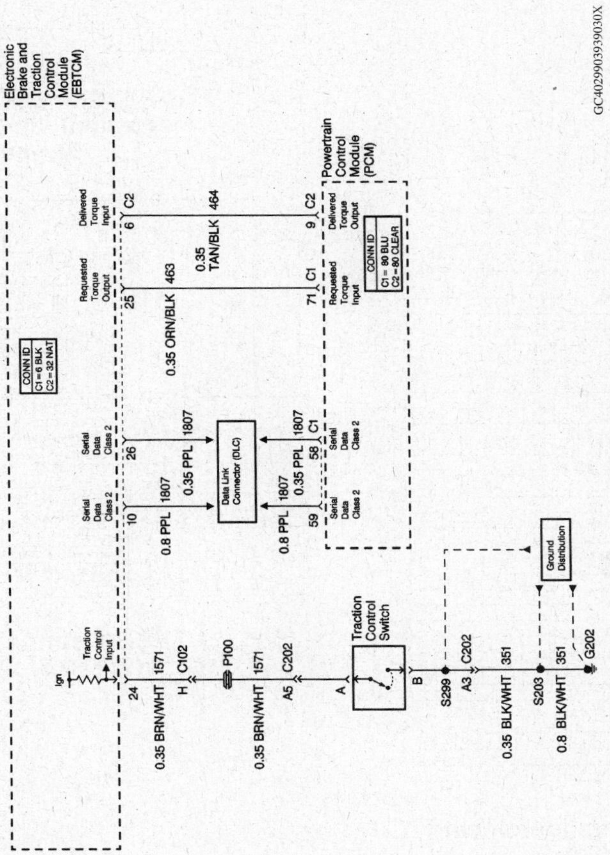

Fig. 24 Wiring diagram (PCM & Traction Control Switch). Park Avenue

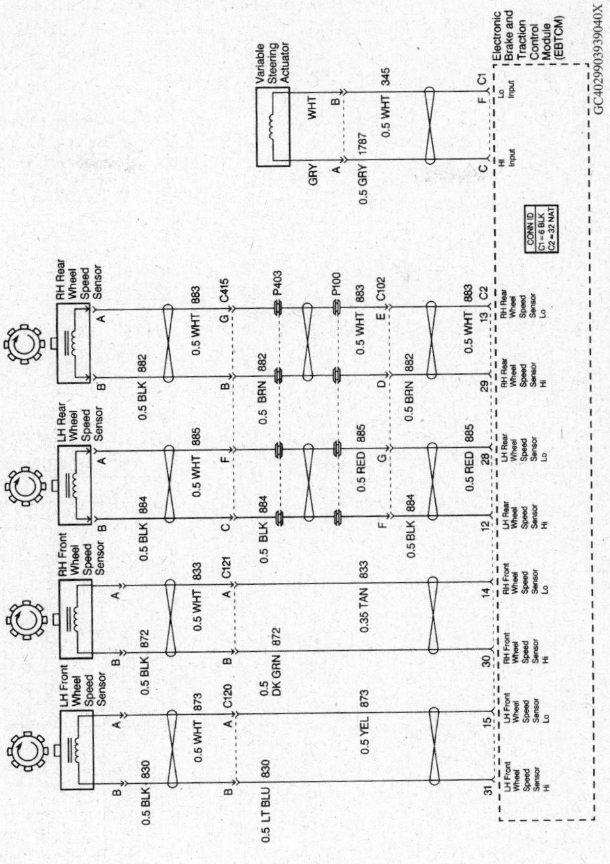

Fig. 25 Wiring diagram (Variable Steering Actuators & Wheel Speed Sensors). Park Avenue

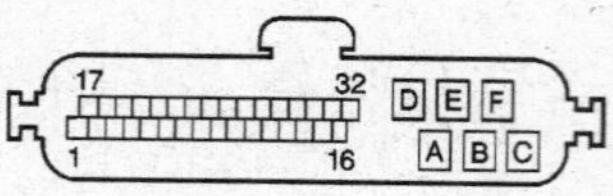

Connector Part Information		• 12160529 (C1) • 6 Way Metri-Pack 280 Series (BLK) • 12129228 (C2) • 32 Way Micro-Pack 100 Series (NAT)	
Pin	**Wire Color**	**Circuit No.**	**Function**
A	BRN	641	Fused Output - IGN
B	BLK	1050	Ground
C	GRY	1787	Feed Motor (High Effort)
D	RED	342	Fused Output (Bat)
E	RED	642	Fused Output (Bat)
F	WHT	345	Feed Motor (Low Effort)
1	ORN/BLK	463	Traction Control System Signal (Torque Desired)
2	BRN/WHT	1571	Traction Control System Switch Signal
3	WHT	17	Stoplamp Switch Output (Oldsmobile, Buick)
3	LT BLU	20	Stoplamp Feed (Pontiac)
4	TAN	848	Brake Pedal Switch Signal (ABS)
5 - 6	—	—	Not Used
7	PPL/WHT	1572	Traction Control System Lamp Output (Failure)
8	LT BLU	830	LF Speed Sensor Signal
9	DK GRN	872	RF Speed Sensor Signal
10	BLK	884	LR Speed Sensor Signal
11	BRN	882	RR Speed Sensor Signal

GC40298039936010X

Fig. 26 EBCM/EBTCM connector terminal identification (Part 1 of 2). Bonneville & LeSabre

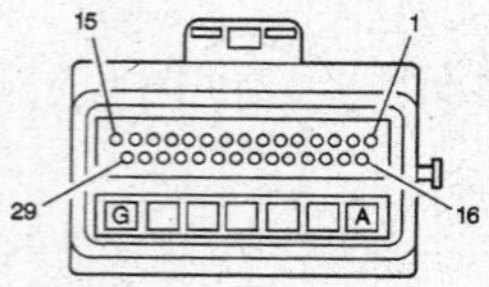

Connector Part Information			• C1 - 15318099 • 7 Way F Metri-Pack 480 Series (BLK) • C2 - 15354984 • 29 Way F Micro-Pack 100 Series (NAT)
Pin	**Wire Color**	**Circuit No.**	**Function**
A	RED	1642	Battery Positive Voltage
B	BRN	641	Ignition 3 voltage
C	GRY	1787	Variable Effort Steering Actuator High Effort Control
D	WHT	345	Variable Effort Steering Actuator Low Effort Control
E	—	—	Not Used
F	BLK/WHT	1251	Ground
G	BLK	1250	Ground
1	—	—	Not Used
2	TAN/BLK	464	Delivered Torque Signal
3	LT GRN	1763	Steering Wheel Position Signal A
4	—	—	Not Used
5	LT GRN/ BLK	1338	Lateral Accelerometer Input (JL4)
6	LT BLU	20	Stop Lamp Supply Voltage
7	—	—	Not Used
8	RED	885	Left Rear Wheel Speed Sensor Low Reference
9	BRN	882	Right Rear Wheel Speed Sensor Signal
10	DK GRN	872	Right Front Wheel Speed Sensor Signal
11	LT BLU	830	Left Front Wheel Speed Sensor Signa
12	ORN/BLK	463	Requested Torque Signal
13	ORN/BLK	556	Low Reference
14	—	—	Not Used
15	—	—	Not Used
16	—	—	Not Used
17	BLK	2626	Brake Pressure Sensor Signal (JL4)
18	LT BLU	1764	Steering Wheel Position Signal B
19	DK BLU	716	Yaw Rate Sensor Signal (JL4)
20	—	—	Not Used
21	LT BLU	1122	ABS/TCS Class 2 Serial Data
22	BLK	884	Left Rear Wheel Speed Sensor Signal
23	WHT	883	Right Rear Wheel Speed Sensor Low Reference

GC4020152535010X

Fig. 27 EBCM connector terminal identification (Part 1 of 2). 2000 Corvette

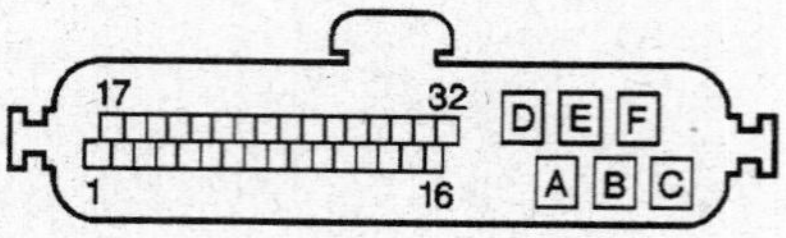

Connector Part Information		• 12160529 (C1) • 6 Way Metri-Pack 280 Series (BLK) • 12129228 (C2) • 32 Way Micro-Pack 100 Series (NAT)	
Pin	**Wire Color**	**Circuit No.**	**Function**
12	—	—	Not Used
13	WHT	852	ABS Signal (Failure)
14	TAN/BLK	464	Traction Control System Signal (Torque Delivered)
15	TAN	800	UART Serial Data Signal
16	BLK	—	Vent Tube
17 - 23	—	—	Not Used
24	YEL	873	LF Speed Sensor Return
25	TAN	833	RF Speed Sensor Return
26	RED	885	LR Speed Sensor Return
27	WHT	883	RR Speed Sensor Return
28 - 29	—	—	Not Used
30	TAN	800	UART Serial Data Signal
31 - 32	—	—	Not Used

GC4029803936020X

Fig. 26 EBCM/EBTCM connector terminal identification (Part 2 of 2). Bonneville & LeSabre

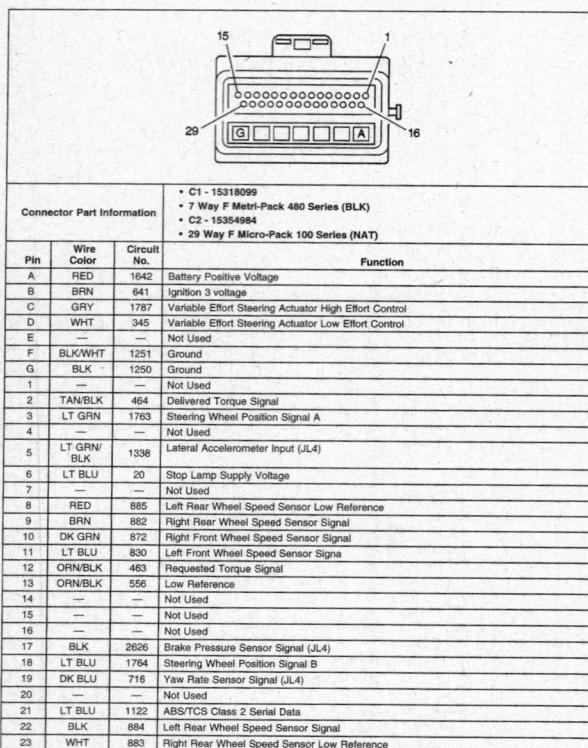

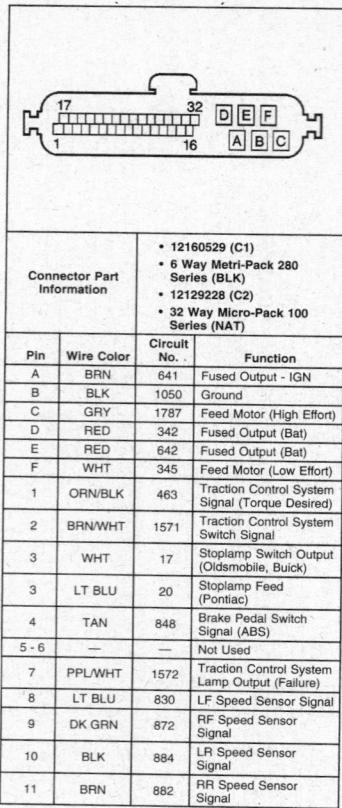

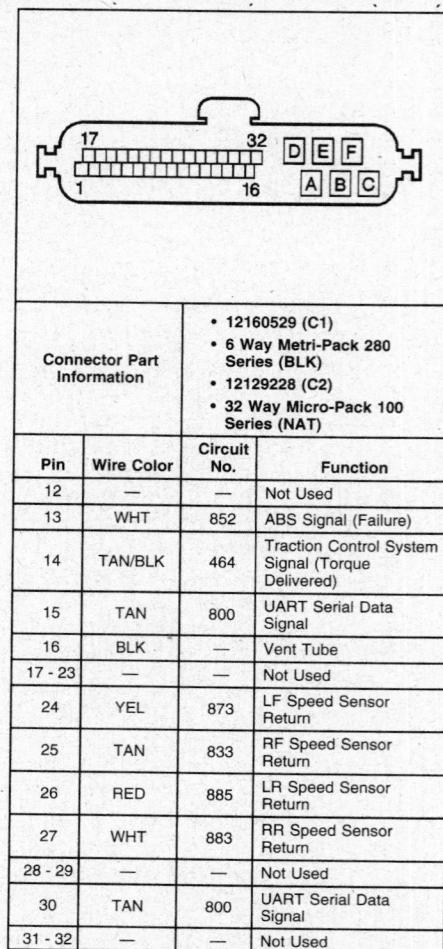

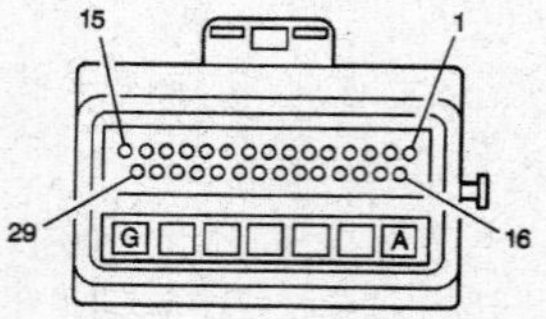

Connector Part Information			• C1 - 15318099 • 7 Way F Metri-Pack 480 Series (BLK) • C2 - 15354984 • 29 Way F Micro-Pack 100 Series (NAT)
Pin	**Wire Color**	**Circuit No.**	**Function**
24	TAN	833	Right Front Wheel Speed Sensor Low Reference
25	YEL	873	Left Front Wheel Speed Sensor Low Reference
26	—	—	Not Used
27	GRY	1056	Steering Wheel Position Sensor 5V Reference Voltage
28	LT BLU	2627	Steering Position Sensor Signal
29	—	—	Not Used

GC4020152535020X

Fig. 27 EBCM connector terminal identification (Part 2 of 2). 2000 Corvette

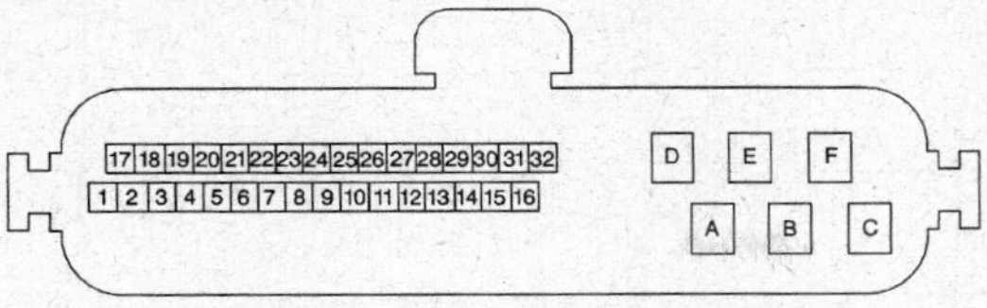

Connector Part Information	• 12129228 • 32 Way Micro-Pack 100 Series (NAT)			Connector Part Information	• 12129228 • 32 Way Micro-Pack 100 Series (NAT)		
Pin	Wire Color	Circuit No.	Function	Pin	Wire Color	Circuit No.	Function
A	PNK	1339	Fused Output (IGN)	15	YEL	873	LF Speed Sensor HI
B	BLK	1651	Ground	16	BLK	—	Vent Tube
C	GRY	1787	Motor Feed (High)	17	WHT	1765	SWPS - Pulse
D	RED	1042	Solenoid Valve Supply	18	WHT	790	Serial Data Signal
E	RED	1042	Pump Motor Supply	19	—	—	Not Used
F	WHT	345	Motor Feed (Low)	20	LT GRN	1763	SWPS - A
1	—	—	Not Used	21	DK BLU	716	Yaw Rate Sensor Signal
2	GRY	791	Serial Data Signal	22	LT BLU	715	Lateral Accelerometer Signal
3	WHT	852	Antilock Indicator	23	LT BLU	1059	SWPS Signal
4	LT BLU	1764	Steering Wheel Position Sensor (SWPS) - B	24	BRN/WHT	1571	TCS Switch Input
5	—	—	Not Used	25	ORN/BLK	463	Requested Torque
6	TAN/BLK	464	Delivered Torque	26	PPL	1807	Class 2 Serial Data
7-8	—	—	Not Used	27	LT GRN/BLK	1338	Sensor Ground
9	LT BLU	20	Brake Switch Input	28	RED	885	LR Speed Sensor LO
10	PPL	1807	Class 2 Serial Data	29	BRN	882	RR Speed Sensor LO
11	GRY/BLK	1337	Yaw Sensor Feed	30	DK GRN	872	RF Speed Sensor LO
12	BLK	884	LR Speed Sensor HI	31	LT BLU	830	LF Speed Sensor LO
13	WHT	883	RR Speed Sensor HI	32	—	—	Not Used
14	TAN	833	RF Speed Sensor HI	—	—	—	—

GC4029803543000X

Fig. 28 EBCM/EBTCM Connector terminal identification. DeVille

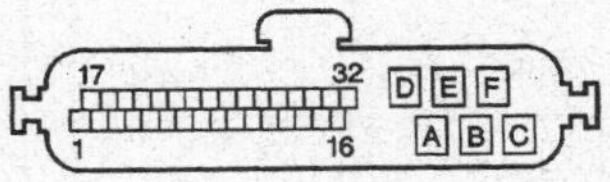

Connector Part Information	• 12129228/12160529 • 32/6 Way F Micro-Pack 100 Series (BLU)		
Pin	Wire Color	Circuit No.	Function
A	BRN	241	Ignition Positive Voltage
B	BLK	1150	Ground
C	GRY	1787	Magna Steer ® (HI)
D	RED	442	Solenoid Valve Supply
E	RED	342	Pump Motor Supply
F	WHT	345	Magna Steer ® (LO)
1	—	—	Not Used
2	GRA	791	ICCS Data Link - Right
3	DK BLU	1537	Antilock Indicator
4	LT BLU	1764	Digital SWPS Phase B
5	—	—	Not Used
6	TAN/BLK	464	Delivered Torque Input
7	WHT	1612	Brake Wear Sensor Signal
8	—	—	Not Used
9	WHT	17	Stoplamp BTSI Switch Input
10	PPL	1807	Class 2 Serial Data Line
11	GRY/BLK	1337	5 Volt Sensor Feed
12	BLK	884	LR Wheel Speed Sensor (HI)
13	WHT	883	RR Wheel Speed Sensor (LO)
14	TAN	833	RF Wheel Speed Sensor (LO)

GC4029803544010X

Fig. 29 EBCM/EBTCM connector terminal identification (Part 1 of 2). Seville

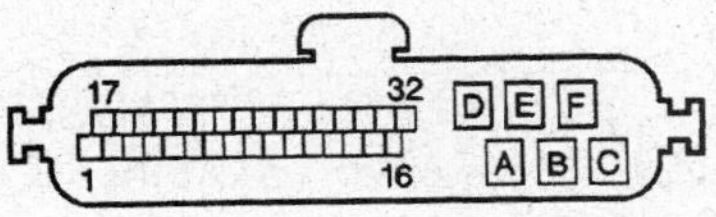

Connector Part Information	• 12129228/12160529 • 32/6 Way F Micro-Pack 100 Series (BLU)		
Pin	Wire Color	Circuit No.	Function
15	YEL	873	LF Wheel Speed Sensor (LO)
16	—	—	Vent Cavity
17	WHT	1765	PWM SWPS Signal
18	WHT	790	ICCS Data Link - Left
19	—	—	Not Used
20	LT GRN	1763	Digital SWPS Phase A
21	DK BLU	716	Yaw Rate Sensor Signal
22	LT BLU	715	Lateral Accelerometer Sensor Signal
23	LT BLU	1059	Analog SWPS Signal
24	—	—	Not Used
25	ORN/BLK	463	Requested Torque Output
26	PPL	1807	Class 2 Serial Data Line
27	LT ORN/BLK	1338	Sensor Return
28	RED	885	LR Wheel Speed Sensor (LO)
29	BRN	882	RR Wheel Speed Sensor (HI)
30	DK GRN	872	RF Wheel Speed Sensor (HI)
31	LT BLU	830	LF Wheel Speed Sensor (HI)
32	—	—	Not Used

GC4029803544020X

Fig. 29 EBCM/EBTCM connector terminal identification (Part 2 of 2). Seville

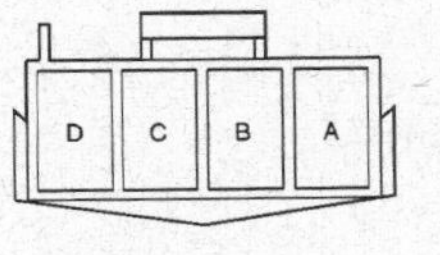

Connector Part Information	• 12033705 • 4 Way F Metri-Pack 280 Series (NAT)		
Pin	Wire Color	Circuit No.	Function
A	PNK	1039	TCC Switch Power Feed
B	PPL	420	TCC Switch Input
C	PNK	1039	ABS Switch Power Feed
D	GRY	847	ABS Brake Switch Input

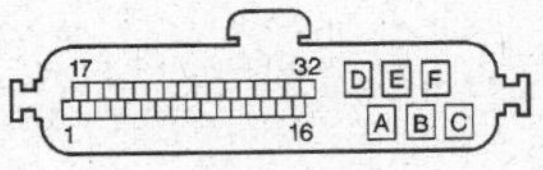

Connector Part Information	• C1 - 12160529 • 6 Way F Metri-Pack 280 Series (BLK) • C2 - 12129228 • 32 Way F Micro-Pack 100 Series (NAT)		
Pin	Wire Color	Circuit No.	Function
A	PNK	241	Fuse Output - Ignition 1
B	BLK	1651	Ground
C	GRY	1787	Variable Effort Steering Actuator Control - High Side
D	RED	1042	Fuse Output - Battery
E	RED	1042	Fuse Output - Battery

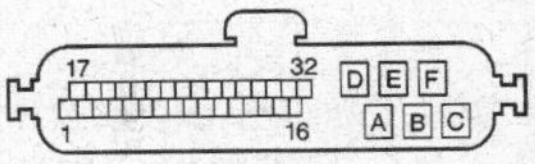

Connector Part Information	• C1 - 12160529 • 6 Way F Metri-Pack 280 Series (BLK) • C2 - 12129228 • 32 Way F Micro-Pack 100 Series (NAT)		
Pin	Wire Color	Circuit No.	Function
F	WHT	345	Variable Effort Steering Actuator Control - Low Side
1	—	—	Not Used
2	GRY	791	Right Normal Force Signal
3	WHT	852	ABS Indicator Signal
4	LT BLU	1764	Digital Steering Wheel Position Signal - Phase B
5	—	—	Not Used
6	TAN/BLK	464	Traction Control System Signal - Torque Delivered
7–8	—	—	Not Used
9	LT BLU	20	Stoplamp Switch Output
10	PPL	1807	Serial Data - Class 2
11	GRY/BLK	1337	Sensor Feed - 5 Volt
12	BLK	884	Wheel Speed Sensor Signal - Left Rear
13	WHT	883	Wheel Speed Sensor Return - Right Rear
14	TAN	833	Wheel Speed Sensor Return - Right Front
15	YEL	873	Wheel Speed Sensor Return - Left Front
16	—	—	Vent Tube
17	WHT	1765	Steering Wheel Position PWM Signal
18	WHT	790	Left Normal Force Signal
19	—	—	Not Used

GC4020152537010X

Fig. 30 EBCM connector terminal identification (Part 1 of 2). Eldorado

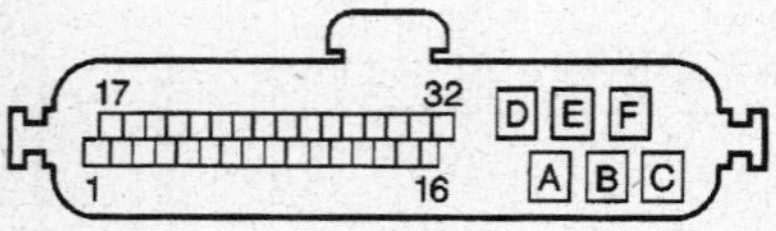

Connector Part Information	• C1 - 12160529 • 6 Way F Metri-Pack 280 Series (BLK) • C2 - 12129228 • 32 Way F Micro-Pack 100 Series (NAT)		
Pin	**Wire Color**	**Circuit No.**	**Function**
20	LT GRN	1763	Digital Steering Wheel Position Signal - Phase A
21	DK BLU	716	Yaw Rate Sensor Signal
22	LT BLU	715	Lateral Accelerometer Signal
23	LT BLU	1059	Analog Steering Wheel Position Signal
24	BRN/WHT	1571	Traction Control Switch Signal
25	ORN/BLK	463	Traction Control System Signal - Torque Desired
26	PPL	1807	Serial Data - Class 2
27	LT GRN/ BLK	1338	Sensor Return
28	RED	885	Wheel Speed Sensor Return - Left Rear
29	BRN	882	Wheel Speed Sensor Signal - Right Rear
30	DK GRN	872	Wheel Speed Sensor Signal - Right Front
31	LT BLU	830	Wheel Speed Sensor Signal - Left Front
32	—	—	Not Used

GC4020152537020X

Fig. 30 EBCM connector terminal identification (Part 2 of 2). Eldorado

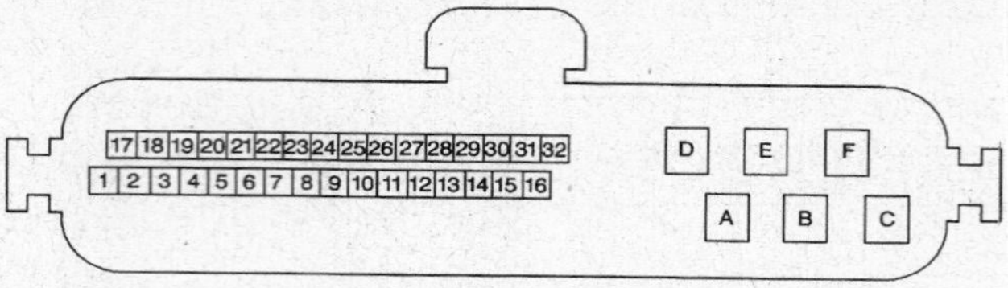

Connector Part Information	• 12129228 • EBCM/EBTCM Connector			Connector Part Information	• 12129228 • EBCM/EBTCM Connector		
Pin	Wire Color	Circuit No.	Function	Pin	Wire Color	Circuit No.	Function
A	BRN	241	Ignition Power	13	WHT	883	Right Rear Wheel Speed Sensor (LO)
B	BLK	1150	Ground	14	TAN	833	Right Front Wheel Speed Sensor (LO)
C	GRA	1787	Variable Steering Solonoid(HI)	15	YEL	873	Left Front Wheel Speed Sensor (LO)
D	RED	342	Solenoid Valve Supply	16	——	——	Vent Tube
E	RED	642	Pump Motor Supply	24	BRN/WHT	1571	Traction Control ON/OFF Input
F	WHT	345	Variable Steering Solonoid(LO)	25	ORG/BLK	463	Requested Torque Output
3	WHT	852	ABS Indicator	26	PPL	1807	Class 2 Serial Data
6	TAN/BLK	464	Delivered Torque Input	28	RED	885	Left Rear Wheel Speed Sensor (LO)
9	LT BLU	20	Stoplamp/BTSI Switch Input	29	BRN	882	Right Rear Wheel Speed Sensor (HI)
10	PPL	1807	Class 2 Serial Data	30	DK GRN	872	Right Front Wheel Speed Sensor (HI)
12	BLK	884	Left Rear Wheel Speed Sensor (HI)	31	LT BLU	830	Left Front Wheel Speed Sensor (HI)

GC4029803530000X

Fig. 31 EBCM/EBTCM connector terminal identification. Park Avenue

DIAGNOSTIC CHART INDEX

Code/Test	Description	Page No.	Fig. No.
BONNEVILLE & LESABRE			
—	ABS Diagnostic System Check	6-316	32
A	ABS Lamp On w/No Code Set	6-344	98
B	ABS Lamp Inoperative w/No Code Set	6-345	100
C	Traction Off Lamp On w/No Code Set	6-346	102
D	Traction Off Lamp Inoperative w/No Code Set	6-346	104
E	Traction Active Lamp On w/No Code Set	6-348	106
F	Traction Active Lamp Inoperative w/No Code Set	6-348	107
G	No Communication w/EBCM/EBTCM	6-348	108
C1211	ABS Lamp Circuit Fault	6-316	34
C1214	Solenoid Valve Relay Contact Or Coil Circuit Open	6-317	36
C1216	Brake Control Relay Coil Circuit Open	6-318	37
C1217	BPMV Pump Motor Relay Contact Circuit Open	6-318	38
C1221	LH Front Wheel Speed Sensor Input Signal Is Zero	6-318	39
C1222	RH Front Wheel Speed Sensor Input Signal Is Zero	6-319	41
C1223	LH Rear Wheel Speed Sensor Input Signal Is Zero	6-320	43
C1224	RH Rear Wheel Speed Sensor Input Signal Is Zero	6-321	45
C1225	LH Excessive Front Wheel Speed Variation	6-321	47
C1226	RH Front Excessive Wheel Speed Variation	6-322	49
C1227	LH Rear Excessive Wheel Speed Variation	6-323	51
C1228	RH Rear Excessive Wheel Speed Variation	6-324	53
C1232	LH Front Wheel Speed Sensor Circuit Open Or Shorted	6-325	55
C1233	RH Front Wheel Speed Sensor Circuit Open Or Shorted	6-326	57
C1234	LH Rear Wheel Speed Sensor Circuit Open Or Shorted	6-328	59
C1235	RH Rear Wheel Speed Sensor Circuit Open Or Shorted	6-329	61
C1236	Low System Supply Voltage	6-330	63
C1237	High System Supply Voltage	6-330	64
C1238	Brake Thermal Model Exceeded	6-331	65
C1242	BPMV Pump Motor Ground Circuit Open	6-331	66
C1243	BPMV Pump Motor Stalled	6-331	67
C1255	EBCM/EBTCM Internal Fault	6-332	68
C1256	EBCM/EBTCM Internal Fault	6-332	69
C1261	LH Front Inlet Valve Solenoid Fault	6-332	70
C1262	LH Front Outlet Valve Solenoid Fault	6-333	71
C1263	RH Front Inlet Valve Solenoid Fault	6-333	72
C1264	RH Front Outlet Valve Solenoid Fault	6-333	73
C1265	LH Rear Inlet Valve Solenoid Fault	6-334	74
C1266	LH Rear Outlet Valve Solenoid Fault	6-334	75
C1267	RH Rear Inlet Valve Fault	6-335	76
C1268	RH Rear Outlet Valve Solenoid Fault	6-335	77
C1271	LH Front TCS Master Cylinder Isolation Valve Fault	6-335	78
C1272	LH Front Prime Valve Fault	6-336	79
C1273	RH Front TCS Master Cylinder Isolation Valve Fault	6-336	80
C1274	RH Front TCS Prime Valve Fault	6-337	81
C1275	Serial Data Fault	6-337	82
C1276	Delivered Torque Signal Circuit Fault	6-337	83
C1277	Requested Torque Signal Circuit Fault	6-339	85
C1278	TCS Temporarily Inhibited By PCM	6-340	87
C1291	Open Brake Lamp Switch Contacts During Decel	6-340	88
C1293	Code C1291 Set In Previous Ignition Cycle	6-341	90
C1294	Brake Lamp Switch Circuit Always Active	6-341	91
C1295	Brake Lamp Switch Circuit Open	6-342	93
CORVETTE			
—	ABS Diagnostic System Check (2000)	6-349	110
—	ABS Indicator Always On (2000)	6-379	176
—	ABS Indicator Inoperative (2000)	6-379	177
A	ABS Lamp On w/No Code Set	6-377	171

Continued

DIAGNOSTIC CHART INDEX—Continued

Continued

DIAGNOSTIC CHART INDEX—Continued

Code/Test	Description	Page No.	Fig. No.
CORVETTE			
C1293	Code C1291/C1292 Set In Current Or Previous Ignition Cycle	6-374	163
C1294	Brake Lamp Switch Circuit Always Active	6-375	164
C1295	Brake Lamp Switch Circuit Open	6-375	165
C1296	Brake Pressure Sensor Circuit Open Or Short	6-375	166
U1016	Loss Of Communications w/PCM	6-376	167
U1255	Generic Loss Of Communications	6-376	168
U1300	Class 2 Short To Ground	6-377	169
U1301	Class 2 Circuit Short To Battery	6-377	170
DEVILLE			
—	ABS Diagnostic System Check	6-379	178
—	No Communications w/EBTCM	6-415	257
—	Traction Off Message On w/No Code Set	6-417	259
—	Traction Off Message Inoperative w/No Code Set	6-418	261
—	Stabilitrak Inoperative w/No Code Set	6-418	263
—	Vehicle Stability Enhancement System Unwanted Activation w/No Code Set	6-419	265
—	Vehicle Stability Enhancement System Excessive Brake Pulsation	6-420	268
C1211	ABS Lamp Circuit Fault	6-380	181
C1214	Solenoid Valve Relay Contact Or Coil Circuit Open	6-381	182
C1217	BPMV Pump Motor Relay Contact Circuit Open	6-382	184
C1221	LH Front Wheel Speed Sensor Input Signal Is Zero	6-383	186
C1222	RH Front Wheel Speed Sensor Input Signal Is Zero	6-383	187
C1223	LH Front Wheel Speed Sensor Input Signal Is Zero	6-384	188
C1224	RH Rear Wheel Speed Sensor Input Signal Is Zero	6-384	189
C1225	LH Front Excessive Wheel Speed Variation	6-384	190
C1226	RH Front Excessive Wheel Speed Variation	6-385	191
C1227	LH Rear Excessive Wheel Speed Variation	6-385	192
C1228	RH Rear Excessive Wheel Speed Variation	6-386	193
C1232	LH Front Wheel Speed Circuit Open Or Shorted	6-387	195
C1233	RH Front Wheel Speed Circuit Open Or Shorted	6-388	197
C1234	LH Rear Wheel Speed Circuit Open Or Shorted	6-390	199
C1235	RH Rear Wheel Speed Circuit Open Or Shorted	6-391	201
C1236	Low System Supply Voltage	6-392	202
C1237	High System Supply Voltage	6-393	204
C1238	Brake Thermal Model Exceeded	6-393	205
C1241	Magnasteer Circuit Fault	6-393	206
C1242	BPMV Pump Motor Ground Circuit Open	6-393	207
C1243	BPMV Pump Motor Stalled	6-394	209
C1252	ICCS 2 Data Link Left Fault	6-395	211
C1253	ICCS 2 Data Link Right Fault	6-395	212
C1255	EBTCM Internal Fault	6-395	213
C1256	EBCM Internal Fault	6-396	214
C1261	LH Front Inlet Valve Solenoid Fault	6-396	215
C1262	LH Front Outlet Solenoid Fault	6-396	216
C1263	RH Front Inlet Valve Solenoid Fault	6-397	218
C1264	RH Front Outlet Valve Solenoid Fault	6-397	219
C1265	LH Rear Inlet Valve Solenoid Fault	6-398	220
C1266	LH Rear Outlet Valve Solenoid Fault	6-398	221
C1267	RH Rear Inlet Valve Solenoid Fault	6-399	222
C1268	RH Rear Outlet Valve Solenoid Fault	6-399	223
C1271	LH TCS Front Master Cylinder Isolation Valve Fault	6-399	224
C1272	LH Front Prime Valve Fault	6-400	225
C1273	RH Front TCS Master Cylinder Isolation Valve Fault	6-400	226
C1274	RH Front TCS Prime Valve Fault	6-401	227
C1276	Delivered Torque Signal Circuit Fault	6-401	228
C1277	Requested Torque Signal Circuit Fault	6-402	230
C1278	TCS Temporarily Inhibited By PCM	6-402	231

Continued

DIAGNOSTIC CHART INDEX—Continued

Code/Test	Description	Page No.	Fig. No.
DEVILLE			
C1281	Stabilitrak Sensors Uncorrelated	6-403	232
C1282	Yaw Rate Sensor Bias Circuit Fault	6-404	234
C1283	Excessive Time To Center Steering	6-405	235
C1284	Lateral Accel Sensor Self Test Fault	6-406	237
C1285	Lateral Accel Sensor Circuit Fault	6-406	238
C1286	Steering/Lateral Accelerometer Sensors Bias Fault	6-407	239
C1287	Steering Sensor Rate Fault	6-408	241
C1288	Steering Sensor Circuit Fault	6-409	243
C1291	Open Brake Lamp Switch Contacts During Decel	6-411	245
C1293	Code C1291 Set In Previous Ignition Cycle	6-412	246
C1294	Brake Lamp Switch Circuit Always Active	6-412	247
C1295	Brake Lamp Switch Circuit Open	6-413	249
C1297	PCM Indicated Brake Extended Travel Switch Failure	6-414	251
C1298	PCM Class 2 Serial Data Link Fault	6-414	252
U1016	Loss Of Communications w/PCM	6-415	254
U1255	Generic Loss Of Communications	6-415	255
U1256	Loss Of Communications w/CVRSS	6-415	256
ELDORADO			
—	ABS Diagnostic System Check	6-421	271
—	ABS Indicator Inoperative	6-446	324
—	ABS Indicator Always On	6-446	325
—	No Communication With EBCM	6-447	326
—	Traction Control Indicator Always On	6-447	327
—	Traction Control Indicator Inoperative	6-448	328
—	Traction Off Message Always On	6-448	329
—	Traction Off Message Inoperative	6-448	330
—	Vehicle Stability Enhancement System Excessive Brake Pulsation	6-449	331
—	Vehicle Stability Enhancement System Inoperative	6-449	332
—	Vehicle Stability Enhancement System Unwanted Activation	6-449	333
C1211	ABS Warning Lamp Fault	6-421	272
C1214	Solenoid Valve Relay Contact Or Coil Circuit Open	6-422	273
C1217	Pump Motor Relay Control Circuit Open	6-422	274
C1221	LF Wheel Speed Input Signal Is 0	6-422	275
C1222	RF Wheel Speed Input Signal Is 0	6-423	276
C1223	LR Wheel Speed Input Signal Is 0	6-423	277
C1224	RR Wheel Speed Input Signal Is 0	6-424	278
C1225	LF Excessive Wheel Speed Variation	6-424	279
C1226	RF Excessive Wheel Speed Variation	6-424	280
C1227	LR Excessive Wheel Speed Variation	6-425	281
C1228	RR Excessive Wheel Speed Variation	6-425	282
C1232	LF Wheel Speed Circuit Open Or Shorted	6-426	283
C1233	RF Wheel Speed Circuit Open Or Shorted	6-426	284
C1234	LR Wheel Speed Circuit Open Or Shorted	6-427	285
C1235	RR Wheel Speed Circuit Open Or Shorted	6-427	286
C1236	Low System Supply Voltage	6-428	287
C1237	High System Supply Voltage	6-429	288
C1238	Brake Thermal Models Exceeded	6-429	289
C1242	BPMV Pump Motor Ground Circuit Open	6-429	290
C1243	BPMV Pump Motor Stalled	6-430	291
C1252	ICCS2 Data Link Left Fault	6-430	292
C1253	ICCS2 Data Link Right Fault	6-431	293
C1255	EBCM Internal Fault	6-431	294
C1256	EBCM Internal Fault	6-432	295
C1261	LF Inlet Valve Solenoid Fault	6-432	296
C1262	LF Outlet Valve Solenoid Fault	6-432	297
C1263	RF Inlet Valve Solenoid Fault	6-433	298

Continued

DIAGNOSTIC CHART INDEX—Continued

Code/Test	Description	Page No.	Fig. No.
ELDORADO			
C1264	RF Outlet Valve Solenoid Fault	6-433	299
C1265	LR Inlet Valve Solenoid Fault	6-433	300
C1266	LR Outlet Valve Solenoid Fault	6-434	301
C1267	RR Inlet Valve Solenoid Fault	6-434	302
C1268	RR Outlet Valve Solenoid Fault	6-435	303
C1271	LF TCS Master Cylinder Isolation Valve Fault	6-435	304
C1272	LF TCS Prime Valve Fault	6-435	305
C1273	RF TCS Master Cylinder Isolation Valve Fault	6-436	306
C1274	RF TCS Prime Valve Fault	6-436	307
C1276	Delivered Torque Signal Circuit Fault	6-437	308
C1277	Requested Torque Signal Circuit Fault	6-437	309
C1278	TCS Temporarily Inhibited By PCM	6-438	310
C1281	Stabilitrak Sensors Uncorrelated	6-438	311
C1282	Yaw Rate Sensor Bias Circuit Fault	6-439	312
C1283	Excessive Time To Center Steering	6-440	313
C1284	Lateral Accelerometer Sensor Self Test Fault	6-440	314
C1285	Lateral Accelerometer Sensor Circuit Fault	6-440	315
C1286	Steering/Lateral Accelerometer Sensor Bias Fault	6-441	316
C1287	Steering Sensor Rate Fault	6-442	317
C1288	Steering Sensor Circuit Fault	6-442	318
C1291	Open Brake Lamp Switch Contacts During Deceleration	6-443	319
C1294	Brake Lamp Switch Circuit Always Active	6-444	320
C1295	Brake Lamp Switch Circuit Open	6-444	321
C1297	PCM Indicated Brake Extended Travel Switch Failure	6-445	322
C1298	PCM Class 2 Serial Data Link Fault	6-445	323
PARK AVENUE			
—	ABS Diagnostic System Check	6-316	33
C1211	ABS Lamp Circuit Fault	6-317	35
C1214	Solenoid Valve Relay Contact Or Coil Circuit Open	6-317	36
C1217	BPMV Pump Motor Relay Contact Circuit Open	6-318	38
C1221	LH Front Wheel Speed Sensor Input Signal Is Zero	6-319	40
C1222	RH Front Wheel Speed Sensor Input Signal Is Zero	6-319	42
C1223	LH Rear Wheel Speed Sensor Input Signal Is Zero	6-320	44
C1224	RH Rear Wheel Speed Sensor Input Signal Is Zero	6-321	46
C1225	LH Front Excessive Wheel Speed Variation	6-322	48
C1226	RH Front Excessive Wheel Speed Variation	6-323	50
C1227	LH Rear Excessive Wheel Speed Variation	6-323	52
C1228	RH Rear Excessive Wheel Speed Variation	6-324	54
C1232	LH Front Wheel Speed Sensor Circuit Open Or Shorted	6-325	56
C1233	RH Front Wheel Speed Sensor Circuit Open Or Shorted	6-327	58
C1234	LH Rear Wheel Speed Sensor Circuit Open Or Shorted	6-328	60
C1235	RH Rear Wheel Speed Sensor Circuit Open Or Shorted	6-329	62
C1236	Low System Supply Voltage	6-330	63
C1237	High System Supply Voltage	6-330	64
C1238	Brake Thermal Model Exceeded	6-331	65
C1242	BPMV Pump Motor Ground Circuit Open	6-331	66
C1243	BPMV Pump Motor Stalled	6-331	67
C1255	EBCM/EBTCM Internal Fault	6-332	68
C1256	EBCM/EBTCM Internal Fault	6-332	69
C1261	LH Front Inlet Valve Solenoid Fault	6-332	70
C1262	LH Front Outlet Valve Solenoid Fault	6-333	71
C1263	RH Front Inlet Valve Solenoid Fault	6-333	72
C1264	RH Front Outlet Valve Solenoid Fault	6-333	73
C1265	LH Rear Inlet Valve Solenoid Fault	6-334	74
C1266	LH Rear Outlet Valve Solenoid Fault	6-334	75
C1267	RH Rear Inlet Valve Fault	6-335	76

Continued

DIAGNOSTIC CHART INDEX—Continued

Code/Test	Description	Page No.	Fig. No.
PARK AVENUE			
C1268	RH Rear Outlet Valve Solenoid Fault	6-335	77
C1271	LH Front TCS Master Cylinder Isolation Valve Fault	6-335	78
C1272	LH Front Prime Valve Fault	6-336	79
C1273	RH Front TCS Master Cylinder Isolation Valve Fault	6-336	80
C1274	RH Front TCS Prime Valve Fault	6-337	81
C1276	Delivered Torque Circuit Fault	6-338	84
C1277	Requested Torque Signal Circuit Fault	6-339	86
C1278	TCS Temporarily Inhibited By PCM	6-340	87
C1291	Open Brake Lamp Switch Contact During Decel	6-341	89
C1293	Code C1291 Set In Previous Ignition Cycle	6-341	90
C1294	Brake Lamp Switch Circuit Always Active	6-342	92
C1295	Brake Lamp Switch Circuit Open	6-343	94
C1298	PCM Class 2 Serial Data Link Fault	6-343	95
U1016	Loss Of Communications w/PCM	6-344	96
U1255	Generic Loss Of Communications	6-344	97
A	ABS Lamp On w/No Code Set	6-345	99
B	ABS Lamp Inoperative w/No Code Set	6-345	101
C	Traction Off Lamp On w/No Code Set	6-346	103
D	Traction Off Lamp Inoperative w/No Code Set	6-347	105
G	No Communication w/EBCM/EBTCM	6-348	109
SEVILLE			
—	ABS Diagnostic System Check	6-379	178
—	ABS Diagnostic System Check & Diagnostic Test Drive	6-380	179
—	No Communications w/EBCM/EBTCM	6-416	258
—	Traction Off Message On w/No Code Set	6-417	260
—	Traction Off Message Inoperative w/No Code Set	6-418	262
—	Stabilitrak Inoperative w/No Code Set	6-419	264
—	Stabilitrak Unwanted Activation w/Code Set	6-419	266
—	Stabilitrak Excessive Brake Pulsation	6-420	267
—	Scan Tool Displays Undefined Code	6-420	269
—	Check Brake Pads Message Always On	6-421	270
C1211	ABS Lamp Circuit Fault	6-380	180
C1214	Solenoid Valve Relay Contact Or Coil Circuit Open	6-381	183
C1217	BPMV Pump Motor Relay Contact Circuit Open	6-382	185
C1225	LH Front Excessive Wheel Speed Variation	6-384	190
C1226	RH Front Excessive Wheel Speed Variation	6-385	191
C1227	LH Rear Excessive Wheel Speed Variation	6-385	192
C1228	RH Rear Excessive Wheel Speed Variation	6-386	193
C1232	LH Front Wheel Speed Circuit Open Or Shorted	6-386	194
C1233	RH Front Wheel Speed Circuit Open Or Shorted	6-387	196
C1234	LH Rear Wheel Speed Circuit Open Or Shorted	6-389	198
C1235	RH Rear Wheel Speed Circuit Open Or Shorted	6-390	200
C1236	Low System Supply Voltage	6-392	203
C1237	High System Supply Voltage	6-393	204
C1238	Brake Thermal Model Exceeded	6-393	205
C1241	Magnasteer Circuit Fault	6-393	206
C1242	BPMV Pump Motor Ground Circuit Open	6-393	208
C1243	BPMV Pump Motor Stalled	6-394	210
C1252	ICCS 2 Data Link Left Fault	6-395	211
C1253	ICCS 2 Data Link Right Fault	6-395	212
C1255	EBTCM Internal Fault	6-395	213
C1256	EBCM Internal Fault	6-396	214
C1261	LH Front Inlet Valve Solenoid Fault	6-396	215
C1262	LH Front Outlet Solenoid Fault	6-397	217
C1263	RH Front Inlet Valve Solenoid Fault	6-397	218
C1264	RH Front Outlet Valve Solenoid Fault	6-397	219

Continued

DIAGNOSTIC CHART INDEX—Continued

Code/Test	Description	Page No.	Fig. No.
SEVILLE			
C1265	LH Rear Inlet Valve Solenoid Fault	6-398	220
C1266	LH Rear Outlet Valve Solenoid Fault	6-398	221
C1267	RH Rear Inlet Valve Solenoid Fault	6-399	222
C1268	RH Rear Outlet Valve Solenoid Fault	6-399	223
C1271	LH TCS Front Master Cylinder Isolation Valve Fault	6-399	224
C1272	LH Front Prime Valve Fault	6-400	225
C1273	RH Front TCS Master Cylinder Isolation Valve Fault	6-400	226
C1274	RH Front TCS Prime Valve Fault	6-401	227
C1276	Delivered Torque Signal Circuit Fault	6-401	229
C1277	Requested Torque Signal Circuit Fault	6-402	230
C1281	ABC Sensors Uncorrelated	6-403	233
C1283	Excessive Time To Center Steering	6-405	236
C1286	Steering/Lateral Accelerometer Sensors Bias Fault	6-408	240
C1287	Steering Sensor Rate Fault	6-409	242
C1288	Steering Sensor Circuit Fault	6-410	244
C1291	Open Brake Lamp Switch Contacts During Decel	6-411	245
C1293	Code C1291 Set In Previous Ignition Cycle	6-412	246
C1294	Brake Lamp Switch Circuit Always Active	6-412	248
C1295	Brake Lamp Switch Circuit Open	6-413	250
C1298	PCM Class 2 Serial Data Link Fault	6-414	253
U1016	Loss Of Communications w/PCM	6-415	254

Step	Action	Value(s)	Yes	No
1	1. Reconnect all previously disconnected components. 2. Cycle the ignition switch from the OFF to RUN position, engine off. 3. Plug a scan tool into the Diagnostic Link Connector (DLC). Does the scan tool communicate with the EBCM/EBTCM?	—	*Go to Step 3*	*Go to Step 2*
2	Does the scan tool communicate with other modules on the UART serial data line?	—	Go to *No Communication with EBCM/EBTCM*	Go to Data Link Connector
3	1. With the scan tool in ABS/TCS Special Functions run the AUTOMATED test. 2. With the scan tool read ABS/TCS DTC(s). Are there any current Diagnostic Trouble Codes?	—	Go to *DTC List* for Applicable DTC Table	*Go to Step 4*
4	Cycle the ignition switch from the OFF to RUN position, engine off. Does the ABS Indicator turn on then turn off after several seconds?	—	*Go to Step 5*	*Go to Step 7*
5	Is this vehicle equipped with Traction Control?	—	*Go to Step 6*	*Go to Step 12*
6	Cycle the ignition switch from the OFF to RUN position, engine off. Does the Traction Off Indicator turn on then turn off after several seconds?	—	*Go to Step 8*	*Go to Step 9*
7	Does the ABS Indicator stay on?	—	Go to *ABS Indicator On No DTC Set*	Go to *ABS Indicator Inoperative with No DTC Set*
8	Is the vehicle an Oldsmobile?	—	*Go to Step 10*	*Go to Step 12*
9	Does the Traction Off Indicator stay on?	—	Go to *Traction Off Indicator On with No DTC Set*	Go to *Traction Off Indicator Inoperative with No DTC Set*
10	Cycle the ignition switch from the OFF to RUN position, engine Off. Does the Traction Active Indicator turn on then turn off after several seconds?	—	*Go to Step 12*	*Go to Step 11*
11	Does the Traction Active Indicator stay on?	—	Go to *Traction Active Indicator On with No DTC Set*	Go to *Traction Active Indicator Inoperative w/No DTC Set*
12	Are there any history DTC(s)?	—	*Go to Step 13*	System OK
13	1. Refer to the appropriate DTC table for the history DTC. 2. Read the diagnostic aids, and the conditions for setting the DTC. 3. Carefully drive the vehicle above 24 Km/h (15 mph) for several minutes, while monitoring a scan tool. Did the history DTC set as a current DTC while the vehicle was being driven?	—	Go to *DTC List* for Applicable DTC Table	System OK

GC4029802690020X

Fig. 32 ABS Diagnostic System Check. Bonneville & LeSabre

Circuit Description

The ABS Indicator driver circuit runs from the Instrument Panel Cluster (IPC) through the Lamp Driver Module (LDM) to the EBCM/EBTCM. The IPC supplies voltage to the ABS indicator. The EBCM/EBTCM controls the ABS indicator through the LDM. The LDM acts as an invertor; when the EBCM/EBTCM supplies a ground for the LDM, the indicator remains off. When the EBCM/EBTCM removes the ground for the LDM, the indicator turns on by using the ground at the LDM terminal D.

Conditions for Setting the DTC

EBCM/EBTCM commands the ABS indicator on and either an open, a short to ground, or a short to voltage is detected in CKT 852.

Action Taken When the DTC Sets

The DTC is stored, but the ABS is not disabled.

Conditions for Clearing the MIL/DTC

- The condition for DTC is no longer present and the scan tool clear DTC function is used.
- 50 ignition cycles have passed with no DTCs detected.

Diagnostic Aids

Perform a thorough inspection of the wiring and connectors. Failure to carefully and fully inspect wiring and connectors may result in misdiagnosis, causing part replacement with reappearance of the malfunction.

Test Description

The number(s) below refer to the step number(s) on the diagnostic table.

2. This step checks if CKT 852 is shorted to voltage.
4. This step checks if CKT 852 is shorted to ground.
6. This step checks for an open in CKT 852.

GC402980271500AX

Fig. 34 Code C1211: ABS Lamp Circuit Fault (Part 1 of 2). Bonneville & LeSabre

Step	Action	Value(s)	Yes	No
1	1. Connect or install all previously disconnected or removed components. 2. Cycle the ignition switch from the OFF to the RUN position with the engine OFF. 3. Plug a Scan Tool into the DLC. Does the Scan Tool communicate with the EBCM/EBTCM?	—	*Go to Step 3*	*Go to Step 2*
2	Does the scan tool communicate with other modules on the class 2 line?	—	Go to *No Communication with EBCM/EBTCM*	Go to Data Link Connector
3	1. With the Scan Tool in the ABS/TCS Special Functions, attempt to run the AUTOMATED Test. 2. Read the ABS/TCS DTCs. Are any DTCs present?	—	Go to the applicable DTC table	*Go to Step 4*
4	Cycle the ignition from the OFF to the RUN position with the engine off. Does the ABS indicator turn On then Off?	—	*Go to Step 6*	*Go to Step 5*
5	Does the ABS indicator stay on?	—	Go to *ABS Indicator On No DTC Set*	Go to *ABS Indicator Inoperative with No DTC Set*
6	Is the vehicle TCS equipped?	—	*Go to Step 7*	*Go to Step 9*
7	Cycle the ignition from the OFF to the RUN position with the engine off. Does the Traction Off indicator turn On then Off?	—	*Go to Step 7*	*Go to Step 6*
8	Does the Traction Off indicator stay on?	—	Refer to *Traction Off Indicator On with No DTC Set*	Refer to *Traction Off Indicator Inoperative with No DTC Set*
9	Are there any history DTCs?	—	*Go to Step 10*	System OK
10	1. Refer to the appropriate DTC table for the history DTC. 2. Read the Diagnostic Aids and the Conditions for setting the DTC. 3. Drive the vehicle above 24 km/h (15 mph) for several minutes while monitoring the Scan Tool for ABS/TCS DTCs. Does the history DTC set as a current DTC while the vehicle is being driven?	—	Go to the applicable DTC table	System OK

GC4029802691000X

Fig. 33 ABS Diagnostic System Check. Park Avenue

Step	Action	Value(s)	Yes	No
1	Was the Diagnostic System Check performed?	—	*Go to Step 2*	Go to *Diagnostic System Check*
2	1. Turn the ignition switch to the OFF position. 2. Disconnect the EBCM/EBTCM. 3. Connect *J 39700* Universal Pinout Box using *J 39700-25* cable adapter to the EBCM/EBTCM harness connector only. 4. Disconnect the LDM. 5. Turn the ignition switch to the RUN position. Do not start the engine. 6. Using *J 39200* DMM, measure the voltage at terminal 13 of *J 39700*. Is the voltage within the specified range in the values column?	Battery volts	*Go to Step 3*	*Go to Step 4*
3	Repair CKT 852 for a short to voltage. Is the repair complete?	—	Go to *Diagnostic System Check*	—
4	1. Turn the ignition switch to the OFF position. 2. Using *J 39200* DMM, measure the resistance between terminal 13 and B of *J 39700*. Is the resistance within the range specified in the values column?	OL (infinite)	*Go to Step 6*	*Go to Step 5*
5	Repair CKT 852 for a short to ground. Is the repair complete?	—	Go to *Diagnostic System Check*	—
6	1. Connect a fused jumper wire between terminals 13 and B of *J 39700*. 2. Using *J 39200* DMM, measure the resistance between the LDM harness connector terminal C and a good ground. Is the resistance within the range specified in the values column?	0-5 Ω	*Go to Step 7*	*Go to Step 8*
7	Replace the EBCM/EBTCM. Is the replacement complete?	—	Go to *Diagnostic System Check*	—
8	Repair an open or high resistance in CKT 852. Is the repair complete?	—	Go to *Diagnostic System Check*	—

GC402980271500BX

Fig. 34 Code C1211: ABS Lamp Circuit Fault (Part 2 of 2). Bonneville & LeSabre

Circuit Description

The instrument cluster controls the operation of the ABS indicator. The EBCM/EBTCM reports the desired status of the ABS indicator via class 2 serial data messages. The ABS indicator signal circuit is a back-up reporting circuit to the class 2 serial data messages. The EBCM/EBTCM supplies ground through the circuit when the ABS is operating properly. When there is a problem with ABS that should turn on the ABS indicator, the EBCM/EBTCM opens the ABS indicator signal circuit. If there is a problem with the ABS class 2 serial data messages, the instrument cluster uses the ABS indicator signal to determine if the ABS indicator should be illuminated. Using the serial data messages and back-up circuit, the instrument cluster decides whether to turn on the ABS indicator.

Conditions for Setting the DTC

The EBCM/EBTCM commands the ABS indicator ON when one of the following conditions are detected:

- An open
- A short to ground
- A short to voltage

Action Taken When the DTC Sets

- A malfunction DTC is stored.
- The ABS is not disabled.
- The ABS indicator remains OFF.

Conditions for Clearing the DTC

- The condition for the DTC is no longer present and you used the scan tool Clear DTC function.
- The EBCM/EBTCM does not detect the DTC in 50 drive cycles.

Diagnostic Aids

- It is very important that a thorough inspection of the wiring and connectors be performed. Failure to carefully and fully inspect wiring and connectors may result in misdiagnosis, causing part replacement with reappearance of the malfunction.
- An intermittent malfunction can be caused by poor connections, broken insulation, or a wire that is broken inside the insulation.
- If an intermittent malfunction exists, refer to *Intermittents and Poor Connections*

Test Description

The numbers below refer to the step numbers on the diagnostic table.

3. This step tests if the instrument cluster can operate the ANTILOCK indicator.
4. This step tests for a short to ground in CKT 852.
6. This step tests for a short to voltage in CKT 852.
7. This step tests for an open in CKT 852.

GC4029903940010X

Fig. 35 Code C1211: ABS Lamp Circuit Fault (Part 1 of 2). Park Avenue

Step	Action	Value(s)	Yes	No
1	Was the ABS Diagnostic System Check performed?	—	Go to *Step 2*	Go to *ABS Diagnostic System Check*
2	1. Turn the ignition switch to the RUN position with the engine OFF. 2. Using a scan tool, read the ABS/TCS and instrument cluster diagnostic trouble codes (DTCs). Is DTC U1300 or DTC U1301 set?	—	Go to *DTC U1300 Class 2 Short to Ground* or *DTC U1301 Class 2 Short to Battery* in Data Link Communications	Go to *Step 3*
3	1. Select SBM special functions on the scan tool. 2. Run the instrument cluster bulb check. Does the ANTILOCK indicator turn ON then OFF?	—	Go to *Step 4*	Go to *Step 10*
4	1. Turn the ignition switch to the OFF position. 2. Disconnect the electronic brake (and traction) control module (EBCM/EBTCM). 3. Connect the *J 39700* universal pinout box using the *J 39700 - 25* cable adapter to the EBCM/EBTCM harness connector only. 4. Disconnect the instrument cluster connector. 5. Using the *J 39200*, measure the resistance between the *J 39700* terminal 3 and terminal B. Is the resistance equal to the specified value?	OL (Infinite)	Go to *Step 6*	Go to *Step 5*
5	Repair the short to ground in CKT 852. Is the repair complete?	—	Go to *ABS Diagnostic System Check*	—
6	1. Turn the ignition switch to the RUN position with the engine OFF. 2. Using the *J 39200*, measure the voltage at terminal 3 of the *J 39700*. Is the voltage more than the specified value?	1 V	Go to *Step 8*	Go to *Step 7*
7	1. Turn the ignition switch to the OFF position. 2. Connect a fused jumper wire between the instrument cluster harness connector terminal B13 and a good ground. 3. Using the *J 39200* digital multimeter (DMM), measure the resistance between the *J 39700* terminal 3 and terminal B. Is the resistance less than the specified value?	5 Ω	Go to *Step 11*	Go to *Step 9*
8	Repair the short to voltage in CKT 852. Is the repair complete?	—	Go to *ABS Diagnostic System Check*	—
9	Repair the open in CKT 852. Is the circuit repair complete?	—	Go to *ABS Diagnostic System Check*	—
10	Suspect the instrument cluster. Is the diagnosis complete?	—	Go to *ABS Diagnostic System Check*	—
11	Replace the EBCM/EBTCM. Is the repair complete?	—	Go to *ABS Diagnostic System Check*	—

GC4029903940020X

Fig. 35 Code C1211: ABS Lamp Circuit Fault (Part 2 of 2). Park Avenue

Circuit Description

The EBCM/EBTCM and the BPMV receive power from three circuits. CKT 642 supplies battery power to the pump motor. CKT 342 supplies ignition power to the solenoid valves, the EBCM/EBTCM, and the pump motor relay coil. CKT 641 supplies battery power to initialize controller operations. CKT 641 also supplies power to the solenoid valve relay coil.

Conditions for Setting the DTC

The solenoid relay is commanded on and the solenoid relay voltage is less than 8.0 volts, and ignition voltage is greater than 10.5 volts

Action Taken When the DTC Sets

- A DTC C1214 is stored
- The ABS/TCS is disabled
- The ABS and the TRACTION OFF indicators turn on

Conditions for Clearing the DTC

- The condition for the DTC is no longer present and the scan tool Clear DTC function is used
- 50 ignition cycles have passed with no DTC(s) detected

Diagnostic Aids

- Thoroughly inspect the wiring and the connectors. Failure to carefully and fully inspect the wiring and the connectors can result in misdiagnosis. Misdiagnosis may cause replacement of parts without repairing the malfunction.
- The following conditions are possible causes of the malfunction:
  - A problem in the power distribution system may result in no battery voltage to CKT 342
  - The ABS SOLENOID fuse is open
  - CKT 342 has a wiring problem, corrosion, or faulty connections
  - There is an internal malfunction in the EBCM/EBTCM or the BPMV
  - The solenoid valve relay is faulty
  - The relays are integral to the EBCM/EBTCM and are not serviceable

Test Description

The numbers below refer to the step numbers on the diagnostic table.

4. This step checks for a short to ground in CKT 342.
5. This step checks for an internal short in the BPMV.
8. This step checks for an open in CKT 342.

GC402980271600AX

Fig. 36 Code C1214: Solenoid Valve Relay Contact Or Coil Circuit Open (Part 1 of 2). Bonneville, LeSabre & Park Avenue

Step	Action	Value(s)	Yes	No
1	Was the Diagnostic System Check performed?	—	*Go to Step 2*	Go to *Diagnostic System Check*
2	Inspect the ABS SOLENOID fuse in the LH MaxiFuse Block. Is the fuse OK?	—	*Go to Step 7*	*Go to Step 3*
3	1. Install a new ABS SOLENOID fuse. 2. Turn the ignition to the RUN position with the engine off. 3. Recheck the ABS SOLENOID fuse. Is the fuse OK?	—	Go to *Diagnostic System Check*	*Go to Step 4*
4	1. Turn the ignition switch to the OFF position. 2. Remove the ABS SOLENOID fuse. 3. Disconnect the EBCM/EBTCM. 4. Connect the *J 39700* Universal Pinout Box using the *J 39700-25* cable adapter to the EBCM/EBTCM harness connector only. 5. Using the *J 39200* DMM, measure the resistance between the *J 39700* terminals D and B. Is the resistance within specifications?	OL (infinite)	*Go to Step 5*	*Go to Step 10*
5	1. Remove the EBCM/EBTCM from the BPMV. 2. Connect the *J 41247* to the BPMV. 3. Measure the resistance between the *J 41247* terminal 7 and the BPMV case. Is the resistance within specifications?	OL (infinite)	*Go to Step 9*	*Go to Step 6*
6	Replace the BPMV. Is the replacement complete?	—	Go to *Diagnostic System Check*	—
7	1. Reinstall the fuse, if removed. 2. Using the *J 39200* DMM, probe between the ABS Solenoid fuse test terminals and a good ground in order to measure the voltage. Is the voltage within specifications?	Battery voltage	*Go to Step 8*	Inspect Power Distribution
8	1. Turn the ignition switch to the OFF position. 2. Disconnect the EBCM/EBTCM. 3. Connect the *J 39700* Universal Pinout Box using the *J 39700-25* cable adapter to the EBCM/EBTCM harness connector only. 4. Using the *J 39200* DMM, measure the voltage at the *J 39700* terminal D. Is the voltage within specifications?	Battery voltage	*Go to Step 9*	*Go to Step 11*
9	Replace the EBCM/EBTCM. Is the replacement complete?	—	Go to *Diagnostic System Check*	—
10	Repair the short to ground in CKT 342. Is the circuit repair complete?	—	Go to *Diagnostic System Check*	—
11	Repair the open or high resistance in CKT 342. Is the circuit repair complete?	—	Go to *Diagnostic System Check*	—

GC402980271600BX

Fig. 36 Code C1214: Solenoid Valve Relay Contact Or Coil Circuit Open (Part 2 of 2). Bonneville, LeSabre & Park Avenue

Circuit Description

The EBCM/EBTCM and the BPMV receive power from three circuits. CKT 642 supplies battery power to the pump motor. CKT 342 supplies ignition power to the solenoid valves, the EBCM/EBTCM, and the pump motor relay coil. CKT 641 supplies battery power to initialize controller operations. CKT 641 also supplies power to the solenoid valve relay coil.

Conditions for Setting the DTC

The solenoid relay is commanded On and the solenoid relay voltage is less than 8.0 volts, and ignition voltage is greater than 10.5 volts

Action Taken When the DTC Sets

- A DTC C1214 is stored
- The ABS/TCS is disabled
- The ABS and the TRACTION OFF indicators turn On

Conditions for Clearing the DTC

- The condition for the DTC is no longer present and the scan tool Clear DTC function is used
- 50 ignition cycles have passed with no DTC(s) detected

Diagnostic Aids

- Thoroughly inspect the wiring and the connectors. Failure to carefully and fully inspect the wiring and the connectors can result in misdiagnosis. Misdiagnosis may cause replacement of parts without repairing the malfunction.
- The relays are integral to the EBCM/EBTCM and are not serviceable.

Step	Action	Value(s)	Yes	No
1	Was the Diagnostic System Check performed?	—	*Go to Step 2*	Go to *Diagnostic System Check*
2	Replace the EBCM/EBTCM. Is the replacement complete?	—	Go to *Diagnostic System Check*	—

GC402980271700 0X

Fig. 37 Code C1216: Brake Control Relay Coil Circuit Open. Bonneville & LeSabre

Step	Action	Value(s)	Yes	No
1	Was the Diagnostic System Check performed?	—	*Go to Step 2*	Go to *Diagnostic System Check*
2	Inspect the ABS MOTOR fuse in the LH MaxiFuse block. Is the fuse OK?	—	*Go to Step 7*	*Go to Step 3*
3	1. Install a new ABS MOTOR fuse. 2. Cycle the ignition from the OFF to the RUN position with the engine off. 3. Using a Scan Tool, select ABS/TCS Special Functions. 4. Run the AUTOMATED Test. 5. Recheck the ABS MOTOR fuse. Is the fuse OK?	—	Go to *Diagnostic System Check*	*Go to Step 4*
4	1. Turn the ignition switch to the OFF position. 2. Remove the ABS MOTOR fuse. 3. Disconnect the EBCM/EBTCM. 4. Disconnect the pump motor ground. 5. Connect the *J 39700* Universal Pinout Box using the *J 39700-25* cable adapter to the EBCM/EBTCM harness connector only. 6. Using the *J 39200* DMM, measure the resistance between the *J 39700* terminals E and B. Is the resistance within specifications?	OL (infinite)	*Go to Step 5*	*Go to Step 10*
5	1. Remove the EBCM/EBTCM from the BPMV. 2. Connect the *J 41247* Pinout Box to the BPMV. 3. Measure the resistance between the *J 41247* terminal 8 and the BPMV case. Is the resistance within specifications?	OL (infinite)	*Go to Step 9*	*Go to Step 6*
6	Replace the BPMV. Is the replacement complete?	—	Go to *Diagnostic System Check*	—
7	1. Reinstall the fuse, if removed. 2. Using the *J 39200* DMM, probe between the ABS Solenoid fuse test terminals and a good ground in order to measure the voltage. Is the voltage within specifications?	Battery voltage	*Go to Step 8*	Inspect Power Distribution
8	1. Turn the ignition switch to the OFF position. 2. Disconnect the EBCM/EBTCM. 3. Connect the *J 39700* Universal Pinout Box using the *J 39700-25* cable adapter to the EBCM/EBTCM harness connector only. 4. Using the *J 39200* DMM, measure the voltage at the *J 39700* terminal E. Is the voltage within specifications?	Battery voltage	*Go to Step 9*	*Go to Step 11*

GC402980271800BX

Fig. 38 Code C1217: BPMV Pump Motor Relay Contact Circuit Open (Part 2 of 3). Bonneville, LeSabre & Park Avenue

Circuit Description

The speed sensor is a single point magnetic pickup that produces an AC signal. The EBCM/EBTCM uses the signal frequency in order to calculate the wheel speed.

Conditions for Setting the DTC

The LF wheel speed equals 0 and the remaining WSS speeds are greater than 8 km/h (5 mph) for 2.5 seconds

Action Taken When the DTC Sets

- A DTC C1221 is stored
- The ABS/TCS is disabled
- The ABS and the TRACTION OFF indicators are turned on

Conditions for Clearing the DTC

- The condition for the DTC is no longer present and the scan tool Clear DTC function is used
- 50 ignition cycles have passed with no DTCs detected

Diagnostic Aids

- Thoroughly inspect the wiring and the connectors. Failure to carefully and fully inspect the wiring and the connectors can result in misdiagnosis. Misdiagnosis may cause replacement of parts without repairing the malfunction.
- The following conditions may cause an intermittent malfunction:
  - Poor connections
  - Broken insulation
  - A broken wire inside the insulation

Test Description

The numbers below refer to step numbers on the diagnostic table.

3. Checks the resistance of the WSS.
5. Checks if the WSS CKTs are shorted together.

GC402980271900AX

Fig. 39 Code C1221: LH Front Wheel Speed Sensor Input Signal Is Zero (Part 1 of 2). Bonneville & LeSabre

Circuit Description

The EBCM/EBTCM and the BPMV receive power from three circuits. CKT 642 supplies battery power to the pump motor. CKT 342 supplies ignition power to the solenoid valves, the EBCM/EBTCM, and the pump motor relay coil. CKT 641 supplies battery power to initialize controller operations. CKT 641 also supplies power to the solenoid valve relay coil.

Conditions for Setting the DTC

The pump motor relay is commanded on and the pump relay voltage is less than 8.0 volts and ignition voltage is more than 10.5 volts

Action Taken When the DTC Sets

- A DTC C1217 is stored
- The ABS/TCS is disabled
- The ABS and the TRACTION OFF indicators are turned on

Conditions for Clearing the DTC

- The condition for the DTC is no longer present and the scan tool Clear DTC function is used
- 50 ignition cycles have passed with no DTCs detected

Diagnostic Aids

- Thoroughly inspect the wiring and the connectors. Failure to carefully and fully inspect the wiring and the connectors can result in misdiagnosis. Misdiagnosis may cause replacement of parts without repairing the malfunction.
- The following conditions are possible causes of the malfunction:
  - A problem in the power distribution system may result in no battery voltage to CKT 642
  - The ABS MOTOR fuse is open
  - CKT 642 has a wiring problem, corrosion, or faulty connections
  - There is an internal malfunction in the EBCM/EBTCM or the BPMV
  - The pump motor relay is faulty
  - The relays are integral to the EBCM/EBTCM and are not serviceable

Test Description

The numbers below refer to the step numbers on the diagnostic table.

4. This step checks for a short to ground in CKT 642.
5. This step checks for an internal short in the BPMV.
8. This step checks for an open in CKT 642.

GC402980271800AX

Fig. 38 Code C1217: BPMV Pump Motor Relay Contact Circuit Open (Part 1 of 3). Bonneville, LeSabre & Park Avenue

Step	Action	Value(s)	Yes	No
9	Replace the EBCM/EBTCM. Is the replacement complete?	—	Go to *Diagnostic System Check*	—
10	Repair the short to ground in CKT 642. Is the circuit repair complete?	—	Go to *Diagnostic System Check*	—
11	Repair the open or high resistance in CKT 642. Is the circuit repair complete?	—	Go to *Diagnostic System Check*	—

GC402980271800CX

Fig. 38 Code C1217: BPMV Pump Motor Relay Contact Circuit Open (Part 3 of 3). Bonneville, LeSabre & Park Avenue

Step	Action	Value(s)	Yes	No
1	Was the Diagnostic System Check performed?	--	*Go to Step 2*	Go to *Diagnostic System Check*
2	1. Inspect the WSS wiring and connectors for damage. 2. Inspect WSS for looseness or damage. Is physical damage of sensor evident?	--	*Go to Step 7*	*Go to Step 3*
3	1. Disconnect the WSS at the sensor pigtail. 2. Using *J 39200* DMM, measure the resistance between terminals A and B of the WSS. Is the resistance within the range specified in the value(s) column?	850-1350Ω	*Go to Step 4*	*Go to Step 7*
4	1. With *J 39200* DMM still connected, select the mV AC scale. 2. Spin the wheel as fast as you can by hand while monitoring the AC output. Is the AC voltage within the range specified in the value(s) column?	Above 100 mV	*Go to Step 5*	*Go to Step 7*
5	1. Disconnect the EBCM/EBTCM harness connector. 2. Install *J 39700* Universal Pinout Box using the *J 39700-25* cable adapter to the EBCM/EBTCM harness connector only. 3. Using *J 39200* DMM, measure resistance between terminals 24 and 8 of the *J 39700*. Is the resistance within the range specified in the value(s) column?	OL (Infinite)	*Go to Step 6*	*Go to Step 8*
6	1. Reconnect all connectors. 2. Carefully test drive vehicle above 24 Km/h (15 mph) for at least 30 seconds while monitoring a scan tool. Does DTC reset as a current DTC?	--	*Go to Step 9*	Go to *Diagnostic System Check*
7	Replace wheel speed sensor. Is the repair complete?	--	*Go to Step 10*	--
8	Repair short between CKT(s) 873 and 830. Is the repair complete?	--	*Go to Step 10*	--
9	Replace EBCM/EBTCM. Is the replacement complete?	--	*Go to Step 10*	--
10	Carefully test drive vehicle above 24 Km/h (15 mph) while monitoring a scan tool for at least 30 seconds. Does the DTC set as a current DTC?	--	*Go to Step 2*	Go to *Diagnostic System Check*

GC402980271900BX

Fig. 39 Code C1221: LH Front Wheel Speed Sensor Input Signal Is Zero (Part 2 of 2). Bonneville & LeSabre

Circuit Description

The speed sensor used on this vehicle is a single point magnetic pickup. This sensor produces an AC signal that the EBCM/EBTCM uses the frequency from to calculate the wheel speed.

Condition For Setting The DTC

- The DTC will set if the LF wheel speed = 0 and the other WSS are greater than 8 Km/h (5 mph) for 2.5 seconds.

Action Taken When The DTC Sets

- A malfunction DTC is stored, ABS/TCS is disabled and the "ABS" and "TRACTION OFF" Indicator lamps are turned "ON."

Conditions for Clearing DTC

- Condition for DTC is no longer present and Scan Tool clear DTC function is used.
- 50 Ignition cycles have passed with no DTC(s) detected.

Diagnostic Aids

- It is very important that a thorough inspection of the wiring and connectors be performed. Failure to carefully and fully inspect wiring and connectors may result in misdiagnosis, causing part replacement with reappearance of the malfunction.
- An intermittent malfunction can be caused by poor connections, broken insulation, or a wire that is broken inside the insulation.

Test Description

The numbers below refer to step numbers on the diagnostic table.

3. Checks the resistance of the WSS.
5. Checks if the WSS CKTs are shorted together.

GC402980271902AX

Fig. 40 Code C1221: LH Front Wheel Speed Sensor Input Signal Is Zero (Part 1 of 2). Park Avenue

Circuit Description

The WSS is a single point magnetic pickup that produces an AC signal. The EBCM/EBTCM uses the signal frequency in order to calculate the wheel speed.

Conditions for Setting the DTC

The RF wheel speed equals 0 and the remaining WSS speeds are greater than 8 km/h (5 mph) for 2.5 seconds

Action Taken When the DTC Sets

- A DTC C1222 is stored
- The ABS/TCS is disabled
- The ABS and the TRACTION OFF indicators are turned on

Conditions for Clearing the DTC

- The condition for the DTC is no longer present and the scan tool Clear DTC function is used
- 50 ignition cycles have passed with no DTCs detected

Diagnostic Aids

- Thoroughly inspect the wiring and the connectors. Failure to carefully and fully inspect the wiring and the connectors can result in misdiagnosis. Misdiagnosis may cause replacement of parts without repairing the malfunction.
- The following conditions may cause an intermittent malfunction:
  - Poor connections
  - Broken insulation
  - A broken wire inside the insulation

Test Description

The numbers below refer to step numbers on the diagnostic table.

3. Checks the resistance of the WSS.
5. Checks if the WSS CKTs are shorted together.

GC402980272000AX

Fig. 41 Code C1222: RH Front Wheel Speed Sensor Input Signal Is Zero (Part 1 of 2). Bonneville & LeSabre

Step	Action	Value(s)	Yes	No
1	Was the Diagnostic System Check performed?	--	*Go to Step 2*	*Go to Diagnostic System Check*
2	1. Inspect the WSS wiring and connectors for damage. 2. Inspect WSS for looseness or damage. Is physical damage of sensor evident?	--	*Go to Step 7*	*Go to Step 3*
3	1. Disconnect the WSS at the sensor pigtail. 2. Using *J 39200* DMM, measure the resistance between terminals A and B of the WSS. Is the resistance within the range specified in the value(s) column?	850-1350Ω	*Go to Step 4*	*Go to Step 7*
4	1. With *J 39200* DMM still connected, select the mV AC scale. 2. Spin the wheel as fast as you can by hand while monitoring the AC output. Is the AC voltage within the range specified in the value(s) column?	Above 100 mV	*Go to Step 5*	*Go to Step 7*
5	1. Disconnect the EBCM/EBTCM harness connector. 2. Install *J 39700* Universal Pinout Box using the *J 39700-25* cable adapter to the EBCM/EBTCM harness connector only. 3. Using *J 39200* DMM, measure resistance between terminals 25 and 9 of the *J 39700*. Is the resistance within the range specified in the value(s) column?	OL (Infinite)	*Go to Step 6*	*Go to Step 8*
6	1. Reconnect all connectors. 2. Carefully test drive vehicle above 24 Km/h (15 mph) for at least 30 seconds while monitoring a scan tool. Does DTC reset as a current DTC?	--	*Go to Step 9*	*Go to Diagnostic System Check*
7	Replace wheel speed sensor. Is the repair complete?	--	*Go to Step 10*	--
8	Repair short between CKT(s) 833 and 872. Is the repair complete?	--	*Go to Step 10*	--
9	Replace EBCM/EBTCM. Is the replacement complete?	--	*Go to Step 10*	--
10	Carefully test drive vehicle above 24 Km/h (15 mph) while monitoring a scan tool for at least 30 seconds. Does the DTC set as a current DTC?	--	*Go to Step 2*	*Go to Diagnostic System Check*

GC402980272000BX

Fig. 41 Code C1222: RH Front Wheel Speed Sensor Input Signal Is Zero (Part 2 of 2). Bonneville & LeSabre

Step	Action	Value(s)	Yes	No
1	Was the ABS Diagnostic System Check performed?	—	Go to *Step 2*	Go to *A Diagnostic System Check*
2	1. Inspect the WSS wiring and connectors for damage. 2. Inspect the WSS for looseness or damage. Is physical damage of the sensor evident?	—	Go to *Step 7*	Go to *Step 3*
3	1. Disconnect the WSS at the sensor pigtail. 2. Using the *J 39200* digital multimeter (DMM), measure the resistance between terminals A and B of the WSS. Is the resistance within the specified range?	850–1350 Ω	Go to *Step 4*	Go to *Step 7*
4	1. With the DMM still connected, select the mV AC scale. 2. Spin the wheel as fast as you can by hand while monitoring the AC output. Is the AC voltage greater than the specified value?	100 mV	Go to *Step 5*	Go to *Step 7*
5	1. Disconnect the EBCM/EBTCM harness connector. 2. Install the *J 39700* universal pinout box using the *J 39700-25* cable adapter to the EBCM/EBTCM harness connector only. 3. Using the DMM, measure the resistance between terminals 15 and 31 of the *J 39700*. Is the resistance within the specified range?	OL (Infinite)	Go to *Step 6*	Go to *Step 8*
6	1. Reconnect all connectors. 2. Carefully test drive the vehicle above 24 Km/h (15 mph) for at least 30 seconds while monitoring a scan tool. Does DTC reset as a current DTC?	—	Go to *Step 9*	Go to *A Diagnostic System Check*
7	Replace the wheel speed sensor. Is the repair complete?	—	Go to *Step 10*	—
8	Repair the short between CKT 873 and CKT 830. Is the repair complete?	—	Go to *Step 10*	—
9	Replace the EBCM/EBTCM. Is the replacement complete?	—	Go to *Step 10*	—
10	Carefully test drive the vehicle above 24 Km/h (15 mph) while monitoring a scan tool for at least 30 seconds. Does the DTC set as a current DTC?	—	Go to *Step 2*	Go to *A Diagnostic System Check*

GC402980271902CX

Fig. 40 Code C1221: LH Front Wheel Speed Sensor Input Signal Is Zero (Part 2 of 2). Park Avenue

Circuit Description

The WSS is a single point magnetic pickup that produces an AC signal. The EBCM/EBTCM uses the signal frequency in order to calculate the wheel speed.

Conditions for Setting the DTC

The RF wheel speed equals 0 and the remaining WSS speeds are greater than 8 km/h (5 mph) for 2.5 seconds

Action Taken When the DTC Sets

- A DTC C1222 is stored
- The ABS/TCS is disabled
- The ABS and the TRACTION OFF indicators are turned on

Conditions for Clearing the DTC

- The condition for the DTC is no longer present and the scan tool Clear DTC function is used
- 50 ignition cycles have passed with no DTCs detected

Diagnostic Aids

- Thoroughly inspect the wiring and the connectors. Failure to carefully and fully inspect the wiring and the connectors can result in misdiagnosis. Misdiagnosis may cause replacement of parts without repairing the malfunction.
- The following conditions may cause an intermittent malfunction:
  - Poor connections
  - Broken insulation
  - A broken wire inside the insulation

Test Description

The numbers below refer to step numbers on the diagnostic table.

3. Checks the resistance of the WSS.
5. Checks if the WSS CKTs are shorted together.

GC402980272002AX

Fig. 42 Code C1222: RH Front Wheel Speed Sensor Input Signal Is Zero (Part 1 of 2). Park Avenue

Step	Action	Value(s)	Yes	No
1	Was the ABS Diagnostic System Check performed?	—	Go to *Step 2*	Go to *A Diagnostic System Check*
2	1. Inspect the WSS wiring and connectors for damage. 2. Inspect the WSS for looseness or damage. Is physical damage of the sensor evident?	—	Go to *Step 7*	Go to *Step 3*
3	1. Disconnect the WSS at the sensor pigtail. 2. Using the *J 39200* digital multimeter (DMM), measure the resistance between terminals A and B of the WSS. Is the resistance within the specified range?	850–1350 Ω	Go to *Step 4*	Go to *Step 7*
4	1. With the DMM still connected, select the mV AC scale. 2. Spin the wheel as fast as you can by hand while monitoring the AC output. Is the AC voltage greater than the specified value?	100 mV	Go to *Step 5*	Go to *Step 7*
5	1. Disconnect the EBCM/EBTCM harness connector. 2. Install the *J 39700* universal pinout box using the *J 39700-25* cable adapter to the EBCM/EBTCM harness connector only. 3. Using the DMM, measure the resistance between terminals 14 and 30 of the *J 39700*. Is the resistance within the specified range?	OL (Infinite)	Go to *Step 6*	Go to *Step 8*
6	1. Reconnect all connectors. 2. Carefully test drive the vehicle above 24 Km/h (15 mph) for at least 30 seconds while monitoring a scan tool. Does DTC reset as a current DTC?	—	Go to *Step 9*	Go to *A Diagnostic System Check*
7	Replace the wheel speed sensor. Is the repair complete?	—	Go to *Step 10*	—
8	Repair the short between CKT 833 and CKT 872. Is the repair complete?	—	Go to *Step 10*	—
9	Replace the EBCM/EBTCM. Is the replacement complete?	—	Go to *Step 10*	—
10	Carefully test drive the vehicle above 24 Km/h (15 mph) while monitoring a scan tool for at least 30 seconds. Does the DTC set as a current DTC?	—	Go to *Step 2*	Go to *A Diagnostic System Check*

GC402980272002CX

Fig. 42 Code C1222: RH Front Wheel Speed Sensor Input Signal Is Zero (Part 2 of 2). Park Avenue

Step	Action	Value(s)	Yes	No
1	Was the Diagnostic System Check performed?	--	*Go to Step 2*	Go to *Diagnostic System Check*
2	1. Inspect the WSS wiring and connectors for damage. 2. Inspect WSS for looseness or damage. Is physical damage of sensor evident?	--	*Go to Step 7*	*Go to Step 3*
3	1. Disconnect the WSS at the sensor pigtail. 2. Using *J 39200* DMM, measure the resistance between terminals A and B of the WSS. Is the resistance within the range specified in the value(s) column?	850-1350Ω	*Go to Step 4*	*Go to Step 7*
4	1. With *J 39200* DMM still connected, select the mV AC scale. 2. Spin the wheel as fast as you can by hand while monitoring the AC output. Is the AC voltage within the range specified in the value(s) column?	Above 100 mV	*Go to Step 5*	*Go to Step 7*
5	1. Disconnect the EBCM/EBTCM harness connector. 2. Install *J 39700* Universal Pinout Box using the *J 39700-25* cable adapter to the EBCM/EBTCM harness connector only. 3. Using *J 39200* DMM, measure resistance between terminals 10 and 28 of the *J 39700*. Is the resistance within the range specified in the value(s) column?	OL (Infinite)	*Go to Step 6*	*Go to Step 8*
6	1. Reconnect all connectors. 2. Carefully test drive vehicle above 24 Km/h (15 mph) for at least 30 seconds while monitoring a scan tool. Does DTC reset as a current DTC?	--	*Go to Step 9*	Go to *Diagnostic System Check*
7	Replace wheel speed sensor. Is the repair complete?	--	*Go to Step 10*	--
8	Repair short between CKT(s) 884 and 885. Is the repair complete?	--	*Go to Step 10*	--
9	Replace EBCM/EBTCM. Is the replacement complete?	--	*Go to Step 10*	--
10	Carefully test drive vehicle above 24 Km/h (15 mph) while monitoring a scan tool for at least 30 seconds. Does the DTC set as a current DTC?	--	*Go to Step 2*	Go to *Diagnostic System Check*

GC402980272100BX

Fig. 43 Code C1223: LH Rear Wheel Speed Sensor Input Signal Is Zero (Part 2 of 2). Bonneville & LeSabre

Circuit Description

The WSS is a single point magnetic pickup that produces an AC signal. The EBCM/EBTCM uses the signal frequency in order to calculate the wheel speed.

Conditions for Setting the DTC

The LR wheel speed equals 0 and the remaining WSS speeds are greater than 8 km/h (5 mph) for 2.5 seconds

Action Taken When the DTC Sets

- A DTC C1223 is stored
- The ABS/TCS is disabled
- The ABS and the TRACTION OFF indicators are turned on

Conditions for Clearing the DTC

- The condition for the DTC is no longer present and the scan tool Clear DTC function is used
- 50 ignition cycles have passed with no DTCs detected

Diagnostic Aids

- Thoroughly inspect the wiring and the connectors. Failure to carefully and fully inspect the wiring and the connectors can result in misdiagnosis. Misdiagnosis may cause replacement of parts without repairing the malfunction.
- The following conditions may cause an intermittent malfunction:
  - Poor connections
  - Broken insulation
  - A broken wire inside the insulation

Test Description

The numbers below refer to step numbers on the diagnostic table.

3. Checks the resistance of the WSS.
5. Checks if the WSS CKTs are shorted together.

GC402980272100AX

Fig. 43 Code C1223: LH Rear Wheel Speed Sensor Input Signal Is Zero (Part 1 of 2). Bonneville & LeSabre

Circuit Description

The WSS is a single point magnetic pickup that produces an AC signal. The EBCM/EBTCM uses the signal frequency in order to calculate the wheel speed.

Conditions for Setting the DTC

The LR wheel speed equals 0 and the remaining WSS speeds are greater than 8 km/h (5 mph) for 2.5 seconds

Action Taken When the DTC Sets

- A DTC C1223 is stored
- The ABS/TCS is disabled
- The ABS and the TRACTION OFF indicators are turned on

Conditions for Clearing the DTC

- The condition for the DTC is no longer present and the scan tool Clear DTC function is used
- 50 ignition cycles have passed with no DTCs detected

Diagnostic Aids

- Thoroughly inspect the wiring and the connectors. Failure to carefully and fully inspect the wiring and the connectors can result in misdiagnosis. Misdiagnosis may cause replacement of parts without repairing the malfunction.
- The following conditions may cause an intermittent malfunction:
  - Poor connections
  - Broken insulation
  - A broken wire inside the insulation

Test Description

The numbers below refer to step numbers on the diagnostic table.

3. Checks the resistance of the WSS.
5. Checks if the WSS CKTs are shorted together.

GC402980272102AX

Fig. 44 Code C1223: LH Rear Wheel Speed Sensor Input Signal Is Zero (Part 1 of 2). Park Avenue

Step	Action	Value(s)	Yes	No
1	Was the ABS Diagnostic System Check performed?	—	Go to *Step 2*	Go to *A Diagnostic System Check*
2	1. Inspect the WSS wiring and connectors for damage. 2. Inspect the WSS for looseness or damage. Is physical damage of the sensor evident?	—	Go to *Step 7*	Go to *Step 3*
3	1. Disconnect the WSS at the sensor pigtail. 2. Using the *J 39200* digital multimeter (DMM), measure the resistance between terminals A and B of the WSS. Is the resistance within the specified range?	850–1350 Ω	Go to *Step 4*	Go to *Step 7*
4	1. With the *J 39200* DMM still connected, select the mV AC scale. 2. Spin the wheel as fast as you can by hand while monitoring the AC output. Is the AC voltage within the range specified in the value(s) column?	100 mV	Go to *Step 5*	Go to *Step 7*
5	1. Disconnect the EBCM/EBTCM harness connector. 2. Install the *J 39700* universal pinout box using the *J 39700-25* cable adapter to the EBCM/EBTCM harness connector only. 3. Using the DMM, measure the resistance between terminals 12 and 28 of the *J 39700*. Is the resistance within the specified range?	OL (Infinite)	Go to *Step 6*	Go to *Step 8*
6	1. Reconnect all connectors. 2. Carefully test drive the vehicle above 24 Km/h (15 mph) for at least 30 seconds while monitoring a scan tool. Does DTC reset as a current DTC?	—	Go to *Step 9*	Go to *A Diagnostic System Check*
7	Replace wheel speed sensor. Is the repair complete?	—	Go to *Step 10*	—
8	Repair the short between CKT 884 and CKT 885. Is the repair complete?	—	Go to *Step 10*	—
9	Replace the EBCM/EBTCM. Is the replacement complete?	—	Go to *Step 10*	—
10	Carefully test drive the vehicle above 24 Km/h (15 mph) while monitoring a scan tool for at least 30 seconds. Does the DTC set as a current DTC?	—	Go to *Step 2*	Go to *A Diagnostic System Check*

GC402980272102CX

Fig. 44 Code C1223: LH Rear Wheel Speed Sensor Input Signal Is Zero (Part 2 of 2). Park Avenue

Circuit Description

The WSS is a single point magnetic pickup that produces an AC signal. The EBCM/EBTCM uses the signal frequency in order to calculate the wheel speed.

Conditions for Setting the DTC

The RR wheel speed equals 0 and the remaining WSS speeds are greater than 8 km/h (5 mph) for 2.5 seconds

Action Taken When the DTC Sets

- A DTC C1224 is stored
- The ABS/TCS is disabled
- The ABS and the TRACTION OFF indicators are turned on

Conditions for Clearing the DTC

- The condition for the DTC is no longer present and the scan tool Clear DTC function is used
- 50 ignition cycles have passed with no DTCs detected

Diagnostic Aids

- Thoroughly inspect the wiring and the connectors. Failure to carefully and fully inspect the wiring and the connectors can result in misdiagnosis. Misdiagnosis may cause replacement of parts without repairing the malfunction.
- The following conditions may cause an intermittent malfunction:
  - Poor connections
  - Broken insulation
  - A broken wire inside the insulation

Test Description

The numbers below refer to step numbers on the diagnostic table.

3. Checks the resistance of the WSS.
5. Checks if the WSS CKTs are shorted together.

GC402980272200AX

Fig. 45 Code C1224: RH Rear Wheel Speed Sensor Input Signal Is Zero (Part 1 of 2). Bonneville & LeSabre

Circuit Description

The WSS is a single point magnetic pickup that produces an AC signal. The EBCM/EBTCM uses the signal frequency in order to calculate the wheel speed.

Conditions for Setting the DTC

The RR wheel speed equals 0 and the remaining WSS speeds are greater than 8 km/h (5 mph) for 2.5 seconds

Action Taken When the DTC Sets

- A DTC C1224 is stored
- The ABS/TCS is disabled
- The ABS and the TRACTION OFF indicators are turned on

Conditions for Clearing the DTC

- The condition for the DTC is no longer present and the scan tool Clear DTC function is used
- 50 ignition cycles have passed with no DTCs detected

Diagnostic Aids

- Thoroughly inspect the wiring and the connectors. Failure to carefully and fully inspect the wiring and the connectors can result in misdiagnosis. Misdiagnosis may cause replacement of parts without repairing the malfunction.
- The following conditions may cause an intermittent malfunction:
  - Poor connections
  - Broken insulation
  - A broken wire inside the insulation

Test Description

The numbers below refer to step numbers on the diagnostic table.

3. Checks the resistance of the WSS.
5. Checks if the WSS CKTs are shorted together.

GC402980272202AX

Fig. 46 Code C1224: RH Rear Wheel Speed Sensor Input Signal Is Zero (Part 1 of 2). Park Avenue

Step	Action	Value(s)	Yes	No
1	Was the ABS Diagnostic System Check performed?	—	Go to *Step 2*	Go to *A Diagnostic System Check*
2	1. Inspect the WSS wiring and connectors for damage. 2. Inspect the WSS for looseness or damage. Is physical damage of the sensor evident?	—	Go to *Step 7*	Go to *Step 3*
3	1. Disconnect the WSS at the sensor pigtail. 2. Using the *J 39200* digital multimeter (DMM), measure the resistance between terminals A and B of the WSS. Is the resistance within the specified range?	850–1350 Ω	Go to *Step 4*	Go to *Step 7*
4	1. With the DMM still connected, select the mV AC scale. 2. Spin the wheel as fast as you can by hand while monitoring the AC output. Is the AC voltage greater than the specified value?	100 mV	Go to *Step 5*	Go to *Step 7*
5	1. Disconnect the EBCM/EBTCM harness connector. 2. Install the *J 39700* universal pinout box using the *J 39700-25* cable adapter to the EBCM/EBTCM harness connector only. 3. Using the DMM, measure the resistance between terminals 13 and 29 of the *J 39700*. Is the resistance within the specified range?	OL (Infinite)	Go to *Step 6*	Go to *Step 8*
6	1. Reconnect all connectors. 2. Carefully test drive the vehicle above 24 Km/h (15 mph) for at least 30 seconds while monitoring a scan tool. Does DTC reset as a current DTC?	—	Go to *Step 9*	Go to *A Diagnostic System Check*
7	Replace the wheel speed sensor. Is the repair complete?	—	Go to *Step 10*	—
8	Repair the short between CKT 882 and CKT 883. Is the repair complete?	—	Go to *Step 10*	—
9	Replace the EBCM/EBTCM. Is the replacement complete?	—	Go to *Step 10*	—
10	Carefully test drive the vehicle above 24 Km/h (15 mph) while monitoring a scan tool for at least 30 seconds. Does the DTC set as a current DTC?	—	Go to *Step 2*	Go to *A Diagnostic System Check*

GC402980272202CX

Fig. 46 Code C1224: RH Rear Wheel Speed Sensor Input Signal Is Zero (Part 2 of 2). Park Avenue

Step	Action	Value(s)	Yes	No
1	Was the Diagnostic System Check performed?	--	*Go to Step 2*	Go to *Diagnostic System Check*
2	1. Inspect the WSS wiring and connectors for damage. 2. Inspect WSS for looseness or damage. Is physical damage of sensor evident?	--	*Go to Step 7*	*Go to Step 3*
3	1. Disconnect the WSS at the sensor pigtail. 2. Using *J 39200* DMM, measure the resistance between terminals A and B of the WSS. Is the resistance within the range specified in the value(s) column?	850-1350Ω	*Go to Step 4*	*Go to Step 7*
4	1. With *J 39200* DMM still connected, select the mV AC scale. 2. Spin the wheel as fast as you can by hand while monitoring the AC output. Is the AC voltage within the range specified in the value(s) column?	Above 100 mV	*Go to Step 5*	*Go to Step 7*
5	1. Disconnect the EBCM/EBTCM harness connector. 2. Install *J 39700* Universal Pinout Box using the *J 39700-25* cable adapter to the EBCM/EBTCM harness connector only. 3. Using *J 39200* DMM, measure resistance between terminals 27 and 11 of the *J 39700*. Is the resistance within the range specified in the value(s) column?	OL (Infinite)	*Go to Step 6*	*Go to Step 8*
6	1. Reconnect all connectors. 2. Carefully test drive vehicle above 24 Km/h (15 mph) for at least 30 seconds while monitoring a scan tool. Does DTC reset as a current DTC?	--	*Go to Step 9*	Go to *Diagnostic System Check*
7	Replace wheel speed sensor. Is the repair complete?	--	*Go to Step 10*	--
8	Repair short between CKT(s) 882 and 883. Is the repair complete?	--	*Go to Step 10*	--
9	Replace EBCM/EBTCM. Is the replacement complete?	--	*Go to Step 10*	--
10	Carefully test drive vehicle above 24 Km/h (15 mph) while monitoring a scan tool for at least 30 seconds. Does the DTC set as a current DTC?	--	*Go to Step 2*	Go to *Diagnostic System Check*

GC402980272200BX

Fig. 45 Code C1224: RH Rear Wheel Speed Sensor Input Signal Is Zero (Part 2 of 2). Bonneville & LeSabre

Circuit Description

The WSS is a single point magnetic pickup that produces an AC signal. The EBCM/EBTCM uses the signal frequency in order to calculate the wheel speed.

Conditions for Setting the DTC

The DTC can be set anytime the brake is not depressed and no wheel speed sensor hardware DTC(s) are present, and the EBCM/EBTCM sees a wheel speed variation of more than 14 Km/h (9 mph) for 2.5 seconds.

- The brake pedal is not pressed
- No WSS hardware DTCs are present
- The EBCM/EBTCM sees a wheel speed variation greater than 14 km/h (9 mph) for 2.5 seconds

Action Taken When the DTC Sets

- A DTC C1225 is stored
- The ABS/TCS is disabled
- The ABS and the TRACTION OFF indicators are turned on

Conditions for Clearing the DTC

- The condition for the DTC is no longer present and the scan tool Clear DTC function is used
- 50 ignition cycles have passed with no DTCs detected

Diagnostic Aids

- Thoroughly inspect the wiring and the connectors. Failure to carefully and fully inspect the wiring and the connectors can result in misdiagnosis. Misdiagnosis may cause replacement of parts without repairing the malfunction.
- The following conditions may cause an intermittent malfunction:
  - Poor connections
  - Broken insulation
  - A broken wire inside the insulation

Test Description

The numbers below refer to step numbers on the diagnostic table.

3. Checks the resistance of the WSS.
5. Checks if the WSS CKTs are shorted together.

GC402980272300AX

Fig. 47 Code C1225: LH Excessive Front Wheel Speed Variation (Part 1 of 2). Bonneville & LeSabre

Step	Action	Value(s)	Yes	No
1	Was the Diagnostic System Check performed?	--	Go to Step 2	Go to Diagnostic System Check
2	1. Inspect the WSS wiring and connectors for damage. 2. Inspect WSS for looseness or damage. Is physical damage of sensor evident?	--	Go to Step 7	Go to Step 3
3	1. Disconnect the WSS at the sensor pigtail. 2. Using J 39200 DMM, measure the resistance between terminals A and B of the WSS. Is the resistance within the range specified in the value(s) column?	850-1350Ω	Go to Step 4	Go to Step 7
4	1. With J 39200 DMM still connected, select the mV AC scale. 2. Spin the wheel as fast as you can by hand while monitoring the AC output. Is the AC voltage within the range specified in the value(s) column?	Above 100 mV	Go to Step 5	Go to Step 7
5	1. Disconnect the EBCM/EBTCM harness connector. 2. Install J 39700 Universal Pinout Box using the J 39700-25 cable adapter to the EBCM/EBTCM harness connector only. 3. Using J 39200 DMM, measure resistance between terminals 24 and 8 of the J 39700. Is the resistance within the range specified in the value(s) column?	OL (Infinite)	Go to Step 6	Go to Step 8
6	1. Reconnect all connectors. 2. Carefully test drive vehicle above 24 Km/h (15 mph) for at least 30 seconds while monitoring a scan tool. Does DTC reset as a current DTC?	--	Go to Step 9	Go to Diagnostic System Check
7	Replace wheel speed sensor. Is the repair complete?	--	Go to Step 10	--
8	Repair short between CKT(s) 873 and 830. Is the repair complete?	--	Go to Step 10	--
9	Replace EBCM/EBTCM. Is the replacement complete?	--	Go to Step 10	--
10	Carefully test drive vehicle above 24 Km/h (15 mph) while monitoring a scan tool for at least 30 seconds. Does the DTC set as a current DTC?	--	Go to Step 2	Go to Diagnostic System Check

GC402980272300BX

Fig. 47 Code C1225: LH Excessive Front Wheel Speed Variation (Part 2 of 2). Bonneville & LeSabre

Step	Action	Value(s)	Yes	No
1	Was the Diagnostic System Check performed?	—	Go to Step 2	Go to ABS Diagnostic System Check
2	1. Inspect the WSS wiring and connectors for damage. 2. Inspect WSS for looseness or damage. Is physical damage of sensor evident?	—	Go to Step 7	Go to Step 3
3	1. Disconnect the WSS at the sensor pigtail. 2. Using J 39200 DMM, measure the resistance between terminals A and B of the WSS. Is the resistance within the range specified in the value(s) column?	850-1350Ω	Go to Step 4	Go to Step 7
4	1. With J 39200 DMM still connected, select the mV AC scale. 2. Spin the wheel as fast as you can by hand while monitoring the AC output. Is the AC voltage within the range specified in the value(s) column?	Above 100 mV	Go to Step 5	Go to Step 7
5	1. Disconnect the EBCM/EBTCM harness connector. 2. Install J 39700 Universal Pinout Box using the J 39700-25 cable adapter to the EBCM/EBTCM harness connector only. 3. Using J 39200 DMM, measure resistance between terminals 15 and 31 of the J 39700. Is the resistance within the range specified in the value(s) column?	OL (Infinite)	Go to Step 6	Go to Step 8
6	1. Reconnect all connectors. 2. Carefully test drive vehicle above 24 Km/h (15 mph) for at least 30 seconds while monitoring a scan tool. Does DTC reset as a current DTC?	—	Go to Step 9	Go to ABS Diagnostic System Check
7	Replace wheel speed sensor. Is the repair complete?	—	Go to Step 10	—
8	Repair short between CKT(s) 873 and 830. Is the repair complete?	—	Go to Step 10	—
9	Replace EBCM/EBTCM. Is the replacement complete?	—	Go to Step 10	—
10	Carefully test drive vehicle above 24 Km/h (15 mph) while monitoring a scan tool for at least 30 seconds. Does the DTC set as a current DTC?	—	Go to Step 2	Go to ABS Diagnostic System Check

GC402980272300CX

Fig. 48 Code C1225: LH Front Excessive Wheel Speed Variation (Part 2 of 2). Park Avenue

Circuit Description

The WSS is a single point magnetic pickup that produces an AC signal. The EBCM/EBTCM uses the signal frequency in order to calculate the wheel speed.

Conditions for Setting the DTC

The DTC can be set anytime the brake is not depressed and no wheel speed sensor hardware DTC(s) are present, and the EBCM/EBTCM sees a wheel speed variation of more than 14 Km/h (9 mph) for 2.5 seconds.

- The brake pedal is not pressed
- No WSS hardware DTCs are present
- The EBCM/EBTCM sees a wheel speed variation greater than 14 km/h (9 mph) for 2.5 seconds

Action Taken When the DTC Sets

- A DTC C1225 is stored
- The ABS/TCS is disabled
- The ABS and the TRACTION OFF indicators are turned on

Conditions for Clearing the DTC

- The condition for the DTC is no longer present and the scan tool Clear DTC function is used
- 50 ignition cycles have passed with no DTCs detected

Diagnostic Aids

- Thoroughly inspect the wiring and the connectors. Failure to carefully and fully inspect the wiring and the connectors can result in misdiagnosis. Misdiagnosis may cause replacement of parts without repairing the malfunction.
- The following conditions may cause an intermittent malfunction:
  - Poor connections
  - Broken insulation
  - A broken wire inside the insulation

Test Description

The numbers below refer to step numbers on the diagnostic table.

3. Checks the resistance of the WSS.
5. Checks if the WSS CKTs are shorted together.

GC402980272302AX

Fig. 48 Code C1225: LH Front Excessive Wheel Speed Variation (Part 1 of 2). Park Avenue

Circuit Description

The WSS is a single point magnetic pickup that produces an AC signal. The EBCM/EBTCM uses the signal frequency in order to calculate the wheel speed.

Conditions for Setting the DTC

The DTC can be set anytime the brake is not depressed and no wheel speed sensor hardware DTC(s) are present, and the EBCM/EBTCM sees a wheel speed variation of more than 14 Km/h (9 mph) for 2.5 seconds.

Action Taken When the DTC Sets

- A DTC C1226 is stored
- The ABS/TCS is disabled
- The ABS and the TRACTION OFF indicators are turned on

Conditions for Clearing the DTC

- The condition for the DTC is no longer present and the scan tool Clear DTC function is used
- 50 ignition cycles have passed with no DTCs detected

Diagnostic Aids

- Thoroughly inspect the wiring and the connectors. Failure to carefully and fully inspect the wiring and the connectors can result in misdiagnosis. Misdiagnosis may cause replacement of parts without repairing the malfunction.
- The following conditions may cause an intermittent malfunction:
  - Poor connections
  - Broken insulation
  - A broken wire inside the insulation

Test Description

The numbers below refer to step numbers on the diagnostic table.

3. Checks the resistance of the WSS.
5. Checks if the WSS CKTs are shorted together.

GC402980272400AX

Fig. 49 Code C1226: RH Front Excessive Wheel Speed Variation (Part 1 of 2). Bonneville & LeSabre

Step	Action	Value(s)	Yes	No
1	Was the Diagnostic System Check performed?	--	Go to Step 2	Go to Diagnostic System Check
2	1. Inspect the WSS wiring and connectors for damage. 2. Inspect WSS for looseness or damage. Is physical damage of sensor evident?	--	Go to Step 7	Go to Step 3
3	1. Disconnect the WSS at the sensor pigtail. 2. Using J 39200 DMM, measure the resistance between terminals A and B of the WSS. Is the resistance within the range specified in the value(s) column?	850-1350Ω	Go to Step 4	Go to Step 7
4	1. With J 39200 DMM still connected, select the mV AC scale. 2. Spin the wheel as fast as you can by hand while monitoring the AC output. Is the AC voltage within the range specified in the value(s) column?	Above 100 mV	Go to Step 5	Go to Step 7
5	1. Disconnect the EBCM/EBTCM harness connector. 2. Install J 39700 Universal Pinout Box using the J 39700-25 cable adapter to the EBCM/EBTCM harness connector only. 3. Using J 39200 DMM, measure resistance between terminals 25 and 9 of the J 39700. Is the resistance within the range specified in the value(s) column?	OL (Infinite)	Go to Step 6	Go to Step 8
6	1. Reconnect all connectors. 2. Carefully test drive vehicle above 24 Km/h (15 mph) for at least 30 seconds while monitoring a scan tool. Does DTC reset as a current DTC?	--	Go to Step 9	Go to Diagnostic System Check
7	Replace wheel speed sensor. Is the repair complete?	--	Go to Step 10	--
8	Repair short between CKT(s) 833 and 872. Is the repair complete?	--	Go to Step 10	--
9	Replace EBCM/EBTCM. Is the replacement complete?	--	Go to Step 10	--
10	Carefully test drive vehicle above 24 Km/h (15 mph) while monitoring a scan tool for at least 30 seconds. Does the DTC set as a current DTC?	--	Go to Step 2	Go to Diagnostic System Check

GC402980272400BX

Fig. 49 Code C1226: RH Front Excessive Wheel Speed Variation (Part 2 of 2). Bonneville & LeSabre

Circuit Description

The WSS is a single point magnetic pickup that produces an AC signal. The EBCM/EBTCM uses the signal frequency in order to calculate the wheel speed.

Conditions for Setting the DTC

The DTC can be set anytime the brake is not depressed and no wheel speed sensor hardware DTC(s) are present, and the EBCM/EBTCM sees a wheel speed variation of more than 14 Km/h (9 mph) for 2.5 seconds.

Action Taken When the DTC Sets

- A DTC C1226 is stored
- The ABS/TCS is disabled
- The ABS and the TRACTION OFF indicators are turned on

Conditions for Clearing the DTC

- The condition for the DTC is no longer present and the scan tool Clear DTC function is used
- 50 ignition cycles have passed with no DTCs detected

Diagnostic Aids

- Thoroughly inspect the wiring and the connectors. Failure to carefully and fully inspect the wiring and the connectors can result in misdiagnosis. Misdiagnosis may cause replacement of parts without repairing the malfunction.
- The following conditions may cause an intermittent malfunction:
  - Poor connections
  - Broken insulation
  - A broken wire inside the insulation

Test Description

The numbers below refer to step numbers on the diagnostic table.

3. Checks the resistance of the WSS.
5. Checks if the WSS CKTs are shorted together.

GC402980272402AX

Fig. 50 Code C1226: RH Front Excessive Wheel Speed Variation (Part 1 of 2). Park Avenue

Step	Action	Value(s)	Yes	No
1	Was the ABS Diagnostic System Check performed?	—	*Go to Step 2*	Go to *A Diagnostic System Check*
2	1. Inspect the WSS wiring and connectors for damage. 2. Inspect the WSS for looseness or damage. Is physical damage of sensor evident?	—	*Go to Step 7*	*Go to Step 3*
3	1. Disconnect the WSS at the sensor pigtail. 2. Using the *J 39200* DMM, measure the resistance between terminals A and B of the WSS. Is the resistance within the specified range?	850-1350Ω	*Go to Step 4*	*Go to Step 7*
4	1. With the *J 39200* DMM still connected, select the mV AC scale. 2. Spin the wheel as fast as you can by hand while monitoring the AC output. Is the AC voltage greater than the specified value?	100 mV	*Go to Step 5*	*Go to Step 7*
5	1. Disconnect the EBCM/EBTCM harness connector. 2. Install the *J 39700* universal pinout box using the *J 39700-25* cable adapter to the EBCM/EBTCM harness connector only. 3. Using the *J 39200* DMM, measure the resistance between terminals 14 and 30 of the *J 39700*. Is the resistance within the specified range?	OL (Infinite)	*Go to Step 6*	*Go to Step 8*
6	1. Reconnect all connectors. 2. Carefully test drive the vehicle above 24 Km/h (15 mph) for at least 30 seconds while monitoring a scan tool. Does DTC reset as a current DTC?	—	*Go to Step 9*	Go to *A Diagnostic System Check*
7	Replace the wheel speed sensor. Is the repair complete?	—	*Go to Step 10*	—
8	Repair the short between CKTs 833 and 872. Is the repair complete?	—	*Go to Step 10*	—
9	Replace the EBCM/EBTCM. Is the replacement complete?	—	*Go to Step 10*	—
10	Carefully test drive the vehicle above 24 Km/h (15 mph) while monitoring a scan tool for at least 30 seconds. Does the DTC set as a current DTC?	—	*Go to Step 2*	Go to *A Diagnostic System Check*

GC402980272402CX

Fig. 50 Code C1226: RH Front Excessive Wheel Speed Variation (Part 2 of 2). Park Avenue

Circuit Description

The WSS is a single point magnetic pickup that produces an AC signal. The EBCM/EBTCM uses the signal frequency in order to calculate the wheel speed.

Conditions for Setting the DTC

The DTC can be set anytime the brake is not depressed and no wheel speed sensor hardware DTC(s) are present, and the EBCM/EBTCM sees a wheel speed variation of more than 14 Km/h (9 mph) for 2.5 seconds.

Action Taken When the DTC Sets

- A DTC C1227 is stored
- The ABS/TCS is disabled
- The ABS and the TRACTION OFF indicators are turned on

Conditions for Clearing the DTC

- The condition for the DTC is no longer present and the scan tool Clear DTC function is used
- 50 ignition cycles have passed with no DTCs detected

Diagnostic Aids

- Thoroughly inspect the wiring and the connectors. Failure to carefully and fully inspect the wiring and the connectors can result in misdiagnosis. Misdiagnosis may cause part replacement without repairing the malfunction.
- The following conditions may cause an intermittent malfunction:
  - Poor connections
  - Broken insulation
  - A broken wire inside the insulation

Test Description

The numbers below refer to step numbers on the diagnostic table.

3. Checks the resistance of the WSS.
5. Checks if the WSS CKTs are shorted together.

GC402980272500AX

Fig. 51 Code C1227: LH Rear Excessive Wheel Speed Variation (Part 1 of 2). Bonneville & LeSabre

Step	Action	Value(s)	Yes	No
1	Was the Diagnostic System Check performed?	--	*Go to Step 2*	Go to *Diagnostic System Check*
2	1. Inspect the WSS wiring and connectors for damage. 2. Inspect WSS for looseness or damage. Is physical damage of sensor evident?	--	*Go to Step 7*	*Go to Step 3*
3	1. Disconnect the WSS at the sensor pigtail. 2. Using *J 39200* DMM, measure the resistance between terminals A and B of the WSS. Is the resistance within the range specified in the value(s) column?	850-1350Ω	*Go to Step 4*	*Go to Step 7*
4	1. With *J 39200* DMM still connected, select the mV AC scale. 2. Spin the wheel as fast as you can by hand while monitoring the AC output. Is the AC voltage within the range specified in the value(s) column?	Above 100 mV	*Go to Step 5*	*Go to Step 7*
5	1. Disconnect the EBCM/EBTCM harness connector. 2. Install *J 39700* Universal Pinout Box using the *J 39700-25* cable adapter to the EBCM/EBTCM harness connector only. 3. Using *J 39200* DMM, measure resistance between terminals 10 and 26 of the *J 39700*. Is the resistance within the range specified in the value(s) column?	OL (Infinite)	*Go to Step 6*	*Go to Step 8*
6	1. Reconnect all connectors. 2. Carefully test drive vehicle above 24 Km/h (15 mph) for at least 30 seconds while monitoring a scan tool. Does DTC reset as a current DTC?	--	*Go to Step 9*	Go to *Diagnostic System Check*
7	Replace wheel speed sensor. Is the repair complete?	--	*Go to Step 10*	--
8	Repair short between CKT(s) 884 and 885. Is the repair complete?	--	*Go to Step 10*	--
9	Replace EBCM/EBTCM. Is the replacement complete?	--	*Go to Step 10*	--
10	Carefully test drive vehicle above 24 Km/h (15 mph) while monitoring a scan tool for at least 30 seconds. Does the DTC set as a current DTC?	--	*Go to Step 2*	Go to *Diagnostic System Check*

GC402980272500BX

Fig. 51 Code C1227: LH Rear Excessive Wheel Speed Variation (Part 2 of 2). Bonneville & LeSabre

Circuit Description

The WSS is a single point magnetic pickup that produces an AC signal. The EBCM/EBTCM uses the signal frequency in order to calculate the wheel speed.

Conditions for Setting the DTC

The DTC can be set anytime the brake is not depressed and no wheel speed sensor hardware DTC(s) are present, and the EBCM/EBTCM sees a wheel speed variation of more than 14 Km/h (9 mph) for 2.5 seconds.

Action Taken When the DTC Sets

- A DTC C1227 is stored
- The ABS/TCS is disabled
- The ABS and the TRACTION OFF indicators are turned on

Conditions for Clearing the DTC

- The condition for the DTC is no longer present and the scan tool Clear DTC function is used
- 50 ignition cycles have passed with no DTCs detected

Diagnostic Aids

- Thoroughly inspect the wiring and the connectors. Failure to carefully and fully inspect the wiring and the connectors can result in misdiagnosis. Misdiagnosis may cause part replacement without repairing the malfunction.
- The following conditions may cause an intermittent malfunction:
  - Poor connections
  - Broken insulation
  - A broken wire inside the insulation
- If an intermittent malfunction exists, Troubleshoot Electrical.

Test Description

The numbers below refer to step numbers on the diagnostic table.

3. Checks the resistance of the WSS.
5. Checks if the WSS CKTs are shorted together.

GC402980272502AX

Fig. 52 Code C1227: LH Rear Excessive Wheel Speed Variation (Part 1 of 2). Park Avenue

Step	Action	Value(s)	Yes	No
1	Was the Diagnostic System Check performed?	—	*Go to Step 2*	Go to *ABS Diagnostic System Check*
2	1. Inspect the WSS wiring and connectors for damage. 2. Inspect WSS for looseness or damage. Is physical damage of sensor evident?	—	*Go to Step 7*	*Go to Step 3*
3	1. Disconnect the WSS at the sensor pigtail. 2. Using *J 39200* DMM, measure the resistance between terminals A and B of the WSS. Is the resistance within the range specified in the value(s) column?	850-1350Ω	*Go to Step 4*	*Go to Step 7*
4	1. With *J 39200* DMM still connected, select the mV AC scale. 2. Spin the wheel as fast as you can by hand while monitoring the AC output. Is the AC voltage within the range specified in the value(s) column?	Above 100 mV	*Go to Step 5*	*Go to Step 7*
5	1. Disconnect the EBCM/EBTCM harness connector. 2. Install *J 39700* Universal Pinout Box using the *J 39700-25* cable adapter to the EBCM/EBTCM harness connector only. 3. Using *J 39200* DMM, measure resistance between terminals 12 and 28 of the *J 39700*. Is the resistance within the range specified in the value(s) column?	OL (Infinite)	*Go to Step 6*	*Go to Step 8*
6	1. Reconnect all connectors. 2. Carefully test drive vehicle above 24 Km/h (15 mph) for at least 30 seconds while monitoring a scan tool. Does DTC reset as a current DTC?	—	*Go to Step 9*	Go to *ABS Diagnostic System Check*
7	Replace wheel speed sensor. Is the repair complete?	—	*Go to Step 10*	—
8	Repair short between CKT(s) 884 and 885. Is the repair complete?	—	*Go to Step 10*	—
9	Replace EBCM/EBTCM. Is the replacement complete?	—	*Go to Step 10*	—
10	Carefully test drive vehicle above 24 Km/h (15 mph) while monitoring a scan tool for at least 30 seconds. Does the DTC set as a current DTC?	—	*Go to Step 2*	Go to *ABS Diagnostic System Check*

GC402980272500CX

Fig. 52 Code C1227: LH Rear Excessive Wheel Speed Variation (Part 2 of 2). Park Avenue

Step	Action	Value(s)	Yes	No
1	Was the Diagnostic System Check performed?	--	*Go to Step 2*	Go to *Diagnostic System Check*
2	1. Inspect the WSS wiring and connectors for damage. 2. Inspect WSS for looseness or damage. Is physical damage of sensor evident?	--	*Go to Step 7*	*Go to Step 3*
3	1. Disconnect the WSS at the sensor pigtail. 2. Using *J 39200* DMM, measure the resistance between terminals A and B of the WSS. Is the resistance within the range specified in the value(s) column?	850-1350Ω	*Go to Step 4*	*Go to Step 7*
4	1. With *J 39200* DMM still connected, select the mV AC scale. 2. Spin the wheel as fast as you can by hand while monitoring the AC output. Is the AC voltage within the range specified in the value(s) column?	Above 100 mV	*Go to Step 5*	*Go to Step 7*
5	1. Disconnect the EBCM/EBTCM harness connector. 2. Install *J 39700* Universal Pinout Box using the *J 39700-25* cable adapter to the EBCM/EBTCM harness connector only. 3. Using *J 39200* DMM, measure resistance between terminals 27 and 11 of the *J 39700*. Is the resistance within the range specified in the value(s) column?	OL (Infinite)	*Go to Step 6*	*Go to Step 8*
6	1. Reconnect all connectors. 2. Carefully test drive vehicle above 24 Km/h (15 mph) for at least 30 seconds while monitoring a scan tool. Does DTC reset as a current DTC?	--	*Go to Step 9*	Go to *Diagnostic System Check*
7	Replace wheel speed sensor. Is the repair complete?	--	*Go to Step 10*	--
8	Repair short between CKT(s) 882 and 883. Is the repair complete?	--	*Go to Step 10*	--
9	Replace EBCM/EBTCM. Is the replacement complete?	--	*Go to Step 10*	--
10	Carefully test drive vehicle above 24 Km/h (15 mph) while monitoring a scan tool for at least 30 seconds. Does the DTC set as a current DTC?	--	*Go to Step 2*	Go to *Diagnostic System Check*

GC402980272600BX

Fig. 53 Code C1228: RH Rear Excessive Wheel Speed Variation (Part 2 of 2). Bonneville & LeSabre

Circuit Description

The WSS is a single point magnetic pickup that produces an AC signal. The EBCM/EBTCM uses the signal frequency in order to calculate the wheel speed.

Conditions for Setting the DTC

The DTC can be set anytime the brake is not depressed and no wheel speed sensor hardware DTC(s) are present, and the EBCM/EBTCM sees a wheel speed variation of more than 14 Km/h (9 mph) for 2.5 seconds.

Action Taken When the DTC Sets

- A DTC C1228 is stored
- The ABS/TCS is disabled
- The ABS and the TRACTION OFF indicators are turned on

Conditions for Clearing the DTC

- The condition for the DTC is no longer present and the scan tool Clear DTC function is used
- 50 ignition cycles have passed with no DTCs detected

Diagnostic Aids

- Thoroughly inspect the wiring and the connectors. Failure to carefully and fully inspect the wiring and the connectors can result in misdiagnosis. Misdiagnosis may cause part replacement without repairing the malfunction.
- The following conditions may cause an intermittent malfunction:
  - Poor connections
  - Broken insulation
  - A broken wire inside the insulation

Test Description

The numbers below refer to step numbers on the diagnostic table.

3. Checks the resistance of the WSS.
5. Checks if the WSS CKTs are shorted together.

GC402980272600AX

Fig. 53 Code C1228: RH Rear Excessive Wheel Speed Variation (Part 1 of 2). Bonneville & LeSabre

Circuit Description

The WSS is a single point magnetic pickup that produces an AC signal. The EBCM/EBTCM uses the signal frequency in order to calculate the wheel speed.

Conditions for Setting the DTC

The DTC can be set anytime the brake is not depressed and no wheel speed sensor hardware DTC(s) are present, and the EBCM/EBTCM sees a wheel speed variation of more than 14 Km/h (9 mph) for 2.5 seconds.

Action Taken When the DTC Sets

- A DTC C1228 is stored
- The ABS/TCS is disabled
- The ABS and the TRACTION OFF indicators are turned on

Conditions for Clearing the DTC

- The condition for the DTC is no longer present and the scan tool Clear DTC function is used
- 50 ignition cycles have passed with no DTCs detected

Diagnostic Aids

- Thoroughly inspect the wiring and the connectors. Failure to carefully and fully inspect the wiring and the connectors can result in misdiagnosis. Misdiagnosis may cause part replacement without repairing the malfunction.
- The following conditions may cause an intermittent malfunction:
  - Poor connections
  - Broken insulation
  - A broken wire inside the insulation

Test Description

The numbers below refer to step numbers on the diagnostic table.

3. Checks the resistance of the WSS.
5. Checks if the WSS CKTs are shorted together.

GC402980272602AX

Fig. 54 Code C1228: RH Rear Excessive Wheel Speed Variation (Part 1 of 2). Park Avenue

Step	Action	Value(s)	Yes	No
1	Was the Diagnostic System Check performed?	—	*Go to Step 2*	Go to *ABS Diagnostic System Check*
2	1. Inspect the WSS wiring and connectors for damage. 2. Inspect WSS for looseness or damage. Is physical damage of sensor evident?	—	*Go to Step 7*	*Go to Step 3*
3	1. Disconnect the WSS at the sensor pigtail. 2. Using *J 39200* DMM, measure the resistance between terminals A and B of the WSS. Is the resistance within the range specified in the value(s) column?	850-1350Ω	*Go to Step 4*	*Go to Step 7*
4	1. With *J 39200* DMM still connected, select the mV AC scale. 2. Spin the wheel as fast as you can by hand while monitoring the AC output. Is the AC voltage within the range specified in the value(s) column?	Above 100 mV	*Go to Step 5*	*Go to Step 7*
5	1. Disconnect the EBCM/EBTCM harness connector. 2. Install *J 39700* Universal Pinout Box using the *J 39700-25* cable adapter to the EBCM/EBTCM harness connector only. 3. Using *J 39200* DMM, measure resistance between terminals 13 and 29 of the *J 39700*. Is the resistance within the range specified in the value(s) column?	OL (Infinite)	*Go to Step 6*	*Go to Step 8*
6	1. Reconnect all connectors. 2. Carefully test drive vehicle above 24 Km/h (15 mph) for at least 30 seconds while monitoring a scan tool. Does DTC reset as a current DTC?	—	*Go to Step 9*	Go to *ABS Diagnostic System Check*
7	Replace wheel speed sensor. Is the repair complete?	—	*Go to Step 10*	—
8	Repair short between CKT(s) 882 and 883. Is the repair complete?	—	*Go to Step 10*	—
9	Replace EBCM/EBTCM. Is the replacement complete?	—	*Go to Step 10*	—
10	Carefully test drive vehicle above 24 Km/h (15 mph) while monitoring a scan tool for at least 30 seconds. Does the DTC set as a current DTC?	—	*Go to Step 2*	Go to *ABS Diagnostic System Check*

GC402980272600CX

Fig. 54 Code C1228: RH Rear Excessive Wheel Speed Variation (Part 2 of 2). Park Avenue

Circuit Description

The WSS is a single point magnetic pickup that produces an AC signal. The EBCM/EBTCM uses the signal frequency in order to calculate the wheel speed.

Conditions for Setting the DTC

The ignition is in the RUN position and the EBCM/EBTCM senses an open, a short to ground, or a short to battery in the LF WSS circuit.

Action Taken When the DTC Sets

- A DTC C1232 is stored
- The ABS/TCS is disabled
- The ABS and the TRACTION OFF indicators are turned on

Conditions for Clearing the DTC

- The condition for the DTC is no longer present and the scan tool clear DTC function is used
- 50 ignition cycles have passed with no DTCs detected

Diagnostic Aids

- Thoroughly inspect the wiring and the connectors. Failure to carefully and fully inspect the wiring and the connectors can result in misdiagnosis. Misdiagnosis may cause replacement of parts without repairing the malfunction.
- The following conditions may cause an intermittent malfunction:
  - Poor connections
  - Broken insulation
  - A broken wire inside the insulation
- If an intermittent malfunction exists, Troubleshoot Electrical

Test Description

The numbers below refer to step numbers on the diagnostic table.

4. Checks for an open in the WSS or WSS CKT.
12. Checks for a short to ground in the WSS or WSS CKT.
19. Checks for a short to voltage in the WSS CKT.
21. Checks for a short to voltage in the WSS CKT.

GC402980272700AX

Fig. 55 Code C1232: LH Front Wheel Speed Sensor Circuit Open Or Shorted (Part 1 of 3). Bonneville & LeSabre

Step	Action	Value(s)	Yes	No
12	Using *J 39200* DMM, measure the resistance between terminals 24 and B of *J 39700*. Is the resistance within the range specified in the value(s) column?	OL (infinite)	*Go to Step 19*	*Go to Step 13*
13	1. Disconnect the LF Wheel Speed Sensor. 2. Using *J 39200* DMM, measure the resistance between terminal A and ground of the Wheel Speed Sensor Connector. Is the resistance within the range specified in the value(s) column?	OL (infinite)	*Go to Step 14*	*Go to Step 11*
14	1. Using *J 39200* DMM, measure the resistance between terminals 8 and B of *J 39700*. Is the resistance within the range specified in the value(s) column?	OL (infinite)	*Go to Step 16*	*Go to Step 15*
15	Repair CKT 830 for a short to ground. Is the repair complete?	—	Go to *Diagnostic System Check*	—
16	Using *J 39200* DMM, measure the resistance between terminals 24 and B of *J 39700*. Is the resistance within the range specified in the value(s) column?	OL (infinite)	*Go to Step 17*	*Go to Step 18*
17	Malfunction is intermittent. Inspect all connectors and harnesses for damage that may result in a short to ground when connected. Is the repair complete?	—	Go to *Diagnostic System Check*	—
18	Repair CKT 873 for a short to ground. Is the repair complete?	—	Go to *Diagnostic System Check*	—
19	1. Disconnect the LF Wheel Speed Sensor. 2. Turn the ignition switch to the RUN position, engine off. 3. Using *J 39200* DMM, measure the voltage at terminal 8 of *J 39700*. Is the voltage within the range specified in the value(s) column?	Above 1V	*Go to Step 20*	*Go to Step 21*
20	Repair CKT 830 for a short to voltage. Is the repair complete?	—	Go to *Diagnostic System Check*	—
21	Using *J 39200* DMM, measure the voltage at terminal 24 of *J 39700*. Is the voltage within the range specified in the value(s) column?	Above 1V	*Go to Step 22*	*Go to Step 23*
22	Repair CKT 873 for a short to voltage. Is the repair complete?	—	Go to *Diagnostic System Check*	—
23	Replace the EBCM/EBTCM. Is the replacement complete?	—	Go to *Diagnostic System Check*	—

GC402980272700CX

Fig. 55 Code C1232: LH Front Wheel Speed Sensor Circuit Open Or Shorted (Part 3 of 3). Bonneville & LeSabre

Step	Action	Value(s)	Yes	No
1	Was the Diagnostic System Check performed?	--	*Go to Step 2*	Go to *Diagnostic System Check*
2	1. Inspect the WSS wiring and connectors for damage. 2. Inspect the WSS for looseness or damage. Is physical damage of sensor evident?	--	*Go to Step 3*	*Go to Step 4*
3	Repair as necessary. Is the repair complete?	—	Go to *Diagnostic System Check*	—
4	1. Turn the ignition switch to the OFF position. 2. Disconnect the EBCM/EBTCM. 3. Install the *J 39700* Universal Pinout Box using the *J 39700-25* cable adapter to the EBCM/EBTCM harness connector only. 4. Using *J 39200* DMM, measure the resistance between terminals 24 and 8 of *J 39700*. Is the resistance within the range specified in the value(s) column?	850 - 1350Ω	*Go to Step 12*	*Go to Step 5*
5	1. Disconnect the LF Wheel Speed Sensor. 2. Using *J 39200* DMM, measure the resistance between terminals A and B of the Wheel Speed Sensor Connector. Is the resistance within the range specified in the value(s) column?	850 - 1350Ω	*Go to Step 6*	*Go to Step 11*
6	1. Connect a jumper between the LF Wheel Speed Sensor harness connector terminal B and ground. 2. Using *J 39200* DMM, measure the resistance between terminals 8 and B of *J 39700*. Is the resistance within the range specified in the value(s) column?	0 - 5Ω	*Go to Step 8*	*Go to Step 7*
7	Repair CKT 830 for an open or high resistance. Is the repair complete?	—	Go to *Diagnostic System Check*	—
8	1. Connect a jumper between the LF Wheel Speed Sensor harness connector terminal A and ground. 2. Using *J 39200* DMM, measure the resistance between terminals 24 and B of *J 39700*. Is the resistance within the range specified in the value(s) column?	0 - 5Ω	*Go to Step 10*	*Go to Step 9*
9	Repair CKT 873 for an open or high resistance. Is the repair complete?	—	Go to *Diagnostic System Check*	—
10	Malfunction is intermittent. Inspect all connectors and harnesses for damage that may result in an open or high resistance when connected. Is the repair complete?	—	Go to *Diagnostic System Check*	—
11	Replace the Wheel Speed Sensor. Is the replacement complete?	—	Go to *Diagnostic System Check*	—

GC402980272700BX

Fig. 55 Code C1232: LH Front Wheel Speed Sensor Circuit Open Or Shorted (Part 2 of 3). Bonneville & LeSabre

Circuit Description

The WSS is a single point magnetic pickup that produces an AC signal. The EBCM/EBTCM uses the signal frequency in order to calculate the wheel speed.

Conditions for Setting the DTC

The ignition is in the RUN position and the EBCM/EBTCM senses an open, a short to ground, or a short to battery in the LF WSS circuit.

Action Taken When the DTC Sets

- A DTC C1232 is stored
- The ABS/TCS is disabled
- The ABS and the TRACTION OFF indicators are turned on

Conditions for Clearing the DTC

- The condition for the DTC is no longer present and the scan tool clear DTC function is used
- 50 ignition cycles have passed with no DTCs detected

Diagnostic Aids

- Thoroughly inspect the wiring and the connectors. Failure to carefully and fully inspect the wiring and the connectors can result in misdiagnosis. Misdiagnosis may cause replacement of parts without repairing the malfunction.
- The following conditions may cause an intermittent malfunction:
  - Poor connections
  - Broken insulation
  - A broken wire inside the insulation

Test Description

The numbers below refer to step numbers on the diagnostic table.

4. Checks for an open in the WSS or WSS CKT.
12. Checks for a short to ground in the WSS or WSS CKT.
19. Checks for a short to voltage in the WSS CKT.
21. Checks for a short to voltage in the WSS CKT.

GC402980272702AX

Fig. 56 Code C1232: LH Front Wheel Speed Sensor Circuit Open Or Shorted (Part 1 of 3). Park Avenue

Step	Action	Value(s)	Yes	No
1	Was the Diagnostic System Check performed?	—	*Go to Step 2*	Go to *ABS Diagnostic System Check*
2	1. Inspect the WSS wiring and connectors for damage. 2. Inspect the WSS for looseness or damage. Is physical damage of sensor evident?	—	*Go to Step 3*	*Go to Step 4*
3	Repair as necessary. Is the repair complete?	—	Go to *ABS Diagnostic System Check*	—
4	1. Turn the ignition switch to the OFF position. 2. Disconnect the EBCM/EBTCM. 3. Install the *J 39700* Universal Pinout Box using the *J 39700-25* cable adapter to the EBCM/EBTCM harness connector only. 4. Using *J 39200* DMM, measure the resistance between terminals 15 and 31 of *J 39700*. Is the resistance within the range specified in the value(s) column?	850 - 1350Ω	*Go to Step 12*	*Go to Step 5*
5	1. Disconnect the LF Wheel Speed Sensor. 2. Using *J 39200* DMM, measure the resistance between terminals A and B of the Wheel Speed Sensor Connector. Is the resistance within the range specified in the value(s) column?	850 - 1350Ω	*Go to Step 6*	*Go to Step 11*
6	1. Connect a jumper between the LF Wheel Speed Sensor harness connector terminal B and ground. 2. Using *J 39200* DMM, measure the resistance between terminals 31 and B of *J 39700*. Is the resistance within the range specified in the value(s) column?	0 - 5Ω	*Go to Step 8*	*Go to Step 7*
7	Repair CKT 830 for an open or high resistance. Is the repair complete?	—	Go to *ABS Diagnostic System Check*	—
8	1. Connect a jumper between the LF Wheel Speed Sensor harness connector terminal A and ground. 2. Using *J 39200* DMM, measure the resistance between terminals 15 and B of *J 39700*. Is the resistance within the range specified in the value(s) column?	0 - 5Ω	*Go to Step 10*	*Go to Step 9*
9	Repair CKT 873 for an open or high resistance. Is the repair complete?	—	Go to *ABS Diagnostic System Check*	—
10	Malfunction is intermittent. Inspect all connectors and harnesses for damage that may result in an open or high resistance when connected. Is the repair complete?	—	Go to *ABS Diagnostic System Check*	—
11	Replace the Wheel Speed Sensor. Is the replacement complete?	—	Go to *ABS Diagnostic System Check*	—

GC402980272700DX

Fig. 56 Code C1232: LH Front Wheel Speed Sensor Circuit Open Or Shorted (Part 2 of 3). Park Avenue

Circuit Description

The WSS is a single point magnetic pickup that produces an AC signal. The EBCM/EBTCM uses the signal frequency in order to calculate the wheel speed.

Conditions for Setting the DTC

The ignition is in the RUN position and the EBCM/EBTCM senses an open, a short to ground, or a short to battery in the RF WSS circuit.

Action Taken When the DTC Sets

- A DTC C1233 is stored.
- The ABS/TCS is disabled.
- The ABS and the TRACTION OFF indicators are turned on.

Conditions for Clearing the DTC

- The condition for the DTC is no longer present and the scan tool clear DTC function is used
- 50 ignition cycles have passed with no DTCs detected.

Diagnostic Aids

- Thoroughly inspect the wiring and the connectors. Failure to carefully and fully inspect the wiring and the connectors can result in misdiagnosis. Misdiagnosis causes reappearance of the malfunction with part replacement.
- The following conditions can cause an intermittent malfunction:
  - Poor connections
  - Broken insulation
  - A broken wire inside the insulation
- If an intermittent malfunction exists, Troubleshoot Electrical

Test Description

The numbers below refer to step numbers on the diagnostic table.

4. Checks for an open in the WSS or WSS CKT.
12. Checks for a short to ground in the WSS or WSS CKT.
19. Checks for a short to voltage in the WSS CKT.
21. Checks for a short to voltage in the WSS CKT.

GC402980272800AX

Fig. 57 Code C1233: RH Front Wheel Speed Sensor Circuit Open Or Shorted (Part 1 of 3). Bonneville & LeSabre

Step	Action	Value(s)	Yes	No
12	Using *J 39200* DMM, measure the resistance between terminals 15 and B of *J 39700*. Is the resistance within the range specified in the value(s) column?	OL (infinite)	*Go to Step 19*	*Go to Step 13*
13	1. Disconnect the LF Wheel Speed Sensor. 2. Using *J 39200* DMM, measure the resistance between terminal A and ground of the Wheel Speed Sensor Connector. Is the resistance within the range specified in the value(s) column?	OL (infinite)	*Go to Step 14*	*Go to Step 11*
14	1. Using *J 39200* DMM, measure the resistance between terminals 31 and B of *J 39700*. Is the resistance within the range specified in the value(s) column?	OL (infinite)	*Go to Step 16*	*Go to Step 15*
15	Repair CKT 830 for a short to ground. Is the repair complete?	—	Go to *ABS Diagnostic System Check*	—
16	Using *J 39200* DMM, measure the resistance between terminals 15 and B of *J 39700*. Is the resistance within the range specified in the value(s) column?	OL (infinite)	*Go to Step 17*	*Go to Step 18*
17	Malfunction is intermittent. Inspect all connectors and harnesses for damage that may result in a short to ground when connected. Is the repair complete?	—	Go to *ABS Diagnostic System Check*	—
18	Repair CKT 873 for a short to ground. Is the repair complete?	—	Go to *ABS Diagnostic System Check*	—
19	1. Disconnect the LF Wheel Speed Sensor. 2. Turn the ignition switch to the RUN position, engine off. 3. Using *J 39200* DMM, measure the voltage at terminal 31 of *J 39700*. Is the voltage within the range specified in the value(s) column?	Above 1V	*Go to Step 20*	*Go to Step 21*
20	Repair CKT 830 for a short to voltage. Is the repair complete?	—	Go to *ABS Diagnostic System Check*	—
21	Using *J 39200* DMM, measure the voltage at terminal 15 of *J 39700*. Is the voltage within the range specified in the value(s) column?	Above 1V	*Go to Step 22*	*Go to Step 23*
22	Repair CKT 873 for a short to voltage. Is the repair complete?	—	Go to *ABS Diagnostic System Check*	—
23	Replace the EBCM/EBTCM. Is the replacement complete?	—	Go to *ABS Diagnostic System Check*	—

GC402980272700EX

Fig. 56 Code C1232: LH Front Wheel Speed Sensor Circuit Open Or Shorted (Part 3 of 3). Park Avenue

Step	Action	Value(s)	Yes	No
1	Was the Diagnostic System Check performed?	—	*Go to Step 2*	Go to *Diagnostic System Check*
2	1. Inspect the WSS wiring and connectors for damage. 2. Inspect the WSS for looseness or damage. Is physical damage of sensor evident?	—	*Go to Step 3*	*Go to Step 4*
3	Repair as necessary. Is the repair complete?	—	Go to *Diagnostic System Check*	—
4	1. Turn the ignition switch to the OFF position. 2. Disconnect the EBCM/EBTCM. 3. Install the *J 39700* Universal Pinout Box using the *J 39700-25* cable adapter to the EBCM/EBTCM harness connector only. 4. Using *J 39200* DMM, measure the resistance between terminals 25 and 9 of *J 39700*. Is the resistance within the range specified in the value(s) column?	850 - 1350Ω	*Go to Step 12*	*Go to Step 5*
5	1. Disconnect the RF Wheel Speed Sensor. 2. Using *J 39200* DMM, measure the resistance between terminals A and B of the Wheel Speed Sensor Connector. Is the resistance within the range specified in the value(s) column?	850 - 1350Ω	*Go to Step 6*	*Go to Step 11*
6	1. Connect a jumper between the RF Wheel Speed Sensor harness connector terminal B and ground. 2. Using *J 39200* DMM, measure the resistance between terminals 9 and B of *J 39700*. Is the resistance within the range specified in the value(s) column?	0 - 5Ω	*Go to Step 8*	*Go to Step 7*
7	Repair CKT 872 for an open or high resistance. Is the repair complete?	—	Go to *Diagnostic System Check*	—
8	1. Connect a jumper between the RF Wheel Speed Sensor harness connector terminal A and ground. 2. Using *J 39200* DMM, measure the resistance between terminals 25 and B of *J 39700*. Is the resistance within the range specified in the value(s) column?	0 - 5Ω	*Go to Step 10*	*Go to Step 9*
9	Repair CKT 833 for an open or high resistance. Is the repair complete?	—	Go to *Diagnostic System Check*	—
10	Malfunction is intermittent. Inspect all connectors and harnesses for damage that may result in an open or high resistance when connected. Is the repair complete?	—	Go to *Diagnostic System Check*	—
11	Replace the Wheel Speed Sensor. Is the replacement complete?	—	Go to *Diagnostic System Check*	—

GC402980272800BX

Fig. 57 Code C1233: RH Front Wheel Speed Sensor Circuit Open Or Shorted (Part 2 of 3). Bonneville & LeSabre

Step	Action	Value(s)	Yes	No
12	Using *J 39200* DMM, measure the resistance between terminals 25 and B of *J 39700*. Is the resistance within the range specified in the value(s) column?	OL (infinite)	*Go to Step 19*	*Go to Step 13*
13	1. Disconnect the RF Wheel Speed Sensor. 2. Using *J 39200* DMM, measure the resistance between terminal A and ground of the Wheel Speed Sensor Connector. Is the resistance within the range specified in the value(s) column?	OL (infinite)	*Go to Step 14*	*Go to Step 11*
14	1. Using *J 39200* DMM, measure the resistance between terminals 9 and B of *J 39700*. Is the resistance within the range specified in the value(s) column?	OL (infinite)	*Go to Step 16*	*Go to Step 15*
15	Repair CKT 872 for a short to ground. Is the repair complete?	—	Go to *Diagnostic System Check*	—
16	Using *J 39200* DMM, measure the resistance between terminals 25 and B of *J 39700*. Is the resistance within the range specified in the value(s) column?	OL (infinite)	*Go to Step 17*	*Go to Step 18*
17	Malfunction is intermittent. Inspect all connectors and harnesses for damage that may result in a short to ground when connected. Is the repair complete?	—	Go to *Diagnostic System Check*	—
18	Repair CKT 833 for a short to ground. Is the repair complete?	—	Go to *Diagnostic System Check*	—
19	1. Disconnect the RF Wheel Speed Sensor. 2. Turn the ignition switch to the RUN position, engine off. 3. Using *J 39200* DMM, measure the voltage at terminal 9 of *J 39700*. Is the voltage within the range specified in the value(s) column?	Above 1V	*Go to Step 20*	*Go to Step 21*
20	Repair CKT 872 for a short to voltage. Is the repair complete?	—	Go to *Diagnostic System Check*	—
21	Using *J 39200* DMM, measure the voltage at terminal 25 of *J 39700*. Is the voltage within the range specified in the value(s) column?	Above 1V	*Go to Step 22*	*Go to Step 23*
22	Repair CKT 833 for a short to voltage. Is the repair complete?	—	Go to *Diagnostic System Check*	—
23	Replace the EBCM/EBTCM. Is the replacement complete?	—	Go to *Diagnostic System Check*	—

GC402980272800CX

Fig. 57 Code C1233: RH Front Wheel Speed Sensor Circuit Open Or Shorted (Part 3 of 3). Bonneville & LeSabre

Step	Action	Value(s)	Yes	No
1	Was the Diagnostic System Check performed?	—	*Go to Step 2*	Go to *ABS Diagnostic System Check*
2	1. Inspect the WSS wiring and connectors for damage. 2. Inspect the WSS for looseness or damage. Is physical damage of sensor evident?	—	*Go to Step 3*	*Go to Step 4*
3	Repair as necessary. Is the repair complete?	—	Go to *ABS Diagnostic System Check*	—
4	1. Turn the ignition switch to the OFF position. 2. Disconnect the EBCM/EBTCM. 3. Install the *J 39700* Universal Pinout Box using the *J 39700-25* cable adapter to the EBCM/EBTCM harness connector only. 4. Using *J 39200* DMM, measure the resistance between terminals 14 and 30 of *J 39700*. Is the resistance within the range specified in the value(s) column?	850 - 1350Ω	*Go to Step 12*	*Go to Step 5*
5	1. Disconnect the RF Wheel Speed Sensor. 2. Using *J 39200* DMM, measure the resistance between terminals A and B of the Wheel Speed Sensor Connector. Is the resistance within the range specified in the value(s) column?	850 - 1350Ω	*Go to Step 6*	*Go to Step 11*
6	1. Connect a jumper between the RF Wheel Speed Sensor harness connector terminal B and ground. 2. Using *J 39200* DMM, measure the resistance between terminals 30 and B of *J 39700*. Is the resistance within the range specified in the value(s) column?	0 - 5Ω	*Go to Step 8*	*Go to Step 7*
7	Repair CKT 872 for an open or high resistance. Is the repair complete?	—	Go to *ABS Diagnostic System Check*	—
8	1. Connect a jumper between the RF Wheel Speed Sensor harness connector terminal A and ground. 2. Using *J 39200* DMM, measure the resistance between terminals 14 and B of *J 39700*. Is the resistance within the range specified in the value(s) column?	0 - 5Ω	*Go to Step 10*	*Go to Step 9*
9	Repair CKT 833 for an open or high resistance. Is the repair complete?	—	Go to *ABS Diagnostic System Check*	—
10	Malfunction is intermittent. Inspect all connectors and harnesses for damage that may result in an open or high resistance when connected. Is the repair complete?	—	Go to *ABS Diagnostic System Check*	—
11	Replace the Wheel Speed Sensor. Is the replacement complete?	—	Go to *ABS Diagnostic System Check*	—

GC402980272800DX

Fig. 58 Code C1233: RH Front Wheel Speed Sensor Circuit Open Or Shorted (Part 2 of 3). Park Avenue

Circuit Description

The WSS is a single point magnetic pickup that produces an AC signal. The EBCM/EBTCM uses the signal frequency in order to calculate the wheel speed.

Conditions for Setting the DTC

The ignition is in the RUN position and the EBCM/EBTCM senses an open, a short to ground, or a short to battery in the RF WSS circuit.

Action Taken When the DTC Sets

- A DTC C1233 is stored.
- The ABS/TCS is disabled.
- The ABS and the TRACTION OFF indicators are turned on.

Conditions for Clearing the DTC

- The condition for the DTC is no longer present and the scan tool clear DTC function is used
- 50 ignition cycles have passed with no DTCs detected.

Diagnostic Aids

- Thoroughly inspect the wiring and the connectors. Failure to carefully and fully inspect the wiring and the connectors can result in misdiagnosis. Misdiagnosis causes reappearance of the malfunction with part replacement.
- The following conditions can cause an intermittent malfunction:
  - Poor connections
  - Broken insulation
  - A broken wire inside the insulation

Test Description

The numbers below refer to step numbers on the diagnostic table.

4. Checks for an open in the WSS or WSS CKT.
12. Checks for a short to ground in the WSS or WSS CKT.
19. Checks for a short to voltage in the WSS CKT.
21. Checks for a short to voltage in the WSS CKT.

GC402980272802AX

Fig. 58 Code C1233: RH Front Wheel Speed Sensor Circuit Open Or Shorted (Part 1 of 3). Park Avenue

Step	Action	Value(s)	Yes	No
12	Using *J 39200* DMM, measure the resistance between terminals 14 and B of *J 39700*. Is the resistance within the range specified in the value(s) column?	OL (infinite)	*Go to Step 19*	*Go to Step 13*
13	1. Disconnect the RF Wheel Speed Sensor. 2. Using *J 39200* DMM, measure the resistance between terminal A and ground of the Wheel Speed Sensor Connector. Is the resistance within the range specified in the value(s) column?	OL (infinite)	*Go to Step 14*	*Go to Step 11*
14	1. Using *J 39200* DMM, measure the resistance between terminals 30 and B of *J 39700*. Is the resistance within the range specified in the value(s) column?	OL (infinite)	*Go to Step 16*	*Go to Step 15*
15	Repair CKT 872 for a short to ground. Refer to Is the repair complete?	—	Go to *ABS Diagnostic System Check*	—
16	Using *J 39200* DMM, measure the resistance between terminals 14 and B of *J 39700*. Is the resistance within the range specified in the value(s) column?	OL (infinite)	*Go to Step 17*	*Go to Step 18*
17	Malfunction is intermittent. Inspect all connectors and harnesses for damage that may result in a short to ground when connected. Is the repair complete?	—	Go to *ABS Diagnostic System Check*	—
18	Repair CKT 833 for a short to ground. Is the repair complete?	—	Go to *ABS Diagnostic System Check*	—
19	1. Disconnect the RF Wheel Speed Sensor. 2. Turn the ignition switch to the RUN position, engine off. 3. Using *J 39200* DMM, measure the voltage at terminal 30 of *J 39700*. Is the voltage within the range specified in the value(s) column?	Above 1V	*Go to Step 20*	*Go to Step 21*
20	Repair CKT 872 for a short to voltage. Is the repair complete?	—	Go to *ABS Diagnostic System Check*	—
21	Using *J 39200* DMM, measure the voltage at terminal 14 of *J 39700*. Is the voltage within the range specified in the value(s) column?	Above 1V	*Go to Step 22*	*Go to Step 23*
22	Repair CKT 833 for a short to voltage. Is the repair complete?	—	Go to *ABS Diagnostic System Check*	—
23	Replace the EBCM/EBTCM. Is the replacement complete?	—	Go to *ABS Diagnostic System Check*	—

GC402980272800EX

Fig. 58 Code C1233: RH Front Wheel Speed Sensor Circuit Open Or Shorted (Part 3 of 3). Park Avenue

Circuit Description

The WSS is a single point magnetic pickup that produces an AC signal. The EBCM/EBTCM uses the signal frequency in order to calculate the wheel speed.

Conditions for Setting the DTC

The ignition is in the RUN position and the EBCM/EBTCM senses an open, a short to ground, or a short to battery in the LR WSS circuit

Action Taken When the DTC Sets

- A DTC C1234 is stored
- The ABS/TCS is disabled
- The ABS and the TRACTION OFF indicators are turned on

Conditions for Clearing the DTC

- The condition for the DTC is no longer present and the scan tool clear DTC function is used
- 50 ignition cycles have passed with no DTCs detected

Diagnostic Aids

- Thoroughly inspect the wiring and the connectors. Failure to carefully and fully inspect the wiring and the connectors can result in misdiagnosis. Misdiagnosis may cause replacement of parts without repairing the malfunction.
- The following conditions may cause an intermittent malfunction:
  - Poor connections
  - Broken insulation
  - A broken wire inside the insulation
- If an intermittent malfunction exists, Troubleshoot Electrical

Test Description

The numbers below refer to step numbers on the diagnostic table.

4. Checks for an open in the WSS or WSS CKT.
12. Checks for a short to ground in the WSS or WSS CKT.
19. Checks for a short to voltage in the WSS CKT.
21. Checks for a short to voltage in the WSS CKT.

GC402980272900AX

Fig. 59 Code C1234: LH Rear Wheel Speed Sensor Circuit Open Or Shorted (Part 1 of 3). Bonneville & LeSabre

Step	Action	Value(s)	Yes	No
13	1. Disconnect the LR Wheel Speed Sensor. 2. Using *J 39200* DMM, measure the resistance between terminal A and ground of the Wheel Speed Sensor Connector. Is the resistance within the range specified in the value(s) column?	OL (infinite)	*Go to Step 14*	*Go to Step 11*
14	1. Using *J 39200* DMM, measure the resistance between terminals 10 and B of *J 39700*. Is the resistance within the range specified in the value(s) column?	OL (infinite)	*Go to Step 16*	*Go to Step 15*
15	Repair CKT 884 for a short to ground. Is the repair complete?	—	Go to *Diagnostic System Check*	—
16	Using *J 39200* DMM, measure the resistance between terminals 26 and B of *J 39700*. Is the resistance within the range specified in the value(s) column?	OL (infinite)	*Go to Step 17*	*Go to Step 18*
17	Malfunction is intermittent. Inspect all connectors and harnesses for damage that may result in a short to ground when connected. Is the repair complete?	—	Go to *Diagnostic System Check*	—
18	Repair CKT 885 for a short to ground. Is the repair complete?	—	Go to *Diagnostic System Check*	—
19	1. Disconnect the LR Wheel Speed Sensor. 2. Turn the ignition switch to the RUN position, engine off. 3. Using *J 39200* DMM, measure the voltage at terminal 10 of *J 39700*. Is the voltage within the range specified in the value(s) column?	Above 1V	*Go to Step 20*	*Go to Step 21*
20	Repair CKT 884 for a short to voltage. Is the repair complete?	—	Go to *Diagnostic System Check*	—
21	Using *J 39200* DMM, measure the voltage at terminal 26 of *J 39700*. Is the voltage within the range specified in the value(s) column?	Above 1V	*Go to Step 22*	*Go to Step 23*
22	Repair CKT 885 for a short to voltage. Is the repair complete?	—	Go to *Diagnostic System Check*	—
23	Replace the EBCM/EBTCM. Is the replacement complete?	—	Go to *Diagnostic System Check*	—

GC402980272900CX

Fig. 59 Code C1234: LH Rear Wheel Speed Sensor Circuit Open Or Shorted (Part 3 of 3). Bonneville & LeSabre

Circuit Description

The WSS is a single point magnetic pickup that produces an AC signal. The EBCM/EBTCM uses the signal frequency in order to calculate the wheel speed.

Conditions for Setting the DTC

The ignition is in the RUN position and the EBCM/EBTCM senses an open, a short to ground, or a short to battery in the LR WSS circuit

Action Taken When the DTC Sets

- A DTC C1234 is stored
- The ABS/TCS is disabled
- The ABS and the TRACTION OFF indicators are turned on

Conditions for Clearing the DTC

- The condition for the DTC is no longer present and the scan tool clear DTC function is used
- 50 ignition cycles have passed with no DTCs detected

Diagnostic Aids

- Thoroughly inspect the wiring and the connectors. Failure to carefully and fully inspect the wiring and the connectors can result in misdiagnosis. Misdiagnosis may cause replacement of parts without repairing the malfunction.
- The following conditions may cause an intermittent malfunction:
  - Poor connections
  - Broken insulation
  - A broken wire inside the insulation

Test Description

The numbers below refer to step numbers on the diagnostic table.

4. Checks for an open in the WSS or WSS CKT.
12. Checks for a short to ground in the WSS or WSS CKT.
19. Checks for a short to voltage in the WSS CKT.
21. Checks for a short to voltage in the WSS CKT.

GC402980272902AX

Fig. 60 Code C1234: LH Rear Wheel Speed Sensor Circuit Open Or Shorted (Part 1 of 3). Park Avenue

Step	Action	Value(s)	Yes	No
1	Was the Diagnostic System Check performed?	—	*Go to Step 2*	Go to *Diagnostic System Check*
2	1. Inspect the WSS wiring and connectors for damage. 2. Inspect the WSS for looseness or damage. Is physical damage of sensor evident?	—	*Go to Step 3*	*Go to Step 4*
3	Repair as necessary. Is the repair complete?	—	Go to *Diagnostic System Check*	—
4	1. Turn the ignition switch to the OFF position. 2. Disconnect the EBCM/EBTCM. 3. Install the *J 39700* Universal Pinout Box using the *J 39700-25* cable adapter to the EBCM/EBTCM harness connector only. 4. Using *J 39200* DMM, measure the resistance between terminals 10 and 26 of *J 39700*. Is the resistance within the range specified in the value(s) column?	850 - 1350Ω	*Go to Step 12*	*Go to Step 5*
5	1. Disconnect the LR Wheel Speed Sensor. 2. Using *J 39200* DMM, measure the resistance between terminals A and B of the Wheel Speed Sensor Connector. Is the resistance within the range specified in the value(s) column?	850 - 1350Ω	*Go to Step 6*	*Go to Step 11*
6	1. Connect a jumper between the LR Wheel Speed Sensor harness connector terminal B and ground. 2. Using *J 39200* DMM, measure the resistance between terminals 10 and B of *J 39700*. Is the resistance within the range specified in the value(s) column?	0 - 5Ω	*Go to Step 8*	*Go to Step 7*
7	Repair CKT 884 for an open or high resistance. Is the repair complete?	—	Go to *Diagnostic System Check*	—
8	1. Connect a jumper between the LR Wheel Speed Sensor harness connector terminal A and ground. 2. Using *J 39200* DMM, measure the resistance between terminals 26 and B of *J 39700*. Is the resistance within the range specified in the value(s) column?	0 - 5Ω	*Go to Step 10*	*Go to Step 9*
9	Repair CKT 885 for an open or high resistance. Is the repair complete?	—	Go to *Diagnostic System Check*	—
10	Malfunction is intermittent. Inspect all connectors and harnesses for damage that may result in an open or high resistance when connected. Is the repair complete?	—	Go to *Diagnostic System Check*	—
11	Replace the Wheel Speed Sensor. Is the replacement complete?	—	Go to *Diagnostic System Check*	—
12	Using *J 39200* DMM, measure the resistance between terminals 26 and B of *J 39700*. Is the resistance within the range specified in the value(s) column?	OL (infinite)	*Go to Step 19*	*Go to Step 13*

GC402980272900BX

Fig. 59 Code C1234: LH Rear Wheel Speed Sensor Circuit Open Or Shorted (Part 2 of 3). Bonneville & LeSabre

Step	Action	Value(s)	Yes	No
1	Was the Diagnostic System Check performed?	—	*Go to Step 2*	Go to *ABS Diagnostic System Check*
2	1. Inspect the WSS wiring and connectors for damage. 2. Inspect the WSS for looseness or damage. Is physical damage of sensor evident?	—	*Go to Step 3*	*Go to Step 4*
3	Repair as necessary. Is the repair complete?	—	Go to *ABS Diagnostic System Check*	—
4	1. Turn the ignition switch to the OFF position. 2. Disconnect the EBCM/EBTCM. 3. Install the *J 39700* Universal Pinout Box using the *J 39700-25* cable adapter to the EBCM/EBTCM harness connector only. 4. Using *J 39200* DMM, measure the resistance between terminals 12 and 28 of *J 39700*. Is the resistance within the range specified in the value(s) column?	850 - 1350Ω	*Go to Step 12*	*Go to Step 5*
5	1. Disconnect the LR Wheel Speed Sensor. 2. Using *J 39200* DMM, measure the resistance between terminals A and B of the Wheel Speed Sensor Connector. Is the resistance within the range specified in the value(s) column?	850 - 1350Ω	*Go to Step 6*	*Go to Step 11*
6	1. Connect a jumper between the LR Wheel Speed Sensor harness connector terminal B and ground. 2. Using *J 39200* DMM, measure the resistance between terminals 12 and B of *J 39700*. Is the resistance within the range specified in the value(s) column?	0 - 5Ω	*Go to Step 8*	*Go to Step 7*
7	Repair CKT 884 for an open or high resistance. Is the repair complete?	—	Go to *ABS Diagnostic System Check*	—
8	1. Connect a jumper between the LR Wheel Speed Sensor harness connector terminal A and ground. 2. Using *J 39200* DMM, measure the resistance between terminals 28 and B of *J 39700*. Is the resistance within the range specified in the value(s) column?	0 - 5Ω	*Go to Step 10*	*Go to Step 9*
9	Repair CKT 885 for an open or high resistance. Is the repair complete?	—	Go to *ABS Diagnostic System Check*	—
10	Malfunction is intermittent. Inspect all connectors and harnesses for damage that may result in an open or high resistance when connected. Is the repair complete?	—	Go to *ABS Diagnostic System Check*	—
11	Replace the Wheel Speed Sensor. Is the replacement complete?	—	Go to *ABS Diagnostic System Check*	—

GC402980272900DX

Fig. 60 Code C1234: LH Rear Wheel Speed Sensor Circuit Open Or Shorted (Part 2 of 3). Park Avenue

Step	Action	Value(s)	Yes	No
12	Using *J 39200* DMM, measure the resistance between terminals 28 and B of *J 39700*. Is the resistance within the range specified in the value(s) column?	OL (infinite)	*Go to Step 19*	*Go to Step 13*
13	1. Disconnect the LR Wheel Speed Sensor. 2. Using *J 39200* DMM, measure the resistance between terminal A and ground of the Wheel Speed Sensor Connector. Is the resistance within the range specified in the value(s) column?	OL (infinite)	*Go to Step 14*	*Go to Step 11*
14	Using *J 39200* DMM, measure the resistance between terminals 12 and B of *J 39700*. Is the resistance within the range specified in the value(s) column?	OL (infinite)	*Go to Step 16*	*Go to Step 15*
15	Repair CKT 884 for a short to ground. Is the repair complete?	—	Go to *ABS Diagnostic System Check*	—
16	Using *J 39200* DMM, measure the resistance between terminals 28 and B of *J 39700*. Is the resistance within the range specified in the value(s) column?	OL (infinite)	*Go to Step 17*	*Go to Step 18*
17	Malfunction is intermittent. Inspect all connectors and harnesses for damage that may result in a short to ground when connected. Is the repair complete?	—	Go to *ABS Diagnostic System Check*	—
18	Repair CKT 885 for a short to ground. Is the repair complete?	—	Go to *ABS Diagnostic System Check*	—
19	1. Disconnect the LR Wheel Speed Sensor. 2. Turn the ignition switch to the RUN position, engine off. 3. Using *J 39200* DMM, measure the voltage at terminal 12 of *J 39700*. Is the voltage within the range specified in the value(s) column?	Above 1V	*Go to Step 20*	*Go to Step 21*
20	Repair CKT 884 for a short to voltage. Is the repair complete?	—	Go to *ABS Diagnostic System Check*	—
21	Using *J 39200* DMM, measure the voltage at terminal 28 of *J 39700*. Is the voltage within the range specified in the value(s) column?	Above 1V	*Go to Step 22*	*Go to Step 23*
22	Repair CKT 885 for a short to voltage. Is the repair complete?	—	Go to *ABS Diagnostic System Check*	—
23	Replace the EBCM/EBTCM. Is the replacement complete?	—	Go to *ABS Diagnostic System Check*	—

GC402980272900EX

Fig. 60 Code C1234: LH Rear Wheel Speed Sensor Circuit Open Or Shorted (Part 3 of 3). Park Avenue

Step	Action	Value(s)	Yes	No
1	Was the Diagnostic System Check performed?	—	*Go to Step 2*	Go to *Diagnostic System Check*
2	1. Inspect the WSS wiring and connectors for damage. 2. Inspect the WSS for looseness or damage. Is physical damage of sensor evident?	—	*Go to Step 3*	*Go to Step 4*
3	Repair as necessary. Is the repair complete?	—	Go to *Diagnostic System Check*	—
4	1. Turn the ignition switch to the OFF position. 2. Disconnect the EBCM/EBTCM. 3. Install the *J 39700* Universal Pinout Box using the *J 39700-25* cable adapter to the EBCM/EBTCM harness connector only. 4. Using *J 39200* DMM, measure the resistance between terminals 27 and 11 of *J 39700*. Is the resistance within the range specified in the value(s) column?	850 - 1350Ω	*Go to Step 12*	*Go to Step 5*
5	1. Disconnect the RR Wheel Speed Sensor. 2. Using *J 39200* DMM, measure the resistance between terminals A and B of the Wheel Speed Sensor Connector. Is the resistance within the range specified in the value(s) column?	850 - 1350Ω	*Go to Step 6*	*Go to Step 11*
6	1. Connect a jumper between the RR Wheel Speed Sensor harness connector terminal B and ground. 2. Using *J 39200* DMM, measure the resistance between terminals 11 and B of *J 39700*. Is the resistance within the range specified in the value(s) column?	0 - 5Ω	*Go to Step 8*	*Go to Step 7*
7	Repair CKT 882 for an open or high resistance. Is the repair complete?	—	Go to *Diagnostic System Check*	—
8	1. Connect a jumper between the RR Wheel Speed Sensor harness connector terminal A and ground. 2. Using *J 39200* DMM, measure the resistance between terminals 27 and B of *J 39700*. Is the resistance within the range specified in the value(s) column?	0 - 5Ω	*Go to Step 10*	*Go to Step 9*
9	Repair CKT 883 for an open or high resistance. Is the repair complete?	—	Go to *Diagnostic System Check*	—
10	Malfunction is intermittent. Inspect all connectors and harnesses for damage that may result in an open or high resistance when connected. Is the repair complete?	—	Go to *Diagnostic System Check*	—
11	Replace the Wheel Speed Sensor. Is the replacement complete?	—	Go to *Diagnostic System Check*	—
12	Using *J 39200* DMM, measure the resistance between terminals 27 and B of *J 39700*. Is the resistance within the range specified in the value(s) column?	OL (infinite)	*Go to Step 19*	*Go to Step 13*

GC402980273000BX

Fig. 61 Code C1235: RH Rear Wheel Speed Sensor Circuit Open Or Shorted (Part 2 of 3). Bonneville & LeSabre

Circuit Description

The WSS a single point magnetic pickup that produces an AC signal. The EBCM/EBTCM uses the signal frequency in order to calculate the wheel speed.

Conditions for Setting the DTC

The ignition is in the RUN position and the EBCM/EBTCM senses an open, a short to ground, or a short to battery in the RR WSS circuit

Action Taken When the DTC Sets

- A DTC C1235 is stored
- The ABS/TCS is disabled
- The ABS and the TRACTION OFF indicators are turned on

Conditions for Clearing the DTC

- The condition for the DTC is no longer present and the scan tool clear DTC function is used
- 50 ignition cycles have passed with no DTCs detected

Diagnostic Aids

- Thoroughly inspect the wiring and the connectors. Failure to carefully and fully inspect the wiring and the connectors can result in misdiagnosis. Misdiagnosis may cause replacement of parts without repairing the malfunction.
- The following conditions may cause an intermittent malfunction:
  - Poor connections
  - Broken insulation
  - A broken wire inside the insulation
- If an intermittent malfunction exists, troubleshoot Electrical

Test Description

The numbers below refer to step numbers on the diagnostic table.

4. Checks for an open in the WSS or WSS CKT.
12. Checks for a short to ground in the WSS or WSS CKT.
19. Checks for a short to voltage in the WSS CKT.
21. Checks for a short to voltage in the WSS CKT.

GC402980273000AX

Fig. 61 Code C1235: RH Rear Wheel Speed Sensor Circuit Open Or Shorted (Part 1 of 3). Bonneville & LeSabre

Step	Action	Value(s)	Yes	No
13	1. Disconnect the RR Wheel Speed Sensor. 2. Using *J 39200* DMM, measure the resistance between terminal A and ground of the Wheel Speed Sensor Connector. Is the resistance within the range specified in the value(s) column?	OL (infinite)	*Go to Step 14*	*Go to Step 11*
14	1. Using *J 39200* DMM, measure the resistance between terminals 11 and B of *J 39700*. Is the resistance within the range specified in the value(s) column?	OL (infinite)	*Go to Step 16*	*Go to Step 15*
15	Repair CKT 882 for a short to ground. Is the repair complete?	—	Go to *Diagnostic System Check*	—
16	Using *J 39200* DMM, measure the resistance between terminals 27 and B of *J 39700*. Is the resistance within the range specified in the value(s) column?	OL (infinite)	*Go to Step 17*	*Go to Step 18*
17	Malfunction is intermittent. Inspect all connectors and harnesses for damage that may result in a short to ground when connected. Is the repair complete?	—	Go to *Diagnostic System Check*	—
18	Repair CKT 883 for a short to ground. Is the repair complete?	—	Go to *Diagnostic System Check*	—
19	1. Disconnect the RR Wheel Speed Sensor. 2. Turn the ignition switch to the RUN position, engine off. 3. Using *J 39200* DMM, measure the voltage at terminal 11 of *J 39700*. Is the voltage within the range specified in the value(s) column?	Above 1V	*Go to Step 20*	*Go to Step 21*
20	Repair CKT 882 for a short to voltage. Is the repair complete?	—	Go to *Diagnostic System Check*	—
21	Using *J 39200* DMM, measure the voltage at terminal 27 of *J 39700*. Is the voltage within the range specified in the value(s) column?	Above 1V	*Go to Step 22*	*Go to Step 23*
22	Repair CKT 883 for a short to voltage. Is the repair complete?	—	Go to *Diagnostic System Check*	—
23	Replace the EBCM/EBTCM. Is the replacement complete?	—	Go to *Diagnostic System Check*	—

GC402980273000CX

Fig. 61 Code C1235: RH Rear Wheel Speed Sensor Circuit Open Or Shorted (Part 3 of 3). Bonneville & LeSabre

Circuit Description

The WSS a single point magnetic pickup that produces an AC signal. The EBCM/EBTCM uses the signal frequency in order to calculate the wheel speed.

Conditions for Setting the DTC

The ignition is in the RUN position and the EBCM/EBTCM senses an open, a short to ground, or a short to battery in the RR WSS circuit

Action Taken When the DTC Sets

- A DTC C1235 is stored
- The ABS/TCS is disabled
- The ABS and the TRACTION OFF indicators are turned on

Conditions for Clearing the DTC

- The condition for the DTC is no longer present and the scan tool clear DTC function is used
- 50 ignition cycles have passed with no DTCs detected

Diagnostic Aids

- Thoroughly inspect the wiring and the connectors. Failure to carefully and fully inspect the wiring and the connectors can result in misdiagnosis. Misdiagnosis may cause replacement of parts without repairing the malfunction.
- The following conditions may cause an intermittent malfunction:
  - Poor connections
  - Broken insulation
  - A broken wire inside the insulation

Test Description

The numbers below refer to step numbers on the diagnostic table.

4. Checks for an open in the WSS or WSS CKT.
12. Checks for a short to ground in the WSS or WSS CKT.
19. Checks for a short to voltage in the WSS CKT.
21. Checks for a short to voltage in the WSS CKT.

GC402980273002AX

Fig. 62 Code C1235: RH Rear Wheel Speed Sensor Circuit Open Or Shorted (Part 1 of 3). Park Avenue

Step	Action	Value(s)	Yes	No
1	Was the ABS Diagnostic System Check performed?	—	*Go to Step 2*	Go to *A Diagnostic System Check*
2	1. Inspect the WSS wiring and connectors for damage. 2. Inspect the WSS for looseness or damage. Is physical damage of sensor evident?	—	*Go to Step 3*	*Go to Step 4*
3	Repair as necessary. Is the repair complete?	—	Go to *A Diagnostic System Check*	—
4	1. Turn the ignition switch to the OFF position. 2. Disconnect the EBCM/EBTCM. 3. Install the *J 39700* universal pinout box using the *J 39700-25* cable adapter to the EBCM/EBTCM harness connector only. 4. Using the *J 39200* DMM, measure the resistance between terminals 13 and 29 of the *J 39700*. Is the resistance within the specified range?	850 – 1350 Ω	*Go to Step 12*	*Go to Step 5*
5	1. Disconnect the RR wheel speed sensor. 2. Using the *J 39200* DMM, measure the resistance between terminals A and B of the wheel speed sensor connector. Is the resistance within the specified range?	850 - 1350 Ω	*Go to Step 6*	*Go to Step 11*
6	1. Connect a jumper between the RR wheel speed sensor harness connector terminal B and ground. 2. Using the *J 39200* DMM, measure the resistance between terminals 29 and B of the *J 39700*. Is the resistance less than the specified value?	0 - 5 Ω	*Go to Step 8*	*Go to Step 7*
7	Repair CKT 882 for an open or high resistance. Is the repair complete?	—	Go to *A Diagnostic System Check*	—
8	1. Connect a jumper between the RR wheel speed sensor harness connector terminal A and ground. 2. Using the *J 39200* DMM, measure the resistance between terminals 13 and B of the *J 39700*. Is the resistance less than the specified value?	0 - 5 Ω	*Go to Step 10*	*Go to Step 9*
9	Repair CKT 883 for an open or high resistance. Is the repair complete?	—	Go to *A Diagnostic System Check*	—
10	Malfunction is intermittent. Inspect all connectors and harnesses for damage that may result in an open or high resistance when connected. Is the repair complete?	—	Go to *A Diagnostic System Check*	—
11	Replace the wheel speed sensor. Is the replacement complete?	—	Go to *A Diagnostic System Check*	—
12	Using the *J 39200* DMM, measure the resistance between terminals 13 and B of the *J 39700*. Is the resistance within the specified range?	OL (infinite)	*Go to Step 19*	*Go to Step 13*
13	1. Disconnect the RR wheel speed sensor. 2. Using *J 39200* DMM, measure the resistance between terminal A and ground of the wheel speed sensor connector. Is the resistance within the specified range?	OL (infinite)	*Go to Step 14*	*Go to Step 11*

GC402980273000DX

Fig. 62 Code C1235: RH Rear Wheel Speed Sensor Circuit Open Or Shorted (Part 2 of 3). Park Avenue

Circuit Description

This circuit monitors the voltage level available to the EBCM/EBTCM. If the voltage drops below 10.5 volts, full performance of the ABS/TCS cannot be guaranteed. During ABS/TCS operation, there are several current requirements that will cause battery voltage to drop. The voltage is monitored prior to ABS/TCS operation in order to indicate good charging system condition and also during ABS/TCS operation when the voltage may drop significantly.

Conditions for Setting the DTC

The vehicle speed is greater than 8 km/h (5 mph) and the battery and ignition voltages are less than 10.5 volts

Action Taken When the DTC Sets

- A DTC C1236 is stored
- The ABS/TCS is disabled
- The ABS and TRACTION OFF indicators are turned on

Conditions for Clearing the DTC

- The condition for the DTC is no longer present and the scan tool clear DTC function is used
- 50 ignition cycles have passed with no DTCs detected

Diagnostic Aids

- Thoroughly inspect the wiring and the connectors. Failure to carefully and fully inspect the wiring and the connectors can result in misdiagnosis. Misdiagnosis may cause replacement of parts without repairing the malfunction.
- Inspect for other low voltage conditions.
- Test the charging system.
- The following conditions are other possible causes of low system voltage:
  - A charging system malfunction
  - Excessive parasitic drain
  - A weak battery
  - A faulty system ground
- If an intermittent malfunction exists, Troubleshoot: Electrical

Test Description

The numbers below refer to the step numbers on the diagnostic table.

4. This step checks for a good ground.
6. This step checks for battery voltage.

GC402980273100AX

Fig. 63 Code C1236: Low System Supply Voltage (Part 1 of 2). Bonneville, LeSabre & Park Avenue

14	Using *J 39200* DMM, measure the resistance between terminals 29 and B of *J 39700*. Is the resistance within the range specified in the value(s) column?	OL (infinite)	*Go to Step 16*	*Go to Step 15*
15	Repair CKT 882 for a short to ground. Is the repair complete?	—	Go to *ABS Diagnostic System Check*	—
16	Using *J 39200* DMM, measure the resistance between terminals 13 and B of *J 39700*. Is the resistance within the range specified in the value(s) column?	OL (infinite)	*Go to Step 17*	*Go to Step 18*
17	Malfunction is intermittent. Inspect all connectors and harnesses for damage that may result in a short to ground when connected. Is the repair complete?	—	Go to *ABS Diagnostic System Check*	—
18	Repair CKT 883 for a short to ground. Is the repair complete?	—	Go to *ABS Diagnostic System Check*	—
19	1. Disconnect the RR Wheel Speed Sensor. 2. Turn the ignition switch to the RUN position, engine off. 3. Using *J 39200* DMM, measure the voltage at terminal 29 of *J 39700*. Is the voltage within the range specified in the value(s) column?	Above 1V	*Go to Step 20*	*Go to Step 21*
20	Repair CKT 882 for a short to voltage. Is the repair complete?	—	Go to *ABS Diagnostic System Check*	—
21	Using *J 39200* DMM, measure the voltage at terminal 13 of *J 39700*. Is the voltage within the range specified in the value(s) column?	Above 1V	*Go to Step 22*	*Go to Step 23*
22	Repair CKT 883 for a short to voltage. Is the repair complete?	—	Go to *ABS Diagnostic System Check*	—
23	Replace the EBCM/EBTCM. Is the replacement complete?	—	Go to *ABS Diagnostic System Check*	—

GC604980273000EX

Fig. 62 Code C1235: RH Rear Wheel Speed Sensor Circuit Open Or Shorted (Part 3 of 3). Park Avenue

Step	Action	Value(s)	Yes	No
1	Was the Diagnostic System Check performed?	—	*Go to Step 2*	Go to *Diagnostic System Check*
2	Check the Charging System. Is the charging system OK?	—	*Go to Step 3*	Charging System Check
3	1. Turn the ignition switch to the OFF position. 2. Disconnect the EBCM/EBTCM harness connector. 3. Inspect the EBCM/EBTCM harness connector and the connector for damage or corrosion. Is there any evidence of damage or corrosion?	—	*Go to Step 7*	*Go to Step 4*
4	1. Install the *J 39700* Universal Pinout Box using the *J 39700-25* cable adapter between the EBCM/EBTCM harness connector and the EBCM/EBTCM. 2. Using the *J 39200* DMM, measure the resistance between the *J 39700* terminal B and a good ground. Is the resistance within specifications?	0-2 Ω	*Go to Step 5*	*Go to Step 8*
5	Measure the voltage between the *J 39700* terminals B and D. Is the voltage within specifications?	More than 10.5 V	*Go to Step 6*	Battery Charging
6	1. Turn the ignition switch to the RUN position with the engine off. 2. Measure the voltage between the *J 39700* terminals A and B. Is the voltage within specifications?	More than 10.5 V	*Go to Step 9*	Battery Charging
7	Repair as necessary. Are the repairs complete?	—	Go to *Diagnostic System Check*	—
8	Repair the open in ground circuit. Is the circuit repair complete?	—	Go to *Diagnostic System Check*	—
9	Replace the EBCM/EBTCM. Is the replacement complete?	—	Go to *Diagnostic System Check*	—

GC402980273100BX

Fig. 63 Code C1236: Low System Supply Voltage (Part 2 of 2). Bonneville, LeSabre & Park Avenue

Circuit Description

This circuit is designed to detect high vehicle voltage levels to the solenoid relay. High voltage may cause damage to the system.

Conditions for Setting the DTC

The vehicle speed is greater than 8 km/h (5 mph) and the battery voltage is more than 17.0 volts

Action Taken When the DTC Sets

- A DTC C1237 is stored
- The ABS/TCS is disabled
- The ABS and TRACTION OFF indicators are turned on

Conditions for Clearing the DTC

- The condition for the DTC is no longer present and the scan tool clear DTC function is used
- 50 ignition cycles have passed with no DTCs detected

Diagnostic Aids

Inspect the battery for overcharging

Test Description

The numbers below refer to the step numbers on the diagnostic table.

2. This step checks to see what the EBCM/EBTCM is reading as the voltage.
3. This step checks the actual battery voltage.

GC402980273200AX

Fig. 64 Code C1237: High System Supply Voltage (Part 1 of 2). Bonneville, LeSabre & Park Avenue

Step	Action	Value(s)	Yes	No
1	Was the Diagnostic System Check performed?	—	*Go to Step 2*	Go to *Diagnostic System Check*
2	1. Turn all accessories off. 2. Start the engine. 3. Using the Scan Tool, select the ABS/TCS DATA LIST. 4. Monitor the battery voltage while running the engine at about 2000 rpm. Is the voltage within specifications?	Less than 17.0 V	*Go to Step 5*	*Go to Step 3*
3	Using the *J 39200* DMM, check the actual battery voltage while running the engine at about 2000 rpm. Is the voltage within specifications?	Less than 17.0 V	*Go to Step 4*	Charging System
4	Test drive the vehicle above 8 km/h (5 mph). Does DTC C1237 reset?	—	*Go to Step 5*	Go to *Diagnostic System Check*
5	Replace the EBCM/EBTCM. Is the replacement complete?	—	Go to *Diagnostic System Check*	—

GC402980273200BX

Fig. 64 Code C1237: High System Supply Voltage (Part 2 of 2). Bonneville, LeSabre & Park Avenue

Step	Action	Value(s)	Yes	No
1	Was the Diagnostic System Check performed?	—	*Go to Step 2*	Go to *Diagnostic System Check*
2	1. Turn the ignition switch to the RUN position with the engine off. 2. Using a scan tool, read the ABS/TCS DTCs. Are there any other DTCs?	—	Go to the appropriate DTC table	*Go to Step 3*
3	1. Allow the vehicle to cool for 30 minutes after driving. 2. Using a scan tool, enter the ABS Data List and read the TCS status. Is the BTM exceeded?	—	*Go to Step 4*	*Go to Step 5*
4	Replace the EBTCM. Is the replacement complete?	—	Go to *Diagnostic System Check*	—
5	Inspect the Stoplamp Switch for misadjustment. Is the switch misadjusted?	—	Adjust Stoplamp Switch	Go to *Diagnostic System Check*

GC402980273300BX

Fig. 65 Code C1238: Brake Thermal Model Exceeded (Part 2 of 2). Bonneville, LeSabre & Park Avenue

Step	Action	Value(s)	Yes	No
1	Was the Diagnostic System Check performed?	—	*Go to Step 2*	Go to *Diagnostic System Check*
2	1. Turn the ignition switch to the OFF position. 2. Using the *J 39200* DMM, measure the resistance between the motor ground stud and a good chassis ground. Is the resistance within specifications?	0-2 Ω	*Go to Step 3*	*Go to Step 8*
3	1. Disconnect the EBCM/EBTCM connector. 2. Remove the EBCM/EBTCM from the BPMV. 3. Inspect the EBCM/EBTCM to BPMV connector for any of the following conditions: • Damage • Corrosion • Poor terminal contact • The presence of brake fluid Is the connector free of the previous conditions?	—	*Go to Step 4*	*Go to Step 5*
4	1. Install the *J 41247* to the BPMV connector. 2. Using the *J 39200* DMM, measure the resistance between the BPMV internal connector terminal 8 and the motor ground stud. Is the resistance within specifications?	0.2 - 10.0 Ω	*Go to Step 6*	*Go to Step 7*
5	1. If corrosion or connector damage is evident, replace the BPMV or the EBCM/EBTCM as necessary. 2. If brake fluid is present, replace the BPMV and the EBCM/EBTCM. Is the replacement complete?	—	Go to *Diagnostic System Check*	—
6	Replace the EBCM/EBTCM. Is the replacement complete?	—	Go to *Diagnostic System Check*	—
7	Replace the BPMV. Is the replacement complete?	—	Go to *Diagnostic System Check*	—
8	Repair the open or high resistance in CKT 1150. Is the circuit repair complete?	—	Go to *Diagnostic System Check*	—

GC402980273400BX

Fig. 66 Code C1242: BPMV Pump Motor Ground Circuit Open (Part 2 of 2). Bonneville, LeSabre & Park Avenue

Circuit Description

The EBTCM monitors the following occurrences in order to calculate the brake rotor temperatures:

- Vehicle speed deceleration
- The ABS/TCS activation
- The brake lamp on times

When the brake rotor temperatures are exceeded, the following events occur:

- The TCS is disabled
- A DTC C1238 is set
- The TRACTION OFF indicator is turned on

If the brake usage is reduced during driving, the brake rotor cooling is calculated and the TCS is enabled.

Conditions for Setting the DTC

DTC C1238 could be set when either driven wheel estimated brake rotor temperature exceeds 375°C (700°F). If either driven wheel estimated brake rotor temperature has exceeded 375°C (700°F) during ABS or normal braking conditions, the code will not be set until the next TCS activation occurs. The code will not be set and TCS will not be disabled if both rotor estimated temperatures have cooled below 275°C (530°F) before the next TCS activation. If either driven wheel brake rotor temperatures has exceeded 375°C (700°F) during TCS then the code will be set immediately, but TCS will not be disabled until the end of the TCS event.

Action Taken When the DTC Sets

- A DTC C1238 is stored
- The TCS is disabled
- The TRACTION OFF indicator is turned on

Conditions for Clearing the DTC

- The condition for the DTC are no longer present and the scan tool clear DTC function is used
- 50 ignition cycles have passed with no DTCs detected

Diagnostic Aids

- The temperatures are estimated figures taken by the EBTCM
- The following conditions are other possible causes of this malfunction:
  - Excessive brake usage
  - Excessive TCS usage
  - A misadjusted or damaged stoplamp/BTSI switch

Test Description

The numbers below refer to the step numbers on the diagnostic table.

3. This step reads the TCS status.

GC402980273300AX

Fig. 65 Code C1238: Brake Thermal Model Exceeded (Part 1 of 2). Bonneville, LeSabre & Park Avenue

Circuit Description

The BPMV pump motor ground is supplied through a ground stud on the pump motor to a good ground.

Conditions for Setting the DTC

The pump relay is commanded off and the pump motor ground CKT 50 resistance is greater than 6900 Ω.

Action Taken When the DTC Sets

- A DTC C1242 is stored
- The ABS/TCS is disabled
- The ABS and the TRACTION OFF indicators are turned on

Conditions for Clearing the DTC

- The condition for the DTC is no longer present and the scan tool clear DTC function is used
- 50 ignition cycles have passed with no DTCs detected

Diagnostic Aids

- Thoroughly inspect the wiring and the connectors. Failure to carefully and fully inspect the wiring and the connectors can result in misdiagnosis. Misdiagnosis may cause replacement of parts without repairing the malfunction.
- The following conditions may cause an intermittent malfunction:
  - Poor connections
  - Broken insulation
  - A broken wire inside the insulation
- If an intermittent malfunction exists, Troubleshoot Electrical

Test Description

The numbers below refer to the step numbers on the diagnostic table.

2. This step checks for a good pump motor ground.
4. This step checks for proper pump motor resistance.

GC402980273400AX

Fig. 66 Code C1242: BPMV Pump Motor Ground Circuit Open (Part 1 of 2). Bonneville, LeSabre & Park Avenue

Circuit Description

When the EBCM/EBTCM grounds the pump motor relay, the relay closes and provides battery voltage to operate the pump.

Conditions for Setting the DTC

The pump motor relay is commanded off after the motor has been on. A malfunction occurred if the pump motor was on, and the EBCM/EBTCM sensed a stuck or slowly turning pump motor

Action Taken When the DTC Sets

- A DTC C1243 is stored
- The ABS/TCS is disabled
- The ABS and the TRACTION OFF indicators are turned on

Conditions for Clearing the DTC

- The condition for the DTC is no longer present and the scan tool clear DTC function is used
- 50 ignition cycles have passed with no DTCs detected

Diagnostic Aids

- Thoroughly inspect the wiring and the connectors. Failure to carefully and fully inspect the wiring and the connectors can result in misdiagnosis. Misdiagnosis may cause replacement of parts without repairing the malfunction.
- The following conditions may cause an intermittent malfunction:
  - Poor connections
  - Broken insulation
  - A broken wire inside the insulation
- If an intermittent malfunction exists, Troubleshoot Electrical

Test Description

The numbers below refer to the step numbers on the diagnostic table.

3. This step checks for a good pump motor ground.
5. This step checks for proper pump motor resistance.

GC402980273500AX

Fig. 67 Code C1243: BPMV Pump Motor Stalled (Part 1 of 2). Bonneville, LeSabre & Park Avenue

Step	Action	Value(s)	Yes	No
1	Was the Diagnostic System Check performed?	—	*Go to Step 2*	Go to *Diagnostic System Check*
2	Is DTC C1217 also set as a current DTC?	—	Go to DTC C1217	*Go to Step 3*
3	1. Turn the ignition switch to the OFF position. 2. Using the *J 39200* DMM, measure the resistance between the motor ground stud and a good ground. Is the resistance within specifications?	0-2 Ω	*Go to Step 4*	*Go to Step 9*
4	1. Disconnect the EBCM/EBTCM connector. 2. Remove the EBCM/EBTCM from the BPMV. 3. Inspect the EBCM/EBTCM to BPMV connector for any of the following conditions: • Damage • Corrosion • Poor terminal contact • The presence of brake fluid Is the connector free of the previous conditions?	—	*Go to Step 5*	*Go to Step 6*
5	1. Install the *J 41247* to the BPMV connector. 2. Using the *J 39200* DMM, measure the resistance between the BPMV internal connector terminal 8 and the motor ground stud. Is the resistance within specifications?	0.2 - 10.0 Ω	*Go to Step 7*	*Go to Step 8*
6	1. If corrosion or connector damage is evident, replace the BPMV or the EBCM/EBTCM as necessary. 2. If brake fluid is present, replace the BPMV and the EBCM/EBTCM. Is the replacement complete?	—	Go to *Diagnostic System Check*	—
7	Replace the EBCM/EBTCM. Is the replacement complete?	—	Go to *Diagnostic System Check*	—
8	Replace the BPMV. Is the replacement complete?	—	Go to *Diagnostic System Check*	—
9	Repair the open or high resistance in ground circuit. Is the circuit repair complete?	—	Go to *Diagnostic System Check*	—

GC402980273500BX

Fig. 67 Code C1243: BPMV Pump Motor Stalled (Part 2 of 2). Bonneville, LeSabre & Park Avenue

Step	Action	Value(s)	Yes	No
1	Was the Diagnostic System Check performed?	—	*Go to Step 2*	Go to *Diagnostic System Check*
2	Are there any other DTCs present besides C1255xx?	—	Go to the appropriate DTC table	*Go to Step 3*
3	1. Turn the ignition switch to the OFF position. 2. Disconnect the EBCM/EBTCM. 3. Inspect for damaged, pushed out, or miswired terminals. Was any damage found?	—	*Go to Step 4*	*Go to Step 5*
4	Repair as necessary. Is the repair complete?	—	Go to *Diagnostic System Check*	—
5	Replace the EBCM/EBTCM. Is the replacement complete?	—	Go to *Diagnostic System Check*	—

GC402980273600BX

Fig. 68 Code C1255: EBCM/EBTCM Internal Fault (Part 2 of 2). Bonneville, LeSabre & Park Avenue

Step	Action	Value(s)	Yes	No
1	Was the Diagnostic System Check performed?	—	*Go to Step 2*	Go to *Diagnostic System Check*
2	Are there any valve DTCs present (C1261 - C1271)?	—	Go to the appropriate DTC table	*Go to Step 3*
3	1. Turn the ignition switch to the OFF position. 2. Disconnect the EBCM/EBTCM. 3. Inspect for damaged, pushed out, or miswired terminals. Was any damage found?	—	*Go to Step 4*	*Go to Step 5*
4	Repair as necessary. Is the repair complete?	—	Go to *Diagnostic System Check*	—
5	Replace the EBCM/EBTCM. Is the replacement complete?	—	Go to *Diagnostic System Check*	—

GC402980273700BX

Fig. 69 Code C1256: EBCM/EBTCM Internal Fault (Part 2 of 2). Bonneville, LeSabre & Park Avenue

Circuit Description

The inlet valve solenoid circuits are supplied with battery power when the ignition is in the RUN position. The EBCM/EBTCM controls the valve functions by grounding the circuit when necessary.

Conditions for Setting the DTC

The EBCM/EBTCM senses a discrepancy such as an open, short to ground, or short to voltage in the circuit.

Action Taken When the DTC Sets

A malfunction DTC is stored, ABS/TCS is disabled and the ABS and TRACTION OFF indicators are turned on.

Conditions for Clearing the DTC

- Condition for DTC is no longer present and scan tool clear DTC function is used.
- Fifty ignition cycles have passed with no DTC(s) detected.

Diagnostic Aids

Make sure the integrity of the connection between the EBCM/EBTCM and the BPMV is secure, tight, and free from corrosion.

Test Description

The numbers below refer to step numbers on the diagnostic table.

3. Checks the resistance value of the solenoid.
4. Checks for a short to ground in the BPMV.
7. Checks for an internal short to voltage.

GC402980273800AX

Fig. 70 Code C1261: LH Front Inlet Valve Solenoid Fault (Part 1 of 2). Bonneville, LeSabre & Park Avenue

Circuit Description

This DTC identifies a malfunction within the EBCM/EBTCM.

Conditions for Setting the DTC

An internal EBCM/EBTCM malfunction exists.

Action Taken When the DTC Sets

- A DTC C1255xx is stored
- Depending on the sub code, the ABS/TCS and/or the MSVA is disabled

Conditions for Clearing the DTC

- The condition for the DTC is no longer present and the scan tool clear DTC function is used
- 50 ignition cycles have passed with no DTCs detected

Diagnostic Aids

- Two more numbers will follow the DTC C1255xx on the Scan Tool, which should be noted along with any other DTCs that may be displayed. These two numbers help engineering to determine the cause of the internal malfunction.
- Inspect that the EBCM/EBTCM to BPMV connection is secure, tight, and free from corrosion.

Test Description

The numbers below refer to the step numbers on the diagnostic table.

3. This step checks for damage.

GC402980273600AX

Fig. 68 Code C1255: EBCM/EBTCM Internal Fault (Part 1 of 2). Bonneville, LeSabre & Park Avenue

Circuit Description

This DTC identifies a malfunction within the EBCM/EBTCM.

Conditions for Setting the DTC

- There is a solenoid short to battery inside the BPMV. If DTCs C1261–C1274 are set along with C1256xx, pursue the solenoid DTCs first.
- There is an internal EBCM/EBTCM malfunction

Action Taken When the DTC Sets

- A DTC C1256xx is stored
- The ABS/TCS is not disabled, and the ABS and TRACTION OFF indicators are not turned on

Conditions for Clearing the DTC

- The condition for the DTC is no longer present and the scan tool clear DTC function is used
- 50 ignition cycles have passed with no DTCs detected

Diagnostic Aids

- Two more numbers will follow the DTC C1256xx on the Scan Tool, which should be noted along with any other DTCs that may be displayed. These two numbers help engineering to determine the cause of the internal malfunction.
- Inspect that the EBCM/EBTCM to BPMV connection is secure, tight, and free from corrosion.

Test Description

The numbers below refer to the step numbers on the diagnostic table.

3. This step checks for damage.

GC402980273700AX

Fig. 69 Code C1256: EBCM/EBTCM Internal Fault (Part 1 of 2). Bonneville, LeSabre & Park Avenue

Step	Action	Value(s)	Yes	No
1	Was the Diagnostic System Check performed?	—	*Go to Step 2*	Go to *Diagnostic System Check*
2	1. Turn the ignition switch to the OFF position. 2. Disconnect the EBCM/EBTCM connector. 3. Remove the EBCM/EBTCM from the BPMV. 4. Inspect the EBCM/EBTCM to BPMV connector for conditions which could cause intermittents such as damage, corrosion, or poor terminal contact. Are internal connectors OK and cavity free of brake fluid?	—	*Go to Step 3*	*Go to Step 6*
3	1. Install *J 41247* BPMV Pinout Box to the BPMV connector. 2. Using *J 39200* DMM, measure the resistance between *J 41247* terminals 14 and 7. Is the resistance within the range specified in the value(s) column?	8 - 12Ω	*Go to Step 4*	*Go to Step 8*
4	Using *J 39200* DMM, measure the resistance between *J 41247* terminal 14 and the BPMV case. Is the resistance within the range specified in the value(s) column?	OL (infinite)	*Go to Step 5*	*Go to Step 8*
5	1. Remove *J 41247*. 2. Reinstall the EBCM/EBTCM to BPMV. 3. Reconnect the EBCM/EBTCM connector. 4. Turn the ignition switch to the RUN position, engine off. Does DTC C1261 reset as a current DTC?	—	*Go to Step 9*	*Go to Step 7*
6	1. If connector corrosion or damage are present, replace BPMV and/or EBCM/EBTCM as necessary. 2. If brake fluid is present, replace both the BPMV and EBCM/EBTCM. Is the repair complete?	—	Go to *Diagnostic System Check*	—
7	Using a scan tool in ABS/TCS Special Functions run the AUTOMATED Test. Does DTC C1261 reset as a current DTC?	—	*Go to Step 8*	Go to *Diagnostic System Check*
8	Replace the BPMV. Is the replacement complete?	—	Go to *Diagnostic System Check*	—
9	Replace the EBCM/EBTCM. Is the replacement complete?	—	Go to *Diagnostic System Check*	—

GC402980273800BX

Fig. 70 Code C1261: LH Front Inlet Valve Solenoid Fault (Part 2 of 2). Bonneville, LeSabre & Park Avenue

Circuit Description

The Outlet valve solenoid circuits are supplied with battery power when the ignition is in the RUN position. The EBCM/EBTCM controls the valve functions by grounding the circuit when necessary.

Conditions for Setting the DTC

The EBCM/EBTCM senses a discrepancy such as an open, short to ground, or short to voltage in the circuit.

Action Taken When the DTC Sets

A malfunction DTC is stored, ABS/TCS is disabled and the ABS and TRACTION OFF Indicators are turned on.

Conditions for Clearing the DTC

- Condition for DTC is no longer present and scan tool clear DTC function is used.
- Fifty ignition cycles have passed with no DTC(s) detected.

Diagnostic Aids

Make sure the integrity of the connection between the EBCM/EBTCM and the BPMV is secure, tight, and free from corrosion.

Test Description

The numbers below refer to step numbers on the diagnostic table.

3. Checks the resistance value of the solenoid.
4. Checks for a short to ground in the BPMV.
7. Checks for an internal short to voltage.

GC402980273900AX

Fig. 71 Code C1262: LH Front Outlet Valve Solenoid Fault (Part 1 of 2). Bonneville, LeSabre & Park Avenue

Circuit Description

The Inlet valve solenoid circuits are supplied with battery power when the ignition is in the RUN position. The EBCM/EBTCM controls the valve functions by grounding the circuit when necessary.

Conditions for Setting the DTC

The EBCM/EBTCM senses a discrepancy such as an open, short to ground, or short to voltage in the circuit.

Action Taken When the DTC Sets

A malfunction DTC is stored, ABS/TCS is disabled and the ABS and TRACTION OFF Indicators are turned on.

Conditions for Clearing the DTC

- Condition for DTC is no longer present and scan tool clear DTC function is used.
- Fifty ignition cycles have passed with no DTC(s) detected.

Diagnostic Aids

Make sure the integrity of the connection between the EBCM/EBTCM and the BPMV is secure, tight, and free from corrosion.

Test Description

The numbers below refer to step numbers on the diagnostic table.

3. Checks the resistance value of the solenoid.
4. Checks for a short to ground in the BPMV.
7. Checks for an internal short to voltage.

GC402980274000AX

Fig. 72 Code C1263: RH Front Inlet Valve Solenoid Fault (Part 1 of 2). Bonneville, LeSabre & Park Avenue

Step	Action	Value(s)	Yes	No
1	Was the Diagnostic System Check performed?	—	*Go to Step 2*	Go to *Diagnostic System Check*
2	1. Turn the ignition switch to the OFF position. 2. Disconnect the EBCM/EBTCM connector. 3. Remove the EBCM/EBTCM from the BPMV. 4. Inspect the EBCM/EBTCM to BPMV connector for conditions which could cause intermittents such as damage, corrosion, or poor terminal contact. Are internal connectors OK and cavity free of brake fluid?	—	*Go to Step 3*	*Go to Step 6*
3	1. Install *J 41247* BPMV Pinout Box to the BPMV connector. 2. Using *J 39200* DMM, measure the resistance between *J 41247* terminals 1 and 7. Is the resistance within the range specified in the value(s) column?	8 - 12Ω	*Go to Step 4*	*Go to Step 8*
4	Using *J 39200* DMM, measure the resistance between *J 41247* terminal 1 and the BPMV case. Is the resistance within the range specified in the value(s) column?	OL (infinite)	*Go to Step 5*	*Go to Step 8*
5	1. Remove *J 41247*. 2. Reinstall the EBCM/EBTCM to BPMV. 3. Reconnect the EBCM/EBTCM connector 4. Turn the ignition switch to the RUN position, engine off. Does DTC C1263 reset as a current DTC?	—	*Go to Step 9*	*Go to Step 7*
6	1. If connector corrosion or damage are present, replace BPMV and/or EBCM/EBTCM as necessary. 2. If brake fluid is present, replace both the BPMV and EBCM/EBTCM. Is the repair complete?	—	Go to *Diagnostic System Check*	—
7	Using a scan tool in ABS/TCS Special Functions run the AUTOMATED Test. Does DTC C1263 reset as a current DTC?	—	*Go to Step 8*	Go to *Diagnostic System Check*
8	Replace the BPMV. Is the replacement complete?	—	Go to *Diagnostic System Check*	—
9	Replace the EBCM/EBTCM. Is the replacement complete?	—	Go to *Diagnostic System Check*	—

GC402980274000BX

Fig. 72 Code C1263: RH Front Inlet Valve Solenoid Fault (Part 2 of 2). Bonneville, LeSabre & Park Avenue

Step	Action	Value(s)	Yes	No
1	Was the Diagnostic System Check performed?	—	*Go to Step 2*	Go to *Diagnostic System Check*
2	1. Turn the ignition switch to the OFF position. 2. Disconnect the EBCM/EBTCM connector. 3. Remove the EBCM/EBTCM from the BPMV. 4. Inspect the EBCM/EBTCM to BPMV connector for conditions which could cause intermittents such as damage, corrosion, or poor terminal contact. Are internal connectors OK and cavity free of brake fluid?	—	*Go to Step 3*	*Go to Step 6*
3	1. Install *J 41247* BPMV Pinout Box to the BPMV connector. 2. Using *J 39200* DMM, measure the resistance between *J 41247* terminals 9 and 7. Is the resistance within the range specified in the value(s) column?	4 - 7Ω	*Go to Step 4*	*Go to Step 8*
4	Using *J 39200* DMM, measure the resistance between *J 41247* terminal 9 and the BPMV case. Is the resistance within the range specified in the value(s) column?	OL (infinite)	*Go to Step 5*	*Go to Step 8*
5	1. Remove *J 41247*. 2. Reinstall the EBCM/EBTCM to BPMV. 3. Reconnect the EBCM/EBTCM connector. 4. Turn the ignition switch to the RUN position, engine off. Does DTC C1262 reset as a current DTC?	—	*Go to Step 9*	*Go to Step 7*
6	1. If connector corrosion or damage are present, replace BPMV and/or EBCM/EBTCM as necessary. If brake fluid is present, replace both the BPMV and EBCM/EBTCM. Is the repair complete?	—	Go to *Diagnostic System Check*	—
7	Using a scan tool in ABS/TCS Special Functions run the AUTOMATED Test. Does DTC C1262 reset as a current DTC?	—	*Go to Step 8*	Go to *Diagnostic System Check*
8	Replace the BPMV. Is the replacement complete?	—	Go to *Diagnostic System Check*	—
9	Replace the EBCM/EBTCM. Is the replacement complete?	—	Go to *Diagnostic System Check*	—

GC402980273900BX

Fig. 71 Code C1262: LH Front Outlet Valve Solenoid Fault (Part 2 of 2). Bonneville, LeSabre & Park Avenue

Circuit Description

The Outlet valve solenoid circuits are supplied with battery power when the ignition is in the RUN position. The EBCM/EBTCM controls the valve functions by grounding the circuit when necessary.

Conditions for Setting the DTC

The EBCM/EBTCM senses a discrepancy such as an open, short to ground, or short to voltage in the circuit.

Action Taken When the DTC Sets

A malfunction DTC is stored, ABS/TCS is disabled and the ABS and TRACTION OFF Indicators are turned on.

Conditions for Clearing the DTC

- Condition for DTC is no longer present and scan tool clear DTC function is used.
- Fifty ignition cycles have passed with no DTC(s) detected.

Diagnostic Aids

Make sure the integrity of the connection between the EBCM/EBTCM and the BPMV is secure, tight, and free from corrosion.

Test Description

The numbers below refer to step numbers on the diagnostic table.

3. Checks the resistance value of the solenoid.
4. Checks for a short to ground in the BPMV.
7. Checks for an internal short to voltage.

GC402980274100AX

Fig. 73 Code C1264: RH Front Outlet Valve Solenoid Fault (Part 1 of 2). Bonneville, LeSabre & Park Avenue

Step	Action	Value(s)	Yes	No
1	Was the Diagnostic System Check performed?	—	*Go to Step 2*	Go to *Diagnostic System Check*
2	1. Turn the ignition switch to the OFF position. 2. Disconnect the EBCM/EBTCM connector. 3. Remove the EBCM/EBTCM from the BPMV. 4. Inspect the EBCM/EBTCM to BPMV connector for conditions which could cause intermittents such as damage, corrosion, or poor terminal contact. Are internal connectors OK and cavity free of brake fluid?	—	*Go to Step 3*	*Go to Step 6*
3	1. Install *J 41247* BPMV Pinout Box to the BPMV connector. 2. Using *J 39200* DMM, measure the resistance between *J 41247* terminals 6 and 7. Is the resistance within the range specified in the value(s) column?	4 - 7Ω	*Go to Step 4*	*Go to Step 8*
4	Using *J 39200* DMM, measure the resistance between *J 41247* terminal 6 and the BPMV case. Is the resistance within the range specified in the value(s) column?	OL (infinite)	*Go to Step 5*	*Go to Step 8*
5	1. Remove *J 41247*. 2. Reinstall the EBCM/EBTCM to BPMV. 3. Reconnect the EBCM/EBTCM connector. 4. Turn the ignition switch to the RUN position, engine off. Does DTC C1264 reset as a current DTC?	—	*Go to Step 9*	*Go to Step 7*
6	1. If connector corrosion or damage are present, replace BPMV and/or EBCM/EBTCM as necessary. 2. If brake fluid is present, replace both the BPMV and EBCM/EBTCM. Is the repair complete?	—	Go to *Diagnostic System Check*	—
7	Using a scan tool in ABS/TCS Special Functions run the AUTOMATED Test. Does DTC C1264 reset as a current DTC?	—	*Go to Step 8*	Go to *Diagnostic System Check*
8	Replace the BPMV. Is the replacement complete?	—	Go to *Diagnostic System Check*	—
9	Replace the EBCM/EBTCM. Is the replacement complete?	—	Go to *Diagnostic System Check*	—

GC402980274100BX

Fig. 73 Code C1264: RH Front Outlet Valve Solenoid Fault (Part 2 of 2). Bonneville, LeSabre & Park Avenue

Step	Action	Value(s)	Yes	No
1	Was the Diagnostic System Check performed?	—	*Go to Step 2*	Go to *Diagnostic System Check*
2	1. Turn the ignition switch to the OFF position. 2. Disconnect the EBCM/EBTCM connector. 3. Remove the EBCM/EBTCM from the BPMV. 4. Inspect the EBCM/EBTCM to BPMV connector for conditions which could cause intermittents such as damage, corrosion, or poor terminal contact. Are internal connectors OK and cavity free of brake fluid?	—	*Go to Step 3*	*Go to Step 6*
3	1. Install *J 41247* BPMV Pinout Box to the BPMV connector. 2. Using *J 39200* DMM, measure the resistance between *J 41247* terminals 2 and 7. Is the resistance within the range specified in the value(s) column?	8 - 12Ω	*Go to Step 4*	*Go to Step 8*
4	Using *J 39200* DMM, measure the resistance between *J 41247* terminal 2 and the BPMV case. Is the resistance within the range specified in the value(s) column?	OL (infinite)	*Go to Step 5*	*Go to Step 8*
5	1. Remove *J 41247*. 2. Reinstall the EBCM/EBTCM to BPMV. 3. Reconnect the EBCM/EBTCM connector. 4. Turn the ignition switch to the RUN position, engine off. Does DTC C1265 reset as a current DTC?	—	*Go to Step 9*	*Go to Step 7*
6	1. If connector corrosion or damage are present, replace BPMV and/or EBCM/EBTCM as necessary. 2. If brake fluid is present, replace both the BPMV and EBCM/EBTCM. Is the repair complete?	—	Go to *Diagnostic System Check*	—
7	Using a scan tool in ABS/TCS Special Functions run the AUTOMATED Test. Does DTC C1265 reset as a current DTC?	—	*Go to Step 8*	Go to *Diagnostic System Check*
8	Replace the BPMV. Is the replacement complete?	—	Go to *Diagnostic System Check*	—
9	Replace the EBCM/EBTCM. Is the replacement complete?	—	Go to *Diagnostic System Check*	—

GC402980274200BX

Fig. 74 Code C1265: LH Rear Inlet Valve Solenoid Fault (Part 2 of 2). Bonneville, LeSabre & Park Avenue

Circuit Description

The Inlet valve solenoid circuits are supplied with battery power when the ignition is in the RUN position. The EBCM/EBTCM controls the valve functions by grounding the circuit when necessary.

Conditions for Setting the DTC

The EBCM/EBTCM senses a discrepancy such as an open, short to ground, or short to voltage in the circuit.

Action Taken When the DTC Sets

A malfunction DTC is stored, ABS/TCS is disabled and the ABS and TRACTION OFF Indicators are turned on.

Conditions for Clearing the DTC

- Condition for DTC is no longer present and scan tool clear DTC function is used.
- Fifty ignition cycles have passed with no DTC(s) detected.

Diagnostic Aids

Make sure the integrity of the connection between the EBCM/EBTCM and the BPMV is secure, tight, and free from corrosion.

Test Description

The numbers below refer to step numbers on the diagnostic table.

3. Checks the resistance value of the solenoid.
4. Checks for a short to ground in the BPMV.
7. Checks for an internal short to voltage.

GC402980274200AX

Fig. 74 Code C1265: LH Rear Inlet Valve Solenoid Fault (Part 1 of 2). Bonneville, LeSabre & Park Avenue

Circuit Description

The Outlet valve solenoid circuits are supplied with battery power when the ignition is in the RUN position. The EBCM/EBTCM controls the valve functions by grounding the circuit when necessary.

Conditions for Setting the DTC

The EBCM/EBTCM senses a discrepancy such as an open, short to ground, or short to voltage in the circuit.

Action Taken When the DTC Sets

A malfunction DTC is stored, ABS/TCS is disabled and the ABS and TRACTION OFF Indicators are turned on.

Conditions for Clearing the DTC

- Condition for DTC is no longer present and scan tool clear DTC function is used.
- Fifty ignition cycles have passed with no DTC(s) detected.

Diagnostic Aids

Make sure the integrity of the connection between the EBCM/EBTCM and the BPMV is secure, tight, and free from corrosion.

Test Description

The numbers below refer to step numbers on the diagnostic table.

3. Checks the resistance value of the solenoid.
4. Checks for a short to ground in the BPMV.
7. Checks for an internal short to voltage.

GC402980274300AX

Fig. 75 Code C1266: LH Rear Outlet Valve Solenoid Fault (Part 1 of 2). Bonneville, LeSabre & Park Avenue

Step	Action	Value(s)	Yes	No
1	Was the Diagnostic System Check performed?	—	*Go to Step 2*	Go to *Diagnostic System Check*
2	1. Turn the ignition switch to the OFF position. 2. Disconnect the EBCM/EBTCM connector. 3. Remove the EBCM/EBTCM from the BPMV. 4. Inspect the EBCM/EBTCM to BPMV connector for conditions which could cause intermittents such as damage, corrosion, or poor terminal contact. Are internal connectors OK and cavity free of brake fluid?	—	*Go to Step 3*	*Go to Step 6*
3	1. Install *J 41247* BPMV Pinout Box to the BPMV connector. 2. Using *J 39200* DMM, measure the resistance between *J 41247* terminals 5 and 7. Is the resistance within the range specified in the value(s) column?	4 - 7Ω	*Go to Step 4*	*Go to Step 8*
4	Using *J 39200* DMM, measure the resistance between *J 41247* terminal 5 and the BPMV case. Is the resistance within the range specified in the value(s) column?	OL (infinite)	*Go to Step 5*	*Go to Step 8*
5	1. Remove *J 41247*. 2. Reinstall the EBCM/EBTCM to BPMV. 3. Reconnect the EBCM/EBTCM connector. 4. Turn the ignition switch to the RUN position, engine off. Does DTC C1266 reset as a current DTC?	—	*Go to Step 9*	*Go to Step 7*
6	1. If connector corrosion or damage are present, replace BPMV and/or EBCM/EBTCM as necessary. 2. If brake fluid is present, replace both the BPMV and EBCM/EBTCM. Is the repair complete?	—	Go to *Diagnostic System Check*	—
7	Using a scan tool in ABS/TCS Special Functions run the AUTOMATED Test. Does DTC C1266 reset as a current DTC?	—	*Go to Step 8*	Go to *Diagnostic System Check*
8	Replace the BPMV. Is the replacement complete?	—	Go to *Diagnostic System Check*	—
9	Replace the EBCM/EBTCM. Is the replacement complete?	—	Go to *Diagnostic System Check*	—

GC402980274300BX

Fig. 75 Code C1266: LH Rear Outlet Valve Solenoid Fault (Part 2 of 2). Bonneville, LeSabre & Park Avenue

Circuit Description

The Inlet valve solenoid circuits are supplied with battery power when the ignition is in the RUN position. The EBCM/EBTCM controls the valve functions by grounding the circuit when necessary.

Conditions for Setting the DTC

The EBCM/EBTCM senses a discrepancy such as an open, short to ground, or short to voltage in the circuit.

Action Taken When the DTC Sets

A malfunction DTC is stored, ABS/TCS is disabled and the ABS and TRACTION OFF indicators are turned on.

Conditions for Clearing the DTC

- Condition for DTC is no longer present and scan tool clear DTC function is used.
- Fifty ignition cycles have passed with no DTC(s) detected.

Diagnostic Aids

Make sure the integrity of the connection between the EBCM/ EBTCM and the BPMV is secure, tight, and free from corrosion.

Test Description

The numbers below refer to step numbers on the diagnostic table.

3. Checks the resistance value of the solenoid.
4. Checks for a short to ground in the BPMV.
7. Checks for an internal short to voltage.

GC402980274400AX

Fig. 76 Code C1267: RH Rear Inlet Valve Fault (Part 1 of 2). Bonneville, LeSabre & Park Avenue

Step	Action	Value(s)	Yes	No
1	Was the Diagnostic System Check performed?	—	*Go to Step 2*	Go to *Diagnostic System Check*
2	1. Turn the ignition switch to the OFF position. 2. Disconnect the EBCM/EBTCM connector. 3. Remove the EBCM/EBTCM from the BPMV. 4. Inspect the EBCM/EBTCM to BPMV connector for conditions which could cause intermittents such as damage, corrosion, or poor terminal contact. Are internal connectors OK and cavity free of brake fluid?	—	*Go to Step 3*	*Go to Step 6*
3	1. Install *J 41247* BPMV Pinout Box to the BPMV connector. 2. Using *J 39200* DMM, measure the resistance between *J 41247* terminals 13 and 7. Is the resistance within the range specified in the value(s) column?	8 - 12Ω	*Go to Step 4*	*Go to Step 8*
4	Using *J 39200* DMM, measure the resistance between *J 41247* terminal 13 and the BPMV case. Is the resistance within the range specified in the value(s) column?	OL (infinite)	*Go to Step 5*	*Go to Step 8*
5	1. Remove *J 41247*. 2. Reinstall the EBCM/EBTCM to BPMV. 3. Reconnect the EBCM/EBTCM connector. 4. Turn the ignition switch to the RUN position, engine off. Does DTC C1267 reset as a current DTC?	—	*Go to Step 9*	*Go to Step 7*
6	1. If connector corrosion or damage are present, replace BPMV and/or EBCM/EBTCM as necessary. 2. If brake fluid is present, replace both the BPMV and EBCM/EBTCM. Is the repair complete?	—	Go to *Diagnostic System Check*	—
7	Using a scan tool in ABS/TCS Special Functions run the AUTOMATED Test. Does DTC C1267 reset as a current DTC?	—	*Go to Step 8*	Go to *Diagnostic System Check*
8	Replace the BPMV. Is the replacement complete?	—	Go to *Diagnostic System Check*	—
9	Replace the EBCM/EBTCM. Is the replacement complete?	—	Go to *Diagnostic System Check*	—

GC402980274400BX

Fig. 76 Code C1267: RH Rear Inlet Valve Fault (Part 2 of 2). Bonneville, LeSabre & Park Avenue

Circuit Description

The Outlet valve solenoid circuits are supplied with battery power when the ignition is in the RUN position. The EBCM/EBTCM controls the valve functions by grounding the circuit when necessary.

Conditions for Setting the DTC

The EBCM/EBTCM senses a discrepancy such as an open, short to ground, or short to voltage in the circuit.

Action Taken When the DTC Sets

A malfunction DTC is stored, ABS/TCS is disabled and the ABS and TRACTION OFF indicators are turned on.

Conditions for Clearing the DTC

- Condition for DTC is no longer present and scan tool clear DTC function is used.
- Fifty ignition cycles have passed with no DTC(s) detected.

Diagnostic Aids

Make sure the integrity of the connection between the EBCM/EBTCM and the BPMV is secure, tight, and free from corrosion.

Test Description

The numbers below refer to step numbers on the diagnostic table.

3. Checks the resistance value of the solenoid.
4. Checks for a short to ground in the BPMV.
7. Checks for an internal short to voltage.

GC402980274500AX

Fig. 77 Code C1268: RH Rear Outlet Valve Solenoid Fault (Part 1 of 2). Bonneville, LeSabre & Park Avenue

Step	Action	Value(s)	Yes	No
1	Was the Diagnostic System Check performed?	—	*Go to Step 2*	Go to *Diagnostic System Check*
2	1. Turn the ignition switch to the OFF position. 2. Disconnect the EBCM/EBTCM connector. 3. Remove the EBCM/EBTCM from the BPMV. 4. Inspect the EBCM/EBTCM to BPMV connector for conditions which could cause intermittents such as damage, corrosion, or poor terminal contact. Are internal connectors OK and cavity free of brake fluid?	—	*Go to Step 3*	*Go to Step 6*
3	1. Install *J 41247* BPMV Pinout Box to the BPMV connector. 2. Using *J 39200* DMM, measure the resistance between *J 41247* terminals 10 and 7. Is the resistance within the range specified in the value(s) column?	4 - 7Ω	*Go to Step 4*	*Go to Step 8*
4	Using *J 39200* DMM, measure the resistance between *J 41247* terminal 10 and the BPMV case. Is the resistance within the range specified in the value(s) column?	OL (infinite)	*Go to Step 5*	*Go to Step 8*
5	1. Remove *J 41247*. 2. Reinstall the EBCM/EBTCM to BPMV. 3. Reconnect the EBCM/EBTCM connector. 4. Turn the ignition switch to the RUN position, engine off. Does DTC C1268 reset as a current DTC?	—	*Go to Step 9*	*Go to Step 7*
6	1. If connector corrosion or damage are present, replace BPMV and/or EBCM/EBTCM as necessary. 2. If brake fluid is present, replace both the BPMV and EBCM/EBTCM. Is the repair complete?	—	Go to *Diagnostic System Check*	—
7	Using a scan tool in ABS/TCS Special Functions run the AUTOMATED Test. Does DTC C1268 reset as a current DTC?	—	*Go to Step 8*	Go to *Diagnostic System Check*
8	Replace the BPMV. Is the replacement complete?	—	Go to *Diagnostic System Check*	—
9	Replace the EBCM/EBTCM. Is the replacement complete?	—	Go to *Diagnostic System Check*	—

GC402980274500BX

Fig. 77 Code C1268: RH Rear Outlet Valve Solenoid Fault (Part 2 of 2). Bonneville, LeSabre & Park Avenue

Circuit Description

The Master Cylinder Isolation valve solenoid circuits are supplied with battery power when the ignition is in the RUN position. The EBTCM controls the valve functions by grounding the circuit when necessary.

Conditions for Setting the DTC

The EBTCM senses a discrepancy such as an open, short to ground, or short to voltage in the circuit.

Action Taken When the DTC Sets

A malfunction DTC is stored, ABS/TCS is disabled and the ABS and TRACTION OFF indicators are turned on.

Conditions for Clearing the DTC

- Condition for DTC is no longer present and scan tool clear DTC function is used.
- Fifty ignition cycles have passed with no DTC(s) detected.

Diagnostic Aids

Make sure the integrity of the connection between the EBTCM and the BPMV is secure, tight, and free from corrosion.

Test Description

The numbers below refer to step numbers on the diagnostic table.

3. Checks the resistance value of the solenoid.
4. Checks for a short to ground in the BPMV.
7. Checks for an internal short to voltage.

GC402980274600AX

Fig. 78 Code C1271: LH Front TCS Master Cylinder Isolation Valve Fault (Part 1 of 2). Bonneville, LeSabre & Park Avenue

Step	Action	Value(s)	Yes	No
1	Was the Diagnostic System Check performed?	—	*Go to Step 2*	Go to *Diagnostic System Check*
2	1. Turn the ignition switch to the OFF position. 2. Disconnect the EBTCM connector. 3. Remove the EBTCM from the BPMV. 4. Inspect the EBTCM to BPMV connector for conditions which could cause intermittents such as damage, corrosion, or poor terminal contact. Are internal connectors OK and cavity free of brake fluid?	—	*Go to Step 3*	*Go to Step 6*
3	1. Install *J 41247* BPMV Pinout Box to the BPMV connector. 2. Using *J 39200* DMM, measure the resistance between *J 41247* terminals 12 and 7. Is the resistance within the range specified in the value(s) column?	8 - 12Ω	*Go to Step 4*	*Go to Step 8*
4	Using *J 39200* DMM, measure the resistance between *J 41247* terminal 12 and the BPMV case. Is the resistance within the range specified in the value(s) column?	OL (infinite)	*Go to Step 5*	*Go to Step 8*
5	1. Remove *J 41247.* 2. Reinstall the EBTCM to BPMV. 3. Reconnect the EBTCM connector. 4. Turn the ignition switch to the RUN position, engine off. Does DTC C1271 reset as a current DTC?	—	*Go to Step 9*	*Go to Step 7*
6	1. If connector corrosion or damage are present, replace BPMV and/or EBTCM as necessary. 2. If brake fluid is present, replace both the BPMV and EBTCM. Is the repair complete?	—	Go to *Diagnostic System Check*	—
7	Using a scan tool in ABS/TCS Special Functions run the AUTOMATED Test. Does DTC C1271 reset as a current DTC?	—	*Go to Step 8*	Go to *Diagnostic System Check*
8	Replace the BPMV. Is the replacement complete?	—	Go to *Diagnostic System Check*	—
9	Replace the EBTCM. Is the replacement complete?	—	Go to *Diagnostic System Check*	—

GC402980274600BX

Fig. 78 Code C1271: LH Front TCS Master Cylinder Isolation Valve Fault (Part 2 of 2). Bonneville, LeSabre & Park Avenue

Step	Action	Value(s)	Yes	No
1	Was the Diagnostic System Check performed?	—	*Go to Step 2*	Go to *Diagnostic System Check*
2	1. Turn the ignition switch to the OFF position. 2. Disconnect the EBTCM connector. 3. Remove the EBTCM from the BPMV. 4. Inspect the EBTCM to BPMV connector for conditions which could cause intermittents such as damage, corrosion, or poor terminal contact. Are internal connectors OK and cavity free of brake fluid?	—	*Go to Step 3*	*Go to Step 6*
3	1. Install *J 41247* BPMV Pinout Box to the BPMV connector. 2. Using *J 39200* DMM, measure the resistance between *J 41247* terminals 11 and 7. Is the resistance within the range specified in the value(s) column?	8 - 12Ω	*Go to Step 4*	*Go to Step 8*
4	Using *J 39200* DMM, measure the resistance between *J 41247* terminal 11 and the BPMV case. Is the resistance within the range specified in the value(s) column?	OL (infinite)	*Go to Step 5*	*Go to Step 8*
5	1. Remove *J 41247.* 2. Reinstall the EBTCM to BPMV. 3. Reconnect the EBTCM connector. 4. Turn the ignition switch to the RUN position, engine off. Does DTC C1272 reset as a current DTC?	—	*Go to Step 9*	*Go to Step 7*
6	1. If connector corrosion or damage are present, replace BPMV and/or EBTCM as necessary. 2. If brake fluid is present, replace both the BPMV and EBTCM. Is the repair complete?	—	Go to *Diagnostic System Check*	—
7	Using a scan tool in ABS/TCS Special Functions run the AUTOMATED Test. Does DTC C1272 reset as a current DTC?	—	*Go to Step 8*	Go to *Diagnostic System Check*
8	Replace the BPMV. Is the replacement complete?	—	Go to *Diagnostic System Check*	—
9	Replace the EBTCM. Is the replacement complete?	—	Go to *Diagnostic System Check*	—

GC402980274700BX

Fig. 79 Code C1272: LH Front Prime Valve Fault (Part 2 of 2). Bonneville, LeSabre & Park Avenue

Circuit Description

The TCS Prime valve solenoid circuits are supplied with battery power when the ignition is in the RUN position. The EBTCM controls the valve functions by grounding the circuit when necessary.

Conditions for Setting the DTC

The EBTCM senses a discrepancy such as an open, short to ground, or short to voltage in the circuit.

Action Taken When the DTC Sets

A malfunction DTC is stored, ABS/TCS is disabled and the ABS and TRACTION OFF Indicators are turned on.

Conditions for Clearing the DTC

- Condition for DTC is no longer present and scan tool clear DTC function is used.
- Fifty ignition cycles have passed with no DTC(s) detected.

Diagnostic Aids

Make sure the integrity of the connection between the EBTCM and the BPMV is secure, tight, and free from corrosion.

Test Description

The numbers below refer to step numbers on the diagnostic table.

3. Checks the resistance value of the solenoid.
4. Checks for a short to ground in the BPMV.
7. Checks for an internal short to voltage.

GC402980274700AX

Fig. 79 Code C1272: LH Front Prime Valve Fault (Part 1 of 2). Bonneville, LeSabre & Park Avenue

Circuit Description

The Master Cylinder Isolation valve solenoid circuits are supplied with battery power when the ignition is in the RUN position. The EBTCM controls the valve functions by grounding the circuit when necessary.

Conditions for Setting the DTC

The EBTCM senses a discrepancy such as an open, short to ground, or short to voltage in the circuit.

Action Taken When the DTC Sets

A malfunction DTC is stored, ABS/TCS is disabled and the ABS and TRACTION OFF Indicators are turned on.

Conditions for Clearing the DTC

- Condition for DTC is no longer present and scan tool clear DTC function is used.
- Fifty ignition cycles have passed with no DTC(s) detected.

Diagnostic Aids

Make sure the integrity of the connection between the EBTCM and the BPMV is secure, tight, and free from corrosion.

Test Description

The numbers below refer to step numbers on the diagnostic table.

3. Checks the resistance value of the solenoid.
4. Checks for a short to ground in the BPMV.
7. Checks for an internal short to voltage.

GC402980274800AX

Fig. 80 Code C1273: RH Front TCS Master Cylinder Isolation Valve Fault (Part 1 of 2). Bonneville, LeSabre & Park Avenue

Step	Action	Value(s)	Yes	No
1	Was the Diagnostic System Check performed?	—	*Go to Step 2*	Go to *Diagnostic System Check*
2	1. Turn the ignition switch to the OFF position. 2. Disconnect the EBTCM connector. 3. Remove the EBTCM from the BPMV. 4. Inspect the EBTCM to BPMV connector for conditions which could cause intermittents such as damage, corrosion, or poor terminal contact. Are internal connectors OK and cavity free of brake fluid?	—	*Go to Step 3*	*Go to Step 6*
3	1. Install *J 41247* BPMV Pinout Box to the BPMV connector. 2. Using *J 39200* DMM, measure the resistance between *J 41247* terminals 3 and 7. Is the resistance within the range specified in the value(s) column?	8 - 12Ω	*Go to Step 4*	*Go to Step 8*
4	Using *J 39200* DMM, measure the resistance between *J 41247* terminal 3 and the BPMV case. Is the resistance within the range specified in the value(s) column?	OL (infinite)	*Go to Step 5*	*Go to Step 8*
5	1. Remove *J 41247.* 2. Reinstall the EBTCM to BPMV. 3. Reconnect the EBTCM connector. 4. Turn the ignition switch to the RUN position, engine off. Does DTC C1273 reset as a current DTC?	—	*Go to Step 9*	*Go to Step 7*
6	1. If connector corrosion or damage are present, replace BPMV and/or EBTCM as necessary. 2. If brake fluid is present, replace both the BPMV and EBTCM. Is the repair complete?	—	Go to *Diagnostic System Check*	—
7	Using a scan tool in ABS/TCS Special Functions run the AUTOMATED Test. Does DTC C1273 reset as a current DTC?	—	*Go to Step 8*	Go to *Diagnostic System Check*
8	Replace the BPMV. Is the replacement complete?	—	Go to *Diagnostic System Check*	—
9	Replace the EBTCM. Is the replacement complete?	—	Go to *Diagnostic System Check*	—

GC402980274800BX

Fig. 80 Code C1273: RH Front TCS Master Cylinder Isolation Valve Fault (Part 2 of 2). Bonneville, LeSabre & Park Avenue

Circuit Description

The TCS Prime valve solenoid circuits are supplied with battery power when the ignition is in the RUN position. The EBTCM controls the valve functions by grounding the circuit when necessary.

Conditions for Setting the DTC

The EBTCM senses a discrepancy such as an open, short to ground, or short to voltage in the circuit.

Action Taken When the DTC Sets

A malfunction DTC is stored, ABS/TCS is disabled and the ABS and TRACTION OFF Indicators are turned on.

Conditions for Clearing the DTC

- Condition for DTC is no longer present and scan tool clear DTC function is used.
- Fifty ignition cycles have passed with no DTC(s) detected.

Diagnostic Aids

Make sure the integrity of the connection between the EBTCM and the BPMV is secure, tight, and free from corrosion.

Test Description

The numbers below refer to step numbers on the diagnostic table.

3. Checks the resistance value of the solenoid.
4. Checks for a short to ground in the BPMV.
7. Checks for an internal short to voltage.

GC402980274900AX

Fig. 81 Code C1274: RH Front TCS Prime Valve Fault (Part 1 of 2). Bonneville, LeSabre & Park Avenue

Step	Action	Value(s)	Yes	No
1	Was the Diagnostic System Check performed?	—	*Go to Step 2*	Go to *Diagnostic System Check*
2	1. Turn the ignition switch to the OFF position. 2. Disconnect the EBTCM connector. 3. Remove the EBTCM from the BPMV. 4. Inspect the EBTCM to BPMV connector for conditions which could cause intermittents such as damage, corrosion, or poor terminal contact. Are internal connectors OK and cavity free of brake fluid?	—	*Go to Step 3*	*Go to Step 6*
3	1. Install *J 41247* BPMV Pinout Box to the BPMV connector. 2. Using *J 39200* DMM, measure the resistance between *J 41247* terminals 4 and 7. Is the resistance within the range specified in the value(s) column?	8 - 12Ω	*Go to Step 4*	*Go to Step 8*
4	Using *J 39200* DMM, measure the resistance between *J 41247* terminal 4 and the BPMV case. Is the resistance within the range specified in the value(s) column?	OL (infinite)	*Go to Step 5*	*Go to Step 8*
5	1. Remove *J 41247*. 2. Reinstall the EBTCM to BPMV. 3. Reconnect the EBTCM connector. 4. Turn the ignition switch to the RUN position, engine off. Does DTC C1274 reset as a current DTC?	—	*Go to Step 9*	*Go to Step 7*
6	1. If connector corrosion or damage are present, replace BPMV and/or EBTCM as necessary. 2. If brake fluid is present, replace both the BPMV and EBTCM. Is the repair complete?	—	Go to *Diagnostic System Check*	—
7	Using a scan tool in ABS/TCS Special Functions run the AUTOMATED Test. Does DTC C1274 reset as a current DTC?	—	*Go to Step 8*	Go to *Diagnostic System Check*
8	Replace the BPMV. Is the replacement complete?	—	Go to *Diagnostic System Check*	—
9	Replace the EBTCM. Is the replacement complete?	—	Go to *Diagnostic System Check*	—

GC402980274900BX

Fig. 81 Code C1274: RH Front TCS Prime Valve Fault (Part 2 of 2). Bonneville, LeSabre & Park Avenue

Circuit Description

The serial data UART allows information to be exchanged from module to module as needed. This is done by the PCM. The PCM requests and sends all of the information that is transmitted via serial data UART. When the scan tool is connected to the serial data UART, the scan tool takes over for the PCM and sends and requests the needed information.

Conditions for Setting the DTC

All of the following conditions occur:

- The ignition is ON.
- A serial data UART message has not been received for 7 seconds.

Action Taken When the DTC Sets

- A malfunction DTC is stored.
- The TCS is disabled.
- The TRACTION OFF indicator is turned ON.
- The ABS remains functional.

Conditions for Clearing the DTC

- The condition for the DTC is no longer present and you used the scan tool Clear DTC function.
- The EBCM/EBTCM does not detect the DTC in 50 drive cycles.

Diagnostic Aids

- It is very important that a thorough inspection of the wiring and connectors be performed. Failure to carefully and fully inspect wiring and connectors may result in misdiagnosis, causing part replacement with reappearance of the malfunction.
- An intermittent malfunction can be caused by poor connections, broken insulation, or a wire that is broken inside the insulation.
- If an intermittent malfunction exists, refer to *Intermittents and Poor Connections*

Test Description

The numbers below refer to the step numbers on the diagnostic table.

5. This step checks for a short to ground.
7. This step checks for an open in CKT 800.
11. This step checks for a short to voltage.

GC4029803937010X

Fig. 82 Code C1275: Serial Data Fault (Part 1 of 2). Bonneville & LeSabre

Step	Action	Value(s)	Yes	No
1	Did you perform the ABS Diagnostic System Check?	—	Go to *Step 2*	Go to *ABS Diagnostic System Check*
2	Is DTC C1276 set as a current DTC?	—	Go to *DTC C1276 Delivered Torque Signal Circuit Malfunction*	Go to *Step 3*
3	Inspect the following grounds in order to ensure that each ground is clean, tight, and free of damage: • G101 • G106 Were any loose, damaged, or corroded grounds found?	—	Go to *Step 4*	Go to *Step 5*
4	Repair the grounds as needed. Did you complete the repair?	—	Go to *ABS Diagnostic System Check*	—
5	1. Turn OFF the ignition. 2. Disconnect the EBCM/EBTCM connector. 3. Install the *J 39700* universal pinout box using the *J 39700 - 25* cable adapter to the EBCM/EBTCM harness connector only. 4. Turn ON the ignition leaving the engine OFF. 5. Use the *J 39200* DMM in order to measure the resistance between the *J 39700* terminal 15 and terminal B. Does the resistance equal the specified value?	OL (infinite)	Go to *Step 7*	Go to *Step 6*
6	Repair a short to ground in CKT 800 (TAN). Did you complete the repair?	—	Go to *ABS Diagnostic System Check*	—
7	1. Disconnect the PCM connector C1. 2. Use the *J 39200* DMM in order to measure the resistance between the *J 39700* terminal 15 and the PCM connector C1 terminal 15. Is the resistance less than the specified value?	5 Ω	Go to *Step 9*	Go to *Step 8*
8	Repair the open in CKT 800 (TAN). Did you complete the repair?	—	Go to *ABS Diagnostic System Check*	—
9	Use the *J 39200* DMM in order to measure the resistance between the *J 39700* terminal 30 and the PCM connector C1 terminal 15. Is the resistance less than the specified value?	5 Ω	Go to *Step 11*	Go to *Step 10*
10	Repair the open in CKT 800 (TAN). Did you complete the repair?	—	Go to *ABS Diagnostic System Check*	—
11	1. Turn ON the ignition leaving the engine OFF. 2. Use the *J 39200* DMM in order to measure the voltage at terminal 15 of the *J 39700*. Is the voltage within the specified range?	Battery Voltage	Go to *Step 12*	Go to *Step 13*
12	Repair a short to battery in CKT 800 (TAN). Did you complete the repair?	—	Go to *ABS Diagnostic System Check*	—
13	Inspect the PCM. Did you complete the repair?	—	Go to *ABS Diagnostic System Check*	—

GC4029803937020X

Fig. 82 Code C1275: Serial Data Fault (Part 2 of 2). Bonneville & LeSabre

Circuit Description

The EBTCM and the PCM simultaneously control the traction control. The PCM sends a DELIVERED TORQUE message via a Pulse Width Modulated (PWM) signal to the EBTCM confirming the delivered torque level for proper TCS operation. The EBTCM supplies the pull up voltage.

Conditions for Setting the DTC

Ignition voltage is present and the PWM signal is out of range or no signal is received for 7 seconds

Action Taken When the DTC Sets

- A DTC C1276 is stored
- The TCS is disabled
- The TRACTION OFF indicator is turned on
- The ABS remains functional

Conditions for Clearing the DTC

- The condition for the DTC is no longer present and the scan tool clear DTC function is used
- 50 ignition cycles have passed with no DTCs detected

Diagnostic Aids

- Thoroughly inspect the wiring and the connectors. Failure to carefully and fully inspect the wiring and the connectors can result in misdiagnosis. Misdiagnosis may cause replacement of parts without repairing the malfunction.
- The following conditions are other possible causes for this malfunction:
  - An open, a short to ground, or a short to voltage in CKT 464
  - A communication frequency problem
  - A communication duty cycle problem
  - A wiring problem, terminal corrosion, or a poor connection in CKT 464
  - The EBTCM is not receiving information from the PCM
- If an intermittent malfunction exists, Troubleshoot Electrical

Test Description

The numbers below refer to the step numbers on the diagnostic table.

4. This step checks for the proper duty cycle.
5. This step checks for the proper frequency.

GC402980275100AX

Fig. 83 Code C1276: Delivered Torque Signal Circuit Fault (Part 1 of 3). Bonneville & LeSabre

Step	Action	Value(s)	Yes	No
1	Was the Diagnostic System Check performed?	—	Go to *Step 2*	Go to *Diagnostic System Check*
2	Check the following grounds, G101, and G106 making sure each ground is clean, tight, and free of damage. Were any loose, damaged, or corroded grounds found?	—	Go to *Step 3*	Go to *Step 4*
3	Repair the grounds as necessary. Is the repair complete?	—	Go to *Diagnostic System Check*	—
4	1. Turn the ignition switch to the OFF position. 2. Disconnect the EBTCM connector. 3. Install the *J 39700* Universal Pinout Box using the *J 39700-25* cable adapter to the EBTCM harness connector and the EBTCM connector. 4. Turn the ignition switch to the RUN position with the engine off. 5. Using the *J 39200* DMM, measure the DC duty cycle between the *J 39700* terminals 14 and B. Is the duty cycle within specifications?	5 - 15%	Go to *Step 5*	Go to *Step 7*
5	Using the *J 39200* DMM, measure the DC Hz between the *J 39700* terminals 14 and B. Is the frequency within specifications?	121 - 134 Hz	Go to *Step 6*	Go to *Step 13*
6	Replace the EBTCM. Is the replacement complete?	—	Go to *Diagnostic System Check*	—
7	1. Turn the ignition switch to the OFF position. 2. Disconnect the PCM connector C1. 3. Turn the ignition switch to the RUN position with the engine off. 4. Using the *J 39200* DMM, measure the voltage between the *J 39700* terminals 14 and B. Is the voltage within specifications?	Battery voltage	Go to *Step 8*	Go to *Step 10*
8	1. Turn the ignition switch to the OFF position. 2. Disconnect the *J 39700-25* cable adapter from the EBTCM, leaving the *J 39700* connected to the EBTCM harness only. 3. Using the *J 39200* DMM, measure the voltage between the *J 39700* terminals 14 and B. Is the voltage within specifications?	More than 1.0 V	Go to *Step 9*	Go to *Step 12*
9	Repair the short to voltage in CKT 464. Is the circuit repair complete?	—	Go to *Diagnostic System Check*	—
10	1. Turn the ignition switch to the OFF position. 2. Using the *J 39200* DMM, measure the resistance between the *J 39700* terminals 14 and B. Is the resistance within specifications?	OL (infinite)	Go to *Step 6*	Go to *Step 11*

GC402980275100BX

Fig. 83 Code C1276: Delivered Torque Signal Circuit Fault (Part 2 of 3). Bonneville & LeSabre

Circuit Description

The EBTCM and the PCM simultaneously control the traction control. The PCM sends a DELIVERED TORQUE message via a Pulse Width Modulated (PWM) signal to the EBTCM confirming the delivered torque level for proper TCS operation. The EBTCM supplies the pull up voltage.

Conditions for Setting the DTC

Ignition voltage is present and the PWM signal is out of range or no signal is received for 7 seconds

Action Taken When the DTC Sets

- A DTC C1276 is stored
- The TCS is disabled
- The TRACTION OFF indicator is turned on
- The ABS remains functional

Conditions for Clearing the DTC

- The condition for the DTC is no longer present and the scan tool clear DTC function is used
- 50 ignition cycles have passed with no DTCs detected

Diagnostic Aids

- Thoroughly inspect the wiring and the connectors. Failure to carefully and fully inspect the wiring and the connectors can result in misdiagnosis. Misdiagnosis may cause replacement of parts without repairing the malfunction.
- The following conditions are other possible causes for this malfunction:
  - An open, a short to ground, or a short to voltage in CKT 464
  - A communication frequency problem
  - A communication duty cycle problem
  - A wiring problem, terminal corrosion, or a poor connection in CKT 464
  - The EBTCM is not receiving information from the PCM

Test Description

The numbers below refer to the step numbers on the diagnostic table.

4. This step checks for the proper duty cycle.
5. This step checks for the proper frequency.

GC402980275102AX

Fig. 84 Code C1276: Delivered Torque Circuit Fault (Part 1 of 3). Park Avenue

Step	Action	Value(s)	Yes	No
11	Repair the short to ground in CKT 464. Is the circuit repair complete?	—	Go to *Diagnostic System Check*	—
12	Using the *J 39200* DMM, measure the resistance between the *J 39700* terminal 14 and the PCM connector C1 terminal 33. Is the resistance within specifications?	0 - 2 Ω	Go to *Step 13*	Go to *Step 14*
13	Suspect the PCM. Is the diagnosis complete?	—	Go to *Diagnostic System Check*	—
14	Repair the open in CKT 464. Is the circuit repair complete?	—	Go to *Diagnostic System Check*	—

GC402980275100CX

Fig. 83 Code C1276: Delivered Torque Signal Circuit Fault (Part 3 of 3). Bonneville & LeSabre

Step	Action	Value(s)	Yes	No
1	Was the Diagnostic System Check performed?	—	Go to *Step 2*	Go to *ABS Diagnostic System Check*
2	Check the following grounds, G101, and G104 making sure each ground is clean, tight, and free of damage. Were any loose, damaged, or corroded grounds found?	—	Go to *Step 3*	Go to *Step 4*
3	Repair the grounds as necessary. Is the repair complete?	—	Go to *ABS Diagnostic System Check*	—
4	1. Turn the ignition switch to the OFF position. 2. Disconnect the EBTCM connector. 3. Install the *J 39700* Universal Pinout Box using the *J 39700-25* cable adapter to the EBTCM harness connector and the EBTCM connector. 4. Turn the ignition switch to the RUN position with the engine off. 5. Using the *J 39200* DMM, measure the DC duty cycle between the *J 39700* terminals 6 and B. Is the duty cycle within specifications?	5 - 20%	Go to *Step 5*	Go to *Step 7*
5	Using the *J 39200* DMM, measure the DC Hz between the *J 39700* terminals 6 and B. Is the frequency within specifications?	121 - 134 Hz	Go to *Step 6*	Go to *Step 13*
6	Replace the EBTCM. Is the replacement complete?	—	Go to *ABS Diagnostic System Check*	—
7	1. Turn the ignition switch to the OFF position. 2. Disconnect the PCM connector C1. 3. Turn the ignition switch to the RUN position with the engine off. 4. Using the *J 39200* DMM, measure the voltage between the *J 39700* terminals 6 and B. Is the voltage within specifications?	More than battery voltage	Go to *Step 8*	Go to *Step 10*
8	1. Turn the ignition switch to the OFF position. 2. Disconnect the *J 39700-25* cable adapter from the EBTCM, leaving the *J 39700* connected to the EBTCM harness only. 3. Using the *J 39200* DMM, measure the voltage between the *J 39700* terminals 6 and B. Is the voltage within specifications?	More than 1.0 V	Go to *Step 9*	Go to *Step 12*
9	Repair the short to voltage in CKT 464. Is the circuit repair complete?	—	Go to *ABS Diagnostic System Check*	—
10	1. Turn the ignition switch to the OFF position. 2. Using the *J 39200* DMM, measure the resistance between the *J 39700* terminals 6 and B. Is the resistance within specifications?	OL (infinite)	Go to *Step 6*	Go to *Step 11*

GC402980275100DX

Fig. 84 Code C1276: Delivered Torque Circuit Fault (Part 2 of 3). Park Avenue

Step	Action	Value(s)	Yes	No
11	Repair the short to ground in CKT 464. Is the circuit repair complete?	—	Go to *ABS Diagnostic System Check*	—
12	Using the *J 39200* DMM, measure the resistance between the *J 39700* terminal 6 and the PCM connector C1 terminal 33. Is the resistance within specifications?	0 - 2 Ω	Go to *Step 13*	Go to *Step 14*
13	Suspect the PCM. Is the diagnosis complete?	—	Go to *ABS Diagnostic System Check*	—
14	Repair the open in CKT 464. Is the circuit repair complete?	—	Go to *ABS Diagnostic System Check*	—

GC402980275100EX

Fig. 84 Code C1276: Delivered Torque Circuit Fault (Part 3 of 3). Park Avenue

Circuit Description

The EBTCM and the PCM simultaneously control the traction control. The PCM receives a REQUESTED TORQUE message via a Pulse Width Modulated (PWM) signal from the EBTCM requesting the desired torque level for proper TCS operation. The PCM supplies the pull up voltage.

Conditions for Setting the DTC

There is an open or short in the REQUESTED TORQUE line between the EBTCM and the PCM or there is a TCS communication malfunction detected by the PCM and indicated to the EBTCM via a PWM message

Action Taken When the DTC Sets

- A DTC C1277 is stored
- The TCS is disabled
- The TRACTION OFF indicator is turned on
- The ABS remains functional

Conditions for Clearing the DTC

- The condition for the DTC is no longer present and the scan tool clear DTC function is used
- 50 ignition cycles have passed with no DTCs detected

Diagnostic Aids

- Thoroughly inspect the wiring and the connectors. Failure to carefully and fully inspect the wiring and the connectors can result in misdiagnosis. Misdiagnosis causes reappearance of the malfunction with part replacement.
- The following conditions are other possible causes for this malfunction:
  - An open, a short to ground, or a short to voltage in CKT 463
  - A communication frequency problem
  - A communication duty cycle problem
  - A wiring problem, terminal corrosion, or a poor connection in CKT 463
  - The PCM is not receiving information from the EBTCM
- If an intermittent malfunction exists, Troubleshoot Electrical

Test Description

The numbers below refer to the step numbers on the diagnostic table.

4. This step checks for the proper duty cycle.
5. This step checks for the proper frequency.

GC402980275200AX

Fig. 85 Code C1277: Requested Torque Signal Circuit Fault (Part 1 of 3). Bonneville & LeSabre

Step	Action	Value(s)	Yes	No
12	Using the *J 39200* DMM, measure the resistance between the *J 39700* terminal 1 and the PCM connector C1 terminal 14. Is the resistance within specifications?	0 - 2 Ω	*Go to Step 13*	*Go to Step 14*
13	Suspect the PCM. Is the diagnosis complete?	—	Go to *Diagnostic System Check*	—
14	Repair the open in CKT 463. Is the circuit repair complete?	—	Go to *Diagnostic System Check*	—

GC402980275200CX

Fig. 85 Code C1277: Requested Torque Signal Circuit Fault (Part 3 of 3). Bonneville & LeSabre

Circuit Description

The EBTCM and the PCM simultaneously control the traction control. The PCM receives a REQUESTED TORQUE message via a Pulse Width Modulated (PWM) signal from the EBTCM requesting the desired torque level for proper TCS operation. The PCM supplies the pull up voltage.

Conditions for Setting the DTC

There is an open or short in the REQUESTED TORQUE line between the EBTCM and the PCM or there is a TCS communication malfunction detected by the PCM and indicated to the EBTCM via a PWM message

Action Taken When the DTC Sets

- A DTC C1277 is stored
- The TCS is disabled
- The TRACTION OFF indicator is turned on
- The ABS remains functional

Conditions for Clearing the DTC

- The condition for the DTC is no longer present and the scan tool clear DTC function is used
- 50 ignition cycles have passed with no DTCs detected

Diagnostic Aids

- Thoroughly inspect the wiring and the connectors. Failure to carefully and fully inspect the wiring and the connectors can result in misdiagnosis. Misdiagnosis causes reappearance of the malfunction with part replacement.
- The following conditions are other possible causes for this malfunction:
  - An open, a short to ground, or a short to voltage in CKT 463
  - A communication frequency problem
  - A communication duty cycle problem
  - A wiring problem, terminal corrosion, or a poor connection in CKT 463
  - The PCM is not receiving information from the EBTCM

Test Description

The numbers below refer to the step numbers on the diagnostic table.

4. This step checks for the proper duty cycle.
5. This step checks for the proper frequency.

GC402980275202AX

Fig. 86 Code C1277: Requested Torque Signal Circuit Fault (Part 1 of 3). Park Avenue

Step	Action	Value(s)	Yes	No
1	Was the Diagnostic System Check performed?	—	*Go to Step 2*	Go to *Diagnostic System Check*
2	Check the following grounds, G101, and G106 making sure each ground is clean tight and free of damage. Were any loose, damaged, or corroded grounds found?	—	*Go to Step 3*	*Go to Step 4*
3	Repair the grounds as necessary. Is the repair complete?	—	Go to *Diagnostic System Check*	—
4	1. Turn the ignition switch to the OFF position. 2. Disconnect the EBTCM connector. 3. Install the *J 39700* Universal Pinout Box using the *J 39700-25* cable adapter to the EBTCM harness connector and the EBTCM connector. 4. Turn the ignition switch to the RUN position with the engine off. 5. Using the *J 39200* DMM, measure the DC duty cycle between the *J 39700* terminals 1 and B. Is the duty cycle within specifications?	85 - 95%	*Go to Step 5*	*Go to Step 6*
5	Using the *J 39200*, measure the DC Hz between the *J 39700* terminals 1 and B. Is the frequency within specifications?	121 - 134 Hz	*Go to Step 13*	*Go to Step 7*
6	1. Turn the ignition switch to the OFF position. 2. Disconnect the *J 39700-25* cable adapter from the EBTCM, leaving the *J 39700* connected to the EBTCM harness only. 3. Using the *J 39200* DMM, measure the voltage between the *J 39700* terminals 1 and B. Is the voltage within specifications?	4.5 - 5.5 V	*Go to Step 7*	*Go to Step 8*
7	Replace the EBTCM. Is the replacement complete?	—	Go to *Diagnostic System Check*	—
8	1. Turn the ignition switch to the OFF position. 2. Disconnect the PCM connector C1. 3. Turn the ignition switch to the RUN position with the engine off. 4. Using the *J 39200* DMM, measure the voltage between the *J 39700* terminals 1 and B. Is the voltage within specifications?	More than 1.0 V	*Go to Step 9*	*Go to Step 10*
9	Repair the short to voltage in CKT 463. Is the circuit repair complete?	—	Go to *Diagnostic System Check*	—
10	1. Turn the ignition switch to the OFF position. 2. Using the *J 39200* DMM, measure the resistance between the *J 39700* terminals 1 and B. Is the resistance within specifications?	OL (infinite)	*Go to Step 12*	*Go to Step 11*
11	Repair the short to ground in CKT 463. Is the circuit repair complete?	—	Go to *Diagnostic System Check*	—

GC402980275200BX

Fig. 85 Code C1277: Requested Torque Signal Circuit Fault (Part 2 of 3). Bonneville & LeSabre

Step	Action	Value(s)	Yes	No
1	Was the Diagnostic System Check performed?	—	*Go to Step 2*	Go to *ABS Diagnostic System Check*
2	Check the following grounds, G101, and G104 making sure each ground is clean tight and free of damage. Were any loose, damaged, or corroded grounds found?	—	*Go to Step 3*	*Go to Step 4*
3	Repair the grounds as necessary. Is the repair complete?	—	Go to *ABS Diagnostic System Check*	—
4	1. Turn the ignition switch to the OFF position. 2. Disconnect the EBTCM connector. 3. Install the *J 39700* Universal Pinout Box using the *J 39700-25* cable adapter to the EBTCM harness connector and the EBTCM connector. 4. Turn the ignition switch to the RUN position with the engine off. 5. Using the *J 39200* DMM, measure the DC duty cycle between the *J 39700* terminals 25 and B. Is the duty cycle within specifications?	85 - 95%	*Go to Step 5*	*Go to Step 6*
5	Using the *J 39200*, measure the DC Hz between the *J 39700* terminals 25 and B. Is the frequency within specifications?	121 - 134 Hz	*Go to Step 13*	*Go to Step 7*
6	1. Turn the ignition switch to the OFF position. 2. Disconnect the *J 39700-25* cable adapter from the EBTCM, leaving the *J 39700* connected to the EBTCM harness only. 3. Using the *J 39200* DMM, measure the voltage between the *J 39700* terminals 25 and B. Is the voltage within specifications?	4.5 - 5.5 V	*Go to Step 7*	*Go to Step 8*
7	Replace the EBTCM. Is the replacement complete?	—	Go to *ABS Diagnostic System Check*	—
8	1. Turn the ignition switch to the OFF position. 2. Disconnect the PCM connector C1. 3. Turn the ignition switch to the RUN position with the engine off. 4. Using the *J 39200* DMM, measure the voltage between the *J 39700* terminals 25 and B. Is the voltage within specifications?	More than 1.0 V	*Go to Step 9*	*Go to Step 10*
9	Repair the short to voltage in CKT 463. Is the circuit repair complete?	—	Go to *ABS Diagnostic System Check*	—
10	1. Turn the ignition switch to the OFF position. 2. Using the *J 39200* DMM, measure the resistance between the *J 39700* terminals 25 and B. Is the resistance within specifications?	OL (infinite)	*Go to Step 12*	*Go to Step 11*

GC402980275200DX

Fig. 86 Code C1277: Requested Torque Signal Circuit Fault (Part 2 of 3). Park Avenue

Step	Action	Value(s)	Yes	No
11	Repair the short to ground in CKT 463. Is the circuit repair complete?	—	Go to *ABS Diagnostic System Check*	—
12	Using the *J 39200* DMM, measure the resistance between the *J 39700* terminal 25 and the PCM connector C1 terminal 14. Is the resistance within specifications?	0 - 2 Ω	*Go to Step 13*	*Go to Step 14*
13	Suspect the PCM. Is the diagnosis complete?	—	Go to *ABS Diagnostic System Check*	—
14	Repair the open in CKT 463. Is the circuit repair complete?	—	Go to *ABS Diagnostic System Check*	—

GC402980275200EX

Fig. 86 Code C1277: Requested Torque Signal Circuit Fault (Part 3 of 3). Park Avenue

Step	Action	Value(s)	Yes	No
1	Was the Diagnostic System Check performed?	—	*Go to Step 2*	Go to *Diagnostic System Check*
2	1. Turn the ignition switch to the RUN position with the engine off. 2. Using a scan tool, read the ABS/TCS DTCs. Are any other DTCs set?	—	Go to the appropriate DTC table	*Go to Step 3*
3	Is DTC C1278 set as a current code?	—	*Go to Step 5*	*Go to Step 4*
4	1. Start the engine and test drive the vehicle at least 16 km/h (10 mph) while monitoring the scan tool for ABS/TCS DTCs. 2. Repeat the above drive cycle sequence two more times. Did DTC C1278 set in the last three drive cycles?	—	*Go to Step 5*	Go to *Diagnostic System Check*
5	Perform the Powertrain OBD System Check. Did the vehicle pass the OBD System Check?	—	Go to Diagnostic Aids	Engine Controls Diagnosis

GC402980275300BX

Fig. 87 Code C1278: TCS Temporarily Inhibited By PCM (Part 2 of 2). Bonneville, LeSabre & Park Avenue

Step	Action	Value(s)	Yes	No
1	Was the Diagnostic System Check performed?	—	*Go to Step 2*	Go to *Diagnostic System Check*
2	Are any WSS DTCs present?	—	Go to the appropriate DTC table	*Go to Step 3*
3	Press the brake pedal. Do the brake lights come on?	—	*Go to Step 4*	*Go to Step 7*
4	1. Turn the ignition switch to the OFF position. 2. Disconnect the EBTCM. 3. Install the *J 39700* Universal Pinout Box using the *J 39700-25* cable adapter to the EBTCM harness connector only. 4. Turn the ignition switch to the RUN position with the engine off. 5. Using the *J 39200* DMM, measure the voltage at the *J 39700* terminal 3 while an assistant presses the brake pedal. Is the voltage within specifications?	Battery voltage	*Go to Step 5*	*Go to Step 6*
5	Replace the EBTCM. Is the replacement complete?	—	Go to *Diagnostic System Check*	—
6	Repair the open or high resistance in CKT 17. Is the circuit repair complete?	—	Go to *Diagnostic System Check*	—
7	Inspect the BRAKE fuse in the I/P Fuse Block. Is the BRAKE fuse OK?	—	*Go to Step 8*	*Go to Step 12*
8	1. Disconnect the Stoplamp/BTSI switch connector. 2. Using the *J 39200* DMM, measure the voltage at the Stoplamp/BTSI switch harness connector terminal A. Is the voltage within specifications?	Battery voltage	*Go to Step 10*	*Go to Step 9*
9	Repair the open in CKT 140. Is the circuit repair complete?	—	Go to *Diagnostic System Check*	—
10	Connect a fused jumper wire between the Stoplamp/BTSI switch harness connector terminals A and B. Do the brake lamps come on?	—	*Go to Step 11*	*Go to Step 6*
11	Adjust or repair the Stoplamp/BTSI switch as necessary. Is the repair complete?	—	Go to *Diagnostic System Check*	—
12	1. Replace the BRAKE fuse. (Do not press the brake pedal.) 2. Check the BRAKE fuse. Is the fuse OK?	—	*Go to Step 14*	*Go to Step 13*
13	Repair the short to ground in CKT 140. Is the circuit repair complete?	—	Go to *Diagnostic System Check*	—

GC402980275400BX

Fig. 88 Code C1291: Open Brake Lamp Switch Contacts During Decel (Part 2 of 3). Bonneville & LeSabre

Circuit Description

The PCM monitors various parameters and will not allow traction control operation if any parameter falls below a specified value.

Conditions for Setting the DTC

The PCM detects a malfunction and then causes TCS shut down until the malfunction has been corrected.

Action Taken When the DTC Sets

- A DTC C1278 is stored (This is a temporary malfunction)
- The TCS is disabled
- The TRACTION OFF indicator is turned on
- If the TCS is no longer inhibited, the indicator will be turned off but the DTC will be stored

Conditions for Clearing the DTC

- The condition for the DTC is no longer present and the scan tool clear DTC function is used
- 50 ignition cycles have passed with no DTCs detected

Diagnostic Aids

This code is for information only. As an aid to the technician, this code indicates that there are no problems in the ABS/TCS system

Test Description

The numbers below refer to the step numbers on the diagnostic table.

4. This step checks if DTC C1278 resets.

GC402980275300AX

Fig. 87 Code C1278: TCS Temporarily Inhibited By PCM (Part 1 of 2). Bonneville, LeSabre & Park Avenue

Circuit Description

This circuit is used to detect an open Stoplamp/BTSI switch in the non-ABS mode. The EBTCM looks for a deceleration rate that would indicate braking action and requires several repeats of this detection method in order to verify this assumption. In each case, the TCS will not be available since the EBTCM sees no Stoplamp/BTSI switch voltage.

Conditions for Setting the DTC

The Stoplamp/BTSI switch remains open for three deceleration cycles.

Action Taken When the DTC Sets

- A DTC C1291 is stored
- The TCS is disabled
- The TRACTION OFF indicator turns on
- The ABS remains functional

Conditions for Clearing the DTC

- The condition for the DTC is no longer present and the scan tool clear DTC function is used
- 50 ignition cycles have passed with no DTCs detected

Diagnostic Aids

- Thoroughly inspect the wiring and the connectors. Failure to carefully and fully inspect the wiring and the connectors can result in misdiagnosis. Misdiagnosis may cause replacement of parts without repairing the malfunction.
- If any WSS DTCs are present, diagnose the WSS DTCs first.
- The following conditions may cause most intermittent malfunctions:
  - Poor connections
  - Rubbed through wire insulation
  - A broken wire inside the insulation
- The following conditions are other possible causes for this malfunction:
  - An open Stoplamp/BTSI switch
  - An open brake fuse
  - A misadjusted Stoplamp/BTSI switch
  - Erratic wheel speeds
  - A wiring problem, terminal corrosion, or a poor connection in the circuit
- If an intermittent malfunction exists, Troubleshoot Electrical

Test Description

The numbers below refer to the step numbers on the diagnostic table.

3. This step checks if the Stoplamp Switch and Power Distribution are OK.
4. This step checks for voltage at the EBTCM.
10. This step checks the Stoplamp Switch.

GC402980275400AX

Fig. 88 Code C1291: Open Brake Lamp Switch Contacts During Decel (Part 1 of 3). Bonneville & LeSabre

Step	Action	Value(s)	Yes	No
14	1. Press the brake pedal. 2. Check the BRAKE fuse. Is the fuse OK?	—	Go to *Diagnostic System Check*	*Go to Step 15*
15	1. Turn the ignition switch to the OFF position. 2. Disconnect the EBTCM. 3. Replace the fuse. 4. Turn the ignition switch to the RUN position with the engine off. 5. Press the brake pedal. 6. Check the BRAKE fuse. Is the fuse OK?	—	*Go to Step 5*	*Go to Step 16*
16	Repair the short to ground in CKT 17. Is the circuit repair complete?	—	Go to *Diagnostic System Check*	—

GC402980275400CX

Fig. 88 Code C1291: Open Brake Lamp Switch Contacts During Decel (Part 3 of 3). Bonneville & LeSabre

Circuit Description

This circuit is used to detect an open Stoplamp/BTSI switch in the non-ABS mode. The EBTCM looks for a deceleration rate that would indicate braking action and requires several repeats of this detection method in order to verify this assumption. In each case, the TCS will not be available since the EBTCM sees no Stoplamp/BTSI switch voltage.

Conditions for Setting the DTC

The Stoplamp/BTSI switch remains open for three deceleration cycles.

Action Taken When the DTC Sets

- A DTC C1291 is stored
- The TCS is disabled
- The TRACTION OFF indicator turns on
- The ABS remains functional

Conditions for Clearing the DTC

- The condition for the DTC is no longer present and the scan tool clear DTC function is used
- 50 ignition cycles have passed with no DTCs detected

Diagnostic Aids

- Thoroughly inspect the wiring and the connectors. Failure to carefully and fully inspect the wiring and the connectors can result in misdiagnosis. Misdiagnosis may cause replacement of parts without repairing the malfunction.
- If any WSS DTCs are present, diagnose the WSS DTCs first.
- The following conditions may cause most intermittent malfunctions:
  - Poor connections
  - Rubbed through wire insulation
  - A broken wire inside the insulation
- The following conditions are other possible causes for this malfunction:
  - An open Stoplamp/BTSI switch
  - An open brake fuse
  - A misadjusted Stoplamp/BTSI switch
  - Erratic wheel speeds
  - A wiring problem, terminal corrosion, or a poor connection in the circuit

Test Description

The numbers below refer to the step numbers on the diagnostic table.

3. This step checks if the Stoplamp Switch and Power Distribution are OK.
4. This step checks for voltage at the EBTCM.
10. This step checks the Stoplamp Switch.

GC402980275402AX

Fig. 89 Code C1291: Open Brake Lamp Switch Contact During Decel (Part 1 of 3). Park Avenue

Step	Action	Value(s)	Yes	No
1	Was the Diagnostic System Check performed?	—	*Go to Step 2*	Go to *ABS Diagnostic System Check*
2	Are any WSS DTCs present?	—	Go to the appropriate DTC table	*Go to Step 3*
3	Press the brake pedal. Do the brake lights come on?	—	*Go to Step 4*	*Go to Step 7*
4	1. Turn the ignition switch to the OFF position. 2. Disconnect the EBTCM. 3. Install the *J 39700* Universal Pinout Box using the *J 39700-25* cable adapter to the EBTCM harness connector only. 4. Turn the ignition switch to the RUN position with the engine off. 5. Using the *J 39200* DMM, measure the voltage at the *J 39700* terminal 9 while an assistant presses the brake pedal. Is the voltage within specifications?	Battery voltage	*Go to Step 5*	*Go to Step 6*
5	Replace the EBTCM. Is the replacement complete?	—	Go to *ABS Diagnostic System Check*	—
6	Repair the open or high resistance in CKT 20. Is the circuit repair complete?	—	Go to *ABS Diagnostic System Check*	—
7	Inspect the STOP fuse in the Underhood Junction Block. Is the BRAKE fuse OK?	—	*Go to Step 8*	*Go to Step 12*
8	1. Disconnect the Stoplamp/BTSI switch connector. 2. Using the *J 39200* DMM, measure the voltage at the Stoplamp/BTSI switch harness connector terminal A. Is the voltage within specifications?	Battery voltage	*Go to Step 10*	*Go to Step 9*
9	Repair the open in CKT 640. Is the circuit repair complete?	—	Go to *ABS Diagnostic System Check*	—
10	Connect a fused jumper wire between the Stoplamp/BTSI switch harness connector terminals A and B. Do the brake lamps come on?	—	*Go to Step 11*	*Go to Step 6*
11	Adjust or repair the Stoplamp/BTSI switch as necessary. Is the repair complete?	—	Go to *ABS Diagnostic System Check*	—
12	1. Replace the STOP fuse. (Do not press the brake pedal.) 2. Check the STOP fuse. Is the fuse OK?	—	*Go to Step 14*	*Go to Step 13*
13	Repair the short to ground in CKT 640. Is the circuit repair complete?	—	Go to *ABS Diagnostic System Check*	—

GC402980275400DX

Fig. 89 Code C1291: Open Brake Lamp Switch Contact During Decel (Part 2 of 3). Park Avenue

Step	Action	Value(s)	Yes	No
14	1. Press the brake pedal. 2. Check the STOP fuse. Is the fuse OK?	—	Go to *ABS Diagnostic System Check*	*Go to Step 15*
15	1. Turn the ignition switch to the OFF position. 2. Disconnect the EBTCM. 3. Replace the fuse. 4. Turn the ignition switch to the RUN position with the engine off. 5. Press the brake pedal. 6. Check the STOP fuse. Is the fuse OK?	—	*Go to Step 5*	*Go to Step 16*
16	Repair the short to ground in CKT 20. Is the circuit repair complete?	—	Go to *ABS Diagnostic System Check*	—

GC402980275400EX

Fig. 89 Code C1291: Open Brake Lamp Switch Contact During Decel (Part 3 of 3). Park Avenue

Circuit Description

This DTC is the second portion of DTC C1291. If DTC C1291 occurred during the last ignition cycle, DTC C1293 becomes a current malfunction during the next ignition cycle, keeping the TCS disabled until a Stoplamp/BTSI switch On state is seen. When a change is seen during an ignition cycle in which DTC C1293 is a current malfunction, DTC C1291 will clear itself at the end of the current ignition cycle, and the TCS will enable at the start of the next ignition cycle. DTC C1293 alone indicates that DTC C1291 occurred previously, but is intermittent, or has been corrected.

Conditions for Setting the DTC

A DTC C1291 was set in the previous ignition cycle.

Action Taken When the DTC Sets

- A DTC C1293 is stored
- The TCS is disabled
- The TRACTION OFF indicator is turned on
- The ABS remains functional

Conditions for Clearing the DTC

- The condition for the DTC is no longer present and the scan tool clear DTC function is used
- 50 ignition cycles have passed with no DTCs detected

Diagnostic Aids

- Thoroughly inspect the wiring and the connectors. Failure to carefully and fully inspect the wiring and the connectors can result in misdiagnosis. Misdiagnosis may cause replacement of parts without repairing the malfunction.
- The following conditions may cause most intermittent malfunctions:
  - Poor connections
  - Rubbed through wire insulation
  - A broken wire inside the insulation
- Verify proper Stoplamp/BTSI switch operation during the Data List of the Scan Tool. As the brake is applied, the data list should display the Stoplamp/BTSI switch on within one inch of travel.

GC402980275500AX

Fig. 90 Code C1293: Code C1291 Set In Previous Ignition Cycle (Part 1 of 2). Bonneville, LeSabre & Park Avenue

Step	Action	Value(s)	Yes	No
1	Was the Diagnostic System Check performed?	—	*Go to Step 2*	Refer to *Diagnostic System Check*
2	1. Turn the ignition switch to the RUN position with the engine off. 2. Using a Scan Tool, read the ABS/TCS DTCs. Is DTC C1291 set as a history or current code?	—	Refer to DTC C1291	Refer to *Diagnostic System Check*

GC402980275500BX

Fig. 90 Code C1293: Code C1291 Set In Previous Ignition Cycle (Part 2 of 2). Bonneville, LeSabre & Park Avenue

Circuit Description

This DTC occurs when the internal self-checking safety logic has determined that the Stoplamp/BTSI switch is continuously on. This is important because the TCS cannot be activated when the Stoplamp/BTSI switch is on.

Conditions for Setting the DTC

A DTC C1294 can be set if the vehicle speed reaches at least 40 km/h (25 mph). A malfunction exists if the brake was never off during two consecutive drive cycles.

Action Taken When the DTC Sets

- A DTC C1294 is stored
- The TCS is disabled
- The TRACTION OFF indicator is turned on
- The ABS remains functional

Conditions for Clearing the DTC

- The condition for the DTC is no longer present and the scan tool clear DTC function is used
- 50 ignition cycles have passed with no DTCs detected

Diagnostic Aids

- Thoroughly inspect the wiring and the connectors. Failure to carefully and fully inspect the wiring and the connectors can result in misdiagnosis. Misdiagnosis may cause replacement of parts without repairing the malfunction.
- The following conditions may cause most intermittent malfunctions:
  - Poor connections
  - Rubbed through wire insulation
  - A broken wire inside the insulation
- The following conditions are other possible causes of this malfunction:
  - A short to voltage in the Stoplamp/BTSI switch circuit
  - A misadjusted or shorted Stoplamp/BTSI switch
- If an intermittent malfunction exists, Troubleshoot Electrical

Test Description

The numbers below refer to the step numbers on the diagnostic table.

4. This step checks for a short to voltage.

GC402980275600AX

Fig. 91 Code C1294: Brake Lamp Switch Circuit Always Active (Part 1 of 2). Bonneville & LeSabre

Step	Action	Value(s)	Yes	No
1	Was the Diagnostic System Check performed?	—	Go to Step 2	Go to Diagnostic System Check
2	Observe the rear brake lamps. Are the rear brake lamps off?	—	Go to Step 4	Go to Step 3
3	Disconnect the Stoplamp/BTSI switch connector. Are the brake lamps on?	—	Go to Step 6	Go to Step 7
4	1. Disconnect the EBTCM harness connector. 2. Install the J 39700 Universal Pinout Box using the J 39700-25 cable adapter to the EBTCM harness connector only. 3. Using the J 39200 DMM, measure the voltage between the J 39700 terminal 3 and ground. Is the voltage within specifications?	More than 1.0 V	Go to Step 6	Go to Step 5
5	1. Turn the ignition switch to the OFF position. 2. Inspect CKT 17 and the EBTCM harness connector for damage which may result in a short to voltage with all connectors connected. 3. Reconnect all connectors. 4. Drive the vehicle for three drive cycles. A drive cycle consists of starting the engine, driving above 40 km/h (25 mph) and back to 0 km/h (0 mph), then turning the ignition switch to the OFF position. Was DTC C1294 set in the last three drive cycles?	—	Go to Step 8	Go to Diagnostic System Check
6	Repair the short to voltage in CKT 17. Is the circuit repair complete?	—	Go to Diagnostic System Check	—
7	Adjust or replace the Stoplamp/BTSI switch as necessary. Is the repair complete?	—	Go to Diagnostic System Check	—
8	Replace the EBTCM. Is the replacement complete?	—	Go to Diagnostic System Check	—

GC402980275600BX

Fig. 91 Code C1294: Brake Lamp Switch Circuit Always Active (Part 2 of 2). Bonneville & LeSabre

Step	Action	Value(s)	Yes	No
1	Was the Diagnostic System Check performed?	—	Go to Step 2	Go to ABS Diagnostic System Check
2	Observe the rear brake lamps. Are the rear brake lamps off?	—	Go to Step 4	Go to Step 3
3	Disconnect the brake lamp switch connector. Are the brake lamps on?	—	Go to Step 6	Go to Step 7
4	1. Disconnect the EBTCM harness connector. 2. Install the J 39700 Universal Pinout Box using the J 39700-25 cable adapter to the EBTCM harness connector only. 3. Using the J 39200 DMM, measure the voltage between the J 39700 terminal 9 and ground. Is the voltage within specifications?	More than 1.0 V	Go to Step 6	Go to Step 5
5	1. Turn the ignition switch to the OFF position. 2. Inspect CKT 20 and the EBTCM harness connector for damage which may result in a short to voltage with all connectors connected. 3. Reconnect all connectors. 4. Drive the vehicle for three drive cycles. A drive cycle consists of starting the engine, driving above 40 km/h (25 mph) and back to 0 km/h (0 mph), then turning the ignition switch to the OFF position. Was DTC C1294 set in the last three drive cycles?	—	Go to Step 8	Go to ABS Diagnostic System Check
6	Repair the short to voltage in CKT 20. Is the circuit repair complete?	—	Go to ABS Diagnostic System Check	—
7	Adjust or replace the Stoplamp/BTSI switch as necessary. Is the repair complete?	—	Go to ABS Diagnostic System Check	—
8	Replace the EBTCM. Is the replacement complete?	—	Go to ABS Diagnostic System Check	—

GC402980275600CX

Fig. 92 Code C1294: Brake Lamp Switch Circuit Always Active (Part 2 of 2). Park Avenue

Circuit Description

This DTC occurs when internal self checking safety logic has determined that the stoplamp/BTSI switch is continuously "ON." This is important because the "TCS" can not be activated when the stoplamp/BTSI switch is "ON."

Condition For Setting The DTC

- DTC C1294 can be set if the vehicle speed reaches at least 40 km/h (25 mph). If the brake was never "OFF" during two consecutive drive cycles, a malfunction exists.

Action Taken When The DTC Sets

- A malfunction DTC is stored, "TCS" is disabled and the "TRACTION OFF" indicator lamp is turned "ON." ABS remains functional.

Conditions for Clearing DTC

- Condition for DTC is no longer present and scan tool clear DTC function is used.
- 50 Ignition cycles have passed with no DTC(s) detected.

Diagnostic Aids

- It is very important that a thorough inspection of the wiring and connectors be performed. Failure to carefully and fully inspect wiring and connectors may result in misdiagnosis, causing part replacement with reappearance of the malfunction.

Possible causes:

- stoplamp/BTSI switch circuit shorted to voltage.
- stoplamp/BTSI switch misadjusted or shorted.
- An "intermittent" malfunction is most likely caused by a poor connection, rubbed through wire insulation, or a wire that is broken inside the insulation.
- If an intermittent malfunction exists.

Test Description

The number below refer to the step number on the diagnostic table.

4. Checks for a short to voltage.

GC402980275602AX

Fig. 92 Code C1294: Brake Lamp Switch Circuit Always Active (Part 1 of 2). Park Avenue

Circuit Description

This DTC is used to identify open Stoplamp/BTSI switch circuitry that prevents the Stoplamp/BTSI switch input to the EBTCM from changing states when the brake is applied. This DTC is used in conjunction with DTC C1291 in order to determine the cause of an open Stoplamp/BTSI switch malfunction.

Conditions for Setting the DTC

DTC C1295 can be set after initialization is completed, if the Stoplamp/BTSI switch input voltage is not within specifications for one second, indicating an open circuit, a malfunction exists.

Action Taken When the DTC Sets

- A DTC C1295 is stored
- The TCS is disabled.
- The TRACTION OFF indicator is turned on
- The ABS remains functional

Conditions for Clearing the DTC

- The condition for the DTC is no longer present and the scan tool Clear DTC function is used
- 50 ignition cycles have passed with no DTCs detected

Diagnostic Aids

- Thoroughly inspect the wiring and the connectors. Failure to carefully and fully inspect the wiring and the connectors may result in misdiagnosis. Misdiagnosis may cause part replacement without repairing the malfunction.
- The following conditions may cause an intermittent malfunction:
  - A poor connection
  - Rubbed through wire insulation
  - A wire broken inside the insulation
- The following conditions are other possible causes for this malfunction:
  - An open in the Stoplamp/BTSI switch input circuit
  - An open in all of the brake lamps
  - An open or maladjusted brake lamp switch
  - A wiring problem, terminal corrosion or a poor connection in the circuit
- If an intermittent malfunction exists. Troubleshoot Electrical

Test Description

The numbers below refer to the step numbers on the diagnostic table.

3. This step checks for voltage at the EBTCM.
9. This step checks for stoplamp/BTSI switch.

GC402980271400AX

Fig. 93 Code C1295: Brake Lamp Switch Circuit Open (Part 1 of 3). Bonneville & LeSabre

Step	Action	Value(s)	Yes	No
1	Was the Diagnostic System Check performed?	—	Go to Step 2	Go to Diagnostic System Check
2	Press the brake pedal. Do the brake lights come on?	—	Go to Step 3	Go to Step 6
3	1. Turn the ignition switch to the OFF position. 2. Disconnect the EBTCM connector. 3. Install the J 39700 Universal Pinout Box using the J 39700-25 cable adapter to the EBTCM harness connector only. 4. Using the J 39200 DMM, measure the voltage at the J 39700 terminals 3 while an assistant presses the brake pedal. Is the voltage within specifications?	Battery voltage	Go to Step 4	Go to Step 5
4	Replace the EBTCM. Is the replacement complete?	—	Go to Diagnostic System Check	—
5	Repair the open or high resistance in CKT 17. Is the circuit repair complete?	—	Go to Diagnostic System Check	—
6	Check the BRAKE fuse in the I/P Fuse Block. Is the fuse OK?	—	Go to Step 7	Go to Step 11
7	1. Disconnect the Stoplamp/BTSI switch connector. 2. Using the J 39200, measure the voltage at the Stoplamp/BTSI switch harness connector terminal A. Is the voltage within specifications?	Battery voltage	Go to Step 9	Go to Step 8
8	Repair the open in CKT 140. Is the circuit repair complete?	—	Go to Diagnostic System Check	—
9	Connect a fused jumper wire between the Stoplamp/BTSI switch harness connector terminals A and B. Do the brake lamps come on?	—	Go to Step 10	Go to Step 5
10	Adjust or repair the Stoplamp/BTSI switch as necessary. Is the repair complete?	—	Go to Diagnostic System Check	—
11	1. Replace the BRAKE fuse. (Do not press the brake pedal.) 2. Check the BRAKE fuse. Is the fuse OK?	—	Go to Step 13	Go to Step 12
12	Repair the short to ground in CKT 140. Is the circuit repair complete?	—	Go to Diagnostic System Check	—
13	1. Press the brake pedal. 2. Check the BRAKE fuse. Is the fuse OK?	—	Go to Diagnostic System Check	Go to Step 14

GC402980271400BX

Fig. 93 Code C1295: Brake Lamp Switch Circuit Open (Part 2 of 3). Bonneville & LeSabre

Step	Action	Value(s)	Yes	No
14	1. Turn the ignition switch to the OFF position. 2. Disconnect the EBTCM. 3. Replace the fuse. 4. Depress the brake pedal. 5. Check the BRAKE fuse. Is the fuse OK?	—	Go to Step 4	Go to Step 15
15	Repair the short to ground in CKT 17. Is the circuit repair complete?	—	Go to Diagnostic System Check	—

GC402980271400CX

Fig. 93 Code C1295: Brake Lamp Switch Circuit Open (Part 3 of 3). Bonneville & LeSabre

Step	Action	Value(s)	Yes	No
1	Was the Diagnostic System Check performed?	—	Go to Step 2	Go to ABS Diagnostic System Check
2	Press the brake pedal. Do the brake lights come on?	—	Go to Step 3	Go to Step 6
3	1. Turn the ignition switch to the OFF position. 2. Disconnect the EBTCM connector. 3. Install the *J 39700* Universal Pinout Box using the *J 39700-25* cable adapter to the EBTCM harness connector only. 4. Using the *J 39200* DMM, measure the voltage at the *J 39700* terminals 9 while an assistant presses the brake pedal. Is the voltage within specifications?	Battery voltage	Go to Step 4	Go to Step 5
4	Replace the EBTCM. Is the replacement complete?	—	Go to ABS Diagnostic System Check	—
5	Repair the open or high resistance in CKT 20. Is the circuit repair complete?	—	Go to ABS Diagnostic System Check	—
6	Check the STOP fuse in the Underhood Junction Block. Is the fuse OK?	—	Go to Step 7	Go to Step 11
7	1. Disconnect the Stoplamp/BTSI switch connector. 2. Using the *J 39200*, measure the voltage at the Stoplamp/BTSI switch harness connector terminal A. Is the voltage within specifications?	Battery voltage	Go to Step 9	Go to Step 8
8	Repair the open in CKT 640. Is the circuit repair complete?	—	Go to ABS Diagnostic System Check	—
9	Connect a fused jumper wire between the Stoplamp/BTSI switch harness connector terminals A and B. Do the brake lamps come on?	—	Go to Step 10	Go to Step 5
10	Adjust or repair the Stoplamp/BTSI switch as necessary. Is the repair complete?	—	Go to ABS Diagnostic System Check	—
11	1. Replace the STOP fuse. (Do not press the brake pedal.) 2. Check the BRAKE fuse. Is the fuse OK?	—	Go to Step 13	Go to Step 12
12	Repair the short to ground in CKT 640. Is the circuit repair complete?	—	Go to ABS Diagnostic System Check	—
13	1. Press the brake pedal. 2. Check the STOP fuse. Is the fuse OK?	—	Go to ABS Diagnostic System Check	Go to Step 14

GC402980271400DX

Fig. 94 Code C1295: Brake Lamp Switch Circuit Open (Part 2 of 3). Park Avenue

Circuit Description

The Class 2 serial data line allows all the modules on the line to transmit information to each other as needed. Each module is assigned an ID and all the information sent out on the line is assigned a priority by which it is received. When the ignition switch is turned to the RUN position each module begins to send and receive information. Each module on the Class 2 serial data line knows what information it needs to send out and what information it should be receiving. What the modules do not know is which module is supposed to send them the information. This information is only learned after the module has received the information it needs along with the ID of the module that sent the information. This information is then remembered until the ignition switch is turned off.

Conditions for Setting the DTC

The ignition switch is in the RUN position and the PCM does not communicate with the EBTCM for 7 seconds

Action Taken When the DTC Sets

- A DTC C1298 is stored
- The TCS is disabled.
- The TRACTION OFF indicator is turned on
- The ABS remains functional

Conditions for Clearing the DTC

- The condition for the DTC is no longer present and the scan tool clear DTC function is used
- 50 ignition cycles have passed with no DTCs detected

Diagnostic Aids

- Thoroughly inspect the wiring and the connectors. Failure to carefully and fully inspect the wiring and the connectors may result in misdiagnosis. Misdiagnosis may cause part replacement without repairing the malfunction.
- The following conditions may cause an intermittent malfunction:
  - A poor connection
  - Rubbed through wire insulation
  - A wire broken inside the insulation

GC402980275800AX

Fig. 95 Code C1298: PCM Class 2 Serial Data Link Fault (Part 1 of 2). Park Avenue

Circuit Description

This DTC is used to identify open Stoplamp/BTSI switch circuitry that prevents the Stoplamp/BTSI switch input to the EBTCM from changing states when the brake is applied. This DTC is used in conjunction with DTC C1291 in order to determine the cause of an open Stoplamp/BTSI switch malfunction.

Conditions for Setting the DTC

DTC C1295 can be set after initialization is completed, if the Stoplamp/BTSI switch input voltage is not within specifications for one second, indicating an open circuit, a malfunction exists.

Action Taken When the DTC Sets

- A DTC C1295 is stored
- The TCS is disabled.
- The TRACTION OFF indicator is turned on
- The ABS remains functional

Conditions for Clearing the DTC

- The condition for the DTC is no longer present and the scan tool Clear DTC function is used
- 50 ignition cycles have passed with no DTCs detected

Diagnostic Aids

- Thoroughly inspect the wiring and the connectors. Failure to carefully and fully inspect the wiring and the connectors may result in misdiagnosis. Misdiagnosis may cause part replacement without repairing the malfunction.
- The following conditions may cause an intermittent malfunction:
  - A poor connection
  - Rubbed through wire insulation
  - A wire broken inside the insulation
- The following conditions are other possible causes for this malfunction:
  - An open in the Stoplamp/BTSI switch input circuit
  - An open in all of the brake lamps
  - An open or maladjusted brake lamp switch
  - A wiring problem, terminal corrosion or a poor connection in the circuit

Test Description

The numbers below refer to the step numbers on the diagnostic table.

3. This step checks for voltage at the EBTCM.
9. This step checks for stoplamp/BTSI switch.

GC402980271402AX

Fig. 94 Code C1295: Brake Lamp Switch Circuit Open (Part 1 of 3). Park Avenue

Step	Action	Value(s)	Yes	No
14	1. Turn the ignition switch to the OFF position. 2. Disconnect the EBTCM. 3. Replace the fuse. 4. Depress the brake pedal. 5. Check the BRAKE fuse. Is the fuse OK?	—	Go to Step 4	Go to Step 15
15	Repair the short to ground in CKT 20. Is the circuit repair complete?	—	Go to ABS Diagnostic System Check	—

GC402980271400EX

Fig. 94 Code C1295: Brake Lamp Switch Circuit Open (Part 3 of 3). Park Avenue

- The following conditions are other possible causes for this malfunction:
  - A Class 2 transmit fault on the EBTCM
  - A Class 2 receiver fault on the PCM
  - Extreme Class 2 bus traffic
  - A wiring problem, terminal corrosion, or a poor connection in the CKT 1807

Test Description

The numbers below refer to the step numbers on the diagnostic table.

5. This step checks to see if the SBM is sending the proper power mode position message.
6. This step checks to see if the EBTCM is sending out the required information on the Class 2 serial data line.

Step	Action	Value(s)	Yes	No
1	Was the Diagnostic System Check performed?	—	Go to Step 2	Refer to ABS Diagnostic System Check
2	Check the following grounds, G101, and G104 making sure each ground is clean tight and free of damage. Were any loose, damaged, or corroded grounds found?	—	Go to Step 3	Go to Step 4
3	Repair the ground(s) as necessary. Is the repair complete?	—	Refer to ABS Diagnostic System Check	—
4	1. Turn the ignition switch to the RUN position with the engine off. 2. Using a Scan Tool, read the ABS/TCS DTCs. Are any of the following DTCs present: U1016, or U1255?	—	Go to Applicable DTC Table	Go to Step 5
5	1. Using a Scan Tool in the ABS/TCS Data List, read the power mode position. 2. While reading the Scan Tool, turn the ignition switch to the following positions: OFF, UNLOCK, RUN, and CRANK. Does the Scan Tool read the proper power mode position?	—	Go to Step 6	Refer to ABS Diagnostic System Check
6	Using a Scan Tool in the Applications Menu, read the Class 2 Normal Mode Message Monitor. Is the EBTCM sending a Class 2 Normal Mode Message?	—	Go to Step 7	Go to Step 8
7	Suspect the PCM. Is the diagnosis complete?	—	Refer to ABS Diagnostic System Check	—
8	Replace the EBTCM. Is the replacement complete?	—	Refer to ABS Diagnostic System Check	—

GC402980275800BX

Fig. 95 Code C1298: PCM Class 2 Serial Data Link Fault (Part 2 of 2). Park Avenue

Circuit Description

The Class 2 serial data line allows all the modules on the line to transmit information to each other as needed. Each module is assigned an ID and all the information sent out on the line is assigned a priority by which it is received. When the ignition switch is turned to the RUN position each module begins to send and receive information. Each module on the Class 2 serial data line knows what information it needs to send out and what information it should be receiving. What the modules do not know is which module is supposed to send them the information. This information is only learned after the module has received the information it needs along with the ID of the module that sent the information. This information is then remembered until the ignition switch is turned off. If the EBTCM looses communication with the Powertrain Control Module (PCM) then DTC U1016 will be set by the EBTCM.

Conditions for Setting the DTC

The DTC can be set any time the ignition is in the RUN position, and the PCM does not communicate with the EBTCM for 5 seconds.

Action Taken When the DTC Sets

A malfunction DTC is stored, TCS is disabled and the TRACTION OFF indicator is turned on. ABS remains functional.

Conditions for Clearing the DTC

- Condition for DTC is no longer present and scan tool clear DTC function is used.
- Fifty ignition cycles have passed with no DTC(s) detected.

Diagnostic Aids

- It is very important that a thorough inspection of the wiring and connectors be performed. Failure to carefully and fully inspect wiring and connectors may result in misdiagnosis, causing part replacement with reappearance of the malfunction.
- An intermittent malfunction is most likely caused by a poor connection, rubbed through wire insulation, or a wire that is broken inside the insulation.

GC402980275900AX

Fig. 96 Code U1016: Loss Of Communications w/PCM (Part 1 of 2). Park Avenue

Step	Action	Value(s)	Yes	No
1	Was the Diagnostic System Check performed?	—	*Go to Step 2*	Go to *ABS Diagnostic System Check*
2	Using a scan tool read the IPC DTC(s). Is DTC U1016 also set as a current IPC DTC?	—	Go to *Powertrain OBD System Check*	*Go to Step 3*
3	Is DTC U1016 set as a current ABS/TCS DTC?	—	*Go to Step 4*	Go to *ABS Diagnostic System Check*
4	Replace the EBTCM. Is the replacement complete?	—	Go to *ABS Diagnostic System Check*	—

GC402980275900BX

Fig. 96 Code U1016: Loss Of Communications w/PCM (Part 2 of 2). Park Avenue

Circuit Description

The Class 2 serial data line allows all the modules on the line to transmit information to each other as needed. Each module is assigned an ID and all the information sent out on the line is assigned a priority by which it is received. When the ignition switch is turned to the RUN position each module begins to send and receive information. Each module on the Class 2 serial data line knows what information it needs to send out and what information it should be receiving. What the modules do not know is which module is supposed to send them the information. This information is only learned after the module has received the information it needs along with the ID of the module that sent the information. This information is then remembered until the ignition switch is turned off. If the EBCM/EBTCM never receives the information or the ID of the module that is supposed to send the information DTC U1255 will be set.

Conditions for Setting the DTC

- The DTC can be set when the ignition is turned to the RUN position, and the EBCM/EBTCM does not receive the PCM ID for 5 seconds.

Action Taken When the DTC Sets

- A malfunction DTC is stored, TCS is disabled and the Traction Control indicator is turned on. ABS remains functional.

Conditions for Clearing the DTC

- Condition for DTC is no longer present and scan tool clear DTC function is used.
- Fifty ignition cycles have passed with no DTC(s) detected.

Diagnostic Aids

- It is very important that a thorough inspection of the wiring and connectors be performed. Failure to carefully and fully inspect wiring and connectors may result in misdiagnosis, causing part replacement with reappearance of the malfunction.
- An intermittent malfunction is most likely caused by a poor connection, rubbed through wire insulation, or a wire that is broken inside the insulation.

Possible Causes

- Class 2 transmit fault on the PCM.
- Class 2 receiver fault on the EBTCM.
- Open Class 2 line.

GC402980276000AX

Fig. 97 Code U1255: Generic Loss Of Communications (Part 1 of 2). Park Avenue

Step	Action	Value(s)	Yes	No
1	Was the Diagnostic System Check performed?	—	*Go to Step 2*	Go to *ABS Diagnostic System Check*
2	1. Turn the ignition switch to the ON position, engine off. 2. Using a scan tool go to the System Selection Menu's Diagnostic Circuit Check and enter the Class 2 Message Monitor. Does the PCM read Active?	—	*Go to Step 3*	Inspect *Powertrain OBD System*
3	Does the IPC read Active?	—	*Go to Step 4*	Inspect Instrument Panel, Gauges and Console
4	Does the BCM read Active?	—	*Go to Step 5*	Inspect BCM Diagnostic System Check in Body Control System
5	Replace EBCM/EBTCM. Is the replacement complete?	—	Go to *ABS Diagnostic System Check*	—

GC402980276000BX

Fig. 97 Code U1255: Generic Loss Of Communications (Part 2 of 2). Park Avenue

Circuit Description

The "ABS" Indicator lamp driver circuit runs from the Instrument Panel Cluster (IPC) through the Lamp Driver Module (LDM) to the EBCM/EBTCM. The IPC supplies voltage to the indicator lamp. The EBCM/EBTCM controls the "ABS" indicator through the LDM. The LDM acts as an invertor when the EBCM/EBTCM supplies a ground for the LDM the indicator lamp remains "OFF." When the EBCM/EBTCM removes the ground for the LDM the indicator lamp turns "ON" by using the ground at the LDM terminal "D."

Diagnostic Aids

- It is very important that a thorough inspection of the wiring and connectors be performed. Failure to carefully and fully inspect wiring and connectors may result in misdiagnosis, causing part replacement with reappearance of the malfunction.
- If the indicator lamp is "ON" then the battery voltage to terminal "B" and the ground at terminal "D" at the LDM are OK.
- If the indicator remains "ON" and there are no DTC(s) then the cause is either CKT 875 shorted to ground, a malfunctioning LDM, or a malfunctioning EBCM/EBTCM.
- If CKT 852 is open, shorted to ground, or shorted to voltage, the EBCM/EBTCM will set a DTC.

Table Test Description

The numbers below refer to step numbers on the diagnostic table.

2. Checks to see if the EBCM/EBTCM is not capable of supplying the ground.
4. Checking to see if CKT 875 is shorted to ground.

GC402970270000AX

Fig. 98 Test A: ABS Lamp On w/No Code Set (Part 1 of 2). Bonneville & LeSabre

Step	Action	Value(s)	Yes	No
1	Was the Diagnostic System Check performed?	—	Go to Step 2	Go to Diagnostic System Check
2	1. Turn the ignition switch to the OFF position. 2. Disconnect the EBCM/EBTCM connector. 3. Connect J 39700 Universal pinout box using J 39700-25 to the EBCM/EBTCM harness only. 4. Connect a fused jumper between terminal 13 and ground terminal B of J 39700 Universal pinout box. 5. Turn the ignition switch to the RUN position, engine OFF. Does the ABS indicator turn OFF?	—	Go to Step 3	Go to Step 4
3	Replace the EBCM/EBTCM. Is the replacement complete?	—	Go to Diagnostic System Check	—
4	1. Turn the ignition switch to the OFF position. 2. Remove the fused jumper. 3. Disconnect the lamp driver module. 4. Turn the ignition switch to the RUN position, engine OFF. Is the ABS indicator ON?	—	Go to Step 5	Go to Step 6
5	Repair CKT 875 for a short to ground. Is the repair complete?	—	Go to Diagnostic System Check	
6	Replace the lamp driver module. Is the replacement complete?	—	Go to Diagnostic System Check	—

GC402970270000BX

Fig. 98 Test A: ABS Lamp On w/No Code Set (Part 2 of 2). Bonneville & LeSabre

Circuit Description

The Instrument Panel Cluster (IPC) turn the ABS Indicator on during the IPC bulb check for approximately 3 seconds when the ignition switch is turned to the RUN position. If the EBCM/EBTCM sets a Diagnostic Trouble Code (DTC) the EBCM/EBTCM sends the IPC the command to turn the ABS Indicator on.

Test Description

The numbers below refer to step numbers on the diagnostic table.

2. Checks if the Instrument Panel Cluster has the ability to turn the ABS indicator off or if the EBCM/EBTCM is sending an incorrect command to turn the ABS indicator on.

Step	Action	Value(s)	Yes	No
DEFINITION: The ABS Indicator does not turn off after the Instrument Panel Cluster (IPC) bulb check and no ABS/TCS DTC(s) set.				
1	Was the Diagnostic System Check performed?	—	*Go to Step 2*	Go to *ABS Diagnostic System Check*
2	Using a scan tool in the ABS/TCS Special Functions attempt to turn off the ABS Indicator. Did the ABS Indicator Turn off?	—	*Go to Step 3*	*Go to Step 4*
3	Replace the EBCM/EBTCM. Is the Replacement complete?	—	Go to *ABS Diagnostic System Check*	—
4	Replace the Instrument Panel Cluster. Is the Replacement complete?	—	Go to *ABS Diagnostic System Check*	—

GC4029802706000X

Fig. 99 Test A: ABS Lamp On w/No Code Set. Park Avenue

Step	Action	Value(s)	Yes	No
1	Was the Diagnostic System Check performed?	—	*Go to Step 2*	Go to *Diagnostic System Check*
2	1. Turn the ignition switch to the OFF position. 2. Disconnect the EBCM/EBTCM. 3. Turn the ignition switch to the RUN position. Do not start the engine. Does the ABS indicator turn on?	—	*Go to Step 16*	*Go to Step 3*
3	1. Turn the ignition switch to the OFF position. 2. Reconnect the EBCM/EBTCM. 3. Check the fuse D1 in the IP Fuse Block. Is the fuse OK?	—	*Go to Step 4*	*Go to Step 5*
4	1. Install the fuse, if removed. 2. Turn the ignition switch to the RUN position. Don't start the engine. 3. Using *J 39200* DMM, check the voltage at the fuse test terminals. Is the voltage within the range specified in the values column?	Battery volts	*Go to Step 6*	Inspect Power Distribution
5	1. Turn the ignition switch to the OFF position. 2. Remove fuse D1. 3. Disconnect the LDM. 4. Using *J 39200* DMM, measure the resistance between terminal B of the LDM harness connector and a good ground. Is the resistance within the range specified in the values column?	OL (infinite)	*Go to Step 9*	*Go to Step 8*
6	1. Turn the ignition switch to the OFF position. 2. Disconnect LDM connector. 3. Turn the ignition switch to the RUN position. Do not start the engine. 4. Using *J 39200* DMM, measure the voltage at terminal B of the LDM harness connector. Is the voltage within the range specified in the value column?	Battery volts	*Go to Step 7*	*Go to Step 17*
7	Using *J 39200* DMM, measure the voltage at terminal E of the LDM harness connector. Is the voltage within the range specified in the values column?	Battery volts	*Go to Step 10*	*Go to Step 11*
8	Repair CKT 39 for a short to ground. Is the repair complete?	—	Go to *Diagnostic System Check*	—
9	1. Replace the fuse. 2. Reconnect the LDM. 3. Turn the ignition switch to the RUN position. Do not start the engine. 4. Recheck fuse D1 in the IP Fuse Block. Is the fuse OK?	—	Go to *Diagnostic System Check*	*Go to Step 12*

GC402980270100BX

Fig. 100 Test B: ABS Lamp Inoperative w/No Code Set (Part 2 of 3). Bonneville & LeSabre

Circuit Description

The ABS Indicator driver circuit runs from the Instrument Panel Cluster (IPC) through the Lamp Driver Module (LDM) to the EBCM/EBTCM. The IPC supplies voltage to the ABS indicator. The EBCM/EBTCM controls the ABS indicator through the LDM. The LDM acts as an inventor. When the EBCM/EBTCM supplies a ground for the LDM the ABS indicator remains Off. When the EBCM/EBTCM removes the ground for the LDM the ABS indicator turns On by using the ground at the LDM terminal D.

Diagnostic Aids

- Perform a thorough inspection of the wiring and connectors. Failure to carefully and fully inspect wiring and connectors may result in misdiagnosis, causing part replacement with reappearance of the malfunction.
- In order for the ABS indicator to come On, there must be battery voltage at terminal B of the LDM and a good ground at terminal D of the LDM.
- If the ABS indicator does not come On and there are no DTCs, then the cause may be one of the following:
  - A malfunctioning LDM
  - CKT 875 is open
  - No power or ground for the LDM
  - A malfunctioning IPC
  - A damaged ABS indicator bulb
- The EBCM/EBTM sets a DTC when CKT 852 is open, shorted to ground, or shorted to voltage
- More than one indicator bulb will be inoperative if the battery feed to the IPC indicators is open

Test Description

The number(s) below refer to the step number(s) on the diagnostic table.

2. This step checks if the EBCM/EBTCM is not capable of removing the ground for CKT 852
5. This step checks for a short to ground in CKT 39.
6. This step checks for voltage at LDM.
7. This step checks for voltage from IPC.
10. This step checks if LDM has a good ground.

GC402980270100AX

Fig. 100 Test B: ABS Lamp Inoperative w/No Code Set (Part 1 of 3). Bonneville & LeSabre

Step	Action	Value(s)	Yes	No
10	1. Turn the ignition switch to the OFF position. 2. Using *J 39200* DMM, measure the resistance between terminal D of the LDM harness connector and a good ground. Is the resistance within the range specified in the values column?	0–2 Ω	*Go to Step 12*	*Go to Step 13*
11	1. Turn the ignition switch to the OFF position. 2. Disconnect IPC connector C1. 3. Connect a fused jumper wire between CKT 875 of the IPC harness connector and a good ground. 4. Using *J 39200* DMM, measure the resistance between the LDM harness connector terminal E and a good ground. Is the resistance within the range specified in the values column?	0–2 Ω	*Go to Step 14*	*Go to Step 15*
12	Replace the LDM. Is the replacement complete?	—	Go to *Diagnostic System Check*	—
13	Repair CKT 1250 for an open. Is the repair complete?	—	Go to *Diagnostic System Check*	—
14	Repair IPC as necessary being sure to check the ABS indicator bulb. Is the repair complete?	—	Go to *Diagnostic System Check*	—
15	Repair an open or high resistance in CKT 875. Is the repair complete?	—	Go to *Diagnostic System Check*	—
16	Replace the EBCM/EBTCM. Is the replacement complete?	—	Go to *Diagnostic System Check*	—
17	Repair an open or high resistance in CKT 39. Is the repair complete?	—	Go to *Diagnostic System Check*	—

GC402980270100CX

Fig. 100 Test B: ABS Lamp Inoperative w/No Code Set (Part 3 of 3). Bonneville & LeSabre

Circuit Description

The instrument cluster turns the ABS indicator ON during the instrument cluster bulb check for approximately 3 seconds when the ignition switch is turned to the RUN position. If the EBCM/EBTCM sets a DTC, the EBCM/EBTCM sends the instrument cluster the command to turn the ABS indicator ON.

Test Description

The numbers below refer to step numbers on the diagnostic table.

2. This step tests if the instrument cluster has the ability to turn the ABS indicator ON.

Step	Action	Value(s)	Yes	No
DEFINITION: The ABS indicator does not come ON during the instrument cluster bulb check.				
1	Was the ABS Diagnostic System Check performed?	—	Go to *Step 2*	Go to *ABS Diagnostic System Check*
2	Using a scan tool in ABS/TCS Special Functions, attempt to turn the ABS indicator ON. Did the ABS indicator turn ON?	—	Go to *Step 3*	Go to *Step 4*
3	Replace the EBCM/EBTCM. Is the repair complete?	—	Go to *ABS Diagnostic System Check*	—
4	Replace the instrument cluster. Is the repair complete?	—	Go to *ABS Diagnostic System Check*	—

GC4029903943000X

Fig. 101 Test B: ABS Lamp Inoperative w/No Code Set. Park Avenue

Circuit Description

If the vehicle is equipped with a U23, or a UH8 IPC, then the TRACTION OFF indicator is controlled by the serial data transmitted over the UART line from the EBTCM to the IPC.

If the vehicle is equipped with and IPC other then those stated above, then the TRACTION OFF indicator driver circuit runs from the IPC through the Lamp Driver Module (LDM) to the EBTCM. The indicator is supplied voltage from the IPC. The EBTCM controls the TRACTION OFF indicator through the LDM. The LDM acts as an invertor, when the EBTCM supplies a ground for the LDM, the indicator remains off. When the EBTCM removes the ground for the LDM, the indicator turns on by using the ground at the LDM terminal D. When the Traction Control switch is pressed, the EBTCM sees the voltage on CKT 1571 go low, the EBTCM disables Traction Control and removes the ground for the TRACTION OFF indicator and the indicator turns on.

Diagnostic Aids

1. Buick uses two clusters: the U23 and the UB3. The U23 TRACTION OFF indicator is controlled by messages over the UART serial data line. The UB3 cluster is hard wired through the LDM to the EBTCM. The EBTCM controls the TRACTION OFF indicator.
2. Oldsmobile uses one cluster: the UH8. The UH8 TRACTION OFF indicator is controlled by the UART serial data line.
3. Pontiac uses three different clusters: the UB3, the U50, and the U2F. All of these clusters are hard wired through the LDM to the EBTCM. The EBTCM controls the TRACTION OFF indicator.
4. If the ABS indicator is on, then the TRACTION OFF indicator will also be on, always check the ABS Indicator first.

Test Description

The number below refer to the step number on the diagnostic table.

2. This step checks to see if the cluster is hard wired, or controlled by serial data.

GC402980269500AX

Fig. 102 Test C: Traction Off Lamp On w/No Code Set (Part 1 of 3). Bonneville & LeSabre

Step	Action	Value(s)	Yes	No
10	Replace the EBTCM. Is the replacement complete?	—	Go to *Diagnostic System Check*	—
11	1. Turn the ignition switch to the OFF position. 2. Disconnect the Lamp Driver Module. 3. Leave the fused jumper wire between terminals 7 and B of *J 39700*. 4. Using *J 39200* DMM, measure the resistance between the LDM harness connector terminal F and a good ground. Is the resistance with the range specified in the values column?	0-2 Ω	*Go to Step 12*	*Go to Step 15*
12	Turn the ignition switch to the RUN position. Do not start the engine. Is the TRACTION OFF indicator on?	—	*Go to Step 13*	*Go to Step 14*
13	Repair CKT 1660 for a short to ground. Is the repair complete?	—	Go to *Diagnostic System Check*	—
14	Replace the LDM. Is the replacement complete?	—	Go to *Diagnostic System Check*	—
15	Repair CKT 1572 for an open. Is the repair complete?	—	Go to *Diagnostic System Check*	—

GC402980269500CX

Fig. 102 Test C: Traction Off Lamp On w/No Code Set (Part 3 of 3). Bonneville & LeSabre

Step	Action	Value(s)	Yes	No
1	Was the Diagnostic System Check performed?	—	*Go to Step 2*	Refer to *ABS Diagnostic System Check*
2	1. Turn the ignition switch to the RUN position with the engine off. 2. Using a Scan Tool, enter ABS Data List. 3. While monitoring the TCS ON/OFF switch status, press and release the TCS switch. Does the switch status change from pressed to released as the TCS switch is pressed and released?	—	*Go to Step 5*	*Go to Step 3*
3	1. Turn the ignition switch to the OFF position. 2. Disconnect the EBTCM. 3. Install the *J 39700* and the *J 39700-25* to the EBTCM harness connector only. 4. Using the *J 39200*, measure the resistance between terminals 24 and B of the *J 39700*. Is the resistance within specifications?	OL	*Go to Step 6*	*Go to Step 4*
4	Repair the short to ground in CKT 1571, being sure to check the traction control switch for a short. Is the circuit repair complete?	—	Refer to *ABS Diagnostic System Check*	—
5	1. Using a Scan Tool, enter the ABS Special Functions. 2. Command the TRACTION OFF indicator off. Did the indicator turn off?	—	*Go to Step 6*	*Go to Step 7*
6	Replace the EBTCM. Is the repair complete?	—	Refer to *ABS Diagnostic System Check*	—
7	Suspect the IPC. Is the diagnosis complete?	—	Refer to *ABS Diagnostic System Check*	—

GC402980270300BX

Fig. 103 Test C: Traction Off Lamp On w/No Code Set (Part 2 of 2). Park Avenue

Step	Action	Value(s)	Yes	No
1	Was the Diagnostic System Check performed?	—	*Go to Step 2*	Go to
2	Is this vehicle equipped with a U23, or a UH8 instrument panel cluster?	—	*Go to Step 3*	*Go to Step 8*
3	1. Turn the ignition switch to the RUN position. Do not start the engine. 2. Use a scan tool in order to enter ABS Data List. 3. While monitoring the TCS ON/OFF Switch status, press and release the TCS switch. Does the switch status change from pressed to released as the TCS switch is pressed and released?	—	*Go to Step 6*	*Go to Step 4*
4	1. Turn the ignition switch to the OFF position. 2. Install *J 39700* Universal Pinout Box using *J 39700-25* cable adapter to the harness connector only. 3. Using *J 39200* DMM, measure the resistance between terminal 2 and B of *J 39700*. Is the resistance within the range specified in the values column?	OL (infinite)	*Go to Step 10*	*Go to Step 5*
5	Repair CKT 1571 for a short to ground. Is the repair complete?	—	Go to *Diagnostic System Check*	—
6	1. Turn the ignition switch to the RUN position. Do no start the engine. 2. With a scan tool in ABS/TCS Special Tests, command the TRACTION OFF indicator off. Does the indicator turn off?	—	*Go to Step 10*	*Go to Step 7*
7	Suspect IPC. Is the diagnosis complete?	—	Go to *Diagnostic System Check*	—
8	1. Turn the ignition switch to the RUN position. Do not start the engine. 2. Use a scan tool in order to enter ABS Data List. 3. While monitoring the TCS ON/OFF Switch status, press and release the TCS switch. Does the switch status change fro pressed to released as the TCS switch is pressed and released?	—	*Go to Step 9*	*Go to Step 4*
9	1. Turn the ignition switch to the OFF position. 2. Disconnect the EBTCM connector. 3. Connect *J 39700* Universal Pinout Box using the *J 39700-25* cable adapter between the EBTCM and the EBTCM harness connector. 4. Connect a fused jumper between the EBTCM connector terminal 7 and ground terminal B. 5. Turn the ignition switch to the RUN position. Do not start the engine. Does the TRACTION OFF indicator turn off?	—	*Go to Step 10*	*Go to Step 11*

GC402980269500BX

Fig. 102 Test C: Traction Off Lamp On w/No Code Set (Part 2 of 3). Bonneville & LeSabre

Circuit Description

The class 2 serial data line from the EBTCM controls the TRACTION OFF indicator. When the EBTCM sees the traction control line go low through the momentary traction control switch, the EBTCM disables the TCS and sends a message to the IPC to turn the TRACTION OFF indicator on. Each time the ignition switch is cycled from the OFF to the RUN position, the TCS is enabled until the traction control switch is pressed.

Diagnostic Aids

- Thoroughly inspect the wiring and the connectors. Failure to carefully and fully inspect the wiring and the connectors may result in misdiagnosis. Misdiagnosis may cause part replacement without repairing the malfunction.
- Inspect all related connectors for corrosion or damage. Repair as necessary.

Test Description

The numbers below refer to the step numbers on the diagnostic table.

3. This step checks for a short to ground in the traction control switch or CKT.
5. This step checks if the IPC has the ability to control the indicator.

GC402980270300AX

Fig. 103 Test C: Traction Off Lamp On w/No Code Set (Part 1 of 2). Park Avenue

Circuit Description

For vehicles equipped with a U23 or a UH8 instrument cluster, the TRACTION OFF indicator is controlled by the EBCM/EBTCM via serial data UART.

For vehicles equipped with a UB3, a U2F, or a U50 instrument cluster, the TRACTION OFF indicator is controlled by the EBCM/EBTCM via the brake lamp driver module. The instrument cluster or remote indicator bank supplies voltage to the indicator. The brake lamp driver module acts as an inverter. When the EBCM/EBTCM supplies ground to the brake lamp driver module, the indicator remains OFF. When the EBCM/EBTCM removes ground from the brake lamp driver module, the brake lamp driver module supplies ground to the TRACTION OFF indicator.

Diagnostic Aids

- Buick uses the U23 and the UB3 instrument clusters.
- Oldsmobile uses the UH8 instrument cluster.
- Pontiac uses the UB3, the U2F, and the U50 instrument clusters.
- It is very important that a thorough inspection of the wiring and connectors be performed. Failure to carefully and fully inspect wiring and connectors may result in misdiagnosis, causing part replacement with reappearance of the malfunction.
- An intermittent malfunction can be caused by poor connections, broken insulation, or a wire that is broken inside the insulation.
- If an intermittent malfunction exists, refer to *Intermittents*

GC4029903938010X

Fig. 104 Test D: Traction Off Lamp Inoperative w/No Code Set (Part 1 of 3). Bonneville & LeSabre

Step	Action	Value(s)	Yes	No
1	Was the Diagnostic System Check performed?	—	Go to Step 2	Go to Diagnostic System Check
2	Is this vehicle equipped with a U23, or a UH8 Instrument cluster?	—	Go to Step 3	Go to Step 9
3	1. Turn the ignition switch to the RUN position, engine OFF. 2. Using a scan tool enter ABS Data List. 3. While monitoring the TCS On/Off Switch status, press and release the TCS switch. Does the switch status change from pressed to released as the TCS switch is pressed and released.	—	Go to Step 4	Go to Step 28
4	Using the scan tool in ABS/TCS Special Tests, command the "TRACTION OFF" indicator ON. Does the indicator come ON?	—	Go to Step 5	Go to Step 6
5	Replace the EBTCM. Is the replacement complete?	—	Go to Diagnostic System Check	—
6	Check the "TRACTION OFF" indicator bulb. Is the bulb OK?	—	Go to Step 7	Go to Step 8
7	Suspect IPC. Refer to SECTION 8A. Is the diagnosis complete?	—	Go to Diagnostic System Check	—
8	Replace the TRACTION OFF indicator bulb. Is the replacement complete?	—	Go to Diagnostic System Check	—
9	1. Turn the ignition switch to the RUN position, engine OFF. 2. Using a scan tool enter ABS Data List. 3. While monitoring the TCS On/Off Switch status, press and release the TCS switch. Does the switch status change from pressed to released as the TCS switch is pressed and released.	—	Go to Step 10	Go to Step 28
10	1. Turn the ignition switch to the OFF position. 2. Disconnect the EBTCM. 3. Turn the ignition switch to the RUN position, engine OFF. Does the TRACTION OFF Indicator come ON?	—	Go to Step 26	Go to Step 11
11	1. Turn the ignition switch to the OFF position. 2. Check fuse D1 in the I/P fuse block. Is the fuse OK?	—	Go to Step 12	Go to Step 13

GC4029903938020X

Fig. 104 Test D: Traction Off Lamp Inoperative w/No Code Set (Part 2 of 3). Bonneville & LeSabre

Step	Action	Value(s)	Yes	No
12	1. Install the fuse, if removed. 2. Turn the ignition switch to the RUN position, engine OFF. 3. Using J 39200, check voltage at the fuse test terminals. Is the voltage within the range specified in the value(s) column?	Battery volts	Go to Step 14	Go to Power Distribution 8A-10
13	1. Turn the ignition switch to the OFF position. 2. Remove fuse D1. 3. Disconnect the LDM. 4. Using J 39200, check the resistance between terminal B of the LDM connector harness side and a good ground. Is the resistance within the range specified in the value(s) column?	OL	Go to Step 17	Go to Step 16
14	1. Turn the ignition switch to the OFF position. 2. Disconnect LDM connector. 3. Turn the Ignition switch to the RUN position, engine OFF. 4. Using J 39200, check the voltage at terminal B of the LDM connector harness side. Is the voltage within the range specified in the value(s) column?	Battery volts	Go to Step 15	Go to Step 27
15	Check voltage at terminal A of the LDM connector harness side. Is the voltage within the range specified in the value(s) column?	Battery volts	Go to Step 18	Go to Step 19
16	Repair CKT 39 for a short to ground. Is the repair complete?	—	Go to Diagnostic System Check	—
17	1. Replace the fuse. 2. Reconnect the LDM. 3. Turn the ignition switch to the RUN position, engine OFF. 4. Recheck fuse D1 in the I/P fuse block. Is the fuse OK?	—	Go to Diagnostic System Check	Go to Step 21
18	1. Turn the ignition switch to the OFF position. 2. Using J 39200, check resistance from terminal D of the LDM connector harness side to a good ground. Is the resistance within the range specified in the value(s) column?	0 - 2 Ω	Go to Step 20	Go to Step 23
19	1. Turn the ignition switch to the OFF position. 2. Disconnect IPC connector C1. 3. Connect a fused jumper wire between CKT 1660 of the IPC connector harness side to a good ground. 4. Using J 39200, check the resistance between the LDM connector harness side terminal A and a good ground. Is the resistance within the range specified in the value(s) column?	0 - 2 Ω	Go to Step 24	Go to Step 25

GC4029903938030X

Fig. 104 Test D: Traction Off Lamp Inoperative w/No Code Set (Part 3 of 3). Bonneville & LeSabre

Circuit Description

The instrument cluster controls the operation of the TRAC OFF indicator. The EBCM/EBTCM receives a traction control input when the traction control switch is pressed. The EBCM/EBTCM disables the TCS then sends a serial data class 2 message to the instrument cluster to turn the TRAC OFF indicator ON. Each time the ignition switch is cycled from the OFF to the RUN position, the TCS is enabled until the traction control switch is pressed.

Diagnostic Aids

- It is very important that a thorough inspection of the wiring and connectors be performed. Failure to carefully and fully inspect wiring and connectors may result in misdiagnosis, causing part replacement with reappearance of the malfunction.
- An intermittent malfunction can be caused by poor connections, broken insulation, or a wire that is broken inside the insulation.
- If an intermittent malfunction exists, refer to *Intermittents and Poor Connections*

Test Description

The number below refers to the step number on the diagnostic table:

2. This step tests if the instrument cluster has the ability to control the indicator.

GC4029903941010X

Fig. 105 Test D: Traction Off Lamp Inoperative w/No Code Set (Part 1 of 2). Park Avenue

Step	Action	Value(s)	Yes	No
1	Was the ABS Diagnostic System Check performed?	—	Go to *Step 2*	Go to *ABS Diagnostic System Check*
2	1. Use a scan tool in order to enter the Instrument Cluster Special Functions. 2. Run the instrument cluster indicator lamp test (WOW the dash). Did the TRAC OFF indicator turn ON then turn OFF?	—	Go to *Step 3*	Go to *Step 7*
3	1. Turn the ignition switch to the OFF position. 2. Disconnect the EBCM/EBTCM. 3. Install the *J 39700* and the *J 39700 - 25* to the EBCM/EBTCM harness connector only. 4. Press and hold the traction control switch. 5. Using the *J 39200*, measure the resistance between terminal 24 and terminal B of the *J 39700*. Is the resistance within the specified range?	5–15 Ω	Go to *Step 6*	Go to *Step 4*
4	1. Disconnect the traction control switch connector. 2. Using the *J 39200*, measure the resistance between terminal 24 of the *J 39700* and the traction control switch connector terminal A. Is the resistance less than the specified value?	5 Ω	Go to *Step 5*	Go to *Step 8*
5	Measure the resistance between the traction control switch connector terminal A and a good ground. Is the resistance less than the specified value?	5 Ω	Go to *Step 9*	Go to *Step 10*
6	Replace the EBCM/EBTCM. Is the repair complete?	—	Go to *ABS Diagnostic System Check*	—
7	Suspect the instrument cluster. Is the diagnosis complete?	—	Go to *ABS Diagnostic System Check*	—
8	Repair the open in CKT 1571. Is the circuit repair complete?	—	Go to *ABS Diagnostic System Check*	—
9	Replace the traction control switch. Is the repair complete?	—	Go to *ABS Diagnostic System Check*	—
10	Repair the open in CKT 351. Is the circuit repair complete?	—	Go to *ABS Diagnostic System Check*	—

GC4029903941020X

Fig. 105 Test D: Traction Off Lamp Inoperative w/No Code Set (Part 2 of 2). Park Avenue

Circuit Description

The TRACTION ACTIVE indicator is used only on Oldsmobile. The TRACTION ACTIVE indicator is controlled by serial data over the UART lines form the EBTCM.

Diagnostic Aids

Perform a through inspection of the wiring and connectors. Failure to carefully and fully inspect wiring and connectors may result in misdiagnosis, causing part replacement with reappearance of the malfunction.

Test Description

The number below refer to the step number on the diagnostic table.

2. This step check if the IPC has the ability to turn the indicator OFF.

Step	Action	Value(s)	Yes	No
1	Was the Diagnostic System Check performed?	—	*Go to Step 2*	Go to *Diagnostic System Check*
2	With a scan tool in ABS/TCS Special Tests command the TRACTION ACTIVE indicator off. Does the TRACTION ACTIVE indicator turn off?	—	*Go to Step 3*	*Go to Step 4*
3	Replace the EBTCM. Is the replacement complete?	—	Go to *Diagnostic System Check*	—
4	Suspect IPC. Is the diagnosis complete?	—	Go to *Diagnostic System Check*	—

GC4029802698000X

Fig. 106 Test E: Traction Active Lamp On w/No Code Set. Bonneville & LeSabre

Circuit Description

The UART serial data link allows information to be exchanged from module to module as needed. This is done by the PCM, the PCM requests and sends all the information that is transmitted on the UART line. When a scan tool is connected to the UART line it takes over for the PCM and sends and requests the needed information.

Diagnostic Aids

- Thoroughly inspect the wiring and the connectors. Failure to carefully and fully inspect the wiring and the connectors can result in misdiagnosis. Misdiagnosis may cause replacement of parts without repairing the malfunction.

Step	Action	Value(s)	Yes	No
DEFINITION: Scan tool can not communicate with the EBCM/EBTCM.				
1	Was the Diagnostic System Check performed?	—	*Go to Step 2*	Go to *Diagnostic System Check*
2	Turn the Ignition switch to the RUN position with the engine off. Can the scan tool communicate with other modules on the UART serial data line, such as the PCM?	—	*Go to Step 3*	Inspect Data Link Connector
3	Inspect the 10A ABS/CCR fuse in the I/P Fuse Block. Is the fuse OK?	—	*Go to Step 4*	*Go to Step 9*
4	Inspect the 40A ABS Solenoid fuse in the LH Maxifuse Block. Is the fuse OK?	—	*Go to Step 12*	*Go to Step 5*

GC402980269700AX

Fig. 108 Test G: No Communication w/EBCM/EBTCM (Part 1 of 3). Bonneville & LeSabre

Step	Action	Value(s)	Yes	No
14	1. Turn the ignition switch to the OFF position. 2. Disconnect the EBCM/EBTCM connector. 3. Connect the *J 39700* Universal Pinout Box using the *J 39700-25* cable adapter to the EBCM/EBTCM harness connector only. 4. Using *J 39200* DMM, measure the resistance between *J 39700* terminal B and a good ground. Is the resistance within the range specified in the value(s) column?	0 - 2Ω	*Go to Step 16*	*Go to Step 15*
15	Repair CKT 1050 or G106 for an open or high resistance. Is the repair complete?	—	Go to *Diagnostic System Check*	—
16	1. Turn the ignition switch to the RUN position, engine off. 2. Using *J 39200* DMM, measure the voltage between *J 39700* terminals A and B. Is the voltage within the range specified in the value(s) column?	Battery Volts	*Go to Step 18*	*Go to Step 17*
17	Repair CKT 641 for an open. Is the repair complete?	—	Go to *Diagnostic System Check*	—
18	Using *J 39200* DMM, measure the voltage between *J 39700* terminals D and B. Is the voltage within the range specified in the value(s) column?	Battery Volts	*Go to Step 7*	*Go to Step 19*
19	Repair CKT 342 for an open. Is the repair complete?	—	Go to *Diagnostic System Check*	—

GC402980269700CX

Fig. 108 Test G: No Communication w/EBCM/EBTCM (Part 3 of 3). Bonneville & LeSabre

Circuit Description

The TRACTION ACTIVE indicator is used only on Oldsmobile. The TRACTION ACTIVE indicator is controlled by serial data over the UART lines form the EBTCM.

Diagnostic Aids

- Perform a through inspection of the wiring and connectors. Failure to carefully and fully inspect wiring and connectors may result in misdiagnosis, causing part replacement with reappearance of the malfunction.
- If the battery feed to the IPC indicators is open, then more than one indicator will be inoperative.

Test Description

The number below refer to the step number on the diagnostic table.

2. This step check if the IPC can turn the indicator on.

Step	Action	Value(s)	Yes	No
1	Was the Diagnostic System Check performed?	—	*Go to Step 2*	Go to *Diagnostic System Check*
2	With a scan tool in ABS/TCS Special Tests command the TRACTION ACTIVE indicator on. Does the TRACTION ACTIVE indicator turn on?	—	*Go to Step 3*	*Go to Step 4*
3	Replace the EBTCM. Is the replacement complete?	—	Go to *Diagnostic System Check*	—
4	Suspect IPC, being sure to check the TRACTION ACTIVE indicator bulb. Is the diagnosis complete?	—	Go to *Diagnostic System Check*	—

GC4029802699000X

Fig. 107 Test F: Traction Active Lamp Inoperative w/No Code Set. Bonneville & LeSabre

Step	Action	Value(s)	Yes	No
5	1. Install a new ABS Solenoid fuse. 2. Recheck the fuse. Is the fuse OK?	—	Go to *Diagnostic System Check*	*Go to Step 6*
6	1. Turn the ignition switch to the OFF position. 2. Remove the ABS Solenoid fuse. 3. Disconnect the EBCM/EBTCM connector. 4. Connect the *J 39700* Universal Pinout Box using the *J 39700-25* cable adapter to the EBCM/EBTCM harness connector only. 5. Using *J 39200* DMM, measure the resistance between terminals D and B of *J 39700*. Is the resistance within the range specified in the value(s) column?	OL (infinite)	*Go to Step 7*	*Go to Step 8*
7	Replace the EBCM/EBTCM. Is the replacement complete?	—	Go to *Diagnostic System Check*	—
8	Repair CKT 342 for a short to ground. Is the repair complete?	—	Go to *Diagnostic System Check*	—
9	1. Install a new 10A ABS/CCR fuse. 2. Cycle the ignition switch from the OFF to RUN position, engine off. 3. Recheck the fuse. Is the fuse OK?	—	Go to *Diagnostic System Check*	*Go to Step 10*
10	1. Turn the ignition switch to the OFF position. 2. Remove the 10A ABS/CCR fuse. 3. Disconnect the EBCM/EBTCM connector. 4. Connect the *J 39700* Universal Pinout Box using the *J 39700-25* cable adapter to the EBCM/EBTCM harness connector only. 5. Using *J 39200* DMM, measure the resistance between terminals A and B of *J 39700*. Is the resistance within the range specified in the value(s) column?	OL (infinite)	*Go to Step 7*	*Go to Step 11*
11	Repair CKT 641 for a short to ground. Is the repair complete?	—	Go to *Diagnostic System Check*	—
12	1. Install the fuses if removed. 2. Turn the ignition switch to the RUN position, engine off. 3. Using *J 39200* DMM, measure the voltage at the 10A ABS/CCR fuse by probing between the fuse test terminals and a good ground. Is the voltage within the range specified within the value(s) column?	Battery Volts	*Go to Step 13*	Power Distribution
13	Using *J 39200* DMM, measure the voltage at the 40A ABS Solenoid fuse by probing between the fuse test terminals and a good ground. Is the voltage within the range specified within the value(s) column?	Battery Volts	*Go to Step 14*	Power Distribution

GC402980269700BX

Fig. 108 Test G: No Communication w/EBCM/EBTCM (Part 2 of 3). Bonneville & LeSabre

Circuit Description

The serial data class 2 allows all of the modules on the line to transmit information to each other as needed. Each module is assigned an ID. All of the information sent out on the line is assigned a priority by which the information is received. When the ignition switch is turned to the RUN position, each module begins to send and receive information. Each module on the serial data class 2 knows what information the module needs to send out and what information the module should be receiving. What the modules do not know is which module is supposed to send the information. This information is only learned after the module has received the information needed along with the ID of the module that sent the information. This information is then remembered until the ignition switch is turned OFF.

GC4029903942010X

Fig. 109 Test G: No Communication w/EBCM/EBTCM (Part 1 of 3). Park Avenue

Step	Action	Value(s)	Yes	No
DEFINITION: Scan tool can not communicate with the EBCM/EBTCM.				
1	Was the ABS Diagnostic System Check performed?	—	Go to *Step 2*	Go to *ABS Diagnostic System Check*
2	Turn the Ignition switch to the RUN position with the engine OFF. Can the scan tool communicate with other modules on serial data class 2, such as the PCM?	—	Go to *Step 3*	Go to *Scan Tool Does Not Communicate w/Class 2 Data*
3	Inspect the 10 A ABS Fuse in the IP fuse block. Is the fuse OK?	—	Go to *Step 4*	Go to *Step 8*
4	Inspect the 40 A ABS SOL Fuse in the underhood maxifuse block. Is the fuse OK?	—	Go to *Step 10*	Go to *Step 5*
5	1. Turn the ignition switch to the OFF position. 2. Remove the ABS SOL Fuse. 3. Disconnect the EBCM/EBTCM connector. 4. Connect the *J 39700* universal pinout box using the *J 39700 - 25* cable adapter to the EBCM/EBTCM harness connector only. 5. Using the *J 39200* digital multimeter (DMM), measure the resistance between terminal D and terminal B of the *J 39700.* Is the resistance equal to the specified value?	OL (Infinite)	Go to *Step 6*	Go to *Step 7*
6	Replace the EBCM/EBTCM. Is the repair complete?	—	Go to *ABS Diagnostic System Check*	—
7	Repair CKT 342 for a short to ground. Is the repair complete?	—	Go to *ABS Diagnostic System Check*	—
8	1. Turn the ignition switch to the OFF position. 2. Remove the 10 A ABS Fuse. 3. Disconnect the EBCM/EBTCM connector. 4. Connect the *J 39700* universal pinout box using the *J 39700 - 25* cable adapter to the EBCM/EBTCM harness connector only. 5. Using the *J 39200* digital multimeter (DMM), measure the resistance between terminal A and terminal B of the *J 39700.* Is the resistance equal to the specified value?	OL (Infinite)	Go to *Step 6*	Go to *Step 9*
9	Repair CKT 441 for a short to ground. Is the repair complete?	—	Go to *ABS Diagnostic System Check*	—
10	1. Install the fuses, if removed. 2. Turn the ignition switch to the RUN position with the engine OFF. 3. Using the *J 39200* DMM, measure the voltage at the 10 A ABS Fuse by probing between the fuse test terminals and a good ground. Is the voltage within the specified range?	Battery Voltage	Go to *Step 11*	*Wiring Repairs*
11	Using the *J 39200* DMM, measure the voltage at the 40 A ABS SOL Fuse by probing between the fuse test terminals and a good ground. Is the voltage within the specified range?	Battery Voltage	Go to *Step 12*	*Wiring Repairs*

GC4029903942020X

Fig. 109 Test G: No Communication w/EBCM/EBTCM (Part 2 of 3). Park Avenue

A Diagnostic System Check - ABS

Step	Action	Value(s)	Yes	No
1	Install a scan tool. Does the scan tool power up?	—	Go to *Step 2*	Go to *Scan Tool Does Not Power Up*
2	1. Reconnect all previously disconnected components. 2. Turn ON the ignition, with the engine OFF. 3. Attempt to establish communications with the EBCM. Does the scan tool communicate with the EBCM?	—	Go to *Step 3*	Go to *Scan Tool Does Not Communicate with Class 2 Device*
3	1. With the scan tool, in ABS/TCS/Active Handling Special Functions in order to run the Automated Test. 2. Select the ABS/TCS/Active Handling display DTC function on the scan tool. Does the scan tool display any DTCs?	—	Go to *Step 4*	Go to *Symptoms*
4	Does the scan tool display any DTCs which begin with a U (i.e. DTC U1016 or U1300)?	—	Go to *Scan Tool Does Not Communicate with Class 2 Device*	Go to *Diagnostic Trouble Code (DTC) List/Type*

GC4020052276000X

Fig. 110 ABS Diagnostic System Check. 2000 Corvette

Step	Action	Value(s)	Yes	No
12	1. Turn the ignition switch to the OFF position. 2. Disconnect the EBCM/EBTCM connector. 3. Connect the *J 39700* universal pinout box using the *J 39700 - 25* cable adapter to the EBCM/EBTCM harness connector only. 4. Using the *J 39200* DMM, measure the resistance between the *J 39700* terminal B and a good ground. Is the resistance less than the specified value?	2 Ω	Go to *Step 14*	Go to *Step 13*
13	Repair CKT 1150 or G104 for an open or high resistance. Is the repair complete?	—	Go to *ABS Diagnostic System Check*	—
14	1. Turn the ignition switch to the RUN position, with the engine OFF. 2. Using the *J 39200* DMM, measure the voltage between the *J 39700* terminal A and terminal B. Is the voltage within the specified range?	Battery Voltage	Go to *Step 16*	Go to *Step 15*
15	Repair CKT 441 for an open. Is the repair complete?	—	Go to *ABS Diagnostic System Check*	—
16	Using the *J 39200* DMM, measure the voltage between the *J 39700* terminal D and terminal B. Is the voltage equal to the specified value?	Battery Voltage	Go to *Step 6*	Go to *Step 17*
17	Repair CKT 342 for an open. an open. Is the repair complete?	—	Go to *ABS Diagnostic System Check*	—

GC4029903942030X

Fig. 109 Test G: No Communication w/EBCM/EBTCM (Part 3 of 3). Park Avenue

Circuit Description

The Traction Control System (TCS) switch circuit provides a ground input to the BCM when the switch is pressed. This input allows the BCM to detect a TCS ON or OFF request. If the BCM detects a ground on the traction control switch signal circuit with the TCS OFF, the BCM will send a message on the serial data line to the EBTCM to turn ON the TCS. If the BCM detects a ground after the TCS is ON, the BCM will send a second message to the EBTCM to turn OFF the TCS. The BCM monitors the TCS switch circuit and determines how long a ground has been applied. If the ground is applied for longer than expected, a malfunction is present and a DTC will set.

Conditions for Setting the DTC

The BCM detects a ground on the traction control switch signal circuit for longer than 60 seconds.

Action Taken When the DTC Sets

- Stores a DTC B2597 in the BCM memory.
- The PCM may disable fuel if vehicle speed is detected.
- No driver warning message will be displayed for this DTC.

Conditions for Clearing the DTC

- The BCM no longer detects a ground on the traction control switch signal circuit for longer than 60 seconds.
- A history DTC will clear after 50 consecutive ignition cycles if the condition for the malfunction is no longer present.
- Use the IPC clearing DTCs feature.
- Use a scan tool.

Diagnostic Aids

- The following conditions may cause an intermittent malfunction:
  - There is an intermittent short to ground in the traction control switch signal circuit.
  - The TCS switch is shorted to ground internally or is sticking.
  - The TCS switch is pressed for longer than 60 seconds.
- If the traction control switch signal circuit is shorted to ground, the TCS could remain ON or OFF at all times depending on whether the TCS was ON or OFF when the malfunction occurred. If the short occurred when the TCS was ON, the TCS will remain OFF at all times. If the short occurred when the TCS was OFF, the TCS will remain ON. The BCM will remember if the TCS was ON or OFF even if the ignition is switched OFF.

GC4020052277010X

Fig. 111 Code B2597: Traction Control System Switch Circuit (Part 1 of 2). 2000 Corvette

- If the DTC is a history DTC, the problem may be intermittent. Perform the tests shown while moving related wiring and connectors. This can often cause the malfunction to occur. Refer to *Intermittents and Poor Connections.*

Test Description

The number(s) below refer to the step number(s) on the diagnostic table.

2. Tests for the normal state of the TCS switch using a scan tool. The scan tool will display the normal state as INACTIVE, and ACTIVE when the switch is activated.
3. Tests if the BCM is able to detect a change in TCS switch state. The scan tool will display the normal state as INACTIVE, and ACTIVE when the switch is activated.
4. Tests for a stuck or shorted TCS switch. If the TCS switch is stuck or shorted, the state will change from ACTIVE to INACTIVE when the TCS switch is disconnected.
5. Tests for a short to ground in the TCS switch signal circuit.
8. When the BCM is replaced, use a scan tool to perform the BCM RPO Reprogram procedure.

Step	Action	Value(s)	Yes	No
1	Did you perform the BCM Diagnostic System Check?	—	Go to *Step 2*	Go to *A Diagnostic System Check - Body Control System*
2	1. Install a scan tool. 2. Turn ON the ignition, with the engine OFF. 3. With a scan tool, observe the TCS Switch parameter in the BCM data list. Does the scan tool display INACTIVE?	—	Go to *Step 3*	Go to *Step 4*
3	1. Activate the TCS switch. 2. With the scan tool, observe the TCS Switch parameter. Does the TCS Switch parameter change state?	—	Go to Diagnostic Aids	Go to *Step 4*
4	1. Turn OFF the ignition. 2. Disconnect the TCS switch. 3. Turn ON the ignition, with the engine OFF. 4. With a scan tool, observe the TCS Switch parameter. Does the scan tool display INACTIVE?	—	Go to *Step 7*	Go to *Step 5*
5	Test the signal circuit of the TCS switch for a short to ground. Did you find and correct the condition?	—	Go to *Step 10*	Go to *Step 6*
6	Inspect for poor connections at the harness connector of the BCM. Did you find and correct the condition?	—	Go to *Step 10*	Go to *Step 8*
7	Inspect for poor connections at the harness connector of the TCS switch. Did you find and correct the condition?	—	Go to *Step 10*	Go to *Step 9*
8	**Important:** Perform the BCM RPO Reprogram procedure. Replace the BCM. Did you complete the replacement?	—	Go to *Step 10*	—
9	Replace the TCS switch. Did you complete the replacement?	—	Go to *Step 10*	—
10	1. Use the scan tool in order to clear the DTCs. 2. Operate the vehicle within the Conditions for Running the DTC as specified in the supporting text. Does the DTC reset?	—	Go to *Step 2*	System OK

GC4020052277020X

Fig. 111 Code B2597: Traction Control System Switch Circuit (Part 2 of 2). 2000 Corvette

Circuit Description

The solenoid valve relay supplies power to the solenoid valves in the BPMV. The solenoid valve relay, located in the EBTCM, is activated whenever the ignition switch is in the ON position and no faults are present. Power is provided to the solenoid valves through the relay from CKT 1242 going into terminal D of the EBTCM. The solenoid valve relay remains engaged until the ignition is turned off or a failure is detected.

Conditions for Setting the DTC

DTC C1214 will set anytime the solenoid valve relay is commanded on and the solenoid valve relay voltage is less than 8 volts, and ignition voltage is greater than 10.5 volts.

Action Taken When the DTC Sets

ABS/TCS/Active Handling
are disabled.

- Indicators that turn on:
  - ABS indicator
  - Car Icon (TCS indicator)
- Messages displayed on the DIC:
  - Service ABS
  - Service Traction System
  - Service Active HNDLG

Conditions for Clearing the DTC

- Condition for DTC is no longer present and scan tool clear DTC function is used.
- Fifty ignition cycles have passed with no DTCs detected.

Diagnostic Aids

- It is very important that a thorough inspection of the wiring and connectors be performed. Failure to carefully and fully inspect wiring and connectors may result in misdiagnosis, causing part replacement with reappearance of the malfunction.
- If an intermittent malfunction exists refer to *Intermittents*
- The Relays are integral to the EBTCM and are not serviceable.

Test Description

The numbers below refer to step numbers on the diagnostic table.

4. Checks for a short to ground in CKT 1242.
5. Checks for an internal short in the BPMV.
8. Checks for an open in CKT 1242.

GC4029803947010X

Fig. 112 Code C1214: Solenoid Valve Relay Contact Or Coil Circuit Open (Part 1 of 2). Corvette

Step	Action	Value(s)	Yes	No
1	Was the Diagnostic System Check performed?	—	*Go to Step 2*	Go to *Diagnostic System Check (ABS)*
2	Inspect fuse 20A ABS ELEC Maxifuse®, in the Underhood Electrical Center. Is the fuse OK?	—	*Go to Step 7*	*Go to Step 3*
3	1. Install a new 20A ABS ELEC Maxifuse®. 2. Cycle the ignition switch from the OFF to ON position, engine off. 3. Recheck the 20A ABS ELEC Maxifuse®. Is the fuse OK?	—	Go to *Diagnostic System Check (ABS)*	*Go to Step 4*
4	1. Turn the Ignition switch to the OFF position. 2. Remove the 20A ABS ELEC Maxifuse®. 3. Disconnect the EBTCM. 4. Connect the *J 39700* Universal Pinout Box using the *J 39700-25* cable adapter to the EBTCM harness connector only. 5. Using *J 39200* DMM measure the resistance between terminals D and B of *J 39700*. Is the resistance within the range specified in the value(s) column?	OL (infinite)	*Go to Step 5*	*Go to Step 10*
5	1. Remove the EBTCM from the BPMV. 2. Connect the *J 41247* Pinout Box to the BPMV. 3. Measure the resistance between the *J 41247* terminal 7 and the BPMV case. Is the resistance within the range specified in the value(s) column?	OL (infinite)	*Go to Step 9*	*Go to Step 6*
6	Replace the BPMV. Is the replacement complete?	—	Go to *Diagnostic System Check (ABS)*	—
7	1. Install the fuse if removed. 2. Using *J 39200* DMM measure the voltage at the 20A ABS ELEC Maxifuse® fuse by probing between the fuse test terminals and a good ground. Is the voltage within the range specified in the value(s) column?	Battery volts	*Go to Step 8*	*Power Distribution*
8	1. Turn the Ignition switch to the OFF position. 2. Disconnect the EBTCM. 3. Connect the *J 39700* Universal Pinout Box using the *J 39700-25* cable adapter to the EBTCM harness connector only. 4. Using *J 39200* DMM measure the voltage at terminal D of *J 39700*. Is the voltage within the range specified in the value(s) column?	Battery volts	*Go to Step 9*	*Go to Step 11*
9	Replace the EBTCM. Is the replacement complete?	—	Go to *Diagnostic System Check (ABS)*	—
10	Repair short to ground in CKT 1242. Is the repair complete?	—	Go to *Diagnostic System Check (ABS)*	—
11	Repair open in CKT 1242. Is the repair complete?	—	Go to *Diagnostic System Check (ABS)*	—

GC4029803947020X

Fig. 112 Code C1214: Solenoid Valve Relay Contact Or Coil Circuit Open (Part 2 of 2). Corvette

Circuit Description

The pump motor is an integral part of the BPMV, while the pump motor relay is integral to the EBTCM. The pump motor relay is not engaged during normal system operation. When an ABS/TCS/Active Handling
operation is required, the EBTCM activates the pump motor relay and battery power is provided to the pump motor.

Conditions for Setting the DTC

DTC C1217 will set anytime the pump motor relay is commanded on and the pump relay voltage is less than 8 volts, and ignition voltage is greater than 10.5 volts.

Action Taken When the DTC Sets

ABS/TCS/Active Handling
are disabled.

- Indicators that turn on:
  - ABS indicator
  - Car Icon (TCS indicator)
- Messages displayed on the DIC:
  - Service ABS
  - Service Traction System
  - Service Active HNDLG

Conditions for Clearing the DTC

- Condition for DTC is no longer present and scan tool clear DTC function is used.
- Fifty ignition cycles have passed with no DTCs detected.

Diagnostic Aids

- It is very important that a thorough inspection of the wiring and connectors be performed. Failure to carefully and fully inspect wiring and connectors may result in misdiagnosis, causing part replacement with reappearance of the malfunction.
- If an intermittent malfunction exists refer to *Intermittents*

Test Description

The numbers below refer to step numbers on the diagnostic table.

4. Checks for a short to ground in CKT 1642.
5. Checks for an internal short in the BPMV.
8. Checks for an open in CKT 1642.

GC4029803948010X

Fig. 113 Code C1217: BPMV Pump Motor Relay Contact Circuit Open (Part 1 of 3). Corvette

Step	Action	Value(s)	Yes	No
1	Was the Diagnostic System Check performed?	—	*Go to Step 2*	Go to *Diagnostic System Check (ABS)*
2	Inspect the 40A ABS Maxifuse®, in the Underhood Electrical Center. Is the fuse OK?	—	*Go to Step 7*	*Go to Step 3*
3	1. Install a new 40A ABS Maxifuse®. 2. Cycle the ignition switch from the OFF to ON position, engine off. 3. Using a scan tool in ABS/TCS or ABS/TCS/Active Handling Special Functions attempt to run the AUTOMATED test. 4. Recheck the 40A ABS Maxifuse® fuse. Is the fuse OK?	—	Go to *Diagnostic System Check (ABS)*	*Go to Step 4*
4	1. Turn the Ignition switch to the OFF position. 2. Remove the 40A ABS Maxifuse®. 3. Disconnect the EBTCM. 4. Disconnect the pump motor ground. 5. Connect the *J 39700* Universal Pinout Box using the *J 39700-25* cable adapter to the EBTCM harness connector only. 6. Using *J 39200* DMM, measure the resistance between terminals E and B of *J 39700*. Is the resistance within the range specified in the value(s) column?	OL (infinite)	*Go to Step 5*	*Go to Step 10*
5	1. Remove the EBTCM from the BPMV. 2. Connect the *J 41247* Pinout Box to the BPMV. 3. Measure the resistance between *J 41247* terminal 8 and the BPMV case. Is the resistance within the range specified in the value(s) column?	OL (infinite)	*Go to Step 9*	*Go to Step 6*
6	Replace the BPMV. Is the replacement complete?	—	Go to *Diagnostic System Check (ABS)*	—
7	1. Install the fuse if removed. 2. Using *J 39200* DMM, measure the voltage at the 40A ABS Maxifuse® fuse by probing between the fuse test terminals and a good ground. Is the voltage within the range specified in the value(s) column?	Battery volts	*Go to Step 8*	*Power Distribution*
8	1. Turn the Ignition switch to the OFF position. 2. Disconnect the EBTCM. 3. Connect *J 39700* Universal Pinout Box using the *J 39700-25* cable adaptor to the EBTCM harness connector only. 4. Using *J 39200* DMM, measure the voltage at terminal E of *J 39700*. Is the voltage within the range specified in the value(s) column?	Battery volts	*Go to Step 9*	*Go to Step 11*

GC4029803948020X

Fig. 113 Code C1217: BPMV Pump Motor Relay Contact Circuit Open (Part 2 of 3). Corvette

Step	Action	Value(s)	Yes	No
9	Replace EBTCM. Is the replacement complete?	—	Go to *Diagnostic System Check (ABS)*	—
10	Repair short to ground in CKT 1642. Is the repair complete?	—	Go to *Diagnostic System Check (ABS)*	—
11	Repair open in CKT 1642. Is the repair complete?	—	Go to *Diagnostic System Check (ABS)*	—

GC4029803948030X

Fig. 113 Code C1217: BPMV Pump Motor Relay Contact Circuit Open (Part 3 of 3). Corvette

Circuit Description

The speed sensor used on this vehicle is a single point magnetic pickup. This sensor produces an AC signal that the EBTCM uses the frequency from to calculate the wheel speed.

Conditions for Setting the DTC

The DTC will set if one wheel speed = 0 and the other WSS are greater than 8 Km/h (5 mph) for 2.5 seconds.

Action Taken When the DTC Sets

A malfunction DTC is stored, ABS/TCS is disabled and the ABS and Traction Control Indicators are turned ON.

Conditions for Clearing the DTC

- Condition for DTC is no longer present and scan tool clear DTC function is used.
- Fifty ignition cycles have passed with no DTC(s) detected.

Diagnostic Aids

- It is very important that a thorough inspection of the wiring and connectors be performed. Failure to carefully and fully inspect wiring and connectors may result in misdiagnosis, causing part replacement with reappearance of the malfunction.
- An intermittent malfunction can be caused by poor connections, broken insulation, or a wire that is broken inside the insulation.

Test Description

The numbers below refer to step numbers on the diagnostic table.

3. Checks the resistance of the WSS.
5. Checks if the WSS CKTs are shorted together.

GC402970263600AX

Fig. 114 Code C1221: LH Front Wheel Speed Sensor Input Signal Is Zero (Part 1 of 2). Corvette

Step	Action	Value(s)	Yes	No
1	Was the Diagnostic System Check performed?	—	*Go to Step 2*	Go to *ABS Diagnostic System Check*
2	1. Inspect the WSS wiring and connectors for damage. 2. Inspect WSS for looseness or damage. Is physical damage of sensor evident?	—	*Go to Step 7*	*Go to Step 3*
3	1. Disconnect the WSS at the sensor pigtail. 2. Using *J 39200* DMM, measure the resistance between terminals A and B of the WSS. Is the resistance within the range specified in the value(s) column?	850-1350Ω	*Go to Step 4*	*Go to Step 7*
4	1. With *J 39200* DMM still connected, select the mV AC scale. 2. Spin the wheel as fast as you can by hand while monitoring the AC output. Is the AC voltage within the range specified in the value(s) column?	Above 100 mV	*Go to Step 5*	*Go to Step 7*
5	1. Disconnect the EBTCM harness connector. 2. Install *J 39700* Universal Pinout Box using the *J 39700-25* cable adapter to the EBTCM harness connector only. 3. Using *J 39200* DMM, measure resistance between terminals 15 and 31 of the *J 39700*. Is the resistance within the range specified in the value(s) column?	OL (Infinite)	*Go to Step 6*	*Go to Step 8*
6	1. Reconnect all connectors. 2. Carefully test drive vehicle above 24 Km/h (15 mph) for at least 30 seconds while monitoring a scan tool. Does DTC reset as a current DTC?	—	*Go to Step 9*	Go to *ABS Diagnostic System Check*
7	Replace wheel speed sensor. Is the repair complete?	—	*Go to Step 10*	—
8	Repair short between CKT(s) 873 and 830. Is the repair complete?	—	*Go to Step 10*	—
9	Replace EBTCM. Is the replacement complete?	—	*Go to Step 10*	—
10	Carefully test drive vehicle above 24 Km/h (15 mph) while monitoring a scan tool for at least 30 seconds. Does the DTC set as a current DTC?	—	*Go to Step 2*	Go to *ABS Diagnostic System Check*

GC402970263600BX

Fig. 114 Code C1221: LH Front Wheel Speed Sensor Input Signal Is Zero (Part 2 of 2). Corvette

Circuit Description

The speed sensor used on this vehicle is a single point magnetic pickup. This sensor produces an AC signal that the EBTCM uses the frequency from to calculate the wheel speed.

Conditions for Setting the DTC

The DTC will set if one wheel speed = 0 and the other WSS are greater than 8 Km/h (5 mph) for 2.5 seconds.

Action Taken When the DTC Sets

A malfunction DTC is stored, ABS/TCS is disabled and the ABS and Traction Control Indicators are turned ON.

Conditions for Clearing the DTC

- Condition for DTC is no longer present and scan tool clear DTC function is used.
- Fifty ignition cycles have passed with no DTC(s) detected.

Diagnostic Aids

- It is very important that a thorough inspection of the wiring and connectors be performed. Failure to carefully and fully inspect wiring and connectors may result in misdiagnosis, causing part replacement with reappearance of the malfunction.

An intermittent malfunction can be caused by poor connections, broken insulation, or a wire that is broken inside the insulation.

Test Description

The numbers below refer to step numbers on the diagnostic table.

3. Checks the resistance of the WSS.
5. Checks if the WSS CKTs are shorted together.

GC402970263700AX

Fig. 115 Code C1222: RH Front Wheel Speed Sensor Input Signal Is Zero (Part 1 of 2). Corvette

Step	Action	Value(s)	Yes	No
1	Was the Diagnostic System Check performed?	—	*Go to Step 2*	Go to *ABS Diagnostic System Check*
2	1. Inspect the WSS wiring and connectors for damage. 2. Inspect WSS for looseness or damage. Is physical damage of sensor evident?	—	*Go to Step 7*	*Go to Step 3*
3	1. Disconnect the WSS at the sensor pigtail. 2. Using *J 39200* DMM, measure the resistance between terminals A and B of the WSS. Is the resistance within the range specified in the value(s) column?	850-1350Ω	*Go to Step 4*	*Go to Step 7*
4	1. With *J 39200* DMM still connected, select the mV AC scale. 2. Spin the wheel as fast as you can by hand while monitoring the AC output. Is the AC voltage within the range specified in the value(s) column?	Above 100 mV	*Go to Step 5*	*Go to Step 7*
5	1. Disconnect the EBTCM harness connector. 2. Install *J 39700* Universal Pinout Box using the *J 39700-25* cable adapter to the EBTCM harness connector only. 3. Using *J 39200* DMM, measure resistance between terminals 14 and 30 of the *J 39700*. Is the resistance within the range specified in the value(s) column?	OL (Infinite)	*Go to Step 6*	*Go to Step 8*
6	1. Reconnect all connectors. 2. Carefully test drive vehicle above 24 Km/h (15 mph) for at least 30 seconds while monitoring a scan tool. Does DTC reset as a current DTC?	—	*Go to Step 9*	Go to *ABS Diagnostic System Check*
7	Replace wheel speed sensor. Is the repair complete?	—	*Go to Step 10*	—
8	Repair short between CKT(s) 833 and 872. Is the repair complete?	—	*Go to Step 10*	—
9	Replace EBTCM. Is the replacement complete?	—	*Go to Step 10*	—
10	Carefully test drive vehicle above 24 Km/h (15 mph) while monitoring a scan tool for at least 30 seconds. Does the DTC set as a current DTC?	—	*Go to Step 2*	Go to *ABS Diagnostic System Check*

GC402970263700BX

Fig. 115 Code C1222: RH Front Wheel Speed Sensor Input Signal Is Zero (Part 2 of 2). Corvette

Circuit Description

The speed sensor used on this vehicle is a single point magnetic pickup. This sensor produces an AC signal that the EBTCM uses the frequency from to calculate the wheel speed.

Conditions for Setting the DTC

The DTC will set if one wheel speed = 0 and the other WSS are greater than 8 Km/h (5 mph) for 2.5 seconds.

Action Taken When the DTC Sets

Malfunction DTC is stored, ABS/TCS is disabled and the ABS and Traction Control Indicators are turned ON.

Conditions for Clearing the DTC

- Condition for DTC is no longer present and scan tool clear DTC function is used.
- Fifty ignition cycles have passed with no DTC(s) detected.

Diagnostic Aids

- It is very important that a thorough inspection of the wiring and connectors be performed. Failure to carefully and fully inspect wiring and connectors may result in misdiagnosis, causing part replacement with reappearance of the malfunction.
- An intermittent malfunction can be caused by poor connections, broken insulation, or a wire that is broken inside the insulation.

Test Description

The numbers below refer to step numbers on the diagnostic table.

3. Checks the resistance of the WSS.
5. Checks if the WSS CKTs are shorted together.

GC402970263800AX

Fig. 116 Code C1223: LH Front Wheel Speed Sensor Input Signal Is Zero (Part 1 of 2). Corvette

Step	Action	Value(s)	Yes	No
1	Was the Diagnostic System Check performed?	—	*Go to Step 2*	Go to *ABS Diagnostic System Check*
2	1. Inspect the WSS wiring and connectors for damage. 2. Inspect WSS for looseness or damage. Is physical damage of sensor evident?	—	*Go to Step 7*	*Go to Step 3*
3	1. Disconnect the WSS at the sensor pigtail. 2. Using *J 39200* DMM, measure the resistance between terminals A and B of the WSS. Is the resistance within the range specified in the value(s) column?	850-1350Ω	*Go to Step 4*	*Go to Step 7*
4	1. With *J 39200* DMM still connected, select the mV AC scale. 2. Spin the wheel as fast as you can by hand while monitoring the AC output. Is the AC voltage within the range specified in the value(s) column?	Above 100 mV	*Go to Step 5*	*Go to Step 7*
5	1. Disconnect the EBTCM harness connector. 2. Install *J 39700* Universal Pinout Box using the *J 39700-25* cable adapter to the EBTCM harness connector only. 3. Using *J 39200* DMM, measure resistance between terminals 12 and 28 of the *J 39700*. Is the resistance within the range specified in the value(s) column?	OL (Infinite)	*Go to Step 6*	*Go to Step 8*
6	1. Reconnect all connectors. 2. Carefully test drive vehicle above 24 Km/h (15 mph) for at least 30 seconds while monitoring a scan tool. Does DTC reset as a current DTC?	—	*Go to Step 9*	Go to *ABS Diagnostic System Check*
7	Replace wheel speed sensor. Is the repair complete?	—	*Go to Step 10*	—
8	Repair short between CKT(s) 884 and 885. Is the repair complete?	—	*Go to Step 10*	—
9	Replace EBTCM. Is the replacement complete?	—	*Go to Step 10*	—
10	Carefully test drive vehicle above 24 Km/h (15 mph) while monitoring a scan tool for at least 30 seconds. Does the DTC set as a current DTC?	—	*Go to Step 2*	Go to *ABS Diagnostic System Check*

GC402970263800BX

Fig. 116 Code C1223: LH Front Wheel Speed Sensor Input Signal Is Zero (Part 2 of 2). Corvette

Step	Action	Value(s)	Yes	No
1	Was the Diagnostic System Check performed?	—	*Go to Step 2*	Go to *ABS Diagnostic System Check*
2	1. Inspect the WSS wiring and connectors for damage. 2. Inspect WSS for looseness or damage. Is physical damage of sensor evident?	—	*Go to Step 7*	*Go to Step 3*
3	1. Disconnect the WSS at the sensor pigtail. 2. Using *J 39200* DMM, measure the resistance between terminals A and B of the WSS. Is the resistance within the range specified in the value(s) column?	850-1350Ω	*Go to Step 4*	*Go to Step 7*
4	1. With *J 39200* DMM still connected, select the mV AC scale. 2. Spin the wheel as fast as you can by hand while monitoring the AC output. Is the AC voltage within the range specified in the value(s) column?	Above 100 mV	*Go to Step 5*	*Go to Step 7*
5	1. Disconnect the EBTCM harness connector. 2. Install *J 39700* Universal Pinout Box using the *J 39700-25* cable adapter to the EBTCM harness connector only. 3. Using *J 39200* DMM, measure resistance between terminals 13 and 29 of the *J 39700*. Is the resistance within the range specified in the value(s) column?	OL (Infinite)	*Go to Step 6*	*Go to Step 8*
6	1. Reconnect all connectors. 2. Carefully test drive vehicle above 24 Km/h (15 mph) for at least 30 seconds while monitoring a scan tool. Does DTC reset as a current DTC?	—	*Go to Step 9*	Go to *ABS Diagnostic System Check*
7	Replace wheel speed sensor. Is the repair complete?	—	*Go to Step 10*	—
8	Repair short between CKT(s) 882 and 883. Is the repair complete?	—	*Go to Step 10*	—
9	Replace EBTCM. Is the replacement complete?	—	*Go to Step 10*	—
10	Carefully test drive vehicle above 24 Km/h (15 mph) while monitoring a scan tool for at least 30 seconds. Does the DTC set as a current DTC?	—	*Go to Step 2*	Go to *ABS Diagnostic System Check*

GC402970263900BX

Fig. 117 Code C1224: RH Read Wheel Speed Sensor Input Signal Is Zero (Part 2 of 2). Corvette

Circuit Description

The speed sensor used on this vehicle is a single point magnetic pickup. This sensor produces an AC signal that the EBTCM uses the frequency from to calculate the wheel speed.

Conditions for Setting the DTC

The DTC will set if one wheel speed = 0 and the other WSS are greater than 8 Km/h (5 mph) for 2.5 seconds.

Action Taken When the DTC Sets

A malfunction DTC is stored, ABS/TCS is disabled and the ABS and Traction Control Indicators are turned ON.

Conditions for Clearing the DTC

- Condition for DTC is no longer present and scan tool clear DTC function is used.
- Fifty ignition cycles have passed with no DTC(s) detected.

Diagnostic Aids

- It is very important that a thorough inspection of the wiring and connectors be performed. Failure to carefully and fully inspect wiring and connectors may result in misdiagnosis, causing part replacement with reappearance of the malfunction.
- An intermittent malfunction can be caused by poor connections, broken insulation, or a wire that is broken inside the insulation.

Test Description

The numbers below refer to step numbers on the diagnostic table.

3. Checks the resistance of the WSS.
5. Checks if the WSS CKTs are shorted together.

GC402970263900AX

Fig. 117 Code C1224: RH Read Wheel Speed Sensor Input Signal Is Zero (Part 1 of 2). Corvette

Circuit Description

The speed sensor used on this vehicle is a single point magnetic pickup. This sensor produces an AC signal that the EBTCM uses the frequency from to calculate the wheel speed.

Conditions for Setting the DTC

The DTC can be set anytime the brake is not depressed and no wheel speed sensor hardware DTC(s) are present, and the EBTCM sees a wheel speed variation of more than 14 Km/h (9 mph) for 2.5 seconds.

Action Taken When the DTC Sets

A malfunction DTC is stored, ABS/TCS is disabled and the ABS and Traction Control Indicators are turned ON.

Conditions for Clearing the DTC

- Condition for DTC is no longer present and scan tool clear DTC function is used.
- Fifty ignition cycles have passed with no DTC(s) detected.

Diagnostic Aids

- It is very important that a thorough inspection of the wiring and connectors be performed. Failure to carefully and fully inspect wiring and connectors may result in misdiagnosis, causing part replacement with reappearance of the malfunction.
- An intermittent malfunction can be caused by poor connections, broken insulation, or a wire that is broken inside the insulation.

Test Description

The numbers below refer to step numbers on the diagnostic table.

3. Checks the resistance of the WSS.
5. Checks if the WSS CKTs are shorted together.

GC402970264000AX

Fig. 118 Code C1225: LH Front Excessive Wheel Speed Variation (Part 1 of 2). Corvette

Step	Action	Value(s)	Yes	No
1	Was the Diagnostic System Check performed?	—	*Go to Step 2*	Go to *ABS Diagnostic System Check*
2	1. Inspect the WSS wiring and connectors for damage. 2. Inspect WSS for looseness or damage. Is physical damage of sensor evident?	—	*Go to Step 7*	*Go to Step 3*
3	1. Disconnect the WSS at the sensor pigtail. 2. Using *J 39200* DMM, measure the resistance between terminals A and B of the WSS. Is the resistance within the range specified in the value(s) column?	850-1350Ω	*Go to Step 4*	*Go to Step 7*
4	1. With *J 39200* DMM still connected, select the mV AC scale. 2. Spin the wheel as fast as you can by hand while monitoring the AC output. Is the AC voltage within the range specified in the value(s) column?	Above 100 mV	*Go to Step 5*	*Go to Step 7*
5	1. Disconnect the EBTCM harness connector. 2. Install *J 39700* Universal Pinout Box using the *J 39700-25* cable adapter to the EBTCM harness connector only. 3. Using *J 39200* DMM, measure resistance between terminals 15 and 31 of the *J 39700*. Is the resistance within the range specified in the value(s) column?	OL (Infinite)	*Go to Step 6*	*Go to Step 8*
6	1. Reconnect all connectors. 2. Carefully test drive vehicle above 24 Km/h (15 mph) for at least 30 seconds while monitoring a scan tool. Does DTC reset as a current DTC?	—	*Go to Step 9*	Go to *ABS Diagnostic System Check*
7	Replace wheel speed sensor. Is the repair complete?	—	*Go to Step 10*	—
8	Repair short between CKT(s) 873 and 830. Is the repair complete?	—	*Go to Step 10*	—
9	Replace EBTCM. Is the replacement complete?	—	*Go to Step 10*	—
10	Carefully test drive vehicle above 24 Km/h (15 mph) while monitoring a scan tool for at least 30 seconds. Does the DTC set as a current DTC?	—	*Go to Step 2*	Go to *ABS Diagnostic System Check*

GC402970264000BX

Fig. 118 Code C1225: LH Front Excessive Wheel Speed Variation (Part 2 of 2). Corvette

Circuit Description

The speed sensor used on this vehicle is a single point magnetic pickup. This sensor produces an AC signal that the EBTCM uses the frequency from to calculate the wheel speed.

Conditions for Setting the DTC

The DTC can be set anytime the brake is not depressed and no wheel speed sensor hardware DTC(s) are present, and the EBTCM sees a wheel speed variation of more than 14 Km/h (9 mph) for 2.5 seconds.

Action Taken When the DTC Sets

A malfunction DTC is stored, ABS/TCS is disabled and the ABS and Traction Control Indicators are turned ON.

Conditions for Clearing the DTC

- Condition for DTC is no longer present and scan tool clear DTC function is used.
- Fifty ignition cycles have passed with no DTC(s) detected.

Diagnostic Aids

- It is very important that a thorough inspection of the wiring and connectors be performed. Failure to carefully and fully inspect wiring and connectors may result in misdiagnosis, causing part replacement with reappearance of the malfunction.
- An intermittent malfunction can be caused by poor connections, broken insulation, or a wire that is broken inside the insulation.

Test Description

The numbers below refer to step numbers on the diagnostic table.

3. Checks the resistance of the WSS.
5. Checks if the WSS CKTs are shorted together.

GC402970264100AX

Fig. 119 Code C1226: RH Rear Excessive Wheel Speed Variation (Part 1 of 2). Corvette

Circuit Description

The speed sensor used on this vehicle is a single point magnetic pickup. This sensor produces an AC signal that the EBTCM uses the frequency from to calculate the wheel speed.

Conditions for Setting the DTC

The DTC can be set anytime the brake is not depressed and no wheel speed sensor hardware DTC(s) are present, and the EBTCM sees a wheel speed variation of more than 14 Km/h (9 mph) for 2.5 seconds.

Action Taken When the DTC Sets

A malfunction DTC is stored, ABS/TCS is disabled and the ABS and Traction Control Indicators are turned ON.

Conditions for Clearing the DTC

- Condition for DTC is no longer present and scan tool clear DTC function is used.
- Fifty ignition cycles have passed with no DTC(s) detected.

Diagnostic Aids

- It is very important that a thorough inspection of the wiring and connectors be performed. Failure to carefully and fully inspect wiring and connectors may result in misdiagnosis, causing part replacement with reappearance of the malfunction.
- An intermittent malfunction can be caused by poor connections, broken insulation, or a wire that is broken inside the insulation.

Test Description

The numbers below refer to step numbers on the diagnostic table.

3. Checks the resistance of the WSS.
5. Checks if the WSS CKTs are shorted together.

GC402970264200AX

Fig. 120 Code C1227: LH Rear Excessive Wheel Speed Variation (Part 1 of 2). Corvette

Step	Action	Value(s)	Yes	No
1	Was the Diagnostic System Check performed?	—	*Go to Step 2*	Go to *ABS Diagnostic System Check*
2	1. Inspect the WSS wiring and connectors for damage. 2. Inspect WSS for looseness or damage. Is physical damage of sensor evident?	—	*Go to Step 7*	*Go to Step 3*
3	1. Disconnect the WSS at the sensor pigtail. 2. Using *J 39200* DMM, measure the resistance between terminals A and B of the WSS. Is the resistance within the range specified in the value(s) column?	850-1350Ω	*Go to Step 4*	*Go to Step 7*
4	1. With *J 39200* DMM still connected, select the mV AC scale. 2. Spin the wheel as fast as you can by hand while monitoring the AC output. Is the AC voltage within the range specified in the value(s) column?	Above 100 mV	*Go to Step 5*	*Go to Step 7*
5	1. Disconnect the EBTCM harness connector. 2. Install *J 39700* Universal Pinout Box using the *J 39700-25* cable adapter to the EBTCM harness connector only. 3. Using *J 39200* DMM, measure resistance between terminals 12 and 28 of the *J 39700*. Is the resistance within the range specified in the value(s) column?	OL (Infinite)	*Go to Step 6*	*Go to Step 8*
6	1. Reconnect all connectors. 2. Carefully test drive vehicle above 24 Km/h (15 mph) for at least 30 seconds while monitoring a scan tool. Does DTC reset as a current DTC?	—	*Go to Step 9*	Go to *ABS Diagnostic System Check*
7	Replace wheel speed sensor. Is the repair complete?	—	*Go to Step 10*	—
8	Repair short between CKT(s) 884 and 885. Is the repair complete?	—	*Go to Step 10*	—
9	Replace EBTCM. Is the replacement complete?	—	*Go to Step 10*	—
10	Carefully test drive vehicle above 24 Km/h (15 mph) while monitoring a scan tool for at least 30 seconds. Does the DTC set as a current DTC?	—	*Go to Step 2*	Go to *ABS Diagnostic System Check*

GC402970264200BX

Fig. 120 Code C1227: LH Rear Excessive Wheel Speed Variation (Part 2 of 2). Corvette

Step	Action	Value(s)	Yes	No
1	Was the Diagnostic System Check performed?	—	*Go to Step 2*	Go to *ABS Diagnostic System Check*
2	1. Inspect the WSS wiring and connectors for damage. 2. Inspect WSS for looseness or damage. Is physical damage of sensor evident?	—	*Go to Step 7*	*Go to Step 3*
3	1. Disconnect the WSS at the sensor pigtail. 2. Using *J 39200* DMM, measure the resistance between terminals A and B of the WSS. Is the resistance within the range specified in the value(s) column?	850-1350Ω	*Go to Step 4*	*Go to Step 7*
4	1. With *J 39200* DMM still connected, select the mV AC scale. 2. Spin the wheel as fast as you can by hand while monitoring the AC output. Is the AC voltage within the range specified in the value(s) column?	Above 100 mV	*Go to Step 5*	*Go to Step 7*
5	1. Disconnect the EBTCM harness connector. 2. Install *J 39700* Universal Pinout Box using the *J 39700-25* cable adapter to the EBTCM harness connector only. 3. Using *J 39200* DMM, measure resistance between terminals 14 and 30 of the *J 39700*. Is the resistance within the range specified in the value(s) column?	OL (Infinite)	*Go to Step 6*	*Go to Step 8*
6	1. Reconnect all connectors. 2. Carefully test drive vehicle above 24 Km/h (15 mph) for at least 30 seconds while monitoring a scan tool. Does DTC reset as a current DTC?	—	*Go to Step 9*	Go to *ABS Diagnostic System Check*
7	Replace wheel speed sensor. Is the repair complete?	—	*Go to Step 10*	—
8	Repair short between CKT(s) 833 and 872. Is the repair complete?	—	*Go to Step 10*	—
9	Replace EBTCM. Is the replacement complete?	—	*Go to Step 10*	—
10	Carefully test drive vehicle above 24 Km/h (15 mph) while monitoring a scan tool for at least 30 seconds. Does the DTC set as a current DTC?	—	*Go to Step 2*	Go to *ABS Diagnostic System Check*

GC402970264100BX

Fig. 119 Code C1226: RH Rear Excessive Wheel Speed Variation (Part 2 of 2). Corvette

Circuit Description

The speed sensor used on this vehicle is a single point magnetic pickup. This sensor produces an AC signal that the EBTCM uses the frequency from to calculate the wheel speed.

Conditions for Setting the DTC

The DTC can be set anytime the brake is not depressed and no wheel speed sensor hardware DTC(s) are present, and the EBTCM sees a wheel speed variation of more than 14 Km/h (9 mph) for 2.5 seconds.

Action Taken When the DTC Sets

A malfunction DTC is stored, ABS/TCS is disabled and the ABS and Traction Control Indicators are turned ON.

Conditions for Clearing the DTC

- Condition for DTC is no longer present and scan tool clear DTC function is used.
- Fifty ignition cycles have passed with no DTC(s) detected.

Diagnostic Aids

- It is very important that a thorough inspection of the wiring and connectors be performed. Failure to carefully and fully inspect wiring and connectors may result in misdiagnosis, causing part replacement with reappearance of the malfunction.
- An intermittent malfunction can be caused by poor connections, broken insulation, or a wire that is broken inside the insulation.

Test Description

The numbers below refer to step numbers on the diagnostic table.

3. Checks the resistance of the WSS.
5. Checks if the WSS CKTs are shorted together.

GC402970264300AX

Fig. 121 Code C1228: RH Read Excessive Wheel Speed Variation (Part 1 of 2). Corvette

Step	Action	Value(s)	Yes	No
1	Was the Diagnostic System Check performed?	—	Go to Step 2	Go to ABS Diagnostic System Check
2	1. Inspect the WSS wiring and connectors for damage. 2. Inspect WSS for looseness or damage. Is physical damage of sensor evident?	—	Go to Step 7	Go to Step 3
3	1. Disconnect the WSS at the sensor pigtail. 2. Using J 39200 DMM, measure the resistance between terminals A and B of the WSS. Is the resistance within the range specified in the value(s) column?	850-1350Ω	Go to Step 4	Go to Step 7
4	1. With J 39200 DMM still connected, select the mV AC scale. 2. Spin the wheel as fast as you can by hand while monitoring the AC output. Is the AC voltage within the range specified in the value(s) column?	Above 100 mV	Go to Step 5	Go to Step 7
5	1. Disconnect the EBTCM harness connector. 2. Install J 39700 Universal Pinout Box using the J 39700-25 cable adapter to the EBTCM harness connector only. 3. Using J 39200 DMM, measure resistance between terminals 13 and 29 of the J 39700. Is the resistance within the range specified in the value(s) column?	OL (Infinite)	Go to Step 6	Go to Step 8
6	1. Reconnect all connectors. 2. Carefully test drive vehicle above 24 Km/h (15 mph) for at least 30 seconds while monitoring a scan tool. Does DTC reset as a current DTC?	—	Go to Step 9	Go to ABS Diagnostic System Check
7	Replace wheel speed sensor. Is the repair complete?	—	Go to Step 10	—
8	Repair short between CKT(s) 882 and 883. Is the repair complete?	—	Go to Step 10	—
9	Replace EBTCM. Is the replacement complete?	—	Go to Step 10	—
10	Carefully test drive vehicle above 24 Km/h (15 mph) while monitoring a scan tool for at least 30 seconds. Does the DTC set as a current DTC?	—	Go to Step 2	Go to ABS Diagnostic System Check

GC402970264300BX

Fig. 121 Code C1228: RH Read Excessive Wheel Speed Variation (Part 2 of 2). Corvette

Step	Action	Value(s)	Yes	No
1	Was the Diagnostic System Check performed?	—	Go to Step 2	Go to ABS Diagnostic System Check
2	1. Inspect the WSS wiring and connectors for damage. 2. Inspect the WSS for looseness or damage. Is physical damage of sensor evident?	—	Go to Step 3	Go to Step 4
3	Repair as necessary. Is the repair complete?	—	Go to ABS Diagnostic System Check	—
4	1. Turn the ignition switch to the OFF position. 2. Disconnect the EBTCM. 3. Install the J 39700 Universal Pinout Box using the J 39700-25 cable adapter to the EBTCM harness connector only. 4. Using J 39200 DMM, measure the resistance between terminals 15 and 31 of J 39700. Is the resistance within the range specified in the value(s) column?	850 - 1350Ω	Go to Step 12	Go to Step 5
5	1. Disconnect the LF Wheel Speed Sensor. 2. Using J 39200 DMM, measure the resistance between terminals A and B of the Wheel Speed Sensor Connector. Is the resistance within the range specified in the value(s) column?	850 - 1350Ω	Go to Step 6	Go to Step 11
6	1. Connect a jumper between the LF Wheel Speed Sensor harness connector terminal A and ground. 2. Using J 39200 DMM, measure the resistance between terminals 31 and B of J 39700. Is the resistance within the range specified in the value(s) column?	0 - 5Ω	Go to Step 8	Go to Step 7
7	Repair CKT 830 for an open or high resistance. Is the repair complete?	—	Go to ABS Diagnostic System Check	—
8	1. Connect a jumper between the LF Wheel Speed Sensor harness connector terminal B and ground. 2. Using J 39200 DMM, measure the resistance between terminals 15 and B of J 39700. Is the resistance within the range specified in the value(s) column?	0 - 5Ω	Go to Step 10	Go to Step 9
9	Repair CKT 873 for an open or high resistance. Is the repair complete?	—	Go to ABS Diagnostic System Check	—
10	Malfunction is intermittent. Inspect all connectors and harnesses for damage that may result in an open or high resistance when connected. Is the repair complete?	—	Go to ABS Diagnostic System Check	—
11	Replace the Wheel Speed Sensor. Is the replacement complete?	—	Go to ABS Diagnostic System Check	—

GC402970264400BX

Fig. 122 Code C1232: LH Front Wheel Speed Circuit Open Or Shorted (Part 2 of 3). Corvette

Circuit Description

The speed sensor used on this vehicle is a single point magnetic pickup. This sensor produces an AC signal that the EBTCM uses the frequency from to calculate the wheel speed.

Conditions for Setting the DTC

The DTC can be set any time the ignition is in the ON position, and the EBTCM senses an open, a short to ground, or a short to battery.

Action Taken When the DTC Sets

A malfunction DTC is stored, ABS/TCS is disabled and the ABS and Traction Control Indicators are turned ON.

Conditions for Clearing the DTC

- Condition for DTC is no longer present and scan tool clear DTC function is used.
- Fifty ignition cycles have passed with no DTC(s) detected.

Diagnostic Aids

- It is very important that a thorough inspection of the wiring and connectors be performed. Failure to carefully and fully inspect wiring and connectors may result in misdiagnosis, causing part replacement with reappearance of the malfunction.
- An intermittent malfunction can be caused by poor connections, broken insulation, or a wire that is broken inside the insulation.

Test Description

The numbers below refer to step numbers on the diagnostic table.

4. Checks for an open in the WSS or WSS CKT.
12. Checks for a short to ground in the WSS or WSS CKT.
19. Checks for a short to voltage in the WSS CKT.
21. Checks for a short to voltage in the WSS CKT.

GC402970264400AX

Fig. 122 Code C1232: LH Front Wheel Speed Circuit Open Or Shorted (Part 1 of 3). Corvette

Step	Action	Value(s)	Yes	No
12	Using J 39200 DMM, measure the resistance between terminals 15 and B of J 39700. Is the resistance within the range specified in the value(s) column?	OL (infinite)	Go to Step 19	Go to Step 13
13	1. Disconnect the LF Wheel Speed Sensor. 2. Using J 39200 DMM, measure the resistance between terminal A and ground of the Wheel Speed Sensor Connector. Is the resistance within the range specified in the value(s) column?	OL (infinite)	Go to Step 14	Go to Step 11
14	1. Using J 39200 DMM, measure the resistance between terminals 31 and B of J 39700. Is the resistance within the range specified in the value(s) column?	OL (infinite)	Go to Step 16	Go to Step 15
15	Repair CKT 830 for a short to ground. Is the repair complete?	—	Go to ABS Diagnostic System Check	—
16	Using J 39200 DMM, measure the resistance between terminals 15 and B of J 39700. Is the resistance within the range specified in the value(s) column?	OL (infinite)	Go to Step 17	Go to Step 18
17	Malfunction is intermittent. Inspect all connectors and harnesses for damage that may result in a short to ground when connected. Is the repair complete?	—	Go to ABS Diagnostic System Check	—
18	Repair CKT 873 for a short to ground. Is the repair complete?	—	Go to ABS Diagnostic System Check	—
19	1. Disconnect the LF Wheel Speed Sensor. 2. Turn the ignition switch to the ON position, engine OFF. 3. Using J 39200 DMM, measure the voltage at terminal 31 of J 39700. Is the voltage within the range specified in the value(s) column?	Above 1V	Go to Step 20	Go to Step 21
20	Repair CKT 830 for a short to voltage. Is the repair complete?	—	Go to ABS Diagnostic System Check	—
21	Using J 39200 DMM, measure the voltage at terminal 15 of J 39700. Is the voltage within the range specified in the value(s) column?	Above 1V	Go to Step 22	Go to Step 23
22	Repair CKT 873 for a short to voltage. Is the repair complete?	—	Go to ABS Diagnostic System Check	—
23	Replace the EBTCM. Is the replacement complete?	—	Go to ABS Diagnostic System Check	—

GC402970264400CX

Fig. 122 Code C1232: LH Front Wheel Speed Circuit Open Or Shorted (Part 3 of 3). Corvette

Circuit Description

The speed sensor used on this vehicle is a single point magnetic pickup. This sensor produces an AC signal that the EBTCM uses the frequency from to calculate the wheel speed.

Conditions for Setting the DTC

The DTC can be set any time the ignition is in the ON position, and the EBTCM senses an open, a short to ground, or a short to battery.

Action Taken When the DTC Sets

A malfunction DTC is stored, ABS/TCS is disabled and the ABS and Traction Control Indicators are turned ON.

Conditions for Clearing the DTC

- Condition for DTC is no longer present and scan tool clear DTC function is used.
- Fifty ignition cycles have passed with no DTC(s) detected.

Diagnostic Aids

- It is very important that a thorough inspection of the wiring and connectors be performed. Failure to carefully and fully inspect wiring and connectors may result in misdiagnosis, causing part replacement with reappearance of the malfunction.
- An intermittent malfunction can be caused by poor connections, broken insulation, or a wire that is broken inside the insulation.

Test Description

The numbers below refer to step numbers on the diagnostic table.

4. Checks for an open in the WSS or WSS CKT.
12. Checks for a short to ground in the WSS or WSS CKT.
19. Checks for a short to voltage in the WSS CKT.
21. Checks for a short to voltage in the WSS CKT.

GC402970264500AX

Fig. 123 Code C1233: RH Front Wheel Speed Circuit Open Or Shorted (Part 1 of 3). Corvette

Step	Action	Value(s)	Yes	No
1	Was the Diagnostic System Check performed?	—	*Go to Step 2*	Go to *ABS Diagnostic System Check*
2	1. Inspect the WSS wiring and connectors for damage. 2. Inspect the WSS for looseness or damage. Is physical damage of sensor evident?	—	*Go to Step 3*	*Go to Step 4*
3	Repair as necessary. Is the repair complete?	—	Go to *ABS Diagnostic System Check*	—
4	1. Turn the ignition switch to the OFF position. 2. Disconnect the EBTCM. 3. Install the *J 39700* Universal Pinout Box using the *J 39700-25* cable adapter to the EBTCM harness connector only. 4. Using *J 39200* DMM, measure the resistance between terminals 14 and 30 of *J 39700*. Is the resistance within the range specified in the value(s) column?	850 - 1350Ω	*Go to Step 12*	*Go to Step 5*
5	1. Disconnect the RF Wheel Speed Sensor. 2. Using *J 39200* DMM, measure the resistance between terminals A and B of the Wheel Speed Sensor Connector. Is the resistance within the range specified in the value(s) column?	850 - 1350Ω	*Go to Step 6*	*Go to Step 11*
6	1. Connect a jumper between the RF Wheel Speed Sensor harness connector terminal A and ground. 2. Using *J 39200* DMM, measure the resistance between terminals 30 and B of *J 39700*. Is the resistance within the range specified in the value(s) column?	0 - 5Ω	*Go to Step 8*	*Go to Step 7*
7	Repair CKT 872 for an open or high resistance. Is the repair complete?	—	Go to *ABS Diagnostic System Check*	—
8	1. Connect a jumper between the RF Wheel Speed Sensor harness connector terminal B and ground. 2. Using *J 39200* DMM, measure the resistance between terminals 14 and B of *J 39700*. Is the resistance within the range specified in the value(s) column?	0 - 5Ω	*Go to Step 10*	*Go to Step 9*
9	Repair CKT 833 for an open or high resistance. Is the repair complete?	—	Go to *ABS Diagnostic System Check*	—
10	Malfunction is intermittent. Inspect all connectors and harnesses for damage that may result in an open or high resistance when connected. Is the repair complete?	—	Go to *ABS Diagnostic System Check*	—
11	Replace the Wheel Speed Sensor. Is the replacement complete?	—	Go to *ABS Diagnostic System Check*	—

GC402970264500BX

Fig. 123 Code C1233: RH Front Wheel Speed Circuit Open Or Shorted (Part 2 of 3). Corvette

Circuit Description

The speed sensor used on this vehicle is a single point magnetic pickup. This sensor produces an AC signal that the EBTCM uses the frequency from to calculate the wheel speed.

Conditions for Setting the DTC

The DTC can be set any time the ignition is in the ON position, and the EBTCM senses an open, a short to ground, or a short to battery.

Action Taken When the DTC Sets

A malfunction DTC is stored, ABS/TCS is disabled and the ABS and Traction Control Indicators are turned ON.

Conditions for Clearing the DTC

- Condition for DTC is no longer present and scan tool clear DTC function is used.
- Fifty ignition cycles have passed with no DTC(s) detected.

Diagnostic Aids

- It is very important that a thorough inspection of the wiring and connectors be performed. Failure to carefully and fully inspect wiring and connectors may result in misdiagnosis, causing part replacement with reappearance of the malfunction.
- An intermittent malfunction can be caused by poor connections, broken insulation, or a wire that is broken inside the insulation.

Test Description

The numbers below refer to step numbers on the diagnostic table.

4. Checks for an open in the WSS or WSS CKT.
12. Checks for a short to ground in the WSS or WSS CKT.
19. Checks for a short to voltage in the WSS CKT.
21. Checks for a short to voltage in the WSS CKT.

GC402970264600AX

Fig. 124 Code C1234: LH Rear Wheel Speed Circuit Open Or Shorted (Part 1 of 3). Corvette

Step	Action	Value(s)	Yes	No
12	Using *J 39200* DMM, measure the resistance between terminals 14 and B of *J 39700*. Is the resistance within the range specified in the value(s) column?	OL (infinite)	*Go to Step 19*	*Go to Step 13*
13	1. Disconnect the RF Wheel Speed Sensor. 2. Using *J 39200* DMM, measure the resistance between terminal A and ground of the Wheel Speed Sensor Connector. Is the resistance within the range specified in the value(s) column?	OL (infinite)	*Go to Step 14*	*Go to Step 11*
14	1. Using *J 39200* DMM, measure the resistance between terminals 30 and B of *J 39700*. Is the resistance within the range specified in the value(s) column?	OL (infinite)	*Go to Step 16*	*Go to Step 15*
15	Repair CKT 872 for a short to ground. Is the repair complete?	—	Go to *ABS Diagnostic System Check*	—
16	Using *J 39200* DMM, measure the resistance between terminals 14 and B of *J 39700*. Is the resistance within the range specified in the value(s) column?	OL (infinite)	*Go to Step 17*	*Go to Step 18*
17	Malfunction is intermittent. Inspect all connectors and harnesses for damage that may result in a short to ground when connected. Is the repair complete?	—	Go to *ABS Diagnostic System Check*	—
18	Repair CKT 833 for a short to ground. Is the repair complete?	—	Go to *ABS Diagnostic System Check*	—
19	1. Disconnect the RF Wheel Speed Sensor. 2. Turn the ignition switch to the ON position, engine OFF. 3. Using *J 39200* DMM, measure the voltage at terminal 30 of *J 39700*. Is the voltage within the range specified in the value(s) column?	Above 1V	*Go to Step 20*	*Go to Step 21*
20	Repair CKT 872 for a short to voltage. Is the repair complete?	—	Go to *ABS Diagnostic System Check*	—
21	Using *J 39200* DMM, measure the voltage at terminal 14 of *J 39700*. Is the voltage within the range specified in the value(s) column?	Above 1V	*Go to Step 22*	*Go to Step 23*
22	Repair CKT 833 for a short to voltage. Is the repair complete?	—	Go to *ABS Diagnostic System Check*	—
23	Replace the EBTCM. Is the replacement complete?	—	Go to *ABS Diagnostic System Check*	—

GC402970264500CX

Fig. 123 Code C1233: RH Front Wheel Speed Circuit Open Or Shorted (Part 3 of 3). Corvette

Step	Action	Value(s)	Yes	No
1	Was the Diagnostic System Check performed?	—	*Go to Step 2*	Go to *ABS Diagnostic System Check*
2	1. Inspect the WSS wiring and connectors for damage. 2. Inspect the WSS for looseness or damage. Is physical damage of sensor evident?	—	*Go to Step 3*	*Go to Step 4*
3	Repair as necessary. Is the repair complete?	—	Go to *ABS Diagnostic System Check*	—
4	1. Turn the ignition switch to the OFF position. 2. Disconnect the EBTCM. 3. Install the *J 39700* Universal Pinout Box using the *J 39700-25* cable adapter to the EBTCM harness connector only. 4. Using *J 39200* DMM, measure the resistance between terminals 12 and 28 of *J 39700*. Is the resistance within the range specified in the value(s) column?	850 - 1350Ω	*Go to Step 12*	*Go to Step 5*
5	1. Disconnect the LR Wheel Speed Sensor. 2. Using *J 39200* DMM, measure the resistance between terminals A and B of the Wheel Speed Sensor Connector. Is the resistance within the range specified in the value(s) column?	850 - 1350Ω	*Go to Step 6*	*Go to Step 11*
6	Using *J 39200* DMM, measure the resistance between terminals 12 of *J 39700* and A of the LR Wheel Speed Sensor harness connector. Is the resistance within the range specified in the value(s) column?	0 - 5Ω	*Go to Step 8*	*Go to Step 7*
7	Repair CKT 884 for an open or high resistance. Is the repair complete?	—	Go to *ABS Diagnostic System Check*	—
8	Using *J 39200* DMM, measure the resistance between terminals 28 of *J 39700* and B of the LR Wheel Speed Sensor harness connector. Is the resistance within the range specified in the value(s) column?	0 - 5Ω	*Go to Step 10*	*Go to Step 9*
9	Repair CKT 885 for an open or high resistance. Is the repair complete?	—	Go to *ABS Diagnostic System Check*	—
10	Malfunction is intermittent. Inspect all connectors and harnesses for damage that may result in an open or high resistance when connected. Is the repair complete?	—	Go to *ABS Diagnostic System Check*	—
11	Replace the Wheel Speed Sensor. Is the replacement complete?	—	Go to *ABS Diagnostic System Check*	—
12	Using *J 39200* DMM, measure the resistance between terminals 28 and B of *J 39700*. Is the resistance within the range specified in the value(s) column?	OL (infinite)	*Go to Step 19*	*Go to Step 13*

GC402970264600BX

Fig. 124 Code C1234: LH Rear Wheel Speed Circuit Open Or Shorted (Part 2 of 3). Corvette

Step	Action	Value(s)	Yes	No
13	1. Disconnect the LR Wheel Speed Sensor. 2. Using *J 39200* DMM, measure the resistance between terminal A and ground of the Wheel Speed Sensor Connector. Is the resistance within the range specified in the value(s) column?	OL (infinite)	*Go to Step 14*	*Go to Step 11*
14	1. Using *J 39200* DMM, measure the resistance between terminals 12 and B of *J 39700*. Is the resistance within the range specified in the value(s) column?	OL (infinite)	*Go to Step 16*	*Go to Step 15*
15	Repair CKT 884 for a short to ground. Is the repair complete?	—	Go to *ABS Diagnostic System Check*	—
16	Using *J 39200* DMM, measure the resistance between terminals 28 and B of *J 39700*. Is the resistance within the range specified in the value(s) column?	OL (infinite)	*Go to Step 17*	*Go to Step 18*
17	Malfunction is intermittent. Inspect all connectors and harnesses for damage that may result in a short to ground when connected. Is the repair complete?	—	Go to *ABS Diagnostic System Check*	—
18	Repair CKT 885 for a short to ground. Is the repair complete?	—	Go to *ABS Diagnostic System Check*	—
19	1. Disconnect the LR Wheel Speed Sensor. 2. Turn the ignition switch to the ON position, engine OFF. 3. Using *J 39200* DMM, measure the voltage at terminal 12 of *J 39700*. Is the voltage within the range specified in the value(s) column?	Above 1V	*Go to Step 20*	*Go to Step 21*
20	Repair CKT 884 for a short to voltage. Is the repair complete?	—	Go to *ABS Diagnostic System Check*	—
21	Using *J 39200* DMM, measure the voltage at terminal 28 of *J 39700*. Is the voltage within the range specified in the value(s) column?	Above 1V	*Go to Step 22*	*Go to Step 23*
22	Repair CKT 885 for a short to voltage. Is the repair complete?	—	Go to *ABS Diagnostic System Check*	—
23	Replace the EBTCM. Is the replacement complete?	—	Go to *ABS Diagnostic System Check*	—

GC402970264600CX

Fig. 124 Code C1234: LH Rear Wheel Speed Circuit Open Or Shorted (Part 3 of 3). Corvette

Step	Action	Value(s)	Yes	No
1	Was the Diagnostic System Check performed?	—	*Go to Step 2*	Go to *ABS Diagnostic System Check*
2	1. Inspect the WSS wiring and connectors for damage. 2. Inspect the WSS for looseness or damage. Is physical damage of sensor evident?	—	*Go to Step 3*	*Go to Step 4*
3	Repair as necessary. Is the repair complete?	—	Go to *ABS Diagnostic System Check*	—
4	1. Turn the ignition switch to the OFF position. 2. Disconnect the EBTCM. 3. Install the *J 39700* Universal Pinout Box using the *J 39700-25* cable adapter to the EBTCM harness connector only. 4. Using *J 39200* DMM, measure the resistance between terminals 13 and 29 of *J 39700*. Is the resistance within the range specified in the value(s) column?	850 - 1350Ω	*Go to Step 12*	*Go to Step 5*
5	1. Disconnect the RR Wheel Speed Sensor. 2. Using *J 39200* DMM, measure the resistance between terminals A and B of the Wheel Speed Sensor Connector. Is the resistance within the range specified in the value(s) column?	850 - 1350Ω	*Go to Step 6*	*Go to Step 11*
6	Using *J 39200* DMM, measure the resistance between terminals 29 of *J 39700* and A of the RR Wheel Speed Sensor harness connector. Is the resistance within the range specified in the value(s) column?	0 - 5Ω	*Go to Step 8*	*Go to Step 7*
7	Repair CKT 882 for an open or high resistance. Is the repair complete?	—	Go to *ABS Diagnostic System Check*	—
8	Using *J 39200* DMM, measure the resistance between terminals 13 of *J 39700* and B of the RR Wheel Speed Sensor harness connector. Is the resistance within the range specified in the value(s) column?	0 - 5Ω	*Go to Step 10*	*Go to Step 9*
9	Repair CKT 883 for an open or high resistance. Is the repair complete?	—	Go to *ABS Diagnostic System Check*	—
10	Malfunction is intermittent. Inspect all connectors and harnesses for damage that may result in an open or high resistance when connected. Is the repair complete?	—	Go to *ABS Diagnostic System Check*	—
11	Replace the Wheel Speed Sensor. Is the replacement complete?	—	Go to *ABS Diagnostic System Check*	—
12	Using *J 39200* DMM, measure the resistance between terminals 13 and B of *J 39700*. Is the resistance within the range specified in the value(s) column?	OL (infinite)	*Go to Step 19*	*Go to Step 13*

GC402970264700BX

Fig. 125 Code C1235: RH Rear Wheel Speed Circuit Open Or Shorted (Part 2 of 3). Corvette

Circuit Description

The speed sensor used on this vehicle is a single point magnetic pickup. This sensor produces an AC signal that the EBTCM uses the frequency from to calculate the wheel speed.

Conditions for Setting the DTC

The DTC can be set any time the ignition is in the ON position, and the EBTCM senses an open, a short to ground, or a short to battery.

Action Taken When the DTC Sets

A malfunction DTC is stored, ABS/TCS is disabled and the ABS and Traction Control Indicators are turned ON.

Conditions for Clearing the DTC

- Condition for DTC is no longer present and scan tool clear DTC function is used.
- Fifty ignition cycles have passed with no DTC(s) detected.

Diagnostic Aids

- It is very important that a thorough inspection of the wiring and connectors be performed. Failure to carefully and fully inspect wiring and connectors may result in misdiagnosis, causing part replacement with reappearance of the malfunction.
- An intermittent malfunction can be caused by poor connections, broken insulation, or a wire that is broken inside the insulation.

Test Description

The numbers below refer to step numbers on the diagnostic table.

4. Checks for an open in the WSS or WSS CKT.
12. Checks for a short to ground in the WSS or WSS CKT.
19. Checks for a short to voltage in the WSS CKT.
21. Checks for a short to voltage in the WSS CKT.

GC402970264700AX

Fig. 125 Code C1235: RH Rear Wheel Speed Circuit Open Or Shorted (Part 1 of 3). Corvette

Step	Action	Value(s)	Yes	No
13	1. Disconnect the RR Wheel Speed Sensor. 2. Using *J 39200* DMM, measure the resistance between terminal A and ground of the Wheel Speed Sensor Connector. Is the resistance within the range specified in the value(s) column?	OL (infinite)	*Go to Step 14*	*Go to Step 11*
14	Using *J 39200* DMM, measure the resistance between terminals 29 and B of *J 39700*. Is the resistance within the range specified in the value(s) column?	OL (infinite)	*Go to Step 16*	*Go to Step 15*
15	Repair CKT 882 for a short to ground. Is the repair complete?	—	Go to *ABS Diagnostic System Check*	—
16	Using *J 39200* DMM, measure the resistance between terminals 13 and B of *J 39700*. Is the resistance within the range specified in the value(s) column?	OL (infinite)	*Go to Step 17*	*Go to Step 18*
17	Malfunction is intermittent. Inspect all connectors and harnesses for damage that may result in a short to ground when connected. Is the repair complete?	—	Go to *ABS Diagnostic System Check*	—
18	Repair CKT 883 for a short to ground. Is the repair complete?	—	Go to *ABS Diagnostic System Check*	—
19	1. Disconnect the RR Wheel Speed Sensor. 2. Turn the ignition switch to the ON position, engine OFF. 3. Using *J 39200* DMM, measure the voltage at terminal 29 of *J 39700*. Is the voltage within the range specified in the value(s) column?	Above 1V	*Go to Step 20*	*Go to Step 21*
20	Repair CKT 882 for a short to voltage. Is the repair complete?	—	Go to *ABS Diagnostic System Check*	—
21	Using *J 39200* DMM, measure the voltage at terminal 13 of *J 39700*. Is the voltage within the range specified in the value(s) column?	Above 1V	*Go to Step 22*	*Go to Step 23*
22	Repair CKT 883 for a short to voltage. Is the repair complete?	—	Go to *ABS Diagnostic System Check*	—
23	Replace the EBTCM. Is the replacement complete?	—	Go to *ABS Diagnostic System Check*	—

GC402970264700CX

Fig. 125 Code C1235: RH Rear Wheel Speed Circuit Open Or Shorted (Part 3 of 3). Corvette

Circuit Description

This circuit is used to monitor the voltage level available to the EBTCM. If the voltage drops below 10.5 volts, full performance of the ABS/TCS/Active Handling (if equipped with RPO JL4) cannot be guaranteed. During ABS/TCS/Active Handling operation, there are several current requirements that will cause battery voltage to drop. Because of this, voltage is monitored prior to ABS/TCS/Active Handling operation to indicate good charging system condition and also during ABS/TCS/Active Handling operation when voltage may drop significantly.

Conditions for Setting the DTC

DTC C1236 can only be set if the vehicle's speed is greater than 8 km/h (5 mph). If both the battery and ignition voltages are less than 10.5 volts, a malfunction DTC will set.

Action Taken When the DTC Sets

ABS/TCS/Active Handling (if equipped with RPO JL4) are disabled.

- Indicators that turn on:
  - ABS indicator
  - Car Icon (TCS indicator)
- Messages displayed on the DIC:
  - Service ABS
  - Service Traction System
  - Service Active HNDLG

Conditions for Clearing the DTC

- Condition for DTC is no longer present and Scan Tool clear DTC function is used.
- 50 Ignition cycles have passed with no DTCs detected.

Diagnostic Aids

- It is very important that a thorough inspection of the wiring and connectors be performed. Failure to carefully and fully inspect wiring and connectors may result in misdiagnosis, causing part replacement with reappearance of the malfunction.
- If an intermittent malfunction exists refer to *Intermittents*
- Check for other low voltage conditions.
- Test the charging system.
- Possible causes for DTC C1236 to set:
  - Charging System Malfunction.
  - Excessive Battery Draw.
  - Weak Battery.
  - Faulty system ground.

GC4029803949010X

Fig. 126 Code C1236: Low System Supply Voltage (Part 1 of 2). Corvette

Test Description

The numbers below refer to step numbers on the diagnostic table.

4. Checks for a good ground.
6. Checks for battery voltage.

Step	Action	Value(s)	Yes	No
1	Was the Diagnostic System Check performed?	—	*Go to Step 2*	Go to *Diagnostic System Check (ABS)*
2	Check the charging system. Is the Charging System OK?	—	*Go to Step 3*	Inspect *Charging System*
3	1. Turn the ignition switch to the OFF position. 2. Disconnect the EBTCM harness connector and inspect both the harness connector and the EBTCM connector for signs of corrosion or damage. Is their evidence of any corrosion or damage?	—	*Go to Step 7*	*Go to Step 4*
4	1. Install *J 39700* Universal Pinout Box using *J 39700-25* cable adapter between the EBTCM harness connector and the EBTCM. 2. Using *J 39200* DMM measure the resistance between terminal B of *J 39700* and a good ground. Is the resistance within the range specified in the value(s) column?	0–2Ω	*Go to Step 5*	*Go to Step 8*
5	Measure the voltage between terminals D and B of *J 39700*. Is the voltage within the range specified in the value(s) column?	Above 10.5 V	*Go to Step 6*	Voltmeter Displays High or Low
6	1. Turn the ignition switch to the ON position, engine off. 2. Measure the voltage at terminals A and B of *J 39700*. Is the voltage within the range specified in the value(s) column?	Above 10.5 V	*Go to Step 9*	Voltmeter Displays High or Low
7	Repair as necessary Is the repair complete?	—	Go to *Diagnostic System Check (ABS)*	—
8	Repair open or high resistance in CKT 1251. Is the repair complete?	—	Go to *Diagnostic System Check (ABS)*	—
9	Replace the EBTCM. Is the replacement complete?	—	Go to *Diagnostic System Check (ABS)*	—

GC4029803949020X

Fig. 126 Code C1236: Low System Supply Voltage (Part 2 of 2). Corvette

Step	Action	Value(s)	Yes	No
1	Was the Diagnostic System Check performed?	—	*Go to Step 2*	Go to *Diagnostic System Check (ABS)*
2	1. Turn all accessories off. 2. Start engine. 3. Using the scan tool select ABS/TCS or ABS/TCS/Active Handling DATA LIST and monitor battery voltage while running engine at approximately 2000 RPM. Is the voltage within the range specified in the Value(s) column?	Less than 17 V	*Go to Step 4*	*Go to Step 3*
3	Check actual battery voltage, using *J 39200* DMM, while running engine at approximately 2000 RPM. Is the voltage within the range specified in the Value(s) column?	Less than 17 V	*Go to Step 4*	Inspect *Charging System*
4	Carefully test drive vehicle above 8 km/h (5 mph). Does DTC C1237 reset as a current DTC?	—	*Go to Step 5*	Go to *Diagnostic System Check (ABS)*
5	Replace the EBTCM. Is repair complete?	—	Go to *Diagnostic System Check (ABS)*	—

GC4029803950020X

Fig. 127 Code C1237: High System Supply Voltage (Part 2 of 2). Corvette

Circuit Description

This circuit is designed to detect high vehicle voltage levels to the solenoid relay. High voltage may cause damage to the system.

Conditions for Setting the DTC

DTC C1237 can only be set if the vehicle's speed is greater than 8 km/h (5 mph). If the battery voltage is greater than 17 volts, a malfunction exists.

Action Taken When the DTC Sets

ABS/TCS/Active Handling are disabled.

- Indicators that turn on:
  - ABS indicator
  - Car Icon (TCS indicator)
- Messages displayed on the DIC:
  - Service ABS
  - Service Traction System
  - Service Active HNDLG

Conditions for Clearing the DTC

- Condition for DTC is no longer present and scan tool clear DTC function is used.
- Fifty ignition cycles have passed with no DTCs detected.

Diagnostic Aids

- If an intermittent malfunction exists refer to *Intermittents*
- Possible causes for DTC C1237 to set:
- Overcharging

Test Description

The numbers below refer to step numbers on the diagnostic table.

2. Checks to see what the EBTCM is reading as the voltage.
3. Checks the actual battery voltage.

GC4029803950010X

Fig. 127 Code C1237: High System Supply Voltage (Part 1 of 2). Corvette

Circuit Description

The BPMV pump motor ground is supplied through a ground stud on the pump motor to a good ground.

Conditions for Setting the DTC

DTC C1242 can be set when the pump relay is commanded off. A malfunction exists if the pump motor ground CKT 1250 resistance is greater than 6900 ohms.

Action Taken When the DTC Sets

ABS/TCS/Active Handling are disabled.

- Indicators that turn on:
  - ABS indicator
  - Car Icon (TCS indicator)
- Messages displayed on the DIC:
  - Service ABS
  - Service Traction System
  - Service Active HNDLG

Conditions for Clearing the DTC

- Condition for DTC is no longer present and scan tool clear DTC function is used.
- Fifty ignition cycles have passed with no DTCs detected.

Diagnostic Aids

- It is very important that a thorough inspection of the wiring and connectors be performed. Failure to carefully and fully inspect wiring and connectors may result in misdiagnosis, causing part replacement with reappearance of the malfunction.
- An intermittent malfunction can be caused by poor connections, broken insulation, or a wire that is broken inside the insulation.
- If an intermittent malfunction exists refer to *Intermittents*

Test Description

The numbers below refer to step numbers on the diagnostic table.

2. Checks for good pump motor ground.
4. Checks for good pump motor ground through the BPMV.

GC4029803951010X

Fig. 128 Code C1242: BPMV Pump Motor Ground Circuit Open (Part 1 of 2). Corvette

Step	Action	Value(s)	Yes	No
1	Was the Diagnostic System Check performed?	—	*Go to Step 2*	Go to *Diagnostic System Check (ABS)*
2	1. Turn the ignition switch to the OFF position. 2. Using *J 39200* DMM, measure resistance between the motor ground stud and a good chassis ground. Is the resistance within the range specified in the Value(s) column?	0–2 Ω	*Go to Step 3*	*Go to Step 8*
3	1. Disconnect the EBTCM connector. 2. Remove the EBTCM from BPMV. 3. Inspect the EBTCM to BPMV connector for conditions which could cause intermittents, such as damage, corrosion, poor terminal contact, or presence of brake fluid. Is connector OK and cavity free of brake fluid?	—	*Go to Step 4*	*Go to Step 5*
4	Using *J 39200* DMM, measure resistance between BPMV internal connector terminal 8 and motor ground stud. Is the resistance within the range specified in the Value(s) column?	0.2–10 Ω	*Go to Step 6*	*Go to Step 7*
5	1. If connector corrosion or damage is evident, replace BPMV and/or EBTCM as necessary. 2. If brake fluid is present, replace BPMV and EBTCM. Is the replacement complete?	—	Go to *Diagnostic System Check (ABS)*	—
6	Replace the EBTCM. Is repair complete?	—	Go to *Diagnostic System Check (ABS)*	—
7	Replace the BPMV. Is repair complete?	—	Go to *Diagnostic System Check (ABS)*	—
8	Repair open or high resistance in CKT 1250. Is repair complete?	—	Go to *Diagnostic System Check (ABS)*	—

GC4029803951020X

Fig. 128 Code C1242: BPMV Pump Motor Ground Circuit Open (Part 2 of 2). Corvette

Circuit Description

When the pump motor relay is grounded by the EBTCM, it closes and provides battery voltage to operate the pump.

Conditions for Setting the DTC

DTC C1243 can be set when the pump motor relay has been commanded off after the pump motor has been on. A malfunction has occurred if the pump motor was on, and the EBTCM sensed a stuck or slowly turning pump motor.

Action Taken When the DTC Sets

ABS/TCS/Active Handling are disabled.

- Indicators that turn on:
  - ABS indicator
  - Car Icon (TCS indicator)
- Messages displayed on the DIC:
  - Service ABS
  - Service Traction System
  - Service Active HNDLG

Conditions for Clearing the DTC

- Condition for DTC is no longer present and scan tool clear DTC function is used.
- Fifty ignition cycles have passed with no DTCs detected.

Diagnostic Aids

- It is very important that a thorough inspection of the wiring and connectors be performed. Failure to carefully and fully inspect wiring and connectors may result in misdiagnosis, causing part replacement with reappearance of the malfunction.
- An intermittent malfunction can be caused by poor connections, broken insulation, or a wire that is broken inside the insulation.
- If an intermittent malfunction exists refer to *Intermittents*

Test Description

The numbers below refer to step numbers on the diagnostic table.

3. Checks for good pump motor ground.
5. Checks for good pump motor ground through the BPMV.

GC4029803952010X

Fig. 129 Code C1243: BPMV Pump Motor Stalled (Part 1 of 2). Corvette

Circuit Description

The EBTCM uses input from the Brake Pressure Sensor for more accurate control during an Active Handling event.

Conditions for Setting the DTC

DTC C1245 can be set after two consecutive ignition cycles if the vehicle speed is greater than 40 Km/h (25 mph) and the Brake Pressure Sensor is always above 100 psi.

Action Taken When the DTC Sets

Active Handling is disabled.

- Indicators that turn on:
  Car Icon (TCS indicator)
- Messages displayed on the DIC:
  Service Active HNDLG

Conditions for Clearing the DTC

- Condition for DTC is no longer present and scan tool clear DTC function is used.
- Fifty ignition cycles have passed with no DTCs detected.

Diagnostic Aids

- It is very important that a thorough inspection of the wiring and connectors be performed. Failure to carefully and fully inspect wiring and connectors may result in misdiagnosis, causing part replacement with reappearance of the malfunction.
- An intermittent malfunction can be caused by poor connections, broken insulation, or a wire that is broken inside the insulation.
- If an intermittent malfunction exists refer to *Intermittents*

Test Description

The number(s) below refer to the step number(s) on the diagnostic table.

2. This step checks for the proper signal state.
4. This step checks for a short to voltage.

GC4029803953010X

Fig. 130 Code C1245: Brake Pressure Sensor Always High (Part 1 of 2). Corvette

Circuit Description

The EBTCM monitors the Brake Pressure Differential Switch to turn off Traction Control and Active Handling if a pressure loss is detected in the hydraulic brake system.

Conditions for Setting the DTC

DTC C1247 can be set anytime, if the EBTCM detects the Brake Pressure Differential Switch has been grounded due to loss of brake pressure or a short to ground.

Action Taken When the DTC Sets

TCS/Active Handling are disabled.

- Indicators that turn on:
  - RED Brake Warning indicator
  - Car Icon (TCS indicator)
- Messages displayed on the DIC:
  - Service Traction System
  - Service Active HNDLG

Conditions for Clearing the DTC

- Condition for DTC is no longer present and scan tool clear DTC function is used.
- Fifty ignition cycles have passed with no DTCs detected.

Diagnostic Aids

- DTC C1247 could be set during a hydraulic brake system bleeding procedure if the ignition switch is in the ON position.
- It is very important that a thorough inspection of the wiring and connectors be performed. Failure to carefully and fully inspect wiring and connectors may result in misdiagnosis, causing part replacement with reappearance of the malfunction.
- An intermittent malfunction can be caused by poor connections, broken insulation, or a wire that is broken inside the insulation.
- If an intermittent malfunction exists refer to *Intermittents*

Test Description

The number(s) below refer to the step number(s) on the diagnostic table.

2. This step checks for a short to ground in the Brake Pressure Differential Switch circuit.
4. This step indicates that the Brake Pressure Differential Switch circuit is operating properly, and the cause of the DTC is a failure in the hydraulic brake system.

GC4029803954010X

Fig. 131 Code C1247: Brake Pressure Differential Switch Activated (Part 1 of 2). Corvette

Step	Action	Value(s)	Yes	No
1	Was the Diagnostic System Check performed?	—	*Go to Step 2*	Go to *Diagnostic System Check (ABS)*
2	Is DTC 1217 also set as a current DTC?	—	Go to *DTC C1217 BPMV Pump Motor Rly Contact CKT Open*	*Go to Step 3*
3	1. Turn the ignition switch to the OFF position. 2. Using the *J 39200* DMM, measure the resistance between the pump motor ground stud and a good chassis ground. Is the resistance within the range specified in the value(s) column?	0–2 Ω	*Go to Step 4*	*Go to Step 9*
4	1. Disconnect the EBTCM connector. 2. Remove the EBTCM from the BPMV. 3. Inspect the EBTCM to BPMV connector for conditions which could cause intermittents, such as damage, corrosion, poor terminal contact, or presence of brake fluid. Is connector OK and cavity free of brake fluid?	—	*Go to Step 5*	*Go to Step 6*
5	1. Install the *J 41247* Pinout Box to the BPMV connector. 2. Using the *J 39200* DMM, measure the resistance between the *J 41247* terminal 8 and the pump motor ground stud. Is the resistance within the range specified in the Value(s) column?	0.2–10 Ω	*Go to Step 7*	*Go to Step 8*
6	1. If connector corrosion or damage is evident, replace BPMV and/or EBTCM as necessary. 2. If brake fluid is present, replace BPMV and EBTCM. Is the replacement complete?	—	Go to *Diagnostic System Check (ABS)*	—
7	Replace the EBTCM. Is the replacement complete?	—	Go to *Diagnostic System Check (ABS)*	—
8	Replace the BPMV. Is the replacement complete?	—	Go to *Diagnostic System Check (ABS)*	—
9	Repair open or high resistance in CKT 1250. Is the repair complete?	—	Go to *Diagnostic System Check (ABS)*	—

GC4029803952020X

Fig. 129 Code C1243: BPMV Pump Motor Stalled (Part 2 of 2). Corvette

Step	Action	Value(s)	Yes	No
1	Was the Diagnostic System Check performed?	—	*Go to Step 2*	Go to *Diagnostic System Check (ABS)*
2	1. Turn the ignition switch to the ON position, engine off. 2. Using a scan tool in ABS/TCS/Active Handling Data List read the Brake Pressure Sensor State. Does the Brake Pressure Sensor State read OFF?	—	*Go to Step 3*	*Go to Step 4*
3	Replace the EBTCM. Is the replacement complete?	—	Go to *Diagnostic System Check (ABS)*	—
4	1. Turn the ignition switch to the OFF position. 2. Disconnect the EBTCM harness connector. 3. Install the *J 39700* Universal Pinout Box using the *J 39700-25* cable adapter to the EBTCM harness connector only. 4. Disconnect the Brake Pressure Sensor connector. 5. Turn the ignition switch to the ON position, engine OFF. 6. Using *J 39200* DMM, measure the voltage at terminal 24 of *J 39700*. Is the voltage within the range specified in the values column?	Above 1.5 V	*Go to Step 5*	*Go to Step 6*
5	Repair CKT 901 for a short to voltage. Is the repair complete?	—	Go to *Diagnostic System Check (ABS)*	—
6	Replace the Brake Pressure Sensor. Is the replacement complete?	—	Go to *Diagnostic System Check (ABS)*	—

GC4029803953020X

Fig. 130 Code C1245: Brake Pressure Sensor Always High (Part 2 of 2). Corvette

Step	Action	Value(s)	Yes	No
1	Was the Diagnostic System Check performed?	—	*Go to Step 2*	Go to *Diagnostic System Check (ABS)*
2	1. Turn the ignition switch to the OFF position. 2. Disconnect the Brake Pressure Differential Switch connector. 3. Turn the ignition switch to the ON position, engine off. Does the Red BRAKE Warning Indicator remain on?	—	*Go to Step 3*	*Go to Step 4*
3	Repair circuit 1659 for a short to ground. Is the repair complete?	—	Go to *Diagnostic System Check (ABS)*	—
4	The Brake Pressure Differential Switch is working properly. Is the repair complete?	—	Go to *Diagnostic System Check (ABS)*	—

GC4029803954020X

Fig. 131 Code C1247: Brake Pressure Differential Switch Activated (Part 2 of 2). Corvette

Circuit Description

The IP monitors the master cylinder fluid level, if the fluid level becomes low the IP will turn on the Red BRAKE Warning indicator to inform the driver to have the hydraulic brake system checked.

Conditions for Setting the DTC

DTC C1248 can be set anytime ignition is present, and a low master cylinder fluid level has been detected by the IP and indicated to the EBTCM by the IP broadcasting a Class 2 message.

Action Taken When the DTC Sets

TCS/Active Handling are disabled.

- Indicators that turn on:
  - RED Brake Warning indicator
  - Car Icon (TCS indicator)
- Messages displayed on the DIC:
  - Service Traction System
  - Service Active HNDLG

Conditions for Clearing the DTC

- Condition for DTC is no longer present and scan tool clear DTC function is used.
- Fifty ignition cycles have passed with no DTCs detected.

Diagnostic Aids

- If an intermittent malfunction exists refer to *Intermittents*
- DTC C1248 is used by the EBTCM for information only. It does not indicate a failure of the ABS/TCS/Active Handling system.

GC4029803955000X

Fig. 132 Code C1248: IPC Indicated Low Brake Fluid. Corvette

Step	Action	Value(s)	Yes	No
1	Was the Diagnostic System Check performed?	—	*Go to Step 2*	Go to *ABS Diagnostic System Check*
2	Are any other DTC(s) present besides C1255xx?	—	Go to Applicable DTC Table	*Go to Step 3*
3	1. Turn the ignition switch to the OFF position. 2. Disconnect the EBTCM. 3. Check for damaged, pushed out, or miswired terminals. Was any damage found?	—	*Go to Step 4*	*Go to Step 5*
4	Repair as necessary. Is the repair complete?	—	Go to *ABS Diagnostic System Check*	—
5	Replace the EBTCM. Is the replacement complete?	—	Go to *ABS Diagnostic System Check*	—

GC402970265200BX

Fig. 133 Code C1255: EBTCM Internal Fault w/ABS/TCS Disabled (Part 2 of 2). Corvette

Step	Action	Value(s)	Yes	No
1	Was the Diagnostic System Check performed?	—	*Go to Step 2*	Go to *ABS Diagnostic System Check*
2	Are any valve solenoid DTC(s) present (C1261 - C1274)?	—	Go to Applicable DTC Table	*Go to Step 3*
3	1. Turn the ignition switch to the OFF position. 2. Disconnect the EBTCM. 3. Check for damaged, pushed out, or miswired terminals. Was any damage found?	—	*Go to Step 4*	*Go to Step 5*
4	Repair as necessary. Is the repair complete?	—	Go to *ABS Diagnostic System Check*	—
5	Replace the EBTCM. Is the replacement complete?	—	Go to *ABS Diagnostic System Check*	—

GC402970265300BX

Fig. 134 Code C1256: EBTCM Internal Fault (Part 2 of 2). Corvette

Circuit Description

The Inlet valve solenoid circuits are supplied with battery power when the ignition is in the ON position. The EBTCM controls the valve functions by grounding the circuit when necessary.

Conditions for Setting the DTC

The EBTCM senses a discrepancy such as an open, short to ground, or short to voltage in the circuit.

Action Taken When the DTC Sets

A malfunction DTC is stored, ABS/TCS is disabled and the ABS and Traction Control Indicaters are turned ON.

Conditions for Clearing the DTC

- Condition for DTC is no longer present and scan tool clear DTC function is used.
- Fifty ignition cycles have passed with no DTC(s) detected.

Diagnostic Aids

- Make sure the integrity of the connection between the EBTCM and the BPMV is secure, tight, and free from corrosion.

Test Description

The numbers below refer to step numbers on the diagnostic table.

3. Checks the resistance value of the solenoid.
4. Checks for a short to ground in the BPMV.
7. Checks for an internal short to voltage.

GC402970265400AX

Fig. 135 Code C1261: LH Front Inlet Valve Solenoid Fault (Part 1 of 2). Corvette

Circuit Description

This DTC identifies a malfunction within the EBTCM.

Conditions for Setting the DTC

DTC C1255xx is set when an internal EBTCM malfunction exists.

Action Taken When the DTC Sets

A malfunction DTC is stored, ABS/TCS is disabled and the ABS and Traction Control Indicators are turned ON.

Conditions for Clearing the DTC

- Condition for DTC is no longer present and scan tool clear DTC function is used.
- Fifty ignition cycles have passed with no DTC(s) detected.

Diagnostic Aids

- When DTC C1255xx is displayed on the Scan Tool, it will be followed by two more numbers which should be noted along with any other DTCs that may be displayed. The additional two numbers displayed with DTC C1255xx are for aiding engineering to determine the cause of the internal malfunction.
- Make sure the integrity of the connection between the EBTCM and the BPMV is secure, tight, and free from corrosion.

GC402970265200AX

Fig. 133 Code C1255: EBTCM Internal Fault w/ABS/TCS Disabled (Part 1 of 2). Corvette

Circuit Description

This DTC identifies a malfunction within the EBTCM.

Conditions for Setting the DTC

- DTC C1256xx can be set when there is a solenoid short to battery inside the BPMV. If DTC(s) C1261 - C1274 are set along with C1256xx then pursue the solenoid DTC(s) first).
- DTC C1256xx can be set when there is an internal EBTCM malfunction.

Action Taken When the DTC Sets

A malfunction DTC is stored, ABS/TCS is not disabled and the ABS and Traction Control indicators are not turned ON.

Conditions for Clearing the DTC

- Condition for DTC is no longer present and scan tool clear DTC function is used.
- Fifty ignition cycles have passed with no DTC(s) detected.

Diagnostic Aids

- When DTC C1256xx is displayed on the Scan Tool, it will be followed by two more numbers which should be noted along with any other DTCs that may be displayed. The additional two numbers displayed with DTC C1256xx are for aiding engineering to determine the cause of the internal malfunction.
- Make sure the integrity of the connection between the EBTCM and the BPMV is secure, tight, and free from corrosion.

GC402970265300AX

Fig. 134 Code C1256: EBTCM Internal Fault (Part 1 of 2). Corvette

Step	Action	Value(s)	Yes	No
1	Was the Diagnostic System Check performed?	—	*Go to Step 2*	Go to *ABS Diagnostic System Check*
2	1. Turn the ignition switch to the OFF position. 2. Disconnect the EBTCM connector. 3. Remove the EBTCM from the BPMV. 4. Inspect the EBTCM to BPMV connector for conditions which could cause intermittents such as damage, corrosion, or poor terminal contact. Are internal connectors OK and cavity free of brake fluid?	—	*Go to Step 3*	*Go to Step 6*
3	1. Install *J 41247* BPMV Pinout Box to the BPMV connector. 2. Using *J 39200* DMM, measure the resistance between *J 41247* terminals 14 and 7. Is the resistance within the range specified in the value(s) column?	8 - 12Ω	*Go to Step 4*	*Go to Step 8*
4	Using *J 39200* DMM, measure the resistance between *J 41247* terminal 14 and the BPMV case. Is the resistance within the range specified in the value(s) column?	OL (infinite)	*Go to Step 5*	*Go to Step 8*
5	1. Remove *J 41247.* 2. Reinstall the EBTCM to BPMV. 3. Reconnect the EBTCM connector. 4. Turn the ignition switch to the ON position, engine OFF. Does DTC C1261 reset as a current DTC?	—	*Go to Step 9*	*Go to Step 7*
6	1. If connector corrosion or damage are present, replace BPMV and/or EBTCM as necessary. 2. If brake fluid is present, replace both the BPMV and EBTCM. Is the repair complete?	—	Go to *ABS Diagnostic System Check*	—
7	Using a scan tool in ABS/TCS Special Functions run the AUTOMATED Test. Does DTC C1261 reset as a current DTC?	—	*Go to Step 8*	Go to *ABS Diagnostic System Check*
8	Replace the BPMV. Is the replacement complete?	—	Go to *ABS Diagnostic System Check*	—
9	Replace the EBTCM. Is the replacement complete?	—	Go to *ABS Diagnostic System Check*	—

GC402970265400BX

Fig. 135 Code C1261: LH Front Inlet Valve Solenoid Fault (Part 2 of 2). Corvette

Circuit Description

The Outlet valve solenoid circuits are supplied with battery power when the ignition is in the ON position. The EBTCM controls the valve functions by grounding the circuit when necessary.

Conditions for Setting the DTC

The EBTCM senses a discrepancy such as an open, short to ground, or short to voltage in the circuit.

Action Taken When the DTC Sets

A malfunction DTC is stored, ABS/TCS is disabled and the ABS and Traction Control Indicators are turned ON.

Conditions for Clearing the DTC

- Condition for DTC is no longer present and scan tool clear DTC function is used.
- Fifty ignition cycles have passed with no DTC(s) detected.

Diagnostic Aids

- Make sure the integrity of the connection between the EBTCM and the BPMV is secure, tight, and free from corrosion.

Test Description

The numbers below refer to step numbers on the diagnostic table.

3. Checks the resistance value of the solenoid.
4. Checks for a short to ground in the BPMV.
7. Checks for an internal short to voltage.

GC402970265500AX

Fig. 136 Code C1262: LH Front Outlet Valve Solenoid Fault (Part 1 of 2). Corvette

Step	Action	Value(s)	Yes	No
1	Was the Diagnostic System Check performed?	—	*Go to Step 2*	*Go to ABS Diagnostic System Check*
2	1. Turn the ignition switch to the OFF position. 2. Disconnect the EBTCM connector. 3. Remove the EBTCM from the BPMV. 4. Inspect the EBTCM to BPMV connector for conditions which could cause intermittents such as damage, corrosion, or poor terminal contact. Are internal connectors OK and cavity free of brake fluid?	—	*Go to Step 3*	*Go to Step 6*
3	1. Install *J 41247* BPMV Pinout Box to the BPMV connector. 2. Using *J 39200* DMM, measure the resistance between *J 41247* terminals 9 and 7. Is the resistance within the range specified in the value(s) column?	4 - 7Ω	*Go to Step 4*	*Go to Step 8*
4	Using *J 39200* DMM, measure the resistance between *J 41247* terminal 9 and the BPMV case. Is the resistance within the range specified in the value(s) column?	OL (infinite)	*Go to Step 5*	*Go to Step 8*
5	1. Remove *J 41247*. 2. Reinstall the EBTCM to BPMV. 3. Reconnect the EBTCM connector. 4. Turn the ignition switch to the ON position, engine OFF. Does DTC C1262 reset as a current DTC?	—	*Go to Step 9*	*Go to Step 7*
6	If connector corrosion or damage are present, replace BPMV and/or EBTCM as necessary. If brake fluid is present, replace both the BPMV and EBTCM. Is the repair complete?	—	*Go to ABS Diagnostic System Check*	—
7	Using a scan tool in ABS/TCS Special Functions run the AUTOMATED Test. Does DTC C1262 reset as a current DTC?	—	*Go to Step 8*	*Go to ABS Diagnostic System Check*
8	Replace the BPMV. Is the replacement complete?	—	*Go to ABS Diagnostic System Check*	—
9	Replace the EBTCM. Is the replacement complete?	—	*Go to ABS Diagnostic System Check*	—

GC402970265500BX

Fig. 136 Code C1262: LH Front Outlet Valve Solenoid Fault (Part 2 of 2). Corvette

Circuit Description

The Inlet valve solenoid circuits are supplied with battery power when the ignition is in the ON position. The EBTCM controls the valve functions by grounding the circuit when necessary.

Conditions for Setting the DTC

The EBTCM senses a discrepancy such as an open, short to ground, or short to voltage in the circuit.

Action Taken When the DTC Sets

A malfunction DTC is stored, ABS/TCS is disabled and the ABS and Traction Control Indicators are turned ON.

Conditions for Clearing the DTC

- Condition for DTC is no longer present and scan tool clear DTC function is used.
- Fifty ignition cycles have passed with no DTC(s) detected.

Diagnostic Aids

- Make sure the integrity of the connection between the EBTCM and the BPMV is secure, tight, and free from corrosion.

Test Description

The numbers below refer to step numbers on the diagnostic table.

3. Checks the resistance value of the solenoid.
4. Checks for a short to ground in the BPMV.
7. Checks for an internal short to voltage.

GC402970265600AX

Fig. 137 Code C1263: RH Front Inlet Valve Solenoid Fault (Part 1 of 2). Corvette

Step	Action	Value(s)	Yes	No
1	Was the Diagnostic System Check performed?	—	*Go to Step 2*	Go to *ABS Diagnostic System Check*
2	1. Turn the ignition switch to the OFF position. 2. Disconnect the EBTCM connector. 3. Remove the EBTCM from the BPMV. 4. Inspect the EBTCM to BPMV connector for conditions which could cause intermittents such as damage, corrosion, or poor terminal contact. Are internal connectors OK and cavity free of brake fluid?	—	*Go to Step 3*	*Go to Step 6*
3	1. Install *J 41247* BPMV Pinout Box to the BPMV connector. 2. Using *J 39200* DMM, measure the resistance between *J 41247* terminals 1 and 7. Is the resistance within the range specified in the value(s) column?	8 - 12Ω	*Go to Step 4*	*Go to Step 8*
4	Using *J 39200* DMM, measure the resistance between *J 41247* terminal 1 and the BPMV case. Is the resistance within the range specified in the value(s) column?	OL (infinite)	*Go to Step 5*	*Go to Step 8*
5	1. Remove *J 41247*. 2. Reinstall the EBTCM to BPMV. 3. Reconnect the EBTCM connector 4. Turn the ignition switch to the ON position, engine OFF. Does DTC C1263 reset as a current DTC?	—	*Go to Step 9*	*Go to Step 7*
6	1. If connector corrosion or damage are present, replace BPMV and/or EBTCM as necessary. 2. If brake fluid is present, replace both the BPMV and EBTCM. Is the repair complete?	—	Go to *ABS Diagnostic System Check*	—
7	Using a scan tool in ABS/TCS Special Functions run the AUTOMATED Test. Does DTC C1263 reset as a current DTC?	—	*Go to Step 8*	Go to *ABS Diagnostic System Check*
8	Replace the BPMV. Is the replacement complete?	—	Go to *ABS Diagnostic System Check*	—
9	Replace the EBTCM. Is the replacement complete?	—	Go to *ABS Diagnostic System Check*	—

GC402970265600BX

Fig. 137 Code C1263: RH Front Inlet Valve Solenoid Fault (Part 2 of 2). Corvette

Circuit Description

The Outlet valve solenoid circuits are supplied with battery power when the ignition is in the ON position. The EBTCM controls the valve functions by grounding the circuit when necessary.

Conditions for Setting the DTC

The EBTCM senses a discrepancy such as an open, short to ground, or short to voltage in the circuit.

Action Taken When the DTC Sets

A malfunction DTC is stored, ABS/TCS is disabled and the ABS and Traction Control Indicators are turned ON.

Conditions for Clearing the DTC

- Condition for DTC is no longer present and scan tool clear DTC function is used.
- Fifty ignition cycles have passed with no DTC(s) detected.

Diagnostic Aids

- Make sure the integrity of the connection between the EBTCM and the BPMV is secure, tight, and free from corrosion.

Test Description

The numbers below refer to step numbers on the diagnostic table.

3. Checks the resistance value of the solenoid.
4. Checks for a short to ground in the BPMV.
7. Checks for an internal short to voltage.

GC402970265700AX

Fig. 138 Code C1264: RH Front Outlet Valve Solenoid Fault (Part 1 of 2). Corvette

Step	Action	Value(s)	Yes	No
1	Was the Diagnostic System Check performed?	—	*Go to Step 2*	Go to *Diagnostic System Check*
2	1. Turn the ignition switch to the OFF position. 2. Disconnect the EBTCM connector. 3. Remove the EBTCM from the BPMV. 4. Inspect the EBTCM to BPMV connector for conditions which could cause intermittents such as damage, corrosion, or poor terminal contact. Are internal connectors OK and cavity free of brake fluid?	—	*Go to Step 3*	*Go to Step 6*
3	1. Install *J 41247* BPMV Pinout Box to the BPMV connector. 2. Using *J 39200* DMM, measure the resistance between *J 41247* terminals 6 and 7. Is the resistance within the range specified in the value(s) column?	4–7 Ω	*Go to Step 4*	*Go to Step 8*
4	Using *J 39200* DMM, measure the resistance between *J 41247* terminal 6 and the BPMV case. Is the resistance within the range specified in the value(s) column?	OL (infinite)	*Go to Step 5*	*Go to Step 8*
5	1. Remove *J 41247*. 2. Reinstall the EBTCM to BPMV. 3. Reconnect the EBTCM connector. 4. Turn the ignition switch to the ON position, engine off. Does DTC C1264 reset as a current DTC?	—	*Go to Step 9*	*Go to Step 7*
6	1. If connector corrosion or damage are present, replace BPMV and/or EBTCM as necessary. 2. If brake fluid is present, replace both the BPMV and EBTCM. Is the repair complete?	—	Go to *Diagnostic System Check*	—
7	Using a scan tool in ABS/TCS Special Functions run the AUTOMATED Test. Does DTC C1264 reset as a current DTC?	—	*Go to Step 8*	Go to *Diagnostic System Check*
8	Replace the BPMV. Is the replacement complete?	—	Go to *Diagnostic System Check*	—
9	Replace the EBTCM. Is the replacement complete?	—	Go to *Diagnostic System Check*	—

GC402970265700BX

Fig. 138 Code C1264: RH Front Outlet Valve Solenoid Fault (Part 2 of 2). Corvette

Circuit Description

The Inlet valve solenoid circuits are supplied with battery power when the ignition is in the ON position. The EBTCM controls the valve functions by grounding the circuit when necessary.

Conditions for Setting the DTC

The EBTCM senses a discrepancy such as an open, short to ground, or short to voltage in the circuit.

Action Taken When the DTC Sets

A malfunction DTC is stored, ABS/TCS is disabled and the ABS and Traction Control Indicators are turned ON.

Conditions for Clearing the DTC

- Condition for DTC is no longer present and scan tool clear DTC function is used.
- Fifty ignition cycles have passed with no DTC(s) detected.

Diagnostic Aids

- Make sure the integrity of the connection between the EBTCM and the BPMV is secure, tight, and free from corrosion.

Test Description

The numbers below refer to step numbers on the diagnostic table.

3. Checks the resistance value of the solenoid.
4. Checks for a short to ground in the BPMV.
7. Checks for an internal short to voltage.

GC402970265800AX

Fig. 139 Code C1265: LH Rear Inlet Valve Solenoid Fault (Part 1 of 2). Corvette

Circuit Description

The Outlet valve solenoid circuits are supplied with battery power when the ignition is in the ON position. The EBTCM controls the valve functions by grounding the circuit when necessary.

Conditions for Setting the DTC

The EBTCM senses a discrepancy such as an open, short to ground, or short to voltage in the circuit.

Action Taken When the DTC Sets

A malfunction DTC is stored, ABS/TCS is disabled and the ABS and Traction Control Indicators are turned ON.

Conditions for Clearing the DTC

- Condition for DTC is no longer present and scan tool clear DTC function is used.
- Fifty ignition cycles have passed with no DTC(s) detected.

Diagnostic Aids

- Make sure the integrity of the connection between the EBTCM and the BPMV is secure, tight, and free from corrosion.

Test Description

The numbers below refer to step numbers on the diagnostic table.

3. Checks the resistance value of the solenoid.
4. Checks for a short to ground in the BPMV.
7. Checks for an internal short to voltage.

GC402970265900AX

Fig. 140 Code C1266: LH Rear Outlet Valve Solenoid Fault (Part 1 of 2). Corvette

Step	Action	Value(s)	Yes	No
1	Was the Diagnostic System Check performed?	—	*Go to Step 2*	Go to *ABS Diagnostic System Check*
2	1. Turn the ignition switch to the OFF position. 2. Disconnect the EBTCM connector. 3. Remove the EBTCM from the BPMV. 4. Inspect the EBTCM to BPMV connector for conditions which could cause intermittents such as damage, corrosion, or poor terminal contact. Are internal connectors OK and cavity free of brake fluid?	—	*Go to Step 3*	*Go to Step 6*
3	1. Install *J 41247* BPMV Pinout Box to the BPMV connector. 2. Using *J 39200* DMM, measure the resistance between *J 41247* terminals 2 and 7. Is the resistance within the range specified in the value(s) column?	8 - 12Ω	*Go to Step 4*	*Go to Step 8*
4	Using *J 39200* DMM, measure the resistance between *J 41247* terminal 2 and the BPMV case. Is the resistance within the range specified in the value(s) column?	OL (infinite)	*Go to Step 5*	*Go to Step 8*
5	1. Remove *J 41247*. 2. Reinstall the EBTCM to BPMV. 3. Reconnect the EBTCM connector. 4. Turn the ignition switch to the ON position, engine OFF. Does DTC C1265 reset as a current DTC?	—	*Go to Step 9*	*Go to Step 7*
6	1. If connector corrosion or damage are present, replace BPMV and/or EBTCM as necessary. 2. If brake fluid is present, replace both the BPMV and EBTCM. Is the repair complete?	—	Go to *ABS Diagnostic System Check*	—
7	Using a scan tool in ABS/TCS Special Functions run the AUTOMATED Test. Does DTC C1265 reset as a current DTC?	—	*Go to Step 8*	Go to *ABS Diagnostic System Check*
8	Replace the BPMV. Is the replacement complete?	—	Go to *ABS Diagnostic System Check*	—
9	Replace the EBTCM. Is the replacement complete?	—	Go to *ABS Diagnostic System Check*	—

GC402970265800BX

Fig. 139 Code C1265: LH Rear Inlet Valve Solenoid Fault (Part 2 of 2). Corvette

Step	Action	Value(s)	Yes	No
1	Was the Diagnostic System Check performed?	—	*Go to Step 2*	Go to *ABS Diagnostic System Check*
2	1. Turn the ignition switch to the OFF position. 2. Disconnect the EBTCM connector. 3. Remove the EBTCM from the BPMV. 4. Inspect the EBTCM to BPMV connector for conditions which could cause intermittents such as damage, corrosion, or poor terminal contact. Are internal connectors OK and cavity free of brake fluid?	—	*Go to Step 3*	*Go to Step 6*
3	1. Install *J 41247* BPMV Pinout Box to the BPMV connector. 2. Using *J 39200* DMM, measure the resistance between *J 41247* terminals 5 and 7. Is the resistance within the range specified in the value(s) column?	4 - 7Ω	*Go to Step 4*	*Go to Step 8*
4	Using *J 39200* DMM, measure the resistance between *J 41247* terminal 5 and the BPMV case. Is the resistance within the range specified in the value(s) column?	OL (infinite)	*Go to Step 5*	*Go to Step 8*
5	1. Remove *J 41247*. 2. Reinstall the EBTCM to BPMV. 3. Reconnect the EBTCM connector. 4. Turn the ignition switch to the ON position, engine OFF Does DTC C1266 reset as a current DTC?	—	*Go to Step 9*	*Go to Step 7*
6	1. If connector corrosion or damage are present, replace BPMV and/or EBTCM as necessary. 2. If brake fluid is present, replace both the BPMV and EBTCM. Is the repair complete?	—	Go to *ABS Diagnostic System Check*	—
7	Using a scan tool in ABS/TCS Special Functions run the AUTOMATED Test. Does DTC C1266 reset as a current DTC?	—	*Go to Step 8*	Go to *ABS Diagnostic System Check*
8	Replace the BPMV. Is the replacement complete?	—	Go to *ABS Diagnostic System Check*	—
9	Replace the EBTCM. Is the replacement complete?	—	Go to *ABS Diagnostic System Check*	—

GC402970265900BX

Fig. 140 Code C1266: LH Rear Outlet Valve Solenoid Fault (Part 2 of 2). Corvette

Circuit Description

The Inlet valve solenoid circuits are supplied with battery power when the ignition is in the ON position. The EBTCM controls the valve functions by grounding the circuit when necessary.

Conditions for Setting the DTC

The EBTCM senses a discrepancy such as an open, short to ground, or short to voltage in the circuit.

Action Taken When the DTC Sets

A malfunction DTC is stored, ABS/TCS is disabled and the ABS and Traction Control Indicators are turned ON.

Conditions for Clearing the DTC

- Condition for DTC is no longer present and scan tool clear DTC function is used.
- Fifty ignition cycles have passed with no DTC(s) detected.

Diagnostic Aids

- Make sure the integrity of the connection between the EBTCM and the BPMV is secure, tight, and free from corrosion.

Test Description

The numbers below refer to step numbers on the diagnostic table.

3. Checks the resistance value of the solenoid.
4. Checks for a short to ground in the BPMV.
7. Checks for an internal short to voltage.

GC402970266000AX

Fig. 141 Code C1267: RH Rear Inlet Valve Solenoid Fault (Part 1 of 2). Corvette

Step	Action	Value(s)	Yes	No
1	Was the Diagnostic System Check performed?	—	*Go to Step 2*	Go to *ABS Diagnostic System Check*
2	1. Turn the ignition switch to the OFF position. 2. Disconnect the EBTCM connector. 3. Remove the EBTCM from the BPMV. 4. Inspect the EBTCM to BPMV connector for conditions which could cause intermittents such as damage, corrosion, or poor terminal contact. Are internal connectors OK and cavity free of brake fluid?	—	*Go to Step 3*	*Go to Step 6*
3	1. Install *J 41247* BPMV Pinout Box to the BPMV connector. 2. Using *J 39200* DMM, measure the resistance between *J 41247* terminals 13 and 7. Is the resistance within the range specified in the value(s) column?	8 - 12Ω	*Go to Step 4*	*Go to Step 8*
4	Using *J 39200* DMM, measure the resistance between *J 41247* terminal 13 and the BPMV case. Is the resistance within the range specified in the value(s) column?	OL (infinite)	*Go to Step 5*	*Go to Step 8*
5	1. Remove *J 41247*. 2. Reinstall the EBTCM to BPMV. 3. Reconnect the EBTCM connector. 4. Turn the ignition switch to the ON position, engine OFF. Does DTC C1267 reset as a current DTC?	—	*Go to Step 9*	*Go to Step 7*
6	1. If connector corrosion or damage are present, replace BPMV and/or EBTCM as necessary. 2. If brake fluid is present, replace both the BPMV and EBTCM. Is the repair complete?	—	Go to *ABS Diagnostic System Check*	—
7	Using a scan tool in ABS/TCS Special Functions run the AUTOMATED Test. Does DTC C1267 reset as a current DTC?	—	*Go to Step 8*	Go to *ABS Diagnostic System Check*
8	Replace the BPMV. Is the replacement complete?	—	Go to *ABS Diagnostic System Check*	—
9	Replace the EBTCM. Is the replacement complete?	—	Go to *ABS Diagnostic System Check*	—

GC402970266000BX

Fig. 141 Code C1267: RH Rear Inlet Valve Solenoid Fault (Part 2 of 2). Corvette

Circuit Description

The Outlet valve solenoid circuits are supplied with battery power when the ignition is in the ON position. The EBTCM controls the valve functions by grounding the circuit when necessary.

Conditions for Setting the DTC

The EBTCM senses a discrepancy such as an open, short to ground, or short to voltage in the circuit.

Action Taken When the DTC Sets

A malfunction DTC is stored, ABS/TCS is disabled and the ABS and Traction Control Indicators are turned ON.

Conditions for Clearing the DTC

- Condition for DTC is no longer present and scan tool clear DTC function is used.
- Fifty ignition cycles have passed with no DTC(s) detected.

Diagnostic Aids

- Make sure the integrity of the connection between the EBTCM and the BPMV is secure, tight, and free from corrosion.

Test Description

The numbers below refer to step numbers on the diagnostic table.

3. Checks the resistance value of the solenoid.
4. Checks for a short to ground in the BPMV.
7. Checks for an internal short to voltage.

GC402970266100AX

Fig. 142 Code C1268: RH Rear Outlet Valve Solenoid Fault (Part 1 of 2). Corvette

Step	Action	Value(s)	Yes	No
1	Was the Diagnostic System Check performed?	—	*Go to Step 2*	Go to *ABS Diagnostic System Check*
2	1. Turn the ignition switch to the OFF position. 2. Disconnect the EBTCM connector. 3. Remove the EBTCM from the BPMV. 4. Inspect the EBTCM to BPMV connector for conditions which could cause intermittents such as damage, corrosion, or poor terminal contact. Are internal connectors OK and cavity free of brake fluid?	—	*Go to Step 3*	*Go to Step 6*
3	1. Install *J 41247* BPMV Pinout Box to the BPMV connector. 2. Using *J 39200* DMM, measure the resistance between *J 41247* terminals 10 and 7. Is the resistance within the range specified in the value(s) column?	4 - 7Ω	*Go to Step 4*	*Go to Step 8*
4	Using *J 39200* DMM, measure the resistance between *J 41247* terminal 10 and the BPMV case. Is the resistance within the range specified in the value(s) column?	OL (infinite)	*Go to Step 5*	*Go to Step 8*
5	1. Remove *J 41247*. 2. Reinstall the EBTCM to BPMV. 3. Reconnect the EBTCM connector. 4. Turn the ignition switch to the ON position, engine OFF. Does DTC C1268 reset as a current DTC?	—	*Go to Step 9*	*Go to Step 7*
6	1. If connector corrosion or damage are present, replace BPMV and/or EBTCM as necessary. 2. If brake fluid is present, replace both the BPMV and EBTCM. Is the repair complete?	—	Go to *ABS Diagnostic System Check*	—
7	Using a scan tool in ABS/TCS Special Functions run the AUTOMATED Test. Does DTC C1268 reset as a current DTC?	—	*Go to Step 8*	Go to *ABS Diagnostic System Check*
8	Replace the BPMV. Is the replacement complete?	—	Go to *ABS Diagnostic System Check*	—
9	Replace the EBTCM. Is the replacement complete?	—	Go to *ABS Diagnostic System Check*	—

GC402970266100BX

Fig. 142 Code C1268: RH Rear Outlet Valve Solenoid Fault (Part 2 of 2). Corvette

Circuit Description

The Master Cylinder Isolation valve solenoid circuits are supplied with battery power when the ignition is in the ON position. The EBTCM controls the valve functions by grounding the circuit when necessary.

Conditions for Setting the DTC

The EBTCM senses a discrepancy such as an open, short to ground, or short to voltage in the circuit.

Action Taken When the DTC Sets

ABS/TCS/Active Handling are disabled.

- Indicators that turn on:
  - ABS indicator
  - Car Icon (TCS indicator)
- Messages displayed on the DIC:
  - Service ABS
  - Service Traction System
  - Service Active HNDLG

Conditions for Clearing the DTC

- Condition for DTC is no longer present and scan tool clear DTC function is used.
- Fifty ignition cycles have passed with no DTCs detected.

Diagnostic Aids

Make sure the integrity of the connection between the EBTCM and the BPMV is secure, tight, and free from corrosion.

Test Description

The numbers below refer to step numbers on the diagnostic table.

3. Checks the resistance value of the solenoid.
4. Checks for a short to ground in the BPMV.
7. Checks for an internal short to voltage.

GC4029803956010X

Fig. 143 Code C1271: Front Master Cylinder Isolation Valve Fault (Part 1 of 2). Corvette

Step	Action	Value(s)	Yes	No
1	Was the Diagnostic System Check performed?	—	*Go to Step 2*	Go to *Diagnostic System Check (ABS)*
2	1. Turn the ignition switch to the OFF position. 2. Disconnect the EBTCM connector. 3. Remove the EBTCM from the BPMV. 4. Inspect the EBTCM to BPMV connector for conditions which could cause intermittents such as damage, corrosion, or poor terminal contact. Are internal connectors OK and cavity free of brake fluid?	—	*Go to Step 3*	*Go to Step 6*
3	1. Install *J 41247* BPMV Pinout Box to the BPMV connector. 2. Using *J 39200* DMM, measure the resistance between *J 41247* terminals 11 and 7. Is the resistance within the range specified in the value(s) column?	8–12 Ω	*Go to Step 4*	*Go to Step 8*
4	Using *J 39200* DMM, measure the resistance between *J 41247* terminal 11 and the BPMV case. Is the resistance within the range specified in the value(s) column?	OL (infinite)	*Go to Step 5*	*Go to Step 8*
5	1. Remove *J 41247*. 2. Reinstall the EBTCM to BPMV. 3. Reconnect the EBTCM connector. 4. Turn the ignition switch to the ON position, engine off. Does DTC C1271 reset as a current DTC?	—	*Go to Step 9*	*Go to Step 7*
6	1. If connector corrosion or damage are present, replace BPMV and/or EBTCM as necessary. 2. If brake fluid is present, replace both the BPMV and EBTCM. Is the repair complete?	—	Go to *Diagnostic System Check (ABS)*	—
7	Using a scan tool in ABS/TCS/Active Handling Special Functions run the AUTOMATED Test. Does DTC C1271 reset as a current DTC?	—	*Go to Step 8*	Go to *Diagnostic System Check (ABS)*
8	Replace the BPMV. Is the replacement complete?	—	Go to *Diagnostic System Check (ABS)*	—
9	Replace the EBTCM. Is the replacement complete?	—	Go to *Diagnostic System Check (ABS)*	—

GC4029803956020X

Fig. 143 Code C1271: Front Master Cylinder Isolation Valve Fault (Part 2 of 2). Corvette

Step	Action	Value(s)	Yes	No
1	Was the Diagnostic System Check performed?	—	*Go to Step 2*	Go to *Diagnostic System Check (ABS)*
2	1. Turn the ignition switch to the OFF position. 2. Disconnect the EBTCM connector. 3. Remove the EBTCM from the BPMV. 4. Inspect the EBTCM to BPMV connector for conditions which could cause intermittents such as damage, corrosion, or poor terminal contact. Are internal connectors OK and cavity free of brake fluid?	—	*Go to Step 3*	*Go to Step 6*
3	1. Install *J 41247* BPMV Pinout Box to the BPMV connector. 2. Using *J 39200* DMM, measure the resistance between *J 41247* terminals 12 and 7. Is the resistance within the range specified in the value(s) column?	8–12 Ω	*Go to Step 4*	*Go to Step 8*
4	Using *J 39200* DMM, measure the resistance between *J 41247* terminal 12 and the BPMV case. Is the resistance within the range specified in the value(s) column?	OL (infinite)	*Go to Step 5*	*Go to Step 8*
5	1. Remove *J 41247*. 2. Reinstall the EBTCM to BPMV. 3. Reconnect the EBTCM connector. 4. Turn the ignition switch to the ON position, engine off. Does DTC C1272 reset as a current DTC?	—	*Go to Step 9*	*Go to Step 7*
6	1. If connector corrosion or damage are present, replace BPMV and/or EBTCM as necessary. 2. If brake fluid is present, replace both the BPMV and EBTCM. Is the repair complete?	—	Go to *Diagnostic System Check (ABS)*	—
7	Using a scan tool in ABS/TCS/Active Handling Special Functions run the AUTOMATED Test. Does DTC C1272 reset as a current DTC?	—	*Go to Step 8*	Go to *Diagnostic System Check (ABS)*
8	Replace the BPMV. Is the replacement complete?	—	Go to *Diagnostic System Check (ABS)*	—
9	Replace the EBTCM. Is the replacement complete?	—	Go to *Diagnostic System Check (ABS)*	—

GC4029803957020X

Fig. 144 Code C1272: Front Prime Valve Fault (Part 2 of 2). Corvette

Circuit Description

The Prime valve solenoid circuits are supplied with battery power when the ignition is in the ON position. The EBTCM controls the valve functions by grounding the circuit when necessary.

Conditions for Setting the DTC

The EBTCM senses a discrepancy such as an open, short to ground, or short to voltage in the circuit.

Action Taken When the DTC Sets

ABS/TCS/Active Handling are disabled.

- Indicators that turn on:
  - ABS indicator
  - Car Icon (TCS indicator)
- Messages displayed on the DIC:
  - Service ABS
  - Service Traction System
  - Service Active HNDLG

Conditions for Clearing the DTC

- Condition for DTC is no longer present and scan tool clear DTC function is used.
- Fifty ignition cycles have passed with no DTCs detected.

Diagnostic Aids

Make sure the integrity of the connection between the EBTCM and the BPMV is secure, tight, and free from corrosion.

Test Description

The numbers below refer to step numbers on the diagnostic table.

3. Checks the resistance value of the solenoid.
4. Checks for a short to ground in the BPMV.
7. Checks for an internal short to voltage.

GC4029803957010X

Fig. 144 Code C1272: Front Prime Valve Fault (Part 1 of 2). Corvette

Circuit Description

The Master Cylinder Isolation valve solenoid circuits are supplied with battery power when the ignition is in the ON position. The EBTCM controls the valve functions by grounding the circuit when necessary.

Conditions for Setting the DTC

The EBTCM senses a discrepancy such as an open, short to ground, or short to voltage in the circuit.

Action Taken When the DTC Sets

ABS/TCS/Active Handling are disabled.

- Indicators that turn on:
  - ABS indicator
  - Car Icon (TCS indicator)
- Messages displayed on the DIC:
  - Service ABS
  - Service Traction System
  - Service Active HNDLG

Conditions for Clearing the DTC

- Condition for DTC is no longer present and scan tool clear DTC function is used.
- Fifty ignition cycles have passed with no DTCs detected.

Diagnostic Aids

Make sure the integrity of the connection between the EBTCM and the BPMV is secure, tight, and free from corrosion.

Test Description

The numbers below refer to step numbers on the diagnostic table.

3. Checks the resistance value of the solenoid.
4. Checks for a short to ground in the BPMV.
7. Checks for an internal short to voltage.

GC4029803958010X

Fig. 145 Code C1273: Rear Master Cylinder Isolation Valve Fault (Part 1 of 2). Corvette

Step	Action	Value(s)	Yes	No
1	Was the Diagnostic System Check performed?	—	*Go to Step 2*	Go to *Diagnostic System Check (ABS)*
2	1. Turn the ignition switch to the OFF position. 2. Disconnect the EBTCM connector. 3. Remove the EBTCM from the BPMV. 4. Inspect the EBTCM to BPMV connector for conditions which could cause intermittents such as damage, corrosion, or poor terminal contact. Are internal connectors OK and cavity free of brake fluid?	—	*Go to Step 3*	*Go to Step 6*
3	1. Install *J 41247* BPMV Pinout Box to the BPMV connector. 2. Using *J 39200* DMM, measure the resistance between *J 41247* terminals 3 and 7. Is the resistance within the range specified in the value(s) column?	8–12 Ω	*Go to Step 4*	*Go to Step 8*
4	Using *J 39200* DMM, measure the resistance between *J 41247* terminal 3 and the BPMV case. Is the resistance within the range specified in the value(s) column?	OL (infinite)	*Go to Step 5*	*Go to Step 8*
5	1. Remove *J 41247*. 2. Reinstall the EBTCM to BPMV. 3. Reconnect the EBTCM connector. 4. Turn the ignition switch to the ON position, engine off. Does DTC C1273 reset as a current DTC?	—	*Go to Step 9*	*Go to Step 7*
6	1. If connector corrosion or damage are present, replace BPMV and/or EBTCM as necessary. 2. If brake fluid is present, replace both the BPMV and EBTCM. Is the repair complete?	—	Go to *Diagnostic System Check (ABS)*	—
7	Using a scan tool in ABS/TCS or ABS/TCS/Active Handling Special Functions run the AUTOMATED Test. Does DTC C1273 reset as a current DTC?	—	*Go to Step 8*	Go to *Diagnostic System Check (ABS)*
8	Replace the BPMV. Is the replacement complete?	—	Go to *Diagnostic System Check (ABS)*	—
9	Replace the EBTCM. Is the replacement complete?	—	Go to *Diagnostic System Check (ABS)*	—

GC4029803958020X

Fig. 145 Code C1273: Rear Master Cylinder Isolation Valve Fault (Part 2 of 2). Corvette

Circuit Description

Traction Control is simultaneously controlled by the EBTCM and the PCM. The PCM sends a DELIVERED TORQUE message via a Pulse Width Modulated (PWM) signal to the EBTCM confirming the delivered torque level for proper Traction Control system operation. The EBTCM supplies the pull up voltage.

Conditions for Setting the DTC

DTC C1276 can be set anytime when ignition voltage is present. A malfunction exists if the PWM signal is out of range or no signal is received for a period of 7 seconds.

Action Taken When the DTC Sets

TCS/Active Handling are disabled.

- Indicators that turn on:
  Car Icon (TCS indicator)
- Messages displayed on the DIC:
  Service Traction System
  Service Active HNDLG

Conditions for Clearing the DTC

- Condition for DTC is no longer present and scan tool clear DTC function is used.
- Fifty ignition cycles have passed with no DTCs detected.

Diagnostic Aids

- It is very important that a thorough inspection of the wiring and connectors be performed. Failure to carefully and fully inspect wiring and connectors may result in misdiagnosis, causing part replacement with reappearance of the malfunction.
- If an intermittent malfunction exists refer to *Intermittents*
- Possible causes for DTC C1276 to set:
  - Open in CKT 464.
  - CKT 464 shorted to ground or voltage.
  - Communication frequency problem.
  - Communication duty cycle problem.
  - CKT 464 has a wiring problem, terminal corrosion, or poor connections.
  - EBTCM not receiving information from the PCM.

Test Description

The numbers below refer to step numbers on the diagnostic table.

4. Checks for proper duty cycle.
5. Checks for proper frequency.

GC4029803959010X

Fig. 146 Code C1276: Delivered Torque Signal Circuit Fault (Part 1 of 3). Corvette

Step	Action	Value(s)	Yes	No
1	Was the Diagnostic System Check performed?	—	*Go to Step 2*	Go to *Diagnostic System Check (ABS)*
2	Check the following grounds, G101 and G106 making sure each ground is clean, tight and free of damage. Were any loose, damaged, or corroded grounds found?	—	*Go to Step 3*	*Go to Step 4*
3	Repair ground as necessary. Is the repair complete?	—	Go to *Diagnostic System Check (ABS)*	—
4	1. Turn the ignition switch to the OFF position. 2. Disconnect the EBTCM connector. 3. Install *J 39700* Universal Pinout Box using the *J 39700-25* cable adapter to the EBTCM harness connector and the EBTCM connector. 4. Turn the ignition switch to the ON position, engine off. 5. Using *J 39200* DMM, measure the DC duty cycle between *J 39700* terminals 6 and B. Is the duty cycle within the range specified in the value(s) column?	5–25 %	*Go to Step 5*	*Go to Step 7*
5	Using *J 39200* DMM, measure the DC Hz between *J 39700* terminals 6 and B. Is the frequency within the range specified in the value(s) column?	121–134 Hz	*Go to Step 6*	*Go to Step 13*
6	Replace the EBTCM. Is the replacement complete?	—	Go to *Diagnostic System Check (ABS)*	—
7	1. Turn the ignition switch to the OFF position. 2. Disconnect the PCM connector C2. 3. Turn the ignition switch to the ON position, engine off. 4. Using *J 39200* DMM, measure the voltage between terminals 6 and B of *J 39700*. Is the voltage within the range specified in the value(s) column?	Battery Volts	*Go to Step 8*	*Go to Step 10*
8	1. Turn the ignition switch to the OFF position. 2. Disconnect the *J 39700-25* cable adapter from the EBTCM leaving the cable adapter connected to the EBTCM harness only. 3. Turn the ignition switch to the ON position, engine off. 4. Using *J 39200* DMM, measure the voltage between terminals 6 and B of *J 39700*. Is the voltage within the range specified in the value(s) column?	Greater than 1V	*Go to Step 9*	*Go to Step 12*
9	Repair CKT 464 for a short to voltage. Is the repair complete?	—	Go to *Diagnostic System Check (ABS)*	—

GC4029803959020X

Fig. 146 Code C1276: Delivered Torque Signal Circuit Fault (Part 2 of 3). Corvette

Step	Action	Value(s)	Yes	No
10	1. Turn the ignition switch to the OFF position. 2. Using *J 39200* DMM, measure the resistance between *J 39700* terminals 6 and B. Is the resistance within the range specified in the value(s) column?	OL (infinite)	*Go to Step 6*	*Go to Step 11*
11	Repair CKT 464 for a short to ground. Is the repair complete?	—	Go to *Diagnostic System Check (ABS)*	—
12	1. Turn the ignition switch to the OFF position. 2. Using *J 39200* DMM, measure the resistance between terminal 6 of *J 39700* and the PCM connector C2 terminal 40. Is the resistance within the range specified in the value(s) column?	0–2 Ω	*Go to Step 13*	*Go to Step 14*
13	Replace PCM. Is the Replacement complete?	—	Go to *Diagnostic System Check (ABS)*	—
14	Repair CKT 464 for an open. Is the repair complete?	—	Go to *Diagnostic System Check (ABS)*	—

GC4029803959030X

Fig. 146 Code C1276: Delivered Torque Signal Circuit Fault (Part 3 of 3). Corvette

Circuit Description

Traction Control is simultaneously controlled by the EBTCM and the PCM. The PCM receives a REQUESTED TORQUE request via a Pulse Width Modulated (PWM) signal from the EBTCM requesting the desired torque level for proper Traction Control system operation. The PCM supplies the pull up voltage.

Conditions for Setting the DTC

There is an open or short in the REQUESTED TORQUE line between the EBTCM and PCM or there is a TCS communication malfunction detected by the PCM and indicated to the EBTCM, by broadcasting a PWM message.

Action Taken When the DTC Sets

TCS/Active Handling are disabled.

- Indicators that turn on:
  Car Icon (TCS indicator)
- Messages displayed on the DIC:
  Service Traction System
  Service Active HNDLG

Conditions for Clearing the DTC

- Condition for DTC is no longer present and scan tool clear DTC function is used.
- Fifty ignition cycles have passed with no DTCs detected.

Diagnostic Aids

- It is very important that a thorough inspection of the wiring and connectors be performed. Failure to carefully and fully inspect wiring and connectors may result in misdiagnosis, causing part replacement with reappearance of the malfunction.
- If an intermittent malfunction exists refer to *Intermittents*
- Possible causes for DTC C1277 to set:
  - Open in CKT 463.
  - CKT 463 shorted to ground or voltage.
  - Communication frequency problem.
  - Communication duty cycle problem.
  - CKT 463 has a wiring problem, terminal corrosion, or poor connections.
  - PCM not receiving information from EBTCM.

GC4029803960010X

Fig. 147 Code C1277: Requested Torque Signal Circuit Fault (Part 1 of 3). Corvette

Test Description

The numbers below refer to step numbers on the diagnostic table.

4. Checks for proper duty cycle.
5. Checks for proper frequency.

Step	Action	Value(s)	Yes	No
1	Was the Diagnostic System Check performed?	—	*Go to Step 2*	Go to *Diagnostic System Check (ABS)*
2	Check the following grounds, G101 and G106 making sure each ground is clean tight and free of damage. Were any loose, damaged, or corroded grounds found?	—	*Go to Step 3*	*Go to Step 4*
3	Repair ground as necessary. Is the repair complete?	—	Go to *Diagnostic System Check (ABS)*	—
4	1. Turn the ignition switch to the OFF position. 2. Disconnect the EBTCM connector. 3. Install *J 39700* Universal Pinout Box using the *J 39700-25* cable adapter to the EBTCM harness connector and the EBTCM connector. 4. Turn the ignition switch to the ON position, engine off. 5. Using *J 39200* DMM, measure the DC duty cycle between *J 39700* terminals 25 and B. Is the duty cycle within the range specified in the value(s) column?	85–95 %	*Go to Step 5*	*Go to Step 6*
5	Using *J 39200* DMM, measure the DC Hz between *J 39700* terminals 25 and B. Is the frequency within the range specified in the value(s) column?	121–134 Hz	*Go to Step 13*	*Go to Step 7*
6	1. Turn the ignition switch to the OFF position. 2. Disconnect *J 39700-25* cable adapter from the EBTCM, leaving *J 39700-25* cable adapter connected to the EBTCM harness connector only. 3. Turn the ignition switch to the ON position, engine off. 4. Using *J 39200* DMM, measure the voltage between terminals 25 and B of *J 39700*. Is the voltage within the range specified in the value(s) column?	4.5–5.5 V	*Go to Step 7*	*Go to Step 8*
7	Replace the EBTCM. Is the replacement complete?	—	Go to *Diagnostic System Check (ABS)*	—
8	1. Turn the ignition switch to the OFF position. 2. Disconnect the PCM connector C1. 3. Turn the ignition switch to the ON position engine off. 4. Using *J 39200* DMM, measure the voltage between terminals 25 and B of *J 39700* Is the voltage within the range specified in the value(s) column?	Greater than 1 V	*Go to Step 9*	*Go to Step 10*

GC4029803960020X

Fig. 147 Code C1277: Requested Torque Signal Circuit Fault (Part 2 of 3). Corvette

Step	Action	Value(s)	Yes	No
9	Repair CKT 463 for a short to voltage. Is the repair complete?	—	Go to *Diagnostic System Check (ABS)*	—
10	1. Turn the ignition switch to the OFF position. 2. Using *J 39200* DMM, measure the resistance between *J 39700* terminals 25 and B. Is the resistance within the range specified in the value(s) column?	OL (infinite)	*Go to Step 12*	*Go to Step 11*
11	Repair CKT 463 for a short to ground. Is the repair complete?	—	Go to *Diagnostic System Check (ABS)*	—
12	Using *J 39200* DMM, measure the resistance between terminal 25 of *J 39700* and the PCM connector C1 terminal 46. Is the resistance within the range specified in the value(s) column?	0–2 Ω	*Go to Step 13*	*Go to Step 14*
13	Replace the PCM. Is the diagnosis complete?	—	Go to *Diagnostic System Check (ABS)*	—
14	Repair CKT 463 for an open. Is the repair complete?	—	Go to *Diagnostic System Check (ABS)*	—

GC4029803960030X

Fig. 147 Code C1277: Requested Torque Signal Circuit Fault (Part 3 of 3). Corvette

Step	Action	Value(s)	Yes	No
1	Was the Diagnostic System Check performed?	—	*Go to Step 2*	Go to *ABS Diagnostic System Check*
2	1. Turn the ignition switch to the ON position, engine OFF. 2. Using a scan tool, read ABS/TCS DTC(s). Are any other DTC(s) set?	—	Go to that DTC table	*Go to Step 3*
3	Is DTC C1278 set as a current code?	—	*Go to Step 5*	*Go to Step 4*
4	1. Start engine and carefully test drive vehicle, achieving at least 16 Km/h (10 mph) while monitoring the scan tool for ABS/TCS DTC(s). 2. Repeat above drive cycle sequence two more times. Did DTC C1278 set in the last three drive cycles	—	*Go to Step 5*	Go to *ABS Diagnostic System Check*
5	Check Powertrain. Did vehicle pass the OBD System Check?	—	Refer to Diagnostic Aids	Check Powertrain.

GC402970266600BX

Fig. 148 Code C1278: TCS Temporarily Inhibited By PCM (Part 2 of 2). Corvette

Action Taken When the DTC Sets

- Magna Steer® is disabled, ABS/TCS remains active.

Conditions for Clearing the DTC

- Condition for DTC is no longer present and scan tool clear DTC function is used.
- Fifty ignition cycles have passed with no DTC(s) detected.

Diagnostic Aids

- If the analog Steering Wheel Position Sensor input is missing then DTC C1288 will set.
- If the Steering Wheel Position Sensor 5 volt supply or the Steering Wheel Position ground is missing DTC C1288 will set.
- It is very important that a thorough inspection of the wiring and connectors be performed. Failure to carefully and fully inspect wiring and connectors may result in misdiagnosis, causing part replacement with reappearance of the malfunction.
- An intermittent malfunction can be caused by poor connections, broken insulation, or a wire that is broken inside the insulation.

Test Description

The numbers below refer to step numbers on the diagnostic table.

3. Checks for the analog voltage to change, if the analog voltage does not change DTC C1281 will set.
4. Checks if the digital Phase A and Phase B are changing state from high to low.
5. checks to see if the analog and digital readings are ± 27° of each other.
31. Checks to see if the EBTCM is supplying the pull up voltage for Phase A.
32. Checks to see if the EBTCM is supplying the pull up voltage for Phase B.
33. Checks to see if the EBTCM is supplying the pull up voltage for the Index pulse.

Step	Action	Value(s)	Yes	No
1	Was the Diagnostic System Check performed?	—	*Go to Step 2*	Go to *ABS Diagnostic System Check*
2	1. Turn the ignition switch to the ON position, engine OFF. 2. Using a scan tool read ABS/TCS DTC(s). Are any of the following DTC(s) present, C1286 or C1288?	—	Go to Applicable DTC table	*Go to Step 3*
3	1. Cycle the ignition switch from the OFF to ON position. 2. Using a scan tool in the Data List monitor the Analog Steer Sensor Voltage as you rotate the steering wheel from left to right. Does the Analog Steer Sensor Voltage change as the steering wheel is rotated?	—	*Go to Step 4*	*Go to Step 6*
4	Using a scan tool in the Data List monitor the Digital HWPS Input as you rotate the steering wheel from left to right Does the Digital HWPS Input change as the steering wheel is rotated?	—	*Go to Step 5*	*Go to Step 10*
5	1. Using a scan tool in the Data List monitor the Analog Steer Sensor Voltage and the Digital HWPS Input. 2. Rotate the steering wheel until the Digital HWPS Input reads 50°. Does the Analog Steer Sensor Voltage read within the range specified in the value(s) column?	2.7 - 3.3V	*Go to Step 7*	*Go to Step 8*

GC402970266700BX

Fig. 149 Code C1281: Steering Sensor Uncorrelated Fault (Part 2 of 5). Corvette

Circuit Description

The PCM monitors various parameters and will not allow Traction Control operation if any parameter falls beyond a predetermined value.

Conditions for Setting the DTC

A malfunction has been detected by the PCM. The PCM then causes TCS shutdown until the malfunction has been corrected.

Action Taken When the DTC Sets

This is a temporary operational malfunction. A malfunction DTC is stored, TCS is disabled and the Traction Control indicator is turned ON. ABS remains functional. If TCS is no longer inhibited the indicator will be turned OFF but the DTC will still be stored.

Conditions for Clearing the DTC

- Condition for DTC is no longer present and scan tool clear DTC function is used.
- Fifty ignition cycles have passed with no DTC(s) detected.

Diagnostic Aids

- This code is for information only. It indicates there are no problems in the ABS/TCS system, is used as an aid to the technician.

GC402970266600AX

Fig. 148 Code C1278: TCS Temporarily Inhibited By PCM (Part 1 of 2). Corvette

Circuit Description

The EBTCM uses four inputs from the Steering Wheel Position sensor:

- Phase A digital input
- Phase B digital input
- Index pulse
- Analog input

This information is used to calculate three things:

1. The front wheels position when centered.
2. The front wheels position when turning.
3. The rate at which the steering wheel is turning.

The EBTCM runs a centering routine when the vehicle speed goes above 30 Km/h (18 mph). When the vehicle reaches 30 Km/h (18 mph), the EBTCM monitors the Steering Wheel Position Sensor inputs (Phase A, Phase B and Analog voltage) to see if the steering wheel is moving. If the steering wheel is not moving for a set period of time then the EBTCM assumes the vehicle is going in a straight line. At this point, the EBTCM looks at the analog voltage signal and reads the voltage. This voltage normally around 2.5V, is then considered the center position and the digital degrees also become zero at the same time. This centering routine is necessary to compensate for wear in the steering and suspension. Wear in the steering and suspension can result in a change in the relationship between the steering wheel and the front tires when driving in a straight line. By running the centering routine the EBTCM can compensate for these changes by changing the digital and analog center position.

The EBTCM uses the digital input (Phase A and Phase B) from the Steering Wheel Position Sensor to calculate the direction the driver of the vehicle is trying to steer during an ABS event. This information is also used to calculate the rate at which the steering wheel is turning to control the amount of effort required from the driver to turn the steering wheel using Magna Steer®.

Conditions for Setting the DTC

- DTC C1281 will set when the digitally derived centered angle differs from the analog derived angle by 27° or more for a period of 5 seconds.
- DTC C1281 will set if the index pulse is not seen between ± 37° or is seen between -185° and -37° or 37° and 185° of steering wheel travel.
- DTC C1281 will set if phase A and or phase B are shorted.

GC402970266700AX

Fig. 149 Code C1281: Steering Sensor Uncorrelated Fault (Part 1 of 5). Corvette

Step	Action	Value(s)	Yes	No
6	1. Turn the Ignition switch to the OFF position. 2. Disconnect the EBTCM. 3. Install the *J 39700* Universal Pinout Box using the *J 39700-25* cable adapter between the EBTCM harness connector and the EBTCM. 4. Turn the ignition switch to the ON position, engine OFF. 5. Using *J 39200* DMM, measure the voltage at terminal 23 of *J 39700* as an assistant rotates the steering wheel. Does the voltage change as the steering wheel is rotated?	—	*Go to Step 9*	*Go to Step 8*
7	Rotate the steering wheel in either direction while monitoring the Digital HWPS Index Pulse with a scan in Data List. Does the Digital HWPS Index Pulse go HIGH within ± 37° of steering center while rotating the steering wheel?	—	*Go to Step 9*	*Go to Step 12*
8	Replace the Steering Wheel Position Sensor. Is the replacement complete?	—	Go to *ABS Diagnostic System Check*	—
9	Replace the EBTCM. Is the replacement complete?	—	Go to *ABS Diagnostic System Check*	—
10	1. Turn the Ignition switch to the OFF position. 2. Disconnect the EBTCM. 3. Install the *J 39700* Universal Pinout Box using the *J 39700-25* cable adapter between the EBTCM harness connector and the EBTCM. 4. Turn the ignition switch to the ON position, engine OFF. 5. Using *J 39200* DMM, measure the voltage at terminal 20 of *J 39700* as an assistant rotates the steering wheel. Does the voltage toggle between 0 and Battery volts as the steering wheel is rotated?	—	*Go to Step 11*	*Go to Step 19*
11	Using *J 39200* DMM, measure the voltage at terminal 4 of *J 39700* as an assistant rotates the steering wheel. Does the voltage toggle between 0 and Battery volts as the steering wheel is rotated?	—	*Go to Step 9*	*Go to Step 25*
12	1. Turn the Ignition switch to the OFF position. 2. Disconnect the EBTCM. 3. Install the *J 39700* Universal Pinout Box using the *J 39700-25* cable adapter between the EBTCM harness connector and the EBTCM. 4. Turn the ignition switch to the ON position, engine OFF. 5. Using *J 39200* DMM, measure the voltage at terminal 19 of *J 39700* as an assistant rotates the steering wheel from the center position to the right. Does the voltage toggle between 0 and Battery volts one time as the steering wheel is rotated to the right?	—	*Go to Step 9*	*Go to Step 13*

GC402970266700CX

Fig. 149 Code C1281: Steering Sensor Uncorrelated Fault (Part 3 of 5). Corvette

Step	Action	Value(s)	Yes	No
13	1. Turn the ignition switch to the OFF position. 2. Disconnect the *J 39700-25* cable adapter from the EBTCM leaving the *J 39700-25* cable adapter connected to the EBTCM harness connector. 3. Disconnect the Steering Wheel Position Sensor connector. 4. Using *J 39200* DMM, measure the resistance between terminals 19 and B of *J 39700*. Is the resistance within the range specified within the value(s) column?	OL (infinite)	*Go to Step 15*	*Go to Step 14*
14	Repair short to ground in CKT 1765. Is the repair complete?	—	Go to *ABS Diagnostic System Check*	—
15	1. Turn the ignition switch to the ON position, engine OFF. 2. Using *J 39200* DMM, measure the voltage at terminal 19 of *J 39700*. Is the voltage within the range specified in the value(s) column?	Above 1V	*Go to Step 16*	*Go to Step 17*
16	Repair short to voltage in CKT 1765. Is the repair complete?	—	Go to *ABS Diagnostic System Check*	—
17	1. Turn the ignition switch to the OFF position. 2. Connect a jumper wire between terminals 19 and B of *J 39700*. 3. Using *J 39200* DMM, measure the resistance between the Steering Wheel Position Sensor harness connector terminal 5 and a good ground. Is the resistance within the range specified in the value(s) column?	0 - 5Ω	*Go to Step 33*	*Go to Step 18*
18	Repair open or high resistance in CKT 1765. Is the repair complete?	—	Go to *ABS Diagnostic System Check*	—
19	1. Turn the ignition switch to the OFF position. 2. Disconnect the *J 39700-25* cable adapter from the EBTCM leaving the *J 39700-25* cable adapter connected to the EBTCM harness connector. 3. Disconnect the Steering Wheel Position Sensor connector. 4. Using *J 39200* DMM, measure the resistance between terminals 20 and B of *J 39700*. Is the resistance within the range specified within the value(s) column?	OL (infinite)	*Go to Step 21*	*Go to Step 20*
20	Repair short to ground in CKT 1763. Is the repair complete?	—	Go to *ABS Diagnostic System Check*	—
21	1. Turn the ignition switch to the On position, engine OFF. 2. Using *J 39200* DMM, measure the voltage at terminal 20 of *J 39700*. Is the voltage within the range specified in the value(s) column?	Above 1V	*Go to Step 22*	*Go to Step 23*

GC402970266700DX

Fig. 149 Code C1281: Steering Sensor Uncorrelated Fault (Part 4 of 5). Corvette

Step	Action	Value(s)	Yes	No
22	Repair short to voltage in CKT 1763. Is the repair complete?	—	Go to *ABS Diagnostic System Check*	—
23	1. Turn the ignition switch to the OFF position. 2. Connect a jumper wire between terminals 20 and B of *J 39700*. 3. Using *J 39200* DMM, measure the resistance between the Steering Wheel Position Sensor harness connector terminal 3 and a good ground. Is the resistance within the range specified in the value(s) column?	0 - 5Ω	*Go to Step 31*	*Go to Step 24*
24	Repair open or high resistance in CKT 1763. Is the repair complete?	—	Go to *ABS Diagnostic System Check*	—
25	1. Turn the ignition switch to the OFF position. 2. Disconnect the *J 39700-25* cable adapter from the EBTCM leaving the *J 39700-25* cable adapter connected to the EBTCM harness connector. 3. Disconnect the Steering Wheel Position Sensor connector. 4. Using *J 39200* DMM, measure the resistance between terminals 4 and B of *J 39700*. Is the resistance within the range specified within the value(s) column?	OL (infinite)	*Go to Step 27*	*Go to Step 26*
26	Repair short to ground in CKT 1764. Is the repair complete?	—	Go to *ABS Diagnostic System Check*	—
27	1. Turn the ignition switch to the ON position, engine OFF. 2. Using *J 39200* DMM, measure the voltage at terminal 4 of *J 39700*. Is the voltage within the range specified in the value(s) column?	Above 1V	*Go to Step 28*	*Go to Step 29*
28	Repair short to voltage in CKT 1764. Is the repair complete?	—	Go to *ABS Diagnostic System Check*	—
29	1. Turn the ignition switch to the OFF position. 2. Connect a jumper wire between terminals 4 and B of *J 39700*. 3. Using *J 39200* DMM, measure the resistance between the Steering Wheel Position Sensor harness connector terminal 4 and a good ground. Is the resistance within the range specified in the value(s) column?	0 - 5Ω	*Go to Step 32*	*Go to Step 30*
30	Repair open or high resistance in CKT 1764. Is the repair complete?	—	Go to *ABS Diagnostic System Check*	—

GC402970266700EX

Fig. 149 Code C1281: Steering Sensor Uncorrelated Fault (Part 5 of 5). Corvette

Circuit Description

Active Handling™ is activated by calculating the driver's desired yaw rate (based on wheel speed sensor inputs, lateral acceleration and steering wheel position information) and compares it to the actual yaw rate as measured by the yaw rate sensor. The difference between these two is the yaw rate error, which is then used to determine the amount of oversteer or understeer. If the yaw rate error becomes too large the system attempts to correct the vehicle's yaw motion by using differential braking on the left or right front and rear wheel brakes. To correct for oversteer differential braking is used on the left or right rear wheel brakes. To correct for understeer differential braking is used on the left or right front wheel brakes.

Conditions for Setting the DTC

- The analog and digital steering sensor do not agree for one second while in an Active Handling™ event.
- DTC C1281 can be set any time after the steering angle has been centered and Active Handling™ is activated. If the Active Handling event occurs for 10 seconds without a sign of the yaw rate error ever changing this code will be set. This is the only condition that will set DTC C1281 by itself.
- DTC C1281 can be set along with DTC C1287. During an Active Handling event the EBTCM does a comparison between the SWPS digital value and the SWPS analog value. If the difference is greater than 20 degrees for 1 second both DTC C1281 and DTC C1287 will be set.
- DTC C1281 can be set along with DTC C1282. During an Active Handling event the EBTCM does a comparison between the actual yaw rate and a yaw rate derived from the difference in output from the front wheel speed sensors during an understeer condition or the rear wheel speed sensors during an oversteer condition. If this yaw rate difference is greater than 10 degrees/seconds for more than 5 seconds DTC C1281 and DTC C1282 will be set. The use of DTC C1281 with DTC C1282 indicates that the road surface (typically ice) may have created an unusually long period where the wheel speed estimate of yaw rate may have been inaccurate due to vehicle sideslip. This means the DTCs may have been falsely set.
- Normal conditions which could cause code C1281 to set include Active Handling™ activation's brought on by aggressive driving on extremely slippery road surfaces for example, spinning the car in one direction for greater than 10 seconds. This means the DTC may have been falsely set due to aggressive driving.

Action Taken When the DTC Sets

ABS and TCS remain enabled, Active Handling™ is disabled.

- Indicators that turn on:
  Car Icon (TCS indicator)
- Messages displayed on the DIC:
  Service Active HNDLG

Conditions for Clearing the DTC

- Condition for DTC is no longer present and scan tool clear DTC function is used.
- Fifty ignition cycles have passed with no DTCs detected.

Diagnostic Aids

- It is very important to check the vehicle for proper alignment. The car should not pull in either direction while driving straight on a flat surface.
- It is very important to find out from the driver when the code was set (when the SERVICE ACTIVE HNDLG message was activated). This information may help to duplicate the failure.
- It is very important that a thorough inspection of the wiring and connectors be performed. Failure to carefully and fully inspect wiring and connectors may result in misdiagnosis, causing part replacement with reappearance of the malfunction.
- An intermittent malfunction is most likely caused by a poor connection, rubbed through wire insulation, or a wire that is broken inside the insulation. Refer to *Intermittents*
- The Snapshot function on the scan tool may help in finding an intermittent DTC C1281.

Test Description

The number(s) below refer to the step number(s) on the diagnostic table.

4. This step checks the accuracy of the analog and digital inputs from the SWPS.
6. This step checks for inaccurate yaw rate sensor input.

GC4029803961010X

Fig. 150 Code C1281: Active Handling Sensors Uncorrelated (Part 1 of 3). Corvette

Step	Action	Value(s)	Yes	No
1	Was the Diagnostic System Check performed?	—	*Go to Step 2*	Go to *Diagnostic System Check (ABS)*
2	Is this vehicle equipped with Active Handling (RPO JL4)?	—	*Go to Step 3*	Go to *DTC C1281 Steering Sensor Uncorrelated Malf*
3	1. Turn the ignition switch to the RUN position, engine OFF. 2. Using a scan tool read ABS/TCS/Active Handling DTC(s). Are any of the following DTC(s) present, C1221-C1235, C1282 or C1287?	—	Go to Applicable DTC table.	*Go to Step 4*
4	Using the scan tool perform the Steering Wheel Position Sensor Test. Is the analog and digital display on the scan tool within plus or minus 5 degrees of each other at the center (zero) position?	—	*Go to Step 6*	*Go to Step 5*
5	Replace the Steering Wheel Position Sensor. Is the replacement complete?	—	*Go to Step 8*	—
6	Carefully drive vehicle above 24 Km/h (15 mph) for 45 seconds in a straight line, while monitoring the Yaw Rate sensor with a scan tool. Is the degrees/second displayed on the scan tool within the range specified in the value(s) column?	0–5 degrees/ second	*Go to Step 8*	*Go to Step 7*

GC4029803961020X

Fig. 150 Code C1281: Active Handling Sensors Uncorrelated (Part 2 of 3). Corvette

Step	Action	Value(s)	Yes	No
7	Replace the Yaw Rate Sensor. Is the replacement complete?	—	*Go to Step 8*	—
8	Perform the Diagnostic Test Drive. Did DTC C1281 set as a current DTC?	—	*Go to Step 9*	Go to *Diagnostic System Check (ABS)*
9	Replace the EBTCM Is the replacement complete?	—	Go to *Diagnostic System Check (ABS)*	—

GC4029803961030X

Fig. 150 Code C1281: Active Handling Sensors Uncorrelated (Part 3 of 3). Corvette

Circuit Description

The yaw rate bias is calculated by the EBTCM any time ignition is present. This value is used to compensate for offsets in the yaw rate sensor output due to temperature changes and manufacturing differences.

Conditions for Setting the DTC

- DTC C1282 can be set any time ignition is present and the yaw rate bias exceeds 7 degrees/seconds.
- DTC C1282 can be set if the measured yaw rate changes by more than 390 degrees/second within one second.
- DTC C1282 can be set if the signal voltage is less than 0.15 volts or greater than 4.85 volts.
- DTC C1282 can be set during an Active Handling event. the EBTCM does a comparison between the actual yaw rate and a yaw rate derived from the difference in output from the front wheel speed sensors during an understeer condition or the rear wheel speed sensors during an oversteer condition. If this yaw rate difference is greater than 10 degrees/seconds for more than 60 seconds DTC C1282 will be set.

Action Taken When the DTC Sets

ABS and TCS remain enabled, Active Handling™ is disabled.

- Indicators that turn on:
  Car Icon (TCS indicator)
- Messages displayed on the DIC:
  Service Active HNDLG

Conditions for Clearing the DTC

- Condition for DTC is no longer present and scan tool clear DTC function is used.
- Fifty ignition cycles have passed with no DTCs detected.

Diagnostic Aids

- It is very important to check the vehicle for proper alignment. The car should not pull in either direction while driving straight on a flat surface.
- When performing the following diagnostic procedure, insure that the vehicle is parked on a level surface.
- It is very important to find out from the driver when the code was set, (when the SERVICE ACTIVE HNDLG message was activated). This information may help to duplicate the failure.
- It is very important that a thorough inspection of the wiring and connectors be performed. Failure to carefully and fully inspect wiring and connectors may result in misdiagnosis, causing part replacement with reappearance of the malfunction.
- It is very important to properly check the 5 volt power supply to the Yaw Rate Sensor. The Yaw Rate Sensor must have at least 4.75 volts, if the Yaw Rate Sensor does not have a stable (not drifting) supply voltage of at least 4.75 volts then DTC C1282 will set.
- An intermittent malfunction is most likely caused by a poor connection, rubbed through wire insulation, or a wire that is broken inside the insulation. Refer to *Intermittents*

Test Description

The number(s) below refer to the step number(s) on the diagnostic table.

24. This step checks for the EBTCM pull up voltage.
25. This step checks for the proper Yaw Rate Sensor signal being sent to the EBTCM.
26. This step checks if the EBTCM can properly interpret the Yaw Rate Sensor signal.

GC4029803962010X

Fig. 151 Code C1282: Yaw Rate Sensor Bias Circuit Fault (Part 1 of 4). Corvette

Step	Action	Value(s)	Yes	No
1	Was the Diagnostic System Check performed?	—	*Go to Step 2*	Go to *Diagnostic System Check (ABS)*
2	1. Turn the ignition switch to the OFF position. 2. Disconnect the EBTCM connector. 3. Install *J 39700* Universal Pinout Box using the *J 39700-25* cable adapter to the EBTCM harness connector only. 4. Using *J 39200* DMM, measure the resistance between *J 39700* terminals 21 and B. Is the resistance within the range specified in the value(s) column?	OL (infinite)	*Go to Step 4*	*Go to Step 3*
3	Repair CKT 910 for a short to ground. Is the repair complete?	—	Go to *Diagnostic System Check (ABS)*	—
4	Using *J 39200* DMM, measure the resistance between *J 39700* terminals 11 and B. Is the resistance within the range specified in the value(s) column?	OL (infinite)	*Go to Step 6*	*Go to Step 5*
5	Repair CKT 1056 for a short to ground. Is the repair complete?	—	Go to *Diagnostic System Check (ABS)*	—
6	1. Disconnect the Yaw Rate Sensor, Lateral Accelerometer, Brake Pressure Sensor, and the SWPS connectors. 2. Using *J 39200* DMM, measure the resistance between *J 39700* terminals 11 and 27. Is the resistance within the range specified in the value(s) column?	OL (infinite)	*Go to Step 8*	*Go to Step 7*
7	Repair short between CKT(s) 556 and 1056. Is the repair complete?	—	Go to *Diagnostic System Check (ABS)*	—
8	Using *J 39200* DMM, measure the resistance between *J 39700* terminals 11 and 21. Is the resistance within the range specified in the value(s) column?	OL (infinite)	*Go to Step 10*	*Go to Step 9*

GC4029803962020X

Fig. 151 Code C1282: Yaw Rate Sensor Bias Circuit Fault (Part 2 of 4). Corvette

Step	Action	Value(s)	Yes	No
9	Repair short between CKT(s) 910 and 1056. Is the repair complete?	—	Go to *Diagnostic System Check (ABS)*	—
10	Using *J 39200* DMM, measure the resistance between *J 39700* terminals 27 and 21. Is the resistance within the range specified in the value(s) column?	OL (infinite)	*Go to Step 12*	*Go to Step 11*
11	Repair short between CKT(s) 556 and 910. Is the repair complete?	—	Go to *Diagnostic System Check (ABS)*	—
12	1. Turn the ignition switch to the ON position, engine OFF. 2. Using *J 39200* DMM, measure the voltage between *J 39700* terminals 21 and B. Is the voltage within the range specified in the value(s) column?	Greater than 1V	*Go to Step 13*	*Go to Step 14*
13	Repair CKT 910 for a short to voltage. Is the repair complete?	—	Go to *Diagnostic System Check (ABS)*	—
14	Using *J 39200* DMM, measure the voltage between *J 39700* terminals 11 and B. Is the voltage within the range specified in the value(s) column?	Greater than 1V	*Go to Step 15*	*Go to Step 16*
15	Repair CKT 1056 for a short to voltage. Is the repair complete?	—	Go to *Diagnostic System Check (ABS)*	—
16	Using *J 39200* DMM, measure the voltage between *J 39700* terminals 27 and B. Is the voltage within the range specified in the value(s) column?	Greater than 1V	*Go to Step 17*	*Go to Step 18*
17	Repair CKT 556 for a short to voltage. Is the repair complete?	—	Go to *Diagnostic System Check (ABS)*	—
18	1. Turn the ignition switch to the OFF position. 2. Connect a fused jumper wire between terminals 21 and B of *J 39700*. 3. Using *J 39200* DMM, measure the resistance between the Yaw Rate Sensor harness connector terminal C and a good ground. Is the resistance within the range specified in the value(s) column?	0–5Ω	*Go to Step 20*	*Go to Step 19*
19	Repair CKT 910 for an open or high resistance. Is the repair complete?	—	Go to *Diagnostic System Check (ABS)*	—
20	1. Connect a fused jumper wire between terminals 27 and B of *J 39700*. 2. Using *J 39200* DMM, measure the resistance between the Yaw Rate Sensor harness connector terminal B and a good ground. Is the resistance within the range specified in the value(s) column?	0–5Ω	*Go to Step 22*	*Go to Step 21*

GC4029803962030X

Fig. 151 Code C1282: Yaw Rate Sensor Bias Circuit Fault (Part 3 of 4). Corvette

Step	Action	Value(s)	Yes	No
21	Repair CKT 556 for an open or high resistance. Is the repair complete?	—	Go to *Diagnostic System Check (ABS)*	—
22	1. Connect a fused jumper wire between terminals 11 and B of *J 39700*. 2. Using *J 39200* DMM, measure the resistance between the Yaw Rate Sensor harness connector terminal A and a good ground. Is the resistance within the range specified in the value(s) column?	0–5Ω	*Go to Step 24*	*Go to Step 23*
23	Repair CKT 1056 for an open or high resistance. Is the repair complete?	—	Go to *Diagnostic System Check (ABS)*	—
24	1. Connect the *J 39700-25* cable adapter between the EBTCM and the EBTCM harness connector. 2. Reconnect the Yaw Rate Sensor. 3. Remove the fused jumper wire from *J 39700*. 4. Turn the ignition switch to the ON position, engine OFF. 5. Using *J 39200* DMM, measure the voltage between *J 39700* terminals 11 and 27. Is the voltage within the range specified in the value(s) column?	4.75–5.25V	*Go to Step 25*	*Go to Step 29*
25	Using *J 39200* DMM, measure the voltage between *J 39700* terminals 21 and 27. Is the voltage within the range specified in the value(s) column?	2.35–2.65V	*Go to Step 26*	*Go to Step 27*
26	Using a scan tool read the Yaw Rate Sensor value in volts. Is the voltage within the range specified in the value(s) column?	2.0–3.0V	*Go to Step 27*	*Go to Step 29*
27	Replace the Yaw Rate Sensor. Is the replacement complete?	—	*Go to Step 28*	—
28	1. Read the diagnostic aids and conditions for setting the DTC. 2. Reconnect all previously disconnected components. 3. Cycle the ignition switch from the OFF to ON position. 4. Carefully drive the vehicle above 24 Km/h (15 mph) for several minutes, while monitoring a scan tool for ABS/TCS/Active Handling DTC(s). Did DTC C1282 set as a current DTC while the vehicle was being driven?	—	*Go to Step 29*	Go to *Diagnostic System Check (ABS)*
29	Replace the EBTCM Is the replacement complete?	—	Go to *Diagnostic System Check (ABS)*	—

GC4029803962040X

Fig. 151 Code C1282: Yaw Rate Sensor Bias Circuit Fault (Part 4 of 4). Corvette

Circuit Description

Steer angle centering is the process by which the EBTCM calibrates the steering sensor output so that it reads zero when the steering wheel is centered. The initial steering wheel center position is calculated after driving 10 Km/h (6 mph) for more than 10 seconds in a straight line on a fairly level surface. The EBTCM uses the Yaw Rate Sensor, Lateral Accelerometer and Wheel Speed Sensors to tell if the vehicle is moving in a straight line. This centering routine is necessary to compensate for wear in the steering and suspension. Wear in the steering and suspension can result in a change in the relationship between the steering wheel and the front wheels. By running the centering routine the EBTCM can compensate for these changes by changing the digital and analog center position.

Conditions for Setting the DTC

The initial steering wheel center position will be determined quickly unless there is a large offset in the yaw sensor or lateral accelerometer output. When this happens the system will believe the steering is far off center even though the vehicle is being driven in a straight line. Under this condition and with a continuous vehicle speed of 40 Km/h (25 mph) or greater for longer than 10 minutes, DTC C1283 will be set.

Action Taken When the DTC Sets

ABS and TCS remain enabled, Active Handling is disabled.

- Indicators that turn on:
  Car Icon (TCS indicator)
- Messages displayed on the DIC:
  Service Active HNDLG
  Service Vehicle Soon

Conditions for Clearing the DTC

- Condition for DTC is no longer present and scan tool clear DTC function is used.
- Fifty ignition cycles have passed with no DTCs detected.

Diagnostic Aids

- It is very important to check the vehicle for proper alignment. The car should not pull in either direction while driving straight on a flat surface.
- It is very important to find out from the driver when the code was set (when the SERVICE ACTIVE HNDLG message was activated). This information may help to duplicate the failure.
- It is very important that a thorough inspection of the wiring and connectors be performed. Failure to carefully and fully inspect wiring and connectors may result in misdiagnosis, causing part replacement with reappearance of the malfunction.

GC4029803963010X

Fig. 152 Code C1283: Excessive Time To Center Steering (Part 1 of 2). Corvette

- An intermittent malfunction is most likely caused by a poor connection, rubbed through wire insulation, or a wire that is broken inside the insulation. Refer to *Intermittents*
- The Snapshot function on the scan tool may help in finding an intermittent DTC C1283.

Test Description

The number(s) below refer to the step number(s) on the diagnostic table.

3. This step checks for the proper Lateral Accelerometer input.
5. This step checks for the proper Yaw Rate Sensor input.

Step	Action	Value(s)	Yes	No
1	Was the Diagnostic System Check performed?	—	*Go to Step 2*	Go to *Diagnostic System Check (ABS)*
2	1. Turn the ignition switch to the ON position, engine OFF. 2. Using a scan tool read ABS/TCS/Active Handling DTC(s). Are any of the following DTC(s) present, C1221-C1235, C1282, C1284, or C1285?	—	Go to the Applicable DTC. Refer to *DTC List*	*Go to Step 3*
3	1. Turn the ignition switch to the OFF position. 2. Disconnect the EBTCM connector. 3. Install *J 39700* Universal Pinout Box using the *J 39700-25* cable adapter to the EBTCM and the EBTCM harness connector. 4. Turn the ignition switch to the ON position, engine OFF. 5. Using *J 39200* DMM, measure the voltage between terminals 22 and B of *J 39700*. Is the voltage within the range specified in the value(s) column?	2.3–2.7V	*Go to Step 5*	*Go to Step 4*
4	Replace the Lateral Accelerometer. Is the replacement complete?	—	Go to *Diagnostic System Check (ABS)*	—
5	Using *J 39200* DMM, measure the voltage between terminals 21 and B of *J 39700*. Is the voltage within the range specified in the value(s) column?	2.3–2.7V	*Go to Step 7*	*Go to Step 6*
6	Replace the Yaw Rate Sensor. Is the replacement complete?	—	Go to *Diagnostic System Check (ABS)*	—
7	1. Read the diagnostic aids and conditions for setting the DTC. 2. Cycle the ignition switch from the OFF to ON position. 3. Carefully drive the vehicle above 40 Km/h (25 mph) for 10 minutes, while monitoring a scan tool for ABS/TCS/Active Handling DTC(s). Did DTC C1283 set as a current DTC?	—	*Go to Step 8*	Go to *Diagnostic System Check (ABS)*
8	Replace the EBTCM. Is the replacement complete?	—	Go to *Diagnostic System Check (ABS)*	—

GC4029803963020X

Fig. 152 Code C1283: Excessive Time To Center Steering (Part 2 of 2). Corvette

Circuit Description

The Lateral Accelerometer performs a Self Test at initialization. The sensor's output will be offset by a fixed amount for a short period of time when the EBTCM powers up. The test will run when the ignition is ON, all 4 wheel speeds are 0 km/h and the steer angle is within 90 degrees of straight ahead.

Conditions for Setting the DTC

The EBTCM will set DTC C1284 if it does not see the expected change in the output of the Lateral Accelerometer soon after initialization.

Action Taken When the DTC Sets

ABS and TCS remain enabled, Active Handling is disabled.

- Indicators that turn on:
  Car Icon (TCS indicator)
- Messages displayed on the DIC:
  Service Active HNDLG

Conditions for Clearing the DTC

- Condition for DTC is no longer present and scan tool clear DTC function is used.
- Fifty ignition cycles have passed with no DTCs detected.

Diagnostic Aids

- It is very important to check the vehicle for proper alignment. The car should not pull in either direction while driving straight on a flat surface.
- It is very important to find out from the driver when the code was set (when the SERVICE ACTIVE HNDLG message was activated). This information may help to duplicate the failure.
- It is very important that a thorough inspection of the wiring and connectors be performed. Failure to carefully and fully inspect wiring and connectors may result in misdiagnosis, causing part replacement with reappearance of the malfunction.
- An intermittent malfunction is most likely caused by a poor connection, rubbed through wire insulation, or a wire that is broken inside the insulation. Refer to *Intermittents*

GC4029803964010X

Fig. 153 Code C1284: Lateral Accelerator Sensor Test Fault (Part 1 of 2). Corvette

Step	Action	Value(s)	Yes	No
1	Was the Diagnostic System Check performed?	—	*Go to Step 2*	Go to *Diagnostic System Check (ABS)*
2	1. Turn the ignition switch to the ON position, engine OFF. 2. Using a scan tool read ABS/TCS/Active Handling DTC(s). Is DTC C1285 set as a current DTC?	—	Go to Applicable DTC table. Refer to *DTC List*	*Go to Step 3*
3	Replace the Lateral Accelerometer. Is the replacement complete?	—	*Go to Step 4*	—
4	1. Read the diagnostic aids and conditions for setting the DTC. 2. Cycle the ignition from the OFF to ON position, engine OFF. 3. With a scan tool read ABS/TCS/Active Handling DTC(s). Did DTC C1284 reset as a current DTC?	—	*Go to Step 5*	Go to *Diagnostic System Check (ABS)*
5	Replace the EBTCM. Is the replacement complete?	—	Go to *Diagnostic System Check (ABS)*	—

GC4029803964020X

Fig. 153 Code C1284: Lateral Accelerator Sensor Test Fault (Part 2 of 2). Corvette

Circuit Description

The output of the Lateral Accelerometer is measured by the EBTCM any time ignition is present. The usable output voltage range for the Lateral Accelerometer is 0.25 - 4.75 volts. The scan tool will report a zero lateral accelerometer signal of 2.5 volts if no sensor bias (offset) is present and the vehicle is on a flat surface.

Conditions for Setting the DTC

DTC C1285 can be set any time the ignition is present and the Lateral Accelerometer voltage is less than 0.15 volts or greater than 4.85 volts for approximately 1 second or more.

Action Taken When the DTC Sets

ABS and TCS remain enabled, Active Handling is disabled.

- Indicators that turn on:
  Car Icon (TCS indicator)
- Messages displayed on the DIC:
  Service Active HNDLG

Conditions for Clearing the DTC

- Condition for DTC is no longer present and scan tool clear DTC function is used.
- Fifty ignition cycles have passed with no DTCs detected.

Diagnostic Aids

- It is very important to find out from the driver when the code was set (when the SERVICE ACTIVE HNDLG message was activated). This information may help to duplicate the failure.
- It is very important that a thorough inspection of the wiring and connectors be performed. Failure to carefully and fully inspect wiring and connectors may result in misdiagnosis, causing part replacement with reappearance of the malfunction.
- An intermittent malfunction is most likely caused by a poor connection, rubbed through wire insulation, or a wire that is broken inside the insulation. Refer to *Intermittents*

Test Description

The number(s) below refer to the step number(s) on the diagnostic table.

24. This step checks for the EBTCM pull up voltage.
25. This step checks for the proper Lateral Accelerometer Sensor signal being sent to the EBTCM.
26. This step checks if the EBTCM can properly interpret the Lateral Accelerometer Sensor signal.

GC4029803965010X

Fig. 154 Code C1285: Lateral Accelerator Sensor Circuit Fault (Part 1 of 4). Corvette

Step	Action	Value(s)	Yes	No
1	Was the Diagnostic System Check performed?	—	*Go to Step 2*	Go to *Diagnostic System Check (ABS)*
2	1. Turn the ignition switch to the OFF position. 2. Disconnect the EBTCM connector. 3. Install *J 39700* Universal Pinout Box using the *J 39700-25* cable adapter to the EBTCM harness connector only. 4. Using *J 39200* DMM, measure the resistance between *J 39700* terminals 22 and B. Is the resistance within the range specified in the value(s) column?	OL (infinite)	*Go to Step 4*	*Go to Step 3*
3	Repair CKT 1338 for a short to ground. Is the repair complete?	—	Go to *Diagnostic System Check (ABS)*	—
4	Using *J 39200* DMM, measure the resistance between *J 39700* terminals 11 and B. Is the resistance within the range specified in the value(s) column?	OL (infinite)	*Go to Step 6*	*Go to Step 5*
5	Repair CKT 1056 for a short to ground. Is the repair complete?	—	Go to *Diagnostic System Check (ABS)*	—
6	1. Disconnect the Yaw Rate Sensor, Lateral Accelerometer, Brake Pressure Sensor, and the SWPS connectors. 2. Using *J 39200* DMM, measure the resistance between *J 39700* terminals 11 and 27. Is the resistance within the range specified in the value(s) column?	OL (infinite)	*Go to Step 8*	*Go to Step 7*
7	Repair short between CKT(s) 556 and 1056. Is the repair complete?	—	Go to *Diagnostic System Check (ABS)*	—
8	Using *J 39200* DMM, measure the resistance between *J 39700* terminals 11 and 22. Is the resistance within the range specified in the value(s) column?	OL (infinite)	*Go to Step 10*	*Go to Step 9*
9	Repair short between CKT(s) 1056 and 1338. Is the repair complete?	—	Go to *Diagnostic System Check (ABS)*	—
10	Using *J 39200* DMM, measure the resistance between *J 39700* terminals 27 and 22. Is the resistance within the range specified in the value(s) column?	OL (infinite)	*Go to Step 12*	*Go to Step 11*
11	Repair short between CKT(s) 1338 and 556. Is the repair complete?	—	Go to *Diagnostic System Check (ABS)*	—
12	1. Turn the ignition switch to the ON position, engine OFF. 2. Using *J 39200* DMM, measure the voltage between *J 39700* terminals 22 and B. Is the voltage within the range specified in the value(s) column?	Greater than 1V	*Go to Step 13*	*Go to Step 14*

GC4029803965020X

Fig. 154 Code C1285: Lateral Accelerator Sensor Circuit Fault (Part 2 of 4). Corvette

Step	Action	Value(s)	Yes	No
13	Repair CKT 1338 for a short to voltage. Is the repair complete?	—	Go to *Diagnostic System Check (ABS)*	—
14	Using *J 39200* DMM, measure the voltage between *J 39700* terminals 11 and B. Is the voltage within the range specified in the value(s) column?	Greater than 1V	*Go to Step 15*	*Go to Step 16*
15	Repair CKT 1056 for a short to voltage. Is the repair complete?	—	Go to *Diagnostic System Check (ABS)*	—
16	Using *J 39200* DMM, measure the voltage between *J 39700* terminals 27 and B. Is the voltage within the range specified in the value(s) column?	Greater than 1V	*Go to Step 17*	*Go to Step 18*
17	Repair CKT 556 for a short to voltage. Is the repair complete?	—	Go to *Diagnostic System Check (ABS)*	—
18	1. Turn the ignition switch to the OFF position. 2. Connect a fused jumper wire between terminals 22 and B of *J 39700*. 3. Using *J 39200* DMM, measure the resistance between the Lateral Accelerometer harness connector terminal B and a good ground. Is the resistance within the range specified in the value(s) column?	0–5Ω	*Go to Step 20*	*Go to Step 19*
19	Repair CKT 1338 for an open or high resistance. Is the repair complete?	—	Go to *Diagnostic System Check (ABS)*	—
20	1. Connect a fused jumper wire between terminals 27 and B of *J 39700*. 2. Using *J 39200* DMM, measure the resistance between the Lateral Accelerometer harness connector terminal C and a good ground. Is the resistance within the range specified in the value(s) column?	0–5Ω	*Go to Step 22*	*Go to Step 21*
21	Repair CKT 556 for an open or high resistance. Is the repair complete?	—	Go to *Diagnostic System Check (ABS)*	—
22	1. Connect a fused jumper wire between terminals 11 and B of *J 39700*. 2. Using *J 39200* DMM, measure the resistance between the Lateral Accelerometer harness connector terminal A and a good ground. Is the resistance within the range specified in the value(s) column?	0–5Ω	*Go to Step 24*	*Go to Step 23*
23	Repair CKT 1056 for an open or high resistance. Is the repair complete?	—	Go to *Diagnostic System Check (ABS)*	—

GC4029803965030X

Fig. 154 Code C1285: Lateral Accelerator Sensor Circuit Fault (Part 3 of 4). Corvette

Step	Action	Value(s)	Yes	No
24	1. Connect the *J 39700-25* cable adapter between the EBTCM and the EBTCM harness connector. 2. Reconnect the Lateral Accelerometer. 3. Remove the fused jumper wire from *J 39700*. 4. Turn the ignition switch to the ON position, engine OFF. 5. Using *J 39200* DMM, measure the voltage between *J 39700* terminals 11 and 27. Is the voltage within the range specified in the value(s) column?	4.75–5.25V	*Go to Step 25*	*Go to Step 29*
25	Using *J 39200* DMM, measure the voltage between *J 39700* terminals 22 and 27. Is the voltage within the range specified in the value(s) column?	2.35–2.65V	*Go to Step 26*	*Go to Step 27*
26	Using a scan tool read the Lateral Accelerometer value in volts. Is the voltage within the range specified in the value(s) column?	2.0–3.0V	*Go to Step 27*	*Go to Step 29*
27	Replace the Lateral Accelerometer. Is the replacement complete?	—	*Go to Step 28*	—
28	1. Read the diagnostic aids and conditions for setting the DTC. 2. Reconnect all previously disconnected components. 3. Cycle the ignition switch from the OFF to ON position. 4. Carefully drive the vehicle above 24 Km/h (15 mph) for several minutes, while monitoring a scan tool for ABS/TCS/Active Handling DTC(s). Did DTC C1285 set as a current DTC while the vehicle was being driven?	—	*Go to Step 29*	Go to *Diagnostic System Check (ABS)*
29	Replace the EBTCM. Is the replacement complete?	—	Go to *Diagnostic System Check (ABS)*	—

GC4029803965040X

Fig. 154 Code C1285: Lateral Accelerator Sensor Circuit Fault (Part 4 of 4). Corvette

Circuit Description

The EBTCM runs a centering routine when the vehicle speed goes above 30 Km/h (18 mph). When the vehicle reaches 30 Km/h (18 mph), the EBTCM monitors the Steering Wheel Position Sensor inputs (Phase A, Phase B and Analog voltage) to see if the steering wheel is moving. If the steering wheel is not moving for a set period of time then the EBTCM assumes the vehicle is going in a straight line. At this point, the EBTCM looks at the analog voltage signal and reads the voltage. This voltage normally around 2.5V, is then considered the center position and the digital degrees also become zero at the same time. This centering routine is necessary to compensate for wear in the steering and suspension. Wear in the steering and suspension can result in a change in the relationship between the steering wheel and the front tires when driving in a straight line. By running the centering routine the EBTCM can compensate for these changes by changing the digital and analog center position.

Conditions for Setting the DTC

- DTC C1286 can be set after the centering routines completion if the bias value is ± 30° from the previous bias value.
- DTC C1286 can also be set at start up if the bias value was out of range on the last ignition cycle.

Action Taken When the DTC Sets

- Magna Steer® is disabled ABS/TCS remains active.

Conditions for Clearing the DTC

- Condition for DTC is no longer present and scan tool clear DTC function is used.
- Fifty ignition cycles have passed with no DTC(s) detected.

Diagnostic Aids

- Possible causes:
  - Steering wheel rotated with steering gear disconnected.
  - Faulty Steering Wheel Position Sensor.
  - Faulty EBTCM.

Test Description

The numbers below refer to the step numbers on the diagnostic table.

4. Recenters the Steering Wheel Position Sensor.

GC402970266800AX

Fig. 155 Code C1286: Steering Sensor Bias Fault (Part 1 of 2). Corvette

Step	Action	Value(s)	Yes	No
1	Was the Diagnostic System Check performed?	—	*Go to Step 2*	Go to *ABS Diagnostic System Check*
2	1. Point the front wheels straight ahead. 2. Using a scan tool check the Steering Wheel Position Sensor Analog voltage. Is the voltage within the range specified within the value(s) column?	2 - 3V	*Go to Step 3*	*Go to Step 4*
3	Replace the EBTCM. Is the repair complete?	—	Go to *ABS Diagnostic System Check*	—
4	1. Turn the ignition switch to the OFF position. 2. Disable the Supplemental Inflatable Restraint (SIR). 3. Remove the Inflatable Restraint Wheel Module Coil. 4. Remove the Intermediate Shaft. 5. Turn the ignition switch to the ON position, engine Off. 6. Using a scan tool monitor the Steering Wheel Position Sensors analog voltage as you rotate the steering column shaft. 7. Turn the steering column shaft until the analog voltage is close to 2.5 volts. Does the analog voltage move to or close to 2.5 volts?	—	*Go to Step 6*	*Go to Step 5*
5	Replace the Steering Wheel Position Sensor. Is the replacement complete?	—	Go to *ABS Diagnostic System Check*	—
6	1. Leave the steering column shaft centered at 2.5 volts. 2. Turn the ignition switch to the OFF position. 3. Install the Intermediate Shaft. 4. Install the Inflatable Restraint Wheel Module Coil. 5. Enable the SIR. Is the repair complete?	—	*Go to Step 7*	—
7	1. Turn the ignition switch to the ON position, engine Off. 2. Using a scan tool clear DTC C1286. 3. Drive vehicle above 30 Km/h (18 mph) for several minutes. 4. Using a scan tool check for DTC C1286. Did DTC C1286 set as a current DTC?	—	*Go to Step 3*	Go to *ABS Diagnostic System Check*

GC402970266800BX

Fig. 155 Code C1286: Steering Sensor Bias Fault (Part 2 of 2). Corvette

Circuit Description

Steer angle centering is the process by which the EBTCM calibrates the steering sensor output so that it reads zero when the steering wheel is centered. The initial steering wheel center position is calculated after driving 10 Km/h (6 mph) for more than 10 seconds in a straight line on a fairly level surface. The EBTCM uses the Yaw Rate Sensor, Lateral Accelerometer and Wheel Speed Sensors to tell if the vehicle is moving in a straight line. This centering routine is necessary to compensate for wear in the steering and suspension. Wear in the steering and suspension can result in a change in the relationship between the steering wheel and the front wheels. By running the centering routine the EBTCM can compensate for these changes by changing the digital and analog center position.

Conditions for Setting the DTC

- DTC C1286 can be set after the centering routines completion if the bias value is plus or minus 40 degrees from the previous bias value.
- DTC C1286 can also be set at start up if the bias value was out of range on the last ignition cycle.

Action Taken When the DTC Sets

ABS and TCS remain enabled, Active Handling™ is disabled.

- Indicators that turn on:
  Car Icon (TCS indicator
- Messages displayed on the DIC:
  Service Active HNDLG
  Service Vehicle Soon

Conditions for Clearing the DTC

- Condition for DTC is no longer present and scan tool clear DTC function is used.
- Fifty ignition cycles have passed with no DTCs detected.

Diagnostic Aids

- It is very important to check the vehicle for proper alignment. The car should not pull in either direction while driving straight on a flat surface.
- It is very important to find out from the driver when the code was set, (when the SERVICE ACTIVE HNDLG message was activated). This information may help to duplicate the failure.
- It is very important that a thorough inspection of the wiring and connectors be performed. Failure to carefully inspect wiring and connectors may result in misdiagnosis, causing part replacement with reappearance of the malfunction.
- An intermittent malfunction is most likely caused by a poor connection, rubbed through wire insulation, or a wire that is broken inside the insulation. Refer to *Intermittents*

Test Description

The numbers below refer to the step numbers on the diagnostic table.

11. Recenters the Steering Wheel Position Sensor.

GC4029803966010X

Fig. 156 Code C1286: Steering Sensor Bias Fault (Part 1 of 3). Corvette

Step	Action	Value(s)	Yes	No
1	Was the Diagnostic System Check performed?	—	*Go to Step 2*	Go to *Diagnostic System Check (ABS)*
2	Is this vehicle equipped with Active Handling ?	—	*Go to Step 3*	Go to *DTC C1286 Steering Sensor Bias Malfunction*
3	Using a scan tool, read ABS/TCS/Active handling DTC(s). Is DTC C1282 or DTC C1284 set as a current DTC?	—	Go to Applicable DTC Table.	*Go to Step 4*
4	1. Point the front wheels straight ahead. 2. Using a scan tool, check the Steering Wheel Position Sensor Analog voltage. Is the voltage within the range specified within the value(s) column?	2–3 V	*Go to Step 5*	*Go to Step 11*
5	Using a scan tool, perform the Steering Wheel Position Sensor Test. Are the analog and digital displays on the scan tool within plus or minus 5 degrees of each other at the center (zero) position?	—	*Go to Step 6*	*Go to Step 12*
6	Perform the Diagnostic Test Drive while monitoring the Yaw Rate Sensor output in degrees/seconds on a scan tool. Refer to *Diagnostic System Check (ABS).* Are the degrees/second displayed on the scan tool within the range specified in the value(s) column?	0–5 degrees/ second	*Go to Step 8*	*Go to Step 7*
7	Replace the Yaw Rate Sensor. Is the replacement complete?	—	*Go to Step 14*	—
8	With the ignition switch in the ON position and the engine off, monitor the Lateral Accelerometer output in voltage using a scan tool. Is the voltage displayed on the scan tool within the range specified in the value(s) column?	2.3–2.7V	*Go to Step 14*	*Go to Step 9*
9	Replace the Lateral Accelerometer. Is the replacement complete?	—	*Go to Step 14*	—
10	Replace the EBTCM. Is the repair complete?	—	Go to *Diagnostic System Check (ABS)*	—

GC4029803966020X

Fig. 156 Code C1286: Steering Sensor Bias Fault (Part 2 of 3). Corvette

Step	Action	Value(s)	Yes	No
11	1. Turn the ignition switch to the OFF position. 2. Disable the Supplemental Inflatable Restraint (SIR). 3. Remove the Inflatable Restraint Wheel Module Coil. 4. Remove the Intermediate Shaft. 5. Turn the ignition switch to the ON position, engine off. 6. Using a scan tool monitor the Steering Wheel Position Sensors analog voltage as you rotate the steering column shaft. 7. Turn the steering column shaft until the analog voltage is close to 2.5 volts. Does the analog voltage move to or close to 2.5 volts?	—	*Go to Step 13*	*Go to Step 12*
12	Replace the Steering Wheel Position Sensor. Is the replacement complete?	—	*Go to Step 14*	—
13	1. Leave the steering column shaft centered at 2.5 volts. 2. Turn the ignition switch to the OFF position. 3. Install the Intermediate Shaft. 4. Install the Inflatable Restraint Wheel Module Coil. 5. Enable the SIR. Is the repair complete?	—	*Go to Step 14*	—
14	1. Turn the ignition switch to the ON position, engine off. 2. Using a scan tool clear DTC C1286. 3. Drive vehicle above 30 Km/h (18 mph) for several minutes. 4. Using a scan tool check for DTC C1286. Did DTC C1286 set as a current DTC?	—	*Go to Step 10*	*Go to Diagnostic System Check (ABS)*

GC4029803966030X

Fig. 156 Code C1286: Steering Sensor Bias Fault (Part 3 of 3). Corvette

Diagnostic Aids

- It is very important that a thorough inspection of the wiring and connectors be performed. Failure to carefully and fully inspect wiring and connectors may result in misdiagnosis, causing part replacement with reappearance of the malfunction.

Test Description

The numbers below refer to the step numbers on the diagnostic table.

2. Checks for normal state change of phase A and Phase B when turning left.
3. Checks for normal state change of phase A and Phase B when turning right.

Step	Action	Value(s)	Yes	No
1	Was the Diagnostic System Check performed?	—	*Go to Step 2*	Go to *ABS Diagnostic System Check*
2	1. Start the engine. 2. Ensure the front wheels are straight. 3. Turn the ignition OFF. 4. Restart the engine. 5. Slowly rotate the steering wheel to the left while monitoring phase A and phase B of the Steering Wheel Position Sensor using a scan tool. Did phase A and phase B change states uniformly as the steering wheel was rotated?	—	*Go to Step 3*	*Go to Step 4*
3	Slowly rotate the steering wheel to the right while monitoring phase A and phase B of the Steering Wheel Position Sensor using a scan tool. Did phase A and phase B change states uniformly as the steering wheel was rotated?	—	*Go to Step 5*	*Go to Step 4*
4	Replace the Steering Wheel Position Sensor. Is the replacement complete?	—	*Go to Step 5*	—
5	1. Read the diagnostic aids and conditions for setting the DTC. 2. Cycle the ignition switch from the OFF to ON position. 3. Start the engine and rotate the steering wheel from left to right while monitoring a scan tool for ABS/TCS DTC(s). Did DTC C1287 set as a current DTC?	—	*Go to Step 6*	Go to *ABS Diagnostic System Check*
6	Replace the EBTCM. Is the replacement complete?	—	Go to *ABS Diagnostic System Check*	—

GC402970266900BX

Fig. 157 Code C1287: Steering Sensor Rate Fault (Part 2 of 2). Corvette

Circuit Description

The EBTCM uses four inputs from the Steering Wheel Position sensor:

- Phase A digital input
- Phase B digital input
- Index pulse
- Analog input

This information is used to calculate three things:

1. The front wheels position when centered.
2. The front wheels position when turning.
3. The rate at which the steering wheel is turning.

The EBTCM runs a centering routine when the vehicle speed goes above 30 Km/h (18 mph). When the vehicle reaches 30 Km/h (18 mph), the EBTCM monitors the Steering Wheel Position Sensor inputs (Phase A, Phase B and Analog voltage) to see if the steering wheel is moving. If the steering wheel is not moving for a set period of time then the EBTCM assumes the vehicle is going in a straight line. At this point, the EBTCM looks at the analog voltage signal and reads the voltage. This voltage normally around 2.5V, is then considered the center position and the digital degrees also become zero at the same time. This centering routine is necessary to compensate for wear in the steering and suspension. Wear in the steering and suspension can result in a change in the relationship between the steering wheel and the front tires when driving in a straight line. By running the centering routine the EBTCM can compensate for these changes by changing the digital and analog center position.

The EBTCM uses the digital input (Phase A and Phase B) from the Steering Wheel Position Sensor to calculate the direction the driver of the vehicle is trying to steer during an ABS event. This information is also used to calculate the rate at which the steering wheel is turning to control the amount of effort required from the driver to turn the steering wheel using Magna Steer®.

Conditions for Setting the DTC

- DTC C1287 can be set any time ignition is present. A fault exists if the steer rate (speed that the steering wheel appears to be turning) exceeds the limits set by the EBTCM.

Action Taken When the DTC Sets

- Magna Steer® is disabled ABS/TCS remains active.

Conditions for Clearing the DTC

- Condition for DTC is no longer present and scan tool clear DTC function is used.
- Fifty ignition cycles have passed with no DTC(s) detected.

GC402970266900AX

Fig. 157 Code C1287: Steering Sensor Rate Fault (Part 1 of 2). Corvette

Circuit Description

The EBTCM uses three inputs from the Steering Wheel Position sensor:

- Phase A digital input
- Phase B digital input
- Analog input

This information is used to calculate three things:

- The front wheels position when centered.
- The front wheels position when turning.
- The vehicles lateral acceleration.

The EBTCM runs a centering routine when the vehicle speed goes above 10 Km/h (6 mph). When the vehicle reaches 10 Km/h (6 mph), the EBTCM monitors the Steering Wheel Position Sensor inputs (Phase A, Phase B and Analog voltage) to see if the steering wheel is moving. If the steering wheel is not moving for a set period of time, then the EBTCM assumes the vehicle is going in a straight line. At this point, the EBTCM looks at the analog voltage signal and reads the voltage. This voltage, normally around 2.5V, is then considered the center position and the digital degrees also become zero at the same time. This centering routine is necessary to compensate for wear in the steering and suspension. Wear in the steering and suspension can result in a change in the relationship between the steering wheel and the front wheels. By running the centering routine the EBTCM can compensate for these changes by changing the digital and analog center position.

The EBTCM uses the digital input (Phase A and Phase B) from the Steering Wheel Position Sensor to calculate the direction the driver of the vehicle is trying to steer during an ABS and Active Handling event. This information is also used to calculate the vehicles lateral acceleration for Magnasteer®2.

Conditions for Setting the DTC

- DTC C1287 can be set any time ignition is present. A fault exists if the steer rate (speed that the steering wheel appears to be turning) exceeds the limits set by the EBTCM.
- DTC C1287 will set if the analog degrees differs from the digital degrees by more than 25 degrees for 5 seconds when the vehicle is not in a Active Handling event, or 1 second if the vehicle is in an Active Handling event.

Action Taken When the DTC Sets

ABS and TCS remain enabled, Active Handling™ is disabled.

- Indicators that turn on:

  Car Icon (TCS indicator

- Messages displayed on the DIC:

  Service Active HNDLG

  Service Vehicle Soon

GC4029803967010X

Fig. 158 Code C1287: Steering Sensor Rate Fault (Part 1 of 2). Corvette

Conditions for Clearing the DTC

- Condition for DTC is no longer present and scan tool clear DTC function is used.
- Fifty ignition cycles have passed with no DTCs detected.

Diagnostic Aids

It is very important that a thorough inspection of the wiring and connectors be performed. Failure to carefully and fully inspect wiring and connectors may result in misdiagnosis, causing part replacement with reappearance of the malfunction.

Test Description

The numbers below refer to the step numbers on the diagnostic table.

3. Checks for normal state change of Phase A and Phase B when turning left.
4. Checks for normal state change of Phase A and Phase B when turning right.

Step	Action	Value(s)	Yes	No
1	Was the Diagnostic System Check performed?	—	*Go to Step 2*	Go to *Diagnostic System Check (ABS)*
2	Is this vehicle equipped with Active Handling?	—	*Go to Step 3*	Go to *DTC C1287 Steering Sensor Rate Malfunction*
3	1. Start the engine. 2. Ensure the front wheels are straight. 3. Turn the ignition OFF. 4. Restart the engine. 5. Slowly rotate the steering wheel to the left while monitoring Phase A and Phase B of the Steering Wheel Position Sensor using a scan tool. Did phase A and phase B change states uniformly as the steering wheel was rotated?	—	*Go to Step 4*	*Go to Step 5*
4	Slowly rotate the steering wheel to the right while monitoring phase A and phase B of the Steering Wheel Position Sensor using a scan tool. Did phase A and phase B change states uniformly as the steering wheel was rotated?	—	*Go to Step 6*	*Go to Step 5*
5	Replace the Steering Wheel Position Sensor. Is the replacement complete?	—	*Go to Step 6*	—
6	1. Read the diagnostic aids and conditions for setting the DTC. 2. Cycle the ignition switch from the OFF to ON position. 3. Start the engine and rotate the steering wheel from left to right while monitoring a scan tool for ABS/TCS/Active Handling DTC(s). Did DTC C1287 set as a current DTC?	—	*Go to Step 7*	Go to *Diagnostic System Check (ABS)*
7	Replace the EBTCM. Is the replacement complete?	—	Go to *Diagnostic System Check (ABS)*	—

GC4029803967020X

Fig. 158 Code C1287: Steering Sensor Rate Fault (Part 2 of 2). Corvette

Step	Action	Value(s)	Yes	No
1	Was the Diagnostic System Check performed?	--	*Go to Step 2*	Go to *ABS Diagnostic System Check*
2	1. Turn the Ignition switch to the OFF position. 2. Disconnect the EBTCM. 3. Install the *J 39700* Universal Pinout Box using the *J 39700-25* cable adapter between the EBTCM harness connector and the EBTCM. 4. Turn the ignition switch to the ON position, engine OFF. 5. Using *J 39200* DMM, measure the voltage at terminal 23 of *J 39700*. Is the voltage within the range specified in the value(s) column?	0.2 - 4.8V	*Go to Step 11*	*Go to Step 3*
3	1. Turn the ignition switch to the OFF position. 2. Disconnect the Steering Wheel Position Sensor connector. 3. Turn the ignition switch to the ON position , engine OFF. 4. Using the *J 39200* DMM, measure the voltage at terminal 1 of the Steering Wheel Position Sensor harness connector. Is the voltage within the range specified in the value(s) column?	4.5 - 5V	*Go to Step 4*	*Go to Step 13*
4	Using *J 39200* DMM, measure the resistance between the Steering Wheel Position Sensor harness connector terminal 2 and a good ground. Is the resistance within the range specified in the value(s) column?	0 - 5Ω	*Go to Step 5*	*Go to Step 17*
5	Using the *J 39200* DMM, measure the voltage at terminal 6 of the Steering Wheel Position Sensor harness connector. Is the voltage within the range specified in the value(s) column?	Above 1V	*Go to Step 6*	*Go to Step 7*
6	Repair CKT 1059 for a short to voltage. Is the repair complete?	—	Go to *ABS Diagnostic System Check*	—
7	1. Turn the ignition switch to the OFF position. 2. Disconnect the *J 39700-25* cable adapter from the EBTCM leaving the *J 39700-25* cable adapter connected to the EBTCM harness connector. 3. Using *J 39200* DMM, measure the resistance between terminals 23 and B of *J 39700*. Is the resistance within the range specified within the value(s) column?	OL (infinite)	*Go to Step 9*	*Go to Step 8*
8	Repair CKT 1059 for a short to ground. Is the repair complete?	—	Go to *ABS Diagnostic System Check*	—

GC402970267000BX

Fig. 159 Code C1288: Steering Sensor Circuit Fault (Part 2 of 3). Corvette

Circuit Description

The Steering Wheel Position Sensor provides the EBTCM with an analog voltage reading from 0.2–4.8V depending on the steering wheel angle. The EBTCM uses the analog voltage for the centering routine. The EBTCM runs a centering routine when the vehicle speed goes above 30 Km/h (18 mph). When the vehicle reaches 30 Km/h (18 mph), the EBTCM monitors the Steering Wheel Position Sensor inputs (Phase A, Phase B and Analog voltage) to see if the steering wheel is moving. If the steering wheel is not moving for a set period of time then the EBTCM assumes the vehicle is going in a straight line. At this point, the EBTCM looks at the analog voltage signal and reads the voltage. This voltage normally around 2.5V, is then considered the center position and the digital degrees also become zero at the same time. This centering routine is necessary to compensate for wear in the steering and suspension. Wear in the steering and suspension can result in a change in the relationship between the steering wheel and the front tires when driving in a straight line. By running the centering routine the EBTCM can compensate for these changes by changing the digital and analog center position.

Conditions for Setting the DTC

The Steering Wheel Position Sensor analog output voltages falls outside 0.2–4.8V range.

Action Taken When the DTC Sets

A malfunction DTC is stored. Magna Steer is disabled ABS/TCS remains active.

Diagnostic Aids

The following are possible causes:

- A Steering Wheel Position Sensor circuit open.
- A Steering Wheel Position Sensor shorted.

Perform an inspection of the wiring and of the connectors. Failure to carefully and fully inspect the wiring and the connectors may result in misdiagnosis. Misdiagnosis causes part replacement with reappearance of the malfunction.

Test Description

The numbers below refer to step numbers on the diagnostic table.

5. Checks for a short to voltage.
7. Checks for a short to ground.
9. Checks for an open.

GC402970267000AX

Fig. 159 Code C1288: Steering Sensor Circuit Fault (Part 1 of 3). Corvette

Step	Action	Value(s)	Yes	No
9	1. Connect a jumper wire between terminals 23 and 27 of *J 39700*. 2. Using *J 39200* DMM, measure the resistance between the Steering Wheel Position Sensors harness connector terminals 2 and 6. Is the resistance within the range specified within the value(s) column?	0 - 5Ω	*Go to Step 12*	*Go to Step 10*
10	Repair CKT 1059 for an open. Is the repair complete?	—	Go to *ABS Diagnostic System Check*	—
11	Replace the EBTCM. Is the replacement complete?	—	Go to *ABS Diagnostic System Check*	—
12	Replace the Steering Wheel Position Sensor. Is the replacement complete?	—	Go to *ABS Diagnostic System Check*	—
13	1. Turn the ignition switch to the OFF position. 2. Disconnect the *J 39700-25* cable adapter from the EBTCM leaving the *J 39700-25* cable adapter connected to the EBTCM harness connector. 3. Connect a jumper wire between terminals 11 and B of *J 39700*. 4. Using *J 39200* DMM, measure the resistance between the Steering Wheel Position Sensor harness connector terminal 1 and a good ground. Is the resistance within the range specified within the value(s) column?	OL (infinite)	*Go to Step 14*	*Go to Step 15*
14	Repair CKT 1056 for an open. Is the repair complete?	—	Go to *ABS Diagnostic System Check*	—
15	1. Remove the jumper wire from *J 39700*. 2. Using *J 39200* DMM, measure the resistance between the Steering Wheel Position Sensor harness connector terminal 1 and a good ground. Is the resistance within the range specified in the values column?	OL (infinite)	*Go to Step 11*	*Go to Step 16*
16	Repair CKT 1056 for a short to ground. Is the repair complete?	—	Go to *ABS Diagnostic System Check*	—
17	Repair CKT 556 for an open or high resistance. Is the repair complete?	—	Go to *ABS Diagnostic System Check*	—

GC402970267000CX

Fig. 159 Code C1288: Steering Sensor Circuit Fault (Part 3 of 3). Corvette

Circuit Description

The Steering Wheel Position Sensor provides the EBTCM with an analog voltage reading from 0.2–4.8V depending on the steering wheel angle. The EBTCM uses the analog voltage for the centering routine. The EBTCM runs a centering routine when the vehicle speed goes above 10 Km/h (6 mph). When the vehicle reaches 10 Km/h (6 mph), the EBTCM monitors the Steering Wheel Position Sensor inputs (Phase A, Phase B and Analog voltage) to see if the steering wheel is moving. If the steering wheel is not moving for a set period of time then the EBTCM assumes the vehicle is going in a straight line. At this point, the EBTCM looks at the analog voltage signal and reads the voltage. This voltage, normally around 2.5V, is then considered the center position and the digital degrees also become zero at the same time. This centering routine is necessary to compensate for wear in the steering and suspension. Wear in the steering and suspension can result in a change in the relationship between the steering wheel and the front wheels. By running the centering routine, the EBTCM can compensate for these changes by changing the digital and analog center position.

Conditions for Setting the DTC

The Steering Wheel Position Sensor analog output voltages falls outside 0.2–4.8V range.

Action Taken When the DTC Sets

ABS and TCS remain enabled, Active Handling™ is disabled.

- Indicators that turn on:
  Car Icon (TCS indicator
- Messages displayed on the DIC:
  Service Active HNDLG
  Service Vehicle Soon

Diagnostic Aids

The following are possible causes:

- A Steering Wheel Position Sensor circuit open.
- A Steering Wheel Position Sensor shorted.

Perform an inspection of the wiring and of the connectors. Failure to carefully inspect the wiring and the connectors may result in misdiagnosis. Misdiagnosis causes part replacement with reappearance of the malfunction.

Test Description

The numbers below refer to step numbers on the diagnostic table.

6. Checks for a short to voltage.
8. Checks for a short to ground.
10. Checks for an open.

GC4029803968010X

Fig. 160 Code C1288: Steering Sensor Circuit Fault (Part 1 of 3). Corvette

Step	Action	Value(s)	Yes	No
1	Was the Diagnostic System Check performed?	—	*Go to Step 2*	Go to *Diagnostic System Check (ABS)*
2	Is this vehicle equipped with Active Handling?	—	*Go to Step 3*	Go to *DTC C1288 Steering Sensor Circuit Malfunction*
3	1. Turn the Ignition switch to the OFF position. 2. Disconnect the EBTCM. 3. Install the *J 39700* Universal Pinout Box using the *J 39700-25* cable adapter between the EBTCM harness connector and the EBTCM. 4. Turn the ignition switch to the ON position, engine off. 5. Using *J 39200* DMM, measure the voltage at terminal 23 of *J 39700*. Is the voltage within the range specified in the value(s) column?	0.2–4.8 V	*Go to Step 12*	*Go to Step 4*
4	1. Turn the ignition switch to the OFF position. 2. Disconnect the Steering Wheel Position Sensor connector. 3. Turn the ignition switch to the ON position, engine off. 4. Using the *J 39200* DMM, measure the voltage at terminal 1 of the Steering Wheel Position Sensor harness connector. Is the voltage within the range specified in the value(s) column?	4.74–5.25 V	*Go to Step 5*	*Go to Step 14*
5	Using *J 39200* DMM, measure the resistance between the Steering Wheel Position Sensor harness connector terminal 2 and a good ground. Is the resistance within the range specified in the value(s) column?	0–5 Ω	*Go to Step 6*	*Go to Step 18*
6	Using the *J 39200* DMM, measure the voltage at terminal 6 of the Steering Wheel Position Sensor harness connector. Is the voltage within the range specified in the value(s) column?	Above 1 V	*Go to Step 7*	*Go to Step 8*
7	Repair CKT 1059 for a short to voltage. Is the repair complete?	—	Go to *Diagnostic System Check (ABS)*	—
8	1. Turn the ignition switch to the OFF position. 2. Disconnect the *J 39700-25* cable adapter from the EBTCM leaving the *J 39700-25* cable adapter connected to the EBTCM harness connector. 3. Using *J 39200* DMM, measure the resistance between terminals 23 and B of *J 39700*. Is the resistance within the range specified within the value(s) column?	OL (infinite)	*Go to Step 10*	*Go to Step 9*
9	Repair CKT 1059 for a short to ground. Is the repair complete?	—	Go to *Diagnostic System Check (ABS)*	—

GC4029803968020X

Fig. 160 Code C1288: Steering Sensor Circuit Fault (Part 2 of 3). Corvette

Step	Action	Value(s)	Yes	No
10	1. Connect a jumper wire between terminals 23 and 27 of *J 39700*. 2. Using *J 39200* DMM, measure the resistance between the Steering Wheel Position Sensors harness connector terminals 2 and 6. Is the resistance within the range specified within the value(s) column?	0–5 Ω	*Go to Step 13*	*Go to Step 11*
11	Repair CKT 1059 for an open. Is the repair complete?	—	Go to *Diagnostic System Check (ABS)*	—
12	Replace the EBTCM. Is the replacement complete?	—	Go to *Diagnostic System Check (ABS)*	—
13	Replace the Steering Wheel Position Sensor. Is the replacement complete?	—	Go to *Diagnostic System Check (ABS)*	—
14	1. Turn the ignition switch to the OFF position. 2. Disconnect the *J 39700-25* cable adapter from the EBTCM leaving the *J 39700-25* cable adapter connected to the EBTCM harness connector. 3. Connect a jumper wire between terminals 11 and B of *J 39700*. 4. Using *J 39200* DMM, measure the resistance between the Steering Wheel Position Sensor harness connector terminal 1 and a good ground. Is the resistance within the range specified within the value(s) column?	0–5Ω	*Go to Step 16*	*Go to Step 15*
15	Repair CKT 1056 for an open or high resistance. Is the repair complete?	—	Go to *Diagnostic System Check (ABS)*	—
16	1. Remove the jumper wire from *J 39700*. 2. Using *J 39200* DMM, measure the resistance between the Steering Wheel Position Sensor harness connector terminal 1 and a good ground. Is the resistance within the range specified in the values column?	OL (infinite)	*Go to Step 12*	*Go to Step 17*
17	Repair CKT 1056 for a short to ground. Is the repair complete?	—	Go to *Diagnostic System Check (ABS)*	—
18	Repair CKT 556 for an open or high resistance. Is the repair complete?	—	Go to *Diagnostic System Check (ABS)*	—

GC4029803968030X

Fig. 160 Code C1288: Steering Sensor Circuit Fault (Part 3 of 3). Corvette

Circuit Description

This circuit is used to detect an open Stoplamp Switch in the non-ABS mode. The EBTCM looks for a deceleration rate that would indicate braking action and verifies this assumption by requiring several repeats of this detection method. In each case, TCS will not be available since no Stoplamp Switch voltage is seen by the EBTCM.

Conditions for Setting the DTC

DTC C1291 is set after the stoplamp switch remains open for three deceleration cycles.

Action Taken When the DTC Sets

A malfunction DTC is stored, TCS is disabled and the Traction Control indicator is turned ON. ABS remains functional.

Conditions for Clearing the DTC

- Condition for DTC is no longer present and scan tool clear DTC function is used.
- Fifty ignition cycles have passed with no DTC(s) detected.

Diagnostic Aids

- It is very important that a thorough inspection of the wiring and connectors be performed. Failure to carefully and fully inspect wiring and connectors may result in misdiagnosis, causing part replacement with reappearance of the malfunction.
- If any Wheel Speed Sensor DTC(s) are present you must diagnose them first.
- An intermittent malfunction is most likely caused by a poor connection, rubbed through wire insulation, or a wire that is broken inside the insulation.
- Possible causes:
  - Open stoplamp switch.
  - Open fuse.
  - Stoplamp switch misadjusted.
  - Erratic Wheel Speeds.
  - Circuit has a wiring problem, terminal corrosion, or poor connections.

Test Description

The numbers below refer to step numbers on the diagnostic table.

3. Checks if Stoplamp Switch and power distribution are OK.
4. Checks for voltage at EBTCM.
10. Checks the Stoplamp Switch.

GC402970267100AX

Fig. 161 Code C1291: Open Brake Lamp Switch Contacts During Deceleration (Part 1 of 3). Corvette

Step	Action	Value(s)	Yes	No
1	Was the Diagnostic System Check performed?	—	*Go to Step 2*	Go to *ABS Diagnostic System Check*
2	Are any Wheel Speed Sensor DTC(s) present?	—	Go to Applicable DTC table	*Go to Step 3*
3	Press the brake pedal. Do the brake lights come on?	—	*Go to Step 4*	*Go to Step 7*
4	1. Turn the ignition switch to the OFF position. 2. Disconnect the EBTCM. 3. Install *J 39700* Universal Pinout Box using *J 39700-25* adapter cable to the EBTCM harness connector only. 4. Turn the ignition switch to the ON position, engine OFF. 5. Using *J 39200* DMM, measure the voltage at terminal 9 of *J 39700* while an assistant presses the brake pedal. Is the voltage within the range specified in the value(s) column?	Battery voltage	*Go to Step 5*	*Go to Step 6*
5	Replace the EBTCM. Is the replacement complete?	—	Go to *ABS Diagnostic System Check*	—
6	Repair open in CKT 20.	—	Go to *ABS Diagnostic System Check*	—
7	Check the STOP/HAZ fuse in the Instrument Panel Electrical Center. Is the fuse OK?	—	*Go to Step 8*	*Go to Step 12*
8	1. Disconnect the Stoplamp switch connector. 2. Using the *J 39200* DMM, measure the voltage at terminal A of the Stoplamp switch harness connector. Is the voltage within the range specified in the value(s) column?	Battery voltage	*Go to Step 10*	*Go to Step 9*
9	Repair CKT 140 for an open. Is the repair complete?	—	Go to *ABS Diagnostic System Check*	—
10	Connect a fused jumper wire between terminals A and B of the Stoplamp switch harness connector. Do the brake lamps come on?	—	*Go to Step 11*	*Go to Step 6*
11	Adjust or repair the Stoplamp switch as necessary. Is the repair complete?	—	Go to *ABS Diagnostic System Check*	—
12	1. Replace the STOP/HAZ fuse. Do not press the brake pedal. 2. Check the STOP/HAZ fuse. Is the fuse OK?	—	*Go to Step 14*	*Go to Step 13*
13	Repair short to ground in CKT 140. Is the repair complete?	—	Go to *ABS Diagnostic System Check*	—

GC402970267100BX

Fig. 161 Code C1291: Open Brake Lamp Switch Contacts During Deceleration (Part 2 of 3). Corvette

Circuit Description

The EBTCM uses input from the Brake Pressure Sensor for more accurate control during an Active Handling event.

Conditions for Setting the DTC

DTC C1292 can be set if three decel cycles occur with the Brake Pressure Sensor pressure reading remains less than 100 psi. A decel cycle includes starting at a speed greater than 24 Km/h (15 mph), then the vehicle must decel at a rate greater than 8 Km/h (5 mph)/second. The vehicle must reach a speed less than 16 Km/h (10 mph).

Action Taken When the DTC Sets

ABS and TCS remain enabled, Active Handling™ is disabled.

- Indicators that turn on:
  Car Icon (TCS indicator)
- Messages displayed on the DIC:
  Service Active HNDLG

Conditions for Clearing the DTC

- Condition for DTC is no longer present and scan tool clear DTC function is used.
- Fifty ignition cycles have passed with no DTCs detected.

Diagnostic Aids

- It is very important that a thorough inspection of the wiring and connectors be performed. Failure to carefully and fully inspect wiring and connectors may result in misdiagnosis, causing part replacement with reappearance of the malfunction.
- An intermittent malfunction can be caused by poor connections, broken insulation, or a wire that is broken inside the insulation.
- If an intermittent malfunction exists refer to *Intermittents*

Test Description

The number(s) below refer to the step number(s) on the diagnostic table.

3. This step checks if the signal from the Brake Pressure Sensor increases as hydraulic pressure increases.

GC4029803969010X

Fig. 162 Code C1292: Low Brake Pressure During Deceleration (Part 1 of 2). Corvette

Step	Action	Value(s)	Yes	No
14	1. Press the brake pedal. 2. Check the STOP/HAZ fuse. Is the fuse OK?	—	Go to *ABS Diagnostic System Check*	*Go to Step 15*
15	1. Turn the ignition switch to the OFF position. 2. Disconnect the EBTCM. 3. Replace the fuse. 4. Press the brake pedal. 5. Check the STOP/HAZ fuse. Is the fuse OK?	—	*Go to Step 5*	*Go to Step 16*
16	Repair CKT 20 for a short to ground. Is the repair complete?	—	Go to *ABS Diagnostic System Check*	—

GC402970267100CX

Fig. 161 Code C1291: Open Brake Lamp Switch Contacts During Deceleration (Part 3 of 3). Corvette

Step	Action	Value(s)	Yes	No
1	Was the Diagnostic System Check performed?	—	*Go to Step 2*	Go to *Diagnostic System Check (ABS)*
2	Are either DTC C1245 or DTC C1296 also set?	—	Go to Applicable DTC Table	*Go to Step 3*
2	1. Turn the ignition switch to the OFF position. 2. Disconnect the EBTCM harness connector. 3. Install the *J 39700* Universal Pinout Box using the *J 39700-25* cable adapter between the EBTCM harness connector and the EBTCM. 4. Turn the ignition switch to the ON position, engine OFF. 5. Using *J 39200* DMM, measure the voltage at terminal 24 of *J 39700*. 6. Slowly press the brake pedal to apply maximum hydraulic pressure. Does the voltage reading on *J 39200* DMM, increase as brake pedal pressure is increased above the range specified in the values column?	2.5V	*Go to Step 4*	*Go to Step 5*
4	Replace the EBTCM. Is the replacement complete?	—	Go to *Diagnostic System Check (ABS)*	—
5	Replace the Brake Pressure Sensor. Is the replacement complete?	—	Go to *Diagnostic System Check (ABS)*	—

GC4029803969020X

Fig. 162 Code C1292: Low Brake Pressure During Deceleration (Part 2 of 2). Corvette

Circuit Description

This DTC is the second portion of DTC C1291. If DTC C1291 occurred during an ignition cycle, DTC C1293 becomes a current malfunction during the next ignition cycle, keeping TCS disabled until a brake switch on state is seen. When a change is seen during an ignition cycle in which DTC C1293 is a current malfunction, DTC C1291 will clear itself at the end of the current ignition cycle, and TCS will enable itself at the start of the next ignition cycle. DTC C1293 alone indicates DTC C1291 occurred previously, but is intermittent, or has been corrected.

Conditions for Setting the DTC

DTC C1293 is set when DTC C1291 was set in the previous or current ignition cycle.

Action Taken When the DTC Sets

ABS remains enabled, TCS/ Active Handling™ are disabled.

- Indicators that turn on:
  Car Icon (TCS indicator
- Messages displayed on the DIC:
  Service Traction System
  Service Active HNDLG

Conditions for Clearing the DTC

- Condition for DTC is no longer present and scan tool clear DTC function is used.
- Fifty ignition cycles have passed with no DTCs detected.

Diagnostic Aids

- It is very important that a thorough inspection of the wiring and connectors be performed. Failure to carefully and fully inspect wiring and connectors may result in misdiagnosis, causing part replacement with reappearance of the malfunction.
- An intermittent malfunction is most likely caused by a poor connection, rubbed through wire insulation, or a wire that is broken inside the insulation.
- Also, verify proper stoplamp switch operation using the Data List of the scan tool. As the brake is applied, the data list should display the stoplamp switch on within 1 inch of travel.
- If an intermittent malfunction exists refer to *Intermittents*

GC4029803970010X

Fig. 163 Code C1293: Code C1291/C1292 Set In Current Or Previous Ignition Cycle (Part 1 of 2). Corvette

Step	Action	Value(s)	Yes	No
1	Was the Diagnostic System Check performed?	—	Go to Step 2	Go to Diagnostic System Check (ABS)
2	1. Turn the ignition switch to the ON position, engine off. 2. Using the scan tool, read ABS/TCS or ABS/TCS/Active Handling DTC(s). Is DTC C1291 set as a history or current code?	—	Go to DTC C1291 Open Brake Lamp Sw Contacts During Decel	Go to Diagnostic System Check (ABS)

GC4029803970020X

Fig. 163 Code C1293: Code C1291/C1292 Set In Current Or Previous Ignition Cycle (Part 2 of 2). Corvette

Step	Action	Value(s)	Yes	No
1	Was the Diagnostic System Check performed?	—	Go to Step 2	Go to ABS Diagnostic System Check
2	Observe rear brake lamps. Are brake lamps OFF?	—	Go to Step 4	Go to Step 3
3	Disconnect the Stoplamp switch connector. Are the brake lamps ON?	—	Go to Step 6	Go to Step 7
4	1. Disconnect the EBTCM harness connector. 2. Install J 39700 Universal Pinout Box using the J 39700-25 adapter cable to the EBTCM harness connector only. 3. Using J 39200 DMM, measure the voltage between the J 39700 terminals 9 and B. Is the voltage within the range specified in the value(s) column?	Greater than 1 V	Go to Step 6	Go to Step 5
5	1. Turn the ignition switch to the OFF position. 2. Inspect CKT 20 and the EBTCM harness connector for damage which may result in a short to voltage with all connector connected. 3. Reconnect all connectors. 4. Carefully drive vehicle for three drive cycles while monitoring a scan tool. A drive cycle consists of starting the engine, driving above 40 km/h (25 mph) back to 0 km/h (0 mph) and then turning the ignition OFF. Was DTC C1294 set in the last three drive cycles?	—	Go to Step 8	Go to ABS Diagnostic System Check
6	Repair short to voltage in CKT 20. Is the repair complete?	—	Go to ABS Diagnostic System Check	—
7	Adjust or replace the Stoplamp switch as necessary. Is the repair complete?	—	Go to ABS Diagnostic System Check	—
8	Replace the EBTCM. Is the replacement complete?	—	Go to ABS Diagnostic System Check	—

GC402970267300BX

Fig. 164 Code C1294: Brake Lamp Switch Circuit Always Active (Part 2 of 2). Corvette

Step	Action	Value(s)	Yes	No
1	Was the Diagnostic System Check performed?	—	Go to Step 2	Go to ABS Diagnostic System Check
2	Press the brake pedal. Do the brake lights come on?	—	Go to Step 3	Go to Step 6
3	1. Turn the ignition switch to the OFF position. 2. Disconnect the EBTCM. 3. Install J 39700 Universal Pinout Box using J 39700-25 adapter cable to the EBTCM harness connector only. 4. Turn the ignition switch to the ON position, engine OFF. 5. Using J 39200 DMM, measure the voltage at terminal 9 of J 39700 while an assistant presses the brake pedal. Is the voltage within the range specified in the value(s) column?	Battery voltage	Go to Step 4	Go to Step 5
4	Replace the EBTCM. Is the replacement complete?	—	Go to ABS Diagnostic System Check	—
5	Repair open in CKT 20.	—	Go to ABS Diagnostic System Check	—
6	Check the STOP/HAZ fuse in the Instrument Panel Electrical Center. Is the fuse OK?	—	Go to Step 7	Go to Step 11
7	1. Disconnect the Stoplamp switch connector. 2. Using the J 39200 DMM, measure the voltage at terminal A of the Stoplamp switch harness connector. Is the voltage within the range specified in the value(s) column?	Battery voltage	Go to Step 9	Go to Step 8
8	Repair CKT 140 for an open. Is the repair complete?	—	Go to ABS Diagnostic System Check	—
9	Connect a fused jumper wire between terminals A and B of the Stoplamp switch harness connector. Do the brake lamps come on?	—	Go to Step 10	Go to Step 5
10	Adjust or repair the Stoplamp switch as necessary. Is the repair complete?	—	Go to ABS Diagnostic System Check	—
11	1. Replace the STOP/HAZ fuse. Do not press the brake pedal. 2. Check the STOP/HAZ fuse. Is the fuse OK?	—	Go to Step 13	Go to Step 12
12	Repair short to ground in CKT 140. Is the repair complete?	—	Go to ABS Diagnostic System Check	—

GC402970267400BX

Fig. 165 Code C1295: Brake Lamp Switch Circuit Open (Part 2 of 3). Corvette

Circuit Description

This DTC occurs when internal self checking safety logic has determined that the Stoplamp Switch is continuously ON. This is important because the TCS can not be activated when the Stoplamp Switch is ON.

Conditions for Setting the DTC

DTC C1294 can be set if the vehicle speed reaches at least 40 km/h (25 mph). If the brake was never OFF during two consecutive drive cycles, a malfunction exists.

Action Taken When the DTC Sets

A malfunction DTC is stored, TCS is disabled and the Traction Control indicator is turned ON.
ABS remains functional.

Conditions for Clearing the DTC

- Condition for DTC is no longer present and scan tool clear DTC function is used.
- Fifty ignition cycles have passed with no DTC(s) detected.

Diagnostic Aids

- It is very important that a thorough inspection of the wiring and connectors be performed. Failure to carefully and fully inspect wiring and connectors may result in misdiagnosis, causing part replacement with reappearance of the malfunction.
- Possible causes:
  - Stoplamp switch circuit shorted to voltage.
  - Stoplamp switch misadjusted or shorted.
  - Binding pedal.

GC402970267300AX

Fig. 164 Code C1294: Brake Lamp Switch Circuit Always Active (Part 1 of 2). Corvette

Circuit Description

This DTC is used to identify open Stoplamp Switch circuitry that prevents the Stoplamp Switch input to the EBTCM from changing states when the brake is applied.

This DTC is used in conjunction with DTC C1291 to determine the cause of an open Stoplamp Switch malfunction.

Conditions for Setting the DTC

DTC C1295 can be set after initialization is completed. If the Stoplamp Switch input voltage is out of specification for one second indicating an open circuit, a malfunction exists.

Action Taken When the DTC Sets

A malfunction DTC is stored, TCS is disabled and the Traction Control indicator is turned ON.
ABS remains functional.

Conditions for Clearing the DTC

- Condition for DTC is no longer present and scan tool clear DTC function is used.
- Fifty ignition cycles have passed with no DTC(s) detected.

Diagnostic Aids

- It is very important that a thorough inspection of the wiring and connectors be performed. Failure to carefully and fully inspect wiring and connectors may result in misdiagnosis, causing part replacement with reappearance of the malfunction.
- Possible causes:
  - Stoplamp switch input circuit open.
  - All brake lamps open.
  - Stoplamp switch open or misadjusted.
  - Open brake lamp ground.
  - Circuit has a wiring problem, terminal corrosion, or poor connections.

Test Description

The numbers below refer to step numbers on the diagnostic table.

3. Checks for voltage at EBTCM.
9. Checks the Stoplamp Switch.

GC402970267400AX

Fig. 165 Code C1295: Brake Lamp Switch Circuit Open (Part 1 of 3). Corvette

Step	Action	Value(s)	Yes	No
13	1. Press the brake pedal. 2. Check the STOP/HAZ fuse. Is the fuse OK?	—	Go to ABS Diagnostic System Check	Go to Step 14
14	1. Turn the ignition switch to the OFF position. 2. Disconnect the EBTCM. 3. Replace the fuse. 4. Press the brake pedal. 5. Check the STOP/HAZ fuse. Is the fuse OK?	—	Go to Step 4	Go to Step 15
15	Repair CKT 20 for a short to ground. Is the repair complete?	—	Go to ABS Diagnostic System Check	—

GC402970267400CX

Fig. 165 Code C1295: Brake Lamp Switch Circuit Open (Part 3 of 3). Corvette

Circuit Description

The EBTCM uses input from the Brake Pressure Sensor for more accurate control during an Active Handling event.

Conditions for Setting the DTC

DTC C1245 can be set anytime the ignition switch is in the ON position, and the signal voltage from the Brake Pressure Sensor is less than 0.20 volts or greater than 4.80 volts.

Action Taken When the DTC Sets

ABS and TCS remain enabled, Active Handling™ is disabled.

- Indicators that turn on:
  Car Icon (TCS indicator)
- Messages displayed on the DIC:
  Service Active HNDLG

Conditions for Clearing the DTC

- Condition for DTC is no longer present and scan tool clear DTC function is used.
- Fifty ignition cycles have passed with no DTCs detected.

Diagnostic Aids

- It is very important that a thorough inspection of the wiring and connectors be performed. Failure to carefully and fully inspect wiring and connectors may result in misdiagnosis, causing part replacement with reappearance of the malfunction.
- An intermittent malfunction can be caused by poor connections, broken insulation, or a wire that is broken inside the insulation.
- If an intermittent malfunction exists refer to *Intermittents*

Test Description

The number(s) below refer to the step number(s) on the diagnostic table.

2. This step checks for the proper signal voltage.
5. This step checks for an open in circuit 901.
7. This step checks for a short to ground in circuit 901.
9. This step checks for an open in circuit 556.
11. This step checks for an open in circuit 1056.

GC4029803971010X

Fig. 166 Code C1296: Brake Pressure Sensor Circuit Open Or Short (Part 1 of 3). Corvette

Step	Action	Value(s)	Yes	No
1	Was the ABS Diagnostic System Check performed?	—	*Go to Step 2*	Go to *Diagnostic System Check (ABS)*
2	Are any other DTCs also set as current DTCs?	—	Go to applicable DTC. Refer to *DTC List*	*Go to Step 3*
3	1. Turn the ignition switch to the OFF position. 2. Disconnect the EBTCM harness connector. 3. Install the *J 39700* Universal Pinout Box using the *J 39700-25* cable adapter between the EBTCM harness connector and the EBTCM. 4. Turn the ignition switch to the ON position, engine OFF. 5. Using *J 39200* DMM, measure the voltage at terminal 24 of *J 39700*. Is the voltage within the range specified in the values column?	0.20 – 4.80V	*Go to Step 4*	*Go to Step 5*
4	Replace the EBTCM. Is the replacement complete?	—	Go to *Diagnostic System Check (ABS)*	—
5	1. Disconnect the Brake Pressure Sensor connector. 2. Disconnect the *J 39700-25* cable adapter from the EBTCM leaving the *J 39700-25* attached to the EBTCM harness connector. 3. Using *J 39200* DMM, measure the resistance between terminal 24 of *J 39700-25* and terminal C of the Brake Pressure Sensor harness connector. Is the resistance within the range specified in the values column?	0 – 5Ω	*Go to Step 7*	*Go to Step 6*
6	Repair CKT 901 for an open. Is the repair complete?	—	Go to *Diagnostic System Check (ABS)*	—
7	Using *J 39200* DMM, measure the resistance between terminal 24 and B of *J 39700-25*. Is the resistance within the range specified in the value(s) column?	OL (infinite)	*Go to Step 9*	*Go to Step 8*
8	Repair CKT 901 for a short to ground. Is the repair complete?	—	Go to *Diagnostic System Check (ABS)*	—
9	Using *J 39200* DMM, measure the resistance between terminal 27 of *J 39700-25* and terminal A of the Brake Pressure Sensor harness connector. Is the resistance within the range specified in the values column?	0 – 5Ω	*Go to Step 11*	*Go to Step 10*
10	Repair CKT 556 between splice S106 and the Brake Pressure Sensor for an open. Is the repair complete?	—	Go to *Diagnostic System Check (ABS)*	—
11	Using *J 39200* DMM, measure the resistance between terminal 11 of *J 39700-25* and terminal B of the Brake Pressure Sensor harness connector. Is the resistance within the range specified in the values column?	0 – 5Ω	*Go to Step 13*	*Go to Step 12*

GC4029803971020X

Fig. 166 Code C1296: Brake Pressure Sensor Circuit Open Or Short (Part 2 of 3). Corvette

Step	Action	Value(s)	Yes	No
12	Repair CKT 1056 between splice S108 and the Brake Pressure Sensor for an open. Is the repair complete?	—	Go to *Diagnostic System Check (ABS)*	—
13	Replace the Brake Pressure Sensor. Is the replacement complete?	—	Go to *Diagnostic System Check (ABS)*	—

GC4029803971030X

Fig. 166 Code C1296: Brake Pressure Sensor Circuit Open Or Short (Part 3 of 3). Corvette

Circuit Description

The Class 2 serial data line allows all the modules on the line to transmit information to each other as needed. Each module is assigned an ID and all the information sent out on the line is assigned a priority by which it is received. When the ignition switch is turned to the ON position each module begins to send and receive information. Each module on the Class 2 serial data line knows what information it needs to send out and what information it should be receiving. What the modules do not know is which module is supposed to send them the information. This information is only learned after the module has received the information it needs along with the ID of the module that sent the information. This information is then remembered until the ignition switch is turned off. If the EBTCM looses communication with the Powertrain Control Module (PCM) then DTC U1016 will be set by the EBTCM.

Conditions for Setting the DTC

- The DTC can be set any time the ignition is in the ON position, and the PCM does not communicate with the EBTCM for 5 seconds.

Action Taken When the DTC Sets

- A malfunction DTC is stored, TCS is disabled and the Traction Control indicator is turned ON. ABS remains functional.

Conditions for Clearing the DTC

- Condition for DTC is no longer present and scan tool clear DTC function is used.
- Fifty ignition cycles have passed with no DTC(s) detected.

Diagnostic Aids

- It is very important that a thorough inspection of the wiring and connectors be performed. Failure to carefully and fully inspect wiring and connectors may result in misdiagnosis, causing part replacement with reappearance of the malfunction.
- An intermittent malfunction is most likely caused by a poor connection, rubbed through wire insulation, or a wire that is broken inside the insulation.

GC402970267500AX

Fig. 167 Code U1016: Loss Of Communications w/PCM (Part 1 of 2). Corvette

Step	Action	Value(s)	Yes	No
1	Was the Diagnostic System Check performed?	—	*Go to Step 2*	Go to *ABS Diagnostic System Check*
2	Using a scan tool read the IPC DTC(s). Is DTC U1016 also set as a current IPC DTC?	—	Inspect powertrain.	*Go to Step 3*
3	Is DTC U1016 set as a current ABS/TCS DTC?	—	*Go to Step 4*	Go to *ABS Diagnostic System Check*
4	Replace the EBTCM. Is the replacement complete?	—	Go to *ABS Diagnostic System Check*	—

GC402970267500BX

Fig. 167 Code U1016: Loss Of Communications w/PCM (Part 2 of 2). Corvette

Circuit Description

The Class 2 serial data line allows all the modules on the line to transmit information to each other as needed. Each module is assigned an ID and all the information sent out on the line is assigned a priority by which it is received. When the ignition switch is turned to the ON position each module begins to send and receive information. Each module on the Class 2 serial data line knows what information it needs to send out and what information it should be receiving. What the modules do not know is which module is supposed to send them the information. This information is only learned after the module has received the information it needs along with the ID of the module that sent the information. This information is then remembered until the ignition switch is turned off. If the EBTCM never recieves the information or the ID of the module that is supposed to send the information DTC U1255 will be set..

Conditions for Setting the DTC

- The DTC can be set when the ignition is turned to the ON position, and the EBTCM does not recieve the PCM ID for 5 seconds.

Action Taken When the DTC Sets

- A malfunction DTC is stored, TCS is disabled and the Traction Control indicator is turned On. ABS remains functional.

Conditions for Clearing the DTC

- Condition for DTC is no longer present and scan tool clear DTC function is used.
- Fifty ignition cycles have passed with no DTC(s) detected.

Diagnostic Aids

- It is very important that a thorough inspection of the wiring and connectors be performed. Failure to carefully and fully inspect wiring and connectors may result in misdiagnosis, causing part replacement with reappearance of the malfunction.
- An intermittent malfunction is most likely caused by a poor connection, rubbed through wire insulation, or a wire that is broken inside the insulation.
  - Class 2 transmit fault on the PCM.
  - Class 2 receiver fault on the EBTCM.
  - Open Class 2 line..

GC402970267600AX

Fig. 168 Code U1255: Generic Loss Of Communications (Part 1 of 2). Corvette

Step	Action	Value(s)	Yes	No
1	Was the Diagnostic System Check performed?	—	*Go to Step 2*	Go to *ABS Diagnostic System Check*
2	1. Turn the ignition switch to the ON position, engine OFF. 2. Using a scan tool go to the System Selection Menu's Diagnostic Circuit Check and enter the Class 2 Message Monitor. Does the PCM/VCM read Active?	—	*Go to Step 3*	Inspect powertrain.
3	Does the IPC read Active?	—	*Go to Step 4*	Inspect instrument panel.
4	Does the RTD read Active?	—	*Go to Step 5*	*Check* Real-Time Damping (RTD)
5	Does the BCM read Active?	—	*Go to Step 6*	*BCM Diagnostic System Check*
6	Replace EBTCM. Is the replacement complete?	—	Go to *ABS Diagnostic System Check*	—

GC402970267600BX

Fig. 168 Code U1255: Generic Loss Of Communications (Part 2 of 2). Corvette

Circuit Description

The Class 2 serial data line allows all the modules on the line to transmit information to each other as needed. Each module is assigned an ID and all the information sent out on the line is assigned a priority by which it is received. When the ignition switch is turned to the ON position each module begins to send and receive information. Each module on the Class 2 serial data line knows what information it needs to send out and what information it should be receiving. What the modules do not know is which module is supposed to send them the information. This information is only learned after the module has received the information it needs along with the ID of the module that sent the information. This information is then remembered until the ignition switch is turned off. If the Class 2 serial data line can not communicate because the data line is shorted to ground then DTC U1300 will set.

Conditions for Setting the DTC

The EBTCM detects a short to ground on the serial data line for 5 seconds or longer. If the failure condition is present reading the DTC using the scan tool will be impossible since the scan tool uses the Class 2 data line to communicate with the EBTCM.

Action Taken When the DTC Sets

ABS remains enabled, TCS/ Active Handling™ are disabled.

- Indicators that turn on:
  Car Icon (TCS indicator
- Messages displayed on the DIC:
  Service Traction System
  Service Active HNDLG

GC4029803972010X

Fig. 169 Code U1300: Class 2 Short To Ground (Part 1 of 2). Corvette

Conditions for Clearing the DTC

- Condition for DTC is no longer present and scan tool clear DTC function is used.
- Fifty ignition cycles have passed with no DTCs detected.

Diagnostic Aids

- If the problem is an intermittent loss of communications. Carefully inspect the serial data line and related components for the following intermittent conditions:
  - There is an intermittent short to ground in the serial data line.
  - Damaged or loose star connector terminals.
- If the serial data line is shorted to ground all systems connected to the same serial data line will not be able to communicate properly.
- If the DTC is a history DTC, the problem may be intermittent. Perform the tests shown while moving related wiring and connectors. This can often cause the malfunction to occur.

Test Description

The numbers below refer to the step numbers on the diagnostic table:

2. This test checks if communications can be established between the scan tool and the other systems connected to the same serial data line.
3. This test will checks for shorts in the serial data line. It also checks for any intermittent malfunctions associated with the serial data line.

Step	Action	Value(s)	Yes	No
1	Was the ABS Diagnostic System Check performed?	—	*Go to Step 2*	Go to *Diagnostic System Check (ABS)*
2	1. Turn the ignition switch to the OFF position. 2. Install a scan tool. 3. Turn the ignition switch to the ON position, engine off. 4. Attempt to establish communications with other systems connected to the same serial data line (PCM, BCM, IPC, etc.). Does the scan tool communicate with other systems?	—	*Go to Step 3*	*Data Link Communications*
3	Check the serial data line for the following intermittent conditions: • Short to ground • Check star connector #1, and #2 make sure the bus bars are properly inserted. • Check for loose or damaged terminals. Was a problem found and repaired?	—	Go to *Diagnostic System Check (ABS)*	System OK

GC4029803972020X

Fig. 169 Code U1300: Class 2 Short To Ground (Part 2 of 2). Corvette

Circuit Description

The Class 2 serial data line allows all the modules on the line to transmit information to each other as needed. Each module is assigned an ID and all the information sent out on the line is assigned a priority by which it is received. When the ignition switch is turned to the ON position each module begins to send and receive information. Each module on the Class 2 serial data line knows what information it needs to send out and what information it should be receiving. What the modules do not know is which module is supposed to send them the information. This information is only learned after the module has received the information it needs along with the ID of the module that sent the information. This information is then remembered until the ignition switch is turned off. If the Class 2 serial data line can not communicate because the data line is shorted to battery then DTC U1301 will set.

Conditions for Setting the DTC

The EBTCM detects a short to battery on the serial data line for 5 seconds or longer. If the failure condition is present reading the DTC using the scan tool will be impossible since the scan tool uses the Class 2 data line to communicate with the EBTCM.

Action Taken When the DTC Sets

ABS remains enabled, TCS/ Active Handling™ are disabled.

- Indicators that turn on:
  Car Icon (TCS indicator
- Messages displayed on the DIC:
  Service Traction System
  Service Active HNDLG

GC4029803973010X

Fig. 170 Code U1301: Class 2 Circuit Short To Battery (Part 1 of 2). Corvette

Conditions for Clearing the DTC

- Condition for DTC is no longer present and scan tool clear DTC function is used.
- Fifty ignition cycles have passed with no DTCs detected.

Diagnostic Aids

- If the problem is an intermittent loss of communications. Carefully inspect the serial data line and related components for the following intermittent conditions:
  - There is an intermittent short to battery in the serial data line.
  - Damaged or loose star connector terminals.
- If the serial data line is shorted to battery all systems connected to the same serial data line will not be able to communicate properly.
- If the DTC is a history DTC, the problem may be intermittent. Perform the tests shown while moving related wiring and connectors. This can often cause the malfunction to occur.

Test Description

The numbers below refer to the step numbers on the diagnostic table:

2. This test checks if communications can be established between the scan tool and the other systems connected to the same serial data line.
3. This test will checks for shorts in the serial data line. It also checks for any intermittent malfunctions associated with the serial data line.

Step	Action	Value(s)	Yes	No
1	Was the ABS Diagnostic System Check performed?	—	*Go to Step 2*	Go to *Diagnostic System Check (ABS)*
2	1. Turn the ignition switch to the OFF position. 2. Install a scan tool. 3. Turn the ignition switch to the ON position, engine off. 4. Attempt to establish communications with other systems connected to the same serial data line (PCM, BCM, IPC, etc.). Does the scan tool communicate with other systems?	—	*Go to Step 3*	*Data Link Communications*
3	Check the serial data line for the following intermittent conditions: • Short to battery • Check star connector #1, and #2 make sure the bus bars are properly inserted. • Check for loose or damaged terminals. Was a problem found and repaired?	—	Go to *Diagnostic System Check (ABS)*	System OK

GC4029803973020X

Fig. 170 Code U1301: Class 2 Circuit Short To Battery (Part 2 of 2). Corvette

Step	Action	Value(s)	Yes	No
DEFINITION: The ABS Indicator does not come On during the IPC bulb check.				
1	Was the Diagnostic System Check performed?	—	*Go to Step 2*	Go to *ABS Diagnostic System Check*
2	Using a scan tool in the Instrument Panel (IPC) Special Functions attempt to turn the ABS Lamp On. Did the ABS Lamp turn On?	—	*Go to Step 3*	*Go to Step 4*
3	Replace the EBTCM. Is the replacement complete?	—	Go to *ABS Diagnostic System Check*	—
4	1. Turn the ignition switch to the OFF position. 2. Check the ABS indicator bulb. Is the ABS Indicator (car icon) bulb OK?	—	*Go to Step 6*	*Go to Step 5*
5	Replace the ABS Indicator bulb. Is the replacement complete?	—	Go to *ABS Diagnostic System Check*	—
6	Replace the Instrument Panel Cluster. Console.	—	Go to *ABS Diagnostic System Check*	—

GC402970268100BX

Fig. 171 Test A: ABS Lamp On w/No Code Set. Corvette

Circuit Description

The Instrument Panel Cluster (IPC) turn the ABS Indicator On during the IPC bulb check for approximately 3 seconds when the ignition switch is turned to the ON position. If the EBTCM sets a Diagnostic Trouble Code (DTC) the EBTCM sends the IPC the command to turn the ABS Indicator On.

Test Description

The numbers below refer to step numbers on the diagnostic table.

2. Checks if the Instrument Panel Cluster has the ability to turn the ABS indicator Off or if the EBTCM is sending an incorrect command to turn the ABS indicator On.

Step	Action	Value(s)	Yes	No
DEFINITION: The ABS Indicator does not turn Off after the Instrument Panel Cluster (IPC) bulb check and no ABS/TCS DTC(s) set.				
1	Was the Diagnostic System Check performed?	—	*Go to Step 2*	Go to *ABS Diagnostic System Check*
2	Using a scan tool in the Instrument Panel Cluster Special Functions attempt to turn OFF the ABS Lamp. Did the ABS Lamp Turn OFF?	—	*Go to Step 3*	*Go to Step 4*
3	Replace the EBTCM. Is the Replacement complete?	—	Go to *ABS Diagnostic System Check*	—
4	Replace the Instrument Panel Cluster. Is the Replacement complete?	—	Go to *ABS Diagnostic System Check*	—

GC4029702680000X

Fig. 172 Test B: ABS Lamp Inoperative w/No Code Set. Corvette

Step	Action	Value(s)	Yes	No
DEFINITION: The Traction Off indicator (car icon) does not come On when the Traction Control Switch is pressed to disable the Traction Control System.				
1	Was the Diagnostic System Check performed?	—	*Go to Step 2*	Go to *ABS Diagnostic System Check*
2	1. Turn the ignition switch to the ON position, engine OFF. 2. Using a scan tool in the Body Control Module Data List read the TCS Switch state as you press and release the TCS Switch. Does the TCS Switch state change properly as the switch is pressed and released?	—	*Go to Step 3*	*Go to Step 9*
3	Using a scan tool in ABS/TCS Special Functions read the TCS Switch Status as you press and release the TCS Switch. Does the TCS Switch state change properly as the switch is pressed and released?	—	*Go to Step 5*	*Go to Step 4*
4	Replace the EBTCM. Is the replacement complete?	—	Go to *ABS Diagnostic System Check*	—
5	Using a scan tool in the Instrument Panel (IPC) Special Functions attempt to turn the Traction Lamp (car icon) On. Did the Traction Lamp turn On?	—	*Go to Step 4*	*Go to Step 6*
6	1. Turn the ignition switch to the OFF position. 2. Check the Traction Off (car icon) indicator bulb. Is the Traction Off Indicator (car icon) bulb OK?	—	*Go to Step 8*	*Go to Step 7*
7	Replace the Traction Off Indicator bulb. Is the replacement complete?	—	Go to *ABS Diagnostic System Check*	—
8	Replace the Instrument Panel Cluster.	—	Go to *ABS Diagnostic System Check*	—
9	1. Remove the Traction Control Switch and disconnect the connector. 2. Using a scan tool in the Body Control Module Data List read the TCS Switch status. 3. Connect a jumper wire between terminals 7 and 5 of the Traction Control Switch harness connector. Does the TCS Switch status read pressed with the jumper wire connected?	—	*Go to Step 10*	*Go to Step 11*
10	Replace the Traction Control Switch. Is the replacement complete?	—	Go to *ABS Diagnostic System Check*	—

GC402970267700BX

Fig. 174 Test D: Traction Off Lamp Inoperative w/No Code Set (Part 1 of 2). Corvette

Circuit Description

The Class 2 serial data line allows all the modules on the line to transmit information to each other as needed. Each module is assigned an ID and all the information sent out on the line is assigned a priority by which it is received. When the ignition switch is turned to the run position each module begins to send and receive information. Each module on the Class 2 serial data line knows what information it needs to send out and what information it should be receiving. What the modules do not know is which module is supposed to send them the information. This information is only learned after the module has received the information it needs along with the ID of the module that sent the information. This information is then remembered until the ignition switch is turned off.

Step	Action	Value(s)	Yes	No
DEFINITION: Scan tool can not communicate with the EBTCM.				
1	Was the Diagnostic System Check performed?	—	*Go to Step 2*	Go to *Diagnostic System Check (ABS)*
2	Can the scan tool communicate with other modules on the Class 2 serial data line, such as the PCM?	—	*Go to Step 3*	*Data Link Communications*
3	Inspect the 10A ABSTRNS fuse in the Underhood Electrical Center. Is the fuse OK?	—	*Go to Step 4*	*Go to Step 9*

GC4029803974010X

Fig. 175 Test E: No Communication w/EBCM/EBTCM (Part 1 of 3). Corvette

Step	Action	Value(s)	Yes	No
DEFINITION: The Traction Off Indicator (car icon) does not turn Off after the Instrument Panel Cluster (IPC) bulb check or after the Traction Control Switch is pressed to turn the Traction Control On after it was disabled.				
1	Was the Diagnostic System Check performed?	—	*Go to Step 2*	Go to *ABS Diagnostic System Check*
2	1. Turn the ignition to the ON position, engine OFF. 2. Using a scan tool check for Body Control Module DTC(s). Is DTC B2597 set in the Body Control Module?	—	*Inspect Traction Control System*	*Go to Step 3*
3	Using a scan tool in the Instrument Panel Cluster Special Functions attempt to turn OFF the Traction Lamp (car icon). Did the Traction Lamp (car icon) Turn OFF?	—	*Go to Step 4*	*Go to Step 5*
4	Replace the EBTCM. Is the Replacement complete?	—	Go to *ABS Diagnostic System Check*	—
5	Replace the Instrument Panel Cluster. Is the Replacement complete?	—	Go to *ABS Diagnostic System Check*	—

GC402970267800BX

Fig. 173 Test C: Traction Off Lamp On w/No Code Set. Corvette

Step	Action	Value(s)	Yes	No
11	1. Turn the ignition switch to the OFF position. 2. Using *J 39200* DMM, measure the resistance between the Traction Control Switch harness connector terminal 5 and ground. Is the resistance within the range specified in the value(s) column?	0 - 5Ω	*Go to Step 13*	*Go to Step 12*
12	Repair CKT 150 for an open or high resistance. Is the repair complete?	—	Go to *ABS Diagnostic System Check*	—
13	1. Disconnect the Body Control Module connector C2. 2. Using *J 39200* DMM, measure the resistance between the Traction Control Switch harness connector terminal 7 and the Body Control Module Connector C2 terminal D15. Is the resistance within the range specified in the value(s) column?	0 - 5Ω	*Go to Step 15*	*Go to Step 14*
14	Repair CKT 1571 for an open or high resistance. Is the repair complete?	—	Go to *ABS Diagnostic System Check*	—
15	Replace the Body Control Module. Is the replacement complete?	—	Go to *ABS Diagnostic System Check*	—

GC402970267700CX

Fig. 174 Test D: Traction Off Lamp Inoperative w/No Code Set (Part 2 of 2). Corvette

Step	Action	Value(s)	Yes	No
4	Inspect the 20A ABS ELEC fuse in the Underhood Electrical Center. Is the fuse OK?	—	*Go to Step 12*	*Go to Step 5*
5	1. Install a new ABS ELEC fuse. 2. Recheck the fuse. Is the fuse OK?	—	Go to *Diagnostic System Check (ABS)*	*Go to Step 6*
6	1. Turn the ignition switch to the OFF position. 2. Remove the ABS ELEC fuse. 3. Disconnect the EBTCM connector. 4. Connect the *J 39700* Universal Pinout Box using the *J 39700-25* cable adapter to the EBTCM harness connector only. 5. Using *J 39200* DMM, measure the resistance between terminals D and B of *J 39700*. Is the resistance within the range specified in the value(s) column?	OL (infinite)	*Go to Step 7*	*Go to Step 8*
7	Replace the EBTCM. Is the replacement complete?	—	Go to *Diagnostic System Check (ABS)*	—
8	Repair CKT 1242 for a short to ground. Is the repair complete?	—	Go to *Diagnostic System Check (ABS)*	—
9	1. Install a new 10A ABSTRNS fuse. 2. Cycle the ignition switch from the OFF to ON position, engine off. 3. Recheck the fuse. Is the fuse OK?	—	Go to *Diagnostic System Check (ABS)*	*Go to Step 10*
10	1. Turn the ignition switch to the OFF position. 2. Remove the 10A ABSTRNS fuse. 3. Disconnect the EBTCM connector. 4. Connect the *J 39700* Universal Pinout Box using the *J 39700-25* cable adapter to the EBTCM harness connector only. 5. Using *J 39200* DMM, measure the resistance between terminals A and B of *J 39700*. Is the resistance within the range specified in the value(s) column?	OL (infinite)	*Go to Step 7*	*Go to Step 11*
11	Repair CKT 641 for a short to ground. Is the repair complete?	—	Go to *Diagnostic System Check (ABS)*	—
12	1. Install the fuses if removed. 2. Turn the ignition switch to the ON position, engine off. 3. Using *J 39200* DMM, measure the voltage at the 10A ABSTRNS fuse by probing between the fuse test terminals and a good ground. Is the voltage within the range specified within the value(s) column?	Battery Volts	*Go to Step 13*	*Power Distribution*

GC4029803974020X

Fig. 175 Test E: No Communication w/EBCM/EBTCM (Part 2 of 3). Corvette

Step	Action	Value(s)	Yes	No
13	Using *J 39200* DMM, measure the voltage at the 20A ABS ELEC fuse by probing between the fuse test terminals and a good ground. Is the voltage within the range specified within the value(s) column?	Battery Volts	*Go to Step 14*	*Power Distribution*
14	1. Turn the ignition switch to the OFF position. 2. Disconnect the EBTCM connector. 3. Connect the *J 39700* Universal Pinout Box using the *J 39700-25* cable adapter to the EBTCM harness connector only. 4. Using *J 39200* DMM, measure the resistance between *J 39700* terminal B and a good ground. Is the resistance within the range specified in the value(s) column?	0–5 Ω	*Go to Step 16*	*Go to Step 15*
15	Repair CKT 1251 or ground G101 for an open or high resistance. Is the repair complete?	—	Go to *Diagnostic System Check (ABS)*	—
16	1. Turn the ignition switch to the ON position, engine off. 2. Using *J 39200* DMM, measure the voltage between *J 39700* terminals A and B. Is the voltage within the range specified in the value(s) column?	Battery Volts	*Go to Step 18*	*Go to Step 17*
17	Repair CKT 641 for an open. Is the repair complete?	—	Go to *Diagnostic System Check (ABS)*	—
18	Using *J 39200* DMM, measure the voltage between *J 39700* terminals D and B. Is the voltage within the range specified in the value(s) column?	Battery Volts	*Go to Step 20*	*Go to Step 19*
19	Repair CKT 1242 for an open. Is the repair complete?	—	Go to *Diagnostic System Check (ABS)*	—
20	1. Turn the ignition switch to the OFF position. 2. Remove the bus bar from the Star Connector 1. 3. Using *J 39200* DMM, measure the resistance between the Star Connector 1 terminal E and terminal 10 of *J 39700*. Is the resistance within the range specified within the values column?	0–5 Ω	*Go to Step 7*	*Go to Step 21*
21	Repair CKT 1122 for an open or high resistance. Is the repair complete?	—	Go to *Diagnostic System Check (ABS)*	—

GC4029803974030X

Fig. 175 Test E: No Communication w/EBCM/EBTCM (Part 3 of 3). Corvette

Circuit Description

The Instrument Panel Cluster (IPC) turn the ABS Indicator on during the IPC bulb check for approximately 3 seconds when the ignition switch is turned to the ON position. If the EBCM sets a Diagnostic Trouble Code (DTC) the EBCM sends the IPC the command to turn the ABS Indicator on.

Test Description

The numbers below refer to step numbers on the diagnostic table.

2. Checks if the IPC has the ability to turn the ABS Indicator on.

GC4020052278010X

Fig. 177 ABS Indicator Inoperative (Part 1 of 2). Corvette

Step	Action	Value(s)	Yes	No
DEFINITION: The ABS Indicator does not come on during the IPC bulb check.				
1	Was the Diagnostic System Check performed?	—	*Go to Step 2*	Go to *A Diagnostic System Check - ABS*
2	Using a scan tool in the Instrument Panel (IPC) Special Functions attempt to turn the ABS Lamp on. Did the ABS Lamp turn on?	—	*Go to Step 3*	*Go to Step 4*
3	Replace the EBCM. Is the replacement complete?	—	Go to *A Diagnostic System Check - ABS*	—
4	1. Turn the ignition switch to the OFF position. 2. Check the ABS indicator bulb. Is the ABS Indicator bulb OK?	—	*Go to Step 6*	*Go to Step 5*
5	Replace the ABS Indicator bulb. Is the replacement complete?	—	Go to *A Diagnostic System Check - ABS*	—
6	Replace the Instrument Panel Cluster. Is the replacement complete?	—	Go to *A Diagnostic System Check - ABS*	—

GC4020052278020X

Fig. 177 ABS Indicator Inoperative (Part 2 of 2). Corvette

Step	Action	Value(s)	Yes	No
DEFINITION: The ABS Indicator does not turn off after the Instrument Panel Cluster (IPC) bulb check and no ABS/TCS DTC(s) set.				
1	Was the Diagnostic System Check performed?	—	*Go to Step 2*	Go to *A Diagnostic System Check - ABS*
2	Using a scan tool in the Instrument Panel Cluster Special Functions attempt to turn off the ABS Lamp. Did the ABS Lamp Turn off?	—	*Go to Step 3*	*Go to Step 4*
3	Replace the EBCM. Is the Replacement complete?	—	Go to *A Diagnostic System Check - ABS*	—
4	Replace the Instrument Panel Cluster. Is the Replacement complete?	—	Go to *A Diagnostic System Check - ABS*	—

GC4020052279000X

Fig. 176 ABS Indicator Always On. Corvette

Circuit Description

The ABS Diagnostic System Check is an organized approach to identify problems associated with the EBTCM. This check must be the starting point for any EBTCM complaint, and will direct you to the next logical step in diagnosing the complaint. The EBTCM is a very reliable component and is not likely the cause of the malfunction. Most system complaints are linked to faulty wiring, connectors, and occasionally to components. Understanding the ABS system and using the tables correctly will reduce diagnostic time and prevent unnecessary parts replacement.

Diagnostic Aids

- An intermittent failure in the electronic system may be very difficult to detect and to accurately diagnose. The EBTCM test for different malfunctions under different vehicle conditions. For this reason, a thorough test drive is often needed in order to repeat a malfunction. If the system malfunction is not repeated during the test drive, a good description of the complaint may be very useful in locating an intermittent malfunction. Faulty electrical connections or wiring causes most intermitting problems. When an intermitting condition is suspected, check the suspected circuits for the following conditions:
  - Poor mating of connector halves or backed out terminals
  - Improperly formed or damaged terminals
  - Wire chafing
  - Poor wire to terminal connections
  - Dirty or corroded terminals
  - Damage to connector bodies
- If the DTC is a history DTC, the problem may be intermittent. Perform the tests shown while moving related wiring and connectors. This can often cause the malfunction to occur. Perform a thorough inspection of all related wiring and connectors pertaining to the history DTC stored.

Step	Action	Value(s)	Yes	No
1	1. Reconnect all previously disconnected components. 2. Cycle the Ignition switch from the OFF to ON position, engine OFF. 3. Plug a scan tool into the diagnostic link connector (DLC). Does the scan tool communicate with the EBTCM?	--	Go to *Step 3*	Go to *Step 2*
2	Does the scan tool communicate with other modules on the class 2 line?	—	Go to *No Communication with EBTCM*	*Does Not Communicate w/Class 2 Data Line*
3	1. Use the scan tool in ABS/TCS Special Functions in order to run the AUTOMATED test. 2. Used the scan tool in order to read ABS/TCS/ICCS DTCs. Are there any current DTCs?	--	Go to *DTC List*	Go to *Step 4*
4	1. Disconnect the scan tool. 2. Cycle the ignition switch from the OFF to ON position. Is the TRACTION OFF message displayed on the DIC?	—	Go to *Traction Off Message On with No DTC Set*	Go to *Step 5*
5	Press the traction control switch to disable traction control. Is the TRACTION OFF message displayed on the DIC?	—	Go to *Step 6*	Go to *Traction Off Message Inoperative with No DTC Set*
6	Are there any history DTCs?	—	Go to *DTC List*	Go to *Step 7*
7	Is the Stabilitrak® inoperative?	—	Go to *Vehicle Stability Enhancement System Inoperative with No DTC Set*	Go to *Step 8*

GC4029803915010X

Fig. 178 ABS Diagnostic System Check (Part 1 of 2). DeVille

Step	Action	Value(s)	Yes	No
8	Is the Stabilitrak® active unwantedly?	—	Go to *Vehicle Stability Enhancement System Unwanted Activation w/ No DTC Set*	Go to *Step 9*
9	Is there excessive brake pedal vibration during Stabilitrak® activation?	--	Go to *Vehicle Stability Enhancement System Excessive Brake Pulsation*	System OK

GC4029803915020X

Fig. 178 ABS Diagnostic System Check (Part 2 of 2). DeVille

Step	Action	Value(s)	Yes	No
8	Is the Stabilitrak® inoperative?	—	Go to *Stabilitrak(R) Inoperative with No DTC Set*	Go to *Step 9*
9	Does the Stabilitrak® activate unwantedly?	—	Go to *Stabilitrak(R) Unwanted Activation w/ No DTC Set*	Go to *Step 10*
10	Does the brake pedal vibrate excessively during Stabilitrak® activation?	—	Go to *Stabilitrak(R) Excessive Brake Pulsation*	System OK

GC4029803887020X

Fig. 179 ABS Diagnostic System Check & Diagnostic Test Drive (Part 2 of 2). Seville

Test Description

The numbers below refer to step numbers on the diagnostic table.

2. Checks if the IPC has the ability to operate the ABS indicator lamp.
3. Checks for a short to ground in CKT 1537.
5. Checks for a short to voltage in CKT 1537.
6. Checks for an open in CKT 1537.

Step	Action	Value(s)	Yes	No
1	Did you perform the Diagnostic System Check?	—	Go to *Step 2*	Go to *Diagnostic System Check*
2	1. Turn OFF the ignition. 2. Turn ON the ignition, with the engine OFF. Did the ABS indicator lamp turn ON then OFF?	—	Go to *Step 3*	Go to *Step 9*
3	1. Turn OFF the ignition. 2. Disconnect the EBTCM. 3. Connect the *J 39700* universal pinout box using the *J 39700-25* cable adapter to the EBTCM harness connector only. 4. Disconnect the IPC connector. 5. Using a *J 39200* DMM, measure the resistance between the *J 39700* terminals 3 and B. Is the resistance within the specified range?	OL (infinite)	Go to *Step 5*	Go to *Step 4*
4	Repair the short to ground in CKT 1537. Did you complete the repair?	—	Go to *Diagnostic System Check*	—
5	1. Turn ON the ignition, with the engine OFF. 2. Using a *J 39200* DMM, measure the voltage between the *J 39700* terminals 3 and B. Is the voltage greater than the specified value?	1 V	Go to *Step 7*	Go to *Step 6*
6	1. Turn OFF the ignition. 2. Connect a fused jumper between the IPC harness connector C2 cavity A5 and a good ground. 3. Using a *J 39200* DMM, measure the resistance between the *J 39700* terminals 3 and B. Is the resistance less than the specified value?	5 Ω	*Go to Step 10*	*Go to Step 8*
7	Repair the short to voltage in CKT 1537. Did you complete the repair?	—	Go to *Diagnostic System Check*	—
8	Repair the open in CKT 1537. Did you complete the repair?	—	Go to *Diagnostic System Check*	—
9	Replace the instrument cluster (IPC). Did you complete the repair?	—	Go to *Diagnostic System Check*	—
10	Replace the EBTCM. Did you complete the repair?	—	Go to *Diagnostic System Check*	—

GC4029803888020X

Fig. 180 Code C1211: ABS Lamp Circuit Fault (Part 2 of 2). Seville

Diagnostic Test Drive

When servicing Stabilitrak® vehicles, test drives will be necessary to allow all tests to be run, and all system functions to be enabled and exercised. A test drive may also be required to duplicate specific DTCs covered in this section. The diagnostic system check (including test drive) should be run when vehicle repairs are complete, to verify the fix.

The diagnostic test drive will vary for ABS/TCS or Stabilitrak® problems.

The following is a suggested Stabilitrak® diagnostic test drive.

1. Read the Diagnostic Aids and the Conditions for Setting the DTC.
2. Reconnect any previously disconnected components.
3. Turn the ignition switch to the OFF, then start the engine.
4. Connect a scan tool to the data link connector (DLC).
5. Monitor the Stabilitrak Steering Angle Is Centered in the ABS/TCS/ICCS Data Display (1) Diagnostics, Data List 2. The scan tool will indicate Yes with the steering wheel centered. Drive the vehicle in a straight line for 45 seconds at 24 Km/h (15 mph) while monitoring the scan tool.
6. Disconnect a scan tool from the data link connector (DLC).
7. Drive the vehicle under the following conditions for at least 10 minutes. At no times should any unlawful or unsafe maneuvers be performed.
   - Highway driving.
   - Rough roads.
   - Perform turning maneuvers (curved freeway entrance ramp, parking lot maneuvers) and high steering angles and yaw rates at low speeds.
   - Verify customers concern and duplicate driving conditions.
   - With the engine still running use the scan tool and check for any DTCs.
   - If any DTCs are set, perform the appropriate DTC table.

Step	Action	Value(s)	Yes	No
1	1. Reconnect all previously disconnected components. 2. Cycle the ignition switch from the OFF to the ON position, with the engine OFF. 3. Connect a scan tool to the data link connector (DLC). Does the scan tool communicate with the EBTCM?	—	Go to *Step 3*	Go to *Step 2*
2	Does the scan tool communicate with other modules on the Class 2 line?	—	Go to *No Communication with EBTCM*	*Data Link Communications*
3	1. With the scan tool in ABS/TCS/ICCS Special Functions, run the Automated Test. 2. With the scan tool, read ABS/TCS/ICCS DTCs. Are there any current Diagnostic Trouble Codes?	—	Go to *Step 4*	Go to *Step 5*
4	Does the scan tool display a DTC that is undefined?	—	Go to *Scan Tool Displays Undefined DTC*	Go to *DTC List*
5	1. Remove the scan tool from the DLC. 2. Cycle the Ignition switch from the OFF to ON position. Does the DIC display the TRACTION OFF message?	—	Go to *Traction Off Message On with No DTC Set*	Go to *Step 6*
6	Press the TCS On/Off switch to disable Traction Control. Does the DIC display the TRACTION OFF message?	—	Go to *Step 7*	Go to *Traction Off Message Inoperative with No DTC Set*
7	Does the DIC display the CHECK BRAKE PADS message?	—	Go to *Check Brake Pads Message Always On*	Go to *Step 8*

GC4029803887010X

Fig. 179 ABS Diagnostic System Check & Diagnostic Test Drive (Part 1 of 2). Seville

Circuit Description

The instrument cluster controls the operation of the ANTILOCK indicator. The EBTCM reports the desired status of the ANTILOCK indicator via serial data class 2 messages. The hard wired circuit is a back-up reporting circuit. The EBTCM supplies ground through the circuit when the ABS is operating properly. Using the serial data messages and back-up circuit, the instrument cluster decides whether to turn on the ANTILOCK indicator.

Conditions for Setting the DTC

All of the following conditions occur:

- The EBTCM commands the ANTILOCK indicator ON.
- The EBTCM detects one of the following conditions in the ANTILOCK indicator control circuit:
  - An open
  - A short to ground
  - A short to voltage

Actions Taken When the DTC Sets

- A malfunction DTC is stored.
- The ABS remains functional.
- For a short, the ABS indicator remains OFF.
- For an open, the ABS indicator is turned ON.

Conditions for Clearing the DTC

- The condition for DTC is no longer present and you used scan tool Clear DTCs function.
- The condition for DTC is no longer present and you used the On-Board Clear DTCs function.
- The EBTCM does not detect the DTC in 50 drive cycles.

Diagnostic Aids

- It is very important that a thorough inspection of the wiring and connectors be performed. Failure to carefully and fully inspect wiring and connectors may result in misdiagnosis, causing part replacement with reappearance of the malfunction.
- An intermittent malfunction can be caused by poor connections, broken insulation, or a wire that is broken inside the insulation.
- If an intermittent malfunction exists, refer to *Intermittents and Poor Connections*

GC4029803888010X

Fig. 180 Code C1211: ABS Lamp Circuit Fault (Part 1 of 2). Seville

Circuit Description

The instrument cluster controls the operation of the ANTILOCK indicator. The EBTCM reports the desired status of the ANTILOCK indicator via serial data class 2 messages. The hard wired circuit is a back-up reporting circuit. The EBTCM supplies ground through the circuit when the ABS is operating properly. Using the serial data messages and back-up circuit, the instrument cluster decides whether to turn on the ANTILOCK indicator.

Conditions for Setting the DTC

All of the following conditions occur:

- The EBTCM commands the ANTILOCK indicator ON.
- The EBTCM detects one of the following conditions in the ANTILOCK indicator control circuit:
  - An open
  - A short to ground
  - A short to voltage

Actions Taken When the DTC Sets

- A malfunction DTC is stored.
- The ABS remains functional.
- For a short, the ABS indicator remains OFF.
- For an open, the ABS indicator is turned ON.

Conditions for Clearing the DTC

- The condition for DTC is no longer present and you used scan tool Clear DTCs function.
- The condition for DTC is no longer present and you used the On-Board Clear DTCs function.
- The EBTCM does not detect the DTC in 50 drive cycles.

Diagnostic Aids

- It is very important that a thorough inspection of the wiring and connectors be performed. Failure to carefully and fully inspect wiring and connectors may result in misdiagnosis, causing part replacement with reappearance of the malfunction.
- An intermittent malfunction can be caused by poor connections, broken insulation, or a wire that is broken inside the insulation.
- If an intermittent malfunction exists, refer to *Intermittents and Poor Connections*

Test Description

The numbers below refer to step numbers on the diagnostic table.

3. This step checks if the instrument cluster has the ability to operate the ABS indicator.
4. This step checks for a short to ground in CKT 852.
6. This step checks for a short to voltage in CKT 852.
7. This step checks for an open in CKT 852.

GC4029903916010X

Fig. 181 Code C1211: ABS Lamp Circuit Fault (Part 1 of 2). DeVille & Eldorado

Step	Action	Value(s)	Yes	No
1	Did you perform the ABS Diagnostic System Check?	--	Go to *Step 2*	Go to *A Diagnostic System Check - ABS*
2	1. Turn ON the ignition, with the engine OFF. 2. Using a scan tool in order to read the ABS/TCS/ICCS DTCs. Are codes U1300 or U1301 present?	--	*DTC U1300 Class 2 Short to Ground* or *DTC U1301 Class 2 Short to Battery*	Go to *Step 3*
3	1. Turn OFF the ignition. 2. Turn ON the ignition, with the engine OFF. Did the ABS indicator turn ON then OFF?	--	Go to *Step 4*	Go to *Step 10*
4	1. Turn OFF the ignition. 2. Disconnect the EBTCM connector. 3. Connect the *J 39700* universal pinout box using the *J 39700-25* cable adapter to the EBTCM harness connector only. 4. Disconnect the instrument cluster connector. 5. Use a *J 39200* DMM in order to measure the resistance between the *J 39700* terminal 3 and terminal B. Is the resistance within the specified range?	OL (Infinite)	Go to *Step 6*	Go to *Step 5*
5	Repair the short to ground in CKT 852. Did you complete the repair?	--	Go to *A Diagnostic System Check - ABS*	--
6	1. Turn ON the ignition, with the engine OFF. 2. Use a *J 39200* DMM in order to measure the voltage between the *J 39700* terminal 3 and terminal B. Is the voltage greater than the specified value?	1 V	Go to *Step 8*	Go to *Step 7*
7	1. Turn OFF the ignition. 2. Connect a fused jumper between the instrument cluster harness connector C2 terminal A5 and a good ground. 3. Use a *J 39200* DMM in order to measure the resistance between the *J 39700* terminal 3 and terminal B. Is the resistance less than the specified value?	5 Ω	Go to *Step 11*	Go to *Step 9*
8	Repair the short to voltage in CKT 852. Did you complete the repair?	--	Go to *A Diagnostic System Check - ABS*	--
9	Repair the open in CKT 852. Did you complete the repair?	--	Go to *A Diagnostic System Check - ABS*	--
10	Inspect the instrument cluster. Did you complete the diagnosis?	--	Go to *A Diagnostic System Check - ABS*	--
11	Replace the EBTCM. Did you complete the repair?	--	Go to *A Diagnostic System Check - ABS*	--

GC4029903916020X

Fig. 181 Code C1211: ABS Lamp Circuit Fault (Part 2 of 2). DeVille & Eldorado

Step	Action	Value(s)	Yes	No
1	Was the Diagnostic System Check performed?	—	*Go to Step 2*	Go to *Diagnostic System Check*
2	Inspect fuse 50A BRAKES Maxifuse®, in the RH Maxifuse block. Is the fuse OK?	—	*Go to Step 7*	*Go to Step 3*
3	1. Install a new 50A BRAKES Maxifuse®. 2. Cycle the ignition switch from the OFF to ON position, engine off. 3. Recheck the 50 A BRAKES Maxifuse®. Is the fuse OK?	—	Go to *Diagnostic System Check*	*Go to Step 4*
4	1. Turn the Ignition switch to the OFF position. 2. Remove the 50A BRAKES Maxifuse®. 3. Disconnect the EBTCM. 4. Connect the *J 39700* Universal Pinout Box using the *J 39700-25* cable adapter to the EBTCM harness connector only. 5. Using *J 39200* DMM measure the resistance between terminals D and B and E and B of *J 39700.* Is the resistance within the range specified in the value(s) column?	OL (infinite)	*Go to Step 5*	*Go to Step 10*
5	1. Remove the EBTCM from the BPMV. 2. Connect the *J 41247* Pinout Box to the BPMV. 3. Measure the resistance between the *J 41247* terminal 7 and the BPMV case. Is the resistance within the range specified in the value(s) column?	OL (infinite)	*Go to Step 9*	*Go to Step 6*
6	Replace the BPMV. Is the replacement complete?	—	Go to *Diagnostic System Check*	—
7	1. Install the fuse if removed. 2. Using *J 39200* DMM measure the voltage at the 50A BRAKES Maxifuse® fuse by probing between the fuse test terminals and a good ground. Is the voltage within the range specified in the value(s) column?	Battery volts	*Go to Step 8*	Inspect Power Distribution
8	1. Turn the Ignition switch to the OFF position. 2. Disconnect the EBTCM. 3. Connect the *J 39700* Universal Pinout Box using the *J 39700-25* cable adapter to the EBTCM harness connector only. 4. Using *J 39200* DMM measure the voltage at terminal D, and at terminal E of *J 39700.* Is the voltage within the range specified in the value(s) column?	Battery volts	*Go to Step 9*	*Go to Step 11*
9	Replace the EBTCM. Is the replacement complete?	—	Go to *Diagnostic System Check*	—

GC402980277600BX

Fig. 182 Code C1214: Solenoid Valve Relay Contact Or Coil Circuit Open (Part 2 of 3). DeVille

Circuit Description

The solenoid valve relay supplies power to the solenoid valves in the BPMV. The solenoid valve relay, located in the EBTCM, is activated whenever the ignition switch is in the ON position and no faults are present. Power is provided to the solenoid valves through the relay from CKT 1042 going into terminal D and E of the EBTCM. The solenoid valve relay remains engaged until the ignition is turned off or a failure is detected.

Conditions for Setting the DTC

DTC C1214 will set anytime the solenoid valve relay is commanded on and the solenoid valve relay voltage is less than 8 volts, and ignition voltage is greater than 10.5 volts.

Action Taken When the DTC Sets

A malfunction DTC is stored, ABS/TCS is disabled and the ABS and Traction Control indicators are turned on.

Conditions for Clearing the DTC

- Condition for DTC is no longer present and scan tool clear DTC function is used.
- Fifty ignition cycles have passed with no DTC(s) detected.

Diagnostic Aids

- It is very important that a thorough inspection of the wiring and connectors be performed. Failure to carefully and fully inspect wiring and connectors may result in misdiagnosis, causing part replacement with reappearance of the malfunction.
- The Relays are integral to the EBTCM and are not serviceable.

Test Description

The numbers below refer to step numbers on the diagnostic table.

4. Checks for a short to ground in CKT 1242.
5. Checks for an internal short in the BPMV.
8. Checks for an open in CKT 1242.

GC402980277600AX

Fig. 182 Code C1214: Solenoid Valve Relay Contact Or Coil Circuit Open (Part 1 of 3). DeVille

Step	Action	Value(s)	Yes	No
10	Repair short to ground in CKT 1042. Is the repair complete?	—	Go to *Diagnostic System Check*	—
11	Repair open in CKT 1042. Is the repair complete?	—	Go to *Diagnostic System Check*	—

GC402980277600CX

Fig. 182 Code C1214: Solenoid Valve Relay Contact Or Coil Circuit Open (Part 3 of 3). DeVille

Circuit Description

The solenoid valve relay supplies power to the solenoid valves. The solenoid valve relay activates when the ignition is ON and when no DTCs are present. Power is supplied to the valve solenoids through the solenoid valve relay via CKT 442. Power is supplied to the pump motor via CKT 342. The ignition input is supplied via CKT 241.

Conditions for Setting the DTC

- The ignition voltage is greater than 10.5 volts.
- The solenoid relay is commanded ON.
- The solenoid relay voltage is less than 8.0 volts.

Action Taken When the DTC Sets

- A malfunction DTC is stored.
- The ABS/TCS/Stabilitrak® is disabled.
- The ABS indicator is turned ON.
- The TRACTION CONTROL indicator is turned ON.
- The DIC displays the SERVICE STABILITY SYS message.

Conditions for Clearing the DTC

- The condition for DTC is no longer present and you used scan tool Clear DTCs function.
- The condition for DTC is no longer present and you used the On-Board Clear DTCs function.
- The EBTCM does not detect the DTC in 50 drive cycles.

Diagnostic Aids

- It is very important that a thorough inspection of the wiring and connectors be performed. Failure to carefully and fully inspect wiring and connectors may result in misdiagnosis, causing part replacement with reappearance of the malfunction.
- An intermittent malfunction can be caused by poor connections, broken insulation, or a wire that is broken inside the insulation.
- If an intermittent malfunction exists, refer to *Intermittents and Poor Connections*
- The relays are integral to the EBTCM and are not serviceable.

GC4029803889010X

Fig. 183 Code C1214: Solenoid Valve Relay Contact Or Coil Circuit Open (Part 1 of 2). Seville

Test Description

The numbers below refer to step numbers on the diagnostic table.

4. Checks for a short to ground in CKT 442.
5. Checks for an internal short in the BPMV.

Step	Action	Value(s)	Yes	No
1	Did you perform the Diagnostic System Check?	—	Go to *Step 2*	Go to *Diagnostic System Check*
2	Check the underhood junction block ABS SOL Fuse for an open. Is the fuse OK?	—	Go to *Step 7*	Go to *Step 3*
3	1. Install a new ABS SOL fuse. 2. Turn OFF the ignition. 3. Turn ON the ignition, with the engine OFF. 4. Recheck the ABS SOL Fuse. Is the fuse OK?	—	Go to *Diagnostic System Check*	Go to *Step 4*
4	1. Turn OFF the ignition. 2. Remove the ABS SOL Fuse. 3. Disconnect the EBTCM. 4. Install the *J 39700* universal pinout box using the *J 39700-25* cable adapter to the EBTCM harness connector only. 5. Using a *J 39200* DMM, measure the resistance between the *J 39700* terminals D and B. Is the resistance within the specified range?	OL (infinite)	Go to *Step 5*	Go to *Step 10*
5	1. Remove the EBTCM from the BPMV. 2. Connect the *J 41247* pinout box to the BPMV. 3. Measure the resistance between the *J 41247* terminal 7 and the BPMV case. Is the resistance within the specified range?	OL (infinite)	Go to *Step 9*	Go to *Step 6*
6	Replace the BPMV. Did you complete the repair?	—	Go to *Diagnostic System Check*	—
7	1. Install the ABS SOL Fuse, if removed. 2. Using a *J 39200* DMM, measure the voltage at the ABS SOL Fuse by probing between the fuse test terminals and a good ground. Is the voltage within the specified range?	Battery Voltage	Go to *Step 8*	*Wiring Repairs*
8	1. Turn OFF the ignition. 2. Disconnect the EBTCM. 3. Install the *J 39700* universal pinout box using the *J 39700-25* cable adapter to the EBTCM harness connector only. 4. Using a *J 39200* DMM, measure the voltage at the *J 39700* terminal D. Is the voltage within the specified range?	Battery Voltage	Go to *Step 9*	Go to *Step 11*
9	Replace the EBTCM. Did you complete the repair?	—	Go to *Diagnostic System Check*	—
10	Repair the short to ground in CKT 442. Did you complete the repair?	—	Go to *Diagnostic System Check*	—
11	Repair the open in CKT 442. Did you complete the repair?	—	Go to *Diagnostic System Check*	—

GC4029803889020X

Fig. 183 Code C1214: Solenoid Valve Relay Contact Or Coil Circuit Open (Part 2 of 2). Seville

Step	Action	Value(s)	Yes	No
1	Was the Diagnostic System Check performed?	—	*Go to Step 2*	Go to *Diagnostic System Check*
2	Inspect the 50A BRAKES Maxifuse® fuse, in the RH Maxifuse block. Is the fuse OK?	—	*Go to Step 7*	*Go to Step 3*
3	1. Install a new 50A BRAKES Maxifuse® fuse. 2. Cycle the ignition switch from the OFF to ON position, engine off. 3. Using a scan tool in ABS/TCS Special Functions attempt to run the AUTOMATED test. 4. Recheck the 50A BRAKES Maxifuse® fuse. Is the fuse OK?	—	Go to *Diagnostic System Check*	*Go to Step 4*
4	1. Turn the Ignition switch to the OFF position. 2. Remove the 50A BRAKES Maxifuse® fuse. 3. Disconnect the EBTCM. 4. Disconnect the pump motor ground. 5. Connect the *J 39700* Universal Pinout Box using the *J 39700-25* cable adapter to the EBTCM harness connector only. 6. Using *J 39200* DMM, measure the resistance between terminals E and B, and D and B, of *J 39700*. Is the resistance within the range specified in the value(s) column?	OL (infinite)	*Go to Step 5*	*Go to Step 10*
5	1. Remove the EBTCM from the BPMV. 2. Connect the *J 41247* Pinout Box to the BPMV. 3. Measure the resistance between *J 41247* terminal 8 and the BPMV case. Is the resistance within the range specified in the value(s) column?	OL (infinite)	*Go to Step 9*	*Go to Step 6*
6	Replace the BPMV. Is the replacement complete?	—	Go to *Diagnostic System Check*	—
7	1. Install the fuse if removed. 2. Using *J 39200* DMM, measure the voltage at the 50A BRAKES Maxifuse® fuse by probing between the fuse test terminals and a good ground. Is the voltage within the range specified in the value(s) column?	Battery volts	*Go to Step 8*	Inspect Power Distribution
8	1. Turn the Ignition switch to the OFF position. 2. Disconnect the EBTCM. 3. Connect *J 39700* Universal Pinout Box using the *J 39700-25* cable adaptor to the EBTCM harness connector only. 4. Using *J 39200* DMM, measure the voltage at terminal E of *J 39700*. Is the voltage within the range specified in the value(s) column?	Battery volts	*Go to Step 9*	*Go to Step 11*
9	Replace EBTCM. Is the replacement complete?	—	Go to *Diagnostic System Check*	—

GC402980277700BX

Fig. 184 Code C1217: BPMV Pump Motor Relay Contact Circuit Open (Part 2 of 3). DeVille

Circuit Description

The pump motor is an integral part of the BPMV, while the pump motor relay is integral to the EBTCM. The pump motor relay is not engaged during normal system operation. When an ABS/TCS operation is required, the EBTCM activates the pump motor relay and battery power is provided to the pump motor.

Conditions for Setting the DTC

DTC C1217 will set anytime the pump motor relay is commanded on and the pump relay voltage is less than 8 volts, and ignition voltage is greater than 10.5 volts.

Action Taken When the DTC Sets

A malfunction DTC is stored, ABS/TCS is disabled and the ABS and Traction Control indicators are turned on.

Conditions for Clearing the DTC

- Condition for DTC is no longer present and scan tool clear DTC function is used.
- Fifty ignition cycles have passed with no DTC(s) detected.

Diagnostic Aids

- It is very important that a thorough inspection of the wiring and connectors be performed. Failure to carefully and fully inspect wiring and connectors may result in misdiagnosis, causing part replacement with reappearance of the malfunction.

Test Description

The numbers below refer to step numbers on the diagnostic table.

4. Checks for a short to ground in CKT 1042.
5. Checks for an internal short in the BPMV.
8. Checks for an open in CKT 1042.

GC402980277700AX

Fig. 184 Code C1217: BPMV Pump Motor Relay Contact Circuit Open (Part 1 of 3). DeVille

Step	Action	Value(s)	Yes	No
10	Repair short to ground in CKT 1042. Is the repair complete?	—	Go to *Diagnostic System Check*	—
11	Repair open in CKT 1042. Is the repair complete?	—	Go to *Diagnostic System Check*	—

GC402980277700CX

Fig. 184 Code C1217: BPMV Pump Motor Relay Contact Circuit Open (Part 3 of 3). DeVille

Circuit Description

The solenoid valve relay supplies power to the solenoid valves. The solenoid valve relay activates when the ignition is ON and when no DTCs are present. Power is supplied to the valve solenoids through the solenoid valve relay via CKT 442. Power is supplied to the pump motor via CKT 342. The ignition input is supplied via CKT 241.

Conditions for Setting the DTC

- The ignition voltage is greater than 10.5 volts.
- The solenoid relay is commanded ON.
- The solenoid relay voltage is less than 8.0 volts.

Action Taken When the DTC Sets

- A malfunction DTC is stored.
- The ABS/TCS/Stabilitrak® is disabled.
- The ABS indicator is turned ON.
- The TRACTION CONTROL indicator is turned ON.
- The DIC displays the SERVICE STABILITY SYS message.

Conditions for Clearing the DTC

- The condition for DTC is no longer present and you used scan tool Clear DTCs function.
- The condition for DTC is no longer present and you used the On-Board Clear DTCs function.
- The EBTCM does not detect the DTC in 50 drive cycles.

Diagnostic Aids

- It is very important that a thorough inspection of the wiring and connectors be performed. Failure to carefully and fully inspect wiring and connectors may result in misdiagnosis, causing part replacement with reappearance of the malfunction.
- An intermittent malfunction can be caused by poor connections, broken insulation, or a wire that is broken inside the insulation.
- If an intermittent malfunction exists, refer to *Intermittents and Poor Connections*
- The relays are integral to the EBTCM and are not serviceable.

GC4029803912010X

Fig. 185 Code C1217: BPMV Pump Motor Relay Contact Circuit Open (Part 1 of 2). Seville

Test Description

The numbers below refer to step numbers on the diagnostic table.

4. Checks for a short to ground in CKT 342.
5. Checks for an internal short in the BPMV.
8. Checks for an open in CKT 342 (RED).

Step	Action	Value(s)	Yes	No
1	Did you perform the Diagnostic System Check?	—	Go to *Step 2*	Go to *Diagnostic System Check*
2	Check the underhood junction block ABS MOTOR Fuse. Is the fuse OK?	—	Go to *Step 7*	Go to *Step 3*
3	1. Install a new ABS MOTOR Fuse. 2. Turn OFF the ignition. 3. Turn ON the ignition, with the engine OFF. 4. Recheck the ABS MOTOR Fuse. Is the fuse OK?	—	Go to *Diagnostic System Check*	Go to *Step 4*
4	1. Turn OFF the ignition. 2. Remove the ABS MOTOR Fuse. 3. Disconnect the EBTCM. 4. Disconnect the pump motor ground. 5. Install the *J 39700* universal pinout box using the *J 39700-25* cable adapter to the EBTCM harness connector only. 6. Using a *J 39200* DMM, measure the resistance between the *J 39700* terminals E and B. Is the resistance within the specified range?	OL (infinite)	Go to *Step 5*	Go to *Step 10*
5	1. Remove the EBTCM from the BPMV. 2. Connect the *J 41247* pinout box to the BPMV. 3. Measure the resistance between *J 41247* terminal 8 and the BPMV case. Is the resistance within the specified range?	OL (infinite)	Go to *Step 9*	Go to *Step 6*
6	Replace the BPMV. Did you complete the repair?	—	Go to *Diagnostic System Check*	—
7	1. Install the ABS MOTOR Fuse, if removed. 2. Using a *J 39200* DMM, measure the voltage at the ABS MOTOR Fuse by probing between the fuse test terminals and a good ground. Is the voltage within the specified range?	Battery Voltage	Go to *Step 8*	Go to *Wiring*
8	1. Turn OFF the ignition. 2. Disconnect the EBTCM. 3. Install the *J 39700* universal pinout box using the *J 39700-25* cable adapter to the EBTCM harness connector only. 4. Using a *J 39200* DMM, measure the voltage at the *J 39700* terminal E. Is the voltage within the specified range?	Battery Voltage	Go to *Step 9*	Go to *Step 11*
9	Replace the EBTCM. Did you complete the repair?	—	Go to *Diagnostic System Check*	—
10	Repair short to ground in CKT 342. Did you complete the repair?	—	Go to *Diagnostic System Check*	—
11	Repair open in CKT 342. Did you complete the repair?	—	Go to *Diagnostic System Check*	—

GC4029803912020X

Fig. 185 Code C1217: BPMV Pump Motor Relay Contact Circuit Open (Part 2 of 2). Seville

Step	Action	Value(s)	Yes	No
1	Was the Diagnostic System Check performed?	—	*Go to Step 2*	Go to *Diagnostic System Check*
2	1. Inspect the WSS wiring and connectors for damage. 2. Inspect WSS for looseness or damage. Is physical damage of sensor evident?	—	*Go to Step 7*	*Go to Step 3*
3	1. Disconnect the WSS at the sensor pigtail. 2. Using *J 39200* DMM, measure the resistance between terminals A and B of the WSS. Is the resistance within the range specified in the value(s) column?	850-1350Ω	*Go to Step 4*	*Go to Step 7*
4	1. With *J 39200* DMM still connected, select the mV AC scale. 2. Spin the wheel as fast as you can by hand while monitoring the AC output. Is the AC voltage within the range specified in the value(s) column?	Above 100 mV	*Go to Step 5*	*Go to Step 7*
5	1. Disconnect the EBTCM harness connector. 2. Install *J 39700* Universal Pinout Box using the *J 39700-25* cable adapter to the EBTCM harness connector only. 3. Using *J 39200* DMM, measure resistance between terminals 15 and 31 of the *J 39700*. Is the resistance within the range specified in the value(s) column?	OL (Infinite)	*Go to Step 6*	*Go to Step 8*
6	1. Reconnect all connectors. 2. Carefully test drive vehicle above 24 Km/h (15 mph) for at least 30 seconds while monitoring a scan tool. Does DTC reset as a current DTC?	—	*Go to Step 9*	Go to *Diagnostic System Check*
7	Replace wheel speed sensor. Is the repair complete?	—	*Go to Step 10*	—
8	Repair short between CKT(s) 873 and 830. Is the repair complete?	—	*Go to Step 10*	—
9	Replace EBTCM. Is the replacement complete?	—	*Go to Step 10*	—
10	Carefully test drive vehicle above 24 Km/h (15 mph) while monitoring a scan tool for at least 30 seconds. Does the DTC set as a current DTC?	—	*Go to Step 2*	Go to *Diagnostic System Check*

GC402980277800BX

Fig. 186 Code C1221: LH Front Wheel Speed Sensor Input Signal Is Zero (Part 2 of 2). DeVille & Seville

Circuit Description

The speed sensor used on this vehicle is a single point magnetic pickup. This sensor produces an AC signal that the EBTCM uses the frequency from to calculate the wheel speed.

Conditions for Setting the DTC

The DTC will set if one wheel speed = 0 and the other WSS are greater than 8 Km/h (5 mph) for 2.5 seconds.

Action Taken When the DTC Sets

A malfunction DTC is stored, ABS/TCS is disabled and the ABS and Traction Control Indicators are turned on.

Conditions for Clearing the DTC

- Condition for DTC is no longer present and scan tool clear DTC function is used.
- Fifty ignition cycles have passed with no DTC(s) detected.

Diagnostic Aids

- It is very important that a thorough inspection of the wiring and connectors be performed. Failure to carefully and fully inspect wiring and connectors may result in misdiagnosis, causing part replacement with reappearance of the malfunction.
- An intermittent malfunction can be caused by poor connections, broken insulation, or a wire that is broken inside the insulation.

Test Description

The numbers below refer to step numbers on the diagnostic table.

3. Checks the resistance of the WSS.
5. Checks if the WSS CKTs are shorted together.

GC402980277800AX

Fig. 186 Code C1221: LH Front Wheel Speed Sensor Input Signal Is Zero (Part 1 of 2). DeVille & Seville

Circuit Description

The speed sensor used on this vehicle is a single point magnetic pickup. This sensor produces an AC signal that the EBTCM uses the frequency from to calculate the wheel speed.

Conditions for Setting the DTC

The DTC will set if one wheel speed = 0 and the other WSS are greater than 8 Km/h (5 mph) for 2.5 seconds.

Action Taken When the DTC Sets

A malfunction DTC is stored, ABS/TCS is disabled and the ABS and Traction Control Indicators are turned on.

Conditions for Clearing the DTC

- Condition for DTC is no longer present and scan tool clear DTC function is used.
- Fifty ignition cycles have passed with no DTC(s) detected.

Diagnostic Aids

- It is very important that a thorough inspection of the wiring and connectors be performed. Failure to carefully and fully inspect wiring and connectors may result in misdiagnosis, causing part replacement with reappearance of the malfunction.
- An intermittent malfunction can be caused by poor connections, broken insulation, or a wire that is broken inside the insulation.

Test Description

The numbers below refer to step numbers on the diagnostic table.

3. Checks the resistance of the WSS.
5. Checks if the WSS CKTs are shorted together.

GC402980277900AX

Fig. 187 Code C1222: RH Front Wheel Speed Sensor Input Signal Is Zero (Part 1 of 2). DeVille & Seville

Step	Action	Value(s)	Yes	No
1	Was the Diagnostic System Check performed?	—	*Go to Step 2*	Go to *Diagnostic System Check*
2	1. Inspect the WSS wiring and connectors for damage. 2. Inspect WSS for looseness or damage. Is physical damage of sensor evident?	—	*Go to Step 7*	*Go to Step 3*
3	1. Disconnect the WSS at the sensor pigtail. 2. Using *J 39200* DMM, measure the resistance between terminals A and B of the WSS. Is the resistance within the range specified in the value(s) column?	850-1350Ω	*Go to Step 4*	*Go to Step 7*
4	1. With *J 39200* DMM still connected, select the mV AC scale. 2. Spin the wheel as fast as you can by hand while monitoring the AC output. Is the AC voltage within the range specified in the value(s) column?	Above 100 mV	*Go to Step 5*	*Go to Step 7*
5	1. Disconnect the EBTCM harness connector. 2. Install *J 39700* Universal Pinout Box using the *J 39700-25* cable adapter to the EBTCM harness connector only. 3. Using *J 39200* DMM, measure resistance between terminals 14 and 30 of the *J 39700*. Is the resistance within the range specified in the value(s) column?	OL (Infinite)	*Go to Step 6*	*Go to Step 8*
6	1. Reconnect all connectors. 2. Carefully test drive vehicle above 24 Km/h (15 mph) for at least 30 seconds while monitoring a scan tool. Does DTC reset as a current DTC?	—	*Go to Step 9*	Go to *Diagnostic System Check*
7	Replace wheel speed sensor. Is the repair complete?	—	*Go to Step 10*	—
8	Repair short between CKT(s) 833 and 872. Is the repair complete?	—	*Go to Step 10*	—
9	Replace EBTCM. Is the replacement complete?	—	*Go to Step 10*	—
10	Carefully test drive vehicle above 24 Km/h (15 mph) while monitoring a scan tool for at least 30 seconds. Does the DTC set as a current DTC?	—	*Go to Step 2*	Go to *Diagnostic System Check*

GC402980277900BX

Fig. 187 Code C1222: RH Front Wheel Speed Sensor Input Signal Is Zero (Part 2 of 2). DeVille & Seville

Circuit Description

The speed sensor used on this vehicle is a single point magnetic pickup. This sensor produces an AC signal that the EBTCM uses the frequency from to calculate the wheel speed.

Conditions for Setting the DTC

The DTC will set if one wheel speed = 0 and the other WSS are greater than 8 Km/h (5 mph) for 2.5 seconds.

Action Taken When the DTC Sets

Malfunction DTC is stored, ABS/TCS is disabled and the ABS and Traction Control Indicators are turned on.

Conditions for Clearing the DTC

- Condition for DTC is no longer present and scan tool clear DTC function is used.
- Fifty ignition cycles have passed with no DTC(s) detected.

Diagnostic Aids

- It is very important that a thorough inspection of the wiring and connectors be performed. Failure to carefully and fully inspect wiring and connectors may result in misdiagnosis, causing part replacement with reappearance of the malfunction.
- An intermittent malfunction can be caused by poor connections, broken insulation, or a wire that is broken inside the insulation.

Test Description

The numbers below refer to step numbers on the diagnostic table.

3. Checks the resistance of the WSS.
5. Checks if the WSS CKTs are shorted together.

GC402980278000AX

Fig. 188 Code C1223: LH Front Wheel Speed Sensor Input Signal Is Zero (Part 1 of 2). DeVille & Seville

Circuit Description

The speed sensor used on this vehicle is a single point magnetic pickup. This sensor produces an AC signal that the EBTCM uses the frequency from to calculate the wheel speed.

Conditions for Setting the DTC

The DTC will set if one wheel speed = 0 and the other WSS are greater than 8 Km/h (5 mph) for 2.5 seconds.

Action Taken When the DTC Sets

A malfunction DTC is stored, ABS/TCS is disabled and the ABS and Traction Control Indicators are turned on.

Conditions for Clearing the DTC

- Condition for DTC is no longer present and scan tool clear DTC function is used.
- Fifty ignition cycles have passed with no DTC(s) detected.

Diagnostic Aids

- It is very important that a thorough inspection of the wiring and connectors be performed. Failure to carefully and fully inspect wiring and connectors may result in misdiagnosis, causing part replacement with reappearance of the malfunction.
- An intermittent malfunction can be caused by poor connections, broken insulation, or a wire that is broken inside the insulation.

Test Description

The numbers below refer to step numbers on the diagnostic table.

3. Checks the resistance of the WSS.
5. Checks if the WSS CKTs are shorted together.

GC402980278100AX

Fig. 189 Code C1224: RH Rear Wheel Speed Sensor Input Signal Is Zero (Part 1 of 2). DeVille & Seville

Step	Action	Value(s)	Yes	No
1	Was the Diagnostic System Check performed?	—	*Go to Step 2*	Go to *Diagnostic System Check*
2	1. Inspect the WSS wiring and connectors for damage. 2. Inspect WSS for looseness or damage. Is physical damage of sensor evident?	—	*Go to Step 7*	*Go to Step 3*
3	1. Disconnect the WSS at the sensor pigtail. 2. Using *J 39200* DMM, measure the resistance between terminals A and B of the WSS. Is the resistance within the range specified in the value(s) column?	850-1350Ω	*Go to Step 4*	*Go to Step 7*
4	1. With *J 39200* DMM still connected, select the mV AC scale. 2. Spin the wheel as fast as you can by hand while monitoring the AC output. Is the AC voltage within the range specified in the value(s) column?	Above 100 mV	*Go to Step 5*	*Go to Step 7*
5	1. Disconnect the EBTCM harness connector. 2. Install *J 39700* Universal Pinout Box using the *J 39700-25* cable adapter to the EBTCM harness connector only. 3. Using *J 39200* DMM, measure resistance between terminals 13 and 29 of the *J 39700*. Is the resistance within the range specified in the value(s) column?	OL (Infinite)	*Go to Step 6*	*Go to Step 8*
6	1. Reconnect all connectors. 2. Carefully test drive vehicle above 24 Km/h (15 mph) for at least 30 seconds while monitoring a scan tool. Does DTC reset as a current DTC?	—	*Go to Step 9*	Go to *Diagnostic System Check*
7	Replace wheel speed sensor. Is the repair complete?	—	*Go to Step 10*	—
8	Repair short between CKT(s) 882 and 883. Is the repair complete?	—	*Go to Step 10*	—
9	Replace EBTCM. Is the replacement complete?	—	*Go to Step 10*	—
10	Carefully test drive vehicle above 24 Km/h (15 mph) while monitoring a scan tool for at least 30 seconds. Does the DTC set as a current DTC?	—	*Go to Step 2*	Go to *Diagnostic System Check*

GC402980278100BX

Fig. 189 Code C1224: RH Rear Wheel Speed Sensor Input Signal Is Zero (Part 2 of 2). DeVille & Seville

Step	Action	Value(s)	Yes	No
1	Was the Diagnostic System Check performed?	—	*Go to Step 2*	Go to *Diagnostic System Check*
2	1. Inspect the WSS wiring and connectors for damage. 2. Inspect WSS for looseness or damage. Is physical damage of sensor evident?	—	*Go to Step 7*	*Go to Step 3*
3	1. Disconnect the WSS at the sensor pigtail. 2. Using *J 39200* DMM, measure the resistance between terminals A and B of the WSS. Is the resistance within the range specified in the value(s) column?	850-1350Ω	*Go to Step 4*	*Go to Step 7*
4	1. With *J 39200* DMM still connected, select the mV AC scale. 2. Spin the wheel as fast as you can by hand while monitoring the AC output. Is the AC voltage within the range specified in the value(s) column?	Above 100 mV	*Go to Step 5*	*Go to Step 7*
5	1. Disconnect the EBTCM harness connector. 2. Install *J 39700* Universal Pinout Box using the *J 39700-25* cable adapter to the EBTCM harness connector only. 3. Using *J 39200* DMM, measure resistance between terminals 12 and 28 of the *J 39700*. Is the resistance within the range specified in the value(s) column?	OL (Infinite)	*Go to Step 6*	*Go to Step 8*
6	1. Reconnect all connectors. 2. Carefully test drive vehicle above 24 Km/h (15 mph) for at least 30 seconds while monitoring a scan tool. Does DTC reset as a current DTC?	—	*Go to Step 9*	Go to *Diagnostic System Check*
7	Replace wheel speed sensor. Is the repair complete?	—	*Go to Step 10*	—
8	Repair short between CKT(s) 884 and 885. Is the repair complete?	—	*Go to Step 10*	—
9	Replace EBTCM. Is the replacement complete?	—	*Go to Step 10*	—
10	Carefully test drive vehicle above 24 Km/h (15 mph) while monitoring a scan tool for at least 30 seconds. Does the DTC set as a current DTC?	—	*Go to Step 2*	Go to *Diagnostic System Check*

GC402980278000BX

Fig. 188 Code C1223: LH Front Wheel Speed Sensor Input Signal Is Zero (Part 2 of 2). DeVille & Seville

Circuit Description

The speed sensor used on this vehicle is a single point magnetic pickup. This sensor produces an AC signal that the EBTCM uses the frequency from to calculate the wheel speed.

Conditions for Setting the DTC

The DTC can be set anytime the brake is not depressed and no wheel speed sensor hardware DTC(s) are present, and the EBTCM sees a wheel speed variation of more than 14 Km/h (9 mph) for 2.5 seconds.

Action Taken When the DTC Sets

A malfunction DTC is stored, ABS/TCS is disabled and the ABS and Traction Control Indicators are turned on.

Conditions for Clearing the DTC

- Condition for DTC is no longer present and scan tool clear DTC function is used.
- Fifty ignition cycles have passed with no DTC(s) detected.

Diagnostic Aids

- It is very important that a thorough inspection of the wiring and connectors be performed. Failure to carefully and fully inspect wiring and connectors may result in misdiagnosis, causing part replacement with reappearance of the malfunction.
- An intermittent malfunction can be caused by poor connections, broken insulation, or a wire that is broken inside the insulation.

Test Description

The numbers below refer to step numbers on the diagnostic table.

3. Checks the resistance of the WSS.
5. Checks if the WSS CKTs are shorted together.

GC402980278200AX

Fig. 190 Code C1225: LH Front Excessive Wheel Speed Variation (Part 1 of 2). DeVille & Seville

Step	Action	Value(s)	Yes	No
1	Was the Diagnostic System Check performed?	—	*Go to Step 2*	Go to *Diagnostic System Check*
2	1. Inspect the WSS wiring and connectors for damage. 2. Inspect WSS for looseness or damage. Is physical damage of sensor evident?	—	*Go to Step 7*	*Go to Step 3*
3	1. Disconnect the WSS at the sensor pigtail. 2. Using *J 39200* DMM, measure the resistance between terminals A and B of the WSS. Is the resistance within the range specified in the value(s) column?	850-1350Ω	*Go to Step 4*	*Go to Step 7*
4	1. With *J 39200* DMM still connected, select the mV AC scale. 2. Spin the wheel as fast as you can by hand while monitoring the AC output. Is the AC voltage within the range specified in the value(s) column?	Above 100 mV	*Go to Step 5*	*Go to Step 7*
5	1. Disconnect the EBTCM harness connector. 2. Install *J 39700* Universal Pinout Box using the *J 39700-25* cable adapter to the EBTCM harness connector only. 3. Using *J 39200* DMM, measure resistance between terminals 15 and 31 of the *J 39700*. Is the resistance within the range specified in the value(s) column?	OL (Infinite)	*Go to Step 6*	*Go to Step 8*
6	1. Reconnect all connectors. 2. Carefully test drive vehicle above 24 Km/h (15 mph) for at least 30 seconds while monitoring a scan tool. Does DTC reset as a current DTC?	—	*Go to Step 9*	Go to *Diagnostic System Check*
7	Replace wheel speed sensor. Is the repair complete?	—	*Go to Step 10*	—
8	Repair short between CKT(s) 873 and 830. Is the repair complete?	—	*Go to Step 10*	—
9	Replace EBTCM. Is the replacement complete?	—	*Go to Step 10*	—
10	Carefully test drive vehicle above 24 Km/h (15 mph) while monitoring a scan tool for at least 30 seconds. Does the DTC set as a current DTC?	—	*Go to Step 2*	Go to *Diagnostic System Check*

GC402980278200BX

Fig. 190 Code C1225: LH Front Excessive Wheel Speed Variation (Part 2 of 2). DeVille & Seville

Step	Action	Value(s)	Yes	No
1	Was the Diagnostic System Check performed?	—	*Go to Step 2*	Go to *Diagnostic System Check*
2	1. Inspect the WSS wiring and connectors for damage. 2. Inspect WSS for looseness or damage. Is physical damage of sensor evident?	—	*Go to Step 7*	*Go to Step 3*
3	1. Disconnect the WSS at the sensor pigtail. 2. Using *J 39200* DMM, measure the resistance between terminals A and B of the WSS. Is the resistance within the range specified in the value(s) column?	850-1350Ω	*Go to Step 4*	*Go to Step 7*
4	1. With *J 39200* DMM still connected, select the mV AC scale. 2. Spin the wheel as fast as you can by hand while monitoring the AC output. Is the AC voltage within the range specified in the value(s) column?	Above 100 mV	*Go to Step 5*	*Go to Step 7*
5	1. Disconnect the EBTCM harness connector. 2. Install *J 39700* Universal Pinout Box using the *J 39700-25* cable adapter to the EBTCM harness connector only. 3. Using *J 39200* DMM, measure resistance between terminals 14 and 30 of the *J 39700*. Is the resistance within the range specified in the value(s) column?	OL (Infinite)	*Go to Step 6*	*Go to Step 8*
6	1. Reconnect all connectors. 2. Carefully test drive vehicle above 24 Km/h (15 mph) for at least 30 seconds while monitoring a scan tool. Does DTC reset as a current DTC?	—	*Go to Step 9*	Go to *Diagnostic System Check*
7	Replace wheel speed sensor. Is the repair complete?	—	*Go to Step 10*	—
8	Repair short between CKT(s) 833 and 872. Is the repair complete?	—	*Go to Step 10*	—
9	Replace EBTCM. Is the replacement complete?	—	*Go to Step 10*	—
10	Carefully test drive vehicle above 24 Km/h (15 mph) while monitoring a scan tool for at least 30 seconds. Does the DTC set as a current DTC?	—	*Go to Step 2*	Go to *Diagnostic System Check*

GC402980278300BX

Fig. 191 Code C1226: RH Front Excessive Wheel Speed Variation (Part 2 of 2). DeVille & Seville

Circuit Description

The speed sensor used on this vehicle is a single point magnetic pickup. This sensor produces an AC signal that the EBTCM uses the frequency from to calculate the wheel speed.

Conditions for Setting the DTC

The DTC can be set anytime the brake is not depressed and no wheel speed sensor hardware DTC(s) are present, and the EBTCM sees a wheel speed variation of more than 14 Km/h (9 mph) for 2.5 seconds.

Action Taken When the DTC Sets

A malfunction DTC is stored, ABS/TCS is disabled and the ABS and Traction Control Indicators are turned on.

Conditions for Clearing the DTC

- Condition for DTC is no longer present and scan tool clear DTC function is used.
- Fifty ignition cycles have passed with no DTC(s) detected.

Diagnostic Aids

- It is very important that a thorough inspection of the wiring and connectors be performed. Failure to carefully and fully inspect wiring and connectors may result in misdiagnosis, causing part replacement with reappearance of the malfunction.
- An intermittent malfunction can be caused by poor connections, broken insulation, or a wire that is broken inside the insulation.

Test Description

The numbers below refer to step numbers on the diagnostic table.

3. Checks the resistance of the WSS.
5. Checks if the WSS CKTs are shorted together.

GC402980278300AX

Fig. 191 Code C1226: RH Front Excessive Wheel Speed Variation (Part 1 of 2). DeVille & Seville

Circuit Description

The speed sensor used on this vehicle is a single point magnetic pickup. This sensor produces an AC signal that the EBTCM uses the frequency from to calculate the wheel speed.

Conditions for Setting the DTC

The DTC can be set anytime the brake is not depressed and no wheel speed sensor hardware DTC(s) are present, and the EBTCM sees a wheel speed variation of more than 14 Km/h (9 mph) for 2.5 seconds.

Action Taken When the DTC Sets

A malfunction DTC is stored, ABS/TCS is disabled and the ABS and Traction Control Indicators are turned on.

Conditions for Clearing the DTC

- Condition for DTC is no longer present and scan tool clear DTC function is used.
- Fifty ignition cycles have passed with no DTC(s) detected.

Diagnostic Aids

- It is very important that a thorough inspection of the wiring and connectors be performed. Failure to carefully and fully inspect wiring and connectors may result in misdiagnosis, causing part replacement with reappearance of the malfunction.
- An intermittent malfunction can be caused by poor connections, broken insulation, or a wire that is broken inside the insulation.

Test Description

The numbers below refer to step numbers on the diagnostic table.

3. Checks the resistance of the WSS.
5. Checks if the WSS CKTs are shorted together.

GC402980278400AX

Fig. 192 Code C1227: LH Rear Excessive Wheel Speed Variation (Part 1 of 2). DeVille & Seville

Step	Action	Value(s)	Yes	No
1	Was the Diagnostic System Check performed?	—	*Go to Step 2*	Go to *Diagnostic System Check*
2	1. Inspect the WSS wiring and connectors for damage. 2. Inspect WSS for looseness or damage. Is physical damage of sensor evident?	—	*Go to Step 7*	*Go to Step 3*
3	1. Disconnect the WSS at the sensor pigtail. 2. Using *J 39200* DMM, measure the resistance between terminals A and B of the WSS. Is the resistance within the range specified in the value(s) column?	850-1350Ω	*Go to Step 4*	*Go to Step 7*
4	1. With *J 39200* DMM still connected, select the mV AC scale. 2. Spin the wheel as fast as you can by hand while monitoring the AC output. Is the AC voltage within the range specified in the value(s) column?	Above 100 mV	*Go to Step 5*	*Go to Step 7*
5	1. Disconnect the EBTCM harness connector. 2. Install *J 39700* Universal Pinout Box using the *J 39700-25* cable adapter to the EBTCM harness connector only. 3. Using *J 39200* DMM, measure resistance between terminals 12 and 28 of the *J 39700*. Is the resistance within the range specified in the value(s) column?	OL (Infinite)	*Go to Step 6*	*Go to Step 8*
6	1. Reconnect all connectors. 2. Carefully test drive vehicle above 24 Km/h (15 mph) for at least 30 seconds while monitoring a scan tool. Does DTC reset as a current DTC?	—	*Go to Step 9*	Go to *Diagnostic System Check*
7	Replace wheel speed sensor. Is the repair complete?	—	*Go to Step 10*	—
8	Repair short between CKT(s) 884 and 885. Is the repair complete?	—	*Go to Step 10*	—
9	Replace EBTCM. Is the replacement complete?	—	*Go to Step 10*	—
10	Carefully test drive vehicle above 24 Km/h (15 mph) while monitoring a scan tool for at least 30 seconds. Does the DTC set as a current DTC?	—	*Go to Step 2*	Go to *Diagnostic System Check*

GC402980278400BX

Fig. 192 Code C1227: LH Rear Excessive Wheel Speed Variation (Part 2 of 2). DeVille & Seville

Circuit Description

The speed sensor used on this vehicle is a single point magnetic pickup. This sensor produces an AC signal that the EBTCM uses the frequency from to calculate the wheel speed.

Conditions for Setting the DTC

The DTC can be set anytime the brake is not depressed and no wheel speed sensor hardware DTC(s) are present, and the EBTCM sees a wheel speed variation of more than 14 Km/h (9 mph) for 2.5 seconds.

Action Taken When the DTC Sets

A malfunction DTC is stored, ABS/TCS is disabled and the ABS and Traction Control Indicators are turned on.

Conditions for Clearing the DTC

- Condition for DTC is no longer present and scan tool clear DTC function is used.
- Fifty ignition cycles have passed with no DTC(s) detected.

Diagnostic Aids

- It is very important that a thorough inspection of the wiring and connectors be performed. Failure to carefully and fully inspect wiring and connectors may result in misdiagnosis, causing part replacement with reappearance of the malfunction.
- An intermittent malfunction can be caused by poor connections, broken insulation, or a wire that is broken inside the insulation.

Test Description

The numbers below refer to step numbers on the diagnostic table.

3. Checks the resistance of the WSS.
5. Checks if the WSS CKTs are shorted together.

GC402980278500AX

Fig. 193 Code C1228: RH Rear Excessive Wheel Speed Variation (Part 1 of 2). DeVille & Seville

Step	Action	Value(s)	Yes	No
1	Was the Diagnostic System Check performed?	—	*Go to Step 2*	Go to *Diagnostic System Check*
2	1. Inspect the WSS wiring and connectors for damage. 2. Inspect WSS for looseness or damage. Is physical damage of sensor evident?	—	*Go to Step 7*	*Go to Step 3*
3	1. Disconnect the WSS at the sensor pigtail. 2. Using *J 39200* DMM, measure the resistance between terminals A and B of the WSS. Is the resistance within the range specified in the value(s) column?	850-1350Ω	*Go to Step 4*	*Go to Step 7*
4	1. With *J 39200* DMM still connected, select the mV AC scale. 2. Spin the wheel as fast as you can by hand while monitoring the AC output. Is the AC voltage within the range specified in the value(s) column?	Above 100 mV	*Go to Step 5*	*Go to Step 7*
5	1. Disconnect the EBTCM harness connector. 2. Install *J 39700* Universal Pinout Box using the *J 39700-25* cable adapter to the EBTCM harness connector only. 3. Using *J 39200* DMM, measure resistance between terminals 13 and 29 of the *J 39700*. Is the resistance within the range specified in the value(s) column?	OL (Infinite)	*Go to Step 6*	*Go to Step 8*
6	1. Reconnect all connectors. 2. Carefully test drive vehicle above 24 Km/h (15 mph) for at least 30 seconds while monitoring a scan tool. Does DTC reset as a current DTC?	—	*Go to Step 9*	Go to *Diagnostic System Check*
7	Replace wheel speed sensor. Is the repair complete?	—	*Go to Step 10*	—
8	Repair short between CKT(s) 882 and 883. Is the repair complete?	—	*Go to Step 10*	—
9	Replace EBTCM. Is the replacement complete?	—	*Go to Step 10*	—
10	Carefully test drive vehicle above 24 Km/h (15 mph) while monitoring a scan tool for at least 30 seconds. Does the DTC set as a current DTC?	—	*Go to Step 2*	Go to *Diagnostic System Check*

GC402980278500BX

Fig. 193 Code C1228: RH Rear Excessive Wheel Speed Variation (Part 2 of 2). DeVille & Seville

Circuit Description

The speed sensor used on this vehicle is a single point magnetic pickup. This sensor produces an AC signal that the EBTCM uses the frequency from to calculate the wheel speed.

Conditions for Setting the DTC

The DTC can be set any time the ignition is in the ON position, and the EBTCM senses an open, a short to ground, or a short to battery.

Action Taken When the DTC Sets

A malfunction DTC is stored, ABS/TCS is disabled and the ABS and Traction Control Indicators are turned on.

Conditions for Clearing the DTC

- Condition for DTC is no longer present and scan tool clear DTC function is used.
- Fifty ignition cycles have passed with no DTC(s) detected.

Diagnostic Aids

- It is very important that a thorough inspection of the wiring and connectors be performed. Failure to carefully and fully inspect wiring and connectors may result in misdiagnosis, causing part replacement with reappearance of the malfunction.
- An intermittent malfunction can be caused by poor connections, broken insulation, or a wire that is broken inside the insulation.

Test Description

The numbers below refer to step numbers on the diagnostic table.

4. Checks for an open in the WSS or WSS CKT.
12. Checks for a short to ground in the WSS or WSS CKT.
19. Checks for a short to voltage in the WSS CKT.
21. Checks for a short to voltage in the WSS CKT.

GC402980278700AX

Fig. 194 Code C1232: LH Front Wheel Speed Circuit Open Or Shorted (Part 1 of 4). Seville

Step	Action	Value(s)	Yes	No
1	Was the Diagnostic System Check performed?	—	*Go to Step 2*	Go to *Diagnostic System Check*
2	1. Inspect the WSS wiring and connectors for damage. 2. Inspect the WSS for looseness or damage. Is physical damage of sensor evident?	—	*Go to Step 3*	*Go to Step 4*
3	Repair as necessary. Is the repair complete?	—	Go to *Diagnostic System Check*	—
4	1. Turn the ignition switch to the OFF position. 2. Disconnect the EBTCM. 3. Install the *J 39700* Universal Pinout Box using the *J 39700-25* cable adapter to the EBTCM harness connector only. 4. Using *J 39200* DMM, measure the resistance between terminals 15 and 31 of *J 39700*. Is the resistance within the range specified in the value(s) column?	850–1350Ω	*Go to Step 12*	*Go to Step 5*
5	1. Disconnect the LF Wheel Speed Sensor. 2. Using *J 39200* DMM, measure the resistance between terminals A and B of the Wheel Speed Sensor Connector. Is the resistance within the range specified in the value(s) column?	850-1350Ω	*Go to Step 6*	*Go to Step 11*
6	1. Connect a jumper between the LF Wheel Speed Sensor harness connector terminal A and ground. 2. Using *J 39200* DMM, measure the resistance between terminals 31 and B of *J 39700*. Is the resistance within the range specified in the value(s) column?	0 - 5Ω	*Go to Step 8*	*Go to Step 7*
7	Repair CKT 830 for an open or high resistance. Is the repair complete?	—	Go to *Diagnostic System Check*	—
8	1. Connect a jumper between the LF Wheel Speed Sensor harness connector terminal B and ground. 2. Using *J 39200* DMM, measure the resistance between terminals 15 and B of *J 39700*. Is the resistance within the range specified in the value(s) column?	0-5Ω	*Go to Step 10*	*Go to Step 9*
9	Repair CKT 873 for an open or high resistance. Is the repair complete?	—	Go to *Diagnostic System Check*	—
10	Malfunction is intermittent. Inspect all connectors and harnesses for damage that may result in an open or high resistance when connected. Is the repair complete?	—	Go to *Diagnostic System Check*	—

GC402980278700BX

Fig. 194 Code C1232: LH Front Wheel Speed Circuit Open Or Shorted (Part 2 of 4). Seville

Step	Action	Value(s)	Yes	No
11	Replace the Wheel Speed Sensor. Is the replacement complete?	—	Go to *Diagnostic System Check*	—
12	Using *J 39200* DMM, measure the resistance between terminals 15 and B of *J 39700*. Is the resistance within the range specified in the value(s) column?	OL (infinite)	*Go to Step 19*	*Go to Step 13*
13	1. Disconnect the LF Wheel Speed Sensor. 2. Using *J 39200* DMM, measure the resistance between terminal A and ground of the Wheel Speed Sensor Connector. Is the resistance within the range specified in the value(s) column?	OL (infinite)	*Go to Step 14*	*Go to Step 11*
14	Using *J 39200* DMM, measure the resistance between terminals 31 and B of *J 39700*. Is the resistance within the range specified in the value(s) column?	OL (infinite)	*Go to Step 16*	*Go to Step 15*
15	Repair CKT 830 for a short to ground. Is the repair complete?	—	Go to *Diagnostic System Check*	—
16	Using *J 39200* DMM, measure the resistance between terminals 15 and B of *J 39700*. Is the resistance within the range specified in the value(s) column?	OL (infinite)	*Go to Step 17*	*Go to Step 18*
17	Malfunction is intermittent. Inspect all connectors and harnesses for damage that may result in a short to ground when connected. Is the repair complete?	—	Go to *Diagnostic System Check*	—
18	Repair CKT 873 for a short to ground. F Is the repair complete?	—	Go to *Diagnostic System Check*	—
19	1. Disconnect the LF Wheel Speed Sensor. 2. Turn the ignition switch to the ON position, engine off. 3. Using *J 39200* DMM, measure the voltage at terminal 31 of *J 39700*. Is the voltage within the range specified in the value(s) column?	Above 1V	*Go to Step 20*	*Go to Step 21*
20	Repair CKT 830 for a short to voltage. Is the repair complete?	—	Go to *Diagnostic System Check*	—

GC402980278700CX

Fig. 194 Code C1232: LH Front Wheel Speed Circuit Open Or Shorted (Part 3 of 4). Seville

Step	Action	Value(s)	Yes	No
21	Using *J 39200* DMM, measure the voltage at terminal 15 of *J 39700*. Is the voltage within the range specified in the value(s) column?	Above 1V	Go to Step 22	Go to Step 23
22	Repair CKT 873 for a short to voltage. Is the repair complete?	—	Go to Diagnostic System Check	—
23	Replace the EBTCM. Is the replacement complete?	—	Go to Diagnostic System Check	—

GC402980278700DX

Fig. 194 Code C1232: LH Front Wheel Speed Circuit Open Or Shorted (Part 4 of 4). Seville

Step	Action	Value(s)	Yes	No
1	Did you perform the ABS Diagnostic System Check?	—	Go to Step 2	Go to A Diagnostic System Check - ABS
2	1. Inspect the wheel speed sensor wiring and connectors for damage. 2. Inspect the wheel speed sensor for looseness or damage. Is physical damage of the sensor or wiring evident?	—	Go to Step 3	Go to Step 4
3	Repair as necessary. Did you complete the repair?	—	Go to A Diagnostic System Check - ABS	—
4	1. Turn OFF the ignition. 2. Disconnect the EBTCM harness connector. 3. Install the *J 39700* universal pinout box using the *J 39700-25* cable adapter to the EBTCM harness connector only. 4. Use a *J 39200* DMM in order to measure the resistance between the *J 39700* terminal 15 and terminal 31. Is the resistance within the specified range?	850–1350 Ω	Go to Step 12	Go to Step 5
5	1. Disconnect the wheel speed sensor connector. 2. Use a *J 39200* DMM in order to measure the resistance between the wheel speed sensor connector terminal A and terminal B. Is the resistance within the specified range?	850–1350 Ω	Go to Step 6	Go to Step 11
6	1. Connect a jumper from the wheel speed sensor harness connector terminal B to ground. 2. Use a *J 39200* DMM in order to measure the resistance between the *J 39700* terminal 31 and terminal B. Is the resistance less than the specified value?	5 Ω	Go to Step 8	Go to Step 7
7	Repair the open or high resistance in CKT 830. Did you complete the repair?	—	Go to A Diagnostic System Check - ABS	—
8	1. Connect a jumper from the wheel speed sensor harness connector terminal A to ground. 2. Use *J 39200* DMM in order to measure the resistance between the *J 39700* terminal 15 and terminal B. Is the resistance less than the specified value?	5 Ω	Go to Step 10	Go to Step 9
9	Repair the open or high resistance in CKT 873. Did you complete the repair?	—	Go to A Diagnostic System Check - ABS	—
10	Malfunction is intermittent. Inspect all connectors and harnesses for damage that may result in an open or high resistance when connected. Did you complete the repair?	—	Go to A Diagnostic System Check - ABS	—
11	Replace the wheel speed sensor. Did you complete the repair?	—	Go to A Diagnostic System Check - ABS	—

GC4029903917020X

Fig. 195 Code C1232: LH Front Wheel Speed Circuit Open Or Shorted (Part 2 of 3). DeVille

Circuit Description

The wheel speed sensor used on this vehicle is a single point magnetic pickup. This sensor produces an AC signal that the EBTCM uses the frequency from to calculate the wheel speed.

Conditions for Setting the DTC

All of the following conditions occur:
- The ignition is ON.
- The EBTCM detects one of the following conditions:
  - An open
  - A short to ground
  - A short to voltage

Action Taken When the DTC Sets

- A malfunction DTC is stored.
- The ABS/TCS/Stabilitrak® is disabled.
- The ABS indicator is turned ON.
- The TRACTION CONTROL indicator is turned ON.
- The DIC displays the SERVICE STABILITY SYS message.

Conditions for Clearing the DTC

- The condition for DTC is no longer present and you used scan tool Clear DTCs function.
- The condition for DTC is no longer present and you used the On-Board Clear DTCs function.
- The EBTCM does not detect the DTC in 50 drive cycles.

Diagnostic Aids

- It is very important that a thorough inspection of the wiring and connectors be performed. Failure to carefully and fully inspect wiring and connectors may result in misdiagnosis, causing part replacement with reappearance of the malfunction.
- An intermittent malfunction can be caused by poor connections, broken insulation, or a wire that is broken inside the insulation.
- If an intermittent malfunction exists, refer to *Intermittents and Poor Connections*

Test Description

The numbers below refer to step numbers on the diagnostic table.

4. This step checks for an open in the wheel speed sensor or circuit.
12. This step checks for a short to ground in the wheel speed sensor or circuit.
19. This step checks for a short to voltage in the wheel speed sensor high circuit.
21. This step checks for a short to voltage in the wheel speed sensor low circuit.

GC4029903917010X

Fig. 195 Code C1232: LH Front Wheel Speed Circuit Open Or Shorted (Part 1 of 3). DeVille

Step	Action	Value(s)	Yes	No
12	Use a *J 39200* DMM in order to measure the resistance between the *J 39700* terminal 15 and terminal B. Is the resistance within the specified range?	OL (Infinite)	Go to Step 19	Go to Step 13
13	1. Disconnect the wheel speed sensor connector. 2. Use a *J 39200* DMM in order to measure the resistance between the left front wheel speed sensor connector terminal A and ground. Is the resistance within the specified range?	OL (Infinite)	Go to Step 14	Go to Step 11
14	Use a *J 39200* DMM in order to measure the resistance between the *J 39700* terminal 31 and terminal B. Is the resistance within the specified range?	OL (Infinite)	Go to Step 16	Go to Step 15
15	Repair the short to ground in CKT 830. Did you complete the repair?	—	Go to A Diagnostic System Check - ABS	—
16	Use a *J 39200* DMM in order to measure the resistance between the *J 39700* terminal 15 and terminal B. Is the resistance within the specified range?	OL (Infinite)	Go to Step 17	Go to Step 18
17	Malfunction is intermittent. Inspect all connectors and harnesses for damage that may result in a short to ground when connected. Refer to *Intermittents and Poor Connections* Did you complete the repair?	—	Go to A Diagnostic System Check - ABS	—
18	Repair the short to ground in CKT 873. Did you complete the repair?	—	Go to A Diagnostic System Check - ABS	—
19	1. Disconnect the wheel speed sensor connector. 2. Turn ON the ignition, with the engine OFF. 3. Use a *J 39200* DMM in order to measure the voltage at the *J 39700* terminal 31. Is the voltage greater than the specified value?	1 V	Go to Step 20	Go to Step 21
20	Repair the short to voltage in CKT 830. Did you complete the repair?	—	Go to A Diagnostic System Check - ABS	—
21	Use a *J 39200* DMM in order to measure the voltage at the *J 39700* terminal 15. Is the voltage greater than the specified value?	1 V	Go to Step 22	Go to Step 23
22	Repair the short to voltage in CKT 873. Did you complete the repair?	—	Go to A Diagnostic System Check - ABS	—
23	Replace the EBTCM. Did you complete the repair?	—	Go to A Diagnostic System Check - ABS	—

GC4029903917030X

Fig. 195 Code C1232: LH Front Wheel Speed Circuit Open Or Shorted (Part 3 of 3). DeVille

Circuit Description

The speed sensor used on this vehicle is a single point magnetic pickup. This sensor produces an AC signal that the EBTCM uses the frequency from to calculate the wheel speed.

Conditions for Setting the DTC

The DTC can be set any time the ignition is in the ON position, and the EBTCM senses an open, a short to ground, or a short to battery.

Action Taken When the DTC Sets

A malfunction DTC is stored, ABS/TCS is disabled and the ABS and Traction Control Indicators are turned on.

Conditions for Clearing the DTC

- Condition for DTC is no longer present and scan tool clear DTC function is used.
- Fifty ignition cycles have passed with no DTC(s) detected.

Diagnostic Aids

- It is very important that a thorough inspection of the wiring and connectors be performed. Failure to carefully and fully inspect wiring and connectors may result in misdiagnosis, causing part replacement with reappearance of the malfunction.
- An intermittent malfunction can be caused by poor connections, broken insulation, or a wire that is broken inside the insulation.

Test Description

The numbers below refer to step numbers on the diagnostic table.

4. Checks for an open in the WSS or WSS CKT.
12. Checks for a short to ground in the WSS or WSS CKT.
19. Checks for a short to voltage in the WSS CKT.
21. Checks for a short to voltage in the WSS CKT.

GC402980278800AX

Fig. 196 Code C1233: RH Front Wheel Speed Circuit Open Or Shorted (Part 1 of 4). Seville

Step	Action	Value(s)	Yes	No
1	Was the Diagnostic System Check performed?	—	*Go to Step 2*	Go to *Diagnostic System Check*
2	1. Inspect the WSS wiring and connectors for damage. 2. Inspect the WSS for looseness or damage. Is physical damage of sensor evident?	—	*Go to Step 3*	*Go to Step 4*
3	Repair as necessary. Is the repair complete?	—	Go to *Diagnostic System Check*	—
4	1. Turn the ignition switch to the OFF position. 2. Disconnect the EBTCM. 3. Install the *J 39700* Universal Pinoput Box using the *J 39700-25* cable adapter to the EBTCM harness connector only. 4. Using *J 39200* DMM, measure the resistance between terminals 14 and 30 of *J 39700.* Is the resistance within the range specified in the value(s) column?	850-1350Ω	*Go to Step 12*	*Go to Step 5*
5	1. Disconnect the RF Wheel Speed Sensor. 2. Using *J 39200* DMM, measure the resistance between terminals A and B of the Wheel Speed Sensor Connector. Is the resistance within the range specified in the value(s) column?	850-1350Ω	*Go to Step 6*	*Go to Step 11*
6	1. Connect a jumper between the RF Wheel Speed Sensor harness connector terminal A and ground. 2. Using *J 39200* DMM, measure the resistance between terminals 30 and B of *J 39700.* Is the resistance within the range specified in the value(s) column?	0-5Ω	*Go to Step 8*	*Go to Step 7*
7	Repair CKT 872 for an open or high resistance. Is the repair complete?	—	Go to *Diagnostic System Check*	—
8	1. Connect a jumper between the RF Wheel Speed Sensor harness connector terminal B and ground. 2. Using *J 39200* DMM, measure the resistance between terminals 14 and B of *J 39700.* Is the resistance within the range specified in the value(s) column?	0-5Ω	*Go to Step 10*	*Go to Step 9*
9	Repair CKT 833 for an open or high resistance. Is the repair complete?	—	Go to *Diagnostic System Check*	—
10	Malfunction is intermittent. Inspect all connectors and harnesses for damage that may result in an open or high resistance when connected. Is the repair complete?	—	Go to *Diagnostic System Check*	—

GC402980278800BX

Fig. 196 Code C1233: RH Front Wheel Speed Circuit Open Or Shorted (Part 2 of 4). Seville

Step	Action	Value(s)	Yes	No
11	Replace the Wheel Speed Sensor. Is the replacement complete?	—	Go to *Diagnostic System Check*	—
12	Using *J 39200* DMM, measure the resistance between terminals 14 and B of *J 39700.* Is the resistance within the range specified in the value(s) column?	OL (infinite)	*Go to Step 19*	*Go to Step 13*
13	1. Disconnect the RF Wheel Speed Sensor. 2. Using *J 39200* DMM, measure the resistance between terminal A and ground of the Wheel Speed Sensor Connector. Is the resistance within the range specified in the value(s) column?	OL (infinite)	*Go to Step 14*	*Go to Step 11*
14	Using *J 39200* DMM, measure the resistance between terminals 30 and B of *J 39700.* Is the resistance within the range specified in the value(s) column?	OL (infinite)	*Go to Step 16*	*Go to Step 15*
15	Repair CKT 872 for a short to ground. Is the repair complete?	—	Go to *Diagnostic System Check*	—
16	Using *J 39200* DMM, measure the resistance between terminals 14 and B of *J 39700.* Is the resistance within the range specified in the value(s) column?	OL (infinite)	*Go to Step 17*	*Go to Step 18*
17	Malfunction is intermittent. Inspect all connectors and harnesses for damage that may result in a short to ground when connected. Is the repair complete?	—	Go to *Diagnostic System Check*	—
18	Repair CKT 833 for a short to ground. Is the repair complete?	—	Go to *Diagnostic System Check*	—
19	1. Disconnect the RF Wheel Speed Sensor. 2. Turn the ignition switch to the ON position, engine off. 3. Using *J 39200* DMM, measure the voltage at terminal 30 of *J 39700.* Is the voltage within the range specified in the value(s) column?	Above 1V	*Go to Step 20*	*Go to Step 21*
20	Repair CKT 872 for a short to voltage. Is the repair complete?	—	Go to *Diagnostic System Check*	—
21	Using *J 39200* DMM, measure the voltage at terminal 14 of *J 39700.* Is the voltage within the range specified in the value(s) column?	Above 1V	*Go to Step 22*	*Go to Step 23*

GC402980278800CX

Fig. 196 Code C1233: RH Front Wheel Speed Circuit Open Or Shorted (Part 3 of 4). Seville

Step	Action	Value(s)	Yes	No
22	Repair CKT 833 for a short to voltage. Is the repair complete?	—	Go to *Diagnostic System Check*	—
23	Replace the EBTCM. Is the replacement complete?	—	Go to *Diagnostic System Check*	—

GC402980278800DX

Fig. 196 Code C1233: RH Front Wheel Speed Circuit Open Or Shorted (Part 4 of 4). Seville

Circuit Description

The wheel speed sensor used on this vehicle is a single point magnetic pickup. This sensor produces an AC signal that the EBTCM uses the frequency from to calculate the wheel speed.

Conditions for Setting the DTC

All of the following conditions occur:

- The ignition is ON.
- The EBTCM detects one of the following conditions:
  - An open
  - A short to ground
  - A short to voltage

Action Taken When the DTC Sets

- A malfunction DTC is stored.
- The ABS/TCS/Stabilitrak® is disabled.
- The ABS indicator is turned ON.
- The TRACTION CONTROL indicator is turned ON.
- The DIC displays the SERVICE STABILITY SYS message.

Conditions for Clearing the DTC

- The condition for DTC is no longer present and you used scan tool Clear DTCs function.
- The condition for DTC is no longer present and you used the On-Board Clear DTCs function.
- The EBTCM does not detect the DTC in 50 drive cycles.

Diagnostic Aids

- It is very important that a thorough inspection of the wiring and connectors be performed. Failure to carefully and fully inspect wiring and connectors may result in misdiagnosis, causing part replacement with reappearance of the malfunction.
- An intermittent malfunction can be caused by poor connections, broken insulation, or a wire that is broken inside the insulation.
- If an intermittent malfunction exists, refer to *Intermittents and Poor Connections*

Test Description

The numbers below refer to step numbers on the diagnostic table.

4. This step checks for an open in the wheel speed sensor or circuit.
12. This step checks for a short to ground in the wheel speed sensor or circuit.
19. This step checks for a short to voltage in the wheel speed sensor high circuit.
21. This step checks for a short to voltage in the wheel speed sensor low circuit

GC4029903918010X

Fig. 197 Code C1233: RH Front Wheel Speed Circuit Open Or Shorted (Part 1 of 3). DeVille

Step	Action	Value(s)	Yes	No
1	Did you perform the ABS Diagnostic System Check?	—	Go to *Step 2*	Go to *A Diagnostic System Check - ABS*
2	1. Inspect the wheel speed sensor wiring and connectors for damage. 2. Inspect the wheel speed sensor for looseness or damage. Is physical damage of the sensor or wiring evident?	—	Go to *Step 3*	Go to *Step 4*
3	Repair as necessary. Did you complete the repair?	—	Go to *A Diagnostic System Check - ABS*	—
4	1. Turn OFF the ignition. 2. Disconnect the EBTCM harness connector. 3. Install the *J 39700* universal pinout box using the *J 39700-25* cable adapter to the EBTCM harness connector only. 4. Use a *J 39200* DMM in order to measure the resistance between the *J 39700* terminal 14 and terminal 30. Is the resistance within the specified range?	850–1350 Ω	Go to *Step 12*	Go to *Step 5*
5	1. Disconnect the wheel speed sensor connector. 2. Use a *J 39200* DMM in order to measure the resistance between the wheel speed sensor connector terminal A and terminal B. Is the resistance within the range specified?	850–1350 Ω	Go to *Step 6*	Go to *Step 11*
6	1. Connect a jumper from the wheel speed sensor harness connector terminal B to ground. 2. Use a *J 39200* DMM in order to measure the resistance between the *J 39700* terminal 30 and terminal B. Is the resistance within less than the specified value?	5 Ω	Go to *Step 8*	Go to *Step 7*
7	Repair the open or high resistance in CKT 872. Did you complete the repair?	—	Go to *A Diagnostic System Check - ABS*	—
8	1. Connect a jumper from the wheel speed sensor harness connector terminal A to ground. 2. Use a *J 39200* DMM in order to measure the resistance between the *J 39700* terminal 14 and terminal B. Is the resistance within less than the specified value?	5 Ω	Go to *Step 10*	Go to *Step 9*
9	Repair the open or high resistance in CKT 833. Did you complete the repair?	—	Go to *A Diagnostic System Check - ABS*	—
10	Malfunction is intermittent. Inspect all connectors and harnesses for damage that may result in an open or high resistance when connected. Did you complete the repair?	—	Go to *A Diagnostic System Check - ABS*	—
11	Replace the wheel speed sensor. Did you complete the repair?	—	Go to *A Diagnostic System Check - ABS*	—

GC4029903918020X

Fig. 197 Code C1233: RH Front Wheel Speed Circuit Open Or Shorted (Part 2 of 3). DeVille

Step	Action	Value(s)	Yes	No
12	Use a *J 39200* DMM in order to measure the resistance between the *J 39700* terminal 14 and terminal B. Is the resistance within the specified range?	OL (Infinite)	Go to *Step 19*	Go to *Step 13*
13	1. Disconnect the wheel speed sensor connector. 2. Use a *J 39200* DMM in order to measure the resistance between the wheel speed sensor connector terminal A and ground. Is the resistance within the specified range?	OL (Infinite)	Go to *Step 14*	Go to *Step 11*
14	Use a *J 39200* DMM in order to measure the resistance between the *J 39700* terminal 30 and terminal B. Is the resistance within the specified range?	OL (Infinite)	Go to *Step 16*	Go to *Step 15*
15	Repair the short to ground in CKT 872. Did you complete the repair?	—	Go to *A Diagnostic System Check - ABS*	—
16	Use a *J 39200* DMM in order to measure the resistance between the *J 39700* terminal 14 and terminal B. Is the resistance within the specified range?	OL (Infinite)	Go to *Step 17*	Go to *Step 18*
17	Malfunction is intermittent. Inspect all connectors and harnesses for damage that may result in a short to ground when connected. Refer to *Intermittents and Poor Connections* Did you complete the repair?	—	Go to *A Diagnostic System Check - ABS*	—
18	Repair the short to ground in CKT 833. Did you complete the repair?	—	Go to *A Diagnostic System Check - ABS*	—
19	1. Disconnect the wheel speed sensor. 2. Turn ON the ignition, with the engine OFF. 3. Use a *J 39200* DMM in order to measure the voltage at the *J 39700* terminal 30. Is the voltage greater than the specified value?	1 V	Go to *Step 20*	Go to *Step 21*
20	Repair the short to voltage in CKT 872. Did you complete the repair?	—	Go to *A Diagnostic System Check - ABS*	—
21	Use a *J 39200* DMM in order to measure the voltage at the *J 39700* terminal 14. Is the voltage greater than the specified value?	1 V	Go to *Step 22*	Go to *Step 23*
22	Repair the short to voltage in CKT 833. Did you complete the repair?	—	Go to *A Diagnostic System Check - ABS*	—
23	Replace the EBTCM. Did you complete the repair?	—	Go to *A Diagnostic System Check - ABS*	—

GC4029903918030X

Fig. 197 Code C1233: RH Front Wheel Speed Circuit Open Or Shorted (Part 3 of 3). DeVille

Step	Action	Value(s)	Yes	No
1	Was the Diagnostic System Check performed?	—	Go to *Step 2*	Go to *Diagnostic System Check*
2	1. Inspect the WSS wiring and connectors for damage. 2. Inspect the WSS for looseness or damage. Is physical damage of sensor evident?	—	Go to *Step 3*	Go to *Step 4*
3	Repair as necessary. Is the repair complete?	—	Go to *Diagnostic System Check*	—
4	1. Turn the ignition switch to the OFF position. 2. Disconnect the EBTCM. 3. Install the *J 39700* Universal Pinout Box using the *J 39700-25* cable adapter to the EBTCM harness connector only. 4. Using *J 39200* DMM, measure the resistance between terminals 12 and 28 of *J 39700*. Is the resistance within the range specified in the value(s) column?	850-1350Ω	Go to *Step 12*	Go to *Step 5*
5	1. Disconnect the LR Wheel Speed Sensor. 2. Using *J 39200* DMM, measure the resistance between terminals A and B of the Wheel Speed Sensor Connector. Is the resistance within the range specified in the value(s) column?	850-1350Ω	Go to *Step 6*	Go to *Step 11*
6	Using *J 39200* DMM, measure the resistance between terminals 12 of *J 39700* and A of the LR Wheel Speed Sensor harness connector. Is the resistance within the range specified in the value(s) column?	0-5Ω	Go to *Step 8*	Go to *Step 7*
7	Repair CKT 884 for an open or high resistance. Is the repair complete?	—	Go to *Diagnostic System Check*	—
8	Using *J 39200* DMM, measure the resistance between terminals 28 of *J 39700* and B of the LR Wheel Speed Sensor harness connector. Is the resistance within the range specified in the value(s) column?	0-5Ω	Go to *Step 10*	Go to *Step 9*
9	Repair CKT 885 for an open or high resistance. Is the repair complete?	—	Go to *Diagnostic System Check*	—
10	Malfunction is intermittent. Inspect all connectors and harnesses for damage that may result in an open or high resistance when connected. Is the repair complete?	—	Go to *Diagnostic System Check*	—

GC402980278900BX

Fig. 198 Code C1234: LH Rear Wheel Speed Circuit Open Or Shorted (Part 2 of 4). Seville

Circuit Description

The speed sensor used on this vehicle is a single point magnetic pickup. This sensor produces an AC signal that the EBTCM uses the frequency from to calculate the wheel speed.

Conditions for Setting the DTC

The DTC can be set any time the ignition is in the ON position, and the EBTCM senses an open, a short to ground, or a short to battery.

Action Taken When the DTC Sets

A malfunction DTC is stored, ABS/TCS is disabled and the ABS and Traction Control Indicators are turned on.

Conditions for Clearing the DTC

- Condition for DTC is no longer present and scan tool clear DTC function is used.
- Fifty ignition cycles have passed with no DTC(s) detected.

Diagnostic Aids

- It is very important that a thorough inspection of the wiring and connectors be performed. Failure to carefully and fully inspect wiring and connectors may result in misdiagnosis, causing part replacement with reappearance of the malfunction.
- An intermittent malfunction can be caused by poor connections, broken insulation, or a wire that is broken inside the insulation.

Test Description

The numbers below refer to step numbers on the diagnostic table.

4. Checks for an open in the WSS or WSS CKT.
12. Checks for a short to ground in the WSS or WSS CKT.
19. Checks for a short to voltage in the WSS CKT.
21. Checks for a short to voltage in the WSS CKT.

GC402980278900AX

Fig. 198 Code C1234: LH Rear Wheel Speed Circuit Open Or Shorted (Part 1 of 4). Seville

Step	Action	Value(s)	Yes	No
11	Replace the Wheel Speed Sensor. Is the replacement complete?	—	Go to *Diagnostic System Check*	—
12	Using *J 39200* DMM, measure the resistance between terminals 28 and B of *J 39700*. Is the resistance within the range specified in the value(s) column?	OL (infinite)	Go to *Step 19*	Go to *Step 13*
13	1. Disconnect the LR Wheel Speed Sensor. 2. Using *J 39200* DMM, measure the resistance between terminal A and ground of the Wheel Speed Sensor Connector. Is the resistance within the range specified in the value(s) column?	OL (infinite)	Go to *Step 14*	Go to *Step 11*
14	Using *J 39200* DMM, measure the resistance between terminals 12 and B of *J 39700*. Is the resistance within the range specified in the value(s) column?	OL (infinite)	Go to *Step 16*	Go to *Step 15*
15	Repair CKT 884 for a short to ground. Is the repair complete?	—	Go to *Diagnostic System Check*	—
16	Using *J 39200* DMM, measure the resistance between terminals 28 and B of *J 39700*. Is the resistance within the range specified in the value(s) column?	OL (infinite)	Go to *Step 17*	Go to *Step 18*
17	Malfunction is intermittent. Inspect all connectors and harnesses for damage that may result in a short to ground when connected. Is the repair complete?	—	Go to *Diagnostic System Check*	—
18	Repair CKT 885 for a short to ground. Is the repair complete?	—	Go to *Diagnostic System Check*	—
19	1. Disconnect the LR Wheel Speed Sensor. 2. Turn the ignition switch to the ON position, engine off. 3. Using *J 39200* DMM, measure the voltage at terminal 12 of *J 39700*. Is the voltage within the range specified in the value(s) column?	Above 1V	Go to *Step 20*	Go to *Step 21*
20	Repair CKT 884 for a short to voltage. Is the repair complete?	—	Go to *Diagnostic System Check*	—
21	Using *J 39200* DMM, measure the voltage at terminal 28 of *J 39700*. Is the voltage within the range specified in the value(s) column?	Above 1V	Go to *Step 22*	Go to *Step 23*

GC402980278900CX

Fig. 198 Code C1234: LH Rear Wheel Speed Circuit Open Or Shorted (Part 3 of 4). Seville

Step	Action	Value(s)	Yes	No
22	Repair CKT 885 for a short to voltage. Is the repair complete?	—	Go to *Diagnostic System Check*	—
23	Replace the EBTCM. Is the replacement complete?	—	Go to *Diagnostic System Check*	—

GC402980278900DX

Fig. 198 Code C1234: LH Rear Wheel Speed Circuit Open Or Shorted (Part 4 of 4). Seville

Circuit Description

The wheel speed sensor used on this vehicle is a single point magnetic pickup. This sensor produces an AC signal that the EBTCM uses the frequency from to calculate the wheel speed.

Conditions for Setting the DTC

All of the following conditions occur:

- The ignition is ON.
- The EBTCM detects one of the following conditions:
  - An open
  - A short to ground
  - A short to voltage

Action Taken When the DTC Sets

- A malfunction DTC is stored.
- The ABS/TCS/Stabilitrak® is disabled.
- The ABS indicator is turned ON.
- The TRACTION CONTROL indicator is turned ON.
- The DIC displays the SERVICE STABILITY SYS message.

Conditions for Clearing the DTC

- The condition for DTC is no longer present and you used scan tool Clear DTCs function.
- The condition for DTC is no longer present and you used the On-Board Clear DTCs function.
- The EBTCM does not detect the DTC in 50 drive cycles.

Diagnostic Aids

- It is very important that a thorough inspection of the wiring and connectors be performed. Failure to carefully and fully inspect wiring and connectors may result in misdiagnosis, causing part replacement with reappearance of the malfunction.
- An intermittent malfunction can be caused by poor connections, broken insulation, or a wire that is broken inside the insulation.
- If an intermittent malfunction exists, refer to *Intermittents and Poor Connections*

Test Description

The numbers below refer to step numbers on the diagnostic table.

4. This step checks for an open in the wheel speed sensor or circuit.
12. This step checks for a short to ground in the wheel speed sensor or circuit.
19. This step checks for a short to voltage in the wheel speed sensor high circuit.
21. This step checks for a short to voltage in the wheel speed sensor low circuit.

GC4029903919010X

Fig. 199 Code C1234: LH Rear Wheel Speed Circuit Open Or Shorted (Part 1 of 3). DeVille

Step	Action	Value(s)	Yes	No
1	Did you perform the ABS Diagnostic System Check?	—	Go to *Step 2*	Go to *A Diagnostic System Check - ABS*
2	1. Inspect the wheel speed sensor wiring and connectors for damage. 2. Inspect the wheel speed sensor for looseness or damage. Is physical damage of the sensor or wiring evident?	—	Go to *Step 3*	Go to *Step 4*
3	Repair as necessary. Did you complete the repair?	—	Go to *A Diagnostic System Check - ABS*	—
4	1. Turn OFF the ignition. 2. Disconnect the EBTCM harness connector. 3. Install the *J 39700* universal pinout box using the *J 39700-25* cable adapter to the EBTCM harness connector only. 4. Disconnect the wheel speed sensor connector. 5. Use a *J 39200* DMM in order to measure the resistance between the *J 39700* terminal 12 and terminal 28. Is the resistance within the specified range?	850–1350 Ω	Go to *Step 12*	Go to *Step 5*
5	1. Disconnect the wheel speed sensor connector. 2. Use a *J 39200* DMM in order to measure the resistance between the wheel speed sensor connector terminal A and terminal B. Is the resistance within the specified range?	850–1350 Ω	Go to *Step 6*	Go to *Step 11*
6	1. Connect a jumper from the wheel speed sensor harness connector terminal A to ground. 2. Use a *J 39200* DMM in order to measure the resistance between the *J 39700* terminal 12 and terminal B. Is the resistance less than the specified value?	5 Ω	Go to *Step 8*	Go to *Step 7*
7	Repair the open or high resistance in CKT 884. Did you complete the repair?	—	Go to *A Diagnostic System Check - ABS*	—
8	1. Connect a jumper from the wheel speed sensor harness connector terminal B to ground. 2. Use *J 39200* DMM in order to measure the resistance between the *J 39700* terminal 28 and terminal B. Is the resistance less than the specified value?	5 Ω	Go to *Step 10*	Go to *Step 9*
9	Repair the open or high resistance in CKT 885. Did you complete the repair?	—	Go to *A Diagnostic System Check - ABS*	—
10	Malfunction is intermittent. Inspect all connectors and harnesses for damage that may result in an open or high resistance when connected. Refer to *Intermittents and Poor Connections* Did you complete the repair?	—	Go to *A Diagnostic System Check - ABS*	—

GC4029903919020X

Fig. 199 Code C1234: LH Rear Wheel Speed Circuit Open Or Shorted (Part 2 of 3). DeVille

Step	Action	Value(s)	Yes	No
11	Replace the wheel speed sensor. Did you complete the repair?	—	Go to *A Diagnostic System Check - ABS*	—
12	Use a *J 39200* DMM in order to measure the resistance between the *J 39700* terminal 28 and terminal B. Is the resistance within the specified range?	OL (Infinite)	Go to *Step 19*	Go to *Step 13*
13	1. Disconnect the wheel speed sensor connector. 2. Use a *J 39200* DMM in order to measure the resistance between the wheel speed sensor connector terminal A and ground. Is the resistance within the specified range?	OL (Infinite)	Go to *Step 14*	Go to *Step 11*
14	Use a *J 39200* DMM in order to measure the resistance between the *J 39700* terminal 12 and terminal B. Is the resistance within the specified range?	OL (Infinite)	Go to *Step 16*	Go to *Step 15*
15	Repair the short to ground in CKT 884. Did you complete the repair?	—	Go to *A Diagnostic System Check - ABS*	—
16	Use a *J 39200* DMM in order to measure the resistance between the *J 39700* terminal 28 and terminal B. Is the resistance within the specified range?	OL (Infinite)	Go to *Step 17*	Go to *Step 18*
17	Malfunction is intermittent. Inspect all connectors and harnesses for damage that may result in a short to ground when connected. Refer to *Intermittents and Poor Connections* Did you complete the repair?	—	Go to *A Diagnostic System Check - ABS*	—
18	Repair the short to ground in CKT 885. Did you complete the repair?	—	Go to *A Diagnostic System Check - ABS*	—
19	1. Disconnect the wheel speed sensor connector. 2. Turn ON the ignition, with the engine OFF. 3. Using a *J 39200* DMM, measure the voltage at the *J 39700* terminal 12. Is the voltage greater than the specified value?	1 V	Go to *Step 20*	Go to *Step 21*
20	Repair the short to voltage in CKT 884. Did you complete the repair?	—	Go to *A Diagnostic System Check - ABS*	—
21	Use a *J 39200* DMM in order to measure the voltage at the *J 39700* terminal 28. Is the voltage greater than the specified value?	1 V	Go to *Step 22*	Go to *Step 23*
22	Repair the short to voltage in CKT 885. Did you complete the repair?	—	Go to *A Diagnostic System Check - ABS*	—
23	Replace the EBTCM. Did you complete the repair?	—	Go to *A Diagnostic System Check - ABS*	—

GC4029903919030X

Fig. 199 Code C1234: LH Rear Wheel Speed Circuit Open Or Shorted (Part 3 of 3). DeVille

Circuit Description

The speed sensor used on this vehicle is a single point magnetic pickup. This sensor produces an AC signal that the EBTCM uses the frequency from to calculate the wheel speed.

Conditions for Setting the DTC

The DTC can be set any time the ignition is in the ON position, and the EBTCM senses an open, a short to ground, or a short to battery.

Action Taken When the DTC Sets

A malfunction DTC is stored, ABS/TCS is disabled and the ABS and Traction Control Indicators are turned on.

Conditions for Clearing the DTC

- Condition for DTC is no longer present and scan tool clear DTC function is used.
- Fifty ignition cycles have passed with no DTC(s) detected.

Diagnostic Aids

- It is very important that a thorough inspection of the wiring and connectors be performed. Failure to carefully and fully inspect wiring and connectors may result in misdiagnosis, causing part replacement with reappearance of the malfunction.
- An intermittent malfunction can be caused by poor connections, broken insulation, or a wire that is broken inside the insulation.

Test Description

The numbers below refer to step numbers on the diagnostic table.

4. Checks for an open in the WSS or WSS CKT.
12. Checks for a short to ground in the WSS or WSS CKT.
19. Checks for a short to voltage in the WSS CKT.
21. Checks for a short to voltage in the WSS CKT.

GC402980279000AX

Fig. 200 Code C1235: RH Rear Wheel Speed Circuit Open Or Shorted (Part 1 of 3). Seville

Step	Action	Value(s)	Yes	No
1	Was the Diagnostic System Check performed?	—	Go to *Step 2*	Go to *Diagnostic System Check*
2	1. Inspect the WSS wiring and connectors for damage. 2. Inspect the WSS for looseness or damage. Is physical damage of sensor evident?	—	Go to *Step 3*	Go to *Step 4*
3	Repair as necessary. Is the repair complete?	—	Go to *Diagnostic System Check*	—
4	1. Turn the ignition switch to the OFF position. 2. Disconnect the EBTCM. 3. Install the *J 39700* Universal Pinout Box using the *J 39700-25* cable adapter to the EBTCM harness connector only. 4. Using *J 39200* DMM, measure the resistance between terminals 13 and 29 of *J 39700*. Is the resistance within the range specified in the value(s) column?	850-1350Ω	Go to *Step 12*	Go to *Step 5*
5	1. Disconnect the RR Wheel Speed Sensor. 2. Using *J 39200* DMM, measure the resistance between terminals A and B of the Wheel Speed Sensor Connector. Is the resistance within the range specified in the value(s) column?	850-1350Ω	Go to *Step 6*	Go to *Step 11*
6	Using *J 39200* DMM, measure the resistance between terminals 29 of *J 39700* and A of the RR Wheel Speed Sensor harness connector. Is the resistance within the range specified in the value(s) column?	0-5Ω	Go to *Step 8*	Go to *Step 7*
7	Repair CKT 882 for an open or high resistance. Is the repair complete?	—	Go to *Diagnostic System Check*	—
8	Using *J 39200* DMM, measure the resistance between terminals 13 of *J 39700* and B of the RR Wheel Speed Sensor harness connector. Is the resistance within the range specified in the value(s) column?	0-5Ω	Go to *Step 10*	Go to *Step 9*
9	Repair CKT 883 for an open or high resistance. Is the repair complete?	—	Go to *Diagnostic System Check*	—
10	Malfunction is intermittent. Inspect all connectors and harnesses for damage that may result in an open or high resistance when connected. Is the repair complete?	—	Go to *Diagnostic System Check*	—
11	Replace the Wheel Speed Sensor. Is the replacement complete?	—	Go to *Diagnostic System Check*	—

GC402980279000BX

Fig. 200 Code C1235: RH Rear Wheel Speed Circuit Open Or Shorted (Part 2 of 3). Seville

Step	Action	Value(s)	Yes	No
12	Using *J 39200* DMM, measure the resistance between terminals 13 and B of *J 39700*. Is the resistance within the range specified in the value(s) column?	OL (infinite)	Go to *Step 19*	Go to *Step 13*
13	1. Disconnect the RR Wheel Speed Sensor. 2. Using *J 39200* DMM, measure the resistance between terminal A and ground of the Wheel Speed Sensor Connector. Is the resistance within the range specified in the value(s) column?	OL (infinite)	Go to *Step 14*	Go to *Step 11*
14	Using *J 39200* DMM, measure the resistance between terminals 29 and B of *J 39700*. Is the resistance within the range specified in the value(s) column?	OL (infinite)	Go to *Step 16*	Go to *Step 15*
15	Repair CKT 882 for a short to ground. Is the repair complete?	—	Go to *Diagnostic System Check*	—
16	Using *J 39200* DMM, measure the resistance between terminals 13 and B of *J 39700*. Is the resistance within the range specified in the value(s) column?	OL (infinite)	Go to *Step 17*	Go to *Step 18*
17	Malfunction is intermittent. Inspect all connectors and harnesses for damage that may result in a short to ground when connected. Is the repair complete?	—	Go to *Diagnostic System Check*	—
18	Repair CKT 883 for a short to ground. Is the repair complete?	—	Go to *Diagnostic System Check*	—
19	1. Disconnect the RR Wheel Speed Sensor. 2. Turn the ignition switch to the ON position, engine off. 3. Using *J 39200* DMM, measure the voltage at terminal 29 of *J 39700*. Is the voltage within the range specified in the value(s) column?	Above 1V	Go to *Step 20*	Go to *Step 21*
20	Repair CKT 882 for a short to voltage. Is the repair complete?	—	Go to *Diagnostic System Check*	—
21	Using *J 39200* DMM, measure the voltage at terminal 13 of *J 39700*. Is the voltage within the range specified in the value(s) column?	Above 1V	Go to *Step 22*	Go to *Step 23*
22	Repair CKT 883 for a short to voltage. Is the repair complete?	—	Go to *Diagnostic System Check*	—
23	Replace the EBTCM. Is the replacement complete?	—	Go to *Diagnostic System Check*	—

GC402980279000CX

Fig. 200 Code C1235: RH Rear Wheel Speed Circuit Open Or Shorted (Part 3 of 3). Seville

Circuit Description

The wheel speed sensor used on this vehicle is a single point magnetic pickup. This sensor produces an AC signal that the EBTCM uses the frequency from to calculate the wheel speed.

Conditions for Setting the DTC

All of the following conditions occur:

- The ignition is ON.
- The EBTCM detects one of the following conditions:
  - An open
  - A short to ground
  - A short to voltage

Action Taken When the DTC Sets

- A malfunction DTC is stored.
- The ABS/TCS/Stabilitrak® is disabled.
- The ABS indicator is turned ON.
- The TRACTION CONTROL indicator is turned ON.
- The DIC displays the SERVICE STABILITY SYS message.

Conditions for Clearing the DTC

- The condition for DTC is no longer present and you used scan tool Clear DTCs function.
- The condition for DTC is no longer present and you used the On-Board Clear DTCs function.
- The EBTCM does not detect the DTC in 50 drive cycles.

Diagnostic Aids

- It is very important that a thorough inspection of the wiring and connectors be performed. Failure to carefully and fully inspect wiring and connectors may result in misdiagnosis, causing part replacement with reappearance of the malfunction.
- An intermittent malfunction can be caused by poor connections, broken insulation, or a wire that is broken inside the insulation.
- If an intermittent malfunction exists, refer to *Intermittents and Poor Connections*

Test Description

The numbers below refer to step numbers on the diagnostic table.

4. This step checks for an open in the wheel speed sensor or circuit.
12. This step checks for a short to ground in the wheel speed sensor or circuit.
19. This step checks for a short to voltage in the wheel speed sensor high circuit.
21. This step checks for a short to voltage in the wheel speed low sensor circuit.

GC4029903920010X

Fig. 201 Code C1235: RH Rear Wheel Speed Circuit Open Or Shorted (Part 1 of 3). DeVille

Step	Action	Value(s)	Yes	No
1	Did you perform the ABS Diagnostic System Check?	—	Go to *Step 2*	Go to *A Diagnostic System Check - ABS*
2	1. Inspect the wheel speed sensor wiring and connectors for damage. 2. Inspect the wheel speed sensor for looseness or damage. Is physical damage of the sensor or wiring evident?	—	Go to *Step 3*	Go to *Step 4*
3	Repair as necessary. Did you complete the repair?	—	Go to *A Diagnostic System Check - ABS*	—
4	1. Turn OFF the ignition. 2. Disconnect the EBTCM harness connector. 3. Install the *J 39700* universal pinout box using the *J 39700-25* cable adapter to the EBTCM harness connector only. 4. Use a *J 39200* DMM in order to measure the resistance between the *J 39700* terminal 13 and terminal 29. Is the resistance within the specified range?	850–1350 Ω	Go to *Step 12*	Go to *Step 5*
5	1. Disconnect the wheel speed sensor connector. 2. Use a *J 39200* DMM in order to measure the resistance between the wheel speed sensor connector terminal A and terminal B. Is the resistance within the specified range?	850–1350 Ω	Go to *Step 6*	Go to *Step 11*
6	1. Connect a jumper from the wheel speed sensor harness connector terminal B to ground. 2. Use a *J 39200* DMM in order to measure the resistance between the *J 39700* terminal 29 and terminal B. Is the resistance less than the specified value?	5 Ω	Go to *Step 8*	Go to *Step 7*
7	Repair the open or high resistance in CKT 882. Did you complete the repair?	—	Go to *A Diagnostic System Check - ABS*	—
8	1. Connect a jumper from the wheel speed sensor harness connector terminal A to ground. 2. Use *J 39200* DMM in order to measure the resistance between the *J 39700* terminal 13 and terminal B. Is the resistance less than the specified value?	5 Ω	Go to *Step 10*	Go to *Step 9*
9	Repair the open or high resistance in CKT 883. Did you complete the repair?	—	Go to *A Diagnostic System Check - ABS*	—
10	The malfunction is intermittent. Inspect all of the connectors and the harnesses for damage that may result in an open or high resistance when connected. Refer to *Intermittents and Poor Connections* Did you complete the repair?	—	Go to *A Diagnostic System Check - ABS*	—

GC4029903920020X

Fig. 201 Code C1235: RH Rear Wheel Speed Circuit Open Or Shorted (Part 2 of 3). DeVille

Step	Action	Value(s)	Yes	No
11	Replace the wheel speed sensor. Did you complete the repair?	—	Go to *A Diagnostic System Check - ABS*	—
12	Use a *J 39200* DMM in order to measure the resistance between the *J 39700* terminal 13 and terminal B. Is the resistance within the specified range?	OL (Infinite)	Go to *Step 19*	Go to *Step 13*
13	1. Disconnect the wheel speed sensor connector. 2. Use a *J 39200* DMM in order to measure the resistance between the wheel speed sensor connector terminal B and ground. Is the resistance within the specified range?	OL (Infinite)	Go to *Step 14*	Go to *Step 11*
14	Use a *J 39200* DMM, in order to measure the resistance between the *J 39700* terminal 29 and terminal B. Is the resistance within the specified range?	OL (Infinite)	Go to *Step 16*	Go to *Step 15*
15	Repair the short to ground in CKT 882. Did you complete the repair?	—	Go to *A Diagnostic System Check - ABS*	—
16	Use a *J 39200* DMM in order to measure the resistance between the *J 39700* terminal 13 and terminal B. Is the resistance within the specified range?	OL (Infinite)	Go to *Step 17*	Go to *Step 18*
17	The malfunction is intermittent. Inspect all of the connectors and the harnesses for damage that may result in a short to ground when connected. Refer to *Intermittents and Poor Connections* Did you complete the repair?	—	Go to *A Diagnostic System Check - ABS*	—
18	Repair the short to ground in CKT 883. Did you complete the repair?	—	Go to *A Diagnostic System Check - ABS*	—
19	1. Disconnect the wheel speed sensor connector. 2. Turn ON the ignition, with the engine OFF. 3. Use a *J 39200* DMM in order to measure the voltage at the *J 39700* terminal 29. Is the voltage greater than the specified value?	1 V	Go to *Step 20*	Go to *Step 21*
20	Repair the short to voltage in CKT 882. Did you complete the repair?	—	Go to *A Diagnostic System Check - ABS*	—
21	Use a *J 39200* DMM in order to measure the voltage at the *J 39700* terminal 13. Is the voltage greater than the specified value?	1 V	Go to *Step 22*	Go to *Step 23*
22	Repair the short to voltage in CKT 883. Did you complete the repair?	—	Go to *A Diagnostic System Check - ABS*	—
23	Replace the EBTCM. Did you complete the repair?	—	Go to *A Diagnostic System Check - ABS*	—

GC4029903920030X

Fig. 201 Code C1235: RH Rear Wheel Speed Circuit Open Or Shorted (Part 3 of 3). DeVille

Step	Action	Value(s)	Yes	No
1	Was the Diagnostic System Check performed?	—	Go to Step 2	Go to the Diagnostic System Check
2	1. Turn the ignition switch to the OFF position. 2. Disconnect EBTCM harness connector and inspect both the harness connector and the EBTCM connector for signs of corrosion or damage. Is there evidence of any corrosion or damage?	—	Go to Step 6	Go to Step 3
3	1. Install the J 39700 universal Pinout Box using the J 39700-25 cable adapter to the EBTCM harness connector only. 2. Using the J 39200, measure resistance between terminal B of the J 39700 and a good ground. Is the resistance within the range specified in the Value(s) column?	0 - 2 Ω	Go to Step 4	Go to Step 7
4	1. Install the J 39700 universal Pinout Box using the J 39700-25 cable adapter to the EBTCM and the EBTCM harness connector. 2. Measure voltage between terminals D and B of the J 39700. Is the voltage within the range specified in the Value(s) column?	Above 10 volts	Go to Step 5	Go to Battery
5	1. Turn the ignition switch to the RUN position; engine is OFF. 2. Measure voltage between terminals A and B of the J 39700. Is the voltage within the range specified in the Value(s) column?	Above 10 volts	Go to Step 8	Go to Battery
6	Repair as necessary. Is repair complete?	—	Go to the Diagnostic System Check	—
7	Repair CKT 1651 for an open. Is the repair complete?	—	Go to the Diagnostic System Check	—
8	Replace the EBTCM Is the replacement complete?	—	Go to the Diagnostic System Check	—

GC402970279100BX

Fig. 202 Code C1236: Low System Supply Voltage (Part 2 of 2). DeVille

Circuit Description

This circuit is used to monitor the voltage level available to the EBTCM. If the voltage drops below 10.5 V, full performance of the ABS/TCS cannot be guaranteed. During ABS/TCS operation, there are several current requirements that will cause battery voltage to drop. Because of this, voltage is monitored prior to ABS/TCS operation to indicate good charging system condition and also during ABS/TCS operation when voltage may drop significantly.

Condition For Setting The DTC

- DTC C1236 can only be set if the vehicle's speed is greater than 8 km/h (5 mph). If both the battery and ignition voltages are less than 10.5 V, a malfunction DTC will set.

Action Taken When the DTC Sets

- A malfunction DTC is stored, ABS/TCS is disabled, and the ABS and TRACTION CONTROL Indicator lamps are turned ON.

Conditions for Clearing the DTC

- Condition for DTC is no longer present and scan tool clear DTC function is used.
- Fifty start cycles have passed with no DTC(s) detected.

Diagnostic Aids

- It is very important that a thorough inspection of the wiring and connectors be performed. Failure to carefully and fully inspect wiring and connectors may result in misdiagnosis, causing part replacement with reappearance of the malfunction.
- An intermittent malfunction is most likely caused by a poor connection, rubbed through insulation, or a wire that is broken inside the insulation.

Test Description

The numbers below refer to step numbers on the diagnostic table.

3. Checks for a good ground.
5. Checks for battery voltage.

GC402970279100AX

Fig. 202 Code C1236: Low System Supply Voltage (Part 1 of 2). DeVille

Circuit Description

This circuit is used to monitor the voltage level available to the EBTCM. If the voltage drops below 10.5 volts, full performance of the ABS/TCS/Stabilitrak® is not guaranteed. During ABS/TCS/Stabilitrak® operation, several current requirements will cause a drop in battery voltage. Prior to ABS/TCS/Stabilitrak® operation, the circuit monitors voltage in order to indicate a good charging system condition. The circuit also monitors the voltage during ABS/TCS/Stabilitrak® operation, when the voltage may drop significantly

Conditions for Setting the DTC

All of the following conditions occur:

- The vehicle speed is greater than 8 km/h (5 mph).
- The battery positive voltage (B+) is less than 10.5 volts.
- The ignition voltage is less than 10.5 volts.

Action Taken When the DTC Sets

- A malfunction DTC is stored.
- The ABS/TCS/Stabilitrak® is disabled.
- The ABS indicator is turned ON.
- The TRACTION CONTROL indicator is turned ON.
- The DIC displays the SERVICE STABILITY SYS message.

Conditions for Clearing the DTC

- The condition for DTC is no longer present and you used scan tool Clear DTCs function.
- The condition for DTC is no longer present and you used the On-Board Clear DTCs function.
- The EBTCM does not detect the DTC in 50 drive cycles.

Diagnostic Aids

- It is very important that a thorough inspection of the wiring and connectors be performed. Failure to carefully and fully inspect wiring and connectors may result in misdiagnosis, causing part replacement with reappearance of the malfunction.
- An intermittent malfunction can be caused by poor connections, broken insulation, or a wire that is broke inside the insulation.
- If an intermittent malfunction exists refer to *Intermittents and Poor Connections*
- Check for other low voltage conditions.
- Test the charging system.

GC4029803891010X

Fig. 203 Code C1236: Low System Supply Voltage (Part 1 of 2). Seville

- Possible low voltage condition causes may include:
  - charging system malfunction
  - excessive battery draw
  - weak battery
  - faulty system ground

Test Description

The numbers below refer to step numbers on the diagnostic table.

4. Checks for a good ground.
6. Checks for battery voltage.

Step	Action	Value(s)	Yes	No
1	Did you perform the Diagnostic System Check?	—	Go to *Step 2*	Go to *Diagnostic System Check*
2	Check the charging system. Is the charging system OK?	—	Go to *Step 3*	*Charging System*
3	1. Turn OFF the ignition. 2. Disconnect the EBTCM harness connector. 3. Inspect both the harness connector and the EBTCM connector for signs of corrosion or damage. Is their evidence of any corrosion or damage?	—	Go to *Step 7*	Go to *Step 4*
4	1. Install the *J 39700* universal pinout box using the *J 39700-25* cable adapter between the EBTCM harness connector and the EBTCM. 2. Using a *J 39200* DMM, measure the resistance between the *J 39700* terminal B and a good ground. Is the resistance less than the specified value?	2 Ω	Go to *Step 5*	Go to *Step 8*
5	Measure the voltage between the *J 39700* terminals D and B. Is the voltage greater than the specified value?	10.5 V	Go to *Step 6*	*Battery Load Test*
6	1. Turn ON the ignition, with the engine OFF. 2. Measure the voltage between the *J 39700* terminals A and B. Is the voltage greater than the specified value?	10.5 V	Go to *Step 9*	*Battery Load Test*
7	Repair as necessary. Did you complete the repair?	—	Go to *Diagnostic System Check*	—
8	Repair the open in CKT 1150. Did you complete the repair?	—	Go to *Diagnostic System Check*	—
9	Replace the EBTCM. Did you complete the repair?	—	Go to *Diagnostic System Check*	—

GC4029803891020X

Fig. 203 Code C1236: Low System Supply Voltage (Part 2 of 2). Seville

Circuit Description

This circuit is designed to detect high vehicle voltage levels to the solenoid relay. High voltage may cause damage to the system.

Conditions for Setting the DTC

DTC C1237 can only be set if the vehicle's speed is greater than 8 km/h (5 mph). If the battery voltage is greater than 17 volts, a malfunction exists.

Action Taken When the DTC Sets

A malfunction DTC is stored, ABS/TCS is disabled and the ABS and Traction Control Indicators are turned on.

Conditions for Clearing the DTC

- Condition for DTC is no longer present and scan tool clear DTC function is used.
- Fifty ignition cycles have passed with no DTC(s) detected.

Diagnostic Aids

- Charging system problems resulting in higher voltage levels will cause DTC C1237 to set:

Test Description

The numbers below refer to step numbers on the diagnostic table.

2. Checks to see what the EBTCM is reading as the voltage.
3. Checks the actual battery voltage.

GC402980279200AX

Fig. 204 Code C1237: High System Supply Voltage (Part 1 of 2). DeVille & Seville

Step	Action	Value(s)	Yes	No
1	Was the Diagnostic System Check performed?	—	*Go to Step 2*	Go to *Diagnostic System Check*
2	1. Turn all accessories off. 2. Start engine. 3. Using the scan tool select ABS/TCS DATA LIST and monitor battery voltage while running engine at approximately 2000 RPM. Is the voltage within the range specified in the value(s) column?	Less than 17 V	*Go to Step 4*	*Go to Step 3*
3	Check actual battery voltage, using *J 39200* DMM, while running engine at approximately 2000 RPM. Is the voltage within the range specified in the value(s) column?	Less than 17 V	*Go to Step 4*	Inspect Starter and Charging System
4	Carefully test drive vehicle above 8 km/h (5 mph). Does DTC C1237 reset as a current DTC?	—	*Go to Step 5*	Go to *Diagnostic System Check*
5	Replace the EBTCM. Is repair complete?	—	Go to *Diagnostic System Check*	—

GC402980279200BX

Fig. 204 Code C1237: High System Supply Voltage (Part 2 of 2). DeVille & Seville

Circuit Description

The EBTCM monitors the following occurrences in order to calculate the brake rotor temperatures:

- Vehicle speed deceleration
- The ABS/TCS activation
- The brake lamp on times

When the brake rotor temperatures are exceeded, the following events occur:

- The TCS is disabled
- A DTC C1238 is set
- The TRACTION OFF indicator is turned on

If the brake usage is reduced during driving, the brake rotor cooling is calculated and the TCS is enabled.

Conditions for Setting the DTC

DTC C1238 could be set when either driven wheel estimated brake rotor temperature exceeds 375°C (700°F). If either driven wheel estimated brake rotor temperature has exceeded 375°C (700°F) during ABS or normal braking conditions, the code will not be set until the next TCS activation occurs. The code will not be set and TCS will not be disabled if both rotor estimated temperatures have cooled below 275°C (530°F) before the next TCS activation. If either driven wheel brake rotor temperatures has exceeded 375°C (700°F) during TCS then the code will be set immediately, but TCS will not be disabled until the end of the TCS event.

Action Taken When the DTC Sets

- A DTC C1238 is stored
- The TCS is disabled
- The TRACTION OFF indicator is turned on

Conditions for Clearing the DTC

- The condition for the DTC are no longer present and the scan tool clear DTC function is used
- 50 ignition cycles have passed with no DTCs detected

Diagnostic Aids

- The temperatures are estimated figures taken by the EBTCM
- The following conditions are other possible causes of this malfunction:
  - Excessive brake usage
  - Excessive TCS usage
  - A misadjusted or damaged stoplamp/BTSI switch.

Test Description

The numbers below refer to the step numbers on the diagnostic table.

3. This step reads the TCS status.

GC402980279300AX

Fig. 205 Code C1238: Brake Thermal Model Exceeded (Part 1 of 2). DeVille & Seville

Step	Action	Value(s)	Yes	No
1	Was the Diagnostic System Check performed?	—	*Go to Step 2*	Go to *Diagnostic System Check*
2	1. Turn the ignition switch to the RUN position with the engine off. 2. Using a Scan Tool, read the ABS/TCS DTCs. Are there any other DTCs?	—	Go to the appropriate DTC table	*Go to Step 3*
3	1. Allow the vehicle to cool for 30 minutes after driving. 2. Using a Scan Tool, enter the ABS Data List and read the TCS status. Is the BTM exceeded?	—	*Go to Step 4*	*Go to Step 5*
4	Replace the EBTCM. Is the replacement complete?	—	Go to *Diagnostic System Check*	—
5	Inspect the stoplamp switch for misadjustment. Is the switch misadjusted?	—	Inspect Stoplamp Switch Adjustment	Go to *Diagnostic System Check*

GC402980279300BX

Fig. 205 Code C1238: Brake Thermal Model Exceeded (Part 2 of 2). DeVille & Seville

Circuit Description

The Speed Dependent Steering System (Magna Steer®), incorporates its controller into the EBTCM. If one or both of the Magna Steer® actuator circuit wires should become open or shorted, a DTC C1241 will set.

Action Taken When the DTC Sets

- A malfunction DTC is stored.
- No ABS/TCS/ICCS indicator lamps or messages are turned ON.
- Magna Steer® is disabled.
- ABS/TCS/ICCS remains functional.
- SERVICE-STEERING SYSTEM message is turned ON.

GC402980279400OX

Fig. 206 Code C1241: Magnasteer Circuit Fault. DeVille & Seville

Circuit Description

The BPMV pump motor ground is supplied through a ground stud on the pump motor to a good ground.

Conditions for Setting the DTC

DTC C1242 can be set when the pump relay is commanded off. A malfunction exists if the pump motor ground CKT 350 resistance is greater than 6900 ohms.

Action Taken When the DTC Sets

A malfunction DTC is stored, ABS/TCS is disabled and the ABS and Traction Control indicators are turned on.

Conditions for Clearing the DTC

- Condition for DTC is no longer present and scan tool clear DTC function is used.
- Fifty ignition cycles have passed with no DTC(s) detected.

Diagnostic Aids

- It is very important that a thorough inspection of the wiring and connectors be performed. Failure to carefully and fully inspect wiring and connectors may result in misdiagnosis, causing part replacement with reappearance of the malfunction.
- An intermittent malfunction can be caused by poor connections, broken insulation, or a wire that is broken inside the insulation.

Test Description

The numbers below refer to step numbers on the diagnostic table.

2. Checks for good pump motor ground.
4. Checks for good pump motor ground through the BPMV.

GC402980279500AX

Fig. 207 Code C1242: BPMV Pump Motor Ground Circuit Open (Part 1 of 2). DeVille

Step	Action	Value(s)	Yes	No
1	Was the Diagnostic System Check performed?	—	*Go to Step 2*	Go to *Diagnostic System Check*
2	1. Turn the ignition switch to the OFF position. 2. Using *J 39200* DMM, measure resistance between the motor ground stud and a good chassis ground. Is the resistance within the range specified in the value(s) column?	0–2 Ω	*Go to Step 3*	*Go to Step 8*
3	1. Disconnect the EBTCM connector. 2. Remove the EBTCM from BPMV. 3. Inspect the EBTCM to BPMV connector for conditions which could cause intermittents, such as damage, corrosion, poor terminal contact, or presence of brake fluid. Is connector OK and cavity free of brake fluid?	—	*Go to Step 4*	*Go to Step 5*
4	Using *J 39200* DMM, measure resistance between BPMV internal connector terminal 8 and motor ground stud. Is the resistance within the range specified in the value(s) column?	0.2–10 Ω	*Go to Step 6*	*Go to Step 7*
5	1. If connector corrosion or damage is evident, replace BPMV and/or EBTCM as necessary. 2. If brake fluid is present, replace BPMV and EBTCM. Is the replacement complete?	—	Go to *Diagnostic System Check*	—
6	Replace the EBTCM. Is repair complete?	—	Go to *Diagnostic System Check*	—
7	Replace the BPMV. Is repair complete?	—	Go to *Diagnostic System Check*	—
8	Repair open or high resistance in CKT 350. Is repair complete?	—	Go to *Diagnostic System Check*	—

GC402980279500BX

Fig. 207 Code C1242: BPMV Pump Motor Ground Circuit Open (Part 2 of 2). DeVille

Circuit Description

The BPMV pump motor ground is supplied through a ground stud on the pump motor to a good ground.

Conditions for Setting the DTC

All of the following conditions occur:

- The pump relay is commanded OFF.
- The pump motor ground resistance is greater than 6900 ohms.

Action Taken When the DTC Sets

- A malfunction DTC is stored.
- The ABS/TCS/Stabilitrak® is disabled.
- The ABS indicator is turned ON.
- The TRACTION CONTROL indicator is turned ON.
- The DIC displays the SERVICE STABILITY SYS message.

Conditions for Clearing the DTC

- The condition for DTC is no longer present and you used scan tool Clear DTCs function.
- The condition for DTC is no longer present and you used the On-Board Clear DTCs function.
- The EBTCM does not detect the DTC in 50 drive cycles.

Diagnostic Aids

- It is very important that a thorough inspection of the wiring and connectors be performed. Failure to carefully and fully inspect wiring and connectors may result in misdiagnosis, causing part replacement with reappearance of the malfunction.
- An intermittent malfunction can be caused by poor connections, broken insulation, or a wire that is broken inside the insulation.
- If an intermittent malfunction exists, refer to *Intermittents and Poor Connections*

GC4029803892010X

Fig. 208 Code C1242: BPMV Pump Motor Ground Circuit Open (Part 1 of 2). Seville

Test Description

The numbers below refer to step numbers on the diagnostic table.

2. Checks for good pump motor ground.
4. Checks for good pump motor ground through the BPMV.

Step	Action	Value(s)	Yes	No
1	Did you perform the Diagnostic System Check?	—	Go to *Step 2*	Go to *Diagnostic System Check*
2	1. Turn OFF the ignition. 2. Using a *J 39200* DMM, measure resistance between the motor ground stud and the battery negative terminal. Is the resistance less than the specified value?	2 Ω	Go to *Step 3*	Go to *Step 8*
3	1. Disconnect the EBTCM connector. 2. Remove the EBTCM from BPMV. 3. Inspect the EBTCM to BPMV connector for conditions which could cause an intermittent, such as damage, corrosion, poor terminal contact, or presence of brake fluid. Does the connector show signs of corrosion or brake fluid?	—	Go to *Step 5*	Go to *Step 4*
4	1. Install the *J 41247* pinout box to the BPMV connector. 2. Using a *J 39200* DMM, measure the resistance between the *J 41247* terminal 8 and the pump motor ground stud. Is the resistance within the specified range?	0.2–10 Ω	Go to *Step 6*	Go to *Step 7*
5	1. If connector corrosion or damage is evident, replace BPMV and/or EBTCM as necessary. 2. If brake fluid is present, replace BPMV and EBTCM. Did you complete the repair?	—	Go to *Diagnostic System Check*	—
6	Replace the EBTCM. Is the repair complete?	—	Go to *Diagnostic System Check*	—
7	Replace the BPMV. Is the repair complete?	—	Go to *Diagnostic System Check*	—
8	Repair open in CKT 1550. Is the repair complete?	—	Go to *Diagnostic System Check*	—

GC4029803892020X

Fig. 208 Code C1242: BPMV Pump Motor Ground Circuit Open (Part 2 of 2). Seville

Step	Action	Value(s)	Yes	No
1	Was the Diagnostic System Check performed?	—	*Go to Step 2*	Go to *Diagnostic System Check*
2	Is DTC 1217 also set as a current DTC?	—	Go to DTC C1217	*Go to Step 3*
3	1. Turn the ignition switch to the OFF position. 2. Using the *J 39200* DMM, measure the resistance between the pump motor ground stud and a good chassis ground. Is the resistance within the range specified in the value(s) column?	0–2 Ω	*Go to Step 4*	*Go to Step 9*
4	1. Disconnect the EBTCM connector. 2. Remove the EBTCM from the BPMV. 3. Inspect the EBTCM to BPMV connector for conditions which could cause intermittents, such as damage, corrosion, poor terminal contact, or presence of brake fluid. Is connector OK and cavity free of brake fluid?	—	*Go to Step 5*	*Go to Step 6*
5	1. Install the *J 41247* Pinout Box to the BPMV connector. 2. Using the *J 39200* DMM, measure the resistance between the *J 41247* terminal 8 and the pump motor ground stud. Is the resistance within the range specified in the value(s) column?	0.2–10 Ω	*Go to Step 7*	*Go to Step 8*
6	If connector corrosion or damage is evident, replace BPMV and/or EBTCM as necessary. Is the replacement complete?	—	Go to *Diagnostic System Check*	—
7	Replace the EBTCM. Is the replacement complete?	—	Go to *Diagnostic System Check*	—
8	Replace the BPMV. Is the replacement complete?	—	Go to *Diagnostic System Check*	—
9	Repair open or high resistance in CKT 350. Is the repair complete?	—	Go to *Diagnostic System Check*	—

GC402980279600BX

Fig. 209 Code C1243: BPMV Pump Motor Stalled (Part 2 of 2). DeVille

Circuit Description

When the pump motor relay is grounded by the EBTCM, it closes and provides battery voltage to operate the pump.

Conditions for Setting the DTC

DTC C1243 can be set when the pump motor relay has been commanded off after the pump motor has been on. A malfunction has occurred if the pump motor was on, and the EBTCM sensed a stuck or slowly turning pump motor.

Action Taken When the DTC Sets

A malfunction DTC is stored, ABS/TCS is disabled and the ABS and Traction Control Indicators are turned on.

Conditions for Clearing the DTC

- Condition for DTC is no longer present and scan tool clear DTC function is used.
- Fifty ignition cycles have passed with no DTC(s) detected.

Diagnostic Aids

- It is very important that a thorough inspection of the wiring and connectors be performed. Failure to carefully and fully inspect wiring and connectors may result in misdiagnosis, causing part replacement with reappearance of the malfunction.
- An intermittent malfunction can be caused by poor connections, broken insulation, or a wire that is broken inside the insulation.

Test Description

The numbers below refer to step numbers on the diagnostic table.

3. Checks for good pump motor ground.
5. Checks for good pump motor ground through the BPMV.

GC402980279600AX

Fig. 209 Code C1243: BPMV Pump Motor Stalled (Part 1 of 2). DeVille

Circuit Description

When the EBTCM grounds the pump motor relay, the relay closes and provides battery voltage in order to operate the pump.

Conditions for Setting the DTC

All of the following conditions occur:

- After the pump motor has been ON, the pump motor relay is commanded OFF.
- The pump motor was ON.
- The EBTCM detected a stalled or slowly turning motor.

Action Taken When the DTC Sets

- A malfunction DTC is stored.
- The ABS/TCS/Stabilitrak® is disabled.
- The ABS indicator is turned ON.
- The TRACTION CONTROL indicator is turned ON.
- The DIC displays the SERVICE STABILITY SYS message.

Conditions for Clearing the DTC

- The condition for DTC is no longer present and you used scan tool Clear DTCs function.
- The condition for DTC is no longer present and you used the On-Board Clear DTCs function.
- The EBTCM does not detect the DTC in 50 drive cycles.

Diagnostic Aids

- It is very important that a thorough inspection of the wiring and connectors be performed. Failure to carefully and fully inspect wiring and connectors may result in misdiagnosis, causing part replacement with reappearance of the malfunction.
- An intermittent malfunction can be caused by poor connections, broken insulation, or a wire that is broken inside the insulation.
- If an intermittent malfunction exists, refer to *Intermittents and Poor Connections*

GC4029803893010X

Fig. 210 Code C1243: BPMV Pump Motor Stalled (Part 1 of 2). Seville

Test Description

The numbers below refer to step numbers on the diagnostic table.

3. Checks for good pump motor ground.
5. Checks for good pump motor ground through the BPMV.

Step	Action	Value(s)	Yes	No
1	Was the Diagnostic System Check performed?	—	Go to *Step 2*	Go to *Diagnostic System Check*
2	Is DTC C1217 also set as a current DTC?	—	Go to *DTC C1217 Pump Motor Relay Contact Circuit Open*	Go to *Step 3*
3	1. Turn OFF the ignition. 2. Using a *J 39200* DMM, measure the resistance between the pump motor ground stud and the battery negative terminal. Is the resistance within the range specified?	2 Ω	Go to *Step 4*	Go to *Step 9*
4	1. Disconnect the EBTCM connector. 2. Remove the EBTCM from BPMV. 3. Inspect the EBTCM to BPMV connector for conditions which could cause an intermittent, such as damage, corrosion, poor terminal contact, or presence of brake fluid. Refer to *Intermittents and Poor Connections* Does the connector show signs of corrosion or brake fluid?	—	Go to *Step 6*	Go to *Step 5*
5	1. Install the *J 41247* pinout box to the BPMV connector. 2. Using a *J 39200* DMM, measure the resistance between the *J 41247* terminal 8 and the pump motor ground stud. Is the resistance within the specified range?	0.2–10 Ω	Go to *Step 7*	Go to *Step 8*
6	1. If connector corrosion or damage is evident, replace BPMV and/or EBTCM as necessary. 2. If brake fluid is present, replace BPMV and EBTCM. Did you complete the repair?	—	Go to *Diagnostic System Check*	—
7	Replace the EBTCM. Is repair complete?	—	Go to *Diagnostic System Check*	—
8	Replace the BPMV. Is the repair complete?	—	Go to *Diagnostic System Check*	—
9	Repair open in CKT 1550. Is the repair complete?	—	Go to *Diagnostic System Check*	—

GC4029803893020X

Fig. 210 Code C1243: BPMV Pump Motor Stalled (Part 2 of 2). Seville

Circuit Description

The CVRSS calculates normal force and transmits a PWM signal to the EBTCM via two dedicated data lines, one right, and one left. The EBTCM supplies the pull up voltage. The EBTCM uses this information to detect rough road conditions and allows for more aggressive braking on rough surfaces.

Conditions for Setting the DTC

The EBTCM measures the PWM duty cycle sent from the CVRSS and checks to see that it is between 10% and 90%. The possible values of duty cycle are 20%, 40%, 60%, and 80%. The CVRSS sends each value twice therefore any normal force value sent to the EBTCM should match either the previous or next normal force value. If either of the above faults are present for more than 5 seconds out of any 10 second period the EBTCM will set a normal force fault.

Action Taken When the DTC Sets

A malfunction DTC is stored and the rough road performance enhancements of ICCS do not function. ABS/TCS/ICCS are still functional.

Conditions for Clearing the DTC

- Condition for DTC is no longer present and scan tool clear DTC function is used.
- 50 ignition cycles have passed with no DTC(s) detected.

Diagnostic Aids

- It is very important that a thorough inspection of the wiring and connectors be performed. Failure to carefully and fully inspect wiring and connectors may result in misdiagnosis, causing part replacement with reappearance of the malfunction.

Step	Action	Value(s)	Yes	No
1	Was the Diagnostic System Check performed?	—	*Go to Step 2*	Go to *Diagnostic System Check*
2	Check the following grounds making sure each ground is clean and torqued to the proper specifications, G102 and G401. Were any loose, damaged, or corroded grounds found?	—	*Go to Step 3*	*Go to Step 4*
3	Repair ground as necessary. Is the repair complete?	—	Go to *Diagnostic System Check*	—
4	1. Turn the ignition switch to the OFF position. 2. Disconnect the EBTCM connector. 3. Install *J 39700* Universal Pinout Box using the *J 39700-25* cable adaptor to the EBTCM harness connector and the EBTCM connector. 4. Turn the ignition switch to the RUN position, engine OFF. 5. Using *J 39200* DMM, measure the DC duty cycle between *J 39700* terminals 18 and B. Is the duty cycle within the range specified in the value(s) column?	10 - 90%	*Go to Step 5*	*Go to Step 6*
5	Replace the EBTCM. Is the replacement complete?	—	Go to *Diagnostic System Check*	—
6	1. Turn the ignition switch to the OFF position. 2. Disconnect the CVRSS connector C1. 3. Turn the ignition switch to the RUN position, engine OFF. 4. Using *J 39200* DMM, measure the voltage between terminals 18 and B of *J 39700*. Is the voltage within the range specified in the value(s) column?	Battery Volts	*Go to Step 7*	*Go to Step 9*

GC402980279700AX

Fig. 211 Code C1252: ICCS 2 Data Link Left Fault (Part 1 of 2). DeVille & Seville

Circuit Description

The CVRSS calculates normal force and transmits a PWM signal to the EBTCM via two dedicated data lines, one right, and one left. The EBTCM supplies the pull up voltage. The EBTCM uses this information to detect rough road conditions and allows for more aggressive braking on rough surfaces.

Conditions for Setting the DTC

The EBTCM measures the PWM duty cycle sent from the CVRSS and checks to see that it is between 10% and 90%. The possible values of duty cycle are 20%, 40%, 60%, and 80%. The CVRSS sends each value twice therefore any normal force value sent to the EBTCM should match either the previous or next normal force value. If either of the above faults are present for more than 5 seconds out of any 10 second period the EBTCM will set a normal force fault.

Action Taken When the DTC Sets

A malfunction DTC is stored and the rough road performance enhancements of ICCS do not function. ABS/TCS/ICCS are still functional.

Conditions for Clearing the DTC

- Condition for DTC is no longer present and scan tool clear DTC function is used.
- 50 ignition cycles have passed with no DTC(s) detected.

Diagnostic Aids

- It is very important that a thorough inspection of the wiring and connectors be performed. Failure to carefully and fully inspect wiring and connectors may result in misdiagnosis, causing part replacement with reappearance of the malfunction.

Step	Action	Value(s)	Yes	No
1	Was the Diagnostic System Check performed?	—	*Go to Step 2*	Go to *Diagnostic System Check*
2	Check the following grounds making sure each ground is clean and torqued to the proper specifications, G102 and G401. Were any loose, damaged, or corroded grounds found?	—	*Go to Step 3*	*Go to Step 4*
3	Repair ground as necessary. Is the repair complete?	—	Go to *Diagnostic System Check*	—
4	1. Turn the ignition switch to the OFF position. 2. Disconnect the EBTCM connector. 3. Install *J 39700* Universal Pinout Box using the *J 39700-25* cable adaptor to the EBTCM harness connector and the EBTCM connector. 4. Turn the ignition switch to the RUN position, engine OFF. 5. Using *J 39200* DMM, measure the DC duty cycle between *J 39700* terminals 2 and B. Is the duty cycle within the range specified in the value(s) column?	10 - 90%	*Go to Step 5*	*Go to Step 6*
5	Replace the EBTCM. Is the replacement complete?	—	Go to *Diagnostic System Check*	—
6	1. Turn the ignition switch to the OFF position. 2. Disconnect the CVRSS connector C1. 3. Turn the ignition switch to the RUN position, engine OFF. 4. Using *J 39200* DMM, measure the voltage between terminals 2 and B of *J 39700*. Is the voltage within the range specified in the value(s) column?	Battery Volts	*Go to Step 7*	*Go to Step 9*

GC402980279800AX

Fig. 212 Code C1253: ICCS 2 Data Link Right Fault (Part 1 of 2). DeVille & Seville

Step	Action	Value(s)	Yes	No
7	1. Turn the ignition switch to the OFF position. 2. Disconnect the *J 39700-25* cable adaptor from the EBTCM leaving the cable adaptor connected to the EBTCM harness only. 3. Turn the ignition switch to the RUN position, engine OFF. 4. Using *J 39200* DMM, measure the voltage between terminals 18 and B of *J 39700* Is the voltage within the range specified in the value(s) column?	Greater than 1V	*Go to Step 8*	*Go to Step 11*
8	Repair CKT 790 for a short to voltage. Is the repair complete?	—	Go to *Diagnostic System Check*	—
9	1. Turn the ignition switch to the OFF position. 2. Using *J 39200* DMM, measure the resistance between *J 39700* terminals 18 and B. Is the resistance within the range specified in the value(s) column?	OL (infinite)	*Go to Step 5*	*Go to Step 10*
10	Repair CKT 790 for a short to ground. Is the repair complete?	—	Go to *Diagnostic System Check*	—
11	Using *J 39200* DMM, measure the resistance between terminal 18 of *J 39700* and the CVRSS connector C1 terminal D15. Is the resistance within the range specified in the value(s) column?	0 - 2Ω	*Go to Step 12*	*Go to Step 13*
12	Suspect CVRSS. Is the diagnosis complete?	—	Go to *Diagnostic System Check*	—
13	Repair CKT 790 for an open. Is the repair complete?	—	Go to *Diagnostic System Check*	—

GC402980279700BX

Fig. 211 Code C1252: ICCS 2 Data Link Left Fault (Part 2 of 2). DeVille & Seville

Step	Action	Value(s)	Yes	No
7	1. Turn the ignition switch to the OFF position. 2. Disconnect the *J 39700-25* cable adaptor from the EBTCM leaving the cable adaptor connected to the EBTCM harness only. 3. Turn the ignition switch to the RUN position, engine OFF. 4. Using *J 39200* DMM, measure the voltage between terminals 2 and B of *J 39700*. Is the voltage within the range specified in the value(s) column?	Greater than 1V	*Go to Step 8*	*Go to Step 11*
8	Repair CKT 791 for a short to voltage. Is the repair complete?	—	Go to *Diagnostic System Check*	—
9	1. Turn the ignition switch to the OFF position. 2. Using *J 39200* DMM, measure the resistance between *J 39700* terminals 2 and B. Is the resistance within the range specified in the value(s) column?	OL (infinite)	*Go to Step 5*	*Go to Step 10*
10	Repair CKT 791 for a short to ground. Is the repair complete?	—	Go to *Diagnostic System Check*	—
11	Using *J 39200* DMM, measure the resistance between terminal 2 of *J 39700* and the CVRSS connector C1 terminal D14. Is the resistance within the range specified in the value(s) column?	0 - 2Ω	*Go to Step 12*	*Go to Step 13*
12	Suspect CVRSS. Is the diagnosis complete?	—	Go to *Diagnostic System Check*	—
13	Repair CKT 791 for an open. Is the repair complete?	—	Go to *Diagnostic System Check*	—

GC402980279800BX

Fig. 212 Code C1253: ICCS 2 Data Link Right Fault (Part 2 of 2). DeVille & Seville

Circuit Description

This DTC identifies a malfunction within the EBTCM.

Conditions for Setting the DTC

DTC C1255xx is set when an internal EBTCM malfunction exists.

Action Taken When the DTC Sets

A malfunction DTC is stored, ABS/TCS is disabled and the ABS and Traction Control Indicators are turned on.

Conditions for Clearing the DTC

- Condition for DTC is no longer present and scan tool clear DTC function is used.
- Fifty ignition cycles have passed with no DTC(s) detected.

Diagnostic Aids

- When DTC C1255xx is displayed on the Scan Tool, it will be followed by two more numbers which should be noted along with any other DTCs that may be displayed. The additional two numbers displayed with DTC C1255xx are for aiding engineering to determine the cause of the internal malfunction.
- Make sure the integrity of the connection between the EBTCM and the BPMV is secure, tight, and free from corrosion.

GC402980279900AX

Fig. 213 Code C1255: EBTCM Internal Fault (Part 1 of 2). DeVille & Seville

Step	Action	Value(s)	Yes	No
1	Was the Diagnostic System Check performed?	—	*Go to Step 2*	Go to *Diagnostic System Check*
2	Are any other DTC(s) present besides C1255xx?	—	Go to Applicable DTC Table	*Go to Step 3*
3	1. Turn the ignition switch to the OFF position. 2. Disconnect the EBTCM. 3. Check for damaged, pushed out, or miswired terminals. Was any damage found?	—	*Go to Step 4*	*Go to Step 5*
4	Repair as necessary. Is the repair complete?	—	Go to *Diagnostic System Check*	—
5	Replace the EBTCM. Is the replacement complete?	—	Go to *Diagnostic System Check*	—

GC402980279900BX

Fig. 213 Code C1255: EBTCM Internal Fault (Part 2 of 2). DeVille & Seville

Step	Action	Value(s)	Yes	No
1	Was the Diagnostic System Check performed?	—	*Go to Step 2*	Go to *Diagnostic System Check*
2	Are any valve solenoid DTC(s) present (C1261 - C1274)?	—	Go to Applicable DTC Table	*Go to Step 3*
3	1. Turn the ignition switch to the OFF position. 2. Disconnect the EBTCM. 3. Check for damaged, pushed out, or miswired terminals. Was any damage found?	—	*Go to Step 4*	*Go to Step 5*
4	Repair as necessary. Is the repair complete?	—	Go to *Diagnostic System Check*	—
5	Replace the EBTCM. Is the replacement complete?	—	Go to *Diagnostic System Check*	—

GC402980280000BX

Fig. 214 Code C1256: EBCM Internal Fault (Part 2 of 2). DeVille & Seville

Step	Action	Value(s)	Yes	No
1	Was the Diagnostic System Check performed?	—	*Go to Step 2*	Go to *Diagnostic System Check*
2	1. Turn the ignition switch to the OFF position. 2. Disconnect the EBTCM connector. 3. Remove the EBTCM from the BPMV. 4. Inspect the EBTCM to BPMV connector for conditions which could cause intermittents such as damage, corrosion, or poor terminal contact. Are internal connectors OK and cavity free of brake fluid?	—	*Go to Step 3*	*Go to Step 6*
3	1. Install *J 41247* BPMV Pinout Box to the BPMV connector. 2. Using *J 39200* DMM, measure the resistance between *J 41247* terminals 14 and 7. Is the resistance within the range specified in the value(s) column?	8 - 12Ω	*Go to Step 4*	*Go to Step 8*
4	Using *J 39200* DMM, measure the resistance between *J 41247* terminal 14 and the BPMV case. Is the resistance within the range specified in the value(s) column?	OL (infinite)	*Go to Step 5*	*Go to Step 8*
5	1. Remove *J 41247*. 2. Reinstall the EBTCM to BPMV. 3. Reconnect the EBTCM connector. 4. Turn the ignition switch to the RUN position, engine off. Does DTC C1261 reset as a current DTC?	—	*Go to Step 9*	*Go to Step 7*
6	1. If connector corrosion or damage are present, replace BPMV and/or EBTCM as necessary. 2. If brake fluid is present, replace both the BPMV and EBTCM. Is the repair complete?	—	Go to *Diagnostic System Check*	—
7	Using a scan tool in ABS/TCS Special Functions run the AUTOMATED Test. Does DTC C1261 reset as a current DTC?	—	*Go to Step 8*	Go to *Diagnostic System Check*
8	Replace the BPMV. Is the replacement complete?	—	Go to *Diagnostic System Check*	—
9	Replace the EBTCM. Is the replacement complete?	—	Go to *Diagnostic System Check*	—

GC402980280100BX

Fig. 215 Code C1261: LH Front Inlet Valve Solenoid Fault (Part 2 of 2). DeVille & Seville

Circuit Description

This DTC identifies a malfunction within the EBTCM.

Conditions for Setting the DTC

- DTC C1256xx can be set when there is a solenoid short to battery inside the BPMV. If DTC(s) C1261 - C1274 are set along with C1256xx then pursue the solenoid DTC(s) first.
- DTC C1256xx can be set when there is an internal EBTCM malfunction.

Action Taken When the DTC Sets

A malfunction DTC is stored, ABS/TCS is not disabled and the ABS and Traction Control indicators are not turned on.

Conditions for Clearing the DTC

- Condition for DTC is no longer present and scan tool clear DTC function is used.
- Fifty ignition cycles have passed with no DTC(s) detected.

Diagnostic Aids

- When DTC C1256xx is displayed on the Scan Tool, it will be followed by two more numbers which should be noted along with any other DTCs that may be displayed. The additional two numbers displayed with DTC C1256xx are for aiding engineering to determine the cause of the internal malfunction.
- Make sure the integrity of the connection between the EBTCM and the BPMV is secure, tight, and free from corrosion.

GC402980280000AX

Fig. 214 Code C1256: EBCM Internal Fault (Part 1 of 2). DeVille & Seville

Circuit Description

The Inlet valve solenoid circuits are supplied with battery power when the ignition is in the RUN position. The EBTCM controls the valve functions by grounding the circuit when necessary.

Conditions for Setting the DTC

The EBTCM senses a discrepancy such as an open, short to ground, or short to voltage in the circuit.

Action Taken When the DTC Sets

A malfunction DTC is stored, ABS/TCS is disabled and the ABS and TRACTION OFF Indicators are turned on.

Conditions for Clearing the DTC

- Condition for DTC is no longer present and scan tool clear DTC function is used.
- Fifty ignition cycles have passed with no DTC(s) detected.

Diagnostic Aids

Make sure the integrity of the connection between the EBTCM and the BPMV is secure, tight, and free from corrosion.

Test Description

The numbers below refer to step numbers on the diagnostic table.

3. Checks the resistance value of the solenoid.
4. Checks for a short to ground in the BPMV.
7. Checks for an internal short to voltage.

GC402980280100AX

Fig. 215 Code C1261: LH Front Inlet Valve Solenoid Fault (Part 1 of 2). DeVille & Seville

Circuit Description

The Outlet valve solenoid circuits are supplied with battery power when the ignition is in the RUN position. The EBTCM controls the valve functions by grounding the circuit when necessary.

Conditions for Setting the DTC

The EBTCM senses a discrepancy such as an open, short to ground, or short to voltage in the circuit.

Action Taken When the DTC Sets

A malfunction DTC is stored, ABS/TCS is disabled and the ABS and TRACTION OFF Indicators are turned on.

Conditions for Clearing the DTC

- Condition for DTC is no longer present and scan tool clear DTC function is used.
- Fifty ignition cycles have passed with no DTC(s) detected.

Diagnostic Aids

Make sure the integrity of the connection between the EBTCM and the BPMV is secure, tight, and free from corrosion.

Test Description

The numbers below refer to step numbers on the diagnostic table.

3. Checks the resistance value of the solenoid.
4. Checks for a short to ground in the BPMV.
7. Checks for an internal short to voltage.

GC4029803914010X

Fig. 216 Code C1262: LH Front Outlet Solenoid Fault (Part 1 of 2). DeVille

Step	Action	Value(s)	Yes	No
1	Was the Diagnostic System Check performed?	—	*Go to Step 2*	Go to *Diagnostic System Check*
2	1. Turn the ignition switch to the OFF position. 2. Disconnect the EBTCM connector. 3. Remove the EBTCM from the BPMV. 4. Inspect the EBTCM to BPMV connector for conditions which could cause intermittents such as damage, corrosion, or poor terminal contact. Are internal connectors OK and cavity free of brake fluid?	—	*Go to Step 3*	*Go to Step 6*
3	1. Install *J 41247* BPMV Pinout Box to the BPMV connector. 2. Using *J 39200* DMM, measure the resistance between *J 41247* terminals 9 and 7. Is the resistance within the range specified in the value(s) column?	4 - 7Ω	*Go to Step 4*	*Go to Step 8*
4	Using *J 39200* DMM, measure the resistance between *J 41247* terminal 9 and the BPMV case. Is the resistance within the range specified in the value(s) column?	OL (infinite)	*Go to Step 5*	*Go to Step 8*
5	1. Remove *J 41247*. 2. Reinstall the EBTCM to BPMV. 3. Reconnect the EBTCM connector. 4. Turn the ignition switch to the RUN position, engine off. Does DTC C1262 reset as a current DTC?	—	*Go to Step 9*	*Go to Step 7*
6	1. If connector corrosion or damage are present, replace BPMV and/or EBTCM as necessary. 2. If brake fluid is present, replace both the BPMV and EBTCM. Is the repair complete?	—	Go to *Diagnostic System Check*	—
7	Using a scan tool in ABS/TCS Special Functions run the AUTOMATED Test. Does DTC C1262 reset as a current DTC?	—	*Go to Step 8*	Go to *Diagnostic System Check*
8	Replace the BPMV. Is the replacement complete?	—	Go to *Diagnostic System Check*	—
9	Replace the EBTCM. Is the replacement complete?	—	Go to *Diagnostic System Check*	—

GC4029803914020X

Fig. 216 Code C1262: LH Front Outlet Solenoid Fault (Part 2 of 2). DeVille

The valve solenoid circuits are supplied with battery power when the ignition is ON. The EBTCM controls the valve functions by grounding the circuit when necessary.

Conditions for Setting the DTC

The EBTCM senses a discrepancy such as an open, short to ground, or short to voltage in the circuit.

Action Taken When the DTC Sets

- A malfunction DTC is stored.
- The ABS/TCS/Stabilitrak® is disabled.
- The ABS indicator is turned ON.
- The TRACTION CONTROL indicator is turned ON.
- The DIC displays the SERVICE STABILITY SYS message.

Conditions for Clearing the DTC

- The condition for DTC is no longer present and you used scan tool Clear DTCs function.
- The condition for DTC is no longer present and you used the On-Board Clear DTCs function.
- The EBTCM does not detect the DTC in 50 drive cycles.

Diagnostic Aids

Make sure the integrity of the connection between the EBTCM and the BPMV is secure, tight, and free from corrosion.

Test Description

The numbers below refer to step numbers on the diagnostic table.

3. Checks the resistance value of the solenoid.
4. Checks for a short to ground in the BPMV.
7. Checks for an internal short to voltage.

GC4029803894010X

Fig. 217 Code C1262: LH Front Outlet Solenoid Fault (Part 1 of 2). Seville

Circuit Description

The Inlet valve solenoid circuits are supplied with battery power when the ignition is in the RUN position. The EBTCM controls the valve functions by grounding the circuit when necessary.

Conditions for Setting the DTC

The EBTCM senses a discrepancy such as an open, short to ground, or short to voltage in the circuit.

Action Taken When the DTC Sets

A malfunction DTC is stored, ABS/TCS is disabled and the ABS and TRACTION OFF Indicators are turned on.

Conditions for Clearing the DTC

- Condition for DTC is no longer present and scan tool clear DTC function is used.
- Fifty ignition cycles have passed with no DTC(s) detected.

Diagnostic Aids

Make sure the integrity of the connection between the EBTCM and the BPMV is secure, tight, and free from corrosion.

Test Description

The numbers below refer to step numbers on the diagnostic table.

3. Checks the resistance value of the solenoid.
4. Checks for a short to ground in the BPMV.
7. Checks for an internal short to voltage.

GC402980280300AX

Fig. 218 Code C1263: RH Front Inlet Valve Solenoid Fault (Part 1 of 2). DeVille & Seville

Step	Action	Value(s)	Yes	No
1	Was the Diagnostic System Check performed?	—	*Go to Step 2*	*Go to Diagnostic System Check*
2	1. Turn the ignition switch to the OFF position. 2. Disconnect the EBTCM connector. 3. Remove the EBTCM from the BPMV. 4. Inspect the EBTCM to BPMV connector for conditions which could cause intermittents such as damage, corrosion, or poor terminal contact. Are internal connectors OK and cavity free of brake fluid?	—	*Go to Step 3*	*Go to Step 6*
3	1. Install *J 41247* BPMV Pinout Box to the BPMV connector. 2. Using *J 39200* DMM, measure the resistance between *J 41247* terminals 1 and 7. Is the resistance within the range specified in the value(s) column?	8 - 12Ω	*Go to Step 4*	*Go to Step 8*
4	Using *J 39200* DMM, measure the resistance between *J 41247* terminal 1 and the BPMV case. Is the resistance within the range specified in the value(s) column?	OL (infinite)	*Go to Step 5*	*Go to Step 8*
5	1. Remove *J 41247*. 2. Reinstall the EBTCM to BPMV. 3. Reconnect the EBTCM connector 4. Turn the ignition switch to the RUN position, engine off. Does DTC C1263 reset as a current DTC?	—	*Go to Step 9*	*Go to Step 7*
6	1. If connector corrosion or damage are present, replace BPMV and/or EBTCM as necessary. 2. If brake fluid is present, replace both the BPMV and EBTCM. Is the repair complete?	—	Go to *Diagnostic System Check*	—
7	Using a scan tool in ABS/TCS Special Functions run the AUTOMATED Test. Does DTC C1263 reset as a current DTC?	—	*Go to Step 8*	Go to *Diagnostic System Check*
8	Replace the BPMV. Is the replacement complete?	—	Go to *Diagnostic System Check*	—
9	Replace the EBTCM. Is the replacement complete?	—	Go to *Diagnostic System Check*	—

GC402980280300BX

Fig. 218 Code C1263: RH Front Inlet Valve Solenoid Fault (Part 2 of 2). DeVille & Seville

Step	Action	Value(s)	Yes	No
1	Did you perform the Diagnostic System Check?	—	Go to *Step 2*	Go to *Diagnostic System Check*
2	1. Turn OFF the ignition. 2. Disconnect the EBTCM harness connector. 3. Remove the EBTCM from the BPMV. 4. Inspect the EBTCM to BPMV connector for conditions which could cause an intermittent such as damage, corrosion, or poor terminal contact. Are the internal connectors good and cavities free of brake fluid?	—	Go to *Step 3*	Go to *Step 6*
3	1. Install the *J 41247* BPMV pinout box to the BPMV connector. 2. Using a *J 39200* DMM, measure the resistance between the *J 41247* terminals 9 and 7. Is the resistance within the specified range?	4–7 Ω	Go to *Step 4*	Go to *Step 8*
4	Using a *J 39200* DMM, measure the resistance between the *J 41247* terminal 9 and the BPMV case. Is the resistance within the specified range?	OL (infinite)	Go to *Step 5*	Go to *Step 8*
5	1. Remove the *J 41247* BPMV pinout box. 2. Reinstall the EBTCM to BPMV. 3. Reconnect the EBTCM harness connector. 4. Connect a scan tool to the data link connector (DLC). 5. Turn ON the ignition, with the engine OFF. 6. Using the scan tool, select ABS/TCS/ICCS Diagnostic Trouble Codes, DTC Information. Does DTC C1262 reset as a current DTC?	—	Go to *Step 9*	Go to *Step 7*
6	• If connector corrosion or damage are present, replace the BPMV and/or the EBTCM as necessary. • If brake fluid is present, replace both the BPMV and the EBTCM. Did you complete the repair?	—	Go to *Diagnostic System Check*	—
7	Using a scan tool in ABS/TCS/ICCS Special Functions, run the Automated Test. Does DTC C1262 reset as a current DTC?	—	Go to *Step 8*	Go to *Diagnostic System Check*
8	Replace the BPMV. Did you complete the repair?	—	Go to *Diagnostic System Check*	—
9	Replace the EBTCM. Did you complete the repair?	—	Go to *Diagnostic System Check*	—

GC4029803894020X

Fig. 217 Code C1262: LH Front Outlet Solenoid Fault (Part 2 of 2). Seville

Circuit Description

The Outlet valve solenoid circuits are supplied with battery power when the ignition is in the RUN position. The EBTCM controls the valve functions by grounding the circuit when necessary.

Conditions for Setting the DTC

The EBTCM senses a discrepancy such as an open, short to ground, or short to voltage in the circuit.

Action Taken When the DTC Sets

A malfunction DTC is stored, ABS/TCS is disabled and the ABS and TRACTION OFF Indicators are turned on.

Conditions for Clearing the DTC

- Condition for DTC is no longer present and scan tool clear DTC function is used.
- Fifty ignition cycles have passed with no DTC(s) detected.

Diagnostic Aids

Make sure the integrity of the connection between the EBTCM and the BPMV is secure, tight, and free from corrosion.

Test Description

The numbers below refer to step numbers on the diagnostic table.

3. Checks the resistance value of the solenoid.
4. Checks for a short to ground in the BPMV.
7. Checks for an internal short to voltage.

GC402980280400AX

Fig. 219 Code C1264: RH Front Outlet Valve Solenoid Fault (Part 1 of 2). DeVille & Seville

Step	Action	Value(s)	Yes	No
1	Was the Diagnostic System Check performed?	—	*Go to Step 2*	Go to *Diagnostic System Check*
2	1. Turn the ignition switch to the OFF position. 2. Disconnect the EBTCM connector. 3. Remove the EBTCM from the BPMV. 4. Inspect the EBTCM to BPMV connector for conditions which could cause intermittents such as damage, corrosion, or poor terminal contact. Are internal connectors OK and cavity free of brake fluid?	—	*Go to Step 3*	*Go to Step 6*
3	1. Install *J 41247* BPMV Pinout Box to the BPMV connector. 2. Using *J 39200* DMM, measure the resistance between *J 41247* terminals 6 and 7. Is the resistance within the range specified in the value(s) column?	4 - 7Ω	*Go to Step 4*	*Go to Step 8*
4	Using *J 39200* DMM, measure the resistance between *J 41247* terminal 6 and the BPMV case. Is the resistance within the range specified in the value(s) column?	OL (infinite)	*Go to Step 5*	*Go to Step 8*
5	1. Remove *J 41247*. 2. Reinstall the EBTCM to BPMV. 3. Reconnect the EBTCM connector. 4. Turn the ignition switch to the RUN position, engine off. Does DTC C1264 reset as a current DTC?	—	*Go to Step 9*	*Go to Step 7*
6	1. If connector corrosion or damage are present, replace BPMV and/or EBTCM as necessary. 2. If brake fluid is present, replace both the BPMV and EBCM/EBTCM. Is the repair complete?	—	Go to *Diagnostic System Check*	—
7	Using a scan tool in ABS/TCS Special Functions run the AUTOMATED Test. Does DTC C1264 reset as a current DTC?	—	*Go to Step 8*	Go to *Diagnostic System Check*
8	Replace the BPMV. Is the replacement complete?	—	Go to *Diagnostic System Check*	—
9	Replace the EBTCM. Is the replacement complete?	—	Go to *Diagnostic System Check*	—

GC402980280400BX

Fig. 219 Code C1264: RH Front Outlet Valve Solenoid Fault (Part 2 of 2). DeVille & Seville

Step	Action	Value(s)	Yes	No
1	Was the Diagnostic System Check performed?	—	*Go to Step 2*	Go to *Diagnostic System Check*
2	1. Turn the ignition switch to the OFF position. 2. Disconnect the EBTCM connector. 3. Remove the EBTCM from the BPMV. 4. Inspect the EBTCM to BPMV connector for conditions which could cause intermittents such as damage, corrosion, or poor terminal contact. Are internal connectors OK and cavity free of brake fluid?	—	*Go to Step 3*	*Go to Step 6*
3	1. Install *J 41247* BPMV Pinout Box to the BPMV connector. 2. Using *J 39200* DMM, measure the resistance between *J 41247* terminals 2 and 7. Is the resistance within the range specified in the value(s) column?	8 - 12Ω	*Go to Step 4*	*Go to Step 8*
4	Using *J 39200* DMM, measure the resistance between *J 41247* terminal 2 and the BPMV case. Is the resistance within the range specified in the value(s) column?	OL (infinite)	*Go to Step 5*	*Go to Step 8*
5	1. Remove *J 41247*. 2. Reinstall the EBTCM to BPMV. 3. Reconnect the EBTCM connector. 4. Turn the ignition switch to the RUN position, engine off. Does DTC C1265 reset as a current DTC?	—	*Go to Step 9*	*Go to Step 7*
6	1. If connector corrosion or damage are present, replace BPMV and/or EBTCM as necessary. 2. If brake fluid is present, replace both the BPMV and EBTCM. Is the repair complete?	—	Go to *Diagnostic System Check*	—
7	Using a scan tool in ABS/TCS Special Functions run the AUTOMATED Test. Does DTC C1265 reset as a current DTC?	—	*Go to Step 8*	Go to *Diagnostic System Check*
8	Replace the BPMV. Is the replacement complete?	—	Go to *Diagnostic System Check*	—
9	Replace the EBCM/EBTCM. Is the replacement complete?	—	Go to *Diagnostic System Check*	—

GC402980280500BX

Fig. 220 Code C1265: LH Rear Inlet Valve Solenoid Fault (Part 2 of 2). DeVille & Seville

Circuit Description

The Inlet valve solenoid circuits are supplied with battery power when the ignition is in the RUN position. The EBTCM controls the valve functions by grounding the circuit when necessary.

Conditions for Setting the DTC

The EBTCM senses a discrepancy such as an open, short to ground, or short to voltage in the circuit.

Action Taken When the DTC Sets

A malfunction DTC is stored, ABS/TCS is disabled and the ABS and TRACTION OFF Indicators are turned on.

Conditions for Clearing the DTC

- Condition for DTC is no longer present and scan tool clear DTC function is used.
- Fifty ignition cycles have passed with no DTC(s) detected.

Diagnostic Aids

Make sure the integrity of the connection between the EBTCM and the BPMV is secure, tight, and free from corrosion.

Test Description

The numbers below refer to step numbers on the diagnostic table.

3. Checks the resistance value of the solenoid.
4. Checks for a short to ground in the BPMV.
7. Checks for an internal short to voltage.

GC402980280500AX

Fig. 220 Code C1265: LH Rear Inlet Valve Solenoid Fault (Part 1 of 2). DeVille & Seville

Circuit Description

The Outlet valve solenoid circuits are supplied with battery power when the ignition is in the RUN position. The EBTCM controls the valve functions by grounding the circuit when necessary.

Conditions for Setting the DTC

The EBTCM senses a discrepancy such as an open, short to ground, or short to voltage in the circuit.

Action Taken When the DTC Sets

A malfunction DTC is stored, ABS/TCS is disabled and the ABS and TRACTION OFF Indicators are turned on.

Conditions for Clearing the DTC

- Condition for DTC is no longer present and scan tool clear DTC function is used.
- Fifty ignition cycles have passed with no DTC(s) detected.

Diagnostic Aids

Make sure the integrity of the connection between the EBTCM and the BPMV is secure, tight, and free from corrosion.

Test Description

The numbers below refer to step numbers on the diagnostic table.

3. Checks the resistance value of the solenoid.
4. Checks for a short to ground in the BPMV.
7. Checks for an internal short to voltage.

GC402980280600AX

Fig. 221 Code C1266: LH Rear Outlet Valve Solenoid Fault (Part 1 of 2). DeVille & Seville

Step	Action	Value(s)	Yes	No
1	Was the Diagnostic System Check performed?	—	*Go to Step 2*	Go to *Diagnostic System Check*
2	1. Turn the ignition switch to the OFF position. 2. Disconnect the EBTCM connector. 3. Remove the EBTCM from the BPMV. 4. Inspect the EBTCM to BPMV connector for conditions which could cause intermittents such as damage, corrosion, or poor terminal contact. Are internal connectors OK and cavity free of brake fluid?	—	*Go to Step 3*	*Go to Step 6*
3	1. Install *J 41247* BPMV Pinout Box to the BPMV connector. 2. Using *J 39200* DMM, measure the resistance between *J 41247* terminals 5 and 7. Is the resistance within the range specified in the value(s) column?	4 - 7Ω	*Go to Step 4*	*Go to Step 8*
4	Using *J 39200* DMM, measure the resistance between *J 41247* terminal 5 and the BPMV case. Is the resistance within the range specified in the value(s) column?	OL (infinite)	*Go to Step 5*	*Go to Step 8*
5	1. Remove *J 41247*. 2. Reinstall the EBTCM to BPMV. 3. Reconnect the EBTCM connector. 4. Turn the ignition switch to the RUN position, engine off Does DTC C1266 reset as a current DTC?	—	*Go to Step 9*	*Go to Step 7*
6	1. If connector corrosion or damage are present, replace BPMV and/or EBTCM as necessary. 2. If brake fluid is present, replace both the BPMV and EBTCM. Is the repair complete?	—	Go to *Diagnostic System Check*	—
7	Using a scan tool in ABS/TCS Special Functions run the AUTOMATED Test. Does DTC C1266 reset as a current DTC?	—	*Go to Step 8*	Go to *Diagnostic System Check*
8	Replace the BPMV. Is the replacement complete?	—	Go to *Diagnostic System Check*	—
9	Replace the EBCM/EBTCM. Is the replacement complete?	—	Go to *Diagnostic System Check*	—

GC402980280600BX

Fig. 221 Code C1266: LH Rear Outlet Valve Solenoid Fault (Part 2 of 2). DeVille & Seville

Circuit Description

The Inlet valve solenoid circuits are supplied with battery power when the ignition is in the RUN position. The EBTCM controls the valve functions by grounding the circuit when necessary.

Conditions for Setting the DTC

The EBTCM senses a discrepancy such as an open, short to ground, or short to voltage in the circuit.

Action Taken When the DTC Sets

A malfunction DTC is stored, ABS/TCS is disabled and the ABS and TRACTION OFF Indicators are turned on.

Conditions for Clearing the DTC

- Condition for DTC is no longer present and scan tool clear DTC function is used.
- Fifty ignition cycles have passed with no DTC(s) detected.

Diagnostic Aids

Make sure the integrity of the connection between the EBTCM and the BPMV is secure, tight, and free from corrosion.

Test Description

The numbers below refer to step numbers on the diagnostic table.

3. Checks the resistance value of the solenoid.
4. Checks for a short to ground in the BPMV.
7. Checks for an internal short to voltage.

GC402980280700AX

Fig. 222 Code C1267: RH Rear Inlet Valve Solenoid Fault (Part 1 of 2). DeVille & Seville

Step	Action	Value(s)	Yes	No
1	Was the Diagnostic System Check performed?	—	*Go to Step 2*	Go to *Diagnostic System Check*
2	1. Turn the ignition switch to the OFF position. 2. Disconnect the EBTCM connector. 3. Remove the EBTCM from the BPMV. 4. Inspect the EBTCM to BPMV connector for conditions which could cause intermittents such as damage, corrosion, or poor terminal contact. Are internal connectors OK and cavity free of brake fluid?	—	*Go to Step 3*	*Go to Step 6*
3	1. Install *J 41247* BPMV Pinout Box to the BPMV connector. 2. Using *J 39200* DMM, measure the resistance between *J 41247* terminals 13 and 7. Is the resistance within the range specified in the value(s) column?	8 - 12Ω	*Go to Step 4*	*Go to Step 8*
4	Using *J 39200* DMM, measure the resistance between *J 41247* terminal 13 and the BPMV case. Is the resistance within the range specified in the value(s) column?	OL (infinite)	*Go to Step 5*	*Go to Step 8*
5	1. Remove *J 41247*. 2. Reinstall the EBTCM to BPMV. 3. Reconnect the EBTCM connector. 4. Turn the ignition switch to the RUN position, engine off. Does DTC C1267 reset as a current DTC?	—	*Go to Step 9*	*Go to Step 7*
6	1. If connector corrosion or damage are present, replace BPMV and/or EBTCM as necessary. 2. If brake fluid is present, replace both the BPMV and EBTCM. Is the repair complete?	—	Go to *Diagnostic System Check*	—
7	Using a scan tool in ABS/TCS Special Functions run the AUTOMATED Test. Does DTC C1267 reset as a current DTC?	—	*Go to Step 8*	Go to *Diagnostic System Check*
8	Replace the BPMV. Is the replacement complete?	—	Go to *Diagnostic System Check*	—
9	Replace the EBCM/EBTCM. Is the replacement complete?	—	Go to *Diagnostic System Check*	—

GC402980280700BX

Fig. 222 Code C1267: RH Rear Inlet Valve Solenoid Fault (Part 2 of 2). DeVille & Seville

Circuit Description

The Outlet valve solenoid circuits are supplied with battery power when the ignition is in the RUN position. The EBTCM controls the valve functions by grounding the circuit when necessary.

Conditions for Setting the DTC

The EBTCM senses a discrepancy such as an open, short to ground, or short to voltage in the circuit.

Action Taken When the DTC Sets

A malfunction DTC is stored, ABS/TCS is disabled and the ABS and TRACTION OFF Indicators are turned on.

Conditions for Clearing the DTC

- Condition for DTC is no longer present and scan tool clear DTC function is used.
- Fifty ignition cycles have passed with no DTC(s) detected.

Diagnostic Aids

Make sure the integrity of the connection between the EBTCM and the BPMV is secure, tight, and free from corrosion.

Test Description

The numbers below refer to step numbers on the diagnostic table.

3. Checks the resistance value of the solenoid.
4. Checks for a short to ground in the BPMV.
7. Checks for an internal short to voltage.

GC402980280800AX

Fig. 223 Code C1268: RH Rear Outlet Valve Solenoid Fault (Part 1 of 2). DeVille & Seville

Step	Action	Value(s)	Yes	No
1	Was the Diagnostic System Check performed?	—	*Go to Step 2*	Go to *Diagnostic System Check*
2	1. Turn the ignition switch to the OFF position. 2. Disconnect the EBTCM connector. 3. Remove the EBTCM from the BPMV. 4. Inspect the EBTCM to BPMV connector for conditions which could cause intermittents such as damage, corrosion, or poor terminal contact. Are internal connectors OK and cavity free of brake fluid?	—	*Go to Step 3*	*Go to Step 6*
3	1. Install *J 41247* BPMV Pinout Box to the BPMV connector. 2. Using *J 39200* DMM, measure the resistance between *J 41247* terminals 10 and 7. Is the resistance within the range specified in the value(s) column?	4 - 7Ω	*Go to Step 4*	*Go to Step 8*
4	Using *J 39200* DMM, measure the resistance between *J 41247* terminal 10 and the BPMV case. Is the resistance within the range specified in the value(s) column?	OL (infinite)	*Go to Step 5*	*Go to Step 8*
5	1. Remove *J 41247*. 2. Reinstall the EBTCM to BPMV. 3. Reconnect the EBTCM connector. 4. Turn the ignition switch to the RUN position, engine off. Does DTC C1268 reset as a current DTC?	—	*Go to Step 9*	*Go to Step 7*
6	1. If connector corrosion or damage are present, replace BPMV and/or EBTCM as necessary. 2. If brake fluid is present, replace both the BPMV and EBTCM. Is the repair complete?	—	Go to *Diagnostic System Check*	—
7	Using a scan tool in ABS/TCS Special Functions run the AUTOMATED Test. Does DTC C1268 reset as a current DTC?	—	*Go to Step 8*	Go to *Diagnostic System Check*
8	Replace the BPMV. Is the replacement complete?	—	Go to *Diagnostic System Check*	—
9	Replace the EBCM/EBTCM. Is the replacement complete?	—	Go to *Diagnostic System Check*	—

GC402980280800BX

Fig. 223 Code C1268: RH Rear Outlet Valve Solenoid Fault (Part 2 of 2). DeVille & Seville

Circuit Description

The Master Cylinder Isolation valve solenoid circuits are supplied with battery power when the ignition is in the RUN position. The EBTCM controls the valve functions by grounding the circuit when necessary.

Conditions for Setting the DTC

The EBTCM senses a discrepancy such as an open, short to ground, or short to voltage in the circuit.

Action Taken When the DTC Sets

A malfunction DTC is stored, ABS/TCS is disabled and the ABS and TRACTION OFF Indicators are turned on.

Conditions for Clearing the DTC

- Condition for DTC is no longer present and scan tool clear DTC function is used.
- Fifty ignition cycles have passed with no DTC(s) detected.

Diagnostic Aids

Make sure the integrity of the connection between the EBTCM and the BPMV is secure, tight, and free from corrosion.

Test Description

The numbers below refer to step numbers on the diagnostic table.

3. Checks the resistance value of the solenoid.
4. Checks for a short to ground in the BPMV.
7. Checks for an internal short to voltage.

GC402980280900AX

Fig. 224 Code C1271: LH TCS Front Master Cylinder Isolation Valve Fault (Part 1 of 2). DeVille & Seville

Step	Action	Value(s)	Yes	No
1	Was the Diagnostic System Check performed?	—	*Go to Step 2*	Go to *Diagnostic System Check*
2	1. Turn the ignition switch to the OFF position. 2. Disconnect the EBTCM connector. 3. Remove the EBTCM from the BPMV. 4. Inspect the EBTCM to BPMV connector for conditions which could cause intermittents such as damage, corrosion, or poor terminal contact. Are internal connectors OK and cavity free of brake fluid?	—	*Go to Step 3*	*Go to Step 6*
3	1. Install *J 41247* BPMV Pinout Box to the BPMV connector. 2. Using *J 39200* DMM, measure the resistance between *J 41247* terminals 12 and 7. Is the resistance within the range specified in the value(s) column?	8 - 12Ω	*Go to Step 4*	*Go to Step 8*
4	Using *J 39200* DMM, measure the resistance between *J 41247* terminal 12 and the BPMV case. Is the resistance within the range specified in the value(s) column?	OL (infinite)	*Go to Step 5*	*Go to Step 8*
5	1. Remove *J 41247*. 2. Reinstall the EBTCM to BPMV. 3. Reconnect the EBTCM connector. 4. Turn the ignition switch to the RUN position, engine off. Does DTC C1271 reset as a current DTC?	—	*Go to Step 9*	*Go to Step 7*
6	1. If connector corrosion or damage are present, replace BPMV and/or EBTCM as necessary. 2. If brake fluid is present, replace both the BPMV and EBTCM. Is the repair complete?	—	Go to *Diagnostic System Check*	—
7	Using a scan tool in ABS/TCS Special Functions run the AUTOMATED Test. Does DTC C1271 reset as a current DTC?	—	*Go to Step 8*	Go to *Diagnostic System Check*
8	Replace the BPMV. Is the replacement complete?	—	Go to *Diagnostic System Check*	—
9	Replace the EBTCM. Is the replacement complete?	—	Go to *Diagnostic System Check*	—

GC402980280900BX

Fig. 224 Code C1271: LH TCS Front Master Cylinder Isolation Valve Fault (Part 2 of 2). DeVille & Seville

Step	Action	Value(s)	Yes	No
1	Was the Diagnostic System Check performed?	—	*Go to Step 2*	Go to *Diagnostic System Check*
2	1. Turn the ignition switch to the OFF position. 2. Disconnect the EBTCM connector. 3. Remove the EBTCM from the BPMV. 4. Inspect the EBTCM to BPMV connector for conditions which could cause intermittents such as damage, corrosion, or poor terminal contact. Are internal connectors OK and cavity free of brake fluid?	—	*Go to Step 3*	*Go to Step 6*
3	1. Install *J 41247* BPMV Pinout Box to the BPMV connector. 2. Using *J 39200* DMM, measure the resistance between *J 41247* terminals 11 and 7. Is the resistance within the range specified in the value(s) column?	8 - 12Ω	*Go to Step 4*	*Go to Step 8*
4	Using *J 39200* DMM, measure the resistance between *J 41247* terminal 11 and the BPMV case. Is the resistance within the range specified in the value(s) column?	OL (infinite)	*Go to Step 5*	*Go to Step 8*
5	1. Remove *J 41247*. 2. Reinstall the EBTCM to BPMV. 3. Reconnect the EBTCM connector. 4. Turn the ignition switch to the RUN position, engine off. Does DTC C1272 reset as a current DTC?	—	*Go to Step 9*	*Go to Step 7*
6	1. If connector corrosion or damage are present, replace BPMV and/or EBTCM as necessary. 2. If brake fluid is present, replace both the BPMV and EBTCM. Is the repair complete?	—	Go to *Diagnostic System Check*	—
7	Using a scan tool in ABS/TCS Special Functions run the AUTOMATED Test. Does DTC C1272 reset as a current DTC?	—	*Go to Step 8*	Go to *Diagnostic System Check*
8	Replace the BPMV. Is the replacement complete?	—	Go to *Diagnostic System Check*	—
9	Replace the EBTCM. Is the replacement complete?	—	Go to *Diagnostic System Check*	—

GC402980281000BX

Fig. 225 Code C1272: LH Front Prime Valve Fault (Part 2 of 2). DeVille & Seville

Circuit Description

The TCS Prime valve solenoid circuits are supplied with battery power when the ignition is in the RUN position. The EBTCM controls the valve functions by grounding the circuit when necessary.

Conditions for Setting the DTC

The EBTCM senses a discrepancy such as an open, short to ground, or short to voltage in the circuit.

Action Taken When the DTC Sets

A malfunction DTC is stored, ABS/TCS is disabled and the ABS and TRACTION OFF Indicators are turned on.

Conditions for Clearing the DTC

- Condition for DTC is no longer present and scan tool clear DTC function is used.
- Fifty ignition cycles have passed with no DTC(s) detected.

Diagnostic Aids

Make sure the integrity of the connection between the EBTCM and the BPMV is secure, tight, and free from corrosion.

Test Description

The numbers below refer to step numbers on the diagnostic table.

3. Checks the resistance value of the solenoid.
4. Checks for a short to ground in the BPMV.
7. Checks for an internal short to voltage.

GC402980281000AX

Fig. 225 Code C1272: LH Front Prime Valve Fault (Part 1 of 2). DeVille & Seville

Circuit Description

The Master Cylinder Isolation valve solenoid circuits are supplied with battery power when the ignition is in the RUN position. The EBTCM controls the valve functions by grounding the circuit when necessary.

Conditions for Setting the DTC

The EBTCM senses a discrepancy such as an open, short to ground, or short to voltage in the circuit.

Action Taken When the DTC Sets

A malfunction DTC is stored, ABS/TCS is disabled and the ABS and TRACTION OFF Indicators are turned on.

Conditions for Clearing the DTC

- Condition for DTC is no longer present and scan tool clear DTC function is used.
- Fifty ignition cycles have passed with no DTC(s) detected.

Diagnostic Aids

Make sure the integrity of the connection between the EBTCM and the BPMV is secure, tight, and free from corrosion.

Test Description

The numbers below refer to step numbers on the diagnostic table.

3. Checks the resistance value of the solenoid.
4. Checks for a short to ground in the BPMV.
7. Checks for an internal short to voltage.

GC402980281100AX

Fig. 226 Code C1273: RH Front TCS Master Cylinder Isolation Valve Fault (Part 1 of 2). DeVille & Seville

Step	Action	Value(s)	Yes	No
1	Was the Diagnostic System Check performed?	—	*Go to Step 2*	Go to *Diagnostic System Check*
2	1. Turn the ignition switch to the OFF position. 2. Disconnect the EBTCM connector. 3. Remove the EBTCM from the BPMV. 4. Inspect the EBTCM to BPMV connector for conditions which could cause intermittents such as damage, corrosion, or poor terminal contact. Are internal connectors OK and cavity free of brake fluid?	—	*Go to Step 3*	*Go to Step 6*
3	1. Install *J 41247* BPMV Pinout Box to the BPMV connector. 2. Using *J 39200* DMM, measure the resistance between *J 41247* terminals 3 and 7. Is the resistance within the range specified in the value(s) column?	8 - 12Ω	*Go to Step 4*	*Go to Step 8*
4	Using *J 39200* DMM, measure the resistance between *J 41247* terminal 3 and the BPMV case. Is the resistance within the range specified in the value(s) column?	OL (infinite)	*Go to Step 5*	*Go to Step 8*
5	1. Remove *J 41247*. 2. Reinstall the EBTCM to BPMV. 3. Reconnect the EBTCM connector. 4. Turn the ignition switch to the RUN position, engine off. Does DTC C1273 reset as a current DTC?	—	*Go to Step 9*	*Go to Step 7*
6	1. If connector corrosion or damage are present, replace BPMV and/or EBTCM as necessary. 2. If brake fluid is present, replace both the BPMV and EBTCM. Is the repair complete?	—	Go to *Diagnostic System Check*	—
7	Using a scan tool in ABS/TCS Special Functions run the AUTOMATED Test. Does DTC C1273 reset as a current DTC?	—	*Go to Step 8*	Go to *Diagnostic System Check*
8	Replace the BPMV. Is the replacement complete?	—	Go to *Diagnostic System Check*	—
9	Replace the EBTCM. Is the replacement complete?	—	Go to *Diagnostic System Check*	—

GC402980281100BX

Fig. 226 Code C1273: RH Front TCS Master Cylinder Isolation Valve Fault (Part 2 of 2). DeVille & Seville

Circuit Description

The TCS Prime valve solenoid circuits are supplied with battery power when the ignition is in the RUN position. The EBTCM controls the valve functions by grounding the circuit when necessary.

Conditions for Setting the DTC

The EBTCM senses a discrepancy such as an open, short to ground, or short to voltage in the circuit.

Action Taken When the DTC Sets

A malfunction DTC is stored, ABS/TCS is disabled and the ABS and TRACTION OFF Indicators are turned on.

Conditions for Clearing the DTC

- Condition for DTC is no longer present and scan tool clear DTC function is used.
- Fifty ignition cycles have passed with no DTC(s) detected.

Diagnostic Aids

Make sure the integrity of the connection between the EBTCM and the BPMV is secure, tight, and free from corrosion.

Test Description

The numbers below refer to step numbers on the diagnostic table.

3. Checks the resistance value of the solenoid.
4. Checks for a short to ground in the BPMV.
7. Checks for an internal short to voltage.

GC402980281200AX

Fig. 227 Code C1274: RH Front TCS Prime Valve Fault (Part 1 of 2). DeVille & Seville

Circuit Description

The EBTCM and the PCM simultaneously controlled the traction control. The PCM sends a Delivered Torque message via a pulse width modulated (PWM) signal to the EBTCM confirming the delivered torque level for proper TCS operation. The EBTCM supplies the pull up voltage.

Conditions for Setting the DTC

The DTC sets if all of the following occur:

- The ignition is ON.
- The PWM signal is out of range or no signal is received for 7 seconds.

Action Taken When the DTC Sets

- A malfunction DTC is stored.
- The TCS is disabled.
- The TRACTION CONTROL indicator is turned ON.
- The ABS remains functional.

Conditions for Clearing the DTC

- The condition for DTC is no longer present and you used scan tool Clear DTCs function.
- The condition for DTC is no longer present and you used the On-Board Clear DTCs function.
- The EBTCM does not detect the DTC in 50 drive cycles.

Diagnostic Aids

- It is very important that a thorough inspection of the wiring and connectors be performed. Failure to carefully and fully inspect wiring and connectors may result in misdiagnosis, causing part replacement with reappearance of the malfunction.
- An intermittent malfunction can be caused by poor connections, broken insulation, or a wire that is broken inside the insulation.
- If an intermittent malfunction exists, refer to *Intermittents and Poor Connections*
- The following conditions can cause this concern:
  - An open circuit.
  - An short to ground or voltage in the circuit.
  - A wiring problem, terminal corrosion, or poor connection in the circuit.
  - A communication frequency problem.
  - A communication duty cycle problem.
  - The EBTCM is not receiving information from the PCM.

Test Description

The numbers below refer to step numbers on the diagnostic table.

4. This step checks for proper duty cycle.
5. This step checks for proper frequency.

GC4029903921010X

Fig. 228 Code C1276: Delivered Torque Signal Circuit Fault (Part 1 of 3). DeVille

Step	Action	Value(s)	Yes	No
1	Did you perform the ABS Diagnostic System Check?	—	Go to *Step 2*	Go to *A Diagnostic System Check - ABS*
2	Inspect the following grounds, ensuring that each ground is clean and torqued to the proper specifications: • G102 • G103 Were any loose, damaged, or corroded grounds found?	—	Go to *Step 3*	Go to *Step 4*
3	Repair the ground as necessary. Did you complete the repair?	—	Go to *A Diagnostic System Check - ABS*	—
4	1. Turn OFF the ignition. 2. Disconnect the EBTCM connector. 3. Install the *J 39700* universal pinout box using the *J 39700-25* cable adapter to the EBTCM harness connector and the EBTCM connector. 4. Turn ON the ignition, with the engine OFF. Use a *J 39200* DMM in order to measure the DC duty cycle between the *J 39700* terminal 6 and terminal B. Is the duty cycle within the specified range?	5–15%	Go to *Step 5*	Go to *Step 7*
5	Use a *J 39200* DMM in order to measure the DC Hz between the *J 39700* terminal 6 and terminal B. Is the frequency within the range specified?	121–134 Hz	Go to *Step 6*	Go to *Step 13*
6	Replace the EBTCM. Did you complete the repair?	—	Go to *A Diagnostic System Check - ABS*	—
7	1. Turn OFF the ignition. 2. Disconnect the PCM connector C2. 3. Turn ON the ignition, with the engine OFF. 4. Use a *J 39200* DMM in order to measure the voltage between terminal 6 and terminal B of the *J 39700*. Is the voltage within the specified range?	Battery Voltage	Go to *Step 8*	Go to *Step 10*
8	1. Turn OFF the ignition. 2. Disconnect the *J 39700-25* cable adaptor from the EBTCM leaving the cable adaptor connected to the EBTCM harness only. 3. Turn ON the ignition, with the engine OFF. 4. Use a *J 39200* DMM in order to measure the voltage between the *J 39700* terminal 6 and terminal B. Is the voltage greater than the specified value?	1 V	Go to *Step 9*	Go to *Step 12*
9	Repair the short to voltage in CKT 464. Did you complete the repair?	—	Go to *A Diagnostic System Check - ABS*	—
10	1. Turn OFF the ignition. 2. Use a *J 39200* DMM in order to measure the resistance between the *J 39700* terminal 6 and terminal B. Is the resistance within the specified range?	OL (Infinite)	Go to *Step 6*	Go to *Step 11*
11	Repair the short to ground in CKT 464. Did you complete the repair?	—	Go to *A Diagnostic System Check - ABS*	—

GC4029903921020X

Fig. 228 Code C1276: Delivered Torque Signal Circuit Fault (Part 2 of 3). DeVille

Step	Action	Value(s)	Yes	No
1	Was the Diagnostic System Check performed?	—	Go to *Step 2*	Go to *Diagnostic System Check*
2	1. Turn the ignition switch to the OFF position. 2. Disconnect the EBTCM connector. 3. Remove the EBTCM from the BPMV. 4. Inspect the EBTCM to BPMV connector for conditions which could cause intermittents such as damage, corrosion, or poor terminal contact. Are internal connectors OK and cavity free of brake fluid?	—	Go to *Step 3*	Go to *Step 6*
3	1. Install *J 41247* BPMV Pinout Box to the BPMV connector. 2. Using *J 39200* DMM, measure the resistance between *J 41247* terminals 4 and 7. Is the resistance within the range specified in the value(s) column?	8 - 12Ω	Go to *Step 4*	Go to *Step 8*
4	Using *J 39200* DMM, measure the resistance between *J 41247* terminal 4 and the BPMV case. Is the resistance within the range specified in the value(s) column?	OL (infinite)	Go to *Step 5*	Go to *Step 8*
5	1. Remove *J 41247*. 2. Reinstall the EBTCM to BPMV. 3. Reconnect the EBTCM connector. 4. Turn the ignition switch to the RUN position, engine off. Does DTC C1274 reset as a current DTC?	—	Go to *Step 9*	Go to *Step 7*
6	1. If connector corrosion or damage are present, replace BPMV and/or EBTCM as necessary. 2. If brake fluid is present, replace both the BPMV and EBTCM. Is the repair complete?	—	Go to *Diagnostic System Check*	—
7	Using a scan tool in ABS/TCS Special Functions run the AUTOMATED Test. Does DTC C1274 reset as a current DTC?	—	Go to *Step 8*	Go to *Diagnostic System Check*
8	Replace the BPMV. Is the replacement complete?	—	Go to *Diagnostic System Check*	—
9	Replace the EBTCM. Is the replacement complete?	—	Go to *Diagnostic System Check*	—

GC402980281200BX

Fig. 227 Code C1274: RH Front TCS Prime Valve Fault (Part 2 of 2). DeVille & Seville

Step	Action	Value(s)	Yes	No
12	Use a *J 39200* DMM in order to measure the resistance between the *J 39700* terminal 6 and the PCM connector C2 terminal 27. Is the resistance less than the specified value?	2 Ω	Go to *Step 13*	Go to *Step 14*
13	Suspect the PCM. Is the diagnosis complete?	—	Go to *A Diagnostic System Check - ABS*	—
14	Repair the open in CKT 464. Did you complete the repair?	—	Go to *A Diagnostic System Check - ABS*	—

GC4029903921030X

Fig. 228 Code C1276: Delivered Torque Signal Circuit Fault (Part 3 of 3). DeVille

Circuit Description

The EBTCM and the PCM simultaneously controlled the traction control. The PCM sends a Delivered Torque message via a pulse width modulated (PWM) signal to the EBTCM confirming the delivered torque level for proper TCS operation. The EBTCM supplies the pull up voltage.

Conditions for Setting the DTC

The DTC sets if all of the following occur:

- The ignition is ON.
- The PWM signal is out of range or no signal is received for 7 seconds.

Action Taken When the DTC Sets

- A malfunction DTC is stored.
- The TCS is disabled.
- The TRACTION CONTROL indicator is turned ON.
- The ABS remains functional.

Conditions for Clearing the DTC

- The condition for DTC is no longer present and you used scan tool Clear DTCs function.
- The condition for DTC is no longer present and you used the On-Board Clear DTCs function.
- The EBTCM does not detect the DTC in 50 drive cycles.

Diagnostic Aids

- It is very important that a thorough inspection of the wiring and connectors be performed. Failure to carefully and fully inspect wiring and connectors may result in misdiagnosis, causing part replacement with reappearance of the malfunction.
- An intermittent malfunction can be caused by poor connections, broken insulation, or a wire that is broken inside the insulation.
- If an intermittent malfunction exists, refer to *Intermittents and Poor Connections*
- The following conditions can cause this concern:
  - An open circuit.
  - An short to ground or voltage in the circuit.
  - A wiring problem, terminal corrosion, or poor connection in the circuit.
  - A communication frequency problem.
  - A communication duty cycle problem.
  - The EBTCM is not receiving information from the PCM.

GC4029803895010X

Fig. 229 Code C1276: Delivered Torque Signal Circuit Fault (Part 1 of 3). Seville

Test Description

The numbers below refer to step numbers on the diagnostic table.

4. Checks for proper duty cycle.
5. Checks for proper frequency.

Step	Action	Value(s)	Yes	No
1	Did you perform the Diagnostic System Check?	—	Go to *Step 2*	Go to *Diagnostic System Check*
2	Check the following grounds, making sure each ground is clean and torqued to the proper specifications: • G102 • G103 Were any loose, damaged, or corroded grounds found?	—	Go to *Step 3*	Go to *Step 4*
3	Repair the ground as necessary. Did you complete the repair?	—	Go to *Diagnostic System Check*	—
4	1. Turn OFF the ignition. 2. Disconnect the EBTCM harness connector. 3. Install the *J 39700* universal pinout box using the *J 39700-25* cable adapter to the EBTCM harness connector and the EBTCM connector. 4. Turn ON the ignition, with the engine OFF. Using a *J 39200* DMM, measure the DC duty cycle between *J 39700* terminals 6 and B. Is the duty cycle within the specified range?	5–15%	Go to *Step 5*	Go to *Step 7*
5	Using a *J 39200* DMM, measure the DC Hz between the *J 39700* terminals 6 and B. Is the frequency within the range specified?	121–134 Hz	Go to *Step 6*	Go to *Step 13*
6	Replace the EBTCM. Did you complete the repair?	—	Go to *Diagnostic System Check*	—
7	1. Turn OFF the ignition. 2. Disconnect the PCM connector C2. 3. Turn ON the ignition, with the engine OFF. 4. Using a *J 39200* DMM, measure the voltage between terminals 6 and B of *J 39700*. Is the voltage within the specified range?	Battery Voltage	Go to *Step 8*	Go to *Step 10*
8	1. Turn OFF the ignition. 2. Disconnect the *J 39700-25* cable adaptor from the EBTCM leaving the cable adaptor connected to the EBTCM harness only. 3. Turn ON the ignition, with the engine OFF. 4. Using a *J 39200* DMM, measure the voltage between the *J 39700* terminals 6 and B. Is the voltage greater than the specified value?	1 V	Go to *Step 9*	Go to *Step 12*
9	Repair the short to voltage in CKT 464. Did you complete the repair?	—	Go to *Diagnostic System Check*	—
10	1. Turn OFF the ignition. 2. Using a *J 39200* DMM, measure the resistance between the *J 39700* terminals 6 and B. Is the resistance within the specified range?	OL (infinite)	Go to *Step 6*	Go to *Step 11*

GC4029803895020X

Fig. 229 Code C1276: Delivered Torque Signal Circuit Fault (Part 2 of 3). Seville

Step	Action	Value(s)	Yes	No
11	Repair the short to ground in CKT 464. Did you complete the repair?	—	Go to *Diagnostic System Check*	—
12	Using a *J 39200* DMM, measure the resistance between the *J 39700* terminal 6 and the PCM connector C2 terminal 27. Is the resistance less than the specified value?	2 Ω	Go to *Step 13*	Go to *Step 14*
13	Suspect PCM. Is the diagnosis complete?	—	Go to *Diagnostic System Check*	—
14	Repair the open in CKT 464. Did you complete the repair?	—	Go to *Diagnostic System Check*	—

GC4029803895030X

Fig. 229 Code C1276: Delivered Torque Signal Circuit Fault (Part 3 of 3). Seville

Circuit Description

The EBTCM and the PCM simultaneously control the traction control. The PCM receives a REQUESTED TORQUE message via a Pulse Width Modulated (PWM) signal from the EBTCM requesting the desired torque level for proper TCS operation. The PCM supplies the pull up voltage.

Conditions for Setting the DTC

There is an open or short in the REQUESTED TORQUE line between the EBTCM and the PCM or there is a TCS communication malfunction detected by the PCM and indicated to the EBTCM via a PWM message.

Action Taken When the DTC Sets

- A DTC C1277 is stored
- The TCS is disabled
- The TRACTION OFF indicator is turned on
- The ABS remains functional.

Conditions for Clearing the DTC

- The condition for the DTC is no longer present and the scan tool clear DTC function is used
- 50 ignition cycles have passed with no DTCs detected.

Diagnostic Aids

- Thoroughly inspect the wiring and the connectors. Failure to carefully and fully inspect the wiring and the connectors can result in misdiagnosis. Misdiagnosis causes reappearance of the malfunction with part replacement.
- The following conditions are other possible causes for this malfunction:
  - An open, a short to ground, or a short to voltage in CKT 463
  - A communication frequency problem
  - A communication duty cycle problem
  - A wiring problem, terminal corrosion, or a poor connection in CKT 463
  - The PCM is not receiving information from the EBTCM.
- If an intermittent malfunction exists, refer to Troubleshooting

Test Description

The numbers below refer to the step numbers on the diagnostic table.

4. This step checks for the proper duty cycle.
5. This step checks for the proper frequency.

GC402980281400AX

Fig. 230 Code C1277: Requested Torque Signal Circuit Fault (Part 1 of 3). DeVille & Seville

Step	Action	Value(s)	Yes	No
1	Was the Diagnostic System Check performed?	—	*Go to Step 2*	Go to *Diagnostic System Check*
2	Check the following grounds, G110, and G107 making sure each ground is clean tight and free of damage. Were any loose, damaged, or corroded grounds found?	—	*Go to Step 3*	*Go to Step 4*
3	Repair the grounds as necessary. Is the repair complete?	—	Go to *Diagnostic System Check*	—
4	1. Turn the ignition switch to the OFF position. 2. Disconnect the EBTCM connector. 3. Install the *J 39700* Universal Pinout Box using the *J 39700-25* cable adapter to the EBTCM harness connector and the EBTCM connector. 4. Turn the ignition switch to the RUN position with the engine off. 5. Using the *J 39200* DMM, measure the DC duty cycle between the *J 39700* terminals 25 and B. Is the duty cycle within specifications?	85 - 95%	*Go to Step 5*	*Go to Step 6*
5	Using the *J 39200*, measure the DC Hz between the *J 39700* terminals 25 and B. Is the frequency within specifications?	121 - 134 Hz	*Go to Step 13*	*Go to Step 7*
6	1. Turn the ignition switch to the OFF position. 2. Disconnect the *J 39700-25* cable adapter from the EBTCM, leaving the *J 39700* connected to the EBTCM harness only. 3. Using the *J 39200* DMM, measure the voltage between the *J 39700* terminals 25 and B. Is the voltage within specifications?	4.5 - 5.5 V	*Go to Step 7*	*Go to Step 8*
7	Replace the EBTCM. Is the replacement complete?	—	Go to *Diagnostic System Check*	—
8	1. Turn the ignition switch to the OFF position. 2. Disconnect the PCM connector C1. 3. Turn the ignition switch to the RUN position with the engine off. 4. Using the *J 39200* DMM, measure the voltage between the *J 39700* terminals 25 and B. Is the voltage within specifications?	More than 1.0 V	*Go to Step 9*	*Go to Step 10*
9	Repair the short to voltage in CKT 463. Is the circuit repair complete?	—	Go to *Diagnostic System Check*	—
10	1. Turn the ignition switch to the OFF position. 2. Using the *J 39200* DMM, measure the resistance between the *J 39700* terminals 25 and B. Is the resistance within specifications?	OL (infinite)	*Go to Step 12*	*Go to Step 11*
11	Repair the short to ground in CKT 463. Is the circuit repair complete?	—	Go to *Diagnostic System Check*	—

GC402980281400BX

Fig. 230 Code C1277: Requested Torque Signal Circuit Fault (Part 2 of 3). DeVille & Seville

Step	Action	Value(s)	Yes	No
12	Using the *J 39200* DMM, measure the resistance between the *J 39700* terminal 25 and the PCM connector C1 terminal 46. Is the resistance within specifications?	0 - 2 Ω	*Go to Step 13*	*Go to Step 14*
13	Suspect the PCM. Is the diagnosis complete?	—	Go to *Diagnostic System Check*	—
14	Repair the open in CKT 463. Is the circuit repair complete?	—	Go to *Diagnostic System Check*	—

GC402980281400CX

Fig. 230 Code C1277: Requested Torque Signal Circuit Fault (Part 3 of 3). DeVille & Seville

Circuit Description

The PCM monitors various parameters and will not allow traction control operation if any parameter falls below a specified value.

Conditions for Setting the DTC

The PCM detects a malfunction and then causes TCS shut down until the malfunction has been corrected.

Action Taken When the DTC Sets

- A DTC C1278 is stored (This is a temporary malfunction)
- The TCS is disabled
- The TRACTION OFF indicator is turned on
- If the TCS is no longer inhibited, the indicator will be turned off but the DTC will be stored

Conditions for Clearing the DTC

- The condition for the DTC is no longer present and the scan tool clear DTC function is used
- 50 ignition cycles have passed with no DTCs detected.

Diagnostic Aids

This code is for information only. As an aid to the technician, this code indicates that there are no problems in the ABS/TCS system

Test Description

The numbers below refer to the step numbers on the diagnostic table.

4. This step checks if DTC C1278 resets.

GC402980281500AX

Fig. 231 Code C1278: TCS Temporarily Inhibited By PCM (Part 1 of 2). DeVille & Seville

Step	Action	Value(s)	Yes	No
1	Was the on Diagnostic System Check performed?	—	*Go to Step 2*	Go to *Diagnostic System Check*
2	1. Turn the ignition switch to the RUN position with the engine off. 2. Using a Scan Tool, read the ABS/TCS DTCs. Are any other DTCs set?	—	Go to the appropriate DTC table	*Go to Step 3*
3	Is DTC C1278 set as a current code?	—	*Go to Step 5*	*Go to Step 4*
4	1. Start the engine and test drive the vehicle at least 16 km/h (10 mph) while monitoring the Scan Tool for ABS/TCS DTCs. 2. Repeat the above drive cycle sequence two more times. Did DTC C1278 set in the last three drive cycles?	—	*Go to Step 5*	Go to *Diagnostic System Check*
5	Perform the Powertrain OBD System Check. Did the vehicle pass the OBD System Check?	—	Go to Diagnostic Aids	Inspect Engine Controls

GC402980281500BX

Fig. 231 Code C1278: TCS Temporarily Inhibited By PCM (Part 2 of 2). DeVille & Seville

Diagnostic Aids

- Check the vehicle for proper alignment. The car should not pull in either direction while driving straight on a flat surface.
- Find out from the driver under what conditions the DTC was set (when the DIC displayed the SERVICE STABILITY SYS message). This information will help to duplicate the failure.
- Thoroughly inspect the wiring and the connectors. An incomplete inspection of the wiring and the connectors may result in a misdiagnosis, causing a part replacement with the reappearance of the malfunction.
- Poor connections, broken insulation, or a break in the wire inside the insulation may cause an intermittent malfunction.
- If an intermittent malfunction exists, refer to *Intermittents and Poor Connections*
- The Snapshot function on the scan tool can help find an intermittent DTC.

Step	Action	Value(s)	Yes	No
1	Did you perform the ABS Diagnostic System Check?	—	Go to *Step 2*	Go to *A Diagnostic System Check - ABS*
2	1. Turn OFF the ignition. 2. Connect a scan tool to the data link connector (DLC). 3. Turn ON the ignition, with the engine OFF. 4. Use the scan tool in order to read ABS/TCS/ICCS DTCs. Are DTCs C1221–C1235 or C1282–C1288 present?	—	Go to *DTC List*	Go to *Step 3*
3	Use the scan tool in order to perform the steering wheel position sensor test. Is the analog and the digital display on the scan tool within 5 degrees of each other at the center (zero) position?	—	Go to *Step 5*	Go to *Step 4*
4	Replace the steering wheel position sensor (SWPS). Did you complete the repair?	—	Go to *Step 7*	—
5	1. Use the scan tool in order to select ABS/TCS/ICCS Data Display (1) Diagnostics, Data List 2. 2. Observe the Yaw Rate Sensor Input parameter. 3. Carefully drive vehicle above 24 km/h (15 mph) for 45 seconds in a straight line. Is the voltage within the specified range?	2.3–2.7 V	Go to *Step 7*	Go to *Step 6*
6	Replace the yaw rate sensor. Did you complete the repair?	—	Go to *Step 7*	—
7	Perform the diagnostic test drive. Did DTC C1281 set as a current DTC?	—	Go to *Step 8*	Go to *A Diagnostic System Check - ABS*
8	Replace the EBTCM. Did you complete the repair?	—	Go to *A Diagnostic System Check - ABS*	—

GC4029903922020X

Fig. 232 Code C1281: Stabilitrak Sensors Uncorrelated (Part 2 of 2). DeVille

Circuit Description

Stabilitrak® is activated by the EBTCM calculating the desired yaw rate and comparing it the actual yaw rate input. The desired yaw rate is calculated from measured steering wheel position, vehicle speed, and lateral acceleration. The difference between the desired yaw rate and actual yaw rate is the yaw rate error, which is a measurement of oversteer or understeer. If the yaw rate error becomes too large, the EBTCM will attempt to correct the vehicle's yaw motion by applying differential braking to the left or right front wheel.

Conditions for Setting the DTC

One of the following conditions occur:

- During Stabilitrak® activation, the analog and digital steering sensor inputs do not agree for 1 second.
- During Stabilitrak® activation, the estimated and actual yaw rates do not agree for 5 seconds.
- The EBTCM checks for this DTC after the steering angle has been centered, during Stabilitrak® activation, and when the vehicle does not have lateral acceleration. The DTC sets when the yaw rate error does not change for 10 seconds.
- In most cases, DTCs C1284–C1287 will set this DTC.
- Normal conditions which could cause this DTC to set include Stabilitrak® activations brought on by aggressive driving on extremely slippery road surfaces. For example, spinning the vehicle in one direction for more than 10 seconds.

Action Taken When the DTC Sets

- A malfunction DTC is stored.
- Stabilitrak® is disabled.
- The DIC displays the SERVICE STABILITY SYS message.
- The ABS/TCS remain functional.

Conditions for Clearing the DTC

- The condition for DTC is no longer present and you used scan tool Clear DTCs function.
- The condition for DTC is no longer present and you used the On-Board Clear DTCs function.
- The EBTCM does not detect the DTC in 50 drive cycles.

GC4029903922010X

Fig. 232 Code C1281: Stabilitrak Sensors Uncorrelated (Part 1 of 2). DeVille

Circuit Description

Stabilitrak® is activated by the EBTCM calculating the desired yaw rate and comparing it the actual yaw rate input. The desired yaw rate is calculated from measured steering wheel position, vehicle speed, and lateral acceleration. The difference between the desired yaw rate and actual yaw rate is the yaw rate error, which is a measurement of oversteer or understeer. If the yaw rate error becomes too large, the EBTCM will attempt to correct the vehicle's yaw motion by applying differential braking to the left or right front wheel.

Conditions for Setting the DTC

One of the following conditions occur:

- During Stabilitrak® activation, the analog and digital steering sensor inputs do not agree for 1 second.
- During Stabilitrak® activation, the estimated and actual yaw rates do not agree for 5 seconds.
- The EBTCM checks for this DTC after the steering angle has been centered, during Stabilitrak® activation, and when the vehicle does not have lateral acceleration. The DTC sets when the yaw rate error does not change for 10 seconds.
- In most cases, DTCs C1284–C1287 will set this DTC.
- Normal conditions which could cause this DTC to set include Stabilitrak® activations brought on by aggressive driving on extremely slippery road surfaces. For example, spinning the vehicle in one direction for more than 10 seconds.

Action Taken When the DTC Sets

- A malfunction DTC is stored.
- Stabilitrak® is disabled.
- The DIC displays the SERVICE STABILITY SYS message.
- The ABS/TCS remain functional.

Conditions for Clearing the DTC

- The condition for DTC is no longer present and you used scan tool Clear DTCs function.
- The condition for DTC is no longer present and you used the On-Board Clear DTCs function.
- The EBTCM does not detect the DTC in 50 drive cycles.

GC4029803896010X

Fig. 233 Code C1281: ABC Sensors Uncorrelated (Part 1 of 2). Seville

Diagnostic Aids

- Check the vehicle for proper alignment. The car should not pull in either direction while driving straight on a flat surface.
- Find out from the driver under what conditions the DTC was set (when the DIC displayed the SERVICE STABILITY SYS message). This information will help to duplicate the failure.
- Thoroughly inspect the wiring and the connectors. An incomplete inspection of the wiring and the connectors may result in a misdiagnosis, causing a part replacement with the reappearance of the malfunction.
- Poor connections, broken insulation, or a break in the wire inside the insulation may cause an intermittent malfunction.
- If an intermittent malfunction exists, refer to *Intermittents and Poor Connections*
- The Snapshot function on the scan tool can help find an intermittent DTC.

Step	Action	Value(s)	Yes	No
1	Did you perform the Diagnostic System Check?	—	Go to *Step 2*	Go to *Diagnostic System Check*
2	1. Turn OFF the ignition. 2. Connect a scan tool to the data link connector (DLC). 3. Turn ON the ignition, with the engine OFF. 4. Using the scan tool, read ABS/TCS/ICCS DTCs. Are DTCs C1221–C1235 or C1282–C1288 present?	—	Go to *DTC List*	Go to *Step 3*
3	Using the scan tool, perform the Steering Wheel Position Sensor Test. Is the analog and digital display on the scan tool within ±5 degrees of each other at the center (zero) position?	—	Go to *Step 5*	Go to *Step 4*
4	Replace the steering wheel position sensor (SWPS). Did you complete the repair?	—	Go to *Step 7*	—
5	1. Using the scan tool, select ABS/TCS/ICCS Data Display (1) Diagnostics, DATA LIST 2. 2. Monitor the Yaw Rate Sensor Input. 3. Carefully drive vehicle above 24 Km/h (15 mph) for 45 seconds in a straight line. Is the voltage within the specified range?	2.3–2.7 V	Go to *Step 7*	Go to *Step 6*
6	Replace the yaw rate sensor. Did you complete the repair?	—	Go to *Step 7*	—
7	Perform the Diagnostic Test Drive. Did DTC C1281 set as a current DTC?	—	Go to *Step 8*	Go to *Diagnostic System Check*
8	Replace the EBTCM. Did you complete the repair?	—	Go to *Diagnostic System Check*	—

GC4029803896020X

Fig. 233 Code C1281: ABC Sensors Uncorrelated (Part 2 of 2). Seville

Circuit Description

The yaw rate bias is calculated by the EBTCM any time ignition is present and the car is standing still. This value is used to compensate for offsets in the yaw rate sensor output due to temperature changes and manufacturing differences. If this bias exceeds ± 5 degrees/second or 0.196 volts then the sensor is assumed to be bad and DTC C1282 will set. The scan tool will report a zero yaw value of 2.5 volts (0 degrees/second) if no offset bias exists.

Conditions for Setting the DTC

- DTC C1282 can be set any time after the steering angle has been centered and the yaw rate sensor voltage is less than 0.15 volts (-67 degrees/second) or greater than 4.85 volts (67 degrees/second.)
- If the measured yaw rate changes by more than 390 degrees/second within one second then DTC C1282 will set.

Action Taken When the DTC Sets

A malfunction DTC is stored, ABS and TCS remain enabled, Stabilitrak™ is disabled and the SERV STABILITY SYS message will be displayed on the DIC.

Conditions for Clearing the DTC

- Condition for DTC is no longer present and scan tool clear DTC function is used.
- Fifty ignition cycles have passed with no DTC(s) detected.

Diagnostic Aids

- If DTC C1281 is set then there is a mismatch between estimated an actual yaw rates.
- It is very important to check the vehicle for proper alignment. The car should not pull in either direction while driving straight on a flat surface.
- When performing the following diagnostic procedure, insure that the vehicle is parked on a level surface.
- It is important to find out from the driver when the code was set, (when the SERV STABILITY SYS message was activated) and what was he doing at the time. This information will help to duplicate the failure.
- It is very important that a thorough inspection of the wiring and connectors be performed. Failure to carefully and fully inspect wiring and connectors may result in misdiagnosis, causing part replacement with reappearance of the malfunction.
- An intermittent malfunction is most likely caused by a poor connection, rubbed through wire insulation, or a wire that is broken inside the insulation.

GC402980281700AX

Fig. 234 Code C1282: Yaw Rate Sensor Bias Circuit Fault (Part 1 of 5). DeVille & Seville

Step	Action	Value(s)	Yes	No
1	Was the Diagnostic System Check performed?	—	*Go to Step 2*	Go to *Diagnostic System Check*
2	1. Turn the ignition switch to the OFF position. 2. Disconnect the EBTCM connector. 3. Install *J 39700* Universal Pinout Box using the *J 39700-25* cable adapter to the EBTCM harness connector only. 4. Using *J 39200* DMM, measure the resistance between *J 39700* terminals 21 and B. Is the resistance within the range specified in the value(s) column?	OL (infinite)	*Go to Step 4*	*Go to Step 3*
3	Repair CKT 716 for a short to ground. Is the repair complete?	—	Go to *Diagnostic System Check*	—
4	Using *J 39200* DMM, measure the resistance between *J 39700* terminals 11 and B. Is the resistance within the range specified in the value(s) column?	OL (infinite)	*Go to Step 6*	*Go to Step 5*
5	Repair CKT 1337 for a short to ground. Is the repair complete?	—	Go to *Diagnostic System Check*	—
6	Using *J 39200* DMM, measure the resistance between *J 39700* terminals 27 and B. Is the resistance within the range specified in the value(s) column?	OL (infinite)	*Go to Step 8*	*Go to Step 7*
7	Repair CKT 1338 for a short to ground. Is the repair complete?	—	Go to *Diagnostic System Check*	—

GC402980281700BX

Fig. 234 Code C1282: Yaw Rate Sensor Bias Circuit Fault (Part 2 of 5). DeVille & Seville

Step	Action	Value(s)	Yes	No
8	Using *J 39200* DMM, measure the resistance between *J 39700* terminals 11 and 27. Is the resistance within the range specified in the value(s) column?	OL (infinite)	*Go to Step 10*	*Go to Step 9*
9	Repair short between CKT(s) 1337 and 1338. Is the repair complete?	—	Go to *Diagnostic System Check*	—
10	Using *J 39200* DMM, measure the resistance between *J 39700* terminals 11 and 21. Is the resistance within the range specified in the value(s) column?	OL (infinite)	*Go to Step 12*	*Go to Step 11*
11	Repair short between CKT(s) 1337 and 716. Is the repair complete?	—	Go to *Diagnostic System Check*	—
12	Using *J 39200* DMM, measure the resistance between *J 39700* terminals 27 and 21. Is the resistance within the range specified in the value(s) column?	OL (infinite)	*Go to Step 14*	*Go to Step 13*
13	Repair short between CKT(s) 1338 and 716. Is the repair complete?	—	Go to *Diagnostic System Check*	—
14	1. Turn the ignition switch to the RUN position, engine OFF. 2. Using *J 39200* DMM, measure the voltage between *J 39700* terminals 21 and B. Is the voltage within the range specified in the value(s) column?	Greater than 1V	*Go to Step 15*	*Go to Step 16*
15	Repair CKT 716 for a short to voltage. Is the repair complete?	—	Go to *Diagnostic System Check*	—
16	Using *J 39200* DMM, measure the voltage between *J 39700* terminals 11 and B. Is the voltage within the range specified in the value(s) column?	Greater than 1V	*Go to Step 17*	*Go to Step 18*
17	Repair CKT 1337 for a short to voltage. Is the repair complete?	—	Go to *Diagnostic System Check*	—
18	Using *J 39200* DMM, measure the voltage between *J 39700* terminals 27 and B. Is the voltage within the range specified in the value(s) column?	Greater than 1V	*Go to Step 19*	*Go to Step 20*
19	Repair CKT 1338 for a short to voltage. Is the repair complete?	—	Go to *Diagnostic System Check*	—

GC402980281700CX

Fig. 234 Code C1282: Yaw Rate Sensor Bias Circuit Fault (Part 3 of 5). DeVille & Seville

Step	Action	Value(s)	Yes	No
20	1. Turn the ignition switch to the OFF position. 2. Connect a fused jumper wire between terminals 21 and B of *J 39700*. 3. Disconnect the Yaw Rate Sensor connector. 4. Using *J 39200* DMM, measure the resistance between the Yaw Rate Sensor harness connector terminal C and a good ground. Is the resistance within the range specified in the value(s) column?	0 - 2Ω	*Go to Step 22*	*Go to Step 21*
21	Repair CKT 716 for an open or high resistance. Is the repair complete?	—	Go to *Diagnostic System Check*	—
22	1. Connect a fused jumper wire between terminals 27 and B of *J 39700*. 2. Using *J 39200* DMM, measure the resistance between the Yaw Rate Sensor harness connector terminal B and a good ground. Is the resistance within the range specified in the value(s) column?	0 - 2Ω	*Go to Step 24*	*Go to Step 23*
23	Repair CKT 1338 for an open or high resistance. Is the repair complete?	—	Go to *Diagnostic System Check*	—
24	1. Connect a fused jumper wire between terminals 11 and B of *J 39700*. 2. Using *J 39200* DMM, measure the resistance between the Yaw Rate Sensor harness connector terminal A and a good ground. Is the resistance within the range specified in the value(s) column?	0 - 2Ω	*Go to Step 26*	*Go to Step 25*
25	Repair CKT 1337 for an open or high resistance. Is the repair complete?	—	Go to *Diagnostic System Check*	—
26	1. Install *J 39700* Universal Pinout Box using the *J 39700-25* cable adapter to the EBTCM and the EBTCM harness connector. 2. Reconnect the Yaw Rate Sensor. 3. Remove the fused jumper wire from *J 39700*. 4. Turn the ignition switch to the RUN position, engine OFF. 5. Using *J 39200* DMM, measure the voltage between *J 39700* terminals 11 and 27. Is the voltage within the range specified in the value(s) column?	4.5 - 5.5V	*Go to Step 27*	*Go to Step 32*
27	Using *J 39200* DMM, measure the voltage between *J 39700* terminals 21 and B. Is the voltage within the range specified in the value(s) column?	2.35 - 2.65V	*Go to Step 28*	*Go to Step 30*
28	Using *J 39200* DMM, measure the voltage between *J 39700* terminals 21 and 27. Is the voltage within the range specified in the value(s) column?	2.35 - 2.65V	*Go to Step 29*	*Go to Step 27*

GC402980281700DX

Fig. 234 Code C1282: Yaw Rate Sensor Bias Circuit Fault (Part 4 of 5). DeVille & Seville

Step	Action	Value(s)	Yes	No
29	Using a scan tool read the Yaw Rate Sensor value in volts. Is the voltage within the range specified in the value(s) column?	2.0 - 3.0V	Go to *Step 30*	Go to *Step 32*
30	Replace the Yaw Rate Sensor. Is the replacement complete?	—	Go to *Step 31*	—
31	1. Read the diagnostic aids and conditions for setting the DTC. 2. Cycle the ignition switch from the OFF to RUN position. 3. Carefully drive the vehicle above 24 Km/h (15 mph) for several minutes, while monitoring a scan tool for ABS/TCS/ICCS DTC(s). Did DTC C1282 set as a current DTC while the vehicle was being driven?	—	Go to *Step 32*	Go to *Diagnostic System Check*
32	Replace the EBTCM. Is the replacement complete?	—	Go to *Diagnostic System Check*	—

GC402980281700EX

Fig. 234 Code C1282: Yaw Rate Sensor Bias Circuit Fault (Part 5 of 5). DeVille & Seville

Step	Action	Value(s)	Yes	No
1	Did you perform the ABS Diagnostic System Check?	—	Go to *Step 2*	Go to *A Diagnostic System Check - ABS*
2	1. Turn OFF the ignition. 2. Connect a scan tool to the data link connector (DLC). 3. Turn ON the ignition, with the engine OFF. 4. Use the scan tool in order to read ABS/TCS/ICCS DTCs. Are DTCs C1221–C1235, C1282, or C1284–C1288 present?	—	Go to *DTC List*	Go to *Step 3*
3	1. Place the steering wheel in the center position so that the front wheels point straight forward. 2. Use the scan tool in order to select the ABS/TCS/ICCS Data Display (1) Diagnostics, Data List 2. 3. Read the analog steering wheel position. Is the voltage within the specified range?	2.05–2.60 V	Go to *Step 5*	Go to *Step 4*
4	Replace the steering wheel position sensor (SWPS). Did you complete the repair?	—	Go to *A Diagnostic System Check - ABS*	—
5	1. Place the vehicle on level ground. 2. Turn OFF the ignition. 3. Disconnect the EBTCM connector. 4. Install the *J 39700* universal pinout box using the *J 39700-25* cable adapter to the EBTCM and the EBTCM harness connector. 5. Turn ON the ignition, with the engine OFF. 6. Use a *J 39200* DMM in order to measure the voltage between the *J 39700* terminal 22 and terminal B. Is the voltage within the specified range?	2.3–2.7 V	Go to *Step 7*	Go to *Step 6*
6	Replace the lateral accelerometer. Did you complete the repair?	—	Go to *A Diagnostic System Check - ABS*	—
7	Use a *J 39200* DMM in order to measure the voltage between the *J 39700* terminal 21 and terminal B. Is the voltage within the specified range?	2.3–2.7 V	Go to *Step 9*	Go to *Step 8*
8	Replace the yaw rate sensor. Did you complete the repair?	—	Go to *A Diagnostic System Check - ABS*	—
9	1. Read Diagnostic Aids and Conditions for Setting the DTC. 2. Turn OFF the ignition. 3. Turn ON the ignition, with the engine OFF. 4. Carefully drive the vehicle above 40 km/h (25 mph) for 10 minutes, while monitoring a scan tool for ABS/TCS/ICCS DTCs. Did DTC C1283 set as a current DTC?	—	Go to *Step 10*	Go to *A Diagnostic System Check - ABS*
10	Replace the EBTCM. Did you complete the repair?	—	Go to *A Diagnostic System Check - ABS*	—

GC4029903923020X

Fig. 235 Code C1283: Excessive Time To Center Steering (Part 2 of 2). DeVille

Circuit Description

Steer angle centering is the process by which the EBTCM calibrates the steering sensor output so that it reads zero when the steering wheel is centered. The initial steering wheel center position is calculated by using the inputs from the yaw rate sensor, the lateral accelerometer, and the wheel speed sensors. The initial steering wheel center position is calculated after driving 10 seconds in a straight line on a level surface at a speed greater than 10 km/h (6 mph).

The initial steering wheel center position will be determined quickly unless there is a large offset in the yaw rate sensor or lateral accelerometer. When this condition occurs, the system will believe that the steering wheel is far off center even though the vehicle is being driven in a straight line.

Conditions for Setting the DTC

All of the following conditions occur:

- The vehicle speed is greater than 40 km/h (25 mph).
- The vehicle has been driven for 10 minutes without completing steer angle centering.

Action Taken When the DTC Sets

- A malfunction DTC is stored.
- Stabilitrak® is disabled.
- The DIC displays the SERVICE STABILITY SYS message.
- The ABS/TCS remain functional.

Conditions for Clearing the DTC

- The condition for DTC is no longer present and you used scan tool Clear DTCs function.
- The condition for DTC is no longer present and you used the On-Board Clear DTCs function.
- The EBTCM does not detect the DTC in 50 drive cycles.

Diagnostic Aids

- Check the vehicle for proper alignment. The car should not pull in either direction while driving straight on a flat surface.
- Find out from the driver under what conditions the DTC was set (when the DIC displayed the SERVICE STABILITY SYS message). This information will help to duplicate the failure.
- Thoroughly inspect the wiring and the connectors. An incomplete inspection of the wiring and the connectors may result in a misdiagnosis, causing a part replacement with the reappearance of the malfunction.
- Poor connections, broken insulation, or a break in the wire inside the insulation may cause an intermittent malfunction.
- If an intermittent malfunction exists, refer to *Intermittents and Poor Connections*
- The Snapshot function on the scan tool can help find an intermittent DTC.

GC4029903923010X

Fig. 235 Code C1283: Excessive Time To Center Steering (Part 1 of 2). DeVille

Circuit Description

Steer angle centering is the process by which the EBTCM calibrates the steering sensor output so that it reads zero when the steering wheel is centered. The initial steering wheel center position is calculated by using the inputs from the yaw rate sensor, the lateral accelerometer, and the wheel speed sensors. The initial steering wheel center position is calculated after driving 10 seconds in a straight line on a level surface at a speed greater than 10 km/h (6 mph).

The initial steering wheel center position will be determined quickly unless there is a large offset in the yaw rate sensor or lateral accelerometer. When this condition occurs, the system will believe that the steering wheel is far off center even though the vehicle is being driven in a straight line.

Conditions for Setting the DTC

All of the following conditions occur:

- The vehicle speed is greater than 40 km/h (25 mph).
- The vehicle has been driven for 10 minutes without completing steer angle centering.

Action Taken When the DTC Sets

- A malfunction DTC is stored.
- Stabilitrak® is disabled.
- The DIC displays the SERVICE STABILITY SYS message.
- The ABS/TCS remain functional.

Conditions for Clearing the DTC

- The condition for DTC is no longer present and you used scan tool Clear DTCs function.
- he condition for DTC is no longer present and you used the On-Board Clear DTCs function.
- The EBTCM does not detect the DTC in 50 drive cycles.

Diagnostic Aids

- Check the vehicle for proper alignment. The car should not pull in either direction while driving straight on a flat surface.
- Find out from the driver under what conditions the DTC was set (when the DIC displayed the SERVICE STABILITY SYS message). This information will help to duplicate the failure.
- Thoroughly inspect the wiring and the connectors. An incomplete inspection of the wiring and the connectors may result in a misdiagnosis, causing a part replacement with the reappearance of the malfunction.
- Poor connections, broken insulation, or a break in the wire inside the insulation may cause an intermittent malfunction.
- If an intermittent malfunction exists, refer to *Intermittents and Poor Connections*
- The Snapshot function on the scan tool can help find an intermittent DTC.

GC4029803897010X

Fig. 236 Code C1283: Excessive Time To Center Steering (Part 1 of 2). Seville

Step	Action	Value(s)	Yes	No
1	Did you perform the Diagnostic System Check?	—	Go to *Step 2*	Go to *Diagnostic System Check*
2	1. Turn OFF the ignition. 2. Connect a scan tool to the data link connector (DLC). 3. Turn ON the ignition, with the engine OFF. 4. Using the scan tool, read ABS/TCS/ICCS DTCs. Are DTCs C1221–C1235, C1282, or C1284–C1288 present?	—	Go to *DTC List*	Go to *Step 3*
3	1. Place the steering wheel in the center position so the front wheels point straight forward. 2. Using the scan tool, select the ABS/TCS/ICCS Data Display (1) Diagnostics, DATA LIST 2. 3. Read the Analog Steering Wheel Position. Is the voltage within the specified range?	2.05–2.60 V	Go to *Step 5*	Go to *Step 4*
4	Replace the steering wheel position sensor (SWPS). Did you complete the repair?	—	Go to *Diagnostic System Check*	—
5	1. Place the vehicle on level ground. 2. Turn OFF the ignition. 3. Disconnect the EBTCM harness connector. 4. Install the *J 39700* universal pinout box using the *J 39700-25* cable adapter to the EBTCM and the EBTCM harness connector. 5. Turn ON the ignition, with the engine OFF. 6. Using a *J 39200* DMM, measure the voltage between the *J 39700* terminals 22 and B. Is the voltage within the specified range?	2.3–2.7 V	Go to *Step 7*	Go to *Step 6*
6	Replace the lateral accelerometer sensor. Did you complete the repair?	—	Go to *Diagnostic System Check*	—
7	Using a *J 39200* DMM, measure the voltage between the *J 39700* terminals 21 and B. Is the voltage within the specified range?	2.3–2.7 V	Go to *Step 9*	Go to *Step 8*
8	Replace the yaw rate sensor. Did you complete the repair?	—	Go to *Diagnostic System Check*	—
9	1. Read Diagnostic Aids and Conditions for Setting the DTC. 2. Cycle the ignition switch from the OFF to ON position. 3. Carefully drive the vehicle above 40 Km/h (25 mph) for 10 minutes, while monitoring a scan tool for ABS/TCS/ICCS DTCs. Did DTC C1283 set as a current DTC?	—	Go to *Step 10*	Go to *Diagnostic System Check*
10	Replace the EBTCM. Did you complete the repair?	—	Go to *Diagnostic System Check*	—

GC4029803897020X

Fig. 236 Code C1283: Excessive Time To Center Steering (Part 2 of 2). Seville

Circuit Description

The Lateral Accelerometer performs a Self Test at initialization. The sensors output will be offset by a fixed amount for a short period of time when the EBTCM powers up. The test will run when the ignition is ON, all 4 wheel speeds are 0 km/h and the steer angle is within 90 degrees of straight ahead.

Conditions for Setting the DTC

The EBTCM will set DTC C1284 if it does not see the expected change in the output of the Lateral Accelerometer soon after initialization.

Action Taken When the DTC Sets

A malfunction DTC is stored, ABS and TCS remain enabled, Stabilitrak™ is disabled and the SERV STABILITY SYS message will be displayed on the DIC.

Conditions for Clearing the DTC

- Condition for DTC is no longer present and scan tool clear DTC function is used.
- Fifty ignition cycles have passed with no DTC(s) detected.

Diagnostic Aids

- When performing the following diagnostic procedure, insure that the vehicle is parked on a level surface and the front wheels are straight ahead.
- It is important to find out from the driver when the code was set, (when the SERV STABILITY SYS message was activated) and what was he doing at the time. This information will help to duplicate the failure.
- It is very important that a thorough inspection of the wiring and connectors be performed. Failure to carefully and fully inspect wiring and connectors may result in misdiagnosis, causing part replacement with reappearance of the malfunction.
- An intermittent malfunction is most likely caused by a poor connection, rubbed through wire insulation, or a wire that is broken inside the insulation.

GC402980281900AX

Fig. 237 Code C1284: Lateral Accel Sensor Self Test Fault (Part 1 of 2). DeVille & Seville

Step	Action	Value(s)	Yes	No
1	Was the Diagnostic System Check performed?	—	*Go to Step 2*	Go to *Diagnostic System Check*
2	1. Turn the ignition switch to the RUN position, engine OFF. 2. Using a scan tool read ABS/TCS/ICCS DTC(s). Are any of the following DTC(s) present, C1221-C1235, C1282 or C1285?	—	Go to Applicable DTC table	*Go to Step 3*
3	Replace the Lateral Accelerometer. Is the replacement complete?	—	*Go to Step 4*	—
4	1. Read the diagnostic aids and conditions for setting the DTC. 2. Cycle the ignition from the OFF to RUN position, engine OFF. 3. With a scan tool read ABS/TCS/ICCS DTC(s). Did DTC C1284 reset as a current DTC?	—	*Go to Step 5*	Go to *Diagnostic System Check*
5	Replace the EBTCM. Is the replacement complete?	—	Go to *Diagnostic System Check*	—

GC402980281900BX

Fig. 237 Code C1284: Lateral Accel Sensor Self Test Fault (Part 2 of 2). DeVille & Seville

Circuit Description

The output of the Lateral Accelerometer is measured by the EBTCM any time ignition is present. The usable output voltage range for the Lateral Accelerometer is 0.25 - 4.75 volts. The scan tool will report a zero lateral accelerometer signal of 2.5 volts if no sensor bias (offset) is present.

Conditions for Setting the DTC

DTC C1285 can be set any time the ignition is present and the Lateral Accelerometer voltage is less than 0.15 volts or greater than 4.85 volts for approximately 1 second or more.

Action Taken When the DTC Sets

A malfunction DTC is stored, ABS and TCS remain enabled, Stabilitrak™ is disabled and the SERV STABILITY SYS message will be displayed on the DIC.

Conditions for Clearing the DTC

- Condition for DTC is no longer present and scan tool clear DTC function is used.
- Fifty ignition cycles have passed with no DTC(s) detected.

Diagnostic Aids

- It is important to find out from the driver when the code was set, (when the SERV STABILITY SYS message was activated) and what was he doing at the time. This information will help to duplicate the failure.
- It is very important that a thorough inspection of the wiring and connectors be performed. Failure to carefully and fully inspect wiring and connectors may result in misdiagnosis, causing part replacement with reappearance of the malfunction.
- An intermittent malfunction is most likely caused by a poor connection, rubbed through wire insulation, or a wire that is broken inside the insulation.

GC402980282000AX

Fig. 238 Code C1285: Lateral Accel Sensor Circuit Fault (Part 1 of 4). DeVille & Seville

Step	Action	Value(s)	Yes	No
1	Was the Diagnostic System Check performed?	—	*Go to Step 2*	Go to *Diagnostic System Check*
2	1. Turn the ignition switch to the OFF position. 2. Disconnect the EBTCM connector. 3. Install *J 39700* Universal Pinout Box using the *J 39700-25* cable adapter to the EBTCM harness connector only. 4. Using *J 39200* DMM, measure the resistance between *J 39700* terminals 22 and B. Is the resistance within the range specified in the value(s) column?	OL (infinite)	*Go to Step 4*	*Go to Step 3*
3	Repair CKT 715 for a short to ground. Is the repair complete?	—	Go to *Diagnostic System Check*	—
4	Using *J 39200* DMM, measure the resistance between *J 39700* terminals 11 and B. Is the resistance within the range specified in the value(s) column?	OL (infinite)	*Go to Step 6*	*Go to Step 5*
5	Repair CKT 1337 for a short to ground. Is the repair complete?	—	Go to *Diagnostic System Check*	—
6	Using *J 39200* DMM, measure the resistance between *J 39700* terminals 27 and B. Is the resistance within the range specified in the value(s) column?	OL (infinite)	*Go to Step 8*	*Go to Step 7*
7	Repair CKT 1338 for a short to ground. Is the repair complete?	—	Go to *Diagnostic System Check*	—
8	Using *J 39200* DMM, measure the resistance between *J 39700* terminals 11 and 27. Is the resistance within the range specified in th value(s) column?	OL (infinite)	*Go to Step 10*	*Go to Step 9*
9	Repair short between CKT(s) 1337 and 1338. Is the repair complete?	—	Go to *Diagnostic System Check*	—
10	Using *J 39200* DMM, measure the resistance between *J 39700* terminals 11 and 22. Is the resistance within the range specified in the value(s) column?	OL (infinite)	*Go to Step 12*	*Go to Step 11*
11	Repair short between CKT(s) 1337 and 715. Is the repair complete?	—	Go to *Diagnostic System Check*	—
12	Using *J 39200* DMM, measure the resistance between *J 39700* terminals 27 and 22. Is the resistance within the range specified in the value(s) column?	OL (infinite)	*Go to Step 14*	*Go to Step 13*
13	Repair short between CKT(s) 1338 and 715. Is the repair complete?	—	Go to *Diagnostic System Check*	—

GC402980282000BX

Fig. 238 Code C1285: Lateral Accel Sensor Circuit Fault (Part 2 of 4). DeVille & Seville

Step	Action	Value(s)	Yes	No
14	1. Turn the ignition switch to the RUN position, engine OFF. 2. Using *J 39200* DMM, measure the voltage between *J 39700* terminals 22 and B. Is the voltage within the range specified in the value(s) column?	Greater than 1V	*Go to Step 15*	*Go to Step 16*
15	Repair CKT 715 for a short to voltage. Is the repair complete?	—	Go to *Diagnostic System Check*	—
16	Using *J 39200* DMM, measure the voltage between *J 39700* terminals 11 and B. Is the voltage within the range specified in the value(s) column?	Greater than 1V	*Go to Step 17*	*Go to Step 18*
17	Repair CKT 1337 for a short to voltage. Is the repair complete?	—	Go to *Diagnostic System Check*	—
18	Using *J 39200* DMM, measure the voltage between *J 39700* terminals 27 and B. Is the voltage within the range specified in the value(s) column?	Greater than 1V	*Go to Step 19*	*Go to Step 20*
19	Repair CKT 1338 for a short to voltage. Is the repair complete?	—	Go to *Diagnostic System Check*	—
20	1. Turn the ignition switch to the OFF position. 2. Connect a fused jumper wire between terminals 22 and B of *J 39700*. 3. Disconnect the Lateral Accelerometer connector. 4. Using *J 39200* DMM, measure the resistance between the Lateral Accelerometer harness connector terminal B and a good ground. Is the resistance within the range specified in the value(s) column?	0 - 2Ω	*Go to Step 22*	*Go to Step 21*
21	Repair CKT 715 for an open or high resistance. Is the repair complete?	—	Go to *Diagnostic System Check*	—
22	1. Connect a fused jumper wire between terminals 27 and B of *J 39700*. 2. Using *J 39200* DMM, measure the resistance between the Lateral Accelerometer harness connector terminal C and a good ground. Is the resistance within the range specified in the value(s) column?	0 - 2Ω	*Go to Step 24*	*Go to Step 23*
23	Repair CKT 1338 for an open or high resistance. Is the repair complete?	—	Go to *Diagnostic System Check*	—
24	1. Connect a fused jumper wire between terminals 11 and B of *J 39700*. 2. Using *J 39200* DMM, measure the resistance between the Lateral Accelerometer harness connector terminal A and a good ground. Is the resistance within the range specified in the value(s) column?	0 - 2Ω	*Go to Step 26*	*Go to Step 25*

GC402980282000CX

Fig. 238 Code C1285: Lateral Accel Sensor Circuit Fault (Part 3 of 4). DeVille & Seville

Circuit Description

The EBTCM learns the steering wheel center position in every drive cycle. Once established, the steering wheel center position should remain fairly constant.

Conditions for Setting the DTC

All of the following conditions occur:

- The steering angle has been centered.
- The center steer angle bias value is more than 20 degrees from the initial center position.

Action Taken When the DTC Sets

- A malfunction DTC is stored.
- Stabilitrak® is disabled.
- The DIC displays the SERVICE STABILITY SYS message.
- The ABS/TCS remain functional.

Conditions for Clearing the DTC

- The condition for DTC is no longer present and you used scan tool Clear DTCs function.
- The condition for DTC is no longer present and you used the On-Board Clear DTCs function.
- The EBTCM does not detect the DTC in 50 drive cycles.

Diagnostic Aids

- Check the vehicle for proper alignment. The car should not pull in either direction while driving straight on a flat surface.
- Find out from the driver under what conditions the DTC was set (when the DIC displayed the SERVICE STABILITY SYS message). This information will help to duplicate the failure.
- Thoroughly inspect the wiring and the connectors. An incomplete inspection of the wiring and the connectors may result in a misdiagnosis, causing a part replacement with the reappearance of the malfunction.
- Poor connections, broken insulation, or a break in the wire inside the insulation may cause an intermittent malfunction.
- If an intermittent malfunction exists, refer to *Intermittents and Poor Connections*
- The Snapshot function on the scan tool can help find an intermittent DTC.

GC4029903924010X

Fig. 239 Code C1286: Steering/Lateral Accelerometer Sensors Bias Fault (Part 1 of 2). DeVille

Step	Action	Value(s)	Yes	No
25	Repair CKT 1337 for an open or high resistance. Is the repair complete?	—	Go to *Diagnostic System Check*	—
26	1. Install *J 39700* Universal Pinout Box using the *J 39700-25* cable adapter to the EBTCM and the EBTCM harness connector. 2. Reconnect the Lateral Accelerometer. 3. Remove the fused jumper wire from *J 39700*. 4. Turn the ignition switch to the RUN position, engine OFF. 5. Using *J 39200* DMM, measure the voltage between *J 39700* terminals 11 and 27. Is the voltage within the range specified in the value(s) column?	4.5 - 5.5V	*Go to Step 27*	*Go to Step 32*
27	Using *J 39200* DMM, measure the voltage between *J 39700* terminals 22 and B. Is the voltage within the range specified in the value(s) column?	2.35 - 2.65V	*Go to Step 28*	*Go to Step 30*
28	Using *J 39200* DMM, measure the voltage between *J 39700* terminals 22 and 27. Is the voltage within the range specified in the value(s) column?	2.35 - 2.65V	*Go to Step 29*	*Go to Step 27*
29	Using a scan tool read the Lateral Accelerometer value in volts. Is the voltage within the range specified in the value(s) column?	2.0 - 3.0V	*Go to Step 30*	*Go to Step 32*
30	Replace the Lateral Accelerometer. Is the replacement complete?	—	*Go to Step 31*	—
31	1. Read the diagnostic aids and conditions for setting the DTC. 2. Cycle the ignition switch from the OFF to RUN position. 3. Carefully drive the vehicle above 24 Km/h (15 mph) for several minutes, while monitoring a scan tool for ABS/TCS/ICCS DTC(s). Did DTC C1285 set as a current DTC while the vehicle was being driven?	—	*Go to Step 32*	Go to *Diagnostic System Check*
32	Replace the EBTCM. Is the replacement complete?	—	Go to *Diagnostic System Check*	—

GC402980282000DX

Fig. 238 Code C1285: Lateral Accel Sensor Circuit Fault (Part 4 of 4). DeVille & Seville

Step	Action	Value(s)	Yes	No
1	Did you perform the ABS Diagnostic System Check?	—	Go to *Step 2*	Go to *A Diagnostic System Check - ABS*
2	1. Turn OFF the ignition. 2. Connect a scan tool to the data link connector (DLC). 3. Turn ON the ignition, with the engine OFF. 4. Use the scan tool in order to read ABS/TCS/ICCS DTCs. Are DTCs C1282–C1285 present?	—	Go to *DTC List*	Go to *Step 3*
3	Perform the steering wheel position sensor test. Is the analog and digital display on the scan tool within 5 degrees of each other at the center (zero) position?	—	Go to *Step 5*	Go to *Step 4*
4	Replace the steering wheel position sensor (SWPS). Did you complete the repair?	—	Go to *Step 9*	—
5	1. Perform the diagnostic test drive. 2. Use the scan tool in order to select the ABS/TCS/ICCS Data Display (1) Diagnostics, Data List 2. 3. Observe the Yaw Rate Sensor Input parameter. Is the voltage within the specified range?	2.3–2.7 V	Go to *Step 7*	Go to *Step 6*
6	Replace the yaw rate sensor. Did you complete the repair?	—	Go to *Step 9*	—
7	1. Turn ON the ignition, with the engine OFF. 2. Use the scan tool in order to select the ABS/TCS/ICCS Data Display (1) Diagnostics, Data List 2. 3. Monitor the Lateral Accelerometer Input parameter. Is the voltage within the specified range?	2.3–2.7 V	Go to *Step 9*	Go to *Step 8*
8	Replace the lateral accelerometer. Did you complete the repair?	—	Go to *Step 9*	—
9	1. Read Diagnostic Aids and Conditions for Setting the DTC. 2. Turn OFF the ignition. 3. Turn ON the ignition, with the engine OFF. 4. With a scan tool read ABS/TCS/ICCS DTCs. Did DTC C1286 reset as a current DTC?	—	Go to *Step 10*	Go to *A Diagnostic System Check - ABS*
10	Replace the EBTCM. Did you complete the repair?	—	Go to *A Diagnostic System Check - ABS*	—

GC4029903924020X

Fig. 239 Code C1286: Steering/Lateral Accelerometer Sensors Bias Fault (Part 2 of 2). DeVille

Circuit Description

The EBTCM learns the steering wheel center position in every drive cycle. Once established, the steering wheel center position should remain fairly constant.

Conditions for Setting the DTC

All of the following conditions occur:

- The steering angle has been centered.
- The center steer angle bias value is more than 20 degrees from the initial center position.

Action Taken When the DTC Sets

- A malfunction DTC is stored.
- Stabilitrak® is disabled.
- The DIC displays the SERVICE STABILITY SYS message.
- The ABS/TCS remain functional.

Conditions for Clearing the DTC

- The condition for DTC is no longer present and you used scan tool Clear DTCs function.
- The condition for DTC is no longer present and you used the On-Board Clear DTCs function.
- The EBTCM does not detect the DTC in 50 drive cycles.

Diagnostic Aids

- Check the vehicle for proper alignment. The car should not pull in either direction while driving straight on a flat surface.
- Find out from the driver under what conditions the DTC was set (when the DIC displayed the SERVICE STABILITY SYS message). This information will help to duplicate the failure.
- Thoroughly inspect the wiring and the connectors. An incomplete inspection of the wiring and the connectors may result in a misdiagnosis, causing a part replacement with the reappearance of the malfunction.
- Poor connections, broken insulation, or a break in the wire inside the insulation may cause an intermittent malfunction.
- If an intermittent malfunction exists, refer to *Intermittents and Poor Connections*
- The Snapshot function on the scan tool can help find an intermittent DTC.

GC4029803898010X

Fig. 240 Code C1286: Steering/Lateral Accelerometer Sensors Bias Fault (Part 1 of 2). Seville

Step	Action	Value(s)	Yes	No
1	Did you perform the Diagnostic System Check?	—	Go to *Step 2*	Go to *Diagnostic System Check*
2	1. Turn OFF the ignition. 2. Connect a scan tool to the data link connector (DLC). 3. Turn ON the ignition, with the engine OFF. 4. Using the scan tool, read ABS/TCS/ICCS DTCs. Are DTCs C1282–C1285 present?	—	Go to *DTC List*	Go to *Step 3*
3	Perform the Steering Wheel Position Sensor Test. Is the analog and digital display on the scan tool within ±5 degrees of each other at the center (zero) position?	—	Go to *Step 5*	Go to *Step 4*
4	Replace the steering wheel position sensor (SWPS). Did you complete the repair?	—	Go to *Step 9*	—
5	1. Perform the Diagnostic Test Drive. 2. Using the scan tool, select the ABS/TCS/ICCS Data Display (1) Diagnostics, DATA LIST 2. 3. Monitor the Yaw Rate Sensor Input. Is the voltage within the specified range?	2.3–2.7 V	Go to *Step 7*	Go to *Step 6*
6	Replace the yaw rate sensor. Did you complete the repair?	—	Go to *Step 9*	—
7	1. Turn ON the ignition, with the engine OFF. 2. Using the scan tool, select the ABS/TCS/ICCS Data Display (1) Diagnostics, DATA LIST 2. 3. Monitor the Lateral Accelerometer Input. Is the voltage within the specified range?	2.3–2.7 V	Go to *Step 9*	Go to *Step 8*
8	Replace the lateral accelerometer. Did you complete the repair?	—	Go to *Step 9*	—
9	1. Read Diagnostic Aids and Conditions for Setting the DTC. 2. Cycle the ignition from the OFF to ON position, engine off. 3. With a scan tool, read ABS/TCS/ICCS DTCs. Did DTC C1286 reset as a current DTC?	—	Go to *Step 10*	Go to *Diagnostic System Check*
10	Replace the EBTCM. Did you complete the repair?	—	Go to *Diagnostic System Check*	—

GC4029803898020X

Fig. 240 Code C1286: Steering/Lateral Accelerometer Sensors Bias Fault (Part 2 of 2). Seville

Circuit Description

The EBTCM learns the steering wheel center position in every drive cycle. Once established, the steering wheel center position should remain fairly constant.

Conditions for Setting the DTC

All of the following conditions occur:

- The ignition is ON.
- The steer rate (speed that the steering wheel appears to be turning) exceeds the limits set by the EBTCM.

Action Taken When the DTC Sets

- A malfunction DTC is stored.
- Stabilitrak® is disabled.
- The DIC displays the SERVICE STABILITY SYS message.
- The ABS/TCS remain functional.

Conditions for Clearing the DTC

- The condition for DTC is no longer present and you used scan tool Clear DTCs function.
- The condition for DTC is no longer present and you used the On-Board Clear DTCs function.
- The EBTCM does not detect the DTC in 50 drive cycles.

Diagnostic Aids

- Check the vehicle for proper alignment. The car should not pull in either direction while driving straight on a flat surface.
- Find out from the driver under what conditions the DTC was set (when the DIC displayed the SERVICE STABILITY SYS message). This information will help to duplicate the failure.
- Thoroughly inspect the wiring and the connectors. An incomplete inspection of the wiring and the connectors may result in a misdiagnosis, causing a part replacement with the reappearance of the malfunction.
- Poor connections, broken insulation, or a break in the wire inside the insulation may cause an intermittent malfunction.
- If an intermittent malfunction exists, refer to *Intermittents and Poor Connections*
- The Snapshot function on the scan tool can help find an intermittent DTC.

GC4029903925010X

Fig. 241 Code C1287: Steering Sensor Rate Fault (Part 1 of 3). DeVille

Step	Action	Value(s)	Yes	No
1	Did you perform the ABS Diagnostic System Check?	—	Go to *Step 2*	Go to *A Diagnostic System Check - ABS*
2	1. Turn OFF the ignition. 2. Connect a scan tool to the data link connector (DLC). 3. Turn ON the ignition, with the engine OFF. 4. Use the scan tool in order to read ABS/TCS/ICCS DTCs. Are DTCs C1282–C1285 present?	—	Go to *DTC List*	Go to *Step 3*
3	1. Start the engine. 2. Ensure the front wheels are straight. 3. Turn OFF the ignition. 4. Restart the engine. 5. Use the scan tool in order to select ABS/TCS/ICCS Data Display (1) Diagnostics, Data List 2. 6. Observe the Digital SWPS Phase A and Digital SWPS Phase B parameters. 7. Slowly rotate the steering wheel to the left. Did Digital SWPS Phase A and Digital SWPS Phase B change states as the steering wheel was rotated?	—	Go to *Step 4*	Go to *Step 6*
4	1. Observe the Digital SWPS Phase A and Digital SWPS Phase B parameters. 2. Slowly rotate the steering wheel to the right. Did Digital SWPS Phase A and Digital SWPS Phase B change states as the steering wheel was rotated?	—	Go to *Step 5*	Go to *Step 6*
5	Perform the Steering Position Sensor Test. Was the Steering Position Sensor Test passed?	—	Go to *Step 21*	Go to *Step 6*
6	1. Turn OFF the ignition. 2. Disconnect the steering wheel position sensor (SWPS) connector. 3. Disconnect the EBTCM connector. 4. Install the *J 39700* universal pinout box using the *J 39700-25* cable adapter to the EBTCM harness connector only. 5. Turn ON the ignition, with the engine OFF. 6. Use a *J 39200* DMM in order to measure the voltage between the *J 39700* terminal 20 and terminal B. Is the voltage greater than the specified value?	1 V	Go to *Step 7*	Go to *Step 8*
7	Repair the short to voltage in CKT 1763. Did you complete the repair?	—	Go to *A Diagnostic System Check - ABS*	—
8	Use a *J 39200* DMM in order to measure the voltage between the *J 39700* terminal 4 and terminal B. Is the voltage greater than the specified value?	1 V	Go to *Step 9*	Go to *Step 10*
9	Repair the short to voltage in CKT 1764. Did you complete the repair?	—	Go to *A Diagnostic System Check - ABS*	—
10	1. Turn OFF the ignition. 2. Use a *J 39200* DMM in order to measure the resistance between the *J 39700* terminal 20 and terminal B. Is the resistance within the specified range?	OL (Infinite)	Go to *Step 12*	Go to *Step 11*

GC4029903925020X

Fig. 241 Code C1287: Steering Sensor Rate Fault (Part 2 of 3). DeVille

Step	Action	Value(s)	Yes	No
11	Repair the short to ground in CKT 1763. Did you complete the repair?	—	Go to *A Diagnostic System Check - ABS*	—
12	Use a *J 39200* DMM in order to measure the resistance between the *J 39700* terminal 4 and terminal B. Is the resistance within the specified range?	OL (Infinite)	Go to *Step 14*	Go to *Step 13*
13	Repair the short to ground in CKT 1764. Did you complete the repair?	—	Go to *A Diagnostic System Check - ABS*	—
14	Use a *J 39200* DMM in order to measure the resistance between the *J 39700* terminal 20 and terminal 4. Is the resistance within the specified range?	OL (Infinite)	Go to *Step 16*	Go to *Step 15*
15	Repair the short between CKT 1763 and CKT 1764. Did you complete the repair?	—	Go to *A Diagnostic System Check - ABS*	—
16	1. Connect a fused jumper between the *J 39700* terminal 20 and terminal B. 2. Disconnect the steering wheel position sensor (SWPS) connector. 3. Use a *J 39200* DMM in order to measure the resistance between the SWPS connector terminal 3 and a good ground. Is the resistance less than the specified value?	2 Ω	Go to *Step 18*	Go to *Step 17*
17	Repair the open in CKT 1763. Did you complete the repair?	—	Go to *A Diagnostic System Check - ABS*	—
18	1. Connect a fused jumper between the *J 39700* terminal 4 and terminal B. 2. Use a *J 39200* DMM in order to measure the resistance between the SWPS connector terminal 4 and a good ground. Is the resistance less than the specified value?	2 Ω	Go to *Step 20*	Go to *Step 19*
19	Repair the open in CKT 1764. Did you complete the repair?	—	Go to *A Diagnostic System Check - ABS*	—
20	Replace the steering wheel position sensor (SWPS). Did you complete the repair?	—	Go to *Step 21*	—
21	1. Read Diagnostic Aids and Conditions for Setting the DTC. 2. Turn OFF the ignition. 3. Turn ON the ignition, with the engine OFF. 4. With a scan tool read ABS/TCS/ICCS DTCs. Did DTC C1287 reset as a current DTC?	—	Go to *Step 22*	Go to *A Diagnostic System Check - ABS*
22	Replace the EBTCM. Did you complete the repair?	—	Go to *A Diagnostic System Check - ABS*	—

GC4029903925030X

Fig. 241 Code C1287: Steering Sensor Rate Fault (Part 3 of 3). DeVille

Step	Action	Value(s)	Yes	No
1	Did you perform the Diagnostic System Check?	—	Go to *Step 2*	Go to *Diagnostic System Check*
2	1. Turn OFF the ignition. 2. Connect a scan tool to the data link connector (DLC). 3. Turn ON the ignition, with the engine OFF. 4. Using the scan tool, read ABS/TCS/ICCS DTCs. Are DTCs C1282–C1285 present?	—	Go to *DTC List*	Go to *Step 3*
3	1. Start the engine. 2. Ensure the front wheels are straight. 3. Turn OFF the ignition. 4. Restart the engine. 5. Using the scan tool, select ABS/TCS/ICCS Data Display (1) Diagnostics, DATA LIST 2. 6. Monitor Digital SWPS Phase A and Digital SWPS Phase B. 7. Slowly rotate the steering wheel to the left. Did Digital SWPS Phase A and Digital SWPS Phase B change states as the steering wheel was rotated?	—	Go to *Step 4*	Go to *Step 6*
4	1. Monitor Digital SWPS Phase A and Digital SWPS Phase B. 2. Slowly rotate the steering wheel to the right. Did Digital SWPS Phase A and Digital SWPS Phase B change states as the steering wheel was rotated?	—	Go to *Step 5*	Go to *Step 6*
5	Perform the Steering Position Sensor Test. Was the Steering Position Sensor Test passed?	—	Go to *Step 21*	Go to *Step 6*
6	1. Turn OFF the ignition. 2. Disconnect the steering wheel position sensor (SWPS) connector. 3. Disconnect the EBTCM harness connector. 4. Install the *J 39700* universal pinout box using the *J 39700-25* cable adapter to the EBTCM harness connector only. 5. Turn ON the ignition, with the engine OFF. 6. Using a *J 39200* DMM, measure the voltage between the *J 39700* terminals 20 and B. Is the voltage greater than the specified value?	1 V	Go to *Step 7*	Go to *Step 8*
7	Repair the short to voltage in CKT 1763. Did you complete the repair?	—	Go to *Diagnostic System Check*	—
8	Using a *J 39200* DMM, measure the voltage between the *J 39700* terminals 4 and B. Is the voltage greater than the specified value?	1 V	Go to *Step 9*	Go to *Step 10*
9	Repair the short to voltage in CKT 1764. Did you complete the repair?	—	Go to *Diagnostic System Check*	—
10	1. Turn OFF the ignition. 2. Using a *J 39200* DMM, measure the resistance between the *J 39700* terminals 20 and B. Is the resistance within the specified range?	OL (infinite)	Go to *Step 12*	Go to *Step 11*
11	Repair the short to ground in CKT 1763. Did you complete the repair?	—	Go to *Diagnostic System Check*	—

GC4029803899020X

Fig. 242 Code C1287: Steering Sensor Rate Fault (Part 2 of 3). Seville

Circuit Description

The EBTCM learns the steering wheel center position in every drive cycle. Once established, the steering wheel center position should remain fairly constant.

Conditions for Setting the DTC

All of the following conditions occur:

- The ignition is ON.
- The steer rate (speed that the steering wheel appears to be turning) exceeds the limits set by the EBTCM.

Action Taken When the DTC Sets

- A malfunction DTC is stored.
- Stabilitrak® is disabled.
- The DIC displays the SERVICE STABILITY SYS message.
- The ABS/TCS remain functional.

Conditions for Clearing the DTC

- The condition for DTC is no longer present and you used scan tool Clear DTCs function.
- The condition for DTC is no longer present and you used the On-Board Clear DTCs function.
- The EBTCM does not detect the DTC in 50 drive cycles.

Diagnostic Aids

- Check the vehicle for proper alignment. The car should not pull in either direction while driving straight on a flat surface.
- Find out from the driver under what conditions the DTC was set (when the DIC displayed the SERVICE STABILITY SYS message). This information will help to duplicate the failure.
- Thoroughly inspect the wiring and the connectors. An incomplete inspection of the wiring and the connectors may result in a misdiagnosis, causing a part replacement with the reappearance of the malfunction.
- Poor connections, broken insulation, or a break in the wire inside the insulation may cause an intermittent malfunction.
- If an intermittent malfunction exists, refer to *Intermittents and Poor Connections*
- The Snapshot function on the scan tool can help find an intermittent DTC.

GC4029803899010X

Fig. 242 Code C1287: Steering Sensor Rate Fault (Part 1 of 3). Seville

Step	Action	Value(s)	Yes	No
12	Using a *J 39200* DMM, measure the resistance between the *J 39700* terminals 4 and B. Is the resistance within the specified range?	OL (infinite)	Go to *Step 14*	Go to *Step 13*
13	Repair the short to ground in CKT 1764. Did you complete the repair?	—	Go to *Diagnostic System Check*	—
14	Using a *J 39200* DMM, measure the resistance between the *J 39700* terminals 20 and 4. Is the resistance within the specified range?	OL (infinite)	Go to *Step 16*	Go to *Step 15*
15	Repair the short between CKT 1763 and CKT 1764. Did you complete the repair?	—	Go to *Diagnostic System Check*	—
16	1. Connect a fused jumper between the *J 39700* terminals 20 and B. 2. Disconnect the steering wheel position sensor (SWPS) connector. 3. Using a *J 39200* DMM, measure the resistance between the SWPS connector terminal 3 and a good ground. Is the resistance less than the specified value?	2 Ω	Go to *Step 18*	Go to *Step 17*
17	Repair the open in CKT 1763. Did you complete the repair?	—	Go to *Diagnostic System Check*	—
18	1. Connect a fused jumper between the *J 39700* terminals 4 and B. 2. Using a *J 39200* DMM, measure the resistance between the SWPS connector terminal 4 and a good ground. Is the resistance less than the specified value?	2 Ω	Go to *Step 20*	Go to *Step 19*
19	Repair the open in CKT 1764. Did you complete the repair?	—	Go to *Diagnostic System Check*	—
20	Replace the steering wheel position sensor (SWPS). Did you complete the repair?	—	Go to *Step 21*	—
21	1. Read Diagnostic Aids and Conditions for Setting the DTC. 2. Cycle the ignition from the OFF to ON position, engine off. 3. With a scan tool read ABS/TCS/ICCS DTCs. Did DTC C1287 reset as a current DTC?	—	Go to *Step 22*	Go to *Diagnostic System Check*
22	Replace the EBTCM. Did you complete the repair?	—	Go to *Diagnostic System Check*	—

GC4029803899030X

Fig. 242 Code C1287: Steering Sensor Rate Fault (Part 3 of 3). Seville

Circuit Description

The steering wheel position sensor produces 2 outputs:

- An analog output.
- A digital output with a resolution of one degree of rotation.

The digital signal output is via 2 lines and is a combination of low and high pulses. By interpreting the relationship of the pulses and the analog input, the EBTCM can determine the direction of steering wheel rotation.

Conditions for Setting the DTC

All of the following conditions occur:

- The vehicle speed is greater than 8 km/h (5 mph).
- One of the folloing conditions occur:
  - The vehicle yaw rate, as measured by the yaw rate sensor, is large enough to cause Stabilitrak® activation, but there have been no pulses from the digital steering sensor indicating movement for a period of 20 seconds prior to a Stabilitrak® event and 0.5 seconds after a Stabilitrak® event.
  - An open or short in the digital steering wheel position sensor phase A circuit.
  - An open or short in the digital steering wheel position sensor phase B circuit.
  - An open or short in the analog steering wheel position sensor circuit.

Action Taken When the DTC Sets

- A malfunction DTC is stored.
- Stabilitrak® is disabled.
- The DIC displays the SERVICE STABILITY SYS message.
- The ABS/TCS remain functional.

Conditions for Clearing the DTC

- The condition for DTC is no longer present and you used scan tool Clear DTCs function.
- The condition for DTC is no longer present and you used the On-Board Clear DTCs function.
- The EBTCM does not detect the DTC in 50 drive cycles.

GC4029903926010X

Fig. 243 Code C1288: Steering Sensor Circuit Fault (Part 1 of 4). DeVille

Diagnostic Aids

- Check the vehicle for proper alignment. The car should not pull in either direction while driving straight on a flat surface.
- Find out from the driver under what conditions the DTC was set (when the DIC displayed the SERVICE STABILITY SYS message). This information will help to duplicate the failure.
- Thoroughly inspect the wiring and the connectors. An incomplete inspection of the wiring and the connectors may result in a misdiagnosis, causing a part replacement with the reappearance of the malfunction.
- Poor connections, broken insulation, or a break in the wire inside the insulation may cause an intermittent malfunction.
- If an intermittent malfunction exists, refer to *Intermittents and Poor Connections*
- The Snapshot function on the scan tool can help find an intermittent DTC.

Step	Action	Value(s)	Yes	No
1	Did you perform the ABS Diagnostic System Check?	—	Go to *Step 2*	Go to *A Diagnostic System Check - ABS*
2	1. Turn OFF the ignition. 2. Disconnect the yaw rate sensor connector. 3. Disconnect the lateral accelerometer connector. 4. Disconnect the steering wheel position sensor (SWPS) connector. 5. Disconnect the EBTCM connector. 6. Install the *J 39700* universal pinout box using the *J 39700-25* cable adapter to the EBTCM harness connector only. 7. Turn ON the ignition, with the engine OFF. 8. Use a *J 39200* DMM in order to measure the voltage between the *J 39700* terminal 23 and terminal B. Is the voltage greater than the specified value?	1 V	Go to *Step 3*	Go to *Step 4*
3	Repair the short to voltage in CKT 1059. Did you complete the repair?	—	Go to *A Diagnostic System Check - ABS*	—
4	Use a *J 39200* DMM in order to measure the voltage between the *J 39700* terminal 11 and terminal B. Is the voltage greater than the specified value?	1 V	Go to *Step 5*	Go to *Step 6*
5	Repair the short to voltage in CKT 1337. Did you complete the repair?	—	Go to *A Diagnostic System Check - ABS*	—
6	Use a *J 39200* DMM in order to measure the voltage between the *J 39700* terminal 27 and terminal B. Is the voltage greater than the specified value?	1 V	Go to *Step 7*	Go to *Step 8*
7	Repair the short to voltage in CKT 1338. Did you complete the repair?	—	Go to *A Diagnostic System Check - ABS*	—
8	Use a *J 39200* DMM in order to measure the resistance between the *J 39700* terminal 23 and terminal B. Is the resistance within the specified range?	OL (Infinite)	Go to *Step 9*	Go to *Step 10*
9	Repair the short to ground in CKT 1059. Did you complete the repair?	—	Go to *A Diagnostic System Check - ABS*	—

GC4029903926020X

Fig. 243 Code C1288: Steering Sensor Circuit Fault (Part 2 of 4). DeVille

Step	Action	Value(s)	Yes	No
24	1. Connect a fused jumper between the *J 39700* terminal 27 and terminal B. 2. Use a *J 39200* DMM in order to measure the resistance between the SWPS connector terminal 2 and a good ground. Is the resistance less than the specified value?	2 Ω	Go to *Step 26*	Go to *Step 25*
25	Repair the open in CKT 1338. Did you complete the repair?	—	Go to *A Diagnostic System Check - ABS*	—
26	Replace the steering wheel position sensor (SWPS). Did you complete the repair?	—	Go to *Step 27*	—
27	1. Read Diagnostic Aids and Conditions for Setting the DTC. 2. Turn OFF the ignition. 3. Turn ON the ignition, with the engine OFF. 4. Carefully drive the vehicle above 24 km/h (15 mph) for several minutes, while monitoring a scan tool for ABS/TCS/ICCS DTCs. Did DTC C1288 set as a current DTC while the vehicle was being driven?	—	Go to *Step 28*	Go to *A Diagnostic System Check - ABS*
28	Replace the EBTCM. Did you complete the repair?	—	Go to *A Diagnostic System Check - ABS*	—

GC4029903926040X

Fig. 243 Code C1288: Steering Sensor Circuit Fault (Part 4 of 4). DeVille

Step	Action	Value(s)	Yes	No
10	Use a *J 39200* DMM in order to measure the resistance between the *J 39700* terminal 11 and terminal B. Is the resistance within the specified range?	OL (Infinite)	Go to *Step 11*	Go to *Step 12*
11	Repair the short to ground in CKT 1337. Did you complete the repair?	—	Go to *A Diagnostic System Check - ABS*	—
12	Use a *J 39200* DMM in order to measure the resistance between the *J 39700* terminal 27 and terminal B. Is the resistance within the specified range?	OL (Infinite)	Go to *Step 13*	Go to *Step 14*
13	Repair the short to ground in CKT 1338. Did you complete the repair?	—	Go to *A Diagnostic System Check - ABS*	—
14	Use a *J 39200* DMM in order to measure the resistance between the *J 39700* terminal 23 and terminal 11. Is the resistance within the specified range?	OL (Infinite)	Go to *Step 16*	Go to *Step 15*
15	Repair the short between CKT 1059. Did you complete the repair?	—	Go to *A Diagnostic System Check - ABS*	—
16	Use a *J 39200* DMM in order to measure the resistance between the *J 39700* terminal 23 and terminal 27. Is the resistance within the specified range?	OL (Infinite)	Go to *Step 18*	Go to *Step 17*
17	Repair the short between CKT 1059 and CKT 1338. Did you complete the repair?	—	Go to *A Diagnostic System Check - ABS*	—
18	Use a *J 39200* DMM in order to measure the resistance between the *J 39700* terminal 11 and terminal 27. Is the resistance within the specified range?	OL (Infinite)	Go to *Step 20*	Go to *Step 19*
19	Repair the short between CKT 1337 and CKT 1338. Did you complete the repair?	—	Go to *A Diagnostic System Check - ABS*	—
20	1. Connect a fused jumper between the *J 39700* terminal 23 and terminal B. 2. Use a *J 39200* DMM in order to measure the resistance between the SWPS connector terminal 6 and a good ground. Is the resistance less than the specified value?	2 Ω	Go to *Step 22*	Go to *Step 21*
21	Repair the open in CKT 1059 between the SWPS and the EBTCM. Did you complete the repair?	—	Go to *A Diagnostic System Check - ABS*	—
22	1. Connect a fused jumper between the *J 39700* terminal 11 and terminal B. 2. Use a *J 39200* DMM in order to measure the resistance between the SWPS connector terminal 1 and a good ground. Is the resistance less than the specified value?	2 Ω	Go to *Step 24*	Go to *Step 23*
23	Repair the open in CKT 1337. Did you complete the repair?	—	Go to *A Diagnostic System Check - ABS*	—

GC4029903926030X

Fig. 243 Code C1288: Steering Sensor Circuit Fault (Part 3 of 4). DeVille

Circuit Description

The steering wheel position sensor produces 2 outputs:

- An analog output.
- A digital output with a resolution of one degree of rotation.

The digital signal output is via 2 lines and is a combination of low and high pulses. By interpreting the relationship of the pulses and the analog input, the EBTCM can determine the direction of steering wheel rotation.

Conditions for Setting the DTC

All of the following conditions occur:

- The vehicle speed is greater than 8 km/h (5 mph).
- One of the following conditions occur:
  - The vehicle yaw rate, as measured by the yaw rate sensor, is large enough to cause Stabilitrak® activation, but there have been no pulses from the digital steering sensor indicating movement for a period of 20 seconds prior to a Stabilitrak® event and 0.5 seconds after a Stabilitrak® event.
  - An open or short in the digital steering wheel position sensor phase A circuit.
  - An open or short in the digital steering wheel position sensor phase B circuit.
  - An open or short in the analog steering wheel position sensor circuit.

Action Taken When the DTC Sets

- A malfunction DTC is stored.
- Stabilitrak® is disabled.
- The DIC displays the SERVICE STABILITY SYS message.
- The ABS/TCS remain functional.

Conditions for Clearing the DTC

- The condition for DTC is no longer present and you used scan tool Clear DTCs function.
- The condition for DTC is no longer present and you used the On-Board Clear DTCs function.
- The EBTCM does not detect the DTC in 50 drive cycles.

GC4029803900010X

Fig. 244 Code C1288: Steering Sensor Circuit Fault (Part 1 of 4). Seville

Diagnostic Aids

- Check the vehicle for proper alignment. The car should not pull in either direction while driving straight on a flat surface.
- Find out from the driver under what conditions the DTC was set (when the DIC displayed the SERVICE STABILITY SYS message). This information will help to duplicate the failure.
- Thoroughly inspect the wiring and the connectors. An incomplete inspection of the wiring and the connectors may result in a misdiagnosis, causing a part replacement with the reappearance of the malfunction.
- Poor connections, broken insulation, or a break in the wire inside the insulation may cause an intermittent malfunction.
- If an intermittent malfunction exists, refer to *Intermittents and Poor Connections*
- The Snapshot function on the scan tool can help find an intermittent DTC.

Step	Action	Value(s)	Yes	No
1	Did you perform the Diagnostic System Check?	—	Go to *Step 2*	Go to *Diagnostic System Check*
2	1. Turn OFF the ignition. 2. Disconnect the yaw rate sensor connector. 3. Disconnect the lateral accelerometer connector. 4. Disconnect the steering wheel position sensor (SWPS) connector. 5. Disconnect the EBTCM harness connector. 6. Install the *J 39700* universal pinout box using the *J 39700-25* cable adapter to the EBTCM harness connector only. 7. Turn ON the ignition, with the engine OFF. 8. Using a *J 39200* DMM, measure the voltage between the *J 39700* terminals 23 and B. Is the voltage greater than the specified value?	1 V	Go to *Step 3*	Go to *Step 4*
3	Repair the short to voltage in CKT 1059. Did you complete the repair?	—	Go to *Diagnostic System Check*	—
4	Using a *J 39200* DMM, measure the voltage between the *J 39700* terminals 11 and B. Is the voltage greater than the specified value?	1 V	Go to *Step 5*	Go to *Step 6*
5	Repair the short to voltage in CKT 1337. Did you complete the repair?	—	Go to *Diagnostic System Check*	—
6	Using a *J 39200* DMM, measure the voltage between the *J 39700* terminals 27 and B. Is the voltage greater than the specified value?	1 V	Go to *Step 7*	Go to *Step 8*
7	Repair the short to voltage in CKT 1338. Did you complete the repair?	—	Go to *Diagnostic System Check*	—
8	Using a *J 39200* DMM, measure the resistance between the *J 39700* terminals 23 and B. Is the resistance within the specified range?	OL (infinite)	Go to *Step 9*	Go to *Step 10*
9	Repair the short to ground in CKT 1059. Did you complete the repair?	—	Go to *Diagnostic System Check*	—
10	Using a *J 39200* DMM, measure the resistance between the *J 39700* terminals 11 and B. Is the resistance within the specified range?	OL (infinite)	Go to *Step 11*	Go to *Step 12*

GC4029803900020X

Fig. 244 Code C1288: Steering Sensor Circuit Fault (Part 2 of 4). Seville

Step	Action	Value(s)	Yes	No
26	Replace the steering wheel position sensor (SWPS). Did you complete the repair?	—	Go to *Step 27*	—
27	1. Read Diagnostic Aids and Conditions for Setting the DTC. 2. Cycle the ignition switch from the OFF to ON position. 3. Carefully drive the vehicle above 24 Km/h (15 mph) for several minutes, while monitoring a scan tool for ABS/TCS/ICCS DTCs. Did DTC C1288 set as a current DTC while the vehicle was being driven?	—	Go to *Step 28*	Go to *Diagnostic System Check*
28	Replace the EBTCM. Did you complete the repair?	—	Go to *Diagnostic System Check*	—

GC4029803900040X

Fig. 244 Code C1288: Steering Sensor Circuit Fault (Part 4 of 4). Seville

Circuit Description

This circuit is used to detect an open stoplamp/BTSI switch in the non-ABS mode. The EBTCM looks for a deceleration rate that would indicate braking action and requires several repeats of this detection method in order to verify this assumption. In each case, the TCS will not be available since the EBTCM sees no stoplamp/BTSI switch voltage.

Conditions for Setting the DTC

The stoplamp/BTSI switch remains open for three deceleration cycles.

Action Taken When the DTC Sets

- A DTC C1291 is stored
- The TCS is disabled
- The TRACTION OFF indicator turns on
- The ABS remains functional

Conditions for Clearing the DTC

- The condition for the DTC is no longer present and the scan tool clear DTC function is used
- 50 ignition cycles have passed with no DTCs detected

Diagnostic Aids

- Thoroughly inspect the wiring and the connectors. Failure to carefully and fully inspect the wiring and the connectors can result in misdiagnosis. Misdiagnosis may cause replacement of parts without repairing the malfunction.
- If any WSS DTCs are present, diagnose the WSS DTCs first.
- The following conditions may cause most intermittent malfunctions:
  - Poor connections
  - Rubbed through wire insulation
  - A broken wire inside the insulation
- The following conditions are other possible causes for this malfunction:
  - An open stoplamp/BTSI switch
  - An open brake fuse
  - A misadjusted stoplamp/BTSI switch
  - Erratic wheel speeds
  - A wiring problem, terminal corrosion, or a poor connection in the circuit.
- If an intermittent malfunction exists, refer to Troubleshooting

GC402980282400AX

Fig. 245 Code C1291: Open Brake Lamp Switch Contacts During Decel (Part 1 of 3). DeVille & Seville

Step	Action	Value(s)	Yes	No
11	Repair the short to ground in CKT 1337. Did you complete the repair?	—	Go to *Diagnostic System Check*	—
12	Using a *J 39200* DMM, measure the resistance between the *J 39700* terminals 27 and B. Is the resistance within the specified range?	OL (infinite)	Go to *Step 13*	Go to *Step 14*
13	Repair the short to ground in CKT 1338. Did you complete the repair?	—	Go to *Diagnostic System Check*	—
14	Using a *J 39200* DMM, measure the resistance between the *J 39700* terminals 23 and 11. Is the resistance within the specified range?	OL (infinite)	Go to *Step 16*	Go to *Step 15*
15	Repair the short between CKT 1059 and CKT 1337. Did you complete the repair?	—	Go to *Diagnostic System Check*	—
16	Using a *J 39200* DMM, measure the resistance between the *J 39700* terminals 23 and 27. Is the resistance within the specified range?	OL (infinite)	Go to *Step 18*	Go to *Step 17*
17	Repair the short between CKT 1059 and CKT 1338. Did you complete the repair?	—	Go to *Diagnostic System Check*	—
18	Using a *J 39200* DMM, measure the resistance between the *J 39700* terminals 11 and 27. Is the resistance within the specified range?	OL (infinite)	Go to *Step 20*	Go to *Step 19*
19	Repair the short between CKT 1337 and CKT 1338. Did you complete the repair?	—	Go to *Diagnostic System Check*	—
20	1. Connect a fused jumper between the *J 39700* terminals 23 and B. 2. Using a *J 39200* DMM, measure the resistance between the SWPS connector terminal 6 and a good ground. Is the resistance less than the specified value?	2 Ω	Go to *Step 22*	Go to *Step 21*
21	Repair the open in CKT 1059. Did you complete the repair?	—	Go to *Diagnostic System Check*	—
22	1. Connect a fused jumper between the *J 39700* terminals 11 and B. 2. Using a *J 39200* DMM, measure the resistance between the SWPS connector terminal 1 and a good ground. Is the resistance less than the specified value?	2 Ω	Go to *Step 24*	Go to *Step 23*
23	Repair the open in CKT 1337. Did you complete the repair?	—	Go to *Diagnostic System Check*	—
24	1. Connect a fused jumper between the *J 39700* terminals 27 and B. 2. Using a *J 39200* DMM, measure the resistance between the SWPS connector terminal 2 and a good ground. Is the resistance less than the specified value?	2 Ω	Go to *Step 26*	Go to *Step 25*
25	Repair the open in CKT 1338. Did you complete the repair?	—	Go to *Diagnostic System Check*	—

GC4029803900030X

Fig. 244 Code C1288: Steering Sensor Circuit Fault (Part 3 of 4). Seville

Test Description

The numbers below refer to the step numbers on the diagnostic table.

3. This step checks if the Stoplamp Switch and Power Distribution are OK.
4. This step checks for voltage at the EBTCM.
10. This step checks the Stoplamp Switch.

Step	Action	Value(s)	Yes	No
1	Was the Diagnostic System Check performed?	—	*Go to Step 2*	Go to *Diagnostic System Check*
2	Are any WSS DTCs present?	—	Go to the appropriate DTC table	*Go to Step 3*
3	Press the brake pedal. Do the brake lights come on?	—	*Go to Step 4*	*Go to Step 7*
4	1. Turn the ignition switch to the OFF position. 2. Disconnect the EBTCM. 3. Install the *J 39700* Universal Pinout Box using the *J 39700-25* cable adapter to the EBTCM harness connector only. 4. Turn the ignition switch to the RUN position with the engine off. 5. Using the *J 39200* DMM, measure the voltage at the *J 39700* terminal 9 while an assistant presses the brake pedal. Is the voltage within specifications?	Battery voltage	*Go to Step 5*	*Go to Step 6*
5	Replace the EBTCM. Is the replacement complete?	—	Go to *Diagnostic System Check*	—
6	Repair the open or high resistance in CKT 20. Is the circuit repair complete?	—	Go to *Diagnostic System Check*	—
7	Inspect the STOP fuse in the engine compartment fuse/relay center. Is the BRAKE fuse OK?	—	*Go to Step 8*	*Go to Step 12*
8	1. Disconnect the Stoplamp/BTSI switch connector. 2. Using the *J 39200* DMM, measure the voltage at the Stoplamp/BTSI switch harness connector terminal A. Is the voltage within specifications?	Battery voltage	*Go to Step 10*	*Go to Step 9*
9	Repair the open in CKT 1540. Is the circuit repair complete?	—	Go to *Diagnostic System Check*	—
10	Connect a fused jumper wire between the Stoplamp/BTSI switch harness connector terminals A and B. Do the brake lamps come on?	—	*Go to Step 11*	*Go to Step 6*
11	Adjust or repair the Stoplamp/BTSI switch as necessary. Is the repair complete?	—	Go to *Diagnostic System Check*	—
12	1. Replace the STOP fuse. (Do not press the brake pedal.) 2. Check the STOP fuse. Is the fuse OK?	—	*Go to Step 14*	*Go to Step 13*

GC402980282400BX

Fig. 245 Code C1291: Open Brake Lamp Switch Contacts During Decel (Part 2 of 3). DeVille & Seville

Step	Action	Value(s)	Yes	No
13	Repair the short to ground in CKT 1540. Is the circuit repair complete?	—	Go to *Diagnostic System Check*	—
14	1. Press the brake pedal. 2. Check the STOP fuse. Is the fuse OK?	—	Go to *Diagnostic System Check*	Go to *Step 15*
15	1. Turn the ignition switch to the OFF position. 2. Disconnect the EBTCM. 3. Replace the fuse. 4. Turn the ignition switch to the RUN position with the engine off. 5. Press the brake pedal. 6. Check the STOP fuse. Is the fuse OK?	—	Go to *Step 5*	Go to *Step 16*
16	Repair the short to ground in CKT 20. Is the circuit repair complete?	—	Go to *Diagnostic System Check*	—

GC402980282400CX

Fig. 245 Code C1291: Open Brake Lamp Switch Contacts During Decel (Part 3 of 3). DeVille & Seville

Step	Action	Value(s)	Yes	No
1	Was the Diagnostic System Check performed?	—	Go to *Step 2*	Refer to *Diagnostic System Check*
2	1. Turn the ignition switch to the RUN position with the engine off. 2. Using a scan tool, read the ABS/TCS DTCs. Is DTC C1291 set as a history or current code?	—	Refer to DTC C1291	Refer to *Diagnostic System Check*

GC402980282500BX

Fig. 246 Code C1293: Code C1291 Set In Previous Ignition Cycle (Part 2 of 2). DeVille & Seville

Step	Action	Value(s)	Yes	No
1	Was the Diagnostic System Check performed?	—	Go to *Step 2*	Go to *Diagnostic System Check*
2	Observe the rear brake lamps. Are the rear brake lamps off?	—	Go to *Step 4*	Go to *Step 3*
3	Disconnect the brake lamp switch connector. Are the brake lamps on?	—	Go to *Step 6*	Go to *Step 7*
4	1. Disconnect the EBTCM harness connector. 2. Install the *J 39700* Universal Pinout Box using the *J 39700-25* cable adapter to the EBTCM harness connector only. 3. Using the *J 39200* DMM, measure the voltage between the *J 39700* terminal 9 and ground. Is the voltage within specifications?	More than 1.0 V	Go to *Step 6*	Go to *Step 5*
5	1. Turn the ignition switch to the OFF position. 2. Inspect CKT 20 and the EBTCM harness connector for damage which may result in a short to voltage with all connectors connected. 3. Reconnect all connectors. 4. Drive the vehicle for three drive cycles. A drive cycle consists of starting the engine, driving above 40 km/h (25 mph) and back to 0 km/h (0 mph), then turning the ignition switch to the OFF position. Was DTC C1294 set in the last three drive cycles?	—	Go to *Step 8*	Go to *Diagnostic System Check*
6	Repair the short to voltage in CKT 20. Is the circuit repair complete?	—	Go to *Diagnostic System Check*	—
7	Adjust or replace the Stoplamp/BTSI switch as necessary. Is the repair complete?	—	Go to *Diagnostic System Check*	—
8	Replace the EBTCM. Is the replacement complete?	—	Go to *Diagnostic System Check*	—

GC402980282600BX

Fig. 247 Code C1294: Brake Lamp Switch Circuit Always Active (Part 2 of 2). DeVille

Circuit Description

This DTC occurs when the internal self-checking safety logic has determined that the stoplamp/BTSI switch is continuously on. The TCS cannot be activated when the stoplamp/BTSI switch is on.

Conditions for Setting the DTC

The DTC sets if the following occur:

- The vehicle speed is greater than 40 km/h (25 mph).
- The brake was never off during 2 consecutive drive cycles.

Action Taken When the DTC Sets

- A malfunction DTC is stored.
- The TCS is disabled.
- The TRACTION CONTROL indicator is turned ON.
- The ABS remains functional.

Conditions for Clearing the DTC

- The condition for DTC is no longer present and you used scan tool Clear DTCs function.
- The condition for DTC is no longer present and you used the On-Board Clear DTCs function.
- The EBTCM does not detect the DTC in 50 drive cycles.

Diagnostic Aids

- It is very important that a thorough inspection of the wiring and connectors be performed. Failure to carefully and fully inspect wiring and connectors may result in misdiagnosis, causing part replacement with reappearance of the malfunction.
- An intermittent malfunction can be caused by poor connections, broken insulation, or a wire that is broken inside the insulation.
- If an intermittent malfunction exists, refer to *Intermittents and Poor Connections*
- This condition may be cause by the following:
  - A short to voltage in the stoplamp/BTSI switch circuit.
  - A misadjusted or shorted stoplamp/BTSI switch.
  - A pedal that is binding.

GC4029803901010X

Fig. 248 Code C1294: Brake Lamp Switch Circuit Always Active (Part 1 of 2). Seville

Circuit Description

This DTC is the second portion of DTC C1291. If DTC C1291 occurred during the last ignition cycle, DTC C1293 becomes a current malfunction during the next ignition cycle, keeping the TCS disabled until a stoplamp/BTSI switch on state is seen. When a change is seen during an ignition cycle in which DTC C1293 is a current malfunction, DTC C1291 will clear itself at the end of the current ignition cycle, and the TCS will enable at the start of the next ignition cycle. DTC C1293 alone indicates that DTC C1291 occurred previously, but is intermittent, or has been corrected.

Conditions for Setting the DTC

A DTC C1291 was set in the previous ignition cycle.

Action Taken When the DTC Sets

- A DTC C1293 is stored
- The TCS is disabled
- The TRACTION OFF indicator is turned on
- The ABS remains functional

Conditions for Clearing the DTC

- The condition for the DTC is no longer present and the scan tool clear DTC function is used
- 50 ignition cycles have passed with no DTCs detected.

Diagnostic Aids

- Thoroughly inspect the wiring and the connectors. Failure to carefully and fully inspect the wiring and the connectors can result in misdiagnosis. Misdiagnosis may cause replacement of parts without repairing the malfunction.
- The following conditions may cause most intermittent malfunctions:
  - Poor connections
  - Rubbed through wire insulation
  - A broken wire inside the insulation
- Verify proper stoplamp/BTSI switch operation during the Data List of the Scan Tool. As the brake is applied, the data list should display the stoplamp/BTSI switch on within an inch of travel.
- If an intermittent malfunction exists, refer to Troubleshooting

Test Description

The numbers below refer to the step numbers on the diagnostic table.

2. This step checks for the proper duty cycle.

GC402980282500AX

Fig. 246 Code C1293: Code C1291 Set In Previous Ignition Cycle (Part 1 of 2). DeVille & Seville

Circuit Description

This DTC occurs when the internal self-checking safety logic has determined that the stoplamp/BTSI switch is continuously on. This is important because the TCS cannot be activated when the stoplamp/BTSI switch is on.

Conditions for Setting the DTC

A DTC C1294 can be set if the vehicle speed reaches at least 40 km/h (25 mph). A malfunction exists if the brake was never off during two consecutive drive cycles.

Action Taken When the DTC Sets

- A DTC C1294 is stored
- The TCS is disabled
- The TRACTION OFF indicator is turned on
- The ABS remains functional

Conditions for Clearing the DTC

- The condition for the DTC is no longer present and the scan tool clear DTC function is used
- 50 ignition cycles have passed with no DTCs detected

Diagnostic Aids

- Thoroughly inspect the wiring and the connectors. Failure to carefully and fully inspect the wiring and the connectors can result in misdiagnosis. Misdiagnosis may cause replacement of parts without repairing the malfunction.
- The following conditions may cause most intermittent malfunctions:
  - Poor connections
  - Rubbed through wire insulation
  - A broken wire inside the insulation
- The following conditions are other possible causes of this malfunction:
  - A short to voltage in the stoplamp/BTSI switch circuit
  - A misadjusted or shorted stoplamp/BTSI switch
- If an intermittent malfunction exists, refer to Troubleshooting

Test Description

The numbers below refer to the step numbers on the diagnostic table.

4. This step checks for a short to voltage.

GC402980282600AX

Fig. 247 Code C1294: Brake Lamp Switch Circuit Always Active (Part 1 of 2). DeVille

Step	Action	Value(s)	Yes	No
1	Did you perform the Diagnostic System Check?	—	Go to *Step 2*	Go to *Diagnostic System Check*
2	Observe the rear brake lamps. Are the brake lamps off?	—	Go to *Step 4*	Go to *Step 3*
3	Disconnect the stoplamp/BTSI switch connector C1. Are the brake lamps still on?	—	Go to *Step 6*	Go to *Step 7*
4	1. Disconnect the EBTCM harness connector. 2. Install the *J 39700* universal pinout box using the *J 39700-25* adapter cable to the EBTCM harness connector only. 3. Using a *J 39200* DMM, measure the voltage between the *J 39700* terminals 9 and B. Is the voltage greater than the specified value?	1 V	Go to *Step 6*	Go to *Step 5*
5	1. Turn OFF the ignition. 2. Inspect CKT 17 and the EBTCM harness connector for damage which may result in a short to voltage with all connectors connected. 3. Reconnect all connectors. 4. Carefully drive vehicle for three drive cycles while monitoring a scan tool. A drive cycle consists of starting the engine, driving above 40 km/h (25 mph) back to 0 km/h (0 mph) and then turning the ignition switch to the OFF position. Was DTC C1294 set in the last three drive cycles?	—	Go to *Step 8*	Go to *Diagnostic System Check*
6	Repair short to voltage in CKT 17. Did you complete the repair?	—	Go to *Diagnostic System Check*	—
7	Adjust or repair the stoplamp/BTSI switch as necessary. Did you complete the repair?	—	Go to *Diagnostic System Check*	—
8	Replace the EBTCM. Did you complete the repair?	—	Go to *Diagnostic System Check*	—

GC4029803901020X

Fig. 248 Code C1294: Brake Lamp Switch Circuit Always Active (Part 2 of 2). Seville

Circuit Description

This DTC is used to identify open stoplamp/BTSI switch circuitry that prevents the stoplamp/BTSI switch input to the EBTCM from changing states when the brake is applied. This DTC is used in conjunction with DTC C1291 in order to determine the cause of an open stoplamp/BTSI switch malfunction.

Conditions for Setting the DTC

DTC C1295 can be set after initialization is completed, if the stoplamp/BTSI switch input voltage is not within specifications for one second, indicating an open circuit, a malfunction exists.

Action Taken When the DTC Sets

- A DTC C1295 is stored
- The TCS is disabled.
- The TRACTION OFF indicator is turned on
- The ABS remains functional

Conditions for Clearing the DTC

- The condition for the DTC is no longer present and the scan tool Clear DTC function is used
- 50 ignition cycles have passed with no DTCs detected

Diagnostic Aids

- Thoroughly inspect the wiring and the connectors. Failure to carefully and fully inspect the wiring and the connectors may result in misdiagnosis. Misdiagnosis may cause part replacement without repairing the malfunction.
- The following conditions may cause an intermittent malfunction:
  - A poor connection
  - Rubbed through wire insulation
  - A wire broken inside the insulation
- The following conditions are other possible causes for this malfunction:
  - An open in the stoplamp/BTSI switch input circuit
  - An open in all of the brake lamps
  - An open or maladjusted brake lamp switch
  - A wiring problem, terminal corrosion or a poor connection in the circuit
- If an intermittent malfunction exists, refer to Troubleshooting

GC402980282700AX

Fig. 249 Code C1295: Brake Lamp Switch Circuit Open (Part 1 of 3). DeVille

Step	Action	Value(s)	Yes	No
13	1. Press the brake pedal. 2. Check the STOP fuse. Is the fuse OK?	—	Go to *Diagnostic System Check*	*Go to Step 14*
14	1. Turn the ignition switch to the OFF position. 2. Disconnect the EBTCM. 3. Replace the fuse. 4. Depress the brake pedal. 5. Check the BRAKE fuse. Is the fuse OK?	—	*Go to Step 4*	*Go to Step 15*
15	Repair the short to ground in CKT 20. Is the circuit repair complete?	—	Go to *Diagnostic System Check*	—

GC402980282700CX

Fig. 249 Code C1295: Brake Lamp Switch Circuit Open (Part 3 of 3). DeVille

Test Description

The numbers below refer to step numbers on the diagnostic table.

3. Checks for voltage at EBTCM.
9. Checks the stoplamp/BTSI switch.

Step	Action	Value(s)	Yes	No
1	Did you perform the Diagnostic System Check?	—	Go to *Step 2*	Go to *Diagnostic System Check*
2	Press the brake pedal. Do the brake lamps turn on?	—	Go to *Step 3*	Go to *Step 6*
3	1. Turn OFF the ignition. 2. Disconnect the EBTCM harness connector. 3. Install the *J 39700* universal pinout box using *J 39700-25* adapter cable to the EBTCM harness connector only. 4. Turn ON the ignition, with the engine OFF. 5. Press the brake pedal. 6. Using a *J 39200* DMM, measure the voltage at the *J 39700* terminal 9. Is the voltage within the specified range?	Battery Voltage	Go to *Step 4*	Go to *Step 5*
4	Replace the EBTCM. Did you complete the repair?	—	Go to *Diagnostic System Check*	—
5	Repair the open in CKT 17. Did you complete the repair?	—	Go to *Diagnostic System Check*	—
6	Check the rear junction block STOP LP Fuse. Is the fuse good?	—	Go to *Step 7*	Go to *Step 11*
7	1. Disconnect the stoplamp/BTSI switch connector C1. 2. Using a *J 39200* DMM, measure the voltage at the stoplamp/BTSI switch harness connector C1 terminal A. Is the voltage within the specified range?	Battery Voltage	Go to *Step 9*	Go to *Step 8*
8	Repair the open in CKT 1640. Did you complete the repair?	—	Go to *Diagnostic System Check*	—
9	Connect a fused jumper wire between the stoplamp/BTSI switch harness connector C1 terminals A and B. Do the brake lamps come on?	—	Go to *Step 10*	Go to *Step 5*
10	Adjust or repair the stoplamp/BTSI switch as necessary. Did you complete the repair?	—	Go to *Diagnostic System Check*	—
11	1. Replace the STOP LP Fuse in the rear junction block. Do not press the brake pedal. 2. Check the STOP LP Fuse. Is the fuse good?	—	Go to *Step 13*	Go to *Step 12*
12	Repair short to ground in CKT 1640. Did you complete the repair?	—	Go to *Diagnostic System Check*	—

GC4029803902020X

Fig. 250 Code C1295: Brake Lamp Switch Circuit Open (Part 2 of 3). Seville

Test Description

The numbers below refer to the step numbers on the diagnostic table.

3. This step checks for voltage at the EBTCM.
9. This step checks for stoplamp/BTSI switch.

Step	Action	Value(s)	Yes	No
1	Was the Diagnostic System Check performed?	—	*Go to Step 2*	Go to *Diagnostic System Check*
2	Press the brake pedal. Do the brake lights come on?	—	*Go to Step 3*	*Go to Step 6*
3	1. Turn the ignition switch to the OFF position. 2. Disconnect the EBTCM connector. 3. Install the *J 39700* Universal Pinout Box using the *J 39700-25* cable adapter to the EBTCM harness connector only. 4. Using the *J 39200* DMM, measure the voltage at the *J 39700* terminals 9 while an assistant presses the brake pedal. Is the voltage within specifications?	Battery voltage	*Go to Step 4*	*Go to Step 5*
4	Replace the EBTCM. Is the replacement complete?	—	Go to *Diagnostic System Check*	—
5	Repair the open or high resistance in CKT 20. Is the circuit repair complete?	—	Go to *Diagnostic System Check*	—
6	Check the STOP fuse in the engine compartment fuse/relay center. Is the fuse OK?	—	*Go to Step 7*	*Go to Step 11*
7	1. Disconnect the Stoplamp/BTSI switch connector. 2. Using the *J 39200*, measure the voltage at the Stoplamp/BTSI switch harness connector terminal A. Is the voltage within specifications?	Battery voltage	*Go to Step 9*	*Go to Step 8*
8	Repair the open in CKT 1540. Is the circuit repair complete?	—	Go to *Diagnostic System Check*	—
9	Connect a fused jumper wire between the Stoplamp/BTSI switch harness connector terminals A and B. Do the brake lamps come on?	—	*Go to Step 10*	*Go to Step 5*
10	Adjust or repair the Stoplamp/BTSI switch as necessary. Is the repair complete?	—	Go to *Diagnostic System Check*	—
11	1. Replace the STOP fuse. (Do not press the brake pedal.) 2. Check the BRAKE fuse. Is the fuse OK?	—	*Go to Step 13*	*Go to Step 12*
12	Repair the short to ground in CKT 1540. Is the circuit repair complete?	—	Go to *Diagnostic System Check*	—

GC402980282700BX

Fig. 249 Code C1295: Brake Lamp Switch Circuit Open (Part 2 of 3). DeVille

Circuit Description

This DTC is used in order to identify open stoplamp/BTSI switch circuitry that prevents the stoplamp/BTSI switch input from changing states when the brake is applied. This DTC is used in conjunction with DTC C1291 in order to determine the cause of an open stoplamp/BTSI switch malfunction.

Conditions for Setting the DTC

This DTC sets after the following occur:

- Initialization is completed.
- The stoplamp/BTSI switch input voltage is out of specification for 1 second (indicating an open circuit).

Action Taken When the DTC Sets

- A malfunction DTC is stored.
- The TCS is disabled.
- The TRACTION CONTROL indicator is turned ON.
- The ABS remains functional.

Conditions for Clearing the DTC

- The condition for DTC is no longer present and you used scan tool Clear DTCs function.
- The condition for DTC is no longer present and you used the On-Board Clear DTCs function.
- The EBTCM does not detect the DTC in 50 drive cycles.

Diagnostic Aids

- It is very important that a thorough inspection of the wiring and connectors be performed. Failure to carefully and fully inspect wiring and connectors may result in misdiagnosis, causing part replacement with reappearance of the malfunction.
- An intermittent malfunction can be caused by poor connections, broken insulation, or a wire that is broken inside the insulation.
- If an intermittent malfunction exists, refer to *Intermittents and Poor Connections*
- This condition may be cause by the following:
  - The stoplamp/BTSI switch circuit is open.
  - All brake lamps are open.
  - The brake lamp switch is open or misadjusted.
  - The brake lamp ground is open.
  - The circuit has a wiring problem, terminal corrosion, or poor connections.

GC4029803902010X

Fig. 250 Code C1295: Brake Lamp Switch Circuit Open (Part 1 of 3). Seville

Step	Action	Value(s)	Yes	No
13	1. Press the brake pedal. 2. Check the rear junction block STOP LP Fuse. Is the fuse good?	—	Go to *Diagnostic System Check*	Go to *Step 14*
14	1. Turn OFF the ignition. 2. Disconnect the EBTCM harness connector. 3. Replace the fuse. 4. Press the brake pedal. 5. Check the rear junction block STOP LP Fuse. Is the fuse good?	—	Go to *Step 4*	Go to *Step 15*
15	Repair short to ground in CKT 17. Did you complete the repair?	—	Go to *Diagnostic System Check*	—

GC4029803902030X

Fig. 250 Code C1295: Brake Lamp Switch Circuit Open (Part 3 of 3). Seville

Circuit Description

The extended travel brake switch is used by the EBTCM to determine if the driver has pressed the brake pedal far enough to initiate moderate braking, as opposed to merely brushing or tapping the pedal. The PCM sends this information to the EBTCM via serial data class 2 messages.

Conditions for Setting the DTC

- The ignition is ON.
- The PCM detects an extended travel brake switch failure. The PCM also set DTC P1575.

Action Taken When the DTC Sets

- A malfunction DTC is stored.
- Stabilitrak® is disabled.
- The DIC displays the SERVICE STABILITY SYS message.
- The ABS/TCS remain functional.

Conditions for Clearing the DTC

- The condition for DTC is no longer present and you used scan tool Clear DTCs function.
- The condition for DTC is no longer present and you used the On-Board Clear DTCs function.
- The EBTCM does not detect the DTC in 50 drive cycles.

GC4029903927010X

Fig. 251 Code C1297: PCM Indicated Brake Extended Travel Switch Failure (Part 1 of 2). DeVille

Diagnostic Aids

- If the extended travel brake switch is not properly adjusted, the driver may experience longer Stabilitrak® brake pedal pulsations before normal brake pedal feel is returned. The Stabilitrak® brake pedal pulsation is different than the ABS brake pedal pulsation. The Stabilitrak® brake pedal pulsation has a much higher frequency and less pedal travel fluctuation.
- It is very important that a thorough inspection of the wiring and connectors be performed. Failure to carefully and fully inspect wiring and connectors may result in misdiagnosis, causing part replacement with reappearance of the malfunction.
- An intermittent malfunction can be caused by poor connections, broken insulation, or a wire that is broken inside the insulation.
- If an intermittent malfunction exists, refer to *Intermittents and Poor Connections Diagnosis* in Wiring Systems.

Step	Action	Value(s)	Yes	No
1	Did you perform the ABS Diagnostic System Check?	—	Go to *Step 2*	Go to *A Diagnostic System Check - ABS*
2	1. Turn OFF the ignition. 2. Connect a scan tool to the data link connector (DLC). 3. Turn ON the ignition, with the engine OFF. 4. Use the scan tool in order to read the powertrain control module (PCM) DTCs. Is DTC P1575 set as a current DTC?	—	*DTC P1575 Extended Travel Brake Switch Circuit*	Go to *Step 3*
3	1. Turn ON the ignition, with the engine OFF. 2. Use the scan tool in order to select ABS/TCS/ICCS Data Display (1) Diagnostics, Data List 2. 3. Monitor the extended travel brake switch. 4. Step on and off the brake pedal with enough force in order to simulate a hard braking condition. As the brake pedal is pressed and released, the scan tool should read Applied and Released. 5. Use a tape measure in order to measure the distance that the brake pedal travels for the scan tool to read Applied. Is the distance within the specified range?	2.5–3.3 cm (1.0–1.3 in)	Go to *A Diagnostic System Check - ABS*	Go to *Step 4*
4	Adjust or repair the extended travel brake switch as necessary. Did you complete the repair?	—	Go to *A Diagnostic System Check - ABS*	—

GC4029903927020X

Fig. 251 Code C1297: PCM Indicated Brake Extended Travel Switch Failure (Part 2 of 2). DeVille

Circuit Description

The Class 2 serial data line allows all the modules on the line to transmit information to each other as needed. Each module is assigned an ID and all the information sent out on the line is assigned a priority by which it is received. When the ignition switch is turned to the RUN position each module begins to send and receive information. Each module on the Class 2 serial data line knows what information it needs to send out and what information it should be receiving. What the modules do not know is which module is supposed to send them the information. This information is only learned after the module has received the information it needs along with the ID of the module that sent the information. This information is then remembered until the ignition switch is turned off. If the EBTCM looses communication with the Powertrain Control Module (PCM) then DTC U1016 will be set by the EBTCM.

Conditions for Setting the DTC

The ignition switch is in the RUN position and the PCM does not communicate with the EBTCM for 7 seconds

Action Taken When the DTC Sets

- A DTC C1298 is stored
- The TCS is disabled.
- The TRACTION OFF indicator is turned on
- The ABS remains functional

Conditions for Clearing the DTC

- The condition for the DTC is no longer present and the scan tool clear DTC function is used
- 50 ignition cycles have passed with no DTCs detected

GC402980282900AX

Fig. 252 Code C1298: PCM Class 2 Serial Data Link Fault (Part 1 of 2). DeVille

Diagnostic Aids

- Thoroughly inspect the wiring and the connectors. Failure to carefully and fully inspect the wiring and the connectors may result in misdiagnosis. Misdiagnosis may cause part replacement without repairing the malfunction.
- The following conditions may cause an intermittent malfunction:
  - A poor connection
  - Rubbed through wire insulation
  - A wire broken inside the insulation
- The following conditions are other possible causes for this malfunction:
  - A Class 2 transmit fault on the EBTCM
  - A Class 2 receiver fault on the PCM
  - Extreme Class 2 bus traffic
  - A wiring problem, terminal corrosion, or a poor connection in the CKT 1807
- If an intermittent malfunction exists, refer to Troubleshooting

Test Description

The numbers below refer to the step numbers on the diagnostic table.

5. This step checks to see if the SBM is sending the proper power mode position message.
6. This step checks to see if the EBTCM is sending out the required information on the Class 2 serial data line.

Step	Action	Value(s)	Yes	No
1	Was the Diagnostic System Check performed?	—	*Go to Step 2*	Refer to *Diagnostic System Check*
2	Check the following grounds, G101, and G104 making sure each ground is clean tight and free of damage. Were any loose, damaged, or corroded grounds found?	—	*Go to Step 3*	*Go to Step 4*
3	Repair the ground(s) as necessary. Is the repair complete?	—	Refer to *Diagnostic System Check*	—
4	1. Turn the ignition switch to the RUN position with the engine off. 2. Using a Scan Tool, read the ABS/TCS DTCs. Are any of the following DTCs present: U1016, or U1255?	—	Go to Applicable DTC Table	*Go to Step 5*
5	1. Using a Scan Tool in the ABS/TCS Data List, read the power mode position. 2. While reading the Scan Tool, turn the ignition switch to the following positions: OFF, UNLOCK, RUN, and CRANK. Does the Scan Tool read the proper power mode position?	—	*Go to Step 6*	Refer to *Diagnostic System Check*
6	Using a Scan Tool in the Applications Menu, read the Class 2 Normal Mode Message Monitor. Is the EBTCM sending a Class 2 Normal Mode Message?	—	*Go to Step 7*	*Go to Step 8*
7	Suspect the PCM. Is the diagnosis complete?	—	Refer to *Diagnostic System Check*	—
8	Replace the EBTCM. Is the replacement complete?	—	Refer to *Diagnostic System Check*	—

GC402980282900BX

Fig. 252 Code C1298: PCM Class 2 Serial Data Link Fault (Part 2 of 2). DeVille

Circuit Description

The serial data serial data allows all of the modules on the line to transmit information to each other as needed. Each module is assigned an ID. All of the information sent out on the line is assigned a priority by which it is received. When the ignition is turned ON, each module begins to send and receive information. Each module on the serial data class 2 knows what information the module needs to send out and what information the module should be receiving. What the modules do not know is which module is supposed to send the information. This information is only learned after the module has received the information needed along with the ID of the module that sent the information. This information is then remembered until the ignition switch is turned off.

Conditions for Setting the DTC

- The ignition is ON.
- The PCM does not receive any messages from the EBTCM for 7 seconds.

Action Taken When the DTC Sets

- A malfunction DTC is stored.
- The TCS is disabled.
- The TRACTION CONTROL indicator is turned ON.
- The ABS remains functional.

Conditions for Clearing the DTC

- The condition for DTC is no longer present and you used scan tool Clear DTCs function.
- The condition for DTC is no longer present and you used the On-Board Clear DTCs function.
- The EBTCM does not detect the DTC in 50 drive cycles.

Diagnostic Aids

- It is very important that a thorough inspection of the wiring and connectors be performed. Failure to carefully and fully inspect wiring and connectors may result in misdiagnosis, causing part replacement with reappearance of the malfunction.
- An intermittent malfunction can be caused by poor connections, broken insulation, or a wire that is broken inside the insulation.
- If an intermittent malfunction exists, refer to *Intermittents and Poor Connections*

GC4029803904010X

Fig. 253 Code C1298: PCM Class 2 Serial Data Link Fault (Part 1 of 2). Seville

Test Description

The numbers below refer to step numbers on the diagnostic table.

5. Checks to see if the dash integration module (DIM) is sending the proper power mode position message.
6. Checks to see if the EBTCM is sending out the required information via serial data class 2.

Step	Action	Value(s)	Yes	No
1	Did you perform the Diagnostic System Check?	—	Go to *Step 2*	Go to *Diagnostic System Check*
2	Check the following grounds, making sure each ground is clean and torqued to the proper specifications: • G102 • G103 Were any loose, damaged, or corroded grounds found?	—	Go to *Step 3*	Go to *Step 4*
3	Repair the ground as necessary. Did you complete the repair?	—	Go to *Diagnostic System Check*	—
4	1. Turn OFF the ignition. 2. Connect a scan tool to the data link connector (DLC). 3. Turn ON the ignition, with the engine OFF. 4. Select ABS/TCS/ICCS Diagnostic Trouble Codes, DTC Information. Are DTCs U1016, U1255, U1300, or U1301 set as history DTCs?	—	Go to *DTC List*	Go to *Step 5*
5	1. Using the scan tool, select Dash Integration Module (DIM) Data Display, Inputs. 2. Monitor the Ignition Switch parameter. 3. Turn the ignition switch to each of the following positions: • OFF • ACC • START • ON Did the scan tool indicate the proper position for each power mode position?	—	Go to *Step 6*	*Body Control Module*
6	Using the scan tool in the Applications menu, read the Class 2 Normal Mode Message Monitor. Is the EBTCM sending a Class 2 Normal Mode Message?	—	Go to *Step 7*	Go to *Step 8*
7	Suspect PCM. Is the PCM diagnosis complete?	—	Go to *Diagnostic System Check*	—
8	Replace the EBTCM. Did you complete the repair?	—	Go to *Diagnostic System Check*	—

GC4029803904020X

Fig. 253 Code C1298: PCM Class 2 Serial Data Link Fault (Part 2 of 2). Seville

Step	Action	Value(s)	Yes	No
1	Was the Diagnostic System Check performed?	—	*Go to Step 2*	Go to *Diagnostic System Check*
2	Using a scan tool read the IPC DTC(s). Is DTC U1016 also set as a current IPC DTC?	—	Go to Powertrain OBD2 System Check	*Go to Step 3*
3	Is DTC U1016 set as a current ABS/TCS DTC?	—	*Go to Step 4*	Go to *Diagnostic System Check*
4	Replace the EBTCM. Is the replacement complete?	—	Go to *Diagnostic System Check*	—

GC402980283000BX

Fig. 254 Code U1016: Loss Of Communications w/PCM (Part 2 of 2). DeVille & Seville

Step	Action	Value(s)	Yes	No
1	Was the Diagnostic System Check performed?	—	Go to Step 2	Go to the Diagnostic System Check
2	1. Turn the ignition switch to the ON position, engine OFF. 2. Using a scan tool, read the Class 2 messages. Is the PCM ACTIVE?	—	Go to Step 3	Inspect Engine Controls
3	Is the IPC ACTIVE?	—	Go to Step 4	Inspect IPC
4	Is the CVRSS ACTIVE?	—	Go to Step 5	Inspect CVRSS
5	Is the PZM ACTIVE?	—	Go to Step 6	Inspect PZM
6	Using a scan tool read the PCM DTCs. Is DTC P1611 also set in the PCM?	—	Inspect the Electronically Controlled Suspension	Go to the Diagnostic System Check

GC402970277400BX

Fig. 255 Code U1255: Generic Loss Of Communications (Part 2 of 2). DeVille

Circuit Description

The Class 2 serial data line allows all the modules on the line to transmit information to each other as needed. Each module is assigned an ID and all the information sent out on the line is assigned a priority by which it is received. When the ignition switch is turned to the RUN position each module begins to send and receive information. Each module on the Class 2 serial data line knows what information it needs to send out and what information it should be receiving. What the modules do not know is which module is supposed to send them the information. This information is only learned after the module has received the information it needs along with the ID of the module that sent the information. This information is then remembered until the ignition switch is turned off. If the EBTCM looses communication with the Powertrain Control Module (PCM) then DTC U1016 will be set by the EBTCM.

Conditions for Setting the DTC

The DTC can be set any time the ignition is in the RUN position, and the PCM does not communicate with the EBTCM for 5 seconds.

Action Taken When the DTC Sets

A malfunction DTC is stored, TCS is disabled and the TRACTION OFF indicator is turned on. ABS remains functional.

Conditions for Clearing the DTC

- Condition for DTC is no longer present and scan tool clear DTC function is used.
- Fifty ignition cycles have passed with no DTC(s) detected.

Diagnostic Aids

- It is very important that a thorough inspection of the wiring and connectors be performed. Failure to carefully and fully inspect wiring and connectors may result in misdiagnosis, causing part replacement with reappearance of the malfunction.
- An intermittent malfunction is most likely caused by a poor connection, rubbed through wire insulation, or a wire that is broken inside the insulation.
- If an intermittent malfunction exists refer lto Troubleshooting

GC402980283000AX

Fig. 254 Code U1016: Loss Of Communications w/PCM (Part 1 of 2). DeVille & Seville

Circuit Description

The Class 2 serial data line allows all the modules on the line to transmit information to each other as needed. Each module is assigned an ID and all the information sent out on the line is assigned a priority by which it is received. When the ignition switch is turned to the ON position each module begins to send and receive information. Each module on the Class 2 serial data line knows what information it needs to send and what information it should be receiving. What the modules do not know is which module is sending the information. The sending module is identified by the ID imbedded information that has been received. The EBTCM retains all of this information until the ignition switch is turned off. If the EBTCM never receives any information, it sets a DTC U1255.

Conditions for setting the DTC

- The DTC can be set when the ignition switch is turned to the ON position, and the EBTCM does not receive the PCM ID for 5 seconds.

Action Taken When the DTC Sets

- A malfunction DTC is stored, ICCS is disabled and the STABILITY REDUCED message is turned ON.

Conditions for Clearing the DTC

- Condition for DTC is no longer present and scan tool clear DTC function is used.
- Fifty start cycles have passed with no DTCs detected.

Diagnostic Aids

- It is very important that a thorough inspection of the wiring and connectors be performed. Failure to carefully and fully inspect wiring and connectors may result in misdiagnosis, causing part replacement with reappearance of the malfunction.
- An intermittent malfunction is most likely caused by a poor connection, rubbed through wire insulation, or a wire that is broken inside the insulation.

GC402970277400AX

Fig. 255 Code U1255: Generic Loss Of Communications (Part 1 of 2). DeVille

DTC U1056 Loss of Communications with CVRSS

Circuit Description

The Class 2 serial data line allows all the modules on the line to transmit information to each other as needed. Each module is assigned an ID and all the information sent out on the line is assigned a priority by which it is received. When the ignition switch is turned to the run position each module begins to send and receive information. Each module on the Class 2 serial data line knows what information it needs to send out and what information it should be receiving. What the modules do not know is which module is supposed to send them the information. This information is only learned after the module has received the information it needs along with the ID of the module that sent the information. This information is then remembered until the ignition switch is turned off. If the EBTCM looses communication with the Continuously Variable Road Sensing Suspension Module (CVRSS) then DTC U1056 will be set by the EBTCM.

Conditions for Setting the DTC

The DTC can be set any time the ignition is in the RUN position, and the CVRSS module does not communicate with the EBTCM for 7 seconds.

Action Taken When the DTC Sets

A malfunction DTC is stored, ABS and TCS remain functional.

Conditions for Clearing the DTC

- Condition for DTC is no longer present and scan tool clear DTC function is used.
- Fifty ignition cycles have passed with no DTC(s) detected.

Diagnostic Aids

- It is very important that a thorough inspection of the wiring and connectors be performed. Failure to carefully and fully inspect wiring and connectors may result in misdiagnosis, causing part replacement with reappearance of the malfunction.
- An intermittent malfunction is most likely caused by a poor connection, rubbed through wire insulation, or a wire that is broken inside the insulation.

Step	Action	Value(s)	Yes	No
1	Was the Diagnostic System Check performed?	—	*Go to Step 2*	Go to *Diagnostic System Check*
2	Using a scan tool read the PCM DTC(s). Is DTC P1611 also set as a current PCM DTC?	—	Inspect Road Sensing Suspension	*Go to Step 3*
3	Is DTC U1056 set as a current ABS/TCS/ICCS DTC?	—	*Go to Step 4*	Go to *Diagnostic System Check*
4	Replace the EBTCM. Is the replacement complete?	—	Go to *Diagnostic System Check*	—

GC4029802831000X

Fig. 256 Code U1256: Loss Of Communications w/CVRSS. DeVille

Circuit Description

The Class 2 serial data line allows all the modules on the line to transmit information to each other as needed. Each module is assigned an ID and all the information sent out on the line is assigned a priority by which it is received. When the ignition switch is turned to the RUN position each module begins to send and receive information. Each module on the Class 2 serial data line knows what information it needs to send out and what information it should be receiving. What the modules do not know is which module is supposed to send them the information. This information is only learned after the module has received the information it needs along with the ID of the module that sent the information. This information is then remembered until the ignition switch is turned off.

GC402980277100AX

Fig. 257 No Communications w/EBTCM (Part 1 of 3). DeVille

Step	Action	Value(s)	Yes	No
DEFINITION: Scan tool can not communicate with the EBTCM.				
1	Was the Diagnostic System Check performed?	—	*Go to Step 2*	*Go to Diagnostic System Check*
2	Turn the Ignition switch to the RUN position with the engine off. Can the scan tool communicate with other modules on the Class 2 serial data line, such as the PCM?	—	*Go to Step 3*	Inspect Data Link Connector
3	Inspect the 10A ABS fuse in the Engine Compartment Fuse/Relay Center. Is the fuse OK?	—	*Go to Step 4*	*Go to Step 9*
4	Inspect the 50A BRAKES Maxifuse in the RH Maxifuse Block. Is the fuse OK?	—	*Go to Step 12*	*Go to Step 5*
5	1. Install a new BRAKES Maxifuse. 2. Recheck the fuse. Is the fuse OK?	—	*Go to Diagnostic System Check*	*Go to Step 6*
6	1. Turn the ignition switch to the OFF position. 2. Remove the BRAKES Maxifuse. 3. Disconnect the EBTCM connector. 4. Connect the *J 39700* Universal Pinout Box using the *J 39700-25* cable adapter to the EBTCM harness connector only. 5. Using *J 39200* DMM, measure the resistance between terminals D and B of *J 39700*. Is the resistance within the range specified in the value(s) column?	OL (infinite)	*Go to Step 7*	*Go to Step 8*
7	Replace the EBTCM. Is the replacement complete?	—	*Go to Diagnostic System Check*	—
8	Repair CKT 1042 for a short to ground. Is the repair complete?	—	*Go to Diagnostic System Check*	—
9	1. Install a new 10A ABS fuse. 2. Cycle the ignition switch from the OFF to RUN position, engine off. 3. Recheck the fuse. Is the fuse OK?	—	*Go to Diagnostic System Check*	*Go to Step 10*
10	1. Turn the ignition switch to the OFF position. 2. Remove the 10A ABS fuse. 3. Disconnect the EBTCM connector. 4. Connect the *J 39700* Universal Pinout Box using the *J 39700-25* cable adapter to the EBTCM harness connector only. 5. Using *J 39200* DMM, measure the resistance between terminals A and B of *J 39700*. Is the resistance within the range specified in the value(s) column?	OL (infinite)	*Go to Step 7*	*Go to Step 11*
11	Repair CKT 1339 for a short to ground. Is the repair complete?	—	*Go to Diagnostic System Check*	—

GC402980277100BX

Fig. 257 No Communications w/EBTCM (Part 2 of 3). DeVille

Step	Action	Value(s)	Yes	No
12	1. Install the fuses if removed. 2. Turn the ignition switch to the RUN position, engine off. 3. Using *J 39200* DMM, measure the voltage at the 10A ABS fuse by probing between the fuse test terminals and a good ground. Is the voltage within the range specified within the value(s) column?	Battery Volts	*Go to Step 13*	Inspect Power Distribution
13	Using *J 39200* DMM, measure the voltage at the 50A BRAKES fuse by probing between the fuse test terminals and a good ground. Is the voltage within the range specified within the value(s) column?	Battery Volts	*Go to Step 14*	Power Distribution
14	1. Turn the ignition switch to the OFF position. 2. Disconnect the EBTCM connector. 3. Connect the *J 39700* Universal Pinout Box using the *J 39700-25* cable adapter to the EBTCM harness connector only. 4. Using *J 39200* DMM, measure the resistance between *J 39700* terminal B and a good ground. Is the resistance within the range specified in the value(s) column?	0 - 2Ω	*Go to Step 16*	*Go to Step 15*
15	Repair CKT 1651 or G110 for an open or high resistance. Is the repair complete?	—	*Go to Diagnostic System Check*	—
16	1. Turn the ignition switch to the RUN position, engine off. 2. Using *J 39200* DMM, measure the voltage between *J 39700* terminals A and B. Is the voltage within the range specified in the value(s) column?	Battery Volts	*Go to Step 18*	*Go to Step 17*
17	Repair CKT 1339 for an open. Is the repair complete?	—	*Go to Diagnostic System Check*	—
18	Using *J 39200* DMM, measure the voltage between *J 39700* terminals D and B. Is the voltage within the range specified in the value(s) column?	Battery Volts	*Go to Step 7*	*Go to Step 19*
19	Repair CKT 1042 for an open. Is the repair complete?	—	*Go to Diagnostic System Check*	—

GC402980277100CX

Fig. 257 No Communications w/EBTCM (Part 3 of 3). DeVille

Circuit Description

The serial data serial data allows all of the modules on the line to transmit information to each other as needed. Each module is assigned an ID. All of the information sent out on the line is assigned a priority by which it is received. When the ignition is turned ON, each module begins to send and receive information. Each module on the serial data class 2 knows what information the module needs to send out and what information the module should be receiving. What the modules do not know is which module is supposed to send the information. This information is only learned after the module has received the information needed along with the ID of the module that sent the information. This information is then remembered until the ignition switch is turned off.

Diagnostic Aids

- It is very important that a thorough inspection of the wiring and connectors be performed. Failure to carefully and fully inspect wiring and connectors may result in misdiagnosis, causing part replacement with reappearance of the malfunction.
- An intermittent malfunction can be caused by poor connections, broken insulation, or a wire that is broken inside the insulation.

GC4029803910010X

Fig. 258 No Communications w/EBCM/EBTCM (Part 1 of 3). Seville

Step	Action	Value(s)	Yes	No
1	Did you perform the Diagnostic System Check?	—	*Go to Step 2*	*Go to Diagnostic System Check*
2	1. Turn OFF the ignition. 2. Connect a scan tool to the data link connector (DLC). 3. Turn ON the ignition, with the engine OFF. 4. Attempt to establish communication with other module on the serial data class 2, such as the PCM. Does the scan tool communicate with any other modules on the serial data class 2?	—	*Go to Step 3*	*Data Link Communications*
3	Check the rear junction block ABS Fuse. Is the fuse good?	—	*Go to Step 4*	*Go to Step 9*
4	Check the underhood junction block ABS SOL Fuse. Is the fuse good?	—	*Go to Step 12*	*Go to Step 5*
5	1. Install a new ABS SOL Fuse in the underhood junction block. 2. Recheck the fuse. Is the fuse good?	—	*Go to Diagnostic System Check*	*Go to Step 6*
6	1. Turn OFF the ignition. 2. Remove the ABS SOL fuse. 3. Disconnect the EBTCM harness connector. 4. Connect the *J 39700* universal pinout box using the *J 39700-25* cable adapter to the EBTCM harness connector only. 5. Using a *J 39200* DMM, measure the resistance between the *J 39700* terminals D and B. Is the resistance within the specified range?	OL (infinite)	*Go to Step 7*	*Go to Step 8*
7	Replace the EBTCM. Did you complete the repair?	—	*Go to Diagnostic System Check*	—
8	Repair the short to ground in CKT 442. Did you complete the repair?	—	*Go to Diagnostic System Check*	—
9	1. Install a new ABS Fuse. 2. Turn OFF the ignition. 3. Turn ON the ignition, with the engine OFF. 4. Recheck the fuse. Is the fuse good?	—	*Go to Diagnostic System Check*	*Go to Step 10*
10	1. Turn OFF the ignition. 2. Remove the ABS Fuse. 3. Disconnect the EBTCM harness connector. 4. Connect the *J 39700* universal pinout box using the *J 39700-25* cable adapter to the EBTCM harness connector only. 5. Using a *J 39200* DMM, measure the resistance between the *J 39700* terminals A and B. Is the resistance within the specified range?	OL (infinite)	*Go to Step 7*	*Go to Step 11*
11	Repair the short to ground in CKT 241. Did you complete the repair?	—	*Go to Diagnostic System Check*	—

GC4029803910020X

Fig. 258 No Communications w/EBCM/EBTCM (Part 2 of 3). Seville

Step	Action	Value(s)	Yes	No
12	1. Install the fuses, if removed. 2. Turn ON the ignition, with the engine OFF. 3. Using a *J 39200* DMM, measure the voltage at the ABS Fuse by probing between the fuse test terminals and a good ground. Is the voltage within the specified range?	Battery Voltage	Go to *Step 13*	Go to *Step 20*
13	Using a *J 39200* DMM, measure the voltage at the ABS SOL Fuse by probing between the fuse test terminals and a good ground. Is the voltage within the specified range?	Battery Voltage	Go to *Step 14*	Go to *Step 21*
14	1. Turn OFF the ignition. 2. Disconnect the EBTCM harness connector. 3. Connect the *J 39700* universal pinout box using the *J 39700-25* cable adapter to the EBTCM harness connector only. 4. Using a *J 39200* DMM, measure the resistance between the *J 39700* terminal B and a good ground. Is the resistance less than the specified value?	2 Ω	Go to *Step 16*	Go to *Step 15*
15	Repair the open in CKT 1150 or G102. Did you complete the repair?	—	Go to *Diagnostic System Check*	—
16	1. Turn ON the ignition, with the engine OFF. 2. Using a *J 39200* DMM, measure the voltage between the *J 39700* terminals A and B. Is the voltage within the specified range?	Battery Voltage	Go to *Step 18*	Go to *Step 17*
17	Repair the open in CKT 241. Did you complete the repair?	—	Go to *Diagnostic System Check*	—
18	Using a *J 39200* DMM, measure the voltage between the *J 39700* terminals D and B. Is the voltage within the specified range?	Battery Voltage	Go to *Step 7*	Go to *Step 19*
19	Repair the open in CKT 442. Did you complete the repair?	—	Go to *Diagnostic System Check*	—
20	Replace the rear junction block. Did you complete the repair?	—	Go to *Diagnostic System Check*	—
21	Replace the underhood junction block. Did you complete the repair?	—	Go to *Diagnostic System Check*	—

GC4029803910030X

Fig. 258 No Communications w/EBCM/EBTCM (Part 3 of 3). Seville

Step	Action	Value(s)	Yes	No
1	Did you perform the ABS Diagnostic System Check?	—	Go to *Step 2*	Go to *A Diagnostic System Check - ABS*
2	1. Turn OFF the ignition. 2. Connect a scan tool to the data link connector (DLC). 3. Turn ON the ignition, with the engine OFF. 4. Use the scan tool in order to select the ABS/TCS/ICCS Data List 2. 5. Monitor the TCS On/Off Switch parameter. 6. Press and then release the traction control switch. Does the scan tool display indicate the parameter changes status?	—	Go to *Step 3*	Go to *Step 4*
3	1. Use the scan tool in order to select the ABS/TCS/ICCS Data List 2. 2. Observe the Traction Off Message Command parameter. 3. Press and then release the traction control switch. Does the scan tool display indicate the parameter changes status?	—	Go to *Step 7*	Go to *Step 8*
4	1. Disconnect the traction control switch connector. 2. Use the scan tool in order to select the ABS/TCS/ICCS Data List 2. 3. Observe the TCS On/Off Switch parameter. Does the scan tool display indicate the parameter is Off?	—	Go to *Step 6*	Go to *Step 5*
5	Repair the short to ground in CKT 1571. Did you complete the repair?	—	Go to *A Diagnostic System Check - ABS*	—
6	Replace the traction control switch. Did you complete the repair?	—	Go to *A Diagnostic System Check - ABS*	—
7	Suspect the instrument cluster. Did you complete the repair?	—	Go to *A Diagnostic System Check - ABS*	—
8	Replace the EBTCM. Did you complete the repair?	—	Go to *A Diagnostic System Check - ABS*	—

GC4029903928020X

Fig. 259 Traction Off Message On w/No Code Set (Part 2 of 2). DeVille

Circuit Description

The TRACTION OFF message is controlled by the EBTCM. When the EBTCM sees the Traction Control Switch Input grounded through the momentary traction control switch, it disables Traction Control and sends a class 2 serial data message to the instrument cluster (IPC) to turn the TRACTION OFF message on. Each time the ignition switch is cycled OFF to ON, Traction Control is enabled.

Diagnostic Aids

- It is very important that a thorough inspection of the wiring and connectors be performed. Failure to carefully and fully inspect wiring and connectors may result in misdiagnosis, causing part replacement with reappearance of the malfunction.
- An intermittent malfunction can be caused by poor connections, broken insulation, or a wire that is broken inside the insulation.
- If an intermittent malfunction exists, refer to *Intermittents and Poor Connections*

Test Description

The numbers below refer to step numbers on the diagnostic table.

2. Checks the state of the traction control switch.
3. Checks the traction control switch and circuit for a short to ground.
4. Checks the instrument cluster for the ability to operate the TRACTION OFF message. The EBTCM sends a serial data class 2 message to the instrument cluster. This test is done to see if the EBTCM can not send the message or the instrument cluster can not receive the message and act on the message properly.

GC4029903928010X

Fig. 259 Traction Off Message On w/No Code Set (Part 1 of 2). DeVille

Circuit Description

The TRACTION OFF message is controlled by the EBTCM. When the IPM sees the Traction Control Disable Input grounded through the momentary traction control disable switch, it sends a Class 2 message to the EBTCM that tells the EBTCM that the traction control disable switch has been pressed. The EBTCM then disables Traction Control and sends a message to the instrument cluster (IPC) to turn the TRACTION OFF message on. Each time the ignition switch is cycled OFF to ON, Traction Control is enabled.

Diagnostic Aids

- It is very important that a thorough inspection of the wiring and connectors be performed. Failure to carefully and fully inspect wiring and connectors may result in misdiagnosis, causing part replacement with reappearance of the malfunction.
- An intermittent malfunction can be caused by poor connections, broken insulation, or a wire that is broken inside the insulation.
- If an intermittent malfunction exists, refer to *Intermittents and Poor Connections*

GC4029803905010X

Fig. 260 Traction Off Message On w/No Code Set (Part 1 of 2). Seville

Test Description

The numbers below refer to step numbers on the diagnostic table.

2. Checks the state of the traction control disable switch.
3. Checks for a stuck traction control disable switch.
4. Checks for short to ground in CKT 1788.

Step	Action	Value(s)	Yes	No
1	Did you perform the Diagnostic System Check?	—	Go to *Step 2*	Go to *Diagnostic System Check*
2	1. Turn OFF the ignition. 2. Connect a scan tool to the data link connector (DLC). 3. Turn ON the ignition, with the engine OFF. 4. Using the scan tool, select Instrument Panel Integration Module (IPM) Data Display, Non-HVAC Data. 5. Monitor TCS Input. Does the scan tool indicate that the traction control disable switch is On?	—	Go to *Step 3*	Go to *Step 7*
3	1. Disconnect the traction control disable switch connector. 2. Using the scan tool, select Instrument Panel Integration Module (IPM) Data Display, Non-HVAC Data. 3. Monitor TCS Input. Does the scan tool indicate that the traction control disable switch is On?	—	Go to *Step 4*	Go to *Step 6*
4	1. Disconnect the IPM connector C1. 2. Using the scan tool, select Instrument Panel Integration Module (IPM) Data Display, Non-HVAC Data. 3. Monitor TCS Input. Does the scan tool indicate that the traction control disable switch is On?	—	Go to *Step 7*	Go to *Step 5*
5	Repair the short to ground in CKT 1788. Did you complete the repair?	—	Go to *Diagnostic System Check*	—
6	Replace the traction control disable switch. Did you complete the repair?	—	Go to *Diagnostic System Check*	—
7	Replace the IPM. Did you complete the repair?	—	Go to *Diagnostic System Check*	—

GC4029803905020X

Fig. 260 Traction Off Message On w/No Code Set (Part 2 of 2). Seville

Circuit Description

The TRACTION OFF message is controlled by the EBTCM. When the EBTCM sees the Traction Control Switch Input grounded through the momentary traction control switch, it disables Traction Control and sends a class 2 serial data message to the instrument cluster (IPC) to turn the TRACTION OFF message on. Each time the ignition switch is cycled OFF to ON, Traction Control is enabled.

Diagnostic Aids

- It is very important that a thorough inspection of the wiring and connectors be performed. Failure to carefully and fully inspect wiring and connectors may result in misdiagnosis, causing part replacement with reappearance of the malfunction.
- An intermittent malfunction can be caused by poor connections, broken insulation, or a wire that is broken inside the insulation.
- If an intermittent malfunction exists, refer to *Intermittents and Poor Connections*

Test Description

The numbers below refer to step numbers on the diagnostic table.

2. Checks the state of the traction control switch.
3. Checks the traction control switch and circuit for a short to ground.
4. Checks the instrument cluster for the ability to operate the TRACTION OFF message. The EBTCM sends a serial data class 2 message to the instrument cluster. This test is done to see if the EBTCM can not send the message or the instrument cluster can not receive the message and act on the message properly.

GC4029903929010X

Fig. 261 Traction Off Message Inoperative w/No Code Set (Part 1 of 3). DeVille

Step	Action	Value(s)	Yes	No
10	Replace the traction control switch. Did you complete the repair?	—	Go to *A Diagnostic System Check - ABS*	—
11	Repair the open in CKT 151. Did you complete the repair?	—	Go to *A Diagnostic System Check - ABS*	—

GC4029903929030X

Fig. 261 Traction Off Message Inoperative w/No Code Set (Part 3 of 3). DeVille

Test Description

The numbers below refer to step numbers on the diagnostic table.

2. Checks if the traction control disable switch is open or inoperative.
4. Checks for an open in CKT 651.
6. Checks for an open in CKT 1788.

Step	Action	Value(s)	Yes	No
1	Did you perform the Diagnostic System Check?	—	Go to *Step 2*	Go to *Diagnostic System Check*
2	1. Turn ON the ignition, with the engine OFF. 2. Remove the traction control disable switch connector. 3. Press and hold the traction control disable switch. 4. Using a *J 39200* DMM, to measure the resistance between the traction control disable switch terminals C and B. Is the resistance less than the specified value?	5 Ω	Go to *Step 4*	Go to *Step 3*
3	Replace the traction control disable switch. Did you complete the repair?	—	Go to *Diagnostic System Check*	—
4	1. Connect a scan tool to the data link connector (DLC). 2. Connect a fused jumper from the traction control disable switch harness connector terminal C to a good ground. 3. Using the scan tool, select Instrument Panel Integration Module (IPM) Data Display, Non-HVAC Data. 4. Monitor TCS Input. Does the scan tool indicate that the traction control disable switch is On?	—	Go to *Step 5*	Go to *Step 6*
5	Repair the open in CKT 651. Did you complete the repair?	—	Go to *Diagnostic System Check*	—
6	1. Disconnect the instrument panel integration module (IPM) connector C1. 2. Using a *J 39200* DMM, measure the resistance between the traction control disable switch harness connector terminal C (LT BLU) and the IPM harness connector C1 terminal C11. Is the resistance less than the specified value?	5 Ω	Go to *Step 8*	Go to *Step 7*
7	Repair the open in CKT 17. Did you complete the repair?	—	Go to *Diagnostic System Check*	—
8	Replace the IPM. Did you complete the repair?	—	Go to *Diagnostic System Check*	—

GC4029803906020X

Fig. 262 Traction Off Message Inoperative w/No Code Set (Part 2 of 2). Seville

Step	Action	Value(s)	Yes	No
1	Did you perform the ABS Diagnostic System Check?	—	Go to *Step 2*	Go to *A Diagnostic System Check - ABS*
2	1. Turn OFF the ignition. 2. Connect a scan tool to the data link connector (DLC). 3. Turn ON the ignition, with the engine OFF. 4. Use the scan tool in order to select the ABS/TCS/ICCS Data List 2. 5. Observe the TCS On/Off Switch parameter. 6. Press and then release the traction control switch. Does the scan tool display indicate the parameter changes status?	—	Go to *Step 3*	Go to *Step 4*
3	1. Use the scan tool in order to select the ABS/TCS/ICCS Data List 2. 2. Observe the Traction Off Message Command parameter. 3. Press and then release the traction control switch. Does the scan tool display indicate the parameter changes status?	—	Go to *Step 7*	Go to *Step 8*
4	1. Turn OFF the ignition. 2. Disconnect the EBTCM connector. 3. Install the *J 39700* universal pinout box using the *J 39700-25* cable adapter to the EBTCM harness connector only. 4. Press and hold the traction control switch. 5. Use the *J 39200* in order to measure the resistance between the *J 39700* terminal 24 and terminal B. Is the resistance within the specified range?	OL (Infinite)	Go to *Step 5*	Go to *Step 8*
5	1. Disconnect the traction control switch connector. 2. Connect a fused jumper from the traction control switch connector terminal A to ground. 3. Use the *J 39200* in order to measure the resistance between the *J 39700* terminal 24 and terminal B. Is the resistance within the specified range?	OL (Infinite)	Go to *Step 9*	Go to *Step 6*
6	1. Use the *J 39200* in order to measure the resistance between the traction control switch terminal A and terminal B. 2. Press and then release the traction control switch. Is the resistance within the specified range?	OL (Infinite)	Go to *Step 10*	Go to *Step 11*
7	Suspect the instrument cluster. Did you complete the repair?	—	Go to *A Diagnostic System Check - ABS*	—
8	Replace the EBTCM. Did you complete the repair?	—	Go to *A Diagnostic System Check - ABS*	—
9	Repair the open in CKT 1571. Did you complete the repair?	—	Go to *A Diagnostic System Check - ABS*	—

GC4029903929020X

Fig. 261 Traction Off Message Inoperative w/No Code Set (Part 2 of 3). DeVille

Circuit Description

The TRACTION OFF message is controlled by the EBTCM. When the IPM sees the Traction Control Disable Input grounded through the momentary traction control disable switch, it sends a Class 2 message to the EBTCM that tells the EBTCM that the traction control disable switch has been pressed. The EBTCM then disables Traction Control and sends a message to the instrument cluster (IPC) to turn the TRACTION OFF message on. Each time the ignition switch is cycled OFF to ON, Traction Control is enabled.

Diagnostic Aids

- It is very important that a thorough inspection of the wiring and connectors be performed. Failure to carefully and fully inspect wiring and connectors may result in misdiagnosis, causing part replacement with reappearance of the malfunction.
- An intermittent malfunction can be caused by poor connections, broken insulation, or a wire that is broken inside the insulation.
- If an intermittent malfunction exists, refer to *Intermittents and Poor Connections*

GC4029803906010X

Fig. 262 Traction Off Message Inoperative w/No Code Set (Part 1 of 2). Seville

Circuit Description

Stabilitrak® activations generally occur during aggressive driving. Perform this test when the Stabilitrak® does not activate when the vehicle is driven aggressively enough to require activation (note that this can be subjective).

Step	Action	Value(s)	Yes	No
1	Did you perform the ABS Diagnostic System Check?	—	Go to *Step 2*	Go to *A Diagnostic System Check - ABS*
2	1. Perform the Diagnostic Test Drive. 2. Use the scan tool in order to observe the Stabilitrak Steering Angle Is Centered in the ABS/TCS/ICCS Data Display (1) Diagnostics, Data List 2. Does the steering angle center within 30 seconds?	—	Go to *A Diagnostic System Check - ABS*	Go to *DTC C1283 Excessive Time to Center Steering*

GC4029903930000X

Fig. 263 Stabilitrak Inoperative w/No Code Set. DeVille

Step	Action	Value(s)	Yes	No
DEFINITION: Stabilitrak® activations generally occur during aggressive driving. Perform this test when the Stabilitrak® does not activate when the vehicle is driven aggressively enough to require activation (note that this can be subjective).				
1	Was the Diagnostic System Check performed?	—	Go to *Step 2*	Go to *Diagnostic System Check*
2	1. Perform the Diagnostic Test Drive. 2. Using the scan tool, monitor the Stabilitrak Steering Angle Is Centered in the ABS/TCS/ICCS Data Display (1) Diagnostics, DATA LIST 2. Has the steering angle been centered within 30 seconds?	—	Go to *Diagnostic System Check*	Go to *DTC C1283 Excessive Time to Center Steering*

GC4029803537000X

Fig. 264 Stabilitrak Inoperative w/No Code Set. Seville

Step	Action	Value(s)	Yes	No
1	Did you perform the ABS Diagnostic System Check?	—	Go to *Step 2*	Go to *A Diagnostic System Check - ABS*
2	Check the mounting of the yaw rate sensor. Is the yaw rate sensor properly secured?	—	Go to *Step 4*	Go to *Step 3*
3	Remount or properly secure the yaw rate sensor. Did you complete the repair?	—	Go to *A Diagnostic System Check - ABS*	—
4	1. Turn OFF the ignition. 2. Connect a scan tool to the data link connector (DLC). 3. Start the engine. 4. Use the scan tool in order to take a snapshot of the yaw rate sensor output. 5. Test drive the vehicle and note the unwanted Stabilitrak® activations. Does the yaw rate sensor output suddenly increase or decrease without rapid turning of the vehicle?	—	Go to *DTC C1282 Yaw Rate Sensor Bias Circuit Malfunction*	Go to *Step 5*
5	1. Ensure that the front wheels are straight. 2. Turn OFF the ignition. 3. Start the engine. 4. Use the scan tool in order to observe the Digital SWPS Phase A and Digital SWPS Phase B in the ABS/TCS/ICCS Data Display (1) Diagnostics, Data List 2. 5. Slowly rotate the steering wheel to the left. Did Phase A and Phase B change states as the steering wheel was rotated?	—	Go to *Step 6*	Go to *Step 8*
6	1. Continue observing the Digital SWPS Phase A and Digital SWPS Phase B in the ABS/TCS/ICCS Data Display (1) Diagnostics, Data List 2. 2. Slowly rotate the steering wheel to the right. Did Phase A and Phase B change states as the steering wheel was rotated?	—	Go to *Step 7*	Go to *Step 8*
7	Perform the Steering Position Sensor Test. Refer to *Scan Tool Diagnostics*. Was the Steering Position Sensor Test passed?	—	Go to *Step 9*	Go to *Step 8*
8	Replace the Steering Wheel Position Sensor. Did you complete the repair?	—	Go to *A Diagnostic System Check - ABS*	—
9	1. Place the vehicle on a level surface. 2. Use the scan tool in order to observe the Lateral Accelerometer Input in the ABS/TCS/ICCS Data Display (1) Diagnostics, Data List 2. Is the Lateral Accelerometer Input voltage within the specified range?	2.3–2.7 V	Go to *Step 14*	Go to *Step 10*
10	Check the mounting of the lateral accelerometer. Is the lateral accelerometer properly secured?	—	Go to *Step 12*	Go to *Step 11*
11	Remount or properly secure the lateral accelerometer. Has the repair been completed?	—	Go to *Step 12*	—

GC4029903931020X

Fig. 265 Vehicle Stability Enhancement System Unwanted Activation w/No Code Set (Part 2 of 3). DeVille

Circuit Description

When Stabilitrak® or TCS activates for longer than 1.5 seconds, there will be an accompanying DIC message. Short activations of either system may occur without any DIC messages. Stabilitrak® activations mostly occur in the turns or bumpy roads without much use of the accelerator pedal. Activations may also occur during aggressive driving. Unwanted Stabilitrak® activations may be caused by the following:

- A loosely mounted yaw rate sensor
- An intermittent faulty steering wheel position sensor
- An intermittent wiring harness problem
- A chassis alignment that is grossly out of specification
- The wrong EBTCM installed
- The wrong steering gear rack installed

GC4029903931010X

Fig. 265 Vehicle Stability Enhancement System Unwanted Activation w/No Code Set (Part 1 of 3). DeVille

Step	Action	Value(s)	Yes	No
12	Use the scan tool in order to observe the Lateral Accelerometer Input in the ABS/TCS/ICCS Data Display (1) Diagnostics, Data List 2. Is the Lateral Accelerometer Input voltage within the specified range?	2.3–2.7 V	Go to *Step 14*	Go to *Step 13*
13	Replace the lateral accelerometer. Has the replacement been completed?	—	Go to *A Diagnostic System Check - ABS*	—
14	Inspect the EBTCM for the proper part number. Is the EBTCM part number correct?	—	Go to *Step 15*	Go to *Step 17*
15	Inspect the power steering gear for the proper part number. Is the power steering gear part number correct?	—	Go to *Step 16*	Go to *Step 18*
16	1. Perform the Diagnostic Test Drive. 2. Inspect for obvious vehicle alignment problems. Is the vehicle alignment proper?	—	Go to *A Diagnostic System Check - ABS*	Go to Wheel Alignment
17	Replace the EBTCM. Did you complete the repair?	—	Go to *A Diagnostic System Check - ABS*	—
18	Replace the power steering gear. Did you complete the repair?	—	Go to *A Diagnostic System Check - ABS*	—

GC4029903931030X

Fig. 265 Vehicle Stability Enhancement System Unwanted Activation w/No Code Set (Part 3 of 3). DeVille

Circuit Description

When Stabilitrak® or TCS activates for longer than 1.5 seconds, there will be an accompanying DIC message. Short activations of either system may occur without any DIC messages. Stabilitrak® activations mostly occur in the turns or bumpy roads without much use of the accelerator pedal. Activations may also occur during aggressive driving. Unwanted Stabilitrak® activations may be caused by the following:

- A loosely mounted yaw rate sensor
- An intermittent faulty steering wheel position sensor
- An intermittent wiring harness problem
- A chassis alignment that is grossly out of specification
- The wrong EBTCM installed
- The wrong steering gear rack installed

GC4029803907010X

Fig. 266 Stabilitrak Unwanted Activation w/Code Set (Part 1 of 3). Seville

Step	Action	Value(s)	Yes	No
1	Did you perform the Diagnostic System Check?	—	Go to *Step 2*	Go to *Diagnostic System Check*
2	Check the mounting of the yaw rate sensor. Is the yaw rate sensor properly secured?	—	Go to *Step 4*	Go to *Step 3*
3	Remount or properly secure the yaw rate sensor. Did you complete the repair?	—	Go to *Diagnostic System Check*	—
4	1. Turn OFF the ignition. 2. Connect a scan tool to the data link connector (DLC). 3. Start the engine. 4. Using the scan tool, take a snapshot of the yaw rate sensor output. 5. Test drive the vehicle and note the unwanted Stabilitrak® activations. Does the yaw rate sensor output suddenly increase or decrease without rapid turning of the vehicle?	—	Go to *DTC C1282 Yaw Rate Sensor Bias Circuit Malfunction*	Go to *Step 5*
5	1. Ensure that the front wheels are straight. 2. Turn OFF the ignition. 3. Start the engine. 4. Using the scan tool, monitor the Digital SWPS Phase A and Digital SWPS Phase B in the ABS/TCS/ICCS Data Display (1) Diagnostics, DATA LIST 2. 5. Slowly rotate the steering wheel to the left. Did Phase A and Phase B change states as the steering wheel was rotated?	—	Go to *Step 6*	Go to *Step 8*
6	1. Continue monitoring the Digital SWPS Phase A and Digital SWPS Phase B in the ABS/TCS/ICCS Data Display (1) Diagnostics, DATA LIST 2. 2. Slowly rotate the steering wheel to the right. Did Phase A and Phase B change states as the steering wheel was rotated?	—	Go to *Step 7*	Go to *Step 8*
7	Perform the Steering Position Sensor Test. Was the Steering Position Sensor Test passed?	—	Go to *Step 9*	Go to *Step 8*
8	Replace the Steering Wheel Position Sensor. Did you complete the repair?	—	Go to *Diagnostic System Check*	—
9	1. Place the vehicle on a level surface. 2. Using the scan tool, display the Lateral Accelerometer Input in the ABS/TCS/ICCS Data Display (1) Diagnostics, DATA LIST 2. Is the Lateral Accelerometer Input voltage within the specified range?	2.3–2.7 V	Go to *Step 14*	Go to *Step 10*
10	Check the mounting of the lateral accelerometer sensor. Is the lateral accelerometer sensor properly secured?	—	Go to *Step 12*	Go to *Step 11*
11	Remount or properly secure the lateral accelerometer. Did you complete the repair?	—	Go to *Step 12*	—
12	Using the scan tool, display the Lateral Accelerometer Input in the ABS/TCS/ICCS Data Display (1) Diagnostics, DATA LIST 2. Is the Lateral Accelerometer Input voltage within the specified range?	2.3–2.7 V	Go to *Step 14*	Go to *Step 13*

GC4029803907020X

Fig. 266 Stabilitrak Unwanted Activation w/Code Set (Part 2 of 3). Seville

Circuit Description

When braking during Stabiltrak® activation, the brake pedal will feel different than the ABS pedal pulsation. The brake pedal pulsates at a higher frequency during Stabilitrak® activation. Perform this test if the brake pedal buzzes excessively during medium braking. Medium braking is defined as greater than 0.3 g or 10 ft/s² (3 m/s²).

GC4029803911010X

Fig. 267 Stabilitrak Excessive Brake Pulsation (Part 1 of 2). Seville

Circuit Description

When braking during Stabiltrak® activation, the brake pedal will feel different than the ABS pedal pulsation. The brake pedal pulsates at a higher frequency during Stabilitrak® activation. Perform this test if the brake pedal buzzes excessively during medium braking. Medium braking is defined as greater than 0.3 g or 10 ft/s² (3 m/s²).

Step	Action	Value(s)	Yes	No
1	Did you perform the ABS Diagnostic System Check?	—	Go to *Step 2*	Go to *A Diagnostic System Check - ABS*
2	1. Turn OFF the ignition. 2. Connect a scan tool to the data link connector (DLC). 3. Turn ON the ignition, with the engine OFF. 4. Check for Powertrain Control Module (PCM) DTCs. Is PCM DTC P1575 set?	—	*DTC P1575 Extended Travel Brake Switch Circuit*	Go to *DTC C1297 PCM Indicated Brake Extended Travel Switch Failure*

GC40299039320000X

Fig. 268 Vehicle Stability Enhancement System Excessive Brake Pulsation. DeVille

Step	Action	Value(s)	Yes	No
13	Replace the lateral accelerometer sensor. Did you complete the repair?	—	Go to *Diagnostic System Check*	—
14	Check the EBTCM for the proper part number. Is the EBTCM part number correct?	—	Go to *Step 15*	Go to *Step 17*
15	Check the power steering gear for the proper part number. Is the power steering gear part number correct?	—	Go to *Step 16*	Go to *Step 18*
16	1. Perform the Diagnostic Test Drive. 2. Check for obvious vehicle alignment problems. Is the vehicle alignment proper?	—	Go to *Diagnostic System Check*	*Alignment Inspection*
17	Replace the EBTCM. Did you complete the repair?	—	Go to *Diagnostic System Check*	—
18	Replace the power steering gear. Did you complete the repair?	—	Go to *Diagnostic System Check*	—

GC4029803907030X

Fig. 266 Stabilitrak Unwanted Activation w/Code Set (Part 3 of 3). Seville

Step	Action	Value(s)	Yes	No
1	Did you perform the ABS Diagnostic System Check?	—	Go to *Step 2*	Go to *A Diagnostic System Check - ABS*
2	1. Turn OFF the ignition. 2. Connect a scan tool to the data link connector (DLC). 3. Turn the ignition switch to the ON position. 4. Check for Powertrain Control Module (PCM) DTCs. Is PCM DTC P1575 set?	—	*DTC P1575 Extended Travel Brake Switch*	Go to *Step 3*
3	1. Turn ON the ignition. 2. Use the scan tool in order to select ABS/TCS/ICCS Data Display (1) Diagnostics, DATA LIST 2. 3. Monitor the Extended Travel Brake Switch. 4. Step on and off the brake pedal with enough force to simulate a hard braking condition. As the brake pedal is pressed and released, the scan tool should read Applied and Released. 5. Use a tape measure in order to measure the distance that the brake pedal travels for the scan tool to read Applied. Is the distance within the specified range?	1.0–1.3 in (2.5–3.3 cm)	Go to *A Diagnostic System Check - ABS*	Go to *Step 4*
4	Adjust or repair the extended travel brake switch as necessary. Did you complete the repair?	—	Go to *A Diagnostic System Check - ABS*	—

GC4029803911020X

Fig. 267 Stabilitrak Excessive Brake Pulsation (Part 2 of 2). Seville

Circuit Description

The scan tool displays a DTC that is not defined in the service manual. The probable cause is an internal malfunction.

Diagnostic Aids

- It is very important that a thorough inspection of the wiring and connectors be performed. Failure to carefully and fully inspect wiring and connectors may result in misdiagnosis, causing part replacement with reappearance of the malfunction.
- An intermittent malfunction can be caused by poor connections, broken insulation, or a wire that is broken inside the insulation.
- If an intermittent malfunction exists, refer to *Intermittents and Poor Connections*

Scan Tool Displays Undefined DTC

Step	Action	Value(s)	Yes	No
1	Did you perform the Diagnostic System Check?	—	Go to *Step 2*	Go to *Diagnostic System Check*
2	1. Turn OFF the ignition. 2. Install a *Scan Tool*. 3. Turn ON the ignition, with the engine OFF. 4. Use the *Scan Tool* in order to clear the DTCs. 5. Turn OFF the ignition. 6. Turn ON the ignition, with the engine OFF. Does the undefined DTC reset?	—	Go to *Step 3*	Go to Diagnostic Aids
3	Replace the EBTCM. Did you complete the repair?	—	Go to *Diagnostic System Check*	—

GC4029803908000X

Fig. 269 Scan Tool Displays Undefined Code. Seville

Step	Action	Value(s)	Yes	No
DEFINITION: The brake sensor input of the EBTCM is normally grounded. The DIC will display the CHANGE BRAKE PADS message when there is an open in the circuit.				
1	Did you perform the Diagnostic System Check?	—	Go to *Step 2*	Go to *Diagnostic System Check*
2	Inspect for wear in the brake pads. Did you find a worn brake pad?	—	Go to *Step 13*	Go to *Step 3*
3	1. Disconnect the RH rear brake pad connector. 2. Connect a fused jumper from the RH rear brake pad connector terminal A to a good ground. Does the CHANGE BRAKE PADS message turn OFF?	—	Go to *Step 11*	Go to *Step 4*
4	1. Disconnect the LH rear brake pad connector. 2. Connect a fused jumper from the LH rear brake pad connector terminal A to a good ground. Does the CHANGE BRAKE PADS message turn OFF?	—	Go to *Step 10*	Go to *Step 5*
5	1. Disconnect the RH front brake pad connector. 2. Connect a fused jumper from the RH front brake pad connector terminal A to a good ground. Does the CHANGE BRAKE PADS message turn OFF?	—	Go to *Step 9*	Go to *Step 6*
6	1. Disconnect the LH front brake pad connector. 2. Connect a fused jumper from the LH front brake pad connector terminal A to a good ground. Does the CHANGE BRAKE PADS message turn OFF?	—	Go to *Step 8*	Go to *Step 7*
7	1. Disconnect the EBTCM connector. 2. Connect the *J 39700* universal pinout box using the *J 39700-25* cable adapter to the EBTCM harness connector only. 3. Disconnect the RH front brake pad connector. 4. Use a *J 39200* in order to measure the resistance from the *J 39700* to the LH front brake pad connector terminal A. Is the resistance less than the specified value?	2 Ω	Go to *Step 12*	Go to *Step 14*
8	1. Disconnect the RH front brake pad connector. 2. Use a *J 39200* in order to measure the resistance from the LH front brake pad connector terminal B to the RH front brake pad connector terminal A. Is the resistance less than the specified value?	2 Ω	Go to *Step 15*	Go to *Step 16*
9	1. Disconnect the LH rear brake pad connector. 2. Use a *J 39200* in order to measure the resistance from the RH front brake pad connector terminal B to the LH rear brake pad connector terminal A. Is the resistance less than the specified value?	2 Ω	Go to *Step 17*	Go to *Step 18*
10	1. Disconnect the RH rear brake pad connector. 2. Use a *J 39200* in order to measure the resistance from the LH rear brake pad connector terminal B to the RH rear brake pad connector terminal A. Is the resistance less than the specified value?	2 Ω	Go to *Step 19*	Go to *Step 20*
11	Use a *J 39200* in order to measure the resistance from the RH rear brake pad connector terminal B to a good ground. Is the resistance less than the specified value?	2 Ω	Go to *Step 21*	Go to *Step 22*
12	Replace the EBTCM. Did you complete the repair?	—	Go to *Diagnostic System Check*	—

GC4029803909010X

Fig. 270 Check Brake Pads Message Always On (Part 1 of 2). Seville

Circuit Description

The ABS Diagnostic System Check is an organized approach to identify problems associated with the EBCM. This check must be the starting point for any EBCM complaint, and will direct you to the next logical step in diagnosing the complaint. The EBCM is a very reliable component and is not likely the cause of the malfunction. Most system complaints are linked to faulty wiring, connectors, and occasionally to components. Understanding the ABS system and using the tables correctly will reduce diagnostic time and prevent unnecessary parts replacement.

Test Description

The numbers below refer to the step numbers on the diagnostic table.

2. Lack of communication may be due to a partial malfunction of the class 2 serial data circuit or due to a total malfunction of the class 2 serial data circuit. The specified procedure will determine the particular condition.
4. The presence of DTCs which begin with "U" indicate some other module is not communicating. The specified procedure will compile all the available information before tests are performed.

Step	Action	Value(s)	Yes	No
1	Install a scan tool. Does the scan tool power up?	—	Go to *Step 2*	*Scan Tool Does Not Power Up*
2	1. Turn ON the ignition, with the engine OFF. 2. Attempt to establish communications with the following control modules. • Continuously variable road sensing suspension (CVRSS) module • Electronic brake control module (EBCM) • Powertrain control module (PCM) • Instrument cluster (IPC) Does the scan tool communicate with all control modules?	—	Go to *Step 3*	*Scan Tool Does Not Communicate with Class 2 Device*
3	Select the display DTCs function on the scan tool for the following control modules: • Continuously variable road sensing suspension (CVRSS) module • Electronic brake control module (EBCM) • Powertrain control module (PCM) • Instrument cluster (IPC) Does the scan tool display any DTCs?	—	Go to *Step 4*	Go to *Symptoms*
4	Does the scan tool display any DTCs which begin with a "U"?	—	*Scan Tool Does Not Communicate with Class 2 Device*	Go to *Step 5*
5	Does the scan tool display DTCs B1552, B1556, B1557, B1981, B1982, or B1983?	—	*Diagnostic Trouble Code (DTC) List/Type* Instrument Panel, Gauges and Console	Go to *Step 6*
6	Does the scan tool display DTCs C0550, C0563, or C0896?	—	*Diagnostic Trouble Code (DTC) List/Type* Road Sensing Suspension - RSS	Go to *Diagnostic Trouble Code (DTC) List/Type*

GC4020051867000X

Fig. 271 ABS Diagnostic System Check. Eldorado

Step	Action	Value(s)	Yes	No
13	Replace the worn brake pad. Did you complete the repair?	—	Go to *Diagnostic System Check*	—
14	Repair the open in CKT 1612. Did you complete the repair?	—	Go to *Diagnostic System Check*	—
15	Replace the LH front brake pad. Did you complete the repair?	—	Go to *Diagnostic System Check*	—
16	Repair the open in CKT 1613. Did you complete the repair?	—	Go to *Diagnostic System Check*	—
17	Replace the RH front brake pad. Did you complete the repair?	—	Go to *Diagnostic System Check*	—
18	Repair the open in CKT 1610. Did you complete the repair?	—	Go to *Diagnostic System Check*	—
19	Replace the LH rear brake pad. Did you complete the repair?	—	Go to *Diagnostic System Check*	—
20	Repair the open in CKT 1611. Did you complete the repair?	—	Go to *Diagnostic System Check*	—
21	Replace the RH rear brake pad. Did you complete the repair?	—	Go to *Diagnostic System Check*	—
22	Repair the open in CKT 850. Did you complete the repair?	—	Go to *Diagnostic System Check*	—

GC4029803909020X

Fig. 270 Check Brake Pads Message Always On (Part 2 of 2). Seville

Circuit Description

The instrument cluster controls the operation of the ABS indicator. The EBCM reports the desired status of the ABS indicator via class 2 serial data messages. The ABS indicator signal circuit is a back-up reporting circuit to the class 2 serial data messages. The EBCM supplies ground through the circuit when the ABS is operating properly. When there is a problem with ABS that should turn on the ABS indicator, the EBCM opens the ABS indicator signal circuit. If there is a problem with the ABS class 2 serial data messages, the instrument cluster uses the ABS indicator signal to determine if the ABS indicator should be illuminated. Using the serial data messages and back-up circuit, the instrument cluster decides whether to turn on the ABS indicator.

Conditions for Running the DTC

The ignition is ON.

Conditions for Setting the DTC

One of the following conditions is present for 2 seconds:

- An open - the ABS indicator signal circuit resistance is greater than 5 kΩ. The condition is detected when the ABS indicator is commanded ON.
- A short to ground - the ABS indicator signal circuit voltage is less than 1.7 volts. The condition is detected when the ABS indicator is commanded ON.
- A short to voltage - the ABS indicator signal circuit voltage is greater than 4.5 volts. The condition is detected when the ABS indicator is commanded OFF.

Action Taken When the DTC Sets

- The ABS remains functional.
- The ABS indicator remains OFF.

GC4020051868010X

Fig. 272 Code C1211: ABS Warning Lamp Fault (Part 1 of 2). Eldorado

Conditions for Clearing the DTC

- The condition for the DTC is no longer present (the DTC is not current) and you used the scan tool Clear DTC function.
- The condition for the DTC is no longer present (the DTC is not current) and you used the On-Board Diagnostics Clear DTC function.
- The EBCM automatically clears the history DTC when a current DTC is not detected in 50 consecutive drive cycles.

Test Description

The numbers below refer to the step numbers on the diagnostic table.

2. This test uses the scan tool to check the normal state of the ABS indicator signal circuit.
3. This test ensures that the instrument cluster can operate the ABS indicator.

Step	Action	Value(s)	Yes	No
1	Did you perform the ABS Diagnostic System Check?	—	Go to *Step 2*	Go to *A Diagnostic System Check - ABS*
2	1. Install a scan tool. 2. Turn ON the igntion, with the engine OFF. 3. With the scan tool, observe the ABS Warning Lamp parameter in the (if equipped) data list. Does the scan tool display Off?	—	Go to *Step 3*	Go to *Step 4*
3	1. Turn OFF the ignition. 2. Turn ON the ignition, with the engine OFF. 3. Observe the ABS indicator on the instrument cluster (IPC) during the bulb check. Does the ABS indicator illuminate during the bulb check?	—	Go to *Step 4*	Go to *Step 6*
4	1. Turn OFF the ignition. 2. Disconnect the EBCM harness connector 3. Connect the *J 39700* universal pinout box using the *J 39700-25* cable adapter to the EBCM harness connector only. 4. Disconnect the instrument cluster harness connector. 5. Test the ABS indicator signal circuit for the following conditions: • An open • A short to ground • A short to voltage • A high resistance Did you find and correct the condition?	—	Go to *Step 9*	Go to *Step 5*
5	Inspect for poor connections at the harness connector of the EBCM. Did you find and correct the condition?	—	Go to *Step 9*	Go to *Step 7*
6	Inspect for poor connections at the harness connector of the instrument cluster (IPC). Did you find and correct the condition?	—	Go to *Step 9*	Go to *Step 8*
7	Replace the EBCM. Did you complete the repair?	—	Go to *Step 9*	—
8	Replace the instrument cluster (IPC). Did you complete the repair?	—	Go to *Step 9*	—
9	1. Use the scan tool in order to clear the DTCs. 2. Operate the vehicle within the Conditions for Running the DTC as specified in the supporting text. Does the DTC reset?	—	Go to *Step 2*	System OK

GC4020051868020X

Fig. 272 Code C1211: ABS Warning Lamp Fault (Part 2 of 2). Eldorado

Circuit Description

The solenoid valve relay is energized when the ignition is ON. The solenoid valve relay supplies voltage to the solenoid valves. This voltage is referred to as the solenoid power voltage. The EBCM controls the solenoid valve by grounding the control circuit.

Conditions for Running the DTC

- The ignition voltage is greater than 10.5 volts.
- The relay is commanded ON.

Conditions for Setting the DTC

The relay voltage is less than 8 volts.

Action Taken When the DTC Sets

If equipped, the following actions occur:

- The EBCM disables the ABS/TCS/VSES for the duration of the ignition cycle.
- The ABS indicator turns ON.
- The TRACTION CONTROL indicator turns ON.
- The DIC displays the SERVICE STABILITY SYS message.

Conditions for Clearing the DTC

- The condition for the DTC is no longer present (the DTC is not current) and you used the scan tool Clear DTC function.
- The condition for the DTC is no longer present (the DTC is not current) and you used the On-Board Diagnostics Clear DTC function.
- The EBCM automatically clears the history DTC when a current DTC is not detected in 50 consecutive drive cycles.

Diagnostic Aids

The relays are integral to the EBCM. The relays are not serviceable.

Test Description

The number below refers to step number on the diagnostic table.

5. This step checks for an internal short in the BPMV.

GC4020051869010X

Fig. 273 Code C1214: Solenoid Valve Relay Contact Or Coil Circuit Open (Part 1 of 2). Eldorado

Circuit Description

The pump motor is grounded through the ground stud on the BPMV. The EBCM controls the pump motor by energizing the pump motor relay. The pump motor relay then supplies voltage to the pump motor. The pump serves 2 purposes:

- Transfers brake fluid from the brake calipers to the master cylinder reservoir during pressure decrease events.
- Transfers brake fluid from the master cylinder reservoir to the brake calipers during pressure increase events.

Conditions for Running the DTC

- The ignition voltage is greater than 10.5 volts.
- The relay is commanded ON.

Conditions for Setting the DTC

The relay voltage is less than 8 volts.

Action Taken When the DTC Sets

If equipped, the following actions occur:

- The EBCM disables the ABS/TCS/VSES for the duration of the ignition cycle.
- The ABS indicator turns ON.
- The TRACTION CONTROL indicator turns ON.
- The DIC displays the SERVICE STABILITY SYS message.

Conditions for Clearing the DTC

- The condition for the DTC is no longer present (the DTC is not current) and you used the scan tool Clear DTC function.
- The condition for the DTC is no longer present (the DTC is not current) and you used the On-Board Diagnostics Clear DTC function.
- The EBCM automatically clears the history DTC when a current DTC is not detected in 50 consecutive drive cycles.

Diagnostic Aids

The relays are integral to the EBCM. The relays are not serviceable.

Test Description

The number below refers to step number on the diagnostic table.

5. This step checks for an internal short in the BPMV.

GC4020051870010X

Fig. 274 Code C1217: Pump Motor Relay Control Circuit Open (Part 1 of 2). Eldorado

Step	Action	Value(s)	Yes	No
1	Did you perform the ABS Diagnostic System Check?	—	Go to *Step 2*	Go to *A Diagnostic System Check - ABS*
2	Inspect the RH underhood fuse block BRAKES (50 A) Fuse. Is the fuse OK?	—	Go to *Step 6*	Go to *Step 3*
3	1. Install a new BRAKES (50 A) Fuse. 2. Turn OFF the ignition. 3. Turn ON the ignition, with the engine OFF. 4. Use a scan tool in order to select ABS/TCS Delco Bosch Special Functions. 5. Run the Automated Test. 6. Inspect the BRAKES (50 A) Fuse. Is the fuse OK?	—	Go to *Intermittents*	Go to *Step 4*
4	1. Turn OFF the ignition. 2. Remove the BRAKES (50 A) Fuse. 3. Disconnect the EBCM connector. 4. Disconnect the BPMV ground. 5. Connect the *J 39700* universal pinout box using the *J 39700-25* cable adapter to the EBCM harness connector only. 6. Test both battery supply circuits for a short to ground. Did you find and correct the condition?	—	Go to *Step 9*	Go to *Step 5*
5	1. Remove the EBCM from the BPMV. 2. Connect the *J 41247* pinout box to the BPMV. 3. Measure the resistance between the solenoid power control circuit and the BPMV case. Is the resistance within the specified range?	OL (Infinite)	Go to *Step 7*	Go to *Step 8*
6	1. Turn OFF the ignition. 2. Remove the BRAKES (50 A) Fuse. 3. Disconnect the EBCM connector. 4. Disconnect the BPMV ground. 5. Connect the *J 39700* universal pinout box using the *J 39700-25* cable adapter to the EBCM harness connector only. 6. Test both battery supply circuits for an open or a high resistance. Did you find and correct the condition?	—	Go to *Step 9*	Go to *Step 7*
7	Replace EBCM. Did you complete the repair?	—	Go to *Step 9*	—
8	Replace the BPMV. Did you complete the repair?	—	Go to *Step 9*	—
9	1. Use the scan tool in order to clear the DTCs. 2. With the scan tool, perform the Automated Test. Does the DTC reset?	—	Go to *Step 2*	System OK

GC4020051870020X

Fig. 274 Code C1217: Pump Motor Relay Control Circuit Open (Part 2 of 2). Eldorado

Step	Action	Value(s)	Yes	No
1	Did you perform the ABS Diagnostic System Check?	—	Go to *Step 2*	Go to *A Diagnostic System Check - ABS*
2	Inspect the RH underhood fuse block BRAKES (50 A) Fuse. Is the fuse OK?	—	Go to *Step 6*	Go to *Step 3*
3	1. Install a new BRAKES (50 A) Fuse. 2. Turn OFF the ignition. 3. Turn ON the ignition, with the engine OFF. 4. Use a scan tool in order to select ABS/TCS Delco Bosch Special Functions. 5. Run the Automated Test. 6. Inspect the BRAKES (50 A) Fuse. Is the fuse OK?	—	Go to *Intermittents*	Go to *Step 4*
4	1. Turn OFF the ignition. 2. Remove the BRAKES (50 A) Fuse. 3. Disconnect the EBCM connector. 4. Disconnect the BPMV ground. 5. Connect the *J 39700* universal pinout box using the *J 39700-25* cable adapter to the EBCM harness connector only. 6. Test both battery supply circuits for a short to ground. Did you find and correct the condition?	—	Go to *Step 9*	Go to *Step 5*
5	1. Remove the EBCM from the BPMV. 2. Connect the *J 41247* pinout box to the BPMV. 3. Measure the resistance between the solenoid power control circuit and the BPMV case. Is the resistance within the specified range?	OL (Infinite)	Go to *Step 7*	Go to *Step 8*
6	1. Turn OFF the ignition. 2. Remove the BRAKES (50 A) Fuse. 3. Disconnect the EBCM connector. 4. Disconnect the BPMV ground. 5. Connect the *J 39700* universal pinout box using the *J 39700-25* cable adapter to the EBCM harness connector only. 6. Test both battery supply circuits for an open or a high resistance. Did you find and correct the condition?	—	Go to *Step 9*	Go to *Step 7*
7	Replace EBCM. Did you complete the repair?	—	Go to *Step 9*	—
8	Replace the BPMV. Did you complete the repair?	—	Go to *Step 9*	—
9	1. Use the scan tool in order to clear the DTCs. 2. With the scan tool, perform the Automated Test. Does the DTC reset?	—	Go to *Step 2*	System OK

GC4020051869020X

Fig. 273 Code C1214: Solenoid Valve Relay Contact Or Coil Circuit Open (Part 2 of 2). Eldorado

Circuit Description

As the wheel spins, the wheel speed sensor produces an AC signal. The EBCM uses the frequency of the AC signal to calculate the wheel speed.

Conditions for Running the DTC

- DTCs C1232–C1235 are not set.
- The brake pedal is not pressed.
- The ABS is not active.

Conditions for Setting the DTC

All of the following conditions exists for 2.5 seconds:

- The suspect wheel speed equals zero.
- The other wheel speeds are greater than 8 km/h (5 mph).
- The other wheel speeds are within 11 km/h (7 mph) of each other.

Action Taken When the DTC Sets

If equipped, the following actions occur:

- The EBCM disables the ABS/TCS/VSES for the duration of the ignition cycle.
- The ABS indicator turns ON.
- The TRACTION CONTROL indicator turns ON.
- The DIC displays the SERVICE STABILITY SYS message.

Conditions for Clearing the DTC

- The condition for the DTC is no longer present (the DTC is not current) and you used the scan tool Clear DTC function.
- The condition for the DTC is no longer present (the DTC is not current) and you used the On-Board Diagnostics Clear DTC function.
- The EBCM automatically clears the history DTC when a current DTC is not detected in 50 consecutive drive cycles.

Diagnostic Aids

Under the following conditions, 2 Wheel Speed Sensor Input is 0 DTCs are set:

- The 2 suspect wheel speeds equal zero for 60 seconds.
- The other wheel speeds are greater than 16 km/h (10 mph).
- The other wheel speeds are within 11 km/h (7 mph) of each other.

Diagnose each wheel speed sensor individually.

Test Description

The numbers below refer to the step numbers on the diagnostic table.

3. This step measures the resistance of the wheel speed sensor.
6. This step tests whether the wheel speed sensor circuits are shorted together.

GC4020051871010X

Fig. 275 Code C1221: LF Wheel Speed Input Signal Is 0 (Part 1 of 2). Eldorado

Step	Action	Value(s)	Yes	No
1	Did you perform the ABS Diagnostic System Check?	—	Go to *Step 2*	Go to *A Diagnostic System Check - ABS*
2	1. Install a scan tool. 2. Carefully drive the vehicle at a speed greater than 8 km/h (5 mph). 3. With the scan tool, observe all of the Wheel Speed parameters in the Delco/Bosch ABS/TCS ICCS (if equipped) data list. Does the scan tool indicate the suspect wheel varies from the speeds of the other wheels?	—	Go to *Step 3*	Go to Diagnostic Aids
3	1. Turn OFF the ignition. 2. Disconnect the wheel speed sensor connector. 3. Measure the resistance across the wheel speed sensor. Does the resistance measure within the specified range?	850–1350 Ω	Go to *Step 4*	Go to *Step 8*
4	1. By hand, spin the wheel. 2. Measure the AC voltage across the wheel speed sensor. Does the AC voltage measure greater than the specified value?	100 mV	Go to *Step 5*	Go to *Step 8*
5	Inspect for poor connections at the harness connector of the wheel speed sensor. Did you find and correct the condition?	—	Go to *Step 10*	Go to *Step 6*
6	1. Disconnect the EBCM harness connector. 2. Install the *J 39700* universal pinout box using the *J 39700-25* cable adapter to the EBCM harness connector only. 3. Test the wheel speed signal circuit for a short to the wheel speed return circuit. Did you find and correct the condition?	—	Go to *Step 10*	Go to *Step 7*
7	Inspect for poor connections at the harness connector of the EBCM. Did you find and correct the condition?	—	Go to *Step 10*	Go to *Step 9*
8	Replace the wheel speed sensor. Did you complete the repair?	—	Go to *Step 10*	—
9	Replace the EBCM. Did you complete the repair?	—	Go to *Step 10*	—
10	1. Use the scan tool in order to clear the DTCs. 2. Operate the vehicle within the Conditions for Running the DTC as specified in the supporting text. Does the DTC reset?	—	Go to *Step 2*	System OK

GC4020051871020X

Fig. 275 Code C1221: LF Wheel Speed Input Signal Is 0 (Part 2 of 2). Eldorado

Step	Action	Value(s)	Yes	No
1	Did you perform the ABS Diagnostic System Check?	—	Go to *Step 2*	Go to *A Diagnostic System Check - ABS*
2	1. Install a scan tool. 2. Carefully drive the vehicle at a speed greater than 8 km/h (5 mph). 3. With the scan tool, observe all of the Wheel Speed parameters in the Delco/Bosch ABS/TCS ICCS (if equipped) data list. Does the scan tool indicate the suspect wheel varies from the speeds of the other wheels?	—	Go to *Step 3*	Go to Diagnostic Aids
3	1. Turn OFF the ignition. 2. Disconnect the wheel speed sensor connector. 3. Measure the resistance across the wheel speed sensor. Does the resistance measure within the specified range?	850–1350 Ω	Go to *Step 4*	Go to *Step 8*
4	1. By hand, spin the wheel. 2. Measure the AC voltage across the wheel speed sensor. Does the AC voltage measure greater than the specified value?	100 mV	Go to *Step 5*	Go to *Step 8*
5	Inspect for poor connections at the harness connector of the wheel speed sensor. Did you find and correct the condition?	—	Go to *Step 10*	Go to *Step 6*
6	1. Disconnect the EBCM harness connector. 2. Install the *J 39700* universal pinout box using the *J 39700-25* cable adapter to the EBCM harness connector only. 3. Test the wheel speed signal circuit for a short to the wheel speed return circuit. Did you find and correct the condition?	—	Go to *Step 10*	Go to *Step 7*
7	Inspect for poor connections at the harness connector of the EBCM. Did you find and correct the condition?	—	Go to *Step 10*	Go to *Step 9*
8	Replace the wheel speed sensor. Did you complete the repair?	—	Go to *Step 10*	—
9	Replace the EBCM. Did you complete the repair?	—	Go to *Step 10*	—
10	1. Use the scan tool in order to clear the DTCs. 2. Operate the vehicle within the Conditions for Running the DTC as specified in the supporting text. Does the DTC reset?	—	Go to *Step 2*	System OK

GC4020051872020X

Fig. 276 Code C1222: RF Wheel Speed Input Signal Is 0 (Part 2 of 2). Eldorado

Circuit Description

As the wheel spins, the wheel speed sensor produces an AC signal. The EBCM uses the frequency of the AC signal to calculate the wheel speed.

Conditions for Running the DTC

- DTCs C1232–C1235 are not set.
- The brake pedal is not pressed.
- The ABS is not active.

Conditions for Setting the DTC

All of the following conditions exists for 2.5 seconds:

- The suspect wheel speed equals zero.
- The other wheel speeds are greater than 8 km/h (5 mph).
- The other wheel speeds are within 11 km/h (7 mph) of each other.

Action Taken When the DTC Sets

If equipped, the following actions occur:

- The EBCM disables the ABS/TCS/VSES for the duration of the ignition cycle.
- The ABS indicator turns ON.
- The TRACTION CONTROL indicator turns ON.
- The DIC displays the SERVICE STABILITY SYS message.

Conditions for Clearing the DTC

- The condition for the DTC is no longer present (the DTC is not current) and you used the scan tool Clear DTC function.
- The condition for the DTC is no longer present (the DTC is not current) and you used the On-Board Diagnostics Clear DTC function.
- The EBCM automatically clears the history DTC when a current DTC is not detected in 50 consecutive drive cycles.

Diagnostic Aids

Under the following conditions, 2 Wheel Speed Sensor Input is 0 DTCs are set:

- The 2 suspect wheel speeds equal zero for 60 seconds.
- The other wheel speeds are greater than 16 km/h (10 mph).
- The other wheel speeds are within 11 km/h (7 mph) of each other.

Diagnose each wheel speed sensor individually.

Test Description

The numbers below refer to the step numbers on the diagnostic table.

3. This step measures the resistance of the wheel speed sensor.
6. This step tests whether the wheel speed sensor circuits are shorted together.

GC4020051872010X

Fig. 276 Code C1222: RF Wheel Speed Input Signal Is 0 (Part 1 of 2). Eldorado

Circuit Description

As the wheel spins, the wheel speed sensor produces an AC signal. The EBCM uses the frequency of the AC signal to calculate the wheel speed.

Conditions for Running the DTC

- DTCs C1232–C1235 are not set.
- The brake pedal is not pressed.
- The ABS is not active.

Conditions for Setting the DTC

All of the following conditions exists for 2.5 seconds:

- The suspect wheel speed equals zero.
- The other wheel speeds are greater than 8 km/h (5 mph).
- The other wheel speeds are within 11 km/h (7 mph) of each other.

Action Taken When the DTC Sets

If equipped, the following actions occur:

- The EBCM disables the ABS/TCS/VSES for the duration of the ignition cycle.
- The ABS indicator turns ON.
- The TRACTION CONTROL indicator turns ON.
- The DIC displays the SERVICE STABILITY SYS message.

Conditions for Clearing the DTC

- The condition for the DTC is no longer present (the DTC is not current) and you used the scan tool Clear DTC function.
- The condition for the DTC is no longer present (the DTC is not current) and you used the On-Board Diagnostics Clear DTC function.
- The EBCM automatically clears the history DTC when a current DTC is not detected in 50 consecutive drive cycles.

Diagnostic Aids

Under the following conditions, 2 Wheel Speed Sensor Input is 0 DTCs are set:

- The 2 suspect wheel speeds equal zero for 60 seconds.
- The other wheel speeds are greater than 16 km/h (10 mph).
- The other wheel speeds are within 11 km/h (7 mph) of each other.

Diagnose each wheel speed sensor individually.

Test Description

The numbers below refer to the step numbers on the diagnostic table.

3. This step measures the resistance of the wheel speed sensor.
6. This step tests whether the wheel speed sensor circuits are shorted together.

GC4020051873010X

Fig. 277 Code C1223: LR Wheel Speed Input Signal Is 0 (Part 1 of 2). Eldorado

Step	Action	Value(s)	Yes	No
1	Did you perform the ABS Diagnostic System Check?	—	Go to *Step 2*	Go to *A Diagnostic System Check - ABS*
2	1. Install a scan tool. 2. Carefully drive the vehicle at a speed greater than 8 km/h (5 mph). 3. With the scan tool, observe all of the Wheel Speed parameters in the Delco/Bosch ABS/TCS ICCS (if equipped) data list. Does the scan tool indicate the suspect wheel varies from the speeds of the other wheels?	—	Go to *Step 3*	Go to Diagnostic Aids
3	1. Turn OFF the ignition. 2. Disconnect the wheel speed sensor connector. 3. Measure the resistance across the wheel speed sensor. Does the resistance measure within the specified range?	850–1350 Ω	Go to *Step 4*	Go to *Step 8*
4	1. By hand, spin the wheel. 2. Measure the AC voltage across the wheel speed sensor. Does the AC voltage measure greater than the specified value?	100 mV	Go to *Step 5*	Go to *Step 8*
5	Inspect for poor connections at the harness connector of the wheel speed sensor. Did you find and correct the condition?	—	Go to *Step 10*	Go to *Step 6*
6	1. Disconnect the EBCM harness connector. 2. Install the *J 39700* universal pinout box using the *J 39700-25* cable adapter to the EBCM harness connector only. 3. Test the wheel speed signal circuit for a short to the wheel speed return circuit. Did you find and correct the condition?	—	Go to *Step 10*	Go to *Step 7*
7	Inspect for poor connections at the harness connector of the EBCM. Did you find and correct the condition?	—	Go to *Step 10*	Go to *Step 9*
8	Replace the wheel speed sensor. Did you complete the repair?	—	Go to *Step 10*	—
9	Replace the EBCM. Did you complete the repair?	—	Go to *Step 10*	—
10	1. Use the scan tool in order to clear the DTCs. 2. Operate the vehicle within the Conditions for Running the DTC as specified in the supporting text. Does the DTC reset?	—	Go to *Step 2*	System OK

GC4020051873020X

Fig. 277 Code C1223: LR Wheel Speed Input Signal Is 0 (Part 2 of 2). Eldorado

Circuit Description

As the wheel spins, the wheel speed sensor produces an AC signal. The EBCM uses the frequency of the AC signal to calculate the wheel speed.

Conditions for Running the DTC

- DTCs C1232–C1235 are not set.
- The brake pedal is not pressed.
- The ABS is not active.

Conditions for Setting the DTC

All of the following conditions exists for 2.5 seconds:

- The suspect wheel speed equals zero.
- The other wheel speeds are greater than 8 km/h (5 mph).
- The other wheel speeds are within 11 km/h (7 mph) of each other.

Action Taken When the DTC Sets

If equipped, the following actions occur:

- The EBCM disables the ABS/TCS/VSES for the duration of the ignition cycle.
- The ABS indicator turns ON.
- The TRACTION CONTROL indicator turns ON.
- The DIC displays the SERVICE STABILITY SYS message.

Conditions for Clearing the DTC

- The condition for the DTC is no longer present (the DTC is not current) and you used the scan tool Clear DTC function.
- The condition for the DTC is no longer present (the DTC is not current) and you used the On-Board Diagnostics Clear DTC function.
- The EBCM automatically clears the history DTC when a current DTC is not detected in 50 consecutive drive cycles.

Diagnostic Aids

Under the following conditions, 2 Wheel Speed Sensor Input is 0 DTCs are set:

- The 2 suspect wheel speeds equal zero for 60 seconds.
- The other wheel speeds are greater than 16 km/h (10 mph).
- The other wheel speeds are within 11 km/h (7 mph) of each other.

Diagnose each wheel speed sensor individually.

Test Description

The numbers below refer to the step numbers on the diagnostic table.

3. This step measures the resistance of the wheel speed sensor.
6. This step tests whether the wheel speed sensor circuits are shorted together.

GC4020051874010X

Fig. 278 Code C1224: RR Wheel Speed Input Signal Is 0 (Part 1 of 2). Eldorado

Step	Action	Value(s)	Yes	No
1	Did you perform the ABS Diagnostic System Check?	—	Go to *Step 2*	Go to *A Diagnostic System Check - ABS*
2	1. Install a scan tool. 2. Carefully drive the vehicle at a speed greater than 8 km/h (5 mph). 3. With the scan tool, observe all of the Wheel Speed parameters in the Delco/Bosch ABS/TCS ICCS (if equipped) data list. Does the scan tool indicate the suspect wheel varies from the speeds of the other wheels?	—	Go to *Step 3*	Go to Diagnostic Aids
3	1. Turn OFF the ignition. 2. Disconnect the wheel speed sensor connector. 3. Measure the resistance across the wheel speed sensor. Does the resistance measure within the specified range?	850–1350 Ω	Go to *Step 4*	Go to *Step 8*
4	1. By hand, spin the wheel. 2. Measure the AC voltage across the wheel speed sensor. Does the AC voltage measure greater than the specified value?	100 mV	Go to *Step 5*	Go to *Step 8*
5	Inspect for poor connections at the harness connector of the wheel speed sensor. Did you find and correct the condition?	—	Go to *Step 10*	Go to *Step 6*
6	1. Disconnect the EBCM harness connector. 2. Install the *J 39700* universal pinout box using the *J 39700-25* cable adapter to the EBCM harness connector only. 3. Test the wheel speed signal circuit for a short to the wheel speed return circuit. Did you find and correct the condition?	—	Go to *Step 10*	Go to *Step 7*
7	Inspect for poor connections at the harness connector of the EBCM. Did you find and correct the condition?	—	Go to *Step 10*	Go to *Step 9*
8	Replace the wheel speed sensor. Did you complete the repair?	—	Go to *Step 10*	—
9	Replace the EBCM. Did you complete the repair?	—	Go to *Step 10*	—
10	1. Use the scan tool in order to clear the DTCs. 2. Operate the vehicle within the Conditions for Running the DTC as specified in the supporting text. Does the DTC reset?	—	Go to *Step 2*	System OK

GC4020051874020X

Fig. 278 Code C1224: RR Wheel Speed Input Signal Is 0 (Part 2 of 2). Eldorado

Circuit Description

As the wheel spins, the wheel speed sensor produces an AC signal. The EBCM uses the frequency of the AC signal to calculate the wheel speed.

Conditions for Running the DTC

- DTCs C1232–C1235 are not set.
- The brake pedal is not pressed.
- The ABS is not active.

Conditions for Setting the DTC

The EBCM detects a wheel speed variation of more than 14 km/h (9 mph) for 2.5 seconds.

Action Taken When the DTC Sets

If equipped, the following actions occur:

- The EBCM disables the ABS/TCS/VSES for the duration of the ignition cycle.
- The ABS indicator turns ON.
- The TRACTION CONTROL indicator turns ON.
- The DIC displays the SERVICE STABILITY SYS message.

Conditions for Clearing the DTC

- The condition for the DTC is no longer present (the DTC is not current) and you used the scan tool Clear DTC function.
- The condition for the DTC is no longer present (the DTC is not current) and you used the On-Board Diagnostics Clear DTC function.
- The EBCM automatically clears the history DTC when a current DTC is not detected in 50 consecutive drive cycles.

Diagnostic Aids

A possible cause of this DTC is electrical noise on the wheel speed sensor harness wiring. Electrical noise could result from the wheel speed sensor wires being routed to close to high energy ignition system components, such as spark plug wires.

Test Description

The numbers below refer to the step numbers on the diagnostic table.

3. This step measures the resistance of the wheel speed sensor.
6. This step tests whether the wheel speed sensor circuits are shorted together.

GC4020051875010X

Fig. 279 Code C1225: LF Excessive Wheel Speed Variation (Part 1 of 2). Eldorado

Step	Action	Value(s)	Yes	No
1	Did you perform the ABS Diagnostic System Check?	—	Go to *Step 2*	Go to *A Diagnostic System Check - ABS*
2	1. Install a scan tool. 2. Carefully drive the vehicle at a speed greater than 8 km/h (5 mph). 3. With the scan tool, observe all of the Wheel Speed parameters in the Delco/Bosch ABS/TCS ICCS (if equipped) data list. Does the scan tool indicate the suspect wheel varies from the speeds of the other wheels?	—	Go to *Step 3*	Go to Diagnostic Aids
3	1. Turn OFF the ignition. 2. Disconnect the wheel speed sensor connector. 3. Measure the resistance across the wheel speed sensor. Does the resistance measure within the specified range?	850–1350 Ω	Go to *Step 4*	Go to *Step 8*
4	1. By hand, spin the wheel. 2. Measure the AC voltage across the wheel speed sensor. Does the AC voltage measure greater than the specified value?	100 mV	Go to *Step 5*	Go to *Step 8*
5	Inspect for poor connections at the harness connector of the wheel speed sensor. Did you find and correct the condition?	—	Go to *Step 10*	Go to *Step 6*
6	1. Disconnect the EBCM harness connector. 2. Install the *J 39700* universal pinout box using the *J 39700-25* cable adapter to the EBCM harness connector only. 3. Test the wheel speed signal circuit for a short to the wheel speed return circuit. Did you find and correct the condition?	—	Go to *Step 10*	Go to *Step 7*
7	Inspect for poor connections at the harness connector of the EBCM. Did you find and correct the condition?	—	Go to *Step 10*	Go to *Step 9*
8	Replace the wheel speed sensor. Did you complete the repair?	—	Go to *Step 10*	—
9	Replace the EBCM. Did you complete the repair?	—	Go to *Step 10*	—
10	1. Use the scan tool in order to clear the DTCs. 2. Operate the vehicle within the Conditions for Running the DTC as specified in the supporting text. Does the DTC reset?	—	Go to *Step 2*	System OK

GC4020051875020X

Fig. 279 Code C1225: LF Excessive Wheel Speed Variation (Part 2 of 2). Eldorado

Circuit Description

As the wheel spins, the wheel speed sensor produces an AC signal. The EBCM uses the frequency of the AC signal to calculate the wheel speed.

Conditions for Running the DTC

- DTCs C1232–C1235 are not set.
- The brake pedal is not pressed.
- The ABS is not active.

Conditions for Setting the DTC

The EBCM detects a wheel speed variation of more than 14 km/h (9 mph) for 2.5 seconds.

Action Taken When the DTC Sets

If equipped, the following actions occur:

- The EBCM disables the ABS/TCS/VSES for the duration of the ignition cycle.
- The ABS indicator turns ON.
- The TRACTION CONTROL indicator turns ON.
- The DIC displays the SERVICE STABILITY SYS message.

Conditions for Clearing the DTC

- The condition for the DTC is no longer present (the DTC is not current) and you used the scan tool Clear DTC function.
- The condition for the DTC is no longer present (the DTC is not current) and you used the On-Board Diagnostics Clear DTC function.
- The EBCM automatically clears the history DTC when a current DTC is not detected in 50 consecutive drive cycles.

Diagnostic Aids

A possible cause of this DTC is electrical noise on the wheel speed sensor harness wiring. Electrical noise could result from the wheel speed sensor wires being routed to close to high energy ignition system components, such as spark plug wires.

Test Description

The numbers below refer to the step numbers on the diagnostic table.

3. This step measures the resistance of the wheel speed sensor.
6. This step tests whether the wheel speed sensor circuits are shorted together.

GC4020051876010X

Fig. 280 Code C1226: RF Excessive Wheel Speed Variation (Part 1 of 2). Eldorado

Step	Action	Value(s)	Yes	No
1	Did you perform the ABS Diagnostic System Check?	—	Go to *Step 2*	Go to *A Diagnostic System Check - ABS*
2	1. Install a scan tool. 2. Carefully drive the vehicle at a speed greater than 8 km/h (5 mph). 3. With the scan tool, observe all of the Wheel Speed parameters in the Delco/Bosch ABS/TCS ICCS (if equipped) data list. Does the scan tool indicate the suspect wheel varies from the speeds of the other wheels?	—	Go to *Step 3*	Go to Diagnostic Aids
3	1. Turn OFF the ignition. 2. Disconnect the wheel speed sensor connector. 3. Measure the resistance across the wheel speed sensor. Does the resistance measure within the specified range?	850–1350 Ω	Go to *Step 4*	Go to *Step 8*
4	1. By hand, spin the wheel. 2. Measure the AC voltage across the wheel speed sensor. Does the AC voltage measure greater than the specified value?	100 mV	Go to *Step 5*	Go to *Step 8*
5	Inspect for poor connections at the harness connector of the wheel speed sensor. Did you find and correct the condition?	—	Go to *Step 10*	Go to *Step 6*
6	1. Disconnect the EBCM harness connector. 2. Install the *J 39700* universal pinout box using the *J 39700-25* cable adapter to the EBCM harness connector only. 3. Test the wheel speed signal circuit for a short to the wheel speed return circuit. Did you find and correct the condition?	—	Go to *Step 10*	Go to *Step 7*
7	Inspect for poor connections at the harness connector of the EBCM. Did you find and correct the condition?	—	Go to *Step 10*	Go to *Step 9*
8	Replace the wheel speed sensor. Did you complete the repair?	—	Go to *Step 10*	—
9	Replace the EBCM. Did you complete the repair?	—	Go to *Step 10*	—
10	1. Use the scan tool in order to clear the DTCs. 2. Operate the vehicle within the Conditions for Running the DTC as specified in the supporting text. Does the DTC reset?	—	Go to *Step 2*	System OK

GC4020051876020X

Fig. 280 Code C1226: RF Excessive Wheel Speed Variation (Part 2 of 2). Eldorado

Step	Action	Value(s)	Yes	No
1	Did you perform the ABS Diagnostic System Check?	—	Go to *Step 2*	Go to *A Diagnostic System Check - ABS*
2	1. Install a scan tool. 2. Carefully drive the vehicle at a speed greater than 8 km/h (5 mph). 3. With the scan tool, observe all of the Wheel Speed parameters in the Delco/Bosch ABS/TCS ICCS (if equipped) data list. Does the scan tool indicate the suspect wheel varies from the speeds of the other wheels?	—	Go to *Step 3*	Go to Diagnostic Aids
3	1. Turn OFF the ignition. 2. Disconnect the wheel speed sensor connector. 3. Measure the resistance across the wheel speed sensor. Does the resistance measure within the specified range?	850–1350 Ω	Go to *Step 4*	Go to *Step 8*
4	1. By hand, spin the wheel. 2. Measure the AC voltage across the wheel speed sensor. Does the AC voltage measure greater than the specified value?	100 mV	Go to *Step 5*	Go to *Step 8*
5	Inspect for poor connections at the harness connector of the wheel speed sensor. Did you find and correct the condition?	—	Go to *Step 10*	Go to *Step 6*
6	1. Disconnect the EBCM harness connector. 2. Install the *J 39700* universal pinout box using the *J 39700-25* cable adapter to the EBCM harness connector only. 3. Test the wheel speed signal circuit for a short to the wheel speed return circuit. Did you find and correct the condition?	—	Go to *Step 10*	Go to *Step 7*
7	Inspect for poor connections at the harness connector of the EBCM. Did you find and correct the condition?	—	Go to *Step 10*	Go to *Step 9*
8	Replace the wheel speed sensor. Did you complete the repair?	—	Go to *Step 10*	—
9	Replace the EBCM. Did you complete the repair?	—	Go to *Step 10*	—
10	1. Use the scan tool in order to clear the DTCs. 2. Operate the vehicle within the Conditions for Running the DTC as specified in the supporting text. Does the DTC reset?	—	Go to *Step 2*	System OK

GC4020051877020X

Fig. 281 Code C1227: LR Excessive Wheel Speed Variation (Part 2 of 2). Eldorado

Circuit Description

As the wheel spins, the wheel speed sensor produces an AC signal. The EBCM uses the frequency of the AC signal to calculate the wheel speed.

Conditions for Running the DTC

- DTCs C1232–C1235 are not set.
- The brake pedal is not pressed.
- The ABS is not active.

Conditions for Setting the DTC

The EBCM detects a wheel speed variation of more than 14 km/h (9 mph) for 2.5 seconds.

Action Taken When the DTC Sets

If equipped, the following actions occur:

- The EBCM disables the ABS/TCS/VSES for the duration of the ignition cycle.
- The ABS indicator turns ON.
- The TRACTION CONTROL indicator turns ON.
- The DIC displays the SERVICE STABILITY SYS message.

Conditions for Clearing the DTC

- The condition for the DTC is no longer present (the DTC is not current) and you used the scan tool Clear DTC function.
- The condition for the DTC is no longer present (the DTC is not current) and you used the On-Board Diagnostics Clear DTC function.
- The EBCM automatically clears the history DTC when a current DTC is not detected in 50 consecutive drive cycles.

Diagnostic Aids

A possible cause of this DTC is electrical noise on the wheel speed sensor harness wiring. Electrical noise could result from the wheel speed sensor wires being routed to close to high energy ignition system components, such as spark plug wires.

Test Description

The numbers below refer to the step numbers on the diagnostic table.

3. This step measures the resistance of the wheel speed sensor.
6. This step tests whether the wheel speed sensor circuits are shorted together.

GC4020051877010X

Fig. 281 Code C1227: LR Excessive Wheel Speed Variation (Part 1 of 2). Eldorado

Circuit Description

As the wheel spins, the wheel speed sensor produces an AC signal. The EBCM uses the frequency of the AC signal to calculate the wheel speed.

Conditions for Running the DTC

- DTCs C1232–C1235 are not set.
- The brake pedal is not pressed.
- The ABS is not active.

Conditions for Setting the DTC

The EBCM detects a wheel speed variation of more than 14 km/h (9 mph) for 2.5 seconds.

Action Taken When the DTC Sets

If equipped, the following actions occur:

- The EBCM disables the ABS/TCS/VSES for the duration of the ignition cycle.
- The ABS indicator turns ON.
- The TRACTION CONTROL indicator turns ON.
- The DIC displays the SERVICE STABILITY SYS message.

Conditions for Clearing the DTC

- The condition for the DTC is no longer present (the DTC is not current) and you used the scan tool Clear DTC function.
- The condition for the DTC is no longer present (the DTC is not current) and you used the On-Board Diagnostics Clear DTC function.
- The EBCM automatically clears the history DTC when a current DTC is not detected in 50 consecutive drive cycles.

Diagnostic Aids

A possible cause of this DTC is electrical noise on the wheel speed sensor harness wiring. Electrical noise could result from the wheel speed sensor wires being routed to close to high energy ignition system components, such as spark plug wires.

Test Description

The numbers below refer to the step numbers on the diagnostic table.

3. This step measures the resistance of the wheel speed sensor.
6. This step tests whether the wheel speed sensor circuits are shorted together.

GC4020051878010X

Fig. 282 Code C1228: RR Excessive Wheel Speed Variation (Part 1 of 2). Eldorado

Step	Action	Value(s)	Yes	No
1	Did you perform the ABS Diagnostic System Check?	—	Go to *Step 2*	Go to *A Diagnostic System Check - ABS*
2	1. Install a scan tool. 2. Carefully drive the vehicle at a speed greater than 8 km/h (5 mph). 3. With the scan tool, observe all of the Wheel Speed parameters in the Delco/Bosch ABS/TCS ICCS (if equipped) data list. Does the scan tool indicate the suspect wheel varies from the speeds of the other wheels?	—	Go to *Step 3*	Go to Diagnostic Aids
3	1. Turn OFF the ignition. 2. Disconnect the wheel speed sensor connector. 3. Measure the resistance across the wheel speed sensor. Does the resistance measure within the specified range?	850–1350 Ω	Go to *Step 4*	Go to *Step 8*
4	1. By hand, spin the wheel. 2. Measure the AC voltage across the wheel speed sensor. Does the AC voltage measure greater than the specified value?	100 mV	Go to *Step 5*	Go to *Step 8*
5	Inspect for poor connections at the harness connector of the wheel speed sensor. Did you find and correct the condition?	—	Go to *Step 10*	Go to *Step 6*
6	1. Disconnect the EBCM harness connector. 2. Install the *J 39700* universal pinout box using the *J 39700-25* cable adapter to the EBCM harness connector only. 3. Test the wheel speed signal circuit for a short to the wheel speed return circuit. Did you find and correct the condition?	—	Go to *Step 10*	Go to *Step 7*
7	Inspect for poor connections at the harness connector of the EBCM. Did you find and correct the condition?	—	Go to *Step 10*	Go to *Step 9*
8	Replace the wheel speed sensor. Did you complete the repair?	—	Go to *Step 10*	—
9	Replace the EBCM. Did you complete the repair?	—	Go to *Step 10*	—
10	1. Use the scan tool in order to clear the DTCs. 2. Operate the vehicle within the Conditions for Running the DTC as specified in the supporting text. Does the DTC reset?	—	Go to *Step 2*	System OK

GC4020051878020X

Fig. 282 Code C1228: RR Excessive Wheel Speed Variation (Part 2 of 2). Eldorado

Circuit Description

As the wheel spins, the wheel speed sensor produces an AC signal. The EBCM uses the frequency of the AC signal to calculate the wheel speed.

Conditions for Running the DTC

The ignition is ON.

Conditions for Setting the DTC

One of the following conditions exists for 0.02 seconds:

- A short to voltage - the wheel speed sensor signal circuit and wheel speed sensor return circuit voltages are both greater than 4.25 volts.
- A short to ground - the wheel speed sensor signal circuit and wheel speed sensor return circuit voltages are both less than 0.75 volts.
- An open - the wheel speed sensor signal circuit voltage is greater than 4.25 volts and wheel speed sensor return circuit voltage is less than 0.75 volts.

Action Taken When the DTC Sets

If equipped, the following actions occur:

- The EBCM disables the ABS/TCS/VSES for the duration of the ignition cycle.
- The ABS indicator turns ON.
- The TRACTION CONTROL indicator turns ON.
- The DIC displays the SERVICE STABILITY SYS message.

Conditions for Clearing the DTC

- The condition for the DTC is no longer present (the DTC is not current) and you used the scan tool Clear DTC function.
- The condition for the DTC is no longer present (the DTC is not current) and you used the On-Board Diagnostics Clear DTC function.
- The EBCM automatically clears the history DTC when a current DTC is not detected in 50 consecutive drive cycles.

Diagnostic Aids

If the customer comments that the ABS indicator is ON only during moist environmental conditions (rain, snow, vehicle wash, etc.), inspect the wheel speed sensor wiring for signs of water intrusion. If the DTC is not current, clear all DTCs and simulate the effects of water intrusion by using the following procedure:

1. Spray the suspected area with a 5% saltwater solution. To create a 5% saltwater solution, add 2 teaspoons of salt to 354 ml (12 oz) of water.
2. Test drive the vehicle over various road surfaces (bumps, turns, etc.) above 40 km/h (25 mph) for at least 30 seconds.
3. If the DTC returns, replace the suspected wheel speed sensor or repair the wheel speed sensor wiring.
4. Rinse the area thoroughly when completed.

GC4020051879010X

Fig. 283 Code C1232: LF Wheel Speed Circuit Open Or Shorted (Part 1 of 3). Eldorado

Test Description

The number below refers to the step number on the diagnostic table.

2. This step tests for an open in the wheel speed sensor and the wheel speed sensor signal circuits.

Step	Action	Value(s)	Yes	No
1	Did you perform the ABS Diagnostic System Check?	—	Go to *Step 2*	Go to *A Diagnostic System Check - ABS*
2	1. Turn OFF the ignition. 2. Disconnect the EBCM harness connector. 3. Install the *J 39700* universal pinout box using the *J 39700-25* cable adapter to the EBCM harness connector only. 4. Measure the resistance at the *J 39700* universal pinout box between the wheel speed sensor signal circuit and the wheel speed sensor return circuit. Does the resistance measure within the specified range?	850–1350 Ω	Go to *Step 6*	Go to *Step 3*
3	1. Disconnect the wheel speed sensor connector. 2. Measure the resistance across the wheel speed sensor. Does the resistance measure within the specified range?	850–1350 Ω	Go to *Step 4*	Go to *Step 12*
4	Test the wheel speed sensor signal circuit for an open. Did you find and correct the condition?	—	Go to *Step 14*	Go to *Step 5*
5	Test the wheel speed sensor return circuit for an open. Did you find and correct the condition?	—	Go to *Step 14*	Go to *Intermittents*
6	Test the wheel speed sensor signal circuit for a short to ground. Did you find and correct the condition?	—	Go to *Step 14*	Go to *Step 7*
7	Test the wheel speed sensor return circuit for a short to ground. Did you find and correct the condition?	—	Go to *Step 14*	Go to *Step 8*
8	Test the wheel speed sensor signal circuit for a short to voltage. Turn ON the ignition, with the engine OFF when you test for a short to voltage. Did you find and correct the condition?	—	Go to *Step 14*	Go to *Step 9*
9	Test the wheel speed sensor return circuit for a short to voltage. Turn ON the ignition, with the engine OFF when you test for a short to voltage. Did you find and correct the condition?	—	Go to *Step 14*	Go to *Step 10*

GC4020051879020X

Fig. 283 Code C1232: LF Wheel Speed Circuit Open Or Shorted (Part 2 of 3). Eldorado

Step	Action	Value(s)	Yes	No
10	Inspect for poor connections at the harness connector of the wheel speed sensor. Did you find and correct the condition?	—	Go to *Step 14*	Go to *Step 11*
11	Inspect for poor connections at the harness connector of the EBCM. Did you find and correct the condition?	—	Go to *Step 14*	Go to *Step 13*
12	Replace the wheel speed sensor. Did you complete the repair?	—	Go to *Step 14*	—
13	Replace the EBCM. Did you complete the repair?	—	Go to *Step 14*	—
14	1. Use the scan tool in order to clear the DTCs. 2. Operate the vehicle within the Conditions for Running the DTC as specified in the supporting text. Does the DTC reset?	—	Go to *Step 2*	System OK

GC4020051879030X

Fig. 283 Code C1232: LF Wheel Speed Circuit Open Or Shorted (Part 3 of 3). Eldorado

Circuit Description

As the wheel spins, the wheel speed sensor produces an AC signal. The EBCM uses the frequency of the AC signal to calculate the wheel speed.

Conditions for Running the DTC

The ignition is ON.

Conditions for Setting the DTC

One of the following conditions exists for 0.02 seconds:

- A short to voltage - the wheel speed sensor signal circuit and wheel speed sensor return circuit voltages are both greater than 4.25 volts.
- A short to ground - the wheel speed sensor signal circuit and wheel speed sensor return circuit voltages are both less than 0.75 volts.
- An open - the wheel speed sensor signal circuit voltage is greater than 4.25 volts and wheel speed sensor return circuit voltage is less than 0.75 volts.

Action Taken When the DTC Sets

If equipped, the following actions occur:

- The EBCM disables the ABS/TCS/VSES for the duration of the ignition cycle.
- The ABS indicator turns ON.
- The TRACTION CONTROL indicator turns ON.
- The DIC displays the SERVICE STABILITY SYS message.

Conditions for Clearing the DTC

- The condition for the DTC is no longer present (the DTC is not current) and you used the scan tool Clear DTC function.
- The condition for the DTC is no longer present (the DTC is not current) and you used the On-Board Diagnostics Clear DTC function.
- The EBCM automatically clears the history DTC when a current DTC is not detected in 50 consecutive drive cycles.

Diagnostic Aids

If the customer comments that the ABS indicator is ON only during moist environmental conditions (rain, snow, vehicle wash, etc.), inspect the wheel speed sensor wiring for signs of water intrusion. If the DTC is not current, clear all DTCs and simulate the effects of water intrusion by using the following procedure:

1. Spray the suspected area with a 5% saltwater solution. To create a 5% saltwater solution, add 2 teaspoons of salt to 354 ml (12 oz) of water.
2. Test drive the vehicle over various road surfaces (bumps, turns, etc.) above 40 km/h (25 mph) for at least 30 seconds.
3. If the DTC returns, replace the suspected wheel speed sensor or repair the wheel speed sensor wiring.
4. Rinse the area thoroughly when completed.

GC4020051880010X

Fig. 284 Code C1233: RF Wheel Speed Circuit Open Or Shorted (Part 1 of 3). Eldorado

Test Description

The number below refers to the step number on the diagnostic table.

2. This step tests for an open in the wheel speed sensor and the wheel speed sensor signal circuits.

Step	Action	Value(s)	Yes	No
1	Did you perform the ABS Diagnostic System Check?	—	Go to *Step 2*	Go to *A Diagnostic System Check - ABS*
2	1. Turn OFF the ignition. 2. Disconnect the EBCM harness connector. 3. Install the *J 39700* universal pinout box using the *J 39700-25* cable adapter to the EBCM harness connector only. 4. Measure the resistance at the *J 39700* universal pinout box between the wheel speed sensor signal circuit and the wheel speed sensor return circuit. Does the resistance measure within the specified range?	850–1350 Ω	Go to *Step 6*	Go to *Step 3*
3	1. Disconnect the wheel speed sensor connector. 2. Measure the resistance across the wheel speed sensor. Does the resistance measure within the specified range?	850–1350 Ω	Go to *Step 4*	Go to *Step 12*
4	Test the wheel speed sensor signal circuit for an open. Did you find and correct the condition?	—	Go to *Step 14*	Go to *Step 5*
5	Test the wheel speed sensor return circuit for an open. Did you find and correct the condition?	—	Go to *Step 14*	Go to *Intermittents*
6	Test the wheel speed sensor signal circuit for a short to ground. Did you find and correct the condition?	—	Go to *Step 14*	Go to *Step 7*
7	Test the wheel speed sensor return circuit for a short to ground. Did you find and correct the condition?	—	Go to *Step 14*	Go to *Step 8*
8	Test the wheel speed sensor signal circuit for a short to voltage. Turn ON the ignition, with the engine OFF when you test for a short to voltage. Did you find and correct the condition?	—	Go to *Step 14*	Go to *Step 9*
9	Test the wheel speed sensor return circuit for a short to voltage. Turn ON the ignition, with the engine OFF when you test for a short to voltage. Did you find and correct the condition?	—	Go to *Step 14*	Go to *Step 10*

GC4020051880020X

Fig. 284 Code C1233: RF Wheel Speed Circuit Open Or Shorted (Part 2 of 3). Eldorado

Step	Action	Value(s)	Yes	No
10	Inspect for poor connections at the harness connector of the wheel speed sensor. Did you find and correct the condition?	—	Go to *Step 14*	Go to *Step 11*
11	Inspect for poor connections at the harness connector of the EBCM. Did you find and correct the condition?	—	Go to *Step 14*	Go to *Step 13*
12	Replace the wheel speed sensor. Did you complete the repair?	—	Go to *Step 14*	—
13	Replace the EBCM. Did you complete the repair?	—	Go to *Step 14*	—
14	1. Use the scan tool in order to clear the DTCs. 2. Operate the vehicle within the Conditions for Running the DTC as specified in the supporting text. Does the DTC reset?	—	Go to *Step 2*	System OK

GC4020051880030X

Fig. 284 Code C1233: RF Wheel Speed Circuit Open Or Shorted (Part 3 of 3). Eldorado

Test Description

The number below refers to the step number on the diagnostic table.

2. This step tests for an open in the wheel speed sensor and the wheel speed sensor signal circuits.

Step	Action	Value(s)	Yes	No
1	Did you perform the ABS Diagnostic System Check?	—	Go to *Step 2*	Go to *A Diagnostic System Check - ABS*
2	1. Turn OFF the ignition. 2. Disconnect the EBCM harness connector. 3. Install the *J 39700* universal pinout box using the *J 39700-25* cable adapter to the EBCM harness connector only. 4. Measure the resistance at the *J 39700* universal pinout box between the wheel speed sensor signal circuit and the wheel speed sensor return circuit. Does the resistance measure within the specified range?	850–1350 Ω	Go to *Step 6*	Go to *Step 3*
3	1. Disconnect the wheel speed sensor connector. 2. Measure the resistance across the wheel speed sensor. Does the resistance measure within the specified range?	850–1350 Ω	Go to *Step 4*	Go to *Step 12*
4	Test the wheel speed sensor signal circuit for an open. Did you find and correct the condition?	—	Go to *Step 14*	Go to *Step 5*
5	Test the wheel speed sensor return circuit for an open. Did you find and correct the condition?	—	Go to *Step 14*	Go to *Intermittents*
6	Test the wheel speed sensor signal circuit for a short to ground. Did you find and correct the condition?	—	Go to *Step 14*	Go to *Step 7*
7	Test the wheel speed sensor return circuit for a short to ground. Did you find and correct the condition?	—	Go to *Step 14*	Go to *Step 8*
8	Test the wheel speed sensor signal circuit for a short to voltage. Turn ON the ignition, with the engine OFF when you test for a short to voltage. Did you find and correct the condition?	—	Go to *Step 14*	Go to *Step 9*
9	Test the wheel speed sensor return circuit for a short to voltage. Turn ON the ignition, with the engine OFF when you test for a short to voltage. Did you find and correct the condition?	—	Go to *Step 14*	Go to *Step 10*

GC4020051881020X

Fig. 285 Code C1234: LR Wheel Speed Circuit Open Or Shorted (Part 2 of 3). Eldorado

Circuit Description

As the wheel spins, the wheel speed sensor produces an AC signal. The EBCM uses the frequency of the AC signal to calculate the wheel speed.

Conditions for Running the DTC

The ignition is ON.

Conditions for Setting the DTC

One of the following conditions exists for 0.02 seconds:

- A short to voltage - the wheel speed sensor signal circuit and wheel speed sensor return circuit voltages are both greater than 4.25 volts.
- A short to ground - the wheel speed sensor signal circuit and wheel speed sensor return circuit voltages are both less than 0.75 volts.
- An open - the wheel speed sensor signal circuit voltage is greater than 4.25 volts and wheel speed sensor return circuit voltage is less than 0.75 volts.

Action Taken When the DTC Sets

If equipped, the following actions occur:

- The EBCM disables the ABS/TCS/VSES for the duration of the ignition cycle.
- The ABS indicator turns ON.
- The TRACTION CONTROL indicator turns ON.
- The DIC displays the SERVICE STABILITY SYS message.

Conditions for Clearing the DTC

- The condition for the DTC is no longer present (the DTC is not current) and you used the scan tool Clear DTC function.
- The condition for the DTC is no longer present (the DTC is not current) and you used the On-Board Diagnostics Clear DTC function.
- The EBCM automatically clears the history DTC when a current DTC is not detected in 50 consecutive drive cycles.

Diagnostic Aids

If the customer comments that the ABS indicator is ON only during moist environmental conditions (rain, snow, vehicle wash, etc.), inspect the wheel speed sensor wiring for signs of water intrusion. If the DTC is not current, clear all DTCs and simulate the effects of water intrusion by using the following procedure:

1. Spray the suspected area with a 5% saltwater solution. To create a 5% saltwater solution, add 2 teaspoons of salt to 354 ml (12 oz) of water.
2. Test drive the vehicle over various road surfaces (bumps, turns, etc.) above 40 km/h (25 mph) for at least 30 seconds.
3. If the DTC returns, replace the suspected wheel speed sensor or repair the wheel speed sensor wiring.
4. Rinse the area thoroughly when completed.

GC4020051881010X

Fig. 285 Code C1234: LR Wheel Speed Circuit Open Or Shorted (Part 1 of 3). Eldorado

Step	Action	Value(s)	Yes	No
10	Inspect for poor connections at the harness connector of the wheel speed sensor. Did you find and correct the condition?	—	Go to *Step 14*	Go to *Step 11*
11	Inspect for poor connections at the harness connector of the EBCM. Did you find and correct the condition?	—	Go to *Step 14*	Go to *Step 13*
12	Replace the wheel speed sensor. Did you complete the repair?	—	Go to *Step 14*	—
13	Replace the EBCM. Did you complete the repair?	—	Go to *Step 14*	—
14	1. Use the scan tool in order to clear the DTCs. 2. Operate the vehicle within the Conditions for Running the DTC as specified in the supporting text. Does the DTC reset?	—	Go to *Step 2*	System OK

GC4020051881030X

Fig. 285 Code C1234: LR Wheel Speed Circuit Open Or Shorted (Part 3 of 3). Eldorado

Circuit Description

As the wheel spins, the wheel speed sensor produces an AC signal. The EBCM uses the frequency of the AC signal to calculate the wheel speed.

Conditions for Running the DTC

The ignition is ON.

Conditions for Setting the DTC

One of the following conditions exists for 0.02 seconds:

- A short to voltage - the wheel speed sensor signal circuit and wheel speed sensor return circuit voltages are both greater than 4.25 volts.
- A short to ground - the wheel speed sensor signal circuit and wheel speed sensor return circuit voltages are both less than 0.75 volts.
- An open - the wheel speed sensor signal circuit voltage is greater than 4.25 volts and wheel speed sensor return circuit voltage is less than 0.75 volts.

Action Taken When the DTC Sets

If equipped, the following actions occur:

- The EBCM disables the ABS/TCS/VSES for the duration of the ignition cycle.
- The ABS indicator turns ON.
- The TRACTION CONTROL indicator turns ON.
- The DIC displays the SERVICE STABILITY SYS message.

Conditions for Clearing the DTC

- The condition for the DTC is no longer present (the DTC is not current) and you used the scan tool Clear DTC function.
- The condition for the DTC is no longer present (the DTC is not current) and you used the On-Board Diagnostics Clear DTC function.
- The EBCM automatically clears the history DTC when a current DTC is not detected in 50 consecutive drive cycles.

Diagnostic Aids

If the customer comments that the ABS indicator is ON only during moist environmental conditions (rain, snow, vehicle wash, etc.), inspect the wheel speed sensor wiring for signs of water intrusion. If the DTC is not current, clear all DTCs and simulate the effects of water intrusion by using the following procedure:

1. Spray the suspected area with a 5% saltwater solution. To create a 5% saltwater solution, add 2 teaspoons of salt to 354 ml (12 oz) of water.
2. Test drive the vehicle over various road surfaces (bumps, turns, etc.) above 40 km/h (25 mph) for at least 30 seconds.
3. If the DTC returns, replace the suspected wheel speed sensor or repair the wheel speed sensor wiring.
4. Rinse the area thoroughly when completed.

GC4020051882010X

Fig. 286 Code C1235: RR Wheel Speed Circuit Open Or Shorted (Part 1 of 3). Eldorado

Test Description

The number below refers to the step number on the diagnostic table.

2. This step tests for an open in the wheel speed sensor and the wheel speed sensor signal circuits.

Step	Action	Value(s)	Yes	No
1	Did you perform the ABS Diagnostic System Check?	—	Go to *Step 2*	Go to *A Diagnostic System Check - ABS*
2	1. Turn OFF the ignition. 2. Disconnect the EBCM harness connector. 3. Install the *J 39700* universal pinout box using the *J 39700-25* cable adapter to the EBCM harness connector only. 4. Measure the resistance at the *J 39700* universal pinout box between the wheel speed sensor signal circuit and the wheel speed sensor return circuit. Does the resistance measure within the specified range?	850–1350 Ω	Go to *Step 6*	Go to *Step 3*
3	1. Disconnect the wheel speed sensor connector. 2. Measure the resistance across the wheel speed sensor. Does the resistance measure within the specified range?	850–1350 Ω	Go to *Step 4*	Go to *Step 12*
4	Test the wheel speed sensor signal circuit for an open. Did you find and correct the condition?	—	Go to *Step 14*	Go to *Step 5*
5	Test the wheel speed sensor return circuit for an open. Did you find and correct the condition?	—	Go to *Step 14*	Go to *Intermittents*
6	Test the wheel speed sensor signal circuit for a short to ground. Did you find and correct the condition?	—	Go to *Step 14*	Go to *Step 7*
7	Test the wheel speed sensor return circuit for a short to ground. Did you find and correct the condition?	—	Go to *Step 14*	Go to *Step 8*
8	Test the wheel speed sensor signal circuit for a short to voltage. Turn ON the ignition, with the engine OFF when you test for a short to voltage. Did you find and correct the condition?	—	Go to *Step 14*	Go to *Step 9*
9	Test the wheel speed sensor return circuit for a short to voltage. Turn ON the ignition, with the engine OFF when you test for a short to voltage. Did you find and correct the condition?	—	Go to *Step 14*	Go to *Step 10*

GC4020051882020X

Fig. 286 Code C1235: RR Wheel Speed Circuit Open Or Shorted (Part 2 of 3). Eldorado

Step	Action	Value(s)	Yes	No
10	Inspect for poor connections at the harness connector of the wheel speed sensor. Did you find and correct the condition?	—	Go to *Step 14*	Go to *Step 11*
11	Inspect for poor connections at the harness connector of the EBCM. Did you find and correct the condition?	—	Go to *Step 14*	Go to *Step 13*
12	Replace the wheel speed sensor. Did you complete the repair?	—	Go to *Step 14*	—
13	Replace the EBCM. Did you complete the repair?	—	Go to *Step 14*	—
14	1. Use the scan tool in order to clear the DTCs. 2. Operate the vehicle within the Conditions for Running the DTC as specified in the supporting text. Does the DTC reset?	—	Go to *Step 2*	System OK

GC4020051882030X

Fig. 286 Code C1235: RR Wheel Speed Circuit Open Or Shorted (Part 3 of 3). Eldorado

Circuit Description

The EBCM monitors the voltage level available for system operation. A low voltage condition prevents the system from operating properly.

Conditions for Running the DTC

The vehicle speed is greater than 8 km/h (5 mph).

Conditions for Setting the DTC

All of the following conditions occur:

- The battery positive voltage (B+) is less than 10.5 volts.
- The ignition voltage is less than 10.5 volts.

Action Taken When the DTC Sets

If equipped, the following actions occur:

- The EBCM disables the ABS/TCS/VSES for the duration of the ignition cycle.
- The ABS indicator turns ON.
- The TRACTION CONTROL indicator turns ON.
- The DIC displays the SERVICE STABILITY SYS message.

Conditions for Clearing the DTC

- The condition for the DTC is no longer present (the DTC is not current) and you used the scan tool Clear DTC function.
- The condition for the DTC is no longer present (the DTC is not current) and you used the On-Board Diagnostics Clear DTC function.
- The EBCM automatically clears the history DTC when a current DTC is not detected in 50 consecutive drive cycles.

Diagnostic Aids

- Test the charging system.

- Possible causes of this DTC are the following conditions:
  - A charging system malfunction
  - An excessive battery draw
  - A weak battery
  - A faulty system ground

GC4020051883010X

Fig. 287 Code C1236: Low System Supply Voltage (Part 1 of 2). Eldorado

Test Description

The numbers below refer to the step numbers on the diagnostic table.

2. This step uses the scan tool to inspect the voltage to the EBCM.
3. This step uses the scan tool to inspect the voltage to the body control module (PZM). A low voltage value in multiple modules indicates a concern in the charging system.
5. This step verifies that the condition is still present.

Step	Action	Value(s)	Yes	No
1	Did you perform the ABS Diagnostic System Check?	—	Go to *Step 2*	Go to *A Diagnostic System Check - ABS*
2	1. Install a scan tool. 2. Start the engine. 3. With the scan tool, observe the Switched System Battery Power parameter in the Delco/Bosch ABS/TCS ICCS (if equipped) data list. Does the scan tool indicate the voltage is greater than the specified value?	10.5 V	Go to Diagnostic Aids	Go to *Step 3*
3	With the scan tool, observe the Battery Voltage parameter in the Body Control Module data list. Does the scan tool indicate the voltage is greater than the specified value?	10.5 V	Go to *Step 4*	*Starting and Charging*
4	1. Turn OFF the ignition. 2. Disconnect the EBCM harness connector. 3. Install the *J 39700* universal pinout box using the *J 39700-25* cable adapter to the EBCM harness connector only. 4. Test the ground circuits of the EBCM including the EBCM ground for a high resistance or an open. Did you find and correct the condition?	—	Go to *Step 7*	Go to *Step 5*
5	1. Reconnect the EBCM harness connector. 2. Turn ON the ignition, with the engine OFF. 3. Use the scan tool in order to clear the DTCs. 4. Operate the vehicle within the Conditions for Running the DTC as specified in the supporting text. Does the DTC reset?	—	Go to *Step 6*	Go to Diagnostic Aids
6	Replace the EBCM. Did you complete the repair?	—	Go to *Step 7*	—
7	1. Use the scan tool in order to clear the DTCs. 2. Operate the vehicle within the Conditions for Running the DTC Does the DTC reset?	—	Go to *Step 2*	System OK

GC4020051883020X

Fig. 287 Code C1236: Low System Supply Voltage (Part 2 of 2). Eldorado

Circuit Description

The EBCM monitors the voltage level available for system operation. If the voltage level is too high, damage may result in the system. When the ECBM detects a high voltage condition, the EBCM turns OFF the solenoid valve relay which removes battery voltage from the solenoid valves.

Conditions for Running the DTC

The vehicle speed is greater than 8 km/h (5 mph).

Conditions for Setting the DTC

The battery positive voltage (B+) is greater than 17 volts.

Action Taken When the DTC Sets

If equipped, the following actions occur:

- The EBCM disables the ABS/TCS/VSES for the duration of the ignition cycle.
- The ABS indicator turns ON.
- The TRACTION CONTROL indicator turns ON.
- The DIC displays the SERVICE STABILITY SYS message.

Conditions for Clearing the DTC

- The condition for the DTC is no longer present (the DTC is not current) and you used the scan tool Clear DTC function.
- The condition for the DTC is no longer present (the DTC is not current) and you used the On-Board Diagnostics Clear DTC function.
- The EBCM automatically clears the history DTC when a current DTC is not detected in 50 consecutive drive cycles.

Diagnostic Aids

A possible cause of this DTC is overcharging.

Test Description

The numbers below refer to the step numbers on the diagnostic table.

2. This step uses the scan tool to inspect the voltage to the EBCM.
3. This step uses the scan tool to inspect the voltage to the body control module (PZM). A high voltage value in multiple modules indicates a concern in the charging system.
4. This step verifies that the condition is still present.

GC4020051884010X

Fig. 288 Code C1237: High System Supply Voltage (Part 1 of 2). Eldorado

Step	Action	Value(s)	Yes	No
1	Did you perform the ABS Diagnostic System Check?	—	Go to *Step 2*	Go to *A Diagnostic System Check - ABS*
2	1. Turn OFF all of the accessories. 2. Install a scan tool. 3. Start the engine. 4. Run the engine at approximately 2000 RPM. 5. With the scan tool, observe the Switched System Battery Power parameter in the Delco/Bosch ABS/TCS ICCS (if equipped) data list. Does the scan tool indicate that the voltage is greater than the specified value?	17 V	Go to *Step 3*	Go to Diagnostic Aids
3	With the scan tool, observe the Battery Voltage parameter in the Body Control Module data list. Does the scan tool indicate the voltage is greater than the specified value?	17 V	Go to *Starting and Charging*	Go to *Step 4*
4	1. Use the scan tool in order to clear the DTCs. 2. Operate the vehicle within the conditions for Running the DTC as specified in the supporting test. Does the DTC reset?	—	Go to *Step 5*	Go to Diagnostic Aids
5	Replace the EBCM. Did you complete the repair?	—	Go to *Step 6*	—
6	1. Use the scan tool in order to clear the DTCs. 2. Operate the vehicle within the conditions for Running the DTC Does the DTC reset?	—	Go to *Step 2*	System OK

GC4020051884020X

Fig. 288 Code C1237: High System Supply Voltage (Part 2 of 2). Eldorado

Circuit Description

The EBCM monitors vehicle speed deceleration, ABS/TCS/VSES activation, and brake lamp on times in order to calculate an estimate of the brake rotor temperatures. If the EBCM calculates that the brake rotor temperatures have exceeded the thermal cutoff point, the EBCM will temporarily suspend the TCS function until the brake rotors cool. This feature is used to maintain braking effectiveness if normal base braking is required. An overly heated brake system could result in brake fade.

The EBCM continues the monitoring of the brake rotor temperatures after the ignition is turned OFF. The EBCM remains awake until the EBCM calculates that the brake rotors cooled sufficiently. The cooling period may take up to 30 minutes.

This DTC sets in order to indicate that the EBCM temporarily disabled TCS and the DIC displays the TRACTION SUSPENDED message. This DTC does not indicate that there is a fault in the TCS system.

Conditions for Running the DTC

The ABS conditions and the braking conditions are normal.

Conditions for Setting the DTC

This DTC sets when the estimated brake rotor temperature of either of the drive wheels exceeds 375°C (700°F). When the estimated brake rotor temperature of either of the drive wheels exceeds 375°C (700°F) during normal braking or normal ABS operations, the DTC does not set until the next TCS activation. The brake rotor temperature can exceed 375°C (700°F) without setting the DTC if a TCS activation has not occurred. When the estimated brake rotor temperature of either of the drive wheels exceeds 375°C (700°F) during a TCS activation, the DTC sets immediately, but the EBCM does not disable TCS until the end of the TCS event.

Action Taken When the DTC Sets

- The EBCM disables the TCS until the DTC becomes a history DTC.
- The DIC displays the TRACTION SUSPENDED message.
- The ABS remains functional.

Conditions for Clearing the DTC

- The current DTC becomes history when the estimated brake rotor temperatures of both drive wheels decreases below 275°C (530°F). The following actions also occur:
  - The EBCM enables TCS.
  - The DIC displays the TRACTION READY message.
- The condition for the DTC is no longer present (the DTC is not current) and you used the scan tool Clear DTC function.
- The condition for the DTC is no longer present (the DTC is not current) and you used the On-Board Diagnostics Clear DTC function.
- The EBCM automatically clears the history DTC when a current DTC is not detected in 50 consecutive drive cycles.

Diagnostic Aids

- With TCS temporarily disabled, the EBCM continues the monitoring of the brake rotor temperatures after the ignition is turned OFF. Turning ON the ignition again while TCS is temporarily disabled will not re-enable TCS.
- The temperature is an estimate calculated by the EBCM.
- Possible causes of this DTC are the following conditions:
  - The brake usage is excessive.
  - The TCS usage is excessive.
  - The stoplamp switch is misaligned or damaged.

Test Description

The numbers below refer to the step numbers on the diagnostic table.

4. This step uses the scan tool to check if the Brake Temp Status (Thermal Model Cutoff) is exceeded.

GC4020051885010X

Fig. 289 Code C1238: Brake Thermal Models Exceeded (Part 1 of 2). Eldorado

Step	Action	Value(s)	Yes	No
1	Did you perform the ABS Diagnostic System Check?	—	Go to *Step 2*	Go to *A Diagnostic System Check - ABS*
2	1. Install a scan tool. 2. Turn ON the ignition, with the engine OFF. 3. Select the Delco/Bosch ABS/TCS ICCS (if equipped) display DTC function on the scan tool. Does the scan tool display a current DTC C1238?	—	Go to *Step 4*	Go to *Step 3*
3	Since most occurrences of this DTC are caused by excessive braking, review with the customer to verify the conditions under which the DTC set. Did vehicle operation cause this DTC to set?	—	Go to Diagnostic Aids	Go to *Step 4*
4	1. Allow 30 minutes from the last time you drove the vehicle for the cooling of the brake rotors. 2. With the scan tool, observe the Brake Temp Status (Thermal Model Cutoff) parameter in the Delco/Bosch ABS/TCS ICCS (if equipped) data list. Does the scan tool display Normal?	—	Go to *Step 6*	Go to *Step 5*
5	Inspect the alignment of the stoplamp switch. Did you find and correct the condition?	—	Go to *Step 8*	Go to *Step 6*
6	1. Use the scan tool in order to clear the DTCs. 2. Operate the vehicle within the Conditions for Running the DTC as specified in the supporting text. Does the DTC reset as a current DTC?	—	Go to *Step 7*	System OK
7	Replace the EBCM. Did you complete the repair?	—	Go to *Step 8*	—
8	1. Use the scan tool in order to clear the DTCs. 2. Operate the vehicle within the Conditions for Running the DTC Does the DTC reset?	—	Go to *Step 2*	System OK

GC4020051885020X

Fig. 289 Code C1238: Brake Thermal Models Exceeded (Part 2 of 2). Eldorado

Circuit Description

The pump motor is grounded through the ground stud on the BPMV. The EBCM controls the pump motor by energizing the pump motor relay. The pump motor relay then supplies voltage to the pump motor. The pump serves 2 purposes:

- Transfers brake fluid from the brake calipers to the master cylinder reservoir during pressure decrease events.
- Transfers brake fluid from the master cylinder reservoir to the brake calipers during pressure increase events.

Conditions for Running the DTC

The pump relay is commanded OFF.

Conditions for Setting the DTC

The pump motor ground resistance is greater than 6900 ohms.

Action Taken When the DTC Sets

If equipped, the following actions occur:

- The EBCM disables the ABS/TCS/VSES for the duration of the ignition cycle.
- The ABS indicator turns ON.
- The TRACTION CONTROL indicator turns ON.
- The DIC displays the SERVICE STABILITY SYS message.

Conditions for Clearing the DTC

- The condition for the DTC is no longer present (the DTC is not current) and you used the scan tool Clear DTC function.
- The condition for the DTC is no longer present (the DTC is not current) and you used the On-Board Diagnostics Clear DTC function.
- The EBCM automatically clears the history DTC when a current DTC is not detected in 50 consecutive drive cycles.

Diagnostic Aids

The pump motor is integral to the BPMV. The pump motor is not serviceable.

Test Description

The numbers below refer to step numbers on the diagnostic table.

2. This step tests the pump motor ground.
4. This step tests the pump motor ground through the BPMV.

GC4020051886010X

Fig. 290 Code C1242: BPMV Pump Motor Ground Circuit Open (Part 1 of 2). Eldorado

Step	Action	Value(s)	Yes	No
1	Did you perform the ABS Diagnostic System Check?	—	Go to *Step 2*	Go to *A Diagnostic System Check - ABS*
2	1. Turn OFF the ignition. 2. Measure resistance between the motor ground stud and the battery negative terminal. Is the resistance less than the specified value?	2 Ω	Go to *Step 3*	Go to *Step 7*
3	1. Disconnect the EBCM connector. 2. Remove the EBCM from BPMV. 3. Inspect the EBCM to BPMV connector for the following conditions, which could cause an intermittent: • Damage • Corrosion • Poor terminal contact • The presence of brake fluid Did you find and correct the condition?	—	Go to *Step 8*	Go to *Step 4*
4	1. Install the *J 41247* BPMV pinout box to the BPMV connector. 2. Measure the resistance between the pump motor control circuit of the *J 41247* BPMV pinout box and the pump motor ground stud. Is the resistance within the specified range?	0.2–10 Ω	Go to *Step 5*	Go to *Step 6*
5	Replace the EBCM. Did you complete the repair?	—	Go to *Step 8*	—
6	Replace the BPMV. Did you complete the repair?	—	Go to *Step 8*	—
7	Repair the open in pump motor ground circuit. Did you complete the repair?	—	Go to *Step 8*	—
8	1. Use the scan tool in order to clear the DTCs. 2. With the scan tool, perform the Automated Test. Does the DTC reset?	—	Go to *Step 2*	System OK

GC4020051886020X

Fig. 290 Code C1242: BPMV Pump Motor Ground Circuit Open (Part 2 of 2). Eldorado

Step	Action	Value(s)	Yes	No
1	Did you perform the ABS Diagnostic System Check?	—	Go to *Step 2*	Go to *A Diagnostic System Check - ABS*
2	1. Turn OFF the ignition. 2. Measure resistance between the motor ground stud and the battery negative terminal. Is the resistance less than the specified value?	2 Ω	Go to *Step 3*	Go to *Step 7*
3	1. Disconnect the EBCM connector. 2. Remove the EBCM from BPMV. 3. Inspect the EBCM to BPMV connector for the following conditions, which could cause an intermittent: • Damage • Corrosion • Poor terminal contact • The presence of brake fluid Did you find and correct the condition?	—	Go to *Step 8*	Go to *Step 4*
4	1. Install the *J 41247* BPMV pinout box to the BPMV connector. 2. Measure the resistance between the pump motor control circuit of the *J 41247* BPMV pinout box and the pump motor ground stud. Is the resistance within the specified range?	0.2–10 Ω	Go to *Step 5*	Go to *Step 6*
5	Replace the EBCM. Did you complete the repair?	—	Go to *Step 8*	—
6	Replace the BPMV. Did you complete the repair?	—	Go to *Step 8*	—
7	Repair the open in pump motor ground circuit. Did you complete the repair?	—	Go to *Step 8*	—
8	1. Use the scan tool in order to clear the DTCs. 2. With the scan tool, perform the Automated Test. Does the DTC reset?	—	Go to *Step 2*	System OK

GC4020051887020X

Fig. 291 Code C1243: BPMV Pump Motor Stalled (Part 2 of 2). Eldorado

Circuit Description

The CVRSS calculates normal force and transmits a PWM signal to the EBCM via two dedicated data lines, one right, and one left. The EBCM supplies the pull up voltage. The EBCM uses this information to detect rough road conditions and allows for more aggressive braking on rough surfaces.

Conditions for Running the DTC

The ignition is ON.

Conditions for Setting the DTC

One of the following conditions are present for more than 5 seconds out of any 10 second period.

- The PWM duty cycle sent from the CVRSS is between 10% and 90%.
- The normal force value sent to the EBCM does not match either the previous or next normal force value. The CVRSS sends each value twice therefore any normal force value should match either the previous or next normal force value. The possible values of the duty cycle are 20%, 40%, 60%, and 80%.

Action Taken When the DTC Sets

- The EBCM disables the rough road detection function of the VSES for the duration of the ignition cycle.
- The ABS/TCS/VSES remains functional.

GC4020051888010X

Fig. 292 Code C1252: ICCS2 Data Link Left Fault (Part 1 of 3). Eldorado

Circuit Description

The pump motor is grounded through the ground stud on the BPMV. The EBCM controls the pump motor by energizing the pump motor relay. The pump motor relay then supplies voltage to the pump motor. The pump serves 2 purposes:

- Transfers brake fluid from the brake calipers to the master cylinder reservoir during pressure decrease events.
- Transfers brake fluid from the master cylinder reservoir to the brake calipers during pressure increase events.

Conditions for Running the DTC

After the pump motor has been ON, the pump motor relay is commanded OFF.

Conditions for Setting the DTC

The pump motor is stalled or turning slowly.

Action Taken When the DTC Sets

If equipped, the following actions occur:

- The EBCM disables the ABS/TCS/VSES for the duration of the ignition cycle.
- The ABS indicator turns ON.
- The TRACTION CONTROL indicator turns ON.
- The DIC displays the SERVICE STABILITY SYS message.

Conditions for Clearing the DTC

- The condition for the DTC is no longer present (the DTC is not current) and you used the scan tool Clear DTC function.
- The condition for the DTC is no longer present (the DTC is not current) and you used the On-Board Diagnostics Clear DTC function.
- The EBCM automatically clears the history DTC when a current DTC is not detected in 50 consecutive drive cycles.

Diagnostic Aids

The pump motor is integral to the BPMV. The pump motor is not serviceable.

Test Description

The numbers below refer to step numbers on the diagnostic table.

2. This step tests the pump motor ground.
4. This step tests the pump motor ground through the BPMV.

GC4020051887010X

Fig. 291 Code C1243: BPMV Pump Motor Stalled (Part 1 of 2). Eldorado

Conditions for Clearing the DTC

- The condition for the DTC is no longer present (the DTC is not current) and you used the scan tool Clear DTC function.
- The condition for the DTC is no longer present (the DTC is not current) and you used the On-Board Diagnostics Clear DTC function.
- The EBCM automatically clears the history DTC when a current DTC is not detected in 50 consecutive drive cycles.

Test Description

The number below refers to the step number on the diagnostic table.

3. This step determines whether the front normal force signal has a valid duty cycle.

Step	Action	Value(s)	Yes	No
1	Did you perform the ABS Diagnostic System Check?	—	Go to *Step 2*	Go to *A Diagnostic System Check - ABS*
2	Inspect the EBCM ground and continuously variable road sensing suspension (CVRSS) module ground, making sure each ground is clean and torqued to the proper specification. Did you find and correct the condition?	—	Go to *Step 11*	Go to *Step 3*
3	1. Install a scan tool. 2. Start the engine. 3. With the scan tool, observe the ICCS2 Data Link parameter in the Delco/Bosch ABS/TCS ICCS2 data list. Does the scan tool display within the specified range?	10–90%	Go to *Intermittents*	Go to *Step 4*
4	1. Turn OFF the ignition. 2. Disconnect the continuously variable road sensing suspension (CVRSS) module harness connector. 3. Turn ON the ignition, with the engine OFF. 4. Measure the voltage from the normal force signal circuit to a good ground. Does the voltage measure near the specified value?	B+	Go to *Step 5*	Go to *Step 6*
5	1. Turn OFF the ignition. 2. Disconnect the EBCM harness connector. 3. Install the *J 39700* universal breakout box using the *J 39700-25* cable adapter to the EBCM harness connector only. 4. Test the normal force signal circuit for a short to voltage. Did you find and correct the condition?	—	Go to *Step 11*	Go to *Step 7*
6	1. Turn OFF the ignition. 2. Disconnect the EBCM harness connector. 3. Install the *J 39700* universal breakout box using the *J 39700-25* cable adapter to the EBCM harness connector only. 4. Test the normal force signal circuit for one of the following conditions: • An open • A high resistance • A short to ground Did you find and correct the condition?	—	Go to *Step 11*	Go to *Step 8*

GC4020051888020X

Fig. 292 Code C1252: ICCS2 Data Link Left Fault (Part 2 of 3). Eldorado

Step	Action	Value(s)	Yes	No
7	Inspect for poor connections the harness connector of the continuously variable road sensing suspension (CVRSS) module. Did you find and correct the condition?	—	Go to *Step 11*	Go to *Step 9*
8	Inspect for poor connections the harness connector of the EBCM. Did you find and correct the condition?	—	Go to *Step 11*	Go to *Step 10*
9	Replace the continuously variable road sensing suspension (CVRSS) module. Did you complete the repair?	—	Go to *Step 11*	—
10	Replace the EBCM. Did you complete the repair?	—	Go to *Step 11*	—
11	1. Use the scan tool in order to clear the DTCs. 2. Operate the vehicle within the Conditions for Running the DTC as specified in the supporting text. Does the DTC reset?	—	Go to *Step 2*	System OK

GC4020051888030X

Fig. 292 Code C1252: ICCS2 Data Link Left Fault (Part 3 of 3). Eldorado

Conditions for Clearing the DTC

- The condition for the DTC is no longer present (the DTC is not current) and you used the scan tool Clear DTC function.
- The condition for the DTC is no longer present (the DTC is not current) and you used the On-Board Diagnostics Clear DTC function.
- The EBCM automatically clears the history DTC when a current DTC is not detected in 50 consecutive drive cycles.

Test Description

The number below refers to the step number on the diagnostic table.

3. This step determines whether the front normal force signal has a valid duty cycle.

Step	Action	Value(s)	Yes	No
1	Did you perform the ABS Diagnostic System Check?	—	Go to *Step 2*	Go to *A Diagnostic System Check - ABS*
2	Inspect the EBCM ground and continuously variable road sensing suspension (CVRSS) module ground, making sure each ground is clean and torqued to the proper specification. Did you find and correct the condition?	—	Go to *Step 11*	Go to *Step 3*
3	1. Install a scan tool. 2. Start the engine. 3. With the scan tool, observe the ICCS2 Data Link parameter in the Delco/Bosch ABS/TCS ICCS2 data list. Does the scan tool display within the specified range?	10–90%	Go to *Intermittents*	Go to *Step 4*
4	1. Turn OFF the ignition. 2. Disconnect the continuously variable road sensing suspension (CVRSS) module harness connector. 3. Turn ON the ignition, with the engine OFF. 4. Measure the voltage from the normal force signal circuit to a good ground. Does the voltage measure near the specified value?	B+	Go to *Step 5*	Go to *Step 6*
5	1. Turn OFF the ignition. 2. Disconnect the EBCM harness connector. 3. Install the *J 39700* universal breakout box using the *J 39700-25* cable adapter to the EBCM harness connector only. 4. Test the normal force signal circuit for a short to voltage. Did you find and correct the condition?	—	Go to *Step 11*	Go to *Step 7*
6	1. Turn OFF the ignition. 2. Disconnect the EBCM harness connector. 3. Install the *J 39700* universal breakout box using the *J 39700-25* cable adapter to the EBCM harness connector only. 4. Test the normal force signal circuit for one of the following conditions: • An open • A high resistance • A short to ground. Did you find and correct the condition?	—	Go to *Step 11*	Go to *Step 8*

GC4020051889020X

Fig. 293 Code C1253: ICCS2 Data Link Right Fault (Part 2 of 3). Eldorado

Circuit Description

The CVRSS calculates normal force and transmits a PWM signal to the EBCM via two dedicated data lines, one right, and one left. The EBCM supplies the pull up voltage. The EBCM uses this information to detect rough road conditions and allows for more aggressive braking on rough surfaces.

Conditions for Running the DTC

The ignition is ON.

Conditions for Setting the DTC

One of the following conditions are present for more than 5 seconds out of any 10 second period.

- The PWM duty cycle sent from the CVRSS is between 10% and 90%.
- The normal force value sent to the EBCM does not match either the previous or next normal force value. The CVRSS sends each value twice therefore any normal force value should match either the previous or next normal force value. The possible values of the duty cycle are 20%, 40%, 60%, and 80%.

Action Taken When the DTC Sets

- The EBCM disables the rough road detection function of the VSES for the duration of the ignition cycle.
- The ABS/TCS/VSES remains functional.

GC4020051889010X

Fig. 293 Code C1253: ICCS2 Data Link Right Fault (Part 1 of 3). Eldorado

Step	Action	Value(s)	Yes	No
7	Inspect for poor connections the harness connector of the continuously variable road sensing suspension (CVRSS) module. Did you find and correct the condition?	—	Go to *Step 11*	Go to *Step 9*
8	Inspect for poor connections the harness connector of the EBCM. Did you find and correct the condition?	—	Go to *Step 11*	Go to *Step 10*
9	Replace the continuously variable road sensing suspension (CVRSS) module. Did you complete the repair?	—	Go to *Step 11*	—
10	Replace the EBCM. Did you complete the repair?	—	Go to *Step 11*	—
11	1. Use the scan tool in order to clear the DTCs. 2. Operate the vehicle within the Conditions for Running the DTC as specified in the supporting text. Does the DTC reset?	—	Go to *Step 2*	System OK

GC4020051889030X

Fig. 293 Code C1253: ICCS2 Data Link Right Fault (Part 3 of 3). Eldorado

Circuit Description

This DTC identifies a malfunction within the EBCM.

Conditions for Running the DTC

The ABS conditions and the braking conditions are normal.

Conditions for Setting the DTC

An internal EBCM malfunction exists.

Action Taken When the DTC Sets

If equipped, the following actions occur:

- The EBCM disables the ABS/TCS/VSES for the duration of the ignition cycle.
- The ABS indicator turns ON.
- The TRACTION CONTROL indicator turns ON.
- The DIC displays the SERVICE STABILITY SYS message.
- For some DTC C1255xx, the EBCM disables the variable effort steering (VES) for the duration of the ignition cycle and the DIC displays the SERVICE STEERING SYS message.

Conditions for Clearing the DTC

- The condition for the DTC is no longer present (the DTC is not current) and you used the scan tool Clear DTC function.
- The condition for the DTC is no longer present (the DTC is not current) and you used the On-Board Diagnostics Clear DTC function.
- The EBCM automatically clears the history DTC when a current DTC is not detected in 50 consecutive drive cycles.

Diagnostic Aids

- When the scan tool displays the DTC, 2 more numbers follow the DTC. Note the 2 numbers and any other DTCs. The 2 numbers with the DTC are an engineering aid in order to determine the cause of the internal malfunction.
- A DTC C1255e2 can be caused by a battery or module disconnect. Inspect for a recent battery disconnect or module connector disconnect before replacing the EBCM.
- A DTC C1255m5 can be set along with any wheel speed sensor DTC. Diagnose any wheel speed sensor DTCs before replacing the EBCM.
- Make sure integrity of the connection between the EBCM and BPMV is secure, tight, and free from corrosion.

Test Description

The number below refers to the step number on the diagnostic table.

2. This step determines whether the DTC is set current.

Step	Action	Value(s)	Yes	No
1	Did you perform the ABS Diagnostic System Check?	—	Go to *Step 2*	Go to *A Diagnostic System Check - ABS*
2	1. Install a scan tool. 2. Turn ON the ignition, with the engine OFF. 3. Use the scan tool in order to clear the DTCs. 4. With the scan tool, perform the Automated Test. Does the DTC reset?	—	Go to *Step 3*	Go to *Step 4*
3	Replace the EBCM. Did you complete the repair?	—	Go to *Step 4*	—
4	1. Use the scan tool in order to clear the DTCs. 2. With the scan tool, perform the Automated Test. Does the DTC reset?	—	Go to *Step 2*	System OK

GC4020051890000X

Fig. 294 Code C1255: EBCM Internal Fault. Eldorado

Circuit Description

This DTC identifies a malfunction within the EBCM.

Conditions for Running the DTC

The ABS conditions and the braking conditions are normal.

Conditions for Setting the DTC

An internal EBCM malfunction exists.

Action Taken When the DTC Sets

- The ABS remains functional.
- The ABS indicator remains OFF.

Conditions for Clearing the DTC

- The condition for the DTC is no longer present (the DTC is not current) and you used the scan tool Clear DTC function.
- The condition for the DTC is no longer present (the DTC is not current) and you used the On-Board Diagnostics Clear DTC function.
- The EBCM automatically clears the history DTC when a current DTC is not detected in 50 consecutive drive cycles.

Diagnostic Aids

- When the scan tool displays the DTC, 2 more numbers follow the DTC. Note the 2 numbers and any other DTCs. The 2 numbers with the DTC are an engineering aid in order to determine the cause of the internal malfunction.
- Make sure the integrity of the connection between the EBCM and the BPMV is secure, tight, and free from corrosion.

Test Description

The number below refers to the step number on the diagnostic table.

2. This step determines whether the DTC is set current.

Step	Action	Value(s)	Yes	No
1	Did you perform the ABS Diagnostic System Check?	—	Go to *Step 2*	Go to *A Diagnostic System Check - ABS*
2	1. Install a scan tool. 2. Turn ON the ignition, with the engine OFF. 3. Use the scan tool in order to clear the DTCs. 4. With the scan tool, perform the Automated Test. Does the DTC reset?	—	Go to *Step 3*	Go to *Step 4*
3	Replace the EBCM. Did you complete the repair?	—	Go to *Step 4*	—
4	1. Use the scan tool in order to clear the DTCs. 2. With the scan tool, perform the Automated Test. Does the DTC reset?	—	Go to *Step 2*	System OK

GC4020051891000X

Fig. 295 Code C1256: EBCM Internal Fault. Eldorado

Step	Action	Value(s)	Yes	No
1	Did you perform the ABS Diagnostic System Check?	—	Go to *Step 2*	Go to *A Diagnostic System Check - ABS*
2	1. Turn OFF the ignition. 2. Disconnect the EBCM connector. 3. Remove the EBCM from the BPMV. 4. Inspect the EBCM to BPMV connector for the following conditions, which could cause an intermittent: • Damage • Corrosion • Poor terminal contact • The presence of brake fluid Did you find and correct the condition?	—	Go to *Step 8*	Go to *Step 3*
3	1. Install the *J 41247* BPMV pinout box to the BPMV connector. 2. Measure the resistance between the solenoid valve control signal circuit and the solenoid power control circuit at *J 41247* BPMV pinout box. Is the resistance within the specified range?	• Inlet Solenoids: 8–12 Ω • Outlet Solenoids: 4–7 Ω • Isolation and Prime Solenoids: 8–12 Ω	Go to *Step 4*	Go to *Step 6*
4	Measure the resistance between the solenoid valve control signal circuit at the *J 41247* BPMV pinout box and the BPMV case. Is the resistance within the specified range?	OL (Infinite)	Go to *Step 5*	Go to *Step 6*
5	1. Remove the *J 41247* BPMV pinout box. 2. Reinstall the EBCM to BPMV. 3. Reconnect the EBCM connector. 4. Install a scan tool. 5. Turn ON the ignition, with the engine OFF. 6. With the scan tool, perform the Automated Test. Does the DTC reset?	—	Go to *Step 7*	Go to *Intermittents*
6	Replace the BPMV. Did you complete the repair?	—	Go to *Step 8*	—
7	Replace the EBCM. Did you complete the repair?	—	Go to *Step 8*	—
8	1. Use the scan tool in order to clear DTCs. 2. With the scan tool, perform the Automated Test. Does the DTC reset?	—	Go to *Step 2*	System OK

GC4020051892020X

Fig. 296 Code C1261: LF Inlet Valve Solenoid Fault (Part 2 of 2). Eldorado

Circuit Description

The solenoid valve relay is energized when the ignition is ON. The solenoid valve relay supplies voltage to the solenoid valves. This voltage is referred to as the solenoid power voltage. The EBCM controls the solenoid valve by grounding the control circuit.

Conditions for Running the DTC

- The solenoid power voltage is greater than 8.0 volts.
- The ignition voltage is greater than 9.0 volts.

Conditions for Setting the DTC

The commanded state of the driver and the actual state of the control circuit do not match for 0.03 seconds.

Action Taken When the DTC Sets

If equipped, the following actions occur:

- The EBCM disables the ABS/TCS/VSES for the duration of the ignition cycle.
- The ABS indicator turns ON.
- The TRACTION CONTROL indicator turns ON.
- The DIC displays the SERVICE STABILITY SYS message.

Conditions for Clearing the DTC

- The condition for the DTC is no longer present (the DTC is not current) and you used the scan tool Clear DTC function.
- The condition for the DTC is no longer present (the DTC is not current) and you used the On-Board Diagnostics Clear DTC function.
- The EBCM automatically clears the history DTC when a current DTC is not detected in 50 consecutive drive cycles.

Diagnostic Aids

- Make sure the integrity of the connection between the EBCM and the BPMV is secure, tight, and free from corrosion.
- The solenoid valves are internal to the BPMV and can not be serviced individually. The solenoid valve circuits are internal to the EBCM and can not be serviced individually.

Test Description

The numbers below refer to step numbers on the diagnostic table.

3. This step tests the resistance value of the solenoid.
4. This step tests for a short to ground in the BPMV.
5. This step determines whether the DTC is current.

GC4020051892010X

Fig. 296 Code C1261: LF Inlet Valve Solenoid Fault (Part 1 of 2). Eldorado

Circuit Description

The solenoid valve relay is energized when the ignition is ON. The solenoid valve relay supplies voltage to the solenoid valves. This voltage is referred to as the solenoid power voltage. The EBCM controls the solenoid valve by grounding the control circuit.

Conditions for Running the DTC

- The solenoid power voltage is greater than 8.0 volts.
- The ignition voltage is greater than 9.0 volts.

Conditions for Setting the DTC

The commanded state of the driver and the actual state of the control circuit do not match for 0.03 seconds.

Action Taken When the DTC Sets

If equipped, the following actions occur:

- The EBCM disables the ABS/TCS/VSES for the duration of the ignition cycle.
- The ABS indicator turns ON.
- The TRACTION CONTROL indicator turns ON.
- The DIC displays the SERVICE STABILITY SYS message.

Conditions for Clearing the DTC

- The condition for the DTC is no longer present (the DTC is not current) and you used the scan tool Clear DTC function.
- The condition for the DTC is no longer present (the DTC is not current) and you used the On-Board Diagnostics Clear DTC function.
- The EBCM automatically clears the history DTC when a current DTC is not detected in 50 consecutive drive cycles.

Diagnostic Aids

- Make sure the integrity of the connection between the EBCM and the BPMV is secure, tight, and free from corrosion.
- The solenoid valves are internal to the BPMV and can not be serviced individually. The solenoid valve circuits are internal to the EBCM and can not be serviced individually.

Test Description

The numbers below refer to step numbers on the diagnostic table.

3. This step tests the resistance value of the solenoid.
4. This step tests for a short to ground in the BPMV.
5. This step determines whether the DTC is current.

GC4020051893010X

Fig. 297 Code C1262: LF Outlet Valve Solenoid Fault (Part 1 of 2). Eldorado

Step	Action	Value(s)	Yes	No
1	Did you perform the ABS Diagnostic System Check?	—	Go to *Step 2*	Go to *A Diagnostic System Check - ABS*
2	1. Turn OFF the ignition. 2. Disconnect the EBCM connector. 3. Remove the EBCM from the BPMV. 4. Inspect the EBCM to BPMV connector for the following conditions, which could cause an intermittent: • Damage • Corrosion • Poor terminal contact • The presence of brake fluid Did you find and correct the condition?	—	Go to *Step 8*	Go to *Step 3*
3	1. Install the *J 41247* BPMV pinout box to the BPMV connector. 2. Measure the resistance between the solenoid valve control signal circuit and the solenoid power control circuit at *J 41247* BPMV pinout box. Is the resistance within the specified range?	• Inlet Solenoids: 8–12 Ω • Outlet Solenoids: 4–7 Ω • Isolation and Prime Solenoids: 8–12 Ω	Go to *Step 4*	Go to *Step 6*
4	Measure the resistance between the solenoid valve control signal circuit at the *J 41247* BPMV pinout box and the BPMV case. Is the resistance within the specified range?	OL (Infinite)	Go to *Step 5*	Go to *Step 6*
5	1. Remove the *J 41247* BPMV pinout box. 2. Reinstall the EBCM to BPMV. 3. Reconnect the EBCM connector. 4. Install a scan tool. 5. Turn ON the ignition, with the engine OFF. 6. With the scan tool, perform the Automated Test. Does the DTC reset?	—	Go to *Step 7*	Go to *Intermittents*
6	Replace the BPMV. Did you complete the repair?	—	Go to *Step 8*	—
7	Replace the EBCM. Did you complete the repair?	—	Go to *Step 8*	—
8	1. Use the scan tool in order to clear DTCs. 2. With the scan tool, perform the Automated Test. Does the DTC reset?	—	Go to *Step 2*	System OK

GC4020051893020X

Fig. 297 Code C1262: LF Outlet Valve Solenoid Fault (Part 2 of 2). Eldorado

Circuit Description

The solenoid valve relay is energized when the ignition is ON. The solenoid valve relay supplies voltage to the solenoid valves. This voltage is referred to as the solenoid power voltage. The EBCM controls the solenoid valve by grounding the control circuit.

Conditions for Running the DTC

- The solenoid power voltage is greater than 8.0 volts.
- The ignition voltage is greater than 9.0 volts.

Conditions for Setting the DTC

The commanded state of the driver and the actual state of the control circuit do not match for 0.03 seconds.

Action Taken When the DTC Sets

If equipped, the following actions occur:

- The EBCM disables the ABS/TCS/VSES for the duration of the ignition cycle.
- The ABS indicator turns ON.
- The TRACTION CONTROL indicator turns ON.
- The DIC displays the SERVICE STABILITY SYS message.

Conditions for Clearing the DTC

- The condition for the DTC is no longer present (the DTC is not current) and you used the scan tool Clear DTC function.
- The condition for the DTC is no longer present (the DTC is not current) and you used the On-Board Diagnostics Clear DTC function.
- The EBCM automatically clears the history DTC when a current DTC is not detected in 50 consecutive drive cycles.

Diagnostic Aids

- Make sure the integrity of the connection between the EBCM and the BPMV is secure, tight, and free from corrosion.
- The solenoid valves are internal to the BPMV and can not be serviced individually. The solenoid valve circuits are internal to the EBCM and can not be serviced individually.

Test Description

The numbers below refer to step numbers on the diagnostic table.

3. This step tests the resistance value of the solenoid.
4. This step tests for a short to ground in the BPMV.
5. This step determines whether the DTC is current.

GC4020051894010X

Fig. 298 Code C1263: RF Inlet Valve Solenoid Fault (Part 1 of 2). Eldorado

Circuit Description

The solenoid valve relay is energized when the ignition is ON. The solenoid valve relay supplies voltage to the solenoid valves. This voltage is referred to as the solenoid power voltage. The EBCM controls the solenoid valve by grounding the control circuit.

Conditions for Running the DTC

- The solenoid power voltage is greater than 8.0 volts.
- The ignition voltage is greater than 9.0 volts.

Conditions for Setting the DTC

The commanded state of the driver and the actual state of the control circuit do not match for 0.03 seconds.

Action Taken When the DTC Sets

If equipped, the following actions occur:

- The EBCM disables the ABS/TCS/VSES for the duration of the ignition cycle.
- The ABS indicator turns ON.
- The TRACTION CONTROL indicator turns ON.
- The DIC displays the SERVICE STABILITY SYS message.

Conditions for Clearing the DTC

- The condition for the DTC is no longer present (the DTC is not current) and you used the scan tool Clear DTC function.
- The condition for the DTC is no longer present (the DTC is not current) and you used the On-Board Diagnostics Clear DTC function.
- The EBCM automatically clears the history DTC when a current DTC is not detected in 50 consecutive drive cycles.

Diagnostic Aids

- Make sure the integrity of the connection between the EBCM and the BPMV is secure, tight, and free from corrosion.
- The solenoid valves are internal to the BPMV and can not be serviced individually. The solenoid valve circuits are internal to the EBCM and can not be serviced individually.

Test Description

The numbers below refer to step numbers on the diagnostic table.

3. This step tests the resistance value of the solenoid.
4. This step tests for a short to ground in the BPMV.
5. This step determines whether the DTC is current.

GC4020051895010X

Fig. 299 Code C1264: RF Outlet Valve Solenoid Fault (Part 1 of 2). Eldorado

Step	Action	Value(s)	Yes	No
1	Did you perform the ABS Diagnostic System Check?	—	Go to *Step 2*	Go to *A Diagnostic System Check - ABS*
2	1. Turn OFF the ignition. 2. Disconnect the EBCM connector. 3. Remove the EBCM from the BPMV. 4. Inspect the EBCM to BPMV connector for the following conditions, which could cause an intermittent: • Damage • Corrosion • Poor terminal contact • The presence of brake fluid Did you find and correct the condition?	—	Go to *Step 8*	Go to *Step 3*
3	1. Install the *J 41247* BPMV pinout box to the BPMV connector. 2. Measure the resistance between the solenoid valve control signal circuit and the solenoid power control circuit at *J 41247* BPMV pinout box. Is the resistance within the specified range?	• Inlet Solenoids: 8–12 Ω • Outlet Solenoids: 4–7 Ω • Isolation and Prime Solenoids: 8–12 Ω	Go to *Step 4*	Go to *Step 6*
4	Measure the resistance between the solenoid valve control signal circuit at the *J 41247* BPMV pinout box and the BPMV case. Is the resistance within the specified range?	OL (Infinite)	Go to *Step 5*	Go to *Step 6*
5	1. Remove the *J 41247* BPMV pinout box. 2. Reinstall the EBCM to BPMV. 3. Reconnect the EBCM connector. 4. Install a scan tool. 5. Turn ON the ignition, with the engine OFF. 6. With the scan tool, perform the Automated Test. Does the DTC reset?	—	Go to *Step 7*	Go to *Intermittents*
6	Replace the BPMV. Did you complete the repair?	—	Go to *Step 8*	—
7	Replace the EBCM. Did you complete the repair?	—	Go to *Step 8*	—
8	1. Use the scan tool in order to clear DTCs. 2. With the scan tool, perform the Automated Test. Does the DTC reset?	—	Go to *Step 2*	System OK

GC4020051895020X

Fig. 299 Code C1264: RF Outlet Valve Solenoid Fault (Part 2 of 2). Eldorado

Step	Action	Value(s)	Yes	No
1	Did you perform the ABS Diagnostic System Check?	—	Go to *Step 2*	Go to *A Diagnostic System Check - ABS*
2	1. Turn OFF the ignition. 2. Disconnect the EBCM connector. 3. Remove the EBCM from the BPMV. 4. Inspect the EBCM to BPMV connector for the following conditions, which could cause an intermittent: • Damage • Corrosion • Poor terminal contact • The presence of brake fluid Did you find and correct the condition?	—	Go to *Step 8*	Go to *Step 3*
3	1. Install the *J 41247* BPMV pinout box to the BPMV connector. 2. Measure the resistance between the solenoid valve control signal circuit and the solenoid power control circuit at *J 41247* BPMV pinout box. Is the resistance within the specified range?	• Inlet Solenoids: 8–12 Ω • Outlet Solenoids: 4–7 Ω • Isolation and Prime Solenoids: 8–12 Ω	Go to *Step 4*	Go to *Step 6*
4	Measure the resistance between the solenoid valve control signal circuit at the *J 41247* BPMV pinout box and the BPMV case. Is the resistance within the specified range?	OL (Infinite)	Go to *Step 5*	Go to *Step 6*
5	1. Remove the *J 41247* BPMV pinout box. 2. Reinstall the EBCM to BPMV. 3. Reconnect the EBCM connector. 4. Install a scan tool. 5. Turn ON the ignition, with the engine OFF. 6. With the scan tool, perform the Automated Test. Does the DTC reset?	—	Go to *Step 7*	Go to *Intermittents*
6	Replace the BPMV. Did you complete the repair?	—	Go to *Step 8*	—
7	Replace the EBCM. Did you complete the repair?	—	Go to *Step 8*	—
8	1. Use the scan tool in order to clear DTCs. 2. With the scan tool, perform the Automated Test. Does the DTC reset?	—	Go to *Step 2*	System OK

GC4020051894020X

Fig. 298 Code C1263: RF Inlet Valve Solenoid Fault (Part 2 of 2). Eldorado

Circuit Description

The solenoid valve relay is energized when the ignition is ON. The solenoid valve relay supplies voltage to the solenoid valves. This voltage is referred to as the solenoid power voltage. The EBCM controls the solenoid valve by grounding the control circuit.

Conditions for Running the DTC

- The solenoid power voltage is greater than 8.0 volts.
- The ignition voltage is greater than 9.0 volts.

Conditions for Setting the DTC

The commanded state of the driver and the actual state of the control circuit do not match for 0.03 seconds.

Action Taken When the DTC Sets

If equipped, the following actions occur:

- The EBCM disables the ABS/TCS/VSES for the duration of the ignition cycle.
- The ABS indicator turns ON.
- The TRACTION CONTROL indicator turns ON.
- The DIC displays the SERVICE STABILITY SYS message.

Conditions for Clearing the DTC

- The condition for the DTC is no longer present (the DTC is not current) and you used the scan tool Clear DTC function.
- The condition for the DTC is no longer present (the DTC is not current) and you used the On-Board Diagnostics Clear DTC function.
- The EBCM automatically clears the history DTC when a current DTC is not detected in 50 consecutive drive cycles.

Diagnostic Aids

- Make sure the integrity of the connection betweer the EBCM and the BPMV is secure, tight, and free from corrosion.
- The solenoid valves are internal to the BPMV anc can not be serviced individually. The solenoid valve circuits are internal to the EBCM and can nc be serviced individually.

Test Description

The numbers below refer to step numbers on the diagnostic table.

3. This step tests the resistance value of the solenoid.
4. This step tests for a short to ground in the BPMV.
5. This step determines whether the DTC is current.

GC4020051896010X

Fig. 300 Code C1265: LR Inlet Valve Solenoid Fault (Part 1 of 2). Eldorado

Step	Action	Value(s)	Yes	No
1	Did you perform the ABS Diagnostic System Check?	—	Go to *Step 2*	Go to *A Diagnostic System Check - ABS*
2	1. Turn OFF the ignition. 2. Disconnect the EBCM connector. 3. Remove the EBCM from the BPMV. 4. Inspect the EBCM to BPMV connector for the following conditions, which could cause an intermittent: • Damage • Corrosion • Poor terminal contact • The presence of brake fluid Did you find and correct the condition?	—	Go to *Step 8*	Go to *Step 3*
3	1. Install the *J 41247* BPMV pinout box to the BPMV connector. 2. Measure the resistance between the solenoid valve control signal circuit and the solenoid power control circuit at *J 41247* BPMV pinout box. Is the resistance within the specified range?	• Inlet Solenoids: 8–12 Ω • Outlet Solenoids: 4–7 Ω • Isolation and Prime Solenoids: 8–12 Ω	Go to *Step 4*	Go to *Step 6*
4	Measure the resistance between the solenoid valve control signal circuit at the *J 41247* BPMV pinout box and the BPMV case. Is the resistance within the specified range?	OL (Infinite)	Go to *Step 5*	Go to *Step 6*
5	1. Remove the *J 41247* BPMV pinout box. 2. Reinstall the EBCM to BPMV. 3. Reconnect the EBCM connector. 4. Install a scan tool. 5. Turn ON the ignition, with the engine OFF. 6. With the scan tool, perform the Automated Test. Does the DTC reset?	—	Go to *Step 7*	Go to *Intermittents*
6	Replace the BPMV. Did you complete the repair?	—	Go to *Step 8*	—
7	Replace the EBCM. Did you complete the repair?	—	Go to *Step 8*	—
8	1. Use the scan tool in order to clear DTCs. 2. With the scan tool, perform the Automated Test. Does the DTC reset?	—	Go to *Step 2*	System OK

GC4020051896020X

Fig. 300 Code C1265: LR Inlet Valve Solenoid Fault (Part 2 of 2). Eldorado

Step	Action	Value(s)	Yes	No
1	Did you perform the ABS Diagnostic System Check?	—	Go to *Step 2*	Go to *A Diagnostic System Check - ABS*
2	1. Turn OFF the ignition. 2. Disconnect the EBCM connector. 3. Remove the EBCM from the BPMV. 4. Inspect the EBCM to BPMV connector for the following conditions, which could cause an intermittent: • Damage • Corrosion • Poor terminal contact • The presence of brake fluid Did you find and correct the condition?	—	Go to *Step 8*	Go to *Step 3*
3	1. Install the *J 41247* BPMV pinout box to the BPMV connector. 2. Measure the resistance between the solenoid valve control signal circuit and the solenoid power control circuit at *J 41247* BPMV pinout box. Is the resistance within the specified range?	• Inlet Solenoids: 8–12 Ω • Outlet Solenoids: 4–7 Ω • Isolation and Prime Solenoids: 8–12 Ω	Go to *Step 4*	Go to *Step 6*
4	Measure the resistance between the solenoid valve control signal circuit at the *J 41247* BPMV pinout box and the BPMV case. Is the resistance within the specified range?	OL (Infinite)	Go to *Step 5*	Go to *Step 6*
5	1. Remove the *J 41247* BPMV pinout box. 2. Reinstall the EBCM to BPMV. 3. Reconnect the EBCM connector. 4. Install a scan tool. 5. Turn ON the ignition, with the engine OFF. 6. With the scan tool, perform the Automated Test. Does the DTC reset?	—	Go to *Step 7*	Go to *Intermittents*
6	Replace the BPMV. Did you complete the repair?	—	Go to *Step 8*	—
7	Replace the EBCM. Did you complete the repair?	—	Go to *Step 8*	—
8	1. Use the scan tool in order to clear DTCs. 2. With the scan tool, perform the Automated Test. Does the DTC reset?	—	Go to *Step 2*	System OK

GC4020051897020X

Fig. 301 Code C1266: LR Outlet Valve Solenoid Fault (Part 2 of 2). Eldorado

Circuit Description

The solenoid valve relay is energized when the ignition is ON. The solenoid valve relay supplies voltage to the solenoid valves. This voltage is referred to as the solenoid power voltage. The EBCM controls the solenoid valve by grounding the control circuit.

Conditions for Running the DTC

- The solenoid power voltage is greater than 8.0 volts.
- The ignition voltage is greater than 9.0 volts.

Conditions for Setting the DTC

The commanded state of the driver and the actual state of the control circuit do not match for 0.03 seconds.

Action Taken When the DTC Sets

If equipped, the following actions occur:

- The EBCM disables the ABS/TCS/VSES for the duration of the ignition cycle.
- The ABS indicator turns ON.
- The TRACTION CONTROL indicator turns ON.
- The DIC displays the SERVICE STABILITY SYS message.

Conditions for Clearing the DTC

- The condition for the DTC is no longer present (the DTC is not current) and you used the scan tool Clear DTC function.
- The condition for the DTC is no longer present (the DTC is not current) and you used the On-Board Diagnostics Clear DTC function.
- The EBCM automatically clears the history DTC when a current DTC is not detected in 50 consecutive drive cycles.

Diagnostic Aids

- Make sure the integrity of the connection between the EBCM and the BPMV is secure, tight, and free from corrosion.
- The solenoid valves are internal to the BPMV and can not be serviced individually. The solenoid valve circuits are internal to the EBCM and can not be serviced individually.

Test Description

The numbers below refer to step numbers on the diagnostic table.

3. This step tests the resistance value of the solenoid.
4. This step tests for a short to ground in the BPMV.
5. This step determines whether the DTC is current.

GC4020051897010X

Fig. 301 Code C1266: LR Outlet Valve Solenoid Fault (Part 1 of 2). Eldorado

Circuit Description

The solenoid valve relay is energized when the ignition is ON. The solenoid valve relay supplies voltage to the solenoid valves. This voltage is referred to as the solenoid power voltage. The EBCM controls the solenoid valve by grounding the control circuit.

Conditions for Running the DTC

- The solenoid power voltage is greater than 8.0 volts.
- The ignition voltage is greater than 9.0 volts.

Conditions for Setting the DTC

The commanded state of the driver and the actual state of the control circuit do not match for 0.03 seconds.

Action Taken When the DTC Sets

If equipped, the following actions occur:

- The EBCM disables the ABS/TCS/VSES for the duration of the ignition cycle.
- The ABS indicator turns ON.
- The TRACTION CONTROL indicator turns ON.
- The DIC displays the SERVICE STABILITY SYS message.

Conditions for Clearing the DTC

- The condition for the DTC is no longer present (the DTC is not current) and you used the scan tool Clear DTC function.
- The condition for the DTC is no longer present (the DTC is not current) and you used the On-Board Diagnostics Clear DTC function.
- The EBCM automatically clears the history DTC when a current DTC is not detected in 50 consecutive drive cycles.

Diagnostic Aids

- Make sure the integrity of the connection between the EBCM and the BPMV is secure, tight, and free from corrosion.
- The solenoid valves are internal to the BPMV and can not be serviced individually. The solenoid valve circuits are internal to the EBCM and can not be serviced individually.

Test Description

The numbers below refer to step numbers on the diagnostic table.

3. This step tests the resistance value of the solenoid.
4. This step tests for a short to ground in the BPMV.
5. This step determines whether the DTC is current.

GC4020051898010X

Fig. 302 Code C1267: RR Inlet Valve Solenoid Fault (Part 1 of 2). Eldorado

Step	Action	Value(s)	Yes	No
1	Did you perform the ABS Diagnostic System Check?	—	Go to *Step 2*	Go to *A Diagnostic System Check - ABS*
2	1. Turn OFF the ignition. 2. Disconnect the EBCM connector. 3. Remove the EBCM from the BPMV. 4. Inspect the EBCM to BPMV connector for the following conditions, which could cause an intermittent: • Damage • Corrosion • Poor terminal contact • The presence of brake fluid Did you find and correct the condition?	—	Go to *Step 8*	Go to *Step 3*
3	1. Install the *J 41247* BPMV pinout box to the BPMV connector. 2. Measure the resistance between the solenoid valve control signal circuit and the solenoid power control circuit at *J 41247* BPMV pinout box. Is the resistance within the specified range?	• Inlet Solenoids: 8–12 Ω • Outlet Solenoids: 4–7 Ω • Isolation and Prime Solenoids: 8–12 Ω	Go to *Step 4*	Go to *Step 6*
4	Measure the resistance between the solenoid valve control signal circuit at the *J 41247* BPMV pinout box and the BPMV case. Is the resistance within the specified range?	OL (Infinite)	Go to *Step 5*	Go to *Step 6*
5	1. Remove the *J 41247* BPMV pinout box. 2. Reinstall the EBCM to BPMV. 3. Reconnect the EBCM connector. 4. Install a scan tool. 5. Turn ON the ignition, with the engine OFF. 6. With the scan tool, perform the Automated Test. Does the DTC reset?	—	Go to *Step 7*	Go to *Intermittents*
6	Replace the BPMV. Did you complete the repair?	—	Go to *Step 8*	—
7	Replace the EBCM. Did you complete the repair?	—	Go to *Step 8*	—
8	1. Use the scan tool in order to clear DTCs. 2. With the scan tool, perform the Automated Test. Does the DTC reset?	—	Go to *Step 2*	System OK

GC4020051898020X

Fig. 302 Code C1267: RR Inlet Valve Solenoid Fault (Part 2 of 2). Eldorado

Circuit Description

The solenoid valve relay is energized when the ignition is ON. The solenoid valve relay supplies voltage to the solenoid valves. This voltage is referred to as the solenoid power voltage. The EBCM controls the solenoid valve by grounding the control circuit.

Conditions for Running the DTC

- The solenoid power voltage is greater than 8.0 volts.
- The ignition voltage is greater than 9.0 volts.

Conditions for Setting the DTC

The commanded state of the driver and the actual state of the control circuit do not match for 0.03 seconds.

Action Taken When the DTC Sets

If equipped, the following actions occur:

- The EBCM disables the ABS/TCS/VSES for the duration of the ignition cycle.
- The ABS indicator turns ON.
- The TRACTION CONTROL indicator turns ON.
- The DIC displays the SERVICE STABILITY SYS message.

Conditions for Clearing the DTC

- The condition for the DTC is no longer present (the DTC is not current) and you used the scan tool Clear DTC function.
- The condition for the DTC is no longer present (the DTC is not current) and you used the On-Board Diagnostics Clear DTC function.
- The EBCM automatically clears the history DTC when a current DTC is not detected in 50 consecutive drive cycles.

Diagnostic Aids

- Make sure the integrity of the connection between the EBCM and the BPMV is secure, tight, and free from corrosion.
- The solenoid valves are internal to the BPMV and can not be serviced individually. The solenoid valve circuits are internal to the EBCM and can not be serviced individually.

Test Description

The numbers below refer to step numbers on the diagnostic table.

3. This step tests the resistance value of the solenoid.
4. This step tests for a short to ground in the BPMV.
5. This step determines whether the DTC is current.

GC4020051899010X

Fig. 303 Code C1268: RR Outlet Valve Solenoid Fault (Part 1 of 2). Eldorado

Step	Action	Value(s)	Yes	No
1	Did you perform the ABS Diagnostic System Check?	—	Go to *Step 2*	Go to *A Diagnostic System Check - ABS*
2	1. Turn OFF the ignition. 2. Disconnect the EBCM connector. 3. Remove the EBCM from the BPMV. 4. Inspect the EBCM to BPMV connector for the following conditions, which could cause an intermittent: • Damage • Corrosion • Poor terminal contact • The presence of brake fluid Did you find and correct the condition?	—	Go to *Step 8*	Go to *Step 3*
3	1. Install the *J 41247* BPMV pinout box to the BPMV connector. 2. Measure the resistance between the solenoid valve control signal circuit and the solenoid power control circuit at *J 41247* BPMV pinout box. Is the resistance within the specified range?	• Inlet Solenoids: 8–12 Ω • Outlet Solenoids: 4–7 Ω • Isolation and Prime Solenoids: 8–12 Ω	Go to *Step 4*	Go to *Step 6*
4	Measure the resistance between the solenoid valve control signal circuit at the *J 41247* BPMV pinout box and the BPMV case. Is the resistance within the specified range?	OL (Infinite)	Go to *Step 5*	Go to *Step 6*
5	1. Remove the *J 41247* BPMV pinout box. 2. Reinstall the EBCM to BPMV. 3. Reconnect the EBCM connector. 4. Install a scan tool. 5. Turn ON the ignition, with the engine OFF. 6. With the scan tool, perform the Automated Test. Does the DTC reset?	—	Go to *Step 7*	Go to *Intermittents*
6	Replace the BPMV. Did you complete the repair?	—	Go to *Step 8*	—
7	Replace the EBCM. Did you complete the repair?	—	Go to *Step 8*	—
8	1. Use the scan tool in order to clear DTCs. 2. With the scan tool, perform the Automated Test. Does the DTC reset?	—	Go to *Step 2*	System OK

GC4020051899020X

Fig. 303 Code C1268: RR Outlet Valve Solenoid Fault (Part 2 of 2). Eldorado

Circuit Description

The solenoid valve relay is energized when the ignition is ON. The solenoid valve relay supplies voltage to the solenoid valves. This voltage is referred to as the solenoid power voltage. The EBCM controls the solenoid valve by grounding the control circuit.

Conditions for Running the DTC

- The solenoid power voltage is greater than 8.0 volts.
- The ignition voltage is greater than 9.0 volts.

Conditions for Setting the DTC

The commanded state of the driver and the actual state of the control circuit do not match for 0.03 seconds.

Action Taken When the DTC Sets

If equipped, the following actions occur:

- The EBCM disables the ABS/TCS/VSES for the duration of the ignition cycle.
- The ABS indicator turns ON.
- The TRACTION CONTROL indicator turns ON.
- The DIC displays the SERVICE STABILITY SYS message.

Conditions for Clearing the DTC

- The condition for the DTC is no longer present (the DTC is not current) and you used the scan tool Clear DTC function.
- The condition for the DTC is no longer present (the DTC is not current) and you used the On-Board Diagnostics Clear DTC function.
- The EBCM automatically clears the history DTC when a current DTC is not detected in 50 consecutive drive cycles.

Diagnostic Aids

- Make sure the integrity of the connection between the EBCM and the BPMV is secure, tight, and free from corrosion.
- The solenoid valves are internal to the BPMV and can not be serviced individually. The solenoid valve circuits are internal to the EBCM and can not be serviced individually.

Test Description

The numbers below refer to step numbers on the diagnostic table.

3. This step tests the resistance value of the solenoid.
4. This step tests for a short to ground in the BPMV.
5. This step determines whether the DTC is current.

GC4020051900010X

Fig. 304 Code C1271: LF TCS Master Cylinder Isolation Valve Fault (Part 1 of 2). Eldorado

Step	Action	Value(s)	Yes	No
1	Did you perform the ABS Diagnostic System Check?	—	Go to *Step 2*	Go to *A Diagnostic System Check - ABS*
2	1. Turn OFF the ignition. 2. Disconnect the EBCM connector. 3. Remove the EBCM from the BPMV. 4. Inspect the EBCM to BPMV connector for the following conditions, which could cause an intermittent: • Damage • Corrosion • Poor terminal contact • The presence of brake fluid Did you find and correct the condition?	—	Go to *Step 8*	Go to *Step 3*
3	1. Install the *J 41247* BPMV pinout box to the BPMV connector. 2. Measure the resistance between the solenoid valve control signal circuit and the solenoid power control circuit at *J 41247* BPMV pinout box. Is the resistance within the specified range?	• Inlet Solenoids: 8–12 Ω • Outlet Solenoids: 4–7 Ω • Isolation and Prime Solenoids: 8–12 Ω	Go to *Step 4*	Go to *Step 6*
4	Measure the resistance between the solenoid valve control signal circuit at the *J 41247* BPMV pinout box and the BPMV case. Is the resistance within the specified range?	OL (Infinite)	Go to *Step 5*	Go to *Step 6*
5	1. Remove the *J 41247* BPMV pinout box. 2. Reinstall the EBCM to BPMV. 3. Reconnect the EBCM connector. 4. Install a scan tool. 5. Turn ON the ignition, with the engine OFF. 6. With the scan tool, perform the Automated Test. Does the DTC reset?	—	Go to *Step 7*	Go to *Intermittent*
6	Replace the BPMV. Did you complete the repair?	—	Go to *Step 8*	—
7	Replace the EBCM. Did you complete the repair?	—	Go to *Step 8*	—
8	1. Use the scan tool in order to clear DTCs. 2. With the scan tool, perform the Automated Test. Does the DTC reset?	—	Go to *Step 2*	System OK

GC4020051900020X

Fig. 304 Code C1271: LF TCS Master Cylinder Isolation Valve Fault (Part 2 of 2). Eldorado

Circuit Description

The solenoid valve relay is energized when the ignition is ON. The solenoid valve relay supplies voltage to the solenoid valves. This voltage is referred to as the solenoid power voltage. The EBCM controls the solenoid valve by grounding the control circuit.

Conditions for Running the DTC

- The solenoid power voltage is greater than 8.0 volts.
- The ignition voltage is greater than 9.0 volts.

Conditions for Setting the DTC

The commanded state of the driver and the actual state of the control circuit do not match for 0.03 seconds.

Action Taken When the DTC Sets

If equipped, the following actions occur:

- The EBCM disables the ABS/TCS/VSES for the duration of the ignition cycle.
- The ABS indicator turns ON.
- The TRACTION CONTROL indicator turns ON.
- The DIC displays the SERVICE STABILITY SYS message.

Conditions for Clearing the DTC

- The condition for the DTC is no longer present (the DTC is not current) and you used the scan tool Clear DTC function.
- The condition for the DTC is no longer present (the DTC is not current) and you used the On-Board Diagnostics Clear DTC function.
- The EBCM automatically clears the history DTC when a current DTC is not detected in 50 consecutive drive cycles.

Diagnostic Aids

- Make sure the integrity of the connection between the EBCM and the BPMV is secure, tight, and free from corrosion.
- The solenoid valves are internal to the BPMV and can not be serviced individually. The solenoid valve circuits are internal to the EBCM and can not be serviced individually.

Test Description

The numbers below refer to step numbers on the diagnostic table.

3. This step tests the resistance value of the solenoid.
4. This step tests for a short to ground in the BPMV.
5. This step determines whether the DTC is current.

GC4020051901010X

Fig. 305 Code C1272: LF TCS Prime Valve Fault (Part 1 of 2). Eldorado

Step	Action	Value(s)	Yes	No
1	Did you perform the ABS Diagnostic System Check?	—	Go to *Step 2*	Go to *A Diagnostic System Check - ABS*
2	1. Turn OFF the ignition. 2. Disconnect the EBCM connector. 3. Remove the EBCM from the BPMV. 4. Inspect the EBCM to BPMV connector for the following conditions, which could cause an intermittent: • Damage • Corrosion • Poor terminal contact • The presence of brake fluid Did you find and correct the condition?	—	Go to *Step 8*	Go to *Step 3*
3	1. Install the *J 41247* BPMV pinout box to the BPMV connector. 2. Measure the resistance between the solenoid valve control signal circuit and the solenoid power control circuit at *J 41247* BPMV pinout box. Is the resistance within the specified range?	• Inlet Solenoids: 8–12 Ω • Outlet Solenoids: 4–7 Ω • Isolation and Prime Solenoids: 8–12 Ω	Go to *Step 4*	Go to *Step 6*
4	Measure the resistance between the solenoid valve control signal circuit at the *J 41247* BPMV pinout box and the BPMV case. Is the resistance within the specified range?	OL (Infinite)	Go to *Step 5*	Go to *Step 6*
5	1. Remove the *J 41247* BPMV pinout box. 2. Reinstall the EBCM to BPMV. 3. Reconnect the EBCM connector. 4. Install a scan tool. 5. Turn ON the ignition, with the engine OFF. 6. With the scan tool, perform the Automated Test. Does the DTC reset?	—	Go to *Step 7*	Go to *Intermittent*
6	Replace the BPMV. Did you complete the repair?	—	Go to *Step 8*	—
7	Replace the EBCM. Did you complete the repair?	—	Go to *Step 8*	—
8	1. Use the scan tool in order to clear DTCs. 2. With the scan tool, perform the Automated Test. Does the DTC reset?	—	Go to *Step 2*	System OK

GC4020051901020X

Fig. 305 Code C1272: LF TCS Prime Valve Fault (Part 2 of 2). Eldorado

Step	Action	Value(s)	Yes	No
1	Did you perform the ABS Diagnostic System Check?	—	Go to *Step 2*	Go to *A Diagnostic System Check - ABS*
2	1. Turn OFF the ignition. 2. Disconnect the EBCM connector. 3. Remove the EBCM from the BPMV. 4. Inspect the EBCM to BPMV connector for the following conditions, which could cause an intermittent: • Damage • Corrosion • Poor terminal contact • The presence of brake fluid Did you find and correct the condition?	—	Go to *Step 8*	Go to *Step 3*
3	1. Install the *J 41247* BPMV pinout box to the BPMV connector. 2. Measure the resistance between the solenoid valve control signal circuit and the solenoid power control circuit at *J 41247* BPMV pinout box. Is the resistance within the specified range?	• Inlet Solenoids: 8–12 Ω • Outlet Solenoids: 4–7 Ω • Isolation and Prime Solenoids: 8–12 Ω	Go to *Step 4*	Go to *Step 6*
4	Measure the resistance between the solenoid valve control signal circuit at the *J 41247* BPMV pinout box and the BPMV case. Is the resistance within the specified range?	OL (Infinite)	Go to *Step 5*	Go to *Step 6*
5	1. Remove the *J 41247* BPMV pinout box. 2. Reinstall the EBCM to BPMV. 3. Reconnect the EBCM connector. 4. Install a scan tool. 5. Turn ON the ignition, with the engine OFF. 6. With the scan tool, perform the Automated Test. Does the DTC reset?	—	Go to *Step 7*	Go to *Intermittent*
6	Replace the BPMV. Did you complete the repair?	—	Go to *Step 8*	—
7	Replace the EBCM. Did you complete the repair?	—	Go to *Step 8*	—
8	1. Use the scan tool in order to clear DTCs. 2. With the scan tool, perform the Automated Test. Does the DTC reset?	—	Go to *Step 2*	System OK

GC4020051902020X

Fig. 306 Code C1273: RF TCS Master Cylinder Isolation Valve Fault (Part 2 of 2). Eldorado

Circuit Description

The solenoid valve relay is energized when the ignition is ON. The solenoid valve relay supplies voltage to the solenoid valves. This voltage is referred to as the solenoid power voltage. The EBCM controls the solenoid valve by grounding the control circuit.

Conditions for Running the DTC

- The solenoid power voltage is greater than 8.0 volts.
- The ignition voltage is greater than 9.0 volts.

Conditions for Setting the DTC

The commanded state of the driver and the actual state of the control circuit do not match for 0.03 seconds.

Action Taken When the DTC Sets

If equipped, the following actions occur:

- The EBCM disables the ABS/TCS/VSES for the duration of the ignition cycle.
- The ABS indicator turns ON.
- The TRACTION CONTROL indicator turns ON.
- The DIC displays the SERVICE STABILITY SYS message.

Conditions for Clearing the DTC

- The condition for the DTC is no longer present (the DTC is not current) and you used the scan tool Clear DTC function.
- The condition for the DTC is no longer present (the DTC is not current) and you used the On-Board Diagnostics Clear DTC function.
- The EBCM automatically clears the history DTC when a current DTC is not detected in 50 consecutive drive cycles.

Diagnostic Aids

- Make sure the integrity of the connection between the EBCM and the BPMV is secure, tight, and free from corrosion.
- The solenoid valves are internal to the BPMV and can not be serviced individually. The solenoid valve circuits are internal to the EBCM and can not be serviced individually.

Test Description

The numbers below refer to step numbers on the diagnostic table.

3. This step tests the resistance value of the solenoid.
4. This step tests for a short to ground in the BPMV.
5. This step determines whether the DTC is current.

GC4020051902010X

Fig. 306 Code C1273: RF TCS Master Cylinder Isolation Valve Fault (Part 1 of 2). Eldorado

Circuit Description

The solenoid valve relay is energized when the ignition is ON. The solenoid valve relay supplies voltage to the solenoid valves. This voltage is referred to as the solenoid power voltage. The EBCM controls the solenoid valve by grounding the control circuit.

Conditions for Running the DTC

- The solenoid power voltage is greater than 8.0 volts.
- The ignition voltage is greater than 9.0 volts.

Conditions for Setting the DTC

The commanded state of the driver and the actual state of the control circuit do not match for 0.03 seconds.

Action Taken When the DTC Sets

If equipped, the following actions occur:

- The EBCM disables the ABS/TCS/VSES for the duration of the ignition cycle.
- The ABS indicator turns ON.
- The TRACTION CONTROL indicator turns ON.
- The DIC displays the SERVICE STABILITY SYS message.

Conditions for Clearing the DTC

- The condition for the DTC is no longer present (the DTC is not current) and you used the scan tool Clear DTC function.
- The condition for the DTC is no longer present (the DTC is not current) and you used the On-Board Diagnostics Clear DTC function.
- The EBCM automatically clears the history DTC when a current DTC is not detected in 50 consecutive drive cycles.

Diagnostic Aids

- Make sure the integrity of the connection between the EBCM and the BPMV is secure, tight, and free from corrosion.
- The solenoid valves are internal to the BPMV and can not be serviced individually. The solenoid valve circuits are internal to the EBCM and can not be serviced individually.

Test Description

The numbers below refer to step numbers on the diagnostic table.

3. This step tests the resistance value of the solenoid.
4. This step tests for a short to ground in the BPMV.
5. This step determines whether the DTC is current.

GC4020051903010X

Fig. 307 Code C1274: RF TCS Prime Valve Fault (Part 1 of 2). Eldorado

Step	Action	Value(s)	Yes	No
1	Did you perform the ABS Diagnostic System Check?	—	Go to *Step 2*	Go to *A Diagnostic System Check - ABS*
2	1. Turn OFF the ignition. 2. Disconnect the EBCM connector. 3. Remove the EBCM from the BPMV. 4. Inspect the EBCM to BPMV connector for the following conditions, which could cause an intermittent: • Damage • Corrosion • Poor terminal contact • The presence of brake fluid Did you find and correct the condition?	—	Go to *Step 8*	Go to *Step 3*
3	1. Install the *J 41247* BPMV pinout box to the BPMV connector. 2. Measure the resistance between the solenoid valve control signal circuit and the solenoid power control circuit at *J 41247* BPMV pinout box. Is the resistance within the specified range?	• Inlet Solenoids: 8–12 Ω • Outlet Solenoids: 4–7 Ω • Isolation and Prime Solenoids: 8–12 Ω	Go to *Step 4*	Go to *Step 6*
4	Measure the resistance between the solenoid valve control signal circuit at the *J 41247* BPMV pinout box and the BPMV case. Is the resistance within the specified range?	OL (Infinite)	Go to *Step 5*	Go to *Step 6*
5	1. Remove the *J 41247* BPMV pinout box. 2. Reinstall the EBCM to BPMV. 3. Reconnect the EBCM connector. 4. Install a scan tool. 5. Turn ON the ignition, with the engine OFF. 6. With the scan tool, perform the Automated Test. Does the DTC reset?	—	Go to *Step 7*	Go to *Intermittent*
6	Replace the BPMV. Did you complete the repair?	—	Go to *Step 8*	—
7	Replace the EBCM. Did you complete the repair?	—	Go to *Step 8*	—
8	1. Use the scan tool in order to clear DTCs. 2. With the scan tool, perform the Automated Test. Does the DTC reset?	—	Go to *Step 2*	System OK

GC4020051903020X

Fig. 307 Code C1274: RF TCS Prime Valve Fault (Part 2 of 2). Eldorado

Conditions for Clearing the DTC

- The condition for the DTC is no longer present (the DTC is not current) and you used the scan tool Clear DTC function.
- The condition for the DTC is no longer present (the DTC is not current) and you used the On-Board Diagnostics Clear DTC function.
- The EBCM automatically clears the history DTC when a current DTC is not detected in 50 consecutive drive cycles.

Diagnostic Aids

The following conditions can cause this concern:

- An open in the delivered torque circuit.
- An short to ground or voltage in the delivered torque circuit.
- A wiring problem, terminal corrosion, or poor connection in the delivered torque circuit.
- A communication frequency problem.
- A communication duty cycle problem.
- The EBCM is not receiving information from the PCM.
- Loose or corroded EBCM ground or PCM ground.

Test Description

The numbers below refer to the step numbers on the diagnostic table.

3. This step uses the scan tool to determine whether the delivered torque signal has a valid duty cycle.
4. This step measures whether the delivered torque signal has a valid duty cycle.
5. This step measures whether the delivered torque signal has a valid frequency.

Step	Action	Value(s)	Yes	No
1	Did you perform the ABS Diagnostic System Check?	—	Go to *Step 2*	Go to *A Diagnostic System Check - ABS*
2	Inspect the EBCM ground and PCM ground, making sure each ground is clean and torqued to the proper specification. Did you find and correct the condition?	—	Go to *Step 13*	Go to *Step 3*
3	1. Install a scan tool. 2. Start the engine. 3. With the scan tool, observe the Delivered Torque parameter in the Delco/Bosch ABS/TCS ICCS (if equipped) data list. Does the scan tool display within the specified range?	5–95%	Go to *Intermittent*	Go to *Step 4*
4	1. Turn OFF the ignition. 2. Disconnect the EBCM harness connector. 3. Install the *J 39700* universal breakout box using the *J 39700-25* cable adapter to the EBCM harness connector and the EBCM connector. 4. Start the engine. 5. Measure the DC duty cycle at the *J 39700* universal pinout box between the delivered torque signal circuit and a good ground. Does the duty cycle measure within the specified range?	5–95%	Go to *Step 5*	Go to *Step 6*
5	Measure the DC Hz at the *J 39700* universal pinout box between the delivered torque signal circuit and a good ground. Does the frequency measure within the specified range?	121–134 Hz	Go to *Step 10*	Go to *Step 9*
6	1. Turn OFF the ignition. 2. Disconnect the powertrain control module (PCM) harness connector. 3. Turn ON the ignition, with the engine OFF. 4. Measure the voltage from the delivered torque signal circuit to a good ground. Does the voltage measure near the specified value?	B+	Go to *Step 7*	Go to *Step 8*

GC4020051904020X

Fig. 308 Code C1276: Delivered Torque Signal Circuit Fault (Part 2 of 3). Eldorado

Circuit Description

The EBCM and the PCM simultaneously control the traction control. The PCM sends a Delivered Torque message via a pulse width modulated (PWM) signal to the EBCM. The duty cycle of the signal is used to determine how much engine torque the PCM is delivering. Normal values are between 10 and 90 percent duty cycle. The signal should be at low values (around 10 percent) at idle and higher values under driving conditions. The EBCM supplies the pull up voltage that the PCM switches to ground to create the signal.

Conditions for Running the DTC

The ignition is ON.

Conditions for Setting the DTC

One of the following conditions occurs:

- The delivered torque PWM signal is less than 5 percent duty cycle or greater than 95 percent duty cycle.
- The EBCM does not receive a delivered torque PWM signal for a period of 7 seconds.

Action Taken When the DTC Sets

- The EBCM disables the TCS for the duration of the ignition cycle.
- The TRACTION CONTROL indicator turns ON.
- The ABS remains functional.

GC4020051904010X

Fig. 308 Code C1276: Delivered Torque Signal Circuit Fault (Part 1 of 3). Eldorado

Step	Action	Value(s)	Yes	No
7	1. Turn OFF the ignition. 2. Disconnect the *J 39700-25* cable adapter from the EBCM connector. 3. Test the delivered torque signal circuit for a short to voltage. Did you find and correct the condition?	—	Go to *Step 13*	Go to *Step 9*
8	1. Turn OFF the ignition. 2. Disconnect the *J 39700-25* cable adapter from the EBCM connector. 3. Test the delivered torque signal circuit for the following conditions: • An open • A short to ground • A high resistance Did you find and correct the condition?	—	Go to *Step 13*	Go to *Step 10*
9	Inspect for poor connections the harness connector of the PCM. Did you find and correct the condition?	—	Go to *Step 13*	Go to *Step 11*
10	Inspect for poor connections the harness connector of the EBCM. Did you find and correct the condition?	—	Go to *Step 13*	Go to *Step 12*
11	**Important:** The replacement PCM must be programmed. Did you find and correct the condition?	—	Go to *Step 13*	—
12	Replace the EBCM. Did you complete the repair?	—	Go to *Step 13*	—
13	1. Use the scan tool in order to clear the DTCs. 2. Operate the vehicle within the Conditions for Running the DTC. Does the DTC reset?	—	Go to *Step 2*	System OK

GC4020051904030X

Fig. 308 Code C1276: Delivered Torque Signal Circuit Fault (Part 3 of 3). Eldorado

Circuit Description

The EBCM and the PCM simultaneously control the traction control. The EBCM sends a Requested Torque message via a pulse width modulated (PWM) signal to the PCM. The duty cycle of the signal is used to determine how much engine torque the EBCM is requesting the PCM to deliver. Normal values are between 10 and 90 percent duty cycle. The signal should be at 90 percent when traction control is not active and at lower values during traction control activations. The PCM supplies the pull up voltage that the EBCM switches to ground to create the signal.

Conditions for Running the DTC

The ignition is ON.

Conditions for Setting the DTC

The PCM diagnoses the requested torque PWM signal circuit and sends a class 2 serial data message to the EBCM indicating a fault is present. The PCM will set DTC P1571 and the EBCM will set DTC C1277. A fault exists in the circuit if the PCM detects one of the following conditions:

- The requested torque PWM signal is less than 5 percent duty cycle or greater than 95 percent duty cycle.
- The requested torque PWM signal is not present for 10 seconds.

Action Taken When the DTC Sets

- The EBCM disables the TCS for the duration of the ignition cycle.
- The TRACTION CONTROL indicator turns ON.
- The ABS remains functional.

GC4020051905010X

Fig. 309 Code C1277: Requested Torque Signal Circuit Fault (Part 1 of 3). Eldorado

Conditions for Clearing the DTC

- The condition for the DTC is no longer present (the DTC is not current) and you used the scan tool Clear DTC function.
- The condition for the DTC is no longer present (the DTC is not current) and you used the On-Board Diagnostics Clear DTC function.
- The EBCM automatically clears the history DTC when a current DTC is not detected in 50 consecutive drive cycles.

Diagnostic Aids

The following conditions can cause this concern:

- An open in the requested torque circuit.
- An short to ground or voltage in the requested torque circuit.
- A wiring problem, terminal corrosion, or poor connection in the requested torque circuit.
- A communication frequency problem.
- A communication duty cycle problem.
- The PCM is not receiving information from the EBCM.
- Loose or corroded EBCM ground or PCM ground.

Test Description

The numbers below refer to the step numbers on the diagnostic table.

4. This step uses the scan tool to determine whether the requested torque signal has a valid duty cycle.
5. This step measures whether the requested torque signal has a valid duty cycle.
6. This step measures whether the EBCM requested torque signal has a valid frequency.

Step	Action	Value(s)	Yes	No
1	Did you perform the ABS Diagnostic System Check?	—	Go to *Step 2*	Go to *A Diagnostic System Check - ABS*
2	1. Install a scan tool. 2. Start the engine. 3. With the scan tool, observe the DTC information parameter in the PCM Diagnostic Trouble Codes (DTCs). Does the scan tool display DTC P1571 as current?	—	*DTC P1571 Traction Control Torque Request Circuit*	Go to *Step 3*
3	Inspect the EBCM ground and PCM ground, making sure each ground is clean and torqued to the proper specification. Did you find and correct the condition?	—	Go to *Step 14*	Go to *Step 4*
4	With the scan tool, observe the Requested Torque parameter in the Delco/Bosch ABS/TCS ICCS (if equipped) data list. Does the scan tool display within the specified range?	5–95%	Go to *Intermittent*	Go to *Step 5*
5	1. Turn OFF the ignition. 2. Disconnect the EBCM harness connector. 3. Install the *J 39700* universal breakout box using the *J 39700-25* cable adapter to the EBCM harness connector and the EBCM connector. 4. Start the engine. 5. Measure the DC duty cycle between the requested torque signal circuit and a good ground. Is the duty cycle within the specified range?	5–95%	Go to *Step 6*	Go to *Step 7*
6	Measure the DC Hz between the requested torque signal circuit and a good ground. Does the frequency measure within the specified range?	121–134 Hz	Go to *Step 11*	Go to *Step 10*

GC4020051905020X

Fig. 309 Code C1277: Requested Torque Signal Circuit Fault (Part 2 of 3). Eldorado

Step	Action	Value(s)	Yes	No
7	1. Turn OFF the ignition. 2. Disconnect the *J 39700-25* cable adapter from the EBCM connector. **Important:** Disconnecting the EBCM connector and turning ON the ignition could cause other modules to set loss of communication DTCs (Uxxxx). Once the EBCM is reconnected, the EBCM may set DTC C1298 PCM Class 2 Serial Data Link Malfunction. 3. Turn ON the ignition, with the engine OFF. 4. Measure the voltage from the requested torque signal circuit to a good ground. Does the voltage measure near or greater than the specified value?	5 V	Go to *Step 8*	Go to *Step 9*
8	1. Turn OFF the ignition. 2. Disconnect the powertrain control module (PCM) harness connector. 3. Test the requested torque signal circuit for a short to voltage. Did you find and correct the condition?	—	Go to *Step 14*	Go to *Step 11*
9	1. Turn OFF the ignition. 2. Disconnect the powertrain control module (PCM) harness connector. 3. Test the requested torque signal circuit for the following conditions: • An open • A short to ground • A high resistance. Did you find and correct the condition?	—	Go to *Step 14*	Go to *Step 10*
10	Inspect for poor connections the harness connector of the PCM. Did you find and correct the condition?	—	Go to *Step 14*	Go to *Step 12*
11	Inspect for poor connections the harness connector of the EBCM. Did you find and correct the condition?	—	Go to *Step 14*	Go to *Step 13*
12	**Important:** The replacement PCM must be programmed. Replace the PCM. Did you find and correct the condition?	—	Go to *Step 14*	—
13	Replace the EBCM. Did you complete the repair?	—	Go to *Step 14*	—
14	1. Use the scan tool in order to clear the DTCs. 2. Operate the vehicle within the Conditions for Running the DTC. Does the DTC reset?	—	Go to *Step 2*	System OK

GC4020051905030X

Fig. 309 Code C1277: Requested Torque Signal Circuit Fault (Part 3 of 3). Eldorado

Circuit Description

The PCM monitors various parameters and will not allow traction control operation if any parameter falls outside a specified range.

Conditions for Running the DTC

The ignition is ON.

Conditions for Setting the DTC

The PCM diagnoses a condition preventing the engine control portion of the traction control function and sends a class 2 message to the EBCM indicating that torque reduction is not allowed. The PCM will typically set a DTC and the EBCM will set this DTC.

Action Taken When the DTC Sets

- The EBCM disables the TCS for the duration of the ignition cycle.
- The TRACTION CONTROL indicator turns ON.
- The ABS remains functional.

Conditions for Clearing the DTC

- The condition for the DTC is no longer present (the DTC is not current) and you used the scan tool Clear DTC function.
- The condition for the DTC is no longer present (the DTC is not current) and you used the On-Board Diagnostics Clear DTC function.
- The EBCM automatically clears the history DTC when a current DTC is not detected in 50 consecutive drive cycles.

Diagnostic Aids

This DTC is for information only. As an aid to the technician, this DTC indicates that there are no problems in the ABS/TCS system.

GC4020051906010X

Fig. 310 Code C1278: TCS Temporarily Inhibited By PCM (Part 1 of 2). Eldorado

Step	Action	Value(s)	Yes	No
1	Did you perform the ABS Diagnostic System Check?	—	Go to *Step 2*	Go to *A Diagnostic System Check - ABS*
2	1. Install a scan tool. 2. Turn ON the ignition, with the engine OFF. 3. With the scan tool, observe the Delco/Bosch ABS/TCS ICCS (if equipped) DTCs. Does the scan tool display DTC C1278 set as a current code?	—	Go to *Step 4*	Go to *Step 3*
3	1. Start the engine. 2. Carefully test drive the vehicle at a speed above the specified value. 3. Use the scan tool in order to monitor the Delco/Bosch ABS/TCS ICCS (if equipped) DTCs. 4. Repeat the drive cycle sequence twice. Did DTC C1278 set in the last 3 tests?	16 km/h (10 mph)	Go to *Step 4*	Go to Diagnostic Aids
4	Inspect the PCM. Did you find and correct the condition?	—	Go to *Step 5*	Go to Diagnostic Aids
5	1. Use the scan tool in order to clear the DTCs. 2. Operate the vehicle within the Conditions for Running the DTC. Does the DTC reset?	—	Go to *Step 2*	System OK

GC4020051906020X

Fig. 310 Code C1278: TCS Temporarily Inhibited By PCM (Part 2 of 2). Eldorado

Circuit Description

The vehicle stability enhancement system (VSES) is activated by the EBCM calculating the desired yaw rate and comparing it to the actual yaw rate input. The desired yaw rate is calculated from measured steering wheel position, vehicle speed, and lateral acceleration. The difference between the desired yaw rate and actual yaw rate is the yaw rate error, which is a measurement of oversteer or understeer. If the yaw rate error becomes too large, the EBCM will attempt to correct the vehicle's yaw motion by applying differential braking to the left or right front wheel.

Conditions for Running the DTC

- The steer angle has been centered.
- The VSES is active.
- The direction (understeer or oversteer) of the yaw rate error has not changed.
- The lateral acceleration is less than 0.5 g.

Conditions for Setting the DTC

One of the following conditions occur:

- The VSES is engaged for 10 seconds with the yaw rate error always in either understeer or oversteer. Under this condition, this DTC will set by itself.
- The yaw rate error is greater than 10 degrees/second for 5 seconds. Under this condition, this DTC will set along with DTC C1282.
- The yaw rate error is greater than 10 degrees/second with the vehicle speed less than 60 km/h (37 mph) and the acceleration pedal is pressed more than 25 percent of the pedal travel range for 1 second during the VSES activation. Under this condition, this DTC will set along with DTC C1282.
- With the steer rate less than 10 degrees/second, the difference between the analog steer angle and digital steer angle is greater than 20 degrees for 1 second. Under this condition, this DTC will set along with DTC C1287.

GC4020051907010X

Fig. 311 Code C1281: Stabilitrak Sensors Uncorrelated (Part 1 of 2). Eldorado

Action Taken When the DTC Sets

- The EBCM disables the VSES for the duration of the ignition cycle.
- The DIC displays the SERVICE STABILITY SYS message.
- The ABS/TCS remains functional.

Conditions for Clearing the DTC

- The condition for the DTC is no longer present (the DTC is not current) and you used the scan tool Clear DTC function.
- The condition for the DTC is no longer present (the DTC is not current) and you used the On-Board Diagnostics Clear DTC function.
- The EBCM automatically clears the history DTC when a current DTC is not detected in 50 consecutive drive cycles.

Diagnostic Aids

- During diagnosis, park the vehicle on a level surface.
- Check the vehicle for proper alignment. The car should not pull in either direction while driving straight on a level surface.
- Find out from the driver under what conditions the DTC was set (when the DIC displayed the SERVICE STABILITY SYS message). This information will help to duplicate the failure.
- The Snapshot function on the scan tool can help find an intermittent DTC.

Test Description

The numbers below refer to the step numbers on the diagnostic table.

2. This step performs the Steering Position Sensor Test to see if the steering wheel position sensor (SWPS) is operating properly.
3. This step checks to see if the yaw rate input parameter is within the valid range.

Step	Action	Value(s)	Yes	No
1	Did you perform the ABS Diagnostic System Check?	—	Go to *Step 2*	Go to *A Diagnostic System Check - ABS*
2	1. Install the scan tool. 2. Turn ON the ignition, with the engine OFF. 3. With the scan tool, perform the Steering Position Sensor Test in Delco/Bosch ABS/TCS ICCS2 Special Functions. Refer to *Scan Tool Diagnostics*. Did the steering wheel position pass the test?	—	Go to *Step 3*	Go to *Step 6*
3	With the scan tool, observe the Yaw Rate Sensor Input parameter in the Delco/Bosch ABS/TCS ICCS2 data list. Does the scan tool display within the specified range?	2.3–2.7 V	Go to *Step 4*	Go to *Step 7*
4	1. Use the scan tool in order to clear the DTCs. 2. Perform the Diagnostic Test Drive. Does the DTC reset?	—	Go to *Step 5*	Go to Diagnostic Aids
5	Replace the EBCM. Did you complete the replacement?	—	Go to *Step 8*	—
6	Replace the steering wheel position sensor (SWPS). Did you complete the replacement?	—	Go to *Step 8*	—
7	Replace the yaw rate sensor. Did you complete the replacement?	—	Go to *Step 8*	—
8	1. Use the scan tool in order to clear the DTCs. 2. Operate the vehicle within the Conditions for Running the DTC. Does the DTC reset?	—	Go to *Step 2*	System OK

GC4020051907020X

Fig. 311 Code C1281: Stabilitrak Sensors Uncorrelated (Part 2 of 2). Eldorado

Conditions for Clearing the DTC

- The condition for the DTC is no longer present (the DTC is not current) and you used the scan tool Clear DTC function.
- The condition for the DTC is no longer present (the DTC is not current) and you used the On-Board Diagnostics Clear DTC function.
- The EBCM automatically clears the history DTC when a current DTC is not detected in 50 consecutive drive cycles.

Diagnostic Aids

- During diagnosis, park the vehicle on a level surface.
- Check the vehicle for proper alignment. The car should not pull in either direction while driving straight on a level surface.
- Find out from the driver under what conditions the DTC was set (when the DIC displayed the SERVICE STABILITY SYS message). This information will help to duplicate the failure.
- The Snapshot function on the scan tool can help find an intermittent DTC.

Test Description

The number below refers to the step number on the diagnostic table.

3. Tests for the proper operation of the circuit in the low voltage range.
4. Tests for the proper operation of the circuit in the high voltage range. If the fuse in the jumper opens when you perform this test, the signal circuit is shorted to ground.
5. Tests for a short to voltage in the 5 volt reference circuit.
6. Tests for a high resistance or an open in the ground circuit.

Step	Action	Value(s)	Yes	No
1	Did you perform the ABS Diagnostic System Check?	—	Go to *Step 2*	Go to *A Diagnostic System Check - ABS*
2	1. Install a scan tool. 2. Turn ON the ignition, with the engine OFF. 3. With the scan tool, observe the Yaw Rate Sensor Input parameter in the Delco/Bosch ABS/TCS ICCS2 data list. Does the scan tool display that the Yaw Rate Sensor Input parameter is within the specified range?	0.15–4.85 V	Go to Diagnostic Aids	Go to *Step 3*
3	1. Turn OFF the ignition. 2. Disconnect the yaw rate sensor connector. 3. Turn ON the ignition, with the engine OFF. 4. With the scan tool, observe the Yaw Rate Sensor Input parameter. Does the scan tool indicate that the Yaw Rate Sensor Input parameter is less than the specified value?	0.15 V	Go to *Step 4*	Go to *Step 10*
4	1. Turn OFF the ignition. 2. Connect a 3 amp fused jumper wire between the 5 volt reference circuit of the yaw rate sensor and the signal circuit of the yaw rate sensor. 3. Turn ON the ignition, with the engine OFF. 4. With the scan tool, observe the Yaw Rate Sensor Input parameter. Does the scan tool indicate that the Yaw Rate Sensor Input parameter is greater than the specified value?	4.85 V	Go to *Step 5*	Go to *Step 8*
5	1. Disconnect the fused jumper wire. 2. Measure the voltage between the 5 volt reference circuit of the yaw rate sensor and the ground circuit of the yaw rate sensor. Does the voltage measure less the specified value?	5 V	Go to *Step 6*	Go to *Step 7*

GC4020051908020X

Fig. 312 Code C1282: Yaw Rate Sensor Bias Circuit Fault (Part 2 of 3). Eldorado

Circuit Description

The vehicle stability enhancement system (VSES) is activated by the EBCM calculating the desired yaw rate and comparing it to the actual yaw rate input. The desired yaw rate is calculated from measured steering wheel position, vehicle speed, and lateral acceleration. The difference between the desired yaw rate and actual yaw rate is the yaw rate error, which is a measurement of oversteer or understeer. If the yaw rate error becomes too large, the EBCM will attempt to correct the vehicle's yaw motion by applying differential braking to the left or right front wheel.

Conditions for Running the DTC

The EBCM performs 4 different tests to detect a DTC condition. The numbers below correspond to the numbers in Conditions for Setting the DTC.

1. The yaw rate sensor bias test runs with the ignition ON.
2. The yaw rate sensor acceleration test runs with the ignition ON.
3. The yaw rate sensor circuit test runs with the vehicle stopped or with the vehicle speed greater than 40 km/h (25 mph).
4. The yaw rate isolation test runs with the VSES active.

Conditions for Setting the DTC

The EBCM performs 4 different tests to detect a DTC condition. The numbers below correspond to the numbers in Conditions for Running the DTC.

1. The yaw rate bias is greater than 7 degrees/second.
2. The yaw rate input change is greater than 390 degrees/second/second.
3. The yaw rate input voltage is less than 0.15 volts or greater than 4.85 volts for 1 second.
4. The yaw rate error is greater than 10 degrees/second for 5 seconds. Under this condition, this DTC will set along with DTC C1281.

Action Taken When the DTC Sets

- The EBCM disables the VSES for the duration of the ignition cycle.
- The DIC displays the SERVICE STABILITY SYS message.
- The ABS/TCS remains functional.

GC4020051908010X

Fig. 312 Code C1282: Yaw Rate Sensor Bias Circuit Fault (Part 1 of 3). Eldorado

Step	Action	Value(s)	Yes	No
6	1. Turn OFF the ignition. 2. Disconnect the negative battery cable. 3. Measure the resistance from the ground circuit of the yaw rate sensor to a good ground. Does the resistance measure less than the specified value?	5 Ω	Go to *Step 12*	Go to *Step 11*
7	Test the 5 volt reference circuit of the yaw rate sensor for a short to voltage. Did you find and correct the condition?	—	Go to *Step 16*	Go to *Step 13*
8	Test the 5 volt reference circuit of the yaw rate sensor for the following conditions: • An open • A short to ground • A high resistance. Did you find and correct the condition?	—	Go to *Step 16*	Go to *Step 9*
9	Test the signal circuit of the yaw rate sensor for the following conditions: • An open • A short to ground • A high resistance. Did you find and correct the condition?	—	Go to *Step 16*	Go to *Step 13*
10	Test the signal circuit of the yaw rate sensor for a short to voltage. Did you find and correct the condition?	—	Go to *Step 16*	Go to *Step 13*
11	1. Disconnect the EBCM harness connector. 2. Install the *J 39700* universal pinout box using the *J 39700-25* cable adapter to the EBCM harness connector only. 3. Test the ground circuit of the yaw rate sensor for a high resistance or an open. Did you find and correct the condition?	—	Go to *Step 16*	Go to *Step 13*
12	Inspect for poor connections at the harness connector of the yaw rate sensor. Did you find and correct the condition?	—	Go to *Step 16*	Go to *Step 14*
13	Inspect for poor connections at the harness connector of the EBCM. Did you find and correct the condition?	—	Go to *Step 16*	Go to *Step 15*
14	Replace the yaw rate sensor. Did you complete the replacement?	—	Go to *Step 16*	—
15	Replace the EBCM. Did you complete the replacement?	—	Go to *Step 16*	—
16	1. Clear the DTCs using the scan tool. 2. Operate the vehicle within the Conditions for Running the DTC as specified in the supporting text. Does the DTC reset?	—	Go to *Step 2*	System OK

GC4020051908030X

Fig. 312 Code C1282: Yaw Rate Sensor Bias Circuit Fault (Part 3 of 3). Eldorado

Circuit Description

The steering wheel position sensor supplies 1 analog input and 2 digital inputs, Phase A and Phase B, to the EBCM. By interpreting the relationship between the inputs, the EBCM can determine the position of the steering wheel and the direction of steering wheel rotation.

Steer angle centering is the process by which the EBCM calibrates the steering sensor output so that the output reads zero when the steering wheel is centered. Using the yaw rate input, lateral accelerometer input, and wheel speed sensor inputs, the initial steering center position is calculated after driving greater than 10 km/h (6 mph) for more than 10 seconds in a straight line on a level surface.

Conditions for Running the DTC

The vehicle speed is greater than 40 km/h (25 mph).

Conditions for Setting the DTC

The vehicle has driven for 10 minutes without completing steer angle centering.

Action Taken When the DTC Sets

- The EBCM disables the VSES for the duration of the ignition cycle.
- The DIC displays the SERVICE STABILITY SYS message.
- The ABS/TCS remains functional.

Conditions for Clearing the DTC

- The condition for the DTC is no longer present (the DTC is not current) and you used the scan tool Clear DTC function.
- The condition for the DTC is no longer present (the DTC is not current) and you used the On-Board Diagnostics Clear DTC function.
- The EBCM automatically clears the history DTC when a current DTC is not detected in 50 consecutive drive cycles.

Diagnostic Aids

- During diagnosis, park the vehicle on a level surface.
- Check the vehicle for proper alignment. The car should not pull in either direction while driving straight on a level surface.
- Find out from the driver under what conditions the DTC was set (when the DIC displayed the SERVICE STABILITY SYS message). This information will help to duplicate the failure.
- The Snapshot function on the scan tool can help find an intermittent DTC.

GC4020051909010X

Fig. 313 Code C1283: Excessive Time To Center Steering (Part 1 of 2). Eldorado

Test Description

The numbers below refer to the step numbers on the diagnostic table.

2. This step performs the Steering Position Sensor Test to see if the steering wheel position sensor (SWPS) is operating properly.
3. This step tests to see if the lateral accelerometer input parameter is within the valid range.
4. This step tests to see if the yaw rate input parameter is within the valid range.

Step	Action	Value(s)	Yes	No
1	Did you perform the ABS Diagnostic System Check?	—	Go to *Step 2*	Go to *A Diagnostic System Check - ABS*
2	1. Install a scan tool. 2. Turn ON the ignition, with the engine OFF. 3. Use the scan tool in order to perform the Steering Position Sensor Test in the Delco/Bosch ABS/TCS ICCS2 Special Functions. Refer to *Scan Tool Diagnostics*. Did the steering wheel position sensor (SWPS) pass the test?	—	Go to *Step 3*	Go to *Step 7*
3	With the scan tool, observe the Lateral Accelerometer Input parameter in the Delco/Bosch ABS/TCS ICCS2 data list. Does the scan tool display within the specified range?	2.3–2.7 V	Go to *Step 4*	Go to *Step 8*
4	With the scan tool, observe the Yaw Rate Sensor Input parameter in the Delco/Bosch ABS/TCS ICCS2 data list. Does the scan tool display within the specified range?	2.3–2.7 V	Go to *Step 5*	Go to *Step 9*
5	1. Use the scan tool in order to clear the DTCs. 2. Perform the Diagnostic Test Drive. Does the DTC reset?	—	Go to *Step 6*	Go to Diagnostic Aids
6	Replace the EBCM. Did you complete the replacement?	—	Go to *Step 10*	—
7	Replace the steering wheel position sensor (SWPS). Did you complete the replacement?	—	Go to *Step 10*	—
8	Replace the lateral accelerometer sensor. Did you complete the replacement?	—	Go to *Step 10*	—
9	Replace the yaw rate sensor. Did you complete the replacement?	—	Go to *Step 10*	—
10	1. Use the scan tool in order to clear the DTCs. 2. Operate the vehicle within the Conditions for Running the DTC. Does the DTC reset?	—	Go to *Step 2*	System OK

GC4020051909020X

Fig. 313 Code C1283: Excessive Time To Center Steering (Part 2 of 2). Eldorado

Circuit Description

The vehicle stability enhancement system (VSES) uses the lateral accelerometer input when calculating the desired yaw rate. The usable output voltage range for the lateral accelerometer is 0.25–4.75 volts. The scan tool will report zero lateral acceleration as 2.5 volts with no sensor bias present.

The lateral accelerometer sensor bias compensates for sensor mounting alignment errors and electronic signal errors.

Conditions for Running the DTC

The EBCM performs 2 different tests to detect a DTC condition. The number below corresponds to the number in Conditions for Setting the DTC.

1. The lateral accelerometer self test is run at initialization. The output of the sensor will be offset by a large fixed amount for a short period of time after ignition power is first applied to the EBCM. The test will run under the following conditions:
   - The ignition is ON.
   - All 4 wheel speeds are 0 km/h (0 mph).
   - The steer angle is within 90 degrees of centered.
   - The period of time between 0.23 seconds and 0.28 seconds after ignition power is first applied to the EBCM.
2. The lateral accelerometer bias test is run with the ignition ON.

Conditions for Setting the DTC

One of the following conditions occurs:

1. The lateral accelerometer signal does not increase by 0.4 g above the normal signal level.
2. The compensated bias value of the lateral accelerometer is greater than 0.3 g.

Action Taken When the DTC Sets

- The EBCM disables the VSES for the duration of the ignition cycle.
- The DIC displays the SERVICE STABILITY SYS message.
- The ABS/TCS remains functional.

Conditions for Clearing the DTC

- The condition for the DTC is no longer present (the DTC is not current) and you used the scan tool Clear DTC function.
- The condition for the DTC is no longer present (the DTC is not current) and you used the On-Board Diagnostics Clear DTC function.
- The EBCM automatically clears the history DTC when a current DTC is not detected in 50 consecutive drive cycles.

GC4020051910010X

Fig. 314 Code C1284: Lateral Accelerometer Sensor Self Test Fault (Part 1 of 2). Eldorado

Diagnostic Aids

- During diagnosis, park the vehicle on a level surface.
- Check the vehicle for proper alignment. The car should not pull in either direction while driving straight on a level surface.
- Find out from the driver under what conditions the DTC was set (when the DIC displayed the SERVICE STABILITY SYS message). This information will help to duplicate the failure.
- The Snapshot function on the scan tool can help find an intermittent DTC.

Step	Action	Value(s)	Yes	No
1	Did you perform the ABS Diagnostic System Check?	—	Go to *Step 2*	Go to *A Diagnostic System Check - ABS*
2	1. Install a scan tool. 2. Turn ON the ignition, with the engine OFF. 3. Use the scan tool in order to clear the DTCs. 4. Perform the Diagnostic Test Drive. Does the DTC reset?	—	Go to *Step 3*	Go to Diagnostic Aids
3	Replace the lateral accelerometer sensor. Did you complete the replacement?	—	Go to *Step 4*	—
4	1. Use the scan tool in order to clear the DTCs. 2. Perform the Diagnostic Test Drive. Does the DTC reset?	—	Go to *Step 5*	Go to Diagnostic Aids
5	Replace the EBCM. Did you complete the replacement?	—	Go to *Step 6*	—
6	1. Use the scan tool in order to clear the DTCs. 2. Operate the vehicle within the Conditions for Running the DTC. Does the DTC reset?	—	Go to *Step 2*	System OK

GC4020051910020X

Fig. 314 Code C1284: Lateral Accelerometer Sensor Self Test Fault (Part 2 of 2). Eldorado

Circuit Description

The vehicle stability enhancement system (VSES) uses the lateral accelerometer input when calculating the desired yaw rate. The usable output voltage range for the lateral accelerometer is 0.25–4.75 volts. The scan tool will report zero lateral acceleration as 2.5 volts with no sensor bias present.

The lateral accelerometer sensor bias compensates for sensor mounting alignment errors and electronic signal errors.

Conditions for Running the DTC

The ignition is ON.

Conditions for Setting the DTC

The lateral accelerometer input voltage is less than 0.15 volts or greater than 4.85 volts for 1 second.

Action Taken When the DTC Sets

- The EBCM disables the VSES for the duration of the ignition cycle.
- The DIC displays the SERVICE STABILITY SYS message.
- The ABS/TCS remains functional.

Conditions for Clearing the DTC

- The condition for the DTC is no longer present (the DTC is not current) and you used the scan tool Clear DTC function.
- The condition for the DTC is no longer present (the DTC is not current) and you used the On-Board Diagnostics Clear DTC function.
- The EBCM automatically clears the history DTC when a current DTC is not detected in 50 consecutive drive cycles.

Diagnostic Aids

- During diagnosis, park the vehicle on a level surface.
- Check the vehicle for proper alignment. The car should not pull in either direction while driving straight on a level surface.
- Find out from the driver under what conditions the DTC was set (when the DIC displayed the SERVICE STABILITY SYS message). This information will help to duplicate the failure.
- The Snapshot function on the scan tool can help find an intermittent DTC.

GC4020051911010X

Fig. 315 Code C1285: Lateral Accelerometer Sensor Circuit Fault (Part 1 of 3). Eldorado

Test Description

The number below refers to the step number on the diagnostic table.

3. Tests for the proper operation of the circuit in the low voltage range.
4. Tests for the proper operation of the circuit in the high voltage range. If the fuse in the jumper opens when you perform this test, the signal circuit is shorted to ground.
5. Tests for a short to voltage in the 5 volt reference circuit.
6. Tests for a high resistance or an open in the ground circuit.

Step	Action	Value(s)	Yes	No
1	Did you perform the ABS Diagnostic System Check?	—	Go to *Step 2*	Go to *A Diagnostic System Check - ABS*
2	1. Install a scan tool. 2. Turn ON the ignition, with the engine OFF. 3. With the scan tool, observe the Lateral Accelerometer Input parameter in the Delco/Bosch ABS/TCS ICCS2 data list. Does the scan tool display that the Lateral Accelerometer Input parameter is within the specified range?	0.15–4.85 V	Go to Diagnostic Aids	*Go to Step 3*
3	1. Turn OFF the ignition. 2. Disconnect the lateral accelerometer sensor connector. 3. Turn ON the ignition, with the engine OFF. 4. With the scan tool, observe the Lateral Accelerometer Input parameter. Does the scan tool indicate that the Lateral Accelerometer Input parameter is less than the specified value?	0.15 V	*Go to Step 4*	*Go to Step 10*
4	1. Turn OFF the ignition. 2. Connect a 3 amp fused jumper wire between the 5 volt reference circuit of the lateral accelerometer sensor and the signal circuit of the lateral accelerometer sensor. 3. Turn ON the ignition, with the engine OFF. 4. With the scan tool, observe the Lateral Accelerometer Input parameter. Does the scan tool indicate that the Lateral Accelerometer Input parameter is greater than the specified value?	4.85 V	*Go to Step 5*	*Go to Step 8*
5	1. Disconnect the fused jumper wire. 2. Measure the voltage between the 5 volt reference circuit of the lateral accelerometer sensor and the ground circuit of the lateral accelerometer. Does the voltage measure less the specified value?	5 V	*Go to Step 6*	*Go to Step 7*
6	1. Turn OFF the ignition. 2. Disconnect the negative battery cable. 3. Measure the resistance from the ground circuit of the lateral accelerometer sensor to a good ground. Does the resistance measure less than the specified value?	5 Ω	*Go to Step 12*	*Go to Step 11*

GC4020051911020X

Fig. 315 Code C1285: Lateral Accelerometer Sensor Circuit Fault (Part 2 of 3). Eldorado

Step	Action	Value(s)	Yes	No
7	Test the 5 volt reference circuit of the lateral accelerometer sensor for a short to voltage. Did you find and correct the condition?	—	*Go to Step 16*	*Go to Step 13*
8	Test the 5 volt reference circuit of the lateral accelerometer sensor for the following conditions: • An open • A short to ground • A high resistance Did you find and correct the condition?	—	*Go to Step 16*	*Go to Step 9*
9	Test the signal circuit of the lateral accelerometer sensor for the following conditions: • An open • A short to ground • A high resistance Did you find and correct the condition?	—	*Go to Step 16*	*Go to Step 13*
10	Test the signal circuit of the lateral accelerometer sensor for a short to voltage. Did you find and correct the condition?	—	*Go to Step 16*	*Go to Step 13*
11	1. Disconnect the EBCM harness connector. 2. Install the *J 39700* universal pinout box using the *J 39700-25* cable adapter to the EBCM harness connector only. 3. Test the ground circuit of the lateral accelerometer sensor for a high resistance or an open. Did you find and correct the condition?	—	*Go to Step 16*	*Go to Step 13*
12	Inspect for poor connections at the harness connector of the lateral accelerometer sensor. Did you find and correct the condition?	—	*Go to Step 16*	*Go to Step 14*
13	Inspect for poor connections at the harness connector of the EBCM. Did you find and correct the condition?	—	*Go to Step 16*	*Go to Step 15*
14	Replace the lateral accelerometer sensor. Did you complete the replacement?	—	*Go to Step 16*	—
15	Replace the EBCM. Did you complete the replacement?	—	*Go to Step 16*	—
16	1. Clear the DTCs using the scan tool. 2. Operate the vehicle within the Conditions for Running the DTC as specified in the supporting text. Does the DTC reset?	—	*Go to Step 2*	System OK

GC4020051911030X

Fig. 315 Code C1285: Lateral Accelerometer Sensor Circuit Fault (Part 3 of 3). Eldorado

Circuit Description

The steering wheel position sensor supplies 1 analog input and 2 digital inputs, Phase A and Phase B, to the EBCM. By interpreting the relationship between the inputs, the EBCM can determine the position of the steering wheel and the direction of steering wheel rotation.

Steer angle centering is the process by which the EBCM calibrates the steering sensor output so that the output reads zero when the steering wheel is centered. Using the yaw rate input, lateral accelerometer input, and wheel speed sensor inputs, the initial steering center position is calculated after driving greater than 10 km/h (6 mph) for more than 10 seconds in a straight line on a level surface.

Conditions for Running the DTC

The steer angle has been centered.

Conditions for Setting the DTC

The steering sensor bias moves greater than 20 degrees after steer centering was accomplished.

Action Taken When the DTC Sets

- The EBCM disables the VSES for the duration of the ignition cycle.
- The DIC displays the SERVICE STABILITY SYS message.
- The ABS/TCS remains functional.

Conditions for Clearing the DTC

- The condition for the DTC is no longer present (the DTC is not current) and you used the scan tool Clear DTC function.
- The condition for the DTC is no longer present (the DTC is not current) and you used the On-Board Diagnostics Clear DTC function.
- The EBCM automatically clears the history DTC when a current DTC is not detected in 50 consecutive drive cycles.

Diagnostic Aids

- During diagnosis, park the vehicle on a level surface.
- Check the vehicle for proper alignment. The car should not pull in either direction while driving straight on a level surface.
- Find out from the driver under what conditions the DTC was set (when the DIC displayed the SERVICE STABILITY SYS message). This information will help to duplicate the failure.
- The Snapshot function on the scan tool can help find an intermittent DTC.

GC4020051912010X

Fig. 316 Code C1286: Steering/Lateral Accelerometer Sensor Bias Fault (Part 1 of 2). Eldorado

Test Description

The numbers below refer to the step numbers on the diagnostic table.

2. This step performs the Steering Position Sensor Test to see if the steering wheel position sensor is operating properly.
3. This step tests to see if the lateral accelerometer input parameter is within the valid range.
4. This step tests to see if the yaw rate input parameter is within the valid range.

Step	Action	Value(s)	Yes	No
1	Did you perform the ABS Diagnostic System Check?	—	Go to *Step 2*	Go to *A Diagnostic System Check - ABS*
2	1. Install a scan tool. 2. Turn ON the ignition, with the engine OFF. 3. Use the scan tool in order to perform the Steering Position Sensor Test in Delco/Bosch ABS/TCS ICCS2 Special Functions. Refer to *Scan Tool Diagnostics*. Did the steering wheel position sensor (SWPS) pass the test?	—	Go to *Step 3*	Go to *Step 7*
3	With the scan tool, observe the Lateral Accelerometer Input parameter in the Delco/Bosch ABS/TCS ICCS2 data list. Does the scan tool display within the specified range?	2.3–2.7 V	Go to *Step 4*	Go to *Step 8*
4	With the scan tool, observe the Yaw Rate Input parameter in the Delco/Bosch ABS/TCS ICCS2 data list. Does the scan tool display within the specified range?	2.3–2.7 V	Go to *Step 5*	Go to *Step 9*
5	1. Use the scan tool in order to clear the DTCs. 2. Perform the Diagnostic Test Drive. Does the DTC reset?	—	Go to *Step 6*	Go to Diagnostic Aids
6	Replace the EBCM. Did you complete the replacement?	—	Go to *Step 10*	—
7	Replace the steering wheel position sensor (SWPS). Did you complete the replacement?	—	Go to *Step 10*	—
8	Replace the lateral accelerometer sensor. Did you complete the replacement?	—	Go to *Step 10*	—
9	Replace the yaw rate sensor. Did you complete the replacement?	—	Go to *Step 10*	—
10	1. Use the scan tool in order to clear the DTCs. 2. Operate the vehicle within the Conditions for Running the DTC. Does the DTC reset?	—	Go to *Step 2*	System OK

GC4020051912020X

Fig. 316 Code C1286: Steering/Lateral Accelerometer Sensor Bias Fault (Part 2 of 2). Eldorado

Circuit Description

The steering wheel position sensor supplies 1 analog input and 2 digital inputs, Phase A and Phase B, to the EBCM. By interpreting the relationship between the inputs, the EBCM can determine the position of the steering wheel and the direction of steering wheel rotation.

Steer angle centering is the process by which the EBCM calibrates the steering sensor output so that the output reads zero when the steering wheel is centered. Using the yaw rate input, lateral accelerometer input, and wheel speed sensor inputs, the initial steering center position is calculated after driving greater than 10 km/h (6 mph) for more than 10 seconds in a straight line on a level surface.

Conditions for Running the DTC

The EBCM performs 3 different tests to detect a DTC condition. The numbers below correspond to the numbers in Conditions for Setting the DTC.

1. The steer sensor rate test runs with the ignition ON.
2. The steer sensor analog mismatch test runs under the following conditions:
   - The digital steer rate is less than 10 degrees/second.
   - The absolute value of the analog steer angle is less than 135 degrees.
3. The analog cross-comparison test runs under the following conditions:
   - The VSES is active.
   - The digital steer rate is less than 10 degrees/second.

Conditions for Setting the DTC

One of the following conditions occur:

1. The steer rate (speed that the steering wheel appears to be turning) is greater than 1000 degrees/second.
2. The difference between the analog steer angle and digital steer angle is greater than 20 degrees continuously for 5 seconds.
3. The difference between the analog steer angle and digital steer angle is greater than 20 degrees for 1 second. Under this condition, this DTC will set along with DTC C1281.

Action Taken When the DTC Sets

- The EBCM disables the VSES for the duration of the ignition cycle.
- The DIC displays the SERVICE STABILITY SYS message.
- The ABS/TCS remains functional.

GC4020051913010X

Fig. 317 Code C1287: Steering Sensor Rate Fault (Part 1 of 3). Eldorado

Step	Action	Value(s)	Yes	No
6	1. Turn OFF the ignition. 2. Disconnect the negative battery cable. 3. Measure the resistance from the ground circuit of the steering wheel position sensor (SWPS) to a good ground. Does the resistance measure less than the specified value?	5 Ω	Go to *Step 12*	Go to *Step 11*
7	Test the 5 volt reference circuit of the steering wheel position sensor (SWPS) for a short to voltage. Did you find and correct the condition?	—	Go to *Step 16*	Go to *Step 13*
8	Test the 5 volt reference circuit of the steering wheel position sensor (SWPS) for the following conditions: • An open • A short to ground • A high resistance Did you find and correct the condition?	—	Go to *Step 16*	Go to *Step 9*
9	Test the signal circuit of the steering wheel position sensor (SWPS) for the following conditions: • An open • A short to ground • A high resistance Did you find and correct the condition?	—	Go to *Step 16*	Go to *Step 13*
10	Test the signal circuit of the steering wheel position sensor (SWPS) for a short to voltage. Did you find and correct the condition?	—	Go to *Step 16*	Go to *Step 13*
11	1. Disconnect the EBCM. 2. Test the ground circuit of the steering wheel position sensor (SWPS) for a high resistance or an open. Did you find and correct the condition?	—	Go to *Step 16*	Go to *Step 13*
12	Inspect for poor connections at the harness connector of the steering wheel position sensor (SWPS). Did you find and correct the condition?	—	Go to *Step 16*	Go to *Step 14*
13	Inspect for poor connections at the harness connector of the EBCM. Did you find and correct the condition?	—	Go to *Step 16*	Go to *Step 15*
14	Replace the steering wheel position sensor (SWPS). Did you complete the replacement?	—	Go to *Step 16*	—
15	Replace the EBCM. Did you complete the replacement?	—	Go to *Step 16*	—
16	1. Use the scan tool in order to clear the DTCs. 2. Operate the vehicle within the Conditions for Running the DTC as specified in the supporting text. Does the DTC reset?	—	Go to *Step 2*	System OK

GC4020051913030X

Fig. 317 Code C1287: Steering Sensor Rate Fault (Part 3 of 3). Eldorado

Conditions for Clearing the DTC

- The condition for the DTC is no longer present (the DTC is not current) and you used the scan tool Clear DTC function.
- The condition for the DTC is no longer present (the DTC is not current) and you used the On-Board Diagnostics Clear DTC function.
- The EBCM automatically clears the history DTC when a current DTC is not detected in 50 consecutive drive cycles.

Diagnostic Aids

- During diagnosis, park the vehicle on a level surface.
- Check the vehicle for proper alignment. The car should not pull in either direction while driving straight on a level surface.
- Find out from the driver under what conditions the DTC was set (when the DIC displayed the SERVICE STABILITY SYS message). This information will help to duplicate the failure.
- The Snapshot function on the scan tool can help find an intermittent DTC.

Test Description

The numbers below refer to the step numbers on the diagnostic table.

3. Tests for the proper operation of the circuit in the low voltage range.
4. Tests for the proper operation of the circuit in the high voltage range. If the fuse in the jumper opens when you perform this test, the signal circuit is shorted to ground.
5. Tests for a short to voltage in the 5 volt reference circuit.
6. Tests for a high resistance or an open in the ground circuit.

Step	Action	Value(s)	Yes	No
1	Did you perform the ABS Diagnostic System Check?	—	Go to *Step 2*	Go to *A Diagnostic System Check - ABS*
2	1. Install a scan tool. 2. Turn ON the ignition, with the engine OFF. 3. With the scan tool, observe the Analog Steering Wheel Position Input parameter in the Delco/Bosch ABS/TCS ICCS2 data list. Does the scan tool indicate that the Analog Steering Wheel Position Input parameter is within the specified range?	0.1-4.9 V	Go to Diagnostic Aids	Go to *Step 3*
3	1. Turn OFF the ignition. 2. Disconnect the steering wheel position sensor (SWPS). 3. Turn ON the ignition, with the engine OFF. 4. With the scan tool, observe the Analog Steering Wheel Position Input parameter. Does the scan tool indicate that the Analog Steering Wheel Position Input parameter is less than the specified value?	0.1 V	Go to *Step 4*	Go to *Step 10*
4	1. Turn OFF the ignition. 2. Connect a 3 amp fused jumper wire between the 5 volt reference circuit of the steering wheel position sensor (SWPS) and the signal circuit of the steering wheel position sensor (SWPS). 3. Turn ON the ignition, with the engine OFF. 4. With the scan tool, observe the Analog Steering Wheel Position Input parameter. Does the scan tool indicate that the Analog Steering Wheel Position Input parameter is greater than the specified value?	4.9 V	Go to *Step 5*	Go to *Step 8*
5	1. Disconnect the fused jumper wire. 2. Measure the voltage between the 5 volt reference circuit of the steering wheel position sensor (SWPS) and the ground circuit of the steering wheel position sensor (SWPS). Does the voltage measure less than the specified value?	5 V	Go to *Step 6*	Go to *Step 7*

GC4020051913020X

Fig. 317 Code C1287: Steering Sensor Rate Fault (Part 2 of 3). Eldorado

Circuit Description

The steering wheel position sensor supplies 1 analog input and 2 digital inputs, Phase A and Phase B, to the EBCM. By interpreting the relationship between the inputs, the EBCM can determine the position of the steering wheel and the direction of steering wheel rotation.

Steer angle centering is the process by which the EBCM calibrates the steering sensor output so that the output reads zero when the steering wheel is centered. Using the yaw rate input, lateral accelerometer input, and wheel speed sensor inputs, the initial steering center position is calculated after driving greater than 10 km/h (6 mph) for more than 10 seconds in a straight line on a level surface.

Conditions for Running the DTC

The ignition is ON.

Conditions for Setting the DTC

One of the following conditions occur:

- The analog steering wheel position sensor signal is greater than 4.9 volts for 0.1 seconds.
- The analog steering wheel position sensor signal is less than 0.1 volts for 0.1 seconds.

Action Taken When the DTC Sets

- The EBCM disables the VSES for the duration of the ignition cycle.
- The DIC displays the SERVICE STABILITY SYS message.
- The ABS/TCS remains functional.

Conditions for Clearing the DTC

- The condition for the DTC is no longer present (the DTC is not current) and you used the scan tool Clear DTC function.
- The condition for the DTC is no longer present (the DTC is not current) and you used the On-Board Diagnostics Clear DTC function.
- The EBCM automatically clears the history DTC when a current DTC is not detected in 50 consecutive drive cycles.

GC4020051914010X

Fig. 318 Code C1288: Steering Sensor Circuit Fault (Part 1 of 3). Eldorado

Diagnostic Aids

- During diagnosis, park the vehicle on a level surface.
- Check the vehicle for proper alignment. The car should not pull in either direction while driving straight on a level surface.
- Find out from the driver under what conditions the DTC was set (when the DIC displayed the SERVICE STABILITY SYS message). This information will help to duplicate the failure.
- The Snapshot function on the scan tool can help find an intermittent DTC.

Test Description

The numbers below refer to the step numbers on the diagnostic table.

3. Tests for the proper operation of the circuit in the low voltage range.
4. Tests for the proper operation of the circuit in the high voltage range. If the fuse in the jumper opens when you perform this test, the signal circuit is shorted to ground.
5. Tests for a short to voltage in the 5 volt reference circuit.
6. Tests for a high resistance or an open in the ground circuit.

Step	Action	Value(s)	Yes	No
1	Did you perform the ABS Diagnostic System Check?	—	Go to *Step 2*	Go to *A Diagnostic System Check - ABS*
2	1. Install a scan tool. 2. Turn ON the ignition, with the engine OFF. 3. With the scan tool, observe the Analog Steering Wheel Position Input parameter in the Delco/Bosch ABS/TCS ICCS2 data list. Does the scan tool indicate that the Analog Steering Wheel Position Input parameter is within the specified range?	0.1-4.9 V	Go to Diagnostic Aids	Go to *Step 3*
3	1. Turn OFF the ignition. 2. Disconnect the steering wheel position sensor (SWPS). 3. Turn ON the ignition, with the engine OFF. 4. With the scan tool, observe the Analog Steering Wheel Position Input parameter. Does the scan tool indicate that the Analog Steering Wheel Position Input parameter is less than the specified value?	0.1 V	Go to *Step 4*	Go to *Step 10*
4	1. Turn OFF the ignition. 2. Connect a 3 amp fused jumper wire between the 5 volt reference circuit of the steering wheel position sensor (SWPS) and the signal circuit of the steering wheel position sensor (SWPS). 3. Turn ON the ignition, with the engine OFF. 4. With the scan tool, observe the Analog Steering Wheel Position Input parameter. Does the scan tool indicate that the Analog Steering Wheel Position Input parameter is greater than the specified value?	4.9 V	Go to *Step 5*	Go to *Step 8*
5	1. Disconnect the fused jumper wire. 2. Measure the voltage between the 5 volt reference circuit of the steering wheel position sensor (SWPS) and the ground circuit of the steering wheel position sensor (SWPS). Does the voltage measure less than the specified value?	5 V	Go to *Step 6*	Go to *Step 7*

GC4020051914020X

Fig. 318 Code C1288: Steering Sensor Circuit Fault (Part 2 of 3). Eldorado

Step	Action	Value(s)	Yes	No
6	1. Turn OFF the ignition. 2. Disconnect the negative battery cable. 3. Measure the resistance from the ground circuit of the steering wheel position sensor (SWPS) to a good ground. Does the resistance measure less than the specified value?	5 Ω	Go to *Step 12*	Go to *Step 11*
7	Test the 5 volt reference circuit of the steering wheel position sensor (SWPS) for a short to voltage. Did you find and correct the condition?	—	Go to *Step 16*	Go to *Step 13*
8	Test the 5 volt reference circuit of the steering wheel position sensor (SWPS) for the following conditions: • An open • A short to ground • A high resistance Did you find and correct the condition?	—	Go to *Step 16*	Go to *Step 9*
9	Test the signal circuit of the steering wheel position sensor (SWPS) for the following conditions: • An open • A short to ground • A high resistance Did you find and correct the condition?	—	Go to *Step 16*	Go to *Step 13*
10	Test the signal circuit of the steering wheel position sensor (SWPS) for a short to voltage. Did you find and correct the condition?	—	Go to *Step 16*	Go to *Step 13*
11	1. Disconnect the EBCM. 2. Test the ground circuit of the steering wheel position sensor (SWPS) for a high resistance or an open. Did you find and correct the condition?	—	Go to *Step 16*	Go to *Step 13*
12	Inspect for poor connections at the harness connector of the steering wheel position sensor (SWPS). Did you find and correct the condition?	—	Go to *Step 16*	Go to *Step 14*
13	Inspect for poor connections at the harness connector of the EBCM. Did you find and correct the condition?	—	Go to *Step 16*	Go to *Step 15*
14	Replace the steering wheel position sensor (SWPS). Did you complete the replacement?	—	Go to *Step 16*	—
15	Replace the EBCM. Did you complete the replacement?	—	Go to *Step 16*	—
16	1. Use the scan tool in order to clear the DTCs. 2. Operate the vehicle within the Conditions for Running the DTC. Does the DTC reset?	—	Go to *Step 2*	System OK

GC4020051914030X

Fig. 318 Code C1288: Steering Sensor Circuit Fault (Part 3 of 3). Eldorado

Circuit Description

The EBCM uses this stoplamp switch circuit for various performance measures within ABS/TCS/VSES. The EBCM detects an open circuit in non-ABS braking. This DTC sets when the EBCM does not detect closure of the brake switch while the car is decelerating at level that indicates the brakes are applied. Several deceleration events without detection of a closed brake switch are required before this DTC is set.

Conditions for Running the DTC

The ABS conditions and the braking conditions are normal.

Conditions for Setting the DTC

The stoplamp switch remains open for 3 deceleration cycles.

Action Taken When the DTC Sets

- The EBCM disables the TCS for the duration of the ignition cycle.
- The TRACTION CONTROL indicator turns ON.
- The ABS remains functional.

Conditions for Clearing the DTC

- The condition for the DTC is no longer present (the DTC is not current) and you used the scan tool Clear DTC function.
- The condition for the DTC is no longer present (the DTC is not current) and you used the On-Board Diagnostics Clear DTC function.
- The EBCM automatically clears the history DTC when a current DTC is not detected in 50 consecutive drive cycles.

GC4020051915010X

Fig. 319 Code C1291: Open Brake Lamp Switch Contacts During Deceleration (Part 1 of 3). Eldorado

Diagnostic Aids

- Diagnose any wheel speed sensor DTCs before continuing with the diagnosis of the DTC.
- A deceleration cycle consists of the following sequence:
  1. The vehicle speed is greater than 24 km/h (15 mph).
  2. The vehicle decelerates more than 8 km/h/second (5 mph/second) for 2 seconds.
  3. The vehicle speed decelerates to less than 16 km/h (10 mph).
- Verify proper stoplamp switch operation using the data list of the scan tool. As the brake is applied, the data list displays the stoplamp switch on within 1 inch of travel.
- Possible causes of this DTC are the following conditions:
  - An open stoplamp switch.
  - The stoplamp switch is misadjusted.
  - An open fuse.
  - Circuit has a wiring problem, terminal corrosion, or poor connections.
  - Erratic wheel speeds.

Test Description

The numbers below refer to the step numbers on the diagnostic table.

3. Tests the circuit for a change in states.
5. Tests for proper operation of the circuit by bypassing the stoplamp/AT shift lock control switch. If the fuse in the jumper opens when you perform this test, the signal circuit of the stoplamp/AT shift lock control switch is shorted to ground.

Step	Action	Value(s)	Yes	No
1	Did you perform the ABS Diagnostic System Check?	—	Go to *Step 2*	Go to *A Diagnostic System Check - ABS*
2	Press the brake pedal. Do the brake lamps turn ON?	—	Go to *Step 3*	Go to *Step 7*
3	1. Install a scan tool. 2. Turn ON the ignition, with the engine OFF. 3. With the scan tool, observe the Brake Light Switch parameter in the Delco/Bosch ABS/TCS ICCS (if equipped). 4. Press the brake pedal. Does the Brake Light Switch parameter change state?	—	Go to Diagnostic Aids	Go to *Step 4*
4	1. Turn OFF the ignition. 2. Inspect the stoplamp/AT shift lock control switch and adjust and/or calibrate if needed. Did you find and correct the condition?	—	Go to *Step 14*	Go to *Step 5*
5	1. Turn OFF the ignition. 2. Disconnect the stoplamp/AT shift lock control switch connector. 3. Connect a 3 amp fused jumper wire between the battery feed of the stoplamp/AT shift lock control switch and the signal circuit of the stoplamp/AT shift lock control switch. 4. Turn ON the ignition, with the engine OFF. 5. With the scan tool, observe the Brake Switch - ABS Input parameter. Does the scan tool display Applied?	—	Go to *Step 11*	Go to *Step 6*

GC4020051915020X

Fig. 319 Code C1291: Open Brake Lamp Switch Contacts During Deceleration (Part 2 of 3). Eldorado

Step	Action	Value(s)	Yes	No
6	Test the signal circuit of the stoplamp/AT shift lock control switch for an open between the EBCM and the splice of the stoplamp switch signal circuit. Did you find and correct the condition?	—	Go to *Step 14*	Go to *Step 10*
7	Test the battery feed circuit of the stoplamp/AT shift lock control switch for a short to ground or an open. Did you find and correct the condition?	—	Go to *Step 14*	Go to *Step 8*
8	Test the signal circuit of the stoplamp/AT shift lock control switch for an open between the stoplamp/AT shift lock control switch and the splice of the stoplamp switch signal circuit. Did you find and correct the condition?	—	Go to *Step 14*	Go to *Step 9*
9	Test the signal circuit of the stoplamp/AT shift lock control switch for a short to ground. Did you find and correct the condition?	—	Go to *Step 14*	Go to *Step 10*
10	Inspect for poor connections at the harness connector of the EBCM. Did you find and correct the condition?	—	Go to *Step 14*	Go to *Step 12*
11	Inspect for poor connections at the harness connector of the stoplamp/AT shift lock control switch. Did you find and correct the condition?	—	Go to *Step 14*	Go to *Step 13*
12	Replace the EBCM. Did you complete the replacement?	—	Go to *Step 14*	—
13	Replace the stoplamp/AT shift lock control switch. Did you complete the replacement?	—	Go to *Step 14*	—
14	1. Use the scan tool in order to clear the DTCs. 2. Operate the vehicle within the Conditions for Running the DTC. Does the DTC reset?	—	Go to *Step 2*	System OK

GC4020051915030X

Fig. 319 Code C1291: Open Brake Lamp Switch Contacts During Deceleration (Part 3 of 3). Eldorado

Test Description

The numbers below refer to the step numbers on the diagnostic table.

2. Test for the current state of the brake switch parameter.

Step	Action	Value(s)	Yes	No
1	Did you perform the ABS Diagnostic System Check?	—	Go to *Step 2*	Go to *A Diagnostic System Check - ABS*
2	1. Install a scan tool. 2. Turn ON the ignition, with the engine OFF. 3. With the scan tool, observe the Brake Light Switch parameter in the Delco/Bosch ABS/TCS ICCS (if equipped) data list. Does the scan tool display Released?	—	Go to *Step 3*	Go to *Step 4*
3	1. Press the brake pedal. 2. With the scan tool, observe the Brake Light Switch parameter. Does the Brake Light Switch parameter change state?	—	Go to Diagnostic Aids	Go to *Step 4*
4	1. Turn OFF the ignition. 2. Inspect the stoplamp/AT shift lock control switch and adjust and/or calibrate if needed. Did you find and correct the condition?	—	Go to *Step 11*	Go to *Step 5*
5	1. Turn OFF the ignition. 2. Disconnect the stoplamp/AT shift lock control switch connector. 3. Turn ON the ignition, with the engine OFF. 4. With the scan tool, observe the Brake Light Switch parameter. Does the scan tool display Released?	—	Go to *Step 8*	Go to *Step 6*
6	Test the signal circuit of the stoplamp/AT shift lock control switch for a short to voltage. Did you find and correct the condition?	—	Go to *Step 11*	Go to *Step 7*
7	Inspect for poor connections at the harness connector of the EBCM. Did you find and correct the condition?	—	Go to *Step 11*	Go to *Step 9*
8	Inspect for poor connections at the harness connector of the stoplamp/AT shift lock control switch. Did you find and correct the condition?	—	Go to *Step 11*	Go to *Step 10*
9	Replace the EBCM. Did you complete the replacement?	—	Go to *Step 11*	—
10	Replace the stoplamp/AT shift lock control switch. Did you complete the replacement?	—	Go to *Step 11*	—
11	1. Use the scan tool in order to clear the DTCs. 2. Operate the vehicle within the Conditions for Running the DTC. Does the DTC reset?	—	Go to *Step 2*	System OK

GC4020051916020X

Fig. 320 Code C1294: Brake Lamp Switch Circuit Always Active (Part 2 of 2). Eldorado

Circuit Description

The EBCM uses this stoplamp switch circuit for various performance measures within ABS/TCS/VSES. This DTC is set if the EBCM has determined that the stoplamp switch is continously ON. The TCS cannot be activated when the stoplamp switch is ON

Conditions for Running the DTC

The vehicle speed is greater than 40 km/h (25 mph).

Conditions for Setting the DTC

The stoplamp switch input was active for 2 consecutive ignition cycles.

Action Taken When the DTC Sets

- The EBCM disables the TCS for the duration of the ignition cycle.
- The TRACTION CONTROL indicator turns ON.
- The ABS remains functional.

Conditions for Clearing the DTC

- The condition for the DTC is no longer present (the DTC is not current) and you used the scan tool Clear DTC function.
- The condition for the DTC is no longer present (the DTC is not current) and you used the On-Board Diagnostics Clear DTC function.
- The EBCM automatically clears the history DTC when a current DTC is not detected in 50 consecutive drive cycles.

Diagnostic Aids

Possible causes of this DTC are the following conditions:

- The stoplamp switch circuit is shorted to voltage.
- The stoplamp switch is misadjusted.
- The stoplamp switch is stuck closed.
- A brake pedal that is binding.

GC4020051916010X

Fig. 320 Code C1294: Brake Lamp Switch Circuit Always Active (Part 1 of 2). Eldorado

Circuit Description

This DTC is used in order to identify open stoplamp switch circuitry that prevents the stoplamp switch input from changing states when the brake is applied.
This DTC is used in conjunction with DTC C1291 in order to determine the cause of an open stoplamp switch malfunction.

Conditions for Running the DTC

This DTC can set at anytime that the EBCM is powered.

Conditions for Setting the DTC

The stoplamp switch input voltage is between 3.4 volts and 5.3 volts for 2 seconds.

Action Taken When the DTC Sets

- The EBCM disables the TCS for the duration of the ignition cycle.
- The TRACTION CONTROL indicator turns ON.
- The ABS remains functional.

Conditions for Clearing the DTC

- The condition for the DTC is no longer present (the DTC is not current) and you used the scan tool Clear DTC function.
- The condition for the DTC is no longer present (the DTC is not current) and you used the On-Board Diagnostics Clear DTC function.
- The EBCM automatically clears the history DTC when a current DTC is not detected in 50 consecutive drive cycles.

GC4020051917010X

Fig. 321 Code C1295: Brake Lamp Switch Circuit Open (Part 1 of 3). Eldorado

Diagnostic Aids

Possible causes of this DTC are the following conditions:

- A signal circuit of the stoplamp switch is open.
- The stoplamp switch is misadjusted.
- Verify proper stoplamp switch operation using the data list of the scan tool. As the brake is applied, the data list displays the stoplamp switch on within 1 inch of travel.
- All brake lamps are open.
- All brake lamp grounds are open.
- Circuit has a wiring problem, terminal corrosion, or poor connections.
- Loose or corroded EBCM ground or PCM ground.
- An internal EBCM problem.

Test Description

The numbers below refer to the step numbers on the diagnostic table.

3. Tests the circuit for a change in states.
5. Tests for proper operation of the circuit by bypassing the stoplamp/AT shift lock control switch. If the fuse in the jumper opens when you perform this test, the signal circuit of the stoplamp/AT shift lock control switch is shorted to ground.

Step	Action	Value(s)	Yes	No
1	Did you perform the ABS Diagnostic System Check?	—	Go to *Step 2*	Go to *A Diagnostic System Check - ABS*
2	Press the brake pedal. Do the brake lamps turn ON?	—	Go to *Step 3*	Go to *Step 7*
3	1. Install a scan tool. 2. Turn ON the ignition, with the engine OFF. 3. With the scan tool, observe the Brake Light Switch parameter in the Delco/Bosch ABS/TCS ICCS (if equipped). 4. Press the brake pedal. Does the Brake Light Switch parameter change state?	—	Go to Diagnostic Aids	Go to *Step 4*
4	1. Turn OFF the ignition. 2. Inspect the stoplamp/AT shift lock control switch and adjust and/or calibrate if needed. Did you find and correct the condition?	—	Go to *Step 14*	Go to *Step 5*
5	1. Turn OFF the ignition. 2. Disconnect the stoplamp/AT shift lock control switch connector. 3. Connect a 3 amp fused jumper wire between the battery feed of the stoplamp/AT shift lock control switch and the signal circuit of the stoplamp/AT shift lock control switch. 4. Turn ON the ignition, with the engine OFF. 5. With the scan tool, observe the Brake Switch - ABS Input parameter. Does the scan tool display Applied?	—	Go to *Step 11*	Go to *Step 6*
6	Test the signal circuit of the stoplamp/AT shift lock control switch for an open between the EBCM and the splice of the stoplamp switch signal circuit. Did you find and correct the condition?	—	Go to *Step 14*	Go to *Step 10*

GC4020051917020X

Fig. 321 Code C1295: Brake Lamp Switch Circuit Open (Part 2 of 3). Eldorado

Step	Action	Value(s)	Yes	No
7	Test the battery feed circuit of the stoplamp/AT shift lock control switch for a short to ground or an open. Did you find and correct the condition?	—	Go to *Step 14*	Go to *Step 8*
8	Test the signal circuit of the stoplamp/AT shift lock control switch for an open between the stoplamp/AT shift lock control switch and the splice of the stoplamp switch signal circuit. Did you find and correct the condition?	—	Go to *Step 14*	Go to *Step 9*
9	Test the signal circuit of the stoplamp/AT shift lock control switch for a short to ground. Did you find and correct the condition?	—	Go to *Step 14*	Go to *Step 10*
10	Inspect for poor connections at the harness connector of the EBCM. Did you find and correct the condition?	—	Go to *Step 14*	Go to *Step 12*
11	Inspect for poor connections at the harness connector of the stoplamp/AT shift lock control switch. Did you find and correct the condition?	—	Go to *Step 14*	Go to *Step 13*
12	Replace the EBCM. Did you complete the replacement?	—	Go to *Step 14*	—
13	Replace the stoplamp/AT shift lock control switch. Did you complete the replacement?	—	Go to *Step 14*	—
14	1. Use the scan tool in order to clear the DTCs. 2. Operate the vehicle within the Conditions for Running the DTC as specified in the supporting text. Does the DTC reset?	—	Go to *Step 2*	System OK

GC4020051917030X

Fig. 321 Code C1295: Brake Lamp Switch Circuit Open (Part 3 of 3). Eldorado

Circuit Description

The extended travel brake switch is used by the EBCM to determine if the driver has pressed the brake pedal far enough to initiate moderate braking, as opposed to merely brushing or tapping the pedal. The PCM sends this information to the EBCM via class 2 serial data messages.

Conditions for Running the DTC

The ignition is ON.

Conditions for Setting the DTC

The PCM detects an extended travel brake switch failure. The PCM also sets DTC P1575.

Action Taken When the DTC Sets

- The EBCM disables the VSES for the duration of the ignition cycle.
- The DIC displays the SERVICE STABILITY SYS message.
- The ABS/TCS remains functional.

Conditions for Clearing the DTC

- The condition for the DTC is no longer present (the DTC is not current) and you used the scan tool Clear DTC function.
- The condition for the DTC is no longer present (the DTC is not current) and you used the On-Board Diagnostics Clear DTC function.
- The EBCM automatically clears the history DTC when a current DTC is not detected in 50 consecutive drive cycles.

Diagnostic Aids

If the extended travel brake switch is not properly adjusted, the driver may experience longer VSES brake pedal pulsations before normal brake pedal feel is returned. The VSES brake pedal pulsation is different than the ABS brake pedal pulsation. The VSES brake pedal pulsation has a much higher frequency and less pedal travel fluctuation.

GC4020051918010X

Fig. 322 Code C1297: PCM Indicated Brake Extended Travel Switch Failure (Part 1 of 2). Eldorado

Step	Action	Value(s)	Yes	No
1	Did you perform the ABS Diagnostic System Check?	—	Go to *Step 2*	Go to *A Diagnostic System Check - ABS*
2	1. Turn OFF the ignition. 2. Install a scan tool. 3. Turn ON the ignition, with the engine OFF. 4. Use the scan tool in order to read the powertrain control module (PCM) DTCs. Is DTC P1575 set as a current DTC?	—	*DTC P1575 Extended Travel Brake Switch Circuit*	Go to *Step 3*
3	1. Turn ON the ignition, with the engine OFF. 2. Observe the Extended Travel Brake Switch parameter in the Delco/Bosch ABS/TCS ICCS (if equipped) data list. 3. Step on and off the brake pedal with enough force in order to simulate a hard braking condition. As the brake pedal is pressed and released, the scan tool should read Applied and Released. 4. Use a tape measure in order to measure the distance that the brake pedal travels for the scan tool to read Applied. Is the distance within the specified range?	2.5–3.3 cm (1.0–1.3 in)	Go to *Step 5*	Go to *Step 4*
4	Adjust or repair the extended travel brake switch as necessary. Did you complete the repair?	—	Go to *Step 5*	—
5	1. Use the scan tool in order to clear the DTCs. 2. Operate the vehicle within the Conditions for Running the DTC. Does the DTC reset?	—	Go to *Step 2*	System OK

GC4020051918020X

Fig. 322 Code C1297: PCM Indicated Brake Extended Travel Switch Failure (Part 2 of 2). Eldorado

Circuit Description

The class 2 serial data line allows all of the modules on the line to transmit information to each other as needed. Each module is assigned an ID. All of the information sent out on the line is assigned a priority by which it is received. When the ignition is turned ON, each module begins to send and receive information. Each module on the class 2 serial data line knows what information the module needs to send out and what information the module should be receiving. What the modules do not know is which module is supposed to send the information. This information is only learned after the module has received the information needed along with the ID of the module that sent the information. This information is then remembered until the ignition switch is turned off.

Conditions for Running the DTC

The ABS conditions and the braking conditions are normal.

Conditions for Setting the DTC

The PCM does not receive any messages from the EBCM for 7 seconds.

Action Taken When the DTC Sets

- The EBCM disables the TCS for the duration of the ignition cycle.
- The TRACTION CONTROL indicator turns ON.
- The ABS remains functional.

Conditions for Clearing the DTC

- The condition for the DTC is no longer present (the DTC is not current) and you used the scan tool Clear DTC function.
- The condition for the DTC is no longer present (the DTC is not current) and you used the On-Board Diagnostics Clear DTC function.
- The EBCM automatically clears the history DTC when a current DTC is not detected in 50 consecutive drive cycles.

Diagnostic Aids

Possible causes of this DTC are the following conditions:

- The EBCM has a class 2 serial data transmit fault.
- The PCM has a class 2 serial data receiver fault.
- The class 2 serial data line has an extremely high amount of traffic.
- Loose or corroded EBCM ground or PCM ground.

Test Description

The number below refers to the step number on the diagnostic table.

2. This step checks to see if the PCM, IPC, or SDM has set DTC U1040.

GC4020051919010X

Fig. 323 Code C1298: PCM Class 2 Serial Data Link Fault (Part 1 of 2). Eldorado

Step	Action	Value(s)	Yes	No
1	Did you perform the ABS Diagnostic System Check?	—	Go to *Step 2*	Go to *A Diagnostic System Check - ABS*
2	1. Install a scan tool. 2. Turn ON the ignition leaving the engine OFF. 3. Select the display DTCs function on the scan tool for the following modules: • Powertrain control module (PCM) • Instrument cluster (IPC) • Inflatable restraint sensing and diagnostic module (SDM) Does the scan tool display DTC U1040?	—	Go to *Scan Tool Does Not Communicate with Class 2 Device in* Data Link Communications	Go to *Step 3*
3	Inspect the EBCM ground and PCM ground, making sure each ground is clean and torqued to the proper specification. Did you find and correct the condition?	—	Go to *Step 8*	Go to *Step 4*
4	1. With the scan tool, observe the System Power Mode parameter in the Data Display 2 Normal Mode in the Delco/Bosch ABS/TCS ICCS (if equipped) data list. 2. Turn the ignition switch to each of the following positions: • OFF • ACC • START • RUN Did the scan tool display the correct ignition switch positions?	—	Go to *Step 5*	*Body Control System*
5	Inpect the PCM. Did you find and correct the condition?	—	Go to *Step 8*	Go to *Step 6*
6	1. Use the scan tool in order to clear the DTCs. 2. Operate the vehicle within the Conditions for Running the DTC as specified in the supporting text. Does the DTC reset?	—	Go to *Step 7*	Go to Diagnostic Aids
7	Replace the EBCM. Did you complete the replacement?	—	Go to *Step 8*	—
8	1. Use the scan tool in order to clear the DTCs. 2. Operate the vehicle within the Conditions for Running the DTC. Does the DTC reset?	—	Go to *Step 2*	System OK

GC4020051919020X

Fig. 323 Code C1298: PCM Class 2 Serial Data Link Fault (Part 2 of 2). Eldorado

Step	Action	Value(s)	Yes	No
1	Did you review the ABS operation and perform the necessary inspections?	—	Go to *Step 2*	Go to *Symptoms*
2	Inspect the EBCM ground, making sure the ground is clean and torqued to the proper specification. Did you find and correct the condition?	—	Go to *Step 9*	Go to *Step 3*
3	1. Install a scan tool. 2. Turn ON the ignition, with the engine OFF. 3. With the scan tool, observe the ABS Warning Lamp parameter in the Delco/Bosch ABS/TCS ICCS (if equipped) data list. Does the scan tool display Off?	—	Go to *Step 4*	Go to *Step 5*
4	1. Turn OFF the ignition. 2. Turn ON the ignition, with the engine OFF. 3. Observe the ABS indicator on the instrument cluster (IPC) during the bulb check. Does the ABS indicator illuminate during the bulb check and then turn OFF?	—	Go to *Step 5*	Go to *Step 6*
5	Inspect for poor connections at the harness connector of the EBCM. Did you find and correct the condition?	—	Go to *Step 9*	Go to *Step 7*
6	Inspect for poor connections at the harness connector of the instrument cluster (IPC). Did you find and correct the condition?	—	Go to *Step 9*	Go to *Step 8*
7	Replace the EBCM. Did you complete the repair?	—	Go to *Step 9*	—
8	Replace the instrument cluster (IPC). Did you complete the repair?	—	Go to *Step 9*	—
9	Operate the system in order to verify the repair. Did you correct the condition?	—	System OK	Go to *Step 2*

GC4020051924020X

Fig. 324 ABS Indicator Inoperative (Part 2 of 2). Eldorado

Circuit Description

The instrument cluster controls the operation of the ABS indicator. The EBCM reports the desired status of the ABS indicator via class 2 serial data messages. The ABS indicator signal circuit is a back-up reporting circuit to the class 2 serial data messages. The EBCM supplies ground through the circuit when the ABS is operating properly. When there is a problem with ABS that should turn on the ABS indicator, the EBCM opens the ABS indicator signal circuit. If there is a problem with the ABS class 2 serial data messages, the instrument cluster uses the ABS indicator signal to determine if the ABS indicator should be illuminated. Using the serial data messages and back-up circuit, the instrument cluster decides whether to turn on the ABS indicator.

Test Description

The numbers below refer to the step numbers on the diagnostic table.

3. This test uses the scan tool to check the normal state of the ABS indicator control.
4. This test ensures that the instrument cluster can operate the ABS indicator.

GC4020051924010X

Fig. 324 ABS Indicator Inoperative (Part 1 of 2). Eldorado

Circuit Description

The instrument cluster controls the operation of the ABS indicator. The EBCM reports the desired status of the ABS indicator via class 2 serial data messages. The ABS indicator signal circuit is a back-up reporting circuit to the class 2 serial data messages. The EBCM supplies ground through the circuit when the ABS is operating properly. When there is a problem with ABS that should turn on the ABS indicator, the EBCM opens the ABS indicator signal circuit. If there is a problem with the ABS class 2 serial data messages, the instrument cluster uses the ABS indicator signal to determine if the ABS indicator should be illuminated. Using the serial data messages and back-up circuit, the instrument cluster decides whether to turn on the ABS indicator.

Test Description

The numbers below refer to the step numbers on the diagnostic table.

3. This test uses the scan tool to check the normal state of the ABS indicator control.
4. This test ensures that the instrument cluster can operate the ABS indicator.

GC4020051925010X

Fig. 325 ABS Indicator Always On (Part 1 of 2). Eldorado

Step	Action	Value(s)	Yes	No
1	Did you review the ABS operation and perform the necessary inspections?	—	Go to *Step 2*	Go to *Symptoms*
2	Inspect the EBCM ground, making sure the ground is clean and torqued to the proper specification. Did you find and correct the condition?	—	Go to *Step 9*	Go to *Step 3*
3	1. Install a scan tool. 2. Turn ON the ignition, with the engine OFF. 3. With the scan tool, observe the ABS Warning Lamp parameter in the Delco/Bosch ABS/TCS ICCS (if equipped) data list. Does the scan tool display Off?	—	Go to *Step 4*	Go to *Step 5*
4	1. Turn OFF the ignition. 2. Turn ON the ignition, with the engine OFF. 3. Observe the ABS indicator on the instrument cluster (IPC) during the bulb check. Does the ABS indicator illuminate during the bulb check and then turn OFF?	—	Go to *Step 5*	Go to *Step 6*
5	Inspect for poor connections at the harness connector of the EBCM. Did you find and correct the condition?	—	Go to *Step 9*	Go to *Step 7*
6	Inspect for poor connections at the harness connector of the instrument cluster (IPC). Did you find and correct the condition?	—	Go to *Step 9*	Go to *Step 8*
7	Replace the EBCM. Did you complete the repair?	—	Go to *Step 9*	—
8	Replace the instrument cluster (IPC). Did you complete the repair?	—	Go to *Step 9*	—
9	Operate the system in order to verify the repair. Did you correct the condition?	—	System OK	Go to *Step 2*

GC4020051925020X

Fig. 325 ABS Indicator Always On (Part 2 of 2). Eldorado

Circuit Description

The class 2 serial data line allows all of the modules on the line to transmit information to each other as needed. Each module is assigned an ID. All of the information sent out on the line is assigned a priority by which it is received. When the ignition is turned ON, each module begins to send and receive information. Each module on the class 2 serial data line knows what information the module needs to send out and what information the module should be receiving. What the modules do not know is which module is supposed to send the information. This information is only learned after the module has received the information needed along with the ID of the module that sent the information. This information is then remembered until the ignition switch is turned off.

GC4020051920010X

Fig. 326 No Communication With EBCM (Part 1 of 3). Eldorado

Step	Action	Value(s)	Yes	No
1	Did you review the ABS operation and perform the necessary inspections?	—	Go to *Step 2*	Go to *Symptoms*
2	1. Turn OFF the ignition. 2. Install a scan tool. 3. Turn ON the ignition, with the engine OFF. 4. Attempt to establish communication with other modules on the class 2 serial data line, such as the PCM. Does the scan tool communicate with any other modules on the class 2 serial data line?	—	Go to *Step 3*	*Scan Tool Does Not Communicate with Class 2 Device*
3	1. Turn OFF the ignition. 2. Inspect the underhood fuse block ABS (10 A) Fuse. Is the fuse good?	—	Go to *Step 4*	Go to *Step 7*
4	Inspect the RH underhood fuse block BRAKES (50 A) Fuse. Is the fuse good?	—	Go to *Step 9*	Go to *Step 5*
5	1. Install a new BRAKES (50 A) Fuse in the RH underhood fuse block. 2. Inspect the new BRAKES (50 A) Fuse. Is the fuse good?	—	Go to *Intermittent*	Go to *Step 6*
6	1. Turn OFF the ignition. 2. Remove the BRAKES (50 A) Fuse from the RH underhood fuse block. 3. Disconnect the EBCM harness connector. 4. Connect the *J 39700* universal pinout box using the *J 39700-25* cable adapter to the EBCM harness connector only. 5. Test the battery voltage circuit for a short to ground. Did you find and correct the condition?	—	Go to *Step 19*	Go to *Step 15*
7	1. Turn OFF the ignition. 2. Install a new ABS (10 A) Fuse in the underhood fuse block. 3. Turn ON the ignition, with the engine OFF. 4. Inspect the new ABS (10 A) Fuse. Is the fuse good?	—	Go to *Intermittent*	Go to *Step 8*
8	1. Turn OFF the ignition. 2. Remove the ABS (10 A) Fuse from the underhood fuse block. 3. Disconnect the EBCM harness connector. 4. Connect the *J 39700* universal pinout box using the *J 39700-25* cable adapter to the EBCM harness connector only. **Important:** Disconnecting the EBCM and turning ON the ignition could cause other modules to set loss of communication DTCs (Uxxxx). Once the EBCM is reconnected, the EBCM may set DTC C1298 PCM Class 2 Serial Data Malfunction. 5. Turn ON the ignition, with the engine OFF. 6. Test the ignition voltage circuit for a short to ground. Did you find and correct the condition?	—	Go to *Step 19*	Go to *Step 15*

GC4020051920020X

Fig. 326 No Communication With EBCM (Part 2 of 3). Eldorado

Step	Action	Value(s)	Yes	No
9	1. Install the fuses, if removed. 2. Turn ON the ignition, with the engine OFF. 3. Measure the voltage at the underhood fuse block ABS (10 A) Fuse by probing between the fuse test terminals and a good ground. Is the voltage within the specified range?	B+	Go to *Step 10*	Go to *Step 17*
10	Measure the voltage at the RH underhood fuse block BRAKES (50 A) Fuse by probing between the fuse test terminals and a good ground. Is the voltage within the specified range?	B+	Go to *Step 11*	Go to *Step 18*
11	Inspect the EBCM ground, making sure the ground is clean and torqued to the proper specification. Did you find and correct the condition?	—	Go to *Step 19*	Go to *Step 12*
12	1. Turn OFF the ignition. 2. Disconnect the EBCM harness connector. 3. Connect the *J 39700* universal pinout box using the *J 39700-25* cable adapter to the EBCM harness connector only. 4. Test the module ground circuit for an open. Did you find and correct the condition?	—	Go to *Step 19*	Go to *Step 13*
13	1. Turn ON the ignition, with the engine OFF. 2. Test the ignition voltage circuit of the EBCM for an open. Did you find and correct the condition?	—	Go to *Step 19*	Go to *Step 14*
14	Test the battery voltage circuit of the EBCM for an open. Did you find and correct the condition?	—	Go to *Step 19*	Go to *Step 15*
15	Inspect for poor connections at the harness connector of the EBCM. Did you find and correct the condition?	—	Go to *Step 19*	Go to *Step 16*
16	Replace the EBCM. Did you complete the repair?	—	Go to *Step 19*	—
17	Replace the underhood fuse block. Did you complete the repair?	—	Go to *Step 19*	—
18	Replace the RH underhood fuse block. Did you complete the repair?	—	Go to *Step 19*	—
19	Operate the system in order to verify the repair. Did you correct the condition?	—	System OK	Go to *Step 2*

GC4020051920030X

Fig. 326 No Communication With EBCM (Part 3 of 3). Eldorado

Circuit Description

The instrument cluster controls the operation of the TRACTION CONTROL indicator. The EBCM reports the desired status of the TRACTION CONTROL indicator via class 2 serial data messages.

Test Description

The numbers below refer to the step numbers on the diagnostic table.

3. This test uses the scan tool to check the normal state of the TRACTION CONTROL indicator control.
4. This test ensures that the instrument cluster can operate the TRACTION CONTROL indicator.

GC4020051926010X

Fig. 327 Traction Control Indicator Always On (Part 1 of 2). Eldorado

Step	Action	Value(s)	Yes	No
1	Did you review the ABS operation and perform the necessary inspections?	—	Go to *Step 2*	Go to *Symptoms*
2	Inspect the EBCM ground, making sure the ground is clean and torqued to the proper specification. Did you find and correct the condition?	—	Go to *Step 9*	Go to *Step 3*
3	1. Install a scan tool. 2. Turn ON the ignition, with the engine OFF. 3. With the scan tool, observe the TCS Warning Lamp parameter in the Delco/Bosch ABS/TCS ICCS (if equipped) data list. Does the scan tool display Off?	—	Go to *Step 4*	Go to *Step 5*
4	1. Turn OFF the ignition. 2. Turn ON the ignition, with the engine OFF. 3. Observe the TRACTION CONTROL indicator on the instrument cluster (IPC) during the bulb check. Does the TRACTION CONTROL indicator illuminate during the bulb check and then turn OFF?	—	Go to *Step 5*	Go to *Step 6*
5	Inspect for poor connections at the harness connector of the EBCM. Did you find and correct the condition?	—	Go to *Step 9*	Go to *Step 7*
6	Inspect for poor connections at the harness connector of the instrument cluster (IPC). Did you find and correct the condition?	—	Go to *Step 9*	Go to *Step 8*
7	Replace the EBCM. Did you complete the repair?	—	Go to *Step 9*	—
8	Replace the instrument cluster (IPC). Did you complete the repair?	—	Go to *Step 9*	—
9	Operate the system in order to verify the repair. Did you correct the condition?	—	System OK	Go to *Step 2*

GC4020051926020X

Fig. 327 Traction Control Indicator Always On (Part 2 of 2). Eldorado

Circuit Description

The instrument cluster controls the operation of the TRACTION CONTROL indicator. The EBCM reports the desired status of the TRACTION CONTROL indicator via class 2 serial data messages.

Test Description

The numbers below refer to the step numbers on the diagnostic table.

3. This test uses the scan tool to check the normal state of the TRACTION CONTROL indicator control.
4. This test ensures that the instrument cluster can operate the TRACTION CONTROL indicator.

GC4020051927010X

Fig. 328 Traction Control Indicator Inoperative (Part 1 of 2). Eldorado

Circuit Description

The TRACTION OFF message on the DIC is controlled by the instrument cluster via class 2 serial data messages from the EBCM. When the EBCM sees the traction control switch input grounded through the momentary traction control switch, it disables traction control and sends a message to the instrument cluster to turn ON the TRACTION OFF message on the DIC. Each time the ignition is cycled from OFF to ON, the traction control system is enabled.

GC4020051928010X

Fig. 329 Traction Off Message Always On (Part 1 of 2). Eldorado

Step	Action	Value(s)	Yes	No
1	Did you review the ABS operation and perform the necessary inspections?	—	Go to *Step 2*	Go to *Symptoms*
2	1. Install a scan tool. 2. Turn ON the ignition, with the engine OFF. 3. With the scan tool, observe the TCS On/Off Status parameter in the Delco/Bosch ABS/TCS ICCS (if equipped) data list. Does the scan tool display Off?	—	Go to *Step 3*	Go to *Step 4*
3	1. Activate the traction control switch. 2. With the scan tool, observe the TCS Switch parameter. Does the TCS On/Off Status parameter change state?	—	Go to *Intermittent*	Go to *Step 4*
4	1. Turn OFF the ignition. 2. Disconnect the traction control switch connector. 3. Turn ON the ignition, with the engine OFF. 4. With the scan tool, observe the TCS On/Off Status parameter. Does the scan tool display Off?	—	Go to *Step 7*	Go to *Step 5*
5	Test the signal circuit of the traction control switch for a short to ground. Did you find and correct the condition?	—	Go to *Step 10*	Go to *Step 6*
6	Inspect for poor connections at the harness connector of the EBCM. Did you find and correct the condition?	—	Go to *Step 10*	Go to *Step 8*
7	Inspect for poor connections at the harness connector of the traction control switch. Did you find and correct the condition?	—	Go to *Step 10*	Go to *Step 9*
8	Replace the EBCM. Did you complete the replacement?	—	Go to *Step 10*	—
9	Replace the traction control switch. Did you complete the replacement?	—	Go to *Step 10*	—
10	Operate the system in order to verify the repair. Did you correct the condition?	—	System OK	Go to *Step 2*

GC4020051928020X

Fig. 329 Traction Off Message Always On (Part 2 of 2). Eldorado

Step	Action	Value(s)	Yes	No
1	Did you review the ABS operation and perform the necessary inspections?	—	Go to *Step 2*	Go to *Symptoms*
2	Inspect the EBCM ground, making sure the ground is clean and torqued to the proper specification. Did you find and correct the condition?	—	Go to *Step 9*	Go to *Step 3*
3	1. Install a scan tool. 2. Turn ON the ignition, with the engine OFF. 3. With the scan tool, observe the TCS Warning Lamp parameter in the Delco/Bosch ABS/TCS ICCS (if equipped) data list. Does the scan tool display Off?	—	Go to *Step 4*	Go to *Step 5*
4	1. Turn OFF the ignition. 2. Turn ON the ignition, with the engine OFF. 3. Observe the TRACTION CONTROL indicator on the instrument cluster (IPC) during the bulb check. Does the TRACTION CONTROL indicator illuminate during the bulb check and then turn OFF?	—	Go to *Step 5*	Go to *Step 6*
5	Inspect for poor connections at the harness connector of the EBCM. Did you find and correct the condition?	—	Go to *Step 9*	Go to *Step 7*
6	Inspect for poor connections at the harness connector of the instrument cluster (IPC). Did you find and correct the condition?	—	Go to *Step 9*	Go to *Step 8*
7	Replace the EBCM. Did you complete the repair?	—	Go to *Step 9*	—
8	Replace the instrument cluster (IPC). Did you complete the repair?	—	Go to *Step 9*	—
9	Operate the system in order to verify the repair. Did you correct the condition?	—	System OK	Go to *Step 2*

GC4020051927020X

Fig. 328 Traction Control Indicator Inoperative (Part 2 of 2). Eldorado

Circuit Description

The TRACTION OFF message on the DIC is controlled by the instrument cluster via class 2 serial data messages from the EBCM. When the EBCM sees the traction control switch input grounded through the momentary traction control switch, it disables traction control and sends a message to the instrument cluster to turn ON the TRACTION OFF message on the DIC. Each time the ignition is cycled from OFF to ON, the traction control system is enabled.

GC4020051929010X

Fig. 330 Traction Off Message Inoperative (Part 1 of 2). Eldorado

Step	Action	Value(s)	Yes	No
1	Did you review the ABS operation and perform the necessary inspections?	—	Go to *Step 2*	Go to *Symptoms*
2	1. Install a scan tool. 2. Turn ON the ignition, with the engine OFF. 3. With the scan tool, observe the TCS On/Off Status parameter in the Delco/Bosch ABS/TCS ICCS (if equipped) data list. 4. Activate the traction control switch. Does the TCS On/Off Status parameter change state?	—	Go to *Intermittent*	Go to *Step 3*
3	1. Turn OFF the ignition. 2. Disconnect the traction control switch connector. 3. Connect a fused jumper from the signal circuit of the traction control switch harness connector to a good ground. 4. Turn ON the ignition, with the engine OFF. 5. With the scan tool, observe the TCS On/Off Status parameter. Does the scan tool display On?	—	Go to *Step 5*	Go to *Step 4*
4	Test the signal circuit of the traction control switch for an open. Did you find and correct the condition?	—	Go to *Step 10*	Go to *Step 6*
5	Test the ground circuit of the traction control switch for an open. Did you find and correct the condition?	—	Go to *Step 10*	Go to *Step 7*
6	Inspect for poor connections at the harness connector of the EBCM. Did you find and correct the condition?	—	Go to *Step 10*	Go to *Step 8*
7	Inspect for poor connections at the harness connector of the traction control switch. Did you find and correct the condition?	—	Go to *Step 10*	Go to *Step 9*
8	Replace the EBCM. Did you complete the replacement?	—	Go to *Step 10*	—
9	Replace the traction control switch. Did you complete the replacement?	—	Go to *Step 10*	—
10	Operate the system in order to verify the repair. Did you correct the condition?	—	System OK	Go to *Step 2*

GC4020051929020X

Fig. 330 Traction Off Message Inoperative (Part 2 of 2). Eldorado

Step	Action	Value(s)	Yes	No
1	Did you review the ABS operation and perform the necessary inspections?	—	Go to *Step 2*	Go to *Symptoms*
2	1. Install a scan tool. 2. Turn ON the ignition, with the engine OFF. 3. Select the powertrain control module (PCM) display DTCs function. Did the scan tool display DTC P1575?	—	*DTC P1575 Extended Travel Brake Switch Circuit*	Go to *Step 3*
3	1. With the scan tool, observe the Extended Travel Brake Switch parameter in the Delco/Bosch ABS/TCS ICCS2 data list. 2. Step on and off the brake pedal with enough force to simulate a hard braking condition. As the brake pedal is pressed and released, the scan tool should read Applied and Released. 3. Use a tape measure in order to measure the distance that the brake pedal travels for the scan tool to read Applied. Does the distance measure within the specified range?	1.0–1.3 in (2.5–3.3 cm)	Go to *Intermittent*	Go to *Step 4*
4	Adjust or repair the extended travel brake switch as necessary. Did you complete the repair?	—	Go to *Step 5*	—
5	Operate the system in order to verify the repair. Did you correct the condition?	—	System OK	Go to *Step 2*

GC4020051923020X

Fig. 331 Vehicle Stability Enhancement System Excessive Brake Pulsation (Part 2 of 2). Eldorado

Circuit Description

When braking during vehicle stability enhancement system (VSES) activation, the brake pedal will feel different than the ABS pedal pulsation. The brake pedal pulsates at a higher frequency during VSES activation. Perform this test if the brake pedal buzzes excessively during medium braking. Medium braking is defined as greater than 0.3 g or 3 m/s^2 (10 ft/s^2).

GC4020051923010X

Fig. 331 Vehicle Stability Enhancement System Excessive Brake Pulsation (Part 1 of 2). Eldorado

Circuit Description

Vehicle stability enhancement system (VSES) activations generally occur during aggressive driving. Perform this test when the VSES does not activate when the vehicle is driven aggressively enough to require activation (this can be subjective).

Step	Action	Value(s)	Yes	No
1	Did you review the ABS operation and perform the necessary inspections?	—	Go to *Step 2*	Go to *Symptoms*
2	1. Install a scan tool. 2. Start the engine. 3. Observe the Stabilitrak Steering Angle Is Centered parameter in the Delco/Bosch ABS/TCS ICCS2 data list. 4. Perform Test Drive. Did the scan tool display Yes within the specified value?	30 seconds	Go to *Intermittent*	Go to *Step 3*
3	Perform the diagnosis for DTC C1283. Did you find and correct the condition?	—	Go to *Step 5*	Go to *Step 4*
4	Replace the EBCM. Did you complete the replacement?	—	Go to *Step 5*	—
5	Operate the system in order to verify the repair. Did you correct the condition?	—	System OK	Go to *Step 2*

GC4020051921000X

Fig. 332 Vehicle Stability Enhancement System Inoperative. Eldorado

Circuit Description

When the vehicle stability enhancement system (VSES) or TCS activates for longer than 1.5 seconds, there will be an accompanying DIC message. Short activations of either system may occur without any DIC messages. The VSES activations mostly occur in the turns or bumpy roads without much use of the accelerator pedal. Activations may also occur during aggressive driving.

Unwanted VSES activations may be caused by the following:

- A loosely mounted yaw rate sensor
- An intermittent faulty steering wheel position sensor
- An intermittent wiring harness problem
- A chassis alignment that is grossly out of specification
- The wrong EBCM installed
- The wrong steering gear rack installed

Step	Action	Value(s)	Yes	No
1	Did you review the ABS operation and perform the necessary inspections?	—	Go to *Step 2*	Go to *Symptoms*
2	Inspect the mounting of the yaw rate sensor. Did you find and correct the condition?	—	Go to *Step 15*	Go to *Step 3*
3	1. Install a scan tool. 2. Start the engine. 3. With the scan tool, observe the Yaw Rate Sensor Input parameter in the Delco/Bosch ABS/TCS ICCS2 data list. 4. Perform the Test Drive. Does the scan tool display suddenly increase or decrease without rapid turning of the vehicle?	—	Go to *Step 4*	Go to *Step 5*

GC4020051922010X

Fig. 333 Vehicle Stability Enhancement System Unwanted Activation (Part 1 of 2). Eldorado

Step	Action	Value(s)	Yes	No
4	Perform the diagnosis for DTC C1282. Did you find and correct the condition?	—	Go to *Step 15*	Go to *Step 12*
5	1. Straighten the front wheels. 2. Observe the Digital SWPS Phase A and Digital SWPS Phase B in the Delco/Bosch ABS/TCS ICCS2 data list. 3. Slowly rotate the steering wheel in both directions. Does the scan tool display change states as the steering wheel was rotated?	—	Go to *Step 6*	Go to *Step 14*
6	Use the scan tool in order to perform the Steering Position Sensor Test in the Delco/Bosch ABS/TCS ICCS2 Special Functions. Did the steering wheel position sensor (SWPS) pass the test?	—	Go to *Step 7*	Go to *Step 14*
7	1. Place the vehicle on a level surface. 2. With the scan tool, observe the Lateral Accelerometer Input parameter in the Delco/Bosch ABS/TCS ICCS2 data list. Does the scan tool display within the specified range?	2.3–2.7 V	Go to *Step 9*	Go to *Step 8*
8	Inspect the mounting of the lateral accelerometer sensor. Did you find and correct the condition?	—	Go to *Step 15*	Go to *Step 9*
9	Inspect the EBCM for the proper part number. Did you find the correct part number?	—	Go to *Step 10*	Go to *Step 12*
10	Inspect the power steering gear for the proper part number. Did you find the correct part number?	—	Go to *Step 11*	Go to *Step 13*
11	Inspect the alignment of the vehicle. Did you find and correct the condition?	—	Go to *Step 15*	Go to *Intermittent*
12	Replace the EBCM. Did you complete the replacement?	—	Go to *Step 15*	—
13	Replace the power steering gear. Did you complete the replacement?	—	Go to *Step 15*	—
14	Replace the steering wheel position sensor (SWPS). Did you complete the replacement?	—	Go to *Step 15*	—
15	Operate the system in order to verify the repair. Did you correct the condition?	—	System OK	Go to *Step 2*

GC4020051922020X

Fig. 333 Vehicle Stability Enhancement System Unwanted Activation (Part 2 of 2). Eldorado

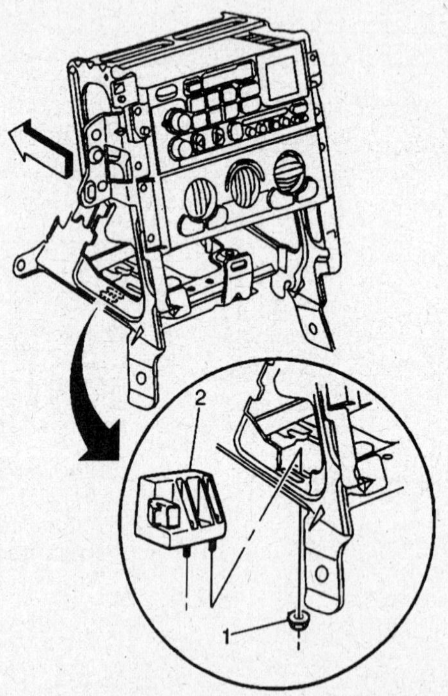

Fig. 334 Yaw rate sensor removal. Corvette

Lucas/Sumitomo

NOTE: On Air Bag Equipped Models, Refer To "Air Bag System Precautions" Located In The Front Of This Manual For System Disarming & Arming Procedures.

NOTE: Refer To "Computer Relearn Procedures" Located In The Front Of This Manual When Battery Power To The Computer Has Been Interrupted.

NOTE: "Electrical Symbol & Wire Color Code Identification" Located In The Front Of This Manual May Be Used As An Aid When Using Wiring Circuits Found In This Section.

INDEX

PRECAUTIONS

Air Bag Systems

Refer to "Air Bag System Precautions" in the front of this manual for system disarming and arming procedures.

Battery Ground Cable

Prior to service, disconnect battery ground cable and isolate as required.

ABS Service

Before performing any repairs on the ABS system, note the following precautions:

1. Before using electric welding equipment, disconnect EBCM.
2. Carefully note routing, position and mounting ABS and TCS wiring, connectors, clips and brackets. ABS and TCS are extremely sensitive to electromagnetic interference.
3. Do not use a fast charger when battery is connected. **Never disconnect battery from system with engine running.**
4. Ignition switch must be in Off position when disconnecting EBCM.
5. Many ABS system components are non-serviceable and must be replaced as assemblies. **Do not disassemble non-serviceable components.**
6. Do not hang other components on wheel speed sensor cables.
7. Do not expose EBCM to temperatures of more than 184°F.
8. Use DOT 3 brake fluid only. Do not use container that has been used with petroleum based fluids or is wet with water. Petroleum based fluids will damage system and water will lower boiling point. Keep fluid containers capped.
9. After replacing any ABS component, inspect system as outlined in "Diagnosis & Testing."

DESCRIPTION

System Operation

The Lucas/Sumitomo system is a hybrid non-integral Anti-lock Braking System (ABS). The system uses a single valve per channel, 4 channel system to reduce the tendency of any wheel to lock-up. ABS operation is available from approximately 4 mph to maximum vehicle speed. During braking, ABS is available from maximum vehicle speed to 3 mph. ABS is used to minimize wheel slipping during braking, allowing for improved vehicle stability and steerability. ABS is accomplished by controlling the hydraulic pressure applied to each front wheel brake and both rear wheel brakes as a pair.

System Components

Refer to **Figs. 1 and 2,** for system component locations.

BRAKE PRESSURE MODULATOR VALVE/ ELECTRONIC BRAKE CONTROL MODULE

The ABS system is controlled by the Electronic Brake Control Module (EBCM). The Brake Pressure Modulator Valve (BPMV) is a compact integrated unit that contains the EBCM, four solenoid valves, four flow control valves in series with each wheel brake hydraulic channel, buffer chambers, pump motor and check valves. The EBCM monitors the speed of each wheel. If any wheel begins to approach lock-up and the brake switch is on, the EBCM controls the motors and solenoids to reduce brake pressure to the wheel approaching lock-up. Once the wheel regains traction, brake pressure is increased until wheel begins to approach lock-up. This cycle repeats until either the vehicle comes to a stop, the brake is released or no wheels approach lock-up. Additionally, the EBCM monitors each input and each output for proper operation. If any system fault is detected, the EBCM will store a Diagnostic Trouble Code (DTC) in nonvolatile memory.

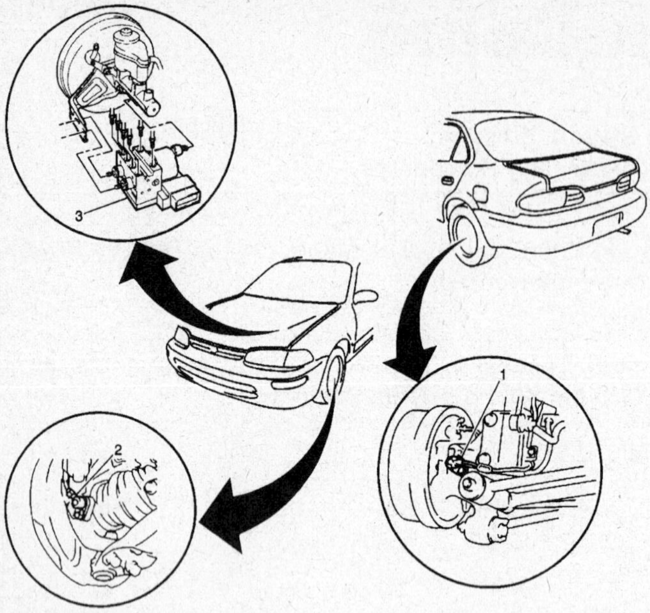

(1) Rear Wheel Speed Sensor
(2) Front Wheel Speed Sensor
(3) Electronic Brake Control Module (EBCM)\Brake Pressure Modulator Valve (BPMV) Assembly

GC4029803584000X

Fig. 1 ABS component location. Prizm

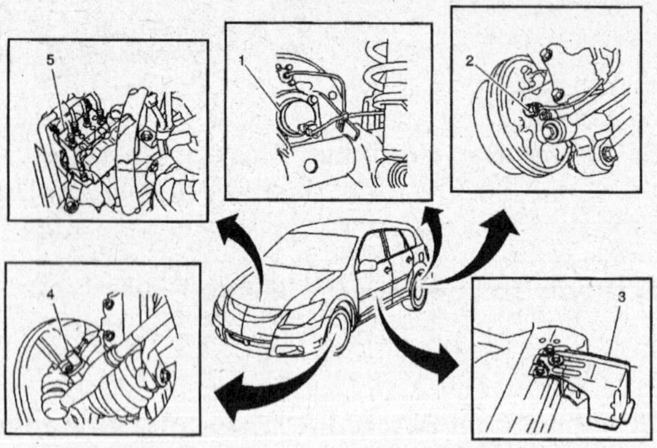

(1) Rear Wheel Speed Sensor FWD
(2) Rear Wheel Speed Sensor AWD
(3) Deceleration Sensor AWD
(4) Front Wheel Speed Sensor
(5) Electronic Brake Control Module (EBCM)/Brake Pressure Modulator Valve (BPMV) Assembly

ARM66GC000000208

Fig. 2 ABS component location. Vibe

WHEEL SPEED SENSORS

The front wheel speed sensors are located on the front steering knuckles. The rear wheel speed sensors are mounted in the rear suspension knuckles. An AC signal is generated by a rotating toothed ring near the sensor pole piece, which produces a magnetic field that increases and decreases in magnitude and frequency proportional to speed. This low voltage signal is sent to the EBCM.

ABS INDICATOR

The ABS indicator turns On light to alert the driver of a fault. When the ABS warning indicator remains On after the 3 second bulb inspection, the ABS is disabled but normal (Non anti-lock) braking will remain.

DIAGNOSIS & TESTING

Accessing Diagnostic Trouble Codes

Diagnostic Trouble Codes (DTC)s may be read using a suitable programed scan tool. There are no provisions for flash code diagnostics.

1. Turn ignition switch to Off position.
2. Connect suitably programmed scan tool to Data Link Connector (DLC), located under lefthand side of instrument panel below steering column.
3. Turn ignition switch to On position.
4. Select DTCs from application menu.
5. Select DTC information on scan tool, then read and record DTCs.

Diagnostic Trouble Code Interpretation

DTCs may be read using a suitably programmed scan tool. There are no flash code diagnostic provisions.

If an ABS fault occurs, the EBCM turns On the ABS warning indicator. The ABS warning indicator remains On for the duration of the ignition cycle in which the EBCM detected the fault and the EBCM stores a DTC. The EBCM stores a SNAP SHOT of several inputs at the time the DTC was detected. This is called enhanced DTC. At the end of ignition cycle (Ignition switch to Lock position), the DTC moves from Current to History. The capture data information is always related to the last DTC set. Retrieve Current, History and Enhance DTC using a scan tool.

Refer to **Figs. 3 and 4,** for diagnostic trouble code interpretation.

Wiring Diagrams

Refer to **Figs. 5 and 6,** for system wiring diagrams.

Diagnostic Tests

PRIZM

Refer to **Figs. 7 through 32,** for diagnostic tests.

VIBE

Refer to **Figs. 33 through 47,** for diagnostic tests.

Intermittents & Poor Connections

Intermittent failures in the anti-lock brake system may be difficult to accurately diagnose. The ABS DTCs which may be stored by the EBCM are not designated as Current or History DTCs. Use the following procedure to assist in intermittent failure diagnosis.

1. Display and clear any ABS DTCs present in EBCM.
2. Attempt to repeat failure condition as follows:
   a. Turn ignition switch to Off position.
   b. Disconnect scan tool. **If scan tool is installed, EBCM will not set DTCs and ABS/TCS functions may not be available.**
   c. Test drive vehicle.
3. After duplicating condition, stop vehicle and display any DTCs stored.
4. If no DTCs were stored refer to "Troubleshooting."
5. If a DTC was stored, inspect related electrical connectors and wiring for the following:
   a. Poor mating of connector halves.
   b. Terminals not fully seated in connector halves.
   c. Improperly formed, or damaged terminals. All connector terminals in a problem circuit should be carefully reformed to increase contact tension.
   d. Poor terminal to wire connection. In most cases, this will require removing wire from connector body.
6. If there is an intermittent warning lamp operation, the following EBCM circuits should be inspected:
   a. Low system voltage. If low voltage is detected at EBCM, ABS lamp will illuminate until normal operating voltage is detected.
   b. Low brake fluid. This condition in BPMV reservoir will cause brake and ABS lamps to illuminate. When

Code	Description
B3449	Stop Lamp Circuit Fault
C0035	Left Front Wheel Speed Circuit Fault
C0036	Left Front Wheel Speed Circuit Range/Performance
C0040	Right Front Wheel Speed Circuit Fault
C0041	Right Front Wheel Speed Circuit Range/Performance
C0045	Left Rear Wheel Speed Circuit Fault
C0046	Left Rear Wheel Speed Circuit Range/Performance
C0050	Right Rear Wheel Speed Circuit Fault
C0051	Right Rear Wheel Speed Circuit Range/Performance
C0060	Left Front ABS Solenoid Number 1 Circuit Fault
C0070	Right Front ABS Solenoid Number 1 Circuit Fault
C0080	Left Rear ABS Solenoid Number 1 Circuit Fault
C0090	Right Rear ABS Solenoid Number 1 Circuit Fault
C0110	Pump Motor Circuit Fault
C0114	Pump Motor Circuit Open
C0116	Pump Motor Relay Circuit Fault
C0121	Valve Relay Circuit Fault
C0125	Valve Relay Circuit Open
C0550	Electronic Brake Control Module Fault
C0899	Device Number 1 Voltage Low
C0900	Device Number 1 Voltage High

Fig. 3 Diagnostic Trouble Code Interpretation. Prizm

Code	Description
C0200	Wheel Speed Sensor Circuit
C0205	Wheel Speed Sensor Circuit
C0210	Wheel Speed Sensor Circuit
C0215	Wheel Speed Sensor Circuit
C0226	Solenoid Circuit Open Or Short
C0236	Solenoid Circuit Open Or Short
C0246	Solenoid Circuit Open Or Short
C0256	Solenoid Circuit Open Or Short
C0273	EBCM Detects Open In Pump Motor Circuit
C0274	EBCM Detects Short In Pump Motor Circuit
C0278	EBCM Detects Valve Relay Off When Commanded On
C0279	EBCM Detects Valve Relay On When Commanded Off
C1235	Wheel Speed Sensor Circuits
C1236	Wheel Speed Sensor Circuits
C1238	Wheel Speed Sensor Circuits
C1239	Wheel Speed Sensor Circuits
C1241	System Voltage
C1243	Deceleration Sensor Ciruit
C1244	Deceleration Sensor Circuit Open Or Short
C1249	Stop Lamp Switch Circuit Open
C1251	EBCM Detects Pump Motor Is Stuck
C1271	Wheel Speed Sensor Circuits
C1272	Wheel Speed Sensor Circuits
C1273	Wheel Speed Sensor Circuits
C1274	Wheel Speed Sensor Circuits
C1275	Wheel Speed Sensor Circuits
C1277	Wheel Speed Sensor Circuits
C1278	Wheel Speed Sensor Circuits
C1279	EBCM Detects Fault In Deceleration Sensor

Fig. 4 Diagnostic Trouble Code Interpretation. Vibe

an acceptable fluid level is registered, lamps will no longer be illuminated.

7. Any condition which results in interruption of power to EBCM or hydraulic unit may cause warning lamps to turn on intermittently. These circuits include main relay, pump motor relay, fuses and related wiring.

Electromagnetic Interference Test

Due to the sensitivity of ABS components to electromagnetic interference, the following inspections should be performed if an intermittent fault is suspected.

1. Inspect for proper installation of wiring harnesses resulting from add on options.
2. Inspect front wheel speed sensor wiring for proper routing away from spark plug wires.

Clearing Diagnostic Trouble Codes

DTCs cannot be cleared by disconnecting the EBCM, battery cables or turning the ignition switch to the Lock position. DTCs can only be cleared with a suitably programmed scan tool, refer to the scan tool manufacturers' instructions for procedure.

SYSTEM SERVICE

Brake System Bleed

PRESSURE BLEED

If the master cylinder or BPMV was replaced, refer to "Auto Bleed" in this section.

1. Ensure level of brake fluid in reservoir is at least ½ full during bleeding operation.
2. Install brake bleeder adapter tool No. J39801, or equivalent, to master cylinder reservoir.
3. Charge pressure bleeder with 20-25 psi of compressed air.
4. Connect pressure bleeder to brake bleeder adapter.
5. Raise and support vehicle.
6. Attach a transparent hose over valve, then submerge other end of hose in a transparent container filled with brake fluid.
7. Loosen bleeder valve in order to purge air from system.
8. **Torque** bleeder valve to 72 inch lbs.
9. Wait 15 seconds.
10. Repeat steps 6 through 8 until all air is removed and air bubbles are no longer present in transparent hose.
11. Repeat steps 6 through 9 until all wheels are bled.
12. Lower vehicle.
13. Ensure brake pedal action is firm. If pedal feels spongy, repeat entire pressure bleeding procedure.
14. Remove pressure bleeder.

MANUAL BLEED

If the master cylinder or BPMV was replaced, refer to "Auto Bleed" in this section.

Bleed the system in the following sequence; right rear, left rear, right front and left front.

1. Turn ignition to Off position.
2. Remove vacuum reserve by applying brakes several times.
3. Remove master cylinder reservoir cap.
4. Fill reservoir to appropriate level, then install cap tightly.
5. Ensure level of brake fluid in reservoir is at least ½ full during bleeding operation.
6. Attach a transparent tube to bleeder plug, then submerge opposite end in a clear container partially filled with brake fluid.
7. Depress brake pedal several times, then hold brake pedal fully depressed.
8. With brake pedal fully depressed, loosen bleeder plug approximately ½ turn. Brake pedal should fall to floor as fluid flows out of bleeder plug into container.
9. Tighten bleeder plug, then slowly release brake pedal.
10. Repeat steps 7 through 9 until air is removed from line and air bubbles are no longer present in container.
11. Fill brake fluid in master cylinder reservoir to MAX mark, then install cap.
12. Pump brake pedal and inspect for fluid leaks.
13. If brake pedal feels spongy, repeat entire bleeding procedure.

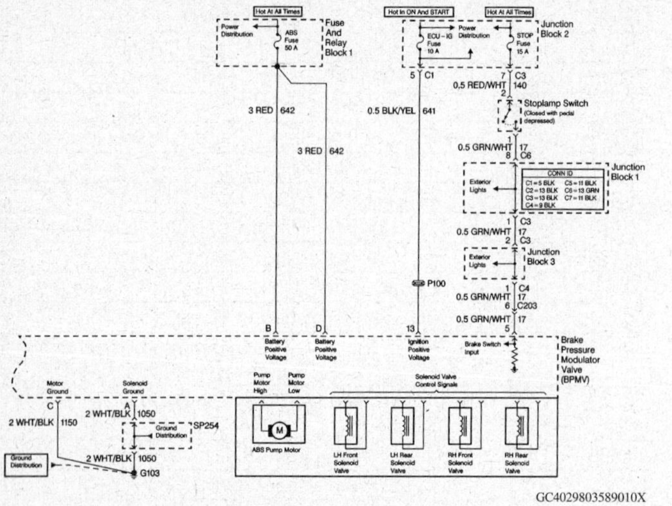

GC4029803589010X

Fig. 5 Wiring diagram (Part 1 of 3). Prizm

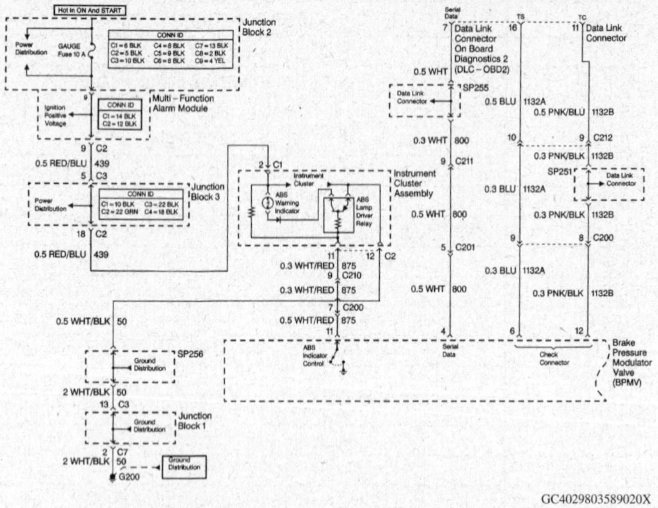

GC4029803589020X

Fig. 5 Wiring diagram (Part 2 of 3). Prizm

14. If brake indicator indicates an unbalanced pressure, repeat entire bleeding procedure.
15. Repeat bleeding procedure at all wheels that require bleeding.
16. Remove bleeding equipment.

AUTO BLEED

This procedure cycles system valves and runs pump in order to purge air from secondary circuits normally closed off during non ABS mode operation and bleeding. The auto bleed procedure is recommended when air ingestion is suspected in secondary circuits, or when the BPMV has been replaced.

Auto bleed procedure may be terminated at any time during process by pressing EXIT button. After pressing EXIT, relieve bleed pressure and disconnect bleed equipment.

1. Raise and support vehicle.
2. Remove tire and wheel assemblies.
3. Inspect brake system for leaks and visual damage.
4. Ensure battery is properly charged.
5. Connect scan tool to DLC.
6. Turn ignition to On position with engine off.
7. Establish communication with ABS system.
8. Select special functions, then the automated bleed procedure.
9. Bleed base brake system as outlined in "Pressure Bleed" in this section.
10. Follow scan tool directions until desired brake pedal height is achieved.
11. If bleed procedure is aborted, proceed as follows:
    a. If a DTC is detected, refer to "Diagnostic Trouble Code Interpretation."
    b. Bleed base brake system as outlined in "Pressure Bleed" in this section.
12. Bleed base brake system a second time. If proper pedal height is not achieved, repeat auto bleed procedure.
13. Disconnect scan tool, then install wheel and tire assemblies.
14. Inspect brake fluid level, then road test vehicle. Ensure brake pedal remains high and firm.

HYDRAULIC SYSTEM FLUSH

If brake fluid is old, rusty or contaminated, or whenever new components are installed in hydraulic system, the system must be flushed. Bleed brakes, allowing at least one quart of clean brake fluid to pass through system. Any rubber components in hydraulic system which were exposed to contaminated fluid must be replaced.

When flushing system, follow steps specified in "Manual Bleed" in this section.

Component Replacement

BRAKE MODULATOR & ELECTRONIC BRAKE CONTROL MODULE (EBCM) ASSEMBLY

PRIZM

1. Remove air cleaner assembly.
2. Disconnect EBCM harness connector (2), **Fig. 48.**

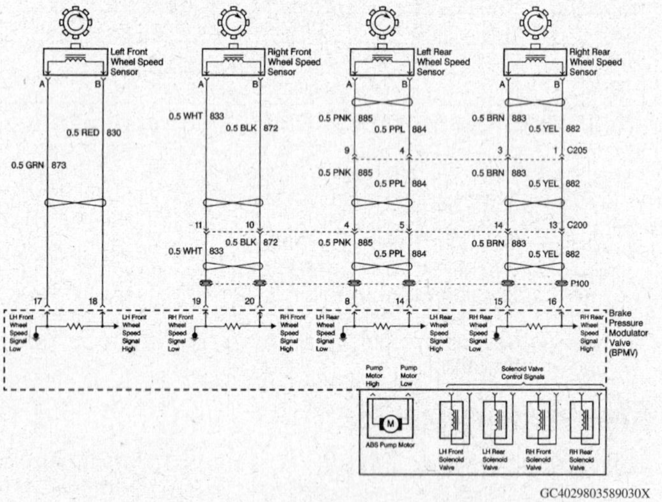

GC4029803589030X

Fig. 5 Wiring diagram (Part 3 of 3). Prizm

3. Remove six brake pipes from BPMV assembly.
4. Plug brake pipes to prevent loss or contamination of brake fluid.
5. Remove three retaining nuts, then the BPMV assembly from bracket.
6. Reverse procedure to install, noting the following:
    a. **Torque** BPMV retaining nuts to 15 ft. lbs.
    b. **Torque** brake pipe fitting nuts to 11 inch lbs.
    c. Bleed brake system as outlined in "Brake System Bleed."
    d. Perform system inspect as outlined in "Troubleshooting."

VIBE

1. Disconnect EBCM electrical connector.
2. Remove six brake hydraulic pipes from modulator assembly. Plug pipes to prevent contamination.
3. Remove brake pressure modulator bracket attaching bolts and nut.
4. Remove modulator and bracket assembly.
5. Remove brake pressure modulator assembly to bracket retaining nuts, then

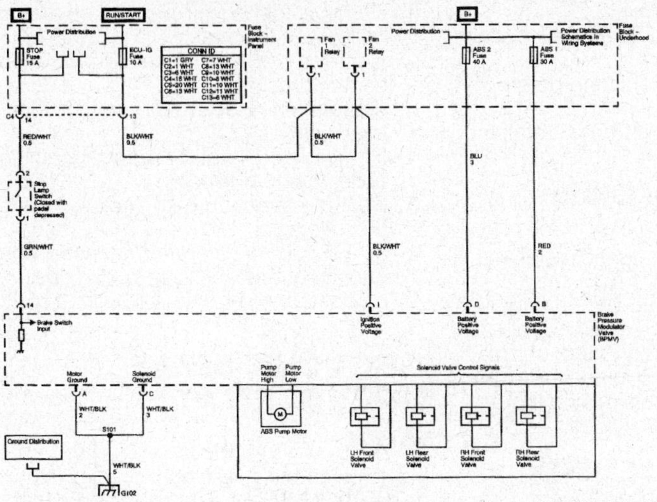

ARM66GC000000170

Fig. 6 Wiring diagram (Part 1 of 4). Vibe

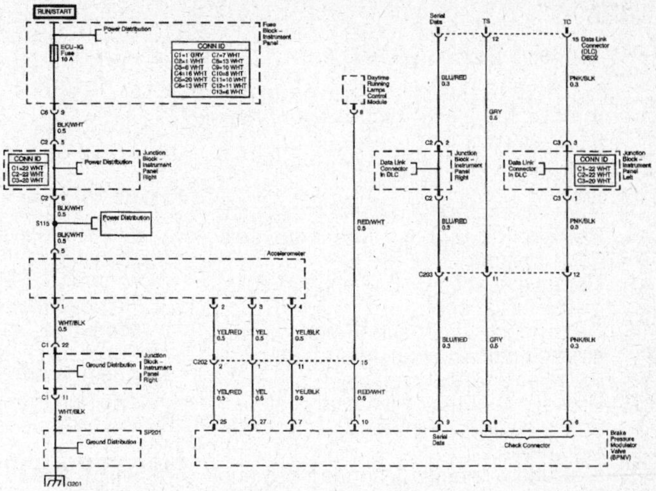

ARM66GC000000171

Fig. 6 Wiring diagram (Part 2 of 4). Vibe

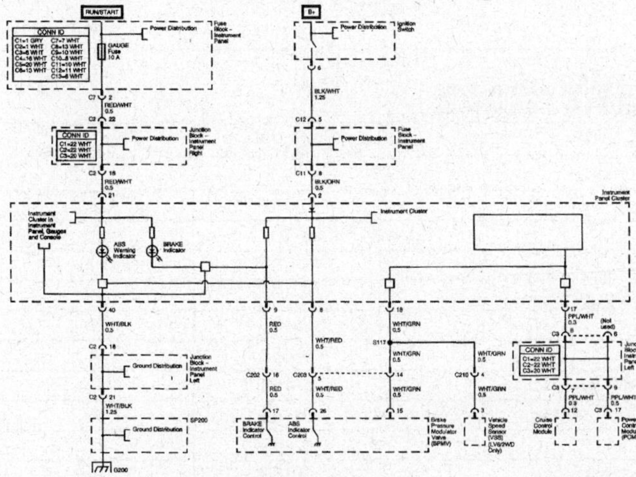

ARM66GC000000172

Fig. 6 Wiring diagram (Part 3 of 4). Vibe

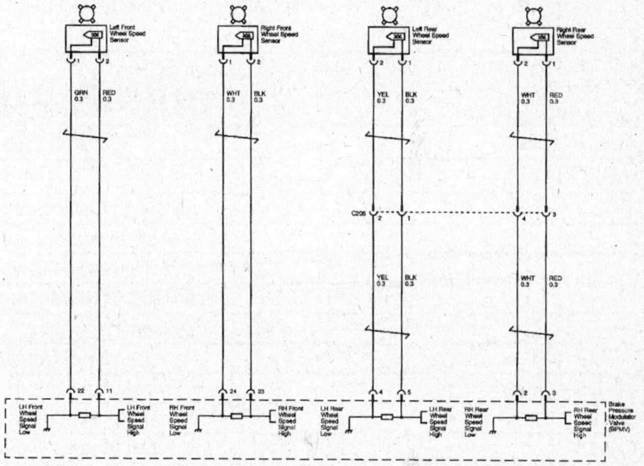

ARM66GC000000173

Fig. 6 Wiring diagram (Part 4 of 4). Vibe

the assembly from bracket.

6. Reverse procedure to install, noting the following:
   a. **Torque** modulator assembly to bracket retaining nuts to 42 inch lbs.
   b. **Torque** modulator bracket attaching bolts and nut to 14 ft. lbs.
   c. **Torque** brake pipe fittings to 11 ft. lbs.

FRONT WHEEL SPEED SENSOR

PRIZM

1. Raise and support vehicle.
2. Remove six retaining bolts and six plastic clips, then the wheel housing.
3. Disconnect wheel speed sensor electrical connector. **Wheel speed sensor is serviceable only as an assembly. Do not attempt to service sensor harness pigtail.**
4. Remove two nuts and clips retaining wheel speed sensor pigtail harness to vehicle.
5. Remove wheel speed sensor retaining bolt, then the sensor from steering knuckle.
6. Reverse procedure to install, noting the following:
   a. **Torque** wheel speed sensor retaining bolt to 72 inch lbs.
   b. **Torque** wheel speed sensor pigtail harness nuts to 48 inch lbs.

VIBE

1. Raise and support vehicle.
2. Remove fender flare from wheelhouse.
3. Remove wheelhouse panel from fender.
4. Disconnect wheel speed sensor electrical connector.
5. Remove wheel speed sensor pigtail electrical harness retaining bolts.
6. Remove wheel speed sensor retaining bolt, then the sensor from steering knuckle.
7. Reverse procedure to install, noting the following:
   a. **Torque** wheel speed sensor retaining to 71 inch lbs.
   b. **Torque** pigtail harness retaining nuts to 21 ft. lbs.

REAR WHEEL SPEED SENSOR

PRIZM

1. Remove rear seat bottom and seat back.
2. Disconnect wheel speed sensor electrical connector. **Wheel speed sensor is serviceable only as an assembly. Do not attempt to service sensor harness pigtail.**
3. Raise and support vehicle.
4. Pull wheel speed sensor pigtail harness out through body, then remove grommet.
5. Remove three wheel speed sensor pigtail harness to vehicle retaining bolts.
6. Remove wheel speed sensor retaining bolt, then the wheel speed sensor from knuckle.
7. Reverse procedure to install, noting the following:
   a. **Torque** wheel speed sensor retaining bolt to 72 inch lbs.
   b. **Torque** wheel speed sensor pigtail harness nuts to 48 inch lbs.

VIBE

All Wheel Drive (AWD)

1. Fold rear seat back cushion down and remove two plastic hinge covers from seat back cushion.
2. Remove trim panel from rear seat back.
3. Remove center rear seat belt retractor.
4. Remove hinge bolts from rear seat back cushion.
5. Remove seat back pivot support bolts, then the rear seat.
6. Disconnect wheel speed sensor harness electrical connector.
7. Raise and support vehicle.
8. Remove fuel tank filler pipe protector attaching bolts, then the fuel tank filler pipe protector.
9. Pull wheel speed sensor harness and grommet through body.
10. Remove wheel speed sensor harness to control arm retaining bolts.
11. Remove wheel speed sensor retaining bolt, then the sensor.
12. Reverse procedure to install, noting the following:
    a. **Torque** sensor retaining bolt to 71 inch lbs.
    b. **Torque** sensor harness retaining bolts to 44 inch lbs.

Front Wheel Drive (FWD)

1. Raise and support vehicle.
2. Disconnect speed sensor electrical connector, **Fig. 49.**
3. Remove rear axle hub and bearing assembly as outlined in "Rear Axle & Suspension" section of "Vibe" chapter.
4. Remove wheel speed sensor from rear axle hub using suitable pulling tool.
5. Reverse procedure to install.

DECELERATION SENSOR

VIBE

The deceleration sensor is located under the lefthand front seat.

1. Remove lefthand front seat retaining bolts, then the seat.
2. Remove bolt from upper deceleration sensor bracket.
3. Disconnect deceleration sensor electrical connector.
4. Remove deceleration sensor retaining bolts, then the sensor.
5. Reverse procedure to install, noting the following:
    a. **Torque** deceleration sensor and sensor bracket bolts to 15 ft. lbs.
    b. **Torque** seat retaining bolts to 35 ft. lbs.

ELECTRONIC BRAKE CONTROL RELAY

PRIZM

The electronic brake control relay is part of the EBCM/BPMV assembly and cannot be serviced separately. Refer to "Brake Modulator Assembly" in this section for service procedure.

DIAGNOSTIC CHART INDEX

Test/Code	Description	Page No.	Fig. No.
PRIZM			
—	ABS Diagnostic System Check	6-458	7
—	ABS Indicator Inoperative	6-467	30
—	ABS Indicator Always On	6-467	31
—	Scan Tool Displays Undefined DTC	6-467	32
—	No Communication With EBCM	6-466	29
B3449	Stop Lamp Circuit Fault	6-458	8
C0035	Left Front Wheel Speed Circuit Fault	6-458	9
C0036	Left Front Wheel Speed Circuit Range/Performance	6-459	10
C0040	Right Front Wheel Speed Circuit Fault	6-459	11
C0041	Right Front Wheel Speed Circuit Range/Performance	6-460	12
C0045	Left Rear Wheel Speed Circuit Fault	6-460	13
C0046	Left Rear Wheel Speed Circuit Range/Performance	6-461	14
C0050	Right Rear Wheel Speed Circuit Fault	6-461	15
C0051	Right Rear Wheel Speed Circuit Range/Performance	6-462	16
C0060	Left Front ABS Solenoid Number 1 Circuit Fault	6-462	17
C0070	Right Front ABS Solenoid Number 1 Circuit Fault	6-463	18
C0080	Left Rear ABS Solenoid Number 1 Circuit Fault	6-463	19
C0090	Right Rear ABS Solenoid Number 1 Circuit Fault	6-463	20
C0110	Pump Motor Circuit Fault	6-463	21
C0114	Pump Motor Circuit Open	6-464	22
C0116	Pump Motor Relay Circuit Fault	6-464	23
C0121	Valve Relay Circuit Fault	6-464	24
C0125	Valve Relay Circuit Open	6-465	25
C0550	Electronic Brake Control Module Fault	6-465	26
C0899	Device Number 1 Voltage Low	6-465	27
C0900	Device Number 1 Voltage High	6-466	28
VIBE			
—	ABS Indicator Always On	6-475	46
—	ABS Indicator Inoperative	6-475	47
—	Diagnostic Circuit Check	6-468	33
C0200	Wheel Speed Sensor Circuit	6-468	34
C0205	Wheel Speed Sensor Circuit	6-468	34
C0210	Wheel Speed Sensor Circuit	6-468	34
C0215	Wheel Speed Sensor Circuit	6-468	34

Continued

DIAGNOSTIC CHART INDEX—Continued

Test/Code	Description	Page No.	Fig. No.
VIBE			
C0226	Solenoid Circuit Open Or Short	6-469	35
C0236	Solenoid Circuit Open Or Short	6-469	35
C0246	Solenoid Circuit Open Or Short	6-469	35
C0256	Solenoid Circuit Open Or Short	6-469	35
C0273	EBCM Detects Open In Pump Motor Circuit	6-469	36
C0274	EBCM Detects Short In Pump Motor Circuit	6-470	37
C0278	EBCM Detects Valve Relay Off When Commanded On	6-470	38
C0279	EBCM Detects Valve Relay On When Commanded Off	6-471	39
C1235	Wheel Speed Sensor Circuits	6-468	34
C1236	Wheel Speed Sensor Circuits	6-468	34
C1238	Wheel Speed Sensor Circuits	6-468	34
C1239	Wheel Speed Sensor Circuits	6-468	34
C1241	System Voltage	6-471	40
C1243	Deceleration Sensor Ciruit	6-472	41
C1244	Deceleration Sensor Circuit Open Or Short	6-473	42
C1249	Stop Lamp Switch Circuit Open	6-473	43
C1251	EBCM Detects Pump Motor Is Stuck	6-474	44
C1271	Wheel Speed Sensor Circuits	6-468	34
C1272	Wheel Speed Sensor Circuits	6-468	34
C1273	Wheel Speed Sensor Circuits	6-468	34
C1274	Wheel Speed Sensor Circuits	6-468	34
C1275	Wheel Speed Sensor Circuits	6-468	34
C1277	Wheel Speed Sensor Circuits	6-468	34
C1278	Wheel Speed Sensor Circuits	6-468	34
C1279	EBCM Detects Fault In Deceleration Sensor	6-474	45

Circuit Description

A Diagnostic System Check – ABS is an organized approach to identify problems associated with the EBCM. This check must be the starting point for any EBCM complaint and will direct you to the next logical step in diagnosing the complaint. The EBCM is a very reliable component and is not likely the cause of the malfunction. Most system complaints are linked to faulty wiring, connectors, and occasionally to components. Understanding the ABS system and using the tables correctly will reduce diagnostic time and prevent unnecessary parts replacement.

Diagnostic Aids

- An intermittent failure in the electronic system may be very difficult to detect and to accurately diagnose. The EBCM tests for different malfunctions under different vehicle conditions. For this reason, a thorough test drive is often needed in order to repeat a malfunction. If the system malfunction is not repeated during the test drive, a good description of the complaint may be very useful in locating an intermittent malfunction. Faulty electrical connections or wiring causes most intermitting problems. When an intermitting condition is suspected, check the suspected circuits for the following conditions:
  - Poor mating of connector halves or backed out terminals
  - Improperly formed or damaged terminals
  - Wire chafing
  - Poor wire to terminal connections
  - Dirty or corroded terminals
  - Damage to connector bodies
- If the DTC is a history DTC, the problem may be intermittent. Perform the tests shown while moving related wiring and connectors. This can often cause the malfunction to occur. Perform a thorough inspection of all related wiring and connectors pertaining to the history DTC stored.

Step	Action	Value(s)	Yes	No
1	1. Reconnect all previously disconnected components. 2. Cycle the Ignition switch from the OFF to ON position, engine OFF. 3. Plug a scan tool into the Data Link Connector (DLC). Does the Scan Tool communicate with the EBCM?	—	Go to *Step 3*	Go to *Step 2*
2	Does the scan tool communicate with other modules on the serial data line?	—	Go to *No Communication with EBCM*	*Scan Tool Does Not Communicate with Components*
3	With the scan tool read ABS DTCs. Are there any current Diagnostic Trouble Codes?	—	Go to Applicable DTC Table	Go to *Step 4*
4	Cycle the ignition switch from the OFF to ON position. Does the ABS Indicator come ON then go OFF after several seconds?	—	Go to *Step 6*	Go to *Step 5*
5	Does the ABS Indicator come ON and stay ON?	—	Go to *ABS Indicator Always On*	Go to *ABS Indicator Inoperative*
6	Are there any History DTCs?	—	Go to *Step 7*	System OK
7	1. Refer to the appropriate DTC table for the History DTC. 2. Read the diagnostic aids, and conditions for setting the DTC. 3. Carefully drive the vehicle above 24 km/h (15 mph) for several minutes while monitoring a scan tool for ABS DTCs. Did the History DTC set as a current DTC while the vehicle was being driven?	—	Go to Applicable DTC Table	System OK

GC4020052285000X

Fig. 7 ABS Diagnostic System Check. Prizm

Inspect the following harness connectors for the following conditions:

- Backed-out terminals
- Improper mating
- Broken locks
- Improperly formed or damaged terminals
- Poor terminal to wiring connections or physical damage to the wiring harness before component replacement:
  - Junction block electrical connectors
  - Stoplamp switch electrical connector
  - EBCM electrical connector

Test Description

The number(s) below refer to the step number(s) on the diagnostic table.

2. This step checks the Stop Lamp Switch status with the switch OFF.
3. This step checks the Stop Lamp Switch status with the switch applied.
4. This step ensures proper adjustment of the Stop Lamp Switch.

Step	Action	Value(s)	Yes	No
1	Did you perform A Diagnostic System Check - ABS?	—	Go to *Step 2*	Go to *A Diagnostic System Check - ABS*
2	1. Install a scan tool. 2. Turn ON the ignition, with the engine OFF. 3. With a scan tool, observe the Brake Switch parameter in the ABS Data List. Does the scan tool display Released?	—	Go to *Step 3*	Go to *Step 4*
3	Press the brake pedal while observing the Brake Switch parameter. Does the Brake Switch parameter change state?	—	Go to Diagnostic Aids	Go to *Step 4*
4	1. Turn OFF the ignition. 2. Inspect the Stop Lamp Switch and adjust if needed. Did you find and correct the condition?	—	Go to *Step 11*	Go to *Step 5*
5	1. Turn OFF the ignition. 2. Disconnect the Stop Lamp Switch. 3. Turn ON the ignition, with the engine OFF. 4. With a scan tool, observe the Brake Switch parameter. Does the scan tool display Released?	—	Go to *Step 8*	Go to *Step 6*
6	Test the Brake Switch circuit for an open or short to ground. Did you find and correct the condition?	—	Go to *Step 11*	Go to *Step 7*
7	Inspect for poor connections at the harness connector of the EBCM. Did you find and correct the condition?	—	Go to *Step 11*	Go to *Step 9*
8	Inspect for poor connections at the harness connector of the EBCM. Did you find and correct the condition?	—	Go to *Step 11*	Go to *Step 10*
9	Replace the Brake Modulator Assembly. Did you complete the replacement?	—	Go to *Step 11*	—
10	Replace the Stop Lamp Switch. Did you complete the replacement?	—	Go to *Step 11*	—
11	1. Use the scan tool in order to clear the DTCs. 2. Operate the vehicle within the Conditions for Running the DTC as specified in the supporting text. Does the DTC reset?	—	Go to *Step 2*	System OK

GC4020052286020X

Fig. 8 Code B3449: Stop Lamp Circuit Fault (Part 2 of 2). Prizm

Circuit Description

The Electronic Brake Control Module (EBCM) monitors brake pedal position through the stoplamp switch. The stoplamp switch is closed when the brake pedal is pressed and the stop lamp switch opens when the brake pedal is released. When the stoplamp switch is closed, the EBCM receives a voltage signal from the stoplamp switch. The stoplamp switch receives power from the STOP fuse.

Conditions for Setting the DTC

- DTC B3449 identifies an open in the stoplamp switch circuit.
- DTC B3449 can be set anytime.

Action Taken When the DTC Sets

The EBCM stores DTC B3449 turns ON the ABS indicator. If this DTC sets during the ABS stop, ABS will remain functional until the vehicle stops. Otherwise ABS is disabled.

Conditions for Clearing the DTC

The condition for the malfunction is no longer present and command the Clear DTC Information function with a scan tool.

Diagnostic Aids

Inspect the following list of items when diagnosing this part of the Antilock Brake System (ABS):

- Open STOP Fuse (possible short to ground in its circuitry)
- Stoplamp switch out of adjustment
- Faulty stoplamp switch (contacts open or closed at the time)
- Open circuit between the stoplamp switch and the EBCM
- Short to voltage between the stoplamp switch and the EBCM

An intermittent malfunction is most likely caused by following conditions:

- A poor connection
- A rubbed through wire insulation
- A wire that is broken inside the insulation

GC4020052286010X

Fig. 8 Code B3449: Stop Lamp Circuit Fault (Part 1 of 2). Prizm

Circuit Description

The wheel speed sensor generates an AC signal. The signal is produced when a toothed ring passes the wheel speed sensor. The frequency of the AC signal is proportional to the wheel speed. The EBCM uses the frequency of the signal in order to calculate the wheel speed.

Conditions for Running the DTC

The ignition is ON.

Conditions for Setting the DTC

DTC C0035 will set when the EBCM detects the following conditions in the wheel speed sensor circuits:

- An open
- A short to voltage
- A short to ground

Action Taken When the DTC Sets

- The EBCM disables the ABS
- The ABS warning indicator turns ON

Conditions for Clearing the DTC

The condition responsible for setting the DTC no longer exists and the Scan Tool Clear DTCs function is used.

Diagnostic Aids

Inspect the following list of items when diagnosing this part of the Antilock Brake System (ABS):

- Faulty electrical circuits (open and or high resistance, short to voltage, or short to ground) between the left front wheel speed sensor and the EBCM
- Faulty left front wheel speed sensor (out of range resistance)

An intermittent malfunction is most likely caused in the following cases:

- A poor connection rubbed through wire insulation
- A wire that is broken inside the insulation

Thoroughly examine any circuitry that is suspected of causing the intermittent complaint for the following conditions:

- Backed-out terminals
- Improper mating
- Broken locks
- Improperly formed or damaged terminals
- Poor terminal to wiring connections or physical damage to the wiring harness

Important: Wheel speed sensor resistance increases with an increase in sensor temperature.

When measuring for a short to ground in a wheel speed sensor wiring circuit, manually switch the *J 39200* (Digital Multimeter) to the Meg-Ohms range. This will ensure a high resistance short to ground can be found.

Test Description

The numbers below refer to the step numbers on the diagnostic table.

4. This step tests the wheel speed sensor for the proper resistance value.
5. This step ensures that the wheel speed sensor generates the proper voltage.
7. This step tests whether the wheel speed sensor circuits are shorted together.

GC4020052287010X

Fig. 9 Code C0035: Left Front Wheel Speed Circuit Fault (Part 1 of 2). Prizm

Step	Action	Value(s)	Yes	No
1	Did you perform A Diagnostic System Check - ABS?	—	Go to *Step 2*	Go to *A Diagnostic System Check - ABS*
2	1. Install a scan tool. 2. Turn ON the ignition. 3. Set up the scan tool Snap Shot feature to trigger for this DTC. 4. Drive the vehicle at a speed greater than the specified value. Does the scan tool indicate that this DTC set?	8 km/h (5 mph)	Go to *Step 3*	Go to *Intermittent*
3	1. Raise and support the vehicle. 2. Disconnect the wheel speed sensor connector. 3. Measure the resistance across the wheel speed sensor. Does the resistance measure within the specified range?	1120–2520 Ω	Go to *Step 4*	Go to *Step 8*
4	1. Spin the wheel. 2. Measure the AC voltage across the wheel speed sensor. Does the AC voltage measure greater than the specified value?	100 mV	Go to *Step 5*	Go to *Step 8*
5	Inspect for poor connections at the harness connector of the wheel speed sensor. Did you find and correct the condition?	—	Go to *Step 10*	Go to *Step 6*
6	Test the wheel speed sensor circuits for the following: 1. An open 2. A short to ground 3. A short to voltage 4. Shorted together Did you find and correct the condition?	—	Go to *Step 10*	Go to *Step 7*
7	Inspect for poor connections at the harness conector for the EBCM. Did you find and correct the condition?	—	Go to *Step 10*	Go to *Step 9*
8	Replace the wheel speed sensor. Did you complete the replacement?	—	Go to *Step 10*	—
9	Replace the Brake Modulator Assembly. Did you complete the replacement?	—	Go to *Step 10*	—
10	1. Use the scan tool in order to clear the DTCs. 2. Operate the vehicle within the Conditions for Running the DTC Does the DTC reset?	—	Go to *Step 2*	System OK

GC4020052287020X

Fig. 9 Code C0035: Left Front Wheel Speed Circuit Fault (Part 2 of 2). Prizm

Test Description

The numbers below refer to the step numbers on the diagnostic table.

4. This step tests the wheel speed sensor for the proper resistance value.
5. This step ensures that the wheel speed sensor generates the proper voltage.
7. This step tests whether the wheel speed sensor circuits are shorted together.

Step	Action	Value(s)	Yes	No
1	Did you perform A Diagnostic System Check - ABS?	—	Go to *Step 2*	Go to *A Diagnostic System Check - ABS*
2	1. Install a scan tool. 2. Turn ON the ignition. 3. Set up the scan tool Snap Shot feature to trigger for this DTC. 4. Drive the vehicle at a speed greater than the specified value. Does the scan tool indicate that this DTC set?	8 km/h (5 mph)	Go to *Step 3*	Go to *Intermittent*
3	1. Raise and support the vehicle. 2. Disconnect the wheel speed sensor connector. 3. Measure the resistance across the wheel speed sensor. Does the resistance measure within the specified range?	1120–2520 Ω	Go to *Step 4*	Go to *Step 8*
4	1. Spin the wheel. 2. Measure the AC voltage across the wheel speed sensor. Does the AC voltage measure greater than the specified value?	100 mV	Go to *Step 5*	Go to *Step 8*
5	Inspect for poor connections at the harness connector of the wheel speed sensor. Did you find and correct the condition?	—	Go to *Step 10*	Go to *Step 6*
6	Test the wheel speed sensor circuits for the following: 1. An open 2. A short to ground 3. A short to voltage 4. Shorted together Did you find and correct the condition?	—	Go to *Step 10*	Go to *Step 7*
7	Inspect for poor connections at the harness conector for the EBCM. Did you find and correct the condition?	—	Go to *Step 10*	Go to *Step 9*
8	Replace the wheel speed sensor. Did you complete the replacement?	—	Go to *Step 10*	—
9	Replace the Brake Modulator Assembly. Did you complete the replacement?	—	Go to *Step 10*	—
10	1. Use the scan tool in order to clear the DTCs. 2. Operate the vehicle within the Conditions for Running the DTC Does the DTC reset?	—	Go to *Step 2*	System OK

GC4020052288020X

Fig. 10 Code C0036: Left Front Wheel Speed Circuit Range/Performance (Part 2 of 2). Prizm

Circuit Description

The wheel speed sensor generates an AC signal. The signal is produced when a toothed ring passes the wheel speed sensor. The frequency of the AC signal is proportional to the wheel speed. The EBCM uses the frequency of the signal in order to calculate the wheel speed.

Conditions for Running the DTC

- No wheel speed sensor circuit hardware malfunctions are present.
- ABS is not active.
- The brake switch is OFF.

Conditions for Setting the DTC

DTC C0036 will set when the EBCM detects a sudden change in the left front wheel speed determined to be unreasonable.

Action Taken When the DTC Sets

- The EBCM disables the ABS
- The ABS warning indicator turns ON

Conditions for Clearing the DTC

- The condition responsible for setting the DTC no longer exists
- The Scan Tool Clear DTCs function is used
- The vehicle is driven at 24km/h (15 mph)

Diagnostic Aids

Inspect for the following when diagnosing this part of the Antilock Brake System (ABS):

- Loose left front wheel speed sensor
- Worn left front suspension and or drivetrain components
- Left front wheel speed sensor physically damaged
- Left front wheel speed sensor reluctor wheel toothed ring damaged

Perform a careful visual inspection of the following items:

- The wheel speed sensor toothed ring
- The left front CV joint
- The left front wheel bearing and left front wheel speed sensor.

An intermittent malfunction is most likely caused in the following cases:

- A poor connection rubbed through wire insulation
- A wire that is broken inside the insulation

If the customer's comments reflect that the ABS indicator lamp is ON only during humid conditions (rain, snow, vehicle wash), thoroughly inspect the left front wheel speed sensor circuitry for signs of water intrusion. Use the following procedure:

Thoroughly inspect any circuitry that is suspected of causing the intermittent complaint for the following conditions:

- Backed-out terminals
- Improper mating
- Broken locks
- Improperly formed or damaged terminals
- Poor terminal to wiring connections
- Physical damage to the wiring harness

Important: Wheel speed sensor resistance increases with an increase in sensor temperature.

When measuring for a short to ground in a wheel speed sensor wiring circuit, manually switch the *J 39200* (Digital Multimeter) to the Meg-Ohms range. This will ensure a high resistance short to ground can be found.

GC4020052288010X

Fig. 10 Code C0036: Left Front Wheel Speed Circuit Range/Performance (Part 1 of 2). Prizm

Circuit Description

The wheel speed sensor generates an AC signal. The signal is produced when a toothed ring passes the wheel speed sensor. The frequency of the AC signal is proportional to the wheel speed. The EBCM uses the frequency of the signal in order to calculate the wheel speed.

Conditions for Running the DTC

The ignition is ON.

Conditions for Setting the DTC

DTC C0040 will set when the EBCM detects the following conditions in the wheel speed sensor circuits:

- An open
- A short to voltage
- A short to ground

Action Taken When the DTC Sets

- The EBCM disables the ABS
- The ABS warning indicator turns ON

Conditions for Clearing the DTC

The condition responsible for setting the DTC no longer exists and the Scan Tool Clear DTCs function is used.

Diagnostic Aids

Inspect the following list of items when diagnosing this part of the Antilock Brake System (ABS):

- Faulty electrical circuits (open, short to voltage, or short to ground) between the right front wheel speed sensor and the EBCM
- Faulty right front wheel speed sensor (out of range resistance)

An intermittent malfunction is most likely caused by a poor connection rubbed thorough wire insulation or a wire that is broken inside the insulation.

If the customer comments reflect that the ABS indicator lamp is ON only during humid conditions (rain, snow, vehicle wash), thoroughly inspect the right front wheel speed sensor circuitry for signs of water intrusion.

Thoroughly examine any intermittent complaint for the following conditions:

- Backed-out terminals
- Improper mating
- Broken locks
- Improperly formed or damaged terminals
- Poor terminal to wiring connections
- Physical damage to the wiring harness

Important: Wheel speed sensor resistance increases with an increase in sensor temperature.

When measuring for a short to ground in a wheel speed sensor wiring circuit, manually switch the J 39200 (Digital Multimeter) to the Meg-Ohms range. This will ensure a high resistance short to ground can be found.

Test Description

The numbers below refer to the step numbers on the diagnostic table.

4. This step tests the wheel speed sensor for the proper resistance value.
5. This step ensures that the wheel speed sensor generates the proper voltage.
7. This step tests whether the wheel speed sensor circuits are shorted together.

GC4020052289010X

Fig. 11 Code C0040: Right Front Wheel Speed Circuit Fault (Part 1 of 2). Prizm

Step	Action	Value(s)	Yes	No
1	Did you perform A Diagnostic System Check - ABS?	—	Go to *Step 2*	Go to *A Diagnostic System Check - ABS*
2	1. Install a scan tool. 2. Turn ON the ignition. 3. Set up the scan tool Snap Shot feature to trigger for this DTC. 4. Drive the vehicle at a speed greater than the specified value. Does the scan tool indicate that this DTC set?	8 km/h (5 mph)	Go to *Step 3*	Go to *Intermittent*
3	1. Raise and support the vehicle. 2. Disconnect the wheel speed sensor connector. 3. Measure the resistance across the wheel speed sensor. Does the resistance measure within the specified range?	1120–2520 Ω	Go to *Step 4*	Go to *Step 8*
4	1. Spin the wheel. 2. Measure the AC voltage across the wheel speed sensor. Does the AC voltage measure greater than the specified value?	100 mV	Go to *Step 5*	Go to *Step 8*
5	Inspect for poor connections at the harness connector of the wheel speed sensor. Did you find and correct the condition?	—	Go to *Step 10*	Go to *Step 6*
6	Test the wheel speed sensor circuits for the following: • An open • A short to ground • A short to voltage • Shorted together Did you find and correct the condition?	—	Go to *Step 10*	Go to *Step 7*
7	Inspect for poor connections at the harness conector for the EBCM. Did you find and correct the condition?	—	Go to *Step 10*	Go to *Step 9*
8	Replace the wheel speed sensor. Did you complete the replacement?	—	Go to *Step 10*	—
9	Replace the Brake Modulator Assembly. Did you complete the replacement?	—	Go to *Step 10*	—
10	1. Use the scan tool in order to clear the DTCs. 2. Operate the vehicle within the Conditions for Running the DTC Does the DTC reset?	—	Go to *Step 2*	System OK

GC4020052289020X

Fig. 11 Code C0040: Right Front Wheel Speed Circuit Fault (Part 2 of 2). Prizm

Test Description

The numbers below refer to the step numbers on the diagnostic table.

4. This step tests the wheel speed sensor for the proper resistance value.
5. This step ensures that the wheel speed sensor generates the proper voltage.
7. This step tests whether the wheel speed sensor circuits are shorted together.

Step	Action	Value(s)	Yes	No
1	Did you perform A Diagnostic System Check - ABS?	—	Go to *Step 2*	Go to *A Diagnostic System Check - ABS*
2	1. Install a scan tool. 2. Turn ON the ignition. 3. Set up the scan tool Snap Shot feature to trigger for this DTC. 4. Drive the vehicle at a speed greater than the specified value. Does the scan tool indicate that this DTC set?	8 km/h (5 mph)	Go to *Step 3*	Go to *Intermittent*
3	1. Raise and support the vehicle. 2. Disconnect the wheel speed sensor connector. 3. Measure the resistance across the wheel speed sensor. Does the resistance measure within the specified range?	1120–2520 Ω	Go to *Step 4*	Go to *Step 8*
4	1. Spin the wheel. 2. Measure the AC voltage across the wheel speed sensor. Does the AC voltage measure greater than the specified value?	100 mV	Go to *Step 5*	Go to *Step 8*
5	Inspect for poor connections at the harness connector of the wheel speed sensor. Did you find and correct the condition?	—	Go to *Step 10*	Go to *Step 6*
6	Test the wheel speed sensor circuits for the following: • An open • A short to ground • A short to voltage • Shorted together Did you find and correct the condition?	—	Go to *Step 10*	Go to *Step 7*
7	Inspect for poor connections at the harness conector for the EBCM. Did you find and correct the condition?	—	Go to *Step 10*	Go to *Step 9*
8	Replace the wheel speed sensor. Did you complete the replacement?	—	Go to *Step 10*	—
9	Replace the Brake Modulator Assembly. Did you complete the replacement?	—	Go to *Step 10*	—
10	1. Use the scan tool in order to clear the DTCs. 2. Operate the vehicle within the Conditions for Running the DTC Does the DTC reset?	—	Go to *Step 2*	System OK

GC4020052290020X

Fig. 12 Code C0041: Right Front Wheel Speed Circuit Range/Performance (Part 2 of 2). Prizm

Circuit Description

The wheel speed sensor generates an AC signal. The signal is produced when a toothed ring passes the wheel speed sensor. The frequency of the AC signal is proportional to the wheel speed. The EBCM uses the frequency of the signal in order to calculate the wheel speed.

Conditions for Running the DTC

- No wheel speed sensor circuit hardware malfunctions are present.
- ABS is not active.
- The brake switch is OFF.

Conditions for Setting the DTC

DTC C0041 will set when the EBCM detects a sudden change in the right front wheel speed determined to be unreasonable.

Action Taken When the DTC Sets

- The EBCM disables the ABS
- The ABS warning indicator turns ON

Conditions for Clearing the DTC

- The condition responsible for setting the DTC no longer exists
- The Scan Tool Clear DTCs function is used
- The vehicle is driven at 24km/h (15 mph)

Diagnostic Aids

Inspect for the following when diagnosing this part of the Antilock Brake System (ABS):

- Loose right front wheel speed sensor
- Worn right front suspension and/or drivetrain components
- Right front wheel speed sensor physically damaged
- Right front wheel speed sensor reluctor wheel toothed ring damaged

Perform a careful visual inspection of the following items:

- The right front wheel speed sensor reluctor wheel toothed ring
- The right front CV joint
- The right front wheel bearing
- The right front wheel speed sensor

If DTC C0041 sets at the same vehicle speed every time and the right front wheel speed variation is noted above this vehicle speed on the scan tool. The right front wheel speed sensor reluctor wheel toothed ring is most likely damaged. This condition may occur at any vehicle speed.

An intermittent malfunction is most likely caused by a poor connection rubbed thorough wire insulation or a wire that is broken inside the insulation.

If the customer comments reflect that the ABS indicator lamp is ON only during humid conditions (rain, snow, vehicle wash), thoroughly inspect the right front wheel speed sensor circuitry for signs of water intrusion.

Thoroughly inspect any circuitry that is suspected or causing the intermittent complaint for the following conditions:

- Backed-out terminals
- Improper mating
- Broken locks
- Improperly formed or damaged terminals
- Poor terminal to wiring connections
- Physical damage to the wiring harness

Important: Wheel speed sensor resistance increases with an increase in sensor temperature.

When measuring for a short to ground in a wheel speed sensor wiring circuit, manually switch the J 39200 (Digital Multimeter) to the Meg-Ohms range. This will ensure a high resistance short to ground can be found.

GC4020052290010X

Fig. 12 Code C0041: Right Front Wheel Speed Circuit Range/Performance (Part 1 of 2). Prizm

Circuit Description

The wheel speed sensor generates an AC signal. The signal is produced when a toothed ring passes the wheel speed sensor. The frequency of the AC signal is proportional to the wheel speed. The EBCM uses the frequency of the signal in order to calculate the wheel speed.

Conditions for Running the DTC

The ignition is ON.

Conditions for Setting the DTC

DTC C0045 will set when the EBCM detects the following conditions in the wheel speed sensor circuits:

- An open
- A short to voltage
- A short to ground

Action Taken When the DTC Sets

- The EBCM disables the ABS
- The ABS warning indicator turns ON

Conditions for Clearing the DTC

The condition responsible for setting the DTC no longer exists and the Scan Tool Clear DTCs function is used.

Diagnostic Aids

Inspect for the following when diagnosing this part of the Antilock Brake System (ABS):

- Faulty electrical circuits (open and or high resistance, short to voltage, or short to ground) between the left rear wheel speed sensor and the EBCM
- Faulty left rear wheel speed sensor (out of range resistance)

An intermittent malfunction is most likely caused by a poor connection rubbed thorough wire insulation or a wire that is broken inside the insulation.

If the customer comments reflect that the ABS indicator lamp is ON only during humid conditions (rain, snow, vehicle wash), thoroughly inspect the left rear wheel speed sensor circuitry for signs of water intrusion.

Thoroughly inspect any intermittent complaint for the following conditions:

- Backed-out terminals
- Improper mating
- Broken locks
- Improperly formed or damaged terminals
- Poor terminal to wiring connections
- Physical damage to the wiring harness

Important: Wheel speed sensor resistance increases with an increase in sensor temperature.

When measuring for a short to ground in a wheel speed sensor wiring circuit, manually switch the J 39200 (Digital Multimeter) to the Meg-Ohms range. This will ensure a high resistance short to ground can be found.

Test Description

The numbers below refer to the step numbers on the diagnostic table.

4. This step tests the wheel speed sensor for the proper resistance value.
5. This step ensures that the wheel speed sensor generates the proper voltage.
7. This step tests whether the wheel speed sensor circuits are shorted together.

GC4020052291010X

Fig. 13 Code C0045: Left Rear Wheel Speed Circuit Fault (Part 1 of 2). Prizm

Step	Action	Value(s)	Yes	No
1	Did you perform A Diagnostic System Check - ABS?	—	Go to *Step 2*	Go to *A Diagnostic System Check - ABS*
2	1. Install a scan tool. 2. Turn ON the ignition. 3. Set up the scan tool Snap Shot feature to trigger for this DTC. 4. Drive the vehicle at a speed greater than the specified value. Does the scan tool indicate that this DTC set?	8 km/h (5 mph)	Go to *Step 3*	Go to *Intermittent*
3	1. Raise and support the vehicle. 2. Disconnect the wheel speed sensor connector. 3. Measure the resistance across the wheel speed sensor. Does the resistance measure within the specified range?	1120–2520 Ω	Go to *Step 4*	Go to *Step 8*
4	1. Spin the wheel. 2. Measure the AC voltage across the wheel speed sensor. Does the AC voltage measure greater than the specified value?	100 mV	Go to *Step 5*	Go to *Step 8*
5	Inspect for poor connections at the harness connector of the wheel speed sensor. Did you find and correct the condition?	—	Go to *Step 10*	Go to *Step 6*
6	Test the wheel speed sensor circuits for the following: • An open • A short to ground • A short to voltage • Shorted together Did you find and correct the condition?	—	Go to *Step 10*	Go to *Step 7*
7	Inspect for poor connections at the harness conector for the EBCM. Did you find and correct the condition?	—	Go to *Step 10*	Go to *Step 9*
8	Replace the wheel speed sensor. Did you complete the replacement?	—	Go to *Step 10*	—
9	Replace the Brake Modulator Assembly. Did you complete the replacement?	—	Go to *Step 10*	—
10	1. Use the scan tool in order to clear the DTCs. 2. Operate the vehicle within the Conditions for Running the DTC Does the DTC reset?	—	Go to *Step 2*	System OK

GC4020052291020X

Fig. 13 Code C0045: Left Rear Wheel Speed Circuit Fault (Part 2 of 2). Prizm

Test Description

The numbers below refer to the step numbers on the diagnostic table.

4. This step tests the wheel speed sensor for the proper resistance value.
5. This step ensures that the wheel speed sensor generates the proper voltage.
7. This step tests whether the wheel speed sensor circuits are shorted together.

Step	Action	Value(s)	Yes	No
1	Did you perform A Diagnostic System Check - ABS?	—	Go to *Step 2*	Go to *A Diagnostic System Check - ABS*
2	1. Install a scan tool. 2. Turn ON the ignition. 3. Set up the scan tool Snap Shot feature to trigger for this DTC. 4. Drive the vehicle at a speed greater than the specified value. Does the scan tool indicate that this DTC set?	8 km/h (5 mph)	Go to *Step 3*	Go to *Intermittent*
3	1. Raise and support the vehicle. 2. Disconnect the wheel speed sensor connector. 3. Measure the resistance across the wheel speed sensor. Does the resistance measure within the specified range?	1120–2520 Ω	Go to *Step 4*	Go to *Step 8*
4	1. Spin the wheel. 2. Measure the AC voltage across the wheel speed sensor. Does the AC voltage measure greater than the specified value?	100 mV	Go to *Step 5*	Go to *Step 8*
5	Inspect for poor connections at the harness connector of the wheel speed sensor. Did you find and correct the condition?	—	Go to *Step 10*	Go to *Step 6*
6	Test the wheel speed sensor circuits for the following: • An open • A short to ground • A short to voltage • Shorted together Did you find and correct the condition?	—	Go to *Step 10*	Go to *Step 7*
7	Inspect for poor connections at the harness conector for the EBCM. Did you find and correct the condition?	—	Go to *Step 10*	Go to *Step 9*
8	Replace the wheel speed sensor. Did you complete the replacement?	—	Go to *Step 10*	—
9	Replace the Brake Modulator Assembly. Did you complete the replacement?	—	Go to *Step 10*	—
10	1. Use the scan tool in order to clear the DTCs. 2. Operate the vehicle within the Conditions for Running the DTC as specified in the supporting text. Does the DTC reset?	—	Go to *Step 2*	System OK

GC4020052292020X

Fig. 14 Code C0046: Left Rear Wheel Speed Circuit Range/Performance (Part 2 of 2). Prizm

Circuit Description

The wheel speed sensor generates an AC signal. The signal is produced when a toothed ring passes the wheel speed sensor. The frequency of the AC signal is proportional to the wheel speed. The EBCM uses the frequency of the signal in order to calculate the wheel speed.

Conditions for Running the DTC

- No wheel speed sensor circuit hardware malfunctions are present.
- ABS is not active.
- The brake switch is OFF.

Conditions for Setting the DTC

DTC C0046 will set when the EBCM detects a sudden change in the left front wheel speed determined to be unreasonable.

Action Taken When the DTC Sets

- The EBCM disables the ABS
- The ABS warning indicator turns ON

Conditions for Clearing the DTC

- The condition responsible for setting the DTC no longer exists
- The Scan Tool Clear DTCs function is used
- The vehicle is driven at 24km/h (15 mph)

Diagnostic Aids

Inspect for the following when diagnosing this part of the Antilock Brake System (ABS):

- Loose left rear wheel speed sensor
- Worn left rear suspension and/or drivetrain components
- Left rear wheel speed sensor physically damaged
- Left rear wheel speed sensor reluctor wheel toothed ring damaged

Perform a careful visual inspection of the following items:

- The left rear wheel speed sensor reluctor wheel toothed ring
- The left rear wheel bearing
- The left rear wheel speed sensor

An intermittent malfunction is most likely caused by a poor connection rubbed thorough wire insulation or a wire that is broken inside the insulation.

If the customer comments reflect that the ABS warning indicator is ON only during humid conditions (rain, snow, vehicle wash), thoroughly inspect the left rear wheel speed sensor circuitry for signs of water intrusion.

Thoroughly inspect any circuitry that is suspected or causing the intermittent complaint for the following conditions:

- Backed-out terminals
- Improper mating
- Broken locks
- Improperly formed or damaged terminals
- Poor terminal to wiring connections
- Physical damage to the wiring harness

Important: Wheel speed sensor resistance increases with an increase in sensor temperature.

When measuring for a short to ground in a wheel speed sensor wiring circuit, manually switch the J 39200 (Digital Multimeter) to the Meg-Ohms range. This will ensure a high resistance short to ground can be found.

GC4020052292010X

Fig. 14 Code C0046: Left Rear Wheel Speed Circuit Range/Performance (Part 1 of 2). Prizm

Circuit Description

The wheel speed sensor generates an AC signal. The signal is produced when a toothed ring passes the wheel speed sensor. The frequency of the AC signal is proportional to the wheel speed. The EBCM uses the frequency of the signal in order to calculate the wheel speed.

Conditions for Running the DTC

The ignition is ON.

Conditions for Setting the DTC

DTC C0050 will set when the EBCM detects the following conditions in the wheel speed sensor circuits:

- An open
- A short to voltage
- A short to ground

Action Taken When the DTC Sets

- The EBCM disables the ABS
- The ABS warning indicator turns ON

Conditions for Clearing the DTC

The condition responsible for setting the DTC no longer exists and the Scan Tool Clear DTCs function is used.

Diagnostic Aids

Inspect for the following when diagnosing this part of the Antilock Brake System (ABS):

- Faulty electrical circuits (open and or high resistance short to voltage or short to ground) between the right rear wheel speed sensor and the EBCM
- Faulty right rear wheel speed sensor (out of range resistance)

An intermittent malfunction is most likely caused by a poor connection rubbed thorough wire insulation or a wire that is broken inside the insulation.

If the customer comments reflect that the ABS indicator lamp is ON only during humid conditions (rain, snow, vehicle wash), thoroughly inspect the right rear wheel speed sensor circuitry for signs of water intrusion.

Thoroughly inspect any circuitry that is suspected or causing the intermittent complaint for the following conditions:

- Backed-out terminals
- Improper mating
- Broken locks
- Improperly formed or damaged terminals
- Poor terminal to wiring connections
- Physical damage to the wiring harness

Important: Wheel speed sensor resistance increases with an increase in sensor temperature.

When measuring for a short to ground in a wheel speed sensor wiring circuit, manually switch the J 39200 (Digital Multimeter) to the Meg-Ohms range. This will ensure a high resistance short to ground can be found.

Test Description

The numbers below refer to the step numbers on the diagnostic table.

4. This step tests the wheel speed sensor for the proper resistance value.
5. This step ensures that the wheel speed sensor generates the proper voltage.
7. This step tests whether the wheel speed sensor circuits are shorted together.

GC4020052293010X

Fig. 15 Code C0050: Right Rear Wheel Speed Circuit Fault (Part 1 of 2). Prizm

Step	Action	Value(s)	Yes	No
1	Did you perform A Diagnostic System Check - ABS?	—	Go to *Step 2*	Go to *A Diagnostic System Check - ABS*
2	1. Install a scan tool. 2. Turn ON the ignition. 3. Set up the scan tool Snap Shot feature to trigger for this DTC. 4. Drive the vehicle at a speed greater than the specified value. Does the scan tool indicate that this DTC set?	8 km/h (5 mph)	Go to *Step 3*	Go to *Intermittent*
3	1. Raise and support the vehicle. 2. Disconnect the wheel speed sensor connector. 3. Measure the resistance across the wheel speed sensor. Does the resistance measure within the specified range?	1120–2520 Ω	Go to *Step 4*	Go to *Step 8*
4	1. Spin the wheel. 2. Measure the AC voltage across the wheel speed sensor. Does the AC voltage measure greater than the specified value?	100 mV	Go to *Step 5*	Go to *Step 8*
5	Inspect for poor connections at the harness connector of the wheel speed sensor. Did you find and correct the condition?	—	Go to *Step 10*	Go to *Step 6*
6	Test the wheel speed sensor circuits for the following: • An open • A short to ground • A short to voltage • Shorted together Did you find and correct the condition?	—	Go to *Step 10*	Go to *Step 7*
7	Inspect for poor connections at the harness conector for the EBCM. Did you find and correct the condition?	—	Go to *Step 10*	Go to *Step 9*
8	Replace the wheel speed sensor. Did you complete the replacement?	—	Go to *Step 10*	—
9	Replace the Brake Modulator Assembly. Did you complete the replacement?	—	Go to *Step 10*	—
10	1. Use the scan tool in order to clear the DTCs. 2. Operate the vehicle within the Conditions for Running the DTC Does the DTC reset?	—	Go to *Step 2*	System OK

GC4020052293020X

Fig. 15 Code C0050: Right Rear Wheel Speed Circuit Fault (Part 2 of 2). Prizm

Test Description

The numbers below refer to the step numbers on the diagnostic table.

4. This step tests the wheel speed sensor for the proper resistance value.
5. This step ensures that the wheel speed sensor generates the proper voltage.
7. This step tests whether the wheel speed sensor circuits are shorted together.

Step	Action	Value(s)	Yes	No
1	Did you perform A Diagnostic System Check - ABS?	—	Go to *Step 2*	Go to *A Diagnostic System Check - ABS*
2	1. Install a scan tool. 2. Turn ON the ignition. 3. Set up the scan tool Snap Shot feature to trigger for this DTC. 4. Drive the vehicle at a speed greater than the specified value. Does the scan tool indicate that this DTC set?	8 km/h (5 mph)	Go to *Step 3*	Go to *Intermittent*
3	1. Raise and support the vehicle. 2. Disconnect the wheel speed sensor connector. 3. Measure the resistance across the wheel speed sensor. Does the resistance measure within the specified range?	1120–2520 Ω	Go to *Step 4*	Go to *Step 8*
4	1. Spin the wheel. 2. Measure the AC voltage across the wheel speed sensor. Does the AC voltage measure greater than the specified value?	100 mV	Go to *Step 5*	Go to *Step 8*
5	Inspect for poor connections at the harness connector of the wheel speed sensor. Did you find and correct the condition?	—	Go to *Step 10*	Go to *Step 6*
6	Test the wheel speed sensor circuits for the following: • An open • A short to ground • A short to voltage • Shorted together Did you find and correct the condition?	—	Go to *Step 10*	Go to *Step 7*
7	Inspect for poor connections at the harness conector for the EBCM. Did you find and correct the condition?	—	Go to *Step 10*	Go to *Step 9*
8	Replace the wheel speed sensor. Did you complete the replacement?	—	Go to *Step 10*	—
9	Replace the Brake Modulator Assembly. Did you complete the replacement?	—	Go to *Step 10*	—
10	1. Use the scan tool in order to clear the DTCs. 2. Operate the vehicle within the Conditions for Running the DTC Does the DTC reset?	—	Go to *Step 2*	System OK

GC4020052294020X

Fig. 16 Code C0051: Right Rear Wheel Speed Circuit Range/Performance (Part 2 of 2). Prizm

Circuit Description

The wheel speed sensor generates an AC signal. The signal is produced when a toothed ring passes the wheel speed sensor. The frequency of the AC signal is proportional to the wheel speed. The EBCM uses the frequency of the signal in order to calculate the wheel speed.

Conditions for Running the DTC

- No wheel speed sensor circuit hardware malfunctions are present.
- ABS is not active.
- The brake switch is OFF.

Conditions for Setting the DTC

DTC C0051 will set when the EBCM detects a sudden change in the right rear wheel speed determined to be unreasonable.

Action Taken When the DTC Sets

- The EBCM disables the ABS
- The ABS warning indicator turns ON

Conditions for Clearing the DTC

- The condition responsible for setting the DTC no longer exists
- The Scan Tool Clear DTCs function is used
- The vehicle is driven at 24km/h (15 mph)

Diagnostic Aids

Inspect for the following when diagnosing this part of the Antilock Brake System (ABS):

- Loose right rear wheel speed sensor
- Worn right rear suspension and or drivetrain components
- Right rear wheel speed sensor physically damaged
- Right rear wheel speed sensor reluctor wheel toothed ring damaged

Perform a careful visual inspection of the following items:

- The right rear wheel speed sensor toothed ring
- The right rear wheel bearing
- The right rear wheel speed sensor

An intermittent malfunction is most likely caused by a poor connection rubbed thorough wire insulation or a wire that is broken inside the insulation.

If the customer comments reflect that the ABS indicator lamp is ON only during humid conditions (rain, snow, vehicle wash), thoroughly inspect the right rear wheel speed sensor circuitry for signs of water intrusion.

Thoroughly inspect any circuitry that is suspected or causing the intermittent complaint for the following conditions:

- Backed-out terminals
- Improper mating
- Broken locks
- Improperly formed or damaged terminals
- Poor terminal to wiring connections
- Physical damage to the wiring harness

Important: Wheel speed sensor resistance increases with an increase in sensor temperature.

When measuring for a short to ground in a wheel speed sensor wiring circuit, manually switch the J 39200 (Digital Multimeter) to the Meg-Ohms range. This will ensure a high resistance short to ground can be found.

GC4020052294010X

Fig. 16 Code C0051: Right Rear Wheel Speed Circuit Range/Performance (Part 1 of 2). Prizm

Circuit Description

The left front solenoid valve is part of Brake Pressure Modulator Valve (BPMV). The BPMV turns ON and OFF the left front solenoid valve as deemed necessary to modulate brake hydraulic pressure to the left front wheel brake during an ABS stop.

Conditions for Running the DTC

DTC 0060 can be set anytime the ignition switch is in the ON position.

Conditions for Setting the DTC

The Electronic Brake Control Module (EBCM) detects an open, a short to voltage, or a short to ground in the left front solenoid circuitry.

Action Taken When the DTC Sets

- The ABS disables
- The ABS warning indicator turns ON

Conditions for Clearing the DTC

The condition responsible for setting the DTC no longer exists and the Scan Tool Clear DTCs function is used.

Diagnostic Aids

If DTC C0125 (Value Relay Circuit Open) is set (current or history DTC), go to the DTC C0125 table first.

Test Description

The numbers below refer to step numbers on the Diagnostic Table.

2. This step determines whether the DTC is current.

GC4020052295010X

Fig. 17 Code C0060: Left Front ABS Solenoid Number 1 Circuit Fault (Part 1 of 2). Prizm

Step	Action	Value(s)	Yes	No
1	Did you perform A Diagnostic System Check - ABS?	—	Go to *Step 2*	Go to *A Diagnostic System Check - ABS*
2	1. Install a scan tool. 2. Turn ON the ignition, with the engine OFF. 3. Use the scan tool in order to clear the DTCs. 4. Using the scan tool, cycle the appropriate solenoid in the Special Functions menu. 5. Read the DTCs. Does the DTC reset?	—	Go to *Step 3*	Go to *Intermittent*
3	1. Test the Solenoid Input circuit for an open, high resistance, or a short to ground. 2. Test the Solenoid Ground circuit for an open or high resistance. Was a problem found and corrected?	—	Go to *A Diagnostic System Check - ABS*	Go to *Step 4*
4	Replace the Brake Modulator Assembly. Is the repair complete?	—	Go to *Step 5*	—
5	1. Use the scan tool in order to clear the DTCs. 2. Using the scan tool, cycle the appropriate solenoid in the Special Functions menu. 3. Read the DTCs. Does the DTC reset?	—	Go to *Step 2*	System OK

GC4020052295020X

Fig. 17 Code C0060: Left Front ABS Solenoid Number 1 Circuit Fault (Part 2 of 2). Prizm

Circuit Description

The right front solenoid valve is part of Brake Pressure Modulator Valve (BPMV). The BPMV turns ON and OFF the right front solenoid valve as deemed necessary to modulate brake hydraulic pressure to the right front wheel brake during an ABS stop.

Conditions for Running the DTC

DTC 0070 can be set anytime the ignition switch is in the ON position.

Conditions for Setting the DTC

The Electronic Brake Control Module (EBCM) detects any of the following in the right front solenoid circuitry:

- an open
- short to ground
- a short to voltage

Action Taken When the DTC Sets

- The ABS disables
- The ABS warning indicator turns ON

Conditions for Clearing the DTC

The condition responsible for setting the DTC no longer exists and the Scan Tool Clear DTCs function is used.

Diagnostic Aids

If DTC C0125 (Value Relay Circuit Open) is set (current or history) go to the DTC C0125 table first.

Test Description

The numbers below refer to step numbers on the Diagnostic Table.

2. This step determines whether the DTC is current.

GC4020052296010X

Fig. 18 Code C0070: Right Front ABS Solenoid Number 1 Circuit Fault (Part 1 of 2). Prizm

Circuit Description

The left rear solenoid valve is part of Brake Pressure Modulator Valve (BPMV). The BPMV turns ON and OFF the left rear solenoid valve as deemed necessary to modulate brake hydraulic pressure to the left rear wheel brake during an ABS stop.

Conditions for Running the DTC

DTC 0080 can be set anytime the ignition switch is in the ON position.

Conditions for Setting the DTC

The Electronic Brake Control Module (EBCM) detects any of the following in the left rear solenoid circuitry:

- an open
- short to ground
- a short to voltage

Action Taken When the DTC Sets

- The ABS disables
- The ABS warning indicator turns ON

Conditions for Clearing the DTC

The condition responsible for setting the DTC no longer exists and the Scan Tool Clear DTCs function is used.

Diagnostic Aids

If DTC C0125 (Value Relay Circuit Open) is set (current or history) go to the DTC C0125 table first.

Test Description

The numbers below refer to step numbers on the Diagnostic Table.

2. This step determines whether the DTC is current.

GC4020052297010X

Fig. 19 Code C0080: Left Rear ABS Solenoid Number 1 Circuit Fault (Part 1 of 2). Prizm

Circuit Description

The right rear solenoid valve is part of Brake Pressure Modulator Valve (BPMV). The BPMV turns ON and OFF the right rear solenoid valve as deemed necessary to modulate brake hydraulic pressure to the right rear wheel brake during an ABS stop.

Conditions for Running the DTC

DTC 0060 can be set anytime the ignition switch is in the ON position.

Conditions for Setting the DTC

The Electronic Brake Control Module (EBCM) detects any of the following in the right rear solenoid circuitry:

- an open
- short to ground
- a short to voltage

Action Taken When the DTC Sets

- The ABS disables
- The ABS warning indicator turns ON

Conditions for Clearing the DTC

The condition responsible for setting the DTC no longer exists and the Scan Tool Clear DTCs function is used.

Diagnostic Aids

If DTC C0125 (Value Relay Circuit Open) is set (current or history) go to the DTC C0125 table first.

Test Description

The numbers below refer to step numbers on the Diagnostic Table.

2. This step determines whether the DTC is current.

GC4020052298010X

Fig. 20 Code C0090: Right Rear ABS Solenoid Number 1 Circuit Fault (Part 1 of 2). Prizm

Step	Action	Value(s)	Yes	No
1	Did you perform A Diagnostic System Check - ABS?	—	Go to *Step 2*	Go to *A Diagnostic System Check - ABS*
2	1. Install a scan tool. 2. Turn ON the ignition, with the engine OFF. 3. Use the scan tool in order to clear the DTCs. 4. Using the scan tool, cycle the appropriate solenoid in the Special Functions menu. 5. Read the DTCs. Does the DTC reset?	—	Go to *Step 3*	Go to *Intermittent*
3	1. Test the Solenoid Input circuit for an open, high resistance, or a short to ground. 2. Test the Solenoid Ground circuit for an open or high resistance. Was a problem found and corrected?	—	Go to *A Diagnostic System Check - ABS*	Go to *Step 4*
4	Replace the Brake Modulator Assembly. Is the repair complete?	—	Go to *Step 5*	—
5	1. Use the scan tool in order to clear the DTCs. 2. Using the scan tool, cycle the appropriate solenoid in the Special Functions menu. 3. Read the DTCs. Does the DTC reset?	—	Go to *Step 2*	System OK

GC4020052298020X

Fig. 20 Code C0090: Right Rear ABS Solenoid Number 1 Circuit Fault (Part 2 of 2). Prizm

Step	Action	Value(s)	Yes	No
1	Did you perform A Diagnostic System Check - ABS?	—	Go to *Step 2*	Go to *A Diagnostic System Check - ABS*
2	1. Install a scan tool. 2. Turn ON the ignition, with the engine OFF. 3. Use the scan tool in order to clear the DTCs. 4. Using the scan tool, cycle the appropriate solenoid in the Special Functions menu. 5. Read the DTCs. Does the DTC reset?	—	Go to *Step 3*	Go to *Testing for Intermittent and Poor Connections*
3	1. Test the Solenoid Input circuit for an open, high resistance, or a short to ground. 2. Test the Solenoid Ground circuit for an open or high resistance. Was a problem found and corrected?	—	Go to *A Diagnostic System Check - ABS*	Go to *Step 4*
4	Replace the Brake Modulator Assembly. Is the repair complete?	—	Go to *Step 5*	—
5	1. Use the scan tool in order to clear the DTCs. 2. Using the scan tool, cycle the appropriate solenoid in the Special Functions menu. 3. Read the DTCs. Does the DTC reset?	—	Go to *Step 2*	System OK

GC4020052296020X

Fig. 18 Code C0070: Right Front ABS Solenoid Number 1 Circuit Fault (Part 2 of 2). Prizm

Step	Action	Value(s)	Yes	No
1	Did you perform A Diagnostic System Check - ABS?	—	Go to *Step 2*	Go to *A Diagnostic System Check - ABS*
2	1. Install a scan tool. 2. Turn ON the ignition, with the engine OFF. 3. Use the scan tool in order to clear the DTCs. 4. Using the scan tool, cycle the appropriate solenoid in the Special Functions menu. 5. Read the DTCs. Does the DTC reset?	—	Go to *Step 3*	Go to *Testing for Intermittent and Poor Connections*
3	1. Test the Solenoid Input circuit for an open, high resistance, or a short to ground. 2. Test the Solenoid Ground circuit for an open or high resistance. Was a problem found and corrected?	—	Go to *A Diagnostic System Check - ABS*	Go to *Step 4*
4	Replace the Brake Modulator Assembly. Is the repair complete?	—	Go to *Step 5*	—
5	1. Use the scan tool in order to clear the DTCs. 2. Using the scan tool, cycle the appropriate solenoid in the Special Functions menu. 3. Read the DTCs. Does the DTC reset?	—	Go to *Step 2*	System OK

GC4020052297020X

Fig. 19 Code C0080: Left Rear ABS Solenoid Number 1 Circuit Fault (Part 2 of 2). Prizm

Circuit Description

The pump motor relay is part of the Electronic Brake Control Module (EBCM). The EBCM turns ON and OFF the pump motor relay as deemed necessary to activate the pump motor.

Conditions for Setting the DTC

The Electronic Brake Control Module (EBCM) detects a stuck pump motor during initialization.

Action Taken When the DTC Sets

- The ABS disables
- The ABS warning indicator turns ON

Conditions for Clearing the DTC

The condition responsible for setting the DTC no longer exists and the Scan Tool Clear DTCs function is used. If the pump motor monitor signal is still incorrect, DTC C0110 will set again as a current DTC and the ABS indicator remain ON.

Diagnostic Aids

If DTC C0114 (Pump Motor Circuit Open) is set (current or history) go to the DTC C0114 table first.

Test Description

The numbers below refer to step numbers on the Diagnostic Table.

2. This step determines whether the DTC is current.

GC4020052299010X

Fig. 21 Code C0110: Pump Motor Circuit Fault (Part 1 of 2). Prizm

Step	Action	Value(s)	Yes	No
1	Did you perform A Diagnostic System Check - ABS?	—	Go to *Step 2*	Go to *A Diagnostic System Check - ABS*
2	1. Install a scan tool. 2. Turn ON the ignition, with the engine OFF. 3. Use the scan tool in order to clear the DTCs. 4. Using the scan tool, cycle the pump motor in the Special Functions menu. 5. Read the DTCs. Does the DTC reset?	—	Go to *Step 3*	Go to *Intermittent*
3	1. Test the Solenoid Input circuit for an open, high resistance, or a short to ground. 2. Test the Solenoid Ground circuit for an open or high resistance. Was a problem found and corrected?	—	Go to *A Diagnostic System Check - ABS*	Go to *Step 4*
4	Replace the Brake Modulator Assembly. Is the repair complete?	—	Go to *Step 5*	—
5	1. Use the scan tool in order to clear the DTCs. 2. Using the scan tool, cycle the pump motor in the Special Functions menu. 3. Read the DTCs. Does the DTC reset?	—	Go to *Step 2*	System OK

GC4020052299020X

Fig. 21 Code C0110: Pump Motor Circuit Fault (Part 2 of 2). Prizm

Step	Action	Value(s)	Yes	No
1	Did you perform A Diagnostic System Check - ABS?	—	Go to *Step 2*	Go to *A Diagnostic System Check - ABS*
2	1. Install a scan tool. 2. Turn ON the ignition, with the engine OFF. 3. Use the scan tool in order to clear the DTCs. 4. Using the scan tool, cycle the pump motor in the Special Functions menu. 5. Read the DTCs. Does the DTC reset?	—	Go to *Step 3*	Go to *Intermittent*
3	1. Test the Pump Motor Input circuit for an open, high resistance, or a short to ground. 2. Test the Motor Ground circuit for an open or high resistance. Was a problem found and corrected?	—	Go to *A Diagnostic System Check - ABS*	Go to *Step 4*
4	Replace the Brake Modulator Assembly. Is the repair complete?	—	Go to *Step 5*	—
5	1. Use the scan tool in order to clear the DTCs. 2. Using the scan tool, cycle the pump motor in the Special Functions menu. 3. Read the DTCs. Does the DTC reset?	—	Go to *Step 2*	System OK

GC4020052300020X

Fig. 22 Code C0114: Pump Motor Circuit Open (Part 2 of 2). Prizm

Step	Action	Value(s)	Yes	No
1	Did you perform A Diagnostic System Check - ABS?	—	Go to *Step 2*	Go to *A Diagnostic System Check - ABS*
2	1. Install a scan tool. 2. Turn ON the ignition, with the engine OFF. 3. Use the scan tool in order to clear the DTCs. 4. Using the scan tool, cycle the pump motor in the Special Functions menu. 5. Read the DTCs. Does the DTC reset?	—	Go to *Step 3*	Go to *Intermittent*
3	1. Test the Pump Motor Input circuit for an open or short to ground. 2. Test the Motor Ground circuit for an open or high resistance. Was a problem found and corrected?	—	Go to *A Diagnostic System Check - ABS*	Go to *Step 4*
4	Replace the Brake Modulator Assembly. Is the repair complete?	—	Go to *Step 5*	—
5	1. Use the scan tool in order to clear the DTCs. 2. Using the scan tool, cycle the pump motor in the Special Functions menu. 3. Read the DTCs. Does the DTC reset?	—	Go to *Step 2*	System OK

GC4020052301020X

Fig. 23 Code C0116: Pump Motor Relay Circuit Fault (Part 2 of 2). Prizm

Circuit Description

The pump motor relay is part of the Electronic Brake Control Module (EBCM). The EBCM turns ON and OFF the pump motor relay as deemed necessary in order to activate the pump motor. The pump motor modulates the brake hydraulic pressure during an ABS stop.

Conditions for Running the DTC

DTC C0114 can be set anytime the pump motor is actuated.

Conditions for Setting the DTC

The Electronic Brake Control Module (EBCM) detects an open in the pump motor circuitry.

Action Taken When the DTC Sets

- The ABS disables
- The ABS warning indicator turns ON

Conditions for Clearing the DTC

The condition responsible for setting the DTC no longer exists and the Scan Tool Clear DTCs function is used. If the pump motor monitor signal is still incorrect, DTC C0114 will set again as a current DTC and the ABS indicator remain ON.

Diagnostic Aids

Inspect the following list of items when diagnosing this part of the Antilock Brake System (ABS):

- The ABS fuse.
- Open or high resistance in the pump motor input circuit.

Inspect the harness connectors for the following conditions:

- Backed-out terminals
- Improper mating
- Broken locks
- Improperly formed or damaged terminals
- Poor terminal to wiring connections or physical damage to the wiring harness

Test Description

The numbers below refer to step numbers on the Diagnostic Table.

2. This step determines whether the DTC is current.

GC4020052300010X

Fig. 22 Code C0114: Pump Motor Circuit Open (Part 1 of 2). Prizm

Circuit Description

The pump motor relay is part of the Electronic Brake Control Module (EBCM). The EBCM turns ON and OFF the pump motor relay as deemed necessary in order to activate the pump motor. The pump motor modulates brake hydraulic pressure during an ABS stop.

Conditions for Running the DTC

DTC C0116 can be set anytime the ignition switch is in the ON position.

Conditions for Setting the DTC

The Electronic Brake Control Module (EBCM) detects an open in the pump motor circuitry.

Action Taken When the DTC Sets

- The ABS disables
- The ABS warning indicator turns ON

Conditions for Clearing the DTC

The condition responsible for setting the DTC no longer exists and the Scan Tool Clear DTCs function is used. Although, after the scan tool erases DTC C0116, the EBCM keeps the ABS indicator ON until the vehicle is driven 10 mph for at least 20 seconds AND the pump motor sends a proper monitor signal to the EBCM. Then the EBCM turns OFF the ABS indicator. If the pump motor monitor signal is still incorrect, DTC C0116 will set again as a current DTC and the ABS indicator remains ON.

Diagnostic Aids

Inspect the ABS fuse when diagnosing this part of the Antilock Brake System (ABS)

Inspect the harness connectors for the following conditions:

- Backed-out terminals
- Improper mating
- Broken locks
- Improperly formed or damaged terminals
- Poor terminal to wiring connections or physical damage to the wiring harness

Test Description

The numbers below refer to step numbers on the Diagnostic Table.

2. This step determines whether the DTC is current.

GC4020052301010X

Fig. 23 Code C0116: Pump Motor Relay Circuit Fault (Part 1 of 2). Prizm

Circuit Description

The valve relay is part of the Electronic Brake Control Module (EBCM). The EBCM turns ON the valve relay when the ignition switch is in the ON position and no malfunction exists in the ABS. The valve relay provides power to the ABS solenoid valves.

Conditions for Running the DTC

DTC C0121 can be set within 3 seconds after the ignition switch is turned to the ON position.

Conditions for Setting the DTC

The Electronic Brake Control Module (EBCM) detects that the valve relay is ON when actually the EBCM commanded the valve relay OFF.

Action Taken When the DTC Sets

- The ABS disables
- The ABS warning indicator turns ON

Conditions for Clearing the DTC

The condition responsible for setting the DTC no longer exists and the Scan Tool Clear DTCs function is used.

Diagnostic Aids

Inspect for the following when diagnosing this part of the Antilock Brake System (ABS):

- The ABS fuse
- Open or high resistance in the pump input circuit (Terminal D)

Inspect the harness connectors for the following conditions:

- Backed-out terminals
- Improper mating
- Broken locks
- Improperly formed or damaged terminals
- Poor terminal to wiring connections or physical damage to the wiring harness

Test Description

The numbers below refer to step numbers on the Diagnostic Table.

2. This step determines whether the DTC is current.

GC4020052302010X

Fig. 24 Code C0121: Valve Relay Circuit Fault (Part 1 of 2). Prizm

Step	Action	Value(s)	Yes	No
1	Did you perform A Diagnostic System Check - ABS?	—	Go to *Step 2*	Go to *A Diagnostic System Check - ABS*
2	1. Install a scan tool. 2. Turn ON the ignition, with the engine OFF. 3. Use the scan tool in order to clear the DTCs. 4. Using the scan tool, cycle the solenoid valves in the Special Functions menu. 5. Read the DTCs. Does the DTC reset?	—	Go to *Step 3*	Go to *Intermittent*
3	Replace the Brake Modulator Assembly. Is the repair complete?	—	Go to *Step 4*	—
4	1. Use the scan tool in order to clear the DTCs. 2. Using the scan tool, cycle the solenoid valves in the Special Functions menu. 3. Read the DTCs. Does the DTC reset?	—	Go to *Step 2*	System OK

GC4020052302020X

Fig. 24 Code C0121: Valve Relay Circuit Fault (Part 2 of 2). Prizm

Step	Action	Value(s)	Yes	No
1	Did you perform A Diagnostic System Check - ABS?	—	Go to *Step 2*	Go to *A Diagnostic System Check - ABS*
2	1. Install a scan tool. 2. Turn ON the ignition, with the engine OFF. 3. Use the scan tool in order to clear the DTCs. 4. Using the scan tool, cycle the solenoid valves in the Special Functions menu. 5. Read the DTCs. Does the DTC reset?	—	Go to *Step 3*	Go to *Intermittent*
3	1. Test the Solenoid Input circuit for an open, high resistance, or a short to ground. 2. Test the Solenoid Ground circuit for an open or high resistance. Was a problem found and corrected?	—	Go to *A Diagnostic System Check - ABS*	Go to *Step 4*
4	Replace the Brake Modulator Assembly. Is the repair complete?	—	Go to *Step 5*	—
5	1. Use the scan tool in order to clear the DTCs. 2. Using the scan tool, cycle the solenoid valves in the Special Functions menu. 3. Read the DTCs. Does the DTC reset?	—	Go to *Step 2*	System OK

GC4020052303020X

Fig. 25 Code C0125: Valve Relay Circuit Open (Part 2 of 2). Prizm

Circuit Description

The Valve relay is part of the Electronic Brake Control Module (EBCM). The EBCM turns ON the valve relay during an ABS stop. The valve relay provides power to the ABS solenoid valves.

Conditions for Running the DTC

DTC C0125 can be set anytime.

Conditions for Setting the DTC

The EBCM detects an open in the valve relay circuitry.

Action Taken When the DTC Sets

- The ABS disables
- The ABS warning indicator turns ON

Conditions for Clearing the DTC

The condition responsible for setting the DTC no longer exists and the Scan Tool Clear DTCs function is used.

Diagnostic Aids

Inspect for the following when diagnosing this part of the Antilock Brake System (ABS):

- Open ABS fuse
- Open or high resistance in the solenoid input circuit
- Open or high resistance in the solenoid ground circuit

Inspect the following harness connectors for the following conditions:

- Backed-out terminals
- Improper mating
- Broken locks
- Improperly formed or damaged terminals
- Poor terminal to wiring connections or physical damage to the wiring harness before component replacement:
  - Junction block electrical connectors
  - Electronic brake control module electrical connector

Test Description

The numbers below refer to step numbers on the Diagnostic Table.

2. This step determines whether the DTC is current.

GC4020052303010X

Fig. 25 Code C0125: Valve Relay Circuit Open (Part 1 of 2). Prizm

System Description

This DTC detects an internal malfunction of the Electronic Brake Control Module (EBCM).

Conditions for Running the DTC

DTC C0550 can be set anytime the ignition switch is in the ON position.

Conditions for Setting the DTC

DTC C0550 is set if the EBCM has an internal malfunction.

Action Taken When the DTC Sets

- The ABS disables
- The ABS warning indicator turns ON

Conditions for Clearing the DTC

The condition responsible for setting the DTC no longer exists and the Scan Tool Clear DTCs function is used.

Diagnostic Aids

Use the enhanced diagnostic function of the Scan Tool in order to measure the frequency of the malfunction.

Clear the DTCs after completing the diagnosis. Test drive the vehicle for three drive cycles in order to verify that the DTC does not reset. Use the following procedure in order to complete one drive cycle:

1. Start the vehicle.
2. Drive the vehicle over 16 km/h (10 mph).
3. Stop the vehicle.
4. Turn the ignition to the OFF position.

Test Description

The numbers below refer to step numbers on the Diagnostic Table.

2. This step determines whether the DTC is current.

Step	Action	Value(s)	Yes	No
1	Did you perform A Diagnostic System Check - ABS?	—	Go to *Step 2*	Go to *A Diagnostic System Check - ABS*
2	1. Install a scan tool. 2. Turn ON the ignition, with the engine OFF. 3. Use the scan tool in order to clear the DTCs. 4. Using the scan tool, cycle the solenoid valves and pump motor in the Special Functions menu. 5. Read the DTCs. Does the DTC reset?	—	Go to *Step 3*	Go to *Intermittent*
3	Replace the Brake Modulator Assembly. Is the repair complete?	—	Go to *Step 4*	—
4	1. Use the scan tool in order to clear the DTCs. 2. Using the scan tool, cycle the solenoid valves and pump motor in the Special Functions menu. 3. Read the DTCs. Does the DTC reset?	—	Go to *Step 2*	System OK

GC4020052304000X

Fig. 26 Code C0550: Electronic Brake Control Module Fault. Prizm

Circuit Description

The Electronic Brake Control Module (EBCM) monitors available voltage level at terminal B.

Conditions for Running the DTC

DTC C0550 can be set anytime the ignition switch is in the ON position.

Conditions for Setting the DTC

This DTC will set if the voltage level at terminal 13 or terminal B is less than 8 volts.

Action Taken When the DTC Sets

- The ABS disables
- The ABS warning indicator turns ON

Conditions for Clearing the DTC

The condition responsible for setting the DTC no longer exists and the Scan Tool Clear DTCs function is used.

Diagnostic Aids

Inspect for the following when diagnosing this part of the Antilock Brake System (ABS):

- Vehicle charging system is not operating properly (low generator output or malfunctioning battery)
- Open or high resistance in the ignition power circuit or the solenoid power input circuit
- Open or high resistance in the solenoid ground circuit

An intermittent malfunction is most likely caused by a poor connection rubbed through wire insulation or a wire that is broken inside the insulation.

Inspect the harness connectors for the following conditions:

- Backed-out terminals
- Improper mating
- Broken locks
- Improperly formed or damaged terminals
- Poor terminal to wiring connections

Test Description

The numbers below refer to the step numbers on the diagnostic table.

2. This step uses the scan tool to check the ignition positive voltage to the EBCM.
3. This step checks the battery positive voltage circuit.
4. This step checks the module ground circuit.

GC4020052305010X

Fig. 27 Code C0899: Device Number 1 Voltage Low (Part 1 of 2). Prizm

Step	Action	Value(s)	Yes	No
1	Did you perform A Diagnostic System Check - ABS?	—	Go to *Step 2*	Go to *A Diagnostic System Check - ABS*
2	1. Install a scan tool. 2. Turn ON the ignition, with the engine OFF. 3. With a scan tool, observe the Ignition Voltage parameter in the ABS Data List. Does the scan tool indicate the ignition voltage is within the specified range?	Battery Voltage	Go to Diagnostic Aids	Go to *Step 3*
3	1. Turn OFF the ignition. 2. Disconnect the EBCM harness connector. 3. Turn ON the ignition, with the engine OFF. 4. Measure the voltage between the Ignition Positive Voltage circuit of the EBCM and a good ground. Does the voltage measure within the specified range?	Battery Voltage	Go to *Step 4*	Go to *Step 5*
4	Measure the voltage between the Ignition Positive Voltage circuit and the module ground circuits of the EBCM. Does the voltage measure within the specified range?	Battery Voltage	Go to *Step 9*	Go to *Step 6*
5	Test the Ignition Positive Voltage circuit of the EBCM for a high resistance, an open, or a short. Did you find and correct the condition?	—	Go to *Step 11*	Go to *Step 8*
6	Test the module ground circuits of the EBCM for a high resistance or an open. Did you find and correct the condition?	—	Go to *Step 11*	Go to *Step 7*
7	Inspect for poor connections or corrosion at the ground G103. Did you find and correct the condition?	—	Go to *Step 11*	Go to *Step 8*
8	Inspect for poor connections at the battery terminals. Did you find and correct the condition?	—	Go to *Step 11*	Go to *Step 9*
9	Inspect for poor connections at the harness connector of the EBCM. Did you find and correct the condition?	—	Go to *Step 11*	Go to *Step 10*
10	Replace the Brake Modulator Assembly. Did you complete the replacement?	—	Go to *Step 11*	—
11	1. Clear the DTCs using the scan tool. 2. Operate the vehicle within the Conditions for Running the DTC Does the DTC reset?	—	Go to *Step 2*	System OK

GC4020052305020X

Fig. 27 Code C0899: Device Number 1 Voltage Low (Part 2 of 2). Prizm

Circuit Description

This DTC is designed to detect high vehicle voltage levels and to protect the Antilock Brake System (ABS) system from high voltage damage.

Conditions for Running the DTC

DTC C0900 can be set anytime the ignition switch is in the ON position.

Conditions for Setting the DTC

Power voltage level circuit is greater than 17.5 volts.

Action Taken When the DTC Sets

- The ABS disables
- The ABS warning indicator turns ON

Conditions for Clearing the DTC

The condition responsible for setting the DTC no longer exists and the Scan Tool Clear DTCs function is used.

Diagnostic Aids

Use the enhanced diagnostic function of the Scan Tool in order to measure the frequency of the malfunction.

Ensure the vehicle's charging system is working properly.

Test Description

The numbers below refer to the step numbers on the diagnostic table.

2. This step uses the scan tool to check the battery positive voltage circuit to the EBCM.
3. This step checks the battery positive voltage supply circuit.

GC4020052306010X

Fig. 28 Code C0900: Device Number 1 Voltage High (Part 1 of 2). Prizm

Step	Action	Value(s)	Yes	No
1	Did you perform A Diagnostic System Check - ABS?	—	Go to *Step 2*	Go to *A Diagnostic System Check - ABS*
2	1. Turn OFF all of the accessories. 2. Install a scan tool. 3. Start the engine. 4. Run the engine at approximately 2000 RPM. 5. With a scan tool, observe the Battery Voltage parameter in the ABS Data List. Does the scan tool indicate that the battery voltage is less than the specified voltage?	17 V	Go to *Step 5*	Go to *Step 3*
3	1. Turn OFF the ignition. 2. Disconnect the EBCM harness connector. 3. Start the engine. 4. Run the engine at approximately 2000 RPM. 5. Measure the voltage at the between the Ignition Positive Voltage circuit of the EBCM and a good ground. Does the voltage measure less than the specified value?	17 V	Go to *Step 4*	*Charging System Check*
4	1. Use the scan tool in order to clear the DTCs. 2. Carefully test drive the vehicle at a speed above 8 km/h (5 mph). Does the DTC reset?	—	Go to *Step 5*	System OK
5	Replace the Brake Modulator Assembly. Did you complete the repair?	—	Go to *Step 6*	—
6	1. Use the scan tool in order to clear the DTCs. 2. Operate the vehicle within the conditions for Running the DTC Does the DTC reset?	—	Go to *Step 2*	System OK

GC4020052306020X

Fig. 28 Code C0900: Device Number 1 Voltage High (Part 2 of 2). Prizm

Circuit Description

The EBCM interfaces with a scan tool through terminal 4 via to Data Link Connector (DLC) terminal 7. A properly set scan tool connected to the DLC can retrieve ABS diagnostic information like Diagnostic Trouble Codes (DTCs) and perform ABS device control for testing purposes.

Diagnostic Aids

Inspect for the following list of items when diagnosing this part of the Antilock Brake System (ABS):

- An open ECU-IG fuse
- An open ABS fuse
- A clean tight G103

The EBCM will not interface with a scan tool if these circuits have excessive resistance:

- The serial data line
- The ignition power circuit
- G103

Ensure that these circuits are in good condition and that no excessive resistance occurs. Also inspect the EBCM electrical connector for poor connector terminal contact.

Test Description

The numbers below refer to the step numbers on the diagnostic table.

2. This test determines if the scan tool can communicate with any other modules on the Class 2 serial data line.
4. Tests for a short to ground in the ignition positive voltage circuit.
6. Tests the EBCM ground circuit for an open or high resistance.
7. Tests the ignition positive voltage circuit for an open or high resistance.

GC4020052307010X

Fig. 29 No Communication With EBCM (Part 1 of 2). Prizm

Step	Action	Value(s)	Yes	No
1	Did you perform A Diagnostic System Check - ABS?	—	Go to *Step 2*	Go to *A Diagnostic System Check - ABS*
2	1. Turn OFF the ignition. 2. Install a scan tool. 3. Turn ON the ignition, with the engine OFF. 4. Attempt to establish communication with other modules on the serial data line, such as the PCM. Does the scan tool communicate with any other modules on the serial data line?	—	Go to *Step 3*	*Scan Tool Does Not Communicate with Components*
3	1. Turn OFF the ignition. 2. Inspect the ECU-IGN Fuse (10A). Is the fuse open?	—	Go to *Step 4*	Go to *Step 5*
4	1. Turn OFF the ignition. 2. Remove the ECU-IGN Fuse (10A) from Junction Block 2. 3. Test the Ignition Positive Voltage circuit for a short to ground. Did you find and correct the condition?	—	Go to *A Diagnostic System Check - ABS*	Go to *Intermittent*
5	Inspect the EBCM ground circuit, making sure that the ground is clean and torqued to the proper specification. Did you find and correct the condition?	—	Go to *A Diagnostic System Check - ABS*	Go to *Step 6*
6	1. Turn OFF the ignition. 2. Test the EBCM ground circuit for an open or high resistance. Did you find and correct the condition?	—	Go to *A Diagnostic System Check - ABS*	Go to *Step 7*
7	Test the Ignition Positive Voltage circuit for an open or high resistance. Did you find and correct the condition?	—	Go to *A Diagnostic System Check - ABS*	Go to *Step 8*
8	Inspect for poor connections at the harness connector of the EBCM. Did you find and correct the condition?	—	Go to *A Diagnostic System Check - ABS*	Go to *Step 9*
9	Replace the Brake Modulator Assembly. Did you complete the replacement?	—	Go to *A Diagnostic System Check - ABS*	—

GC4020052307020X

Fig. 29 No Communication With EBCM (Part 2 of 2). Prizm

Circuit Description

The Electronic Brake Control Module (EBCM) turns OFF the ABS warning indicator by grounding terminal 11 after Initilization.

The ABS warning indicator is connected to the gauge fuse. This circuit has power when the ignition switch is in the ON or START positions.

When the ignition switch is turned to the ON position, the EBCM turns ON the ABS warning indicator for 3 seconds for a bulb check. If the EBCM detects a malfunction, the ABS warning indicator will stay ON to warn the driver that the ABS is disabled and it needs service.

Diagnostic Aids

Inspect for the following when diagnosing this part of the Antilock Brake System (ABS):

- Open gauge fuse
- Open ABS warning indicator bulb filament
- Open or poor G103
- Open within Instrument panel gage cluster printed circuit

Inspect the following harness connectors:

- For backed-out terminals
- For improper mating
- For broken locks
- For improperly formed or damaged terminals
- For poor terminal to wiring connections
- For physical damage to the wiring harness before component replacement:
  - Instrument panel gage cluster electrical connectors
  - Junction block electrical connectors
  - EBCM electrical connector

Test Description

The number(s) below refer to the step number(s) on the diagnostic table.

2. Tests for power distribution to the instrument panel gage cluster.
3. Tests for power distribution to the EBCM (ignition power).
4. Tests for power distribution to the EBCM for motor and solenoids.
5. Tests for proper ground to the EBCM.

GC4020052308010X

Fig. 30 ABS Indicator Inoperative (Part 1 of 2). Prizm

Step	Action	Value(s)	Yes	No
1	Did you perform A Diagnostic System Check - ABS?	—	Go to *Step 2*	Go to *A Diagnostic System Check - ABS*
2	Test the ABS Indicator I/P input circuit for an open or short to ground. Was a problem found and corrected?	—	Go to *A Diagnostic System Check - ABS*	Go to *Step 3*
3	Test the Ignition Positive Voltage circuit for an open or short to ground. Was a problem found and corrected?	—	Go to *A Diagnostic System Check - ABS*	Go to *Step 4*
4	Test the Solenoid Input and the Pump Motor Input circuits for an open or short to ground. Was a problem found and corrected?	—	Go to *A Diagnostic System Check - ABS*	Go to *Step 5*
5	Test the Solenoid Ground and the Pump Motor Ground circuits for an open or high resistance. Was a problem found and corrected?	—	Go to *A Diagnostic System Check - ABS*	Go to *Step 6*
6	Test the ABS Indicator Control circuit for an open or short to ground. Was a problem found and corrected?	—	Go to *A Diagnostic System Check - ABS*	Go to *Step 7*
7	1. Remove the instrument panel gage cluster. 2. Remove and inspect the ABS indicator bulb filament. Is the ABS indicator bulb filament open?	—	Go to *Step 8*	Go to *Step 9*
8	Replace the ABS indicator bulb. Is the repair complete?	—	Go to *A Diagnostic System Check - ABS*	—
9	1. Replace the Antilock Indicator Driver Module. 2. Clear all DTCs. 3. Test drive the vehicle at 24 km/h (15 mph) for 30 seconds. 4. Using the scan tool, check for DTCs. Does the DTC reset?	—	Go to *Step 10*	Go to *A Diagnostic System Check - ABS*
10	Replace the Brake Modulator Assembly. Is the repair complete?	—	Go to *A Diagnostic System Check - ABS*	—

GC4020052308020X

Fig. 30 ABS Indicator Inoperative (Part 2 of 2). Prizm

Circuit Description

The Electronic Brake Control Module (EBCM) turns ON the ABS warning indicator by grounding terminal 11.

The ABS warning indicator is connected to the gauge fuse. This circuit has power when the ignition switch is in the ON or START positions.

When the ignition switch is turned to the ON position, the EBCM turns ON the ABS warning indicator for 3 seconds for a bulb check. If the EBCM detects a malfunction the ABS warning indicator will stay ON to warn the driver that the ABS is disabled and needs service.

Diagnostic Aids

Inspect for a short to ground between the EBCM and the instrument cluster.

Inspect the following harness connectors for improperly formed or damaged terminals or physical damage to the wiring harness before component replacement:

- The EBCM electrical connector
- The Instrument panel gauge cluster electrical connector

The ABS indicator will remain ON until the vehicle is road tested after the repair of the following Diagnostic Trouble Codes:

- C0036
- C0041
- C0046
- C0051
- C0110
- C0114
- C0116

Test Description

The number(s) below refer to the step number(s) on the diagnostic table.

2. After repairs that set a certain DTCs (refer to Diagnostic Aids for specific DTCs) even after clearing DTCs the ABS will keep the ABS indicator ON until a road test is performed to confirm proper system operation.
3. Determines whether there is a short to ground in the ABS indicator circuit or a malfunctioning EBCM.
4. Refer to Diagnostic Aids for a list of DTCs that need road test confirmation before the ABS indicator is turned OFF.
5. A short to ground in the ABS Indicator Control circuit will keep the ABS indicator ON.

GC4020052309010X

Fig. 31 ABS Indicator Always On (Part 1 of 2). Prizm

Step	Action	Value(s)	Yes	No
1	Did you perform A Diagnostic System Check - ABS?	—	Go to *Step 2*	Go to *A Diagnostic System Check - ABS*
2	1. Turn the ignition switch to the LOCK position. 2. Disconnect the scan tool if one is connected to the OBD2 Data Link Connector (DLC). 3. Turn the ignition switch to the ON position. 4. Test drive the vehicle at 24 km/h (15 mph) for 30 seconds. 5. Stop the vehicle. Is the ABS indicator ON?	—	Go to *Step 3*	Go to *Step 4*
3	1. Turn the ignition switch to the LOCK position. 2. Disconnect the Electronic Brake Control Module (EBCM) electrical connector. 3. Turn the ignition switch to the ON position. Is the ABS indicator ON?	—	Go to *Step 5*	Go to *Step 6*
4	The malfunction that caused the EBCM to turn ON the ABS indicator is no longer present. When a specific DTC is deleted (after the malfunction that set the DTC is corrected or no longer present), the EBCM will keep the ABS indicator ON until the vehicle is road tested for repair confirmation. In other words, the DTC itself is erased but the ABS indicator remains on until the vehicle is road tested after repairs. Refer to Diagnostic Aids for additional information. Is the action complete?	—	Go to *A Diagnostic System Check - ABS*	—
5	Test the ABS Indicator Control circuit for an open or short to ground. Was a problem found and corrected?	—	Go to *A Diagnostic System Check - ABS*	Go to *Step 6*
6	1. Replace the Antilock Indicator Driver Module. 2. Clear all DTCs. 3. Test drive the vehicle at 24 km/h (15 mph) for 30 seconds. 4. Using the scan tool, check for DTCs. Did the DTC reset?	—	Go to *Step 7*	Go to *A Diagnostic System Check - ABS*
7	Replace the Brake Modulator Assembly. Is the repair complete?	—	Go to *A Diagnostic System Check - ABS*	—

GC4020052309020X

Fig. 31 ABS Indicator Always On (Part 2 of 2). Prizm

Circuit Description

The Electronic Brake Control Module (EBCM) interfaces with a scan tool through terminal 4 via the OBD2 Data Link Connector (DLC) terminal 7. A properly set scan tool connected to the DLC can retrieve ABS diagnostic information like Diagnostic Trouble Codes (DTCs) and perform ABS device control for testing purposes.

Diagnostic Aids

Inspect the following list of items when diagnosing this part of the Antilock Brake System (ABS):

- Scan tool in good working order
- Scan tool with correct software

Test Description

The number(s) below refer to the step number(s) on the diagnostic table.

2. Performs undefined DTC confirmation.
3. Performs undefined DTC confirmation with a known good scan tool.

Step	Action	Value(s)	Yes	No
1	Did you perform A Diagnostic System Check - ABS?	—	Go to *Step 2*	Go to *A Diagnostic System Check - ABS*
2	1. Turn the ignition switch to the LOCK position. 2. Connect a scan tool to the OBD2 Data Link Connector (DLC). 3. Turn the ignition switch to the ON position. 4. Select Diagnostic Trouble Codes (DTCs) from Application Menu on the scan tool. 5. Select DTC Information on the scan tool. 6. Record the undefined DTCs. 7. Turn the ignition switch to the LOCK position. 8. Disconnect the scan tool from the DLC. 9. Test drive the vehicle at 24 km/h (15 mph) for 30 seconds. 10. When driving conditions permit, perform an ABS stop and bring the vehicle to a complete stop. 11. Connect a scan tool to the Data Link Connector (DLC). 12. Select Diagnostic Trouble Codes (DTCs) from Application Menu on the scan tool. 13. Select DTC Information on the scan tool. 14. Select Current DTC on the scan tool. Does the undefined DTC reset?	—	Go to *Step 3*	Go to *Step 5*
3	1. Disconnect the scan tool from the DLC. 2. Connect a known-good scan tool to the OBD2 Data Link Connector (DLC). 3. Turn the ignition switch to the ON position. 4. Select the Diagnostic Trouble Codes (DTCs) from Application Menu on scan tool. 5. Select DTC Information on the scan tool. 6. Read DTCs on the scan tool. Does the undefined DTC reset?	—	Go to *Step 4*	Go to *Step 5*
4	Replace the brake pressure modulator valve assembly. Is the repair complete?	—	Go to *A Diagnostic System Check - ABS*	—
5	A malfunction is not present at this time. Is the action complete?	—	Go to *A Diagnostic System Check - ABS*	—

GC4020052310000X

Fig. 32 Scan Tool Displays Undefined DTC. Prizm

Diagnostic Aids

- An intermittent Malfunction in the electronic system may be very difficult to detect and to accurately diagnose. The EBCM tests for different malfunctions under different vehicle conditions. For this reason, a thorough test drive is often needed in order to repeat a malfunction. If the system malfunction is not repeated during the test drive, a good description of the complaint may be very useful in locating an intermittent malfunction. Faulty electrical connections or wiring causes most intermittent problems. When an intermittent condition is suspected, check the suspect circuits for the following conditions:
  - Poor mating of connector halves or backed out terminals
  - Improperly formed or damaged terminals
  - Wire chafing
  - Poor wire to terminal connections
  - Dirty or corroded terminals
  - Damage to connector bodies
- If the DTC is a history DTC, the problem may be intermittent. Perform the tests shown while moving related wiring and connectors. This can often cause the malfunction to occur. Perform a thorough inspection of all related wiring and connectors pertaining to the history DTC stored. Refer to Testing for Intermittent and Poor Connections in Wiring Systems.

Test Description

The number(s) below refer to the step number(s) on the diagnostic table.

2. Lack of communication may be due to a malfunction of the class 2 serial data circuit.

Step	Action	Yes	No
Schematic Reference: ABS Schematics			
1	Install a scan tool. Does the scan tool power up?	Go to Step 2	Data Link Communications
2	1. Turn ON the ignition, with the engine OFF. 2. Attempt to establish communication with the EBCM. Does the scan tool communicate with the EBCM?	Go to Step 3	Data Link Communications
3	Select the ABS display DTCs function on the scan tool. Does the scan tool display any DTCs?	Go to Diagnostic Trouble Code (DTC)	Go to Symptoms - Antilock Brake System

ARM66GC000000174

Fig. 33 Diagnostic Circuit Check. Vibe

Conditions for Clearing the DTC

C0205, C0210, C0215, and C0220

The condition responsible for setting the DTC no longer exists and the scan tool Clear DTCs function is used.

C1235, C1236, C1238, and C1239

The condition responsible for setting the DTC no longer exists and the scan tool Clear DTCs function is used.

C1271, C1272, C1273, and C1274

The condition responsible for setting the DTC no longer exists and the scan tool Clear DTCs function is used.

C1275, C1276, C1277, and C1278

- The condition responsible for setting the DTC no longer exists and the scan tool Clear DTCs function is used.
- After the DTC is cleared, the ABS indicator will remain ON until the vehicle is road tested to verify the repair. Once the vehicle has been driven at a speed above 16 km/h (10 mph) for 20 seconds with no malfunctions present, the EBCM will turn OFF the ABS indicator.

Diagnostic Aids

Thoroughly inspect the wiring and the connectors. An incomplete inspection of the wiring and the connectors may result in a misdiagnosis, causing a part replacement with the reappearance of the malfunction.

The following are possible causes of the malfunction:

- A short to ground or a short to voltage in the wheel speed sensor circuitry
- An open or high resistance in the wheel speed sensor circuitry
- A malfunctioning wheel speed sensor
- A malfunctioning wheel speed sensor rotor
- An internal EBCM malfunction

Test Description

The numbers below refer to the step numbers on the diagnostic table.

3. This step tests the wheel speed sensor for the proper resistance value.

ARM66GC000000176

Fig. 34 Codes C0200–C0215, C1235–C1239 & C1271–C1278: Wheel Speed Sensor Circuits (Part 2 of 4). Vibe

As the wheel spins, the wheel speed sensor produces an alternating current (AC) signal. The electronic brake control module (EBCM) uses the frequency of the AC signal to calculate the wheel speed.

Conditions for Running the DTC

C0200, C0205, C0210, and C0215

The ignition is in the ON position.

C1235, C1236, C1238, and C1239

- The ignition is in the ON position.
- Vehicle speed of 20 km/h (12 mph) or more.

C1271, C1272, C1273, and C1274

- The ignition is in the ON position.
- Vehicle speed of 20 km/h (12 mph) or more.

C1275, C1276, C1277, and C1278

- The ignition is in the ON position.
- Vehicle speed of 20 km/h (12 mph) or more.

Conditions for Setting the DTC

C0200, C0205, C0210, and C0215

The EBCM detects one of the following conditions in the wheel speed sensor circuits:

- An open
- A short to ground
- A short to voltage

C1235, C1236, C1238, and C1239

The EBCM detects noise in the wheel speed sensor signal for more than 5 seconds.

C1271, C1272, C1273, and C1274

The EBCM detects low output voltage of the wheel speed sensor.

C1275, C1276, C1277, and C1278

The EBCM detects a rapid change in the wheel speed which is determined to be unreasonable.

Action Taken When the DTC Sets

The following actions occur:

- The EBCM disables the antilock brake system (ABS) for the duration of the ignition cycle.
- The ABS indicator turns ON.

ARM66GC000000175

Fig. 34 Codes C0200–C0215, C1235–C1239 & C1271–C1278: Wheel Speed Sensor Circuits (Part 1 of 4). Vibe

Step	Action	Value(s)	Yes	No
1	Did you perform A Diagnostic System Check - ABS?	--	Go to Step 2	Go to Diagnostic System Check -
2	1. Install a scan tool. 2. Turn ON the ignition, with the engine OFF. **Important** Interruption or loss of communication with the scan tool may occur if speed exceeds 56 km/h (35 mph). 3. Drive the vehicle at a speed greater than the specified value for 30 seconds. Does the scan tool indicate that this wheel speed DTC set?	45 km/h (28 mph)	Go to Step 3	Go to Diagnostic Aids
3	1. Raise and support the vehicle. 2. Disconnect the wheel speed sensor connector. 3. Measure the resistance across the wheel speed sensor. Does the resistance measure within the specified range?	920-1220 ohms	Go to Step 4	Go to Step 10
4	Measure the resistance between the wheel speed sensor terminals and ground. Does the resistance measure greater than specified?	Greater than 1 M ohms	Go to Step 5	Go to Step 10
5	Inspect for poor connections at the harness connector of the wheel speed sensor. Did you find and correct the condition?	--	Go to Step 13	Go to Step 6

ARM66GC000000177

Fig. 34 Codes C0200–C0215, C1235–C1239 & C1271–C1278: Wheel Speed Sensor Circuits (Part 3 of 4). Vibe

6	1. Disconnect the EBCM harness connector. 2. Test the wheel speed sensor circuits for the following: o An open o A short to ground o A short to voltage o Shorted together Did you find and correct the condition?	-	Go to Step 13	Go to Step 7
7	Inspect for poor connections at the harness connector for the EBCM. Did you find and correct the condition?	-	Go to Step 13	Go to Step 8
8	Inspect the wheel speed sensor for damage. Is the wheel speed sensor damaged?	-	Go to Step 10	Go to Step 9
9	Inspect the wheel speed sensor rotor for damage. Is the wheel speed sensor rotor damaged?	-	Go to Step 11	Go to Step 12
10	Replace the wheel speed sensor. Did you complete the replacement?	-	Go to Step 13	--
11	Replace the wheel speed sensor rotor. Did you complete the replacement?	-	Go to Step 13	--
12	Replace the brake pressure modulator valve (BPMV). Did you complete the replacement?	-	Go to Step 13	--
13	1. Use the scan tool in order to clear the DTCs. 2. Operate the vehicle within the Conditions for Running the DTC as specified in the supporting text. Does the DTC reset?	-	Go to Step 2	System OK

ARM66GC000000178

Fig. 34 Codes C0200–C0215, C1235–C1239 & C1271–C1278: Wheel Speed Sensor Circuits (Part 4 of 4). Vibe

Step	Action	Yes	No
1	Did you perform A Diagnostic System Check - ABS?	Go to Step 2	Go to Diagnostic System Check
2	Is DTC C0278 also set?	Go to DTC C0278	Go to Step 3
3	Is DTC C0279 also set?	Go to DTC C0279	Go to Step 4
4	1. Install a scan tool. 2. Turn ON the ignition, with the engine OFF. 3. Use the scan tool in order to clear the DTCs. 4. Using the scan tool, cycle the appropriate solenoid in the Special Functions menu. 5. Read the DTCs. Does the DTC reset?	Go to Step 5	Go to Diagnostic Aids
5	Replace the Brake Pressure Modulator Valve (BPMV). Did you complete the replacement?	Go to Step 6	--
6	1. Use the scan tool in order to clear the DTCs. 2. Operate the vehicle within the Conditions for Running the DTC as specified in the supporting text. Does the DTC reset?	Go to Step 2	System OK

ARM66GC000000180

Fig. 35 Codes C0226–C0256: Solenoid Circuit Open Or Short (Part 2 of 2). Vibe

The solenoid valves are part of the brake pressure modulator valve (BPMV). The BPMV turns ON and OFF the solenoid valves as deemed necessary to modulate hydraulic pressure to the wheel brakes during an antilock brake system (ABS) stop.

Conditions for Running the DTC

DTC's C0226 - C0256 can be set anytime the ignition switch is in the ON position.

Conditions for Setting the DTC

The electronic brake control module (EBCM) detects one of the following conditions in the solenoid circuitry:

- An open
- A short to ground
- A short to voltage

Action Taken When the DTC Sets

- The ABS is disabled.
- The ABS warning indicator turns ON.

Conditions for Clearing the DTC

The condition responsible for setting the DTC no longer exists and the Scan Tool Clear DTCs function is used.

Diagnostic Aids

Thoroughly inspect the wiring and the connectors. An incomplete inspection of the wiring and the connectors may result in a misdiagnosis, causing a part replacement with the reappearance of the malfunction.

The following are possible causes of the malfunction:

- An open, high resistance, or a short to ground in the battery positive voltage circuits
- An open or high resistance in the solenoid ground circuit
- An internal EBCM malfunction

Test Description

The numbers below refer to step numbers on the diagnostic table.

4. This step determines if the DTC is current.

ARM66GC000000179

Fig. 35 Codes C0226–C0256: Solenoid Circuit Open Or Short (Part 1 of 2). Vibe

Circuit Description

The pump motor relay is part of the electronic brake control module (EBCM). The EBCM turns ON and OFF the pump motor relay as deemed necessary in order to activate the pump motor. The pump motor modulates brake hydraulic pressure during an antilock brake system (ABS) stop.

Conditions for Running the DTC

DTC C0273 can be set anytime the ignition switch is in the ON position.

Conditions for Setting the DTC

The electronic brake control module (EBCM) detects an open in the pump motor circuitry.

Action Taken When the DTC Sets

- The ABS is disabled.
- The ABS warning indicator turns ON.

Conditions for Clearing the DTC

- The condition responsible for setting the DTC no longer exists and the scan tool Clear DTCs function is used.
- After the DTC is cleared, the ABS indicator will remain ON until the vehicle is road tested to verify the repair. Once the vehicle has been driven at a speed above 16 km/h (10 mph) for 20 seconds with no malfunctions present, the EBCM will turn OFF the ABS indicator.

Diagnostic Aids

Thoroughly inspect the wiring and the connectors. An incomplete inspection of the wiring and the connectors may result in a misdiagnosis, causing a part replacement with the reappearance of the malfunction.

The following are possible causes of the malfunction:

- An open or high resistance in the battery positive voltage circuit
- An open or high resistance in the motor ground circuit
- An internal EBCM malfunction

Test Description

The number below refers to the step number on the diagnostic table.

2. This step determines if the DTC is current.

ARM66GC000000181

Fig. 36 Code C0273: EBCM Detects Open In Pump Motor Circuit (Part 1 of 2). Vibe

Step	Action	Yes	No
1	Did you perform A Diagnostic System Check - ABS?	Go to Step 2	Go to Diagnostic System Check
2	1. Install a scan tool. 2. Turn ON the ignition, with the engine OFF. 3. Use the scan tool in order to clear the DTCs. 4. Using the scan tool, cycle the pump motor in the Special Functions menu. 5. Read the DTCs. Does the DTC reset?	Go to Step 3	Go to Diagnostic Aids
3	Test the ABS No. 2 fuse for continuity. Is continuity present?	Go to Step 4	Go to Step 5
4	1. Test the battery positive voltage circuit for an open or high resistance. 2. Test the motor ground circuit for an open or high resistance. Did you find and correct the condition?	Go to Step 8	Go to Step 6
5	Test the battery positive voltage circuit for a short to ground. Did you find and correct the condition?	Go to Step 8	Go to Step 7
6	Replace the brake pressure modulator valve (BPMV). Did you complete the replacement?	Go to Step 8	--
7	Replace the ABS No. 2 fuse. Did you complete the replacement?	Go to Step 8	--
8	1. Use the scan tool in order to clear the DTCs. 2. Operate the vehicle within the Conditions for Running the DTC as specified in the supporting text. Does the DTC reset?	Go to Step 2	System OK

ARM66GC000000182

Fig. 36 Code C0273: EBCM Detects Open In Pump Motor Circuit (Part 2 of 2). Vibe

Step	Action	Yes	No
1	Did you perform A Diagnostic System Check - ABS?	Go to Step 2	Go to Diagnostic System Check
2	1. Install a scan tool. 2. Turn ON the ignition, with the engine OFF. 3. Use the scan tool in order to clear the DTCs. 4. Using the scan tool, cycle the pump motor in the Special Functions menu. 5. Read the DTCs. Does the DTC reset?	Go to Step 3	Go to Diagnostic Aids
3	Test the battery positive voltage circuit for a short to ground. Did you find and correct the condition?	Go to Step 5	Go to Step 4
4	Replace the brake pressure modulator valve (BPMV). Did you complete the replacement?	Go to Step 5	--
5	1. Use the scan tool in order to clear the DTCs. 2. Operate the vehicle within the Conditions for Running the DTC as specified in the supporting text. Does the DTC reset?	Go to Step 2	System OK

ARM66GC000000184

Fig. 37 Code C0274: EBCM Detects Short In Pump Motor Circuit (Part 2 of 2). Vibe

Circuit Description

The pump motor relay is part of the electronic brake control module (EBCM). The EBCM turns ON and OFF the pump motor relay as deemed necessary in order to activate the pump motor. The pump motor modulates brake hydraulic pressure during an antilock brake system (ABS) stop.

Conditions for Running the DTC

DTC C0274 can be set anytime the ignition switch is in the ON position.

Conditions for Setting the DTC

The electronic brake control module (EBCM) detects an short in the pump motor circuitry.

Action Taken When the DTC Sets

- The ABS is disabled.
- The ABS warning indicator turns ON.

Conditions for Clearing the DTC

- The condition responsible for setting the DTC no longer exists and the scan tool Clear DTCs function is used.
- After the DTC is cleared, the ABS indicator will remain ON until the vehicle is road tested to verify the repair. Once the vehicle has been driven at a speed above 16 km/h (10 mph) for 20 seconds with no malfunctions present, the EBCM will turn OFF the ABS indicator.

Diagnostic Aids

Thoroughly inspect the wiring and the connectors. An incomplete inspection of the wiring and the connectors may result in a misdiagnosis, causing a part replacement with the reappearance of the malfunction.

The following are possible causes of the malfunction:

- A short to ground in the battery positive voltage circuit
- An internal EBCM malfunction

Test Description

The number below refers to the step number on the diagnostic table.

2. This step determines if the DTC is current.

ARM66GC000000183

Fig. 37 Code C0274: EBCM Detects Short In Pump Motor Circuit (Part 1 of 2). Vibe

Circuit Description

The valve relay is part of the electronic brake control module (EBCM). The EBCM turns ON the valve relay when the ignition switch is in the ON position and no malfunction exists in the ABS. The valve relay provides power to the antilock brake system (ABS) solenoid valves.

Conditions for Running the DTC

DTC C0278 can be set anytime the ignition switch is turned to the ON position.

Conditions for Setting the DTC

The EBCM detects that the valve relay is OFF when actually the EBCM commanded the valve relay ON.

Action Taken When the DTC Sets

- The ABS is disabled.
- The ABS warning indicator turns ON.

Conditions for Clearing the DTC

The condition responsible for setting the DTC no longer exists and the scan tool Clear DTCs function is used.

Diagnostic Aids

Thoroughly inspect the wiring and the connectors. An incomplete inspection of the wiring and the connectors may result in a misdiagnosis, causing a part replacement with the reappearance of the malfunction.

The following are possible causes of the malfunction:

- An open or high resistance in the battery positive voltage circuit
- An open or high resistance in the motor ground circuit
- An internal EBCM malfunction

Test Description

The number below refers to the step number on the diagnostic table.

2. This step determines if the DTC is current.

ARM66GC000000185

Fig. 38 Code C0278: EBCM Detects Valve Relay Off When Commanded On (Part 1 of 2). Vibe

Step	Action	Yes	No
1	Did you perform A Diagnostic System Check - ABS?	Go to Step 2	Go to Diagnostic System Check
2	1. Install a scan tool. 2. Turn ON the ignition, with the engine OFF. 3. Use the scan tool in order to clear the DTCs. 4. Using the scan tool, cycle the solenoid valves in the Special Functions menu. 5. Read the DTCs. Does the DTC reset?	Go to Step 3	Go to Diagnostic Aids
3	Test The ABS No. 1 fuse for continuity. Is continuity present?	Go to Step 4	Go to Step 5
4	1. Test the battery positive voltage circuit for an open or high resistance. 2. Test the motor ground circuit for an open or high resistance. Did you find and correct the condition?	Go to Step 7	Go to Step 6
5	Test the battery positive voltage circuit for a short to ground. Did you find and correct the condition?	Go to Step 8	Go to Step 7
6	Replace the brake pressure modulator valve (BPMV). Did you complete the replacement?	Go to Step 8	--
7	Replace the ABS No. 1 fuse. Did you complete the replacement?	Go to Step 8	--
5	1. Use the scan tool in order to clear the DTCs. 2. Operate the vehicle within the Conditions for Running the DTC as specified in the supporting text. Does the DTC reset?	Go to Step 2	System OK

ARM66GC000000186

Fig. 38 Code C0278: EBCM Detects Valve Relay Off When Commanded On (Part 2 of 2). Vibe

Step	Action	Yes	No
1	Did you perform A Diagnostic System Check - ABS?	Go to Step 2	Go to Diagnostic System Check
2	1. Install a scan tool. 2. Turn ON the ignition, with the engine OFF. 3. Use the scan tool in order to clear the DTCs. 4. Using the scan tool, cycle the solenoid valves in the Special Functions menu. 5. Read the DTCs. Does the DTC reset?	Go to Step 3	Go to Diagnostic Aids
3	Test the battery positive voltage circuit for short to gound. Did you find and correct the condition?	Go to Step 5	Go to Step 4
4	Replace the brake pressure modulator valve (BPMV). Did you complete the replacement?	Go to Step 5	--
5	1. Use the scan tool in order to clear the DTCs. 2. Operate the vehicle within the Conditions for Running the DTC as specified in the supporting text. Does the DTC reset?	Go to Step 2	System OK

ARM66GC000000188

Fig. 39 Code C0279: EBCM Detects Valve Relay On When Commanded Off (Part 2 of 2). Vibe

Circuit Description

The valve relay is part of the electronic brake control module (EBCM). The EBCM turns ON the valve relay when the ignition switch is in the ON position and no malfunction exists in the antilock brake system (ABS). The valve relay provides power to the ABS solenoid valves.

Conditions for Running the DTC

DTC C0279 can be set any time the ignition switch is in the ON position.

Conditions for Setting the DTC

The EBCM detects that the valve relay is ON when actually the EBCM commanded the valve relay OFF.

Action Taken When the DTC Sets

- The ABS is disabled.
- The ABS warning indicator turns ON.

Conditions for Clearing the DTC

The condition responsible for setting the DTC no longer exists and the scan tool Clear DTCs function is used.

Diagnostic Aids

Thoroughly inspect the wiring and the connectors. An incomplete inspection of the wiring and the connectors may result in a misdiagnosis, causing a part replacement with the reappearance of the malfunction.

The following are possible causes of the malfunction:

- A short to ground in the battery positive voltage circuit
- An internal EBCM malfunction

Test Description

The number below refers to the step number on the diagnostic table.

2. This step determines if the DTC is current.

ARM66GC000000187

Fig. 39 Code C0279: EBCM Detects Valve Relay On When Commanded Off (Part 1 of 2). Vibe

Circuit Description

The electronic brake control module (EBCM) monitors the ignition positive voltage level available for antilock brake system (ABS) operation.

Conditions for Running the DTC

The vehicle speed is greater than 3 km/h (2 mph).

Conditions for Setting the DTC

- The ignition positive voltage is less than 8.5 volts for 10 seconds.
- The battery positive voltage is greater than 19.0 volts for 1 second.

Action Taken When the DTC Sets

- The ABS is disabled.
- The ABS warning indicator turns ON.

Conditions for Clearing the DTC

The condition responsible for setting the DTC no longer exists and the scan tool Clear DTCs function is used.

Diagnostic Aids

Thoroughly inspect the wiring and the connectors. An incomplete inspection of the wiring and the connectors may result in a misdiagnosis, causing a part replacement with the reappearance of the malfunction.

The following are possible causes of the malfunction:

- Low battery voltage
- High battery voltage
- An open or high resistance in the ignition positive voltage circuit
- An open or high resistance in the motor or solenoid ground circuits
- An internal EBCM malfunction

Test Description

The numbers below refer to the step numbers on the diagnostic table.

2. This step uses the scan tool to test the ignition positive voltage circuit to the EBCM.
3. This step tests the ignition positive voltage supply circuit.
4. This step uses the scan tool to test the ignition positive voltage to the EBCM.

ARM66GC000000189

Fig. 40 Code C1241: System Voltage (Part 1 of 3). Vibe

Step	Action	Value(s)	Yes	No
1	Did you perform A Diagnostic System Check - ABS?	--	Go to Step 2	Go to Diagnostic System Check -
2	1. Turn OFF all of the accessories. 2. Install a scan tool. 3. Start the engine. 4. Run the engine at approximately 2000 RPM. 5. With a scan tool, observe the Ignition Voltage parameter in the ABS data list. Does the scan tool indicate that the ignition voltage is within the specified voltage?	High	Go to Step 3	Go to Step 4
3	1. Turn OFF the ignition. 2. Disconnect the EBCM harness connector. 3. Start the engine. 4. Run the engine at approximately 2000 RPM. 5. Measure the voltage between the ignition positive voltage circuit of the EBCM and a good ground. Does the voltage measure less than the specified value?	17 V	Go to Step 12	Engine Electrical
4	1. Turn ON the ignition, with the engine OFF. 2. With a scan tool, observe the Ignition Voltage parameter in the ABS data list. Does the scan tool indicate the ignition voltage is within the specified range?	Normal	Go to Diagnostic Aids	Go to Step 5
5	1. Turn OFF the ignition. 2. Disconnect the EBCM harness connector. 3. Turn ON the ignition, with the engine OFF. 4. Measure the voltage between the ignition positive voltage circuit of the EBCM and a good ground. Does the voltage measure within the specified range?	Battery Voltage	Go to Step 6	Go to Step 7
6	Measure the voltage between the ignition positive voltage circuit and the module ground circuit of the EBCM. Does the voltage measure within the specified range?	Battery Voltage	Go to Step 11	Go to Step 8

ARM66GC000000190

Fig. 40 Code C1241: System Voltage (Part 2 of 3). Vibe

Circuit Description

The electronic brake control module (EBCM) monitors the deceleration of the vehicle for antilock brake system (ABS) operation.

Conditions for Running the DTC

The vehicle speed is greater than 5 km/h (3 mph).

Conditions for Setting the DTC

- A vehicle forward or backward G force of 0.4 or greater is detected with brake pedal not depressed.
- The sensor input does not change at 1 cycle for 16 consecutive times.

Action Taken When the DTC Sets

The ABS warning indicator turns ON.

Conditions for Clearing the DTC

The condition responsible for setting the DTC no longer exists and the scan tool Clear DTCs function is used.

Diagnostic Aids

Thoroughly inspect the wiring and the connectors. An incomplete inspection of the wiring and the connectors may result in a misdiagnosis, causing a part replacement with the reappearance of the malfunction.

The following are possible causes of the malfunction:

- An open or short in deceleration sensor to EBCM wiring circuits
- An open or high resistance in the ignition positive voltage circuit
- An open or high resistance in the deceleration sensor ground circuit
- A deceleration sensor malfunction
- An internal EBCM malfunction

Test Description

The numbers below refer to the step numbers on the diagnostic table.

2. This step uses the scan tool to test the ignition positive voltage circuit to the EBCM.

ARM66GC000000192

Fig. 41 Code C1243: Deceleration Sensor Ciruit (Part 1 of 2). Vibe

7	Test the ignition positive voltage circuit of the EBCM for a high resistance, an open, or a short. Did you find and correct the condition?	-	Go to Step 13	Go to Step 10
8	Test the motor and solenoid ground circuits of the EBCM for a high resistance or an open. Did you find and correct the condition?	-	Go to Step 13	Go to Step 9
9	Inspect for poor connections or corrosion at the ground G102. Did you find and correct the condition?	-	Go to Step 13	Go to Step 10
10	Inspect for poor connections at the battery terminals. Did you find and correct the condition?	-	Go to Step 13	Go to Step 11
11	Inspect for poor connections at the harness connector of the EBCM. Did you find and correct the condition?	-	Go to Step 13	Go to Step 12
12	Replace the brake pressure modulator valve (BPMV). Did you complete the replacement?	-	Go to Step 13	--
13	1. Use the scan tool in order to clear the DTCs. 2. Operate the vehicle within the Conditions for Running the DTC as specified in the supporting text. Does the DTC reset?	-	Go to Step 2	System OK

ARM66GC000000191

Fig. 40 Code C1241: System Voltage (Part 3 of 3). Vibe

Step	Action	Value(s)	Yes	No
1	Did you perform A Diagnostic System Check - ABS?	--	Go to Step 2	Go to Diagnostic System Check -
2	1. Turn ON the ignition, with the engine OFF. 2. With a scan tool, observe the deceleration sensor parameter in the ABS data list. Does the scan tool indicate the deceleration sensor is within the specified range?	Low	Go to Diagnostic Aids	Go to Step 3
3	Test the deceleration sensor circuits of the EBCM for a high resistance, an open, or a short. Did you find and correct the condition?	--	Go to Step 7	Go to Step 4
4	Test the voltage of the deceleration sensor circuits of the EBCM to a good ground. Is the voltage within the specified range?	Terminal GS1 and GS2: approximately 5 V Terminal GST: switching 0 to 12 V	Go to Step 5	Go to Step 6
5	Replace the Deceleration Sensor. Did you complete the replacement?	--	Go to Step 7	--
6	Replace the Brake Pressure Modulator Valve (BPMV). Did you complete the replacement?	--	Go to Step 7	--
7	1. Use the scan tool in order to clear the DTCs. 2. Operate the vehicle within the Conditions for Running the DTC as specified in the supporting text. Does the DTC reset?	--	Go to Step 2	System OK

ARM66GC000000193

Fig. 41 Code C1243: Deceleration Sensor (Part 2 of 2). Vibe

Circuit Description

The electronic brake control module (EBCM) monitors the deceleration of the vehicle for antilock brake system (ABS) operation.

Conditions for Running the DTC

The vehicle speed is greater than 5 km/h (3 mph).

Conditions for Setting the DTC

The EBCM detects an open or a short in the deceleration sensor circuitry.

Action Taken When the DTC Sets

The ABS warning indicator turns ON.

Conditions for Clearing the DTC

The condition responsible for setting the DTC no longer exists and the scan tool Clear DTCs function is used.

Diagnostic Aids

Thoroughly inspect the wiring and the connectors. An incomplete inspection of the wiring and the connectors may result in a misdiagnosis, causing a part replacement with the reappearance of the malfunction.

The following are possible causes of the malfunction:

- An open or short in deceleration sensor to EBCM wiring circuits
- An open or high resistance in the ignition positive voltage circuit
- An open or high resistance in the deceleration sensor ground circuit
- A deceleration sensor malfunction
- An internal EBCM malfunction

Test Description

The numbers below refer to the step numbers on the diagnostic table.

2. This step uses the scan tool to test the ignition positive voltage circuit to the EBCM.

ARM66GC000000194

Fig. 42 Code C1244: Deceleration Sensor Circuit Open Or Short (Part 1 of 2). Vibe

Step	Action	Value(s)	Yes	No
1	Did you perform A Diagnostic System Check - ABS?	--	Go to Step 2	Go to Diagnostic System Check -
2	1. Turn ON the ignition, with the engine OFF. 2. With a scan tool, observe the deceleration sensor parameter in the ABS data list. Does the scan tool indicate the deceleration sensor is within the specified range?	Low	Go to Diagnostic Aids	Go to Step 3
3	Test the deceleration sensor circuits of the EBCM for a high resistance, an open, or a short. Did you find and correct the condition?	--	Go to Step 7	Go to Step 4
4	Test the voltage of the deceleration sensor circuits of the EBCM to a good ground. Is the voltage within the specified range?	Terminal GS1 and GS2: approximately 5 V Terminal GST: switching between 0 and 12 V	Go to Step 5	Go to Step 6
5	Replace the deceleration sensor. Did you complete the replacement?	--	Go to Step 7	--
6	Replace the brake pressure modulator valve (BPMV). Did you complete the replacement?	--	Go to Step 7	--
7	1. Use the scan tool in order to clear the DTCs. 2. Operate the vehicle within the Conditions for Running the DTC as specified in the supporting text. Does the DTC reset?	--	Go to Step 2	System OK

ARM66GC000000195

Fig. 42 Code C1244: Deceleration Sensor Circuit Open Or Short (Part 2 of 2). Vibe

Circuit Description

The electronic brake control module (EBCM) monitors brake pedal position through the stop lamp switch. The stop lamp switch is closed when the brake pedal is pressed and the stop lamp switch opens when the brake pedal is released. When the stop lamp switch is closed, the EBCM receives a voltage signal from the stop lamp switch. The stop lamp switch receives power from the STOP fuse.

Conditions for Running the DTC

DTC C1249 can be set anytime.

Conditions for Setting the DTC

The EBCM detects an open in the stop lamp switch circuit.

Action Taken When the DTC Sets

The EBCM turns ON the ABS indicator. If this DTC sets during an ABS event, the ABS will remain functional until the vehicle stops. Otherwise the ABS is disabled.

Conditions for Clearing the DTC

The condition responsible for setting the DTC no longer exists and the scan tool Clear DTCs function is used.

Diagnostic Aids

Thoroughly inspect the wiring and the connectors. An incomplete inspection of the wiring and the connectors may result in a misdiagnosis, causing a part replacement with the reappearance of the malfunction.

The following are possible causes of the malfunction:

- An open STOP fuse, possible short to ground in its circuitry
- Misadjusted stop lamp switch
- Faulty stop lamp switch
- Open or high resistance in the brake switch input circuit
- Short to voltage in the brake switch input circuit
- An internal EBCM malfunction

Test Description

The number(s) below refer to the step number(s) on the diagnostic table.

2. This step inspects the Stop Lamp Switch status with the switch OFF.
3. This step inspects the Stop Lamp Switch status with the switch applied.

ARM66GC000000196

Fig. 43 Code C1249: Stop Lamp Switch Circuit Open (Part 1 of 3). Vibe

Step	Action	Yes	No
1	Did you perform A Diagnostic System Check - ABS?	Go to Step 2	Go to Diagnostic System Check
2	1. Install a scan tool. 2. Turn ON the ignition, with the engine OFF. 3. With a scan tool, observe the Brake Switch parameter in the ABS Data List. Does the scan tool display Released?	Go to Step 3	Go to Step 4
3	Press the brake pedal while observing the Brake Switch parameter. Does the Brake Switch parameter change state?	Go to Diagnostic Aids	Go to Step 4
4	1. Turn OFF the ignition. 2. Inspect the stop lamp switch and adjust if needed. Did you find and correct the condition?	Go to Step 11	Go to Step 5
5	1. Turn OFF the ignition. 2. Disconnect the stop lamp switch. 3. Turn ON the ignition, with the engine OFF. 4. With a scan tool, observe the Brake Switch parameter. Does the scan tool display Released?	Go to Step 8	Go to Step 6
6	Test the Brake Switch circuit for an open or short to ground. Did you find and correct the condition?	Go to Step 11	Go to Step 7

ARM66GC000000197

Fig. 43 Code C1249: Stop Lamp Switch Circuit Open (Part 2 of 3). Vibe

7	Inspect for poor connections at the harness connector of the EBCM. Did you find and correct the condition?	Go to Step 11	Go to Step 9
8	Inspect for poor connections at the harness connector of the EBCM. Did you find and correct the condition?	Go to Step 11	Go to Step 10
9	Replace the brake pressure modulator valve (BPMV). Did you complete the replacement?	Go to Step 11	--
10	Replace the stop lamp switch. Did you complete the replacement?	Go to Step 11	--
11	1. Use the scan tool in order to clear the DTCs. 2. Operate the vehicle within the Conditions for Running the DTC as specified in the supporting text. Does the DTC reset?	Go to Step 2	System OK

ARM66GC000000198

Fig. 43 Code C1249: Stop Lamp Switch Circuit Open (Part 3 of 3). Vibe

Step	Action	Yes	No
1	Did you perform A Diagnostic System Check - ABS?	Go to Step 2	Go to Diagnostic System Check -
2	1. Install a scan tool. 2. Turn ON the ignition, with the engine OFF. 3. Use the scan tool in order to clear the DTCs. 4. Using the scan tool, cycle the pump motor in the Special Functions menu. 5. Read the DTCs. Does the DTC reset?	Go to Step 3	Go to Diagnostic Aids
3	1. Test the battery positive voltage circuits for an open, high resistance, or a short to ground. 2. Test the motor ground circuit for an open or high resistance. Did you find and correct the condition?	Go to Step 5	Go to Step 4
4	Replace the brake pressure modulator valve (BPMV). Did you complete the replacement?	Go to Step 5	--
5	1. Use the scan tool in order to clear the DTCs. 2. Operate the vehicle within the Conditions for Running the DTC as specified in the supporting text. Does the DTC reset?	Go to Step 2	System OK

ARM66GC000000200

Fig. 44 Code C1251: EBCM Detects Pump Motor Is Stuck (Part 2 of 2). Vibe

Circuit Description

The pump motor relay is part of the electronic brake control module (EBCM). The EBCM turns ON and OFF the pump motor relay as deemed necessary to activate the pump motor.

Conditions for Running the DTC

DTC C1251 can be set anytime the pump motor is actuated.

Conditions for Setting the DTC

The EBCM detects a stuck pump motor.

Action Taken When the DTC Sets

- The ABS is disabled.
- The ABS warning indicator turns ON.

Conditions for Clearing the DTC

- The condition responsible for setting the DTC no longer exists and the scan tool Clear DTCs function is used.
- After the DTC is cleared, the ABS indicator will remain ON until the vehicle is road tested to verify the repair. Once the vehicle has been driven at a speed above 16 km/h (10 mph) for 20 seconds with no malfunctions present, the EBCM will turn OFF the ABS indicator.

Diagnostic Aids

Thoroughly inspect the wiring and the connectors. An incomplete inspection of the wiring and the connectors may result in a misdiagnosis, causing a part replacement with the reappearance of the malfunction.

The following are possible causes of the malfunction:

- An open, high resistance, or a short to ground in the battery positive voltage circuits
- An open or high resistance in the motor ground circuit
- An internal EBCM malfunction

Test Description

The number below refers to the step number on the diagnostic table.

2. This step determines if the DTC is current.

ARM66GC000000199

Fig. 44 Code C1251: EBCM Detects Pump Motor Is Stuck (Part 1 of 2). Vibe

Circuit Description

The electronic brake control module (EBCM) monitors the deceleration of the vehicle for antilock brake system (ABS) operation.

Conditions for Running the DTC

The ignition is in the ON position.

Conditions for Setting the DTC

The EBCM detects a malfunfunction in the deceleration sensor.

Action Taken When the DTC Sets

The ABS warning indicator turns ON.

Conditions for Clearing the DTC

The condition responsible for setting the DTC no longer exists and the scan tool Clear DTCs function is used.

Diagnostic Aids

Thoroughly inspect the wiring and the connectors. An incomplete inspection of the wiring and the connectors may result in a misdiagnosis, causing a part replacement with the reappearance of the malfunction.

The following are possible causes of the malfunction:

- An open or short in deceleration sensor to EBCM wiring circuits
- An open or high resistance in the ignition positive voltage circuit
- An open or high resistance in the deceleration sensor ground circuit
- A deceleration sensor malfunction
- An internal EBCM malfunction

Test Description

The numbers below refer to the step numbers on the diagnostic table.

2. This step uses the scan tool to test the ignition positive voltage circuit to the EBCM.

ARM66GC000000201

Fig. 45 Code C1279: EBCM Detects Fault In Deceleration Sensor (Part 1 of 2). Vibe

Step	Action	Value(s)	Yes	No
1	Did you perform A Diagnostic System Check - ABS?	--	Go to Step 2	Go to Diagnostic System Check -
2	1. Turn ON the ignition, with the engine OFF. 2. With a scan tool, observe the deceleration sensor parameter in the ABS data list. Does the scan tool indicate the deceleration sensor is within the specified range?	Low	Go to Diagnostic Aids	Go to Step 3
3	Test the deceleration sensor circuits of the EBCM for a high resistance, an open, or a short. Did you find and correct the condition?	--	Go to Step 7	Go to Step 4
4	Test the voltage of the deceleration sensor circuits of the EBCM to a good ground. Is the voltage within the specified range?	Terminal GS1 and GS2: approximately 5 V Terminal GST: switching 0 to 12 V	Go to Step 5	Go to Step 6
5	Replace the deceleration sensor. Did you complete the replacement?	--	Go to Step 7	--
6	Replace the brake pressure modulator valve (BPMV). Did you complete the replacement?	--	Go to Step 7	--
7	1. Use the scan tool in order to clear the DTCs. 2. Operate the vehicle within the Conditions for Running the DTC as specified in the supporting text. Does the DTC reset?	--	Go to Step 2	System OK

ARM66GC000000202

Fig. 45 Code C1279: EBCM Detects Fault In Deceleration Sensor (Part 2 of 2). Vibe

Step	Action	Yes	No
1	Did you perform A Diagnostic System Check - ABS?	Go to Step 2	Go to Diagnostic System Check
2	1. Turn OFF the ignition. 2. Disconnect the EBCM electrical connector. 3. Turn ON the ignition, with the engine OFF. Is the ABS indicator ON?	Go to Step 3	Go to Diagnostic Aids
3	1. Test the battery positive circuit for an open or short to ground. 2. Test the motor ground circuit for an open or high resistance. Did you find and correct the condition?	Go to Step 8	Go to Step 4
4	Test the ABS indicator control circuit for a open or high resistance. Did you find and correct the condition?	Go to Step 8	Go to Step 5
5	Apply a ground to the ABS indicator control circuit. Is the ABS indicator ON?	Go to Step 6	Go to Step 7
6	Replace the instrument panel cluster assembly. Did you complete the replacement?	Go to Step 8	--
7	Replace the brake pressure modulator valve (BPMV). Is the repair complete?	Go to Step 8	--
8	Operate the system in order to verify the repair. Did you correct the condition?	System OK	Go to Step 2

ARM66GC000000204

Fig. 46 ABS Indicator Always On (Part 2 of 2). Vibe

Circuit Description

The electronic brake control module (EBCM) turns ON the antilock brake system (ABS) indicator by opening the ABS indicator control circuit. The ABS indicator is connected to the GAUGE fuse. This circuit has power when the ignition switch is in the ON or START positions. When the ignition switch is turned to the ON position, the EBCM turns ON the ABS indicator for 3 seconds for a bulb check. If the EBCM detects a malfunction, the ABS indicator will stay ON to warn the driver that the ABS is disabled and needs service.

Diagnostic Aids

Thoroughly inspect the wiring and the connectors. An incomplete inspection of the wiring and the connectors may result in a misdiagnosis, causing a part replacement with the reappearance of the malfunction.

The following are possible causes of the malfunction:

- The connector is off the EBCM.
- An open or high resistance in the ABS indicator control circuit
- An internal EBCM malfunction

Test Description

The number(s) below refer to the step number(s) on the diagnostic table.

4. An open in the ABS indicator control circuit will keep the ABS indicator ON.

ARM66GC000000203

Fig. 46 ABS Indicator Always On (Part 1 of 2). Vibe

Circuit Description

The electronic brake control module (EBCM) turns ON the antilock brake system (ABS) indicator by opening the ABS indicator control circuit. The ABS indicator is connected to the GAUGE fuse. This circuit has power when the ignition switch is in the ON or START positions. When the ignition switch is turned to the ON position, the EBCM turns ON the ABS indicator for 3 seconds for a bulb check. If the EBCM detects a malfunction, the ABS indicator will stay ON to warn the driver that the ABS is disabled and needs service.

Diagnostic Aids

Thoroughly inspect the wiring and the connectors. An incomplete inspection of the wiring and the connectors may result in a misdiagnosis, causing a part replacement with the reappearance of the malfunction.

The following are possible causes of the malfunction:

- An open in the ABS Indicator Control circuit.
- An internal EBCM malfunction.
- A malfunctioning Instrument Cluster Panel Assembly.

Test Description

The number(s) below refer to the step number(s) on the diagnostic table.

3. Determines if the malfunction is caused by an internal EBCM malfunction.

ARM66GC000000205

Fig. 47 ABS Indicator Inoperative (Part 1 of 2). Vibe

Step	Action	Yes	No
1	Did you perform A Diagnostic System Check - ABS?	Go to Step 2	Go to Diagnostic System Check
2	Do any of the other instrument cluster indicators or gages function?	Go to Step 3	Instrument Panel, Gages, and Console
3	1. Turn OFF the ignition. 2. Disconnect the EBCM electrical connector. 3. Turn ON the ignition, with the engine OFF. Does the ABS indicator turn ON?	Go to Step 6	Go to Step 4
4	Test the ABS indicator control circuit for a short to ground. Did you find and correct the condition?	Go to Step 7	Go to Step 5
5	Replace the instrument panel cluster assembly. Did you complete the replacement?	Go to Step 7	--
6	Replace the brake pressure modulator valve (BPMV). Is the repair complete?	Go to Step 7	--
7	Operate the system in order to verify the repair. Did you correct the condition?	System OK	Go to Step 2

ARM66GC000000206

Fig. 47 ABS Indicator Inoperative (Part 2 of 2). Vibe

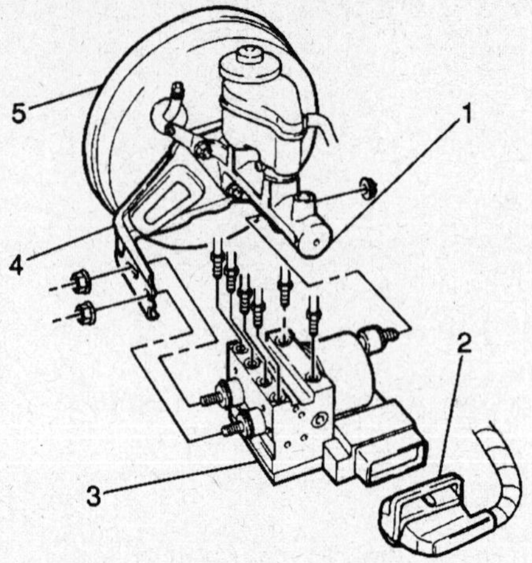

(1) Master Cylinder
(2) BPMV Wiring Harness Connector
(3) EBCM/BPMV Assembly
(4) EBCM/BPMV Mounting Bracket
(5) Brake Vacuum Booster

GC4029803583000X

Fig. 48 Brake modulator replacement

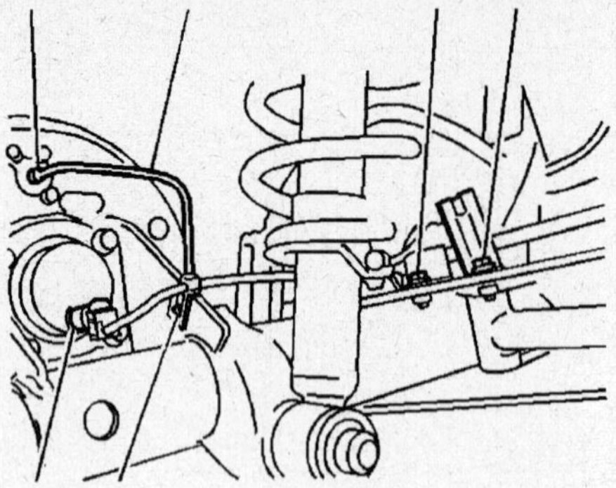

ARM66GC000000207

Fig. 49 Rear wheel speed sensor. Vibe w/FWD

Delphi DBC 7

NOTE: On Air Bag Equipped Models, Refer To "Air Bag System Precautions" Located In The Front Of This Manual For System Disarming & Arming Procedures.

NOTE: Refer To "Computer Relearn Procedures" Located In The Front Of This Manual When Battery Power To The Computer Has Been Interrupted.

NOTE: "Electrical Symbol & Wire Color Code Identification" Located In The Front Of This Manual May Be Used As An Aid When Using Wiring Circuits Found In This Section.

INDEX

PRECAUTIONS

Air Bag Systems

Refer to "Air Bag System Precautions" in the front of this manual for system disarming and arming procedures.

Battery Ground Cable

Prior to service, disconnect battery ground cable and isolate as required.

ABS Service

Before performing any repairs on the ABS system, note the following precautions:

1. Before using electric welding equipment, disconnect EBCM.
2. Carefully note routing, position and mounting ABS and TCS wiring, connectors, clips and brackets. ABS and TCS are extremely sensitive to electromagnetic interference.
3. Do not use a fast charger when battery is connected. **Never disconnect battery from system with engine running.**
4. Ignition switch must be in Off position when disconnecting EBCM.
5. Many ABS system components are non-serviceable and must be replaced as assemblies. **Do not disassemble non-serviceable components.**
6. Do not hang other components on wheel speed sensor cables.
7. Do not expose EBCM to temperatures of more than 184°F.
8. Use DOT 3 brake fluid only. Do not use container that has been used with petroleum based fluids or is wet with water. Petroleum based fluids will damage system and water will lower boiling point. Keep fluid containers capped.
9. After replacing any ABS component, inspect system as outlined in "Diagnosis & Testing."

DESCRIPTION

System Operation

ANTI-LOCK BRAKE SYSTEM (ABS)

The ABS system will control hydraulic pressure in the individual wheel circuits to prevent any wheel from slipping. A separate hydraulic line and specific solenoid valves are provided for each wheel. The ABS can decrease, hold or increase hydraulic pressure to each wheel brake. However, it cannot increase hydraulic pressure above what the master cylinder is transmitting.

ENHANCED TRACTION SYSTEM (ETS)

The ETS limits wheel slip during acceleration when one or more of the drive wheels are accelerating too rapidly and the brake switch is off. The EBCM monitors wheel speed slip through the ABS Wheel Speed Sensors (WSS), and then processes the sensor data and sends a desired wheel torque valve to the Powertrain Control Module (PCM) via a class 2 serial data line signal. The PCM then calculates and employs control of the wheel slip/wheel torque by utilizing one of the three following methods; retarding ignition timing, shutting off up to three injectors or up-shifting the transmission.

The ETS is enabled when the Traction Control switch is in the On position and the Trac Off lamp is not lit, and the catalytic

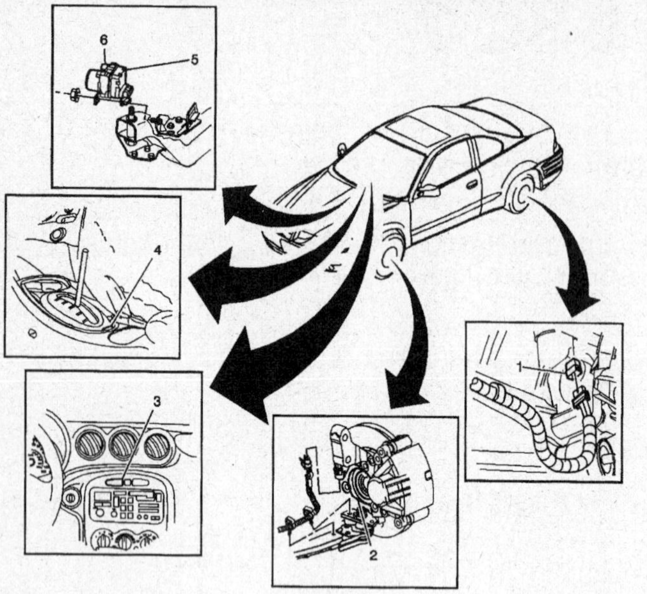

(1) Wheel Speed Sensor (WSS) - LR
(2) Wheel Speed Sensor (WSS) - LF
(3) Traction Control Switch
(4) Traction Control Switch
(5) Electronic Brake Control Module (EBCM)
(6) Brake Pressure Modulator Valve (BPMV)

ARM66GC000000546

Fig. 1 ABS components. Alero, Grand Am & Malibu

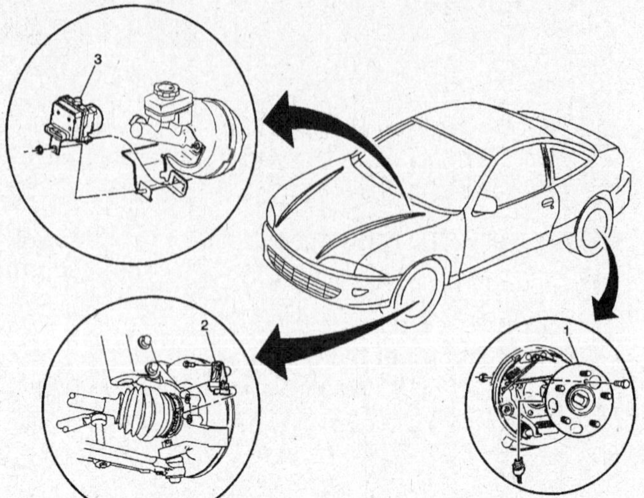

(1) Wheel Speed Sensor - LR.RR Similar
(2) Wheel Speed Sensor - LF,RF Similar
(3) EBCM/BPMV Assembly

ARM66GC000000547

Fig. 2 ABS components. Cavalier & Sunfire

converter and the engine coolant temperatures are within normal operating ranges. The ETS will be disable under the following conditions; EBCM senses a valid brake switch input, parking brake is engaged, catalytic converter temperature rises above normal range, engine coolant temperature is outside normal operating range, PCM sets a Diagnostic Trouble Code (DTC) that turns on Check Engine lamp or EBCM sets any DTC that effects ETS operation.

TRACTION CONTROL SYSTEM (TCS)

When the EBCM detects one or both front wheels rotating faster than the rear wheels, it will request the Powertrain Control Module (PCM) reduce torque applied to drive wheels. The PCM retards the timing and turns off the supercharger (if equipped) and fuel injectors similar to ETS system. The EBCM applies the front brakes in order to reduce front wheel torque. Once the front wheels begin rotating at the same speed as the rear wheels, the system will return full control to the driver.

System Components

Refer to **Figs. 1 through 4,** for system component locations.

BRAKE PRESSURE MODULATOR VALVE (BPMV)

The BPMV is mounted on the driver's side of the engine compartment. It provides brake fluid modulation for the individual wheel circuits during anti-lock braking. With the exception of the Electronic Brake Control Module (EBCM), the BPMV is an integral, non-serviceable component.

ELECTRONIC BRAKE CONTROL MODULE (EBCM) MODULE

The EBCM detects wheel slip tendencies and wheel speed differences. The EBCM controls the brake system while in anti-lock or traction control models, controls Magnetic Steering Variable Assist System (MSVA) and monitors system for proper electrical operation.

The EBCM continuously inspects each wheel speed to determine if any wheel is beginning to slip. If a wheel slip tendency is detected, the EBCM commands the appropriate valve positions to modulate the brake fluid pressure in some or all of the hydraulic circuits. The system controls hydraulic circuits until the slipping tendency is no longer present.

The EBCM also continuously monitors the ABS, ETS and TCS for proper operation. If an error is detected, the EBCM can disable the ABS, ETS or TCS and turn on the ABS, Low Trac and Trac Off indicators.

TRACTION CONTROL SYSTEM (TRAC) ON/OFF SWITCH

The TRAC switch allows the driver to turn off the ETS or TCS.

WHEEL SPEED SENSORS (WSS)

Each wheel speed sensor transmits wheel speed information to the EBCM via a small AC voltage. This voltage is generated by magnetic induction caused by passing a toothed sensor ring (part of the integral hub/bearing assembly) past a stationary sensor. The signal is transmitted to the EBCM through shielded wiring to reduce electro-magnetic interference that can cause false or noisy WSS inputs.

DIAGNOSIS & TESTING

Accessing Diagnostic Trouble Codes

Diagnostic Trouble Codes (DTCs) may be read using a suitably programed scan tool. There are no provisions for flash code diagnostics.

1. Turn ignition switch to Off position.
2. Connect suitably programmed scan tool connected to Data Link Connector (DLC), located under lefthand side of instrument panel below steering column.
3. Turn ignition switch to On position.
4. Select scan tool Special Functions.
5. Select and run Automated Test.
6. Record all DTCs.

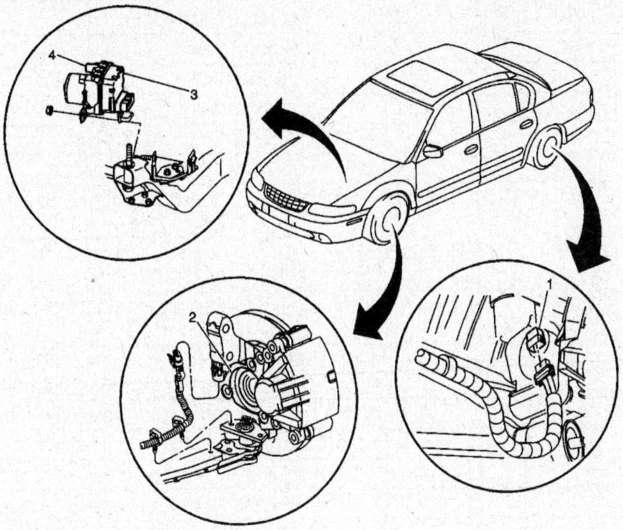

(1) Rear Wheel Speed Sensor
(2) Front Wheel Speed Sensor
(3) Electronic Brake Control Module (EBCM)
(4) Brake Pressure Modulator Valve (BPMV)

ARM66GC000000548

Fig. 3 ABS components. Century, Impala, Monte Carlo & Regal

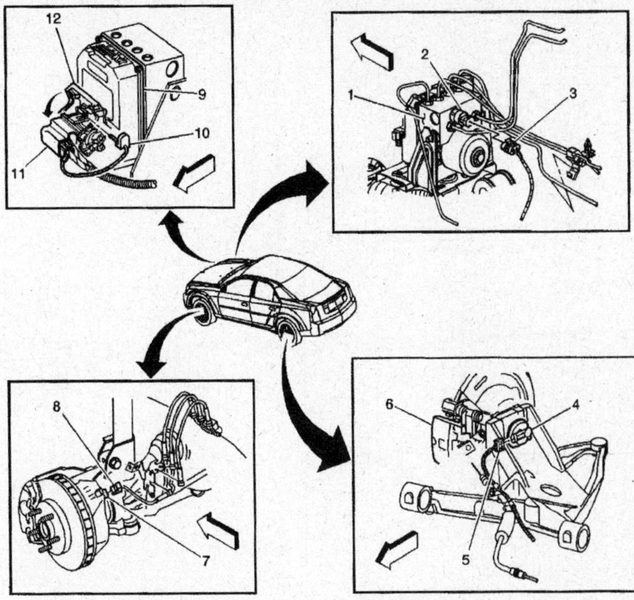

(1) Brake Pressure Modulator Valve (BPMV)
(2) Brake Fluid Pressure Sensor
(3) Brake Fluid Pressure Sensor Connector
(4) Wheel Speed Sensor-RR (LR Similar)
(5) Wheel Speed Sensor Connector-RR (LR Similar)
(6) Brake Caliper-LF
(7) Wheel Speed Sensor-LF (RF Similar)
(8) Wheel Speed Sensor Connector-LF (RF Similar)
(9) Electronic Brake Control Module (EBCM)
(10) EBCM Connector Position Assurance Retainer
(11) EBCM Connector
(12) EBCM Connector Lock

ARM66GC000000209

Fig. 4 ABS components (Part 1 of 2). CTS

Diagnostic Trouble Code Interpretation

Diagnostic Trouble Codes (DTCs) may be read using a suitably programmed scan tool. There are no flash code diagnostic provisions.

Connector numbers, circuit numbers and wire codes for individual models may vary from those printed in DTC flowcharts and circuit diagrams. Always refer to wiring circuits and connector terminal identification diagrams included for individual models in order to determine correct wire codes and connector or circuit numbers prior to proceeding with DTC flowcharts.

If no DTCs are present, or if mechanical component DTCs are present, perform automated modulator test using the scan tool to isolate the cause of the problem. If the failure is intermittent and not reproducible, test drive vehicle while using the automatic snapshot feature of the scan tool. Perform normal acceleration, stopping and turning maneuvers. If this does not reproduce the fault, perform an ABS stop from approximately 30–50 mph while triggering an ABS DTC. If failure still will not reproduce, use enhanced diagnostic information found in CODE HISTORY to determine whether or not this failure should be further diagnosed.

Refer to **Fig. 5,** for Diagnostic Trouble Code (DTC) identification.

Wiring Diagrams

ALERO & GRAND AM

Refer to **Figs. 6 and 7,** for wiring diagrams.

CAVALIER & SUNFIRE

Refer to **Fig. 8,** for wiring diagrams.

CENTURY & REGAL

Refer to **Fig. 9,** for wiring diagrams.

CTS

Refer to **Fig. 10,** for wiring diagrams.

IMPALA & MONTE CARLO

Refer to **Fig. 11,** for wiring diagrams.

MALIBU

Refer to **Fig. 12,** for wiring diagrams.

EBCM Terminal Identification

Refer to **Figs. 13 through 17,** for EBCM connector terminal identification.

Diagnostic Tests

ALERO, CAVALIER, GRAND AM, MALIBU & SUNFIRE

Refer to **Figs. 18 through 38,** for diagnostic tests. dummy text dummy text dummy text

CENTURY, IMPALA, MONTE CARLO & REGAL

Refer to **Figs. 39 through 66,** for diagnostic tests.

CTS

Refer to **Figs. 67 through 98,** for diagnostic tests.

Intermittents & Poor Connections

Intermittent failures in the anti-lock brake system may be difficult to accurately diagnose. The ABS Diagnostic Trouble Codes (DTCs) which may be stored by the EBCM are not designated as Current or History DTCs. These DTCs can be helpful in diagnosing intermittent conditions.

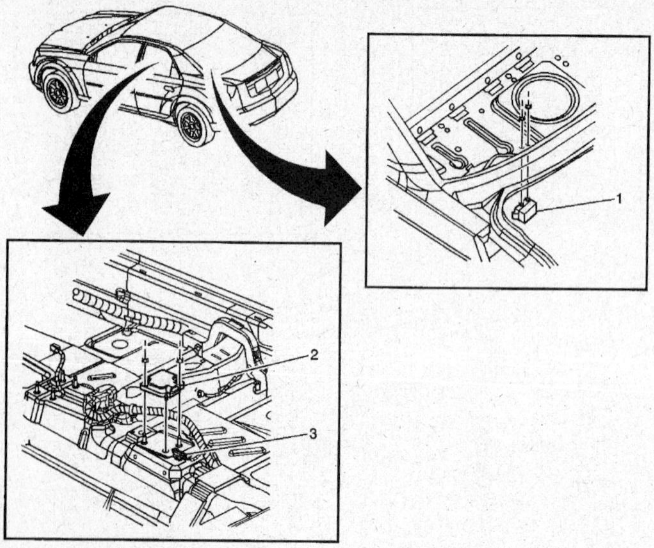

(1) Yaw Rate Sensor
(2) Lateral Accelerometer Sensor
(3) Lateral Accelerometer Sensor Connector

ARM66GC000000210

Fig. 4 ABS components (Part 2 of 2). CTS

Code	Description
B2747	Traction Control Switch Circuit Low
C1214	Solenoid Valve Relay Or Coil Circuit Open
C1216	EBCM Command Pressure Release Too Long
C1217	Pump Motor Shorted To Ground
C1218	Pump Motor Circuit Short To Voltage
C1221	Lefthand Front Wheel Speed Sensor Input Signal Is Zero
C1222	Righthand Front Wheel Speed Sensor Input Signal Is Zero
C1223	Lefthand Rear Wheel Speed Sensor Input Signal Is Zero
C1224	Righthand Rear Wheel Speed Sensor Input Signal Is Zero
C1225	Lefthand Front Excessive Wheel Speed Variation
C1226	Righthand Front Excessive Wheel Speed Variation
C1227	Lefthand Rear Excessive Wheel Speed Variation
C1228	Righthand Rear Excessive Wheel Speed Variation
C1232	Lefthand Front Wheel Circuit Open Or Shorted
C1233	Righthand Front Wheel Circuit Open Or Shorted
C1234	Lefthand Rear Wheel Circuit Open Or Shorted
C1235	Righthand Rear Wheel Circuit Open Or Shorted
C1236	Low System Supply Voltage
C1237	High System Supply Voltage
C1238	Bake Thermal Model Exceeded

Fig. 5 DTC identification (Part 1 of 2)

If an intermittent condition is being diagnosed, the ABS system can be used in the following manner to help isolate the suspected circuit.

1. Display and clear any ABS DTCs present in EBCM.
2. Attempt to repeat failure condition, noting following:
   a. Turn ignition switch to Off position.
   b. Disconnect scan tool. **If scan tool is installed, EBCM will not set DTCs and ABS/TCS functions may not be available.**
   c. Test drive vehicle.
3. After duplicating condition, stop vehicle and display any DTCs stored.
4. If no DTCs were stored refer to "Troubleshooting."
5. If a DTC was stored, inspect electrical connections and wiring for the circuit involves as follows:
   a. Poor mating of connector halves.
   b. Terminals not fully seated in connector halves.
   c. Improperly formed, or damaged terminals. All connector terminals in a problem circuit should be carefully reformed to increase contact tension.
   d. Poor terminal to wire connection. In most cases, this will require removing wire from connector body.
6. If there is an intermittent warning lamp operation, the following EBCM circuits should be inspected:
   a. Low system voltage. If low voltage is detected at EBCM, Anti-lock lamp will illuminate until normal operating voltage is detected.
   b. Low brake fluid. This condition in Pressure Modulator Valve (PMV) reservoir will cause Brake and Anti-lock lamps to illuminate. When an acceptable fluid level is registered, lamps will no longer be illuminated.
7. Any condition which results in interruption of power to EBCM or hydraulic unit may cause warning lamps to turn on intermittently. These circuits include main relay, pump motor relay, fuses and related wiring.

Electromagnetic Interference Test

Due to the sensitivity of ABS components to electromagnetic interference, the following inspections should be performed if an intermittent fault is suspected.

1. Inspect for proper installation of wiring harnesses resulting from add on options.
2. Visually inspect wheel speed sensor and toothed sensor ring for looseness, damage, accumulation of foreign material and proper mounting. Replace damaged components, remove any foreign material and properly attach all components.
3. Ensure front wheel speed sensor wiring is routed away from spark plug wires.
4. Measure resistance of spark plug wires. If resistance is greater than 30,000 ohms for any wire, replace spark plug wires.
5. While test driving vehicle, monitor wheel speeds with scan tool. If any wheel speed drops or displays an erratic speed, refer to appropriate wheel speed sensor DTC.

Clearing Diagnostic Trouble Codes

Diagnostic Trouble Codes (DTCs) cannot be cleared by disconnecting EBCM or battery cables. Follow scan tool instructions to clear DTCs. DTCs can also be cleared by cycling vehicle power 100 times without a particular fault reappearing. After that particular DTC is erased from the EBCM memory, the ignition cycle counter will be reset to zero.

SYSTEM SERVICE

Brake System Bleed

In most circumstances a manual brake bleed is all that is required. Automated ABS bleeding is required under the following conditions: when manual bleeding does not achieve desired pedal height or feel; brake pressure modulator valve (BPMV) replacement; extreme loss of brake fluid; air ingestion is suspected.

MANUAL BLEED

Use suitable container to catch fluid.

1. Clean reservoir cover and surrounding area.
2. Remove cover, fill fluid reservoir and install cover.
3. Attach one end of a clear plastic hose to rear hydraulic modulator bleeder valve, then submerge other end of hose in a clear container partially filled with brake fluid.
4. Slowly open bleeder valve ½–¾ turn.
5. Press brake pedal and hold until fluid begins to flow.
6. Close valve when fluid flows without air bubbles, then release brake pedal pressure.
7. Repeat procedure on forward bleeder valve. **This will ensure assembly is full of fluid. Complete air bleeding**

Code	Description
C1242	Pump Motor Circuit Open
C1243	BPMV Pump Motor Stalled
C1247	Low Brake Fluid Detected
C1254	Abnormal Shutdown Detected
C1255	EBCM Internal Fault
C1256	EBCM Internal Fault
C1261	Lefthand Front Inlet Valve Solenoid Fault
C1262	Lefthand Front Outlet Valve Solenoid Fault
C1263	Righthand Front Inlet Valve Solenoid Fault
C1264	Righthand Front Outlet Valve Solenoid Fault
C1265	Lefthand Rear Inlet Valve Solenoid Fault
C1266	Lefthand Rear Outlet Valve Solenoid Fault
C1267	Righthand Rear Inlet Valve Solenoid Fault
C1268	Righthand Rear Outlet Valve Solenoid Fault
C1275	PCM Requested ETS To Be Disabled
C1276	Delivered Torque Signal Circuit Fault
C1277	Requested Torque Signal Circuit Fault
C1278	TCS Temporarily Inhibited By PCM
C1291	Open Brake Lamp Switch Contacts During Decel
C1293	C1291 Set Current/Previous Ignition Cycle
C1294	Brake Lamp Switch Always Active
C1295	Brake Lamp Switch Circuit Open
C1298	PCM Class 2 Serial Data Link Fault

Fig. 5 DTC identification (Part 2 of 2)

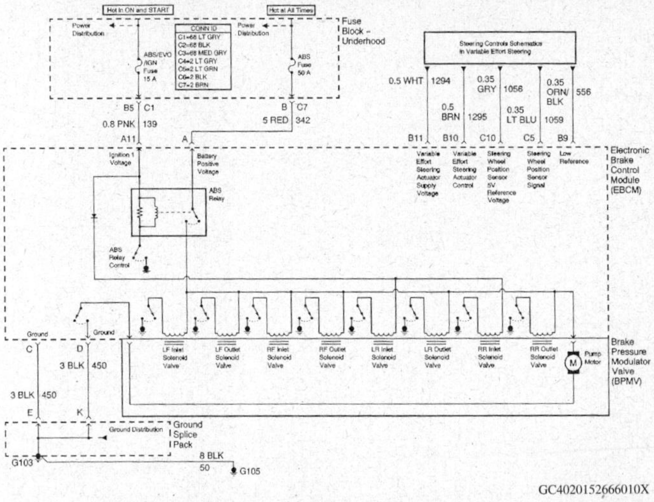

Fig. 6 Wiring diagram (Part 1 of 4). 2001–02 Alero & Grand Am

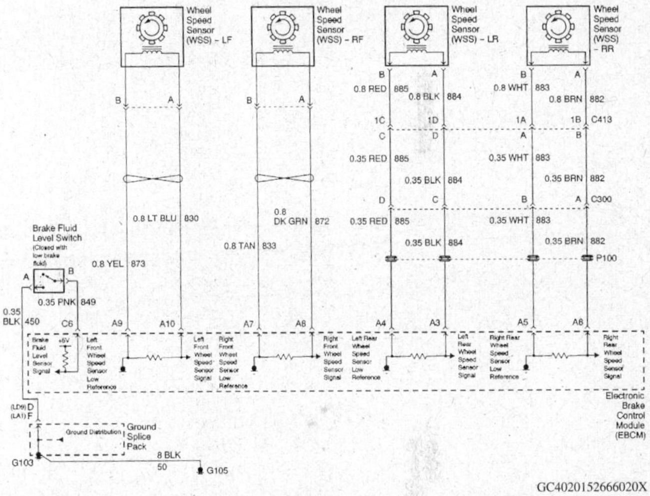

Fig. 6 Wiring diagram (Part 2 of 4). 2001–02 Alero & Grand Am

will be conducted after individual wheel brakes have been bled.

8. Remove cover and fill fluid reservoir, then install cover.
9. Raise and support vehicle, then bleed brakes as follows:
   a. Attach one end of bleeder hose to righthand rear wheel bleeder valve, then submerge other end of hose in a clear container partially filled with brake fluid.
   b. Open bleeder valve and slowly press brake pedal until fluid begins to flow.
   c. Close valve and release brake pedal pressure, then wait at least five seconds.
   d. Repeat steps "b" and "c" until brake pedal feels firm at half travel and no air bubbles are observed in container.
   e. Repeat procedure on lefthand rear, righthand front and lefthand front wheels, in turn.
10. Lower vehicle and fill fluid reservoir.
11. Attach one end of a clear plastic hose to rear hydraulic modulator bleeder valve, then submerge other end of hose in a clear container partially filled with brake fluid.
12. Slowly open bleeder valve ½–¾ turn.
13. Press brake pedal and hold until fluid begins to flow.
14. Close valve when fluid flows without air bubbles, then release brake pedal pressure. Repeat this step until no air bubbles are seen in container.
15. Repeat steps 11 through 14, on forward bleeder valve.
16. Fill fluid reservoir.
17. Turn ignition switch to the Run position and apply brake pedal with moderate force. If pedal travel is not excessive and pedal feels firm and constant, proceed to next step. If pedal still fills soft, repeat bleed procedure.
18. Start engine and apply brake pedal with moderate force. If pedal travel is not excessive and feels firm and constant, proceed to step 19. If pedal is soft or has excessive travel, proceed as follows:
   a. Use scan tool to release and apply motors 2–3 times.
   b. Cycle solenoids 5–10 times.
   c. Apply front and rear motors to ensure pistons are at upper most position.
   d. Repeat bleeding procedure.
19. Road test vehicle by starting engine and drive vehicle at six mph for five seconds.
20. Stop vehicle and turn ignition switch to Lock position.
21. Start engine and drive vehicle at six mph for five seconds. If pedal travel is not excessive and pedal feels firm and constant, proceed to next step. If pedal is soft or has excessive travel, repeat bleed procedure.
22. Road test vehicle, making several non-ABS stops at moderate speed to ensure proper braking function. Allow brakes to cool between stops.

AUTOMATED BLEED

Pressure bleeding equipment must have a rubber diaphragm between air supply and brake fluid to prevent air, moisture and other contaminants from entering system.

1. Ensure battery is fully charged, then connect suitably programed scan tool to Data Link Connector (DLC).
2. Access current and history Diagnostic Trouble Codes (DTCs). Repair all DTCs.
3. Visually inspect system for damage and leaks. Repair as required.
4. Raise and support vehicle, then turn ignition switch to Off position.
5. Remove all tire and wheel assemblies.
6. Connect suitable pressure bleeding tool according to manufacturers instructions.
7. Turn ignition switch to On position. Do not start engine.
8. Connect suitably programed scan tool

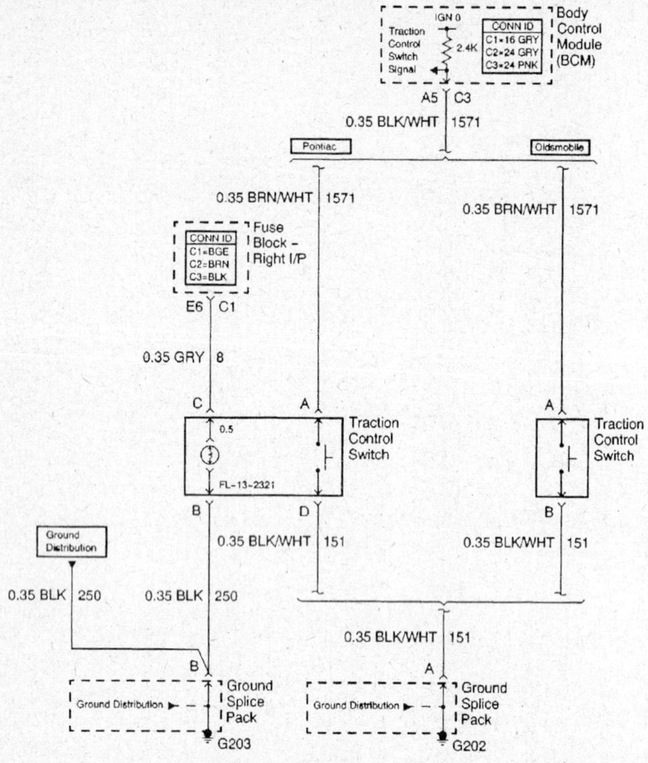

Fig. 6 Wiring diagram (Part 3 of 4). 2001–02 Alero & Grand Am

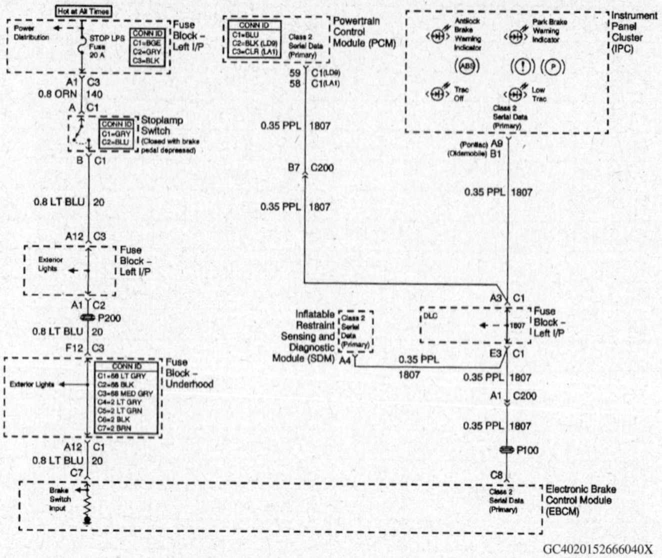

Fig. 6 Wiring diagram (Part 4 of 4). 2001–02 Alero & Grand Am

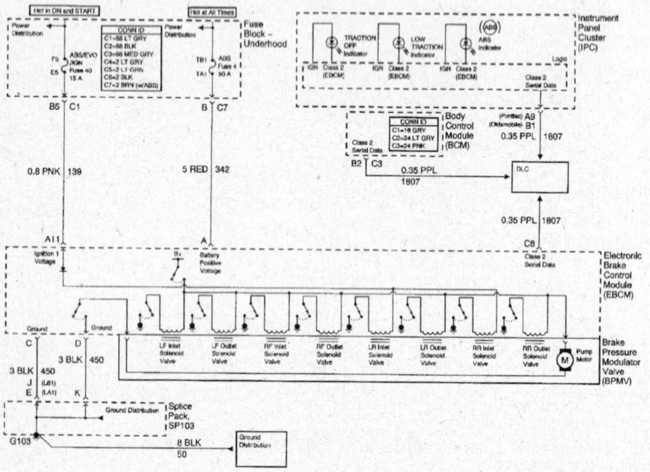

Fig. 7 Wiring diagram (Part 1 of 3). 2003–04 Alero & Grand Am

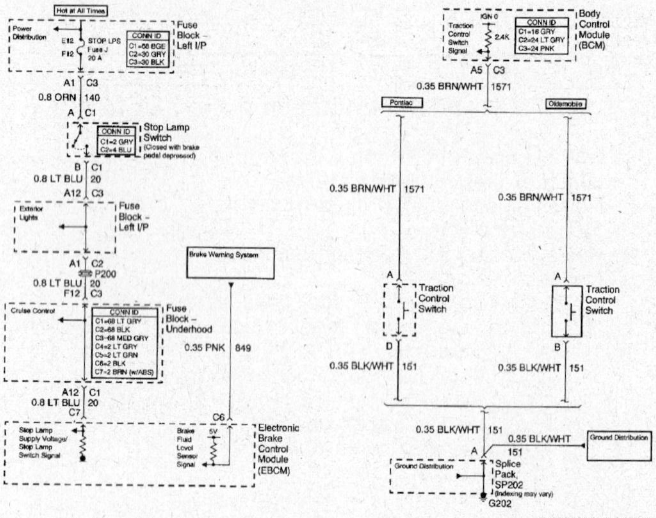

Fig. 7 Wiring diagram (Part 2 of 3). 2003–04 Alero & Grand Am

and establish ABS system communications.

9. Pressurize bleeding tool to 30–35 psi.
10. Ensure all bleeder screws are closed, then select scan tool Automated Bleed Procedure and follow instructions.
11. Automated bleed procedure will cycle and pump front release valves for one minute.
12. After cycle has stopped, scan tool will enter cool down mode and display three minute timer.
13. After following scan tool bleed procedure, press brake pedal to determine height and feel. Repeat procedure until pedal is acceptable.
14. Remove scan tool, then install tire and wheel assemblies.
15. Lower vehicle, then inspect and adjust master cylinder brake fluid level.

HYDRAULIC SYSTEM FLUSH

If brake fluid is old, rusty or contaminated, or whenever new components are installed in hydraulic system, the system must be flushed. Bleed brakes, allowing at least one quart of clean brake fluid to pass through system. Any rubber components in hydraulic system which were exposed to contaminated fluid must be replaced.

PRESSURE FLUSH

Pressure bleeding equipment must have a rubber diaphragm between air supply and brake fluid to prevent air, moisture and other contaminants from entering system.

1. Clean reservoir cover and surrounding area.
2. Remove cover and reservoir fluid.
3. Fill reservoir with clean DOT 3 brake fluid.
4. Attach bleeding adapter tool No. J-35589, or equivalent, to brake fluid reservoir and pressure bleeding equipment.
5. Pressurize bleeding equipment to 5–10 psi and wait 30 seconds to ensure there are no leaks.
6. Pressurize equipment to 30–35 psi.

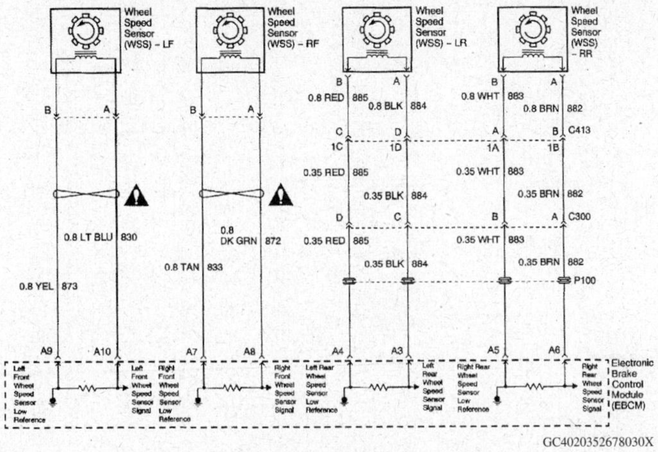

Fig. 7 Wiring diagram (Part 3 of 3). 2003–04 Alero & Grand Am

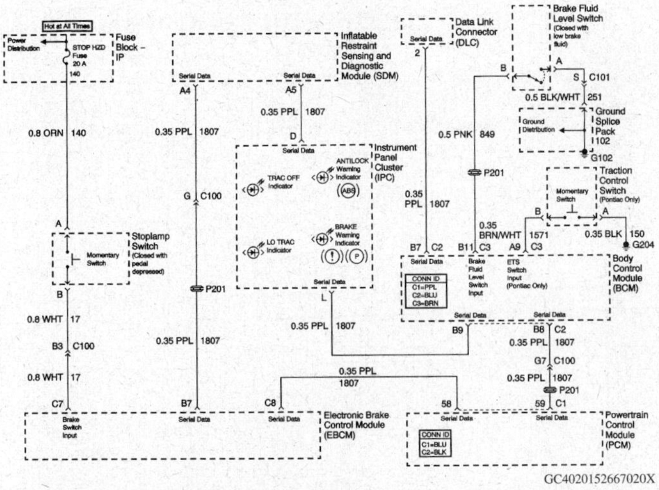

Fig. 8 Wiring diagram (Part 2 of 3). Cavalier & Sunfire

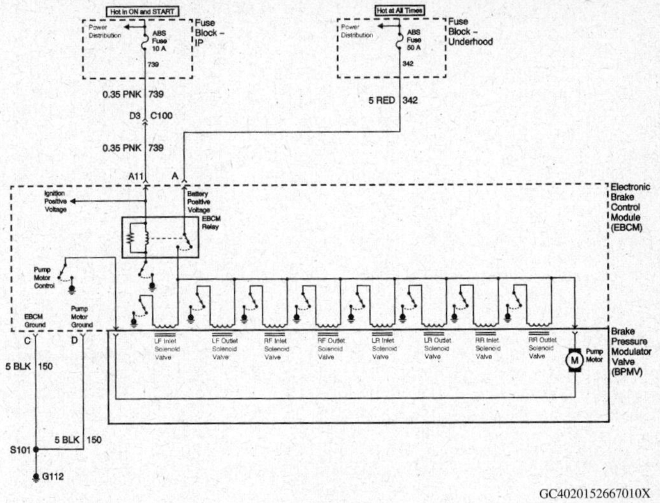

Fig. 8 Wiring diagram (Part 1 of 3). Cavalier & Sunfire

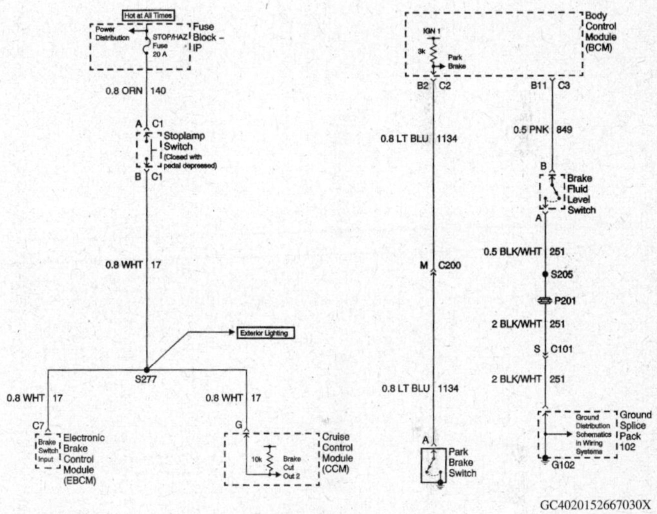

Fig. 8 Wiring diagram (Part 3 of 3). Cavalier & Sunfire

7. Attach clear plastic hose to rear hydraulic modulator bleeder valve. Place other end in suitable container to collect draining brake fluid. **Do not submerge hose end in fluid.**
8. Slowly open bleeder valve and allow fluid to flow until clean brake fluid flows.
9. Close valve and repeat procedure on forward bleeder valve.
10. **Torque** bleeder valves to 84 inch lbs.
11. Raise and support vehicle.
12. Attach bleeder hose to righthand rear wheel bleeder valve. Place other end in container to collect draining brake fluid. **Do not submerge hose end in fluid.**
13. Slowly open bleeder valve and allow fluid to flow until clean brake fluid flows, or until at least eight ounces of fluid is collected.
14. Close valve and repeat procedure on lefthand rear, righthand front and lefthand front wheels, in turn.
15. Lower vehicle and remove bleeder adapter tool.
16. Replace brake hose assemblies, master cylinder rubber components, brake caliper and wheel cylinder boots and seals, hydraulic modulator and ABS solenoids.
17. Repeat flushing procedure.
18. Inspect and correct reservoir fluid level.
19. Install reservoir cap and bleed system.

MANUAL FLUSH

Use suitable container and/or shop rags to catch fluid.

1. Clean reservoir cover and surrounding area.
2. Remove cover and reservoir fluid.
3. Fill reservoir with clean DOT 3 brake fluid.
4. Attach clear plastic hose to rearward hydraulic modulator bleeder valve. Place other end in container to collect draining brake fluid. **Do not submerge hose end in fluid.**
5. Open bleeder valve ½–1 turn.
6. Press brake pedal until fluid begins to flow.
7. Close valve and release brake pedal pressure.
8. Repeat previous steps until clean brake fluid flows, or until at least four ounces of fluid is collected.
9. Close valve and repeat procedure on forward bleeder valve.
10. **Torque** bleeder valves to 84 inch lbs.
11. Inspect and correct reservoir fluid level.
12. Install reservoir cap and bleed system.
13. Raise and support vehicle.
14. Attach bleeder hose to righthand rear wheel bleeder valve. Place other end in container to collect draining brake fluid. **Do not submerge hose end in fluid.**
15. Open bleeder valve and slowly press brake pedal until fluid begins to flow.
16. Close valve and release brake pedal pressure.
17. Repeat previous steps until clean brake fluid flows, or until at least eight ounces of fluid is collected.
18. Close valve and repeat procedure on lefthand rear, righthand front and lefthand front wheels, in turn.
19. Lower vehicle.
20. Replace brake hose assemblies, master cylinder rubber components, brake

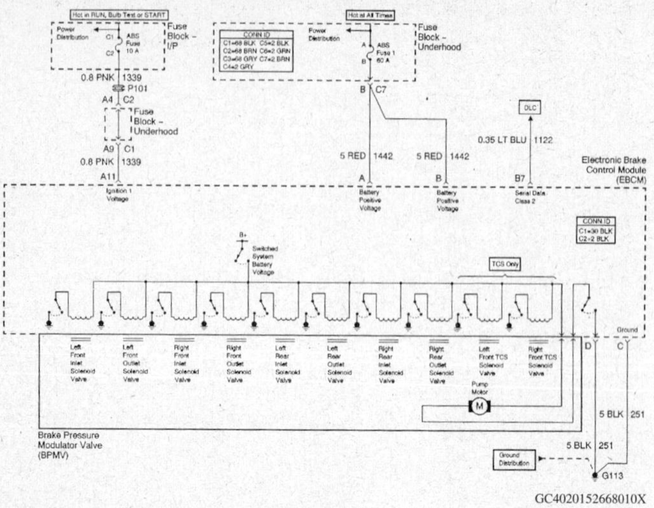

Fig. 9 Wiring diagram (Part 1 of 4). Century & Regal

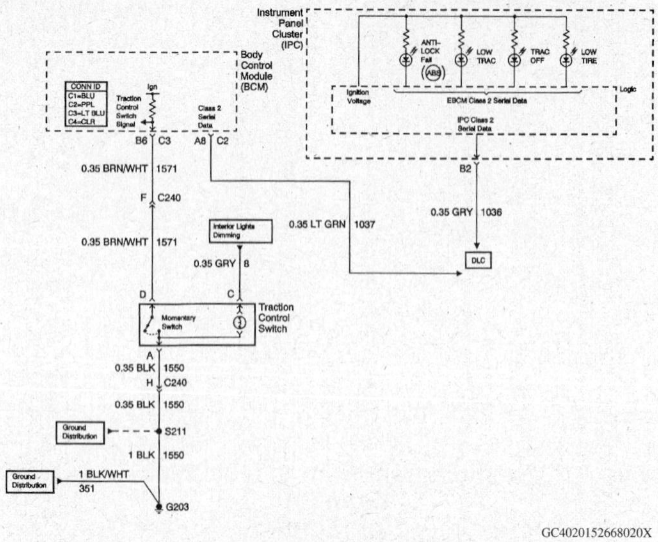

Fig. 9 Wiring diagram (Part 2 of 4). Century & Regal

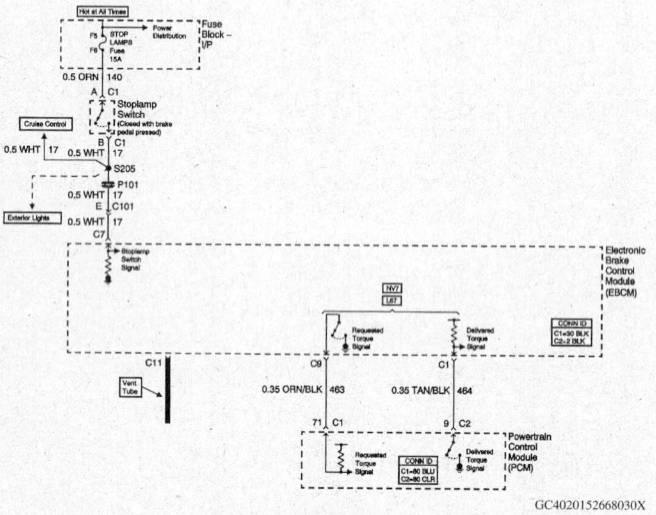

Fig. 9 Wiring diagram (Part 3 of 4). Century & Regal

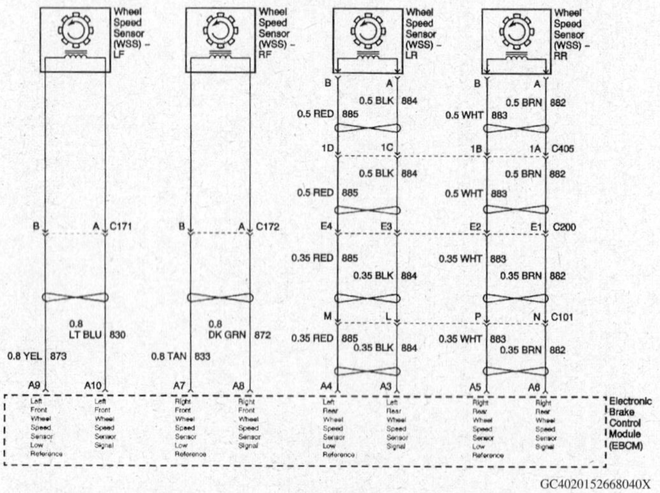

Fig. 9 Wiring diagram (Part 4 of 4). Century & Regal

caliper and wheel cylinder boots and seals, hydraulic modulator and ABS solenoids.

21. Repeat flushing procedure.
22. Inspect and correct reservoir fluid level.
23. Install reservoir cap and bleed system.

Component Replacement

BRAKE PRESSURE MODULATOR VALVE (BPMV)

ALERO & GRAND AM

The BPMV cannot be repaired. The complete unit must be replaced.

Before removing the brake modulator assembly it will be required to use a suitably programmed scan tool to perform the "Gear Tension Relief" function. This function will relieve the retained load on the brake modulator assembly.

1. Remove battery and battery tray.
2. Drain cooling system, then remove radiator inlet hose.
3. Disconnect brake solenoid valve and brake motor pack electrical connectors.
4. Disconnect wheel cylinder to brake modulator pipes from modulator.
5. Disconnect master cylinder to proportioning valve brake pipes from proportioning valve.
6. Remove brake modulator assembly to bracket mounting nut, then the modulator assembly from bracket.
7. Reverse procedure to install, noting the following:
   a. **Torque** modulator assembly to bracket mounting nut to 22 ft. lbs.
   b. **Torque** master cylinder to proportioning valve pipe fittings to 12 ft. lbs.
   c. **Torque** wheel cylinder to brake modulator brake pipe fittings to 18 ft. lbs.
   d. Bleed brake system as outlined in "Brake System Bleed."

CAVALIER & SUNFIRE

The BPMV cannot be repaired. The complete unit must be replaced.

1. Remove Connector Position Assurance (CPA) cover from Electronic Brake Control Module (EBCM) electrical connector.
2. Disconnect EBCM connector.
3. Disconnect caliper and wheel cylinder brake pipes from BPMV. Position pipes aside.
4. Disconnect master cylinder to BPMV pipes. Position pipes aside.
5. Remove BPMV/EBCM assembly to lower mounting bracket retaining nut, then the BPMV/EBCM assembly from engine compartment.
6. Remove BPMV to EBCM attaching screws, then separate BPMV from EBCM.
7. Reverse procedure to install, noting the following:
   a. **Torque** BPMV to EBCM attaching screws to 44 inch lbs.
   b. **Torque** BPMV/EBCM assembly to bracket retaining nut to 84 inch lbs.

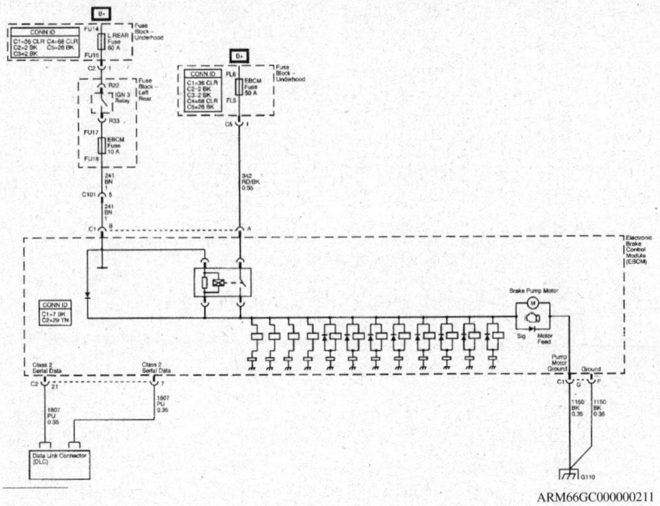

Fig. 10 Wiring diagram (Part 1 of 4). CTS

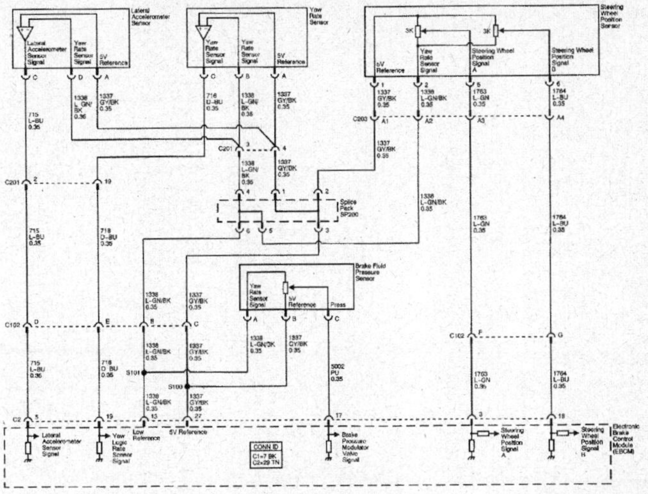

Fig. 10 Wiring diagram (Part 2 of 4). CTS

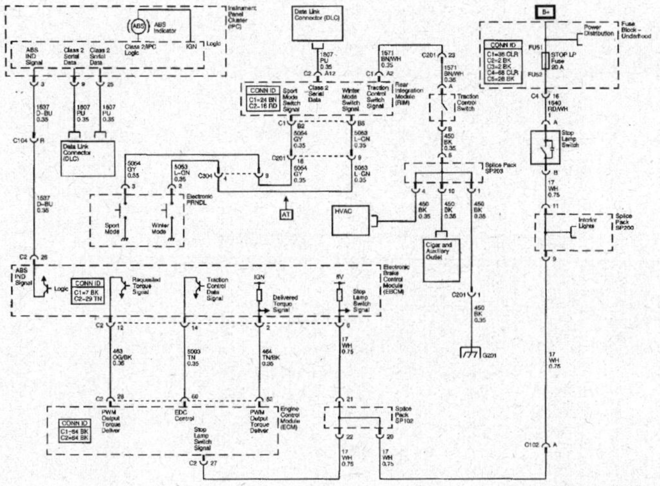

Fig. 10 Wiring diagram (Part 3 of 4). CTS

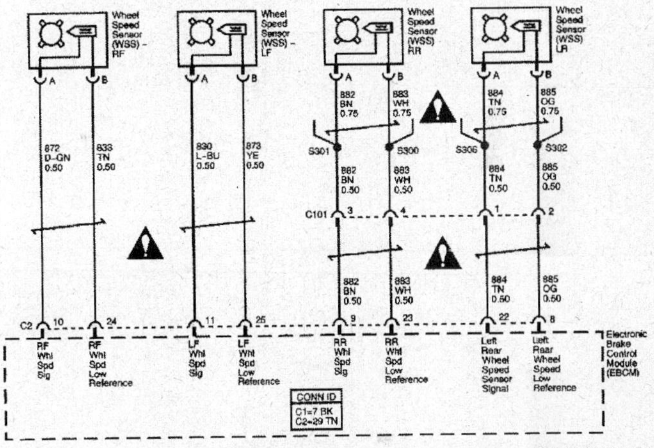

Fig. 10 Wiring diagram (Part 4 of 4). CTS

c. **Torque** BPMV brake pipe fittings to 18 ft. lbs.
d. Bleed brake system as outlined in "Brake System Bleed."

CENTURY, IMPALA, MONTE CARLO & REGAL

The BPMV cannot be repaired. The complete unit must be replaced.

1. Turn ignition switch to Off position.
2. Remove cruise control module mounting bolts and position module aside.
3. Disengage and push down on locking tab, then move closing connector cover to open position and disconnect EBCM harness connector.
4. Note location of hydraulic brake pipes for installation reference.
5. Disconnect and cover brake pipes, then swing pipes out of way. **Do not disconnect pipes from master cylinder.**
6. Protect vehicle exterior from possible brake fluid spillage.
7. Remove mounting bolts, then the BPMV with EBCM from bracket.
8. Reverse procedure to install, noting the following:
   a. **Torque** mounting bolts and nuts to 84 inch lbs.
   b. **Torque** strut tower mounting nut to 26 inch lbs.
   c. **Torque** pipe fittings to 18 ft. lbs.
   d. Bleed brake system as outlined in "Brake System Bleed."

CTS

The BPMV cannot be repaired. The complete unit must be replaced.

1. Turn ignition switch to Off.
2. Disconnect coolant bypass hose from radiator and position aside.
3. Remove master cylinder brake pipes from BPMV.
4. Remove wheel brake pipes from BPMV.
5. Disconnect brake fluid pressure sensor electrical connector.
6. Remove Connector Position Assurance (CPA) retainer from EBCM connector.
7. Disconnect EBCM electrical connector.
8. Remove BPMV/EBCM assembly to bracket retaining nuts, then the assembly from bracket.
9. Remove and discard BPMV to EBCM attaching screws and separate BPMV from EBCM.
10. Reverse procedure to install, noting the following:
    a. **Torque** BPMV to EBCM attaching screws to 44 inch lbs.
    b. **Torque** BPMV/EBCM to bracket retaining nuts to 89 inch lbs.
    c. **Torque** brake pipe to BPMV fittings to 18 ft. lbs.
    d. Bleed brake system as outlined in "Brake System Bleed."

MALIBU

The BPMV cannot be repaired, the complete unit must be replaced.

1. Turn ignition switch to Off position.
2. Remove battery and tray.
3. Note hydraulic brake pipe locations for installation reference.
4. Disconnect and cover brake pipes.
5. Raise and support vehicle, then remove front and left engine splash shields.
6. Disengage and push down on locking tab, then move closing connector cover to open position and disconnect EBCM harness connector.
7. Remove mounting bolts, then the

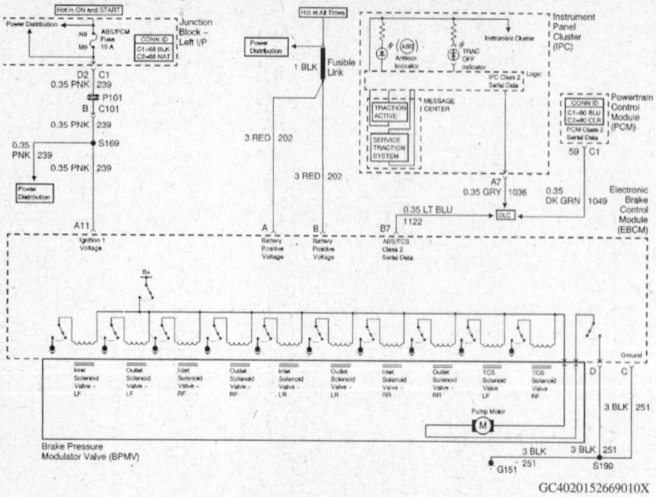

Fig. 11 Wiring diagram (Part 1 of 4). Impala & Monte Carlo

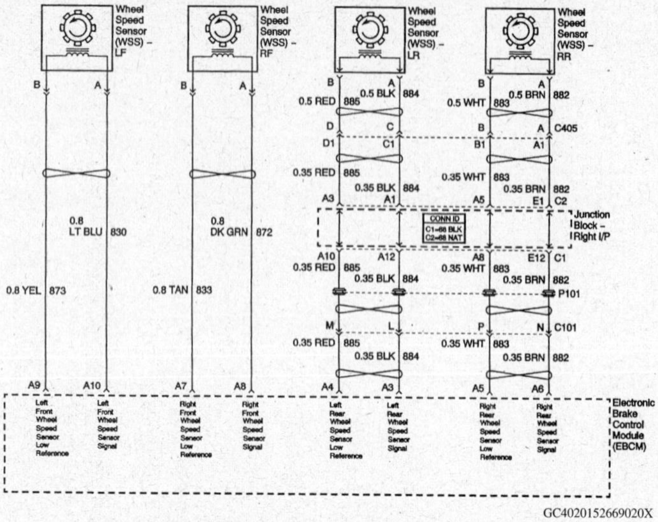

Fig. 11 Wiring diagram (Part 2 of 4). Impala & Monte Carlo

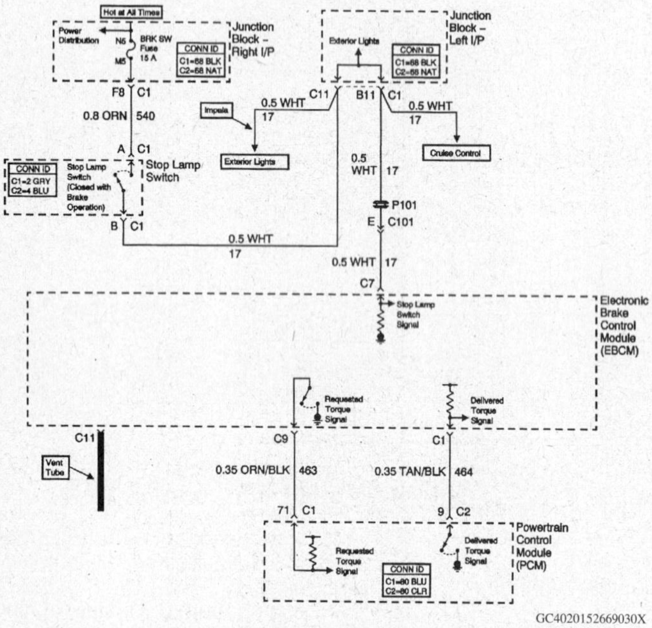

Fig. 11 Wiring diagram (Part 3 of 4). Impala & Monte Carlo

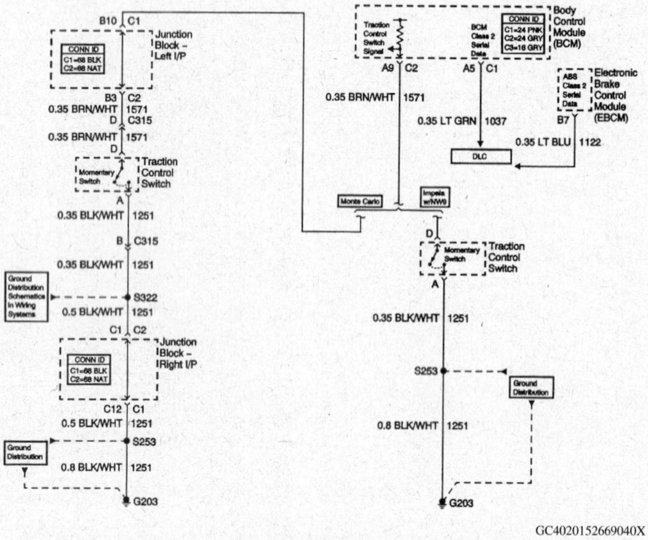

Fig. 11 Wiring diagram (Part 4 of 4). Impala & Monte Carlo

BPMV with EBCM from bracket.

8. Reverse procedure to install, noting the following:
   a. **Torque** mounting bolts and nuts to 84 inch lbs.
   b. **Torque** pipe fittings to 18 ft. lbs.
   c. Bleed brake system as outlined in "Brake System Bleed."

BPMV BRACKET

ALERO, CAVALIER, GRAND AM & SUNFIRE

1. Remove BPMV as outlined in "Brake Pressure Modulator Valve."
2. Remove master cylinder mounting nuts.
3. Move master cylinder forward enough to clear vacuum brake booster studs.
4. Remove lower BPMV bracket from vacuum brake booster.
5. Reverse procedure to install. **Torque** master cylinder mounting nuts to 20 ft. lbs.

CENTURY, IMPALA, MONTE CARLO & REGAL

1. Remove BPMV as outlined in "Brake Pressure Modulator Valve."
2. Remove lower mounting nuts and bolt, then the mounting nut at top of strut tower.
3. Remove bracket.
4. Reverse procedure to install, noting the following:
   a. **Torque** lower mounting nuts and bolt to 84 inch lbs.
   b. **Torque** top nut to 26 inch lbs.

MALIBU

1. Remove BPMV as outlined in "Brake Pressure Modulator Valve."
2. Remove mounting bolts and bracket.
3. Reverse procedure to install. **Torque** mounting bolts to 18 ft. lbs.

ELECTRONIC BRAKE CONTROL MODULE (EBCM)

ALERO, CAVALIER, CENTURY, GRAND AM, IMPALA, MONTE CARLO, REGAL & SUNBIRD

1. Turn ignition switch to Off position.
2. Remove BPMV as outlined in "Brake Pressure Modulator Valve."
3. Disconnect EBCM harness connector.
4. Brush any dirt/debris from assembly.
5. Remove attaching screws.
6. Separate EBCM from BPMV by gently pulling apart.
7. Reverse procedure to install. **Torque** attaching screws to 44 inch lbs.

CTS

The BPMV cannot be repaired. The complete unit must be replaced.

1. Turn ignition switch to Off position.
2. Disconnect coolant bypass valve from radiator and position aside.

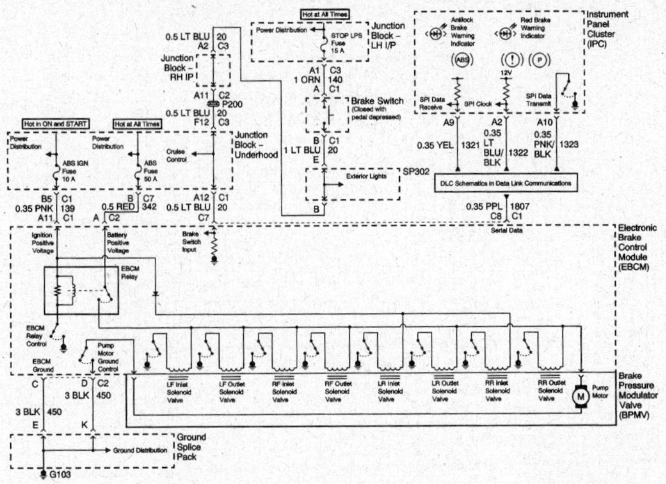

GC4020152670010X

Fig. 12 Wiring diagram (Part 1 of 2). Malibu

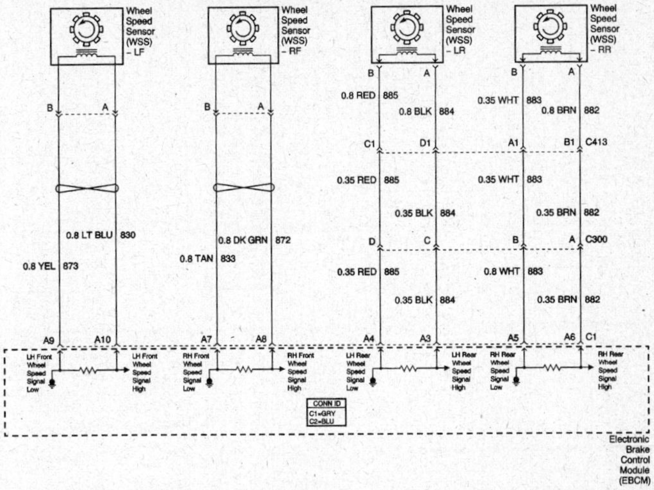

GC4020152670020X

Fig. 12 Wiring diagram (Part 2 of 2). Malibu

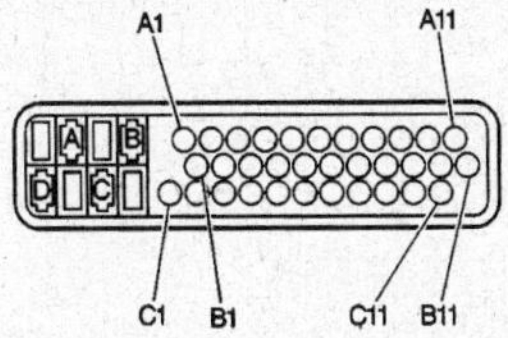

Connector Part Information		• 15336549 • 37-Way F Micro-Pack 100 Series (BLK)	
Pin	Wire Color	Circuit No.	Function
A	RED	342	Battery Positive Voltage
A1–A2	—	—	Not Used
A3	BLK	884	Left Rear Wheel Speed Sensor Signal
A4	RED	885	Left Rear Wheel Speed Sensor Low Reference
A5	WHT	883	Right Rear Wheel Speed Sensor Low Reference
A6	BRN	882	Right Rear Wheel Speed Sensor Signal
A7	TAN	833	Right Front Wheel Speed Sensor Low Reference
A8	DK GRN	872	Right Front Wheel Speed Sensor Signal
A9	YEL	873	Left Front Wheel Speed Sensor Signal
A10	LT BLU	830	Left Front Wheel Speed Sensor Signal
A11	PNK	139	Ignition 1 Voltage
B	—	—	Not Used
B1–B8	—	—	Not Used
B9	ORN/BLK	556	Low Reference
B10	BRN	1295	Variable Effort Steering Actuator Control
B11	WHT	1294	Variable Effort Steering Actuator Supply Voltage
C	BLK	450	Ground
C1–C4	—	—	Not Used
C5	LT BLU	1059	Steering Wheel Position Sensor Signal
C6	PNK	849	Brake Fluid Level Sensor Signal

Connector Part Information		• 15336549 • 37-Way F Micro-Pack 100 Series (BLK)	
Pin	Wire Color	Circuit No.	Function
C7	LT BLU	20	Stop Lamp Supply Voltage
C8	PPL	1807	Class 2 Serial Data (Primary)
C9	—	—	Not Used
C10	GRY	1056	Steering Wheel Position Sensor 5V Reference Voltage
C11	—	—	Not Used
D	BLK	450	Ground

GC4020152671000X

Fig. 13 EBCM terminal identification. Alero & Grand Am

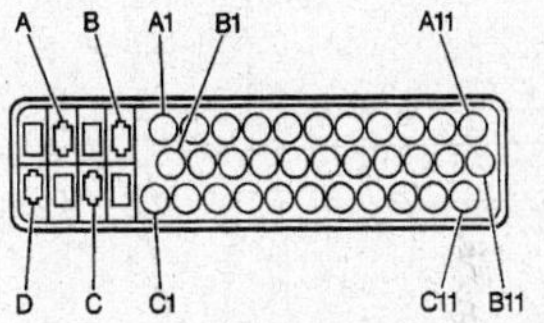

Connector Part Information		• 12167668 • 37-Way F Micro-Pack Series (BLK)	
Pin	Wire Color	Circuit No.	Function
A1-A2	—	—	Not Used
A3	TAN	884	Left Rear Wheel Speed Sensor Signal
A4	ORN	885	Left Rear Wheel Speed Sensor Low Reference
A5	WHT	883	Right Rear Wheel Speed Sensor Low Reference
A6	BRN	882	Right Rear Wheel Speed Sensor Signal
A7	TAN	833	Right Front Wheel Speed Sensor Low Reference
A8	DK GRN	872	Right Front Wheel Speed Sensor Signal
A9	YEL	873	Left Front Wheel Speed Sensor Low Reference
A10	LT BLU	830	Left Front Wheel Speed Sensor Signal
A11	PNK	739	Ignition 1 Voltage
B1-B11	—	—	Not Used
C1-C6	—	—	Not Used
C7	WHT	17	Stop Lamp Switch Signal
C8	PPL	1807	Class 2 Serial Data (Primary)
C9-C10	—	—	Not Used
C11	—	—	Vent Hose
A	RED/BLK	342	Battery Positive Voltage
B	—	—	Not Used
C	BLK	150	Ground
D	BLK	150	Ground

GC4020152672000X

Fig. 14 EBCM terminal identification. Cavalier & Sunfire

3. Remove Connector Position Assurance (CPA) retainer from EBCM connector.
4. Disconnect EBCM connector.
5. Remove and discard two upper EBCM to BPMV screws.
6. Raise and support vehicle.
7. Remove front air deflector.
8. Remove and discard two lower EBCM to BPMV attaching screws.
9. Lower vehicle, then separate EBCM from BPMV.
10. Reverse procedure to install. **Torque** new EBCM to BPMV attaching screws to 44 inch lbs.

WHEEL SPEED SENSOR

ALERO, CAVALIER, GRAND AM & SUNFIRE

Front

1. Raise and support vehicle.
2. Disconnect speed sensor electrical connector.
3. Remove mounting bolt.
4. If locating pin breaks off and remains in knuckle, proceed as follows:
   a. Remove brake rotor.
   b. Remove broken pin using suitable blunt punch.
   c. Clean hole using suitable sand paper wrapped around a screwdriver.
5. Remove speed sensor. If sensor will not slide out of knuckle, proceed as follows:
   a. Remove brake rotor.
   b. Remove sensor using suitable blunt punch.

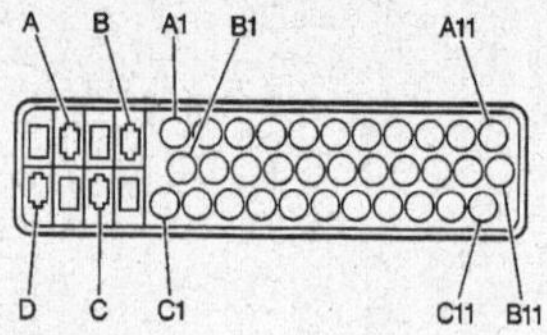

Connector Part Information	• 15336549 • 37-Way F Mixed Series (BLK)		
Pin	**Wire Color**	**Circuit No.**	**Function**
A1-A2	—	—	Not Used
A3	BLK	884	Wheel Speed Sensor Signal - Left Rear (Signal HI)
A4	RED	885	Wheel Speed Sensor Return - Left Rear (Signal LO)
A5	WHT	883	Wheel Speed Sensor Return - Right Rear (Signal LO)
A6	BRN	882	Wheel Speed Sensor Signal - Right Rear (Signal HI)
A7	TAN	833	Wheel Speed Sensor Return - Right Front (Signal LO)
A8	DK GRN	872	Wheel Speed Sensor Signal - Right Front (Signal HI)
A9	YEL	873	Wheel Speed Sensor Return - Left Front (Signal LO)
A10	LT BLU	830	Wheel Speed Sensor Signal - Left Front (Signal HI)
A11	PNK	1339	Fused Output - IGN 1
B1-B6	—	—	Not Used
B7	LT BLU	1122	Class 2 Serial Data Signal
B8-B9	—	—	Not Used
B10	WHT	345	Magnetic Steering Variable Assist Motor Feed - Low Effort
B11	GRY	1787	Magnetic Steering Variable Assist Motor Feed - High Effort
C1-C6	—	—	Not Used (w/RPO L36)
C1	TAN/BLK	464	Traction Control System Signal - Torque Delivered (w/RPO L67)
C2-C6	—	—	Not Used (w/RPO L67)
C7	WHT	17	Stop Lamp Switch Output

Connector Part Information	• 15336549 • 37-Way F Mixed Series (BLK)		
Pin	**Wire Color**	**Circuit No.**	**Function**
C8-C10	—	—	Not Used (w/RPO L36)
C8	—	—	Not Used (w/RPO L67)
C9	ORN/BLK	463	Traction Control System Signal - Torque Desired (w/RPO L67)
C10	—	—	Not Used (w/RPO L67)
C11	—	3000	Vacuum Hose Vent
A	RED	1442	Fused Output - Battery
B	RED	1442	Fused Output - Battery
C	BLK	251	Ground - Clean
D	BLK	251	Ground - Clean

GC4020152673000X

Fig. 15 EBCM terminal identification. Century & Regal

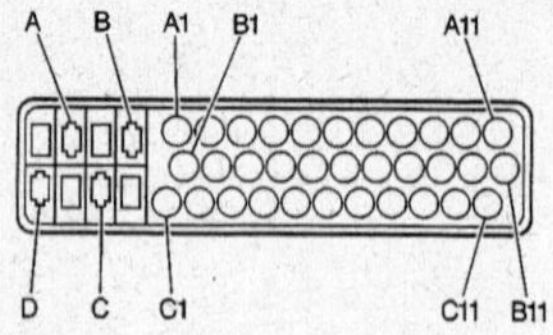

Connector Part Information	• 15317510 • 33 Way F Micro-Pack 100 W Series (RED)		
Pin	**Wire Color**	**Circuit No.**	**Function**
A1-A2	—	—	Not Used
A3	BLK	884	Wheel Speed Sensor Signal -LR
A4	RED	885	Wheel Speed Sensor Return-LR
A5	WHT	883	Wheel Speed Sensor Signal-RR
A6	BRN	882	Wheel Speed Sensor Return-RR
A7	TAN	833	Wheel Speed Sensor Return-RF
A8	DK GRN	872	Wheel Speed Sensor Signal-RF
A9	YEL	873	Wheel Speed Sensor Return-LF
A10	LT BLU	830	Wheel Speed Sensor Signal-LF
A11	PNK	239	Fuse Output -IGN 1
B1-B6	—	—	Not Used
B7	LT BLU	1122	SDS-Class B to ABS/TCS
B8-B11	—	—	Not Used
C1	TAN/BLK	464	TCS-Signal -Torque Delivered
C2-C6	—	—	Not Used
C7	WHT	17	Stoplamp Switch Output
C8	—	—	Not Used
C9	ORN/BLK	463	TCS-Signal-Torque Desired
C10	—	—	Not Used
C11	—	3000	Vent Tube

Connector Part Information	• 15336549 • 4 Way F GT 280 (BLK)		
Pin	**Wire Color**	**Circuit No.**	**Function**
A	RED	202	Fuse Output-BATTERY
B	RED	202	Fuse Output-BATTERY
C	BLK/WHT	251	Ground-Clean
D	BLK/WHT	251	Ground-Clean

GC4020152674000X

Fig. 16 EBCM terminal identification. Impala & Monte Carlo

6. Reverse procedure to install. **Torque** mounting bolt to 107 inch lbs.

Rear

The wheel speed sensor and ring are an integral part of the hub and bearing assembly. Refer to the "Rear Axle & Suspension" section of the "Cavalier & Sunfire" chassis chapter for hub and bearing assembly replacement.

CENTURY, IMPALA, MONTE CARLO & REGAL

The wheel speed sensor and ring are an integral part of the hub and bearing assembly. Refer to the "Front Suspension & Steering" and "Rear Axle & Suspension" sections of the "Century, Grand Prix, Impala, Intrigue, Lumina, Monte Carlo & Regal" chassis chapter for hub and bearing assembly replacement.

CTS

The wheel speed sensor and ring are an integral part of the hub and bearing assembly. Refer to the "Front Suspension & Steering" and "Rear Axle & Suspension" sections of the "CTS" chassis chapter for hub and bearing assembly replacement.

MALIBU

The wheel speed sensor and ring are an integral part of the hub and bearing assembly. Refer to the "Front Suspension & Steering" and "Rear Axle & Suspension" sections of the "Alero, Grand Am, Malibu & Skylark," chassis chapter for hub and bearing assembly replacement.

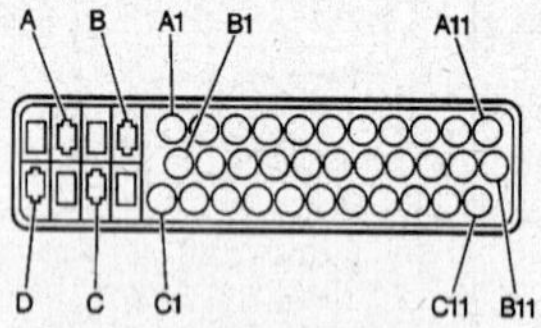

Connector Part Information	• 12167668 • 37-Way F Micro-Pack Series (BLK)		
Pin	**Wire Color**	**Circuit No.**	**Function**
A1-A2	—	—	Not Used
A3	BLK	884	Left Rear Wheel Speed Sensor Signal
A4	RED	885	Left Rear Wheel Speed Sensor Low Reference
A5	WHT	883	Right Rear Wheel Speed Sensor Low Reference
A6	BRN	882	Right Rear Wheel Speed Sensor Signal
A7	TAN	833	Right Front Wheel Speed Sensor Low Reference
A8	DK GRN	872	Right Front Wheel Speed Sensor Signal
A9	YEL	873	Left Front Wheel Speed Sensor Low Reference
A10	LT BLU	830	Left Front Wheel Speed Sensor Signal
A11	PNK	139	Ignition 1 Voltage
B1-B11	—	—	Not Used
C1-C6	—	—	Not Used
C7	LT BLU	20	Stop Lamp Supply Voltage
C8	PPL	1807	Class 2 Serial Data (Primary)
C9-C10	—	—	Not Used
C11	—	—	Not Used
A	RED	342	Battery Positive Voltage
B	—	—	Not Used
C	BLK	450	Ground
D	BLK	450	Ground

GC4020152675000X

Fig. 17 EBCM terminal identification. Malibu

DIAGNOSTIC CHART INDEX

Code	Description	Page No.	Fig. No.
ALERO, CAVALIER, GRAND AM, MALIBU & SUNFIRE			
—	ABS Indicator Always On	6-496	32
—	ABS Indicator Inoperative	6-496	33
—	Diagnostic System Check	6-491	18
—	Low Traction Indicator Always On	6-497	35
—	Low Traction Indicator Inoperative	6-497	36
—	No Communication w/EBCM	6-497	34
—	Traction Off Indicator Always On	6-498	37
—	Traction Off Indicator Inoperative	6-498	38
C1214	System Relay Control Or Coil Circuit Open	6-491	19
C1217	Pump Motor Shorted To Ground	6-491	20
C1218	Pump Motor Circuit Shorted To Voltage Or Motor Ground Open	6-492	21
C1221–C1235	Wheel Speed Sensor Circuits	6-492	22
C1236	Low System Supply Voltage	6-493	23
C1237	High System Supply Voltage	6-494	24
C1242	Pump Motor Circuit Open Or Pump Motor Stalled	6-494	25
C1243	Pump Motor Circuit Open Or Pump Motor Stalled	6-494	25
C1254	Abnormal Shutdown Detected	6-494	26
C1255	EBCM Internal Fault	6-495	27
C1256	EBCM Internal Fault	6-495	27
C1261–C1268	Inlet & Outlet Valve Solenoid Fault	6-495	28
C1275	PCM Requested ETS To Be Disabled	6-495	29
C1278	ETS Temporarily Inhibited By PCM	6-496	30
C1295	Brake Lamp Switch Circuit Open	6-496	31
CENTURY, IMPALA, MONTE CARLO & REGAL			
—	ABS Indicator Always On	6-507	61
—	ABS Indicator Inoperative	6-508	62
—	Diagnostic System Check	6-498	39
—	Low Traction Control Indicator Always On	6-508	63
—	Low Traction Control Indicator Inoperative	6-508	64
—	Traction Indicator Always On	6-508	65
—	Traction Indicator Inoperative	6-509	66
B2747	Traction Control Switch Circuit Low	6-499	40
C1214	Solenoid Valve Relay Contact Or Coil Circuit Open	6-499	41
C1216	EBCM Commanded Pressure Release Too Long	6-500	42
C1217	Pump Motor Shorted To Ground	6-500	43
C1218	Pump Motor Circuit Short To Voltage	6-500	44
C1221–C1235	Wheel Speed Sensors	6-501	45
C1236	Low System Supply Voltage	6-501	46
C1237	High System Supply Voltage	6-502	47
C1238	Brake Thermal Model Exceeded	6-502	48
C1242	Pump Motor Circuit Open & Pump Motor Is Stalled	6-503	49
C1243	Pump Motor Circuit Open & Pump Motor Is Stalled	6-503	49
C1248	Dynamic Rear Proportioning System	6-503	50
C1254	Abnormal Shutdown Detected	6-503	51
C1255	EBCM Internal Fault	6-504	52
C1256	EBCM Internal Fault	6-504	52
C1261–C1274	Inlet Or Outlet Solenoid Valve Fault	6-504	53
C1275	PCM Requested ETS To Be Disabled	6-504	54
C1276	Delivered Torque Signal Circuit Fault	6-505	55
C1277	Requested Torque Signal Circuit Fault	6-505	56
C1278	TCS Temporarily Inhibited By PCM	6-506	57
C1291	Open Brake Lamp Switch Contacts During Decel	6-506	58
C1293	Open Brake Lamp Switch Contacts During Decel	6-506	58
C1294	Brake Lamp Switch Circuit Always Active	6-506	59
C1295	Brake Lamp Switch Circuit Open	6-507	60
P1571	Requested Torque Signal Circuit Fault	6-505	56

Continued

DIAGNOSTIC CHART INDEX—Continued

Code	Description	Page No.	Fig. No.
CENTURY, IMPALA, MONTE CARLO & REGAL			
P1644	Delivered Torque Signal Circuit Fault	6-505	55
P1689	Delivered Torque Signal Circuit Fault	6-505	55
CTS			
—	ABS Indicator Always On	6-528	90
—	ABS Indicator Inoperative	6-529	91
—	Diagnostic Circuit Check	6-509	67
—	Traction Control Indicator Always On	6-529	92
—	Traction Control Indicator Inoperative	6-530	93
—	Traction Off Indicator Always On	6-530	94
—	Traction Off Indicator Inoperative	6-530	95
—	Vehicle Stability Enhancement System Excessive Brake Pulsation	6-532	98
—	Vehicle Stability Enhancement System Unwanted Activation	6-532	97
—	Vehicle Stability Enhancement System Inoperative	6-531	96
C1211	ABS Serial Data Message	6-510	68
C1214	System Voltage	6-510	69
C1217	Pump Motor Voltage Too High Or Low	6-511	70
C1218	Commanded Pump Motor Voltage Too High Or Low	6-511	71
C1221–C1235	Wheel Speed Sensors	6-512	72
C1242	Pump Motor Circuit Or Pump Motor Stalled	6-513	73
C1243	Pump Motor Circuit Or Pump Motor Stalled	6-513	73
C1244	Engine Drag Control (DEC) Circuit	6-514	74
C1248	Dynamic Rear Proportioning System	6-515	75
C1254	Abnormal Shutdown Detected	6-515	76
C1255	Internal EBCM Fault	6-516	77
C1256	Internal EBCM Fault	6-516	77
C1261–C1274	System Relay	6-516	78
C1276	Delivered Torque Signal Circuit Fault	6-517	79
C1277	Requested Torque Signal Circuit Fault	6-518	80
C1278	Traction Control Torque Reduction Is Not Allowed	6-519	81
C1281	Steering Sensor Circuit	6-519	82
C1283	Steering Sensor Circuit	6-519	82
C1282	YAW Rate Input Error	6-520	83
C1284	Lateral Accelerometer Sensor Circuit Fault	6-522	84
C1285	Lateral Accelerometer Sensor Circuit Fault	6-522	84
C1286	Steering Sensor Circuit	6-519	82
C1287	Vehicle Stability System Steer Rate Fault	6-523	85
C1288	Vehicle Stability System Steer Rate Fault	6-523	85
C1291	Stop Lamp Switch Circuit	6-525	86
C1292	Brake Pressure Sensor Circuit	6-526	87
C1293	Brake Pressure Sensor Circuit	6-526	87
C1294	Stop Lamp Switch	6-527	88
C1295	Stop Lamp Switch Input Voltage	6-528	89
C1296	Brake Pressure Sensor Circuit	6-526	87
P0856	Requested Torque Signal Circuit Fault	6-518	80
P1644	Delivered Torque Signal Circuit Fault	6-517	79
P1689	Delivered Torque Signal Circuit Fault	6-517	79

System Description

The diagnostic system check is an organized method of identifying any problems caused by a malfunction in either of the following systems:

- The Antilock Brake System (ABS)
- The Enhanced Traction System (ETS)

The service technician must begin diagnosis of any ABS or ETS complaint with the diagnostic system check.

The diagnostic system check directs the service technician to the next logical step in diagnosing the complaint.

Diagnostic Process

Use the following ordered procedure when servicing the ABS/ETS.

Failure to use the following procedure may cause the loss of important diagnostic data. Failure to use the following procedure may lead to difficult and time-consuming diagnostic procedures.

1. Use the following procedure to perform a vehicle preliminary diagnostic inspection:
   - Inspect the brake master cylinder fluid reservoir:
     - Verify that the brake fluid level is correct.
     - Inspect the master cylinder for contamination.
   - Inspect the ABS and the brake system for the following conditions:
     - Leaks
     - Wiring damage
   - Inspect the brake components of all four wheels:
     - Verify that no drag exists.
     - Verify that the brake apply operation is correct.
   - Inspect for worn or damaged wheel bearings. Worn or damaged wheel bearings may cause a wheel to "wobble".
   - Inspect the wheel speed sensors and the wheel speed sensor wiring:
     - Verify that all of the sensors are solidly attached.
     - Inspect for wiring damage, especially at vehicle attachment points.
   - Inspect the outer CV joint:
     - Verify that the outer CV joint is aligned correctly.
     - Verify that the outer CV joint operates correctly.
   - Inspect the tires. Verify that the tires meet legal tread depth requirements.
2. If any DTCs are displayed, select DTC History.
   - 2.1. Determine which malfunction occurred most recently.
   - 2.2. Diagnose and repair the most recent malfunction first.
3. Determine if the following conditions exist:
   - No DTCs are present.
   - There are malfunctions in the mechanical components.
   - The failure is intermittent and cannot be reproduced.
4. If the above conditions exist, attempt to reproduce the malfunction:
   - 4.1. Use the automatic snapshot feature of the Scan Tool while test driving the vehicle. Perform normal acceleration, stopping, and turning maneuvers during the test drive.
   - 4.2. If the test drive does not reproduce the malfunction, perform an ABS stop:
     - Perform the stop on a low coefficient surface (such as gravel).
     - Perform the stop from a speed of 48–80 km/h (30–50 mph).
     - Trigger the snapshot mode on any ABS DTC while performing the stop.
   - 4.3. If the ABS stop does not reproduce the malfunction, use the enhanced diagnostic information in the DTC History in order to determine if further diagnosis is needed. This determination will be based on the frequency of failure.
5. Clear the ABS/ETS DTCs after all of the system malfunctions have been corrected.

Diagnostic Aids

Diagnosing DTCs in the correct order is very important. Failure to diagnose DTCs in the order specified may result in the following:

- Extended diagnostic time
- Incorrect diagnosis
- Incorrect parts replacement

GC4020051822010X

Fig. 18 Diagnostic System Check (Part 1 of 2). Alero, Cavalier, Grand Am, Malibu & Sunfire

Step	Action	Value(s)	Yes	No
1	1. Reconnect all previously disconnected components. 2. Cycle the Ignition switch from the OFF to the ON position, engine OFF. 3. Plug the *Scan Tool* into the Data Link Connector (DLC), Does the Scan Tool communicate with the EBCM?	—	*Go to Step 3*	*Go to Step 2*
2	Does the scan tool communicate with other modules on the serial data line?	—	Go to *No Communication with EBCM*	Go to Data Link Communications
3	With the scan tool read ABS DTCs. Are there any current Diagnostic Trouble Codes?	–	Go to Applicable DTC Table	*Go to Step 4*
4	Cycle the ignition switch from the OFF to the ON position. Does the ABS Indicator come ON then go OFF after several seconds?	—	*Go to Step 6*	*Go to Step 5*
5	Does the ABS Warning Indicator come ON and stay ON?	—	Go to *ABS Indicator Always On*	Go to *ABS Indicator Inoperative*
6	Are there any history DTCs?	—	*Go to Step 7*	System OK
7	1. Refer to the appropriate DTC table for the history DTC. 2. Read the diagnostic aids, and conditions for setting the DTC. 3. Carefully drive the vehicle above 24 km/h (15 mph) for several minutes while monitoring a scan tool for ABS DTCs. Did the history DTC set as a current DTC while the vehicle was being driven?	—	Go to Applicable DTC Table	System OK

GC4020051822000X

Fig. 18 Diagnostic System Check (Part 2 of 2). Alero, Cavalier, Grand Am, Malibu & Sunfire

Circuit Description

The system relay is energized when the ignition is ON. The system relay supplies voltage to the solenoid valves and the pump motor. This voltage is referred to as the system voltage.

The EBCM controls each solenoid valve by grounding the solenoid.

The EBCM controls the pump motor by grounding the control circuit. The pump serves 2 purposes:

- Transfers brake fluid from the brake calipers to the master cylinder reservoir during pressure decrease events.
- Transfers brake fluid from the master cylinder reservoir to the brake calipers during pressure increase events.

Conditions for Running the DTC

- The ignition voltage is greater than 10.5 volts.
- The system relay is commanded ON.
- For Criteria 2, one of the following conditions exists:
  - The pump motor is OFF.
  - During initialization, the pump motor is ON.

Conditions for Setting the DTC

One of the following conditions exists for 0.23 seconds:

Criteria 1

The system voltage is less than 8 volts.

Criteria 2

The difference between the ignition voltage and system voltage is greater than 1.9 volts.

Action Taken When the DTC Sets

- The EBCM disables the ABS for the duration of the ignition cycle.
- The ABS indicator turns ON.
- The DRP does not function optimally.

Conditions for Clearing the DTC

- The condition for the DTC is no longer present (the DTC is not current) and you used the scan tool Clear DTC function.
- The EBCM automatically clears the history DTC when a current DTC is not detected in 100 consecutive drive cycles.

Diagnostic Aids

The system relay is integral to the EBCM. The relay is not serviceable.

Test Description

The number below refers to the step number on the diagnostic table.

2. Determines whether the DTC is current.

Step	Action	Value(s)	Yes	No
1	Did you perform the ABS Diagnostic System Check?	—	Go to *Step 2*	Go to *Diagnostic System Check*
2	1. Install a scan tool. 2. Turn ON the ignition, with the engine OFF. 3. Use the scan tool in order to clear the DTCs. 4. With the scan tool, perform the Automated Test. Does the DTC reset as a current DTC?	—	Go to *Step 3*	Go to *Intermittent*
3	1. Remove the EBCM from the BPMV. 2. Measure the resistance between each pump motor control circuit of the BPMV and the housing of the BPMV. Does the DMM display the specified value?	OL	Go to *Step 5*	Go to *Step 4*
4	Replace the EBCM and the BPMV. Did you complete the repair?	—	Go to *Step 6*	—
5	Replace the EBCM. Did you complete the repair?	—	Go to *Step 6*	—
6	1. Use the scan tool in order to clear the DTCs. 2. With the scan tool, perform the Automated Test. Does the DTC reset?	—	Go to *Step 2*	System OK

GC4020352679000X

Fig. 19 Code C1214: System Relay Control Or Coil Circuit Open. Alero, Cavalier, Grand Am, Malibu & Sunfire

Circuit Description

The system relay is energized when the ignition is ON. The system relay supplies voltage to the solenoid valves and the pump motor. This voltage is referred to as the system voltage.

The EBCM controls each solenoid valve by grounding the solenoid.

The EBCM controls the pump motor by grounding the control circuit. The pump serves 2 purposes:

- Transfers brake fluid from the brake calipers to the master cylinder reservoir during pressure decrease events.
- Transfers brake fluid from the master cylinder reservoir to the brake calipers during pressure increase events.

Conditions for Running the DTC

- The pump motor has been commanded OFF for 1 second.
- The system voltage is greater than 9.36 volts.

Conditions for Setting the DTC

One of the following conditions exists for 0.2 seconds:

- The voltage across the pump motor is greater than 10.2 volts.
- The pump motor low side voltage is less than 2.7 volts.

Action Taken When the DTC Sets

- The EBCM disables the ABS for the duration of the ignition cycle.
- The ABS indicator turns ON.
- The DRP does not function optimally.

Conditions for Clearing the DTC

- The condition for the DTC is no longer present (the DTC is not current) and you used the scan tool Clear DTC function.
- The EBCM automatically clears the history DTC when a current DTC is not detected in 100 consecutive drive cycles.

Diagnostic Aids

- This DTC determines if there is a short in the pump motor control circuit.
- The pump motor is integral to the BPMV. The pump motor is not serviceable.

Test Description

The number below refers to the step number on the diagnostic table.

3. Tests the pump motor circuits of the BPMV for a short to the housing of the BPMV.

GC4020352680010X

Fig. 20 Code C1217: Pump Motor Shorted To Ground (Part 1 of 2). Alero, Cavalier, Grand Am, Malibu & Sunfire

Step	Action	Value(s)	Yes	No
1	Did you perform the ABS Diagnostic System Check?	—	Go to *Step 2*	Go to *Diagnostic System Check*
2	1. Turn OFF the ignition. **Important:** Removing battery voltage or ground from the EBCM will result in the following conditions: • Loss of the TIM learned tire inflation configuration parameters in the EBCM • The EBCM sets DTC C1245 When the diagnosis is complete, inspect the tire pressures and perform the TIM reset. 2. Disconnect the EBCM harness connector. 3. Connect the *J 39700* universal pinout box using the *J 39700-99* cable adapter to the EBCM harness connector only. 4. Test both ground circuits of the EBCM including the EBCM ground for a high resistance or an open. Did you find and correct the condition?	—	Go to *Step 8*	Go to *Step 3*
3	1. Remove the EBCM from the BPMV. 2. Measure the resistance from both pump motor control circuits of the BPMV to the housing of the BPMV. Does the resistance measure less than the specified value?	5 Ω	Go to *Step 4*	Go to *Step 5*
4	Inspect for poor connections at the connector of the BPMV. Did you find and correct the condition?	—	Go to *Step 8*	Go to *Step 6*
5	Inspect for poor connections at the harness connector of the EBCM. Did you find and correct the condition?	—	Go to *Step 8*	Go to *Step 7*
6	Replace the BPMV. Did you complete the repair?	—	Go to *Step 8*	—
7	Replace the EBCM. Did you complete the repair?	—	Go to *Step 8*	—
8	1. Use the scan tool in order to clear the DTCs. 2. With the scan tool, perform the Automated Test. Does the DTC reset?	—	Go to *Step 2*	System OK

GC4020352680020X

Fig. 20 Code C1217: Pump Motor Shorted To Ground (Part 2 of 2). Alero, Cavalier, Grand Am, Malibu & Sunfire

Step	Action	Yes	No
1	Did you perform the ABS Diagnostic System Check?	Go to *Step 2*	Go to *Diagnostic System Check*
2	1. Use the scan tool in order to clear the DTCs. 2. With the scan tool, perform the Automated Test. Does the DTC reset?	Go to *Step 3*	Go to *Intermittent*
3	1. Remove the EBCM from the BPMV. 2. Inspect the EBCM to BPMV connector for conditions which could cause an intermittent, such as damage, corrosion, poor terminal contact, or presence of brake fluid. Is connector OK and cavity free of brake fluid?	Go to *Step 5*	Go to *Step 4*
4	1. If connector corrosion or damage is evident, replace BPMV and/or EBCM as necessary. 2. If brake fluid is present, replace both BPMV and EBCM. Did you complete the repair?	Go to *Step 9*	—
5	1. Connect the EBCM harness to the EBCM with the BPMV still separated. 2. Connect a test lamp between the pump motor circuits, internal EBCM side, using the *J 35616-A* Connector Test Adapter Kit. 3. With the scan tool, perform the Automated Bleed. Does the test lamp illuminate?	Go to *Step 8*	Go to *Step 6*
6	1. Turn OFF the ignition. **Important:** Removing battery voltage or ground from the EBCM will result in the following conditions: • Loss of the TIM learned tire inflation configuration parameters in the EBCM • The EBCM sets DTC C1245 When the diagnosis is complete, inspect the tire pressures and perform the TIM reset. 2. Disconnect the EBCM connector. 3. Connect the *J 39700* universal pinout box using the *J 39700-99* cable adapter to the EBCM harness connector only. 4. Test both ground circuits of the EBCM including the EBCM ground for a high resistance or an open. Did you find and correct the condition?	Go to *Step 9*	Go to *Step 7*
7	Replace the EBCM. Did you complete the repair?	Go to *Step 9*	—
8	Replace the BPMV. Did you complete the repair?	Go to *Step 9*	—
9	1. Use the scan tool in order to clear the DTCs. 2. With the scan tool, perform the Automated Test. Does the DTC reset?	Go to *Step 2*	System OK

GC4020352681020X

Fig. 21 Code C1218: Pump Motor Circuit Shorted To Voltage Or Motor Ground Open (Part 2 of 2). 2003–04 Alero & Grand Am

Circuit Description

The system relay is energized when the ignition is ON. The system relay supplies voltage to the solenoid valves and the pump motor. This voltage is referred to as the system voltage.

The EBCM controls each solenoid valve by grounding the solenoid.

The EBCM controls the pump motor by grounding the control circuit. The pump serves 2 purposes:

- Transfers brake fluid from the brake calipers to the master cylinder reservoir during pressure decrease events.
- Transfers brake fluid from the master cylinder reservoir to the brake calipers during pressure increase events.

Conditions for Running the DTC

- The pump motor is commanded ON.
- The system voltage is greater than 8 volts.

Conditions for Setting the DTC

One of the following conditions exists for 0.16 seconds:

- With the commanded pump motor voltage less than the system voltage, the actual pump motor voltage is 3 volts less than the commanded voltage.
- With the commanded pump motor voltage greater than the system voltage, the actual pump motor voltage is less than 8 volts.

Action Taken When the DTC Sets

- The EBCM disables the ABS for the duration of the ignition cycle.
- The ABS indicator turns ON.
- The DRP does not function optimally.

Conditions for Clearing the DTC

- The condition for the DTC is no longer present (the DTC is not current) and you used the scan tool Clear DTC function.
- The EBCM automatically clears the history DTC when a current DTC is not detected in 100 consecutive drive cycles.

Diagnostic Aids

The pump motor is integral to the BPMV. The pump motor is not serviceable.

Test Description

The number below refers to the step number on the diagnostic table.

5. Tests the ability of the EBCM to control the pump motor. If the test lamp illuminates, the pump motor circuit within the EBCM is good.

GC4020352681010X

Fig. 21 Code C1218: Pump Motor Circuit Shorted To Voltage Or Motor Ground Open (Part 1 of 2). Alero, Cavalier, Grand Am, Malibu & Sunfire

Circuit Description

As the wheel spins, the wheel speed sensor produces an AC signal. The EBCM uses the frequency of the AC signal to calculate the wheel speed.

Conditions for Running the DTC

C1221 through C1228

- DTCs C1232 through C1235 are not set.
- The brake pedal is not pressed.
- The ABS is not active.

C1232 through C1235

The ignition is ON.

Conditions for Setting the DTC

C1221 through C1224

All of the following conditions exists for 2.5 seconds:

- The suspect wheel speed equals zero.
- The other wheel speeds are greater than 8 km/h (5 mph).
- The other wheel speeds are within 11 km/h (7 mph) of each other.

C1225 through C1228

The EBCM detects a rapid variation in the wheel speed. The wheel speed changes by 16 km/h or more in 0.01 second. The change must occur 3 times with no more than 0.2 seconds between occurrences.

C1232 through C1235

One of the following conditions exists for 0.02 seconds:

- A short to voltage - the wheel speed sensor signal circuit and wheel speed sensor return circuit voltages are both greater than 4.25 volts.
- A short to ground - the wheel speed sensor signal circuit and wheel speed sensor return circuit voltages are both less than 0.75 volts.
- An open - the wheel speed sensor signal circuit voltage is greater than 4.25 volts and wheel speed sensor return circuit voltage is less than 0.75 volts.

Action Taken When the DTC Sets

If equipped, the following actions occur:

- The EBCM disables the ABS/TCS for the duration of the ignition cycle.
- The EBCM temporarily suspends the TIM monitoring function while the DTC is set.
- The ABS indicator turns ON.
- The Traction Off indicator turns ON.
- The DRP does not function optimally unless a DTC for the other wheel speed sensor on the same axle is also set, then the EBCM disables the DRP for the duration of the ignition cycle.
- When the EBCM disables DRP, the red Brake warning indicator turns ON.

Conditions for Clearing the DTC

- The condition for the DTC is no longer present (the DTC is not current) and you used the scan tool Clear DTC function.
- The EBCM automatically clears the history DTC when a current DTC is not detected in 100 consecutive drive cycles.

Diagnostic Aids

C1221 through C1224

Under the following conditions, 2 Wheel Speed Sensor Input is 0 DTCs are set:

- The 2 suspect wheel speeds equal zero for 60 seconds.
- The other wheel speeds are greater than 16 km/h (10 mph).
- The other wheel speeds are within 11 km/h (7 mph) of each other.

Diagnose each wheel speed sensor individually.

C1225 through C1228

A possible cause of this DTC is electrical noise on the wheel speed sensor harness wiring. Electrical noise could result from the wheel speed sensor wires being routed to close to high energy ignition system components, such as spark plug wires.

C1232 through C1235

If the customer comments that the ABS indicator is ON only during moist environmental conditions (rain, snow, vehicle wash, etc.), inspect the wheel speed sensor wiring for signs of water intrusion. If the DTC is not current, clear all DTCs and simulate the effects of water intrusion by using the following procedure:

1. Spray the suspected area with a 5 percent saltwater solution. To create a 5 percent saltwater solution, add 2 teaspoons (9.9 ml) of salt to 354 ml (12 oz) of water.
2. Test drive the vehicle over various road surfaces (bumps, turns, etc.) above 40 km/h (25 mph) for at least 30 seconds.
3. If the DTC returns, replace the suspected wheel speed sensor or repair the wheel speed sensor wiring.
4. Rinse the area thoroughly when completed.

Test Description

The numbers below refer to the step numbers on the diagnostic table.

4. Measures the resistance of the wheel speed sensor in order to determine if the sensor has a valid resistance value.
5. Ensures that the wheel speed sensor is generating a valid AC voltage output.

GC4020352682010X

Fig. 22 Codes C1221–C1235: Wheel Speed Sensor Circuits (Part 1 of 3). Alero, Cavalier, Grand Am, Malibu & Sunfire

Step	Action	Value(s)	Yes	No
1	Did you perform the ABS Diagnostic System Check?	—	Go to *Step 2*	Go to *Diagnostic System Check*
2	1. Install a scan tool. 2. Turn ON the ignition. 3. Set up the scan tool snap shot feature to trigger for this DTC. 4. Drive the vehicle at a speed greater than the specified value. Does the scan tool indicate that this wheel speed DTC set?	8 km/h (5 mph)	Go to *Step 3*	Go to *Intermittent*
3	1. Raise and support the vehicle. 2. Disconnect the wheel speed sensor connector. 3. Measure the resistance across the wheel speed sensor. Does the resistance measure within the specified range?	Front: 1040–1160 Ω Rear: 1044–1276 Ω	Go to *Step 4*	Go to *Step 8*
4	1. Spin the wheel. 2. Measure the AC voltage across the wheel speed sensor. Does the AC voltage measure greater than the specified value?	100 mV	Go to *Step 5*	Go to *Step 8*
5	Inspect for poor connections at the harness connector of the wheel speed sensor. Did you find and correct the condition?	—	Go to *Step 10*	Go to *Step 6*
6	**Important:** Removing battery voltage or ground from the EBCM will result in the following conditions: • Loss of the TIM learned tire inflation configuration parameters in the EBCM • The EBCM sets DTC C1245 When the diagnosis is complete, inspect the tire pressures and perform the TIM reset. 1. Disconnect the EBCM harness connector. 2. Install the *J 39700* universal pinout box using the *J 39700-99* cable adapter to the EBCM harness connector only. 3. Test the wheel speed sensor circuits for the following: • An open • A short to ground • A short to voltage • Shorted together Did you find and correct the condition?	—	Go to *Step 10*	Go to *Step 7*

GC4020352682020X

Fig. 22 Codes C1221–C1235: Wheel Speed Sensor Circuits (Part 2 of 3). Alero, Cavalier, Grand Am, Malibu & Sunfire

Step	Action	Value(s)	Yes	No
7	Inspect for poor connections at the harness connector for the EBCM. Did you find and correct the condition?	—	Go to *Step 10*	Go to *Step 9*
8	Replace the wheel speed sensor. Did you complete the repair?	—	Go to *Step 10*	—
9	Replace the EBCM. Did you complete the repair?	—	Go to *Step 10*	—
10	1. Use the scan tool in order to clear the DTCs. 2. Operate the vehicle within the Conditions for Running the DTC as specified in the supporting text. Does the DTC reset?	—	Go to *Step 2*	System OK

GC4020352682030X

Fig. 22 Codes C1221–C1235: Wheel Speed Sensor Circuits (Part 3 of 3). Alero, Cavalier, Grand Am, Malibu & Sunfire

Circuit Description

The EBCM monitors the voltage level available for system operation. A low voltage condition prevents the system from operating properly.

Conditions for Running the DTC

- The vehicle speed is greater than 8 km/h (5 mph).
- The ignition voltage is less than 10.5 volts.
- The system relay is commanded ON.

Conditions for Setting the DTC

One of the following conditions exists for 0.72 seconds:

- During initialization or when the system is inactive, the system voltage is less than 10.5 volts.
- During the system operation, the system voltage is less than 9.3 volts.

Action Taken When the DTC Sets

- The EBCM disables the ABS for the duration of the ignition cycle.
- The ABS indicator turns ON.
- The DRP does not function optimally.

Conditions for Clearing the DTC

- The condition for the DTC is no longer present (the DTC is not current) and you used the scan tool Clear DTC function.
- The EBCM automatically clears the history DTC when a current DTC is not detected in 100 consecutive drive cycles.

Diagnostic Aids

- Test the charging system.
- Possible causes of this DTC are the following conditions:
  - A charging system malfunction
  - An excessive battery draw
  - A weak battery
  - A faulty system ground

Test Description

2. Use the scan tool in order to inspect the voltage to the EBCM.
3. Use the scan tool in order to inspect the voltage to the body control module. A low voltage value in multiple modules indicates a concern in the charging system.
5. Verifies that the condition is still present.

GC4020352683010X

Fig. 23 Code C1236: Low System Supply Voltage (Part 1 of 2). Alero, Cavalier, Grand Am, Malibu & Sunfire

Step	Action	Value(s)	Yes	No
1	Did you perform the ABS Diagnostic System Check?	—	Go to *Step 2*	Go to *Diagnostic System Check*
2	1. Install a scan tool. 2. Start the engine. 3. With a scan tool, observe the Switched Battery Voltage parameter in ABS data list. Does the scan tool indicate the voltage is greater than the specified value?	10.5 V	Go to Diagnostic Aids	Go to *Step 3*
3	With a scan tool, observe the Battery Voltage parameter in the Body Control Module data list. Does the scan tool indicate the voltage is greater than the specified value?	10.5 V	Go to *Step 4*	Engine Electrical
4	1. Turn OFF the ignition. **Important:** Removing battery voltage or ground from the EBCM will result in the following conditions: • Loss of the TIM learned tire inflation configuration parameters in the EBCM • The EBCM sets DTC C1245 When the diagnosis is complete, inspect the tire pressures and perform the TIM reset. 2. Disconnect the EBCM harness connector. 3. Install the *J 39700* universal pinout box using the *J 39700-99* cable adaptor to the EBCM harness connector only. 4. Test the ground circuits of the EBCM including the EBCM ground for a high resistance or an open. Did you find and correct the condition?	—	Go to *Step 7*	Go to *Step 5*
5	1. Reconnect the EBCM harness connector. 2. Turn ON the ignition, with the engine OFF. 3. Use the scan tool in order to clear the DTCs. 4. Operate the vehicle within the Conditions for Running the DTC as specified in the supporting text. Does the DTC reset?	—	Go to *Step 6*	Go to Diagnostic Aids
6	Replace the EBCM. Did you complete the repair?	—	Go to *Step 7*	—
7	1. Use the scan tool in order to clear the DTCs. 2. Operate the vehicle within the Conditions for Running the DTC as specified in the supporting text. Does the DTC reset?	—	Go to *Step 2*	System OK

GC4020352683020X

Fig. 23 Code C1236: Low System Supply Voltage (Part 2 of 2). Alero, Cavalier, Grand Am, Malibu & Sunfire

Circuit Description

The EBCM monitors the voltage level available for system operation. If the voltage level is too high, damage may result in the system. When the EBCM detects a high voltage condition, the EBCM turns OFF the system relay which removes battery voltage from the solenoid valves and pump motor.

Conditions for Running the DTC

The vehicle speed is greater than 8 km/h (5 mph).

Conditions for Setting the DTC

The system voltage is greater than 17 volts for 0.7 seconds.

Action Taken When the DTC Sets

- The EBCM disables the ABS for the duration of the ignition cycle.
- The ABS indicator turns ON.
- The DRP does not function optimally.

Conditions for Clearing the DTC

- The condition for the DTC is no longer present (the DTC is not current) and you used the scan tool Clear DTC function.
- The EBCM automatically clears the history DTC when a current DTC is not detected in 100 consecutive drive cycles.

Diagnostic Aids

A possible cause of this DTC is overcharging.

Test Description

2. Use the scan tool in order to inspect the voltage to the EBCM.
3. Use the scan tool in order to inspect the voltage to the body control module. A high voltage value in multiple modules indicates a concern in the charging system.
4. Verifies that the condition is still present.

Step	Action	Value(s)	Yes	No
1	Did you perform the ABS Diagnostic System Check?	—	Go to *Step 2*	Go to *Diagnostic System Check*
2	1. Turn OFF all of the accessories. 2. Install a scan tool. 3. Start the engine. 4. Run the engine at approximately 2000 RPM. 5. With a scan tool, observe the Switched Battery Voltage parameter in ABS data list. Does the scan tool indicate that the voltage is greater than the specified value?	16.3 V	Go to *Step 3*	Go to Diagnostic Aids
3	With a scan tool, observe the Battery Voltage parameter in the Body Control Module data list. Does the scan tool indicate the voltage is greater than the specified value?	16.3 V	Engine Electrical	Go to *Step 4*
4	1. Use the scan tool in order to clear the DTCs. 2. Operate the vehicle within the Conditions for Running the DTC as specified in the supporting text. Does the DTC reset?	—	Go to *Step 5*	Go to Diagnostic Aids
5	Replace the EBCM. Did you complete the repair?	—	Go to *Step 6*	—
6	1. Use the scan tool in order to clear the DTCs. 2. Operate the vehicle within the conditions for Running the DTC as specified in the supporting text. Does the DTC reset?	—	Go to *Step 2*	System OK

GC4020352684000X

Fig. 24 Code C1237: High System Supply Voltage. Alero, Cavalier, Grand Am, Malibu & Sunfire

Step	Action	Yes	No
1	Did you perform the ABS Diagnostic System Check?	Go to *Step 2*	Go to *Diagnostic System Check*
2	1. Use the scan tool in order to clear the DTCs. 2. With the scan tool, perform the Automated Test. Does the DTC reset?	Go to *Step 3*	Go to *Intermittent*
3	1. Remove the EBCM from the BPMV. 2. Inspect the EBCM to BPMV connector for conditions which could cause an intermittent, such as damage, corrosion, poor terminal contact, or presence of brake fluid. Is connector OK and cavity free of brake fluid?	Go to *Step 5*	Go to *Step 4*
4	1. If connector corrosion or damage is evident, replace BPMV and/or EBCM as necessary. 2. If brake fluid is present, replace both BPMV and EBCM. Did you complete the repair?	Go to *Step 8*	—
5	1. Connect the EBCM harness to the EBCM with the BPMV still separated. 2. Connect a test lamp between the pump motor circuits, internal EBCM side, using the *J 35616-A* Connector Test Adapter Kit. 3. With the scan tool, perform the Automated Bleed. Does the test lamp illuminate?	Go to *Step 7*	Go to *Step 6*
6	Replace the EBCM. Did you complete the repair?	Go to *Step 8*	—
7	Replace the BPMV. Did you complete the repair?	Go to *Step 8*	—
8	1. Use the scan tool in order to clear the DTCs. 2. With the scan tool, perform the Automated Test. Does the DTC reset?	Go to *Step 2*	System OK

GC4020352685020X

Fig. 25 Codes C1242 & C1243: Pump Motor Circuit Open Or Pump Motor Stalled (Part 2 of 2). Alero, Cavalier, Grand Am, Malibu & Sunfire

Circuit Description

The system relay is energized when the ignition is ON. The system relay supplies voltage to the solenoid valves and the pump motor. This voltage is referred to as the system voltage.

The EBCM controls each solenoid valve by grounding the solenoid.

The EBCM controls the pump motor by grounding the control circuit. The pump serves 2 purposes:

- Transfers brake fluid from the brake calipers to the master cylinder reservoir during pressure decrease events.
- Transfers brake fluid from the master cylinder reservoir to the brake calipers during pressure increase events.

Conditions for Running the DTC

C1242

- The system voltage is greater than 8.0 volts.
- The system relay is ON.
- The pump motor is commanded OFF.

C1243

- The pump motor is ON for at least 0.3 seconds.
- The system relay is ON.

Conditions for Setting the DTC

C1242

The voltage across the pump motor is between 1.7 to 10.2 volts for 2 seconds.

C1243

The pump motor is stalled or turning slowly.

Action Taken When the DTC Sets

- The EBCM disables the ABS for the duration of the ignition cycle.
- The ABS indicator turns ON.
- The DRP does not function optimally.

Conditions for Clearing the DTC

- The condition for the DTC is no longer present (the DTC is not current) and you used the scan tool Clear DTC function.
- The EBCM automatically clears the history DTC when a current DTC is not detected in 100 consecutive drive cycles.

Diagnostic Aids

The pump motor is integral to the BPMV. The pump motor is not serviceable.

Test Description

The number below refers to the step number on the diagnostic table.

5. Tests the ability of the EBCM to control the pump motor. If the test lamp illuminates, the pump motor circuit within the EBCM is good.

GC4020352685010X

Fig. 25 Codes C1242 & C1243: Pump Motor Circuit Open Or Pump Motor Stalled (Part 1 of 2). Alero, Cavalier, Grand Am, Malibu & Sunfire

Circuit Description

The microprocessor contains a data storage area (keep alive memory) which can save pertinent data when the ignition is turned OFF. The keep alive memory (KAM) data is lost if battery power or module ground is removed from the module. The KAM area is an integral part of the microprocessor and cannot be serviced separately.

Conditions for Running the DTC

The ABS conditions and the braking conditions are normal.

Conditions for Setting the DTC

The microprocessor calculates a checksum on those areas of memory that hold critical operation data. This is done at a regular interval and is called the periodic checksum. The microprocessor also calculates a checksum on these memory locations when ever new data is written to them. This is called the running checksum.

To check the keep alive memory (KAM), the microprocessor compares the periodic checksum to the running checksum. If they do not match, the microprocessor sets the DTC.

Action Taken When the DTC Sets

If equipped, the following actions occur:

- The EBCM disables the DRP/ABS/TCS for the duration of the ignition cycle.
- The EBCM disables the variable effort steering (VES) for the duration of the ignition cycle.
- The ABS indicator turns ON.
- The Traction Off indicator turns ON.
- The EBCM will not send serial data messages.
- The EBCM will not send the requested torque output to the PCM.

Conditions for Clearing the DTC

- The condition for the DTC is no longer present (the DTC is not current) and you used the scan tool Clear DTC function.
- The EBCM automatically clears the history DTC when a current DTC is not detected in 100 consecutive drive cycles.

Diagnostic Aids

Possible causes of this DTC are the following conditions:

- A loss of battery ground.
- A disconnected battery.
- A running reset. (A running reset is detected when the keep alive memory check sum is not updated properly.)
- A sudden drop in the system voltage to less than 5 volts.
- Long extended engine cranks that cause the battery voltage to drop.
- Poor power or ground connections.
- An internal EBCM malfunction.

Test Description

The numbers below refer to the step numbers on the diagnostic table.

2. Tests for an open in the ground circuits of the body control module.
4. Verifies the proper operation of the charging system.
6. Determines whether the DTC resets.

GC4020352686010X

Fig. 26 Code C1254: Abnormal Shutdown Detected (Part 1 of 2). Alero, Cavalier, Grand Am, Malibu & Sunfire

Step	Action	Yes	No
1	Did you perform the ABS Diagnostic System Check?	Go to *Step 2*	Go to *Diagnostic System Check*
2	1. Turn OFF the ignition. **Important:** Removing battery voltage or ground from the EBCM will result in the following conditions: • Loss of the TIM learned tire inflation configuration parameters in the EBCM • The EBCM sets DTC C1245 When the diagnosis is complete, inspect the tire pressures and perform the TIM reset. 2. Disconnect the EBCM harness connector. 3. Install the *J 39700* universal breakout box using the *J 39700-99* cable adapter to the EBCM harness connector only. 4. Test the module ground circuit of the EBCM for a high resistance or an open. Did you find and correct the condition?	Go to *Step 8*	Go to *Step 3*
3	Has the battery been disconnected recently?	Go to *Step 8*	Go to *Step 4*
4	Test the charging system. Did you find and correct the condition?	Go to *Step 8*	Go to *Step 5*
5	Inspect for poor connections at the harness connector of the EBCM. Did you find and correct the condition?	Go to *Step 8*	Go to *Step 6*
6	1. Use the scan tool in order to clear the DTCs. 2. With the scan tool, perform the Automated Test. Does the DTC reset?	Go to *Step 7*	Go to *Intermittent*
7	Replace the EBCM. Did you complete the repair?	Go to *Step 8*	—
8	1. Use the scan tool in order to clear the DTCs. 2. With the scan tool, perform the Automated Test. Does the DTC reset?	Go to *Step 2*	System OK

GC4020352686020X

Fig. 26 Code C1254: Abnormal Shutdown Detected (Part 2 of 2). Alero, Cavalier, Grand Am, Malibu & Sunfire

Circuit Description

The system relay is energized when the ignition is ON. The system relay supplies voltage to the valve solenoids and the pump motor. This voltage is referred to as the system voltage. The EBCM microprocessor activates the valve solenoids by grounding the control circuit.

Conditions for Running the DTC

- The system voltage is greater than 8.0 volts.
- The ignition voltage is greater than 9.0 volts.

Conditions for Setting the DTC

The commanded state of the driver and the actual state of the control circuit do not match for 0.03 seconds.

Action Taken When the DTC Sets

- The EBCM disables the ABS for the duration of the ignition cycle.
- The ABS indicator turns ON.
- The DRP does not function optimally.
- For DTC C1265 or C1267, the red Brake warning indicator turns ON. When both DTCs C1265 and C1267 are set or a wheel speed sensor DTC for the other wheel on the same axle is also set, the EBCM disables the DRP for the duration of the ignition cycle.

Conditions for Clearing the DTC

- The condition for the DTC is no longer present (the DTC is not current) and you used the scan tool Clear DTC function.
- The EBCM automatically clears the history DTC when a current DTC is not detected in 100 consecutive drive cycles.

Diagnostic Aids

The solenoid valve circuit is internal to the EBCM. The solenoid valve circuit is not diagnosable external to the EBCM. The DTC sets when there is a malfunction in the solenoid circuit internal to the EBCM.

Test Description

The number below refers to the step number on the diagnostic table.

2. Determines whether the DTC is current.

Step	Action	Yes	No
1	Did you perform the ABS Diagnostic System Check?	Go to *Step 2*	Go to *Diagnostic System Check*
2	1. Install a scan tool. 2. Turn ON the ignition, with the engine OFF. 3. Use the scan tool in order to clear the DTCs. 4. With the scan tool, perform the Automated Test. Does the DTC reset as a current DTC?	Go to *Step 3*	Go to *Intermittent*
3	Replace the EBCM. Did you complete the repair?	Go to *Step 4*	—
4	1. Use the scan tool in order to clear the DTCs. 2. With the scan tool, perform the Automated Test. Does the DTC reset?	Go to *Step 2*	System OK

GC4020352688000X

Fig. 28 Codes C1261–C1268: Inlet & Outlet Valve Solenoid Fault. Alero, Cavalier, Grand Am, Malibu & Sunfire

Circuit Description

This DTC identifies a malfunction within the EBCM.

Conditions for Running the DTC

The ABS conditions and the braking conditions are normal.

Conditions for Setting the DTC

An internal EBCM malfunction exists.

Action Taken When the DTC Sets

C1255

If equipped, the following actions occur:

- The EBCM disables the ABS for the duration of the ignition cycle.
- The DRP does function optimally.
- The ABS indicator turns ON.
- For some DTC C1255xx, the EBCM disables the TCS for the duration of the ignition cycle and the Traction Off indicator turns ON.
- For some DTC C1255xx, the EBCM disables the variable effort steering (VES) for the duration of the ignition cycle.
- For some DTC C1255xx, the EBCM temporarily suspends the TIM monitoring function while the DTC is set.
- For some DTC C1255xx, the EBCM disables the DRP for the duration of the ignition cycle.
- When the EBCM disables the DRP, the red Brake warning indicator turns ON.

C1256

- The ABS remains functional.
- The ABS indicator remains OFF.

Conditions for Clearing the DTC

- The condition for the DTC is no longer present (the DTC is not current) and you used the scan tool Clear DTC function.
- The EBCM automatically clears the history DTC when a current DTC is not detected in 100 consecutive drive cycles.

Diagnostic Aids

The scan tool displays 2 additional characters after the DTC. Take note of the 2 character code and any other DTCs that are set. The 2 character code is an engineering aid used in order to determine the cause of the internal malfunction.

Test Description

The number below refers to the step number on the diagnostic table.

2. Determines whether the DTC is current.

Step	Action	Yes	No
1	Did you perform the ABS Diagnostic System Check?	Go to *Step 2*	Go to *Diagnostic System Check*
2	1. Install a scan tool. 2. Turn ON the ignition, with the engine OFF. 3. Use the scan tool in order to clear the DTCs. 4. With the scan tool, perform the Automated Test. Does the DTC reset as a current DTC?	Go to *Step 3*	Go to *Intermittent*
3	Replace the EBCM. Did you complete the repair?	Go to *Step 4*	—
4	1. Use the scan tool in order to clear the DTCs. 2. With the scan tool, perform the Automated Test. Does the DTC reset?	Go to *Step 2*	System OK

GC4020352687000X

Fig. 27 Codes C1255 & C1256: EBCM Internal Fault. Alero, Cavalier, Grand Am, Malibu & Sunfire

Circuit Description

The PCM monitors various parameters and will not allow ETS operation if any parameter falls outside a specified range.

Conditions for Running the DTC

The ignition is ON.

Conditions for Setting the DTC

A malfunction has been detected by the PCM which would inhibit ETS operation.

Action Taken When the DTC Sets

- The EBCM disables the ETS for the duration of the ignition cycle.
- The TRAC OFF indicator turns ON.
- The ABS will remain functional.

Conditions for Clearing the DTC

- The condition for setting the DTC is no longer present and the scan tool Clear DTCs function is used.
- The EBCM automatically clears the history DTC when a current DTC is not detected in 100 consecutive drive cycles.

Diagnostic Aids

- Thoroughly inspect the wiring and the connectors. An incomplete inspection of the wiring and the connectors may result in a misdiagnosis, causing a part replacement with the reappearance of the malfunction.

GC4020051853010X

Fig. 29 Codes C1275: PCM Requested ETS To Be Disabled (Part 1 of 2). 2001–02 Alero & Grand Am

Step	Action	Value(s)	Yes	No
1	Did you perform the ABS Diagnostic System Check?	—	Go to *Step 2*	Go to *A Diagnostic System Check - ABS*
2	1. Turn OFF the ignition. 2. Install a scan tool. 3. Turn ON the ignition, with the engine OFF. 4. With a scan tool, observe the DTC Information. Does the scan tool display any other ABS DTCs?	—	Go to DTC List	Go to *Step 3*
3	Is DTC C1275 set as a current code?	—	Go to *Step 5*	Go to *Step 4*
4	1. Start the engine. 2. Carefully test drive the vehicle at a speed above the specified value. Use the scan tool in order to monitor the ABS DTCs. 3. Repeat the drive cycle sequence twice. Did DTC C1275 set in the last 2 tests?	16 km/h (10 mph)	Go to *Step 5*	System OK
5	Inspect the PCM. Did you find and correct the condition?	—	Go to *Step 6*	Go to Diagnostic Aids
6	1. Use the scan tool in order to clear the DTCs. 2. Operate the vehicle within the Conditions for Running the DTC as specified in the supporting text. Does the DTC reset?	—	Go to *Step 2*	System OK

GC4020051853020X

Fig. 29 Codes C1275: PCM Requested ETS To Be Disabled (Part 2 of 2). 2001–02 Alero & Grand Am

Circuit Description

The PCM monitors various parameters and will not allow ETS operation if any parameter falls outside a specified range.

Conditions for Running the DTC

The ignition is ON.

Conditions for Setting the DTC

A malfunction has been detected by the PCM which would inhibit ETS operation.

Action Taken When the DTC Sets

- The EBCM disables the ETS for the duration of the ignition cycle.
- The TRAC OFF indicator turns ON.
- The ABS will remain functional.

Conditions for Clearing the DTC

- The condition for setting the DTC is no longer present and the scan tool Clear DTCs function is used.
- The EBCM automatically clears the history DTC when a current DTC is not detected in 100 consecutive drive cycles.

Diagnostic Aids

- Thoroughly inspect the wiring and the connectors. An incomplete inspection of the wiring and the connectors may result in a misdiagnosis, causing a part replacement with the reappearance of the malfunction.

GC4020051854010X

Fig. 30 Codes C1278: ETS Temporarily Inhibited By PCM (Part 1 of 2). 2001–02 Alero & Grand Am

Step	Action	Value(s)	Yes	No
1	Did you perform the ABS Diagnostic System Check?	—	Go to *Step 2*	Go to *A Diagnostic System Check - ABS*
2	1. Turn OFF the ignition. 2. Install a scan tool. 3. Turn ON the ignition, with the engine OFF. 4. With a scan tool, observe the DTC Information. Does the scan tool display any other ABS DTCs?	—	Go to *Diagnostic Trouble Code (DTC) List*	Go to *Step 3*
3	Is DTC C1278 set as a current code?	—	Go to *Step 5*	Go to *Step 4*
4	1. Start the engine. 2. Carefully test drive the vehicle at a speed above the specified value. Use the scan tool in order to monitor the ABS DTCs. 3. Repeat the drive cycle sequence twice. Did DTC C1278 set in the last 2 tests?	16 km/h (10 mph)	Go to *Step 5*	System OK
5	Inspect the PCM. Did you find and correct the condition?	—	Go to *Step 6*	Go to *Diagnostic Aids*
6	1. Use the scan tool in order to clear the DTCs. 2. Operate the vehicle within the Conditions for Running the DTC as specified in the supporting text. Does the DTC reset?	—	Go to *Step 2*	System OK

GC4020051854020X

Fig. 30 Codes C1278: ETS Temporarily Inhibited By PCM (Part 2 of 2). 2001–02 Alero & Grand Am

Circuit Description

The EBCM sources 5 volts on the stoplamp switch signal circuit when the stoplamp switch is inactive. The voltage is supplied a ground path through the stoplamp bulbs.

Conditions for Running the DTC

The ignition is ON.

Conditions for Setting the DTC

The stoplamp switch input voltage is between 1.73 volts and 5.28 volts for 2 seconds.

Action Taken When the DTC Sets

- The ABS remains functional.
- The ABS indicator remains OFF.

Conditions for Clearing the DTC

- The condition for the DTC is no longer present (the DTC is not current) and you used the scan tool Clear DTC function.
- The EBCM automatically clears the history DTC when a current DTC is not detected in 100 consecutive drive cycles.

Diagnostic Aids

Possible causes of this DTC are the following conditions:

- A signal circuit of the stoplamp switch is open.
- The stoplamp switch is misadjusted.
- Verify proper stoplamp switch operation using the data list of the scan tool. As the brake is applied, the data list displays the stoplamp switch on within 2.54 cm (1 in) of travel.
- All brake lamps are open.
- All brake lamp grounds are open.
- Circuit has a wiring problem, terminal corrosion, or poor connections.
- Loose or corroded EBCM ground or PCM ground.
- An internal EBCM problem.

Test Description

The numbers below refer to the step numbers on the diagnostic table.

3. This DTC detects an open stoplamp switch signal circuit from the stoplamp side of the splice pack to the EBCM.
4. The EBCM sources 5 volts on the stoplamp switch signal circuit. This small voltage has a ground path through the stoplamp bulbs. This DTC sets if the path to ground is open.

GC4020352689010X

Fig. 31 Code C1295: Brake Lamp Switch Circuit Open (Part 1 of 2). Alero, Cavalier, Grand Am, Malibu & Sunfire

Step	Action	Yes	No
1	Did you perform the ABS Diagnostic System Check?	Go to *Step 2*	Go to *Diagnostic System Check*
2	1. Press the brake pedal. 2. With the scan tool, observe the Brake Switch Status parameter in the ABS data list. Does the Brake Switch Status parameter display Applied?	Go to *Step 4*	Go to *Step 3*
3	Test the signal circuit of the stoplamp switch for an open. Did you find and correct the condition?	Go to *Step 9*	Go to *Step 7*
4	Press the brake pedal. Are all of the stoplamps OFF?	Go to *Step 5*	Go to Diagnostic Aids
5	Test the feed circuit of the stoplamps for an open or high resistance. Did you find and correct the condition?	Go to *Step 9*	Go to *Step 6*
6	Test the ground circuit of the stoplamps for an open or high resistance. Did you find and correct the condition?	Go to *Step 9*	Go to Diagnostic Aids
7	Inspect for poor connections at the harness connector of the EBCM. Did you find and correct the condition?	Go to *Step 9*	Go to *Step 8*
8	Replace the EBCM. Did you complete the replacement?	Go to *Step 9*	—
9	1. Use the scan tool in order to clear the DTCs. 2. Operate the vehicle within the Conditions for Running the DTC as specified in the supporting text. Does the DTC reset?	Go to *Step 2*	System OK

GC4020352689020X

Fig. 31 Code C1295: Brake Lamp Switch Circuit Open (Part 2 of 2). Alero, Cavalier, Grand Am, Malibu & Sunfire

ABS Indicator Always On

Circuit Description

The instrument cluster controls the operation of the ABS indicator. The EBCM reports the desired status of the ABS indicator via serial data messages.

Test Description

The numbers below refer to the step numbers on the diagnostic table.

3. Use the scan tool to check the normal state of the ABS indicator control circuit.
4. Ensures that the instrument panel cluster (IPC) can operate the ABS indicator.

Step	Action	Yes	No
1	Did you perform the ABS Diagnostic System Check?	Go to *Step 2*	Go to *Diagnostic System Check - ABS*
2	Inspect the EBCM ground, making sure the ground is clean and torqued to the proper specification. Did you find and correct the condition?	Go to *Step 9*	Go to *Step 3*
3	1. Install a scan tool. 2. Turn ON the ignition, with the engine OFF. 3. With a scan tool, observe the ABS Warning Lamp parameter in the ABS data list. Does the scan tool display Off?	Go to *Step 4*	Go to *Step 5*
4	1. Turn OFF the ignition. 2. Turn ON the ignition, with the engine OFF. 3. Observe the ABS indicator on the instrument panel cluster (IPC) during the displays test. Does the ABS indicator illuminate during the displays test and then turn OFF?	Go to *Intermittent and Poor Connections*	Go to *Step 6*
5	Inspect for poor connections at the harness connector of the EBCM. Did you find and correct the condition?	Go to *Step 9*	Go to *Step 7*
6	Inspect for poor connections at the harness connector of the IPC. Did you find and correct the condition?	Go to *Step 9*	Go to *Step 8*
7	Replace the EBCM. Did you complete the repair?	Go to *Step 9*	—
8	Replace the instrument panel cluster (IPC). Did you complete the repair?	Go to *Step 9*	—
9	Operate the system in order to verify the repair. Did you correct the condition?	System OK	Go to *Step 2*

GC4020352690000X

Fig. 32 ABS Indicator Always On. Alero, Cavalier, Grand Am, Malibu & Sunfire

Circuit Description

The instrument cluster controls the operation of the ABS indicator. The EBCM reports the desired status of the ABS indicator via serial data messages.

Test Description

The numbers below refer to the step numbers on the diagnostic table.

3. Use the scan tool to check the normal state of the ABS indicator control circuit.
4. Ensures that the instrument panel cluster (IPC) can operate the ABS indicator.

Step	Action	Yes	No
1	Did you perform the ABS Diagnostic System Check?	Go to *Step 2*	Go to *Diagnostic System Check*
2	Inspect the EBCM ground, making sure the ground is clean and torqued to the proper specification. Did you find and correct the condition?	Go to *Step 9*	Go to *Step 3*
3	1. Install a scan tool. 2. Turn ON the ignition, with the engine OFF. 3. With a scan tool, observe the ABS Warning Lamp parameter in the ABS data list. Does the scan tool display Off?	Go to *Step 4*	Go to *Step 5*
4	1. Turn OFF the ignition. 2. Turn ON the ignition, with the engine OFF. 3. Observe the ABS indicator on the instrument panel cluster (IPC) during the displays test. Does the ABS indicator illuminate during the displays test and then turn OFF?	Go to *Intermittent and Poor Connections*	Go to *Step 6*
5	Inspect for poor connections at the harness connector of the EBCM. Did you find and correct the condition?	Go to *Step 9*	Go to *Step 7*
6	Inspect for poor connections at the harness connector of the IPC. Did you find and correct the condition?	Go to *Step 9*	Go to *Step 8*
7	Replace the EBCM. Did you complete the repair?	Go to *Step 9*	—
8	Replace the instrument panel cluster (IPC). Did you complete the repair?	Go to *Step 9*	—
9	Operate the system in order to verify the repair. Did you correct the condition?	System OK	Go to *Step 2*

GC4020352691000X

Fig. 33 ABS Indicator Inoperative. Alero, Cavalier, Grand Am, Malibu & Sunfire

Circuit Description

The Class 2 serial data line allows all of the modules on the line to transmit information to each other as needed. Each module is assigned an ID. All of the information sent out on the line is assigned a priority by which it is received. When the ignition is turned ON, each module begins to send and receive information. Each module on the Class 2 serial data line knows what information the module needs to send out and what information the module should be receiving. What the modules do not know is which module is supposed to send the information. This information is only learned after the module has received the information needed along with the ID of the module that sent the information. This information is then remembered until the ignition switch is turned off.

Diagnostic Aids

- The following are possible causes:
  - An open or short in the Class 2 serial data line.
  - An open in the ignition positive voltage circuit.
  - An open in the EBCM ground circuit.
  - An internal EBCM malfunction.
- Thoroughly inspect the wiring and the connectors An incomplete inspection of the wiring and the connectors may result in a misdiagnosis, causing a part replacement with the reappearance of the malfunction.

Test Description

The numbers below refer to the step numbers on the diagnostic table.

2. This test determines if the scan tool can communicate with any other modules on the Class 2 serial data line.
4. Tests for a short to ground in the ignition positive voltage circuit.
6. Tests the EBCM ground circuit for an open or high resistance.
7. Tests the ignition positive voltage circuit for an open or high resistance.

GC4020051859010X

Fig. 34 No Communication w/EBCM (Part 1 of 2). Cavalier, Malibu & Sunfire

Step	Action	Value(s)	Yes	No
1	Did you perform the ABS Diagnostic System Check?	—	Go to *Step 2*	Go to *A Diagnostic System Check - ABS*
2	1. Turn OFF the ignition. 2. Install a scan tool. 3. Turn ON the ignition, with the engine OFF. 4. Attempt to establish communication with other modules on the Class 2 serial data line, such as the PCM. Does the scan tool communicate with any other modules on the Class 2 serial data line?	—	Go to *Step 3*	Go to *Does Not Communicate with Class 2 Device*
3	1. Turn OFF the ignition. 2. Inspect the Fuse Block ABS fuse (10A). Is the fuse open?	—	Go to *Step 4*	Go to *Step 5*
4	1. Turn OFF the ignition. 2. Remove the ABS fuse (10A) from the Fuse Block. 3. Disconnect the EBCM harness connector. 4. Connect the *J 39700* universal pinout box using the *J 39700-99* cable adapter to the EBCM harness connector only. 5. Test the ignition positive voltage circuit for a short to ground. Did you find and correct the condition?	—	Go to *A Diagnostic System Check - ABS*	Go to *Intermittents*
5	Inspect the EBCM ground G112, making sure that the ground is clean and torqued to the proper specification. Did you find and correct the condition?	—	Go to *A Diagnostic System Check - ABS*	Go to *Step 6*
6	1. Turn OFF the ignition. 2. Disconnect the EBCM harness connector. 3. Connect the *J 39700* universal pinout box using the *J 39700-99* cable adapter to the EBCM harness connector only. 4. Test the EBCM ground circuit for an open or high resistance. Did you find and correct the condition?	—	Go to *A Diagnostic System Check - ABS*	Go to *Step 7*
7	Test the ignition positive voltage circuit for an open or high resistance. Did you find and correct the condition?	—	Go to *A Diagnostic System Check - ABS*	Go to *Step 8*
8	Inspect for poor connections at the harness connector of the EBCM. Did you find and correct the condition?	—	Go to *A Diagnostic System Check - ABS*	Go to *Step 9*
9	Replace the EBCM. Did you complete the replacement?	—	Go to *A Diagnostic System Check - ABS*	—

GC4020051859020X

Fig. 34 No Communication w/EBCM (Part 2 of 2). Cavalier, Malibu & Sunfire

Low Traction Indicator Always On

Circuit Description

The Low Traction indicator is controlled by the instrument cluster via serial data messages from the EBCM. When the ABS or TCS is active for 0.5 seconds, the EBCM commands the instrument cluster to turn ON the Low Traction indicator.

The Low Traction indicator will also turn ON during the instrument cluster bulb check. When the ignition switch is turned to ON, the Low Traction indicator will turn ON for approximately 3 seconds and then turn OFF.

Test Description

The numbers below refer to the step numbers on the diagnostic table.

2. Use the scan tool to check the normal state of the Low Traction indicator control.
3. Ensures that the instrument cluster can operate the Low Traction indicator.

Step	Action	Value(s)	Yes	No
1	Did you perform the ABS Diagnostic System Check?	—	Go to *Step 2*	Go to *Diagnostic System Check*
2	1. Install a scan tool. 2. Turn ON the ignition, with the engine OFF. 3. With a scan tool, observe the ETS Active Lamp parameter in the ETS data list. Does the scan tool display Off?	—	Go to *Step 3*	Go to *Step 4*
3	1. Turn OFF the ignition. 2. Turn ON the ignition, with the engine OFF. 3. Observe the Low Traction indicator on the instrument cluster (IPC) during the bulb check. Does the Low Traction indicator illuminate during the bulb check and then turn OFF?	—	Go to *Intermittent and Poor Connections*	Go to *Step 5*
4	Inspect for poor connections at the harness connector of the EBCM. Did you find and correct the condition?	—	Go to *Step 8*	Go to *Step 6*
5	Inspect for poor connections at the harness connector of the instrument cluster (IPC). Did you find and correct the condition?	—	Go to *Step 8*	Go to *Step 7*
6	Replace the EBCM. Did you complete the repair?	—	Go to *Step 8*	—
7	Replace the instrument cluster (IPC). Did you complete the repair?	—	Go to *Step 8*	—
8	Operate the system in order to verify the repair. Did you correct the condition?	—	System OK	Go to *Step 2*

GC4020352692000X

Fig. 35 Low Traction Indicator Always On. Alero, Cavalier, Grand Am, Malibu & Sunfire

Circuit Description

The Low Traction indicator is controlled by the instrument cluster via serial data messages from the EBCM. When the ABS or TCS is active for 0.5 seconds, the EBCM commands the instrument cluster to turn ON the Low Traction indicator.

The Low Traction indicator will also turn ON during the instrument cluster bulb check. When the ignition switch is turned to ON, the Low Traction indicator will turn ON for approximately 3 seconds and then turn OFF.

Test Description

The numbers below refer to the step numbers on the diagnostic table.

2. Use the scan tool to check the normal state of the Low Traction indicator control.
3. Ensures that the instrument cluster can operate the Low Traction indicator.

Step	Action	Value(s)	Yes	No
1	Did you perform the ABS Diagnostic System Check?	—	Go to *Step 2*	Go to *Diagnostic System Check*
2	1. Install a scan tool. 2. Turn ON the ignition, with the engine OFF. 3. With a scan tool, observe the ETS Active Lamp parameter in the ETS data list. Does the scan tool display Off?	—	Go to *Step 3*	Go to *Step 4*
3	1. Turn OFF the ignition. 2. Turn ON the ignition, with the engine OFF. 3. Observe the Low Traction indicator on the instrument cluster (IPC) during the bulb check. Does the Low Traction indicator illuminate during the bulb check and then turn OFF?	—	Go to *Intermittent and Poor Connections*	Go to *Step 5*
4	Inspect for poor connections at the harness connector of the EBCM. *Connection* Did you find and correct the condition?	—	Go to *Step 8*	Go to *Step 6*
5	Inspect for poor connections at the harness connector of the instrument cluster (IPC). Did you find and correct the condition?	—	Go to *Step 8*	Go to *Step 7*
6	Replace the EBCM. Did you complete the repair?	—	Go to *Step 8*	—
7	Replace the instrument cluster (IPC). Did you complete the repair?	—	Go to *Step 8*	—
8	Operate the system in order to verify the repair. Did you correct the condition?	—	System OK	Go to *Step 2*

GC4020352693000X

Fig. 36 Low Traction Indicator Inoperative. Alero, Cavalier, Grand Am, Malibu & Sunfire

Circuit Description

The Traction Off indicator is controlled by the instrument cluster via serial data messages from the EBCM. When the body control module sees the traction control switch input grounded through the momentary traction control switch, it sends a serial data message to the EBCM that tells the EBCM that the traction control switch has been pressed. The EBCM then disables traction control and sends a serial data message to the instrument cluster to turn the Traction Off indicator ON. Each time the ignition is cycled from OFF to ON, the traction control system is enabled.

The following conditions will cause the Traction Off indicator to illuminate:

- The EBCM has disabled the TCS due to a DTC.
- The driver manually disabling the TCS via the traction control switch.
- The instrument cluster bulb check. When the ignition switch is turned to ON, the Traction Off indicator will turn on for approximately 3 seconds and then turn OFF.

Test Description

The numbers below refer to the step numbers on the diagnostic table.

2. Use the scan tool to check the normal state of the Traction Off indicator control.
3. Ensures that the instrument cluster can operate the Traction Off indicator.

Step	Action	Value(s)	Yes	No
1	Did you perform the ABS Diagnostic System Check?	—	Go to *Step 2*	Go to *Diagnostic System Check*
2	1. Install a scan tool. 2. Turn ON the ignition, with the engine OFF. 3. With a scan tool, observe the ETS Warning Lamp parameter in the ETS data list. Does the scan tool display Off?	—	Go to *Step 3*	Go to *Step 4*
3	1. Turn OFF the ignition. 2. Turn ON the ignition, with the engine OFF. 3. Observe the Traction Off indicator on the instrument cluster (IPC) during the bulb check. Does the Traction Off indicator illuminate during the bulb check and then turn OFF?	—	Go to *Intermittent and Poor Connections*	Go to *Step 5*
4	Inspect for poor connections at the harness connector of the EBCM. Did you find and correct the condition?	—	Go to *Step 8*	Go to *Step 6*
5	Inspect for poor connections at the harness connector of the instrument cluster (IPC). Did you find and correct the condition?	—	Go to *Step 8*	Go to *Step 7*
6	Replace the EBCM. Did you complete the repair?	—	Go to *Step 8*	—
7	Replace the instrument cluster (IPC). Did you complete the repair?	—	Go to *Step 8*	—
8	Operate the system in order to verify the repair. Did you correct the condition?	—	System OK	Go to *Step 2*

GC4020352694000X

Fig. 37 Traction Off Indicator Always On. Alero, Cavalier, Grand Am, Malibu & Sunfire

Step	Action	Value(s)	Yes	No
7	1. Turn OFF the ignition. 2. Disconnect the traction control switch connector. 3. Connect a 3 amp fused jumper from the signal circuit of the traction control switch to the ground circuit of the traction control switch. 4. Turn ON the ignition, with the engine OFF. 5. With a scan tool, observe the Traction Switch parameter. Does the scan tool display On?	—	Go to *Step 12*	Go to *Step 9*
8	Test the signal circuit of the traction control switch for a short to ground. Did you find and correct the condition?	—	Go to *Step 19*	Go to *Step 11*
9	Test the signal circuit of the traction control switch for an open or high resistance. Did you find and correct the condition?	—	Go to *Step 19*	Go to *Step 10*
10	Test the ground circuit of the traction control switch for an open or high resistance. Did you find and correct the condition?	—	Go to *Step 19*	Go to *Step 11*
11	Inspect for poor connections at the harness connector of the body control module. Did you find and correct the condition?	—	Go to *Step 19*	Go to *Step 15*
12	Inspect for poor connections at the harness connector of the traction control switch. Did you find and correct the condition?	—	Go to *Step 19*	Go to *Step 16*
13	Inspect for poor connections at the harness connector of the EBCM. Did you find and correct the condition?	—	Go to *Step 19*	Go to *Step 17*
14	Inspect for poor connections at the harness connector of the instrument cluster (IPC). Did you find and correct the condition?	—	Go to *Step 19*	Go to *Step 18*
15	**Important:** Perform the setup procedure for the body control module. Replace the body control module. Did you complete the replacement?	—	Go to *Step 19*	—
16	Replace the traction control switch. Did you complete the replacement?	—	Go to *Step 19*	—
17	Replace the EBCM. Did you complete the repair?	—	Go to *Step 19*	—
18	Replace the instrument cluster (IPC). Did you complete the repair?	—	Go to *Step 19*	—
19	Operate the system in order to verify the repair. Did you correct the condition?	—	System OK	Go to *Step 2*

GC4020352695020X

Fig. 38 Traction Off Indicator Inoperative (Part 2 of 2). Alero, Cavalier, Grand Am, Malibu & Sunfire

Circuit Description

The Traction Off indicator is controlled by the instrument cluster via serial data messages from the EBCM. When the body control module sees the traction control switch input grounded through the momentary traction control switch, it sends a serial data message to the EBCM that tells the EBCM that the traction control switch has been pressed. The EBCM then disables traction control and sends a serial data message to the instrument cluster to turn the Traction Off indicator ON. Each time the ignition is cycled from OFF to ON, the traction control system is enabled.

The following conditions will cause the Traction Off indicator to illuminate:

- The EBCM has disabled the TCS due to a DTC.
- The driver manually disabling the TCS via the traction control switch.
- The instrument cluster bulb check. When the ignition switch is turned to ON, the Traction Off indicator will turn on for approximately 3 seconds and then turn OFF.

Test Description

The numbers below refer to the step numbers on the diagnostic table.

2. Use the scan tool to check the normal state of the Traction Off indicator control.
3. Ensures that the instrument cluster can operate the Traction Off indicator.

Step	Action	Value(s)	Yes	No
1	Did you perform the ABS Diagnostic System Check?	—	Go to *Step 2*	Go to *Diagnostic System Check - ABS*
2	1. Install a scan tool. 2. Turn ON the ignition, with the engine OFF. 3. With a scan tool, observe the ETS Warning Lamp parameter in the ETS data list. Does the scan tool display Off?	—	Go to *Step 3*	Go to *Step 13*
3	1. Turn OFF the ignition. 2. Turn ON the ignition, with the engine OFF. 3. Observe the Traction Off indicator on the instrument cluster (IPC) during the bulb check. Does the Traction Off indicator illuminate during the bulb check and then turn OFF?	—	Go to *Step 4*	Go to *Step 14*
4	1. Turn OFF the ignition. 2. Install a scan tool. 3. Turn ON the ignition, with the engine OFF. 4. With a scan tool, observe the Traction Switch parameter in the Body Control Module data list. 5. Activate the traction control switch. Does the Traction Switch parameter change state?	—	Go to *Intermittent and Poor Connections*	Go to *Step 5*
5	Does the scan indicate that the Traction Switch parameter is On?	—	Go to *Step 6*	Go to *Step 7*
6	1. Turn OFF the ignition. 2. Disconnect the traction control switch connector. 3. Turn ON the ignition, with the engine OFF. 4. With a scan tool, observe the Traction Switch parameter. Does the scan tool display Off?	—	Go to *Step 12*	Go to *Step 8*

GC4020352695010X

Fig. 38 Traction Off Indicator Inoperative (Part 1 of 2). Alero, Cavalier, Grand Am, Malibu & Sunfire

Circuit Description

The EBCM Diagnostic System Check is an organized approach to identify problems associated with the Anti Lock Brake System. The EBCM is a very reliable component and is not likely the cause of the malfunction. Most system complaints are linked to faulty wiring, connectors, and occasionally to components. Understanding the ABS system and using the tables correctly will reduce diagnostic time and prevent unnecessary parts replacement.

GC4020052025010X

Fig. 39 Diagnostic System Check (Part 1 of 2). Century, Impala, Monte Carlo & Regal

Diagnostic Aids

- An intermittent failure in the electronic system may be very difficult to detect and to accurately diagnose. The EBCM tests for different malfunctions under different vehicle conditions. For this reason, a thorough test drive is often needed in order to repeat a malfunction. If the system malfunction is not repeated during the test drive, a good description of the complaint may be very useful in locating an intermittent malfunction. Faulty electrical connections or wiring causes most intermittent problems. When an intermittent condition is suspected, check the suspected circuits for the following conditions:
  - Poor mating of connector halves or backed out terminals
  - Improperly formed or damaged terminals
  - Wire chafing
  - Poor wire to terminal connections
  - Dirty or corroded terminals
  - Damage to connector bodies
- If the DTC is a history DTC, the problem may be intermittent. Perform the tests shown while moving related wiring and connectors. This can often cause the malfunction to occur. Perform a thorough inspection of all related wiring and connectors pertaining to the history DTC stored.

Step	Action	Value(s)	Yes	No
1	Install a scan tool. Does the scan tool power up?	—	Go to *Step 2*	*Scan Tool Does Not Communicate with Class 2 Device*
2	1. Turn ON the ignition, with the engine OFF. 2. Attempt to establish communications with the PCM and BCM control modules. Does the scan tool communicate with the PCM and BCM control modules?	—	Go to *Step 3*	*Scan Tool Does Not Communicate with Class 2 Device*
3	Select the ABS control module display DTC function on the scan tool. Does the scan tool display any DTCs?	—	Go to *Step 4*	Go to *Symptoms*
4	Does the scan tool display any DTCs which begin with the letter "U"?	—	*Scan Tool Does Not Communicate with Class 2 Device*	Go to *Diagnostic Trouble Code (DTC) List/Type* for the Applicable DTC

GC4020052025020X

Fig. 39 Diagnostic System Check (Part 2 of 2). Century, Impala, Monte Carlo & Regal

Step	Action	Yes	No
1	Did you perform the ABS Diagnostic System Check?	Go to *Step 2*	Go to *Diagnostic System Check - ABS*
2	1. Install a scan tool. 2. Turn ON the ignition, with the engine OFF. 3. With a scan tool, observe the TCS Switch parameter in the BCM data list. Does the scan tool display Off?	Go to *Step 3*	Go to *Step 4*
3	1. Activate the TCS switch. 2. With the scan tool, observe the TCS Switch parameter. Does the TCS Switch parameter change state?	Go to Diagnostic Aids	Go to *Step 4*
4	1. Turn OFF the ignition. 2. Disconnect the TCS switch. 3. Turn ON the ignition, with the engine OFF. 4. With a scan tool, observe the TCS Switch parameter. Does the scan tool display Off?	Go to *Step 7*	Go to *Step 5*
5	Test the signal circuit of the TCS switch for a short to ground. Did you find and correct the condition?	Go to *Step 10*	Go to *Step 6*
6	Inspect for poor connections at the harness connector of the BCM. Did you find and correct the condition?	Go to *Step 10*	Go to *Step 8*
7	Inspect for poor connections at the harness connector of the TCS switch. Did you find and correct the condition?	Go to *Step 10*	Go to *Step 9*
8	**Important:** Perform the setup procedure for the BCM. Replace the BCM. Did you complete the repair?	Go to *Step 10*	—
9	Replace the traction control switch. Did you complete the repair?	Go to *Step 10*	—
10	1. Use the scan tool in order to clear the DTCs. 2. Operate the vehicle within the Conditions for Running the DTC as specified in the supporting text. Does the DTC reset?	Go to *Step 2*	System OK

GC4020052696020X

Fig. 40 Code B2747: Traction Control Switch Circuit Low (Part 2 of 2). Century, Impala, Monte Carlo & Regal

Circuit Description

The Traction Off indicator is controlled by the instrument cluster via serial data messages from the EBCM. When the body control module sees the traction control switch input grounded through the momentary traction control switch, it sends a serial data message to the EBCM that tells the EBCM that the traction control switch has been pressed. The EBCM then disables traction control and sends a serial data message to the instrument cluster to turn the Traction Off indicator ON. Each time the ignition is cycled from OFF to ON, the traction control system is enabled.

The following conditions will cause the Traction Off indicator to illuminate:

- The EBCM has disabled the TCS due to a DTC.
- The driver manually disabling the TCS via the traction control switch.
- The instrument cluster bulb check. When the ignition switch is turned to ON, the Traction Off indicator will turn on for approximately 3 seconds and then turn OFF.

Conditions for Running the DTC

The ignition is ON.

Conditions for Setting the DTC

The BCM detects a ground on the traction control switch signal circuit for longer than 60 seconds.

Action Taken When the DTC Sets

- The ABS remains functional.
- The ABS indicator remains OFF.

Conditions for Clearing the DTC

- The condition for the DTC is no longer present (the DTC is not current) and you used the scan tool Clear DTC function.
- The BCM automatically clears the history DTC when a current DTC is not detected in 100 consecutive ignition cycles.

Test Description

The numbers below refer to the step numbers on the diagnostic table.

2. Tests for the normal state of the TCS switch using a scan tool.
3. Tests if the BCM is able to detect a change in TCS switch state.
4. Tests for a stuck or shorted TCS switch. If the TCS switch is stuck or shorted, the state will change from On to Off when the TCS switch is disconnected.
5. Tests for a short to ground in the TCS switch signal circuit.
8. When the BCM is replaced, use a scan tool to perform the setup procedure for the BCM.

GC4020052696010X

Fig. 40 Code B2747: Traction Control Switch Circuit Low (Part 1 of 2). Century, Impala, Monte Carlo & Regal

Circuit Description

The system relay is energized when the ignition is ON. The system relay supplies voltage to the solenoid valves and the pump motor. This voltage is referred to as the system voltage.

The EBCM controls each solenoid valve by grounding the solenoid.

The EBCM controls the pump motor by grounding the control circuit. The pump serves 2 purposes:

- Transfers brake fluid from the brake calipers to the master cylinder reservoir during pressure decrease events.
- Transfers brake fluid from the master cylinder reservoir to the brake calipers during pressure increase events.

Conditions for Running the DTC

- The ignition voltage is greater than 10.8 volts.
- The system relay is commanded ON.
- For Criteria 2, one of the following conditions exists:
  - The pump motor is OFF.
  - During initialization, the pump motor is ON.

Conditions for Setting the DTC

One of the following conditions exists for 0.23 seconds:

Criteria 1

The system voltage is less than 8 volts.

Criteria 2

The difference between the ignition voltage and system voltage is greater than 1.9 volts.

Action Taken When the DTC Sets

If equipped, the following actions occur:

- The EBCM disables the ABS for the duration of the ignition cycle.
- The EBCM disables the TCS (w/NW9) for the duration of the ignition cycle.
- The DRP does not function optimally, or with ignition voltage less than 8.5 volts, the EBCM disables the DRP for the duration of the ignition cycle.
- The ABS indicator turns ON.
- The Traction Off indicator turns ON.

Conditions for Clearing the DTC

- The condition for the DTC is no longer present (the DTC is not current) and you used the scan tool Clear DTC function.
- The EBCM automatically clears the history DTC when a current DTC is not detected in 100 consecutive drive cycles.

Diagnostic Aids

The system relay is integral to the EBCM. The relay is not serviceable.

Test Description

The number below refers to the step number on the diagnostic table.

2. Determines whether the DTC is current.

Step	Action	Value(s)	Yes	No
1	Did you perform the ABS Diagnostic System Check?	—	Go to *Step 2*	Go to *Diagnostic System Check - ABS*
2	1. Install a scan tool. 2. Turn ON the ignition, with the engine OFF. 3. Use the scan tool in order to clear the DTCs. 4. With the scan tool, perform the Automated Test. Does the DTC reset as a current DTC?	—	Go to *Step 3*	Go to *Intermittent and Poor Connections*
3	1. Remove the EBCM from the BPMV. 2. Measure the resistance between each pump motor control circuit of the BPMV and the housing of the BPMV. Does the DMM display the specified value?	OL	Go to *Step 5*	Go to *Step 4*
4	Replace the EBCM and the BPMV. Did you complete the repair?	—	Go to *Step 6*	—
5	Replace the EBCM. Did you complete the repair?	—	Go to *Step 6*	—
6	1. Use the scan tool in order to clear the DTCs. 2. With the scan tool, perform the Automated Test. Does the DTC reset?	—	Go to *Step 2*	System OK

GC4020052697000X

Fig. 41 Code C1214: Solenoid Valve Relay Contact Or Coil Circuit Open. Century, Impala, Monte Carlo & Regal

Circuit Description

The EBCM monitors the On/Off state of each solenoid and recognizes when the ABS is in pressure decrease too long. This fault indicates that the EBCM was unable to decrease brake pressure enough to a certain wheel to prevent excessive wheel slip.

Conditions for Running the DTC

- The ABS is active.
- The wheel speed is less than 5 km/h (3 mph).

Conditions for Setting the DTC

The solenoid of the wheel is releasing for greater than 1 second.

Action Taken When the DTC Sets

If equipped, the following actions occur:

- The EBCM disables the ABS for the duration of the ignition cycle.
- The EBCM disables the TCS (w/NW9) for the duration of the ignition cycle.
- The ABS indicator turns ON.
- The Traction Off indicator turns ON.

Conditions for Clearing the DTC

- The condition for the DTC is no longer present (the DTC is not current) and you used the scan tool Clear DTC function.
- The EBCM automatically clears the history DTC when a current DTC is not detected in 100 consecutive drive cycles.

Diagnostic Aids

Possible causes of this DTC are the following conditions:

- A contaminated hydraulic unit.
- An intermittent wheel speed sensor.
- A sticking solenoid.
- Excessive brake drag or high resistance in base brake system.
- Suspension system irregularities.

Step	Action	Value(s)	Yes	No
1	Did you perform the ABS Diagnostic System Check?	—	Go to *Step 2*	Go to *Diagnostic System Check*
2	1. Install a scan tool. 2. Turn ON the ignition, with the ignition OFF. 3. With a scan tool, observe the DTC Information parameter in the ABS Diagnostic Trouble Codes (DTCs). Does the scan tool display any other ABS DTCs relating to wheel speed sensor or solenoid valve operation?	—	Go to *Diagnostic Trouble Code*	Go to *Step 3*
3	With a scan tool, monitor all of the wheel speed sensor in the ABS Data Display while decelerating the vehicle from 56 to 0 km/h (35 to 0 mph). Do any of the wheel speeds indicate erratic or intermittent operation?	—	Go to *Diagnostic Trouble Code (DTC)*	Go to *Step 4*
4	Inspect the base brake system for the following conditions: • Brake fluid contamination. • Excessive brake drag. • Suspension system irregularities. Did you find and correct the condition?	—	Go to *Step 7*	Go to *Step 5*
5	1. Use the scan tool in order to clear the DTCs. 2. With the scan tool, perform the Automated Test. Does the DTC reset as a current DTC?	—	Go to *Step 6*	System OK
6	Replace the BPMV. Did you complete the repair?	—	Go to *Step 7*	—
7	1. Use the scan tool in order to clear the DTCs. 2. With the scan tool, perform the Automated Test. Does the DTC reset?	—	Go to *Step 2*	System OK

GC4020052698000X

Fig. 42 Code C1216: EBCM Commanded Pressure Release Too Long. Century, Impala, Monte Carlo & Regal

Step	Action	Value(s)	Yes	No
1	Did you perform the ABS Diagnostic System Check?	—	Go to *Step 2*	Go to *Diagnostic System Check*
2	1. Turn OFF the ignition. **Important:** Removing battery voltage or ground from the EBCM will result in the following conditions: • Loss of the TIM learned tire inflation configuration parameters in the EBCM • The EBCM sets DTC C1245 When the diagnosis is complete, inspect the tire pressures and perform the TIM reset. 2. Disconnect the EBCM harness connector. 3. Connect the *J 39700* universal pinout box using the *J 39700-99* cable adapter to the EBCM harness connector only. 4. Test both ground circuits of the EBCM including the EBCM ground for a high resistance or an open. Did you find and correct the condition?	—	Go to *Step 8*	Go to *Step 3*
3	1. Remove the EBCM from the BPMV. 2. Measure the resistance from both pump motor control circuits of the BPMV to the housing of the BPMV. Does the resistance measure less than the specified value?	5 Ω	Go to *Step 4*	Go to *Step 5*
4	Inspect for poor connections at the connector of the BPMV. Did you find and correct the condition?	—	Go to *Step 8*	Go to *Step 6*
5	Inspect for poor connections at the harness connector of the EBCM. Did you find and correct the condition?	—	Go to *Step 8*	Go to *Step 7*
6	Replace the BPMV. Did you complete the repair?	—	Go to *Step 8*	—
7	Replace the EBCM. Did you complete the repair?	—	Go to *Step 8*	—
8	1. Use the scan tool in order to clear the DTCs. 2. With the scan tool, perform the Automated Test. Does the DTC reset?	—	Go to *Step 2*	System OK

GC4020052699020X

Fig. 43 Code C1217: Pump Motor Shorted To Ground (Part 2 of 2). Century, Impala, Monte Carlo & Regal

Circuit Description

The system relay is energized when the ignition is ON. The system relay supplies voltage to the solenoid valves and the pump motor. This voltage is referred to as the system voltage.

The EBCM controls each solenoid valve by grounding the solenoid.

The EBCM controls the pump motor by grounding the control circuit. The pump serves 2 purposes:

- Transfers brake fluid from the brake calipers to the master cylinder reservoir during pressure decrease events.
- Transfers brake fluid from the master cylinder reservoir to the brake calipers during pressure increase events.

Conditions for Running the DTC

- The pump motor has been commanded OFF for 1 second.
- The system voltage is greater than 9.36 volts.

Conditions for Setting the DTC

One of the following conditions exists for 0.2 seconds:

- The voltage across the pump motor is greater than 10.2 volts.
- The pump motor low side voltage is less than 2.7 volts.

Action Taken When the DTC Sets

If equipped, the following actions occur:

- The EBCM disables the ABS for the duration of the ignition cycle.
- The EBCM disables the TCS (w/NW9) for the duration of the ignition cycle.
- The DRP does not function optimally, or with ignition voltage less than 8.5 volts, the EBCM disables the DRP for the duration of the ignition cycle.
- The ABS indicator turns ON.
- The Traction Off indicator turns ON.

Conditions for Clearing the DTC

- The condition for the DTC is no longer present (the DTC is not current) and you used the scan tool Clear DTC function.
- The EBCM automatically clears the history DTC when a current DTC is not detected in 100 consecutive drive cycles.

Diagnostic Aids

- This DTC determines if there is a short in the pump motor control circuit.
- The pump motor is integral to the BPMV. The pump motor is not serviceable.

Test Description

The number below refers to the step number on the diagnostic table.

3. Tests the pump motor circuits of the BPMV for a short to the housing of the BPMV.

GC4020052699010X

Fig. 43 Code C1217: Pump Motor Shorted To Ground (Part 1 of 2). Century, Impala, Monte Carlo & Regal

Circuit Description

The system relay is energized when the ignition is ON. The system relay supplies voltage to the solenoid valves and the pump motor. This voltage is referred to as the system voltage.

The EBCM controls each solenoid valve by grounding the solenoid.

The EBCM controls the pump motor by grounding the control circuit. The pump serves 2 purposes:

- Transfers brake fluid from the brake calipers to the master cylinder reservoir during pressure decrease events.
- Transfers brake fluid from the master cylinder reservoir to the brake calipers during pressure increase events.

Conditions for Running the DTC

- The pump motor is commanded ON.
- The system voltage is greater than 8 volts.

Conditions for Setting the DTC

One of the following conditions exists for 0.16 seconds:

- With the commanded pump motor voltage less than the system voltage, the actual pump motor voltage is 3 volts less than the commanded voltage.
- With the commanded pump motor voltage greater than the system voltage, the actual pump motor voltage is less than 8 volts.

Action Taken When the DTC Sets

If equipped, the following actions occur:

- The EBCM disables the ABS for the duration of the ignition cycle.
- The EBCM disables the TCS (w/NW9) for the duration of the ignition cycle.
- The DRP does not function optimally, or with ignition voltage less than 8.5 volts, the EBCM disables the DRP for the duration of the ignition cycle.
- The ABS indicator turns ON.
- The Traction Off indicator turns ON.

Conditions for Clearing the DTC

- The condition for the DTC is no longer present (the DTC is not current) and you used the scan tool Clear DTC function.
- The EBCM automatically clears the history DTC when a current DTC is not detected in 100 consecutive drive cycles.

Diagnostic Aids

The pump motor is integral to the BPMV. The pump motor is not serviceable.

Test Description

The number below refers to the step number on the diagnostic table.

5. Tests the ability of the EBCM to control the pump motor. If the test lamp illuminates, the pump motor circuit within the EBCM is good.

GC4020052700010X

Fig. 44 Code C1218: Pump Motor Circuit Short To Voltage (Part 1 of 2). Century, Impala, Monte Carlo & Regal

Step	Action	Yes	No
1	Did you perform the ABS Diagnostic System Check?	Go to *Step 2*	Go to *Diagnostic System Check*
2	1. Use the scan tool in order to clear the DTCs. 2. With the scan tool, perform the Automated Test. Does the DTC reset?	Go to *Step 3*	Go to *Intermittent and Poor Connections*
3	1. Remove the EBCM from the BPMV. 2. Inspect the EBCM to BPMV connector for conditions which could cause an intermittent, such as damage, corrosion, poor terminal contact, or presence of brake fluid. Is connector OK and cavity free of brake fluid?	Go to *Step 5*	Go to *Step 4*
4	1. If connector corrosion or damage is evident, replace BPMV and/or EBCM as necessary. 2. If brake fluid is present, replace both BPMV and EBCM. Did you complete the repair?	Go to *Step 9*	—
5	1. Connect the EBCM harness to the EBCM with the BPMV still separated. 2. Connect a test lamp between the pump motor circuits, internal EBCM side, using the *J 35616-A* Connector Test Adapter Kit. 3. With the scan tool, perform the Automated Bleed. Does the test lamp illuminate?	Go to *Step 8*	Go to *Step 6*
6	1. Turn OFF the ignition. **Important:** Removing battery voltage or ground from the EBCM will result in the following conditions: • Loss of the TIM learned tire inflation configuration parameters in the EBCM • The EBCM sets DTC C1245 When the diagnosis is complete, inspect the tire pressures and perform the TIM reset. 2. Disconnect the EBCM connector. 3. Connect the *J 39700* universal pinout box using the *J 39700-99* cable adapter to the EBCM harness connector only. 4. Test both ground circuits of the EBCM including the EBCM ground for a high resistance or an open. Did you find and correct the condition?	Go to *Step 9*	Go to *Step 7*
7	Replace the EBCM. Did you complete the repair?	Go to *Step 9*	—
8	Replace the BPMV. Did you complete the repair?	Go to *Step 9*	—
9	1. Use the scan tool in order to clear the DTCs. 2. With the scan tool, perform the Automated Test. Does the DTC reset?	Go to *Step 2*	System OK

GC4020052700020X

Fig. 44 Code C1218: Pump Motor Circuit Short To Voltage (Part 2 of 2). Century, Impala, Monte Carlo & Regal

Circuit Description

As the wheel spins, the wheel speed sensor produces an AC signal. The EBCM uses the frequency of the AC signal to calculate the wheel speed.

Conditions for Running the DTC

C1221 through C1228

- DTCs C1232 through C1235 are not set.
- The brake pedal is not pressed.
- The ABS is not active.

C1232 through C1235

The ignition is ON.

Conditions for Setting the DTC

C1221 through C1224

All of the following conditions exists for 2.5 seconds:

- The suspect wheel speed equals zero.
- The other wheel speeds are greater than 8 km/h (5 mph).
- The other wheel speeds are within 11 km/h (7 mph) of each other.

C1225 through C1228

The EBCM detects a rapid variation in the wheel speed. The wheel speed changes by 24 km/h or more in 0.01 second. The change must occur 5 times with no more than 1 second between occurrences.

C1232 through C1235

One of the following conditions exists for 0.02 seconds:

- A short to voltage - the wheel speed sensor signal circuit and wheel speed sensor return circuit voltages are both greater than 4.25 volts.
- A short to ground - the wheel speed sensor signal circuit and wheel speed sensor return circuit voltages are both less than 0.75 volts.
- An open - the wheel speed sensor signal circuit voltage is greater than 4.25 volts and wheel speed sensor return circuit voltage is less than 0.75 volts.

Action Taken When the DTC Sets

If equipped, the following actions occur:

- The EBCM disables the ABS/TCS for the duration of the ignition cycle.
- The EBCM temporarily suspends the TIM monitoring function while the DTC is set.
- The DRP does not function optimally.
- The ABS indicator turns ON.
- The Traction Off indicator turns ON.

Conditions for Clearing the DTC

- The condition for the DTC is no longer present (the DTC is not current) and you used the scan tool Clear DTC function.
- The EBCM automatically clears the history DTC when a current DTC is not detected in 100 consecutive drive cycles.

Diagnostic Aids

C1221 through C1224

Under the following conditions, 2 Wheel Speed Sensor Input is 0 DTCs are set:

- The 2 suspect wheel speeds equal zero for 20 seconds.
- The other wheel speeds are greater than 16 km/h (10 mph).
- The other wheel speeds are within 11 km/h (7 mph) of each other.

Diagnose each wheel speed sensor individually.

C1225 through C1228

A possible cause of this DTC is electrical noise on the wheel speed sensor harness wiring. Electrical noise could result from the wheel speed sensor wires being routed to close to high energy ignition system components, such as spark plug wires.

C1232 through C1235

If the customer comments that the ABS indicator is ON only during moist environmental conditions (rain, snow, vehicle wash, etc.), inspect the wheel speed sensor wiring for signs of water intrusion. If the DTC is not current, clear all DTCs and simulate the effects of water intrusion by using the following procedure:

1. Spray the suspected area with a 5 percent saltwater solution. To create a 5 percent saltwater solution, add 2 teaspoons of salt to 354 ml (12 oz) of water.
2. Test drive the vehicle over various road surfaces (bumps, turns, etc.) above 40 km/h (25 mph) for at least 30 seconds.
3. If the DTC returns, replace the suspected wheel speed sensor or repair the wheel speed sensor wiring.
4. Rinse the area thoroughly when completed.

Test Description

The numbers below refer to the step numbers on the diagnostic table.

4. Measures the resistance of the wheel speed sensor in order to determine if the sensor has a valid resistance value.
5. Ensures that the wheel speed sensor is generating a valid AC voltage output.

GC4020052701010X

Fig. 45 Codes C1221–C1235: Wheel Speed Sensors (Part 1 of 2). Century, Impala, Monte Carlo & Regal

Step	Action	Value(s)	Yes	No
1	Did you perform the ABS Diagnostic System Check?	—	Go to *Step 2*	Go to *Diagnostic System Check*
2	1. Install a scan tool. 2. Turn ON the ignition. 3. Set up the scan tool snap shot feature to trigger for this DTC. 4. Drive the vehicle at a speed greater than the specified value. Does the scan tool indicate that this wheel speed DTC set?	8 km/h (5 mph)	Go to *Step 3*	Go to *Intermittent and Poor Connections*
3	1. Raise and support the vehicle. 2. Disconnect the wheel speed sensor connector. 3. Measure the resistance across the wheel speed sensor. Does the resistance measure within the specified range?	850–1350 Ω	Go to *Step 4*	Go to *Step 8*
4	1. Spin the wheel. 2. Measure the AC voltage across the wheel speed sensor. Does the AC voltage measure greater than the specified value?	100 mV	Go to *Step 5*	Go to *Step 8*
5	Inspect for poor connections at the harness connector of the wheel speed sensor. Did you find and correct the condition?	—	Go to *Step 10*	Go to *Step 6*
6	**Important:** Removing battery voltage or ground from the EBCM will result in the following conditions: • Loss of the TIM learned tire inflation configuration parameters in the EBCM • The EBCM sets DTC C1245 When the diagnosis is complete, inspect the tire pressures and perform the TIM reset. 1. Disconnect the EBCM harness connector. 2. Install the *J 39700* universal pinout box using the *J 39700-99* cable adapter to the EBCM harness connector only. 3. Test the wheel speed sensor circuits for the following: • An open • A short to ground • A short to voltage • Shorted together Did you find and correct the condition?	—	Go to *Step 10*	Go to *Step 7*

GC4020052701020X

Fig. 45 Codes C1221–C1235: Wheel Speed Sensors (Part 2 of 2). Century, Impala, Monte Carlo & Regal

Circuit Description

The EBCM monitors the voltage level available for system operation. A low voltage condition prevents the system from operating properly.

Conditions for Running the DTC

- The vehicle speed is greater than 8 km/h (5 mph).
- The ignition voltage is less than 10.8 volts.
- The system relay is commanded ON.

Conditions for Setting the DTC

One of the following conditions exists for 0.72 seconds:

- During initialization or when the system is inactive, the system voltage is less than 10.8 volts.
- During the system operation, the system voltage is less than 9.36 volts.

Action Taken When the DTC Sets

If equipped, the following actions occur:

- The EBCM disables the ABS for the duration of the ignition cycle.
- The EBCM disables the TCS (w/NW9) for the duration of the ignition cycle.
- The DRP does not function optimally, or with ignition voltage less than 8.5 volts, the EBCM disables the DRP for the duration of the ignition cycle.
- The ABS indicator turns ON.
- The Traction Off indicator turns ON.

Conditions for Clearing the DTC

- The condition for the DTC is no longer present (the DTC is not current) and you used the scan tool Clear DTC function.
- The EBCM automatically clears the history DTC when a current DTC is not detected in 100 consecutive drive cycles.

Diagnostic Aids

- Test the charging system. Refer to *Diagnostic System Check - Engine Electrical*
- Possible causes of this DTC are the following conditions:
  - A charging system malfunction
  - An excessive battery draw
  - A weak battery
  - A faulty system ground

Test Description

2. Use the scan tool in order to inspect the voltage to the EBCM.
3. Use the scan tool in order to inspect the voltage to the body control module. A low voltage value in multiple modules indicates a concern in the charging system.
5. Verifies that the condition is still present.

GC4020052702010X

Fig. 46 Code C1236: Low System Supply Voltage (Part 1 of 2). Century, Impala, Monte Carlo & Regal

Step	Action	Value(s)	Yes	No
1	Did you perform the ABS Diagnostic System Check?	—	Go to *Step 2*	Go to *Diagnostic System Check*
2	1. Install a scan tool. 2. Start the engine. 3. With a scan tool, observe the Switched Battery Voltage parameter in ABS data list. Does the scan tool indicate the voltage is greater than the specified value?	10.5 V	Go to Diagnostic Aids	Go to *Step 3*
3	With a scan tool, observe the Battery Voltage parameter in the Body Control Module data list. Does the scan tool indicate the voltage is greater than the specified value?	10.5 V	Go to *Step 4*	Engine Electrical
4	1. Turn OFF the ignition. **Important:** Removing battery voltage or ground from the EBCM will result in the following conditions: • Loss of the TIM learned tire inflation configuration parameters in the EBCM • The EBCM sets DTC C1245 When the diagnosis is complete, inspect the tire pressures and perform the TIM reset. 2. Disconnect the EBCM harness connector. 3. Install the *J 39700* universal pinout box using the *J 39700-99* cable adaptor to the EBCM harness connector only. 4. Test the ground circuits of the EBCM including the EBCM ground for a high resistance or an open. Did you find and correct the condition?	—	Go to *Step 7*	Go to *Step 5*
5	1. Reconnect the EBCM harness connector. 2. Turn ON the ignition, with the engine OFF. 3. Use the scan tool in order to clear the DTCs. 4. Operate the vehicle within the Conditions for Running the DTC as specified in the supporting text. Does the DTC reset?	—	Go to *Step 6*	Go to Diagnostic Aids
6	Replace the EBCM. Did you complete the repair?	—	Go to *Step 7*	—
7	1. Use the scan tool in order to clear the DTCs. 2. Operate the vehicle within the Conditions for Running the DTC as specified in the supporting text. Does the DTC reset?	—	Go to *Step 2*	System OK

GC4020052702020X

Fig. 46 Code C1236: Low System Supply Voltage (Part 2 of 2). Century, Impala, Monte Carlo & Regal

Circuit Description

The EBCM monitors the voltage level available for system operation. If the voltage level is too high, damage may result in the system. When the EBCM detects a high voltage condition, the EBCM turns OFF the system relay which removes battery voltage from the solenoid valves and pump motor.

Conditions for Running the DTC

The vehicle speed is greater than 8 km/h (5 mph).

Conditions for Setting the DTC

The system voltage is greater than 17 volts for 0.7 seconds.

Action Taken When the DTC Sets

If equipped, the following actions occur:

- The EBCM disables the ABS for the duration of the ignition cycle.
- The EBCM disables the TCS (w/NW9) for the duration of the ignition cycle.
- The DRP does not function optimally, or with ignition voltage less than 8.5 volts, the EBCM disables the DRP for the duration of the ignition cycle.
- The ABS indicator turns ON.
- The Traction Off indicator turns ON.

Conditions for Clearing the DTC

- The condition for the DTC is no longer present (the DTC is not current) and you used the scan tool Clear DTC function.
- The EBCM automatically clears the history DTC when a current DTC is not detected in 100 consecutive drive cycles.

Diagnostic Aids

A possible cause of this DTC is overcharging.

Test Description

2. Use the scan tool in order to inspect the voltage to the EBCM.
3. Use the scan tool in order to inspect the voltage to the body control module. A high voltage value in multiple modules indicates a concern in the charging system.
4. Verifies that the condition is still present.

Step	Action	Value(s)	Yes	No
1	Did you perform the ABS Diagnostic System Check?	—	Go to *Step 2*	Go to *Diagnostic System Check*
2	1. Turn OFF all of the accessories. 2. Install a scan tool. 3. Start the engine. 4. Run the engine at approximately 2000 RPM. 5. With a scan tool, observe the Switched Battery Voltage parameter in ABS data list. Does the scan tool indicate that the voltage is greater than the specified value?	16.3 V	Go to *Step 3*	Go to Diagnostic Aids
3	With a scan tool, observe the Battery Voltage parameter in the Body Control Module data list. Does the scan tool indicate the voltage is greater than the specified value?	16.3 V	Engine Electrical	Go to *Step 4*
4	1. Use the scan tool in order to clear the DTCs. 2. Operate the vehicle within the Conditions for Running the DTC as specified in the supporting text. Does the DTC reset?	—	Go to *Step 5*	Go to Diagnostic Aids
5	Replace the EBCM. Did you complete the repair?	—	Go to *Step 6*	—
6	1. Use the scan tool in order to clear the DTCs. 2. Operate the vehicle within the conditions for Running the DTC as specified in the supporting test. Does the DTC reset?	—	Go to *Step 2*	System OK

GC4020052703000X

Fig. 47 Code C1237: High System Supply Voltage. Century, Impala, Monte Carlo & Regal

Circuit Description

The EBCM monitors vehicle speed deceleration, system activation, and stoplamp switch active times in order to calculate an estimate of the brake rotor temperatures. If the EBCM calculates that the brake rotor temperatures have exceeded the thermal cutoff point, the EBCM will temporarily suspend the TCS function until the brake rotors cool. This feature is used to maintain braking effectiveness if normal base braking is required. An overly heated brake system could result in brake fade.

The EBCM continues calculating the brake rotor temperatures after the ignition is turned OFF. The EBCM remains awake until the EBCM calculates that the brake rotors cooled sufficiently. The cooling period may take up to 30 minutes.

Conditions for Running the DTC

The ABS conditions and the braking conditions are normal.

Conditions for Setting the DTC

This DTC sets when the estimated brake rotor temperature of either of the drive wheels exceeds 375°C (700°F). When the estimated brake rotor temperature of either of the drive wheels exceeds 375°C (700°F) during normal braking or normal ABS operations, the DTC does not set until the next TCS activation. The brake rotor temperature can exceed 375°C (700°F) without setting the DTC if a TCS activation has not occurred. When the estimated brake rotor temperature of either of the drive wheels exceeds 375°C (700°F) during a TCS activation, the DTC sets immediately, but the EBCM does not disable TCS until the end of the TCS event.

Action Taken When the DTC Sets

- The EBCM disables the TCS until the DTC becomes a history DTC.
- The Traction Off indicator turns ON.
- The ABS remains functional.

Conditions for Clearing the DTC

- The current DTC becomes history when the estimated brake rotor temperatures of both drive wheels decreases below 275°C (530°F). The EBCM also enables TCS.
- The condition for the DTC is no longer present (the DTC is not current) and you used the scan tool Clear DTC function.
- The EBCM automatically clears the history DTC when a current DTC is not detected in 100 consecutive drive cycles.

Diagnostic Aids

- With TCS temporarily disabled, the EBCM continues calculating the brake rotor temperatures after the ignition is turned OFF. Turning ON the ignition again while TCS is temporarily disabled will not re-enable TCS.
- The temperature is an estimate calculated by the EBCM.
- Possible causes of this DTC are the following conditions:
  - The brake usage is excessive.
  - The TCS usage is excessive.
  - The stoplamp switch is misaligned or damaged.

Test Description

The number below refers to the step number on the diagnostic table.

4. Use the scan tool in order to verify that the Brake Thermal Model is exceeded.

GC4020052704010X

Fig. 48 Code C1238: Brake Thermal Model Exceeded (Part 1 of 2). Century, Impala, Monte Carlo & Regal

Step	Action	Yes	No
1	Did you perform the ABS Diagnostic System Check?	Go to *Step 2*	Go to *Diagnostic System Check*
2	1. Install a scan tool. 2. Turn ON the ignition, with the engine OFF. 3. Select the display DTCs function on the scan tool for the EBCM. Does the scan tool display that this DTC is set current?	Go to *Step 4*	Go to *Step 3*
3	Since most occurrences of this DTC are caused by excessive braking, review with the customer to verify the conditions under which the DTC set. Did vehicle operation cause this DTC to set?	Go to Diagnostic Aids	Go to *Step 4*
4	1. Allow 30 minutes from the last time you drove the vehicle for the cooling of the brake rotors. 2. With a scan tool, observe the Brake Temp Status parameter in the ABS/TCS data list. Does the scan tool display Normal?	Go to *Step 6*	Go to *Step 5*
5	Inspect the alignment of the stoplamp switch. Did you find and correct the condition?	Go to *Step 8*	Go to *Step 6*
6	1. Use the scan tool in order to clear the DTCs. 2. Operate the vehicle within the Conditions for Running the DTC as specified in the supporting text. Does the DTC reset as a current DTC?	Go to *Step 7*	System OK
7	Replace the EBCM. Did you complete the repair?	Go to *Step 8*	—
8	1. Use the scan tool in order to clear the DTCs. 2. Operate the vehicle within the Conditions for Running the DTC as specified in the supporting text. Does the DTC reset?	Go to *Step 2*	System OK

GC4020052704020X

Fig. 48 Code C1238: Brake Thermal Model Exceeded (Part 2 of 2). Century, Impala, Monte Carlo & Regal

Circuit Description

The system relay is energized when the ignition is ON. The system relay supplies voltage to the solenoid valves and the pump motor. This voltage is referred to as the system voltage.

The EBCM controls each solenoid valve by grounding the solenoid.

The EBCM controls the pump motor by grounding the control circuit. The pump serves 2 purposes:

- Transfers brake fluid from the brake calipers to the master cylinder reservoir during pressure decrease events.
- Transfers brake fluid from the master cylinder reservoir to the brake calipers during pressure increase events.

Conditions for Running the DTC

C1242

- The system voltage is greater than 8.0 volts.
- The system relay is ON.
- The pump motor is commanded OFF.

C1243

- The pump motor is ON for at least 0.3 seconds.
- The system relay is ON.

Conditions for Setting the DTC

C1242

The voltage across the pump motor is between 1.7 to 10.2 volts for 2 seconds.

C1243

The pump motor is stalled or turning slowly.

Action Taken When the DTC Sets

If equipped, the following actions occur:

- The EBCM disables the ABS for the duration of the ignition cycle.
- The EBCM disables the TCS (w/NW9) for the duration of the ignition cycle.
- The DRP does not function optimally, or with ignition voltage less than 8.5 volts, the EBCM disables the DRP for the duration of the ignition cycle.
- The ABS indicator turns ON.
- The Traction Off indicator turns ON.

Conditions for Clearing the DTC

- The condition for the DTC is no longer present (the DTC is not current) and you used the scan tool Clear DTC function.
- The EBCM automatically clears the history DTC when a current DTC is not detected in 100 consecutive drive cycles.

Diagnostic Aids

The pump motor is integral to the BPMV. The pump motor is not serviceable.

Test Description

The number below refers to the step number on the diagnostic table.

5. Tests the ability of the EBCM to control the pump motor. If the test lamp illuminates, the pump motor circuit within the EBCM is good.

GC4020052705010X

Fig. 49 Codes C1242 & C1243: Pump Motor Circuit Open & Pump Motor Is Stalled (Part 1 of 2). Century, Impala, Monte Carlo & Regal

Step	Action	Yes	No
1	Did you perform the ABS Diagnostic System Check?	Go to *Step 2*	Go to *Diagnostic System Check*
2	1. Use the scan tool in order to clear the DTCs. 2. With the scan tool, perform the Automated Test. Does the DTC reset?	Go to *Step 3*	Go to *Intermittent and Poor Connections*
3	1. Remove the EBCM from the BPMV. 2. Inspect the EBCM to BPMV connector for conditions which could cause an intermittent, such as damage, corrosion, poor terminal contact, or presence of brake fluid. Is connector OK and cavity free of brake fluid?	Go to *Step 5*	Go to *Step 4*
4	1. If connector corrosion or damage is evident, replace BPMV and/or EBCM as necessary. 2. If brake fluid is present, replace both BPMV and EBCM. Did you complete the repair?	Go to *Step 8*	—
5	1. Connect the EBCM harness to the EBCM with the BPMV still separated. 2. Connect a test lamp between the pump motor circuits, internal EBCM side, using the *J 35616-A* Connector Test Adapter Kit. 3. With the scan tool, perform the Automated Bleed. Does the test lamp illuminate?	Go to *Step 7*	Go to *Step 6*
6	Replace the EBCM. Did you complete the repair?	Go to *Step 8*	—
7	Replace the BPMV. Did you complete the repair?	Go to *Step 8*	—
8	1. Use the scan tool in order to clear the DTCs. 2. With the scan tool, perform the Automated Test. Does the DTC reset?	Go to *Step 2*	System OK

GC4020052705020X

Fig. 49 Codes C1242 & C1243: Pump Motor Circuit Open & Pump Motor Is Stalled (Part 2 of 2). Century, Impala, Monte Carlo & Regal

Circuit Description

The dynamic rear proportioning (DRP) is a control system that replaces the hydraulic proportioning function of the mechanical proportioning valve in the base brake system. The DRP control system is part of the operating software in the EBCM. The DRP uses active control with the existing ABS in order to regulate the vehicle's rear brake pressure.

Conditions for Running the DTC

One or more faults have been detected by the EBCM in the ABS/TCS systems.

Conditions for Setting the DTC

One of the following conditions exits:

- DTC C1236 sets and ignition voltage is less than 8.5 volts.
- DTC C1254 or C1255 sets.
- DTCs C1265 and C1267 set.
- Two wheel speed sensor DTCs on the same axle set.

Action Taken When the DTC Sets

- The EBCM disables the DRP for the duration of the ignition cycle.
- The red Brake warning indicator turns ON.

Conditions for Clearing the DTC

- The condition for the DTC is no longer present (the DTC is not current) and you used the scan tool Clear DTC function.
- The EBCM automatically clears the history DTC when a current DTC is not detected in 100 consecutive drive cycles.

Diagnostic Aids

- Use this DTC in order to differentiate which of the following conditions is present:
  - The EBCM turned ON the red Brake warning indicator.
  - The instrument cluster turned ON the red Brake warning indicator due to low brake fluid in the master cylinder reservoir.
  - The body control module turned ON the red Brake warning indicator due to the application of the park brake.
- Diagnose any other ABS DTCs that set along with this DTC.

Test Description

The number below refers to the step number on the diagnostic table.

2. Verifies whether other ABS/TCS DTCs are set.

Step	Action	Yes	No
1	Did you perform the ABS Diagnostic System Check?	Go to *Step 2*	Go to *Diagnostic System Check*
2	1. Install a scan tool. 2. Turn ON the ignition, with the engine OFF. 3. Select the display DTCs function on the scan tool for the EBCM. Does the scan tool display any ABS/TCS DTCs?	Go to *Diagnostic Trouble Code (DTC) List*	Go to *Step 3*
3	1. Use the scan tool in order to clear the DTCs. 2. Operate the vehicle within the Conditions for Running the DTC as specified in the supporting text. Does the DTC reset?	Go to *Step 2*	Go to *Intermittent and Poor Connections*

GC4020052706000X

Fig. 50 Code C1248: C1236, C1254, C1255, C1265 Or C1267 Are Set, Or 2 Wheel Speed Sensor Codes On Same Axle Are Set. Century, Impala, Monte Carlo & Regal

Circuit Description

The microprocessor contains a data storage area (keep alive memory) which can save pertinent data when the ignition is turned OFF. The keep alive memory (KAM) data is lost if battery power or module ground is removed from the module. The KAM area is an integral part of the microprocessor and cannot be serviced separately.

Conditions for Running the DTC

The ABS conditions and the braking conditions are normal.

Conditions for Setting the DTC

The microprocessor calculates a checksum on those areas of memory that hold critical operation data. This is done at a regular interval and is called the periodic checksum. The microprocessor also calculates a checksum on these memory locations when ever new data is written to them. This is called the running checksum.

To check the keep alive memory (KAM), the microprocessor compares the periodic checksum to the running checksum. If they do not match, the microprocessor sets the DTC.

Action Taken When the DTC Sets

If equipped, the following actions occur:

- The EBCM disables the DRP/ABS/TCS for the duration of the ignition cycle.
- The EBCM disables the variable effort steering (VES) for the duration of the ignition cycle.
- The ABS indicator turns ON.
- The Traction Off indicator turns ON.
- The EBCM will not send serial data messages.
- The EBCM will not send the requested torque output to the PCM.

Conditions for Clearing the DTC

- The condition for the DTC is no longer present (the DTC is not current) and you used the scan tool Clear DTC function.
- The EBCM automatically clears the history DTC when a current DTC is not detected in 100 consecutive drive cycles.

Diagnostic Aids

Possible causes of this DTC are the following conditions:

- A loss of battery ground.
- A disconnected battery.
- A running reset. (A running reset is detected when the keep alive memory check sum is not updated properly.)
- A sudden drop in the system voltage to less than 5 volts.
- Long extended engine cranks that cause the battery voltage to drop.
- Poor power or ground connections.
- An internal EBCM malfunction.

Test Description

The numbers below refer to the step numbers on the diagnostic table.

2. Tests for an open in the ground circuits of the body control module.
4. Verifies the proper operation of the charging system.
6. Determines whether the DTC resets.

GC4020052707010X

Fig. 51 Code C1254: Abnormal Shutdown Detected (Part 1 of 2). Century, Impala, Monte Carlo & Regal

Step	Action	Yes	No
1	Did you perform the ABS Diagnostic System Check?	Go to *Step 2*	Go to *Diagnostic System Check*
2	1. Turn OFF the ignition. **Important:** Removing battery voltage or ground from the EBCM will result in the following conditions: • Loss of the TIM learned tire inflation configuration parameters in the EBCM • The EBCM sets DTC C1245 When the diagnosis is complete, inspect the tire pressures and perform the TIM reset. Refer to *Tire Pressure Monitor Reset Procedure* in Tire Pressure Monitoring. 2. Disconnect the EBCM harness connector. 3. Install the *J 39700* universal breakout box using the *J 39700-99* cable adapter to the EBCM harness connector only. 4. Test the module ground circuit of the EBCM for a high resistance or an open. Did you find and correct the condition?	Go to *Step 8*	Go to *Step 3*
3	Has the battery been disconnected recently?	Go to *Step 8*	Go to *Step 4*
4	Test the charging system. Did you find and correct the condition?	Go to *Step 8*	Go to *Step 5*
5	Inspect for poor connections at the harness connector of the EBCM. Did you find and correct the condition?	Go to *Step 8*	Go to *Step 6*
6	1. Use the scan tool in order to clear the DTCs. 2. With the scan tool, perform the Automated Test. Does the DTC reset?	Go to *Step 7*	Go to *Intermittent and Poor Connections*
7	Replace the EBCM. Did you complete the repair?	Go to *Step 8*	—
8	1. Use the scan tool in order to clear the DTCs. 2. With the scan tool, perform the Automated Test. Does the DTC reset?	Go to *Step 2*	System OK

GC4020052707020X

Fig. 51 Code C1254: Abnormal Shutdown Detected (Part 2 of 2). Century, Impala, Monte Carlo & Regal

Circuit Description

This DTC identifies a malfunction within the EBCM.

Conditions for Running the DTC

The ABS conditions and the braking conditions are normal.

Conditions for Setting the DTC

An internal EBCM malfunction exists.

Action Taken When the DTC Sets

C1255

If equipped, the following actions occur:

- The EBCM disables the DRP/ABS/TCS for the duration of the ignition cycle.
- The EBCM disables the variable effort steering (VES) for the duration of the ignition cycle.
- The EBCM temporarily suspends the TIM monitoring function while the DTC is set.
- The ABS indicator turns ON.
- The Traction Off indicator turns ON.

C1256

- The ABS remains functional.
- The ABS indicator remains OFF.

Conditions for Clearing the DTC

- The condition for the DTC is no longer present (the DTC is not current) and you used the scan tool Clear DTC function.
- The EBCM automatically clears the history DTC when a current DTC is not detected in 100 consecutive drive cycles.

Diagnostic Aids

The scan tool displays 2 additional characters after the DTC. Take note of the 2 character code and any other DTCs that are set. The 2 character code is an engineering aid used in order to determine the cause of the internal malfunction.

Test Description

The number below refers to the step number on the diagnostic table.

2. Determines whether the DTC is current.

Step	Action	Yes	No
1	Did you perform the ABS Diagnostic System Check?	Go to *Step 2*	Go to *Diagnostic System Check*
2	1. Install a scan tool. 2. Turn ON the ignition, with the engine OFF. 3. Use the scan tool in order to clear the DTCs. 4. With the scan tool, perform the Automated Test. Does the DTC reset as a current DTC?	Go to *Step 3*	Go to *Intermittent and Poor Connections*
3	Replace the EBCM. Did you complete the repair?	Go to *Step 4*	—
4	1. Use the scan tool in order to clear the DTCs. 2. With the scan tool, perform the Automated Test. Does the DTC reset?	Go to *Step 2*	System OK

GC4020052708000X

Fig. 52 Codes C1255 & C1256: EBCM Internal Fault. Century, Impala, Monte Carlo & Regal

Circuit Description

The system relay is energized when the ignition is ON. The system relay supplies voltage to the solenoid valves and the pump motor. This voltage is referred to as the system voltage. The EBCM controls the solenoid valve by grounding the control circuit.

Conditions for Running the DTC

- The system voltage is greater than 8.0 volts.
- The ignition voltage is greater than 9.0 volts.

Conditions for Setting the DTC

The commanded state of the driver and the actual state of the control circuit do not match for 0.03 seconds.

Action Taken When the DTC Sets

If equipped, the following actions occur:

- The EBCM disables the ABS for the duration of the ignition cycle.
- The EBCM disables the TCS (w/NW9) for the duration of the ignition cycle.
- The DRP does not function optimally, or with ignition voltage less than 8.5 volts, the EBCM disables the DRP for the duration of the ignition cycle.
- The ABS indicator turns ON.
- The Traction Off indicator turns ON.

Conditions for Clearing the DTC

- The condition for the DTC is no longer present (the DTC is not current) and you used the scan tool Clear DTC function.
- The EBCM automatically clears the history DTC when a current DTC is not detected in 100 consecutive drive cycles.

Diagnostic Aids

The solenoid valve circuit is internal to the EBCM. The solenoid valve circuit is not diagnosable external to the EBCM. The DTC sets when there is a malfunction in the solenoid circuit internal to the EBCM.

Test Description

The number below refers to the step number on the diagnostic table.

2. Determines whether the DTC is current.

Step	Action	Yes	No
1	Did you perform the ABS Diagnostic System Check?	Go to *Step 2*	Go to *Diagnostic System Check*
2	1. Install a scan tool. 2. Turn ON the ignition, with the engine OFF. 3. Use the scan tool in order to clear the DTCs. 4. With the scan tool, perform the Automated Test. Does the DTC reset as a current DTC?	Go to *Step 3*	Go to *Intermittent and Poor Connections*
3	Replace the EBCM. Refer to *Electronic Brake Control Module (EBCM) Replacement.* Did you complete the repair?	Go to *Step 4*	—
4	1. Use the scan tool in order to clear the DTCs. 2. With the scan tool, perform the Automated Test. Does the DTC reset?	Go to *Step 2*	System OK

GC4020052709000X

Fig. 53 Codes C1261–C1274: Inlet Or Outlet Solenoid Valve Fault. Century, Impala, Monte Carlo & Regal

Circuit Description

The PCM monitors various parameters and will not allow operation of the Enhanced Traction system (ETS) if any PCM parameter falls below a predetermined value.

Conditions for Running the DTC

The ignition is ON.

Conditions for Setting the DTC

The PCM detects a malfunction and then causes the ETS to shutdown until the malfunction is corrected.

Action Taken When the DTC Sets

- A DTC C1275 is stored.
- The ETS is disabled.
- The TRAC OFF indicator is turned ON.
- The ABS remains functional.
- If the ETS is no longer inhibited, the indicator lamp will be turned OFF but the DTC will still be stored.

Conditions for Clearing the DTC

- The condition for the DTC is no longer present and the scan tool clear DTC function is used
- 100 ignition cycles have passed with no DTCs detected

Diagnostic Aids

Check for PCM DTCs. If no PCM DTC is stored, DTC C1275 may have set due to a hot engine or a hot transaxle (both normal conditions). No repairs should be made to the ETS System. ETS will remain disabled until the EBTCM receives a traction allowed message from the PCM. When the EBTCM receives this message, it re-enables the ETS and turns OFF the TRAC OFF indicator. Any further references for diagnosis should be taken from Engine Controls.

GC4020052062010X

Fig. 54 Code C1275: PCM Requested ETS To Be Disabled (Part 1 of 2). Century, Impala, Monte Carlo & Regal

Step	Action	Value(s)	Yes	No
1	Did you perform the ABS Diagnostic System Check?	—	*Go to Step 2*	*Go to A Diagnostic System Check - ABS*
2	1. Turn the ignition switch to the RUN position, engine off. 2. Use the Scan Tool in order to read the DTCs. Make note of the DTCs. Are any other ABS or PCM DTCs set?	—	*Go to Diagnostic Trouble Code (DTC) List/Type*	*Go to Step 3*
3	1. Clear the DTCs. 2. Turn the ignition switch to the OFF position. 3. Turn the ignition switch to the RUN position, engine off. Does DTC C1275 reset?	—	*Go to Step 5*	*Go to Step 4*
4	1. Start the engine and test drive the vehicle at a speed of at least 16 km/h (10 mph). 2. Initiate an enhanced traction assisted take off. 3. Repeat the above drive cycle sequence two more times. Did the DTC C1275 set in these last three drive cycles?	—	*Go to Step 5*	System OK
5	Perform a Powertrain OBD System Check. Did the vehicle pass the OBD system check?	—	*Go to Step 6*	*Go to Diagnostic Trouble Code (DTC) List/Type*
6	Replace the EBCM Is the repair complete?	—	*Go to Step 7*	—
7	1. Use the scan tool in order to clear the DTCs. 2. Operate the vehicle within the Conditions for Running the DTC Does the DTC reset?	—	*Go to Step 2*	System OK

GC4020052062020X

Fig. 54 Code C1275: PCM Requested ETS To Be Disabled (Part 2 of 2). Century, Impala, Monte Carlo & Regal

Circuit Description

The EBCM and the PCM simultaneously control the traction control. The PCM reduces the amount of torque supplied to the drive wheels by retarding spark timing and selectively turning off fuel injectors. The EBCM actively applies the brakes to the front wheels in order to reduce torque.

The EBCM sends a requested torque message via a pulse width modulated (PWM) signal to the PCM. The duty cycle of the signal is used to determine how much engine torque the EBCM is requesting the PCM to deliver. Normal values are between 10 and 90 percent duty cycle. The signal should be at 90 percent when traction control is not active and at lower values during traction control activations. The PCM supplies a pull up voltage of 5 volts that the EBCM switches to ground to create the signal.

The PCM sends a delivered torque message via a pulse width modulated (PWM) signal to the EBCM. The duty cycle of the signal is used to determine how much engine torque the PCM is delivering. Normal values are between 10 and 90 percent duty cycle. The signal should be at low values (around 10 percent) at idle and higher values under driving conditions. The EBCM supplies a pull up voltage of 12 volts that the PCM switches to ground to create the signal.

When certain PCM DTCs are set, the PCM will not be able to perform the torque reduction portion of traction control. A serial data message is sent to the EBCM indicating that traction control is not allowed.

Conditions for Running the DTC

The engine is running.

Conditions for Setting the DTC

C1276

One of the following conditions exists:

- The EBCM detects that delivered torque signal is out of the valid range.
- The EBCM does not receive the delivered torque signal.

P1644 or P1689

The PCM detects that the delivered torque signal voltage is invalid.

Action Taken When the DTC Sets

- The EBCM disables the TCS for the duration of the ignition cycle.
- The PCM will store conditions which were present when the DTC set as Fail Records data only.
- The Traction Off indicator turns ON.
- The ABS remains functional.

Conditions for Clearing the DTC

- The condition for the DTC is no longer present (the DTC is not current) and you used the scan tool Clear DTC function.
- The EBCM automatically clears the history DTC when a current DTC is not detected in 100 consecutive drive cycles.
- The PCM automatically clears the history DTC when a current DTC is not detected in 40 consecutive warm-up cycles.

Diagnostic Aids

The following conditions can cause this concern:

- An open in the delivered torque circuit.
- An short to ground or voltage in the delivered torque circuit.
- A wiring problem, terminal corrosion, or poor connection in the delivered torque circuit.
- A communication frequency problem.
- A communication duty cycle problem.
- The EBCM is not receiving information from the PCM.
- Loose or corroded EBCM ground or PCM ground.

Test Description

The numbers below refer to the step numbers on the diagnostic table.

3. Use the scan tool in order to determine if the delivered torque signal has a valid duty cycle.
9. This vehicle is equipped with a PCM which uses an Electrically Erasable Programmable Read Only Memory (EEPROM). When replacing the PCM, the replacement PCM must be programmed.

Step	Action	Value(s)	Yes	No
1	Did you perform the ABS Diagnostic System Check?	—	Go to *Step 2*	Go to *Diagnostic System Check*
2	Inspect the EBCM ground and PCM ground, making sure each ground is clean and torqued to the proper specification. Did you find and correct the condition?	—	Go to *Step 11*	Go to *Step 3*

GC4020052710010X

Fig. 55 Codes C1276, P1644 & P1689: Delivered Torque Signal Circuit Fault (Part 1 of 2). Century, Impala, Monte Carlo & Regal

Step	Action	Value(s)	Yes	No
3	1. Install a scan tool. 2. Start the engine. 3. With a scan tool, observe the PCM to EBTCM Delivered parameter in the TCS data list. Does the scan tool display the specified value?	90%	Go to *Step 4*	Go to *Intermittent and Poor Connections*
4	1. Turn OFF the ignition. 2. Disconnect the EBCM harness connector. 3. Install the *J 39700* universal breakout box using the *J 39700-99* cable adapter to the EBCM harness connector and the EBCM connector. 4. Disconnect the powertrain control module (PCM) harness connector. 5. Turn ON the ignition, with the engine OFF. 6. Measure the voltage from the delivered torque signal circuit to a good ground. Does the voltage measure near the specified value?	B+	Go to *Step 5*	Go to *Step 6*
5	1. Turn OFF the ignition. 2. Disconnect the *J 39700-99* cable adapter from the EBCM connector. 3. Turn ON the ignition, with the engine OFF. 4. Test the delivered torque signal circuit for a short to voltage. Did you find and correct the condition?	—	Go to *Step 11*	Go to *Step 7*
6	1. Turn OFF the ignition. 2. Disconnect the *J 39700-99* cable adapter from the EBCM connector. 3. Test the delivered torque signal circuit for the following conditions: • An open • A short to ground • A high resistance Did you find and correct the condition?	—	Go to *Step 11*	Go to *Step 8*
7	Inspect for poor connections the harness connector of the PCM. Did you find and correct the condition?	—	Go to *Step 11*	Go to *Step 9*
8	Inspect for poor connections the harness connector of the EBCM. Did you find and correct the condition?	—	Go to *Step 11*	Go to *Step 10*
9	**Important:** The replacement PCM must be programmed. Replace the PCM. Did you complete the repair?	—	Go to *Step 11*	—
10	Replace the EBCM. Did you complete the repair?	—	Go to *Step 11*	—
11	1. Use the scan tool in order to clear the DTCs. 2. Operate the vehicle within the Conditions for Running the DTC as specified in the supporting text. Does the DTC reset?	—	Go to *Step 2*	System OK

GC4020052710020X

Fig. 55 Codes C1276, P1644 & P1689: Delivered Torque Signal Circuit Fault (Part 2 of 2). Century, Impala, Monte Carlo & Regal

Circuit Description

The EBCM and the PCM simultaneously control the traction control. The PCM reduces the amount of torque supplied to the drive wheels by retarding spark timing and selectively turning off fuel injectors. The EBCM actively applies the brakes to the front wheels in order to reduce torque.

The EBCM sends a requested torque message via a pulse width modulated (PWM) signal to the PCM. The duty cycle of the signal is used to determine how much engine torque the EBCM is requesting the PCM to deliver. Normal values are between 10 and 90 percent duty cycle. The signal should be at 90 percent when traction control is not active and at lower values during traction control activations. The PCM supplies a pull up voltage of 5 volts that the EBCM switches to ground to create the signal.

The PCM sends a delivered torque message via a pulse width modulated (PWM) signal to the EBCM. The duty cycle of the signal is used to determine how much engine torque the PCM is delivering. Normal values are between 10 and 90 percent duty cycle. The signal should be at low values (around 10 percent) at idle and higher values under driving conditions. The EBCM supplies a pull up voltage of 12 volts that the PCM switches to ground to create the signal.

When certain PCM DTCs are set, the PCM will not be able to perform the torque reduction portion of traction control. A serial data message is sent to the EBCM indicating that traction control is not allowed.

Conditions for Running the DTC

The engine is running.

Conditions for Setting the DTC

C1277

The PCM diagnoses the requested torque signal circuit and sends a serial data message to the EBCM indicating a fault is present.

P1571

One of the following conditions exists:

- The PCM detects that requested torque signal is out of the valid range.
- The PCM does not receive the requested torque signal.

Action Taken When the DTC Sets

- The EBCM disables the TCS for the duration of the ignition cycle.
- The PCM will store conditions which were present when the DTC set as Fail Records data only.
- The Traction Off indicator turns ON.
- The ABS remains functional.

Conditions for Clearing the DTC

- The condition for the DTC is no longer present (the DTC is not current) and you used the scan tool Clear DTC function.
- The EBCM automatically clears the history DTC when a current DTC is not detected in 100 consecutive drive cycles.
- The PCM automatically clears the history DTC when a current DTC is not detected in 40 consecutive warm-up cycles.

Diagnostic Aids

The following conditions can cause this concern:

- An open in the delivered torque circuit.
- An short to ground or voltage in the delivered torque circuit.
- A wiring problem, terminal corrosion, or poor connection in the delivered torque circuit.
- A communication frequency problem.
- A communication duty cycle problem.
- The EBCM is not receiving information from the PCM.
- Loose or corroded EBCM ground or PCM ground.

Test Description

The numbers below refer to the step numbers on the diagnostic table.

3. Use the scan tool in order to determine if the requested torque signal has a valid duty cycle.
4. Measure the requested torque signal in order to determine if the signal has a valid duty cycle.
5. Measure the requested torque signal in order to determine if the signal has a valid frequency.
11. This vehicle is equipped with a PCM which uses an Electrically Erasable Programmable Read Only Memory (EEPROM). When replacing the PCM, the replacement PCM must be programmed.

GC4020052711010X

Fig. 56 Codes C1277 & P1571: Requested Torque Signal Circuit Fault (Part 1 of 3). Century, Impala, Monte Carlo & Regal

Step	Action	Value(s)	Yes	No
1	Did you perform the ABS Diagnostic System Check?	—	Go to *Step 2*	Go to *Diagnostic System Check*
2	Inspect the EBCM ground and PCM ground, making sure each ground is clean and torqued to the proper specification. Did you find and correct the condition?	—	Go to *Step 13*	Go to *Step 3*
3	1. Install a scan tool. 2. Start the engine. 3. With the scan tool, observe the Torque Request Signal parameter in the Powertrain Control Module data list. Does the scan tool display less than the specified value?	100%	Go to *Intermittent and Poor Connections*	Go to *Step 4*
4	1. Turn OFF the ignition. 2. Disconnect the EBCM harness connector. 3. Install the *J 39700* universal breakout box using the *J 39700-99* cable adapter to the EBCM harness connector and the EBCM connector. 4. Start the engine. 5. Measure the DC duty cycle between the requested torque signal circuit and a good ground. Is the duty cycle within the specified range?	5–95%	Go to *Step 5*	Go to *Step 6*
5	Measure the DC Hz between the requested torque signal circuit and a good ground. Does the frequency measure within the specified range?	121–134 Hz	Go to *Step 8*	Go to *Step 6*
6	1. Turn OFF the ignition. 2. Disconnect the *J 39700-99* cable adapter from the EBCM connector. **Important:** Disconnecting the EBCM connector and turning ON the ignition could cause other modules to set loss of communication DTCs (Uxxxx). Once the EBCM is reconnected, the EBCM may set DTC C1298. 3. Turn ON the ignition, with the engine OFF. 4. Measure the voltage from the requested torque signal circuit to a good ground. Does the voltage measure within the specified range?	4 – 6 V	Go to *Step 10*	Go to *Step 7*
7	1. Turn OFF the ignition. 2. Disconnect the powertrain control module (PCM) harness connector. 3. Test the requested torque signal circuit for the following conditions: • A short to voltage • A short to ground Did you find and correct the condition?	—	Go to *Step 13*	Go to *Step 10*

GC4020052711020X

Fig. 56 Codes C1277 & P1571: Requested Torque Signal Circuit Fault (Part 2 of 3). Century, Impala, Monte Carlo & Regal

Step	Action	Value(s)	Yes	No
8	1. Turn OFF the ignition. 2. Disconnect the powertrain control module (PCM) harness connector. 3. Test the requested torque signal circuit for the following conditions: • An open • A high resistance Did you find and correct the condition?	—	Go to *Step 13*	Go to *Step 9*
9	Inspect for poor connections the harness connector of the PCM. Did you find and correct the condition?	—	Go to *Step 13*	Go to *Step 11*
10	Inspect for poor connections the harness connector of the EBCM. Did you find and correct the condition?	—	Go to *Step 13*	Go to *Step 12*
11	**Important:** The replacement PCM must be programmed. Replace the PCM. Did you complete the repair?	—	Go to *Step 13*	—
12	Replace the EBCM. Did you complete the repair?	—	Go to *Step 13*	—
13	1. Use the scan tool in order to clear the DTCs. 2. Operate the vehicle within the Conditions for Running the DTC as specified in the supporting text. Does the DTC reset?	—	Go to *Step 2*	System OK

GC4020052711030X

Fig. 56 Codes C1277 & P1571: Requested Torque Signal Circuit Fault (Part 3 of 3). Century, Impala, Monte Carlo & Regal

Circuit Description

The stoplamp switch signal informs the EBCM when the brake pedal is pressed.

Conditions for Running the DTC

The ABS conditions and the braking conditions are normal.

Conditions for Setting the DTC

C1291

The stoplamp switch remains open for 3 deceleration cycles.

C1293

A DTC C1291 was set in a previous ignition cycle.

Action Taken When the DTC Sets

- The EBCM disables the TCS for the duration of the ignition cycle.
- The Traction Off indicator turns ON.
- The ABS remains functional.

Conditions for Clearing the DTC

- The condition for the DTC is no longer present (the DTC is not current) and you used the scan tool Clear DTC function.
- The EBCM automatically clears the history DTC when a current DTC is not detected in 100 consecutive drive cycles.

Diagnostic Aids

- Diagnose any wheel speed sensor DTCs before continuing with the diagnosis of the DTC.
- A deceleration cycle consists of the following sequence:
  1. The vehicle speed is greater than 24 km/h (15 mph).
  2. The vehicle decelerates more than 8 km/h/second (5 mph/second) for 2 seconds.
  3. The vehicle speed decelerates to less than 16 km/h (10 mph).
- Verify proper stoplamp switch operation using the data list of the scan tool. As the brake is applied, the data list displays the stoplamp switch on within 2.54 cm (1 in) of travel.
- Possible causes of this DTC are the following conditions:
  - An open stoplamp switch
  - The stoplamp switch is misadjusted
  - An open fuse
  - Circuit has a wiring problem, terminal corrosion, or poor connections
  - Erratic wheel speeds

Test Description

The numbers below refer to the step numbers on the diagnostic table.

3. Tests the circuit for a change in states.
5. Tests for proper operation of the circuit by bypassing the stoplamp switch. If the fuse in the jumper opens when you perform this test, the signal circuit of the stoplamp switch is shorted to ground.

Step	Action	Yes	No
1	Did you perform the ABS Diagnostic System Check?	Go to *Step 2*	Go to *Diagnostic System Check*
2	Press the brake pedal. Do the brake lamps turn ON?	Go to *Step 3*	Go to *Step 7*
3	1. Press the brake pedal. 2. With a scan tool, observe the Brake Switch Status parameter in the ABS data list. Does the Brake Switch Status parameter change state?	Go to Diagnostic Aids	Go to *Step 4*
4	1. Turn OFF the ignition. 2. Inspect the stoplamp switch and adjust and/or calibrate if needed. Did you find and correct the condition?	Go to *Step 14*	Go to *Step 5*

GC4020052712010X

Fig. 58 Codes C1291 & C1293: Open Brake Lamp Switch Contacts During Decel (Part 1 of 2). Century, Impala, Monte Carlo & Regal

Circuit Description

The PCM monitors various parameters and will not allow traction control operation if any parameter falls below a specified value.

Conditions for Running the DTC

The ignition is ON.

Conditions for Setting the DTC

The PCM detects a malfunction and then causes TCS shut down until the malfunction has been corrected.

Action Taken When the DTC Sets

- A DTC C1278 is stored (This is a temporary malfunction)
- The TCS is disabled
- The TRACTION OFF indicator is turned on
- ABS remains functional.

Conditions for Clearing the DTC

- The condition for the DTC is no longer present and the scan tool clear DTC function is used
- 100 ignition cycles have passed with no DTCs detected

Diagnostic Aids

This code is for information only. As an aid to the technician, this code indicates that there are no problems in the ABS/ETS/TCS system. Any further references for diagnostic information should be taken from Engine Controls.

Step	Action	Value(s)	Yes	No
1	Did you perform the ABS Diagnostic System Check?	—	*Powertrain On Board Diagnostic*	Go to *A Diagnostic System Check - ABS*

GC4020052065000X

Fig. 57 Code C1278: TCS Temporarily Inhibited By PCM. Century, Impala, Monte Carlo & Regal

Step	Action	Yes	No
5	1. Turn OFF the ignition. 2. Disconnect the stoplamp switch connector. 3. Connect a 3 amp fused jumper wire between the battery positive voltage circuit of the stoplamp switch and the signal circuit of the stoplamp switch. 4. Turn ON the ignition, with the engine OFF. 5. With a scan tool, observe the Brake Switch Status parameter. Does the scan tool display Applied?	Go to *Step 11*	Go to *Step 6*
6	Test the signal circuit of the stoplamp switch for an open between the splice pack of the stoplamp signal circuit and the EBCM. Did you find and correct the condition?	Go to *Step 14*	Go to *Step 10*
7	Test the battery positive voltage circuit of the stoplamp switch for a short to ground or an open. Did you find and correct the condition?	Go to *Step 14*	Go to *Step 8*
8	Test the signal circuit of the stoplamp switch for an open between the stoplamp switch and the splice of the stoplamp signal circuit. Did you find and correct the condition?	Go to *Step 14*	Go to *Step 9*
9	Test the signal circuit of the stoplamp switch for a short to ground. Did you find and correct the condition?	Go to *Step 14*	Go to *Step 10*
10	Inspect for poor connections at the harness connector of the EBCM. Did you find and correct the condition?	Go to *Step 14*	Go to *Step 12*
11	Inspect for poor connections at the harness connector of the stoplamp switch. Did you find and correct the condition?	Go to *Step 14*	Go to *Step 13*
12	Replace the EBCM. Did you complete the repair?	Go to *Step 14*	—
13	Replace the stoplamp switch. Did you complete the repair?	Go to *Step 14*	—
14	1. Use the scan tool in order to clear the DTCs. 2. Operate the vehicle within the Conditions for Running the DTC as specified in the supporting text. Does the DTC reset?	Go to *Step 2*	System OK

GC4020052712020X

Fig. 58 Codes C1291 & C1293: Open Brake Lamp Switch Contacts During Decel (Part 2 of 2). Century, Impala, Monte Carlo & Regal

Circuit Description

The stoplamp switch signal informs the EBCM when the brake pedal is pressed.

Conditions for Running the DTC

The vehicle speed is greater than 40 km/h (25 mph).

Conditions for Setting the DTC

The stoplamp switch input was active for 2 consecutive ignition cycles.

Action Taken When the DTC Sets

- The EBCM disables the TCS for the duration of the ignition cycle.
- The Traction Off indicator turns ON.
- The ABS remains functional.

Conditions for Clearing the DTC

- The condition for the DTC is no longer present (the DTC is not current) and you used the scan tool Clear DTC function.
- The EBCM automatically clears the history DTC when a current DTC is not detected in 100 consecutive drive cycles.

Diagnostic Aids

Possible causes of this DTC are the following conditions:

- The stoplamp switch circuit is shorted to voltage.
- The stoplamp switch is misadjusted.
- The stoplamp switch is stuck closed.
- A brake pedal that is binding.

Test Description

The number below refers to the step number on the diagnostic table.

2. Test for the current state of the brake lamp switch parameter.

GC4020052713010X

Fig. 59 Code C1294: Brake Lamp Switch Circuit Always Active (Part 1 of 2). Century, Impala, Monte Carlo & Regal

Step	Action	Yes	No
1	Did you perform the ABS Diagnostic System Check?	Go to *Step 2*	Go to *Diagnostic System Check*
2	1. Install a scan tool. 2. Turn ON the ignition, with the engine OFF. 3. With a scan tool, observe the Brake Switch Status parameter in the ABS data list. Does the scan tool display Released?	Go to *Step 3*	Go to *Step 4*
3	1. Press the brake pedal. 2. With a scan tool, observe the Brake Switch Status parameter. Does the Brake Switch Status parameter change state?	Go to Diagnostic Aids	Go to *Step 4*
4	1. Turn OFF the ignition. 2. Inspect the stoplamp switch and adjust and/or calibrate if needed. Did you find and correct the condition?	Go to *Step 11*	Go to *Step 5*
5	1. Turn OFF the ignition. 2. Disconnect the stoplamp switch connector. 3. Turn ON the ignition, with the engine OFF. 4. With a scan tool, observe the Brake Switch Status parameter. Does the scan tool display Released?	Go to *Step 8*	Go to *Step 6*
6	Test the stoplamp switch signal circuit for a short to voltage. Did you find and correct the condition?	Go to *Step 11*	Go to *Step 7*
7	Inspect for poor connections at the harness connector of the EBCM. Did you find and correct the condition?	Go to *Step 11*	Go to *Step 9*
8	Inspect for poor connections at the harness connector of the stoplamp switch. *Connections* and Did you find and correct the condition?	Go to *Step 11*	Go to *Step 10*
9	Replace the EBCM. Did you complete the repair?	Go to *Step 11*	—
10	Replace the stoplamp switch. Did you complete the repair?	Go to *Step 11*	—
11	1. Use the scan tool in order to clear the DTCs. 2. Operate the vehicle within the Conditions for Running the DTC as specified in the supporting text. Does the DTC reset?	Go to *Step 2*	System OK

GC4020052713020X

Fig. 59 Code C1294: Brake Lamp Switch Circuit Always Active (Part 2 of 2). Century, Impala, Monte Carlo & Regal

Step	Action	Yes	No
7	Inspect for poor connections at the harness connector of the EBCM. Did you find and correct the condition?	Go to *Step 9*	Go to *Step 8*
8	Replace the EBCM. Did you complete the replacement?	Go to *Step 9*	—
9	1. Use the scan tool in order to clear the DTCs. 2. Operate the vehicle within the Conditions for Running the DTC as specified in the supporting text. Does the DTC reset?	Go to *Step 2*	System OK

GC4020052714020X

Fig. 60 Code C1295: Brake Lamp Switch Circuit Open (Part 2 of 2). Century, Impala, Monte Carlo & Regal

Circuit Description

The EBCM sources 5 volts on the stoplamp switch signal circuit when the stoplamp switch is inactive. The voltage is supplied a ground path through the stoplamp bulbs.

Conditions for Running the DTC

The ignition is ON.

Conditions for Setting the DTC

The stoplamp switch input voltage is between 2.2 volts and 5.0 volts for 2 seconds.

Action Taken When the DTC Sets

- The EBCM disables the TCS for the duration of the ignition cycle.
- The Traction Off indicator turns ON.
- The ABS remains functional.

Conditions for Clearing the DTC

- The condition for the DTC is no longer present (the DTC is not current) and you used the scan tool Clear DTC function.
- The EBCM automatically clears the history DTC when a current DTC is not detected in 100 consecutive drive cycles.

Diagnostic Aids

Possible causes of this DTC are the following conditions:

- A signal circuit of the stoplamp switch is open.
- The stoplamp switch is misadjusted.
- Verify proper stoplamp switch operation using the data list of the scan tool. As the brake is applied, the data list displays the stoplamp switch on within 2.54 cm (1 in) of travel.
- All brake lamps are open.
- All brake lamp grounds are open.
- Circuit has a wiring problem, terminal corrosion, or poor connections.
- Loose or corroded EBCM ground or PCM ground.
- An internal EBCM problem.

Test Description

The numbers below refer to the step numbers on the diagnostic table.

3. This DTC detects an open stoplamp switch signal circuit from the stoplamp side of the splice pack to the EBCM.
4. The EBCM sources 5 volts on the stoplamp switch signal circuit. This small voltage has a ground path through the stoplamp bulbs. This DTC sets if the path to ground is open.

Step	Action	Yes	No
1	Did you perform the ABS Diagnostic System Check?	Go to *Step 2*	Go to *Diagnostic System Check*
2	1. Press the brake pedal. 2. With the scan tool, observe the Brake Switch Status parameter in the ABS data list. Does the Brake Switch Status parameter display Applied?	Go to *Step 4*	Go to *Step 3*
3	Test the signal circuit of the stoplamp switch for an open. Did you find and correct the condition?	Go to *Step 9*	Go to *Step 7*
4	Press the brake pedal. Are all of the stoplamps OFF?	Go to *Step 5*	Go to Diagnostic Aids
5	Test the feed circuit of the stoplamps for an open or high resistance. Did you find and correct the condition?	Go to *Step 9*	Go to *Step 6*
6	Test the ground circuit of the stoplamps for an open or high resistance. Did you find and correct the condition?	Go to *Step 9*	Go to Diagnostic Aids

GC4020052714010X

Fig. 60 Code C1295: Brake Lamp Switch Circuit Open (Part 1 of 2). Century, Impala, Monte Carlo & Regal

Circuit Description

The instrument cluster controls the operation of the ABS indicator. The EBCM reports the desired status of the ABS indicator via serial data messages.

Test Description

The numbers below refer to the step numbers on the diagnostic table.

3. Use the scan tool to check the normal state of the ABS indicator control circuit.
4. Ensures that the instrument panel cluster (IPC) can operate the ABS indicator.

Step	Action	Yes	No
1	Did you perform the ABS Diagnostic System Check?	Go to *Step 2*	Go to *Diagnostic System Check*
2	Inspect the EBCM ground, making sure the ground is clean and torqued to the proper specification. Did you find and correct the condition?	Go to *Step 9*	Go to *Step 3*
3	1. Install a scan tool. 2. Turn ON the ignition, with the engine OFF. 3. With a scan tool, observe the ABS Warning Lamp parameter in the ABS data list. Does the scan tool display Off?	Go to *Step 4*	Go to *Step 5*
4	1. Turn OFF the ignition. 2. Turn ON the ignition, with the engine OFF. 3. Observe the ABS indicator on the instrument panel cluster (IPC) during the displays test. Does the ABS indicator illuminate during the displays test and then turn OFF?	Go to *Intermittent and Poor Connections*	Go to *Step 6*
5	Inspect for poor connections at the harness connector of the EBCM. Did you find and correct the condition?	Go to *Step 9*	Go to *Step 7*
6	Inspect for poor connections at the harness connector of the IPC. Did you find and correct the condition?	Go to *Step 9*	Go to *Step 8*
7	Replace the EBCM. Did you complete the repair?	Go to *Step 9*	—
8	Replace the instrument panel cluster (IPC). Did you complete the repair?	Go to *Step 9*	—
9	Operate the system in order to verify the repair. Did you correct the condition?	System OK	Go to *Step 2*

GC4020052715000X

Fig. 61 ABS Indicator Always On. Century, Impala, Monte Carlo & Regal

Step	Action	Yes	No
1	Did you perform the ABS Diagnostic System Check?	Go to *Step 2*	Go to *Diagnostic System Check*
2	Inspect the EBCM ground, making sure the ground is clean and torqued to the proper specification. Did you find and correct the condition?	Go to *Step 9*	Go to *Step 3*
3	1. Install a scan tool. 2. Turn ON the ignition, with the engine OFF. 3. With a scan tool, observe the ABS Warning Lamp parameter in the ABS data list. Does the scan tool display Off?	Go to *Step 4*	Go to *Step 5*
4	1. Turn OFF the ignition. 2. Turn ON the ignition, with the engine OFF. 3. Observe the ABS indicator on the instrument panel cluster (IPC) during the displays test. Does the ABS indicator illuminate during the displays test and then turn OFF?	Go to *Intermittent and Poor Connections*	Go to *Step 6*
5	Inspect for poor connections at the harness connector of the EBCM. Did you find and correct the condition?	Go to *Step 9*	Go to *Step 7*
6	Inspect for poor connections at the harness connector of the IPC. Did you find and correct the condition?	Go to *Step 9*	Go to *Step 8*
7	Replace the EBCM. Did you complete the repair?	Go to *Step 9*	—
8	Replace the instrument panel cluster (IPC). Did you complete the repair?	Go to *Step 9*	—
9	Operate the system in order to verify the repair. Did you correct the condition?	System OK	Go to *Step 2*

GC4020052716000X

Fig. 62 ABS Indicator Inoperative. Century, Impala, Monte Carlo & Regal

Circuit Description

The Low Traction indicator is controlled by the instrument cluster via serial data messages from the EBCM. When the ABS or TCS is active for 0.5 seconds, the EBCM commands the instrument cluster to turn ON the Low Traction indicator.

The Low Traction indicator will also turn ON during the instrument cluster bulb check. When the ignition switch is turned to ON, the Low Traction indicator will turn ON for approximately 3 seconds and then turn OFF.

Test Description

The numbers below refer to the step numbers on the diagnostic table.

2. Use the scan tool to check the normal state of the Low Traction indicator control.
3. Ensures that the instrument cluster can operate the Low Traction indicator.

Step	Action	Value(s)	Yes	No
1	Did you perform the ABS Diagnostic System Check?	—	Go to *Step 2*	Go to *Diagnostic System Check*
2	1. Install a scan tool. 2. Turn ON the ignition, with the engine OFF. 3. With a scan tool, observe the ETS Active Lamp parameter in the ETS data list. Does the scan tool display Off?	—	Go to *Step 3*	Go to *Step 4*
3	1. Turn OFF the ignition. 2. Turn ON the ignition, with the engine OFF. 3. Observe the Low Traction indicator on the instrument cluster (IPC) during the bulb check. Does the Low Traction indicator illuminate during the bulb check and then turn OFF?	—	Go to *Intermittent and Poor Connections*	Go to *Step 5*
4	Inspect for poor connections at the harness connector of the EBCM. Did you find and correct the condition?	—	Go to *Step 8*	Go to *Step 6*
5	Inspect for poor connections at the harness connector of the instrument cluster (IPC). Did you find and correct the condition?	—	Go to *Step 8*	Go to *Step 7*
6	Replace the EBCM. Did you complete the repair?	—	Go to *Step 8*	—
7	Replace the instrument cluster (IPC). Did you complete the repair?	—	Go to *Step 8*	—
8	Operate the system in order to verify the repair. Did you correct the condition?	—	System OK	Go to *Step 2*

GC4020052718000X

Fig. 64 Low Traction Control Indicator Inoperative. Century, Impala, Monte Carlo & Regal

Circuit Description

The Low Traction indicator is controlled by the instrument cluster via serial data messages from the EBCM. When the ABS or TCS is active for 0.5 seconds, the EBCM commands the instrument cluster to turn ON the Low Traction indicator.

The Low Traction indicator will also turn ON during the instrument cluster bulb check. When the ignition switch is turned to ON, the Low Traction indicator will turn ON for approximately 3 seconds and then turn OFF.

Test Description

The numbers below refer to the step numbers on the diagnostic table.

2. Use the scan tool to check the normal state of the Low Traction indicator control.
3. Ensures that the instrument cluster can operate the Low Traction indicator.

Step	Action	Value(s)	Yes	No
1	Did you perform the ABS Diagnostic System Check?	—	Go to *Step 2*	Go to *Diagnostic System Check*
2	1. Install a scan tool. 2. Turn ON the ignition, with the engine OFF. 3. With a scan tool, observe the ETS Active Lamp parameter in the ETS data list. Does the scan tool display Off?	—	Go to *Step 3*	Go to *Step 4*
3	1. Turn OFF the ignition. 2. Turn ON the ignition, with the engine OFF. 3. Observe the Low Traction indicator on the instrument cluster (IPC) during the bulb check. Does the Low Traction indicator illuminate during the bulb check and then turn OFF?	—	Go to *Intermittent and Poor Connections*	Go to *Step 5*
4	Inspect for poor connections at the harness connector of the EBCM. Did you find and correct the condition?	—	Go to *Step 8*	Go to *Step 6*
5	Inspect for poor connections at the harness connector of the instrument cluster (IPC). Did you find and correct the condition?	—	Go to *Step 8*	Go to *Step 7*
6	Replace the EBCM. Did you complete the repair?	—	Go to *Step 8*	—
7	Replace the instrument cluster (IPC). Did you complete the repair?	—	Go to *Step 8*	—
8	Operate the system in order to verify the repair. Did you correct the condition?	—	System OK	Go to *Step 2*

GC4020052717000X

Fig. 63 Low Traction Control Indicator Always On. Century, Impala, Monte Carlo & Regal

Circuit Description

The Traction Off indicator is controlled by the instrument cluster via serial data messages from the EBCM. When the body control module sees the traction control switch input grounded through the momentary traction control switch, it sends a serial data message to the EBCM that tells the EBCM that the traction control switch has been pressed. The EBCM then disables traction control and sends a serial data message to the instrument cluster to turn the Traction Off indicator ON. Each time the ignition is cycled from OFF to ON, the traction control system is enabled.

The following conditions will cause the Traction Off indicator to illuminate:

- The EBCM has disabled the TCS due to a DTC.
- The driver manually disabling the TCS via the traction control switch.
- The instrument cluster bulb check. When the ignition switch is turned to ON, the Traction Off indicator will turn on for approximately 3 seconds and then turn OFF.

Test Description

The numbers below refer to the step numbers on the diagnostic table.

2. Use the scan tool to check the normal state of the Traction Off indicator control.
3. Ensures that the instrument cluster can operate the Traction Off indicator.

Step	Action	Value(s)	Yes	No
1	Did you perform the ABS Diagnostic System Check?	—	Go to *Step 2*	Go to *Diagnostic System Check*
2	1. Install a scan tool. 2. Turn ON the ignition, with the engine OFF. 3. With a scan tool, observe the TCS Warning Lamp parameter in the TCS data list (w/NW9) or ETS Warning Lamp parameter in the ETS data list (w/NW7). Does the scan tool display Off?	—	Go to *Step 3*	Go to *Step 4*
3	1. Turn OFF the ignition. 2. Turn ON the ignition, with the engine OFF. 3. Observe the Traction Off indicator on the instrument cluster (IPC) during the bulb check. Does the Traction Off indicator illuminate during the bulb check and then turn OFF?	—	Go to *Intermittent and Poor Connections*	Go to *Step 5*
4	Inspect for poor connections at the harness connector of the EBCM. Did you find and correct the condition?	—	Go to *Step 8*	Go to *Step 6*
5	Inspect for poor connections at the harness connector of the instrument cluster (IPC). Did you find and correct the condition?	—	Go to *Step 8*	Go to *Step 7*
6	Replace the EBCM. Did you complete the repair?	—	Go to *Step 8*	—
7	Replace the instrument cluster (IPC). Did you complete the repair?	—	Go to *Step 8*	—
8	Operate the system in order to verify the repair. Did you correct the condition?	—	System OK	Go to *Step 2*

GC4020052719000X

Fig. 65 Traction Indicator Always On. Century, Impala, Monte Carlo & Regal

Circuit Description

The Traction Off indicator is controlled by the instrument cluster via serial data messages from the EBCM. When the body control module sees the traction control switch input grounded through the momentary traction control switch, it sends a serial data message to the EBCM that tells the EBCM that the traction control switch has been pressed. The EBCM then disables traction control and sends a serial data message to the instrument cluster to turn the Traction Off indicator ON. Each time the ignition is cycled from OFF to ON, the traction control system is enabled.

The following conditions will cause the Traction Off indicator to illuminate:

- The EBCM has disabled the TCS due to a DTC.
- The driver manually disabling the TCS via the traction control switch.
- The instrument cluster bulb check. When the ignition switch is turned to ON, the Traction Off indicator will turn on for approximately 3 seconds and then turn OFF.

Test Description

The numbers below refer to the step numbers on the diagnostic table.

2. Use the scan tool to check the normal state of the Traction Off indicator control.
3. Ensures that the instrument cluster can operate the Traction Off indicator.

Step	Action	Value(s)	Yes	No
1	Did you perform the ABS Diagnostic System Check?	—	Go to *Step 2*	Go to *Diagnostic System Check*
2	1. Install a scan tool. 2. Turn ON the ignition, with the engine OFF. 3. With a scan tool, observe the TCS Warning Lamp parameter in the TCS data list) or ETS Warning Lamp parameter in the ETS data list (w/NW7). Does the scan tool display Off?	—	Go to *Step 3*	Go to *Step 10*
3	1. Turn OFF the ignition. 2. Turn ON the ignition, with the engine OFF. 3. Observe the Traction Off indicator on the instrument cluster (IPC) during the bulb check. Does the Traction Off indicator illuminate during the bulb check and then turn OFF?	—	Go to *Step 4*	Go to *Step 11*
4	1. Turn OFF the ignition. 2. Install a scan tool. 3. Turn ON the ignition, with the engine OFF. 4. With a scan tool, observe the TCS Switch parameter in the Body Control Module data list. 5. Activate the traction control switch. Does the TCS Switch parameter change state?	—	Go to *Intermittent and Poor Connections*	Go to *Step 5*
5	1. Turn OFF the ignition. 2. Disconnect the traction control switch connector. 3. Connect a 3 amp fused jumper from the signal circuit of the traction control switch to the ground circuit of the traction control switch. 4. Turn ON the ignition, with the engine OFF. 5. With a scan tool, observe the TCS Switch parameter. Does the scan tool display On?	—	Go to *Step 9*	Go to *Step 6*

GC4020052720010X

Fig. 66 Traction Indicator Inoperative (Part 1 of 2). Century, Impala, Monte Carlo & Regal

Step	Action	Value(s)	Yes	No
6	Test the signal circuit of the traction control switch for an open or high resistance. Did you find and correct the condition?	—	Go to *Step 16*	Go to *Step 7*
7	Test the ground circuit of the traction control switch for an open or high resistance. Did you find and correct the condition?	—	Go to *Step 16*	Go to *Step 8*
8	Inspect for poor connections at the harness connector of the body control module (BCM). Did you find and correct the condition?	—	Go to *Step 16*	Go to *Step 12*
9	Inspect for poor connections at the harness connector of the traction control switch. Did you find and correct the condition?	—	Go to *Step 16*	Go to *Step 13*
10	Inspect for poor connections at the harness connector of the EBCM. Did you find and correct the condition?	—	Go to *Step 16*	Go to *Step 14*
11	Inspect for poor connections at the harness connector of the instrument cluster (IPC). Did you find and correct the condition?	—	Go to *Step 16*	Go to *Step 15*
12	**Important:** Perform the setup procedure for the body control module. Replace the body control module (BCM). Did you complete the replacement?	—	Go to *Step 16*	—
13	Replace the traction control switch. Did you complete the replacement?	—	Go to *Step 16*	—
14	Replace the EBCM. Did you complete the repair?	—	Go to *Step 16*	—
15	Replace the instrument cluster (IPC). Did you complete the repair?	—	Go to *Step 16*	—
16	Operate the system in order to verify the repair. Did you correct the condition?	—	System OK	Go to *Step 2*

GC4020052720020X

Fig. 66 Traction Indicator Inoperative (Part 2 of 2). Century, Impala, Monte Carlo & Regal

Circuit Description

The ABS Diagnostic System Check is an organized approach to identify problems associated with the EBCM. This check must be the starting point for any EBCM complaint, and will direct you to the next logical step in diagnosing the complaint. The EBCM is a very reliable component and is not likely the cause of the malfunction. Most system complaints are linked to faulty wiring, connectors, and occasionally to components. Understanding the ABS system and using the tables correctly will reduce diagnostic time and prevent unnecessary parts replacement.

Test Description

The numbers below refer to the step numbers on the diagnostic table.

2. Lack of communication may be due to a partial malfunction of the serial data circuit or due to a total malfunction of the serial data circuit. The specified procedure will determine the particular condition.
4. The presence of DTCs which begin with "U" indicate some other module is not communicating. The specified procedure will compile all the available information before tests are performed.

Step	Action	Yes	No
1	Install a scan tool. Does the scan tool power up?	Go to Step 2	Data Link Communications
2	1. Turn ON the ignition, with the engine OFF. 2. Attempt to establish communication with the following control modules: o Dash integration module (DIM) o Electronic brake control module (EBCM) o Instrument panel cluster (IPC) o Powertrain control module (PCM) o Rear integration module (RIM) Does the scan tool communicate with all control modules?	Go to Step 3	Data Link Communications

ARM66GC000000215

Fig. 67 Diagnostic Circuit Check (Part 1 of 2). CTS

3	Select the display DTCs function on the scan tool for the following control modules: • Dash integration module (DIM) • Electronic brake control module (EBCM) • Instrument panel cluster (IPC) • Powertrain control module (PCM) • Rear integration module (RIM) Does the scan tool display any DTCs?	Go to Step 4	Antilock Brake System
4	Does the scan tool display any DTCs which begin with a "U"?	Data Link Communications	Go to Step 5
5	Does the scan tool display DTC B1000, B1004, B1007, B1009, or B1020?	Body Control System	Go to Step 6
6	Does the scan tool display DTC B1327, B1328, B1513, or B1514?	Engine Electrical	Go to Diagnostic Trouble Code (DTC)

ARM66GC000000216

Fig. 67 Diagnostic Circuit Check (Part 2 of 2). CTS

Circuit Description

The instrument cluster controls the operation of the ABS indicator. The EBCM reports the desired status of the ABS indicator via serial data messages. The ABS indicator signal circuit is a back-up reporting circuit to the serial data messages. The EBCM supplies ground through the circuit when the ABS is operating properly. When there is a problem with ABS that should turn on the ABS indicator, the EBCM opens the ABS indicator signal circuit. If there is a problem with the ABS serial data messages, the instrument cluster uses the ABS indicator signal to determine if the ABS indicator should be illuminated. Using the serial data messages and back-up circuit, the instrument cluster decides whether to turn on the ABS indicator.

Conditions for Running the DTC

The ignition is ON.

Conditions for Setting the DTC

- The ABS indicator lamp is commanded OFF.
- Voltage on the ABS indicator lamp circuit is greater than approximately 4.5 volts for 2 seconds.

Action Taken When the DTC Sets

- The ABS remains functional.
- The ABS indicator may remain OFF.

Conditions for Clearing the DTC

- The condition for the DTC is no longer present and the DTC is cleared with a scan tool.
- The EBCM automatically clears the history DTC when a current DTC is not detected in 100 consecutive drive cycles.

Diagnostic Aids

A possible cause of this DTC is a short to battery in the ABS indicator signal circuit.

Test Description

The numbers below refer to the step numbers on the diagnostic table.

2. Use the scan tool to verify the normal state of the ABS indicator signal circuit.

3. Ensure that the instrument cluster can operate the ABS indicator.

ARM66GC000000217

Fig. 68 Code C1211: ABS Serial Data Message (Part 1 of 3). CTS

Step	Action	Yes	No
1	Did you perform the ABS Diagnostic System Check?	Go to Step 2	Go to Diagnostic System Checl
2	1. Install a scan tool. 2. Turn ON the ignition, with the engine OFF. 3. With a scan tool, observe the ABS Warning Indicator parameter in the DRP/ABS/TCS data list. Does the scan tool display Off?	Go to Step 3	Go to Step 4
3	1. Turn OFF the ignition. 2. Turn ON the ignition, with the engine OFF. 3. Observe the ABS indicator on the instrument cluster (IPC) during the bulb check. Does the ABS indicator illuminate during the bulb check?	Go to Step 4	Go to Step 6
4	1. Turn OFF the ignition. 2. Disconnect the EBCM harness connector. 3. Connect the J 39700 Universal Pinout Box using the J 39700-300 Cable Adapter to the EBCM harness connector only. 4. Disconnect the instrument cluster harness connector. 5. Test the ABS indicator signal circuit for a short to voltage. Did you find and correct the condition?	Go to Step 9	Go to Step 5

ARM66GC000000218

Fig. 68 Code C1211: ABS Serial Data Message (Part 2 of 3) . CTS

5	Inspect for poor connections at the harness connector of the EBCM. Did you find and correct the condition?	Go to Step 9	Go to Step 7
6	Inspect for poor connections at the harness connector of the instrument cluster. Did you find and correct the condition?	Go to Step 9	Go to Step 8
7	**Important** Perform the setup procedure for the EBCM. An unprogrammed EBCM will result in the following conditions: • Inoperative or poorly functioning system operations • The EBCM sets DTC C1248 and DTC C1255m3. Replace the EBCM. Did you complete the repair?	Go to Step 9	--
8	Replace the instrument cluster (IPC). Did you complete the repair?	Go to Step 9	--
9	1. Use the scan tool in order to clear the DTCs. 2. Operate the vehicle within the Conditions for Running the DTC as specified in the supporting text. Does the DTC reset?	Go to Step 2	System OK

ARM66GC000000219

Fig. 68 Code C1211: ABS Serial Data Message (Part 3 of 3). CTS

Circuit Description

The system relay is energized when the ignition is ON. The system relay supplies voltage to the solenoid valves and the pump motor. This voltage is referred to as the system voltage.

The EBCM controls each solenoid valve by grounding the solenoid.

The EBCM controls the pump motor by grounding the control circuit. The pump serves 2 purposes:

- Transfers brake fluid from the brake calipers to the master cylinder reservoir during pressure decrease events.
- Transfers brake fluid from the master cylinder reservoir to the brake calipers during pressure increase events.

Conditions for Running the DTC

- The ignition is ON.
- The system relay is commanded ON.

Conditions for Setting the DTC

Both of the following conditions exist for 0.23 seconds:

- Ignition voltage is greater than 10.5 volts
- System voltage is less than 8.0 volts

Action Taken When the DTC Sets

If equipped, the following actions occur:

- The EBCM disables the ABS/DRP/TCS/VSES for the duration of the ignition cycle.
- The ABS indicator turns ON.
- The Traction Off indicator turns ON.
- The DIC displays the Service Traction System message.
- The DIC displays the Service Stability System message.
- The EBCM will also set DTC C1248.
- The red Brake warning indicator turns ON.

Conditions for Clearing the DTC

- The condition for the DTC is no longer present and the DTC is cleared with a scan tool.
- The EBCM automatically clears the history DTC when a current DTC is not detected in 100 consecutive drive cycles.

Diagnostic Aids

The system relay is integral to the EBCM. The relay is not serviceable.

ARM66GC000000220

Fig. 69 Code C1214: System Voltage (Part 1 of 2). CTS

Step	Action	Value	Yes	No
1	Did you perform the ABS Diagnostic System Check?	--	Go to Step 2	Go to Diagnostic System Check
2	1. Install a scan tool. 2. Turn ON the ignition, with the engine OFF. 3. Use the scan tool in order to clear the DTCs. 4. With the scan tool, perform the Automated Test. Does the DTC reset as a current DTC?	--	Go to Step 3	Test for Intermittent and Poor Connections
3	1. Remove the EBCM from the BPMV. Refer to Electronic Brake Control Module (EBCM) Replacement . 2. Measure the resistance between each pump motor control circuit of the BPMV and the housing of the BPMV. Does the DMM display the specified value?	OL	Go to Step 5	Go to Step 4
4	Replace the EBCM and the BPMV. Did you complete the repair?	--	Go to Step 6	--
5	Replace the EBCM. Did you complete the repair?	--	Go to Step 6	--
6	1. Use the scan tool in order to clear the DTCs. 2. With the scan tool, perform the Automated Test. Does the DTC reset?	--	Go to Step 2	System OK

ARM66GC000000221

Fig. 69 Code C1214: System Voltage (Part 2 of 2). CTS

Step	Action	Value (s)	Yes	No
1	Did you perform the ABS Diagnostic System Check?	--	Go to Step 2	Go to Diagnostic System Check -
2	1. Turn OFF the ignition. 2. Disconnect the EBCM harness connector. 3. Connect the J 39700 universal pinout box using the J 39700-300 cable adapter to the EBCM harness connector only. 4. Test both ground circuits of the EBCM including the EBCM ground for a high resistance or an open. Did you find and correct the condition?	--	Go to Step 8	Go to Step 3
3	1. Remove the EBCM from the BPMV. 2. Measure the resistance from both pump motor control circuits of the BPMV to the housing of the BPMV. Does the resistance measure less than the specified value?	5 ohms	Go to Step 4	Go to Step 5
4	Inspect for poor connections at the connector of the BPMV. Did you find and correct the condition?	--	Go to Step 8	Go to Step 6
5	Inspect for poor connections at the harness connector of the EBCM. Did you find and correct the condition?	--	Go to Step 8	Go to Step 7
6	Replace the BPMV. Did you complete the repair?	--	Go to Step 8	--
7	Replace the EBCM. Did you complete the repair?	--	Go to Step 8	--
8	1. Use the scan tool in order to clear the DTCs. 2. With the scan tool, perform the Automated Test. Does the DTC reset?	--	Go to Step 2	System OK

ARM66GC000000223

Fig. 70 Code C1217: Pump Motor Voltage Too High Or Low (Part 2 of 2). CTS

Circuit Description

The system relay is energized when the ignition is ON. The system relay supplies voltage to the solenoid valves and the pump motor. This voltage is referred to as the system voltage.

The EBCM controls each solenoid valve by grounding the solenoid.

The EBCM controls the pump motor by grounding the control circuit. The pump serves 2 purposes:

- Transfers brake fluid from the brake calipers to the master cylinder reservoir during pressure decrease events.
- Transfers brake fluid from the master cylinder reservoir to the brake calipers during pressure increase events.

Conditions for Running the DTC

- The pump motor has been commanded OFF for 1 second.
- The system voltage is greater than 9.36 volts.

Conditions for Setting the DTC

One of the following conditions exists for 0.2 seconds:

- The voltage across the pump motor is greater than 10.2 volts.
- The pump motor low side voltage is less than 2.7 volts.

Action Taken When the DTC Sets

If equipped, the following actions occur:

- The EBCM disables the DRP/ABS/TCS/VSES for the duration of the ignition cycle.
- The ABS indicator turns ON.
- The Traction Off indicator turns ON.
- The DIC displays the Service Stability System message.
- The EBCM will also set DTC C1248.
- The red Brake warning indicator turns ON.

Conditions for Clearing the DTC

- The condition for the DTC is no longer present and the DTC is cleared with a scan tool.
- The EBCM automatically clears the history DTC when a current DTC is not detected in 100 consecutive drive cycles.

Diagnostic Aids

- This DTC determines if there is a short in the pump motor control circuit.
- The pump motor is integral to the BPMV. The pump motor is not serviceable.

ARM66GC000000222

Fig. 70 Code C1217: Pump Motor Voltage Too High Or Low (Part 1 of 2). CTS

Circuit Description

The system relay is energized when the ignition is ON. The system relay supplies voltage to the solenoid valves and the pump motor. This voltage is referred to as the system voltage.

The EBCM controls each solenoid valve by grounding the solenoid.

The EBCM controls the pump motor by grounding the control circuit. The pump serves 2 purposes:

- Transfers brake fluid from the brake calipers to the master cylinder reservoir during pressure decrease events.
- Transfers brake fluid from the master cylinder reservoir to the brake calipers during pressure increase events.

Conditions for Running the DTC

- The pump motor is commanded ON.
- The system voltage is greater than 8 volts.

Conditions for Setting the DTC

One of the following conditions exists for 0.16 seconds:

- With the commanded pump motor voltage less than the system voltage, the actual pump motor voltage is 3 volts less than the commanded voltage.
- With the commanded pump motor voltage greater than the system voltage, the actual pump motor voltage is less than 8 volts.

Action Taken When the DTC Sets

If equipped, the following actions occur:

- The EBCM disables the ABS/TCS/VSES for the duration of the ignition cycle.
- The DRP does not function optimally.
- The ABS indicator turns ON.
- The Traction Off indicator turns ON.
- The DIC displays the Service Stability System message.

Conditions for Clearing the DTC

- The condition for the DTC is no longer present and the DTC is cleared with a scan tool.
- The EBCM automatically clears the history DTC when a current DTC is not detected in 100 consecutive drive cycles.

Diagnostic Aids

The pump motor is integral to the BPMV. The pump motor is not serviceable.

ARM66GC000000224

Fig. 71 Code C1218: Commanded Pump Motor Voltage Too High Or Low (Part 1 of 3). CTS

Step	Action	Value (s)	Yes	No
1	Did you perform the ABS Diagnostic System Check?	--	Go to Step 2	Go to Diagnostic System Check
2	1. Use the scan tool in order to clear the DTCs. 2. With the scan tool, perform the Automated Test. Does the DTC reset?	--	Go to Step 3	Test for Intermittent and Poor Connections
3	1. Remove the EBCM from the BPMV. 2. Inspect the EBCM to BPMV connector for conditions which could cause an intermittent, such as damage, corrosion, poor terminal contact, or presence of brake fluid. Is connector OK and cavity free of brake fluid?	--	Go to Step 5	Go to Step 4
4	1. If connector corrosion or damage is evident, replace BPMV and/or EBCM as necessary. 2. If brake fluid is present, replace both BPMV and EBCM. Did you complete the repair?	--	Go to Step 9	--
5	1. Connect the EBCM harness to the EBCM with the BPMV still separated. 2. Connect a test lamp between the pump motor circuits, internal EBCM side, using the J 35616-A Connector Test Adapter Kit . 3. With the scan tool, perform the Automated Bleed. Does the test lamp illuminate?	--	Go to Step 8	Go to Step 6
6	1. Turn OFF the ignition. 2. Disconnect the EBCM connector. 3. Connect the J 39700 universal pinout box using the J 39700-300 cable adapter to the EBCM harness connector only. 4. Test both ground circuits of the EBCM including the EBCM ground for a high resistance or an open. Did you find and correct the condition?	--	Go to Step 9	Go to Step 7

ARM66GC000000225

Fig. 71 Code C1218: Commanded Pump Motor Voltage Too High Or Low (Part 2 of 3). CTS

Circuit Description

As the wheel spins, the wheel speed sensor produces an AC signal. The EBCM uses the frequency of the AC signal to calculate the wheel speed.

Conditions for Running the DTC

C1221 through C1228

- DTCs C1232 through C1235 are not set.
- The brake pedal is not pressed.
- The ABS is not active.

C1232 through C1235

The ignition is ON.

Conditions for Setting the DTC

C1221 through C1224

All of the following conditions exists for 2.5 seconds:

- The suspect wheel speed equals zero.
- The other wheel speeds are greater than 8 km/h (5 mph).
- The other wheel speeds are within 11 km/h (7 mph) of each other.

C1225 through C1228

The EBCM detects a rapid variation in the wheel speed. The wheel speed changes by 16 km/h (10 mph) or more in 0.01 second. The change must occur 3 times with no more than 0.2 seconds between occurrences.

C1232 through C1235

One of the following conditions exists for 0.02 seconds:

- A short to voltage - the wheel speed sensor signal circuit and wheel speed sensor return circuit voltages are both greater than 4.25 volts.
- A short to ground - the wheel speed sensor signal circuit and wheel speed sensor return circuit voltages are both less than 0.75 volts.
- An open - the wheel speed sensor signal circuit voltage is greater than 4.25 volts and wheel speed sensor return circuit voltage is less than 0.75 volts.

Action Taken When the DTC Sets

If equipped, the following actions occur:

- The EBCM disables the ABS/EDC/TCS/VSES for the duration of the ignition cycle.
- The DRP does not function optimally.
- The ABS indicator turns ON.

ARM66GC000000227

Fig. 72 Codes C1221–C1235: Wheel Speed Sensors (Part 1 of 4). CTS

7	Replace the EBCM. Did you complete the repair?	--	Go to Step 9	--
8	Replace the BPMV. Did you complete the repair?	--	Go to Step 9	--
9	1. Use the scan tool in order to clear the DTCs. 2. With the scan tool, perform the Automated Test. Does the DTC reset?	--	Go to Step 2	System OK

ARM66GC000000226

Fig. 71 Code C1218: Commanded Pump Motor Voltage Too High Or Low (Part 3 of 3). CTS

Conditions for Clearing the DTC

- The condition for the DTC is no longer present and the DTC is cleared with a scan tool.
- The EBCM automatically clears the history DTC when a current DTC is not detected in 100 consecutive drive cycles.

Diagnostic Aids

C1221 through C1224

Under the following conditions, 2 Wheel Speed Sensor Input is 0 DTCs are set:

- The 2 suspect wheel speeds equal zero for 20 seconds.
- The other wheel speeds are greater than 16 km/h (10 mph).
- The other wheel speeds are within 11 km/h (7 mph) of each other.

Diagnose each wheel speed sensor individually.

C1225 through C1228

A possible cause of this DTC is electrical noise on the wheel speed sensor harness wiring. Electrical noise could result from the wheel speed sensor wires being routed to close to high energy ignition system components, such as spark plug wires.

C1232 through C1235

If the customer comments that the ABS indicator is ON only during moist environmental conditions: rain, snow, vehicle wash, etc., inspect the wheel speed sensor wiring for signs of water intrusion. If the DTC is not current, clear all DTCs and simulate the effects of water intrusion by using the following procedure:

1. Spray the suspected area with a 5 percent saltwater solution. To create a 5 percent saltwater solution, add 2 teaspoons of salt to 8 fl oz of water (10 g of salt to 200 ml of water).
2. Test drive the vehicle over various road surfaces: bumps, turns, etc., above 40 km/h (25 mph) for at least 30 seconds.
3. If the DTC returns, replace the suspected wheel speed sensor or repair the wheel speed sensor wiring.
4. Rinse the area thoroughly when completed.

Test Description

The numbers below refer to the step numbers on the diagnostic table.

4. Measures the resistance of the wheel speed sensor in order to determine if the sensor has a valid resistance value.

5. Ensures that the wheel speed sensor is generating a valid AC voltage output.

ARM66GC000000228

Fig. 72 Codes C1221–C1235: Wheel Speed Sensors (Part 2 of 4). CTS

Step	Action	Value(s)	Yes	No
1	Did you perform the ABS Diagnostic System Check?	--	Go to Step 2	Go to Diagnostic System Check
2	1. Install a scan tool. 2. Turn ON the ignition. 3. Set up the scan tool snap shot feature to trigger for this DTC. 4. Drive the vehicle at a speed greater than the specified value. Does the scan tool indicate that this wheel speed DTC set?	8 km/h (5 mph)	Go to Step 3	Test for Intermittent and Poor Connections
3	1. Raise and support the vehicle. 2. Disconnect the wheel speed sensor connector. 3. Measure the resistance across the wheel speed sensor. Does the resistance measure within the specified range?	850-1350 ohms	Go to Step 4	Go to Step 8
4	1. Spin the wheel. 2. Measure the AC voltage across the wheel speed sensor. Does the AC voltage measure greater than the specified value?	100 mV	Go to Step 5	Go to Step 8
5	Inspect for poor connections at the harness connector of the wheel speed sensor. Did you find and correct the condition?	--	Go to Step 10	Go to Step 6

ARM66GC000000229

Fig. 72 Codes C1221–C1235: Wheel Speed Sensors (Part 3 of 4). CTS

6	1. Disconnect the EBCM harness connector. 2. Install the J 39700 universal pinout box using the J 39700-300 cable adapter to the EBCM harness connector only. 3. Test the wheel speed sensor circuits for the following: o An open o A short to ground o A short to voltage o Shorted together Did you find and correct the condition?	--	Go to Step 10	Go to Step 7
7	Inspect for poor connections at the harness connector for the EBCM. Did you find and correct the condition?	--	Go to Step 10	Go to Step 9
8	Replace the wheel speed sensor. Did you complete the repair?	--	Go to Step 10	--
9	Replace the EBCM. Did you complete the repair?	--	Go to Step 10	--
10	1. Use the scan tool in order to clear the DTCs. 2. Operate the vehicle within the Conditions for Running the DTC as specified in the supporting text. Does the DTC reset?	--	Go to Step 2	System OK

ARM66GC000000230

Fig. 72 Codes C1221–C1235: Wheel Speed Sensors (Part 4 of 4). CTS

Circuit Description

The system relay is energized when the ignition is ON. The system relay supplies voltage to the solenoid valves and the pump motor. This voltage is referred to as the system voltage.

The EBCM controls each solenoid valve by grounding the solenoid.

The EBCM controls the pump motor by grounding the control circuit. The pump serves 2 purposes:

- Transfers brake fluid from the brake calipers to the master cylinder reservoir during pressure decrease events.
- Transfers brake fluid from the master cylinder reservoir to the brake calipers during pressure increase events.

Conditions for Running the DTC

C1242

- The system voltage is greater than 8.0 volts.
- The system relay is ON.
- The pump motor is commanded OFF.

C1243

- The pump motor is ON for at least 0.3 seconds.
- The system relay is ON.

Conditions for Setting the DTC

C1242

The voltage across the pump motor is between 1.7 - 10.2 volts for 2 seconds.

C1243

The pump motor is stalled or turning slowly.

ARM66GC000000231

Fig. 73 Codes C1242 & C1243: Pump Motor Circuit Or Pump Motor Stalled (Part 1 of 3). CTS

Action Taken When the DTC Sets

If equipped, the following actions occur:

- The EBCM disables the ABS/TCS/VSES for the duration of the ignition cycle.
- The DRP does not function optimally.
- The ABS indicator turns ON.
- The Traction Off indicator turns ON.
- The DIC displays the Service Stability System message.

Conditions for Clearing the DTC

- The condition for the DTC is no longer present and the DTC is cleared with a scan tool.
- The EBCM automatically clears the history DTC when a current DTC is not detected in 100 consecutive drive cycles.

Diagnostic Aids

The pump motor is integral to the BPMV. The pump motor is not serviceable.

Test Description

The number below refers to the step number on the diagnostic table.

5. Tests the ability of the EBCM to control the pump motor. If the test lamp illuminates, the pump motor circuit within the EBCM is good.

ARM66GC000000232

Fig. 73 Codes C1242 & C1243: Pump Motor Circuit Or Pump Motor Stalled (Part 2 of 3). CTS

Step	Action	Yes	No
1	Did you perform the ABS Diagnostic System Check?	Go to Step 2	Go to Diagnostic System Check
2	1. Use the scan tool in order to clear the DTCs. 2. With the scan tool, perform the Automated Test. Does the DTC reset?	Go to Step 3	Test for Intermittent and Poor Connections
3	1. Remove the EBCM from the BPMV. Refer to Electronic Brake Control Module (EBCM) Replacement . 2. Inspect the EBCM to BPMV connector for conditions which could cause an intermittent, such as damage, corrosion, poor terminal contact, or presence of brake fluid. Is the connector OK and the cavity free of brake fluid?	Go to Step 5	Go to Step 4
4	1. If connector corrosion or damage is evident, replace BPMV and/or EBCM as necessary. 2. If brake fluid is present, replace both BPMV and EBCM. Did you complete the repair?	Go to Step 8	--
5	1. Connect the EBCM harness to the EBCM with the BPMV still separated. 2. Connect a test lamp between the pump motor circuits, internal EBCM side, using the J 35616-A GM terminal test kit . 3. With the scan tool, perform the Automated Bleed. Does the test lamp illuminate?	Go to Step 7	Go to Step 6
6	Replace the EBCM. Did you complete the repair?	Go to Step 8	--
7	Replace the BPMV. Did you complete the repair?	Go to Step 8	--
8	1. Use the scan tool in order to clear the DTCs. 2. With the scan tool, perform the Automated Test. Does the DTC reset?	Go to Step 2	System OK

ARM66GC000000233

Fig. 73 Codes C1242 & C1243: Pump Motor Circuit Or Pump Motor Stalled (Part 3 of 3). CTS

Step	Action	Value (s)	Yes	No
1	Did you perform the ABS Diagnostic System Check?	--	Go to Step 2	Go to Diagnostic System Check -
2	Inspect the EBCM ground and PCM ground, making sure each ground is clean and torqued to the proper specification. Did you find and correct the condition?	--	Go to Step 10	Go to Step 3
3	1. Disconnect the EBCM harness connector. 2. Install the J 39700 universal pinout box using the J 39700-300 cable adapter to the EBCM harness connector and the EBCM connector. 3. Disconnect the powertrain control module (PCM) harness connector. 4. Turn ON the ignition, with the engine OFF. 5. Measure the voltage from the engine drag control signal circuit to a good ground. Does the voltage measure near the specified value?	B+	Go to Step 4	Go to Step 5
4	1. Turn OFF the ignition. 2. Disconnect the J 39700-300 cable adapter from the EBCM connector. 3. Turn ON the ignition, with the engine OFF. 4. Test the engine drag control signal circuit for a short to voltage. Did you find and correct the condition?	--	Go to Step 10	Go to Step 6
5	1. Turn OFF the ignition. 2. Disconnect the J 39700-300 cable adapter from the EBCM connector. 3. Test the engine drag control signal circuit for the following conditions: o An open o A short to ground o A high resistance Did you find and correct the condition?	--	Go to Step 10	Go to Step 7

ARM66GC000000235

Fig. 74 Code C1244: Engine Drag Control (DEC) Circuit (Part 2 of 3). CTS

Circuit Description

Engine drag control (EDC) The EBCM sends a engine drag control (EDC) request via a dedicated data line. The PCM supplies a pull up voltage of 5 volts that the EBCM switches to ground to create the signal.

Conditions for Running the DTC

The engine is running.

Conditions for Setting the DTC

The EBCM receives a serial data message from the PCM indicating that the EDC circuit has failed.

Action Taken When the DTC Sets

- The EBCM disables the EDC for the duration of the ignition cycle.
- The DIC displays the Service Stability System message.
- The ABS/TCS remains functional.

Conditions for Clearing the DTC

- The condition for the DTC is no longer present and the DTC is cleared with a scan tool.
- The EBCM automatically clears the history DTC when a current DTC is not detected in 100 consecutive drive cycles.

Diagnostic Aids

The following conditions can cause this concern:

- An open in the EDC control circuit.
- An short to ground or voltage in the EDC control circuit.
- A wiring problem, terminal corrosion, or poor connection in the EDC control circuit.

Test Description

The numbers below refer to the step numbers on the diagnostic table.

9. This vehicle is equipped with a PCM which uses an Electrically Erasable Programmable Read Only Memory (EEPROM). When replacing the PCM, the replacement PCM must be programmed.

ARM66GC000000234

Fig. 74 Code C1244: Engine Drag Control (DEC) Circuit (Part 1 of 3). CTS

6	Inspect for poor connections the harness connector of the PCM. Did you find and correct the condition?	-	Go to Step 10	Go to Step 8
7	Inspect for poor connections the harness connector of the EBCM. Did you find and correct the condition?	-	Go to Step 10	Go to Step 9
8	**Important** The replacement PCM must be programmed. Replace the PCM. Did you complete the repair?	-	Go to Step 10	--
9	Replace the EBCM. Did you complete the repair?	-	Go to Step 10	--
10	1. Use the scan tool in order to clear the DTCs. 2. Operate the vehicle within the Conditions for Running the DTC as specified in the supporting text. Does the DTC reset?	-	Go to Step 2	System OK

ARM66GC000000236

Fig. 74 Code C1244: Engine Drag Control (DEC) Circuit (Part 3 of 3). CTS

Circuit Description

The dynamic rear proportioning (DRP) is a control system that replaces the hydraulic proportioning function of the mechanical proportioning valve in the base brake system. The DRP control system is part of the operating software in the EBCM. The DRP uses active control with the existing ABS in order to regulate the vehicle's rear brake pressure.

Conditions for Running the DTC

One or more faults have been detected by the EBCM in the ABS/TCS systems.

Conditions for Setting the DTC

One of the following conditions exists:

- DTC C1214, C1217, C1237, C1254, C1255, C1261-1268, or C1271-1274 sets.
- DTC C1236 sets and the system voltage is less than 8.5 volts.
- Two wheel speed sensor DTCs on the same axle set.

Action Taken When the DTC Sets

- The EBCM disables the DRP for the duration of the ignition cycle.
- The red Brake warning indicator turns ON.

Conditions for Clearing the DTC

- The condition for the DTC is no longer present and the DTC is cleared with a scan tool.
- The EBCM automatically clears the history DTC when a current DTC is not detected in 100 consecutive drive cycles.

Diagnostic Aids

- Use this DTC in order to differentiate which of the following conditions is present:
  - The EBCM turned ON the red Brake warning indicator.
  - The instrument cluster turned ON the red Brake warning indicator due to low brake fluid in the master cylinder reservoir.
  - The instrument cluster turned ON the red Brake warning indicator due to the application of the park brake.
- Diagnose any other ABS DTCs that set along with this DTC.

Test Description

The number below refers to the step number on the diagnostic table.

2. Verifies whether other ABS/TCS/VSES DTCs are set.

ARM66GC000000237

Fig. 75 Code C1248: Dynamic Rear Proportioning System (Part 1 of 2). CTS

Circuit Description

The microprocessor contains a data storage area, keep alive memory, which can save pertinent data when the ignition is turned OFF. The keep alive memory (KAM) data is lost if battery power or module ground is removed from the module. The KAM area is an integral part of the microprocessor and cannot be serviced separately.

Conditions for Running the DTC

The ABS conditions and the braking conditions are normal.

Conditions for Setting the DTC

The microprocessor calculates a checksum on those areas of memory that hold critical operation data. This is done at a regular interval and is called the periodic checksum. The microprocessor also calculates a checksum on these memory locations when ever new data is written to them. This is called the running checksum.

To check the keep alive memory (KAM), the microprocessor compares the periodic checksum to the running checksum. If they do not match, the microprocessor sets the DTC.

Action Taken When the DTC Sets

If equipped, the following actions occur:

- The EBCM disables the ABS/DRP/EDC/TCS/VSES for the duration of the ignition cycle.
- The EBCM disables the variable effort steering (VES) for the duration of the ignition cycle.
- The ABS indicator turns ON.
- The Traction Off indicator turns ON.
- The DIC displays the Service Stability System message.
- The red Brake warning indicator turns ON.
- The EBCM will also set DTC C1248.
- The EBCM will not send serial data messages.
- The EBCM will not send the requested torque output to the PCM.

ARM66GC000000239

Fig. 76 Code C1254: Abnormal Shutdown Detected (Part 1 of 3). CTS

Step	Action	Yes	No
1	Did you perform the ABS Diagnostic System Check?	Go to Step 2	Go to Diagnostic System Check
2	1. Install a scan tool. 2. Turn ON the ignition, with the engine OFF. 3. Select the display DTCs function on the scan tool for the EBCM. Does the scan tool display any ABS/TCS/VSES DTCs?	Go to Diagnostic Trouble Code (DTC)	Go to Step 3
3	1. Use the scan tool in order to clear the DTCs. 2. Operate the vehicle within the Conditions for Running the DTC as specified in the supporting text. Does the DTC reset?	Go to Step 2	Test for Intermittent and Poor Connections

ARM66GC000000238

Fig. 75 Code C1248: Dynamic Rear Proportioning System (Part 2 of 2). CTS

Conditions for Clearing the DTC

- The condition for the DTC is no longer present and the DTC is cleared with a scan tool.
- The EBCM automatically clears the history DTC when a current DTC is not detected in 100 consecutive drive cycles.

Diagnostic Aids

Possible causes of this DTC are the following conditions:

- A loss of battery ground
- A disconnected battery
- A running reset A running reset is detected when the keep alive memory check sum is not updated properly.
- A sudden drop in the system voltage to less than 5 volts
- Long extended engine cranks that cause the battery voltage to drop
- Poor power or ground connections
- An internal EBCM malfunction

Test Description

The numbers below refer to the step numbers on the diagnostic table.

2. Tests for an open in the ground circuits of the body control module.

4. Verifies the proper operation of the charging system.

6. Determines whether the DTC resets.

ARM66GC000000240

Fig. 76 Code C1254: Abnormal Shutdown Detected (Part 2 of 3). CTS

Step	Action	Value (s)	Yes	No
1	Did you perform the ABS Diagnostic System Check?	--	Go to Step 2	Go to Diagnostic System Check
2	1. Turn OFF the ignition. 2. Disconnect the EBCM harness connector. 3. Install the J 39700 universal pinout box using the J 39700-300 cable adapter to the EBCM harness connector only. 4. Test the module ground circuit of the EBCM for a high resistance or an open. Did you find and correct the condition?	--	Go to Step 8	Go to Step 3
3	Has the battery been disconnected recently?	--	Go to Step 8	Go to Step 4
4	Test the charging system. Did you find and correct the condition?	--	Go to Step 8	Go to Step 5
5	Inspect for poor connections at the harness connector of the EBCM. Did you find and correct the condition?	--	Go to Step 8	Go to Step 6
6	1. Use the scan tool in order to clear the DTCs. 2. With the scan tool, perform the Automated Test. Does the DTC reset?	--	Go to Step 7	Test for Intermittent and Poor Connections
7	Replace the EBCM. Refer to Electronic Brake Control Module (EBCM) Replacement . Did you complete the repair?	--	Go to Step 8	--
8	1. Use the scan tool in order to clear the DTCs. 2. With the scan tool, perform the Automated Test. Does the DTC reset?	--	Go to Step 2	System OK

ARM66GC000000241

Fig. 76 Code C1254: Abnormal Shutdown Detected (Part 3 of 3). CTS

Step	Action	Yes	No
1	Did you perform the ABS Diagnostic System Check?	Go to Step 2	Go to Diagnostic System Check -
2	1. Install a scan tool. 2. Turn ON the ignition, with the engine OFF. 3. Use the scan tool in order to clear the DTCs. 4. With the scan tool, perform the Automated Test. Does the DTC reset as a current DTC?	Go to Step 3	Test for Intermittent and Poor Connections
3	Replace the EBCM. Did you complete the repair?	Go to Step 4	--
4	1. Use the scan tool in order to clear the DTCs. 2. With the scan tool, perform the Automated Test. Does the DTC reset?	Go to Step 2	System OK

ARM66GC000000243

Fig. 77 Codes C1255 & C1256: Internal EBCM Fault (Part 2 of 2). CTS

Circuit Description

This DTC identifies a malfunction within the EBCM.

Conditions for Running the DTC

The ABS conditions and the braking conditions are normal.

Conditions for Setting the DTC

An internal EBCM malfunction exists.

Action Taken When the DTC Sets

C1255

If equipped, the following actions occur:

- The EBCM disables the ABS/DRP/EDC/TCS/VSES for the duration of the ignition cycle.
- The EBCM disables the variable effort steering (VES) for the duration of the ignition cycle.
- The ABS indicator turns ON.
- The Traction Off indicator turns ON.
- The red Brake warning indicator turns ON.
- The DIC displays the Service Stability System message.
- The EBCM will also set DTC C1248.

C1256

- The ABS remains functional.
- The ABS indicator remains OFF.

Conditions for Clearing the DTC

- The condition for the DTC is no longer present and the DTC is cleared with a scan tool.
- The EBCM automatically clears the history DTC when a current DTC is not detected in 100 consecutive drive cycles.

Diagnostic Aids

The scan tool displays 2 additional characters after the DTC. Take note of the 2 character code and any other DTCs that are set. The 2 character code is an engineering aid used in order to determine the cause of the internal malfunction.

Test Description

The number below refers to the step number on the diagnostic table.

2. Determines whether the DTC is current.

ARM66GC000000242

Fig. 77 Codes C1255 & C1256: Internal EBCM Fault (Part 1 of 2). CTS

Circuit Description

The system relay is energized when the ignition is ON. The system relay supplies voltage to the valve solenoids and the pump motor. This voltage is referred to as the system voltage. The EBCM microprocessor activates the valve solenoids by grounding the control circuit.

Conditions for Running the DTC

- The system voltage is greater than 8 volts.
- The ignition voltage is greater than 9 volts.

Conditions for Setting the DTC

The commanded state of the driver and the actual state of the control circuit do not match for 0.03 seconds.

Action Taken When the DTC Sets

If equipped, the following actions occur:

- The EBCM disables the DRP/ABS/TCS/VSES for the duration of the ignition cycle.
- The ABS indicator turns ON.
- The Traction Off indicator turns ON.
- The DIC displays the Service Stability System message.
- The EBCM will also set DTC C1248.
- The red Brake warning indicator turns ON.

Conditions for Clearing the DTC

- The condition for the DTC is no longer present and the DTC is cleared with a scan tool.
- The EBCM automatically clears the history DTC when a current DTC is not detected in 100 consecutive drive cycles.

Diagnostic Aids

The solenoid valve circuit is internal to the EBCM. The solenoid valve circuit is not diagnosable external to the EBCM. The DTC sets when there is a malfunction in the solenoid circuit internal to the EBCM.

Test Description

The number below refers to the step number on the diagnostic table.

2. Determines whether the DTC is current.

ARM66GC000000244

Fig. 78 Codes C1261–C1274: System Relay (Part 1 of 2). CTS

Step	Action	Yes	No
Schematic Reference: ABS Schematics			
1	Did you perform the ABS Diagnostic System Check?	Go to Step 2	Go to Diagnostic System Check -
2	1. Install a scan tool. 2. Turn ON the ignition, with the engine OFF. 3. Use the scan tool in order to clear the DTCs. 4. With the scan tool, perform the Automated Test. Does the DTC reset as a current DTC?	Go to Step 3	Test for Intermittent and Poor Connections
3	Replace the EBCM. Did you complete the repair?	Go to Step 4	--
4	1. Use the scan tool in order to clear the DTCs. 2. With the scan tool, perform the Automated Test. Does the DTC reset?	Go to Step 2	System OK

ARM66GC000000245

Fig. 78 Codes C1261–C1274: System Relay (Part 2 of 2). CTS

Action Taken When the DTC Sets

- The EBCM disables the EDC/TCS for the duration of the ignition cycle.
- The PCM will store conditions which were present when the DTC set as Fail Records data only.
- The Traction Off indicator turns ON.
- The ABS remains functional.

Conditions for Clearing the DTC

- The condition for the DTC is no longer present and you used the scan tool Clear DTC function.
- The EBCM automatically clears the history DTC when a current DTC is not detected in 100 consecutive drive cycles.
- The PCM automatically clears the history DTC when a current DTC is not detected in 40 consecutive warm-up cycles.

Diagnostic Aids

The following conditions can cause this concern:

- An open in the delivered torque circuit.
- An short to ground or voltage in the delivered torque circuit.
- A wiring problem, terminal corrosion, or poor connection in the delivered torque circuit.
- A communication frequency problem.
- A communication duty cycle problem.
- The EBCM is not receiving information from the PCM.
- Loose or corroded EBCM ground or PCM ground.

Test Description

The numbers below refer to the step numbers on the diagnostic table.

3. Use the scan tool in order to determine if the delivered torque signal has a valid duty cycle.

9. This vehicle is equipped with a PCM which uses an Electrically Erasable Programmable Read Only Memory (EEPROM). When replacing the PCM, the replacement PCM must be programmed.

ARM66GC000000247

Fig. 79 Codes C1276, P1644 & P1689: Delivered Torque Signal Circuit Fault (Part 2 of 4). CTS

Circuit Description

The EBCM and the PCM simultaneously control the traction control. The PCM reduces the amount of torque supplied to the drive wheels by retarding spark timing and selectively turning off fuel injectors. The EBCM actively applies the brakes to the front wheels in order to reduce torque.

The EBCM sends a requested torque message via a pulse width modulated (PWM) signal to the PCM. The duty cycle of the signal is used to determine how much engine torque the EBCM is requesting the PCM to deliver. Normal values are between 10 and 90 percent duty cycle. The signal should be at 90 percent when traction control is not active and at lower values during traction control activations. The PCM supplies a pull up voltage of 5 volts that the EBCM switches to ground to create the signal.

The PCM sends a delivered torque message via a pulse width modulated (PWM) signal to the EBCM. The duty cycle of the signal is used to determine how much engine torque the PCM is delivering. Normal values are between 10 and 90 percent duty cycle. The signal should be at low values (around 10 percent) at idle and higher values under driving conditions. The EBCM supplies a pull up voltage of 12 volts that the PCM switches to ground to create the signal.

When certain PCM DTCs are set, the PCM will not be able to perform the torque reduction portion of traction control. A serial data message is sent to the EBCM indicating that traction control is not allowed.

Conditions for Running the DTC

The engine is running.

Conditions for Setting the DTC

C1276

One of the following conditions exists:

- The EBCM detects that delivered torque signal is out of the valid range.
- The EBCM does not receive the delivered torque signal.

P1644 or P1689

The PCM detects that the delivered torque signal voltage is invalid.

ARM66GC000000246

Fig. 79 Codes C1276, P1644 & P1689: Delivered Torque Signal Circuit Fault (Part 1 of 4). CTS

Step	Action	Value (s)	Yes	No
1	Did you perform the ABS Diagnostic System Check?	--	Go to Step 2	Go to Diagnostic System Check
2	Inspect the EBCM ground and PCM ground, making sure each ground is clean and torqued to the proper specification. Did you find and correct the condition?	--	Go to Step 11	Go to Step 3
3	1. Install a scan tool. 2. Start the engine. 3. With a scan tool, observe the Delivered Torque PWM Duty Cycle parameter in the DRP/ABS/TCS data list. Does the scan tool display the specified value?	90%	Go to Step 4	Test for Intermittent and Poor Connections
4	1. Turn OFF the ignition. 2. Disconnect the EBCM harness connector. 3. Install the J 39700 universal pinout box using the J 39700-300 cable adapter to the EBCM harness connector and the EBCM connector. 4. Disconnect the powertrain control module (PCM) harness connector. 5. Turn ON the ignition, with the engine OFF. 6. Measure the voltage from the delivered torque signal circuit to a good ground. Does the voltage measure near the specified value?	B+	Go to Step 5	Go to Step 6
5	1. Turn OFF the ignition. 2. Disconnect the J 39700-300 cable adapter from the EBCM connector. 3. Turn ON the ignition, with the engine OFF. 4. Test the delivered torque signal circuit for a short to voltage. Did you find and correct the condition?	--	Go to Step 11	Go to Step 7

ARM66GC000000248

Fig. 79 Codes C1276, P1644 & P1689: Delivered Torque Signal Circuit Fault (Part 3 of 4). CTS

6	1. Turn OFF the ignition. 2. Disconnect the J 39700-300 cable adapter from the EBCM connector. 3. Test the delivered torque signal circuit for the following conditions: o An open o A short to ground o A high resistance Did you find and correct the condition?	-	Go to Step 11	Go to Step 8
7	Inspect for poor connections the harness connector of the PCM. Did you find and correct the condition?	-	Go to Step 11	Go to Step 9
8	Inspect for poor connections the harness connector of the EBCM. Did you find and correct the condition?	-	Go to Step 11	Go to Step 10
9	**Important** The replacement PCM must be programmed. Replace the PCM. Did you complete the repair?	-	Go to Step 11	--
10	Replace the EBCM. Did you complete the repair?	-	Go to Step 11	--
11	1. Use the scan tool in order to clear the DTCs. 2. Operate the vehicle within the Conditions for Running the DTC as specified in the supporting text. Does the DTC reset?	-	Go to Step 2	System OK

ARM66GC000000249

Fig. 79 Codes C1276, P1644 & P1689: Delivered Torque Signal Circuit Fault (Part 4 of 4). CTS

Conditions for Clearing the DTC

- The condition for the DTC is no longer present and you used the scan tool Clear DTC function
- The EBCM automatically clears the history DTC when a current DTC is not detected in 100 consecutive drive cycles.
- The PCM automatically clears the history DTC when a current DTC is not detected in 40 consecutive warm-up cycles.

Diagnostic Aids

The following conditions can cause this concern:

- An open in the delivered torque circuit.
- An short to ground or voltage in the delivered torque circuit.
- A wiring problem, terminal corrosion, or poor connection in the delivered torque circuit.
- A communication frequency problem.
- A communication duty cycle problem.
- The EBCM is not receiving information from the PCM.
- Loose or corroded EBCM ground or PCM ground.

Test Description

The numbers below refer to the step numbers on the diagnostic table.

3. Use the scan tool in order to determine if the requested torque signal has a valid duty cycle.
4. Measure the requested torque signal in order to determine if the signal has a valid duty cycle.
5. Measure the requested torque signal in order to determine if the signal has a valid frequency.
11. This vehicle is equipped with a PCM which uses an Electrically Erasable Programmable Read Only Memory (EEPROM). When replacing the PCM, the replacement PCM must be programmed.

ARM66GC000000483

Fig. 80 Codes C1277 & P0856: Requested Torque Signal Circuit Fault (Part 2 of 5). CTS

Circuit Description

The EBCM and the PCM simultaneously control the traction control. The PCM reduces the amount of torque supplied to the drive wheels by retarding spark timing and selectively turning off fuel injectors. The EBCM actively applies the brakes to the front wheels in order to reduce torque.

The EBCM sends a requested torque message via a pulse width modulated (PWM) signal to the PCM. The duty cycle of the signal is used to determine how much engine torque the EBCM is requesting the PCM to deliver. Normal values are between 10 and 90 percent duty cycle. The signal should be at 90 percent when traction control is not active and at lower values during traction control activations. The PCM supplies a pull up voltage of 5 volts that the EBCM switches to ground to create the signal.

The PCM sends a delivered torque message via a pulse width modulated (PWM) signal to the EBCM. The duty cycle of the signal is used to determine how much engine torque the PCM is delivering. Normal values are between 10 and 90 percent duty cycle. The signal should be at low values (around 10 percent) at idle and higher values under driving conditions. The EBCM supplies a pull up voltage of 12 volts that the PCM switches to ground to create the signal.

When certain PCM DTCs are set, the PCM will not be able to perform the torque reduction portion of traction control. A serial data message is sent to the EBCM indicating that traction control is not allowed.

Conditions for Running the DTC

The engine is running.

Conditions for Setting the DTC

C1277

The PCM diagnoses the requested torque signal circuit and sends a serial data message to the EBCM indicating that a fault is present.

Action Taken When the DTC Sets

- The EBCM disables the EDC/TCS for the duration of the ignition cycle.
- The Traction Off indicator turns ON.
- The ABS remains functional.

ARM66GC000000482

Fig. 80 Codes C1277 & P0856: Requested Torque Signal Circuit Fault (Part 1 of 5). CTS

Step	Action	Value (s)	Yes	No
1	Did you perform the ABS Diagnostic System Check?	--	Go to Step 2	Go to Diagnostic System Check
2	Inspect the EBCM ground and PCM ground, making sure each ground is clean and torqued to the proper specification. Refer to Circuit Testing and Wiring Repairs in Wiring Systems. Did you find and correct the condition?	--	Go to Step 13	Go to Step 3
3	1. Install a scan tool. 2. Start the engine. 3. With a scan tool, observe the Torque Request Signal parameter in the Powertrain Control Module data list. Does the scan display less than the specified value?	100%	Test for Intermittent and Poor Connections	Go to Step 4
4	1. Turn OFF the ignition. 2. Disconnect the EBCM harness connector. 3. Install the J 39700 universal breakout box using the J 39700-300 cable adapter to the EBCM harness connector and the EBCM connector. 4. Start the engine. 5. Measure the DC duty cycle between the requested torque signal circuit and a good ground. Is the duty cycle within the specified range?	5-95%	Go to Step 5	Go to Step 6
5	Measure the DC frequency between the requested torque signal circuit and a good ground. Does the frequency measure within the specified range?	121-134 Hz	Go to Step 8	Go to Step 6

ARM66GC000000484

Fig. 80 Codes C1277 & P0856: Requested Torque Signal Circuit Fault (Part 3 of 5). CTS

5	Measure the DC frequency between the requested torque signal circuit and a good ground. Does the frequency measure within the specified range?	121-134 Hz	Go to Step 8	Go to Step 6
6	1. Turn OFF the ignition. 2. Disconnect the J 39700-300 cable adapter from the EBCM connector. 3. Turn ON the ignition, with the engine OFF. 4. Measure the voltage from the requested torque signal circuit to a good ground. Does the voltage measure within the specified range?	4-6 V	Go to Step 10	Go to Step 7
7	1. Turn OFF the ignition. 2. Disconnect the powertrain control module (PCM) harness connector. 3. Test the requested torque signal circuit for the following conditions: o A short to voltage o A short to ground Did you find and correct the condition?	--	Go to Step 13	Go to Step 10
8	1. Turn OFF the ignition. 2. Disconnect the powertrain control module (PCM) harness connector. 3. Test the requested torque signal circuit for the following conditions: o An open o A high resistance Did you find and correct the condition?	--	Go to Step 13	Go to Step 9

ARM66GC000000485

Fig. 80 Codes C1277 & P0856: Requested Torque Signal Circuit Fault (Part 4 of 5). CTS

Circuit Description

The EBCM and the PCM simultaneously control the traction control. The PCM reduces the amount of torque supplied to the drive wheels by retarding spark timing and selectively turning off fuel injectors. The EBCM actively applies the brakes to the front wheels in order to reduce torque.

The EBCM sends a requested torque message via a pulse width modulated (PWM) signal to the PCM. The duty cycle of the signal is used to determine how much engine torque the EBCM is requesting the PCM to deliver. Normal values are between 10 and 90 percent duty cycle. The signal should be at 90 percent when traction control is not active and at lower values during traction control activations. The PCM supplies a pull up voltage of 5 volts that the EBCM switches to ground to create the signal.

The PCM sends a delivered torque message via a pulse width modulated (PWM) signal to the EBCM. The duty cycle of the signal is used to determine how much engine torque the PCM is delivering. Normal values are between 10 and 90 percent duty cycle. The signal should be at low values (around 10 percent) at idle and higher values under driving conditions. The EBCM supplies a pull up voltage of 12 volts that the PCM switches to ground to create the signal.

When certain PCM DTCs are set, the PCM will not be able to perform the torque reduction portion of traction control. A serial data message is sent to the EBCM indicating that traction control is not allowed.

Conditions for Running the DTC

The ignition is ON.

Conditions for Setting the DTC

The PCM diagnoses a condition preventing the engine control portion of the traction control function and sends a serial data message to the EBCM indicating that torque reduction is not allowed. The PCM will typically set a DTC and the EBCM will set this DTC.

Action Taken When the DTC Sets

- The EBCM disables the EDC/TCS for the duration of the ignition cycle.
- The Traction Off indicator turns ON.
- The ABS remains functional.

Conditions for Clearing the DTC

- The condition for the DTC is no longer present and the DTC is cleared with a scan tool.
- The EBCM automatically clears the history DTC when a current DTC is not detected in 100 consecutive drive cycles.

Diagnostic Aids

This DTC is for information only. As an aid to the technician, this DTC indicates that there are no problems in the ABS/TCS system.

ARM66GC000000487

Fig. 81 Code C1278: Traction Control Torque Reduction Is Not Allowed (Part 1 of 2). CTS

9	Inspect for poor connections the harness connector of the PCM. Did you find and correct the condition?	-	Go to Step 13	Go to Step 11
10	Inspect for poor connections the harness connector of the EBCM. Did you find and correct the condition?	-	Go to Step 13	Go to Step 12
11	**Important** The replacement PCM must be programmed. Replace the PCM. Did you complete the repair?	-	Go to Step 13	--
12	Replace the EBCM. Did you complete the repair?	-	Go to Step 13	--
13	1. Use the scan tool in order to clear the DTCs. 2. Operate the vehicle within the Conditions for Running the DTC as specified in the supporting text. Does the DTC reset?	-	Go to Step 2	System OK

ARM66GC000000486

Fig. 80 Codes C1277 & P0856: Requested Torque Signal Circuit Fault (Part 5 of 5). CTS

Step	Action	Value (s)	Yes	No
1	Did you perform the ABS Diagnostic System Check?	--	Engine Control Module (ECM)	Go to Diagnostic System Check -

ARM66GC000000488

Fig. 81 Code C1278: Traction Control Torque Reduction Is Not Allowed (Part 2 of 2). CTS

Circuit Description

The vehicle stability enhancement system (VSES) adds an additional level of vehicle control to the EBCM.

Yaw rate is the rate of rotation about the vehicle's vertical axis. The VSES is activated when the EBCM determines that the desired yaw rate does not match the actual yaw rate as measured by the yaw rate sensor.

The desired yaw rate is calculated from the following parameters:

- The position of the steering wheel
- The speed of the vehicle
- The lateral, or sideways, acceleration of the vehicle

The difference between the desired yaw rate and the actual yaw rate is the yaw rate error, which is a measurement of oversteer or understeer. If the yaw rate error becomes too large, the EBCM attempts to correct the vehicle's yaw motion by applying differential braking to the appropriate wheel. The amount of differential braking applied is based on both the yaw rate error and side slip rate error.

The VSES activations generally occur during aggressive driving, in turns or on bumpy roads without much use of the accelerator pedal. When braking during VSES activation, the pedal pulsations feel different than the ABS pedal pulsations. The brake pedal pulsates at a higher frequency during VSES activation.

The usable output voltage range for the lateral accelerometer and yaw rate sensors is 0.25-4.75 volts. The scan tool will report zero lateral acceleration or yaw rate as 2.5 volts with no sensor bias present. The sensor bias compensates for sensor mounting alignment errors, electronic signal errors, temperature changes, and manufacturing differences.

The steering wheel position sensor supplies two analog inputs to the EBCM. The two input signals are approximately 90 degrees out of phase. By interpreting the relationship between the two inputs, the EBCM can determine the position of the steering wheel and the direction of steering wheel rotation.

Steer angle centering is the process by which the EBCM calibrates the steering sensor output so that the output reads zero when the steering wheel is centered. Using the yaw rate input, lateral accelerometer input, and wheel speed sensor inputs, the initial steering center position is calculated after driving faster than 10 km/h (6 mph) for more than 10 seconds in a straight line on a level surface.

Conditions for Running the DTC

C1281

- The steer angle has been centered.
- The VSES is active.
- The direction (understeer or oversteer) of the delta velocity error has not changed.
- The centered lateral acceleration value is less than 0.5 g.
- The yaw rate error is less than 6 degrees/second.

ARM66GC000000489

Fig. 82 Codes C1281, C1283 & C1286: Steering Sensor Circuit (Part 1 of 4). CTS

Conditions for Running the DTC

C1281

- The steer angle has been centered.
- The VSES is active.
- The direction (understeer or oversteer) of the delta velocity error has not changed.
- The centered lateral acceleration value is less than 0.5 g.
- The yaw rate error is less than 6 degrees/second.
- The side slip error is greater than 1.8 meters/second*second.

C1283

The vehicle speed is greater than 40 km/h (25 mph).

C1286

The steer angle has been centered.

Conditions for Setting the DTC

C1281

One of the following conditions exists:

- The VSES is engaged for 10 seconds with a constant understeer or oversteer condition. Under this condition, this DTC will set by itself.
- The yaw rate error is greater than 10 degrees/second for 5 seconds. Under this condition, this DTC will set along with DTC C1282.
- The yaw rate error is greater than 10 degrees/second with the vehicle speed less than 60 km/h (37 mph) and the acceleration pedal is pressed more than 25 percent of the pedal travel range for 1 second during the VSES activation. Under this condition, this DTC will set along with DTC C1282.
- With the yaw rate less than 8 degrees/second, the side slip error is greater than 4.9 meters/second^2 for 5 seconds. Under this condition, this DTC will set along with DTC C1284.
- With the steer rate less than 80 degrees/second, the difference between the 2 steering sensor signals (Phase A and Phase B) is greater than 20 degrees for 1 second. Under this condition, this DTC will set along with DTC C1287.

C1283

The vehicle has been driven for 10 minutes without completing steer angle centering.

C1286

The steering sensor bias moves more than 40 degrees after steer centering was accomplished.

ARM66GC000000490

Fig. 82 Codes C1281, C1283 & C1286: Steering Sensor Circuit (Part 2 of 4). CTS

Step	Action	Value (s)	Yes	No
1	Did you perform the ABS Diagnostic System Check?	--	Go to Step 2	Go to Diagnostic System Check
2	1. Install a scan tool. 2. Turn ON the ignition, with the engine OFF. 3. With the scan tool, perform the Steering Position Sensor Test. Did the SWPS pass the test?	--	Go to Step 3	Go to Step 7
3	With a scan tool, observe the Lateral Accelerometer Input parameter in the VSES data list. Does the scan tool display within the specified range?	2.3-2.7 V	Go to Step 4	Go to Step 8
4	With a scan tool, observe the Yaw Rate Sensor Input parameter in the VSES data list. Does the scan tool display within the specified range?	2.3-2.7 V	Go to Step 5	Go to Step 9
5	1. Use the scan tool in order to clear the DTCs. 2. Perform the Diagnostic Test Drive. Does the DTC reset?	--	Go to Step 6	Go to Diagnostic Aids
6	Replace the EBCM. Did you complete the repair?	--	Go to Step 10	--
7	Replace the steering wheel position sensor (SWPS). Did you complete the replacement?	--	Go to Step 10	--
8	Replace the lateral accelerometer sensor. Did you complete the replacement?	--	Go to Step 10	--
9	Replace the yaw rate sensor. Did you complete the replacement?	--	Go to Step 10	--
10	1. Use the scan tool in order to clear the DTCs. 2. Operate the vehicle within the Conditions for Running the DTC as specified in the supporting text. Does the DTC reset?	--	Go to Step 2	System OK

ARM66GC000000492

Fig. 82 Codes C1281, C1283 & C1286: Steering Sensor Circuit (Part 4 of 4). CTS

Action Taken When the DTC Sets

- The EBCM disables the VSES for the duration of the ignition cycle.
- The DIC displays the Service Stability System message.
- The ABS/TCS remains functional.

Conditions for Clearing the DTC

- The condition for the DTC is no longer present (the DTC is not current) and you used the scan tool Clear DTC function.
- The condition for the DTC is no longer present (the DTC is not current) and you used the On-Board Diagnostics Clear DTC function.
- The EBCM automatically clears the history DTC when a current DTC is not detected in 100 consecutive drive cycles.

Diagnostic Aids

- During diagnosis, park the vehicle on a level surface.
- Check the vehicle for proper alignment. The car should not pull in either direction while driving straight on a level surface.
- Find out from the driver under what conditions the DTC was set (when the DIC displayed the Service Stability System message). This information will help to duplicate the failure.
- The Snapshot function on the scan tool can help find an intermittent DTC.

Test Description

The numbers below refer to the step numbers on the diagnostic table.

2. Perform the Steering Position Sensor Test in order to verify that the steering wheel position sensor (SWPS) is operating properly.
3. Verify that the lateral accelerometer input parameter is within the valid range.
4. Verify that the yaw rate input parameter is within the valid range.

ARM66GC000000491

Fig. 82 Codes C1281, C1283 & C1286: Steering Sensor Circuit (Part 3 of 4). CTS

Circuit Description

The vehicle stability enhancement system (VSES) is activated by the EBCM calculating the desired yaw rate and comparing it to the actual yaw rate input. The desired yaw rate is calculated from measured steering wheel position, vehicle speed, and lateral acceleration. The difference between the desired yaw rate and actual yaw rate is the yaw rate error, which is a measurement of oversteer or understeer. If the yaw rate error becomes too large, the EBCM will attempt to correct the vehicle's yaw motion by applying differential braking to the left or right front wheel.

The amount of differential braking applied to the left or right front wheel is based on both the yaw rate error and side slip rate error. The side slip rate error is a function of the lateral acceleration minus the product of the yaw rate and vehicle speed. The yaw rate error and side slip rate error are combined to produce the total delta velocity error. When the delta velocity error becomes too large and the VSES system activates, the driver's steering inputs combined with the differential braking will attempt to bring the delta velocity error toward zero.

The VSES activations generally occur during aggressive driving, in the turns or bumpy roads without much use of the accelerator pedal. When braking during VSES activation, the brake pedal will feel different than the ABS pedal pulsation. The brake pedal pulsates at a higher frequency during VSES activation.

The usable output voltage range for the lateral accelerometer and yaw rate sensors is 0.25-4.75 volts. The scan tool will report zero lateral acceleration or yaw rate as 2.5 volts with no sensor bias present. The sensor bias compensates for sensor mounting alignment errors, electronic signal errors, temperature changes, and manufacturing differences.

The steering wheel position sensor supplies 2 analog inputs, Phase A and Phase B, to the EBCM. The 2 input signals are approximately 90 degrees out of phase. By interpreting the relationship between the 2 inputs, the EBCM can determine the position of the steering wheel and the direction of steering wheel rotation.

Steer angle centering is the process by which the EBCM calibrates the steering sensor output so that the output reads zero when the steering wheel is centered. Using the yaw rate input, lateral accelerometer input, and wheel speed sensor inputs, the initial steering center position is calculated after driving greater than 10 km/h (6 mph) for more than 10 seconds in a straight line on a level surface.

Conditions for Running the DTC

The EBCM performs 6 different tests to detect a DTC condition. The numbers below correspond to the numbers in Conditions for Setting the DTC.

1. The yaw rate sensor bias test runs with the ignition ON.
2. The yaw rate sensor acceleration test runs with the ignition ON.
3. The yaw rate sensor circuit test runs with the vehicle stopped or with the vehicle speed greater than 45 km/h (28 mph).
4. The yaw rate isolation test runs with the following conditions:
   - The brake pedal is not pressed.
   - The ABS is not active.

ARM66GC000000493

Fig. 83 Code C1282: YAW Rate Input Error (Part 1 of 6). CTS

Conditions for Running the DTC

The EBCM performs 6 different tests to detect a DTC condition. The numbers below correspond to the numbers in Conditions for Setting the DTC.

1. The yaw rate sensor bias test runs with the ignition ON.
2. The yaw rate sensor acceleration test runs with the ignition ON.
3. The yaw rate sensor circuit test runs with the vehicle stopped or with the vehicle speed greater than 45 km/h (28 mph).
4. The yaw rate isolation test runs with the following conditions:
   - The brake pedal is not pressed.
   - The ABS is not active.
   - The vehicle speed is greater than 5 km/h (3 mph).
5. The above yaw rate isolation test run with the VSES active.
6. The false activation test runs with the VSES active.

Conditions for Setting the DTC

The EBCM performs 6 different tests to detect a DTC condition. The numbers below correspond to the numbers in Conditions for Running the DTC.

1. The yaw rate bias is greater than 7 degrees/second.
2. The yaw rate input change is greater than 390 degrees/second/second.
3. The yaw rate input voltage is less than 0.15 volts or greater than 4.85 volts for 1 second.
4. The yaw rate error is greater than 10 degrees/second 30 times within a drive cycle.
5. The yaw rate error is greater than 10 degrees/second for 5 seconds. Under this condition, this DTC will set along with DTC C1281.
6. The yaw rate error is greater than 10 degrees/second with the vehicle speed less than 60 km/h (37 mph) and the acceleration pedal is pressed more than 25 percent of the pedal travel range for 1 second during the VSES activation. Under this condition, this DTC will set along with DTC C1281.

Action Taken When the DTC Sets

- The EBCM disables the VSES for the duration of the ignition cycle.
- The DIC displays the Service Stability System message.
- The ABS/TCS remains functional.

Conditions for Clearing the DTC

- The condition for the DTC is no longer present (the DTC is not current) and you used the scan tool Clear DTC function.
- The condition for the DTC is no longer present (the DTC is not current) and you used the On-Board Diagnostics Clear DTC function.
- The EBCM automatically clears the history DTC when a current DTC is not detected in 100 consecutive drive cycles.

ARM66GC000000494

Fig. 83 Code C1282: YAW Rate Input Error (Part 2 of 6). CTS

Step	Action	Values	Yes	No
1	Did you perform the ABS Diagnostic System Check?	--	Go to Step 2	Go to Diagnostic System Check -
2	1. Install a scan tool. 2. Turn ON the ignition, with the engine OFF. 3. With a scan tool, observe the Yaw Rate Sensor Input parameter in the VSES data list. Does the scan tool display that the Yaw Rate Sensor Input parameter is within the specified range?	0.15-4.85 V	Go to Step 6	Go to Step 3
3	1. Turn OFF the ignition. 2. Disconnect the yaw rate sensor connector. 3. Turn ON the ignition, with the engine OFF. 4. With the scan tool, observe the Yaw Rate Sensor Input parameter. Does the scan tool display that the Yaw Rate Sensor Input parameter is less than the specified value?	0.15 V	Go to Step 4	Go to Step 10
4	1. Turn OFF the ignition. 2. Connect a 3 amp fused jumper wire between the 5 volt reference circuit of the yaw rate sensor and the signal circuit of the yaw rate sensor. 3. Turn ON the ignition, with the engine OFF. 4. With the scan tool, observe the Yaw Rate Sensor Input parameter. Does the scan tool display that the Yaw Rate Sensor Input parameter is greater than the specified value?	4.85 V	Go to Step 5	Go to Step 8
5	1. Disconnect the fused jumper wire. 2. Measure the voltage between the 5 volt reference circuit of the yaw rate sensor and the low reference circuit of the yaw rate sensor. Does the voltage measure less the specified value?	5 V	Go to Step 12	Go to Step 7
6	Does the scan tool display that the Yaw Rate Sensor Input parameter is within the specified range?	2.3-2.7 V	Go to Diagnostic Aids	Go to Step 11
7	Test the 5 volt reference circuit of the yaw rate sensor for a short to voltage. Did you find and correct the condition?	--	Go to Step 16	Go to Step 13

ARM66GC000000496

Fig. 83 Code C1282: YAW Rate Input Error (Part 4 of 6). CTS

Diagnostic Aids

- During diagnosis, park the vehicle on a level surface.
- Check the vehicle for proper alignment. The car should not pull in either direction while driving straight on a level surface.
- Find out from the driver under what conditions the DTC was set (when the DIC displayed the Service Stability System message). This information will help to duplicate the failure.
- The Snapshot function on the scan tool can help find an intermittent DTC.

Test Description

The numbers below refer to the step numbers on the diagnostic table.

3. Tests for the proper operation of the circuit in the low voltage range.

4. Tests for the proper operation of the circuit in the high voltage range. If the fuse in the jumper opens when you perform this test, the signal circuit is shorted to ground.

5. Tests for a short to voltage in the 5 volt reference circuit.

6. Tests the bias voltage of the yaw rate sensor.

ARM66GC000000495

Fig. 83 Code C1282: YAW Rate Input Error (Part 3 of 6). CTS

8	Test the 5 volt reference circuit of the yaw rate sensor for the following conditions: • An open • A short to ground • A high resistance Did you find and correct the condition?	-	Go to Step 16	Go to Step 9
9	Test the signal circuit of the yaw rate sensor for the following conditions: • An open • A short to ground • A high resistance Did you find and correct the condition?	-	Go to Step 16	Go to Step 13
10	Test the signal circuit of the yaw rate sensor for a short to voltage. Did you find and correct the condition?	-	Go to Step 16	Go to Step 13
11	1. Disconnect the EBCM harness connector. 2. Install the J 39700 universal pinout box using the J 39700-300 cable adapter to the EBCM harness connector only. 3. Test the low reference circuit of the yaw rate sensor for a high resistance or an open. Did you find and correct the condition?	-	Go to Step 16	Go to Step 12

ARM66GC000000497

Fig. 83 Code C1282: YAW Rate Input Error (Part 5 of 6). CTS

12	Inspect for poor connections at the harness connector of the yaw rate sensor. Did you find and correct the condition?	-	Go to Step 16	Go to Step 14
13	Inspect for poor connections at the harness connector of the EBCM. Did you find and correct the condition?	-	Go to Step 16	Go to Step 15
14	Replace the yaw rate sensor. Did you complete the repair?	-	Go to Step 16	--
15	Replace the EBCM. Did you complete the repair?	-	Go to Step 16	--
16	1. Clear the DTCs using the scan tool. 2. Operate the vehicle within the Conditions for Running the DTC as specified in the supporting text. Does the DTC reset?	-	Go to Step 2	System OK

ARM66GC000000498

Fig. 83 Code C1282: YAW Rate Input Error (Part 6 of 6). CTS

Circuit Description

The vehicle stability enhancement system (VSES) is activated by the EBCM calculating the desired yaw rate and comparing it to the actual yaw rate input. The desired yaw rate is calculated from measured steering wheel position, vehicle speed, and lateral acceleration. The difference between the desired yaw rate and actual yaw rate is the yaw rate error, which is a measurement of oversteer or understeer. If the yaw rate error becomes too large, the EBCM will attempt to correct the vehicle's yaw motion by applying differential braking to the left or right front wheel.

The amount of differential braking applied to the left or right front wheel is based on both the yaw rate error and side slip rate error. The side slip rate error is a function of the lateral acceleration minus the product of the yaw rate and vehicle speed. The yaw rate error and side slip rate error are combined to produce the total delta velocity error. When the delta velocity error becomes too large and the VSES system activates, the driver's steering inputs combined with the differential braking will attempt to bring the delta velocity error toward zero.

The VSES activations generally occur during aggressive driving, in the turns or bumpy roads without much use of the accelerator pedal. When braking during VSES activation, the brake pedal will feel different than the ABS pedal pulsation. The brake pedal pulsates at a higher frequency during VSES activation.

The usable output voltage range for the lateral accelerometer and yaw rate sensors is 0.25-4.75 volts. The scan tool will report zero lateral acceleration or yaw rate as 2.5 volts with no sensor bias present. The sensor bias compensates for sensor mounting alignment errors, electronic signal errors, temperature changes, and manufacturing differences.

The steering wheel position sensor supplies 2 analog inputs, Phase A and Phase B, to the EBCM. The 2 input signals are approximately 90 degrees out of phase. By interpreting the relationship between the 2 inputs, the EBCM can determine the position of the steering wheel and the direction of steering wheel rotation.

Steer angle centering is the process by which the EBCM calibrates the steering sensor output so that the output reads zero when the steering wheel is centered. Using the yaw rate input, lateral accelerometer input, and wheel speed sensor inputs, the initial steering center position is calculated after driving greater than 10 km/h (6 mph) for more than 10 seconds in a straight line on a level surface.

Conditions for Running the DTC

The ignition is ON.

ARM66GC000000499

Fig. 84 Codes C1284 & C1285: Lateral Accelerometer Sensor Circuit Fault (Part 1 of 6). CTS

Conditions for Setting the DTC

C1284

The EBCM performs 6 different tests to detect a DTC condition. The numbers below correspond to the numbers in Conditions for Running the DTC.

1. The compensated bias value of the lateral accelerometer sensor is greater than 0.3 g.
2. The lateral accelerometer sensor performs a self test that results in an offset of 0.5 g. The EBCM compares the sensor output during the self test with the output following the test. The DTC sets when the lateral acceleration immediately following the self test is greater than the self test output minus 0.4 g.
3. The lateral jerk is greater than 18.5 g/second for 0.12 seconds more than 2 times within the ignition cycle.
4. The lateral acceleration is 0.4 g for 0.25 seconds.
5. The side slip error is greater than 0.5 g 30 times within a drive cycle.
6. The side slip error is greater than 0.5 g for 5 seconds. Under this condition, this DTC will set along with DTC C1281.

C1285

The lateral accelerometer input voltage is less than 0.15 volts or greater than 4.85 volts for 1 second.

Action Taken When the DTC Sets

- The EBCM disables the VSES for the duration of the ignition cycle.
- The DIC displays the Service Stability System message.
- The ABS/TCS remains functional.

Conditions for Clearing the DTC

- The condition for the DTC is no longer present (the DTC is not current) and you used the scan tool Clear DTC function.
- The condition for the DTC is no longer present (the DTC is not current) and you used the On-Board Diagnostics Clear DTC function.
- The EBCM automatically clears the history DTC when a current DTC is not detected in 100 consecutive drive cycles.

ARM66GC000000500

Fig. 84 Codes C1284 & C1285: Lateral Accelerometer Sensor Circuit Fault (Part 2 of 6). CTS

Diagnostic Aids

- During diagnosis, park the vehicle on a level surface.
- Check the vehicle for proper alignment. The car should not pull in either direction while driving straight on a level surface.
- Find out from the driver under what conditions the DTC was set (when the DIC displayed the Service Stability System message). This information will help to duplicate the failure.
- The Snapshot function on the scan tool can help find an intermittent DTC.

Test Description

The numbers below refer to the step numbers on the diagnostic table.

3. Tests for the proper operation of the circuit in the low voltage range.
4. Tests for the proper operation of the circuit in the high voltage range. If the fuse in the jumper opens when you perform this test, the signal circuit is shorted to ground.
5. Tests for a short to voltage in the 5 volt reference circuit.
6. Tests the bias voltage of the lateral accelerometer sensor.

ARM66GC000000501

Fig. 84 Codes C1284 & C1285: Lateral Accelerometer Sensor Circuit Fault (Part 3 of 6). CTS

Step	Action	Values	Yes	No
1	Did you perform the ABS Diagnostic System Check?	--	Go to Step 2	Go to Diagnostic System Check -
2	1. Install a scan tool. 2. Turn ON the ignition, with the engine OFF. 3. With a scan tool, observe the Lateral Accelerometer Input parameter in the VSES data list. Does the scan tool display that the Lateral Accelerometer Input parameter is within the specified range?	0.15-4.85 V	Go to Step 6	Go to Step 3
3	1. Turn OFF the ignition. 2. Disconnect the lateral accelerometer sensor connector. 3. Turn ON the ignition, with the engine OFF. 4. With the scan tool, observe the Lateral Accelerometer Input parameter. Does the scan tool display that the Lateral Accelerometer Input parameter is less than the specified value?	0.15 V	Go to Step 4	Go to Step 10
4	1. Turn OFF the ignition. 2. Connect a 3 amp fused jumper wire between the 5 volt reference circuit of the lateral accelerometer sensor and the signal circuit of the lateral accelerometer sensor. 3. Turn ON the ignition, with the engine OFF. 4. With the scan tool, observe the Lateral Accelerometer Input parameter. Does the scan tool display that the Lateral Accelerometer Input parameter is greater than the specified value?	4.85 V	Go to Step 5	Go to Step 8
5	1. Disconnect the fused jumper wire. 2. Measure the voltage between the 5 volt reference circuit of the lateral accelerometer sensor and the low reference circuit of the lateral accelerometer. Does the voltage measure less the specified value?	5 V	Go to Step 12	Go to Step 7

ARM66GC000000502

Fig. 84 Codes C1284 & C1285: Lateral Accelerometer Sensor Circuit Fault (Part 4 of 6). CTS

6	Does the scan tool display that the Lateral Accelerometer Input parameter is within the specified range?	2.3-2.7 V	Go to Diagnostic Aids	Go to Step 11
7	Test the 5 volt reference circuit of the lateral accelerometer sensor for a short to voltage. Did you find and correct the condition?	--	Go to Step 16	Go to Step 13
8	Test the 5 volt reference circuit of the lateral accelerometer sensor for the following conditions: • An open • A short to ground • A high resistance Did you find and correct the condition?	--	Go to Step 16	Go to Step 9
9	Test the signal circuit of the lateral accelerometer sensor for the following conditions: • An open • A short to ground • A high resistance Did you find and correct the condition?	--	Go to Step 16	Go to Step 13

ARM66GC000000503

Fig. 84 Codes C1284 & C1285: Lateral Accelerometer Sensor Circuit Fault (Part 5 of 6). CTS

10	Test the signal circuit of the lateral accelerometer sensor for a short to voltage. Did you find and correct the condition?	-	Go to Step 16	Go to Step 13
11	1. Disconnect the EBCM harness connector. 2. Install the J 39700 universal pinout box using the J 39700-300 cable adapter to the EBCM harness connector only. 3. Test the low reference circuit of the lateral accelerometer sensor for a high resistance or an open. Did you find and correct the condition?	-	Go to Step 16	Go to Step 12
12	Inspect for poor connections at the harness connector of the lateral accelerometer sensor. Did you find and correct the condition?	-	Go to Step 16	Go to Step 14
13	Inspect for poor connections at the harness connector of the EBCM. Did you find and correct the condition?	-	Go to Step 16	Go to Step 15
14	Replace the lateral accelerometer sensor. Did you complete the repair?	-	Go to Step 16	--
15	Replace the EBCM. Did you complete the repair?	-	Go to Step 16	--
16	1. Clear the DTCs using the scan tool. 2. Operate the vehicle within the Conditions for Running the DTC as specified in the supporting text. Does the DTC reset?	-	Go to Step 2	System OK

ARM66GC000000504

Fig. 84 Codes C1284 & C1285: Lateral Accelerometer Sensor Circuit Fault (Part 6 of 6). CTS

Circuit Description

The vehicle stability enhancement system (VSES) is activated by the EBCM calculating the desired yaw rate and comparing it to the actual yaw rate input. The desired yaw rate is calculated from measured steering wheel position, vehicle speed, and lateral acceleration. The difference between the desired yaw rate and actual yaw rate is the yaw rate error, which is a measurement of oversteer or understeer. If the yaw rate error becomes too large, the EBCM will attempt to correct the vehicle's yaw motion by applying differential braking to the left or right front wheel.

The amount of differential braking applied to the left or right front wheel is based on both the yaw rate error and side slip rate error. The side slip rate error is a function of the lateral acceleration minus the product of the yaw rate and vehicle speed. The yaw rate error and side slip rate error are combined to produce the total delta velocity error. When the delta velocity error becomes too large and the VSES system activates, the driver's steering inputs combined with the differential braking will attempt to bring the delta velocity error toward zero.

The VSES activations generally occur during aggressive driving, in the turns or bumpy roads without much use of the accelerator pedal. When braking during VSES activation, the brake pedal will feel different than the ABS pedal pulsation. The brake pedal pulsates at a higher frequency during VSES activation.

The usable output voltage range for the lateral accelerometer and yaw rate sensors is 0.25-4.75 volts. The scan tool will report zero lateral acceleration or yaw rate as 2.5 volts with no sensor bias present. The sensor bias compensates for sensor mounting alignment errors, electronic signal errors, temperature changes, and manufacturing differences.

The steering wheel position sensor supplies 2 analog inputs, Phase A and Phase B, to the EBCM. The 2 input signals are approximately 90 degrees out of phase. By interpreting the relationship between the 2 inputs, the EBCM can determine the position of the steering wheel and the direction of steering wheel rotation.

Steer angle centering is the process by which the EBCM calibrates the steering sensor output so that the output reads zero when the steering wheel is centered. Using the yaw rate input, lateral accelerometer input, and wheel speed sensor inputs, the initial steering center position is calculated after driving greater than 10 km/h (6 mph) for more than 10 seconds in a straight line on a level surface.

Conditions for Running the DTC

The ignition is ON.

Conditions for Setting the DTC

C1287

One of the following conditions exists:

- The steering wheel position sensor is synchronized and the steer rate (speed that the steering wheel appears to be turning) is greater than 1100 degrees/second.

ARM66GC000000505

Fig. 85 Codes C1287 & C1288: Vehicle Stability System Steer Rate Fault (Part 1 of 7). CTS

Conditions for Running the DTC

The ignition is ON.

Conditions for Setting the DTC

C1287

One of the following conditions exists:

- The steering wheel position sensor is synchronized and the steer rate (speed that the steering wheel appears to be turning) is greater than 1100 degrees/second.
- The steer rate is less than 80 degrees/second and the difference in the phase angle between Phase A and Phase B is greater than 20 degrees.
- The 2 steering sensor signals (Phase A and Phase B) do not agree for 1 second. Under this condition, this DTC will set along with DTC C1281.

C1288

One of the following conditions exists:

- Both Phase A and Phase B are greater than 4.9 volts for 1.6 seconds.
- Both Phase A and Phase B are less than 0.2 volts for 1.6 seconds.
- The difference in the changes in Phase A and Phase B is greater than 35.2 degrees for 9.76 milliseconds.

Action Taken When the DTC Sets

- The EBCM disables the VSES for the duration of the ignition cycle.
- The DIC displays the Service Stability System message.
- The ABS/TCS remains functional.

Conditions for Clearing the DTC

- The condition for the DTC is no longer present (the DTC is not current) and you used the scan tool Clear DTC function.
- The condition for the DTC is no longer present (the DTC is not current) and you used the On-Board Diagnostics Clear DTC function.
- The EBCM automatically clears the history DTC when a current DTC is not detected in 100 consecutive drive cycles.

Diagnostic Aids

- During diagnosis, park the vehicle on a level surface.
- Check the vehicle for proper alignment. The car should not pull in either direction while driving straight on a level surface.
- Find out from the driver under what conditions the DTC was set (when the DIC displayed the Service Stability System message). This information will help to duplicate the failure.
- The Snapshot function on the scan tool can help find an intermittent DTC.

ARM66GC000000506

Fig. 85 Codes C1287 & C1288: Vehicle Stability System Steer Rate Fault (Part 2 of 7). CTS

Test Description

The numbers below refer to the step numbers on the diagnostic table.

2. Perform the Steering Position Sensor Test in order to verify if the steering wheel position sensor (SWPS) is operating properly.
3. Tests for the proper operation of the steering wheel position signal A circuit in the low voltage range.
4. Tests for the proper operation of the steering wheel position signal B circuit in the low voltage range.
5. Tests for the proper operation of the steering wheel position signal A circuit in the high voltage range. If the fuse in the jumper opens when you perform this test, the signal circuit is shorted to ground.
6. Tests for the proper operation of the steering wheel position signal B circuit in the high voltage range. If the fuse in the jumper opens when you perform this test, the signal circuit is shorted to ground.
7. Tests for a short to voltage in the 5 volt reference circuit.
8. Tests for a high resistance or an open in the low reference circuit.

ARM66GC000000507

Fig. 85 Codes C1287 & C1288: Vehicle Stability System Steer Rate Fault (Part 3 of 7). CTS

Step	Action	Value (s)	Yes	No
1	Did you perform the ABS Diagnostic System Check?	--	Go to Step 2	Go to Diagnostic System Check -
2	1. Install a scan tool. 2. Turn ON the ignition, with the engine OFF. 3. With the scan tool, perform the Steering Position Sensor Test. Did the SWPS pass the test?	--	Go to Diagnostic Aids	Go to Step 3
3	1. Turn OFF the ignition. 2. Disconnect the steering wheel position sensor (SWPS) connector. 3. Turn ON the ignition, with the engine OFF. 4. With the scan tool, observe the Dual Analog SWPS Input A parameter in the VSES data list. Does the scan tool indicate the Dual Analog SWPS Input A parameter is less than the specified value?	0.2 V	Go to Step 4	Go to Step 13
4	With the scan tool, observe the Dual Analog SWPS Input B parameter. Does the scan tool indicate the Dual Analog SWPS Input B parameter is less than the specified value?	0.2 V	Go to Step 5	Go to Step 14
5	1. Turn OFF the ignition. 2. Connect a 3 amp fused jumper wire between the 5 volt reference circuit of the steering wheel position sensor (SWPS) and the signal A circuit of the steering wheel position sensor (SWPS). 3. Turn ON the ignition, with the engine OFF. 4. With the scan tool, observe the Dual Analog SWPS Input A parameter. Does the scan tool indicate that the Dual Analog SWPS Input A parameter is greater than the specified value?	4.9 V	Go to Step 6	Go to Step 10

ARM66GC000000508

Fig. 85 Codes C1287 & C1288: Vehicle Stability System Steer Rate Fault (Part 4 of 7). CTS

6	1. Turn OFF the ignition. 2. Disconnect the fused jumper wire. 3. Connect a 3 amp fused jumper wire between the 5 volt reference circuit of the steering wheel position sensor (SWPS) and the signal B circuit of the steering wheel position sensor (SWPS). 4. Turn ON the ignition, with the engine OFF. 5. With the scan tool, observe the Dual Analog SWPS Input B parameter. Does the scan tool indicate that the Dual Analog SWPS Input B parameter is greater than the specified value?	4.9 V	Go to Step 7	Go to Step 10
7	1. Disconnect the fused jumper wire. 2. Measure the voltage between the 5 volt reference circuit of the steering wheel position sensor (SWPS) and the low reference circuit of the steering wheel position sensor (SWPS). Does the voltage measure less the specified value?	5 V	Go to Step 8	Go to Step 9
8	1. Turn OFF the ignition. 2. Disconnect the negative battery cable. 3. Measure the resistance from the low reference circuit of the steering wheel position sensor (SWPS) to a good ground. Does the resistance measure less than the specified value?	5 ohms	Go to Step 16	Go to Step 15
9	Test the 5 volt reference circuit of the steering wheel position sensor (SWPS) for a short to voltage. Did you find and correct the condition?	--	Go to Step 20	Go to Step 17
10	Test the 5 volt reference circuit of the steering wheel position sensor (SWPS) for the following conditions: • An open • A short to ground • A high resistance Did you find and correct the condition?	--	Go to Step 20	Go to Step 11

ARM66GC000000509

Fig. 85 Codes C1287 & C1288: Vehicle Stability System Steer Rate Fault (Part 5 of 7). CTS

11	Test the signal A circuit of the steering wheel position sensor (SWPS) for the following conditions: • An open • A short to ground • A high resistance Did you find and correct the condition?	-	Go to Step 20	Go to Step 12
12	Test the signal B circuit of the steering wheel position sensor (SWPS) for the following conditions: • An open • A short to ground • A high resistance Did you find and correct the condition?	-	Go to Step 20	Go to Step 17
13	Test the signal A circuit of the steering wheel position sensor (SWPS) for a short to voltage. Did you find and correct the condition?	-	Go to Step 20	Go to Step 17
14	Test the signal B circuit of the steering wheel position sensor (SWPS) for a short to voltage. Did you find and correct the condition?	-	Go to Step 20	Go to Step 17
15	1. Disconnect the EBCM harness connector. 2. Install the J 39700 universal pinout box using the J 39700-300 cable adapter to the EBCM harness connector only. 3. Test the low reference circuit of the steering wheel position sensor (SWPS) for a high resistance or an open. Did you find and correct the condition?	-	Go to Step 20	Go to Step 17
16	Inspect for poor connections at the harness connector of the steering wheel position sensor (SWPS). Did you find and correct the condition?	-	Go to Step 20	Go to Step 18

ARM66GC000000510

Fig. 85 Codes C1287 & C1288: Vehicle Stability System Steer Rate Fault (Part 6 of 7). CTS

17	Inspect for poor connections at the harness connector of the EBCM. Did you find and correct the condition?	Go to Step 20	Go to Step 19
18	Replace the steering wheel position sensor (SWPS). Did you complete the repair?	Go to Step 20	--
19	Replace the EBCM. Did you complete the repair?	Go to Step 20	--
20	1. Clear the DTCs using the scan tool. 2. Operate the vehicle within the Conditions for Running the DTC as specified in the supporting text. Does the DTC reset?	Go to Step 2	System OK

ARM66GC000000511

Fig. 85 Codes C1287 & C1288: Vehicle Stability System Steer Rate Fault (Part 7 of 7). CTS

Step	Action	Yes	No
1	Did you perform the ABS Diagnostic System Check?	Go to Step 2	Go to Diagnostic System Check -
2	Press the brake pedal. Do the brake lamps turn ON?	Go to Step 3	Go to Step 7
3	1. Press the brake pedal. 2. With a scan tool, observe the Stop Lamp Switch parameter in the DRP/ABS/TCS data list. Does the Stop Lamp Switch parameter change state?	Go to Diagnostic Aids	Go to Step 4
4	1. Turn OFF the ignition. 2. Inspect the stop lamp switch and adjust and/or calibrate if needed. Did you find and correct the condition?	Go to Step 14	Go to Step 5
5	1. Turn OFF the ignition. 2. Disconnect the stop lamp switch connector. 3. Connect a 3 amp fused jumper wire between the battery positive voltage circuit of the stop lamp switch and the signal circuit of the stop lamp switch. 4. Turn ON the ignition, with the engine OFF. 5. With a scan tool, observe the Stop Lamp Switch parameter. Does the scan tool display Applied?	Go to Step 11	Go to Step 6
6	Test the signal circuit of the stop lamp switch for an open between the splice pack of the stop lamp signal circuit and the EBCM. Did you find and correct the condition?	Go to Step 14	Go to Step 10
7	Test the battery positive voltage circuit of the stop lamp switch for a short to ground or an open. Did you find and correct the condition?	Go to Step 14	Go to Step 8

ARM66GC000000513

Fig. 86 Code C1291: Stop Lamp Switch Circuit (Part 2 of 3). CTS

Circuit Description

The stop lamp switch signal informs the EBCM when the brake pedal is pressed.

Conditions for Running the DTC

The ABS conditions and the braking conditions are normal.

Conditions for Setting the DTC

The stoplamp switch remains open for 3 deceleration cycles.

Action Taken When the DTC Sets

- The EBCM disables the EDC/TCS for the duration of the ignition cycle.
- The Traction Off indicator turns ON.
- The ABS remains functional.

Conditions for Clearing the DTC

- The condition for the DTC is no longer present (the DTC is not current) and you used the scan tool Clear DTC function.
- The condition for the DTC is no longer present (the DTC is not current) and you used the On-Board Diagnostics Clear DTC function.
- The EBCM automatically clears the history DTC when a current DTC is not detected in 100 consecutive drive cycles.

Diagnostic Aids

- Diagnose any wheel speed sensor DTCs before continuing with the diagnosis of the DTC.
- A deceleration cycle consists of the following sequence:
  1. The vehicle speed is greater than 24 km/h (15 mph).
  2. The vehicle decelerates more than 8 km/h/second (5 mph/second) for 2 seconds.
  3. The vehicle speed decelerates to less than 16 km/h (10 mph).
- Verify proper stop lamp switch operation using the data list of the scan tool. As the brake is applied, the data list displays the stop lamp switch on within 2.54 cm (1 in) of travel.
- Possible causes of this DTC are the following conditions:
  - An open stop lamp switch
  - The stop lamp switch is misadjusted
  - An open fuse
  - Circuit has a wiring problem, terminal corrosion, or poor connections
  - Erratic wheel speeds

Test Description

The numbers below refer to the step numbers on the diagnostic table.

3. Tests the circuit for a change in states.

5. Tests for proper operation of the circuit by bypassing the stop lamp switch. If the fuse in the jumper opens when you perform this test, the signal circuit of the stop lamp switch is shorted to

ARM66GC000000512

Fig. 86 Code C1291: Stop Lamp Switch Circuit (Part 1 of 3). CTS

8	Test the signal circuit of the stop lamp switch for an open between the stop lamp switch and the splice of the stop lamp signal circuit. Did you find and correct the condition?	Go to Step 14	Go to Step 9
9	Test the signal circuit of the stop lamp switch for a short to ground. Did you find and correct the condition?	Go to Step 14	Go to Step 10
10	Inspect for poor connections at the harness connector of the EBCM. Did you find and correct the condition?	Go to Step 14	Go to Step 12
11	Inspect for poor connections at the harness connector of the stop lamp switch. Did you find and correct the condition?	Go to Step 14	Go to Step 13
12	Replace the EBCM. Did you complete the repair?	Go to Step 14	--
13	Replace the stop lamp switch. Did you complete the repair?	Go to Step 14	--
14	1. Use the scan tool in order to clear the DTCs. 2. Operate the vehicle within the Conditions for Running the DTC as specified in the supporting text. Does the DTC reset?	Go to Step 2	System OK

ARM66GC000000514

Fig. 86 Code C1291: Stop Lamp Switch Circuit (Part 3 of 3). CTS

Circuit Description

The EBCM uses the input from the brake fluid pressure sensor for more accurate braking control during VSES.

Conditions for Running the DTC

C1292

The ignition is ON.

C1293

The vehicle speed is greater than 40 km/h (25 mph).

C1296

The ignition is ON for 1.2 seconds.

Conditions for Setting the DTC

C1292

The brake fluid pressure is less than 345 kPa (50 psi) for 3 deceleration cycles.

C1293

The brake fluid pressure is greater than 552 kPa (80 psi) for 2 consecutive ignition cycles.

C1296

One of the following conditions exists:

- The brake fluid pressure sensor signal is greater than 4.9 volts for 2 minutes.
- The brake fluid pressure sensor signal is less than 0.14 volts for 0.1 seconds.

Action Taken When the DTC Sets

- The EBCM disables the VSES for the duration of the ignition cycle.
- The DIC displays the Service Stability System message.
- The ABS/TCS remains functional.

ARM66GC000000515

Fig. 87 Codes C1292, C1293 & C1296: Brake Pressure Sensor Circuit (Part 1 of 5). CTS

Conditions for Clearing the DTC

- The condition for the DTC is no longer present (the DTC is not current) and you used the scan tool Clear DTC function.
- The condition for the DTC is no longer present (the DTC is not current) and you used the On-Board Diagnostics Clear DTC function.
- The EBCM automatically clears the history DTC when a current DTC is not detected in 100 consecutive drive cycles.

Diagnostic Aids

- Find out from the driver under what conditions the DTC was set (when the DIC displayed the Service Active Handling message). This information will help to duplicate the failure.
- The Snapshot function on the scan tool can help find an intermittent DTC.
- A deceleration cycle consists of the following sequence:
  1. The vehicle speed is greater than 24 km/h (15 mph).
  2. The vehicle decelerates more than 8 km/h/second (5 mph/second) for 2 seconds.
  3. The vehicle speed decelerates to less than 16 km/h (10 mph).

Test Description

The numbers below refer to the step numbers on the diagnostic table.

3. Tests for the proper operation of the circuit in the low voltage range.
4. Tests for the proper operation of the circuit in the high voltage range. If the fuse in the jumper opens when you perform this test, the signal circuit is shorted to ground.
5. Tests for a short to voltage in the 5 volt reference circuit.
6. Tests for a high resistance or an open in the low reference circuit.

ARM66GC000000516

Fig. 87 Codes C1292, C1293 & C1296: Brake Pressure Sensor Circuit (Part 2 of 5). CTS

Step	Action	Value (s)	Yes	No
1	Did you perform the ABS Diagnostic System Check?	--	Go to Step 2	Go to Diagnostic System Check -
2	1. Install a scan tool. 2. Turn ON the ignition, with the engine OFF. 3. With a scan tool, observe the Master Cylinder Pressure Sensor Input parameter in the DRP/ABS/TCS data list. Does the scan tool display that the Master Cylinder Pressure Sensor Input parameter is within the specified range?	0.14-4.9 V	Go to Diagnostic Aids	Go to Step 3
3	1. Turn OFF the ignition. 2. Disconnect the brake fluid pressure sensor connector. 3. Turn ON the ignition, with the engine OFF. 4. With the scan tool, observe the Master Cylinder Pressure Sensor Input parameter. Does the scan tool indicate that the Master Cylinder Pressure Sensor Input parameter is less than the specified value?	0.14 V	Go to Step 4	Go to Step 10
4	1. Turn OFF the ignition. 2. Connect a 3 amp fused jumper wire between the 5 volt reference circuit of the brake fluid pressure sensor and the signal circuit of the brake fluid pressure sensor. 3. Turn ON the ignition, with the engine OFF. 4. With the scan tool, observe the Master Cylinder Pressure Sensor Input parameter. Does the scan tool indicate that the Master Cylinder Pressure Sensor Input parameter is greater than the specified value?	4.9 V	Go to Step 5	Go to Step 8
5	1. Disconnect the fused jumper wire. 2. Measure the voltage between the 5 volt reference circuit of the brake fluid pressure sensor and the low reference circuit of the brake fluid pressure sensor. Does the voltage measure less the specified value?	5 V	Go to Step 6	Go to Step 7

ARM66GC000000517

Fig. 87 Codes C1292, C1293 & C1296: Brake Pressure Sensor Circuit (Part 3 of 5). CTS

6	1. Turn OFF the ignition. 2. Disconnect the negative battery cable. 3. Measure the resistance from the low reference circuit of the brake fluid pressure sensor to a good ground. Does the resistance measure less than the specified value?	5 ohms	Go to Step 12	Go to Step 11
7	Test the 5 volt reference circuit of the brake fluid pressure sensor for a short to voltage. Did you find and correct the condition?	--	Go to Step 16	Go to Step 13
8	Test the 5 volt reference circuit of the brake fluid pressure sensor for the following conditions: • An open • A short to ground • A high resistance Did you find and correct the condition?	--	Go to Step 16	Go to Step 9
9	Test the signal circuit of the brake fluid pressure sensor for the following conditions: • An open • A short to ground • A high resistance Did you find and correct the condition?	--	Go to Step 16	Go to Step 13
10	Test the signal circuit of the brake fluid pressure sensor for a short to voltage. Did you find and correct the condition?	--	Go to Step 16	Go to Step 13

ARM66GC000000518

Fig. 87 Codes C1292, C1293 & C1296: Brake Pressure Sensor Circuit (Part 4 of 5). CTS

11	1. Disconnect the EBCM harness connector. 2. Install the J 39700 universal pinout box using the J 39700-300 cable adapter to the EBCM harness connector only. 3. Test the low reference circuit of the brake fluid pressure sensor for a high resistance or an open. Did you find and correct the condition?	-	Go to Step 16	Go to Step 13
12	Inspect for poor connections at the harness connector of the brake fluid pressure sensor. Did you find and correct the condition?	-	Go to Step 16	Go to Step 14
13	Inspect for poor connections at the harness connector of the EBCM. Did you find and correct the condition?	-	Go to Step 16	Go to Step 15
14	Replace the brake fluid pressure sensor. Did you complete the repair?	-	Go to Step 16	--
15	Replace the EBCM. Did you complete the repair?	-	Go to Step 16	--
16	1. Clear the DTCs using the scan tool. 2. Operate the vehicle within the Conditions for Running the DTC as specified in the supporting text. Does the DTC reset?	-	Go to Step 2	System OK

ARM66GC000000519

Fig. 87 Codes C1292, C1293 & C1296: Brake Pressure Sensor Circuit (Part 5 of 5). CTS

Step	Action	Yes	No
1	Did you perform the ABS Diagnostic System Check?	Go to Step 2	Go to Diagnostic System Check -
2	1. Install a scan tool. 2. Turn ON the ignition, with the engine OFF. 3. With a scan tool, observe the Stop Lamp Switch parameter in the DRP/ABS/TCS data list. Does the scan tool display Released?	Go to Step 3	Go to Step 4
3	1. Press the brake pedal. 2. With a scan tool, observe the Stop Lamp Switch parameter. Does the Stop Lamp Switch parameter change state?	Go to Diagnostic Aids	Go to Step 4
4	1. Turn OFF the ignition. 2. Inspect the stop lamp switch and adjust and/or calibrate if needed. Did you find and correct the condition?	Go to Step 11	Go to Step 5
5	1. Turn OFF the ignition. 2. Disconnect the stop lamp switch connector. 3. Turn ON the ignition, with the engine OFF. 4. With a scan tool, observe the Stop Lamp Switch parameter. Does the scan tool display Released?	Go to Step 8	Go to Step 6
6	Test the stop lamp switch signal circuit for a short to voltage. Did you find and correct the condition?	Go to Step 11	Go to Step 7

ARM66GC000000521

Fig. 88 Code C1294: Stop Lamp Switch (Part 2 of 3). CTS

Circuit Description

The stop lamp switch signal informs the EBCM when the brake pedal is pressed.

Conditions for Running the DTC

The vehicle speed is greater than 40 km/h (25 mph).

Conditions for Setting the DTC

The stop lamp switch input was active for 2 consecutive ignition cycles.

Action Taken When the DTC Sets

- The EBCM disables the EDC/TCS for the duration of the ignition cycle.
- The Traction Off indicator turns ON.
- The ABS remains functional.

Conditions for Clearing the DTC

- The condition for the DTC is no longer present and the DTC is cleared with a scan tool.
- The EBCM automatically clears the history DTC when a current DTC is not detected in 100 consecutive drive cycles.

Diagnostic Aids

Possible causes of this DTC are the following conditions:

- The stop lamp switch circuit is shorted to voltage.
- The stop lamp switch is misadjusted.
- The stop lamp switch is stuck closed.
- A brake pedal that is binding.

Test Description

The number below refers to the step number on the diagnostic table.

2. Test for the current state of the brake lamp switch parameter.

ARM66GC000000520

Fig. 88 Code C1294: Stop Lamp Switch (Part 1 of 3). CTS

7	Inspect for poor connections at the harness connector of the EBCM. Did you find and correct the condition?	Go to Step 11	Go to Step 9
8	Inspect for poor connections at the harness connector of the stop lamp switch. Did you find and correct the condition?	Go to Step 11	Go to Step 10
9	Replace the EBCM. Did you complete the repair?	Go to Step 11	--
10	Replace the stop lamp switch. Did you complete the repair?	Go to Step 11	--
11	1. Use the scan tool in order to clear the DTCs. 2. Operate the vehicle within the Conditions for Running the DTC as specified in the supporting text. Does the DTC reset?	Go to Step 2	System OK

ARM66GC000000522

Fig. 88 Code C1294: Stop Lamp Switch (Part 3 of 3). CTS

Circuit Description

The EBCM sources 5 volts on the stop lamp switch signal circuit when the stop lamp switch is inactive. The voltage is supplied a ground path through the stop lamp bulbs.

Conditions for Running the DTC

The ignition is ON.

Conditions for Setting the DTC

The stoplamp switch input voltage is between 1.87 and 5.28 volts for 2 seconds.

Action Taken When the DTC Sets

- The EBCM disables the EDC/TCS for the duration of the ignition cycle.
- The Traction Off indicator turns ON.
- The ABS remains functional.

Conditions for Clearing the DTC

- The condition for the DTC is no longer present and the DTC is cleared with a scan tool.
- The EBCM automatically clears the history DTC when a current DTC is not detected in 100 consecutive drive cycles.

Diagnostic Aids

Possible causes of this DTC are the following conditions:

- A signal circuit of the stop lamp switch is open.
- The stop lamp switch is misadjusted.
- Verify proper stop lamp switch operation using the data list of the scan tool. As the brake is applied, the data list displays the stop lamp switch ON within 2.54 cm (1 in) of travel.
- All brake lamps are open.
- All brake lamp grounds are open.
- Circuit has a wiring problem, terminal corrosion, or poor connections.
- Loose or corroded EBCM ground or PCM ground.
- An internal EBCM problem.

Test Description

The numbers below refer to the step numbers on the diagnostic table.

3. This DTC detects an open stoplamp switch signal circuit from the stoplamp side of the splice pack to the EBCM.

4. The EBCM sources 5 volts on the stoplamp switch signal circuit. This small voltage has a ground path through the stoplamp bulbs. This DTC sets if the path to ground is open.

ARM66GC000000523

Fig. 89 Code C1295: Stop Lamp Switch Input Voltage (Part 1 of 2). CTS

Step	Action	Yes	No
1	Did you perform the ABS Diagnostic System Check?	Go to Step 2	Go to Diagnostic System Check -
2	1. Press the brake pedal. 2. With the scan tool, observe the Stop Lamp Switch parameter in the DRP/ABS/TCS data list. Does the Stop Lamp Switch parameter display Applied?	Go to Step 4	Go to Step 3
3	Test the signal circuit of the stop lamp switch for an open. Did you find and correct the condition?	Go to Step 9	Go to Step 7
4	Press the brake pedal. Are all of the stop lamps OFF?	Go to Step 5	Go to Diagnostic Aids
5	Test the feed circuit of the stop lamps for an open or high resistance. Did you find and correct the condition?	Go to Step 9	Go to Step 6
6	Test the ground circuit of the stop lamps for an open or high resistance. Did you find and correct the condition?	Go to Step 9	Go to Diagnostic Aids
7	Inspect for poor connections at the harness connector of the EBCM. Did you find and correct the condition?	Go to Step 9	Go to Step 8
8	Replace the EBCM. Did you complete the replacement?	Go to Step 9	--
9	1. Use the scan tool in order to clear the DTCs. 2. Operate the vehicle within the Conditions for Running the DTC as specified in the supporting text. Does the DTC reset?	Go to Step 2	System OK

ARM66GC000000524

Fig. 89 Code C1295: Stop Lamp Switch Input Voltage (Part 2 of 2). CTS

Circuit Description

The instrument cluster controls the operation of the ABS indicator. The EBCM reports the desired status of the ABS indicator via serial data messages. The ABS indicator signal circuit is a back-up reporting circuit to the serial data messages. The EBCM supplies ground through the circuit when the ABS is operating properly. When there is a problem with ABS that should turn on the ABS indicator, the EBCM opens the ABS indicator signal circuit. If there is a problem with the ABS serial data messages, the instrument cluster uses the ABS indicator signal to determine if the ABS indicator should be illuminated. Using the serial data messages and back-up circuit, the instrument cluster decides whether to turn on the ABS indicator.

Test Description

The numbers below refer to the step numbers on the diagnostic table.

3. Use the scan tool to check the normal state of the ABS indicator control circuit.

4. Ensures that the instrument panel cluster (IPC) can operate the ABS indicator.

Step	Action	Value (s)	Yes	No
1	Did you perform the ABS Diagnostic System Check?	--	Go to Step 2	Go to Diagnostic System Check -
2	Inspect the EBCM ground, making sure the ground is clean and torqued to the proper specification. Did you find and correct the condition?	--	Go to Step 9	Go to Step 3
3	1. Install a scan tool. 2. Turn ON the ignition, with the engine OFF. 3. With a scan tool, observe the ABS Warning Indicator parameter in the DRP/ABS/TCS data list. Does the scan tool display Off?	--	Go to Step 4	Go to Step 5

ARM66GC000000525

Fig. 90 ABS Indicator Always On (Part 1 of 2). CTS

4	1. Turn OFF the ignition. 2. Turn ON the ignition, with the engine OFF. 3. Observe the ABS indicator on the instrument panel cluster (IPC) during the displays test. Does the ABS indicator illuminate during the displays test and then turn OFF?	-	Test for Intermittent and Poor Connections	Go to Step 6
5	Inspect for poor connections at the harness connector of the EBCM. Did you find and correct the condition?	-	Go to Step 9	Go to Step 7
6	Inspect for poor connections at the harness connector of the IPC. Did you find and correct the condition?	-	Go to Step 9	Go to Step 8
7	Replace the EBCM. Did you complete the repair?	-	Go to Step 9	--
8	**Important** Perform the setup procedure for the replacement IPC. Replace the instrument panel cluster (IPC). Did you complete the repair?	-	Go to Step 9	--
9	Operate the system in order to verify the repair. Did you correct the condition?	-	System OK	Go to Step 2

ARM66GC000000526

Fig. 90 ABS Indicator Always On (Part 2 of 2). CTS

Circuit Description

The instrument cluster controls the operation of the ABS indicator. The EBCM reports the desired status of the ABS indicator via serial data messages. The ABS indicator signal circuit is a back-up reporting circuit to the serial data messages. The EBCM supplies ground through the circuit when the ABS is operating properly. When there is a problem with ABS that should turn on the ABS indicator, the EBCM opens the ABS indicator signal circuit. If there is a problem with the ABS serial data messages, the instrument cluster uses the ABS indicator signal to determine if the ABS indicator should be illuminated. Using the serial data messages and back-up circuit, the instrument cluster decides whether to turn on the ABS indicator.

Test Description

The numbers below refer to the step numbers on the diagnostic table.

3. Use the scan tool to check the normal state of the ABS indicator control circuit.
4. Ensures that the instrument panel cluster (IPC) can operate the ABS indicator.

Step	Action	Value (s)	Yes	No
1	Did you perform the ABS Diagnostic System Check?	--	Go to Step 2	Go to Diagnostic System Check -
2	Inspect the EBCM ground, making sure the ground is clean and torqued to the proper specification. Did you find and correct the condition?	--	Go to Step 9	Go to Step 3
3	1. Install a scan tool. 2. Turn ON the ignition, with the engine OFF. 3. With a scan tool, observe the ABS Warning Indicator parameter in the DRP/ABS/TCS data list. Does the scan tool display Off?	--	Go to Step 4	Go to Step 5

ARM66GC000000527

Fig. 91 ABS Indicator Inoperative (Part 1 of 2). CTS

4	1. Turn OFF the ignition. 2. Turn ON the ignition, with the engine OFF. 3. Observe the ABS indicator on the instrument panel cluster (IPC) during the displays test. Does the ABS indicator illuminate during the displays test and then turn OFF?	-	Test for Intermittent and Poor Connections	Go to Step 6
5	Inspect for poor connections at the harness connector of the EBCM. Did you find and correct the condition?	-	Go to Step 9	Go to Step 7
6	Inspect for poor connections at the harness connector of the IPC. Did you find and correct the condition?	-	Go to Step 9	Go to Step 8
7	Replace the EBCM. Did you complete the repair?	-	Go to Step 9	--
8	**Important** Perform the setup procedure for the replacement IPC. Replace the instrument panel cluster (IPC). Did you complete the repair?	-	Go to Step 9	--
9	Operate the system in order to verify the repair. Did you correct the condition?	-	System OK	Go to Step 2

ARM66GC000000528

Fig. 91 ABS Indicator Inoperative (Part 2 of 2). CTS

Circuit Description

The Traction Control indicator is controlled by the instrument cluster (IPC) via serial data messages from the EBCM. The EBCM send a serial data message to the IPC to illuminate the Traction Control indicator when the EBCM has disabled TCS due to a DTC. The Traction Control indicator will also turn ON during the instrument cluster bulb check. When the ignition switch is turned to ON, the Traction Control indicator will turn ON for approximately 3 seconds and then turn OFF.

Test Description

The numbers below refer to the step numbers on the diagnostic table.

2. Use the scan tool to check the normal state of the Traction Control indicator control.
3. Ensures that the instrument cluster can operate the Traction Control indicator.

ARM66GC000000529

Fig. 92 Traction Control Indicator Always On (Part 1 of 2). CTS

Step	Action	Yes	No
1	Did you perform the ABS Diagnostic System Check?	Go to Step 2	Go to Diagnostic System Check -
2	1. Install a scan tool. 2. Turn ON the ignition, with the engine OFF. 3. With a scan tool, observe the TCS Warning Indicator/Message parameter in the DRP/ABS/TCS data list. Does the scan tool display Off?	Go to Step 3	Go to Step 4
3	1. Turn OFF the ignition. 2. Turn ON the ignition, with the engine OFF. 3. Observe the Traction Control indicator on the instrument cluster (IPC) during the bulb check. Does the Traction Control indicator illuminate during the bulb check and then turn OFF?	Test for Intermittent and Poor Connections	Go to Step 5
4	Inspect for poor connections at the harness connector of the EBCM. Did you find and correct the condition?	Go to Step 8	Go to Step 6
5	Inspect for poor connections at the harness connector of the instrument cluster (IPC). Did you find and correct the condition?	Go to Step 8	Go to Step 7
6	Replace the EBCM. Did you complete the repair?	Go to Step 8	--
7	Replace the instrument cluster (IPC). Did you complete the repair?	Go to Step 8	--
8	Operate the system in order to verify the repair. Did you correct the condition?	System OK	Go to Step 2

ARM66GC000000530

Fig. 92 Traction Control Indicator Always On (Part 2 of 2). CTS

Circuit Description

The Traction Control indicator is controlled by the instrument cluster (IPC) via serial data messages from the EBCM. The EBCM send a serial data message to the IPC to illuminate the Traction Control indicator when the EBCM has disabled TCS due to a DTC. The Traction Control indicator will also turn ON during the instrument cluster bulb check. When the ignition switch is turned to ON, the Traction Control indicator will turn ON for approximately 3 seconds and then turn OFF.

Test Description

The numbers below refer to the step numbers on the diagnostic table.

2. Use the scan tool to check the normal state of the Traction Control indicator control.
3. Ensures that the instrument cluster can operate the Traction Control indicator.

ARM66GC000000531

Fig. 93 Traction Control Indicator Inoperative (Part 1 of 2). CTS

Circuit Description

The Traction Off indicator is controlled by the instrument cluster via serial data messages from the EBCM. When the RIM sees the traction control switch input grounded through the momentary traction control switch, it sends a serial data message to the EBCM that tells the EBCM that the traction control switch has been pressed. The EBCM then disables traction control and sends a serial data message to the instrument cluster to turn on the Traction Off indicator on the instrument panel. Each time the ignition is cycled from OFF to ON, the traction control system is enabled.

Test Description

The numbers below refer to the step numbers on the diagnostic table.

2. Use the scan tool to check the normal state of the Traction Off indicator control.
3. Ensures that the instrument cluster can operate the Traction Off indicator.

ARM66GC000000533

Fig. 94 Traction Off Indicator Always On (Part 1 of 2). CTS

Step	Action	Yes	No
1	Did you perform the ABS Diagnostic System Check?	Go to Step 2	Go to Diagnostic System Check -
2	1. Install a scan tool. 2. Turn ON the ignition, with the engine OFF. 3. With a scan tool, observe the TCS Warning Indicator/Message parameter in the DRP/ABS/TCS data list. Does the scan tool display Off?	Go to Step 3	Go to Step 4
3	1. Turn OFF the ignition. 2. Turn ON the ignition, with the engine OFF. 3. Observe the Traction Off indicator on the instrument panel cluster (IPC) during the bulb check. Does the Traction Off indicator illuminate during the bulb check and then turn OFF?	Test for Intermittent and Poor Connections	Go to Step 5
4	Inspect for poor connections at the harness connector of the EBCM. Did you find and correct the condition?	Go to Step 8	Go to Step 6
5	Inspect for poor connections at the harness connector of the instrument panel cluster (IPC). Did you find and correct the condition?	Go to Step 8	Go to Step 7
6	Replace the EBCM. Did you complete the repair?	Go to Step 8	--
7	Replace the instrument panel cluster (IPC). Did you complete the repair?	Go to Step 8	--
8	Operate the system in order to verify the repair. Did you correct the condition?	System OK	Go to Step 2

ARM66GC000000534

Fig. 94 Traction Off Indicator Always On (Part 2 of 2). CTS

Step	Action	Yes	No
1	Did you perform the ABS Diagnostic System Check?	Go to Step 2	Go to Diagnostic System Check -
2	1. Install a scan tool. 2. Turn ON the ignition, with the engine OFF. 3. With a scan tool, observe the TCS Warning Indicator/Message parameter in the DRP/ABS/TCS data list. Does the scan tool display Off?	Go to Step 3	Go to Step 4
3	1. Turn OFF the ignition. 2. Turn ON the ignition, with the engine OFF. 3. Observe the Traction Control indicator on the instrument cluster (IPC) during the bulb check. Does the Traction Control indicator illuminate during the bulb check and then turn OFF?	Test for Intermittent and Poor Connections	Go to Step 5
4	Inspect for poor connections at the harness connector of the EBCM. Did you find and correct the condition?	Go to Step 8	Go to Step 6
5	Inspect for poor connections at the harness connector of the instrument cluster (IPC). Did you find and correct the condition?	Go to Step 8	Go to Step 7
6	Replace the EBCM. Did you complete the repair?	Go to Step 8	--
7	Replace the instrument cluster (IPC). Did you complete the repair?	Go to Step 8	--
8	Operate the system in order to verify the repair. Did you correct the condition?	System OK	Go to Step 2

ARM66GC000000532

Fig. 93 Traction Control Indicator Inoperative (Part 2 of 2). CTS

Circuit Description

The Traction Off indicator is controlled by the instrument cluster via serial data messages from the EBCM. When the RIM sees the traction control switch input grounded through the momentary traction control switch, it sends a serial data message to the EBCM that tells the EBCM that the traction control switch has been pressed. The EBCM then disables traction control and sends a serial data message to the instrument cluster to turn on the Traction Off indicator on the instrument panel. Each time the ignition is cycled from OFF to ON, the traction control system is enabled.

Test Description

The numbers below refer to the step numbers on the diagnostic table.

2. Use the scan tool to check the normal state of the Traction Off control.
3. Ensures that the instrument cluster can operate the Traction Off indicator.

Step	Action	Yes	No
1	Did you perform the ABS Diagnostic System Check?	Go to Step 2	Go to Diagnostic System Check -
2	1. Install a scan tool. 2. Turn ON the ignition, with the engine OFF. 3. With a scan tool, observe the TCS Warning Indicator/Message parameter in the DRP/ABS/TCS data list. Does the scan tool display Off?	Go to Step 3	Go to Step 10
3	1. Turn OFF the ignition. 2. Turn ON the ignition, with the engine OFF. 3. Observe the Traction Off indicator on the instrument panel cluster (IPC) during the bulb check. Does the Traction Off indicator illuminate during the bulb check and then turn OFF?	Go to Step 4	Go to Step 11

ARM66GC000000535

Fig. 95 Traction Off Indicator Inoperative (Part 1 of 3). CTS

4	1. Turn OFF the ignition. 2. Install a scan tool. 3. Turn ON the ignition, with the engine OFF. 4. With a scan tool, observe the TCS On/Off Switch parameter in the Rear Integration Module data list. 5. Activate the traction control switch. Does the TCS On/Off Switch parameter change state?	Test for Intermittent and Poor Connections	Go to Step 5
5	1. Turn OFF the ignition. 2. Disconnect the traction control switch connector. 3. Connect a 3 amp fused jumper from the signal circuit of the traction control switch to the ground circuit of the traction control switch. 4. Turn ON the ignition, with the engine OFF. 5. With a scan tool, observe the TCS Switch State parameter. Does the scan tool display On?	Go to Step 9	Go to Step 6
6	Test the signal circuit of the traction control switch for an open or high resistance. Did you find and correct the condition?	Go to Step 16	Go to Step 7
7	Test the ground circuit of the traction control switch for an open or high resistance. Did you find and correct the condition?	Go to Step 16	Go to Step 8
8	Inspect for poor connections at the harness connector of the rear integration module (RIM). Did you find and correct the condition?	Go to Step 16	Go to Step 12
9	Inspect for poor connections at the harness connector of the traction control switch. Did you find and correct the condition?	Go to Step 16	Go to Step 13

ARM66GC000000536

Fig. 95 Traction Off Indicator Inoperative (Part 2 of 3). CTS

Circuit Description

The vehicle stability enhancement system (VSES) is activated by the EBCM calculating the desired yaw rate and comparing it to the actual yaw rate input. The desired yaw rate is calculated from measured steering wheel position, vehicle speed, and lateral acceleration. The difference between the desired yaw rate and actual yaw rate is the yaw rate error, which is a measurement of oversteer or understeer. If the yaw rate error becomes too large, the EBCM will attempt to correct the vehicle's yaw motion by applying differential braking to the left or right front wheel.

The VSES activations generally occur during aggressive driving, in the turns or bumpy roads without much use of the accelerator pedal. When braking during VSES activation, the brake pedal will feel different than the ABS pedal pulsation. The brake pedal pulsates at a higher frequency during VSES activation.

The usable output voltage range for the lateral accelerometer and yaw rate sensors is 0.25-4.75 volts. The scan tool will report zero lateral acceleration or yaw rate as 2.5 volts with no sensor bias present. The sensor bias compensates for sensor mounting alignment errors, electronic signal errors, temperature changes, and manufacturing differences.

The steering wheel position sensor supplies 2 analog inputs, Phase A and Phase B, to the EBCM. The 2 input signals are approximately 90 degrees out of phase. By interpreting the relationship between the 2 inputs, the EBCM can determine the position of the steering wheel and the direction of steering wheel rotation.

Steer angle centering is the process by which the EBCM calibrates the steering sensor output so that the output reads zero when the steering wheel is centered. Using the yaw rate input, lateral accelerometer input, and wheel speed sensor inputs, the initial steering center position is calculated after driving greater than 10 km/h (6 mph) for more than 10 seconds in a straight line on a level surface.

Test Description

The numbers below refer to the step numbers on the diagnostic table.

3. Perform the Steering Position Sensor Test in order to verify if the steering wheel position sensor (SWPS) is operating properly.
4. Verify that the lateral accelerometer input parameter is within the valid range.
5. Verify that the yaw rate input parameter is within the valid range.

ARM66GC000000538

Fig. 96 Vehicle Stability Enhancement System Inoperative (Part 1 of 3). CTS

10	Inspect for poor connections at the harness connector of the EBCM. Did you find and correct the condition?	Go to Step 16	Go to Step 14
11	Inspect for poor connections at the harness connector of the instrument panel cluster (IPC). Did you find and correct the condition?	Go to Step 16	Go to Step 15
12	Replace the rear integration module (RIM). Did you complete the replacement?	Go to Step 16	--
13	Replace the traction control switch. Did you complete the replacement?	Go to Step 16	--
14	Replace the EBCM. Did you complete the repair?	Go to Step 16	--
15	Replace the instrument panel cluster (IPC). Did you complete the repair?	Go to Step 16	--
16	Operate the system in order to verify the repair. Did you correct the condition?	System OK	Go to Step 2

ARM66GC000000537

Fig. 95 Traction Off Indicator Inoperative (Part 3 of 3). CTS

Step	Action	Value(s)	Yes	No
1	Did you perform the ABS Diagnostic System Check?	--	Go to Step 2	Go to Diagnostic System Check -
2	1. Install a scan tool. 2. Start the engine. 3. Observe the VSES Is Centered parameter in the VSES data list. 4. Perform the Diagnostic Test Drive. Refer to Diagnostic Test Drive . Did the scan tool display Yes within the specified value?	30 seconds	Test for Intermittent and Poor Connections	Go to Step 3
3	With the scan tool, perform the With the scan tool, perform the Steering Position Sensor Test. Did the SWPS pass the test?	--	Go to Step 4	Go to Step 7
4	With a scan tool, observe the Lateral Accelerometer Input parameter in the VSES data list. Does the scan tool display within the specified range?	2.3-2.7 V	Go to Step 5	Go to Step 8
5	With a scan tool, observe the Yaw Rate Sensor Input parameter in the VSES data list. Does the scan tool display within the specified range?	2.3-2.7 V	Go to Step 6	Go to Step 9

ARM66GC000000539

Fig. 96 Vehicle Stability Enhancement System Inoperative (Part 2 of 3). CTS

6	Replace the EBCM. Did you complete the replacement?	-	Go to Step 10	--
7	Replace the steering wheel position sensor (SWPS). Did you complete the replacement?	-	Go to Step 10	--
8	Replace the lateral accelerometer sensor. Did you complete the replacement?	-	Go to Step 10	--
9	Replace the yaw rate sensor. Did you complete the replacement?	-	Go to Step 10	--
10	Operate the system in order to verify the repair. Did you correct the condition?	-	System OK	Go to Step 2

ARM66GC000000540

Fig. 96 Vehicle Stability Enhancement System Inoperative (Part 3 of 3). CTS

Circuit Description

The vehicle stability enhancement system (VSES) is activated by the EBCM calculating the desired yaw rate and comparing it to the actual yaw rate input. The desired yaw rate is calculated from measured steering wheel position, vehicle speed, and lateral acceleration. The difference between the desired yaw rate and actual yaw rate is the yaw rate error, which is a measurement of oversteer or understeer. If the yaw rate error becomes too large, the EBCM will attempt to correct the vehicle's yaw motion by applying differential braking to the left or right front wheel.

The VSES activations generally occur during aggressive driving, in the turns or bumpy roads without much use of the accelerator pedal. When braking during VSES activation, the brake pedal will feel different than the ABS pedal pulsation. The brake pedal pulsates at a higher frequency during VSES activation.

The usable output voltage range for the lateral accelerometer and yaw rate sensors is 0.25-4.75 volts. The scan tool will report zero lateral acceleration or yaw rate as 2.5 volts with no sensor bias present. The sensor bias compensates for sensor mounting alignment errors, electronic signal errors, temperature changes, and manufacturing differences.

The steering wheel position sensor supplies 2 analog inputs, Phase A and Phase B, to the EBCM. The 2 input signals are approximately 90 degrees out of phase. By interpreting the relationship between the 2 inputs, the EBCM can determine the position of the steering wheel and the direction of steering wheel rotation.

Steer angle centering is the process by which the EBCM calibrates the steering sensor output so that the output reads zero when the steering wheel is centered. Using the yaw rate input, lateral accelerometer input, and wheel speed sensor inputs, the initial steering center position is calculated after driving greater than 10 km/h (6 mph) for more than 10 seconds in a straight line on a level surface.

Test Description

The number below refers to the step number on the diagnostic table.

6. Perform the Steering Position Sensor Test in order to verify if the steering wheel position sensor (SWPS) is operating properly.

ARM66GC000000541

Fig. 97 Vehicle Stability Enhancement System Unwanted Activation (Part 1 of 3). CTS

Step	Action	Value (s)	Yes	No
1	Did you perform the ABS Diagnostic System Check?	--	Go to Step 2	Go to Diagnostic System Check - ABS
2	Inspect the mounting of the yaw rate sensor. Did you find and correct the condition?	--	Go to Step 15	Go to Step 3
3	1. Install a scan tool. 2. Start the engine. 3. With a scan tool, observe the Yaw Rate Sensor Input parameter in the VSES data list. 4. Perform the Diagnostic Test Drive. Does the scan tool display suddenly increase or decrease without rapid turning of the vehicle?	--	Go to Step 4	Go to Step 5
4	Perform the diagnosis for DTC C1282. Refer to DTC C1282 . Did you find and correct the condition?	--	Go to Step 15	Go to Step 12
5	1. Straighten the front wheels. 2. Observe the Dual Analog SWPS Input A and Dual Analog SWPS Input B in the DRP/ABS/TCS data list. 3. Slowly rotate the steering wheel in both directions. Does the scan tool display change states as the steering wheel was rotated?	--	Go to Step 6	Go to Step 14
6	With the scan tool, perform the Steering Position Sensor Test. Did the SWPS pass the test?	--	Go to Step 7	Go to Step 14
7	1. Place the vehicle on a level surface. 2. With a scan tool, observe the Lateral Accelerometer Input parameter in the VSES data list. Does the scan tool display within the specified range?	2.3-2.7 V	Go to Step 9	Go to Step 8

ARM66GC000000542

Fig. 97 Vehicle Stability Enhancement System Unwanted Activation (Part 2 of 3). CTS

8	Inspect the mounting of the lateral accelerometer sensor. Did you find and correct the condition?	-	Go to Step 15	Go to Step 9
9	Inspect the EBCM for the proper part number. Did you find the correct part number?	-	Go to Step 10	Go to Step 12
10	Inspect the power steering gear for the proper part number. Did you find the correct part number?	-	Go to Step 11	Go to Step 13
11	Inspect the alignment of the vehicle. Did you find and correct the condition?	-	Go to Step 15	Test for Intermittent and Poor Connections
12	Replace the EBCM. Did you complete the repair?	-	Go to Step 15	--
13	Replace the power steering gear. Did you complete the repair?	-	Go to Step 15	--
14	Replace the steering wheel position sensor (SWPS). Did you complete the repair?	-	Go to Step 15	--
15	Operate the system in order to verify the repair. Did you correct the condition?	-	System OK	Go to Step 2

ARM66GC000000543

Fig. 97 Vehicle Stability Enhancement System Unwanted Activation (Part 3 of 3). CTS

Circuit Description

The vehicle stability enhancement system (VSES) is activated by the EBCM calculating the desired yaw rate and comparing it to the actual yaw rate input. The desired yaw rate is calculated from measured steering wheel position, vehicle speed, and lateral acceleration. The difference between the desired yaw rate and actual yaw rate is the yaw rate error, which is a measurement of oversteer or understeer. If the yaw rate error becomes too large, the EBCM will attempt to correct the vehicle's yaw motion by applying differential braking to the left or right front wheel.

The VSES activations generally occur during aggressive driving, in the turns or bumpy roads without much use of the accelerator pedal. When braking during VSES activation, the brake pedal will feel different than the ABS pedal pulsation. The brake pedal pulsates at a higher frequency during VSES activation.

The usable output voltage range for the lateral accelerometer and yaw rate sensors is 0.25-4.75 volts. The scan tool will report zero lateral acceleration or yaw rate as 2.5 volts with no sensor bias present. The sensor bias compensates for sensor mounting alignment errors, electronic signal errors, temperature changes, and manufacturing differences.

The steering wheel position sensor supplies 2 analog inputs, Phase A and Phase B, to the EBCM. The 2 input signals are approximately 90 degrees out of phase. By interpreting the relationship between the 2 inputs, the EBCM can determine the position of the steering wheel and the direction of steering wheel rotation.

Steer angle centering is the process by which the EBCM calibrates the steering sensor output so that the output reads zero when the steering wheel is centered. Using the yaw rate input, lateral accelerometer input, and wheel speed sensor inputs, the initial steering center position is calculated after driving greater than 10 km/h (6 mph) for more than 10 seconds in a straight line on a level surface.

ARM66GC000000544

Fig. 98 Vehicle Stability Enhancement System Excessive Brake Pulsation (Part 1 of 2). CTS

Step	Action	Value(s)	Yes	No
1	Did you perform the ABS Diagnostic System Check?	--	Go to Step 2	Go to Diagnostic System Check
2	1. With a scan tool, observe the Stop Lamp Switch parameter in the DRP/ABS/TCS data list. 2. Step on and off the brake pedal with enough force to simulate a hard braking condition. As the brake pedal is pressed and released, the scan tool should read Applied and Released. 3. Use a tape measure in order to measure the distance that the brake pedal travels for the scan tool to read Applied. Does the distance measure within the specified range?	2.5-3.3 cm (1.0-1.3 in)	Test for Intermittent and Poor Connections	Go to Step 3
3	Adjust or repair the extended travel brake switch as necessary. Did you complete the repair?	--	Go to Step 4	--
4	Operate the system in order to verify the repair. Did you correct the condition?	--	System OK	Go to Step 2

ARM66GC000000545

Fig. 98 Vehicle Stability Enhancement System Excessive Brake Pulsation (Part 2 of 2). CTS

Delco/Bosch Type 5.3

NOTE: On Air Bag Equipped Models, Refer To "Air Bag System Precautions" Located In The Front Of This Manual For System Disarming & Arming Procedures.

NOTE: Refer To "Computer Relearn Procedures" Located In The Front Of This Manual When Battery Power To The Computer Has Been Interrupted.

NOTE: "Electrical Symbol & Wire Color Code Identification" Located In The Front Of This Manual May Be Used As An Aid When Using Wiring Circuits Found In This Section.

INDEX

PRECAUTIONS

Air Bag Systems

Refer to "Air Bag System Precautions" in the front of this manual for system disarming and arming procedures.

Battery Ground Cable

Prior to service, disconnect battery ground cable and isolate as required.

ABS Service

Before performing any repairs on the ABS system, note the following precautions:

1. Before using electric welding equipment, disconnect EBCM.
2. Carefully note routing, position and mounting ABS and TCS wiring, connectors, clips and brackets. ABS and TCS are extremely sensitive to electromagnetic interference.
3. Do not use a fast charger when battery is connected. **Never disconnect battery from system with engine running.**
4. Ignition switch must be in Off position when disconnecting EBCM.
5. Many ABS system components are non-serviceable and must be replaced as assemblies. **Do not disassemble non-serviceable components.**
6. Do not hang other components on wheel speed sensor cables.
7. Do not expose EBCM to temperatures of more than 184°F.
8. Use DOT 3 brake fluid only. Do not use container that has been used with petroleum based fluids or is wet with water. Petroleum based fluids will damage system and water will lower boiling point. Keep fluid containers capped.
9. After replacing any ABS component, inspect system as outlined in "Diagnosis & Testing."

DESCRIPTION

System Operation

The Anti-Lock Brake System (ABS) minimizes wheel lock-up during heavy braking. The ABS monitors each wheel's speed and controls brake fluid pressure to each wheel independently. A separate hydraulic line and solenoid valve for each wheel allows hydraulic pressure to be modulated, preventing wheel lock-up. The ABS can decrease, hold or increase hydraulic pressure.

The system continuously monitors all components, using several methods to determine faults and notify the driver of faults. When the engine is started, the ABS electrical circuit is inspected. As the vehicle reaches four mph, the Brake Pressure Modulator Valve (BPMV) is inspected. The driver is informed of faults when the system illuminates either the Brake and/or ABS lamps.

If the Brake warning lamp is lit, brake system conditions may result in reduced braking ability. If the ABS indicator lamp is lit, an ABS fault has been detected and the anti-lock and traction control functions are turned off. If only the ABS indicator lamp is on, normal braking with full power assist is available without anti-lock. If both lamps are on, there may be a hydraulic brake system problem.

The Traction Control System (TCS) system also monitors rear wheel speed and compares it to front wheel speed. If front wheel speed is excessive, the TCS will activate. When the TCS activates, it signals the Powertrain Control Module (PCM) to retard timing, selectively turn off fuel injectors and/or apply front brakes to reduce drive

Description
DTC C1211 ABS Indicator Lamp Circuit Malfunction
DTC C1214 System Relay Contact or Coil Circuit Open
DTC C1217 Pump Motor Shorted to Ground
DTC C1218 Pump Motor Circuit Shorted to Voltage or Motor Ground Open
DTC C1221 LF Wheel Speed Sensor Input Signal is 0
DTC C1222 RF Wheel Speed Sensor Input Signal is 0
DTC C1223 LR Wheel Speed Sensor Input Signal is 0
DTC C1224 RR Wheel Speed Sensor Input Signal is 0
DTC C1225 LF Excessive Wheel Speed Variation
DTC C1226 RF Excessive Wheel Speed Variation
DTC C1227 LR Excessive Wheel Speed Variation
DTC C1228 RR Excessive Wheel Speed Variation
DTC C1232 LF Wheel Speed Circuit Open or Shorted
DTC C1233 RF Wheel Speed Circuit Open or Shorted
DTC C1234 LR Wheel Speed Circuit Open or Shorted
DTC C1235 RR Wheel Speed Circuit Open or Shorted
DTC C1236 Low System Supply Voltage
DTC C1237 High System Supply Voltage
DTC C1238 Brake Thermal Model Exceeded
DTC C1241 Variable Effort Steering Circuit Malfunction in Variable Effort Steering
DTC C1242 Pump Motor Circuit Open
DTC C1243 BPMV Pump Motor Stalled
DTC C1245 Low Tire Pressure Detected in Tire Pressure Monitoring
DTC C1248 EBCM Turned the Red Brake Warning Indicator On
DTC C1254 Abnormal Shutdown Detected
DTC C1255 EBCM Internal Malfunction
DTC C1256 EBCM Internal Malfunction
DTC C1261 LF Inlet Valve Solenoid Malfunction
DTC C1262 LF Outlet Valve Solenoid Malfunction
DTC C1263 RF Inlet Valve Solenoid Malfunction
DTC C1264 RF Outlet Valve Solenoid Malfunction
DTC C1265 LR Inlet Valve Solenoid Malfunction
DTC C1266 LR Outlet Valve Solenoid Malfunction
DTC C1267 RR Inlet Valve Solenoid Malfunction
DTC C1268 RR Outlet Valve Solenoid Malfunction

GC4020152600010X

Fig. 1 DTC identification (Part 1 of 2)

Description
DTC C1271 LF TCS Master Cylinder Isolation Valve Malfunction
DTC C1272 LF TCS Prime Valve Malfunction
DTC C1273 RF TCS Master Cylinder Isolation Valve Malfunction
DTC C1274 RF TCS Prime Valve Malfunction
DTC C1276 Delivered Torque Signal Circuit Malfunction
DTC C1277 Requested Torque Signal Circuit Malfunction
DTC C1278 TCS Temporarily Inhibited By PCM
DTC C1281 VSES Sensors Uncorrelated
DTC C1282 Yaw Rate Sensor Bias Circuit Malfunction
DTC C1283 Excessive Time to Center Steering
DTC C1284 Lateral Accelerometer Sensor Bias Malfunction
DTC C1285 Lateral Accelerometer Sensor Circuit Malfunction
DTC C1286 Steering Sensor Bias Malfunction
DTC C1287 Steering Sensor Rate Malfunction
DTC C1288 Steering Sensor Circuit Malfunction
DTC C1291 Open Brake Lamp Switch Contacts During Deceleration
DTC C1293 Code C1291 Set in Previous Ignition Cycle
DTC C1294 Brake Lamp Switch Circuit Always Active
DTC C1295 Brake Lamp Switch Circuit Open
DTC C1298 PCM Class 2 Serial Data Link Malfunction
DTC P1571 Traction Control Torque Request Circuit in Engine Controls
DTC P1689 Traction Control Delivered Torque Output Circuit in Engine Controls
DTC U1016 Loss of Communications with PCM Go to *Scan Tool Does Not Communicate with Class 2 Device*
DTC U1040 Loss of Communications with ABS Go to *Scan Tool Does Not Communicate with Class 2 Device*
DTC U1064 Loss of Communications with SBM Go to *Scan Tool Does Not Communicate with Class 2 Device*
DTC U1088 Loss of Communications with SDM Go to *Scan Tool Does Not Communicate with Class 2 Device*
DTC U1096 Loss of Communications with IPC Go to *Scan Tool Does Not Communicate with Class 2 Device*
DTC U1152 Loss of Communications with HCM Go to *Scan Tool Does Not Communicate with Class 2 Device*
DTC U1160 Loss of Communications with DDM Go to *Scan Tool Does Not Communicate with Class 2 Device*
DTC U1255 Class 2 Data Link Malfunction Go to *Scan Tool Does Not Communicate with Class 2 Device*
DTC U1300 Class 2 Data Link Low Go to *Scan Tool Does Not Communicate with Class 2 Device*
DTC U1301 Class 2 Data Link High Go to *Scan Tool Does Not Communicate with Class 2 Device*

GC4020152600020X

Fig. 1 DTC identification (Part 2 of 2)

wheel torque and improve traction and stability. This function may to turned on or off by the driver.

System Components

BRAKE PRESSURE MODULATOR VALVE (BPMV)

The Brake Pressure Modulator Valve (BPMV), mounted on the front lefthand side of the engine compartment, provides brake fluid modulation for individual wheel circuits during anti-lock operations. The BPMV can also apply the brakes during traction control mode.

The BPMV is not serviceable. The BPMV contains a small pump motor to circulate brake fluid back to the master cylinder. Also integrated into the BPMV are the solenoid valves which can increase, decrease or hold brake hydraulic pressure. There are also two non-serviceable relays in the BPMV for the pump motor and solenoid valve.

ELECTRONIC BRAKE CONTROL MODULE (EBCM)

The Electronic Brake Control Module (EBCM) is a microprocessor which monitors wheel speed and the Brake Pressure Modulator Valve (BPMV) electrical status. It is located between the BPMV and the master cylinder, on the front lefthand side of the engine compartment.

The EBCM detects wheel locking tendencies and rotating speed differences, controls anti-lock brake operations, commands traction control torque reduction and monitors system electrical operations. The EBCM also controls Diagnostic Trouble Code (DTC) displays.

WHEEL SPEED SENSORS

Wheel speed sensors transmit wheel speed information to the EBCM with voltage generated by magnetic induction caused by passing a toothed sensor ring past a stationary sensor. The wheel speed sensors are not adjustable.

The front wheel speed sensors are mounted in the hub and bearing assembly and the rear wheel speed sensors are mounted in the bearing assembly.

DIAGNOSIS & TESTING

Accessing Diagnostic Trouble Codes

1. Turn ignition switch to Off position.
2. Connect suitably programmed scan tool connected to Data Link Connector (DLC), located on lefthand side of instrument panel below steering column.
3. Turn ignition switch to On position.
4. Select scan tool's Special Functions.

5. Select and run Automated Test.
6. Note Diagnostic Trouble Codes (DTCs).

Diagnostic Trouble Code Interpretation

Refer to **Fig. 1,** for Diagnostic Trouble Code (DTC) identification and description.

Wiring Diagrams

AURORA, BONNEVILLE & LESABRE

Refer to **Fig. 2,** for system wiring circuits.

DEVILLE & SEVILLE

Refer to **Figs. 3 and 4,** for system wiring circuits.

PARK AVENUE

Refer to **Fig. 5,** for system wiring circuits.

EBCM Connector Views

Refer to **Figs. 6 through 8,** for EBCM connector views.

Diagnostic Tests

AURORA, BONNEVILLE, LESABRE & PARK AVENUE

Refer to **Figs. 9 through 71,** for diagnostic tests.

DEVILLE & SEVILLE

Refer to **Figs. 72 through 105,** for diagnostic tests.

Clearing Diagnostic Trouble Codes

Connect a suitably programmed scan tool to Data Link Connector (DLC), and follow manufacturer's instructions.

Intermittents & Poor Connections

Intermittent failures in the anti-lock brake system may be difficult to accurately diagnose. The ABS Diagnostic Trouble Codes (DTCs) which may be stored by the EBCM are not designated as Current or History DTCs. These DTCs can be helpful in diagnosing intermittent conditions.

If an intermittent condition is being diagnosed, the ABS system can be used in the following manner to help isolate the suspected circuit.

1. Display and clear any ABS DTCs present in EBCM, then turn ignition off and disconnect scan tool. **If scan tool is installed, EBCM will not set DTCs and ABS/TCS functions may not be available.**
2. Test drive vehicle and attempt to duplicate the intermittent condition.
3. After duplicating condition, stop vehicle and display any DTCs stored.
4. If a DTC was stored, inspect affected circuit and electrical connectors for the following:
   a. Poor mating of connector halves.
   b. Terminals not fully seated in connector halves.
   c. Improperly formed, or damaged terminals. All connector terminals in a problem circuit should be carefully reformed to increase contact tension.
   d. Poor terminal to wire connection. In most cases, this will require removing wire from connector body.
5. If there is an intermittent warning lamp operation, the following EBCM circuits should be inspected:
   a. Low system voltage. If low voltage is detected at EBCM, Anti-lock lamp will illuminate until normal operating voltage is detected.
   b. Low brake fluid. This condition in Pressure Modulator Valve (PMV) reservoir will cause Brake and Antilock lamps to illuminate. When an acceptable fluid level is registered, lamps will no longer be on.
6. Any condition which results in interruption of power to EBCM or hydraulic unit may cause warning lamps to turn on intermittently. These circuits include main relay, pump motor relay, fuses and related wiring.

Ignition Cycle Default

If vehicle power is cycled 100 times without a particular fault reappearing, that particular DTC will be erased from the EBCM memory, and ignition cycle counter will be reset to zero.

Electromagnetic Interference Test

Due to the sensitivity of ABS components to electromagnetic interference, the following inspects should be performed is an intermittent fault is suspected.

1. Inspect for proper installation of wiring harnesses resulting from add on options.
2. Visually inspect wheel speed sensor and toothed sensor ring for looseness, damage, accumulation of foreign material and proper mounting. Replace damaged components, remove any foreign material and properly attach all components.
3. Ensure front wheel speed sensor wiring is routed away from spark plug wires.
4. Measure spark plug wire resistance. If resistance is greater than 30,000 ohms for any wire, replace spark plug wires.
5. While test driving vehicle, use a properly programmed scan tool to monitor wheel speeds. If any wheel speed drops or displays an erratic speed, refer to appropriated wheel speed sensor DTC.

SYSTEM SERVICE

Brake System Bleed

AUTO BLEED

Perform manual or pressure bleeding as outlined in "Manual Bleed" or "Pressure Bleed" before auto bleeding system.

1. Turn ignition switch to Off position.
2. Raise and support vehicle, then remove all tire and wheel assemblies.
3. Inspect brake system for leaks and damage.
4. Ensure battery is fully charged.
5. Connect suitable programmed scan tool to Data Link Connector (DLC) located on lefthand side of instrument panel below steering column.
6. Turn ignition switch to On position. Do not start engine.
7. Establish scan tool communications by selecting ABS/TCS, Special Functions and Automated Bleed Procedure.
8. Bleed system as outlined in "Manual Bleed" or "Pressure Bleed."
9. Follow scan tool instructions until desired brake pedal height is obtained. Inspect pedal for firmness.

MANUAL BLEED

1. Remove vacuum reserve by pumping brakes several times with engine off.
2. Fill master cylinder reservoir with clean brake fluid.
3. Inspect fluid level often during bleeding procedure, do not let reservoir fall below half full.
4. If required, bleed master cylinder as follows:
   a. Disconnect forward brake line from master cylinder.
   b. Allow brake fluid to flow from forward port, then connect and tighten brake line.
   c. Slowly depress brake pedal one time and hold.
   d. Loosen front brake line connection and purge air from master cylinder.
   e. Tighten connection and slowly release brake pedal.
   f. Wait 15 seconds and repeat until all air is purged from forward brake line connection.
   g. Disconnect rear brake line from master cylinder and allow brake fluid to flow from port.
   h. Slowly depress brake pedal one time and hold.
   i. Loosen rear brake line connection and purge air from master cylinder.
   j. Tighten connection and slowly release brake pedal.
   k. Wait 15 seconds and repeat until all air is purged from forward brake line connection.
5. Bleed calipers in following order: righthand rear, lefthand rear, righthand front and lefthand front.
6. Place one end of a transparent tube over bleeder valve and other end of tube into a transparent container with clean brake fluid.
7. Slowly depress brake pedal one time and hold.

8. Loosen bleeder valve and purge air, then tighten bleeder screw and slowly release pedal. Repeat until all air is purged from system.
9. **Torque** bleed screws to 115 inch lbs.
10. If brake pedal is spongy, auto bleed modulator as outlined in "Auto Bleed" and repeat bleeding procedure.

PRESSURE BLEED

1. Loosen and slightly tighten bleeder valves at all four wheels. Repair any broken, stripped or frozen valves at this time.
2. Replace master cylinder reservoir cap with suitable pressure bleeding adapter.
3. Charge bleeder to 30–35 psi and connect hose to adapter.
4. Raise and support vehicle.
5. Bleed calipers in following order: righthand rear, lefthand rear, righthand front and lefthand front.
6. Place one end of a transparent tube over bleeder valve and other end of tube in a transparent container partially filled with clean brake fluid.
7. Open bleeder screw at least ¾ turn and allow fluid to flow until air is purged. Pump brake pedal while pressure bleeding.
8. Close bleed screw and **torque** to 115 inch lbs.
9. If brake pedal is spongy, auto bleed modulator as outlined in "Auto Bleed" and repeat bleeding procedure.

Component Replacement

BRAKE PRESSURE MODULATOR VALVE (BPMV)

BONNEVILLE, LESABRE & PARK AVENUE

The Brake Pressure Modulator Valve (BPMV) cannot be repaired. The complete unit must be replaced. **With the exception of the EBCM screws, no screws on the BPMV may be loosened. If screws are loosened, it will not be possible to get brake circuits leak tight.**

1. Turn ignition switch to the OFF position.
2. Remove air cleaner assembly.
3. Disconnect EBCM wiring harness and BPMV motor ground cable.
4. Remove brake pipe fittings. Note location for installation reference.
5. Remove mounting bolts and separate EBCM from BPMV.
6. Reverse procedure to install, noting the following:
   a. **Torque** mounting bolts to 35 inch lbs.
   b. **Torque** brake pipe fittings to 11 ft. lbs.
   c. Bleed brake hydraulic system as outlined in "Brake System Bleed."

AURORA, DEVILLE & SEVILLE

1. Turn ignition off, then raise and support vehicle.
2. Remove left front tire and wheel assembly.
3. Remove splash shield from inside wheelwell.
4. Loosen pinch clamp, then remove exhaust hose from secondary AIR pump.
5. Remove air inlet hose/filter from AIR pump.
6. Disconnect AIR pump electrical connector.
7. Loosen AIR to cradle bracket nuts, then remove upper AIR pump to cradle bolt.
8. Remove AIR pump from cradle bracket.
9. Rotate EBCM connector tab up to unlocked position, then disconnect EBCM electrical connector.
10. Mark brake pipes for installation reference, then remove brake pipes from BPMV.
11. Remove BPMV to bracket retaining nuts, then remove EBCM/BPMV assembly from bracket.
12. Remove BPMV to EBCM attaching screws, then separate BPMV from EBCM.
13. Reverse procedure to install, noting the following:
    a. **Torque** BPMV to EBCM attaching screws to 28 inch lbs.
    b. **Torque** BPMV to bracket attaching bolts to 89 inch lbs.
    c. **Torque** all brake pipe connections to 11 ft. lbs.
    d. Bleed brake system.

ELECTRONIC BRAKE CONTROL MODULE (EBCM)

Refer to "Brake Pressure Modulator Valve (BPMV)" for replacement procedure. If replacing EBCM with a new unit, the new unit will have to be programmed using the latest available software.

WHEEL SPEED SENSOR

The wheel speed sensors are integral with the hub and bearing assembly. To replace the sensors, refer to "Hub & Bearing, Replace" in either the "Rear Suspension" or "Front Suspension & Steering" section of the appropriate chassis chapter.

LATERAL ACCELEROMETER SENSOR

1. Turn ignition switch to the OFF position.
2. Remove rear seat cushion.
3. Disconnect lateral accelerator sensor electrical connector, **Fig. 106.**
4. Remove accelerator retaining bolts, then the accelerator.
5. Reverse procedure to install.

YAW RATE SENSOR

1. Turn ignition switch to the OFF position.
2. Remove rear shelf trim panel.
3. Remove yaw rate sensor retaining nuts, **Fig. 107.**
4. Disconnect yaw rate sensor electrical connector, then remove sensor.
5. Reverse procedure to install.

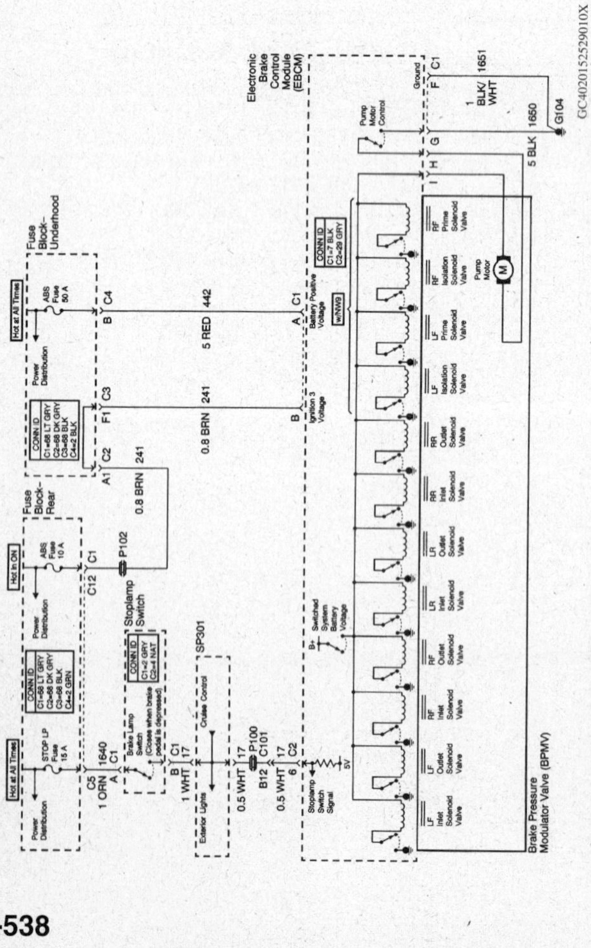

Fig. 2 Wiring diagram (Part 1 of 5). Aurora, Bonneville & LeSabre

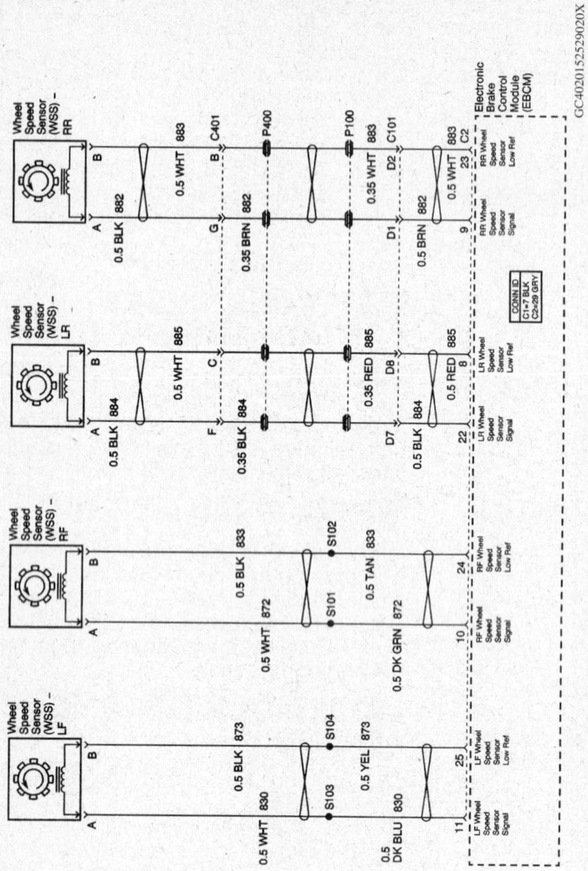

Fig. 2 Wiring diagram (Part 2 of 5). Aurora, Bonneville & LeSabre

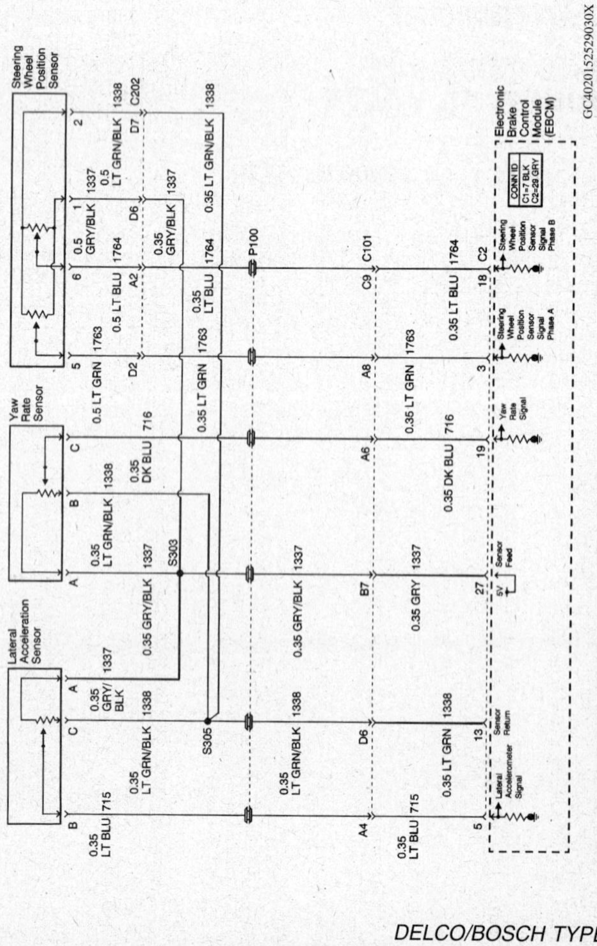

Fig. 2 Wiring diagram (Part 3 of 5). Aurora, Bonneville & LeSabre

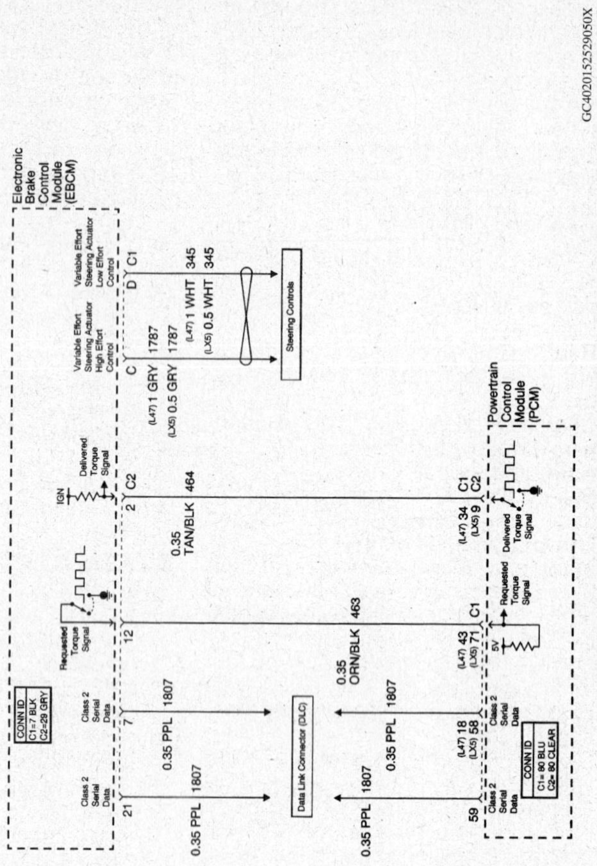

Fig. 2 Wiring diagram (Part 4 of 5). Aurora

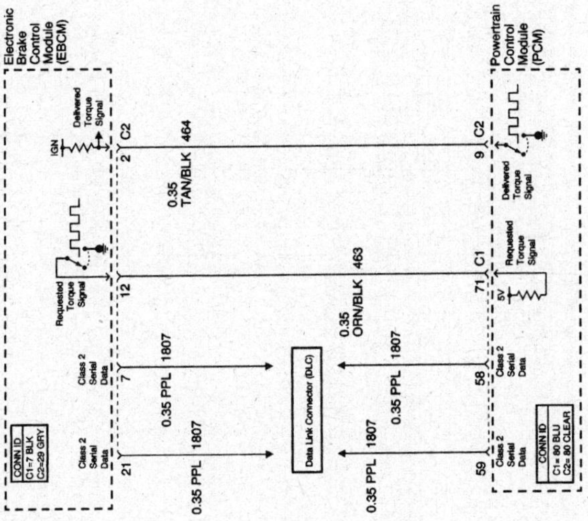

Fig. 2 Wiring diagram (Part 4 of 5). LeSabre

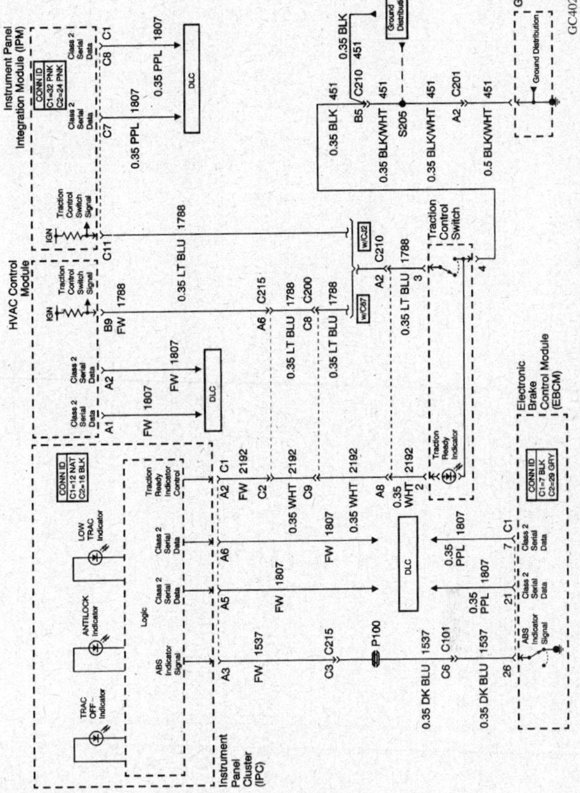

Fig. 2 Wiring diagram (Part 5 of 5). Bonneville

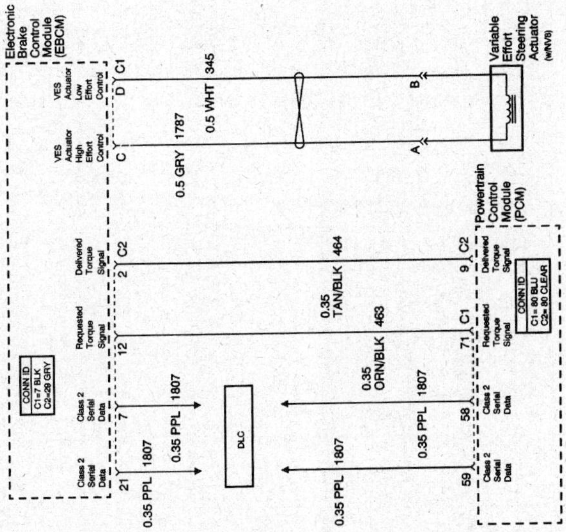

Fig. 2 Wiring diagram (Part 4 of 5). Bonneville

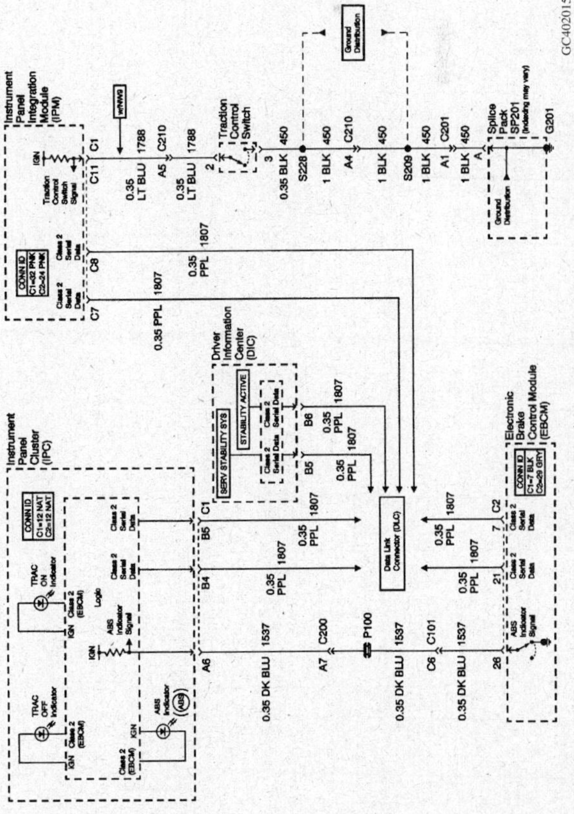

Fig. 2 Wiring diagram (Part 5 of 5). Aurora

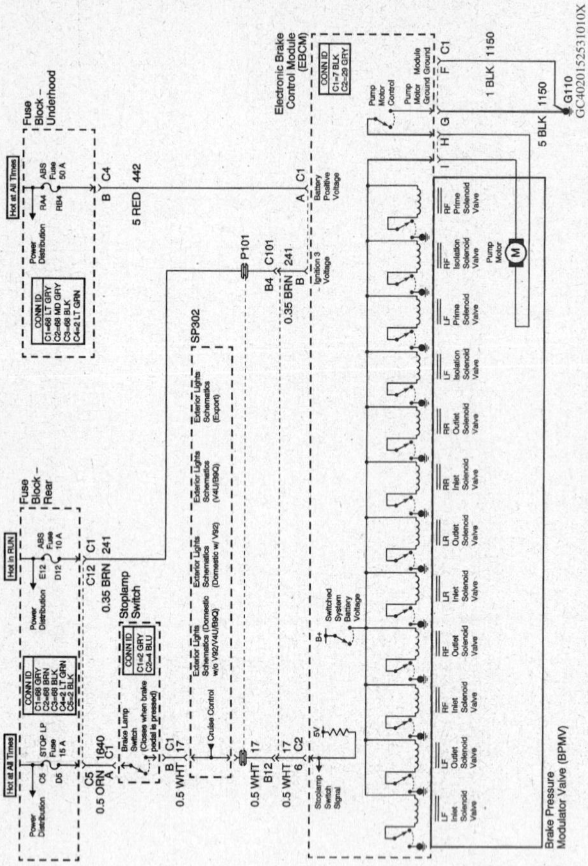

Fig. 3 Wiring diagram (Part 1 of 5). DeVille

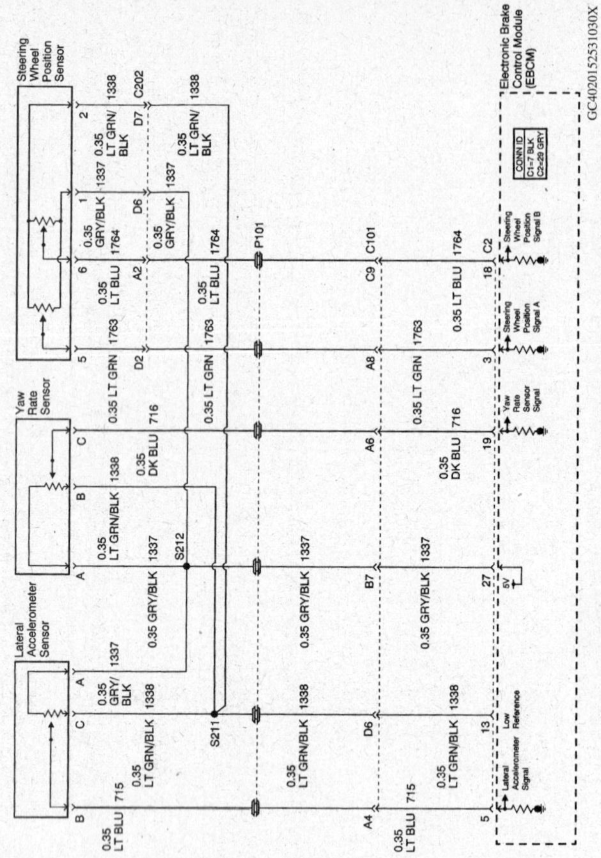

Fig. 3 Wiring diagram (Part 3 of 5). DeVille

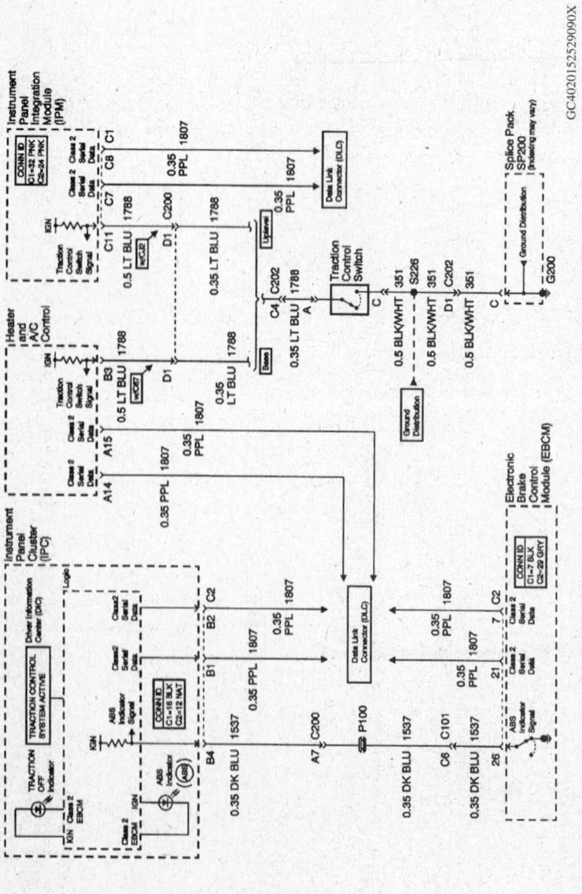

Fig. 2 Wiring diagram (Part 5 of 5). LeSabre

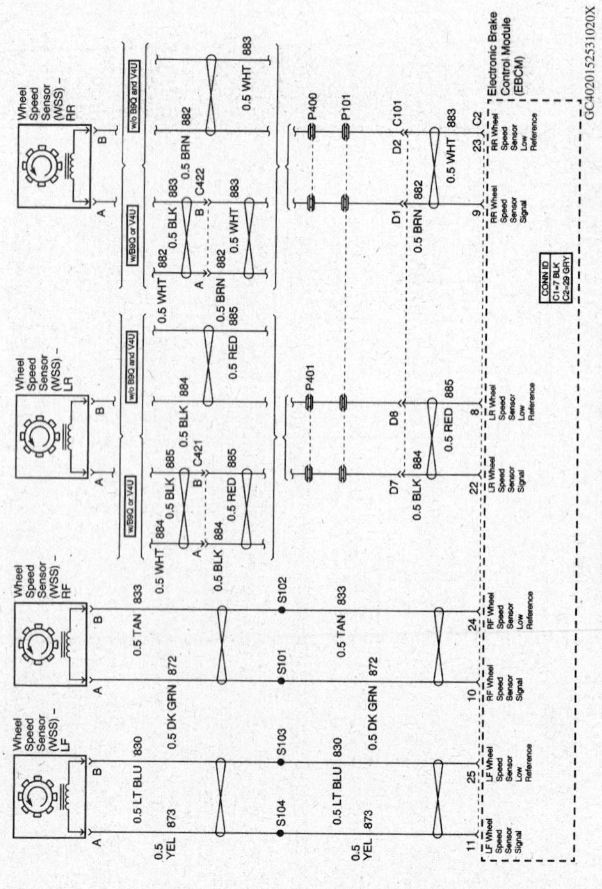

Fig. 3 Wiring diagram (Part 2 of 5). DeVille

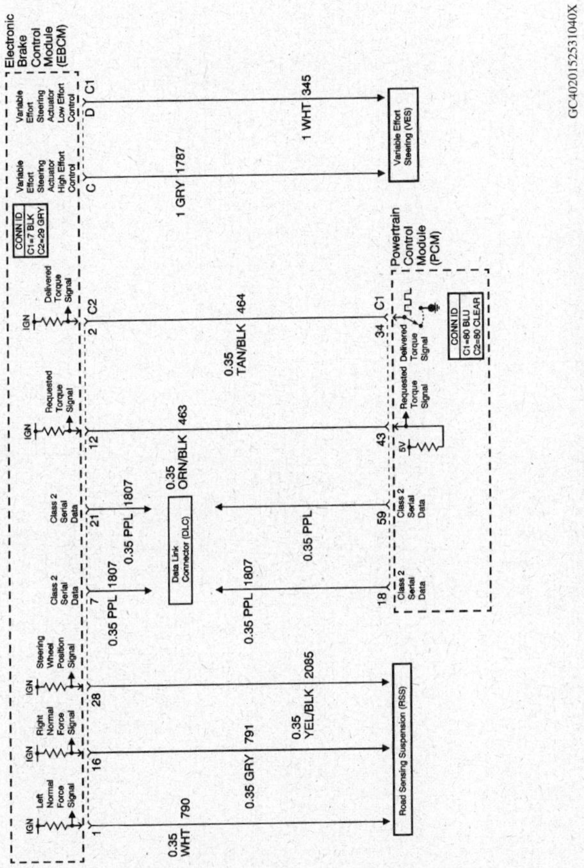

Fig. 3 Wiring diagram (Part 4 of 5). DeVille

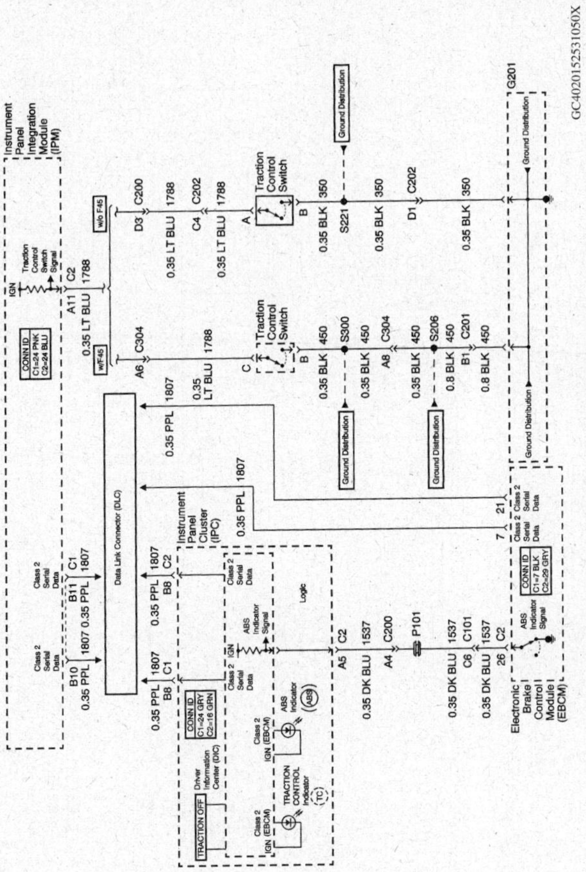

Fig. 3 Wiring diagram (Part 5 of 5). DeVille

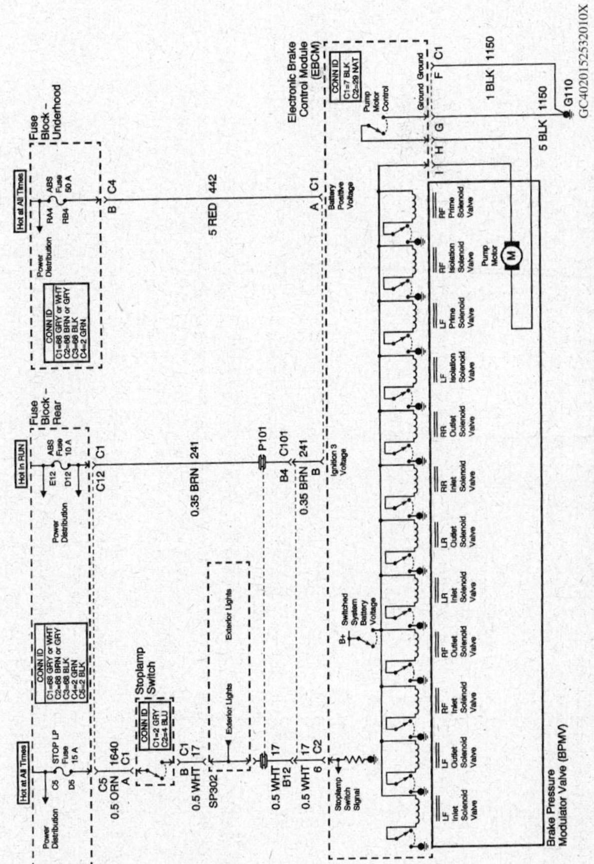

Fig. 4 Wiring diagram (Part 1 of 5). Seville

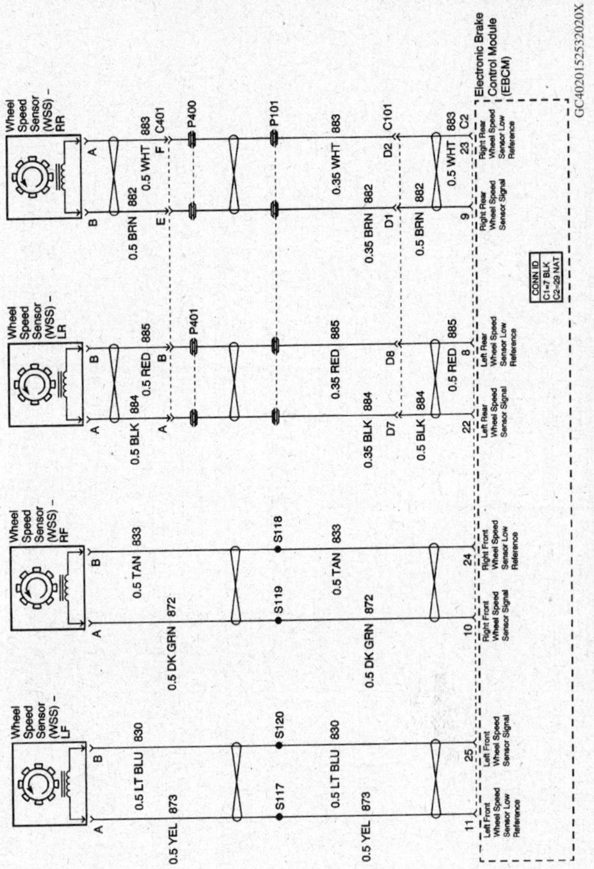

Fig. 4 Wiring diagram (Part 2 of 5). Seville

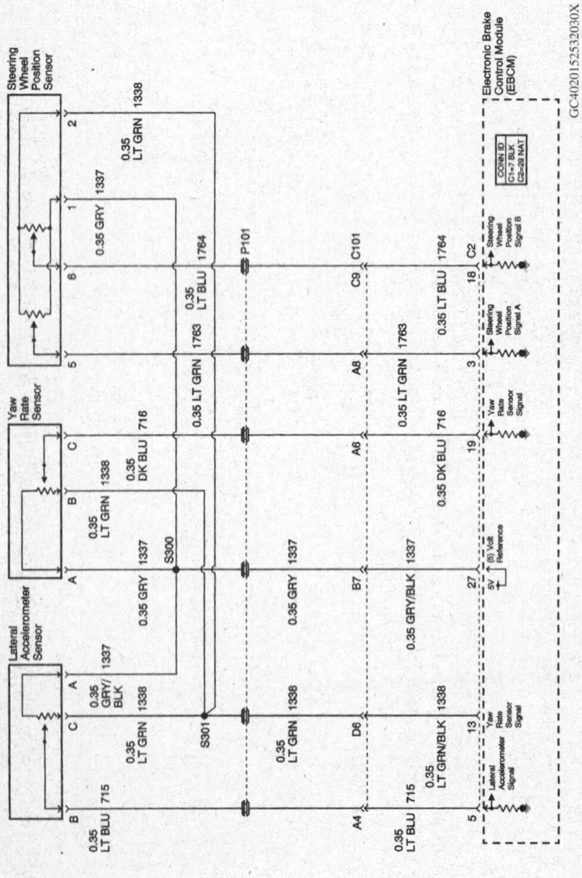

Fig. 4 Wiring diagram (Part 3 of 5). Seville

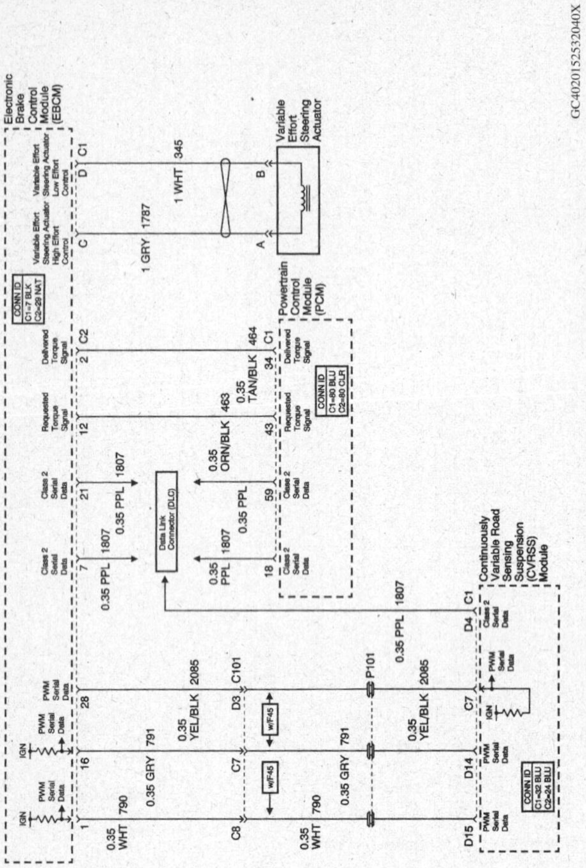

CC4020152532030X

Fig. 4 Wiring diagram (Part 4 of 5). Seville

CC4020152532040X

Fig. 4 Wiring diagram (Part 5 of 5). Seville

CC4020152532050X

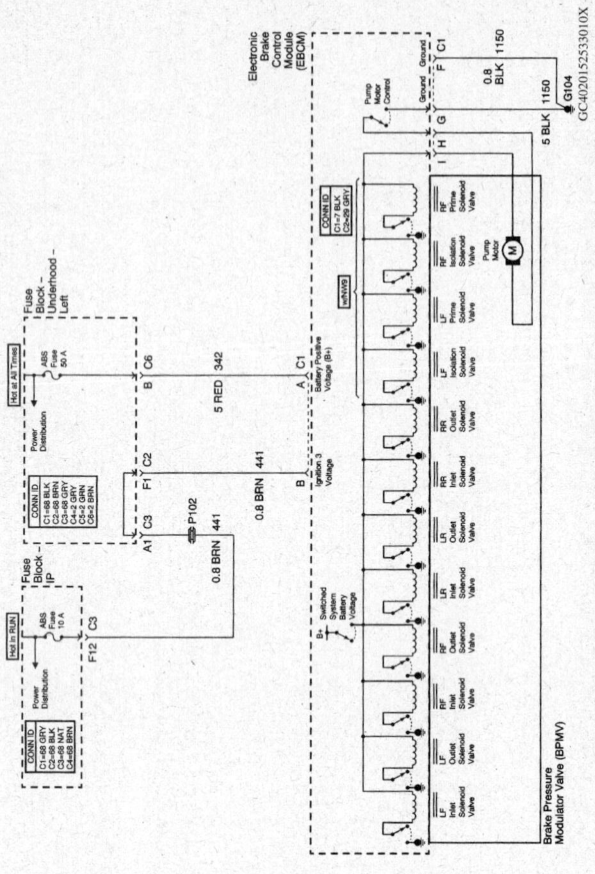

Fig. 5 Wiring diagram (Part 1 of 5). Park Avenue

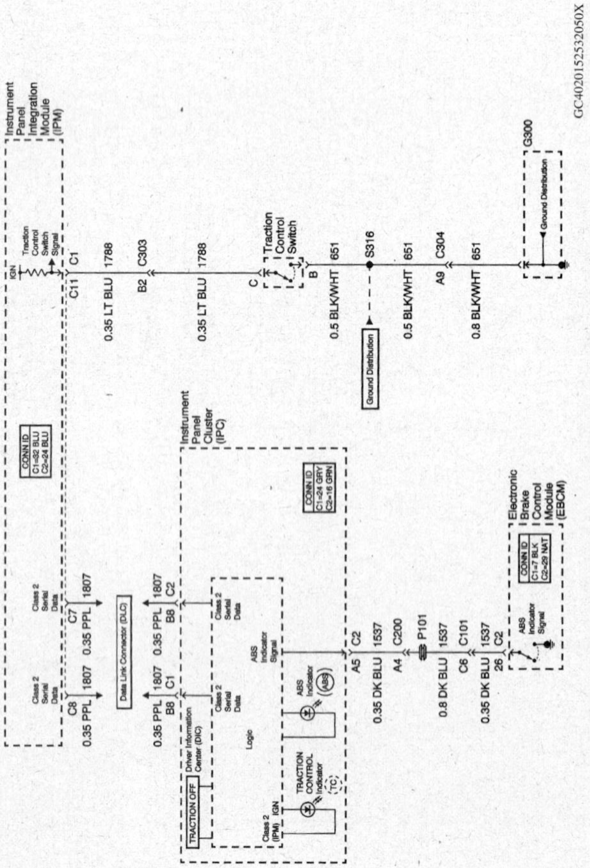

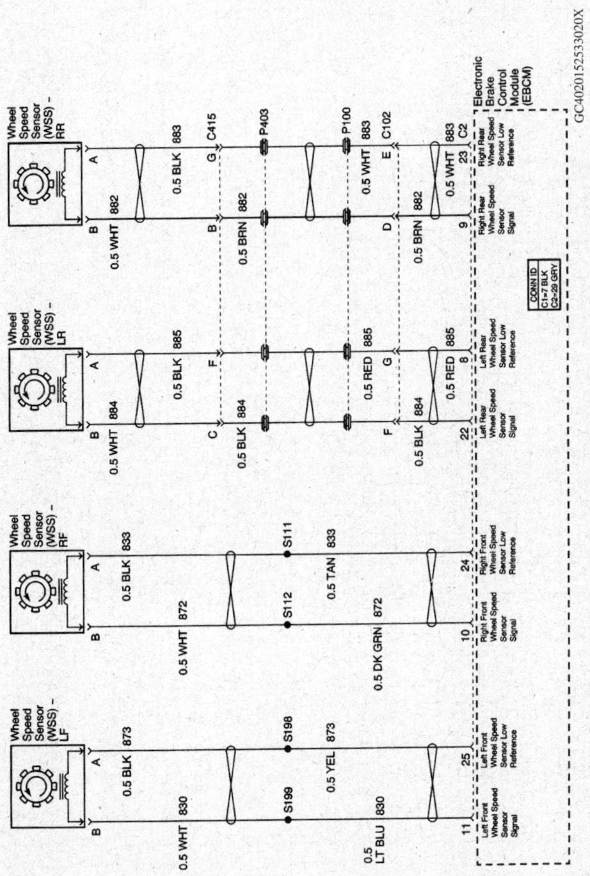

Fig. 5 Wiring diagram (Part 2 of 5). Park Avenue

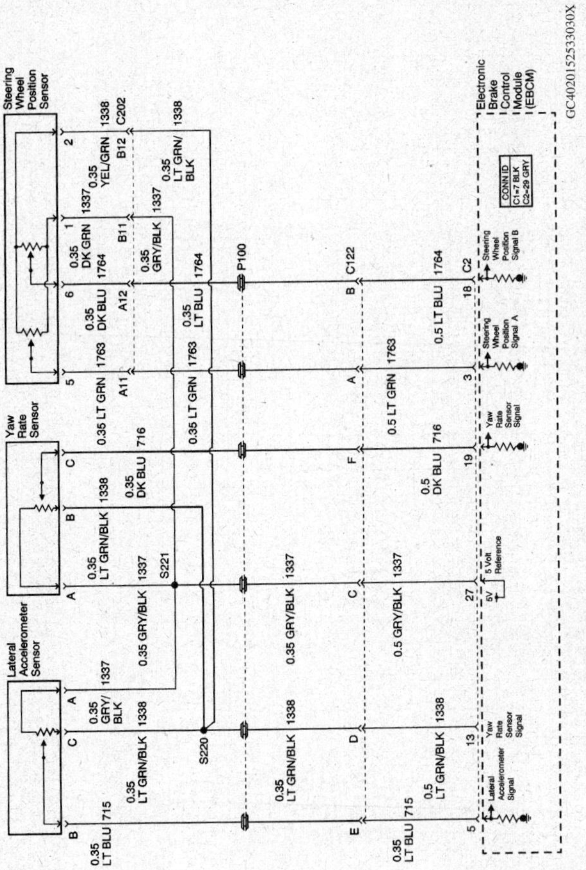

Fig. 5 Wiring diagram (Part 3 of 5). Park Avenue

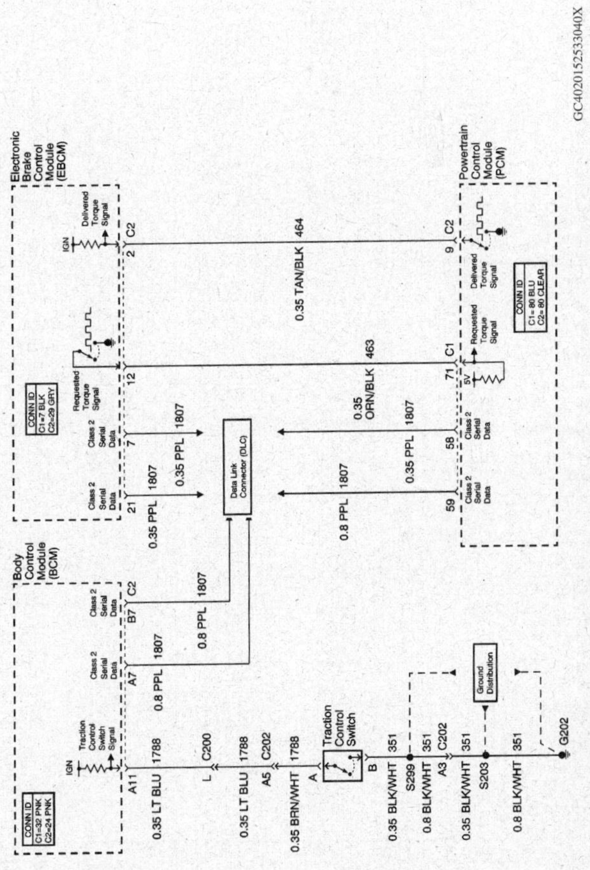

Fig. 5 Wiring diagram (Part 4 of 5). Park Avenue

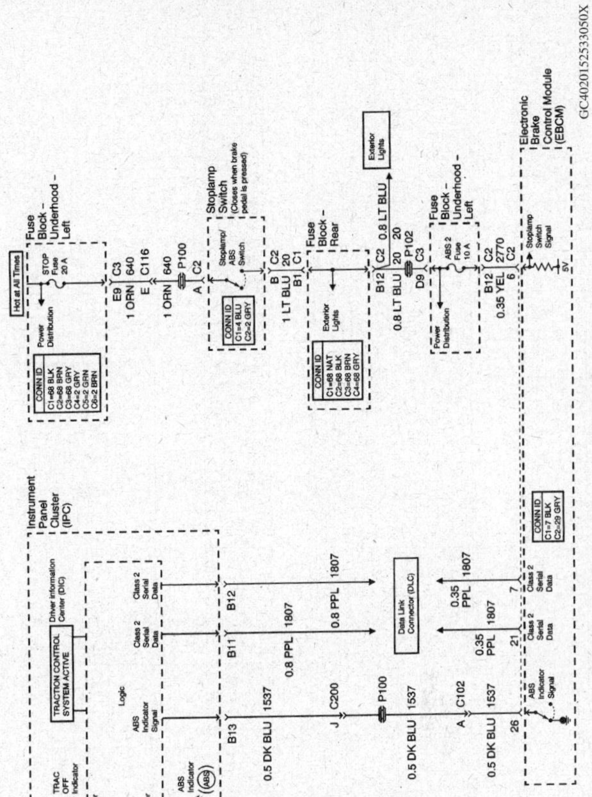

Fig. 5 Wiring diagram (Part 5 of 5). Park Avenue

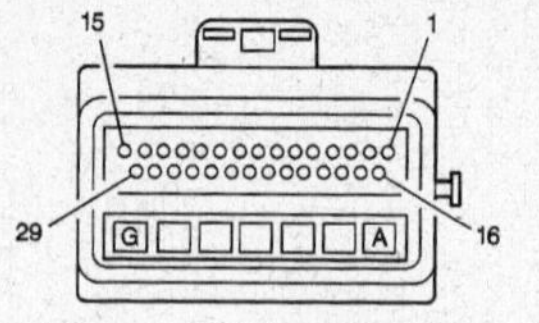

Connector Part Information	• C1 - 15318099 • 7 Way F Metri-Pack 480 Series (BLK) • C2 - 15356700 • 29 Way F Micro-Pack 100 Series (GRY)		
Pin	**Wire Color**	**Circuit No.**	**Function**
A	RED	442	Battery Positive Voltage
B	BRN	241	Ignition 3 Voltage
C	GRY	1787	Variable Effort Steering Actuator High Effort Control (w/NV8)
D	WHT	345	Variable Effort Steering Actuator Low Effort Control (w/NV8)
E	—	—	Vent Tube
F	BLK/WHT	1651	Ground
G	BLK	1650	Ground
1	—	—	Not Used
2	TAN/BLK	464	Delivered Torque Signal (w/NW9)
3	LT GRN	1763	Steering Wheel Position Signal A (w/JL4)
4	—	—	Not Used
5	LT BLU	715	Lateral Accelerometer Signal (w/JL4)
6	WHT	17	Stoplamp Switch Signal (w/NW9)
7	PPL	1807	Class 2 Serial Data
8	RED	885	Left Rear Wheel Speed Sensor Low Reference
9	BRN	882	Right Rear Wheel Speed Sensor Signal

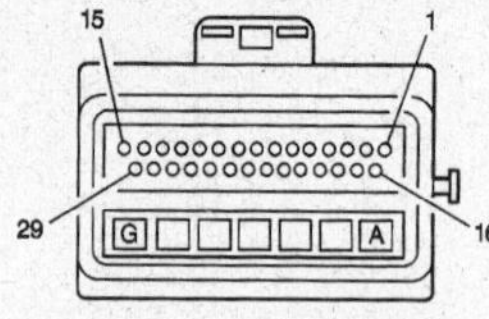

Connector Part Information	• C1 - 15318099 • 7 Way F Metri-Pack 480 Series (BLK) • C2 - 15356700 • 29 Way F Micro-Pack 100 Series (GRY)		
Pin	**Wire Color**	**Circuit No.**	**Function**
10	DK GRN	872	Right Front Wheel Speed Sensor Signal
11	DK BLU	830	Left Front Wheel Speed Sensor Signal
12	ORN/BLK	463	Requested Torque Signal (w/NW9)
13	LT GRN	1338	Low Reference (w/JL4)
14–17	—	—	Not Used
18	LT BLU	1764	Steering Wheel Position Signal B (w/JL4)
19	DK BLU	716	Yaw Rate Sensor Signal (w/JL4)
20	—	—	Not Used
21	PPL	1807	Class 2 Serial Data
22	BLK	884	Left Rear Wheel Speed Sensor Signal
23	WHT	883	Right Rear Wheel Speed Sensor Low Reference
24	TAN	833	Right Front Wheel Speed Sensor Low Reference
25	YEL	873	Left Front Wheel Speed Sensor Low Reference
26	DK BLU	1537	ABS Indicator Signal
27	GRY	1337	5 V Reference (w/JL4)
28–29	—	—	Not Used

GC4020152534000X

Fig. 6 EBCM connector terminal identification. Aurora, Bonneville & LeSabre

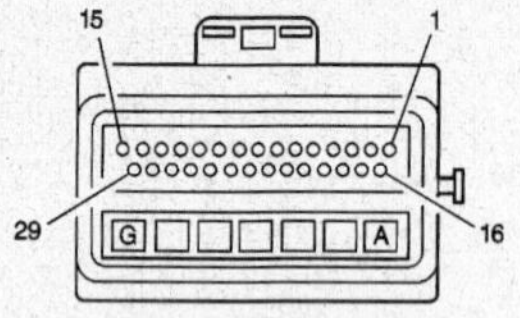

Connector Part Information	• C1 - 15318099 • 7 Way F Metri-Pack 480 Series (BLK) • C2 - 15356700 • 29 Way F Micro-Pack 100 Series (NAT)		
Pin	**Wire Color**	**Circuit No.**	**Function**
A	RED	442	Battery Positive Voltage
B	BRN	241	Ignition 3 Voltage
C	GRY	1787	Variable Effort Steering Actuator High Effort Control
D	WHT	345	Variable Effort Steering Actuator Low Effort Control
E	—	—	Vent Tube
F - G	BLK	1150	Ground
1	WHT	790	PWM Serial Data
2	TAN/BLK	464	Delivered Torque Signal
3	LT GRN	1763	Steering Wheel Position Signal A
4	WHT	1612	Left Front Brake Lining Wear Sensor Signal
5	LT BLU	715	Lateral Accelerometer Signal
6	WHT	17	Stop Lamp Switch Signal
7	PPL	1807	Class 2 Serial Data (Primary)
8	RED	885	Left Rear Wheel Speed Sensor Low Reference
9	BRN	882	Right Rear Wheel Speed Sensor Signal
10	DK GRN	872	Right Front Wheel Speed Sensor Signal

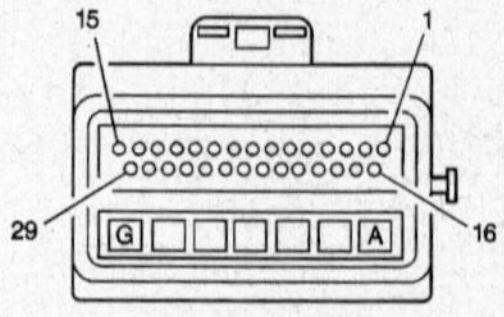

Connector Part Information	• C1 - 15318099 • 7 Way F Metri-Pack 480 Series (BLK) • C2 - 15356700 • 29 Way F Micro-Pack 100 Series (NAT)		
Pin	**Wire Color**	**Circuit No.**	**Function**
11	YEL	873	Left Front Wheel Speed Sensor Low Reference
12	ORN/BLK	463	Requested Torque Signal
13	LT GRN/ BLK	1338	Yaw Rate Sensor Signal
14–15	—	—	Not Used
16	GRY	791	PWM Serial Data
17	—	—	Not Used
18	LT BLU	1764	Steering Wheel Position Signal B
19	DK BLU	716	Yaw Rate Sensor Signal
20	—	—	Not Used
21	PPL	1807	Class 2 Serial Data (Primary)
22	BLK	884	Left Rear Wheel Speed Sensor Signal
23	WHT	883	Right Rear Wheel Speed Sensor Low Reference
24	TAN	833	Right Front Wheel Speed Sensor Low Reference
25	LT BLU	830	Left Front Wheel Speed Sensor Signal
26	DK BLU	1537	ABS Indicator Signal
27	GRY/BLK	1337	5 Volt Reference
28	YEL/BLK	2085	PWM Serial Data
29	—	—	Not Used

GC4020152536000X

Fig. 7 EBCM connector terminal identification. DeVille & Seville

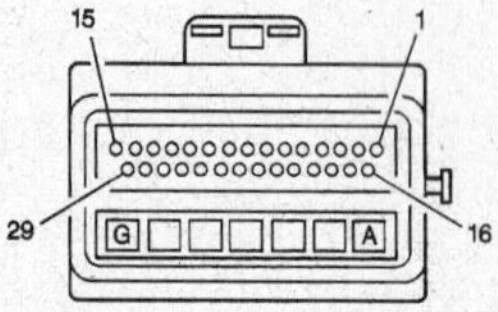

Connector Part Information	• C1 - 15318099 • 7 Way F Metri-Pack 480 Series (BLK) • C2 - 15354984 • 29 Way F Micro-Pack 100 Series (NAT) • C2 - 15356700 • 29 Way F Micro-Pack 100 Series (GRY)		
Pin	**Wire Color**	**Circuit No.**	**Function**
A	RED	342	Fuse Output - Battery
B	BRN	441	Fuse Output - Ignition 3
C	GRY	1787	Variable Effort Steering Motor Control - High Side (w/NV8)
D	WHT	345	Variable Effort Steering Motor Control - Low Side (w/NV8)
E	—	—	Vent Tube
F	BLK	1651	Ground - Module
G	BLK	1650	Ground - Pump Motor
1	—	—	Not Used
2	TAN/BLK	464	Traction Control System Signal - Torque Delivered (w/NW9)
3	LT GRN	1763	Steering Wheel Position Signal - Phase A (w/JL4)
4	—	—	Not Used
5	LT BLU	715	Lateral Accelerometer Signal (w/JL4)
6	YEL	2770	Fuse Output - Stoplamp Switch (w/NW9)
7	PPL	1807	Serial Data - Class 2
8	RED	885	Wheel Speed Sensor Return - Left Rear
9	BRN	882	Wheel Speed Sensor Signal - Right Rear
10	DK GRN	872	Wheel Speed Sensor Signal - Right Front

Connector Part Information	• C1 - 15318099 • 7 Way F Metri-Pack 480 Series (BLK) • C2 - 15354984 • 29 Way F Micro-Pack 100 Series (NAT) • C2 - 15356700 • 29 Way F Micro-Pack 100 Series (GRY)		
Pin	**Wire Color**	**Circuit No.**	**Function**
11	LT BLU	830	Wheel Speed Sensor Signal - Left Front
12	ORN/BLK	463	Traction Control System Signal - Torque Desired (w/NW9)
13	LT GRN/ BLK	1338	Sensor Return (w/JL4)
14–17	—	—	Not Used
18	LT BLU	1764	Steering Wheel Position Signal - Phase B (w/JL4)
19	DK BLU	716	Yaw Rate Sensor Signal (w/JL4)
20	—	—	Not Used
21	PPL	1807	Serial Data - Class 2
22	BLK	884	Wheel Speed Sensor Signal - Left Rear
23	WHT	883	Wheel Speed Sensor Return - Right Rear
24	TAN	833	Wheel Speed Sensor Return - Right Front
25	YEL	873	Wheel Speed Sensor Return - Left Front
26	DK BLU	1537	ABS Indicator Lamp Output
27	GRY/BLK	1337	Sensor Feed - 5 V (w/JL4)
28–29	—	—	Not Used

GC4020152538000X

Fig. 8 EBCM connector terminal identification. Park Avenue

DIAGNOSTIC CHART INDEX

Code	Description	Page No.	Fig. No.
AURORA, BONNEVILLE, LESABRE & PARK AVENUE			
—	ABS Symptoms (Aurora)	6-560	34
—	ABS Indicator Always On (Aurora)	6-560	35
—	ABS Indicator Inoperative (Aurora)	6-561	36
—	Traction Active Indicator Always On (Aurora)	6-561	37
—	Traction Active Indicator Inoperative (Aurora)	6-561	38
—	Traction Off Indicator Always On (Aurora)	6-561	39
—	Traction Off Indicator Inoperative (Aurora)	6-562	40
—	Vehicle Stability Enhancement System Inoperative (Aurora)	6-562	41
—	Vehicle Stability Enhancement System Unwanted Activation (Aurora)	6-563	42
—	Vehicle Stability Enhancement System Excessive Brake Pulsation (Aurora)	6-563	43
—	ABS Symptoms (Bonneville)	6-563	44
—	ABS Indicator Always On (Bonneville)	6-564	45
—	ABS Indicator Inoperative (Bonneville)	6-564	46
—	Low Traction Indicator Always On (Bonneville)	6-565	47
—	Low Traction Indicator Inoperative (Bonneville)	6-565	48
—	Traction Off Indicator Always On (Bonneville)	6-565	49
—	Traction Off Indicator Inoperative (Bonneville)	6-565	50
—	Traction Ready Indicator Always On (Bonneville)	6-566	51
—	Traction Ready Indicator Inoperative (Bonneville)	6-566	52
—	Vehicle Stability Enhancement System Inoperative (Bonneville)	6-566	53
—	Vehicle Stability Enhancement System Unwanted Activation (Bonneville)	6-567	54
—	Vehicle Stability Enhancement System Excessive Brake Pulsation (Bonneville)	6-567	55
—	ABS Symptoms (LeSabre)	6-568	56
—	ABS Indicator Always On (LeSabre)	6-568	57
—	ABS Indicator Inoperative (LeSabre)	6-568	58
—	Traction Off Indicator Always On (LeSabre)	6-568	59
—	Traction Off Indicator Inoperative (LeSabre)	6-569	60
—	Vehicle Stability Enhancement System Inoperative (LeSabre)	6-569	61
—	Vehicle Stability Enhancement System Unwanted Activation (LeSabre)	6-570	62
—	Vehicle Stability Enhancement System Excessive Pulsation (LeSabre)	6-570	63
—	ABS Symptoms (Park Avenue)	6-570	64
—	ABS Indicator Always On (Park Avenue)	6-570	65
—	ABS Indicator Inoperative (Park Avenue)	6-571	66
—	Traction Off Indicator Always On (Park Avenue)	6-571	67
—	Traction Off Indicator Inoperative (Park Avenue)	6-571	68
—	Vehicle Stability Enhancement System Inoperative (Park Avenue)	6-572	69
—	Vehicle Stability Enhancement System Unwanted Activation (Park Avenue)	6-572	70
—	Vehicle Stability Enhancement System Excessive Brake Pulsation (Park Avenue)	6-573	71
—	Diagnostic System Check (Aurora, Bonneville & LeSabre)	6-548	9
—	Diagnostic System Check (Park Avenue)	6-548	10
C1211	ABS Lamp Circuit Fault	6-548	11
C1214	System Relay Contact Or Coil Circuit Open	6-549	12
C1217	Pump Motor Shorted To Ground	6-549	13
C1218	Pump Motor Circuit Open	6-550	14
C1221	LH Front Wheel Speed Sensor Signal is zero	6-550	15
C1222	RH Front Wheel Speed Sensor Signal Is Zero	6-550	15
C1223	LH Rear Wheel Speed Sensor Signal Is Zero	6-550	15
C1224	RH Rear Wheel Speed Sensor Signal Is Zero	6-550	15
C1225	LH Front Excessive Wheel Speed Variation	6-550	15
C1226	RH Front Excessive Wheel Speed Variation	6-550	15
C1227	LH Rear Excessive Wheel Speed Variation	6-550	15
C1228	RH Rear Excessive Wheel Speed Variation	6-550	15
C1232	LH Front Wheel Speed Sensor Circuit Open Or Shorted	6-550	15
C1233	RH Front Wheel Speed Sensor Circuit Open Or Shorted	6-550	15
C1234	LH Rear Wheel Speed Sensor Circuit Open Or Shorted	6-550	15
C1235	RH Rear Wheel Speed Sensor Circuit Open Or Shorted	6-550	15

Continued

DIAGNOSTIC CHART INDEX—Continued

Code	Description	Page No.	Fig. No.
AURORA, BONNEVILLE, LESABRE & PARK AVENUE			
C1236	Low System Supply Voltage	6-551	16
C1237	High System Supply Voltage	6-551	17
C1238	Brake Thermal Model Exceeded	6-552	18
C1242	Pump Motor Circuit Open	6-552	19
C1243	BPMV Pump Motor Stalled	6-552	19
C1248	Brake Warning Indicator Fault	6-553	20
C1254	Abnormal Shutdown Detected	6-553	21
C1255	EBCM Internal Fault	6-553	22
C1256	EBCM Internal Fault	6-553	22
C1261	LH Front Inlet Valve Solenoid Fault	6-554	23
C1262	LH Front Outlet Valve Solenoid Fault	6-554	23
C1263	RH Front Inlet Valve Solenoid Fault	6-554	23
C1264	RH Front Outlet Valve Solenoid Fault	6-554	23
C1265	LH Rear Inlet Valve Solenoid Fault	6-554	23
C1266	LH Rear Outlet Valve Solenoid Fault	6-554	23
C1267	RH Rear Inlet Valve Solenoid Fault	6-554	23
C1268	RH Rear Outlet Valve Solenoid Fault	6-554	23
C1271	LH Front TCS Master Cylinder Isolation Valve Fault	6-554	23
C1272	LH Front TCS Prime Valve Fault	6-554	23
C1273	RH Front TCS Master Cylinder Isolation Valve Fault	6-554	23
C1274	RH Front TCS Prime Valve Fault	6-554	23
C1276	Delivered Torque Signal Circuit Fault	6-554	24
C1277	Requested Torque Signal Circuit Fault	6-555	25
C1278	TCS Temporarily inhibited By PCM	6-555	26
C1281	VSES Sensors Uncorrelated	6-556	27
C1282	Yaw Rate Sensor Bias Circuit Fault	6-556	28
C1283	VSES Sensors Uncorrelated	6-556	27
C1284	Lateral Accelerometer Sensor Circuit Fault	6-557	29
C1285	Lateral Accelerometer Sensor Circuit Fault	6-557	29
C1286	VSES Sensors Uncorrelated	6-556	27
C1287	Steering Sensor Circuit Fault	6-558	30
C1288	Steering Sensor Circuit Fault	6-558	30
C1291	Open Brake Lamp Switch Contacts During Deceleration	6-559	31
C1293	Open Brake Lamp Switch Contacts During Deceleration	6-559	31
C1294	Brake Lamp Switch Circuit Always Active	6-559	32
C1295	Brake Lamp Switch Circuit Open	6-560	33
DEVILLE & SEVILLE			
—	ABS Symptoms	6-585	97
—	ABS Indicator Always On	6-586	98
—	ABS Indicator Inoperative	6-586	99
—	Traction Control Indicator Always On	6-586	100
—	Traction Control Indicator Inoperative	6-586	101
—	Traction Off Indicator Inoperative	6-587	102
—	Vehicle Stability Enhancement System Inoperative	6-587	103
—	Vehicle Stability Enhancement System Unwanted Activation	6-588	104
—	Vehicle Stability Enhancement System Excessive Brake Pulsation	6-588	105
—	Diagnostic System Check	6-573	72
C1211	ABS Indicator Lamp Circuit Fault	6-573	73
C1214	System Relay Contact Or Coil Circuit Open	6-574	74
C1217	Pump Motor Shorted To Ground	6-574	75
C1218	Pump Motor Circuit Shorted To Voltage Or Motor Ground Open	6-575	76
C1221	LH Front Wheel Speed Sensor Signal Is Zero	6-575	77
C1222	RH Front Wheel Speed Sensor Signal Is Zero	6-575	77
C1223	LH Rear Wheel Speed Sensor Signal Is Zero	6-575	77
C1224	RH Rear Wheel Speed Sensor Signal Is Zero	6-575	77
C1225	LH Front Excessive Wheel Speed Variation	6-575	77

Continued

DIAGNOSTIC CHART INDEX—Continued

Code	Description	Page No.	Fig. No.
DEVILLE & SEVILLE			
C1226	RH Front Excessive Wheel Speed Variation	6-575	77
C1227	LH Rear Excessive Wheel Speed Variation	6-575	77
C1228	RH Rear Excessive Wheel Speed Variation	6-575	77
C1232	LH Front Wheel Speed Sensor Circuit Open Or Shorted	6-575	77
C1233	RH Front Wheel Speed Sensor Circuit Open Or Shorted	6-575	77
C1234	LH Rear Wheel Speed Sensor Circuit Open Or Shorted	6-575	77
C1235	RH Rear Wheel Speed Sensor Circuit Open Or Shorted	6-575	77
C1236	Low System Supply Voltage	6-576	78
C1237	High System Supply Voltage	6-576	79
C1238	Brake Thermal Model Exceeded	6-577	80
C1242	Pump Motor Circuit Open	6-577	81
C1243	BPMV Pump Motor Stalled	6-577	81
C1248	EBCM Turned Red Brake Warning Indicator On	6-578	82
C1251	RSS Indicated Fault	6-578	83
C1254	Abnormal Shutdown Detected	6-578	84
C1255	EBCM Internal Fault	6-579	85
C1256	EBCM Internal Fault	6-579	85
C1261	LH Front Inlet Valve Solenoid Fault	6-579	86
C1262	LH Front Outlet Valve Solenoid Fault	6-579	86
C1263	RH Front Inlet Valve Solenoid Fault	6-579	86
C1264	RH Front Outlet Valve Solenoid Fault	6-579	86
C1265	LH Rear Inlet Valve Solenoid Fault	6-579	86
C1266	LH Rear Outlet Valve Solenoid Fault	6-579	86
C1267	RH Rear Inlet Valve Solenoid Fault	6-579	86
C1268	RH Rear Outlet Valve Solenoid Fault	6-579	86
C1271	LH Front TCS Master Cylinder Isolation Valve Fault	6-579	86
C1272	LH Front TCS Prime Valve Fault	6-579	86
C1273	RH Front TCS Master Cylinder Isolation Valve Fault	6-579	86
C1274	RH Front TCS Prime Valve Fault	6-579	86
C1276	Delivered Torque Signal Circuit Fault	6-579	87
C1277	Requested Torque Signal Circuit Fault	6-580	88
C1278	TCS Temporarily Inhibited By PCM	6-580	89
C1281	VSES Sensors Uncorrelated	6-581	90
C1282	Yaw Rate Sensor Bias Circuit Fault	6-581	91
C1283	Excessive Time To Center Steering	6-581	90
C1284	Lateral Accelerometer Sensor Circuit Fault	6-582	92
C1285	Lateral Accelerometer Sensor Circuit Fault	6-582	92
C1286	Steering Sensor Bias Fault	6-581	90
C1287	Steering Sensor Rate Fault	6-583	93
C1288	Steering Sensor Circuit Fault	6-583	93
C1291	Open Brake Lamp Switch Contacts During Deceleration	6-584	94
C1293	Open Brake Lamp Switch Contacts During Deceleration	6-584	94
C1294	Brake Lamp Switch Circuit Always Active	6-584	95
C1295	Brake Lamp Switch Circuit Open	6-585	96

Circuit Description

The ABS Diagnostic System Check is an organized approach to identify problems associated with the EBCM. This check must be the starting point for any

EBCM complaint, and will direct you to the next logical step in diagnosing the complaint. The EBCM is a very reliable component and is not likely the cause of the malfunction. Most system complaints are linked to faulty wiring, connectors, and occasionally to components. Understanding the ABS system and using the tables correctly will reduce diagnostic time and prevent unnecessary parts replacement.

Test Description

The numbers below refer to the step numbers on the diagnostic table.

2. Lack of communication may be due to a partial malfunction of the serial data circuit or due to a total malfunction of the serial data circuit. The specified procedure will determine the particular condition.
4. The presence of DTCs which begin with "U" indicate some other module is not communicating. The specified procedure will compile all the available information before tests are performed.

Step	Action	Yes	No
1	Install a scan tool. Does the scan tool power up?	Go to *Step 2*	*Diagnose* Data Link Communications
2	1. Turn ON the ignition, with the engine OFF. 2. Attempt to establish communication with the following control modules: • Driver information center (DIC) • Electronic brake control module (EBCM) • Instrument panel cluster (IPC) • Instrument panel integration module (IPM) • Powertrain control module (PCM) Does the scan tool communicate with all control modules?	Go to *Step 3*	*Diagnose* Data Link Communications
3	Select the display DTCs function on the scan tool for the following control modules: • Driver information center (DIC) • Electronic brake control module (EBCM) • Instrument panel cluster (IPC) • Instrument panel integration module (IPM) • Powertrain control module (PCM) Does the scan tool display any DTCs?	Go to *Step 4*	Go to *Symptoms Antilock Brake System*
4	Does the scan tool display any DTCs which begin with a "U"?	*Diagnose* Data Link Communications	Go to *Step 5*
5	Does the scan tool display DTC B1000, B1004, B1007, B1009, or B1010?	*Diagnose* Body Control System	Go to *Step 6*
6	Does the scan tool display DTC B1327, B1513, or B1514?	*Diagnose* Engine Electrical	Go to *Diagnostic Trouble Code (DTC) List*

GC4020152539000X

Fig. 9 Diagnostic System Check. Aurora, Bonneville & LeSabre

Circuit Description

The ABS Diagnostic System Check is an organized approach to identify problems associated with the EBCM. This check must be the starting point for any EBCM complaint, and will direct you to the next logical step in diagnosing the complaint. The EBCM is a very reliable component and is not likely the cause of the malfunction. Most system complaints are linked to faulty wiring, connectors, and occasionally to components. Understanding the ABS system and using the tables correctly will reduce diagnostic time and prevent unnecessary parts replacement.

Test Description

The numbers below refer to the step numbers on the diagnostic table.

2. Lack of communication may be due to a partial malfunction of the serial data circuit or due to a total malfunction of the serial data circuit. The specified procedure will determine the particular condition.
4. The presence of DTCs which begin with "U" indicate some other module is not communicating. The specified procedure will compile all the available information before tests are performed.

A Diagnostic System Check - ABS

Step	Action	Yes	No
1	Install a scan tool. Does the scan tool power up?	Go to *Step 2*	*Diagnose* Data Link Communications
2	1. Turn ON the ignition, with the engine OFF. 2. Attempt to establish communication with the following control modules: • The body control module • The electronic brake control module (EBCM) • The instrument panel cluster (IPC) • The powertrain control module (PCM) Does the scan tool communicate with all control modules?	Go to *Step 3*	*Diagnose* Data Link Communications
3	Select the display DTCs function on the scan tool for the following control modules: • The body control module • The electronic brake control module (EBCM) • The instrument panel cluster (IPC) • The powertrain control module (PCM) Does the scan tool display any DTCs?	Go to *Step 4*	Go to *Symptoms - Antilock Brake System*
4	Does the scan tool display any DTCs which begin with a "U"?	*Diagnose* Data Link Communications	Go to *Step 5*
5	Does the scan tool display DTC B1652, B1656, B1657, or B1658?	*Diagnose* Body Control System	Go to *Step 6*
6	Does the scan tool display DTC B1982 or B1983?	*Diagnose* Engine Electrical	Go to *Diagnostic Trouble Code (DTC) List*

GC4020152540000X

Fig. 10 Diagnostic System Check. Park Avenue

Circuit Description

The instrument cluster controls the operation of the ABS indicator. The EBCM reports the desired status of the ABS indicator via serial data messages. The ABS indicator signal circuit is a back-up reporting circuit to the serial data messages. The EBCM supplies ground through the circuit when the ABS is operating properly. When there is a problem with ABS that should turn on the ABS indicator, the EBCM opens the ABS indicator signal circuit. If there is a problem with the ABS serial data messages, the instrument cluster uses the ABS indicator signal to determine if the ABS indicator should be illuminated. Using the serial data messages and back-up circuit, the instrument cluster decides whether to turn on the ABS indicator.

Conditions for Running the DTC

The EBCM commands the indicator OFF.

Conditions for Setting the DTC

The ABS indicator signal circuit voltage is greater than 4.5 volts for 2 seconds.

Action Taken When the DTC Sets

- The ABS remains functional.
- The ABS indicator remains OFF.

Conditions for Clearing the DTC

- The condition for the DTC is no longer present (the DTC is not current) and you used the scan tool Clear DTC function.
- The EBCM automatically clears the history DTC when a current DTC is not detected in 100 consecutive drive cycles.

Diagnostic Aids

A possible cause of this DTC is a short to battery in the ABS indicator signal circuit.

Test Description

The numbers below refer to the step numbers on the diagnostic table.

2. Use the scan tool to verify the normal state of the ABS indicator signal circuit.
3. Ensure that the instrument cluster can operate the ABS indicator.

GC4020152541010X

Fig. 11 Code C1211: ABS Lamp Circuit Fault (Part 1 of 2). Aurora, Bonneville, LeSabre & Park Avenue

Step	Action	Yes	No
1	Did you perform the ABS Diagnostic System Check?	Go to *Step 2*	Go to *Diagnostic System Check - ABS*
2	1. Install a scan tool. 2. Turn ON the ignition, with the engine OFF. 3. With a scan tool, observe the ABS Warning Indicator parameter in the DRP/ABS/TCS data list. Does the scan tool display Off?	Go to *Step 3*	Go to *Step 4*
3	1. Turn OFF the ignition. 2. Turn ON the ignition, with the engine OFF. 3. Observe the ABS indicator on the instrument cluster (IPC) during the bulb check. Does the ABS indicator illuminate during the bulb check?	Go to *Step 4*	Go to *Step 6*
4	1. Turn OFF the ignition. **Important:** Removing battery voltage or ground from the EBCM will result in the following conditions: • Loss of the TIM learned tire inflation configuration parameters in the EBCM • The EBCM sets DTC C1245. When the diagnosis is complete, inspect the tire pressures and perform the TIM reset. 2. Disconnect the EBCM harness connector. 3. Connect the *J 39700* Universal Pinout Box using the *J 39700-300* Cable Adapter to the EBCM harness connector only. 4. Disconnect the instrument cluster harness connector. 5. Test the ABS indicator signal circuit for a short to voltage. Did you find and correct the condition?	Go to *Step 9*	Go to *Step 5*
5	Inspect for poor connections at the harness connector of the EBCM. Did you find and correct the condition?	Go to *Step 9*	Go to *Step 7*
6	Inspect for poor connections at the harness connector of the instrument cluster. Did you find and correct the condition?	Go to *Step 9*	Go to *Step 8*
7	**Important:** Perform the setup procedure for the EBCM. An unprogrammed EBCM will result in the following conditions: • Inoperative or poorly functioning system operations • The EBCM sets DTC C1248 and DTC C1255m3. Replace the EBCM. Did you complete the repair?	Go to *Step 9*	—
8	Replace the instrument cluster (IPC). Did you complete the repair?	Go to *Step 9*	—
9	1. Use the scan tool in order to clear the DTCs. 2. Operate the vehicle within the Conditions for Running the DTC as specified in the supporting text. Does the DTC reset?	Go to *Step 2*	System OK

GC4020152541020X

Fig. 11 Code C1211: ABS Lamp Circuit Fault (Part 2 of 2). Aurora, Bonneville, LeSabre & Park Avenue

Circuit Description

The system relay is energized when the ignition is ON. The system relay supplies voltage to the solenoid valves and the pump motor. This voltage is referred to as the system voltage.

The EBCM controls each solenoid valve by grounding the solenoid.

The EBCM controls the pump motor by grounding the control circuit. The pump serves 2 purposes:

- Transfers brake fluid from the brake calipers to the master cylinder reservoir during pressure decrease events.
- Transfers brake fluid from the master cylinder reservoir to the brake calipers during pressure increase events.

Conditions for Running the DTC

- The ignition voltage is greater than 10.5 volts.
- The system relay is commanded ON.

Conditions for Setting the DTC

The system voltage is less than 8 volts for 0.23 seconds.

Action Taken When the DTC Sets

If equipped, the following actions occur:

- The EBCM disables the DRP/ABS/TCS/VSES for the duration of the ignition cycle.
- The ABS indicator turns ON.
- The Traction Off indicator turns ON.
- The DIC displays the Service Stability System message.
- The EBCM will also set DTC C1248.
- The red Brake warning indicator turns ON.

Conditions for Clearing the DTC

- The condition for the DTC is no longer present (the DTC is not current) and you used the scan tool Clear DTC function.
- The EBCM automatically clears the history DTC when a current DTC is not detected in 100 consecutive drive cycles.

Diagnostic Aids

The system relay is integral to the EBCM. The relay is not serviceable.

Test Description

The number below refers to the step number on the diagnostic table.

2. Determines whether the DTC is current.

GC4020152542010X

Fig. 12 Code C1214: System Relay Contact Or Coil Circuit Open (Part 1 of 2). Aurora, Bonneville, LeSabre & Park Avenue

Step	Action	Value(s)	Yes	No
1	Did you perform the ABS Diagnostic System Check?	—	Go to *Step 2*	Go to *Diagnostic System Check - ABS*
2	1. Install a scan tool. 2. Turn ON the ignition, with the engine OFF. 3. Use the scan tool in order to clear the DTCs. 4. With the scan tool, perform the Automated Test. Does the DTC reset as a current DTC?	—	Go to *Step 3*	*Test for Intermittent*
3	1. Disconnect the pump motor harness pigtail connector of the brake pressure modulator valve (BPMV). 2. Measure the resistance between each pump motor control circuit and the housing of the BPMV at the pump motor harness pigtail connector of the BPMV. Does the DMM display the specified value?	OL	Go to *Step 5*	Go to *Step 4*
4	**Important:** Perform the setup procedure for the EBCM. An unprogrammed EBCM will result in the following conditions: • Inoperative or poorly functioning system operations • The EBCM sets DTC C1248 and DTC C1255m3 Replace the EBCM and the BPMV. Did you complete the repair?	—	Go to *Step 6*	—
5	**Important:** Perform the setup procedure for the EBCM. An unprogrammed EBCM will result in the following conditions: • Inoperative or poorly functioning system operations • The EBCM sets DTC C1248 and DTC C1255m3. Replace the EBCM. Did you complete the repair?	—	Go to *Step 6*	—
6	1. Use the scan tool in order to clear the DTCs. 2. With the scan tool, perform the Automated Test. Does the DTC reset?	—	Go to *Step 2*	System OK

GC4020152542020X

Fig. 12 Code C1214: System Relay Contact Or Coil Circuit Open (Part 2 of 2). Aurora, Bonneville, LeSabre & Park Avenue

Circuit Description

The system relay is energized when the ignition is ON. The system relay supplies voltage to the solenoid valves and the pump motor. This voltage is referred to as the system voltage.

The EBCM controls each solenoid valve by grounding the solenoid.

The EBCM controls the pump motor by grounding the control circuit. The pump serves 2 purposes:

- Transfers brake fluid from the brake calipers to the master cylinder reservoir during pressure decrease events.
- Transfers brake fluid from the master cylinder reservoir to the brake calipers during pressure increase events.

Conditions for Running the DTC

- The pump motor has been commanded OFF for 1 second.
- The system voltage is greater than 9 volts.

Conditions for Setting the DTC

One of the following conditions exists for 0.2 seconds:

- The voltage across the pump motor is greater than 10.2 volts.
- The pump motor low side voltage is less than 2.7 volts.

Action Taken When the DTC Sets

If equipped, the following actions occur:

- The EBCM disables the DRP/ABS/TCS/VSES for the duration of the ignition cycle.
- The ABS indicator turns ON.
- The Traction Off indicator turns ON.
- The DIC displays the Service Stability System message.
- The EBCM will also set DTC C1248.
- The red Brake warning indicator turns ON.

Conditions for Clearing the DTC

- The condition for the DTC is no longer present (the DTC is not current) and you used the scan tool Clear DTC function.
- The EBCM automatically clears the history DTC when a current DTC is not detected in 100 consecutive drive cycles.

Diagnostic Aids

- This DTC determines if there is a short in the pump motor control circuit.
- The pump motor is integral to the BPMV. The pump motor is not serviceable.

Test Description

The number below refers to the step number on the diagnostic table.

3. Tests the pump motor circuits of the BPMV for a short to the housing of the BPMV. The wiring from the BPMV to the EBCM should not be repaired.

GC4020152543010X

Fig. 13 Code C1217: Pump Motor Shorted To Ground (Part 1 of 2). Aurora, Bonneville, LeSabre & Park Avenue

Step	Action	Value(s)	Yes	No
1	Did you perform the ABS Diagnostic System Check?	—	Go to *Step 2*	Go to *Diagnostic System Check - ABS*
2	1. Turn OFF the ignition. **Important:** Removing battery voltage or ground from the EBCM will result in the following conditions: • Loss of the TIM learned tire inflation configuration parameters in the EBCM • The EBCM sets DTC C1245. When the diagnosis is complete, inspect the tire pressures and perform the TIM reset. 2. Disconnect the EBCM harness connector. 3. Connect the *J 39700* Universal Pinout Box using the *J 39700-300* Cable Adapter to the EBCM harness connector only. 4. Test both ground circuits of the EBCM including the EBCM ground for a high resistance or an open. Did you find and correct the condition?	—	Go to *Step 8*	Go to *Step 3*
3	1. Disconnect the pump motor harness pigtail connector of the BPMV. 2. Measure the resistance between each pump motor control circuit and the housing of the BPMV at the pump motor harness pigtail connector of the BPMV. Does the resistance measure less than the specified value?	5 Ω	Go to *Step 4*	Go to *Step 5*
4	Inspect for poor connections at the pump motor harness pigtail connector of the BPMV. Did you find and correct the condition?	—	Go to *Step 8*	Go to *Step 6*
5	Inspect for poor connections at the harness connector of the EBCM. Did you find and correct the condition?	—	Go to *Step 8*	Go to *Step 7*
6	Replace the BPMV. Did you complete the repair?	—	Go to *Step 8*	—
7	**Important:** Perform the setup procedure for the EBCM. An unprogrammed EBCM will result in the following conditions: • Inoperative or poorly functioning system operations • The EBCM sets DTC C1248 and DTC C1255m3. Replace the EBCM. Did you complete the repair?	—	Go to *Step 8*	—
8	1. Use the scan tool in order to clear the DTCs. 2. With the scan tool, perform the Automated Test. Does the DTC reset?	—	Go to *Step 2*	System OK

GC4020152543020X

Fig. 13 Code C1217: Pump Motor Shorted To Ground (Part 2 of 2). Aurora, Bonneville, LeSabre & Park Avenue

Circuit Description

The system relay is energized when the ignition is ON. The system relay supplies voltage to the solenoid valves and the pump motor. This voltage is referred to as the system voltage.

The EBCM controls each solenoid valve by grounding the solenoid.

The EBCM controls the pump motor by grounding the control circuit. The pump serves 2 purposes:

- Transfers brake fluid from the brake calipers to the master cylinder reservoir during pressure decrease events.
- Transfers brake fluid from the master cylinder reservoir to the brake calipers during pressure increase events.

Conditions for Running the DTC

- The pump motor is commanded ON.
- The system voltage is greater than 8 volts.

Conditions for Setting the DTC

One of the following conditions exists for 0.5 seconds:

- With the commanded pump motor voltage less than the system voltage, the actual pump motor voltage is 3 volts less than the commanded voltage.
- With the commanded pump motor voltage greater than the system voltage, the actual pump motor voltage is less than 8 volts.

Action Taken When the DTC Sets

If equipped, the following actions occur:

- The EBCM disables the ABS/TCS/VSES for the duration of the ignition cycle.
- The DRP does not function optimally.
- The ABS indicator turns ON.
- The Traction Off indicator turns ON.
- The DIC displays the Service Stability System message.

Conditions for Clearing the DTC

- The condition for the DTC is no longer present (the DTC is not current) and you used the scan tool Clear DTC function.
- The EBCM automatically clears the history DTC when a current DTC is not detected in 100 consecutive drive cycles.

Diagnostic Aids

The pump motor is integral to the BPMV. The pump motor is not serviceable.

Test Description

The number below refers to the step number on the diagnostic table.

3. Tests the ability of the EBCM to control the pump motor. If the test lamp illuminates, the pump motor circuit within the EBCM is good.

GC4020152544010X

Fig. 14 Code C1218: Pump Motor Circuit Open (Part 1 of 2). Aurora, Bonneville, LeSabre & Park Avenue

Step	Action	Yes	No
1	Did you perform the ABS Diagnostic System Check?	Go to *Step 2*	Go to *Diagnostic System Check - ABS*
2	1. Install a scan tool. 2. Turn ON the ignition, with the engine OFF. 3. Use the scan tool in order to clear the DTCs. 4. With the scan tool, perform the Automated Test. Does the DTC reset?	Go to *Step 3*	*Test for Intermittent*
3	1. Turn OFF the ignition. 2. Disconnect the pump motor harness pigtail connector of the BPMV. 3. Connect a test lamp between the pump motor circuits at the pump motor connector of the EBCM. 4. Use the scan tool in order to clear the DTCs. 5. With the scan tool, perform the Pump Motor Test. Does the test lamp illuminate?	Go to *Step 5*	Go to *Step 4*
4	1. Turn OFF the ignition. **Important:** Removing battery voltage or ground from the EBCM will result in the following conditions: • Loss of the TIM learned tire inflation configuration parameters in the EBCM • The EBCM sets DTC C1245. When the diagnosis is complete, inspect the tire pressures and perform the TIM reset. 2. Disconnect the EBCM harness connector. 3. Connect the *J 39700* Universal Pinout Box using the *J 39700-300* Cable Adapter to the EBCM harness connector only. 4. Test both ground circuits of the EBCM including the EBCM ground for a high resistance or an open. Did you find and correct the condition?	Go to *Step 9*	Go to *Step 6*
5	Inspect for poor connections at the pump motor harness pigtail connector of the BPMV. Did you find and correct the condition?	Go to *Step 9*	Go to *Step 7*
6	Inspect for poor connections at the harness connector of the EBCM. Did you find and correct the condition?	Go to *Step 9*	Go to *Step 8*
7	Replace the BPMV. Did you complete the repair?	Go to *Step 9*	—
8	**Important:** Perform the setup procedure for the EBCM. An unprogrammed EBCM will result in the following conditions: • Inoperative or poorly functioning system operations • The EBCM sets DTC C1248 and DTC C1255m3. Replace the EBCM. Did you complete the repair?	Go to *Step 9*	—
9	1. Use the scan tool in order to clear the DTCs. 2. With the scan tool, perform the Automated Test. Does the DTC reset?	Go to *Step 2*	System OK

GC4020152544020X

Fig. 14 Code C1218: Pump Motor Circuit Open (Part 2 of 2). Aurora, Bonneville, LeSabre & Park Avenue

Circuit Description

As the wheel spins, the wheel speed sensor produces an AC signal. The EBCM uses the frequency of the AC signal to calculate the wheel speed.

Conditions for Running the DTC

C1221 through C1228

- DTCs C1232 through C1235 are not set.
- The brake pedal is not pressed.
- The ABS is not active.

C1232 through C1235

The ignition is ON.

Conditions for Setting the DTC

C1221 through C1224

All of the following conditions exists for 2.5 seconds:

- The suspect wheel speed equals zero.
- The other wheel speeds are greater than 8 km/h (5 mph).
- The other wheel speeds are within 11 km/h (7 mph) of each other.

C1225 through C1228

The EBCM detects a rapid variation in the wheel speed. The wheel speed changes by 16 km/h or more in 0.01 second. The change must occur 3 times with no more than 0.2 seconds between occurrences.

C1232 through C1235

One of the following conditions exists for 0.02 seconds:

- A short to voltage - the wheel speed sensor signal circuit and wheel speed sensor return circuit voltages are both greater than 4.25 volts.
- A short to ground - the wheel speed sensor signal circuit and wheel speed sensor return circuit voltages are both less than 0.75 volts.
- An open - the wheel speed sensor signal circuit voltage is greater than 4.25 volts and wheel speed sensor return circuit voltage is less than 0.75 volts.

Action Taken When the DTC Sets

If equipped, the following actions occur:

- The EBCM disables the ABS/TCS/VSES for the duration of the ignition cycle.
- The EBCM temporarily suspends the TIM monitoring function while the DTC is set.
- The DRP does not function optimally.
- The ABS indicator turns ON.
- The Traction Off indicator turns ON.
- The DIC displays the Service Stability System message.

Conditions for Clearing the DTC

- The condition for the DTC is no longer present (the DTC is not current) and you used the scan tool Clear DTC function.
- The EBCM automatically clears the history DTC when a current DTC is not detected in 100 consecutive drive cycles.

Diagnostic Aids

C1221 through C1224

Under the following conditions, 2 Wheel Speed Sensor Input is 0 DTCs are set:

- The 2 suspect wheel speeds equal zero for 60 seconds.
- The other wheel speeds are greater than 16 km/h (10 mph).
- The other wheel speeds are within 11 km/h (7 mph) of each other.

Diagnose each wheel speed sensor individually.

C1225 through C1228

A possible cause of this DTC is electrical noise on the wheel speed sensor harness wiring. Electrical noise could result from the wheel speed sensor wires being routed to close to high energy ignition system components, such as spark plug wires.

C1232 through C1235

If the customer comments that the ABS indicator is ON only during moist environmental conditions (rain, snow, vehicle wash, etc.), inspect the wheel speed sensor wiring for signs of water intrusion. If the DTC is not current, clear all DTCs and simulate the effects of water intrusion by using the following procedure:

1. Spray the suspected area with a 5 percent saltwater solution. To create a 5 percent saltwater solution, add 2 teaspoons (9.9 ml) of salt to 354 ml (12 oz) of water.
2. Test drive the vehicle over various road surfaces (bumps, turns, etc.) above 40 km/h (25 mph) for at least 30 seconds.
3. If the DTC returns, replace the suspected wheel speed sensor or repair the wheel speed sensor wiring.
4. Rinse the area thoroughly when completed.

Test Description

The numbers below refer to the step numbers on the diagnostic table.

3. Measure the resistance of the wheel speed sensor in order to determine if the sensor has a valid resistance value.
4. Ensures that the wheel speed sensor is generating a valid AC voltage output.

GC4020152545010X

Fig. 15 Codes C1221-C1235: Wheel Speed Sensor Fault (Part 1 of 3). Aurora, Bonneville, LeSabre & Park Avenue

Step	Action	Value(s)	Yes	No
1	Did you perform the ABS Diagnostic System Check?	—	Go to *Step 2*	Go to *Diagnostic System Check - ABS*
2	1. Install a scan tool. 2. Turn ON the ignition. 3. Set up the scan tool snap shot feature to trigger for this DTC. 4. Drive the vehicle at a speed greater than the specified value. Does the scan tool indicate that this wheel speed DTC set?	8 km/h (5 mph)	Go to *Step 3*	Go to Diagnostic Aids
3	1. Raise and support the vehicle. 2. Disconnect the wheel speed sensor connector. 3. Measure the resistance across the wheel speed sensor. Does the resistance measure within the specified range?	850–1350 Ω	Go to *Step 4*	Go to *Step 8*
4	1. Spin the wheel. 2. Measure the AC voltage across the wheel speed sensor. Does the AC voltage measure greater than the specified value?	100 mV	Go to *Step 5*	Go to *Step 8*
5	Inspect for poor connections at the harness connector of the wheel speed sensor. Did you find and correct the condition?	—	Go to *Step 10*	Go to *Step 6*
6	**Important:** Removing battery voltage or ground from the EBCM will result is the following conditions: • Loss of the TIM learned tire inflation configuration parameters in the EBCM • The EBCM sets DTC C1245. When the diagnosis is complete, inspect the tire pressures and perform the TIM reset. 1. Disconnect the EBCM harness connector. 2. Install the *J 39700* Universal Pinout Box using the *J 39700-300* Cable Adapter to the EBCM harness connector only. 3. Test the wheel speed sensor circuits for the following: • An open • A short to ground • A short to voltage • Shorted together Did you find and correct the condition?	—	Go to *Step 10*	Go to *Step 7*

GC4020152545020X

Fig. 15 Codes C1221-C1235: Wheel Speed Sensor Fault (Part 2 of 3). Aurora, Bonneville, LeSabre & Park Avenue

Step	Action	Value(s)	Yes	No
7	Inspect for poor connections at the harness connector for the EBCM. Did you find and correct the condition?	—	Go to *Step 10*	Go to *Step 9*
8	Replace the wheel speed sensor. Did you complete the replacement?	—	Go to *Step 10*	—
9	**Important:** Perform the setup procedure for the EBCM. An unprogrammed EBCM will result in the following conditions: • Inoperative or poorly functioning system operations • The EBCM sets DTC C1248 and DTC C1255m3. Replace the EBCM. Did you complete the repair?	—	Go to *Step 10*	—
10	1. Use the scan tool in order to clear the DTCs. 2. Operate the vehicle within the Conditions for Running the DTC as specified in the supporting text. Does the DTC reset?	—	Go to *Step 2*	System OK

GC4020152545030X

Fig. 15 Codes C1221-C1235: Wheel Speed Sensor Fault (Part 3 of 3). Aurora, Bonneville, LeSabre & Park Avenue

Step	Action	Value(s)	Yes	No
1	Did you perform the ABS Diagnostic System Check?	—	Go to *Step 2*	Go to *Diagnostic System Check - ABS*
2	1. Install a scan tool. 2. Start the engine. 3. With a scan tool, observe the Switched System Battery Voltage parameter in DRP/ABS/TCS data list. Does the scan tool indicate the voltage is greater than the specified value?	10.5 V	Go to Diagnostic Aids	Go to *Step 3*
3	With a scan tool, observe the Battery Voltage parameter in Dash Integration Module data list. Does the scan tool indicate the voltage is greater than the specified value?	10.5 V	Go to *Step 4*	*Diagnose* Engine Electrical
4	1. Turn OFF the ignition. **Important:** Removing battery voltage or ground from the EBCM will result in the following conditions: • Loss of the TIM learned tire inflation configuration parameters in the EBCM • The EBCM sets DTC C1245. When the diagnosis is complete, inspect the tire pressures and perform the TIM reset. 2. Disconnect the EBCM harness connector. 3. Install the *J 39700* Universal Pinout Box using the *J 39700-300* Cable Adaptor to the EBCM harness connector only. 4. Test the ground circuits of the EBCM including the EBCM ground for a high resistance or an open. Did you find and correct the condition?	—	Go to *Step 7*	Go to *Step 5*
5	1. Reconnect the EBCM harness connector. 2. Turn ON the ignition, with the engine OFF. 3. Use the scan tool in order to clear the DTCs. 4. Operate the vehicle within the Conditions for Running the DTC as specified in the supporting text. Does the DTC reset?	—	Go to *Step 6*	Go to Diagnostic Aids
6	**Important:** Perform the setup procedure for the EBCM. An unprogrammed EBCM will result in the following conditions: • Inoperative or poorly functioning system operations • The EBCM sets DTC C1248 and DTC C1255m3. Replace the EBCM. Did you complete the repair?	—	Go to *Step 7*	—
7	1. Use the scan tool in order to clear the DTCs. 2. Operate the vehicle within the Conditions for Running the DTC as specified in the supporting text. Does the DTC reset?	—	Go to *Step 2*	System OK

GC4020152546020X

Fig. 16 Code C1236: Low System Supply Voltage (Part 2 of 2). Aurora, Bonneville, LeSabre & Park Avenue

Circuit Description

The EBCM monitors the voltage level available for system operation. A low voltage condition prevents the system from operating properly.

Conditions for Running the DTC

- The vehicle speed is greater than 8 km/h (5 mph).
- The ignition voltage is less than 10.5 volts.
- The system relay is commanded ON.

Conditions for Setting the DTC

One of the following conditions exists for 0.72 seconds:

- During initialization or when the system is inactive, the system voltage is less than 10.5 volts.
- During the system operation, the system voltage is less than 9.0 volts.

Action Taken When the DTC Sets

If equipped, the following actions occur:

- The EBCM disables the ABS/TCS/VSES for the duration of the ignition cycle.
- The ABS indicator turns ON.
- The Traction Off indicator turns ON.
- The DIC displays the Service Stability System message.
- The DRP does not function optimally, or with system voltage less than 8.5 volts, the EBCM disables the DRP for the duration of the ignition cycle.
- When the EBCM disables the DRP, the following actions also occur:
  - The EBCM will also set DTC C1248.
  - The red Brake warning indicator turns ON.

Conditions for Clearing the DTC

- The condition for the DTC is no longer present (the DTC is not current) and you used the scan tool Clear DTC function.
- The EBCM automatically clears the history DTC when a current DTC is not detected in 100 consecutive drive cycles.

Diagnostic Aids

- Test the charging system.
- Possible causes of this DTC are the following conditions:
  - A charging system malfunction
  - An excessive battery draw
  - A weak battery
  - A faulty system ground

Test Description

The numbers below refer to the step numbers on the diagnostic table.

2. Use the scan tool in order to inspect the voltage to the EBCM.
3. Use the scan tool in order to inspect the voltage to the dash integration module (DIM). A low voltage value in multiple modules indicates a concern in the charging system.
5. Verifies that the condition is still present.

GC4020152546010X

Fig. 16 Code C1236: Low System Supply Voltage (Part 1 of 2). Aurora, Bonneville, LeSabre & Park Avenue

Circuit Description

The EBCM monitors the voltage level available for system operation. If the voltage level is too high, damage may result in the system. When the EBCM detects a high voltage condition, the EBCM turns OFF the system relay which removes battery voltage from the solenoid valves and pump motor.

Conditions for Running the DTC

The vehicle speed is greater than 8 km/h (5 mph).

Conditions for Setting the DTC

The system voltage is greater than 16.4 volts for 0.72 seconds.

Action Taken When the DTC Sets

If equipped, the following actions occur:

- The EBCM disables the DRP/ABS/TCS/VSES for the duration of the ignition cycle.
- The ABS indicator turns ON.
- The Traction Off indicator turns ON.
- The DIC displays the Service Stability System message.
- The EBCM will also set DTC C1248.
- The red Brake warning indicator turns ON.

Conditions for Clearing the DTC

- The condition for the DTC is no longer present (the DTC is not current) and you used the scan tool Clear DTC function.
- The EBCM automatically clears the history DTC when a current DTC is not detected in 100 consecutive drive cycles.

Diagnostic Aids

A possible cause of this DTC is overcharging.

Test Description

The numbers below refer to the step numbers on the diagnostic table.

2. Use the scan tool in order to inspect the voltage to the EBCM.
3. Use the scan tool in order to inspect the voltage to the dash integration module (DIM). A high voltage value in multiple modules indicates a concern in the charging system.
4. Verifies that the condition is still present.

GC4020152547010X

Fig. 17 Code C1237: High System Supply Voltage (Part 1 of 2). Aurora, Bonneville, LeSabre & Park Avenue

Step	Action	Value(s)	Yes	No
1	Did you perform the ABS Diagnostic System Check?	—	Go to *Step 2*	Go to *Diagnostic System Check - ABS*
2	1. Turn OFF all of the accessories. 2. Install a scan tool. 3. Start the engine. 4. Run the engine at approximately 2000 RPM. 5. With a scan tool, observe the Switched System Battery Voltage parameter in the DRP/ABS/TCS data list. Does the scan tool indicate that the voltage is greater than the specified value?	16.4 V	Go to *Step 3*	Go to Diagnostic Aids
3	With a scan tool, observe the Battery Voltage parameter in Dash Integration Module data list. Does the scan tool indicate the voltage is greater than the specified value?	16.4 V	*Diagnose* Engine Electrical	Go to *Step 4*
4	1. Use the scan tool in order to clear the DTCs. 2. Operate the vehicle within the conditions for Running the DTC as specified in the supporting text. Does the DTC reset?	—	Go to *Step 5*	Go to Diagnostic Aids
5	**Important:** Perform the setup procedure for the EBCM. An unprogrammed EBCM will result in the following conditions: • Inoperative or poorly functioning system operations • The EBCM sets DTC C1248 and DTC C1255m3. Replace the EBCM. Did you complete the repair?	—	Go to *Step 6*	—
6	1. Use the scan tool in order to clear the DTCs. 2. Operate the vehicle within the conditions for Running the DTC as specified in the supporting text. Does the DTC reset?	—	Go to *Step 2*	System OK

GC4020152547020X

Fig. 17 Code C1237: High System Supply Voltage (Part 2 of 2). Aurora, Bonneville, LeSabre & Park Avenue

Circuit Description

The EBCM monitors vehicle speed deceleration, system activation, and stoplamp switch active times in order to calculate an estimate of the brake rotor temperatures. If the EBCM calculates that the brake rotor temperatures have exceeded the thermal cutoff point, the EBCM will temporarily suspend the TCS function until the brake rotors cool. This feature is used to maintain braking effectiveness if normal base braking is required. An overly heated brake system could result in brake fade.

The EBCM continues calculating the brake rotor temperatures after the ignition is turned OFF. The EBCM remains awake until the EBCM calculates that the brake rotors cooled sufficiently. The cooling period may take up to 30 minutes.

Conditions for Running the DTC

The ABS conditions and the braking conditions are normal.

Conditions for Setting the DTC

This DTC sets when the estimated brake rotor temperature of either of the drive wheels exceeds 375°C (700°F). When the estimated brake rotor temperature of either of the drive wheels exceeds 375°C (700°F) during normal braking or normal ABS operations, the DTC does not set until the next TCS activation. The brake rotor temperature can exceed 375°C (700°F) without setting the DTC if a TCS activation has not occurred. When the estimated brake rotor temperature of either of the drive wheels exceeds 375°C (700°F) during a TCS activation, the DTC sets immediately, but the EBCM does not disable TCS until the end of the TCS event.

Action Taken When the DTC Sets

- The EBCM disables the TCS until the DTC becomes a history DTC.
- The Traction Off indicator turns ON.
- The ABS remains functional.

Conditions for Clearing the DTC

- The current DTC becomes history when the estimated brake rotor temperatures of both drive wheels decreases below 275°C (530°F). The EBCM also enables TCS.
- The condition for the DTC is no longer present (the DTC is not current) and you used the scan tool Clear DTC function.
- The EBCM automatically clears the history DTC when a current DTC is not detected in 100 consecutive drive cycles.

Diagnostic Aids

- With TCS temporarily disabled, the EBCM continues calculating the brake rotor temperatures after the ignition is turned OFF. Turning ON the ignition again while TCS is temporarily disabled will not re-enable TCS.
- The temperature is an estimate calculated by the EBCM.
- Possible causes of this DTC are the following conditions:
  - The brake usage is excessive.
  - The TCS usage is excessive.
  - The stoplamp switch is misaligned or damaged.

Test Description

The number below refers to the step number on the diagnostic table.

4. Use the scan tool in order to verify that the Brake Thermal Model is exceeded.

GC4020152548010X

Fig. 18 Code C1238: Brake Thermal Model Exceeded (Part 1 of 2). Aurora, Bonneville, LeSabre & Park Avenue

Step	Action	Yes	No
1	Did you perform the ABS Diagnostic System Check?	Go to *Step 2*	Go to *Diagnostic System Check - ABS*
2	1. Install a scan tool. 2. Turn ON the ignition, with the engine OFF. 3. Select the display DTCs function on the scan tool for the EBCM. Does the scan tool display that this DTC is set current?	Go to *Step 4*	Go to *Step 3*
3	Since most occurrences of this DTC are caused by excessive braking, review with the customer to verify the conditions under which the DTC set. Did vehicle operation cause this DTC to set?	Go to Diagnostic Aids	Go to *Step 4*
4	1. Allow 30 minutes from the last time you drove the vehicle for the cooling of the brake rotors. 2. With a scan tool, observe the Brake Temp Status parameter in the DRP/ABS/TCS data list. Does the scan tool display Normal?	Go to *Step 6*	Go to *Step 5*
5	Inspect the alignment of the stoplamp switch. Did you find and correct the condition?	Go to *Step 8*	Go to *Step 6*
6	1. Use the scan tool in order to clear the DTCs. 2. Operate the vehicle within the Conditions for Running the DTC as specified in the supporting text. Does the DTC reset as a current DTC?	Go to *Step 7*	System OK
7	**Important:** Perform the setup procedure for the EBCM. An unprogrammed EBCM will result in the following conditions: • Inoperative or poorly functioning system operations • The EBCM sets DTC C1248 and DTC C1255m3. Replace the EBCM. Did you complete the repair?	Go to *Step 8*	—
8	1. Use the scan tool in order to clear the DTCs. 2. Operate the vehicle within the Conditions for Running the DTC as specified in the supporting text. Does the DTC reset?	Go to *Step 2*	System OK

GC4020152548020X

Fig. 18 Code C1238: Brake Thermal Model Exceeded (Part 2 of 2). Aurora, Bonneville, LeSabre & Park Avenue

Circuit Description

The system relay is energized when the ignition is ON. The system relay supplies voltage to the solenoid valves and the pump motor. This voltage is referred to as the system voltage.

The EBCM controls each solenoid valve by grounding the solenoid.

The EBCM controls the pump motor by grounding the control circuit. The pump serves 2 purposes:

- Transfers brake fluid from the brake calipers to the master cylinder reservoir during pressure decrease events.
- Transfers brake fluid from the master cylinder reservoir to the brake calipers during pressure increase events.

Conditions for Running the DTC

C1242

- The system voltage is greater than 8.0 volts.
- The system relay is ON.
- The pump motor is commanded OFF.

C1243

- The pump motor is ON for at least 0.3 seconds.
- The system relay is ON.

Conditions for Setting the DTC

C1242

The voltage across the pump motor is between 1.7–10.2 volts for 2 seconds.

C1243

The pump motor is stalled or turning slowly.

Action Taken When the DTC Sets

If equipped, the following actions occur:

- The EBCM disables the ABS/TCS/VSES for the duration of the ignition cycle.
- The DRP does not function optimally.
- The ABS indicator turns ON.
- The Traction Off indicator turns ON.
- The DIC displays the Service Stability System message.

Conditions for Clearing the DTC

- The condition for the DTC is no longer present (the DTC is not current) and you used the scan tool Clear DTC function.
- The EBCM automatically clears the history DTC when a current DTC is not detected in 100 consecutive drive cycles.

Diagnostic Aids

The pump motor is integral to the BPMV. The pump motor is not serviceable.

Test Description

The number below refers to the step number on the diagnostic table.

3. Tests the ability of the EBCM to control the pump motor. If the test lamp illuminates, the pump motor circuit within the EBCM is good.

GC4020152549010X

Fig. 19 Code C1242 Or C1243: BPMV Pump Motor Circuit Fault (Part 1 of 2). Aurora, Bonneville, LeSabre & Park Avenue

Step	Action	Yes	No
1	Did you perform the ABS Diagnostic System Check?	Go to *Step 2*	Go to *Diagnostic System Check - ABS*
2	1. Install a scan tool. 2. Turn ON the ignition, with the engine OFF. 3. Use the scan tool in order to clear the DTCs. 4. With the scan tool, perform the Automated Test. Does the DTC reset?	Go to *Step 3*	*Test for Intermittent*
3	1. Turn OFF the ignition. 2. Disconnect the pump motor harness pigtail connector of the BPMV. 3. Connect a test lamp between the pump motor circuits at the pump motor connector of the EBCM using the *J 35616-A* Connector Test Adapter Kit. 4. Use the scan tool in order to clear the DTCs. 5. With the scan tool, perform the Pump Motor Test. Does the test lamp illuminate?	Go to *Step 4*	Go to *Step 5*
4	Inspect for poor connections at the pump motor harness pigtail connector of the BPMV. Did you find and correct the condition?	Go to *Step 8*	Go to *Step 6*
5	Inspect for poor connections at the harness connector of the EBCM. Did you find and correct the condition?	Go to *Step 8*	Go to *Step 7*
6	Replace the BPMV. Did you complete the repair?	Go to *Step 8*	—
7	**Important:** Perform the setup procedure for the EBCM. An unprogrammed EBCM will result in the following conditions: • Inoperative or poorly functioning system operations • The EBCM sets DTC C1248 and DTC C1255m3. Replace the EBCM. Did you complete the repair?	Go to *Step 8*	—
8	1. Use the scan tool in order to clear the DTCs. 2. With the scan tool, perform the Automated Test. Does the DTC reset?	Go to *Step 2*	System OK

GC4020152549020X

Fig. 19 Code C1242 Or C1243: BPMV Pump Motor Circuit Fault (Part 2 of 2). Aurora, Bonneville, LeSabre & Park Avenue

Circuit Description

The dynamic rear proportioning (DRP) is a control system that replaces the hydraulic proportioning function of the mechanical proportioning valve in the base brake system. The DRP control system is part of the operating software in the EBCM. The DRP uses active control with the existing ABS in order to regulate the vehicle's rear brake pressure.

Conditions for Running the DTC

One or more faults have been detected by the EBCM in the ABS/TCS systems.

Conditions for Setting the DTC

One of the following conditions exists:

- DTC C1214, C1217, C1237, C1254, C1255, C1261–1268, or C1271–1274 sets.
- DTC C1236 sets and the system voltage is less than 8.5 volts.
- Two wheel speed sensor DTCs on the same axle set.

Action Taken When the DTC Sets

- The EBCM disables the DRP for the duration of the ignition cycle.
- The red Brake warning indicator turns ON.

Conditions for Clearing the DTC

- The condition for the DTC is no longer present (the DTC is not current) and you used the scan tool Clear DTC function.
- The EBCM automatically clears the history DTC when a current DTC is not detected in 100 consecutive drive cycles.

Diagnostic Aids

- Use this DTC in order to differentiate which of the following conditions is present:
  - The EBCM turned ON the red Brake warning indicator.
  - The instrument cluster turned ON the red Brake warning indicator due to low brake fluid in the master cylinder reservoir.
  - The instrument cluster turned ON the red Brake warning indicator due to the application of the park brake.
- Diagnose any other ABS DTCs that set along with this DTC.

Test Description

The number below refers to the step number on the diagnostic table.

2. Verifies whether other ABS/TCS/VSES DTCs are set.

Step	Action	Yes	No
1	Did you perform the ABS Diagnostic System Check?	Go to *Step 2*	Go to *Diagnostic System Check - ABS*
2	1. Install a scan tool. 2. Turn ON the ignition, with the engine OFF. 3. Select the display DTCs function on the scan tool for the EBCM. Does the scan tool display any ABS/TCS/VSES DTCs?	Go to *Diagnostic Trouble Code (DTC) List*	Go to *Step 3*
3	1. Use the scan tool in order to clear the DTCs. 2. Operate the vehicle within the Conditions for Running the DTC as specified in the supporting text. Does the DTC reset?	Go to *Step 2*	*Test for Intermittent*

GC4020152550000X

Fig. 20 Code C1248: Brake Warning Indicator Fault. Aurora, Bonneville, LeSabre & Park Avenue

Step	Action	Yes	No
1	Did you perform the ABS Diagnostic System Check?	Go to *Step 2*	Go to *Diagnostic System Check - ABS*
2	1. Turn OFF the ignition. **Important:** Removing battery voltage or ground from the EBCM will result in the following conditions: • Loss of the TIM learned tire inflation configuration parameters in the EBCM • The EBCM sets DTC C1245. When the diagnosis is complete, inspect the tire pressures and perform the TIM reset. 2. Disconnect the EBCM harness connector. 3. Install the *J 39700* Universal Pinout Box using the *J 39700-300* Cable Adapter to the EBCM harness connector only. 4. Test both ground circuits of the EBCM including the EBCM ground for a high resistance or an open. Did you find and correct the condition?	Go to *Step 8*	Go to *Step 3*
3	Has the battery been disconnected recently?	Go to *Step 8*	Go to *Step 4*
4	Test the charging system. Did you find and correct the condition?	Go to *Step 8*	Go to *Step 5*
5	Inspect for poor connections at the harness connector of the EBCM. Did you find and correct the condition?	Go to *Step 8*	Go to *Step 6*
6	1. Use the scan tool in order to clear the DTCs. 2. With the scan tool, perform the Automated Test. Does the DTC reset?	Go to *Step 7*	*Test for Intermittent*
7	**Important:** Perform the setup procedure for the EBCM. An unprogrammed EBCM will result in the following conditions: • Inoperative or poorly functioning system operations • The EBCM sets DTC C1248 and DTC C1255m3. Replace the EBCM. Did you complete the repair?	Go to *Step 8*	—
8	1. Use the scan tool in order to clear the DTCs. 2. With the scan tool, perform the Automated Test. Does the DTC reset?	Go to *Step 2*	System OK

GC4020152551020X

Fig. 21 Code C1254: Abnormal Shutdown Detected (Part 2 of 2). Aurora, Bonneville, LeSabre & Park Avenue

Circuit Description

The microprocessor contains a data storage area (keep alive memory) which can save pertinent data when the ignition is turned OFF. The keep alive memory (KAM) data is lost if battery power or module ground is removed from the module. The KAM area is an integral part of the microprocessor and cannot be serviced separately.

Conditions for Running the DTC

The ABS conditions and the braking conditions are normal.

Conditions for Setting the DTC

The microprocessor calculates a checksum on those areas of memory that hold critical operation data. This is done at a regular interval and is called the periodic checksum. The microprocessor also calculates a checksum on these memory locations when ever new data is written to them. This is called the running checksum.

To check the keep alive memory (KAM), the microprocessor compares the periodic checksum to the running checksum. If they do not match, the microprocessor sets the DTC.

Action Taken When the DTC Sets

If equipped, the following actions occur:

- The EBCM disables the DRP/ABS/TCS/VSES/TIM for the duration of the ignition cycle.
- The EBCM disables the variable effort steering (VES) for the duration of the ignition cycle.
- The ABS indicator turns ON.
- The Traction Off indicator turns ON.
- The DIC displays the Service Stability System message.
- The red Brake warning indicator turns ON.
- The EBCM will also set DTC C1245 and DTC C1248.
- The EBCM will not send serial data messages.
- The EBCM will not send the requested torque output to the PCM.

Conditions for Clearing the DTC

- The condition for the DTC is no longer present (the DTC is not current) and you used the scan tool Clear DTC function.
- The EBCM automatically clears the history DTC when a current DTC is not detected in 100 consecutive drive cycles.

Diagnostic Aids

Possible causes of this DTC are the following conditions:

- A loss of battery ground
- A disconnected battery
- A running reset (A running reset is detected when the keep alive memory check sum is not updated properly.)
- A sudden drop in the system voltage to less than 5 volts
- Long extended engine cranks that cause the battery voltage to drop
- Poor power or ground connections.
- An internal EBCM malfunction.

Test Description

The numbers below refer to the step numbers on the diagnostic table.

2. Tests for an open in the ground circuits of the EBCM.
4. Verifies the proper operation of the charging system.
6. Determines whether the DTC resets.

GC4020152551010X

Fig. 21 Code C1254: Abnormal Shutdown Detected (Part 1 of 2). Aurora, Bonneville, LeSabre & Park Avenue

Circuit Description

This DTC identifies a malfunction within the EBCM.

Conditions for Running the DTC

The ABS conditions and the braking conditions are normal.

Conditions for Setting the DTC

An internal EBCM malfunction exists.

Action Taken When the DTC Sets

C1255

If equipped, the following actions occur:

- The EBCM disables the DRP/ABS/TCS/VSES for the duration of the ignition cycle.
- The ABS indicator turns ON.
- The Traction Off indicator turns ON.
- The red Brake warning indicator turns ON.
- The DIC displays the Service Stability System message.
- The EBCM will also set DTC C1248.
- For some DTC C1255xx, the EBCM disables the variable effort steering (VES) for the duration of the ignition cycle.
- For some DTC C1255xx, the EBCM temporarily suspends the TIM monitoring function while the DTC is set.

C1256

- The ABS remains functional.
- The ABS indicator remains OFF.

Conditions for Clearing the DTC

- The condition for the DTC is no longer present (the DTC is not current) and you used the scan tool Clear DTC function.
- The EBCM automatically clears the history DTC when a current DTC is not detected in 100 consecutive drive cycles.

Diagnostic Aids

- The scan tool displays 2 additional characters after the DTC. Take note of the 2 character code and any other DTCs that are set. The 2 character code is an engineering aid used in order to determine the cause of the internal malfunction.
- When the scan tool displays DTC C1255m3, the EBCM has not been programmed. Perform the setup procedure for the EBCM.

Test Description

The number below refers to the step number on the diagnostic table.

2. Determines whether the DTC is current.

Step	Action	Yes	No
1	Did you perform the ABS Diagnostic System Check?	Go to *Step 2*	Go to *Diagnostic System Check - ABS*
2	1. Install a scan tool. 2. Turn ON the ignition, with the engine OFF. 3. Use the scan tool in order to clear the DTCs. 4. With the scan tool, perform the Automated Test. Does the DTC reset as a current DTC?	Go to *Step 3*	*Test for Intermittent*
3	**Important:** Perform the setup procedure for the EBCM. An unprogrammed EBCM will result in the following conditions: • Inoperative or poorly functioning system operations • The EBCM sets DTC C1248 and DTC C1255m3. Replace the EBCM. Did you complete the repair?	Go to *Step 4*	—
4	1. Use the scan tool in order to clear the DTCs. 2. With the scan tool, perform the Automated Test. Does the DTC reset?	Go to *Step 2*	System OK

GC4020152552000X

Fig. 22 Code C1255 Or C1256: EBCM Internal Fault. Aurora, Bonneville, LeSabre & Park Avenue

Circuit Description

The system relay is energized when the ignition is ON. The system relay supplies voltage to the solenoid valves and the pump motor. This voltage is referred to as the system voltage. The EBCM controls the solenoid valve by grounding the control circuit.

Conditions for Running the DTC

- The system voltage is greater than 8.0 volts.
- The ignition voltage is greater than 9.0 volts.

Conditions for Setting the DTC

The commanded state of the driver and the actual state of the control circuit do not match for 0.03 seconds.

Action Taken When the DTC Sets

If equipped, the following actions occur:

- The EBCM disables the DRP/ABS/TCS/VSES for the duration of the ignition cycle.
- The ABS indicator turns ON.
- The Traction Off indicator turns ON.
- The DIC displays the Service Stability System message.
- The EBCM will also set DTC C1248.
- The red Brake warning indicator turns ON.

Conditions for Clearing the DTC

- The condition for the DTC is no longer present (the DTC is not current) and you used the scan tool Clear DTC function.
- The EBCM automatically clears the history DTC when a current DTC is not detected in 100 consecutive drive cycles.

Diagnostic Aids

The solenoid valve circuit is internal to the EBCM. The solenoid valve circuit is not diagnosable external to the EBCM. The DTC sets when there is a malfunction in the solenoid circuit internal to the EBCM.

Test Description

The number below refers to the step number on the diagnostic table.

2. Determines whether the DTC is current.

Step	Action	Yes	No
1	Did you perform the ABS Diagnostic System Check?	Go to *Step 2*	Go to *Diagnostic System Check - ABS*
2	1. Install a scan tool. 2. Turn ON the ignition, with the engine OFF. 3. Use the scan tool in order to clear the DTCs. 4. With the scan tool, perform the Automated Test. Does the DTC reset as a current DTC?	Go to *Step 3*	*Test for Intermittent*
3	**Important:** Perform the setup procedure for the EBCM. An unprogrammed EBCM will result in the following conditions: • Inoperative or poorly functioning system operations • The EBCM sets DTC C1248 and DTC C1255m3. Replace the EBCM. Did you complete the repair?	Go to *Step 4*	—
4	1. Use the scan tool in order to clear the DTCs. 2. With the scan tool, perform the Automated Test. Does the DTC reset?	Go to *Step 2*	System OK

GC4020152553000X

Fig. 23 Codes C1261-C1274: Solenoid Valve Fault. Aurora, Bonneville, LeSabre & Park Avenue

Step	Action	Value(s)	Yes	No
1	Did you perform the ABS Diagnostic System Check?	—	Go to *Step 2*	Go to *Diagnostic System Check - ABS*
2	Inspect the EBCM ground and PCM ground, making sure each ground is clean and torqued to the proper specification. Did you find and correct the condition?	—	Go to *Step 11*	Go to *Step 3*
3	1. Install a scan tool. 2. Start the engine. 3. With a scan tool, observe the Delivered Torque parameter in the DRP/ABS/TCS data list. Does the scan tool display the specified value?	90%	Go to *Step 4*	*Test for Intermittent*
4	1. Turn OFF the ignition. **Important:** Removing battery voltage or ground from the EBCM will result in the following conditions: • Loss of the TIM learned tire inflation configuration parameters in the EBCM • The EBCM sets DTC C1245. When the diagnosis is complete, inspect the tire pressures and perform the TIM reset. 2. Disconnect the EBCM harness connector. 3. Install the *J 39700* universal breakout box using the *J 39700-300* cable adapter to the EBCM harness connector and the EBCM connector. 4. Disconnect the powertrain control module (PCM) harness connector. 5. Turn ON the ignition, with the engine OFF. 6. Measure the voltage from the delivered torque signal circuit to a good ground. Does the voltage measure near the specified value?	B+	Go to *Step 5*	Go to *Step 6*
5	1. Turn OFF the ignition. 2. Disconnect the *J 39700-300* cable adapter from the EBCM connector. 3. Turn ON the ignition, with the engine OFF. 4. Test the delivered torque signal circuit for a short to voltage. Did you find and correct the condition?	—	Go to *Step 11*	Go to *Step 7*
6	1. Turn OFF the ignition. 2. Disconnect the *J 39700-300* cable adapter from the EBCM connector. 3. Test the delivered torque signal circuit for the following conditions: • An open • A short to ground • A high resistance Did you find and correct the condition?	—	Go to *Step 11*	Go to *Step 8*

GC4020152554020X

Fig. 24 Code C1276: Delivered Torque Signal Circuit Fault (Part 2 of 3). Aurora, Bonneville, LeSabre & Park Avenue

Circuit Description

The EBCM and the PCM simultaneously control the traction control. The PCM reduces the amount of torque supplied to the drive wheels by retarding spark timing and selectively turning off fuel injectors. The EBCM actively applies the brakes to the front wheels in order to reduce torque.

The EBCM sends a requested torque message via a pulse width modulated (PWM) signal to the PCM. The duty cycle of the signal is used to determine how much engine torque the EBCM is requesting the PCM to deliver. Normal values are between 10 and 90 percent duty cycle. The signal should be at 90 percent when traction control is not active and at lower values during traction control activations. The PCM supplies a pull up voltage of 5 volts that the EBCM switches to ground to create the signal.

The PCM sends a delivered torque message via a pulse width modulated (PWM) signal to the EBCM. The duty cycle of the signal is used to determine how much engine torque the PCM is delivering. Normal values are between 10 and 90 percent duty cycle. The signal should be at low values (around 10 percent) at idle and higher values under driving conditions. The EBCM supplies a pull up voltage of 12 volts that the PCM switches to ground to create the signal.

When certain PCM DTCs are set, the PCM will not be able to perform the torque reduction portion of traction control. A serial data message is sent to the EBCM indicating that traction control is not allowed.

Conditions for Running the DTC

The engine is running.

Conditions for Setting the DTC

C1276

One of the following conditions exists:

- The EBCM detects that delivered torque signal is out of the valid range.
- The EBCM does not receive the delivered torque signal.

P1644 or P1689

The PCM detects that the delivered torque signal voltage is invalid.

Action Taken When the DTC Sets

- The EBCM disables the TCS for the duration of the ignition cycle.
- The PCM will store conditions which were present when the DTC set as Fail Records data only.
- The Traction Off indicator turns ON.
- The ABS remains functional.

Conditions for Clearing the DTC

- The condition for the DTC is no longer present (the DTC is not current) and you used the scan tool Clear DTC function.
- The EBCM automatically clears the history DTC when a current DTC is not detected in 100 consecutive drive cycles.
- The PCM automatically clears the history DTC when a current DTC is not detected in 40 consecutive warm-up cycles.

Diagnostic Aids

The following conditions can cause this concern:

- An open in the delivered torque circuit.
- An short to ground or voltage in the delivered torque circuit.
- A wiring problem, terminal corrosion, or poor connection in the delivered torque circuit.
- A communication frequency problem.
- A communication duty cycle problem.
- The EBCM is not receiving information from the PCM.
- Loose or corroded EBCM ground or PCM ground.

Test Description

The numbers below refer to the step numbers on the diagnostic table.

3. Use the scan tool in order to determine if the delivered torque signal has a valid duty cycle.
9. This vehicle is equipped with a PCM which uses an Electrically Erasable Programmable Read Only Memory (EEPROM). When replacing the PCM, the replacement PCM must be programmed.

GC4020152554010X

Fig. 24 Code C1276: Delivered Torque Signal Circuit Fault (Part 1 of 3). Aurora, Bonneville, LeSabre & Park Avenue

Step	Action	Value(s)	Yes	No
7	Inspect for poor connections the harness connector of the PCM. Did you find and correct the condition?	—	Go to *Step 11*	Go to *Step 9*
8	Inspect for poor connections the harness connector of the EBCM. Did you find and correct the condition?	—	Go to *Step 11*	Go to *Step 10*
9	**Important:** The replacement PCM must be programmed. Replace the PCM. Did you complete the repair?	—	Go to *Step 11*	—
10	**Important:** Perform the setup procedure for the EBCM. An unprogrammed EBCM will result in the following conditions: • Inoperative or poorly functioning system operations • The EBCM sets DTC C1248 and DTC C1255m3. Replace the EBCM. Did you complete the repair?	—	Go to *Step 11*	—
11	1. Use the scan tool in order to clear the DTCs. 2. Operate the vehicle within the Conditions for Running the DTC as specified in the supporting text. Does the DTC reset?	—	Go to *Step 2*	System OK

GC4020152554030X

Fig. 24 Code C1276: Delivered Torque Signal Circuit Fault (Part 3 of 3). Aurora, Bonneville, LeSabre & Park Avenue

Circuit Description

The EBCM and the PCM simultaneously control the traction control. The PCM reduces the amount of torque supplied to the drive wheels by retarding spark timing and selectively turning off fuel injectors. The EBCM actively applies the brakes to the front wheels in order to reduce torque.

The EBCM sends a requested torque message via a pulse width modulated (PWM) signal to the PCM. The duty cycle of the signal is used to determine how much engine torque the EBCM is requesting the PCM to deliver. Normal values are between 10 and 90 percent duty cycle. The signal should be at 90 percent when traction control is not active and at lower values during traction control activations. The PCM supplies a pull up voltage of 5 volts that the EBCM switches to ground to create the signal.

The PCM sends a delivered torque message via a pulse width modulated (PWM) signal to the EBCM. The duty cycle of the signal is used to determine how much engine torque the PCM is delivering. Normal values are between 10 and 90 percent duty cycle. The signal should be at low values (around 10 percent) at idle and higher values under driving conditions. The EBCM supplies a pull up voltage of 12 volts that the PCM switches to ground to create the signal.

When certain PCM DTCs are set, the PCM will not be able to perform the torque reduction portion of traction control. A serial data message is sent to the EBCM indicating that traction control is not allowed.

Conditions for Running the DTC

The engine is running.

Conditions for Setting the DTC

C1277

The PCM diagnoses the requested torque signal circuit and sends a serial data message to the EBCM indicating a fault is present.

P1571

One of the following conditions exists:

- The PCM detects that requested torque signal is out of the valid range.
- The PCM does not receive the requested torque signal.

Action Taken When the DTC Sets

- The EBCM disables the TCS for the duration of the ignition cycle.
- The PCM will store conditions which were present when the DTC set as Fail Records data only.
- The Traction Off indicator turns ON.
- The ABS remains functional.

Conditions for Clearing the DTC

- The condition for the DTC is no longer present (the DTC is not current) and you used the scan tool Clear DTC function.
- The EBCM automatically clears the history DTC when a current DTC is not detected in 100 consecutive drive cycles.
- The PCM automatically clears the history DTC when a current DTC is not detected in 40 consecutive warm-up cycles.

Diagnostic Aids

The following conditions can cause this concern:

- An open in the requested torque circuit.
- An short to ground or voltage in the requested torque circuit.
- A wiring problem, terminal corrosion, or poor connection in the requested torque circuit.
- A communication frequency problem.
- A communication duty cycle problem.
- The PCM is not receiving information from the EBCM.
- Loose or corroded EBCM ground or PCM ground.

A DTC P1571 may set along with several other PCM DTCs if the key is held in the CRANK position while the engine is running. The starter lockout function of the PCM is enabled several seconds after the engine is running and prevents the starter from engaging while the engine is running. This will cause a partial loss of power to some components and systems.

Test Description

The numbers below refer to the step numbers on the diagnostic table.

3. Use the scan tool in order to determine if the requested torque signal has a valid duty cycle.
4. Measure the requested torque signal in order to determine if the signal has a valid duty cycle.
5. Measure the requested torque signal in order to determine if the signal has a valid frequency.
11. This vehicle is equipped with a PCM which uses an Electrically Erasable Programmable Read Only Memory (EEPROM). When replacing the PCM, the replacement PCM must be programmed.

GC4020152554040X

Fig. 25 Code C1277: Requested Torque Signal Circuit Fault (Part 1 of 3). Aurora, Bonneville, LeSabre & Park Avenue

Step	Action	Value(s)	Yes	No
1	Did you perform the ABS Diagnostic System Check?	—	Go to *Step 2*	Go to *Diagnostic System Check - ABS*
2	Inspect the EBCM ground and PCM ground, making sure each ground is clean and torqued to the proper specification. Did you find and correct the condition?	—	Go to *Step 13*	Go to *Step 3*
3	1. Install a scan tool. 2. Start the engine. 3. With a scan, observe the Torque Request Signal parameter in the Powertrain Control Module data list. Does the scan display less than the specified value?	100%	*Test for Intermittent*	Go to *Step 4*
4	1. Turn OFF the ignition. **Important:** Removing battery voltage or ground from the EBCM will result in the following conditions: • Loss of the TIM learned tire inflation configuration parameters in the EBCM • The EBCM sets DTC C1245 When the diagnosis is complete, inspect the tire pressures and perform the TIM reset. 2. Disconnect the EBCM harness connector. 3. Install the *J 39700* universal breakout box using the *J 39700-300* cable adapter to the EBCM harness connector and the EBCM connector. 4. Start the engine. 5. Measure the DC duty cycle between the requested torque signal circuit and a good ground. Is the duty cycle within the specified range?	5–95%	Go to *Step 5*	Go to *Step 6*
5	Measure the DC Hz between the requested torque signal circuit and a good ground. Does the frequency measure within the specified range?	121–134 Hz	Go to *Step 8*	Go to *Step 6*
6	1. Turn OFF the ignition. 2. Disconnect the *J 39700-300* cable adapter from the EBCM connector. **Important:** Disconnecting the EBCM connector and turning ON the ignition could cause other modules to set loss of communication DTCs (Uxxxx). Once the EBCM is reconnected, the EBCM may set DTC C1245 or DTC C1298. 3. Turn ON the ignition, with the engine OFF. 4. Measure the voltage from the requested torque signal circuit to a good ground. Does the voltage measure within the specified range?	4–6 V	Go to *Step 10*	Go to *Step 7*

GC4020152554050X

Fig. 25 Code C1277: Requested Torque Signal Circuit Fault (Part 2 of 3). Aurora, Bonneville, LeSabre & Park Avenue

Step	Action	Value(s)	Yes	No
7	1. Turn OFF the ignition. 2. Disconnect the powertrain control module (PCM) harness connector. 3. Test the requested torque signal circuit for the following conditions: • A short to voltage • A short to ground Did you find and correct the condition?	—	Go to *Step 13*	Go to *Step 10*
8	1. Turn OFF the ignition. 2. Disconnect the powertrain control module (PCM) harness connector. 3. Test the requested torque signal circuit for the following conditions: • An open • A high resistance Did you find and correct the condition?	—	Go to *Step 13*	Go to *Step 9*
9	Inspect for poor connections the harness connector of the PCM. Did you find and correct the condition?	—	Go to *Step 13*	Go to *Step 11*
10	Inspect for poor connections the harness connector of the EBCM. Did you find and correct the condition?	—	Go to *Step 13*	Go to *Step 12*
11	**Important:** The replacement PCM must be programmed. Replace the PCM. Did you complete the repair?	—	Go to *Step 13*	—
12	**Important:** Perform the setup procedure for the EBCM. An unprogrammed EBCM will result in the following conditions: • Inoperative or poorly functioning system operations • The EBCM sets DTC C1248 and DTC C1255m3. Replace the EBCM. Did you complete the repair?	—	Go to *Step 13*	—
13	1. Use the scan tool in order to clear the DTCs. 2. Operate the vehicle within the Conditions for Running the DTC as specified in the supporting text. Does the DTC reset?	—	Go to *Step 2*	System OK

GC4020152554060X

Fig. 25 Code C1277: Requested Torque Signal Circuit Fault (Part 3 of 3). Aurora, Bonneville, LeSabre & Park Avenue

Circuit Description

The EBCM and the PCM simultaneously control the traction control. The PCM reduces the amount of torque supplied to the drive wheels by retarding spark timing and selectively turning off fuel injectors. The EBCM actively applies the brakes to the front wheels in order to reduce torque.

The EBCM sends a requested torque message via a pulse width modulated (PWM) signal to the PCM. The duty cycle of the signal is used to determine how much engine torque the EBCM is requesting the PCM to deliver. Normal values are between 10 and 90 percent duty cycle. The signal should be at 90 percent when traction control is not active and at lower values during traction control activations. The PCM supplies a pull up voltage of 5 volts that the EBCM switches to ground to create the signal.

The PCM sends a delivered torque message via a pulse width modulated (PWM) signal to the EBCM. The duty cycle of the signal is used to determine how much engine torque the PCM is delivering. Normal values are between 10 and 90 percent duty cycle. The signal should be at low values (around 10 percent) at idle and higher values under driving conditions. The EBCM supplies a pull up voltage of 12 volts that the PCM switches to ground to create the signal.

When certain PCM DTCs are set, the PCM will not be able to perform the torque reduction portion of traction control. A serial data message is sent to the EBCM indicating that traction control is not allowed.

Conditions for Running the DTC

The ignition is ON.

Conditions for Setting the DTC

The PCM diagnoses a condition preventing the engine control portion of the traction control function and sends a serial data message to the EBCM indicating that torque reduction is not allowed. The PCM will typically set a DTC and the EBCM will set this DTC.

Action Taken When the DTC Sets

- The EBCM disables the TCS for the duration of the ignition cycle.
- The Traction Off indicator turns ON.
- The ABS remains functional.

Conditions for Clearing the DTC

- The condition for the DTC is no longer present (the DTC is not current) and you used the scan tool Clear DTC function.
- The EBCM automatically clears the history DTC when a current DTC is not detected in 100 consecutive drive cycles.

Diagnostic Aids

This DTC is for information only. As an aid to the technician, this DTC indicates that there are no problems in the ABS/TCS system.

Step	Action	Yes	No
1	Did you perform the ABS Diagnostic System Check?	*Diagnose Engine Controls*	Go to *Diagnostic System Check - ABS*

GC4020152555000X

Fig. 26 Code C1278: TCS Temporarily Inhibited By PCM. Aurora, Bonneville, LeSabre & Park Avenue

Circuit Description

The vehicle stability enhancement system (VSES) is activated by the EBCM calculating the desired yaw rate and comparing it to the actual yaw rate input. The desired yaw rate is calculated from measured steering wheel position, vehicle speed, and lateral acceleration. The difference between the desired yaw rate and actual yaw rate is the yaw rate error, which is a measurement of oversteer or understeer. If the yaw rate error becomes too large, the EBCM will attempt to correct the vehicle's yaw motion by applying differential braking to the left or right front wheel.

The VSES activations generally occur during aggressive driving, in the turns or bumpy roads without much use of the accelerator pedal. When braking during VSES activation, the brake pedal will feel different than the ABS pedal pulsation. The brake pedal pulsates at a higher frequency during VSES activation.

The usable output voltage range for the lateral accelerometer and yaw rate sensors is 0.25–4.75 volts. The scan tool will report zero lateral acceleration or yaw rate as 2.5 volts with no sensor bias present. The sensor bias compensates for sensor mounting alignment errors, electronic signal errors, temperature changes, and manufacturing differences.

The steering wheel position sensor supplies 2 analog inputs, Phase A and Phase B, to the EBCM. The 2 input signals are approximately 90 degrees out of phase. By interpreting the relationship between the 2 inputs, the EBCM can determine the position of the steering wheel and the direction of steering wheel rotation.

Steer angle centering is the process by which the EBCM calibrates the steering sensor output so that the output reads zero when the steering wheel is centered. Using the yaw rate input, lateral accelerometer input, and wheel speed sensor inputs, the initial steering center position is calculated after driving greater than 10 km/h (6 mph) for more than 10 seconds in a straight line on a level surface.

Conditions for Running the DTC

C1281

- The steer angle has been centered.
- The VSES is active.
- The direction (understeer or oversteer) of the yaw rate error has not changed.
- The centered lateral acceleration value is less than 0.5 g.

C1283

The vehicle speed is greater than 40 km/h (25 mph).

C1286

The steer angle has been centered.

Conditions for Setting the DTC

C1281

One of the following conditions exists:

- The VSES is engaged for 10 seconds with the yaw rate error always in either understeer or oversteer. Under this condition, this DTC will set by itself.
- The yaw rate error is greater than 10 degrees/second for 5 seconds. Under this condition, this DTC will set along with DTC C1282.
- The yaw rate error is greater than 10 degrees/second with the vehicle speed less than 60 km/h (37 mph) and the acceleration pedal is pressed more than 25 percent of the pedal travel range for 1 second during the VSES activation. Under this condition, this DTC will set along with DTC C1282.
- With the steer rate less than 80 degrees/second, the difference between the 2 steering sensor signals (Phase A and Phase B) is greater than 20 degrees for 1 second. Under this condition, this DTC will set along with DTC C1287.

C1283

The vehicle has driven for 10 minutes without completing steer angle centering.

C1286

The steering sensor bias moves greater than 40 degrees after steer centering was accomplished.

Action Taken When the DTC Sets

- The EBCM disables the VSES for the duration of the ignition cycle.
- The DIC displays the Service Stability System message.
- The ABS/TCS remains functional.

Conditions for Clearing the DTC

- The condition for the DTC is no longer present (the DTC is not current) and you used the scan tool Clear DTC function.
- The EBCM automatically clears the history DTC when a current DTC is not detected in 100 consecutive drive cycles.

Diagnostic Aids

- During diagnosis, park the vehicle on a level surface.
- Check the vehicle for proper alignment. The car should not pull in either direction while driving straight on a level surface.
- Find out from the driver under what conditions the DTC was set (when the DIC displayed the Service Stability System message). This information will help to duplicate the failure.
- The Snapshot function on the scan tool can help find an intermittent DTC.

GC4020152555010X

Fig. 27 Codes C1281, C1283 Or C1286: VSES Sensors Uncorrelated (Part 1 of 2). Aurora, Bonneville, LeSabre & Park Avenue

Test Description

The numbers below refer to the step numbers on the diagnostic table.

2. Perform the Steering Position Sensor Test in order to verify that the steering wheel position sensor (SWPS) is operating properly.
3. Verify that the lateral accelerometer input parameter is within the valid range.
4. Verify that the yaw rate input parameter is within the valid range.

Step	Action	Value(s)	Yes	No
1	Did you perform the ABS Diagnostic System Check?	—	Go to *Step 2*	Go to *Diagnostic System Check - ABS*
2	1. Install a scan tool. 2. Turn ON the ignition, with the engine OFF. 3. With the scan tool, perform the Steering Position Sensor Test. Did the SWPS pass the test?	—	Go to *Step 3*	Go to *Step 7*
3	With a scan tool, observe the Lateral Accelerometer Input parameter in the VSES data list. Does the scan tool display within the specified range?	2.3–2.7 V	Go to *Step 4*	Go to *Step 8*
4	With a scan tool, observe the Yaw Rate Sensor Input parameter in the VSES data list. Does the scan tool display within the specified range?	2.3–2.7 V	Go to *Step 5*	Go to *Step 9*
5	1. Use the scan tool in order to clear the DTCs. 2. Perform the Diagnostic Test Drive. Does the DTC reset?	—	Go to *Step 6*	Go to Diagnostic Aids
6	**Important:** Perform the setup procedure for the EBCM. An unprogrammed EBCM will result in the following conditions: • Inoperative or poorly functioning system operations • The EBCM sets DTC C1248 and DTC C1255m3. Replace the EBCM. Did you complete the repair?	—	Go to *Step 10*	—
7	Replace the steering wheel position sensor (SWPS). Did you complete the replacement?	—	Go to *Step 10*	—
8	Replace the lateral accelerometer sensor. Did you complete the replacement?	—	Go to *Step 10*	—
9	Replace the yaw rate sensor. Did you complete the replacement?	—	Go to *Step 10*	—
10	1. Use the scan tool in order to clear the DTCs. 2. Operate the vehicle within the Conditions for Running the DTC as specified in the supporting text. Does the DTC reset?	—	Go to *Step 2*	System OK

GC4020152555020X

Fig. 27 Codes C1281, C1283 Or C1286: VSES Sensors Uncorrelated (Part 2 of 2). Aurora, Bonneville, LeSabre & Park Avenue

Circuit Description

The vehicle stability enhancement system (VSES) is activated by the EBCM calculating the desired yaw rate and comparing it to the actual yaw rate input. The desired yaw rate is calculated from measured steering wheel position, vehicle speed, and lateral acceleration. The difference between the desired yaw rate and actual yaw rate is the yaw rate error, which is a measurement of oversteer or understeer. If the yaw rate error becomes too large, the EBCM will attempt to correct the vehicle's yaw motion by applying differential braking to the left or right front wheel.

The VSES activations generally occur during aggressive driving, in the turns or bumpy roads without much use of the accelerator pedal. When braking during VSES activation, the brake pedal will feel different than the ABS pedal pulsation. The brake pedal pulsates at a higher frequency during VSES activation.

The usable output voltage range for the lateral accelerometer and yaw rate sensors is 0.25–4.75 volts. The scan tool will report zero lateral acceleration or yaw rate as 2.5 volts with no sensor bias present. The sensor bias compensates for sensor mounting alignment errors, electronic signal errors, temperature changes, and manufacturing differences.

The steering wheel position sensor supplies 2 analog inputs, Phase A and Phase B, to the EBCM. The 2 input signals are approximately 90 degrees out of phase. By interpreting the relationship between the 2 inputs, the EBCM can determine the position of the steering wheel and the direction of steering wheel rotation.

Steer angle centering is the process by which the EBCM calibrates the steering sensor output so that the output reads zero when the steering wheel is centered. Using the yaw rate input, lateral accelerometer input, and wheel speed sensor inputs, the initial steering center position is calculated after driving greater than 10 km/h (6 mph) for more than 10 seconds in a straight line on a level surface.

Conditions for Running the DTC

The EBCM performs 6 different tests to detect a DTC condition. The numbers below correspond to the numbers in Conditions for Setting the DTC.

1. The yaw rate sensor bias test runs with the ignition ON.
2. The yaw rate sensor acceleration test runs with the ignition ON.
3. The yaw rate sensor circuit test runs with the vehicle stopped or with the vehicle speed greater than 45 km/h (28 mph).
4. The yaw rate isolation test runs with the following conditions:
   - The brake pedal is not pressed.
   - The ABS is not active.
   - The vehicle speed is greater than 5 km/h (3 mph).
5. The above yaw rate isolation test run with the VSES active.
6. The false activation test runs with the VSES active.

Conditions for Setting the DTC

The EBCM performs 6 different tests to detect a DTC condition. The numbers below correspond to the numbers in Conditions for Running the DTC.

1. The yaw rate bias is greater than 7 degrees/second.
2. The yaw rate input change is greater than 390 degrees/second/second.
3. The yaw rate input voltage is less than 0.15 volts or greater than 4.85 volts for 1 second.
4. The yaw rate error is greater than 10 degrees/second 30 times within a drive cycle.
5. The yaw rate error is greater than 10 degrees/second for 5 seconds. Under this condition, this DTC will set along with DTC C1281.
6. The yaw rate error is greater than 10 degrees/second with the vehicle speed less than 60 km/h (37 mph) and the acceleration pedal is pressed more than 25 percent of the pedal travel range for 1 second during the VSES activation. Under this condition, this DTC will set along with DTC C1281.

Action Taken When the DTC Sets

- The EBCM disables the VSES for the duration of the ignition cycle.
- The DIC displays the Service Stability System message.
- The ABS/TCS remains functional.

Conditions for Clearing the DTC

- The condition for the DTC is no longer present (the DTC is not current) and you used the scan tool Clear DTC function.
- The EBCM automatically clears the history DTC when a current DTC is not detected in 100 consecutive drive cycles.

Diagnostic Aids

- During diagnosis, park the vehicle on a level surface.
- Check the vehicle for proper alignment. The car should not pull in either direction while driving straight on a level surface.
- Find out from the driver under what conditions the DTC was set (when the DIC displayed the Service Stability System message). This information will help to duplicate the failure.
- The Snapshot function on the scan tool can help find an intermittent DTC.

GC4020152556010X

Fig. 28 Code C1282: Yaw Rate Sensor Bias Circuit Fault (Part 1 of 3). Aurora, Bonneville, LeSabre & Park Avenue

Test Description

The number below refers to the step number on the diagnostic table.

3. Tests for the proper operation of the circuit in the low voltage range.
4. Tests for the proper operation of the circuit in the high voltage range. If the fuse in the jumper opens when you perform this test, the signal circuit is shorted to ground.
5. Tests for a short to voltage in the 5 volt reference circuit.
6. Tests the bias voltage of the yaw rate sensor.

Step	Action	Value(s)	Yes	No
1	Did you perform the ABS Diagnostic System Check?	—	Go to *Step 2*	Go to *Diagnostic System Check - ABS*
2	1. Install a scan tool. 2. Turn ON the ignition, with the engine OFF. 3. With a scan tool, observe the Yaw Rate Sensor Input parameter in the VSES data list. Does the scan tool display that the Yaw Rate Sensor Input parameter is within the specified range?	0.15–4.85 V	Go to *Step 6*	Go to *Step 3*
3	1. Turn OFF the ignition. 2. Disconnect the yaw rate sensor connector. 3. Turn ON the ignition, with the engine OFF. 4. With the scan tool, observe the Yaw Rate Sensor Input parameter. Does the scan tool display that the Yaw Rate Sensor Input parameter is less than the specified value?	0.15 V	Go to *Step 4*	Go to *Step 10*
4	1. Turn OFF the ignition. 2. Connect a 3 amp fused jumper wire between the 5 volt reference circuit of the yaw rate sensor and the signal circuit of the yaw rate sensor. 3. Turn ON the ignition, with the engine OFF. 4. With the scan tool, observe the Yaw Rate Sensor Input parameter. Does the scan tool display that the Yaw Rate Sensor Input parameter is greater than the specified value?	4.85 V	Go to *Step 5*	Go to *Step 8*
5	1. Disconnect the fused jumper wire. 2. Measure the voltage between the 5 volt reference circuit of the yaw rate sensor and the low reference circuit of the yaw rate sensor. Does the voltage measure less the specified value?	5 V	Go to *Step 12*	Go to *Step 7*
6	Does the scan tool display that the Yaw Rate Sensor Input parameter is within the specified range?	2.3–2.7 V	Go to Diagnostic Aids	Go to *Step 11*
7	Test the 5 volt reference circuit of the yaw rate sensor for a short to voltage. Did you find and correct the condition?	—	Go to *Step 16*	Go to *Step 13*
8	Test the 5 volt reference circuit of the yaw rate sensor for the following conditions: • An open • A short to ground • A high resistance Did you find and correct the condition?	—	Go to *Step 16*	Go to *Step 9*

GC4020152556020X

Fig. 28 Code C1282: Yaw Rate Sensor Bias Circuit Fault (Part 2 of 3). Aurora, Bonneville, LeSabre & Park Avenue

Step	Action	Value(s)	Yes	No
9	Test the signal circuit of the yaw rate sensor for the following conditions: • An open • A short to ground • A high resistance Did you find and correct the condition?	—	Go to *Step 16*	Go to *Step 13*
10	Test the signal circuit of the yaw rate sensor for a short to voltage. Did you find and correct the condition?	—	Go to *Step 16*	Go to *Step 13*
11	**Important:** Removing battery voltage or ground from the EBCM will result in the following conditions: • Loss of the TIM learned tire inflation configuration parameters in the EBCM • The EBCM sets DTC C1245. When the diagnosis is complete, inspect the tire pressures and perform the TIM reset. 1. Disconnect the EBCM harness connector. 2. Install the *J 39700* Universal Pinout Box using the *J 39700-300* Cable Adapter to the EBCM harness connector only. 3. Test the low reference circuit of the yaw rate sensor for a high resistance or an open. Did you find and correct the condition?	—	Go to *Step 16*	Go to *Step 12*
12	Inspect for poor connections at the harness connector of the yaw rate sensor. Did you find and correct the condition?	—	Go to *Step 16*	Go to *Step 14*
13	Inspect for poor connections at the harness connector of the EBCM. Did you find and correct the condition?	—	Go to *Step 16*	Go to *Step 15*
14	Replace the yaw rate sensor. Did you complete the repair?	—	Go to *Step 16*	—
15	**Important:** Perform the setup procedure for the EBCM. An unprogrammed EBCM will result in the following conditions: • Inoperative or poorly functioning system operations • The EBCM sets DTC C1248 and DTC C1255m3. Replace the EBCM. Did you complete the repair?	—	Go to *Step 16*	—
16	1. Clear the DTCs using the scan tool. 2. Operate the vehicle within the Conditions for Running the DTC as specified in the supporting text. Does the DTC reset?	—	Go to *Step 2*	System OK

GC4020152556030X

Fig. 28 Code C1282: Yaw Rate Sensor Bias Circuit Fault (Part 3 of 3). Aurora, Bonneville, LeSabre & Park Avenue

Circuit Description

The vehicle stability enhancement system (VSES) is activated by the EBCM calculating the desired yaw rate and comparing it to the actual yaw rate input. The desired yaw rate is calculated from measured steering wheel position, vehicle speed, and lateral acceleration. The difference between the desired yaw rate and actual yaw rate is the yaw rate error, which is a measurement of oversteer or understeer. If the yaw rate error becomes too large, the EBCM will attempt to correct the vehicle's yaw motion by applying differential braking to the left or right front wheel.

The VSES activations generally occur during aggressive driving, in the turns or bumpy roads without much use of the accelerator pedal. When braking during VSES activation, the brake pedal will feel different than the ABS pedal pulsation. The brake pedal pulsates at a higher frequency during VSES activation.

The usable output voltage range for the lateral accelerometer and yaw rate sensors is 0.25–4.75 volts. The scan tool will report zero lateral acceleration or yaw rate as 2.5 volts with no sensor bias present. The sensor bias compensates for sensor mounting alignment errors, electronic signal errors, temperature changes, and manufacturing differences.

The steering wheel position sensor supplies 2 analog inputs, Phase A and Phase B, to the EBCM. The 2 input signals are approximately 90 degrees out of phase. By interpreting the relationship between the 2 inputs, the EBCM can determine the position of the steering wheel and the direction of steering wheel rotation.

Steer angle centering is the process by which the EBCM calibrates the steering sensor output so that the output reads zero when the steering wheel is centered. Using the yaw rate input, lateral accelerometer input, and wheel speed sensor inputs, the initial steering center position is calculated after driving greater than 10 km/h (6 mph) for more than 10 seconds in a straight line on a level surface.

Conditions for Running the DTC

The ignition is ON.

Conditions for Setting the DTC

C1284

The compensated bias value of the lateral accelerometer is greater than 0.3 g.

C1285

The lateral accelerometer input voltage is less than 0.15 volts or greater than 4.85 volts for 1 second.

Action Taken When the DTC Sets

- The EBCM disables the VSES for the duration of the ignition cycle.
- The DIC displays the Service Stability System message.
- The ABS/TCS remains functional.

Conditions for Clearing the DTC

- The condition for the DTC is no longer present (the DTC is not current) and you used the scan tool Clear DTC function.
- The EBCM automatically clears the history DTC when a current DTC is not detected in 100 consecutive drive cycles.

Diagnostic Aids

- During diagnosis, park the vehicle on a level surface.
- Check the vehicle for proper alignment. The car should not pull in either direction while driving straight on a level surface.
- Find out from the driver under what conditions the DTC was set (when the DIC displayed the Service Stability System message). This information will help to duplicate the failure.
- The Snapshot function on the scan tool can help find an intermittent DTC.

Test Description

The numbers below refer to the step numbers on the diagnostic table.

3. Tests for the proper operation of the circuit in the low voltage range.
4. Tests for the proper operation of the circuit in the high voltage range. If the fuse in the jumper opens when you perform this test, the signal circuit is shorted to ground.
5. Tests for a short to voltage in the 5 volt reference circuit.
6. Tests the bias voltage of the lateral accelerometer sensor.

GC4020152557010X

Fig. 29 Code C1284 Or C1285: Lateral Accelerometer Sensor Circuit Fault (Part 1 of 3). Aurora, Bonneville, LeSabre & Park Avenue

Step	Action	Value(s)	Yes	No
1	Did you perform the ABS Diagnostic System Check?	—	Go to *Step 2*	Go to *Diagnostic System Check - ABS*
2	1. Install a scan tool. 2. Turn ON the ignition, with the engine OFF. 3. With a scan tool, observe the Lateral Accelerometer Input parameter in the VSES data list. Does the scan tool display that the Lateral Accelerometer Input parameter is within the specified range?	0.15–4.85 V	Go to *Step 6*	Go to *Step 3*
3	1. Turn OFF the ignition. 2. Disconnect the lateral accelerometer sensor connector. 3. Turn ON the ignition, with the engine OFF. 4. With the scan tool, observe the Lateral Accelerometer Input parameter. Does the scan tool display that the Lateral Accelerometer Input parameter is less than the specified value?	0.15 V	Go to *Step 4*	Go to *Step 10*
4	1. Turn OFF the ignition. 2. Connect a 3 amp fused jumper wire between the 5 volt reference circuit of the lateral accelerometer sensor and the signal circuit of the lateral accelerometer sensor. 3. Turn ON the ignition, with the engine OFF. 4. With the scan tool, observe the Lateral Accelerometer Input parameter. Does the scan tool display that the Lateral Accelerometer Input parameter is greater than the specified value?	4.85 V	Go to *Step 5*	Go to *Step 8*
5	1. Disconnect the fused jumper wire. 2. Measure the voltage between the 5 volt reference circuit of the lateral accelerometer sensor and the low reference circuit of the lateral accelerometer. Does the voltage measure less the specified value?	5 V	Go to *Step 12*	Go to *Step 7*
6	Does the scan tool display the Lateral Accelerometer Input parameter is within the specified range?	2.3–2.7 V	Go to Diagnostic Aids	Go to *Step 11*
7	Test the 5 volt reference circuit of the lateral accelerometer sensor for a short to voltage. Did you find and correct the condition?	—	Go to *Step 16*	Go to *Step 13*
8	Test the 5 volt reference circuit of the lateral accelerometer sensor for the following conditions: • An open • A short to ground • A high resistance Did you find and correct the condition?	—	Go to *Step 16*	Go to *Step 9*
9	Test the signal circuit of the lateral accelerometer sensor for the following conditions: • An open • A short to ground • A high resistance Did you find and correct the condition?	—	Go to *Step 16*	Go to *Step 13*

GC4020152557020X

Fig. 29 Code C1284 Or C1285: Lateral Accelerometer Sensor Circuit Fault (Part 2 of 3). Aurora, Bonneville, LeSabre & Park Avenue

Step	Action	Value(s)	Yes	No
10	Test the signal circuit of the lateral accelerometer sensor for a short to voltage. Did you find and correct the condition?	—	Go to *Step 16*	Go to *Step 13*
11	**Important:** Removing battery voltage or ground from the EBCM will result in the following conditions: • Loss of the TIM learned tire inflation configuration parameters in the EBCM • The EBCM sets DTC C1245. When the diagnosis is complete, inspect the tire pressures and perform the TIM reset. 1. Disconnect the EBCM harness connector. 2. Install the *J 39700* Universal Pinout Box using the *J 39700-300* Cable Adapter to the EBCM harness connector only. 3. Test the low reference circuit of the lateral accelerometer sensor for a high resistance or an open. Did you find and correct the condition?	—	Go to *Step 16*	Go to *Step 12*
12	Inspect for poor connections at the harness connector of the lateral accelerometer sensor. Did you find and correct the condition?	—	Go to *Step 16*	Go to *Step 14*
13	Inspect for poor connections at the harness connector of the EBCM. Did you find and correct the condition?	—	Go to *Step 16*	Go to *Step 15*
14	Replace the lateral accelerometer sensor. Did you complete the repair?	—	Go to *Step 16*	—
15	**Important:** Perform the setup procedure for the EBCM. An unprogrammed EBCM will result in the following conditions: • Inoperative or poorly functioning system operations • The EBCM sets DTC C1248 and DTC C1255m3. Replace the EBCM. Did you complete the repair?	—	Go to *Step 16*	—
16	1. Clear the DTCs using the scan tool. 2. Operate the vehicle within the Conditions for Running the DTC as specified in the supporting text. Does the DTC reset?	—	Go to *Step 2*	System OK

GC4020152557030X

Fig. 29 Code C1284 Or C1285: Lateral Accelerometer Sensor Circuit Fault (Part 3 of 3). Aurora, Bonneville, LeSabre & Park Avenue

Circuit Description

The vehicle stability enhancement system (VSES) is activated by the EBCM calculating the desired yaw rate and comparing it to the actual yaw rate input. The desired yaw rate is calculated from measured steering wheel position, vehicle speed, and lateral acceleration. The difference between the desired yaw rate and actual yaw rate is the yaw rate error, which is a measurement of oversteer or understeer. If the yaw rate error becomes too large, the EBCM will attempt to correct the vehicle's yaw motion by applying differential braking to the left or right front wheel.

The VSES activations generally occur during aggressive driving, in the turns or bumpy roads without much use of the accelerator pedal. When braking during VSES activation, the brake pedal will feel different than the ABS pedal pulsation. The brake pedal pulsates at a higher frequency during VSES activation.

The usable output voltage range for the lateral accelerometer and yaw rate sensors is 0.25–4.75 volts. The scan tool will report zero lateral acceleration or yaw rate as 2.5 volts with no sensor bias present. The sensor bias compensates for sensor mounting alignment errors, electronic signal errors, temperature changes, and manufacturing differences.

The steering wheel position sensor supplies 2 analog inputs, Phase A and Phase B, to the EBCM. The 2 input signals are approximately 90 degrees out of phase. By interpreting the relationship between the 2 inputs, the EBCM can determine the position of the steering wheel and the direction of steering wheel rotation.

Steer angle centering is the process by which the EBCM calibrates the steering sensor output so that the output reads zero when the steering wheel is centered. Using the yaw rate input, lateral accelerometer input, and wheel speed sensor inputs, the initial steering center position is calculated after driving greater than 10 km/h (6 mph) for more than 10 seconds in a straight line on a level surface.

Conditions for Running the DTC

The ignition is ON.

Conditions for Setting the DTC

C1287

One of the following conditions exists:

- The steering wheel position sensor is synchronized and the steer rate (speed that the steering wheel appears to be turning) is greater than 1100 degrees/second.
- The steer rate is less than 80 degrees/second and the difference in the phase angle between Phase A and Phase B is greater than 20 degrees.
- The 2 steering sensor signals (Phase A and Phase B) do not agree for 1 second. Under this condition, this DTC will set along with DTC C1281.

C1288

One of the following conditions exists:

- Both Phase A and Phase B are greater than 4.9 volts for 1.6 seconds.
- Both Phase A and Phase B are less than 0.2 volts for 1.6 seconds.
- The difference in the changes in Phase A and Phase B is greater than 35.2 degrees for 9.76 milliseconds.

Action Taken When the DTC Sets

- The EBCM disables the VSES for the duration of the ignition cycle.
- The DIC displays the Service Stability System message.
- The ABS/TCS remains functional.

Conditions for Clearing the DTC

- The condition for the DTC is no longer present (the DTC is not current) and you used the scan tool Clear DTC function.
- The EBCM automatically clears the history DTC when a current DTC is not detected in 100 consecutive drive cycles.

Diagnostic Aids

- During diagnosis, park the vehicle on a level surface.
- Check the vehicle for proper alignment. The car should not pull in either direction while driving straight on a level surface.
- Find out from the driver under what conditions the DTC was set (when the DIC displayed the Service Stability System message). This information will help to duplicate the failure.
- The Snapshot function on the scan tool can help find an intermittent DTC.

Test Description

The numbers below refer to the step numbers on the diagnostic table.

2. Perform the Steering Position Sensor Test in order to verify if the steering wheel position sensor (SWPS) is operating properly.
3. Tests for the proper operation of the steering wheel position signal A circuit in the low voltage range.
4. Tests for the proper operation of the steering wheel position signal B circuit in the low voltage range.

GC4020152558010X

Fig. 30 Code C1287 Or C1288: Steering Sensor Circuit Fault (Part 1 of 4). Aurora, Bonneville, LeSabre & Park Avenue

5. Tests for the proper operation of the steering wheel position signal A circuit in the high voltage range. If the fuse in the jumper opens when you perform this test, the signal circuit is shorted to ground.
6. Tests for the proper operation of the steering wheel position signal B circuit in the high voltage range. If the fuse in the jumper opens when you perform this test, the signal circuit is shorted to ground.
7. Tests for a short to voltage in the 5 volt reference circuit.
8. Tests for a high resistance or an open in the low reference circuit.

Step	Action	Value(s)	Yes	No
Schematic Reference: *ABS Schematics*				
1	Did you perform the ABS Diagnostic System Check?	—	Go to *Step 2*	Go to *Diagnostic System Check - ABS*
2	1. Install a scan tool. 2. Turn ON the ignition, with the engine OFF. 3. With the scan tool, perform the Steering Position Sensor Test. Did the SWPS pass the test?	—	Go to Diagnostic Aids	Go to *Step 3*
3	1. Turn OFF the ignition. 2. Disconnect the steering wheel position sensor (SWPS) connector. 3. Turn ON the ignition, with the engine OFF. 4. With the scan tool, observe the Dual Analog SWPS Input A parameter in the VSES data list. Does the scan tool indicate the Dual Analog SWPS Input A parameter is less than the specified value?	0.2 V	Go to *Step 4*	Go to *Step 13*
4	With the scan tool, observe the Dual Analog SWPS Input B parameter. Does the scan tool indicate the Dual Analog SWPS Input B parameter is less than the specified value?	0.2 V	Go to *Step 5*	Go to *Step 14*
5	1. Turn OFF the ignition. 2. Connect a 3 amp fused jumper wire between the 5 volt reference circuit of the steering wheel position sensor (SWPS) and the signal A circuit of the steering wheel position sensor (SWPS). 3. Turn ON the ignition, with the engine OFF. 4. With the scan tool, observe the Dual Analog SWPS Input A parameter. Does the scan tool indicate that the Dual Analog SWPS Input A parameter is greater than the specified value?	4.9 V	Go to *Step 6*	Go to *Step 10*
6	1. Turn OFF the ignition. 2. Disconnect the fused jumper wire. 3. Connect a 3 amp fused jumper wire between the 5 volt reference circuit of the steering wheel position sensor (SWPS) and the signal B circuit of the steering wheel position sensor (SWPS). 4. Turn ON the ignition, with the engine OFF. 5. With the scan tool, observe the Dual Analog SWPS Input B parameter. Does the scan tool indicate that the Dual Analog SWPS Input B parameter is greater than the specified value?	4.9 V	Go to *Step 7*	Go to *Step 10*

GC4020152558020X

Fig. 30 Code C1287 Or C1288: Steering Sensor Circuit Fault (Part 2 of 4). Aurora, Bonneville, LeSabre & Park Avenue

Step	Action	Value(s)	Yes	No
7	1. Disconnect the fused jumper wire. 2. Measure the voltage between the 5 volt reference circuit of the steering wheel position sensor (SWPS) and the low reference circuit of the steering wheel position sensor (SWPS). Does the voltage measure less the specified value?	5 V	Go to *Step 8*	Go to *Step 9*
8	1. Turn OFF the ignition. 2. Disconnect the negative battery cable. 3. Measure the resistance from the low reference circuit of the steering wheel position sensor (SWPS) to a good ground. Does the resistance measure less than the specified value?	5 Ω	Go to *Step 16*	Go to *Step 15*
9	Test the 5 volt reference circuit of the steering wheel position sensor (SWPS) for a short to voltage. Did you find and correct the condition?	—	Go to *Step 20*	Go to *Step 17*
10	Test the 5 volt reference circuit of the steering wheel position sensor (SWPS) for the following conditions: • An open • A short to ground • A high resistance Did you find and correct the condition?	—	Go to *Step 20*	Go to *Step 11*
11	Test the signal A circuit of the steering wheel position sensor (SWPS) for the following conditions: • An open • A short to ground • A high resistance Did you find and correct the condition?	—	Go to *Step 20*	Go to *Step 12*
12	Test the signal B circuit of the steering wheel position sensor (SWPS) for the following conditions: • An open • A short to ground • A high resistance Did you find and correct the condition?	—	Go to *Step 20*	Go to *Step 17*
13	Test the signal A circuit of the steering wheel position sensor (SWPS) for a short to voltage. Did you find and correct the condition?	—	Go to *Step 20*	Go to *Step 17*
14	Test the signal B circuit of the steering wheel position sensor (SWPS) for a short to voltage. Did you find and correct the condition?	—	Go to *Step 20*	Go to *Step 17*

GC4020152558030X

Fig. 30 Code C1287 Or C1288: Steering Sensor Circuit Fault (Part 3 of 4). Aurora, Bonneville, LeSabre & Park Avenue

Step	Action	Value(s)	Yes	No
15	**Important:** Removing battery voltage or ground from the EBCM will result in the following conditions: • Loss of the TIM learned tire inflation configuration parameters in the EBCM • The EBCM sets DTC C1245. When the diagnosis is complete, inspect the tire pressures and perform the TIM reset when. 1. Disconnect the EBCM harness connector. 2. Install the *J 39700* Universal Pinout Box using the *J 39700-300* Cable Adapter to the EBCM harness connector only. 3. Test the low reference circuit of the steering wheel position sensor (SWPS) for a high resistance or an open. Did you find and correct the condition?	—	Go to *Step 20*	Go to *Step 17*
16	Inspect for poor connections at the harness connector of the steering wheel position sensor (SWPS). Did you find and correct the condition?	—	Go to *Step 20*	Go to *Step 18*
17	Inspect for poor connections at the harness connector of the EBCM Did you find and correct the condition?	—	Go to *Step 20*	Go to *Step 19*
18	Replace the steering wheel position sensor (SWPS). Did you complete the repair?	—	Go to *Step 20*	—
19	**Important:** Perform the setup procedure for the EBCM. An unprogrammed EBCM will result in the following conditions: • Inoperative or poorly functioning system operations • The EBCM sets DTC C1248 and DTC C1255m3. Replace the EBCM. Did you complete the repair?	—	Go to *Step 20*	—
20	1. Clear the DTCs using the scan tool. 2. Operate the vehicle within the Conditions for Running the DTC as specified in the supporting text. Does the DTC reset?	—	Go to *Step 2*	System OK

GC4020152558040X

Fig. 30 Code C1287 Or C1288: Steering Sensor Circuit Fault (Part 4 of 4). Aurora, Bonneville, LeSabre & Park Avenue

Circuit Description

The stoplamp switch signal informs the EBCM when the brake pedal is pressed.

Conditions for Running the DTC

The ABS conditions and the braking conditions are normal.

Conditions for Setting the DTC

C1291

The stoplamp switch remains open for 3 deceleration cycles.

C1293

A DTC C1291 was set in a previous ignition cycle.

Action Taken When the DTC Sets

- The EBCM disables the TCS for the duration of the ignition cycle.
- The Traction Off indicator turns ON.
- The ABS remains functional.

Conditions for Clearing the DTC

- The condition for the DTC is no longer present (the DTC is not current) and you used the scan tool Clear DTC function.
- The EBCM automatically clears the history DTC when a current DTC is not detected in 100 consecutive drive cycles.

Diagnostic Aids

- Diagnose any wheel speed sensor DTCs before continuing with the diagnosis of the DTC.
- A deceleration cycle consists of the following sequence:
  1. The vehicle speed is greater than 24 km/h (15 mph).
  2. The vehicle decelerates more than 8 km/h/second (5 mph/second) for 2 seconds.
  3. The vehicle speed decelerates to less than 16 km/h (10 mph).
- Verify proper stoplamp switch operation using the data list of the scan tool. As the brake is applied, the data list displays the stoplamp switch on within 2.54 cm (1 in) of travel.
- Possible causes of this DTC are the following conditions:
  - An open stoplamp switch
  - The stoplamp switch is misadjusted
  - An open fuse
  - Circuit has a wiring problem, terminal corrosion, or poor connections
  - Erratic wheel speeds

Test Description

The numbers below refer to the step numbers on the diagnostic table.

3. Tests the circuit for a change in states.
5. Tests for proper operation of the circuit by bypassing the stoplamp switch. If the fuse in the jumper opens when you perform this test, the signal circuit of the stoplamp switch is shorted to ground.

Step	Action	Yes	No
Schematic Reference: *ABS Schematics*			
1	Did you perform the ABS Diagnostic System Check?	Go to *Step 2*	Go to *Diagnostic System Check - ABS*
2	Press the brake pedal. Do the brake lamps turn ON?	Go to *Step 3*	Go to *Step 7*
3	1. Press the brake pedal. 2. With a scan tool, observe the Stop Lamp Switch parameter in the DRP/ABS/TCS data list. Does the Stop Lamp Switch parameter change state?	Go to Diagnostic Aids	Go to *Step 4*

GC4020152559010X

Fig. 31 Code C1291 Or C1293: Open Brake Lamp Switch Contacts During Deceleration (Part 1 of 2). Aurora, Bonneville, LeSabre & Park Avenue

Step	Action	Yes	No
4	1. Turn OFF the ignition. 2. Inspect the stoplamp switch and adjust and/or calibrate if needed. Did you find and correct the condition?	Go to *Step 14*	Go to *Step 5*
5	1. Turn OFF the ignition. 2. Disconnect the stoplamp switch connector. 3. Connect a 3 amp fused jumper wire between the battery positive voltage circuit of the stoplamp switch and the signal circuit of the stoplamp switch. 4. Turn ON the ignition, with the engine OFF. 5. With a scan tool, observe the Stop Lamp Switch parameter. Does the scan tool display Applied?	Go to *Step 11*	Go to *Step 6*
6	Test the signal circuit of the stoplamp switch for an open between the splice pack of the stoplamp signal circuit and the EBCM. Did you find and correct the condition?	Go to *Step 14*	Go to *Step 10*
7	Test the battery positive voltage circuit of the stoplamp switch for a short to ground or an open. Did you find and correct the condition?	Go to *Step 14*	Go to *Step 8*
8	Test the signal circuit of the stoplamp switch for an open between the stoplamp switch and the splice of the stoplamp signal circuit. Did you find and correct the condition?	Go to *Step 14*	Go to *Step 9*
9	Test the signal circuit of the stoplamp switch for a short to ground. Did you find and correct the condition?	Go to *Step 14*	Go to *Step 10*
10	Inspect for poor connections at the harness connector of the EBCM. Did you find and correct the condition?	Go to *Step 14*	Go to *Step 12*
11	Inspect for poor connections at the harness connector of the stoplamp switch. Did you find and correct the condition?	Go to *Step 14*	Go to *Step 13*
12	**Important:** Perform the setup procedure for the EBCM. An unprogrammed EBCM will result in the following conditions: • Inoperative or poorly functioning system operations • The EBCM sets DTC C1248 and DTC C1255m3. Replace the EBCM. Did you complete the repair?	Go to *Step 14*	—
13	Replace the stoplamp switch. Did you complete the repair?	Go to *Step 14*	—
14	1. Use the scan tool in order to clear the DTCs. 2. Operate the vehicle within the Conditions for Running the DTC as specified in the supporting text. Does the DTC reset?	Go to *Step 2*	System OK

GC4020152559020X

Fig. 31 Code C1291 Or C1293: Open Brake Lamp Switch Contacts During Deceleration (Part 2 of 2). Aurora, Bonneville, LeSabre & Park Avenue

Circuit Description

The stoplamp switch signal informs the EBCM when the brake pedal is pressed.

Conditions for Running the DTC

The vehicle speed is greater than 40 km/h (25 mph).

Conditions for Setting the DTC

The stoplamp switch input was active for 2 consecutive ignition cycles.

Action Taken When the DTC Sets

- The EBCM disables the TCS for the duration of the ignition cycle.
- The Traction Off indicator turns ON.
- The ABS remains functional.

Conditions for Clearing the DTC

- The condition for the DTC is no longer present (the DTC is not current) and you used the scan tool Clear DTC function.
- The EBCM automatically clears the history DTC when a current DTC is not detected in 100 consecutive drive cycles.

Diagnostic Aids

Possible causes of this DTC are the following conditions:

- The stoplamp switch circuit is shorted to voltage
- The stoplamp switch is misadjusted.
- The stoplamp switch is stuck closed.
- A brake pedal that is binding.

Test Description

The number below refers to the step number on the diagnostic table.

2. Test for the current state of the stoplamp switch parameter.

GC4020152560010X

Fig. 32 Code C1294: Brake Lamp Switch Circuit Always Active (Part 1 of 2). Aurora, Bonneville, LeSabre & Park Avenue

Step	Action	Yes	No
1	Did you perform the ABS Diagnostic System Check?	Go to *Step 2*	Go to *Diagnostic System Check - ABS*
2	1. Install a scan tool. 2. Turn ON the ignition, with the engine OFF. 3. With a scan tool, observe the Stop Lamp Switch parameter in the DRP/ABS/TCS data list. Does the scan tool display Released?	Go to *Step 3*	Go to *Step 4*
3	1. Press the brake pedal. 2. With a scan tool, observe the Stop Lamp Switch parameter. Does the Stop Lamp Switch parameter change state?	Go to Diagnostic Aids	Go to *Step 4*
4	1. Turn OFF the ignition. 2. Inspect the stoplamp switch and adjust and/or calibrate if needed. Did you find and correct the condition?	Go to *Step 11*	Go to *Step 5*
5	1. Turn OFF the ignition. 2. Disconnect the stoplamp switch connector. 3. Turn ON the ignition, with the engine OFF. 4. With a scan tool, observe the Stop Lamp Switch parameter. Does the scan tool display Released?	Go to *Step 8*	Go to *Step 6*
6	Test the stoplamp switch signal circuit for a short to voltage. Did you find and correct the condition?	Go to *Step 11*	Go to *Step 7*
7	Inspect for poor connections at the harness connector of the EBCM. Did you find and correct the condition?	Go to *Step 11*	Go to *Step 9*
8	Inspect for poor connections at the harness connector of the stoplamp switch. Did you find and correct the condition?	Go to *Step 11*	Go to *Step 10*
9	**Important:** Perform the setup procedure for the EBCM. An unprogrammed EBCM will result in the following conditions: • Inoperative or poorly functioning system operations • The EBCM sets DTC C1248 and DTC C1255m3. Replace the EBCM. Did you complete the repair?	Go to *Step 11*	—
10	Replace the stoplamp switch. Did you complete the repair?	Go to *Step 11*	—
11	1. Use the scan tool in order to clear the DTCs. 2. Operate the vehicle within the Conditions for Running the DTC as specified in the supporting text. Does the DTC reset?	Go to *Step 2*	System OK

GC4020152560020X

Fig. 32 Code C1294: Brake Lamp Switch Circuit Always Active (Part 2 of 2). Aurora, Bonneville, LeSabre & Park Avenue

Circuit Description

The EBCM sources 5 volts on the stoplamp switch signal circuit when the stoplamp switch is inactive. The voltage is supplied a ground path through the stoplamp bulbs.

Conditions for Running the DTC

The ignition is ON.

Conditions for Setting the DTC

The stoplamp switch input voltage is between 2.1 volts and 5.3 volts for 2 seconds.

Action Taken When the DTC Sets

- The EBCM disables the TCS for the duration of the ignition cycle.
- The Traction Off indicator turns ON.
- The ABS remains functional.

Conditions for Clearing the DTC

- The condition for the DTC is no longer present (the DTC is not current) and you used the scan tool Clear DTC function.
- The EBCM automatically clears the history DTC when a current DTC is not detected in 100 consecutive drive cycles.

Diagnostic Aids

Possible causes of this DTC are the following conditions:

- A signal circuit of the stoplamp switch is open.
- The stoplamp switch is misadjusted.
- Verify proper stoplamp switch operation using the data list of the scan tool. As the brake is applied, the data list displays the stoplamp switch on within 2.54 cm (1 in) of travel.
- All brake lamps are open.
- All brake lamp grounds are open.
- Circuit has a wiring problem, terminal corrosion, or poor connections.
- Loose or corroded EBCM ground or PCM ground.
- An internal EBCM problem.

Test Description

The numbers below refer to the step numbers on the diagnostic table.

3. This DTC detects an open stoplamp switch signal circuit from the stoplamp side of the splice pack to the EBCM.
4. The EBCM sources 5 volts on the stoplamp switch signal circuit. This small voltage has a ground path through the stoplamp bulbs. This DTC sets if the path to ground is open.

Step	Action	Yes	No
Schematic Reference: *ABS Schematics*			
1	Did you perform the ABS Diagnostic System Check?	Go to *Step 2*	Go to *Diagnostic System Check - ABS*
2	1. Press the brake pedal. 2. With the scan tool, observe the Stop Lamp Switch parameter in the DRP/ABS/TCS data list. Does the Stop Lamp Switch parameter display Applied?	Go to *Step 4*	Go to *Step 3*
3	Test the signal circuit of the stoplamp switch for an open or high resistance. Did you find and correct the condition?	Go to *Step 9*	Go to *Step 7*
4	Press the brake pedal. Are all of the stoplamps OFF?	Go to *Step 5*	Go to Diagnostic Aids
5	Test the feed circuit of the stoplamps for an open or high resistance. Did you find and correct the condition?	Go to *Step 9*	Go to *Step 6*
6	Test the ground circuit for the stoplamps for an open or high resistance. Did you find and correct the condition?	Go to *Step 9*	Go to Diagnostic Aids

GC4020152561010X

Fig. 33 Code C1295: Brake Lamp Switch Circuit Open (Part 1 of 2). Aurora, Bonneville, LeSabre & Park Avenue

Important: The following steps must be completed before using the symptom tables.

1. Perform the *Diagnostic System Check - ABS* before using the Symptom Tables in order to verify that all of the following are true:
   - There are no DTCs set.
   - The control module(s) can communicate via the serial data link.
2. Review the system operation in order to familiarize yourself with the system functions.

Visual/Physical Inspection

- Inspect for aftermarket devices which could affect the operation of the antilock brake system.
- Inspect the easily accessible or visible system components for obvious damage or conditions which could cause the symptom.
- Inspect the master cylinder reservoir for the proper brake fluid level.

Intermittent

Faulty electrical connections or wiring may be the cause of intermittent conditions.

Symptom List

Refer to a symptom diagnostic procedure from the following list in order to diagnose the symptom:

- *ABS Indicator Always On*
- *ABS Indicator Inoperative*
- *Traction Active Indicator Always On*
- *Traction Active Indicator Inoperative*
- *Traction Off Indicator Always On*
- *Traction Off Indicator Inoperative*
- *Vehicle Stability Enhancement System Inoperative*
- *Vehicle Stability Enhancement System Unwanted Activation*
- *Vehicle Stability Enhancement System Excessive Brake Pulsation*

GC4020152562000X

Fig. 34 ABS Symptoms. Aurora

Step	Action	Yes	No
7	Inspect for poor connections at the harness connector of the EBCM. Did you find and correct the condition?	Go to *Step 9*	Go to *Step 8*
8	**Important:** Perform the setup procedure for the EBCM. An unprogrammed EBCM will result in the following conditions: • Inoperative or poorly functioning system operations • The EBCM sets DTC C1248 and DTC C1255m3. Replace the EBCM. Did you complete the repair?	Go to *Step 9*	—
9	1. Use the scan tool in order to clear the DTCs. 2. Operate the vehicle within the Conditions for Running the DTC as specified in the supporting text. Does the DTC reset?	Go to *Step 2*	System OK

GC4020152561020X

Fig. 33 Code C1295: Brake Lamp Switch Circuit Open (Part 2 of 2). Aurora, Bonneville, LeSabre & Park Avenue

Circuit Description

The instrument cluster controls the operation of the ABS indicator. The EBCM reports the desired status of the ABS indicator via serial data messages. The ABS indicator signal circuit is a back-up reporting circuit to the serial data messages. The EBCM supplies ground through the circuit when the ABS is operating properly. When there is a problem with ABS that should turn on the ABS indicator, the EBCM opens the ABS indicator signal circuit. If there is a problem with the ABS serial data messages, the instrument cluster uses the ABS indicator signal to determine if the ABS indicator should be illuminated. Using the serial data messages and back-up circuit, the instrument cluster decides whether to turn on the ABS indicator.

Test Description

The numbers below refer to the step numbers on the diagnostic table.

3. Use the scan tool to check the normal state of the ABS indicator control circuit.
4. Ensures that the instrument cluster can operate the ABS indicator.

Step	Action	Yes	No
1	Did you perform the ABS Diagnostic System Check?	Go to *Step 2*	Go to *Diagnostic System Check - ABS*
2	Inspect the EBCM ground, making sure the ground is clean and torqued to the proper specification. Did you find and correct the condition?	Go to *Step 9*	Go to *Step 3*
3	1. Install a scan tool. 2. Turn ON the ignition, with the engine OFF. 3. With a scan tool, observe the ABS Warning Indicator parameter in the DRP/ABS/TCS data list. Does the scan tool display Off?	Go to *Step 4*	Go to *Step 5*
4	1. Turn OFF the ignition. 2. Turn ON the ignition, with the engine OFF. 3. Observe the ABS indicator on the instrument cluster (IPC) during the bulb check. Does the ABS indicator illuminate during the bulb check and then turn OFF?	*Test for Intermittent*	Go to *Step 6*
5	Inspect for poor connections at the harness connector of the EBCM. Did you find and correct the condition?	Go to *Step 9*	Go to *Step 7*
6	Inspect for poor connections at the harness connector of the instrument cluster (IPC). Did you find and correct the condition?	Go to *Step 9*	Go to *Step 8*
7	**Important:** Perform the setup procedure for the EBCM. An unprogrammed EBCM will result in the following conditions: • Inoperative or poorly functioning system operations • The EBCM sets DTC C1248 and DTC C1255m3. Replace the EBCM. Did you complete the repair?	Go to *Step 9*	—
8	Replace the instrument cluster (IPC). Did you complete the repair?	Go to *Step 9*	—
9	Operate the system in order to verify the repair. Did you correct the condition?	System OK	Go to *Step 2*

GC4020152563000X

Fig. 35 ABS Indicator Always On. Aurora

Circuit Description

The instrument cluster controls the operation of the ABS indicator. The EBCM reports the desired status of the ABS indicator via serial data messages. The ABS indicator signal circuit is a back-up reporting circuit to the serial data messages. The EBCM supplies ground through the circuit when the ABS is operating properly. When there is a problem with ABS that should turn on the ABS indicator, the EBCM opens the ABS indicator signal circuit. If there is a problem with the ABS serial data messages, the instrument cluster uses the ABS indicator signal to determine if the ABS indicator should be illuminated. Using the serial data messages and back-up circuit, the instrument cluster decides whether to turn on the ABS indicator.

Test Description

The numbers below refer to the step numbers on the diagnostic table.

3. Use the scan tool to check the normal state of the ABS indicator control circuit.
4. Ensures that the instrument cluster can operate the ABS indicator.

Step	Action	Yes	No
1	Did you perform the ABS Diagnostic System Check?	Go to *Step 2*	Go to *Diagnostic System Check - ABS*
2	Inspect the EBCM ground, making sure the ground is clean and torqued to the proper specification. Did you find and correct the condition?	Go to *Step 9*	Go to *Step 3*
3	1. Install a scan tool. 2. Turn ON the ignition, with the engine OFF. 3. With a scan tool, observe the ABS Warning Indicator parameter in the DRP/ABS/TCS data list. Does the scan tool display Off?	Go to *Step 4*	Go to *Step 5*
4	1. Turn OFF the ignition. 2. Turn ON the ignition, with the engine OFF. 3. Observe the ABS indicator on the instrument cluster (IPC) during the bulb check. Does the ABS indicator illuminate during the bulb check and then turn OFF?	*Test for Intermittent*	Go to *Step 6*
5	Inspect for poor connections at the harness connector of the EBCM. Did you find and correct the condition?	Go to *Step 9*	Go to *Step 7*
6	Inspect for poor connections at the harness connector of the instrument cluster (IPC). Did you find and correct the condition?	Go to *Step 9*	Go to *Step 8*
7	**Important:** Perform the setup procedure for the EBCM. An unprogrammed EBCM will result in the following conditions: • Inoperative or poorly functioning system operations • The EBCM sets DTC C1248 and DTC C1255m3. Replace the EBCM. Did you complete the repair?	Go to *Step 9*	—
8	Replace the instrument cluster (IPC). Did you complete the repair?	Go to *Step 9*	—
9	Operate the system in order to verify the repair. Did you correct the condition?	System OK	Go to *Step 2*

GC4020152564000X

Fig. 36 ABS Indicator Inoperative. Aurora

Circuit Description

The Traction Active indicator is controlled by the instrument cluster via serial data messages from the EBCM. When the TCS is active for 3 seconds, the EBCM commands the instrument cluster to turn ON the Traction Active indicator.

The Traction Active indicator will also turn ON during the instrument cluster bulb check. When the ignition switch is turned to ON, the Traction Active indicator will turn on for approximately 3 seconds and then turn OFF.

Test Description

The numbers below refer to the step numbers on the diagnostic table.

2. Use the scan tool to check the normal state of the Traction Active indicator control.
3. Ensures that the instrument cluster can operate the Traction Active indicator.

Step	Action	Yes	No
1	Did you perform the ABS Diagnostic System Check?	Go to *Step 2*	Go to *Diagnostic System Check - ABS*
2	1. Install a scan tool. 2. Turn ON the ignition, with the engine OFF. 3. With a scan tool, observe the TCS Active Indicator/Message parameter in the DRP/ABS/TCS data list. Does the scan tool display Off?	Go to *Step 3*	Go to *Step 4*
3	1. Turn OFF the ignition. 2. Turn ON the ignition, with the engine OFF. 3. Observe the Traction Active indicator on the instrument cluster (IPC) during the bulb check. Does the Traction Active indicator illuminate during the bulb check and then turn OFF?	*Test for Intermittent*	Go to *Step 5*
4	Inspect for poor connections at the harness connector of the EBCM. Did you find and correct the condition?	Go to *Step 8*	Go to *Step 6*
5	Inspect for poor connections at the harness connector of the instrument cluster (IPC). Did you find and correct the condition?	Go to *Step 8*	Go to *Step 7*
6	**Important:** Perform the setup procedure for the EBCM. An unprogrammed EBCM will result in the following conditions: • Inoperative or poorly functioning system operations • The EBCM sets DTC C1248 and DTC C1255m3. Replace the EBCM. Did you complete the repair?	Go to *Step 8*	—
7	Replace the instrument cluster (IPC). Did you complete the repair?	Go to *Step 8*	—
8	Operate the system in order to verify the repair. Did you correct the condition?	System OK	Go to *Step 2*

GC4020152566000X

Fig. 38 Traction Active Indicator Inoperative. Aurora

Circuit Description

The Traction Active indicator is controlled by the instrument cluster via serial data messages from the EBCM. When the TCS is active for 3 seconds, the EBCM commands the instrument cluster to turn ON the Traction Active indicator.

The Traction Active indicator will also turn ON during the instrument cluster bulb check. When the ignition switch is turned to ON, the Traction Active indicator will turn on for approximately 3 seconds and then turn OFF.

Test Description

The numbers below refer to the step numbers on the diagnostic table.

2. Use the scan tool to check the normal state of the Traction Active indicator control.
3. Ensures that the instrument cluster can operate the Traction Active indicator.

Step	Action	Yes	No
1	Did you perform the ABS Diagnostic System Check?	Go to *Step 2*	Go to *Diagnostic System Check - ABS*
2	1. Install a scan tool. 2. Turn ON the ignition, with the engine OFF. 3. With a scan tool, observe the TCS Active Indicator/Message parameter in the DRP/ABS/TCS data list. Does the scan tool display Off?	Go to *Step 3*	Go to *Step 4*
3	1. Turn OFF the ignition. 2. Turn ON the ignition, with the engine OFF. 3. Observe the Traction Active indicator on the instrument cluster (IPC) during the bulb check. Does the Traction Active indicator illuminate during the bulb check and then turn OFF?	*Test for Intermittent*	Go to *Step 5*
4	Inspect for poor connections at the harness connector of the EBCM. Did you find and correct the condition?	Go to *Step 8*	Go to *Step 6*
5	Inspect for poor connections at the harness connector of the instrument cluster (IPC). Did you find and correct the condition?	Go to *Step 8*	Go to *Step 7*
6	**Important:** Perform the setup procedure for the EBCM. An unprogrammed EBCM will result in the following conditions: • Inoperative or poorly functioning system operations • The EBCM sets DTC C1248 and DTC C1255m3. Replace the EBCM. Did you complete the repair?	Go to *Step 8*	—
7	Replace the instrument cluster (IPC). Did you complete the repair?	Go to *Step 8*	—
8	Operate the system in order to verify the repair. Did you correct the condition?	System OK	Go to *Step 2*

GC4020152565000X

Fig. 37 Traction Active Indicator Always On. Aurora

Circuit Description

The Traction Off indicator is controlled by the instrument cluster via serial data messages from the EBCM. When the IPM sees the traction control switch input grounded through the momentary traction control switch, it sends a serial data message to the EBCM that tells the EBCM that the traction control switch has been pressed. The EBCM then disables traction control and sends a serial data message to the instrument cluster to turn the Traction Off indicator ON. Each time the ignition is cycled from OFF to ON, the traction control system is enabled.

The following conditions will cause the Traction Off indicator to illuminate:

- The EBCM has disabled the TCS due to a DTC.
- The driver manually disabling the TCS via the traction control switch.
- The instrument cluster bulb check. When the ignition switch is turned to ON, the Traction Off indicator will turn on for approximately 3 seconds and then turn OFF.

Test Description

The numbers below refer to the step numbers on the diagnostic table.

2. Use the scan tool to check the normal state of the Traction Off indicator control.
3. Ensures that the instrument cluster can operate the Traction Off indicator.

Step	Action	Yes	No
1	Did you perform the ABS Diagnostic System Check?	Go to *Step 2*	Go to *Diagnostic System Check - ABS*
2	1. Install a scan tool. 2. Turn ON the ignition, with the engine OFF. 3. With a scan tool, observe the TCS Warning Indicator/Message parameter in the DRP/ABS/TCS data list. Does the scan tool display Off?	Go to *Step 3*	Go to *Step 4*
3	1. Turn OFF the ignition. 2. Turn ON the ignition, with the engine OFF. 3. Observe the Traction Off indicator on the instrument cluster (IPC) during the bulb check. Does the Traction Off indicator illuminate during the bulb check and then turn OFF?	*Test for Intermittent*	Go to *Step 5*
4	Inspect for poor connections at the harness connector of the EBCM. Did you find and correct the condition?	Go to *Step 8*	Go to *Step 6*
5	Inspect for poor connections at the harness connector of the instrument cluster (IPC). Did you find and correct the condition?	Go to *Step 8*	Go to *Step 7*
6	**Important:** Perform the setup procedure for the EBCM. An unprogrammed EBCM will result in the following conditions: • Inoperative or poorly functioning system operations • The EBCM sets DTC C1248 and DTC C1255m3. Replace the EBCM. Did you complete the repair?	Go to *Step 8*	—
7	Replace the instrument cluster (IPC). Did you complete the repair?	Go to *Step 8*	—
8	Operate the system in order to verify the repair. Did you correct the condition?	System OK	Go to *Step 2*

GC4020152567000X

Fig. 39 Traction Off Indicator Always On. Aurora

Circuit Description

The Traction Off indicator is controlled by the instrument cluster via serial data messages from the EBCM. When the IPM sees the traction control switch input grounded through the momentary traction control switch, it sends a serial data message to the EBCM that tells the EBCM that the traction control switch has been pressed. The EBCM then disables traction control and sends a serial data message to the instrument cluster to turn the Traction Off indicator ON. Each time the ignition is cycled from OFF to ON, the traction control system is enabled.

The following conditions will cause the Traction Off indicator to illuminate:

- The EBCM has disabled the TCS due to a DTC.
- The driver manually disabling the TCS via the traction control switch.
- The instrument cluster bulb check. When the ignition switch is turned to ON, the Traction Off indicator will turn on for approximately 3 seconds and then turn OFF.

Test Description

The numbers below refer to the step numbers on the diagnostic table.

2. Use the scan tool to check the normal state of the Traction Off indicator control.
3. Ensures that the instrument cluster can operate the Traction Off indicator.

Step	Action	Yes	No
1	Did you perform the ABS Diagnostic System Check?	Go to *Step 2*	Go to *Diagnostic System Check - ABS*
2	1. Install a scan tool. 2. Turn ON the ignition, with the engine OFF. 3. With a scan tool, observe the TCS Warning Indicator/Message parameter in the DRP/ABS/TCS data list. Does the scan tool display Off?	Go to *Step 3*	Go to *Step 13*
3	1. Turn OFF the ignition. 2. Turn ON the ignition, with the engine OFF. 3. Observe the Traction Off indicator on the instrument cluster (IPC) during the bulb check. Does the Traction Off indicator illuminate during the bulb check and then turn OFF?	Go to *Step 4*	Go to *Step 14*
4	1. Turn OFF the ignition. 2. Install a scan tool. 3. Turn ON the ignition, with the engine OFF. 4. With a scan tool, observe the TCS Switch parameter in the Instrument Panel Module data list. 5. Activate the traction control switch. Does the TCS Switch parameter change state?	*Test for Intermittent*	Go to *Step 5*
5	Does the scan indicate that the TCS Switch parameter is On?	Go to *Step 6*	Go to *Step 7*
6	1. Turn OFF the ignition. 2. Disconnect the traction control switch connector. 3. Turn ON the ignition, with the engine OFF. 4. With a scan tool, observe the TCS Switch parameter. Does the scan tool display Off?	Go to *Step 12*	Go to *Step 8*

GC4020152568010X

Fig. 40 Traction Off Indicator Inoperative (Part 1 of 2). Aurora

Step	Action	Yes	No
7	1. Turn OFF the ignition. 2. Disconnect the traction control switch connector. 3. Connect a 3 amp fused jumper from the signal circuit of the traction control switch to the ground circuit of the traction control switch. 4. Turn ON the ignition, with the engine OFF. 5. With a scan tool, observe the TCS Switch parameter. Does the scan tool display On?	Go to *Step 12*	Go to *Step 9*
8	Test the signal circuit of the traction control switch for a short to ground. Did you find and correct the condition?	Go to *Step 19*	Go to *Step 11*
9	Test the signal circuit of the traction control switch for an open or high resistance. Did you find and correct the condition?	Go to *Step 19*	Go to *Step 10*
10	Test the ground circuit of the traction control switch for an open or high resistance. Did you find and correct the condition?	Go to *Step 19*	Go to *Step 11*
11	Inspect for poor connections at the harness connector of the instrument panel module (IPM). Did you find and correct the condition?	Go to *Step 19*	Go to *Step 15*
12	Inspect for poor connections at the harness connector of the traction control switch. Did you find and correct the condition?	Go to *Step 19*	Go to *Step 16*
13	Inspect for poor connections at the harness connector of the EBCM. Did you find and correct the condition?	Go to *Step 19*	Go to *Step 17*
14	Inspect for poor connections at the harness connector of the instrument cluster (IPC). Did you find and correct the condition?	Go to *Step 19*	Go to *Step 18*
15	Replace the instrument panel module (IPM). Did you complete the replacement?	Go to *Step 19*	—
16	Replace the traction control switch. Did you complete the replacement?	Go to *Step 19*	—
17	**Important:** Perform the setup procedure for the EBCM. An unprogrammed EBCM will result in the following conditions: • Inoperative or poorly functioning system operations • The EBCM sets DTC C1248 and DTC C1255m3. Replace the EBCM. Did you complete the repair?	Go to *Step 19*	—
18	Replace the instrument cluster (IPC). Did you complete the repair?	Go to *Step 19*	—
19	Operate the system in order to verify the repair. Did you correct the condition?	System OK	Go to *Step 2*

GC4020152568020X

Fig. 40 Traction Off Indicator Inoperative (Part 2 of 2). Aurora

Circuit Description

The vehicle stability enhancement system (VSES) is activated by the EBCM calculating the desired yaw rate and comparing it to the actual yaw rate input. The desired yaw rate is calculated from measured steering wheel position, vehicle speed, and lateral acceleration. The difference between the desired yaw rate and actual yaw rate is the yaw rate error, which is a measurement of oversteer or understeer. If the yaw rate error becomes too large, the EBCM will attempt to correct the vehicle's yaw motion by applying differential braking to the left or right front wheel.

The VSES activations generally occur during aggressive driving, in the turns or bumpy roads without much use of the accelerator pedal. When braking during VSES activation, the brake pedal will feel different than the ABS pedal pulsation. The brake pedal pulsates at a higher frequency during VSES activation.

The usable output voltage range for the lateral accelerometer and yaw rate sensors is 0.25–4.75 volts. The scan tool will report zero lateral acceleration or yaw rate as 2.5 volts with no sensor bias present. The sensor bias compensates for sensor mounting alignment errors, electronic signal errors, temperature changes, and manufacturing differences.

The steering wheel position sensor supplies 2 analog inputs, Phase A and Phase B, to the EBCM. The 2 input signals are approximately 90 degrees out of phase. By interpreting the relationship between the 2 inputs, the EBCM can determine the position of the steering wheel and the direction of steering wheel rotation.

Steer angle centering is the process by which the EBCM calibrates the steering sensor output so that the output reads zero when the steering wheel is centered. Using the yaw rate input, lateral accelerometer input, and wheel speed sensor inputs, the initial steering center position is calculated after driving greater than 10 km/h (6 mph) for more than 10 seconds in a straight line on a level surface.

Test Description

The numbers below refer to the step numbers on the diagnostic table.

3. Perform the Steering Position Sensor Test in order to verify if the steering wheel position sensor (SWPS) is operating properly.
4. Verify that the lateral accelerometer input parameter is within the valid range.
5. Verify that the yaw rate input parameter is within the valid range.

GC4020152570010X

Fig. 41 Vehicle Stability Enhancement System Inoperative (Part 1 of 2). Aurora

Step	Action	Value(s)	Yes	No
1	Did you perform the ABS Diagnostic System Check?	—	Go to *Step 2*	Go to *Diagnostic System Check - ABS*
2	1. Install a scan tool. 2. Start the engine. 3. Observe the VSES Is Centered parameter in the VSES data list. 4. Perform the Diagnostic Test Drive. Did the scan tool display Yes within the specified value?	30 seconds	*Test for Intermittent*	Go to *Step 3*
3	With the scan tool, perform the Steering Position Sensor Test. Did the SWPS pass the test?	—	Go to *Step 4*	Go to *Step 7*
4	With a scan tool, observe the Lateral Accelerometer Input parameter in the VSES data list. Does the scan tool display within the specified range?	2.3–2.7 V	Go to *Step 5*	Go to *Step 8*
5	With a scan tool, observe the Yaw Rate Sensor Input parameter in the VSES data list. Does the scan tool display within the specified range?	2.3–2.7 V	Go to *Step 6*	Go to *Step 9*
6	**Important:** Perform the setup procedure for the EBCM. An unprogrammed EBCM will result in the following conditions: • Inoperative or poorly functioning system operations • The EBCM sets DTC C1248 and DTC C1255m3. Replace the EBCM. Did you complete the repair?	—	Go to *Step 10*	—
7	Replace the steering wheel position sensor (SWPS). Did you complete the replacement?	—	Go to *Step 10*	—
8	Replace the lateral accelerometer sensor. Did you complete the replacement?	—	Go to *Step 10*	—
9	Replace the yaw rate sensor. Did you complete the replacement?	—	Go to *Step 10*	—
10	Operate the system in order to verify the repair. Did you correct the condition?	—	System OK	Go to *Step 2*

GC4020152570020X

Fig. 41 Vehicle Stability Enhancement System Inoperative (Part 2 of 2). Aurora

Circuit Description

The vehicle stability enhancement system (VSES) is activated by the EBCM calculating the desired yaw rate and comparing it to the actual yaw rate input. The desired yaw rate is calculated from measured steering wheel position, vehicle speed, and lateral acceleration. The difference between the desired yaw rate and actual yaw rate is the yaw rate error, which is a measurement of oversteer or understeer. If the yaw rate error becomes too large, the EBCM will attempt to correct the vehicle's yaw motion by applying differential braking to the left or right front wheel.

The VSES activations generally occur during aggressive driving, in the turns or bumpy roads without much use of the accelerator pedal. When braking during VSES activation, the brake pedal will feel different than the ABS pedal pulsation. The brake pedal pulsates at a higher frequency during VSES activation.

The usable output voltage range for the lateral accelerometer and yaw rate sensors is 0.25–4.75 volts. The scan tool will report zero lateral acceleration or yaw rate as 2.5 volts with no sensor bias present.

The sensor bias compensates for sensor mounting alignment errors, electronic signal errors, temperature changes, and manufacturing differences.

The steering wheel position sensor supplies 2 analog inputs, Phase A and Phase B, to the EBCM. The 2 input signals are approximately 90 degrees out of phase. By interpreting the relationship between the 2 inputs, the EBCM can determine the position of the steering wheel and the direction of steering wheel rotation.

Steer angle centering is the process by which the EBCM calibrates the steering sensor output so that the output reads zero when the steering wheel is centered. Using the yaw rate input, lateral accelerometer input, and wheel speed sensor inputs, the initial steering center position is calculated after driving greater than 10 km/h (6 mph) for more than 10 seconds in a straight line on a level surface.

Test Description

The number below refers to the step number on the diagnostic table.

6. Perform the Steering Position Sensor Test in order to verify if the steering wheel position sensor (SWPS) is operating properly.

GC4020152571010X

Fig. 42 Vehicle Stability Enhancement System Unwanted Activation (Part 1 of 3). Aurora

Step	Action	Value(s)	Yes	No
12	**Important:** Perform the setup procedure for the EBCM. An unprogrammed EBCM will result in the following conditions: • Inoperative or poorly functioning system operations • The EBCM sets DTC C1248 and DTC C1255m3. Replace the EBCM. Did you complete the repair?	—	Go to *Step 15*	—
13	Replace the power steering gear. Did you complete the repair?	—	Go to *Step 15*	—
14	Replace the steering wheel position sensor (SWPS). Did you complete the repair?	—	Go to *Step 15*	—
15	Operate the system in order to verify the repair. Did you correct the condition?	—	System OK	Go to *Step 2*

GC4020152571030X

Fig. 42 Vehicle Stability Enhancement System Unwanted Activation (Part 3 of 3). Aurora

Circuit Description

The vehicle stability enhancement system (VSES) is activated by the EBCM calculating the desired yaw rate and comparing it to the actual yaw rate input. The desired yaw rate is calculated from measured steering wheel position, vehicle speed, and lateral acceleration. The difference between the desired yaw rate and actual yaw rate is the yaw rate error, which is a measurement of oversteer or understeer. If the yaw rate error becomes too large, the EBCM will attempt to correct the vehicle's yaw motion by applying differential braking to the left or right front wheel.

The VSES activations generally occur during aggressive driving, in the turns or bumpy roads without much use of the accelerator pedal. When braking during VSES activation, the brake pedal will feel different than the ABS pedal pulsation. The brake pedal pulsates at a higher frequency during VSES activation.

The usable output voltage range for the lateral accelerometer and yaw rate sensors is 0.25–4.75 volts. The scan tool will report zero lateral acceleration or yaw rate as 2.5 volts with no sensor bias present.

The sensor bias compensates for sensor mounting alignment errors, electronic signal errors, temperature changes, and manufacturing differences.

The steering wheel position sensor supplies 2 analog inputs, Phase A and Phase B, to the EBCM. The 2 input signals are approximately 90 degrees out of phase. By interpreting the relationship between the 2 inputs, the EBCM can determine the position of the steering wheel and the direction of steering wheel rotation.

Steer angle centering is the process by which the EBCM calibrates the steering sensor output so that the output reads zero when the steering wheel is centered. Using the yaw rate input, lateral accelerometer input, and wheel speed sensor inputs, the initial steering center position is calculated after driving greater than 10 km/h (6 mph) for more than 10 seconds in a straight line on a level surface.

Step	Action	Value(s)	Yes	No
1	Did you perform the ABS Diagnostic System Check?	—	Go to *Step 2*	Go to *Diagnostic System Check - ABS*
2	1. Install a scan tool. 2. Turn ON the ignition, with the engine OFF. 3. Select the powertrain control module (PCM) display DTCs function. Does the scan tool display DTC P1575?	—	Go to *DTC P1575*	Go to *Step 3*
3	1. With a scan tool, observe the Extended Travel Brake Switch parameter in the DRP/ABS/TCS data list. 2. Step on and off the brake pedal with enough force to simulate a hard braking condition. As the brake pedal is pressed and released, the scan tool should read Applied and Released. 3. Use a tape measure in order to measure the distance that the brake pedal travels for the scan tool to read Applied. Does the distance measure within the specified range?	2.5–3.3 cm (1.0–1.3 in)	*Test for Intermittent*	Go to *Step 4*
4	Adjust or repair the extended travel brake switch as necessary. Did you complete the repair?	—	Go to *Step 5*	—
5	Operate the system in order to verify the repair. Did you correct the condition?	—	System OK	Go to *Step 2*

GC4020152572000X

Fig. 43 Vehicle Stability Enhancement System Excessive Brake Pulsation. Aurora

Step	Action	Value(s)	Yes	No
1	Did you perform the ABS Diagnostic System Check?	—	Go to *Step 2*	Go to *Diagnostic System Check - ABS*
2	Inspect the mounting of the yaw rate sensor. Did you find and correct the condition?	—	Go to *Step 15*	Go to *Step 3*
3	1. Install a scan tool. 2. Start the engine. 3. With a scan tool, observe the Yaw Rate Sensor Input parameter in the VSES data list. 4. Perform the Diagnostic Test Drive. Does the scan tool display suddenly increase or decrease without rapid turning of the vehicle?	—	Go to *Step 4*	Go to *Step 5*
4	Perform the diagnosis for DTC C1282. Did you find and correct the condition?	—	Go to *Step 15*	Go to *Step 12*
5	1. Straighten the front wheels. 2. Observe the Dual Analog SWPS Input A and Dual Analog SWPS Input B in the VSES data list. 3. Slowly rotate the steering wheel in both directions. Does the scan tool display change states as the steering wheel was rotated?	—	Go to *Step 6*	Go to *Step 14*
6	With the scan tool, perform the Steering Position Sensor Test. Did the SWPS pass the test?	—	Go to *Step 7*	Go to *Step 14*
7	1. Place the vehicle on a level surface. 2. With a scan tool, observe the Lateral Accelerometer Input parameter in the VSES data list. Does the scan tool display within the specified range?	2.3–2.7 V	Go to *Step 9*	Go to *Step 8*
8	Inspect the mounting of the lateral accelerometer sensor. Did you find and correct the condition?	—	Go to *Step 15*	Go to *Step 9*
9	Inspect the EBCM for the proper part number. Did you find the correct part number?	—	Go to *Step 10*	Go to *Step 12*
10	Inspect the power steering gear for the proper part number. Did you find the correct part number?	—	Go to *Step 11*	Go to *Step 13*
11	Inspect the alignment of the vehicle. Did you find and correct the condition?	—	Go to *Step 15*	*Test for Intermittent*

GC4020152571020X

Fig. 42 Vehicle Stability Enhancement System Unwanted Activation (Part 2 of 3). Aurora

Important: The following steps must be completed before using the symptom tables.

1. Perform the *Diagnostic System Check - ABS* before using the Symptom Tables in order to verify that all of the following are true:
   - There are no DTCs set.
   - The control module(s) can communicate via the serial data link.
2. Review the system operation in order to familiarize yourself with the system functions.

Visual/Physical Inspection

- Inspect for aftermarket devices which could affect the operation of the antilock brake system.
- Inspect the easily accessible or visible system components for obvious damage or conditions which could cause the symptom.
- Inspect the master cylinder reservoir for the proper brake fluid level.

Intermittent

Faulty electrical connections or wiring may be the cause of intermittent conditions.

Symptom List

Refer to a symptom diagnostic procedure from the following list in order to diagnose the symptom:

- *ABS Indicator Always On*
- *ABS Indicator Inoperative*
- *Low Traction Indicator Always On*
- *Low Traction Indicator Inoperative*

GC4020152573010X

Fig. 44 ABS Symptoms (Part 1 of 2). Bonneville

- *Traction Off Indicator Always On*
- *Traction Off Indicator Inoperative*
- *Traction Ready Indicator Always On*
- *Traction Ready Indicator Inoperative*
- *Vehicle Stability Enhancement System Inoperative*
- *Vehicle Stability Enhancement System Unwanted Activation*
- *Vehicle Stability Enhancement System Excessive Brake Pulsation*

GC4020152573020X

Fig. 44 ABS Symptoms (Part 2 of 2). Bonneville

Step	Action	Yes	No
1	Did you perform the ABS Diagnostic System Check?	Go to *Step 2*	Go to *Diagnostic System Check - ABS*
2	Inspect the EBCM ground, making sure the ground is clean and torqued to the proper specification. Did you find and correct the condition?	Go to *Step 9*	Go to *Step 3*
3	1. Install a scan tool. 2. Turn ON the ignition, with the engine OFF. 3. With a scan tool, observe the ABS Warning Indicator parameter in the DRP/ABS/TCS data list. Does the scan tool display Off?	Go to *Step 4*	Go to *Step 5*
4	1. Turn OFF the ignition. 2. Turn ON the ignition, with the engine OFF. 3. Observe the ABS indicator on the instrument cluster (IPC) during the bulb check. Does the ABS indicator illuminate during the bulb check and then turn OFF?	*Test for Intermittent*	Go to *Step 6*
5	Inspect for poor connections at the harness connector of the EBCM. Did you find and correct the condition?	Go to *Step 9*	Go to *Step 7*
6	Inspect for poor connections at the harness connector of the instrument cluster (IPC). Did you find and correct the condition?	Go to *Step 9*	Go to *Step 8*
7	**Important:** Perform the setup procedure for the EBCM. An unprogrammed EBCM will result in the following conditions: • Inoperative or poorly functioning system operations • The EBCM sets DTC C1248 and DTC C1255m3. Replace the EBCM. Did you complete the repair?	Go to *Step 9*	—
8	Replace the instrument cluster (IPC). Did you complete the repair?	Go to *Step 9*	—
9	Operate the system in order to verify the repair. Did you correct the condition?	System OK	Go to *Step 2*

GC4020152574020X

Fig. 45 ABS Indicator Always On (Part 2 of 2). Bonneville

Circuit Description

The instrument cluster controls the operation of the ABS indicator. The EBCM reports the desired status of the ABS indicator via serial data messages. The ABS indicator signal circuit is a back-up reporting circuit to the serial data messages. The EBCM supplies ground through the circuit when the ABS is operating properly. When there is a problem with ABS that should turn on the ABS indicator, the EBCM opens the ABS indicator signal circuit. If there is a problem with the ABS serial data messages, the instrument cluster uses the ABS indicator signal to determine if the ABS indicator should be illuminated. Using the serial data messages and back-up circuit, the instrument cluster decides whether to turn on the ABS indicator.

Test Description

The numbers below refer to the step numbers on the diagnostic table.

3. Use the scan tool to check the normal state of the ABS indicator control circuit.
4. Ensures that the instrument cluster can operate the ABS indicator.

GC4020152574010X

Fig. 45 ABS Indicator Always On (Part 1 of 2). Bonneville

Circuit Description

The instrument cluster controls the operation of the ABS indicator. The EBCM reports the desired status of the ABS indicator via serial data messages. The ABS indicator signal circuit is a back-up reporting circuit to the serial data messages. The EBCM supplies ground through the circuit when the ABS is operating properly. When there is a problem with ABS that should turn on the ABS indicator, the EBCM opens the ABS indicator signal circuit. If there is a problem with the ABS serial data messages, the instrument cluster uses the ABS indicator signal to determine if the ABS indicator should be illuminated. Using the serial data messages and back-up circuit, the instrument cluster decides whether to turn on the ABS indicator.

Test Description

The numbers below refer to the step numbers on the diagnostic table.

3. Use the scan tool to check the normal state of the ABS indicator control circuit.
4. Ensures that the instrument cluster can operate the ABS indicator.

Step	Action	Yes	No
1	Did you perform the ABS Diagnostic System Check?	Go to *Step 2*	Go to *Diagnostic System Check - ABS*
2	Inspect the EBCM ground, making sure the ground is clean and torqued to the proper specification. Did you find and correct the condition?	Go to *Step 9*	Go to *Step 3*
3	1. Install a scan tool. 2. Turn ON the ignition, with the engine OFF. 3. With a scan tool, observe the ABS Warning Indicator parameter in the DRP/ABS/TCS data list. Does the scan tool display Off?	Go to *Step 4*	Go to *Step 5*
4	1. Turn OFF the ignition. 2. Turn ON the ignition, with the engine OFF. 3. Observe the ABS indicator on the instrument cluster (IPC) during the bulb check. Does the ABS indicator illuminate during the bulb check and then turn OFF?	*Test for Intermittent*	Go to *Step 6*
5	Inspect for poor connections at the harness connector of the EBCM. Did you find and correct the condition?	Go to *Step 9*	Go to *Step 7*
6	Inspect for poor connections at the harness connector of the instrument cluster (IPC). Did you find and correct the condition?	Go to *Step 9*	Go to *Step 8*
7	**Important:** Perform the setup procedure for the EBCM. An unprogrammed EBCM will result in the following conditions: • Inoperative or poorly functioning system operations • The EBCM sets DTC C1248 and DTC C1255m3. Replace the EBCM. Did you complete the repair?	Go to *Step 9*	—
8	Replace the instrument cluster (IPC). Did you complete the repair?	Go to *Step 9*	—
9	Operate the system in order to verify the repair. Did you correct the condition?	System OK	Go to *Step 2*

GC4020152575000X

Fig. 46 ABS Indicator Inoperative. Bonneville

Circuit Description

The Low Traction indicator is controlled by the instrument cluster via serial data messages from the EBCM. When the ABS, TCS, or VSES is active for 0.5 seconds, the EBCM commands the instrument cluster to turn ON the Low Traction indicator.

The Low Traction indicator will also turn ON during the instrument cluster bulb check. When the ignition switch is turned to ON, the Low Traction indicator will turn ON for approximately 3 seconds and then turn OFF.

Test Description

The numbers below refer to the step numbers on the diagnostic table.

2. Use the scan tool to check the normal state of the Low Traction indicator control.
3. Ensures that the instrument cluster can operate the Low Traction indicator.

Step	Action	Value(s)	Yes	No
1	Did you perform the ABS Diagnostic System Check?	—	Go to *Step 2*	Go to *Diagnostic System Check - ABS*
2	1. Install a scan tool. 2. Turn ON the ignition, with the engine OFF. 3. With a scan tool, observe the TCS Active Indicator/Message parameter in the DRP/ABS/TCS data list. Does the scan tool display Off?	—	Go to *Step 3*	Go to *Step 4*
3	1. Turn OFF the ignition. 2. Turn ON the ignition, with the engine OFF. 3. Observe the Low Traction indicator on the instrument cluster (IPC) during the bulb check. Does the Low Traction indicator illuminate during the bulb check and then turn OFF?	—	*Test for Intermittent*	Go to *Step 5*
4	Inspect for poor connections at the harness connector of the EBCM. Did you find and correct the condition?	—	Go to *Step 8*	Go to *Step 6*
5	Inspect for poor connections at the harness connector of the instrument cluster (IPC). Did you find and correct the condition?	—	Go to *Step 8*	Go to *Step 7*
6	**Important:** Perform the setup procedure for the EBCM. An unprogrammed EBCM will result in the following conditions: • Inoperative or poorly functioning system operations • The EBCM sets DTC C1248 and DTC C1255m3 Replace the EBCM. Did you complete the repair?	—	Go to *Step 8*	—
7	Replace the instrument cluster (IPC). Did you complete the repair?	—	Go to *Step 8*	—
8	Operate the system in order to verify the repair. Did you correct the condition?	—	System OK	Go to *Step 2*

GC4020152576000X

Fig. 47 Low Traction Indicator Always On. Bonneville

Circuit Description

The Low Traction indicator is controlled by the instrument cluster via serial data messages from the EBCM. When the ABS, TCS, or VSES is active for 0.5 seconds, the EBCM commands the instrument cluster to turn ON the Low Traction indicator.

The Low Traction indicator will also turn ON during the instrument cluster bulb check. When the ignition switch is turned to ON, the Low Traction indicator will turn ON for approximately 3 seconds and then turn OFF.

Test Description

The numbers below refer to the step numbers on the diagnostic table.

2. Use the scan tool to check the normal state of the Low Traction indicator control.
3. Ensures that the instrument cluster can operate the Low Traction indicator.

Step	Action	Value(s)	Yes	No
1	Did you perform the ABS Diagnostic System Check?	—	Go to *Step 2*	Go to *Diagnostic System Check - ABS*
2	1. Install a scan tool. 2. Turn ON the ignition, with the engine OFF. 3. With a scan tool, observe the TCS Active Indicator/Message parameter in the DRP/ABS/TCS data list. Does the scan tool display Off?	—	Go to *Step 3*	Go to *Step 4*
3	1. Turn OFF the ignition. 2. Turn ON the ignition, with the engine OFF. 3. Observe the Low Traction indicator on the instrument cluster (IPC) during the bulb check. Does the Low Traction indicator illuminate during the bulb check and then turn OFF?	—	*Test for Intermittent*	Go to *Step 5*
4	Inspect for poor connections at the harness connector of the EBCM. Did you find and correct the condition?	—	Go to *Step 8*	Go to *Step 6*
5	Inspect for poor connections at the harness connector of the instrument cluster (IPC). Did you find and correct the condition?	—	Go to *Step 8*	Go to *Step 7*
6	**Important:** Perform the setup procedure for the EBCM. An unprogrammed EBCM will result in the following conditions: • Inoperative or poorly functioning system operations • The EBCM sets DTC C1248 and DTC C1255m3 Replace the EBCM. Did you complete the repair?	—	Go to *Step 8*	—
7	Replace the instrument cluster (IPC). Did you complete the repair?	—	Go to *Step 8*	—
8	Operate the system in order to verify the repair. Did you correct the condition?	—	System OK	Go to *Step 2*

GC4020152577000X

Fig. 48 Low Traction Indicator Inoperative. Bonneville

Circuit Description

The Traction Off indicator is controlled by the instrument cluster via serial data messages from the EBCM. When the heater and A/C control (w/C67) or the instrument panel module (IPM) (w/CJ2) sees the traction control switch input grounded through the momentary traction control switch, it sends a serial data message to the EBCM that tells the EBCM that the traction control switch has been pressed. The EBCM then disables traction control and sends a message to the instrument cluster to turn the Traction Off indicator ON. Each time the ignition is cycled from OFF to ON, the traction control system is enabled.

The following conditions will cause the Traction Off indicator to illuminate:

- The EBCM has disabled the TCS due to a DTC.
- The driver manually disabling the TCS via the traction control switch.
- The instrument cluster bulb check. When the ignition switch is turned to ON, the Traction Off indicator will turn on for approximately 3 seconds and then turn OFF.

Test Description

The numbers below refer to the step numbers on the diagnostic table.

2. Use the scan tool to check the normal state of the Traction Off indicator control.
3. Ensures that the instrument cluster can operate the Traction Off indicator.

Step	Action	Yes	No
1	Did you perform the ABS Diagnostic System Check?	Go to *Step 2*	Go to *Diagnostic System Check - ABS*
2	1. Install a scan tool. 2. Turn ON the ignition, with the engine OFF. 3. With a scan tool, observe the TCS Warning Indicator/Message parameter in the DRP/ABS/TCS data list. Does the scan tool display Off?	Go to *Step 3*	Go to *Step 4*
3	1. Turn OFF the ignition. 2. Turn ON the ignition, with the engine OFF. 3. Observe the Traction Off indicator on the instrument cluster (IPC) during the bulb check. Does the Traction Off indicator illuminate during the bulb check and then turn OFF?	*Test for Intermittent*	Go to *Step 5*
4	Inspect for poor connections at the harness connector of the EBCM. Did you find and correct the condition?	Go to *Step 8*	Go to *Step 6*
5	Inspect for poor connections at the harness connector of the instrument cluster (IPC). Did you find and correct the condition?	Go to *Step 8*	Go to *Step 7*
6	**Important:** Perform the setup procedure for the EBCM. An unprogrammed EBCM will result in the following conditions: • Inoperative or poorly functioning system operations • The EBCM sets DTC C1248 and DTC C1255m3. Replace the EBCM. Did you complete the repair?	Go to *Step 8*	—
7	Replace the instrument cluster (IPC). Did you complete the repair?	Go to *Step 8*	—
8	Operate the system in order to verify the repair. Did you correct the condition?	System OK	Go to *Step 2*

GC4020152578000X

Fig. 49 Traction Off Indicator Always On. Bonneville

Circuit Description

The Traction Off indicator is controlled by the instrument cluster via serial data messages from the EBCM. When the heater and A/C control (w/C67) or the instrument panel module (IPM) (w/CJ2) sees the traction control switch input grounded through the momentary traction control switch, it sends a serial data message to the EBCM that tells the EBCM that the traction control switch has been pressed. The EBCM then disables traction control and sends a message to the instrument cluster to turn the Traction Off indicator ON. Each time the ignition is cycled from OFF to ON, the traction control system is enabled.

The following conditions will cause the Traction Off indicator to illuminate:

- The EBCM has disabled the TCS due to a DTC.
- The driver manually disabling the TCS via the traction control switch.
- The instrument cluster bulb check. When the ignition switch is turned to ON, the Traction Off indicator will turn on for approximately 3 seconds and then turn OFF.

Test Description

The numbers below refer to the step numbers on the diagnostic table.

2. Use the scan tool to check the normal state of the Traction Off indicator control.
3. Ensures that the instrument cluster can operate the Traction Off indicator.

Step	Action	Value(s)	Yes	No
1	Did you perform the ABS Diagnostic System Check?	—	Go to *Step 2*	Go to *Diagnostic System Check - ABS*
2	1. Install a scan tool. 2. Turn ON the ignition, with the engine OFF. 3. With a scan tool, observe the TCS Warning Indicator/Message parameter in the DRP/ABS/TCS data list. Does the scan tool display Off?	—	Go to *Step 3*	Go to *Step 13*
3	1. Turn OFF the ignition. 2. Turn ON the ignition, with the engine OFF. 3. Observe the Traction Off indicator on the instrument cluster (IPC) during the bulb check. Does the Traction Off indicator illuminate during the bulb check and then turn OFF?	—	Go to *Step 4*	Go to *Step 14*
4	1. Turn OFF the ignition. 2. Install a scan tool. 3. Turn ON the ignition, with the engine OFF. 4. With a scan tool, observe the TCS Switch parameter in the Climate Control Panel (w/C67) data list or the Instrument Panel Module (w/CJ2) data list. 5. Activate the traction control switch. Does the TCS Switch parameter change state?	—	*Test for Intermittent*	Go to *Step 5*
5	Does the scan indicate that the TCS Switch parameter is On?	—	Go to *Step 6*	Go to *Step 7*
6	1. Turn OFF the ignition. 2. Disconnect the traction control switch connector. 3. Turn ON the ignition, with the engine OFF. 4. With a scan tool, observe the TCS Switch parameter. Does the scan tool display Off?	—	Go to *Step 12*	Go to *Step 8*
7	1. Turn OFF the ignition. 2. Disconnect the traction control switch connector. 3. Connect a 3 amp fused jumper from the signal circuit of the traction control switch to the ground circuit of the traction control switch. 4. Turn ON the ignition, with the engine OFF. 5. With a scan tool, observe the TCS Switch parameter. Does the scan tool display On?	—	Go to *Step 12*	Go to *Step 9*

GC4020152579010X

Fig. 50 Traction Off Indicator Inoperative (Part 1 of 2). Bonneville

Step	Action	Value(s)	Yes	No
8	Test the signal circuit of the traction control switch for a short to ground. Did you find and correct the condition?	—	Go to *Step 19*	Go to *Step 11*
9	Test the signal circuit of the traction control switch for an open or high resistance. Did you find and correct the condition?	—	Go to *Step 19*	Go to *Step 10*
10	Test the ground circuit of the traction control switch for an open or high resistance. Did you find and correct the condition?	—	Go to *Step 19*	Go to *Step 11*
11	Inspect for poor connections at the harness connector of the heater and A/C control (w/C67) or the instrument panel module (IPM) (w/CJ2). Did you find and correct the condition?	—	Go to *Step 19*	Go to *Step 15*
12	Inspect for poor connections at the harness connector of the traction control switch. Did you find and correct the condition?	—	Go to *Step 19*	Go to *Step 16*
13	Inspect for poor connections at the harness connector of the EBCM. Did you find and correct the condition?	—	Go to *Step 19*	Go to *Step 17*
14	Inspect for poor connections at the harness connector of the instrument cluster (IPC). Did you find and correct the condition?	—	Go to *Step 19*	Go to *Step 18*
15	Replace the heater and A/C control (w/C67) or the instrument panel module (IPM) (w/CJ2). Did you complete the replacement?	—	Go to *Step 19*	—
16	Replace the traction control switch. Did you complete the replacement?	—	Go to *Step 19*	—
17	**Important:** Perform the setup procedure for the EBCM. An unprogrammed EBCM will result in the following conditions: • Inoperative or poorly functioning system operations • The EBCM sets DTC C1248 and DTC C1255m3 Replace the EBCM. Did you complete the repair?	—	Go to *Step 19*	—
18	Replace the instrument cluster (IPC). Did you complete the repair?	—	Go to *Step 19*	—
19	Operate the system in order to verify the repair. Did you correct the condition?	—	System OK	Go to *Step 2*

GC4020152579020X

Fig. 50 Traction Off Indicator Inoperative (Part 2 of 2). Bonneville

Circuit Description

The Traction Ready indicator is located on the traction control switch and is controlled by the instrument cluster via serial data messages from the EBCM. The indicator is illuminated when the traction control system (TCS) is ready to be activated, if necessary. When the EBCM disables the TCS, it sends a serial data message to the instrument cluster. The instrument cluster then turns OFF the Traction Ready indicator. Each time the ignition is cycled from OFF to ON, the TCS is enabled.

Step	Action	Value(s)	Yes	No
1	Did you perform the ABS Diagnostic System Check?	—	Go to *Step 2*	Go to *Diagnostic System Check - ABS*
2	1. Turn OFF the ignition. 2. Disconnect the traction control switch. 3. Turn ON the ignition, with the engine OFF. 4. Measure the voltage from the traction ready indicator control circuit of the traction control switch to the ground circuit of the traction control switch. Does the voltage measure near the specified value?	B+	Go to *Step 5*	Go to *Step 3*
3	Test the ground circuit of the traction control switch for an open. Did you find and correct the condition?	—	Go to *Step 9*	Go to *Step 4*
4	Test the traction ready indicator control circuit of the traction control switch for the following conditions: • An open • A short to ground • A high resistance Did you find and correct the condition?	—	Go to *Step 9*	Go to *Step 6*
5	Inspect for poor connections at the harness connector of the traction control switch. Did you find and correct the condition?	—	Go to *Step 9*	Go to *Step 7*
6	Inspect for poor connections at the harness connector of the instrument cluster (IPC). Did you find and correct the condition?	—	Go to *Step 9*	Go to *Step 8*
7	Replace the traction control switch. Did you complete the repair?	—	Go to *Step 9*	—
8	Replace the instrument cluster (IPC). Did you complete the repair?	—	Go to *Step 9*	—
9	Operate the system in order to verify the repair. Did you correct the condition?	—	System OK	Go to *Step 2*

GC4020152581000X

Fig. 52 Traction Ready Indicator Inoperative. Bonneville

Circuit Description

The Traction Ready indicator is located on the traction control switch and is controlled by the instrument cluster via serial data messages from the EBCM. The indicator is illuminated when the traction control system (TCS) is ready to be activated, if necessary. When the EBCM disables the TCS, it sends a serial data message to the instrument cluster. The instrument cluster then turns OFF the Traction Ready indicator. Each time the ignition is cycled from OFF to ON, the TCS is enabled.

Step	Action	Value(s)	Yes	No
1	Did you perform the ABS Diagnostic System Check?	—	Go to *Step 2*	Go to *Diagnostic System Check - ABS*
2	1. Turn OFF the ignition. 2. Disconnect the instrument cluster. 3. Turn ON the ignition, with the engine OFF. Does the Traction Ready indicator turn OFF?	—	Go to *Step 5*	Go to *Step 3*
3	Test the traction ready indicator control circuit of the traction control switch for an short to voltage. Did you find and correct the condition?	—	Go to *Step 8*	Go to *Step 4*
4	Inspect for poor connections at the harness connector of the traction control switch. Did you find and correct the condition?	—	Go to *Step 8*	Go to *Step 6*
5	Inspect for poor connections at the harness connector of the instrument cluster (IPC). Did you find and correct the condition?	—	Go to *Step 8*	Go to *Step 7*
6	Replace the traction control switch. Did you complete the repair?	—	Go to *Step 8*	—
7	Replace the instrument cluster (IPC). Did you complete the repiar?	—	Go to *Step 8*	—
8	Operate the system in order to verify the repair. Did you correct the condition?	—	System OK	Go to *Step 2*

GC4020152580000X

Fig. 51 Traction Ready Indicator Always On. Bonneville

Circuit Description

The vehicle stability enhancement system (VSES) is activated by the EBCM calculating the desired yaw rate and comparing it to the actual yaw rate input. The desired yaw rate is calculated from measured steering wheel position, vehicle speed, and lateral acceleration. The difference between the desired yaw rate and actual yaw rate is the yaw rate error, which is a measurement of oversteer or understeer. If the yaw rate error becomes too large, the EBCM will attempt to correct the vehicle's yaw motion by applying differential braking to the left or right front wheel.

The VSES activations generally occur during aggressive driving, in the turns or bumpy roads without much use of the accelerator pedal. When braking during VSES activation, the brake pedal will feel different than the ABS pedal pulsation. The brake pedal pulsates at a higher frequency during VSES activation.

The usable output voltage range for the lateral accelerometer and yaw rate sensors is 0.25–4.75 volts. The scan tool will report zero lateral acceleration or yaw rate as 2.5 volts with no sensor bias present. The sensor bias compensates for sensor mounting alignment errors, electronic signal errors, temperature changes, and manufacturing differences.

The steering wheel position sensor supplies 2 analog inputs, Phase A and Phase B, to the EBCM. The 2 input signals are approximately 90 degrees out of phase. By interpreting the relationship between the 2 inputs, the EBCM can determine the position of the steering wheel and the direction of steering wheel rotation.

Steer angle centering is the process by which the EBCM calibrates the steering sensor output so that the output reads zero when the steering wheel is centered. Using the yaw rate input, lateral accelerometer input, and wheel speed sensor inputs, the initial steering center position is calculated after driving greater than 10 km/h (6 mph) for more than 10 seconds in a straight line on a level surface.

Test Description

The numbers below refer to the step numbers on the diagnostic table.

3. Perform the Steering Position Sensor Test in order to verify if the steering wheel position sensor (SWPS) is operating properly.
4. Verify that the lateral accelerometer input parameter is within the valid range.
5. Verify that the yaw rate input parameter is within the valid range.

GC4020152582010X

Fig. 53 Vehicle Stability Enhancement System Inoperative (Part 1 of 2). Bonneville

Step	Action	Value(s)	Yes	No
1	Did you perform the ABS Diagnostic System Check?	—	Go to *Step 2*	Go to *Diagnostic System Check - ABS*
2	1. Install a scan tool. 2. Start the engine. 3. Observe the VSES Is Centered parameter in the VSES data list. 4. Perform the Diagnostic Test Drive. Did the scan tool display Yes within the specified value?	30 seconds	*Test for Intermittent*	Go to *Step 3*
3	With the scan tool, perform the Steering Position Sensor Test. Did the SWPS pass the test?	—	Go to *Step 4*	Go to *Step 7*
4	With a scan tool, observe the Lateral Accelerometer Input parameter in the VSES data list. Does the scan tool display within the specified range?	2.3–2.7 V	Go to *Step 5*	Go to *Step 8*
5	With a scan tool, observe the Yaw Rate Sensor Input parameter in the VSES data list. Does the scan tool display within the specified range?	2.3–2.7 V	Go to *Step 6*	Go to *Step 9*
6	**Important:** Perform the setup procedure for the EBCM. An unprogrammed EBCM will result in the following conditions: • Inoperative or poorly functioning system operations • The EBCM sets DTC C1248 and DTC C1255m3. Replace the EBCM. Did you complete the repair?	—	Go to *Step 10*	—
7	Replace the steering wheel position sensor (SWPS). Did you complete the replacement?	—	Go to *Step 10*	—
8	Replace the lateral accelerometer sensor. Did you complete the replacement?	—	Go to *Step 10*	—
9	Replace the yaw rate sensor. Did you complete the replacement?	—	Go to *Step 10*	—
10	Operate the system in order to verify the repair. Did you correct the condition?	—	System OK	Go to *Step 2*

GC4020152582020X

Fig. 53 Vehicle Stability Enhancement System Inoperative (Part 2 of 2). Bonneville

Step	Action	Value(s)	Yes	No
7	1. Place the vehicle on a level surface. 2. With a scan tool, observe the Lateral Accelerometer Input parameter in the VSES data list. Does the scan tool display within the specified range?	2.3–2.7 V	Go to *Step 9*	Go to *Step 8*
8	Inspect the mounting of the lateral accelerometer sensor. Did you find and correct the condition?	—	Go to *Step 15*	Go to *Step 9*
9	Inspect the EBCM for the proper part number. Did you find the correct part number?	—	Go to *Step 10*	Go to *Step 12*
10	Inspect the power steering gear for the proper part number. Did you find the correct part number?	—	Go to *Step 11*	Go to *Step 13*
11	Inspect the alignment of the vehicle. Did you find and correct the condition?	—	Go to *Step 15*	*Test for Intermittent*
12	**Important:** Perform the setup procedure for the EBCM. An unprogrammed EBCM will result in the following conditions: • Inoperative or poorly functioning system operations • The EBCM sets DTC C1248 and DTC C1255m3. Replace the EBCM. Did you complete the repair?	—	Go to *Step 15*	—
13	Replace the power steering gear. Did you complete the repair?	—	Go to *Step 15*	—
14	Replace the steering wheel position sensor (SWPS). Did you complete the repair?	—	Go to *Step 15*	—
15	Operate the system in order to verify the repair. Did you correct the condition?	—	System OK	Go to *Step 2*

GC4020152583020X

Fig. 54 Vehicle Stability Enhancement System Unwanted Activation (Part 2 of 2). Bonneville

Circuit Description

The vehicle stability enhancement system (VSES) is activated by the EBCM calculating the desired yaw rate and comparing it to the actual yaw rate input. The desired yaw rate is calculated from measured steering wheel position, vehicle speed, and lateral acceleration. The difference between the desired yaw rate and actual yaw rate is the yaw rate error, which is a measurement of oversteer or understeer. If the yaw rate error becomes too large, the EBCM will attempt to correct the vehicle's yaw motion by applying differential braking to the left or right front wheel.

The VSES activations generally occur during aggressive driving, in the turns or bumpy roads without much use of the accelerator pedal. When braking during VSES activation, the brake pedal will feel different than the ABS pedal pulsation. The brake pedal pulsates at a higher frequency during VSES activation.

The usable output voltage range for the lateral accelerometer and yaw rate sensors is 0.25–4.75 volts. The scan tool will report zero lateral acceleration or yaw rate as 2.5 volts with no sensor bias present. The sensor bias compensates for sensor mounting alignment errors, electronic signal errors, temperature changes, and manufacturing differences.

The steering wheel position sensor supplies 2 analog inputs, Phase A and Phase B, to the EBCM. The 2 input signals are approximately 90 degrees out of phase. By interpreting the relationship between the 2 inputs, the EBCM can determine the position of the steering wheel and the direction of steering wheel rotation.

Steer angle centering is the process by which the EBCM calibrates the steering sensor output so that the output reads zero when the steering wheel is centered. Using the yaw rate input, lateral accelerometer input, and wheel speed sensor inputs, the initial steering center position is calculated after driving greater than 10 km/h (6 mph) for more than 10 seconds in a straight line on a level surface.

Test Description

The number below refers to the step number on the diagnostic table.

6. Perform the Steering Position Sensor Test in order to verify if the steering wheel position sensor (SWPS) is operating properly.

Step	Action	Value(s)	Yes	No
1	Did you perform the ABS Diagnostic System Check?	—	Go to *Step 2*	Go to *Diagnostic System Check - ABS*
2	Inspect the mounting of the yaw rate sensor. Did you find and correct the condition?	—	Go to *Step 15*	Go to *Step 3*
3	1. Install a scan tool. 2. Start the engine. 3. With a scan tool, observe the Yaw Rate Sensor Input parameter in the VSES data list. 4. Perform the Diagnostic Test Drive. Does the scan tool display suddenly increase or decrease without rapid turning of the vehicle?	—	Go to *Step 4*	Go to *Step 5*
4	Perform the diagnosis for DTC C1282. Did you find and correct the condition?	—	Go to *Step 15*	Go to *Step 12*
5	1. Straighten the front wheels. 2. Observe the Dual Analog SWPS Input A and Dual Analog SWPS Input B in the VSES data list. 3. Slowly rotate the steering wheel in both directions. Does the scan tool display change states as the steering wheel was rotated?	—	Go to *Step 6*	Go to *Step 14*
6	With the scan tool, perform the Steering Position Sensor Test. Did the SWPS pass the test?	—	Go to *Step 7*	Go to *Step 14*

GC4020152583010X

Fig. 54 Vehicle Stability Enhancement System Unwanted Activation (Part 1 of 2). Bonneville

Circuit Description

The vehicle stability enhancement system (VSES) is activated by the EBCM calculating the desired yaw rate and comparing it to the actual yaw rate input. The desired yaw rate is calculated from measured steering wheel position, vehicle speed, and lateral acceleration. The difference between the desired yaw rate and actual yaw rate is the yaw rate error, which is a measurement of oversteer or understeer. If the yaw rate error becomes too large, the EBCM will attempt to correct the vehicle's yaw motion by applying differential braking to the left or right front wheel.

The VSES activations generally occur during aggressive driving, in the turns or bumpy roads without much use of the accelerator pedal. When braking during VSES activation, the brake pedal will feel different than the ABS pedal pulsation. The brake pedal pulsates at a higher frequency during VSES activation.

The usable output voltage range for the lateral accelerometer and yaw rate sensors is 0.25–4.75 volts. The scan tool will report zero lateral acceleration or yaw rate as 2.5 volts with no sensor bias present. The sensor bias compensates for sensor mounting alignment errors, electronic signal errors, temperature changes, and manufacturing differences.

The steering wheel position sensor supplies 2 analog inputs, Phase A and Phase B, to the EBCM. The 2 input signals are approximately 90 degrees out of phase. By interpreting the relationship between the 2 inputs, the EBCM can determine the position of the steering wheel and the direction of steering wheel rotation.

Steer angle centering is the process by which the EBCM calibrates the steering sensor output so that the output reads zero when the steering wheel is centered. Using the yaw rate input, lateral accelerometer input, and wheel speed sensor inputs, the initial steering center position is calculated after driving greater than 10 km/h (6 mph) for more than 10 seconds in a straight line on a level surface.

Step	Action	Value(s)	Yes	No
1	Did you perform the ABS Diagnostic System Check?	—	Go to *Step 2*	Go to *Diagnostic System Check - ABS*
2	1. Install a scan tool. 2. Turn ON the ignition, with the engine OFF. 3. Select the display DTCs function on the scan tool for the powertrain control module (PCM). Does the scan tool display DTC P1575?	—	*Diagnose Engine Controls*	Go to *Step 3*
3	1. With a scan tool, observe the Extended Travel Brake Switch parameter in the DRP/ABS/TCS data list. 2. Step on and off the brake pedal with enough force to simulate a hard braking condition. As the brake pedal is pressed and released, the scan tool should read Applied and Released. 3. Use a tape measure in order to measure the distance that the brake pedal travels for the scan tool to read Applied. Does the distance measure within the specified range?	1.0–1.3 in (2.5–3.3 cm)	*Test for Intermittent*	Go to *Step 4*
4	Adjust or repair the extended travel brake switch as necessary. Did you complete the repair?	—	Go to *Step 5*	—
5	Operate the system in order to verify the repair. Did you correct the condition?	—	System OK	Go to *Step 2*

GC4020152584000X

Fig. 55 Vehicle Stability Enhancement System Excessive Brake Pulsation. Bonneville

Important: The following steps must be completed before using the symptom tables.

1. Perform the *Diagnostic System Check - ABS* before using the Symptom Tables in order to verify that all of the following are true:
   - There are no DTCs set.
   - The control module(s) can communicate via the serial data link.
2. Review the system operation in order to familiarize yourself with the system functions.

Visual/Physical Inspection

- Inspect for aftermarket devices which could affect the operation of the antilock brake system.
- Inspect the easily accessible or visible system components for obvious damage or conditions which could cause the symptom.
- Inspect the master cylinder reservoir for the proper brake fluid level.

Intermittent

Faulty electrical connections or wiring may be the cause of intermittent conditions.

Symptom List

Refer to a symptom diagnostic procedure from the following list in order to diagnose the symptom:

- *ABS Indicator Always On*
- *ABS Indicator Inoperative*
- *Traction Off Indicator Always On*
- *Traction Off Indicator Inoperative*
- *Vehicle Stability Enhancement System Inoperative*
- *Vehicle Stability Enhancement System Unwanted Activation*
- *Vehicle Stability Enhancement System Excessive Brake Pulsation*

GC4020152585000X

Fig. 56 ABS Symptoms. LeSabre

Circuit Description

The instrument cluster controls the operation of the ABS indicator. The EBCM reports the desired status of the ABS indicator via serial data messages. The ABS indicator signal circuit is a back-up reporting circuit to the serial data messages. The EBCM supplies ground through the circuit when the ABS is operating properly. When there is a problem with ABS that should turn on the ABS indicator, the EBCM opens the ABS indicator signal circuit. If there is a problem with the ABS serial data messages, the instrument cluster uses the ABS indicator signal to determine if the ABS indicator should be illuminated. Using the serial data messages and back-up circuit, the instrument cluster decides whether to turn on the ABS indicator.

Test Description

The numbers below refer to the step numbers on the diagnostic table.

3. Use the scan tool to check the normal state of the ABS indicator control circuit.
4. Ensures that the instrument cluster can operate the ABS indicator.

Step	Action	Yes	No
1	Did you perform the ABS Diagnostic System Check?	Go to *Step 2*	Go to *Diagnostic System Check - ABS*
2	Inspect the EBCM ground, making sure the ground is clean and torqued to the proper specification. Did you find and correct the condition?	Go to *Step 9*	Go to *Step 3*
3	1. Install a scan tool. 2. Turn ON the ignition, with the engine OFF. 3. With a scan tool, observe the ABS Warning Indicator parameter in the DRP/ABS/TCS data list. Does the scan tool display Off?	Go to *Step 4*	Go to *Step 5*
4	1. Turn OFF the ignition. 2. Turn ON the ignition, with the engine OFF. 3. Observe the ABS indicator on the instrument cluster (IPC) during the bulb check. Does the ABS indicator illuminate during the bulb check and then turn OFF?	*Test for Intermittent*	Go to *Step 6*
5	Inspect for poor connections at the harness connector of the EBCM. Did you find and correct the condition?	Go to *Step 9*	Go to *Step 7*
6	Inspect for poor connections at the harness connector of the instrument cluster (IPC). Did you find and correct the condition?	Go to *Step 9*	Go to *Step 8*
7	**Important:** Perform the setup procedure for the EBCM. An unprogrammed EBCM will result in the following conditions: • Inoperative or poorly functioning system operations • The EBCM sets DTC C1248 and DTC C1255m3. Replace the EBCM. Did you complete the repair?	Go to *Step 9*	—
8	Replace the instrument cluster (IPC). Did you complete the repair?	Go to *Step 9*	—
9	Operate the system in order to verify the repair. Did you correct the condition?	System OK	Go to *Step 2*

GC4020152587000X

Fig. 58 ABS Indicator Inoperative. LeSabre

Circuit Description

The instrument cluster controls the operation of the ABS indicator. The EBCM reports the desired status of the ABS indicator via serial data messages. The ABS indicator signal circuit is a back-up reporting circuit to the serial data messages. The EBCM supplies ground through the circuit when the ABS is operating properly. When there is a problem with ABS that should turn on the ABS indicator, the EBCM opens the ABS indicator signal circuit. If there is a problem with the ABS serial data messages, the instrument cluster uses the ABS indicator signal to determine if the ABS indicator should be illuminated. Using the serial data messages and back-up circuit, the instrument cluster decides whether to turn on the ABS indicator.

Test Description

The numbers below refer to the step numbers on the diagnostic table.

3. Use the scan tool to check the normal state of the ABS indicator control circuit.
4. Ensures that the instrument cluster can operate the ABS indicator.

Step	Action	Yes	No
1	Did you perform the ABS Diagnostic System Check?	Go to *Step 2*	Go to *Diagnostic System Check - ABS*
2	Inspect the EBCM ground, making sure the ground is clean and torqued to the proper specification. Did you find and correct the condition?	Go to *Step 9*	Go to *Step 3*
3	1. Install a scan tool. 2. Turn ON the ignition, with the engine OFF. 3. With a scan tool, observe the ABS Warning Indicator parameter in the DRP/ABS/TCS data list. Does the scan tool display Off?	Go to *Step 4*	Go to *Step 5*
4	1. Turn OFF the ignition. 2. Turn ON the ignition, with the engine OFF. 3. Observe the ABS indicator on the instrument cluster (IPC) during the bulb check. Does the ABS indicator illuminate during the bulb check and then turn OFF?	*Test for Intermittent*	Go to *Step 6*
5	Inspect for poor connections at the harness connector of the EBCM. Did you find and correct the condition?	Go to *Step 9*	Go to *Step 7*
6	Inspect for poor connections at the harness connector of the instrument cluster (IPC). Did you find and correct the condition?	Go to *Step 9*	Go to *Step 8*
7	**Important:** Perform the setup procedure for the EBCM. An unprogrammed EBCM will result in the following conditions: • Inoperative or poorly functioning system operations • The EBCM sets DTC C1248 and DTC C1255m3. Replace the EBCM. Did you complete the repair?	Go to *Step 9*	—
8	Replace the instrument cluster (IPC). Did you complete the repair?	Go to *Step 9*	—
9	Operate the system in order to verify the repair. Did you correct the condition?	System OK	Go to *Step 2*

GC4020152586000X

Fig. 57 ABS Indicator Always On. LeSabre

Circuit Description

The Traction Off indicator is controlled by the instrument cluster via serial data messages from the EBCM. When the heater and A/C control (w/C67) or the instrument panel module (IPM) (w/CJ2) sees the traction control switch input grounded through the momentary traction control switch, it sends a serial data message to the EBCM that tells the EBCM that the traction control switch has been pressed. The EBCM then disables traction control and sends a message to the instrument cluster to turn the Traction Off indicator ON. Each time the ignition is cycled from OFF to ON, the traction control system is enabled.

The following conditions will cause the Traction Off indicator to illuminate:

- The EBCM has disabled the TCS due to a DTC.
- The driver manually disabling the TCS via the traction control switch.
- The instrument cluster bulb check. When the ignition switch is turned to ON, the Traction Off indicator will turn on for approximately 3 seconds and then turn OFF.

Test Description

The numbers below refer to the step numbers on the diagnostic table.

2. Use the scan tool to check the normal state of the Traction Off indicator control.
3. Ensures that the instrument cluster can operate the Traction Off indicator.

Step	Action	Yes	No
1	Did you perform the ABS Diagnostic System Check?	Go to *Step 2*	Go to *Diagnostic System Check - ABS*
2	1. Install a scan tool. 2. Turn ON the ignition, with the engine OFF. 3. With a scan tool, observe the TCS Warning Indicator/Message parameter in the DRP/ABS/TCS data list. Does the scan tool display Off?	Go to *Step 3*	Go to *Step 4*
3	1. Turn OFF the ignition. 2. Turn ON the ignition, with the engine OFF. 3. Observe the Traction Off indicator on the instrument cluster (IPC) during the bulb check. Does the Traction Off indicator illuminate during the bulb check and then turn OFF?	*Test for Intermittent*	Go to *Step 5*
4	Inspect for poor connections at the harness connector of the EBCM. Did you find and correct the condition?	Go to *Step 8*	Go to *Step 6*
5	Inspect for poor connections at the harness connector of the instrument cluster (IPC). Did you find and correct the condition?	Go to *Step 8*	Go to *Step 7*
6	**Important:** Perform the setup procedure for the EBCM. An unprogrammed EBCM will result in the following conditions: • Inoperative or poorly functioning system operations • The EBCM sets DTC C1248 and DTC C1255m3. Replace the EBCM. Did you complete the repair?	Go to *Step 8*	—
7	Replace the instrument cluster (IPC). Did you complete the repair?	Go to *Step 8*	—
8	Operate the system in order to verify the repair. Did you correct the condition?	System OK	Go to *Step 2*

GC4020152588000X

Fig. 59 Traction Off Indicator Always On. LeSabre

Circuit Description

The Traction Off indicator is controlled by the instrument cluster via serial data messages from the EBCM. When the heater and A/C control (w/C67) or the instrument panel module (IPM) (w/CJ2) sees the traction control switch input grounded through the momentary traction control switch, it sends a serial data message to the EBCM that tells the EBCM that the traction control switch has been pressed. The EBCM then disables traction control and sends a message to the instrument cluster to turn the Traction Off indicator ON. Each time the ignition is cycled from OFF to ON, the traction control system is enabled.

The following conditions will cause the Traction Off indicator to illuminate:

- The EBCM has disabled the TCS due to a DTC.
- The driver manually disabling the TCS via the traction control switch.
- The instrument cluster bulb check. When the ignition switch is turned to ON, the Traction Off indicator will turn on for approximately 3 seconds and then turn OFF.

Test Description

The numbers below refer to the step numbers on the diagnostic table.

2. Use the scan tool to check the normal state of the Traction Off indicator control.
3. Ensures that the instrument cluster can operate the Traction Off indicator.

Step	Action	Value(s)	Yes	No
1	Did you perform the ABS Diagnostic System Check?	—	Go to *Step 2*	Go to *Diagnostic System Check - ABS*
2	1. Install a scan tool. 2. Turn ON the ignition, with the engine OFF. 3. With a scan tool, observe the TCS Warning Indicator/Message parameter in the DRP/ABS/TCS data list. Does the scan tool display Off?	—	Go to *Step 3*	Go to *Step 13*
3	1. Turn OFF the ignition. 2. Turn ON the ignition, with the engine OFF. 3. Observe the Traction Off indicator on the instrument cluster (IPC) during the bulb check. Does the Traction Off indicator illuminate during the bulb check and then turn OFF?	—	Go to *Step 4*	Go to *Step 14*
4	1. Turn OFF the ignition. 2. Install a scan tool. 3. Turn ON the ignition, with the engine OFF. 4. With a scan tool, observe the TCS Switch parameter in the Climate Control Panel (w/C67) data list or the Instrument Panel Module (w/CJ2) data list. 5. Activate the traction control switch. Does the TCS Switch parameter change state?	—	*Test for Intermittent*	Go to *Step 5*
5	Does the scan indicate that the TCS Switch parameter is On?	—	Go to *Step 6*	Go to *Step 7*
6	1. Turn OFF the ignition. 2. Disconnect the traction control switch connector. 3. Turn ON the ignition, with the engine OFF. 4. With a scan tool, observe the TCS Switch parameter. Does the scan tool display Off?	—	Go to *Step 12*	Go to *Step 8*
7	1. Turn OFF the ignition. 2. Disconnect the traction control switch connector. 3. Connect a 3 amp fused jumper from the signal circuit of the traction control switch to the ground circuit of the traction control switch. 4. Turn ON the ignition, with the engine OFF. 5. With a scan tool, observe the TCS Switch parameter. Does the scan tool display On?	—	Go to *Step 12*	Go to *Step 9*

GC4020152589010X

Fig. 60 Traction Off Indicator Inoperative (Part 1 of 2). LeSabre

Step	Action	Value(s)	Yes	No
8	Test the signal circuit of the traction control switch for a short to ground. Did you find and correct the condition?	—	Go to *Step 19*	Go to *Step 11*
9	Test the signal circuit of the traction control switch for an open or high resistance. Did you find and correct the condition?	—	Go to *Step 19*	Go to *Step 10*
10	Test the ground circuit of the traction control switch for an open or high resistance. Did you find and correct the condition?	—	Go to *Step 19*	Go to *Step 11*
11	Inspect for poor connections at the harness connector of the heater and A/C control (w/C67) or the instrument panel module (IPM) (w/CJ2). Did you find and correct the condition?	—	Go to *Step 19*	Go to *Step 15*
12	Inspect for poor connections at the harness connector of the traction control switch. Did you find and correct the condition?	—	Go to *Step 19*	Go to *Step 16*
13	Inspect for poor connections at the harness connector of the EBCM. Did you find and correct the condition?	—	Go to *Step 19*	Go to *Step 17*
14	Inspect for poor connections at the harness connector of the instrument cluster (IPC). Did you find and correct the condition?	—	Go to *Step 19*	Go to *Step 18*
15	Replace the heater and A/C control (w/C67) or the instrument panel module (IPM) (w/CJ2). Did you complete the replacement?	—	Go to *Step 19*	—
16	Replace the traction control switch. Did you complete the replacement?	—	Go to *Step 19*	—
17	**Important:** Perform the setup procedure for the EBCM. An unprogrammed EBCM will result in the following conditions: • Inoperative or poorly functioning system operations • The EBCM sets DTC C1248 and DTC C1255m3 Replace the EBCM. Did you complete the repair?	—	Go to *Step 19*	—
18	Replace the instrument cluster (IPC). Did you complete the repair?	—	Go to *Step 19*	—
19	Operate the system in order to verify the repair. Did you correct the condition?	—	System OK	Go to *Step 2*

GC4020152589020X

Fig. 60 Traction Off Indicator Inoperative (Part 2 of 2). LeSabre

Circuit Description

The vehicle stability enhancement system (VSES) is activated by the EBCM calculating the desired yaw rate and comparing it to the actual yaw rate input. The desired yaw rate is calculated from measured steering wheel position, vehicle speed, and lateral acceleration. The difference between the desired yaw rate and actual yaw rate is the yaw rate error, which is a measurement of oversteer or understeer. If the yaw rate error becomes too large, the EBCM will attempt to correct the vehicle's yaw motion by applying differential braking to the left or right front wheel.

The VSES activations generally occur during aggressive driving, in the turns or bumpy roads without much use of the accelerator pedal. When braking during VSES activation, the brake pedal will feel different than the ABS pedal pulsation. The brake pedal pulsates at a higher frequency during VSES activation.

The usable output voltage range for the lateral accelerometer and yaw rate sensors is 0.25–4.75 volts. The scan tool will report zero lateral acceleration or yaw rate as 2.5 volts with no sensor bias present. The sensor bias compensates for sensor mounting alignment errors, electronic signal errors, temperature changes, and manufacturing differences.

The steering wheel position sensor supplies 2 analog inputs, Phase A and Phase B, to the EBCM. The 2 input signals are approximately 90 degrees out of phase. By interpreting the relationship between the 2 inputs, the EBCM can determine the position of the steering wheel and the direction of steering wheel rotation.

Steer angle centering is the process by which the EBCM calibrates the steering sensor output so that the output reads zero when the steering wheel is centered. Using the yaw rate input, lateral accelerometer input, and wheel speed sensor inputs, the initial steering center position is calculated after driving greater than 10 km/h (6 mph) for more than 10 seconds in a straight line on a level surface.

Test Description

The numbers below refer to the step numbers on the diagnostic table.

3. Perform the Steering Position Sensor Test in order to verify if the steering wheel position sensor (SWPS) is operating properly.
4. Verify that the lateral accelerometer input parameter is within the valid range.
5. Verify that the yaw rate input parameter is within the valid range.

GC4020152590010X

Fig. 61 Vehicle Stability Enhancement System Inoperative (Part 1 of 2). LeSabre

Step	Action	Value(s)	Yes	No
1	Did you perform the ABS Diagnostic System Check?	—	Go to *Step 2*	Go to *Diagnostic System Check - ABS*
2	1. Install a scan tool. 2. Start the engine. 3. Observe the VSES Is Centered parameter in the VSES data list. 4. Perform the Diagnostic Test Drive. Did the scan tool display Yes within the specified value?	30 seconds	*Test for Intermittent*	Go to *Step 3*
3	With the scan tool, perform the Steering Position Sensor Test. Did the SWPS pass the test?	—	Go to *Step 4*	Go to *Step 7*
4	With a scan tool, observe the Lateral Accelerometer Input parameter in the VSES data list. Does the scan tool display within the specified range?	2.3–2.7 V	Go to *Step 5*	Go to *Step 8*
5	With a scan tool, observe the Yaw Rate Sensor Input parameter in the VSES data list. Does the scan tool display within the specified range?	2.3–2.7 V	Go to *Step 6*	Go to *Step 9*
6	**Important:** Perform the setup procedure for the EBCM. An unprogrammed EBCM will result in the following conditions: • Inoperative or poorly functioning system operations • The EBCM sets DTC C1248 and DTC C1255m3. Replace the EBCM. Did you complete the repair?	—	Go to *Step 10*	—
7	Replace the steering wheel position sensor (SWPS). Did you complete the replacement?	—	Go to *Step 10*	—
8	Replace the lateral accelerometer sensor. Did you complete the replacement?	—	Go to *Step 10*	—
9	Replace the yaw rate sensor. Did you complete the replacement?	—	Go to *Step 10*	—
10	Operate the system in order to verify the repair. Did you correct the condition?	—	System OK	Go to *Step 2*

GC4020152590020X

Fig. 61 Vehicle Stability Enhancement System Inoperative (Part 2 of 2). LeSabre

Circuit Description

The vehicle stability enhancement system (VSES) is activated by the EBCM calculating the desired yaw rate and comparing it to the actual yaw rate input. The desired yaw rate is calculated from measured steering wheel position, vehicle speed, and lateral acceleration. The difference between the desired yaw rate and actual yaw rate is the yaw rate error, which is a measurement of oversteer or understeer. If the yaw rate error becomes too large, the EBCM will attempt to correct the vehicle's yaw motion by applying differential braking to the left or right front wheel.

The VSES activations generally occur during aggressive driving, in the turns or bumpy roads without much use of the accelerator pedal. When braking during VSES activation, the brake pedal will feel different than the ABS pedal pulsation. The brake pedal pulsates at a higher frequency during VSES activation.

The usable output voltage range for the lateral accelerometer and yaw rate sensors is 0.25–4.75 volts. The scan tool will report zero lateral acceleration or yaw rate as 2.5 volts with no sensor bias present. The sensor bias compensates for sensor mounting alignment errors, electronic signal errors, temperature changes, and manufacturing differences.

The steering wheel position sensor supplies 2 analog inputs, Phase A and Phase B, to the EBCM. The 2 input signals are approximately 90 degrees out of phase. By interpreting the relationship between the 2 inputs, the EBCM can determine the position of the steering wheel and the direction of steering wheel rotation.

Steer angle centering is the process by which the EBCM calibrates the steering sensor output so that the output reads zero when the steering wheel is centered. Using the yaw rate input, lateral accelerometer input, and wheel speed sensor inputs, the initial steering center position is calculated after driving greater than 10 km/h (6 mph) for more than 10 seconds in a straight line on a level surface.

Test Description

The number below refers to the step number on the diagnostic table.

6. Perform the Steering Position Sensor Test in order to verify if the steering wheel position sensor (SWPS) is operating properly.

Step	Action	Value(s)	Yes	No
1	Did you perform the ABS Diagnostic System Check?	—	Go to *Step 2*	Go to *Diagnostic System Check - ABS*
2	Inspect the mounting of the yaw rate sensor. Did you find and correct the condition?	—	Go to *Step 15*	Go to *Step 3*
3	1. Install a scan tool. 2. Start the engine. 3. With a scan tool, observe the Yaw Rate Sensor Input parameter in the VSES data list. 4. Perform the Diagnostic Test Drive. Does the scan tool display suddenly increase or decrease without rapid turning of the vehicle?	—	Go to *Step 4*	Go to *Step 5*
4	Perform the diagnosis for DTC C1282. Did you find and correct the condition?	—	Go to *Step 15*	Go to *Step 12*
5	1. Straighten the front wheels. 2. Observe the Dual Analog SWPS Input A and Dual Analog SWPS Input B in the VSES data list. 3. Slowly rotate the steering wheel in both directions. Does the scan tool display change states as the steering wheel was rotated?	—	Go to *Step 6*	Go to *Step 14*
6	With the scan tool, perform the Steering Position Sensor Test. Did the SWPS pass the test?	—	Go to *Step 7*	Go to *Step 14*
7	1. Place the vehicle on a level surface. 2. With a scan tool, observe the Lateral Accelerometer Input parameter in the VSES data list. Does the scan tool display within the specified range?	2.3–2.7 V	Go to *Step 9*	Go to *Step 8*

GC4020152591010X

Fig. 62 Vehicle Stability Enhancement System Unwanted Activation (Part 1 of 2). LeSabre

Circuit Description

The vehicle stability enhancement system (VSES) is activated by the EBCM calculating the desired yaw rate and comparing it to the actual yaw rate input. The desired yaw rate is calculated from measured steering wheel position, vehicle speed, and lateral acceleration. The difference between the desired yaw rate and actual yaw rate is the yaw rate error, which is a measurement of oversteer or understeer. If the yaw rate error becomes too large, the EBCM will attempt to correct the vehicle's yaw motion by applying differential braking to the left or right front wheel.

The VSES activations generally occur during aggressive driving, in the turns or bumpy roads without much use of the accelerator pedal. When braking during VSES activation, the brake pedal will feel different than the ABS pedal pulsation. The brake pedal pulsates at a higher frequency during VSES activation.

The usable output voltage range for the lateral accelerometer and yaw rate sensors is 0.25–4.75 volts. The scan tool will report zero lateral acceleration or yaw rate as 2.5 volts with no sensor bias present. The sensor bias compensates for sensor mounting alignment errors, electronic signal errors, temperature changes, and manufacturing differences.

The steering wheel position sensor supplies 2 analog inputs, Phase A and Phase B, to the EBCM. The 2 input signals are approximately 90 degrees out of phase. By interpreting the relationship between the 2 inputs, the EBCM can determine the position of the steering wheel and the direction of steering wheel rotation.

Steer angle centering is the process by which the EBCM calibrates the steering sensor output so that the output reads zero when the steering wheel is centered. Using the yaw rate input, lateral accelerometer input, and wheel speed sensor inputs, the initial steering center position is calculated after driving greater than 10 km/h (6 mph) for more than 10 seconds in a straight line on a level surface.

Step	Action	Value(s)	Yes	No
Schematic Reference: *ABS Schematics*				
1	Did you perform the ABS Diagnostic System Check?	—	Go to *Step 2*	Go to *Diagnostic System Check - ABS*
2	1. Install a scan tool. 2. Turn ON the ignition, with the engine OFF. 3. Select the display DTCs function on the scan tool for the powertrain control module (PCM). Does the scan tool display DTC P1575?	—	*Diagnose Engine Controls*	Go to *Step 3*
3	1. With a scan tool, observe the Extended Travel Brake Switch parameter in the DRP/ABS/TCS data list. 2. Step on and off the brake pedal with enough force to simulate a hard braking condition. As the brake pedal is pressed and released, the scan tool should read Applied and Released. 3. Use a tape measure in order to measure the distance that the brake pedal travels for the scan tool to read Applied. Does the distance measure within the specified range?	1.0–1.3 in (2.5–3.3 cm)	*Test for Intermittent*	Go to *Step 4*
4	Adjust or repair the extended travel brake switch as necessary. Did you complete the repair?	—	Go to *Step 5*	—
5	Operate the system in order to verify the repair. Did you correct the condition?	—	System OK	Go to *Step 2*

GC4020152592000X

Fig. 63 Vehicle Stability Enhancement System Excessive Pulsation. LeSabre

Step	Action	Value(s)	Yes	No
8	Inspect the mounting of the lateral accelerometer sensor. Did you find and correct the condition?	—	Go to *Step 15*	Go to *Step 9*
9	Inspect the EBCM for the proper part number. Did you find the correct part number?	—	Go to *Step 10*	Go to *Step 12*
10	Inspect the power steering gear for the proper part number. Did you find the correct part number?	—	Go to *Step 11*	Go to *Step 13*
11	Inspect the alignment of the vehicle. Did you find and correct the condition?	—	Go to *Step 15*	*Test for Intermittent*
12	**Important:** Perform the setup procedure for the EBCM. An unprogrammed EBCM will result in the following conditions: • Inoperative or poorly functioning system operations • The EBCM sets DTC C1248 and DTC C1255m3. Replace the EBCM. Did you complete the repair?	—	Go to *Step 15*	—
13	Replace the power steering gear. Did you complete the repair?	—	Go to *Step 15*	—
14	Replace the steering wheel position sensor (SWPS). Did you complete the repair?	—	Go to *Step 15*	—
15	Operate the system in order to verify the repair. Did you correct the condition?	—	System OK	Go to *Step 2*

GC4020152591020X

Fig. 62 Vehicle Stability Enhancement System Unwanted Activation (Part 2 of 2). LeSabre

Important: The following steps must be completed before using the symptom tables.

1. Perform the *A Diagnostic System Check - ABS* before using the Symptom Tables in order to verify that all of the following are true:
   - There are no DTCs set.
   - The control module(s) can communicate via the serial data link.
2. Review the system operation in order to familiarize yourself with the system functions. Refer to the following:
   - *ABS Description*
   - *ABS Operation*

Visual/Physical Inspection

- Inspect for aftermarket devices which could affect the operation of the antilock brake system.
- Inspect the easily accessible or visible system components for obvious damage or conditions which could cause the symptom.
- Inspect the master cylinder reservoir for the proper brake fluid level.

Intermittent

Faulty electrical connections or wiring may be the cause of intermittent conditions.

Symptom List

Refer to a symptom diagnostic procedure from the following list in order to diagnose the symptom:

- *No Communication with EBCM*
- *Vehicle Stability Enhancement System Inoperative*
- *Vehicle Stability Enhancement System Unwanted Activation*
- *Vehicle Stability Enhancement System Excessive Brake Pulsation*
- *ABS Indicator Always On*
- *ABS Indicator Inoperative*
- *TRAC OFF Indicator Always On*
- *TRAC OFF Indicator Inoperative*

GC4020152569000X

Fig. 64 ABS Symptoms. Park Avenue

Circuit Description

The instrument cluster controls the operation of the ABS indicator. The EBCM reports the desired status of the ABS indicator via serial data messages. The ABS indicator signal circuit is a back-up reporting circuit to the serial data messages. The EBCM supplies ground through the circuit when the ABS is operating properly. When there is a problem with ABS that should turn on the ABS indicator, the EBCM opens the ABS indicator signal circuit. If there is a problem with the ABS serial data messages, the instrument cluster uses the ABS indicator signal to determine if the ABS indicator should be illuminated. Using the serial data messages and back-up circuit, the instrument cluster decides whether to turn on the ABS indicator.

Test Description

The numbers below refer to the step numbers on the diagnostic table.

3. Use the scan tool to check the normal state of the ABS indicator control circuit.
4. Ensures that the instrument cluster can operate the ABS indicator.

Step	Action	Yes	No
1	Did you perform the ABS Diagnostic System Check?	Go to *Step 2*	Go to *A Diagnostic System Check - ABS*
2	Inspect the EBCM ground, making sure the ground is clean and torqued to the proper specification. Did you find and correct the condition?	Go to *Step 9*	Go to *Step 3*
3	1. Install a scan tool. 2. Turn ON the ignition, with the engine OFF. 3. With a scan tool, observe the ABS Warning Indicator parameter in the DRP/ABS/TCS data list. Does the scan tool display Off?	Go to *Step 4*	Go to *Step 5*
4	1. Turn OFF the ignition. 2. Turn ON the ignition, with the engine OFF. 3. Observe the ABS indicator on the instrument cluster (IPC) during the bulb check. Does the ABS indicator illuminate during the bulb check and then turn OFF?	*Test for Intermittent*	Go to *Step 6*
5	Inspect for poor connections at the harness connector of the EBCM. Did you find and correct the condition?	Go to *Step 9*	Go to *Step 7*
6	Inspect for poor connections at the harness connector of the instrument cluster (IPC). Did you find and correct the condition?	Go to *Step 9*	Go to *Step 8*
7	**Important:** Perform the setup procedure for the EBCM. An unprogrammed EBCM will result in the following conditions: • Inoperative or poorly functioning system operations • The EBCM sets DTC C1248 and DTC C1255m3. Replace the EBCM. Did you complete the repair?	Go to *Step 9*	—
8	Replace the instrument cluster (IPC). Did you complete the repair?	Go to *Step 9*	—
9	Operate the system in order to verify the repair. Did you correct the condition?	System OK	Go to *Step 2*

GC4020152593000X

Fig. 65 ABS Indicator Always On. Park Avenue

Circuit Description

The instrument cluster controls the operation of the ABS indicator. The EBCM reports the desired status of the ABS indicator via serial data messages. The ABS indicator signal circuit is a back-up reporting circuit to the serial data messages. The EBCM supplies ground through the circuit when the ABS is operating properly. When there is a problem with ABS that should turn on the ABS indicator, the EBCM opens the ABS indicator signal circuit. If there is a problem with the ABS serial data messages, the instrument cluster uses the ABS indicator signal to determine if the ABS indicator should be illuminated. Using the serial data messages and back-up circuit, the instrument cluster decides whether to turn on the ABS indicator.

Test Description

The numbers below refer to the step numbers on the diagnostic table.

3. Use the scan tool to check the normal state of the ABS indicator control circuit.
4. Ensures that the instrument cluster can operate the ABS indicator.

Step	Action	Yes	No
1	Did you perform the ABS Diagnostic System Check?	Go to *Step 2*	Go to *A Diagnostic System Check - ABS*
2	Inspect the EBCM ground, making sure the ground is clean and torqued to the proper specification. Did you find and correct the condition?	Go to *Step 9*	Go to *Step 3*
3	1. Install a scan tool. 2. Turn ON the ignition, with the engine OFF. 3. With a scan tool, observe the ABS Warning Indicator parameter in the DRP/ABS/TCS data list. Does the scan tool display Off?	Go to *Step 4*	Go to *Step 5*
4	1. Turn OFF the ignition. 2. Turn ON the ignition, with the engine OFF. 3. Observe the ABS indicator on the instrument cluster (IPC) during the bulb check. Does the ABS indicator illuminate during the bulb check and then turn OFF?	*Test for Intermittent*	Go to *Step 6*
5	Inspect for poor connections at the harness connector of the EBCM. Did you find and correct the condition?	Go to *Step 9*	Go to *Step 7*
6	Inspect for poor connections at the harness connector of the instrument cluster (IPC). Did you find and correct the condition?	Go to *Step 9*	Go to *Step 8*
7	**Important:** Perform the setup procedure for the EBCM. An unprogrammed EBCM will result in the following conditions: • Inoperative or poorly functioning system operations • The EBCM sets DTC C1248 and DTC C1255m3. Replace the EBCM. Did you complete the repair?	Go to *Step 9*	—
8	Replace the instrument cluster (IPC). Did you complete the repair?	Go to *Step 9*	—
9	Operate the system in order to verify the repair. Did you correct the condition?	System OK	Go to *Step 2*

GC4020152594000X

Fig. 66 ABS Indicator Inoperative. Park Avenue

Circuit Description

The Traction Off indicator is controlled by the instrument cluster via serial data messages from the EBCM. When the body control module sees the traction control switch input grounded through the momentary traction control switch, it sends a serial data message to the EBCM that tells the EBCM that the traction control switch has been pressed. The EBCM then disables traction control and sends a serial data message to the instrument cluster to turn the Traction Off indicator ON. Each time the ignition is cycled from OFF to ON, the traction control system is enabled.

The following conditions will cause the Traction Off indicator to illuminate:

- The EBCM has disabled the TCS due to a DTC.
- The driver manually disabling the TCS via the traction control switch.
- The instrument cluster bulb check. When the ignition switch is turned to ON, the Traction Off indicator will turn on for approximately 3 seconds and then turn OFF.

Test Description

The numbers below refer to the step numbers on the diagnostic table.

2. Use the scan tool to check the normal state of the Traction Off indicator control.
3. Ensures that the instrument cluster can operate the Traction Off indicator.

Step	Action	Yes	No
Schematic Reference: *ABS Schematics*			
1	Did you perform the ABS Diagnostic System Check?	Go to *Step 2*	Go to *A Diagnostic System Check - ABS*
2	1. Install a scan tool. 2. Turn ON the ignition, with the engine OFF. 3. With a scan tool, observe the TCS Warning Indicator/Message parameter in the DRP/ABS/TCS data list. Does the scan tool display Off?	Go to *Step 3*	Go to *Step 4*
3	1. Turn OFF the ignition. 2. Turn ON the ignition, with the engine OFF. 3. Observe the Traction Off indicator on the instrument cluster (IPC) during the bulb check. Does the Traction Off indicator illuminate during the bulb check and then turn OFF?	*Test for Intermittent*	Go to *Step 5*
4	Inspect for poor connections at the harness connector of the EBCM. Did you find and correct the condition?	Go to *Step 8*	Go to *Step 6*
5	Inspect for poor connections at the harness connector of the instrument cluster (IPC). Did you find and correct the condition?	Go to *Step 8*	Go to *Step 7*
6	**Important:** Perform the setup procedure for the EBCM. An unprogrammed EBCM will result in the following conditions: • Inoperative or poorly functioning system operations • The EBCM sets DTC C1248 and DTC C1255m3. Replace the EBCM. Did you complete the repair?	Go to *Step 8*	—
7	Replace the instrument cluster (IPC). Did you complete the repair?	Go to *Step 8*	—
8	Operate the system in order to verify the repair. Did you correct the condition?	System OK	Go to *Step 2*

GC4020152595000X

Fig. 67 Traction Off Indicator Always On. Park Avenue

Circuit Description

The Traction Off indicator is controlled by the instrument cluster via serial data messages from the EBCM. When the body control module sees the traction control switch input grounded through the momentary traction control switch, it sends a serial data message to the EBCM that tells the EBCM that the traction control switch has been pressed. The EBCM then disables traction control and sends a serial data message to the instrument cluster to turn the Traction Off indicator ON. Each time the ignition is cycled from OFF to ON, the traction control system is enabled.

The following conditions will cause the Traction Off indicator to illuminate:

- The EBCM has disabled the TCS due to a DTC.
- The driver manually disabling the TCS via the traction control switch.
- The instrument cluster bulb check. When the ignition switch is turned to ON, the Traction Off indicator will turn on for approximately 3 seconds and then turn OFF.

Test Description

The numbers below refer to the step numbers on the diagnostic table.

2. Use the scan tool to check the normal state of the Traction Off indicator control.
3. Ensures that the instrument cluster can operate the Traction Off indicator.

Step	Action	Yes	No
1	Did you perform the ABS Diagnostic System Check?	Go to *Step 2*	Go to *A Diagnostic System Check - ABS*
2	1. Install a scan tool. 2. Turn ON the ignition, with the engine OFF. 3. With a scan tool, observe the TCS Warning Indicator/Message parameter in the DRP/ABS/TCS data list. Does the scan tool display Off?	Go to *Step 3*	Go to *Step 13*
3	1. Turn OFF the ignition. 2. Turn ON the ignition, with the engine OFF. 3. Observe the Traction Off indicator on the instrument cluster (IPC) during the bulb check. Does the Traction Off indicator illuminate during the bulb check and then turn OFF?	Go to *Step 4*	Go to *Step 14*
4	1. Turn OFF the ignition. 2. Install a scan tool. 3. Turn ON the ignition, with the engine OFF. 4. With a scan tool, observe the Traction Switch parameter in the Body Control Module data list. 5. Activate the traction control switch. Does the Traction Switch parameter change state?	*Test for Intermittent*	Go to *Step 5*
5	Does the scan indicate that the Traction Switch parameter is On?	Go to *Step 6*	Go to *Step 7*
6	1. Turn OFF the ignition. 2. Disconnect the traction control switch connector. 3. Turn ON the ignition, with the engine OFF. 4. With a scan tool, observe the Traction Switch parameter. Does the scan tool display Off?	Go to *Step 12*	Go to *Step 8*
7	1. Turn OFF the ignition. 2. Disconnect the traction control switch connector. 3. Connect a 3 amp fused jumper from the signal circuit of the traction control switch to the ground circuit of the traction control switch. 4. Turn ON the ignition, with the engine OFF. 5. With a scan tool, observe the Traction Switch parameter. Does the scan tool display On?	Go to *Step 12*	Go to *Step 9*

GC4020152596010X

Fig. 68 Traction Off Indicator Inoperative (Part 1 of 2). Park Avenue

Step	Action	Yes	No
8	Test the signal circuit of the traction control switch for a short to ground. Did you find and correct the condition?	Go to *Step 19*	Go to *Step 11*
9	Test the signal circuit of the traction control switch for an open or high resistance. Did you find and correct the condition?	Go to *Step 19*	Go to *Step 10*
10	Test the ground circuit of the traction control switch for an open or high resistance. Did you find and correct the condition?	Go to *Step 19*	Go to *Step 11*
11	Inspect for poor connections at the harness connector of the body control module (SBM). Did you find and correct the condition?	Go to *Step 19*	Go to *Step 15*
12	Inspect for poor connections at the harness connector of the traction control switch. Did you find and correct the condition?	Go to *Step 19*	Go to *Step 16*
13	Inspect for poor connections at the harness connector of the EBCM. Did you find and correct the condition?	Go to *Step 19*	Go to *Step 17*
14	Inspect for poor connections at the harness connector of the instrument cluster (IPC). Did you find and correct the condition?	Go to *Step 19*	Go to *Step 18*
15	Replace the body control module (SBM). Did you complete the replacement?	Go to *Step 19*	—
16	Replace the traction control switch. Did you complete the replacement?	Go to *Step 19*	—
17	**Important:** Perform the setup procedure for the EBCM. An unprogrammed EBCM will result in the following conditions: • Inoperative or poorly functioning system operations • The EBCM sets DTC C1248 and DTC C1255m3. Replace the EBCM. Did you complete the repair?	Go to *Step 19*	—
18	Replace the instrument cluster (IPC). Did you complete the repair?	Go to *Step 19*	—
19	Operate the system in order to verify the repair. Did you correct the condition?	System OK	Go to *Step 2*

GC4020152596020X

Fig. 68 Traction Off Indicator Inoperative (Part 2 of 2). Park Avenue

Circuit Description

The vehicle stability enhancement system (VSES) is activated by the EBCM calculating the desired yaw rate and comparing it to the actual yaw rate input. The desired yaw rate is calculated from measured steering wheel position, vehicle speed, and lateral acceleration. The difference between the desired yaw rate and actual yaw rate is the yaw rate error, which is a measurement of oversteer or understeer. If the yaw rate error becomes too large, the EBCM will attempt to correct the vehicle's yaw motion by applying differential braking to the left or right front wheel.

The VSES activations generally occur during aggressive driving, in the turns or bumpy roads without much use of the accelerator pedal. When braking during VSES activation, the brake pedal will feel different than the ABS pedal pulsation. The brake pedal pulsates at a higher frequency during VSES activation.

The usable output voltage range for the lateral accelerometer and yaw rate sensors is 0.25–4.75 volts. The scan tool will report zero lateral acceleration or yaw rate as 2.5 volts with no sensor bias present. The sensor bias compensates for sensor mounting alignment errors, electronic signal errors, temperature changes, and manufacturing differences.

The steering wheel position sensor supplies 2 analog inputs, Phase A and Phase B, to the EBCM. The 2 input signals are approximately 90 degrees out of phase. By interpreting the relationship between the 2 inputs, the EBCM can determine the position of the steering wheel and the direction of steering wheel rotation.

Steer angle centering is the process by which the EBCM calibrates the steering sensor output so that the output reads zero when the steering wheel is centered. Using the yaw rate input, lateral accelerometer input, and wheel speed sensor inputs, the initial steering center position is calculated after driving greater than 10 km/h (6 mph) for more than 10 seconds in a straight line on a level surface.

Test Description

The numbers below refer to the step numbers on the diagnostic table.

3. Perform the Steering Position Sensor Test in order to verify if the steering wheel position sensor (SWPS) is operating properly.
4. Verify that the lateral accelerometer input parameter is within the valid range.
5. Verify that the yaw rate input parameter is within the valid range.

GC4020152597010X

Fig. 69 Vehicle Stability Enhancement System Inoperative (Part 1 of 2). Park Avenue

Step	Action	Value(s)	Yes	No
1	Did you perform the ABS Diagnostic System Check?	—	Go to *Step 2*	Go to *A Diagnostic System Check - ABS*
2	1. Install a scan tool. 2. Start the engine. 3. Observe the VSES Is Centered parameter in the VSES data list. 4. Perform the Diagnostic Test Drive. Did the scan tool display Yes within the specified value?	30 seconds	*Test for Intermittent*	Go to *Step 3*
3	With the scan tool, perform the Steering Position Sensor Test. Did the SWPS pass the test?	—	Go to *Step 4*	Go to *Step 7*
4	With a scan tool, observe the Lateral Accelerometer Input parameter in the VSES data list. Does the scan tool display within the specified range?	2.3–2.7 V	Go to *Step 5*	Go to *Step 8*
5	With a scan tool, observe the Yaw Rate Sensor Input parameter in the VSES data list. Does the scan tool display within the specified range?	2.3–2.7 V	Go to *Step 6*	Go to *Step 9*
6	**Important:** Perform the setup procedure for the EBCM. An unprogrammed EBCM will result in the following conditions: • Inoperative or poorly functioning system operations • The EBCM sets DTC C1248 and DTC C1255m3. Replace the EBCM. Did you complete the repair?	—	Go to *Step 10*	—
7	Replace the steering wheel position sensor (SWPS). Did you complete the replacement?	—	Go to *Step 10*	—
8	Replace the lateral accelerometer sensor. Did you complete the replacement?	—	Go to *Step 10*	—
9	Replace the yaw rate sensor. Did you complete the replacement?	—	Go to *Step 10*	—
10	Operate the system in order to verify the repair. Did you correct the condition?	—	System OK	Go to *Step 2*

GC4020152597020X

Fig. 69 Vehicle Stability Enhancement System Inoperative (Part 2 of 2). Park Avenue

Circuit Description

The vehicle stability enhancement system (VSES) is activated by the EBCM calculating the desired yaw rate and comparing it to the actual yaw rate input. The desired yaw rate is calculated from measured steering wheel position, vehicle speed, and lateral acceleration. The difference between the desired yaw rate and actual yaw rate is the yaw rate error, which is a measurement of oversteer or understeer. If the yaw rate error becomes too large, the EBCM will attempt to correct the vehicle's yaw motion by applying differential braking to the left or right front wheel.

The VSES activations generally occur during aggressive driving, in the turns or bumpy roads without much use of the accelerator pedal. When braking during VSES activation, the brake pedal will feel different than the ABS pedal pulsation. The brake pedal pulsates at a higher frequency during VSES activation.

The usable output voltage range for the lateral accelerometer and yaw rate sensors is 0.25–4.75 volts. The scan tool will report zero lateral acceleration or yaw rate as 2.5 volts with no sensor bias present. The sensor bias compensates for sensor mounting alignment errors, electronic signal errors, temperature changes, and manufacturing differences.

The steering wheel position sensor supplies 2 analog inputs, Phase A and Phase B, to the EBCM. The 2 input signals are approximately 90 degrees out of phase. By interpreting the relationship between the 2 inputs, the EBCM can determine the position of the steering wheel and the direction of steering wheel rotation.

Steer angle centering is the process by which the EBCM calibrates the steering sensor output so that the output reads zero when the steering wheel is centered. Using the yaw rate input, lateral accelerometer input, and wheel speed sensor inputs, the initial steering center position is calculated after driving greater than 10 km/h (6 mph) for more than 10 seconds in a straight line on a level surface.

Test Description

The number below refers to the step number on the diagnostic table.

6. Perform the Steering Position Sensor Test in order to verify if the steering wheel position sensor (SWPS) is operating properly.

Step	Action	Value(s)	Yes	No
1	Did you perform the ABS Diagnostic System Check?	—	Go to *Step 2*	Go to *A Diagnostic System Check - ABS*
2	Inspect the mounting of the yaw rate sensor. Did you find and correct the condition?	—	Go to *Step 15*	Go to *Step 3*
3	1. Install a scan tool. 2. Start the engine. 3. With a scan tool, observe the Yaw Rate Sensor Input parameter in the VSES data list. 4. Perform the Diagnostic Test Drive. Does the scan tool display suddenly increase or decrease without rapid turning of the vehicle?	—	Go to *Step 4*	Go to *Step 5*
4	Perform the diagnosis for DTC C1282. Did you find and correct the condition?	—	Go to *Step 15*	Go to *Step 12*
5	1. Straighten the front wheels. 2. Observe the Dual Analog SWPS Input A and Dual Analog SWPS Input B in the VSES data list. 3. Slowly rotate the steering wheel in both directions. Does the scan tool display change states as the steering wheel was rotated?	—	Go to *Step 6*	Go to *Step 14*
6	With the scan tool, perform the Steering Position Sensor Test. Did the SWPS pass the test?	—	Go to *Step 7*	Go to *Step 14*

GC4020152598010X

Fig. 70 Vehicle Stability Enhancement System Unwanted Activation (Part 1 of 2). Park Avenue

Step	Action	Value(s)	Yes	No
7	1. Place the vehicle on a level surface. 2. With a scan tool, observe the Lateral Accelerometer Input parameter in the VSES data list. Does the scan tool display within the specified range?	2.3–2.7 V	Go to *Step 9*	Go to *Step 8*
8	Inspect the mounting of the lateral accelerometer sensor. Did you find and correct the condition?	—	Go to *Step 15*	Go to *Step 9*
9	Inspect the EBCM for the proper part number. Did you find the correct part number?	—	Go to *Step 10*	Go to *Step 12*
10	Inspect the power steering gear for the proper part number. Did you find the correct part number?	—	Go to *Step 11*	Go to *Step 13*
11	Inspect the alignment of the vehicle. Did you find and correct the condition?	—	Go to *Step 15*	*Test for Intermittent*
12	**Important:** Perform the setup procedure for the EBCM. An unprogrammed EBCM will result in the following conditions: • Inoperative or poorly functioning system operations • The EBCM sets DTC C1248 and DTC C1255m3. Replace the EBCM. Did you complete the repair?	—	Go to *Step 15*	—
13	Replace the power steering gear. Did you complete the repair?	—	Go to *Step 15*	—
14	Replace the steering wheel position sensor (SWPS). Did you complete the repair?	—	Go to *Step 15*	—
15	Operate the system in order to verify the repair. Did you correct the condition?	—	System OK	Go to *Step 2*

GC4020152598020X

Fig. 70 Vehicle Stability Enhancement System Unwanted Activation (Part 2 of 2). Park Avenue

Circuit Description

The vehicle stability enhancement system (VSES) is activated by the EBCM calculating the desired yaw rate and comparing it to the actual yaw rate input. The desired yaw rate is calculated from measured steering wheel position, vehicle speed, and lateral acceleration. The difference between the desired yaw rate and actual yaw rate is the yaw rate error, which is a measurement of oversteer or understeer. If the yaw rate error becomes too large, the EBCM will attempt to correct the vehicle's yaw motion by applying differential braking to the left or right front wheel.

The VSES activations generally occur during aggressive driving, in the turns or bumpy roads without much use of the accelerator pedal. When braking during VSES activation, the brake pedal will feel different than the ABS pedal pulsation. The brake pedal pulsates at a higher frequency during VSES activation.

The usable output voltage range for the lateral accelerometer and yaw rate sensors is 0.25–4.75 volts. The scan tool will report zero lateral acceleration or yaw rate as 2.5 volts with no sensor bias present. The sensor bias compensates for sensor mounting alignment errors, electronic signal errors, temperature changes, and manufacturing differences.

The steering wheel position sensor supplies 2 analog inputs, Phase A and Phase B, to the EBCM. The 2 input signals are approximately 90 degrees out of phase. By interpreting the relationship between the 2 inputs, the EBCM can determine the position of the steering wheel and the direction of steering wheel rotation.

Steer angle centering is the process by which the EBCM calibrates the steering sensor output so that the output reads zero when the steering wheel is centered. Using the yaw rate input, lateral accelerometer input, and wheel speed sensor inputs, the initial steering center position is calculated after driving greater than 10 km/h (6 mph) for more than 10 seconds in a straight line on a level surface.

Step	Action	Value(s)	Yes	No
1	Did you perform the ABS Diagnostic System Check?	—	Go to *Step 2*	Go to *A Diagnostic System Check - ABS*
2	1. Install a scan tool. 2. Turn ON the ignition, with the engine OFF. 3. Select the display DTCs function on the scan tool for the powertrain control module (PCM). Does the scan tool display DTC P1575?	—	*Diagnose Engine Controls*	Go to *Step 3*
3	1. With a scan tool, observe the Extended Travel Brake Switch parameter in the DRP/ABS/TCS data list. 2. Step on and off the brake pedal with enough force to simulate a hard braking condition. As the brake pedal is pressed and released, the scan tool should read Applied and Released. 3. Use a tape measure in order to measure the distance that the brake pedal travels for the scan tool to read Applied. Does the distance measure within the specified range?	1.0–1.3 in (2.5–3.3 cm)	*Test for Intermittent*	Go to *Step 4*
4	Adjust or repair the extended travel brake switch as necessary. Did you complete the repair?	—	Go to *Step 5*	—
5	Operate the system in order to verify the repair. Did you correct the condition?	—	System OK	Go to *Step 2*

GC4020152599000X

Fig. 71 Vehicle Stability Enhancement System Excessive Brake Pulsation. Park Avenue

Circuit Description

The ABS Diagnostic System Check is an organized approach to identify problems associated with the EBCM. This check must be the starting point for any EBCM complaint, and will direct you to the next logical step in diagnosing the complaint. The EBCM is a very reliable component and is not likely the cause of the malfunction. Most system complaints are linked to faulty wiring, connectors, and occasionally to components. Understanding the ABS system and using the tables correctly will reduce diagnostic time and prevent unnecessary parts replacement.

Test Description

The numbers below refer to the step numbers on the diagnostic table.

2. Lack of communication may be due to a partial malfunction of the serial data circuit or due to a total malfunction of the serial data circuit. The specified procedure will determine the particular condition.
4. The presence of DTCs which begin with "U" indicate some other module is not communicating. The specified procedure will compile all the available information before tests are performed.

Step	Action	Yes	No
1	Install a scan tool. Does the scan tool power up?	Go to *Step 2*	*Diagnose* Data Link Communications
2	1. Turn ON the ignition, with the engine OFF. 2. Attempt to establish communication with the following control modules: • Electronic brake control module (EBCM) • Electronic suspension control module • Instrument panel cluster (IPC) • HVAC control module (Instrument panel module) • Powertrain control module (PCM) Does the scan tool communicate with all control modules?	Go to *Step 3*	*Diagnose* Data Link Communications
3	Select the display DTCs function on the scan tool for the following control modules: • Electronic brake control module (EBCM) • Electronic suspension control module • Instrument panel cluster (IPC) • HVAC control module (Instrument panel module) • Powertrain control module (PCM) Does the scan tool display any DTCs?	Go to *Step 4*	Go to *Symptoms - Antilock Brake System*
4	Does the scan tool display any DTCs which begin with a "U"?	*Diagnose* Data Link Communications	Go to *Step 5*
5	Does the scan tool display DTC B1000, B1004, B1007, B1009, B1013, or B1014?	*Diagnose* Body Control System	Go to *Step 6*
6	Does the scan tool display DTC B1327, B1513, or B1514?	*Diagnose* Engine Electrical	Go to *Diagnostic Trouble Code (DTC) List*

GC4020152633000X

Fig. 72 Diagnostic System Check. DeVille & Seville

Circuit Description

The instrument cluster controls the operation of the ABS indicator. The EBCM reports the desired status of the ABS indicator via serial data messages. The ABS indicator signal circuit is a back-up reporting circuit to the serial data messages. The EBCM supplies ground through the circuit when the ABS is operating properly. When there is a problem with ABS that should turn on the ABS indicator, the EBCM opens the ABS indicator signal circuit. If there is a problem with the ABS serial data messages, the instrument cluster uses the ABS indicator signal to determine if the ABS indicator should be illuminated. Using the serial data messages and back-up circuit, the instrument cluster decides whether to turn on the ABS indicator.

Conditions for Running the DTC

The EBCM commands the indicator OFF.

Conditions for Setting the DTC

The ABS indicator signal circuit voltage is greater than 4.5 volts for 2 seconds.

Action Taken When the DTC Sets

- The ABS remains functional.
- The ABS indicator remains OFF.

Conditions for Clearing the DTC

- The condition for the DTC is no longer present (the DTC is not current) and you used the scan tool Clear DTC function.
- The condition for the DTC is no longer present (the DTC is not current) and you used the On-Board Diagnostics Clear DTC function.
- The EBCM automatically clears the history DTC when a current DTC is not detected in 100 consecutive drive cycles.

Diagnostic Aids

A possible cause of this DTC is a short to battery in the ABS indicator signal circuit.

Test Description

The numbers below refer to the step numbers on the diagnostic table.

2. Use the scan tool to verify the normal state of the ABS indicator signal circuit.
3. Ensure that the instrument cluster can operate the ABS indicator.

GC4020152634010X

Fig. 73 Code C1211: ABS Indicator Lamp Circuit Fault (Part 1 of 2). DeVille & Seville

Step	Action	Yes	No
1	Did you perform the ABS Diagnostic System Check?	Go to *Step 2*	Go to *Diagnostic System Check - ABS*
2	1. Install a scan tool. 2. Turn ON the ignition, with the engine OFF. 3. With a scan tool, observe the ABS Warning Indicator parameter in the DRP/ABS/TCS data list. Does the scan tool display Off?	Go to *Step 3*	Go to *Step 4*
3	1. Turn OFF the ignition. 2. Turn ON the ignition, with the engine OFF. 3. Observe the ABS indicator on the instrument cluster (IPC) during the bulb check. Does the ABS indicator illuminate during the bulb check?	Go to *Step 4*	Go to *Step 6*
4	1. Turn OFF the ignition. 2. Disconnect the EBCM harness connector 3. Connect the *J 39700* universal pinout box using the *J 39700-300* cable adapter to the EBCM harness connector only. 4. Disconnect the instrument cluster harness connector. 5. Test the ABS indicator signal circuit for a short to voltage. Did you find and correct the condition?	Go to *Step 9*	Go to *Step 5*
5	Inspect for poor connections at the harness connector of the EBCM. Did you find and correct the condition?	Go to *Step 9*	Go to *Step 7*
6	Inspect for poor connections at the harness connector of the instrument cluster. Did you find and correct the condition?	Go to *Step 9*	Go to *Step 8*
7	**Important:** Perform the setup procedure for the EBCM. An unprogrammed EBCM will result in the following conditions: • Inoperative or poorly functioning system operations • The EBCM sets DTC C1248 and DTC C1255m3 Replace the EBCM. Did you complete the repair?	Go to *Step 9*	—
8	Replace the instrument cluster (IPC). Did you complete the repair?	Go to *Step 9*	—
9	1. Use the scan tool in order to clear the DTCs. 2. Operate the vehicle within the Conditions for Running the DTC as specified in the supporting text. Does the DTC reset?	Go to *Step 2*	System OK

GC4020152634020X

Fig. 73 Code C1211: ABS Indicator Lamp Circuit Fault (Part 2 of 2). DeVille & Seville

Circuit Description

The system relay is energized when the ignition is ON. The system relay supplies voltage to the solenoid valves and the pump motor. This voltage is referred to as the system voltage.

The EBCM controls each solenoid valve by grounding the solenoid.

The EBCM controls the pump motor by grounding the control circuit. The pump serves 2 purposes:

- Transfers brake fluid from the brake calipers to the master cylinder reservoir during pressure decrease events.
- Transfers brake fluid from the master cylinder reservoir to the brake calipers during pressure increase events.

Conditions for Running the DTC

- The ignition voltage is greater than 10.5 volts.
- The system relay is commanded ON.

Conditions for Setting the DTC

The system voltage is less than 8 volts for 0.23 seconds.

Action Taken When the DTC Sets

If equipped, the following actions occur:

- The EBCM disables the DRP/ABS/TCS/VSES for the duration of the ignition cycle.
- The ABS indicator turns ON.
- The Traction Control indicator turns ON.
- The DIC displays the Service Stability System message.
- The EBCM will also set DTC C1248.
- The red Brake warning indicator turns ON.

Conditions for Clearing the DTC

- The condition for the DTC is no longer present (the DTC is not current) and you used the scan tool Clear DTC function.
- The condition for the DTC is no longer present (the DTC is not current) and you used the On-Board Diagnostics Clear DTC function.
- The EBCM automatically clears the history DTC when a current DTC is not detected in 100 consecutive drive cycles.

Diagnostic Aids

The system relay is integral to the EBCM. The relay is not serviceable.

Test Description

The number below refers to the step number on the diagnostic table.

2. Determines whether the DTC is current.

GC4020152635010X

Fig. 74 Code C1214: System Relay Contact Or Coil Circuit Open (Part 1 of 2). DeVille & Seville

Step	Action	Value(s)	Yes	No
1	Did you perform the ABS Diagnostic System Check?	—	Go to *Step 2*	Go to *Diagnostic System Check - ABS*
2	1. Install a scan tool. 2. Turn ON the ignition, with the engine OFF. 3. Use the scan tool in order to clear the DTCs. 4. With the scan tool, perform the Automated Test. Does the DTC reset as a current DTC?	—	Go to *Step 3*	*Test for Intermittent*
3	1. Disconnect the pump motor harness pigtail connector of the brake pressure modulator valve (BPMV). 2. Measure the resistance between each pump motor control circuit and the housing of the BPMV at the pump motor harness pigtail connector of the BPMV. Does the DMM display the specified value?	OL	Go to *Step 5*	Go to *Step 4*
4	**Important:** Perform the setup procedure for the EBCM. An unprogrammed EBCM will result in the following conditions: • Inoperative or poorly functioning system operations • The EBCM sets DTC C1248 and DTC C1255m3 Replace the EBCM and the BPMV. Did you complete the repair?	—	Go to *Step 6*	—
5	**Important:** Perform the setup procedure for the EBCM. An unprogrammed EBCM will result in the following conditions: • Inoperative or poorly functioning system operations • The EBCM sets DTC C1248 and DTC C1255m3 Replace the EBCM. Did you complete the repair?	—	Go to *Step 6*	—
6	1. Use the scan tool in order to clear the DTCs. 2. With the scan tool, perform the Automated Test. Does the DTC reset?	—	Go to *Step 2*	System OK

GC4020152635020X

Fig. 74 Code C1214: System Relay Contact Or Coil Circuit Open (Part 2 of 2). DeVille & Seville

Circuit Description

The system relay is energized when the ignition is ON. The system relay supplies voltage to the solenoid valves and the pump motor. This voltage is referred to as the system voltage.

The EBCM controls each solenoid valve by grounding the solenoid.

The EBCM controls the pump motor by grounding the control circuit. The pump serves 2 purposes:

- Transfers brake fluid from the brake calipers to the master cylinder reservoir during pressure decrease events.
- Transfers brake fluid from the master cylinder reservoir to the brake calipers during pressure increase events.

Conditions for Running the DTC

- The pump motor has been commanded OFF for 1 second.
- The system voltage is greater than 9 volts.

Conditions for Setting the DTC

One of the following conditions exists for 0.2 seconds:

- The voltage across the pump motor is greater than 10.2 volts.
- The pump motor low side voltage is less than 2.7 volts.

Action Taken When the DTC Sets

If equipped, the following actions occur:

- The EBCM disables the DRP/ABS/TCS/VSES for the duration of the ignition cycle.
- The ABS indicator turns ON.
- The Traction Control indicator turns ON.
- The DIC displays the Service Stability System message.
- The EBCM will also set DTC C1248.
- The red Brake warning indicator turns ON.

Conditions for Clearing the DTC

- The condition for the DTC is no longer present (the DTC is not current) and you used the scan tool Clear DTC function.
- The condition for the DTC is no longer present (the DTC is not current) and you used the On-Board Diagnostics Clear DTC function.
- The EBCM automatically clears the history DTC when a current DTC is not detected in 100 consecutive drive cycles.

Diagnostic Aids

- This DTC determines if there is a short in the pump motor control circuit.
- The pump motor is integral to the BPMV. The pump motor is not serviceable.

Test Description

The number below refers to the step number on the diagnostic table.

3. Tests the pump motor circuits of the BPMV for a short to the housing of the BPMV. The wiring from the BPMV to the EBCM should not be repaired.

GC4020152636010X

Fig. 75 Code C1217: Pump Motor Shorted To Ground (Part 1 of 2). DeVille & Seville

Step	Action	Value(s)	Yes	No
1	Did you perform the ABS Diagnostic System Check?	—	Go to *Step 2*	Go to *Diagnostic System Check - ABS*
2	1. Turn OFF the ignition. 2. Disconnect the EBCM harness connector 3. Connect the *J 39700* universal pinout box using the *J 39700-300* cable adapter to the EBCM harness connector only. 4. Test both ground circuits of the EBCM including the EBCM ground for a high resistance or an open. Did you find and correct the condition?	—	Go to *Step 8*	Go to *Step 3*
3	1. Disconnect the pump motor harness pigtail connector of the BPMV. 2. Measure the resistance between each pump motor control circuit and the housing of the BPMV at the pump motor harness pigtail connector of the BPMV. Does the resistance measure less than the specified value?	5 Ω	Go to *Step 4*	Go to *Step 5*
4	Inspect for poor connections at the pump motor pigtail connector of the BPMV. Did you find and correct the condition?	—	Go to *Step 8*	Go to *Step 6*
5	Inspect for poor connections at the harness connector of the EBCM. Did you find and correct the condition?	—	Go to *Step 8*	Go to *Step 7*
6	Replace the BPMV. Did you complete the repair?	—	Go to *Step 8*	—
7	**Important:** Perform the setup procedure for the EBCM. An unprogrammed EBCM will result in the following conditions: • Inoperative or poorly functioning system operations • The EBCM sets DTC C1248 and DTC C1255m3 Replace the EBCM. Did you complete the repair?	—	Go to *Step 8*	—
8	1. Use the scan tool in order to clear the DTCs. 2. With the scan tool, perform the Automated Test. Does the DTC reset?	—	Go to *Step 2*	System OK

GC4020152636020X

Fig. 75 Code C1217: Pump Motor Shorted To Ground (Part 2 of 2). DeVille & Seville

Circuit Description

The system relay is energized when the ignition is ON. The system relay supplies voltage to the solenoid valves and the pump motor. This voltage is referred to as the system voltage.

The EBCM controls each solenoid valve by grounding the solenoid.

The EBCM controls the pump motor by grounding the control circuit. The pump serves 2 purposes:

- Transfers brake fluid from the brake calipers to the master cylinder reservoir during pressure decrease events.
- Transfers brake fluid from the master cylinder reservoir to the brake calipers during pressure increase events.

Conditions for Running the DTC

- The pump motor is commanded ON.
- The system voltage is greater than 8 volts.

Conditions for Setting the DTC

One of the following conditions exists for 0.5 seconds:

- With the commanded pump motor voltage less than the system voltage, the actual pump motor voltage is 3 volts less than the commanded voltage.
- With the commanded pump motor voltage greater than the system voltage, the actual pump motor voltage is less than 8 volts.

Action Taken When the DTC Sets

If equipped, the following actions occur:

- The EBCM disables the ABS/TCS/VSES for the duration of the ignition cycle.
- The DRP does not function optimally.
- The ABS indicator turns ON.
- The Traction Control indicator turns ON.
- The DIC displays the Service Stability System message.

Conditions for Clearing the DTC

- The condition for the DTC is no longer present (the DTC is not current) and you used the scan tool Clear DTC function.
- The condition for the DTC is no longer present (the DTC is not current) and you used the On-Board Diagnostics Clear DTC function.
- The EBCM automatically clears the history DTC when a current DTC is not detected in 100 consecutive drive cycles.

Diagnostic Aids

The pump motor is integral to the BPMV. The pump motor is not serviceable.

Test Description

The number below refers to the step number on the diagnostic table.

3. Tests the ability of the EBCM to control the pump motor. If the test lamp illuminates, the pump motor circuit within the EBCM is good.

GC4020152637010X

Fig. 76 Code C1218: Pump Motor Circuit Shorted To Voltage Or Motor Ground Open (Part 1 of 2). DeVille & Seville

Step	Action	Yes	No
1	Did you perform the ABS Diagnostic System Check?	Go to *Step 2*	Go to *Diagnostic System Check - ABS*
2	1. Install a scan tool. 2. Turn ON the ignition, with the engine OFF. 3. Use the scan tool in order to clear the DTCs. 4. With the scan tool, perform the Automated Test. Does the DTC reset?	Go to *Step 3*	*Test for Intermittent*
3	1. Turn OFF the ignition. 2. Disconnect the pump motor harness pigtail connector of the BPMV. 3. Connect a test lamp between the pump motor circuits at the pump motor connector of the EBCM using the *J 35616-A* connector test adapter kit. 4. Use the scan tool in order to clear the DTCs. 5. With the scan tool, perform the Pump Motor Test. Does the test lamp illuminate?	Go to *Step 5*	Go to *Step 4*
4	1. Turn OFF the ignition. 2. Disconnect the EBCM harness connector. 3. Connect the *J 39700* universal pinout box using the *J 39700-300* cable adapter to the EBCM harness connector only. 4. Test both ground circuits of the EBCM including the EBCM ground for a high resistance or an open. Did you find and correct the condition?	Go to *Step 9*	Go to *Step 6*
5	Inspect for poor connections at the pump motor harness pigtail connector of the BPMV. Did you find and correct the condition?	Go to *Step 9*	Go to *Step 7*
6	Inspect for poor connections at the harness connector of the EBCM. Did you find and correct the condition?	Go to *Step 9*	Go to *Step 8*
7	Replace the BPMV. Did you complete the repair?	Go to *Step 9*	—
8	**Important:** Perform the setup procedure for the EBCM. An unprogrammed EBCM will result in the following conditions: • Inoperative or poorly functioning system operations • The EBCM sets DTC C1248 and DTC C1255m3 Replace the EBCM. Did you complete the repair?	Go to *Step 9*	—
9	1. Use the scan tool in order to clear the DTCs. 2. With the scan tool, perform the Automated Test. Does the DTC reset?	Go to *Step 2*	System OK

GC4020152637020X

Fig. 76 Code C1218: Pump Motor Circuit Shorted To Voltage Or Motor Ground Open (Part 2 of 2). DeVille & Seville

Circuit Description

As the wheel spins, the wheel speed sensor produces an AC signal. The EBCM uses the frequency of the AC signal to calculate the wheel speed.

Conditions for Running the DTC

C1221 through C1228

- DTCs C1232 through C1235 are not set.
- The brake pedal is not pressed.
- The ABS is not active.

C1232 through C1235

The ignition is ON.

Conditions for Setting the DTC

C1221 through C1224

All of the following conditions exists for 2.5 seconds:

- The suspect wheel speed equals zero.
- The other wheel speeds are greater than 8 km/h (5 mph).
- The other wheel speeds are within 11 km/h (7 mph) of each other.

C1225 through C1228

The EBCM detects a rapid variation in the wheel speed. The wheel speed changes by 16 km/h (10 mph) or more in 0.01 second. The change must occur 3 times with no more than 0.2 seconds between occurrences.

C1232 through C1235

One of the following conditions exists for 0.02 seconds:

- A short to voltage - the wheel speed sensor signal circuit and wheel speed sensor return circuit voltages are both greater than 4.25 volts.
- A short to ground - the wheel speed sensor signal circuit and wheel speed sensor return circuit voltages are both less than 0.75 volts.
- An open - the wheel speed sensor signal circuit voltage is greater than 4.25 volts and wheel speed sensor return circuit voltage is less than 0.75 volts.

Action Taken When the DTC Sets

If equipped, the following actions occur:

- The EBCM disables the ABS/TCS/VSES for the duration of the ignition cycle.
- The DRP does not function optimally.
- The ABS indicator turns ON.
- The Traction Control indicator turns ON.
- The DIC displays the Service Stability System message.

Conditions for Clearing the DTC

- The condition for the DTC is no longer present (the DTC is not current) and you used the scan tool Clear DTC function.
- The condition for the DTC is no longer present (the DTC is not current) and you used the On-Board Diagnostics Clear DTC function.
- The EBCM automatically clears the history DTC when a current DTC is not detected in 100 consecutive drive cycles.

Diagnostic Aids

C1221 through C1224

Under the following conditions, 2 Wheel Speed Sensor Input is 0 DTCs are set:

- The 2 suspect wheel speeds equal zero for 60 seconds.
- The other wheel speeds are greater than 16 km/h (10 mph).
- The other wheel speeds are within 11 km/h (7 mph) of each other.

Diagnose each wheel speed sensor individually.

C1225 through C1228

A possible cause of this DTC is electrical noise on the wheel speed sensor harness wiring. Electrical noise could result from the wheel speed sensor wires being routed to close to high energy ignition system components, such as spark plug wires.

C1232 through C1235

If the customer comments that the ABS indicator is ON only during moist environmental conditions (rain, snow, vehicle wash, etc.), inspect the wheel speed sensor wiring for signs of water intrusion. If the DTC is not current, clear all DTCs and simulate the effects of water intrusion by using the following procedure:

1. Spray the suspected area with a 5 percent saltwater solution. To create a 5 percent saltwater solution, add 2 teaspoons (9.9 ml) of salt to 354 ml (12 oz) of water.
2. Test drive the vehicle over various road surfaces (bumps, turns, etc.) above 40 km/h (25 mph) for at least 30 seconds.
3. If the DTC returns, replace the suspected wheel speed sensor or repair the wheel speed sensor wiring.
4. Rinse the area thoroughly when completed.

Test Description

The numbers below refer to the step numbers on the diagnostic table.

3. Measure the resistance of the wheel speed sensor in order to determine if the sensor has a valid resistance value.
4. Ensures that the wheel speed sensor is generating a valid AC voltage output.

GC4020152638010X

Fig. 77 Codes C1221-C1235: Wheel Speed Sensor (Part 1 of 3). DeVille & Seville

Step	Action	Value(s)	Yes	No
1	Did you perform the ABS Diagnostic System Check?	—	Go to *Step 2*	Go to *Diagnostic System Check - ABS*
2	1. Install a scan tool. 2. Turn ON the ignition. 3. Set up the scan tool snap shot feature to trigger for this DTC. 4. Drive the vehicle at a speed greater than the specified value. Does the scan tool indicate that this wheel speed DTC set?	8 km/h (5 mph)	Go to *Step 3*	Go to Diagnostic Aids
3	1. Raise and support the vehicle. 2. Disconnect the wheel speed sensor connector. 3. Measure the resistance across the wheel speed sensor. Does the resistance measure within the specified range?	850–1350 Ω	Go to *Step 4*	Go to *Step 8*
4	1. Spin the wheel. 2. Measure the AC voltage across the wheel speed sensor. Does the AC voltage measure greater than the specified value?	100 mV	Go to *Step 5*	Go to *Step 8*
5	Inspect for poor connections at the harness connector of the wheel speed sensor. Did you find and correct the condition?	—	Go to *Step 10*	Go to *Step 6*
6	1. Disconnect the EBCM harness connector. 2. Install the *J 39700* universal pinout box using the *J 39700-300* cable adapter to the EBCM harness connector only. 3. Test the wheel speed sensor circuits for the following: • An open • A short to ground • A short to voltage • Shorted together Did you find and correct the condition?	—	Go to *Step 10*	Go to *Step 7*
7	Inspect for poor connections at the harness connector for the EBCM. Did you find and correct the condition?	—	Go to *Step 10*	Go to *Step 9*

GC4020152638020X

Fig. 77 Codes C1221-C1235: Wheel Speed Sensor (Part 2 of 3). DeVille & Seville

Step	Action	Value(s)	Yes	No
8	Replace the wheel speed sensor. Did you complete the repair?	—	Go to *Step 10*	—
9	**Important:** Perform the setup procedure for the EBCM. An unprogrammed EBCM will result in the following conditions: • Inoperative or poorly functioning system operations • The EBCM sets DTC C1248 and DTC C1255m3 Replace the EBCM. Did you complete the repair?	—	Go to *Step 10*	—
10	1. Use the scan tool in order to clear the DTCs. 2. Operate the vehicle within the Conditions for Running the DTC as specified in the supporting text. Does the DTC reset?	—	Go to *Step 2*	System OK

GC4020152638030X

Fig. 77 Codes C1221-C1235: Wheel Speed Sensor (Part 3 of 3). DeVille & Seville

Step	Action	Value(s)	Yes	No
1	Did you perform the ABS Diagnostic System Check?	—	Go to *Step 2*	Go to *Diagnostic System Check - ABS*
2	1. Install a scan tool. 2. Start the engine. 3. With a scan tool, observe the Switched System Battery Voltage parameter in DRP/ABS/TCS data list. Does the scan tool indicate the voltage is greater than the specified value?	10.5 V	Go to Diagnostic Aids	Go to *Step 3*
3	With a scan tool, observe the Battery Voltage parameter in Dash Integration Module data list. Does the scan tool indicate the voltage is greater than the specified value?	10.5 V	Go to *Step 4*	*Diagnose* Engine Electrical
4	1. Turn OFF the ignition. 2. Disconnect the EBCM harness connector. 3. Install the *J 39700* universal pinout box using the *J 39700-300* cable adaptor to the EBCM harness connector only. 4. Test the ground circuits of the EBCM including the EBCM ground for a high resistance or an open. Did you find and correct the condition?	—	Go to *Step 7*	Go to *Step 5*
5	1. Reconnect the EBCM harness connector. 2. Turn ON the ignition, with the engine OFF. 3. Use the scan tool in order to clear the DTCs. 4. Operate the vehicle within the Conditions for Running the DTC as specified in the supporting text. Does the DTC reset?	—	Go to *Step 6*	Go to Diagnostic Aids
6	**Important:** Perform the setup procedure for the EBCM. An unprogrammed EBCM will result in the following conditions: • Inoperative or poorly functioning system operations • The EBCM sets DTC C1248 and DTC C1255m3 Replace the EBCM. Did you complete the repair?	—	Go to *Step 7*	—
7	1. Use the scan tool in order to clear the DTCs. 2. Operate the vehicle within the Conditions for Running the DTC as specified in the supporting text. Does the DTC reset?	—	Go to *Step 2*	System OK

GC4020152639020X

Fig. 78 Code C1236: Low System Supply Voltage (Part 2 of 2). DeVille & Seville

Circuit Description

The EBCM monitors the voltage level available for system operation. A low voltage condition prevents the system from operating properly.

Conditions for Running the DTC

- The vehicle speed is greater than 8 km/h (5 mph).
- The ignition voltage is less than 10.5 volts.
- The system relay is commanded ON.

Conditions for Setting the DTC

One of the following conditions exists for 0.72 seconds:

- During initialization or when the system is inactive, the system voltage is less than 10.5 volts.
- During the system operation, the system voltage is less than 9.0 volts.

Action Taken When the DTC Sets

If equipped, the following actions occur:

- The EBCM disables the ABS/TCS/VSES for the duration of the ignition cycle.
- The ABS indicator turns ON.
- The Traction Control indicator turns ON.
- The DIC displays the Service Stability System message.
- The DRP does not function optimally, or with system voltage less than 8.5 volts, the EBCM disables the DRP for the duration of the ignition cycle.
- When the EBCM disables the DRP, the following actions also occur:
  - The EBCM will also set DTC C1248.
  - The red Brake warning indicator turns ON.

Conditions for Clearing the DTC

- The condition for the DTC is no longer present (the DTC is not current) and you used the scan tool Clear DTC function.
- The condition for the DTC is no longer present (the DTC is not current) and you used the On-Board Diagnostics Clear DTC function.
- The EBCM automatically clears the history DTC when a current DTC is not detected in 100 consecutive drive cycles.

Diagnostic Aids

- Test the charging system. Refer to *Diagnostic System Check - Engine Electrical*
- Possible causes of this DTC are the following conditions:
  - A charging system malfunction
  - An excessive battery draw
  - A weak battery
  - A faulty system ground

Test Description

The numbers below refer to the step numbers on the diagnostic table.

2. Use the scan tool in order to inspect the voltage to the EBCM.
3. Use the scan tool in order to inspect the voltage to the dash integration module (DIM). A low voltage value in multiple modules indicates a concern in the charging system.
5. Verifies that the condition is still present.

GC4020152639010X

Fig. 78 Code C1236: Low System Supply Voltage (Part 1 of 2). DeVille & Seville

Circuit Description

The EBCM monitors the voltage level available for system operation. If the voltage level is too high, damage may result in the system. When the EBCM detects a high voltage condition, the EBCM turns OFF the system relay which removes battery voltage from the solenoid valves and pump motor.

Conditions for Running the DTC

The vehicle speed is greater than 8 km/h (5 mph).

Conditions for Setting the DTC

The system voltage is greater than 16.4 volts for 0.72 seconds.

Action Taken When the DTC Sets

If equipped, the following actions occur:

- The EBCM disables the DRP/ABS/TCS/VSES for the duration of the ignition cycle.
- The ABS indicator turns ON.
- The Traction Control indicator turns ON.
- The DIC displays the Service Stability System message.
- The EBCM will also set DTC C1248.
- The red Brake warning indicator turns ON.

Conditions for Clearing the DTC

- The condition for the DTC is no longer present (the DTC is not current) and you used the scan tool Clear DTC function.
- The condition for the DTC is no longer present (the DTC is not current) and you used the On-Board Diagnostics Clear DTC function.
- The EBCM automatically clears the history DTC when a current DTC is not detected in 100 consecutive drive cycles.

Diagnostic Aids

A possible cause of this DTC is overcharging.

Test Description

The numbers below refer to the step numbers on the diagnostic table.

2. Use the scan tool in order to inspect the voltage to the EBCM.
3. Use the scan tool in order to inspect the voltage to the dash integration module (DIM). A high voltage value in multiple modules indicates a concern in the charging system.
4. Verifies that the condition is still present.

Step	Action	Value(s)	Yes	No
1	Did you perform the ABS Diagnostic System Check?	—	Go to *Step 2*	Go to *Diagnostic System Check - ABS*
2	1. Turn OFF all of the accessories. 2. Install a scan tool. 3. Start the engine. 4. Run the engine at approximately 2,000 RPM. 5. With a scan tool, observe the Switched System Battery Voltage parameter in the DRP/ABS/TCS data list. Does the scan tool indicate that the voltage is greater than the specified value?	16.4 V	Go to *Step 3*	Go to Diagnostic Aids
3	With a scan tool, observe the Battery Voltage parameter in Dash Integration Module data list. Does the scan tool indicate the voltage is greater than the specified value?	16.4 V	*Diagnose* Engine Electrical	Go to *Step 4*
4	1. Use the scan tool in order to clear the DTCs. 2. Operate the vehicle within the conditions for Running the DTC as specified in the supporting test. Does the DTC reset?	—	Go to *Step 5*	Go to Diagnostic Aids
5	**Important:** Perform the setup procedure for the EBCM. An unprogrammed EBCM will result in the following conditions: • Inoperative or poorly functioning system operations • The EBCM sets DTC C1248 and DTC C1255m3 Replace the EBCM. Did you complete the repair?	—	Go to *Step 6*	—
6	1. Use the scan tool in order to clear the DTCs. 2. Operate the vehicle within the conditions for Running the DTC as specified in the supporting test. Does the DTC reset?	—	Go to *Step 2*	System OK

GC4020152640000X

Fig. 79 Code C1237: High System Supply Voltage. DeVille & Seville

Circuit Description

The EBCM monitors vehicle speed deceleration, system activation, and stoplamp switch active times in order to calculate an estimate of the brake rotor temperatures. If the EBCM calculates that the brake rotor temperatures have exceeded the thermal cutoff point, the EBCM will temporarily suspend the TCS function until the brake rotors cool. This feature is used to maintain braking effectiveness if normal base braking is required. An overly heated brake system could result in brake fade.

The EBCM continues calculating the brake rotor temperatures after the ignition is turned OFF. The EBCM remains awake until the EBCM calculates that the brake rotors cooled sufficiently. The cooling period may take up to 30 minutes.

Conditions for Running the DTC

The ABS conditions and the braking conditions are normal.

Conditions for Setting the DTC

This DTC sets when the estimated brake rotor temperature of either of the drive wheels exceeds 375°C (700°F). When the estimated brake rotor temperature of either of the drive wheels exceeds 375°C (700°F) during normal braking or normal ABS operations, the DTC does not set until the next TCS activation. The brake rotor temperature can exceed 375°C (700°F) without setting the DTC if a TCS activation has not occurred. When the estimated brake rotor temperature of either of the drive wheels exceeds 375°C (700°F) during a TCS activation, the DTC sets immediately, but the EBCM does not disable TCS until the end of the TCS event.

Action Taken When the DTC Sets

- The EBCM disables the TCS until the DTC becomes a history DTC.
- The DIC displays the Traction Suspended message.
- The ABS remains functional.

Conditions for Clearing the DTC

- The current DTC becomes history when the estimated brake rotor temperatures of both drive wheels decreases below 275°C (530°F). The following actions also occur:
  - The EBCM enables TCS.
  - The DIC displays the Traction Ready message.
- The condition for the DTC is no longer present (the DTC is not current) and you used the scan tool Clear DTC function.
- The condition for the DTC is no longer present (the DTC is not current) and you used the On-Board Diagnostics Clear DTC function.
- The EBCM automatically clears the history DTC when a current DTC is not detected in 100 consecutive drive cycles.

Diagnostic Aids

- With TCS temporarily disabled, the EBCM continues calculating the brake rotor temperatures after the ignition is turned OFF. Turning ON the ignition again while TCS is temporarily disabled will not re-enable TCS.
- The temperature is an estimate calculated by the EBCM.
- Possible causes of this DTC are the following conditions:
  - The brake usage is excessive.
  - The TCS usage is excessive.
  - The stoplamp switch is misaligned or damaged.

Test Description

The number below refers to the step number on the diagnostic table.

4. Use the scan tool in order to verify that the Brake Thermal Model is exceeded.

GC4020152641010X

Fig. 80 Code C1238: Brake Thermal Model Exceeded (Part 1 of 2). DeVille & Seville

Step	Action	Yes	No
1	Did you perform the ABS Diagnostic System Check?	Go to *Step 2*	Go to *Diagnostic System Check - ABS*
2	1. Install a scan tool. 2. Turn ON the ignition, with the engine OFF. 3. Select the display DTCs function on the scan tool for the EBCM. Does the scan tool display that this DTC is set current?	Go to *Step 4*	Go to *Step 3*
3	Since most occurrences of this DTC are caused by excessive braking, review with the customer to verify the conditions under which the DTC set. Did vehicle operation cause this DTC to set?	Go to Diagnostic Aids	Go to *Step 4*
4	1. Allow 30 minutes from the last time you drove the vehicle for the cooling of the brake rotors. 2. With a scan tool, observe the Brake Temp Status parameter in the DRP/ABS/TCS data list. Does the scan tool display Normal?	Go to *Step 6*	Go to *Step 5*
5	Inspect the alignment of the stoplamp switch. Did you find and correct the condition?	Go to *Step 8*	Go to *Step 6*
6	1. Use the scan tool in order to clear the DTCs. 2. Operate the vehicle within the Conditions for Running the DTC as specified in the supporting text. Does the DTC reset as a current DTC?	Go to *Step 7*	System OK
7	**Important:** Perform the setup procedure for the EBCM. An unprogrammed EBCM will result in the following conditions: • Inoperative or poorly functioning system operations • The EBCM sets DTC C1248 and DTC C1255m3 Replace the EBCM. Did you complete the repair?	Go to *Step 8*	—
8	1. Use the scan tool in order to clear the DTCs. 2. Operate the vehicle within the Conditions for Running the DTC as specified in the supporting text. Does the DTC reset?	Go to *Step 2*	System OK

GC4020152641020X

Fig. 80 Code C1238: Brake Thermal Model Exceeded (Part 2 of 2). DeVille & Seville

Circuit Description

The system relay is energized when the ignition is ON. The system relay supplies voltage to the solenoid valves and the pump motor. This voltage is referred to as the system voltage.

The EBCM controls each solenoid valve by grounding the solenoid.

The EBCM controls the pump motor by grounding the control circuit. The pump serves 2 purposes:

- Transfers brake fluid from the brake calipers to the master cylinder reservoir during pressure decrease events.
- Transfers brake fluid from the master cylinder reservoir to the brake calipers during pressure increase events.

Conditions for Running the DTC

C1242

- The system voltage is greater than 8.0 volts.
- The system relay is ON.
- The pump motor is commanded OFF.

C1243

- The pump motor is ON for at least 0.3 seconds.
- The system relay is ON.

Conditions for Setting the DTC

C1242

The voltage across the pump motor is between 1.7 – 10.2 volts for 2 seconds.

C1243

The pump motor is stalled or turning slowly.

Action Taken When the DTC Sets

If equipped, the following actions occur:

- The EBCM disables the ABS/TCS/VSES for the duration of the ignition cycle.
- The DRP does not function optimally.
- The ABS indicator turns ON.
- The Traction Control indicator turns ON.
- The DIC displays the Service Stability System message.

Conditions for Clearing the DTC

- The condition for the DTC is no longer present (the DTC is not current) and you used the scan tool Clear DTC function.
- The condition for the DTC is no longer present (the DTC is not current) and you used the On-Board Diagnostics Clear DTC function.
- The EBCM automatically clears the history DTC when a current DTC is not detected in 100 consecutive drive cycles.

Diagnostic Aids

The pump motor is integral to the BPMV. The pump motor is not serviceable.

Test Description

The number below refers to the step number on the diagnostic table.

3. Tests the ability of the EBCM to control the pump motor. If the test lamp illuminates, the pump motor circuit within the EBCM is good.

GC4020152642010X

Fig. 81 Code C1242 Or C1243: BPMV Pump Motor Circuit Fault (Part 1 of 2). DeVille & Seville

Step	Action	Yes	No
1	Did you perform the ABS Diagnostic System Check?	Go to *Step 2*	Go to *Diagnostic System Check - ABS*
2	1. Install a scan tool. 2. Turn ON the ignition, with the engine OFF. 3. Use the scan tool in order to clear the DTCs. 4. With the scan tool, perform the Automated Test. Does the DTC reset?	Go to *Step 3*	*Test for Intermittent*
3	1. Turn OFF the ignition. 2. Disconnect the pump motor harness pigtail connector of the BPMV. 3. Connect a test lamp between the pump motor circuits at the pump motor connector of the EBCM using the *J 35616-A* Connector Test Adapter Kit. 4. Use the scan tool in order to clear the DTCs. 5. With the scan tool, perform the Pump Motor Test. Does the test lamp illuminate?	Go to *Step 4*	Go to *Step 5*
4	Inspect for poor connections at the pump motor harness pigtail connector of the BPMV. Did you find and correct the condition?	Go to *Step 8*	Go to *Step 6*
5	Inspect for poor connections at the harness connector of the EBCM. Did you find and correct the condition?	Go to *Step 8*	Go to *Step 7*
6	Replace the BPMV. Did you complete the repair?	Go to *Step 8*	—
7	**Important:** Perform the setup procedure for the EBCM. An unprogrammed EBCM will result in the following conditions: • Inoperative or poorly functioning system operations • The EBCM sets DTC C1248 and DTC C1255m3 Replace the EBCM. Did you complete the repair?	Go to *Step 8*	—
8	1. Use the scan tool in order to clear the DTCs. 2. With the scan tool, perform the Automated Test. Does the DTC reset?	Go to *Step 2*	System OK

GC4020152642020X

Fig. 81 Code C1242 Or C1243: BPMV Pump Motor Circuit Fault (Part 2 of 2). DeVille & Seville

Circuit Description

The dynamic rear proportioning (DRP) is a control system that replaces the hydraulic proportioning function of the mechanical proportioning valve in the base brake system. The DRP control system is part of the operating software in the EBCM. The DRP uses active control with the existing ABS in order to regulate the vehicle's rear brake pressure.

Conditions for Running the DTC

One or more faults have been detected by the EBCM in the ABS/TCS systems.

Conditions for Setting the DTC

One of the following conditions exists:

- DTC C1214, C1217, C1237, C1254, C1255, C1261–1268, or C1271–1274 sets.
- DTC C1236 sets and the system voltage is less than 8.5 volts.
- Two wheel speed sensor DTCs on the same axle set.

Action Taken When the DTC Sets

- The EBCM disables the DRP for the duration of the ignition cycle.
- The red Brake warning indicator turns ON.

Conditions for Clearing the DTC

- The condition for the DTC is no longer present (the DTC is not current) and you used the scan tool Clear DTC function.
- The condition for the DTC is no longer present (the DTC is not current) and you used the On-Board Diagnostics Clear DTC function.
- The EBCM automatically clears the history DTC when a current DTC is not detected in 100 consecutive drive cycles.

Diagnostic Aids

- Use this DTC in order to differentiate which of the following conditions is present:
  - The EBCM turned ON the red Brake warning indicator.
  - The instrument cluster turned ON the red Brake warning indicator due to low brake fluid in the master cylinder reservoir.
  - The instrument cluster turned ON the red Brake warning indicator due to the application of the park brake.
- Diagnose any other ABS DTCs that set along with this DTC.

Test Description

The number below refers to the step number on the diagnostic table.

2. Verifies whether other ABS/TCS/VSES DTCs are set.

Step	Action	Yes	No
1	Did you perform the ABS Diagnostic System Check?	Go to *Step 2*	Go to *Diagnostic System Check - ABS*
2	1. Install a scan tool. 2. Turn ON the ignition, with the engine OFF. 3. Select the display DTCs function on the scan tool for the EBCM. Does the scan tool display any ABS/TCS/VSES DTCs?	Go to *Diagnostic Trouble Code (DTC) List*	Go to *Step 3*
3	1. Use the scan tool in order to clear the DTCs. 2. Operate the vehicle within the Conditions for Running the DTC as specified in the supporting text. Does the DTC reset?	Go to *Step 2*	*Test for Intermittent*

GC4020152643000X

Fig. 82 Code C1248: EBCM Turned Red Brake Warning Indicator On. DeVille & Seville

Circuit Description

The CVRSS calculates normal force and transmits a PWM signal to the EBCM via two dedicated data lines, one right, and one left. The EBCM supplies the pull up voltage. The EBCM uses this information to detect rough road conditions and allows for more aggressive braking on rough surfaces.

Conditions for Running the DTC

The ignition is ON.

Conditions for Setting the DTC

The CVRSS diagnoses a condition in the road sensing suspension system and sends a serial data message to the EBCM. The CVRSS will typically set a DTC and the EBCM will set this DTC.

Action Taken When the DTC Sets

- The EBCM disables the rough road detection function of the VSES for the duration of the ignition cycle.
- The ABS/TCS/VSES remains functional.

Conditions for Clearing the DTC

- The condition for the DTC is no longer present (the DTC is not current) and you used the scan tool Clear DTC function.
- The condition for the DTC is no longer present (the DTC is not current) and you used the On-Board Diagnostics Clear DTC function.
- The EBCM automatically clears the history DTC when a current DTC is not detected in 100 consecutive drive cycles.

Diagnostic Aids

This DTC is for information only. As an aid to the technician, this DTC indicates that there are no problems in the ABS/TCS system.

Step	Action	Yes	No
1	Did you perform the ABS Diagnostic System Check?	Go to *Diagnostic System Check*	Go to *Diagnostic System Check - ABS*

GC4020152644000X

Fig. 83 Code C1251: RSS Indicated Fault. DeVille & Seville

Circuit Description

The microprocessor contains a data storage area (keep alive memory) which can save pertinent data when the ignition is turned OFF. The keep alive memory (KAM) data is lost if battery power or module ground is removed from the module. The KAM area is an integral part of the microprocessor and cannot be serviced separately.

Conditions for Running the DTC

The ABS conditions and the braking conditions are normal.

Conditions for Setting the DTC

The microprocessor calculates a checksum on those areas of memory that hold critical operation data. This is done at a regular interval and is called the periodic checksum. The microprocessor also calculates a checksum on these memory locations when ever new data is written to them. This is called the running checksum.

To check the keep alive memory (KAM), the microprocessor compares the periodic checksum to the running checksum. If they do not match, the microprocessor sets the DTC.

Action Taken When the DTC Sets

If equipped, the following actions occur:

- The EBCM disables the DRP/ABS/TCS/VSES for the duration of the ignition cycle.
- The EBCM disables the variable effort steering (VES) for the duration of the ignition cycle.
- The ABS indicator turns ON.
- The Traction Control indicator turns ON.
- The DIC displays the Service Stability System and Service Steering System messages.
- The red Brake warning indicator turns ON.
- The EBCM will also set DTC C1248.
- The EBCM will not send serial data messages.
- The EBCM will not send the requested torque output to the PCM.
- The EBCM will not send the steering angle PWM output to the electronic suspension control module.

Conditions for Clearing the DTC

- The condition for the DTC is no longer present (the DTC is not current) and you used the scan tool Clear DTC function.
- The condition for the DTC is no longer present (the DTC is not current) and you used the On-Board Diagnostics Clear DTC function.
- The EBCM automatically clears the history DTC when a current DTC is not detected in 100 consecutive drive cycles.

Diagnostic Aids

Possible causes of this DTC are the following conditions:

- A loss of battery ground.
- A disconnected battery.
- A running reset. (A running reset is detected when the keep alive memory check sum is not updated properly.)
- A sudden drop in the system voltage to less than 5 volts.
- Long extended engine cranks that cause the battery voltage to drop.
- Poor power or ground connections.
- An internal EBCM malfunction.

Test Description

The numbers below refer to the step numbers on the diagnostic table.

2. Tests for an open in the ground circuits of the EBCM.
4. Verifies the proper operation of the charging system.
6. Determines whether the DTC resets.

GC4020152645010X

Fig. 84 Code C1254: Abnormal Shutdown Detected (Part 1 of 2). DeVille & Seville

Step	Action	Yes	No
1	Did you perform the ABS Diagnostic System Check?	Go to *Step 2*	Go to *Diagnostic System Check - ABS*
2	1. Turn OFF the ignition. 2. Disconnect the EBCM harness connector. 3. Install the *J 39700* universal breakout box using the *J 39700-300* cable adapter to the EBCM harness connector only. 4. Test both ground circuits of the EBCM including the EBCM ground for a high resistance or an open. Did you find and correct the condition?	Go to *Step 8*	Go to *Step 3*
3	Has the battery been disconnected recently?	Go to *Step 8*	Go to *Step 4*
4	Test the charging system. Did you find and correct the condition?	Go to *Step 8*	Go to *Step 5*
5	Inspect for poor connections at the harness connector of the EBCM. Did you find and correct the condition?	Go to *Step 8*	Go to *Step 6*
6	1. Use the scan tool in order to clear the DTCs. 2. With the scan tool, perform the Automated Test. Does the DTC reset?	Go to *Step 7*	*Test for Intermittent*
7	**Important:** Perform the setup procedure for the EBCM. An unprogrammed EBCM will result in the following conditions: • Inoperative or poorly functioning system operations • The EBCM sets DTC C1248 and DTC C1255m3 Replace the EBCM. Did you complete the repair?	Go to *Step 8*	—
8	1. Use the scan tool in order to clear the DTCs. 2. With the scan tool, perform the Automated Test. Does the DTC reset?	Go to *Step 2*	System OK

GC4020152645020X

Fig. 84 Code C1254: Abnormal Shutdown Detected (Part 2 of 2). DeVille & Seville

Circuit Description

This DTC identifies a malfunction within the EBCM.

Conditions for Running the DTC

The ABS conditions and the braking conditions are normal.

Conditions for Setting the DTC

An internal EBCM malfunction exists.

Action Taken When the DTC Sets

C1255

If equipped, the following actions occur:

- The EBCM disables the DRP/ABS/TCS/VSES for the duration of the ignition cycle.
- The ABS indicator turns ON.
- The Traction Control indicator turns ON.
- The red Brake warning indicator turns ON.
- The DIC displays the Service Stability System message.
- The EBCM will also set DTC C1248.
- For some DTC C1255xx, the EBCM disables the variable effort steering (VES) for the duration of the ignition cycle and the DIC displays the Service Steering System message.

C1256

- The ABS remains functional.
- The ABS indicator remains OFF.

Conditions for Clearing the DTC

- The condition for the DTC is no longer present (the DTC is not current) and you used the scan tool Clear DTC function.
- The condition for the DTC is no longer present (the DTC is not current) and you used the On-Board Diagnostics Clear DTC function.
- The EBCM automatically clears the history DTC when a current DTC is not detected in 100 consecutive drive cycles.

Diagnostic Aids

- The scan tool displays 2 additional characters after the DTC. Take note of the 2 character code and any other DTCs that are set. The 2 character code is an engineering aid used in order to determine the cause of the internal malfunction.
- When the scan tool displays DTC C1255m3, the EBCM has not been programmed. Perform the setup procedure for the EBCM.

Test Description

The number below refers to the step number on the diagnostic table.

2. Determines whether the DTC is current.

Step	Action	Yes	No
1	Did you perform the ABS Diagnostic System Check?	Go to *Step 2*	Go to *Diagnostic System Check - ABS*
2	1. Install a scan tool. 2. Turn ON the ignition, with the engine OFF. 3. Use the scan tool in order to clear the DTCs. 4. With the scan tool, perform the Automated Test. Does the DTC reset as a current DTC?	Go to *Step 3*	*Test for Intermittent*
3	**Important:** Perform the setup procedure for the EBCM. An unprogrammed EBCM will result in the following conditions: • Inoperative or poorly functioning system operations • The EBCM sets DTC C1248 and DTC C1255m3 Replace the EBCM. Did you complete the repair?	Go to *Step 4*	—
4	1. Use the scan tool in order to clear the DTCs. 2. With the scan tool, perform the Automated Test. Does the DTC reset?	Go to *Step 2*	System OK

GC4020152646010X

Fig. 85 Code C1255 Or C1256: EBCM Internal Fault. DeVille & Seville

Circuit Description

The system relay is energized when the ignition is ON. The system relay supplies voltage to the valve solenoids and the pump motor. This voltage is referred to as the system voltage. The EBCM microprocessor activates the valve solenoids by grounding the control circuit.

Conditions for Running the DTC

- The system voltage is greater than 8 volts.
- The ignition voltage is greater than 9 volts.

Conditions for Setting the DTC

The commanded state of the driver and the actual state of the control circuit do not match for 0.03 seconds.

Action Taken When the DTC Sets

If equipped, the following actions occur:

- The EBCM disables the DRP/ABS/TCS/VSES for the duration of the ignition cycle.
- The ABS indicator turns ON.
- The Traction Control indicator turns ON.
- The DIC displays the Service Stability System message.
- The EBCM will also set DTC C1248.
- The red Brake warning indicator turns ON

Conditions for Clearing the DTC

- The condition for the DTC is no longer present (the DTC is not current) and you used the scan tool Clear DTC function.
- The condition for the DTC is no longer present (the DTC is not current) and you used the On-Board Diagnostics Clear DTC function.
- The EBCM automatically clears the history DTC when a current DTC is not detected in 100 consecutive drive cycles.

Diagnostic Aids

The solenoid valve circuit is internal to the EBCM. The solenoid valve circuit is not diagnosable external to the EBCM. The DTC sets when there is a malfunction in the solenoid circuit internal to the EBCM.

Test Description

The number below refers to the step number on the diagnostic table.

2. Determines whether the DTC is current.

Step	Action	Yes	No
1	Did you perform the ABS Diagnostic System Check?	Go to *Step 2*	Go to *Diagnostic System Check - ABS*
2	1. Install a scan tool. 2. Turn ON the ignition, with the engine OFF. 3. Use the scan tool in order to clear the DTCs. 4. With the scan tool, perform the Automated Test. Does the DTC reset as a current DTC?	Go to *Step 3*	*Test for Intermittent*
3	**Important:** Perform the setup procedure for the EBCM. An unprogrammed EBCM will result in the following conditions: • Inoperative or poorly functioning system operations • The EBCM sets DTC C1248 and DTC C1255m3 Replace the EBCM. Did you complete the repair?	Go to *Step 4*	—
4	1. Use the scan tool in order to clear the DTCs. 2. With the scan tool, perform the Automated Test. Does the DTC reset?	Go to *Step 2*	System OK

GC4020152646020X

Fig. 86 Codes C1261-C1274: Valve Solenoid Fault. DeVille & Seville

Circuit Description

The EBCM and the PCM simultaneously control the traction control. The PCM reduces the amount of torque supplied to the drive wheels by retarding spark timing and selectively turning off fuel injectors. The EBCM actively applies the brakes to the front wheels in order to reduce torque.

The EBCM sends a requested torque message via a pulse width modulated (PWM) signal to the PCM. The duty cycle of the signal is used to determine how much engine torque the EBCM is requesting the PCM to deliver. Normal values are between 10 and 90 percent duty cycle. The signal should be at 90 percent when traction control is not active and at lower values during traction control activations. The PCM supplies a pull up voltage of 5 volts that the EBCM switches to ground to create the signal.

The PCM sends a delivered torque message via a pulse width modulated (PWM) signal to the EBCM. The duty cycle of the signal is used to determine how much engine torque the PCM is delivering. Normal values are between 10 and 90 percent duty cycle. The signal should be at low values (around 10 percent) at idle and higher values under driving conditions. The EBCM supplies a pull up voltage of 12 volts that the PCM switches to ground to create the signal.

When certain PCM DTCs are set, the PCM will not be able to perform the torque reduction portion of traction control. A serial data message is sent to the EBCM indicating that traction control is not allowed.

Conditions for Running the DTC

The engine is running.

Conditions for Setting the DTC

C1276

One of the following conditions exists:

- The EBCM detects that delivered torque signal is out of the valid range.
- The EBCM does not receive the delivered torque signal.

P1644 or P1689

The PCM detects that the delivered torque signal voltage is invalid.

Action Taken When the DTC Sets

- The EBCM disables the TCS for the duration of the ignition cycle.
- The PCM will store conditions which were present when the DTC set as Fail Records data only.
- The Traction Control indicator turns ON.
- The ABS remains functional.

Conditions for Clearing the DTC

- The condition for the DTC is no longer present (the DTC is not current) and you used the scan tool Clear DTC function.
- The condition for the DTC is no longer present (the DTC is not current) and you used the On-Board Diagnostics Clear DTC function.
- The EBCM automatically clears the history DTC when a current DTC is not detected in 100 consecutive drive cycles.
- The PCM automatically clears the history DTC when a current DTC is not detected in 40 consecutive warm-up cycles.

Diagnostic Aids

The following conditions can cause this concern:

- An open in the delivered torque circuit.
- An short to ground or voltage in the delivered torque circuit.
- A wiring problem, terminal corrosion, or poor connection in the delivered torque circuit.
- A communication frequency problem.
- A communication duty cycle problem.
- The EBCM is not receiving information from the PCM.
- Loose or corroded EBCM ground or PCM ground.

Test Description

The numbers below refer to the step numbers on the diagnostic table.

3. Use the scan tool in order to determine if the delivered torque signal has a valid duty cycle.
9. This vehicle is equipped with a PCM which uses an Electrically Erasable Programmable Read Only Memory (EEPROM). When replacing the PCM, the replacement PCM must be programmed.

Step	Action	Value(s)	Yes	No
1	Did you perform the ABS Diagnostic System Check?	—	Go to *Step 2*	Go to *Diagnostic System Check - ABS*
2	Inspect the EBCM ground and PCM ground, making sure each ground is clean and torqued to the proper specification. Did you find and correct the condition?	—	Go to *Step 11*	Go to *Step 3*
3	1. Install a scan tool. 2. Start the engine. 3. With a scan tool, observe the Delivered Torque parameter in the DRP/ABS/TCS data list. Does the scan tool display the specified value?	90%	Go to *Step 4*	*Test for Intermittent*

GC4020152647010X

Fig. 87 Code C1276: Delivered Torque Signal Circuit Fault (Part 1 of 2). DeVille & Seville

Step	Action	Value(s)	Yes	No
4	1. Turn OFF the ignition. 2. Disconnect the EBCM harness connector. 3. Install the *J 39700* universal breakout box using the *J 39700-300* cable adapter to the EBCM harness connector and the EBCM connector. 4. Disconnect the powertrain control module (PCM) harness connector. 5. Turn ON the ignition, with the engine OFF. 6. Measure the voltage from the delivered torque signal circuit to a good ground. Does the voltage measure near the specified value?	B+	Go to *Step 5*	Go to *Step 6*
5	1. Turn OFF the ignition. 2. Disconnect the *J 39700-300* cable adapter from the EBCM connector. 3. Turn ON the ignition, with the engine OFF. 4. Test the delivered torque signal circuit for a short to voltage. Did you find and correct the condition?	—	Go to *Step 11*	Go to *Step 7*
6	1. Turn OFF the ignition. 2. Disconnect the *J 39700-300* cable adapter from the EBCM connector. 3. Test the delivered torque signal circuit for the following conditions: • An open • A short to ground • A high resistance Did you find and correct the condition?	—	Go to *Step 11*	Go to *Step 8*
7	Inspect for poor connections the harness connector of the PCM. Did you find and correct the condition?	—	Go to *Step 11*	Go to *Step 9*
8	Inspect for poor connections the harness connector of the EBCM. Did you find and correct the condition?	—	Go to *Step 11*	Go to *Step 10*
9	**Important:** The replacement PCM must be programmed. Replace the PCM. Did you complete the repair?	—	Go to *Step 11*	—
10	**Important:** Perform the setup procedure for the EBCM. An unprogrammed EBCM will result in the following conditions: • Inoperative or poorly functioning system operations • The EBCM sets DTC C1248 and DTC C1255m3 Replace the EBCM. Did you complete the repair?	—	Go to *Step 11*	—
11	1. Use the scan tool in order to clear the DTCs. 2. Operate the vehicle within the Conditions for Running the DTC as specified in the supporting text. Does the DTC reset?	—	Go to *Step 2*	System OK

GC4020152647020X

Fig. 87 Code C1276: Delivered Torque Signal Circuit Fault (Part 2 of 2). DeVille & Seville

Circuit Description

The EBCM and the PCM simultaneously control the traction control. The PCM reduces the amount of torque supplied to the drive wheels by retarding spark timing and selectively turning off fuel injectors. The EBCM actively applies the brakes to the front wheels in order to reduce torque.

The EBCM sends a requested torque message via a pulse width modulated (PWM) signal to the PCM. The duty cycle of the signal is used to determine how much engine torque the EBCM is requesting the PCM to deliver. Normal values are between 10 and 90 percent duty cycle. The signal should be at 90 percent when traction control is not active and at lower values during traction control activations. The PCM supplies a pull up voltage of 5 volts that the EBCM switches to ground to create the signal.

The PCM sends a delivered torque message via a pulse width modulated (PWM) signal to the EBCM. The duty cycle of the signal is used to determine how much engine torque the PCM is delivering. Normal values are between 10 and 90 percent duty cycle. The signal should be at low values (around 10 percent) at idle and higher values under driving conditions. The EBCM supplies a pull up voltage of 12 volts that the PCM switches to ground to create the signal.

When certain PCM DTCs are set, the PCM will not be able to perform the torque reduction portion of traction control. A serial data message is sent to the EBCM indicating that traction control is not allowed.

Conditions for Running the DTC

The engine is running.

Conditions for Setting the DTC

C1277

The PCM diagnoses the requested torque signal circuit and sends a serial data message to the EBCM indicating a fault is present.

P1571

One of the following conditions exists:

- The PCM detects that requested torque signal is out of the valid range.
- The PCM does not receive the requested torque signal.

Action Taken When the DTC Sets

- The EBCM disables the TCS for the duration of the ignition cycle.
- The PCM will store conditions which were present when the DTC set as Fail Records data only.
- The Traction Control indicator turns ON.
- The ABS remains functional.

Conditions for Clearing the DTC

- The condition for the DTC is no longer present (the DTC is not current) and you used the scan tool Clear DTC function.
- The condition for the DTC is no longer present (the DTC is not current) and you used the On-Board Diagnostics Clear DTC function.
- The EBCM automatically clears the history DTC when a current DTC is not detected in 100 consecutive drive cycles.
- The PCM automatically clears the history DTC when a current DTC is not detected in 40 consecutive warm-up cycles.

Diagnostic Aids

The following conditions can cause this concern:

- An open in the requested torque circuit.
- An short to ground or voltage in the requested torque circuit.
- A wiring problem, terminal corrosion, or poor connection in the requested torque circuit.
- A communication frequency problem.
- A communication duty cycle problem.
- The PCM is not receiving information from the EBCM.
- Loose or corroded EBCM ground or PCM ground.

A DTC P1571 may set along with several other PCM DTCs if the key is held in the CRANK position while the engine is running. The starter lockout function of the PCM is enabled several seconds after the engine is running and prevents the starter from engaging while the engine is running. This will cause a partial loss of power to some components and systems.

Test Description

The numbers below refer to the step numbers on the diagnostic table.

3. Use the scan tool in order to determine if the requested torque signal has a valid duty cycle.
4. Measure the requested torque signal in order to determine if the signal has a valid duty cycle.
5. Measure the requested torque signal in order to determine if the signal has a valid frequency.
11. This vehicle is equipped with a PCM which uses an Electrically Erasable Programmable Read Only Memory (EEPROM). When replacing the PCM, the replacement PCM must be programmed.

GC4020152648010X

Fig. 88 Code C1277: Requested Torque Signal Circuit Fault (Part 1 of 3). DeVille & Seville

Step	Action	Value(s)	Yes	No
1	Did you perform the ABS Diagnostic System Check?	—	Go to *Step 2*	Go to *Diagnostic System Check - ABS*
2	Inspect the EBCM ground and PCM ground, making sure each ground is clean and torqued to the proper specification. Did you find and correct the condition?	—	Go to *Step 13*	Go to *Step 3*
3	1. Install a scan tool. 2. Start the engine. 3. With a scan, observe the Torque Request Signal parameter in the Powertrain Control Module data list. Does the scan display less than the specified value?	—	*Test for Intermittent*	Go to *Step 4*
4	1. Turn OFF the ignition. 2. Disconnect the EBCM harness connector. 3. Install the *J 39700* universal breakout box using the *J 39700-300* cable adapter to the EBCM harness connector and the EBCM connector. 4. Start the engine. 5. Measure the DC duty cycle between the requested torque signal circuit and a good ground. Is the duty cycle within the specified range?	5–95%	Go to *Step 5*	Go to *Step 6*
5	Measure the DC Hz between the requested torque signal circuit and a good ground. Does the frequency measure within the specified range?	121–134 Hz	Go to *Step 8*	Go to *Step 6*
6	1. Turn OFF the ignition. 2. Disconnect the *J 39700-300* cable adapter from the EBCM connector. **Important:** Disconnecting the EBCM connector and turning ON the ignition could cause other modules to set loss of communication DTCs (Uxxxx). Once the EBCM is reconnected, the EBCM may set DTC C1298. 3. Turn ON the ignition, with the engine OFF. 4. Measure the voltage from the requested torque signal circuit to a good ground. Does the voltage measure within the specified range?	4–6 V	Go to *Step 10*	Go to *Step 7*
7	1. Turn OFF the ignition. 2. Disconnect the powertrain control module (PCM) harness connector. 3. Test the requested torque signal circuit for the following conditions: • A short to voltage • A short to ground Did you find and correct the condition?	—	Go to *Step 13*	Go to *Step 10*

GC4020152648020X

Fig. 88 Code C1277: Requested Torque Signal Circuit Fault (Part 2 of 3). DeVille & Seville

Step	Action	Value(s)	Yes	No
8	1. Turn OFF the ignition. 2. Disconnect the powertrain control module (PCM) harness connector. 3. Test the requested torque signal circuit for the following conditions: • An open • A high resistance Did you find and correct the condition?	—	Go to *Step 13*	Go to *Step 9*
9	Inspect for poor connections the harness connector of the PCM. Did you find and correct the condition?	—	Go to *Step 13*	Go to *Step 11*
10	Inspect for poor connections the harness connector of the EBCM. Did you find and correct the condition?	—	Go to *Step 13*	Go to *Step 12*
11	**Important:** The replacement PCM must be programmed. Replace the PCM. Did you complete the repair?	—	Go to *Step 13*	—
12	**Important:** Perform the setup procedure for the EBCM. An unprogrammed EBCM will result in the following conditions: • Inoperative or poorly functioning system operations • The EBCM sets DTC C1248 and DTC C1255m3 Replace the EBCM. Did you complete the repair?	—	Go to *Step 13*	—
13	1. Use the scan tool in order to clear the DTCs. 2. Operate the vehicle within the Conditions for Running the DTC as specified in the supporting text. Does the DTC reset?	—	Go to *Step 2*	System OK

GC4020152648030X

Fig. 88 Code C1277: Requested Torque Signal Circuit Fault (Part 3 of 3). DeVille & Seville

Circuit Description

The EBCM and the PCM simultaneously control the traction control. The PCM reduces the amount of torque supplied to the drive wheels by retarding spark timing and selectively turning off fuel injectors. The EBCM actively applies the brakes to the front wheels in order to reduce torque.

The EBCM sends a requested torque message via a pulse width modulated (PWM) signal to the PCM. The duty cycle of the signal is used to determine how much engine torque the EBCM is requesting the PCM to deliver. Normal values are between 10 and 90 percent duty cycle. The signal should be at 90 percent when traction control is not active and at lower values during traction control activations. The PCM supplies a pull up voltage of 5 volts that the EBCM switches to ground to create the signal.

The PCM sends a delivered torque message via a pulse width modulated (PWM) signal to the EBCM. The duty cycle of the signal is used to determine how much engine torque the PCM is delivering. Normal values are between 10 and 90 percent duty cycle. The signal should be at low values (around 10 percent) at idle and higher values under driving conditions. The EBCM supplies a pull up voltage of 12 volts that the PCM switches to ground to create the signal.

When certain PCM DTCs are set, the PCM will not be able to perform the torque reduction portion of traction control. A serial data message is sent to the EBCM indicating that traction control is not allowed.

Conditions for Running the DTC

The ignition is ON.

Conditions for Setting the DTC

The PCM diagnoses a condition preventing the engine control portion of the traction control function and sends a serial data message to the EBCM indicating that torque reduction is not allowed. The PCM will typically set a DTC and the EBCM will set this DTC.

Action Taken When the DTC Sets

- The EBCM disables the TCS for the duration of the ignition cycle.
- The Traction Control indicator turns ON.
- The ABS remains functional.

Conditions for Clearing the DTC

- The condition for the DTC is no longer present (the DTC is not current) and you used the scan tool Clear DTC function.
- The condition for the DTC is no longer present (the DTC is not current) and you used the On-Board Diagnostics Clear DTC function.
- The EBCM automatically clears the history DTC when a current DTC is not detected in 100 consecutive drive cycles.

Diagnostic Aids

This DTC is for information only. As an aid to the technician, this DTC indicates that there are no problems in the ABS/TCS system.

DTC C1278

Step	Action	Yes	No
Schematic Reference: *ABS Schematics*			
1	Did you perform the ABS Diagnostic System Check?	*Diagnose Engine Controls*	Go to *Diagnostic System Check - ABS*

GC4020152649000X

Fig. 89 Code C1278: TCS Temporarily Inhibited By PCM. DeVille & Seville

Circuit Description

The vehicle stability enhancement system (VSES) is activated by the EBCM calculating the desired yaw rate and comparing it to the actual yaw rate input. The desired yaw rate is calculated from measured steering wheel position, vehicle speed, and lateral acceleration. The difference between the desired yaw rate and actual yaw rate is the yaw rate error, which is a measurement of oversteer or understeer. If the yaw rate error becomes too large, the EBCM will attempt to correct the vehicle's yaw motion by applying differential braking to the left or right front wheel.

The amount of differential braking applied to the left or right front wheel is based on both the yaw rate error and side slip rate error. The side slip rate error is a function of the lateral acceleration minus the product of the yaw rate and vehicle speed. The yaw rate error and side slip rate error are combined to produce the total delta velocity error. When the delta velocity error becomes too large and the VSES system activates, the driver's steering inputs combined with the differential braking will attempt to bring the delta velocity error toward zero.

The VSES activations generally occur during aggressive driving, in the turns or bumpy roads without much use of the accelerator pedal. When braking during VSES activation, the brake pedal will feel different than the ABS pedal pulsation. The brake pedal pulsates at a higher frequency during VSES activation.

The usable output voltage range for the lateral accelerometer and yaw rate sensors is 0.25–4.75 volts. The scan tool will report zero lateral acceleration or yaw rate as 2.5 volts with no sensor bias present. The sensor bias compensates for sensor mounting alignment errors, electronic signal errors, temperature changes, and manufacturing differences.

The steering wheel position sensor supplies 2 analog inputs, Phase A and Phase B, to the EBCM. The 2 input signals are approximately 90 degrees out of phase. By interpreting the relationship between the 2 inputs, the EBCM can determine the position of the steering wheel and the direction of steering wheel rotation.

Steer angle centering is the process by which the EBCM calibrates the steering sensor output so that the output reads zero when the steering wheel is centered. Using the yaw rate input, lateral accelerometer input, and wheel speed sensor inputs, the initial steering center position is calculated after driving greater than 10 km/h (6 mph) for more than 10 seconds in a straight line on a level surface.

Conditions for Running the DTC

C1281

- The steer angle has been centered.
- The VSES is active.
- The direction (understeer or oversteer) of the delta velocity error has not changed.
- The centered lateral acceleration value is less than 0.5 g.
- The yaw rate error is less than 5.8 degrees/second.
- The side slip error is greater than 1.8 meters/second*second.

C1283

The vehicle speed is greater than 40 km/h (25 mph).

C1286

The steer angle has been centered.

Conditions for Setting the DTC

C1281

One of the following conditions exists:

- The VSES is engaged for 10 seconds with the delta velocity error always in either understeer or oversteer. Under this condition, this DTC will set by itself.
- The yaw rate error is greater than 10 degrees/second for 5 seconds. Under this condition, this DTC will set along with DTC C1282.
- The yaw rate error is greater than 10 degrees/second with the vehicle speed less than 60 km/h (37 mph) and the acceleration pedal is pressed more than 25 percent of the pedal travel range for 1 second during the VSES activation. Under this condition, this DTC will set along with DTC C1282.
- With the yaw rate less than 8 degrees/second, the side slip error is greater than 4.9 meters/second*second for 5 seconds. Under this condition, this DTC will set along with DTC C1284.
- With the steer rate less than 80 degrees/second, the difference between the 2 steering sensor signals (Phase A and Phase B) is greater than 20 degrees for 1 second. Under this condition, this DTC will set along with DTC C1287.

C1283

The vehicle has driven for 10 minutes without completing steer angle centering.

C1286

The steering sensor bias moves greater than 40 degrees after steer centering was accomplished.

GC4020152650010X

Fig. 90 Codes C1281, C1283 Or C1286: VSES Sensors Uncorrelated (Part 1 of 3). DeVille & Seville

Action Taken When the DTC Sets

- The EBCM disables the VSES for the duration of the ignition cycle.
- The DIC displays the Service Stability System message.
- The ABS/TCS remains functional.

Conditions for Clearing the DTC

- The condition for the DTC is no longer present (the DTC is not current) and you used the scan tool Clear DTC function.
- The condition for the DTC is no longer present (the DTC is not current) and you used the On-Board Diagnostics Clear DTC function.
- The EBCM automatically clears the history DTC when a current DTC is not detected in 100 consecutive drive cycles.

Diagnostic Aids

- During diagnosis, park the vehicle on a level surface.
- Check the vehicle for proper alignment. The car should not pull in either direction while driving straight on a level surface.
- Find out from the driver under what conditions the DTC was set (when the DIC displayed the Service Stability System message). This information will help to duplicate the failure.
- The Snapshot function on the scan tool can help find an intermittent DTC.

Test Description

The numbers below refer to the step numbers on the diagnostic table.

2. Perform the Steering Position Sensor Test in order to verify that the steering wheel position sensor (SWPS) is operating properly.
3. Verify that the lateral accelerometer input parameter is within the valid range.
4. Verify that the yaw rate input parameter is within the valid range.

Step	Action	Value(s)	Yes	No
1	Did you perform the ABS Diagnostic System Check?	—	Go to *Step 2*	Go to *Diagnostic System Check - ABS*
2	1. Install a scan tool. 2. Turn ON the ignition, with the engine OFF. 3. With the scan tool, perform the Steering Position Sensor Test. Did the SWPS pass the test?	—	Go to *Step 3*	Go to *Step 7*
3	With a scan tool, observe the Lateral Accelerometer Input parameter in the VSES data list. Does the scan tool display within the specified range?	2.3–2.7 V	Go to *Step 4*	Go to *Step 8*
4	With a scan tool, observe the Yaw Rate Sensor Input parameter in the VSES data list. Does the scan tool display within the specified range?	2.3–2.7 V	Go to *Step 5*	Go to *Step 9*
5	1. Use the scan tool in order to clear the DTCs. 2. Perform the Diagnostic Test Drive. Does the DTC reset?	—	Go to *Step 6*	Go to Diagnostic Aids

GC4020152650020X

Fig. 90 Codes C1281, C1283 Or C1286: VSES Sensors Uncorrelated (Part 2 of 3). DeVille & Seville

Step	Action	Value(s)	Yes	No
6	**Important:** Perform the setup procedure for the EBCM. An unprogrammed EBCM will result in the following conditions: • Inoperative or poorly functioning system operations • The EBCM sets DTC C1248 and DTC C1255m3 Replace the EBCM. Did you complete the repair?	—	Go to *Step 10*	—
7	Replace the steering wheel position sensor (SWPS). Did you complete the replacement?	—	Go to *Step 10*	—
8	Replace the lateral accelerometer sensor. Did you complete the replacement?	—	Go to *Step 10*	—
9	Replace the yaw rate sensor. Did you complete the replacement?	—	Go to *Step 10*	—
10	1. Use the scan tool in order to clear the DTCs. 2. Operate the vehicle within the Conditions for Running the DTC as specified in the supporting text. Does the DTC reset?	—	Go to *Step 2*	System OK

GC4020152650030X

Fig. 90 Codes C1281, C1283 Or C1286: VSES Sensors Uncorrelated (Part 3 of 3). DeVille & Seville

Circuit Description

The vehicle stability enhancement system (VSES) is activated by the EBCM calculating the desired yaw rate and comparing it to the actual yaw rate input. The desired yaw rate is calculated from measured steering wheel position, vehicle speed, and lateral acceleration. The difference between the desired yaw rate and actual yaw rate is the yaw rate error, which is a measurement of oversteer or understeer. If the yaw rate error becomes too large, the EBCM will attempt to correct the vehicle's yaw motion by applying differential braking to the left or right front wheel.

The amount of differential braking applied to the left or right front wheel is based on both the yaw rate error and side slip rate error. The side slip rate error is a function of the lateral acceleration minus the product of the yaw rate and vehicle speed. The yaw rate error and side slip rate error are combined to produce the total delta velocity error. When the delta velocity error becomes too large and the VSES system activates, the driver's steering inputs combined with the differential braking will attempt to bring the delta velocity error toward zero.

The VSES activations generally occur during aggressive driving, in the turns or bumpy roads without much use of the accelerator pedal. When braking during VSES activation, the brake pedal will feel different than the ABS pedal pulsation. The brake pedal pulsates at a higher frequency during VSES activation.

The usable output voltage range for the lateral accelerometer and yaw rate sensors is 0.25–4.75 volts. The scan tool will report zero lateral acceleration or yaw rate as 2.5 volts with no sensor bias present. The sensor bias compensates for sensor mounting alignment errors, electronic signal errors, temperature changes, and manufacturing differences.

The steering wheel position sensor supplies 2 analog inputs, Phase A and Phase B, to the EBCM. The 2 input signals are approximately 90 degrees out of phase. By interpreting the relationship between the 2 inputs, the EBCM can determine the position of the steering wheel and the direction of steering wheel rotation.

Steer angle centering is the process by which the EBCM calibrates the steering sensor output so that the output reads zero when the steering wheel is centered. Using the yaw rate input, lateral accelerometer input, and wheel speed sensor inputs, the initial steering center position is calculated after driving greater than 10 km/h (6 mph) for more than 10 seconds in a straight line on a level surface.

Conditions for Running the DTC

The EBCM performs 6 different tests to detect a DTC condition. The numbers below correspond to the numbers in Conditions for Setting the DTC.

1. The yaw rate sensor bias test runs with the ignition ON.
2. The yaw rate sensor acceleration test runs with the ignition ON.
3. The yaw rate sensor circuit test runs with the vehicle stopped or with the vehicle speed greater than 45 km/h (28 mph).
4. The yaw rate isolation test runs with the following conditions:
   - The brake pedal is not pressed.
   - The ABS is not active.
   - The vehicle speed is greater than 5 km/h (3 mph).
5. The above yaw rate isolation test run with the VSES active.
6. The false activation test runs with the VSES active.

Conditions for Setting the DTC

The EBCM performs 6 different tests to detect a DTC condition. The numbers below correspond to the numbers in Conditions for Running the DTC.

1. The yaw rate bias is greater than 7 degrees/second.
2. The yaw rate input change is greater than 390 degrees/second/second.
3. The yaw rate input voltage is less than 0.15 volts or greater than 4.85 volts for 1 second.
4. The yaw rate error is greater than 10 degrees/second 30 times within a drive cycle.
5. The yaw rate error is greater than 10 degrees/second for 5 seconds. Under this condition, this DTC will set along with DTC C1281.
6. The yaw rate error is greater than 10 degrees/second with the vehicle speed less than 60 km/h (37 mph) and the acceleration pedal is pressed more than 25 percent of the pedal travel range for 1 second during the VSES activation. Under this condition, this DTC will set along with DTC C1281.

Action Taken When the DTC Sets

- The EBCM disables the VSES for the duration of the ignition cycle.
- The DIC displays the Service Stability System message.
- The ABS/TCS remains functional.

GC4020152651010X

Fig. 91 Code C1282: Yaw Rate Sensor Bias Circuit Fault (Part 1 of 3). DeVille & Seville

Conditions for Clearing the DTC

- The condition for the DTC is no longer present (the DTC is not current) and you used the scan tool Clear DTC function.
- The condition for the DTC is no longer present (the DTC is not current) and you used the On-Board Diagnostics Clear DTC function.
- The EBCM automatically clears the history DTC when a current DTC is not detected in 100 consecutive drive cycles.

Diagnostic Aids

- During diagnosis, park the vehicle on a level surface.
- Check the vehicle for proper alignment. The car should not pull in either direction while driving straight on a level surface.
- Find out from the driver under what conditions the DTC was set (when the DIC displayed the Service Stability System message). This information will help to duplicate the failure.
- The Snapshot function on the scan tool can help find an intermittent DTC.

Test Description

The number below refers to the step number on the diagnostic table.

3. Tests for the proper operation of the circuit in the low voltage range.
4. Tests for the proper operation of the circuit in the high voltage range. If the fuse in the jumper opens when you perform this test, the signal circuit is shorted to ground.
5. Tests for a short to voltage in the 5 volt reference circuit.
6. Tests the bias voltage of the yaw rate sensor.

Step	Action	Value(s)	Yes	No
1	Did you perform the ABS Diagnostic System Check?	—	Go to *Step 2*	Go to *Diagnostic System Check - ABS*
2	1. Install a scan tool. 2. Turn ON the ignition, with the engine OFF. 3. With a scan tool, observe the Yaw Rate Sensor Input parameter in the VSES data list. Does the scan tool display that the Yaw Rate Sensor Input parameter is within the specified range?	0.15–4.85 V	Go to *Step 6*	Go to *Step 3*
3	1. Turn OFF the ignition. 2. Disconnect the yaw rate sensor connector. 3. Turn ON the ignition, with the engine OFF. 4. With the scan tool, observe the Yaw Rate Sensor Input parameter. Does the scan tool display that the Yaw Rate Sensor Input parameter is less than the specified value?	0.15 V	Go to *Step 4*	Go to *Step 10*
4	1. Turn OFF the ignition. 2. Connect a 3 amp fused jumper wire between the 5 volt reference circuit of the yaw rate sensor and the signal circuit of the yaw rate sensor. 3. Turn ON the ignition, with the engine OFF. 4. With the scan tool, observe the Yaw Rate Sensor Input parameter. Does the scan tool display that the Yaw Rate Sensor Input parameter is greater than the specified value?	4.85 V	Go to *Step 5*	Go to *Step 8*
5	1. Disconnect the fused jumper wire. 2. Measure the voltage between the 5 volt reference circuit of the yaw rate sensor and the low reference circuit of the yaw rate sensor. Does the voltage measure less the specified value?	5 V	Go to *Step 12*	Go to *Step 7*
6	Does the scan tool display that the Yaw Rate Sensor Input parameter is within the specified range?	2.3–2.7 V	Go to Diagnostic Aids	Go to *Step 11*
7	Test the 5 volt reference circuit of the yaw rate sensor for a short to voltage. Did you find and correct the condition?	—	Go to *Step 16*	Go to *Step 13*

GC4020152651020X

Fig. 91 Code C1282: Yaw Rate Sensor Bias Circuit Fault (Part 2 of 3). DeVille & Seville

Step	Action	Value(s)	Yes	No
8	Test the 5 volt reference circuit of the yaw rate sensor for the following conditions: • An open • A short to ground • A high resistance Did you find and correct the condition?	—	Go to *Step 16*	Go to *Step 9*
9	Test the signal circuit of the yaw rate sensor for the following conditions: • An open • A short to ground • A high resistance Did you find and correct the condition?	—	Go to *Step 16*	Go to *Step 13*
10	Test the signal circuit of the yaw rate sensor for a short to voltage. Did you find and correct the condition?	—	Go to *Step 16*	Go to *Step 13*
11	1. Disconnect the EBCM harness connector. 2. Install the *J 39700* universal pinout box using the *J 39700-300* cable adapter to the EBCM harness connector only. 3. Test the low reference circuit of the yaw rate sensor for a high resistance or an open. Did you find and correct the condition?	—	Go to *Step 16*	Go to *Step 12*
12	Inspect for poor connections at the harness connector of the yaw rate sensor. Did you find and correct the condition?	—	Go to *Step 16*	Go to *Step 14*
13	Inspect for poor connections at the harness connector of the EBCM. Did you find and correct the condition?	—	Go to *Step 16*	Go to *Step 15*
14	Replace the yaw rate sensor. Did you complete the repair?	—	Go to *Step 16*	—
15	**Important:** Perform the setup procedure for the EBCM. An unprogrammed EBCM will result in the following conditions: • Inoperative or poorly functioning system operations • The EBCM sets DTC C1248 and DTC C1255m3 Replace the EBCM. Did you complete the repair?	—	Go to *Step 16*	—
16	1. Clear the DTCs using the scan tool. 2. Operate the vehicle within the Conditions for Running the DTC as specified in the supporting text. Does the DTC reset?	—	Go to *Step 2*	System OK

GC4020152651030X

Fig. 91 Code C1282: Yaw Rate Sensor Bias Circuit Fault (Part 3 of 3). DeVille & Seville

Circuit Description

The vehicle stability enhancement system (VSES) is activated by the EBCM calculating the desired yaw rate and comparing it to the actual yaw rate input. The desired yaw rate is calculated from measured steering wheel position, vehicle speed, and lateral acceleration. The difference between the desired yaw rate and actual yaw rate is the yaw rate error, which is a measurement of oversteer or understeer. If the yaw rate error becomes too large, the EBCM will attempt to correct the vehicle's yaw motion by applying differential braking to the left or right front wheel.

The amount of differential braking applied to the left or right front wheel is based on both the yaw rate error and side slip rate error. The side slip rate error is a function of the lateral acceleration minus the product of the yaw rate and vehicle speed. The yaw rate error and side slip rate error are combined to produce the total delta velocity error. When the delta velocity error becomes too large and the VSES system activates, the driver's steering inputs combined with the differential braking will attempt to bring the delta velocity error toward zero.

The VSES activations generally occur during aggressive driving, in the turns or bumpy roads without much use of the accelerator pedal. When braking during VSES activation, the brake pedal will feel different than the ABS pedal pulsation. The brake pedal pulsates at a higher frequency during VSES activation.

The usable output voltage range for the lateral accelerometer and yaw rate sensors is 0.25–4.75 volts. The scan tool will report zero lateral acceleration or yaw rate as 2.5 volts with no sensor bias present. The sensor bias compensates for sensor mounting alignment errors, electronic signal errors, temperature changes, and manufacturing differences.

The steering wheel position sensor supplies 2 analog inputs, Phase A and Phase B, to the EBCM. The 2 input signals are approximately 90 degrees out of phase. By interpreting the relationship between the 2 inputs, the EBCM can determine the position of the steering wheel and the direction of steering wheel rotation.

Steer angle centering is the process by which the EBCM calibrates the steering sensor output so that the output reads zero when the steering wheel is centered. Using the yaw rate input, lateral accelerometer input, and wheel speed sensor inputs, the initial steering center position is calculated after driving greater than 10 km/h (6 mph) for more than 10 seconds in a straight line on a level surface.

Conditions for Running the DTC

C1284

The EBCM performs 6 different tests to detect a DTC condition. The numbers below correspond to the numbers in Conditions for Setting the DTC.

1. The lateral accelerometer sensor bias test runs with the ignition ON.
2. The lateral accelerometer sensor self test runs with the following conditions:
   - The ignition is ON.
   - The vehicle is stopped.
3. The lateral accelerometer sensor jerk test runs with the ignition ON.
4. The centered lateral accelerometer sensor test runs with the following conditions:
   - The ignition is ON.
   - The vehicle is stopped.
5. The lateral accelerometer sensor isolation test, runs with the following conditions:
   - The ignition is ON.
   - DTC C1282 is not set.
   - The yaw rate is less than 8 degrees/second.
6. The above lateral accelerometer sensor isolation test run with the VSES active.

C1285

The ignition is ON.

Conditions for Setting the DTC

C1284

The EBCM performs 6 different tests to detect a DTC condition. The numbers below correspond to the numbers in Conditions for Running the DTC.

1. The compensated bias value of the lateral accelerometer sensor is greater than 0.3 g.
2. The lateral accelerometer sensor performs a self test that results in an offset of 0.5 g. The EBCM compares the sensor output during the self test with the output following the test. The DTC sets when the lateral acceleration immediately following the self test is 0.8 g.
3. The lateral jerk is greater than 19 g/second for 0.01 seconds.
4. The lateral acceleration is 0.4 g for 0.25 seconds.
5. The side slip error is greater than 4.9 meters/second*second 30 times within a drive cycle.
6. The side slip error is greater than 4.9 meters/second*second for 5 seconds. Under this condition, this DTC will set along with DTC C1281.

C1285

The lateral accelerometer input voltage is less than 0.15 volts or greater than 4.85 volts for 1 second.

GC4020152652010X

Fig. 92 Code C1284 Or C1285: Lateral Accelerometer Sensor Circuit Fault (Part 1 of 3). DeVille & Seville

Action Taken When the DTC Sets

- The EBCM disables the VSES for the duration of the ignition cycle.
- The DIC displays the Service Stability System message.
- The ABS/TCS remains functional.

Conditions for Clearing the DTC

- The condition for the DTC is no longer present (the DTC is not current) and you used the scan tool Clear DTC function.
- The condition for the DTC is no longer present (the DTC is not current) and you used the On-Board Diagnostics Clear DTC function.
- The EBCM automatically clears the history DTC when a current DTC is not detected in 100 consecutive drive cycles.

Diagnostic Aids

- During diagnosis, park the vehicle on a level surface.
- Check the vehicle for proper alignment. The car should not pull in either direction while driving straight on a level surface.
- Find out from the driver under what conditions the DTC was set (when the DIC displayed the Service Stability System message). This information will help to duplicate the failure.
- The Snapshot function on the scan tool can help find an intermittent DTC.

Test Description

The number below refers to the step number on the diagnostic table.

3. Tests for the proper operation of the circuit in the low voltage range.
4. Tests for the proper operation of the circuit in the high voltage range. If the fuse in the jumper opens when you perform this test, the signal circuit is shorted to ground.
5. Tests for a short to voltage in the 5 volt reference circuit.
6. Tests the bias voltage of the lateral accelerometer sensor.

Step	Action	Value(s)	Yes	No
1	Did you perform the ABS Diagnostic System Check?	—	Go to *Step 2*	Go to *Diagnostic System Check - ABS*
2	1. Install a scan tool. 2. Turn ON the ignition, with the engine OFF. 3. With a scan tool, observe the Lateral Accelerometer Input parameter in the VSES data list. Does the scan tool display that the Lateral Accelerometer Input parameter is within the specified range?	0.15–4.85 V	Go to *Step 6*	Go to *Step 3*
3	1. Turn OFF the ignition. 2. Disconnect the lateral accelerometer sensor connector. 3. Turn ON the ignition, with the engine OFF. 4. With the scan tool, observe the Lateral Accelerometer Input parameter. Does the scan tool display that the Lateral Accelerometer Input parameter is less than the specified value?	0.15 V	Go to *Step 4*	Go to *Step 10*
4	1. Turn OFF the ignition. 2. Connect a 3 amp fused jumper wire between the 5 volt reference circuit of the lateral accelerometer sensor and the signal circuit of the lateral accelerometer sensor. 3. Turn ON the ignition, with the engine OFF. 4. With the scan tool, observe the Lateral Accelerometer Input parameter. Does the scan tool display that the Lateral Accelerometer Input parameter is greater than the specified value?	4.85 V	Go to *Step 5*	Go to *Step 8*
5	1. Disconnect the fused jumper wire. 2. Measure the voltage between the 5 volt reference circuit of the lateral accelerometer sensor and the low reference circuit of the lateral accelerometer. Does the voltage measure less the specified value?	5 V	Go to *Step 12*	Go to *Step 7*

GC4020152652020X

Fig. 92 Code C1284 Or C1285: Lateral Accelerometer Sensor Circuit Fault (Part 2 of 3). DeVille & Seville

Step	Action	Value(s)	Yes	No
6	Does the scan tool display that the Lateral Accelerometer Input parameter is within the specified range?	2.3–2.7 V	Go to Diagnostic Aids	Go to *Step 11*
7	Test the 5 volt reference circuit of the lateral accelerometer sensor for a short to voltage. Did you find and correct the condition?	—	Go to *Step 16*	Go to *Step 13*
8	Test the 5 volt reference circuit of the lateral accelerometer sensor for the following conditions: • An open • A short to ground • A high resistance Did you find and correct the condition?	—	Go to *Step 16*	Go to *Step 9*
9	Test the signal circuit of the lateral accelerometer sensor for the following conditions: • An open • A short to ground • A high resistance Did you find and correct the condition?	—	Go to *Step 16*	Go to *Step 13*
10	Test the signal circuit of the lateral accelerometer sensor for a short to voltage. Did you find and correct the condition?	—	Go to *Step 16*	Go to *Step 13*
11	1. Disconnect the EBCM harness connector. 2. Install the *J 39700* universal pinout box using the *J 39700-300* cable adapter to the EBCM harness connector only. 3. Test the low reference circuit of the lateral accelerometer sensor for a high resistance or an open. Did you find and correct the condition?	—	Go to *Step 16*	Go to *Step 12*
12	Inspect for poor connections at the harness connector of the lateral accelerometer sensor. Did you find and correct the condition?	—	Go to *Step 16*	Go to *Step 14*
13	Inspect for poor connections at the harness connector of the EBCM. Did you find and correct the condition?	—	Go to *Step 16*	Go to *Step 15*
14	Replace the lateral accelerometer sensor. Did you complete the repair?	—	Go to *Step 16*	—
15	**Important:** Perform the setup procedure for the EBCM. An unprogrammed EBCM will result in the following conditions: • Inoperative or poorly functioning system operations • The EBCM sets DTC C1248 and DTC C1255m3 Replace the EBCM. Did you complete the repair?	—	Go to *Step 16*	—
16	1. Clear the DTCs using the scan tool. 2. Operate the vehicle within the Conditions for Running the DTC as specified in the supporting text. Does the DTC reset?	—	Go to *Step 2*	System OK

GC4020152652030X

Fig. 92 Code C1284 Or C1285: Lateral Accelerometer Sensor Circuit Fault (Part 3 of 3). DeVille & Seville

Circuit Description

The vehicle stability enhancement system (VSES) is activated by the EBCM calculating the desired yaw rate and comparing it to the actual yaw rate input. The desired yaw rate is calculated from measured steering wheel position, vehicle speed, and lateral acceleration. The difference between the desired yaw rate and actual yaw rate is the yaw rate error, which is a measurement of oversteer or understeer. If the yaw rate error becomes too large, the EBCM will attempt to correct the vehicle's yaw motion by applying differential braking to the left or right front wheel.

The amount of differential braking applied to the left or right front wheel is based on both the yaw rate error and side slip rate error. The side slip rate error is a function of the lateral acceleration minus the product of the yaw rate and vehicle speed. The yaw rate error and side slip rate error are combined to produce the total delta velocity error. When the delta velocity error becomes too large and the VSES system activates, the driver's steering inputs combined with the differential braking will attempt to bring the delta velocity error toward zero.

The VSES activations generally occur during aggressive driving, in the turns or bumpy roads without much use of the accelerator pedal. When braking during VSES activation, the brake pedal will feel different than the ABS pedal pulsation. The brake pedal pulsates at a higher frequency during VSES activation.

The usable output voltage range for the lateral accelerometer and yaw rate sensors is 0.25–4.75 volts. The scan tool will report zero lateral acceleration or yaw rate as 2.5 volts with no sensor bias present. The sensor bias compensates for sensor mounting alignment errors, electronic signal errors, temperature changes, and manufacturing differences.

The steering wheel position sensor supplies 2 analog inputs, Phase A and Phase B, to the EBCM. The 2 input signals are approximately 90 degrees out of phase. By interpreting the relationship between the 2 inputs, the EBCM can determine the position of the steering wheel and the direction of steering wheel rotation.

Steer angle centering is the process by which the EBCM calibrates the steering sensor output so that the output reads zero when the steering wheel is centered. Using the yaw rate input, lateral accelerometer input, and wheel speed sensor inputs, the initial steering center position is calculated after driving greater than 10 km/h (6 mph) for more than 10 seconds in a straight line on a level surface.

Conditions for Running the DTC

The ignition is ON.

Conditions for Setting the DTC

C1287

One of the following conditions exists:

- The steering wheel position sensor is synchronized and the steer rate (speed that the steering wheel appears to be turning) is greater than 1100 degrees/second.
- The steer rate is less than 80 degrees/second and the difference in the phase angle between Phase A and Phase B is greater than 20 degrees.
- The 2 steering sensor signals (Phase A and Phase B) do not agree for 1 second. Under this condition, this DTC will set along with DTC C1281.

C1288

One of the following conditions exists:

- Both Phase A and Phase B are greater than 4.9 volts for 1.6 seconds.
- Both Phase A and Phase B are less than 0.2 volts for 1.6 seconds.
- The difference in the changes in Phase A and Phase B is greater than 35.2 degrees for 9.76 milliseconds.

Action Taken When the DTC Sets

- The EBCM disables the VSES for the duration of the ignition cycle.
- The DIC displays the Service Stability System message.
- The ABS/TCS remains functional.

Conditions for Clearing the DTC

- The condition for the DTC is no longer present (the DTC is not current) and you used the scan tool Clear DTC function.
- The condition for the DTC is no longer present (the DTC is not current) and you used the On-Board Diagnostics Clear DTC function.
- The EBCM automatically clears the history DTC when a current DTC is not detected in 100 consecutive drive cycles.

Diagnostic Aids

- During diagnosis, park the vehicle on a level surface.
- Check the vehicle for proper alignment. The car should not pull in either direction while driving straight on a level surface.
- Find out from the driver under what conditions the DTC was set (when the DIC displayed the Service Stability System message). This information will help to duplicate the failure.
- The Snapshot function on the scan tool can help find an intermittent DTC.

GC4020152653010X

Fig. 93 Code C1287 Or C1288: Steering Sensor Circuit Fault (Part 1 of 4). DeVille & Seville

Test Description

The numbers below refer to the step numbers on the diagnostic table.

2. Perform the Steering Position Sensor Test in order to verify if the steering wheel position sensor (SWPS) is operating properly.
3. Tests for the proper operation of the steering wheel position signal A circuit in the low voltage range.
4. Tests for the proper operation of the steering wheel position signal B circuit in the low voltage range.
5. Tests for the proper operation of the steering wheel position signal A circuit in the high voltage range. If the fuse in the jumper opens when you perform this test, the signal circuit is shorted to ground.
6. Tests for the proper operation of the steering wheel position signal B circuit in the high voltage range. If the fuse in the jumper opens when you perform this test, the signal circuit is shorted to ground.
7. Tests for a short to voltage in the 5 volt reference circuit.
8. Tests for a high resistance or an open in the low reference circuit.

Step	Action	Value(s)	Yes	No
1	Did you perform the ABS Diagnostic System Check?	—	Go to *Step 2*	Go to *Diagnostic System Check - ABS*
2	1. Install a scan tool. 2. Turn ON the ignition, with the engine OFF. 3. With the scan tool, perform the Steering Position Sensor Test. Did the SWPS pass the test?	—	Go to Diagnostic Aids	Go to *Step 3*
3	1. Turn OFF the ignition. 2. Disconnect the steering wheel position sensor (SWPS) connector. 3. Turn ON the ignition, with the engine OFF. 4. With the scan tool, observe the Dual Analog SWPS Input A parameter in the VSES data list. Does the scan tool indicate the Dual Analog SWPS Input A parameter is less than the specified value?	0.2 V	Go to *Step 4*	Go to *Step 13*
4	With the scan tool, observe the Dual Analog SWPS Input B parameter. Does the scan tool indicate the Dual Analog SWPS Input B parameter is less than the specified value?	0.2 V	Go to *Step 5*	Go to *Step 14*
5	1. Turn OFF the ignition. 2. Connect a 3 amp fused jumper wire between the 5 volt reference circuit of the steering wheel position sensor (SWPS) and the signal A circuit of the steering wheel position sensor (SWPS). 3. Turn ON the ignition, with the engine OFF. 4. With the scan tool, observe the Dual Analog SWPS Input A parameter. Does the scan tool indicate that the Dual Analog SWPS Input A parameter is greater than the specified value?	4.9 V	Go to *Step 6*	Go to *Step 10*

GC4020152653020X

Fig. 93 Code C1287 Or C1288: Steering Sensor Circuit Fault (Part 2 of 4). DeVille & Seville

Step	Action	Value(s)	Yes	No
6	1. Turn OFF the ignition. 2. Disconnect the fused jumper wire. 3. Connect a 3 amp fused jumper wire between the 5 volt reference circuit of the steering wheel position sensor (SWPS) and the signal B circuit of the steering wheel position sensor (SWPS). 4. Turn ON the ignition, with the engine OFF. 5. With the scan tool, observe the Dual Analog SWPS Input B parameter. Does the scan tool indicate that the Dual Analog SWPS Input B parameter is greater than the specified value?	4.9 V	Go to *Step 7*	Go to *Step 10*
7	1. Disconnect the fused jumper wire. 2. Measure the voltage between the 5 volt reference circuit of the steering wheel position sensor (SWPS) and the low reference circuit of the steering wheel position sensor (SWPS). Does the voltage measure less the specified value?	5 V	Go to *Step 8*	Go to *Step 9*
8	1. Turn OFF the ignition. 2. Disconnect the negative battery cable. 3. Measure the resistance from the low reference circuit of the steering wheel position sensor (SWPS) to a good ground. Does the resistance measure less than the specified value?	5 Ω	Go to *Step 16*	Go to *Step 15*
9	Test the 5 volt reference circuit of the steering wheel position sensor (SWPS) for a short to voltage. Did you find and correct the condition?	—	Go to *Step 20*	Go to *Step 17*
10	Test the 5 volt reference circuit of the steering wheel position sensor (SWPS) for the following conditions: • An open • A short to ground • A high resistance Did you find and correct the condition?	—	Go to *Step 20*	Go to *Step 11*
11	Test the signal A circuit of the steering wheel position sensor (SWPS) for the following conditions: • An open • A short to ground • A high resistance Did you find and correct the condition?	—	Go to *Step 20*	Go to *Step 12*
12	Test the signal B circuit of the steering wheel position sensor (SWPS) for the following conditions: • An open • A short to ground • A high resistance Did you find and correct the condition?	—	Go to *Step 20*	Go to *Step 17*
13	Test the signal A circuit of the steering wheel position sensor (SWPS) for a short to voltage. Did you find and correct the condition?	—	Go to *Step 20*	Go to *Step 17*

GC4020152653030X

Fig. 93 Code C1287 Or C1288: Steering Sensor Circuit Fault (Part 3 of 4). DeVille & Seville

Step	Action	Value(s)	Yes	No
14	Test the signal B circuit of the steering wheel position sensor (SWPS) for a short to voltage. Did you find and correct the condition?	—	Go to Step 20	Go to Step 17
15	1. Disconnect the EBCM harness connector. 2. Install the J 39700 universal pinout box using the J 39700-300 cable adapter to the EBCM harness connector only. 3. Test the low reference circuit of the steering wheel position sensor (SWPS) for a high resistance or an open. Did you find and correct the condition?	—	Go to Step 20	Go to Step 17
16	Inspect for poor connections at the harness connector of the steering wheel position sensor (SWPS). Did you find and correct the condition?	—	Go to Step 20	Go to Step 18
17	Inspect for poor connections at the harness connector of the EBCM. Did you find and correct the condition?	—	Go to Step 20	Go to Step 19
18	Replace the steering wheel position sensor (SWPS). Did you complete the repair?	—	Go to Step 20	—
19	**Important:** Perform the setup procedure for the EBCM. An unprogrammed EBCM will result in the following conditions: • Inoperative or poorly functioning system operations • The EBCM sets DTC C1248 and DTC C1255m3 Replace the EBCM. Did you complete the repair?	—	Go to Step 20	—
20	1. Clear the DTCs using the scan tool. 2. Operate the vehicle within the Conditions for Running the DTC as specified in the supporting text. Does the DTC reset?	—	Go to Step 2	System OK

GC4020152653040X

Fig. 93 Code C1287 Or C1288: Steering Sensor Circuit Fault (Part 4 of 4). DeVille & Seville

Step	Action	Yes	No
5	1. Turn OFF the ignition. 2. Disconnect the stoplamp switch connector. 3. Connect a 3 amp fused jumper wire between the battery positive voltage circuit of the stoplamp switch and the signal circuit of the stoplamp switch. 4. Turn ON the ignition, with the engine OFF. 5. With a scan tool, observe the Stop Lamp Switch parameter. Does the scan tool display Applied?	Go to Step 11	Go to Step 6
6	Test the signal circuit of the stoplamp switch for an open between the splice pack of the stoplamp signal circuit and the EBCM. Did you find and correct the condition?	Go to Step 14	Go to Step 10
7	Test the battery positive voltage circuit of the stoplamp switch for a short to ground or an open. Did you find and correct the condition?	Go to Step 14	Go to Step 8
8	Test the signal circuit of the stoplamp switch for an open between the stoplamp switch and the splice of the stoplamp signal circuit. Did you find and correct the condition?	Go to Step 14	Go to Step 9
9	Test the signal circuit of the stoplamp switch for a short to ground. Did you find and correct the condition?	Go to Step 14	Go to Step 10
10	Inspect for poor connections at the harness connector of the EBCM. Did you find and correct the condition?	Go to Step 14	Go to Step 12
11	Inspect for poor connections at the harness connector of the stoplamp switch. Did you find and correct the condition?	Go to Step 14	Go to Step 13
12	**Important:** Perform the setup procedure for the EBCM. An unprogrammed EBCM will result in the following conditions: • Inoperative or poorly functioning system operations • The EBCM sets DTC C1248 and DTC C1255m3 Replace the EBCM. Did you complete the repair?	Go to Step 14	—
13	Replace the stoplamp switch. Did you complete the repair?	Go to Step 14	—
14	1. Use the scan tool in order to clear the DTCs. 2. Operate the vehicle within the Conditions for Running the DTC as specified in the supporting text. Does the DTC reset?	Go to Step 2	System OK

GC4020152654020X

Fig. 94 Code C1291 Or C1293: Open Brake Lamp Switch Contacts During Deceleration (Part 2 of 2). DeVille & Seville

Circuit Description

The stoplamp switch signal informs the EBCM when the brake pedal is pressed.

Conditions for Running the DTC

The ABS conditions and the braking conditions are normal.

Conditions for Setting the DTC

C1291

The stoplamp switch remains open for 3 deceleration cycles.

C1293

A DTC C1291 was set in a previous ignition cycle.

Action Taken When the DTC Sets

- The EBCM disables the TCS for the duration of the ignition cycle.
- The Traction Control indicator turns ON.
- The ABS remains functional.

Conditions for Clearing the DTC

- The condition for the DTC is no longer present (the DTC is not current) and you used the scan tool Clear DTC function.
- The condition for the DTC is no longer present (the DTC is not current) and you used the On-Board Diagnostics Clear DTC function.
- The EBCM automatically clears the history DTC when a current DTC is not detected in 100 consecutive drive cycles.

Diagnostic Aids

- Diagnose any wheel speed sensor DTCs before continuing with the diagnosis of the DTC.
- A deceleration cycle consists of the following sequence:
  1. The vehicle speed is greater than 24 km/h (15 mph).
  2. The vehicle decelerates more than 8 km/h/second (5 mph/second) for 2 seconds.
  3. The vehicle speed decelerates to less than 16 km/h (10 mph).
- Verify proper stoplamp switch operation using the data list of the scan tool. As the brake is applied, the data list displays the stoplamp switch on within 2.54 cm (1 in) of travel.
- Possible causes of this DTC are the following conditions:
  - An open stoplamp switch
  - The stoplamp switch is misadjusted
  - An open fuse
  - Circuit has a wiring problem, terminal corrosion, or poor connections
  - Erratic wheel speeds

Test Description

The numbers below refer to the step numbers on the diagnostic table.

3. Tests the circuit for a change in states.
5. Tests for proper operation of the circuit by bypassing the stoplamp switch. If the fuse in the jumper opens when you perform this test, the signal circuit of the stoplamp switch is shorted to ground.

Step	Action	Yes	No
1	Did you perform the ABS Diagnostic System Check?	Go to Step 2	Go to Diagnostic System Check - ABS
2	Press the brake pedal. Do the brake lamps turn ON?	Go to Step 3	Go to Step 7
3	1. Press the brake pedal. 2. With a scan tool, observe the Stop Lamp Switch parameter in the DRP/ABS/TCS data list. Does the Stop Lamp Switch parameter change state?	Go to Diagnostic Aids	Go to Step 4
4	1. Turn OFF the ignition. 2. Inspect the stoplamp switch and adjust and/or calibrate if needed. Did you find and correct the condition?	Go to Step 14	Go to Step 5

GC4020152654010X

Fig. 94 Code C1291 Or C1293: Open Brake Lamp Switch Contacts During Deceleration (Part 1 of 2). DeVille & Seville

Circuit Description

The stoplamp switch signal informs the EBCM when the brake pedal is pressed.

Conditions for Running the DTC

The vehicle speed is greater than 40 km/h (25 mph).

Conditions for Setting the DTC

The stoplamp switch input was active for 2 consecutive ignition cycles.

Action Taken When the DTC Sets

- The EBCM disables the TCS for the duration of the ignition cycle.
- The Traction Control indicator turns ON.
- The ABS remains functional.

Conditions for Clearing the DTC

- The condition for the DTC is no longer present (the DTC is not current) and you used the scan tool Clear DTC function.
- The condition for the DTC is no longer present (the DTC is not current) and you used the On-Board Diagnostics Clear DTC function.
- The EBCM automatically clears the history DTC when a current DTC is not detected in 100 consecutive drive cycles.

Diagnostic Aids

Possible causes of this DTC are the following conditions:

- The stoplamp switch circuit is shorted to voltage.
- The stoplamp switch is misadjusted.
- The stoplamp switch is stuck closed.
- A brake pedal that is binding.

Test Description

The number below refers to the step number on the diagnostic table.

2. Test for the current state of the stoplamp switch parameter.

GC4020152655010X

Fig. 95 Code C1294: Brake Lamp Switch Circuit Always On (Part 1 of 2). DeVille & Seville

Step	Action	Yes	No
1	Did you perform the ABS Diagnostic System Check?	Go to *Step 2*	Go to *Diagnostic System Check - ABS*
2	1. Install a scan tool. 2. Turn ON the ignition, with the engine OFF. 3. With a scan tool, observe the Stop Lamp Switch parameter in the DRP/ABS/TCS data list. Does the scan tool display Released?	Go to *Step 3*	Go to *Step 4*
3	1. Press the brake pedal. 2. With a scan tool, observe the Stop Lamp Switch parameter. Does the Stop Lamp Switch parameter change state?	Go to Diagnostic Aids	Go to *Step 4*
4	1. Turn OFF the ignition. 2. Inspect the stoplamp switch and adjust and/or calibrate if needed. Did you find and correct the condition?	Go to *Step 11*	Go to *Step 5*
5	1. Turn OFF the ignition. 2. Disconnect the stoplamp switch connector. 3. Turn ON the ignition, with the engine OFF. 4. With a scan tool, observe the Stop Lamp Switch parameter. Does the scan tool display Released?	Go to *Step 8*	Go to *Step 6*
6	Test the stoplamp switch signal circuit for a short to voltage. Did you find and correct the condition?	Go to *Step 11*	Go to *Step 7*
7	Inspect for poor connections at the harness connector of the EBCM. Did you find and correct the condition?	Go to *Step 11*	Go to *Step 9*
8	Inspect for poor connections at the harness connector of the stoplamp switch. Did you find and correct the condition?	Go to *Step 11*	Go to *Step 10*
9	**Important:** Perform the setup procedure for the EBCM. An unprogrammed EBCM will result in the following conditions: • Inoperative or poorly functioning system operations • The EBCM sets DTC C1248 and DTC C1255m3 Replace the EBCM. Did you complete the repair?	Go to *Step 11*	—
10	Replace the stoplamp switch. Did you complete the repair?	Go to *Step 11*	—
11	1. Use the scan tool in order to clear the DTCs. 2. Operate the vehicle within the Conditions for Running the DTC as specified in the supporting text. Does the DTC reset?	Go to *Step 2*	System OK

GC4020152655020X

Fig. 95 Code C1294: Brake Lamp Switch Circuit Always On (Part 2 of 2). DeVille & Seville

Step	Action	Yes	No
7	Inspect for poor connections at the harness connector of the EBCM. Did you find and correct the condition?	Go to *Step 9*	Go to *Step 8*
8	**Important:** Perform the setup procedure for the EBCM. An unprogrammed EBCM will result in the following conditions: • Inoperative or poorly functioning system operations • The EBCM sets DTC C1248 and DTC C1255m3 Replace the EBCM. Did you complete the repair?	Go to *Step 9*	—
9	1. Use the scan tool in order to clear the DTCs. 2. Operate the vehicle within the Conditions for Running the DTC as specified in the supporting text. Does the DTC reset?	Go to *Step 2*	System OK

Symptoms - Antilock Brake System

Important: The following steps must be completed before using the symptom tables.

1. Perform the *Diagnostic System Check - ABS* before using the Symptom Tables in order to verify that all of the following are true:
   - There are no DTCs set.
   - The control module(s) can communicate via the serial data link.
2. Review the system operation in order to familiarize yourself with the system functions.

Visual/Physical Inspection

- Inspect for aftermarket devices which could affect the operation of the antilock brake system.
- Inspect the easily accessible or visible system components for obvious damage or conditions which could cause the symptom.
- Inspect the master cylinder reservoir for the proper brake fluid level.

Intermittent

Faulty electrical connections or wiring may be the cause of intermittent conditions.

Symptom List

Refer to a symptom diagnostic procedure from the following list in order to diagnose the symptom:

- *ABS Indicator Always On*
- *ABS Indicator Inoperative*
- *Traction Control Indicator Always On*
- *Traction Control Indicator Inoperative*
- *Traction Off Indicator Inoperative*
- *Vehicle Stability Enhancement System Inoperative (w/JL4)*
- *Vehicle Stability Enhancement System Unwanted Activation (w/JL4)*
- *Vehicle Stability Enhancement System Excessive Brake Pulsation (w/JL4)*

GC4020152656020X

Fig. 96 Code C1295: Brake Lamp Switch Circuit Open (Part 2 of 2). DeVille & Seville

Circuit Description

The EBCM sources 5 volts on the stoplamp switch signal circuit when the stoplamp switch is inactive. The voltage is supplied a ground path through the stoplamp bulbs.

Conditions for Running the DTC

The ignition is ON.

Conditions for Setting the DTC

The stoplamp switch input voltage is between 2.1 volts and 5.3 volts for 2 seconds.

Action Taken When the DTC Sets

- The EBCM disables the TCS for the duration of the ignition cycle.
- The Traction Control indicator turns ON.
- The ABS remains functional.

Conditions for Clearing the DTC

- The condition for the DTC is no longer present (the DTC is not current) and you used the scan tool Clear DTC function.
- The condition for the DTC is no longer present (the DTC is not current) and you used the On-Board Diagnostics Clear DTC function.
- The EBCM automatically clears the history DTC when a current DTC is not detected in 100 consecutive drive cycles.

Diagnostic Aids

Possible causes of this DTC are the following conditions:

- A signal circuit of the stoplamp switch is open.
- The stoplamp switch is misadjusted.
- Verify proper stoplamp switch operation using the data list of the scan tool. As the brake is applied, the data list displays the stoplamp switch on within 2.54 cm (1 in) of travel.
- All brake lamps are open.
- All brake lamp grounds are open.
- Circuit has a wiring problem, terminal corrosion, or poor connections.
- Loose or corroded EBCM ground or PCM ground.
- An internal EBCM problem.

Test Description

The numbers below refer to the step numbers on the diagnostic table.

3. This DTC detects an open stoplamp switch signal circuit from the stoplamp side of the splice pack to the EBCM.
4. The EBCM sources 5 volts on the stoplamp switch signal circuit. This small voltage has a ground path through the stoplamp bulbs. This DTC sets if the path to ground is open.

Step	Action	Yes	No
1	Did you perform the ABS Diagnostic System Check?	Go to *Step 2*	Go to *Diagnostic System Check - ABS*
2	1. Press the brake pedal. 2. With the scan tool, observe the Stop Lamp Switch parameter in the DRP/ABS/TCS data list. Does the Stop Lamp Switch parameter display Applied?	Go to *Step 4*	Go to *Step 3*
3	Test the signal circuit of the stoplamp switch for an open or high resistance. Did you find and correct the condition?	Go to *Step 9*	Go to *Step 7*
4	Press the brake pedal. Are all of the stoplamps OFF?	Go to *Step 5*	Go to Diagnostic Aids
5	Test the feed circuit of the stoplamps for an open or high resistance. Did you find and correct the condition?	Go to *Step 9*	Go to *Step 6*
6	Test the ground circuit for the stoplamps for an open or high resistance. Did you find and correct the condition?	Go to *Step 9*	Go to Diagnostic Aids

GC4020152656010X

Fig. 96 Code C1295: Brake Lamp Switch Circuit Open (Part 1 of 2). DeVille & Seville

Symptoms - Antilock Brake System

Important: The following steps must be completed before using the symptom tables.

1. Perform the *Diagnostic System Check - ABS* before using the Symptom Tables in order to verify that all of the following are true:
   - There are no DTCs set.
   - The control module(s) can communicate via the serial data link.
2. Review the system operation in order to familiarize yourself with the system functions.

Visual/Physical Inspection

- Inspect for aftermarket devices which could affect the operation of the antilock brake system.
- Inspect the easily accessible or visible system components for obvious damage or conditions which could cause the symptom.
- Inspect the master cylinder reservoir for the proper brake fluid level.

Intermittent

Faulty electrical connections or wiring may be the cause of intermittent conditions.

Symptom List

Refer to a symptom diagnostic procedure from the following list in order to diagnose the symptom:

- *ABS Indicator Always On*
- *ABS Indicator Inoperative*
- *Traction Control Indicator Always On*
- *Traction Control Indicator Inoperative*
- *Traction Off Indicator Inoperative*
- *Vehicle Stability Enhancement System Inoperative (w/JL4)*
- *Vehicle Stability Enhancement System Unwanted Activation (w/JL4)*
- *Vehicle Stability Enhancement System Excessive Brake Pulsation (w/JL4)*

GC4020152657000X

Fig. 97 ABS Symptoms. DeVille & Seville

Circuit Description

The instrument cluster controls the operation of the ABS indicator. The EBCM reports the desired status of the ABS indicator via serial data messages. The ABS indicator signal circuit is a back-up reporting circuit to the serial data messages. The EBCM supplies ground through the circuit when the ABS is operating properly. When there is a problem with ABS that should turn on the ABS indicator, the EBCM opens the ABS indicator signal circuit. If there is a problem with the ABS serial data messages, the instrument cluster uses the ABS indicator signal to determine if the ABS indicator should be illuminated. Using the serial data messages and back-up circuit, the instrument cluster decides whether to turn on the ABS indicator.

Test Description

The numbers below refer to the step numbers on the diagnostic table.

3. Use the scan tool to check the normal state of the ABS indicator control circuit.
4. Ensures that the instrument cluster can operate the ABS indicator.

Step	Action	Yes	No
	Schematic Reference: *ABS Schematics*		
1	Did you perform the ABS Diagnostic System Check?	Go to *Step 2*	Go to *Diagnostic System Check - ABS*
2	Inspect the EBCM ground, making sure the ground is clean and torqued to the proper specification. Refer to *Circuit Testing* and *Wiring Repairs* in Wiring Systems. Did you find and correct the condition?	Go to *Step 9*	Go to *Step 3*
3	1. Install a scan tool. 2. Turn ON the ignition, with the engine OFF. 3. With a scan tool, observe the ABS Warning Indicator parameter in the DRP/ABS/TCS data list. Does the scan tool display Off?	Go to *Step 4*	Go to *Step 5*
4	1. Turn OFF the ignition. 2. Turn ON the ignition, with the engine OFF. 3. Observe the ABS indicator on the instrument cluster (IPC) during the bulb check. Does the ABS indicator illuminate during the bulb check and then turn OFF?	*Test for Intermittent*	Go to *Step 6*
5	Inspect for poor connections at the harness connector of the EBCM. Did you find and correct the condition?	Go to *Step 9*	Go to *Step 7*
6	Inspect for poor connections at the harness connector of the instrument cluster (IPC). Did you find and correct the condition?	Go to *Step 9*	Go to *Step 8*
7	**Important:** Perform the setup procedure for the EBCM. An unprogrammed EBCM will result in the following conditions: • Inoperative or poorly functioning system operations • The EBCM sets DTC C1248 and DTC C1255m3 Replace the EBCM. Did you complete the repair?	Go to *Step 9*	—
8	Replace the instrument cluster (IPC). Did you complete the repair?	Go to *Step 9*	—
9	Operate the system in order to verify the repair. Did you correct the condition?	System OK	Go to *Step 2*

GC4020152658000X

Fig. 98 ABS Indicator Always On. Deville & Seville

Circuit Description

The instrument cluster controls the operation of the ABS indicator. The EBCM reports the desired status of the ABS indicator via serial data messages. The ABS indicator signal circuit is a back-up reporting circuit to the serial data messages. The EBCM supplies ground through the circuit when the ABS is operating properly. When there is a problem with ABS that should turn on the ABS indicator, the EBCM opens the ABS indicator signal circuit. If there is a problem with the ABS serial data messages, the instrument cluster uses the ABS indicator signal to determine if the ABS indicator should be illuminated. Using the serial data messages and back-up circuit, the instrument cluster decides whether to turn on the ABS indicator.

Test Description

The numbers below refer to the step numbers on the diagnostic table.

3. Use the scan tool to check the normal state of the ABS indicator control circuit.
4. Ensures that the instrument cluster can operate the ABS indicator.

Step	Action	Yes	No
1	Did you perform the ABS Diagnostic System Check?	Go to *Step 2*	Go to *Diagnostic System Check - ABS*
2	Inspect the EBCM ground, making sure the ground is clean and torqued to the proper specification. Did you find and correct the condition?	Go to *Step 9*	Go to *Step 3*
3	1. Install a scan tool. 2. Turn ON the ignition, with the engine OFF. 3. With a scan tool, observe the ABS Warning Indicator parameter in the DRP/ABS/TCS data list. Does the scan tool display Off?	Go to *Step 4*	Go to *Step 5*
4	1. Turn OFF the ignition. 2. Turn ON the ignition, with the engine OFF. 3. Observe the ABS indicator on the instrument cluster (IPC) during the bulb check. Does the ABS indicator illuminate during the bulb check and then turn OFF?	*Test for Intermittent*	Go to *Step 6*
5	Inspect for poor connections at the harness connector of the EBCM. Did you find and correct the condition?	Go to *Step 9*	Go to *Step 7*
6	Inspect for poor connections at the harness connector of the instrument cluster (IPC). Did you find and correct the condition?	Go to *Step 9*	Go to *Step 8*
7	**Important:** Perform the setup procedure for the EBCM. An unprogrammed EBCM will result in the following conditions: • Inoperative or poorly functioning system operations • The EBCM sets DTC C1248 and DTC C1255m3 Replace the EBCM. Did you complete the repair?	Go to *Step 9*	—
8	Replace the instrument cluster (IPC). Did you complete the repair?	Go to *Step 9*	—
9	Operate the system in order to verify the repair. Did you correct the condition?	System OK	Go to *Step 2*

GC4020152659000X

Fig. 99 ABS Indicator Inoperative. DeVille & Seville

Circuit Description

The Traction Control indicator is controlled by the instrument cluster (IPC) via serial data messages from the EBCM. The EBCM send a serial data message to the IPC to illuminate the Traction Control indicator when the EBCM has disabled TCS due to a DTC. The Traction Control indicator will also turn ON during the instrument cluster bulb check. When the ignition switch is turned to ON, the Traction Control indicator will turn ON for approximately 3 seconds and then turn OFF.

Test Description

The numbers below refer to the step numbers on the diagnostic table.

2. Use the scan tool to check the normal state of the Traction Control indicator control.
3. Ensures that the instrument cluster can operate the Traction Control indicator.

Step	Action	Yes	No
1	Did you perform the ABS Diagnostic System Check?	Go to *Step 2*	Go to *Diagnostic System Check - ABS*
2	1. Install a scan tool. 2. Turn ON the ignition, with the engine OFF. 3. With a scan tool, observe the TCS Warning Indicator/Message parameter in the DRP/ABS/TCS data list. Does the scan tool display Off?	Go to *Step 3*	Go to *Step 4*
3	1. Turn OFF the ignition. 2. Turn ON the ignition, with the engine OFF. 3. Observe the Traction Control indicator on the instrument cluster (IPC) during the bulb check. Does the Traction Control indicator illuminate during the bulb check and then turn OFF?	*Test for Intermittent*	Go to *Step 5*
4	Inspect for poor connections at the harness connector of the EBCM. Did you find and correct the condition?	Go to *Step 8*	Go to *Step 6*
5	Inspect for poor connections at the harness connector of the instrument cluster (IPC). Did you find and correct the condition?	Go to *Step 8*	Go to *Step 7*
6	**Important:** Perform the setup procedure for the EBCM. An unprogrammed EBCM will result in the following conditions: • Inoperative or poorly functioning system operations • The EBCM sets DTC C1248 and DTC C1255m3 Replace the EBCM. Did you complete the repair?	Go to *Step 8*	—
7	Replace the instrument cluster (IPC). Did you complete the repair?	Go to *Step 8*	—
8	Operate the system in order to verify the repair. Did you correct the condition?	System OK	Go to *Step 2*

GC4020152660000X

Fig. 100 Traction Control Indicator Always On. DeVille & Seville

Circuit Description

The Traction Control indicator is controlled by the instrument cluster (IPC) via serial data messages from the EBCM. The EBCM send a serial data message to the IPC to illuminate the Traction Control indicator when the EBCM has disabled TCS due to a DTC. The Traction Control indicator will also turn ON during the instrument cluster bulb check. When the ignition switch is turned to ON, the Traction Control indicator will turn ON for approximately 3 seconds and then turn OFF.

Test Description

The numbers below refer to the step numbers on the diagnostic table.

2. Use the scan tool to check the normal state of the Traction Control indicator control.
3. Ensures that the instrument cluster can operate the Traction Control indicator.

Step	Action	Yes	No
1	Did you perform the ABS Diagnostic System Check?	Go to *Step 2*	Go to *Diagnostic System Check - ABS*
2	1. Install a scan tool. 2. Turn ON the ignition, with the engine OFF. 3. With a scan tool, observe the TCS Warning Indicator/Message parameter in the DRP/ABS/TCS data list. Does the scan tool display Off?	Go to *Step 3*	Go to *Step 4*
3	1. Turn OFF the ignition. 2. Turn ON the ignition, with the engine OFF. 3. Observe the Traction Control indicator on the instrument cluster (IPC) during the bulb check. Does the Traction Control indicator illuminate during the bulb check and then turn OFF?	*Test for Intermittent*	Go to *Step 5*
4	Inspect for poor connections at the harness connector of the EBCM. Did you find and correct the condition?	Go to *Step 8*	Go to *Step 6*
5	Inspect for poor connections at the harness connector of the instrument cluster (IPC). Did you find and correct the condition?	Go to *Step 8*	Go to *Step 7*
6	**Important:** Perform the setup procedure for the EBCM. An unprogrammed EBCM will result in the following conditions: • Inoperative or poorly functioning system operations • The EBCM sets DTC C1248 and DTC C1255m3 Replace the EBCM. Did you complete the repair?	Go to *Step 8*	—
7	Replace the instrument cluster (IPC). Did you complete the repair?	Go to *Step 8*	—
8	Operate the system in order to verify the repair. Did you correct the condition?	System OK	Go to *Step 2*

GC4020152661000X

Fig. 101 Traction Control Indicator Inoperative. DeVille & Seville

Circuit Description

The Traction Off message on the DIC is controlled by the instrument cluster via serial data messages from the EBCM. When the IPM sees the traction control switch input grounded through the momentary traction control switch, it sends a serial data message to the EBCM that tells the EBCM that the traction control switch has been pressed. The EBCM then disables traction control and sends a serial data message to the instrument cluster to display the Traction Off message on the DIC. Each time the ignition is cycled from OFF to ON, the traction control system is enabled.

Step	Action	Yes	No
1	Did you perform the ABS Diagnostic System Check?	Go to *Step 2*	Go to *Diagnostic System Check - ABS*
2	1. Turn OFF the ignition. 2. Install a scan tool. 3. Turn ON the ignition, with the engine OFF. 4. With a scan tool, observe the TCS Switch parameter in the Instrument Panel Module data list. 5. Activate the traction control switch. Does the TCS Switch parameter change state?	*Test for Intermittent*	Go to *Step 3*
3	Does the scan indicate that the TCS Switch parameter is On?	Go to *Step 4*	Go to *Step 5*
4	1. Turn OFF the ignition. 2. Disconnect the traction control switch connector. 3. Turn ON the ignition, with the engine OFF. 4. With a scan tool, observe the TCS Switch parameter. Does the scan tool display Off?	Go to *Step 10*	Go to *Step 6*
5	1. Turn OFF the ignition. 2. Disconnect the traction control switch connector. 3. Connect a 3 amp fused jumper from the signal circuit of the traction control switch to the ground circuit of the traction control switch. 4. Turn ON the ignition, with the engine OFF. 5. With a scan tool, observe the TCS Switch parameter. Does the scan tool display On?	Go to *Step 10*	Go to *Step 7*
6	Test the signal circuit of the traction control switch for a short to ground. Did you find and correct the condition?	Go to *Step 13*	Go to *Step 9*
7	Test the signal circuit of the traction control switch for an open or high resistance. Did you find and correct the condition?	Go to *Step 13*	Go to *Step 8*

GC4020152662010X

Fig. 102 Traction Off Indicator Inoperative (Part 1 of 2). DeVille & Seville

Step	Action	Yes	No
8	Test the ground circuit of the traction control switch for an open or high resistance. Did you find and correct the condition?	Go to *Step 13*	Go to *Step 9*
9	Inspect for poor connections at the harness connector of the instrument panel module (IPM). Did you find and correct the condition?	Go to *Step 13*	Go to *Step 11*
10	Inspect for poor connections at the harness connector of the traction control switch. Did you find and correct the condition?	Go to *Step 13*	Go to *Step 12*
11	Replace the instrument panel module (IPM). Did you complete the replacement?	Go to *Step 13*	—
12	Replace the traction control switch. Did you complete the replacement?	Go to *Step 13*	—
13	Operate the system in order to verify the repair. Did you correct the condition?	System OK	Go to *Step 2*

GC4020152662020X

Fig. 102 Traction Off Indicator Inoperative (Part 2 of 2). DeVille & Seville

Circuit Description

The vehicle stability enhancement system (VSES) is activated by the EBCM calculating the desired yaw rate and comparing it to the actual yaw rate input. The desired yaw rate is calculated from measured steering wheel position, vehicle speed, and lateral acceleration. The difference between the desired yaw rate and actual yaw rate is the yaw rate error, which is a measurement of oversteer or understeer. If the yaw rate error becomes too large, the EBCM will attempt to correct the vehicle's yaw motion by applying differential braking to the left or right front wheel.

The amount of differential braking applied to the left or right front wheel is based on both the yaw rate error and side slip rate error. The side slip rate error is a function of the lateral acceleration minus the product of the yaw rate and vehicle speed. The yaw rate error and side slip rate error are combined to produce the total delta velocity error. When the delta velocity error becomes too large and the VSES system activates, the driver's steering inputs combined with the differential braking will attempt to bring the delta velocity error toward zero.

The VSES activations generally occur during aggressive driving, in the turns or bumpy roads without much use of the accelerator pedal. When braking during VSES activation, the brake pedal will feel different than the ABS pedal pulsation. The brake pedal pulsates at a higher frequency during VSES activation.

The usable output voltage range for the lateral accelerometer and yaw rate sensors is 0.25–4.75 volts. The scan tool will report zero lateral acceleration or yaw rate as 2.5 volts with no sensor bias present. The sensor bias compensates for sensor mounting alignment errors, electronic signal errors, temperature changes, and manufacturing differences.

The steering wheel position sensor supplies 2 analog inputs, Phase A and Phase B, to the EBCM. The 2 input signals are approximately 90 degrees out of phase. By interpreting the relationship between the 2 inputs, the EBCM can determine the position of the steering wheel and the direction of steering wheel rotation.

Steer angle centering is the process by which the EBCM calibrates the steering sensor output so that the output reads zero when the steering wheel is centered. Using the yaw rate input, lateral accelerometer input, and wheel speed sensor inputs, the initial steering center position is calculated after driving greater than 10 km/h (6 mph) for more than 10 seconds in a straight line on a level surface.

Test Description

The numbers below refer to the step numbers on the diagnostic table.

3. Perform the Steering Position Sensor Test in order to verify if the steering wheel position sensor (SWPS) is operating properly.
4. Verify that the lateral accelerometer input parameter is within the valid range.
5. Verify that the yaw rate input parameter is within the valid range.

GC4020152663010X

Fig. 103 Vehicle Stability Enhancement System Inoperative (Part 1 of 2). DeVille & Seville

Step	Action	Value(s)	Yes	No
1	Did you perform the ABS Diagnostic System Check?	—	Go to *Step 2*	Go to *Diagnostic System Check - ABS*
2	1. Install a scan tool. 2. Start the engine. 3. Observe the VSES Is Centered parameter in the VSES data list. 4. Perform the Diagnostic Test Drive. Did the scan tool display Yes within the specified value?	30 seconds	*Test for Intermittent*	Go to *Step 3*
3	With the scan tool, perform the Steering Position Sensor Test. Did the SWPS pass the test?	—	Go to *Step 4*	Go to *Step 7*
4	With a scan tool, observe the Lateral Accelerometer Input parameter in the VSES data list. Does the scan tool display within the specified range?	2.3–2.7 V	Go to *Step 5*	Go to *Step 8*
5	With a scan tool, observe the Yaw Rate Sensor Input parameter in the VSES data list. Does the scan tool display within the specified range?	2.3–2.7 V	Go to *Step 6*	Go to *Step 9*
6	**Important:** Perform the setup procedure for the EBCM. An unprogrammed EBCM will result in the following conditions: • Inoperative or poorly functioning system operations • The EBCM sets DTC C1248 and DTC C1255m3 Replace the EBCM. Did you complete the repair?	—	Go to *Step 10*	—
7	Replace the steering wheel position sensor (SWPS). Did you complete the replacement?	—	Go to *Step 10*	—
8	Replace the lateral accelerometer sensor. Did you complete the replacement?	—	Go to *Step 10*	—
9	Replace the yaw rate sensor. Did you complete the replacement?	—	Go to *Step 10*	—
10	Operate the system in order to verify the repair. Did you correct the condition?	—	System OK	Go to *Step 2*

GC4020152663020X

Fig. 103 Vehicle Stability Enhancement System Inoperative (Part 2 of 2). DeVille & Seville

Circuit Description

The vehicle stability enhancement system (VSES) is activated by the EBCM calculating the desired yaw rate and comparing it to the actual yaw rate input. The desired yaw rate is calculated from measured steering wheel position, vehicle speed, and lateral acceleration. The difference between the desired yaw rate and actual yaw rate is the yaw rate error, which is a measurement of oversteer or understeer. If the yaw rate error becomes too large, the EBCM will attempt to correct the vehicle's yaw motion by applying differential braking to the left or right front wheel.

The amount of differential braking applied to the left or right front wheel is based on both the yaw rate error and side slip rate error. The side slip rate error is a function of the lateral acceleration minus the product of the yaw rate and vehicle speed. The yaw rate error and side slip rate error are combined to produce the total delta velocity error. When the delta velocity error becomes too large and the VSES system activates, the driver's steering inputs combined with the differential braking will attempt to bring the delta velocity error toward zero.

The VSES activations generally occur during aggressive driving, in the turns or bumpy roads without much use of the accelerator pedal. When braking during VSES activation, the brake pedal will feel different than the ABS pedal pulsation. The brake pedal pulsates at a higher frequency during VSES activation.

The usable output voltage range for the lateral accelerometer and yaw rate sensors is 0.25–4.75 volts. The scan tool will report zero lateral acceleration or yaw rate as 2.5 volts with no sensor bias present. The sensor bias compensates for sensor mounting alignment errors, electronic signal errors, temperature changes, and manufacturing differences.

The steering wheel position sensor supplies 2 analog inputs, Phase A and Phase B, to the EBCM. The 2 input signals are approximately 90 degrees out of phase. By interpreting the relationship between the 2 inputs, the EBCM can determine the position of the steering wheel and the direction of steering wheel rotation.

Steer angle centering is the process by which the EBCM calibrates the steering sensor output so that the output reads zero when the steering wheel is centered. Using the yaw rate input, lateral accelerometer input, and wheel speed sensor inputs, the initial steering center position is calculated after driving greater than 10 km/h (6 mph) for more than 10 seconds in a straight line on a level surface.

Test Description

The number below refers to the step number on the diagnostic table.

6. Perform the Steering Position Sensor Test in order to verify if the steering wheel position sensor (SWPS) is operating properly.

Step	Action	Value(s)	Yes	No
1	Did you perform the ABS Diagnostic System Check?	—	Go to *Step 2*	Go to *Diagnostic System Check - ABS*
2	Inspect the mounting of the yaw rate sensor. Did you find and correct the condition?	—	Go to *Step 15*	Go to *Step 3*
3	1. Install a scan tool. 2. Start the engine. 3. With a scan tool, observe the Yaw Rate Sensor Input parameter in the VSES data list. 4. Perform the Diagnostic Test Drive. Does the scan tool display suddenly increase or decrease without rapid turning of the vehicle?	—	Go to *Step 4*	Go to *Step 5*
4	Perform the diagnosis for DTC C1282. Did you find and correct the condition?	—	Go to *Step 15*	Go to *Step 12*

GC4020152664010X

Fig. 104 Vehicle Stability Enhancement System Unwanted Activation (Part 1 of 2). DeVille & Seville

Step	Action	Value(s)	Yes	No
5	1. Straighten the front wheels. 2. Observe the Dual Analog SWPS Input A and Dual Analog SWPS Input B in the VSES data list. 3. Slowly rotate the steering wheel in both directions. Does the scan tool display change states as the steering wheel was rotated?	—	Go to *Step 6*	Go to *Step 14*
6	With the scan tool, perform the Steering Position Sensor Test. Did the SWPS pass the test?	—	Go to *Step 7*	Go to *Step 14*
7	1. Place the vehicle on a level surface. 2. With a scan tool, observe the Lateral Accelerometer Input parameter in the VSES data list. Does the scan tool display within the specified range?	2.3–2.7 V	Go to *Step 9*	Go to *Step 8*
8	Inspect the mounting of the lateral accelerometer sensor. Did you find and correct the condition?	—	Go to *Step 15*	Go to *Step 9*
9	Inspect the EBCM for the proper part number. Did you find the correct part number?	—	Go to *Step 10*	Go to *Step 12*
10	Inspect the power steering gear for the proper part number. Did you find the correct part number?	—	Go to *Step 11*	Go to *Step 13*
11	Inspect the alignment of the vehicle. Did you find and correct the condition?	—	Go to *Step 15*	*Test for Intermittent*
12	**Important:** Perform the setup procedure for the EBCM. An unprogrammed EBCM will result in the following conditions: • Inoperative or poorly functioning system operations • The EBCM sets DTC C1248 and DTC C1255m3 Replace the EBCM. Did you complete the repair?	—	Go to *Step 15*	—
13	Replace the power steering gear. Did you complete the repair?	—	Go to *Step 15*	—
14	Replace the steering wheel position sensor (SWPS). Did you complete the repair?	—	Go to *Step 15*	—
15	Operate the system in order to verify the repair. Did you correct the condition?	—	System OK	Go to *Step 2*

GC4020152664020X

Fig. 104 Vehicle Stability Enhancement System Unwanted Activation (Part 2 of 2). DeVille & Seville

Circuit Description

The vehicle stability enhancement system (VSES) is activated by the EBCM calculating the desired yaw rate and comparing it to the actual yaw rate input. The desired yaw rate is calculated from measured steering wheel position, vehicle speed, and lateral acceleration. The difference between the desired yaw rate and actual yaw rate is the yaw rate error, which is a measurement of oversteer or understeer. If the yaw rate error becomes too large, the EBCM will attempt to correct the vehicle's yaw motion by applying differential braking to the left or right front wheel.

The amount of differential braking applied to the left or right front wheel is based on both the yaw rate error and side slip rate error. The side slip rate error is a function of the lateral acceleration minus the product of the yaw rate and vehicle speed. The yaw rate error and side slip rate error are combined to produce the total delta velocity error. When the delta velocity error becomes too large and the VSES system activates, the driver's steering inputs combined with the differential braking will attempt to bring the delta velocity error toward zero.

The VSES activations generally occur during aggressive driving, in the turns or bumpy roads without much use of the accelerator pedal.

When braking during VSES activation, the brake pedal will feel different than the ABS pedal pulsation. The brake pedal pulsates at a higher frequency during VSES activation.

The usable output voltage range for the lateral accelerometer and yaw rate sensors is 0.25–4.75 volts. The scan tool will report zero lateral acceleration or yaw rate as 2.5 volts with no sensor bias present. The sensor bias compensates for sensor mounting alignment errors, electronic signal errors, temperature changes, and manufacturing differences.

The steering wheel position sensor supplies 2 analog inputs, Phase A and Phase B, to the EBCM. The 2 input signals are approximately 90 degrees out of phase. By interpreting the relationship between the 2 inputs, the EBCM can determine the position of the steering wheel and the direction of steering wheel rotation.

Steer angle centering is the process by which the EBCM calibrates the steering sensor output so that the output reads zero when the steering wheel is centered. Using the yaw rate input, lateral accelerometer input, and wheel speed sensor inputs, the initial steering center position is calculated after driving greater than 10 km/h (6 mph) for more than 10 seconds in a straight line on a level surface.

Step	Action	Value(s)	Yes	No
1	Did you perform the ABS Diagnostic System Check?	—	Go to *Step 2*	Go to *Diagnostic System Check - ABS*
2	1. Install a scan tool. 2. Turn ON the ignition, with the engine OFF. 3. Select the display DTCs function on the scan tool for the powertrain control module (PCM). Does the scan tool display DTC P1575?	—	*Diagnose Engine Controls*	Go to *Step 3*
3	1. With a scan tool, observe the Extended Travel Brake Switch parameter in the DRP/ABS/TCS data list. 2. Step on and off the brake pedal with enough force to simulate a hard braking condition. As the brake pedal is pressed and released, the scan tool should read Applied and Released. 3. Use a tape measure in order to measure the distance that the brake pedal travels for the scan tool to read Applied. Does the distance measure within the specified range?	2.5–3.3 cm (1.0–1.3 in)	*Test for Intermittent*	Go to *Step 4*
4	Adjust or repair the extended travel brake switch as necessary. Did you complete the repair?	—	Go to *Step 5*	—
5	Operate the system in order to verify the repair. Did you correct the condition?	—	System OK	Go to *Step 2*

GC4020152665000X

Fig. 105 Vehicle Stability Enhancement System Excessive Brake Pulsation. DeVille & Seville

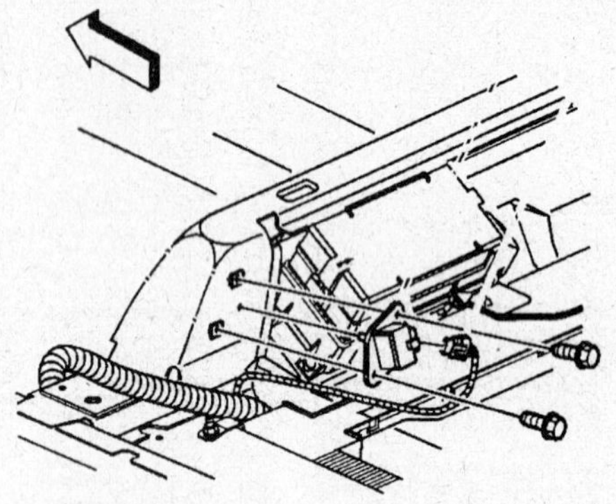

GC4020004039000X

Fig. 106 Lateral accelerometer sensor removal

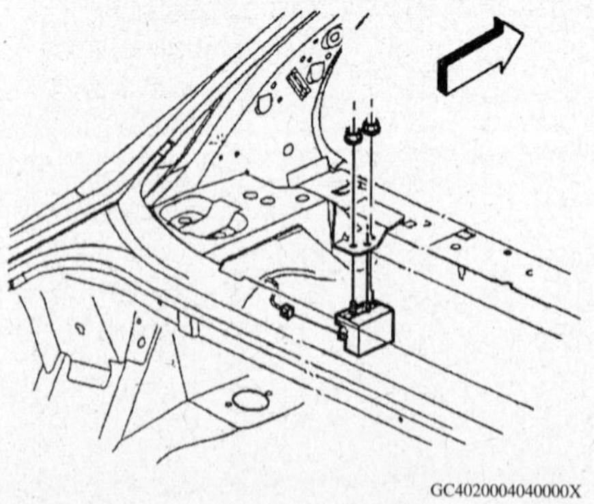

GC4020004040000X

Fig. 107 Yaw rate sensor removal

Saturn

NOTE: On Air Bag Equipped Models, Refer To "Air Bag System Precautions" Located In The Front Of This Manual For System Disarming & Arming Procedures.

NOTE: Refer To "Computer Relearn Procedures" Located In The Front Of This Manual When Battery Power To The Computer Has Been Interrupted.

NOTE: "Electrical Symbol & Wire Color Code Identification" Located In The Front Of This Manual May Be Used As An Aid When Using Wiring Circuits Found In This Section.

INDEX

PRECAUTIONS

Air Bag Systems

Refer to "Air Bag System Precautions" in the front of this manual for system disarming and arming procedures.

Battery Ground Cable

Prior to service, disconnect battery ground cable and isolate as required.

DESCRIPTION

System Operation

The Anti-Lock Brake System (ABS) minimizes wheel lockup during heavy braking on most road surfaces. The system performs this function by monitoring wheel speed and controlling the brake fluid pressure during braking. This allows the driver to retain directional stability and better steering capability.

Anti-Lock Telltale Lamp & Red Brake Warning Lamp

The Anti-Lock Telltale lamp, located in the instrument cluster, has several functions. If the lamp comes on solid, a fault has occurred and the ABS system has been disabled and should be serviced as soon as possible. If the telltale lamp is flashing, a fault has occurred, but the ABS system is still operational. The vehicle should still be serviced as soon as possible. Because the telltale lamp is also used to perform a bulb and system inspection, it will come on with the key on and the engine not running. When the engine is started, the lamp will turn off after approximately three seconds. If the lamp remains on or begins to flash, the self-diagnostic system has detected a fault.

The red brake warning lamp will light if master cylinder brake fluid level is low or if parking brake switch is closed; it is activated by the ABCM.

Low Traction Telltale Lamp

The Low Traction telltale lamp, located in the instrument cluster will come on whenever the Traction Control System (TCS) is in operation. The telltale lamp will remain On for 3–4 seconds after the TCS activity has completed. The telltale does not operate during an ABS activation.

TROUBLESHOOTING

Anti-Lock System

Refer to "Hydraulic Brake Systems" for anti-lock system troubleshooting procedures.

Traction Control System

Refer to **Figs. 1 through 3,** for traction control troubleshooting.

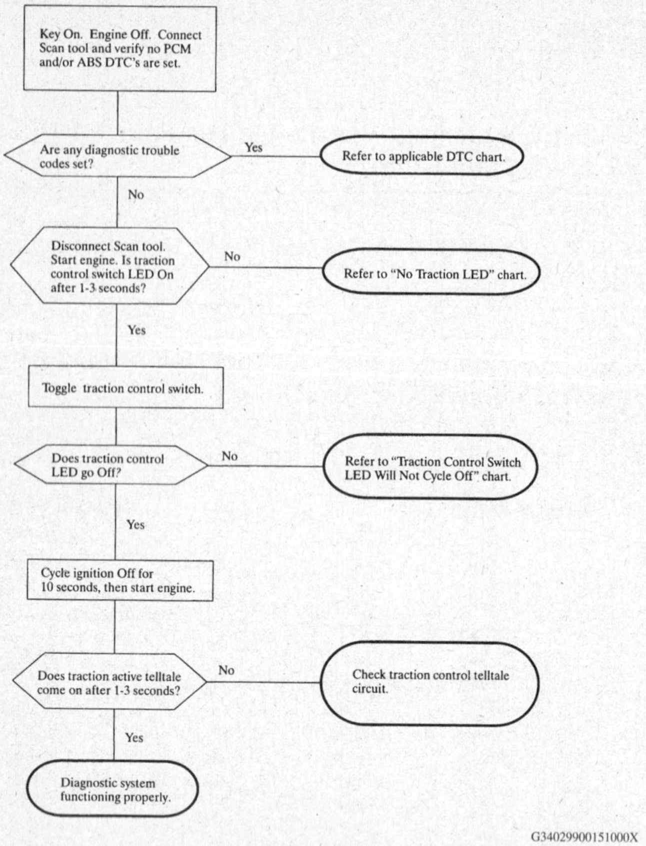

Fig. 1 Traction Control: Diagnostic Inspection. S-Series

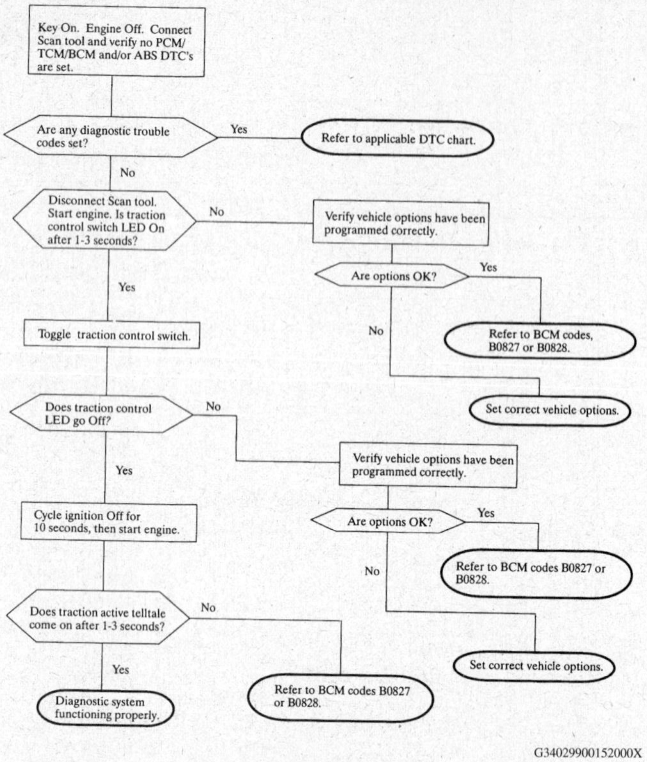

Fig. 2 Traction Control: Diagnostic Inspection. L-Series

DIAGNOSIS & TESTING

Accessing Diagnostic Trouble Codes

Connect a suitably programmed scan tool to the Data Link Connector (DLC), and follow manufacturer's instructions.

Diagnostic Trouble Code Interpretation

Refer to the "Diagnostic Chart Index" for DTC identification and description.

Wiring Diagrams & Connector Pin Identification

ION

When performing ABS system troubleshooting, diagnosis and testing, refer to wiring circuit, **Figs. 4 through 6,** and anti-lock brake system connector terminal and pin identification, **Figs. 7 through 10.**

L-SERIES

When performing ABS system troubleshooting, diagnosis and testing, refer to wiring circuits, **Figs. 11 and 12,** and anti-lock brake system connector terminal and pin identification, **Figs. 13 through 15.**

S-SERIES

When performing ABS system troubleshooting, diagnosis and testing, refer to wiring circuits, **Fig. 16,** and anti-lock brake system connector terminal and pin identification, **Figs. 17 and 18.**

Diagnostic Tests

ION

Refer to **Figs. 19 through 41,** for diagnostic trouble code diagnosis.

L-SERIES

Refer to **Figs. 42 through 60,** for diagnostic trouble code diagnosis.

S-SERIES

Refer to **Figs. 61 through 80,** for diagnostic trouble code diagnosis.

Clearing Diagnostic Trouble Codes

LESS SCAN TOOL

Current diagnostic trouble codes are cleared every time the ignition is turned off. To clear Malf History (Past Diagnostic Trouble Codes), select "Clear Codes" function on the scan tool. Past diagnostic trouble codes will clear themselves after 100 ignition cycles with no fault occurring. **Disconnecting power to the ABCM has no effect on stored diagnostic trouble codes.**

WITH SCAN TOOL

Connect a suitably programmed scan tool to Data Link Connector (DLC), and follow manufacturer's instruction.

Intermittent Fault Conditions

Intermittent faults are a common source of misdiagnosis when accessing diagnostic trouble codes. Most intermittent faults are caused by loose or damaged electrical wiring and connectors. The scan tool can be used in several ways to aid in intermittent diagnosis. Connect the scan tool to the DLC connector, then manipulate wiring harnesses or components while observing the scan tool. Leaving scan tool connected to the DLC connector, drive vehicle under conditions similar to those present when the ABS fault first occurred. If the problem seems to be related to certain parameters that can be inspected with the scan tool, they should be inspected at this time. If there does not seem to be any correlation between the problem and any specific circuit, the scan tool can be inspected on each position, watching for a period of time to see if there is any change in the readings that would indicate an intermittent fault.

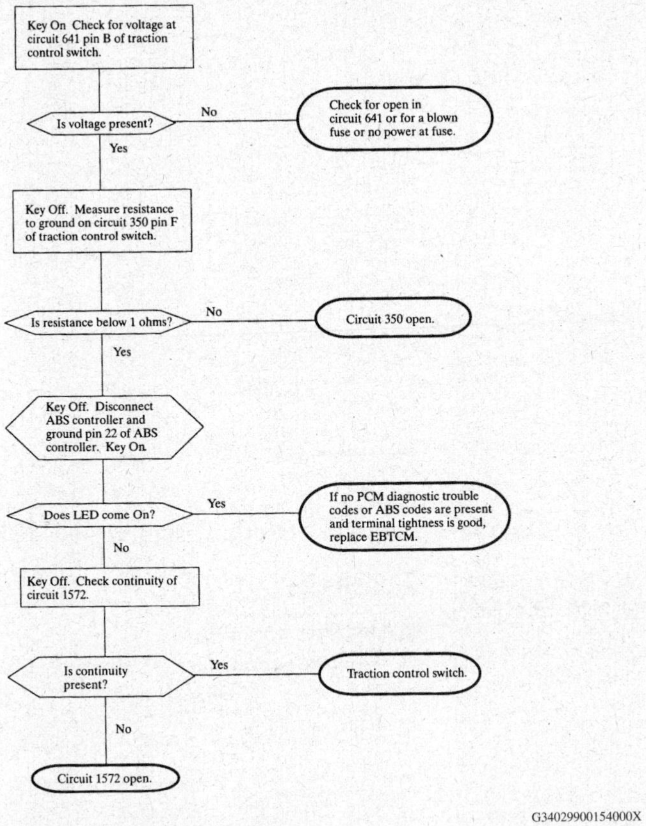

Fig. 3 Traction Control: No Traction Led. S-Series

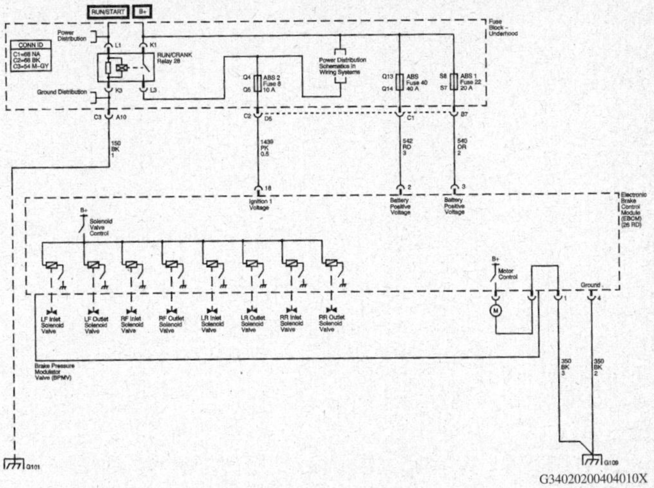

Fig. 4 Wiring diagram (Part 1 of 3). ION

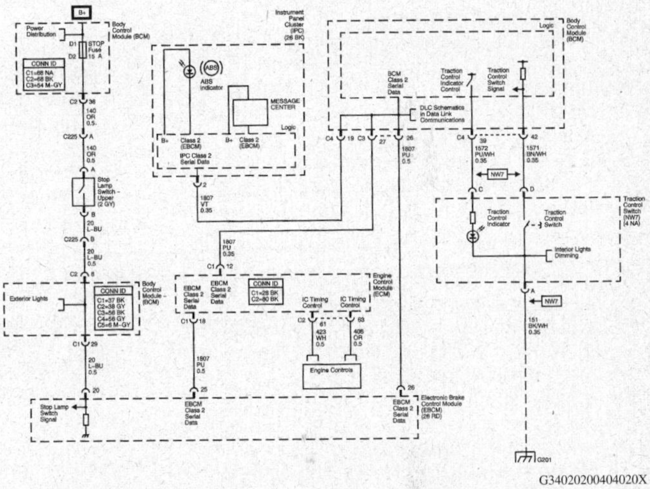

Fig. 4 Wiring diagram (Part 2 of 3). ION

SYSTEM SERVICE

Brake System Bleed

ION

This vehicle is equipped with two types of hydraulic brake pipe flares and components, there is a first design and a second design, **Fig. 81. Do not mis-match flare types or component, damage and or fluid leaks may occur.**

AUTOMATED

This procedure requires a scan tool to cycle the system solenoid valves and runs the ABS pump to purge air from the secondary system. The automated bleed procedure opens the secondary system circuits allowing trapped air to flow outward toward brake corner components such as wheel cylinders and calipers.

1. Ensure battery is fully charged, then connect a suitably programmed scan tool to Data Link Connector (DLC).
2. Fill master cylinder with suitable DOT 3 brake fluid.
3. Turn ignition switch to On position, then raise and support vehicle.
4. Remove all four wheel/tire assemblies.
5. Follow scan tool manufacturers' instructions to communicate with ABS system.
6. Scan tool will request a base brake system pressure bleed, bleed system as outlined in "Brake System Bleed" in this section.
7. Follow scan tool instructions until desired brake pedal height is achieved, then depress brake pedal to inspect for firmness.
8. Remove scan tool and all base brake bleed procedure components, then install wheel/tire assemblies and lower vehicle.

MANUAL

1. With ignition switch in Off position, depress pedal 3–5 times to deplete power booster reserve.
2. Fill master cylinder with suitable Dot 3 brake fluid.
3. Loosen front brake pipe at master cylinder and allow a small amount of fluid to gravity flow from port.
4. Tighten front master cylinder brake pipe securely.
5. With help from an assistant, depress brake pedal slowly, maintaining steady pressure on pedal.
6. Loosen front brake pipe at master cylinder to purge air from port.
7. With brake pedal still depressed, tighten brake fitting, then slowly release pedal.
8. Wait 15 seconds, then repeat steps 5 through 7 until air is removed from (front) secondary master cylinder bore, refer to **Fig. 81,** for tightening specifications.
9. Loosen rear brake pipe at master cylinder and allow a small amount of fluid to gravity flow from port.
10. Repeat steps 5 through 7 until air is removed from (rear) primary master cylinder bore, refer to **Fig. 81,** for tightening specifications.
11. Attach a bleeder hose to righthand rear bleeder screw, then insert other end of hose into a suitable clear container.
12. Loosen bleeder screw and apply brake pedal slowly and hold.
13. Tighten bleeder screw and release brake pedal.
14. Repeat steps 11 and 12 until all air is removed.
15. Repeat steps 11 through 13 in the following order; lefthand front, lefthand rear and righthand front. **Torque** wheel cylinder bleeder screws to 71 inch lbs. **Torque** caliper bleeder screws to 97 inch lbs.

PRESSURE

1. Clean area around master cylinder reservoir cap.

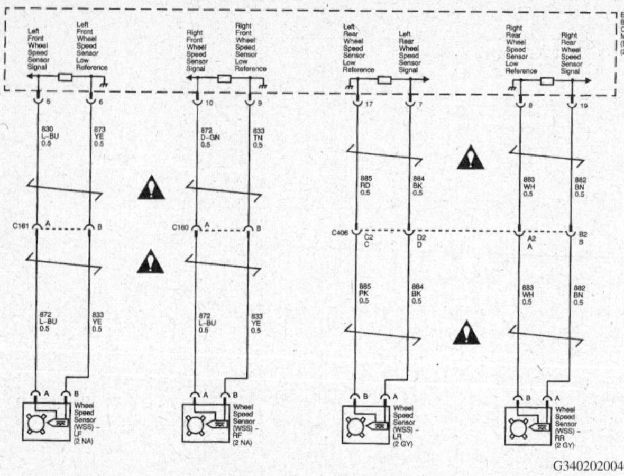

Fig. 4 Wiring diagram (Part 3 of 3). ION

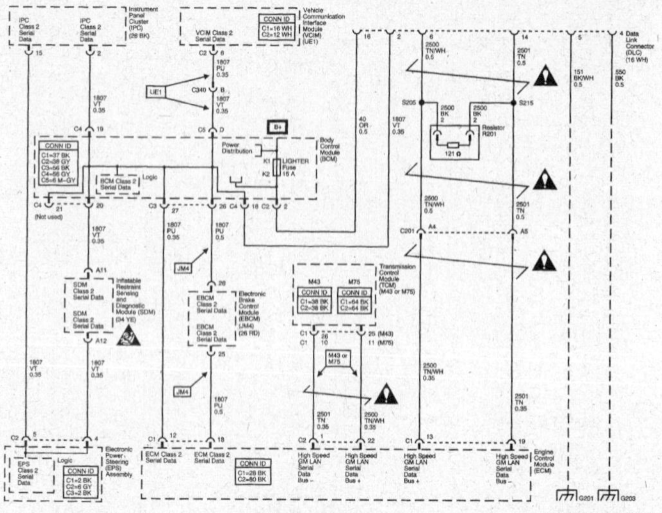

Fig. 5 Data link communications wiring circuit. ION

2. With ignition switch in Off position, depress pedal 3–5 times to deplete power booster reserve.
3. Fill master cylinder with suitable Dot 3 brake fluid.
4. Install brake bleed adapter tool No. J-44894–A, or equivalent, to fluid reservoir.
5. Connect pressure bleeder tool No. J 29532, or equivalent, to adapter and pressurize to 25–30 psi. Wait approximately 30 seconds, then inspect for leaks.
6. Loosen master cylinder front brake line fitting and allow fluid to flow from fitting until all air is removed from front (secondary) cylinder bore. Refer to **Fig. 81,** for tightening specifications.
7. Loosen master cylinder rear brake line fitting and allow fluid to flow from fitting until all air is removed from rear cylinder bore. Refer to **Fig. 81,** for tightening specifications.
8. Attach a clear tube to righthand rear bleeder screw.
9. Loosen screw and allow fluid to flow from fitting until all air is removed. **Torque** wheel cylinder bleeder screws to 71 inch lbs. **Torque** caliper bleeder screws to 97 inch lbs.
10. Repeat steps 8 and 9 in the following order; lefthand front, lefthand rear and righthand front.

L-SERIES

It is not required or recommended to bleed the Anti-Lock Brake Control Module (ABCM) or the Electronic Brake Traction Control Module (EBTCM). Bleeding may induce air into the brake hydraulic system.

MANUAL

1. Fill master cylinder with Dot 3 brake fluid.
2. Loosen front brake pipe at master cylinder and allow fluid to flow from port.
3. Tighten front brake pipe, then loosen brake pipe ¼ turn.
4. Depress brake pedal slowly until fluid is seen coming from fitting.
5. With brake pedal still depressed, tighten brake fitting, then slowly release pedal.
6. Repeat steps 3 through 5 until air is removed from (front) secondary master cylinder bore, **torque** brake fitting to 12 ft. lbs.
7. Loosen rear brake pipe at master cylinder and allow fluid to flow from port.
8. Repeat steps 3 through 5 until air is removed from (rear) primary master cylinder bore, **torque** brake fitting to 12 ft. lbs.
9. Attach a bleeder hose to righthand rear bleeder screw, then insert other end of hose into a suitable clear container.
10. Loosen bleeder screw and apply brake pedal slowly and hold.
11. Tighten bleeder screw and release brake pedal.
12. Repeat steps 9 and 10 until all air is removed.
13. Repeat steps 9 through 12 in the following order; lefthand front, lefthand rear and righthand front. **Torque** bleeder screws to 71 inch lbs.

PRESSURE

1. Clean area around master cylinder reservoir cap.
2. Fill master cylinder with Dot 3 brake fluid.
3. Install brake bleed adapter tool No. J-43915, or equivalent, to fluid reservoir.
4. Connect pressure bleeder tool No. J 29532, or equivalent, to adapter and pressurize to 20–25 psi.
5. Loosen master cylinder front brake line fitting and allow fluid to flow from fitting until all air is removed from front (secondary) cylinder bore. **Torque** fitting to 12 ft. lbs.
6. Loosen master cylinder rear brake line fitting and allow fluid to flow from fitting until all air is removed from rear cylinder bore. **Torque** fitting to 12 ft. lbs.
7. Attach a clear tube to righthand rear bleeder screw.
8. Loosen screw and allow fluid to flow from fitting until all air is removed. **Torque** bleeder screw to 71 inch lbs.
9. Repeat steps 7 and 8 in the following order; lefthand front, lefthand rear and righthand front.

S-SERIES

MANUAL

1. Ensure battery is fully charged, then connect a suitably programmed scan tool to Data Link Connector (DLC).
2. Fill master cylinder with DOT 3 brake fluid.
3. Turn ignition switch to the RUN position, then raise and support vehicle.
4. Follow scan tool manufacturers' instructions to communicate with ABS system.
5. Attach a clear bleed hose to righthand rear wheel bleeder screw, then insert other end of bleed hose into a clear container.
6. Slowly apply brake pedal and hold in position.
7. Scan tool should instruct operator to open righthand rear brake screw.
8. Press START button on scan tool and open bleeder screw simultaneously. **During the first part of the automated bleed procedure the pump will cycle for 60 seconds. After cycling the pump, the scan tool will go into a cool-down mode for 180 seconds. The scan tool will display the timer. The automated bleed procedure will not continue until the timer has expired.**
9. When brake pedal reaches floor, close bleeder screw.
10. Release brake pedal, then slowly apply and hold brake pedal in position again and hold, then open bleeder screw. Repeat procedure as many times as required to remove air from system.
11. Repeat steps 8 through 10 in the following order; lefthand rear, righthand front and lefthand front.
12. **Torque** rear bleeder screws to 66 inch lbs.
13. **Torque** front bleeder screws to 97 inch lbs.

PRESSURE

This system uses an automated brake bleed procedure. It is required to have a

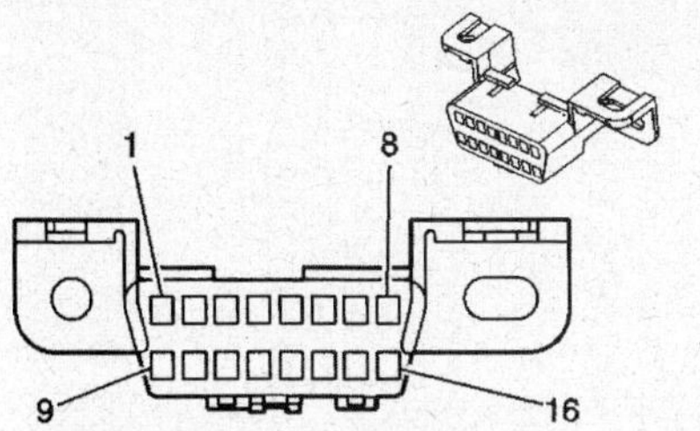

Connector Part Information	• 179631-1 • 16 Way F (WH)		
Pin	Wire Color	Circuit No.	Function
1	—	—	Not Used
2	VT	1807	Class 2 Serial Data
3	—	—	Not Used
4	BK	550	Ground
5	BK/WH	151	Ground
6	TN/WH	2500	High Speed GM LAN Serial Data Bus+
7–13	—	—	Not Used
14	TN	2501	High Speed GM LAN Serial Data Bus-
15	—	—	Not Used
16	OR	40	Battery Positive Voltage

G34020200413000X

Fig. 6 Data link communications connector terminal identification. ION

suitably programmed scan tool to complete this procedure.

1. Ensure battery is fully charged, then connect a suitably programmed scan tool to Data Link Connector (DLC).
2. Fill master cylinder with DOT 3 brake fluid.
3. Connect pressure bleeder tool No. J 29532, or equivalent, to master cylinder and pressurize to 35 psi.
4. Turn ignition switch to the RUN position, then follow scan tool manufacturers' instructions to communicate with ABS system.
5. Select CONTINUE on scan tool to begin bleed procedure. **During the first part of the automated bleed procedure the pump will cycle for 60 seconds. After cycling the pump, the scan tool will go into a cool-down mode for 180 seconds. The scan tool will display the timer. The automated bleed procedure will not continue until the timer has expired.**
6. Raise and support vehicle.
7. Attach a clear bleed hose to righthand rear wheel bleeder screw, then insert other end of bleed hose into a clear container.
8. Open bleeder screw, then press START button on scan tool.
9. Scan tool will cycle both release valves and pump motor for 60 seconds. Once scan tool is done cycling designated wheel cylinder or caliper, close bleeder screw.
10. Repeat steps 7 through 9 in the following order; lefthand rear, righthand front and lefthand front.
11. Repeat entire bleed procedure steps 7 through 10.
12. **Torque** rear bleeder screws to 66 inch lbs.
13. **Torque** front bleeder screws to 97 inch lbs.

Component Replacement

ELECTRONIC BRAKE CONTROL MODULE (EBCM)

ION

1. Clean area around EBCM and Brake Pressure Modulator Valve (BPMV) of dirt and foreign material.
2. With ignition switch in Off position, disconnect EBCM electrical connector.
3. Remove four EBCM retaining bolts, then separate EBCM from BPMV by gently pulling them apart, **Fig. 82.**
4. Reverse procedure to install noting the following:
   a. Clean EBCM and BPMV matting surfaces with suitable denatured alcohol.
   b. Install EBCM onto BPMV, ensure EBCM terminals are properly aligned with BPMV terminals.
   c. Install four ECBM retaining bolts, then tighten bolts in a criss-cross pattern, then **torque** to 27 inch lbs.
   d. Connect ECBM electrical connector.

ANTI-LOCK BRAKE CONTROL MODULE (ABCM) & ELECTRONIC BRAKE TRACTION CONTROL MODULE (EBTCM)

L-SERIES

1. Remove brake pipe fittings from Brake Pressure Modulator Valve (BPMV).
2. Disconnect brake pipe fittings from master cylinder.
3. Disconnect EBTCM electrical connector.
4. Remove ABS control assembly mounting nuts and bracket.
5. Remove ABS control assembly from vehicle.
6. Disconnect pump motor electrical connector.
7. Remove EBTCM to BPMV attaching screws, then separate control module from BPMV.
8. Reverse procedure to install, noting the following:
   a. **Torque** control assembly to bracket nuts to 15 ft. lbs.

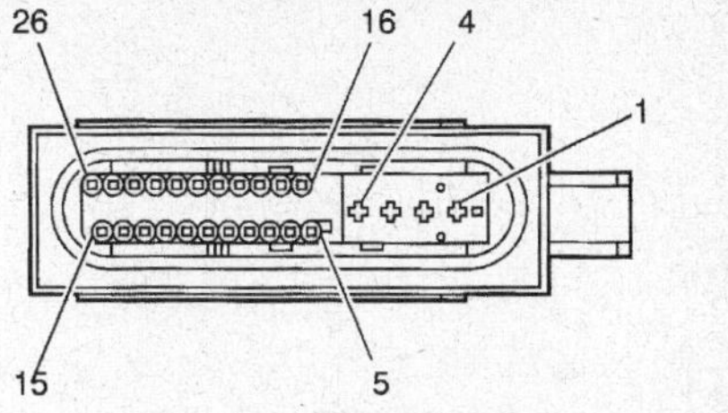

Connector Part Information	• 1-928404-410 • 26–Way F Bosch (BK)		
Pin	Wire Color	Circuit No.	Function
1	BK	350	Ground
2	RD	542	Battery Positive Voltage
3	OR	540	Battery Positive Voltage
4	BK	350	Ground
5	L-BU	830	Left Front Wheel Speed Sensor Signal
6	YE	873	Left Front Wheel Speed Sensor Low Reference
7	BK	884	Left Rear Wheel Speed Sensor Signal
8	WH	883	Right Rear Wheel Speed Sensor Low Reference
9	TN	833	Right Front Wheel Speed Sensor Low Reference
10	D-GN	872	Right Front Wheel Speed Sensor Signal
11–16	—	—	Not Used
17	RD	885	Left Rear Wheel Speed Sensor Low Reference
18	PK	1439	Ignition 1 Voltage
19	BN	882	Right Rear Wheel Speed Sensor Signal
20	L-BU	20	Stop Lamp Switch Signal
21–24	—	—	Not Used
25	PU	1807	EBCM Class 2 Serial Data
26	PU	1807	EBCM Class 2 Serial Data

G34020200405000X

Fig. 7 Electronic brake control module connector terminal identification. ION

   b. **Torque** all brake pipe fittings to 13 ft. lbs.
   c. **Perform manual hydraulic brake system bleed procedure only**, as outlined in "Brake System Bleed" in "System Service." It is not required or recommended to bleed ABCM/EBTCM controller, air may be induced into system.

S-SERIES

1. Remove air cleaner housing and air induction hose from throttle body.
2. Remove Powertrain Control Module (PCM) retaining bolts.
3. Disconnect PCM electrical connector, then position PCM aside.
4. Disconnect ABS control module electrical connector, then remove ABS

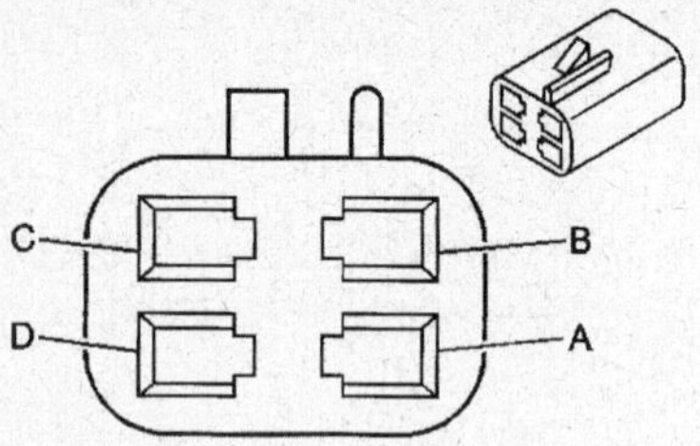

Connector Part Information		• 12089248 • 4-Way F Metri-Pack 150 Series (BK)	
Pin	Wire Color	Circuit No.	Function
A	BK/WH	151	Ground
B	GY	8	Instrument Panel Lamp Supply Voltage - 1
C	PU/WH	1572	Traction Control Indicator Control
D	BN/WH	1571	Traction Control Switch Signal

G34020200406000X

Fig. 8 Traction control switch connector terminal identification. ION

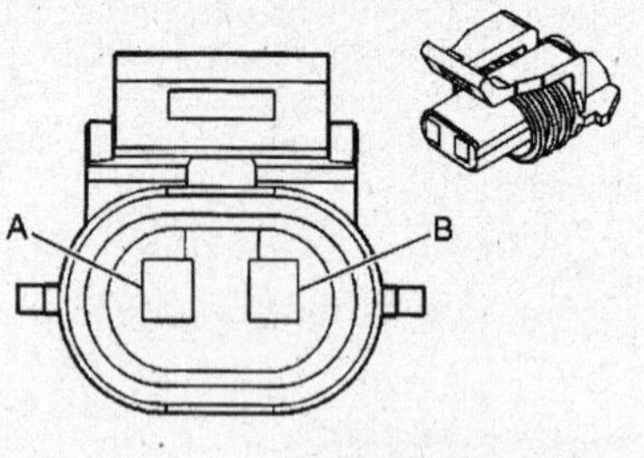

Connector Part Information		• 12052644 • 2-Way F Metri-Pack 150 Series Sealed (GY)	
Pin	Wire Color	Circuit No.	Function
A	L-BU	872	Left Front Wheel Speed Sensor Signal
B	YE	833	Left Front Wheel Speed Sensor Low Reference

G34020200407000X

Fig. 9 Front wheel speed sensor connector terminal identification. ION

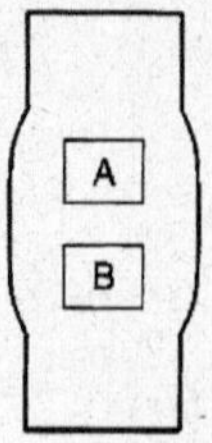

Connector Part Information		• 15305168 • 2-Way F (GY)	
Pin	Wire Color	Circuit No.	Function
A	BK	884	Left Rear Wheel Speed Sensor Signal
B	RD	885	Left Rear Wheel Speed Sensor Low Reference

G34020200408000X

Fig. 10 Rear wheel speed sensor connector terminal identification. ION

control module to brake pressure modulator attaching screws.

5. Pull control module away from modulator.
6. Reverse procedure to install, noting the following:
   a. **Torque** control module to brake pressure modulator attaching screws to 35–53 inch lbs.
   b. **Torque** PCM retaining bolts to 53 inch lbs.

BRAKE PRESSURE MODULATOR VALVE (BPMV)

ION

This vehicle is equipped with two types of hydraulic brake pipe flares and components, there is a first design and a second design **Fig. 81. Do not mis-match flare types or components, damage and or fluid leaks may occur.**

1. Remove EBCM as outlined under, "Electronic Brake Control Module (EBCM)" in this section.
2. Clean area around (BPMV) of dirt and foreign material.
3. Place a suitable shop towel or equivalent, under BPMV to retain any fluid loss.
4. Mark positions of BPMV hydraulic pipe assemblies for installation reference.
5. Disconnect caliper and wheel cylinder to BPMV hydraulic pipes **Fig. 83,** then cap ends to prevent fluid loss and contamination.
6. Disconnect master cylinder to BPMV hydraulic pipes, then cap ends to prevent fluid loss and contamination.
7. install caps in modulator assembly hydraulic pipe openings to prevent fluid loss and contamination.
8. Remove two BPMV assembly insulator nuts to mounting bracket, then BPMV assembly.
9. Reverse procedure to install noting the following:
   a. Install BPMV assembly to bracket, **torque** mounting nuts to 71 inch lbs.
   b. Remove plugs from hydraulic pipes and BPMV pipe openings.
   c. Install hydraulic pipes, using paint mark references for proper pipe locations.
   d. Refer to **Fig. 81,** for tightening specifications.
   e. Perform automated brake system bleed as outlined under, "Brake System Bleed" in the "System Services" section.

L-SERIES

Refer to "Anti-Lock Brake Control Module (ABCM) & Electronic Brake Traction Control Module (EBTCM)" for BPMV replacement procedure.

S-SERIES

1. Remove air cleaner housing and air induction hose from throttle body.
2. Remove Powertrain Control Module (PCM) retaining bolts.
3. Disconnect PCM electrical connector, then position PCM aside.
4. Disconnect brake fluid level switch and control module electrical connectors.
5. Remove brake pipe fittings from Brake Pressure Modulator Valve (BPMV).
6. Remove ABS control assembly to rail attaching bolt, then the control assembly from vehicle.
7. Remove control module to BPMV attaching screws, then separate control module from BPMV.
8. Reverse procedure to install, noting the following:
   a. **Torque** control module to brake pressure modulator attaching screws to 35–53 inch lbs.
   b. **Torque** PCM retaining bolts to 53 inch lbs.
   c. Bleed brake hydraulic system as outlined in "Brake System Bleed" in "System Service."

TRACTION CONTROL SWITCH

ION

1. Remove instrument panel accessory trim plate as outlined under, "Dash Panel Service" in this manual.
2. Carefully release traction control switch retaining clips.
3. Disconnect electrical connector, then remove switch.
4. Reverse procedure to install.

L-SERIES

1. Remove instrument panel center trim plate by gently rearward on top of trim plate to release retaining clips.
2. Tilt trim panel to access traction control switch electrical connector, disconnect electrical connector.
3. Release locking tabs on traction control switch, then remove switch through front of center trim plate.
4. Reverse procedure to install.

S-SERIES

1. Lift upward on lefthand side of switch assembly to release locking tabs retaining switch to dash panel.
2. Disconnect electrical connector, then remove switch assembly.
3. Reverse procedure to install.

FRONT WHEEL SPEED SENSOR

1. Raise and support vehicle.
2. Disconnect wheel speed sensor electrical connector, **Fig. 84.**
3. Remove wheel speed sensor to steering knuckle Torx head bolt, then the wheel speed sensor. **When removing speed sensor, be careful not to damage speed sensor ring. Even a minor scratch on sensor ring can cause a loss of ABS operation. Front speed sensor has a locating pin which may become stuck in steering knuckle. This pin may separate from sensor during removal and remain in knuckle. If this pin**

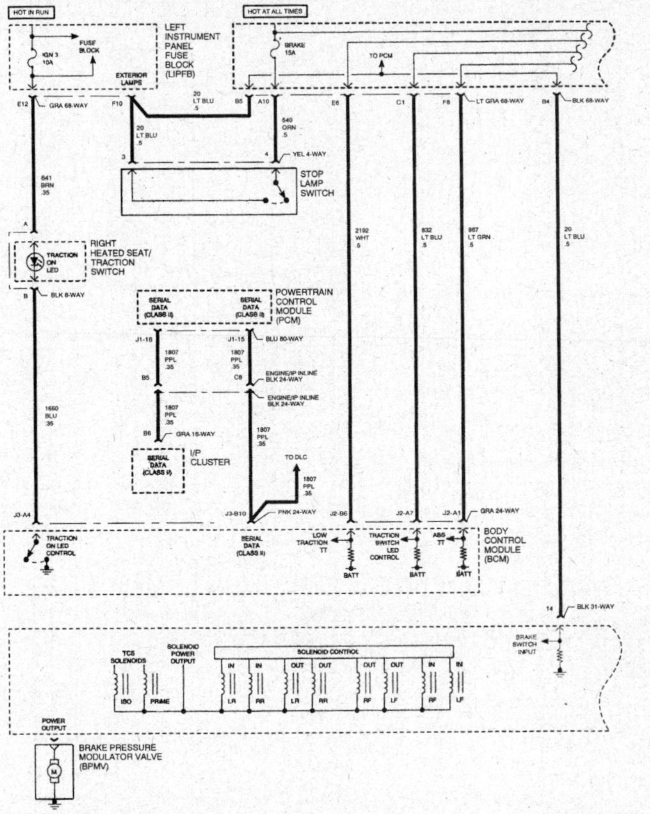

Fig. 11 Wiring diagram (Part 1 of 4). L-Series w/2.2L engine

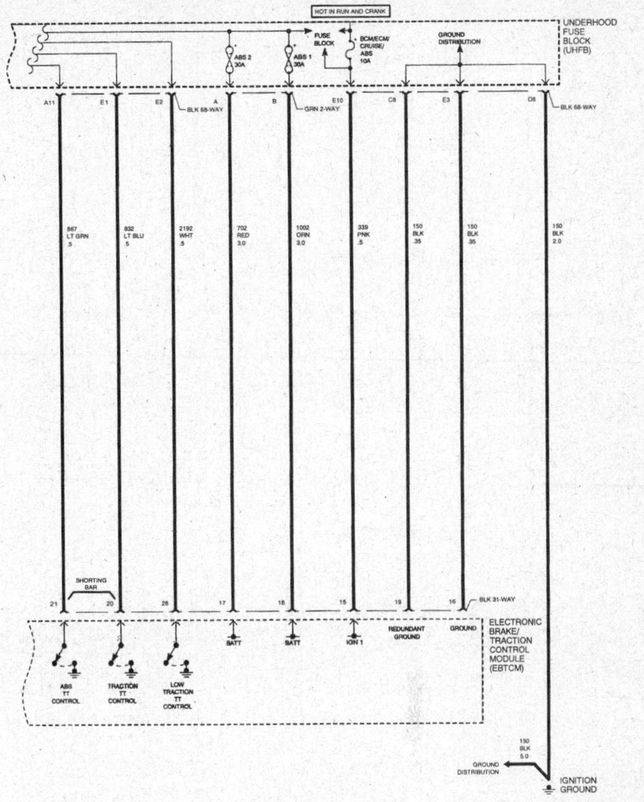

Fig. 11 Wiring diagram (Part 2 of 4). L-Series w/2.2L engine

cannot be pulled out of knuckle it must be drilled out using an 8mm drill bit. Be careful not to enlarge pin hole when drilling pin out of knuckle.

4. Reverse procedure to install. **Torque** Torx head bolt to 89 inch lbs.

REAR WHEEL SPEED SENSOR

ION

The rear wheel speed sensor is contained within the hub and bearing assembly. The sensor cannot be serviced separately.

1. Raise and support vehicle, then remove wheel and tire assembly.
2. Disconnect wheel speed sensor electrical connector, **Fig. 85.**
3. Remove rear brake drum.
4. Remove plug from brake actuator access hole, use access hole to install a support for backing plate, **Fig. 85.**
5. Remove hub/bearing assembly mounting nuts, hub/bearing assembly.
6. Reverse procedure to install noting the following:
   a. **Torque** hub/bearing assembly mounting bolts to 37 ft. lbs.
   b. Remove support and install backing plate plug and brake drum.
   c. Connect wheel speed sensor electrical connector.
   d. Install wheel and tire assembly, then lower vehicle.

L-SERIES

The rear wheel speed sensor is contained within the hub and bearing assembly. The sensor cannot be serviced separately.

1. Raise and support vehicle, then remove wheel and tire assembly.
2. Disconnect sensor electrical connector.
3. **On models equipped with disc brakes,** proceed as follows:
   a. Remove caliper assembly attaching bolts and suspend caliper assembly aside.
   b. Remove brake rotor attaching bolts, then the brake rotor.
4. **On models equipped with drum brakes,** remove drum attaching bolts, then the brake drum.
5. **On all models,** remove hub to rear axle control arm retaining nuts, then the hub assembly. Discard nuts.
6. Reverse procedure to install, noting the following:
   a. **Torque** hub to rear axle control arm retaining nuts to 37 ft. lbs.
   b. **Torque** brake drum/rotor attaching bolts to 35 inch lbs.
   c. **On models equipped with disc brakes, torque** caliper attaching bolts to 59 ft. lbs.

S-SERIES

Disc Brake

The rear wheel speed sensor is contained within the hub and bearing assembly. The sensor cannot be serviced separately.

1. Raise and support vehicle.
2. Remove wheel, then disconnect electrical connector from speed sensor.
3. Remove two caliper to knuckle mounting bolts, then suspend caliper from strut spring with wire.
4. Remove rotor from hub, then four hub to knuckle attaching bolts, **Fig. 86.**
5. Remove hub and bearing assembly.
6. Reverse procedure to install, **torque** hub to knuckle bolts and caliper to knuckle bolts to 63 ft. lbs.

Drum Brake

The rear wheel speed sensor is contained within the hub and bearing assembly. The sensor cannot be serviced separately.

1. Raise and support vehicle. then remove tire and wheel assembly.
2. Disconnect speed sensor electrical connector.
3. Remove brake drum, then the hub to knuckle attaching bolts.
4. Remove hub and bearing assembly.
5. Reverse procedure to install, noting the following:
   a. **Torque** hub to knuckle attaching bolts to 53 ft. lbs.
   b. **Torque** wheel lug nut to 103 ft. lbs.

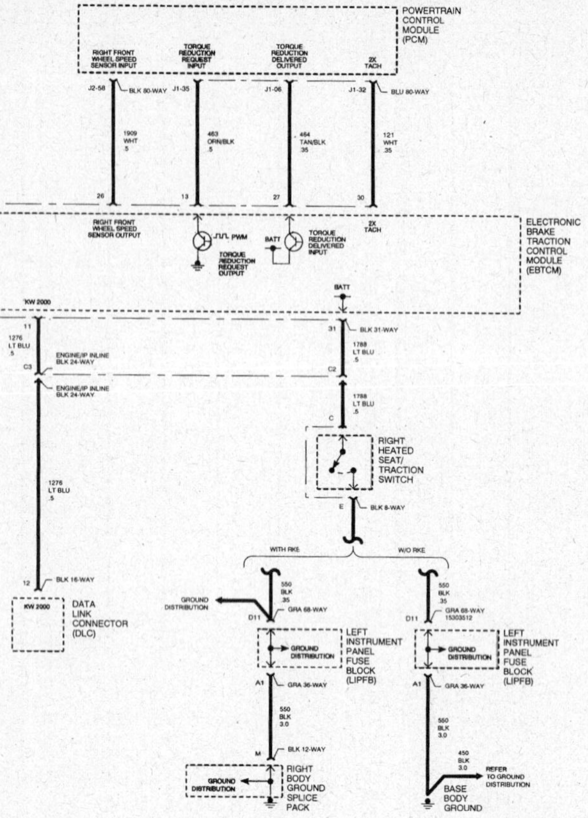

G34020000231030X

Fig. 11 Wiring diagram (Part 3 of 4). L-Series w/2.2L engine

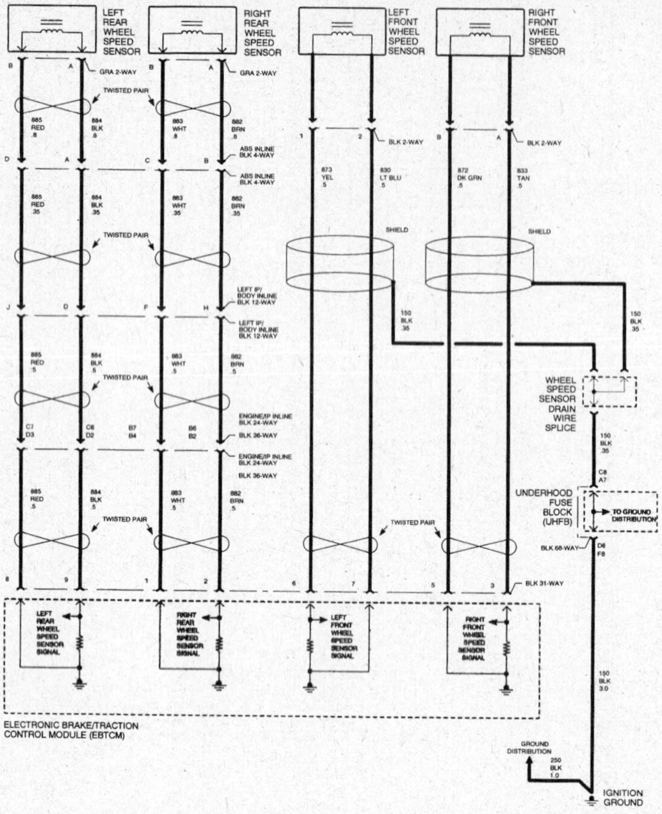

G34020000231040X

Fig. 11 Wiring diagram (Part 4 of 4). L-Series w/2.2L engine

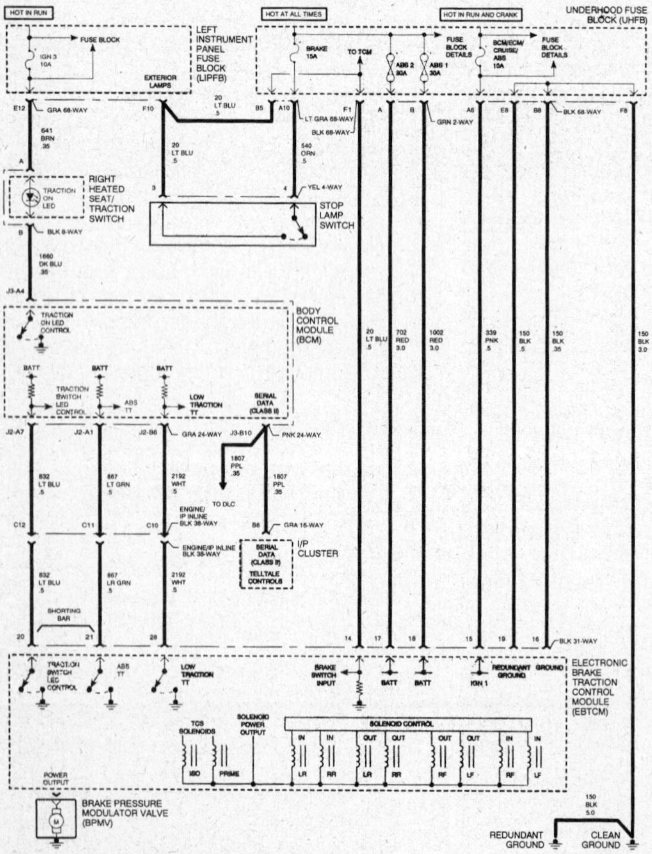

G34020000232010X

Fig. 12 Wiring diagram (Part 1 of 3). L-Series w/3.0L engine

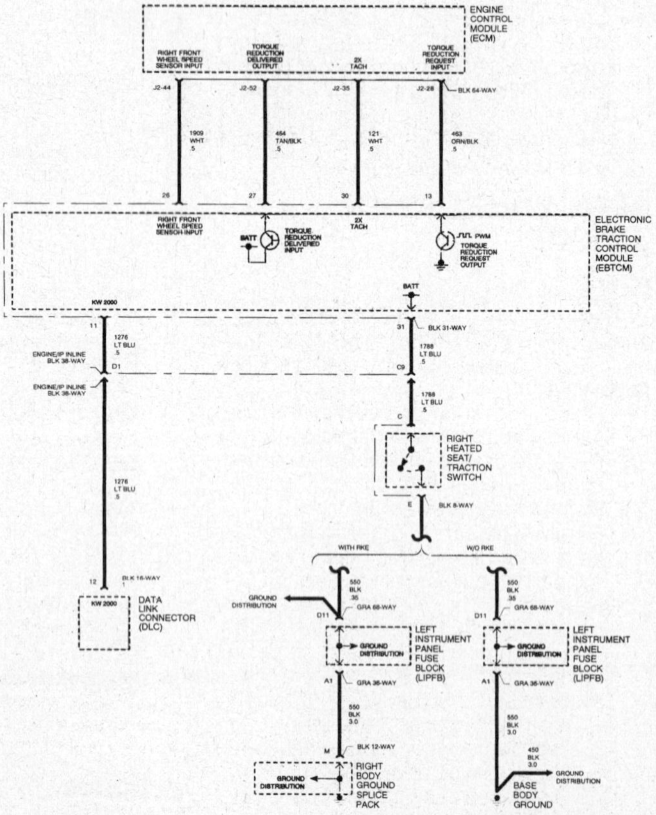

G34020000232020X

Fig. 12 Wiring diagram (Part 2 of 3). L-Series w/3.0L engine

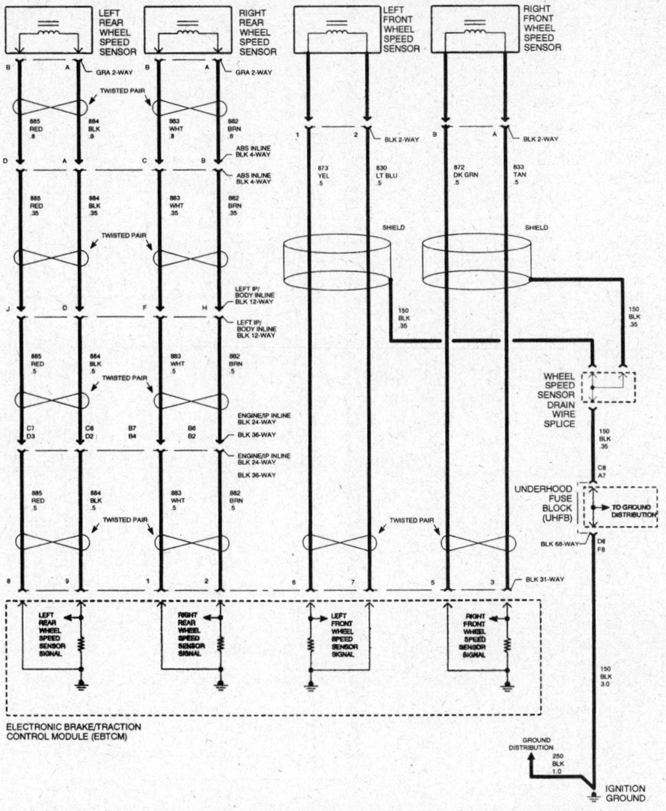

G34020000232030X

Fig. 12 Wiring diagram (Part 3 of 3). L-Series w/3.0L engine

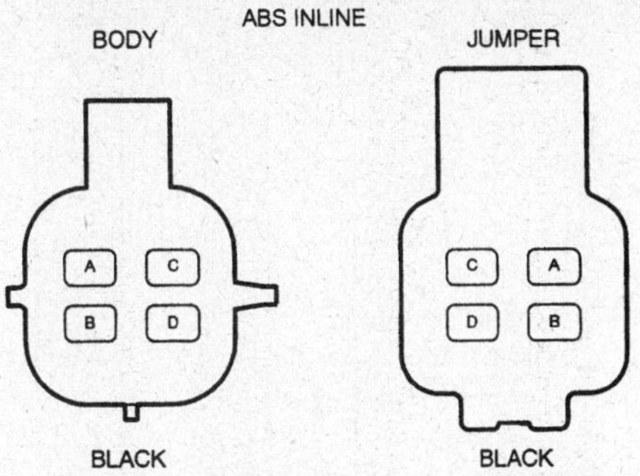

G34020000273000X

Fig. 13 ABS Inline connector terminal identification. L-Series

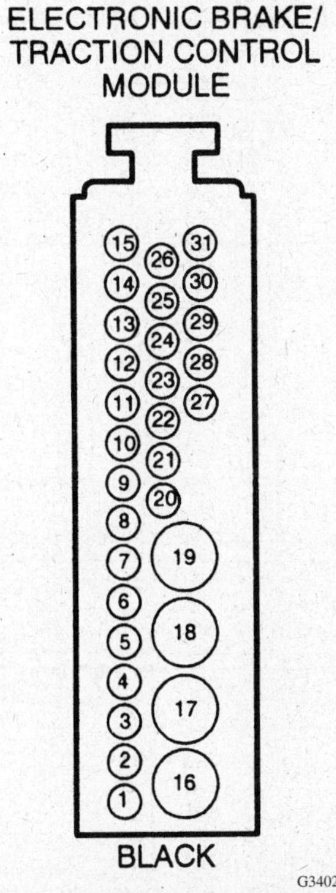

G34020000274000X

Fig. 14 Electronic brake/traction control module connector terminal identification. L-Series

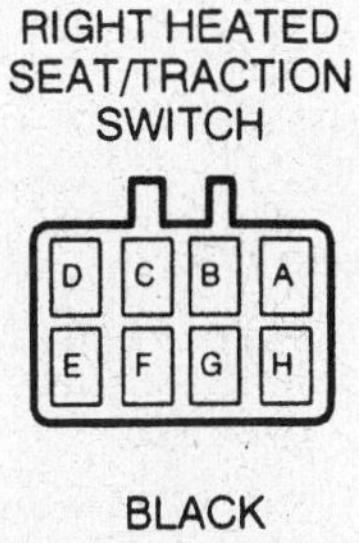

G34020000275000X

Fig. 15 RH heated seat/traction control switch connector terminal identification. L-Series

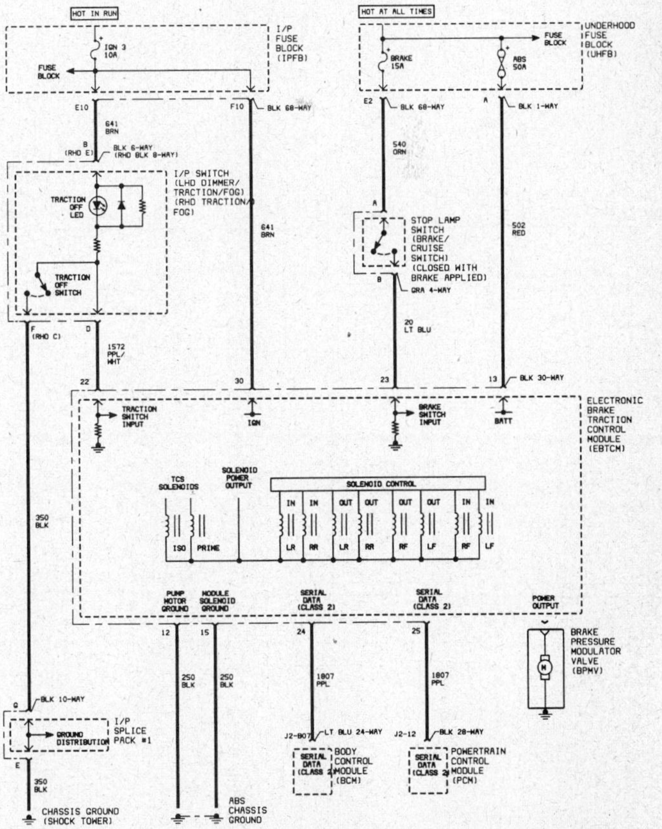

G34029900155010X

Fig. 16 Wiring diagram (Part 1 of 2). S-Series

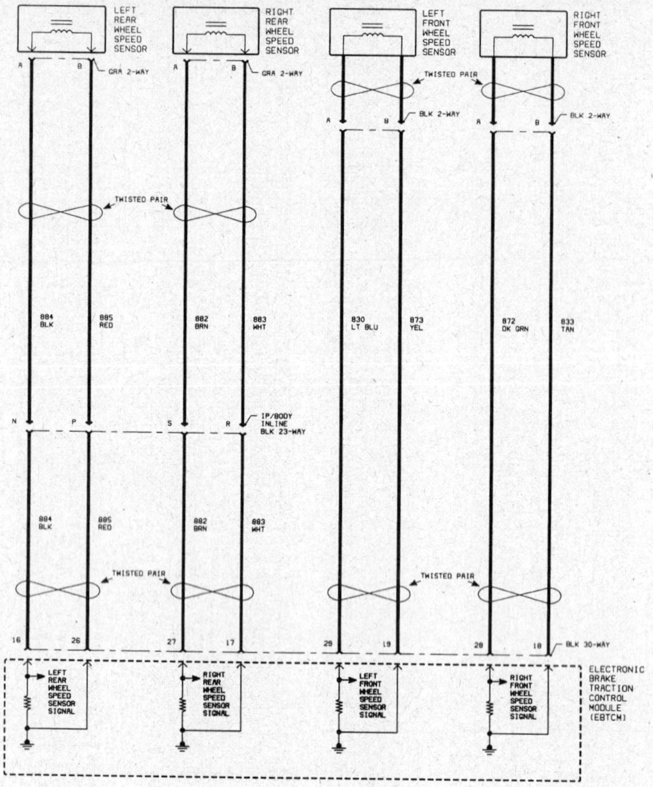

G34029900155020X

Fig. 16 Wiring diagram (Part 2 of 2). S-Series

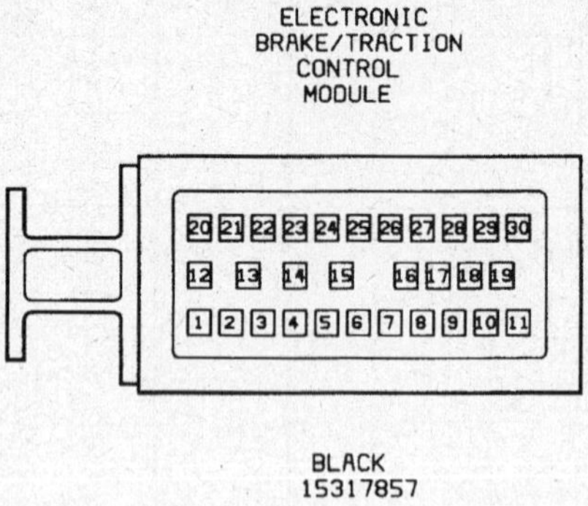

G34029900157000X

Fig. 17 Electronic brake/traction control module connector terminal identification. S-Series

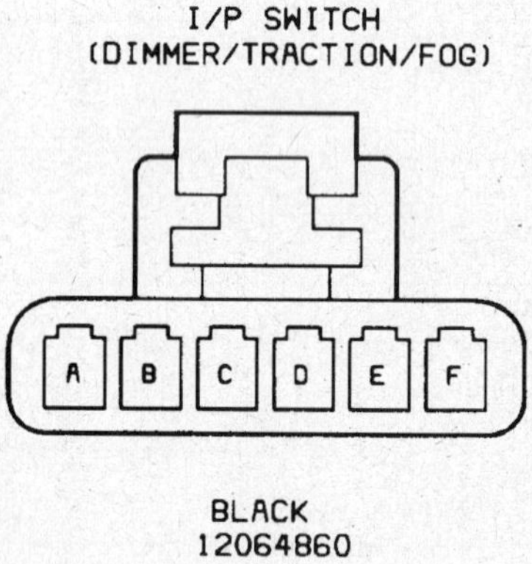

G34029900158000X

Fig. 18 Traction controller 6-pin connector terminal identification. S-Series

DIAGNOSTIC CHART INDEX

Code	Description	Page No.	Fig. No.
ION			
—	ABS Indicator Always On	6-601	19
—	ABS Indicator Inoperative	6-601	20
—	Brake Warning Indicator Always On	6-601	21
—	Brake Warning Indicator Inoperative	6-601	22
—	Diagnostic System Check ABS	6-602	23
—	Diagnostic System Check Hydraulic Brakes	6-602	24
—	Scan Tool Does Not Communicate With Class 2 Device	6-602	25
—	Scan Tool Does Not Power Up	6-603	26
—	Symptoms Anti-Lock Brake System	6-603	27
—	Symptoms Hydraulic Brakes	6-604	28
—	Traction Control Indicator Always On	6-604	29
—	Traction Control Indicator Inoperative	6-604	30
C0035-C0051	Wheel Speed Sensor Fault	6-604	31
C0060-C0095	ABS Solenoid Circuit Fault	6-605	32
C0110	ABS Pump Motor Failure	6-605	33
C0121	Solenoid Valve Relay Valve Fault	6-606	34
C0129	Brake Fluid Level Low Or Brake Fluid Level Switch Fault	6-606	35
C0267	Brake Fluid Level Low Or Brake Fluid Level Switch Fault	6-606	35
C0161	ABS/TCS Brake Switch Fault	6-606	36
C0245	Wheel Speed Sensor Signal Incorrect	6-607	37
C0550	ECU Fault	6-607	38
C0896	System Voltage To High/Low	6-608	39
U1000 & U1255	Class 2 Serial Data Circuit Communication Error	6-608	40
U1300, U1301 & U1305	Class 2 Serial Data Circuit Signal Error	6-609	41
L -SERIES			
—	TRAC Switch LED Inoperative	6-609	42
B0827	Traction Control System Off Indicator Circuit Low	6-610	43
B0828	Traction Control System Off Indicator Circuit High	6-610	44
C0035	LH Front Wheel Speed Sensor Fault	6-610	45
C0040	RH Front Wheel Speed Sensor Fault	6-611	46
C0045	LH Rear Wheel Speed Sensor Fault	6-612	47
C0050	RH Rear Wheel Speed Sensor Fault	6-612	48
C0060	LH Front ABS Solenoid No. 1 Circuit Fault	6-613	49
C0065	LH Front ABS Solenoid No. 2 Circuit Fault	6-613	49
C0070	RH Front ABS Solenoid No. 1 Circuit Fault	6-613	49
C0075	RH Front ABS Solenoid No. 2 Circuit Fault	6-613	49
C0080	LH Rear ABS Solenoid No. 1 Circuit Fault	6-613	49
C0085	LH Rear ABS Solenoid No. 2 Circuit Fault	6-613	49
C0090	RH Rear ABS Solenoid No. 1 Circuit Fault	6-613	49
C0095	RH Rear ABS Solenoid No. 2 Circuit Fault	6-613	49
C0110	Pump Motor Fault	6-613	50
C0121	Valve Relay Circuit Fault	6-613	51
C0141	LH TCS Solenoid No. 1 Fault	6-613	52
C0146	LH TCS Solenoid No. 2 Fault	6-613	52
C0151	RH TCS Solenoid No. 1 Fault	6-613	52
C0156	RH TCS Solenoid No. 2 Fault	6-613	52
C0161	ABS/TCS Brake Switch Circuit Fault	6-613	53
C0236	TCS RPM Signal Circuit Fault	6-614	54
C0241	PWM Delivered Torque Reduction Fault	6-614	55
C0244	PWM Delivered Torque Fault	6-615	56
C0245	Wheel Speed Sensor Frequency Error	6-615	57
C0550	ECU Fault	6-615	58
C0551	Option Configuration Error	6-615	59
C0896	System High/Low Voltage	6-615	60

Continued

DIAGNOSTIC CHART INDEX—Continued

Code	Description	Page No.	Fig. No.
S-SERIES			
—	No Traction LED	6-616	62
—	Traction Control Diagnostic Check	6-615	61
—	Traction Control Switch LED Will Not Cycle Off	6-616	63
C0035	Wheel Speed Sensor Circuit Fault	6-616	64
C0036	Wheel Speed Circuit Range Performance	6-617	65
C0037	Wheel Speed Sensor Circuit Low	6-617	66
C0040	Wheel Speed Sensor Circuit Fault	6-616	64
C0041	Wheel Speed Circuit Range Performance	6-617	65
C0042	Wheel Speed Sensor Circuit Low	6-617	66
C0045	Wheel Speed Sensor Circuit Fault	6-616	64
C0046	Wheel Speed Circuit Range Performance	6-617	65
C0047	Wheel Speed Sensor Circuit Low	6-617	66
C0050	Wheel Speed Sensor Circuit Fault	6-616	64
C0051	Wheel Speed Circuit Range Performance	6-617	65
C0052	Wheel Speed Sensor Circuit Low	6-617	66
C0060	Solenoid Circuit Fault	6-618	67
C0065	Solenoid Circuit Fault	6-618	67
C0070	Solenoid Circuit Fault	6-618	67
C0075	Solenoid Circuit Fault	6-618	67
C0080	Lefthand Rear Solenoid No. 1 Circuit Fault	6-618	68
C0085	Solenoid Circuit Fault	6-618	67
C0090	Righthand Rear Solenoid No. 1 Circuit Fault	6-618	69
C0095	Solenoid Circuit Fault	6-618	67
C0112	Pump Motor Circuit Low	6-618	70
C0113	Pump Motor Circuit High	6-618	71
C0114	Pump Motor Circuit Open	6-619	72
C0115	Pump Motor Fault	6-619	73
C0124	Valve Relay Circuit High	6-619	74
C0125	Valve Relay Circuit Open	6-620	75
C0165	ABS/TCS Brake Switch Circuit Open	6-620	76
C0550	ECU Fault	6-621	77
C0552	Improper Shutdown	6-621	78
C0899	Device No. 1 Voltage Low	6-621	79
C0900	Device No. 1 Voltage High	6-622	80

Circuit Description

The instrument panel cluster (IPC) turns the ABS Indicator on during the IPC bulb check for approximately 3 seconds when the ignition switch is turned to the ON position. If the EBCM sets a diagnostic trouble code (DTC) the EBCM sends a class 2 message to the body control module (BCM) and the (BCM) sends a class 2 message to the (IPC) to command the ABS indicator on.

Diagnostic Aids

- It is very important that a thorough inspection of the wiring and connectors be performed. Failure to carefully and fully inspect wiring and connectors may result in misdiagnosis, causing part replacement with reappearance of the malfunction.
- Thoroughly inspect any circuitry that may be causing the complaint for the following conditions:
  - Backed out terminals
  - Improper mating
  - Broken locks
  - Improperly formed or damaged terminals
  - Poor terminal-to-wiring connections
  - Physical damage to the wiring harness
- The following conditions may cause an intermittent malfunction:
  - A poor connection
  - Rubbed-through wire insulation
  - A broken wire inside the insulation
- If an intermittent malfunction exists refer to *Intermittent Fault Conditions*

Test Description

The number(s) below refer to the step numbers on the diagnostic table.

2. Confirm if the scan tool can turn on and off all the indicator lamps in the instrument cluster.
4. Verify if the circuits going to the instrument cluster or the cluster is at fault.

Step	Action	Yes	No
1	Did you perform the Diagnostic System Check?	Go to *Step 2*	Go to *Diagnostic System Check - ABS*
2	1. Using a scan tool, select the Brake Control Module, Special Functions mode. 2. Select Output Control, Solenoid Test. 3. Select ABS Telltale Indicator. 4. In the ABS Telltale test mode you can turn the instrument panel indicators on or off. All indicators will turn ON when commanded on. Does the ABS indicator turn on then off?	Go to *Step 3*	Go to *Step 4*
3	Replace the *Electronic Brake Control Module (EBCM)* Is the replacement complete?	Go to *Diagnostic System Check - ABS*	—
4	1. Disconnect the instrument cluster and connect a test light across the appropriate power and ground terminals. 2. With the test light OFF, repair the open in power or ground circuit to cluster 3. With the test light ON, check the connector for poor connection to cluster. 4. If OK, replace the instrument cluster. Is the instrument cluster replacement complete?	Go to *Diagnostic System Check - ABS*	—

G34020200414000X

Fig. 19 ABS Indicator Always On. ION

Circuit Description

The instrument panel cluster (IPC) turns the ABS indicator on during the IPC bulb check for approximately 3 seconds when the ignition switch is turned to the ON position. If the electronic brake control module sets a diagnostic trouble code (DTC) the EBCM sends a class 2 message to the body control module (BCM) and the (BCM) sends a class 2 message to the IPC to command the ABS indicator on.

Diagnostic Aids

- It is very important that a thorough inspection of the wiring and connectors be performed. Failure to carefully and fully inspect wiring and connectors may result in misdiagnosis, causing part replacement with reappearance of the malfunction.
- Thoroughly inspect any circuitry that may be causing the complaint for the following conditions:
  - Backed out terminals
  - Improper mating
  - Broken locks
  - Improperly formed or damaged terminals
  - Poor terminal-to-wiring connections
  - Physical damage to the wiring harness
- The following conditions may cause an intermittent malfunction:
  - A poor connection
  - Rubbed-through wire insulation
  - A broken wire inside the insulation
- If an intermittent malfunction exists refer to *Intermittent Fault Conditions*

Test Description

The numbers below refer to the step numbers on the diagnostic table.

2. Confirm if the scan tool can turn on and off all the indicator lamps in the instrument cluster.
4. Verify if the circuits going to the instrument cluster or the cluster is at fault.

Step	Action	Yes	No
1	Did you perform the Diagnostic System Check?	Go to *Step 2*	Go to *Diagnostic System Check - ABS*
2	1. Using a scan tool, select the Brake Control Module, Special Functions mode, Output Control. 2. Select Solenoid Test. 3. Select ABS Telltale Indicator. 4. In the ABS Telltale Test mode you can turn the instrument panel indicators ON or OFF. All indicators will turn ON when commanded on. Does the ABS Indicator turn on then off?	Go to *Step 3*	Go to*Step 4*
3	Replace the ABS module. Is the replacement complete?	Go to *Diagnostic System Check - ABS*	—
4	1. Disconnect the instrument cluster and connect a test light across the appropriate power and ground terminals. 2. With the test light OFF, repair the open in power or ground circuit to cluster. 3. With the test light ON, check the connector for poor connection to the cluster. 4. If OK, replace the instrument cluster. Is the instrument cluster replacement complete?	Go to *Diagnostic System Check - ABS*	—

G34020200415000X

Fig. 20 ABS Indicator Inoperative. ION

Step	Action	Yes	No
1	Did you perform the Hydraulic Brake Diagnostic System Check?	Go to *Step 2*	Go to *Diagnostic System Check - Hydraulic Brakes*
2	1. Turn ON the ignition, with the engine OFF. 2. Release the park brake. 3. With a scan tool, observe the Park Brake Switch parameter in the Body Control Module data list. Does the scan tool indicate that the Park Brake Switch parameter is Off?	*Test for Intermittent and Poor Connections*	Go to *Step 3*
3	1. Turn OFF the ignition. 2. Disconnect the park brake switch. 3. Turn ON the ignition, with the engine OFF. 4. With a scan tool, observe the Park Brake Switch parameter. Does the scan tool indicate that the Park Brake Switch parameter is Off?	Go to *Step 5*	Go to *Step 4*
4	Test the signal circuit of the park brake switch for a short to ground. Did you find and correct the condition?	Go to *Step 9*	Go to *Step 6*
5	Inspect for poor connections at the harness connector of the park brake switch. Did you find and correct the condition?	Go to *Step 9*	Go to *Step 7*
6	Inspect for poor connections at the harness connector of the body control module (BCM). Did you find and correct the condition?	Go to *Step 9*	Go to *Step 8*
7	Replace the park brake switch. Did you complete the repair?	Go to *Step 9*	—
8	Replace the body control module (BCM). Did you complete the repair?	Go to *Step 9*	—
9	Operate the system in order to verify the repair. Did you correct the condition?	System OK	Go to *Step 2*

G34020200427000X

Fig. 21 Brake Warning Indicator Always On. ION

Step	Action	Yes	No
1	Did you perform the Hydraulic Brake Diagnostic System Check?	Go to *Step 2*	Go to *Diagnostic System Check - Hydraulic Brakes*
2	1. Turn ON the ignition, with the engine OFF. 2. Release the park brake. 3. With a scan tool, observe the Park Brake Switch parameter in the Body Control Module data list. Does the scan tool indicate that the Park Brake Switch parameter is Off?	*Test for Intermittent and Poor Connections*	Go to *Step 3*
3	1. Turn OFF the ignition. 2. Disconnect the park brake switch. 3. Turn ON the ignition, with the engine OFF. 4. With a scan tool, observe the Park Brake Switch parameter. Does the scan tool indicate that the Park Brake Switch parameter is Off?	Go to *Step 5*	Go to *Step 4*
4	Test the signal circuit of the park brake switch for a short to ground. Did you find and correct the condition?	Go to *Step 9*	Go to *Step 6*
5	Inspect for poor connections at the harness connector of the park brake switch. Did you find and correct the condition?	Go to *Step 9*	Go to *Step 7*
6	Inspect for poor connections at the harness connector of the body control module (BCM). Did you find and correct the condition?	Go to *Step 9*	Go to *Step 8*
7	Replace the park brake switch. Did you complete the repair?	Go to *Step 9*	—
8	Replace the body control module (BCM). Did you complete the repair?	Go to *Step 9*	—
9	Operate the system in order to verify the repair. Did you correct the condition?	System OK	Go to *Step 2*

G34020200428000X

Fig. 22 Brake Warning Indicator Inoperative. ION

Circuit Description

The ABS Diagnostic System Check is an organized approach to identify problems associated with the EBCM. This check must be the starting point for any EBCM complaint, and will direct you to the next logical step in diagnosing the complaint. The EBCM is a very reliable component and is not likely the cause of the malfunction. Most system complaints are linked to faulty wiring, connectors, and occasionally to components. Understanding the ABS system and using the tables correctly will reduce diagnostic time and prevent unnecessary parts replacement.

Step	Action	Yes	No
1	Install a scan tool. Does the scan tool power up?	Go to *Step 2*	Go to *Scan Tool Does Not Power Up*
2	1. Turn ON the ignition, with the engine OFF. 2. Attempt to establish communication with the following control modules: • Body control module (BCM) • Electronic brake control module (EBCM) • Instrument panel module (IPC) • Powertrain control module (PCM) Does the scan tool communicate with all control modules?	Go to *Step 3*	Go to *Scan Tool Does Not Communicate with Class 2 Device*
3	Select the display DTCs function on the scan tool for the following control modules: • Body control module (BCM) • Electronic brake control module (EBCM) • Instrument panel module (IPC) • Powertrain control module (PCM) Does the scan tool display any DTCs?	Go to *Step 4*	Go to *Symptoms - Antilock Brake System*
4	Does the scan tool display any DTCs which begin with a "U"?	Go to *Scan Tool Does Not Communicate with Class 2 Device*	Go to *Step 5*
5	Does the scan tool display DTC B1000 or B1001?	Go to *Diagnostic Trouble Code (DTC)*	Go to *Step 6*
6	Does the scan tool display DTC B1327 or B1328?	Go to *Diagnostic Trouble Code (DTC)*	Go to *Diagnostic Trouble Code (DTC)*

G34020200409000X

Fig. 23 Diagnostic System Check ABS. ION

Circuit Description

Modules connected to the class 2 serial data circuit monitor for serial data communications during normal vehicle operation. Operating information and commands are exchanged among the modules. Connecting a scan tool to the DLC allows communication with the modules for diagnostic purposes.

Diagnostic Aids

The engine will not start when there is a total loss of class 2 serial data communication while the ignition is OFF. The GMLAN bus can not be used to analyze a malfunction on the Class 2 serial data bus. The following conditions will cause a total loss of class 2 serial data communication:

- A class 2 serial data circuit shorted to ground.
- A class 2 serial data circuit shorted to voltage.
- An internal condition within a module or connector on the class 2 serial data circuit, that causes a short to voltage or ground to the class 2 serial data circuit.

Test Description

The numbers below refer to the step numbers on the diagnostic table.

2. A partial loss of communication in the class 2 serial data circuit uses a different procedure than a total loss of communication of the class 2 serial data circuit.
4. The following DTCs may be retrieved with a history status. These DTCs are not the cause of the present condition.
   - U1300
   - U1301
   - U1305
6. A State of Health DTC with a history status may be present along with a U1000 or U1255 with a current status. This indicates that the malfunction occurred when the ignition was on.
10. Normal class 2 serial data communication cannot take place until the power mode master (PMM) module sends the appropriate power mode message. If the PMM does not send a wake-up message, other modules on the class 2 serial data circuit may not communicate.
12. This step will isolate a wiring problem or a module malfunction.
13. An open circuit at this point will cause a loss of communication with the vehicle.
14. This step analyzes the specific branch circuit for a malfunction.
19. If there are no current DTCs that begin with the letter "U", the communication concern has been repaired.
20. The communication concern may have prevented diagnosis of the customer complaint.

Step	Action	Yes	No
1	Install a scan tool. Does the scan tool power up?	Go to *Step 2*	Go to *Scan Tool Does Not Power Up*
2	1. Turn ON the ignition, with the engine OFF. 2. Attempt to communicate with each module on the class 2 serial data circuit. If using a Tech 2, obtain this information using the Class 2 Message Monitor feature. Does the scan tool communicate with any module on the class 2 serial data circuit?	Go to *Step 3*	Go to *Step 8*
3	1. Select the Display DTCs function for each module. If using a Tech 2, use the Class 2 DTC Check feature in order to determine which modules do have DTCs set. 2. Record all of the displayed DTCs, the DTC status and the module which set the DTC. Did you record any DTCs in the range of U1000 to U1305?	Go to *Step 4*	Go to *Step 7*
4	Are history DTCs U1300, U1301 or U1305 retrieved from any module?	Go to *Step 5*	Go to *Step 6*

G34020200411010X

Fig. 25 Scan Tool Does Not Communicate With Class 2 Device (Part 1 of 4). ION

Test Description

The numbers below refer to the step numbers on the diagnostic table.

2. Lack of communication may be due to a partial malfunction of the serial data circuit or due to a total malfunction of the serial data circuit. The specified procedure will determine the particular condition.
4. The presence of DTCs which begin with "U" indicate some other module is not communicating. The specified procedure will compile the available information before tests are performed.

Step	Action	Yes	No
1	Install a scan tool. Does the scan tool power up?	Go to *Step 2*	Go to *Scan Tool Does Not Power Up*
2	1. Turn ON the ignition, with the engine OFF. 2. Attempt to establish communication with the following control modules: • Electronic brake control module (EBCM) • Body control module (BCM) Does the scan tool communicate with all control modules?	Go to *Step 3*	Go to *Scan Tool Does Not Communicate with Class 2 Device*
3	Select the display DTCs function on the scan tool for the following control modules: • Electronic brake control module (EBCM) • Body control module (BCM) Does the scan tool display any DTCs?	Go to *Step 4*	Go to *Symptoms - Hydraulic Brakes*
4	Does the scan tool display any DTCs which begin with a "U"?	Go to *Scan Tool Does Not Communicate with Class 2 Device*	Go to *Step 5*
5	Does the scan tool display DTC B1000?	Go to *Diagnostic Trouble Code (DTC)*	Go to *Step 6*
6	Does the scan tool display DTC P0562, or P0621?	Go to *Diagnostic Trouble Code (DTC)*	Go to *Diagnostic Trouble Code (DTC)*

G34020200426000X

Fig. 24 Diagnostic System Check Hydraulic Brakes. ION

Step	Action	Yes	No
5	**Important:** Turn ON the ignition, with the engine OFF, when testing for a short to voltage. Use the DMM MIN/MAX function to capture intermittent conditions. Test the class 2 serial data circuit for an intermittent short to ground or an intermittent short to voltage. Did you find and correct the condition?	Go to *Step 18*	Go to *Step 6*
6	Are U1000 or U1255 the only DTCs displayed in the previously specified range?	Go to *DTC U1000 and U1255*	Go to *DTC U1001-U1254*
7	Diagnose the non communicating module by using the DTC U1001 — U1254 Lost Communications with XXX procedure for the module which is not communicating. The DTC U1001 — U1254 Lost Communications with XXX procedure will determine which module is not communicating. Did you complete the action?	Replace Body Control Module	—
8	1. Turn OFF the ignition. 2. Disconnect the scan tool from the data link connector (DLC). 3. Inspect for poor connections and terminal tension at the DLC. Did you find and correct the condition?	Replace Body Control Module	Go to *Step 9*
9	Test the ground circuits of the DLC for an open or high resistance. Did you find and correct the condition?	Replace Body Control Module	Go to *Step 10*
10	1. Isolate the power mode master (PMM) module from all other modules on the class 2 serial data circuit by backing out only the class 2 serial data terminals from the PMM harness connectors, except for the one class 2 serial data circuit that is routed to the DLC, pin 2. To identify which module is the PMM 2. Reconnect all of the PMM harness connectors with the extracted class 2 serial data circuit terminals. 3. Turn the ignition On, with the engine Off. 4. Attempt to communicate with the PMM. Does the scan tool communicate with the PMM?	Go to *Step 12*	Go to *Step 11*

G34020200411020X

Fig. 25 Scan Tool Does Not Communicate With Class 2 Device (Part 2 of 4). ION

Step	Action	Yes	No
11	1. Test the class 2 serial data circuits between the DLC and the PMM for the following conditions. Turn ON the ignition when testing for a short to voltage: • High resistance • Open • Short to ground • Short to voltage 2. Test the following circuits of the PMM for an open or high resistance: • The battery positive voltage input circuits • The battery positive voltage output circuits • The ignition voltage input circuits • The ignition voltage output circuits • The switched battery positive voltage supply circuits • The ground circuits Did you find and correct the condition?	Go to *Step 18*	Go to Step *Step 17*
12	Perform the following for each class 2 serial data branch circuit, in order to determine if the concern is located within the class 2 serial data branch circuits or the modules connected to the class 2 bus: 1. Turn OFF the ignition. 2. One at a time, replace each terminal in the PMM harness connectors. 3. Turn ON the ignition, with the engine OFF. 4. Attempt to communicate with any module connected to the class 2 serial data branch circuit after reinstalling it's class 2 serial data terminal. 5. Record which branch of the class 2 serial data circuit causes a loss of communication if one occurs in the above items. Does the scan tool communicate with all modules connected to the class 2 serial data circuit after all the branch circuits have been reconnected?	Go to *Step 13*	Go to *Step 14*
13	Inspect for poor connections and terminal tension at the harness connector of the PMM harness connector that contains the discreet class 2 serial data circuit for the DLC. Did you complete the action?	Go to *Step 18*	—
14	1. Turn OFF the ignition. 2. Using the record made in step 12, identify each module on that branch of the class 2 serial data circuit and disconnect there harness connectors containing the class 2 serial data circuits. 3. Using the record made in step 12 again, test the branch circuits that caused a No Com with class 2 for the following. Turn ON the ignition when testing for a short to voltage: • Short to ground • Short to voltage Did you find and correct the problem?	Go to *Step 18*	Go to *Step 15*

G34020200411030X

Fig. 25 Scan Tool Does Not Communicate With Class 2 Device (Part 3 of 4). ION

Step	Action	Yes	No
15	The concern is a malfunctioning module on the class 2 serial data branch circuit recorded in step 12. 1. Turn OFF the ignition. 2. One at a time, starting with the first module on the malfunctioning class 2 serial data branch circuit closest to the PMM, start attaching modules back onto that branch circuit. 3. Turn ON the ignition, with the engine OFF. 4. Attempt to communicate with the reinstalled modules connected to the malfunctioning branch. 5. Repeat items 1 through 4 attempting to lose communication. If communication is lost, record the last module reconnected proceed down the table and discontinue the repeating of items 1 through 4. Does the scan tool communicate with all the modules connected to the class 2 serial data circuit?	Go to *Step 18*	Go to *Step 1*
16	Inspect for poor connections and terminal tension at the harness connector of the reconnected module that causes a loss of communication. Did you find and correct the condition?	Go to *Step 18*	Go to *Step 17*
17	**Important:** Perform the module setup procedure if required. Replace the suspect module. Did you complete the replacement?	Go to *Step 18*	—
18	1. Connect all of the modules. 2. Connect all the connectors. 3. Install a scan tool. 4. Turn ON the ignition leaving the engine OFF. **Important:** The scan tool may require a power up reset before communication will occur due to a short on the class 2 serial data circuit. Turn off or disconnect the scan tool before you display DTCs. 5. Wait for 10 seconds. 6. Select the display DTCs function for each module. If using a Tech 2, use the Class 2 DTC Check feature in order to determine which modules do have DTCs set. 7. Record all of the displayed DTCs and the DTC status. Did your record any DTCs which begin with a letter U and with a current status?	Go to *Step 20*	Go to *Step 19*
19	Did you record any DTCs which do not begin with a letter "U"?	Go to *Step 20*	Go to *Step 22*
20	Diagnose the DTCs as directed by the diagnostic procedures for the particular module or concern. Did you complete the action?	Go to *Step 21*	—
21	Did you diagnose all of the DTCs?	Go to *Step 22*	Go to *Step 20*
22	Clear the DTCs using the scan tool. Did you complete the action?	Replace Body Control Module	—

G34020200411040X

Fig. 25 Scan Tool Does Not Communicate With Class 2 Device (Part 4 of 4). ION

Circuit Description

The data link connector (DLC) is a standardized 16 cavity connector. Connector design and location is dictated by an industry wide standard, and is required to provide the following:

- Scan tool power battery positive voltage at terminal 16.
- Scan tool power ground at terminal 4.
- Common signal ground at terminal 5.

The scan tool will power up with the ignition OFF. Some modules however, will not communicate unless the ignition is ON and the power mode master (PMM) module sends the appropriate power mode message.

Test Description

The number below refers to the step number on the diagnostic table.

4. If the battery positive voltage and ground circuits of the DLC are functioning properly. The malfunction must be due to the scan tool.

Step	Action	Yes	No
1	Test the battery positive voltage circuit of the DLC for an open or a short to ground. Did you find and correct the condition?	Replace Body Control Module	Go to *Step 2*
2	Test the ground circuit from pin 4 of the DLC for an open or high resistance. Did you find and correct the condition?	Replace Body Control Module	Go to *Step 3*
3	Inspect for poor connections and terminal tension at the DLC. Did you find and correct the condition?	Replace Body Control Module	Go to *Step 4*
4	The scan tool may be malfunctioning. Refer to the scan tool user guide. Did you obtain a properly operating scan tool?	Replace Body Control Module	—

G34020200410000X

Fig. 26 Scan Tool Does Not Power Up. ION

Symptoms - Antilock Brake System

Important: The following steps must be completed before using the symptom tables.

1. Perform the *Diagnostic System Check - ABS* before using the Symptom Tables in order to verify that all of the following are true:
   - There are no DTCs set.
   - The control module(s) can communicate via the serial data link.
2. Review the system operation in order to familiarize yourself with the system functions.

Visual/Physical Inspection

- Inspect for aftermarket devices which could affect the operation of the antilock brake system.
- Inspect the easily accessible or visible system components for obvious damage or conditions which could cause the symptom.
- Inspect the master cylinder reservoir for the proper fluid level.

Intermittent

Faulty electrical connections or wiring may be the cause of intermittent conditions. Test for *Intermittent and Poor Connections*

Symptom List

Refer to a symptom diagnostic procedure from the following list in order to diagnose the symptom:

- *ABS Indicator Always On*
- *ABS Indicator Inoperative*
- *Traction Control Indicator Always On*
- *Traction Control Indicator Inoperative*

G34020200433000X

Fig. 27 Symptoms Anti-Lock Brake System. ION

Important: The following steps must be completed before using the symptom tables.

1. Perform the *Brake System Vehicle Road Test* before using the hydraulic brake symptom tables in order to duplicate the customer's concern.
2. Review the system operation in order to familiarize yourself with the system functions. Refer to the following:
   - *Brake Warning System*
   - *Hydraulic Brake System*
   - *Brake Assist System*
   - *Disc Brake System*

Visual/Physical Inspection

- Inspect for aftermarket devices which could affect the operation of the Hydraulic Brake System.
- Inspect the easily accessible or visible system components for obvious damage or conditions which could cause the symptom.

Intermittent

Faulty electrical connections or wiring may be the cause of intermittent conditions. Test for *Intermittent and Poor Connections*

Symptom List

Refer to a symptom diagnostic procedure from the following list in order to diagnose the symptom:

- *Brake Warning Indicator Always On*
- *Brake Warning Indicator Inoperative*
- *Brake Pulsation*
- *Braking Action Uneven - Pulls to One Side*
- *Braking Action Uneven - Front to Rear*
- *Brake Pedal Excessive Travel*
- *Brake Pedal Excessive Effort*
- *Brake System Slow Release*
- *Brake Fluid Loss*

G34020200429000X

Fig. 28 Symptoms Hydraulic Brakes. ION

Circuit Description

When the TCS is enabled, the body control module (BCM) illuminates the TRAC switch LED. The BCM will send a Class 2 data message to the electronic brake control module (EBCM) indicated that traction control is requested. If the traction control is disabled, the BCM will send a Class 2 data message to the EBCM indication that traction control is disabled. The TRAC switch is normally open switch. When the TRAC switch is pressed, the switch signal circuit is grounded to the BCM and the traction control LED indicator changes states.

The following conditions will cause the TRAC OFF to display in the IPC, and the LED indicator to turn off:

- The EBCM has disabled the TCS due to a DTC.
- The EBCM has disabled the TCS due to a overheated ABS/TCS hydraulic unit.
- The instrument cluster bulb check. When the ignition switch is turned to ON, the TRAC OFF indicator will turn on for approximately 5 seconds and then turn OFF.

Diagnostic Aids

- It is very important that a thorough inspection of the wiring and connectors be performed. Failure to carefully and fully inspect wiring and connectors may result in misdiagnosis, causing part replacement with reappearance of the malfunction.
- Thoroughly inspect any circuitry that may be causing the complaint for the following conditions:
  - Backed out terminals
  - Improper mating
  - Broken locks
  - Improperly formed or damaged terminals
  - Poor terminal-to-wiring connections
  - Physical damage to the wiring harness
- The following conditions may cause an intermittent malfunction:
  - A poor connection
  - Rubbed-through wire insulation
  - A broken wire inside the insulation
- If an intermittent malfunction exists refer to *Intermittent Fault Conditions*

Test Description

The number(s) below refer to the step number(s) on the diagnostic table.

2. Confirm if the scan tool can turn on and off all the indicator lamps in the instrument cluster.
4. Verify if the circuits going to the instrument Cluster or the cluster is at fault.

Step	Action	Yes	No
1	Did you perform the Diagnostic System Check?	Go to *Step 2*	Go to *Diagnostic System Check - ABS*
2	1. Using a scan tool, select the Body Control Module Special Functions mode. 2. Select Chassis Data Displays Test in Output Control. 3. In the Displays Test mode you can turn the TRAC OFF Switch LED indicator on or off. All indicators will turn ON when commanded ON. Does the TRAC OFF Switch LED Indicator turn on?	Go to *Step 4*	Go to *Step 3*
3	1. Using a scan tool, select the BCM Data Display mode. 2. Select Chassis Data Display. 3. In the Displays Test mode, monitor the TRAC LED indicator. Press the TRAC switch. The LED should change states. Does the scan tool display ON with TRAC switch pressed?	Go to *Step 8*	Go to *Step 7*
4	Measure the voltage at the TRAC switch between terminal D and ground. Is voltage present?	Go to *Step 6*	Go to *Step 5*
5	Test the traction control switch signal circuit for an open. Did you find and correct the condition?	Go to *Step 12*	—

G34020200417010X

Fig. 30 Traction Control Indicator Inoperative (Part 1 of 2). ION

Step	Action	Yes	No
6	Activate the TRAC OFF switch, switch activated. Measure the voltage at the TRAC switch between terminal A and ground. Is voltage present?	Go to Diagnostic Aids	Go to *Step 10*
7	Test the traction control switch ground circuit for an open. Did you find and correct the condition?	Go to *Step 12*	Go to *Step 11*
8	Measure the voltage at the TRAC switch between terminal C and ground. Is voltage present?	Go to *Step 10*	Go to *Step 9*
9	Test the traction control indicator control circuit for an open or short to ground. Did you find and correct the condition?	Go to *Step 12*	—
10	Replace the traction control switch. Did you find and correct the condition?	Go to *Step 12*	—
11	Replace the BCM. Is the replacement complete?	Go to *Step 12*	—
12	Operate the system in order to verify the repair. Did you correct the condition?	System OK	Go to *Step 2*

G34020200417020X

Fig. 30 Traction Control Indicator Inoperative (Part 2 of 2). ION

Circuit Description

When the TCS is enabled, the body control module (BCM) illuminates the TRAC switch LED. The BCM will send a Class 2 data message to the electronic brake control module (EBCM) indicated that traction control is requested. If the traction control is disabled, the BCM will send a Class 2 data message to the EBCM indication that traction control is disabled. The TRAC switch is normally open switch. When the TRAC switch is pressed, the switch signal circuit is grounded to the BCM and the traction control LED indicator changes states.

The following conditions will cause the TRAC OFF to display in the IPC, and the LED indicator to turn off:

- The EBCM has disabled the TCS due to a DTC.
- The EBCM has disabled the TCS due to a overheated ABS/TCS hydraulic unit.
- The instrument cluster bulb check. When the ignition switch is turned to ON, the TRAC OFF indicator will turn on for approximately 5 seconds and then turn OFF.

Diagnostic Aids

- It is very important that a thorough inspection of the wiring and connectors be performed. Failure to carefully and fully inspect wiring and connectors may result in misdiagnosis, causing part replacement with reappearance of the malfunction.
- Thoroughly inspect any circuitry that may be causing the complaint for the following conditions:
  - Backed out terminals
  - Improper mating
  - Broken locks
  - Improperly formed or damaged terminals
  - Poor terminal-to-wiring connections
  - Physical damage to the wiring harness
- The following conditions may cause an intermittent malfunction:
  - A poor connection
  - Rubbed-through wire insulation
  - A broken wire inside the insulation
- If an intermittent malfunction exists refer to *Intermittent Fault Conditions*

Test Description

The number(s) below refer to the step number(s) on the diagnostic table.

2. Confirms if the scan tool can monitor the on and off the Traction Control Switch LED indicator.
4. Verify if the circuits going to the Traction Control Switch is at fault.

Step	Action	Yes	No
1	Did you perform the Diagnostic System Check?	Go to *Step 2*	Go to *Diagnostic System Check - ABS*
2	1. Using a scan tool, select the BCM Data Display mode. 2. Select Chassis Data Display. 3. In the Displays Test mode, monitor the TRAC switch LED indicator. Press the TRAC switch. The LED should change states. Does the TRAC switch LED display on the scan tool change when pressed?	Go to *Step 3*	Go to *Step 4*
3	Test the traction control indicator control circuit for a short to voltage. Did you find and correct the condition?	Go to *Step 6*	Go to *Step 5*
4	Test the Traction Control Switch Signal circuit or Traction Control Switch for an open. Did you find and correct the condition?	Go to *Step 6*	Intermittent Fault Conditions
5	Replace the BCM. Is the replacement complete?	Go to *Step 6*	—
6	Operate the system in order to verify the repair. Did you correct the condition?	System OK	Go to *Step 2*

G34020200416000X

Fig. 29 Traction Control Indicator Always On. ION

Circuit Description

The wheel speed sensor produces an alternating current signal whose amplitude and frequency vary, depending on the velocity of the wheel. The electronic brake control module uses the frequency of the AC signal to calculate the wheel speed.

Conditions for Running the DTC

C0035 C0040 C0045 C0050

The ignition is ON.

C0036 C0041 C0046 C0051

- Vehicle speed is over 43 km/h (26 mph).
- The brake pedal is not pressed.
- The ABS is not active.

Conditions for Setting the DTC

C0035 C0040 C0045 C0050

One of the following conditions exists for 0.02 seconds:

- A short to voltage — in the wheel speed sensor signal circuit.
- An open — in the wheel speed sensor signal circuit.

C0036 C0041 C0046 C0051

All of the following conditions exists for 0.01 seconds:

- The DTC will set if one wheel speed = 0, and the other WSS are greater than 43 km/h (26 mph)
- The DTC will set if during drive off, one wheel speed = 0, and the other WSS are greater than 12 km/h (7.5 mph)
- A short to ground - the wheel speed sensor signal circuit is shorted to ground

Action Taken When the DTC Sets

If equipped, the following actions occur:

- The EBCM disables the ABS/TCS for the duration of the ignition cycle
- A DTC malfunction will set
- The ABS indicator turns ON
- The traction control switch LED will turn OFF

Conditions for Clearing the DTC

- The condition for the DTC is no longer present and you used the scan tool Clear DTC function.
- The EBCM automatically clears the history DTC when a current DTC is not detected in 100 consecutive drive cycles.

Diagnostic Aids

C0035 C0040 C0045 C0050

If the customer comments that the ABS indicator is ON only during moist environmental conditions (rain, snow, vehicle wash, etc.), inspect the wheel speed sensor wiring for signs of water intrusion. If the DTC is not current, clear all DTCs and simulate the effects of water intrusion by using the following procedure:

1. Spray the suspected area with a 5 percent saltwater solution. To create a 5 percent saltwater solution, add 2 teaspoons of salt to 354 ml (12 oz) of water.
2. Test drive the vehicle over various road surfaces (bumps, turns, etc.) above 43 km/h (26 mph) for at least 30 seconds.
3. If the DTC returns, replace the suspected wheel speed sensor or repair the wheel speed sensor wiring.
4. Rinse the area thoroughly when completed.

C0036 C0041 C0046 C0051

A possible cause of this DTC is electrical noise on the wheel speed sensor harness wiring. Electrical noise could result from the wheel speed sensor wires being routed to close to high energy ignition system components, such as spark plug wires.

Test Description

The numbers below refer to the step numbers on the diagnostic table.

3. This step tests the wheel speed sensor for the proper resistance value.
4. This step ensures that the wheel speed sensor generates the proper voltage.

G34020200418010X

Fig. 31 Codes C0035-C0051: Wheel Speed Sensor Fault (Part 1 of 2). ION

Step	Action	Value(s)	Yes	No
1	Did you perform the ABS Diagnostic System Check?	—	Go to *Step 2*	Go to *Diagnostic System Check - ABS*
2	1. Install a scan tool. 2. Turn ON the ignition. 3. Set up the scan tool snap shot feature to trigger for this DTC. 4. Drive the vehicle at a speed greater than the specified value. Does the scan tool indicate that this wheel speed DTC set?	43 km/h (26 mph)	Go to *Step 3*	Go to Diagnostic Aids
3	1. Raise and support the vehicle. 2. Disconnect the wheel speed sensor connector. 3. Measure the resistance across the wheel speed sensor. Does the resistance measure within the specified range?	800–1700 Ω	Go to *Step 4*	Go to *Step 8*
4	1. Spin the wheel. 2. Measure the AC voltage across the wheel speed sensor. Does the AC voltage measure greater than the specified value?	100 mV	Go to *Step 5*	Go to *Step 8*
5	Inspect for poor connections at the harness connector of the wheel speed sensor. Did you find and correct the condition?	—	Go to *Step 10*	Go to *Step 6*
6	1. Disconnect the EBCM harness connector. 2. Connect the DMM between the sensor signal and the ground circuit of the EBCM connector. 3. Test the wheel speed sensor circuits for the following: • An open • A short to ground • A short to voltage • Shorted together Did you find and correct the condition?	—	Go to *Step 10*	Go to *Step 7*
7	Inspect for poor connections at the harness connector for the EBCM. Did you find and correct the condition?	—	Go to *Step 10*	Go to *Step 9*
8	Replace the wheel speed sensor. Did you complete the replacement?	—	Go to *Step 10*	—
9	Replace the EBCM. Did you complete the repair?	—	Go to *Step 10*	—
10	1. Use the scan tool in order to clear the DTCs. 2. Operate the vehicle within the Conditions for Running the DTC as specified in the supporting text. Does the DTC reset?	—	Go to *Step 2*	System OK

G34020200418020X

Fig. 31 Codes C0035-C0051: Wheel Speed Sensor Fault (Part 2 of 2). ION

Circuit Description

The inlet and outlet valve solenoid circuits are supplied with battery power when the ignition is in the ON position. The electronic brake control module controls the valve functions by grounding the circuit when necessary.

Conditions for Running the DTC

- The DTC can set anytime the ignition switch is in the ON position.
- The DTC can set when the vehicle speed is greater than 15 km/h (9 mph).

Conditions for Setting the DTC

The DTC will set when the EBCM detects one of the following internal to the EBCM only:

- An open in the solenoid coil or circuit.
- A short to ground in the solenoid coil or circuit.
- A short to voltage in the solenoid coil or circuit.

Action Taken When the DTC Sets

If equipped, the following actions occur:

- The EBCM disables the ABS/TCS/DRP for the duration of the ignition cycle.
- A malfunction DTC will set.
- The ABS indicator turns ON.
- The traction control switch LED indicator turns OFF.

Conditions for Clearing the DTC

- The condition for the DTC is no longer present and you used the scan tool Clear DTC function.
- The EBCM automatically clears the history DTC when a current DTC is not detected in 100 consecutive drive cycles.

Diagnostic Aids

The solenoid valve circuit and the solenoid coil are internal to the EBCM. No part of the solenoid circuit is diagnosable external to the EBCM. The DTC sets when there is a malfunction in the solenoid circuit internal to the EBCM only.

Test Description

The numbers below refer to step numbers on the diagnostic table.

2. This step determines if the DTC is current.

Step	Action	Yes	No
1	Did you perform the Diagnostic System Check?	Go to *Step 2*	Go to *Diagnostic System Check - ABS*
2	1. Using a scan tool clear the DTC. 2. Remove the scan tool from the data link connector. 3. Carefully drive the vehicle above 15 km/h (9 mph) for several minutes. 4. Turn the ignition switch to the OFF position. 5. Install a scan tool. 6. Turn the ignition switch to the ON position, engine off. 7. Using the scan tool in Diagnostic Trouble Codes, retrieve current DTCs. Did any one of the DTCs C0060-C0095 reset as a current DTC?	Go to *Step 3*	Go to *Testing for Intermittent and Poor Connections*
3	Replace the EBCM. Is the repair complete?	Go to *Step 4*	—
4	1. Use the scan tool in order to clear the DTCs. 2. Operate the vehicle within the Conditions for Running the DTC as specification in the supporting text. Does the DTC reset?	Go to *Step 2*	System OK

G34020200419000X

Fig. 32 Codes C0060-C0095: ABS Solenoid Circuit Fault. ION

Circuit Description

The pump motor is an integral part of the brake pressure modulator valve, while the pump motor relay is integral to the electronic brake control module. The pump motor relay is not engaged during normal system operation. When ABS or TCS operation is required the EBCM activates the pump motor relay and battery power is provided to the pump motor.

Conditions for Running the DTC

- The ignition switch is in the ON position.
- Initialization is complete.

Conditions for Setting the DTC

- Pump motor voltage is not present 100 milliseconds after activation of the pump motor relay.
- Pump motor voltage is present for more than 5 seconds with no activation of the pump motor relay.
- Pump motor voltage is not present for 40 milliseconds after the pump motor relay is commanded off.

Action Taken When the DTC Sets

If equipped, the following actions occur:

- The EBCM disables the ABS/TCS for the duration of the ignition cycle.
- A malfunction DTC will set.
- The ABS indicator turns ON.
- The traction control switch LED indicator turns OFF.

Conditions for Clearing the DTC

- The condition for the DTC is no longer present and you used the scan tool Clear DTC function.
- The EBCM automatically clears the history DTC when a current DTC is not detected in 100 consecutive drive cycles.

Diagnostic Aids

- It is very important that a thorough inspection of the wiring and connectors be performed. Failure to carefully and fully inspect wiring and connectors may result in misdiagnosis, causing part replacement with reappearance of the malfunction.
- Thoroughly inspect any circuitry that may be causing the complaint for the following conditions:
  - Backed out terminals
  - Improper mating
  - Broken locks
  - Improperly formed or damaged terminals
  - Poor terminal-to-wiring connections
  - Physical damage to the wiring harness
- The following conditions may cause an intermittent malfunction:
  - A poor connection
  - Rubbed-through wire insulation
  - A broken wire inside the insulation
- If an intermittent malfunction exists *Test for Intermittent and Poor Connections*

Test Description

The number below refers to the step number on the diagnostic table.

3. This step tests the pump motor circuits of the BPMV for a short to the housing of the BPMV. The wiring from the BPMV to the EBCM should not be repaired.

G34020200420010X

Fig. 33 Code C0110: ABS Pump Motor Failure (Part 1 of 2). ION

Step	Action	Value(s)	Yes	No
1	Did you perform the ABS Diagnostic System Check?	—	Go to *Step 2*	Go to *Diagnostic System Check - ABS*
2	1. Disconnect the EBCM harness connector. 2. Test both ground circuits of the EBCM including the EBCM ground for a high resistance or an open. 3. Test the Battery Positive Voltage circuits for an open, high resistance, or a short to ground. Did you find and correct the condition?	—	Go to *Step 8*	Go to *Step 3*
3	1. Disconnect the pump motor harness pigtail connector of the BPMV. 2. Measure the resistance between each pump motor control circuit and the housing of the BPMV at the pump motor harness pigtail connector of the BPMV. Does the resistance measure less than the specified value?	5 Ω	Go to *Step 4*	Go to *Step 5*
4	Inspect for poor connections at the pump motor harness pigtail connector of the BPMV. Did you find and correct the condition?	—	Go to *Step 8*	Go to *Step 6*
5	Inspect for poor connections at the harness connector of the EBCM. Did you find and correct the condition?	—	Go to *Step 8*	Go to *Step 7*
6	Replace the BPMV. Did you complete the repair?	—	Go to *Step 8*	—
7	Replace the EBCM. Did you complete the repair?	—	Go to *Step 8*	—
8	1. Use the scan tool in order to clear the DTCs. 2. Operate the vehicle within the conditions for Running the DTC as specified in the supporting text. Does the DTC reset?	—	Go to *Step 2*	System OK

G34020200420020X

Fig. 33 Code C0110: ABS Pump Motor Failure (Part 2 of 2). ION

- If an intermittent malfunction exists, *Test for Intermittent and Poor Connections*
- The solenoid valve relay is an integral part of the EBCM and is not serviced separately.

Test Description

The number below refers to step number on the diagnostic table.

2. This step determines if the DTC is current.

Step	Action	Yes	No
1	Did you perform the Diagnostic System Check?	Go to *Step 2*	Go to *Diagnostic System Check - ABS*
2	1. Install a scan tool. 2. Turn ON the ignition, with the engine OFF. 3. Use the scan tool in order to clear the DTCs. Does the DTC reset?	Go to *Step 3*	Go to Diagnostic Aids
3	1. Disconnect the EBCM harness connector. 2. Test the battery positive voltage circuit for an open, high resistance, or a short to ground. Did you find and correct the condition?	Go to *Step 5*	Go to *Step 4*
4	Replace the electronic brake control Module (EBCM). Did you complete the replacement?	Go to *Step 5*	—
5	1. Use the scan tool in order to clear the DTCs. 2. Operate the vehicle within the Conditions for Running the DTC as specified in the supporting text. Does the DTC reset?	Go to *Step 2*	System OK

G34020200421000X

Fig. 34 Code C0121: Solenoid Valve Relay Valve Fault. ION

Step	Action	Yes	No
1	Did you perform the hydraulic brake Diagnostic System Check?	Go to *Step 2*	Go to *Diagnostic System Check - Hydraulic Brakes*
2	1. Use a scan tool in order to clear the DTCs. 2. Operate the vehicle within the Conditions for Running the DTC as specified in the supporting text. Does the DTC C0129 or C0267 set as current?	Go to *Step 3*	Go to Diagnostic Aids
3	Inspect the brake fluid level in the master cylinder reservoir. Did you find and correct the condition?	Go to *Step 8*	Go to *Step 4*
4	1. Disconnect the brake fluid level switch harness connector. 2. Use the scan tool to observe the Brake Fluid Level status. Does the scan tool display Low?	Go to *Step 6*	Go to *Step 5*
5	Replace the brake fluid level switch. Did you complete the replacement?	Go to *Step 8*	—
6	1. Turn OFF the ignition. 2. Disconnect the BCM harness connector. 3. Test the brake warning indicator supply voltage circuit for a short to ground, short to voltage, or open. Did you find and correct the condition?	Go to *Step 8*	Go to *Step 7*
7	Replace the BCM. Did you complete the replacement?	Go to *Step 8*	—
8	1. Use the scan tool in order to clear the DTCs. 2. Operate the vehicle within the Conditions for Running the DTC as specified in the supporting text. Does the DTC reset?	Go to *Step 3*	System OK

G34020200425020X

Fig. 35 Codes C0129 & C0267: Brake Fluid Level Low Or Brake Fluid Level Switch Fault (Part 2 of 2). ION

Circuit Description

The stop lamp switch is a normally open switch, when the brake pedal is depressed the electronic brake control module will sense battery voltage. This allows the EBCM to determine the state of the brake lamps.

Conditions for Running the DTC

- The ignition switch is ON.
- The DTC can be set after system initialization.

Conditions for Setting the DTC

- EBCM detects battery voltage at all times.
- EBCM never detects battery voltage from feed circuit.
- Both brake lamps are faulty.

Action Taken When the DTC Sets

If equipped, the following actions occur:

- The EBCM disables the ABS/TCS for the duration of the ignition cycle.
- A malfunction DTC will set.
- The ABS indicator turns ON.
- The traction control switch LED will turn OFF
- The following conditions may cause an intermittent malfunction:
  - A poor connection
  - Rubbed-through wire insulation
  - A broken wire inside the insulation
- If an intermittent malfunction exists *Test for Intermittent and Poor Connections*

Test Description

The numbers below refer to the step numbers on the diagnostic table.

3. This DTC detects an open stop lamp switch signal circuit from the stop lamp side of the switch to the BCM and out to the EBCM.

Conditions for Clearing the DTC

- The condition for the DTC is no longer present and you used the scan tool Clear DTC function.
- The EBCM automatically clears the history DTC when a current DTC is not detected in 100 consecutive drive cycles.

Diagnostic Aids

- It is very important that a thorough inspection of the wiring and connectors be performed. Failure to carefully and fully inspect wiring and connectors may result in misdiagnosis, causing part replacement with reappearance of the malfunction.
- Thoroughly inspect any circuitry that may be causing the complaint for the following conditions:
  - Backed out terminals
  - Improper mating
  - Broken locks
  - Improperly formed or damaged terminals
  - Poor terminal-to-wiring connections
  - Physical damage to the wiring harness

4. The EBCM sources 5 volts on the stop lamp switch signal circuit. This small voltage has a ground path through the stop lamp bulbs. This DTC sets if the path to ground is open.
7. With the scan tool, test for the current state of the brake lamp switch parameter.
10. Test the stop lamp signal circuit for a short to voltage.

G34020200422010X

Fig. 36 Code C0161: ABS/TCS Brake Switch Fault (Part 1 of 2). ION

Circuit Description

The body control module (BCM) monitors the brake fluid level in the master cylinder reservoir via the brake fluid level switch.

Conditions for Running the DTC

The ignition switch is in the ON position for 60 seconds or more.

Conditions for Setting the DTC

- The BCM detects a low brake fluid level condition for more then 60 seconds.
- The BCM detects a short to voltage in the brake fluid level signal circuit.
- The BCM detects an open in the brake fluid level signal circuit.

Action Taken When the DTC Sets

The red brake warning indicator turns ON.

Conditions for Clearing the DTC

The conditions for setting the DTC are no longer present and you use the scan tool Clear DTCs function.

Diagnostic Aids

A lower than normal brake fluid level in the master cylinder may cause the brake fluid level switch to close when the vehicle makes sharp turns or sudden stops. Low brake fluid level may be caused by a brake fluid leak or worn disc brake pads.

Thoroughly inspect connections or circuitry that may cause an intermittent malfunction. *Test for Intermittent and Poor Connections*

G34020200425010X

Fig. 35 Codes C0129 & C0267: Brake Fluid Level Low Or Brake Fluid Level Switch Fault (Part 1 of 2). ION

Step	Action	Yes	No
1	Did you perform the ABS Diagnostic System Check?	Go to *Step 2*	Go to *Diagnostic System Check - ABS*
2	1. Press the brake pedal. 2. With the scan tool, observe the Brake Switch Status parameter in the ABS data list. Does the Brake Switch Status parameter display Applied?	Go to *Step 4*	Go to *Step 3*
3	Test the signal circuit of the stop lamp switch for an open. Did you find and correct the condition?	Go to *Step 15*	Go to *Step 11*
4	Press the brake pedal. Are all of the stop lamps OFF?	Go to *Step 5*	Go to *Step 7*
5	Test the feed circuit of the stop lamps for an open or high resistance. Did you find and correct the condition?	Go to *Step 15*	Go to *Step 6*
6	Test the stop lamp switch circuits for an open or high resistance. Did you find and correct the condition?	Go to *Step 15*	Go to Diagnostic Aids
7	1. Press the brake pedal. 2. With a scan tool, observe the Brake Switch Status parameter. Does the Brake Switch Status parameter change state?	Go to Diagnostic Aids	Go to *Step 8*
8	1. Turn OFF the ignition. 2. Inspect the stop lamp switch and adjust and/or calibrate if needed. Did you find and correct the condition?	Go to *Step 15*	Go to *Step 9*
9	1. Turn OFF the ignition switch. 2. Disconnect the stop lamp switch connector. 3. Turn ON the ignition, with the engine OFF. 4. With a scan tool, observe the Brake Switch Status parameter. Does the scan tool display Released?	Go to *Step 11*	Go to *Step 10*
10	Test the stop lamp signal circuit for a short to voltage. Did you find and correct the condition?	Go to *Step 15*	Go to *Step 12*
11	Inspect for poor connections at the harness connector of the stop lamp switch. Did you find and correct the condition?	Go to *Step 15*	Go to *Step 13*
12	Inspect for poor connections at the harness connector of the EBCM. Did you find and correct the condition?	Go to *Step 15*	Go to *Step 14*
13	Replace the stop lamp switch. Did you complete the repair?	Go to *Step 15*	—
14	Replace the EBCM. Did you complete the replacement?	Go to *Step 15*	—
15	1. Use the scan tool in order to clear the DTCs. 2. Operate the vehicle within the Conditions for Running the DTC as specified in the supporting text. Does the DTC reset?	Go to *Step 2*	System OK

G34020200422020X

Fig. 36 Code C0161: ABS/TCS Brake Switch Fault (Part 2 of 2). ION

Circuit Description

As the wheel spins, the wheel speed sensor produces an alternating current signal. The electronic brake control module uses the frequency of the AC signal to calculate the wheel speed.

Conditions for Running the DTC

- The ignition switch is ON.
- The DTC can be set after system initialization.

Conditions for Setting the DTC

- The EBCM detects a deviation between the left and right rear wheel speeds of greater than 6 km/h (3.75 mph) at a vehicle speed of less than 100 km/h (62 mph) on vehicles equipped with TCS.
- The EBCM detects a deviation between the left and right front wheel speeds of greater than 10 km/h (6.25 mph) at a vehicle speed of less than 100 km/h (62 mph).
- The EBCM detects a deviation between the left and right rear wheel speeds of greater than 6 percent of the vehicle speed at greater than 100 km/h (62 mph) on vehicles equipped with TCS.
- The EBCM detects a deviation between the left and right front wheel speeds of greater than 4 km/h plus 6 percent of the vehicle speed at greater than 100 km/h (62 mph).

This DTC will set when the EBCM cannot specifically identify which wheel speed sensor is causing the malfunction. If the EBCM can identify the specific wheel speed sensor causing the malfunction, DTC C0245 will become a history DTC, and the DTC associated with the sensor (DTC C0036, DTC C0041, DTC C0046, DTC C0051, or DTC C0056) will be set concurrent with DTC C0245.

Under the following conditions, 2 Wheel Speed Sensor Input is 0 DTCs are set:

- The 2 suspect wheel speeds equal zero for 10–20 seconds.
- The other wheel speeds are greater than 16 km/h (10 mph).
- The other wheel speeds are within 11 km/h (7 mph) of each other.

Diagnose each wheel speed sensor individually.

Action Taken When the DTC Sets

If equipped, the following actions occur:

- A malfunction DTC stores
- The ABS/TCS disables
- The amber ABS indicator turn on
- The traction control switch LED will turn off

Conditions for Clearing the DTC

- The condition for the DTC is no longer present and you used the scan tool Clear DTC function.
- The EBCM automatically clears the history DTC when a current DTC is not detected in 100 consecutive drive cycles.

Diagnostic Aids

- It is very important that a thorough inspection of the wiring and connectors be performed. Failure to carefully and fully inspect wiring and connectors may result in misdiagnosis, causing part replacement with reappearance of the malfunction.
- Thoroughly inspect any circuitry that may be causing the complaint for the following conditions:
  - Backed out terminals
  - Improper mating
  - Broken locks
  - Improperly formed or damaged terminals
  - Poor terminal-to-wiring connections
  - Physical damage to the wiring harness
- The following conditions may cause an intermittent malfunction:
  - A poor connection
  - Rubbed-through wire insulation
  - A broken wire inside the insulation
- If the customer's comments reflect that the amber ABS/TCS indicator is on only during moist environmental conditions (rain, snow, vehicle wash), inspect all the wheel speed sensor circuitry for signs of water intrusion. If the DTC is not current, clear all DTCs and simulate the effects of water intrusion by using the following procedure:
  1. Spray the suspected area with a five percent saltwater solution.

     Add two teaspoons of salt to twelve ounces of water to make a five percent saltwater solution.
  2. Test drive the vehicle over various road surfaces (bumps, turns, etc.) above 43 km/h (26 mph) for at least 30 seconds.
  3. If the DTC returns, replace the suspected harness.
- If an intermittent malfunction exists *Test for Intermittent and Poor Connections*

G34020200423010X

Fig. 37 Code C0245: Wheel Speed Sensor Signal Incorrect (Part 1 of 3). ION

Test Description

The numbers below refer to step numbers on the diagnostic table.

2. If DTC C0245 is a history code, this step checks if a specific Wheel Speed Circuit Malfunction DTC is set concurrently with DTC C0245.
7. This step checks if the wheel speed sensor harness is routed in close proximity to the spark plug wires.
9. In this step, if the scan tool can record any erroneous wheel speed sensor signals, diagnose that sensor(s) first.

Step	Action	Yes	No
1	Did you perform the diagnostic system check?	Go to *Step 2*	Go to *Diagnostic System Check - ABS*
2	Is the following DTC(s) set concurrently with a history DTC C0245? • DTC C0036 • DTC C0041 • DTC C0046 • DTC C0051 • DTC C0056	Go to *Diagnostic Trouble Code (DTC)*	Go to *Step 3*
3	Inspect the wheel speed sensor for physical damage. Is physical damage of the wheel speed sensor evident?	Go to *Step 4*	Go to *Step 5*
4	Replace the wheel speed sensor. Is the replacement complete?	Go to *Step 14*	—
5	Inspect the wiring harness for physical damage. Is physical damage of the wiring harness evident?	Go to *Step 6*	Go to *Step 7*
6	Repair the wiring harness or connector. Is the replacement complete?	Go to *Step 14*	—
7	Inspect wiring harness for proper routing of the wheel speed sensor harness. verify that the wheel speed sensor harness is routed away from the spark plug wires. Is the wheel speed sensor harness properly routed?	Go to *Step 9*	Go to *Step 8*
8	Reroute the wheel speed sensor harness away from the spark plug wires. Is the reroute complete?	Go to *Step 14*	—
9	1. Install a scan tool. 2. Turn the ignition switch to the RUN position. 3. Set the scan tool to Snap Shot Auto Trigger mode and monitor the wheel speed sensors. 4. Carefully drive the vehicle above 43 km/h (26 mph) for several minutes. Did the scan tool trigger on any of the wheel speed sensors?	Go to *Step 10*	Go to *Step 11*
10	Note which wheel speed sensor triggered the scan tool. Follow the appropriate Wheel Speed Sensor Malfunction DTC table for the wheel speed sensor that triggered. Is the repair complete?	Go to *Step 14*	—

G34020200423020X

Fig. 37 Code C0245: Wheel Speed Sensor Signal Incorrect (Part 2 of 3). ION

Step	Action	Yes	No
11	1. Reconnect all previously disconnected components. 2. Using a scan tool clear the DTC. 3. Remove the scan tool from the DLC. 4. Carefully drive the vehicle above 43 km/h (26 mph) for several minutes. Does the DTC reset as a current DTC?	Go to *Step 13*	Go to *Step 12*
12	Malfunction is intermittent. Inspect all connectors and harnesses for damage that may result in an open or high resistance when connected. Is the repair complete?	Go to *Step 14*	—
13	Replace the EBCM. Is the replacement complete?	Go to *Step 14*	—
14	1. Use the scan tool in order to clear the DTCs. 2. Operate the vehicle within the conditions for running the DTC as specified in the supporting text. Does the DTC reset?	Go to *Step 2*	System OK

G34020200423030X

Fig. 37 Code C0245: Wheel Speed Sensor Signal Incorrect (Part 3 of 3). ION

Circuit Description

The internal fault detection is handled inside the control module. No external circuits are involved.

Conditions for Running the DTC

The microprocessor runs the program to detect an internal fault when power up is commanded. The only requirements are voltage and ground. This program runs even if the voltage is out of the valid operating range.

Conditions for Setting the DTC

- The control module detects an internal write malfunction.
- The control module detects an internal checksum malfunction.

Action Taken When the DTC Sets

If equipped, the following module specific actions may occur:

- The ABS indicator turns on.
- The BRAKE Warning indicator turns on.
- The SERVICE 4WD indicator turns on and the system will be disabled.
- The Service 4 Wheel Steering indicator turns on and the system will be disabled.
- The SERVICE RIDE SYS or SERVICE RIDE CONTROL message is displayed.
- The SERVICE SUSPENSION SYS message is displayed.
- The TCS indicator turns on.

Conditions for Clearing the DTC

- A current DTC clears when the malfunction is no longer present.
- A history DTC clears when the module ignition cycle counter reaches the reset threshold, without a repeat of the malfunction.

Diagnostic Aids

- This DTC may be stored as a history DTC without affecting the operation of the module. If stored only as a history DTC and not retrieved as a current DTC, do not replace the module.
- If this DTC is retrieved as both a current and history DTC, replace the module.

Step	Action	Yes	No
1	Did you perform the Diagnostic System Check for the system exhibiting the symptom?	Go to *Step 2*	Replace Body Control Module
2	1. Install a scan tool. 2. Turn ON the ignition, with the engine OFF. 3. Retrieve DTCs. Is DTC retrieved as a current DTC?	Go to *Step 3*	Go to Diagnostic Aids
3	**Important:** Perform the programming or setup procedure for the module if required. Replace the control module setting the DTC as current. Did you complete the replacement?	Go to *Step 4*	—
4	1. Use the scan tool in order to clear the DTCs. 2. Operate the vehicle within the Conditions for Running the DTC as specified in the supporting text. Does the DTC reset?	Go to *Step 2*	System OK

G34020200430000X

Fig. 38 Code C0550: ECU Fault. ION

Circuit Description

The electronic brake control module is required to operate within a specified range of voltage to function properly. During ABS and TCS operation, there are current requirements that will cause the voltage to drop. Because of this, voltage is monitored out of ABS/TCS control to indicate a good charging system condition, and also during ABS/TCS control when voltage may drop significantly. The EBCM also monitors for high voltage conditions which could damage the EBCM.

Conditions for Running the DTC

- The ignition switch is ON.
- The DTC can be set after system initialization.

Conditions for Setting the DTC

- The EBCM operating voltage falls below 9.4 volts out of ABS/TCS control, or 9.2 volts during ABS/TCS control.
- The EBCM operating voltage rises above 16.9 volts.
- The low voltage or the high voltage is detected for more than 500 milliseconds with the vehicle speed above 6 km/h (3.6 mph).
- Thoroughly inspect any circuitry that may be causing the complaint for the following conditions:
  - Backed out terminals
  - Improper mating
  - Broken locks
  - Improperly formed or damaged terminals
  - Poor terminal-to-wiring connections
  - Physical damage to the wiring harness
- The following conditions may cause an intermittent malfunction:
  - A poor connection
  - Rubbed-through wire insulation
  - A broken wire inside the insulation

Action Taken When the DTC Sets

If equipped, the following actions occur:

- A malfunction DTC is stored.
- The ABS and the Traction Control indicators are turned on.
- The ABS/TCS is disabled.

Conditions for Clearing the DTC

- The condition for the DTC is no longer present and you used the scan tool Clear DTC function.
- The EBCM automatically clears the history DTC when a current DTC is not detected in 100 consecutive drive cycles.

Diagnostic Aids

- It is very important that a thorough inspection of the wiring and connectors be performed. Failure to carefully and fully inspect wiring and connectors may result in misdiagnosis, causing part replacement with reappearance of the malfunction.
- If an intermittent malfunction exists, *Test for Intermittent and Poor Connections*

Test Description

The numbers below refer to the step numbers on the diagnostic table.

2. This step checks if the voltage is above the maximum of the range.
4. Step 4 checks if the voltage is below the minimum of the range.
6. This step checks for the integrity of the ground circuit.

G34020200424010X

Fig. 39 Code C0896: System Voltage To High/Low (Part 1 of 2). ION

Step	Action	Value(s)	Yes	No
1	Did you perform the Diagnostic System Check?	—	Go to *Step 2*	Go to *Diagnostic System Check - ABS*
2	1. Turn all the accessories off. 2. Install a scan tool. 3. Start the engine. 4. Use the scan tool to monitor the battery voltage while running the engine at approximately 2000 RPM. Is the monitored battery voltage within the specified range?	0–16.9 V	Go to *Step 4*	Go to *Step 3*
3	Use a DMM to measure the voltage between the battery positive terminal and ground. Is the voltage within the specified range?	0–16.9 V	Go to *Step 5*	*Engine Electrical*
4	Continue to monitor the battery voltage with the scan tool while running the engine at approximately 2000 RPM. Is the monitored battery voltage within the specified range?	0–9.4 V	Go to *Step 6*	Go to *Step 5*
5	1. Turn the ignition switch to the OFF position. 2. Disconnect the scan tool if still connected. 3. Test drive the vehicle above 6 km/h (3.5 mph). — Did DTC C0896 reset?	—	Go to *Step 10*	Go to *Diagnostic System Check - ABS*
6	1. Turn the ignition switch to the OFF position. 2. Disconnect the EBCM connector. 3. Use a DMM to measure the resistance between the connector terminal 4 and a good ground. Is the resistance within the specified range?	0–5 Ω	Go to *Step 8*	Go to *Step 7*
7	Repair open or high resistance in the ground circuit. Is the repair complete?	—	Go to *Step 11*	—
8	1. Turn the ignition switch to the RUN position. 2. Use a DMM to measure the voltage between terminal 18 and 4. Is the voltage within the specified range?	Above 9.4 V	Go to *Step 9*	*Engine Electrical*
9	1. Turn the ignition switch to the OFF position. 2. Reconnect the EBCM connector. 3. Disconnect the scan tool if the scan tool is still connected. 4. Test drive the vehicle above 6 km/h (3.5 mph). Did DTC C0896 reset?	—	Go to *Step 10*	Go to *Step 11*
10	Replace the EBCM. Is the repair complete?	—	Go to *Step 11*	—
11	1. Use the scan tool in order to clear the DTCs. 2. Operate the vehicle within the Conditions for Running the DTC as specified in the supporting text. Does the DTC reset?	—	Go to *Step 2*	System OK

G34020200424020X

Fig. 39 Code C0896: System Voltage To High/Low (Part 2 of 2). ION

Circuit Description

Modules connected to the class 2 serial data circuit monitor for serial data communications during normal vehicle operation. Operating information and commands are exchanged among the modules. When a module receives a message for a critical operating parameter, the module records the ID number of the module which sent the message for State of Health monitoring, Node Alive messages. A critical operating parameter is one which, when not received, requires that the module use a default value for that parameter. When a module does not associate an ID number with at least one critical parameter within about 5.5 seconds of beginning serial data communication, DTC U1000 or U1255 is set. When more than one critical parameter does not have an ID number associated with it, the DTC will only be reported once.

The table below list the modules on the Class 2 Serial Data Circuit that will set a U1000 or U1255 and should be actively communicating the previously described messages on the Class 2 Serial Data Circuit.

Control Module	ID Number
Body Control Module (BCM)	064
Electronic Brake Control Module (EBCM)	040
Engine Control Module (ECM)	016
Electronic Power Steering (EPS)	048
Instrument Panel Cluster (IPC)	096
Sensing and Diagnostic Module (SDM)	088
Vehicle Communication Interface Module (VCIM)	(151)

Conditions for Running the DTC

The ignition switch run power mode is selected.

The modules voltage supply is within normal operating value, approximately 9–16 volts.

Conditions for Setting the DTC

At least one critical operating parameter has not been associated with a modules assigned ID number within about 5.5 seconds after beginning serial data communication.

Action Taken When the DTC Sets

The SERVICE VEHICLE SOON indicator illuminates.

The module will use default values for the missing parameters.

Conditions for Clearing the DTC

- A current DTC will clear when all critical operating parameters for the module have been associated with an ID number, or at the end of the current ignition cycle.
- A history DTC clears when the module ignition cycle counter reaches the reset threshold, without a repeat of the malfunction.

Diagnostic Aids

When a malfunction such as a open fuse to a module occurs while modules are communicating, a Loss of XXX Communication DTC is set as current. When the modules stop communicating, ignition is turned off, the current Loss of XXX Communication DTC is cleared but the history DTC remains. When the modules begin to communicate again, the ignition is turned on, the module with the open fuse will not be learned by the other modules so U1000 or U1255 is set current by the other modules. If the malfunction occurs when the modules are not communicating, only U1000 or U1255 is set.

Test Description

The numbers below refer to the step numbers on the diagnostic table.

1. A DTC U1001 – U1254 "Lost Communications with XXX" with a history status may indicate the cause of U1000 or U1255.
2. The modules not communicating are the likely cause of U1000 or U1255. The modules that are available on the class 2 serial data circuit are listed in the Circuit Description.
7. The module which was not communicating due to a poor connection to the class 2 serial data circuit may have set DTC U1001 – U1254 "Lost Communications with XXX" for those modules that it was monitoring.
9. The modules which can communicate indicate the module which cannot communicate. You must clear the serial data communication DTCs from these modules to avoid future misdiagnosis.
12. If all modules are communicating, the module which set U1000 or U1255 may have done so due to some other condition.
14. The module which set U1000 or U1255 is the likely cause of the malfunction.

G34020200431010X

Fig. 40 Codes U1000 & U1255: Class 2 Serial Data Circuit Communication Error (Part 1 of 4). ION

Step	Action	Yes	No
1	1. Install a scan tool. 2. Turn ON the ignition, with the engine OFF. 3. Record the DTCs set in by each module. If using a Tech 2, use the Class 2 DTC Check feature to determine which modules have DTCs set. Did you record any DTCs in the range of U1001-U1254 with a history status?	Go to *Diagnostic Trouble Code (DTC)*	Go to *Step 2*
2	1. Turn ON the ignition, with the engine OFF. 2. Attempt to communicate with each module on the class 2 serial data circuit. If using a Tech 2, obtain this information using the class 2 Message Monitor feature. 3. Record all of the modules communicating on the class 2 serial data circuit. 4. Compare the list of modules which are communicating to the list given in Circuit Description. Does any module on the class 2 serial data circuit not communicate?	Go to *Step 3*	Go to *Step 12*
3	Test the circuits of the module that is not communicating for an open or short to ground. Did you find and correct the condition?	Go to *Step 8*	Go to *Step 4*
4	1. Turn OFF the ignition. 2. Test the ground circuits of the module that is not communicating for an open. Did you find and correct the condition?	Go to *Step 8*	Go to *Step 5*
5	**Important:** Inspect all connectors in the serial data communications circuit. 1. Turn OFF the ignition. 2. Test the class 2 serial data circuits of the module that is not communicating for an open. Did you find and correct the condition?	Go to *Step 8*	Go to *Step 6*

G34020200431020X

Fig. 40 Codes U1000 & U1255: Class 2 Serial Data Circuit Communication Error (Part 2 of 4). ION

Step	Action	Yes	No
6	Inspect the harness connector of the module that is not communicating for poor connections and terminal tension at the following circuits: • The battery positive voltage input circuits • The switched battery positive voltage supply • The battery positive voltage output circuits • The ignition voltage input circuits • The ignition voltage output circuits • The ground circuits • The class 2 serial data circuits Refer to the following: • *Control Module References* • *Test for Intermittent and Poor Connections* • *Connector Repairs* Did you find and correct the condition?	Go to *Step 8*	Go to *Step 7*
7	**Important:** Perform the module programming or setup procedure if required. Replace the module that is not communicating. Did you complete the replacement?	Go to *Step 10*	—
8	1. Install a scan tool. 2. Turn ON the ignition, with the engine OFF. 3. Select the Display DTCs function for the module which was not communicating. Does the scan tool display any DTCs which do not begin with a "U"?	Use applicable diagnostic for the system or module that set	Go to *Step 9*
9	Use the scan tool in order to clear the DTCs. Did you complete the action?	Go to *Step 10*	—
10	Select the Display DTCs function for the modules which had U1000 or U1255 set as a current DTC. Does the scan tool display DTCs which do not begin with a "U"?	Use applicable diagnostic for the system or module that set	Go to *Step 11*
11	Use the scan tool in order to clear the DTCs. Did you complete the action?	System OK	—
12	Did you record any other DTCs for the modules which had U1000 or U1255 set as a current DTC?	Use applicable diagnostic for the system or module that set	Go to *Step 13*

G34020200431030X

Fig. 40 Codes U1000 & U1255: Class 2 Serial Data Circuit Communication Error (Part 3 of 4). ION

Circuit Description

Modules connected to the class 2 serial data circuit monitor for serial data communications during normal vehicle operation. Operating information and commands are exchanged among the modules. In addition to this, Node Alive messages are transmitted by each module on the class 2 serial data circuit about once every 2 seconds. When the module detects one of the following conditions on the class 2 serial data circuit for approximately 3 seconds, the setting of all other class 2 serial communication DTCs is inhibited and a DTC will set.

DTC	Condition
U1300	Low voltage on the class 2 serial data circuit.
U1301	High voltage on the class 2 serial data circuit.
U1305	Either high or low voltage on the class 2 serial data circuit. Some modules will set DTC U1305 if they are not capable of distinguishing between a short to battery voltage or ground.

Conditions for Running the DTCs

- Voltage supplied to the module is in the normal operating voltage range.
- The vehicle power mode requires serial data communication to occur.

Conditions for Setting the DTCs

- No valid messages are detected on the class 2 serial data circuit.
- The voltage level detected on the class 2 serial data circuit is in one of the following conditions:
  - High
  - Low
- The above conditions are met for approximately 3 seconds.

Action Taken When the DTCs Sets

The module uses default values for all parameters received on the class 2 serial data circuit.

Conditions for Clearing the DTC

- A current DTC clears when the malfunction is no longer present.
- A history DTC clears when the module ignition cycle counter reaches the reset threshold, without a repeat of the malfunction.

Diagnostic Aids

- These DTCs cannot be retrieved with a current status. Diagnosis of current DTCs is accomplished via the symptom, Scan Tool Does Not Communicate with a Class 2 Device. Refer to *Scan Tool Does Not Communicate with Class 2 Device*
- An intermittent condition is likely to be caused by a short on the class 2 serial data circuit. Use the Scan Tool Does Not Communicate with a Class 2 Device procedure in order to isolate an intermittent condition. Refer to *Scan Tool Does Not Communicate with Class 2 Device*

G34020200432000X

Fig. 41 Codes U1300, U1301 & U1305: Class 2 Serial Data Circuit Signal Error. ION

Step	Action	Yes	No
13	1. Install a scan tool. 2. Turn ON the ignition, with the engine OFF. 3. Use the scan tool in order to clear the DTCs. 4. Turn OFF the ignition for at least 5 seconds. 5. Turn ON the ignition with the engine OFF. 6. Select the Display DTCs function. Does the scan tool display U1000 or U1255 set as a current DTC?	Go to *Step 14*	Go to Diagnostic Aids
14	**Important:** Perform the module programming or setup procedure if required. Replace the module which had U1000 or U1255 set as a current DTC. Did you complete the replacement?	System OK	—

G34020200431040X

Fig. 40 Codes U1000 & U1255: Class 2 Serial Data Circuit Communication Error (Part 4 of 4). ION

When TCS is enabled, the TRAC LED request from the EBTCM to the BCM (circuit 832) is at battery voltage and the BCM grounds circuit 1660. This action turns the TRAC LED On; indicating that TCS is available.

When the driver disables TCS by depressing the TRAC switch, the EBTCM grounds circuit 832. In response, the BCM turns the LED Off by removing the ground on circuit 1660.

DIAGNOSTIC AIDS

- If TRAC LED is On at all times with no DTC, check circuit 832 for short to voltage.
- If TRAC LED is Off at all times, refer to the following chart.

G34020000234010X

Fig. 42 TRAC Switch LED Inoperative (Part 1 of 2). L-Series

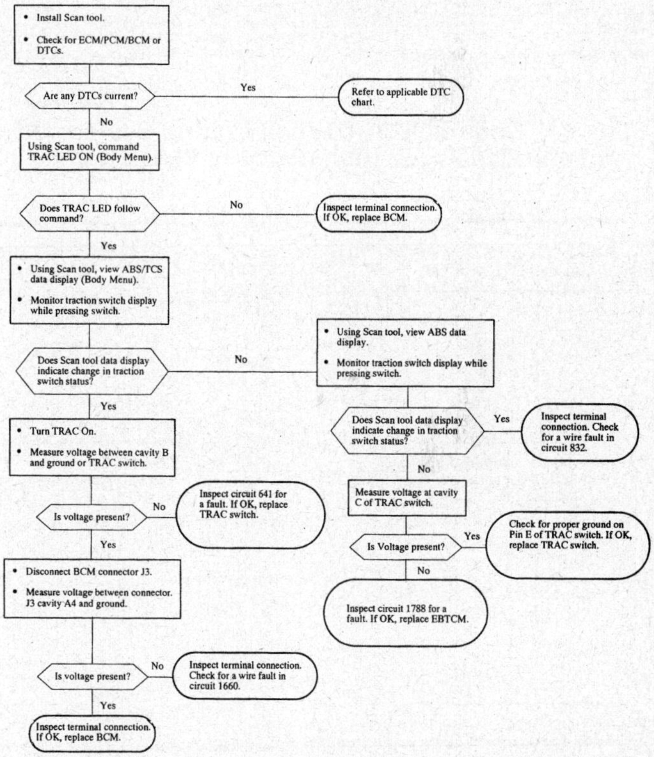

G34020000234020X

Fig. 42 TRAC Switch LED Inoperative (Part 2 of 2). L-Series

When TCS is enabled, the TRAC LED request from the EBTCM to the BCM (circuit 832) is at battery voltage and the BCM grounds circuit 1660. This action turns the TRAC LED On, indicating that TCS is available.

When the driver disables TCS by depressing the TRAC switch, the EBTCM grounds circuit 832. In response, the BCM turns the LED Off by removing the ground on circuit 1660.

DTC PARAMETERS

DTC B0827 will set:

- If the driver depresses the TRAC switch with the ignition in the RUN position and circuit 1660 is open or shorted to ground.
- If circuit 641 is open.

IMPORTANT: The EBTCM does not test circuit 832 for malfunction.

IMPORTANT: DTC B0827 will not illuminate a telltale.

Two different failure modes can exist when B0827 is set:

- If the TRAC LED is Off, check circuit 641 for open.
- Output from BCM is Off.
- Condition must be present for 30 seconds.
- Short-to-ground or Open on 1660 or 1641.
- No telltale will illuminate.
- If the TRAC LED is always On, check circuit 1660 for short to ground.

DIAGNOSTIC AIDS

Inspect wiring, components, and connector for the following conditions:

- Proper connection.
- Backed-out terminals.
- Broken connector locks.
- Corrosion in connectors/terminals.
- Burned, chafed or pinched wires.
- Broken wire inside insulation.
- Loose components.

G34020000235010X

Fig. 43 Code B0827: Traction Control System Off Indicator Circuit Low (Part 1 of 2). L-Series

When TCS is enabled, the TRAC LED request from the EBTCM to the BCM (circuit 832) is at battery voltage and the BCM grounds circuit 1660. This action turns the TRAC LED On, indicating that TCS is available.

When the driver disables TCS by depressing the TRAC switch, the EBTCM grounds circuit 832. In response, the BCM turns the LED Off by removing the ground on circuit 1660.

DTC PARAMETERS

DTC B0828 will set:

- If the driver depresses the TRAC switch with the ignition in the RUN position and circuit 1660 is shorted to voltage.

IMPORTANT: The EBTCM does not test circuit 832 for malfunction.

IMPORTANT: DTC B0828 will not illuminate a telltale.

- Output from BCM is On.

DIAGNOSTIC AIDS

Inspect wiring, components, and connectors for the following conditions:

- Proper connection.
- Backed-out terminals.
- Broken connector locks.
- Corrosion in connectors/terminals.
- Burned, chafed, or pinched wires.
- Broken wire inside insulation.
- Loose components.

G34020000236010X

Fig. 44 Code B0828: Traction Control System Off Indicator Circuit High (Part 1 of 2). L-Series

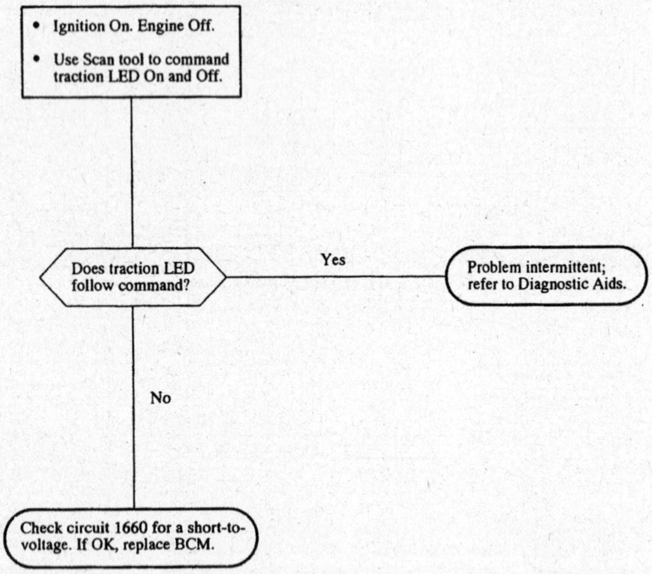

G34020000236020X

Fig. 44 Code B0828: Traction Control System Off Indicator Circuit High (Part 2 of 2). L-Series

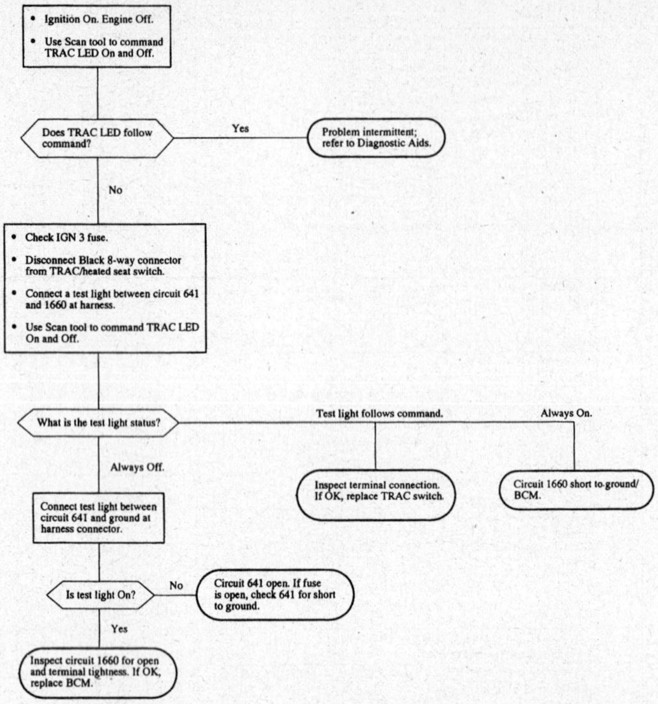

G34020000235020X

Fig. 43 Code B0827: Traction Control System Off Indicator Circuit Low (Part 2 of 2). L-Series

The wheel speed sensor produces an AC voltage whose amplitude and frequency vary, depending on the velocity of the wheel. The EBTCM uses this voltage signal to calculate wheel speed.

DTC PARAMETERS

DTC C0035 will set if:

- Left front wheel speed circuit is open, grounded, or shorted to battery.
- Left front wheel speed = zero, while other wheel speeds are greater than 40 km/h (25 mph) for 10 ms.
- This code can set anytime after the key is turned to the RUN position.

When the DTC sets, the EBTCM will disable ABS and Traction Control and turn On the ABS telltale.

If two or more wheel speed faults occur, dynamic rear proportioning (DRP) is disabled for the entire ignition cycle.

DIAGNOSTIC AIDS

Inspect wiring, components and connectors for the following conditions:

- Proper connection.
- Backed-out terminals.
- Broken connector locks.
- Corrosion in connectors/terminals.
- Burned, chafed, or pinched wiring.
- Broken wire inside insulation.
- Loose components.

Possible causes for DTC C0035 to set:

- Damaged or missing teeth on the wheel speed sensor ring.
- Large grooves or gouges, or build-up of foreign material in the gaps between the wheel speed sensor ring teeth.
- A worn front hub bearing assembly, or worn inner axle bearing which could allow the sensor to toothed ring gap to change excessively.

G34020000237010X

Fig. 45 Code C0035: LH Front Wheel Speed Sensor Fault (Part 1 of 3). L-Series

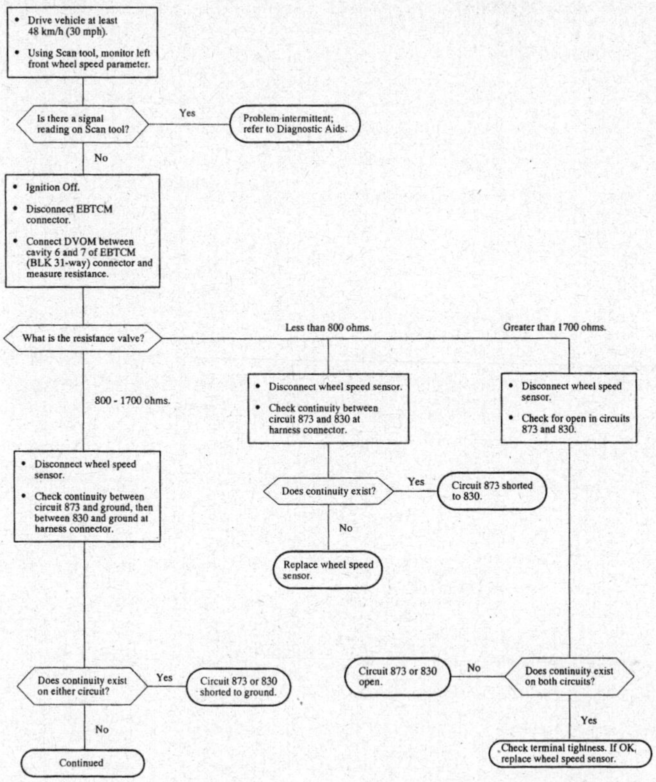

G34020000237020X

Fig. 45 Code C0035: LH Front Wheel Speed Sensor Fault (Part 2 of 3). L-Series

The wheel speed sensor produces an AC voltage whose amplitude and frequency vary, depending on the velocity of the wheel. The EBTCM uses this voltage signal to calculate wheel speed.

DTC PARAMETERS

DTC C0040 will set if the following conditions exist:

- Right front wheel speed circuit is open, grounded, or shorted to battery.
- Right front wheel speed = zero, while other wheel speeds are greater than 40 km/h (25 mph) for 10 ms.
- This code can set anytime after the key is turned to the RUN position.

When the DTC sets, the EBTCM will disable ABS and Traction Control and turn ON the antilock telltale.

If two or more wheel speed faults occur, dynamic rear proportioning (DRP) is disabled for the entire ignition cycle.

DIAGNOSTIC AIDS

Inspect wiring, components, and connectors for the following:

- Poor Connection.
- Backed-out terminals.
- Broken connector locks.
- Corrosion in connectors/terminals.
- Burned, chafed, or pinched wiring.
- Broken wire inside insulation.
- Loose components.

Possible causes for DTC C0040 to set:

- Damaged or missing teeth on the wheel speed sensor ring.
- Large grooves or gouges, or build-up of foreign material in the gaps between the wheel speed sensor ring teeth.
- A worn front hub bearing assembly, or worn inner axle bearing which could allow the sensor to toothed ring gap to change excessively.

G34020000238010X

Fig. 46 Code C0040: RH Front Wheel Speed Sensor Fault (Part 1 of 3). L-Series

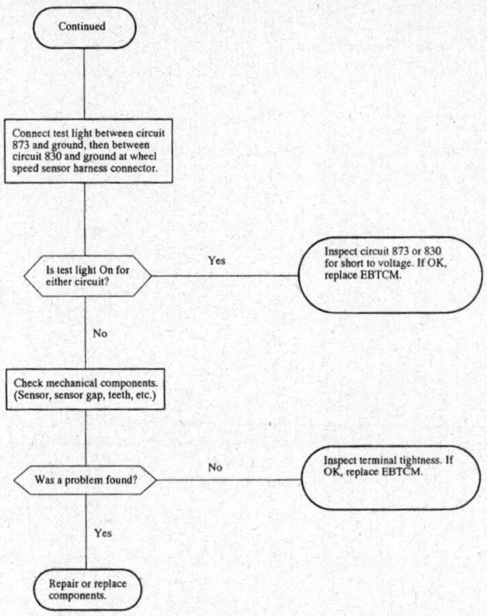

G34020000237030X

Fig. 45 Code C0035: LH Front Wheel Speed Sensor Fault (Part 3 of 3). L-Series

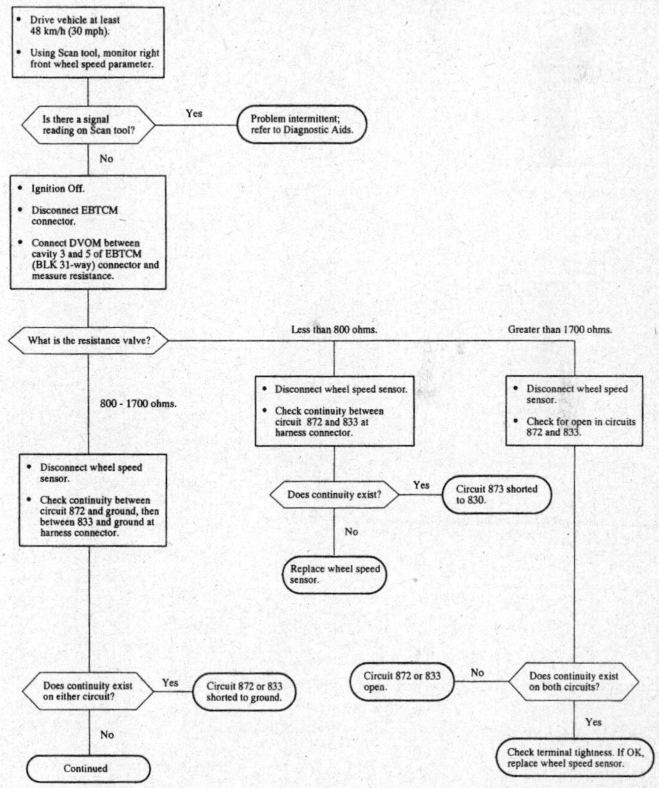

G34020000238020X

Fig. 46 Code C0040: RH Front Wheel Speed Sensor Fault (Part 2 of 3). L-Series

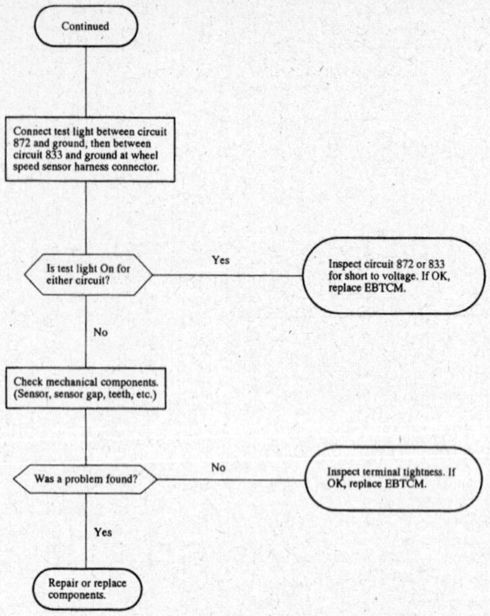

G34020000238030X

Fig. 46 Code C0040: RH Front Wheel Speed Sensor Fault (Part 3 of 3). L-Series

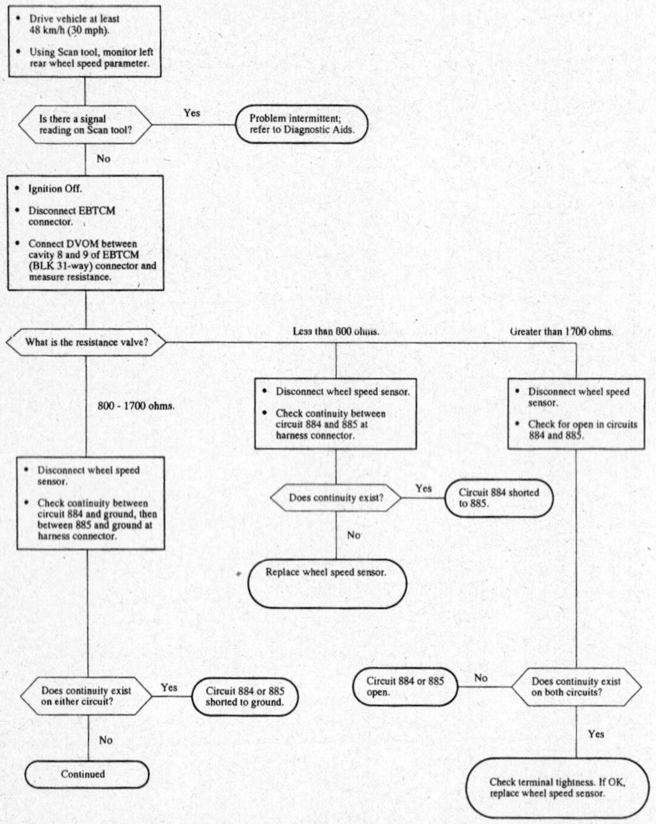

G34020000239020X

Fig. 47 Code C0045: LH Rear Wheel Speed Sensor Fault (Part 2 of 3). L-Series

The wheel speed sensor produces an AC voltage whose amplitude and frequency vary, depending on the velocity of the wheel. The EBTCM uses this voltage signal to calculate wheel speed.

DTC PARAMETERS

DTC C0045 will set if the following conditions exist:

- Left rear wheel speed circuit is open, grounded, or shorted to battery.
- Left rear wheel speed = zero, while other wheel speeds are greater than 40 km/h (25 mph) for 10 ms.
- This code can set anytime after the key is turned to the RUN position.

When the DTC sets, the EBTCM will disable ABS and Traction Control and turn ON the antilock telltale.

If two or more wheel speed faults occur, dynamic rear proportioning (DRP) is disabled for the entire ignition cycle.

DIAGNOSTIC AIDS

Inspect wiring, components, and connectors for the following:

- Proper connection.
- Backed-out terminals.
- Broken connector locks.
- Corrosion in connectors/terminals.
- Burned, chafed or pinched wiring.
- Broken wire inside insulation.
- Loose components.

Possible causes for DTC C0045 to set:

- Damaged or missing teeth on the wheel speed sensor ring.
- Large grooves or gouges, or build-up of foreign material in the gaps between the wheel speed sensor ring teeth.
- A worn rear hub bearing assembly, or worn inner axle bearing which could allow the sensor to toothed ring gap to change excessively.

G34020000239010X

Fig. 47 Code C0045: LH Rear Wheel Speed Sensor Fault (Part 1 of 3). L-Series

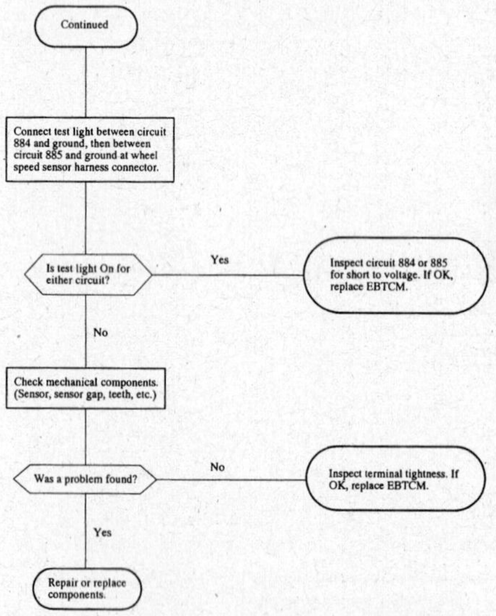

G34020000239030X

Fig. 47 Code C0045: LH Rear Wheel Speed Sensor Fault (Part 3 of 3). L-Series

The wheel speed sensor produces an AC voltage whose amplitude and frequency vary, depending on the velocity of the wheel. The EBTCM uses this voltage signal to calculate wheel speed.

DTC PARAMETERS

DTC C0050 will set if the following conditions exist:

- Right rear wheel speed circuit is open, grounded, or shorted to battery.
- Right rear wheel speed = zero, while other wheel speeds are greater than 40 km/h (25 mph) for 10 ms.
- This code can set anytime after the key is turned to the RUN position.

When the DTC sets, the EBTCM will disable ABS and Traction Control and turn ON the antilock telltale.

If two or more wheel speed faults occur, dynamic rear proportioning (DRP) is disabled for the entire ignition cycle.

DIAGNOSTIC AIDS

Inspect wiring, components, and connectors for the following:

- Proper connection.
- Backed-out terminals.
- Broken connector locks.
- Corrosion in connectors/terminals.
- Burned, chafed, or pinched wiring.
- Broken wire inside insulation.
- Loose components.

Possible causes for DTC C0050 to set:

- Damaged or missing teeth on the wheel speed sensor ring.
- Large grooves or gouges, or build-up of foreign material in the gaps between the wheel speed sensor ring teeth.
- A worn rear hub bearing assembly, or worn inner axle bearing which could allow the sensor to toothed ring gap to change excessively.

G34020000240010X

Fig. 48 Code C0050: RH Rear Wheel Speed Sensor Fault (Part 1 of 3). L Series

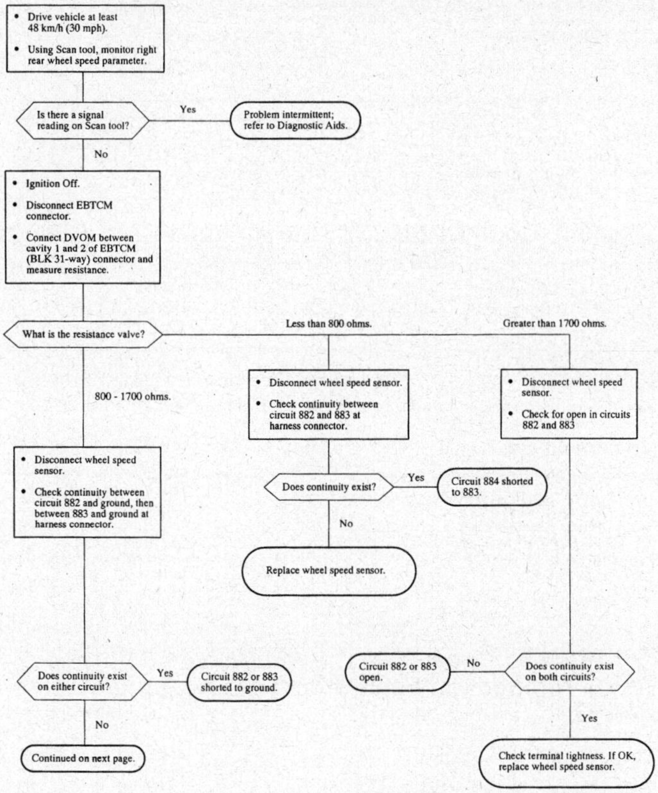

G34020000240020X

Fig. 48 Code C0050: RH Rear Wheel Speed Sensor Fault (Part 2 of 3). L-Series

The UHFB supplies the solenoid circuits with battery voltage when the ignition is in the RUN position. The ABS control module (EBTCM) controls valve function by grounding the solenoid circuit when necessary.

The #1 solenoids are outlet valves. The #2 solenoids are inlet valves.

DTC PARAMETERS

DTC will set if the ABS control module detects an open, short to ground, or short to voltage on the solenoid circuit(s) inside the control module.

When any of the above DTCs set:

- The ABS telltale will be On.
- The ABS control module will disable ABS, TCS and DRP.

DIAGNOSTIC AIDS

The ABS control module must be replaced.

IMPORTANT: New ABS control modules will automatically set DTC C0551 when installed. To clear DTC C0551, new modules must be configured with the correct engine and transmission option bit.

G34020000241000X

Fig. 49 Codes C0060, C0065, C0070, C0075, C0080, C0085, C0090 & C0095: ABS Solenoid Circuit Fault. L-Series

The ABS control module uses a relay to control valve solenoids. When ignition is in the Run position, the module energizes the relay winding to switch battery voltage that supplies the solenoids. The module will disable the relay when ignition is Off, or a fault is detected.

DTC PARAMETERS

DTC C0121 will set if:

- If the control module commands the relay On, but does not sense battery voltage at the solenoids.
- If the control module commands the relay Off, and senses battery voltage at the solenoids.

When DTC C0121 sets:

- The ABS telltale will be On.
- The ABS control module will disable ABS, TCS, and DRP.

DIAGNOSTIC AIDS

This relay is inside the ABS control module and is NOT serviceable.

IMPORTANT: An open in circuits 1002 or 702 will set this DTC.

G34020000243010X

Fig. 51 Code C0121: Valve Relay Circuit Fault (Part 1 of 2). L-Series

The UHFB supplies the solenoid circuits with battery voltage when the ignition is in the RUN position. The ABS control module (EBTCM) controls valve function by grounding the solenoid circuit when necessary.

The #1 solenoids are prime valves. The #2 solenoids are isolation valves.

DTC PARAMETERS

DTC will set if the ABS control module detects an open, short to ground or short to voltage on the solenoid circuit(s) inside the control module.

When any of the above DTCs set:

- The ABS telltale will be On.
- The ABS control module will disable ABS, TCS, and DRP.

DIAGNOSTIC AIDS

The ABS control module must be replaced.

IMPORTANT: New ABS control modules will automatically set DTC C0551 when installed. To clear DTC C0551, new modules must be configured with the correct engine and transmission option bit.

G34020000244000X

Fig. 52 Codes C0141, C0146, C0151 & C0156: TCS Solenoid Fault. L-Series

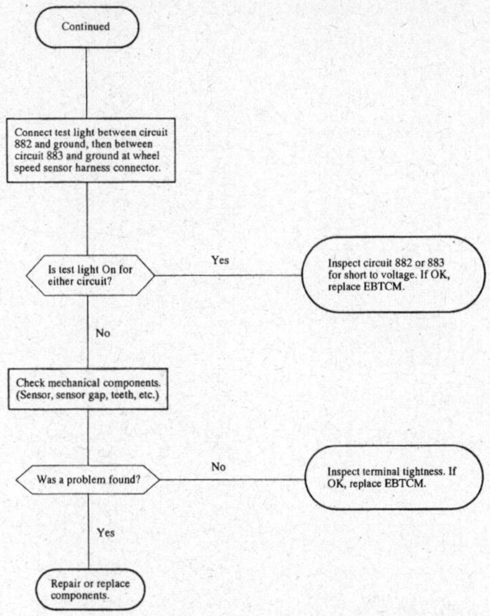

G34020000240030X

Fig. 48 Code C0050: RH Rear Wheel Speed Sensor Fault (Part 3 of 3). L-Series

During an ABS or TCS event, the ABS control module energizes the pump motor relay winding to switch battery voltage to the pump motor. This relay and motor is not used during normal braking.

DTC PARAMETERS

DTC C0110 will set if:

- If the control module commands the relay On, but does not sense battery voltage at the motor.
- If the control module commands the relay Off, and senses battery voltage at the motor.

When DTC C0110 sets:

- The ABS telltale will be On.
- The ABS control module will disable ABS, TCS, and DRP.

DIAGNOSTIC AIDS

The pump relay and motor are NOT serviceable.

The valve assembly (with control module) must be replaced.

G34020000242000X

Fig. 50 Code C0110: Pump Motor Fault. L-Series

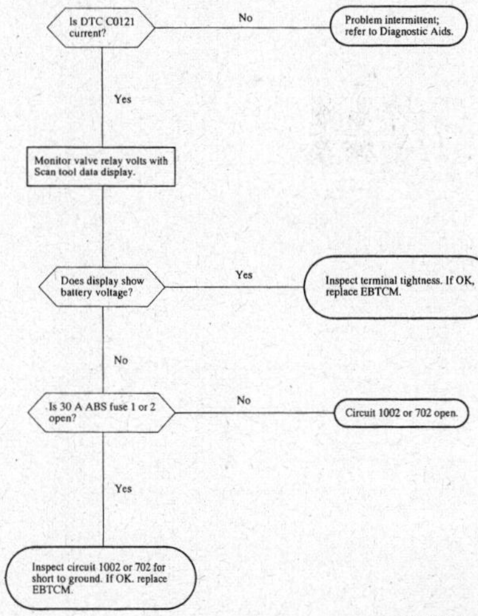

G34020000243020X

Fig. 51 Code C0121: Valve Relay Circuit Fault (Part 2 of 2). L-Series

The normally-open stop lamp switch supplies battery voltage to the ABS control module when the brake pedal is depressed.

DTC PARAMETERS

IMPORTANT: When DTC C0161 sets the ABS control module will NOT disable ABS, TCS, and DRP.

DTC will set if the ABS control module detects an open in circuit 20.

DIAGNOSTIC AIDS

Inspect wiring, components, and connectors for the following:

- Proper connection.
- Backed-out terminals.
- Broken connector locks.
- Corrosion in connectors/terminals.
- Burned, chafed, or pinched wiring.
- Broken wire inside insulation.
- Loose components.
- Both brake lamp bulbs burned out.

G34020000245010X

Fig. 53 Code C0161: ABS/TCS Brake Switch Circuit Fault (Part 1 of 2). L-Series

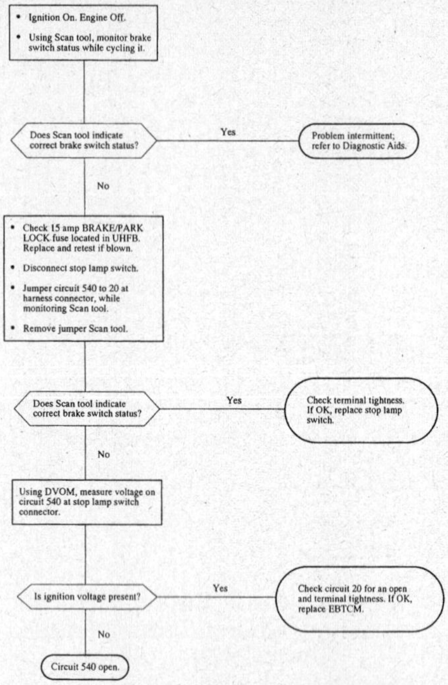

G34020000245020X

Fig. 53 Code C0161: ABS/TCS Brake Switch Circuit Fault (Part 2 of 2). L-Series

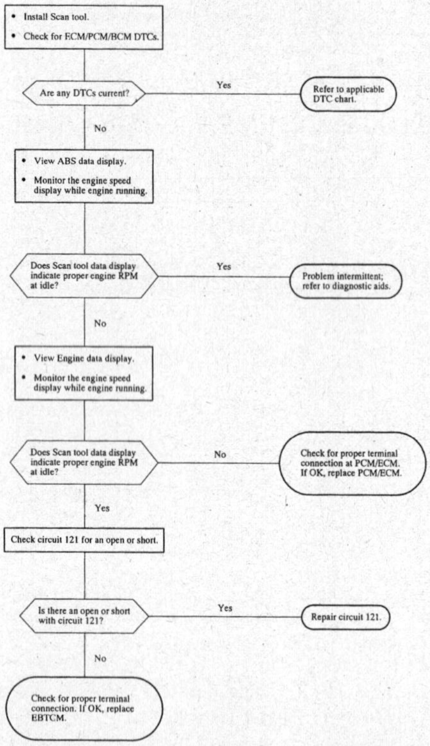

G34020000246020X

Fig. 54 Code C0236: TCS RPM Signal Circuit Fault (Part 2 of 2). L-Series

The PCM/ECM provides the EBTCM with engine RPM data so that it can determine traction control operation.

DTC PARAMETERS

DTC C0236 will set if the following conditions exist:

- Circuit 121 is open or shorted.
- The EBTCM does not receive a RPM signal one second after engine has been started.

When DTC C0236 sets:

- Traction control will be disabled.
- The traction Off indicator turns ON.
- The ABS remains functional.

DIAGNOSTIC AIDS

Possible causes for DTC C0236 to set:

- Open in circuit 121.
- Circuit 121 is shorted to ground or voltage.
- Improper connection, terminal corrosion, backed-out terminals, or damaged wire insulation.
- EBTCM not receiving signal from PCM/ECM.

G34020000246010X

Fig. 54 Code C0236: TCS RPM Signal Circuit Fault (Part 1 of 2). L-Series

The EBTCM and the PCM/ECM simultaneously control the traction control. The PCM/ECM reduces the amount of torque supplied to the drive wheels by retarding spark timing and selectively turning off fuel injectors. The EBTCM actively applies the brakes to the front wheels in order to reduce torque.

The EBTCM sends a requested torque message via pulse width modulated (PWM) signal to the PCM/ECM. The duty cycle of the signal is used to determine how much engine torque the EBTCM is requesting to the PCM/ECM to deliver. Normal values are between 10 and 90 percent duty cycle. The signal should be at 90 percent when traction control is not active and at lower values during traction control activations. The PCM/ECM supplies a pull up voltage of 5 volts that the EBTCM switches to ground to create the signal.

DTC PARAMETERS

DTC C0241 will set if the following conditions exist:

- The PCM/ECM does not receive the requested torque signal (open or shorted circuit).
- An incorrect requested torque signal is detected by the PCM/ECM. A PWM signal is sent back to the EBTCM via the delivered torque circuit.

When DTC C0241 sets:

- Traction control will be disabled.
- The traction Off indicator turns ON.
- The ABS remains functional.

DIAGNOSTIC AIDS

Possible causes for DTC C0241 to set:

- Open in the requested torque circuit.
- Requested torque circuit shorted to ground or voltage.
- Requested torque circuit has a wiring problem, terminal corrosion, or poor connection.
- PCM/ECM not receiving information from EBTCM.

G34020000247010X

Fig. 55 Code C0241: PWM Delivered Torque Reduction Fault (Part 1 of 2). L-Series

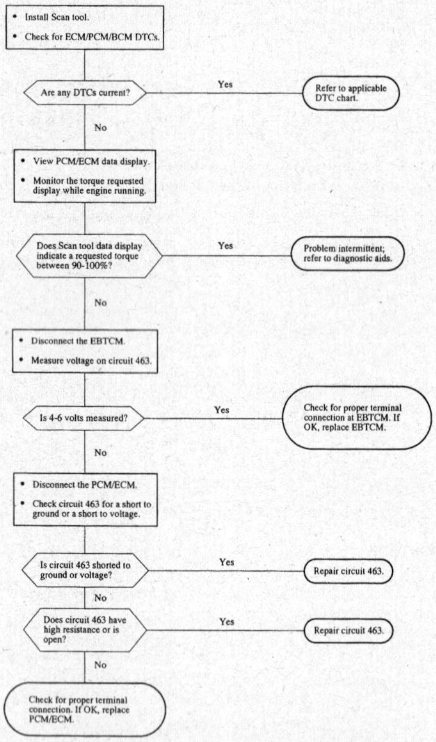

G34020000247020X

Fig. 55 Code C0241: PWM Delivered Torque Reduction Fault (Part 2 of 2). L-Series

The EBTCM and the PCM/ECM simultaneously control the traction control. The PCM/ECM reduces the amount of torque supplied to the drive wheels by retarding spark timing and selectively turning off fuel injectors. The EBTCM actively applies the brakes to the front wheels in order to reduce torque.

The PCM/ECM sends a delivered torque message via pulse width modulated (PWM) signal to the EBTCM. The duty cycle of the signal is used to determine how much engine torque the PCM/ECM is delivering. Normal values are between 10 and 90 percent duty cycle. The signal should be at low values (around 10 percent) at idle and higher values under driving conditions. The EBTCM supplies a pull-up voltage of 12 volts that the PCM/ECM switches to ground to create the signal.

DTC PARAMETERS

DTC C0244 will set if the following conditions exist:

- The EBTCM does not receive the delivered torque signal (open or shorted circuit).
- An incorrect delivered torque signal is detected by the EBTCM.

When DTC C0244 sets:

- Traction control will be disabled.
- The traction Off indicator turns ON.
- The ABS remains functional.

DIAGNOSTIC AIDS

Possible causes for DTC C0244 to set:

- Open in the delivered torque circuit.
- Delivered torque circuit shorted to ground or voltage.
- Delivered torque circuit has a wiring problem, terminal corrosion, or poor connection.
- EBTCM not receiving signal from PCM/ECM.

G34020000248010X

Fig. 56 Code C0244: PWM Delivered Torque Fault (Part 1 of 2). L-Series

ABS equipped vehicles have wheel speed sensors at all four wheels. The front wheel speed sensors monitor the speed of each wheel by placing a magnetic coupling next to a toothed ring mounted on the axle of each wheel. The rear wheel speed sensors monitor speed of each wheel with a magnetic coupling and a toothed ring internal to the wheel bearings. These sensors produce an AC signal that the electronic brake traction control module (EBTCM) uses to calculate wheel speed. The signal frequency changes with the wheel speed. DTC C0245 will set when the EBTCM cannot specifically identify which wheel speed sensor is causing the malfunction, DTC C0245 will be in history and the DTC associated with the malfunctioning sensor will be set along with DTC C0245.

DTC PARAMETERS

DTC C0245 will set if the following conditions exist:

- The EBTCM detects a deviation between left and right rear wheel speeds of greater than 6 km/h (3.75 mph) at a vehicle speed of less than 100 km/h (62 mph) on vehicles equipped with TCS.
- The EBTCM detects a deviation between left and right front wheel speeds of greater than 10 km/h (6.25 mph) at a vehicle speed of less than 100 km/h (62 mph).
- The EBTCM detects a deviation between left and right rear wheel speeds of greater than 6% of vehicle speed at greater than 100 km/h (62 mph) on vehicles equipped with TCS.
- The EBTCM detects a deviation between left and right front wheel speeds of greater than 4 km/h plus 6% of vehicle speed at greater than 100 km/h (62 mph).
- When this DTC sets the EBTCM will disable ABS, Traction Control and Dynamic Rear Proportioning and turn ON the antilock telltale.

DIAGNOSTIC AIDS

- It is very important to thoroughly inspect wiring components and connectors. Failure to carefully and fully inspect wiring and connectors may result in misdiagnosis, causing part replacement with reappearance of the malfunction.
- Inspect any circuitry that may be causing the complaint for the following conditions:
  - Backed out terminals.
  - Improper mating.
  - Broken connector locks.
  - Improperly formed or damaged terminals.
  - Poor terminal-to-wiring connections.
  - Physical damage to the wiring harness.
- The following conditions may cause an intermittent malfunction:
  - A poor connection.
  - Rubbed-through wire insulation.
  - A broken wire inside the insulation.
- Possible causes for DTC C0245 to set:
  - Damaged or missing teeth on one or more if the wheel speed sensor rings.
  - Large grooves or gouges, or buildup of foreign material in the gaps between the wheel speed sensor ring teeth.
  - A worn front hub bearing assembly, or worn inner axle bearing which allow the sensor to toothed ring gap to change excessively.

G34020000249000X

Fig. 57 Code C0245: Wheel Speed Sensor Frequency Error. L-Series

DTC PARAMETERS

DTC C0551 will set if ABS control module option configuration bit does not match vehicle.

When DTC P0551 sets:

- The TRAC switch LED is commanded Off.
- The ABS control module will disable TCS.

DIAGNOSTIC AIDS

IMPORTANT: When C0551 sets, TCS is disabled for the entire ignition cycle.

IMPORTANT: New ABS control modules will automatically set DTC C0551 when installed. To clear DTC C0551, new modules must be configured with the correct engine and transmission option bit.

G34020000251000X

Fig. 59 Code C0551: Option Configuration Error. L-Series

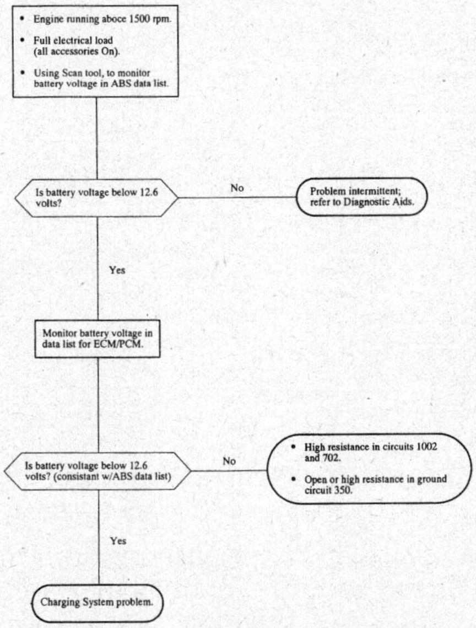

G34020000252020X

Fig. 60 Code C0896: System High/Low Voltage (Part 2 of 2). L-Series

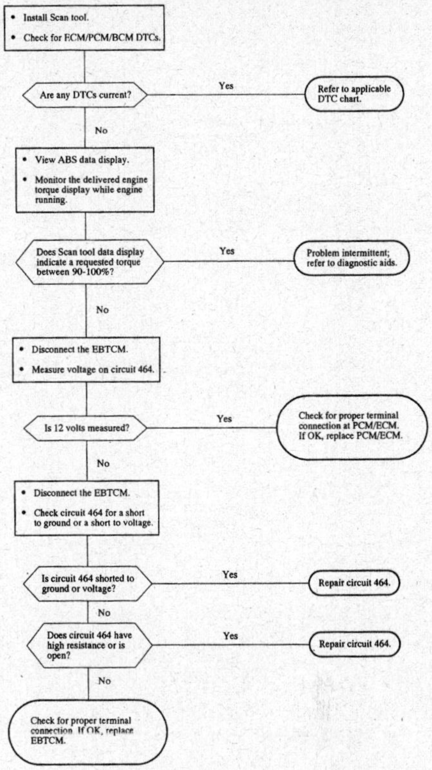

G34020000248020X

Fig. 56 Code C0244: PWM Delivered Torque Fault (Part 2 of 2). L-Series

DTC PARAMETERS

DTC C0550 will set if the ABS control module detects an internal fault.

When DTC C0550 sets:

- The ABS telltale will be On.
- The ABS control module will disable ABS, TCS, and DRP.

DIAGNOSTIC AIDS

The ABS control module must be replaced.

IMPORTANT: New ABS control modules will automatically set DTC C0551 when installed. To clear DTC C0551, new modules must be configured with the correct engine and transmission option bit.

G34020000250000X

Fig. 58 Code C0050: ECU Fault. L-Series

DTC PARAMETERS

DTC C0896 will set if the battery voltage drops below 9.4 volts or exceeds 17.4 volts while vehicle speed is above 4 mph.

When DTC C0896 sets:

- The ABS telltale will be On.
- The ABS control module will disable ABS, TCS, and DRP.

DIAGNOSTIC AIDS

IMPORTANT: If battery voltage returns to normal levels (9.4 – 17.4 volts) within the same ignition cycle, the ABS control module will enable ABS/TCS/DRP and will turn the ABS telltale Off.

IMPORTANT: An open in circuit 1008 or 702 will NOT set this DTC.

Use the Scan tool to observe battery voltage display.

G34020000252010X

Fig. 60 Code C0896: System High/Low Voltage (Part 1 of 2). L-Series

The TCS is enabled every time the ignition is switched On. The TRAC switch LED will be On to advise the driver that TCS is available. The TRAC LED will be Off if the driver disabled TCS by depressing the TRAC switch or if the ABS control module disables TCS because an applicable DTC is set.

G34020000253010X

Fig. 61 Traction Control Diagnostic Check (Part 1 of 2). S-Series

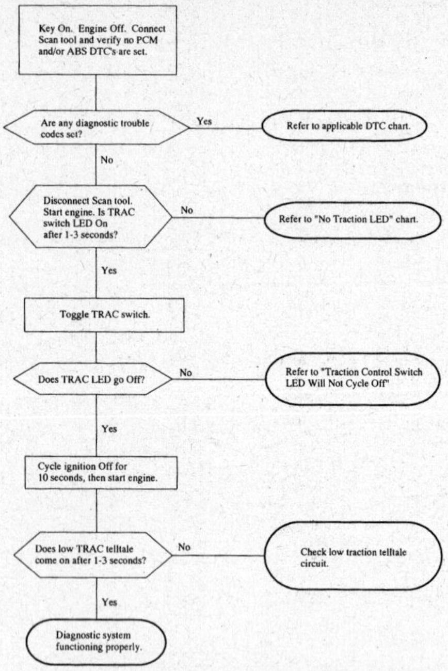

G34020000253020X

Fig. 61 Traction Control Diagnostic Check (Part 2 of 2). S-Series

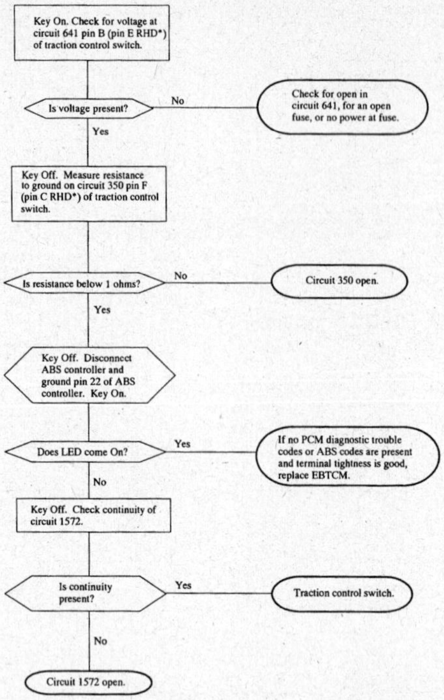

G34020000254000X

Fig. 62 No Traction LED. S-Series

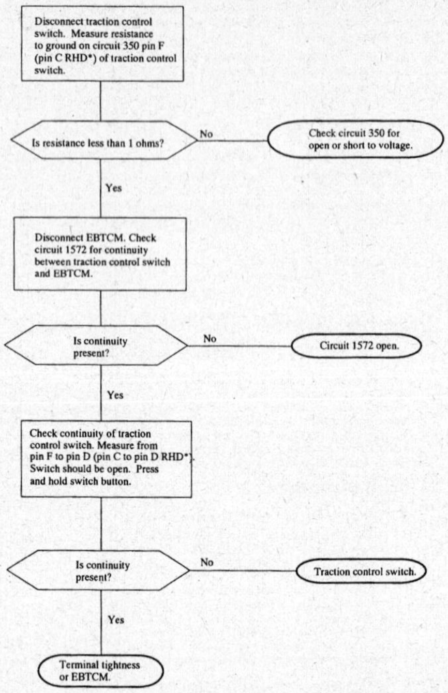

G34020000255000X

Fig. 63 Traction Control Switch LED Will Not Cycle Off. S-Series

The wheel speed sensor produces an AC voltage whose amplitude and frequency vary, depending upon the velocity of the wheel. The ABS control module (EBTCM) uses this voltage signal to calculate wheel speed.

DTC PARAMETERS

DTC will set if:

- The ABS control module detects that a wheel speed circuit is open, grounded or shorted to battery while ignition is in RUN.

When DTC sets:

- The ABS telltale will be On.
- The control module will disable ABS.

DIAGNOSTIC AIDS

The inline connectors at wheel speed sensors are the most likely area for opens and shorts.

When diagnosing intermittent conditions, use the Scan tool to observe parameters while test driving or wiggling a wire harness.

G34020000256010X

Fig. 64 Codes C0035, C0040, C0045 & C0050: Wheel Speed Sensor Circuit Fault (Part 1 of 3). S-Series

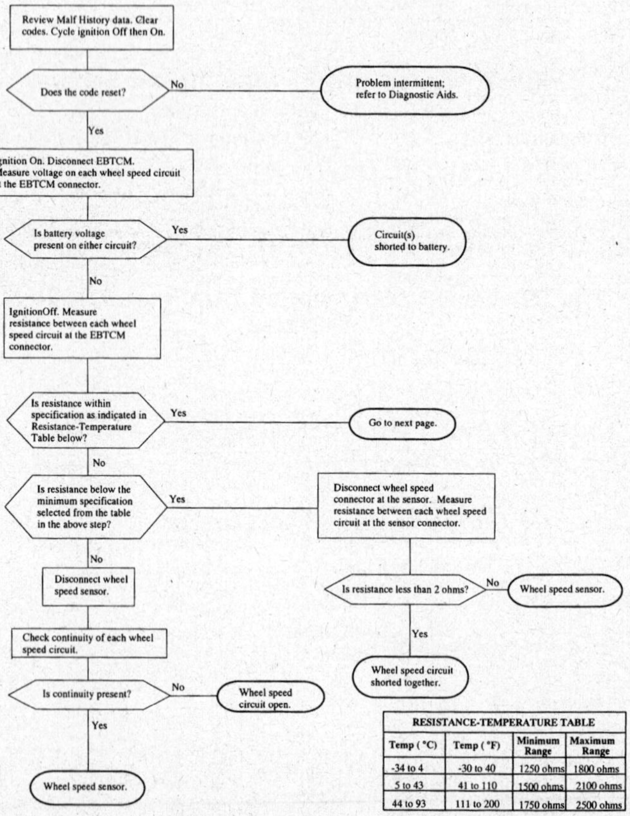

RESISTANCE-TEMPERATURE TABLE

Temp (°C)	Temp (°F)	Minimum Range	Maximum Range
-34 to 4	-30 to 40	1250 ohms	1800 ohms
5 to 43	41 to 110	1500 ohms	2100 ohms
44 to 93	111 to 200	1750 ohms	2500 ohms

G34020000256020X

Fig. 64 Codes C0035, C0040, C0045 & C0050: Wheel Speed Sensor Circuit Fault (Part 2 of 3). S-Series

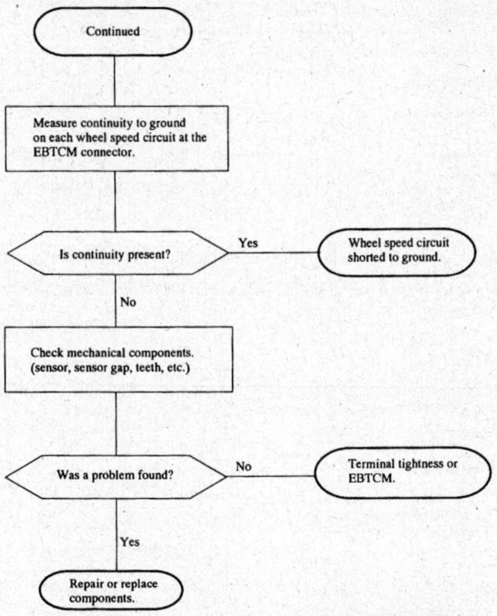

G34020000256030X

Fig. 64 Codes C0035, C0040, C0045 & C0050: Wheel Speed Sensor Circuit Fault (Part 3 of 3). S-Series

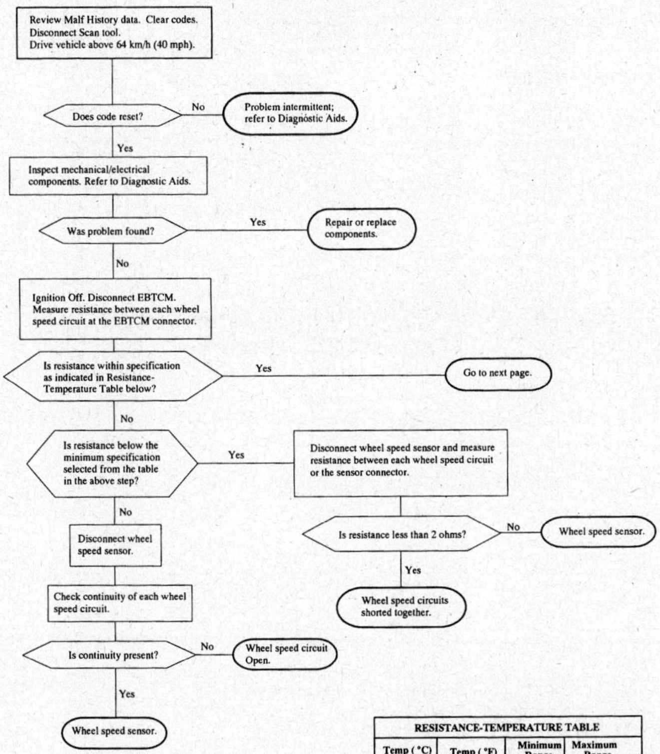

RESISTANCE-TEMPERATURE TABLE

Temp (°C)	Temp (°F)	Minimum Range	Maximum Range
-34 to 4	-30 to 40	1250 ohms	1800 ohms
5 to 43	41 to 110	1500 ohms	2100 ohms
44 to 93	111 to 200	1750 ohms	2500 ohms

G34020000257020X

Fig. 65 Codes C0036, C0041, C0046 & C0051: Wheel Speed Circuit Range Performance (Part 2 of 3). S-Series

The wheel speed sensor produces an AC voltage whose amplitude and frequency vary, depending upon the velocity of the wheel. The ABS control module (EBTCM) uses this voltage signal to calculate wheel speed.

DTC PARAMETERS

DTC will set if:

- One wheel speed changes 16 km/h (10 mph) or more in .01 seconds.
- A wheel speed sensor circuit malfunction is not set for the same wheel speed sensor.
- The change must occur three times with 1 second between each occurrence.

When DTC sets:

- The ABS telltale will be On.
- The control module will disable ABS.

DIAGNOSTIC AIDS

Possible causes for DTC to set:

- Wheel speed sensor or circuit intermittently open or shorted.
- Excessive sensor air gap.
- No air gap (pole strike).
- Low sensor output.
- Loose sensor.
- Worn suspension or drivetrain components.
- Damaged tooth or teeth on speed ring.
- Electrical noise induced on wheel speed circuit.
- Brake switch always Off (Open).
- Large grooves, gouges, or foreign material in speed ring.
- A worn front hub bearing or inner axle bearing.

G34020000257010X

Fig. 65 Codes C0036, C0041, C0046 & C0051: Wheel Speed Circuit Range Performance (Part 1 of 3). S-Series

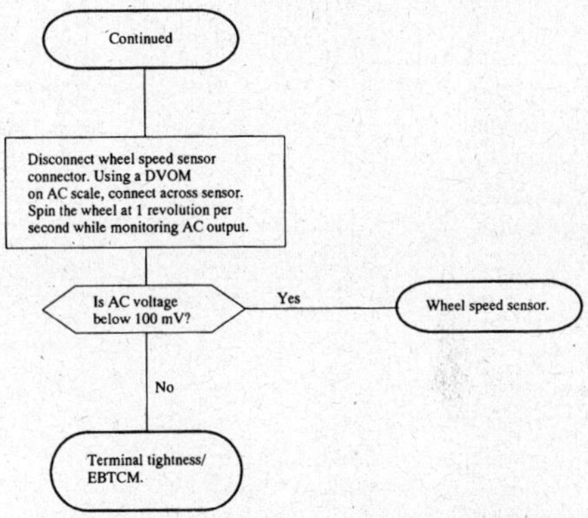

G34020000257030X

Fig. 65 Codes C0036, C0041, C0046 & C0051: Wheel Speed Circuit Range Performance (Part 3 of 3). S-Series

The wheel speed sensor produces an AC voltage whose amplitude and frequency vary, depending upon the velocity of the wheel. The ABS control module (EBTCM) uses this voltage signal to calculate wheel speed.

DTC PARAMETERS

DTC will set if:

- A wheel speed = 0 km/h (0 mph) and the other three wheel speeds are greater than 8 kph (5 mph) for 2.5 seconds and no wheel speed sensor circuit malfunction DTCs are set.

When DTC sets:

- The ABS telltale will be On.
- The control module will disable ABS.

DIAGNOSTIC AIDS

The inline connectors at wheel speed sensors are the most likely area for opens and shorts.

When diagnosing intermittent conditions, use the Scan tool to observe parameters while testing driving or wiggling a wire harness. Compare parameters with those on a known good system.

Possible causes for DTC to set:

- Wheel speed sensor has low or not output.
- Excessive air gap.
- No speed ring.
- Wheel speed sensor shorted.

G34020000258010X

Fig. 66 Codes C0037, C0042, C0047 & C0052: Wheel Speed Sensor Circuit Low (Part 1 of 2). S-Series

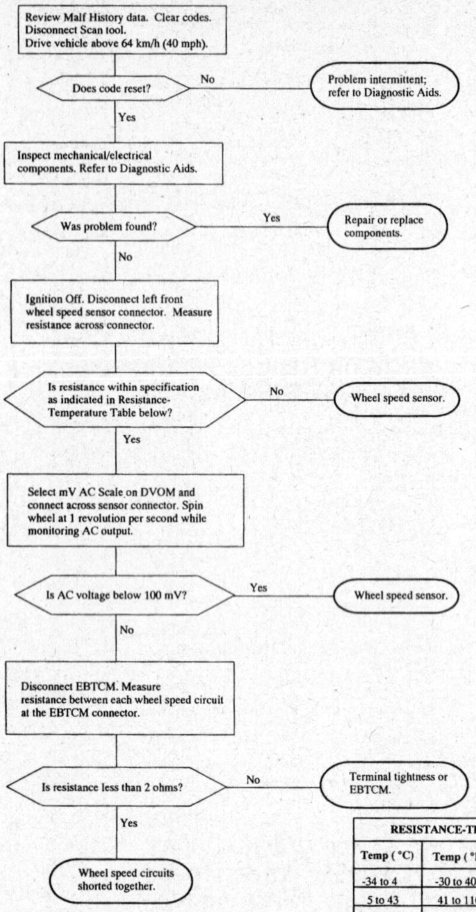

RESISTANCE-TEMPERATURE TABLE

Temp (°C)	Temp (°F)	Minimum Range	Maximum Range
-34 to 4	-30 to 40	1250 ohms	1800 ohms
5 to 43	41 to 110	1500 ohms	2100 ohms
44 to 93	111 to 200	1750 ohms	2500 ohms

G34020000258020X

Fig. 66 Codes C0037, C0042, C0047 & C0052: Wheel Speed Sensor Circuit Low (Part 2 of 2). S-Series

The UHFB supplies the solenoid circuits with battery voltage when the ignition is in run. The ABS control module (EBTCM) controls valve function by grounding the solenoid circuit when necessary.

#1 solenoids are outlet valves.

DTC PARAMETERS

DTC will set if the ABS control module detects an open, short to ground or short to voltage on the solenoid circuit(s) inside the control module.

When DTC C0080 sets:

- The ABS telltale will be on.
- The red BRAKE telltale will be On.
- Dynamic rear proportioning (DRP) will only be functional on one rear wheel. If a RR solenoid or RR wheel speed DTC sets with DTC C0080, then DRP is disabled.

DIAGNOSTIC AIDS

The ABS control module must be replaced.

G34020000260000X

Fig. 68 Code C0080: Lefthand Rear Solenoid No. 1 Circuit Fault. S-Series

The UHFB supplies the solenoid circuits with battery voltage when the ignition is in run. The ABS control module (EBTCM) controls valve function by grounding the solenoid circuit when necessary.

#1 solenoids are outlet valves. #2 solenoids are inlet valves.

DTC PARAMETERS

DTC will set if the ABS control module detects an open, short to ground or short to voltage on the solenoid circuit(s) inside the control module.

When any of the above DTCs set:

- The ABS telltale will be on.
- The ABS control module will disable ABS.
- Dynamic Rear Proportioning (DRP) limited to hold function only.

DIAGNOSTIC AIDS

The ABS control module must be replaced.

G34020000259000X

Fig. 67 Codes C0060, C0065, C0070, C0075, C0085 & C0095: Solenoid Circuit Fault. S-Series

The UHFB supplies the solenoid circuits with battery voltage when the ignition is in run. The ABS control module (EBTCM) controls valve function by grounding the solenoid circuit when necessary.

#1 solenoids are outlet valves.

DTC PARAMETERS

DTC will set if the ABS control module detects an open, short to ground or short to voltage on the solenoid circuit(s) inside the control module.

When DTC C0090 sets:

- The ABS telltale will be on.
- The red BRAKE telltale will be On.
- The ABS control module will disable ABS.
- Dynamic rear proportioning (DRP) will only be functional on one rear wheel. If a LR solenoid or LR wheel speed DTC sets with DTC C0080, then DRP is disabled.

DIAGNOSTIC AIDS

The ABS control module must be replaced.

G34020000261000X

Fig. 69 Code C0090: Righthand Rear Solenoid No. 1 Circuit Fault. S-Series

The pump motor is part of the valve assembly (BPMV). The system relay and pump motor driver is located in the electronic ABS control module (EBTCM). The system relay supplies power to the solenoids and pump motor whenever the ignition switch is in the RUN position. The pump motor driver switches the pump motor on during ABS operation.

DTC PARAMETERS

DTC C0112 will set if:

- System voltage is greater than 9 volts and the voltage across the pump is greater than 10 volts when the pump has been off of one second.
- Pump low side voltage is less than or equal to 2.7 volts for .2 seconds when the pump has been off for one second.

When the trouble code sets, ABS is disabled and the antilock telltale is turned On.

Dynamic rear proportioning (DRP) will only have the hold function.

DIAGNOSTIC AIDS

- It is very important to thoroughly inspect wiring components and connectors. Failure to inspect wiring and connectors may result in misdiagnosis, causing part replacement with a reoccuring malfunction.

Possible causes for DTC C0112 to set:

- Motor is shorted to ground.
- Failed EBTCM motor driver.

G34020000262010X

Fig. 70 Code C0112: Pump Motor Circuit Low (Part 1 of 2). S-Series

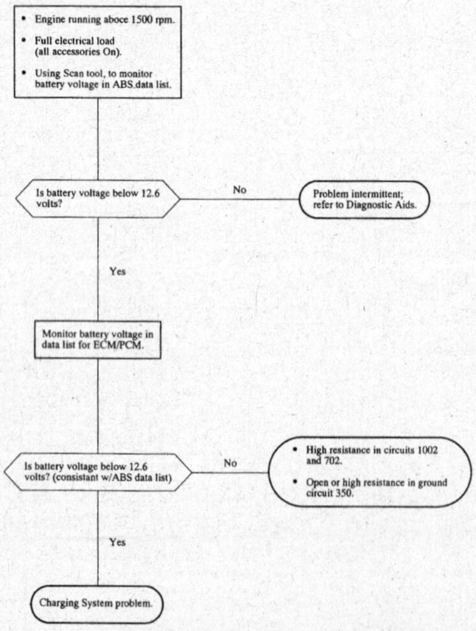

G34020000262020X

Fig. 70 Code C0112: Pump Motor Circuit Low (Part 2 of 2). S-Series

The pump motor is part of the valve assembly (BPMV). The system relay and pump motor driver is located in the Electronic ABS control module (EBTCM). The system relay supplies power to the solenoids and pump motor whenever the ignition switch is in the RUN position. The pump motor driver switches the pump motor on during ABS operation.

DTC PARAMETERS

DTC C0113 will set if:

- The voltage across the pump is 3 volts less than the commanded pump voltage and the commanded pump voltage is less than the system voltage. System voltage is greater than 8 volts and the pump is commanded on.
- The voltage across the pump is less than 8 volts and the commanded pump voltage is greater than or equal to system voltage. System voltage is greater than 8 volts and the pump is commanded on.

When the trouble code sets, ABS is disabled and the antilock telltale is turned On.

Dynamic rear proportioning (DRP) will only have the hold function.

DIAGNOSTIC AIDS

- It is very important to thoroughly inspect wiring components and connectors. Failure to inspect wiring and connectors may result in misdiagnosis, causing part replacement with a reoccuring malfunction.

Possible causes for DTC C0113 to set:

- Motor is shorted to battery.
- Motor ground is open.
- Motor ground has high resistance.
- Failed EBTCM motor driver.

G34020000263010X

Fig. 71 Code C0113: Pump Motor Circuit High (Part 1 of 2). S-Series

The pump motor is part of the valve assembly (BPMV). The system relay and pump motor driver is located in the Electronic ABS control module (EBTCM). The system relay supplies power to the solenoids and pump motor whenever the ignition switch is in the RUN position. The pump motor driver switches the pump motor on during ABS operation.

DTC PARAMETERS

DTC C0114 will set if:

- System voltage is greater than 8 volts, the system relay is on and the pump is commanded off.
- Voltage across the pump is between 1.6 and 10 volts for 2 seconds.

When the trouble code sets, ABS is disabled and the antilock telltale is turned On.

Dynamic rear proportioning (DRP) will only have the hold function.

DIAGNOSTIC AIDS

- It is very important to thoroughly inspect wiring components and connectors. Failure to inspect wiring and connectors may result in misdiagnosis, causing part replacement with a reoccuring malfunction.

Possible causes for DTC C0114 to set:

- Pump motor open.
- Pump motor (internal) circuit open.

G34020000264010X

Fig. 72 Code C0114: Pump Motor Circuit Open (Part 1 of 2). S-Series

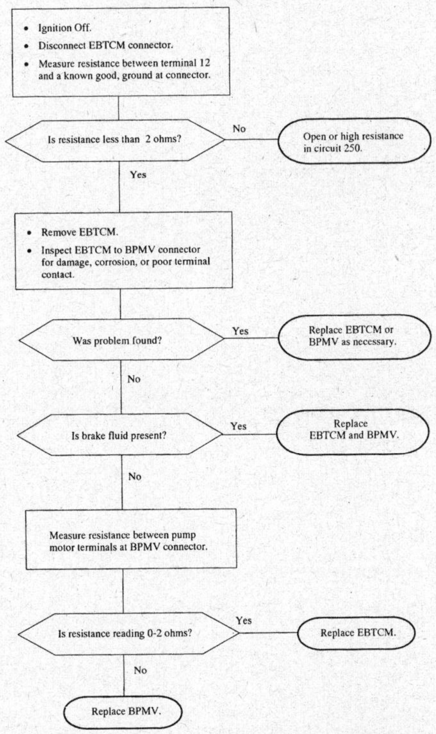

G34020000264020X

Fig. 72 Code C0114: Pump Motor Circuit Open (Part 2 of 2). S-Series

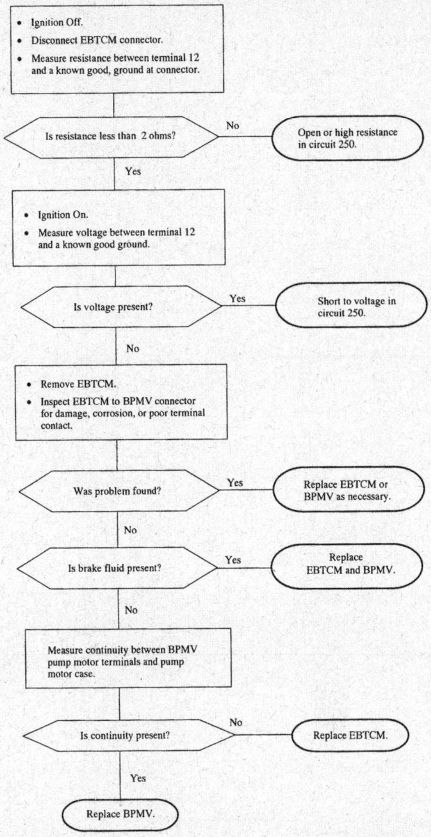

G34020000263020X

Fig. 71 Code C0113: Pump Motor Circuit High (Part 2 of 2). S-Series

The pump motor is part of the valve assembly (BPMV). The system relay and pump motor driver is located in the Electronic ABS control module (EBTCM). The system relay supplies power to the solenoids and pump motor whenever the ignition switch is in the RUN position. The pump motor driver switches the pump motor on during ABS operation.

DTC PARAMETERS

DTC C0115 will set if:

- The EBTCM senses a stalled or slow turning pump motor.

When the trouble code sets, ABS is disabled and the antilock telltale is turned On.

Dynamic rear proportioning (DRP) will only have the hold function.

DIAGNOSTIC AIDS

- It is very important to thoroughly inspect wiring components and connectors. Failure to inspect wiring and connectors may result in misdiagnosis, causing part replacement with a reoccuring malfunction.

Possible causes for DTC C0115 to set:

- Pump motor is stuck.
- Pump motor turns too slowly. (Could be due to corroded motor or contaminated pump circuit.)
- Pump motor has high resistance.

G34020000265010X

Fig. 73 Code C0115: Pump Motor Fault (Part 1 of 2). S-Series

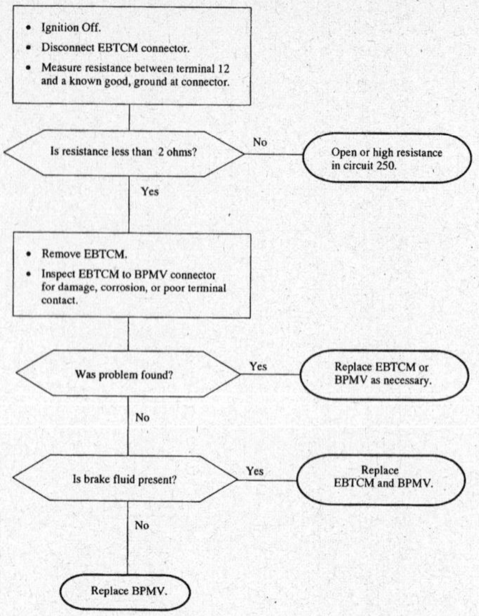

G34020000265020X

Fig. 73 Code C0115: Pump Motor Fault (Part 2 of 2). S-Series

The ABS enable relay is inside the ABS control module (EBTCM) and provides shut-down capability in the event of a system failure.

DTC PARAMETERS

DTC C0124 will set if:

- Enable relay is stuck on when commanded Off.

ABS and dynamic rear proportioning (DRP) will be fully functional.

The wrench light will be turned On.

DIAGNOSTIC AIDS

- The ABS Control Module must be replaced.

G34020000266000X

Fig. 74 Code C0124: Valve Relay Circuit High. S-Series

The solenoid valve relay supplies power to the solenoid valve coils in the electronic brake and traction control module (EBTCM). The solenoid valve relay, located in the EBTCM, is activated whenever the ignition switch is in the RUN position and no faults are present. The solenoid valve relay remains engaged until the ignition is turned Off or a failure is detected.

DTC PARAMETERS

DTC C0125 will set if:

- ETCM commands relay on, ignition voltage is greater than 11 volts and switch solenoid relay voltage is less than 8 volts for .23 seconds.

When this trouble code sets, the EBTCM will disable ABS, and turn On the antilock telltale.

Dynamic rear proportioning will only have the hold function.

DIAGNOSTIC AIDS

- It is very important to thoroughly inspect wiring components and connectors. Failure to carefully and fully inspect wiring and connectors may result in misdiagnosis, causing part replacement with reappearance of the malfunction.
- Inspect any circuitry that may be causing the complaint for the following conditions:
  - Backed out terminals
  - Improper mating
  - Broken connector locks
  - Corrosion in connectors/terminals
  - Rubbed through wire insulation
  - Broken wire inside insulation
  - Loose components

Possible causes for DTC C0125 to set:

- Poor EBTCM connection or terminal mattings.
- Internal EBTCM solenoid relay contacts open.
- Internal EBTCM circuit open or high resistance
- Internal EBTCM solenoid relay coil or relay coil circuit open.

G34020000267010X

Fig. 75 Code C0125: Valve Relay Circuit Open (Part 1 of 3). S-Series

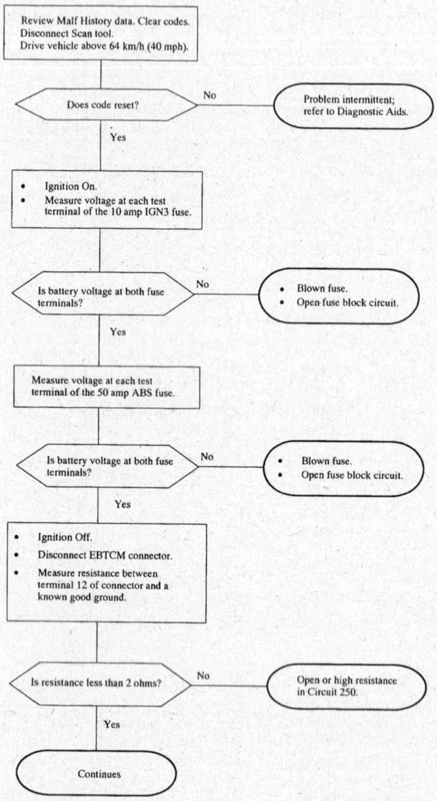

G34020000267020X

Fig. 75 Code C0125: Valve Relay Circuit Open (Part 2 of 3). S-Series

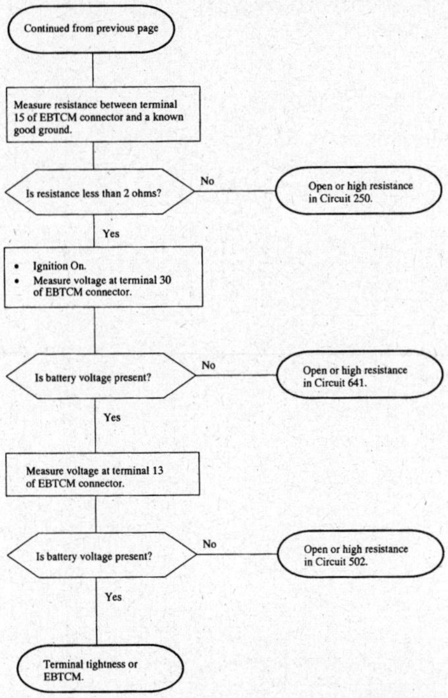

G34020000267030X

Fig. 75 Code C0125: Valve Relay Circuit Open (Part 3 of 3). S-Series

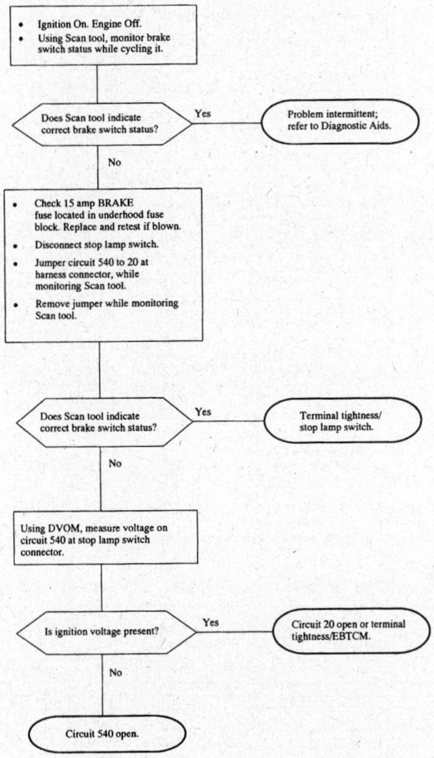

G34020000268020X

Fig. 76 Code C0165: ABS/TCS Brake Switch Circuit Open (Part 2 of 2). S-Series

The stoplamp switch indicates brake pedal status to the ABS control module (EBTCM). The normally open stop lamp switch interrupts voltage to the EBTCM. Applying brake pedal "closes" switch and supplies voltage on circuit 20 to the EBTCM.

DTC PARAMETERS

DTC C0165 will set if:

- The EBTCM senses an open condition in the brake switch input, all brake lamps, or brake lamp grounds for 2 seconds.

Open brake switch circuit may result in possible false setting of wheel speed codes C0036, C0041, C0046, or C0051.

The wrench light will be turned On.

DIAGNOSTIC AIDS

- It is very important to thoroughly inspect wiring components and connectors. Failure to carefully and fully inspect wiring and connectors may result in misdiagnosis, causing part replacement with reappearance of the malfunction.
- Inspect any circuitry that may be causing the complaint for the following conditions:
  - Backed out terminals
  - Improper mating
  - Broken connector locks
  - Improperly formed or damaged terminals
  - Poor terminal-to-wiring connections.
  - Physical damage to the wiring harness.
- The following conditions may cause an intermittent malfunction:
  - A poor connection
  - Rubbed-through wire insulation
  - A broken wire inside the insulation

Possible causes for DTC C0165 to set:

- Brake switch input circuit open.
- All brake lamps open.
- All brake lamp grounds open.
- Internal EBTCM problems.

G34020000268010X

Fig. 76 Code C0165: ABS/TCS Brake Switch Circuit Open (Part 1 of 2). S-Series

DTC PARAMETERS

DTC C0550 will set if:

- An internal malfunction exists.

When this trouble code sets, the ABS Control Module will disable ABS, traction control and dynamic rear proportioning and turn On the antilock and RED brake telltale

DIAGNOSTIC AIDS

- The ABS control module must be replaced.

G34020000269000X

Fig. 77 Code C0550: ECU Fault. S-Series

In a normal key down situation the ABS control module performs a sequence of internal processes to get ready for the next ignition cycle.

DTC PARAMETERS

DTC C0552 will set if:

- There is a sudden loss of power or ground during EBTCM operation that causes a running reset.
- 4 running reset occur.

When this trouble code sets the EBTCM will disable ABS and turn On the antilock telltale.

Dynamic rear proportioning will be disabled and the RED brake telltale turned On.

DIAGNOSTIC AIDS

Possible causes for DTC 0552 to set:

- Loss of EBTCM ground.
- Battery power is lost while EBTCM is operating. (ignition voltage present)
- Sudden drop in voltage. (less than 5 volts)

Monitor Scan tool for low ignition or battery voltage while cranking and driving the vehicle.

G34020000270010X

Fig. 78 Code C0552: Improper Shutdown (Part 1 of 3). S-Series

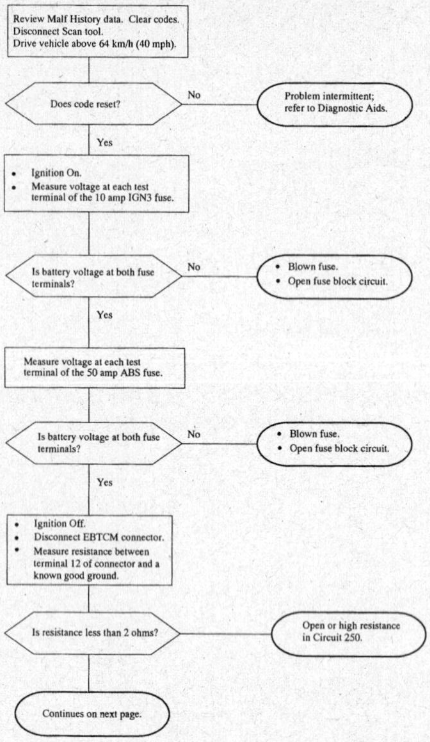

G34020000270020X

Fig. 78 Code C0552: Improper Shutdown (Part 2 of 3). S-Series

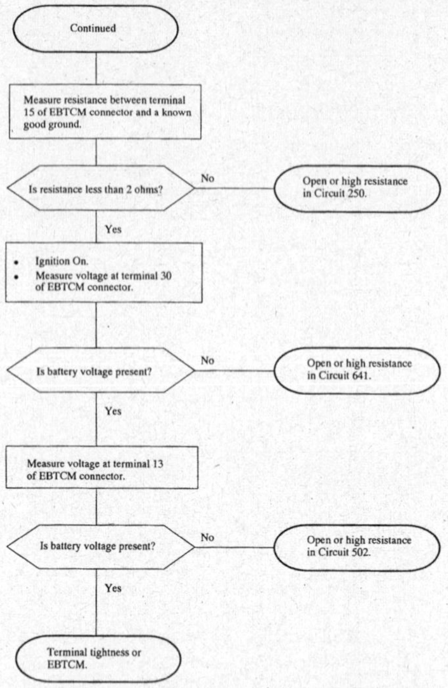

G34020000270030X

Fig. 78 Code C0552: Improper Shutdown (Part 3 of 3). S-Series

The ABS control module (EBTCM) functions properly within a specified range of voltage. During ABS operation there are current requirements that will cause the system voltage to drop. Because of this, the EBTCM continuously monitors system voltage.

DTC PARAMETERS

DTC C0899 will set if:

Vehicle speed is greater than 8 km/h (5 mph), ignition voltage is less than or equal to 11.2 volts, the solenoid relay is commanded on and one of the following conditions exists for .72 seconds:

- System is not in ABS, (pump off) and system voltage is less than or equal to 11.2 volts.
- During initialization system voltage is less than or equal to 11.2 volts.
- System is in ABS stop (pump running) system voltage is less than or equal to 9.6 volts.

When this trouble code sets, the EBTCM will disable ABS and turn On the antilock telltale.

Dynamic rear proportioning (DRP) will only have the hold function unless system voltage is less than 8 volts, then DRP will be disabled and the RED brake telltale turned on.

DIAGNOSTIC AIDS

Check for the following conditions:

- Poor connection or damaged harness. Inspect the wiring harness for damage. If the harness appears to be OK, observe the battery voltage display on the scan tool while moving connectors and wiring related ABS dash harness, and engine harness. A change in display will indicate the location of fault.

Possible causes for DTC C0899 to set:

- Charging system malfunction
- Excessive battery draw
- Weak battery
- Loose or corroded ground
- Loose or corroded battery terminals

G34020000271010X

Fig. 79 Code C0899: Device No. 1 Voltage Low (Part 1 of 3). S-Series

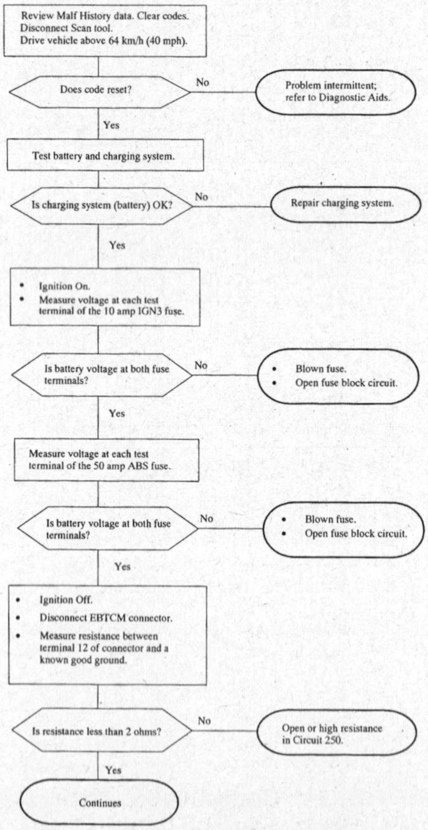

G34020000271020X

Fig. 79 Code C0899: Device No. 1 Voltage Low (Part 2 of 3). S-Series

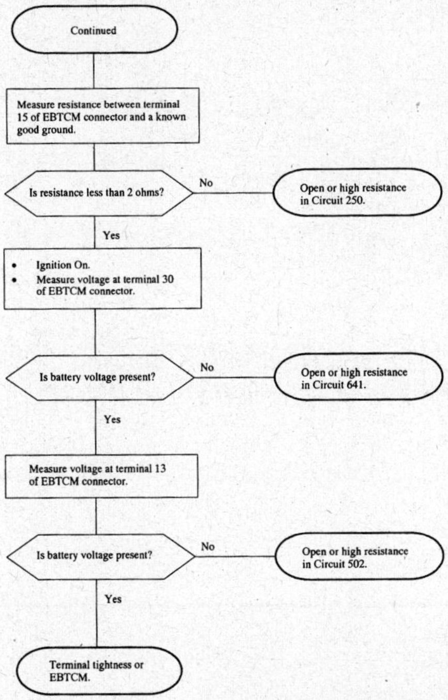

G34020000271030X

Fig. 79 Code C0899: Device No. 1 Voltage Low (Part 3 of 3). S-Series

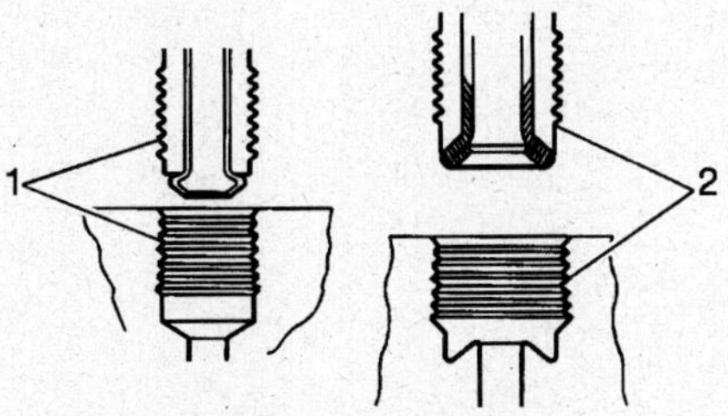

1- FIRST DESIGN, ISO FLARE, TIGHTEN TO 14 FT. LBS.

2- SECOND DESIGN, DOUBLE INVERTED FLARE, TIGHTEN TO 13 FT. LBS.

G34020200434000X

Fig. 81 Hydraulic brake pipe flare designs & tightening specifications. ION

The ABS control module (EBTCM) functions properly within a specified range of voltage. During ABS and traction control operation there are current requirements that will cause the system voltage to drop. Because of this, the EBTCM continuously monitors system voltage for a good charging system and for a high voltage that could damage the system.

DTC PARAMETERS

DTC C0900 will set if:

Vehicle speed is greater than 8 km/h (5 mph), and solenoid relay voltage is greater than 19 volts for .72 seconds:

When this trouble code sets, the EBTCM will disable ABS and turn On the antilock telltale.

Dynamic rear proportioning (DRP) will only have the hold function.

DIAGNOSTIC AIDS

Check for following conditions:

- Charging system malfunction

G34020000272000X

Fig. 80 Code C0900: Device No. 1 Voltage High. S-Series

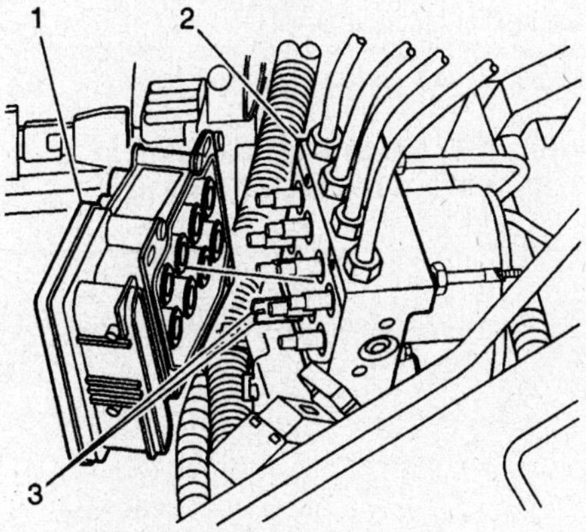

1- ELECTRONIC BRAKE CONTROL MODULE (EBCM)

2- BRAKE PRESSURE MODULATOR VALVE (BPMV)

3- ELECTRICAL TERMINALS

G34020200435000X

Fig. 82 Electronic Brake Control Module (EBCM) replacement. ION

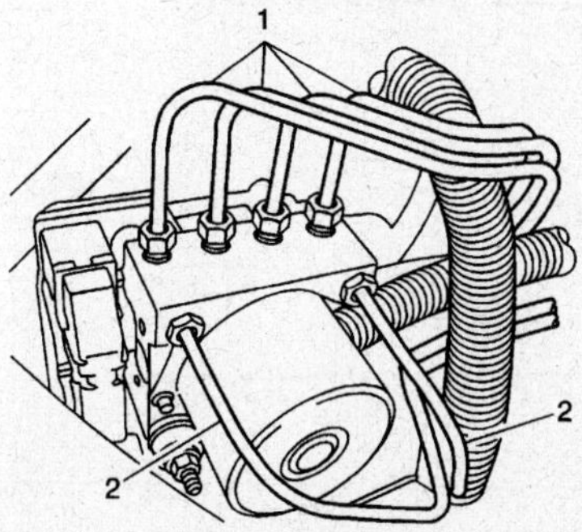

1- CALIPER & WHEEL CYLINDER HYDRAULIC PIPES

2- MASTER CYLINDER HYDRAULIC PIPES

G34020200436000X

Fig. 83 Brake Pressure Modulator Valve (BPMV) hydraulic pipe locations. ION

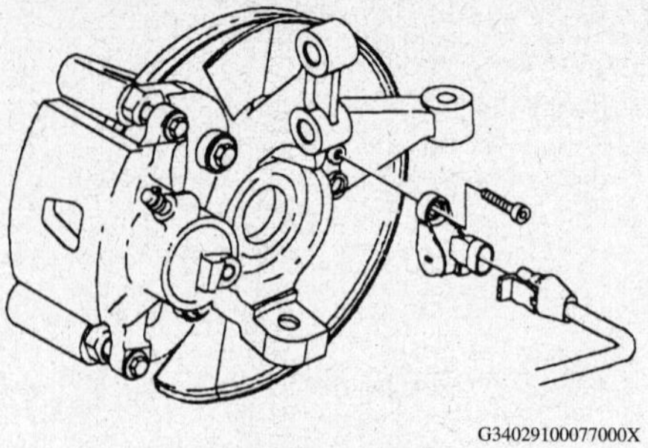

Fig. 84 Front speed sensor replacement

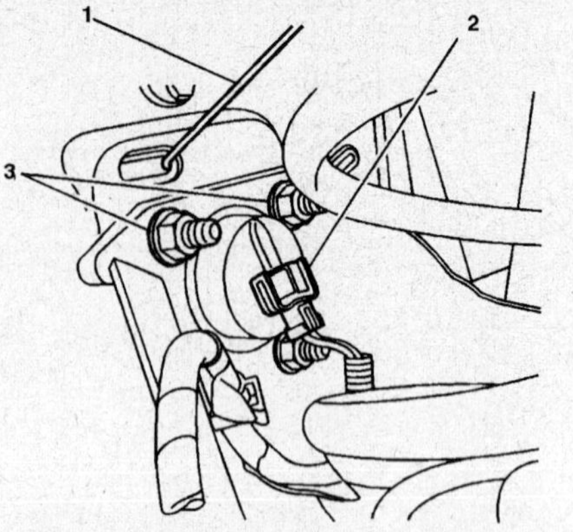

1- BACKING PLATE SUPPORT
2- WHEEL SPEED SENSOR ELECTRICAL CONNECTOR
3- HUB/BEARING ASSEMBLY MOUNTING BOLTS

G34020200437000X

Fig. 85 Rear hub & bearing assembly replacement. ION

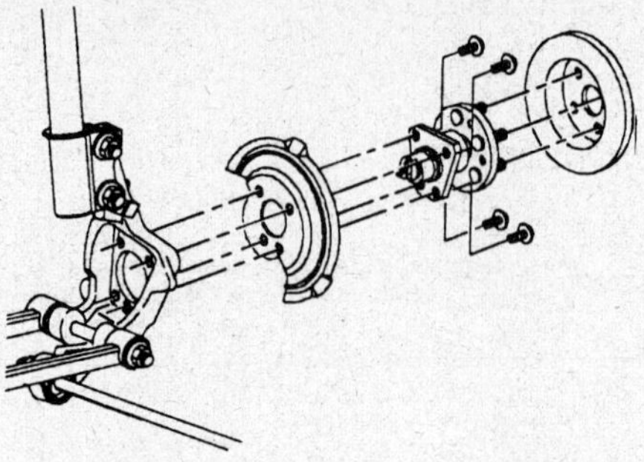

Fig. 86 Rear hub & bearing assembly replacement. S-Series

TIRE PRESSURE MONITORING SYSTEM

INDEX

PRECAUTIONS

Air Bag Systems

Refer to "Air Bag System Precautions" in the front of this manual for system disarming and arming procedures.

Battery Ground Cable

Prior to service, disconnect battery ground cable and isolate as required.

DESCRIPTION

The tire pressure monitor (TPM) system alerts the driver when a large change in the pressure of one tire exists. The system detects a tire pressure condition while the vehicle is in motion, once a tire pressure condition is detected, the system alerts the driver whenever the ignition is turned On.

The TPM system uses electronic brake control module, wheel speed sensors, data messages and instrument cluster to perform system functions as required.

DIAGNOSIS & TESTING

Accessing Diagnostic Trouble Codes

Connect a suitably programmed scan tool to Data Link Connector (DLC) and follow manufacturer's instructions.

Wiring Diagrams

ALERO & GRAND AM

Refer to **Figs. 1 through 3,** for tire pressure monitoring system wiring.

AURORA

Refer to **Fig. 4,** for tire pressure monitoring system wiring.

BONNEVILLE

Refer to **Figs. 5 and 6,** for tire pressure monitoring system wiring.

CENTURY & REGAL

Refer to **Figs. 7 and 8,** for tire pressure monitoring system wiring.

CORVETTE

Refer to **Figs. 9 and 10,** for tire pressure monitoring system wiring.

DEVILLE & SEVILLE

Refer to **Figs. 11 and 12,** for tire pressure monitoring system wiring.

IMPALA & MONTE CARLO

Refer to **Figs. 13 and 14,** for tire pressure monitoring system wiring.

LESABRE & PARK AVENUE

Refer to **Fig. 15,** for tire pressure monitoring system wiring.

Diagnostic Tests

ALERO & GRAND AM

Refer to **Figs. 16 through 23,** for tire pressure monitoring system diagnostic test procedures.

AURORA

Refer to **Figs. 24 and 25,** for tire pressure monitoring system diagnostic test procedures.

BONNEVILLE

Refer to **Figs. 26 through 31,** for tire pressure monitoring system diagnostic test procedures.

CENTURY & REGAL

Refer to **Figs. 32 through 41,** for tire pressure monitoring system diagnostic test procedures.

CORVETTE

Refer to **Figs. 42 through 52,** for tire pressure monitoring system diagnostic test procedures.

DEVILLE & SEVILLE

Refer to **Figs. 53 and 54,** for tire pressure monitoring system diagnostic test procedures.

IMPALA & MONTE CARLO

Refer to **Figs. 55 through 58,** for tire pressure monitoring system diagnostic test procedures.

LESABRE & PARK AVENUE

Refer to **Figs. 59 and 60,** for tire pressure monitoring system diagnostic test procedures.

Clearing Diagnostic Trouble Codes

Connect a suitably programmed scan tool to Data Link Connector (DLC), and follow manufacturer's instructions.

Intermittent & Poor Connections

INTERMITTENTS

Most intermittents are caused by faulty electrical connections or wiring. Inspect for the following:

1. Wiring broken inside insulation.
2. Poor connection between male and female terminal at connector.

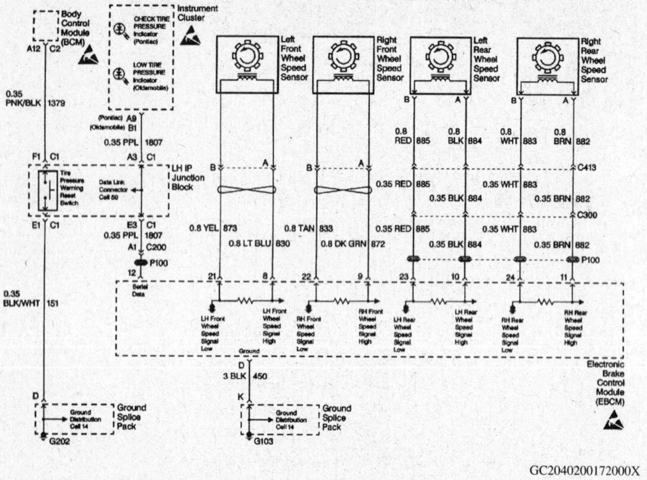

Fig. 1 Wiring diagram. 2000 Alero & Grand Am

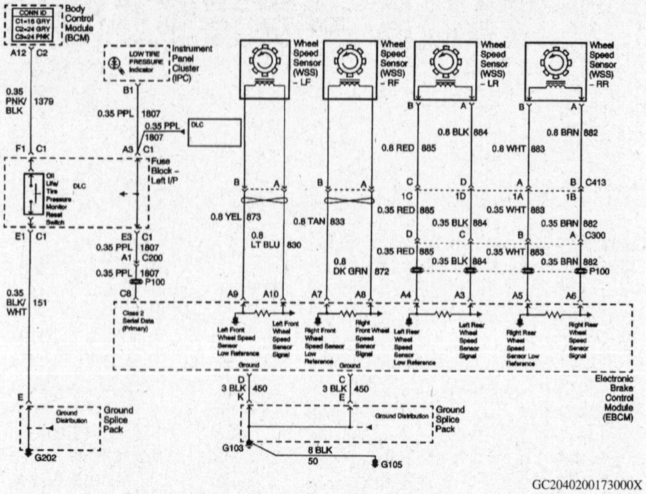

Fig. 2 Wiring diagram. 2001 Alero & Grand Am

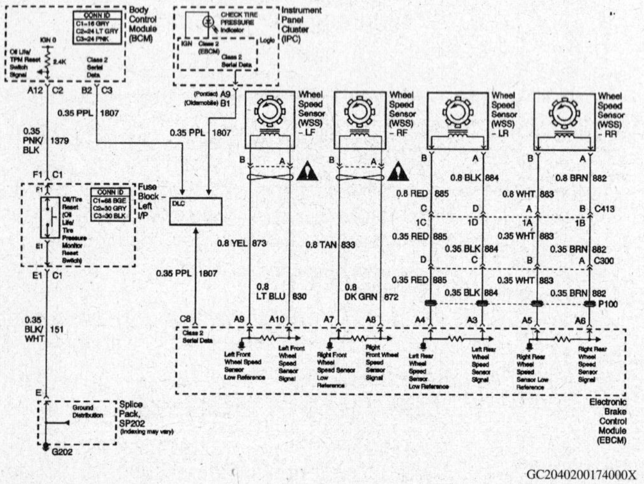

Fig. 3 Wiring diagram. 2002–04 Alero & Grand Am

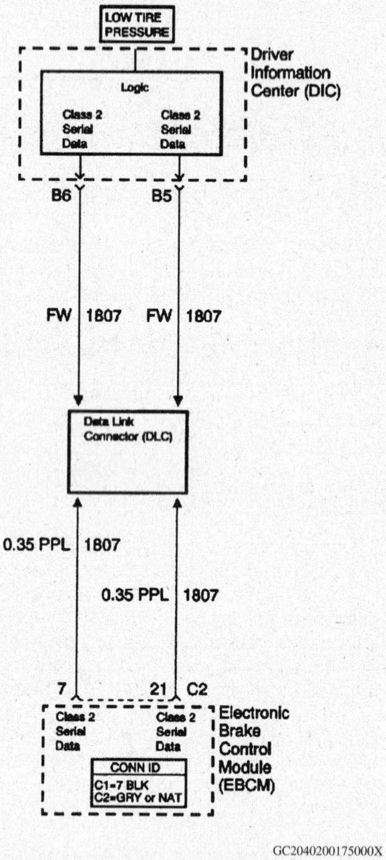

Fig. 4 Wiring diagram. Aurora

3. Poor terminal to wire connection. Some conditions which fall under this are:
   a. Poor crimps.
   b. Poor solder joints.
   c. Crimping over wire insulation rather than wire.
   d. Corrosion in wire to terminal contact.
4. Wire insulation which is rubbed through. This causes an intermittent short as bare area touches other wiring or components.

POOR CONNECTIONS

1. It is important to test terminal contact at component and any inline connectors before replacing suspect component.
2. Mating terminals must be inspected to ensure good terminal contact.
3. Poor connection between male and female terminal at a connector may be result of contamination or deformation.
4. Contamination may be caused by:
   a. Connector halves being improperly connected.
   b. Missing or damaged seal.
   c. Damaged connector.
   d. Exposing terminals to moisture and dirt.
5. Deformation is caused by:
   a. Probing connector terminal mating side without proper adapter.
   b. Improperly joining connector halves.
   c. Repeatedly separating and joining connector halves.

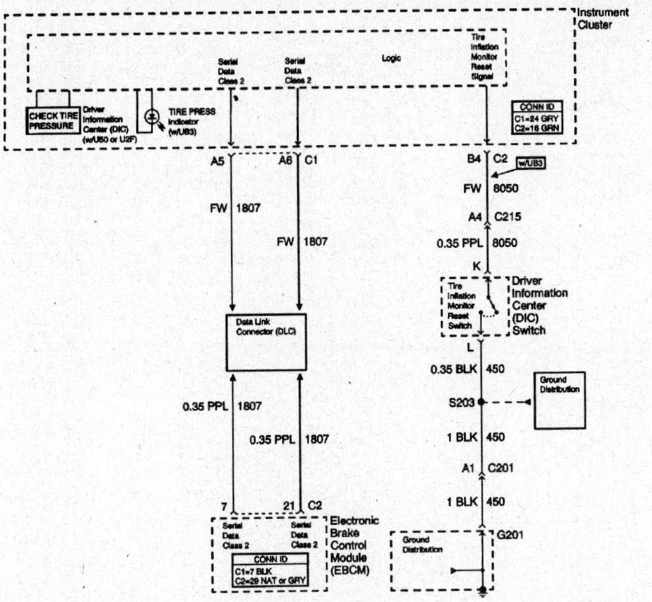

GC2040200176000X

Fig. 5 Wiring diagram. 2000 Bonneville

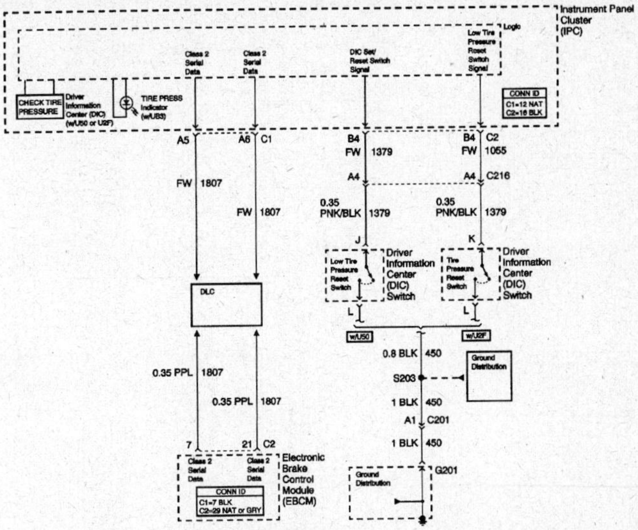

GC2040200177000X

Fig. 6 Wiring diagram. 2001–04 Bonneville

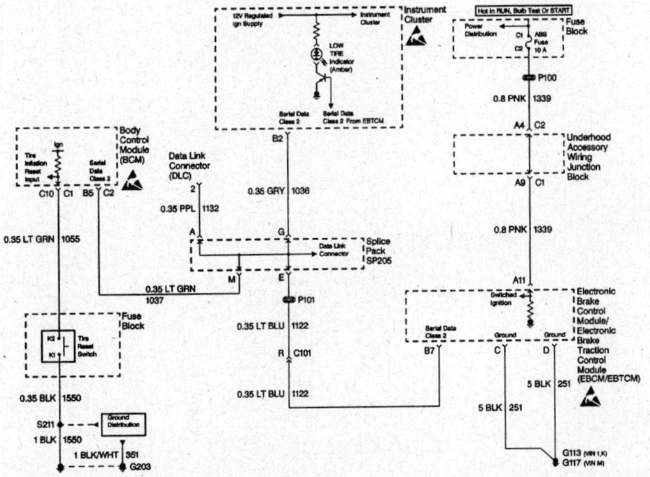

GC2040200178000X

Fig. 7 Wiring diagram (Part 1 of 2). 2000 Century & Regal

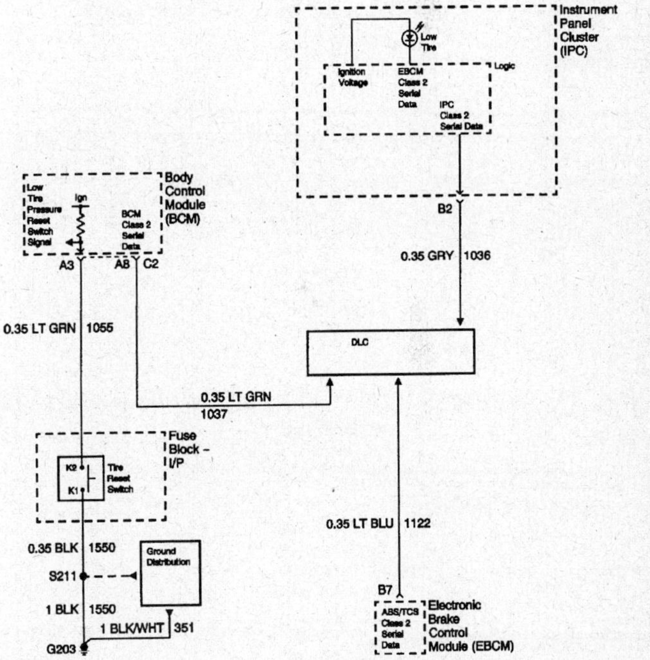

GC2040200180000X

Fig. 8 Wiring diagram. 2001–04 Century & Regal

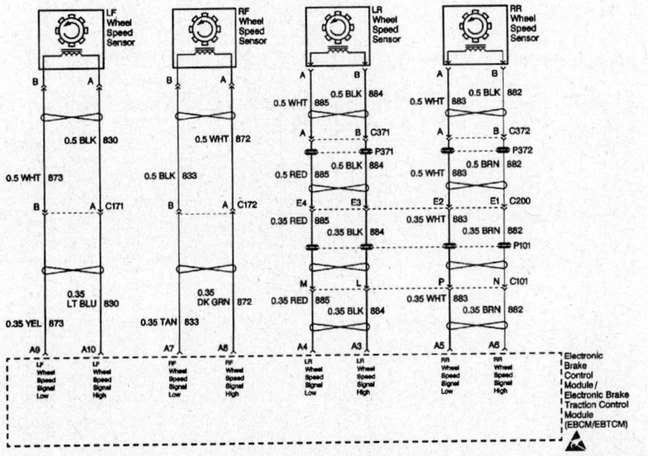

GC2040200179000X

Fig. 7 Wiring diagram (Part 2 of 2). 2000 Century & Regal

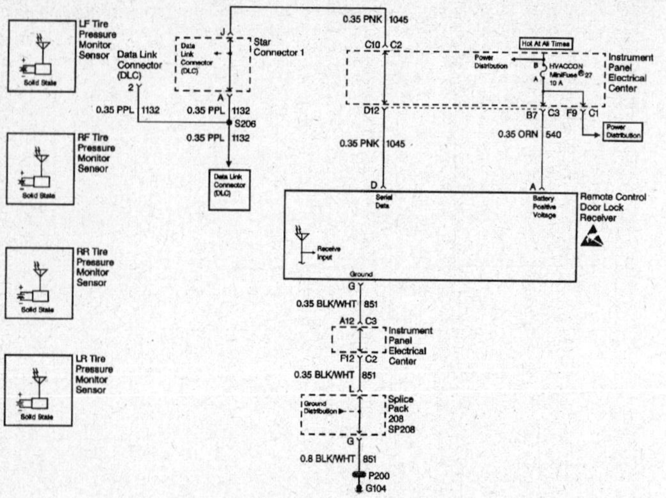

GC2040200181000X

Fig. 9 Wiring diagram. 2000 Corvette

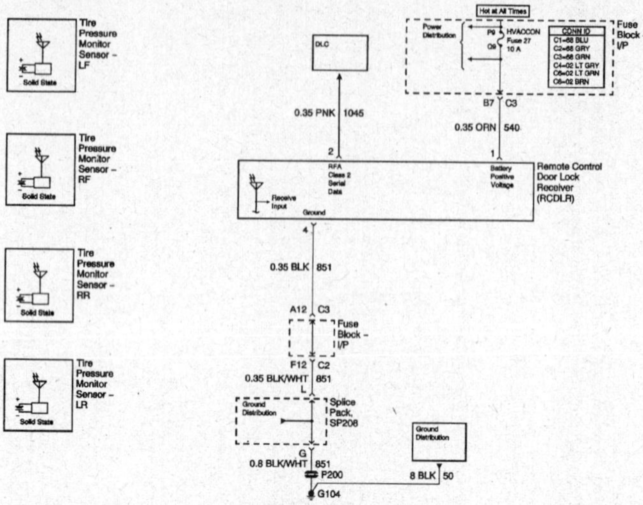

GC2040200182000X

Fig. 10 Wiring diagram. 2001–04 Corvette

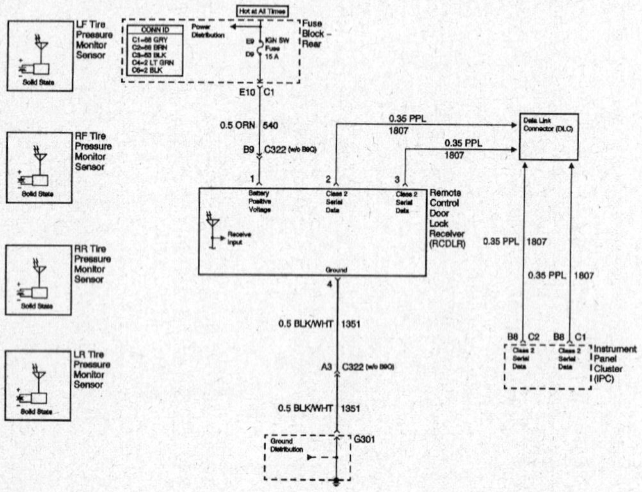

GC2040200183000X

Fig. 11 Wiring diagram. 2001–02 Deville & 2001–04 Seville

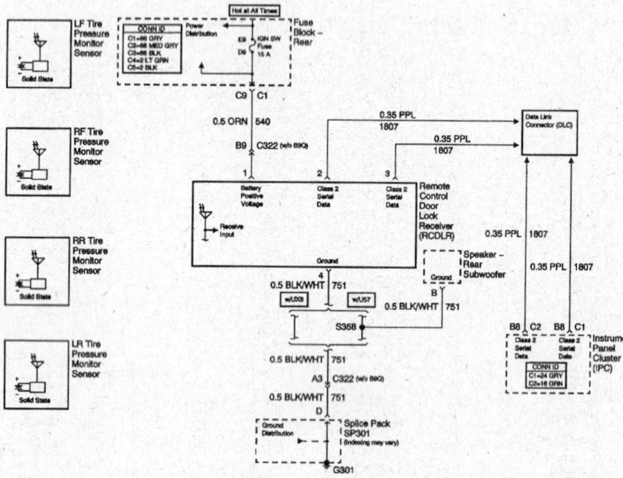

GC2040200184000X

Fig. 12 Wiring diagram. 2003–04 Deville

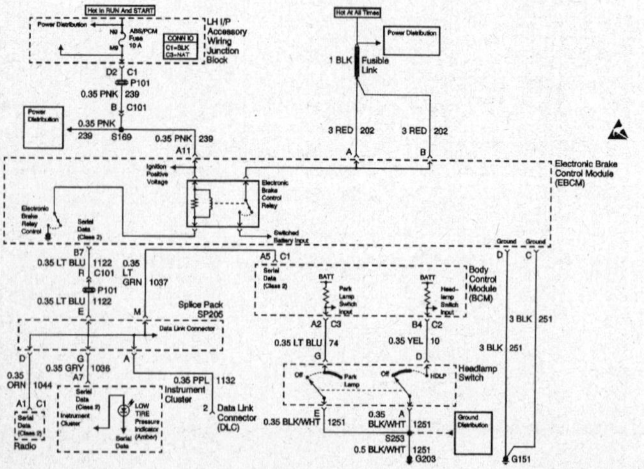

GC2040200185000X

Fig. 13 Wiring diagram (Part 1 of 2). 2000 Impala & Monte Carlo

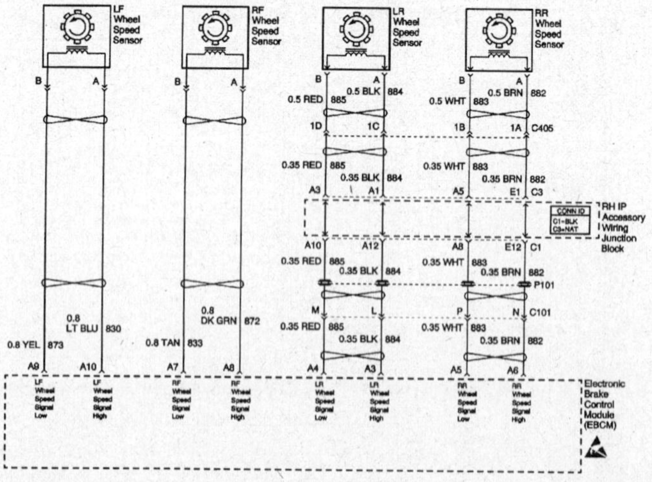

GC2040200186000X

Fig. 13 Wiring diagram (Part 2 of 2). 2000 Impala & Monte Carlo

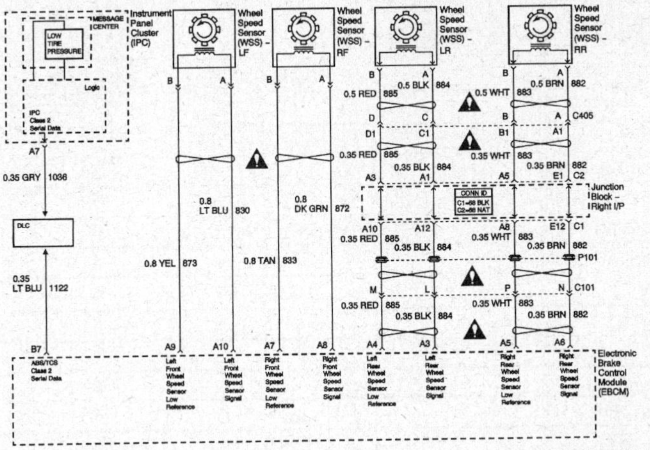

GC2040200187000X

Fig. 14 Wiring diagram. 2001–04 Impala & Monte Carlo

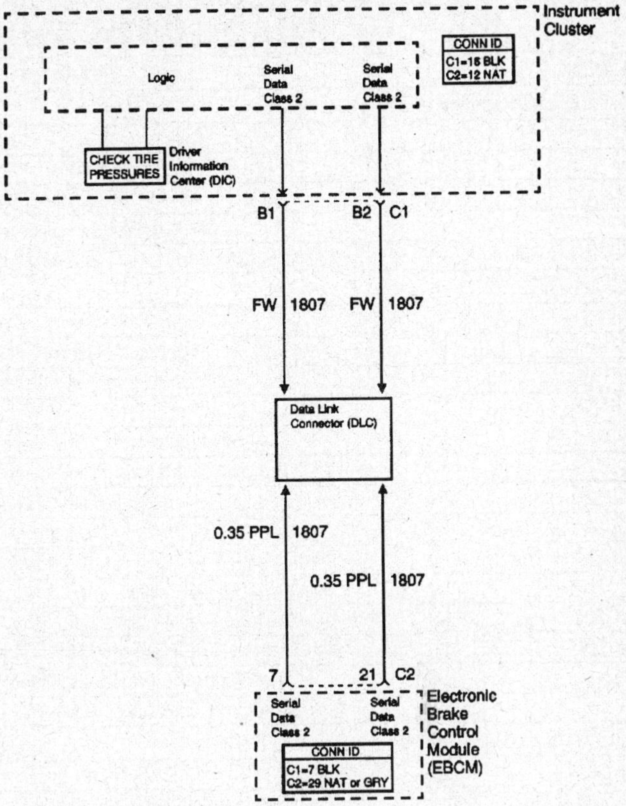

GC2040200189000X

Fig. 15 Wiring diagram. LeSabre & Park Avenue

DIAGNOSTIC CHART INDEX

Code	Description	Page No.	Fig. No.
ALERO & GRAND AM			
—	Diagnostic System Check (2000)	7-7	16
—	Diagnostic System Check (2001–04)	7-7	17
C1245	Low Tire Pressure Detected	7-7	18
—	Low Tire Pressure Indicator Always On (2000)	7-7	19
—	Low Tire Pressure Indicator Always On (2001–04)	7-8	20
—	Low Tire Pressure Indicator Inoperative (2000)	7-8	21
—	Low Tire Pressure Indicator Inoperative (2001–04)	7-8	22
—	Low Tire Pressure Indicator Does Not Reset	7-8	23
AURORA			
—	Diagnostic System Check	7-9	24
C1245	Low Tire Pressure Detected	7-9	25
BONNEVILLE			
—	Diagnostic System Check	7-9	26
B2818	Low Tire Pressure System Reset Circuit Low	7-10	27
C1245	Low Tire Pressure Detected	7-10	28
—	Low Tire Pressure Indicator Always On	7-10	29
—	Low Tire Pressure Indicator Inoperative	7-10	30
—	Low Tire Pressure Indicator Does Not Reset	7-11	31
CENTURY & REGAL			
—	Diagnostic System Check (2000)	7-11	32
—	Diagnostic System Check (2001–04)	7-11	33
B2818	Low Tire Pressure Detected (2000)	7-12	34
B2818	Low Tire Pressure Detected (2000)	7-12	34
B2818	Low Tire Pressure Detected (2001–04)	7-12	35
C1245	Low Tire Pressure Detected (2000)	7-13	36

Continued

DIAGNOSTIC CHART INDEX—Continued

Step	Action	Normal Result(s)	Abnormal Result (s)*
1	Check the pressure in all tires to ensure they are within 2 psi of one another. Turn the ignition switch to the ON position.	CHECK TIRE PRESSURE (Pontiac) or LOW TIRE PRESSURE (Oldsmobile) message is not displayed.	Low Tire Pressure Indicator Always On
2	Check all tire pressures. Tire pressures are not within 12 psi of one another. Turn the ignition switch to the ON position.	CHECK TIRE PRESSURE (Pontiac) or LOW TIRE PRESSURE (Oldsmobile) message is displayed.	Low Tire Pressure Indicator Inoperative
* Refer to the appropriate symptom diagnostic table for the applicable abnormal result.			

GC2040200190000X

Fig. 16 Diagnostic System Check. 2000 Alero & Grand Am

Step	Action	Yes	No
1	Install a scan tool. Does the scan tool power up?	Go to Step 2	Scan Tool Does Not Power Up
2	1. Turn ON the ignition, with the engine OFF. 2. Attempt to establish communications with the Electronic Brake Control Module (EBCM). Does the scan tool communicate with the EBCM?	Go to Step 3	Scan Tool Does Not Communicate with Class 2 Device
3	Select the ABS Diagnostic Trouble Codes DTC function on the scan tool. Does the scan tool display any DTCs that begin with a "U"?	Diagnostic Trouble Code (DTC) List	Go to Step 4
4	Does the scan tool display any ABS DTCs?	Go to Diagnostic System Check	Go to Step 5
5	Does the scan tool display DTC C1245?	Go to DTC C1245	System OK

GC2040200191000X

Fig. 17 Diagnostic System Check. 2001–04 Alero & Grand Am

Step	Action	Yes	No
1	Did you perform the Tire Pressure Monitor Diagnostic System Check?	Go to Step 2	Go to Diagnostic System Check -
2	1. Install a scan tool. 2. Turn ON the ignition, with the engine OFF. 3. With a scan tool, monitor the DTC Information for DTC C1245 in the TIM Diagnostic Trouble Codes (DTCs) selection. Does the scan tool indicate that DTC C1245 is current?	Go to Step 3	Go to Diagnostic Aids
3	Since some occurrences of this DTC are caused by driving conditions, or tire size differences, review the TPM system with the customer to verify the conditions under which the DTC set. Did driving conditions, or tire size cause the DTC to set?	Go to Step 5	Go to Step 4
4	1. Calibrate the TPM system. 2. Use the scan tool in order to clear the DTC. 3. Operate the vehicle within the Conditions for Running the DTC as specified in the supporting text. Does the DTC reset as a current DTC?	Go to Diagnostic Aids	System OK
5	Inspect the tire pressures and adjust to manufacturer's specification if needed. Calibrate the TPM system if tire pressures were adjusted. Did you complete the repair?	System OK	--

GC2040200192000X

Fig. 18 Code C1245: Low Tire Pressure Detected. Alero & Grand Am

Step	Action	Yes	No
1	Did you perform the Tire Inflation Monitoring System Diagnostic System Check?	Go to Step 2	Go to Diagnostic System Check -
2	Did you perform the Tire Inflation Monitoring Reset Procedure and System Re-learn Process test drive?	Go to Step 3	Go to Tire Inflation Monitoring System
3	1. Connect a scan tool. 2. Turn the ignition switch to the ON position. 3. Select TIM Data from the Data Display menu on the scan tool. 4. View Low Tire Pressure Data. Is the Low Tire Pressure Warning ON?	Go to Step 4	Go to Step 5
4	Replace the EBCM. Did you complete the repair?	Go to Diagnostic System Check -	--
5	Replace the Instrument Cluster. Did you complete the repair?	Go to Diagnostic System Check -	--

GC2040200193000X

Fig. 19 Low Tire Pressure Indicator Always On. 2000 Alero & Grand Am

Step	Action	Yes	No
1	Did you perform the TPM Diagnostic System Check?	Go to Step 2	Go to Diagnostic System Check -
2	1. Turn OFF the ignition. 2. Turn ON the ignition, with the engine OFF. 3. Observe the tire pressure indicator on the systems monitor, or the instrument Panel cluster (IPC) during the bulb check. Does the indicator illuminate during the bulb check and then turn OFF?	Go to Intermittent and Poor Connections	Go to Step 3
3	Replace the IPC. Did you complete the replacement?	Go to Step 4	--
4	Operate the system in order to verify the repair. Did you correct the condition?	System OK	Go to Step 2

GC2040200194000X

Fig. 20 Low Tire Pressure Indicator Always On. 2001–04 Alero & Grand Am

Step	Action	Yes	No
1	Did you perform the TPM Diagnostic System Check?	Go to Step 2	Go to Diagnostic System Check -
2	1. Turn OFF the ignition. 2. Turn ON the ignition, with the engine OFF. 3. Observe the tire pressure indicator on the systems monitor, or the Instrument Panel Cluster (IPC) during the bulb check. Does the warning indicator illuminate during the bulb check?	Go to Intermittent and Poor Connections	Go to Step 3
3	Replace the IPC. Did you complete the replacement?	Go to Step 4	--
4	Operate the system in order to verify the repair. Did you correct the condition?	System OK	Go to Step 2

GC2040200196000X

Fig. 22 Low Tire Pressure Indicator Inoperative. 2001–04 Alero & Grand Am

Step	Action	Yes	No
1	Did you perform the Tire Inflation Monitoring System Diagnostic System Check?	Go to Step 2	Go to Diagnostic System Check -
2	Did you perform the Tire Inflation Monitoring Reset Procedure and System Re-learn Process test drive?	Go to Step 3	Go to Tire Inflation Monitoring System
3	1. Lower the tire pressure of one tire by 15 psi. 2. Connect a scan tool. 3. Select TIM Data from the Data Display menu on the scan tool. 4. Drive the vehicle for about 25 minutes on a smooth, straight, paved road at a constant speed above 15 MPH. 5. View the Low Tire Pressure data. Is the LOW TIRE PRESSURE Warning ON?	Go to Step 5	Go to Step 4
4	Replace the EBCM. Did you complete the repair?	Go to Diagnostic System Check -	--
5	Replace the Instrument Cluster. Did you complete the repair?	Go to Diagnostic System Check -	--

GC2040200195000X

Fig. 21 Low Tire Pressure Indicator Inoperative. 2000 Alero & Grand Am

Step	Action	Yes	No
1	Did you perform the TPM Diagnostic System Check?	Go to Step 2	Go to Diagnostic System Check -
2	1. Install a scan tool. 2. Turn ON the ignition, with the engine OFF. 3. With a scan tool, observe the TIM Reset Switch parameter in the Chassis data display list. 4. Press the tire pressure monitor reset switch. Does the scan tool display On when the switch is pressed?	Go to Intermittent and Poor Connections	Go to Step 3
3	1. Turn OFF the ignition. 2. Disconnect the oil life/TIM reset switch. 3. Connect a 3 amp fused jumper wire between the tire pressure monitor reset signal circuit of the reset switch and a good ground. 4. Turn ON the ignition, with the engine OFF. 5. With a scan tool, observe the TIM Reset Switch parameter. Does the scan tool display On?	Go to Step 6	Go to Step 4

GC2040200197010X

Fig. 23 Low Tire Pressure Indicator Does Not Reset (Part 1 of 2). Alero & Grand Am

4	Test the tire pressure monitor reset signal circuit of the reset switch for a high resistance or an open. Did you find and correct the condition?	Go to Step 10	Go to Step 5
5	Test the ground circuit of the TIM reset switch for a high resistance or an open. Did you find and correct the condition?	Go to Step 10	Go to Step 7
6	Inspect for poor connections at the harness connector of the TIM reset switch. Did you find and correct the condition?	Go to Step 10	Go to Step 8
7	Inspect for poor connections at the harness connector of the instrument cluster (IPC). Did you find and correct the condition?	Go to Step 10	Go to Step 9
8	Replace the TIM reset switch. Did you complete the replacement?	Go to Step 10	--
9	Replace the IPC. Did you complete the replacement?	Go to Step 10	--
10	Operate the system in order to verify the repair. Did you correct the condition?	System OK	Go to Step 2

GC2040200197020X

Fig. 23 Low Tire Pressure Indicator Does Not Reset (Part 2 of 2). Alero & Grand Am

Step	Action	Value (s)	Yes	No
1	Did you perform the Tire Pressure Monitoring Diagnostic System Check?	--	Go to Step 2	Go to Diagnostic System Check -
2	1. Install a scan tool. 2. Turn ON the ignition, with the engine OFF. 3. With a scan tool, monitor the DTC Information for DTC C1245 in the DRP/ABS/TCS/TIM/VSES (if equipped) Diagnostic Trouble Codes (DTCs). Does the scan tool indicate that DTC C1245 is current?	--	Go to Step 3	Go to Diagnostic Aids
3	Since most occurrences of this DTC are caused by low tire pressure, review the TIM system with the customer to verify the conditions under which the DTC set. Did tire inflation cause this DTC to set?	--	Go to Step 5	Go to Step 4
4	1. Perform the tire inflation monitoring reset. 2. Use the scan tool in order to clear the DTCs. 3. Operate the vehicle within the Conditions for Running the DTC as specified in the supporting text. Does the DTC reset as a current DTC?	--	Go to Diagnostic Aids	System OK
5	Inspect the tire pressures and adjust if needed Perform the tire inflation monitoring reset if tire pressures were adjusted. Did you complete the repair?	--	System OK	--

GC2040200199000X

Fig. 25 Code C1245: Low Tire Pressure Detected. Aurora

Step	Action	Yes	No
1	Install a scan tool. Does the scan tool power up?	Go to Step 2	Scan Tool Does Not Power Up
2	1. Turn ON the ignition, with the engine OFF. 2. Attempt to establish communications with the EBCM. Does the scan tool communicate with the EBCM?	Go to Step 3	Scan Tool Does Not Communicate with Class 2 Device in Data Link Communications
3	Select the DRP/ABS/TCS/TIM/VSES (if equipped) display DTC function on the scan tool. Does the scan tool display any ABS DTCs?	Diagnostic System Check - ABS	Go to Step 4
4	Does the scan tool display DTC C1245?	Go to DTC C1245	System OK

GC2040200198000X

Fig. 24 Diagnostic System Check. Aurora

Step	Action	Value (s)	Yes	No
1	Install a scan tool. Does the scan tool power up?	--	Go to Step 2	Scan Tool Does Not Power Up
2	1. Turn ON the ignition, with the engine OFF. 2. Attempt to establish communications with the following control modules: o Electronic brake control module (EBCM) o Instrument cluster (IPC) Does the scan tool communicate with the control modules listed above?	--	Go to Step 3	Scan Tool Does Not Communicate with Class 2 Device
3	Select the DRP/ABS/TCS/TIM/VSES display DTC function on the scan tool. Does the scan tool display any DRP/ABS/TCS/VSES DTCs?	--	Go to Diagnostic System Check -	Go to Step 4
4	Does the scan tool display DTC C1245?	--	Go to DTC C1245 Low Tire Pressure Detected	Go to Step 5
5	Select the instrument cluster (IPC) display DTC function on the scan tool. Does the scan tool display DTC B2818?	--	Go to DTC B2818 Low Tire Pressure System Reset Circuit Low	Go to Symptoms

GC2040200200000X

Fig. 26 Diagnostic System Check. Bonneville

Step	Action	Value (s)	Yes	No
1	Did you perform the TPM Diagnostic System Check?	--	Go to Step 2	Go to Diagnostic System Check
2	1. Install a scan tool. 2. Turn ON the ignition, with the engine OFF. 3. With a scan tool, select the BCM Diagnostic Trouble Codes (DTC) function. Does the scan tool display DTC B2818 as current?	--	Go to Step 3	Intermittent and Poor Connections
3	1. Turn OFF the ignition. 2. Disconnect the reset switch. 3. Turn ON the ignition, with the engine OFF 4. With the scan tool, observe the Tire Reset Switch, w/Systems Monitor, or the DIC Reset Button, w/DIC, data parameter in the IPC Data list. Does the scan tool display OFF?	--	Go to Step 6	Go to Step 4
4	Test the signal circuit of the reset switch for a short to ground. Did you find and correct the condition?	--	Go to Step 7	Go to Step 5
5	Replace the IPC. Did you complete the replacement?	--	Go to Step 7	--
6	Replace the reset switch. Did you complete the replacement?	--	Go to Step 7	--
7	1. Use the scan tool in order to clear the DTC. 2. Operate the vehicle within the Conditions for Running the DTC as specified in the supporting text. Does the DTC reset?	--	Go to Step 2	System OK

GC2040200201000X

Fig. 27 Code B2818: Low Tire Pressure System Reset Circuit Low. Bonneville

Step	Action	Value (s)	Yes	No
1	Did you perform the TIM Diagnostic System Check?	--	Go to Step 2	Go to Diagnostic System Check -
2	1. Turn OFF the ignition. 2. Turn ON the ignition, with the engine OFF. 3. Observe the TIRE PRESS indicator on the systems monitor of the instrument cluster (IPC) during the bulb check. Does the TIRE PRESS indicator illuminate during the bulb check and then turn OFF?	--	Intermittent and Poor Connections	Go to Step 3
3	Replace the instrument cluster (IPC). Did you complete the replacement?	--	Go to Step 4	--
4	Operate the system in order to verify the repair. Did you correct the condition?	--	System OK	Go to Step 2

GC2040200203000X

Fig. 29 Low Tire Pressure Indicator Always On. Bonneville

Step	Action	Yes	No
1	Did you perform the Tire Pressure Monitor Diagnostic System Check?	Go to Step 2	Go to Diagnostic System Check -
2	1. Install a scan tool. 2. Turn ON the ignition, with the engine OFF. 3. With a scan tool, select the TIM Diagnostic Trouble Codes (DTCs) function. Does the scan tool indicate that DTC C1245 is current?	Go to Step 3	Go to Diagnostic Aids
3	Since some occurrences of this DTC are caused by driving conditions, or tire size difference, review the TPM system with the customer to verify the conditions under which the DTC set. Did driving conditions, or tire size cause this DTC to set?	Go to Step 4	Go to Step 5
4	1. Calibrate the TPM system. 2. Use the scan tool in order to clear the DTCs. 3. Operate the vehicle within the Conditions for Running the DTC as specified in the supporting text. Does the DTC reset as a current DTC?	Go to Step 5	System OK
5	Inspect the tire pressures and adjust to manufacturers specification if needed. Calibrate the TPM system if tire pressures were adjusted. Did you complete the repair?	System OK	--

GC2040200202000X

Fig. 28 Code C1245: Low Tire Pressure Detected. Bonneville

Step	Action	Value (s)	Yes	No
1	Did you perform the TIM Diagnostic System Check?	--	Go to Step 2	Go to Diagnostic System Check -
2	1. Turn OFF the ignition. 2. Turn ON the ignition, with the engine OFF. 3. Observe the TIRE PRESS indicator on the systems monitor of the instrument cluster (IPC) during the bulb check. Does the TIRE PRESS indicator illuminate during the bulb check?	--	Intermittent and Poor Connections	Go to Step 3
3	Replace the instrument cluster (IPC). Did you complete the replacement?	--	Go to Step 4	--
4	Operate the system in order to verify the repair. Did you correct the condition?	--	System OK	Go to Step 2

GC2040200204000X

Fig. 30 Low Tire Pressure Indicator Inoperative. Bonneville

Step	Action	Value(s)	Yes	No
1	Did you perform the TPM Diagnostic System Check?	--	Go to Step 2	Go to Diagnostic System Check -
2	1. Install a scan tool. 2. Turn ON the ignition, with the engine OFF. 3. With a scan tool, observe the Tire Reset Switch parameter in the IPC data list. 4. Press the TIRE PRESS RESET switch. Does the scan tool display On when the switch is pressed?	--	Intermittent and Poor Connections	Go to Step 3
3	1. Turn OFF the ignition. 2. Disconnect the reset switch. 3. Connect a 3 amp fused jumper wire between the harness connector of the reset switch signal circuit and a good ground. 4. Turn ON the ignition, with the engine OFF. 5. With a scan tool, observe the Tire Reset Switch parameter. Does the scan tool display On?	--	Go to Step 6	Go to Step 4
4	Test the reset switch signal circuit for a high resistance or an open. Did you find and correct the condition?	--	Go to Step 10	Go to Step 5
5	Test the ground circuit of the reset switch for a high resistance or an open. Did you find and correct the condition?	--	Go to Step 10	Go to Step 7

GC2040200205010X

Fig. 31 Low Tire Pressure Indicator Does Not Reset (Part 1 of 2). Bonneville

Step	Action	Value(s)	Yes	No
1	Install a scan tool. Does the scan tool power up?	--	Go to Step 2	Scan Tool Does Not Power Up
2	1. Turn ON the ignition, with the engine OFF. 2. Attempt to establish communications with the EBCM. Does the scan tool communicate with the EBCM?	--	Go to Step 3	Scan Tool Does Not Communicate with Class 2 Device
3	Select the ABS-TCS-TIM (if equipped) display DTC function on the scan tool. Does the scan tool display any ABS DTCs, except DTC B2818?	--	Go to Diagnostic Trouble Code (DTC)	Go to Symptoms

GC2040200206000X

Fig. 32 Diagnostic System Check. 2000 Century & Regal

6	Inspect for poor connections at the harness connector of the reset switch. Did you find and correct the condition?	--	Go to Step 10	Go to Step 8
7	Inspect for poor connections at the harness connector of the instrument cluster (IPC). Did you find and correct the condition?	--	Go to Step 10	Go to Step 9
8	Replace the reset switch. Did you complete the replacement?	--	Go to Step 10	--
9	Replace the IPC. Did you complete the replacement?	--	Go to Step 10	--
10	Operate the system in order to verify the repair. Did you correct the condition?	--	System OK	Go to Step 2

GC2040200205020X

Fig. 31 Low Tire Pressure Indicator Does Not Reset (Part 2 of 2). Bonneville

Step	Action	Yes	No
1	Install a scan tool. Does the scan tool power up?	Go to Step 2	Scan Tool Does Not Power Up
2	1. Turn ON the ignition, with the engine OFF. 2. Attempt to establish communications with the Electronic Brake Control Module (EBCM). Does the scan tool communicate with the EBCM?	Go to Step 3	Scan Tool Does Not Communicate with Class 2 Device
3	Select the ABS Diagnostic Trouble Codes DTC function on the scan tool. Does the scan tool display any DTCs that begin with a "U"?	Go to Diagnostic Trouble Code (DTC)	Go to Step 4
4	Does the scan tool display any ABS DTCs?	Go to Diagnostic System Check	Go to Step 5
5	Does the scan tool display DTC C1245?	Go to DTC C1245	System OK

GC2040200207000X

Fig. 33 Diagnostic System Check. 2001–04 Century & Regal

Step	Action	Value (s)	Yes	No
1	Was the BCM Diagnostic System Check performed?	--	Go to Step 2	Go to Diagnostic System Check -
2	1. Turn the ignition switch to the OFF position. 2. Disconnect the Body Control Module (BCM) connector C1. 3. Turn the ignition switch to the ON position. 4. Using a test light connect between the BCM harness connector C1 terminal C10 and B+. 5. Press and hold the tire reset switch. Does the test light illuminate?	--	Go to Step 3	Go to Step 4
3	1. Leave the test light in the same location from the previous step. 2. Disconnect the Tire Inflation Reset Switch. Does the test light illuminate?	--	Go to Step 5	Go to Step 6
4	1. Turn the ignition switch in the OFF position. 2. Reinstall connectors/components removed. 3. Turn the ignition switch in the ON position. 4. Clear DTCs. 5. Wait 5 minutes. 6. Check for DTCs. Does B2818 reset as a current DTC?	--	Go to Step 7	Go to Step 8

GC2040200208010X

Fig. 34 Code B2818: Low Tire Pressure Detected (Part 1 of 2). 2000 Century & Regal

5	Repair a short to ground in circuit 1055 between the BCM connector C1 terminal C10 and the tire inflation reset switch connector terminal K2. Is the repair complete?	--	Go to Step 9	--
6	Replace the tire inflation reset switch. Is the repair complete?	--	Go to Step 9	--
7	1. Replace the BCM. 2. After replacing the BCM, perform the Setup New BCM procedure. Is the repair complete?	--	Go to Step 9	--
8	The malfunction is not present. Is the repair complete?	--	Go to Step 9	--
9	1. Turn the ignition switch to the OFF position. 2. Reinstall connectors/components removed. 3. Turn the ignition switch to the On position. Are all repair complete?	--	System OK	Go to Diagnostic System Check -

GC2040200208020X

Fig. 34 Code B2818: Low Tire Pressure Detected (Part 2 of 2). 2000 Century & Regal

Step	Action	Yes	No
1	Did you perform the Tire Pressure Monitor Diagnostic System Check?	Go to Step 2	Go to Diagnostic System Check -
2	1. Install a scan tool. 2. Turn ON the ignition, with the engine OFF. 3. With a scan tool, observe the TIM Reset Switch data parameter in the TIM data list. Does the scan tool display Released?	Go to Step 3	Go to Step 4
3	1. Depress the RESET switch. 2. With the scan tool, observe the TIM Reset Switch data parameter. Does the TIM Reset Switch data parameter change states?	Test for Intermittent and Poor Connections	Go to Step 4
4	1. Turn OFF the ignition. 2. Disconnect the BCM harness connector. 3. disconnect the Low Tire Pressure Reset Switch Signal circuit from the BCM harness connector. 4. Reconnect the BCM harness connector to the BCM. 5. Turn ON the ignition, with the engine OFF. 6. With a scan tool, observe the TIM Reset Switch data parameter. Does the scan tool display Released?	Go to Step 5	Go to Step 6
5	Test the signal circuit of the RESET switch for a short to ground. Did you find and correct the condition?	Go to Step 8	Go to Step 7
6	Replace the BCM. Did you complete the replacement?	Go to Step 8	--

GC2040200209010X

Fig. 35 Code B2818: Low Tire Pressure Detected (Part 1 of 2). 2001–04 Century & Regal

7	Replace the RESET switch. Did you complete the replacement?	Go to Step 8	--
8	1. Use the scan tool in order to clear the DTCs. 2. Operate the vehicle within the Conditions for Running the DTC as specified in the supporting text. Does the DTC reset?	Go to Step 2	System OK

GC2040200209020X

Fig. 35 Code B2818: Low Tire Pressure Detected (Part 2 of 2). 2001–04 Century & Regal

Step	Action	Value (s)	Yes	No
1	Did you perform the TPM Diagnostic System Check?	--	Go to Step 2	Go to Diagnostic System Check -
2	1. Install a scan tool. 2. Turn ON the ignition, with the engine OFF. 3. With a scan tool, monitor the DTC Information for DTC C1245 in the ABS/TCS/TIM (if equipped) Diagnostic Trouble Codes (DTCs). Does the scan tool indicate that DTC C1245 is current?	--	Go to Step 3	Go to Diagnostic Aids
3	Since most occurrences of this DTC are caused by low tire pressure, review the TIM system with the customer to verify the conditions under which the DTC set. Did tire inflation cause this DTC to set?	--	Go to Step 4	Go to Diagnostic Aids
4	1. Inspect the tire pressures and adjust if needed. Perform the tire inflation monitoring reset if tire pressures were adjusted. 2. Use the scan tool in order to clear the DTCs. 3. Operate the vehicle within the Conditions for Running the DTC as specified in the supporting text. Does the DTC reset as a current DTC?	--	Go to Diagnostic Aids	System OK

GC2040200211000X

Fig. 36 Code C1245: Low Tire Pressure Detected. 2000 Century & Regal

Step	Action	Yes	No
1	Did you perform the Tire Pressure Monitor Diagnostic System Check?	Go to Step 2	Go to Diagnostic System Check -
2	1. Install a scan tool. 2. Turn ON the ignition, with the engine OFF. 3. With a scan tool, select the Diagnostic Trouble Codes (DTCs) function. Does the scan tool indicate that DTC C1245 is current?	Go to Step 3	Go to Diagnostic Aids
3	Since some occurrences of this DTC are caused by driving conditions, or different tire size, review the TPM system with the customer to verify the conditions under which the DTC set. Did driving conditions, or tire size cause this DTC to set?	Go to Step 5	Go to Step 4
4	1. Calibrate the TPM system. 2. Use the scan tool in order to clear the DTCs. 3. Operate the vehicle within the Conditions for Running the DTC as specified in the supporting text. Does the DTC reset as a current DTC?	Go to Step 5	System OK
5	Inspect the tire pressures and set to manufacturers specification if needed. Calibrate the TPM system if tire pressures were adjusted. Did you complete the repair?	System OK	--

GC2040200212000X

Fig. 37 Code C1245: Low Tire Pressure Detected. 2001–04 Century & Regal

Step	Action	Value (s)	Yes	No
1	Perform the tire pressure reset procedure. Does the LOW TIRE indicator turn off?	--	System OK	Go to Step 2
2	Check for BCM DTCs. Are there any BCM DTCs present?	--	Go to Diagnostic System Check	Go to Step 3
3	Check for Instrument Cluster DTC's. Are there any instrument cluster DTCs present?	--	Go to Diagnostic Starting Point	Go to Step 4
4	Operate the system which the Symptom occurred. Is the symptom still present?	--	Go To Diagnostic Aids	System OK

GC2040200214000X

Fig. 38 Low Tire Pressure Indicator Always On. 2000–01 Century & Regal

Step	Action	Yes	No
1	Did you perform the TPM Diagnostic System Check?	Go to Step 2	Go to Diagnostic System Check
2	1. Turn OFF the ignition. 2. Turn ON the ignition, with the engine OFF. 3. Observe the tire pressure indicator on the systems monitor, or the instrument Panel cluster (IPC) during the bulb check. Does the indicator illuminate during the bulb check and then turn OFF?	Go to Testing for Intermittent and Poor Connections	Go to Step 3
3	Replace the IPC. Did you complete the replacement?	Go to Step 4	--
4	Operate the system in order to verify the repair. Did you correct the condition?	System OK	Go to Step 2

GC2040200215000X

Fig. 39 Low Tire Pressure Indicator Always On. 2002–04 Century & Regal

Step	Action	Yes	No
1	Did you perform the TPM Diagnostic System Check?	Go to Step 2	Go to Diagnostic System Check -
2	1. Turn OFF the ignition. 2. Turn ON the ignition, with the engine OFF. 3. Observe the tire pressure indicator on the systems monitor, or the Instrument Panel Cluster (IPC) during the bulb check. Does the warning indicator illuminate during the bulb check?	Testing for Intermittent and Poor Connections	Go to Step 3
3	Replace the IPC. Did you complete the replacement?	Go to Step 4	--
4	Operate the system in order to verify the repair. Did you correct the condition?	System OK	Go to Step 2

GC2040200217000X

Fig. 40 Low Tire Pressure Indicator Inoperative. Century & Regal

Step	Action	Yes	No
1	Did you perform the Tire Pressure Monitor Diagnostic System Check?	Go to Step 2	Diagnostic System Check -
2	1. Install a scan tool. 2. Turn ON the ignition, with the engine OFF. 3. With a scan tool, observe the TIM Reset Switch parameter in the TIM data list. 4. Press the RESET switch. Does the scan tool display Pressed when the switch is pressed?	Testing for Intermittent and Poor Connections	Go to Step 3
3	1. Turn OFF the ignition. 2. Disconnect the reset switch signal circuit from the IP Fuse Block. 3. Connect a 3 amp fused jumper wire between the reset switch signal circuit and a good ground. 4. Turn ON the ignition, with the engine OFF. 5. With a scan tool, observe the TIM Reset Switch parameter. Does the scan tool display Pressed?	Go to Step 5	Go to Step 4
4	Test the reset switch signal circuit for a high resistance or an open. Did you find and correct the condition?	Go to Step 10	Go to Step 7

GC2040200218010X

Fig. 41 Low Tire Pressure Indicator Does Not Reset (Part 1 of 2). Century & Regal

Step	Action	Yes	No
5	Test the ground circuit of the TIM reset switch for a high resistance or an open. Did you find and correct the condition?	Go to Step 10	Go to Step 6
6	Inspect for poor connections at the harness connector of the TIM reset switch. Did you find and correct the condition?	Go to Step 10	Go to Step 8
7	Inspect for poor connections at the harness connector of the Body Control Module (BCM). Did you find and correct the condition?	Go to Step 10	Go to Step 9
8	Replace the TIM reset switch. Did you complete the replacement?	Go to Step 10	--
9	Replace the BCM. Did you complete the replacement?	Go to Step 10	--
10	Operate the system in order to verify the repair. Did you correct the condition?	System OK	Go to Step 2

GC2040200218020X

Fig. 41 Low Tire Pressure Indicator Does Not Reset (Part 2 of 2). Century & Regal

Step	Action	Yes	No
1	Install a scan tool. Does the scan tool power up?	Go to Step 2	Scan Tool Does Not Power Up
2	1. Turn ON the ignition, with the engine OFF. 2. Attempt to establish communication with the RFA system. Does the scan tool communicate with the RFA system?	Go to Step 3	Scan Tool Does Not Communicate with Class 2 Device
3	Select the RFA display DTCs function on the scan tool. Does the scan tool display any DTCs?	Go to Step 4	the Applicable Symptom Table
4	Does the scan tool display any DTCs which begin with a "U"?	Scan Tool Does Not Communicate with Class 2 Device	Go to Diagnostic Trouble Code (DTC)

GC2040200221000X

Fig. 42 Diagnostic System Check. 2000 Corvette

Step	Action	Yes	No
1	Install a scan tool. Does the scan tool power up?	Go to Step 2	Scan Tool Does Not Power Up
2	1. Turn ON the ignition, with the engine OFF. 2. Attempt to establish communication with the RCDLR. Does the scan tool communicate with the RCDLR?	Go to Step 3	Go to Scan Tool Does Not Communicate with Class 2 Device
3	Select the RKE Diagnostic Trouble Codes (DTC) function on the scan tool. Does the scan tool display any DTCs that begin with a "U"?	Go to Diagnostic Trouble Code (DTC)	Go to Step 4
4	Does the scan tool display any RKE DTCs?	Go to Diagnostic Trouble Code (DTC)	Go to Step 5
5	Does the scan tool display any TPM DTCs?	Go to Diagnostic Trouble Code (DTC)	System OK

GC2040200222000X

Fig. 43 Diagnostic System Check. 2001–04 Corvette

Step	Action	Value (s)	Yes	No
1	Were you sent here from the TPM Diagnostic System Check?	--	Go to Step 2	Go to Diagnostic System Check
2	Using the buttons on the DIC, enter the TIRE TRAINING mode. Can the programming be successfully accessed through the IPC?	--	Go to Step 3	Go to Diagnostic System Check
3	Program all TPM sensors. Was the left front TPM sensor programming successful?	--	Go to Step 6	Go to Step 4
4	1. Replace the left front TPM sensor. 2. Program all the TPM sensors. Is the replacement complete?	--	Go to Step 5	--

GC2040200225010X

Fig. 44 Code C2100: Lefthand Front TPM Sensor Fault (Part 1 of 2). 2000 Corvette

5	1. Clear the DTCs. 2. Road test the vehicle above 24 km/h (15 mph) for 20 minutes. Does DTC C2100 reset?	--	Go to Step 7	System OK
6	1. Clear the DTCs. 2. Road test the vehicle above 24 km/h (15 mph) for 20 minutes. Does DTC C2100 reset?	--	Go to Step 4	System OK
7	1. Replace the remote control door lock receiver. 2. Program all TPM sensors. 3. Program the RFA transmitters. Is the replacement complete?	--	Go to Step 8	--
8	1. Turn the ignition to OFF. 2. Install any components or connectors that were removed. 3. Clear all DTCs. Are the repairs complete?	--	Go to Diagnostic System Check	--

GC2040200225020X

Fig. 44 Code C2100: Lefthand Front TPM Sensor Fault (Part 2 of 2). 2000 Corvette

Step	Action	Value (s)	Yes	No
1	Were you sent here from the TPM Diagnostic System Check?	--	Go to Step 2	Go to Diagnostic System Check
2	Using the buttons on the DIC, enter the TIRE TRAINING mode. Can the programming be successfully accessed through the IPC?	--	Go to Step 3	Go to Diagnostic System Check
3	Program all TPM sensors. Was the right front TPM sensor programming successful?	--	Go to Step 6	Go to Step 4
4	1. Replace the right front TPM sensor. 2. Program all the TPM sensors. Is the replacement complete?	--	Go to Step 5	--

GC2040200226010X

Fig. 45 Code C2105: Righthand Front TPM Sensor Fault (Part 1 of 2). 2000 Corvette

5	1. Clear the DTCs. 2. Road test the vehicle above 24 km/h (15 mph) for 20 minutes. Does DTC C2105 reset?	--	Go to Step 7	System OK
6	1. Clear the DTCs. 2. Road test the vehicle above 24 km/h (15 mph) for 20 minutes. Does DTC C2105 reset?	--	Go to Step 4	System OK
7	1. Replace the remote control door lock receiver. 2. Program all TPM sensors. 3. Program the RFA transmitters. Is the replacement complete?	--	Go to Step 8	--
8	1. Turn the ignition to OFF. 2. Install any components or connectors that were removed. 3. Clear all DTCs. Are the repairs complete?	--	Go to Diagnostic System Check	--

GC2040200226020X

Fig. 45 Code C2105: Righthand Front TPM Sensor Fault (Part 2 of 2). 2000 Corvette

Step	Action	Value (s)	Yes	No
1	Were you sent here from the TPM Diagnostic System Check?	--	Go to Step 2	Go to Diagnostic System Check
2	Using the buttons on the DIC, enter the TIRE TRAINING mode. Can the programming be successfully accessed through the IPC?	--	Go to Step 3	Go to Diagnostic System Check
3	Program all TPM sensors. Was the right rear TPM sensor programming successful?	--	Go to Step 6	Go to Step 4
4	1. Replace the right rear TPM sensor. 2. Program all the TPM sensors. Is the replacement complete?	--	Go to Step 5	--

GC2040200227010X

Fig. 46 Code C2110: Righthand Rear TPM Sensor Fault (Part 1 of 2). 2000 Corvette

5	1. Clear the DTCs. 2. Road test the vehicle above 24 km/h (15 mph) for 20 minutes. Does DTC C2110 reset?	--	Go to Step 7	System OK
6	1. Clear the DTCs. 2. Road test the vehicle above 24 km/h (15 mph) for 20 minutes. Does DTC C2110 reset?	--	Go to Step 4	System OK
7	1. Replace the remote control door lock receiver. 2. Program all TPM sensors. 3. Program the RFA transmitters. Is the replacement complete?	--	Go to Step 8	--
8	1. Turn the ignition to OFF. 2. Install any components or connectors that were removed. 3. Clear all DTCs. Are the repairs complete?	--	Go to Diagnostic System Check	--

GC2040200227020X

Fig. 46 Code C2110: Righthand Rear TPM Sensor Fault (Part 2 of 2). 2000 Corvette

Step	Action	Value (s)	Yes	No
1	Were you sent here from the TPM Diagnostic System Check?	--	Go to Step 2	Go to Diagnostic System Check
2	Using the buttons on the DIC, enter the TIRE TRAINING mode. Can the programming be successfully accessed through the IPC?	--	Go to Step 3	Go to Diagnostic System Check
3	Program all TPM sensors. Was the left rear TPM sensor programming successful?	--	Go to Step 6	Go to Step 4
4	1. Replace the left rear TPM sensor. 2. Program all the TPM sensors. Is the replacement complete?	--	Go to Step 5	--

GC2040200228010X

Fig. 47 Code C2115: Lefthand Rear TPM Sensor Fault (Part 1 of 2). 2000 Corvette

5	1. Clear the DTCs. 2. Road test the vehicle above 24 km/h (15 mph) for 20 minutes. Does DTC C2115 reset?	--	Go to Step 7	System OK
6	1. Clear the DTCs. 2. Road test the vehicle above 24 km/h (15 mph) for 20 minutes. Does DTC C2115 reset?	--	Go to Step 4	System OK
7	1. Replace the remote control door lock receiver. 2. Program all TPM sensors. 3. Program the RFA transmitters. Is the replacement complete?	--	Go to Step 8	--
8	1. Turn the ignition to OFF. 2. Install any components or connectors that were removed. 3. Clear all DTCs. Are the repairs complete?	--	Go to Diagnostic System Check	--

GC2040200228020X

Fig. 47 Code C2115: Lefthand Rear TPM Sensor Fault (Part 2 of 2). 2000 Corvette

7	1. Replace the remote control door lock receiver. 2. Program all TPM sensors. 3. Program the RFA transmitters. Is the replacement complete?	--	Go to Step 8	--
8	1. Turn the ignition to OFF. 2. Install any components or connectors that were removed. 3. Clear all DTCs. Are the repairs complete?	--	Go to Diagnostic System Check	--

GC2040200229020X

Fig. 48 Code C2120: TPM System Fault (Part 2 of 2). 2000 Corvette

Step	Action	Value (s)	Yes	No
1	Were you sent here from the TPM Diagnostic System Check?	--	Go to Step 2	Go to Diagnostic System Check
2	Using the RESET button on the DIC, enter the TIRE TRAINING mode. Can the reprogramming be successfully accessed through the IPC?	--	Go to Step 3	Go to Diagnostic System Check
3	Program all TPM sensors. Was the programming successful?	--	Go to Step 5	Go to Step 4
4	Inspect all wheels for missing or damaged TPM sensors. Are all sensors on the vehicle and undamaged?	--	Go to Step 7	Go to Step 6
5	1. Clear the DTCs. 2. Road test the vehicle above 24 km/h (15 mph) for 20 minutes. Does DTC C2120 reset?	--	Go to Step 7	System OK
6	1. Replace the damaged or missing TPM sensor(s). 2. Program all TPM sensors. Is the replacement complete?	--	Go to Step 8	--

GC2040200229010X

Fig. 48 Code C2120: TPM System Fault (Part 1 of 2). 2000 Corvette

Step	Action	Value (s)	Yes	No
1	Were you sent here from the TPM Diagnostic System Check?	--	Go to Step 2	Go to Diagnostic System Check
2	Using the buttons on the DIC, enter the TIRE TRAINING mode. Can the programming be successfully accessed through the IPC?	--	Go to Step 3	Go to Diagnostic System Check
3	Program all TPM sensors. Was the programming successful?	--	Go to Step 5	Go to Step 4
4	Inspect all wheels for missing or damaged TPM sensors. Are all sensors on the vehicle and undamaged?	--	Go to Step 9	Go to Step 7
5	1. Clear all DTCs. 2. Road test the vehicle above 24 km/h (15 mph) for 20 minutes. Does DTC C2121 reset?	--	Go to Step 9	Go to Step 6
6	1. Select the display RFA DTC function with the scan tool. 2. Check for RFA DTC B2805. Is DTC B2805 stored?	--	Go to Step 8	System OK

GC2040200230010X

Fig. 49 Code C2121: TPM System Programming Fault (Part 1 of 2). 2000 Corvette

7	1. Replace the damaged or missing TPM sensor(s). 2. Program all TPM sensors. Is the replacement complete?	--	Go to Step 10	--
8	Program the RFA transmitters. Refer to Transmitter Programming/Synchronization in Keyless Entry. Was the programming successful?	--	Go to Step 10	Go to Diagnostic System Check
9	1. Replace the remote control door lock receiver. 2. Program all TPM sensors. 3. Program the RFA transmitters. Is the replacement complete?	--	Go to Step 10	--
10	1. Turn the ignition to OFF. 2. Install any components or connectors that were removed. 3. Clear all DTCs. Are the repairs complete?	--	Go to Diagnostic System Check	--

GC2040200230020X

Fig. 49 Code C2121: TPM System Programming Fault (Part 2 of 2). 2000 Corvette

5	Replace the TPM sensor. Did you complete the replacement?	Go to Step 6	System OK
6	1. Use the scan tool in order to clear the DTCs. 2. Operate the vehicle within normal operating conditions. Does the DTC reset?	Go to Step 7	System OK
7	1. Replace the RCDLR. 2. Program the TPM sensors. Refer to Tire Pressure Monitoring Sensor Programming. 3. Operate the vehicle within normal operating conditions. Does the DTC reset?	Go to Diagnostic Aids	System OK

GC2040200231020X

Fig. 50 Codes C0750, C0755, C0760 & C0765: No Current Tire Pressure Information Transmitted (Part 2 of 2). 2001–04 Corvette

Step	Action	Yes	No
1	Did you perform the TPM Diagnostic System Check?	Go to Step 2	Go to Diagnostic System Check -
2	1. Install a scan tool. 2. Turn ON the ignition, with the engine OFF. 3. With a scan tool, select the Remote Function Actuation (RFA) system Diagnostic Trouble Codes (DTC) function. Does the scan tool indicate that DTC C0750, C0755, C0760 or C0765 is current?	Go to Step 3	Go to Diagnostic Aids
3	Since some occurrences of this DTC are caused by radio interference, or driving conditions, review the TPM system with the customer to verify the conditions under which the DTC set. Did radio interference, or driving conditions cause this DTC to set?	Go to Diagnostic Aids	Go to Step 4
4	1. Clear the DTCs. 2. Reprogram all the TPM sensors. 3. Operate the vehicle within normal operating conditions. Does the DTC reset?	Go to Step 5	System OK

GC2040200231010X

Fig. 50 Codes C0750, C0755, C0760 & C0765: No Current Tire Pressure Information Transmitted (Part 1 of 2). 2001–04 Corvette

Diagnosis on the Tire Pressure Monitor (TPM) system is done by reading DTC stored in the receiver's memory. TPM DTCs can only be displayed through the Instrument Panel Cluster (IPC) display (on-board diagnostic capabilities), or by using a scan tool. Most all information in this section will refer to the scan tool for diagnostic support. Refer to Scan Tool Diagnostics . The TPM system relies on the same receiver as the Remote Function Actuation (RFA) system, therefore TPM DTCs will be displayed in addition to RFA DTCs. For more information on the RFA system. Refer to Remote Keyless Entry Diagnostic Information in Keyless Entry.

The TPM system uses information from other systems in order to execute some functions. Therefore, before further diagnosis, review the general information on how the TPM system operates and how each system interacts with the TPM. For example, the TPM system uses barometric pressure information from the Powertrain Control Module (PCM) to compensate for different altitudes. If tire pressure readings are inaccurate a good starting point would be to monitor barometric pressure readings from the PCM. This can determine if the PCM is sending the correct barometric pressure data to the TPM system.

Use a scan tool in order to diagnose the TPM system when referred to in diagnostic procedures. In addition to displaying DTCs, the TPM system displays the input status and the data values used. Any of these features can be selected using the scan tool.

Become very familiar with the TPM system capabilities and diagnostic features. These self-diagnostic features are referenced in the DTC tables and are very useful in diagnosing non-DTC setting malfunctions as well.

Replace the receiver only if the diagnostic procedures specifically direct you to do so. Check for wiring problems first. Then check the system for further problems. Most system malfunctions are traceable to faulty wiring and connectors, and occasionally components. The receiver very reliable and not the likely cause of a system malfunction. Receiver replacement before a complete diagnosis will usually result in a recurrence of the original complaint malfunction.

SERVICE TIRE WARN SYS Message

GC2040200223010X

Fig. 51 Tire Pressure Monitoring System Diagnosis (Part 1 of 2). 2000 Corvette

The TPM system does not have an indicator lamp or a specific message in order to indicate a malfunction. When the TPM system indicates a malfunction, the receiver sends a message through the serial data line to the IPC to display the SERVICE TIRE WARN SYS message. Further diagnosis of the TPM system is done through reading the DTCs or through the use of a scan tool.

DTCs Current and History

The TPM system stores DTCs as either current or history codes. DTCs for the TPM system are accessed through RFA system. Most TPM system malfunctions will set a DTC and display the SERVICE TIRE WARN SYS message on the IPC. Other TPM malfunctions will only set a DTC and not display a fault message and must be read using a scan tool. History DTCs are intermittent malfunctions and be diagnosed different then current DTCs. Refer to Intermittents and Poor Connections.

TPM System Specifications

Application	Specification
FLAT TIRE	Under 34 kPa (5 psi)
HIGH TIRE PRESSURE	Over 289 kPa (42 psi)
LOW TIRE PRESSURE	34-172 kPa (5-25 psi)
Normal Range	173-289 kPa (25-42 psi)
Tire Pressure Sensor Range	0-427 kPa (0-62 psi)
Vehicle Minimum Speed for Sensor Transmission	16-24 km/h (10-15 mph)

GC2040200223020X

Fig. 51 Tire Pressure Monitoring System Diagnosis (Part 2 of 2). 2000 Corvette

Step	Action	Value (s)	Yes	No
5	1. Road test the vehicle above 40 km/h (25 mph) for 5 minutes or until the tire pressure data is displayed on the IPC. 2. Select the RFA data display function with the scan tool. 3. Read the tire pressure data. Are all tire pressure readings within specifications?	34-289 kPa (5-42 psi)	Go to Diagnostic System Check -	Go to Step 6
6	1. Replace the appropriate TPM sensor. 2. Program all TPM sensors. Is the replacement complete?	--	Go to Step 8	--
7	1. Add or remove air to the tires as needed. 2. Using the RESET button on the DIC, clear the tire pressure warning messages. Are the tire pressure readings OK?	--	Go to Step 3	--
8	1. Turn the ignition to OFF. 2. Install or connect any components or connectors that were removed or disconnected. 3. Clear all DTCs. Are all DTCs cleared?	--	Go to Diagnostic System Check -	--

GC2040200224020X

Fig. 52 Service Tire Warning Message Displayed (Part 2 of 2). 2000 Corvette

Step	Action	Value (s)	Yes	No
1	Were you sent here from the TPM Diagnostic System Check?	--	Go to Step 2	Go to Diagnostic System Check -
2	**Important** Inspect that the tire pressure gage is properly calibrated in order to ensure the most accurate readings. Using a tire pressure gage, measure and record each tire pressure. Is the tire pressure OK?	--	Go to Step 3	Go to Step 7
3	Road test the vehicle above 40 km/h (25 mph) for 5 minutes or until the tire pressure data is displayed on the IPC. Are all tire pressure readings within specifications?	34-289 kPa (5-42 psi)	Go to Step 4	Go to Step 5
4	Check for any of the following tire pressure warning messages displayed on the IPC: 1. HIGH TIRE PRESSURE 2. LOW TIRE PRESSURE 3. FLAT TIRE Are any of these messages displayed?	--	Go to Step 5	System OK

GC2040200224010X

Fig. 52 Service Tire Warning Message Displayed (Part 1 of 2). 2000 Corvette

Step	Action	Yes	No
1	Install a scan tool. Does the scan tool power up?	Go to Step 2	Scan Tool Does Not Power Up
2	1. Turn ON the ignition, with the engine OFF. 2. Attempt to establish communication with the RCDLR. Does the scan tool communicate with the RCDLR?	Go to Step 3	Scan Tool Does Not Communicate with Class 2 Device
3	Select the RKE Diagnostic Trouble Codes (DTC) function on the scan tool. Does the scan tool display any DTCs that begin with a "U"?	Go to Diagnostic Trouble Code (DTC)	Go to Step 4
4	Does the scan tool display any RKE DTCs?	Go to Diagnostic Trouble Code (DTC)	Go to Step 5
5	Does the scan tool display any TPM DTCs?	Go to Diagnostic Trouble Code (DTC)	System OK

GC2040200232000X

Fig. 53 Diagnostic System Check. Deville & Seville

Step	Action	Yes	No
1	Did you perform the TPM Diagnostic System Check?	Go to Step 2	Go to Diagnostic System Check -
2	1. Install a scan tool. 2. Turn ON the ignition, with the engine OFF. 3. With a scan tool, select the Diagnostic Trouble Code (DTC) function in Tire Pressure Monitor . Does the scan tool indicate that DTC C0750, C0755, C0760, or C0765 is current?	Go to Step 3	Go to Diagnostic Aids
3	Since some occurrences of this DTC are caused by radio frequency interference, or driving conditions, review the TPM system with the customer to verify the conditions under which the DTC set. Did vehicle operation cause this DTC to set?	Go to Diagnostic Aids	Go to Step 4
4	With the scan tool, observe the suspect sensor's Tire Pressure Sensor Battery Status data parameter in the Tire Pressure Monitor Data Display list. Does the scan tool indicate that the sensor battery status is OK?	Go to Step 5	Go to Step 6

GC2040200233010X

Fig. 54 Codes C0750, C0755, C0760 & C0765: No Current Tire Pressure Information Transmitted (Part 1 of 2). Deville & Seville

5	1. Use the scan tool in order to clear the DTCs. 2. Operate the vehicle within normal operating conditions. Does the DTC reset?	Go to Step 6	System OK
6	Replace the TPM sensor. Did you complete the replacement?	Go to Step 7	System OK
7	1. Use the scan tool in order to clear the DTCs. 2. Operate the vehicle within normal operating conditions. Does the DTC reset?	Go to Step 8	System OK
8	1. Replace the RCDLR. 2. Program the TPM sensors. 3. Operate the vehicle within normal operating conditions. Does the DTC reset?	Go to Diagnostic Aids	System OK

GC2040200233020X

Fig. 54 Codes C0750, C0755, C0760 & C0765: No Current Tire Pressure Information Transmitted (Part 2 of 2). Deville & Seville

Step	Action	Value (s)	Yes	No
1	Install a scan tool. Does the scan tool power up?	--	Go to Step 2	Scan Tool Does Not Power Up in Data Link Communications
2	1. Turn ON the ignition, with the engine OFF. 2. Attempt to establish communications with the EBCM. Does the scan tool communicate with the EBCM?	--	Go to Step 3	Scan Tool Does Not Communicate with Class 2 Device
3	Select the ABS-TCS-TPM (if equipped) display DTC function on the scan tool. Does the scan tool display any ABS DTCs, except DTC C1245?	--	Go to Diagnostic System Check -	Go to Diagnostic Trouble Code (DTC)

GC2040200234000X

Fig. 55 Diagnostic System Check. Impala & Monte Carlo

Step	Action	Value (s)	Yes	No
1	Did you perform the TPM Diagnostic System Check?	--	Go to Step 2	Go to Diagnostic System Check -
2	1. Install a scan tool. 2. Turn ON the ignition, with the engine OFF. 3. With a scan tool, monitor the DTC Information for DTC C1245 in the ABS/TCS/TPM (if equipped) Diagnostic Trouble Codes (DTCs). Does the scan tool indicate that DTC C1245 is current?	--	Go to Step 3	Go to Diagnostic Aids
3	Since most occurrences of this DTC are caused by low tire pressure, review the TPM system with the customer to verify the conditions under which the DTC set. Did vehicle operation cause this DTC to set?	--	Go to Step 5	Go to Step 4
4	1. Perform the tire inflation monitoring reset if tire pressures were adjusted. 2. Use the scan tool in order to clear the DTCs. 3. Operate the vehicle within the Conditions for Running the DTC as specified in the supporting text. Does the DTC reset as a current DTC?	--	Go to Diagnostic Aids	System OK
5	Inspect the tire pressures and adjust if needed. Perform the tire inflation monitoring reset if tire pressures were adjusted. Did you complete the repair?	--	System OK	--

GC2040200235000X

Fig. 56 Code C1245: Low Tire Pressure Detected. Impala & Monte Carlo

Step	Action	Value (s)	Yes	No
1	Perform both tire pressure reset procedures. Does the LOW TIRE PRESSURE indicator turn off?	--	System OK	Go to Step 2
2	Inspect for Instrument Cluster DTC's. Are there any instrument cluster DTCs present?	--	Go to Diagnostic System Check -	Go to Step 3
3	Operate the system in order to verify the repair. Did you correct the condition?	--	System OK	Go to Step 2

GC2040200236000X

Fig. 57 Low Tire Pressure Indicator Always On. Impala & Monte Carlo

Step	Action	Yes	No
1	Install a scan tool. Does the scan tool power up?	Go to Step 2	Scan Tool Does Not Power Up
2	1. Turn ON the ignition, with the engine OFF. 2. Attempt to establish communications with the Electronic Brake Control Module (EBCM). Does the scan tool communicate with the EBCM?	Go to Step 3	Scan Tool Does Not Communicate with Class 2 Device
3	Select the ABS Diagnostic Trouble Codes DTC function on the scan tool. Does the scan tool display any DTCs that begin with a "U"?	Go to Diagnostic Trouble Code (DTC)	Go to Step 4
4	Does the scan tool display any ABS DTCs?	Go to Diagnostic System Check	Go to Step 5
5	Does the scan tool display DTC C1245?	Go to DTC C1245	System OK

GC2040200239000X

Fig. 59 Diagnostic System Check. LeSabre & Park Avenue

Step	Action	Value (s)	Yes	No
1	Was the Diagnostic System Check-Tire Pressure Monitor performed?	--	Go to Step 2	Go to Diagnostic System Check -
2	1. Turn the ignition switch to RUN. 2. Observe LOW TIRE indicator in the instrument panel. Does the indicator turn on for approximately 3 seconds and then turn off?	--	System OK	Go to Step 3
3	Replace the I/P Cluster. Did you complete the replacement?	--	Go to Step 4	--
4	Operate the system in order to verify the repair. Did you correct the condition?	--	System OK	Go to DTC C1245 Low Tire Pressure Detected

GC2040200237000X

Fig. 58 Low Tire Pressure Indicator Inoperative. Impala & Monte Carlo

Step	Action	Yes	No
1	Did you perform the Tire Pressure Monitor Diagnostic System Check?	Go to Step 2	Go to Diagnostic System Check -
2	1. Install a scan tool. 2. Turn ON the ignition, with the engine OFF. 3. With a scan tool, select the ABS Diagnostic Trouble Codes (DTCs) function. Does the scan tool indicate that DTC C1245 is current?	Go to Step 3	Go to Diagnostic Aids
3	Since some occurrences of this DTC are caused by driving condition, or tire size difference, review the TPM system with the customer to verify the conditions under which the DTC set. Did driving conditions, or tire size cause this DTC to set?	Go to Step 4	Go to Step 5
4	1. Calibrate the TPM system. 2. Use the scan tool in order to clear the DTCs. 3. Operate the vehicle within the Conditions for Running the DTC as specified in the supporting text. Does the DTC reset as a current DTC?	Go to Diagnostic Aids	System OK
5	Inspect the tire pressures and adjust to manufacturers specification if needed. Calibrate the TPM system if tire pressures were adjusted. Did you complete the repair?	System OK	--

GC2040200242000X

Fig. 60 Code C1245: Low Tire Pressure Detected. LeSabre & Park Avenue

COMPONENT SERVICE

Pressure Monitor Sensor Programming

ALERO & GRAND AM

The "Tire Low Tire Pressure" indicator will be turn On when the pressure in one of the tires is 12 psi. lower or higher then the other three tires.

1. Inflate all tires to specifications.
2. Place ignition switch in the On position.
3. Depress RESET button located on driver side instrument panel fuse box.
4. The OIL CHANGE indicator should begin to flash.
5. Press RESET button again, the CHANGE OIL indicator should go Off and the LOW TIRE PRESSURE indicator should begin to flash.
6. Depress RESET button until a chime sounds and the LOW TIRE PRESSURE indicator turns Off.

AURORA

The "Tire Low Tire Pressure" indicator will be turn On when the pressure in one of the tires is 12 psi. lower or higher then the other three tires.

1. Inflate all tires to specifications.
2. Place ignition switch in the On position.
3. Press SELECT right arrow button until GAUGE is displayed.
4. Press SELECT down arrow button until TIRE PRESSURE is displayed.
5. Depress RESET button for 3 seconds until TIRE PRESSURE RESET is displayed.
6. Release the RESET button, TIRE PRESSURE NORMAL should be displayed.

BONNEVILLE

2000-01

Using System Monitor

The "Tire Low Tire Pressure" indicator will be turn On when the pressure in one of the tires is 10 psi. lower or higher then the other three tires.

1. Inflate all tires to specifications.
2. Place ignition switch in the On position.
3. Depress and hold TIRE RESET button until TIRE PRESS indicator begins to flash.
4. Release the button, the TIRE PRESS indicator should turn Off.

Using Drive Information Control (DIC)

The "Tire Low Tire Pressure" indicator will be turn On when the pressure in one of the tires is 10 psi. lower or higher then the other three tires.

1. Inflate all tires to specifications.
2. Place ignition switch in the On position.
3. Press MODE button until TIRE PRESS is displayed.
4. Press RESET button until TIRE PRESS RESET is displayed.
5. Release the RESET button, TIRE PRESS NORMAL should be displayed.

2002-04

Tire Driver Information Center (DIC) will display Normal when tire pressure is normal. When low tire pressure is detected the DIC will display Low Tire Pressure.

1. Inflate all tires to specifications.
2. Place ignition switch in the On position.
3. Depress DIC SET button for 3 seconds.
4. The DIC will display TIRE PRESSURE RESET for 3 seconds indicating the monitor has been reset.

CENTURY & REGAL

The "Tire Low Tire Pressure" indicator will be turn On when the pressure in one of the tires is 12 psi. lower or higher then the other three tires.

1. Inflate all tires to vehicle manufacturers specifications.
2. Place ignition switch in the On position.
3. Depress RESET button located on passenger side instrument panel fuse box.
4. The LOW TIRE indicator should flash 3 times and turn Off.

CORVETTE

The tire pressure monitor will display the 4 tire pressure on the Driver Information Center (DIC) while the vehicle is being driven. If the system detects a tire pressure above 42 psi., the HIGH TIRE PRESSURE message will be displayed on the DIC. If the system detects a tire pressure between 5 and 25 psi., LOW TIRE PRESSURE will be displayed. If a tire pressure below 5 psi. is detected, FLAT TIRE will be displayed followed by two chime sounds and the message MAX. SPEED 55 MPH and REDUCED HANDLING. After servicing or inflating tire to recommended pressure, press DIC RESET button to clear DIC warning messages.

DEVILLE & SEVILLE

If system detects proper tire pressure, TIRE OK will be displayed on the Driver Information Control (DIC). If the system detects a tire pressure above 38 psi., the TIRE HIGH message will be displayed, if the system detects a tire pressure below 25 psi., TIRE LOW will be displayed followed by CHECK TIRE PRESSURE. Inflating tire to recommended pressure will clear the tire message.

IMPALA & MONTE CARLO

USING RDS RADIO

The "Tire Low Tire Pressure" indicator will be turn On when the pressure in one of the tires is 12 psi. lower or higher then the other three tires.

1. Inflate all tires to specifications.
2. Place ignition switch in the On position.
3. Place radio in Off position.
4. Depress and hold DISP button until SETTINGS is displayed.
5. Press SEEK up or down buttons until TIRE MON is displayed.
6. Press PREV or NEXT buttons until RESET is displayed.
7. Press DISP button, a chime will sound and DONE will be displayed.
8. Scroll menu until EXIT is displayed, then press DISP button. A chime will sound to indicate system exit from TIRE MON.

2002-04

Using Light Switch

The "Tire Low Tire Pressure" indicator will be turn On when the pressure in one of the tires is 12 psi. lower or higher then the other three tires.

1. Inflate all tires to specifications.
2. Place ignition switch in the On position.
3. Cycle the light switch from Off to Parking Lamps 3 times within 5 seconds.

LESABRE & PARK AVENUE

2000

1. Inflate all tires to specifications.
2. Place ignition switch in the On position.
3. Press GAUGE button until TIRE PRESSURE LOW, CHECK TIRES is displayed.
4. Press RESET button until TIRE PRESSURE NORMAL is displayed.

2001-04

The "Tire Low Tire Pressure" indicator will be turn On when the pressure in one of the tires is 12 psi. lower or higher then the other three tires.

1. Inflate all tires to specifications.
2. Place ignition switch in the On position.
3. Press GAUGE INFO button until TIRE PRESSURE is displayed.
4. Depress and hold RESET button until TIRE PRESSURE RESET is displayed.
5. Release RESET button, TIRE PRESSURE NORMAL should be displayed.

Pressure Monitor Sensor Replacement

Ensure cap and valve are placed in a dry and clean location after removal. The cap is aluminum and valve is nickel plated to prevent corrosion and are not to be substituted with any other material.

When using a machine to separate tire and bead from wheel, position bead breaking tool 90° from valve stem to ensure sensor is not damaged.

1. Raise and support vehicle using suitable lift.
2. Remove tire and wheel assembly, then the tire from wheel.
3. Remove TPM sensor nut, then the sensor.
4. Reverse procedure to install

TIGHTENING SPECIFICATIONS

Component	Torque Ft. Lbs.
Sensor Nut	35①
Wheel Lug Nuts	100

① — Inch lbs.

ACTIVE SUSPENSION SYSTEMS

TABLE OF CONTENTS

Application Chart

Model	Year	Type
Aurora	2000–04	Automatic Level Control
Bonneville, LeSabre & Park Avenue	2000–04	Automatic Level Control
Catera	2000–01	Automatic Level Control
Corvette	2000–04	Real Time Damping
DeVille	2000–04	Automatic Level Control
		Continuously Variable Road Sensing Suspension
Eldorado	2000–02	Automatic Level Control
		Continuously Variable Road Sensing Suspension
Seville	2000–04	Automatic Level Control
		Continuously Variable Road Sensing Suspension

Automatic Level Control (ALC)

NOTE: On Air Bag Equipped Models, Refer To "Air Bag System Precautions" Located In The Front Of This Manual For System Disarming & Arming Procedures.

NOTE: Refer To "Computer Relearn Procedures" Located In The Front Of This Manual When Battery Power To The Computer Has Been Interrupted.

NOTE: "Electrical Symbol & Wire Color Code Identification" Located In The Front Of This Manual May Be Used As An Aid When Using Wiring Circuits Found In This Section.

INDEX

PRECAUTIONS

Air Bag Systems

Refer to "Air Bag System Precautions" in front of this manual for system arming and disarming procedures.

Battery Ground Cable

Prior to service, disconnect battery ground cable and isolate as required.

DESCRIPTION

The Automatic Level Control (ALC) and Electronic Level Control (ELC) system adjusts rear trim height in response to changes in vehicle loading. This system consists of an air compressor assembly, air dryer, exhaust solenoid, compressor relay, height sensor, air adjustable shocks and air tubing. The compressor is activated when the ignition is On and weight is added to the vehicle. The exhaust solenoid is connected directly to the positive side of the battery, enabling the system to exhaust with the ignition Off and when excess weight is removed.

System Components

COMPRESSOR

This assembly is a positive displacement air pump powered by a 12-volt DC permanent magnet motor. The air compressor head casting contains intake and exhaust valves plus a solenoid operated exhaust valve which releases air from the system when energized. Air compressor intake air is drawn through an intake air hose and filter. The air compressor is a serviceable part mounted to a bracket.

AIR DRYER

The air dryer, attached to the compressor outlet, performs two system functions. The dryer contains a dry chemical that absorbs moisture from the air before it is delivered to the struts. Moisture is removed from the air dryer and returned to the atmosphere when system is being exhausted. The air dryer also contains a valve arrangement that maintains a minimum air pressure of 7–14 psi in the struts.

EXHAUST SOLENOID

The exhaust solenoid is located in the compressor head assembly and provides two functions. When energized, it exhausts air from the rear struts. It also acts as a pressure relief valve to limit maximum pressure output of the compressor.

COMPRESSOR RELAY

The compressor relay is controlled by the height sensor and completes the 12-volt circuit to the compressor.

HEIGHT SENSOR

The solid state sensor detects height changes at the rear of the vehicle, in turn, controls the functions of the compressor and exhaust solenoid. To prevent energizing the compressor relay or exhaust solenoid during normal ride motions, the sensor circuit provides a fixed delay before ground is completed to either circuit.

The sensor limits compressor run time and exhaust solenoid energized time to a range of 4.5–7.5 minutes. This prevents continuous compressor operation in case of a severe system leak or continuous exhaust solenoid operation. The timer circuitry is reset whenever the ignition is cycled On and Off, or the sensor exhaust or compress output signal changes.

The sensor is mounted to the lefthand front side of the rear suspension support assembly. The actuation arm is attached to the lefthand rear control arm by a short link.

AIR ADJUSTABLE SHOCKS

The rear air adjustable shock absorbers are constructed with a rubber like air sleeve attached to the dust tube and reservoir. This sleeve forms a flexible chamber which extends the shock absorber when pressure in the chamber is increased. When air pressure is reduced, the weight of the vehicle collapses the shock absorber. in order to maintain proper operation and reliability of the air adjustable shock absorbers, a system pressure from 7–14 psi must be maintained at all times.

System Operation

When a load is added to the vehicle, the body is moved down causing the height sensor arm to rotate upward. This movement activates the internal timing circuit which, after a predetermined delay of 17–27 seconds, then provides ground to complete the compressor relay circuit. When the relay circuit is energized, the circuit to the compressor is complete, allowing the compressor to send pressurized air to the shocks.

As the shocks inflate, the vehicle body moves upward, causing the sensor arm to rotate downward. Once the body reaches its original height, the sensor opens the compressor relay circuit and shuts the compressor Off.

When a load is removed from vehicle, the body rises, causing the sensor actuating arm to rotate downward. This activates the internal timing circuit. After the initial fixed delay, the sensor provides a ground to complete the exhaust solenoid circuit, energizing the solenoid. Air starts exhausting out of the shock absorbers, back through the air dryer and exhaust solenoid valve, and into the atmosphere.

As the vehicle body lowers, the height sensor arm is rotated upward until the vehicle reaches its original height. When this height is reached, the sensor opens the exhaust solenoid circuit which prevents air from escaping.

The height sensor position is inspected when the ignition is turned On. If the height sensor indicates that it is not required to raise or lower the vehicle, the internal timer circuit is activated. After 40 seconds, the compressor will run for four seconds. This ensures the shocks are filled with the proper residual pressure (7–14 psi). If weight is added or removed from the vehicle during this 40 second delay, the air replenishment cycle will be overridden and the vehicle will raise or lower after normal delay.

ADJUSTMENTS

When repair or adjustment procedures require vehicle to be raised on a hoist, it is important that the rear axle assembly remains in the normal trim height position at all times. When a frame contact hoist is used, two additional jack stands should be used to support the rear axle or control arms in the normal trim height position.

Height Sensor

The link should be properly attached to the sensor arm and track bar, when making this adjustment.

1. Loosen lock bolt securing metal arm to height sensor plastic arm.
2. To raise vehicle trim height, move plastic arm upward and tighten lock bolt.
3. To lower vehicle trim height, loosen lock bolt securing metal arm to height sensor plastic arm, then move plastic arm down.
4. If adjustment cannot be made, inspect for correct sensor.

DIAGNOSIS & TESTING

When diagnostic procedures require vehicle to be raised on a hoist, it is important that the rear axle assembly remains in the normal trim height position at all times. When a frame contact hoist is used, two additional jack stands should be used to support the rear axle or control arms in the normal trim height position.

Wiring Diagrams

Refer to **Figs. 1 through 12,** for ALC wiring diagrams.

Diagnostic Tests

AURORA, BONNEVILLE & LESABRE

Refer to **Figs. 13 through 20,** for diagnostic test procedures.

CATERA

Refer to **Figs. 21 through 34,** for system diagnostic tests.

DEVILLE

Refer to **Figs. 35 through 43,** for system diagnostic tests.

ELDORADO

2000–01

Refer to **Figs. 44 through 51,** for system diagnostic tests.

2002

Refer to **Figs. 52 through 61,** for diagnostic test procedures.

PARK AVENUE

Refer to **Figs. 62 and 63,** for diagnostic test procedures.

SEVILLE

2000-01

Refer to **Figs. 64 through 70,** for diagnostic test procedures.

2002-04

Refer to **Figs. 52 through 61,** for diagnostic test procedures.

Component Testing

RESIDUAL AIR CHECK

1. Remove air line from dryer fitting and attach air line from pressure gauge tool No. J 22124-A, or equivalent, to dryer fitting, **Fig. 71.**
2. Disconnect electrical connection to pump and jumper 12-volt dark green wire terminal to run compressor. Pump should run until a pressure of 100 psi is reached.
3. Disconnect wiring from compressor exhaust solenoid and jumper 12-volt to one terminal and ground other terminal to the exhaust system.
4. Air should be exhausted from system until gauge indicates 7–14 psi.

COMPRESSOR/DRYER PERFORMANCE TEST

1. Disconnect wiring from compressor motor and exhaust solenoid terminals.
2. Disconnect existing pressure line from dryer and attach pressure gauge tool No. J 22124-A, or equivalent, to dryer fitting.
3. Connect an ammeter to 12-volt source and to compressor.
4. Operate compressor and note the following:
   a. Current draw should not exceed 14 amps.
   b. When gauge reads at least 100 psi, turn compressor Off by disconnecting power supply and observe if pressure leaks down. Compressor should not leak below 90 psi. If compressor is permitted to run until it reaches maximum output pressure of 180 psi, solenoid exhaust valve will act as a relief valve. Resulting leak down when compressor is shutoff will indicate a false leak.
   c. Refer to chart outlined in **Fig. 72,** if compressor fails to meet specification.
   d. If performance is satisfactory, install compressor and connect wiring and air lines.

ELC SYSTEM LEAK TEST

1. Install pressure gauge tool No. J 22124-A, or equivalent, into ELC system between dryer assembly and pressure regulator valve. Install so shutoff valve is on compressor side of gauge.
2. With shutoff valve open, apply service air pressure through service valve on gauge until gauge reads 100 psi.
3. If leak is indicated, close shutoff valve and continue to observe for pressure drop. Closing valve isolates compressor from rest of system.
4. If gauge pressure continues to drop, leak is outside compressor. Leak test all connections with soap and water or suitable leak test solution.
5. If gauge pressure does not continue to drop, leak is in compressor. Refer to **Fig. 73,** to inspect compressor for leaks.
6. If pressure builds up rapidly but vehicle does not raise, inspect for pinched air lines and stuck or binding shocks.

HEIGHT SENSOR OPERATIONAL CHECK

1. Turn ignition Off, then On. This will reset height sensor timer circuits.
2. Raise vehicle on hoist. Ensure rear wheels or axle housing are supported and that vehicle is at proper trim height.
3. Disconnect link from height sensor arm, then ensure sensor wiring and harness ground are connected properly.
4. Move sensor arm upward. There should be a delay of 8–15 seconds before compressor turns on and shocks start to inflate. As soon as shocks start to fill, stop compressor by moving sensor arm down.
5. Move sensor arm down below position where compressor stopped. There should be a delay of 8–15 seconds before shocks start to deflate and vehicle lowers.

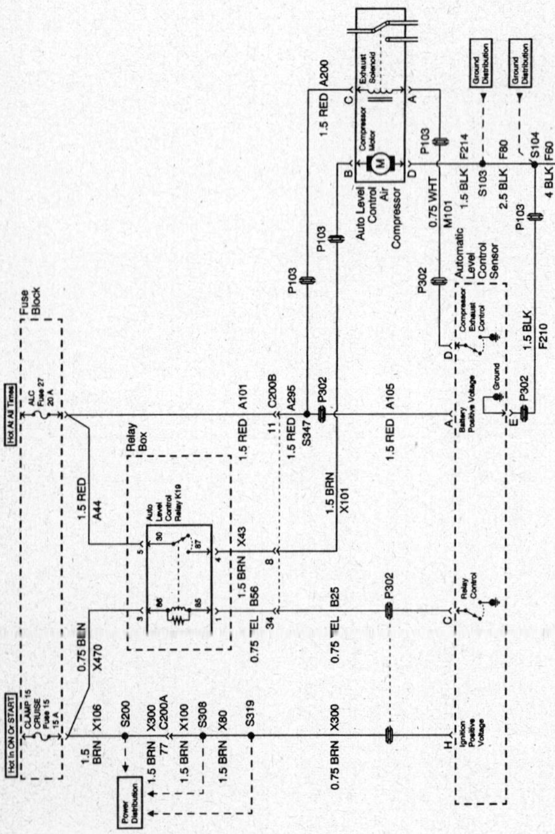

GC20198003000010X

Fig. 1 Wiring diagram (Part 1 of 2). Catera

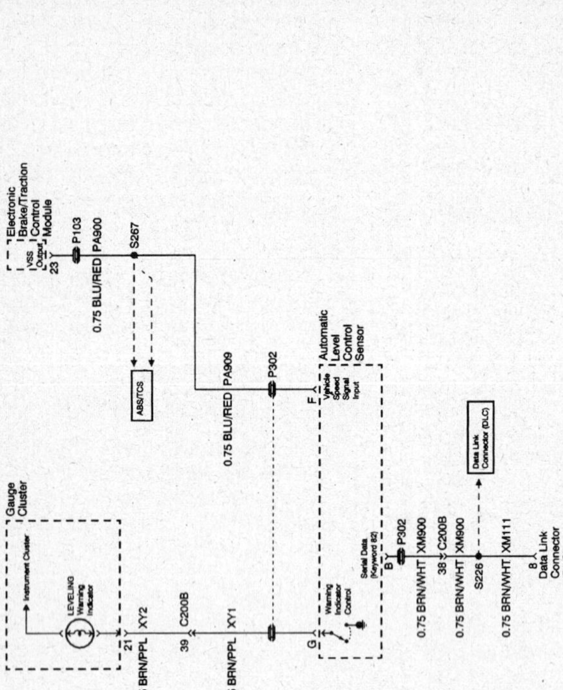

GC20198003000020X

Fig. 1 Wiring diagram (Part 2 of 2). Catera

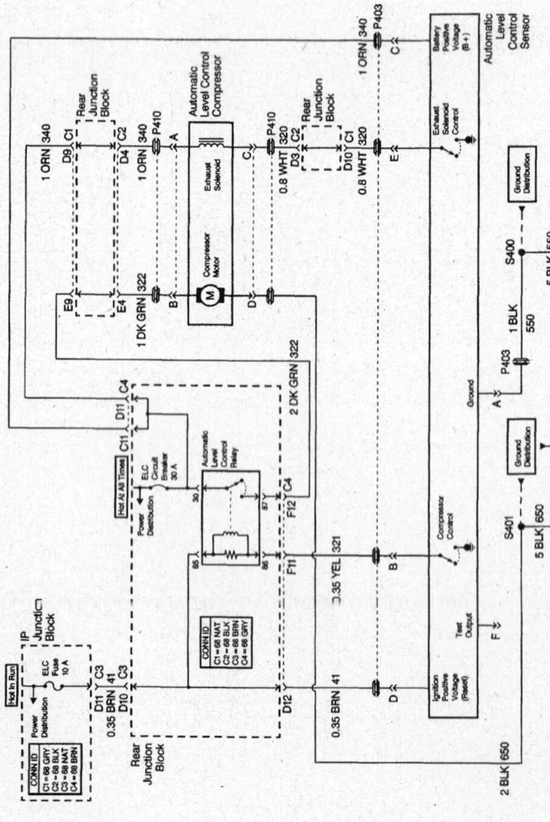

GC20198003210000X

Fig. 2 Wiring diagram. Park Avenue

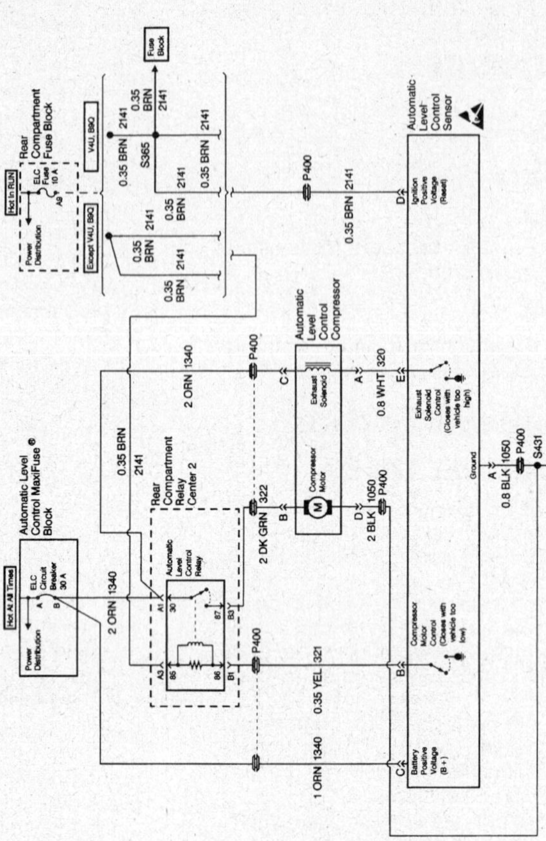

GC20198002900000X

Fig. 3 Wiring diagram. 2000–01 Eldorado Less Road Sensing Suspension

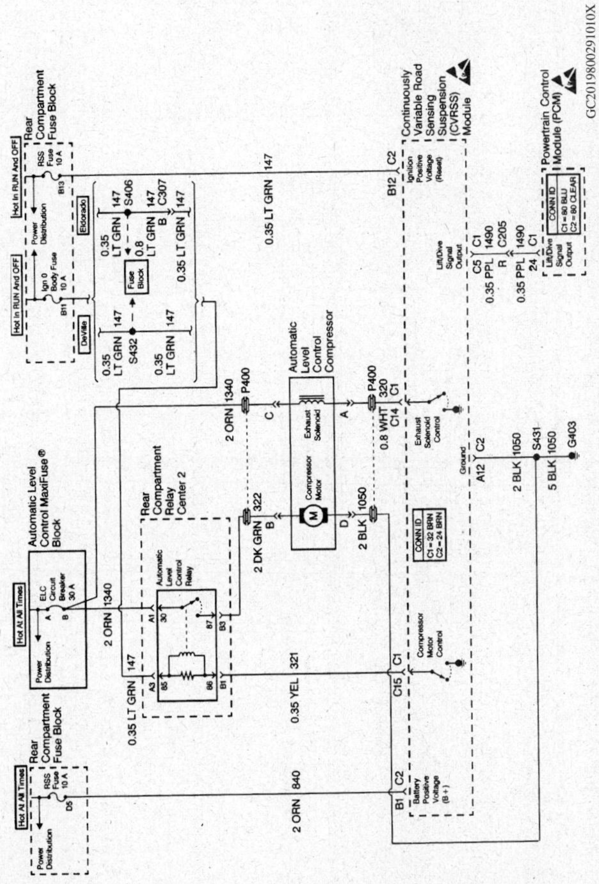

Fig. 4 Wiring diagram (Part 1 of 2). 2000–01 Eldorado w/Road Sensing Suspension

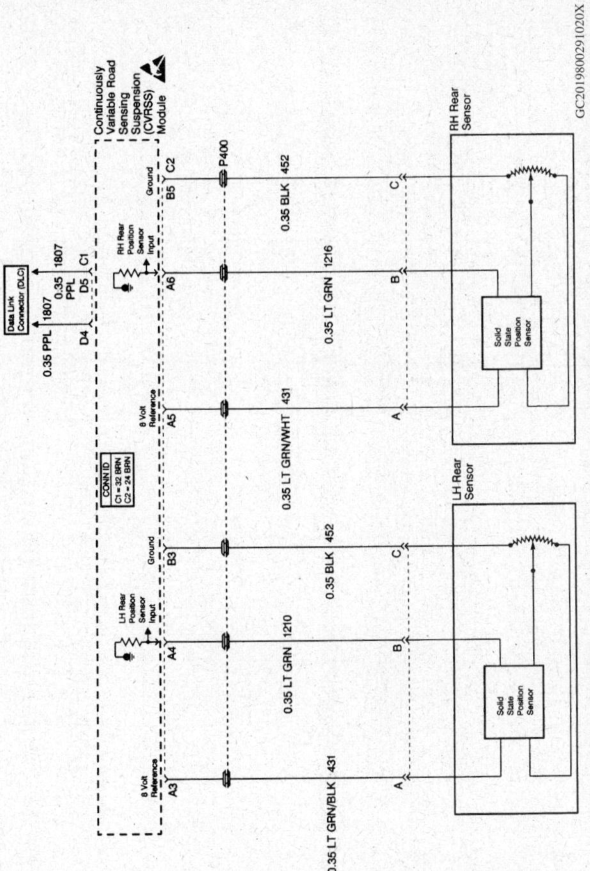

Fig. 4 Wiring diagram (Part 2 of 2). 2000–01 Eldorado w/Road Sensing Suspension

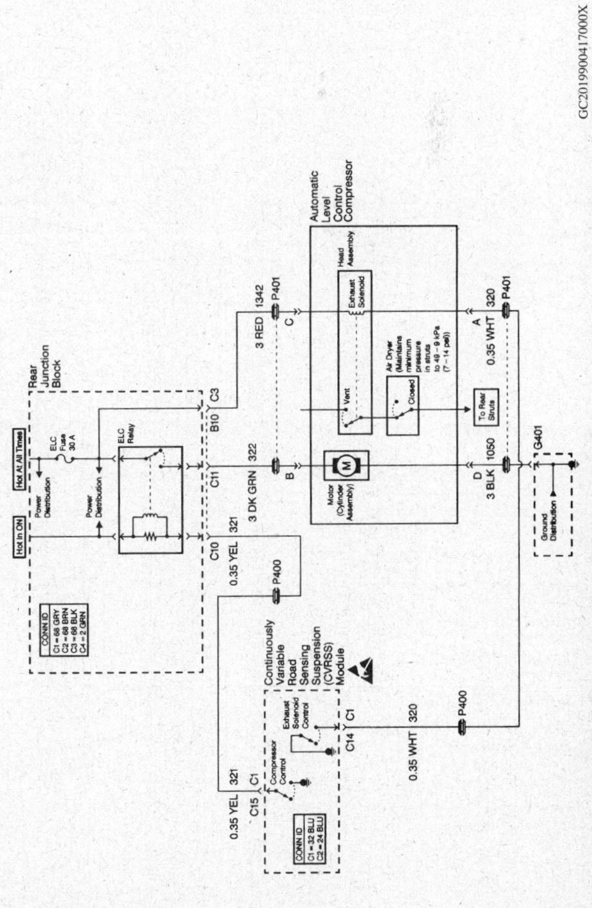

Fig. 5 Wiring diagram. 2000–01 Seville w/Road Sensing Suspension

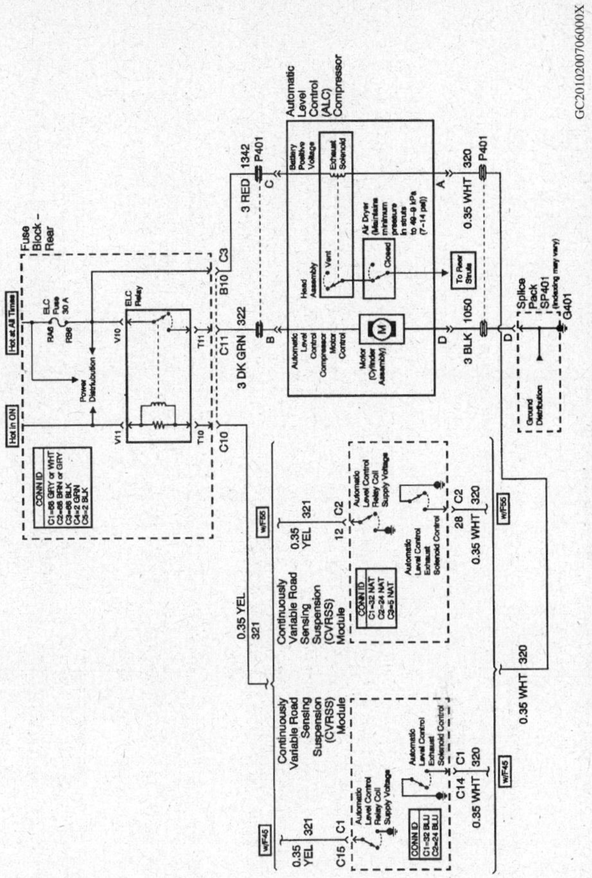

Fig. 6 Wiring diagram. 2002–04 Seville w/Road Sensing Suspension

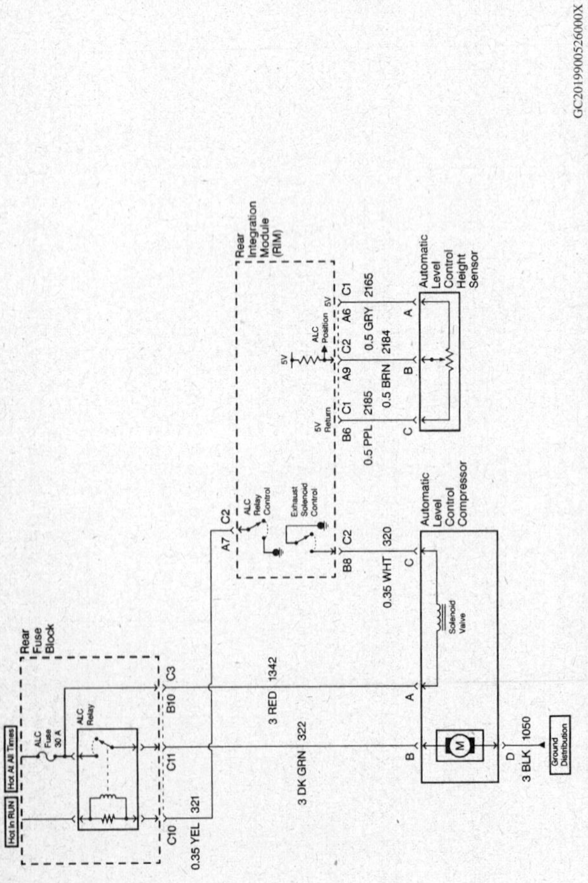

Fig. 7 Wiring diagram. Aurora, Bonneville & LeSabre

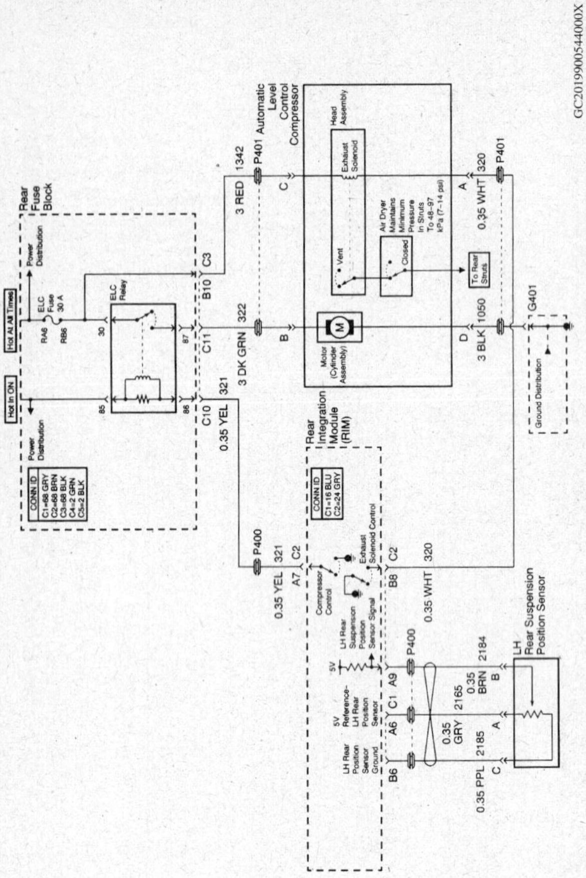

Fig. 8 Wiring diagram. DeVille & 2002 Eldorado Less Road Sensing Suspension

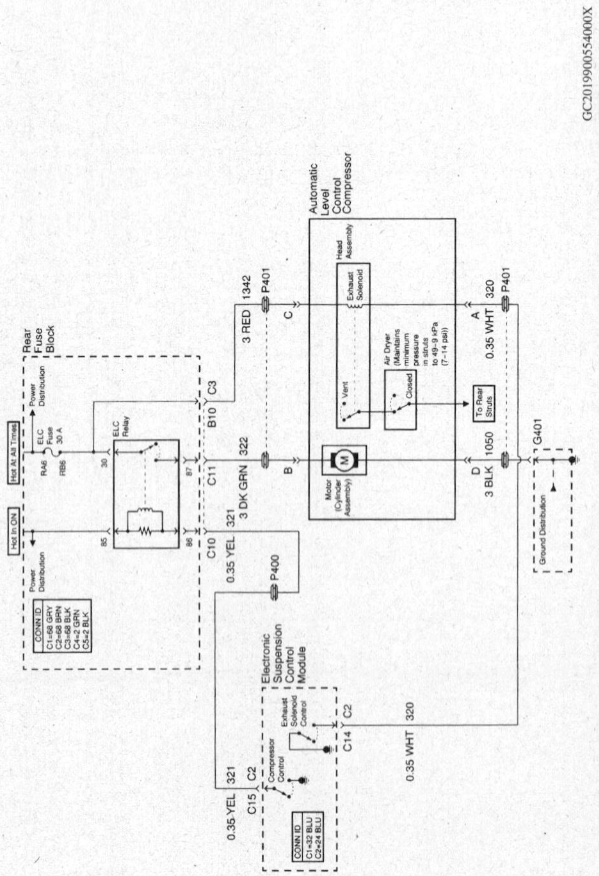

Fig. 9 Wiring diagram. DeVille & 2002 Eldorado w/Road Sensing Suspension

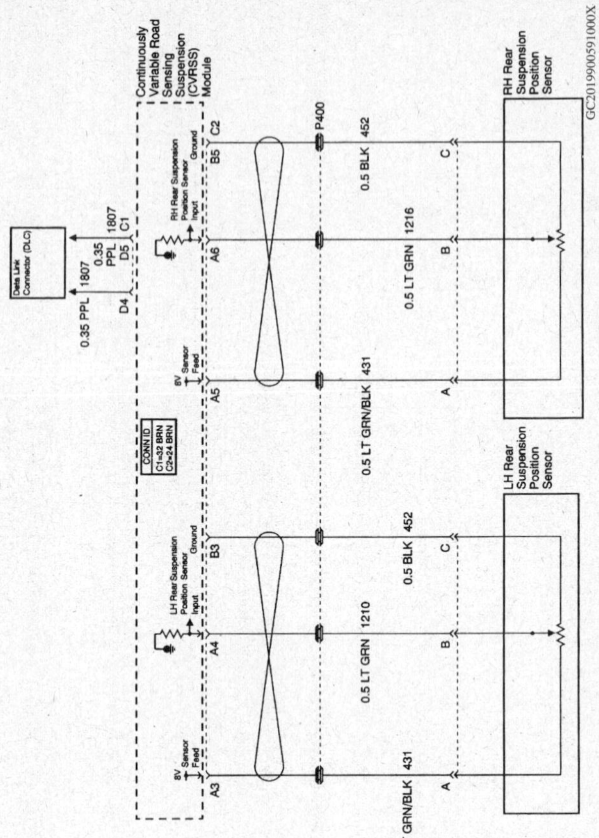

Fig. 10 Wiring diagram (Rear Suspension Sensors). DeVille & 2002 Eldorado

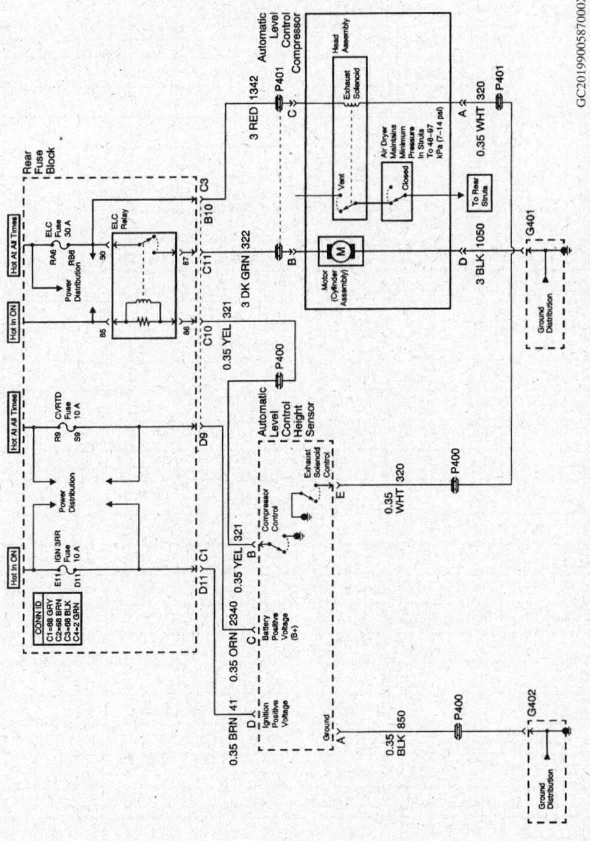

GC2019900587000X

Fig. 11 Wiring diagram. Seville Less Road Sensing Suspension

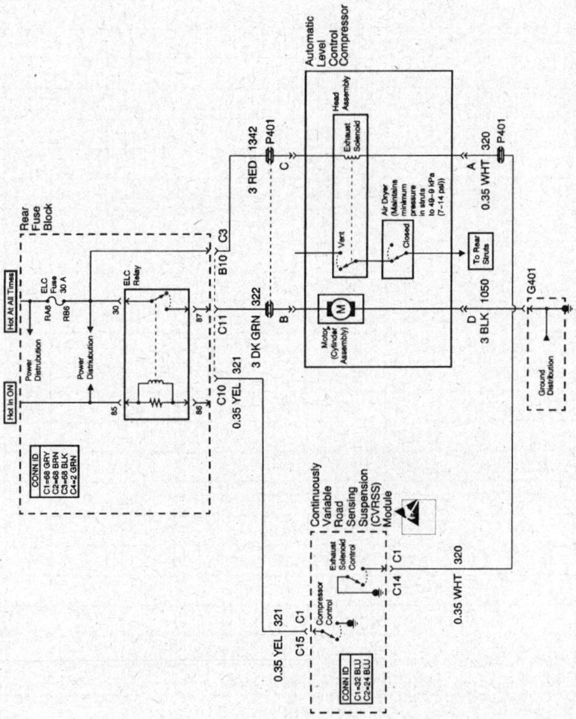

GC2019900588000X

Fig. 12 Wiring diagram. Seville w/Road Sensing Suspension

DIAGNOSTIC CHART INDEX

Code/Test	Description	Page No.	Fig. No.
AURORA			
—	System Check	8-10	13
C0625	Level Control Suspension Sensor Fault	8-10	14
C0628	Level Control Position Sensor Circuit High	8-10	15
C0660	Level Control Exhaust Valve Circuit Fault	8-11	16
C0663	Level Control Exhaust Valve Circuit High	8-11	17
C0697	Level Control Accy Inflator Switch Fault	8-11	18
1	Rear Of Vehicle High	8-11	19
2	Rear Of Vehicle Low	8-12	20
BONNEVILLE & LESABRE			
—	System Check	8-10	13
C0625	Level Control Suspension Sensor Fault	8-10	14
C0628	Level Control Position Sensor Circuit High	8-10	15
C0660	Level Control Exhaust Valve Circuit Fault	8-11	16
C0663	Level Control Exhaust Valve Circuit High	8-11	17
C0697	Level Control Accy Inflator Switch Fault	8-11	18
1	Rear Of Vehicle High	8-11	19
2	Rear Of Vehicle Low	8-12	20
CATERA			
—	ALC Suspension System Check	8-12	21
—	ALC Compressor Inoperative	8-13	22
—	ALC System Operation Check	8-13	23
01	General Sensor Fault	8-14	24
02	Instantaneous Battery Voltage Out Of Range	8-14	25
03	Filtered Battery Voltage Out Of Range	8-14	26
04	Compressor Relay Short To Ground/Open	8-14	27
05	Compressor Relay Short To Battery	8-14	28
06	Exhaust Valve Short To Ground/Open Circuit	8-14	29
07	Exhaust Valve Short To Battery	8-14	30
08	Warning Lamp Short To Ground/Open Circuit	8-15	31
09	Warning Lamp Short To Battery	8-15	32
10	Intake Accumulator Fault	8-15	33
11	Exhaust Accumulator Fault	8-15	34
DEVILLE			
—	System Check	8-15	35
C0625	Level Control Suspension Sensor Fault	8-15	36
C0628	Level Control Position Sensor Circuit High	8-16	37
C0655	Level Control Compressor Relay Fault	8-16	38
C0658	Level Control Compressor Relay Circuit High	8-16	39
C0660	Level Control Exhaust Valve Circuit Fault	8-17	40
C0663	Level Control Exhaust Valve Circuit High	8-17	41
1	Rear Of Vehicle High	8-17	42
2	Rear Of Vehicle Low	8-18	43
2000–01 ELDORADO			
—	ALC System Operation Check (Less Road Sensing Suspension)	8-18	44
—	ALC System Operation Check (With Road Sensing Suspension)	8-18	45
1	ALC System Leak Test	8-18	46
2	Rear Of Vehicle High (Less Road Sensing Suspension)	8-19	47
3	Rear Of Vehicle High (With Road Sensing Suspension)	8-20	48
4	Rear Of Vehicle Low (Less Road Sensing Suspension)	8-20	49
5	Rear Of Vehicle Low (With Road Sensing Suspension)	8-21	50
6	Height Sensor Operational Check	8-21	51
2002 ELDORADO			
—	ALC System Check	8-22	52
1	ALC Air Compressor Performance Test	8-24	55
2	ALC System Leak Test	8-24	56

Continued

DIAGNOSTIC CHART INDEX—Continued

Step	Action	Yes	No
1	Install a scan tool. Does the scan tool power up?	Go to Step 2	Inspect Data Link Communications
2	1. Turn ON the ignition, with the engine OFF. 2. Attempt to establish communication with the Rear Integrated Module (RIM). Does the scan tool communicate with the RIM?	Go to Step 3	Inspect Data Link Communications
3	Check for DTCs. Does the scan tool display any DTCs?	Diagnose & repair as necessary	Go to Symptoms - Automatic Level Control

GC2010000718000X

Fig. 13 System Check. Aurora, Bonneville & LeSabre

Step	Action	Value(s)	Yes	No
7	Test the signal circuit of the suspension position sensor for a short to ground, high resistance, or an open. Did you find and correct the condition?	—	Go to Step 13	Go to Step 10
8	Test the ground circuit of the suspension position sensor for a high resistance, or an open. Did you find and correct the condition?	—	Go to Step 13	Go to Step 10
9	Inspect for poor connections at the harness connector of the suspension position sensor. Did you find and correct the condition?	—	Go to Step 13	Go to Step 11
10	Inspect for poor connections at the harness connector of the RIM. Did you find and correct the condition?	—	Go to Step 13	Go to Step 12
11	Replace the suspension position sensor. Did you complete the replacement?	—	Go to Step 13	—
12	Replace the RIM.	—	Go to Step 13	—
13	1. Clear the DTCs using the scan tool. 2. Operate the vehicle within the Conditions for Running the DTC as specified in the supporting text. Does the DTC reset?	—	Go to Step 2	—

GC2019900537020X

Fig. 14 Code C0625: Level Control Suspension Sensor Fault (Part 2 of 2). Aurora, Bonneville & LeSabre

Step	Action	Value(s)	Yes	No
1	Did you perform A Diagnostic System Check - Automatic Level Control?	—	Go to Step 2	Go to Automatic Level Control Diagnostic System Check
2	1. Install a scan tool. 2. Turn ON the ignition leaving the engine OFF. 3. With a scan tool, observe the Suspension Position Sensor parameter in the Body Control Module data list using the scan tool. Does the scan tool indicate the voltage is within the specified range?	0.25—4.75 V	Go to Diagnostic Aids	Go to Step 3
3	1. Turn OFF the ignition. 2. Disconnect the suspension position sensor. 3. Turn ON the ignition leaving the engine OFF. 4. With a scan tool, observe the suspension position sensor voltage parameter. Does the scan tool indicate that the voltage parameter is greater than the specified value?	0 V	Go to Step 4	Go to Step 10
4	Measure the voltage of the suspension position sensor signal circuit to ground. Does the scan tool indicate that the voltage parameter is greater than the specified value?	5 V	Go to Step 6	Go to Step 5
5	Measure the voltage of the suspension position sensor reference circuit to ground. Does the scan tool indicate that the parameter is greater than the specified value?	5 V	Go to Step 7	Go to Step 8
6	Test the 5–volt signal circuit of the suspension position sensor for a short to voltage. Did you find and correct the condition?	—	Go to Step 14	Go to Step 11
7	Test the 5–volt reference circuit of the suspension position sensor for a short to voltage. Did you find and correct the condition?	—	Go to Step 14	Go to Step 11
8	Measure the resistance of the suspension position sensor ground circuit to ground. Is the resistance greater than the specified value?	5 Ω	Go to Step 9	Go to Step 10

GC2019900538010X

Fig. 15 Code C0628: Level Control Position Sensor Circuit High (Part 1 of 2). Aurora, Bonneville & LeSabre

Step	Action	Value(s)	Yes	No
1	Did you perform A Diagnostic System Check - Automatic Level Control?	—	Go to Step 2	Go to Automatic Level Control Diagnostic System Check
2	1. Install a scan tool. 2. Turn ON the ignition leaving the engine OFF. 3. Observe the Suspension Sensor data parameter in the Body Control Module data list using the scan tool. Does the scan tool indicate the voltage is within the specified range?	0.5–4.5 V	Go to Diagnostic Aids	Go to Step 3
3	1. Turn OFF the ignition. 2. Disconnect the suspension position sensor. 3. Turn ON the ignition leaving the engine OFF. 4. Measure the voltage from the suspension position sensor 5 volt reference circuit to a good ground. Does the voltage measure near the specified value?	5 V	Go to Step 4	Go to Step 6
4	1. Turn OFF the ignition. 2. Connect a 3–amp fused jumper wire between the 5 volt reference circuit of the suspension position sensor and the signal circuit of the suspension position sensor. 3. Turn ON the ignition, with the engine OFF. 4. With a scan tool, observe the suspension position sensor parameter. Does the scan tool indicate that the suspension position sensor voltage is greater than the specified value?	4.75 V	Go to Step 5	Go to Step 7
5	1. Disconnect the fused jumper wire. 2. Measure the voltage between the 5–volt reference circuit of the suspension position sensor and the ground circuit of the suspension position sensor. Does the voltage measure less than the specified value?	4.75 V	Go to Step 8	Go to Step 9
6	Test the 5–volt reference circuit of the suspension position sensor for a short to ground or an open. Did you find and correct the condition?	—	Go to Step 13	Go to Step 10

GC2019900537010X

Fig. 14 Code C0625: Level Control Suspension Sensor Fault (Part 1 of 2). Aurora, Bonneville & LeSabre

Step	Action	Value(s)	Yes	No
9	Repair the open circuit or short to voltage on the suspension position sensor ground circuit. Did you find and correct the condition?	—	Go to Step 14	—
10	Inspect for poor connections at the harness connector of the suspension position sensor. Did you find and correct the condition?	—	Go to Step 14	Go to Step 12
11	Inspect for poor connections at the harness connector of the RIM. Did you find and correct the condition?	—	Go to Step 14	Go to Step 13
12	Replace the suspension position sensor. **Important:** Perform the ALC relearn procedure. Did you complete the replacement?	—	Go to Step 14	—
13	Replace the RIM. **Important:** Perform the ALC relearn procedure. Did you complete the replacement?	—	Go to Step 14	—
14	1. Clear the DTCs using the scan tool. 2. Operate the vehicle within the Conditions for Running the DTC as specified in the supporting text. Does the DTC reset?	—	Go to Step 2	System OK

GC2019900538020X

Fig. 15 Code C0628: Level Control Position Sensor Circuit High (Part 2 of 2). Aurora, Bonneville & LeSabre

Step	Action	Value(s)	Yes	No
1	Did you perform A Diagnostic System Check - Automatic Level Control ?	—	Go to Step 2	Go to Automatic Level Control Diagnostic System Check
2	1. Install a scan tool. 2. Turn ON the ignition leaving the engine OFF. 3. With a scan tool, command the ALC exhaust solenoid ON and OFF. Does the exhaust solenoid valve turn ON and OFF with each command?	—	Go to Diagnostic Aids	Go to Step 3
3	1. Turn OFF the ignition. 2. Disconnect the ALC exhaust solenoid valve. 3. Turn ON the ignition, with the engine OFF. 4. Probe the coil side feed circuit of the exhaust solenoid valve harness connector with a test lamp that is connected to a good ground. Does the test lamp illuminate?	—	Go to Step 4	Go to Step 10
4	1. Connect a test lamp between the control circuit of the exhaust solenoid valve harness connector and the coil side feed circuit of the exhaust solenoid harness connector. 2. With a scan tool, command the exhaust solenoid valve ON and OFF. Does the test lamp turn ON and OFF with each command?	—	Go to Step 8	Go to Step 5
5	Does the test lamp remain illuminated with each command?	—	Go to Step 7	Go to Step 6
6	Test the control circuit of the exhaust solenoid valve for a short to voltage or an open. Did you find and correct the condition?	—	Go to Step 13	Go to Step 9
7	Test the control circuit of the exhaust solenoid valve for a short to ground. Did you find and correct the condition?	—	Go to Step 13	Go to Step 9
8	Inspect for poor connections at the exhaust solenoid. Did you find and correct the condition?	—	Go to Step 13	Go to Step 11
9	Inspect for poor connections at the harness connector for the RIM. Did you find and correct the condition?	—	Go to Step 13	Go to Step 12
10	Repair the coil side feed circuit of the exhaust solenoid valve. Did you complete the repair?	—	Go to Step 13	—
11	Replace the compressor head assembly. Did you complete the replacement?	—	Go to Step 13	—
12	Replace the RIM. Did you complete the replacement?	—	Go to Step 13	—
13	1. Use the scan tool in order to clear the DTC's. 2. Operate the vehicle within the Conditions for Running the DTC as specified in the supporting text. Does the DTC reset?	—	Go to Step 2	System OK

GC2019900539000X

Fig. 16 Code C0660: Level Control Exhaust Valve Circuit Fault. Aurora, Bonneville & LeSabre

Step	Action	Value(s)	Yes	No
1	Did you perform A Diagnostic System Check - Automatic Level Control ?	—	Go to Step 2	Go to Automatic Level Control Diagnostic System Check
2	1. Install a scan tool. 2. Turn ON the ignition leaving the engine OFF. 3. Clear all of the DTCs with the scan tool. Does the DTC reappear within 10 seconds?	—	Go to Step 3	Go to Diagnostic aids
3	1. Disconnect the accessory inflator switch. 2. Turn on the ignition leaving the engine OFF. 3. Observe the accessory inflator switch with the scan tool. Does the scan tool indicate idle?	—	Go to Step 6	Go to Step 4
4	Test the automatic level control accessory inflator switch input circut for a short. Did you find and correct the condition?	—	Go to Step 9	Go to Step 5
5	Inspect for poor connections/terminal tension at the rear intergration module (RIM). Did you find and correct the condition?	—	Go to step 9	Go to Step 7
6	Inspect for poor connections/ terminal tension at the automatic level control accessory inflator switch harness. Did you find and correct the condition?	—	Go to Step 9	Go to Step 8
7	Replace the RIM. Did you complete the replacement?	—	Go to Step 10	—
8	Replace the automatic level control accessory inflator switch. Did you complete the replacement?	—	Go to Step 9	—
9	Clear the DTCs using the scan tool. Did you complete the action?	—	Go to Step 10	—
10	Operate the vehicle within the conditions for running the DTCs as specified in the supporting text Does the DTC reset?	—	Go to Step 2	—

GC2019900541000X

Fig. 18 Code C0697: Level Control Accy Inflator Switch Fault. Aurora, Bonneville & LeSabre

Step	Action Connect	Value(s)	Yes	No
1	Did you perform A Diagnostic System Check - Automatic Level Control ?	—	Go to Step 2	Go to Automatic Level Control Diagnostic System Check
2	1. Install a scan tool 2. Turn ON the ignition, with the engine OFF. 3. With a scan tool, command the ALC exhaust solenoid valve ON and OFF. Does the exhaust solenoid valve turn ON and OFF with each command?	—	Go to Diagnostic Aids	Go to Step 3
3	1. Turn OFF the ignition. 2. Disconnect the exhaust solenoid valve harness connector. 3. Turn ON the ignition, with the engine OFF. 4. Connect a test lamp between the control circuit of the exhaust solenoid harness connector and the coil side feed circuit of the exhaust solenoid harness connector. 5. With a scan tool, command the exhaust solenoid ON and OFF. Does the test lamp turn ON and OFF with each command?	—	Go to Step 6	Go to Step 4
4	Does the test lamp remain OFF with each command?	—	Go to Step 5	Go to Step 7
5	Test the exhaust solenoid control circuit for a short to voltage.	—	Go to Step 10	Go to Step 7
6	Inspect for poor connections at the exhaust valve solenoid harness connector. Did you find and correct the condition?	—	Go to Step 10	Go to Step 8
7	Inspect for poor connections at the RIM. Did you find and correct the condition?	—	Go to Step 10	Go to Step 9
8	Replace the compressor head assembly. Did you complete the replacement?	—	Go to Step 10	—
9	Replace the RIM. Did you complete the replacement?	—	Go to Step 10	—
10	1. Use the scan tool in order to clear the DTC's. 2. Operate the vehicle within the Conditions for Running the DTC as specified in the supporting text. Did the DTC reset?	—	Go to Step 2	System OK

GC2019900540000X

Fig. 17 Code C0663: Level Control Exhaust Valve Circuit High. Aurora, Bonneville & LeSabre

Step	Action	Value(s)	Yes	No
DEFINITION: Rear Suspension Height High				
1	Did you perform A Diagnostic System Check - Automatic Level Control?	—	Go to Step 2	Go to Automatic Level Control Diagnostic System Check
2	1. Install a scan tool. 2. Turn ON the ignition, with the engine OFF. 3. With the scan tool, observe the suspension position sensor in the RIM. Does the scan tool indicate that the suspension position sensor is within the specified range?	.25–2.5 V	Go to Step 3	Go to Step 8
3	With the scan tool command the exhaust solenoid open, to vent the system (an audible hiss sound may be heard). Did the ALC system vent and the vehicle lower?	—	Go to Step 4	Go to Step 6
4	Observe the suspension position sensor reading on the scan tool. Did the suspension position sensor reading change?	—	Go to Step 8	Go to Step 5

GC2019900542010X

Fig. 19 Test 1: Rear Of Vehicle High (Part 1 of 2). Aurora, Bonneville & LeSabre

Step	Action	Value(s)	Yes	No
5	**Important:** The vehicle must be raised on a drive on lift. Full vehicle weight must be on the rear tires. Care must be used when disconnecting and retaining the suspension position sensor link. If the link is allowed to travel freely a false DTC may be set. 1. Disconnect the suspension position sensor actuating link. 2. Move the position sensor link up, so that it is approximately 45 degrees above level to the floor and retain it there. 3. With a scan tool, observe the suspension position sensor parameter. Did the suspension position sensor reading change?	—	Go to *Step 8*	Go to *Step 9*
6	**Important:** The vehicle must be raised on a drive on lift. Full vehicle weight must be on the rear tires. 1. Raise and support the vehicle. 2. Disconnect the air tube assembly from the drier. Did the ALC system vent and the vehicle lower?	—	Go to *Step 10*	Go to *Step 7*
7	Disconnect the air tube assembly from the shocks. Did the system vent and the vehicle lower?	—	Go to *Step 11*	Go to *Step 12*
8	Perform the ALC relearn procedure. Did you complete the procedure?	—	Go to *Step 15*	—
9	Inspect for poor connections/ terminal tension at the harness connector of the suspension position sensor. Did you find and correct the condition?	—	Go to *Step 15*	Go to *Step 13*
10	Inspect for poor connections/ terminal tension at the harness connector of the Automatic Level Control Compressor Assembly. Did you find and correct the condition?	—	Go to *Step 15*	Go to *Step 14*
11	Replace the air tube assembly. Did you complete the replacement?	—	Go to *Step 15*	—
12	Replace the shock that did not lower. Did you complete the replacement?	—	Go to *Step 15*	—
13	Replace the suspension position sensor. Did you complete the replacement?	—	Go to *Step 15*	—
14	Replace the automatic level control compressor head assembly. Did you complete the replacement?	—	Go to *Step 15*	—
15	Operate the vehicle within the conditions for enabling the automatic level control. Does the ALC operate correctly?	—	System OK	Go to *Step 2*

GC2019900542020X

Fig. 19 Test 1: Rear Of Vehicle High (Part 2 of 2). Aurora, Bonneville & LeSabre

Step	Action	Value(s)	Yes	No
12	Inspect for poor connections at the ALC compressor assembly. Did you find and correct the condition?	—	Go to *Step 19*	Go to *Step 17*
13	Inspect for poor connections at the harness connector of the rear integration module (RIM). Did you find and correct the condition?	—	Go to *Step 19*	Go to *Step 18*
14	Repair the high resistance/ open ALC compressor ground circuit. Did you complete the repair?	—	Go to *Step 19*	—
15	Repair the coil side feed circuit of the ALC relay. Did you complete the repair?	—	Go to *Step 19*	—
16	Replace the ALC relay. Did you complete the replacement?	—	Go to *Step 19*	—
17	Replace the ALC compressor assembly. Did you complete the replacement?	—	Go to *Step 19*	—
18	Replace the RIM. Did you complete the replacement?	—	Go to *Step 19*	—
19	Operate the system to verify the repair. Does the system operate normally?	—	System OK	Go to *Step 2*

GC2019900543020X

Fig. 20 Test 2: Rear Of Vehicle Low (Part 2 of 2). Aurora, Bonneville & LeSabre

Step	Action	Value(s)	Yes	No
1	Did you perform A Diagnostic System Check - Automatic Level Control?	—	Go to *Step 2*	Go to *Automatic Level Control Diagnostic System Check*
2	1. Install a scan tool. 2. Turn ON the ignition, with the engine OFF. 3. With a scan tool, command the ALC relay ON and OFF. Does the ALC relay turn ON and OFF with each command?	—	Go to *Step 8*	Go to *Step 3*
3	1. Turn OFF the ignition. 2. Disconnect the ALC relay. 3. Turn ON the ignition, with the engine OFF. 4. Probe the coil side feed circuit of the ALC relay with a test lamp that is connected to a good ground. Does the test lamp illuminate?	—	Go to *Step 4*	Go to *Step 15*
4	1. Connect a test lamp between the control circuit of the ALC relay and the coil side feed circuit of the ALC relay. 2. With a scan tool, command the ALC relay ON and OFF. Does the test lamp turn ON and OFF with each command?	—	Go to *Step 11*	Go to *Step 5*
5	Does the test lamp remain illuminated with each command?	—	Go to *Step 7*	Go to *Step 6*
6	Test the control circuit of the ALC relay for a short to voltage or an open. Did you find and correct the condition?	—	Go to *Step 19*	Go to *Step 13*
7	Test the control circuit of the ALC for a short to ground. Did you find and correct the condition?	—	Go to *Step 19*	Go to *Step 13*
8	1. Turn OFF the ignition. 2. Disconnect the ALC compressor motor. 3. Turn ON the ignition, with the engine OFF. 4. Probe the ALC compressor motor battery positive feed circuit with a test lamp connected to a good ground. 5. With a scan tool, command the ALC relay ON. Did the test lamp illuminate?	—	Go to *Step 9*	Go to *Step 13*
9	1. Turn OFF the ignition. 2. Disconnect the negitive battery cable. 3. Measure the resistance of the ALC compressor ground circuit to a good ground. Is the resistance lower than the specified value?	5 Ω	Go to *Step 12*	Go to *Step 14*
10	Test the ALC compressor motor battery positive feed circuit for an open. Did you find and correct the condition?	—	Go to *Step 19*	Go to *Step 11*
11	Inspect for poor connections at the ALC relay. Did you find and correct the condition?	—	Go to *Step 19*	Go to *Step 16*

GC2019900543010X

Fig. 20 Test 2: Rear Of Vehicle Low (Part 1 of 2). Aurora, Bonneville & LeSabre

Step	Action	Value(s)	Yes	No
1	1. Check vehicle trim height. 2. Reset the automatic level control (ALC) system by cycling the ignition. 3. Place a 136 kg (300 lb) weight in the rear compartment. 4. Turn the ignition switch to the ON position. 5. Check the operation of the rear suspension leveling air compressor. Does the compressor activate after 25 seconds?	—	*Go to Step 2*	*Go to Step 9*
2	Did the compressor remain active longer than 3 minutes?	—	*Go to Step 3*	*Go to Step 4*
3	Go to the *ALC System Operation Check* for diagnosis. Is the repair procedure complete?	—	System OK	—
4	Did the rear of the vehicle return to the original trim height?	—	*Go to Step 6*	*Go to Step 5*
5	Go to *Height Sensor Operational Check* for diagnosis. Is the repair procedure complete?	—	System OK	—
6	1. Remove the 136 kg (300 lb) weight from the rear compartment. 2. Check the operation of the exhaust solenoid valve. Does the valve activate after 25 seconds?	—	*Go to Step 7*	*Go to Step 9*
7	Check the vehicle trim height after 5 minutes. Did the rear of the vehicle return to the original trim height?	—	*Go to Step 9*	*Go to Step 8*
8	Go to *ALC Compressor Inoperative - No DTC Set* for diagnosis. Is the repair procedure complete?	—	System OK	—

GC2019800301010X

Fig. 21 ALC Suspension System Check (Part 1 of 2). Catera

Step	Action	Value(s)	Yes	No
9	1. Turn the ignition switch to the OFF position. 2. Install the scan tool. 3. Establish communication with the Automatic Level Control (ALC) Sensor. Does the scan tool communicate with the ALC Sensor?	—	*Go to Step 11*	*Go to Step 10*
10	Go to *Scan Tool Does Not Communicate with ALC Sensor* for diagnosis. Is the repair procedure complete?	—	System OK	—
11	Are any current DTCs displayed?	—	*Go to Step 12*	*Go to Step 13*
12	Go to the *DTC List* for the applicable DTC for diagnosis. Is the repair procedure complete?	—	System OK	—
13	Are any history or intermittent DTCs displayed?	—	*Go to Step 14*	System OK
14	1. There is an intermittent problem within the system. 2. Go to the Diagnostic Aids relating to the DTC for diagnosis. Is the repair procedure complete?	—	System OK	—

GC2019800301020X

Fig. 21 ALC Suspension System Check (Part 2 of 2). Catera

Step	Action	Value(s)	Yes	No
7	Replace the rear suspension leveling air compressor relay K19. Is the replacement complete?	—	*Go to Step 11*	—
8	Connect a test lamp between terminal B and terminal D of the rear suspension leveling air compressor connector. Does the test lamp light?	—	*Go to Step 10*	*Go to Step 9*
9	Locate and repair an open or high resistance in circuit F214. Is the repair complete?	—	*Go to Step 11*	—
10	Repair or replace the rear suspension leveling air compressor. Is the repair or replacement complete?	—	*Go to Step 11*	—
11	1. Connect all of the connectors that were disconnected. 2. Check the ALC system operation. Does the ALC system operate properly?	—	System OK	*Go to Step 1*

GC2019800302020X

Fig. 22 ALC Compressor Inoperative (Part 2 of 2). Catera

Step	Action	Value(s)	Yes	No
6	1. Shut off the compressor when the pressure reaches 80 psi. 2. Monitor the gauge for one minute. Did the pressure leak down?	—	*Go to Step 10*	*Go to Step 7*
7	1. Connect the *Pressure Gauge* to the right rear shock absorber. Ensure the toggle valve on the *Pressure Gauge* is away from the shock absorber. 2. Close the toggle valve. 3. Pressurize the shock absorber at the toggle valve on the *Pressure Gauge* to 80 psi. 4. Monitor the gauge for one minute. Did the system leak down?	—	*Go to Step 11*	*Go to Step 8*
8	1. Use the toggle valve on the *Pressure Gauge* to slowly release the air pressure. 2. Disconnect the *Pressure Gauge* from the right rear shock absorber. 3. Connect the *Pressure Gauge* to the left rear shock absorber. 4. Pressurize the *Pressure Gauge* to 80 psi. 5. Monitor the gauge for one minute. Did the pressure leak down?	—	*Go to Step 12*	*Go to Step 9*
9	1. Use the toggle valve on the *Pressure Gauge* to slowly release the air pressure. 2. Disconnect the *Pressure Gauge* from the left rear shock absorber. 3. Connect the *Pressure Gauge*, inline, at the tee near the rear of the vehicle. 4. Reconnect the air tube to the ALC dryer. 5. Open the toggle valve on the *Pressure Gauge*. 6. Use shop air to pressurize the system to 80 psi at the service connection of the *Pressure Gauge* 7. Monitor the pressure gauge for one minute. Did the pressure leak down?	—	*Go to Step 14*	*Go to Step 20*
10	Replace the following components: • Replace the ALC compressor. • Replace the air tube. Are the replacements complete?	—	*Go to Step 20*	—
11	1. Slowly open the toggle valve on the *Pressure Gauge* to relieve the air pressure. 2. Replace the right rear shock absorber. 3. Reconnect all the air tube connections. Is the shock absorber replaced and are all the air tube connections reconnected?	—	*Go to Step 20*	—

GC2019800311020X

Fig. 23 ALC System Operation Check (Part 2 of 3). Catera

Step	Action	Value(s)	Yes	No
1	Was the Automatic Level Control (ALC) System Check performed?	—	*Go to Step 2*	*Go to ALC Suspension System Check.*
2	1. Remove the rear suspension leveling air compressor relay K19 form the relay box. 2. Turn the ignition switch to the ON position. 3. Use the DMM to measure the voltage between terminal 5 of the relay box and a good ground. Is the measured voltage within the specified value?	B+	*Go to Step 4*	*Go to Step 3*
3	Locate and repair an open or high resistance in circuit A44. Is the repair complete?	—	*Go to Step 4*	—
4	Connect a fused jumper wire between terminal 5 and terminal 4 of the relay box. Does the rear suspension leveling air compressor activate?	—	*Go to Step 7*	*Go to Step 5*
5	1. Disconnect the rear suspension leveling air compressor connector. 2. Use the DMM to measure the voltage between terminal B of the rear suspension leveling air compressor connector and a good ground. Is the measured voltage within the specified value?	B+	*Go to Step 7*	*Go to Step 6*
6	Locate and repair an open or high resistance in circuits X43 and/or X101. Is the repair complete?	—	*Go to Step 8*	—

GC2019800302010X

Fig. 22 ALC Compressor Inoperative (Part 1 of 2). Catera

Step	Action	Value(s)	Yes	No
1	Has the ALC compressor assembly and the air tube been replaced?	—	*Go to Step 7*	*Go to Step 2*
2	1. Raise and support the vehicle. 2. Inspect the air tubes running from the ALC compressor to both rear shock absorbers. 3. Inspect the air tube connection at the ALC air dryer. Are the air tubes damaged and/or disconnected?	—	*Go to Step 13*	*Go to Step 3*
3	Squeeze the left rear shock absorber in the middle of the air sleeve. Did the air sleeve slightly compress?	—	*Go to Step 5*	*Go to Step 4*
4	1. Operate the ALC system for 60 seconds. 2. Use a soap bubble solution to test the air tube-to-air dryer connection for leaks. Is a leak evident?	—	*Go to Step 20*	*Go to Step 5*
5	1. Disconnect the air tube from the ALC dryer. 2. Connect the *Pressure Gauge* to the ALC dryer. 3. Close the toggle valve on the *Pressure Gauge*. 4. Operate the ALC compressor. Did the pressure build to the specified value?	80 psi	*Go to Step 6*	*Go to Step 10*

GC2019800311010X

Fig. 23 ALC System Operation Check (Part 1 of 3). Catera

Step	Action	Value(s)	Yes	No
12	1. Slowly open the toggle valve on the *Pressure Gauge* to relieve the air pressure. 2. Replace the left rear shock absorber. 3. Reconnect all the air tube connections. Is the shock absorber replaced and are all the air tube connections reconnected?	—	*Go to Step 20*	—
13	Are any of the air tubes damaged?	—	*Go to Step 14*	*Go to Step 18*
14	Replace the air tube that runs from the air dryer to the two rear shock absorbers. Is the replacement complete?	—	*Go to Step 15*	—
15	1. Remove the ALC air dryer from the compressor assembly. 2. Shake the ALC air dryer with the head connection down. Did water/moisture come out of the ALC air dryer when it was shaken?	—	*Go to Step 16*	*Go to Step 17*
16	Replace the ALC air dryer. Is the replacement complete?	—	*Go to Step 17*	—
17	Replace the compressor head. Is the replacement complete?	—	*Go to Step 18*	—
18	1. Install the ALC compressor on the vehicle. 2. Reconnect all the air tube connections. Is the ALC compressor reinstalled and are all the air tube connections reconnected?	—	*Go to Step 20*	—
19	Repair the air tube-to-air dryer connection leak. Is the repair complete?	—	*Go to Step 20*	—
20	1. Reconnect all the connectors previously removed. 2. Reconnect all the components previously removed. 3. Clear all the codes with the ignition ON and with the engine OFF. 4. Wait for at least 5 minutes. Is the rear of the vehicle trim level?	—	System OK	—

GC2019800311030X

Fig. 23 ALC System Operation Check (Part 3 of 3). Catera

Conditions for Setting the DTC

This DTC is set when the automatic level control sensor detects an internal hardware or software error. Examples of these errors are listed below.

- Position data out of range
- History code block error
- Trim-set block error
- Calibration block error
- A/D conversion error
- Ram integrity error
- Read/Write to EEPROM error

Action Taken When the DTC Sets

The LEVELING indicator lamp will flash while this DTC is present. The function of the ALC system may be degraded or disabled, depending upon which error has been detected.

Conditions for Clearing the DTC

The position data out of range and the A/D conversion error are checked continuously and can be recovered from during the same ignition cycle. All other errors are checked during the start up self test at each ignition cycle. The DTC will clear when no error is detected and the cause for the error has been repaired.

Diagnostic Aids

- Cycle the ignition.
- Use the scan tool to re-check for DTC 01.
- If DTC 01 is still present, replace the automatic level control sensor.

GC2019800326000X

Fig. 24 Code 01: General Sensor Fault. Catera

Conditions for Setting the DTC

This code is set when the vehicle's battery voltage momentarily goes above 16.0 V.

Action Taken When the DTC Sets

The detection of leveling output, and the position out-of-range malfunctions are disabled. This is necessary to prevent erroneous detection of malfunction conditions due to engine crank or unusual system voltage conditions.

Conditions for Clearing the DTC

- The DTC will clear when battery voltage returns to its nominal range.
- Using a scan tool.

Diagnostic Aids

- The battery system should be checked for proper functionality.
- This code does not require the replacing of the Automatic Level Control (ALC) sensor.
- This code will not cause the LEVELING indicator lamp to flash.
- Make sure that the automatic leveling control sensor is receiving the correct voltage.
- Make sure that the ALC sensor has a good ground.

GC2019800327000X

Fig. 25 Code 02: Instantaneous Battery Voltage Out Of Range. Catera

Conditions for Setting the DTC

This code sets when the vehicle's battery voltage is continuously above 16.5 V or below 9.0 V.

Action Taken When the DTC Sets

During this period of voltage out-of-range, the detection of leveling output and position out-of-range malfunction, the air replacement cycle (ARC), intake and exhaust activities are disabled. This is necessary to prevent erroneous detection of malfunction conditions due to engine crank or unusual system voltage conditions.

Conditions for Clearing the DTC

- The DTC will clear when the battery voltage returns to its nominal range.
- Using a scan tool.

Diagnostic Aids

- The battery system should be checked for proper functionality.
- This code does not require the replacing of the automatic level control sensor.
- This code will not cause the LEVELING indicator lamp to flash.
- Make sure that the automatic leveling control sensor is receiving the correct voltage.
- Make sure that the automatic leveling control sensor has a good ground.

GC2019800328000X

Fig. 26 Code 03: Filtered Battery Voltage Out Of Range. Catera

Step	Action	Value(s)	Yes	No
1	Did you perform the Automatic Level Control (ALC) Diagnostic System Check?	—	*Go to Step 2*	Go to *Automatic Level Control Diagnostic System Check*
2	1. Disconnect the auto level control relay K19 from the relay box. 2. Turn ON the ignition, with the engine OFF. 3. Measure the voltage between the ignition 1 voltage circuit of the auto level control relay K19 and ground. Is the measured voltage within the specified value?	B+	*Go to Step 4*	*Go to Step 3*
3	Repair the open, high resistance or short to ground in the ignition 1 voltage circuit of the auto level control relay K19. Is the repair complete?	—	*Go to Step 9*	—
4	1. Turn OFF the ignition. 2. Disconnect the automatic level control (ALC) sensor. 3. Connect a fused jumper wire between the ignition 1 voltage circuit of the auto level control relay K19 and the control circuit of the auto level control relay K19 at the relay box. 4. Turn ON the ignition, with the engine OFF. 5. Measure the voltage between the control circuit of the auto level control relay K19 at the sensor and ground. Is the measured voltage near the specified value?	12 V	*Go to Step 6*	*Go to Step 5*
5	Repair the open, high resistance, or short to ground in the control circuit of the auto level control relay K19. Is the repair complete?	—	*Go to Step 9*	—
6	Measure the resistance between the ignition 1 voltage circuit of the auto level control relay K19 and the control circuit of the auto level control relay K19 at the relay box. Is the measured resistance within the specified value?	80 Ω-85 Ω	*Go to Step 8*	*Go to Step 7*
7	Replace the auto level control relay K19. Is the repair complete?	—	*Go to Step 9*	—
8	Replace the ALC sensor. Is the repair complete?	—	*Go to Step 9*	—
9	Operate the system in order to verify the repair. Did you correct the condition?	—	System OK	*Go to Step 2*

GC2010100638000X

Fig. 27 Code 04: Compressor Relay Short To Ground/Open. Catera

Step	Action	Value(s)	Yes	No
1	Did you perform the Automatic Level Control (ALC) Diagnostic System Check?	—	*Go to Step 2*	Go to *Automatic Level Control Diagnostic System Check*
2	1. Disconnect the auto level control relay K19 from the relay box. 2. Turn ON the ignition, with the engine OFF. 3. Measure the voltage between the low control circuit of the auto level control relay K19 and ground. Is the voltage near the specified range?	12 V	*Go to Step 3*	*Go to Step 4*
3	Repair a short to B+ in the low control circuit of the auto level control relay K19. Is the repair complete?	—	*Go to Step 5*	—
4	Replace the ALC sensor. Is the repair complete?	—	*Go to Step 5*	—
5	Operate the system in order to verify the repair. Did you correct the condition?	—	System OK	*Go to Step 2*

GC2010100639000X

Fig. 28 Code 05: Compressor Relay Short To Battery. Catera

Step	Action	Value(s)	Yes	No
1	Did you perform the Automatic Level Control (ALC) Diagnostic System Check?	—	*Go to Step 2*	Go to *Automatic Level Control Diagnostic System Check*
2	1. Disconnect the auto level control air compressor connector. 2. Measure the voltage between the auto level control air compressor connector terminal C and ground. Is the voltage near the specified value?	12 V	*Go to Step 4*	*Go to Step 3*
3	Repair an open, high resistance or a short to ground in the battery positive voltage circuit of the auto level control air compressor. Is the repair complete?	—	*Go to Step 10*	—
4	1. Disconnect the ALC sensor connector. 2. Connect a fused jumper between the disconnected auto level control air compressor connector terminals C and A. 3. Measure the voltage between the ALC sensor connector terminal D and ground. Is the voltage near the specified value?	12 V	*Go to Step 6*	*Go to Step 5*
5	Repair an open, high resistance or a short to ground in the compressor exhaust control circuit. Is the repair complete?	—	*Go to Step 10*	—
6	Measure the resistance between terminals C and A of the auto level control air compressor. Is the resistance reading within the specified value?	25 Ω–35 Ω	*Go to Step 7*	*Go to Step 8*
7	1. Connect all of the connectors that were disconnected. 2. Install a scan tool. 3. Turn ON the ignition, with the engine OFF. 4. Use the scan tool in order to clear DTCs. 5. Wait at least 5 minutes. Does the LEVELING indicator lamp flash?	—	*Go to Step 9*	*Go to Step 10*
8	Replace the complete air compressor head. Did you complete the replacement?	—	*Go to Step 10*	—
9	Replace the ALC sensor. Is the repair complete?	—	*Go to Step 10*	—
10	Operate the system in order to verify the repair. Did you correct the condition?	—	System OK	*Go to Step 2*

GC2010100640000X

Fig. 29 Code 06: Exhaust Valve Short To Ground/ Open Circuit. Catera

Step	Action	Value(s)	Yes	No
1	Did you perform the Automatic Level Control (ALC) Diagnostic System Check?	—	*Go to Step 2*	Go to *Automatic Level Control Diagnostic System Check*
2	1. Disconnect the auto level control air compressor connector. 2. Measure the voltage between the harness side of the air compressor connector terminal A and ground. Does the voltage measure greater than the specified value?	0.1 V	*Go to Step 3*	*Go to Step 4*
3	Repair a short to voltage in the control circuit of the exhaust solenoid valve. Is the repair complete?	—	*Go to Step 8*	—
4	Measure the resistance between terminals C and A of the auto level control air compressor at the air compressor. Is the resistance reading within the specified value?	25 Ω–35 Ω	*Go to Step 5*	*Go to Step 7*
5	1. Connect all of the connectors that were disconnected. 2. Install a scan tool. 3. Turn ON the ignition, with the engine OFF. 4. Use the scan tool in order to clear DTCs. 5. Wait at least 5 minutes. Is the LEVELING indicator lamp flashing?	—	*Go to Step 6*	*Go to Step 8*
6	Replace the ALC sensor. Is the repair complete?	—	*Go to Step 8*	—
7	Replace the air compressor head. Did you complete the replacement?	—	*Go to Step 8*	—
8	Operate the system in order to verify the repair. Did you correct the condition?	—	System OK	*Go to Step 2*

GC2010100641000X

Fig. 30 Code 07: Exhaust Valve Short To Battery. Catera

Step	Action	Value(s)	Yes	No
1	Did you perform the Automatic Level Control (ALC) Diagnostic System Check?	—	*Go to Step 2*	Go to *Automatic Level Control Diagnostic System Check*
2	1. Disconnect the ALC sensor connector. 2. Turn ON the ignition, with the engine OFF. Is the LEVELING indicator lamp illuminated?	—	*Go to Step 3*	*Go to Step 4*
3	Repair a short to ground in the control circuit of the LEVELING indicator lamp. Is the repair complete?	—	*Go to Step 7*	—
4	Connect a fused jumper wire between the ALC sensor connector terminal G and ground. Is the LEVELING indicator lamp illuminated?	—	*Go to Step 6*	*Go to Step 5*
5	Repair an open in the control circuit of the LEVELING indicator lamp. Is the repair complete?	—	*Go to Step 7*	—
6	Replace the ALC sensor. Is the repair complete?	—	*Go to Step 7*	—
7	Operate the system in order to verify the repair. Did you correct the condition?	—	System OK	*Go to Step 2*

GC2010100642000X

Fig. 31 Code 08: Warning Lamp Short To Ground/ Open Circuit. Catera

Step	Action	Value(s)	Yes	No
1	Was the system leak test performed?	—	*Go to Step 2*	Go to *ALC Suspension System Check.*
2	Disconnect the rear suspension leveling air compressor relay K19 from the relay box. Is the rear suspension leveling air compressor still active?	—	*Go to Step 4*	*Go to Step 3*
3	Replace the rear suspension leveling air compressor relay K19. Is the replacement complete?	—	*Go to Step 4*	—
4	1. Turn the ignition switch to the OFF position. 2. Connect all of the connectors that were disconnected. 3. Reinstall all of the components that were removed. 4. Turn the ignition switch to the ON position. 5. Wait for at least 15 seconds. Does the LEVELING indicator lamp flash?	—	*Go to Step 1*	System OK

GC2019800309000X

Fig. 33 Code 10: Intake Accumulator Fault. Catera

Step	Action	Yes	No
1	Install a scan tool. Does the scan tool power up?	Go to *Step 2*	Go to *Scan Tool Does Not Power Up*
2	1. Turn ON the ignition, with the engine OFF. 2. Attempt to establish communication with the Rear Integrated Module (RIM). Does the scan tool communicate with the RIM?	Go to *Step 3*	Go to *Scan Tool Does Not Communicate with Class 2 Device*
3	Select the automatic level control display DTC function on the scan tool. Does the scan tool display any DTCs?	Go to *Step 4*	Go to *Symptoms*
4	Does the scan tool display any DTCs which begin with a "U"?	Go to *Scan Tool Does Not Communicate with Class 2 Device*	Go to *Step 5*
5	Does the scan tool display DTC B1007 or B1009?	Go to *Diagnostic Trouble Code (DTC) List/Type (RIM)*	Go to *Step 6*
6	Does the scan tool display DTC B1327?	Go to *Diagnostic Trouble Code (DTC) List/Type*	Go to *Step 7*
7	Does the scan tool display any other DTC's for the RIM module?	Go to *Diagnostic Trouble Code (DTC) List/Type*	Go to *Symptoms*

GC2019900545000X

Fig. 35 System Check. DeVille

Step	Action	Value(s)	Yes	No
1	Did you perform the Automatic Level Control (ALC) Diagnostic System Check?	—	*Go to Step 2*	Go to *Automatic Level Control Diagnostic System Check*
2	1. Disconnect the automatic level control (ALC) sensor connector. 2. Measure the voltage between the ALC sensor connector terminal G and ground. Is the voltage reading greater than the specified value?	0.1 V	*Go to Step 3*	*Go to Step 4*
3	Repair a short to voltage in the control circuit of the LEVELING indicator lamp. Is the repair complete?	—	*Go to Step 5*	—
4	Replace the ALC sensor. Is the repair complete?	—	*Go to Step 5*	—
5	Operate the system in order to verify the repair. Did you correct the condition?	—	System OK	*Go to Step 2*

GC2010100643000X

Fig. 32 Code 09: Warning Lamp Short To Battery. Catera

Step	Action	Value(s)	Yes	No
1	Did you perform the Automatic Level Control (ALC) Diagnostic System Check?	—	*Go to Step 2*	Go to *Automatic Level Control Diagnostic System Check*
2	Inspect the automatic level control (ALC) sensor actuating arm and link rod for abnormalities. Were any abnormalities found?	—	*Go to Step 5*	*Go to Step 3*
3	1. Disconnect the link rod. 2. Turn ON the ignition, with the engine OFF. 3. Push up on the ALC sensor actuating arm until the compressor activates. 4. Operate the compressor for 60 seconds. 5. Push down on the ALC sensor actuating arm until the exhaust solenoid valve clicks. Does the exhaust solenoid valve click?	—	*Go to Step 4*	*Go to Step 6*
4	Is air exhausting from the air compressor air filter?	—	Go to Diagnostic Aids	*Go to Step 7*
5	1. Replace the ALC sensor if the actuating arm is damaged. 2. Replace the link rod if damaged. Did you complete the replacement?	—	*Go to Step 8*	—
6	Inspect for poor connections at the ALC sensor. Did you find and correct the condition?	—	*Go to Step 8*	*Go to Step 5*
7	Inspect the air filter and all tubing for blockage. Did you find and correct the condition?	—	*Go to Step 8*	*Go to Step 9*
8	Operate the system in order to verify the repair. Did you find and correct the condition?	—	System OK	*Go to Step 3*
9	Replace the auto level control air compressor. Did you complete the replacement?	—	*Go to Step 8*	—

GC2010100644000X

Fig. 34 Code 11: Exhaust Accumulator Fault. Catera

Step	Action	Value(s)	Yes	No
1	Did you perform the Automatic Level Control Diagnostic System Check?	—	*Go to Step 2*	Go to *Automatic Level Control Diagnostic System Check*
2	1. Install a scan tool. 2. Turn ON the ignition leaving the engine OFF. 3. Observe the Suspension Sensor data parameter in the Body Control Module data list using the scan tool. Does the scan tool indicate the voltage is within the specified range?	.5–4.75 V	Go to Diagnostic Aids	*Go to Step 3*
3	1. Turn OFF the ignition. 2. Disconnect the suspension position sensor. 3. Turn ON the ignition leaving the engine OFF. 4. Measure the voltage from the suspension position sensor 5 volt reference circuit to a good ground. Does the voltage measure near the specified value?	5 V	*Go to Step 4*	*Go to Step 7*
4	1. Turn OFF the ignition. 2. Connect a 3–amp fused jumper wire between the 5 volt reference circuit of the suspension position sensor and the signal circuit of the suspension position sensor. 3. Turn ON the ignition, with the engine OFF. 4. With a scan tool, observe the suspension position sensor parameter. Does the scan tool indicate that the suspension position sensor voltage is greater than the specified value?	4.75 V	*Go to Step 5*	*Go to Step 8*
5	1. Disconnect the fused jumper wire. 2. Measure the voltage between the 5–volt reference circuit of the suspension position sensor and the ground circuit of the suspension position sensor. Does the voltage measure less than the specified value?	4.75 V	*Go to Step 6*	*Go to Step 9*
6	1. Turn OFF the ignition. 2. Disconnect the negative battery cable. 3. Measure the resistance from the ground circuit of the suspension position sensor to a good ground. Does the resistance measure less than the specified value?	5 Ω	*Go to Step 11*	*Go to Step 10*
7	Test the 5–volt reference circuit of the suspension position sensor for a short to ground, high resistance, or an open. Did you find and correct the condition?	—	*Go to Step 15*	*Go to Step 12*
8	Test the 5–volt signal circuit of the suspension position sensor for a short to ground, high resistance, or an open. Did you find and correct the condition?	—	*Go to Step 15*	*Go to Step 12*
9	Test the signal circuit of the suspension position sensor for a short to voltage. Did you find and correct the condition?	—	*Go to Step 15*	*Go to Step 12*
10	1. Disconnect the RIM. 2. Test the ground circuit of the suspension position sensor for a high resistance, or an open. Did you find and correct the condition?	—	*Go to Step 15*	*Go to Step 12*

GC2019900546010X

Fig. 36 Code C0625: Level Control Suspension Sensor Fault (Part 1 of 2). DeVille

Step	Action	Value(s)	Yes	No
11	Inspect for poor connections at the harness connector of the suspension position sensor. Did you find and correct the condition?	—	Go to Step 15	Go to Step 13
12	Inspect for poor connections at the harness connector of the RIM. Did you find and correct the condition?	—	Go to Step 15	Go to Step 14
13	Replace the suspension position sensor. Did you complete the replacement?	—	Go to Step 15	—
14	Replace the RIM. Did you complete the replacement?	—	Go to Step 15	—
15	1. Clear the DTCs using the scan tool. 2. Operate the vehicle within the Conditions for Running the DTC as specified in the supporting text. Does the DTC reset?	—	Go to Step 2	System OK

GC2019900546020X

Fig. 36 Code C0625: Level Control Suspension Sensor Fault (Part 2 of 2). DeVille

Step	Action	Value(s)	Yes	No
13	Replace the RIM. Perform the ALC relearn procedure. Did you complete the replacement?	—	Go to Step 14	—
14	1. Clear the DTCs using the scan tool. 2. Operate the vehicle within the Conditions for Running the DTC as specified in the supporting text. Does the DTC reset?	—	Go to Step 2	System OK

GC2019900547020X

Fig. 37 Code C0628: Level Control Position Sensor Circuit High (Part 2 of 2). DeVille

Step	Action	Value(s)	Yes	No
1	Did you perform the Automatic Level Control Diagnostic System Check?	—	Go to Step 2	Go to Automatic Level Control Diagnostic System Check
2	1. Install a scan tool. 2. Turn ON the ignition, with the engine OFF. 3. With a scan tool, command the level control compressor relay ON and OFF. Does the level control compressor relay turn ON and OFF with each command?	—	Go to Diagnostic Aids	Go to Step 3
3	1. Turn OFF the ignition. 2. Disconnect the level control compressor relay. 3. Turn ON the ignition, with the engine OFF. 4. Probe the coil side feed circuit of the level control compressor relay with a test lamp that is connected to a good ground. Does the test lamp illuminate?	—	Go to Step 4	Go to Step 10
4	1. Connect a test lamp between the control circuit of the level control relay and the coil side feed circuit of the level control compressor relay. 2. With a scan tool, command the level control compressor relay ON and OFF. Does the test lamp turn ON and OFF with each command?	—	Go to Step 8	Go to Step 5
5	Does the test lamp remain illuminated with each command?	—	Go to Step 7	Go to Step 6
6	Test the control circuit of the level control compressor relay for a short to voltage or an open. Did you find and correct the condition?	—	Go to Step 13	Go to Step 9
7	Test the control circuit of the level control compressor relay for a short to ground. Did you find and correct the condition?	—	Go to Step 13	Go to Step 9
8	Inspect for poor connections at the level control compressor relay. Did you find and correct the condition?	—	Go to Step 13	Go to Step 11
9	Inspect for poor connections at the harness connector of the RIM. Did you find and correct the condition?	—	Go to Step 13	Go to Step 12
10	Repair the coil side feed circuit of the level control compressor relay. Did you complete the repair?	—	Go to Step 13	—
11	Replace the level control compressor relay Did you complete the replacement?	—	Go to Step 13	—
12	Replace the RIM. Did you complete the replacement?	—	Go to Step 13	—
13	1. Use the scan tool in order to clear the DTCs. 2. Operate the vehicle within the Conditions for Running the DTC as specified in the supporting text. Does the DTC reset?	—	Go to Step 2	System OK

GC2019900548000X

Fig. 38 Code C0655: Level Control Compressor Relay Fault. DeVille

Step	Action	Value(s)	Yes	No
1	Did you perform the Automatic Level Control Diagnostic System Check?	—	Go to Step 2	Go to Automatic Level Control Diagnostic System Check
2	1. Install a scan tool. 2. Turn ON the ignition leaving the engine OFF. 3. With a scan tool, observe the Suspension Position Sensor parameter in the Body Control Module data list using the scan tool. Does the scan tool indicate the voltage is within the specified range?	.25—4.75 V	Go to Diagnostic Aids	Go to Step 3
3	1. Turn OFF the ignition. 2. Disconnect the suspension position sensor. 3. Turn ON the ignition leaving the engine OFF. 4. With a scan tool, observe the suspension position sensor voltage parameter. Does the scan tool indicate that the voltage parameter is greater than the specified value?	0 V	Go to Step 4	Go to Step 10
4	Measure the voltage of the suspension position sensor signal circuit to ground. Does the scan tool indicate that the voltage parameter is greater than the specified value?	5 V	Go to Step 6	Go to Step 5
5	Measure the voltage of the suspension position sensor reference circuit to ground. Does the scan tool indicate that the parameter is greater than the specified value?	5 V	Go to Step 7	Go to Step 8
6	Test the 5-volt signal circuit of the suspension position sensor for a short to voltage. Did you find and correct the condition?	—	Go to Step 14	Go to Step 11
7	Test the 5-volt reference circuit of the suspension position sensor for a short to voltage. Did you find and correct the condition?	—	Go to Step 14	Go to Step 11
8	Measure the resistance of the suspension position sensor ground circuit to ground. Is the resistance greater than the specified value?	5 Ω	Go to Step 9	Go to Step 10
9	Repair the open circuit or short to voltage on the suspension position sensor ground circuit. Did you find and correct the condition?	—	Go to Step 14	—
10	Inspect for poor connections at the harness connector of the suspension position sensor. Did you find and correct the condition?	—	Go to Step 14	Go to Step 12
11	Inspect for poor connections at the harness connector of the RIM. Did you find and correct the condition?	—	Go to Step 14	Go to Step 13
12	Replace the suspension position sensor. Perform the ALC relearn procedure. Did you complete the replacement?	—	Go to Step 14	—

GC2019900547010X

Fig. 37 Code C0628: Level Control Position Sensor Circuit High (Part 1 of 2). DeVille

Step	Action	Value(s)	Yes	No
1	Did you perform the Automatic Level Control Diagnostic System Check?	—	Go to Step 2	Go to Automatic Level Control Diagnostic System Check
2	1. Install a scan tool. 2. Turn ON the ignition, with the engine OFF. 3. With a scan tool, command the level control compressor relay ON and OFF. Does the level control compressor relay turn ON and OFF with each command?	—	Go to Diagnostic Aids	Go to Step 3
3	1. Turn OFF the ignition. 2. Disconnect the level control compressor relay. 3. Turn ON the ignition, with the engine OFF. 4. Probe the coil side feed circuit of the level control compressor relay with a test lamp that is connected to a good ground. Does the test lamp illuminate?	—	Go to Step 4	Go to Step 10
4	1. Connect a test lamp between the control circuit of the level control relay and the coil side feed circuit of the level control compressor relay. 2. With a scan tool, command the level control compressor relay ON and OFF. Does the test lamp turn ON and OFF with each command?	—	Go to Step 8	Go to Step 5
5	Does the test lamp remain illuminated with each command?	—	Go to Step 7	Go to Step 6
6	Test the control circuit of the level control compressor relay for a short to voltage. Did you find and correct the condition?	—	Go to Step 13	Go to Step 9
7	Test the control circuit of the level control compressor relay for a short to ground. Did you find and correct the condition?	—	Go to Step 13	Go to Step 9
8	Inspect for poor connections at the level control compressor relay. Did you find and correct the condition?	—	Go to Step 13	Go to Step 11
9	Inspect for poor connections at the harness connector of the RIM. Did you find and correct the condition?	—	Go to Step 13	Go to Step 12
10	Repair the coil side feed circuit of the level control compressor relay. Did you complete the repair?	—	Go to Step 13	—
11	Replace the level control compressor relay Did you complete the replacement?	—	Go to Step 13	—
12	Replace the RIM. Did you complete the replacement?	—	Go to Step 13	—
13	1. Use the scan tool in order to clear the DTCs. 2. Operate the vehicle within the Conditions for Running the DTC as specified in the supporting text. Does the DTC reset?	—	Go to Step 2	System OK

GC2019900549000X

Fig. 39 Code C0658: Level Control Compressor Relay Circuit High. DeVille

Step	Action	Value(s)	Yes	No
1	Did you perform the Automatic Level Control Diagnostic System Check?	—	Go to Step 2	Go to Automatic Level Control Diagnostic System Check
2	1. Install a scan tool. 2. Turn ON the ignition leaving the engine OFF. 3. With a scan tool, command the ALC exhaust solenoid ON and OFF. Does the exhaust solenoid valve turn ON and OFF with each command?	—	Go to Diagnostic Aids	Go to Step 3
3	1. Turn OFF the ignition. 2. Disconnect the ALC exhaust solenoid valve. 3. Turn ON the ignition, with the engine OFF. 4. Probe the coil side feed circuit of the exhaust solenoid valve harness connector with a test lamp that is connected to a good ground. Does the test lamp illuminate?	—	Go to Step 4	Go to Step 10
4	1. Connect a test lamp between the control circuit of the exhaust solenoid valve harness connector and the coil side feed circuit of the exhaust solenoid harness connector. 2. With a scan tool, command the exhaust solenoid valve ON and OFF. Does the test lamp turn ON and OFF with each command?	—	Go to Step 8	Go to Step 5
5	Does the test lamp remain illuminated with each command?	—	Go to Step 7	Go to Step 6
6	Test the control circuit of the exhaust solenoid valve for a short to voltage or an open. Did you find and correct the condition?	—	Go to Step 13	Go to Step 9
7	Test the control circuit of the exhaust solenoid valve for a short to ground. Did you find and correct the condition?	—	Go to Step 13	Go to Step 9
8	Inspect for poor connections at the exhaust solenoid. Did you find and correct the condition?	—	Go to Step 13	Go to Step 11
9	Inspect for poor connections at the harness connector for the RIM. Did you find and correct the condition?	—	Go to Step 13	Go to Step 12
10	Repair the coil side feed circuit of the exhaust solenoid valve. Did you complete the repair?	—	Go to Step 13	—
11	Replace the compressor head assembly. Did you complete the replacement?	—	Go to Step 13	—
12	Replace the RIM. Did you complete the replacement?	—	Go to Step 13	—
13	1. Use the scan tool in order to clear the DTC's. 2. Operate the vehicle within the Conditions for Running the DTC as specified in the supporting text. Does the DTC reset?	—	Go to Step 2	System OK

GC2019900550000X

Fig. 40 Code C0660: Level Control Exhaust Valve Circuit Fault. DeVille

Step	Action	Value(s)	Yes	No
1	Did you perform the ALC Diagnostic System Check	—	Go to Step 2	Go to Automatic Level Control Diagnostic System Check
2	1. Install a scan tool. 2. Turn ON the ignition, with the engine OFF. 3. With the scan tool, observe the suspension position sensor in the RIM. Does the scan tool indicate that the suspension position sensor is within the specified range?	25–2.5 V	Go to Step 3	Go to Step 8
3	With the scan tool command the exhaust solenoid open, to vent the system (an audible hiss sound may be heard). Did the ALC system vent and the vehicle lower?	—	Go to Step 4	Go to Step 6
4	Observe the suspension position sensor reading on the scan tool. Did the suspension position sensor reading change?	—	Go to Step 8	Go to Step 5
5	**Important:** The vehicle must be raised on a drive on lift. Full vehicle weight must be on the rear tires. Care must be used when disconnecting and retaining the suspension position sensor link. If the link is allowed to travel freely, a false DTC may be set. 1. Disconnect the suspension position sensor actuating link. 2. Move the position sensor link up, so that it is approximately 45 degrees above level to the floor and retain it there. 3. With a scan tool, observe the suspension position sensor parameter. Did the suspension position sensor reading change?	—	Go to Step 8	Go to Step 9
6	**Important:** The vehicle must be raised on a drive on lift. Full vehicle weight must be on the rear tires. 1. Raise and support the vehicle. 2. Disconnect the air tube assembly from the drier. Did the ALC system vent and the vehicle lower?	—	Go to Step 10	Go to Step 7
7	Disconnect the air tube assembly from the drier. Did the vehicle lower?	—	Go to Step 11	Go to Step 12

GC2019900552010X

Fig. 42 Test 1: Rear Of Vehicle High (Part 1 of 2). DeVille

Step	Action	Value(s)	Yes	No
1	Did you perform the Automatic Level Control Diagnostic System Check?	—	Go to Step 2	Go to Automatic Level Control/ Diagnostic System Check.
2	1. Install a scan tool 2. Turn ON the ignition, with the engine OFF. 3. With a scan tool, command the ALC exhaust solenoid valve ON and OFF. Does the exhaust solenoid valve turn ON and OFF with each command?	—	Go to Diagnostic Aids	Go to Step 3
3	1. Turn OFF the ignition. 2. Disconnect the exhaust solenoid valve harness connector. 3. Turn ON the ignition, with the engine OFF. 4. Connect a test lamp between the control circuit of the exhaust solenoid harness connector and the coil side feed circuit of the exhaust solenoid harness connector. 5. With a scan tool, command the exhaust solenoid ON and OFF. Does the test lamp turn ON and OFF with each command?	—	Go to Step 6	Go to Step 4
4	Does the test lamp remain OFF with each command?	—	Go to Step 5	Go to Step 7
5	Test the exhaust solenoid control circuit for a short to voltage. Did you find and correct the condition?	—	Go to Step 10	Go to Step 7
6	Inspect for poor connections at the exhaust valve solenoid harness connector. Did you find and correct the condition?	—	Go to Step 10	Go to Step 8
7	Inspect for poor connections at the RIM. Did you find and correct the condition?	—	Go to Step 10	Go to Step 9
8	Replace the compressor head assembly. Did you complete the replacement?	—	Go to Step 10	—
9	Replace the RIM. Did you complete the replacement?	—	Go to Step 10	—
10	1. Use the scan tool in order to clear the DTC's. 2. Operate the vehicle within the Conditions for Running the DTC as specified in the supporting text. Did the DTC reset?	—	Go to Step 2	System OK

GC2019900551000X

Fig. 41 Code C0663: Level Control Exhaust Valve Circuit High. DeVille

Step	Action	Value(s)	Yes	No
8	Perform the ALC relearn procedure. Did you complete the procedure?	—	Go to Step 15	—
9	Inspect the poor connections/ terminal tension at the harness connector of the suspension position sensor. Did you find and correct the condition?	—	Go to Step 15	Go to Step 13
10	Inspect for poor connections/ terminal tension at the harness connector of the Automatic Level Control Compressor Assembly. Did you find and correct the condition?	—	Go to Step 15	Go to Step 14
11	Replace the air tube assembly. Did you complete the replacement?	—	Go to Step 15	—
12	Replace the shock that did not lower. Did you complete the replacement?	—	Go to Step 15	—
13	Replace the suspension position sensor. Did you complete the replacement?	—	Go to Step 15	—
14	Replace the automatic level control compressor head assembly. Did you complete the replacement?	—	Go to Step 15	—
15	Operate the vehicle within the conditions for enabling the automatic level control. Does the ALC operate correctly?	—	System OK	Go to Step 2

GC2019900552020X

Fig. 42 Test 1: Rear Of Vehicle High (Part 2 of 2). DeVille

Step	Action	Value(s)	Yes	No
1	**Important:** Perform a close visual inspection of all air lines, connectors and components. Did you perform the Automatic Level Control (ALC) Diagnostic System Check?	—	Go to *Step 2*	Go to *Automatic Level Control Diagnostic System Check*
2	1. Install a scan tool. 2. Turn ON the ignition, with the engine OFF. 3. With a scan tool, command the ALC relay ON and OFF. Does the ALC relay turn ON and OFF with each command?	—	Go to *Step 8*	Go to *Step 3*
3	1. Turn OFF the ignition. 2. Disconnect the ALC relay. 3. Turn ON the ignition, with the engine OFF. 4. Probe the coil side feed circuit of the ALC relay with a test lamp that is connected to a good ground. Does the test lamp illuminate?	—	Go to *Step 4*	Go to *Step 15*
4	1. Connect a test lamp between the control circuit of the ALC relay and the coil side feed circuit of the ALC relay. 2. With a scan tool, command the ALC relay ON and OFF. Does the test lamp turn ON and OFF with each command?	—	Go to *Step 11*	Go to *Step 5*
5	Does the test lamp remain illuminated with each command?	—	Go to *Step 7*	Go to *Step 6*

GC2019900553010X

Fig. 43 Test 2: Rear Of Vehicle Low (Part 1 of 2). DeVille

Step	Action	Normal Result(s)	Abnormal Result(s)*
1	Turn the ignition switch to the ON position.	After approximately 35-55 seconds, the air compressor runs for 3-5 seconds. NOTE: This action may be overridden by the height sensor if a load has been added or removed from the vehicle.	• The air compressor cycles on and off frequently. If no air leaks are present, go to *Rear of Vehicle Low (w/o Road Sensing Suspension).* • The air compressor runs excessively. Check for a disconnected or damaged air tube or a damaged strut. If OK, go to *Rear of Vehicle Low (w/o Road Sensing Suspension).*
2	Add a 300 lb. load to the luggage compartment.	After a 17-27 second delay, the air compressor runs and the rear of the vehicle rises to the correct trim height.	• The air compressor cycles on and off frequently. If no air leaks are present, go to *Rear of Vehicle Low (w/o Road Sensing Suspension).* • The air compressor runs excessively. Check for a disconnected or damaged air tube or a damaged strut. If OK, go to *Rear of Vehicle Low (w/o Road Sensing Suspension).*
3	Turn the ignition switch to the OFF position. Remove the load from the luggage compartment.	After a 17-27 second delay, a hiss of escaping air may be heard, and the rear of the vehicle lowers to the correct trim height.	—

* Refer to the appropriate symptom diagnostic table for the applicable abnormal result.

GC2019800292000X

Fig. 44 ALC System Operation Check. 2000–01 Eldorado Less Road Sensing Suspension

Step	Action	Normal Result(s)	Abnormal Result(s)*
1	1. Turn the ignition ON with the engine off. 2. Clear the CVRSS codes. Refer to *Clearing DTCs.* 3. Wait for 90 seconds. 4. Check for CVRSS codes using the On-Board Diagnostics. Refer to *Displaying DTCs.*	No CVRSS codes are present.	One of the following DTCs is displayed as HISTORY or CURRENT: • C1735 • C1736 • C1737 • C1738 If one of the above DTCs is displayed, go to the appropriate diagnostic table.
2	Turn the ignition switch to the ON position.	After a delay, the air compressor runs for 3-5 seconds. NOTE: This action may be overridden if a load has been added or removed from the vehicle.	• The air compressor cycles on and off frequently. If no air leaks are present, go to *Rear of Vehicle Low (with Road Sensing Suspension).* • The air compressor runs excessively. Check for a disconnected or damaged air tube or a damaged strut. If OK, go to *Rear of Vehicle Low (with Road Sensing Suspension).*
3	Add a 300 lb. load to the luggage compartment.	After a delay, the air compressor runs and the rear of the vehicle rises to the correct trim height. Refer to *Trim Height* in Suspension General Diagnostics.	• The air compressor cycles on and off frequently. If no air leaks are present, go to *Rear of Vehicle Low (with Road Sensing Suspension).* • The air compressor runs excessively. Check for a disconnected or damaged air tube or a damaged strut. If OK, go to *Rear of Vehicle Low (with Road Sensing Suspension).*
4	Turn the ignition switch to the OFF position. Remove the load from the luggage compartment.	After a delay, a hiss of escaping air may be heard, and the rear of the vehicle lowers to the correct trim height. Refer to *Trim Height* in Suspension General Diagnostics.	—

* Refer to the appropriate symptom diagnostic table for the applicable abnormal result.

GC2019800293000X

Fig. 45 ALC System Operation Check. 2000–01 Eldorado Less Road Sensing Suspension

Step	Action	Value(s)	Yes	No
6	Test the control circuit of the ALC relay for a short to voltage or an open. Did you find and correct the condition?	—	Go to *Step 19*	Go to *Step 13*
7	Test the control circuit of the ALC for a short to ground. Did you find and correct the condition?	—	Go to *Step 19*	Go to *Step 13*
8	1. Turn OFF the ignition. 2. Disconnect the ALC compressor motor. 3. Turn ON the ignition, with the engine OFF. 4. Probe the ALC compressor motor battery positive feed circuit with a test lamp connected to a good ground. 5. With a scan tool, command the ALC relay ON. Did the test lamp illuminate?	—	Go to *Step 9*	Go to *Step 13*
9	1. Turn OFF the ignition. 2. Disconnect the negitive battery cable. 3. Measure the resistance of the ALC compressor ground circuit to a good ground. Is the resistance lower than the specified value?	5 Ω	Go to *Step 12*	Go to *Step 14*
10	Test the ALC compressor motor battery positive feed circuit for an open. Did you find and correct the condition?	—	Go to *Step 19*	Go to *Step 11*
11	Inspect for poor connections at the ALC relay. Did you find and correct the condition?	—	Go to *Step 19*	Go to *Step 16*
12	Inspect for poor connections at the ALC compressor assembly. Did you find and correct the condition?	—	Go to *Step 19*	Go to *Step 17*
13	Inspect for poor connections at the harness connector of the Rear Integration Module (RIM). Did you find and correct the condition?	—	Go to *Step 19*	Go to *Step 18*
14	Repair the high resistance/ open ALC compressor ground circuit. Did you complete the repair?	—	Go to *Step 19*	—
15	Repair the coil side feed circuit of the ALC relay. Did you complete the repair?	—	Go to *Step 19*	—
16	Replace the ALC relay. Did you complete the replacement?	—	Go to *Step 19*	—
17	Replace the ALC compressor assembly. Did you complete the replacement?	—	Go to *Step 19*	—
18	Replace the RIM.	—	Go to *Step 19*	—
19	Operate the system to verify the repair. Does the system operate normally?	—	System OK	Go to *Step 2*

GC2019900553020X

Fig. 43 Test 2: Rear Of Vehicle Low (Part 2 of 2). DeVille

Step	Action	Value(s)	Yes	No
1	Has the ALC air compressor assembly and the air tube been replaced?	—	Go to *Step 7*	Go to *Step 2*
2	1. Raise the vehicle. 2. Inspect the air tubes running from the ALC air compressor to both of the rear shock absorbers. 3. Inspect the air tube connection at the ALC air dryer. Are the air tubes damaged or disconnected?	—	Go to *Step 13*	Go to *Step 3*
3	Squeeze the left rear shock absorber in the middle of the air sleeve. Can the air sleeve be slightly compressed?	—	Go to *Step 5*	Go to *Step 4*

GC2019800294010X

Fig. 46 Test 1: ALC System Leak Test (Part 1 of 4). 2000–01 Eldorado

Step	Action	Value(s)	Yes	No
4	1. Turn the ignition OFF. 2. Connect a scan tool to the DLC. 3. Turn the ignition ON with the engine OFF. 4. Under the SUSPENSION option, activate the ALC air compressor. 5. Operate the ALC air compressor for 60 seconds. 6. Using a soap bubble solution, test the air tube-to-air dryer connection for leaks. Was a leak found and repaired?	—	Go to *Step 16*	Go to *Step 5*
5	1. Turn the ignition OFF. 2. Disconnect the air tube from the ALC air dryer. 3. Connect the *J 22124-B* adapter and gage to the ALC air dryer. 4. Close the *J 22124-B* gage toggle valve. 5. Disconnect connector C1 from the CVRSS control module. 6. Turn the ignition ON with the engine OFF. ***Caution: This will activate the ALC compressor.*** 7. Connect pin C15 of CVRSS connector C1 (harness side) to ground using a jumper wire. Does the pressure build up to 80 psi?	80 psi	Go to *Step 6*	Go to *Step 10*
6	1. When the pressure reaches 80 psi, shut off the air compressor by removing the jumper from pin C15. 2. Monitor the pressure gage for 1 minute. Does the pressure leak down?	—	Go to *Step 10*	Go to *Step 7*
7	1. Connect *J 22124-B* adapter tube and gage to the right rear shock absorber. The *J 22124-B* gage toggle valve should be on the side away from the shock absorber. 2. Close the *J 22124-B* gage toggle valve. 3. Input shop air into the *J 22124-B* gage schrader valve until the pressure gage reads 80 psi. 4. Monitor the pressure gage for 1 minute. Does the pressure leak down?	—	Go to *Step 11*	Go to *Step 8*
8	1. Slowly open the *J 22124-B* gage toggle valve to release air pressure. 2. Disconnect the *J 22124-B* adapter tube from the right rear shock absorber. 3. Connect the *J 22124-B* adapter tube with gage to the left rear shock absorber. The *J 22124-B* gage toggle valve should be on the side away from the shock absorber. 4. Close the *J 22124-B* gage toggle valve. 5. Input shop air into the *J 22124-B* gage schrader valve until the pressure gage reads 80 psi. 6. Monitor the pressure gage for 1 minute. Does the pressure leak down?	—	Go to *Step 12*	Go to *Step 9*

GC2019800294020X

Fig. 46 Test 1: ALC System Leak Test (Part 2 of 4). 2000–01 Eldorado

Step	Action	Value(s)	Yes	No
18	1. Install the ALC air compressor assembly on the vehicle. 2. Reconnect all of the air tube connectors. Have all of the air tubes been reconnected?	—	Go to *Step 19*	—
19	1. Turn the ignition OFF. 2. Reconnect all of the connectors and/or components that were removed. 3. Turn the ignition ON with the engine OFF. 4. Clear the CVRSS DTCs. 5. Wait for at least 5 minutes. Is the rear of the vehicle trim (level)?	—	System OK	—

GC2019800294040X

Fig. 46 Test 1: ALC System Leak Test (Part 4 of 4). 2000–01 Eldorado

Step	Action	Value(s)	Yes	No
DEFINITION: The rear of the vehicle is above trim height. This diagnostic procedure only applies to vehicles without Road Sensing Suspension.				
1	Is any aftermarket equipment installed on the vehicle that could affect the ALC system?	—	Go to *Step 2*	Go to *Step 4*
2	Check the aftermarket equipment to ensure that it is not affecting ALC performance. Is the aftermarket equipment affecting the ALC performance?	—	Go to *Step 3*	Go to *Step 4*
3	Correct the condition. Is the condition corrected?	—	Go to *ALC System Operation Check (w/o Road Sensing Suspension)*	—
4	Check the ELC fuse in the rear compartment fuse Block and the ALC circuit breaker in the ALC MaxiFuse Block® for an open (blown) or tripped (open) condition. Is the fuse open or the circuit breaker tripped?	—	Go to *Step 5*	Go to *Step 6*
5	Replace the fuse or reset the circuit breaker. NOTE: If the fuse is open (blown) repeatedly, check CKT 2141 (BRN) for a short circuit to ground condition. If the circuit breaker trips repeatedly, check CKT 1340 (ORN) for a short circuit to ground condition. Is the replacement complete?	—	Go to *ALC System Operation Check (w/o Road Sensing Suspension)*	—
6	Check the height sensor and link for proper connection and damage. Are the height sensor and link properly connected and in good condition?	—	Go to *Step 8*	Go to *Step 7*
7	Reconnect or replace the height sensor or link. Is the repair or replacement complete?	—	Go to *ALC System Operation Check (w/o Road Sensing Suspension)*	—

GC2019800295010X

Fig. 47 Test 2: Rear Of Vehicle High (Part 1 of 3). 2000–01 Eldorado Less Road Sensing Suspension

Step	Action	Value(s)	Yes	No
9	1. Slowly open the *J 22124-B* gage toggle valve to release air pressure. 2. Disconnect the *J 22124-B* adapter tube from the gage and from the left rear shock absorber. 3. Connect the *J 22124-B* gage to the left rear and right rear air tube connectors. 4. Reconnect the air tube to the ALC air dryer. 5. Open the *J 22124-B* gage toggle valve. 6. Input shop air into the *J 22124-B* gage schrader valve until the pressure gage reads 80 psi. 7. Monitor the pressure gage for 1 minute. Does the pressure leak down?	—	Go to *Step 14*	Go to *Step 19*
10	1. Replace the ALC air compressor assembly. 2. Replace the air tube. Are the replacements complete?	—	Go to *Step 19*	—
11	1. Replace the right rear shock absorber. 2. Reconnect all the air tube connectors. Is the shock absorber replaced and are all the air tube connections made?	—	Go to *Step 19*	—
12	1. Slowly open the *J 22124-B* gage toggle valve to release the air pressure. 2. Replace the left rear shock absorber. 3. Reconnect all of the air tube connectors. Is the shock absorber replaced and are all of the air tube connections made?	—	Go to *Step 19*	—
13	Are any of the air tubes damaged?	—	Go to *Step 14*	Go to *Step 18*
14	Replace the air tube that runs from the air dryer to the two rear shock absorbers. Is the replacement complete?	—	Go to *Step 15*	—
15	1. Remove the ALC dryer from the air compressor assembly. 2. Shake the ALC air dryer with the head-connection end down. Does moisture come out of the ALC air dryer when it is shaken?	—	Go to *Step 16*	Go to *Step 17*
16	Replace the ALC air dryer. Is the replacement complete?	—	Go to *Step 17*	—
17	Replace the air compressor head. Is the replacement complete?	—	Go to *Step 18*	—

GC2019800294030X

Fig. 46 Test 1: ALC System Leak Test (Part 3 of 4). 2000–01 Eldorado

Step	Action	Value(s)	Yes	No
8	1. Turn the ignition switch to the ON position. **Important:** The vehicle must be raised on a drive-on lift or be supported at the rear under the rear axle. Full vehicle weight must be on the rear suspension. 2. Raise the vehicle. 3. Disconnect the link from the height sensor. 4. Move the height sensor lever down so that it is approximately 45 degrees below level (to the floor) and hold it there. Will the rear of the vehicle lower to trim level or below? NOTE: The height sensor has a 17 to 27 second delay period before the exhaust solenoid is activated.	—	Go to *Step 9*	Go to *Step 10*
9	Adjust the height sensor. Is trim height at the rear underbody points correct?	Trim Height	Go to *ALC System Operation Check*	Repeat this *Step*
10	Move the height sensor lever up so that it is approximately 45 degrees above level (to the floor) and hold it there for a minimum of 27 seconds (17 to 27 seconds is the height sensor delay period). Does the air compressor come on?	—	Go to *Step 11*	Go to *Height Sensor Operational Check*
11	Disconnect the air tube from the air dryer. Will the rear of the vehicle lower to trim level or below?	—	Go to *Step 19*	Go to *Step 12*
12	1. Connect the link to the height sensor lever. 2. Disconnect the air tube from both struts. Will the rear of the vehicle lower to trim level or below?	—	Go to *Step 13*	Go to *Step 14*
13	Replace the air tube. Is the replacement complete?	—	Go to *ALC System Operation Check (w/o Road Sensing Suspension)*	—
14	Is the vehicle uneven (more than 12 mm (0.5 in) from side to side at the rear?	—	Go to *Step 16*	Go to *Step 15*
15	Replace both rear springs. Is the trim height at the rear underbody points correct?	Trim Height	Go to *ALC System Operation Check (w/o Road Sensing Suspension)*	—
16	1. Note which side of the vehicle is high. 2. Bounce the rear of the vehicle three times. Is the vehicle still uneven more than 12 mm (0.5 in) from side to side at the rear?	—	Go to *Step 17*	Go to *Step 18*
17	Replace the rear spring on the side of the vehicle that is high. Is the trim height at the rear underbody points correct?	Trim Height	Go to *ALC System Operation Check (w/o Road Sensing Suspension)*	Repeat this *Diagnostic Table*
18	Replace the rear shock absorber on the side of the vehicle that is high. Is the trim height at the rear underbody points correct?	Trim Height	Go to *ALC System Operation Check (w/o Road Sensing Suspension)*	Repeat this *Diagnostic Table*

GC2019800295020X

Fig. 47 Test 2: Rear Of Vehicle High (Part 2 of 3). 2000–01 Eldorado Less Road Sensing Suspension

Step	Action	Value(s)	Yes	No
19	1. Raise the rear of the vehicle up as much as possible by holding the height sensor up. NOTE: The height sensor has a 17 to 27 second delay period before the air compressor is activated. 2. Reconnect the link to the height sensor. 3. Disconnect the air compressor electrical connector. 4. Check for continuity between terminals C and A of the air compressor connector. Is continuity present?	Continuity	Go to *Step 21*	Go to *Step 20*
20	Replace the air compressor head. Is the replacement complete?	—	Go to *ALC System Operation Check (w/o Road Sensing Suspension)*	—
21	Measure the voltage between the air compressor electrical connector (vehicle side), terminal C and ground. Is battery voltage present?	Battery Voltage	Go to*Step 23*	Go to*Step 22*
22	Repair the open circuit condition in CKT 2141 (BRN). Is the repair complete?	—	Go to *ALC System Operation Check (w/o Road Sensing Suspension)*	—
23	1. Cycle the ignition switch and return it to the ON position. 2. Measure the voltage from the air compressor electrical connector (vehicle side), terminal C to the same connector, terminal A. NOTE: The link must be connected. Voltage will not be present within 17 to 27 seconds of the ignition switch cycle (height sensor delay). Voltage will not be present after approximately seven minutes. Is battery voltage present?	Battery Voltage	Go to *Step 25*	Go to *Step 24*
24	Check for an open circuit condition in circuit 320 (WHT). Also, check for a poor connection at the height sensor connector. Was an open circuit or poor connection found and repaired?	—	Go to *ALC System Operation Check (w/o Road Sensing Suspension)*	Go to *Height Sensor Operational Check*
25	Replace the air compressor head. Is the replacement complete?	—	Go to *ALC System Operation Check (w/o Road Sensing Suspension)*	—

GC2019800295030X

Fig. 47 Test 2: Rear Of Vehicle High (Part 3 of 3). 2000–01 Eldorado Less Road Sensing Suspension

Step	Action	Value(s)	Yes	No
10	1. Turn the ignition OFF. 2. Replace the ALC air compressor assembly. 3. Install the ALC intake air filter on the vehicle body. Are all of the replacements and/or installations complete?	—	Go to *Step 13*	—
11	1. Turn the ignition OFF. 2. Connect the scan tool. 3. Turn the ignition ON with the engine OFF. 4. Perform the ALC Trim Height Adjustment. Has the ALC Trim Height Adjustment been completed?	—	Go to *Step 13*	—
12	Replace the air tube going from the air dryer to both the rear shock absorbers. Is the replacement complete?	—	Go to *Step 13*	—
13	1. Turn the ignition OFF. 2. Turn the ignition ON with the engine OFF. 3. Wait for at least 5 minutes. Is the rear of the vehicle trim (level)?	—	System OK	—

GC2019800296020X

Fig. 48 Test 3: Rear Of Vehicle High (Part 2 of 2). 2000–01 Eldorado w/Road Sensing Suspension

Step	Action	Value(s)	Yes	No
DEFINITION: The rear of the vehicle will not raise, is always low, or leaks down when the vehicle is not used. This diagnostic procedure only applies to vehicles without Road Sensing Suspension.				
1	Is any aftermarket equipment installed on the vehicle that could affect the ALC system?	—	Go to *Step 2*	Go to *Step 4*
2	Check the aftermarket equipment to ensure that it is not affecting ALC performance. Is the aftermarket equipment affecting the ALC performance?	—	Go to *Step 3*	Go to *Step 4*
3	Correct the condition. Is the condition corrected?	—	Go to *ALC System Operation Check (w/o Road Sensing Suspension)*	—
4	Check the ELC fuse in the rear compartment fuse block and the ALC circuit breaker in the ALC MaxiFuse® Block for an open (blown) or tripped (open) condition. Is the fuse open or the circuit breaker tripped?	—	Go to *Step 5*	Go to *Step 6*
5	Replace the fuse or reset the circuit breaker. NOTE: If the fuse is open (blown) repeatedly, check CKT 2141 (BRN) for a short circuit to ground condition. If the circuit breaker trips repeatedly, check CKT 1340 (ORN) for a short circuit to ground condition. Is the replacement or reset complete?	—	Go to *ALC System Operation Check (w/o Road Sensing Suspension)*	—
6	Check the height sensor and link for proper connection and damage. Are the height sensor and the link properly connected and in good condition?	—	Go to *Step 8*	Go to *Step 7*

GC2019800297010X

Fig. 49 Test 4: Rear Of Vehicle Low (Part 1 of 4). 2000–01 Eldorado Less Road Sensing Suspension

Step	Action	Value(s)	Yes	No
1	Was the ALC System Check performed?	—	Go to *Step 2*	Go to *ALC System Operation Check (with Road Sensing Suspension)*
2	1. Turn the ignition ON with the engine OFF. 2. Listen for the ALC air compressor to activate. Is the ALC air compressor running for more than 5 minutes?	5 minutes	Go to *Step 3*	Go to *Step 6*
3	1. Turn the ignition OFF 2. Remove the ALC compressor relay. 3. Turn the ignition ON with the engine OFF. Is the air compressor running?	—	Go to *Step 4*	Go to *Step 5*
4	1. Turn the ignition OFF. 2. Reinstall the ALC compressor relay. 3. Repair the short to voltage in CKT 322. Is the repair complete?	—	Go to *Step 13*	—
5	1. Turn the ignition OFF. 2. Replace the ALC compressor relay. Is the replacement complete?	—	Go to *Step 13*	—
6	Inspect the left and right rear position sensors for damage and disconnected links. Are any damaged sensors or disconnected links present?	—	Go to *Step 7*	Go to *Step 8*
7	Replace the damaged rear position sensor or reconnect the link. Is the replacement complete?	—	Go to *Step 13*	—
8	1. Remove the ALC intake filter from the vehicle body (do not remove it from the ALC air compressor or hose). 2. Using the scan tool, cycle output ALC compressor. 3. After 1 minute, stop cycling. 4. Cycle the ALC exhaust while checking to see if air is exiting the ALC intake air filter. Is air exiting the ALC intake air filter?	—	Go to *Step 11*	Go to *Step 9*
9	1. Stop exhausting. 2. Disconnect the air tubes from both rear shock absorbers. 3. Connect the *J 22124-B* gage to both (between) the air tubes. 4. Open the *J 22124-B* gage toggle valve. 5. Disconnect the air tube from the ALC air dryer. 6. Apply shop air to the *J 22124-B* gage schrader valve. Is air exiting both of the air tubes at the ALC air dryer connection?	—	Go to *Step 10*	Go to *Step 12*

GC2019800296010X

Fig. 48 Test 3: Rear Of Vehicle High (Part 1 of 2). 2000–01 Eldorado w/Road Sensing Suspension

Step	Action	Value(s)	Yes	No
7	Reconnect or replace the height sensor or the link. Is the repair or replacement complete?	—	Go to *ALC System Operation Check (w/o Road Sensing Suspension)*	—
8	Does the vehicle leak down when the vehicle is not used for an extended period of time (overnight), but then come up to normal trim height with vehicle use?	—	Go to *Step 28*	Go to *Step 9*
9	1. Turn the ignition switch to the ON position. 2. Add approximately 300 lbs of weight to the rear of the vehicle. Does the rear of the vehicle rise and not leak down? NOTE: Allow 27 seconds for the air compressor to start and then additional time for the struts to inflate.	—	Go to *Step 10*	Go to *Step 12*
10	Is the trim height at the rear underbody points correct?	Trim Height	Go to *ALC System Operation Check (w/o Road Sensing Suspension)*	Go to *Step 11*
11	Adjust the height sensor. Is trim height at the rear underbody points correct?	Trim Height	Go to *ALC System Operation Check (w/o Road Sensing Suspension)*	*Repeat this Step*
12	Did the air compressor operate when weight was added?	—	Go to *Step 28*	Go to *Step 13*
13	1. Disconnect the height sensor electrical connector. 2. Turn the ignition switch to the ON position. 3. Connect a fused jumper from the height sensor connector (vehicle side) terminal B to ground. Is the air compressor operating?	—	Go to *Height Sensor Operational Check*	Go to *Step 14*
14	1. Turn the ignition switch to the OFF position. 2. Connect the height sensor electrical connector. 3. Remove the ALC relay from the rear compartment relay center #2. 4. Turn the ignition switch to the ON position. 5. Measure the voltage from terminal A3 to ground. Is battery voltage present?	Battery Voltage	Go to *Step 16*	Go to *Step 15*
15	Repair the open circuit condition in circuit 2141 (BRN). Is the replacement or repair complete?	—	Go to *ALC System Operation Check (w/o Road Sensing Suspension)*	—
16	Measure the voltage from terminal A1 to ground (this terminal is HOT AT ALL TIMES). Is battery voltage present?	Battery Voltage	Go to*Step 18*	Go to *Step 17*
17	Repair the open circuit condition in circuit 1340 (ORN) between the ALC MaxiFuse® block and the rear compartment relay center #2. Is the repair complete?	—	Go to *ALC System Operation Check (w/o Road Sensing Suspension)*	—

GC2019800297020X

Fig. 49 Test 4: Rear Of Vehicle Low (Part 2 of 4). 2000–01 Eldorado Less Road Sensing Suspension

Step	Action	Value(s)	Yes	No
18	1. Connect a voltmeter between the terminals where relay pins 85 and 86 were removed. 2. Turn the ignition switch to the ON position. NOTE: The ignition switch must be cycled if the ignition was left on from the previous step. Is battery voltage present after 17 to 27 seconds (17 to 27 seconds is the height sensor delay period).	Battery Voltage	Go to *Step 20*	Go to *Step 19*
19	Check for a poor connection at the height sensor connector, terminal B, or an open-circuit condition in circuit 321 (YEL). Was a poor connection or open-circuit condition found and corrected?	—	Go to *ALC System Operation Check (w/o Road Sensing Suspension)*	Go to *Height Sensor Operational Check*
20	Connect a 30-amp fused jumper between terminals A1 and B3. Is the air compressor operating?	—	Go to *Step 21*	Go to *Step 22*
21	Replace the ELC relay. Is the replacement complete?	—	Go to *ALC System Operation Check (w/o Road Sensing Suspension)*	—
22	1. Leave the jumper from the previous step in place. 2. Disconnect the air compressor electrical connector. 3. Measure the voltage from the air compressor electrical connector (vehicle side), terminal B, to ground. Is battery voltage present?	Battery Voltage	Go to *Step 24*	Go to *Step 23*
23	Repair the open-circuit condition in circuit 322 (DK GRN). Is the repair complete?	—	Go to *ALC System Operation Check (w/o Road Sensing Suspension)*	—
24	1. Leave the jumper from the previous step in place. 2. Measure the voltage from the air compressor connector (vehicle side), terminal B, to the same connector, terminal D. Is battery voltage present?	Battery Voltage	Go to *Step 26*	Go to *Step 25*
25	Repair the open-circuit condition in CKT 1050 (BLK). Is the repair complete?	—	Go to *ALC System Operation Check (w/o Road Sensing Suspension)*	—
26	1. Disconnect the jumper and install the ALC relay. 2. Jumper the air compressor connector (compressor side), terminal D, to ground. 3. Jumper the air compressor connector (compressor side), terminal B to B+ using a 30–amp fused jumper wire. Is the air compressor operating?	—	Go to *Step 13*	Go to *Step 27*
27	Replace the air compressor. Is the replacement complete?	—	Go to *ALC System Operation Check (w/o Road Sensing Suspension)*	—

GC2019800297030X

Fig. 49 Test 4: Rear Of Vehicle Low (Part 3 of 4). 2000–01 Eldorado Less Road Sensing Suspension

Step	Action	Value(s)	Yes	No
1	Was the ALC System Check performed?	—	Go to *Step 2*	Go to *ALC System Operation Check (with Road Sensing Suspension)*
2	1. Turn the ignition ON with the engine OFF. 2. Listen for the ALC air compressor to activate. Does the air compressor come on within 30 seconds?	30 seconds	Go to *Step 9*	Go to *Step 3*
3	1. Turn the ignition OFF. 2. Disconnect the ALC connector from the ALC air compressor assembly. 3. Disconnect connector C1 from the CVRSS control module. 4. Turn the ignition ON. 5. Connect pin C15 of CVRSS connector C1 (harness side) to ground using a jumper wire. 6. Measure the voltage between pin B of the ALC air compressor connector (harness side) and ground. Does the voltmeter display a voltage greater than 10 volts?	10 volts	Go to *Step 4*	Go to *Step 7*
4	1. Remove the jumper wire from pin C15. 2. Turn the ignition OFF. 3. Check for continuity between pin D of the ALC air compressor connector (harness side) and ground. Is there continuity?	—	Go to *Step 6*	Go to *Step 5*
5	1. Turn the ignition OFF. 2. Repair the open circuit condition in CKT 1050. Is the repair complete?	—	Go to *ALC System Operation Check (with Road Sensing Suspension)*	—
6	1. Replace the ALC air compressor assembly. 2. Replace the air tube. Is the repair complete?	—	Go to *Step 12*	—
7	1. Remove the jumper wire from pin C15. 2. Turn the ignition OFF. 3. Check for the following: • tripped (open) ALC circuit breaker • blown (open) IGN-0-BODY fuse • open CKT 322 • open CKT 321 • open CKT 1340 • open CKT 147 Was a problem found?	—	Go to *Step 8*	—

GC2019800298010X

Fig. 50 Test 5: Rear Of Vehicle Low (Part 1 of 2). 2000–01 Eldorado w/Road Sensing Suspension

Step	Action	Value(s)	Yes	No
28	Check the following: • Rear struts for a leaking air sleeve. • Air tube for kinks or pinched tubes. • Air tubes for a disconnected condition • All air tube connections using soap and water. Was a leak or damage found and corrected?	—	Go to *ALC System Operation Check (w/o Road Sensing Suspension)*	Go to *Step 29*
29	1. Disconnect the air tube from the air dryer. 2. Connect the *J 22124-B* adapter tube to the air dryer. 3. Connect the *J 22124-B* gage to the *J 22124-B* adapter tube with the toggle valve on the opposite side (away from the air compressor) and closed. 4. Disconnect the air compressor electrical connector. 5. Jumper the air compressor electrical connector (compressor side), terminal A to ground. 6. Jumper the air compressor electrical connector (compressor side), terminal C, to B+ using a 30-amp fused jumper wire. 7. Allow the air compressor to operate until the pressure reaches 690 kPa (100 psi). 8. Disconnect the jumper from terminal A when 690 kPa (100 psi) is reached. Is the air compressor able to reach it 690 kPa (100 psi)?	690 kPa (100 psi)	Go to *Step 31*	Go to *Step 30*
30	Replace the air compressor. Is the replacement complete?	—	Go to *ALC System Operation Check (w/o Road Sensing Suspension)*	—
31	Does the air pressure reading on the *J 22124-B* stay at 690 kPa (100 psi)?	690 kPa (100 psi)	Go to *Step 32*	Go to *Air Compressor Leak Test*
32	The air tube or a shock absorber is leaking. Replace the component with the leak. Is the replacement complete?	—	Go to *ALC System Operation Check (w/o Road Sensing Suspension)*	—

GC2019800297040X

Fig. 49 Test 4: Rear Of Vehicle Low (Part 4 of 4). 2000–01 Eldorado Less Road Sensing Suspension

Step	Action	Value(s)	Yes	No
8	Repair the open circuit condition or reset/replace the circuit breaker/fuse. NOTE: A tripped circuit breaker may indicate: • no head relief – check for CVRSS codes • faulty air compressor • a short to ground in CKT 1340 Is the repair complete?	—	Go to *ALC System Operation Check (with Road Sensing Suspension)*	—
9	Inspect the left and right rear position sensors for damage and disconnected links. Are any damaged sensors or disconnected links present?	—	Go to *Step 13*	Go to *Step 10*
10	Perform the ALC System Leak Test. Is a leak present?	—	Go to *Step 11*	Go to *Step 12*
11	Repair the leak in the ALC System. Is the repair complete?	—	Go to *Step 14*	—
12	1. Turn the ignition OFF. 2. Connect the scan tool to the DLC. 3. Turn the ignition ON with engine OFF. 4. Perform the ALC Trim Height Adjustment. Has the ALC trim height adjustment been completed?	—	Go to *Step 14*	—
13	Replace the damaged rear position sensor or reconnect the link. Is the replacement complete?	—	Go to *ALC System Operation Check (with Road Sensing Suspension)*	—
14	1. Reconnect all of the connectors that were removed. 2. Clear the CVRSS DTCs. 3. Wait for at least 5 minutes. Is the rear of the vehicle trim (level)?	—	System OK	—

GC2019800298020X

Fig. 50 Test 5: Rear Of Vehicle Low (Part 2 of 2). 2000–01 Eldorado w/Road Sensing Suspension

Step	Action	Value(s)	Yes	No
	DEFINITION: This test checks the condition of the height sensor and the height sensor supply and ground circuits. This diagnostic procedure only applies to vehicles without Road Sensing Suspension.			
1	1. Disconnect the height sensor connector. 2. Measure the voltage from the height sensor connector (vehicle side), terminal C to ground. Is battery voltage measured?	Battery Voltage	Go to *Step 3*	Go to *Step 2*
2	**Important:** Ensure that the ALC circuit breaker is not tripped (open). Repair the open in circuit 1340 (ORN) between the ALC MaxiFuse® Block and the height sensor. Is the repair or replacement complete?	—	Go to *ALC System Operation Check (w/o Road Sensing Suspension)*	—

GC2019800299010X

Fig. 51 Test 6: Height Sensor Operational Check (Part 1 of 3). 2000–01 Eldorado

Step	Action	Value(s)	Yes	No
3	Measure the voltage from the height sensor connector (vehicle side), terminal C to the same connector, terminal A. Is battery voltage measured?	Battery Voltage	Go to *Step 5*	Go to *Step 4*
4	Repair the open circuit condition in CKT 1050 (BLK). Is the repair complete?	—	Go to *ALC System Operation Check (w/o Road Sensing Suspension)*	—
5	1. Turn the ignition switch to the ON position. 2. Measure the voltage from the height sensor connector (vehicle side), terminal D to the same connector, terminal A. Is battery voltage measured?	Battery Voltage	Go to *Step 7*	Go to *Step 6*
6	**Important:** Ensure that the ELC fuse is not open (blown). Repair the open circuit condition in CKT 2141 (BRN). Is the repair complete?	—	Go to *ALC System Operation Check (w/o Road Sensing Suspension)*	—
7	1. Check the height sensor connector for proper terminal contact. 2. Connect the height sensor connector. 3. Cycle ignition switch and return ignition switch to ON. Does the air compressor operate for 3 to 5 seconds after an initial 35 to 55 second delay?	—	Go to *Step 9*	Go to *Step 8*
8	Replace the height sensor. Is the replacement complete?	—	Go to *ALC System Operation Check (w/o Road Sensing Suspension)*	—
9	1. Raise the vehicle. NOTE: The vehicle must be raised on a drive-on lift or be supported at the rear under the rear axle. Full vehicle weight must be on the rear axle. 2. Disconnect the link from the position sensor. 3. Move the height sensor arm up so that it is approximately 45 degrees above level (to the floor). Does the air compressor run after the 17 to 27 second delay?	—	Go to *Step 11*	Go to *Step 10*
10	Replace the height sensor. Is the replacement complete?	—	Go to *ALC System Operation Check (w/o Road Sensing Suspension)*	—

GC2019800299020X

Fig. 51 Test 6: Height Sensor Operational Check (Part 2 of 3). 2000–01 Eldorado

Test Description

The numbers below refer to the step numbers on the diagnostic table.

2. Lack of communication may be due to a partial malfunction of the class 2 serial data circuit or due to a total malfunction of the class 2 serial data circuit. The specified procedure will determine the particular condition.

4. The presence of DTCs which begin with "U" indicate some other module is not communicating. The specified procedure will compile all the available information before tests are performed.

Step	Action	Yes	No
1	Install a scan tool. Does the scan tool power up?	Go to Step 2	Inspect DCL Connector & Scan Tool
2	1. Turn ON the ignition, with the engine OFF. 2. Attempt to establish communication with the following modules: o Continuously Variable Road Sensing Suspension (CVRSS) Module o Electronic Brake Control Module (EBCM) o Powertrain Control Module (PCM) Does the scan tool communicate with all of the listed control modules?	Go to Step 3	Inspect DCL Connector & Wiring
3	**Important** The engine may start during the following step. Turn OFF the engine as soon as you have observed the Crank power mode. 1. Access the Ignition Switch parameter in the body control module (BCM) inputs data display list. 2. Rotate the ignition switch through all positions while observing the ignition switch power mode parameter. Does the ignition switch parameter reading match the ignition switch position for all switch positions?	Go to Step 4	Go to Power Mode Mismatch

GC2010200707010X

Fig. 52 ALC System Check (Part 1 of 2). 2002 Eldorado & 2002–04 Seville

Step	Action	Value(s)	Yes	No
11	Move the height sensor down slowly until the air compressor stops. Does the air compressor stop?	—	Go to *Step 13*	Go to *Step 12*
12	Replace the height sensor. Is the replacement complete?	—	Go to *ALC System Operation Check (w/o Road Sensing Suspension)*	—
13	Move the height sensor arm down so that it is approximately 45 degrees below level (to the floor). After a 17 to 27 second delay, does air escape from the air compressor as the vehicle begins to lower?	—	Go to *Step 15*	Go to *Step 14*
14	Replace the height sensor. Is the replacement complete?	—	Go to *ALC System Operation Check (w/o Road Sensing Suspension)*	—
15	Adjust the height sensor. Is the adjustment complete?	—	Go to *ALC System Operation Check (w/o Road Sensing Suspension)*	—

GC2019800299030X

Fig. 51 Test 6: Height Sensor Operational Check (Part 3 of 3). 2000–01 Eldorado

Step	Action	Yes	No
4	Select the display DTCs function on the scan tool for the following modules: • Continuously Variable Road Sensing Suspension (CVRSS) • Electronic Brake Control (EBCM) • Powertrain Control (PCM) Does the scan tool display any DTCs?	Go to Step 5	Go to Tests Automatic Level Control
5	Does the scan tool display any DTCs which begin with a "U"?	Inspect DCL Connector & Wiring	Go to Step 6
6	Does the scan tool display any PCM DTCs?	Go to MOTOR's "Domestic Engine Performance & Driveability Manual"	Go to Step 7
7	Does the scan tool display any EBCM DTCs?	Go To Anti-Lock Brake	Go to Step 8
8	Does the scan tool display any of the following DTCs? C0657, C0658, C0662, C0663	Go to Diagnostic Trouble Code (DTC) List	Go to Road Sensing Suspension

GC2010200707020X

Fig. 52 ALC System Check (Part 2 of 2). 2002 Eldorado & 2002–04 Seville

Circuit Description W/F45 Road Sensing Suspension

The Automatic Level Control compressor is switched ON and OFF using an Electronic Level Control (ELC) compressor relay which is controlled by the Electronic Suspension Control (ESC) module. The ESC module circuitry provides a switched path to ground whenever compressor activity is required. This drive circuit is also continually monitored to determine if the voltage level agrees with the commanded state.

Conditions for Running the DTC

The ignition is ON.

Conditions for Setting the DTC

DTC C0657

The following conditions must be present to set the DTC:

- The ESC module detects voltage less than a preset value in the compressor motor control circuit during a compressor OFF state test.
- The fault is detected during three consecutive ignition cycles, or during the same ignition cycle after clearing the DTC with a scan tool.

DTC C0658

The following conditions must be present to set the DTC:

- The ESC module detects voltage greater than a preset value in the compressor motor control circuit during a compressor ON state test.
- The fault is detected during three consecutive ignition cycles, or during the same ignition cycle after clearing the DTC with a scan tool.

Action Taken When the DTC Sets

The ELC compressor relay output drive is disabled for the remainder of the ignition cycle.

Conditions for Clearing the MIL/DTC

- The scan tool can be used to clear the DTC.
- The DTC is saved as history when the ESC module no longer sees an out of range voltage condition in the compressor motor control circuit. The DTC will clear if the fault does not return after 50 consecutive ignition cycles.

Diagnostic Aids

These DTCs are set only by electrical problems with the ELC compressor relay coil circuit.

GC2010200708010X

Fig. 53 Codes C0657 & C0658: Compressor Motor Control Circuit Voltage (Part 1 of 3). 2002 Eldorado & 2002–04 Seville

Compressor motor problems and pneumatic leakage problems do not set these DTCs.

Test Description

The numbers below refer to the step numbers on the diagnostic table.

2. Tests for voltage in the Automatic Level Control relay coil supply voltage circuit.
3. Tests for a short to voltage in the Automatic Level Control relay coil supply voltage circuit.

Step	Action	Yes	No
1	Did you perform the Automatic Level Control Diagnostic System Check?	Go to Step 2	Go to System Check
2	1. Disconnect the ESC module connector. 2. Turn ON the ignition, with the engine OFF. 3. Connect a test lamp between the Automatic Level Control (ALC) relay coil supply voltage circuit and a good ground. Does the test lamp illuminate?	Go to Step 3	Go to Step 4
3	1. Turn OFF the ignition. 2. Disconnect the ELC Relay. 3. Turn ON the ignition, with the engine OFF. 4. Connect a test lamp between the ALC relay coil supply voltage circuit and a good ground. Does the test lamp illuminate?	Go to Step 7	Go to Step 6
4	Test the ALC relay coil supply voltage circuit for a short to ground or an open. Did you find and correct the condition?	Go to Step 10	Go to Step 5
5	Inspect for poor connections at the ELC Relay. Did you find and correct the condition?	Go to Step 10	Go to Step 8
6	Inspect for poor connections at the harness connector of the ESC module. Did you find and correct the condition?	Go to Step 10	Go to Step 9
7	Repair the short to voltage in the ALC relay coil supply voltage circuit. Did you complete the repair?	Go to Step 10	--

GC2010200708020X

Fig. 53 Codes C0657 & C0658: Compressor Motor Control Circuit Voltage (Part 2 of 3). 2002 Eldorado & 2002–04 Seville

Circuit Description W/F45 Road Sensing Suspension

The Automatic Level Control exhaust solenoid valve is switched ON or OFF by the Electronic Suspension Control (ESC) module. The ESC module provides a ground whenever exhaust activity is required and during a head-relief sequence which occurs before each compressor start-up. This drive output from the ESC module is continually monitored to determine if the voltage level agrees with the commanded state.

Conditions for Running the DTC

The ignition is ON.

Conditions for Setting the DTC

DTC C0662

The following conditions must be present to set the DTC:

- The ESC module detects voltage less than a preset value in the exhaust solenoid control circuit during an exhaust solenoid valve OFF state test.
- The fault is detected during three consecutive ignition cycles, or during the same ignition cycle after clearing the DTC with a scan tool.

DTC C0663

The following conditions must be present to set the DTC:

- The ESC module detects voltage greater than a preset value in the exhaust solenoid control circuit during an exhaust solenoid valve ON state test.
- The fault is detected during three consecutive ignition cycles, or during the same ignition cycle after clearing the DTC with a scan tool.

Action Taken When the DTC Sets

- ALL rear leveling activity for the remainder of the ignition cycle will be disabled.
- The SERVICE SUSPENSION SYSTEM message will be displayed.

Conditions for Clearing the MIL/DTC

- The scan tool can be used to clear the DTC.
- The DTC is saved as history when the ESC module no longer sees an out of range voltage condition in the exhaust solenoid control circuit. The DTC will clear if the fault does not return after 50 consecutive ignition cycles.

Diagnostic Aids

GC2010200709010X

Fig. 54 Codes C0662 & C0663: Exhaust Solenoid Control Circuit Voltage (Part 1 of 3). 2002 Eldorado & 2002–04 Seville

Step	Action	Yes	No
8	Replace the ELC Relay. Did you complete the replacement?	Go to Step 10	--
9	Replace the ESC module. Did you complete the replacement?	Go to Step 10	--
10	1. Use the scan tool in order to clear the DTCs . 2. Operate the vehicle within the Conditions for Running the DTC as specified in the supporting text. Does the DTC reset?	Go to Step 2	System OK

GC2010200708030X

Fig. 53 Codes C0657 & C0658: Compressor Motor Control Circuit Voltage (Part 3 of 3). 2002 Eldorado & 2002–04 Seville

Diagnostic Aids

These DTCs are set only by electrical problems with the ELC exhaust solenoid control circuit. Pneumatic blockage problems do not set these DTCs.

A temporary compressor overload, such as high head pressure during a cold start, may cause the ELC fuse to open. This is one possible cause of DTC C0662.

Test Description

The numbers below refer to the step numbers on the diagnostic table.

2. Tests for voltage in the ALC exhaust solenoid control circuit.
3. Tests for a short to voltage in the ALC exhaust solenoid control circuit.
4. Tests for voltage in the battery positive voltage circuit of the ALC compressor in order to isolate a short to ground or an open.

Step	Action	Yes	No
1	Did you perform the Automatic Level Control Diagnostic System Check?	Go to Step 2	Go to System Check
2	1. Disconnect the ESC module connector. 2. Turn ON the ignition, with the engine OFF. 3. Connect a test lamp between the ALC exhaust solenoid control circuit and a good ground. Does the test lamp illuminate?	Go to Step 3	Go to Step 4
3	1. Turn OFF the ignition. 2. Disconnect the ALC compressor connector. 3. Turn ON the ignition, with the engine OFF. 4. Connect a test lamp between the ALC exhaust solenoid control circuit and a good ground. Does the test lamp illuminate?	Go to Step 9	Go to Step 7
4	1. Turn OFF the ignition. 2. Disconnect the ALC compressor connector. 3. Turn ON the ignition, with the engine OFF. 4. Connect a test lamp between the battery positive voltage circuit of the ALC compressor and a good ground. Does the test lamp illuminate?	Go to Step 5	Go to Step 8
5	Test the ALC exhaust solenoid control circuit for a short to ground or an open. Did you find and correct the condition?	Go to Step 12	Go to Step 6

GC2010200709020X

Fig. 54 Codes C0662 & C0663: Exhaust Solenoid Control Circuit Voltage (Part 2 of 3). 2002 Eldorado & 2002–04 Seville

Step	Action	Yes	No
6	Inspect for poor connections at the ALC compressor connector. Did you find and correct the condition?	Go to Step 12	Go to Step 10
7	Inspect for poor connections at the ESC module. Did you find and correct the condition?	Go to Step 12	Go to Step 11
8	Repair the short to ground or the open in the battery positive voltage circuit of the ALC compressor connector. Did you complete the repair?	Go to Step 12	--
9	Repair the short to voltage in the ALC exhaust solenoid control circuit. Did you complete the repair?	Go to Step 12	--
10	Replace the ALC compressor head. Did you complete the replacement?	Go to Step 12	--
11	Replace the ESC module. Did you complete the replacement?	Go to Step 12	--
12	1. Use the scan tool in order to clear the DTCs . 2. Operate the vehicle within the Conditions for Running the DTC as specified in the supporting text. Does the DTC reset?	Go to Step 2	System OK

GC2010200709030X

Fig. 54 Codes C0662 & C0663: Exhaust Solenoid Control Circuit Voltage (Part 3 of 3). 2002 Eldorado & 2002–04 Seville

Step	Action	Yes	No
3	Reapply the service air and monitor the automatic level control air compressor assembly for leaks. Does the pressure leak down below 620 kPa (110 psi)?	Go to Step 4	System OK
4	Replace the automatic level control air compressor. Was the repair completed?	Go to Step 3	--
5	Monitor the J 22124-B pressure gage for 1 minute. Does the pressure leak down below 620 kPa (90 psi)?	Go to Step 2	System OK

GC2010200711020X

Fig. 55 ALC Air Compressor Performance Test (Part 2 of 2). 2002 Eldorado & 2002–04 Seville

Step	Action	Yes	No
1	Did you review the ALC System Description and Operation and perform the necessary inspections?	Go to Step 2	Go to Automatic Level Control Tests
2	1. Disconnect the air tube from the air dryer. 2. Connect the air tube to the J 22124-B on the side opposite the toggle valve. 3. Close the toggle valve. 4. Apply service air pressure to J 22124-B service valve until the gage reads 550 kPa (80 psi). 5. Monitor the J 22124-B gage pressure for 1 minute. Does the system maintain pressure?	System OK	Go to Step 3
3	Inspect the shock absorber air sleeves for air leakage using soapy water. Did you find an air leak?	Go to Step 5	Go to Step 4
4	Inspect the air tubes and connections for air leakage using soapy water. Did you find and correct the condition?	Go to Step 6	--
5	Replace the shock absorbers. Did you complete the replacement?	Go to Step 6	--
6	Operate the system in order to verify the repair. Did you correct the condition?	System OK	Go to Step 2

GC2010200712000X

Fig. 56 ALC System Leak Test. 2002 Eldorado & 2002–04 Seville

Step	Action	Yes	No
1	1. Disconnect the air line from the automatic level control air dryer. 2. Connect the automatic level control air dryer to the J 22124-B using the adapter J 22124-98 on the side opposite of the toggle valve. Close the toggle valve in the down position. 3. With Road sensor Suspension A. Turn on the Ignition with eng OFF. B. Activate the automatic level control compressor with the scan tool. 4. With Road sensor Suspension A. Disconnect the automatic level control module. B. Connect a 3 amp fused jumper wire between the automatic level control relay coil supply voltage and ground. C. This step will activate the automatic level control compressor motor. 5. Allow the automatic level control air compressor to run until the J 22124-B gage pressure reads at least 750 kPa (110 psi). 6. Deactivate the automatic level control air compressor. Does the automatic level control air compressor develop at least 750 kPa (110 psi)? The automatic level control air compressor may leak down as low as 620 kPa (90 psi) after deactivating. This is an acceptable level.	Go to Step 5	Go to Step 2
2	1. Apply service air to the J 22124-B service valve until the gage reads 690 kPa (100 psi). 2. Using a soap bubble solution, check for leaks in the automatic level control air compressor assembly: o The automatic level control air dryer O-ring casting bore. o The automatic level control air dryer. Replace the automatic level control air dryer. o The automatic level control air compressor head cover bolts. **Tighten** Tighten the automatic level control air compressor head cover bolts as required to 6 N·m (53 lb in). o The automatic level control air compressor head casting air intake and exhaust opening. Replace the automatic level control air compressor head if you find a leak. o Around the edge of the solenoid valve terminal housing. Replace the automatic level control air compressor head if you find a leak. o Around the edge of the cover gasket. If you find a leak, check the tightness of the cover bolts before you replace the gasket. 3. Complete repairs as necessary. Did you find and repair any leaks?	Go to Step 3	Go to Step 4

GC2010200711010X

Fig. 55 ALC Air Compressor Performance Test (Part 1 of 2). 2002 Eldorado & 2002–04 Seville

Step	Action	Yes	No
1	Did you perform the necessary inspections?	Go to Step 2	Go to Automatic Level Control
2	1. Disconnect the auto level control sensor connector. 2. Connect a test lamp between the battery positive voltage circuit of the ALC sensor and a good ground. Does the test lamp illuminate?	Go to Step 3	Go to Step 10
3	Connect a test lamp between the battery positive voltage circuit and the ground circuit of the ALC sensor. Does the test lamp illuminate?	Go to Step 4	Go to Step 11
4	1. Turn ON the ignition, with the engine OFF. 2. Connect a test lamp between the ignition 1 voltage circuit of the ALC sensor and a good ground. Does the test lamp illuminate?	Go to Step 5	Go to Step 12
5	Connect a 10 A fused jumper between the automatic level control exhaust solenoid control circuit of the ALC sensor and a good ground. Does the exhaust solenoid activate and vent air?	Go to Step 14	Go to Step 6
6	Inspect the fuse in the jumper wire. Did the fuse in the jumper open?	Go to Step 13	Go to Step 7
7	1. Leave the 10 A fused jumper connected. 2. Disconnect the ALC air compressor connector. 3. Connect a test lamp between the battery positive voltage circuit and the automatic level control exhaust solenoid control circuit of the ALC compressor. Does the test lamp illuminate?	Go to Step 15	Go to Step 8
8	Test the automatic level control exhaust solenoid control circuit for an open. Did you find and correct the condition?	Go to Step 16	Go to Step 9

GC2010200713010X

Fig. 57 Rear Of Vehicle High (Part 1 of 2). 2002 Eldorado & 2002–04 Seville Less Road Sensing Suspension

Step	Action	Yes	No
9	Repair the open in the battery positive voltage circuit of the ALC compressor. Did you complete the repair?	Go to Step 16	--
10	Repair the open in the battery positive voltage circuit of the ALC sensor. Did you complete the repair?	Go to Step 16	--
11	Repair the open in the automatic level control sensor ground circuit. Did you complete the repair?	Go to Step 16	--
12	Repair the open in the ignition 1 voltage circuit of the ALC sensor. Did you complete the repair?	Go to Step 16	--
13	Repair the short to voltage in the automatic level control exhaust solenoid control circuit. Did you complete the repair?	Go to Step 16	--
14	Replace the auto level control sensor. Did you complete the replacement?	Go to Step 16	--
15	Replace the auto level control air compressor head. Did you complete the replacement?	Go to Step 16	--
16	Operate the system in order to verify the repair. Did you correct the condition?	System OK	Go to Step 2

GC2010200713020X

Fig. 57 Rear Of Vehicle High (Part 2 of 2). 2002 Eldorado & 2002–04 Seville Less Road Sensing Suspension

Step	Action	Yes	No
9	1. Disconnect the air tubes from both rear shock absorbers. 2. Connect the Special Tools ALC pressure gage between both air tubes. 3. Open the gage toggle valve. 4. Disconnect the air tube from the ALC air dryer. 5. Apply shop air to the gage schrader valve. Is air exiting both of the air tubes at the ALC air dryer connection?	Go to Step 10	Go to Step 12
10	1. Turn the ignition OFF. 2. Replace the ALC air compressor assembly. 3. Install the ALC intake air filter on the vehicle body. Are all of the replacements and/or installations complete?	Go to Step 13	--
11	1. Turn the ignition OFF. 2. Connect the scan tool. 3. Turn the ignition ON with the engine OFF. 4. Perform the CVRSS/ALC recalibration procedure. Has the recalibration procedure been completed?	Go to Step 13	--
12	Replace the air tube going from the air dryer to both rear shock absorbers. Is the repair complete?	Go to Step 13	--
13	1. Turn the ignition OFF. 2. Turn the ignition ON with the engine OFF. 3. Wait for at least 5 minutes. Is the rear of the vehicle at trim level?	Go to Step 14	Go to Step 2
14	Operate the system in order to verify the repair. Did you correct the condition?	System OK	Go to Step 2

GC2010200714020X

Fig. 58 Rear Of Vehicle High (Part 2 of 2). 2002 Eldorado & 2002–04 Seville w/Road Sensing Suspension

Step	Action	Yes	No
1	Did you perform the Automatic Level Control (ALC) Diagnostic System Check?	Go to Step 2	Go to System Check
2	1. Turn the ignition ON with the engine OFF. 2. Listen for the ALC air compressor to activate. Is the ALC air compressor running for more than 5 minutes?	Go to Step 3	Go to Step 6
3	1. Turn the ignition OFF. 2. Remove the ALC compressor relay. 3. Turn the ignition ON with the engine OFF. Is the air compressor running?	Go to Step 4	Go to Step 5
4	1. Turn the ignition OFF. 2. Reinstall the ALC compressor relay. 3. Repair the short to voltage in the ALC air compressor motor control circuit. Is the repair complete?	Go to Step 13	--
5	1. Turn the ignition OFF. 2. Replace the ALC air compressor relay. Is the repair complete?	Go to Step 13	--
6	Inspect the left and right rear position sensors for damage and disconnected links. Are any damaged sensors or disconnected links present?	Go to Step 7	Go to Step 8
7	Replace the damaged rear position sensor or reconnect the link. Is the repair complete?	Go to Step 13	--
8	1. Remove the ALC intake filter from the vehicle body. Do not remove it from the ALC air compressor or hose. 2. Using the scan tool, cycle ALC air compressor. 3. After 1 minute, stop cycling. 4. Cycle the ALC exhaust solenoid while checking to see if air is exiting the ALC intake air filter. Is air exiting the ALC intake air filter?	Go to Step 11	Go to Step 9

GC2010200714010X

Fig. 58 Rear Of Vehicle High (Part 1 of 2). 2002 Eldorado & 2002–04 Seville w/Road Sensing Suspension

Step	Action	Yes	No
1	Did you perform the necessary inspections?	Go to Step 2	Go to - Automatic Level Control Test
2	1. Turn ON the ignition, with the engine OFF. 2. Add a load of 135 kg (300 lbs) to the rear of the vehicle. Does the automatic level control (ALC) compressor operate?	Go to Step 3	Go to Step 4
3	Does the rear of the vehicle rise and not leak down?	Go to Automatic Level Control Sensor Adjustment	Go to - Automatic Level Control Test
4	1. Disconnect the automatic level control sensor connector. 2. Connect a test lamp between the battery positive voltage circuit of the automatic level control (ALC) sensor and a good ground. Does the test lamp illuminate?	Go to Step 5	Go to Step 14
5	Connect a test lamp between the battery positive voltage circuit and the ground circuit of the ALC sensor. Does the test lamp illuminate?	Go to Step 6	Go to Step 15
6	Connect a test lamp between the automatic level control relay coil supply voltage circuit and a good ground. Does the test lamp illuminate?	Go to Step 7	Go to Step 11
7	Connect a 10 amp fused jumper wire between the automatic level control relay coil supply voltage circuit and a good ground. Does the ALC activate?	Go to Step 16	Go to Step 8

GC2010200715010X

Fig. 59 Rear Of Vehicle Low (Part 1 of 3). 2002 Eldorado & 2002–04 Seville Less Road Sensing Suspension

Step	Action	Yes	No
8	1. Leave the 10 amp fused jumper wire connected between the automatic level control relay coil supply voltage circuit and a good ground 2. Disconnect the ALC compressor connector. 3. Connect a test lamp between the automatic level control compressor motor control circuit and a good ground. Does the test lamp illuminate?	Go to Step 10	Go to Step 9
9	Test the automatic level control compressor motor control circuit for a short to ground or an open. Did you find and correct the condition?	Go to Step 19	Go to Step 13
10	Test the ALC compressor harness for a poor connection or an open. Did you find and correct the condition?	Go to Step 19	Go to Step 18
11	Test the automatic level control relay coil supply voltage circuit for a short to ground or an open. Did you find and correct the condition?	Go to Step 19	Go to Step 12
12	Test the ignition 1 voltage circuit to the ELC relay for a short to ground or an open. Did you find and correct the condition?	Go to Step 19	Go to Step 17
13	Test the battery positive voltage circuit to the ELC relay for a short to ground or an open. Did you find and correct the condition?	Go to Step 19	Go to Step 17
14	Repair the open in the battery positive voltage circuit to the ALC sensor. Did you complete the repair?	Go to Step 19	--
15	Repair the open in the ALC sensor ground circuit. Did you complete the repair?	Go to Step 19	--
16	Replace the ALC sensor. Did you complete the replacement?	Go to Step 19	--

GC2010200715020X

Fig. 59 Rear Of Vehicle Low (Part 2 of 3). 2002 Eldorado & 2002–04 Seville Less Road Sensing Suspension

Step	Action	Yes	No
1	Did you perform the Automatic Level Control (ALC) System Check?	Go to Step 2	Go to Diagnostic System Check - Automatic Level Control
2	1. Turn the ignition ON with the engine OFF. 2. Listen for the ALC air compressor to activate. Does the air compressor come on within 30 seconds?	Go to Step 8	Go to Step 3
3	1. Turn the ignition OFF. 2. Disconnect the ALC connector from the ALC air compressor assembly. 3. Disconnect the Electronic Suspension Module connector. 4. Turn the ignition ON. 5. Connect a fused jumper between the ALC relay coil supply voltage circuit and ground. 6. Measure the voltage between the ALC compressor motor control circuit and ground. Does the voltmeter display a voltage greater than 10 volts?	Go to Step 4	Go to Step 6
4	1. Remove the fused jumper wire. 2. Turn the ignition OFF. 3. Test the ground circuit of the ALC air compressor connector for a ground. Did you find and correct the condition?	Go to Step 13	Go to Step 5
5	Replace the ALC air compressor assembly. Is the repair complete?	Go to Step 11	--
6	1. Remove the fused jumper wire. 2. Turn the ignition OFF. 3. Check for the following: o Open ELC fuse o Bad ELC relay o Open circuit in ALC air compressor motor control circuit o Open circuit in ALC relay coil supply voltage circuit Was a problem found?	Go to Step 7	--

GC2010200716010X

Fig. 60 Rear Of Vehicle Low (Part 1 of 2). 2002 Eldorado & 2002–04 Seville w/Road Sensing Suspension

Step	Action	Yes	No
17	Replace the ELC relay. Did you complete the replacement?	Go to Step 19	--
18	Replace the ALC compressor. Did you complete the replacement?	Go to Step 19	--
19	Operate the system in order to verify the repair. Did you correct the condition?	System OK	Go to Step 1

GC2010200715030X

Fig. 59 Rear Of Vehicle Low (Part 3 of 3). 2002 Eldorado & 2002–04 Seville Less Road Sensing Suspension

Step	Action	Yes	No
7	**Important** A open fuse may indicate: • No head relief--check for ALC codes. • A faulty air compressor • A short to ground in the exhaust solenoid battery positive circuit Repair the short to ground in the ALC compressor battery positive circuit or replace the fuse. Is the repair complete?	Go to Step 13	--
8	Inspect the left and right rear position sensors for damage and disconnected links. Are any damaged sensors or disconnected links present?	Go to Step 12	Go to Step 9
9	Perform the ALC System Leak Test. Is a leak present?	Go to Step 10	Go to Step 11
10	Repair the leak in the ALC System. Is the repair complete?	Go to Step 13	--
11	1. Turn the ignition OFF. 2. Connect the scan tool. 3. Turn the ignition ON with engine OFF. 4. Perform the CVRSS/ALC recalibration procedure. Has the recalibration been completed?	Go to Step 13	--
12	Replace the damaged rear position sensor or reconnect the link. Is the replacement complete?	Go to Step 13	--
13	Operate the system in order to verify the repair. Did you correct the condition?	System OK	Go to Step 1

GC2010200716020X

Fig. 60 Rear Of Vehicle Low (Part 2 of 2). 2002 Eldorado & 2002–04 Seville w/Road Sensing Suspension

Circuit Description

Normal vehicle class 2 communications and module operations will not begin until the system power mode has been identified. Discrete wires from the ignition switch contacts are monitored by the power mode master (PMM) module in order to determine the correct power mode. The PMM communicates the system power mode to all class 2 modules on the class 2 serial data line.

Test Description

The numbers below refer to the step numbers on the diagnostic table.

6. This step tests for battery voltage on the signal circuits that are not required.
7. This step tests for no battery voltage on the required signal circuits.
8. If any ignition switch parameters that should be inactive in the present ignition switch position are active, 2 ignition switch signal circuits may be shorted together.
9. This step eliminates open circuits as the cause of the malfunction.

Step	Action	Yes	No
Important: Open the driver door and leave it open during this test. This will disable the RAP power mode and eliminate this power mode from the power mode parameter list.			
1	1. Install a scan tool. 2. Turn OFF the ignition. 3. With a scan tool, under the Diagnostic Circuit Check menu observe the Class 2 Power Mode parameter. Does the displayed power mode parameter match the actual ignition switch position?	Go to Step 2	Go to Step 6

GC2010200717010X

Fig. 61 Power Mode Mismatch (Part 1 of 4). 2002 Eldorado & 2002–04 Seville

Step	Action	Yes	No
2	1. Turn the ignition switch to the UNLOCK position. 2. With a scan tool, under the Diagnostic Circuit Check menu observe the Class 2 Power Mode parameter. Does the displayed power mode parameter match the actual ignition switch position?	Go to Step 3	Go to Step 6
3	1. Turn ON the ignition, with the engine OFF. 2. With a scan tool, under the Diagnostic Circuit Check menu observe the Class 2 Power Mode parameter. Does the displayed power mode parameter match the actual ignition switch position?	Go to Step 4	Go to Step 6
4	**Important:** The engine may start during this procedure. Turn the ignition OFF after verifying this power mode. 1. Turn the ignition switch to the CRANK position. 2. With a scan tool, under the Diagnostic Circuit Check menu observe the Class 2 Power Mode parameter. Does the displayed power mode parameter match the actual ignition switch position?	Go to Step 5	Go to Step 6
5	1. Turn the ignition switch to the ACCY position. 2. With a scan tool, under the Diagnostic Circuit Check menu observe the Class 2 Power Mode parameter. Does the displayed power mode parameter match the actual ignition switch position?	Intermittent and Poor Connections	Go to Step 6
6	**Important:** The engine may start during this procedure. Turn the ignition OFF after verifying this power mode. 1. Turn OFF the ignition. 2. Disconnect the PMM. 3. Hold the ignition switch in the position that indicated the incorrect power mode. 4. With a test lamp attached to a good ground, test the PMM ignition switch inputs for voltage. Is voltage present on only the inputs specified for the ignition switch position?	Go to Step 7	Go to Step 8

GC2010200717020X

Fig. 61 Power Mode Mismatch (Part 2 of 4). 2002 Eldorado & 2002–04 Seville

Step	Action	Yes	No
13	**Important:** After replacement of the PMM perform the set up procedure if required. Replace the PMM. Did you complete the replacement?	Go to Step 14	--
14	**Important:** The engine may start during this procedure. Turn the ignition OFF after verifying all power modes. 1. Reconnect all disconnected components. 2. With a scan tool, under the Diagnostic Circuit Check menu observe the Class 2 Power Mode parameter. 3. Cycle the ignition switch through all possible positions one at a time. Does the displayed power mode parameter match the actual ignition switch position?	System OK	Go to Step 1

GC2010200717040X

Fig. 61 Power Mode Mismatch (Part 4 of 4). 2002 Eldorado & 2002–04 Seville

Step	Action	Yes	No
7	**Important:** The engine may start during this procedure. Turn the ignition OFF after verifying this power mode. 1. Hold the ignition switch in the position that indicated the incorrect power mode. 2. With a test lamp attached to a good ground, test the PMM ignition switch inputs for voltage. Is voltage not present on any inputs specified for the ignition switch position?	Go to Step 9	Go to Step 11
8	1. Disconnect the ignition switch. 2. Test the PMM ignition switch input circuits for a short to voltage. 3. Test the PMM ignition switch circuits for a short between circuits. Did you find and correct the condition?	Go to Step 14	Go to Step 10
9	1. Disconnect the ignition switch. 2. Test the PMM ignition switch input circuits for an open. Did you find and correct the condition?	Go to Step 14	Go to Step 10
10	Inspect for poor connections and terminal tension at the harness connector of the ignition switch. Did you find and correct the condition?	Go to Step 14	Go to Step 12
11	Inspect for poor connections and terminal tension at the harness connector of the PMM. Did you find and correct the condition?	Go to Step 14	Go to Step 13
12	Replace the ignition switch. Did you complete the replacement?	Go to Step 14	--

GC2010200717030X

Fig. 61 Power Mode Mismatch (Part 3 of 4). 2002 Eldorado & 2002–04 Seville

Step	Action	Value(s)	Yes	No
1	Did you review the Automatic Level Control (ALC) System Operation?		Go to Step 2	Go to Automatic Level Control System Operation
2	**Important** **The vehicle must be raised on a drive on hoist.** 1 Raise and support the vehicle. 2 Disconnect the ALC position sensor harness connector. 3 Using a test lamp connected to a good ground, probe the position sensor harness connector battery positive voltage terminal. Does the test lamp illuminate?		Go to Step 3	Go to Step 12
3	Connect a test lamp between the position sensor harness connector positive battery voltage terminal and the position sensor harness connector ground terminal. Does the test lamp illuminate?		Go to Step 4	Go to Step 13
4	Using a 3 amp fused jumper wire, jumper the position sensor harness connector exhaust solenoid control circuit to a good ground. Did the exhaust solenoid click?		Go to Step 5	Go to Step 8
5	Did the vehicle lower?		Go to Step 6	Go to Step 10
6	Check the ALC position sensor adjustment. Is the adjustment OK?		Go to Step 14	Go to Step 7
7	Readjust the ALC position sensor. Did you complete the adjustment?		Go to Step 20	

GC2019900624010X

Fig. 62 Test 1: Rear Of Vehicle High (Part 1 of 3). Park Avenue

Step	Action	Value(s)	Yes	No
8	Test the ALC exhaust solenoid feed circuit for a open circuit or a short to ground. Did you find and correct the condition?		Go to Step 20	Go to Step 9
9	Test the ALC exhaust solenoid control circuit for a open circuit or a short to ground. Did you find and correct the condition?		Go to Step 20	Go to Step 15
10	Disconnect the air tube assembly from the drier. Did the vehicle lower?		Go to Step 15	Go to Step 11
11	Disconnect the air tube assembly from the shocks. Did the vehicle lower?		Go to Step 16	Go to Step 17
12	Repair open circuit or short to ground on the position sensor positive battery circuit. Did you complete the repair?		Go to Step 20	
13	Repair open circuit or short to voltage on the position sensor ground circuit. Did you complete the repair?		Go to Step 20	
14	Inspect for poor connections / terminal tension at the harness connector for the ALC position sensor. Did you find and correct the condition?		Go to Step 20	Go to Step 18
15	Inspect for poor connections / terminal tension at the harness connector for the ALC exhaust solenoid. Did you find and correct the condition?		Go to Step 20	Go to Step 19
16	Replace the air tube assembly. Did you complete the replacement?		Go to Step 20	

GC2019900624020X

Fig. 62 Test 1: Rear Of Vehicle High (Part 2 of 3). Park Avenue

Step	Action	Value(s)	Yes	No
1	Did you review the Automatic Level Control (ALC) Operation?		Go to Step 2	Go to Automatic Level Control System Operation
2	**Important** **The vehicle must be raised on a drive on hoist.** 1 Raise and support the vehicle. 2 Carefully inspect the air tube assembly,shocks, position sensor,link and compressor assembly for leaks and damage. **Were any leaks or damage found?**		Go to Step 3	Go to Step 4
3	Repair or replace any damaged or leaking components. Is the repair complete?		Go to Step 27	

GC2019900625010X

Fig. 63 Test 2: Rear Of Vehicle Low (Part 1 of 4). Park Avenue

Step	Action	Value(s)	Yes	No
11	Test the ALC relay coil side feed circuit for a open circuit or a short to ground. Did you find and correct the condition?		Go to Step 27	Go to Step 12
12	Test the ALC compressor motor control circuit for an open circuit or a short to voltage. Did you find and correct the condition?		Go to Step 27	Go to Step 21
13	Test the ALC compressor motor feed circuit for a open circuit or a short to ground. Did you find and correct the condition?		Go to Step 27	Go to Step 14
14	Test the ALC relay supply circuit for an open circuit or a short to ground. Did you find and correct the condition?		Go to Step 27	Go to Step 21
15	Check the ALC position sensor adjustment. Is the adjustment OK		Go to Step 22	Go to Step 16
16	Readjust the ALC position sensor. Did you complete the adjustment?		Go to Step 27	
17	Repair open circuit or short to ground on position sensor battery positive circuit. Did you complete the repair?		Go to Step 27	
18	Repair open circuit or short to voltage on the position sensor ground circuit. Did you complete the repair?		Go to Step 27	

GC2019900625030X

Fig. 63 Test 2: Rear Of Vehicle Low (Part 3 of 4). Park Avenue

Step	Action	Value(s)	Yes	No
17	Replace the shock that did not lower. Did you complete the replacement?		Go to Step 20	
18	Replace the ALC position sensor. Did you complete the replacement		Go to Step 20	
19	Replace the ALC compressor head assembly. Did you complete the replacement?		Go to Step 20	
20	Operate the vehicle within the conditions for enabling the automatic level control. Does the ALC operate properly?		System OK	Go to Step 2

GC2019900624030X

Fig. 62 Test 1: Rear Of Vehicle High (Part 3 of 3). Park Avenue

Step	Action	Value(s)	Yes	No
4	1 Disconnect the ALC position sensor harness connector. 2 Using a test lamp connected to a good ground, probe the position sensor harness battery positive voltage circuit. Does the test lamp illuminate?		Go to Step 5	Go to Step 17
5	Connect a test lamp between the position sensor harness connector battery positive voltage terminal and position sensor ground terminal. Does the test lamp illuminate?		Go to Step 6	Go to Step 18
6	1 Turn ON the ignition, with the engine OFF. 2 Using a test lamp connected to a good ground, probe the position sensor harness connector ignition positive voltage circuit. Does the test lamp illuminate?		Go to Step 7	Go to Step 19
7	Using a 3 amp fused jumper wire, jumper the position sensor harness connector compressor motor control circuit to a good ground. Does the ALC compressor engage?		Go to Step 15	Go to Step 8
8	Did the ALC relay click?		Go to Step 9	Go to Step 11
9	1 Disconnect the ALC compressor harness connector. 2 Using a test lamp connected to a good ground, probe the ALC compressor motor feed circuit. Does the test lamp illuminate?		Go to Step 10	Go to Step 13
10	Connect a test lamp between the compressor motor harness connector compressor feed circuit and the compressor ground circuit. Does the test lamp illuminate?		Go to Step 23	Go to Step 20

GC2019900625020X

Fig. 63 Test 2: Rear Of Vehicle Low (Part 2 of 4). Park Avenue

Step	Action	Value(s)	Yes	No
19	Repair open circuit or short to ground on the position sensor ignition positive voltage circuit. Did you complete the repair?		Go to Step 27	
20	Repair open circuit or short to voltage on the ALC compressor ground circuit. Did you find and correct the condition?		Go to Step 27	
21	Inspect for poor connections / terminal tension at the ALC relay. Did you find and correct the condition?		Go to Step 27	Go to Step 24
22	Inspect for poor connections / terminal tension at the ALC Position Sensor. Did you find and correct the condition?		Go to Step 27	Go to Step 25
23	Inspect for poor connections / terminal tension at the ALC Compressor Assembly. Did you find and correct the condition?		Go to Step 27	Go to Step 26
24	Replace the ALC relay. Did you complete the replacement?		Go to Step 27	
25	Replace the ALC Position Sensor. Did you complete the replacement?		Go to Step 27	
26	Replace the ALC Compressor. Did you complete the replacement?		Go to Step 27	
27	Operate the vehicle within the conditions for enabling the automatic level control. Does the ALC operate correctly?		System OK	Go to Step 2

GC2019900625040X

Fig. 63 Test 2: Rear Of Vehicle Low (Part 4 of 4). Park Avenue

Step	Action	Normal Result(s)	Abnormal Result(s)
1	Turn the ignition to the ON position.	After approximately 35–55 seconds, the air compressor runs for 3–5 seconds. **Important:** This action may be overridden by the height sensor if a load has been added or removed from the vehicle.	• The air compressor cycles on and off frequently. If no air leaks are present, go to *Rear of Vehicle Low (w/o Road Sensing Suspension).* • The air compressor runs excessively. Check for a disconnected or damaged air tube or a damaged shock absorber. If OK, go to *Rear of Vehicle Low (w/o Road Sensing Suspension).*
2	Add a 136 kg (300 lb) load to the luggage compartment.	After a 17–27 second delay, the air compressor runs and the rear of the vehicle rises to the correct trim height.	• The air compressor cycles on and off frequently. If no air leaks are present, go to *Rear of Vehicle Low (w/o Road Sensing Suspension).* • The air compressor runs excessively. Check for a disconnected or damaged air tube or a damaged shock absorber. If OK, go to *Rear of Vehicle Low (w/o Road Sensing Suspension).*
3	1. Turn the ignition to the OFF position. 2. Remove the load from the luggage compartment.	After a 17–27 second delay, a hiss of escaping air may be heard, and the rear of the vehicle lowers to the correct trim height.	The exhaust solenoid does not energize after a 17-27 second delay and the rear of the vehicle remains above the correct trim height. Refer to *Rear of Vehicle High (w/o Road Sensing Suspension).*

GC2019900424000X

Fig. 64 ALC System Operation Check. 2000–01 Seville Less Road Sensing Suspension

Step	Action	Value(s)	Yes	No
1	Is any aftermarket equipment installed on the vehicle that could affect the ALC system?	—	Go to *Step 2*	Go to *Step 4*
2	Check the aftermarket equipment to ensure that it is not affecting ALC performance. Is the aftermarket equipment affecting the ALC performance?	—	Go to *Step 3*	Go to *Step 4*
3	Correct the condition. Is the condition corrected?	—	Go to *ALC System Operation Check (w/o Road Sensing Suspension)*	—
4	Check the ELC fuse for an open (blown) condition. Is the fuse open?	—	Go to *Step 5*	Go to *Step 6*
5	**Important:** If the fuse is open (blown) repeatedly, check circuit 1342 (RED) for a short circuit condition to ground. Replace the fuse. Is the replacement complete?	—	Go to *ALC System Operation Check (w/o Road Sensing Suspension)*	—
6	Check the height sensor and link for proper connection and damage. Are the height sensor and link properly connected and in good condition?	—	Go to *Step 8*	Go to *Step 7*
7	Reconnect or replace the height sensor or link. Is the repair or replacement complete?	—	Go to *ALC System Operation Check (w/o Road Sensing Suspension)*	—

GC2019900426010X

Fig. 66 Test 1: Rear Of Vehicle High (Part 1 of 3). 2000–01 Seville Less Road Sensing Suspension

Step	Action	Value(s)	Yes	No
8	1. Turn the ignition to the ON position. **Important:** The vehicle must be raised on a drive-on lift. Full vehicle weight must be on the rear tires. 2. Raise the vehicle. 3. Disconnect the link from the height sensor. **Important:** The height sensor has a 17–27 second delay period before the exhaust solenoid is activated. 4. Move the height sensor lever down so that it is approximately 45 degrees below level (to the floor) and hold it there. Will the rear of the vehicle lower to trim level or below?	—	Go to *Step 9*	Go to *Step 10*
9	Adjust the height sensor. Is trim height at the rear underbody points correct?	—	Go to *ALC System Operation Check (w/o Road Sensing Suspension)*	Repeat *Step 9*
10	Move the height sensor lever up so that it is approximately 45 degrees above level (to the floor) and hold it there for a minimum of 27 seconds (17–27 seconds is the height sensor delay period). Does the air compressor come on?	—	Go to *Step 11*	Go to *Height Sensor Operational Check*
11	Disconnect the air tube from the air dryer. Will the rear of the vehicle lower to trim level or below?	—	Go to *Step 19*	Go to *Step 12*
12	1. Connect the link to the height sensor lever. 2. Disconnect the air tube from both shock absorbers. Will the rear of the vehicle lower to trim level or below?	—	Go to *Step 13*	Go to *Step 14*
13	Replace the air tube. Is the replacement complete?	—	Go to *ALC System Operation Check (w/o Road Sensing Suspension)*	—
14	Is the vehicle uneven (more than 19 mm (0.75 in) from side to side at the rear?	—	Go to *Step 16*	Go to *Step 15*
15	Replace both rear springs. Is the trim height at the rear underbody points correct?	—	Go to *ALC System Operation Check (w/o Road Sensing Suspension)*	—
16	1. Observe which side of the vehicle is high. 2. Bounce the rear of the vehicle three times. Is the vehicle still uneven more than 19 mm (0.75 in) from side to side at the rear?	—	Go to *Step 17*	Go to *Step 18*
17	Replace the rear spring on the side of the vehicle that is high. Is the trim height at the rear underbody points correct?	—	Go to *ALC System Operation Check (w/o Road Sensing Suspension)*	Repeat this *Diagnostic Table*

GC2019900426020X

Fig. 66 Test 1: Rear Of Vehicle High (Part 2 of 3). 2000–01 Seville Less Road Sensing Suspension

Step	Action	Normal Result(s)	Abnormal Result(s)
1	1. Turn the ignition ON with the engine off. 2. Clear the CVRSS DTCs. 3. Check for CVRSS DTCs using the On-Board Diagnostics.	No CVRSS DTCs are present.	One of the following DTCs is displayed as HISTORY or CURRENT: • C1735 • C1736 • C1737 • C1738 If one of the above DTCs is displayed, go to the appropriate diagnostic table.
2	Turn the ignition to the ON position.	After a delay, the air compressor runs for 3–5 seconds. **Important:** This action may be overridden if a load has been added or removed from the vehicle.	• The air compressor cycles on and off frequently. If no air leaks are present, go to *Rear of Vehicle Low (with Road Sensing Suspension).* • The air compressor runs excessively. Check for a disconnected or damaged air tube or a damaged strut. If OK, go to *Rear of Vehicle Low (with Road Sensing Suspension).*
3	Add a 136 kg (300 lb) load to the luggage compartment.	After a delay, the air compressor runs and the rear of the vehicle rises to the correct trim height. Refer to *Trim Height* in Suspension General Diagnostics.	• The air compressor cycles on and off frequently. If no air leaks are present, go to *Rear of Vehicle Low (with Road Sensing Suspension).* • The air compressor runs excessively. Check for a disconnected or damaged air tube or a damaged strut. If OK, go to *Rear of Vehicle Low (with Road Sensing Suspension).*
4	1. Turn the ignition to the OFF position. 2. Remove the load from the luggage compartment.	After a delay, a hiss of escaping air may be heard, and the rear of the vehicle lowers to the correct trim height. Refer to *Trim Height* in Suspension General Diagnostics.	The exhaust solenoid does not energize after a 17-27 second delay and the rear of the vehicle remains above the correct trim height. Refer to *Rear of Vehicle High (with Road Sensing Suspension).*

GC2019900425000X

Fig. 65 ALC System Operation Check. 2000–01 Seville w/Road Sensing Suspension

Step	Action	Value(s)	Yes	No
18	Replace the rear shock absorber on the side of the vehicle that is high. Is the trim height at the rear underbody points correct?	—	Go to *ALC System Operation Check (w/o Road Sensing Suspension)*	Repeat this *Diagnostic Table*
19	**Important:** The height sensor has a 17–27 second delay period before the air compressor is activated. 1. Raise the rear of the vehicle up as much as possible by holding the height sensor up. 2. Reconnect the link to the height sensor. 3. Disconnect the air compressor electrical connector. 4. Check for continuity between terminals A and C of the air compressor connector. Is continuity present?	—	Go to *Step 21*	Go to *Step 20*
20	Replace the air compressor head. Is the replacement complete?	—	Go to *ALC System Operation Check (w/o Road Sensing Suspension)*	—
21	Measure the voltage between the air compressor electrical connector (vehicle side), terminal C and ground. Is battery voltage present?	10.5–15 V	Go to *Step 23*	Go to *Step 22*
22	Check for a poor connection at the rear junction block. If the connections are OK, repair the open circuit condition in circuit 1342. Is the repair complete?	—	Go to *ALC System Operation Check (w/o Road Sensing Suspension)*	—
23	1. Cycle the ignition switch and return it to the ON position. **Important:** The link must be connected. Voltage will not be present within 17–27 seconds of the ignition switch cycle (height sensor delay). Voltage will not be present after approximately seven minutes. 2. Measure the voltage from the air compressor electrical connector (vehicle side), terminal A to the same connector, terminal C. Is battery voltage present?	10.5–15 V	Go to *Step 25*	Go to *Step 24*
24	Check for an open circuit condition in circuit 320. Also, check for a poor connection at the rear junction block and at the height sensor connector. Was an open circuit condition or poor connection condition found and repaired?	—	Go to *ALC System Operation Check (w/o Road Sensing Suspension)*	Go to *Height Sensor Operational Check*
25	Replace the air compressor head. Is the replacement complete?	—	Go to *ALC System Operation Check (w/o Road Sensing Suspension)*	—

GC2019900426030X

Fig. 66 Test 1: Rear Of Vehicle High (Part 3 of 3). 2000–01 Seville Less Road Sensing Suspension

Step	Action	Value(s)	Yes	No
1	Was the ALC System Check performed?	—	Go to *Step 2*	Go to *ALC System Operation Check (with Road Sensing Suspension)*
2	1. Turn the ignition ON with the engine OFF. 2. Listen for the ALC air compressor to activate. Is the ALC air compressor running for more than 5 minutes?	—	Go to *Step 3*	Go to *Step 6*
3	1. Turn the ignition OFF 2. Remove the ELC compressor relay. 3. Turn the ignition ON with the engine OFF. Is the air compressor running?	—	Go to *Step 4*	Go to *Step 5*
4	1. Turn the ignition OFF. 2. Reinstall the ELC compressor relay. 3. Repair the short to voltage in circuit 322. Is the repair complete?	—	Go to *Step 13*	—
5	1. Turn the ignition OFF. 2. Replace the ELC compressor relay. Is the replacement complete?	—	Go to *Step 13*	—
6	Inspect the left and right rear position sensors for damage and disconnected links. Are any damaged sensors or disconnected links present?	—	Go to *Step 7*	Go to *Step 8*
7	Replace the damaged rear position sensor or reconnect the link. Is the replacement complete?	—	Go to *Step 13*	—
8	1. Remove the ALC intake filter from the vehicle body (do not remove it from the ALC air compressor or hose). 2. Using the scan tool, cycle output ALC compressor. 3. After 1 minute, stop cycling. 4. Cycle the ALC exhaust while checking to see if air is exiting the ALC intake air filter. Is air exiting the ALC intake air filter?	—	Go to *Step 11*	Go to *Step 9*
9	1. Stop exhausting. 2. Disconnect the air tubes from both rear shock absorbers. 3. Connect the *J 22124-B* pressure gage to both (between) the air tubes. 4. Open the *J 22124-B* pressure gage toggle valve. 5. Disconnect the air tube from the ALC air dryer. 6. Apply shop air to the *J 22124-B* pressure gage schrader valve. Is air exiting both of the air tubes at the ALC air dryer connection?	—	Go to *Step 10*	Go to *Step 12*
10	1. Turn the ignition OFF. 2. Replace the ALC air compressor assembly. 3. Install the ALC intake air filter on the vehicle body. Are all of the replacements and/or installations complete?	—	Go to *Step 13*	—

GC2019900427010X

Fig. 67 Test 1: Rear Of Vehicle High (Part 1 of 2). 2000–01 Seville w/Road Sensing Suspension

Step	Action	Value(s)	Yes	No
1	Is any aftermarket equipment installed on the vehicle that could affect the ALC system?	—	Go to *Step 2*	Go to *Step 4*
2	Check the aftermarket equipment to ensure that it is not affecting ALC performance. Is the aftermarket equipment affecting the ALC performance?	—	Go to *Step 3*	Go to *Step 4*
3	Correct the condition. Is the condition corrected?	—	Go to *ALC System Operation Check (w/o Road Sensing Suspension)*	—
4	Check the IGN 3 fuse and ELC fuse for an open (blown) condition. Is the fuse open?	—	Go to *Step 5*	Go to *Step 6*
5	**Important:** If the fuse is open (blown) repeatedly, check circuit 41 (BRN) or circuit 1342 (RED) for a short circuit to ground condition. Replace the fuse. Is the replacement or repair complete?	—	Go to *ALC System Operation Check (w/o Road Sensing Suspension)*	—
6	Check the height sensor and link for proper connection and damage. Are the height sensor and the link properly connected and in good condition?	—	Go to *Step 8*	Go to *Step 7*
7	Reconnect or replace the height sensor or the link. Is the repair or replacement complete?	—	Go to *ALC System Operation Check (w/o Road Sensing Suspension)*	—
8	Does the vehicle leak down when the vehicle is not used for an extended period of time (overnight), but then come up to normal trim height with vehicle use?	—	Go to *Step 28*	Go to *Step 9*

GC2019900428010X

Fig. 68 Test 2: Rear Of Vehicle Low (Part 1 of 5). 2000–01 Seville Less Road Sensing Suspension

Step	Action	Value(s)	Yes	No
11	1. Turn the ignition OFF. 2. Connect the scan tool. 3. Turn the ignition ON with the engine OFF. 4. Perform the ALC Trim Height Adjustment. Has the ALC Trim Height Adjustment been completed?	—	Go to *Step 13*	—
12	Replace the air tube going from the air dryer to both the rear shock absorbers. Is the replacement complete?	—	Go to *Step 13*	—
13	1. Turn the ignition OFF. 2. Turn the ignition ON with the engine OFF. 3. Wait for at least 5 minutes. Is the rear of the vehicle trim (level)?	—	System OK	—

GC2019900427020X

Fig. 67 Test 1: Rear Of Vehicle High (Part 2 of 2). 2000–01 Seville w/Road Sensing Suspension

Step	Action	Value(s)	Yes	No
9	1. Turn the ignition switch to the ON position. 2. Add approximately 136 kg (300 lbs) of weight to the rear of the vehicle. **Important:** Allow 27 seconds for the air compressor to start and then additional time for the shock absorbers to inflate. Does the rear of the vehicle rise and not leak down?	—	Go to *Step 10*	Go to *Step 12*
10	Is the trim height at the rear underbody points correct?	—	Go to *ALC System Operation Check (w/o Road Sensing Suspension)*	Go to *Step 11*
11	Adjust the height sensor. Is trim height at the rear underbody points correct?	—	Go to *ALC System Operation Check (w/o Road Sensing Suspension)*	*Repeat this Step*
12	Did the air compressor operate when weight was added?	—	Go to *Step 28*	Go to *Step 13*
13	1. Disconnect the height sensor electrical connector. 2. Turn the ignition switch to the ON position. 3. Connect a fused jumper from the height sensor connector (vehicle side) terminal B to ground. Is the air compressor operating?	—	Go to *Height Sensor Operational Check*	Go to *Step 14*
14	1. Turn the ignition switch to the OFF position. 2. Connect the height sensor electrical connector. 3. Remove the ELC relay from the rear junction block. 4. Turn the ignition switch to the ON position. 5. Measure the voltage from the right rear terminal (where relay pin 85 was removed) to ground. Is voltage above the specified value?	10.5 V	Go to *Step 16*	Go to *Step 15*
15	Check for an open ELC fuse, or for an open circuit to the fuse or in the rear junction block. Repair the open circuit or replace the ELC fuse or the rear junction block as required. Is the repair or replacement complete?	—	Go to *ALC System Operation Check (w/o Road Sensing Suspension)*	—
16	Measure the voltage from the right front terminal (where relay pin 30 was removed) to ground (this terminal is hot at all times). Is voltage more than the specified value?	10.5 V	Go to *Step 18*	Go to *Step 17*
17	Replace the rear junction block. Is the replacement complete?	—	Go to *ALC System Operation Check (w/o Road Sensing Suspension)*	—

GC2019900428020X

Fig. 68 Test 2: Rear Of Vehicle Low (Part 2 of 5). 2000–01 Seville Less Road Sensing Suspension

Step	Action	Value(s)	Yes	No
18	1. Remove the ELC relay. 2. Connect a voltmeter between the right rear terminal and left front terminal (where relay pins 85 and 86 were removed). **Important:** The ignition switch must be cycled if the ignition was left on from the previous step. 3. Turn the ignition switch to the ON position. Does voltage exceed the specified voltage after 17–27 seconds (17–27 seconds is the height sensor delay period)?	10.5 V	Go to *Step 20*	Go to *Step 19*
19	Check for a poor connection at the height sensor connector, terminal B, or an open circuit condition in circuit 321. Was a poor connection or open circuit condition found and corrected?	—	Go to *ALC System Operation Check (w/o Road Sensing Suspension)*	Go to *Height Sensor Operational Check*
20	Connect a 30-amp fused jumper between the right front terminal and the left rear terminal (where relay pins 30 and 87 were removed). Is the air compressor operating?	—	Go to *Step 21*	Go to *Step 22*
21	Replace the ELC relay. Is the replacement complete?	—	Go to *ALC System Operation Check (w/o Road Sensing Suspension)*	—
22	1. Leave the jumper from the previous step in place. 2. Disconnect the air compressor electrical connector. 3. Measure the voltage from the air compressor electrical connector (vehicle side), terminal B, to ground. Is voltage more than the specified value?	10.5 V	Go to *Step 24*	Go to *Step 23*
23	1. Check the rear junction block connectors for a poor connection. 2. If the connections are OK, repair the open circuit condition in circuit 322. Is the repair complete?	—	Go to *ALC System Operation Check (w/o Road Sensing Suspension)*	—
24	1. Leave the jumper from the previous step in place. 2. Measure the voltage from the air compressor connector (vehicle side), terminal B, to the same connector, terminal D. Is voltage more than the specified value?	10.5–15 V	Go to *Step 26*	Go to *Step 25*
25	Repair the open circuit condition in circuit 1050. Is the repair complete?	—	Go to *ALC System Operation Check (w/o Road Sensing Suspension)*	—
26	1. Disconnect the jumper and install the ALC relay. 2. Jumper the air compressor connector (compressor side), terminal D, to ground. 3. Jumper the air compressor connector (compressor side), terminal B to B+ using a 30-amp fused jumper wire. Is the air compressor operating?	—	Go to*Step 13*	Go to *Step 27*

GC2019900428030X

Fig. 68 Test 2: Rear Of Vehicle Low (Part 3 of 5). 2000–01 Seville Less Road Sensing Suspension

Step	Action	Value(s)	Yes	No
27	Replace the air compressor. Is the replacement complete?	—	Go to *ALC System Operation Check (w/o Road Sensing Suspension)*	—
28	Check the following: **Important:** If the air sleeve is worn through, perform the residual air pressure check. • Rear shock absorbers for a leaking air sleeve. • Air tube for kinks or pinched tubes. • Air tube for a disconnected condition at the shock absorbers or at the air dryer. • All air tube connections using soap and water. Was a leak or damage found and corrected?	—	Go to *ALC System Operation Check (w/o Road Sensing Suspension)*	Go to *Step 29*
29	1. Disconnect the air tube from the air dryer. 2. Connect the *J 22124-91* pressure gage adapter to the air dryer. 3. Connect the *J 22124-B* pressure gage to the *J 22124-91* pressure gage adapter with the toggle valve on the opposite side (away from the air compressor) and closed. 4. Disconnect the air compressor electrical connector. 5. Jumper the air compressor electrical connector (compressor side), terminal D to ground. 6. Jumper the air compressor electrical connector (compressor side), terminal B, to B+ using a 30-amp fused jumper wire. 7. Allow the air compressor to operate until the pressure reaches 690 kPa (100 psi). 8. Disconnect the jumper from terminal D when 690 kPa (100 psi) is reached. Is the air compressor able to reach it 690 kPa (100 psi)?	690 kPa (100 psi)	Go to *Step 31*	Go to *Step 30*
30	Replace the air compressor. Is the replacement complete?	—	Go to *ALC System Operation Check (w/o Road Sensing Suspension)*	—
31	Does the air pressure reading on the *J 22124-B* pressure gage stay at 690 kPa (100 psi)?	690 kPa (100 psi)	Go to *Step 32*	Go to *Air Compressor Leak Test*
32	1. Open the *J 22124-B* pressure gage toggle valve. 2. Disconnect the vehicle air tube from the LH rear shock absorber. 3. Connect the *J 22124-B* pressure gage adapter tube to the LH rear shock absorber and to the *J 22124-B* pressure gage. 4. Reconnect the ground jumper to the air compressor connector terminal D (terminal B should still be connected to B+). Is the air compressor able to reach 690 kPa (100 psi) and then maintain 690 kPa (100 psi) after the jumper is disconnected from terminal D?	690 kPa (100 psi)	Go to *Step 34*	Go to *Step 33*

GC2019900428040X

Fig. 68 Test 2: Rear Of Vehicle Low (Part 4 of 5). 2000–01 Seville Less Road Sensing Suspension

Step	Action	Value(s)	Yes	No
1	Was the ALC System Check performed?	—	Go to *Step 2*	Go to *ALC System Operation Check (with Road Sensing Suspension)*
2	1. Turn the ignition ON with the engine OFF. 2. Listen for the ALC air compressor to activate. Does the air compressor come on within 30 seconds?	30 seconds	Go to *Step 9*	Go to *Step 3*
3	1. Turn the ignition OFF. 2. Disconnect the ALC connector from the ALC air compressor assembly. 3. Disconnect connector C1 from the CVRSS control module. 4. Turn the ignition ON. 5. Connect pin C15 of CVRSS connector C1 (harness side) to ground using a jumper wire. 6. Measure the voltage between pin B of the ALC air compressor connector (harness side) and ground. Is the voltage greater than the specified value?	10 volts	Go to *Step 4*	Go to *Step 7*
4	1. Remove the jumper wire from pin C15. 2. Turn the ignition OFF. 3. Check for continuity between pin D of the ALC air compressor connector (harness side) and ground. Is there continuity?	—	Go to *Step 6*	Go to *Step 5*
5	1. Turn the ignition OFF. 2. Repair the open circuit condition in circuit 1050. Is the repair complete?	—	Go to *ALC System Operation Check (with Road Sensing Suspension)*	—
6	1. Replace the ALC air compressor assembly. 2. Replace the air tube. Is the repair complete?	—	Go to *Step 12*	—
7	1. Remove the jumper wire from pin C15. 2. Turn the ignition OFF. 3. Check for the following: • open (blown) ELC fuse • open circuit 322 • open circuit 321 • open circuit in the Rear Junction Block Was a problem found?	—	Go to *Step 8*	—
8	Repair the open circuit condition or replace the fuse. Is the repair complete?	—	Go to *ALC System Operation Check (with Road Sensing Suspension)*	—
9	Inspect the left and right rear position sensors for damage and disconnected links. Are any damaged sensors or disconnected links present?	—	Go to *Step 13*	Go to *Step 10*
10	Perform the ALC System Leak Test. Is a leak present?	—	Go to *Step 11*	Go to *Step 12*

GC2019900429010X

Fig. 69 Test 2: Rear Of Vehicle Low (Part 1 of 2). 2000–01 Seville w/Road Sensing Suspension

Step	Action	Value(s)	Yes	No
33	Replace the LH rear shock absorber.	—	Go to *ALC System Operation Check (w/o Road Sensing Suspension)*	—
34	1. Disconnect the adapter tube from the LH rear shock absorber. 2. Connect the vehicle air tube to the LH rear shock absorber. 3. Disconnect the vehicle air tube from the RH rear shock absorber. 4. Connect the adapter tube to the RH rear shock absorber. 5. Reconnect the ground jumper to the air compressor connector terminal D (terminal B should still be connected to B+). Is the air compressor able to reach 690 kPa (100 psi)?	690 kPa (100 psi)	Go to *Step 36*	Go to *Step 35*
35	Replace the RH rear shock absorber. Is the replacement complete?	—	Go to *ALC System Operation Check (w/o Road Sensing Suspension)*	—
36	1. Disconnect the adapter tube from the RH rear shock absorber and the *J 22124-B* pressure gage. Do not connect the vehicle air tube. 2. Disconnect the *J 22124-91* pressure gage adapter from the air dryer and the *J 22124-B* pressure gage. 3. Connect the vehicle air tube to the air dryer. 4. Connect the *J 22124-B* pressure gage to the vehicle air tube at the RH rear shock absorber. The *J 22124-B* pressure gage toggle valve must be on the side of the gage away from the air tube. 5. Close the *J 22124-B* pressure gage toggle valve. 6. Reconnect the ground jumper to the air compressor connector terminal D (terminal B should still be connected to B+). Is the air compressor able to reach 690 kPa (100 psi) and then maintain 690 kPa (100 psi) after the jumper is disconnected from terminal D?	690 kPa (100 psi)	Go to *Step 38*	Go to *Step 37*
37	Replace the air tube. Is the replacement complete?	—	Go to *ALC System Operation Check (w/o Road Sensing Suspension)*	—
38	Check for a binding rear shock absorber. Was a binding shock absorber found and replaced?	—	Go to *ALC System Operation Check (w/o Road Sensing Suspension)*	—

GC2019900428050X

Fig. 68 Test 2: Rear Of Vehicle Low (Part 5 of 5). 2000–01 Seville Less Road Sensing Suspension

Step	Action	Value(s)	Yes	No
11	Repair the leak in the ALC System. Is the repair complete?	—	Go to *Step 14*	—
12	1. Turn the ignition OFF. 2. Connect the scan tool to the DLC. 3. Turn the ignition switch ON with engine OFF. 4. Perform the ALC Trim Height Adjustment. Has the ALC trim height adjustment been completed?	—	Go to *Step 14*	—
13	Replace the damaged rear position sensor or reconnect the link. Is the replacement complete?	—	Go to *ALC System Operation Check (with Road Sensing Suspension)*	—
14	1. Reconnect all of the connectors that were removed. 2. Clear the CVRSS DTCs. 3. Wait for at least 5 minutes. Is the rear of the vehicle trim height correct?	—	System OK	Go to *Step 12*

GC2019900429020X

Fig. 69 Test 2: Rear Of Vehicle Low (Part 2 of 2). 2000–01 Seville w/Road Sensing Suspension

Step	Action	Value(s)	Yes	No
1	1. Disconnect the height sensor electrical connector. 2. Measure the voltage from the height sensor connector (vehicle side), terminal C to ground. Is voltage greater than the specified value?	10.0 V	Go to *Step 3*	Go to *Step 2*
2	Repair the open circuit condition in circuit 2340 (ORN) between the height sensor and the rear junction block. Is the repair complete?	—	Go to *ALC System Operation Check (w/o Road Sensing Suspension)*	—
3	Measure the voltage from the height sensor connector (vehicle side), terminal C to the same connector, terminal A. Is voltage greater than the specified value?	10.0 V	Go to *Step 5*	Go to *Step 4*
4	Repair the open circuit condition in circuit 850 (BLK). Is the repair complete?	—	Go to *ALC System Operation Check (w/o Road Sensing Suspension)*	—
5	1. Turn the ignition switch to the ON position. 2. Measure the voltage from the height sensor connector (vehicle side), terminal D to the same connector, terminal A. Is voltage greater than the specified value?	10.0 V	Go to *Step 7*	Go to *Step 6*
6	Repair the open circuit condition in circuit 41 (BRN). Is the repair complete?	—	Go to *ALC System Operation Check (w/o Road Sensing Suspension)*	—

GC2019900430010X

Fig. 70 Test 3: Height Sensor Operational Check (Part 1 of 2). 2000–01 Seville

Step	Action	Value(s)	Yes	No
7	1. Check the height sensor connector for proper terminal contact. 2. Reconnect the height sensor connector. 3. Cycle the ignition switch and return the ignition switch to ON. 4. Observe the compressor operation for one of the following actions. • The air compressor operates for 3 to 5 seconds after an initial 35 to 55 second delay? • The exhaust solenoid valve opens after a 17 to 27 second delay, then the air compressor operates for 3 to 5 seconds after an additional 15 to 35 second delay. • The air compressor operates after a 17 to 27 second delay. Was one of the compressor actions observed?	—	Go to *Step 9*	Go to *Step 8*
8	Replace the height sensor. Is the replacement complete?	—	Go to *ALC System Operation Check (w/o Road Sensing Suspension)*	—
9	**Important:** The vehicle must be raised on a drive-on lift. The full vehicle weight must be on the rear tires. 1. Raise the vehicle. 2. Disconnect the link from the position sensor. 3. Move the height sensor arm up so that it is approximately 45 degrees above level (to the floor). Does the air compressor run after the 17–27 second delay?	—	Go to *Step 11*	Go to *Step 10*
10	Replace the height sensor. Is the replacement complete?	—	Go to *ALC System Operation Check (w/o Road Sensing Suspension)*	—
11	Move the height sensor down slowly until the air compressor stops. Does the air compressor stop?	—	Go to *Step 13*	Go to *Step 12*
12	Replace the height sensor. Is the replacement complete?	—	Go to *ALC System Operation Check (w/o Road Sensing Suspension)*	—
13	Move the height sensor arm down so that it is approximately 45 degrees below level (to the floor). After a 17–27 second delay, does air escape from the air compressor as the vehicle begins to lower?	—	Go to *Step 15*	Go to *Step 14*
14	Replace the height sensor. Is the replacement complete?	—	Go to *ALC System Operation Check (w/o Road Sensing Suspension)*	—
15	Adjust the height sensor. Is the adjustment complete?	—	Go to *ALC System Operation Check (w/o Road Sensing Suspension)*	—

GC2019900430020X

Fig. 70 Test 3: Height Sensor Operational Check (Part 2 of 2). 2000–01 Seville

MALFUNCTION	CORRECTION
1. Compressor runs but current draw exceeds 14 amps.	1. Replace compressor.
2. Compressor inoperative	2. Replace compressor.
3. Compressor output less than 758 kPa (110 psi)	3. Perform compressor/dryer leak test, if no leak is found, replace compressor.
4. Pressure leaks down to 0 kPa (0 psi)	4. Perform compressor/dryer leak test, and make corrections as required.
5. Pressure build up ok, but leaks down below 60 kPa (90 psi) before holding steady. (Does not go to 0 psi.)	5. Replace head assembly

GC2019100126000X

Fig. 72 Compressor/Dryer Troubleshooting Chart

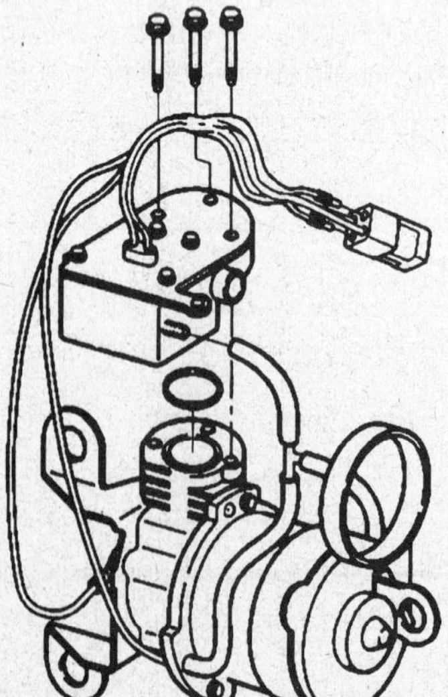

GC2019100066000A

Fig. 74 Disassembled view air compressor

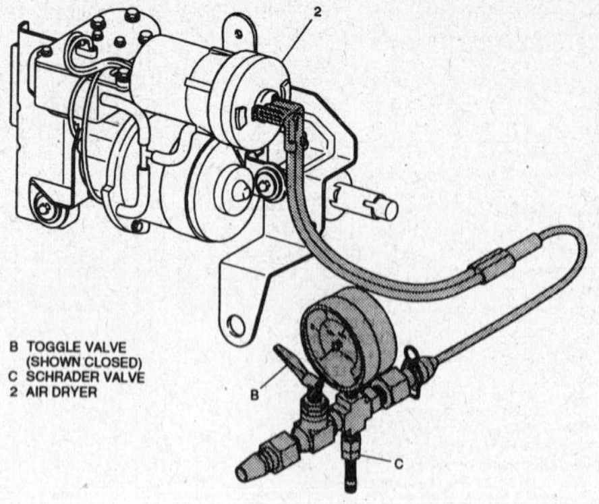

GC2019100062000A

Fig. 71 Compressor Performance Inspection

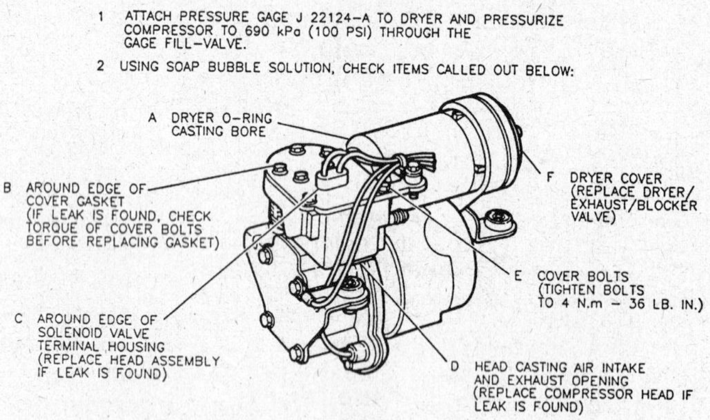

GC2019100063000X

Fig. 73 Compressor Leak Inspection

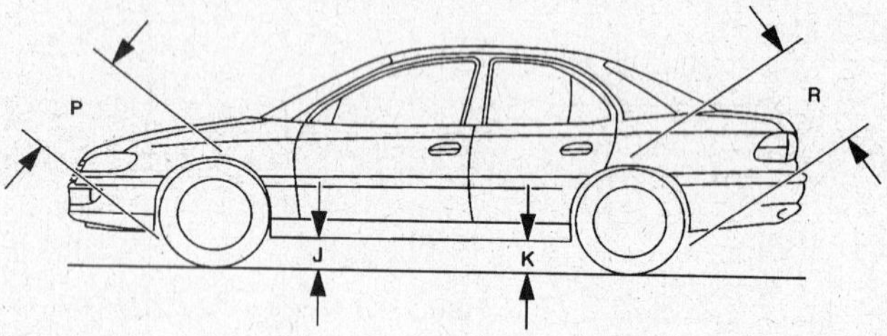

GC2019900623000X

Fig. 75 Vehicle trim height measurements. Catera

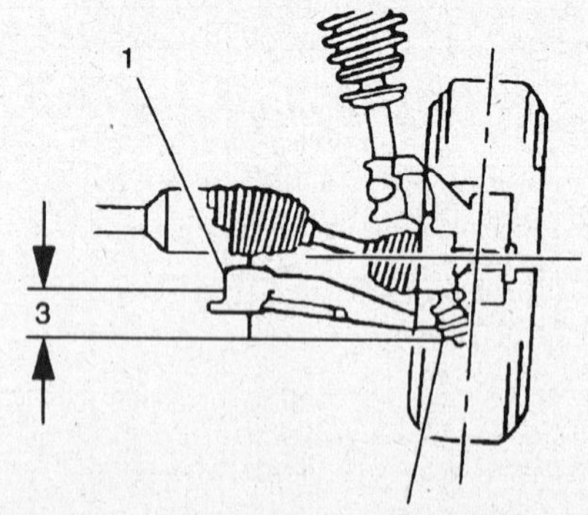

Measure the distance between the lowest point on the ball joint housing and the centerline of the control arm bolt. This distance (3) should be 30-50 mm (1 3/16 to 2 in).

GC2019900513010X

Fig. 76 Vehicle trim height measurements (Part 1 of 4). Park Avenue

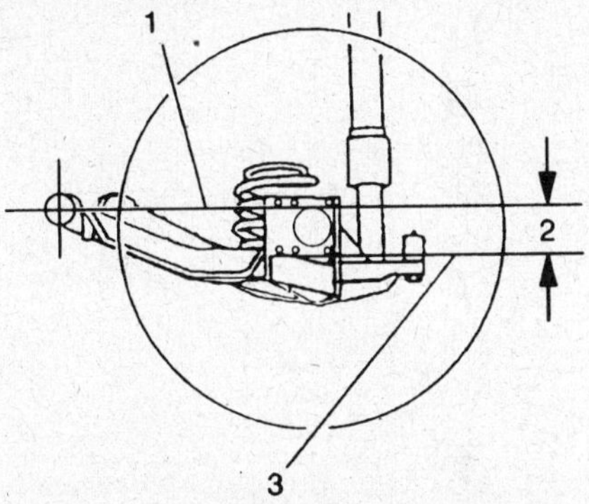

Measure the distance from the bottom of the control arm wheel bearing face to the centerline of the outboard control arm bolt. This distance (2) should be 76-96 mm (3-3 3/4 in).

GC2019900513020X

Fig. 76 Vehicle trim height measurements (Part 2 of 4). Park Avenue

SYSTEM SERVICE

When repair or adjustment procedures require vehicle to be raised on a hoist, it is important that the rear axle assembly remains in the normal trim height position at all times. When a frame contact hoist is used, two additional jack stands should be used to support the rear axle or control arms in the normal trim height position.

Air Compressor Service

DISASSEMBLE

1. Remove compressor cover screws, then the compressor cover and gasket, **Fig. 74.**
2. Remove compressor head and solenoid assembly.
3. Remove two filters, exhaust valve, spring and air dryer O-ring from head assembly.
4. Remove solenoid from head by lifting slightly and sliding to dryer outlet side.
5. Remove O-ring from solenoid assembly.
6. Remove head gasket from cylinder assembly.
7. Remove four mounting bracket screws, then the bracket and gasket. Note position of ground wire for installation.

ASSEMBLE

1. Install gasket and mounting bracket, then the ground wire and screws.
2. Install head gasket on cylinder assembly.
3. Install O-ring on solenoid assembly, then the solenoid in head with valve opposite air dryer outlet.
4. Install two filters, exhaust valve and spring on head assembly.
5. Install gasket and cover on head assembly, then four short cover screws.
6. Install head and cover assembly to cylinder assembly using three long screws. **Torque** all screws in sequence, **Fig. 74,** to 53 inch lbs.
7. Install air dryer O-ring on compressor.

Vehicle Trim Height Inspection

Trim heights are checked with tires at recommended pressure, fuel tank at capacity, front seat in rear position, no passengers and trunk empty, except for spare tire and jack.

Specifications are as follows:

CATERA

Measure trim height as outlined in **Fig. 75.**

1. Trim height should be as follows:
   a. P = 27⁵⁄₁₆ inches.
   b. J = 6⅞ inches.
   c. K = 6½ inches.
   d. R = 27⁵⁄₁₆ inches.

EXCEPT CATERA

Refer to **Figs. 76 through 79,** for trim height measurements.

Vehicle Trim Height Adjustment

1. Loosen locknut securing metal arm to height sensor plastic arm, **Fig. 80.**
2. To increase trim height, move plastic actuator arm upward and tighten locknut.
3. To decrease trim height, move plastic actuator arm downward and tighten locknut.
4. If proper adjustment cannot be made, ensure correct height sensor is installed.

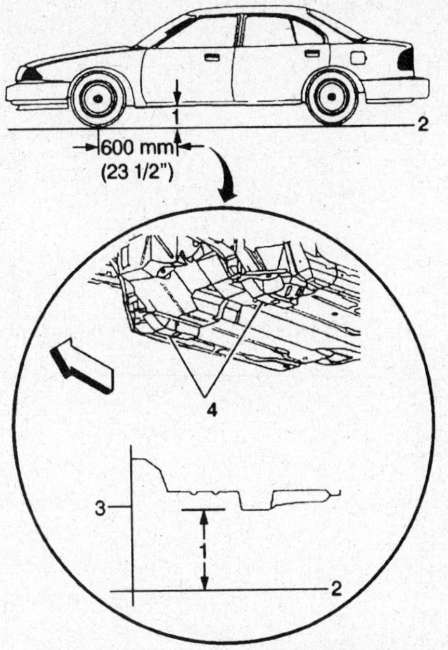

Measure the distance (1) from the ground (2) to the front underbody points (4). This distance (1) should be 164-184 mm (6 7/16 to 7 1/4 in)

GC2019900513030X

Fig. 76 Vehicle trim height measurements (Part 3 of 4). Park Avenue

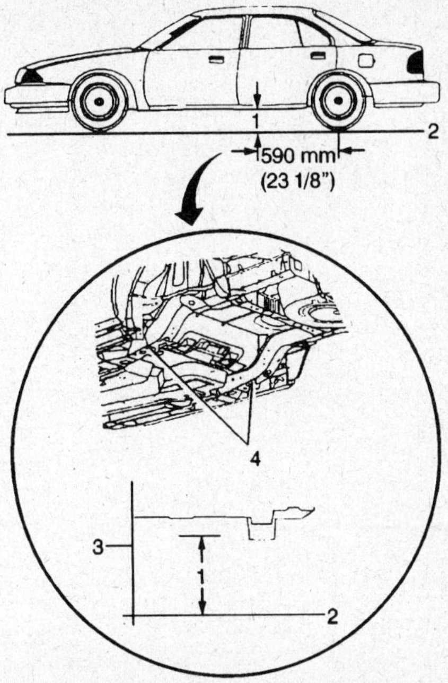

Measure the distance (1) from the ground (2) to the rear underbody points (4). This distance (1) 213-233 mm (8 3/8 to 9 3/16 in)

The maximum variation side-to-side and front-to-rear is 19 mm (3/4 in).

GC2019900513040X

Fig. 76 Vehicle trim height measurements (Part 4 of 4). Park Avenue

COMPONENT REPLACEMENT

When repair or adjustment procedures require that vehicle be raised on a hoist, it is important that the rear axle assembly remains in the normal trim height position at all times. When a frame contact hoist is used, two additional jack stands should be used to support the rear axle or control arms in the normal trim height position.

Compressor & Bracket Assembly

1. Raise and support vehicle.
2. Clean areas surrounding air fittings to prevent contamination from entering ALC system.
3. Disconnect air tube from air drier.
4. Remove bolt and harness tie with air tube from compressor bracket.
5. Remove intake air filter from vehicle.
6. Remove vehicle harness connector from air compressor connector.
7. Remove nuts and bolts, then the compressor assembly.
8. Slide air compressor connector off of connector anchor.
9. Remove heat shield from air compressor bracket.

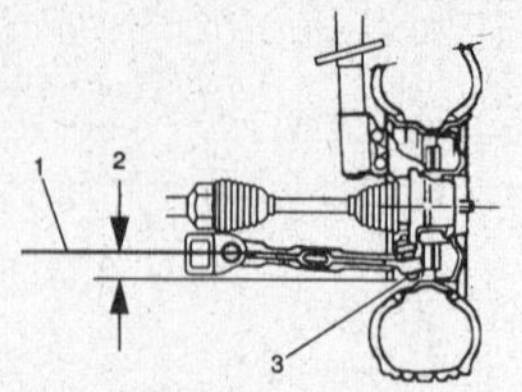

Measure the clearance (2) between the centerline of the bushing bolt and the lowest point on the ball joint housing (3) (excluding the grease fitting).
- The clearance (2) should measure 50 mm (1.97 in) on the Eldorado.
- The clearance (2) should measure 51 mm (2.01 in) on the Deville

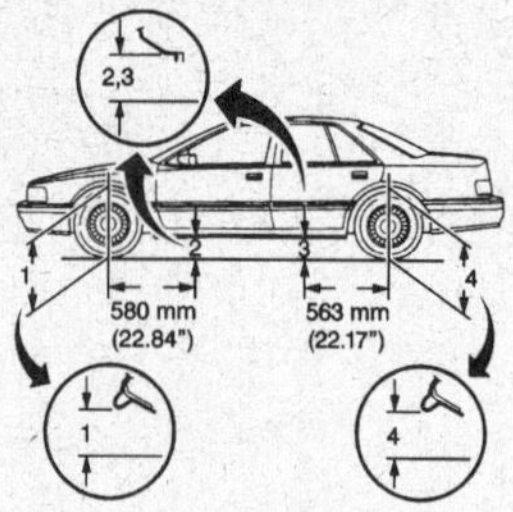

Measure the clearances (1–4) between the underbody and the ground.
- The clearance (1) should measure 715 mm (28.15 in) on the Eldorado.
- The clearance (2) should measure 220 mm (8.66 in) on the Eldorado.
- The clearance (3) should measure 214 mm (8.43 in) on the Eldorado.
- The clearance (4) should measure 709 mm (27.91 in) on the Eldorado.
- The clearance (1) should measure 707 mm (27.83 in) on the Deville.
- The clearance (2) should measure 192 mm (7.56 in) on the Deville.
- The clearance (3) should measure 202 mm (7.95 in) on the Deville.
- The clearance (4) should measure 543 mm (21.38 in) on the Deville.

Verify that all of the above clearances measure within the maximum variation from the specified values.

All measurements are plus or minus 10 mm (0.04 in).

Maximum variation side-to-side is 12 mm (0.05 in).

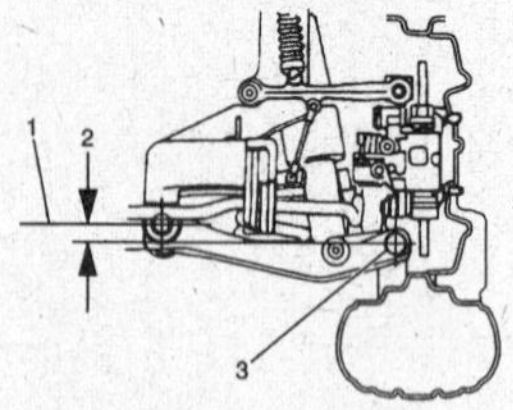

Measure the clearance (2) between the centerline of the front inner bearing bushing bolt (3) and the centerline of the front outer bushing bolt (this measurement should be taken on the front side of the rear suspension assembly).
- The clearance (2) should measure 29 mm (1.14 in) on the Eldorado.
- The clearance (2) should measure 37 mm (1.46 in) on the Deville.

GC2019900518000X

Fig. 77 Vehicle trim height measurements. Eldorado

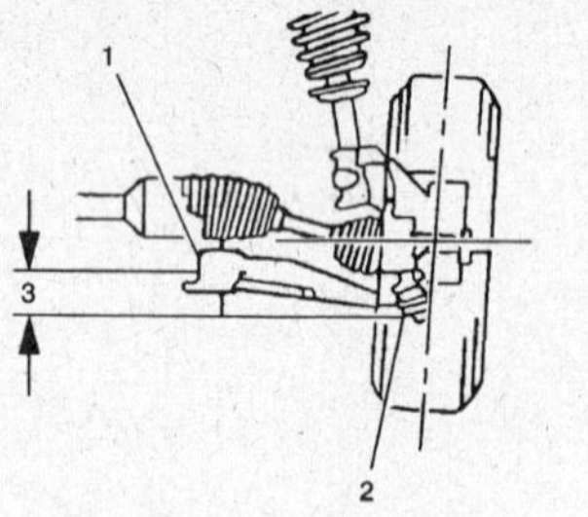

Measure the distance between the lowest point on the ball joint housing and the centerline of the control arm bolt. This distance (3) should be 40 mm (1.57 in) (With KS) and 30 mm (1.18 in) (With KY).

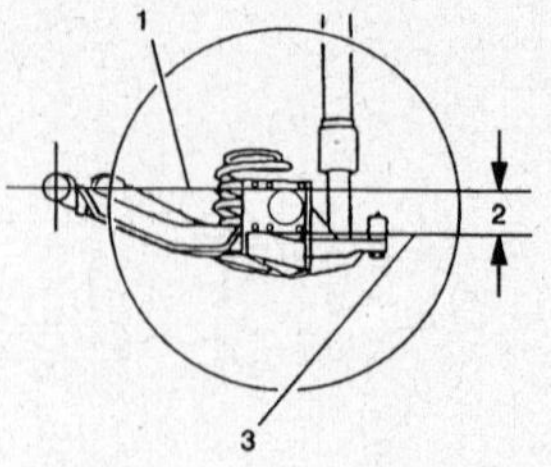

Measure the distance from the bottom of the control arm wheel bearing face to the centerline of the outboard control arm bolt. This distance (2) should be 86 mm (3.39 in) (With KS) and 76 mm (2.99 in) (With KY).

Measure the distance from the ground to the lower most portion of the front unibody frame. This distance should be 179 mm (7.05 in) (With KS) and 169 mm (6.65 in) (With KY)

Measure the distance from the ground to the lower most portion of the rear unibody frame. This distance should be 229 mm (9.02 in) (With KS) and 218 mm (8.58 in) (With KY)

If vehicle trim height is out of specifications, locate damaged or worn component and repair.

GC2019900519000X

Fig. 78 Vehicle trim height measurements. Seville

10. Remove compressor from mounting bracket, then the air drier from compressor.
11. Remove air hose from compressor in two places.
12. Remove two brackets from compressor.
13. Reverse procedure to install.

Air Dryer

1. Remove compressor as outlined in "Compressor & Bracket Assembly."
2. Rotate dryer retainer spring 90° and pull dryer and O-ring out of compressor head assembly, **Fig. 81.**
3. Reverse procedure to install.

Air Tube

1. Raise and support vehicle.
2. Clean air tube connector and surrounding areas to prevent contamination of ALC system.
3. Remove air tube from air drier.
4. Remove bolt and harness tie from air compressor bracket.
5. Remove both rear wheels.
6. Disconnect air tube from righthand and lefthand shock absorbers by rotating spring clip 90° out of slot, then pulling connector from shock absorber.
7. Remove two metal clips from air tube and from vehicle.
8. Remove air tube with clips from vehicle.
9. Reverse procedure to install, noting the following:
   a. Ensure air tube is routed correctly and all fasteners are used.
   b. Lubricate O-rings with silicone lubricant.
   c. Connect air tubes to rear shocks by rotating spring clips 90° into slots then pushing air tubes into fittings until spring clip snaps into groove.
   d. Before driving vehicle, turn ignition on and wait approximately 45 seconds to allow system to execute ARC, ensuring that shock absorbers are filled with residual pressure.

Compressor Head Assembly

1. Remove air compressor assembly from vehicle.
2. Slide air compressor connector away from compressor and off of anchor.
3. Remove heat shield from compressor.
4. Remove air drier.
5. Remove bolt and harness tie.
6. Remove two harness ties and wire wrap from harness.
7. Remove two wire terminals from air compressor connector.
8. Note wire colors and position for installation reference.
9. Remove air hose from air compressor head.
10. Remove three bolts, then the air compressor head, **Fig. 82.**
11. Remove gasket from compressor head or compressor assembly.
12. Reverse procedure to install, noting the following:
    a. Install new gasket on compressor assembly.
    b. Install compressor head on compressor assembly and **torque** mounting bolts to 53 inch lbs.

Solenoid Valve Assembly

If solenoid valve assembly requires replacement, it should be replaced with compressor head assembly. Refer to "Compressor Head Assembly"

Height Sensor & Bracket

1. Raise and support vehicle.
2. Disconnect harness from sensor electrical connector by squeezing oval sides of connector lock to release locking tabs.
3. Remove link from height sensor arm, then remove sensor mounting screws or nuts and sensor.
4. Remove sensor mounting bracket to underbody attaching screws and remove bracket.
5. Reverse procedure to install, noting the following:
   a. When connecting harness to sensor electrical connector, push connector into sensor plug until sloped shoulder on rear edge of boss is visible in plug slot. Push oval connector lock onto plug until its two locking tabs snap over shoulder of sensor plug.
   b. Perform height sensor operational inspection and adjustment procedure as outlined in "Vehicle Trim Height Adjustment."

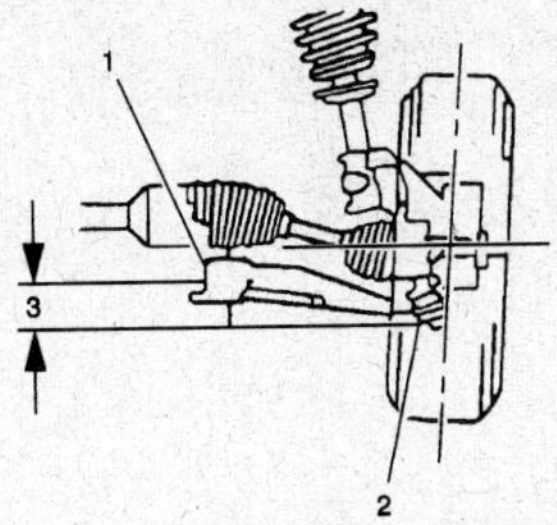

Measure the distance between the lowest point on the ball joint housing and the centerline of the control arm bolt. This distance (3) should be 30 - 50 mm (1 3/16 to 2 in).

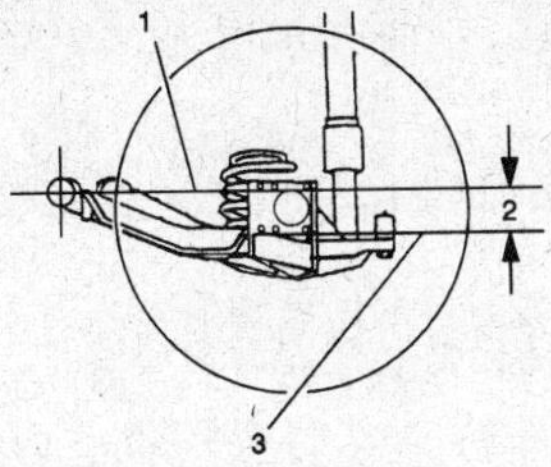

Measure the distance from the bottom of the control arm wheel bearing face to the centerline of the outboard control arm bolt. This distance (2) should be 76 - 96 mm (3 - 3 3/4 in).

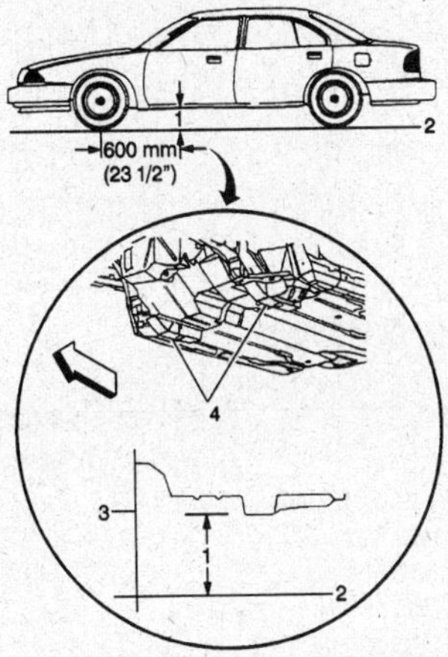

Measure the distance (1) from the ground (2) to the front underbody points (4). This distance (1) should be 164 - 184 mm (6 7/16 to 7 1/4 in)

GC2019900534010X

Fig. 79 Vehicle trim height measurements (Part 1 of 2). Aurora, Bonneville, DeVille & LeSabre

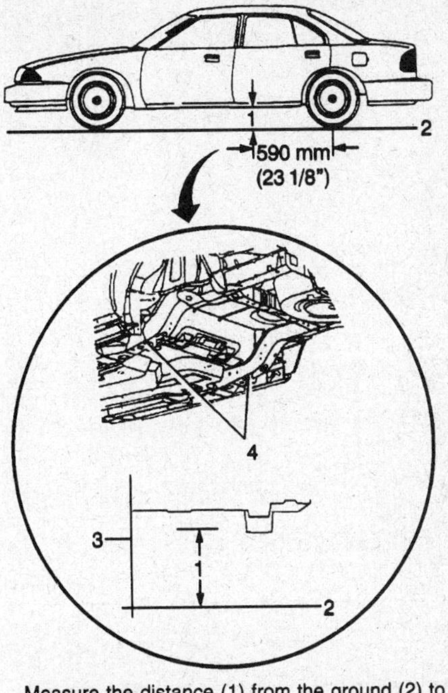

Measure the distance (1) from the ground (2) to the rear underbody points (4). This distance (1) 213 - 233 mm (8 3/8 to 9 3/16 in)

The maximum variation side-to-side and front-to-rear is 19 mm (3/4 in).

GC2019900534020X

Fig. 79 Vehicle trim height measurements (Part 2 of 2). Aurora, Bonneville, DeVille & LeSabre

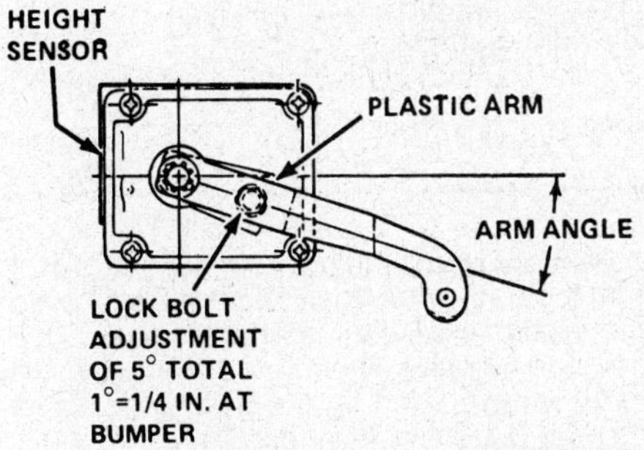

GC2019100084000X

Fig. 80 Vehicle trim height adjustment

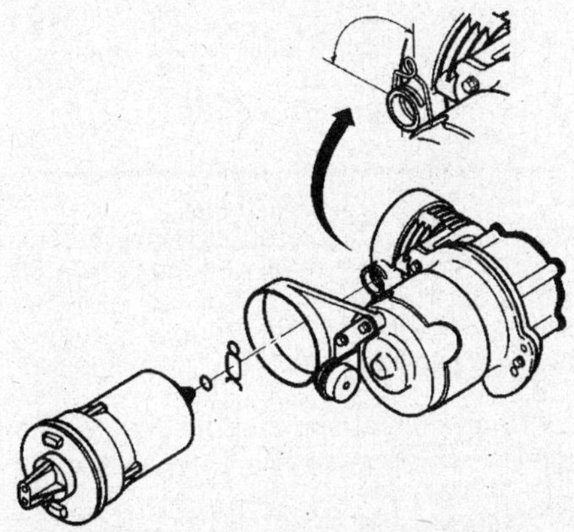

GC2010100645000X

Fig. 81 Air drier replacement

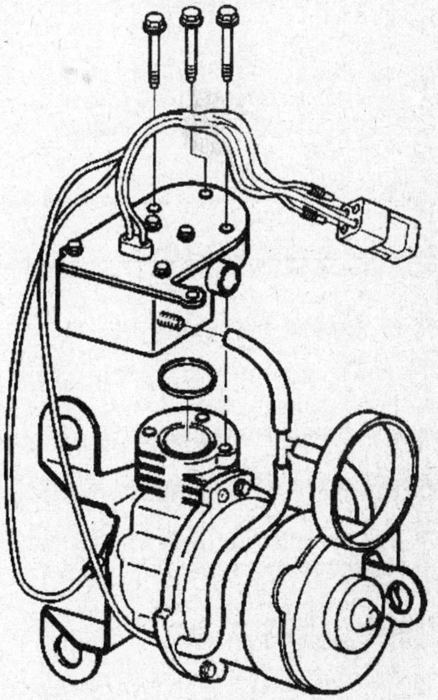

GC2010100646000X

Fig. 82 Air compressor head replacement

Continuously Variable Road Sensing Suspension & Real Time Damping

NOTE: On Air Bag Equipped Models, Refer To "Air Bag System Precautions" Located In The Front Of This Manual For System Disarming & Arming Procedures.

NOTE: Refer To "Computer Relearn Procedures" Located In The Front Of This Manual When Battery Power To The Computer Has Been Interrupted.

NOTE: "Electrical Symbol & Wire Color Code Identification" Located In The Front Of This Manual May Be Used As An Aid When Using Wiring Circuits Found In This Section.

INDEX

PRECAUTIONS

Air Bag Systems

Refer to "Air Bag System Precautions" in the front of this manual for system disarming and arming procedures.

Battery Ground Cable

Prior to service, disconnect battery ground cable and isolate as required.

DESCRIPTION

The Continuously Variable Road Sensing Suspension (CVRSS), Road Sensing Suspension (RSS) and Real Time Damping (RTD) systems, **Fig. 1,** controls damping forces in the shock absorbers and struts in response to various road and driving conditions. The system is capable of making these changes within 10–15 milliseconds.

The sensing module receives the following inputs; vertical acceleration, wheel to body position, vehicle speed and lift/dive. The sensing module evaluates the input data and uses it to control the solenoid valves in each of the dampers independently to provide varied levels of suspension control.

The system also controls the Speed Sensitive Steering (SSS) system and Electronic Level Control (ELC) system. The SSS system changes driver steering effort based on vehicle speed. The ELC system maintains proper vehicle trim height under various vehicle loading conditions.

System Components

SENSING MODULE

The sensing module located on the right-hand rear of the passenger compartment, behind the rear seat back. Controls the Sensing Suspension, Speed Sensitive Steering and Electronic Level Control Systems.

POSITION SENSORS

Position sensors are mounted at each corner of the vehicle between a control arm and the body. The position sensors provide the system with relative wheel to body position and velocity. The rear position sensors input is also used by the Electronic Level Control (ELC) system for trim height information.

ACCELEROMETER

An accelerometer is mounted on each corner of the vehicle. The accelerometer supplies the controller with the vertical acceleration of the body.

SPEED SENSOR

Vehicle speed input is received from the Powertrain Control Module (PCM) and is used to determine the amount of damper control and steering assist required.

LIFT/DIVE

Lift/dive input is received from the Powertrain Control Module (PCM). When the system receives a lift or dive signal it will adjust the suspension system to the firm position on all corners. The lift signal is

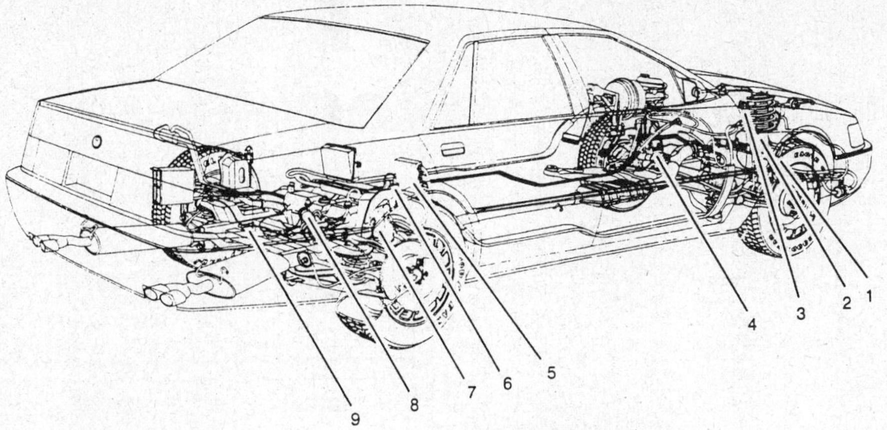

1 FRONT POSITION SENSOR
2 FRONT STRUT
3 FRONT ACCELEROMETER
4 SPEED SENSITIVE STEERING SOLENOID
5 RSS MODULE
6 REAR POSITION SENSOR
7 REAR SHOCK
8 ELC COMPRESSOR
9 REAR ACCELEROMETER
10 RESISTOR MODULE (NOT VISIBLE)

Fig. 1 Road Sensing Suspension (RSS) system

calculated in the PCM based of throttle position, transmission gear and vehicle speed. The dive signal, calculated by the PCM, inspects the rate of change in vehicle speed.

DAMPER

The damper contains a solenoid valve that is controlled by the sensing module. The solenoid provides two levels of damping, firm and soft. The soft mode is accomplished by switching the solenoid to the "ON" state, causing the damper oil to bypass the main damper valving. The firm mode is accomplished by switching the solenoid to the "OFF" state causing the damper oil to flow through the main damper valving. Each mode is much softer/firmer than a passive damper would be. The solenoid is an integral part of the damper and cannot be serviced separately.

SENSING RESISTOR MODULE

The sensing resistor module is located in the luggage compartment in the righthand quarter panel, external to the sensing module and consists of four resistors inside a ceramic material. When a solenoid is switched to the "ON" state, full system voltage is applied for a short period of time to quickly activate the solenoid. It is undesirable to maintain this high current to the solenoid any longer than required, therefore a resistor is put into the circuit. This "Hold" mode provides enough current to hold the solenoid in the "ON" position.

STEERING SOLENOID

The steering solenoid valve is a device that is controlled to vary power assist levels. The solenoid is driven by the controller using pulse width modulation (varying the amount of time the solenoid is on) as a function of the vehicle speed. When the solenoid is in the "OFF" position, the vehicle will have full power steering assist.

ELECTRONIC LEVEL CONTROL (ELC) SYSTEM

The ELC system automatically adjusts the rear trim height in response to vehicle loading. On vehicles with the 4.6L engine, the height sensing function is performed by the rear position sensors. Rear trim height information is input from the rear position sensors to the control module which controls the ELC compressor and exhaust solenoid information. Refer to "Electronic Level Controls" for system operation and on vehicle service.

Intermittent/Poor Connections

Most electrical intermittences are caused by faulty connections, poor grounds, poorly seated harness wiring, dirt/corrosion and chafed wires. The CVRSS module is a reliable component and is seldom the cause of the problem. The "Service Ride Control" message may illuminate intermittently if the battery voltage is not within 10–16 volts or if power has been interrupted.

DIAGNOSIS & TESTING

Accessing Diagnostic Trouble Codes

Connect a suitably programmed scan tool to Data Link Connector (DLC), and follow manufacturer's instructions.

Wiring Diagrams

Refer to **Figs 2 through 5,** for wiring diagrams.

Diagnostic Trouble Code Interpretation

The sensing control module continually monitors operating conditions for possible system faults. By comparing system conditions against standard operating limits, certain circuit and component faults can be detected. A four digit alpha-numeric diagnostic trouble code is stored in the computer memory when a problem is detected by this self diagnostic system.

Diagnostic Tests

BONNEVILLE & LESABRE

Refer to **Figs. 6 through 14,** for diagnostic tests.

CORVETTE

Refer to **Figs. 15 through 27,** for diagnostic test procedures.

DEVILLE, ELDORADO & SEVILLE

Refer to **Figs. 28 through 40,** for diagnostic test procedures.

Clearing Diagnostic Trouble Codes

Connect a suitably programmed scan tool to Data Link Connector (DLC), and follow manufacturer's instructions.

Intermittents

Most intermittent fault conditions are caused by poor electrical connections or improperly routed wiring harnesses. These conditions can usually be located by performing a thorough visual inspection of the system or by road testing the vehicle while monitoring the suspected circuit.

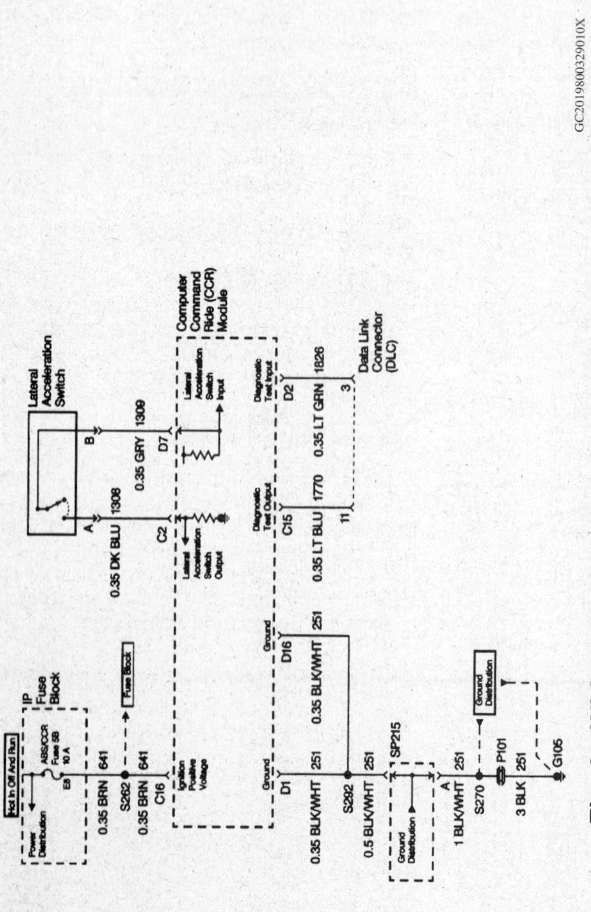

Fig. 2 Wiring diagram (Part 1 of 3). Bonneville & LeSabre

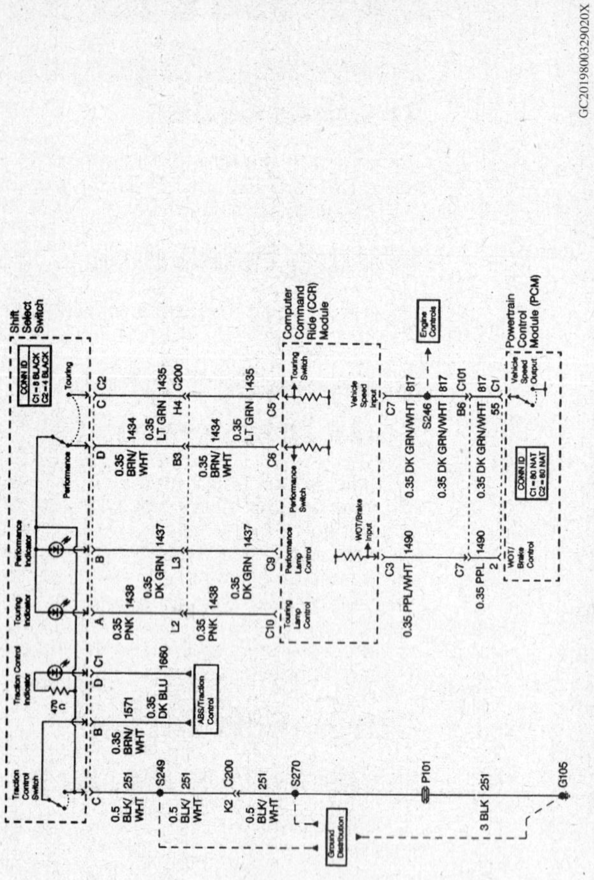

Fig. 2 Wiring diagram (Part 2 of 3). Bonneville & LeSabre

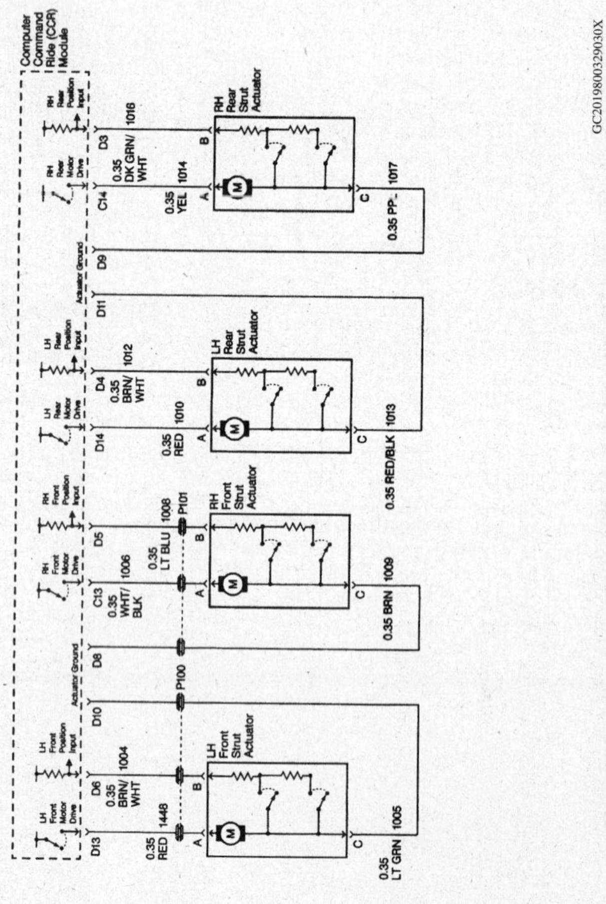

Fig. 2 Wiring diagram (Part 3 of 3). Bonneville & LeSabre

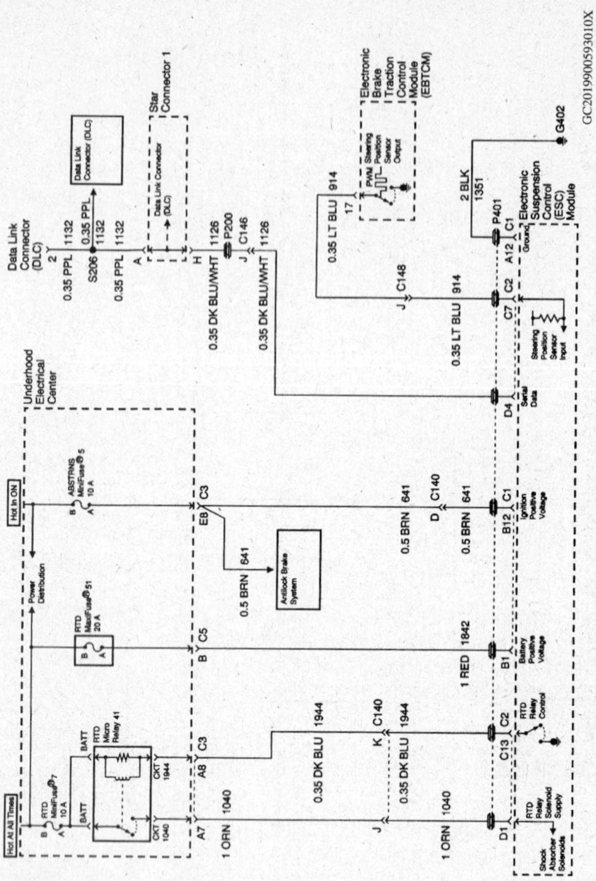

Fig. 3 Wiring diagram (Part 1 of 4). Corvette

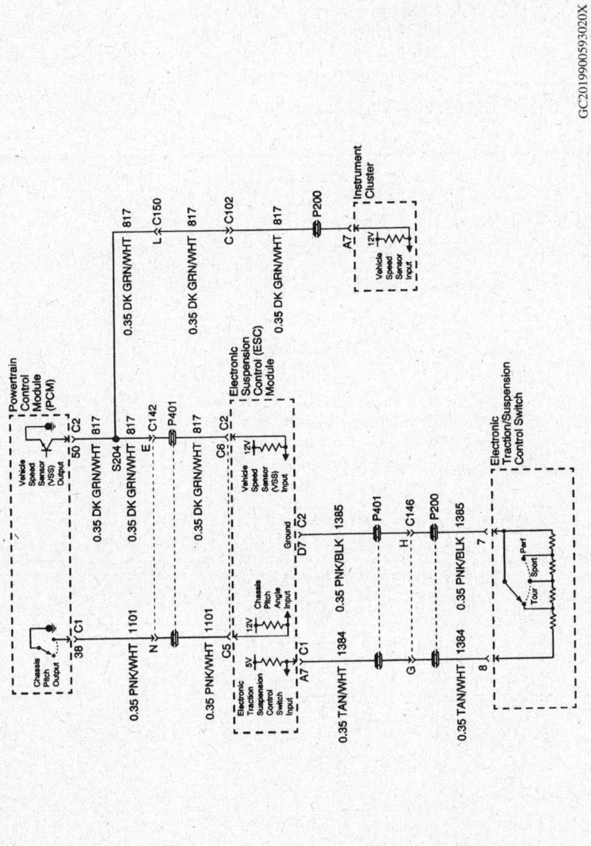

GC2019900593020X

Fig. 3 Wiring diagram (Part 2 of 4). Corvette

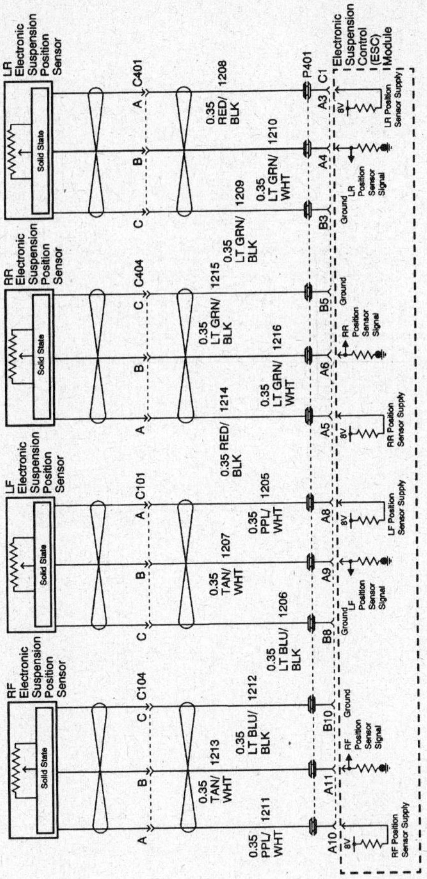

GC2019900593030X

Fig. 3 Wiring diagram (Part 3 of 4). Corvette

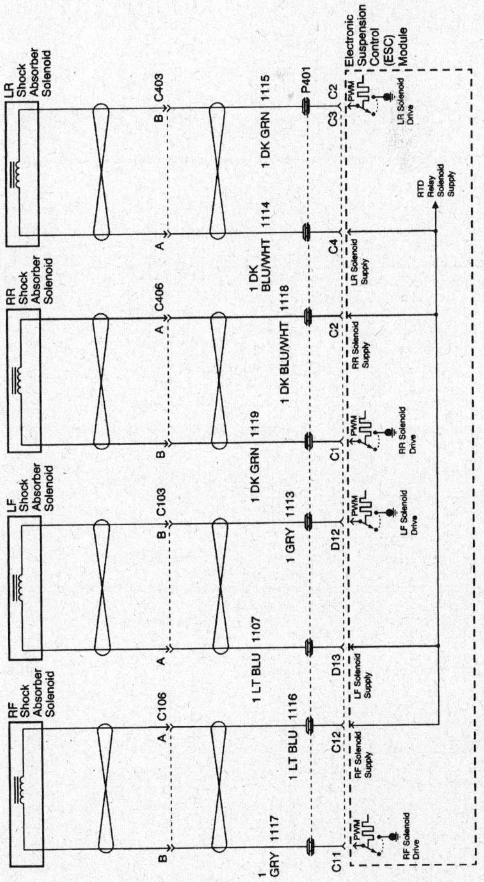

GC2019900593040X

Fig. 3 Wiring diagram (Part 4 of 4). Corvette

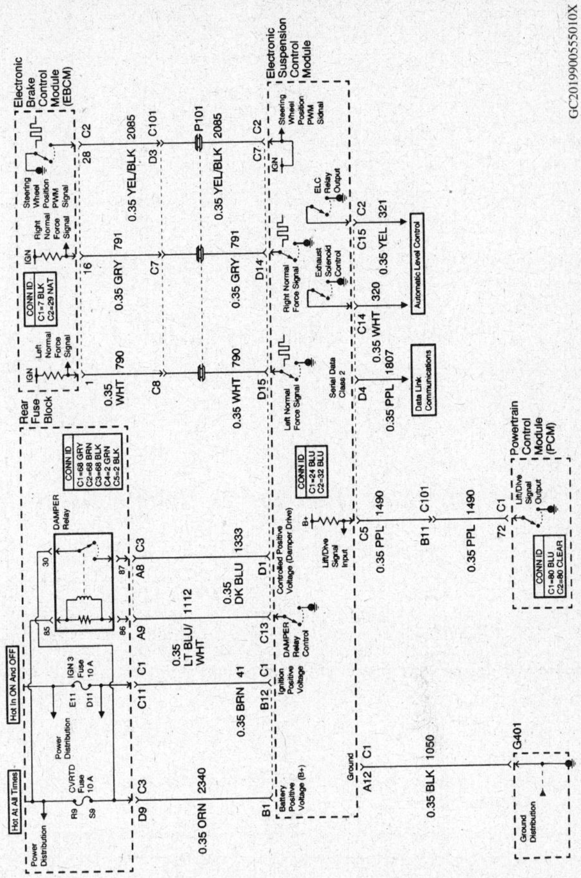

GC2019900555010X

Fig. 4 Wiring diagram (Part 1 of 2). DeVille & Seville

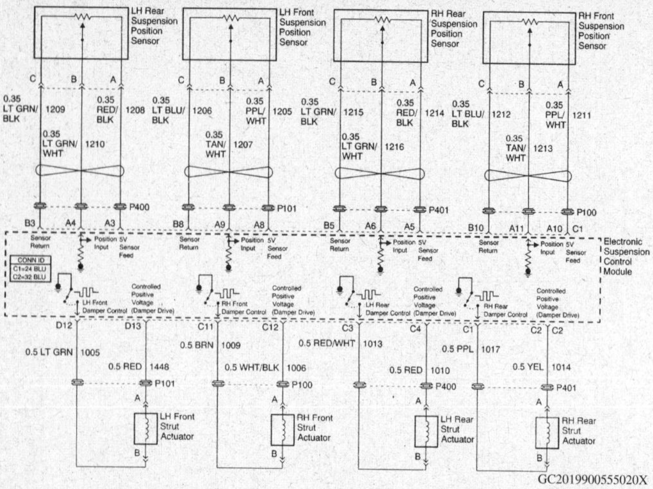

Fig. 4 Wiring diagram (Part 2 of 2). DeVille & Seville

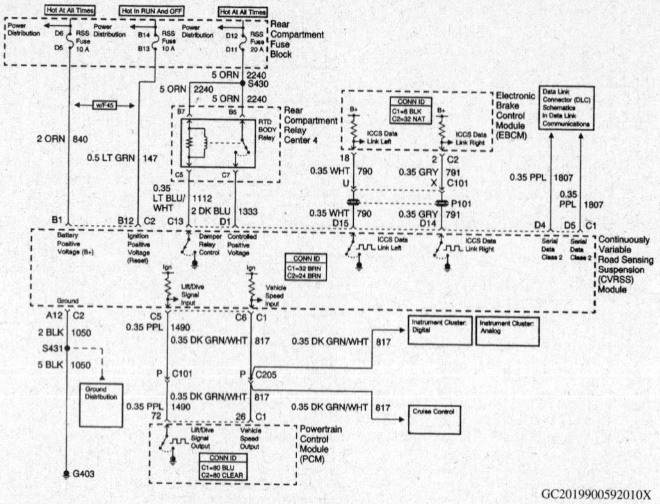

Fig. 5 Wiring diagram (Part 1 of 2). Eldorado

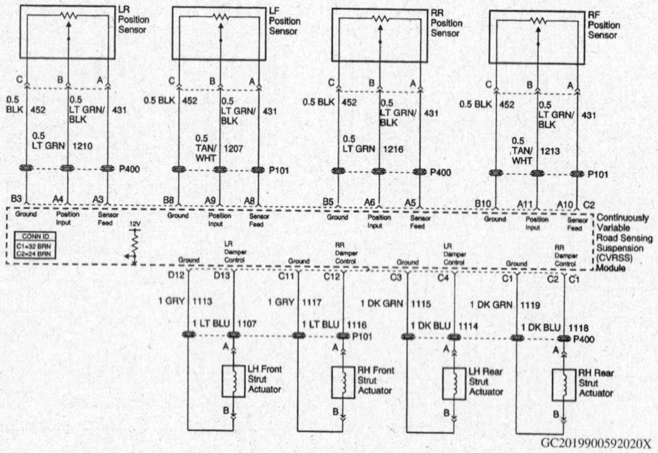

Fig. 5 Wiring diagram (Part 2 of 2). Eldorado

DIAGNOSTIC CHART INDEX

Code	Description	Page No.	Fig. No.
BONNEVILLE & LESABRE			
—	Diagnostic System Check	8-43	6
23	Lefthand Front Actuator Position Error	8-43	7
24	Righthand Front Actuator Position Error	8-43	8
25	Lefthand Rear Actuator Position Error	8-44	9
26	Righthand Rear Actuator Position Error	8-45	10
31	Lift Or Dive Signal Error	8-45	11
32	Lateral Accelerator Switch Error	8-46	12
33	Drive Select Switch Input Error	8-46	13
34	Vehicle Speed Sensor Signal Error	8-47	14
CORVETTE			
—	System Check	8-47	15
B2795	Suspension Control Select Switch Circuit Fault	8-47	16
B3577	Suspension Control Select Switch Contact Fault	8-47	17
C0550	ECU Fault	8-47	18
C0563	Calibration ROM Checksum Error	8-47	19
C0577	Shock Solenoid Circuit Fault	8-48	20
C0578	Shock Solenoid Circuit Fault	8-48	20
C0579	Shock Solenoid Circuit Fault	8-48	20
C0582	Shock Solenoid Circuit Fault	8-48	20
C0583	Shock Solenoid Circuit Fault	8-48	20
C0584	Shock Solenoid Circuit Fault	8-48	20
C0587	Shock Solenoid Circuit Fault	8-48	20
C0588	Shock Solenoid Circuit Fault	8-48	20
C0589	Shock Solenoid Circuit Fault	8-48	20
C0592	Shock Solenoid Circuit Fault	8-48	20
C0593	Shock Solenoid Circuit Fault	8-48	20
C0594	Shock Solenoid Circuit Fault	8-48	20
C0615	Position Sensor Fault	8-48	21
C0620	Position Sensor Fault	8-48	21
C0625	Position Sensor Fault	8-48	21
C0630	Position Sensor Fault	8-48	21
C0665	Chassis Pitch Signal Circuit Fault	8-48	22
C0690	Damper Control Relay Circuit Fault	8-49	23
C0691	Damper Control Relay Circuit Range	8-49	24
C0693	Damper Control Relay Circuit High	8-49	25
C0695	Position Sensor Supply Voltage Fault	8-49	26
C0710	Steering Position Signal Fault	8-50	27
DEVILLE & ELDORADO			
—	System Check	8-50	28
C0550	ECU Fault	8-50	29
C0563	Calibration ROM Checksum Error	8-50	30
C0577	Solenoid Circuit Fault	8-50	31
C0578	Solenoid Circuit Fault	8-50	31
C0579	Solenoid Circuit Fault	8-50	31
C0582	Solenoid Circuit Fault	8-50	31
C0583	Solenoid Circuit Fault	8-50	31
C0584	Solenoid Circuit Fault	8-50	31
C0587	Solenoid Circuit Fault	8-50	31
C0588	Solenoid Circuit Fault	8-50	31
C0589	Solenoid Circuit Fault	8-50	31
C0592	Solenoid Circuit Fault	8-50	31
C0593	Solenoid Circuit Fault	8-50	31
C0594	Solenoid Circuit Fault	8-50	31
C0615	Position Sensor Fault	8-51	32
C0620	Position Sensor Fault	8-51	32
C0625	Position Sensor Fault	8-51	32

Continued

DIAGNOSTIC CHART INDEX—Continued

Code	Description	Page No.	Fig. No.
DEVILLE & ELDORADO			
C0630	Position Sensor Fault	8-51	32
C0635	Normal Force Signal Circuit Fault	8-51	33
C0638	Normal Force Signal Circuit Fault	8-51	33
C0640	Normal Force Signal Circuit Fault	8-51	33
C0643	Normal Force Signal Circuit Fault	8-51	33
C0657	Level Control Compressor Circuit Fault	8-51	34
C0658	Level Control Compressor Circuit Fault	8-51	34
C0662	Level Control Exhaust Valve Circuit Fault	8-52	35
C0663	Level Control Exhaust Valve Circuit Fault	8-52	35
C0665	Chassis Pitch Signal Circuit Fault	8-52	36
C0690	Damper Control Relay Circuit Fault	8-52	37
C0691	Damper Control Relay Circuit Fault	8-52	37
C0693	Damper Control Relay Circuit Fault	8-52	37
C0696	Position Sensor Overcurrent	8-53	38
C0710	Steering Position Signal Fault	8-53	39
C0896	Device Voltage Range/Performance	8-53	40
C1252	Normal Force Signal Circuit Fault	8-51	33
C1253	Normal Force Signal Circuit Fault	8-51	33
SEVILLE			
—	System Check	8-50	28
C0550	ECU Fault	8-50	29
C0563	Calibration ROM Checksum Error	8-50	30
C0577	Solenoid Circruit Fault	8-50	31
C0578	Solenoid Circruit Fault	8-50	31
C0579	Solenoid Circruit Fault	8-50	31
C0582	Solenoid Circruit Fault	8-50	31
C0583	Solenoid Circruit Fault	8-50	31
C0584	Solenoid Circruit Fault	8-50	31
C0587	Solenoid Circruit Fault	8-50	31
C0588	Solenoid Circruit Fault	8-50	31
C0589	Solenoid Circruit Fault	8-50	31
C0592	Solenoid Circruit Fault	8-50	31
C0593	Solenoid Circruit Fault	8-50	31
C0594	Solenoid Circruit Fault	8-50	31
C0615	Position Sensor Fault	8-51	32
C0620	Position Sensor Fault	8-51	32
C0625	Position Sensor Fault	8-51	32
C0630	Position Sensor Fault	8-51	32
C0635	Normal Force Signal Circuit Fault	8-51	33
C0638	Normal Force Signal Circuit Fault	8-51	33
C0640	Normal Force Signal Circuit Fault	8-51	33
C0643	Normal Force Signal Circuit Fault	8-51	33
C0657	Level Control Compressor Circuit Fault	8-51	34
C0658	Level Control Compressor Circuit Fault	8-51	34
C0662	Level Control Exhaust Valve Circuit Fault	8-52	35
C0663	Level Control Exhaust Valve Circuit Fault	8-52	35
C0665	Chassis Pitch Signal Circuit Fault	8-52	36
C0690	Damper Control Relay Circuit Fault	8-52	37
C0691	Damper Control Relay Circuit Fault	8-52	37
C0693	Damper Control Relay Circuit Fault	8-52	37
C0696	Position Sensor Overcurrent	8-53	38
C0710	Steering Position Signal Fault	8-53	39
C0896	Device Voltage Range/Performance	8-53	40
C1252	Normal Force Signal Circuit Fault	8-51	33
C1253	Normal Force Signal Circuit Fault	8-51	33

Step	Action	Value(s)	Yes	No
1	1. Turn the ignition ON. 2. Connect pins 3 and 4 of DLC connector to enter diagnostics. 3. Check and record the codes. 4. Exit diagnostics. 5. Clear error codes. 6. Enter Diagnostics. Are any error codes present?	—	Go to *Step 2*	If codes were previously set, refer to the appropriate diagnosis chart
2	Is there a single code set?	—	Refer to the appropriate error code diagnosis chart.	Go to *Step 3*
3	1. Disconnect the control module. 2. Check the resistance from drive to ground on each strut. • LF strut – pin D13 to pin D10 • RF strut – pin C13 to pin D8 • LR strut – pin D14 to pin D11 • RR strut – pin C14 to pin D9 • Resistance values should be between 20Ω and 60Ω Does the resistance value on each strut match the resistance values of the other struts?	Ω	Repeat this *system check*	Go to *Step 4*
4	Check the connector and strut cavity of the unmatching strut for the following: • Connector alignment • Moisture • Dirt Are strut cavities and connectors free from moisture and dirt and connected properly?	—	Repeat this *system check*	Go to *Step 5*
5	1. Clean and dry the connector and strut cavity. 2. Reconnect the connector to the strut. Are strut cavities and connectors free from moisture and dirt and connected properly?	—	Repeat this *system check*	—

GC2019800330000X

Fig. 6 Diagnostic System Check. Bonneville & LeSabre

Step	Action	Value(s)	Yes	No
10	1. Reconnect the control module. 2. Backprobe the control module connector with a digital voltmeter between pins D13 and D10. 3. Turn the ignition ON. Does the voltage go high (B+) for approximately the first 2-6 seconds after the key is turned on?	Voltage	Go to *Step 18*	Go to *Step 11*
11	Replace the control module. Is the replacement complete?	—	Go to *RTD Diagnostic System Check*	—
12	Is the resistance greater than 60 Ω?	Ω	Go to *Step 13*	—
13	Check the resistance in circuit 1448 from the control module to the strut. Is the resistance greater than 2 Ω?	Ω	Go to *Step 14*	Go to *Step 15*
14	Repair the open in circuit 1448. Is the repair complete?	—	Go to *RTD Diagnostic System Check*	—
15	Check resistance in circuit 1005 from the control module to the strut. Is the resistance greater than 2 Ω?	Ω	Go to *Step 16*	Go to *Step 17*
16	Repair open in circuit 1005. Is the repair complete?	—	Go to *RTD Diagnostic System Check*	—
17	Replace the strut. Is the replacement complete?	—	Go to *RTD Diagnostic System Check*	—
18	1. Install a 6.6 K Ω resistor between pins D2 and D16. 2. Measure the voltage between pins D6 and D10. Is the voltage less than 0.5 volts with no fluctuation?	Voltage	Go to *Step 21*	Go to *Step 19*
19	Is the voltage more than 0.5 volts, but less than 4.5 volts with no fluctuation?	Voltage	Go to *Step 20*	Go to *Step 23*
20	Replace the strut. Is the replacement complete?	—	Go to *RTD Diagnostic System Check*	—
21	1. Turn the ignition OFF. 2. Measure the resistance between pins D6 and D10 of wiring harness connector. Is the resistance greater than 100 Ω?	Ω	Go to *Step 22*	Go to *Step 29*
22	Replace the control module. Is the replacement complete?	—	Go to *RTD Diagnostic System Check*	—
23	Is the voltage greater than 4.5 volts with no fluctuation?	—	Go to *Step 26*	Go to *Step 24*
24	Does the voltage fluctuate between 1,3,and 5 volts?	Voltage	Go to *Step 25*	Repeat this *diagnosis chart*
25	Normal operation. Check for intermittents. Is an intermittent condition present?	—	Go to *Intermittents and Poor Connections*	—
26	1. Disconnect the control module. 2. Check the resistance in circuit 1004 from the control module to the strut connector. Is the resistance greater than 2 Ω?	Ω	Go to *Step 27*	Go to *Step 28*

GC2019800331020X

Fig. 7 Code 23: Lefthand Front Actuator Position Error (Part 2 of 3). Bonneville & LeSabre

Step	Action	Value(s)	Yes	No
1	1. Perform the *RTD Diagnostic System Check*. 2. Turn the ignition OFF. 3. Disconnect the control module. 4. Measure the resistance between pins D13 and D10 of wiring harness connector. Is the resistance between 0-2 Ω?	Ω	Go to *Step 2*	Go to *Step 5*
2	Disconnect the strut connector and measure the resistance between pins D13 and D10 again. Is the resistance greater than 2 Ω?	Ω	Go to *Step 3*	Go to *Step 4*
3	Replace the strut. Is the replacement complete?	—	Go to *RTD Diagnostic System Check*	—
4	Repair short to ground in circuit 1448. Is the repair complete?	—	Go to *RTD Diagnostic System Check*	—
5	Is the resistance between 3-19 Ω?	Ω	Go to *Step 6*	Go to *Step 9*
6	Check the strut connector for corrosion, moisture or foreign material. Is corrosion, moisture, or foreign material present?	—	Go to *Step 8*	Go to *Step 7*
7	Replace the strut. Is the replacement complete?	—	Go to *RTD Diagnostic System Check*	—
8	Clean or repair as necessary. Is the repair complete?	—	Go to *RTD Diagnostic System Check*	—
9	Is the resistance between 20-60 Ω?	Ω	Go to *Step 10*	Go to *Step 12*

GC2019800331010X

Fig. 7 Code 23: Lefthand Front Actuator Position Error (Part 1 of 3). Bonneville & LeSabre

Step	Action	Value(s)	Yes	No
27	Repair the open in circuit 1004. Is the repair complete?	—	Go to *RTD Diagnostic System Check*	—
28	Replace the strut. Is the replacement complete?	—	Go to *RTD Diagnostic System Check*	—
29	1. Disconnect the strut connector. 2. Measure the resistance between pins D6 and D10 of the wiring harness connector. Is the resistance greater than 100 Ω?	Ω	Go to *Step 30*	Go to *Step 31*
30	Replace the strut. Is the replacement complete?	—	Go to *RTD Diagnostic System Check*	—
31	1. Disconnect the control module. 2. Measure the resistance between pins D6 and D10 of the control module connector. Is the resistance greater than 20,000 Ω?	Ω	Go to *Step 33*	Go to *Step 32*
32	Replace the control module. Is the replacement complete?	—	Go to *RTD Diagnostic System Check*	—
33	**Important:** The control module connector and the strut connector must be disconnected. Measure the resistance between pin D6 and pin D10 of the wiring harness connector. Is the resistance greater than 100 Ω?	Ω	Go to *Step 34*	Go to *Step 35*
34	Repair short in circuit 1004 to ground. Is the repair complete?	—	Go to *RTD Diagnostic System Check*	—
35	Repair the short in circuit 1004 to 1005. Is the repair complete?	—	Go to *RTD Diagnostic System Check*	—

GC2019800331030X

Fig. 7 Code 23: Lefthand Front Actuator Position Error (Part 3 of 3). Bonneville & LeSabre

Step	Action	Value(s)	Yes	No
1	1. Perform the *RTD Diagnostic System Check*. 2. Turn the ignition OFF. 3. Disconnect the control module. 4. Measure the resistance between pins C13 and D8 of wiring harness connector. Is the resistance between 0-2 Ω?	Ω	Go to *Step 2*	Go to *Step 5*
2	Disconnect the strut connector and measure the resistance between pins C13 and D8 again. Is the resistance greater than 2 Ω?	Ω	Go to *Step 3*	Go to *Step 4*
3	Replace the strut. Is the replacement complete?	—	Go to *RTD Diagnostic System Check*	—
4	Repair short to ground in circuit 1006. Is the repair complete?	—	Go to *RTD Diagnostic System Check*	—
5	Is the resistance between 3-19 Ω?	Ω	Go to *Step 6*	Go to *Step 9*
6	Check the strut connector for corrosion, moisture or foreign material. Is corrosion, moisture, or foreign material present?	—	Go to *Step 8*	Go to *Step 7*
7	Replace the strut. Is the replacement complete?	—	Go to *RTD Diagnostic System Check*	—
8	Clean or repair as necessary. Is the repair complete?	—	Go to *RTD Diagnostic System Check*	—
9	Is the resistance between 20-60 Ω?	Ω	Go to *Step 10*	Go to *Step 12*

GC2019800332010X

Fig. 8 Code 24: Righthand Front Actuator Position Error (Part 1 of 3). Bonneville & LeSabre

Step	Action	Value(s)	Yes	No
10	1. Reconnect the control module. 2. Backprobe the control module connector with a digital voltmeter between pins C13 and D8. 3. Turn the ignition ON. Does the voltage go high (B+) for approximately the first 2-6 seconds after the key is turned on?	Voltage	Go to *Step 18*	Go to *Step 11*
11	Replace the control module. Is the replacement complete?	—	Go to *RTD Diagnostic System Check*	—
12	Is the resistance greater than 60 Ω?	Ω	Go to*Step 13*	—
13	Check the resistance in circuit 1006 from the control module to the strut. Is the resistance greater than 2 Ω?	Ω	Go to *Step 14*	Go to *Step 15*
14	Repair the open in circuit 1006. Is the repair complete?	—	Go to *RTD Diagnostic System Check*	—
15	Check resistance in circuit 1009 from the control module to the strut. Is the resistance greater than 2 Ω?	Ω	Go to *Step 16*	Go to *Step 17*
16	Repair open in circuit 1009. Is the repair complete?	—	Go to *RTD Diagnostic System Check*	—
17	Replace the strut. Is the replacement complete?	—	Go to *RTD Diagnostic System Check*	—
18	1. Install a 6.6 K Ω resistor between pins D2 and D16. 2. Measure the voltage between pins D5 and D8. Is the voltage less than 0.5 volts with no fluctuation?	Voltage	Go to *Step 21*	Go to *Step 19*
19	Is the voltage more than 0.5 volts, but less than 4.5 volts with no fluctuation?	Voltage	Go to*Step 20*	Go to *Step 23*
20	Replace the strut. Is the replacement complete?	—	Go to *RTD Diagnostic System Check*	—
21	1. Turn the ignition OFF. 2. Measure the resistance between pins D5 and D8 of wiring harness connector. Is the resistance greater than 100 Ω?	Ω	Go to *Step 22*	Go to*Step 29*
22	Replace the control module. Is the replacement complete?	—	Go to *RTD Diagnostic System Check*	—
23	Is the voltage greater than 4.5 volts with no fluctuation?	—	Go to *Step 26*	Go to *Step 24*
24	Does the voltage fluctuate between 1,3,and 5 volts?	Voltage	Go to *Step 25*	Repeat this *diagnosis chart*
25	Normal operation. Check for intermittents. Is an intermittent condition present?	—	Go to *Intermittents and Poor Connections*	—
26	1. Disconnect the control module. 2. Check the resistance in circuit 1008 from the control module to the strut connector. Is the resistance greater than 2 Ω?	Ω	Go to*Step 27*	Go to*Step 28*

GC2019800332020X

Fig. 8 Code 24: Righthand Front Actuator Position Error (Part 2 of 3). Bonneville & LeSabre

Step	Action	Value(s)	Yes	No
1	1. Perform the *RTD Diagnostic System Check.* 2. Turn the ignition OFF. 3. Disconnect the control module. 4. Measure the resistance between pins D14 and D11 of wiring harness connector. Is the resistance between 0-2 Ω?	Ω	Go to *Step 2*	Go to *Step 5*
2	Disconnect the strut connector and measure the resistance between pins D14 and D11 again. Is the resistance greater than 2 Ω?	Ω	Go to *Step 3*	Go to *Step 4*
3	Replace the strut. Is the replacement complete?	—	Go to *RTD Diagnostic System Check*	—
4	Repair short to ground in circuit 1010. Is the repair complete?	—	Go to *RTD Diagnostic System Check*	—
5	Is the resistance between 3-19 Ω?	Ω	Go to *Step 6*	Go to *Step 9*
6	Check the strut connector for corrosion, moisture or foreign material. Is corrosion, moisture, or foreign material present?	—	Go to *Step 8*	Go to *Step 7*
7	Replace the strut. Is the replacement complete?	—	Go to *RTD Diagnostic System Check*	—
8	Clean or repair as necessary. Is the repair complete?	—	Go to *RTD Diagnostic System Check*	—
9	Is the resistance between 20-60 Ω?	Ω	Go to *Step 10*	Go to *Step 12*

GC2019800333010X

Fig. 9 Code 25: Lefthand Rear Actuator Position Error (Part 1 of 3). Bonneville & LeSabre

Step	Action	Value(s)	Yes	No
27	Repair the open in circuit 1008. Is the repair complete?	—	Go to *RTD Diagnostic System Check*	—
28	Replace the strut. Is the replacement complete?	—	Go to *RTD Diagnostic System Check*	—
29	1. Disconnect the strut connector. 2. Measure the resistance between pins D5 and D8 of the wiring harness connector. Is the resistance greater than 100 Ω?	Ω	Go to *Step 30*	Go to *Step 31*
30	Replace the strut. Is the replacement complete?	—	Go to *RTD Diagnostic System Check*	—
31	1. Disconnect the control module. 2. Measure the resistance between pins D5 and D8 of the control module connector. Is the resistance greater than 20,000 Ω?	Ω	Go to *Step 33*	Go to*Step 32*
32	Replace the control module. Is the replacement complete?	—	Go to *RTD Diagnostic System Check*	—
33	**Important:** The control module connector and the strut connector must not be connected. Measure the resistance between pins D5 and D8 of the control module connector. Is the resistance greater than 100 Ω?	Ω	Go to *Step 34*	Go to *Step 35*
34	Repair short in circuit 1008 to ground. Is the repair complete?	—	Go to *RTD Diagnostic System Check*	—
35	Repair the short in circuit 1008 to 1009. Is the repair complete?	—	Go to *RTD Diagnostic System Check*	—

GC2019800332030X

Fig. 8 Code 24: Righthand Front Actuator Position Error (Part 3 of 3). Bonneville & LeSabre

Step	Action	Value(s)	Yes	No
10	1. Reconnect the control module. 2. Backprobe the control module connector with a digital voltmeter between pins D14 and D11. 3. Turn the ignition ON. Does the voltage go high (B+) for approximately the first 2-6 seconds after the key is turned on?	Voltage	Go to *Step 18*	Go to *Step 11*
11	Replace the control module. Is the replacement complete?	—	Go to *RTD Diagnostic System Check*	—
12	Is the resistance greater than 60 Ω?	Ω	Go to*Step 13*	—
13	Check the resistance in circuit 1010 from the control module to the strut. Is the resistance greater than 2 Ω?	Ω	Go to *Step 14*	Go to *Step 15*
14	Repair the open in circuit 1010. Is the repair complete?	—	Go to *RTD Diagnostic System Check*	—
15	Check resistance in circuit 1013 from the control module to the strut. Is the resistance greater than 2 Ω?	Ω	Go to *Step 16*	Go to *Step 17*
16	Repair open in circuit 1013. Is the repair complete?	—	Go to *RTD Diagnostic System Check*	—
17	Replace the strut. Is the replacement complete?	—	Go to *RTD Diagnostic System Check*	—
18	1. Install a 6.6 K Ω resistor between pins D2 and D16. 2. Measure the voltage between pins D4 and D11. Is the voltage less than 0.5 volts with no fluctuation?	Voltage	Go to *Step 21*	Go to *Step 19*
19	Is the voltage more than 0.5 volts, but less than 4.5 volts with no fluctuation?	Voltage	Go to*Step 20*	Go to *Step 23*
20	Replace the strut. Is the replacement complete?	—	Go to *RTD Diagnostic System Check*	—
21	1. Turn the ignition OFF. 2. Measure the resistance between pins D4 and D11 of wiring harness connector. Is the resistance greater than 100 Ω?	Ω	Go to *Step 22*	Go to*Step 29*
22	Replace the control module. Is the replacement complete?	—	Go to *RTD Diagnostic System Check*	—
23	Is the voltage greater than 4.5 volts with no fluctuation?	—	Go to *Step 26*	Go to *Step 24*
24	Does the voltage fluctuate between 1,3,and 5 volts?	Voltage	Go to *Step 25*	Repeat this *diagnosis chart*
25	Normal operation. Check for intermittents. Is an intermittent condition present?	—	Go to *Intermittents and Poor Connections*	—
26	1. Disconnect the control module. 2. Check the resistance in circuit 1012 from the control module to the strut connector. Is the resistance greater than 2 Ω?	Ω	Go to*Step 27*	Go to*Step 28*

GC2019800333020X

Fig. 9 Code 25: Lefthand Rear Actuator Position Error (Part 2 of 3). Bonneville & LeSabre

Step	Action	Value(s)	Yes	No
27	Repair the open in circuit 1012. Is the repair complete?	—	Go to *RTD Diagnostic System Check*	—
28	Replace the strut. Is the replacement complete?	—	Go to *RTD Diagnostic System Check*	—
29	1. Disconnect the strut connector. 2. Measure the resistance between pins D4 and D11 of the wiring harness connector. Is the resistance greater than 100 Ω?	Ω	Go to *Step 30*	Go to *Step 31*
30	Replace the strut. Is the replacement complete?	—	Go to *RTD Diagnostic System Check*	—
31	1. Disconnect the control module. 2. Measure the resistance between pins D4 and D11 of the control module connector. Is the resistance greater than 20,000 Ω?	Ω	Go to *Step 33*	Go to*Step 32*
32	Replace the control module. Is the replacement complete?	—	Go to *RTD Diagnostic System Check*	—
33	**Important:** The control module connector and the strut connector must be disconnected. Measure the resistance between pin D4 and pin D11 of the wiring harness connector. Is the resistance greater than 100 Ω?	Ω	Go to *Step 34*	Go to *Step 35*
34	Repair short in circuit 1012 to ground. Is the repair complete?	—	Go to *RTD Diagnostic System Check*	—
35	Repair the short in circuit 1012 to 1013. Is the repair complete?	—	Go to *RTD Diagnostic System Check*	—

GC2019800333030X

Fig. 9 Code 25: Lefthand Rear Actuator Position Error (Part 3 of 3). Bonneville & LeSabre

Step	Action	Value(s)	Yes	No
10	1. Reconnect the control module. 2. Backprobe the control module connector with a digital voltmeter between pins C14 and D9. 3. Turn the ignition ON. Does the voltage go high (B+) for approximately the first 2-6 seconds after the key is turned on?	Voltage	Go to *Step 18*	Go to *Step 11*
11	Replace the control module. Is the replacement complete?	—	Go to *RTD Diagnostic System Check*	—
12	Is the resistance greater than 60 Ω?	Ω	Go to*Step 13*	—
13	Check the resistance in circuit 1014 from the control module to the strut. Is the resistance greater than 2 Ω?	Ω	Go to *Step 14*	Go to *Step 15*
14	Repair the open in circuit 1014. Is the repair complete?	—	Go to *RTD Diagnostic System Check*	—
15	Check resistance in circuit 1017 from the control module to the strut. Is the resistance greater than 2 Ω?	Ω	Go to *Step 16*	Go to *Step 17*
16	Repair open in circuit 1017. Is the repair complete?	—	Go to *RTD Diagnostic System Check*	—
17	Replace the strut. Is the replacement complete?	—	Go to *RTD Diagnostic System Check*	—
18	1. Install a 6.6 K Ω resistor between pins D2 and D16. 2. Measure the voltage between pins D3 and D9. Is the voltage less than 0.5 volts with no fluctuation?	Voltage	Go to *Step 21*	Go to *Step 19*
19	Is the voltage more than 0.5 volts, but less than 4.5 volts with no fluctuation?	Voltage	Go to*Step 20*	Go to *Step 23*
20	Replace the strut. Is the replacement complete?	—	Go to *RTD Diagnostic System Check*	—
21	1. Turn the ignition OFF. 2. Measure the resistance between pins D3 and D9 of wiring harness connector. Is the resistance greater than 100 Ω?	Ω	Go to *Step 22*	Go to*Step 29*
22	Replace the control module. Is the replacement complete?	—	Go to *RTD Diagnostic System Check*	—
23	Is the voltage greater than 4.5 volts with no fluctuation?	—	Go to *Step 26*	Go to *Step 24*
24	Does the voltage fluctuate between 1,3,and 5 volts?	Voltage	Go to *Step 25*	Repeat this *diagnosis chart*
25	Normal operation. Check for intermittents. Is an intermittent condition present?	—	Go to *Intermittents and Poor Connections*	—
26	1. Disconnect the control module. 2. Check the resistance in circuit 1016 from the control module to the strut connector. Is the resistance greater than 2 Ω?	Ω	Go to*Step 27*	Go to*Step 28*

GC2019800334020X

Fig. 10 Code 26: Righthand Rear Actuator Position Error (Part 2 of 3). Bonneville & LeSabre

Step	Action	Value(s)	Yes	No
1	1. Perform the *RTD Diagnostic System Check.* 2. Turn the ignition OFF. 3. Disconnect the control module. 4. Measure the resistance between pins C14 and D9 of wiring harness connector. Is the resistance between 0-2 Ω?	Ω	Go to *Step 2*	Go to *Step 5*
2	Disconnect the strut connector and measure the resistance between pins C14 and D9 again. Is the resistance greater than 2 Ω?	Ω	Go to *Step 3*	Go to *Step 4*
3	Replace the strut. Is the replacement complete?	—	Go to *RTD Diagnostic System Check*	—
4	Repair short to ground in circuit 1014. Is the repair complete?	—	Go to *RTD Diagnostic System Check*	—
5	Is the resistance between 3-19 Ω?	Ω	Go to *Step 6*	Go to *Step 9*
6	Check the strut connector for corrosion, moisture or foreign material. Is corrosion, moisture, or foreign material present?	—	Go to *Step 8*	Go to *Step 7*
7	Replace the strut. Is the replacement complete?	—	Go to *RTD Diagnostic System Check*	—
8	Clean or repair as necessary. Is the repair complete?	—	Go to *RTD Diagnostic System Check*	—
9	Is the resistance between 20-60 Ω?	Ω	Go to *Step 10*	Go to *Step 12*

GC2019800334010X

Fig. 10 Code 26: Righthand Rear Actuator Position Error (Part 1 of 3). Bonneville & LeSabre

Step	Action	Value(s)	Yes	No
27	Repair the open in circuit 1016. Is the repair complete?	—	Go to *RTD Diagnostic System Check*	—
28	Replace the strut. Is the replacment complete?	—	Go to *RTD Diagnostic System Check*	—
29	1. Disconnect the strut connector. 2. Measure the resistance between pins D3 and D9 of the wiring harness connector. Is the resistance greater than 100 Ω?	Ω	Go to *Step 30*	Go to *Step 31*
30	Replace the strut. Is the replacement complete?	—	Go to *RTD Diagnostic System Check*	—
31	1. Disconnect the control module. 2. Measure the resistance between pins D3 and D9 of the control module connector. Is the resistance greater than 20,000 Ω?	Ω	Go to *Step 33*	Go to*Step 32*
32	Replace the control module. Is the replacement complete?	—	Go to *RTD Diagnostic System Check*	—
33	**Important:** The control module connector and the strut connector must be disconnected. Measure the resistance between pin D3 and pin D9 of the wiring harness connector. Is the resistance greater than 100 Ω?	Ω	Go to *Step 34*	Go to *Step 35*
34	Repair short in circuit 1016 to ground. Is the repair complete?	—	Go to *RTD Diagnostic System Check*	—
35	Repair the short in circuit 1016 to 1017. Is the repair complete?	—	Go to *RTD Diagnostic System Check*	—

GC2019800334030X

Fig. 10 Code 26: Righthand Rear Actuator Position Error (Part 3 of 3). Bonneville & LeSabre

Step	Action	Value(s)	Yes	No
1	1. Perform the *RTD Diagnostic System Check.* 2. Turn the ignition OFF. 3. Backprobe control module pin C3 to pin D16 with a digital voltmeter. 4. Turn the ignition ON. 5. Monitor the voltage for at least 20 seconds. Is the voltage always low?	—	Go to *Step 2*	Go to *Step 7*
2	1. Disconnect the PCM connector 3. 2. Check the voltage from control module pin C3 to pin D16. Does the voltage stay low?	—	Go to *Step 4*	Go to *Step 3*
3	Replace the PCM. Is the replacement complete?	—	Go to *RTD Diagnostic System Check*	—
4	Check for a short circuit to ground condition in CKT 1490. Is the circuit OK?	—	Go to *Step 5*	Go to *Step 6*
5	Replace the control module. Is the replacement complete?	—	Go to *RTD Diagnostic System Check*	—
6	Repair the short circuit to ground condition in CKT 1490. Is the repair complete?	—	Go to *RTD Diagnostic System Check*	—
7	Does the voltage start low and then go high for 10 seconds?	—	Go to *Step 8*	Go to *Step 9*
8	Normal operation. Check for intermittents. Were any intermittents found?	—	Go to *Intermittents and Poor Connections*	Go to *RTD Diagnostic System Check*

GC2019800335010X

Fig. 11 Code 31: Lift Or Dive Signal Error (Part 1 of 2). Bonneville & LeSabre

Step	Action	Value(s)	Yes	No
9	Jump PCM pin 3E6 to ground and continue to monitor the voltage at control module pin C3. Does the voltage stay high?	—	Go to *Step 11*	Go to *Step 10*
10	Replace the PCM. Is the replacement complete?	—	Go to *RTD Diagnostic System Check*	—
11	Check for an open circuit condition or short circuit to battery condition in circuit 1490. Was an open circuit condition or short circuit to battery condition found in CKT 1490?	—	Go to *Step 12*	Go to*Step 13*
12	Repair CKT 1490. Is the repair complete?	—	Go to *RTD Diagnostic System Check*	—
13	Replace the module. Is the replacement complete?	—	Go to *RTD Diagnostic System Check*	—

GC2019800335020X

Fig. 11 Code 31: Lift Or Dive Signal Error (Part 2 of 2). Bonneville & LeSabre

Step	Action	Value(s)	Yes	No
15	1. Disconnect the control module. 2. Measure the resistance between pins D7 and C2 of the wiring harness connector. Is the resistance less than 100 Ω?	Ω	Go to *Step 16*	Go to *Step 17*
16	Replace the control module. Is the replacement complete?	—	Go to *RTD Diagnostic System Check*	—
17	Disconnect the lateral accelerator switch and measure the resistance across the switch terminals. Is the resistance less than 100 Ω?	Ω	Go to *Step 18*	Go to *Step 19*
18	Repair the open circuit condition in circuit 1308 or 1309. Is the repair complete?	—	Go to *RTD Diagnostic System Check*	—
19	Replace the lateral accelerator switch. Is the replacement complete?	—	Go to *RTD Diagnostic System Check*	—
20	Repair the short circuit to ignition/battery condition in circuit 1308 or 1309. Is the repair complete?	—	Go to *RTD Diagnostic System Check*	—

GC2019800336020X

Fig. 12 Code 32: Lateral Accelerator Switch Error (Part 2 of 2). Bonneville & LeSabre

Step	Action	Value(s)	Yes	No
1	1. Turn the ignition OFF. 2. Disconnect the control module. 3. Place the driver select switch in the TOURING setting. 4. Measure the resistance between pins C5 and ground of wiring harness connector. Is the resistance greater than 10 Ω?	Ω	Go to *Step 2*	Go to *Step 7*
2	Check the resistance in circuit 1435 from the control module to the driver select switch. Is the resistance greater than 10 Ω	Ω	Go to *Step 3*	Go to *Step 4*
3	Repair the open circuit condition in circuit 1435. Is the repair complete?	—	Go to *RTD Diagnostic System Check*	—
4	Check the resistance in the circuit from the drivers switch to ground. Is the resistance greater than 10 Ω?	Ω	Go to *Step 5*	Go to *Step 6*
5	Repair the open circuit condition in circuit 1436. Is the repair complete?	—	Go to *RTD Diagnostic System Check*	—
6	Replace the driver select switch. Is the repair complete?	—	Go to *RTD Diagnostic System Check*	—
7	Measure the resistance between pins C6 and ground of wiring harness connector. Is the resistance greater than 500 Ω?	500 Ω	Go to *Step 8*	Go to *Step 16*
8	Measure the resistance between pins C6 and D16 of wiring harness connector. Is the resistance greater than 500 Ω?	500 Ω	Go to *Step 10*	Go to *Step 9*
9	Repair the short in circuit 1434. Is the repair complete?	—	Go to *RTD Diagnostic System Check*	—
10	1. Place the driver select switch in the PERFORM setting. 2. Measure the resistance between pins C6 and ground of wiring harness connector. Is the resistance greater than 10 Ω?	Ω	Go to *Step 11*	Go to*Step 19*
11	Check the resistance in circuit 1434 from the control module to the driver select switch. Is the resistance greater than 10 Ω?	Ω	Go to *Step 12*	Go to *Step 13*
12	Repair the open in circuit 1434. Is the repair complete?	—	Go to *RTD Diagnostic System Check*	—

GC2019800337010X

Fig. 13 Code 33: Drive Select Switch Input Error (Part 1 of 2). Bonneville & LeSabre

Step	Action	Value(s)	Yes	No
1	• Turn the ignition ON (car level). • Backprobe the control module connector with a digital voltmeter. Measure the voltage from pin D7 to pin D16 (ground). Is less than 1 volt measured?	Voltage	Go to *Step 2*	Go to *Step 7*
2	1. Turn the ignition OFF. 2. Disconnect the control module connector. 3. Check the resistance between pins D7 and D16 of the wiring harness connector. Is the resistance greater than 1 Ω?	Ω	Go to *Step 4*	Go to *Step 3*
3	Repair the short circuit to ground condition in CKT 1309 (pin D7). Is the repair complete?	—	Go to *RTD Diagnostic System Check*	—
4	Check the resistance between pins C2 and D16. Is the resistance greater than 1 Ω	Ω	Go to *Step 5*	Go to *Step 6*
5	Replace the control module. Is the replacement complete?	—	Go to *RTD Diagnostic System Check*	—
6	Repair the short circuit to ground condition in circuit 1308 (pin C2). Is the repair complete?	—	Go to *RTD Diagnostic System Check*	—
7	Is more than 1 volt, but less than 2.5 volts measured?	volt	Go to *Step 8*	Go to *Step 11*
8	1. Clear error codes. 2. Enter diagnostics. Is code 32 still set?	—	Go to *Step 9*	Go to *Step 10*
9	Replace the control module. Is the replacement complete?	—	Go to *RTD Diagnostic System Check*	—
10	Replace the lateral accelerator switch. Is the replacement complete?	—	Go to *RTD Diagnostic System Check*	—
11	Is more than 2.5 volts, but less than 4.2 volts measured?	volts	Go to *Step 12*	Go to *Step 13*
12	Replace the lateral accelerator switch. Is the replacement complete?	—	Go to *RTD Diagnostic System Check*	—
13	Is more than 4.2 volts, but less than 5.5 volts measured?	volts	Go to *Step 15*	Go to *Step 14*
14	Check circuits 1308 and 1309 for a short circuit to ignition/battery condition. Is a short circuit to ignition/battery condition present?	—	Go to *Step 20*	—

GC2019800336010X

Fig. 12 Code 32: Lateral Accelerator Switch Error (Part 1 of 2). Bonneville & LeSabre

Step	Action	Value(s)	Yes	No
13	Check the resistance in the circuit from driver select switch to ground. Is the resistance greater than 10 Ω?	Ω	Go to *Step 14*	Go to *Step 15*
14	Repair the open in circuit 1436. Is the repair complete?	—	Go to *RTD Diagnostic System Check*	—
15	Replace the driver select switch. Is the replacement complete?	—	Go to *RTD Diagnostic System Check*	—
16	1. Disconnect the driver select switch. 2. Measure the resistance between pins C6 and ground of wiring harness connector. Is the resistance greater than 500 Ω?	Ω	Go to *Step 17*	Go to *Step 18*
17	Replace the driver select switch. Is the replacement complete?	—	Go to *RTD Diagnostic System Check*	—
18	Repair the short in circuit 1434. Is the repair complete?	—	Go to *RTD Diagnostic System Check*	—
19	Measure the resistance between pins C5 and ground of the wiring harness connector. Is the resistance greater than 500 Ω?	Ω	Go to *Step 20*	Go to *Step 23*
20	Measure the resistance between pins C5 and D16 of the wiring harness connector. Is the resistance greater than 500 Ω?	Ω	Go to *Step 21*	Go to *Step 22*
21	Replace the control module. Is the replacement complete?	—	Go to *RTD Diagnostic System Check*	—
22	Repair the short in circuit 1435. Is the repair complete?	—	Go to *RTD Diagnostic System Check*	—
23	1. Disconnect the driver select switch. 2. Measure the resistance between pins C5 and ground of wiring harness connector. Is the resistance greater than 500 Ω?	—	Go to *Step 24*	Go to *Step 25*
24	Replace the driver select switch. Is the replacement complete?	—	Go to *RTD Diagnostic System Check*	—
25	Repair the short in circuit 1435. Is the repair complete?	—	Go to *RTD Diagnostic System Check*	—

GC2019800337020X

Fig. 13 Code 33: Drive Select Switch Input Error (Part 2 of 2). Bonneville & LeSabre

Step	Action	Value(s)	Yes	No
1	Is PCM code 24 set?	—	Follow PCM diagnostics to repair	Go to *Step 2*
2	1. Disconnect the Control Module. 2. Check CKT 817 by measuring the resistance from the PCM to the Control Module Connector pin C7. Is the resistance greater than the specified value?	2 Ω	Go to *Step 3*	Go to *Step 4*
3	Repair the open circuit condition in CKT 817. Is the repair complete?	—	Go to *RTD Diagnostic System Check*	—
4	Check CKT 817 for a short circuit to ground condition by measuring the resistance between the wiring harness pin C7 and ground. Is the resistance greater than the specified value?	100 Ω	Go to *Step 6*	Go to *Step 5*
5	Repair the short circuit to ground condition in CKT 817. Is the repair complete?	—	Go to *RTD Diagnostic System Check*	—
6	Check for a short to voltage in CKT 817. Is a short to voltage present?	—	Go to *Step 7*	Go to *Step 8*
7	Replace the control module. Is the control module replacement complete?	—	Go to *RTD Diagnostic System Check*	—
8	Repair short to voltage in CKT 817. Is the repair complete?	—	Go to *RTD Diagnostic System Check*	—

GC2019900512000X

Fig. 14 Code 34: Vehicle Speed Sensor Signal Error. Bonneville & LeSabre

Step	Action	Value(s)	Yes	No
1	Did you perform the RTD Diagnostic System Check?	—	Go to *Step 2*	Go to *System Check -*
2	1. Install a scan tool. 2. Turn ON the ignition, engine OFF. 3. With a scan tool, observe the Suspension Control Select Switch parameter in the RTD data list in the following switch positions: • PERF • SPORT • TOUR Does the scan tool indicate that the Suspension Control Select Switch parameter is within the specified range?	PERF: 0.5–1.5 V SPORT: 1.5–2.5 V TOUR: 2.5–3.5 V	Intermittents	Go to *Step 3*
3	1. Turn OFF the ignition. 2. Disconnect the suspension control switch. 3. Turn ON the ignition, with the engine OFF. 4. With a scan tool, observe the Suspension Control Select Switch data parameter. Does the scan tool indicate that the Suspension Control Select Switch data parameter is greater than the specified value?	4.5 V	Go to *Step 4*	Go to *Step 5*
4	1. Turn OFF the ignition. 2. Connect a 3 amp fused jumper wire between the signal circuit of the suspension control switch and the ground circuit of the suspension control switch. 3. Turn ON the ignition, with the engine OFF. 4. With a scan tool, observe the Suspension Control Select Switch parameter. Does the scan tool indicate that the Suspension Control Select Switch parameter is less than the specified value?	0.5 V	Go to *Step 8*	Go to *Step 6*
5	Test the signal circuit of the suspension control switch for a short to ground. Did you find and correct the condition?	—	Go to *Step 12*	Go to *Step 9*
6	Test the signal circuit of the suspension control switch for a short to voltage, a high resistance, or an open. Did you find and correct the condition?	—	Go to *Step 12*	Go to *Step 7*
7	Test the ground circuit of the suspension control switch for a high resistance or an open. Did you find and correct the condition?	—	Go to *Step 12*	Go to *Step 9*
8	Inspect for poor connections at the harness connector of the suspension control switch. Did you find and correct the condition?	—	Go to *Step 12*	Go to *Step 10*
9	Inspect for poor connections at the harness connector of the ESC module. Did you find and correct the condition?	—	Go to *Step 12*	Go to *Step 11*
10	Replace the Suspension Control Select switch. Did you complete the replacement?	—	Go to *Step 12*	—
11	Replace the ESC. Did you complete the replacement?	—	Go to *Step 12*	—
12	1. Use the scan tool in order to clear the DTCs. 2. Operate the vehicle within the Conditions for Running the DTC as specified in the supporting text. Does the DTC reset?	—	Go to *Step 2*	System OK

GC2010000720000X

Fig. 16 Code B2795: Suspension Control Select Switch Circuit Fault. Corvette

Step	Action	Value(s)	Yes	No
9	Inspect for poor connections at the harness connector of the ESC module. Did you find and correct the condition?	—	Go to *Step 12*	Go to *Step 11*
10	Replace the Suspension Control Select switch. Did you complete the replacement?	—	Go to *Step 12*	—
11	Replace the ESC. Did you complete the replacement?	—	Go to *Step 12*	—
12	1. Use the scan tool in order to clear the DTCs. 2. Operate the vehicle within the Conditions for Running the DTC as specified in the supporting text. Does the DTC reset?	—	Go to *Step 2*	System OK

GC2010000721020X

Fig. 17 Code B3577: Suspension Control Select Switch Contact Fault (Part 2 of 2). Corvette

Step	Action	Yes	No
1	Install a scan tool. Does the scan tool power up?	Go to Step 2	Go to Scan Tool Does Not Power Up
2	1 Turn ON the ignition, with the engine OFF. 2 Attempt to establish communication with the RTD system. Does the scan tool communicate with the RTD system?	Go to Step 3	Go to Scan Tool Does Not Communicate with Class 2 Device
3	Select the RTD display DTCs function on the scan tool. Does the scan tool display any DTCs?	Go to Step 4	Go to the Applicable Symptom Table
4	Does the scan tool display any DTCs which begin with a "U"?	Go to Scan Tool Does Not Communicate with Class 2 Device	Go to Diagnostic Trouble Code (DTC) List/Type

GC2019900594000X

Fig. 15 System Check. Corvette

Step	Action	Value(s)	Yes	No
1	Did you perform the RTD Diagnostic System Check?	—	Go to *Step 2*	Go to *System Check*
2	1. Install a scan tool. 2. Turn ON the ignition, engine OFF. 3. With a scan tool, observe the Suspension Control Select Switch parameter in the RTD data list in the following switch positions: • PERF • SPORT • TOUR Does the scan tool indicate that the Suspension Control Select Switch parameter is within the specified range?	PERF: 0.5–1.5 V SPORT: 1.5–2.5 V TOUR: 2.5–3.5 V	Intermittent	Go to *Step 3*
3	1. Turn OFF the ignition. 2. Disconnect the suspension control switch. 3. Turn ON the ignition, with the engine OFF. 4. With a scan tool, observe the Suspension Control Select Switch data parameter. Does the scan tool indicate that the Suspension Control Select Switch data parameter is greater than the specified value?	4.5 V	Go to *Step 4*	Go to *Step 5*
4	1. Turn OFF the ignition. 2. Connect a 3 amp fused jumper wire between the signal circuit of the suspension control switch and the ground circuit of the suspension control switch. 3. Turn ON the ignition, with the engine OFF. 4. With a scan tool, observe the Suspension Control Select Switch parameter. Does the scan tool indicate that the Suspension Control Select Switch parameter is less than the specified value?	0.5 V	Go to *Step 8*	Go to *Step 6*
5	Test the signal circuit of the suspension control switch for a short to ground. Did you find and correct the condition?	—	Go to *Step 12*	Go to *Step 9*
6	Test the signal circuit of the suspension control switch for a short to voltage, a high resistance, or an open. Did you find and correct the condition?	—	Go to *Step 12*	Go to *Step 7*
7	Test the ground circuit of the suspension control switch for a high resistance or an open. Did you find and correct the condition?	—	Go to *Step 12*	Go to *Step 9*
8	Inspect for poor connections at the harness connector of the suspension control switch. Did you find and correct the condition?	—	Go to *Step 12*	Go to *Step 10*

GC2010000721010X

Fig. 17 Code B3577: Suspension Control Select Switch Contact Fault (Part 1 of 2). Corvette

Step	Action	Yes	No
1	Did you perform the RTD Diagnostic System Check?	Go to *Step 2*	Go to *System Check*
2	Replace the ESC module. Did you complete the replacement?	System OK	—

GC2010000722000X

Fig. 18 Code C0550: ECU Fault. Corvette

Step	Action	Yes	No
1	Did you perform the RTD Diagnostic System Check?	Go to *Step 2*	Go to *Diagnostic System Check - Real Time Damping*
2	Replace the ESC module. Did you complete the replacement?	System OK	—

GC2010000723000X

Fig. 19 Code C0563: Calibration ROM Checksum Error. Corvette

Step	Action	Value(s)	Yes	No
1	Did you perform the RTD Diagnostic System Check?	—	Go to Step 2	Go to System Check
2	1. Disconnect the shock absorber connector. 2. Measure the resistance of the shock absorber solenoid. Does the resistance measure within the specified value?	9.5 – 15.5 Ω	Go to Step 3	Go to Step 11
3	1. Turn ON the ignition, with the engine OFF. 2. Probe the supply circuit of the shock absorber solenoid with a test lamp that is connected to a good ground. Does the test lamp illuminate?	—	Go to Step 4	Go to Step 10
4	1. Connect a test lamp between the control circuit of the shock absorber solenoid and the supply circuit of the shock absorber solenoid. 2. With a scan tool, command the shock absorber solenoid ON and OFF. Does the test lamp turn ON and OFF with each command?	—	Go to Step 8	Go to Step 5
5	Does the test lamp remain illuminated with each command?	—	Go to Step 7	Go to Step 6
6	Test the control circuit of the shock absorber solenoid far an open or short to voltage. Did you find and correct the condition?	—	Go to Step 13	Go to Step 9
7	Test the control circuit of the shock absorber solenoid far a short to ground. Did you find and correct the condition?	—	Go to Step 13	Go to Step 9
8	Inspect for poor connections at the harness connector shock absorber solenoid. Did you find and correct the condition?	—	Go to Step 13	Go to Step 11
9	Inspect for poor connections at the harness connector of the ESC module. Did you find and correct the condition?	—	Go to Step 13	Go to Step 12
10	Repair the supply circuit of the shock absorber solenoid. Did you complete the repair?	—	Go to Step 13	—
11	Replace the applicable shock absorber Did you complete the replacement?	—	Go to Step 13	—
12	Replace the ESC module. Did you complete the replacement?	—	Go to Step 13	—
13	1. Use the scan tool in order to clear the DTCs. Does the DTC reset?	—	Go to Step 2	System OK

GC2010000724000X

Fig. 20 Codes C0577, C0578, C0579, C0582, C0583, C0584, C0587, C0588, C0589, C0592, C0593 & C0594: Shock Solenoid Circuit Fault. Corvette

Step	Action	Value(s)	Yes	No
11	1. Disconnect the ESC module. 2. Test the ground circuit of the position sensor for a high resistance or an open. Did you find and correct the condition?	—	Go to Step 16	Go to Step 13
12	Inspect for poor connections at the harness connector of the position sensor. Did you find and correct the condition?	—	Go to Step 16	Go to Step 14
13	Inspect for poor connections at the harness connector of the ESC module. Did you find and correct the condition?	—	Go to Step 16	Go to Step 15
14	Replace the applicable position sensor. Did you complete the replacement?	—	Go to Step 16	—
15	Replace the ESC module. Did you complete the replacement?	—	Go to Step 16	—
16	1. Use the scan tool in order to clear the DTCs. 2. Operate the vehicle within the Conditions for Running the DTC as specified in the supporting text. Does the DTC reset?	—	Go to Step 2	System OK

GC2010000725020X

Fig. 21 Codes C0615, C0620, C0625 & C0630: Position Sensor Fault (Part 2 of 2). Corvette

Step	Action	Value(s)	Yes	No
1	Did you perform the RTD Diagnostic System Check?	—	Go to Step 2	Go to Diagnostic System Check - Real Time Damping
2	1. Install a scan tool. 2. Turn ON the ignition, with the engine OFF. 3. With the scan tool, observe the Position Sensor data parameter in the RTD data list. Does the scan tool indicate that the Position Sensor data parameter is within the specified range?	0.35 – 4.75 V	Go to Diagnostic Aids	Go to Step 3
3	1. Turn OFF the ignition. 2. Disconnect the position sensor. 3. Turn ON the ignition, with the engine OFF. 4. With a scan tool, observe the Position Sensor data parameter. Does the scan tool indicate that the Position Sensor data parameter is less than the specified value?	0.35 V	Go to Step 4	Go to Step 10
4	1. Turn OFF the ignition. 2. Connect a 3 amp fused jumper wire between the 8 volt reference circuit of the position sensor and the signal circuit of the position sensor. 3. Turn ON the ignition, with the engine OFF. 4. With a scan tool, observe the Position Sensor data parameter. Does the scan tool indicate the Position Sensor data parameter is greater than the specified value?	4.75 V	Go to Step 5	Go to Step 8
5	1. Disconnect the fused jumper wire. 2. Measure the voltage between the 8 volt reference circuit of the position sensor and the ground circuit of the position sensor. Does the voltage measure less than the specified value?	8 V	Go to Step 6	Go to Step 7
6	1. Turn OFF the ignition. 2. Measure the resistance from the ground circuit of the position sensor to a good ground. Does the resistance measure less than the specified value?	5 Ω	Go to Step 12	Go to Step 11
7	Test the 8 volt reference circuit of the position sensor for a short to voltage. Did you find and correct the condition?	—	Go to Step 16	Go to Step 13
8	Test the 8 volt reference circuit of the position sensor for a short to ground, a high resistance, or an open. Did you find and correct the condition?	—	Go to Step 16	Go to Step 9
9	Test the signal circuit of the position sensor for a short to ground, a high resistance, or an open. Did you find and correct the condition?	—	Go to Step 16	Go to Step 13
10	Test the signal circuit of the position sensor for a short to voltage. Did you find and correct the condition?	—	Go to Step 16	Go to Step 13

GC2010000725010X

Fig. 21 Codes C0615, C0620, C0625 & C0630: Position Sensor Fault (Part 1 of 2). Corvette

Step	Action	Yes	No
1	Did you perform the RTD Diagnostic System Check?	Go to Step 2	Go to System Check
2	1. Install a scan tool. 2. Turn ON the ignition, with the engine OFF. 3. With a scan tool, observe the Chassis Pitch Angle parameter in the RTD data list. Does the scan tool display Inactive?	Go to Step 4	Go to Step 3
3	1. Turn OFF the ignition. 2. Disconnect the FCM. 3. Turn ON the ignition, with the engine OFF. 4. With a scan tool, observe the Chassis Pitch Angle parameter. Does the scan tool display Inactive?	Go to Step 8	Go to Step 6
4	1. Turn OFF the ignition. 2. Disconnect the PCM connectors. 3. Connect a 3 amp fused jumper wire between the chassis pitch angle circuit at the PCM connector and a good ground. 4. Turn ON the ignition, with the engine OFF. 5. With a scan tool, observe the Chassis Pitch Angle data parameter. Does the scan tool display Active?	Go to Step 8	Go to Step 5
5	Test the Chassis Pitch Angle circuit for an open or short to voltage. Did you find and correct the condition?	Go to Step 11	Go to Step 7
6	Test the Chassis Pitch Angle circuit for a short to ground. Did you find and correct the condition?	Go to Step 11	Go to Step 7
7	Inspect for poor connections at the harness connector of the ESC module. Did you find and correct the condition?	Go to Step 11	Go to Step 9
8	Inspect for poor connections at the harness connector of the PCM. Did you find and correct the condition?	Go to Step 11	Go to Step 10
9	Replace the ESC module. Did you complete the replacement?	Go to Step 11	—
10	**Important:** Perform the set up procedure for the PCM. Replace the PCM. Did you complete the replacement?	Go to Step 11	—
11	1. Use the scan tool in order to clear the DTCs. 2. Operate the vehicle within the Conditions for Running the DTC as specified in the supporting text. Does the DTC reset?	Go to Step 2	System OK

GC2010000726000X

Fig. 22 Code C0665: Chassis Pitch Signal Circuit Fault. Corvette

Step	Action	Yes	No
1	Did you perform the RTD Diagnostic System Check?	Go to *Step 2*	Go to *System Check -*
2	1. Install a scan tool. 2. Turn ON the ignition, with the engine OFF. 3. Select RTD display DTC function on the scan tool. Does the scan tool display DTC C0691 or C0693?	Go to *Diagnostic Trouble Code (DTC)*	Go to *Step 3*
3	Does the scan tool display DTC C0577, C0582, C0587 or C0592?	Go to *Diagnostic Trouble Code (DTC)*	Go to *Step 4*
4	1. Turn OFF the ignition. 2. Disconnect the RTD relay. 3. Turn ON the ignition, with the engine OFF. 4. Probe the feed circuit of the RTD relay with a test lamp that is connected to a good ground. Does the test lamp illuminate?	Go to *Step 5*	Go to *Step 7*
5	Test the solenoid supply circuit of the RTD relay for a short to ground or an open. Did you find and correct the condition?	Go to *Step 9*	Go to *Step 6*
6	Inspect for poor connections at the RTD relay. Did you find and correct the condition?	Go to *Step 9*	Go to *Step 8*
7	Repair the feed circuit of the RTD relay. Did you complete the repair?	Go to *Step 9*	—
8	Replace the RTD relay. Did you complete the replacement?	Go to *Step 9*	—
9	1. Use the scan tool in order to clear the DTCs. 2. Operate the vehicle within the Conditions for Setting the DTC as specified in the supporting text. Does the DTC reset?	Go to *Step 2*	System OK

GC2010000727000X

Fig. 23 Code C0690: Damper Control Relay Circuit Fault. Corvette

Step	Action	Yes	No
1	Did you perform the RTD Diagnostic System Check?	Go to *Step 2*	Go to *System Check*
2	1. Turn OFF the ignition. 2. Disconnect the RTD relay. 3. Turn ON the ignition, with the engine OFF. 4. Probe the coil side feed circuit of the RTD relay with a test lamp that is connected to a good ground. Does the test lamp illuminate?	Go to *Step 3*	Go to *Step 9*
3	1. Connect a test lamp between the control circuit of the RTD relay and the coil side feed circuit of the RTD relay. 2. Turn the ignition ON and OFF. Does the test lamp turn ON and OFF when the ignition is cycled?	Go to *Step 7*	Go to *Step 4*
4	Does the test lamp remain illuminated when the ignition is turned ON and OFF?	Go to *Step 6*	Go to *Step 5*
5	Test the control circuit of the RTD relay for an open. Did you find and correct the condition?	Go to *Step 12*	Go to *Step 8*
6	Test the control circuit of the RTD relay for a short to ground. Did you find and correct the condition?	Go to *Step 12*	Go to *Step 8*
7	Inspect for poor connections at the RTD relay. Did you find and correct the condition?	Go to *Step 12*	Go to *Step 10*
8	Inspect for poor connections at the harness connector of the ESC module. Did you find and correct the condition?	Go to *Step 12*	Go to *Step 11*
9	Repair the coil side feed circuit of the RTD relay. Did you complete the repair?	Go to *Step 12*	—
10	Replace the RTD relay. Did you complete the replacement?	Go to *Step 12*	—
11	Replace the ESC module. Did you complete the replacement?	Go to *Step 12*	—
12	1. Use the scan tool in order to clear the DTCs. Does the DTC reset?	Go to *Step 2*	System OK

GC2010000728000X

Fig. 24 Code C0691: Damper Control Relay Circuit Range. Corvette

Step	Action	Yes	No
1	Did you perform the RTD Diagnostic System Check?	Go to *Step 2*	Go to *System Check*
2	1. Turn OFF the ignition. 2. Disconnect the RTD relay. 3. Turn ON the ignition, with the engine OFF. 4. Probe the coil side feed circuit of the RTD relay with a test lamp that is connected to a good ground. Does the test lamp illuminate?	Go to *Step 3*	Go to *Step 9*
3	1. Connect a test lamp between the control circuit of the RTD relay and the coil side feed circuit of the RTD relay. 2. Turn the ignition ON and OFF. Does the test lamp turn ON and OFF when the ignition is cycled?	Go to *Step 7*	Go to *Step 4*
4	Does the test lamp remain illuminated when the ignition is turned ON and OFF?	Go to *Step 6*	Go to *Step 5*
5	Test the control circuit of the RTD relay for a short to voltage. Did you find and correct the condition?	Go to *Step 12*	Go to *Step 8*
6	Test the control circuit of the RTD relay for a short to ground. Did you find and correct the condition?	Go to *Step 12*	Go to *Step 8*
7	Inspect for poor connections at the RTD relay. Did you find and correct the condition?	Go to *Step 12*	Go to *Step 10*
8	Inspect for poor connections at the harness connector of the ESC module. Did you find and correct the condition?	Go to *Step 12*	Go to *Step 11*
9	Repair the coil side feed circuit of the RTD relay. Did you complete the repair?	Go to *Step 12*	—
10	Replace the RTD relay. Did you complete the replacement?	Go to *Step 12*	—
11	Replace the ESC module. Did you complete the replacement?	Go to *Step 12*	—
12	1. Use the scan tool in order to clear the DTCs. 2. Operate the vehicle within the Conditions for Setting the DTC as specified in the supporting text. Does the DTC reset?	Go to *Step 2*	System OK

GC2010000729000X

Fig. 25 Code C0693: Damper Control Relay Circuit High. Corvette

Step	Action	Value(s)	Yes	No
1	Did you perform the RTD Diagnostic System Check?	—	Go to *Step 2*	Go to *System Check*
2	1. Install a scan tool. 2. Turn ON the ignition, with the engine OFF. 3. With the scan tool, observe all four Position Sensor data parameters in the RTD data list. Does the scan tool indicate that all four Position Sensor data parameters are within the specified range?	0 - 0.2 V	Go to *Step 3*	Go to *Step 6*
3	1. Turn OFF the ignition. 2. Disconnect all four position sensors. 3. Turn ON the ignition, with the engine OFF. 4. Use the scan tool in order to clear the DTCs. Does the DTC reset?	—	Go to *Step 5*	Go to *Step 4*
4	Reconnect each position sensor one at a time and observe if the DTC resets after each sensor is reconnected. Does the DTC reset?	—	Go to *Step 7*	System OK
5	Test the 8 volt reference circuit of all position sensors for a short to ground. Did you find and correct the condition?	—	Go to *Step 9*	Go to *Step 8*
6	Test the 8 volt reference circuit of all position sensors for a short to voltage. Did you find and correct the condition?	—	Go to *Step 9*	Go to Diagnostic Aids
7	Replace the applicable position sensor. Did you complete the replacement?	—	Go to *Step 9*	—
8	Replace the ESC module. Did you complete the replacement?	—	Go to *Step 9*	—
9	1. Use the scan tool in order to clear the DTCs. Does the DTC reset?	—	Go to *Step 2*	System OK

GC2010000730000X

Fig. 26 Code C0695: Position Sensor Supply Voltage Fault. Corvette

Step	Action	Value(s)	Yes	No
1	Did you perform the RTD Diagnostic System Check?	—	Go to *Step 2*	Go to *Real Time Damping*
2	1. Install a scan tool. 2. Turn ON the ignition, with the engine OFF. 3. Select ABS display DTC function on the scan tool. Does the scan tool display DTC C1281, C1286, or C1287?	—	Go to Antilock Brake System	Go to *Step 3*
3	With the scan tool, observe the Steering Position PWM data parameter in the RTD data list while turning the steering wheel. Does the scan tool indicate that the Steering Position PWM parameter is within the specified range when the steering wheel is turned?	0–10 ms	Go to Diagnostic Aids	Go to *Step 4*
4	1. Turn OFF the ignition. 2. Disconnect the ESC module. 3. Turn ON the ignition, with the engine OFF. 4. Measure the voltage from the steering position sensor signal circuit and to a good ground. Does the voltage measure within the specified range?	10.0–13.0 V	Go to *Step 6*	Go to *Step 5*
5	Test the signal circuit of the steering position sensor for an open, short to ground or short to voltage. Did you find and correct the condition?	—	Go to *Step 10*	Go to *Step 7*
6	Inspect for poor connections at the harness connector of the ESC module. Did you find and correct the condition?	—	Go to *Step 10*	Go to *Step 8*
7	Inspect for poor connections at the harness connector of the EBCM. Did you find and correct the condition?	—	Go to *Step 10*	Go to *Step 9*
8	Replace the ESC module. Did you complete the replacement?	—	Go to *Step 10*	—
9	Replace the EBCM. Did you complete the replacement?	—	Go to *Step 10*	—
10	1. Use the scan tool in order to clear the DTCs. Does the DTC reset?	—	Go to *Step 2*	System OK

GC2010000731000X

Fig. 27 Code C0710: Steering Position Signal Fault. Corvette

Step	Action	Value(s)	Yes	No
1	Did you perform the Road Sensing Suspension Diagnostic System Check?	—	Go to *Step 2*	Go to *System Check*
2	Inspect for DTC C0550. Is DTC C0550 displayed as a CURRENT fault (not a HISTORY fault)?	—	Go to *Step 5*	Go to *Step 3*
3	1. Use the scan tool in order to clear the DTCs. 2. Operate the vehicle within the Conditions for Running the DTC as specified in the supporting text. Does the DTC reset?	—	Go to *Step 5*	Go to *Step 4*
4	Has this vehicle been serviced for DTC C0550 previously?	—	Go to *Step 5*	Go to *Step 6*
5	**Important:** Perform the set up procedure for the ESC module. Replace the ESC module. Did you complete the replacement?	—	Go to *Step 6*	—
6	1. Use the scan tool in order to clear the DTCs. Does the DTC reset?	—	Go to *Step 2*	System OK

GC2010000735000X

Fig. 29 Code C0550: ECU Fault. DeVille, Eldorado & Seville

Step	Action	Value(s)	Yes	No
1	Did you perform the Road Sensing Suspension Diagnostic System Check?	—	Go to *Step 2*	Go to *System Check*
2	1. Install the scan tool. 2. Turn the ignition ON with the engine off. 3. Calibrate the ESC module using the scan tool. 4. Use the scan tool to clear the DTCs. 5. Operate the vehicle within the Conditions for Running the DTC as specified in the supporting text. Does the DTC reset?	—	Go to *Step 3*	System OK
3	1. Calibrate the ESC module using the scan tool. 2. Use the scan tool to clear the DTCs. 3. Operate the vehicle within the Conditions for Running the DTC as specified in the supporting text. Does the DTC reset?	—	Go to *Step 4*	System OK
4	**Important:** Perform the set up and calibration procedure for the ESC module. Replace the ESC module. Did you complete the replacement?	—	Go to *Step 5*	—
5	1. Use the scan tool in order to clear the DTCs. Does the DTC reset?	—	Go to *Step 2*	System OK

GC2010000736000X

Fig. 30 Code C0563: Calibration ROM Checksum Error. DeVille, Eldorado & Seville

Step	Action	Yes	No
1	Install a scan tool. Does the scan tool power up?	Go to *Step 2*	Data Link Communications
2	1. Turn ON the ignition, with the engine OFF. 2. Attempt to establish communication with the following modules: • Electronic Suspension Control (ESC) Module • Electronic Brake Control Module (EBCM) • Powertrain Control Module (PCM) Does the scan tool communicate with all of the listed control modules?	Go to *Step 3*	Data Link Communications
3	Select the display DTCs function on the scan tool for the following modules: • ESC Module • Electronic Brake Control Module (EBCM) • Powertrain Control Module (PCM) Does the scan tool display any DTCs?	Go to *Step 4*	Go to *Intermittent*
4	Does the scan tool display any DTCs which begin with a "U"?	Data Link Communications	Go to *Step 5*
5	Does the scan tool display any PCM DTCs?	Go to MOTOR's Domestic Engine Performance & Driveability Manual	Go to *Step 6*
6	Does the scan tool display any EBCM DTCs?	Go to Go to ABS Traction Control	Go to *Step 7*
7	Does the scan tool display DTC C0550?	Go to *DTC C0550*	Go to *Step 8*
8	Does the scan tool display DTC C0563?	Go to *DTC C0563*	Go to *Step 9*
9	Does the scan tool display DTC C0696?	Go to *DTC C0696*	Go to *Step 10*
10	Does the scan tool display DTC C0896?	Go to *DTC C0896*	Go to *Diagnostic Trouble Code (DTC)*

GC2010000734000X

Fig. 28 System Check. DeVille, Eldorado & Seville

Step	Action	Value(s)	Yes	No
1	Did you perform the Road Sensing Suspension Diagnostic System Check?	—	Go to *Step 2*	Go to *System Check*
2	1. Disconnect the strut actuator connector. 2. Measure the resistance of the strut actuator. Does the resistance measure within the specified value?	9.5– 15.5 Ω	Go to *Step 3*	Go to *Step 8*
3	1. Turn ON the ignition, with the engine OFF. 2. Connect a test lamp between the strut motor increase damping circuit of the strut actuator and a good ground. Does the test lamp illuminate?	—	Go to *Step 4*	Go to *Step 5*
4	Test the strut motor decrease damping circuit of the strut actuator for a short to ground, a short to voltage, or an open. Did you find and correct the condition?	—	Go to *Step 10*	Go to *Step 7*
5	Test the strut motor increase damping circuit of the strut actuator for a short to ground or an open. Did you complete the repair?	—	Go to *Step 10*	Go to *Step 7*
6	Inspect for poor connections at the harness connector of the strut actuator. Did you find and correct the condition?	—	Go to *Step 10*	Go to *Step 7*
7	Inspect for poor connections at the harness connector of the Electronic Suspension Control (ESC) module. Did you find and correct the condition?	—	Go to *Step 10*	Go to *Step 9*
8	Replace the strut/shock absorber. Did you complete the replacement?	—	Go to *Step 10*	—
9	Replace the Electronic Suspension Control (ESC) module. Did you complete the replacement?	—	Go to *Step 10*	—
10	1. Use the scan tool in order to clear the DTCs. Does the DTC reset?	—	Go to *Step 2*	System OK

GC2010000737000X

Fig. 31 Codes C0577, C0578, C0579, C0582, C0583, C0584, C0587, C0588, C0589, C0592, C0593 & C0594: Solenoid Circuit Fault. DeVille, Eldorado & Seville

Step	Action	Value(s)	Yes	No
1	Did you perform the Road Sensing Suspension Diagnostic System Check?	—	Go to *Step 2*	Go to *System Check -*
2	1. Install a scan tool. 2. Turn ON the ignition, with the engine OFF. 3. With the scan tool, observe the position sensor data parameter in the ESC module data list. Does the scan tool indicate that the position sensor data parameter is within the specified range?	0.35 - 4.75 V	Go to *Diagnostic Aids*	Go to *Step 3*
3	1. Turn OFF the ignition. 2. Disconnect the position sensor. 3. Turn ON the ignition, with the engine OFF. 4. With a scan tool, observe the position sensor data parameter. Does the scan tool indicate that the position sensor data parameter is less than the specified value?	0.35 V	Go to *Step 4*	Go to *Step 8*
4	Measure the voltage between the 5 volt reference circuit of the position sensor and a good ground. Does the voltage measure near the specified value?	5 V	Go to *Step 5*	Go to *Step 6*

GC2010000738010X

Fig. 32 Codes C0615, C0620, C0625 & C0630: Position Sensor Fault (Part 1 of 2). DeVille, Eldorado & Seville

Step	Action	Value(s)	Yes	No
5	1. Turn OFF the ignition. 2. Connect a 3 amp fused jumper wire between the 5 volt reference circuit of the position sensor and the signal circuit of the position sensor. 3. Turn ON the ignition, with the engine OFF. 4. With a scan tool, observe the position sensor data parameter. Does the scan tool indicate that the position sensor data parameter is greater than the specified value?	4.75 V	Go to *Step 7*	Go to *Step 9*
6	Does the voltage measure greater than the specified value?	5.625 V	Go to *Step 10*	Go to *Step 11*
7	1. Disconnect the fused jumper wire. 2. Measure the voltage between the 5 volt reference circuit of the position sensor and the low reference circuit of the position sensor. Does the voltage measure less than the specified value?	3.75 V	Go to *Step 12*	Go to *Step 13*
8	Test the signal circuit of the position sensor for a short to voltage. Did you find and correct the condition?	—	Go to *Step 17*	Go to *Step 14*
9	Test the signal circuit of the position sensor for a short to ground, high resistance, or an open. Did you find and correct the condition?	—	Go to *Step 17*	Go to *Step 14*
10	Test the 5 volt reference circuit of the position sensor for a short to voltage. Did you find and correct the condition?	—	Go to *Step 17*	Go to *Step 14*
11	Test the 5 volt reference circuit of the position sensor for a short to ground, high resistance, or an open. Did you find and correct the condition?	—	Go to *Step 17*	Go to *Step 14*
12	Test the low reference circuit of the position sensor for high resistance or an open. Did you find and correct the condition?	—	Go to *Step 17*	Go to *Step 14*
13	Inspect for poor connections at the harness connector of the position sensor. Did you find and correct the condition?	—	Go to *Step 17*	Go to *Step 15*
14	Inspect for poor connections at the harness connector of the ESC module. Did you find and correct the condition?	—	Go to *Step 17*	Go to *Step 16*
15	Replace the position sensor. Did you complete the replacement?	—	Go to *Step 17*	—
16	**Important:** Perform the set up procedure for the ESC module. Replace the ESC module. Did you complete the replacement?	—	Go to *Step 17*	—
17	1. Use the scan tool in order to clear the DTCs. Does the DTC reset?	—	Go to *Step 2*	System OK

GC2010000738020X

Fig. 32 Codes C0615, C0620, C0625 & C0630: Position Sensor Fault (Part 2 of 2). DeVille, Eldorado & Seville

Step	Action	Value(s)	Yes	No
1	Did you perform the Road Sensing Suspension Diagnostic System Check?	—	Go to *Step 2*	Go to *System Check*
2	1. Install a scan tool. 2. Start the engine. 3. Observe the Front Normal Force parameter in the VSES/CVRSS data list. Does the scan tool display within the specified range?	10–90%	Go to *Intermittent*	Go to *Step 3*
3	1. Turn OFF the ignition. 2. Disconnect the Electronic Suspension Control (ESC) module connector. 3. Turn ON the ignition, with the engine OFF. 4. Measure the voltage from the normal force signal circuit to a good ground. Does the voltage measure near the specified value?	B+	Go to *Step 5*	Go to *Step 4*
4	Test the normal force signal circuit for high resistance, a short to ground, or an open. Did you find and correct the condition?	—	Go to *Step 10*	Go to *Step 6*
5	Test the normal force signal circuit for a short to voltage. Did you find and correct the condition?	—	Go to *Step 10*	Go to *Step 7*
6	Inspect for poor connections at the harness connector of the Electronic Brake Control module (EBCM). Did you find and correct the condition?	—	Go to *Step 10*	Go to *Step 8*
7	Inspect for poor connections at the harness connector of the Electronic Suspension Control (ESC) module. Did you find and correct the condition?	—	Go to *Step 10*	Go to *Step 9*
8	Replace the EBCM. Did you complete the replacement?	—	Go to *Step 10*	—
9	**Important:** Perform the set up and calibration procedure for the Electronic Suspension Control (ESC) module. Replace the Electronic Suspension Control (ESC) module. Did you complete the replacement?	—	Go to *Step 10*	—
10	1. Use the scan tool in order to clear the DTCs. Does the DTC reset?	—	Go to *Step 2*	System OK

GC2010000739000X

Fig. 33 Codes C0635, C0638, C0640, C0643, C1252 & C1253: Normal Force Signal Circuit Fault. DeVille, Eldorado & Seville

Step	Action	Value(s)	Yes	No
1	Did you perform the Road Sensing Suspension Diagnostic System Check?	—	Go to *Step 2*	Go to *System Check -*
2	1. Disconnect the Electronic Suspension Control (ESC) module connector. 2. Turn ON the ignition, with the engine OFF. 3. Connect a test lamp between the Automatic Level Contol (ALC) relay coil supply voltage circuit of the ESC module and a good ground. Does the test lamp illuminate?	—	Go to *Step 3*	Go to *Step 4*
3	1. Turn OFF the ignition. 2. Disconnect the ELC Relay. 3. Turn ON the ignition, with the engine OFF. 4. Connect a test lamp between the ALC relay coil supply voltage circuit of the ESC module and a good ground. Does the test lamp illuminate?	—	Go to *Step 7*	Go to *Step 6*
4	Test the ALC relay coil supply voltage circuit of the ESC module for a short to ground or an open. Did you find and correct the condition?	—	Go to *Step 10*	Go to *Step 5*
5	Inspect for poor connections at the ELC Relay Did you find and correct the condition?	—	Go to *Step 10*	Go to *Step 8*
6	Inspect for poor connections at the harness connector of the Electronic Suspension Control (ESC) module. Did you find and correct the condition?	—	Go to *Step 10*	Go to *Step 9*
7	Repair the short to voltage in the ALC relay coil supply voltage circuit. Did you complete the repair?	—	Go to *Step 10*	—
8	Replace the ELC Relay. Did you complete the replacement?	—	Go to *Step 10*	—
9	Replace the Electronic Suspension Control (ESC) module. Did you complete the replacement?	—	Go to *Step 10*	—
10	1. Use the scan tool in order to clear the DTCs. Does the DTC reset?	—	Go to *Step 2*	System OK

GC2010000740000X

Fig. 34 Codes C0657 & C0658: Level Control Compressor Circuit Fault. DeVille, Eldorado & Seville

Step	Action	Value(s)	Yes	No
1	Did you perform the Road Sensing Suspension Diagnostic System Check?	—	Go to *Step 2*	Go to *System Check*
2	1. Disconnect the ESC module connector. 2. Turn ON the ignition, with the engine OFF. 3. Connect a test lamp between the ALC exhaust solenoid control circuit of the ESC module and a good ground. Does the test lamp illuminate?	—	Go to *Step 3*	Go to *Step 4*
3	1. Turn OFF the ignition. 2. Disconnect the ALC compressor connector. 3. Turn ON the ignition, with the engine OFF. 4. Connect a test lamp between the ALC exhaust solenoid control circuit of the ESC module and a good ground. Does the test lamp illuminate?	—	Go to *Step 9*	Go to *Step 7*

GC2010000741010X

Fig. 35 Codes C0662 & C0663: Level Control Exhaust Valve Circuit Fault (Part 1 of 2). DeVille, Eldorado & Seville

Step	Action	Value(s)	Yes	No
1	Did you perform the Road Sensing Suspension Diagnostic System Check?	—	Go to *Step 2*	Go to *System Check*
2	Measure the voltage by probing from the chassis pitch signal circuit of the ESC module to a good ground. Does the voltage measure near the specified value?	5 V	Go to *Step 3*	Go to *Step 4*
3	1. Observe the voltage reading. 2. Turn ON the ignition, with the engine OFF. Does the voltage momentarily drop near the specified value within 31 seconds?	1 V	Go to Intermittents	Go to *Step 5*
4	Does the voltage measure near the specified value?	B+	Go to *Step 8*	Go to *Step 6*
5	Test the chassis pitch signal circuit for a short to ground or an open. Did you find and correct the condition?	—	Go to *Step 11*	Go to *Step 7*
6	Inspect for poor connections at the harness connector of the ESC module. Did you find and correct the condition?	—	Go to *Step 11*	Go to *Step 9*
7	Inspect for poor connections at the harness connector of the PCM. Did you find and correct the condition?	—	Go to *Step 11*	Go to *Step 10*
8	Repair the short to voltage in the chassis pitch signal circuit. Did you complete the repair?	—	Go to *Step 11*	—
9	**Important:** Perform the set up procedure for the ESC module. Replace the ESC module. Did you complete the replacement?	—	Go to *Step 11*	—
10	Replace the PCM. Did you complete the replacement?	—	Go to *Step 11*	—
11	1. Use the scan tool in order to clear the DTCs. Does the DTC reset?	—	Go to *Step 2*	System OK

GC2010000742000X

Fig. 36 Code C0665: Chassis Pitch Signal Circuit Fault. DeVille, Eldorado & Seville

Step	Action	Value(s)	Yes	No
4	1. Turn OFF the ignition. 2. Disconnect the ALC compressor connector. 3. Turn ON the ignition, with the engine OFF. 4. Connect a test lamp between the battery positive voltage circuit of the ALC compressor and a good ground. Does the test lamp illuminate?	—	Go to *Step 5*	Go to *Step 8*
5	Test the ALC exhaust solenoid control circuit for a short to ground or an open. Did you find and correct the condition?	—	Go to *Step 12*	Go to *Step 6*
6	Inspect for poor connections at the ALC compressor connector. Did you find and correct the condition?	—	Go to *Step 12*	Go to *Step 10*
7	Inspect for poor connections at the Electronic Suspension Control (ESC) module. Did you find and correct the condition?	—	Go to *Step 12*	Go to *Step 11*
8	Repair the short to ground or the open in the battery positive voltage circuit of the ALC compressor connector. Did you complete the repair?	—	Go to *Step 12*	—
9	Repair the short to voltage in the ALC exhaust solenoid control circuit. Did you complete the repair?	—	Go to *Step 12*	—
10	Replace the ALC compressor head. Did you complete the replacement?	—	Go to *Step 12*	—
11	Replace the Electronic Suspension Control (ESC) module. Did you complete the replacement?	—	Go to *Step 12*	—
12	1. Use the scan tool in order to clear the DTCs. Does the DTC reset?	—	Go to *Step 2*	System OK

GC2010000741020X

Fig. 35 Codes C0662 & C0663: Level Control Exhaust Valve Circuit Fault (Part 2 of 2). DeVille, Eldorado & Seville

Step	Action	Value(s)	Yes	No
1	Did you perform the Road Sensing Suspension Diagnostic System Check?	—	Go to *Step 2*	Go to *System Check*
2	1. Disconnect the ESC module connector. 2. Connect a test lamp between the damping relay coil control circuit of the ESC module connector and a good ground. Does the test lamp illuminate?	—	Go to *Step 3*	Go to *Step 7*
3	1. Remove the damper relay. 2. Connect a test lamp between the damping relay coil control circuit of the ESC module connector and a good ground. Does the test lamp illuminate?	—	Go to *Step 9*	Go to *Step 4*
4	Connect a test lamp between the damper drive relay circuit of the ESC module connector and a good ground. Does the test lamp illuminate?	—	Go to *Step 10*	Go to *Step 5*
5	1. Install the damper relay. 2. Connect a 10 amp fused jumper wire between the damping relay coil control circuit of the ESC module connector and a good ground. 3. Connect a test lamp between the damper drive relay circuit of the ESC module connector and a good ground. Does the test lamp illuminate?	—	Go to *Step 8*	Go to *Step 6*
6	Test the damper drive relay circuit for an open. Did you find and correct the condition?	—	Go to *Step 13*	Go to *Step 11*
7	Test the damping relay coil control circuit for a short to ground or an open. Did you find and correct the condition?	—	Go to *Step 13*	Go to *Step 11*
8	Inspect for poor connections at the harness connector of the ESC module. Did you find and correct the condition?	—	Go to *Step 13*	Go to *Step 12*
9	Repair the short to voltage in the damping relay coil control circuit. Did you complete the repair?	—	Go to *Step 13*	—
10	Repair the short to voltage in the damper drive relay circuit. Did you complete the repair?	Go to *Step 13*	—	
11	Replace the damper relay. Did you complete the replacement?	—	Go to *Step 13*	—
12	Replace the ESC module. Did you complete the replacement?	—	Go to *Step 13*	—
13	1. Use the scan tool in order to clear the DTCs. Does the DTC reset?	—	Go to *Step 2*	System OK

GC2010000743000X

Fig. 37 Codes C0690, C0691 & C0693: Damper Control Relay Circuit Fault. DeVille, Eldorado & Seville

Step	Action	Value(s)	Yes	No
1	Did you perform the Road Sensing Suspension Diagnostic System Check?	—	Go to *Step 2*	Go to *System Check -*
2	1. Turn ON the ignition, with the engine OFF. 2. Measure the voltage from the 5 V reference circuit of the ESC module to the left rear position sensor by backprobing the ESC module connector. Does the voltage measure less than the specified value?	3.75 V	Go to *Step 4*	Go to *Step 3*
3	Does the voltage measure greater than the specified value?	5.625 V	Go to *Step 6*	Go to *Step 7*
4	Test the 5 V reference circuit of each position sensor for a short to ground. Did you find and correct the condition?	—	Go to *Step 8*	Go to *Step 5*
5	Test for a short between the 5 V reference circuit and the ground circuit of each position sensor. Did you find and correct the condition?	—	Go to *Step 8*	Go to *Step 7*
6	Test the 5 V reference circuit of each position sensor for a short to voltage. Did you find and correct the condition?	—	Go to *Step 8*	Go to *Step 7*
7	**Important:** Perform the set up and calibration procedure for the ESC module. Replace the ESC module. Did you complete the replacement?	—	Go to *Step 8*	—
8	1. Use the scan tool in order to clear the DTCs. Does the DTC reset?	—	Go to *Step 2*	System OK

GC2010000744000X

Fig. 38 Code C0696: Position Sensor Overcurrent. DeVille, Eldorado & Seville

Step	Action	Value(s)	Yes	No
1	Did you perform the Road Sensing Suspension Diagnostic System Check?	—	Go to *Step 2*	Go to *System Check -*
2	1. Install a scan tool. 2. Turn ON the ignition, with the engine OFF. 3. With a scan tool, observe the Steering Position PWM parameter in the ESC module data list. Does the scan tool indicate that the Steering Position PWM Parameter is within the specified range?	0–10 ms.	Go to *Step 3*	Go to *Step 4*
3	1. Activate the Steering Position PWM input. 2. With the scan tool, observe the Steering Position PWM data parameter while turning the steering wheel. Does the Steering Position PWM data parameter change state while the steering wheel is turned?	—	Go to Intermittents	Go to *Step 4*
4	1. Turn OFF the ignition. 2. Disconnect the EBCM. 3. Turn ON the ignition, with the engine OFF. 4. With a scan tool, observe the Steering Position PWM data parameter. Does the scan tool indicate that the Steering Position PWM Parameter is within the specified range?	0–10 ms.	Go to *Step 7*	Go to *Step 5*
5	Test the signal circuit of the EBCM for a short to ground. Did you find and correct the condition?	—	Go to *Step 10*	Go to *Step 6*
6	Inspect for poor connections at the harness connector of the ESC module. Did you find and correct the condition?	—	Go to *Step 10*	Go to *Step 8*
7	Inspect for poor connections at the harness connector of the EBCM. Did you find and correct the condition?	—	Go to *Step 10*	Go to *Step 9*
8	**Important:** Perform the set up procedure for the ESC module. Replace the ESC module. Did you complete the replacement?	—	Go to *Step 10*	—
9	Replace the EBCM. Did you complete the replacement?	—	Go to *Step 10*	—
10	1. Use the scan tool in order to clear the DTCs. Does the DTC reset?	—	Go to *Step 2*	System OK

GC2010000745000X

Fig. 39 Code C0710: Steering Position Signal Fault. DeVille, Eldorado & Seville

Step	Action	Value(s)	Yes	No
1	Measure the voltage in the ESC module battery positive voltage circuit. Does the voltage the measure within the specified values?	9-15.5 V	Go to *Step 3*	Go to *Step 2*
2	Test for high resistance, a short to ground or an open in the battery positive voltage circuit of the ESC module. Did you find and correct the condition?	—	Go to *Step 7*	Go to *System Check*
3	1. Use the scan tool in order to clear the DTCs. 2. Operate the vehicle within the Conditions for Running the DTC as specified in the supporting text. Does the DTC reset?	—	Go to *Step 4*	Go to *Step 6*
4	Inspect for poor connections at the harness connector of the ESC module. Did you find and correct the condition?	—	Go to *Step 7*	Go to *Step 5*
5	Replace the ESC module. Did you complete the replacement?	—	Go to *Step 7*	—
6	Inspect for poor connections at the harness connector of the ESC module. Did you find and correct the condition?	—	Go to *Step 7*	Go to Diagnostic Aids
7	1. Use the scan tool in order to clear the DTCs. Does the DTC reset?	—	Go to *Step 2*	System OK

GC2010000746000X

Fig. 40 Code C0896: Device Voltage Range/ Performance. DeVille, Eldorado & Seville

SYSTEM SERVICE

Trim Height Adjustment

To adjust vehicle trim height, a TECH II, or equivalent, scan tool is required.

1. Place vehicle on a level surface, with doors closed and no passengers or extra weight in vehicle.
2. If any rear position sensor or rear damper codes are set, they must be repaired prior to adjusting trim height.
3. Inspect rear position sensor values in diagnostics to ensure they are in normal range. If parameters are not within normal range, inspect for bent position sensor brackets or disconnected sensors.
4. Inspect fuel level reading in IPC (data parameter ID40) and round up to nearest gallon.
5. Connect a suitably programmed TECH II, or equivalent, scan tool to DLC connector, then run ignition key to the "ON" position.
6. Adjust trim height per scan tool instructions, then remove scan tool from vehicle.

COMPONENT REPLACEMENT

Module Calibration

If the module is replaced on a convertible model that does not have an EEPROM number, use the following procedure to calibrate the module.

1. Ensure scan tool has latest chassis application card.
2. Connect scan tool to DLC.
3. Turn ignition On.
4. Select RTD from chassis menu and follow scan tool instructions.

Electronic Suspension Control (ESC) Module

BONNEVILLE, DEVILLE, ELDORADO, LESABRE & SEVILLE

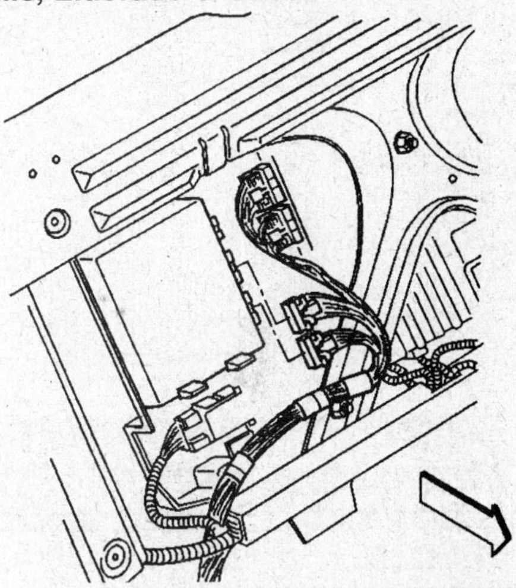

GC2019800747000X

Fig. 41 ESC module replacement. Bonneville, DeVille, Eldorado, LeSabre & Seville

1. Remove trim panel from luggage compartment to gain access to rear electronics compartment.
2. Disconnect control module electrical connectors, **Fig. 41.**
3. Remove control module from electronics bay.
4. Reverse procedure to install.

CORVETTE

After replacing the sensing module it will be required to calibrate the new module. A TECH II, or equivalent, scan tool, is required to calibrate the new module.

1. Raise lefthand side rear compartment lid.
2. Push down on ESC module **Fig. 42.**
3. Disconnect ESC module connectors.
4. Reverse procedure to install.

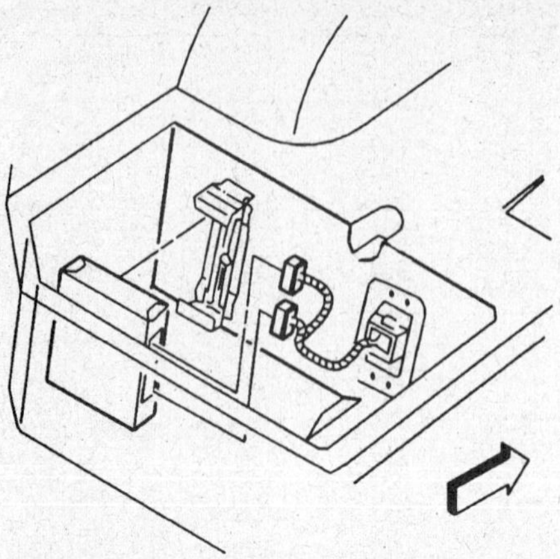

GC2019900621000X

Fig. 42 ESC module replacement. Corvette

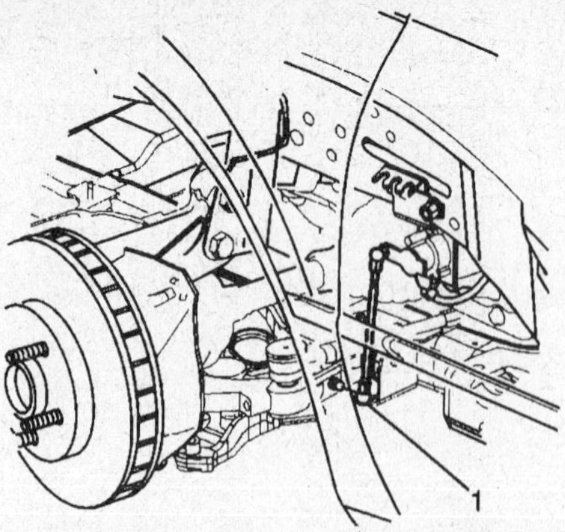

GC2019100122000A

Fig. 43 Front position sensor replacement. Bonneville, DeVille, Eldorado, LeSabre & Seville

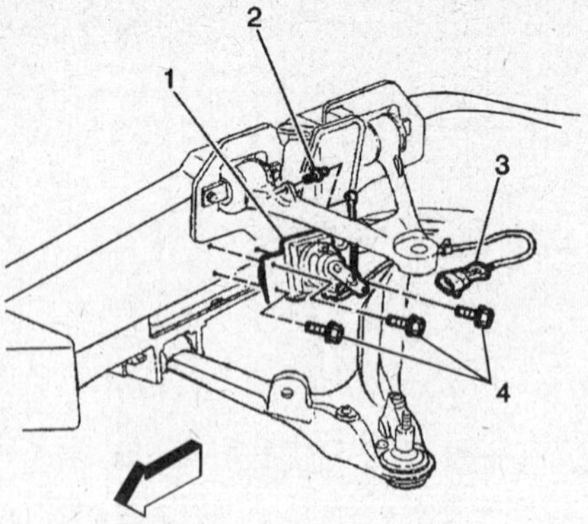

1- Front Position Sensor
2- Control Arm Link Stud
3- Connector
4- Mounting Bolts

GC2010000732000X

Fig. 44 Front position sensor replacement. Corvette

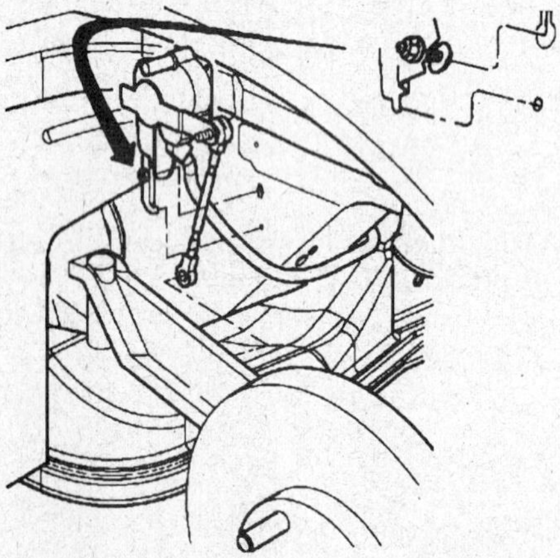

GC2019100123000A

Fig. 45 Rear position sensor replacement. Bonneville, DeVille, Eldorado, LeSabre & Seville

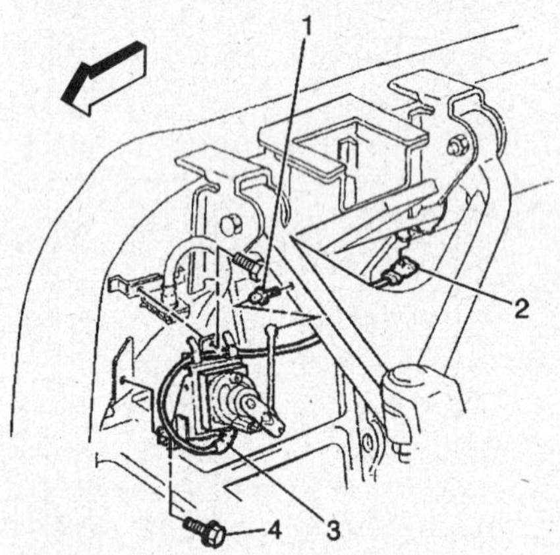

1- Rear Position Sensor
2- Cotrol Arm Link Stud
3- Connector
4- Mounting Bolts

GC2010000733000X

Fig. 46 Rear position sensor replacement. Corvette

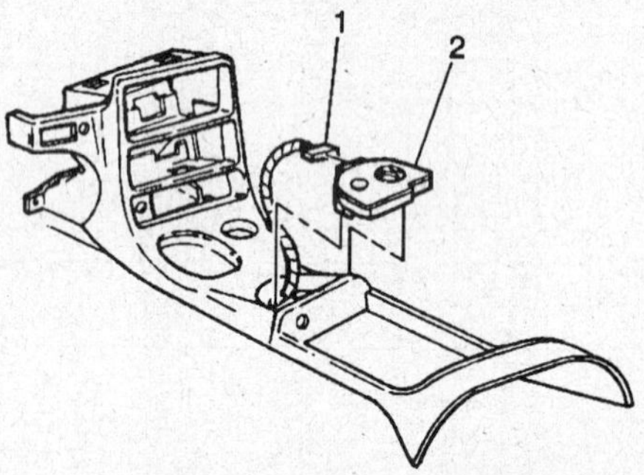

GC2019900622000X

Fig. 47 Electronic suspension ride control switch replacement

Front Position Sensor

BONNEVILLE, DEVILLE, ELDORADO, LESABRE & SEVILLE

1. Raise and support vehicle.
2. Remove wheel and tire assembly.
3. Disconnect position sensor electrical connector, **Fig. 43.**
4. Disconnect wires from frame rail.
5. Unlatch sensor locking tabs and remove position sensor from upper and lower ball studs.
6. Reverse procedure to install.

CORVETTE

1. Raise and support vehicle, then remove wheel and tire assembly.
2. Disconnect position sensor electrical connector, **Fig. 44.**
3. Remove position sensor harness retainers.
4. Remove position sensor link from control arm link stud.
5. Remove position sensor mounting bolts, then the position sensor.
6. Reverse procedure to install. **Torque** sensor mounting bolts to 26 inch lbs.

Rear Position Sensor

BONNEVILLE, DEVILLE, ELDORADO, LESABRE & SEVILLE

1. Raise and support vehicle.
2. Remove wheel and tire assembly.
3. Disconnect sensor electrical connector, **Fig. 45.**
4. Disconnect wires from suspension support.
5. Unlatch sensor locking tabs and remove position sensor from upper and lower ball studs.
6. Reverse procedure to install.

CORVETTE

1. Raise and support vehicle, then remove wheel and tire assembly.
2. Disconnect position sensor electrical connector, **Fig. 46.**
3. Remove position sensor harness retainers.
4. Remove position sensor link from control arm link stud.
5. Remove position sensor mounting bolts, then the position sensor.
6. Reverse procedure to install. **Torque** sensor mounting bolts to 26 inch lbs.

Electronic Suspension Ride Control Switch

1. Turn Off ignition switch.
2. Open center console door.
3. Pull up on switch assembly from rear in order to release mounting clips, **Fig. 47.**
4. Disconnect harness connector.
5. Remove switch assembly.
6. Reverse procedures to install.

DECIMAL & MILLIMETER EQUIVALENTS

Inch	Inch	mm
1/64	.015625	.397
1/32	.03125	.794
3/64	.046875	1.191
1/16	.0625	1.587
5/64	.078125	1.984
3/32	.09375	2.381
7/64	.109375	2.778
1/8	.125	3.175
9/64	.140625	3.572
5/32	.15625	3.969
11/64	.17185	4.366
3/16	.1875	4.762
13/64	.203125	5.159
7/32	.21875	5.556
15/64	.234375	5.953
1/4	.25	6.350
17/64	.265626	6.747
9/32	.28125	7.144
19/64	.296875	7.541
5/16	.3125	7.937
21/64	.328125	8.334
11/32	.34375	8.731

Inch	Inch	mm
23/64	.359375	9.128
3/8	.375	9.525
25/64	.390625	9.922
13/32	.40625	10.319
27/64	.421875	10.716
7/16	.4375	11.113
29/64	.453125	11.509
15/32	.46875	11.906
31/64	.484375	12.303
1/2	.5	12.700
33/64	.515625	13.097
17/32	.53125	13.494
35/64	.546875	13.890
9/16	.5625	14.287
37/64	.578125	14.684
19/32	.59375	15.081
39/64	.609375	15.478
5/8	.625	15.875
41/64	.640625	16.272
21/32	.65625	16.669
43/64	.671875	17.065

Inch	Inch	mm
11/16	.6875	17.462
45/64	.703125	17.859
23/32	.71875	18.265
47/64	.734375	18.653
3/4	.75	19.505
49/64	.765625	19.447
25/32	.78125	19.884
51/64	.796875	20.240
13/16	.8125	20.637
53/64	.828125	21.034
27/32	.84375	21.431
55/64	.859375	21.828
7/8	.875	22.225
57/64	.890625	22.622
29/32	.90625	23.019
59/64	.921875	23.415
15/16	.9375	23.812
61/64	.953125	24.209
31/32	.96875	24.606
63/64	.984375	25.003
1	1	25.400

Special Service Tools

Throughout this manual references are made to and illustrations may depict the use of special tools required to perform certain jobs. These special tools can generally be ordered through the dealers of the make vehicle being serviced. It is also suggested that you check with local automotive supply firms as they also supply tools manufactured by other firms that will assist in the performance of these jobs. The vehicle manufacturers special tools are supplied by:

Chrysler Corporation . . . . Miller Special Tools
OTC Division
28635 Mound Rd.
Warren, Michigan 48092-3499

Ford Motor Company . . . . SPX Corporation, OTC
Attn: Ford Rotunda
28635 Mound Rd.
Warren, Michigan 48092-3499

General Motors Corporation . . . . Kent-Moore
SPX Corporation
28635 Mound Rd.
Warren, Michigan 48092-3499

MANUAL INFORMATION LOCATOR

Operation/Subject/Topic	Auto Repair Manual, Vol. 1	Auto Repair Manual, Vol. 2	Domestic Engine Performance & Driveability Manual
Active Suspension System	—	X	—
Air Bags	—	X	—
Air Bag System Precautions	X	X	X
Air Conditioning	X	—	—
AIR Systems	—	—	X
All-Wheel Drive Systems	X	—	—
Alternator Specifications	X	—	—
Alternator Systems	X	—	—
Anti-Lock Brake Systems	—	X	—
Automatic Seat Belts	—	X	—
Axle Shaft Service	X	—	—
Back-Up Light Switch, Replace	X	—	—
Balance Shaft Service	X	—	—
Ball Joint Service	X	—	—
Belt Tension Data	X	—	—
Blower Motor, Replace	X	—	—
Brake Booster Service	X	—	—
Brake Service	X	—	—
Camber Adjustment	X	—	—
Camshaft Service	X	—	—
Capacity Data	X	—	—
Caster Adjustment	X	—	—
Catalytic Converters	—	—	X
Coil Pack, Replace	X	—	X
Coil Spring, Replace	X	—	—
Compression Check	X	—	X
Compression Pressures	X	—	X
Computer Relearn Procedures	X	X	X
Computerized Engine Control Systems	—	—	X
Control Arm Service	X	—	—
Cooling System Bleed	X	—	—
Cooling System Data	X	—	—
Crankshaft Pulley, Replace	X	—	—
Crankshaft Rear Oil Seal Service	X	—	—
Cruise Control Systems	—	X	—
Cylinder Block Specifications	X	—	—
Cylinder Head Service	X	—	—
Cylinder Head Specifications	X	—	—
Cylinder Head, Replace	X	—	—
Cylinder Liner, Replace	X	—	—
Dash Panel Service	—	X	—
Differential Service	X	—	—
Dimmer Switch, Replace	X	—	—
Disc Brake Service	X	—	—
Distributor Service	—	—	X
Distributor, Replace	X	—	X
Distributorless Ignition Systems	—	—	X
Drive Axle Service	X	—	—
Drive Belt Tension Data	X	—	—
Drum Brake Service	X	—	—
EGR System	—	—	X
Electric Engine Cooling Fans	X	—	—
Electric Fuel Pumps	X	—	X
Electrical Symbol Identification	X	X	X
Electronic Fuel Injection	—	—	X
Electronic Ignition	—	—	X
Electronic Instrumentation	—	—	X
Electronic Level Controls	—	X	—
Emission Control Application Charts	—	—	X
Emission Controls	—	—	X
Emission Vacuum Hose Routings	—	—	X
Engine Compartment Reference Diagrams	—	—	X

Operation/Subject/Topic	Auto Repair Manual, Vol. 1	Auto Repair Manual, Vol. 2	Domestic Engine Performance & Driveability Manual
Engine Cooling Fans	X	—	—
Engine Control Module, Replace	—	—	X
Engine Control Unit, Replace	—	—	X
Engine Front Cover Service	X	—	—
Engine Mounts, Replace	X	—	—
Engine Oil Seal Service	X	—	—
Engine Rebuilding Specifications	X	—	—
Engine Repairs	X	—	—
Engine Sensor Location	—	—	X
Engine Sensor Replacement	—	—	X
Engine Sensor Specifications	—	—	X
Engine System Identification Charts	—	—	X
Engine Tightening Specifications	X	—	—
Engine, Replace	X	—	—
Evaporator Core, Replace	X	—	—
Exhaust Gas Recirculation (EGR) Systems	—	—	X
Exhaust Manifold, Replace	X	—	—
Fast Idle Speed Adjustment	—	—	X
Federal Air Quality Standards	—	—	X
Flasher Location	X	—	—
Front Drive Axle Service	X	—	—
Front Wheel Alignment	X	—	—
Fuel Control System Identification	—	—	X
Fuel Filter, Replace	X	—	—
Fuel Injection Systems	—	—	X
Fuel Injector Cleaning Procedures	—	—	X
Fuel Injector, Replace	—	—	X
Fuel Pump Pressure Specifications	X	—	X
Fuel Pump Pressure Test	—	—	X
Fuel Pump Relay Location	X	—	X
Fuel Pump Replacement	X	—	X
Fuse Panel Location	X	—	—
General Engine Specifications	X	—	—
Headlight Switch, Replace	X	—	—
Heated Air Cleaners	—	—	X
Heater Core, Replace	X	—	—
Hub & Bearing Assembly Service	X	—	—
Hydraulic Brake System Service	X	—	—
Hydraulic Engine Cooling Fans	X	—	—
Hydraulic Valve LIfter Service	X	—	—
Idle Mixture Adjustments	—	—	X
Idle Speed Adjustments	—	—	X
Ignition Lock, Replace	X	—	—
Ignition Switch, Replace	X	—	—
Ignition System Application	—	—	X
Ignition Timing Procedures	—	—	X
Instrument Cluster, Replace	X	—	—
Intake Manifold, Replace	X	—	—
Intermittent Malfunction Computer Diagnosis	—	—	X
Knock Sensor, Replace	—	—	X
Leaf Spring, Replace	X	—	—
Lift Point Illustrations	X	X	—
Locking Differential Service	X	—	—
Locking Hub Service	X	—	—
Lower Ball Joint, Replace	X	—	—
Lower Control Arm Service	X	—	—
Lubricant Data	X	—	—
MacPherson Strut Service	X	—	—
Main & Rod Bearing Specifications	X	—	—
Maintenance & Warning Lamp Reset Procedures	X	X	X